D1311319

PETERSON'S GRADUATE PROGRAMS IN BUSINESS, EDUCATION, INFORMATION STUDIES, LAW & SOCIAL WORK

2013

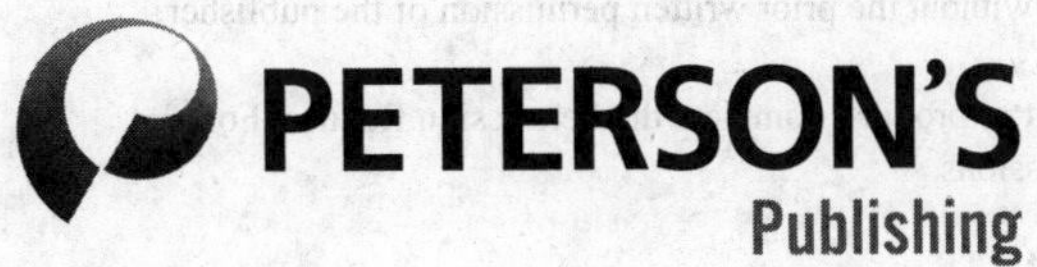

About Peterson's Publishing

Peterson's Publishing provides the accurate, dependable, high-quality education content and guidance you need to succeed. No matter where you are on your academic or professional path, you can rely on Peterson's print and digital publications for the most up-to-date education exploration data, expert test-prep tools, and top-notch career success resources—everything you need to achieve your goals.

Visit us online at **www.petersonspublishing.com** and let Peterson's help you achieve your goals.

For more information, contact Peterson's Publishing, 2000 Lenox Drive, Lawrenceville, NJ 08648; 800-338-3282 Ext. 54229; or find us on the World Wide Web at www.petersonspublishing.com.

Bernadette Webster, Managing Editor; Jill C. Schwartz, Editor; Ken Britschge, Research Project Manager; Amanda Ortiz, Amy L. Weber, Research Associates; Phyllis Johnson, Software Engineer; Ray Golaszewski, Publishing Operations Manager; Linda M. Williams, Composition Manager; Carrie Hansen, Christine Lucht, Bailey Williams, Client Fulfillment Team

ISSN 1093-8443
ISBN-13: 978-0-7689-3625-4
ISBN-10: 0-7689-3625-X

Printed in the United States of America

10 9 8 7 6 5 4 3 2 1   15 14 13

Forty-seventh Edition

CONTENTS

A Note from the Peterson's Editors

The six volumes of Peterson's *Graduate and Professional Programs*, the only annually updated reference work of its kind, provide wideranging information on the graduate and professional programs offered by accredited colleges and universities in the United States, U.S. territories, and Canada and by those institutions outside the United States that are accredited by U.S. accrediting bodies. Nearly 36,000 individual academic and professional programs at more than 2,200 institutions are listed. Peterson's *Graduate and Professional Programs* have been used for more than forty years by prospective graduate and professional students, placement counselors, faculty advisers, and all others interested in postbaccalaureate education.

Graduate & Professional Programs: An Overview contains information on institutions as a whole, while the other books in the series are devoted to specific academic and professional fields:

Graduate Programs in the Humanities, Arts & Social Sciences
Graduate Programs in the Biological/Biomedical Sciences & Health-Related Medical Professions
Graduate Programs in the Physical Sciences, Mathematics, Agricultural Sciences, the Environment & Natural Resources
Graduate Programs in Engineering & Applied Sciences
Graduate Programs in Business, Education, Information Studies, Law & Social Work

The books may be used individually or as a set. For example, if you have chosen a field of study but do not know what institution you want to attend or if you have a college or university in mind but have not chosen an academic field of study, it is best to begin with the Overview guide.

Graduate & Professional Programs: An Overview presents several directories to help you identify programs of study that might interest you; you can then research those programs further in the other books in the series by using the Directory of Graduate and Professional Programs by Field, which lists 500 fields and gives the names of those institutions that offer graduate degree programs in each.

For geographical or financial reasons, you may be interested in attending a particular institution and will want to know what it has to offer. You should turn to the Directory of Institutions and Their Offerings, which lists the degree programs available at each institution. As in the Directory of Graduate and Professional Programs by Field, the level of degrees offered is also indicated. All books in the series include advice on graduate education, including topics such as admissions tests, financial aid, and accreditation. **The Graduate Adviser** includes two essays and information about accreditation. The first essay, "The Admissions Process," discusses general admission requirements, admission tests, factors to consider when selecting a graduate school or program, when and how to apply, and how admission decisions are made. Special information for international students and tips for minority students are also included. The second essay, "Financial Support," is an overview of the broad range of support available at the graduate level. Fellowships, scholarships, and grants; assistantships and internships; federal and private loan programs, as well as Federal Work-Study; and the GI bill are detailed. This essay concludes with advice on applying for need-based financial aid. "Accreditation and Accrediting Agencies" gives information on accreditation and its purpose and lists institutional accrediting agencies first and then specialized accrediting agencies relevant to each volume's specific fields of study.

With information on more than 44,000 graduate programs in more than 500 disciplines, Peterson's *Graduate and Professional Programs* give you all the information you need about the programs that are of interest to you in three formats: **Profiles** (capsule summaries of basic information), **Displays** (information that an institution or program wants to emphasize), and **Close-Ups** (written by administrators, with more expansive information than the **Profiles**, emphasizing different aspects of the programs). By using these various formats of program information, coupled with **Appendixes** and **Indexes** covering directories and subject areas for all six books, you will find that these guides provide the most comprehensive, accurate, and up-to-date graduate study information available.

Find Us on Facebook®

Join the grad school conversation on Facebook® at www.facebook.com/petersonspublishing. Peterson's expert resources are available to help you as you search for the right graduate program for you.

Peterson's publishes a full line of resources with information you need to guide you through the graduate admissions process. Peterson's publications can be found at college libraries and career centers and your local bookstore or library—or visit us on the Web at www.petersonspublishing.com. Peterson's books are now also available as eBooks.

Colleges and universities will be pleased to know that Peterson's helped you in your selection. Admissions staff members are more than happy to answer questions, address specific problems, and help in any way they can. The editors at Peterson's wish you great success in your graduate program search!

THE GRADUATE ADVISER

The Admissions Process

Generalizations about graduate admissions practices are not always helpful because each institution has its own set of guidelines and procedures. Nevertheless, some broad statements can be made about the admissions process that may help you plan your strategy.

Factors Involved in Selecting a Graduate School or Program

Selecting a graduate school and a specific program of study is a complex matter. Quality of the faculty; program and course offerings; the nature, size, and location of the institution; admission requirements; cost; and the availability of financial assistance are among the many factors that affect one's choice of institution. Other considerations are job placement and achievements of the program's graduates and the institution's resources, such as libraries, laboratories, and computer facilities. If you are to make the best possible choice, you need to learn as much as you can about the schools and programs you are considering before you apply.

The following steps may help you narrow your choices.

- Talk to alumni of the programs or institutions you are considering to get their impressions of how well they were prepared for work in their fields of study.
- Remember that graduate school requirements change, so be sure to get the most up-to-date information possible.
- Talk to department faculty members and the graduate adviser at your undergraduate institution. They often have information about programs of study at other institutions.
- Visit the Web sites of the graduate schools in which you are interested to request a graduate catalog. Contact the department chair in your chosen field of study for additional information about the department and the field.
- Visit as many campuses as possible. Call ahead for an appointment with the graduate adviser in your field of interest and be sure to check out the facilities and talk to students.

General Requirements

Graduate schools and departments have requirements that applicants for admission must meet. Typically, these requirements include undergraduate transcripts (which provide information about undergraduate grade point average and course work applied toward a major), admission test scores, and letters of recommendation. Most graduate programs also ask for an essay or personal statement that describes your personal reasons for seeking graduate study. In some fields, such as art and music, portfolios or auditions may be required in addition to other evidence of talent. Some institutions require that the applicant have an undergraduate degree in the same subject as the intended graduate major.

Most institutions evaluate each applicant on the basis of the applicant's total record, and the weight accorded any given factor varies widely from institution to institution and from program to program.

The Application Process

You should begin the application process at least one year before you expect to begin your graduate study. Find out the application deadline for each institution (many are provided in the **Profile** section of this guide). Go to the institution's Web site and find out if you can apply online. If not, request a paper application form. Fill out this form thoroughly and neatly. Assume that the school needs all the information it is requesting and that the admissions officer will be sensitive to the neatness and overall quality of what you submit. Do not supply more information than the school requires.

The institution may ask at least one question that will require a threeor four-paragraph answer. Compose your response on the assumption that the admissions officer is interested in both what you think and how you express yourself. Keep your statement brief and to the point, but, at the same time, include all pertinent information about your past experiences and your educational goals. Individual statements vary greatly in style and content, which helps admissions officers differentiate among applicants. Many graduate departments give considerable weight to the statement in making their admissions decisions, so be sure to take the time to prepare a thoughtful and concise statement.

If recommendations are a part of the admissions requirements, carefully choose the individuals you ask to write them. It is generally best to ask current or former professors to write the recommendations, provided they are able to attest to your intellectual ability and motivation for doing the work required of a graduate student. It is advisable to provide stamped, preaddressed envelopes to people being asked to submit recommendations on your behalf.

Completed applications, including references, transcripts, and admission test scores, should be received at the institution by the specified date.

Be advised that institutions do not usually make admissions decisions until all materials have been received. Enclose a self-addressed postcard with your application, requesting confirmation of receipt. Allow at least ten days for the return of the postcard before making further inquiries.

If you plan to apply for financial support, it is imperative that you file your application early.

ADMISSION TESTS

The major testing program used in graduate admissions is the Graduate Record Examinations (GRE) testing program, sponsored by the GRE Board and administered by Educational Testing Service, Princeton, New Jersey.

The Graduate Record Examinations testing program consists of a General Test and eight Subject Tests. The General Test measures critical thinking, verbal reasoning, quantitative reasoning, and analytical writing skills. It is offered as an Internet-based test (iBT) in the United States, Canada, and many other countries.

The Graduate Record Examinations testing program consists of the revised General Test and eight Subject Tests. The GRE® revised General Test, introduced in August 2011, features a new test-taker friendly design and new question types. It reflects the kind of thinking students need to do in graduate or business school and demonstrates that students are indeed ready for graduate-level work.

- **Verbal Reasoning**—Measures ability to analyze and evaluate written material and synthesize information obtained from it, analyze relationships among component parts of sentences, and recognize relationships among words and concepts.
- **Quantitative Reasoning**—Measures problem-solving ability, focusing on basic concepts of arithmetic, algebra, geometry, and data analysis.
- **Analytical Writing**—Measures critical thinking and analytical writing skills, specifically the ability to articulate and support complex ideas clearly and effectively.

The GRE® revised General Test is available at about 700 test centers in more than 160 countries. It is offered as a computer-based test year-round at most locations around the world and as a paper-based test up to three times a year in areas where computer-based testing is not available.

Three scores are reported on the revised General Test:

1. A **Verbal Reasoning score** is reported on a 130–170 score scale, in 1-point increments.
2. A **Quantitative Reasoning score** is reported on a 130–170 score scale, in 1-point increments.

3 An **Analytical Writing score** is reported on a 0–6 score level, in half-point increments.

The GRE Subject Tests measure achievement and assume undergraduate majors or extensive background in the following eight disciplines:

- Biochemistry, Cell and Molecular Biology
- Biology
- Chemistry
- Computer Science
- Literature in English
- Mathematics
- Physics
- Psychology

The Subject Tests are available three times per year as paper-based administrations around the world. Testing time is approximately 2 hours and 50 minutes. You can obtain more information about the GRE by visiting the ETS Web site at www.ets.org or consulting the *GRE Information and Registration Bulletin.* The *Bulletin* can be obtained at many undergraduate colleges. You can also download it from the ETS Web site or obtain it by contacting Graduate Record Examinations, Educational Testing Service, P.O. Box 6000, Princeton, NJ 08541-6000; phone: 609-771-7670.

If you expect to apply for admission to a program that requires any of the GRE tests, you should select a test date well in advance of the application deadline. Scores on the computer-based General Test are reported within ten to fifteen days; scores on the paper-based Subject Tests are reported within six weeks.

Another testing program, the Miller Analogies Test (MAT), is administered at more than 500 Controlled Testing Centers, licensed by Harcourt Assessment, Inc., in the United States, Canada, and other countries. The MAT computer-based test is now available. Testing time is 60 minutes. The test consists of 120 partial analogies. You can obtain the *Candidate Information Booklet,* which contains a list of test centers and instructions for taking the test, from http://www.milleranalogies.com or by calling 800-622-3231 (toll-free).

Check the specific requirements of the programs to which you are applying.

How Admission Decisions Are Made

The program you apply to is directly involved in the admissions process. Although the final decision is usually made by the graduate dean (or an associate) or the faculty admissions committee, recommendations from faculty members in your intended field are important. At some institutions, an interview is incorporated into the decision process.

A Special Note for International Students

In addition to the steps already described, there are some special considerations for international students who intend to apply for graduate study in the United States. All graduate schools require an indication of competence in English. The purpose of the Test of English as a Foreign Language (TOEFL) is to evaluate the English proficiency of people who are nonnative speakers of English and want to study at colleges and universities where English is the language of instruction. The TOEFL is administered by Educational Testing Service (ETS) under the general direction of a policy board established by the College Board and the Graduate Record Examinations Board.

The TOEFL iBT assesses the four basic language skills: listening, reading, writing, and speaking. It was administered for the first time in September 2005, and ETS continues to introduce the TOEFL iBT in selected cities. The Internet-based test is administered at secure, official test centers. The testing time is approximately 4 hours. Because the TOEFL iBT includes a speaking section, the Test of Spoken English (TSE) is no longer needed.

The TOEFL is also offered in the paper-based format in areas of the world where Internet-based testing is not available. The paper-based TOEFL consists of three sections—listening comprehension,structure and written expression, and reading comprehension. The testing time is approximately 3 hours. The Test of Written English (TWE) is also given. The TWE is a 30-minute essay that measures the examinee's ability to compose in English. Examinees receive a TWE score separate from their TOEFL score. The *Information Bulletin* contains information on local fees and registration procedures.

The TOEFL® paper-based test (TOEFL PBT) began being phased out in mid-2012. For those who may have taken the TOEFL PBT, scores remain valid for two years after the test date. The Test of Written English (TWE) is also given. The TWE is a 30-minute essay that measures the examinee's ability to compose in English. Examinees receive a TWE score separate from their TOEFL score. The Information Bulletin contains information on local fees and registration procedures.

Additional information and registration materials are available from TOEFL Services, Educational Testing Service, P.O. Box 6151, Princeton, New Jersey 08541-6151. Phone: 609-771-7100. Web site: www.toefl.org.

International students should apply especially early because of the number of steps required to complete the admissions process. Furthermore, many United States graduate schools have a limited number of spaces for international students, and many more students apply than the schools can accommodate.

International students may find financial assistance from institutions very limited. The U.S. government requires international applicants to submit a certification of support, which is a statement attesting to the applicant's financial resources. In addition, international students *must* have health insurance coverage.

Tips for Minority Students

Indicators of a university's values in terms of diversity are found both in its recruitment programs and its resources directed to student success. Important questions: Does the institution vigorously recruit minorities for its graduate programs? Is there funding available to help with the costs associated with visiting the school? Are minorities represented in the institution's brochures or Web site or on their faculty rolls? What campus-based resources or services (including assistance in locating housing or career counseling and placement) are available? Is funding available to members of underrepresented groups?

At the program level, it is particularly important for minority students to investigate the "climate" of a program under consideration. How many minority students are enrolled and how many have graduated? What opportunities are there to work with diverse faculty and mentors whose research interests match yours? How are conflicts resolved or concerns addressed? How interested are faculty in building strong and supportive relations with students? "Climate" concerns should be addressed by posing questions to various individuals, including faculty members, current students, and alumni.

Information is also available through various organizations, such as the Hispanic Association of Colleges & Universities (HACU), and publications such as *Diverse Issues in Higher Education* and *Hispanic Outlook* magazine. There are also books devoted to this topic, such as *The Multicultural Student's Guide to Colleges* by Robert Mitchell.

Financial Support

The range of financial support at the graduate level is very broad. The following descriptions will give you a general idea of what you might expect and what will be expected of you as a financial support recipient.

Fellowships, Scholarships, and Grants

These are usually outright awards of a few hundred to many thousands of dollars with no service to the institution required in return. Fellowships and scholarships are usually awarded on the basis of merit and are highly competitive. Grants are made on the basis of financial need or special talent in a field of study. Many fellowships, scholarships, and grants not only cover tuition, fees, and supplies but also include stipends for living expenses with allowances for dependents. However, the terms of each should be examined because some do not permit recipients to supplement their income with outside work. Fellowships, scholarships, and grants may vary in the number of years for which they are awarded.

In addition to the availability of these funds at the university or program level, many excellent fellowship programs are available at the national level and may be applied for before and during enrollment in a graduate program. A listing of many of these programs can be found at the Council of Graduate Schools' Web site: http://www. cgsnet.org. There is a wealth of information in the "Programs" and "Awards" sections.

Assistantships and Internships

Many graduate students receive financial support through assistantships, particularly involving teaching or research duties. It is important to recognize that such appointments should not be viewed simply as employment relationships but rather should constitute an integral and important part of a student's graduate education. As such, the appointments should be accompanied by strong faculty mentoring and increasingly responsible apprenticeship experiences. The specific nature of these appointments in a given program should be considered in selecting that graduate program.

TEACHING ASSISTANTSHIPS

These usually provide a salary and full or partial tuition remission and may also provide health benefits. Unlike fellowships, scholarships, and grants, which require no service to the institution, teaching assistantships require recipients to provide the institution with a specific amount of undergraduate teaching, ideally related to the student's field of study. Some teaching assistants are limited to grading papers, compiling bibliographies, taking notes, or monitoring laboratories. At some graduate schools, teaching assistants must carry lighter course loads than regular full-time students.

RESEARCH ASSISTANTSHIPS

These are very similar to teaching assistantships in the manner in which financial assistance is provided. The difference is that recipients are given basic research assignments in their disciplines rather than teaching responsibilities. The work required is normally related to the student's field of study; in most instances, the assistantship supports the student's thesis or dissertation research.

ADMINISTRATIVE INTERNSHIPS

These are similar to assistantships in application of financial assistance funds, but the student is given an assignment on a part-time basis, usually as a special assistant with one of the university's administrative offices. The assignment may not necessarily be directly related to the recipient's discipline.

RESIDENCE HALL AND COUNSELING ASSISTANTSHIPS

These assistantships are frequently assigned to graduate students in psychology, counseling, and social work, but they may be offered to students in other disciplines, especially if the student has worked in this capacity during his or her undergraduate years. Duties can vary from being available in a dean's office for a specific number of hours for consultation with undergraduates to living in campus residences and being responsible for both counseling and administrative tasks or advising student activity groups. Residence hall assistantships often include a room and board allowance and, in some cases, tuition assistance and stipends. Contact the Housing and Student Life Office for more information.

Health Insurance

The availability and affordability of health insurance is an important issue and one that should be considered in an applicant's choice of institution and program. While often included with assistantships and fellowships, this is not always the case and, even if provided, the benefits may be limited. It is important to note that the U.S. government requires international students to have health insurance.

The GI Bill

This provides financial assistance for students who are veterans of the United States armed forces. If you are a veteran, contact your local Veterans Administration office to determine your eligibility and to get full details about benefits. There are a number of programs that offer educational benefits to current military enlistees. Some states have tuition assistance programs for members of the National Guard. Contact the VA office at the college for more information.

Federal Work-Study Program (FWS)

Employment is another way some students finance their graduate studies. The federally funded Federal Work-Study Program provides eligible students with employment opportunities, usually in public and private nonprofit organizations. Federal funds pay up to 75 percent of the wages, with the remainder paid by the employing agency. FWS is available to graduate students who demonstrate financial need. Not all schools have these funds, and some only award them to undergraduates. Each school sets its application deadline and workstudy earnings limits. Wages vary and are related to the type of work done. You must file the Free Application for Federal Student Aid (FAFSA) to be eligible for this program.

Loans

Many graduate students borrow to finance their graduate programs when other sources of assistance (which do not have to be repaid) prove insufficient. You should always read and understand the terms of any loan program before submitting your application.

FEDERAL DIRECT LOANS

Federal Direct Stafford Loans. The Federal Direct Stafford Loan Program offers 6.8 percent interest rate loans to students with the Department of Education acting as the lender.

There are two components of the Federal Stafford Loan program. Under the *subsidized* component (for loans with enrollment prior to July 1, 2012) of the program, the federal government pays the interest on the loan while you are enrolled in graduate school on at least a half-time basis, as well as during any period of deferment. Under the *unsubsidized* component of the program, you pay the interest on the loan from the day proceeds are issued. Eligibility for the federal subsidy is based on demonstrated financial need as determined by the financial aid office from the information you provide on the FAFSA. A cosigner is not required, since the loan is not based on creditworthiness.

Although *unsubsidized* Federal Direct Stafford Loans may not be as desirable as *subsidized* Federal Direct Stafford Loans from the student's perspective, they are a useful source of support for those who may not qualify for the subsidized loans or who need additional financial assistance.

Graduate students may borrow up to $20,500 per year through the Direct Stafford Loan Program, up to a cumulative maximum of $138,500, including undergraduate borrowing. This may include up to $8,500 in *subsidized* Direct Stafford Loans annually, depending on eligibility, up to a cumulative maximum of $65,500, including undergraduate borrowing. The amount of the loan borrowed through the *unsubsidized* Direct Stafford Loan Program equals the total amount of the loan (as much as $20,500) minus your eligibility for a *subsidized* Direct Loan (as much as $8,500). You may borrow up to the cost of attendance at the school in which you are enrolled or will attend, minus estimated financial assistance from other federal, state, and private sources, up to a maximum of $20,500.

Direct Stafford Graduate Loans made on or after July 1, 2006, carry a fixed interest rate of 6.8% both for in-school and in-repayment borrowers.

A fee is deducted from the loan proceeds upon disbursement. Loans with a first disbursement on or after July 1, 2010 but before July 1, 2012, have a borrower origination fee of 1 percent. For loans disbursed after July 1, 2012, these fee deductions no longer apply. The Budget Control Act of 2011, signed into law on August 2, 2011, eliminates Direct Subsidized Loan eligibility for graduate and professional students for periods of enrollment beginning on or after July 1, 2012 and terminates the authority of the Department of Education to offer most repayment incentives to Direct Loan borrowers for loans disbursed on or after July 1, 2012.

Under the *subsidized* Federal Direct Stafford Loan Program, repayment begins six months after your last date of enrollment on at least a half-time basis. Under the *unsubsidized* program, repayment of interest begins within thirty days from disbursement of the loan proceeds, and repayment of the principal begins six months after your last enrollment on at least a half-time basis. Some borrowers may choose to defer interest payments while they are in school. The accrued interest is added to the loan balance when the borrower begins repayment. There are several repayment options.

Federal Perkins Loans. The Federal Perkins Loan is available to students demonstrating financial need and is administered directly by the school. Not all schools have these funds, and some may award them to undergraduates only. Eligibility is determined from the information you provide on the FAFSA. The school will notify you of your eligibility.

Eligible graduate students may borrow up to $6,000 per year, up to a maximum of $40,000, including undergraduate borrowing (even if your previous Perkins Loans have been repaid). The interest rate for Federal Perkins Loans is 5 percent, and no interest accrues while you remain in school at least half-time. There are no guarantee, loan, or disbursement fees. Repayment begins nine months after your last date of enrollment on at least a half-time basis and may extend over a maximum of ten years with no prepayment penalty.

Federal Direct Graduate PLUS Loans. Effective July 1, 2006, graduate and professional students are eligible for Graduate PLUS loans. This program allows students to borrow up to the cost of attendance, less any other aid received. These loans have a fixed interest rate of 7.9 percent, and interest begins to accrue at the time of disbursement. The PLUS loans do involve a credit check; a PLUS borrower may obtain a loan with a cosigner if his or her credit is not good enough. Grad PLUS loans may be deferred while a student in school and for the six months following a drop below half-time enrollment. For more information, contact your college financial aid office.

Deferring Your Federal Loan Repayments. If you borrowed under the Federal Direct Stafford Loan Program, Federal Direct PLUS Loan Program, or the Federal Perkins Loan Program for previous undergraduate or graduate study, your payments may be deferred when you return to graduate school, depending on when you borrowed and under which program.

There are other deferment options available if you are temporarily unable to repay your loan. Information about these deferments is provided at your entrance and exit interviews. If you believe you are eligible for a deferment of your loan payments, you must contact your lender or loan servicer to request a deferment. The deferment must be filed prior to the time your payment is due, and it must be refiled when it expires if you remain eligible for deferment at that time.

SUPPLEMENTAL (PRIVATE) LOANS

Many lending institutions offer supplemental loan programs and other financing plans, such as the ones described here, to students seeking additional assistance in meeting their education expenses. Some loan programs target all types of graduate students; others are designed specifically for business, law, or medical students. In addition, you can use private loans not specifically designed for education to help finance your graduate degree.

If you are considering borrowing through a supplemental or private loan program, you should carefully consider the terms and be sure to "read the fine print." Check with the program sponsor for the most current terms that will be applicable to the amounts you intend to borrow for graduate study. Most supplemental loan programs for graduate study offer unsubsidized, credit-based loans. In general, a credit-ready borrower is one who has a satisfactory credit history or no credit history at all. A creditworthy borrower generally must pass a credit test to be eligible to borrow or act as a cosigner for the loan funds.

Many supplemental loan programs have minimum and maximum annual loan limits. Some offer amounts equal to the cost of attendance minus any other aid you will receive for graduate study. If you are planning to borrow for several years of graduate study, consider whether there is a cumulative or aggregate limit on the amount you may borrow. Often this cumulative or aggregate limit will include any amounts you borrowed and have not repaid for undergraduate or previous graduate study.

The combination of the annual interest rate, loan fees, and the repayment terms you choose will determine how much you will repay over time. Compare these features in combination before you decide which loan program to use. Some loans offer interest rates that are adjusted monthly, some quarterly, some annually. Some offer interest rates that are lower during the in-school, grace, and deferment periods and then increase when you begin repayment. Some programs include a loan "origination" fee, which is usually deducted from the principal amount you receive when the loan is disbursed and must be repaid along with the interest and other principal when you graduate, withdraw from school, or drop below half-time study. Sometimes the loan fees are reduced if you borrow with a qualified cosigner. Some programs allow you to defer interest and/or principal payments while you are enrolled in graduate school. Many programs allow you to capitalize your interest payments; the interest due on your loan is added to the outstanding balance of your loan, so you don't have to repay immediately, but this increases the amount you owe. Other programs allow you to pay the interest as you go, which reduces the amount you later have to repay. The private loan market is very competitive, and your financial aid office can help you evaluate these programs.

Applying for Need-Based Financial Aid

Schools that award federal and institutional financial assistance based on need will require you to complete the FAFSA and, in some cases, an institutional financial aid application.

If you are applying for federal student assistance, you **must** complete the FAFSA. A service of the U.S. Department of Education, the FAFSA is free to all applicants. Most applicants apply online at www.fafsa.ed.gov. Paper applications are available at the financial aid office of your local college.

After your FAFSA information has been processed, you will receive a Student Aid Report (SAR). If you provided an e-mail address on the

FAFSA, this will be sent to you electronically; otherwise, it will be mailed to your home address.

Follow the instructions on the SAR if you need to correct information reported on your original application. If your situation changes after you file your FAFSA, contact your financial aid officer to discuss amending your information. You can also appeal your financial aid award if you have extenuating circumstances.

If you would like more information on federal student financial aid, visit the FAFSA Web site or download the most recent version of *Funding Education Beyond High School: The Guide to Federal Student Aid* at http://studentaid.ed.gov/students/publications/student_guide/index.html. This guide is also available in Spanish.

The U.S. Department of Education also has a toll-free number for questions concerning federal student aid programs. The number is 1-800-4-FED AID (1-800-433-3243). If you are hearing impaired, call toll-free, 1-800-730-8913.

Summary

Remember that these are generalized statements about financial assistance at the graduate level. Because each institution allots its aid differently, you should communicate directly with the school and the specific department of interest to you. It is not unusual, for example, to find that an endowment vested within a specific department supports one or more fellowships. You may fit its requirements and specifications precisely.

Accreditation and Accrediting Agencies

Colleges and universities in the United States, and their individual academic and professional programs, are accredited by nongovernmental agencies concerned with monitoring the quality of education in this country. Agencies with both regional and national jurisdictions grant accreditation to institutions as a whole, while specialized bodies acting on a nationwide basis—often national professional associations— grant accreditation to departments and programs in specific fields.

Institutional and specialized accrediting agencies share the same basic concerns: the purpose an academic unit—whether university or program—has set for itself and how well it fulfills that purpose, the adequacy of its financial and other resources, the quality of its academic offerings, and the level of services it provides. Agencies that grant institutional accreditation take a broader view, of course, and examine university-wide or college-wide services with which a specialized agency may not concern itself.

Both types of agencies follow the same general procedures when considering an application for accreditation. The academic unit prepares a self-evaluation, focusing on the concerns mentioned above and usually including an assessment of both its strengths and weaknesses; a team of representatives of the accrediting body reviews this evaluation, visits the campus, and makes its own report; and finally, the accrediting body makes a decision on the application. Often, even when accreditation is granted, the agency makes a recommendation regarding how the institution or program can improve. All institutions and programs are also reviewed every few years to determine whether they continue to meet established standards; if they do not, they may lose their accreditation.

Accrediting agencies themselves are reviewed and evaluated periodically by the U.S. Department of Education and the Council for Higher Education Accreditation (CHEA). Recognized agencies adhere to certain standards and practices, and their authority in matters of accreditation is widely accepted in the educational community.

This does not mean, however, that accreditation is a simple matter, either for schools wishing to become accredited or for students deciding where to apply. Indeed, in certain fields the very meaning and methods of accreditation are the subject of a good deal of debate. For their part, those applying to graduate school should be aware of the safeguards provided by regional accreditation, especially in terms of degree acceptance and institutional longevity. Beyond this, applicants should understand the role that specialized accreditation plays in their field, as this varies considerably from one discipline to another. In certain professional fields, it is necessary to have graduated from a program that is accredited in order to be eligible for a license to practice, and in some fields the federal government also makes this a hiring requirement. In other disciplines, however, accreditation is not as essential, and there can be excellent programs that are not accredited. In fact, some programs choose not to seek accreditation, although most do.

Institutions and programs that present themselves for accreditation are sometimes granted the status of candidate for accreditation, or what is known as "preaccreditation." This may happen, for example, when an academic unit is too new to have met all the requirements for accreditation. Such status signifies initial recognition and indicates that the school or program in question is working to fulfill all requirements; it does not, however, guarantee that accreditation will be granted.

Institutional Accrediting Agencies—Regional

MIDDLE STATES ASSOCIATION OF COLLEGES AND SCHOOLS
Accredits institutions in Delaware, District of Columbia, Maryland, New Jersey, New York, Pennsylvania, Puerto Rico, and the Virgin Islands.
Dr. Elizabeth Sibolski, President
Middle States Commission on Higher Education
3624 Market Street, Second Floor West
Philadelphia, Pennsylvania 19104
Phone: 267-284-5000
Fax: 215-662-5501
E-mail: info@msche.org
Web: www.msche.org

NEW ENGLAND ASSOCIATION OF SCHOOLS AND COLLEGES
Accredits institutions in Connecticut, Maine, Massachusetts, New Hampshire, Rhode Island, and Vermont.
Barbara E. Brittingham, Director
Commission on Institutions of Higher Education
209 Burlington Road, Suite 201
Bedford, Massachusetts 01730-1433
Phone: 781-271-0022
Fax: 781-271-0950
E-mail: kwillis@neasc.org
Web: http://cihe.neasc.org

NORTH CENTRAL ASSOCIATION OF COLLEGES AND SCHOOLS
Accredits institutions in Arizona, Arkansas, Colorado, Illinois, Indiana, Iowa, Kansas, Michigan, Minnesota, Missouri, Nebraska, New Mexico, North Dakota, Ohio, Oklahoma, South Dakota, West Virginia, Wisconsin, and Wyoming.
Dr. Sylvia Manning, President
The Higher Learning Commission
230 South LaSalle Street, Suite 7-500
Chicago, Illinois 60604-1413
Phone: 312-263-0456
Fax: 312-263-7462
E-mail: smanning@hlcommission.org
Web: www.ncahlc.org

NORTHWEST COMMISSION ON COLLEGES AND UNIVERSITIES
Accredits institutions in Alaska, Idaho, Montana, Nevada, Oregon, Utah, and Washington.
Dr. Sandra E. Elman, President
8060 165th Avenue, NE, Suite 100
Redmond, Washington 98052
Phone: 425-558-4224
Fax: 425-376-0596
E-mail: selman@nwccu.org
Web: www.nwccu.org

SOUTHERN ASSOCIATION OF COLLEGES AND SCHOOLS
Accredits institutions in Alabama, Florida, Georgia, Kentucky, Louisiana, Mississippi, North Carolina, South Carolina, Tennessee, Texas, and Virginia.
Belle S. Wheelan, President
Commission on Colleges
1866 Southern Lane
Decatur, Georgia 30033-4097
Phone: 404-679-4500
Fax: 404-679-4558
E-mail: questions@sacscoc.org
Web: www.sacscoc.org

WESTERN ASSOCIATION OF SCHOOLS AND COLLEGES
Accredits institutions in California, Guam, and Hawaii.
Ralph A. Wolff, President and Executive Director
Accrediting Commission for Senior Colleges and Universities
985 Atlantic Avenue, Suite 100
Alameda, California 94501
Phone: 510-748-9001
Fax: 510-748-9797
E-mail: wascsr@wascsenior.org
Web: www.wascweb.org/org

Institutional Accrediting Agencies—Other

ACCREDITING COUNCIL FOR INDEPENDENT COLLEGES AND SCHOOLS
Albert C. Gray, Ph.D., Executive Director and CEO
750 First Street, NE, Suite 980
Washington, DC 20002-4241
Phone: 202-336-6780
Fax: 202-842-2593
E-mail: info@acics.org
Web: www.acics.org

DISTANCE EDUCATION AND TRAINING COUNCIL (DETC)
Accrediting Commission
Michael P. Lambert, Executive Director
1601 18th Street, NW, Suite 2
Washington, DC 20009
Phone: 202-234-5100
Fax: 202-332-1386
E-mail: Brianna@detc.org
Web: www.detc.org

Specialized Accrediting Agencies

ACUPUNCTURE AND ORIENTAL MEDICINE
William W. Goding, M.Ed., RRT, Interim Executive Director
Accreditation Commission for Acupuncture and Oriental Medicine
14502 Greenview Drive, Suite 300B
Laurel, Maryland 20708
Phone: 301-313-0855
Fax: 301-313-0912
E-mail: coordinator@acaom.org
Web: www.acaom.org

ART AND DESIGN
Samuel Hope, Executive Director
Karen P. Moynahan, Associate Director
National Association of Schools of Art and Design (NASAD)
Commission on Accreditation
11250 Roger Bacon Drive, Suite 21
Reston, Virginia 20190-5243
Phone: 703-437-0700
Fax: 703-437-6312
E-mail: info@arts-accredit.org
Web: http://nasad.arts-accredit.org/

BUSINESS
Jerry Trapnell, Executive Vice President/Chief Accreditation Officer
AACSB International—The Association to Advance Collegiate Schools of Business
777 South Harbour Island Boulevard, Suite 750
Tampa, Florida 33602
Phone: 813-769-6500
Fax: 813-769-6559
E-mail: jerryt@aacsb.edu
Web: www.aacsb.edu

CHIROPRACTIC
S. Ray Bennett, Director of Accreditation Services
Council on Chiropractic Education (CCE)
Commission on Accreditation
8049 North 85th Way
Scottsdale, Arizona 85258-4321
Phone: 480-443-8877
Fax: 480-483-7333
E-mail: cce@cce-usa.org
Web: www.cce-usa.org

CLINICAL LABORATORY SCIENCES
Dianne M. Cearlock, Ph.D., Chief Executive Officer
National Accrediting Agency for Clinical Laboratory Sciences
5600 North River Road, Suite 720
Rosemont, Illinois 60018-5119
Phone: 773-714-8880
Fax: 773-714-8886
E-mail: info@naacls.org
Web: www.naacls.org

CLINICAL PASTORAL EDUCATION
Deryck Durston, Interim Executive Director
Association for Clinical Pastoral Education, Inc.
1549 Claremont Road, Suite 103
Decatur, Georgia 30033-4611
Phone: 404-320-1472
Fax: 404-320-0849
E-mail: acpe@acpe.edu
Web: www.acpe.edu

DANCE
Samuel Hope, Executive Director
Karen P. Moynahan, Associate Director
National Association of Schools of Dance (NASD)
Commission on Accreditation
11250 Roger Bacon Drive, Suite 21
Reston, Virginia 20190-5248
Phone: 703-437-0700
Fax: 703-437-6312
E-mail: info@arts-accredit.org
Web: http://nasd.arts-accredit.org

DENTISTRY
Anthony Ziebert, Director
Commission on Dental Accreditation
American Dental Association
211 East Chicago Avenue, Suite 1900
Chicago, Illinois 60611
Phone: 312-440-4643
E-mail: accreditation@ada.org
Web: www.ada.org

DIETETICS
Ulric K. Chung, Ph.D., Executive Director
American Dietetic Association
Commission on Accreditation for Dietetics Education (CADE-ADA)
120 South Riverside Plaza, Suite 2000
Chicago, Illinois 60606-6995
Phone: 800-877-1600
Fax: 312-899-4817
E-mail: cade@eatright.org
Web: www.eatright.org/cade

ENGINEERING
Michael Milligan, Ph.D., PE, Executive Director
Accreditation Board for Engineering and Technology, Inc. (ABET)
111 Market Place, Suite 1050
Baltimore, Maryland 21202
Phone: 410-347-7700
Fax: 410-625-2238
E-mail: accreditation@abet.org
Web: www.abet.org

FORESTRY
Carol L. Redelsheimer
Director of Science and Education
5400 Grosvenor Lane
Bethesda, Maryland 20814-2198
Phone: 301-897-8720 Ext. 123
Fax: 301-897-3690
E-mail: redelsheimerc@safnet.org
Web: www.safnet.org

HEALTH SERVICES ADMINISTRATION
Commission on Accreditation of Healthcare Management Education (CAHME)
John S. Lloyd, President and CEO
2111 Wilson Boulevard, Suite 700
Arlington, Virginia 22201
Phone: 703-351-5010
Fax: 703-991-5989
E-mail: info@cahme.org
Web: www.cahme.org

INTERIOR DESIGN
Holly Mattson, Executive Director
Council for Interior Design Accreditation
206 Grandview Avenue, Suite 350
Grand Rapids, Michigan 49503-4014
Phone: 616-458-0400
Fax: 616-458-0460
E-mail: info@accredit-id.org
Web: www.accredit-id.org

JOURNALISM AND MASS COMMUNICATIONS
Susanne Shaw, Executive Director
Accrediting Council on Education in Journalism and Mass Communications (ACEJMC)
School of Journalism
Stauffer-Flint Hall
University of Kansas
1435 Jayhawk Boulevard
Lawrence, Kansas 66045-7575
Phone: 785-864-3973
Fax: 785-864-5225
E-mail: sshaw@ku.edu
Web: www2.ku.edu/~acejmc

LANDSCAPE ARCHITECTURE
Ronald C. Leighton, Executive Director
Landscape Architectural Accreditation Board (LAAB)
American Society of Landscape Architects (ASLA)
636 Eye Street, NW
Washington, DC 20001-3736
Phone: 202-898-2444
Fax: 202-898-1185
E-mail: info@asla.org
Web: www.asla.org

LAW
Hulett H. Askew, Consultant on Legal Education
American Bar Association
321 North Clark Street, 21st Floor
Chicago, Illinois 60654
Phone: 312-988-6738
Fax: 312-988-5681
E-mail: legaled@americanbar.org
Web: www.abanet.org/legaled/

LIBRARY
Karen O'Brien, Director
Office for Accreditation
American Library Association
50 East Huron Street
Chicago, Illinois 60611
Phone: 800-545-2433 Ext. 2432
Fax: 312-280-2433
E-mail: accred@ala.org
Web: www.ala.org/accreditation/

MARRIAGE AND FAMILY THERAPY
Tanya A. Tamarkin, Director of Educational Affairs
Commission on Accreditation for Marriage and Family Therapy Education
American Association for Marriage and Family Therapy
112 South Alfred Street
Alexandria, Virginia 22314-3061
Phone: 703-838-9808
Fax: 703-838-9805
E-mail: coamfte@aamft.org
Web: www.aamft.org

MEDICAL ILLUSTRATION
Commission on Accreditation of Allied Health Education Programs (CAAHEP)
Kathleen Megivern, Executive Director
1361 Park Street
Clearwater, Florida 33756
Phone: 727-210-2350
Fax: 727-210-2354
E-mail: mail@caahep.org
Web: www.caahep.org

MEDICINE
Liaison Committee on Medical Education (LCME)
In odd-numbered years beginning each July 1, contact:
Barbara Barzansky, Ph.D., LCME Secretary
American Medical Association
Council on Medical Education
515 North State Street
Chicago, Illinois 60654
Phone: 312-464-4933
Fax: 312-464-5830
E-mail: cme@aamc.org
Web: www.ama-assn.org

In even-numbered years beginning each July 1, contact:
Dan Hunt, M.D., LCME Secretary
Association of American Medical Colleges
2450 N Street, NW Washington, DC 20037
Phone: 202-828-0596
Fax: 202-828-1125
E-mail: dhunt@aamc.org
Web: www.lcme.org

MUSIC
Samuel Hope, Executive Director
Karen P. Moynahan, Associate Director
National Association of Schools of Music (NASM)
Commission on Accreditation
11250 Roger Bacon Drive, Suite 21
Reston, Virginia 20190-5248
Phone: 703-437-0700
Fax: 703-437-6312
E-mail: info@arts-accredit.org
Web: http://nasm.arts-accredit.org/

NATUROPATHIC MEDICINE
Daniel Seitz, J.D., Ed.D., Executive Director
Council on Naturopathic Medical Education
P.O. Box 178
Great Barrington, Massachusetts 01230
Phone: 413-528-8877
Fax: 413-528-8880
E-mail: council@cnme.org
Web: www.cnme.org

NURSE ANESTHESIA
Francis R. Gerbasi, Executive Director
Council on Accreditation of Nurse Anesthesia Educational Programs
American Association of Nurse Anesthetists
222 South Prospect Avenue, Suite 304
Park Ridge, Illinois 60068
Phone: 847-692-7050 Ext. 1154
Fax: 847-692-6968
E-mail: fgerbasi@aana.com
Web: http://home.coa.us.com

NURSE EDUCATION
Jennifer L. Butlin, Director
Commission on Collegiate Nursing Education (CCNE)
One Dupont Circle, NW, Suite 530
Washington, DC 20036-1120
Phone: 202-887-6791
Fax: 202-887-8476
E-mail: jbutlin@aacn.nche.edu
Web: www.aacn.nche.edu/accreditation

NURSE MIDWIFERY
Lorrie Kaplan, Executive Director
Accreditation Commission for Midwifery Education
American College of Nurse-Midwives
Nurse-Midwifery Program
8403 Colesville Road, Suite 1550
Silver Spring, Maryland 20910
Phone: 240-485-1800
Fax: 240-485-1818
E-mail: lkaplan@acnm.org
Web: www.midwife.org/acme.cfm

Jo Anne Myers-Ciecko, MPH, Executive Director
Midwifery Education Accreditation Council
P.O. Box 984
La Conner, Washington 98257
Phone: 360-466-2080
Fax: 480-907-2936
E-mail: info@meacschools.org
Web: www.meacschools.org

NURSE PRACTITIONER
Gay Johnson, Acting CEO
National Association of Nurse Practitioners in Women's Health
Council on Accreditation
505 C Street, NE Washington, DC 20002
Phone: 202-543-9693 Ext. 1
Fax: 202-543-9858
E-mail: info@npwh.org
Web: www.npwh.org

NURSING
Sharon J. Tanner, Ed.D., RN, Executive Director
National League for Nursing Accrediting Commission (NLNAC)
3343 Peachtree Road, NE, Suite 500
Atlanta, Georgia 30326
Phone: 404-975-5000
Fax: 404-975-5020
E-mail: nlnac@nlnac.org
Web: www.nlnac.org

OCCUPATIONAL THERAPY
Neil Harvison, Ph.D., OTR/L
Director of Accreditation and Academic Affairs
The American Occupational Therapy Association
4720 Montgomery Lane
P.O. Box 31220
Bethesda, Maryland 20824-1220
Phone: 301-652-2682 Ext. 2912
Fax: 301-652-7711
E-mail: accred@aota.org
Web: www.aota.org

OPTOMETRY
Joyce L. Urbeck, Administrative Director
Accreditation Council on Optometric Education
American Optometric Association (AOA)
243 North Lindbergh Boulevard
St. Louis, Missouri 63141
Phone: 314-991-4000 Ext. 246
Fax: 314-991-4101
E-mail: acoe@aoa.org
Web: www.theacoe.org

OSTEOPATHIC MEDICINE
Konrad C. Miskowicz-Retz, Ph.D., CAE
Director, Department of Education
Commission on Osteopathic College Accreditation
American Osteopathic Association
142 East Ontario Street
Chicago, Illinois 60611
Phone: 312-202-8048
Fax: 312-202-8202
E-mail: kretz@osteopathic.org
Web: www.osteopathic.org

PHARMACY
Peter H. Vlasses, Executive Director
Accreditation Council for Pharmacy Education
20 North Clark Street, Suite 2500
Chicago, Illinois 60602-5109
Phone: 312-664-3575
Fax: 312-664-4652
E-mail: csinfo@acpe-accredit.org
Web: www.acpe-accredit.org

PHYSICAL THERAPY
Mary Jane Harris, Director
Commission on Accreditation in Physical Therapy Education (CAPTE)
American Physical Therapy Association (APTA)
1111 North Fairfax Street
Alexandria, Virginia 22314
Phone: 703-706-3245
Fax: 703-706-3387
E-mail: accreditation@apta.org
Web: www.capteonline.org

PHYSICIAN ASSISTANT STUDIES
John E. McCarty, Executive Director
Accreditation Review Commission on Education for the Physician Assistant, Inc. (ARC-PA)
12000 Findley Road, Suite 150
Johns Creek, Georgia 30097
Phone: 770-476-1224
Fax: 770-476-1738
E-mail: arc-pa@arc-pa.org
Web: www.arc-pa.org

PLANNING
Shonagh Merits, Executive Director
American Institute of Certified Planners/Association of Collegiate Schools of Planning/American Planning Association
Planning Accreditation Board (PAB)
53 W. Jackson Boulevard, Suite 1315
Chicago, Illinois 60604
Phone: 312-334-1271
Fax: 312-334-1273
E-mail: smerits@planningaccreditationboard.org
Web: www.planningaccreditationboard.org

PODIATRIC MEDICINE
Alan R. Tinkleman, Executive Director
Council on Podiatric Medical Education (CPME)
American Podiatric Medical Association
9312 Old Georgetown Road
Bethesda, Maryland 20814-1621
Phone: 301-571-9200
Fax: 301-571-4903
E-mail: artinkleman@apma.org
Web: www.cpme.org

PSYCHOLOGY AND COUNSELING
Susan Zlotlow, Executive Director
Office of Program Consultation and Accreditation
American Psychological Association
750 First Street, NE Washington, DC 20002-4242
Phone: 202-336-5979
Fax: 202-336-5978
E-mail: apaaccred@apa.org
Web: www.apa.org/ed/accreditation

Carol L. Bobby, Executive Director
Council for Accreditation of Counseling and Related Educational Programs (CACREP)
1001 North Fairfax Street, Suite 510
Alexandria, Virginia 22314
Phone: 703-535-5990
Fax: 703-739-6209
E-mail: cacrep@cacrep.org
Web: www.cacrep.org

PUBLIC AFFAIRS AND ADMINISTRATION
Crystal Calarusse, Executive Director
Commission on Peer Review and Accreditation
National Association of Schools of Public Affairs and Administration
1029 Vermont Avenue, NW, Suite 1100
Washington, DC 20005
Phone: 202-628-8965
Fax: 202-626-4978
E-mail: copra@naspaa.org
Web: www.naspaa.org

PUBLIC HEALTH
Laura Rasar King, M.P.H., CHES, Executive Director
Council on Education for Public Health
800 Eye Street, NW, Suite 202
Washington, DC 20001-3710
Phone: 202-789-1050
Fax: 202-789-1895
E-mail: Lking@ceph.org
Web: www.ceph.org

REHABILITATION EDUCATION
Dr. Tom Evenson, Executive Director
Council on Rehabilitation Education (CORE)
Commission on Standards and Accreditation
1699 Woodfield Road, Suite 300
Schaumburg, Illinois 60173
Phone: 847-944-1345
Fax: 847-944-1324
E-mail: evenson@unt.edu
Web: www.core-rehab.org

SOCIAL WORK
Stephen M. Holloway, Director of Accreditation
Commission on Accreditation
Council on Social Work Education
1701 Duke Street, Suite 200
Alexandria, Virginia 22314
Phone: 703-683-8080
Fax: 703-683-8099
E-mail: sholloway@cswe.org
Web: www.cswe.org

SPEECH-LANGUAGE PATHOLOGY AND AUDIOLOGY
Patrima L. Tice, Director of Credentialing
American Speech-Language-Hearing Association
Council on Academic Accreditation in Audiology and SpeechLanguage Pathology
2200 Research Boulevard
Rockville, Maryland 20850-3289
Phone: 301-296-5796
Fax: 301-296-8750
E-mail: ptice@asha.org
Web: www.asha.org/academic/accreditation/default.htm

TECHNOLOGY
Michale S. McComis, Ed.D., Executive Director
Accrediting Commission of Career Schools and Colleges
2101 Wilson Boulevard, Suite 302
Arlington, Virginia 22201
Phone: 703-247-4212
Fax: 703-247-4533
E-mail: mccomis@accsc.org
Web: www.accsc.org

TEACHER EDUCATION
James G. Cibulka, President
National Council for Accreditation of Teacher Education
2010 Massachusetts Avenue, NW, Suite 500
Washington, DC 20036-1023
Phone: 202-466-7496
Fax: 202-296-6620
E-mail: ncate@ncate.org
Web: www.ncate.org

Mark LaCelle-Peterson, President
Teacher Education Accreditation Council (TEAC)
Accreditation Committee
One Dupont Circle, Suite 320
Washington, DC 20036-0110
Phone: 202-831-0400
Fax: 202-831-3013
E-mail: teac@teac.org
Web: www.teac.org

THEATER
Samuel Hope, Executive Director
Karen P. Moynahan, Associate Director
National Association of Schools of Theatre Commission on Accreditation
11250 Roger Bacon Drive, Suite 21
Reston, Virginia 20190
Phone: 703-437-0700
Fax: 703-437-6312
E-mail: info@arts-accredit.org
Web: http://nast.arts-accredit.org/

THEOLOGY

Bernard Fryshman, Executive Vice President
Association of Advanced Rabbinical and Talmudic Schools (AARTS)
Accreditation Commission
11 Broadway, Suite 405
New York, New York 10004
Phone: 212-363-1991
Fax: 212-533-5335
E-mail: BFryshman@nyit.edu

Daniel O. Aleshire, Executive Director
Association of Theological Schools in the United States and Canada (ATS)
Commission on Accrediting
10 Summit Park Drive
Pittsburgh, Pennsylvania 15275-1110
Phone: 412-788-6505
Fax: 412-788-6510
E-mail: ats@ats.edu
Web: www.ats.edu

Paul Boatner, President
Transnational Association of Christian Colleges and Schools (TRACS)
Accreditation Commission
15935 Forest Road
Forest, Virginia 24551
Phone: 434-525-9539
Fax: 434-525-9538
E-mail: info@tracs.org
Web: www.tracs.org

VETERINARY MEDICINE

Dave Granstrom, Executive Director
Education and Research Division
American Veterinary Medical Association (AVMA)
Council on Education
1931 North Meacham Road, Suite 100
Schaumburg, Illinois 60173
Phone: 847-925-8070 Ext. 6674
Fax: 847-925-9329
E-mail: info@avma.org
Web: www.avma.org

How to Use These Guides

As you identify the particular programs and institutions that interest you, you can use both the ***Graduate & Professional Programs: An Overview*** volume and the specialized volumes in the series to obtain detailed information.

- ***Graduate Programs in the Physical Sciences, Mathematics, Agricultural Sciences, the Environment & Natural Resources***
- ***Graduate Programs in Engineering & Applied Sciences***
- ***Graduate Programs the Humanities, Arts & Social Sciences***
- ***Graduate Programs in the Biological/Biomedical Sciences & Health-Related Professions***
- ***Graduate Programs in Business, Education, Information Studies, Law & Social Work***

Each of the specialized volumes in the series is divided into sections that contain one or more directories devoted to programs in a particular field. If you do not find a directory devoted to your field of interest in a specific volume, consult "Directories and Subject Areas" (located at the end of each volume). After you have identified the correct volume, consult the "Directories and Subject Areas in This Book" index, which shows (as does the more general directory) what directories cover subjects not specifically named in a directory or section title.

Each of the specialized volumes in the series has a number of general directories. These directories have entries for the largest unit at an institution granting graduate degrees in that field. For example, the general Engineering and Applied Sciences directory in the ***Graduate Programs in Engineering & Applied Sciences*** volume consists of **Profiles** for colleges, schools, and departments of engineering and applied sciences.

General directories are followed by other directories, or sections, that give more detailed information about programs in particular areas of the general field that has been covered. The general Engineering and Applied Sciences directory, in the previous example, is followed by nineteen sections with directories in specific areas of engineering, such as Chemical Engineering, Industrial/Management Engineering, and Mechanical Engineering.

Because of the broad nature of many fields, any system of organization is bound to involve a certain amount of overlap. Environmental studies, for example, is a field whose various aspects are studied in several types of departments and schools. Readers interested in such studies will find information on relevant programs in the ***Graduate Programs in the Biological/Biomedical Sciences & Health-Related Professions*** volume under Ecology and Environmental Biology and Environmental and Occupational Health; in the ***Graduate Programs in the Physical Sciences, Mathematics, Agricultural Sciences, the Environment & Natural Resources*** volume under Environmental Management and Policy and Natural Resources; and in the ***Graduate Programs in Engineering & Applied Sciences*** volume under Energy Management and Policy and Environmental Engineering. To help you find all of the programs of interest to you, the introduction to each section within the specialized volumes includes, if applicable, a paragraph suggesting other sections and directories with information on related areas of study.

Directory of Institutions with Programs in Business, Education, Information Studies, Law & Social Work

This directory lists institutions in alphabetical order and includes beneath each name the academic fields in which each institution offers graduate programs. The degree level in each field is also indicated, provided that the institution has supplied that information in response to Peterson's Annual Survey of Graduate and Professional Institutions.

An M indicates that a master's degree program is offered; a D indicates that a doctoral degree program is offered; a P indicates that the first professional degree is offered; an O signifies that other advanced degrees (e.g., certificates or specialist degrees) are offered; and an * (asterisk) indicates that a **Close-Up** and/or **Display** is located in this volume. See the index, "Close-Ups and Displays," for the specific page number.

Profiles of Academic and Professional Programs in the Specialized Volumes

Each section of **Profiles** has a table of contents that lists the Program Directories, **Displays**, and **Close-Ups.** Program Directories consist of the **Profiles** of programs in the relevant fields, with **Displays** following if programs have chosen to include them. **Close-Ups,** which are more individualized statements, again if programs have chosen to submit them, are also listed.

The **Profiles** found in the 500 directories in the specialized volumes provide basic data about the graduate units in capsule form for quick reference. To make these directories as useful as possible, **Profiles** are generally listed for an institution's smallest academic unit within a subject area. In other words, if an institution has a College of Liberal Arts that administers many related programs, the **Profile** for the individual program (e.g., Program in History), not the entire College, appears in the directory.

There are some programs that do not fit into any current directory and are not given individual **Profiles**. The directory structure is reviewed annually in order to keep this number to a minimum and to accommodate major trends in graduate education.

The following outline describes the **Profile** information found in the guides and explains how best to use that information. Any item that does not apply to or was not provided by a graduate unit is omitted from its listing. The format of the **Profiles** is constant, making it easy to compare one institution with another and one program with another.

Identifying Information. The institution's name, in boldface type, is followed by a complete listing of the administrative structure for that field of study. (For example, University of Akron, Buchtel College of Arts and Sciences, Department of Theoretical and Applied Mathematics, Program in Mathematics.) The last unit listed is the one to which all information in the **Profile** pertains. The institution's city, state, and zip code follow.

Offerings. Each field of study offered by the unit is listed with all postbaccalaureate degrees awarded. Degrees that are not preceded by a specific concentration are awarded in the general field listed in the unit name. Frequently, fields of study are broken down into subspecializations, and those appear following the degrees awarded; for example, "Offerings in secondary education (M.Ed.), including English education, mathematics education, science education." Students enrolled in the M.Ed. program would be able to specialize in any of the three fields mentioned.

Professional Accreditation. Some **Profiles** indicate whether a program is professionally accredited. Because it is possible for a program to receive or lose professional accreditation at any time, students entering fields in which accreditation is important to a career should verify the status of programs by contacting either the chairperson or the appropriate accrediting association.

Jointly Offered Degrees. Explanatory statements concerning programs that are offered in cooperation with other institutions are included in the list of degrees offered. This occurs most commonly on a regional basis (for example, two state universities offering a cooperative Ph.D. in special education) or where the specialized nature of the institutions encourages joint efforts (a J.D./M.B.A. offered by a law school at an institution with no formal business programs and an institution with a business school but lacking a law school). Only programs that are truly cooperative are listed; those involving only limited course work at another institution are not. Interested students should contact the heads of such units for further information.

Part-Time and Evening/Weekend Programs. When information regarding the availability of part-time or evening/weekend study appears in the **Profile**, it means that students are able to earn a degree exclusively through such study.

Postbaccalaureate Distance Learning Degrees. A post-baccalaureate distance learning degree program signifies that course requirements can be fulfilled with minimal or no on-campus study.

Faculty. Figures on the number of faculty members actively involved with graduate students through teaching or research are separated into full- and part-time as well as men and women whenever the information has been supplied.

Students. Figures for the number of students enrolled in graduate and professional programs pertain to the semester of highest enrollment from the 2011–12 academic year. These figures are broken down into full- and part-time and men and women whenever the data have been supplied. Information on the number of matriculated students enrolled in the unit who are members of a minority group or are international students appears here. The average age of the matriculated students is followed by the number of applicants, the percentage accepted, and the number enrolled for fall 2011.

Degrees Awarded. The number of degrees awarded in the calendar year is listed. Many doctoral programs offer a terminal master's degree if students leave the program after completing only part of the requirements for a doctoral degree; that is indicated here. All degrees are classified into one of four types: master's, doctoral, first professional, and other advanced degrees. A unit may award one or several degrees at a given level; however, the data are only collected by type and may therefore represent several different degree programs.

Degree Requirements. The information in this section is also broken down by type of degree, and all information for a degree level pertains to all degrees of that type unless otherwise specified. Degree requirements are collected in a simplified form to provide some very basic information on the nature of the program and on foreign language, thesis or dissertation, comprehensive exam, and registration requirements. Many units also provide a short list of additional requirements, such as fieldwork or an internship. For complete information on graduation requirements, contact the graduate school or program directly.

Entrance Requirements. Entrance requirements are broken down into the four degree levels of master's, doctoral, first professional, and other advanced degrees. Within each level, information may be provided in two basic categories: entrance exams and other requirements. The entrance exams are identified by the standard acronyms used by the testing agencies, unless they are not well known. Other entrance requirements are quite varied, but they often contain an undergraduate or graduate grade point average (GPA). Unless otherwise stated, the GPA is calculated on a 4.0 scale and is listed as a minimum required for admission. Additional exam requirements/recommendations for international students may be listed here. Application deadlines for domestic and international students, the application fee, and whether electronic applications are accepted may be listed here. Note that the deadline should be used for reference only; these dates are subject to change, and students interested in applying should always contact the graduate unit directly about application procedures and deadlines.

Expenses. The typical cost of study for the 2011–12 academic year is given in two basic categories: tuition and fees. Cost of study may be quite complex at a graduate institution. There are often sliding scales for part-time study, a different cost for first-year students, and other variables that make it impossible to completely cover the cost of study for each graduate program. To provide the most usable information, figures are given for full-time study for a full year where available and for part-time study in terms of a per-unit rate (per credit, per semester hour, etc.). Occasionally, variances may be noted in tuition and fees for reasons such as the type of program, whether courses are taken during the day or evening, whether courses are at the master's or doctoral level, or other institution-specific reasons. Expenses are usually subject to change; for exact costs at any given time, contact your chosen schools and programs directly. Keep in mind that the tuition of Canadian institutions is usually given in Canadian dollars.

Financial Support. This section contains data on the number of awards administered by the institution and given to graduate students during the 2011–12 academic year. The first figure given represents the total number of students receiving financial support enrolled in that unit. If the unit has provided information on graduate appointments, these are broken down into three major categories: fellowships give money to graduate students to cover the cost of study and living expenses and are not based on a work obligation or research commitment, research assistantships provide stipends to graduate students for assistance in a formal research project with a faculty member, and teaching assistantships provide stipends to graduate students for teaching or for assisting faculty members in teaching undergraduate classes. Within each category, figures are given for the total number of awards, the average yearly amount per award, and whether full or partial tuition reimbursements are awarded. In addition to graduate appointments, the availability of several other financial aid sources is covered in this section. Tuition waivers are routinely part of a graduate appointment, but units sometimes waive part or all of a student's tuition even if a graduate appointment is not available. Federal WorkStudy is made available to students who demonstrate need and meet the federal guidelines; this form of aid normally includes 10 or more hours of work per week in an office of the institution. Institutionally sponsored loans are low-interest loans available to graduate students to cover both educational and living expenses. Career-related internships or fieldwork offer money to students who are participating in a formal off-campus research project or practicum. Grants, scholarships, traineeships, unspecified assistantships, and other awards may also be noted. The availability of financial support to part-time students is also indicated here.

Some programs list the financial aid application deadline and the forms that need to be completed for students to be eligible for financial awards. There are two forms: FAFSA, the Free Application for Federal Student Aid, which is required for federal aid, and the CSS PROFILE®.

Faculty Research. Each unit has the opportunity to list several keyword phrases describing the current research involving faculty members and graduate students. Space limitations prevent the unit from listing complete information on all research programs. The total expenditure for funded research from the previous academic year may also be included.

Unit Head and Application Contact. The head of the graduate program for each unit is listed with academic title and telephone and fax numbers and e-mail address if available. In addition to the unit head, many graduate programs list a separate contact for application and admission information, which follows the listing for the unit head. If no unit head or application contact is given, you should contact the overall institution for information on graduate admissions.

Displays and Close-Ups

The **Displays** and **Close-Ups** are supplementary insertions submitted by deans, chairs, and other administrators who wish to offer an additional, more individualized statement to readers. A number of graduate school and program administrators have attached a **Display** ad near the **Profile** listing. Here you will find information that an institution or program wants to emphasize. The **Close-Ups** are by their very nature more expansive and flexible than the **Profiles**, and the administrators who have written them may emphasize different aspects of their programs. All of the **Close-Ups** are organized in the same way (with the exception of a few that describe research and training opportunities instead of degree programs), and in each one you will find information on the same basic topics, such as programs of study, research facilities, tuition and fees, financial aid, and application procedures. If an institution or program has submitted a **Close-Up**, a boldface cross-reference appears below its **Profile**. As with the **Displays**, all of the **Close-Ups** in the guides have been submitted by choice; the absence of a **Display** or **Close-Up** does not reflect any type of editorial judgment on the part of Peterson's, and their presence in the guides should not be taken as an indication of status, quality, or approval. Statements regarding a university's objectives and accomplishments are a reflection of its own beliefs and are not the opinions of the Peterson's editors.

Appendixes

This section contains two appendixes. The first, "Institutional Changes Since the 2012 Edition," lists institutions that have closed, merged, or changed their name or status since the last edition of the guides. The second, "Abbreviations Used in the Guides," gives abbreviations of degree names, along with what those abbreviations stand for. These appendixes are identical in all six volumes of ***Peterson's Graduate and Professional Programs***.

Indexes

There are three indexes presented here. The first index, "Close-Ups and Displays," gives page references for all programs that have chosen to place **Close-Ups** and **Displays** in this volume. It is arranged alphabetically by institution; within institutions, the arrangement is alphabetical by subject area. It is not an index to all programs in the book's directories of **Profiles**; readers must refer to the directories themselves for **Profile** information on programs that have not submitted the additional, more individualized statements. The second index, "Directories and Subject Areas in Other Books in This Series", gives book references for the directories in the specialized volumes and also includes cross-references for subject area names not used in the directory structure, for example, "Computing Technology (see Computer Science)." The third index, "Directories and Subject Areas in This Book," gives page references for the directories in this volume and cross-references for subject area names not used in this volume's directory structure.

Data Collection Procedures

The information published in the directories and **Profiles** of all the books is collected through Peterson's Annual Survey of Graduate and Professional Institutions. The survey is sent each spring to nearly 2,400 institutions offering postbaccalaureate degree programs, including accredited institutions in the United States, U.S. territories, and Canada and those institutions outside the United States that are accredited by U.S. accrediting bodies. Deans and other administrators complete these surveys, providing information on programs in the 500 academic and professional fields covered in the guides as well as overall institutional information. While every effort has been made to ensure the accuracy and completeness of the data, information is sometimes unavailable or changes occur after publication deadlines. All usable information received in time for publication has been included. The omission of any particular item from a directory or **Profile** signifies either that the item is not applicable to the institution or program or that information was not available. **Profiles** of programs scheduled to begin during the 2012–13 academic year cannot, obviously, include statistics on enrollment or, in many cases, the number of faculty members. If no usable data were submitted by an institution, its name, address, and program name appear in order to indicate the availability of graduate work.

Criteria for Inclusion in This Guide

To be included in this guide, an institution must have full accreditation or be a candidate for accreditation (preaccreditation) status by an institutional or specialized accrediting body recognized by the U.S. Department of Education or the Council for Higher Education Accreditation (CHEA). Institutional accrediting bodies, which review each institution as a whole, include the six regional associations of schools and colleges (Middle States, New England, North Central, Northwest, Southern, and Western), each of which is responsible for a specified portion of the United States and its territories. Other institutional accrediting bodies are national in scope and accredit specific kinds of institutions (e.g., Bible colleges, independent colleges, and rabbinical and Talmudic schools). Program registration by the New York State Board of Regents is considered to be the equivalent of institutional accreditation, since the board requires that all programs offered by an institution meet its standards before recognition is granted. A Canadian institution must be chartered and authorized to grant degrees by the provincial government, affiliated with a chartered institution, or accredited by a recognized U.S. accrediting body. This guide also includes institutions outside the United States that are accredited by these U.S. accrediting bodies. There are recognized specialized or professional accrediting bodies in more than fifty different fields, each of which is authorized to accredit institutions or specific programs in its particular field. For specialized institutions that offer programs in one field only, we designate this to be the equivalent of institutional accreditation. A full explanation of the accrediting process and complete information on recognized institutional (regional and national) and specialized accrediting bodies can be found online at www.chea.org or at www.ed.gov/admins/finaid/accred/index.html.

NOTICE: Certain portions of or information contained in this book have been submitted and paid for by the educational institution identified, and such institutions take full responsibility for the accuracy, timeliness, completeness and functionality of such contents. Such portions or information include (i) each display ad that comprises a half page of information covering a single educational institution or program and (ii) each two-page description or Close-Up of a graduate school or program that appear in the different sections of this guide. The "Close-Ups and Displays" are listed in various sections throughout the book.

DIRECTORY OF INSTITUTIONS WITH PROGRAMS IN BUSINESS, EDUCATION, INFORMATION STUDIES, LAW & SOCIAL WORK

ABILENE CHRISTIAN UNIVERSITY
Accounting M
Curriculum and Instruction M
Education—General M,O
Educational Leadership and Administration M,O
Educational Media/Instructional Technology M,O
Higher Education M
Human Resources Development M
Human Services M,O
Social Work M

ACADEMY OF ART UNIVERSITY
Advertising and Public Relations M
Art Education M

ACADIA UNIVERSITY
Counselor Education M
Curriculum and Instruction M
Education—General M
Educational Leadership and Administration M
Educational Media/Instructional Technology M
Kinesiology and Movement Studies M
Mathematics Education M
Recreation and Park Management M
Science Education M
Social Sciences Education M
Special Education M

ADAMS STATE UNIVERSITY
Counselor Education M
Education—General M
Physical Education M
Special Education M

ADELPHI UNIVERSITY
Accounting M
Art Education M
Business Administration and Management—General M*
Early Childhood Education M,O
Education—General M,D,O*
Educational Leadership and Administration M,O
Educational Media/Instructional Technology M,O
Electronic Commerce M
Elementary Education M
English as a Second Language M,O
Finance and Banking M
Health Education M,O
Human Resources Management M,O
Management Information Systems M,O
Marketing M
Physical Education M,O
Reading Education M
Secondary Education M
Social Work M,D*
Special Education M,O

ADLER GRADUATE SCHOOL
Counselor Education M,O
Human Resources Development M,O

AIR FORCE INSTITUTE OF TECHNOLOGY
Logistics M,D
Management Information Systems M

ALABAMA AGRICULTURAL AND MECHANICAL UNIVERSITY
Business Administration and Management—General M
Counselor Education M,O
Early Childhood Education M,O
Education—General M,O
Educational Leadership and Administration M,O
Elementary Education M,O
Human Resources Management M,O
Marketing M
Music Education M
Physical Education M
Secondary Education M,O
Social Work M
Special Education M,O
Vocational and Technical Education M

ALABAMA STATE UNIVERSITY
Accounting M
Counselor Education M,O
Early Childhood Education M,O
Educational Leadership and Administration M,D,O
Educational Media/Instructional Technology M,O
Educational Policy M,D,O
Elementary Education M,O
English Education M,O
Health Education M
Mathematics Education M,O
Physical Education M
Science Education M,O
Secondary Education M,O
Social Sciences Education M,O
Special Education M

ALASKA PACIFIC UNIVERSITY
Business Administration and Management—General M
Education—General M
Elementary Education M
Environmental Education M
Investment Management M,O
Middle School Education M

ALBANY LAW SCHOOL
Law M,D

ALBANY STATE UNIVERSITY
Accounting M
Business Administration and Management—General M
Counselor Education M,O
Early Childhood Education M,O
Education—General M,O
Educational Leadership and Administration M,O
English Education M
Health Education M,O
Human Resources Management M
Mathematics Education M
Middle School Education M,O
Physical Education M,O
Science Education M
Social Work M
Special Education M,O

ALBERTUS MAGNUS COLLEGE
Business Administration and Management—General M
Education—General M
Human Services M

ALBRIGHT COLLEGE
Early Childhood Education M
Education—General M
Elementary Education M
English as a Second Language M
Special Education M

ALCORN STATE UNIVERSITY
Agricultural Education M,O
Business Administration and Management—General M
Counselor Education M,O
Education—General M,O
Elementary Education M,O
Health Education M,O
Physical Education M,O
Secondary Education M,O
Special Education M,O
Vocational and Technical Education M,O

ALFRED UNIVERSITY
Business Administration and Management—General M
Counselor Education M,D,O
Education—General M
Mathematics Education M
Reading Education M

ALLEN COLLEGE
Health Education M,D,O

ALLIANT INTERNATIONAL UNIVERSITY–FRESNO
Education—General M
Educational Leadership and Administration D
English as a Second Language M,O

ALLIANT INTERNATIONAL UNIVERSITY–IRVINE
Education—General M,O
Educational Leadership and Administration M,D,O
Educational Media/Instructional Technology M,O
Educational Psychology M,D,O
English as a Second Language M,D
Higher Education M,D,O
Multilingual and Multicultural Education M,O
Special Education M,O

ALLIANT INTERNATIONAL UNIVERSITY–LOS ANGELES
Business Administration and Management—General D
Education—General M,O
Educational Leadership and Administration M,O
Educational Psychology M,D,O
Student Affairs M,D,O

ALLIANT INTERNATIONAL UNIVERSITY–MÉXICO CITY
Business Administration and Management—General M
Education—General M
Educational Leadership and Administration M
International Business M

ALLIANT INTERNATIONAL UNIVERSITY–SACRAMENTO
Education—General M,O

ALLIANT INTERNATIONAL UNIVERSITY–SAN DIEGO
Business Administration and Management—General M
Education—General M,O
Educational Leadership and Administration M,D,O
Educational Psychology M,D,O
English as a Second Language M,D,O
Higher Education M,D,O
Student Affairs M,D,O

ALLIANT INTERNATIONAL UNIVERSITY–SAN FRANCISCO
Business Administration and Management—General M
Counselor Education M
Education—General M,O
Educational Leadership and Administration M,D,O
Educational Psychology M,D,O
Higher Education M,D,O
Law D
Multilingual and Multicultural Education M,O
Special Education M,O
Sustainability Management M

ALVERNIA UNIVERSITY
Business Administration and Management—General M
Education—General M
Organizational Management D
Urban Education M

ALVERNO COLLEGE
Adult Education M
Business Administration and Management—General M
Education—General M
Educational Leadership and Administration M
Educational Media/Instructional Technology M
Reading Education M
Science Education M

AMBERTON UNIVERSITY
Business Administration and Management—General M
Human Resources Development M
Human Resources Management M

THE AMERICAN COLLEGE
Business Administration and Management—General M
Finance and Banking M
Organizational Management M

AMERICAN COLLEGE OF EDUCATION
Curriculum and Instruction M
Education—General M
Educational Leadership and Administration M
Educational Media/Instructional Technology M
English as a Second Language M
Multilingual and Multicultural Education M

AMERICAN COLLEGE OF THESSALONIKI
Business Administration and Management—General M,O
Entrepreneurship M,O
Finance and Banking M,O
Marketing M,O

AMERICAN GRADUATE UNIVERSITY
Business Administration and Management—General M,O
Project Management M,O

AMERICAN INTERCONTINENTAL UNIVERSITY ATLANTA
International Business M
Management Information Systems M

AMERICAN INTERCONTINENTAL UNIVERSITY BUCKHEAD CAMPUS
Accounting M
Business Administration and Management—General M
Finance and Banking M
Marketing M

AMERICAN INTERCONTINENTAL UNIVERSITY HOUSTON
Business Administration and Management—General M

AMERICAN INTERCONTINENTAL UNIVERSITY LONDON
Business Administration and Management—General M
International Business M
Management Information Systems M

AMERICAN INTERCONTINENTAL UNIVERSITY ONLINE
Accounting M
Business Administration and Management—General M
Curriculum and Instruction M
Education—General M
Educational Leadership and Administration M
Educational Measurement and Evaluation M
Educational Media/Instructional Technology M
Finance and Banking M
Human Resources Management M
Industrial and Manufacturing Management M
International Business M
Marketing M
Project Management M

AMERICAN INTERCONTINENTAL UNIVERSITY SOUTH FLORIDA
Accounting M
Business Administration and Management—General M
Educational Media/Instructional Technology M
Finance and Banking M
Human Resources Management M
International Business M
Marketing M

AMERICAN INTERNATIONAL COLLEGE
Accounting M
Business Administration and Management—General M
Counselor Education M,D,O
Early Childhood Education M,D,O
Education—General M,D,O
Educational Leadership and Administration M,D,O
Educational Psychology M,D
Elementary Education M,D,O
Finance and Banking M
Hospitality Management M
Human Resources Development M
International Business M
Management Information Systems M
Marketing M
Middle School Education M,D,O
Nonprofit Management M
Organizational Management M
Reading Education M,D,O
Secondary Education M,D,O
Special Education M,D,O
Taxation M

AMERICAN JEWISH UNIVERSITY
Business Administration and Management—General M
Education—General M
Nonprofit Management M
Social Work M

AMERICAN PUBLIC UNIVERSITY SYSTEM
Accounting M
Business Administration and Management—General M
Counselor Education M
Curriculum and Instruction M
Distance Education Development M
Education—General M
Educational Leadership and Administration M
Elementary Education M
English as a Second Language M
Entrepreneurship M
Exercise and Sports Science M
Finance and Banking M
Human Resources Management M
International Business M
Legal and Justice Studies M
Logistics M
Management Information Systems M
Management Strategy and Policy M
Marketing M
Nonprofit Management M
Organizational Management M
Project Management M
Reading Education M
Secondary Education M
Social Sciences Education M
Special Education M
Sports Management M
Transportation Management M

AMERICAN SENTINEL UNIVERSITY
Business Administration and Management—General M
Management Information Systems M

AMERICAN UNIVERSITY
Accounting M,O
Business Administration and Management—General M,D,O
Curriculum and Instruction M,O
Early Childhood Education M,O
Education—General M,O
Elementary Education M,O
English as a Second Language M,O
Entrepreneurship M,D,O
Exercise and Sports Science M,O
Finance and Banking M,D,O
Health Education M,O
Human Resources Management M,O
International and Comparative Education M
International Business O
Law M,D,O
Legal and Justice Studies M,D,O
Management Information Systems M,D,O
Marketing M,O
Nonprofit Management M,D,O
Organizational Management M
Real Estate M,O
Secondary Education M,O
Special Education M
Sustainability Management M
Taxation M,O

THE AMERICAN UNIVERSITY IN CAIRO
Business Administration and Management—General M,O
English as a Second Language M,O
Foreign Languages Education M
Industrial and Manufacturing Management M
International and Comparative Education M
Law M
Management Information Systems M

THE AMERICAN UNIVERSITY IN DUBAI
Business Administration and Management—General M
Finance and Banking M
International Business M
Marketing M

THE AMERICAN UNIVERSITY OF ATHENS
Business Administration and Management—General M

AMERICAN UNIVERSITY OF BEIRUT
Business Administration and Management—General M
Education—General M

THE AMERICAN UNIVERSITY OF PARIS
Business Administration and Management—General M
International Business M
Law M

AMERICAN UNIVERSITY OF PUERTO RICO
Art Education M
Education—General M
Elementary Education M
Physical Education M
Science Education M
Special Education M

AMERICAN UNIVERSITY OF SHARJAH
Business Administration and Management—General M
English as a Second Language M

AMRIDGE UNIVERSITY
Counselor Education M,D

Organizational Behavior M,D
Organizational Management M,D

ANAHEIM UNIVERSITY
Business Administration and Management—General M,O
English as a Second Language M,O
Sustainability Management M,O

ANDERSON UNIVERSITY (IN)
Accounting M,D
Business Administration and Management—General M,D
Education—General M

ANDERSON UNIVERSITY (SC)
Business Administration and Management—General M
Education—General M

ANDOVER NEWTON THEOLOGICAL SCHOOL
Religious Education M,D

ANDREWS UNIVERSITY
Accounting M
Curriculum and Instruction M,D,O
Education—General M,D,O
Educational Leadership and Administration M,D,O
Educational Psychology M,D
Elementary Education M,D,O
English as a Second Language M,D,O
English Education M,D,O
Finance and Banking M
Foreign Languages Education M,D,O
Higher Education M,D,O
Human Services M
Religious Education M,D,O
Science Education M,D,O
Secondary Education M,D,O
Social Sciences Education M,D,O
Social Work M
Special Education M

ANGELO STATE UNIVERSITY
Accounting M
Business Administration and Management—General M
Counselor Education M
Curriculum and Instruction M
Education—General M
Educational Leadership and Administration M,O
Higher Education M
Special Education M
Sports Management M

ANNA MARIA COLLEGE
Art Education M
Business Administration and Management—General M,O
Early Childhood Education M,O
Education—General M,O
Elementary Education M,O
English Education M,O

ANTIOCH UNIVERSITY LOS ANGELES
Business Administration and Management—General M
Education—General M
Human Resources Development M
Organizational Management M

ANTIOCH UNIVERSITY MIDWEST
Business Administration and Management—General M
Education—General M
Management Strategy and Policy M

ANTIOCH UNIVERSITY NEW ENGLAND
Business Administration and Management—General M
Early Childhood Education M
Education—General M
Educational Leadership and Administration M
Elementary Education M
Environmental Education M
Foundations and Philosophy of Education M
Organizational Management M,O
Science Education M
Sustainability Management M

ANTIOCH UNIVERSITY SANTA BARBARA
Education—General M
Organizational Management M

ANTIOCH UNIVERSITY SEATTLE
Business Administration and Management—General M
Education—General M
Organizational Management M

APPALACHIAN SCHOOL OF LAW
Law D

APPALACHIAN STATE UNIVERSITY
Accounting M
Business Administration and Management—General M
Counselor Education M
Curriculum and Instruction M
Educational Leadership and Administration M,D,O
Educational Media/Instructional Technology M,O
Elementary Education M
English Education M
Exercise and Sports Science M
Foreign Languages Education M
Higher Education M,O
Library Science M,O
Mathematics Education M
Middle School Education M
Music Education M
Reading Education M
Science Education M
Social Sciences Education M
Social Work M
Special Education M
Student Affairs M
Taxation M
Vocational and Technical Education M

AQUINAS COLLEGE
Business Administration and Management—General M
Education—General M
Marketing M
Organizational Management M
Sustainability Management M

ARCADIA UNIVERSITY
Art Education M,D,O
Business Administration and Management—General M
Computer Education M,D,O
Curriculum and Instruction M,D,O
Early Childhood Education M,D,O
Education—General M,D,O
Educational Leadership and Administration M,D,O
Educational Media/Instructional Technology M,D,O
Elementary Education M,D,O
English Education M,D,O
Environmental Education M,D,O
Health Education M
Mathematics Education M,D,O
Music Education M,D,O
Reading Education M,D,O
Science Education M,D,O
Secondary Education M,D,O
Social Sciences Education M,D,O
Special Education M,D,O

ARGOSY UNIVERSITY, ATLANTA
Accounting M,D
Business Administration and Management—General M,D*
Counselor Education M,D,O
Education—General M,D,O
Educational Leadership and Administration M,D,O*
Educational Media/Instructional Technology M,D,O
Elementary Education M,D,O
Finance and Banking M,D
Higher Education M,D,O
International Business M,D
Management Information Systems M,D
Marketing M,D
Secondary Education M,D,O

ARGOSY UNIVERSITY, CHICAGO
Accounting M,D
Adult Education M,D,O
Business Administration and Management—General M,D*
Community College Education M,D,O
Counselor Education D
Education—General M,D,O*
Educational Leadership and Administration M,D,O
Elementary Education M,D,O
Finance and Banking M,D
Higher Education M,D,O
International Business M,D
Management Information Systems M,D
Marketing M,D
Organizational Behavior D
Organizational Management D
Secondary Education M,D,O
Sustainability Management M,D

ARGOSY UNIVERSITY, DALLAS
Accounting M,D,O
Business Administration and Management—General M,D,O*
Counselor Education D
Education—General M,D*
Educational Leadership and Administration M,D
Finance and Banking M,D,O
Higher Education M,D
International Business M,D,O
Management Information Systems M,D,O
Marketing M,D,O
Sustainability Management M,D,O

ARGOSY UNIVERSITY, DENVER
Accounting M,D
Business Administration and Management—General M,D*
Community College Education M,D
Counselor Education M,D
Education—General M,D*
Educational Leadership and Administration M,D
Educational Media/Instructional Technology M,D
Elementary Education M,D
Finance and Banking M,D
Higher Education M,D
International Business M,D
Management Information Systems M,D
Marketing M,D
Organizational Management M,D
Sustainability Management M,D

ARGOSY UNIVERSITY, HAWAI`I
Accounting M,D,O
Adult Education M,D
Business Administration and Management—General M,D,O*
Education—General M,D*
Educational Leadership and Administration M,D
Elementary Education M,D
Finance and Banking M,D,O
Higher Education M,D
International Business M,D,O
Management Information Systems M,D,O
Marketing M,D,O
Organizational Management D
Secondary Education M,D
Sustainability Management M,D,O

ARGOSY UNIVERSITY, INLAND EMPIRE
Accounting M,D
Business Administration and Management—General M,D*
Community College Education M,D
Education—General M,D
Educational Leadership and Administration M,D*
Elementary Education M,D
Finance and Banking M,D
Higher Education M,D
International Business M,D
Management Information Systems M,D
Marketing M,D
Organizational Management M,D
Secondary Education M,D
Sustainability Management M,D

ARGOSY UNIVERSITY, LOS ANGELES
Accounting M,D
Business Administration and Management—General M,D*
Community College Education M,D
Education—General M,D*
Educational Leadership and Administration M,D
Elementary Education M,D
Finance and Banking M,D
Higher Education M,D
International Business M,D
Management Information Systems M,D
Marketing M,D
Organizational Management M,D
Secondary Education M,D
Sustainability Management M,D

ARGOSY UNIVERSITY, NASHVILLE
Accounting M,D
Business Administration and Management—General M,D*
Counselor Education D
Education—General M,D,O
Educational Leadership and Administration M,D,O*
Educational Media/Instructional Technology M,D,O
Elementary Education M,D,O
Finance and Banking M,D
Higher Education M,D,O
International Business M,D
Management Information Systems M,D
Marketing M,D
Secondary Education M,D,O

ARGOSY UNIVERSITY, ORANGE COUNTY
Accounting M,D,O
Business Administration and Management—General M,D,O*
Community College Education M,D
Education—General M,D*
Educational Leadership and Administration M,D
Educational Media/Instructional Technology M,D
Elementary Education M,D
Finance and Banking M,D,O
Higher Education M,D
International Business M,D,O
Management Information Systems M,D,O
Marketing M,D,O
Organizational Management D
Secondary Education M,D
Sustainability Management M,D,O

ARGOSY UNIVERSITY, PHOENIX
Accounting M,D
Adult Education M,D,O
Business Administration and Management—General M,D*
Community College Education M,D,O
Education—General M,D,O*
Educational Leadership and Administration M,D,O
Educational Media/Instructional Technology M,D,O
Elementary Education M,D,O
Finance and Banking M,D
Higher Education M,D,O
International Business M,D
Management Information Systems M,D
Marketing M,D
Secondary Education M,D,O
Sustainability Management M,D

ARGOSY UNIVERSITY, SALT LAKE CITY
Accounting M,D
Business Administration and Management—General M,D*
Counselor Education M,D*
Education—General M,D*
Educational Leadership and Administration M,D
Finance and Banking M,D
International Business M,D
Management Information Systems M,D
Marketing M,D
Sustainability Management M,D

ARGOSY UNIVERSITY, SAN DIEGO
Accounting M,D
Business Administration and Management—General M,D*
Community College Education M,D
Education—General M,D*
Educational Leadership and Administration M,D
Elementary Education M,D
Finance and Banking M,D
Higher Education M,D
International Business M,D
Management Information Systems M,D
Marketing M,D
Organizational Management M,D
Secondary Education M,D

ARGOSY UNIVERSITY, SAN FRANCISCO BAY AREA
Accounting M,D
Business Administration and Management—General M,D*
Community College Education M,D
Education—General M,D*
Educational Leadership and Administration M,D
Educational Media/Instructional Technology M,D
Elementary Education M,D
Finance and Banking M,D
Higher Education M,D
International Business M,D
Management Information Systems M,D
Marketing M,D
Organizational Management M,D
Secondary Education M,D
Sustainability Management M,D

ARGOSY UNIVERSITY, SARASOTA
Accounting M,D,O
Business Administration and Management—General M,D,O*
Counselor Education M,D,O
Education—General M,D,O*
Educational Leadership and Administration M,D,O
Educational Media/Instructional Technology M,D,O
Elementary Education M,D,O
Finance and Banking M,D,O
Higher Education M,D,O
International Business M,D,O
Management Information Systems M,D,O
Marketing M,D,O
Organizational Management M,D,O
Secondary Education M,D,O
Sustainability Management M,D,O

ARGOSY UNIVERSITY, SCHAUMBURG
Accounting M,D,O
Business Administration and Management—General M,D,O*
Community College Education M,D,O
Counselor Education M,D,O
Education—General M,D,O*
Educational Leadership and Administration M,D,O
Elementary Education M,D,O
Finance and Banking M,D,O
Higher Education M,D,O
International Business M,D,O
Management Information Systems M,D,O
Marketing M,D,O
Secondary Education M,D,O
Sustainability Management M,D,O

ARGOSY UNIVERSITY, SEATTLE
Accounting M,D
Adult Education M,D
Business Administration and Management—General M,D*
Community College Education M,D
Education—General M,D*
Educational Leadership and Administration M,D
Educational Media/Instructional Technology M,D
Elementary Education M,D
Finance and Banking M,D
Higher Education M,D
International Business M,D
Management Information Systems M,D
Marketing M,D
Organizational Management M,D
Secondary Education M,D
Sustainability Management M,D

ARGOSY UNIVERSITY, TAMPA
Accounting M,D
Business Administration and Management—General M,D*
Community College Education M,D,O
Counselor Education M,D,O
Education—General M,D,O*
Educational Leadership and Administration M,D,O
Elementary Education M,D,O
Finance and Banking M,D
Higher Education M,D,O
International Business M,D
Management Information Systems M,D
Marketing M,D
Organizational Management M,D
Secondary Education M,D,O
Sustainability Management M,D

ARGOSY UNIVERSITY, TWIN CITIES
Accounting M,D
Business Administration and Management—General M,D*
Education—General M,D,O*
Educational Leadership and Administration M,D,O
Educational Media/Instructional Technology M,D,O

*M—master's degree; P—first professional degree; D—doctorate; O—other advanced degree; *Close-Up and/or Display*

Elementary Education M,D,O
Finance and Banking M,D
Higher Education M,D,O
International Business M,D
Management Information Systems M,D
Marketing M,D
Organizational Management M,D
Secondary Education M,D,O
Sustainability Management M,D

ARGOSY UNIVERSITY, WASHINGTON DC
Accounting M,D,O
Business Administration and Management—General M,D,O*
Community College Education M,D,O
Counselor Education M,D,O
Education—General M,D,O*
Educational Leadership and Administration M,D,O
Elementary Education M,D,O
Finance and Banking M,D,O
Higher Education M,D,O
International Business M,D,O
Management Information Systems M,D,O
Marketing M,D,O
Organizational Management M,D,O
Secondary Education M,D,O
Sustainability Management M,D,O

ARIZONA STATE UNIVERSITY
Accounting M,D
Art Education M,D
Aviation Management M
Business Administration and Management—General M,D
Counselor Education M,D
Curriculum and Instruction M,D
Education—General M,D,O
Educational Leadership and Administration M,D
Educational Media/Instructional Technology M,D,O
Educational Policy D
Elementary Education M,D
English as a Second Language M,D,O
Entrepreneurship M
Exercise and Sports Science M,D,O
Finance and Banking M,D
Foreign Languages Education M,D
Foundations and Philosophy of Education M
Health Education D
Higher Education M,D
Kinesiology and Movement Studies M,D,O
Law M,D
Legal and Justice Studies M,D,O
Management Information Systems M,D
Marketing M,D
Mathematics Education M,D
Music Education M,D
Nonprofit Management M,D,O
Physical Education M,D
Real Estate M
Recreation and Park Management M,D,O
Secondary Education M,D
Social Work M,D,O
Special Education M,D
Supply Chain Management M,D
Travel and Tourism M,D,O

ARKANSAS STATE UNIVERSITY
Accounting M
Agricultural Education M,O
Business Administration and Management—General M
Business Education M,O
Community College Education M,D,O
Counselor Education M,O
Curriculum and Instruction M,D,O
Early Childhood Education M,D,O
Education of the Gifted M,D,O
Education—General M,D,O
Educational Leadership and Administration M,D,O
Electronic Commerce M,O
Elementary Education M,O
English Education M,O
Exercise and Sports Science M,O
Health Education M,O
Management Information Systems M
Mathematics Education M,O
Middle School Education M,O
Music Education M,O
Physical Education M,O
Reading Education M,O
Science Education M,O
Social Sciences Education M,O
Social Work M,O
Special Education M,D,O
Sports Management M,O
Student Affairs M,O

ARKANSAS TECH UNIVERSITY
Counselor Education M,O
Curriculum and Instruction M,O
Education—General M,O
Educational Leadership and Administration M,O
Educational Media/Instructional Technology M,O
Elementary Education M,O
English as a Second Language M
English Education M
Physical Education M,O
Student Affairs M,O

ARMSTRONG ATLANTIC STATE UNIVERSITY
Adult Education M
Athletic Training and Sports Medicine M
Business Education M
Curriculum and Instruction M
Early Childhood Education M
Education—General M
Elementary Education M
English Education M
Exercise and Sports Science M
Mathematics Education M
Middle School Education M
Science Education M
Secondary Education M
Social Sciences Education M
Special Education M

ART ACADEMY OF CINCINNATI
Art Education M

ASBURY THEOLOGICAL SEMINARY
Religious Education M,D,O

ASBURY UNIVERSITY
Educational Leadership and Administration M
English as a Second Language M
Mathematics Education M
Reading Education M
Science Education M
Social Sciences Education M
Social Work M
Special Education M

ASHLAND THEOLOGICAL SEMINARY
Counselor Education M,D,O

ASHLAND UNIVERSITY
Business Administration and Management—General M
Curriculum and Instruction M
Education of the Gifted M
Education—General M,D
Educational Leadership and Administration M,D
Educational Media/Instructional Technology M
Exercise and Sports Science M
Foundations and Philosophy of Education M
Physical Education M
Reading Education M
Special Education M
Sports Management M
Student Affairs M

ASHWORTH COLLEGE
Business Administration and Management—General M
Human Resources Management M
International Business M
Marketing M

ASPEN UNIVERSITY
Business Administration and Management—General M,O
Finance and Banking M,O
Management Information Systems M,O
Project Management M,O

ASSUMPTION COLLEGE
Accounting M,O
Business Administration and Management—General M,O
Finance and Banking M,O
Human Resources Management M,O
International Business M,O
Marketing M,O
Nonprofit Management M,O
Social Work M,O
Special Education M,O

ATHABASCA UNIVERSITY
Adult Education M
Business Administration and Management—General M,O
Counselor Education M,O
Distance Education Development M,O
Education—General M,O
Organizational Management M,O
Project Management M,O

ATLANTA'S JOHN MARSHALL LAW SCHOOL
Law M,D

A.T. STILL UNIVERSITY OF HEALTH SCIENCES
Athletic Training and Sports Medicine M,D
Health Education M,D
Kinesiology and Movement Studies M,D

AUBURN UNIVERSITY
Accounting M
Adult Education M,D,O
Business Administration and Management—General M,D
Business Education M,D,O
Curriculum and Instruction M,D,O
Early Childhood Education M,D,O
Education—General M,D,O
Educational Leadership and Administration M,D,O
Educational Media/Instructional Technology M,D,O
Educational Psychology M,D,O
Elementary Education M,D,O
English Education M,D,O
Exercise and Sports Science M,D,O
Finance and Banking M
Foreign Languages Education M,D,O
Health Education M,D,O
Higher Education M,D,O
Hospitality Management M,D,O
Human Resources Management M,D
Kinesiology and Movement Studies M,D,O
Management Information Systems M,D
Mathematics Education M,D,O
Music Education M,D,O
Physical Education M,D,O
Reading Education M,D,O
Real Estate M
Science Education M,D,O
Secondary Education M,D,O
Social Sciences Education M,D,O
Special Education M,D

AUBURN UNIVERSITY MONTGOMERY
Business Administration and Management—General M
Counselor Education M,O
Early Childhood Education M,O
Education—General M,O
Educational Leadership and Administration M,O
Elementary Education M,O
Physical Education M,O
Reading Education M,O
Secondary Education M,O
Special Education M,O

AUGSBURG COLLEGE
Business Administration and Management—General M
Education—General M
Organizational Management M
Social Work M

AUGUSTANA COLLEGE
Education—General M
Sports Management M

AUGUSTA STATE UNIVERSITY
Business Administration and Management—General M
Counselor Education M
Curriculum and Instruction M
Education—General M,O
Educational Leadership and Administration M,O
Health Education M
Physical Education M
Secondary Education M,O
Special Education M,O

AURORA UNIVERSITY
Business Administration and Management—General M
Curriculum and Instruction M,D
Early Childhood Education M,D
Education—General M,D
Educational Leadership and Administration M,D
Educational Media/Instructional Technology M,D
Elementary Education M,D
Mathematics Education M,D
Reading Education M,D
Recreation and Park Management M
Science Education M
Social Work M,D
Special Education M,D

AUSTIN COLLEGE
Art Education M
Education—General M
Elementary Education M
Middle School Education M
Music Education M
Physical Education M
Secondary Education M

AUSTIN PEAY STATE UNIVERSITY
Business Administration and Management—General M
Counselor Education M,O
Curriculum and Instruction M,O
Education—General M,O
Educational Leadership and Administration M,O
Elementary Education M,O
Exercise and Sports Science M
Health Education M
Music Education M
Reading Education M,O
Secondary Education M,O
Social Work M
Special Education M,O

AVE MARIA SCHOOL OF LAW
Law D

AVERETT UNIVERSITY
Business Administration and Management—General M
Curriculum and Instruction M
Education—General M
English Education M

AVILA UNIVERSITY
Accounting M
Business Administration and Management—General M
Education—General M,O
English as a Second Language M,O
Finance and Banking M
International Business M
Management Information Systems M
Marketing M
Organizational Management M

AZUSA PACIFIC UNIVERSITY
Business Administration and Management—General M
Counselor Education M
Curriculum and Instruction M
Education—General M,D,O
Educational Leadership and Administration M,D
Educational Media/Instructional Technology M
English as a Second Language M
Entrepreneurship M
Finance and Banking M
Foundations and Philosophy of Education M
Higher Education M,D
Human Resources Development M
Human Resources Management M
International Business M
Library Science M,O
Management Strategy and Policy M
Marketing M
Multilingual and Multicultural Education M
Music Education M
Nonprofit Management M
Organizational Management M
Physical Education M
Religious Education M
Social Work M
Special Education M
Student Affairs M

BABSON COLLEGE
Accounting M,O
Business Administration and Management—General M,O
Entrepreneurship M,O

BAKER COLLEGE CENTER FOR GRADUATE STUDIES - ONLINE
Accounting M,D
Business Administration and Management—General M,D
Finance and Banking M,D
Human Resources Management M,D
Management Information Systems M,D
Marketing M,D

BAKER UNIVERSITY
Business Administration and Management—General M
Education—General M,D

BAKKE GRADUATE UNIVERSITY
Business Administration and Management—General M,D
Entrepreneurship M,D
Urban Education M,D

BALDWIN WALLACE UNIVERSITY
Accounting M
Business Administration and Management—General M
Education—General M
Educational Leadership and Administration M
Educational Media/Instructional Technology M
Entrepreneurship M
Human Resources Management M
International Business M
Reading Education M
Special Education M
Sustainability Management M

BALL STATE UNIVERSITY
Accounting M
Actuarial Science M
Adult Education M,D
Advertising and Public Relations M
Business Administration and Management—General M
Business Education M
Curriculum and Instruction M,O
Education—General M,D,O
Educational Leadership and Administration M,D,O
Educational Psychology M,D,O
Elementary Education M,D
English as a Second Language M,D
Exercise and Sports Science D
Foundations and Philosophy of Education D
Higher Education M,D
Mathematics Education M,D
Music Education M,D
Physical Education M,D
Science Education M,D
Secondary Education M,D
Special Education M,D,O
Vocational and Technical Education M

BANK STREET COLLEGE OF EDUCATION
Early Childhood Education M
Education—General M
Educational Leadership and Administration M
Elementary Education M
Foundations and Philosophy of Education M
Mathematics Education M
Multilingual and Multicultural Education M
Museum Education M
Reading Education M
Special Education M

BAPTIST BIBLE COLLEGE OF PENNSYLVANIA
Counselor Education M
Education—General M
Religious Education M,D

BAPTIST THEOLOGICAL SEMINARY AT RICHMOND
Religious Education M,D

BARD COLLEGE
Education—General M
Sustainability Management M,O

BARRY UNIVERSITY
Accounting M
Athletic Training and Sports Medicine M
Business Administration and Management—General M,O
Counselor Education M,D,O
Curriculum and Instruction D,O
Distance Education Development O
Early Childhood Education M,D,O
Education of the Gifted M,D,O
Education—General M,D,O
Educational Leadership and Administration M,D,O
Educational Media/Instructional Technology M,D,O
Elementary Education M,D,O
English as a Second Language M,D,O

Program	Degrees
Exercise and Sports Science	M
Finance and Banking	O
Higher Education	M,D
Human Resources Development	M,D
Human Resources Management	O
International Business	O
Kinesiology and Movement Studies	M
Law	D
Management Information Systems	O
Marketing	O
Reading Education	M,D,O
Social Work	M,D
Special Education	M,D,O
Sports Management	M

BAYAMÓN CENTRAL UNIVERSITY

Program	Degrees
Accounting	M
Business Administration and Management—General	M
Counselor Education	M,O
Early Childhood Education	M,O
Education—General	M,O
Educational Leadership and Administration	M,O
Elementary Education	M,O
Finance and Banking	M
Marketing	M
Special Education	M,O

BAYLOR UNIVERSITY

Program	Degrees
Accounting	M
Business Administration and Management—General	M
Curriculum and Instruction	M,D
Education of the Gifted	M,D,O
Education—General	M,D,O
Educational Leadership and Administration	M,O
Educational Psychology	M,D,O
Exercise and Sports Science	M,D
Health Education	M,D
Law	D
Management Information Systems	M,D
Physical Education	M,D
Social Work	M
Special Education	M,D,O

BAY PATH COLLEGE

Program	Degrees
Educational Leadership and Administration	M
Entrepreneurship	M
Higher Education	M
Management Information Systems	M
Nonprofit Management	M
Special Education	M,O

BELHAVEN UNIVERSITY (MS)

Program	Degrees
Business Administration and Management—General	M
Education—General	M
Elementary Education	M
Multilingual and Multicultural Education	M
Secondary Education	M

BELLARMINE UNIVERSITY

Program	Degrees
Business Administration and Management—General	M
Early Childhood Education	M,D,O
Education—General	M,D,O
Educational Leadership and Administration	M,D,O
Management Information Systems	M
Middle School Education	M,D,O
Reading Education	M,D,O
Secondary Education	M,D,O
Special Education	M,D,O

BELLEVUE UNIVERSITY

Program	Degrees
Business Administration and Management—General	M,D
Counselor Education	M
Educational Media/Instructional Technology	M
Finance and Banking	M,D
Human Resources Management	M,D
Human Services	M
Management Information Systems	M
Organizational Management	M
Project Management	M

BELMONT UNIVERSITY

Program	Degrees
Business Administration and Management—General	M
Early Childhood Education	M
Education—General	M
Elementary Education	M
English Education	M
Law	D
Mathematics Education	M
Middle School Education	M
Music Education	M
Science Education	M
Secondary Education	M
Social Sciences Education	M
Special Education	M
Sports Management	M

BEMIDJI STATE UNIVERSITY

Program	Degrees
Education—General	M
Mathematics Education	M
Special Education	M

BENEDICTINE COLLEGE

Program	Degrees
Business Administration and Management—General	M
Educational Leadership and Administration	M

BENEDICTINE UNIVERSITY

Program	Degrees
Accounting	M
Business Administration and Management—General	M
Curriculum and Instruction	M
Education—General	M
Educational Leadership and Administration	M,D
Elementary Education	M
Entrepreneurship	M
Exercise and Sports Science	M
Finance and Banking	M
Health Education	M
Higher Education	D
Human Resources Management	M
International Business	M
Logistics	M
Management Information Systems	M
Marketing	M
Organizational Behavior	M
Organizational Management	M,D
Reading Education	M
Science Education	M
Secondary Education	M
Special Education	M

BENEDICTINE UNIVERSITY AT SPRINGFIELD

Program	Degrees
Business Administration and Management—General	M
Elementary Education	M
Organizational Behavior	M
Organizational Management	M,D
Reading Education	M

BENNINGTON COLLEGE

Program	Degrees
Education—General	M
Foreign Languages Education	M
Multilingual and Multicultural Education	M

BENTLEY UNIVERSITY

Program	Degrees
Accounting	M,D
Business Administration and Management—General	M,D,O
Finance and Banking	M
Marketing	M
Taxation	M

BERNARD M. BARUCH COLLEGE OF THE CITY UNIVERSITY OF NEW YORK

Program	Degrees
Accounting	M,D
Business Administration and Management—General	M,D,O
Educational Leadership and Administration	M,O
Entrepreneurship	M,D
Finance and Banking	M,D
Higher Education	M
Human Resources Management	M,D
Industrial and Manufacturing Management	M,D
International Business	M,D
Management Information Systems	M,D
Marketing	M,D
Nonprofit Management	M
Organizational Behavior	M,D
Quantitative Analysis	M
Real Estate	M
Sustainability Management	M,D
Taxation	M

BERRY COLLEGE

Program	Degrees
Business Administration and Management—General	M
Curriculum and Instruction	O
Early Childhood Education	M
Education—General	M,O
Educational Leadership and Administration	O
Middle School Education	M
Reading Education	M
Secondary Education	M

BETHEL COLLEGE

Program	Degrees
Business Administration and Management—General	M
Education—General	M

BETHEL SEMINARY

Program	Degrees
Religious Education	M,D,O

BETHEL UNIVERSITY (MN)

Program	Degrees
Business Administration and Management—General	M,D,O
Education—General	M,D,O
Educational Leadership and Administration	M,D,O
Elementary Education	M,D,O
Higher Education	M,D,O
Organizational Management	M,D,O
Reading Education	M,D,O
Secondary Education	M,D,O
Special Education	M,D,O

BETHEL UNIVERSITY (TN)

Program	Degrees
Business Administration and Management—General	M
Educational Leadership and Administration	M

BIOLA UNIVERSITY

Program	Degrees
Business Administration and Management—General	M
Education—General	O
English as a Second Language	M,D,O
Religious Education	M,D,O
Science Education	M
Special Education	O

BISHOP'S UNIVERSITY

Program	Degrees
Education—General	M,O
English as a Second Language	M,O

BLACK HILLS STATE UNIVERSITY

Program	Degrees
Business Administration and Management—General	M
Curriculum and Instruction	M
Management Strategy and Policy	M

BLOOMSBURG UNIVERSITY OF PENNSYLVANIA

Program	Degrees
Accounting	M
Athletic Training and Sports Medicine	M
Business Administration and Management—General	M
Business Education	M
Counselor Education	M
Curriculum and Instruction	M
Early Childhood Education	M
Education—General	M
Educational Media/Instructional Technology	M
Elementary Education	M
Exercise and Sports Science	M
Reading Education	M
Science Education	M
Special Education	M
Student Affairs	M

BLUE MOUNTAIN COLLEGE

Program	Degrees
Elementary Education	M

BLUFFTON UNIVERSITY

Program	Degrees
Business Administration and Management—General	M
Education—General	M
Organizational Management	M

BOB JONES UNIVERSITY

Program	Degrees
Accounting	M,D,O
Business Administration and Management—General	M,D,O
Counselor Education	M,D,O
Curriculum and Instruction	M,D,O
Educational Leadership and Administration	M,D,O
Elementary Education	M,D,O
English Education	M,D,O
Mathematics Education	M,D,O
Music Education	M,D,O
Secondary Education	M,D,O
Social Sciences Education	M,D,O
Special Education	M,D,O
Student Affairs	M,D,O

BOISE STATE UNIVERSITY

Program	Degrees
Accounting	M
Art Education	M
Business Administration and Management—General	M
Counselor Education	M
Curriculum and Instruction	D
Early Childhood Education	M
Education—General	M,D
Educational Leadership and Administration	M,D
Educational Media/Instructional Technology	M
Exercise and Sports Science	M
Management Information Systems	M
Music Education	M
Physical Education	M
Reading Education	M
Science Education	M,D
Social Work	M
Special Education	M
Taxation	M

BORICUA COLLEGE

Program	Degrees
Human Services	M

BOSTON COLLEGE

Program	Degrees
Accounting	M
Business Administration and Management—General	M
Counselor Education	M,D
Curriculum and Instruction	M,D,O
Early Childhood Education	M
Education—General	M,D,O
Educational Leadership and Administration	M,D,O
Educational Measurement and Evaluation	M,D
Educational Psychology	M,D
Elementary Education	M,D
Finance and Banking	M,D
Higher Education	M,D
Law	D
Organizational Behavior	D
Organizational Management	D
Reading Education	M,O
Religious Education	M,D,O
Science Education	M,D
Secondary Education	M
Social Work	M,D
Special Education	M,O

THE BOSTON CONSERVATORY

Program	Degrees
Music Education	M,O

BOSTON UNIVERSITY

Program	Degrees
Actuarial Science	M
Advertising and Public Relations	M
Art Education	M
Athletic Training and Sports Medicine	D
Business Administration and Management—General	M,D
Education—General	M,D,O
Electronic Commerce	M
Finance and Banking	M,D
Health Law	M
Intellectual Property Law	M,D
International Business	M
Investment Management	M,D
Law	M,D
Legal and Justice Studies	M
Management Information Systems	M
Management Strategy and Policy	M
Music Education	M,D
Project Management	M
Social Work	M,D
Taxation	M,D
Travel and Tourism	M

BOWIE STATE UNIVERSITY

Program	Degrees
Business Administration and Management—General	M
Counselor Education	M
Education—General	M
Educational Leadership and Administration	M,D
Elementary Education	M
Human Resources Development	M
Management Information Systems	M,O
Reading Education	M
Secondary Education	M
Special Education	M

BOWLING GREEN STATE UNIVERSITY

Program	Degrees
Accounting	M
Art Education	M
Business Administration and Management—General	M
Business Education	M
Counselor Education	M
Curriculum and Instruction	M
Early Childhood Education	M
Education of the Gifted	M
Educational Leadership and Administration	M,D,O
Educational Media/Instructional Technology	M
Foreign Languages Education	M
Higher Education	D
International and Comparative Education	M
Kinesiology and Movement Studies	M
Leisure Studies	M
Mathematics Education	M,D
Music Education	M,D
Organizational Management	M
Reading Education	M,O
Recreation and Park Management	M
Science Education	M
Special Education	M
Sports Management	M
Student Affairs	M
Vocational and Technical Education	M

BRADLEY UNIVERSITY

Program	Degrees
Accounting	M
Business Administration and Management—General	M
Counselor Education	M
Curriculum and Instruction	M,O
Education—General	M,D,O
Educational Leadership and Administration	M

BRANDEIS UNIVERSITY

Program	Degrees
Business Administration and Management—General	M
Elementary Education	M
Entrepreneurship	M
Finance and Banking	M
Health Education	D
Human Services	M
International Business	M,D
Management Information Systems	M
Nonprofit Management	M
Project Management	M
Religious Education	M
Secondary Education	M
Sustainability Management	M,D

BRANDMAN UNIVERSITY

Program	Degrees
Business Administration and Management—General	M
Counselor Education	M
Education—General	M
Educational Leadership and Administration	M
Human Resources Management	M
Organizational Management	M
Special Education	M

BRANDON UNIVERSITY

Program	Degrees
Counselor Education	M,O
Curriculum and Instruction	M,O
Education—General	M,O
Educational Leadership and Administration	M,O
Music Education	M
Special Education	M,O

BRENAU UNIVERSITY

Program	Degrees
Accounting	M
Business Administration and Management—General	M
Early Childhood Education	M,O
Education—General	M,O
Middle School Education	M,O
Organizational Management	M
Project Management	M
Secondary Education	M,O
Special Education	M,O

BRESCIA UNIVERSITY

Program	Degrees
Business Administration and Management—General	M
Curriculum and Instruction	M

BRIAR CLIFF UNIVERSITY

Program	Degrees
Human Resources Management	M

BRIDGEWATER STATE UNIVERSITY

Program	Degrees
Accounting	M
Art Education	M
Business Administration and Management—General	M
Counselor Education	M,O
Early Childhood Education	M
Education—General	M,O
Educational Leadership and Administration	M,O

*M—master's degree; P—first professional degree; D—doctorate; O—other advanced degree; *Close-Up and/or Display*

Educational Media/Instructional Technology M
Elementary Education M
Finance and Banking M
Mathematics Education M
Physical Education M
Reading Education M,O
Science Education M
Secondary Education M
Social Sciences Education M
Social Work M
Special Education M

BRIERCREST SEMINARY
Business Administration and Management—General M
Organizational Management M

BRIGHAM YOUNG UNIVERSITY
Accounting M
Art Education M
Athletic Training and Sports Medicine M,D
Business Administration and Management—General M
Education—General M,D,O
Educational Leadership and Administration M,D
Educational Media/Instructional Technology M,D
Educational Psychology M,D
English as a Second Language M
Exercise and Sports Science M,D
Finance and Banking M
Foreign Languages Education M
Foundations and Philosophy of Education M,D
Health Education M
Human Resources Management M
Law M,D
Management Information Systems M
Mathematics Education M
Music Education M
Nonprofit Management M
Reading Education M
Recreation and Park Management M
Religious Education M
Science Education M,D
Social Work M
Special Education M,D,O

BROADVIEW UNIVERSITY–WEST JORDAN
Business Administration and Management—General M
Management Information Systems M

BROCK UNIVERSITY
Accounting M
Business Administration and Management—General M
Education—General M,D
English as a Second Language M
Legal and Justice Studies M

BROOKLYN COLLEGE OF THE CITY UNIVERSITY OF NEW YORK
Accounting M
Art Education M,O
Counselor Education M,O
Early Childhood Education M
Education—General M,O
Educational Leadership and Administration M
Elementary Education M
English Education M,O
Environmental Education M
Exercise and Sports Science M
Finance and Banking M
Foreign Languages Education M,O
Health Education M,O
International Business M
Mathematics Education M,O
Middle School Education M,O
Multilingual and Multicultural Education M
Music Education M,D,O
Organizational Behavior M
Physical Education M,O
Science Education M,O
Secondary Education M,O
Social Sciences Education M,O
Special Education M
Sports Management M

BROOKLYN LAW SCHOOL
Law D

BROWN UNIVERSITY
Education—General M
Elementary Education M
English Education M
Multilingual and Multicultural Education M,D
Science Education M
Secondary Education M
Social Sciences Education M
Urban Education M

BRYAN COLLEGE
Business Administration and Management—General M

BRYANT UNIVERSITY
Accounting M
Business Administration and Management—General M
Taxation M

BRYN MAWR COLLEGE
Social Work M,D

BUCKNELL UNIVERSITY
Education—General M
Student Affairs M

BUENA VISTA UNIVERSITY
Counselor Education M
Curriculum and Instruction M
Education—General M
English as a Second Language M

BUFFALO STATE COLLEGE, STATE UNIVERSITY OF NEW YORK
Adult Education M,O
Art Education M
Business Education M
Early Childhood Education M
Educational Leadership and Administration O
Educational Media/Instructional Technology M
Elementary Education M
English Education M
Human Resources Management M,O
Mathematics Education M
Multilingual and Multicultural Education M
Reading Education M
Science Education M
Social Sciences Education M
Special Education M
Student Affairs M
Vocational and Technical Education M

BUTLER UNIVERSITY
Accounting M
Business Administration and Management—General M
Counselor Education M
Education—General M
Educational Leadership and Administration M
Elementary Education M
Music Education M
Reading Education M
Secondary Education M
Special Education M

CABRINI COLLEGE
Education—General M
Organizational Management M

CAIRN UNIVERSITY
Education—General M
Educational Leadership and Administration M
Organizational Management M

CALDWELL COLLEGE
Accounting M
Business Administration and Management—General M
Counselor Education M,O
Curriculum and Instruction M,O
Education—General M,O
Educational Leadership and Administration M,O
Reading Education M,O
Special Education M,O

CALIFORNIA BAPTIST UNIVERSITY
Accounting M
Athletic Training and Sports Medicine M
Business Administration and Management—General M
Counselor Education M
Curriculum and Instruction M
Education—General M
Educational Leadership and Administration M
Educational Media/Instructional Technology M
English as a Second Language M
English Education M
Exercise and Sports Science M
International and Comparative Education M
Music Education M
Physical Education M
Reading Education M
Special Education M
Sports Management M
Vocational and Technical Education M

CALIFORNIA COAST UNIVERSITY
Business Administration and Management—General M
Curriculum and Instruction M,D
Education—General M,D
Educational Leadership and Administration M,D
Educational Psychology M,D
Human Resources Management M
Marketing M
Organizational Management M,D

CALIFORNIA COLLEGE OF THE ARTS
Finance and Banking M
Organizational Management M

CALIFORNIA INTERCONTINENTAL UNIVERSITY
Business Administration and Management—General M,D
Entertainment Management M
Entrepreneurship M,D
Finance and Banking M,D
Human Resources Management M,D
International Business M,D
Management Information Systems M,D
Marketing M,D
Organizational Management M,D
Project Management M,D
Quality Management M,D

CALIFORNIA INTERNATIONAL BUSINESS UNIVERSITY
Business Administration and Management—General M,D

CALIFORNIA LUTHERAN UNIVERSITY
Business Administration and Management—General M,O
Counselor Education M
Education—General M,D
Educational Leadership and Administration M,D
Elementary Education M,D
Entrepreneurship M,O
Finance and Banking M,O
Higher Education M,D
International Business M,O
Management Information Systems M,O
Marketing M,O
Middle School Education M,D
Nonprofit Management M,O
Organizational Behavior M,O
Special Education M,D

CALIFORNIA MARITIME ACADEMY
Transportation Management M

CALIFORNIA MIRAMAR UNIVERSITY
Business Administration and Management—General M
Management Strategy and Policy M
Taxation M

CALIFORNIA NATIONAL UNIVERSITY FOR ADVANCED STUDIES
Business Administration and Management—General M

CALIFORNIA POLYTECHNIC STATE UNIVERSITY, SAN LUIS OBISPO
Agricultural Education M
Business Administration and Management—General M
Education—General M
Industrial and Manufacturing Management M
Kinesiology and Movement Studies M
Taxation M

CALIFORNIA STATE POLYTECHNIC UNIVERSITY, POMONA
Accounting M
Business Administration and Management—General M
Education—General M
Kinesiology and Movement Studies M
Management Information Systems M

CALIFORNIA STATE UNIVERSITY, BAKERSFIELD
Business Administration and Management—General M
Counselor Education M
Education—General M,O
Educational Leadership and Administration M
Mathematics Education M
Middle School Education M
Secondary Education M
Social Work M
Special Education M
Student Affairs M

CALIFORNIA STATE UNIVERSITY CHANNEL ISLANDS
Business Administration and Management—General M
Educational Leadership and Administration M

CALIFORNIA STATE UNIVERSITY, CHICO
Business Administration and Management—General M
Curriculum and Instruction M
Educational Leadership and Administration M
English as a Second Language M
Foreign Languages Education M
Kinesiology and Movement Studies M
Mathematics Education M
Recreation and Park Management M
Social Sciences Education M
Social Work M
Special Education M

CALIFORNIA STATE UNIVERSITY, DOMINGUEZ HILLS
Business Administration and Management—General M
Computer Education M,O
Counselor Education M
Curriculum and Instruction M
Education—General M,O
Educational Leadership and Administration M
Educational Media/Instructional Technology M,O
English as a Second Language M,O
International and Comparative Education M
Mathematics Education M
Multilingual and Multicultural Education M
Physical Education M
Quality Management M
Science Education M
Social Work M
Special Education M

CALIFORNIA STATE UNIVERSITY, EAST BAY
Accounting M
Actuarial Science M
Business Administration and Management—General M
Counselor Education M
Distance Education Development M
Early Childhood Education M
Education—General M
Educational Leadership and Administration M,D
Educational Media/Instructional Technology M
English as a Second Language M
Entrepreneurship M
Finance and Banking M
Human Resources Management M
Industrial and Manufacturing Management M
International Business M
Management Information Systems M
Management Strategy and Policy M
Marketing M
Mathematics Education M
Organizational Management M
Physical Education M
Reading Education M
Recreation and Park Management M
Social Sciences Education M
Social Work M
Special Education M
Supply Chain Management M
Taxation M
Travel and Tourism M
Urban Education M,D

CALIFORNIA STATE UNIVERSITY, FRESNO
Accounting M
Business Administration and Management—General M
Counselor Education M
Curriculum and Instruction M
Early Childhood Education M
Education—General M,D
Educational Leadership and Administration M,D
English as a Second Language M
Exercise and Sports Science M
Kinesiology and Movement Studies M
Mathematics Education M
Music Education M
Reading Education M
Social Sciences Education M
Social Work M
Special Education M

CALIFORNIA STATE UNIVERSITY, FULLERTON
Accounting M
Advertising and Public Relations M
Business Administration and Management—General M
Counselor Education M
Educational Leadership and Administration M,D
Educational Media/Instructional Technology M
Electronic Commerce M
Elementary Education M
English as a Second Language M
Entrepreneurship M
Finance and Banking M
International Business M
Management Information Systems M
Marketing M
Mathematics Education M
Middle School Education M
Multilingual and Multicultural Education M
Music Education M
Physical Education M
Reading Education M
Science Education M
Secondary Education M
Social Work M
Special Education M
Taxation M
Travel and Tourism M

CALIFORNIA STATE UNIVERSITY, LONG BEACH
Art Education M
Athletic Training and Sports Medicine M
Business Administration and Management—General M
Counselor Education M
Education—General M,D
Educational Leadership and Administration M,D
Educational Psychology M
Elementary Education M
English as a Second Language M
Exercise and Sports Science M
Health Education M
Higher Education M
Hospitality Management M
Kinesiology and Movement Studies M
Leisure Studies M
Logistics M
Mathematics Education M
Physical Education M
Recreation and Park Management M
Science Education M
Secondary Education M
Social Work M
Special Education M
Sports Management M
Student Affairs M

CALIFORNIA STATE UNIVERSITY, LOS ANGELES
Accounting M
Art Education M
Business Administration and Management—General M
Counselor Education M,D
Education—General M,D
Elementary Education M
Finance and Banking M
Health Education M
International Business M
Kinesiology and Movement Studies M
Management Information Systems M
Marketing M
Music Education M
Physical Education M
Reading Education M
Secondary Education M
Social Work M

Special Education M,D
Taxation M

CALIFORNIA STATE UNIVERSITY, MONTEREY BAY
Business Administration and Management—General M
Education—General M
Educational Media/Instructional Technology M
Management Information Systems M
Social Work M

CALIFORNIA STATE UNIVERSITY, NORTHRIDGE
Art Education M
Business Administration and Management—General M
Counselor Education M
Curriculum and Instruction M
Early Childhood Education M
Education—General M,D
Educational Leadership and Administration M,D
Educational Media/Instructional Technology M
Educational Psychology M
Elementary Education M
English Education M
Hospitality Management M
Kinesiology and Movement Studies M
Mathematics Education M
Multilingual and Multicultural Education M
Music Education M
Reading Education M
Recreation and Park Management M
Science Education M
Secondary Education M
Social Work M
Special Education M
Taxation M
Travel and Tourism M

CALIFORNIA STATE UNIVERSITY, SACRAMENTO
Accounting M
Business Administration and Management—General M
Counselor Education M
Curriculum and Instruction M
Early Childhood Education M
Education—General M
Educational Leadership and Administration M
English as a Second Language M
Foreign Languages Education M
Human Resources Development M
Human Resources Management M
Human Services M
Multilingual and Multicultural Education M
Physical Education M
Reading Education M
Real Estate M
Recreation and Park Management M
Social Work M
Special Education M
Vocational and Technical Education M

CALIFORNIA STATE UNIVERSITY, SAN BERNARDINO
Accounting M
Business Administration and Management—General M
Counselor Education M
Curriculum and Instruction M
Education—General M,D
Educational Leadership and Administration M,D
Educational Media/Instructional Technology M
English as a Second Language M,D
English Education M,D
Entrepreneurship M
Finance and Banking M
Health Education M
International Business M
Kinesiology and Movement Studies M
Management Information Systems M
Marketing M
Mathematics Education M
Multilingual and Multicultural Education M
Reading Education M
Science Education M
Secondary Education M,D
Social Sciences Education M,D
Social Work M
Special Education M
Supply Chain Management M
Vocational and Technical Education M

CALIFORNIA STATE UNIVERSITY, SAN MARCOS
Business Administration and Management—General M
Education—General M

CALIFORNIA STATE UNIVERSITY, STANISLAUS
Business Administration and Management—General M
Community College Education D
Counselor Education M
Curriculum and Instruction M
Education—General M,D,O
Educational Leadership and Administration M,D
Educational Media/Instructional Technology M
Elementary Education M

English as a Second Language M,O
Multilingual and Multicultural Education M
Physical Education M
Reading Education M
Secondary Education M
Social Work M
Special Education M

CALIFORNIA UNIVERSITY OF PENNSYLVANIA
Athletic Training and Sports Medicine M
Business Administration and Management—General M
Counselor Education M
Education—General M
Educational Leadership and Administration M
Elementary Education M
Exercise and Sports Science M
Legal and Justice Studies M
Reading Education M
Secondary Education M
Social Work M
Special Education M
Sports Management M
Vocational and Technical Education M

CALIFORNIA WESTERN SCHOOL OF LAW
Accounting M,D
Law M,D

CALUMET COLLEGE OF SAINT JOSEPH
Educational Leadership and Administration M
Quality Management M

CALVIN COLLEGE
Curriculum and Instruction M
Education—General M
Educational Leadership and Administration M
Reading Education M
Special Education M

CALVIN THEOLOGICAL SEMINARY
Religious Education M,D

CAMBRIDGE COLLEGE
Business Administration and Management—General M
Counselor Education M,D,O
Curriculum and Instruction M,D,O
Early Childhood Education M,D,O
Education—General M,D,O
Educational Leadership and Administration M,D,O
Educational Measurement and Evaluation M,D,O
Educational Media/Instructional Technology M,D,O
Elementary Education M,D,O
English as a Second Language M,D,O
Entrepreneurship M
Health Education M,D,O
Home Economics Education M,D,O
Mathematics Education M,D,O
Middle School Education M,D,O
Nonprofit Management M
Organizational Management M
Reading Education M,D,O
Science Education M,D,O
Social Sciences Education M,D,O
Special Education M,D,O

CAMERON UNIVERSITY
Business Administration and Management—General M
Education—General M
Educational Leadership and Administration M
Entrepreneurship M

CAMPBELLSVILLE UNIVERSITY
Business Administration and Management—General M
Curriculum and Instruction M
Education—General M
Music Education M
Organizational Management M
Social Work
Special Education M

CAMPBELL UNIVERSITY
Business Administration and Management—General M
Counselor Education M
Education—General M
Educational Leadership and Administration M
Elementary Education M
English Education M
Law D
Mathematics Education M
Middle School Education M
Physical Education M
Religious Education M,D
Secondary Education M
Social Sciences Education M

CANISIUS COLLEGE
Accounting M
Business Administration and Management—General M
Business Education M
Counselor Education M
Early Childhood Education M
Education of the Gifted M,O
Education—General M,O
Educational Leadership and Administration M,O
Elementary Education M,O
International Business M

Kinesiology and Movement Studies M
Marketing M
Middle School Education M
Physical Education M
Reading Education M,O
Secondary Education M,O
Special Education M,O
Sports Management M
Student Affairs M,O

CAPE BRETON UNIVERSITY
Business Administration and Management—General M

CAPELLA UNIVERSITY
Accounting M,D,O
Adult Education M,D,O
Business Administration and Management—General M,D,O
Curriculum and Instruction M,D,O
Education—General M,D,O
Educational Leadership and Administration M,D,O
Educational Media/Instructional Technology M,D,O
Educational Psychology M,D,O
Elementary Education M,D,O
Finance and Banking M,D,O
Higher Education M,D,O
Human Resources Management M,D,O
Human Services M,D,O
Management Information Systems M,D,O
Marketing M,D,O
Middle School Education M,D,O
Multilingual and Multicultural Education M,D,O
Nonprofit Management M,D,O
Organizational Management M,D,O
Project Management M,D,O
Reading Education M,D,O

CAPITAL UNIVERSITY
Business Administration and Management—General M
Entrepreneurship M
Finance and Banking M
Law M,D
Legal and Justice Studies M
Marketing M
Music Education M
Taxation M

CAPITOL COLLEGE
Business Administration and Management—General M
Management Information Systems M

CARDINAL STRITCH UNIVERSITY
Business Administration and Management—General M
Computer Education M
Education—General M,D
Educational Leadership and Administration M,D
Educational Media/Instructional Technology M
English as a Second Language M
Reading Education M
Special Education M
Sports Management M
Urban Education M,D

CARIBBEAN UNIVERSITY
Curriculum and Instruction M,D
Early Childhood Education M,D
Education—General M,D
Educational Leadership and Administration M,D
Educational Media/Instructional Technology M,D
Elementary Education M,D
English Education M,D
Foreign Languages Education M,D
Human Resources Management M,D
Mathematics Education M,D
Physical Education M,D
Science Education M,D
Social Sciences Education M,D
Special Education M,D

CARLETON UNIVERSITY
Business Administration and Management—General M,D
Legal and Justice Studies M,D
Social Work M

CARLOS ALBIZU UNIVERSITY, MIAMI CAMPUS
Business Administration and Management—General M,D
Education of the Gifted M,D
English as a Second Language M,D
Entrepreneurship M,D
Nonprofit Management M,D
Organizational Management M,D
Special Education M,D

CARLOW UNIVERSITY
Art Education M
Business Administration and Management—General M
Counselor Education M
Early Childhood Education M
Education—General M
Educational Media/Instructional Technology M
Entrepreneurship M
Middle School Education M
Organizational Management M,D
Secondary Education M
Special Education M

CARNEGIE MELLON UNIVERSITY
Accounting D

Business Administration and Management—General M,D
Education—General M,D
Electronic Commerce M
Entertainment Management M
Entrepreneurship D
Finance and Banking D
Industrial and Manufacturing Management M,D
Management Information Systems M,D
Marketing D
Music Education M
Organizational Behavior D

CARROLL UNIVERSITY
Business Administration and Management—General M
Education—General M

CARSON-NEWMAN COLLEGE
Business Administration and Management—General M
Counselor Education M
Curriculum and Instruction M
Education—General M
Educational Leadership and Administration M
Elementary Education M
English as a Second Language M
Secondary Education M

CARTHAGE COLLEGE
Art Education M,O
Counselor Education M,O
Education of the Gifted M,O
Education—General M,O
Educational Leadership and Administration M,O
English Education M,O
Reading Education M,O
Science Education M,O
Social Sciences Education M,O

CASE WESTERN RESERVE UNIVERSITY
Accounting M,D
Art Education M
Business Administration and Management—General M,D
Finance and Banking M,D
Human Resources Management M
Industrial and Manufacturing Management M,D
Intellectual Property Law M,D
Law M,D
Legal and Justice Studies M,D
Logistics M,D
Management Information Systems M,D
Management Strategy and Policy M
Marketing M,D
Music Education M,D
Nonprofit Management M,O
Organizational Behavior M,D
Quality Management M,D
Social Work M,D
Supply Chain Management M

CASTLETON STATE COLLEGE
Curriculum and Instruction M
Education—General M,O
Educational Leadership and Administration M,O
Reading Education M,O
Special Education M,O

CATAWBA COLLEGE
Education—General M
Elementary Education M

THE CATHOLIC UNIVERSITY OF AMERICA
Accounting M
Business Administration and Management—General M
Education—General M,D,O
Educational Leadership and Administration M,D,O
Educational Policy M,D,O
Educational Psychology M,D,O
Human Resources Management M
Information Studies M
Law D
Legal and Justice Studies D,O
Library Science M
Secondary Education M,D,O
Social Work M,D
Special Education M,D,O

CEDAR CREST COLLEGE
Education—General M

CEDARVILLE UNIVERSITY
Education—General M
Educational Leadership and Administration M

CENTENARY COLLEGE
Accounting M
Business Administration and Management—General M
Education—General M
Educational Leadership and Administration M
Special Education M

CENTENARY COLLEGE OF LOUISIANA
Business Administration and Management—General M
Curriculum and Instruction M
Education—General M
Educational Leadership and Administration M
Elementary Education M
Secondary Education M

*M—master's degree; P—first professional degree; D—doctorate; O—other advanced degree; *Close-Up and/or Display*

CENTRAL CONNECTICUT STATE UNIVERSITY
- Actuarial Science M,O
- Advertising and Public Relations M,O
- Art Education M,O
- Counselor Education M,O
- Early Childhood Education M
- Education—General M,D,O
- Educational Leadership and Administration M,D,O
- Educational Media/Instructional Technology M
- Elementary Education M,O
- English as a Second Language M,O
- Exercise and Sports Science M,O
- Foreign Languages Education M,O
- Foundations and Philosophy of Education M
- Industrial and Manufacturing Management M,O
- Information Studies M
- Logistics M,O
- Music Education M,O
- Physical Education M,O
- Reading Education M,O
- Science Education M,O
- Secondary Education M
- Special Education M,O
- Supply Chain Management M,O
- Vocational and Technical Education M,O

CENTRAL EUROPEAN UNIVERSITY
- Business Administration and Management—General M
- Finance and Banking M,D
- International Business M,D
- Law M,D
- Legal and Justice Studies M,D
- Management Information Systems M
- Marketing M
- Real Estate M

CENTRAL METHODIST UNIVERSITY
- Counselor Education M
- Education—General M

CENTRAL MICHIGAN UNIVERSITY
- Accounting M
- Adult Education M,O
- Business Administration and Management—General M,O
- Community College Education M,O
- Counselor Education M
- Curriculum and Instruction M,D,O
- Early Childhood Education M,O
- Education—General M,D,O
- Educational Leadership and Administration M,D,O
- Educational Media/Instructional Technology M,D,O
- Elementary Education M,O
- English as a Second Language M
- Exercise and Sports Science M,D
- Finance and Banking M
- Higher Education M,D,O
- Human Resources Management M,O
- Industrial and Manufacturing Management M
- International Business M,O
- Leisure Studies M
- Logistics M,O
- Management Information Systems M,O
- Marketing M
- Mathematics Education M,D
- Middle School Education M
- Music Education M
- Physical Education M
- Reading Education M,O
- Recreation and Park Management M,O
- Science Education M
- Secondary Education M,O
- Special Education M,O
- Sports Management M,O
- Student Affairs M,D,O

CENTRAL STATE UNIVERSITY
- Education—General M

CENTRAL WASHINGTON UNIVERSITY
- Accounting M
- Counselor Education M
- Curriculum and Instruction M
- Education—General M
- Educational Leadership and Administration M
- English as a Second Language M
- Exercise and Sports Science M
- Foundations and Philosophy of Education M
- Health Education M
- Home Economics Education M
- Physical Education M
- Reading Education M
- Special Education M
- Sports Management M
- Vocational and Technical Education M

CHADRON STATE COLLEGE
- Business Administration and Management—General M
- Business Education M,O
- Counselor Education M,O
- Education—General M,O
- Educational Leadership and Administration M,O
- Elementary Education M,O
- English Education M,O
- Secondary Education M,O
- Social Sciences Education M,O

CHAMINADE UNIVERSITY OF HONOLULU
- Accounting M
- Business Administration and Management—General M
- Education—General M
- Educational Leadership and Administration M
- Elementary Education M
- English Education M
- Mathematics Education M
- Nonprofit Management M
- Science Education M
- Secondary Education M
- Social Sciences Education M
- Special Education M

CHAMPLAIN COLLEGE
- Business Administration and Management—General M
- Education—General M
- Law M

CHANCELLOR UNIVERSITY
- Business Administration and Management—General M

CHAPMAN UNIVERSITY
- Business Administration and Management—General M
- Counselor Education M,D,O
- Curriculum and Instruction M,D,O
- Education—General M,D,O
- Educational Psychology M,D,O
- Elementary Education M,D,O
- Environmental Law M,D
- Law M,D
- Secondary Education M,D,O
- Special Education M,D,O
- Taxation M,D

CHARLESTON SOUTHERN UNIVERSITY
- Accounting M
- Business Administration and Management—General M
- Education—General M
- Educational Leadership and Administration M
- Elementary Education M
- Finance and Banking M
- Management Information Systems M
- Organizational Management M
- Secondary Education M

CHARLOTTE SCHOOL OF LAW
- Law D

CHATHAM UNIVERSITY
- Accounting M
- Art Education M
- Business Administration and Management—General M
- Early Childhood Education M
- Education—General M
- Elementary Education M
- English Education M
- Environmental Education M
- Mathematics Education M
- Science Education M
- Secondary Education M
- Social Sciences Education M
- Special Education M
- Sustainability Management M

CHESTNUT HILL COLLEGE
- Early Childhood Education M
- Education—General M
- Educational Leadership and Administration M
- Educational Media/Instructional Technology M,O
- Human Services M,O
- Middle School Education M
- Secondary Education M

CHEYNEY UNIVERSITY OF PENNSYLVANIA
- Adult Education M
- Early Childhood Education O
- Education—General M,O
- Educational Leadership and Administration M,O
- Elementary Education M
- Special Education M

THE CHICAGO SCHOOL OF PROFESSIONAL PSYCHOLOGY
- Counselor Education M,D

CHICAGO STATE UNIVERSITY
- Counselor Education M
- Early Childhood Education M
- Education—General M,D
- Educational Leadership and Administration M,D
- Educational Media/Instructional Technology M
- Elementary Education M
- Foundations and Philosophy of Education M
- Higher Education M,D
- Library Science M
- Middle School Education M
- Multilingual and Multicultural Education M
- Physical Education M
- Reading Education M
- Secondary Education M
- Social Work M
- Special Education M
- Vocational and Technical Education M

CHOWAN UNIVERSITY
- Education—General M

CHRISTIAN BROTHERS UNIVERSITY
- Business Administration and Management—General M,O
- Education—General M
- Educational Leadership and Administration M
- Finance and Banking M,O
- Project Management M,O

CHRISTOPHER NEWPORT UNIVERSITY
- Art Education M
- Computer Education M
- Education—General M
- Elementary Education M
- English as a Second Language M
- English Education M
- Foreign Languages Education M
- Mathematics Education M
- Music Education M
- Science Education M
- Secondary Education M
- Social Sciences Education M

THE CITADEL, THE MILITARY COLLEGE OF SOUTH CAROLINA
- Business Administration and Management—General M
- Counselor Education M,O
- Education—General M,O
- Educational Leadership and Administration M,O
- Elementary Education M
- English Education M
- Health Education M
- Mathematics Education M
- Physical Education M
- Project Management M
- Reading Education M
- Science Education M
- Secondary Education M
- Social Sciences Education M
- Student Affairs M

CITY COLLEGE OF THE CITY UNIVERSITY OF NEW YORK
- Early Childhood Education M
- Education—General M,O
- Educational Leadership and Administration M,O
- English Education M,O
- Mathematics Education M,O
- Middle School Education M,O
- Multilingual and Multicultural Education M
- Reading Education M
- Science Education M
- Secondary Education M,O
- Social Sciences Education M,O
- Special Education M,O

CITY UNIVERSITY OF NEW YORK SCHOOL OF LAW
- Law D

CITY UNIVERSITY OF SEATTLE
- Accounting M,O
- Business Administration and Management—General M,O
- Curriculum and Instruction M,D,O
- Education—General M,D,O
- Educational Leadership and Administration M,D,O
- Elementary Education M,D,O
- Finance and Banking M,D,O
- Higher Education M,D,O
- Human Resources Management M,O
- International Business M,O
- Management Information Systems M,O
- Marketing M,O
- Organizational Management M,D,O
- Project Management M,O
- Reading Education M,D,O
- Special Education M,D,O
- Sustainability Management M,O

CLAFLIN UNIVERSITY
- Business Administration and Management—General M

CLAREMONT GRADUATE UNIVERSITY
- Archives/Archival Administration M,D,O
- Business Administration and Management—General M,D,O
- Education—General M,D,O
- Educational Leadership and Administration M,D,O
- Educational Measurement and Evaluation M,D,O
- Electronic Commerce M,D,O
- Higher Education M,D,O
- Human Resources Development M,D,O
- Human Resources Management M
- Management Information Systems M,D,O
- Management Strategy and Policy M,D,O
- Special Education M,D,O
- Student Affairs M,D,O
- Urban Education M,D,O

CLAREMONT MCKENNA COLLEGE
- Finance and Banking M

CLAREMONT SCHOOL OF THEOLOGY
- Religious Education M,D

CLARION UNIVERSITY OF PENNSYLVANIA
- Advertising and Public Relations M,O
- Business Administration and Management—General M
- Curriculum and Instruction M,O
- Early Childhood Education M,O
- Education—General M,O
- Educational Media/Instructional Technology M,O
- English Education M,O
- Foreign Languages Education M,O
- Library Science M,O
- Mathematics Education M,O
- Reading Education M,O
- Science Education M,O
- Special Education M,O
- Vocational and Technical Education M,O

CLARK ATLANTA UNIVERSITY
- Accounting M
- Business Administration and Management—General M
- Counselor Education M
- Curriculum and Instruction M
- Education—General M,D,O
- Educational Leadership and Administration M,D,O
- Educational Psychology M
- Mathematics Education M
- Science Education M
- Social Work M,D
- Special Education M

CLARKE UNIVERSITY
- Business Administration and Management—General M
- Early Childhood Education M
- Education—General M
- Educational Leadership and Administration M
- Educational Media/Instructional Technology M
- Reading Education M
- Special Education M

CLARKSON UNIVERSITY
- Business Administration and Management—General M

CLARK UNIVERSITY
- Accounting M
- Business Administration and Management—General M
- Education—General M
- Finance and Banking M
- International Business M
- Management Information Systems M
- Marketing M

CLAYTON STATE UNIVERSITY
- Accounting M
- Archives/Archival Administration M
- Business Administration and Management—General M
- Education—General M
- English Education M
- International Business M
- Mathematics Education M
- Supply Chain Management M

CLEARWATER CHRISTIAN COLLEGE
- Educational Leadership and Administration M

CLEARY UNIVERSITY
- Accounting M,O
- Business Administration and Management—General M,O
- Finance and Banking M,O
- Nonprofit Management M,O
- Organizational Management M,O
- Sustainability Management M,O

CLEMSON UNIVERSITY
- Accounting M
- Agricultural Education M
- Business Administration and Management—General M
- Counselor Education M
- Curriculum and Instruction D
- Early Childhood Education M
- Education—General M,D,O
- Educational Leadership and Administration M,D,O
- Elementary Education M
- English Education M
- Entrepreneurship M
- Higher Education D
- Human Resources Development M
- Human Resources Management M
- Marketing M
- Mathematics Education M
- Middle School Education M
- Reading Education M
- Real Estate M
- Recreation and Park Management M,D
- Science Education M
- Secondary Education M
- Social Sciences Education M
- Special Education M
- Student Affairs M
- Travel and Tourism M,D

CLEVELAND STATE UNIVERSITY
- Accounting M
- Adult Education M,O
- Art Education M
- Business Administration and Management—General M,D
- Counselor Education M,D,O
- Early Childhood Education M
- Education of Students with Severe/Multiple Disabilities M
- Education—General M,D,O
- Educational Leadership and Administration M,D,O
- English as a Second Language M
- Exercise and Sports Science M
- Finance and Banking M,D,O
- Foreign Languages Education M
- Health Education M
- Human Resources Management M
- Industrial and Manufacturing Management D
- International Business M,D,O
- Law M,D,O
- Management Information Systems M,D
- Marketing M,D,O
- Mathematics Education M
- Middle School Education M
- Music Education M
- Nonprofit Management M,O
- Organizational Management M,O
- Physical Education M
- Real Estate M,D,O
- Science Education M
- Social Work M

Special Education M
Sports Management M
Taxation M
Urban Education M,D

COASTAL CAROLINA UNIVERSITY
Accounting M
Business Administration and Management—General M
Education—General M
Educational Leadership and Administration M

COE COLLEGE
Education—General M

COGSWELL POLYTECHNICAL COLLEGE
Entrepreneurship M

COLGATE UNIVERSITY
Secondary Education M

THE COLLEGE AT BROCKPORT, STATE UNIVERSITY OF NEW YORK
Accounting M
Counselor Education M,O
Curriculum and Instruction M
Education—General M,O
Educational Leadership and Administration O
English Education M
Foreign Languages Education M,O
Health Education M
Leisure Studies M
Mathematics Education M
Middle School Education M
Multilingual and Multicultural Education M,O
Nonprofit Management M,O
Physical Education M,O
Reading Education M
Recreation and Park Management M
Science Education M
Social Sciences Education M
Social Work M
Sports Management M,O

COLLEGE FOR FINANCIAL PLANNING
Finance and Banking M

COLLEGE OF CHARLESTON
Accounting M
Business Administration and Management—General M
Early Childhood Education M
Education—General M,O
Elementary Education M
English as a Second Language O
Foreign Languages Education M
Management Information Systems M
Mathematics Education M
Music Education M
Science Education M
Special Education M

THE COLLEGE OF IDAHO
Education—General M

COLLEGE OF MOUNT ST. JOSEPH
Art Education M
Early Childhood Education M
Education—General M
Educational Leadership and Administration M
Middle School Education M
Multilingual and Multicultural Education M
Music Education M
Organizational Management M
Reading Education M
Religious Education M,O
Secondary Education M

COLLEGE OF MOUNT SAINT VINCENT
Education—General M,O
Educational Media/Instructional Technology M,O
Middle School Education M,O
Multilingual and Multicultural Education M,O
Urban Education M,O

THE COLLEGE OF NEW JERSEY
Counselor Education M
Early Childhood Education M
Education—General M,O
Educational Leadership and Administration M,O
Elementary Education M
English as a Second Language M,O
Health Education M
International and Comparative Education M,O
Physical Education M
Reading Education M,O
Secondary Education M,O
Special Education M,O

THE COLLEGE OF NEW ROCHELLE
Art Education M
Early Childhood Education M
Education of the Gifted M,O
Education—General M,O
Educational Leadership and Administration M,O
Elementary Education M
English as a Second Language M,O
Human Resources Development M
Multilingual and Multicultural Education M,O
Reading Education M
Special Education M

COLLEGE OF SAINT ELIZABETH
Business Administration and Management—General M
Education—General M,D,O
Educational Leadership and Administration M,D,O
Educational Media/Instructional Technology M,D,O
Higher Education M,O
Student Affairs M,O

COLLEGE OF ST. JOSEPH
Business Administration and Management—General M
Counselor Education M
Education—General M
Elementary Education M
English Education M
Reading Education M
Secondary Education M
Social Sciences Education M
Special Education M

COLLEGE OF SAINT MARY
Education—General M
Educational Leadership and Administration M
Educational Measurement and Evaluation M
English as a Second Language M
Health Education D
Organizational Management M

THE COLLEGE OF SAINT ROSE
Accounting M
Art Education M,O
Business Administration and Management—General M
Business Education M,O
Counselor Education M
Curriculum and Instruction M,O
Early Childhood Education M,O
Education—General M,O
Educational Leadership and Administration M,O
Educational Media/Instructional Technology M,O
Educational Psychology M,O
Elementary Education M,O
Multilingual and Multicultural Education M,O
Music Education M,O
Nonprofit Management O
Reading Education M,O
Secondary Education M,O
Special Education M,O
Student Affairs M,O

THE COLLEGE OF ST. SCHOLASTICA
Business Administration and Management—General M,O
Education—General M,O
Exercise and Sports Science M
Management Information Systems M,O

COLLEGE OF STATEN ISLAND OF THE CITY UNIVERSITY OF NEW YORK
Business Administration and Management—General M
Education—General M,O
Educational Leadership and Administration O
Elementary Education M
Secondary Education M
Special Education M

THE COLLEGE OF WILLIAM AND MARY
Accounting M
Business Administration and Management—General M
Counselor Education M,D
Curriculum and Instruction M,D
Education of the Gifted M
Education—General M,D,O
Educational Leadership and Administration M,D
Educational Media/Instructional Technology M,D
Educational Policy M,D
Elementary Education M
English Education M
Foreign Languages Education M
Law M,D
Mathematics Education M
Reading Education M
Science Education M
Secondary Education M
Social Sciences Education M
Special Education M

COLLÈGE UNIVERSITAIRE DE SAINT-BONIFACE
Education—General M

COLORADO CHRISTIAN UNIVERSITY
Business Administration and Management—General M
Business Education M
Curriculum and Instruction M
Distance Education Development M
Early Childhood Education M
Education—General M
Educational Media/Instructional Technology M
Elementary Education M
Project Management M
Special Education M

THE COLORADO COLLEGE
Art Education M
Education—General M
Elementary Education M
English Education M
Foreign Languages Education M
Mathematics Education M
Music Education M
Science Education M
Secondary Education M
Social Sciences Education M

COLORADO MESA UNIVERSITY
Business Administration and Management—General M
Education—General M
Educational Leadership and Administration M
English as a Second Language M

COLORADO STATE UNIVERSITY
Accounting M
Adult Education M,D
Advertising and Public Relations M,D
Business Administration and Management—General M
Community College Education M,D
Counselor Education M,D
Education—General M,D
Educational Leadership and Administration M,D
Exercise and Sports Science M,D
Finance and Banking M
Foreign Languages Education M
Management Information Systems M
Organizational Management M
Recreation and Park Management M,D
Social Work M,D
Student Affairs M,D
Sustainability Management M
Vocational and Technical Education M,D

COLORADO STATE UNIVERSITY–PUEBLO
Art Education M
Business Administration and Management—General M
Education—General M
Educational Media/Instructional Technology M
Foreign Languages Education M
Health Education M
Music Education M
Physical Education M
Special Education M

COLORADO TECHNICAL UNIVERSITY COLORADO SPRINGS
Accounting M,D
Business Administration and Management—General M,D
Finance and Banking M,D
Human Resources Management M,D
Industrial and Manufacturing Management M,D
Logistics M,D
Marketing M,D
Project Management M,D

COLORADO TECHNICAL UNIVERSITY DENVER SOUTH
Accounting M
Business Administration and Management—General M
Finance and Banking M
Human Resources Management M
Industrial and Manufacturing Management M
Marketing M
Project Management M

COLORADO TECHNICAL UNIVERSITY SIOUX FALLS
Business Administration and Management—General M
Human Resources Management M
Management Information Systems M
Organizational Management M
Project Management M

COLUMBIA COLLEGE (MO)
Business Administration and Management—General M
Education—General M

COLUMBIA COLLEGE (SC)
Education—General M
Elementary Education M
Organizational Behavior M,O

COLUMBIA COLLEGE CHICAGO
Education—General M
Elementary Education M
English Education M
Entertainment Management M
Multilingual and Multicultural Education M
Urban Education M

COLUMBIA INTERNATIONAL UNIVERSITY
Counselor Education M,D,O
Curriculum and Instruction M,D,O
Early Childhood Education M,D,O
Education—General M,D,O
Educational Leadership and Administration M,D,O
Educational Media/Instructional Technology M,D,O
Elementary Education M,D,O
English as a Second Language M,D,O
Higher Education M,D,O
Multilingual and Multicultural Education M,D,O
Religious Education M,D,O
Special Education M,D,O

COLUMBIA SOUTHERN UNIVERSITY
Business Administration and Management—General M,D
Electronic Commerce M
Finance and Banking M
Hospitality Management M
Human Resources Management M
International Business M
Marketing M

COLUMBIA UNIVERSITY
Accounting M,D
Actuarial Science M
Archives/Archival Administration M
Business Administration and Management—General M,D
Entrepreneurship M
Finance and Banking M,D
Human Resources Management M
Information Studies M
International Business M
Kinesiology and Movement Studies M,D
Law M,D
Marketing M,D
Nonprofit Management M
Real Estate M
Science Education M,D,O
Social Work M,D
Sports Management M
Sustainability Management M

COLUMBUS STATE UNIVERSITY
Art Education M
Business Administration and Management—General M,O
Counselor Education M,D,O
Curriculum and Instruction M,D,O
Early Childhood Education M,O
Education—General M,D,O
Educational Leadership and Administration M,D,O
Educational Media/Instructional Technology M,O
English Education M,O
Health Education M,O
Higher Education M,D,O
Mathematics Education M,O
Middle School Education M,O
Music Education M,O
Organizational Management M,O
Physical Education M,O
Science Education M,O
Secondary Education M,O
Social Sciences Education M,O
Special Education M,O

CONCORDIA COLLEGE
Education—General M
Foreign Languages Education M

CONCORDIA UNIVERSITY (CA)
Business Administration and Management—General M
Counselor Education M
Curriculum and Instruction M
Education—General M
Educational Leadership and Administration M
Physical Education M
Sports Management M

CONCORDIA UNIVERSITY (CANADA)
Accounting M,D,O
Adult Education M,O
Art Education M,D
Aviation Management M,D,O
Business Administration and Management—General M,D,O
Education—General M,D,O
Educational Media/Instructional Technology M,D,O
English as a Second Language M,O
Exercise and Sports Science M
Investment Management M,D,O
Mathematics Education M,D
Organizational Management M
Sports Management M,D,O
Transportation Management M,D,O

CONCORDIA UNIVERSITY (OR)
Business Administration and Management—General M
Curriculum and Instruction M
Education—General M
Educational Leadership and Administration M
Elementary Education M
Secondary Education M

CONCORDIA UNIVERSITY ANN ARBOR
Curriculum and Instruction M
Educational Leadership and Administration M
Organizational Management M

CONCORDIA UNIVERSITY CHICAGO
Business Administration and Management—General M
Counselor Education M,O
Curriculum and Instruction M
Early Childhood Education M,D
Education—General M
Educational Leadership and Administration M,D,O
Educational Media/Instructional Technology M
Elementary Education M
Exercise and Sports Science M
Human Services M
Reading Education M
Religious Education M
Secondary Education M

CONCORDIA UNIVERSITY, NEBRASKA
Early Childhood Education M
Education—General M

*M—master's degree; P—first professional degree; D—doctorate; O—other advanced degree; *Close-Up and/or Display*

- Educational Leadership and Administration M
- Elementary Education M
- Reading Education M
- Religious Education M
- Secondary Education M

CONCORDIA UNIVERSITY, ST. PAUL
- Business Administration and Management—General M
- Curriculum and Instruction M,O
- Early Childhood Education M,O
- Education—General M,O
- Educational Leadership and Administration M,O
- Educational Media/Instructional Technology M,O
- Human Resources Management M
- Organizational Management M
- Reading Education M,O
- Religious Education M,O
- Special Education M,O
- Sports Management M,O

CONCORDIA UNIVERSITY TEXAS
- Education—General M

CONCORDIA UNIVERSITY WISCONSIN
- Art Education M
- Business Administration and Management—General M
- Counselor Education M
- Curriculum and Instruction M
- Early Childhood Education M
- Education—General M
- Educational Leadership and Administration M
- Environmental Education M
- Finance and Banking M
- Human Resources Management M
- Human Services M,D
- International Business M
- Management Information Systems M
- Marketing M
- Reading Education M
- Special Education M
- Student Affairs M

CONCORD LAW SCHOOL
- Law D

CONCORD UNIVERSITY
- Educational Leadership and Administration M
- Reading Education M
- Social Sciences Education M

CONSERVATORIO DE MUSICA
- Music Education M

CONVERSE COLLEGE
- Art Education M,O
- Curriculum and Instruction O
- Early Childhood Education M,O
- Education of the Gifted M
- Education—General M,O
- Educational Leadership and Administration M,O
- Elementary Education M
- English Education M
- Mathematics Education M
- Music Education M
- Science Education M
- Secondary Education M
- Social Sciences Education M
- Special Education M

COPENHAGEN BUSINESS SCHOOL
- Business Administration and Management—General M,D
- International Business M,D
- Logistics M,D
- Management Information Systems M,D

COPPIN STATE UNIVERSITY
- Adult Education M
- Curriculum and Instruction M
- Education—General M
- Human Services M
- Reading Education M
- Special Education M

CORBAN UNIVERSITY
- Business Administration and Management—General M
- Education—General M
- Nonprofit Management M

CORCORAN COLLEGE OF ART AND DESIGN
- Art Education M

CORNELL UNIVERSITY
- Accounting D
- Adult Education M,D
- Agricultural Education M,D
- Business Administration and Management—General M,D
- Curriculum and Instruction M,D
- Education—General M,D
- Facilities Management M
- Finance and Banking D
- Foreign Languages Education M,D
- Hospitality Management M,D
- Human Resources Management M,D
- Information Studies D
- Law M,D
- Marketing D
- Mathematics Education M,D
- Organizational Behavior M,D
- Real Estate M
- Science Education M,D
- Social Work M,D

CORNERSTONE UNIVERSITY
- Business Administration and Management—General M,O
- Education—General M,O
- English as a Second Language M,O

COVENANT COLLEGE
- Education—General M

CREIGHTON UNIVERSITY
- Business Administration and Management—General M
- Counselor Education M
- Education—General M,D
- Educational Leadership and Administration M,D
- Elementary Education M
- Law M,D,O
- Management Information Systems M
- Secondary Education M
- Special Education M
- Student Affairs M

CUMBERLAND UNIVERSITY
- Business Administration and Management—General M
- Education—General M

CURRY COLLEGE
- Business Administration and Management—General M,O
- Education—General M,O
- Elementary Education M,O
- Finance and Banking M,O
- Foundations and Philosophy of Education M,O
- Reading Education M,O
- Special Education M,O

DAEMEN COLLEGE
- Accounting M
- Business Administration and Management—General M
- Early Childhood Education M
- Education—General M
- International Business M
- Management Information Systems M
- Marketing M
- Middle School Education M
- Nonprofit Management M
- Special Education M

DAKOTA STATE UNIVERSITY
- Education—General M
- Educational Media/Instructional Technology M

DAKOTA WESLEYAN UNIVERSITY
- Curriculum and Instruction M
- Education—General M
- Educational Leadership and Administration M
- Secondary Education M

DALHOUSIE UNIVERSITY
- Business Administration and Management—General M,O
- Electronic Commerce M,D
- Finance and Banking M
- Health Education M
- Information Studies M
- Kinesiology and Movement Studies M
- Law M,D
- Leisure Studies M
- Library Science M
- Management Information Systems M
- Social Work M

DALLAS BAPTIST UNIVERSITY
- Accounting M
- Business Administration and Management—General M
- Counselor Education M,O
- Curriculum and Instruction M
- Distance Education Development M
- Early Childhood Education M
- Education—General M
- Educational Leadership and Administration M
- Elementary Education M
- English as a Second Language M
- Entrepreneurship M
- Finance and Banking M
- Higher Education M
- Human Resources Management M
- International Business M
- Kinesiology and Movement Studies M
- Management Information Systems M
- Marketing M
- Nonprofit Management M
- Project Management M
- Reading Education M
- Religious Education M
- Secondary Education M

DALLAS THEOLOGICAL SEMINARY
- Adult Education M,D,O
- Educational Leadership and Administration M,D,O
- Religious Education M,D,O

DANIEL WEBSTER COLLEGE
- Aviation Management M
- Business Administration and Management—General M

DARTMOUTH COLLEGE
- Business Administration and Management—General M

DAVENPORT UNIVERSITY
- Accounting M
- Business Administration and Management—General M
- Finance and Banking M
- Human Resources Management M
- Management Strategy and Policy M
- Marketing M

DAVENPORT UNIVERSITY
- Accounting M
- Business Administration and Management—General M
- Finance and Banking M
- Human Resources Management M
- Management Strategy and Policy M

DAVENPORT UNIVERSITY
- Accounting M
- Business Administration and Management—General M
- Finance and Banking M
- Human Resources Management M

DEFIANCE COLLEGE
- Adult Education M
- Business Administration and Management—General M
- Education—General M
- Management Strategy and Policy M
- Secondary Education M
- Special Education M
- Sports Management M

DELAWARE STATE UNIVERSITY
- Adult Education M
- Art Education M
- Business Administration and Management—General M
- Curriculum and Instruction M
- Education—General M,D
- Educational Leadership and Administration M,D
- Exercise and Sports Science M
- Foreign Languages Education M
- Mathematics Education M
- Reading Education M
- Science Education M,D
- Social Work M
- Special Education M

DELAWARE VALLEY COLLEGE
- Accounting M
- Business Administration and Management—General M
- Curriculum and Instruction M
- Educational Leadership and Administration M
- Educational Media/Instructional Technology M
- International Business M

DELTA STATE UNIVERSITY
- Accounting M
- Aviation Management M
- Business Administration and Management—General M
- Counselor Education M,D
- Education—General M,D,O
- Educational Leadership and Administration M,D,O
- Elementary Education M,D,O
- English Education M
- Exercise and Sports Science M
- Health Education M
- Higher Education D
- Physical Education M
- Recreation and Park Management M
- Secondary Education M
- Social Sciences Education M
- Special Education M

DEPAUL UNIVERSITY
- Accounting M
- Actuarial Science M,O
- Adult Education M
- Advertising and Public Relations M
- Business Administration and Management—General M
- Counselor Education M,D
- Curriculum and Instruction M,D
- Early Childhood Education M,D
- Education—General M,D
- Educational Leadership and Administration M,D
- Electronic Commerce M,D
- Elementary Education M,D
- English as a Second Language M,O
- Entrepreneurship M
- Finance and Banking M,O
- Foreign Languages Education M,D
- Foundations and Philosophy of Education M,D
- Health Law M,D,O
- Human Resources Management M
- Industrial and Manufacturing Management M
- Intellectual Property Law M,D
- International Business M
- Law M,D
- Management Information Systems M,D
- Management Strategy and Policy M
- Marketing M
- Mathematics Education M,O
- Multilingual and Multicultural Education M,D
- Music Education M,O
- Nonprofit Management M,O
- Physical Education M,D
- Reading Education M,D
- Real Estate M
- Secondary Education M,D
- Social Work M
- Special Education M,D
- Student Affairs M,D
- Taxation M

DEREE - THE AMERICAN COLLEGE OF GREECE
- Marketing M

DESALES UNIVERSITY
- Accounting M
- Business Administration and Management—General M
- Education—General M
- Educational Media/Instructional Technology M
- English as a Second Language M
- Finance and Banking M
- Human Resources Management M
- Management Information Systems M
- Marketing M
- Project Management M
- Special Education M

DEVRY COLLEGE OF NEW YORK
- Business Administration and Management—General M

DEVRY UNIVERSITY
- Business Administration and Management—General M,O

DEVRY UNIVERSITY
- Accounting M
- Business Administration and Management—General M
- Finance and Banking M
- Human Resources Management M
- Management Information Systems M
- Project Management M

DEVRY UNIVERSITY ONLINE
- Business Administration and Management—General M

DOANE COLLEGE
- Business Administration and Management—General M
- Counselor Education M
- Curriculum and Instruction M
- Education—General M
- Educational Leadership and Administration M

DOMINICAN COLLEGE
- Business Administration and Management—General M
- Education—General M
- Elementary Education M
- Special Education M

DOMINICAN UNIVERSITY
- Accounting M
- Business Administration and Management—General M
- Curriculum and Instruction M
- Early Childhood Education M
- Education—General M
- Educational Leadership and Administration M
- Elementary Education M
- English as a Second Language M
- Information Studies M,D,O
- Library Science M,D,O
- Organizational Management M
- Reading Education M
- Social Work M
- Special Education M

DOMINICAN UNIVERSITY OF CALIFORNIA
- Business Administration and Management—General M
- Education—General M,O
- International Business M
- Management Strategy and Policy M
- Special Education M,O
- Sustainability Management M

DORDT COLLEGE
- Education—General M

DOWLING COLLEGE
- Aviation Management M,O
- Business Administration and Management—General M,O
- Early Childhood Education M,D,O
- Education of the Gifted M,D,O
- Education—General M,D,O
- Educational Leadership and Administration M,D,O
- Educational Media/Instructional Technology M,D,O
- Educational Psychology M,D,O
- Entertainment Management M,O
- Finance and Banking M,O
- Human Resources Management M,O
- Management Information Systems M,O
- Marketing M,O
- Middle School Education M,D,O
- Project Management M,O
- Reading Education M,D,O
- Special Education M,D,O
- Sports Management M,D,O

DRAKE UNIVERSITY
- Business Administration and Management—General M
- Education—General M,D,O
- Law D

DREW UNIVERSITY
- Education—General M
- Foreign Languages Education M
- Mathematics Education M
- Science Education M
- Social Sciences Education M

DREXEL UNIVERSITY
- Accounting M,D,O
- Archives/Archival Administration M
- Business Administration and Management—General M,D,O
- Curriculum and Instruction M
- Education—General M,D
- Educational Leadership and Administration M,D
- Educational Media/Instructional Technology M,D
- Finance and Banking M,D,O
- Higher Education M
- Hospitality Management M
- Human Resources Development M
- Information Studies M
- International and Comparative Education M
- Library Science M,D,O
- Management Strategy and Policy M,D,O

Marketing M,D,O
Mathematics Education M
Organizational Behavior M,D,O
Project Management M
Quantitative Analysis M,D,O
Real Estate M
Special Education M
Sports Management M

DRURY UNIVERSITY
Business Administration and Management—General M
Education of the Gifted M
Education—General M
Educational Media/Instructional Technology M
Elementary Education M
Human Services M
Mathematics Education M
Middle School Education M
Reading Education M
Secondary Education M
Special Education M

DUKE UNIVERSITY
Business Administration and Management—General M,D
Education—General M
Law M,D

DUQUESNE UNIVERSITY
Business Administration and Management—General M*
Computer Education M,D,O
Counselor Education M,D,O
Curriculum and Instruction M,O
Early Childhood Education M
Education—General M,D,O
Educational Leadership and Administration M,D,O
Educational Measurement and Evaluation M,D,O
Educational Media/Instructional Technology M,D,O
English as a Second Language M
English Education M,D,O
Foreign Languages Education M,D,O
Foundations and Philosophy of Education M
International Business M
Law M,D
Management Information Systems M
Management Strategy and Policy M
Mathematics Education M,D,O
Music Education M,O
Organizational Management M
Reading Education M
Science Education M
Secondary Education M
Social Sciences Education M,D,O
Special Education M
Sports Management M

D'YOUVILLE COLLEGE
Business Administration and Management—General M
Education—General M,O
Educational Leadership and Administration D
Elementary Education M,O
Health Education D
International Business M
Secondary Education M,O
Special Education M,O

EARLHAM COLLEGE
Education—General M

EAST CAROLINA UNIVERSITY
Accounting M
Adult Education M,D
Athletic Training and Sports Medicine M
Business Administration and Management—General M,D,O
Business Education M
Community College Education M,O
Computer Education M,O
Counselor Education M,D
Curriculum and Instruction M,O
Distance Education Development M,O
Early Childhood Education M,D
Education—General M,D,O
Educational Leadership and Administration M,D,O
Educational Media/Instructional Technology M,O
Elementary Education M,O
English as a Second Language M,D,O
English Education M,O
Exercise and Sports Science M,D,O
Health Education M
Higher Education M,D
Industrial and Manufacturing Management M,D,O
Kinesiology and Movement Studies M,D,O
Leisure Studies M,O
Library Science M
Logistics M,D,O
Management Information Systems M,D,O
Mathematics Education M,O
Middle School Education M,O
Music Education M,O
Physical Education M,D,O
Quality Management M,D,O
Reading Education M,O
Recreation and Park Management M,O
Science Education M,O
Social Sciences Education M
Social Work M,O
Special Education M,O
Sports Management M,D,O
Vocational and Technical Education M

EAST CENTRAL UNIVERSITY
Counselor Education M
Education—General M
Human Resources Management M

EASTERN CONNECTICUT STATE UNIVERSITY
Early Childhood Education M
Education—General M
Educational Media/Instructional Technology M
Elementary Education M
Organizational Management M
Reading Education M
Science Education M
Secondary Education M

EASTERN ILLINOIS UNIVERSITY
Accounting M,O
Art Education M
Business Administration and Management—General M,O
Community College Education M
Counselor Education M
Early Childhood Education M
Education—General M,O
Educational Leadership and Administration M,O
Elementary Education M
Exercise and Sports Science M
Kinesiology and Movement Studies M
Mathematics Education M
Middle School Education M
Music Education M
Special Education M
Student Affairs M

EASTERN KENTUCKY UNIVERSITY
Agricultural Education M
Art Education M
Business Administration and Management—General M
Business Education M
Counselor Education M
Curriculum and Instruction M
Education—General M
Educational Leadership and Administration M
Elementary Education M
English Education M
Health Education M
Higher Education M
Home Economics Education M
Library Science M
Mathematics Education M
Music Education M
Physical Education M
Recreation and Park Management M
Science Education M
Secondary Education M
Social Sciences Education M
Special Education M
Sports Management M
Vocational and Technical Education M

EASTERN MENNONITE UNIVERSITY
Business Administration and Management—General M
Education—General M

EASTERN MICHIGAN UNIVERSITY
Accounting M
Art Education M
Athletic Training and Sports Medicine M,O
Business Administration and Management—General M,O
Counselor Education M,O
Curriculum and Instruction M
Developmental Education M,O
Early Childhood Education M
Education—General M,D,O
Educational Leadership and Administration M,D,O
Educational Measurement and Evaluation M,O
Educational Media/Instructional Technology M,O
Educational Psychology M,O
Electronic Commerce M,O
Elementary Education M
English as a Second Language M,O
English Education M,O
Entrepreneurship M,O
Exercise and Sports Science M
Finance and Banking M,O
Foundations and Philosophy of Education M
Health Education M
Hospitality Management M,O
Human Resources Management M,O
Human Services O
International Business M,O
Kinesiology and Movement Studies M
Management Information Systems M,O
Marketing M,O
Mathematics Education M
Middle School Education M
Multilingual and Multicultural Education M,D,O
Music Education M
Nonprofit Management M,O
Organizational Management M,O
Physical Education M
Quality Management M,O
Reading Education M
Science Education M
Secondary Education M
Social Work M
Special Education M,O
Sports Management M
Supply Chain Management M,O
Travel and Tourism M,O
Vocational and Technical Education M

EASTERN NAZARENE COLLEGE
Business Administration and Management—General M
Early Childhood Education M,O
Education—General M,O
Educational Leadership and Administration M,O
Elementary Education M,O
English as a Second Language M,O
Middle School Education M,O
Reading Education M,O
Secondary Education M,O
Special Education M,O

EASTERN NEW MEXICO UNIVERSITY
Business Administration and Management—General M
Counselor Education M
Curriculum and Instruction M
Early Childhood Education M
Education—General M
Educational Leadership and Administration M
Educational Media/Instructional Technology M
Elementary Education M
English as a Second Language M
Exercise and Sports Science M
Human Services M
Multilingual and Multicultural Education M
Physical Education M
Reading Education M
Science Education M
Secondary Education M
Special Education M
Sports Management M
Vocational and Technical Education M

EASTERN OREGON UNIVERSITY
Business Administration and Management—General M
Education—General M
Elementary Education M
Secondary Education M

EASTERN UNIVERSITY
Business Administration and Management—General M
Counselor Education M,O
Education—General M,O
Health Education M
Multilingual and Multicultural Education M
Nonprofit Management M
Organizational Management M,D

EASTERN WASHINGTON UNIVERSITY
Adult Education M
Business Administration and Management—General M
Computer Education M
Counselor Education M
Curriculum and Instruction M
Early Childhood Education M
Education—General M
Educational Leadership and Administration M
Educational Media/Instructional Technology M
Elementary Education M
English as a Second Language M
Exercise and Sports Science M
Foreign Languages Education M
Foundations and Philosophy of Education M
Mathematics Education M
Music Education M
Physical Education M
Reading Education M
Recreation and Park Management M
Secondary Education M
Social Work M
Special Education M
Sports Management M

EAST STROUDSBURG UNIVERSITY OF PENNSYLVANIA
Education—General M
Educational Media/Instructional Technology M
Elementary Education M
Exercise and Sports Science M
Health Education M
Hospitality Management M
Physical Education M
Reading Education M
Science Education M
Secondary Education M
Social Sciences Education M
Special Education M
Sports Management M
Travel and Tourism M

EAST TENNESSEE STATE UNIVERSITY
Accounting M
Archives/Archival Administration M,O
Business Administration and Management—General M,O
Counselor Education M,D
Curriculum and Instruction M,O
Early Childhood Education M,D
Education—General M,D,O
Educational Leadership and Administration M,D,O
Educational Media/Instructional Technology M,O
Elementary Education M,O
English as a Second Language M,O
Entrepreneurship M,O
Exercise and Sports Science M,D
Finance and Banking M,O
Higher Education M,D
Library Science M,O
Management Information Systems M
Management Strategy and Policy M,O
Middle School Education M,O
Nonprofit Management M,O
Physical Education M,D
Reading Education M,O
Secondary Education M,O
Social Work M
Special Education M,D
Sports Management M,D

ECOLE HÔTELIÈRE DE LAUSANNE
Hospitality Management M

EDGEWOOD COLLEGE
Accounting M
Adult Education M,D,O
Business Administration and Management—General M
Education—General M,D,O
Educational Leadership and Administration M,D,O
English as a Second Language M,D,O
Finance and Banking M
Marketing M
Multilingual and Multicultural Education M,D,O
Organizational Management M
Reading Education M,D,O
Special Education M,D,O
Sustainability Management M,D,O

EDINBORO UNIVERSITY OF PENNSYLVANIA
Counselor Education M,O
Early Childhood Education M,O
Education—General M,O
Educational Leadership and Administration M,O
Educational Psychology M,O
Elementary Education M,O
Middle School Education M
Reading Education M,O
Secondary Education M
Social Work M
Special Education M,O

ELIZABETH CITY STATE UNIVERSITY
Education—General M
Educational Leadership and Administration M
Elementary Education M

ELLIS UNIVERSITY
Accounting M
Business Administration and Management—General M
Early Childhood Education M
Education—General M
Educational Leadership and Administration M
Educational Media/Instructional Technology M
Electronic Commerce M
Finance and Banking M
International Business M
Management Information Systems M
Marketing M
Project Management M

ELMHURST COLLEGE
Accounting M
Business Administration and Management—General M
Educational Leadership and Administration M
Management Information Systems M
Special Education M
Supply Chain Management M

ELMS COLLEGE
Early Childhood Education M,O
Education—General M,O
Elementary Education M,O
English as a Second Language M,O
English Education M,O
Foreign Languages Education M,O
Reading Education M,O
Science Education M,O
Secondary Education M,O
Special Education M,O

ELON UNIVERSITY
Business Administration and Management—General M
Education of the Gifted M
Education—General M
Elementary Education M
Law D
Special Education M

EMBRY-RIDDLE AERONAUTICAL UNIVERSITY–DAYTONA
Aviation Management M*
Business Administration and Management—General M

EMBRY-RIDDLE AERONAUTICAL UNIVERSITY–WORLDWIDE
Aviation Management M,O
Business Administration and Management—General M,O
Education—General M
Industrial and Manufacturing Management M,O
Logistics M,O
Project Management M,O
Supply Chain Management M,O
Transportation Management M,O

*M—master's degree; P—first professional degree; D—doctorate; O—other advanced degree; *Close-Up and/or Display*

EMERSON COLLEGE
Advertising and Public Relations M
International Business M
Marketing M

EMMANUEL CHRISTIAN SEMINARY
Religious Education M,D

EMMANUEL COLLEGE (UNITED STATES)
Business Administration and Management—General M,O
Education—General M,O
Educational Leadership and Administration M,O
Elementary Education M,O
Human Resources Management M,O
Secondary Education M,O

EMORY & HENRY COLLEGE
Education—General M
Organizational Management M
Reading Education M

EMORY UNIVERSITY
Accounting D
Business Administration and Management—General M,D
Education—General M,D
Finance and Banking D
Health Education M,D
Law M,D,O
Management Information Systems D
Marketing D
Middle School Education M,D
Organizational Management D
Secondary Education M,D

EMPORIA STATE UNIVERSITY
Archives/Archival Administration M,D,O
Business Administration and Management—General M
Business Education M
Counselor Education M
Curriculum and Instruction M
Early Childhood Education M
Education of the Gifted M
Education—General M,O
Educational Leadership and Administration M
Educational Media/Instructional Technology M
Elementary Education M
English as a Second Language M
Information Studies M,D,O
Library Science M,D,O
Music Education M
Physical Education M
Reading Education M
Social Sciences Education M
Special Education M

ENDICOTT COLLEGE
Art Education M
Business Administration and Management—General M
Distance Education Development M
Early Childhood Education M
Elementary Education M
Hospitality Management M
Management Information Systems M
Organizational Management M
Reading Education M
Secondary Education M
Special Education M
Sports Management M

ERIKSON INSTITUTE
Early Childhood Education M,D
English as a Second Language M,O

ESSEC BUSINESS SCHOOL
Business Administration and Management—General M,D
Hospitality Management M,D
International Business M,D

EVANGEL UNIVERSITY
Counselor Education M
Education—General M
Educational Leadership and Administration M
Organizational Management M
Reading Education M
Secondary Education M

EVEREST UNIVERSITY
Accounting M
Business Administration and Management—General M
Human Resources Management M
International Business M

EVEREST UNIVERSITY
Business Administration and Management—General M

EVEREST UNIVERSITY
Business Administration and Management—General M

EVEREST UNIVERSITY
Accounting M
Business Administration and Management—General M
Human Resources Management M
International Business M

EVEREST UNIVERSITY
Business Administration and Management—General M

EVEREST UNIVERSITY
Business Administration and Management—General M

EVEREST UNIVERSITY
Business Administration and Management—General M

EVERGLADES UNIVERSITY
Business Administration and Management—General M

THE EVERGREEN STATE COLLEGE
Education—General M

EXCELSIOR COLLEGE
Business Administration and Management—General M,O

FACULTAD DE DERECHO EUGENIO MARÍA DE HOSTOS
Law D

FAIRFIELD UNIVERSITY
Accounting M,O
Business Administration and Management—General M,O
Counselor Education M,O
Education—General M,O
Educational Media/Instructional Technology M,O
Elementary Education M,O
English as a Second Language M,O
Entrepreneurship M,O
Finance and Banking M,O
Foundations and Philosophy of Education M,O
Human Resources Management M,O
International Business M,O
Management Information Systems M,O
Marketing M,O
Multilingual and Multicultural Education M,O
Special Education M,O
Taxation M,O

FAIRLEIGH DICKINSON UNIVERSITY, COLLEGE AT FLORHAM
Accounting M
Business Administration and Management—General M,O
Education—General M,O
Educational Leadership and Administration M
Educational Media/Instructional Technology M,O
Entrepreneurship M,O
Finance and Banking M,O
Hospitality Management M
Human Resources Management M
International Business M,O
Marketing M,O
Organizational Behavior M,O
Organizational Management M,O
Reading Education M,O
Sports Management M
Sustainability Management O
Taxation M,O

FAIRLEIGH DICKINSON UNIVERSITY, METROPOLITAN CAMPUS
Accounting M,O
Business Administration and Management—General M,O
Curriculum and Instruction M
Education—General M,O
Educational Leadership and Administration M
Educational Media/Instructional Technology M,O
Electronic Commerce M
Entrepreneurship M,O
Finance and Banking M,O
Foundations and Philosophy of Education M
Hospitality Management M
Human Resources Management M,O
International Business M
Management Information Systems M,O
Marketing M,O
Multilingual and Multicultural Education M
Nonprofit Management M,O
Reading Education M,O
Science Education M
Special Education M
Sports Management M
Taxation M

FAIRMONT STATE UNIVERSITY
Business Administration and Management—General M
Distance Education Development M
Education—General M
Educational Leadership and Administration M
Educational Media/Instructional Technology M
Exercise and Sports Science M
Human Services M
Reading Education M
Special Education M

FASHION INSTITUTE OF TECHNOLOGY
Business Administration and Management—General M*
Marketing M*

FAULKNER UNIVERSITY
Business Administration and Management—General M
Counselor Education M
Education—General M
Law D

FAYETTEVILLE STATE UNIVERSITY
Business Administration and Management—General M
Educational Leadership and Administration M,D
Elementary Education M
Middle School Education M
Reading Education M
Secondary Education M
Social Sciences Education M
Social Work M

FELICIAN COLLEGE
Business Administration and Management—General M*
Education—General M,O*
Educational Leadership and Administration M,O
Entrepreneurship M
Religious Education M,O

FERRIS STATE UNIVERSITY
Business Administration and Management—General M
Community College Education D
Curriculum and Instruction M
Developmental Education M
Education—General M
Educational Leadership and Administration M,D
Educational Media/Instructional Technology M
Elementary Education M
Human Services M
Management Information Systems M
Project Management M
Reading Education M
Special Education M

FIELDING GRADUATE UNIVERSITY
Community College Education M,D,O
Educational Leadership and Administration M,D,O
Educational Media/Instructional Technology M,D,O
Higher Education M,D,O
Legal and Justice Studies M,D,O
Organizational Management M,D,O

FITCHBURG STATE UNIVERSITY
Accounting M
Art Education M,O
Business Administration and Management—General M
Counselor Education M
Curriculum and Instruction M
Early Childhood Education M
Educational Leadership and Administration M,O
Educational Media/Instructional Technology M,O
Elementary Education M
English Education M,O
Higher Education M,O
Human Resources Management M
Middle School Education M
Science Education M,O
Secondary Education M
Social Sciences Education M,O
Special Education M
Vocational and Technical Education M

FIVE TOWNS COLLEGE
Music Education M,D

FLORIDA AGRICULTURAL AND MECHANICAL UNIVERSITY
Accounting M
Adult Education M,D
Business Administration and Management—General M
Business Education M
Counselor Education M,D
Early Childhood Education M
Education—General M,D
Educational Leadership and Administration M,D
Elementary Education M
English Education M
Finance and Banking M
Health Education M
Law D
Management Information Systems M
Marketing M
Mathematics Education M
Physical Education M
Recreation and Park Management M
Science Education M
Secondary Education M
Social Sciences Education M
Social Work M
Vocational and Technical Education M

FLORIDA ATLANTIC UNIVERSITY
Accounting M,D
Adult Education M,D,O
Art Education M
Business Administration and Management—General M,D,O
Counselor Education M,D,O
Curriculum and Instruction M,D,O
Early Childhood Education M,D,O
Education—General M,D,O
Educational Leadership and Administration M,D,O
Elementary Education M
English as a Second Language M,D,O
English Education M
Entrepreneurship M,D
Environmental Education M
Exercise and Sports Science M
Foundations and Philosophy of Education M
Higher Education M,D,O
International Business M,D
Management Information Systems M
Multilingual and Multicultural Education M,D,O
Nonprofit Management M
Reading Education M
Social Work M
Special Education M,D
Taxation M
Travel and Tourism M,O

FLORIDA COASTAL SCHOOL OF LAW
Law D

FLORIDA GULF COAST UNIVERSITY
Accounting M
Business Administration and Management—General M
Counselor Education M
Curriculum and Instruction M,D,O
Education—General M,D,O
Educational Leadership and Administration M,D,O
Educational Media/Instructional Technology M,D,O
English Education M,D,O
Reading Education M
Social Work M
Special Education M
Taxation M

FLORIDA INSTITUTE OF TECHNOLOGY
Accounting M
Business Administration and Management—General M
Computer Education M,D,O
Electronic Commerce M,D,O
Elementary Education M,D,O
Environmental Education M,D,O
Finance and Banking M
Human Resources Management M
International Business M
Logistics M
Management Information Systems M,D
Marketing M
Mathematics Education M,D,O
Organizational Behavior M,D
Project Management M
Quality Management M
Science Education M,D,O
Supply Chain Management M
Transportation Management M

FLORIDA INTERNATIONAL UNIVERSITY
Accounting M
Adult Education M,D,O
Art Education M,D,O
Athletic Training and Sports Medicine M
Business Administration and Management—General M,D
Counselor Education M,D,O
Curriculum and Instruction M,D,O
Early Childhood Education M,D,O
Education—General M,D,O
Educational Leadership and Administration M,D,O
Educational Media/Instructional Technology M,D,O
Elementary Education M,D,O
English as a Second Language M,D,O
English Education M,D,O
Finance and Banking M
Foreign Languages Education M,D,O
Higher Education M,D,O
Hospitality Management M
Human Resources Development M,D,O
Human Resources Management M
International and Comparative Education M,D,O
International Business M
Law D
Management Information Systems M
Mathematics Education M,D,O
Multilingual and Multicultural Education M,D,O
Music Education M
Physical Education M,D,O
Reading Education M,D,O
Real Estate M
Recreation and Park Management M,D,O
Science Education M,D,O
Social Sciences Education M,D,O
Social Work M,D
Special Education M,D,O
Sports Management M,D,O
Taxation M
Urban Education M,D,O

FLORIDA MEMORIAL UNIVERSITY
Business Administration and Management—General M
Education—General M
Elementary Education M
Reading Education M
Special Education M

FLORIDA SOUTHERN COLLEGE
Business Administration and Management—General M
Education—General M

FLORIDA STATE UNIVERSITY
Accounting M,D
Art Education M,D,O
Business Administration and Management—General M,D
Counselor Education M,D,O
Distance Education Development M,D
Early Childhood Education M,D,O
Education—General M,D,O
Educational Leadership and Administration M,D,O
Educational Measurement and Evaluation M,D,O
Educational Media/Instructional Technology M,D,O
Educational Policy M,D,O
Educational Psychology M,D,O
Elementary Education M,D,O
English Education M,D,O
Environmental Law M,D
Exercise and Sports Science M,D
Finance and Banking M,D
Foundations and Philosophy of Education M,D,O
Health Education M,D
Higher Education M,D,O

Human Resources Development M,D,O
Information Studies M,D,O
Insurance M,D
International and Comparative Education M,D,O
Law M,D
Library Science M,D,O
Management Information Systems M,D
Management Strategy and Policy M,D
Marketing M,D
Mathematics Education M,D,O
Music Education M,D
Organizational Behavior M,D
Physical Education M,D,O
Reading Education M,D,O
Recreation and Park Management M,D,O
Science Education M,D,O
Social Sciences Education M
Social Work M,D
Special Education M,D,O
Sports Management M,D,O
Taxation M,D

FONTBONNE UNIVERSITY
Accounting M
Business Administration and Management—General M
Computer Education M
Education—General M
Special Education M
Taxation M

FORDHAM UNIVERSITY
Accounting M
Adult Education M,D,O
Business Administration and Management—General M
Counselor Education M,D,O
Curriculum and Instruction M,D,O
Early Childhood Education M,D,O
Education—General M,D,O
Educational Leadership and Administration M,D,O
Educational Psychology M,D,O
Elementary Education M,D,O
English as a Second Language M,D,O
Finance and Banking M
Human Resources Management M,D,O
Intellectual Property Law M,D
Law M,D
Management Information Systems M
Marketing M
Multilingual and Multicultural Education M,D,O
Reading Education M,D,O
Religious Education M,D,O
Secondary Education M,D,O
Social Work M,D
Special Education M,D,O
Taxation M

FORT HAYS STATE UNIVERSITY
Business Administration and Management—General M
Counselor Education M
Education—General M,O
Educational Leadership and Administration M,O
Educational Media/Instructional Technology M
Health Education M
Physical Education M
Special Education M

FORT VALLEY STATE UNIVERSITY
Counselor Education M,O

FRAMINGHAM STATE UNIVERSITY
Business Administration and Management—General M
Curriculum and Instruction M
Early Childhood Education M
Educational Leadership and Administration M
Educational Media/Instructional Technology M
Elementary Education M
English as a Second Language M
English Education M
Foreign Languages Education M
Health Education M
Human Resources Management M
Mathematics Education M
Reading Education M
Social Sciences Education M
Special Education M

FRANCISCAN UNIVERSITY OF STEUBENVILLE
Business Administration and Management—General M
Curriculum and Instruction M
Education—General M
Educational Leadership and Administration M

FRANCIS MARION UNIVERSITY
Business Administration and Management—General M
Early Childhood Education M
Education—General M
Elementary Education M
Secondary Education M
Special Education M

FRANKLIN PIERCE UNIVERSITY
Business Administration and Management—General M,D,O
Curriculum and Instruction M,D,O
Human Resources Management M,D,O
Management Information Systems M,D,O
Management Strategy and Policy M,D,O
Special Education M,D,O
Sports Management M,D,O
Sustainability Management M,D,O

FRANKLIN UNIVERSITY
Accounting M
Business Administration and Management—General M
Educational Media/Instructional Technology M
Marketing M

FREED-HARDEMAN UNIVERSITY
Accounting M
Business Administration and Management—General M
Counselor Education M,O
Curriculum and Instruction M,O
Education—General M,O
Educational Leadership and Administration M,O
Management Strategy and Policy M
Special Education M,O

FRESNO PACIFIC UNIVERSITY
Business Administration and Management—General M
Counselor Education M
Curriculum and Instruction M
Education of Students with Severe/Multiple Disabilities M
Education—General M
Educational Leadership and Administration M
Educational Media/Instructional Technology M
Elementary Education M
English as a Second Language M
Kinesiology and Movement Studies M
Mathematics Education M
Middle School Education M
Multilingual and Multicultural Education M
Reading Education M
Science Education M
Secondary Education M
Special Education M
Student Affairs M

FRIENDS UNIVERSITY
Accounting M
Business Administration and Management—General M
Education—General M
Human Resources Development M
Industrial and Manufacturing Management M
International Business M
Law M
Management Information Systems M

FROSTBURG STATE UNIVERSITY
Business Administration and Management—General M
Counselor Education M
Curriculum and Instruction M
Education—General M
Educational Leadership and Administration M
Educational Media/Instructional Technology M
Elementary Education M
Reading Education M
Recreation and Park Management M
Secondary Education M
Special Education M

FULL SAIL UNIVERSITY
Business Administration and Management—General M
Educational Media/Instructional Technology M
Entertainment Management M
Marketing M

FURMAN UNIVERSITY
Curriculum and Instruction M,O
Early Childhood Education M,O
Education—General M,O
Educational Leadership and Administration M,O
English as a Second Language M,O
Reading Education M,O
Special Education M,O

GALLAUDET UNIVERSITY
Counselor Education M,D,O
Early Childhood Education M,D,O
Education—General M,D,O
Elementary Education M,D,O
International and Comparative Education M,D,O
Secondary Education M,D,O
Social Work M,D,O
Special Education M,D,O

GANNON UNIVERSITY
Accounting O
Business Administration and Management—General M,O
Counselor Education M,O
Curriculum and Instruction M
Early Childhood Education M
Education—General M,D,O
Educational Leadership and Administration M,D,O
Educational Media/Instructional Technology M
English as a Second Language O
Environmental Education M
Finance and Banking O
Human Resources Management O
Investment Management O
Marketing O
Organizational Management D,O
Reading Education M,O
Science Education M

GARDNER-WEBB UNIVERSITY
Business Administration and Management—General M
Curriculum and Instruction D
Education—General M,D
Educational Leadership and Administration M,D
Elementary Education M
English Education M
Exercise and Sports Science M
Middle School Education M
Physical Education M
Religious Education M,D

GARRETT-EVANGELICAL THEOLOGICAL SEMINARY
Religious Education M,D

GENEVA COLLEGE
Business Administration and Management—General M
Counselor Education M
Education—General M
Educational Leadership and Administration M
Higher Education M
Organizational Management M
Reading Education M
Special Education M

GEORGE FOX UNIVERSITY
Business Administration and Management—General M,D
Counselor Education M,O
Curriculum and Instruction M,D,O
Education—General M,D,O
Educational Leadership and Administration M,D,O
Educational Media/Instructional Technology M,D,O
English as a Second Language M,D,O
Finance and Banking M,D
Higher Education M,D,O
Human Resources Management M,D
Marketing M,D
Multilingual and Multicultural Education M,D
Organizational Management M,D
Reading Education M,D,O
Religious Education M,D,O
Secondary Education M,D,O

GEORGE MASON UNIVERSITY
Accounting M
Actuarial Science M,D,O
Advertising and Public Relations M,O
Art Education M,O
Business Administration and Management—General M
Community College Education M,D,O
Counselor Education M
Curriculum and Instruction M
Education—General M,D,O
Educational Leadership and Administration M
Educational Measurement and Evaluation M
Educational Psychology M,O
Electronic Commerce M,D,O
English as a Second Language M,D,O
Entrepreneurship M,O
Exercise and Sports Science M
Foreign Languages Education M
Higher Education D,O
Human Resources Management M
International and Comparative Education M
International Business M
Law M,D
Logistics M,O
Management Information Systems M,D,O
Music Education M,D,O
Nonprofit Management M,D,O
Organizational Management M
Project Management M,O
Real Estate M
Recreation and Park Management M
Social Work M
Special Education M
Sports Management M
Transportation Management M,O

GEORGETOWN COLLEGE
Education—General M
Reading Education M
Special Education M

GEORGETOWN UNIVERSITY
Advertising and Public Relations M
Business Administration and Management—General M
English as a Second Language M,D,O
Finance and Banking D
Health Law M,D
Human Resources Management M,D
Industrial and Manufacturing Management D
International Business M,D
Law M,D
Multilingual and Multicultural Education M,D,O
Real Estate M,D
Sports Management M,D
Taxation M,D

THE GEORGE WASHINGTON UNIVERSITY
Accounting M,D
Adult Education O
Business Administration and Management—General M,D,O
Counselor Education M,D,O
Curriculum and Instruction M,D,O
Distance Education Development O
Early Childhood Education M
Education—General M,D,O
Educational Leadership and Administration M,D,O
Educational Media/Instructional Technology M,O
Educational Policy M,D
Elementary Education M
Exercise and Sports Science M
Finance and Banking M,D
Foundations and Philosophy of Education O
Higher Education M,D,O
Hospitality Management M,O
Human Resources Development M,O
Human Resources Management M,D
International and Comparative Education M
International Business M,D
Investment Management M,D
Law M,D
Legal and Justice Studies M,O
Management Information Systems M,D
Management Strategy and Policy M,D
Marketing M,D
Multilingual and Multicultural Education M,D,O
Museum Education M
Organizational Management M,D,O
Project Management M,D
Reading Education O
Real Estate M,D
Secondary Education M
Special Education M,D,O
Sports Management M,O
Travel and Tourism M,O
Vocational and Technical Education O

GEORGIA COLLEGE & STATE UNIVERSITY
Accounting M
Business Administration and Management—General M
Curriculum and Instruction M,O
Early Childhood Education M,O
Education—General M,O
Educational Leadership and Administration M,O
Educational Media/Instructional Technology M,O
Exercise and Sports Science M
Health Education M
Kinesiology and Movement Studies M
Library Science M,O
Logistics M
Management Information Systems M
Middle School Education M,O
Music Education M
Physical Education M
Recreation and Park Management M
Secondary Education M,O
Special Education M,O

GEORGIA INSTITUTE OF TECHNOLOGY
Accounting M,D,O
Business Administration and Management—General M,D,O
Electronic Commerce M,O
Entrepreneurship M,O
Finance and Banking M,D,O
International Business M,O
Management Information Systems M,D,O
Management Strategy and Policy M,D,O
Marketing M,D,O
Organizational Behavior M,D,O

GEORGIAN COURT UNIVERSITY
Business Administration and Management—General M
Education—General M
Educational Leadership and Administration M,O
Religious Education M,O

GEORGIA SOUTHERN UNIVERSITY
Accounting M
Art Education M
Business Administration and Management—General M
Business Education M
Counselor Education M,O
Curriculum and Instruction M,D
Early Childhood Education M,O
Education—General M,D,O
Educational Leadership and Administration M,D,O
Educational Media/Instructional Technology M
English Education M
Foreign Languages Education M
Health Education M,D
Higher Education M
Home Economics Education M
Kinesiology and Movement Studies M
Logistics D
Management Information Systems O
Mathematics Education M
Middle School Education M
Reading Education M
Science Education M
Social Sciences Education M
Special Education M
Sports Management M
Supply Chain Management D

*M—master's degree; P—first professional degree; D—doctorate; O—other advanced degree; *Close-Up and/or Display*

GEORGIA SOUTHWESTERN STATE UNIVERSITY
- Business Administration and Management—General M
- Early Childhood Education M,O
- Education—General M,O
- Health Education M,O
- Middle School Education M,O
- Physical Education M,O
- Reading Education M,O
- Secondary Education M,O
- Special Education M,O

GEORGIA STATE UNIVERSITY
- Accounting M,D,O
- Actuarial Science M
- Art Education M,D,O
- Athletic Training and Sports Medicine M
- Business Administration and Management—General M,D
- Counselor Education M,D,O
- Early Childhood Education M,D,O
- Education of Students with Severe/Multiple Disabilities M
- Education—General M,D,O
- Educational Leadership and Administration M,D,O
- Educational Measurement and Evaluation M,D
- Educational Media/Instructional Technology M,D,O
- Educational Policy M,D,O
- Educational Psychology M,D
- English as a Second Language M,D,O
- English Education M,D,O
- Entrepreneurship M,D
- Exercise and Sports Science M
- Finance and Banking M,D,O
- Foundations and Philosophy of Education M,D
- Health Education M
- Human Resources Management M,D
- Human Services M
- Insurance M,D,O
- International Business M
- Kinesiology and Movement Studies D
- Law D
- Management Information Systems M,D
- Management Strategy and Policy M,D
- Marketing M,D
- Mathematics Education M,D,O
- Middle School Education M,O
- Music Education M,D,O
- Nonprofit Management M,D,O
- Organizational Management M,D
- Physical Education M
- Quantitative Analysis M,D
- Reading Education M,D,O
- Real Estate M,D,O
- Science Education M,D,O
- Secondary Education M,D,O
- Social Sciences Education M,D,O
- Social Work M
- Special Education M,D
- Sports Management M
- Taxation M

GLION INSTITUTE OF HIGHER EDUCATION
- Hospitality Management M

GLOBAL UNIVERSITY
- Religious Education M

GLOBE UNIVERSITY–WOODBURY
- Business Administration and Management—General M
- Management Information Systems M

GODDARD COLLEGE
- Business Administration and Management—General M
- Education—General M
- Sustainability Management M

GOLDEN GATE BAPTIST THEOLOGICAL SEMINARY
- Early Childhood Education M,D,O
- Educational Leadership and Administration M,D,O

GOLDEN GATE UNIVERSITY
- Accounting M,D,O
- Advertising and Public Relations M,D,O
- Business Administration and Management—General M,D,O
- Environmental Law M,D
- Finance and Banking M,D,O
- Human Resources Management M,D,O
- Intellectual Property Law M,D
- International Business M,D,O
- Law M,D
- Legal and Justice Studies M,D,O
- Management Information Systems M,D,O
- Marketing M,D,O
- Supply Chain Management M,D,O
- Taxation M,D,O

GOLDEY-BEACOM COLLEGE
- Business Administration and Management—General M
- Finance and Banking M
- Human Resources Management M
- International Business M
- Management Information Systems M
- Marketing M
- Taxation M

GONZAGA UNIVERSITY
- Accounting M
- Business Administration and Management—General M
- Education—General M
- Educational Leadership and Administration M,D
- English as a Second Language M
- Law D
- Organizational Management M
- Reading Education M
- Special Education M
- Sports Management M

GORDON COLLEGE
- Education—General M
- Music Education M

GOSHEN COLLEGE
- Environmental Education M

GOUCHER COLLEGE
- Education—General M

GOVERNORS STATE UNIVERSITY
- Accounting M
- Business Administration and Management—General M
- Early Childhood Education M
- Education—General M
- Educational Leadership and Administration M
- Educational Media/Instructional Technology M
- Legal and Justice Studies M
- Management Information Systems M
- Reading Education M
- Social Work M
- Special Education M

GRACELAND UNIVERSITY (IA)
- Education—General M
- Educational Leadership and Administration M
- Educational Media/Instructional Technology M
- Special Education M

GRADUATE INSTITUTE OF APPLIED LINGUISTICS
- Multilingual and Multicultural Education M,O

GRADUATE SCHOOL AND UNIVERSITY CENTER OF THE CITY UNIVERSITY OF NEW YORK
- Accounting D
- Business Administration and Management—General D
- Educational Psychology D
- Finance and Banking D
- Management Information Systems D
- Organizational Behavior D
- Social Work D
- Urban Education D

GRAMBLING STATE UNIVERSITY
- Counselor Education M,D
- Curriculum and Instruction M,D
- Developmental Education M,D
- Education—General M,D
- Educational Leadership and Administration M,D
- Educational Media/Instructional Technology M,D
- Higher Education M,D
- Human Resources Management M
- Mathematics Education M,D
- Reading Education M,D
- Science Education M,D
- Social Sciences Education M,D
- Social Work M
- Sports Management M
- Student Affairs M,D

GRAND CANYON UNIVERSITY
- Accounting M
- Business Administration and Management—General M,D
- Counselor Education M
- Curriculum and Instruction M
- Education—General M,D
- Educational Leadership and Administration M,D
- Elementary Education M
- Entrepreneurship M
- Finance and Banking M
- Health Education D
- Higher Education D
- Human Resources Management M
- Management Information Systems M
- Marketing M
- Organizational Management D
- Secondary Education M
- Special Education M

GRAND RAPIDS THEOLOGICAL SEMINARY OF CORNERSTONE UNIVERSITY
- Religious Education M

GRAND VALLEY STATE UNIVERSITY
- Accounting M
- Adult Education M,O
- Business Administration and Management—General M
- Curriculum and Instruction M
- Early Childhood Education M,O
- Education—General M,O
- Educational Leadership and Administration M,O
- Educational Media/Instructional Technology M,O
- Elementary Education M,O
- English as a Second Language M,O
- English Education M
- Higher Education M,O
- Management Information Systems M
- Middle School Education M,O
- Reading Education M
- Secondary Education M,O
- Social Work M
- Special Education M
- Taxation M

GRAND VIEW UNIVERSITY
- Business Administration and Management—General M
- Education—General M
- Organizational Management M

GRANITE STATE COLLEGE
- Project Management M

GRANTHAM UNIVERSITY
- Business Administration and Management—General M
- Human Resources Development M
- Management Information Systems M
- Management Strategy and Policy M
- Organizational Management M
- Project Management M

GRATZ COLLEGE
- Education—General M
- Educational Media/Instructional Technology O
- Nonprofit Management O
- Religious Education M,D,O
- Social Work M,O

GREEN MOUNTAIN COLLEGE
- Business Administration and Management—General M

GREENSBORO COLLEGE
- Education—General M
- Elementary Education M
- English as a Second Language M
- Special Education M

GREENVILLE COLLEGE
- Education—General M
- Elementary Education M
- Secondary Education M

GWYNEDD-MERCY COLLEGE
- Business Administration and Management—General M
- Counselor Education M
- Education—General M
- Educational Leadership and Administration M
- Reading Education M
- Special Education M

HAMLINE UNIVERSITY
- Business Administration and Management—General M,D
- Education—General M,D
- English as a Second Language M,D
- Environmental Education M,D
- Law M,D
- Nonprofit Management M,D
- Reading Education M,D
- Science Education M,D

HAMPTON UNIVERSITY
- Business Administration and Management—General M,D
- Counselor Education M
- Early Childhood Education M
- Education of the Gifted M
- Education—General M
- Educational Leadership and Administration M,D
- Elementary Education M
- Middle School Education M
- Music Education M
- Secondary Education M
- Special Education M
- Student Affairs M

HANNIBAL-LAGRANGE UNIVERSITY
- Education—General M
- Reading Education M

HARDING UNIVERSITY
- Art Education M,O
- Business Administration and Management—General M
- Counselor Education M,O
- Early Childhood Education M,O
- Education—General M,O
- Educational Leadership and Administration M,O
- Elementary Education M,O
- English as a Second Language M,O
- English Education M,O
- Foreign Languages Education M,O
- Health Education M,O
- International Business M
- Mathematics Education M,O
- Organizational Management M
- Reading Education M,O
- Secondary Education M,O
- Social Sciences Education M,O
- Special Education M,O

HARDIN-SIMMONS UNIVERSITY
- Business Administration and Management—General M
- Counselor Education M
- Education of the Gifted M
- Education—General M
- Kinesiology and Movement Studies M
- Music Education M
- Reading Education M
- Recreation and Park Management M
- Science Education M,D

HARRISBURG UNIVERSITY OF SCIENCE AND TECHNOLOGY
- Educational Media/Instructional Technology M
- Entrepreneurship M
- Management Information Systems M
- Project Management M

HARRISON MIDDLETON UNIVERSITY
- Education—General M,D
- Legal and Justice Studies M,D
- Science Education M,D

HARVARD UNIVERSITY
- Accounting D
- Art Education M
- Business Administration and Management—General M,D,O
- Curriculum and Instruction M
- Education—General M,D
- Educational Leadership and Administration M,D
- Educational Measurement and Evaluation D
- Educational Media/Instructional Technology M,O
- Educational Policy M
- Educational Psychology M
- Foundations and Philosophy of Education M,O
- Higher Education D
- Industrial and Manufacturing Management D
- International and Comparative Education M
- Law M,D
- Legal and Justice Studies D
- Management Strategy and Policy D
- Marketing D
- Mathematics Education M,O
- Multilingual and Multicultural Education D
- Organizational Behavior D
- Reading Education M
- Science Education M

HASTINGS COLLEGE
- Education—General M

HAWAI'I PACIFIC UNIVERSITY
- Accounting M
- Business Administration and Management—General M*
- Electronic Commerce M*
- Elementary Education M*
- English as a Second Language M*
- Finance and Banking M*
- Human Resources Management M*
- International Business M
- Management Information Systems M*
- Marketing M
- Organizational Management M*
- Secondary Education M*
- Social Work M*
- Travel and Tourism M

HEBREW COLLEGE
- Early Childhood Education M,O
- Education—General M,O
- Middle School Education M,O
- Music Education M,O
- Religious Education M,O
- Special Education M,O

HEBREW UNION COLLEGE–JEWISH INSTITUTE OF RELIGION (NY)
- Education—General M
- Nonprofit Management M
- Religious Education M

HEC MONTREAL
- Accounting M,O
- Business Administration and Management—General M,D,O
- Electronic Commerce M,O
- Finance and Banking M,O
- Human Resources Management M
- Industrial and Manufacturing Management M
- International Business M
- Logistics M
- Management Information Systems M
- Management Strategy and Policy M
- Marketing M
- Organizational Management M
- Supply Chain Management M,O
- Taxation M,O

HEIDELBERG UNIVERSITY
- Business Administration and Management—General M
- Education—General M
- Music Education M

HENDERSON STATE UNIVERSITY
- Business Administration and Management—General M
- Counselor Education M
- Curriculum and Instruction M
- Early Childhood Education M
- Education—General M,O
- Educational Leadership and Administration M,O
- Middle School Education M
- Physical Education M
- Reading Education M
- Special Education M
- Sports Management M

HENDRIX COLLEGE
- Accounting M

HERITAGE UNIVERSITY
- Counselor Education M
- Education—General M
- Educational Leadership and Administration M
- English as a Second Language M
- Multilingual and Multicultural Education M
- Reading Education M
- Science Education M
- Special Education M

HERZING UNIVERSITY ONLINE
- Accounting M
- Business Administration and Management—General M
- Human Resources Management M

- Marketing M
- Project Management M

HIGH POINT UNIVERSITY
- Business Administration and Management—General M
- Education—General M
- Educational Leadership and Administration M
- Elementary Education M
- Mathematics Education M
- Nonprofit Management M
- Secondary Education M
- Special Education M

HODGES UNIVERSITY
- Business Administration and Management—General M
- Education—General M
- Legal and Justice Studies M
- Management Information Systems M

HOFSTRA UNIVERSITY
- Accounting M,O
- Art Education M,O
- Business Administration and Management—General M,O
- Business Education M,O
- Counselor Education M,O
- Early Childhood Education M,D,O
- Education—General M,D,O
- Educational Leadership and Administration M,D,O
- Educational Media/Instructional Technology M,O
- Educational Policy M,D,O
- Elementary Education M,D,O
- English as a Second Language M,O
- English Education M,O
- Entertainment Management M,O
- Exercise and Sports Science M,O
- Finance and Banking M,O
- Foreign Languages Education M,O
- Foundations and Philosophy of Education M,D,O
- Health Education M,O
- Higher Education M,D,O
- Human Resources Management M,O
- International Business M,O
- Investment Management M,O
- Law M,D
- Legal and Justice Studies M,O
- Management Information Systems M,O
- Marketing Research M,O
- Marketing M,O
- Mathematics Education M,O
- Middle School Education M,O
- Multilingual and Multicultural Education M,O
- Music Education M,O
- Physical Education M,O
- Quality Management M,O
- Reading Education M,D,O
- Real Estate M,O
- Science Education M,O
- Secondary Education M,D,O
- Social Sciences Education M,D,O
- Special Education M,D,O
- Sports Management M,O
- Taxation M,O

HOLLINS UNIVERSITY
- Education—General M
- Legal and Justice Studies M,O

HOLY FAMILY UNIVERSITY
- Business Administration and Management—General M*
- Education—General M*
- Educational Leadership and Administration M
- Elementary Education M
- Finance and Banking M
- Human Resources Management M*
- Management Information Systems M*
- Reading Education M
- Secondary Education M
- Special Education M

HOLY NAMES UNIVERSITY
- Business Administration and Management—General M
- Education—General M,O
- Educational Psychology M,O
- English as a Second Language M,O
- Finance and Banking M
- Marketing M
- Music Education M,O
- Special Education M,O
- Sports Management M
- Urban Education M,O

HOOD COLLEGE
- Accounting M
- Business Administration and Management—General M
- Curriculum and Instruction M,O
- Early Childhood Education M,O
- Education—General M,O
- Educational Leadership and Administration M,O
- Elementary Education M,O
- Finance and Banking M
- Human Resources Management M
- Management Information Systems M
- Marketing M
- Mathematics Education M,O
- Middle School Education M,O
- Reading Education M,O
- Science Education M,O
- Secondary Education M,O
- Special Education M,O

HOPE INTERNATIONAL UNIVERSITY
- Education—General M
- Educational Leadership and Administration M
- Elementary Education M
- International Business M
- Marketing M
- Nonprofit Management M
- Secondary Education M

HOUSTON BAPTIST UNIVERSITY
- Accounting M
- Business Administration and Management—General M
- Counselor Education M
- Curriculum and Instruction M
- Education—General M
- Educational Leadership and Administration M
- Educational Measurement and Evaluation M
- English as a Second Language M
- Human Resources Management M
- Reading Education M

HOWARD PAYNE UNIVERSITY
- Educational Leadership and Administration M

HOWARD UNIVERSITY
- Accounting M
- Business Administration and Management—General M
- Counselor Education M,D
- Early Childhood Education M
- Education—General M,D
- Educational Leadership and Administration M,D,O
- Educational Psychology D
- Elementary Education M
- Exercise and Sports Science M
- Finance and Banking M
- Health Education M
- Human Resources Management M
- International Business M
- Law M,D
- Leisure Studies M
- Management Information Systems M
- Marketing M
- Multilingual and Multicultural Education M,D
- Music Education M
- Physical Education M
- Secondary Education M
- Social Work M,D
- Special Education M
- Sports Management M
- Supply Chain Management M

HULT INTERNATIONAL BUSINESS SCHOOL (UNITED STATES)
- Business Administration and Management—General M
- Entrepreneurship M
- Finance and Banking M
- International Business M
- Marketing M

HUMBOLDT STATE UNIVERSITY
- Athletic Training and Sports Medicine M
- Business Administration and Management—General M
- Education—General M
- English Education M
- Exercise and Sports Science M
- Kinesiology and Movement Studies M
- Physical Education M
- Social Work M

HUMPHREYS COLLEGE
- Law D

HUNTER COLLEGE OF THE CITY UNIVERSITY OF NEW YORK
- Accounting M
- Counselor Education M
- Early Childhood Education M,O
- Education of Students with Severe/Multiple Disabilities M
- Education—General M,O
- Educational Leadership and Administration O
- Elementary Education M
- English as a Second Language M
- English Education M
- Foreign Languages Education M
- Mathematics Education M
- Multilingual and Multicultural Education M
- Music Education M
- Reading Education M,O
- Science Education M,O
- Secondary Education M
- Social Sciences Education M
- Social Work M,D
- Special Education M

HUNTINGTON UNIVERSITY
- Education—General M

HUSSON UNIVERSITY
- Business Administration and Management—General M
- Counselor Education M
- Hospitality Management M
- Nonprofit Management M

ICR GRADUATE SCHOOL
- Science Education M

IDAHO STATE UNIVERSITY
- Business Administration and Management—General M,O
- Counselor Education M,D,O
- Curriculum and Instruction M,O
- Education—General M,D,O
- Educational Leadership and Administration M,D,O
- Educational Media/Instructional Technology M,D,O
- Elementary Education M,O
- English as a Second Language M,D,O
- Health Education M
- Management Information Systems M,O
- Mathematics Education M,D
- Physical Education M
- Reading Education M,O
- Secondary Education M,O
- Special Education M,D,O
- Vocational and Technical Education M

ILLINOIS INSTITUTE OF TECHNOLOGY
- Business Administration and Management—General M,D
- Finance and Banking M,D
- Human Resources Development M,D
- Industrial and Manufacturing Management M
- Law M,D
- Management Information Systems M,D
- Marketing M,D
- Mathematics Education M,D
- Science Education M,D
- Sustainability Management M
- Taxation M,D

ILLINOIS STATE UNIVERSITY
- Accounting M
- Business Administration and Management—General M
- Curriculum and Instruction M,D
- Education—General M,D
- Educational Leadership and Administration M,D
- Educational Policy M,D
- Educational Psychology M,D,O
- Health Education M
- Higher Education M,D
- Management Information Systems M
- Mathematics Education D
- Physical Education M
- Reading Education M
- Social Work M
- Special Education M,D
- Student Affairs M

IMCA–INTERNATIONAL MANAGEMENT CENTRES ASSOCIATION
- Business Administration and Management—General M

IMMACULATA UNIVERSITY
- Advertising and Public Relations M
- Counselor Education M,D,O
- Educational Leadership and Administration M,D,O
- Elementary Education M,D,O
- Multilingual and Multicultural Education M
- Organizational Management M
- Secondary Education M,D,O
- Special Education M,D,O

INDEPENDENCE UNIVERSITY
- Business Administration and Management—General M

INDIANA STATE UNIVERSITY
- Athletic Training and Sports Medicine M
- Business Administration and Management—General M
- Counselor Education M,D,O
- Curriculum and Instruction M,D
- Early Childhood Education M
- Education—General M,D,O
- Educational Leadership and Administration M,D,O
- Educational Media/Instructional Technology M,D
- Elementary Education M
- English as a Second Language M,O
- English Education M
- Exercise and Sports Science M
- Health Education M
- Higher Education M,D,O
- Home Economics Education M
- Human Resources Development M
- Mathematics Education M
- Multilingual and Multicultural Education M,O
- Physical Education M
- Science Education M,D
- Sports Management M
- Student Affairs M,D,O
- Vocational and Technical Education M

INDIANA TECH
- Accounting M
- Business Administration and Management—General M
- Human Resources Development M
- Human Resources Management M
- International Business D
- Marketing M
- Organizational Management M
- Science Education M

INDIANA UNIVERSITY BLOOMINGTON
- Art Education M,D,O
- Athletic Training and Sports Medicine M,D
- Business Administration and Management—General M,D
- Counselor Education M,D,O
- Curriculum and Instruction M,D,O
- Education—General M,D,O
- Educational Leadership and Administration M,D,O
- Educational Measurement and Evaluation M,D,O
- Educational Media/Instructional Technology M,D
- Educational Policy M,D,O
- Educational Psychology M,D,O
- Elementary Education M,D,O
- English as a Second Language M,D,O
- Exercise and Sports Science M,D
- Finance and Banking M,D,O
- Foreign Languages Education M,D
- Foundations and Philosophy of Education M,D,O
- Health Education M,D
- Higher Education M,D,O
- Information Studies M,D,O
- International and Comparative Education M,D,O
- Kinesiology and Movement Studies M,D
- Law M,D,O
- Leisure Studies M,D
- Library Science M,D,O
- Management Information Systems M,D,O
- Mathematics Education M,D,O
- Multilingual and Multicultural Education M,D
- Nonprofit Management M,D,O
- Organizational Management M,D,O
- Physical Education M,D,O
- Reading Education M,D,O
- Recreation and Park Management M,D
- Science Education M,D,O
- Secondary Education M,D,O
- Social Sciences Education M,D,O
- Special Education M,D,O
- Sports Management M,D
- Sustainability Management M,D,O
- Travel and Tourism M,D

INDIANA UNIVERSITY EAST
- Education—General M
- Social Work M

INDIANA UNIVERSITY KOKOMO
- Business Administration and Management—General M
- Education—General M
- Elementary Education M

INDIANA UNIVERSITY NORTHWEST
- Accounting M,O
- Business Administration and Management—General M,O
- Education—General M
- Elementary Education M
- Secondary Education M
- Social Work M

INDIANA UNIVERSITY OF PENNSYLVANIA
- Adult Education M,D
- Business Administration and Management—General M
- Business Education M
- Counselor Education M
- Curriculum and Instruction M,D
- Education—General M,D,O
- Educational Leadership and Administration D,O
- Educational Media/Instructional Technology M,D
- Educational Psychology M,O
- Elementary Education M
- English as a Second Language M,D
- English Education M,D
- Exercise and Sports Science M
- Facilities Management M
- Health Education M
- Higher Education M
- Human Resources Development M
- Mathematics Education M
- Music Education M
- Physical Education M
- Reading Education M
- Special Education M
- Sports Management M
- Student Affairs M
- Vocational and Technical Education M

INDIANA UNIVERSITY–PURDUE UNIVERSITY FORT WAYNE
- Business Administration and Management—General M
- Counselor Education M
- Education—General M,O
- Educational Leadership and Administration M,O
- Elementary Education M
- English as a Second Language M,O
- English Education M,O
- Facilities Management M,O
- Mathematics Education M,O
- Organizational Management M,O
- Secondary Education M
- Special Education M,O

INDIANA UNIVERSITY–PURDUE UNIVERSITY INDIANAPOLIS
- Accounting M
- Adult Education M
- Art Education M
- Business Administration and Management—General M
- Computer Education M
- Counselor Education M
- Curriculum and Instruction M,O
- Early Childhood Education M,O
- Education—General M,O
- Educational Leadership and Administration M,O
- English as a Second Language M,O
- English Education M,O
- Foreign Languages Education M,O

*M—master's degree; P—first professional degree; D—doctorate; O—other advanced degree; *Close-Up and/or Display*

- Health Education M,D
- Higher Education M,O
- Law M,D
- Library Science M,O
- Mathematics Education M
- Nonprofit Management M,O
- Organizational Management M,O
- Physical Education M
- Reading Education M,O
- Social Work M,D,O
- Special Education M,O
- Student Affairs M,O

INDIANA UNIVERSITY SOUTH BEND
- Accounting M
- Art Education M
- Business Administration and Management—General M
- Counselor Education M
- Education—General M
- Elementary Education M
- Management Information Systems M
- Nonprofit Management M,O
- Secondary Education M
- Social Work M
- Special Education M

INDIANA UNIVERSITY SOUTHEAST
- Business Administration and Management—General M
- Counselor Education M
- Education—General M
- Elementary Education M
- Finance and Banking M
- Secondary Education M

INDIANA WESLEYAN UNIVERSITY
- Accounting M
- Business Administration and Management—General M
- Counselor Education M
- Educational Leadership and Administration M,O
- Higher Education M
- Human Resources Management M
- Organizational Management D

INSTITUTE FOR CHRISTIAN STUDIES
- Education—General M,D

INSTITUTE FOR CLINICAL SOCIAL WORK
- Social Work D

INSTITUTO CENTROAMERICANO DE ADMINISTRACIÓN DE EMPRESAS
- Business Administration and Management—General M
- Finance and Banking M
- Real Estate M

INSTITUTO TECNOLOGICO DE SANTO DOMINGO
- Accounting M,O
- Adult Education M,O
- Business Administration and Management—General M,O
- Education—General M,O
- Educational Leadership and Administration M,O
- Educational Psychology M,O
- Environmental Education M,D,O
- Finance and Banking M,O
- Human Resources Management M,O
- Industrial and Manufacturing Management M,O
- International Business M,O
- Marketing M,O
- Organizational Management M,O
- Quality Management M,O
- Quantitative Analysis M,O
- Secondary Education M,O
- Social Sciences Education M,O
- Taxation M,O
- Transportation Management M,O

INSTITUTO TECNOLÓGICO Y DE ESTUDIOS SUPERIORES DE MONTERREY, CAMPUS CENTRAL DE VERACRUZ
- Business Administration and Management—General M
- Education—General M
- Educational Leadership and Administration M
- Educational Media/Instructional Technology M
- Electronic Commerce M
- Finance and Banking M
- International Business M
- Management Information Systems M
- Marketing M

INSTITUTO TECNOLÓGICO Y DE ESTUDIOS SUPERIORES DE MONTERREY, CAMPUS CHIHUAHUA
- International Business M,O

INSTITUTO TECNOLÓGICO Y DE ESTUDIOS SUPERIORES DE MONTERREY, CAMPUS CIUDAD DE MÉXICO
- Business Administration and Management—General M,D
- Education—General M,D
- Educational Media/Instructional Technology M,D
- Finance and Banking M,D
- International Business M,D
- Law O
- Management Information Systems M,D
- Quality Management M,D

INSTITUTO TECNOLÓGICO Y DE ESTUDIOS SUPERIORES DE MONTERREY, CAMPUS CIUDAD JUÁREZ
- Business Administration and Management—General M
- Education—General M
- Educational Leadership and Administration M
- Educational Media/Instructional Technology M,D
- Electronic Commerce M
- Management Information Systems M
- Quality Management M

INSTITUTO TECNOLÓGICO Y DE ESTUDIOS SUPERIORES DE MONTERREY, CAMPUS CIUDAD OBREGÓN
- Business Administration and Management—General M
- Developmental Education M
- Education—General M
- Finance and Banking M
- Management Information Systems M
- Marketing M
- Mathematics Education M

INSTITUTO TECNOLÓGICO Y DE ESTUDIOS SUPERIORES DE MONTERREY, CAMPUS CUERNAVACA
- Business Administration and Management—General M
- Finance and Banking M
- Human Resources Management M
- International Business M
- Marketing M

INSTITUTO TECNOLÓGICO Y DE ESTUDIOS SUPERIORES DE MONTERREY, CAMPUS ESTADO DE MÉXICO
- Business Administration and Management—General M,D
- Education—General M,D
- Educational Leadership and Administration M,D
- Educational Media/Instructional Technology M,D
- Electronic Commerce M,D
- Finance and Banking M,D
- Industrial and Manufacturing Management M,D
- Management Information Systems M,D
- Marketing M,D
- Quality Management M,D

INSTITUTO TECNOLÓGICO Y DE ESTUDIOS SUPERIORES DE MONTERREY, CAMPUS GUADALAJARA
- Business Administration and Management—General M
- Finance and Banking M

INSTITUTO TECNOLÓGICO Y DE ESTUDIOS SUPERIORES DE MONTERREY, CAMPUS IRAPUATO
- Business Administration and Management—General M,D
- Education—General M,D
- Educational Leadership and Administration M,D
- Educational Media/Instructional Technology M,D
- Electronic Commerce M,D
- Finance and Banking M,D
- Industrial and Manufacturing Management M,D
- International Business M,D
- Library Science M,D
- Management Information Systems M,D
- Marketing Research M,D
- Quality Management M,D

INSTITUTO TECNOLÓGICO Y DE ESTUDIOS SUPERIORES DE MONTERREY, CAMPUS LAGUNA
- Business Administration and Management—General M
- Management Information Systems M

INSTITUTO TECNOLÓGICO Y DE ESTUDIOS SUPERIORES DE MONTERREY, CAMPUS LEÓN
- Business Administration and Management—General M

INSTITUTO TECNOLÓGICO Y DE ESTUDIOS SUPERIORES DE MONTERREY, CAMPUS MONTERREY
- Business Administration and Management—General M,D
- Finance and Banking M
- International Business M
- Marketing M
- Science Education M,D

INSTITUTO TECNOLÓGICO Y DE ESTUDIOS SUPERIORES DE MONTERREY, CAMPUS QUERÉTARO
- Business Administration and Management—General M

INSTITUTO TECNOLÓGICO Y DE ESTUDIOS SUPERIORES DE MONTERREY, CAMPUS SONORA NORTE
- Business Administration and Management—General M
- Education—General M

INSTITUTO TECNOLÓGICO Y DE ESTUDIOS SUPERIORES DE MONTERREY, CAMPUS TOLUCA
- Business Administration and Management—General M

INTER AMERICAN UNIVERSITY OF PUERTO RICO, AGUADILLA CAMPUS
- Accounting M
- Business Administration and Management—General M
- Educational Leadership and Administration M
- Elementary Education M
- Finance and Banking M
- Human Resources Management M
- Management Information Systems M
- Marketing M

INTER AMERICAN UNIVERSITY OF PUERTO RICO, ARECIBO CAMPUS
- Accounting M
- Business Administration and Management—General M
- Counselor Education M
- Curriculum and Instruction M
- Education—General M
- Educational Leadership and Administration M
- Elementary Education M
- English as a Second Language M
- Finance and Banking M
- Foreign Languages Education M
- Human Resources Management M
- Mathematics Education M
- Science Education M
- Social Sciences Education M

INTER AMERICAN UNIVERSITY OF PUERTO RICO, BARRANQUITAS CAMPUS
- Accounting M
- Business Administration and Management—General M
- Curriculum and Instruction M
- Education—General M
- Educational Leadership and Administration M
- Elementary Education M
- English as a Second Language M
- Finance and Banking M
- Foreign Languages Education M
- Library Science M
- Mathematics Education M
- Science Education M
- Social Sciences Education M
- Special Education M

INTER AMERICAN UNIVERSITY OF PUERTO RICO, BAYAMÓN CAMPUS
- Human Resources Management M

INTER AMERICAN UNIVERSITY OF PUERTO RICO, GUAYAMA CAMPUS
- Business Administration and Management—General M
- Early Childhood Education M
- Elementary Education M
- Marketing M

INTER AMERICAN UNIVERSITY OF PUERTO RICO, METROPOLITAN CAMPUS
- Accounting M
- Athletic Training and Sports Medicine M
- Business Administration and Management—General M
- Business Education M
- Counselor Education M,D
- Curriculum and Instruction M,D
- Education—General M,D
- Educational Leadership and Administration M,D
- Educational Media/Instructional Technology M
- Elementary Education M
- English as a Second Language M
- Exercise and Sports Science M
- Finance and Banking M
- Foreign Languages Education M
- Health Education M
- Higher Education M
- Human Resources Development M
- Human Resources Management M
- Industrial and Manufacturing Management M
- International Business M,D
- Management Information Systems M
- Marketing M
- Mathematics Education M
- Music Education M
- Physical Education M
- Religious Education D
- Science Education M
- Social Sciences Education M
- Social Work M
- Special Education M
- Vocational and Technical Education M

INTER AMERICAN UNIVERSITY OF PUERTO RICO, PONCE CAMPUS
- Accounting M
- Elementary Education M
- English as a Second Language M
- Finance and Banking M
- Human Resources Management M
- Marketing M
- Mathematics Education M
- Science Education M
- Social Sciences Education M

INTER AMERICAN UNIVERSITY OF PUERTO RICO, SAN GERMÁN CAMPUS
- Accounting M,D
- Business Administration and Management—General M,D
- Business Education M
- Counselor Education M
- Curriculum and Instruction D
- Elementary Education M
- English as a Second Language M
- Finance and Banking M,D
- Health Education M
- Human Resources Development M,D
- Human Resources Management M,D
- Industrial and Manufacturing Management M,D
- Kinesiology and Movement Studies M
- Library Science M
- Marketing M,D
- Mathematics Education M
- Music Education M
- Physical Education M
- Science Education M
- Special Education M

INTER AMERICAN UNIVERSITY OF PUERTO RICO SCHOOL OF LAW
- Law D

INTERNATIONAL BAPTIST COLLEGE
- Education—General M

INTERNATIONAL COLLEGE OF THE CAYMAN ISLANDS
- Business Administration and Management—General M
- Business Education M
- Human Resources Management M

INTERNATIONAL TECHNOLOGICAL UNIVERSITY
- Business Administration and Management—General M
- Industrial and Manufacturing Management M

THE INTERNATIONAL UNIVERSITY OF MONACO
- Business Administration and Management—General M
- Entrepreneurship M
- Finance and Banking M
- International Business M
- Marketing M

IONA COLLEGE
- Accounting M,O
- Advertising and Public Relations M,O
- Business Administration and Management—General M,O
- Early Childhood Education M
- Education—General M
- Educational Leadership and Administration M
- Elementary Education M
- English Education M
- Finance and Banking M,O
- Foreign Languages Education M
- Human Resources Management M,O
- International Business M,O
- Marketing M,O
- Mathematics Education M
- Nonprofit Management M,O
- Reading Education M
- Science Education M
- Secondary Education M
- Social Sciences Education M
- Special Education M

IOWA STATE UNIVERSITY OF SCIENCE AND TECHNOLOGY
- Accounting M
- Agricultural Education M,D
- Counselor Education M,D
- Curriculum and Instruction M,D
- Educational Leadership and Administration M,D
- Educational Measurement and Evaluation M,D
- Educational Media/Instructional Technology M,D
- Elementary Education M,D
- English as a Second Language M
- Exercise and Sports Science M
- Foundations and Philosophy of Education M,D
- Higher Education M,D
- Home Economics Education M,D
- Hospitality Management M,D
- Human Resources Development M,D
- Kinesiology and Movement Studies M,D
- Management Information Systems M,D
- Mathematics Education M,D
- Science Education M
- Special Education M,D
- Student Affairs M,D
- Transportation Management M
- Vocational and Technical Education M,D

ITHACA COLLEGE
- Accounting M
- Business Administration and Management—General M
- Elementary Education M
- English Education M
- Exercise and Sports Science M
- Foreign Languages Education M
- Health Education M
- Mathematics Education M
- Music Education M
- Physical Education M
- Science Education M
- Secondary Education M
- Social Sciences Education M
- Sports Management M

ITT TECHNICAL INSTITUTE (IN)
- Business Administration and Management—General M

JACKSON STATE UNIVERSITY
- Accounting M

- Business Administration and Management—General M,D
- Counselor Education M
- Early Childhood Education M,D,O
- Education—General M,D,O
- Educational Leadership and Administration M,D,O
- Educational Media/Instructional Technology M,D,O
- Elementary Education M,D,O
- English Education M
- Health Education M
- Mathematics Education M
- Music Education M
- Physical Education M
- Science Education M
- Secondary Education M,D,O
- Social Work M,D
- Special Education M,O
- Vocational and Technical Education M

JACKSONVILLE STATE UNIVERSITY
- Business Administration and Management—General M
- Counselor Education M
- Early Childhood Education M
- Education—General M,O
- Educational Leadership and Administration M,O
- Educational Media/Instructional Technology M
- Elementary Education M
- Physical Education M,O
- Reading Education M
- Secondary Education M
- Special Education M

JACKSONVILLE UNIVERSITY
- Business Administration and Management—General M
- Education—General M
- Educational Leadership and Administration M
- Organizational Management M
- Sports Management M

JAMES MADISON UNIVERSITY
- Accounting M
- Art Education M
- Business Administration and Management—General M
- Early Childhood Education M
- Educational Leadership and Administration M
- Elementary Education M
- Health Education M
- Kinesiology and Movement Studies M
- Middle School Education M
- Music Education M,D
- Reading Education M
- Secondary Education M
- Special Education M
- Vocational and Technical Education M

THE JEWISH THEOLOGICAL SEMINARY
- Religious Education M,D

JEWISH UNIVERSITY OF AMERICA
- Religious Education M,D

JOHN BROWN UNIVERSITY
- Business Administration and Management—General M
- Counselor Education M
- Educational Leadership and Administration M
- Higher Education M

JOHN CARROLL UNIVERSITY
- Accounting M
- Business Administration and Management—General M
- Counselor Education M,O
- Early Childhood Education M
- Education—General M
- Educational Leadership and Administration M
- Educational Psychology M
- Middle School Education M
- Nonprofit Management M
- Science Education M
- Secondary Education M

JOHN F. KENNEDY UNIVERSITY
- Business Administration and Management—General M,O
- Education—General M
- Health Education M
- Human Resources Development M,O
- Law D
- Organizational Management M,O

JOHN JAY COLLEGE OF CRIMINAL JUSTICE OF THE CITY UNIVERSITY OF NEW YORK
- Legal and Justice Studies M,D
- Organizational Behavior M,D

JOHN MARSHALL LAW SCHOOL
- Intellectual Property Law M,D
- International Business M,D
- Law M,D
- Legal and Justice Studies M,D
- Management Information Systems M,D
- Real Estate M,D
- Taxation M,D

THE JOHNS HOPKINS UNIVERSITY
- Adult Education M,O
- Business Administration and Management—General M,O
- Counselor Education M,O
- Curriculum and Instruction M,O
- Early Childhood Education M,D,O
- Education of the Gifted M,D,O
- Education—General M,D,O
- Educational Leadership and Administration M,D,O
- Educational Media/Instructional Technology M,D,O
- Educational Psychology M,O
- Elementary Education M,O
- English as a Second Language M,D,O
- English Education M,O
- Finance and Banking M,O
- Foreign Languages Education M,O
- Health Education M,D,O
- Human Resources Development M,O
- Investment Management M,O
- Management Information Systems M,O
- Marketing M
- Mathematics Education M,O
- Reading Education M,D,O
- Real Estate M,O
- Science Education M,O
- Secondary Education M,O
- Social Sciences Education M,O
- Special Education M,D,O
- Urban Education M,O

JOHNSON & WALES UNIVERSITY
- Accounting M
- Business Education M
- Education—General M
- Educational Leadership and Administration D
- Elementary Education M,D
- Higher Education D
- Hospitality Management M
- International Business M
- Secondary Education M,D
- Special Education M

JOHNSON STATE COLLEGE
- Counselor Education M
- Curriculum and Instruction M
- Education of the Gifted M
- Education—General M
- Reading Education M
- Science Education M
- Secondary Education M
- Special Education M

JOHNSON UNIVERSITY
- Education—General M
- Educational Media/Instructional Technology M

JONES INTERNATIONAL UNIVERSITY
- Accounting M
- Adult Education M
- Business Administration and Management—General M
- Curriculum and Instruction M
- Distance Education Development M
- Education—General M
- Educational Leadership and Administration M
- Educational Media/Instructional Technology M
- Elementary Education M
- Entrepreneurship M
- Finance and Banking M
- Higher Education M
- Organizational Management M
- Project Management M
- Secondary Education M

THE JUDGE ADVOCATE GENERAL'S SCHOOL, U.S. ARMY
- Law M

JUDSON UNIVERSITY
- Education—General M
- English as a Second Language M
- Organizational Management M
- Reading Education M

KANSAS STATE UNIVERSITY
- Accounting M
- Adult Education M,D
- Advertising and Public Relations M
- Business Administration and Management—General M
- Counselor Education M,D
- Curriculum and Instruction M,D
- Early Childhood Education M
- Education—General M,D
- Educational Leadership and Administration M,D
- Educational Media/Instructional Technology M,D
- Elementary Education M,D
- English as a Second Language M,D
- English Education M,D
- Higher Education M,D
- Hospitality Management M,D
- Human Services M
- Industrial and Manufacturing Management M
- Kinesiology and Movement Studies M
- Marketing M
- Mathematics Education M,D
- Middle School Education M,D
- Music Education M
- Reading Education M,D
- Science Education M,D
- Secondary Education M,D
- Social Sciences Education M,D
- Special Education M,D
- Student Affairs M,D
- Vocational and Technical Education M,D

KANSAS WESLEYAN UNIVERSITY
- Business Administration and Management—General M
- Sports Management M

KAPLAN UNIVERSITY, DAVENPORT CAMPUS
- Business Administration and Management—General M
- Education—General M
- Educational Leadership and Administration M
- Educational Media/Instructional Technology M
- Entrepreneurship M
- Finance and Banking M
- Higher Education M
- Human Resources Management M
- International Business M
- Law M
- Legal and Justice Studies M,O
- Logistics M
- Management Information Systems M
- Marketing M
- Mathematics Education M
- Organizational Management M
- Project Management M
- Reading Education M
- Science Education M
- Secondary Education M
- Special Education M
- Student Affairs M
- Supply Chain Management M

KEAN UNIVERSITY
- Accounting M
- Adult Education M
- Art Education M
- Business Administration and Management—General M
- Counselor Education M
- Curriculum and Instruction M
- Early Childhood Education M
- Education—General M
- Educational Leadership and Administration M,D
- English as a Second Language M
- Exercise and Sports Science M
- Foreign Languages Education M
- International Business M
- Management Information Systems M
- Mathematics Education M
- Multilingual and Multicultural Education M
- Nonprofit Management M
- Reading Education M
- Science Education M
- Social Work M
- Special Education M
- Urban Education D

KEENE STATE COLLEGE
- Counselor Education M,O
- Curriculum and Instruction M,O
- Education—General M,O
- Educational Leadership and Administration M,O
- Special Education M,O

KEISER UNIVERSITY
- Accounting M
- Business Administration and Management—General M,D
- Education—General M
- Educational Leadership and Administration M,D
- Educational Media/Instructional Technology D
- International Business M,D
- Marketing M,D
- Organizational Management D

KENNESAW STATE UNIVERSITY
- Accounting M
- Art Education M
- Business Administration and Management—General M,D
- Early Childhood Education M
- Education—General M,D,O
- Educational Leadership and Administration M,D,O
- Educational Media/Instructional Technology M
- Elementary Education M
- English as a Second Language M
- English Education M
- Exercise and Sports Science M
- Mathematics Education M
- Middle School Education M
- Science Education M
- Secondary Education M
- Social Work M
- Special Education M

KENT STATE UNIVERSITY
- Accounting M,D
- Art Education M
- Athletic Training and Sports Medicine M,D
- Business Administration and Management—General M
- Computer Education M
- Counselor Education M,D,O
- Curriculum and Instruction M,D,O
- Early Childhood Education M,D,O
- Education of the Gifted M,D,O
- Education—General M,D,O
- Educational Leadership and Administration M,D,O
- Educational Measurement and Evaluation M,D
- Educational Media/Instructional Technology M
- Educational Psychology M,D
- English as a Second Language M,D
- English Education M,D
- Exercise and Sports Science M,D
- Finance and Banking D
- Foreign Languages Education M,D
- Foundations and Philosophy of Education M,D
- Health Education M,D
- Higher Education M,D,O
- Hospitality Management M
- Human Services M,D,O
- Library Science M
- Management Information Systems D
- Marketing D
- Middle School Education M
- Music Education M,D
- Reading Education M
- Recreation and Park Management M
- Secondary Education M
- Special Education M,D,O
- Sports Management M
- Student Affairs M
- Travel and Tourism M
- Vocational and Technical Education M

KENT STATE UNIVERSITY AT STARK
- Business Administration and Management—General M
- Curriculum and Instruction M
- Education—General M

KENTUCKY STATE UNIVERSITY
- Business Administration and Management—General M
- Human Resources Development M
- Management Information Systems M
- Nonprofit Management M
- Special Education M

KETTERING UNIVERSITY
- Business Administration and Management—General M

KEUKA COLLEGE
- Business Administration and Management—General M
- Early Childhood Education M

KING COLLEGE
- Business Administration and Management—General M

KING'S COLLEGE
- Business Administration and Management—General M
- Reading Education M

KUTZTOWN UNIVERSITY OF PENNSYLVANIA
- Art Education M
- Business Administration and Management—General M
- Counselor Education M
- Curriculum and Instruction M
- Education—General M
- Educational Leadership and Administration M
- Educational Media/Instructional Technology M
- Elementary Education M
- English Education M
- Library Science M
- Mathematics Education M
- Reading Education M
- Science Education M
- Secondary Education M
- Social Sciences Education M
- Social Work M

LAGRANGE COLLEGE
- Curriculum and Instruction M,O
- Education—General M,O
- Middle School Education M,O
- Organizational Management M
- Secondary Education M,O

LAKE ERIE COLLEGE
- Business Administration and Management—General M
- Curriculum and Instruction M
- Education—General M
- Educational Leadership and Administration M
- Reading Education M

LAKE ERIE COLLEGE OF OSTEOPATHIC MEDICINE
- Health Education M,D,O

LAKE FOREST COLLEGE
- Education—General M

LAKE FOREST GRADUATE SCHOOL OF MANAGEMENT
- Business Administration and Management—General M
- Finance and Banking M
- International Business M
- Marketing M
- Organizational Behavior M

LAKEHEAD UNIVERSITY
- Education—General M,D
- Exercise and Sports Science M
- Kinesiology and Movement Studies M
- Social Work M

LAKEHEAD UNIVERSITY–ORILLIA
- Business Administration and Management—General M

LAKELAND COLLEGE
- Accounting M
- Business Administration and Management—General M
- Counselor Education M
- Education—General M
- Finance and Banking M
- Project Management M

*M—master's degree; P—first professional degree; D—doctorate; O—other advanced degree; *Close-Up and/or Display*

LAMAR UNIVERSITY
Accounting M
Business Administration and Management—General M
Counselor Education M,D,O
Education—General M,D,O
Educational Leadership and Administration M,D,O
Educational Media/Instructional Technology M,D,O
Entrepreneurship M
Finance and Banking M
Kinesiology and Movement Studies M
Management Strategy and Policy M
Music Education M
Special Education M,D,O
Student Affairs M,O

LANCASTER BIBLE COLLEGE
Counselor Education M,D
Elementary Education M,D
Secondary Education M,D
Special Education M,D

LANCASTER THEOLOGICAL SEMINARY
Religious Education M,D,O

LANDER UNIVERSITY
Curriculum and Instruction M
Education—General M
Elementary Education M

LANGSTON UNIVERSITY
Education—General M
Elementary Education M
English as a Second Language M
Multilingual and Multicultural Education M
Urban Education M

LA ROCHE COLLEGE
Human Resources Management M,O

LA SALLE UNIVERSITY
Business Administration and Management—General M,O
Education—General M
Educational Media/Instructional Technology M

LASELL COLLEGE
Advertising and Public Relations M,O
Business Administration and Management—General M,O
Education—General M
Elementary Education M
Hospitality Management M,O
Human Resources Management M,O
Marketing M,O
Nonprofit Management M,O
Project Management M,O
Special Education M
Sports Management M,O

LA SIERRA UNIVERSITY
Accounting M,O
Advertising and Public Relations M
Business Administration and Management—General M,O
Counselor Education M,O
Curriculum and Instruction M,D,O
Education—General M,D,O
Educational Leadership and Administration M,D,O
Educational Psychology M,O
Finance and Banking M,O
Human Resources Management M,O
Marketing M,O
Religious Education M

LAURA AND ALVIN SIEGAL COLLEGE OF JUDAIC STUDIES
Religious Education M

LAUREL UNIVERSITY
Business Administration and Management—General M

LAURENTIAN UNIVERSITY
Business Administration and Management—General M
Science Education O
Social Work M

LAWRENCE TECHNOLOGICAL UNIVERSITY
Business Administration and Management—General M,D
Educational Media/Instructional Technology M
Industrial and Manufacturing Management M,D
International Business M,D
Management Information Systems M,D
Project Management M,D
Science Education M

LEBANESE AMERICAN UNIVERSITY
Business Administration and Management—General M

LEBANON VALLEY COLLEGE
Business Administration and Management—General M
Music Education M
Science Education M

LEE UNIVERSITY
Counselor Education M
Education—General M,O
Educational Leadership and Administration M,O
Elementary Education M,O
Music Education M
Secondary Education M,O
Special Education M,O
Student Affairs M

LEHIGH UNIVERSITY
Accounting M
Business Administration and Management—General M,D,O
Counselor Education M,D,O
Curriculum and Instruction M,D,O
Education—General M,D,O
Educational Leadership and Administration M,D,O
Educational Media/Instructional Technology M,D,O
Elementary Education M,D,O
English as a Second Language M,O
Environmental Law M,O
Finance and Banking M
Human Services M,D,O
International and Comparative Education M,O
Project Management M,D,O
Quantitative Analysis M
Special Education M,D,O
Student Affairs M,D,O
Supply Chain Management M,D,O

LEHMAN COLLEGE OF THE CITY UNIVERSITY OF NEW YORK
Accounting M
Business Education M
Counselor Education M
Early Childhood Education M
Education—General M
Elementary Education M
English as a Second Language M
English Education M
Health Education M
Mathematics Education M
Multilingual and Multicultural Education M
Music Education M
Reading Education M
Recreation and Park Management M
Science Education M
Social Sciences Education M
Special Education M

LE MOYNE COLLEGE
Business Administration and Management—General M
Early Childhood Education M,O
Education—General M,O
Educational Leadership and Administration M,O
Elementary Education M,O
English as a Second Language M,O
English Education M,O
Middle School Education M,O
Reading Education M,O
Secondary Education M,O
Social Sciences Education M,O
Special Education M,O

LENOIR-RHYNE UNIVERSITY
Accounting M
Athletic Training and Sports Medicine M
Business Administration and Management—General M
Counselor Education M
Early Childhood Education M
Education—General M
Entrepreneurship M

LESLEY UNIVERSITY
Art Education M,D,O
Computer Education M,D,O
Curriculum and Instruction M,D,O
Early Childhood Education M,D,O
Education—General M,D,O
Elementary Education M,D,O
Environmental Education M,D,O
Middle School Education M,D,O
Reading Education M,D,O
Science Education M,D,O
Special Education M,D,O

LETOURNEAU UNIVERSITY
Business Administration and Management—General M
Education—General M
Management Strategy and Policy M

LEWIS & CLARK COLLEGE
Curriculum and Instruction M
Early Childhood Education M
Educational Leadership and Administration D,O
Elementary Education M
Environmental Law M,D
Law M,D
Middle School Education M
Secondary Education M
Special Education M

LEWIS UNIVERSITY
Accounting M
Aviation Management M
Business Administration and Management—General M
Counselor Education M
Early Childhood Education M,D,O
Education—General M,D,O
Educational Leadership and Administration M,D,O
Educational Media/Instructional Technology M
Electronic Commerce M
Elementary Education M
English as a Second Language M
Finance and Banking M
Higher Education M
Human Resources Management M
International Business M
Management Information Systems M
Marketing M
Mathematics Education M
Nonprofit Management M
Organizational Management M
Project Management M
Reading Education M
Science Education M
Secondary Education M
Social Sciences Education M
Special Education M
Student Affairs M

LIBERTY UNIVERSITY
Business Administration and Management—General M
Counselor Education M,D,O
Curriculum and Instruction M,D,O
Distance Education Development M,D,O
Early Childhood Education M,D,O
Education of the Gifted M,D,O
Education—General M,D,O
Educational Leadership and Administration M,D,O
Educational Media/Instructional Technology M,D,O
Elementary Education M,D,O
Exercise and Sports Science M,D,O
Human Services M,D
Law D
Mathematics Education M,D,O
Middle School Education M,D,O
Reading Education M,D,O
Secondary Education M,D,O
Special Education M,D,O
Sports Management M,D,O

LIFE UNIVERSITY
Exercise and Sports Science M

LIM COLLEGE
Business Administration and Management—General M
Entrepreneurship M

LINCOLN CHRISTIAN SEMINARY
Religious Education M,D

LINCOLN MEMORIAL UNIVERSITY
Business Administration and Management—General M
Counselor Education M,D,O
Curriculum and Instruction M,D,O
Education—General M,D,O
Educational Leadership and Administration M,D,O
English Education M,D,O
Higher Education M,D,O
Human Resources Development M,D,O
Law D

LINCOLN UNIVERSITY (CA)
Business Administration and Management—General M,D
Finance and Banking M,D
Human Resources Management M,D
International Business M,D
Investment Management M,D
Management Information Systems M,D

LINCOLN UNIVERSITY (MO)
Accounting M,O
Business Administration and Management—General M,O
Counselor Education M,O
Educational Leadership and Administration M,O
Elementary Education M,O
Entrepreneurship M,O
Secondary Education M,O
Special Education M,O

LINCOLN UNIVERSITY (PA)
Business Administration and Management—General M
Early Childhood Education M
Elementary Education M
Finance and Banking M
Human Resources Management M
Human Services M
Reading Education M

LINDENWOOD UNIVERSITY
Accounting M
Business Administration and Management—General M,O
Education—General M,D,O
Educational Leadership and Administration M,D,O
Educational Media/Instructional Technology M,D,O
English as a Second Language M,D,O
Entrepreneurship M
Finance and Banking M
Human Resources Management M,O
Human Services M
International Business M
Management Information Systems M,O
Marketing M
Nonprofit Management M
Physical Education M,D,O
Sports Management M
Supply Chain Management M

LIPSCOMB UNIVERSITY
Accounting M
Business Administration and Management—General M
Education—General M,D
Educational Leadership and Administration M,D
Educational Media/Instructional Technology M,D
Exercise and Sports Science M
Finance and Banking M
Human Resources Management M
Mathematics Education M,D
Nonprofit Management M
Organizational Management M
Special Education M,D
Sports Management M
Sustainability Management M

LOCK HAVEN UNIVERSITY OF PENNSYLVANIA
Education—General M
Elementary Education M

LOGAN UNIVERSITY–COLLEGE OF CHIROPRACTIC
Exercise and Sports Science M

LOMA LINDA UNIVERSITY
Counselor Education M,D,O
Health Education M,D
Social Work M,D

LONG ISLAND UNIVERSITY–BRENTWOOD CAMPUS
Counselor Education M
Early Childhood Education M
Education—General M
Reading Education M
Special Education M

LONG ISLAND UNIVERSITY–BROOKLYN CAMPUS
Accounting M
Athletic Training and Sports Medicine M
Business Administration and Management—General M
Counselor Education M,O
Education—General M,O
Educational Leadership and Administration M
Educational Media/Instructional Technology M
Elementary Education M
English as a Second Language M
English Education M
Exercise and Sports Science M
Health Education M
Human Resources Management M
Mathematics Education M
Multilingual and Multicultural Education M
Physical Education M
Reading Education M
Special Education M
Taxation M

LONG ISLAND UNIVERSITY–C. W. POST CAMPUS
Accounting M,O
Archives/Archival Administration M,D,O
Art Education M
Business Administration and Management—General M,O
Computer Education M
Counselor Education M
Early Childhood Education M
Education—General M,D,O
Educational Leadership and Administration M,D,O
Educational Media/Instructional Technology M
Elementary Education M
English as a Second Language M
English Education M
Finance and Banking M,O
Foreign Languages Education M
Information Studies M,D,O
International Business M,O
Library Science M,D,O
Management Information Systems M,O
Marketing M,O
Mathematics Education M
Middle School Education M
Multilingual and Multicultural Education M
Music Education M
Nonprofit Management M,O
Reading Education M
Science Education M
Secondary Education M
Social Work M
Special Education M
Taxation M,O

LONG ISLAND UNIVERSITY–HUDSON AT ROCKLAND
Business Administration and Management—General M,O
Counselor Education M
Early Childhood Education M
Educational Leadership and Administration M,O
Elementary Education M
Entrepreneurship M,O
Finance and Banking M,O
Reading Education M
Secondary Education M
Special Education M

LONG ISLAND UNIVERSITY–HUDSON AT WESTCHESTER
Business Administration and Management—General M
Counselor Education M
Early Childhood Education M
Education—General M,O
Educational Psychology M
Elementary Education M
English as a Second Language M,O
Information Studies M
Library Science M
Multilingual and Multicultural Education M,O
Reading Education M,O
Secondary Education M,O
Special Education M,O

LONG ISLAND UNIVERSITY–RIVERHEAD
Early Childhood Education M
Education—General M,O
Elementary Education M
Reading Education M
Special Education M

LONGWOOD UNIVERSITY
- Business Administration and Management—General M
- Counselor Education M
- Education—General M
- Educational Leadership and Administration M
- Educational Media/Instructional Technology M
- Elementary Education M
- English Education M
- Reading Education M
- Secondary Education M
- Special Education M

LORAS COLLEGE
- Educational Leadership and Administration M
- Special Education M

LOUISIANA STATE UNIVERSITY AND AGRICULTURAL AND MECHANICAL COLLEGE
- Accounting M,D
- Agricultural Education M,D
- Business Administration and Management—General M,D
- Business Education M,D
- Counselor Education M,D,O
- Education—General M,D,O
- Educational Leadership and Administration M,D,O
- Educational Measurement and Evaluation M,D,O
- Educational Media/Instructional Technology M,D,O
- Elementary Education M,D,O
- Finance and Banking M,D
- Higher Education M,D,O
- Home Economics Education M,D
- Human Resources Development M,D
- Information Studies M
- International and Comparative Education M,D
- Kinesiology and Movement Studies M,D
- Law M,D
- Library Science M
- Management Information Systems M,D
- Marketing D
- Music Education M,D
- Secondary Education M,D,O
- Social Work M,D
- Vocational and Technical Education M,D

LOUISIANA STATE UNIVERSITY IN SHREVEPORT
- Business Administration and Management—General M
- Counselor Education M
- Curriculum and Instruction M
- Education—General M
- Educational Leadership and Administration M
- Human Services M
- Kinesiology and Movement Studies M

LOUISIANA TECH UNIVERSITY
- Accounting M,D
- Business Administration and Management—General M,D
- Business Education M,D
- Counselor Education M,D
- Curriculum and Instruction M,D
- Education—General M,D
- Educational Leadership and Administration M,D
- English Education M,D
- Exercise and Sports Science M
- Finance and Banking M,D
- Foreign Languages Education M,D
- Health Education M,D
- Marketing M,D
- Mathematics Education M,D
- Physical Education M,D
- Science Education M,D
- Secondary Education M,D
- Social Sciences Education M,D
- Special Education M,D

LOURDES UNIVERSITY
- Education—General M
- Educational Media/Instructional Technology M
- Organizational Management M

LOYOLA MARYMOUNT UNIVERSITY
- Business Administration and Management—General M
- Counselor Education M
- Early Childhood Education M
- Education—General M,D
- Educational Leadership and Administration M,D
- Elementary Education M
- Law M,D
- Mathematics Education M
- Multilingual and Multicultural Education M
- Reading Education M
- Religious Education M
- Secondary Education M
- Special Education M
- Taxation M,D
- Urban Education M

LOYOLA UNIVERSITY CHICAGO
- Accounting M
- Business Administration and Management—General M
- Counselor Education M,D
- Curriculum and Instruction M,O
- Education—General M,D,O
- Educational Leadership and Administration M,D,O
- Educational Measurement and Evaluation M,D
- Educational Media/Instructional Technology M,O
- Educational Policy M,D
- Educational Psychology M
- Elementary Education M,O
- English as a Second Language M,O
- Finance and Banking M
- Health Law M,D
- Higher Education M,D
- Human Resources Management M,D
- Law M,D
- Legal and Justice Studies M,D
- Management Information Systems M,D
- Marketing M
- Mathematics Education M,O
- Reading Education M,O
- Religious Education M,O
- Science Education M,O
- Secondary Education M,O
- Social Work M,D,O
- Special Education M,O
- Taxation M,D

LOYOLA UNIVERSITY MARYLAND
- Accounting M
- Business Administration and Management—General M
- Counselor Education M,O
- Curriculum and Instruction M,O
- Early Childhood Education M,O
- Education—General M,O
- Educational Leadership and Administration M,O
- Educational Media/Instructional Technology M
- Elementary Education M,O
- English Education M
- Finance and Banking M
- International Business M
- Management Information Systems M
- Marketing M
- Mathematics Education M
- Middle School Education M,O
- Reading Education M,O
- Science Education M
- Secondary Education M,O
- Special Education M,O

LOYOLA UNIVERSITY NEW ORLEANS
- Business Administration and Management—General M
- Counselor Education M
- Law M,D

LUTHER RICE UNIVERSITY
- Religious Education M,D

LYNCHBURG COLLEGE
- Business Administration and Management—General M
- Counselor Education M
- Curriculum and Instruction M
- Education—General M,D
- Educational Leadership and Administration M,D
- Reading Education M
- Science Education M
- Special Education M

LYNDON STATE COLLEGE
- Counselor Education M
- Curriculum and Instruction M
- Education—General M
- Reading Education M
- Science Education M
- Special Education M

LYNN UNIVERSITY
- Aviation Management M
- Business Administration and Management—General M
- Education of the Gifted M,D
- Education—General M,D
- Educational Leadership and Administration M,D
- Hospitality Management M
- International Business M
- Investment Management M
- Marketing M
- Special Education M,D
- Sports Management M

MAASTRICHT SCHOOL OF MANAGEMENT
- Business Administration and Management—General M,D
- Facilities Management M,D
- Sustainability Management M,D

MADONNA UNIVERSITY
- Business Administration and Management—General M
- Education—General M
- Educational Leadership and Administration M
- English as a Second Language M
- International Business M
- Quality Management M
- Reading Education M
- Special Education M

MAHARISHI UNIVERSITY OF MANAGEMENT
- Accounting M,D
- Business Administration and Management—General M,D
- Education—General M
- Elementary Education M
- Secondary Education M
- Sustainability Management M,D

MAINE MARITIME ACADEMY
- International Business M,O
- Logistics M,O
- Supply Chain Management M,O
- Transportation Management M,O

MALONE UNIVERSITY
- Business Administration and Management—General M
- Counselor Education M
- Curriculum and Instruction M
- Education—General M
- Educational Leadership and Administration M
- Organizational Management M
- Reading Education M
- Special Education M

MANCHESTER COLLEGE
- Athletic Training and Sports Medicine M
- Education—General M

MANHATTAN COLLEGE
- Counselor Education M,O
- Early Childhood Education M,O
- Education—General M,O
- Educational Leadership and Administration M,O
- Multilingual and Multicultural Education M,O
- Special Education M,O
- Student Affairs M,O

MANHATTANVILLE COLLEGE
- Art Education M
- Early Childhood Education M
- Education—General M,D*
- Educational Leadership and Administration M,D
- Elementary Education M
- English as a Second Language M
- English Education M
- Exercise and Sports Science M
- Finance and Banking M
- Foreign Languages Education M
- Human Resources Development M
- International Business M
- Management Strategy and Policy M
- Marketing M
- Mathematics Education M
- Middle School Education M
- Music Education M
- Organizational Management M
- Reading Education M
- Science Education M
- Secondary Education M
- Social Sciences Education M
- Special Education M
- Sports Management M

MANSFIELD UNIVERSITY OF PENNSYLVANIA
- Art Education M
- Education—General M
- Elementary Education M
- Information Studies M
- Library Science M
- Organizational Management M
- Secondary Education M
- Special Education M

MAPLE SPRINGS BAPTIST BIBLE COLLEGE AND SEMINARY
- Religious Education M,D,O

MARIAN UNIVERSITY (IN)
- Education—General M

MARIAN UNIVERSITY (WI)
- Business Administration and Management—General M
- Education—General M,D
- Educational Leadership and Administration M,D
- Organizational Management M
- Quality Management M

MARIETTA COLLEGE
- Education—General M

MARIST COLLEGE
- Business Administration and Management—General M,O
- Education—General M,O
- Industrial and Manufacturing Management M,O
- Management Information Systems M,O

MARLBORO COLLEGE
- Business Administration and Management—General M
- Computer Education M
- Education—General M
- Educational Media/Instructional Technology M
- Legal and Justice Studies M
- Project Management M,O
- Sustainability Management M

MARQUETTE UNIVERSITY
- Accounting M
- Advertising and Public Relations M,O
- Business Administration and Management—General M,O
- Counselor Education M,D
- Curriculum and Instruction M,D,O
- Education—General M,D,O
- Educational Leadership and Administration M,D,O
- Educational Policy M,D,O
- Elementary Education M,D,O
- Entrepreneurship M,O
- Finance and Banking M,O
- Foreign Languages Education M,D,O
- Foundations and Philosophy of Education M,D,O
- Human Resources Development M
- Human Resources Management M,O
- Industrial and Manufacturing Management M,O
- International Business M,O
- Law D
- Management Information Systems M,O
- Marketing Research M
- Marketing M,O
- Mathematics Education M,D
- Nonprofit Management M,O
- Reading Education M,D,O
- Real Estate M
- Secondary Education M,D,O
- Sports Management M,O
- Student Affairs M,D,O
- Supply Chain Management M,O

MARSHALL UNIVERSITY
- Accounting M
- Adult Education M
- Business Administration and Management—General M
- Counselor Education M,O
- Early Childhood Education M
- Education—General M,D,O
- Educational Leadership and Administration M,D,O
- Elementary Education M
- Exercise and Sports Science M
- Health Education M
- Human Resources Management M
- Reading Education M,O
- Secondary Education M
- Special Education M
- Sports Management M
- Vocational and Technical Education M

MARTIN LUTHER COLLEGE
- Curriculum and Instruction M
- Education—General M
- Educational Leadership and Administration M
- Special Education M

MARY BALDWIN COLLEGE
- Education—General M
- Elementary Education M
- Middle School Education M

MARYGROVE COLLEGE
- Education—General M
- Educational Leadership and Administration M
- Elementary Education M
- Human Resources Management M
- Legal and Justice Studies M
- Reading Education M
- Secondary Education M
- Urban Education M

MARYLAND INSTITUTE COLLEGE OF ART
- Art Education M
- Business Administration and Management—General M

MARYLHURST UNIVERSITY
- Business Administration and Management—General M
- Education—General M
- Finance and Banking M
- Marketing M
- Nonprofit Management M
- Organizational Behavior M
- Real Estate M

MARYMOUNT UNIVERSITY
- Business Administration and Management—General M,O
- Counselor Education M
- Education—General M
- Educational Leadership and Administration M,O
- Elementary Education M
- English as a Second Language M
- Human Resources Management M,O
- Legal and Justice Studies M,O
- Management Information Systems M,O
- Organizational Management M,O
- Project Management M,O
- Secondary Education M
- Special Education M

MARYVILLE UNIVERSITY OF SAINT LOUIS
- Accounting M,O
- Actuarial Science M
- Art Education M,D
- Business Administration and Management—General M,O
- Business Education M,D
- Early Childhood Education M,D
- Education of the Gifted M,D
- Education—General M,D
- Educational Leadership and Administration M,D
- Elementary Education M,D
- Entertainment Management M,O
- Higher Education M,D
- Marketing M,O
- Middle School Education M,D
- Organizational Management M,O
- Project Management M,O
- Reading Education M,D
- Secondary Education M,D
- Sports Management M,O

MARYWOOD UNIVERSITY
- Art Education M
- Business Administration and Management—General M

*M—master's degree; P—first professional degree; D—doctorate; O—other advanced degree; *Close-Up and/or Display*

Counselor Education M
Early Childhood Education M
Education—General M
Educational Leadership and Administration M,D
Elementary Education M
Exercise and Sports Science M
Finance and Banking M
Health Education D
Higher Education M,D
Investment Management M
Management Information Systems M
Music Education M
Nonprofit Management M
Reading Education M
Secondary Education M
Social Work M,D
Special Education M

MASSACHUSETTS COLLEGE OF ART AND DESIGN
Art Education M,O
Education—General M

MASSACHUSETTS COLLEGE OF LIBERAL ARTS
Curriculum and Instruction M
Education—General M
Educational Leadership and Administration M
Reading Education M
Special Education M

MASSACHUSETTS INSTITUTE OF TECHNOLOGY
Business Administration and Management—General M,D
Logistics M,D
Real Estate M

MASSACHUSETTS MARITIME ACADEMY
Facilities Management M

MASSACHUSETTS SCHOOL OF LAW AT ANDOVER
Law D

MASSACHUSETTS SCHOOL OF PROFESSIONAL PSYCHOLOGY
Student Affairs M,D,O

MCDANIEL COLLEGE
Counselor Education M
Curriculum and Instruction M
Educational Leadership and Administration M
Educational Media/Instructional Technology M
Elementary Education M
Human Resources Development M
Human Services M
Library Science M
Physical Education M
Reading Education M
Secondary Education M
Special Education M

MCGILL UNIVERSITY
Accounting M,D,O
Business Administration and Management—General M,D,O
Curriculum and Instruction M,D,O
Education—General M,D,O
Educational Leadership and Administration M,D,O
Educational Psychology M,D,O
Entrepreneurship M,D,O
Finance and Banking M,D,O
Foreign Languages Education M,D,O
Foundations and Philosophy of Education M,D,O
Industrial and Manufacturing Management M,D,O
Information Studies M,D,O
International Business M,D,O
Kinesiology and Movement Studies M,D,O
Law M,D,O
Library Science M,D,O
Management Information Systems M,D,O
Management Strategy and Policy M,D,O
Marketing M,D,O
Music Education M,D
Physical Education M,D,O
Social Work M,D,O
Transportation Management M,D

MCKENDREE UNIVERSITY
Business Administration and Management—General M
Education—General M
Educational Leadership and Administration M
Higher Education M
Human Resources Management M
International Business M
Music Education M
Special Education M

MCMASTER UNIVERSITY
Business Administration and Management—General M,D
Human Resources Management M,D
Kinesiology and Movement Studies M,D
Management Information Systems D
Social Work M

MCNEESE STATE UNIVERSITY
Accounting M
Business Administration and Management—General M
Counselor Education M
Curriculum and Instruction M
Early Childhood Education M
Educational Leadership and Administration M,O
Educational Measurement and Evaluation M
Educational Media/Instructional Technology M,O
Elementary Education M
Exercise and Sports Science M
Music Education M,O
Reading Education M
Science Education M
Secondary Education M
Special Education M

MEDAILLE COLLEGE
Business Administration and Management—General M
Curriculum and Instruction M
Education—General M
Elementary Education M
Organizational Management M
Reading Education M
Secondary Education M
Special Education M

MELBOURNE BUSINESS SCHOOL
Business Administration and Management—General M,D,O
Marketing M,D,O

MEMORIAL UNIVERSITY OF NEWFOUNDLAND
Adult Education M,D,O
Business Administration and Management—General M
Curriculum and Instruction M,D,O
Education—General M,D,O
Educational Leadership and Administration M,D,O
Educational Media/Instructional Technology M,D,O
Educational Psychology M,D,O
Exercise and Sports Science M
Kinesiology and Movement Studies M
Physical Education M
Social Work M

MEMPHIS COLLEGE OF ART
Art Education M

MERCER UNIVERSITY
Accounting M
Business Administration and Management—General M
Counselor Education M,D
Curriculum and Instruction M,D,O
Early Childhood Education M,D,O
Education—General M,D,O
Educational Leadership and Administration M,D,O
Higher Education M,D,O
Law D
Middle School Education M,D,O
Reading Education M,D,O
Secondary Education M,D,O

MERCY COLLEGE
Accounting M
Business Administration and Management—General M
Counselor Education M,O
Early Childhood Education M,O
Education—General M,O
Educational Leadership and Administration M,O
Electronic Commerce M,O
Elementary Education M,O
English as a Second Language M,O
Human Resources Management M,O
Middle School Education M
Multilingual and Multicultural Education M,O
Organizational Management M
Reading Education M
Secondary Education M
Special Education M,O
Urban Education M

MERCYHURST COLLEGE
Accounting M,O
Educational Leadership and Administration M,O
Entrepreneurship M,O
Exercise and Sports Science M
Higher Education M,O
Human Resources Management M,O
Multilingual and Multicultural Education M,O
Nonprofit Management M,O
Organizational Management M,O
Secondary Education M,O
Special Education M,O
Sports Management M,O

MEREDITH COLLEGE
Business Administration and Management—General M
Education—General M

MERRIMACK COLLEGE
Business Administration and Management—General M
Early Childhood Education M,O
Education—General M,O
Educational Leadership and Administration M,O
Elementary Education M,O
English as a Second Language M,O
Higher Education M,O
Middle School Education M,O
Reading Education M,O
Secondary Education M,O
Special Education M,O

MESSIAH COLLEGE
Art Education M
Counselor Education M,O
English as a Second Language M
Higher Education M
Special Education M
Sports Management M
Student Affairs M

METHODIST UNIVERSITY
Business Administration and Management—General M

METROPOLITAN COLLEGE OF NEW YORK
Business Administration and Management—General M
Elementary Education M

METROPOLITAN STATE UNIVERSITY
Business Administration and Management—General M,D,O
Information Studies M,D,O
Management Information Systems M,D,O
Nonprofit Management M,D,O
Project Management M,D,O

MGH INSTITUTE OF HEALTH PROFESSIONS
Reading Education M,O

MIAMI UNIVERSITY
Accounting M
Art Education M
Business Administration and Management—General M
Curriculum and Instruction M,D
Early Childhood Education M
Education—General M,D,O
Educational Leadership and Administration M,D
Educational Media/Instructional Technology M,O
Educational Psychology M,O
Elementary Education M
Exercise and Sports Science M
Higher Education M,D
Mathematics Education M
Music Education M
Reading Education M
Secondary Education M
Special Education M,O
Student Affairs M,D

MICHIGAN SCHOOL OF PROFESSIONAL PSYCHOLOGY
Educational Psychology M,D

MICHIGAN STATE UNIVERSITY
Accounting M,D
Adult Education M,D,O
Advertising and Public Relations M,D
Business Administration and Management—General M,D
Counselor Education M,D,O
Curriculum and Instruction M,D,O
Education—General M,D,O
Educational Leadership and Administration M,D,O
Educational Measurement and Evaluation M,D,O
Educational Media/Instructional Technology M,D,O
Educational Policy D
Educational Psychology M,D,O
English as a Second Language M,D
Finance and Banking M,D
Foreign Languages Education D
Higher Education M,D,O
Hospitality Management M
Human Resources Management M,D
Kinesiology and Movement Studies M,D
Management Information Systems M,D
Marketing M,D
Mathematics Education M,D
Music Education M,D
Reading Education M
Recreation and Park Management M,D
Science Education M,D
Social Sciences Education M,D
Social Work M,D
Special Education M,D,O
Supply Chain Management M,D

MICHIGAN STATE UNIVERSITY COLLEGE OF LAW
Law M,D
Legal and Justice Studies M,D

MICHIGAN TECHNOLOGICAL UNIVERSITY
Business Administration and Management—General M
Entrepreneurship O
Science Education M,D
Sustainability Management O

MID-AMERICA CHRISTIAN UNIVERSITY
Business Administration and Management—General M
Organizational Management M

MIDAMERICA NAZARENE UNIVERSITY
Business Administration and Management—General M
Education—General M
Educational Media/Instructional Technology M
English as a Second Language M
Finance and Banking M
International Business M
Nonprofit Management M
Organizational Management M
Special Education M

MIDDLE TENNESSEE STATE UNIVERSITY
Accounting M
Aviation Management M
Business Administration and Management—General M
Business Education M
Counselor Education M,O
Curriculum and Instruction M,O
Early Childhood Education M,O
Education—General M,D,O
Educational Leadership and Administration M,O
Educational Media/Instructional Technology M,O
Elementary Education M,O
English as a Second Language M,O
Exercise and Sports Science M,D
Foreign Languages Education M
Health Education M
Management Information Systems M
Management Strategy and Policy M,O
Marketing M
Mathematics Education M,D
Middle School Education M,O
Physical Education M
Reading Education M,D
Recreation and Park Management M
Science Education M
Secondary Education M,O
Social Work M
Special Education M
Vocational and Technical Education M

MIDWAY COLLEGE
Business Administration and Management—General M
Organizational Management M

MIDWESTERN BAPTIST THEOLOGICAL SEMINARY
Religious Education M,D,O

MIDWESTERN STATE UNIVERSITY
Business Administration and Management—General M
Counselor Education M
Curriculum and Instruction M
Education—General M
Educational Leadership and Administration M
Educational Media/Instructional Technology M
Human Resources Development M
Kinesiology and Movement Studies M
Reading Education M
Special Education M

MILLERSVILLE UNIVERSITY OF PENNSYLVANIA
Art Education M
Early Childhood Education M
Education of the Gifted M
Education—General M
Elementary Education M
English Education M
Foundations and Philosophy of Education M
Mathematics Education M
Reading Education M
Social Work M
Special Education M
Sports Management M
Vocational and Technical Education M

MILLIGAN COLLEGE
Business Administration and Management—General M
Education—General M

MILLIKIN UNIVERSITY
Business Administration and Management—General M

MILLSAPS COLLEGE
Accounting M
Business Administration and Management—General M

MILLS COLLEGE
Art Education M,D
Business Administration and Management—General M
Curriculum and Instruction M,D
Early Childhood Education M,D
Education—General M,D
Educational Leadership and Administration M,D
Elementary Education M,D
English Education M,D
Foreign Languages Education M,D
Health Education M,D
Mathematics Education M,D
Science Education M,D
Secondary Education M,D
Social Sciences Education M,D

MILWAUKEE SCHOOL OF ENGINEERING
Business Administration and Management—General M
Industrial and Manufacturing Management M
International Business M
Marketing M

MINNESOTA STATE UNIVERSITY MANKATO
Art Education M
Business Administration and Management—General M
Counselor Education M,D,O
Curriculum and Instruction M,O
Early Childhood Education M,O
Education—General M,D,O
Educational Leadership and Administration M
Educational Media/Instructional Technology M,O
Elementary Education M,O
English as a Second Language M,O
English Education M,O
Health Education M,O
Higher Education M,O
Human Services M
Management Information Systems M,O

Mathematics Education M
Multilingual and Multicultural Education M,O
Physical Education M
Science Education M
Secondary Education M,O
Social Sciences Education M
Social Work M
Special Education M,O
Student Affairs M,D,O

MINNESOTA STATE UNIVERSITY MOORHEAD
Counselor Education M
Curriculum and Instruction M
Education—General M,O
Educational Leadership and Administration M,O
Human Services M,O
Reading Education M
Special Education M

MINOT STATE UNIVERSITY
Business Administration and Management—General M
Early Childhood Education M
Education of Students with Severe/Multiple Disabilities M
Elementary Education M
Management Information Systems M
Mathematics Education M
Music Education M
Science Education M
Special Education M

MISERICORDIA UNIVERSITY
Business Administration and Management—General M
Curriculum and Instruction M
Education—General M
Organizational Management M

MISSISSIPPI COLLEGE
Accounting M,O
Advertising and Public Relations M
Art Education M,D,O
Business Administration and Management—General M,O
Business Education M,D,O
Computer Education M,D,O
Counselor Education M,D,O
Curriculum and Instruction M,D,O
Education—General M,D,O
Educational Leadership and Administration M,D,O
Elementary Education M,D,O
English as a Second Language M
English Education M,D,O
Finance and Banking M,O
Higher Education M,D,O
Kinesiology and Movement Studies M
Law D,O
Legal and Justice Studies M,O
Mathematics Education M,D,O
Music Education M
Science Education M,D,O
Secondary Education M,D,O
Social Sciences Education M,D,O
Special Education M,D,O

MISSISSIPPI STATE UNIVERSITY
Accounting M,D
Agricultural Education M,D
Business Administration and Management—General M,D
Counselor Education M,D,O
Curriculum and Instruction M,D,O
Education—General M,D,O
Educational Leadership and Administration M,D,O
Educational Media/Instructional Technology M,D,O
Educational Psychology M,D,O
Elementary Education M,D,O
Finance and Banking M,D
Foreign Languages Education M
Human Resources Development M,D,O
Kinesiology and Movement Studies M
Management Information Systems M,D
Marketing M,D
Middle School Education M,D,O
Physical Education M
Project Management M
Science Education M,D,O
Secondary Education M,D,O
Special Education M,D,O
Student Affairs M,D,O
Taxation M,D

MISSISSIPPI UNIVERSITY FOR WOMEN
Curriculum and Instruction M
Education of the Gifted M
Education—General M
Educational Leadership and Administration M
Health Education M
Reading Education M

MISSISSIPPI VALLEY STATE UNIVERSITY
Education—General M
Elementary Education M

MISSOURI BAPTIST UNIVERSITY
Business Administration and Management—General M,O
Counselor Education M,O
Education—General M,O
Educational Leadership and Administration M,O

MISSOURI SOUTHERN STATE UNIVERSITY
Business Administration and Management—General M
Early Childhood Education M
Education—General M
Educational Media/Instructional Technology M

MISSOURI STATE UNIVERSITY
Accounting M
Business Administration and Management—General M
Counselor Education M,O
Curriculum and Instruction M
Early Childhood Education M
Educational Leadership and Administration M,O
Educational Media/Instructional Technology M
Elementary Education M,O
Foreign Languages Education M
Higher Education M
Management Information Systems M
Music Education M
Physical Education M
Project Management M
Reading Education M
Science Education M
Secondary Education M,O
Social Sciences Education M
Social Work M
Special Education M,D
Sports Management M
Student Affairs M

MISSOURI UNIVERSITY OF SCIENCE AND TECHNOLOGY
Mathematics Education M,D

MISSOURI WESTERN STATE UNIVERSITY
Educational Measurement and Evaluation M
English as a Second Language M
Management Information Systems M
Special Education M

MOLLOY COLLEGE
Accounting M
Business Administration and Management—General M
Education—General M,O
Finance and Banking M
Social Work M

MONMOUTH UNIVERSITY
Accounting M,O
Advertising and Public Relations M,O
Business Administration and Management—General M,O*
Education—General M,O
Educational Leadership and Administration M,O
Elementary Education M,O
English as a Second Language M,O
Finance and Banking M,O
Reading Education M,O
Real Estate M,O
Secondary Education M,O
Social Work M,O
Special Education M,O

MONROE COLLEGE
Business Administration and Management—General M

MONTANA STATE UNIVERSITY
Accounting M
Adult Education M,D,O
Agricultural Education M
Curriculum and Instruction M,D,O
Education—General M,D,O
Educational Leadership and Administration M,D,O
Health Education M
Higher Education M,D,O
Home Economics Education M
Mathematics Education M,D
Vocational and Technical Education M,D,O

MONTANA STATE UNIVERSITY BILLINGS
Advertising and Public Relations M
Athletic Training and Sports Medicine M
Counselor Education M
Curriculum and Instruction M
Early Childhood Education M
Education—General M,O
Educational Media/Instructional Technology M
Human Services M
Physical Education M
Reading Education M
Secondary Education M
Special Education M
Sports Management M

MONTANA STATE UNIVERSITY–NORTHERN
Counselor Education M
Education—General M

MONTANA TECH OF THE UNIVERSITY OF MONTANA
Project Management M

MONTCLAIR STATE UNIVERSITY
Accounting M,O
Advertising and Public Relations M
Archives/Archival Administration M
Art Education M
Business Administration and Management—General M,O

Counselor Education M,D,O
Curriculum and Instruction M,D,O
Early Childhood Education M
Education—General M,D,O
Educational Leadership and Administration M,D
Educational Media/Instructional Technology O
Elementary Education M
English as a Second Language M,O
English Education M,O
Environmental Education M,O
Exercise and Sports Science M,O
Finance and Banking M,O
Foreign Languages Education M
Foundations and Philosophy of Education D,O
Health Education M
Intellectual Property Law M,O
International Business O
Law M,O
Legal and Justice Studies O
Management Information Systems M,O
Marketing M,O
Mathematics Education M,D
Music Education M
Physical Education M
Reading Education M,O
Science Education M,O
Special Education M,O
Sports Management M

MONTEREY INSTITUTE OF INTERNATIONAL STUDIES
Business Administration and Management—General M
English as a Second Language M
Foreign Languages Education M
International Business M

MONTREAT COLLEGE
Business Administration and Management—General M
Environmental Education M

MOODY THEOLOGICAL SEMINARYMICHIGAN
Religious Education M,O

MOORE COLLEGE OF ART & DESIGN
Art Education M

MORAVIAN COLLEGE
Accounting M
Business Administration and Management—General M
Curriculum and Instruction M
Human Resources Development M
Human Resources Management M
Supply Chain Management M

MOREHEAD STATE UNIVERSITY
Adult Education M,O
Art Education M
Business Administration and Management—General M
Business Education M,O
Counselor Education M,O
Curriculum and Instruction M,O
Education of the Gifted M,O
Education—General M,O
Educational Leadership and Administration M,O
Educational Media/Instructional Technology M,O
Elementary Education M,O
English Education M,O
Exercise and Sports Science M
Foreign Languages Education M,O
Health Education M
Higher Education M,O
International and Comparative Education M,O
Management Information Systems M
Mathematics Education M
Middle School Education M,O
Music Education M
Physical Education M
Reading Education M,O
Science Education M
Secondary Education M,O
Social Sciences Education M,O
Special Education M,O
Sports Management M
Vocational and Technical Education M,O

MOREHOUSE SCHOOL OF MEDICINE
Health Education M

MORGAN STATE UNIVERSITY
Business Administration and Management—General D
Community College Education D
Education—General M,D
Educational Leadership and Administration M,D
Elementary Education M
Higher Education D
Mathematics Education M,D
Middle School Education M
Science Education M,D
Secondary Education M
Social Work M,D
Transportation Management M,D
Urban Education M,D

MORNINGSIDE COLLEGE
Education—General M
Special Education M

MORRISON UNIVERSITY
Business Administration and Management—General M

MOUNTAIN STATE UNIVERSITY
Management Strategy and Policy M
Organizational Management D

MOUNT ALOYSIUS COLLEGE
Business Administration and Management—General M
Education—General M

MOUNT IDA COLLEGE
Business Administration and Management—General M

MOUNT MARTY COLLEGE
Business Administration and Management—General M

MOUNT MARY COLLEGE
Business Administration and Management—General M
Counselor Education M
Education—General M
Health Education M

MOUNT MERCY UNIVERSITY
Business Administration and Management—General M
Education—General M
Reading Education M
Special Education M

MOUNT SAINT MARY COLLEGE
Business Administration and Management—General M
Early Childhood Education M,O
Education—General M,O
Elementary Education M,O
Finance and Banking M
Middle School Education M,O
Reading Education M,O
Secondary Education M,O
Special Education M,O

MOUNT ST. MARY'S COLLEGE
Business Administration and Management—General M
Education—General M,O
Educational Leadership and Administration M,O
Elementary Education M
Entrepreneurship M
Nonprofit Management M
Organizational Management M
Project Management M
Secondary Education, M
Special Education M,O

MOUNT ST. MARY'S UNIVERSITY
Business Administration and Management—General M
Education—General M

MOUNT SAINT VINCENT UNIVERSITY
Adult Education M
Curriculum and Instruction M
Education—General M
Educational Psychology M
Elementary Education M
English as a Second Language M
Foundations and Philosophy of Education M
Middle School Education M
Reading Education M
Special Education M

MOUNT VERNON NAZARENE UNIVERSITY
Business Administration and Management—General M
Education—General M

MULTNOMAH UNIVERSITY
Counselor Education M
Education—General M
English as a Second Language M

MURRAY STATE UNIVERSITY
Accounting M
Agricultural Education M
Business Administration and Management—General M
Counselor Education M,O
Early Childhood Education M
Education—General M,D,O
Educational Leadership and Administration M,O
Elementary Education M,O
English as a Second Language M
Exercise and Sports Science M
Human Services M
Leisure Studies M
Middle School Education M,O
Music Education M
Physical Education M,O
Reading Education M,O
Secondary Education M,O
Special Education M
Vocational and Technical Education M

MUSKINGUM UNIVERSITY
Education—General M

NAROPA UNIVERSITY
Counselor Education M
Education—General M
Recreation and Park Management M

NATIONAL AMERICAN UNIVERSITY
Business Administration and Management—General M

THE NATIONAL GRADUATE SCHOOL OF QUALITY MANAGEMENT
Quality Management M,D

NATIONAL LOUIS UNIVERSITY
Adult Education M,D,O

*M—master's degree; P—first professional degree; D—doctorate; O—other advanced degree; *Close-Up and/or Display*

Business Administration and Management—General M
Counselor Education M,D,O
Curriculum and Instruction M,D,O
Developmental Education M,D,O
Early Childhood Education M,D,O
Education—General M,D,O
Educational Leadership and Administration M,D,O
Educational Media/Instructional Technology M,D,O
Educational Psychology M,D,O
Elementary Education M,D,O
English Education M,D,O
Human Resources Development M
Human Resources Management M
Human Services M,D,O
Mathematics Education M,D,O
Reading Education M,D,O
Science Education M,D,O
Secondary Education M,D,O
Special Education M,D,O

NATIONAL UNIVERSITY
Accounting M,O
Business Administration and Management—General M,O
Counselor Education M
Early Childhood Education M,O
Education—General M,O
Educational Leadership and Administration M,O
Educational Media/Instructional Technology M,O
Elementary Education M,O
Finance and Banking M,O
Higher Education M
Human Resources Management M
Human Services M,O
International Business M
Management Information Systems M
Organizational Management M
Project Management M,O
Secondary Education M,O
Special Education M,O
Sustainability Management M,O

NAVAL POSTGRADUATE SCHOOL
Business Administration and Management—General M
Finance and Banking M
Logistics M
Management Information Systems M,D,O
Supply Chain Management M
Transportation Management M

NAZARETH COLLEGE OF ROCHESTER
Art Education M
Business Administration and Management—General M
Business Education M
Early Childhood Education M
Education—General M
Educational Media/Instructional Technology M
Elementary Education M
English as a Second Language M
Human Resources Management M
Middle School Education M
Music Education M
Reading Education M
Social Work M

NEUMANN UNIVERSITY
Education—General M
Educational Leadership and Administration D
Management Strategy and Policy M
Sports Management M

NEW CHARTER UNIVERSITY
Business Administration and Management—General M
Finance and Banking M

NEW ENGLAND COLLEGE
Accounting M
Business Administration and Management—General M
Education—General M,D
Educational Leadership and Administration M,D
Higher Education M,D
Human Services M
Management Strategy and Policy M
Marketing M
Nonprofit Management M
Project Management M
Recreation and Park Management M
Special Education M,D
Sports Management M

NEW ENGLAND COLLEGE OF BUSINESS AND FINANCE
Finance and Banking M

NEW ENGLAND INSTITUTE OF TECHNOLOGY
Management Information Systems M

NEW ENGLAND LAW–BOSTON
Law M,D

NEW JERSEY CITY UNIVERSITY
Accounting M
Art Education M
Business Administration and Management—General M
Early Childhood Education M
Educational Leadership and Administration M
Educational Media/Instructional Technology M
Educational Psychology M,O
Elementary Education M
English as a Second Language M
Finance and Banking M
Health Education M
Mathematics Education M
Multilingual and Multicultural Education M
Music Education M
Reading Education M
Secondary Education M
Special Education M
Urban Education M

NEW JERSEY INSTITUTE OF TECHNOLOGY
Business Administration and Management—General M
International Business M
Management Information Systems M,D
Transportation Management M,D

NEWMAN THEOLOGICAL COLLEGE
Educational Leadership and Administration M,O
Religious Education M,O

NEWMAN UNIVERSITY
Business Administration and Management—General M
Curriculum and Instruction M
Education—General M
Educational Leadership and Administration M
English as a Second Language M
Finance and Banking M
International Business M
Management Information Systems M
Organizational Management M
Reading Education M
Social Work M

NEW MEXICO HIGHLANDS UNIVERSITY
Business Administration and Management—General M
Counselor Education M
Curriculum and Instruction M
Education—General M
Educational Leadership and Administration M
Exercise and Sports Science M
Health Education M
Human Resources Management M
International Business M
Management Information Systems M
Nonprofit Management M
Social Work M
Special Education M
Sports Management M

NEW MEXICO INSTITUTE OF MINING AND TECHNOLOGY
Science Education M

NEW MEXICO STATE UNIVERSITY
Accounting M
Agricultural Education M
Business Administration and Management—General M,D
Counselor Education M,D,O
Curriculum and Instruction M,D
Distance Education Development O
Education—General M,D,O
Educational Leadership and Administration M,D
Finance and Banking O
Health Education M
Marketing D
Multilingual and Multicultural Education M,D
Music Education M
Social Work M
Special Education M,D

NEW ORLEANS BAPTIST THEOLOGICAL SEMINARY
Religious Education M,D

THE NEW SCHOOL
English as a Second Language M
Finance and Banking M,D
Nonprofit Management M
Organizational Management M
Sustainability Management M

NEW YORK INSTITUTE OF TECHNOLOGY
Accounting M,O
Business Administration and Management—General M,O
Counselor Education M
Distance Education Development M,O
Education—General M,O
Educational Leadership and Administration O
Educational Media/Instructional Technology M,O
Elementary Education M
Finance and Banking M,O
Human Resources Management M,O
International Business M,O
Management Information Systems M,O
Marketing M,O

NEW YORK LAW SCHOOL
Finance and Banking M,D
Law M,D*
Taxation M,D

NEW YORK MEDICAL COLLEGE
Health Education O

NEW YORK UNIVERSITY
Accounting M,D
Advertising and Public Relations M
Archives/Archival Administration M,D,O
Art Education M
Business Administration and Management—General M,D,O
Business Education M,O
Counselor Education M,D,O
Curriculum and Instruction M,D,O
Early Childhood Education M,D
Education—General M,D,O
Educational Leadership and Administration M,D,O
Educational Media/Instructional Technology M,D,O
Educational Policy M,D
Educational Psychology M,D
Elementary Education M,D
English as a Second Language M,D,O
English Education M,D,O
Environmental Education M
Finance and Banking M,D,O
Foreign Languages Education M,D,O
Foundations and Philosophy of Education M,D
Higher Education M,D
Hospitality Management M,D,O
Human Resources Development M,O
Human Resources Management M,D,O
International and Comparative Education M,D,O
International Business M,D,O
Kinesiology and Movement Studies M,D,O
Law M,D,O
Legal and Justice Studies M,D
Management Information Systems M,D,O
Management Strategy and Policy M,D,O
Marketing M,D,O
Mathematics Education M
Multilingual and Multicultural Education M,D,O
Music Education M,D,O
Nonprofit Management M,D,O
Organizational Behavior M,D
Organizational Management M,D
Quantitative Analysis M,D,O
Reading Education M
Real Estate M,O
Science Education M
Secondary Education M,D,O
Social Sciences Education M,D,O
Social Work M,D
Special Education M,D
Sports Management M,O
Student Affairs M,D
Taxation M,D,O
Travel and Tourism M,O

NIAGARA UNIVERSITY
Business Administration and Management—General M
Counselor Education M,O
Early Childhood Education M,O
Education—General M,D,O
Educational Leadership and Administration M,O
Elementary Education M,O
Foundations and Philosophy of Education M
Middle School Education M,O
Reading Education M
Secondary Education M,O
Special Education M,O

NICHOLLS STATE UNIVERSITY
Business Administration and Management—General M
Counselor Education M
Curriculum and Instruction M
Education—General M
Educational Leadership and Administration M
Mathematics Education M

NICHOLS COLLEGE
Business Administration and Management—General M
Sports Management M

THE NIGERIAN BAPTIST THEOLOGICAL SEMINARY
Religious Education M,D,O

NIPISSING UNIVERSITY
Education—General M,O

NORFOLK STATE UNIVERSITY
Early Childhood Education M
Education of Students with Severe/Multiple Disabilities M
Education—General M
Educational Leadership and Administration M
Music Education M
Secondary Education M
Social Work M,D
Special Education M
Urban Education M

NORTH CAROLINA AGRICULTURAL AND TECHNICAL STATE UNIVERSITY
Adult Education M
Agricultural Education M
Counselor Education M
Early Childhood Education M
Education—General M
Educational Leadership and Administration M
Educational Media/Instructional Technology M
Elementary Education M
English Education M
Health Education M
Management Information Systems M
Physical Education M
Reading Education M
Science Education M
Secondary Education M
Social Work M
Vocational and Technical Education M

NORTH CAROLINA CENTRAL UNIVERSITY
Business Administration and Management—General M
Counselor Education M
Curriculum and Instruction M
Education—General M
Educational Leadership and Administration M
Educational Media/Instructional Technology M
Elementary Education M
Information Studies M
Law D
Library Science M
Mathematics Education M
Middle School Education M
Physical Education M
Recreation and Park Management M
Special Education M
Sports Management M

NORTH CAROLINA STATE UNIVERSITY
Accounting M
Adult Education M,D
Agricultural Education M,O
Business Administration and Management—General M*
Business Education M
Community College Education M,D
Counselor Education M,D
Curriculum and Instruction M,D
Developmental Education M,D,O
Education—General M,D,O
Educational Leadership and Administration M,D
Educational Measurement and Evaluation D
Educational Media/Instructional Technology M,D
Elementary Education M
English Education M
Entrepreneurship M
Higher Education M,D
Human Resources Development M
Mathematics Education M,D
Middle School Education M
Nonprofit Management M,D,O
Recreation and Park Management M,D
Science Education M,D
Secondary Education M
Social Sciences Education M
Social Work M
Special Education M
Sports Management M,D
Supply Chain Management M
Travel and Tourism M,D

NORTH CENTRAL COLLEGE
Business Administration and Management—General M
Curriculum and Instruction M
Education—General M
Educational Leadership and Administration M
Finance and Banking M
Human Resources Management M
Management Information Systems M
Management Strategy and Policy M
Marketing M
Nonprofit Management M
Organizational Management M
Sports Management M

NORTHCENTRAL UNIVERSITY
Business Administration and Management—General M,D,O
Education—General M,D,O

NORTH DAKOTA STATE UNIVERSITY
Adult Education M,D,O
Agricultural Education M
Business Administration and Management—General M
Counselor Education M,D
Education—General M,D,O
Educational Leadership and Administration M,O
Exercise and Sports Science M
Higher Education O
Logistics M,D
Mathematics Education M,D,O
Music Education M,D,O
Physical Education M,D,O
Science Education M,D,O
Social Sciences Education M,D,O
Sports Management M
Transportation Management M,D
Vocational and Technical Education M,D,O

NORTHEASTERN ILLINOIS UNIVERSITY
Accounting M
Business Administration and Management—General M
Counselor Education M
Education of the Gifted M
Education—General M
Educational Leadership and Administration M
English as a Second Language M
English Education M
Finance and Banking M
Human Resources Development M
Marketing M
Mathematics Education M
Multilingual and Multicultural Education M
Reading Education M
Special Education M
Urban Education M

NORTHEASTERN STATE UNIVERSITY
Accounting M
Business Administration and Management—General M
Counselor Education M
Early Childhood Education M
Education—General M
Educational Leadership and Administration M

Program	Degrees
Educational Media/Instructional Technology	M
Finance and Banking	M
Foundations and Philosophy of Education	M
Health Education	M
Higher Education	M
Industrial and Manufacturing Management	M
Mathematics Education	M
Reading Education	M
Science Education	M

NORTHEASTERN UNIVERSITY

Program	Degrees
Accounting	M
Business Administration and Management—General	M,O
Counselor Education	M,O
Entrepreneurship	M
Exercise and Sports Science	M
Law	D
Legal and Justice Studies	M,D
Management Information Systems	M,D
Student Affairs	M,O

NORTHERN ARIZONA UNIVERSITY

Program	Degrees
Business Administration and Management—General	M
Community College Education	M,D,O
Counselor Education	M,D,O
Curriculum and Instruction	M,D,O
Early Childhood Education	M
Education—General	M,D,O
Educational Leadership and Administration	M,D,O
Educational Media/Instructional Technology	M,D,O
Educational Psychology	M,D,O
Elementary Education	M
English as a Second Language	M,D,O
English Education	M,D,O
Foreign Languages Education	M
Foundations and Philosophy of Education	M,D,O
Higher Education	M,D,O
Mathematics Education	M,O
Multilingual and Multicultural Education	M,D,O
Science Education	M,O
Secondary Education	M
Special Education	M,D,O
Student Affairs	M,D,O
Vocational and Technical Education	M,D,O

NORTHERN ILLINOIS UNIVERSITY

Program	Degrees
Accounting	M
Adult Education	M,D
Business Administration and Management—General	M
Counselor Education	M,D
Curriculum and Instruction	M,D
Early Childhood Education	M,D
Education—General	M,D,O
Educational Leadership and Administration	M,D,O
Educational Media/Instructional Technology	M,D
Educational Psychology	M,D,O
Elementary Education	M,D
Foundations and Philosophy of Education	M,D,O
Higher Education	M,D
Industrial and Manufacturing Management	M
Law	D
Management Information Systems	M
Physical Education	M
Reading Education	M,D
Secondary Education	M,D
Special Education	M,D
Sports Management	M
Taxation	M

NORTHERN KENTUCKY UNIVERSITY

Program	Degrees
Accounting	M,O
Advertising and Public Relations	M,O
Business Administration and Management—General	M,O
Counselor Education	M,O
Education—General	M,D,O
Educational Leadership and Administration	M,D,O
Law	D
Nonprofit Management	M,O
Organizational Management	M
Social Work	M
Special Education	M,O
Student Affairs	M,O
Taxation	M,O

NORTHERN MICHIGAN UNIVERSITY

Program	Degrees
Counselor Education	M
Education—General	M,O
Educational Leadership and Administration	M,O
Elementary Education	M
Exercise and Sports Science	M
Reading Education	M,O
Science Education	M
Secondary Education	M
Special Education	M

NORTHERN STATE UNIVERSITY

Program	Degrees
Counselor Education	M
Education—General	M
Educational Leadership and Administration	M
Educational Media/Instructional Technology	M
Elementary Education	M
Health Education	M
Physical Education	M
Secondary Education	M

NORTH GEORGIA COLLEGE & STATE UNIVERSITY

Program	Degrees
Art Education	M,O
Business Administration and Management—General	M
Early Childhood Education	M,O
Education—General	M,O
Educational Leadership and Administration	M,O
English Education	M,O
Mathematics Education	M,O
Middle School Education	M,O
Physical Education	M,O
Secondary Education	M,O
Social Sciences Education	M,O

NORTH GREENVILLE UNIVERSITY

Program	Degrees
Education—General	M,D
Finance and Banking	M,D
Human Resources Management	M,D

NORTH PARK UNIVERSITY

Program	Degrees
Business Administration and Management—General	M
Education—General	M
Nonprofit Management	M

NORTHWEST CHRISTIAN UNIVERSITY

Program	Degrees
Business Administration and Management—General	M
Counselor Education	M
Education—General	M

NORTHWESTERN COLLEGE

Program	Degrees
Organizational Management	M

NORTHWESTERN OKLAHOMA STATE UNIVERSITY

Program	Degrees
Adult Education	M
Counselor Education	M
Curriculum and Instruction	M
Education—General	M
Educational Leadership and Administration	M
Elementary Education	M
Reading Education	M
Secondary Education	M

NORTHWESTERN POLYTECHNIC UNIVERSITY

Program	Degrees
Business Administration and Management—General	M

NORTHWESTERN STATE UNIVERSITY OF LOUISIANA

Program	Degrees
Adult Education	M
Counselor Education	M,O
Curriculum and Instruction	M
Early Childhood Education	M
Education—General	M,O
Educational Leadership and Administration	M,O
Educational Media/Instructional Technology	M,O
Elementary Education	M,O
Health Education	M
Middle School Education	M,O
Reading Education	M,O
Secondary Education	M,O
Special Education	M,O
Student Affairs	M

NORTHWESTERN UNIVERSITY

Program	Degrees
Accounting	D
Advertising and Public Relations	M
Business Administration and Management—General	M
Education—General	M,D*
Educational Media/Instructional Technology	M,D
Electronic Commerce	M
Elementary Education	M
Finance and Banking	D
Higher Education	M
Kinesiology and Movement Studies	D
Law	M,D,O
Management Information Systems	M
Management Strategy and Policy	M,D
Marketing	M,D
Music Education	M,D
Organizational Behavior	M,D
Organizational Management	M,D
Project Management	M
Secondary Education	M
Sports Management	M
Taxation	M,D

NORTHWEST MISSOURI STATE UNIVERSITY

Program	Degrees
Agricultural Education	M
Business Administration and Management—General	M
Counselor Education	M
Early Childhood Education	M
Education—General	M,O
Educational Leadership and Administration	M,O
Educational Media/Instructional Technology	M
Elementary Education	M,O
English as a Second Language	M,O
English Education	M
Health Education	M
Higher Education	M,O
Management Information Systems	M
Mathematics Education	M
Middle School Education	M
Music Education	M
Physical Education	M
Reading Education	M
Recreation and Park Management	M
Science Education	M
Secondary Education	M,O
Social Sciences Education	M
Special Education	M

NORTHWEST NAZARENE UNIVERSITY

Program	Degrees
Business Administration and Management—General	M
Counselor Education	M
Curriculum and Instruction	M,D,O
Education—General	M,D,O
Educational Leadership and Administration	M,D,O
Reading Education	M,D,O
Religious Education	M
Social Work	M
Special Education	M,D,O

NORTHWEST UNIVERSITY

Program	Degrees
Business Administration and Management—General	M
Education—General	M
Organizational Management	M

NORTHWOOD UNIVERSITY, MICHIGAN CAMPUS

Program	Degrees
Business Administration and Management—General	M

NORWICH UNIVERSITY

Program	Degrees
Business Administration and Management—General	M
Finance and Banking	M
International Business	M
Management Information Systems	M
Organizational Management	M
Project Management	M
Science Education	M

NOTRE DAME COLLEGE (OH)

Program	Degrees
Reading Education	M,O
Special Education	M,O

NOTRE DAME DE NAMUR UNIVERSITY

Program	Degrees
Business Administration and Management—General	M
Curriculum and Instruction	M,O
Education—General	M,O
Educational Leadership and Administration	M,O
Educational Media/Instructional Technology	M,O
English as a Second Language	M,O
Finance and Banking	M
Human Resources Management	M
Marketing	M
Special Education	M,O

NOTRE DAME OF MARYLAND UNIVERSITY

Program	Degrees
Business Administration and Management—General	M
Education—General	M
Educational Leadership and Administration	M,D
English as a Second Language	M
Nonprofit Management	M

NOVA SOUTHEASTERN UNIVERSITY

Program	Degrees
Accounting	M,D
Business Administration and Management—General	M,D
Counselor Education	M,D,O
Distance Education Development	M,D,O
Education—General	M,D,O
Educational Media/Instructional Technology	M,D,O
Health Law	M,D,O
Human Resources Management	M,D
Human Services	M,D
International Business	M,D
Law	M,D,O
Legal and Justice Studies	M,D,O
Management Information Systems	M,D
Real Estate	M,D
Student Affairs	M,D,O
Taxation	M,D

NYACK COLLEGE

Program	Degrees
Business Administration and Management—General	M
Counselor Education	M
Elementary Education	M
Organizational Management	M
Special Education	M

OAKLAND CITY UNIVERSITY

Program	Degrees
Business Administration and Management—General	M
Education—General	M,D
Educational Leadership and Administration	M,D

OAKLAND UNIVERSITY

Program	Degrees
Accounting	M,O
Business Administration and Management—General	M,O
Early Childhood Education	M,D,O
Education—General	M,D,O
Educational Leadership and Administration	M,D,O
Educational Media/Instructional Technology	O
English as a Second Language	M,O
Entrepreneurship	M,O
Exercise and Sports Science	M,O
Finance and Banking	M,O
Foundations and Philosophy of Education	M
Higher Education	M,D,O
Human Resources Development	M
Human Resources Management	M,O
Industrial and Manufacturing Management	M,O
International Business	M,O
Management Information Systems	M,O

Program	Degrees
Marketing	M,O
Mathematics Education	M,D,O
Music Education	M,D
Reading Education	M,D,O
Secondary Education	M
Special Education	M,O

OCCIDENTAL COLLEGE

Program	Degrees
Education—General	M
Elementary Education	M
English Education	M
Foreign Languages Education	M
Mathematics Education	M
Science Education	M
Secondary Education	M
Social Sciences Education	M

OGLALA LAKOTA COLLEGE

Program	Degrees
Business Administration and Management—General	M
Educational Leadership and Administration	M

OGLETHORPE UNIVERSITY

Program	Degrees
Early Childhood Education	M
Education—General	M

OHIO DOMINICAN UNIVERSITY

Program	Degrees
Business Administration and Management—General	M
Education—General	M
English as a Second Language	M

OHIO NORTHERN UNIVERSITY

Program	Degrees
Law	M,D

THE OHIO STATE UNIVERSITY

Program	Degrees
Accounting	M,D
Agricultural Education	M,D
Art Education	M,D
Business Administration and Management—General	M,D
Education—General	M,D
Educational Leadership and Administration	M,D
Educational Policy	M,D
Hospitality Management	M,D
Human Resources Management	M,D
Law	M,D
Logistics	M
Management Information Systems	M,D
Marketing	M,D
Physical Education	M,D
Social Work	M,D

THE OHIO STATE UNIVERSITY AT LIMA

Program	Degrees
Early Childhood Education	M
Education—General	M
Middle School Education	M
Social Work	M

THE OHIO STATE UNIVERSITY AT MARION

Program	Degrees
Early Childhood Education	M
Education—General	M
Middle School Education	M

THE OHIO STATE UNIVERSITY–MANSFIELD CAMPUS

Program	Degrees
Early Childhood Education	M
Education—General	M
Middle School Education	M
Social Work	M

THE OHIO STATE UNIVERSITY–NEWARK CAMPUS

Program	Degrees
Early Childhood Education	M
Education—General	M
Middle School Education	M
Social Work	M

OHIO UNIVERSITY

Program	Degrees
Athletic Training and Sports Medicine	M
Business Administration and Management—General	M
Computer Education	M,D
Counselor Education	M,D
Curriculum and Instruction	M,D
Education—General	M,D
Educational Leadership and Administration	M,D
Educational Measurement and Evaluation	M,D
Educational Media/Instructional Technology	M,D
English as a Second Language	M
Exercise and Sports Science	M,D
Finance and Banking	M
Higher Education	M,D
Mathematics Education	M,D
Middle School Education	M,D
Multilingual and Multicultural Education	M,D
Music Education	M,O
Physical Education	M
Reading Education	M,D
Recreation and Park Management	M
Science Education	M
Secondary Education	M,D
Social Sciences Education	M,D
Social Work	M
Special Education	M,D
Sports Management	M
Student Affairs	M,D

OHIO VALLEY UNIVERSITY

Program	Degrees
Education—General	M

OKLAHOMA CITY UNIVERSITY

Program	Degrees
Accounting	M
Business Administration and Management—General	M
Early Childhood Education	M
Elementary Education	M
English as a Second Language	M

*M—master's degree; P—first professional degree; D—doctorate; O—other advanced degree; *Close-Up and/or Display*

Finance and Banking M
International Business M
Law D
Management Information Systems M
Marketing M
Nonprofit Management M

OKLAHOMA STATE UNIVERSITY
Accounting M,D
Agricultural Education M,D
Business Administration and Management—General M,D
Curriculum and Instruction M,D
Education—General M,D,O
Educational Leadership and Administration M,D
Educational Psychology M,D,O
Finance and Banking M,D
Health Education M,D,O
Higher Education M,D
Hospitality Management M,D
Management Information Systems M,D
Marketing M,D
Mathematics Education M,D
Music Education M
Quantitative Analysis M,D

OLD DOMINION UNIVERSITY
Accounting M
Athletic Training and Sports Medicine M
Business Administration and Management—General M,D
Business Education M,D
Community College Education M,D
Counselor Education M,D,O
Curriculum and Instruction M,D
Early Childhood Education M,D
Education—General M,D,O
Educational Leadership and Administration M,D,O
Educational Media/Instructional Technology M,D
Elementary Education M
Exercise and Sports Science M
Finance and Banking M,D
Higher Education M,D,O
International Business M
Kinesiology and Movement Studies D
Library Science M
Management Information Systems M
Marketing D
Middle School Education M
Music Education M
Physical Education M
Reading Education M,D
Recreation and Park Management M
Science Education M
Secondary Education M
Special Education M,D
Sports Management M
Travel and Tourism M
Vocational and Technical Education M,D

OLIVET COLLEGE
Education—General M

OLIVET NAZARENE UNIVERSITY
Business Administration and Management—General M
Curriculum and Instruction M
Education—General M
Educational Leadership and Administration M
Elementary Education M
Library Science M
Organizational Management M
Reading Education M
Secondary Education M

ORAL ROBERTS UNIVERSITY
Accounting M
Business Administration and Management—General M
Curriculum and Instruction M,D
Education—General M,D
Educational Leadership and Administration M,D
Entrepreneurship M
Finance and Banking M
Higher Education M,D
International Business M
Marketing M
Nonprofit Management M
Religious Education M,D

OREGON STATE UNIVERSITY
Adult Education M
Agricultural Education M
Business Administration and Management—General M,O
Counselor Education M,D
Education—General M,D
Educational Leadership and Administration M
Elementary Education M
Exercise and Sports Science M,D
Kinesiology and Movement Studies M,D
Mathematics Education M,D
Music Education M
Physical Education M,D
Science Education M,D
Student Affairs M

OREGON STATE UNIVERSITY–CASCADES
Education—General M

OTTAWA UNIVERSITY
Business Administration and Management—General M
Counselor Education M
Curriculum and Instruction M
Early Childhood Education M
Education—General M
Educational Leadership and Administration M

Educational Media/Instructional Technology M
Elementary Education M
Finance and Banking M
Human Resources Development M
Human Resources Management M
Marketing M
Special Education M

OTTERBEIN UNIVERSITY
Business Administration and Management—General M
Education—General M

OUR LADY OF HOLY CROSS COLLEGE
Counselor Education M
Curriculum and Instruction M
Education—General M
Educational Leadership and Administration M

OUR LADY OF THE LAKE UNIVERSITY OF SAN ANTONIO
Accounting M
Business Administration and Management—General M
Counselor Education M
Curriculum and Instruction M
Early Childhood Education M
Education—General M,D
Educational Leadership and Administration M
Educational Media/Instructional Technology M
Elementary Education M
English as a Second Language M
English Education M
Finance and Banking M
Management Information Systems M
Mathematics Education M
Middle School Education M
Multilingual and Multicultural Education M
Nonprofit Management M
Organizational Management M,D
Reading Education M
Science Education M
Secondary Education M
Social Work M
Special Education M
Vocational and Technical Education M

OXFORD GRADUATE SCHOOL
Organizational Management M,D

PACE UNIVERSITY
Accounting M
Business Administration and Management—General M,D,O
Early Childhood Education M,O
Education—General M,O
Educational Leadership and Administration M,O
Educational Media/Instructional Technology M,O
Electronic Commerce M,D,O
Elementary Education M,O
Entrepreneurship M
Environmental Law M,D
Finance and Banking M
Human Resources Management M
International Business M
Investment Management M
Law M,D
Legal and Justice Studies M,D
Management Information Systems M
Management Strategy and Policy M
Marketing Research M
Marketing M
Nonprofit Management M
Reading Education M,O
Special Education M,O
Taxation M

PACIFIC LUTHERAN UNIVERSITY
Business Administration and Management—General M
Curriculum and Instruction M
Education—General M
Educational Leadership and Administration M

PACIFIC STATES UNIVERSITY
Accounting M,D
Business Administration and Management—General M,D
Finance and Banking M,D
International Business M,D
Management Information Systems M,D
Real Estate M,D

PACIFIC UNION COLLEGE
Education—General M
Elementary Education M
Secondary Education M

PACIFIC UNIVERSITY
Early Childhood Education M
Education—General M
Elementary Education M
Middle School Education M
Secondary Education M
Special Education M

PALM BEACH ATLANTIC UNIVERSITY
Business Administration and Management—General M
Counselor Education M
Education—General M
Organizational Management M

PARK UNIVERSITY
Business Administration and Management—General M
Education—General M
Educational Leadership and Administration M
Entrepreneurship M

International Business M
Law M
Management Information Systems M
Middle School Education M
Multilingual and Multicultural Education M
Nonprofit Management M
Secondary Education M
Special Education M

PENN STATE DICKINSON SCHOOL OF LAW
Law M,D

PENN STATE ERIE, THE BEHREND COLLEGE
Business Administration and Management—General M
Project Management M

PENN STATE GREAT VALLEY
Business Administration and Management—General M
Education—General M
Finance and Banking M
Human Resources Development M
Special Education M

PENN STATE HARRISBURG
Business Administration and Management—General M
Curriculum and Instruction M
Developmental Education M
Education—General M
Health Education M
Management Information Systems M
Reading Education M

PENN STATE UNIVERSITY PARK
Adult Education M,D,O
Agricultural Education M,D,O
Business Administration and Management—General M,D
Counselor Education M,D,O
Curriculum and Instruction M,D,O
Education—General M,D,O
Educational Leadership and Administration M,D,O
Educational Media/Instructional Technology M,D,O
Educational Policy M,D,O
Educational Psychology M,D,O
Higher Education M,D,O
Hospitality Management M,D
Human Resources Development M,D,O
Human Resources Management M
Industrial and Manufacturing Management M
Kinesiology and Movement Studies M,D,O
Leisure Studies M,D
Music Education M,D,O
Quality Management M
Recreation and Park Management M,D
Special Education M,D,O
Student Affairs M,D,O
Travel and Tourism M,D
Vocational and Technical Education M,D,O

PEPPERDINE UNIVERSITY
Business Administration and Management—General M
Education—General M,D
Educational Leadership and Administration M,D
Educational Media/Instructional Technology M,D
Finance and Banking M
International Business M
Law D
Organizational Management M

PERU STATE COLLEGE
Curriculum and Instruction M
Education—General M
Entrepreneurship M
Organizational Management M

PFEIFFER UNIVERSITY
Business Administration and Management—General M
Elementary Education M
Organizational Management M
Religious Education M

PHILADELPHIA UNIVERSITY
Business Administration and Management—General M
Finance and Banking M
International Business M
Marketing M
Taxation M

PHILLIPS GRADUATE INSTITUTE
Counselor Education M
Organizational Behavior D

PHILLIPS THEOLOGICAL SEMINARY
Business Administration and Management—General M,D
Higher Education M,D
Religious Education M,D
Social Work M,D

PIEDMONT COLLEGE
Business Administration and Management—General M
Early Childhood Education M,D,O
Education—General M,D,O
Educational Leadership and Administration M,D,O
Middle School Education M,D,O
Secondary Education M,D,O
Special Education M,D,O

PITTSBURG STATE UNIVERSITY
Accounting M
Art Education M

Business Administration and Management—General M
Community College Education O
Counselor Education M
Early Childhood Education M
Education—General M,O
Educational Leadership and Administration M,O
Educational Media/Instructional Technology M
Elementary Education M
Higher Education M,O
Human Resources Development M
Music Education M
Physical Education M
Reading Education M
Secondary Education M
Special Education M
Vocational and Technical Education M,O

PLYMOUTH STATE UNIVERSITY
Adult Education D
Athletic Training and Sports Medicine M
Business Administration and Management—General M
Counselor Education M
Education—General O
Educational Leadership and Administration M
Elementary Education M
English Education M
Health Education M
Mathematics Education M
Middle School Education M
Reading Education M
Science Education M
Secondary Education M
Special Education M,D,O

POINT LOMA NAZARENE UNIVERSITY
Business Administration and Management—General M
Education—General M,O

POINT PARK UNIVERSITY
Business Administration and Management—General M
Curriculum and Instruction M
Education—General M
Educational Leadership and Administration M
Organizational Management M
Special Education M

POLYTECHNIC INSTITUTE OF NEW YORK UNIVERSITY
Business Administration and Management—General M,D,O
Electronic Commerce M,D,O
Entrepreneurship M,D,O
Finance and Banking M,O
Human Resources Management M,D,O
Management Information Systems M,D,O
Organizational Behavior M,O
Project Management M,D,O
Transportation Management M

POLYTECHNIC INSTITUTE OF NYU, WESTCHESTER GRADUATE CENTER
Business Administration and Management—General M

POLYTECHNIC UNIVERSITY OF PUERTO RICO
Business Administration and Management—General M
Industrial and Manufacturing Management M
International Business M
Management Information Systems M

POLYTECHNIC UNIVERSITY OF PUERTO RICO, MIAMI CAMPUS
Accounting M
Business Administration and Management—General M
Finance and Banking M
Human Resources Management M
Industrial and Manufacturing Management M
International Business M
Logistics M
Marketing M
Project Management M
Supply Chain Management M

POLYTECHNIC UNIVERSITY OF PUERTO RICO, ORLANDO CAMPUS
Accounting M
Business Administration and Management—General M
Finance and Banking M
Human Resources Management M
Industrial and Manufacturing Management M
International Business M

PONTIFICAL CATHOLIC UNIVERSITY OF PUERTO RICO
Accounting M,O
Business Administration and Management—General M,D,O
Business Education M,D
Counselor Education M
Curriculum and Instruction M,D
Education—General M,D
Educational Leadership and Administration D
Educational Psychology M
English as a Second Language M
Finance and Banking M
Human Resources Management M,O
Human Services M,D
International Business M
Law D
Logistics O
Management Information Systems M,O

Marketing M
Religious Education M
Social Work M
Transportation Management O

PONTIFICIA UNIVERSIDAD CATOLICA MADRE Y MAESTRA
Business Administration and Management—General M
Early Childhood Education M
Entrepreneurship M
Finance and Banking M
Hospitality Management M
Human Resources Management M
Insurance M
International Business M
Law M
Logistics M
Management Strategy and Policy M
Marketing M
Real Estate M
Travel and Tourism M

PORTLAND STATE UNIVERSITY
Adult Education M,D
Business Administration and Management—General M,D,O
Counselor Education M,D
Curriculum and Instruction M,D
Early Childhood Education M,D
Education—General M,D
Educational Leadership and Administration M,D
Educational Media/Instructional Technology M,D
Elementary Education M,D
English as a Second Language M
Finance and Banking M
Foreign Languages Education M
Health Education M,O
Higher Education M,D
Industrial and Manufacturing Management M,D
International Business M
Mathematics Education M,D
Music Education M
Reading Education M,D
Science Education M,D
Secondary Education M,D
Social Sciences Education M
Social Work M,D
Special Education M,D

POST UNIVERSITY
Business Administration and Management—General M
Education—General M
Educational Media/Instructional Technology M
Entrepreneurship M
Finance and Banking M
Human Services M
Marketing M

PRAIRIE VIEW A&M UNIVERSITY
Accounting M
Business Administration and Management—General M
Counselor Education M,D
Curriculum and Instruction M
Education—General M,D
Educational Leadership and Administration M,D
Health Education M
Legal and Justice Studies M,D
Management Information Systems M,D
Physical Education M
Special Education M

PRATT INSTITUTE
Archives/Archival Administration M,O
Art Education M,O
Facilities Management M
Information Studies M,O*
Library Science M,O
Special Education M

PRESCOTT COLLEGE
Counselor Education M,D
Early Childhood Education M,D
Education—General M,D
Educational Leadership and Administration M,D
Elementary Education M,D
Environmental Education M,D
Leisure Studies M
Secondary Education M,D
Special Education M,D

PRINCETON UNIVERSITY
Finance and Banking M

PROVIDENCE COLLEGE
Accounting M
Business Administration and Management—General M
Counselor Education M
Educational Leadership and Administration M
Elementary Education M
Entrepreneurship M
Finance and Banking M
International Business M
Marketing M
Mathematics Education M
Nonprofit Management M
Reading Education M
Secondary Education M
Special Education M

PROVIDENCE COLLEGE AND THEOLOGICAL SEMINARY
English as a Second Language M,D,O
Religious Education M,D,O
Student Affairs M,D,O

PURDUE UNIVERSITY
Agricultural Education M,D,O
Art Education M,D,O
Business Administration and Management—General M,D
Counselor Education M,D,O
Curriculum and Instruction M,D,O
Education of the Gifted M,D,O
Education—General M,D,O
Educational Leadership and Administration M,D,O
Educational Media/Instructional Technology M,D,O
Educational Psychology M,D,O
Elementary Education M,D,O
English Education M,D,O
Exercise and Sports Science M,D
Finance and Banking M
Foreign Languages Education M,D,O
Foundations and Philosophy of Education M,D,O
Health Education M,D
Higher Education M,D,O
Home Economics Education M,D,O
Hospitality Management M,D
Human Resources Management M,D
Industrial and Manufacturing Management M
International Business M
Kinesiology and Movement Studies M,D
Mathematics Education M,D,O
Organizational Behavior D
Physical Education M,D
Quantitative Analysis M,D
Reading Education M,D,O
Science Education M,D,O
Social Sciences Education M,D,O
Special Education M,D,O
Sports Management M,D
Travel and Tourism M,D
Vocational and Technical Education M,D,O

PURDUE UNIVERSITY CALUMET
Accounting M
Business Administration and Management—General M
Counselor Education M
Education—General M
Educational Leadership and Administration M
Educational Media/Instructional Technology M
Human Services M
Mathematics Education M
Science Education M
Special Education M

PURDUE UNIVERSITY NORTH CENTRAL
Education—General M
Elementary Education M

QUEENS COLLEGE OF THE CITY UNIVERSITY OF NEW YORK
Accounting M
Art Education M,O
Counselor Education M
Early Childhood Education M,O
Education—General M,O
Educational Leadership and Administration O
Elementary Education M,O
English as a Second Language M
English Education M,O
Exercise and Sports Science M
Foreign Languages Education M,O
Home Economics Education M
Information Studies M,O
Library Science M,O
Mathematics Education M,O
Multilingual and Multicultural Education M,O
Music Education M,O
Reading Education M
Science Education M,O
Secondary Education M,O
Social Sciences Education M,O
Special Education M

QUEEN'S UNIVERSITY AT KINGSTON
Business Administration and Management—General M
Education—General M,D
Entrepreneurship M
Exercise and Sports Science M,D
Finance and Banking M
Information Studies M,D
Law M,D
Legal and Justice Studies M,D
Marketing M
Project Management M

QUEENS UNIVERSITY OF CHARLOTTE
Business Administration and Management—General M
Education—General M
Educational Leadership and Administration M
Elementary Education M
Reading Education M

QUINCY UNIVERSITY
Business Administration and Management—General M
Counselor Education M
Curriculum and Instruction M
Education—General M
Educational Leadership and Administration M
Human Resources Management M
Reading Education M
Special Education M

QUINNIPIAC UNIVERSITY
Advertising and Public Relations M
Business Administration and Management—General M
Education—General M,O
Educational Leadership and Administration M,O
Elementary Education M
English Education M
Finance and Banking M
Foreign Languages Education M
Health Law M,D
Investment Management M
Law M,D
Management Information Systems M
Marketing M
Mathematics Education M
Middle School Education M
Organizational Management M
Science Education M
Secondary Education M
Social Sciences Education M
Supply Chain Management M

RADFORD UNIVERSITY
Business Administration and Management—General M
Counselor Education M
Early Childhood Education M
Education—General M
Educational Leadership and Administration M
Music Education M
Reading Education M
Social Work M
Special Education M

RAMAPO COLLEGE OF NEW JERSEY
Business Administration and Management—General M
Educational Leadership and Administration M
Educational Media/Instructional Technology M

RANDOLPH COLLEGE
Curriculum and Instruction M
Education—General M
Special Education M

REFORMED THEOLOGICAL SEMINARY–JACKSON CAMPUS
Religious Education M,D,O

REGENT'S AMERICAN COLLEGE LONDON
Business Administration and Management—General M
Finance and Banking M
Human Resources Management M
International Business M
Management Information Systems M
Marketing M

REGENT UNIVERSITY
Adult Education M,D,O
Business Administration and Management—General M,D,O
Counselor Education M,D,O
Distance Education Development M,D,O
Education—General M,D,O
Educational Leadership and Administration M,D,O
Educational Measurement and Evaluation M,D,O
Educational Psychology M,D,O
Elementary Education M,D,O
English as a Second Language M,D,O
Entrepreneurship M,D,O
Higher Education M,D,O
Human Resources Development M,D,O
Law M,D
Legal and Justice Studies M,D
Management Strategy and Policy M,D,O
Mathematics Education M,D,O
Nonprofit Management M
Organizational Management M,D,O
Reading Education M,D,O
Religious Education M,D,O
Special Education M,D,O
Student Affairs M,D,O

REGIS COLLEGE (MA)
Education—General M
Elementary Education M
Quality Management M
Reading Education M
Special Education M

REGIS UNIVERSITY
Accounting M,O
Adult Education M,O
Business Administration and Management—General M,O
Curriculum and Instruction M,O
Education—General M,O
Educational Leadership and Administration M,O
Educational Media/Instructional Technology M,O
Electronic Commerce M,O
Finance and Banking M,O
Foundations and Philosophy of Education M,O
Human Resources Management M,O
Industrial and Manufacturing Management M,O
International Business M,O
Management Information Systems M,O
Management Strategy and Policy M,O
Marketing M,O
Nonprofit Management M,O
Organizational Management M,O
Project Management M,O
Reading Education M,O
Science Education M,O
Special Education M,O

REINHARDT UNIVERSITY
Business Administration and Management—General M
Early Childhood Education M
Education—General M
Music Education M

RENSSELAER AT HARTFORD
Business Administration and Management—General M

RENSSELAER POLYTECHNIC INSTITUTE
Business Administration and Management—General M,D
Entrepreneurship M,D

RHODE ISLAND COLLEGE
Accounting M,O
Art Education M
Counselor Education M,O
Early Childhood Education M
Education—General D
Educational Leadership and Administration M,O
Elementary Education M
English as a Second Language M
English Education M
Finance and Banking M,O
Foreign Languages Education M
Health Education M,O
Mathematics Education M
Music Education M
Physical Education M,O
Reading Education M
Secondary Education M
Social Sciences Education M
Social Work M
Special Education M,O

RHODE ISLAND SCHOOL OF DESIGN
Art Education M

RHODES COLLEGE
Accounting M

RICE UNIVERSITY
Business Administration and Management—General M
Education—General M
Science Education M,D

THE RICHARD STOCKTON COLLEGE OF NEW JERSEY
Business Administration and Management—General M
Education—General M
Educational Leadership and Administration M
Educational Media/Instructional Technology M
Social Work M

RIDER UNIVERSITY
Accounting M
Business Administration and Management—General M
Business Education O
Counselor Education M,O
Curriculum and Instruction M,O
Education—General M,O
Educational Leadership and Administration M,O
Elementary Education O
English as a Second Language O
English Education O
Foreign Languages Education O
Mathematics Education O
Music Education M
Organizational Management M
Reading Education M,O
Science Education O
Social Sciences Education O
Special Education M,O

RIVIER UNIVERSITY
Business Administration and Management—General M
Counselor Education M,D,O
Curriculum and Instruction M,D,O
Early Childhood Education M,D,O
Education—General M,D,O
Educational Leadership and Administration M,D,O
Elementary Education M,D,O
Foreign Languages Education M
Management Information Systems M
Reading Education M,D,O
Social Sciences Education M
Special Education M,D,O

ROBERT MORRIS UNIVERSITY
Business Administration and Management—General M
Business Education M,D,O
Education—General M,D,O
Educational Leadership and Administration M,D,O
Human Resources Management M
Management Information Systems M,D
Nonprofit Management M
Organizational Management M,D
Project Management M,D
Sports Management M,D,O
Taxation M

ROBERT MORRIS UNIVERSITY ILLINOIS
Accounting M

*M—master's degree; P—first professional degree; D—doctorate; O—other advanced degree; *Close-Up and/or Display*

Business Administration and Management—General M
Educational Leadership and Administration M
Finance and Banking M
Higher Education M
Human Resources Management M
Management Information Systems M
Sports Management M

ROBERTS WESLEYAN COLLEGE
Business Administration and Management—General M,O
Counselor Education M,O
Early Childhood Education M,O
Education—General M,O
Human Services M
Management Strategy and Policy M,O
Marketing M,O
Middle School Education M,O
Nonprofit Management M,O
Reading Education M,O
Secondary Education M,O
Social Work M
Special Education M,O
Urban Education M,O

ROCHESTER COLLEGE
Religious Education M

ROCHESTER INSTITUTE OF TECHNOLOGY
Accounting M
Art Education M
Business Administration and Management—General M
Entrepreneurship M
Finance and Banking M
Hospitality Management M
Human Resources Development M
Industrial and Manufacturing Management M
International Business M
Management Information Systems M
Project Management O
Secondary Education M
Special Education M
Sustainability Management M,D
Travel and Tourism M

ROCKFORD COLLEGE
Business Administration and Management—General M
Early Childhood Education M
Education—General M
Elementary Education M
Reading Education M
Secondary Education M
Special Education M

ROCKHURST UNIVERSITY
Business Administration and Management—General M
Education—General M

ROCKY MOUNTAIN COLLEGE
Accounting M
Educational Leadership and Administration M

ROCKY MOUNTAIN UNIVERSITY OF HEALTH PROFESSIONS
Athletic Training and Sports Medicine D
Exercise and Sports Science D

ROGER WILLIAMS UNIVERSITY
Education—General M
Elementary Education M
Law D
Reading Education M

ROLLINS COLLEGE
Business Administration and Management—General M
Counselor Education M
Education—General M
Elementary Education M
Entrepreneurship M
Finance and Banking M
Human Resources Development M
Human Resources Management M
International Business M
Marketing M

ROOSEVELT UNIVERSITY
Accounting M
Actuarial Science M
Business Administration and Management—General M
Counselor Education M
Early Childhood Education M
Education—General M,D
Educational Leadership and Administration M
Elementary Education M
Hospitality Management M
Human Resources Development M
Human Resources Management M
International Business M
Management Information Systems M
Marketing M
Music Education M,O
Organizational Management M,D
Reading Education M
Real Estate M,O
Secondary Education M
Special Education M

ROSALIND FRANKLIN UNIVERSITY OF MEDICINE AND SCIENCE
Health Education M

ROSEMAN UNIVERSITY OF HEALTH SCIENCES
Business Administration and Management—General M

ROSEMONT COLLEGE
Business Administration and Management—General M
Counselor Education M
Education—General M
Elementary Education M
Human Services M

ROWAN UNIVERSITY
Accounting M
Advertising and Public Relations M
Business Administration and Management—General M*
Counselor Education M
Curriculum and Instruction M
Education—General M,D,O
Educational Leadership and Administration M,D,O
Elementary Education M
English as a Second Language O
Entrepreneurship M
Finance and Banking M
Foreign Languages Education M
Higher Education M
Library Science M
Management Information Systems M
Marketing M
Multilingual and Multicultural Education O
Project Management M
Reading Education M
Secondary Education M
Special Education M

ROYAL MILITARY COLLEGE OF CANADA
Business Administration and Management—General M

ROYAL ROADS UNIVERSITY
Advertising and Public Relations O
Business Administration and Management—General M,O
Environmental Education M,O
Hospitality Management M,O
Human Resources Management M,O
Project Management O
Travel and Tourism M,O

RUTGERS, THE STATE UNIVERSITY OF NEW JERSEY, CAMDEN
Business Administration and Management—General M
Educational Leadership and Administration M
Educational Policy D
Law D
Mathematics Education M

RUTGERS, THE STATE UNIVERSITY OF NEW JERSEY, NEWARK
Accounting D
Business Administration and Management—General M,D
Finance and Banking D
Human Resources Management M,D
International Business D
Law D
Management Information Systems D
Marketing D
Organizational Management D
Supply Chain Management D

RUTGERS, THE STATE UNIVERSITY OF NEW JERSEY, NEW BRUNSWICK
Counselor Education M
Developmental Education M
Early Childhood Education M,D
Education—General M,D
Educational Leadership and Administration M,D
Educational Measurement and Evaluation M
Educational Policy D
Educational Psychology M,D
Elementary Education M,D
English as a Second Language M,D
English Education M
Foreign Languages Education M,D
Foundations and Philosophy of Education M,D
Human Resources Management M,D
Information Studies M,D
Legal and Justice Studies D
Library Science M,D
Mathematics Education M,D
Multilingual and Multicultural Education M,D
Music Education M,D,O
Quality Management M,D
Reading Education M,D
Science Education M,D
Social Sciences Education M,D
Social Work M,D
Special Education M,D
Student Affairs M

SACRED HEART UNIVERSITY
Accounting M
Advertising and Public Relations M
Business Administration and Management—General M
Education—General M,O
Educational Leadership and Administration M,O
Educational Media/Instructional Technology M,O
Elementary Education M,O
Exercise and Sports Science M
Finance and Banking M
Management Information Systems M,O
Marketing M
Reading Education M,O
Secondary Education M,O

SAGE GRADUATE SCHOOL
Art Education M
Business Administration and Management—General M
Counselor Education M,O
Education—General M,D,O
Educational Leadership and Administration D
Elementary Education M
English Education M
Finance and Banking M
Health Education M
Human Resources Management M
Management Strategy and Policy M
Marketing M
Mathematics Education M
Organizational Management M
Reading Education M
Social Sciences Education M
Special Education M

SAGINAW VALLEY STATE UNIVERSITY
Business Administration and Management—General M
Distance Education Development M
Early Childhood Education M
Education—General M,O
Educational Leadership and Administration M,O
Educational Media/Instructional Technology M
Elementary Education M
Middle School Education M
Physical Education M
Reading Education M
Science Education M
Secondary Education M
Special Education M

ST. AMBROSE UNIVERSITY
Accounting M
Business Administration and Management—General M,D
Education—General M
Educational Leadership and Administration M
Human Resources Management M,D
Organizational Management M
Social Work M
Special Education M

ST. AUGUSTINE'S SEMINARY OF TORONTO
Religious Education M,O

ST. BONAVENTURE UNIVERSITY
Business Administration and Management—General M
Counselor Education M,O
Early Childhood Education M
Education of the Gifted M
Education—General M,O
Educational Leadership and Administration M,O
Marketing M
Middle School Education M
Reading Education M
Secondary Education M
Special Education M

ST. CATHARINE COLLEGE
Organizational Management M

ST. CATHERINE UNIVERSITY
Curriculum and Instruction M
Education—General M
Information Studies M
Library Science M
Organizational Management M
Social Work M

ST. CLOUD STATE UNIVERSITY
Business Administration and Management—General M
Counselor Education M
Curriculum and Instruction M
Education—General M,D
Educational Leadership and Administration M,D
Educational Media/Instructional Technology M
English as a Second Language M
Exercise and Sports Science M
Higher Education M,D
Music Education M
Nonprofit Management M
Physical Education M
Social Work M
Special Education M
Sports Management M
Student Affairs M

ST. EDWARD'S UNIVERSITY
Accounting M,O
Business Administration and Management—General M,O
Education—General M,O
Educational Leadership and Administration M,O
Educational Media/Instructional Technology M,O
Finance and Banking M,O
International Business M,O
Management Information Systems M
Marketing M,O
Organizational Management M
Project Management M,O
Special Education M,O
Sports Management M,O
Student Affairs M

ST. FRANCIS COLLEGE
Accounting M

SAINT FRANCIS UNIVERSITY
Business Administration and Management—General M
Education—General M
Educational Leadership and Administration M
Health Education M
Human Resources Management M
Reading Education M

ST. FRANCIS XAVIER UNIVERSITY
Adult Education M
Curriculum and Instruction M
Education—General M
Educational Leadership and Administration M

ST. JOHN FISHER COLLEGE
Business Administration and Management—General M
Education—General M,D,O
Educational Leadership and Administration M,D
Elementary Education M
English Education M
Foreign Languages Education M
Human Resources Development M
Mathematics Education M
Middle School Education M
Reading Education M
Science Education M
Social Sciences Education M
Special Education M,O

ST. JOHN'S UNIVERSITY (NY)
Accounting M,O
Actuarial Science M
Business Administration and Management—General M,O
Counselor Education M,O
Early Childhood Education M
Education—General M,D,O
Educational Leadership and Administration M,D,O
Elementary Education M
English as a Second Language M,O
Finance and Banking M,O
Information Studies M,O
Insurance M
International Business M,O
Investment Management M,O
Law D
Legal and Justice Studies M
Library Science M,O
Management Information Systems M,O
Management Strategy and Policy M,O
Marketing M,O
Middle School Education M,O
Multilingual and Multicultural Education M
Quantitative Analysis M,O
Reading Education M,D,O
Secondary Education M
Special Education M,O
Sports Management M
Taxation M,O

ST. JOSEPH'S COLLEGE, LONG ISLAND CAMPUS
Accounting M
Business Administration and Management—General M,O
Early Childhood Education M
Human Resources Management M,O
Organizational Management M,O
Reading Education M
Special Education M

ST. JOSEPH'S COLLEGE, NEW YORK
Accounting M
Business Administration and Management—General M*
Early Childhood Education M
Education—General M*
Human Services M*
Reading Education M
Special Education M

SAINT JOSEPH'S COLLEGE OF MAINE
Accounting M
Adult Education M
Business Administration and Management—General M
Education—General M
Educational Leadership and Administration M
Health Education M

SAINT JOSEPH'S UNIVERSITY
Accounting M
Adult Education M,O
Business Administration and Management—General M,O
Curriculum and Instruction M,D,O
Education—General M,D,O
Educational Leadership and Administration M,D,O
Educational Media/Instructional Technology M,D,O
Elementary Education M,D,O
English as a Second Language M,D,O
Finance and Banking M
Health Education M,O
Human Resources Management M*
International Business M
Law M,O
Management Information Systems M*
Management Strategy and Policy M
Marketing M
Middle School Education M,D,O
Organizational Management M,O
Reading Education M,D,O
Secondary Education M,D,O
Special Education M,D,O

ST. LAWRENCE UNIVERSITY
Counselor Education M,O
Education—General M,O
Educational Leadership and Administration M,O

SAINT LEO UNIVERSITY
Accounting M
Business Administration and Management—General M
Curriculum and Instruction M,O
Education of the Gifted M,O
Education—General M,O
Educational Leadership and Administration M,O
Educational Media/Instructional Technology M,O
Higher Education M,O
Human Resources Management M
Legal and Justice Studies M
Marketing M
Reading Education M,O
Social Work M
Sports Management M

SAINT LOUIS UNIVERSITY
Accounting M
Athletic Training and Sports Medicine M,D
Business Administration and Management—General M
Counselor Education M,D,O
Curriculum and Instruction M,D
Education—General M,D
Educational Leadership and Administration M,D,O
Finance and Banking M
Foundations and Philosophy of Education M,D
Higher Education M,D,O
International Business M,D
Law M,D
Organizational Management M,D,O
Social Work M
Special Education M,D
Student Affairs M,D,O

SAINT MARTIN'S UNIVERSITY
Business Administration and Management—General M
Counselor Education M
Education—General M
Educational Leadership and Administration M
English as a Second Language M
Reading Education M
Special Education M

SAINT MARY-OF-THE-WOODS COLLEGE
Management Strategy and Policy M

SAINT MARY'S COLLEGE OF CALIFORNIA
Business Administration and Management—General M
Counselor Education M
Curriculum and Instruction M
Early Childhood Education M
Education—General M,D
Educational Leadership and Administration M,D
Exercise and Sports Science M
Finance and Banking M
Investment Management M
Kinesiology and Movement Studies M
Reading Education M
Special Education M
Sports Management M

ST. MARY'S COLLEGE OF MARYLAND
Education—General M

SAINT MARY'S UNIVERSITY (CANADA)
Business Administration and Management—General M,D

ST. MARY'S UNIVERSITY (UNITED STATES)
Accounting M
Business Administration and Management—General M
Counselor Education D
Education—General M,O
Educational Leadership and Administration M,O
Finance and Banking M
Human Services M,D,O
International Business M
Law D
Reading Education M

SAINT MARY'S UNIVERSITY OF MINNESOTA
Business Administration and Management—General M
Education of the Gifted M,O
Education—General M,O
Educational Leadership and Administration M,D,O
Elementary Education M,O
Human Resources Management M
International Business M
Organizational Management M
Project Management M,O
Reading Education M,O
Religious Education M
Secondary Education M,O
Special Education M,O

SAINT MICHAEL'S COLLEGE
Art Education M,O
Business Administration and Management—General M,O
Curriculum and Instruction M,O
Education—General M,O
Educational Leadership and Administration M,O
Educational Media/Instructional Technology M,O
English as a Second Language M,O
Reading Education M,O
Special Education M,O

ST. NORBERT COLLEGE
Education—General M

SAINT PETER'S UNIVERSITY
Accounting M
Business Administration and Management—General M
Counselor Education M,O
Education—General M,D,O
Educational Leadership and Administration M,D
Elementary Education M,O
Finance and Banking M
Human Resources Management M
International Business M
Management Information Systems M
Marketing M
Mathematics Education M,D,O
Middle School Education M,O
Reading Education M,O
Secondary Education M,O
Special Education M,O

SAINTS CYRIL AND METHODIUS SEMINARY
Religious Education M

ST. THOMAS AQUINAS COLLEGE
Business Administration and Management—General M
Education—General M,O
Educational Leadership and Administration M,O
Elementary Education M,O
Finance and Banking M
Marketing M
Middle School Education M,O
Reading Education M,O
Secondary Education M,O
Special Education M,O

ST. THOMAS UNIVERSITY
Accounting M,O
Business Administration and Management—General M,O
Counselor Education M,O
Education of the Gifted M,D,O
Education—General M,D,O
Educational Leadership and Administration M,D,O
Educational Media/Instructional Technology M,D,O
Elementary Education M,D,O
English as a Second Language M,D,O
Human Resources Management M,O
International Business M,O
Law M,D
Reading Education M,D,O
Special Education M,D,O
Sports Management M,O
Taxation M,D

SAINT VINCENT COLLEGE
Curriculum and Instruction M
Education—General M
Educational Leadership and Administration M
Educational Media/Instructional Technology M
Environmental Education M
Special Education M

ST. VLADIMIR'S ORTHODOX THEOLOGICAL SEMINARY
Religious Education M,D

SAINT XAVIER UNIVERSITY
Business Administration and Management—General M,O
Counselor Education M
Curriculum and Instruction M
Early Childhood Education M
Education—General M
Educational Leadership and Administration M
Educational Media/Instructional Technology M
Elementary Education M
English as a Second Language M
Finance and Banking M,O
Foreign Languages Education M
Marketing M,O
Music Education M
Project Management M,O
Reading Education M
Science Education M
Secondary Education M
Special Education M

SALEM COLLEGE
Art Education M
Counselor Education M
Education—General M
Elementary Education M
English as a Second Language M
Middle School Education M
Music Education M
Reading Education M
Secondary Education M
Special Education M

SALEM INTERNATIONAL UNIVERSITY
Business Administration and Management—General M
Curriculum and Instruction M
Education—General M
Educational Leadership and Administration M
International Business M

SALEM STATE UNIVERSITY
Art Education M
Business Administration and Management—General M
Counselor Education M
Early Childhood Education M
Educational Leadership and Administration M
Educational Media/Instructional Technology M
Elementary Education M
English as a Second Language M
English Education M
Higher Education M
Mathematics Education M
Middle School Education M
Physical Education M
Reading Education M
Science Education M
Secondary Education M
Social Work M
Special Education M

SALISBURY UNIVERSITY
Accounting M
Business Administration and Management—General M
Education—General M
Educational Leadership and Administration M
English as a Second Language M
Mathematics Education M
Reading Education M
Social Work M

SALUS UNIVERSITY
Special Education M,O

SALVE REGINA UNIVERSITY
Business Administration and Management—General M,O
Business Education M,O
Human Resources Development M,O
Human Resources Management M,O
Management Strategy and Policy M,O
Organizational Management M,O

SAMFORD UNIVERSITY
Business Administration and Management—General M
Early Childhood Education M,D,O
Education of the Gifted M,D,O
Education—General M,D,O
Educational Leadership and Administration M,D,O
Elementary Education M,D,O
Law M,D
Music Education M
Secondary Education M,D,O

SAM HOUSTON STATE UNIVERSITY
Accounting M
Business Administration and Management—General M
Counselor Education M,D
Curriculum and Instruction M
Developmental Education M,D
Education—General M,D
Educational Leadership and Administration M,D
Educational Media/Instructional Technology M
Finance and Banking M
Higher Education M,D
Kinesiology and Movement Studies M
Library Science M
Project Management M
Reading Education M,D
Special Education M,D

SAN DIEGO STATE UNIVERSITY
Accounting M
Advertising and Public Relations M
Business Administration and Management—General M
Counselor Education M
Curriculum and Instruction M
Education—General M,D
Educational Leadership and Administration M
Educational Media/Instructional Technology M,D
Elementary Education M,D
English as a Second Language M,O
Entrepreneurship M
Exercise and Sports Science M
Finance and Banking M
Higher Education M
Human Resources Management M
Kinesiology and Movement Studies M
Management Information Systems M
Marketing M
Mathematics Education M,D
Multilingual and Multicultural Education M,D
Music Education M
Reading Education M
Science Education M,D
Secondary Education M
Social Work M
Special Education M
Sports Management M

SAN FRANCISCO STATE UNIVERSITY
Accounting M
Adult Education M,O
Business Administration and Management—General M
Early Childhood Education M,D,O
Education—General M,D,O
Educational Leadership and Administration M,D,O
Educational Media/Instructional Technology M,O
Elementary Education M
English as a Second Language M
English Education M,O
Exercise and Sports Science M
Health Education M
Kinesiology and Movement Studies M
Legal and Justice Studies M
Leisure Studies M
Mathematics Education M
Music Education M
Nonprofit Management M
Reading Education M,O
Recreation and Park Management M
Secondary Education M
Social Work M
Special Education M,O

SAN JOAQUIN COLLEGE OF LAW
Law D

SAN JOSE STATE UNIVERSITY
Accounting M
Business Administration and Management—General M
Counselor Education M
Curriculum and Instruction M,O
Education—General M,O
Educational Leadership and Administration M
Elementary Education M,O
English as a Second Language M,O
Health Education M,O
Higher Education M
Industrial and Manufacturing Management M
Information Studies M,D
Kinesiology and Movement Studies M
Library Science M,D
Management Information Systems M
Mathematics Education M
Quality Management M
Reading Education M,O
Recreation and Park Management M
Science Education M
Secondary Education O
Social Work M,O
Special Education M
Student Affairs M
Taxation M
Transportation Management M

SANTA CLARA UNIVERSITY
Accounting M
Business Administration and Management—General M
Counselor Education M
Education—General M,O
Educational Leadership and Administration M,O
Entrepreneurship M
Finance and Banking M
Intellectual Property Law M,D,O
International Business M
Law M,D,O
Management Information Systems M
Marketing M
Organizational Management M
Supply Chain Management M

SANTA FE UNIVERSITY OF ART AND DESIGN
Education—General M

SARAH LAWRENCE COLLEGE
Education—General M

SAVANNAH COLLEGE OF ART AND DESIGN
Advertising and Public Relations M
Education—General M

SAVANNAH STATE UNIVERSITY
Business Administration and Management—General M
Social Work M

SAYBROOK UNIVERSITY
Organizational Behavior M,D
Organizational Management M,D

SCHILLER INTERNATIONAL UNIVERSITY (GERMANY)
Business Administration and Management—General M
International Business M
Management Information Systems M

SCHILLER INTERNATIONAL UNIVERSITY
Business Administration and Management—General M
International Business M

SCHILLER INTERNATIONAL UNIVERSITY (SPAIN)
Business Administration and Management—General M
International Business M

SCHILLER INTERNATIONAL UNIVERSITY
Business Administration and Management—General M
International Business M

SCHILLER INTERNATIONAL UNIVERSITY (UNITED STATES)
Business Administration and Management—General M
Finance and Banking M
Hospitality Management M
International Business M

*M—master's degree; P—first professional degree; D—doctorate; O—other advanced degree; *Close-Up and/or Display*

Management Information Systems M
Travel and Tourism M

SCHOOL OF THE ART INSTITUTE OF CHICAGO
Art Education M

SCHOOL OF THE MUSEUM OF FINE ARTS, BOSTON
Art Education M,O

SCHOOL OF VISUAL ARTS (NY)
Art Education M

SCHREINER UNIVERSITY
Business Administration and Management—General M
Education—General M

SEATTLE PACIFIC UNIVERSITY
Business Administration and Management—General M
Counselor Education M,D,O
Curriculum and Instruction M
Educational Leadership and Administration M,D,O
English as a Second Language M
Management Information Systems M
Reading Education M
Secondary Education M,O

SEATTLE UNIVERSITY
Accounting M
Adult Education M,O
Business Administration and Management—General M,O
Counselor Education M,O
Curriculum and Instruction M,O
Education—General M,D,O
Educational Leadership and Administration M,D,O
English as a Second Language M,O
Finance and Banking M,O
Law D
Organizational Management M,O
Reading Education M,O
Special Education M,O
Sports Management M

SETON HALL UNIVERSITY
Accounting M,O
Athletic Training and Sports Medicine M
Business Administration and Management—General M,O
Education—General M,D,O
Educational Leadership and Administration D,O
Educational Measurement and Evaluation M,D,O
Educational Media/Instructional Technology M
Finance and Banking M
Health Law M,D
Higher Education D
International Business M,O
Law M,D
Marketing M
Museum Education M
Nonprofit Management M,O
Special Education M
Sports Management M
Student Affairs M
Supply Chain Management M
Taxation M,O

SETON HILL UNIVERSITY
Business Administration and Management—General M,O
Education—General M,O
Elementary Education M,O
Entrepreneurship M,O
Middle School Education M,O
Special Education M,O

SHASTA BIBLE COLLEGE
Educational Leadership and Administration M
Religious Education M

SHAWNEE STATE UNIVERSITY
Curriculum and Instruction M
Education—General M

SHAW UNIVERSITY
Curriculum and Instruction M

SHENANDOAH UNIVERSITY
Athletic Training and Sports Medicine M,O
Business Administration and Management—General M,O
Education—General M,D,O
Music Education M,D,O

SHEPHERD UNIVERSITY
Curriculum and Instruction M

SHIPPENSBURG UNIVERSITY OF PENNSYLVANIA
Business Administration and Management—General M,O
Counselor Education M,O
Curriculum and Instruction M
Early Childhood Education M
Education—General M,O
Educational Leadership and Administration M
Elementary Education M
English Education M
Foreign Languages Education M
Higher Education M
Management Information Systems M
Mathematics Education M
Middle School Education M
Organizational Management M
Reading Education M
Science Education M
Social Work M
Special Education M

SHORTER UNIVERSITY
Accounting M
Business Administration and Management—General M
Curriculum and Instruction M

SIENA HEIGHTS UNIVERSITY
Early Childhood Education M
Education—General M
Educational Leadership and Administration M
Elementary Education M
Mathematics Education M
Middle School Education M
Reading Education M
Secondary Education M

SIERRA NEVADA COLLEGE
Education—General M
Educational Leadership and Administration M
Elementary Education M
Secondary Education M

SILICON VALLEY UNIVERSITY
Business Administration and Management—General M

SILVER LAKE COLLEGE OF THE HOLY FAMILY
Business Administration and Management—General M
Education—General M
Educational Leadership and Administration M
Music Education M
Organizational Behavior M
Special Education M

SIMMONS COLLEGE
Archives/Archival Administration M,D,O
Business Administration and Management—General M,O
Education—General M,D,O
Educational Leadership and Administration M,D,O
Educational Media/Instructional Technology M,D,O
English as a Second Language M,D,O
Entrepreneurship M,O
Health Education M,D,O
Information Studies M,D,O
Library Science M,D,O
Reading Education M,D,O
Social Work M,D,O
Special Education M,D,O
Urban Education M,D,O

SIMON FRASER UNIVERSITY
Actuarial Science M,D
Art Education M,D
Business Administration and Management—General M,D
Counselor Education M,D
Curriculum and Instruction M,D
Education—General M,D
Educational Leadership and Administration M,D
Educational Media/Instructional Technology M,D
Educational Psychology M,D
English as a Second Language M,D
Finance and Banking M,D
Foundations and Philosophy of Education M,D
International Business M,D
Kinesiology and Movement Studies M,D
Mathematics Education M,D

SIMPSON COLLEGE
Education—General M
Secondary Education M

SIMPSON UNIVERSITY
Education—General M
Educational Leadership and Administration M

SINTE GLESKA UNIVERSITY
Education—General M
Elementary Education M

SIT GRADUATE INSTITUTE
Business Administration and Management—General M
English as a Second Language M
International and Comparative Education M
International Business M

SLIPPERY ROCK UNIVERSITY OF PENNSYLVANIA
Counselor Education M
Education—General M
Educational Leadership and Administration M
Elementary Education M
English Education M
Environmental Education M
Mathematics Education M
Physical Education M
Reading Education M
Recreation and Park Management M
Science Education M
Secondary Education M
Social Sciences Education M
Special Education M

SMITH COLLEGE
Education—General M
Elementary Education M
English Education M
Exercise and Sports Science M
Foreign Languages Education M
Mathematics Education M
Middle School Education M
Science Education M
Secondary Education M
Social Sciences Education M
Social Work M,D
Special Education M

SOJOURNER-DOUGLASS COLLEGE
Human Services M
Reading Education M
Urban Education M

SOKA UNIVERSITY OF AMERICA
English as a Second Language O
Foreign Languages Education O

SONOMA STATE UNIVERSITY
Business Administration and Management—General M
Counselor Education M
Education—General M,D,O
Kinesiology and Movement Studies M
Special Education M,D,O

SOUTH CAROLINA STATE UNIVERSITY
Business Education M,D,O
Counselor Education M,D,O
Early Childhood Education M,D,O
Education—General M,D,O
Educational Leadership and Administration M,D,O
Elementary Education M,D,O
English Education M,D,O
Entrepreneurship M
Home Economics Education M,D,O
Human Services M,O
Mathematics Education M,D,O
Science Education M,D,O
Secondary Education M,D,O
Social Sciences Education M,D,O
Special Education M,D,O
Vocational and Technical Education M,D,O

SOUTH DAKOTA STATE UNIVERSITY
Counselor Education M
Curriculum and Instruction M
Education—General M,D
Educational Leadership and Administration M
Health Education M
Hospitality Management M,D
Physical Education M
Recreation and Park Management M

SOUTHEASTERN BAPTIST THEOLOGICAL SEMINARY
Religious Education M,D

SOUTHEASTERN LOUISIANA UNIVERSITY
Accounting M
Business Administration and Management—General M
Counselor Education M
Curriculum and Instruction M
Education—General M,D
Educational Leadership and Administration M,D
Educational Media/Instructional Technology M
Elementary Education M
English Education M
Health Education M
Kinesiology and Movement Studies M
Reading Education M
Special Education M

SOUTHEASTERN OKLAHOMA STATE UNIVERSITY
Aviation Management M
Business Administration and Management—General M
Counselor Education M
Education—General M
Educational Leadership and Administration M
Management Information Systems M
Mathematics Education M
Reading Education M
Special Education M

SOUTHEASTERN UNIVERSITY (FL)
Business Administration and Management—General M
Counselor Education M
Education—General M
Educational Leadership and Administration M
Elementary Education M
Human Services M

SOUTHEAST MISSOURI STATE UNIVERSITY
Accounting M
Business Administration and Management—General M
Counselor Education M,O
Educational Leadership and Administration M,O
Educational Media/Instructional Technology M
Elementary Education M,O
English as a Second Language M
Entrepreneurship M
Exercise and Sports Science M
Finance and Banking M
Foundations and Philosophy of Education M
Higher Education M,O
Industrial and Manufacturing Management M
International Business M
Leisure Studies M
Middle School Education M
Science Education M
Secondary Education M,O
Special Education M
Sports Management M

SOUTHERN ADVENTIST UNIVERSITY
Accounting M
Business Administration and Management—General M
Counselor Education M
Education—General M
Educational Leadership and Administration M
Finance and Banking M
Marketing M
Nonprofit Management M
Reading Education M
Recreation and Park Management M
Religious Education M
Social Work M

SOUTHERN ARKANSAS UNIVERSITY–MAGNOLIA
Business Administration and Management—General M
Counselor Education M
Curriculum and Instruction M
Education—General M
Educational Leadership and Administration M
Elementary Education M
English as a Second Language M
Kinesiology and Movement Studies M
Library Science M
Middle School Education M
Reading Education M
Secondary Education M

SOUTHERN BAPTIST THEOLOGICAL SEMINARY
Higher Education M,D
Religious Education M,D

SOUTHERN CONNECTICUT STATE UNIVERSITY
Art Education M
Business Administration and Management—General M
Counselor Education M,O
Education—General M,D,O
Educational Leadership and Administration M,D,O
Educational Measurement and Evaluation M,D,O
Elementary Education M,O
English as a Second Language M,O
Environmental Education M,O
Exercise and Sports Science M
Foundations and Philosophy of Education M,D,O
Health Education M
Information Studies M,O
Leisure Studies M
Library Science M,O
Multilingual and Multicultural Education M
Physical Education M
Reading Education M,O
Recreation and Park Management M
Science Education M,O
Social Work M
Special Education M,O

SOUTHERN EVANGELICAL SEMINARY
Religious Education M,D,O

SOUTHERN ILLINOIS UNIVERSITY CARBONDALE
Accounting M,D
Business Administration and Management—General M,D
Counselor Education M,D
Curriculum and Instruction M,D
Education—General M,D
Educational Leadership and Administration M,D
Educational Measurement and Evaluation M,D
Educational Psychology M,D
English as a Second Language M,D
Health Education M,D
Health Law M
Higher Education M
Law M,D
Legal and Justice Studies M
Music Education M
Physical Education M
Recreation and Park Management M
Social Work M
Special Education M
Vocational and Technical Education M,D

SOUTHERN ILLINOIS UNIVERSITY EDWARDSVILLE
Accounting M
Art Education M
Business Administration and Management—General M
Curriculum and Instruction M
Education—General M,D,O
Educational Leadership and Administration M,D,O
Educational Media/Instructional Technology M,O
English as a Second Language M,O
English Education M,O
Finance and Banking M
Foreign Languages Education M
Foundations and Philosophy of Education M
Health Education M
Higher Education M
Kinesiology and Movement Studies M
Management Information Systems M
Marketing Research M
Mathematics Education M
Music Education M,O
Physical Education M
Project Management M
Reading Education M,O
Science Education M
Secondary Education M
Social Sciences Education M

Social Work M
Special Education M,O
Taxation M

SOUTHERN METHODIST UNIVERSITY
Accounting M
Advertising and Public Relations M
Business Administration and Management—General M
Counselor Education M,O
Education of the Gifted M,D,O
Education—General M,D,O
Entrepreneurship M
Finance and Banking M
Law M,D
Management Information Systems M
Management Strategy and Policy M
Marketing M
Multilingual and Multicultural Education M,D,O
Music Education M,O
Real Estate M
Taxation M,D

SOUTHERN NAZARENE UNIVERSITY
Business Administration and Management—General M

SOUTHERN NEW HAMPSHIRE UNIVERSITY
Accounting M,D,O
Business Administration and Management—General M,D,O
Business Education M,O
Computer Education M,O
Curriculum and Instruction M,O
Education—General M,O
Educational Leadership and Administration M,O
Elementary Education M,O
English as a Second Language M,O
Finance and Banking M,D,O
Hospitality Management M,D,O
Human Resources Development M,O
Human Resources Management M,D,O
International Business M,D,O
Management Information Systems M,D,O
Marketing M,D,O
Nonprofit Management M,D,O
Organizational Management M,D,O
Project Management M,D,O
Secondary Education M,O
Special Education M,O
Sports Management M,D,O
Taxation M,D,O
Vocational and Technical Education M,O

SOUTHERN OREGON UNIVERSITY
Business Administration and Management—General M
Early Childhood Education M
Education—General M
Educational Leadership and Administration M
Elementary Education M
Environmental Education M
Foreign Languages Education M
Reading Education M
Secondary Education M
Special Education M

SOUTHERN POLYTECHNIC STATE UNIVERSITY
Accounting M,O
Business Administration and Management—General M,O
Educational Media/Instructional Technology M,O
Quality Management M,O

SOUTHERN UNIVERSITY AND AGRICULTURAL AND MECHANICAL COLLEGE
Business Administration and Management—General M
Counselor Education M
Education—General M,D
Educational Leadership and Administration M
Educational Media/Instructional Technology M
Elementary Education M
Law D
Mathematics Education D
Recreation and Park Management M
Science Education D
Secondary Education M
Special Education M,D

SOUTHERN UNIVERSITY AT NEW ORLEANS
Management Information Systems M
Social Work M

SOUTHERN UTAH UNIVERSITY
Accounting M
Business Administration and Management—General M
Education—General M
Exercise and Sports Science M

SOUTHERN WESLEYAN UNIVERSITY
Business Administration and Management—General M
Education—General M

SOUTH TEXAS COLLEGE OF LAW
Law D

SOUTH UNIVERSITY (AL)
Business Administration and Management—General M*

SOUTH UNIVERSITY (FL)
Business Administration and Management—General M*

SOUTH UNIVERSITY (FL)
Business Administration and Management—General M*

SOUTH UNIVERSITY (GA)
Business Administration and Management—General M*
Entrepreneurship M
Hospitality Management M
Sustainability Management M

SOUTH UNIVERSITY (MI)
Business Administration and Management—General M*

SOUTH UNIVERSITY (SC)
Business Administration and Management—General M*

SOUTH UNIVERSITY (TX)
Business Administration and Management—General M*

SOUTH UNIVERSITY (VA)
Business Administration and Management—General M*

SOUTH UNIVERSITY (VA)
Business Administration and Management—General M*

SOUTHWEST BAPTIST UNIVERSITY
Business Administration and Management—General M
Education—General M,O
Educational Leadership and Administration M,O

SOUTHWESTERN ADVENTIST UNIVERSITY
Accounting M
Business Administration and Management—General M
Curriculum and Instruction M
Education—General M
Educational Leadership and Administration M
Finance and Banking M
Reading Education M

SOUTHWESTERN ASSEMBLIES OF GOD UNIVERSITY
Curriculum and Instruction M
Education—General M
Educational Leadership and Administration M
Religious Education M
Secondary Education M

SOUTHWESTERN BAPTIST THEOLOGICAL SEMINARY
Religious Education M,D,O

SOUTHWESTERN COLLEGE (KS)
Accounting M
Business Administration and Management—General M
Curriculum and Instruction M,D
Education—General M,D
Music Education M
Organizational Management M
Special Education M,D

SOUTHWESTERN LAW SCHOOL
Law M,D

SOUTHWESTERN OKLAHOMA STATE UNIVERSITY
Art Education M
Business Administration and Management—General M
Counselor Education M
Early Childhood Education M
Education—General M
Educational Leadership and Administration M
Educational Measurement and Evaluation M
Elementary Education M
English Education M
Kinesiology and Movement Studies M
Mathematics Education M
Music Education M
Recreation and Park Management M
Science Education M
Secondary Education M
Social Sciences Education M
Special Education M

SOUTHWEST MINNESOTA STATE UNIVERSITY
Business Administration and Management—General M
Early Childhood Education M
Education—General M
Educational Leadership and Administration M
English as a Second Language M
Marketing M
Mathematics Education M
Reading Education M
Special Education M

SOUTHWEST UNIVERSITY
Business Administration and Management—General M
Organizational Management M

SPALDING UNIVERSITY
Business Administration and Management—General M
Counselor Education M
Education—General M,D
Educational Leadership and Administration M,D
Elementary Education M
Middle School Education M
Secondary Education M
Social Work M
Special Education M

SPERTUS INSTITUTE OF JEWISH STUDIES
Nonprofit Management M
Religious Education M

SPRING ARBOR UNIVERSITY
Business Administration and Management—General M
Education—General M
Organizational Management M
Reading Education M
Special Education M

SPRINGFIELD COLLEGE
Athletic Training and Sports Medicine M,D
Counselor Education M,O
Early Childhood Education M
Education—General M
Educational Leadership and Administration M
Elementary Education M
Exercise and Sports Science M,D
Health Education M,D,O
Human Services M
Organizational Management M
Physical Education M,D,O
Recreation and Park Management M
Secondary Education M
Social Work M
Special Education M
Sports Management M,D,O
Student Affairs M,O

SPRING HILL COLLEGE
Business Administration and Management—General M
Early Childhood Education M
Education—General M
Elementary Education M
Foundations and Philosophy of Education M
Secondary Education M
Social Sciences Education M,O

STANFORD UNIVERSITY
Art Education M,D
Business Administration and Management—General M,D
Computer Education M,D
Curriculum and Instruction M,D
Education—General M,D
Educational Leadership and Administration M,D
Educational Measurement and Evaluation M,D
Educational Psychology D
English Education M,D
Foreign Languages Education M
Foundations and Philosophy of Education M,D
Higher Education M,D
International and Comparative Education M,D
Law M,D
Mathematics Education M,D
Science Education M,D
Social Sciences Education M,D

STATE UNIVERSITY OF NEW YORK AT BINGHAMTON
Accounting M,D
Business Administration and Management—General M,D
Early Childhood Education M,D
Education—General M,D
Educational Leadership and Administration M
English Education M
Finance and Banking M,D
Foreign Languages Education M
Foundations and Philosophy of Education D
Legal and Justice Studies M,D
Mathematics Education M
Reading Education M
Science Education M
Secondary Education M
Social Sciences Education M
Social Work M
Special Education M
Student Affairs M

STATE UNIVERSITY OF NEW YORK AT FREDONIA
Education—General M,O
Educational Leadership and Administration O
Elementary Education M
English as a Second Language M
Music Education M
Reading Education M
Science Education M
Secondary Education M

STATE UNIVERSITY OF NEW YORK AT NEW PALTZ
Accounting M
Art Education M
Business Administration and Management—General M
Counselor Education M
Early Childhood Education M
Education—General M,O
Educational Leadership and Administration M,O
Elementary Education M
English as a Second Language M
English Education M
Multilingual and Multicultural Education M
Reading Education M
Science Education M
Secondary Education M
Social Sciences Education M
Special Education M

STATE UNIVERSITY OF NEW YORK AT OSWEGO
Agricultural Education M
Art Education M
Business Administration and Management—General M
Business Education M
Early Childhood Education M
Education—General M,O
Educational Leadership and Administration O
Elementary Education M
Middle School Education M
Reading Education M
Secondary Education M
Special Education M
Vocational and Technical Education M

STATE UNIVERSITY OF NEW YORK AT PLATTSBURGH
Counselor Education M,O
Curriculum and Instruction M
Early Childhood Education O
Educational Leadership and Administration O
Elementary Education M
English Education M
Foreign Languages Education M
Mathematics Education M
Organizational Management M
Reading Education M
Science Education M
Secondary Education M
Social Sciences Education M
Special Education M
Student Affairs M,O

STATE UNIVERSITY OF NEW YORK COLLEGE AT CORTLAND
Early Childhood Education M
Education—General M,O
Educational Leadership and Administration O
English as a Second Language M
English Education M
Exercise and Sports Science M
Foreign Languages Education M
Health Education M
Mathematics Education M
Physical Education M
Reading Education M
Recreation and Park Management M
Science Education M
Secondary Education M
Social Sciences Education M
Special Education M
Sports Management M

STATE UNIVERSITY OF NEW YORK COLLEGE AT GENESEO
Accounting M
Business Administration and Management—General M
Early Childhood Education M
Education—General M
Elementary Education M
Multilingual and Multicultural Education M
Reading Education M
Secondary Education M

STATE UNIVERSITY OF NEW YORK COLLEGE AT OLD WESTBURY
Accounting M

STATE UNIVERSITY OF NEW YORK COLLEGE AT ONEONTA
Counselor Education M,O
Education—General M,O
Educational Media/Instructional Technology M,O
Educational Psychology M,O
Elementary Education M
Home Economics Education M
Middle School Education M
Reading Education M
Secondary Education M
Special Education M,O

STATE UNIVERSITY OF NEW YORK COLLEGE AT POTSDAM
Curriculum and Instruction M
Early Childhood Education M
Educational Media/Instructional Technology M
Elementary Education M
Mathematics Education M
Middle School Education M
Music Education M
Organizational Management M
Reading Education M
Science Education M
Secondary Education M
Social Sciences Education M
Special Education M

STATE UNIVERSITY OF NEW YORK COLLEGE OF ENVIRONMENTAL SCIENCE AND FORESTRY
Sustainability Management M,D

*M—master's degree; P—first professional degree; D—doctorate; O—other advanced degree; *Close-Up and/or Display*

STATE UNIVERSITY OF NEW YORK EMPIRE STATE COLLEGE
Business Administration and Management—General M
Education—General M

STATE UNIVERSITY OF NEW YORK INSTITUTE OF TECHNOLOGY
Accounting M

STATE UNIVERSITY OF NEW YORK MARITIME COLLEGE
Transportation Management M

STEPHEN F. AUSTIN STATE UNIVERSITY
Accounting M
Agricultural Education M
Athletic Training and Sports Medicine M
Business Administration and Management—General M
Counselor Education M
Early Childhood Education M
Education—General M,D
Educational Leadership and Administration M,D
Elementary Education M
Kinesiology and Movement Studies M
Marketing M
Mathematics Education M
Secondary Education M,D
Social Work M
Special Education M

STEPHENS COLLEGE
Business Administration and Management—General M
Counselor Education M
Curriculum and Instruction M

STETSON UNIVERSITY
Accounting M
Business Administration and Management—General M
Counselor Education M
Education—General M,O
Educational Leadership and Administration M,O
Law M,D
Reading Education M

STEVENS INSTITUTE OF TECHNOLOGY
Business Administration and Management—General M
Electronic Commerce M,O
Entrepreneurship M,O
Finance and Banking M
Human Resources Management M
Industrial and Manufacturing Management M
International Business M
Logistics M,D,O
Management Information Systems M,D,O
Management Strategy and Policy M,O
Project Management M,O
Quality Management M,O

STONY BROOK UNIVERSITY, STATE UNIVERSITY OF NEW YORK
Business Administration and Management—General M,O
Computer Education M
Educational Leadership and Administration M,O
Educational Media/Instructional Technology M,O
English as a Second Language M
English Education M,D,O
Finance and Banking M,O
Foreign Languages Education M,O
Human Resources Management M,O
Management Information Systems M,D,O
Marketing M,O
Mathematics Education M,O
Physical Education M,O
Science Education M,D,O
Social Sciences Education M,O
Social Work M,D

STRATFORD UNIVERSITY (MD)
Hospitality Management M

STRATFORD UNIVERSITY (VA)
Accounting M
Business Administration and Management—General M
Entrepreneurship M
Management Information Systems M

STRAYER UNIVERSITY
Accounting M
Business Administration and Management—General M
Education—General M
Educational Media/Instructional Technology M
Finance and Banking M
Hospitality Management M
Human Resources Management M
Management Information Systems M
Marketing M
Supply Chain Management M
Taxation M
Travel and Tourism M

SUFFOLK UNIVERSITY
Accounting M,O
Adult Education M,O
Advertising and Public Relations M
Business Administration and Management—General M,O
Counselor Education M,O
Education—General M,O
Educational Leadership and Administration M,O
Entrepreneurship M,O
Finance and Banking M,O
Foundations and Philosophy of Education M,O
Health Education M
Health Law M,D
Human Resources Development M,O
Intellectual Property Law M,D
International Business M,D,O
Law M,D
Management Strategy and Policy M,O
Marketing M,O
Middle School Education M,O
Nonprofit Management M,O
Organizational Behavior M,O
Organizational Management M,O
Secondary Education M,O
Taxation M,O

SULLIVAN UNIVERSITY
Business Administration and Management—General M,D

SUL ROSS STATE UNIVERSITY
Art Education M
Business Administration and Management—General M
Counselor Education M
Education—General M
Educational Leadership and Administration M
Educational Measurement and Evaluation M
Elementary Education M
Multilingual and Multicultural Education M
Physical Education M
Reading Education M
Secondary Education M

SWEET BRIAR COLLEGE
Education—General M

SYRACUSE UNIVERSITY
Accounting M,D
Adult Education O
Advertising and Public Relations M
Art Education M,O
Business Administration and Management—General M,D
Counselor Education M,D
Curriculum and Instruction M,D,O
Early Childhood Education M
Education of Students with Severe/Multiple Disabilities M
Education—General M,D,O
Educational Leadership and Administration M,D,O
Educational Measurement and Evaluation M,D,O
Educational Media/Instructional Technology M,O
English as a Second Language M,O
English Education M
Entrepreneurship M,D
Exercise and Sports Science M
Finance and Banking M,D
Foundations and Philosophy of Education M,D
Higher Education M,D
Human Resources Development D
Industrial and Manufacturing Management D
Information Studies M,D*
Law D
Library Science M,O
Management Information Systems M,D,O
Management Strategy and Policy D
Marketing M,D
Mathematics Education M,D
Music Education M
Organizational Behavior D
Organizational Management O
Quantitative Analysis D
Reading Education M,D
Science Education M,D
Social Sciences Education M
Social Work M
Special Education M,D
Sports Management M
Student Affairs M
Supply Chain Management M,D
Travel and Tourism M

TABOR COLLEGE
Accounting M
Business Administration and Management—General M

TAFT LAW SCHOOL
Law M,D
Legal and Justice Studies M,D
Taxation M,D

TARLETON STATE UNIVERSITY
Accounting M
Agricultural Education M
Business Administration and Management—General M
Counselor Education M,O
Curriculum and Instruction M
Education—General M,D,O
Educational Leadership and Administration M,D,O
Finance and Banking M
Human Resources Management M
Management Information Systems M
Music Education M
Physical Education M
Secondary Education M,O
Special Education M,O

TAYLOR COLLEGE AND SEMINARY
English as a Second Language M,O

TAYLOR UNIVERSITY
Business Administration and Management—General M
Higher Education M
International Business M
Management Strategy and Policy M

TEACHER EDUCATION UNIVERSITY
Counselor Education M
Education—General M
Educational Leadership and Administration M
Educational Media/Instructional Technology M
Elementary Education M

TEACHERS COLLEGE, COLUMBIA UNIVERSITY
Adult Education M,D
Art Education M,D
Computer Education M
Counselor Education M
Curriculum and Instruction M,D
Early Childhood Education M,D
Education of Students with Severe/Multiple Disabilities M
Education of the Gifted M,D
Education—General M,D,O
Educational Leadership and Administration M,D
Educational Measurement and Evaluation M,D
Educational Media/Instructional Technology M,D
Educational Psychology M,D
Elementary Education M,D,O
English as a Second Language M,D
English Education M,D
Foundations and Philosophy of Education M,D
Health Education M,D
Higher Education M,D
International and Comparative Education M,D
Kinesiology and Movement Studies M,D
Mathematics Education M,D
Multilingual and Multicultural Education M
Music Education M,D
Organizational Management M
Physical Education M,D
Reading Education M
Science Education M,D
Social Sciences Education M,D
Special Education M,D,O
Student Affairs M,D
Urban Education D

TÉLÉ-UNIVERSITÉ
Distance Education Development M,D
Finance and Banking M,D

TEMPLE BAPTIST SEMINARY
Religious Education M,D

TEMPLE UNIVERSITY
Accounting M,D
Actuarial Science M
Art Education M
Business Administration and Management—General M,D
Early Childhood Education M,D
Education—General M,D
Educational Leadership and Administration M,D
Educational Psychology M,D
Elementary Education M,D
English as a Second Language M,D
English Education M,D
Entrepreneurship D
Finance and Banking M,D
Foreign Languages Education M,D
Health Education M,D
Hospitality Management M,D
Human Resources Management M
Insurance D
International Business M,D
Kinesiology and Movement Studies M,D
Law M,D
Legal and Justice Studies M,D
Leisure Studies M
Management Information Systems D
Management Strategy and Policy D
Marketing M,D
Mathematics Education M,D
Music Education M,D
Physical Education M,D
Reading Education M,D
Recreation and Park Management M,D
Science Education M,D
Social Work M,D
Special Education M,D
Sports Management M,D
Taxation M,D
Travel and Tourism M
Urban Education M,D
Vocational and Technical Education M,D

TENNESSEE STATE UNIVERSITY
Business Administration and Management—General M
Counselor Education M,D
Curriculum and Instruction M,D
Education—General M,D,O
Educational Leadership and Administration M,D,O
Elementary Education M,D
Exercise and Sports Science M
Music Education M
Physical Education M
Special Education M,D

TENNESSEE TECHNOLOGICAL UNIVERSITY
Accounting M
Business Administration and Management—General M
Curriculum and Instruction M,O
Early Childhood Education M,O
Education of the Gifted D
Education—General M,D,O
Educational Leadership and Administration M,O
Educational Measurement and Evaluation D
Educational Psychology M,O
Elementary Education M,O
Finance and Banking M
Health Education M
Human Resources Management M
Insurance M
International Business M
Kinesiology and Movement Studies M
Library Science M
Management Information Systems M
Management Strategy and Policy M
Music Education M,D,O
Physical Education M
Reading Education M,D,O
Secondary Education M,O
Special Education M,O

TENNESSEE TEMPLE UNIVERSITY
Curriculum and Instruction M
Education—General M
Educational Leadership and Administration M

TEXAS A&M HEALTH SCIENCE CENTER
Health Education M

TEXAS A&M INTERNATIONAL UNIVERSITY
Accounting M
Business Administration and Management—General M
Counselor Education M
Curriculum and Instruction M
Education—General M
Educational Leadership and Administration M
Finance and Banking M
Foreign Languages Education M,D
International Business M
Management Information Systems M
Special Education M

TEXAS A&M UNIVERSITY
Accounting M,D
Adult Education M,D
Agricultural Education M,D
Business Administration and Management—General M,D
Curriculum and Instruction M,D
Education—General M,D
Educational Leadership and Administration M,D
Educational Measurement and Evaluation M,D
Educational Media/Instructional Technology M,D
Educational Psychology M,D
English as a Second Language M,D
English Education M,D
Finance and Banking M,D
Health Education M,D
Higher Education M,D
Human Resources Development M,D
Human Resources Management M,D
Industrial and Manufacturing Management M,D
Kinesiology and Movement Studies M,D
Management Information Systems M,D
Marketing M,D
Mathematics Education M,D
Multilingual and Multicultural Education M,D
Nonprofit Management M,O
Physical Education M,D
Reading Education M,D
Recreation and Park Management M,D
Science Education M,D
Special Education M,D
Sports Management M,D
Urban Education M,D

TEXAS A&M UNIVERSITY AT GALVESTON
Transportation Management M

TEXAS A&M UNIVERSITY–COMMERCE
Accounting M
Agricultural Education M
Business Administration and Management—General M
Counselor Education M,D
Early Childhood Education M,D
Education—General M,D
Educational Leadership and Administration M,D
Educational Media/Instructional Technology M,D
Elementary Education M,D
English as a Second Language M,D
English Education M,D
Exercise and Sports Science M,D
Finance and Banking M
Health Education M,D
Higher Education M,D
Kinesiology and Movement Studies M,D
Marketing M
Multilingual and Multicultural Education M,D
Music Education M,D
Physical Education M,D
Reading Education M,D
Secondary Education M,D
Social Sciences Education M
Social Work M
Special Education M,D

TEXAS A&M UNIVERSITY–CORPUS CHRISTI
Accounting M
Business Administration and Management—General M

Counselor Education M,D
Curriculum and Instruction M,D
Early Childhood Education M,D
Education—General M,D
Educational Leadership and Administration M,D
Educational Media/Instructional Technology M,D
Elementary Education M
International Business M
Kinesiology and Movement Studies M,D
Mathematics Education M
Reading Education M,D
Secondary Education M
Special Education M

TEXAS A&M UNIVERSITY–KINGSVILLE
Adult Education M
Agricultural Education M
Business Administration and Management—General M
Counselor Education M
Early Childhood Education M
Education—General M,D
Educational Leadership and Administration M,D
Elementary Education M
English as a Second Language M
Foreign Languages Education M
Health Education M
Higher Education D
Kinesiology and Movement Studies M
Multilingual and Multicultural Education M,D
Music Education M
Reading Education M
Secondary Education M
Special Education M

TEXAS A&M UNIVERSITY–SAN ANTONIO
Accounting M
Business Administration and Management—General M
Counselor Education M
Early Childhood Education M
Educational Leadership and Administration M
Educational Measurement and Evaluation M
Finance and Banking M
Human Resources Management M
International Business M
Kinesiology and Movement Studies M
Management Information Systems M
Multilingual and Multicultural Education M
Project Management M
Reading Education M
Special Education M
Supply Chain Management M

TEXAS A&M UNIVERSITY–TEXARKANA
Accounting M
Adult Education M
Business Administration and Management—General M
Curriculum and Instruction M
Education—General M
Educational Leadership and Administration M
Educational Media/Instructional Technology M
Special Education M

TEXAS CHRISTIAN UNIVERSITY
Accounting M
Advertising and Public Relations M
Business Administration and Management—General M,D
Counselor Education M,D,O
Curriculum and Instruction M,D
Education—General M,D,O
Educational Leadership and Administration M,D,O
Educational Psychology M,D,O
Elementary Education M
Higher Education D
Kinesiology and Movement Studies M
Middle School Education M
Music Education M,D,O
Science Education M,D
Secondary Education M
Special Education M

TEXAS SOUTHERN UNIVERSITY
Business Administration and Management—General M
Counselor Education M,D
Curriculum and Instruction M,D
Education—General M,D
Educational Leadership and Administration M,D
Health Education M
Higher Education M,D
Human Services M
Law D
Management Information Systems M
Multilingual and Multicultural Education M,D
Physical Education M
Secondary Education M,D
Transportation Management M

TEXAS STATE UNIVERSITY–SAN MARCOS
Accounting M
Adult Education M,D
Agricultural Education M
Athletic Training and Sports Medicine M
Business Administration and Management—General M
Counselor Education M
Education—General M,D,O
Educational Leadership and Administration M,D
Educational Media/Instructional Technology M
Elementary Education M
Health Education M
Higher Education M
Legal and Justice Studies M
Leisure Studies M
Management Information Systems M
Mathematics Education M,D
Multilingual and Multicultural Education M
Music Education M
Physical Education M
Reading Education M
Recreation and Park Management M
Science Education M
Secondary Education M
Social Sciences Education D
Social Work M
Special Education M
Student Affairs M
Vocational and Technical Education M

TEXAS TECH UNIVERSITY
Accounting M,D
Agricultural Education M,D
Art Education M
Business Administration and Management—General M,D
Counselor Education M,D
Curriculum and Instruction M,D
Education—General M,D
Educational Leadership and Administration M,D
Educational Media/Instructional Technology M,D
Educational Psychology M,D
Elementary Education M,D
Entrepreneurship M
Exercise and Sports Science M
Finance and Banking M,D
Higher Education M,D
Home Economics Education M,D
Hospitality Management M,D
Industrial and Manufacturing Management M,D
International Business M
Law M,D
Management Information Systems M,D
Marketing M,D
Multilingual and Multicultural Education M,D
Music Education M,D
Quantitative Analysis M,D
Reading Education M,D
Real Estate M
Secondary Education M,D
Special Education M,D
Taxation M,D

TEXAS TECH UNIVERSITY HEALTH SCIENCES CENTER
Athletic Training and Sports Medicine M

TEXAS WESLEYAN UNIVERSITY
Business Administration and Management—General M
Counselor Education M,D
Education—General M,D
Law D

TEXAS WOMAN'S UNIVERSITY
Business Administration and Management—General M
Counselor Education M,D
Curriculum and Instruction M,D
Early Childhood Education M,D
Education—General M,D
Educational Leadership and Administration M,D
Exercise and Sports Science M,D
Health Education M,D
Kinesiology and Movement Studies M,D
Library Science M,D
Mathematics Education M
Physical Education M,D
Reading Education M,D
Special Education M,D
Sports Management M,D

THOMAS COLLEGE
Business Administration and Management—General M
Business Education M
Computer Education M
Human Resources Management M

THOMAS EDISON STATE COLLEGE
Business Administration and Management—General M
Distance Education Development O
Educational Leadership and Administration M
Educational Media/Instructional Technology O
Human Resources Management M,O
Organizational Management O

THOMAS JEFFERSON SCHOOL OF LAW
Law D

THOMAS JEFFERSON UNIVERSITY
Health Education M,D,O

THOMAS M. COOLEY LAW SCHOOL
Environmental Law M,D
Finance and Banking M,D
Insurance M,D
Intellectual Property Law M,D
Law M,D
Legal and Justice Studies M,D
Taxation M,D

THOMAS MORE COLLEGE
Business Administration and Management—General M
Education—General M

THOMAS UNIVERSITY
Business Administration and Management—General M
Education—General M
Human Services M

THOMPSON RIVERS UNIVERSITY
Business Administration and Management—General M
Education—General M
Social Work M

THUNDERBIRD SCHOOL OF GLOBAL MANAGEMENT
Business Administration and Management—General M
International Business M

TIFFIN UNIVERSITY
Business Administration and Management—General M
Finance and Banking M
Human Resources Management M
International Business M
Marketing M
Sports Management M

TOURO COLLEGE
Counselor Education M
Education of the Gifted M,O
Education—General M,O
Educational Leadership and Administration M,O
Educational Media/Instructional Technology M,O
English as a Second Language M,O
Law M,D
Legal and Justice Studies M,D
Management Information Systems M
Mathematics Education M,O
Multilingual and Multicultural Education M,O
Reading Education M,O
Social Work M
Special Education M,O

TOURO UNIVERSITY
Education—General M,D

TOWSON UNIVERSITY
Accounting M
Art Education M,O
Early Childhood Education M,O
Education—General M
Educational Media/Instructional Technology M,D
Elementary Education M
Human Resources Development M
Kinesiology and Movement Studies M
Management Information Systems M,D,O
Management Strategy and Policy O
Mathematics Education M
Music Education M,O
Organizational Behavior O
Reading Education M,O
Religious Education M,D,O
Secondary Education M
Special Education M,O

TREVECCA NAZARENE UNIVERSITY
Business Administration and Management—General M
Counselor Education M,D
Curriculum and Instruction M
Education—General M,D
Educational Leadership and Administration M,D
Elementary Education M
English as a Second Language M
Library Science M
Organizational Management M
Secondary Education M
Special Education M,D

TRIDENT UNIVERSITY INTERNATIONAL
Adult Education M
Business Administration and Management—General M,D
Early Childhood Education M
Education—General M,D
Educational Leadership and Administration M,D
Educational Media/Instructional Technology M,D
Finance and Banking M,D
Health Education M,D,O
Higher Education M,D
Human Resources Management M,D
International Business M,D
Legal and Justice Studies M,D,O
Logistics M,D
Management Information Systems M,D,O
Marketing M,D
Project Management M,D
Quality Management M,D,O
Reading Education M

TRINITY BAPTIST COLLEGE
Educational Leadership and Administration M
Special Education M

TRINITY INTERNATIONAL UNIVERSITY
Business Administration and Management—General M,D,O
Education—General M
Educational Leadership and Administration M
Law D
Religious Education M,D,O

TRINITY LUTHERAN SEMINARY
Religious Education M

TRINITY UNIVERSITY
Accounting M
Business Administration and Management—General M
Education—General M
Educational Leadership and Administration M

TRINITY WASHINGTON UNIVERSITY
Business Administration and Management—General M
Counselor Education M
Curriculum and Instruction M
Early Childhood Education M
Education—General M
Educational Leadership and Administration M
Elementary Education M
English as a Second Language M
English Education M
Human Resources Management M
Nonprofit Management M
Organizational Management M
Reading Education M
Secondary Education M
Social Sciences Education M
Special Education M

TRINITY WESTERN UNIVERSITY
Business Administration and Management—General M
Educational Leadership and Administration M,O
English as a Second Language M
International Business M
Nonprofit Management M,O
Organizational Management M,O

TROPICAL AGRICULTURE RESEARCH AND HIGHER EDUCATION CENTER
Travel and Tourism M,D

TROY UNIVERSITY
Accounting M
Adult Education M
Art Education M
Business Administration and Management—General M
Computer Education M
Counselor Education M,O
Early Childhood Education M,O
Education of the Gifted M
Education—General M,O
Educational Leadership and Administration M,O
Educational Media/Instructional Technology M
Elementary Education M,O
English Education M
Exercise and Sports Science M
Finance and Banking M
Foundations and Philosophy of Education M
Higher Education M
Hospitality Management M
Human Resources Management M
International Business M
Management Information Systems M
Mathematics Education M
Music Education M
Nonprofit Management M
Organizational Management M
Physical Education M
Reading Education M
Science Education M
Secondary Education M
Social Sciences Education M
Social Work M,O
Sports Management M
Taxation M,O

TRUMAN STATE UNIVERSITY
Accounting M
Education—General M

TUFTS UNIVERSITY
Early Childhood Education M,D,O
Education—General M,D,O
International Business M,D
Law M,D
Management Strategy and Policy O
Middle School Education M,D
Nonprofit Management O
Secondary Education M,D

TULANE UNIVERSITY
Business Administration and Management—General M,D
Health Education M
Law M,D
Social Work M

TUSCULUM COLLEGE
Adult Education M
Education—General M
Organizational Management M

UNIFICATION THEOLOGICAL SEMINARY
Religious Education M,D

UNION COLLEGE (KY)
Education—General M
Educational Leadership and Administration M
Elementary Education M
Health Education M

*M—master's degree; P—first professional degree; D—doctorate; O—other advanced degree; *Close-Up and/or Display*

Middle School Education M
Music Education M
Physical Education M
Reading Education M
Secondary Education M
Special Education M

UNION GRADUATE COLLEGE
Business Administration and Management—General M,O
Education—General M,O
Educational Leadership and Administration M,O
English Education M,O
Finance and Banking M,O
Foreign Languages Education M,O
Health Law M,O
Human Resources Management M,O
Mathematics Education M,O
Middle School Education M,O
Science Education M,O
Social Sciences Education M,O

UNION INSTITUTE & UNIVERSITY
Adult Education M,D,O
Counselor Education M,D,O
Curriculum and Instruction M,D,O
Education—General M,D,O
Educational Leadership and Administration M,D,O
Educational Psychology M,D,O
Higher Education M,D,O
Reading Education M,D,O

UNION PRESBYTERIAN SEMINARY
Religious Education M,D

UNION UNIVERSITY
Business Administration and Management—General M
Education—General M,D,O
Educational Leadership and Administration M,D,O
Higher Education M,D,O

UNITED STATES INTERNATIONAL UNIVERSITY
Business Administration and Management—General M
Entrepreneurship M
Finance and Banking M
Human Resources Management M
International Business M
Management Information Systems M
Management Strategy and Policy M
Marketing M
Organizational Management M

UNITED STATES SPORTS ACADEMY
Athletic Training and Sports Medicine M
Exercise and Sports Science M
Physical Education M
Sports Management M,D

UNITED STATES UNIVERSITY
Business Administration and Management—General M
Early Childhood Education M
Education—General M
Educational Leadership and Administration M
Foreign Languages Education M
Health Education M
Higher Education M
Special Education M

UNIVERSIDAD ADVENTISTA DE LAS ANTILLAS
Curriculum and Instruction M
Educational Leadership and Administration M
Health Education M

UNIVERSIDAD AUTONOMA DE GUADALAJARA
Advertising and Public Relations M,D
Business Administration and Management—General M,D
Education—General M,D
Entertainment Management M,D
International Business M,D
Law M,D
Legal and Justice Studies M,D
Marketing Research M,D
Mathematics Education M,D

UNIVERSIDAD CENTRAL DEL ESTE
Finance and Banking M
Higher Education M
Human Resources Development M
Law D

UNIVERSIDAD DE IBEROAMERICA
Educational Psychology M,D

UNIVERSIDAD DE LAS AMERICAS, A.C.
Business Administration and Management—General M
Education—General M
Finance and Banking M
Marketing Research M
Organizational Behavior M
Quality Management M

UNIVERSIDAD DE LAS AMÉRICAS–PUEBLA
Business Administration and Management—General M
Education—General M
Finance and Banking M
Industrial and Manufacturing Management M

UNIVERSIDAD DEL ESTE
Accounting M
Adult Education M
Business Administration and Management—General M
Electronic Commerce M
Elementary Education M
English as a Second Language M
Foreign Languages Education M
Human Resources Management M
Management Information Systems M
Management Strategy and Policy M
Social Work M
Special Education M

UNIVERSIDAD DEL TURABO
Accounting M
Athletic Training and Sports Medicine M
Business Administration and Management—General M,D
Counselor Education M
Curriculum and Instruction M,D
Early Childhood Education M
Education—General M,D,O
Educational Leadership and Administration M,D,O
English as a Second Language M
Human Resources Management M
Human Services M
Information Studies M
Library Science M,O
Logistics M
Management Information Systems D
Marketing M
Physical Education M
Project Management M
Quality Management M
Special Education M

UNIVERSIDAD FLET
Education—General M

UNIVERSIDAD IBEROAMERICANA
Business Administration and Management—General M,D
Educational Leadership and Administration M,D
Human Resources Development M,D
Law M,D
Marketing M,D
Real Estate M,D
Special Education M,D

UNIVERSIDAD METROPOLITANA
Accounting M
Adult Education M
Business Administration and Management—General M
Curriculum and Instruction M
Education—General M
Educational Leadership and Administration M
Elementary Education M
Finance and Banking M
Human Resources Management M
International Business M
Leisure Studies M
Management Information Systems M
Marketing M
Physical Education M
Recreation and Park Management M
Secondary Education M
Special Education M

UNIVERSIDAD NACIONAL PEDRO HENRIQUEZ URENA
Project Management M
Science Education M

UNIVERSITÉ DE MONCTON
Business Administration and Management—General M
Counselor Education M
Education—General M
Educational Leadership and Administration M
Educational Psychology M
Social Work M

UNIVERSITÉ DE MONTRÉAL
Curriculum and Instruction M,D,O
Education—General M,D,O
Educational Leadership and Administration M,D,O
Educational Psychology M,D,O
Electronic Commerce M,D
Human Services D
Information Studies M,D,O
Kinesiology and Movement Studies M,D,O
Law M,D,O
Library Science M,D
Physical Education M,D,O
Social Work O
Taxation M,D,O

UNIVERSITÉ DE SHERBROOKE
Accounting M
Business Administration and Management—General M,D,O
Education—General M,O
Educational Leadership and Administration M
Electronic Commerce M
Elementary Education M,O
Finance and Banking M
Health Law M,D,O
Higher Education M,O
International Business M
Kinesiology and Movement Studies M,O
Law M,D,O
Management Information Systems M,O
Marketing M
Organizational Behavior M
Physical Education M,O
Social Work M
Special Education M,O
Taxation M,O

UNIVERSITÉ DU QUÉBEC À CHICOUTIMI
Business Administration and Management—General M
Education—General M,D
Project Management M

UNIVERSITÉ DU QUÉBEC À MONTRÉAL
Accounting M,O
Actuarial Science O
Business Administration and Management—General M,D,O
Education—General M,D,O
Environmental Education M,D,O
Finance and Banking O
Kinesiology and Movement Studies M
Law O
Management Information Systems M
Project Management M,O
Social Work M

UNIVERSITÉ DU QUÉBEC À RIMOUSKI
Business Administration and Management—General M,O
Education—General M,D,O
Project Management M,O

UNIVERSITÉ DU QUÉBEC À TROIS-RIVIÈRES
Accounting M
Business Administration and Management—General M,D
Education—General M,D
Educational Leadership and Administration O
Educational Psychology M,D
Finance and Banking O
Leisure Studies M,O
Physical Education M
Travel and Tourism M,O

UNIVERSITÉ DU QUÉBEC, ÉCOLE NATIONALE D'ADMINISTRATION PUBLIQUE
International Business M,O

UNIVERSITÉ DU QUÉBEC EN ABITIBI-TÉMISCAMINGUE
Business Administration and Management—General M
Education—General M,D,O
Project Management M,O
Social Work M

UNIVERSITÉ DU QUÉBEC EN OUTAOUAIS
Accounting M,O
Adult Education O
Education—General M,D,O
Educational Psychology M
Finance and Banking M,O
Foreign Languages Education O
Project Management M,O
Social Work M

UNIVERSITÉ LAVAL
Accounting M,O
Advertising and Public Relations O
Business Administration and Management—General M,D,O
Counselor Education M,D
Curriculum and Instruction M,D
Education—General M,D,O
Educational Leadership and Administration M,D,O
Educational Measurement and Evaluation M,D,O
Educational Media/Instructional Technology M,D
Educational Psychology M,D
Electronic Commerce M,O
Entrepreneurship M,O
Facilities Management M,O
Finance and Banking M,O
International Business M,O
Kinesiology and Movement Studies M,D
Law M,D,O
Legal and Justice Studies O
Management Information Systems M,O
Marketing M,O
Music Education M,D
Organizational Management M,D
Social Work M,D

UNIVERSITY AT ALBANY, STATE UNIVERSITY OF NEW YORK
Accounting M
Business Administration and Management—General M
Counselor Education M,D,O
Curriculum and Instruction M,D,O
Education—General M,D,O
Educational Leadership and Administration M,D,O
Educational Measurement and Evaluation M,D,O
Educational Media/Instructional Technology M,D,O
Educational Psychology M,D,O
Finance and Banking M
Human Resources Management M
Information Studies M,O
Marketing M
Mathematics Education M,D
Reading Education M,D,O
Science Education M,D
Social Work M,D
Special Education M
Taxation M

UNIVERSITY AT BUFFALO, THE STATE UNIVERSITY OF NEW YORK
Accounting M,D
Business Administration and Management—General M,D
Counselor Education M,D,O
Early Childhood Education M,D,O
Education of the Gifted M,D,O
Education—General M,D,O
Educational Leadership and Administration M,D,O
Educational Media/Instructional Technology M,D,O
Educational Psychology M,D,O
Electronic Commerce M,D,O
Elementary Education M,D,O
English as a Second Language M,D,O
English Education M,D,O
Exercise and Sports Science M,D,O
Finance and Banking M,D
Foreign Languages Education M,D,O
Foundations and Philosophy of Education M,D,O
Higher Education M,D,O
Human Resources Management M,D,O
Information Studies M,O
International Business M,D,O
Law M,D
Library Science M,O
Logistics M,D
Management Information Systems M,D,O
Mathematics Education M,D,O
Multilingual and Multicultural Education M,D,O
Music Education M,D,O
Reading Education M,D,O
Science Education M,D,O
Social Sciences Education M,D,O
Social Work M,D*
Special Education M,D,O

THE UNIVERSITY OF AKRON
Accounting M
Business Administration and Management—General M
Counselor Education M,D
Education—General M,D
Educational Leadership and Administration M,D
Electronic Commerce M
Elementary Education M,D
Entrepreneurship M
Exercise and Sports Science M
Finance and Banking M
Higher Education M
Human Resources Management M
International Business M
Law M,D
Management Information Systems M
Marketing M
Music Education M
Physical Education M
Secondary Education M,D
Social Work M
Special Education M
Supply Chain Management M
Taxation M
Vocational and Technical Education M

THE UNIVERSITY OF ALABAMA
Accounting M,D
Advertising and Public Relations M
Business Administration and Management—General M,D
Counselor Education M,D,O
Education of the Gifted M,D,O
Educational Leadership and Administration M,D,O
Elementary Education M,D,O
English as a Second Language M,D
Exercise and Sports Science M,D
Finance and Banking M,D
Health Education M,D
Higher Education M,D
Hospitality Management M
Industrial and Manufacturing Management M,D
Information Studies M,D
Kinesiology and Movement Studies M,D
Law M,D
Library Science M,D
Marketing M,D
Music Education M,D,O
Physical Education M,D
Quality Management M
Secondary Education M,D,O
Social Work M,D
Special Education M,D,O
Sports Management M,D
Taxation M,D

THE UNIVERSITY OF ALABAMA AT BIRMINGHAM
Accounting M
Art Education M
Business Administration and Management—General M
Counselor Education M
Curriculum and Instruction O
Early Childhood Education M,D
Education—General M,D,O
Educational Leadership and Administration M,D,O
Elementary Education M
Health Education M,D
Physical Education M
Secondary Education M
Special Education M

THE UNIVERSITY OF ALABAMA IN HUNTSVILLE
Accounting M,O
Business Administration and Management—General M,O
English Education M,O
Entrepreneurship M,O
Finance and Banking M,O
Human Resources Management M,O
Logistics M,O
Management Information Systems M,O
Marketing M,O
Mathematics Education M,D
Project Management M,O
Reading Education M,O
Science Education M,D
Social Sciences Education M
Supply Chain Management M,O
Taxation M

UNIVERSITY OF ALASKA ANCHORAGE
Adult Education M
Business Administration and Management—General M
Counselor Education M
Early Childhood Education M,O
Education—General M,O
Educational Leadership and Administration M,O
Logistics M,O
Project Management M
Social Work M,O
Special Education M,O

UNIVERSITY OF ALASKA FAIRBANKS
Business Administration and Management—General M
Counselor Education M
Curriculum and Instruction M,O
Education—General M,O
Elementary Education M,O
English Education M,O
Finance and Banking M
Multilingual and Multicultural Education M,O
Music Education M
Reading Education M,O
Secondary Education M,O
Special Education M,O

UNIVERSITY OF ALASKA SOUTHEAST
Business Administration and Management—General M
Early Childhood Education M
Education—General M
Educational Media/Instructional Technology M
Elementary Education M
Secondary Education M

UNIVERSITY OF ALBERTA
Accounting D
Adult Education M,D,O
Business Administration and Management—General M,D
Counselor Education M,D
Educational Leadership and Administration M,D,O
Educational Media/Instructional Technology M,D
Educational Policy M,D,O
Educational Psychology M,D
Elementary Education M,D
English as a Second Language M,D
Exercise and Sports Science M,D
Finance and Banking M,D
Information Studies M
International Business M
Law M,D
Library Science M
Marketing D
Multilingual and Multicultural Education M
Organizational Management D
Physical Education M,D
Recreation and Park Management M,D
Secondary Education M,D
Special Education M,D
Sports Management M

THE UNIVERSITY OF ARIZONA
Accounting M
Agricultural Education M
Art Education M
Business Administration and Management—General M,D
Counselor Education M,D
Education—General M,D,O
Educational Leadership and Administration M,D,O
Educational Psychology M,D,O
English as a Second Language M,D
English Education D
Finance and Banking M,D
Higher Education M,D
Information Studies M,D
Law M,D
Library Science M,D
Management Information Systems M
Management Strategy and Policy D
Marketing M,D
Multilingual and Multicultural Education M,D,O
Music Education M,D
Reading Education M,D,O
Special Education M,D,O

UNIVERSITY OF ARKANSAS
Accounting M
Agricultural Education M
Athletic Training and Sports Medicine M
Business Administration and Management—General M,D
Counselor Education M,D,O
Curriculum and Instruction D
Early Childhood Education M
Education—General M,D,O
Educational Leadership and Administration M,D,O
Educational Measurement and Evaluation M,D
Educational Media/Instructional Technology M
Educational Policy D
Elementary Education M,O
Health Education M,D
Higher Education M,D,O
Industrial and Manufacturing Management M
Kinesiology and Movement Studies M,D
Law M,D
Management Information Systems M
Mathematics Education M
Middle School Education M,D,O
Physical Education M
Recreation and Park Management M,D
Secondary Education M,O
Social Work M
Special Education M
Vocational and Technical Education M,D

UNIVERSITY OF ARKANSAS AT LITTLE ROCK
Accounting M,O
Adult Education M
Art Education M
Business Administration and Management—General M,O
Counselor Education M
Early Childhood Education M
Education of the Gifted M
Education—General M,D,O
Educational Leadership and Administration M,D,O
Educational Media/Instructional Technology M
English as a Second Language M
Foreign Languages Education M
Higher Education D
Law D
Management Information Systems M,O
Middle School Education M
Nonprofit Management O
Reading Education M,O
Secondary Education M
Social Work M
Special Education M,O
Taxation M,O

UNIVERSITY OF ARKANSAS AT MONTICELLO
Education—General M
Educational Leadership and Administration M

UNIVERSITY OF ARKANSAS AT PINE BLUFF
Early Childhood Education M
Education—General M
English Education M
Mathematics Education M
Physical Education M
Science Education M
Secondary Education M
Social Sciences Education M

UNIVERSITY OF ATLANTA
Business Administration and Management—General M,D,O
Educational Leadership and Administration M,D,O
Law M,D,O
Management Information Systems M,D,O
Project Management M,D,O

UNIVERSITY OF BALTIMORE
Accounting M,O
Business Administration and Management—General M,O
Finance and Banking M
Human Services M
Law M,D
Legal and Justice Studies M
Management Information Systems M,O
Marketing M
Taxation M,D

UNIVERSITY OF BRIDGEPORT
Accounting M
Business Administration and Management—General M
Computer Education M,D,O
Early Childhood Education M,D,O
Education—General M,D,O
Educational Leadership and Administration M,D,O
Elementary Education M,D,O
Entrepreneurship M
Finance and Banking M
Human Resources Development M
Human Resources Management M
Human Services M
Industrial and Manufacturing Management M
International and Comparative Education M,D,O
International Business M
Management Information Systems M
Marketing M
Middle School Education M,D,O
Music Education M,D,O
Reading Education M,D,O
Secondary Education M,D,O
Student Affairs M

THE UNIVERSITY OF BRITISH COLUMBIA
Accounting D
Adult Education M,D
Archives/Archival Administration M,D
Art Education M,D
Business Administration and Management—General M,D
Business Education M,D
Curriculum and Instruction M,D
Early Childhood Education M,D
Education—General M,D,O
Educational Leadership and Administration M,D
Educational Measurement and Evaluation M,D,O
Educational Policy M,D
English as a Second Language M,D
Finance and Banking D
Foundations and Philosophy of Education M,D
Higher Education M,D
Home Economics Education M,D
Information Studies M,D
International Business D
Kinesiology and Movement Studies M,D
Law M,D
Library Science M,D
Management Information Systems D
Management Strategy and Policy D
Marketing D
Mathematics Education M,D
Music Education M,D
Organizational Behavior D
Physical Education M,D
Quantitative Analysis M,D
Reading Education M,D
Science Education M,D
Social Sciences Education M,D
Social Work M,D
Special Education M,D,O
Transportation Management D
Vocational and Technical Education M,D

UNIVERSITY OF CALGARY
Business Administration and Management—General M,D
Curriculum and Instruction M,D,O
Education of the Gifted M,D,O
Educational Leadership and Administration M,D,O
Educational Measurement and Evaluation M,D,O
Educational Media/Instructional Technology M,D,O
English as a Second Language M,D,O
Environmental Law M,O
Exercise and Sports Science M,D
Foreign Languages Education M,D,O
Foundations and Philosophy of Education M,D,O
Health Education M,D
Higher Education M,D,O
Kinesiology and Movement Studies M,D
Law M,D,O
Legal and Justice Studies M,O
Management Strategy and Policy M,D
Social Work M,D,O
Special Education M,D
Vocational and Technical Education M,D,O

UNIVERSITY OF CALIFORNIA, BERKELEY
Accounting D,O
Business Administration and Management—General M,D,O
Education—General M,D,O
English as a Second Language O
Facilities Management O
Finance and Banking D,O
Human Resources Management O
Industrial and Manufacturing Management D
Information Studies M,D
International Business O
Law M,D
Legal and Justice Studies D
Management Information Systems O
Marketing D,O
Mathematics Education M,D
Organizational Behavior D
Project Management O
Real Estate D
Science Education M,D
Social Work M,D
Special Education M,D
Sustainability Management O

UNIVERSITY OF CALIFORNIA, DAVIS
Business Administration and Management—General M
Curriculum and Instruction M,D
Education—General M,D
Educational Psychology M,D
Exercise and Sports Science M
Law M,D
Transportation Management M,D

UNIVERSITY OF CALIFORNIA, HASTINGS COLLEGE OF THE LAW
Law M,D

UNIVERSITY OF CALIFORNIA, IRVINE
Business Administration and Management—General M,D
Education—General M,D
Educational Leadership and Administration M,D
Elementary Education M,D
Foreign Languages Education M,D
Law D
Secondary Education M,D

UNIVERSITY OF CALIFORNIA, LOS ANGELES
Accounting M,D
Archives/Archival Administration M,D,O
Business Administration and Management—General M,D*
Education—General M,D
Educational Leadership and Administration D
English as a Second Language M,D,O
Finance and Banking M,D
Human Resources Development M,D
Industrial and Manufacturing Management M,D
Information Studies M,D,O
International Business M,D
Law M,D
Library Science M,D,O
Management Information Systems M,D
Management Strategy and Policy M,D
Marketing M,D
Organizational Behavior M,D
Social Work M,D
Special Education D

UNIVERSITY OF CALIFORNIA, RIVERSIDE
Archives/Archival Administration M,D
Business Administration and Management—General M
Education—General M,D
Educational Leadership and Administration M,D
Educational Psychology M,D
Foundations and Philosophy of Education M,D
Higher Education M,D
Multilingual and Multicultural Education M,D
Reading Education M,D
Special Education M,D

UNIVERSITY OF CALIFORNIA, SAN DIEGO
Business Administration and Management—General M
Education—General M,D
Health Law M
Law M
Legal and Justice Studies M
Mathematics Education D
Science Education D

UNIVERSITY OF CALIFORNIA, SANTA BARBARA
Education—General M,D,O
Educational Leadership and Administration M,D,O
Educational Measurement and Evaluation M,D,O
International and Comparative Education M,D,O
Quantitative Analysis M,D
Special Education M,D,O
Transportation Management M,D

UNIVERSITY OF CALIFORNIA, SANTA CRUZ
Education—General M,D
Finance and Banking M
Management Information Systems M,D
Social Sciences Education M

UNIVERSITY OF CENTRAL ARKANSAS
Accounting M
Business Administration and Management—General M
Counselor Education M
Education—General M,O
Educational Leadership and Administration M,O
Educational Media/Instructional Technology M
Foreign Languages Education M
Health Education M
Kinesiology and Movement Studies M
Library Science M
Mathematics Education M
Music Education M,O
Organizational Management D
Reading Education M
Special Education M
Student Affairs M

UNIVERSITY OF CENTRAL FLORIDA
Accounting M
Actuarial Science M,O
Art Education M
Business Administration and Management—General M,D,O
Community College Education M,D,O
Counselor Education M,D,O
Early Childhood Education M
Education of the Gifted M,O
Educational Leadership and Administration M,D,O
Educational Media/Instructional Technology M,D,O
Elementary Education M,D
English as a Second Language M,D,O
English Education M
Entrepreneurship M,O
Exercise and Sports Science M,D
Higher Education M,D
Hospitality Management M,O
International and Comparative Education M,O
Mathematics Education M,D,O
Middle School Education M
Nonprofit Management M,O
Reading Education M,D,O
Science Education M,D,O
Social Sciences Education M,D
Social Work M,O
Special Education M,D,O
Sports Management M
Student Affairs M,D
Taxation M
Travel and Tourism M,O
Urban Education M,O
Vocational and Technical Education M

UNIVERSITY OF CENTRAL MISSOURI
Accounting M
Business Administration and Management—General M
Counselor Education M,D,O
Curriculum and Instruction M,D,O
Education—General M,D,O
Educational Leadership and Administration M,D,O

*M—master's degree; P—first professional degree; D—doctorate; O—other advanced degree; *Close-Up and/or Display*

Educational Media/Instructional Technology	M,D,O
Elementary Education	M,D,O
English as a Second Language	M
Exercise and Sports Science	M
Finance and Banking	M
Foundations and Philosophy of Education	M,D,O
Human Services	M,D,O
Industrial and Manufacturing Management	M,D
Library Science	M,D,O
Management Information Systems	M
Management Strategy and Policy	M
Marketing	M
Physical Education	M
Reading Education	M,D,O
Secondary Education	M,D,O
Special Education	M,D,O
Student Affairs	M,D,O
Vocational and Technical Education	M,D,O

UNIVERSITY OF CENTRAL OKLAHOMA

Adult Education	M
Athletic Training and Sports Medicine	M
Computer Education	M
Counselor Education	M
Early Childhood Education	M
Education—General	M
Educational Leadership and Administration	M
Educational Media/Instructional Technology	M
Elementary Education	M
English as a Second Language	M
Health Education	M
Higher Education	M
Home Economics Education	M
Library Science	M
Mathematics Education	M
Music Education	M
Reading Education	M
Secondary Education	M
Special Education	M

UNIVERSITY OF CHARLESTON

Accounting	M
Business Administration and Management—General	M
Legal and Justice Studies	M

UNIVERSITY OF CHICAGO

Accounting	M,D,O
Business Administration and Management—General	M,D,O
Entrepreneurship	M,D,O
Finance and Banking	M,D,O
Human Resources Management	M,D,O
International Business	M,D,O
Law	M,D
Management Strategy and Policy	M,D,O
Marketing	M,D,O
Organizational Behavior	M,D,O
Science Education	D
Social Work	M,D
Urban Education	M

UNIVERSITY OF CINCINNATI

Accounting	M,D
Adult Education	M,D,O
Art Education	M
Business Administration and Management—General	M,D
Counselor Education	M,D,O
Curriculum and Instruction	M,D
Early Childhood Education	M
Education—General	M,D,O
Educational Leadership and Administration	M,D,O
Elementary Education	M
English as a Second Language	M,D,O
Finance and Banking	D
Foundations and Philosophy of Education	M,D
Health Education	M,D
Industrial and Manufacturing Management	D
Law	D
Management Information Systems	M,D
Marketing	M,D
Mathematics Education	M,D
Music Education	M
Organizational Management	M
Quantitative Analysis	M,D
Reading Education	M,D
Science Education	M,D,O
Secondary Education	M
Social Sciences Education	M,D,O
Social Work	M
Special Education	M,D

UNIVERSITY OF COLORADO AT COLORADO SPRINGS

Athletic Training and Sports Medicine	M
Business Administration and Management—General	M
Counselor Education	M,D
Curriculum and Instruction	M,D
Education—General	M,D
Educational Leadership and Administration	M,D
Human Services	M,D
Special Education	M,D

UNIVERSITY OF COLORADO BOULDER

Accounting	M,D
Business Administration and Management—General	M
Curriculum and Instruction	M,D
Education—General	M,D
Educational Measurement and Evaluation	D
Educational Policy	M,D
Educational Psychology	M,D
Entrepreneurship	M,D
Finance and Banking	M,D
Kinesiology and Movement Studies	M,D
Law	D
Management Information Systems	M,D
Marketing	M,D
Multilingual and Multicultural Education	M,D
Music Education	M,D
Organizational Management	M,D

UNIVERSITY OF COLORADO DENVER

Accounting	M
Adult Education	M
Business Administration and Management—General	M
Counselor Education	M
Distance Education Development	M
Early Childhood Education	M,D
Education—General	M,D,O
Educational Leadership and Administration	M,D,O
Educational Measurement and Evaluation	M,D,O
Educational Media/Instructional Technology	M
Educational Policy	D
Educational Psychology	M,O
Electronic Commerce	M
Elementary Education	M
English Education	M
Entertainment Management	M
Entrepreneurship	M,D
Environmental Education	M
Environmental Law	M,D
Finance and Banking	M
Health Education	M,D
Human Resources Management	M
Insurance	M
International Business	M
Investment Management	M
Management Information Systems	M,D
Management Strategy and Policy	M
Marketing Research	M
Marketing	M
Mathematics Education	M,D
Multilingual and Multicultural Education	M
Nonprofit Management	M,D
Quantitative Analysis	M
Reading Education	M
Science Education	M,D
Secondary Education	M
Special Education	M,D
Sports Management	M
Sustainability Management	M

UNIVERSITY OF CONNECTICUT

Accounting	M,D
Actuarial Science	M,D
Adult Education	M,D
Agricultural Education	M,D,O
Business Administration and Management—General	M,D*
Counselor Education	M,D,O
Education of the Gifted	M,D,O
Education—General	M,D,O
Educational Leadership and Administration	D,O
Educational Measurement and Evaluation	M,D,O
Educational Media/Instructional Technology	M,D,O
Educational Psychology	M,D,O
Elementary Education	M,D,O
English Education	M,D,O
Exercise and Sports Science	M,D
Finance and Banking	M,D,O
Foreign Languages Education	M,D,O
Foundations and Philosophy of Education	D
Higher Education	M
Human Resources Development	M
Human Resources Management	M
Law	D
Leisure Studies	M,D
Marketing	M,D
Mathematics Education	M,D,O
Multilingual and Multicultural Education	M,D,O
Music Education	M,D,O
Nonprofit Management	M,O
Quantitative Analysis	M,O
Reading Education	M,D,O
Science Education	M,D
Secondary Education	M,D,O
Social Sciences Education	M,D,O
Special Education	M,D,O

UNIVERSITY OF DALLAS

Accounting	M
Business Administration and Management—General	M
Entertainment Management	M
Finance and Banking	M
Human Resources Management	M
International Business	M
Logistics	M
Management Information Systems	M
Management Strategy and Policy	M
Marketing	M
Organizational Management	M
Project Management	M
Sports Management	M
Supply Chain Management	M

UNIVERSITY OF DAYTON

Accounting	M
Art Education	M
Business Administration and Management—General	M
Counselor Education	M,O
Early Childhood Education	M
Educational Leadership and Administration	M,D,O
Educational Media/Instructional Technology	M
Exercise and Sports Science	M,D
Finance and Banking	M
Law	M,D
Marketing	M
Mathematics Education	M
Middle School Education	M
Music Education	M
Physical Education	M,D
Reading Education	M
Secondary Education	M
Special Education	M
Student Affairs	M,O

UNIVERSITY OF DELAWARE

Accounting	M
Agricultural Education	M
Business Administration and Management—General	M,D
Business Education	M,D
Curriculum and Instruction	M,D,O
Education—General	M,D,O
Educational Leadership and Administration	M,D,O
English as a Second Language	M,D,O
Entrepreneurship	M,D
Finance and Banking	M
Foreign Languages Education	M
Higher Education	M,D,O
Hospitality Management	M
Kinesiology and Movement Studies	M,D
Management Information Systems	M
Multilingual and Multicultural Education	M,D,O
Music Education	M

UNIVERSITY OF DENVER

Accounting	M
Advertising and Public Relations	M,O
Business Administration and Management—General	M
Curriculum and Instruction	M,D,O
Education—General	M,D,O
Educational Leadership and Administration	M,D,O
Educational Policy	M,D,O
Finance and Banking	M
Health Law	M,O
Higher Education	M,D,O
Human Resources Development	M,O
Human Resources Management	M,O
International Business	M,D,O
Law	M,D,O
Legal and Justice Studies	M,O
Library Science	M,D,O
Management Information Systems	M,O
Management Strategy and Policy	M
Marketing	M
Music Education	M,O
Organizational Management	M,O
Project Management	M,O
Real Estate	M
Social Work	M,D,O
Taxation	M

UNIVERSITY OF DETROIT MERCY

Business Administration and Management—General	M,O
Computer Education	M
Counselor Education	M
Curriculum and Instruction	M
Education—General	M
Educational Leadership and Administration	M
Law	D
Management Information Systems	M
Mathematics Education	M
Special Education	M

UNIVERSITY OF DUBUQUE

Business Administration and Management—General	M

UNIVERSITY OF EVANSVILLE

Business Administration and Management—General	M
Education—General	M

THE UNIVERSITY OF FINDLAY

Athletic Training and Sports Medicine	M
Business Administration and Management—General	M
Early Childhood Education	M
Education—General	M
Educational Leadership and Administration	M
Educational Media/Instructional Technology	M
English as a Second Language	M
Hospitality Management	M
Multilingual and Multicultural Education	M
Organizational Management	M
Reading Education	M
Science Education	M
Special Education	M

UNIVERSITY OF FLORIDA

Accounting	M,D
Advertising and Public Relations	M
Agricultural Education	M,D
Athletic Training and Sports Medicine	M,D
Business Administration and Management—General	M,D
Counselor Education	M,D,O
Curriculum and Instruction	M,D,O
Early Childhood Education	M,D,O
Education—General	M,D,O
Educational Leadership and Administration	M,D,O
Educational Measurement and Evaluation	M,D,O
Educational Psychology	M,D,O
Electronic Commerce	M
Elementary Education	M,D,O
English as a Second Language	M,D,O
English Education	M,D,O
Environmental Law	M,D
Exercise and Sports Science	M,D
Finance and Banking	M,D,O
Foundations and Philosophy of Education	M,D,O
Health Education	M,D,O
Higher Education	M,D,O
Human Resources Management	M
Insurance	M,D,O
International Business	M,D
Kinesiology and Movement Studies	M,D
Law	M,D
Management Information Systems	M,D
Management Strategy and Policy	M
Marketing	M,D
Mathematics Education	M,D,O
Multilingual and Multicultural Education	M,D,O
Music Education	M,D
Physical Education	M,D
Quantitative Analysis	M
Reading Education	M,D,O
Real Estate	M,D,O
Recreation and Park Management	M,D
Science Education	M,D,O
Social Sciences Education	M,D,O
Special Education	M,D,O
Sports Management	M,D
Student Affairs	M,D,O
Supply Chain Management	M,D
Taxation	M,D

UNIVERSITY OF GEORGIA

Accounting	M
Adult Education	M,D,O
Agricultural Education	M
Art Education	M,D,O
Business Administration and Management—General	M,D
Counselor Education	M,D,O
Early Childhood Education	M,D,O
Education—General	M,D,O
Educational Leadership and Administration	M,D,O
Educational Media/Instructional Technology	M,D,O
Educational Policy	M,D,O
Educational Psychology	M,D,O
Elementary Education	M,D,O
English Education	M,D,O
Foreign Languages Education	M,D,O
Foundations and Philosophy of Education	M,D,O
Health Education	M,D
Higher Education	D
Human Resources Management	M,D,O
Kinesiology and Movement Studies	M,D
Law	M,D
Leisure Studies	M,D,O
Management Information Systems	D
Mathematics Education	M,D,O
Middle School Education	M,D,O
Music Education	M,D,O
Nonprofit Management	M,D,O
Physical Education	M,D
Reading Education	M,D,O
Science Education	M,D,O
Social Sciences Education	M,D,O
Social Work	M,D,O
Special Education	M,D,O
Student Affairs	M,D,O
Vocational and Technical Education	M,D,O

UNIVERSITY OF GREAT FALLS

Education—General	M
Human Services	M
Secondary Education	M

UNIVERSITY OF GUAM

Business Administration and Management—General	M
Counselor Education	M
Education—General	M
Educational Leadership and Administration	M
English as a Second Language	M
Reading Education	M
Secondary Education	M
Social Work	M
Special Education	M

UNIVERSITY OF GUELPH

Business Administration and Management—General	M,D
Hospitality Management	M
Organizational Management	M

UNIVERSITY OF HARTFORD

Accounting	M,O
Business Administration and Management—General	M
Counselor Education	M,O
Early Childhood Education	M
Education—General	M,D,O
Educational Leadership and Administration	D,O
Educational Media/Instructional Technology	M
Elementary Education	M
Music Education	M,D,O
Organizational Behavior	M
Taxation	M,O

UNIVERSITY OF HAWAII AT HILO

Education—General	M
Foreign Languages Education	M,D

UNIVERSITY OF HAWAII AT MANOA

Accounting	M,D
Business Administration and Management—General	M
Curriculum and Instruction	M,D
Early Childhood Education	M
Education—General	M,D,O
Educational Leadership and Administration	M,D

Program	Degrees
Educational Media/Instructional Technology	M,D
Educational Policy	D
Educational Psychology	M,D
English as a Second Language	M,D,O
Entrepreneurship	M,O
Finance and Banking	M,D
Foreign Languages Education	M,D,O
Foundations and Philosophy of Education	M,D
Human Resources Management	M
Information Studies	M,O
International Business	M,D
Kinesiology and Movement Studies	M,D
Law	M,D,O
Library Science	M,O
Management Information Systems	M,D,O
Marketing	M,D
Organizational Behavior	M
Organizational Management	M,D
Real Estate	M
Social Work	M,D
Special Education	M,D
Taxation	M
Travel and Tourism	M

UNIVERSITY OF HOUSTON

Program	Degrees
Accounting	M,D
Advertising and Public Relations	M
Business Administration and Management—General	M,D
Curriculum and Instruction	M,D
Education—General	M,D
Educational Leadership and Administration	M,D
Educational Psychology	M,D
Environmental Law	M,D
Exercise and Sports Science	M,D
Finance and Banking	M
Foundations and Philosophy of Education	M,D
Health Education	M,D
Health Law	M,D
Higher Education	M,D
Hospitality Management	M
Human Resources Development	M
Intellectual Property Law	M,D
Kinesiology and Movement Studies	M,D
Law	M,D
Logistics	M
Marketing	D
Music Education	M,D
Physical Education	M,D
Project Management	M
Social Work	M,D
Special Education	M,D
Supply Chain Management	M
Taxation	M,D

UNIVERSITY OF HOUSTON–CLEAR LAKE

Program	Degrees
Accounting	M
Business Administration and Management—General	M
Counselor Education	M
Curriculum and Instruction	M
Early Childhood Education	M
Education—General	M,D
Educational Leadership and Administration	M,D
Educational Media/Instructional Technology	M
Exercise and Sports Science	M
Finance and Banking	M
Foundations and Philosophy of Education	M
Human Resources Management	M
Library Science	M
Management Information Systems	M
Multilingual and Multicultural Education	M
Reading Education	M

UNIVERSITY OF HOUSTON–DOWNTOWN

Program	Degrees
Business Administration and Management—General	M
Curriculum and Instruction	M
Elementary Education	M
Multilingual and Multicultural Education	M
Secondary Education	M
Urban Education	M

UNIVERSITY OF HOUSTON–VICTORIA

Program	Degrees
Accounting	M
Business Administration and Management—General	M
Counselor Education	M
Curriculum and Instruction	M
Education—General	M
Educational Leadership and Administration	M
Entrepreneurship	M
Finance and Banking	M
International Business	M
Marketing	M
Special Education	M

UNIVERSITY OF IDAHO

Program	Degrees
Accounting	M
Agricultural Education	M
Art Education	M
Athletic Training and Sports Medicine	M,D
Business Administration and Management—General	M
Counselor Education	M
Curriculum and Instruction	M,O
Education—General	M,D,O
Educational Leadership and Administration	M,O
English as a Second Language	M
Environmental Law	D
Law	D
Physical Education	M
Recreation and Park Management	M
Special Education	M

UNIVERSITY OF ILLINOIS AT CHICAGO

Program	Degrees
Accounting	M
Business Administration and Management—General	M,D
Curriculum and Instruction	M,D
Education—General	M,D
Educational Leadership and Administration	M,D
Educational Policy	M,D
Educational Psychology	D
Elementary Education	M,D
English as a Second Language	M
English Education	M,D
Health Education	M
Kinesiology and Movement Studies	M,D
Management Information Systems	M,D
Mathematics Education	M
Multilingual and Multicultural Education	M,D
Quantitative Analysis	M,D
Reading Education	M,D
Real Estate	M
Secondary Education	M,D
Social Work	M,D
Special Education	M,D
Urban Education	M,D

UNIVERSITY OF ILLINOIS AT SPRINGFIELD

Program	Degrees
Accounting	M
Business Administration and Management—General	M
Education—General	M
Educational Leadership and Administration	M
Human Services	M
Legal and Justice Studies	M
Management Information Systems	M

UNIVERSITY OF ILLINOIS AT URBANA–CHAMPAIGN

Program	Degrees
Accounting	M,D
Actuarial Science	M,D
Advertising and Public Relations	M
Agricultural Education	M,D
Art Education	M,D
Business Administration and Management—General	M,D
Counselor Education	M,D,O
Curriculum and Instruction	M,D,O
Education of Students with Severe/Multiple Disabilities	M,D,O
Education—General	M,D,O
Educational Leadership and Administration	M,D,O
Educational Policy	M,D,O
Educational Psychology	M,D,O
English as a Second Language	M,D
Finance and Banking	M,D
Foreign Languages Education	M,D
Human Resources Development	M,D,O
Human Resources Management	M,D,O
Information Studies	M,D,O
Kinesiology and Movement Studies	M,D
Law	M,D
Leisure Studies	M,D
Library Science	M,D,O
Management Strategy and Policy	M,D,O
Mathematics Education	M,D
Music Education	M,D
Science Education	M,D
Social Work	M,D
Special Education	M,D,O
Taxation	M,D
Vocational and Technical Education	M,D,O

UNIVERSITY OF INDIANAPOLIS

Program	Degrees
Art Education	M
Business Administration and Management—General	M,O
Curriculum and Instruction	M
Education—General	M
Educational Leadership and Administration	M
Elementary Education	M
English Education	M
Foreign Languages Education	M
Mathematics Education	M
Physical Education	M
Science Education	M
Secondary Education	M
Social Sciences Education	M

THE UNIVERSITY OF IOWA

Program	Degrees
Accounting	M,D
Actuarial Science	M,D
Art Education	M,D
Business Administration and Management—General	M,D
Counselor Education	M,D
Curriculum and Instruction	M,D
Developmental Education	M,D
Early Childhood Education	M,D
Education—General	M,D,O
Educational Leadership and Administration	M,D,O
Educational Measurement and Evaluation	M,D,O
Educational Policy	M,D,O
Educational Psychology	M,D,O
Elementary Education	M,D
English Education	M,D
Exercise and Sports Science	M,D
Finance and Banking	M,D
Foreign Languages Education	M,D
Foundations and Philosophy of Education	M,D,O
Higher Education	M,D,O
Information Studies	M
Investment Management	M
Law	M,D
Leisure Studies	M
Library Science	M
Management Strategy and Policy	M
Marketing	M,D
Mathematics Education	M,D
Physical Education	M,D
Recreation and Park Management	M
Science Education	M,D
Secondary Education	M,D
Social Sciences Education	M,D
Social Work	M,D
Special Education	M,D
Sports Management	M
Student Affairs	M,D

THE UNIVERSITY OF KANSAS

Program	Degrees
Accounting	M
Art Education	M
Business Administration and Management—General	M,D
Curriculum and Instruction	M,D
Education—General	M,D,O
Educational Leadership and Administration	M,D
Educational Measurement and Evaluation	M,D
Educational Policy	D
Educational Psychology	M,D
Facilities Management	M,D,O
Foundations and Philosophy of Education	D
Health Education	M,D,O
Higher Education	M,D
Law	D
Management Information Systems	M,D
Music Education	M,D
Organizational Management	M,D,O
Physical Education	M,D
Social Work	M,D
Special Education	M,D

UNIVERSITY OF KENTUCKY

Program	Degrees
Accounting	M
Art Education	M
Business Administration and Management—General	M,D
Curriculum and Instruction	M,D
Early Childhood Education	M,D
Education—General	M,D,O
Educational Leadership and Administration	M,D,O
Educational Measurement and Evaluation	M,D
Educational Media/Instructional Technology	M,D
Educational Policy	M,D
Educational Psychology	M,D,O
Exercise and Sports Science	M,D
Foreign Languages Education	M
Higher Education	M,D
Hospitality Management	M
International Business	M
Kinesiology and Movement Studies	M,D
Law	D
Library Science	M*
Middle School Education	M,D
Music Education	M,D
Social Work	M,D
Special Education	M,D
Vocational and Technical Education	M

UNIVERSITY OF LA VERNE

Program	Degrees
Accounting	M
Business Administration and Management—General	M,O
Counselor Education	M,O
Education—General	M,O
Educational Leadership and Administration	M,D,O
Finance and Banking	M
International Business	M
Law	D
Management Information Systems	M
Marketing	M
Multilingual and Multicultural Education	O
Nonprofit Management	M,O
Organizational Management	M,D,O
Reading Education	M,O
Student Affairs	M

UNIVERSITY OF LETHBRIDGE

Program	Degrees
Accounting	M,D
Business Administration and Management—General	M,D
Education—General	M,D
Educational Leadership and Administration	M,D
Exercise and Sports Science	M,D
Finance and Banking	M,D
Human Resources Management	M,D
International Business	M,D
Kinesiology and Movement Studies	M,D
Management Information Systems	M,D
Management Strategy and Policy	M,D

UNIVERSITY OF LOUISIANA AT LAFAYETTE

Program	Degrees
Business Administration and Management—General	M
Counselor Education	M
Curriculum and Instruction	M
Education of the Gifted	M
Education—General	M,D
Educational Leadership and Administration	M,D
Music Education	M

UNIVERSITY OF LOUISIANA AT MONROE

Program	Degrees
Business Administration and Management—General	M
Counselor Education	M
Curriculum and Instruction	M,D
Education of the Gifted	M,D
Education—General	M,D,O
Educational Leadership and Administration	D
Educational Measurement and Evaluation	M,D
Elementary Education	M,D
Exercise and Sports Science	M
Middle School Education	M
Reading Education	M,D
Secondary Education	M

UNIVERSITY OF LOUISVILLE

Program	Degrees
Accounting	M
Art Education	M,D
Business Administration and Management—General	M
Counselor Education	M,D
Curriculum and Instruction	M,D
Early Childhood Education	M,D
Education—General	M,D,O
Educational Leadership and Administration	M,D,O
Educational Psychology	M,D
Elementary Education	M,D
Entrepreneurship	M,D
Exercise and Sports Science	M
Health Education	M,D
Higher Education	M,D,O
Human Resources Development	M,D,O
Human Resources Management	M,D
International Business	M
Law	D
Logistics	M,D,O
Middle School Education	M,D
Music Education	M,D
Nonprofit Management	M,D
Physical Education	M
Reading Education	M,D
Secondary Education	M,D
Social Work	M,D,O
Special Education	M,D
Sports Management	M
Student Affairs	M,D
Supply Chain Management	M,D,O

UNIVERSITY OF MAINE

Program	Degrees
Accounting	M
Business Administration and Management—General	M
Counselor Education	M,D,O
Curriculum and Instruction	M
Education—General	M,D,O
Educational Leadership and Administration	M,D,O
Educational Media/Instructional Technology	M
Elementary Education	M,O
English Education	M
Exercise and Sports Science	M
Finance and Banking	M
Foreign Languages Education	M
Higher Education	M,D,O
Kinesiology and Movement Studies	M
Management Information Systems	M
Mathematics Education	M
Physical Education	M
Reading Education	M,D,O
Science Education	M,O
Secondary Education	M,O
Social Sciences Education	M,O
Social Work	M
Special Education	M,O
Sustainability Management	M

UNIVERSITY OF MAINE AT FARMINGTON

Program	Degrees
Early Childhood Education	M
Education—General	M
Educational Leadership and Administration	M

UNIVERSITY OF MANAGEMENT AND TECHNOLOGY

Program	Degrees
Business Administration and Management—General	M,D,O
Management Information Systems	M,O
Project Management	M,D,O

THE UNIVERSITY OF MANCHESTER

Program	Degrees
Accounting	M,D
Actuarial Science	M,D
Business Administration and Management—General	M,D
Education—General	M,D
Educational Psychology	M,D
English as a Second Language	M,D
Health Law	M,D
Industrial and Manufacturing Management	M,D
Law	M,D
Social Work	M,D

UNIVERSITY OF MANITOBA

Program	Degrees
Adult Education	M
Archives/Archival Administration	M,D
Business Administration and Management—General	M,D
Counselor Education	M
Curriculum and Instruction	M
Education—General	M,D
Educational Leadership and Administration	M

*M—master's degree; P—first professional degree; D—doctorate; O—other advanced degree; *Close-Up and/or Display*

Program	Degrees
Educational Psychology	M
English as a Second Language	M
English Education	M
Foundations and Philosophy of Education	M
Higher Education	M
Kinesiology and Movement Studies	M
Law	M
Physical Education	M
Recreation and Park Management	M
Social Work	M,D
Special Education	M

UNIVERSITY OF MARY

Program	Degrees
Accounting	M
Business Administration and Management—General	M
Curriculum and Instruction	M
Early Childhood Education	M
Education—General	M
Educational Leadership and Administration	M
Higher Education	M
Human Resources Management	M
Management Strategy and Policy	M
Project Management	M
Reading Education	M
Special Education	M
Student Affairs	M

UNIVERSITY OF MARY HARDIN-BAYLOR

Program	Degrees
Accounting	M
Business Administration and Management—General	M
Counselor Education	M
Curriculum and Instruction	M,D
Education—General	M,D
Educational Leadership and Administration	M,D
Management Information Systems	M

UNIVERSITY OF MARYLAND, BALTIMORE

Program	Degrees
Law	M,D
Social Work	M,D

UNIVERSITY OF MARYLAND, BALTIMORE COUNTY

Program	Degrees
Art Education	M
Curriculum and Instruction	M,O
Distance Education Development	M,O
Early Childhood Education	M
Education—General	M,O
Educational Media/Instructional Technology	M,O
Educational Policy	M,D
Elementary Education	M
English as a Second Language	M,O
English Education	M
Foreign Languages Education	M
Health Education	M,O
Human Services	M,D
Mathematics Education	M
Multilingual and Multicultural Education	M,D
Music Education	M
Science Education	M
Secondary Education	M
Social Sciences Education	M

UNIVERSITY OF MARYLAND, COLLEGE PARK

Program	Degrees
Advertising and Public Relations	M,D
Business Administration and Management—General	M,D
Counselor Education	M,D,O
Curriculum and Instruction	M,D,O
Early Childhood Education	M,D
Education—General	M,D,O
Educational Leadership and Administration	M,D,O
Educational Measurement and Evaluation	M,D
Educational Media/Instructional Technology	M,D,O
Educational Policy	M,D
Educational Psychology	M,D
English as a Second Language	M,D,O
Foreign Languages Education	D
Foundations and Philosophy of Education	M,D,O
Health Education	M,D
Higher Education	M,D
Information Studies	M,D
International and Comparative Education	M,D
Kinesiology and Movement Studies	M,D
Law	
Library Science	
Music Education	M,D
Reading Education	M,D,O
Real Estate	M
Secondary Education	M,D,O
Social Work	
Special Education	M,D,O
Student Affairs	M,D,O

UNIVERSITY OF MARYLAND EASTERN SHORE

Program	Degrees
Counselor Education	M
Education—General	M
Educational Leadership and Administration	D
Organizational Management	D
Special Education	M
Vocational and Technical Education	M

UNIVERSITY OF MARYLAND UNIVERSITY COLLEGE

Program	Degrees
Accounting	M,O
Business Administration and Management—General	M,D,O
Distance Education Development	M,O
Education—General	M
Finance and Banking	M,O
International Business	M,O
Management Information Systems	M,O

UNIVERSITY OF MARY WASHINGTON

Program	Degrees
Business Administration and Management—General	M
Education—General	M
Management Information Systems	M

UNIVERSITY OF MASSACHUSETTS AMHERST

Program	Degrees
Accounting	M,D
Art Education	M
Business Administration and Management—General	M,D
Counselor Education	M,D,O
Early Childhood Education	M,D,O
Education—General	M,D,O
Educational Leadership and Administration	M,D,O
Educational Measurement and Evaluation	M,D,O
Educational Media/Instructional Technology	M,D,O
Educational Policy	M,D,O
Elementary Education	M,D,O
English as a Second Language	M,D,O
Entertainment Management	M
Finance and Banking	M,D
Foreign Languages Education	M
Health Education	M
Higher Education	M,D,O
Hospitality Management	M,D
International and Comparative Education	M,D,O
Kinesiology and Movement Studies	M,D
Management Strategy and Policy	M,D
Marketing	M,D
Multilingual and Multicultural Education	M,D,O
Music Education	M,D
Organizational Management	M,D
Reading Education	M,D,O
Science Education	M,D,O
Secondary Education	M,D,O
Special Education	M,D,O
Sports Management	M,D
Travel and Tourism	M,D

UNIVERSITY OF MASSACHUSETTS BOSTON

Program	Degrees
Archives/Archival Administration	M
Business Administration and Management—General	M
Counselor Education	M,O
Curriculum and Instruction	M
Education—General	M,D,O
Educational Leadership and Administration	M,D,O
Elementary Education	M,D,O
English as a Second Language	M
Foreign Languages Education	M
Higher Education	M,D,O
Human Services	M
Multilingual and Multicultural Education	M
Secondary Education	M,D,O
Special Education	M
Urban Education	M,D,O

UNIVERSITY OF MASSACHUSETTS DARTMOUTH

Program	Degrees
Accounting	M,O
Art Education	M
Business Administration and Management—General	M,O
Education—General	M,O
Educational Policy	M,O
Elementary Education	M,O
Finance and Banking	M,O
International Business	M,O
Law	D
Marketing	M,O
Mathematics Education	D
Middle School Education	M,O
Organizational Management	M,O
Secondary Education	M,O
Supply Chain Management	M,O

UNIVERSITY OF MASSACHUSETTS LOWELL

Program	Degrees
Business Administration and Management—General	M,O
Curriculum and Instruction	M,D,O
Education—General	M,D,O
Educational Leadership and Administration	M,D,O
Entrepreneurship	M,O
Mathematics Education	M,D,O
Music Education	M
Reading Education	M,D,O
Science Education	M,D,O

UNIVERSITY OF MEDICINE AND DENTISTRY OF NEW JERSEY

Program	Degrees
Health Education	M,D,O
Kinesiology and Movement Studies	M,D
Quantitative Analysis	M,O

UNIVERSITY OF MEMPHIS

Program	Degrees
Accounting	M,D
Adult Education	M,D
Business Administration and Management—General	M,D
Counselor Education	M,D
Curriculum and Instruction	M,D
Early Childhood Education	M,D
Education—General	M,D,O
Educational Leadership and Administration	M,D
Educational Measurement and Evaluation	M,D
Educational Media/Instructional Technology	M,D
Educational Psychology	M,D
Elementary Education	M,D
English as a Second Language	M,D,O
Exercise and Sports Science	M
Finance and Banking	M,D
Higher Education	M,D
International Business	M,D
Law	D
Leisure Studies	M
Management Information Systems	M,D
Marketing	M,D
Middle School Education	M,D
Music Education	M,D
Nonprofit Management	M
Physical Education	M
Reading Education	M,D
Real Estate	M,D
Secondary Education	M,D
Special Education	M,D
Supply Chain Management	M,D
Taxation	M

UNIVERSITY OF MIAMI

Program	Degrees
Accounting	M
Advertising and Public Relations	M,D
Athletic Training and Sports Medicine	M,D
Business Administration and Management—General	M
Counselor Education	M,O
Early Childhood Education	M,O
Education—General	M,D,O
Educational Measurement and Evaluation	M,D
Exercise and Sports Science	M,D
Finance and Banking	M
Higher Education	M,D,O
International Business	M
Law	M,D,O
Management Information Systems	M
Marketing	M
Mathematics Education	D
Multilingual and Multicultural Education	D
Music Education	M,D,O
Reading Education	D
Real Estate	M,D,O
Science Education	D
Special Education	M,D,O
Sports Management	M
Taxation	M,D,O

UNIVERSITY OF MICHIGAN

Program	Degrees
Archives/Archival Administration	M,D
Business Administration and Management—General	D
Education—General	D
Educational Media/Instructional Technology	M,D
English Education	D
Foreign Languages Education	M,D
Health Education	M,D
Information Studies	M,D
Kinesiology and Movement Studies	M,D
Law	M,D
Library Science	M,D
Music Education	M,D,O
Real Estate	M,O
Social Work	M,D
Sports Management	M,D
Taxation	M,D

UNIVERSITY OF MICHIGAN–DEARBORN

Program	Degrees
Accounting	M
Business Administration and Management—General	M
Curriculum and Instruction	D
Education—General	M,D
Educational Leadership and Administration	M,D
Educational Psychology	D
Finance and Banking	M
International Business	M
Management Information Systems	M
Management Strategy and Policy	M
Marketing	M
Project Management	M
Science Education	M
Special Education	M,D
Supply Chain Management	M
Urban Education	M

UNIVERSITY OF MICHIGAN–FLINT

Program	Degrees
Business Administration and Management—General	M
Education—General	M
Educational Media/Instructional Technology	M
Elementary Education	M
Health Education	M
Reading Education	M
Special Education	M

UNIVERSITY OF MINNESOTA, DULUTH

Program	Degrees
Business Administration and Management—General	M
Education—General	D
Music Education	M
Social Work	M

UNIVERSITY OF MINNESOTA, TWIN CITIES CAMPUS

Program	Degrees
Accounting	M,D
Adult Education	M,D,O
Agricultural Education	M,D
Art Education	M,D,O
Business Administration and Management—General	M,D
Business Education	M,D
Counselor Education	M,D,O
Curriculum and Instruction	M,D,O
Early Childhood Education	M,D,O
Education of the Gifted	M,D,O
Education—General	M,D,O
Educational Leadership and Administration	M,D
Educational Measurement and Evaluation	M,D
Educational Media/Instructional Technology	M,D,O
Educational Policy	M,D,O
Educational Psychology	M,D,O
Elementary Education	M,D,O
English as a Second Language	M
English Education	M
Environmental Education	M,D,O
Exercise and Sports Science	M,D,O
Finance and Banking	M,D
Foreign Languages Education	M
Foundations and Philosophy of Education	M,D,O
Higher Education	M,D
Human Resources Development	M,D,O
Human Resources Management	M,D
Industrial and Manufacturing Management	D
International and Comparative Education	M,D
Kinesiology and Movement Studies	M,D
Law	M,D
Leisure Studies	M,D
Management Information Systems	M,D
Management Strategy and Policy	D
Marketing	M,D
Mathematics Education	M
Multilingual and Multicultural Education	M
Physical Education	M,D,O
Quantitative Analysis	M,D,O
Reading Education	M,D,O
Recreation and Park Management	M,D
Science Education	M
Social Sciences Education	M
Social Work	M,D
Special Education	M,D,O
Sports Management	M,D,O
Student Affairs	M,D,O
Supply Chain Management	M
Taxation	M
Vocational and Technical Education	M,D,O

UNIVERSITY OF MISSISSIPPI

Program	Degrees
Accounting	M,D
Art Education	M
Business Administration and Management—General	M,D
Counselor Education	M,D,O
Curriculum and Instruction	M,D,O
Education—General	M,D,O
Educational Leadership and Administration	M,D,O
Exercise and Sports Science	M,D
Higher Education	M,D,O
Law	D
Legal and Justice Studies	M
Leisure Studies	M,D
Management Information Systems	M,D
Recreation and Park Management	M,D
Social Work	M
Student Affairs	M,D,O
Taxation	M,D

UNIVERSITY OF MISSOURI

Program	Degrees
Accounting	M,D
Adult Education	M,D,O
Agricultural Education	M,D,O
Art Education	M,D,O
Business Administration and Management—General	M,D
Business Education	M,D,O
Curriculum and Instruction	M,D,O
Early Childhood Education	M,D,O
Education of the Gifted	M,D
Education—General	M,D,O
Educational Leadership and Administration	M,D,O
Educational Media/Instructional Technology	M,D,O
Educational Psychology	M,D,O
Elementary Education	M,D,O
English Education	M,D,O
Exercise and Sports Science	M,D
Foreign Languages Education	M,D,O
Health Education	M,D,O
Higher Education	M,D,O
Hospitality Management	M,D
Information Studies	M,D,O
Law	M,D
Library Science	M,D,O
Mathematics Education	M,D,O
Music Education	M,D,O
Nonprofit Management	M,D,O
Organizational Management	M,D,O
Reading Education	M,D,O
Recreation and Park Management	M
Science Education	M,D,O
Social Sciences Education	M,D,O
Social Work	M
Special Education	M,D
Vocational and Technical Education	M,D,O

UNIVERSITY OF MISSOURI–KANSAS CITY

Program	Degrees
Accounting	M,D
Business Administration and Management—General	M,D
Curriculum and Instruction	M,D,O
Education—General	M,D,O
Educational Leadership and Administration	M,D,O
Entrepreneurship	M,D
Finance and Banking	M,D
Law	M,D
Music Education	M,D
Reading Education	M,D,O
Real Estate	M,D
Social Work	M
Special Education	M,D,O
Taxation	M,D

UNIVERSITY OF MISSOURI–ST. LOUIS

Program	Degrees
Accounting	M,D,O
Adult Education	M,D,O

Business Administration and Management—General M,D,O
Counselor Education M,D
Curriculum and Instruction M,D
Early Childhood Education M,O
Education—General M,D,O
Educational Leadership and Administration M,D,O
Educational Measurement and Evaluation M,O
Educational Psychology D
Elementary Education M,O
English as a Second Language M,O
Finance and Banking M,D,O
Higher Education M,D,O
Human Resources Development M,O
Human Resources Management M,D,O
Industrial and Manufacturing Management M,D,O
Logistics M,D,O
Management Information Systems M,D,O
Marketing M,D,O
Middle School Education M,O
Music Education M
Nonprofit Management M,O
Reading Education M,O
Secondary Education M,O
Social Work M,O
Special Education M,O
Supply Chain Management M,D,O

UNIVERSITY OF MOBILE
Business Administration and Management—General M
Education—General M

THE UNIVERSITY OF MONTANA
Accounting M
Business Administration and Management—General M
Counselor Education M,D,O
Curriculum and Instruction M,D
Education—General M,D,O
Educational Leadership and Administration M,D,O
English Education M
Exercise and Sports Science M
Health Education M
Law D
Mathematics Education M,D
Music Education M
Physical Education M
Recreation and Park Management M,D
Social Work M

UNIVERSITY OF MONTEVALLO
Business Administration and Management—General M
Counselor Education M
Education—General M,O
Educational Leadership and Administration M,O
Elementary Education M
Secondary Education M

UNIVERSITY OF NEBRASKA AT KEARNEY
Art Education M
Business Administration and Management—General M
Counselor Education M,O
Curriculum and Instruction M
Education—General M,O
Educational Leadership and Administration M,O
Educational Media/Instructional Technology M
Exercise and Sports Science M
Foreign Languages Education M
Music Education M
Physical Education M
Reading Education M
Science Education M
Special Education M

UNIVERSITY OF NEBRASKA AT OMAHA
Accounting M
Athletic Training and Sports Medicine M
Business Administration and Management—General M
Counselor Education M
Education—General M,D,O
Educational Leadership and Administration M,D,O
Educational Media/Instructional Technology M,O
Educational Psychology M,D,O
Elementary Education M
English as a Second Language M,O
Foreign Languages Education M
Health Education M
Human Resources Development M,O
Management Information Systems M,D,O
Physical Education M
Project Management M,D,O
Reading Education M
Recreation and Park Management M
Secondary Education M
Social Work M
Special Education M
Urban Education M,O

UNIVERSITY OF NEBRASKA–LINCOLN
Accounting M,D
Actuarial Science M
Adult Education M,D,O
Advertising and Public Relations M,D
Agricultural Education M
Business Administration and Management—General M,D
Curriculum and Instruction M,D,O
Early Childhood Education M,D
Educational Leadership and Administration M,D,O
Educational Measurement and Evaluation M,D,O
Educational Psychology M,D,O
Exercise and Sports Science M,D
Finance and Banking M,D
Home Economics Education M,D
Law M,D
Legal and Justice Studies M
Management Information Systems M
Marketing M,D
Music Education M,D
Special Education M,D,O
Vocational and Technical Education M,D,O

UNIVERSITY OF NEVADA, LAS VEGAS
Accounting M,O
Business Administration and Management—General M
Counselor Education M,D,O
Curriculum and Instruction M,D,O
Early Childhood Education M,D,O
Education—General M,D,O
Educational Leadership and Administration M,D,O
Educational Media/Instructional Technology M,D,O
Educational Psychology M,D,O
Entrepreneurship O
Exercise and Sports Science M
Finance and Banking O
Higher Education M,D,O
Hospitality Management M,D
Human Resources Development M,D,O
Kinesiology and Movement Studies M
Law D
Leisure Studies M
Management Information Systems M,O
Nonprofit Management M,D,O
Organizational Management M,D,O
Physical Education M,D
Social Work M,O
Special Education M,D,O
Sports Management M,D

UNIVERSITY OF NEVADA, RENO
Accounting M
Business Administration and Management—General M
Counselor Education M,D,O
Curriculum and Instruction D
Education—General M,D,O
Educational Leadership and Administration M,D,O
Educational Psychology M,D,O
Elementary Education M
English as a Second Language M
Finance and Banking M
Foreign Languages Education M
Legal and Justice Studies M,D
Management Information Systems M
Mathematics Education M
Reading Education M,D
Secondary Education M
Social Work M
Special Education M,D

UNIVERSITY OF NEW BRUNSWICK FREDERICTON
Business Administration and Management—General M
Education—General M,D
Entrepreneurship M
Exercise and Sports Science M
Marketing M,D
Physical Education M
Recreation and Park Management M
Sports Management M

UNIVERSITY OF NEW BRUNSWICK SAINT JOHN
Business Administration and Management—General M
Electronic Commerce M
International Business M

UNIVERSITY OF NEW ENGLAND
Curriculum and Instruction M,O
Education—General M,O
Educational Leadership and Administration M,O
Educational Measurement and Evaluation M,O
Health Education M
Reading Education M,O
Social Work M,O
Special Education M,O

UNIVERSITY OF NEW HAMPSHIRE
Accounting M
Business Administration and Management—General M,O
Counselor Education M,O
Early Childhood Education M
Education—General M,D,O
Educational Leadership and Administration M,O
Elementary Education M
English Education M,D
Environmental Education M
Higher Education M
Kinesiology and Movement Studies M,O
Law M,D,O
Legal and Justice Studies M
Logistics M,D
Management Information Systems M,O
Mathematics Education M,D,O
Music Education M,O
Physical Education M,O
Recreation and Park Management M,O
Science Education M,D
Secondary Education M
Social Work M,O
Special Education M,O

UNIVERSITY OF NEW HAVEN
Accounting M,O
Business Administration and Management—General M,O
Education—General M
Facilities Management M,O
Finance and Banking M,O
Human Resources Management M,O
Industrial and Manufacturing Management M
International Business M,O
Management Strategy and Policy M,O
Marketing M,O
Organizational Management M,O
Sports Management M,O
Taxation M,O

UNIVERSITY OF NEW MEXICO
Accounting M
Art Education M
Business Administration and Management—General M
Counselor Education M,D
Curriculum and Instruction O
Early Childhood Education D
Education—General M,D,O
Educational Leadership and Administration M,D,O
Educational Media/Instructional Technology M,D,O
Educational Psychology M,D
Elementary Education M
English as a Second Language M,D
English Education M,D
Exercise and Sports Science M,D
Finance and Banking M,D
Foundations and Philosophy of Education M,D
Health Education M
Higher Education O
Human Resources Management M,D
International Business M
Law D
Management Information Systems M
Management Strategy and Policy M
Marketing M
Multilingual and Multicultural Education M,D
Music Education M
Organizational Management M
Physical Education M,D
Reading Education M,D
Science Education O
Secondary Education M
Special Education M,D,O
Sports Management M,D
Taxation M

UNIVERSITY OF NEW ORLEANS
Accounting M
Business Administration and Management—General M
Counselor Education M,D,O
Curriculum and Instruction M,D,O
Education—General M,D,O
Educational Leadership and Administration M,D,O
Finance and Banking M,D
Hospitality Management M
Special Education M,D,O
Taxation M
Travel and Tourism M

UNIVERSITY OF NORTH ALABAMA
Business Administration and Management—General M
Counselor Education M
Education—General M,O
Educational Leadership and Administration O
Elementary Education M
Exercise and Sports Science M
Kinesiology and Movement Studies M
Physical Education M
Secondary Education M
Special Education M

THE UNIVERSITY OF NORTH CAROLINA AT CHAPEL HILL
Accounting M,D
Athletic Training and Sports Medicine M
Business Administration and Management—General M,D
Counselor Education M
Curriculum and Instruction M,D
Early Childhood Education M,D
Education—General M,D
Educational Leadership and Administration M,D
Educational Measurement and Evaluation M,D
Educational Psychology M,D
English as a Second Language M
English Education M
Exercise and Sports Science M
Finance and Banking D
Foreign Languages Education M
Health Education M,D
Information Studies M,D,O
Kinesiology and Movement Studies M,D
Law D
Library Science M,D,O
Management Information Systems D
Management Strategy and Policy D
Marketing D
Mathematics Education M
Music Education M
Organizational Behavior D
Physical Education M
Reading Education M,D
Science Education M
Secondary Education M
Social Sciences Education M
Social Work M,D
Sports Management M

THE UNIVERSITY OF NORTH CAROLINA AT CHARLOTTE
Accounting M
Advertising and Public Relations M,O
Art Education M,D
Business Administration and Management—General M,O
Counselor Education M,D,O
Curriculum and Instruction M,D
Education of the Gifted M,D,O
Educational Leadership and Administration M,D
Educational Media/Instructional Technology M,D
Elementary Education M
English Education M,O
Exercise and Sports Science M
Finance and Banking M,O
Kinesiology and Movement Studies M
Management Information Systems M
Marketing M
Mathematics Education M,D
Middle School Education M,D
Music Education M,D
Nonprofit Management M,O
Reading Education M
Real Estate M,O
Secondary Education M,D
Social Sciences Education M
Social Work M
Special Education M,D,O
Supply Chain Management M

THE UNIVERSITY OF NORTH CAROLINA AT GREENSBORO
Accounting M,O
Adult Education M,D,O
Business Administration and Management—General M,O
Counselor Education M,D,O
Curriculum and Instruction M,D,O
Early Childhood Education M,D,O
Education—General M,D,O
Educational Leadership and Administration M,D,O
Educational Measurement and Evaluation D
Educational Media/Instructional Technology M,D,O
Elementary Education D
English as a Second Language M,D,O
English Education M,D
Exercise and Sports Science M,D
Finance and Banking M,O
Foreign Languages Education M,D,O
Higher Education D
Information Studies M
Library Science M
Management Information Systems M,D,O
Marketing M,D
Mathematics Education M,D,O
Middle School Education M,D,O
Multilingual and Multicultural Education M,D,O
Music Education M,D
Nonprofit Management M,O
Reading Education M,D,O
Recreation and Park Management M
Science Education M,D,O
Social Sciences Education M,D,O
Social Work M
Special Education M,D,O
Supply Chain Management M,D,O
Taxation M,O

THE UNIVERSITY OF NORTH CAROLINA AT PEMBROKE
Art Education M
Business Administration and Management—General M
Counselor Education M
Education—General M
Educational Leadership and Administration M
Elementary Education M
English Education M
Mathematics Education M
Middle School Education M
Music Education M
Physical Education M
Reading Education M
Science Education M
Social Sciences Education M

THE UNIVERSITY OF NORTH CAROLINA WILMINGTON
Accounting M
Business Administration and Management—General M
Curriculum and Instruction M
Education—General M,D
Educational Leadership and Administration M,D
Educational Media/Instructional Technology M
Elementary Education M
Environmental Education M
Middle School Education M
Reading Education M
Secondary Education M
Social Work M

UNIVERSITY OF NORTH DAKOTA
Accounting M

*M—master's degree; P—first professional degree; D—doctorate; O—other advanced degree; *Close-Up and/or Display*

Business Administration and Management—General M
Early Childhood Education M
Education—General M,D,O
Educational Leadership and Administration M,D,O
Educational Measurement and Evaluation D
Educational Media/Instructional Technology M
Elementary Education M,D
Kinesiology and Movement Studies M
Law D
Music Education M,D
Reading Education M
Secondary Education D
Social Work M
Special Education M,D

UNIVERSITY OF NORTHERN BRITISH COLUMBIA
Education—General M,D,O
Social Work M,D,O

UNIVERSITY OF NORTHERN COLORADO
Accounting M
Counselor Education M,D
Early Childhood Education M,D
Education—General M,D,O
Educational Leadership and Administration M,D,O
Educational Measurement and Evaluation M,D
Educational Media/Instructional Technology M,D
Educational Psychology M,D
Exercise and Sports Science M,D
Foreign Languages Education M
Health Education M
Higher Education D
Library Science M
Mathematics Education M,D
Music Education M,D
Physical Education M,D
Reading Education M
Science Education M,D
Special Education M,D
Sports Management M,D
Student Affairs D

UNIVERSITY OF NORTHERN IOWA
Accounting M
Actuarial Science M
Art Education M
Athletic Training and Sports Medicine M,D
Business Administration and Management—General M
Counselor Education M
Curriculum and Instruction D
Early Childhood Education M
Education of the Gifted M
Education—General M,D,O
Educational Leadership and Administration M,D
Educational Media/Instructional Technology M
Educational Psychology M,O
Elementary Education M
English as a Second Language M
English Education M
Foreign Languages Education M
Health Education M,D
Higher Education M
Human Services M,D
Kinesiology and Movement Studies M
Leisure Studies M,D
Mathematics Education M
Middle School Education M
Music Education M
Nonprofit Management M
Physical Education M
Reading Education M
Science Education M
Secondary Education M
Social Work M
Special Education M,D
Student Affairs M
Vocational and Technical Education M,D

UNIVERSITY OF NORTH FLORIDA
Accounting M
Adult Education M
Business Administration and Management—General M
Counselor Education M,D
Education—General M,D
Educational Leadership and Administration M,D
Educational Media/Instructional Technology M,D
Electronic Commerce M
Elementary Education M
English as a Second Language M
Exercise and Sports Science M,D
Finance and Banking M
Human Resources Management M
International Business M
Logistics M
Management Information Systems M
Nonprofit Management M,O
Reading Education M
Secondary Education M
Special Education M
Sports Management M,D

UNIVERSITY OF NORTH TEXAS
Accounting M,D
Art Education M,D,O
Business Administration and Management—General M,D
Computer Education M,D
Counselor Education M,D,O
Curriculum and Instruction M,D
Early Childhood Education M,D,O
Education—General M,D,O
Educational Leadership and Administration M,D
Educational Measurement and Evaluation D
Educational Media/Instructional Technology M,D
Educational Psychology M
Finance and Banking M,D
Higher Education M,D,O
Hospitality Management M
Information Studies M,D
International and Comparative Education M,D
Kinesiology and Movement Studies M
Leisure Studies M,O
Library Science M,D
Management Information Systems M,D
Marketing D
Music Education M,D
Quantitative Analysis M,D
Reading Education M,D
Real Estate M,D
Recreation and Park Management M,O
Secondary Education M,O
Special Education M,D,O
Taxation M,D
Vocational and Technical Education M,D

UNIVERSITY OF NORTH TEXAS HEALTH SCIENCE CENTER AT FORT WORTH
Science Education M,D

UNIVERSITY OF NOTRE DAME
Accounting M
Business Administration and Management—General M
Education—General M
Law M,D
Nonprofit Management M
Taxation M

UNIVERSITY OF OKLAHOMA
Accounting M
Adult Education M,D
Advertising and Public Relations M
Business Administration and Management—General M,D*
Curriculum and Instruction M,D,O
Early Childhood Education M,D,O
Education—General M,D,O
Educational Leadership and Administration M,D,O
Educational Measurement and Evaluation M,D
Educational Media/Instructional Technology M,D
Educational Psychology M,D
Elementary Education M,D,O
English Education M,D,O
Exercise and Sports Science M,D
Higher Education M,D,O
Human Resources Development M,O
Human Resources Management M,O
Human Services M,O
Information Studies M,O
Law M,D
Legal and Justice Studies M,O
Library Science M,O
Management Information Systems M,O
Mathematics Education M,D,O
Multilingual and Multicultural Education M,D,O
Music Education M,D
Organizational Behavior M
Project Management M
Reading Education M,D,O
Science Education M,D,O
Secondary Education M,D,O
Social Sciences Education M,D,O
Social Work M
Special Education M,D

UNIVERSITY OF OKLAHOMA HEALTH SCIENCES CENTER
Health Education D
Reading Education M,D,O
Special Education M,D,O

UNIVERSITY OF OREGON
Accounting M,D
Business Administration and Management—General M,D
Education—General M,D
Finance and Banking D
Law M,D
Management Information Systems M
Marketing D
Music Education M,D
Quantitative Analysis M,D

UNIVERSITY OF OTTAWA
Business Administration and Management—General M*
Education—General M,D,O
Electronic Commerce M,D,O
Finance and Banking D,O
Kinesiology and Movement Studies M,D
Law M,D
Music Education M,O
Project Management M,O
Social Work M

UNIVERSITY OF PENNSYLVANIA
Accounting M,D
Business Administration and Management—General M,D
Education—General M,D*
Educational Leadership and Administration M,D
Educational Measurement and Evaluation M,D
Educational Media/Instructional Technology M
Educational Policy M,D
Elementary Education M
English as a Second Language M,D
English Education M,D
Finance and Banking M,D
Foundations and Philosophy of Education M,D
Higher Education M,D
Insurance M,D
International and Comparative Education M,D
International Business M
Law M,D
Legal and Justice Studies M,D
Management Information Systems M,D
Marketing M,D
Multilingual and Multicultural Education M
Reading Education M
Real Estate M,D
Secondary Education M
Social Work M,D
Urban Education M

UNIVERSITY OF PHOENIX–ATLANTA CAMPUS
Accounting M
Business Administration and Management—General M
Human Resources Management M
International Business M
Management Information Systems M
Marketing M

UNIVERSITY OF PHOENIX–AUGUSTA CAMPUS
Accounting M
Business Administration and Management—General M
Human Resources Management M
International Business M
Management Information Systems M
Marketing M

UNIVERSITY OF PHOENIX–AUSTIN CAMPUS
Accounting M
Business Administration and Management—General M
Curriculum and Instruction M
Education—General M
Electronic Commerce M
Human Resources Management M
International Business M
Management Information Systems M
Marketing M

UNIVERSITY OF PHOENIX–BAY AREA CAMPUS
Accounting M,D
Adult Education M,D,O
Business Administration and Management—General M,D
Early Childhood Education M,D,O
Education—General M,D,O
Educational Leadership and Administration M,D,O
Elementary Education M,D,O
Higher Education M,D,O
Human Resources Management M,D
International Business M,D
Management Information Systems M,D
Marketing M,D
Organizational Management M,D
Project Management M,D
Secondary Education M,D,O
Special Education M,D,O

UNIVERSITY OF PHOENIX–BIRMINGHAM CAMPUS
Accounting M
Business Administration and Management—General M
Human Resources Management M
International Business M
Management Information Systems M
Marketing M

UNIVERSITY OF PHOENIX–BOSTON CAMPUS
Business Administration and Management—General M
International Business M
Management Information Systems M

UNIVERSITY OF PHOENIX–CENTRAL FLORIDA CAMPUS
Accounting M
Business Administration and Management—General M
Computer Education M
Curriculum and Instruction M
Early Childhood Education M
Education—General M
Educational Leadership and Administration M
Elementary Education M
Human Resources Management M
International Business M
Management Information Systems M
Marketing M
Mathematics Education M
Secondary Education M

UNIVERSITY OF PHOENIX–CENTRAL MASSACHUSETTS CAMPUS
Business Administration and Management—General M
Education—General M

UNIVERSITY OF PHOENIX–CENTRAL VALLEY CAMPUS
Accounting M
Business Administration and Management—General M
Computer Education M
Curriculum and Instruction M
Education—General M
Elementary Education M
Human Resources Management M
International Business M
Management Information Systems M
Marketing M
Secondary Education M

UNIVERSITY OF PHOENIX–CHARLOTTE CAMPUS
Accounting M
Business Administration and Management—General M
Health Education M
International Business M
Management Information Systems M

UNIVERSITY OF PHOENIX–CHATTANOOGA CAMPUS
Accounting M
Business Administration and Management—General M
Curriculum and Instruction M
Education—General M
Educational Leadership and Administration M
Elementary Education M
Human Resources Management M
International Business M
Management Information Systems M
Marketing M
Secondary Education M

UNIVERSITY OF PHOENIX–CHEYENNE CAMPUS
Business Administration and Management—General M
Human Resources Management M
International Business M
Management Information Systems M
Marketing M

UNIVERSITY OF PHOENIX–CHICAGO CAMPUS
Business Administration and Management—General M
Electronic Commerce M
Human Resources Management M
International Business M
Management Information Systems M

UNIVERSITY OF PHOENIX–CINCINNATI CAMPUS
Accounting M
Business Administration and Management—General M
Electronic Commerce M
Human Resources Management M
International Business M
Management Information Systems M
Marketing M

UNIVERSITY OF PHOENIX–CLEVELAND CAMPUS
Accounting M
Business Administration and Management—General M
Human Resources Management M
International Business M
Management Information Systems M
Marketing M

UNIVERSITY OF PHOENIX–COLUMBIA CAMPUS
Business Administration and Management—General M

UNIVERSITY OF PHOENIX–COLUMBUS GEORGIA CAMPUS
Accounting M
Business Administration and Management—General M
Electronic Commerce M
Human Resources Management M
International Business M
Management Information Systems M
Marketing M

UNIVERSITY OF PHOENIX–COLUMBUS OHIO CAMPUS
Accounting M
Business Administration and Management—General M
Human Resources Management M
International Business M
Management Information Systems M
Marketing M

UNIVERSITY OF PHOENIX–DALLAS CAMPUS
Accounting M
Business Administration and Management—General M
Curriculum and Instruction M
Education—General M
Electronic Commerce M
Human Resources Management M
International Business M
Management Information Systems M
Marketing M

UNIVERSITY OF PHOENIX–DENVER CAMPUS
Accounting M
Business Administration and Management—General M
Curriculum and Instruction M
Education—General M
Educational Leadership and Administration M
Electronic Commerce M
Elementary Education M
Human Resources Management M
International Business M
Management Information Systems M
Marketing M
Secondary Education M

UNIVERSITY OF PHOENIX–DES MOINES CAMPUS
- Accounting M
- Business Administration and Management—General M
- Health Education M,D
- Human Resources Management M
- International Business M
- Management Information Systems M
- Marketing M

UNIVERSITY OF PHOENIX–EASTERN WASHINGTON CAMPUS
- Accounting M
- Business Administration and Management—General M
- Human Resources Management M
- Management Information Systems M
- Marketing M

UNIVERSITY OF PHOENIX–FAIRFIELD COUNTY CAMPUS
- Business Administration and Management—General M

UNIVERSITY OF PHOENIX–HARRISBURG CAMPUS
- Accounting M
- Business Administration and Management—General M
- Human Resources Management M
- International Business M
- Management Information Systems M
- Marketing M

UNIVERSITY OF PHOENIX–HAWAII CAMPUS
- Accounting M
- Business Administration and Management—General M
- Curriculum and Instruction M
- Education—General M
- Educational Leadership and Administration M
- Elementary Education M
- Human Resources Management M
- International Business M
- Management Information Systems M
- Marketing M
- Secondary Education M
- Special Education M

UNIVERSITY OF PHOENIX–HOUSTON CAMPUS
- Accounting M
- Business Administration and Management—General M
- Curriculum and Instruction M
- Education—General M
- Electronic Commerce M
- Human Resources Management M
- International Business M
- Management Information Systems M
- Marketing M

UNIVERSITY OF PHOENIX–IDAHO CAMPUS
- Accounting M
- Business Administration and Management—General M
- Curriculum and Instruction M
- Education—General M
- Educational Leadership and Administration M
- Elementary Education M
- Human Resources Management M
- International Business M
- Management Information Systems M
- Marketing M
- Secondary Education M

UNIVERSITY OF PHOENIX–INDIANAPOLIS CAMPUS
- Accounting M
- Business Administration and Management—General M
- Education—General M
- Elementary Education M
- Human Resources Management M
- International Business M
- Management Information Systems M
- Marketing M
- Secondary Education M

UNIVERSITY OF PHOENIX–JERSEY CITY CAMPUS
- Accounting M
- Business Administration and Management—General M
- Human Resources Management M
- International Business M
- Management Information Systems M
- Marketing M

UNIVERSITY OF PHOENIX–KANSAS CITY CAMPUS
- Accounting M
- Business Administration and Management—General M
- Education—General M
- Educational Leadership and Administration M
- Human Resources Management M
- International Business M
- Marketing M

UNIVERSITY OF PHOENIX–LAS VEGAS CAMPUS
- Accounting M
- Business Administration and Management—General M
- Counselor Education M
- Curriculum and Instruction M
- Education—General M
- Educational Leadership and Administration M
- Elementary Education M
- Human Resources Management M
- International Business M
- Management Information Systems M
- Marketing M

UNIVERSITY OF PHOENIX–LITTLE ROCK CAMPUS
- Business Administration and Management—General M

UNIVERSITY OF PHOENIX–LOUISIANA CAMPUS
- Accounting M
- Business Administration and Management—General M
- Curriculum and Instruction M
- Early Childhood Education M
- Education—General M
- Human Resources Management M
- International Business M
- Management Information Systems M
- Marketing M

UNIVERSITY OF PHOENIX–LOUISVILLE CAMPUS
- Business Administration and Management—General M

UNIVERSITY OF PHOENIX–MADISON CAMPUS
- Accounting M
- Business Administration and Management—General M
- Curriculum and Instruction D,O
- Education—General D,O
- Educational Leadership and Administration D,O
- Electronic Commerce M
- Higher Education D,O
- Human Resources Management M
- International Business M
- Management Information Systems M
- Marketing M

UNIVERSITY OF PHOENIX–MARYLAND CAMPUS
- Business Administration and Management—General M
- International Business M

UNIVERSITY OF PHOENIX–MEMPHIS CAMPUS
- Accounting M
- Business Administration and Management—General M
- Curriculum and Instruction M
- Education—General M
- Educational Leadership and Administration M
- Electronic Commerce M
- Elementary Education M
- Human Resources Management M
- International Business M
- Management Information Systems M
- Marketing M
- Secondary Education M

UNIVERSITY OF PHOENIX–METRO DETROIT CAMPUS
- Education—General M
- Educational Leadership and Administration M
- Elementary Education M
- Management Information Systems M
- Secondary Education M
- Special Education M

UNIVERSITY OF PHOENIX–MILWAUKEE CAMPUS
- Accounting M,D
- Business Administration and Management—General M,D
- Curriculum and Instruction M,D,O
- Education—General M,D,O
- Educational Leadership and Administration M,D,O
- English as a Second Language M,D,O
- Health Education M,D
- Higher Education M,D,O
- Human Resources Management M,D
- Management Information Systems M,D
- Organizational Management M,D

UNIVERSITY OF PHOENIX–MINNEAPOLIS/ST. LOUIS PARK CAMPUS
- Accounting M
- Business Administration and Management—General M
- Human Resources Management M
- Human Services M
- International Business M
- Marketing M

UNIVERSITY OF PHOENIX–NASHVILLE CAMPUS
- Business Administration and Management—General M
- Curriculum and Instruction M
- Education—General M
- Educational Leadership and Administration M
- Elementary Education M
- Human Resources Management M
- Management Information Systems M
- Secondary Education M

UNIVERSITY OF PHOENIX–NEW MEXICO CAMPUS
- Accounting M
- Business Administration and Management—General M
- Counselor Education M
- Curriculum and Instruction M
- Education—General M
- Educational Leadership and Administration M
- Electronic Commerce M
- Elementary Education M
- Human Resources Management M
- International Business M
- Management Information Systems M
- Marketing M
- Secondary Education M

UNIVERSITY OF PHOENIX–NORTHERN NEVADA CAMPUS
- Accounting M
- Business Administration and Management—General M
- Curriculum and Instruction M
- Education—General M
- Educational Leadership and Administration M
- Elementary Education M
- Human Resources Management M
- International Business M
- Management Information Systems M
- Marketing M
- Secondary Education M

UNIVERSITY OF PHOENIX–NORTHERN VIRGINIA CAMPUS
- Accounting M
- Business Administration and Management—General M
- Education—General M
- Educational Leadership and Administration M
- Management Information Systems M

UNIVERSITY OF PHOENIX–NORTH FLORIDA CAMPUS
- Accounting M
- Business Administration and Management—General M
- Computer Education M
- Curriculum and Instruction M
- Early Childhood Education M
- Education—General M
- Educational Leadership and Administration M
- Elementary Education M
- Human Resources Management M
- International Business M
- Management Information Systems M
- Marketing M
- Mathematics Education M
- Secondary Education M

UNIVERSITY OF PHOENIX–NORTHWEST ARKANSAS CAMPUS
- Accounting M
- Business Administration and Management—General M
- Human Resources Management M
- International Business M
- Management Information Systems M
- Marketing M

UNIVERSITY OF PHOENIX–OKLAHOMA CITY CAMPUS
- Accounting M
- Business Administration and Management—General M
- Electronic Commerce M
- Human Resources Management M
- International Business M
- Management Information Systems M
- Marketing M

UNIVERSITY OF PHOENIX–OMAHA CAMPUS
- Accounting M
- Adult Education M
- Business Administration and Management—General M
- Computer Education M
- Curriculum and Instruction M
- Education—General M
- Educational Leadership and Administration M
- Elementary Education M
- English as a Second Language M
- English Education M
- Human Resources Management M
- International Business M
- Management Information Systems M
- Marketing M
- Mathematics Education M
- Secondary Education M
- Special Education M

UNIVERSITY OF PHOENIX–ONLINE CAMPUS
- Accounting M,O
- Adult Education M,O
- Business Administration and Management—General M,D,O
- Computer Education M,O
- Curriculum and Instruction M,D,O
- Early Childhood Education M,O
- Education—General M,O
- Educational Leadership and Administration M,D,O
- Educational Media/Instructional Technology D,O
- Elementary Education M,O
- English Education M,O
- Health Education M,O
- Higher Education D,O
- Human Resources Management M,O
- International Business M,O
- Management Information Systems M
- Marketing M,O
- Mathematics Education M,O
- Middle School Education M,O
- Organizational Management M,D,O
- Project Management M,O
- Reading Education M,O
- Science Education M,O
- Secondary Education M,O
- Special Education M,O

UNIVERSITY OF PHOENIX–OREGON CAMPUS
- Accounting M
- Business Administration and Management—General M
- Curriculum and Instruction M
- Early Childhood Education M
- Education—General M
- Elementary Education M
- Human Resources Management M
- International Business M
- Management Information Systems M
- Marketing M
- Middle School Education M
- Secondary Education M

UNIVERSITY OF PHOENIX–PHILADELPHIA CAMPUS
- Accounting M
- Business Administration and Management—General M
- Human Resources Management M
- International Business M
- Management Information Systems M
- Marketing M

UNIVERSITY OF PHOENIX–PHOENIX MAIN CAMPUS
- Accounting M,O
- Adult Education M
- Business Administration and Management—General M,O
- Counselor Education M
- Curriculum and Instruction M
- Early Childhood Education M
- Education—General M
- Educational Leadership and Administration M
- Elementary Education M
- Health Education M,O
- Human Resources Management M,O
- International Business M,O
- Marketing M,O
- Project Management M,O
- Reading Education M
- Secondary Education M
- Special Education M
- Vocational and Technical Education M

UNIVERSITY OF PHOENIX–PITTSBURGH CAMPUS
- Accounting M
- Business Administration and Management—General M
- Electronic Commerce M
- Human Resources Management M
- International Business M
- Management Information Systems M
- Marketing M

UNIVERSITY OF PHOENIX–PUERTO RICO CAMPUS
- Accounting M
- Business Administration and Management—General M
- Early Childhood Education M
- Education—General M
- Educational Leadership and Administration M
- Entrepreneurship M
- Human Resources Management M
- Human Services M
- International Business M
- Marketing M
- Project Management M

UNIVERSITY OF PHOENIX–RALEIGH CAMPUS
- Accounting M
- Business Administration and Management—General M
- Electronic Commerce M
- Health Education M,D
- Human Resources Management M
- International Business M
- Management Information Systems M
- Marketing M

UNIVERSITY OF PHOENIX–RICHMOND CAMPUS
- Accounting M
- Business Administration and Management—General M
- Curriculum and Instruction M
- Education—General M
- Educational Leadership and Administration M
- Human Resources Management M
- International Business M
- Management Information Systems M
- Marketing M

UNIVERSITY OF PHOENIX–SACRAMENTO VALLEY CAMPUS
- Accounting M
- Adult Education M,O
- Business Administration and Management—General M
- Curriculum and Instruction M,O
- Education—General M,O
- Elementary Education M,O
- Human Resources Management M

*M—master's degree; P—first professional degree; D—doctorate; O—other advanced degree; *Close-Up and/or Display*

International Business M
Management Information Systems M
Marketing M
Secondary Education M,O

UNIVERSITY OF PHOENIX–ST. LOUIS CAMPUS
Accounting M
Business Administration and Management—General M
Human Resources Management M
International Business M
Management Information Systems M
Marketing M

UNIVERSITY OF PHOENIX–SAN ANTONIO CAMPUS
Accounting M
Business Administration and Management—General M
Curriculum and Instruction M
Electronic Commerce M
Human Resources Management M
International Business M
Management Information Systems M
Marketing M

UNIVERSITY OF PHOENIX–SAN DIEGO CAMPUS
Accounting M
Business Administration and Management—General M
Computer Education M
Curriculum and Instruction M
Education—General M
Elementary Education M
English as a Second Language M
Human Resources Management M
International Business M
Management Information Systems M
Marketing M
Secondary Education M

UNIVERSITY OF PHOENIX–SAVANNAH CAMPUS
Accounting M
Business Administration and Management—General M
Human Resources Management M
International Business M
Management Information Systems M
Marketing M

UNIVERSITY OF PHOENIX–SOUTHERN ARIZONA CAMPUS
Accounting M
Adult Education M,O
Business Administration and Management—General M
Counselor Education M,O
Curriculum and Instruction M,O
Education—General M,O
Educational Leadership and Administration M,O
Educational Psychology M,O
Elementary Education M,O
Human Resources Management M
International Business M
Management Information Systems M
Marketing M
Secondary Education M,O
Special Education M,O

UNIVERSITY OF PHOENIX–SOUTHERN CALIFORNIA CAMPUS
Accounting M
Adult Education M,O
Business Administration and Management—General M
Counselor Education M
Education—General M,O
Educational Leadership and Administration M,O
Human Resources Management M
International Business M
Management Information Systems M
Marketing M
Project Management M

UNIVERSITY OF PHOENIX–SOUTHERN COLORADO CAMPUS
Accounting M
Business Administration and Management—General M
Curriculum and Instruction M,O
Education—General M,O
Educational Leadership and Administration M,O
Elementary Education M,O
Health Education M
Human Resources Management M
International Business M
Management Information Systems M
Marketing M
Secondary Education M,O

UNIVERSITY OF PHOENIX–SOUTH FLORIDA CAMPUS
Accounting M
Business Administration and Management—General M
Computer Education M
Curriculum and Instruction M
Early Childhood Education M
Education—General M
Educational Leadership and Administration M
Elementary Education M
Human Resources Management M
International Business M
Management Information Systems M
Marketing M
Mathematics Education M
Secondary Education M

UNIVERSITY OF PHOENIX–SPRINGFIELD CAMPUS
Accounting M
Business Administration and Management—General M
Computer Education M
Curriculum and Instruction M
Education—General M
Educational Leadership and Administration M
English as a Second Language M
English Education M
Human Resources Management M
International Business M
Management Information Systems M
Marketing M
Mathematics Education M

UNIVERSITY OF PHOENIX–TULSA CAMPUS
Accounting M
Business Administration and Management—General M
Human Resources Management M
International Business M
Management Information Systems M
Marketing M

UNIVERSITY OF PHOENIX–UTAH CAMPUS
Accounting M
Business Administration and Management—General M
Curriculum and Instruction M
Education—General M
Educational Leadership and Administration M
Elementary Education M
Human Resources Management M
International Business M
Management Information Systems M
Marketing M
Secondary Education M
Special Education M

UNIVERSITY OF PHOENIX–VANCOUVER CAMPUS
Accounting M
Business Administration and Management—General M
Computer Education M
Curriculum and Instruction M
Education—General M
Educational Leadership and Administration M
Human Resources Management M
International Business M
Management Information Systems M
Marketing M

UNIVERSITY OF PHOENIX–WASHINGTON CAMPUS
Business Administration and Management—General M

UNIVERSITY OF PHOENIX–WASHINGTON D.C. CAMPUS
Accounting M,D
Adult Education M,D,O
Business Administration and Management—General M,D
Computer Education M,D,O
Curriculum and Instruction M,D,O
Early Childhood Education M,D,O
Education—General M,D,O
Educational Leadership and Administration M,D,O
Educational Media/Instructional Technology M,D,O
Elementary Education M,D,O
English as a Second Language M,D,O
English Education M,D,O
Health Education M,D
Higher Education M,D,O
Human Resources Management M,D
Management Information Systems M,D
Mathematics Education M,D,O
Organizational Management M,D
Secondary Education M,D,O
Special Education M,D,O

UNIVERSITY OF PHOENIX–WEST FLORIDA CAMPUS
Accounting M
Business Administration and Management—General M
Computer Education M
Curriculum and Instruction M
Early Childhood Education M
Education—General M
Educational Leadership and Administration M
Educational Media/Instructional Technology M
Elementary Education M
Human Resources Management M
International Business M
Management Information Systems M
Marketing M
Mathematics Education M
Secondary Education M

UNIVERSITY OF PHOENIX–WEST MICHIGAN CAMPUS
Business Administration and Management—General M

UNIVERSITY OF PHOENIX–WICHITA CAMPUS
Business Administration and Management—General M

UNIVERSITY OF PITTSBURGH
Accounting M,D
Athletic Training and Sports Medicine M
Business Administration and Management—General M,D,O
Early Childhood Education M,D
Education—General M,D
Educational Leadership and Administration M,D
Educational Measurement and Evaluation M,D
Educational Policy D
Elementary Education M,D
English as a Second Language O
English Education M,D
Environmental Law M,O
Exercise and Sports Science M,D
Finance and Banking M,D,O
Foreign Languages Education M,D
Foundations and Philosophy of Education M,D
Health Education M,D,O
Health Law M,O
Higher Education M,D
Human Resources Management M,D,O
Industrial and Manufacturing Management M,O
Information Studies M,D,O
Intellectual Property Law M,O
International and Comparative Education M,D
International Business M
Law M,D,O
Legal and Justice Studies M,O
Library Science M,D,O
Management Information Systems M,D,O
Management Strategy and Policy M,O
Marketing M,D,O
Mathematics Education M,D
Nonprofit Management M
Organizational Behavior M,D,O
Quantitative Analysis D
Reading Education M,D
Science Education M,D
Secondary Education M,D
Social Sciences Education M,D
Social Work M,D,O
Special Education M,D

UNIVERSITY OF PORTLAND
Business Administration and Management—General M
Education—General M
Entrepreneurship M
Finance and Banking M
Marketing M
Nonprofit Management M
Sustainability Management M

UNIVERSITY OF PRINCE EDWARD ISLAND
Education—General M
Educational Leadership and Administration M

UNIVERSITY OF PUERTO RICO, MAYAGÜEZ CAMPUS
Agricultural Education M
Business Administration and Management—General M
English Education M
Finance and Banking M
Human Resources Management M
Industrial and Manufacturing Management M
Physical Education M

UNIVERSITY OF PUERTO RICO, MEDICAL SCIENCES CAMPUS
Health Education M
Special Education O

UNIVERSITY OF PUERTO RICO, RÍO PIEDRAS
Accounting M,D
Business Administration and Management—General M,D
Counselor Education M,D
Curriculum and Instruction M,D
Early Childhood Education M
Education—General M,D
Educational Leadership and Administration M,D
Educational Measurement and Evaluation M
English as a Second Language M
Exercise and Sports Science M
Finance and Banking M,D
Foreign Languages Education M,D
Human Resources Management M,D
Industrial and Manufacturing Management M,D
Information Studies M,O
International Business M,D
Law M,D
Library Science M,O
Marketing M,D
Mathematics Education M,D
Quantitative Analysis M,D
Science Education M,D
Social Sciences Education M,D
Social Work M,D
Special Education M

UNIVERSITY OF PUGET SOUND
Counselor Education M
Education—General M
Elementary Education M
Secondary Education M

UNIVERSITY OF REDLANDS
Business Administration and Management—General M
Education—General M,D,O
Management Information Systems M

UNIVERSITY OF REGINA
Adult Education M
Business Administration and Management—General M,O
Curriculum and Instruction M
Education—General M,D,O
Educational Leadership and Administration M
Educational Psychology M
Human Resources Development M
Human Resources Management M,O
International Business M,O
Kinesiology and Movement Studies M,D
Organizational Management M,D
Project Management M,O
Social Work M

UNIVERSITY OF RHODE ISLAND
Accounting M,D
Adult Education M,D
Business Administration and Management—General M,D
Education—General M,D
Elementary Education M,D
Exercise and Sports Science M,D
Finance and Banking M,D
Health Education M
Human Resources Management M
Industrial and Manufacturing Management M,D
Information Studies M
Library Science M
Marketing M,D
Music Education M,D
Physical Education M
Reading Education M,D
Recreation and Park Management M
Secondary Education M,D
Special Education M,D
Student Affairs M
Supply Chain Management M,D

UNIVERSITY OF RICHMOND
Business Administration and Management—General M
Law D

UNIVERSITY OF RIO GRANDE
Art Education M
Education—General M
Mathematics Education M
Reading Education M
Special Education M

UNIVERSITY OF ROCHESTER
Accounting M
Business Administration and Management—General M,D
Counselor Education M,D
Curriculum and Instruction M,D
Education—General M,D
Educational Leadership and Administration M,D
Educational Policy M,D
Entrepreneurship M
Foundations and Philosophy of Education D
Higher Education M,D
Music Education M,D
Student Affairs M

UNIVERSITY OF ST. FRANCIS (IL)
Art Education M,D
Business Administration and Management—General M
Business Education M
Curriculum and Instruction M,D
Education—General M,D
Educational Leadership and Administration M,D
Elementary Education M,D
English Education M,D
Mathematics Education M,D
Reading Education M,D
Science Education M,D
Secondary Education M,D
Social Sciences Education M,D
Social Work M,O
Special Education M,D

UNIVERSITY OF SAINT FRANCIS (IN)
Business Administration and Management—General M
Counselor Education M
Education—General M
Special Education M

UNIVERSITY OF SAINT JOSEPH
Business Administration and Management—General M
Counselor Education M
Education—General M
Special Education M,O

UNIVERSITY OF SAINT MARY
Business Administration and Management—General M
Curriculum and Instruction M
Education—General M
Special Education M

UNIVERSITY OF ST. MICHAEL'S COLLEGE
Religious Education M,D,O

UNIVERSITY OF ST. THOMAS (MN)
Accounting M
Business Administration and Management—General M
Curriculum and Instruction M,O
Early Childhood Education M,O
Education of the Gifted M,O
Education—General M,D,O
Educational Leadership and Administration M,D,O
Educational Media/Instructional Technology M,D,O
Educational Policy M,D,O
Elementary Education M,O

Program	Degrees
English as a Second Language	M,O
Human Resources Management	M,D,O
Law	D
Management Information Systems	M,O
Mathematics Education	M,O
Multilingual and Multicultural Education	M,O
Music Education	M
Organizational Management	M,D,O
Reading Education	M,O
Real Estate	M
Religious Education	M
Secondary Education	M,O
Social Work	M
Special Education	M,O
Student Affairs	M,D,O

UNIVERSITY OF ST. THOMAS (TX)

Program	Degrees
Business Administration and Management—General	M
Counselor Education	M
Curriculum and Instruction	M
Education—General	M
Educational Leadership and Administration	M
Educational Measurement and Evaluation	M
Elementary Education	M
English as a Second Language	M
Multilingual and Multicultural Education	M
Reading Education	M
Religious Education	M
Secondary Education	M
Special Education	M

UNIVERSITY OF SAN DIEGO

Program	Degrees
Accounting	M
Business Administration and Management—General	M
Counselor Education	M
Curriculum and Instruction	M
Education—General	M,D,O
Educational Leadership and Administration	M,D,O
English as a Second Language	M
Higher Education	M,D,O
International Business	M
Law	M,D,O
Legal and Justice Studies	M,D,O
Nonprofit Management	M,D,O
Reading Education	M
Real Estate	M
Special Education	M
Supply Chain Management	M,O
Taxation	M,D,O

UNIVERSITY OF SAN FRANCISCO

Program	Degrees
Business Administration and Management—General	M
Counselor Education	M,D
Curriculum and Instruction	M,D
Education—General	M,D
Educational Leadership and Administration	M,D
Educational Media/Instructional Technology	M,D
Electronic Commerce	M
English as a Second Language	M,D
Entrepreneurship	M
Finance and Banking	M
Intellectual Property Law	M
International and Comparative Education	M,D
International Business	M
Investment Management	M
Law	M,D
Management Information Systems	M
Marketing	M
Multilingual and Multicultural Education	M,D
Nonprofit Management	M
Organizational Management	M
Project Management	M
Reading Education	M,D
Religious Education	M,D
Sports Management	M

UNIVERSITY OF SASKATCHEWAN

Program	Degrees
Accounting	M
Business Administration and Management—General	M
Curriculum and Instruction	M,D,O
Education—General	M,D,O
Educational Leadership and Administration	M,D,O
Educational Psychology	M,D,O
Finance and Banking	M
Foundations and Philosophy of Education	M,D,O
International Business	M,D
Kinesiology and Movement Studies	M,D
Law	M,D
Marketing	M
Special Education	M,D,O
Sustainability Management	M

THE UNIVERSITY OF SCRANTON

Program	Degrees
Accounting	M
Business Administration and Management—General	M
Counselor Education	M
Curriculum and Instruction	M
Early Childhood Education	M
Education—General	M
Educational Leadership and Administration	M
Elementary Education	M
English as a Second Language	M
Finance and Banking	M
Human Resources Development	M
Human Resources Management	M
International Business	M
Management Information Systems	M
Marketing	M
Organizational Management	M
Reading Education	M
Secondary Education	M
Special Education	M

UNIVERSITY OF SIOUX FALLS

Program	Degrees
Business Administration and Management—General	M
Education—General	M,O
Educational Leadership and Administration	M,O
Educational Media/Instructional Technology	M,O
Entrepreneurship	M
Marketing	M
Reading Education	M,O

UNIVERSITY OF SOUTH AFRICA

Program	Degrees
Accounting	M,D
Adult Education	M,D
Business Administration and Management—General	M,D
Counselor Education	M,D
Curriculum and Instruction	M,D
Education—General	M,D
Educational Leadership and Administration	M,D
Educational Media/Instructional Technology	M,D
Educational Psychology	M,D
English as a Second Language	M,D
Environmental Education	M,D
Foundations and Philosophy of Education	M,D
Health Education	M,D
Human Resources Development	M,D
International and Comparative Education	M,D
Law	M,D
Logistics	M,D
Management Information Systems	M
Marketing	M,D
Mathematics Education	M,D
Quantitative Analysis	M,D
Real Estate	M,D
Science Education	M,D
Social Work	M,D
Travel and Tourism	M,D
Vocational and Technical Education	M,D

UNIVERSITY OF SOUTH ALABAMA

Program	Degrees
Accounting	M
Business Administration and Management—General	M
Counselor Education	M,D
Early Childhood Education	M,O
Education—General	M,D,O
Educational Leadership and Administration	M,O
Educational Media/Instructional Technology	M,D
Elementary Education	M,O
Exercise and Sports Science	M
Health Education	M
Leisure Studies	M
Management Information Systems	M
Physical Education	M
Reading Education	M,O
Recreation and Park Management	M
Science Education	M,O
Secondary Education	M,O
Special Education	M,O

UNIVERSITY OF SOUTH CAROLINA

Program	Degrees
Accounting	M
Archives/Archival Administration	M,O
Art Education	M,D
Business Administration and Management—General	M,D
Business Education	M,D
Counselor Education	D,O
Curriculum and Instruction	D
Early Childhood Education	M,D
Education—General	M,D,O
Educational Leadership and Administration	M,D,O
Educational Measurement and Evaluation	M,D
Educational Media/Instructional Technology	M
Educational Psychology	M,D
Elementary Education	M,D
English as a Second Language	M,D,O
English Education	M,D
Entertainment Management	M
Exercise and Sports Science	M,D
Foreign Languages Education	M,D
Foundations and Philosophy of Education	D
Health Education	M,D,O
Higher Education	M
Hospitality Management	M
Human Resources Management	M
Information Studies	M,D,O
International Business	M
Law	D
Library Science	M,D,O
Mathematics Education	M,D
Music Education	M,D,O
Physical Education	M,D
Reading Education	M,D
Science Education	M,D
Secondary Education	M,D
Social Sciences Education	M,D
Social Work	M,D
Special Education	M,D
Sports Management	M
Student Affairs	M
Travel and Tourism	M

UNIVERSITY OF SOUTH CAROLINA AIKEN

Program	Degrees
Educational Media/Instructional Technology	M

UNIVERSITY OF SOUTH CAROLINA UPSTATE

Program	Degrees
Early Childhood Education	M
Education—General	M
Elementary Education	M
Special Education	M

THE UNIVERSITY OF SOUTH DAKOTA

Program	Degrees
Accounting	M
Business Administration and Management—General	M
Counselor Education	M,D,O
Curriculum and Instruction	M,D,O
Education—General	M,D,O
Educational Leadership and Administration	M,D,O
Educational Media/Instructional Technology	M,O
Educational Psychology	M,D,O
Elementary Education	M
Exercise and Sports Science	M
Kinesiology and Movement Studies	M
Law	D
Secondary Education	M
Special Education	M

UNIVERSITY OF SOUTHERN CALIFORNIA

Program	Degrees
Accounting	M
Advertising and Public Relations	M
Business Administration and Management—General	M,D
Counselor Education	M
Education—General	M,D
Educational Leadership and Administration	D
Educational Policy	D
Educational Psychology	D
English as a Second Language	M
Health Education	M
Higher Education	D
Kinesiology and Movement Studies	M,D
Law	M,D
Multilingual and Multicultural Education	D
Music Education	M,D,O
Nonprofit Management	M,O
Organizational Management	M
Quantitative Analysis	M,D
Real Estate	M
Social Work	M,D
Student Affairs	M
Supply Chain Management	M,D,O
Taxation	M
Urban Education	D

UNIVERSITY OF SOUTHERN INDIANA

Program	Degrees
Business Administration and Management—General	M
Education—General	M
Elementary Education	M
Industrial and Manufacturing Management	M
Secondary Education	M
Social Work	M

UNIVERSITY OF SOUTHERN MAINE

Program	Degrees
Accounting	M
Adult Education	M,O
Business Administration and Management—General	M
Counselor Education	M,O
Education of the Gifted	M,O
Education—General	M,D,O
Educational Leadership and Administration	M,O
Educational Psychology	M,O
English as a Second Language	M,O
Finance and Banking	M
Higher Education	M,O
Law	D
Middle School Education	M,O
Nonprofit Management	M,O
Reading Education	M,O
Social Work	M
Special Education	M,O
Sports Management	M,O
Sustainability Management	M

UNIVERSITY OF SOUTHERN MISSISSIPPI

Program	Degrees
Accounting	M
Adult Education	M,D,O
Advertising and Public Relations	M,D
Business Administration and Management—General	M
Community College Education	M,D,O
Counselor Education	M,D,O
Curriculum and Instruction	M,D,O
Early Childhood Education	M,D,O
Education of the Gifted	M,D,O
Education—General	M,D,O
Educational Leadership and Administration	M,D,O
Educational Measurement and Evaluation	M,D,O
Elementary Education	M,D,O
Exercise and Sports Science	M,D
Foreign Languages Education	M
Health Education	M
Higher Education	M,D,O
Leisure Studies	M,D
Library Science	M
Management Information Systems	M
Mathematics Education	M,D
Music Education	M,D
Physical Education	M,D
Reading Education	M,D,O
Recreation and Park Management	M,D
Science Education	M,D
Secondary Education	M,D,O
Social Sciences Education	M,D,O
Social Work	M
Special Education	M,D,O
Sports Management	M,D
Student Affairs	M,D,O
Vocational and Technical Education	M

UNIVERSITY OF SOUTH FLORIDA

Program	Degrees
Accounting	M,D
Adult Education	M,D,O
Business Administration and Management—General	M,D
Community College Education	M,D,O
Counselor Education	M,D,O
Curriculum and Instruction	M,D,O
Early Childhood Education	M,D,O
Education of the Gifted	M,D,O
Education—General	M,D,O
Educational Leadership and Administration	M,D,O
Educational Measurement and Evaluation	M,D,O
Educational Media/Instructional Technology	M,D,O
Elementary Education	M,D,O
English as a Second Language	M,D,O
English Education	M,D,O
Entrepreneurship	M,O
Exercise and Sports Science	M
Finance and Banking	M,D
Foreign Languages Education	M,D,O
Higher Education	M,D,O
Information Studies	M
Library Science	M
Management Information Systems	M,D
Marketing	M,D
Mathematics Education	M,D,O
Music Education	M,D
Physical Education	M
Reading Education	M,D,O
Real Estate	M
Science Education	M,D,O
Secondary Education	M,D,O
Social Sciences Education	M,D,O
Social Work	M,D
Special Education	M,D
Student Affairs	M,D,O
Vocational and Technical Education	M,D,O

UNIVERSITY OF SOUTH FLORIDA–POLYTECHNIC

Program	Degrees
Business Administration and Management—General	M
Counselor Education	M
Educational Leadership and Administration	M
Management Information Systems	M
Reading Education	M

UNIVERSITY OF SOUTH FLORIDA–ST. PETERSBURG CAMPUS

Program	Degrees
Business Administration and Management—General	M
Education—General	M
Educational Leadership and Administration	M
Elementary Education	M
English Education	M
Mathematics Education	M
Middle School Education	M
Reading Education	M
Science Education	M

UNIVERSITY OF SOUTH FLORIDA SARASOTA-MANATEE

Program	Degrees
Business Administration and Management—General	M
Curriculum and Instruction	M
Education—General	M
Educational Leadership and Administration	M
Elementary Education	M
English as a Second Language	M
Hospitality Management	M
Reading Education	M
Social Work	M

THE UNIVERSITY OF TAMPA

Program	Degrees
Accounting	M
Business Administration and Management—General	M
Curriculum and Instruction	M
Education—General	M
Educational Leadership and Administration	M
Entrepreneurship	M
Finance and Banking	M
International Business	M
Management Information Systems	M
Marketing	M
Nonprofit Management	M

THE UNIVERSITY OF TENNESSEE

Program	Degrees
Accounting	M,D
Adult Education	M,D
Advertising and Public Relations	M,D
Agricultural Education	M
Art Education	M,D,O
Athletic Training and Sports Medicine	M,D
Business Administration and Management—General	M,D
Counselor Education	M,D,O
Curriculum and Instruction	M,D,O
Early Childhood Education	M,D,O
Education—General	M,D,O
Educational Leadership and Administration	M,D,O
Educational Measurement and Evaluation	M,D,O

*M—master's degree; P—first professional degree; D—doctorate; O—other advanced degree; *Close-Up and/or Display*

- Educational Media/Instructional Technology M,D,O
- Educational Psychology M,D,O
- Elementary Education M,D,O
- English as a Second Language M,D,O
- English Education M,D,O
- Exercise and Sports Science M,D,O
- Finance and Banking M,D
- Foreign Languages Education M,D,O
- Foundations and Philosophy of Education M,D,O
- Health Education M
- Hospitality Management M
- Human Resources Development M
- Industrial and Manufacturing Management M,D
- Kinesiology and Movement Studies M,D
- Law D
- Leisure Studies M,D
- Logistics M,D
- Marketing M,D
- Mathematics Education M,D,O
- Multilingual and Multicultural Education M,D,O
- Music Education M
- Reading Education M,D,O
- Recreation and Park Management M,D
- Science Education M,D,O
- Secondary Education M,D,O
- Social Sciences Education M,D,O
- Social Work M,D
- Special Education M,D,O
- Sports Management M,D
- Student Affairs M
- Transportation Management M,D
- Travel and Tourism M

THE UNIVERSITY OF TENNESSEE AT CHATTANOOGA

- Accounting M
- Athletic Training and Sports Medicine M
- Business Administration and Management—General M
- Counselor Education M,D,O
- Education—General M,D,O
- Educational Leadership and Administration M,D,O
- Educational Media/Instructional Technology M,D,O
- Elementary Education M,D,O
- Music Education M
- Nonprofit Management M,O
- Physical Education M
- Project Management M,O
- Quality Management M,O
- Secondary Education M,D,O
- Special Education M,D,O

THE UNIVERSITY OF TENNESSEE AT MARTIN

- Business Administration and Management—General M
- Counselor Education M
- Education—General M
- Educational Leadership and Administration M

THE UNIVERSITY OF TEXAS AT ARLINGTON

- Accounting M,D
- Business Administration and Management—General M,D
- Curriculum and Instruction M
- Education—General M,D
- Educational Leadership and Administration M,D
- Educational Policy M,D
- English as a Second Language M
- Exercise and Sports Science M
- Finance and Banking M,D
- Higher Education M,D
- Human Resources Management M
- Industrial and Manufacturing Management M,D
- Logistics M,D
- Management Information Systems M,D
- Marketing Research M,D
- Marketing M,D
- Mathematics Education M,D
- Multilingual and Multicultural Education M,D
- Music Education M
- Quantitative Analysis M,D
- Real Estate M,D
- Social Work M,D
- Taxation M,D

THE UNIVERSITY OF TEXAS AT AUSTIN

- Accounting M,D
- Actuarial Science M,D
- Advertising and Public Relations M,D
- Art Education M
- Business Administration and Management—General M,D
- Counselor Education M,D
- Curriculum and Instruction M,D
- Early Childhood Education M,D
- Education—General M,D
- Educational Leadership and Administration M,D
- Educational Media/Instructional Technology M,D
- Educational Psychology M,D
- Entrepreneurship M
- Exercise and Sports Science M,D
- Finance and Banking M,D
- Health Education M,D
- Industrial and Manufacturing Management M,D
- Information Studies M,D,O
- Kinesiology and Movement Studies M,D
- Law M,D
- Management Information Systems M,D
- Marketing M,D
- Multilingual and Multicultural Education M,D
- Music Education M,D
- Physical Education M,D
- Quantitative Analysis M,D
- Reading Education M,D
- Social Work M,D
- Special Education M,D
- Supply Chain Management M,D

THE UNIVERSITY OF TEXAS AT BROWNSVILLE

- Business Administration and Management—General M
- Counselor Education M
- Curriculum and Instruction M
- Early Childhood Education M
- Education—General M
- Educational Leadership and Administration M
- Educational Media/Instructional Technology M
- English as a Second Language M
- Multilingual and Multicultural Education M
- Reading Education M
- Special Education M

THE UNIVERSITY OF TEXAS AT DALLAS

- Accounting M,D
- Business Administration and Management—General M,D*
- Electronic Commerce M
- Entrepreneurship M
- Finance and Banking M,D
- International Business M,D
- Investment Management M
- Law M,D
- Management Information Systems M,D
- Management Strategy and Policy M,D
- Marketing M,D
- Mathematics Education M
- Organizational Management M
- Project Management M
- Real Estate M
- Science Education M
- Supply Chain Management M
- Taxation M

THE UNIVERSITY OF TEXAS AT EL PASO

- Accounting M
- Art Education M
- Business Administration and Management—General M,D,O*
- Counselor Education M
- Curriculum and Instruction M,D
- Education—General M,D
- Educational Leadership and Administration M,D
- Educational Measurement and Evaluation M
- Educational Psychology M
- English as a Second Language M,O
- English Education M,D,O
- International Business M,D,O
- Kinesiology and Movement Studies M
- Mathematics Education M
- Multilingual and Multicultural Education M,D,O
- Music Education M
- Reading Education M,D
- Science Education M
- Social Work M
- Special Education M

THE UNIVERSITY OF TEXAS AT SAN ANTONIO

- Accounting M,D
- Adult Education M,D
- Business Administration and Management—General M,D
- Counselor Education M,D
- Curriculum and Instruction M,D
- Early Childhood Education M,D
- Educational Leadership and Administration M,D
- Educational Media/Instructional Technology M,D
- Educational Psychology M,D
- English as a Second Language M,D
- Finance and Banking M,D
- Health Education M
- Higher Education M,D
- International Business M,D
- Kinesiology and Movement Studies M
- Management Information Systems M,D
- Marketing M,D
- Mathematics Education M
- Multilingual and Multicultural Education M,D
- Organizational Management M,D
- Reading Education M,D
- Social Work M
- Special Education M,D
- Taxation M,D

THE UNIVERSITY OF TEXAS AT TYLER

- Business Administration and Management—General M
- Early Childhood Education M
- Educational Leadership and Administration M
- Health Education M
- Human Resources Development M,D
- Industrial and Manufacturing Management M,D
- Kinesiology and Movement Studies M
- Reading Education M
- Special Education M
- Vocational and Technical Education M,D

THE UNIVERSITY OF TEXAS OF THE PERMIAN BASIN

- Accounting M
- Business Administration and Management—General M
- Counselor Education M
- Early Childhood Education M
- Education—General M
- Educational Leadership and Administration M
- English as a Second Language M
- Foundations and Philosophy of Education M
- Kinesiology and Movement Studies M
- Reading Education M
- Special Education M

THE UNIVERSITY OF TEXAS–PAN AMERICAN

- Accounting M
- Advertising and Public Relations M,O
- Business Administration and Management—General M,D
- Counselor Education M
- Early Childhood Education M
- Education of the Gifted M
- Education—General M,D
- Educational Leadership and Administration M,D
- Educational Measurement and Evaluation M
- Educational Psychology M
- Elementary Education M
- English as a Second Language M
- Finance and Banking M,D
- Kinesiology and Movement Studies M
- Management Information Systems M
- Marketing M,D
- Mathematics Education M
- Multilingual and Multicultural Education M
- Music Education M
- Reading Education M
- Secondary Education M
- Social Work M
- Special Education M

THE UNIVERSITY OF THE ARTS

- Art Education M
- Museum Education M
- Music Education M

UNIVERSITY OF THE CUMBERLANDS

- Business Administration and Management—General M
- Business Education M,D,O
- Counselor Education M,D,O
- Education—General M,D,O
- Educational Leadership and Administration M,D,O
- Elementary Education M,D,O
- Marketing M,D,O
- Middle School Education M,D,O
- Reading Education M,D,O
- Secondary Education M,D,O
- Special Education M,D,O
- Student Affairs M,D,O

UNIVERSITY OF THE DISTRICT OF COLUMBIA

- Business Administration and Management—General M
- Counselor Education M
- Early Childhood Education M
- Education—General M
- Law M,D
- Legal and Justice Studies M,D
- Mathematics Education M
- Special Education M

UNIVERSITY OF THE INCARNATE WORD

- Accounting M
- Adult Education M,D,O
- Business Administration and Management—General M,O
- Early Childhood Education M,D
- Education—General M,D
- Educational Leadership and Administration M,D
- Educational Media/Instructional Technology M,D,O
- Elementary Education M
- Entrepreneurship M,D
- Higher Education M,D
- International Business M,D
- Kinesiology and Movement Studies M,D
- Multilingual and Multicultural Education M,D
- Organizational Management M,D,O
- Physical Education M,O
- Project Management M,O
- Reading Education M,O
- Science Education M
- Secondary Education M
- Special Education M,D
- Sports Management M,O

UNIVERSITY OF THE PACIFIC

- Business Administration and Management—General M
- Curriculum and Instruction M,D
- Education—General M,D,O
- Educational Leadership and Administration M,D
- Educational Psychology M,D,O
- Exercise and Sports Science M
- Law M,D
- Legal and Justice Studies M,D
- Music Education M
- Special Education M,D
- Taxation M,D

UNIVERSITY OF THE SACRED HEART

- Accounting M,O
- Advertising and Public Relations M
- Business Administration and Management—General M,O
- Early Childhood Education M,O
- Education—General M,O
- Educational Media/Instructional Technology M
- English Education M,O
- Foreign Languages Education M,O
- Human Resources Management M
- Legal and Justice Studies M
- Management Information Systems M
- Marketing M
- Mathematics Education M,O
- Nonprofit Management M
- Taxation M

UNIVERSITY OF THE SOUTHWEST

- Business Administration and Management—General M
- Counselor Education M
- Curriculum and Instruction M
- Early Childhood Education M
- Education—General M
- Educational Leadership and Administration M
- English as a Second Language M
- Multilingual and Multicultural Education M
- Special Education M
- Sports Management M

UNIVERSITY OF THE VIRGIN ISLANDS

- Business Administration and Management—General M
- Education—General M
- Mathematics Education M

UNIVERSITY OF THE WEST

- Business Administration and Management—General M
- Finance and Banking M
- International Business M
- Management Information Systems M
- Nonprofit Management M

THE UNIVERSITY OF TOLEDO

- Accounting M
- Art Education M,D,O
- Business Administration and Management—General M,D,O
- Business Education M,D,O
- Counselor Education M,D,O
- Curriculum and Instruction M,D,O
- Early Childhood Education M,D
- Education of the Gifted M,D,O
- Education—General M,D,O
- Educational Leadership and Administration M,D,O
- Educational Measurement and Evaluation M,D,O
- Educational Media/Instructional Technology M,D,O
- Educational Psychology M,D,O
- English as a Second Language M,D,O
- English Education M,D,O
- Entrepreneurship M
- Exercise and Sports Science M,D
- Finance and Banking M
- Foreign Languages Education M,D,O
- Foundations and Philosophy of Education M,D,O
- Health Education M,D,O
- Higher Education M,D,O
- Human Resources Management M
- Industrial and Manufacturing Management M,D,O
- Law D
- Leisure Studies M,D
- Management Information Systems M,D,O
- Mathematics Education M,D,O
- Middle School Education M,D,O
- Music Education M,D,O
- Nonprofit Management M,O
- Physical Education M,D
- Recreation and Park Management M,D
- Science Education M,D,O
- Secondary Education M,D,O
- Social Sciences Education M,D,O
- Social Work M,O
- Special Education M,D
- Supply Chain Management M,D,O
- Vocational and Technical Education M,D,O

UNIVERSITY OF TORONTO

- Business Administration and Management—General M,D
- Education—General M,D
- Finance and Banking M
- Human Resources Management M,D
- Information Studies M,D
- Law M,D
- Music Education M,D
- Physical Education M,D
- Social Work M,D

UNIVERSITY OF TULSA

- Accounting M
- Business Administration and Management—General M
- Education—General M
- Elementary Education M
- English Education M
- Environmental Law M,D,O
- Finance and Banking M
- Health Law M,D,O
- International Business M
- Investment Management M
- Law M,D,O
- Management Information Systems M
- Mathematics Education M
- Science Education M
- Secondary Education M
- Taxation M

UNIVERSITY OF UTAH

- Accounting M,D
- Art Education M
- Business Administration and Management—General M,D
- Counselor Education M,D

Early Childhood Education M,D
Education—General M,D
Educational Leadership and Administration M,D
Educational Media/Instructional Technology M,D
Educational Psychology M,D
Elementary Education M,D
Exercise and Sports Science M,D
Finance and Banking M,D
Foreign Languages Education M,D
Foundations and Philosophy of Education M,D
Health Education M,D
Law M,D
Leisure Studies M,D
Management Information Systems M
Reading Education M,D
Real Estate M,D
Recreation and Park Management M,D
Science Education M,D
Secondary Education M,D
Social Work M,D
Special Education M,D

UNIVERSITY OF VERMONT
Accounting M
Business Administration and Management—General M
Counselor Education M
Curriculum and Instruction M
Education—General M,D
Educational Leadership and Administration M,D
Foreign Languages Education M
Mathematics Education M,D
Reading Education M
Science Education M,D
Social Work M
Special Education M

UNIVERSITY OF VICTORIA
Art Education M,D
Business Administration and Management—General M
Counselor Education M,D
Curriculum and Instruction M,D
Early Childhood Education M,D
Education—General M,D
Educational Leadership and Administration M,D
Educational Measurement and Evaluation M,D
Educational Psychology M,D
English Education M,D
Environmental Education M,D
Foreign Languages Education M
Foundations and Philosophy of Education M,D
Kinesiology and Movement Studies M
Law M,D
Leisure Studies M
Mathematics Education M,D
Music Education M,D
Physical Education M
Reading Education M,D
Science Education M,D
Social Sciences Education M,D
Social Work M
Special Education M,D
Vocational and Technical Education M,D

UNIVERSITY OF VIRGINIA
Accounting M
Business Administration and Management—General M,D
Counselor Education M,D,O
Curriculum and Instruction M,D,O
Early Childhood Education M,D,O
Education of the Gifted M,D,O
Education—General M,D,O
Educational Leadership and Administration M,D,O
Educational Measurement and Evaluation M,D,O
Educational Media/Instructional Technology M,D,O
Educational Psychology M,D,O
Elementary Education M,D,O
English Education M,D,O
Finance and Banking M
Foreign Languages Education M,D,O
Health Education M,D
Higher Education M,D,O
Kinesiology and Movement Studies M,D
Law M,D
Management Information Systems M
Marketing D
Mathematics Education M,D,O
Physical Education M,D
Reading Education M,D,O
Science Education M,D,O
Social Sciences Education M,D,O
Special Education M,D,O
Student Affairs M,D,O

UNIVERSITY OF WASHINGTON
Accounting M,D
Business Administration and Management—General M,D
Business Education M,D
Curriculum and Instruction M,D
Education—General M,D
Educational Leadership and Administration M,D
Educational Measurement and Evaluation M,D
Educational Media/Instructional Technology M,D
Educational Policy M,D
Educational Psychology M,D
English as a Second Language M,D
English Education M,D
Finance and Banking M,D
Foundations and Philosophy of Education M,D
Higher Education M,D
Intellectual Property Law M,D
International Business M,D,O
Law M,D
Legal and Justice Studies M,D
Library Science M,D
Logistics M,D,O
Mathematics Education M,D
Multilingual and Multicultural Education M,D
Music Education M,D
Physical Education M,D
Reading Education M,D
Science Education M,D
Social Sciences Education M,D
Social Work M,D
Special Education M,D
Taxation M,D
Transportation Management M,D,O

UNIVERSITY OF WASHINGTON, BOTHELL
Business Administration and Management—General M
Education—General M
Educational Leadership and Administration M
Middle School Education M
Secondary Education M

UNIVERSITY OF WASHINGTON, TACOMA
Accounting M
Business Administration and Management—General M
Education—General M
Educational Leadership and Administration M
Elementary Education M
Finance and Banking M
Mathematics Education M
Science Education M
Social Work M
Special Education M

UNIVERSITY OF WATERLOO
Accounting M,D
Actuarial Science M,D
Business Administration and Management—General M
Entrepreneurship M
Finance and Banking M,D
Health Education M,D
Kinesiology and Movement Studies M,D
Leisure Studies M,D
Recreation and Park Management M,D
Taxation M,D
Travel and Tourism M

THE UNIVERSITY OF WEST ALABAMA
Adult Education M
Counselor Education M
Curriculum and Instruction M
Early Childhood Education M
Education—General M
Educational Leadership and Administration M
Educational Media/Instructional Technology M
Elementary Education M
Secondary Education M
Special Education M
Student Affairs M

THE UNIVERSITY OF WESTERN ONTARIO
Business Administration and Management—General M,D
Curriculum and Instruction M
Education—General M
Educational Policy M
Educational Psychology M
Entrepreneurship M,D
Finance and Banking M,D
Information Studies M,D
International Business M,D
Kinesiology and Movement Studies M,D
Law M,D,O
Library Science M,D
Management Strategy and Policy M,D
Marketing M,D
Special Education M

UNIVERSITY OF WEST FLORIDA
Accounting M
Business Administration and Management—General M,O
Counselor Education M,O
Curriculum and Instruction M,D,O
Early Childhood Education M,O
Education—General D
Educational Leadership and Administration M,D,O
Educational Media/Instructional Technology M,D
Elementary Education M
Exercise and Sports Science M,O
Health Education M
Leisure Studies M
Management Strategy and Policy M,O
Middle School Education M,O
Multilingual and Multicultural Education D
Physical Education M
Reading Education M
Science Education M,D
Secondary Education M,D
Social Sciences Education D
Social Work M
Special Education M
Student Affairs M,O
Vocational and Technical Education M,D,O

UNIVERSITY OF WEST GEORGIA
Accounting M
Art Education M,O
Business Administration and Management—General M
Business Education M,O
Counselor Education M,D,O
Early Childhood Education M,O
Education—General M,D,O
Educational Leadership and Administration M,O
Educational Media/Instructional Technology M,O
English as a Second Language M,D,O
English Education M,O
Foreign Languages Education M,O
Mathematics Education M,O
Middle School Education M,O
Music Education M
Physical Education M,O
Reading Education M,D,O
Science Education M,O
Secondary Education M,O
Social Sciences Education M,O
Special Education M,D,O
Sports Management M,O

UNIVERSITY OF WINDSOR
Business Administration and Management—General M
Education—General M,D
Kinesiology and Movement Studies M
Legal and Justice Studies M
Social Work M

UNIVERSITY OF WISCONSIN–EAU CLAIRE
Business Administration and Management—General M
Education—General M
Elementary Education M
Library Science M
Reading Education M
Secondary Education M
Special Education M

UNIVERSITY OF WISCONSIN–GREEN BAY
Business Administration and Management—General M
Education—General M
Social Work M

UNIVERSITY OF WISCONSIN–LA CROSSE
Athletic Training and Sports Medicine M
Business Administration and Management—General M
Education—General M
Elementary Education M
Exercise and Sports Science M
Health Education M
Higher Education M
Physical Education M
Recreation and Park Management M
Secondary Education M
Special Education M
Student Affairs M

UNIVERSITY OF WISCONSIN–MADISON
Accounting M,D
Actuarial Science M
Art Education M,D
Business Administration and Management—General M
Counselor Education M
Curriculum and Instruction M,D
Education—General M,D,O
Educational Leadership and Administration M,D,O
Educational Policy M,D,O
Educational Psychology M,D
Finance and Banking M,D
Foreign Languages Education M,D
Human Resources Management M,D
Information Studies M,D
Insurance M,D
Investment Management D
Kinesiology and Movement Studies M,D
Law M,D
Legal and Justice Studies M,D
Library Science M,D
Management Information Systems D
Marketing Research M
Marketing D
Mathematics Education M,D
Music Education M,D
Real Estate M,D
Science Education M,D
Social Work M,D
Special Education M,D
Supply Chain Management M
Taxation M

UNIVERSITY OF WISCONSIN–MILWAUKEE
Adult Education D
Archives/Archival Administration M,D,O
Art Education M
Business Administration and Management—General M,D,O
Counselor Education M,D
Curriculum and Instruction M,D
Early Childhood Education M
Education—General M,D,O
Educational Leadership and Administration M,D,O
Educational Measurement and Evaluation M,D
Educational Media/Instructional Technology D
Educational Psychology M,D
Elementary Education M
English as a Second Language M,D,O
Foundations and Philosophy of Education M,D
Health Education M,D,O
Higher Education M,O
Human Resources Development M,O
Information Studies M,D,O
International Business M,O
Investment Management M,D,O
Kinesiology and Movement Studies M
Library Science M,D,O
Middle School Education M
Multilingual and Multicultural Education D
Music Education M,O
Nonprofit Management M,D,O
Reading Education M
Real Estate M,O
Recreation and Park Management M,O
Secondary Education M
Social Work M,D,O
Special Education M,D,O
Taxation M,D,O
Urban Education D

UNIVERSITY OF WISCONSIN–OSHKOSH
Business Administration and Management—General M
Counselor Education M
Curriculum and Instruction M
Early Childhood Education M
Education—General M
Educational Leadership and Administration M
International Business M
Mathematics Education M
Reading Education M
Social Work M
Special Education M

UNIVERSITY OF WISCONSIN–PARKSIDE
Business Administration and Management—General M

UNIVERSITY OF WISCONSIN–PLATTEVILLE
Adult Education M
Counselor Education M
Education—General M
Elementary Education M
English Education M
Middle School Education M
Project Management M
Secondary Education M

UNIVERSITY OF WISCONSIN–RIVER FALLS
Agricultural Education M
Business Administration and Management—General M
Counselor Education M,O
Education—General M
Elementary Education M
English as a Second Language M
Mathematics Education M
Reading Education M
Science Education M
Social Sciences Education M

UNIVERSITY OF WISCONSIN–STEVENS POINT
Advertising and Public Relations M
Business Administration and Management—General M
Counselor Education M
Education—General M
Educational Leadership and Administration M
Elementary Education M
Music Education M
Reading Education M
Science Education M
Special Education M

UNIVERSITY OF WISCONSIN–STOUT
Education—General M,O
Human Resources Development M
Vocational and Technical Education M,O

UNIVERSITY OF WISCONSIN–SUPERIOR
Art Education M
Counselor Education M
Curriculum and Instruction M
Education—General M
Educational Leadership and Administration M,O
Reading Education M
Special Education M

UNIVERSITY OF WISCONSIN–WHITEWATER
Accounting M
Business Administration and Management—General M
Business Education M
Counselor Education M
Curriculum and Instruction M
Education of the Gifted M
Education—General M
Educational Leadership and Administration M
Exercise and Sports Science M
Finance and Banking M
Higher Education M
Human Resources Management M
International Business M
Library Science M
Marketing M

*M—master's degree; P—first professional degree; D—doctorate; O—other advanced degree; *Close-Up and/or Display*

Multilingual and Multicultural Education M
Physical Education M
Reading Education M
Secondary Education M
Special Education M
Supply Chain Management M

UNIVERSITY OF WYOMING
Accounting M
Business Administration and Management—General M
Counselor Education M,D
Curriculum and Instruction M,D
Educational Leadership and Administration M,D,O
Educational Media/Instructional Technology M,D
Exercise and Sports Science M
Finance and Banking M
Health Education M
Kinesiology and Movement Studies M
Law D
Mathematics Education M,D
Music Education M
Physical Education M
Science Education M
Social Work M
Special Education M,D,O
Student Affairs M,D

UPPER IOWA UNIVERSITY
Accounting M
Business Administration and Management—General M
Education—General M
Educational Leadership and Administration M
Finance and Banking M
Higher Education M
Human Resources Management M
Human Services M
International Business M
Organizational Management M
Quality Management M

URBANA UNIVERSITY
Business Administration and Management—General M
Education—General M

URSULINE COLLEGE
Art Education M
Business Administration and Management—General M
Early Childhood Education M
Education—General M
Educational Leadership and Administration M
Mathematics Education M
Middle School Education M
Reading Education M
Science Education M
Social Sciences Education M
Special Education M

UTAH STATE UNIVERSITY
Accounting M
Agricultural Education M
Business Administration and Management—General M
Business Education M,D
Counselor Education M,D
Curriculum and Instruction D
Education—General M,D,O
Educational Measurement and Evaluation M,D
Educational Media/Instructional Technology M,D,O
Elementary Education M
Health Education M
Home Economics Education M
Human Resources Management M
Management Information Systems M,D
Multilingual and Multicultural Education M
Physical Education M
Recreation and Park Management M,D
Secondary Education M
Special Education M,D,O
Vocational and Technical Education M

UTAH VALLEY UNIVERSITY
Accounting M
Business Administration and Management—General M
Education—General M

UTICA COLLEGE
Accounting M
Education—General M,O

VALDOSTA STATE UNIVERSITY
Business Administration and Management—General M
Counselor Education M,O
Early Childhood Education M,O
Educational Leadership and Administration M,D,O
Information Studies M
Library Science M
Middle School Education M,O
Secondary Education M,O
Social Work M
Special Education M,O

VALLEY CITY STATE UNIVERSITY
Education—General M
Educational Media/Instructional Technology M
English as a Second Language M
Library Science M
Vocational and Technical Education M

VALPARAISO UNIVERSITY
Business Administration and Management—General M,O
Counselor Education
Education—General M
Educational Leadership and Administration M
English as a Second Language M,O
Entertainment Management M
Finance and Banking M
International Business M
Law M,D
Legal and Justice Studies O
Management Information Systems M
Sports Management M

VANCOUVER ISLAND UNIVERSITY
Business Administration and Management—General M
Finance and Banking M
International Business M
Marketing M

VANDERBILT UNIVERSITY
Accounting M
Business Administration and Management—General M
Counselor Education M
Education—General M,D*
Educational Leadership and Administration M,D
Educational Measurement and Evaluation M,D
Educational Policy M,D
Elementary Education M
English Education M
Finance and Banking M
Foreign Languages Education M,D
Higher Education M,D
International and Comparative Education M,D
Law M,D
Multilingual and Multicultural Education M,D
Organizational Management M,D
Reading Education M
Science Education M,D
Secondary Education M
Special Education M,D
Urban Education M

VANDERCOOK COLLEGE OF MUSIC
Music Education M

VANGUARD UNIVERSITY OF SOUTHERN CALIFORNIA
Business Administration and Management—General M
Education—General M

VAUGHN COLLEGE OF AERONAUTICS AND TECHNOLOGY
Aviation Management M

VERMONT LAW SCHOOL
Environmental Law M
Law D
Legal and Justice Studies M

VILLANOVA UNIVERSITY
Accounting M
Business Administration and Management—General M
Counselor Education M
Education—General M
Educational Leadership and Administration M
Finance and Banking M
Human Resources Development M
International Business M
Law D
Management Information Systems M
Management Strategy and Policy M
Marketing M
Real Estate M
Secondary Education M
Taxation M

VIRGINIA COLLEGE AT BIRMINGHAM
Business Administration and Management—General M

VIRGINIA COMMONWEALTH UNIVERSITY
Accounting M,D
Adult Education M
Advertising and Public Relations M
Art Education M
Athletic Training and Sports Medicine M
Business Administration and Management—General M,O
Counselor Education M
Early Childhood Education M,O
Education—General M,D,O
Educational Leadership and Administration D
Educational Measurement and Evaluation D
Educational Media/Instructional Technology M
Educational Policy D
Educational Psychology D
Elementary Education M,O
Exercise and Sports Science M
Finance and Banking M
Health Education M,O
Human Resources Development M
Industrial and Manufacturing Management M
Insurance M
Management Information Systems M,D
Management Strategy and Policy M
Marketing M
Music Education M
Nonprofit Management M,O
Physical Education M,D,O
Quantitative Analysis M
Reading Education M,O
Real Estate M,O
Recreation and Park Management M
Secondary Education M,O
Social Work M,D
Special Education M,D,O
Student Affairs M
Urban Education D

VIRGINIA INTERNATIONAL UNIVERSITY
Accounting M,O
Business Administration and Management—General M,O
English as a Second Language M,O
Finance and Banking M,O
Human Resources Management M,O
International Business M,O
Logistics M,O
Management Information Systems M,O
Marketing M,O

VIRGINIA POLYTECHNIC INSTITUTE AND STATE UNIVERSITY
Accounting M,D
Agricultural Education M,D
Business Administration and Management—General M,D
Counselor Education M,D,O
Curriculum and Instruction M,D,O
Distance Education Development M,O
Education—General M,O
Educational Leadership and Administration M,D,O
Educational Measurement and Evaluation M,D,O
Educational Media/Instructional Technology M,O
Educational Policy M,D,O
Finance and Banking M,D
Foreign Languages Education M
Higher Education M,D,O
Hospitality Management M,D
Management Information Systems M,D,O
Marketing M,D
Mathematics Education D,O
Nonprofit Management M,D,O
Quantitative Analysis M,O
Social Sciences Education D,O
Travel and Tourism M,D
Vocational and Technical Education M,D,O

VIRGINIA STATE UNIVERSITY
Education—General M,O
Educational Leadership and Administration M,D
Health Education M
Mathematics Education M
Vocational and Technical Education M,O

VITERBO UNIVERSITY
Business Administration and Management—General M
Education—General M

WAGNER COLLEGE
Accounting M
Business Administration and Management—General M
Early Childhood Education M
Education—General M,O
Educational Leadership and Administration M,O
Elementary Education M
Finance and Banking M
International Business M
Marketing M
Middle School Education M
Reading Education M
Secondary Education M

WAKE FOREST UNIVERSITY
Accounting M
Business Administration and Management—General M
Counselor Education M
Education—General M
Entrepreneurship M
Exercise and Sports Science M
Finance and Banking M
Industrial and Manufacturing Management M
Law M,D
Marketing M
Secondary Education M
Taxation M

WALDEN UNIVERSITY
Accounting M,D,O
Adult Education M,D,O
Business Administration and Management—General M,D,O
Community College Education M,D,O
Counselor Education M,D
Curriculum and Instruction M,D,O
Developmental Education M,D,O
Distance Education Development M,D,O
Early Childhood Education M,D,O
Education—General M,D,O
Educational Leadership and Administration M,D,O
Educational Measurement and Evaluation M,D,O
Educational Media/Instructional Technology M,D,O
Educational Policy M,D,O
Educational Psychology M,D,O
Elementary Education M,D,O
English as a Second Language M,D,O
Entrepreneurship M,D,O
Finance and Banking M,D,O
Health Education M,D,O
Higher Education M,D,O
Human Resources Development M,D,O
Human Resources Management M,D,O
Human Services M,D
International and Comparative Education M,D,O
International Business M,D,O
Law M,D,O
Management Information Systems M,D,O
Management Strategy and Policy M,D,O
Marketing M,D,O
Mathematics Education M,D,O
Middle School Education M,D,O
Multilingual and Multicultural Education M,D,O
Nonprofit Management M,D,O
Organizational Management M,D,O
Project Management M,D,O
Reading Education M,D,O
Science Education M,D,O
Secondary Education M,D,O
Social Work M,D
Special Education M,D,O
Supply Chain Management M,D,O
Sustainability Management M,D,O

WALLA WALLA UNIVERSITY
Curriculum and Instruction M
Education—General M
Educational Leadership and Administration M
Reading Education M
Social Work M
Special Education M

WALSH COLLEGE OF ACCOUNTANCY AND BUSINESS ADMINISTRATION
Accounting M
Business Administration and Management—General M
Finance and Banking M
Management Information Systems M
Taxation M

WALSH UNIVERSITY
Business Administration and Management—General M
Counselor Education M
Education—General M
Marketing M
Religious Education M

WARNER PACIFIC COLLEGE
Business Administration and Management—General M
Education—General M
Organizational Management M

WARNER UNIVERSITY
Business Administration and Management—General M
Education—General M

WASHBURN UNIVERSITY
Business Administration and Management—General M
Curriculum and Instruction M
Education—General M
Educational Leadership and Administration M
Law D
Reading Education M
Social Work M
Special Education M

WASHINGTON ADVENTIST UNIVERSITY
Business Administration and Management—General M

WASHINGTON AND LEE UNIVERSITY
Law M,D

WASHINGTON STATE UNIVERSITY
Accounting M,D
Business Administration and Management—General M,D
Curriculum and Instruction M,D
Education—General M,D,O
Educational Leadership and Administration M,D
Educational Psychology M,D,O
Elementary Education M,D
English Education M,D
Exercise and Sports Science M,D
Finance and Banking M,D
Foreign Languages Education M
Higher Education M,D,O
Industrial and Manufacturing Management M,D
International Business M,D,O
Management Information Systems M,D
Marketing M,D
Mathematics Education M,D
Multilingual and Multicultural Education M,D
Music Education M
Reading Education M,D
Secondary Education M,D
Sports Management M,D,O
Student Affairs M,D,O
Taxation M

WASHINGTON STATE UNIVERSITY SPOKANE
Education—General M,O
Educational Leadership and Administration M,O
Exercise and Sports Science M

WASHINGTON STATE UNIVERSITY TRI-CITIES
Business Administration and Management—General M
Counselor Education M,D
Education—General M,D
Educational Leadership and Administration M,D
Reading Education M,D
Secondary Education M,D

WASHINGTON STATE UNIVERSITY VANCOUVER
Business Administration and Management—General M
Education—General M,D

WASHINGTON UNIVERSITY IN ST. LOUIS
Accounting M
Business Administration and Management—General M,D
Education—General M,D
Educational Measurement and Evaluation D
Elementary Education M
Finance and Banking M
Kinesiology and Movement Studies D
Law M,D
Secondary Education M
Social Work M,D
Special Education M,D
Supply Chain Management M

WAYLAND BAPTIST UNIVERSITY
Business Administration and Management—General M
Education—General M
Educational Leadership and Administration M
Educational Media/Instructional Technology M
Higher Education M
Human Resources Management M
International Business M
Management Information Systems M
Organizational Management M
Special Education M

WAYNESBURG UNIVERSITY
Business Administration and Management—General M,D
Education—General M,D
Educational Media/Instructional Technology M,D
Finance and Banking M,D
Human Resources Management M,D
Organizational Management M,D
Special Education M,D

WAYNE STATE COLLEGE
Business Administration and Management—General M
Business Education M
Counselor Education M
Curriculum and Instruction M
Early Childhood Education M
Education—General M,O
Educational Leadership and Administration M,O
Elementary Education M
English as a Second Language M
English Education M
Exercise and Sports Science M
Home Economics Education M
Mathematics Education M
Music Education M
Organizational Management M
Physical Education M
Science Education M
Social Sciences Education M
Special Education M
Sports Management M
Vocational and Technical Education M

WAYNE STATE UNIVERSITY
Accounting M,D,O
Advertising and Public Relations M,D,O
Archives/Archival Administration M,D,O
Art Education M,D,O
Business Administration and Management—General M,D,O*
Counselor Education M,D,O
Curriculum and Instruction M,D,O
Distance Education Development M,D,O
Early Childhood Education M,D,O
Education—General M,D,O
Educational Leadership and Administration M,D,O
Educational Measurement and Evaluation M,D,O
Educational Media/Instructional Technology M,D,O
Educational Policy M,D,O
Educational Psychology M,D,O
Elementary Education M,D,O
English as a Second Language M,D,O
English Education M,D,O
Exercise and Sports Science M,D
Finance and Banking M,D
Foreign Languages Education M,D,O
Foundations and Philosophy of Education M,D,O
Health Education M,D
Higher Education M,D,O
Human Resources Management M,D
Industrial and Manufacturing Management M,D
Information Studies M,D,O
Kinesiology and Movement Studies M,D,O
Law M,D,O
Library Science M,O
Management Information Systems M,D,O
Mathematics Education M,D,O
Multilingual and Multicultural Education M,D,O
Music Education M,O
Nonprofit Management M
Organizational Behavior M
Organizational Management M
Physical Education M,D
Reading Education M,D,O
Science Education M,D,O
Secondary Education M,D,O
Social Sciences Education M,D,O
Social Work M,D,O
Special Education M,D,O
Sports Management M,D
Taxation M,D,O

Urban Education M,O
Vocational and Technical Education M,D,O

WEBBER INTERNATIONAL UNIVERSITY
Accounting M
Business Administration and Management—General M
Sports Management M

WEBER STATE UNIVERSITY
Accounting M
Athletic Training and Sports Medicine M
Business Administration and Management—General M
Curriculum and Instruction M
Education—General M
Legal and Justice Studies M
Taxation M

WEBSTER UNIVERSITY
Advertising and Public Relations M
Business Administration and Management—General M,D,O
Early Childhood Education M
Education—General M,O
Educational Leadership and Administration M,O
Educational Media/Instructional Technology M,O
English as a Second Language M
Finance and Banking M
Human Resources Development M,D,O
Human Resources Management M,D,O
Intellectual Property Law M,O
International Business M
Legal and Justice Studies M
Management Information Systems M,D,O
Marketing M,D,O
Mathematics Education M,O
Music Education M
Nonprofit Management M,D,O
Organizational Management M
Quality Management M,D,O
Social Sciences Education M,O
Special Education M,O

WESLEYAN COLLEGE
Business Administration and Management—General M
Early Childhood Education M
Education—General M

WESLEY BIBLICAL SEMINARY
Religious Education M

WESLEY COLLEGE
Business Administration and Management—General M
Education—General M

WEST CHESTER UNIVERSITY OF PENNSYLVANIA
Athletic Training and Sports Medicine M
Business Administration and Management—General M,O
Counselor Education M,O
Early Childhood Education M,O
Education—General M,O
Educational Media/Instructional Technology M,O
Electronic Commerce M,O
Elementary Education M,O
English as a Second Language M,O
Entrepreneurship M,O
Exercise and Sports Science M
Finance and Banking M,O
Foreign Languages Education M,O
Health Education M,O
Human Resources Management M,O
Kinesiology and Movement Studies M
Management Information Systems M,O
Middle School Education M,O
Music Education M,O
Nonprofit Management M,O
Physical Education M,O
Reading Education M,O
Science Education M,O
Secondary Education M,O
Social Work M,O
Special Education M,O
Sports Management M

WESTERN CAROLINA UNIVERSITY
Accounting M
Business Administration and Management—General M
Community College Education M,D,O
Counselor Education M,O
Education—General M,D,O
Educational Leadership and Administration M,D,O
English as a Second Language M
Entrepreneurship M
Higher Education M,D,O
Human Resources Development M
Physical Education M,D,O
Project Management M
Social Work M

WESTERN CONNECTICUT STATE UNIVERSITY
Accounting M
Business Administration and Management—General M
Counselor Education M
Curriculum and Instruction M
Education—General M,D
Educational Leadership and Administration D
Educational Media/Instructional Technology M
English as a Second Language M
English Education M
Mathematics Education M

Music Education M
Reading Education M
Science Education M
Secondary Education M
Special Education M

WESTERN GOVERNORS UNIVERSITY
Business Administration and Management—General M
Education—General M,O
Educational Leadership and Administration M,O
Educational Measurement and Evaluation M,O
Educational Media/Instructional Technology M,O
Elementary Education M,O
English Education M,O
Higher Education M,O
Management Information Systems M
Management Strategy and Policy M
Mathematics Education M,O
Science Education M,O
Social Sciences Education M,O
Special Education M,O

WESTERN ILLINOIS UNIVERSITY
Accounting M
Business Administration and Management—General M
Counselor Education M
Distance Education Development M,O
Education—General M,D,O
Educational Leadership and Administration M,D,O
Educational Media/Instructional Technology M,O
Elementary Education M
English as a Second Language M,O
Foundations and Philosophy of Education M,O
Health Education M,O
Kinesiology and Movement Studies M
Reading Education M
Recreation and Park Management M
Special Education M
Sports Management M
Student Affairs M
Travel and Tourism M

WESTERN INTERNATIONAL UNIVERSITY
Business Administration and Management—General M
Finance and Banking M
International Business M
Management Information Systems M
Management Strategy and Policy M
Marketing M
Organizational Behavior M
Organizational Management M

WESTERN KENTUCKY UNIVERSITY
Adult Education M,D,O
Art Education M
Business Administration and Management—General M
Counselor Education M,O
Early Childhood Education M,O
Educational Leadership and Administration M,D,O
Educational Media/Instructional Technology M,O
Elementary Education M,O
English as a Second Language M
English Education M
Foreign Languages Education M
Higher Education M
Middle School Education M,O
Music Education M
Physical Education M
Reading Education M
Recreation and Park Management M
Secondary Education M,O
Social Work M
Special Education M,O
Sports Management M
Student Affairs M

WESTERN MICHIGAN UNIVERSITY
Accounting M
Art Education M
Athletic Training and Sports Medicine M
Business Administration and Management—General M
Counselor Education M,D,O
Education—General M,D,O
Educational Leadership and Administration M,D,O
Educational Measurement and Evaluation M,D,O
Educational Media/Instructional Technology M,D,O
English Education M,D
Exercise and Sports Science M
Finance and Banking M
Health Education D
Human Resources Development M,D
Mathematics Education M,D
Music Education M,D
Nonprofit Management M,D,O
Physical Education M,D
Reading Education M,D
Science Education M,D
Social Work M
Special Education M,D
Sports Management M
Vocational and Technical Education M

WESTERN NEW ENGLAND UNIVERSITY
Accounting M
Business Administration and Management—General M

Elementary Education M
English Education M
Law M,D
Mathematics Education M
Sports Management M

WESTERN NEW MEXICO UNIVERSITY
Business Administration and Management—General M
Counselor Education M
Education—General M
Educational Leadership and Administration M
Elementary Education M
English as a Second Language M
Multilingual and Multicultural Education M
Reading Education M
Secondary Education M
Social Work M
Special Education M

WESTERN OREGON UNIVERSITY
Early Childhood Education M
Education—General M
Educational Media/Instructional Technology M
Health Education M
Mathematics Education M
Multilingual and Multicultural Education M
Science Education M
Secondary Education M
Social Sciences Education M
Special Education M

WESTERN SEMINARY
Human Resources Development M

WESTERN STATE COLLEGE OF COLORADO
Education—General M
Educational Leadership and Administration M
Reading Education M

WESTERN STATE UNIVERSITY COLLEGE OF LAW
Law D

WESTERN UNIVERSITY OF HEALTH SCIENCES
Health Education M

WESTERN WASHINGTON UNIVERSITY
Adult Education M
Business Administration and Management—General M
Counselor Education M
Education of the Gifted M
Education—General M
Educational Leadership and Administration M
Elementary Education M
Environmental Education M
Exercise and Sports Science M
Higher Education M
Physical Education M
Science Education M
Secondary Education M

WESTFIELD STATE UNIVERSITY
Counselor Education M
Early Childhood Education M
Education—General M,O
Educational Leadership and Administration M,O
Educational Media/Instructional Technology M
Elementary Education M
Physical Education M
Reading Education M
Secondary Education M
Special Education M
Vocational and Technical Education M,O

WEST LIBERTY UNIVERSITY
Education—General M

WESTMINSTER COLLEGE (PA)
Counselor Education M,O
Education—General M,O
Educational Leadership and Administration M,O
Reading Education M,O

WESTMINSTER COLLEGE (UT)
Accounting M,O
Business Administration and Management—General M,O
Education—General M

WEST TEXAS A&M UNIVERSITY
Accounting M
Business Administration and Management—General M
Counselor Education M
Curriculum and Instruction M
Education—General M
Educational Leadership and Administration M
Educational Measurement and Evaluation M
Educational Media/Instructional Technology M
Exercise and Sports Science M
Finance and Banking M
Reading Education M
Special Education M

WEST VIRGINIA UNIVERSITY
Accounting M
Agricultural Education M,D
Art Education M
Athletic Training and Sports Medicine M,D

*M—master's degree; P—first professional degree; D—doctorate; O—other advanced degree; *Close-Up and/or Display*

Business Administration and Management—General M
Counselor Education M
Curriculum and Instruction M,D
Early Childhood Education M,D
Education of Students with Severe/Multiple Disabilities M,D
Education of the Gifted M,D
Education—General M,D
Educational Leadership and Administration M,D
Educational Media/Instructional Technology M,D
Educational Psychology M
Elementary Education M
English as a Second Language M
Environmental Education M,D
Exercise and Sports Science M,D
Health Education M,D
Higher Education M,D
Human Services M
Law D
Legal and Justice Studies M
Marketing M,O
Mathematics Education M,D
Music Education M,D
Physical Education M,D
Reading Education M
Recreation and Park Management M
Secondary Education M,D
Social Work M
Special Education M,D
Sports Management M,D

WEST VIRGINIA WESLEYAN COLLEGE
Athletic Training and Sports Medicine M
Business Administration and Management—General M
Education—General M

WHEATON COLLEGE
Education—General M
Elementary Education M
English as a Second Language M,O
Religious Education M
Secondary Education M

WHEELING JESUIT UNIVERSITY
Accounting M
Business Administration and Management—General M
Educational Leadership and Administration M
Organizational Management M

WHEELOCK COLLEGE
Early Childhood Education M
Education—General M
Educational Leadership and Administration M
Elementary Education M
Reading Education M
Social Work M
Special Education M

WHITTIER COLLEGE
Education—General M
Educational Leadership and Administration M
Elementary Education M
Law M,D
Legal and Justice Studies M,D
Secondary Education M

WHITWORTH UNIVERSITY
Counselor Education M
Education of the Gifted M
Education—General M
Educational Leadership and Administration M
Elementary Education M
International Business M
Secondary Education M
Special Education M

WHU - OTTO BEISHEIM SCHOOL OF MANAGEMENT
Business Administration and Management—General M

WICHITA STATE UNIVERSITY
Accounting M
Business Administration and Management—General M
Counselor Education M,D,O
Curriculum and Instruction M
Early Childhood Education M
Education of the Gifted M
Education—General M,D,O
Educational Leadership and Administration M,D,O
Educational Psychology M,D,O
Exercise and Sports Science M
Human Services M
Music Education M
Social Work M
Special Education M
Sports Management M

WIDENER UNIVERSITY
Accounting M
Adult Education M,D
Business Administration and Management—General M
Counselor Education M,D
Early Childhood Education M,D
Education—General M,D
Educational Leadership and Administration M,D
Educational Media/Instructional Technology M,D
Educational Psychology M,D
Elementary Education M,D
English Education M,D
Foundations and Philosophy of Education M,D
Health Education M,D
Health Law M,D
Human Resources Management M
Law M,D
Mathematics Education M,D
Middle School Education M,D
Reading Education M,D
Science Education M,D
Social Sciences Education M,D
Social Work M,D
Special Education M,D
Taxation M

WILFRID LAURIER UNIVERSITY
Accounting M,D
Business Administration and Management—General M,D
Finance and Banking M,D
Human Resources Management M,D
Kinesiology and Movement Studies M
Legal and Justice Studies D
Marketing M,D
Organizational Behavior M,D
Organizational Management M,D
Physical Education M
Social Work M,D
Supply Chain Management M,D

WILKES UNIVERSITY
Accounting M
Business Administration and Management—General M
Computer Education M,D
Curriculum and Instruction M,D
Distance Education Development M,D
Early Childhood Education M,D
Education—General M,D
Educational Leadership and Administration M,D
Educational Measurement and Evaluation M,D
Educational Media/Instructional Technology M,D
English as a Second Language M,D
English Education M,D
Entrepreneurship M
Finance and Banking M
Higher Education M,D
Human Resources Management M
Industrial and Manufacturing Management M
International Business M
Marketing M
Mathematics Education M,D
Organizational Management M
Reading Education M,D
Science Education M,D
Secondary Education M,D
Social Sciences Education M,D
Special Education M,D

WILLAMETTE UNIVERSITY
Business Administration and Management—General M
Education—General M
Law M,D
Reading Education M
Special Education M

WILLIAM CAREY UNIVERSITY
Art Education M,O
Business Administration and Management—General M
Education of the Gifted M,O
Education—General M,O
Elementary Education M,O
English Education M,O
Secondary Education M,O
Social Sciences Education M,O
Special Education M,O

WILLIAM HOWARD TAFT UNIVERSITY
Education—General M
Taxation M

WILLIAM MITCHELL COLLEGE OF LAW
Law M,D

WILLIAM PATERSON UNIVERSITY OF NEW JERSEY
Business Administration and Management—General M
Counselor Education M
Education—General M
Educational Leadership and Administration M
Reading Education M
Special Education M

WILLIAM WOODS UNIVERSITY
Curriculum and Instruction M,O
Educational Leadership and Administration M,O
Elementary Education M,O
Human Resources Development M,O
Physical Education M,O
Secondary Education M,O
Special Education M,O

WILMINGTON COLLEGE
Education—General M
Reading Education M
Special Education M

WILMINGTON UNIVERSITY
Accounting M,D
Business Administration and Management—General M,D
Counselor Education M,D
Education of the Gifted M,D
Education—General M,D
Educational Leadership and Administration M,D
Educational Media/Instructional Technology M,D
Elementary Education M,D
English as a Second Language M,D
Finance and Banking M,D
Higher Education M,D
Human Resources Management M,D
Human Services M,D
Management Information Systems M,D
Marketing M,D
Organizational Management M,D
Reading Education M,D
Secondary Education M,D
Special Education M,D
Vocational and Technical Education M,D

WILSON COLLEGE
Education—General M
Elementary Education M
Secondary Education M

WINGATE UNIVERSITY
Business Administration and Management—General M
Community College Education M,D
Education—General M,D
Educational Leadership and Administration M,D
Elementary Education M,D
Health Education M,D
Physical Education M,D
Sports Management M,D

WINONA STATE UNIVERSITY
Counselor Education M
Education—General M
Educational Leadership and Administration M,O
Recreation and Park Management M,O
Special Education M
Sports Management M,O

WINSTON-SALEM STATE UNIVERSITY
Business Administration and Management—General M
Elementary Education M
Management Information Systems M

WINTHROP UNIVERSITY
Art Education M
Business Administration and Management—General M
Counselor Education M
Education—General M
Educational Leadership and Administration M
Middle School Education M
Music Education M
Physical Education M
Project Management M,O
Reading Education M
Secondary Education M
Social Work M
Special Education M

WITTENBERG UNIVERSITY
Education—General M

WOODBURY UNIVERSITY
Business Administration and Management—General M
Organizational Management M

WORCESTER POLYTECHNIC INSTITUTE
Business Administration and Management—General M,O
Educational Media/Instructional Technology M,D
Management Information Systems M,O
Marketing M,O
Organizational Management M,O

WORCESTER STATE UNIVERSITY
Accounting M
Business Administration and Management—General M
Early Childhood Education M
Education—General M,O
Educational Leadership and Administration M,O
Elementary Education M
English Education M
Foreign Languages Education M
Health Education M
Middle School Education M,O
Nonprofit Management M
Organizational Management M
Reading Education M,O
Secondary Education M
Social Sciences Education M
Special Education M,O

WRIGHT STATE UNIVERSITY
Accounting M
Adult Education O
Business Administration and Management—General M
Business Education M
Computer Education M
Counselor Education M
Curriculum and Instruction M,O
Early Childhood Education M
Education of the Gifted M
Education—General M,O
Educational Leadership and Administration M,O
Elementary Education M
English as a Second Language M
Finance and Banking M
Health Education M
Higher Education M,O
International and Comparative Education M
International Business M
Library Science M
Logistics M
Management Information Systems M
Marketing M
Mathematics Education M
Middle School Education M
Music Education M
Physical Education M
Project Management M
Recreation and Park Management M
Science Education M
Secondary Education M
Special Education M
Supply Chain Management M
Vocational and Technical Education M

XAVIER UNIVERSITY
Business Administration and Management—General M
Counselor Education M
Early Childhood Education M
Education—General M
Educational Leadership and Administration M
Elementary Education M
Finance and Banking M
Health Law M
Human Resources Development M
International Business M
Management Information Systems M
Management Strategy and Policy M
Marketing M
Multilingual and Multicultural Education M
Reading Education M
Religious Education M
Secondary Education M
Special Education M
Sports Management M

XAVIER UNIVERSITY OF LOUISIANA
Counselor Education M
Curriculum and Instruction M
Education—General M
Educational Leadership and Administration M

YALE UNIVERSITY
Accounting D
Business Administration and Management—General M,D
Finance and Banking D
Law M,D
Marketing D
Organizational Management D

YESHIVA UNIVERSITY
Accounting M
Educational Leadership and Administration M,D,O
Intellectual Property Law M,D
Law M,D
Religious Education M,D,O
Social Work M,D*

YORK COLLEGE OF PENNSYLVANIA
Accounting M
Business Administration and Management—General M
Education—General M
Educational Leadership and Administration M
Finance and Banking M
Marketing M
Reading Education M

YORKTOWN UNIVERSITY
Business Administration and Management—General M
Entrepreneurship M
Sports Management M

YORK UNIVERSITY
Business Administration and Management—General M,D*
Education—General M,D
Finance and Banking M,D
Human Resources Management M,D
International Business M,D
Kinesiology and Movement Studies M,D
Law M,D
Social Work M,D

YOUNGSTOWN STATE UNIVERSITY
Accounting M
Business Administration and Management—General M,O
Counselor Education M
Curriculum and Instruction M
Early Childhood Education M
Education of the Gifted M
Education—General M,D
Educational Leadership and Administration M,D
Educational Media/Instructional Technology M
Finance and Banking M
Human Services M
Marketing M
Mathematics Education M
Middle School Education M
Music Education M
Reading Education M
Science Education M
Secondary Education M
Special Education M

ACADEMIC AND PROFESSIONAL PROGRAMS IN BUSINESS

Section 1
Business Administration and Management

This section contains a directory of institutions offering graduate work in business administration and management, followed by in-depth entries submitted by institutions that chose to prepare detailed program descriptions. Additional information about programs listed in the directory but not augmented by an in-depth entry may be obtained by writing directly to the dean of a graduate school or chair of a department at the address given in the directory.

For programs offering related work, see also in this book Sections 2–18, *Education (Business Education)*, and *Sports Management.* In the other guides in this series:

Graduate Programs in the Humanities, Arts & Social Sciences

See *Art and Art History (Arts Administration), Economics, Family and Consumer Sciences (Consumer Economics), Political Science and International Affairs, Psychology (Industrial and Organizational Psychology),* and *Public, Regional, and Industrial Affairs (Industrial and Labor Relations)*

Graduate Programs in the Biological/Biomedical Sciences & Health-Related Medical Professions

See *Health Services and Nursing (Nursing and Healthcare Administration)*

Graduate Programs in the Physical Sciences, Mathematics, Agricultural Sciences, the Environment & Natural Resources

See *Environmental Sciences and Management (Environmental Management and Policy)* and *Mathematical Sciences*

Graduate Programs in Engineering & Applied Sciences

See *Computer Science and Information Technology, Civil and Environmental Engineering (Construction Engineering and Management), Industrial Engineering,* and *Management of Engineering and Technology*

CONTENTS

Program Directory

Displays and Close-Ups

See also:

Business Administration and Management—General

Adelphi University, Robert B. Willumstad School of Business, Graduate Opportunity for Accelerated Learning MBA Program, Garden City, NY 11530-0701. Offers accounting (MBA); finance (MBA). *Accreditation:* AACSB. Part-time and evening/weekend programs available. *Students:* 13 full-time (7 women), 23 part-time (7 women); includes 17 minority (7 Black or African American, non-Hispanic/Latino; 6 Asian, non-Hispanic/Latino; 4 Hispanic/Latino), 2 international. Average age 41. In 2011, 14 master's awarded. *Entrance requirements:* For master's, GMAT, 2 letters of recommendation, four years managerial experience, letter of sponsorship from current place of employment, resume. Additional exam requirements/recommendations for international students: Required—TOEFL (minimum score 550 paper-based; 213 computer-based; 80 iBT). *Application deadline:* For fall admission, 4/1 for international students; for spring admission, 11/1 for international students. Applications are processed on a rolling basis. Application fee: $50. Electronic applications accepted. *Expenses: Tuition:* Full-time $29,600; part-time $930 per credit. *Required fees:* $1100. *Financial support:* Research assistantships with full and partial tuition reimbursements, career-related internships or fieldwork, Federal Work-Study, institutionally sponsored loans, scholarships/grants, and unspecified assistantships available. Financial award application deadline: 3/1; financial award applicants required to submit FAFSA. *Faculty research:* Capital market, executive compensation, business ethics, classical value theory, labor economics. *Unit head:* Rakesh Gupta, Chairperson, 516-877-4670, Fax: 516-877-4607, E-mail: gradbusinquiries@adelphi.edu. *Application contact:* Christine Murphy, Director of Admissions, 516-877-3050, Fax: 516-877-3039, E-mail: graduateadmissions@adelphi.edu.

Adelphi University, Robert B. Willumstad School of Business, MBA Program, Garden City, NY 11530-0701. Offers finance (MBA); management information systems (MBA); management/human resource management (MBA); marketing/e-commerce (MBA). *Accreditation:* AACSB. Part-time and evening/weekend programs available. *Students:* 258 full-time (121 women), 111 part-time (58 women); includes 67 minority (22 Black or African American, non-Hispanic/Latino; 18 Asian, non-Hispanic/Latino; 24 Hispanic/Latino; 3 Two or more races, non-Hispanic/Latino), 172 international. Average age 28. In 2011, 111 master's awarded. *Degree requirements:* For master's, capstone course. *Entrance requirements:* For master's, GMAT, 2 letters of recommendation. Additional exam requirements/recommendations for international students: Required—TOEFL (minimum score 550 paper-based; 213 computer-based; 80 iBT). *Application deadline:* For fall admission, 4/1 for international students; for spring admission, 11/1 for international students. Applications are processed on a rolling basis. Application fee: $50. Electronic applications accepted. *Expenses: Tuition:* Full-time $29,600; part-time $930 per credit. *Required fees:* $1100. *Financial support:* Research assistantships with full and partial tuition reimbursements, career-related internships or fieldwork, Federal Work-Study, institutionally sponsored loans, scholarships/grants, and unspecified assistantships available. Financial award application deadline: 3/1; financial award applicants required to submit FAFSA. *Faculty research:* Supply chain management, distribution channels, productivity benchmark analysis, data envelopment analysis, financial portfolio analysis. *Unit head:* Rakesh Gupta, 516-877-4670, Fax: 516-877-4607, E-mail: gradbusinquiries@adelphi.edu. *Application contact:* Christine Murphy, Director of Admissions, 516-877-3050, Fax: 516-877-3039, E-mail: graduateadmissions@adelphi.edu. Web site: http://business.adelphi.edu/degree-programs/graduate-degree-programs/m-b-a/.

See Display below and Close-Up on page 177.

Alabama Agricultural and Mechanical University, School of Graduate Studies, School of Business, Department of Management and Marketing, Huntsville, AL 35811. Offers MBA. Part-time and evening/weekend programs available. *Degree requirements:* For master's, comprehensive exam, thesis optional. *Entrance requirements:* For master's, GMAT, minimum undergraduate GPA of 2.5. Additional exam requirements/recommendations for international students: Required—TOEFL (minimum score 500 paper-based; 173 computer-based; 61 iBT). Electronic applications accepted. *Faculty research:* Consumer behavior of blacks, small business marketing, economics of education, China in transition, international economics.

Alaska Pacific University, Graduate Programs, Business Administration Department, Program in Business Administration, Anchorage, AK 99508-4672. Offers business administration (MBA); health services administration (MBA). Part-time and evening/weekend programs available. *Degree requirements:* For master's, capstone course. *Entrance requirements:* For master's, GMAT or GRE General Test, minimum GPA of 3.0.

Albany State University, College of Business, Albany, GA 31705-2717. Offers accounting (MBA); general (MBA); healthcare (MBA). *Accreditation:* ACBSP. Part-time and evening/weekend programs available. *Faculty:* 3 full-time (0 women), 1 part-time/adjunct (0 women). *Students:* 4 full-time (2 women), 22 part-time (16 women); includes 24 minority (all Black or African American, non-Hispanic/Latino), 1 international. Average age 33. 22 applicants, 77% accepted, 9 enrolled. In 2011, 5 master's awarded. *Degree requirements:* For master's, comprehensive exam, internship, 3 hours of physical education. *Entrance requirements:* For master's, GMAT (minimum score of 450)/GRE (minimum score of 800) for those without earned master's degree or higher, minimum undergraduate GPA of 2.5, 2 letters of reference, official transcript, pre-entrance medical record and certificate of immunization. *Application deadline:* For fall admission, 6/1 for domestic students, 5/1 for international students; for spring admission, 11/1 for domestic students, 10/1 for international students. Applications are processed on a rolling basis. Application fee: $20. Electronic applications accepted. *Expenses:* Tuition, state resident: full-time $3204; part-time $178 per credit hour. Tuition, nonresident: full-time $12,816; part-time $712 per credit hour. *Required fees:* $379 per semester. *Financial support:* Application deadline: 4/15; applicants required to submit FAFSA. *Faculty research:* Diversity issues, ancestry, understanding finance through use of technology. *Unit head:* Dr. Fidelis Ikem, Interim Dean, 229-430-7009, Fax: 229-430-5119, E-mail: fidelis.ikem@asurams.edu. *Application contact:* Jeffrey Pierce, II, Graduate Counselor, 229-430-4646, Fax: 229-430-4105, E-mail: jeffrey.pierce@asurams.edu. Web site: http://asu-sacs.asurams.edu/ASUCatalog/Graduate/index.html.

Albertus Magnus College, Master of Arts in Leadership Program, New Haven, CT 06511-1189. Offers MA. Part-time and evening/weekend programs available. *Faculty:* 3 full-time (0 women), 8 part-time/adjunct (5 women). *Students:* 15 full-time (11 women), 8 part-time (all women); includes 7 minority (6 Black or African American, non-Hispanic/ Latino; 1 Hispanic/Latino). 30 applicants, 83% accepted, 23 enrolled. In 2011, 17 master's awarded. *Degree requirements:* For master's, thesis optional. *Entrance requirements:* For master's, interview. Additional exam requirements/recommendations for international students: Recommended—TOEFL. Application fee: $50. *Faculty research:* Leadership, quality management, employee motivation. *Unit head:* Dr. Howard Fero, Director, 203-773-4424, E-mail: hfero@albertus.edu. *Application contact:* Annette Bosley-Boyce, 203-773-8512, Fax: 203-773-5257, E-mail: leadership@ albertus.edu.

Albertus Magnus College, Master of Business Administration Program, New Haven, CT 06511-1189. Offers business administration (MBA). Program also offered in East Hartford, CT. Part-time and evening/weekend programs available. Postbaccalaureate distance learning degree programs offered (no on-campus study). *Faculty:* 7 full-time (2 women), 24 part-time/adjunct (6 women). *Students:* 228 full-time (131 women), 19 part-time (9 women); includes 74 minority (61 Black or African American, non-Hispanic/ Latino; 2 American Indian or Alaska Native, non-Hispanic/Latino; 1 Asian, non-Hispanic/ Latino; 10 Hispanic/Latino). Average age 35. 52 applicants, 100% accepted, 52 enrolled. In 2011, 112 master's awarded. *Degree requirements:* For master's, thesis, capstone project. *Entrance requirements:* For master's, 3 years of management or related experience, minimum GPA of 2.5. Additional exam requirements/recommendations for international students: Required—TOEFL. *Application deadline:* Applications are processed on a rolling basis. Application fee: $50. *Financial support:* Available to part-time students. *Faculty research:* Finance, project management, accounting, business administration. *Unit head:* Dr. Wayne Gineo, Director, MBA Programs, 203-777-7100, E-mail: wgineo@albertus.edu. *Application contact:* Dr. Irene Rios, Dean of New Dimensions, 203-777-7100, Fax: 203-777-9906, E-mail: irios@albertus.edu. Web site: http://www.albertus.edu/index.html.

Alcorn State University, School of Graduate Studies, School of Business, Natchez, MS 39122-8399. Offers MBA.

Alfred University, Graduate School, College of Business, Alfred, NY 14802-1205. Offers business administration (MBA). *Accreditation:* AACSB. Part-time programs available. *Entrance requirements:* For master's, GMAT. Additional exam requirements/ recommendations for international students: Required—TOEFL (minimum score 590 paper-based; 243 computer-based; 90 iBT), IELTS (minimum score 6.5). Electronic applications accepted. *Faculty research:* Regional economic development, activity-based costing, nonprofit consumer behavior.

Alliant International University–Los Angeles, Marshall Goldsmith School of Management, Business Division, Alhambra, CA 91803-1360. Offers DBA. *Unit head:* Dr. Jim Goodrich, Systemwide Dean, 866-825-5426, Fax: 858-552-1974, E-mail: admissions@alliant.edu. *Application contact:* Alliant International University Central Contact Center, 866-U-ALLIANT, Fax: 858-635-4555, E-mail: admissions@alliant.edu.

Alliant International University–México City, School of Management, Mexico City, Mexico. Offers business administration (MBA); international business administration (MIBA); international studies (MA), including international relations. Part-time and evening/weekend programs available. *Faculty:* 7 part-time/adjunct (3 women). *Students:* 9. Average age 33. In 2011, 9 master's awarded. *Degree requirements:* For master's, thesis (for some programs). *Entrance requirements:* For master's, GMAT or GRE (depending on program), minimum GPA of 3.0, letters of recommendation. Additional exam requirements/recommendations for international students: Required—TOEFL (minimum score 550 paper-based; 213 computer-based), TWE (minimum score 5). *Application deadline:* For fall admission, 8/1 priority date for domestic students, 8/1 for international students; for spring admission, 12/1 priority date for domestic students, 12/ 1 for international students. Applications are processed on a rolling basis. Application fee: $45. Electronic applications accepted. *Financial support:* Research assistantships, teaching assistantships, career-related internships or fieldwork, Federal Work-Study, institutionally sponsored loans, and scholarships/grants available. Support available to part-time students. Financial award application deadline: 2/15; financial award applicants required to submit FAFSA. *Faculty research:* Global economy, international relations. *Unit head:* Dr. Chet Haskell, Dean, 858-635-4696, E-mail: contacto@ alliantmexico.com. *Application contact:* Lesly Gutierrez Garcia, Coordinator of Admissions and Student Services, (+5255) 5525-7651, E-mail: contacto@ alliantmexico.com. Web site: http://www.alliantmexico.com.

Alliant International University–San Diego, Alliant School of Management, Business and Management Division, San Diego, CA 92131-1799. Offers business administration (MBA); MBA/MA; MBA/PhD. Part-time and evening/weekend programs available. *Faculty:* 8 full-time (3 women), 7 part-time/adjunct (1 woman). *Students:* 50 full-time (27 women), 57 part-time (25 women); includes 23 minority (8 Black or African American, non-Hispanic/Latino; 8 Asian, non-Hispanic/Latino; 7 Hispanic/Latino), 38 international. Average age 37. In 2011, 28 master's awarded. *Entrance requirements:* For master's, GMAT or GRE, minimum GPA of 2.75. Additional exam requirements/recommendations for international students: Required—TOEFL (minimum score 550 paper-based; 213 computer-based), TWE (minimum score 5). *Application deadline:* For fall admission, 8/1 priority date for domestic students, 8/1 for international students; for spring admission, 12/1 priority date for domestic students, 12/1 for international students. Applications are processed on a rolling basis. Application fee: $55. Electronic applications accepted. Tuition and fees vary according to degree level and program. *Financial support:* Research assistantships, teaching assistantships, career-related internships or fieldwork, Federal Work-Study, institutionally sponsored loans, scholarships/grants, and tuition waivers (partial) available. Support available to part-time students. Financial award application deadline: 2/15; financial award applicants required to submit FAFSA. *Faculty research:* Financial and commodity markets; market micro-structures; risk measurement, virtual teams, sustainable work environments. *Unit head:* Dr. Rachna Kumar, Program Director, 858-635-4551, Fax: 855-635-4739, E-mail: admissions@ alliant.edu. *Application contact:* Alliant International University Central Contact Center, 866-U-ALLIANT, Fax: 858-635-4555, E-mail: admissions@alliant.edu. Web site: http:// www.alliant.edu/usicb.

Alliant International University–San Francisco, School of Management, Presidio School of Management, San Francisco, CA 94133-1221. Offers sustainable management (MBA, MPA). Part-time programs available. *Faculty:* 6 full-time (3 women), 15 part-time/adjunct (8 women). *Students:* 175 full-time (88 women), 61 part-time (26 women); includes 15 minority (10 Asian, non-Hispanic/Latino; 5 Two or more races, non-Hispanic/Latino). Average age 35. *Entrance requirements:* For master's, letters of reference, essay. Additional exam requirements/recommendations for international students: Required—TOEFL (minimum score 100 iBT). *Application deadline:* For fall admission, 3/9 priority date for domestic students. Applications are processed on a rolling basis. Electronic applications accepted. *Financial support:* Application deadline: 3/9; applicants required to submit FAFSA. *Faculty research:* Sustainable management, renewable energy and clean technology, ecological economics, social entrepreneurship, urban sustainability. *Unit head:* Dr. Edward Quevedo, Interim Dean, 415-561-6555, E-mail: info@presidioedu.org. *Application contact:* Bethany Baugh, Director of Admissions, 415-561-6555, E-mail: admissions@presidioedu.org.

Alvernia University, Graduate Studies, Department of Business, Reading, PA 19607-1799. Offers MBA. *Accreditation:* ACBSP. Part-time and evening/weekend programs available. *Degree requirements:* For master's, thesis optional. *Entrance requirements:* For master's, GMAT, GRE, or MAT. Electronic applications accepted.

Alverno College, School of Business, Milwaukee, WI 53234-3922. Offers MBA. Evening/weekend programs available. *Faculty:* 4 full-time (all women), 3 part-time/ adjunct (2 women). *Students:* 85 full-time (71 women), 3 part-time (all women); includes 24 minority (10 Black or African American, non-Hispanic/Latino; 2 Asian, non-Hispanic/ Latino; 10 Hispanic/Latino; 2 Two or more races, non-Hispanic/Latino), 1 international. Average age 37. 57 applicants, 49% accepted, 21 enrolled. In 2011, 31 master's awarded. *Entrance requirements:* For master's, 3 or more years relevant work experience. Additional exam requirements/recommendations for international students: Required—TOEFL. *Application deadline:* For fall admission, 7/15 priority date for domestic students, 7/15 for international students; for spring admission, 12/15 priority date for domestic students, 12/15 for international students. Applications are processed on a rolling basis. Application fee: $0. Electronic applications accepted. Application fee is waived when completed online. *Expenses:* Contact institution. *Financial support:* Federal Work-Study available. Support available to part-time students. Financial award application deadline: 4/15; financial award applicants required to submit FAFSA. *Unit head:* Patricia Jensen, MBA Program Director, 414-382-6321, E-mail: patricia.jensen@ alverno.edu. *Application contact:* Christy Stone, Director of Graduate and Adult Recruitment, 414-382-6108, Fax: 414-382-6354, E-mail: christy.stone@alverno.edu.

Amberton University, Graduate School, Department of Business Administration, Garland, TX 75041-5595. Offers general business (MBA); management (MBA). Part-time and evening/weekend programs available. *Entrance requirements:* For master's, minimum GPA of 3.0.

The American College, Graduate Programs, Bryn Mawr, PA 19010-2105. Offers financial services (MSFS); leadership (MSM). Part-time and evening/weekend programs available. Postbaccalaureate distance learning degree programs offered (minimal on-campus study). Electronic applications accepted. *Faculty research:* Retirement counseling, social security, aging, family composition, inflation.

American College of Thessaloniki, Department of Business Administration, Pylea, Greece. Offers banking and finance (MBA); entrepreneurship (MBA, Certificate); finance (Certificate); management (MBA, Certificate); marketing (MBA, Certificate). Part-time and evening/weekend programs available. *Degree requirements:* For master's, thesis. *Entrance requirements:* For master's, bachelor's degree. Additional exam requirements/ recommendations for international students: Recommended—TOEFL. Electronic applications accepted.

American Graduate University, Program in Acquisition Management, Covina, CA 91724. Offers MAM, Certificate. Part-time programs available. Postbaccalaureate distance learning degree programs offered (no on-campus study). *Faculty:* 2 full-time (1 woman), 15 part-time/adjunct (2 women). *Students:* 326 part-time. In 2011, 37 master's awarded. *Degree requirements:* For master's, comprehensive exam, thesis (for some programs). *Entrance requirements:* For master's, undergraduate degree from institution accredited by accrediting agency recognized by the U.S. Department of Education. Additional exam requirements/recommendations for international students: Required—TOEFL. *Application deadline:* Applications are processed on a rolling basis. Application fee: $50. Electronic applications accepted. *Expenses: Tuition:* Part-time $275 per credit. *Unit head:* Paul McDonald, President, 626-966-4576 Ext. 1006, E-mail: paulmcdonald@ agu.edu. *Application contact:* Marie Sirney, Admissions Director, 626-966-4576 Ext. 1003, Fax: 626-915-1709, E-mail: mariesirney@agu.edu.

American Graduate University, Program in Business Administration, Covina, CA 91724. Offers MBA. Part-time programs available. Postbaccalaureate distance learning degree programs offered (no on-campus study). *Faculty:* 2 full-time (1 woman), 15 part-time/adjunct (2 women). *Students:* 226 part-time. In 2011, 15 master's awarded. *Degree requirements:* For master's, thesis. *Entrance requirements:* For master's, undergraduate degree from institution accredited by accrediting agency recognized by the U.S. Department of Education. Additional exam requirements/recommendations for international students: Required—TOEFL. *Application deadline:* Applications are processed on a rolling basis. Application fee: $50. Electronic applications accepted. *Expenses: Tuition:* Part-time $275 per credit. *Unit head:* Paul McDonald, President, 626-966-4576 Ext. 1006, E-mail: paulmcdonald@agu.edu. *Application contact:* Marie J. Sirney, Executive Vice President, 626-966-4576, Fax: 626-915-1709, E-mail: mariesirney@agu.edu.

American Graduate University, Program in Contract Management, Covina, CA 91724. Offers MCM, Certificate. Part-time programs available. Postbaccalaureate distance learning degree programs offered (no on-campus study). *Faculty:* 2 full-time (1 woman), 15 part-time/adjunct (2 women). *Students:* 116 part-time. In 2011, 18 master's awarded. *Degree requirements:* For master's, comprehensive exam (for some programs), thesis (for some programs). *Entrance requirements:* For master's, undergraduate degree from institution accredited by accrediting agency recognized by the U.S. Department of Education. Additional exam requirements/recommendations for international students: Required—TOEFL. *Application deadline:* Applications are processed on a rolling basis. Application fee: $50. Electronic applications accepted. *Expenses: Tuition:* Part-time $275 per credit. *Unit head:* Paul McDonald, President, 626-966-4576 Ext. 1006, E-mail: paulmcdonald@agu.edu. *Application contact:* Marie Sirney, 626-966-4576 Ext. 1003, Fax: 626-915-1709, E-mail: mariesirney@agu.edu.

American InterContinental University Buckhead Campus, Program in Business Administration, Atlanta, GA 30326-1016. Offers accounting and finance (MBA); management (MBA); marketing (MBA). Evening/weekend programs available. Postbaccalaureate distance learning degree programs offered. *Entrance requirements:* For master's, minimum cumulative undergraduate GPA of 2.0. Additional exam requirements/recommendations for international students: Required—TOEFL (minimum score 530 paper-based; 230 computer-based). Electronic applications accepted. *Faculty research:* Leadership management, international advertising.

American InterContinental University Houston, School of Business, Houston, TX 77042. Offers management (MBA).

American InterContinental University London, Program in Business Administration, London, United Kingdom. Offers international business (MBA). *Degree requirements:* For master's, thesis optional. *Entrance requirements:* For master's, interview, professional experience. Additional exam requirements/recommendations for international students: Required—TOEFL or IELTS recommended. Electronic applications accepted.

American InterContinental University Online, Program in Business Administration, Hoffman Estates, IL 60192. Offers accounting and finance (MBA); finance (MBA); healthcare management (MBA); human resource management (MBA); international business (MBA); management (MBA); marketing (MBA); operations management (MBA); organizational psychology and development (MBA); project management (MBA). Evening/weekend programs available. Postbaccalaureate distance learning degree

requirements/recommendations for international students: Required—TOEFL (minimum score 550 paper-based; 213 computer-based). Electronic applications accepted.

American InterContinental University South Florida, Program in International Business, Weston, FL 33326. Offers accounting and finance (MBA); human resource management (MBA); management (MBA); marketing (MBA). Part-time and evening/weekend programs available. Postbaccalaureate distance learning degree programs offered. Electronic applications accepted.

American International College, School of Business Administration, Springfield, MA 01109-3189. Offers MBA, MPA, MS, MSAT. Part-time and evening/weekend programs available. Postbaccalaureate distance learning degree programs offered (minimal on-campus study). *Degree requirements:* For master's, comprehensive exam (for some programs), thesis (for some programs). *Entrance requirements:* For master's, GMAT, BA or BS, minimum GPA of 2.75. Additional exam requirements/recommendations for international students: Required—TOEFL (minimum score 550 paper-based; 213 computer-based; 80 iBT).

American Jewish University, Graduate School of Nonprofit Management, Program in Business Administration, Bel Air, CA 90077-1599. Offers general nonprofit administration (MBA); Jewish nonprofit administration (MBA). Part-time and evening/weekend programs available. *Degree requirements:* For master's, thesis, internship. *Entrance requirements:* For master's, GMAT or GRE General Test, interview, minimum undergraduate GPA of 3.0. Additional exam requirements/recommendations for international students: Required—TOEFL (minimum score 550 paper-based; 247 computer-based).

American Public University System, AMU/APU Graduate Programs, Charles Town, WV 25414. Offers accounting (MBA, MS); administration and supervision (M Ed); criminal justice (MA); emergency and disaster management (MA); entrepreneurship (MBA); environmental policy and management (MS), including environmental planning, environmental sustainability, fish and wildlife management, general (MA, MS), global environmental management; finance (MBA); general (MBA); global business management (MBA); guidance and counseling (M Ed); history (MA), including American history, ancient and classical history, European history, global history, military and diplomatic history, public history; homeland security (MA); homeland security resource allocation (MBA); humanities (MA); information technology (MS), including digital forensics, enterprise software development, information assurance and security, IT project management; information technology management (MBA); intelligence studies (MA), including criminal intelligence, general (MA, MS), homeland security, intelligence analysis, intelligence collection, intelligence operations, terrorism studies; international relations and conflict resolution (MA), including comparative and security issues, conflict resolution, international and transnational security issues, peacekeeping; legal studies (MA); management (MA), including defense management, general (MA, MS), human resource management, organizational leadership, public administration, reverse logistics, strategic consulting; marketing (MBA); military history (MA), including American military history, American revolution, civil war, war since 1946, World War II; military studies (MA), including air warfare, asymmetrical warfare, joint warfare, land warfare, naval warfare, strategic leadership; national security studies (MA), including general (MA, MS), homeland security, regional security studies, security and intelligence analysis, terrorism studies; nonprofit management (MBA); political science (MA), including American politics and government, comparative government and development, public policy; psychology (MA); public administration (MA, MPA), including disaster management (MPA), environmental policy (MA), health policy (MPA), human resources (MPA), national security (MPA), organizational management (MPA), security management (MPA); public health (MA, MPH), including emergency management (MPH), environmental health (MPH), public administration (MA); reverse logistics management (MA); security management (MA); space studies (MS), including aerospace science, planetary science; sports and health sciences (MS); sports management (MS), including coaching theory and strategy, sports administration; teaching (M Ed), including curriculum and instruction for elementary teachers, elementary, elementary reading, English language learners, instructional leadership, online learning, secondary social sciences, special education; transportation and logistics management (MA), including maritime engineering management. Programs offered via distance learning only. Part-time and evening/weekend programs available. Postbaccalaureate distance learning degree programs offered (no on-campus study). *Faculty:* 445 full-time (241 women), 1,360 part-time/adjunct (617 women). *Students:* 688 full-time (338 women), 10,168 part-time (3,706 women); includes 3,130 minority (1,007 Black or African American, non-Hispanic/Latino; 103 American Indian or Alaska Native, non-Hispanic/Latino; 825 Asian, non-Hispanic/Latino; 810 Hispanic/Latino; 51 Native Hawaiian or other Pacific Islander, non-Hispanic/Latino; 334 Two or more races, non-Hispanic/Latino), 134 international. Average age 35. In 2011, 2,386 master's awarded. *Degree requirements:* For master's, comprehensive exam or practicum. *Entrance requirements:* For master's, official transcript showing earned bachelor's degree from institution accredited by recognized accrediting body. Additional exam requirements/recommendations for international students: Required—TOEFL (minimum score 550 paper-based; 213 computer-based), IELTS (minimum score 6.5). *Application deadline:* Applications are processed on a rolling basis. Application fee: $0. Electronic applications accepted. *Expenses: Tuition:* Part-time $325 per credit hour. *Financial support:* Applicants required to submit FAFSA. *Faculty research:* Military history, criminal justice, management performance, national security. *Unit head:* Dr. Karan Powell, Executive Vice President and Provost, 877-468-6268, Fax: 304-724-3780. *Application contact:* Terry Grant, Vice President of Enrollment Management, 877-468-6268, Fax: 304-724-3780, E-mail: info@apus.edu. Web site: http://www.apus.edu.

American Sentinel University, Graduate Programs, Aurora, CO 80014. Offers business administration (MBA); business intelligence (MS); computer science (MSCS); health information management (MS); healthcare (MBA); information systems (MSIS); nursing (MSN). Part-time and evening/weekend programs available. Postbaccalaureate distance learning degree programs offered (no on-campus study). *Entrance requirements:* Additional exam requirements/recommendations for international students: Required—TOEFL (minimum score 600 paper-based; 215 computer-based). Electronic applications accepted.

American University, Kogod School of Business, Master of Business Administration Program, Washington, DC 20016-8044. Offers accounting (MBA); consulting (MBA), including business systems consulting, management consulting; entrepreneurship (MBA); entrepreneurship (Certificate); finance (MBA); global emerging markets (MBA); leadership and strategic human capital management (MBA); marketing (MBA); real estate (MBA); MBA/JD; MBA/LL M; MBA/MA. Part-time and evening/weekend programs available. *Faculty:* 13 full-time (6 women). *Students:* 96 full-time (43 women), 104 part-time (35 women); includes 49 minority (14 Black or African American, non-Hispanic/Latino; 16 Asian, non-Hispanic/Latino; 16 Hispanic/Latino; 1 Native Hawaiian or other Pacific Islander, non-Hispanic/Latino; 2 Two or more races, non-Hispanic/Latino), 22 international. Average age 29. 340 applicants, 52% accepted, 52 enrolled. In 2011, 124 master's awarded. *Entrance requirements:* For master's, GMAT, resume, personal statement, interview. Additional exam requirements/recommendations for international students: Required—TOEFL. *Application deadline:* For fall admission, 2/1 priority date for domestic students; for spring admission, 10/1 priority date for domestic students. Applications are processed on a rolling basis. Application fee: $100. *Expenses:* Contact institution. *Financial support:* In 2011–12, 19 students received support. Fellowships, research assistantships with partial tuition reimbursements available, career-related internships or fieldwork, Federal Work-Study, and institutionally sponsored loans available. Support available to part-time students. Financial award application deadline: 2/1. *Faculty research:* Information technology, decision-aiding methodology, negotiation. *Unit head:* Dr. Stevan R. Holmberg, Chair, 202-885-1921, Fax: 202-885-1916, E-mail: sholmbe@american.edu. *Application contact:* Shannon Demko, Director of Admissions, 202-885-1968, Fax: 202-885-1078, E-mail: demko@american.edu. Web site: http://www.american.edu/kogod/.

American University, School of Public Affairs, Department of Public Administration, Washington, DC 20016-8070. Offers key executive leadership (MPA); leadership for organizational change (Certificate); non-profit management (Certificate); organization development (MSOD); public administration (MPA, PhD); public financial management (Certificate); public management (Certificate); public policy (MPP, Certificate), including public policy (MPP), public policy analysis (Certificate); public policy analysis (Certificate); LL M/MPA; MPA/JD; MPP/JD; MPP/LL M. Part-time and evening/weekend programs available. *Faculty:* 28 full-time (13 women), 14 part-time/adjunct (4 women). *Students:* 232 full-time (145 women), 240 part-time (145 women); includes 111 minority (62 Black or African American, non-Hispanic/Latino; 6 American Indian or Alaska Native, non-Hispanic/Latino; 21 Asian, non-Hispanic/Latino; 15 Hispanic/Latino; 7 Two or more races, non-Hispanic/Latino), 42 international. Average age 30. 809 applicants, 69% accepted, 172 enrolled. In 2011, 171 master's, 4 doctorates, 14 other advanced degrees awarded. *Degree requirements:* For master's, comprehensive exam; for doctorate, comprehensive exam, thesis/dissertation. *Entrance requirements:* For master's, GRE, statement of purpose; 2 recommendations, resume; for doctorate, GRE, 3 recommendations, statement of purpose, resume, writing sample; for Certificate, bachelor's degree. Additional exam requirements/recommendations for international students: Required—TOEFL. *Application deadline:* For fall admission, 2/1 for domestic students; for spring admission, 11/1 for domestic students. Application fee: $55. *Expenses: Tuition:* Full-time $24,264; part-time $1348 per credit hour. *Required fees:* $430. Tuition and fees vary according to course load and program. *Financial support:* Fellowships, research assistantships, teaching assistantships, career-related internships or fieldwork, Federal Work-Study, and institutionally sponsored loans available. Financial award application deadline: 2/1. *Faculty research:* Urban management, conservation politics, state and local budgeting, tax policy. *Unit head:* Dr. Jocelyn Johnston, Chair, 202-885-2608, Fax: 202-885-2347, E-mail: johnston@american.edu. *Application contact:* Brenda Manley, Admissions and Financial Aid Manager, 202-885-6202, Fax: 202-885-2355, E-mail: bmanley@american.edu. Web site: http://www.american.edu/spa/dpap/.

The American University in Cairo, School of Business, New Cairo 11835, Egypt. Offers business administration (MBA, Diploma); economics (MA). Part-time programs available. *Faculty:* 21 full-time (4 women), 6 part-time/adjunct (2 women). *Students:* 104 full-time (28 women), 102 part-time (61 women). 289 applicants, 46% accepted, 48 enrolled. In 2011, 85 master's awarded. *Degree requirements:* For master's, thesis (for some programs). *Entrance requirements:* For master's, English entrance exam, GMAT, GRE. Additional exam requirements/recommendations for international students: Required—TOEFL (minimum score 450 paper-based; 133 computer-based; 45 iBT). *Application deadline:* For fall admission, 2/1 priority date for domestic students, 2/1 for international students; for spring admission, 11/1 priority date for domestic students, 11/1 for international students. Applications are processed on a rolling basis. Application fee: $50. Electronic applications accepted. *Expenses: Tuition:* Part-time $932 per credit hour. Tuition and fees vary according to course load, degree level and program. *Financial support:* Fellowships with partial tuition reimbursements, research assistantships, teaching assistantships, career-related internships or fieldwork, scholarships/grants, and unspecified assistantships available. Financial award application deadline: 5/12; financial award applicants required to submit CSS PROFILE. *Faculty research:* Marketing and quality management, banking operations management, strategic planning. *Unit head:* Dr. Sherif Kamel, Dean, 20-2-2615-3290, E-mail: skamel@aucegypt.edu. *Application contact:* Wesley Clark, Director of North American Admissions and Financial Aid, 212-646-810-9433 Ext. 4547, E-mail: wclark@aucnyo.edu. Web site: http://www.aucegypt.edu/Business/Pages/default.aspx.

The American University in Dubai, Master in Business Administration Program, Dubai, United Arab Emirates. Offers general (MBA); healthcare management (MBA); international finance (MBA); international marketing (MBA); management of construction enterprises (MBA). Part-time and evening/weekend programs available. *Degree requirements:* For master's, thesis optional. *Entrance requirements:* For master's, GMAT, Interview. Additional exam requirements/recommendations for international students: Required—TOEFL (minimum score 550 paper-based; 213 computer-based; 79 iBT). Electronic applications accepted.

The American University of Athens, School of Graduate Studies, Athens, Greece. Offers biomedical sciences (MS); business (MBA); business communication (MA); computer sciences (MS); engineering and applied sciences (MS); politics and policy making (MA); systems engineering (MS); telecommunications (MS). *Entrance requirements:* For master's, resume, 2 recommendation letters. Additional exam requirements/recommendations for international students: Required—TOEFL (minimum score 550 paper-based; 213 computer-based). *Faculty research:* Nanotechnology, environmental sciences, rock mechanics, human skin studies, Monte Carlo algorithms and software.

American University of Beirut, Graduate Programs, Olayan School of Business, The Executive MBA Program, Beirut, Lebanon. Offers EMBA. *Faculty:* 14 full-time (4 women), 4 part-time/adjunct (1 woman). *Students:* 39 full-time (5 women). Average age 41. 40 applicants, 48% accepted, 18 enrolled. In 2011, 25 master's awarded. *Degree requirements:* For master's, one foreign language. *Entrance requirements:* For master's, analytical exam (developed and administered in-house), letters of recommendation, interview. Additional exam requirements/recommendations for international students: Required—TOEFL (minimum score 585 paper-based; 90 iBT), IELTS. *Application deadline:* Applications are processed on a rolling basis. Application fee: $75. *Expenses: Tuition:* Full-time $12,780; part-time $710 per credit. Tuition and fees vary according to course load and program. *Faculty research:* Capital acquisition/mergers and acquisition, corporate governance and financial reporting, corporate social responsibility, revenue management models in the cargo and cruise ship industries, inventory models. *Unit head:* Riad Dimeshkie, Director, 961-1350000 Ext. 3724, Fax: 961-1750214, E-mail: rd28@aub.edu.lb. *Application contact:* Rula Murtada-Karam, Executive MBA Officer, 961-1350000 Ext. 3946, Fax: 961-1750214, E-mail: rm04@aub.edu.lb.

American University of Beirut, Graduate Programs, Olayan School of Business, The MBA Program, Beirut, Lebanon. Offers MBA. Part-time and evening/weekend programs available. *Faculty:* 9 full-time (3 women), 3 part-time/adjunct (0 women). *Students:* 36 full-time (26 women), 42 part-time (23 women). Average age 28. 103 applicants, 25% accepted, 17 enrolled. In 2011, 26 master's awarded. *Degree requirements:* For master's, one foreign language, thesis (for some programs), final project (for full-time students). *Entrance requirements:* For master's, GMAT (minimum score of 570), letters of recommendation. Additional exam requirements/recommendations for international students: Required—TOEFL (minimum score 600 paper-based; 250 computer-based; 100 iBT), IELTS (minimum score 7.5). *Application deadline:* For fall admission, 2/20 for domestic and international students; for spring admission, 11/15 for domestic and international students. Application fee: $50. *Expenses: Tuition:* Full-time $12,780; part-time $710 per credit. Tuition and fees vary according to course load and program. *Financial support:* In 2011–12, 29 students received support. Scholarships/grants and unspecified assistantships available. Support available to part-time students. Financial award application deadline: 2/20. *Faculty research:* Capital acquisition/mergers and acquisition, corporate governance and financial reporting, organizational behavior, entrepreneurship, corporate social responsibility, corporate finance. *Unit head:* Dr. Salim Chahine, Director, 961-1374374 Ext. 3722, Fax: 961-1750214, E-mail: sc09@aub.edu.lb. *Application contact:* Dr. Salim Kanaan, Director, Admissions Office, 961-1350000 Ext. 2594, Fax: 961-1750775, E-mail: sk00@aub.edu.lb. Web site: http://sb.aub.edu.lb.

The American University of Paris, Graduate Programs, Paris, France. Offers cross-cultural and sustainable business management (MA); cultural translation (MA); global communications (MA); global communications and civil society (MA); international affairs, conflict resolution and civil society development (MA); Middle East and Islamic studies (MA); Middle East and Islamic studies and international affairs (MA); public policy and international affairs (MA); public policy and international law (MA). *Faculty:* 14 full-time (3 women). *Students:* 142 full-time (98 women), 59 part-time (41 women). *Degree requirements:* For master's, thesis. *Entrance requirements:* For master's, minimum undergraduate GPA of 3.0. Additional exam requirements/recommendations for international students: Recommended—TOEFL, IELTS. *Application deadline:* For fall admission, 4/15 for international students; for spring admission, 11/15 for international students. Applications are processed on a rolling basis. Application fee: $75. Electronic applications accepted. Tuition and fees charges are reported in euros. *Expenses: Tuition:* Full-time 25,060 euros; part-time 784 euros per credit. *Required fees:* 784 euros per credit. *Financial support:* Scholarships/grants available. Financial award applicants required to submit FAFSA. *Unit head:* Dr. Celeste Schenck, President, 33 1 40 62 06 59, E-mail: president@aup.fr. *Application contact:* International Admissions Counselor, 33-1 40 62 07 20, Fax: 33-1 47 05 34 32, E-mail: admissions@aup.edu. Web site: http://aup.edu/main/academics/graduate.htm.

American University of Sharjah, Graduate Programs, Sharjah, United Arab Emirates. Offers business (EMBA, GEMPA, MBA); chemical engineering (MS Ch E); civil engineering (MSCE); computer engineering (MS); electrical engineering (MSEE); mechanical engineering (MSME); mechatronics engineering (MS); public administration (MPA); teaching English to speakers of other languages (MA); translation and interpreting (MA); urban planning (MUP). Part-time and evening/weekend programs available. *Entrance requirements:* For master's, GMAT (MBA). Additional exam requirements/recommendations for international students: Required—TOEFL (minimum score 550 paper-based; 213 computer-based; 80 iBT), TWE (minimum score 5). Electronic applications accepted. *Faculty research:* Chemical engineering, civil engineering, computer engineering, electrical engineering, linguistics, translation.

Anaheim University, Programs in Business Administration, Anaheim, CA 92806-5150. Offers online global (MBA); online green (MBA); professional (MBA); sustainable management (Certificate, Diploma). Postbaccalaureate distance learning degree programs offered.

Anderson University, College of Business, Anderson, SC 29621-4035. Offers MBA. *Accreditation:* ACBSP.

Anderson University, Falls School of Business, Anderson, IN 46012-3495. Offers accountancy (MA); business administration (MBA, DBA). *Accreditation:* ACBSP.

Angelo State University, College of Graduate Studies, College of Business, Department of Management and Marketing, San Angelo, TX 76909. Offers business administration (MBA). *Accreditation:* ACBSP. Part-time and evening/weekend programs available. *Faculty:* 6 full-time (1 woman). *Students:* 13 full-time (4 women), 27 part-time (12 women); includes 2 minority (1 Black or African American, non-Hispanic/Latino; 1 Hispanic/Latino), 3 international. Average age 28. 26 applicants, 50% accepted, 10 enrolled. In 2011, 14 master's awarded. *Entrance requirements:* For master's, GMAT or GRE. Additional exam requirements/recommendations for international students: Required—TOEFL or IELTS. *Application deadline:* For fall admission, 7/15 priority date for domestic students, 6/10 for international students; for spring admission, 12/1 priority date for domestic students, 11/1 for international students. Applications are processed on a rolling basis. Application fee: $40 ($50 for international students). Electronic applications accepted. *Financial support:* In 2011–12, 21 students received support. Career-related internships or fieldwork, Federal Work-Study, and scholarships/grants available. Support available to part-time students. Financial award application deadline: 3/1; financial award applicants required to submit FAFSA. *Unit head:* Dr. Tom F. Badgett, Department Head, 325-942-2383 Ext. 225, Fax: 325-942-2384, E-mail: tom.badgett@angelo.edu. *Application contact:* Dr. Carol B. Diminnie, Graduate Advisor, 325-942-2383 Ext. 229, Fax: 325-942-2194, E-mail: carol.diminnie@angelo.edu. Web site: http://www.angelo.edu/dept/management_marketing/.

Anna Maria College, Graduate Division, Program in Business Administration, Paxton, MA 01612. Offers MBA, AC. Part-time and evening/weekend programs available. *Degree requirements:* For master's, capstone project. *Entrance requirements:* For master's, minimum GPA of 2.7. Additional exam requirements/recommendations for international students: Required—TOEFL (minimum score 500 paper-based). Electronic applications accepted. *Faculty research:* Management organization.

Antioch University Los Angeles, Graduate Programs, Program in Organizational Management, Culver City, CA 90230. Offers human resource development (MA); leadership (MA); organizational development (MA). Part-time and evening/weekend programs available. *Entrance requirements:* For master's, interview. Additional exam requirements/recommendations for international students: Required—TOEFL. *Faculty research:* Systems thinking and chaos theory, technology and organizational structure, nonprofit management, power and empowerment.

Antioch University Midwest, Graduate Programs, Individualized Liberal and Professional Studies Program, Yellow Springs, OH 45387-1609. Offers liberal and professional studies (MA), including counseling, creative writing, education, liberal studies, management, modern literature, psychology, visual arts. Part-time and evening/weekend programs available. Postbaccalaureate distance learning degree programs offered (minimal on-campus study). *Faculty:* 2 full-time (1 woman), 2 part-time/adjunct (both women). *Students:* 25 full-time (16 women), 38 part-time (30 women); includes 17 minority (15 Black or African American, non-Hispanic/Latino; 2 Hispanic/Latino). Average age 38. 13 applicants, 69% accepted, 5 enrolled. In 2011, 17 master's awarded. *Degree requirements:* For master's, thesis or alternative. *Entrance requirements:* For master's, resume, goal statement, interview. *Application deadline:* For fall admission, 8/1 for domestic students; for winter admission, 12/1 for domestic students; for spring admission, 3/10 for domestic students. Applications are processed on a rolling basis. Application fee: $50. Electronic applications accepted. *Expenses:* Contact institution. *Financial support:* Federal Work-Study available. Financial award applicants required to submit FAFSA. *Unit head:* Dr. Joseph Cronin, Chair, 937-769-1894, Fax: 937-769-1807, E-mail: jcronin@antioch.edu. *Application contact:* Deena Kent-Hummel, Director of Admissions, 937-769-1800, Fax: 937-769-1804, E-mail: dkent@antioch.edu.

Antioch University Midwest, Graduate Programs, Program in Management and Leading Change, Yellow Springs, OH 45387-1609. Offers MA. Part-time and evening/weekend programs available. Postbaccalaureate distance learning degree programs offered (minimal on-campus study). *Faculty:* 3 part-time/adjunct (2 women). *Students:* 24 full-time (15 women), 2 part-time (both women); includes 12 minority (11 Black or African American, non-Hispanic/Latino; 1 Hispanic/Latino). Average age 38. 44 applicants, 66% accepted, 21 enrolled. In 2011, 21 master's awarded. *Entrance requirements:* For master's, resume, goal statement, interview. *Application deadline:* For fall admission, 9/1 for domestic students; for winter admission, 12/1 for domestic students; for spring admission, 3/10 for domestic students. Applications are processed on a rolling basis. Application fee: $50. Electronic applications accepted. *Expenses:* Contact institution. *Financial support:* Federal Work-Study available. Financial award applicants required to submit FAFSA. *Unit head:* Dr. Stephen Brzezinski, Chair, 937-769-1860, Fax: 937-769-1807, E-mail: sbrzezinski@antioch.edu. *Application contact:* Deena Kent-Hummel, Director of Admissions, 937-769-1816, Fax: 937-769-1804, E-mail: dkent@antioch.edu. Web site: http://midwest.antioch.edu.

Antioch University New England, Graduate School, Department of Organization and Management, Program in Organizational and Environmental Sustainability (Green MBA), Keene, NH 03431-3552. Offers MBA. Part-time programs available. *Entrance requirements:* For master's, GRE, resume, 3 letters of recommendation. Additional exam requirements/recommendations for international students: Required—TOEFL (minimum score 600 paper-based; 250 computer-based).

Antioch University Seattle, Graduate Programs, Center for Creative Change, Seattle, WA 98121-1814. Offers environment and community (MA); management (MS); organizational psychology (MA); strategic communications (MA); whole system design (MA). Evening/weekend programs available. Electronic applications accepted. *Expenses:* Contact institution.

Appalachian State University, Cratis D. Williams Graduate School, Program in Business Administration, Boone, NC 28608. Offers general management (MBA). *Accreditation:* AACSB. Part-time programs available. Postbaccalaureate distance learning degree programs offered (no on-campus study). *Faculty:* 34 full-time (8 women), 6 part-time/adjunct (0 women). *Students:* 44 full-time (16 women), 26 part-time (11 women); includes 11 minority (1 Black or African American, non-Hispanic/Latino; 2 American Indian or Alaska Native, non-Hispanic/Latino; 8 Asian, non-Hispanic/Latino), 2 international. 71 applicants, 89% accepted, 38 enrolled. In 2011, 35 master's awarded. *Degree requirements:* For master's, comprehensive exam. *Entrance requirements:* For master's, GMAT, 3 letters of recommendation. Additional exam requirements/recommendations for international students: Required—TOEFL (minimum score 550 paper-based; 230 computer-based; 79 iBT), IELTS (minimum score 6.5). *Application deadline:* For fall admission, 3/1 for domestic students, 2/1 for international students; for spring admission, 7/1 for international students. Applications are processed on a rolling basis. Application fee: $55. Electronic applications accepted. *Expenses:* Tuition, state resident: full-time $4040; part-time $180 per semester hour. Tuition, nonresident: full-time $15,900; part-time $760 per semester hour. *Required fees:* $2500; $20 per semester hour. Tuition and fees vary according to campus/location. *Financial support:* In 2011–12, 10 research assistantships (averaging $8,000 per year) were awarded; fellowships, teaching assistantships, career-related internships or fieldwork, Federal Work-Study, scholarships/grants, and unspecified assistantships also available. Financial award application deadline: 4/1; financial award applicants required to submit FAFSA. *Total annual research expenditures:* $800,000. *Unit head:* Dr. Joseph Cazier, Director and Assistant Dean, College of Business, 828-262-2922, E-mail: cazierja@appstate.edu. *Application contact:* Sandy Krause, Director of Admissions, 828-262-2130, Fax: 828-262-2709, E-mail: krausesl@appstate.edu. Web site: http://www.mba.appstate.edu.

Aquinas College, School of Management, Grand Rapids, MI 49506-1799. Offers health care administration (M Mgt); marketing management (M Mgt); organizational leadership (M Min); sustainable business (M Mgt, MSB). Part-time and evening/weekend programs available. *Faculty:* 11 full-time (3 women), 7 part-time/adjunct (0 women). *Students:* 12 full-time (6 women), 56 part-time (32 women); includes 7 minority (3 Black or African American, non-Hispanic/Latino; 1 Asian, non-Hispanic/Latino; 3 Hispanic/Latino). *Entrance requirements:* For master's, GMAT, minimum undergraduate GPA of 2.75, 2 years of work experience. Additional exam requirements/recommendations for international students: Required—TOEFL (minimum score 550 paper-based; 213 computer-based). *Application deadline:* Applications are processed on a rolling basis. *Expenses:* Contact institution. *Financial support:* Scholarships/grants available. Support available to part-time students. Financial award application deadline: 3/15; financial award applicants required to submit FAFSA. *Unit head:* Brian DiVita, Director, 616-632-2922, Fax: 616-732-4489. *Application contact:* Lynn Atkins-Rykert, Administrative Assistant, 616-632-2924, Fax: 616-732-4489, E-mail: atkinlyn@aquinas.edu.

Arcadia University, Graduate Studies, Program in Business Administration, Glenside, PA 19038-3295. Offers IMBA, MBA. *Accreditation:* ACBSP. *Students:* 40 full-time (8 women), 131 part-time (61 women); includes 23 minority (16 Black or African American, non-Hispanic/Latino; 6 Asian, non-Hispanic/Latino; 1 Hispanic/Latino), 88 international. Average age 36. In 2011, 31 master's awarded. Application fee: $50. *Expenses:* Contact institution. *Unit head:* Dr. Tony Muscia, Executive Director, 215-579-2789. *Application contact:* Office of Enrollment Management, 215-572-2910, Fax: 215-572-4049, E-mail: admiss@arcadia.edu.

Argosy University, Atlanta, College of Business, Atlanta, GA 30328. Offers accounting (DBA); corporate compliance (MBA); customized professional concentration (MBA, DBA); finance (MBA); healthcare administration (MBA); information systems (DBA); information systems management (MBA); international business (MBA, DBA); management (MBA, MSM, DBA); marketing (MBA, DBA).

See Close-Up on page 179.

Argosy University, Chicago, College of Business, Chicago, IL 60601. Offers accounting (DBA); customized professional concentration (MBA, DBA); finance (MBA); fraud examination (MBA); global business sustainability (DBA); healthcare administration (MBA); information systems (DBA); information systems management (MBA); international business (MBA, DBA); management (MBA, MSM, DBA); marketing (MBA, DBA); organizational leadership (Ed D); public administration (MBA); sustainable management (MBA). Postbaccalaureate distance learning degree programs offered (minimal on-campus study).

See Close-Up on page 181.

Argosy University, Dallas, College of Business, Farmers Branch, TX 75244. Offers accounting (DBA, AGC); corporate compliance (MBA, Graduate Certificate); customized professional concentration (MBA); finance (MBA, Graduate Certificate); fraud examination (MBA, Graduate Certificate); global business sustainability (DBA, AGC); healthcare administration (Graduate Certificate); healthcare management (MBA); information systems (MBA, DBA, AGC); information systems management (Graduate Certificate); international business (MBA, DBA, AGC, Graduate Certificate);

management (MBA, DBA, AGC, Graduate Certificate); marketing (MBA, DBA, AGC, Graduate Certificate); public administration (MBA, Graduate Certificate); sustainable management (MBA, Graduate Certificate).

See Close-Up on page 183.

Argosy University, Denver, College of Business, Denver, CO 80231. Offers accounting (DBA); corporate compliance (MBA); customized professional concentration (MBA, DBA); finance (MBA); fraud examination (MBA); global business sustainability (DBA); healthcare administration (MBA); information systems (DBA); information systems management (MBA); international business (MBA, DBA); management (MBA, MSM, DBA); marketing (MBA, DBA); organizational leadership (Ed D); public administration (MBA); sustainable management (MBA).

See Close-Up on page 185.

Argosy University, Hawai`i, College of Business, Honolulu, HI 96813. Offers accounting (DBA); corporate compliance (MBA); customized professional concentration (MBA, DBA); finance (MBA, Certificate); fraud examination (MBA); global business sustainability (DBA); healthcare administration (MBA, Certificate); information systems (DBA); information systems management (MBA, Certificate); international business (MBA, DBA, Certificate); management (MBA, MSM, DBA); marketing (MBA, DBA, Certificate); organizational leadership (Ed D); public administration (MBA); sustainable management (MBA).

See Close-Up on page 187.

Argosy University, Inland Empire, College of Business, San Bernardino, CA 92408. Offers accounting (DBA); corporate compliance (MBA); customized professional concentration (MBA, DBA); finance (MBA); fraud examination (MBA); global business sustainability (DBA); healthcare administration (MBA); information systems (DBA); information systems management (MBA); international business (MBA, DBA); management (MBA, MSM, DBA); marketing (MBA, DBA); organizational leadership (Ed D); public administration (MBA); sustainable management (MBA).

See Close-Up on page 189.

Argosy University, Los Angeles, College of Business, Santa Monica, CA 90045. Offers accounting (DBA); corporate compliance (MBA); customized professional concentration (MBA, DBA); finance (MBA); fraud examination (MBA); global business sustainability (DBA); healthcare administration (MBA); information systems (DBA); information systems management (MBA); international business (MBA, DBA); management (MBA, MSM, DBA); marketing (MBA, DBA); organizational leadership (Ed D); public administration (MBA); sustainable management (MBA).

See Close-Up on page 191.

Argosy University, Nashville, College of Business, Nashville, TN 37214. Offers accounting (DBA); customized professional concentration (MBA, DBA); finance (MBA); healthcare administration (MBA); information systems (MBA, DBA); international business (MBA, DBA); management (MBA, MSM, DBA); marketing (MBA, DBA).

See Close-Up on page 193.

Argosy University, Orange County, College of Business, Orange, CA 92868. Offers accounting (DBA, Adv C); corporate compliance (MBA); customized professional concentration (MBA, DBA); finance (MBA, Certificate); fraud examination (MBA); global business sustainability (DBA); healthcare administration (MBA, Certificate); information systems (DBA, Adv C, Certificate); information systems management (MBA); international business (MBA, DBA, Adv C, Certificate); management (MBA, MSM, DBA, Adv C); marketing (MBA, DBA, Adv C, Certificate); organizational leadership (Ed D); public administration (MBA, Certificate); sustainable management (MBA).

See Close-Up on page 195.

Argosy University, Phoenix, College of Business, Phoenix, AZ 85021. Offers accounting (DBA); corporate compliance (MBA); customized professional concentration (MBA, DBA); finance (MBA); fraud examination (MBA); global business sustainability (DBA); healthcare administration (MBA); information systems (DBA); information systems management (MBA); international business (MBA, DBA); management (MBA, DBA); marketing (MBA, DBA); public administration (MBA); sustainable management (MBA).

See Close-Up on page 197.

Argosy University, Salt Lake City, College of Business, Draper, UT 84020. Offers accounting (DBA); corporate compliance (MBA); customized professional concentration (MBA, DBA); finance (MBA); fraud examination (MBA); global business sustainability (DBA); healthcare administration (MBA); information systems (DBA); information systems management (MBA); international business (MBA, DBA); management (MBA, DBA); marketing (MBA, DBA); public administration (MBA); sustainable management (MBA).

See Close-Up on page 199.

Argosy University, San Diego, College of Business, San Diego, CA 92108. Offers accounting (DBA); corporate compliance (MBA); customized professional concentration (MBA, DBA); finance (MBA); fraud examination (MBA); global business sustainability (DBA); information systems (DBA); information systems management (MBA); international business (MBA, DBA); management (MBA, MSM, DBA); marketing (MBA, DBA); organizational leadership (Ed D); public administration (MBA).

See Close-Up on page 201.

Argosy University, San Francisco Bay Area, College of Business, Alameda, CA 94501. Offers accounting (DBA); corporate compliance (MBA); customized professional concentration (MBA, DBA); finance (MBA); fraud examination (MBA); global business sustainability (DBA); healthcare administration (MBA); information systems (DBA); information systems management (MBA); international business (MBA, DBA); management (MBA, MSM, DBA); marketing (MBA, DBA); organizational leadership (Ed D); public administration (MBA); sustainable management (MBA).

See Close-Up on page 203.

Argosy University, Sarasota, College of Business, Sarasota, FL 34235. Offers accounting (DBA, Adv C); corporate compliance (MBA, DBA, Certificate); customized professional concentration (MBA, DBA); finance (MBA, Certificate); fraud examination (MBA, Certificate); global business sustainability (DBA, Adv C); healthcare administration (MBA, Certificate); information systems (DBA, Adv C, Certificate); information systems management (MBA); international business (MBA, DBA, Adv C, Certificate); management (MBA, MSM, DBA, Adv C, Certificate); marketing (MBA, DBA, Adv C, Certificate); organizational leadership (Ed D); public administration (MBA, Certificate); sustainable management (MBA, Certificate).

See Close-Up on page 205.

Argosy University, Schaumburg, College of Business, Schaumburg, IL 60173-5403. Offers accounting (DBA, Adv C); customized professional concentration (MBA, DBA); finance (MBA, Certificate); fraud examination (MBA); global business sustainability (DBA); healthcare administration (MBA, Certificate); information systems (DBA, Adv C, Certificate); information systems management (MBA); international business (MBA, DBA, Adv C, Certificate); management (MBA, MSM, DBA, Adv C, Certificate); marketing (MBA, DBA, Adv C, Certificate); organizational leadership (Ed D); public administration (MBA); sustainable management (MBA).

See Close-Up on page 207.

Argosy University, Seattle, College of Business, Seattle, WA 98121. Offers accounting (DBA); corporate compliance (MBA); customized professional concentration (MBA, DBA); finance (MBA); fraud examination (MBA); global business sustainability (DBA); healthcare administration (MBA); information systems (DBA); information systems management (MBA); international business (MBA, DBA); management (MBA, MSM, DBA); marketing (MBA, DBA); organizational leadership (Ed D); public administration (MBA); sustainable management (MBA).

See Close-Up on page 209.

Argosy University, Tampa, College of Business, Tampa, FL 33607. Offers accounting (DBA); corporate compliance (MBA); customized professional concentration (MBA, DBA); finance (MBA); fraud examination (MBA); global business sustainability (DBA); healthcare administration (MBA); information systems (DBA); information systems management (MBA); international business (MBA, DBA); management (MBA, MSM, DBA); marketing (MBA, DBA); organizational leadership (Ed D); public administration (MBA); sustainable management (MBA).

See Close-Up on page 211.

Argosy University, Twin Cities, College of Business, Eagan, MN 55121. Offers accounting (DBA); customized professional concentration (MBA, DBA); finance (MBA); fraud examination (MBA); global business sustainability (DBA); healthcare administration (MBA); information systems (DBA); information systems management (MBA); international business (MBA, DBA); management (MBA, MSM, DBA); marketing (MBA, DBA); organizational leadership (Ed D); public administration (MBA); sustainable management (MBA).

See Close-Up on page 213.

Argosy University, Washington DC, College of Business, Arlington, VA 22209. Offers accounting (DBA); customized professional concentration (MBA, DBA); finance (MBA); fraud examination (MBA); global business sustainability (DBA); healthcare administration (MBA); information systems (DBA); information systems management (MBA); international business (MBA, DBA, Certificate); management (MBA, MSM, DBA); marketing (MBA, DBA, Certificate); organizational leadership (Ed D); public administration (MBA); sustainable management (MBA).

See Close-Up on page 215.

Arizona State University, W. P. Carey School of Business, Program in Business Administration, Tempe, AZ 85287-4906. Offers accountancy (PhD); agribusiness (PhD); business administration (MBA); finance (PhD); financial management and markets (MBA); information management (MBA); information systems (PhD); management (PhD); marketing (PhD); strategic marketing and services leadership (MBA); supply chain financial management (MBA); supply chain management (MBA, PhD); JD/MBA; MBA/M Acc; MBA/M Arch. *Accreditation:* AACSB. Part-time and evening/weekend programs available. Postbaccalaureate distance learning degree programs offered (minimal on-campus study). Terminal master's awarded for partial completion of doctoral program. *Degree requirements:* For master's, thesis or alternative, internship, interactive Program of Study (iPOS) submitted before completing 50 percent of required credit hours; for doctorate, comprehensive exam, thesis/dissertation, interactive Program of Study (iPOS) submitted before completing 50 percent of required credit hours. *Entrance requirements:* For master's, GMAT, minimum GPA of 3.0 in last 2 years of work leading to bachelor's degree, 2 letters of recommendation, professional resume, official transcripts, 3 essays; for doctorate, GMAT or GRE, minimum GPA of 3.0 in last 2 years of work leading to bachelor's degree, 3 letters of recommendation, resume, personal statement/essay. Additional exam requirements/recommendations for international students: Required—TOEFL (minimum score 550 paper-based; 213 computer-based; 80 iBT), IELTS (minimum score 6.5). Electronic applications accepted. *Expenses:* Contact institution.

Arkansas State University, Graduate School, College of Business, Department of Economics and Finance, Jonesboro, State University, AR 72467. Offers business administration (MBA). *Accreditation:* AACSB. Part-time programs available. *Faculty:* 10 full-time (1 woman). *Students:* 73 full-time (31 women), 89 part-time (39 women); includes 8 minority (5 Black or African American, non-Hispanic/Latino; 2 Asian, non-Hispanic/Latino; 1 Two or more races, non-Hispanic/Latino), 85 international. Average age 27. 162 applicants, 85% accepted, 77 enrolled. In 2011, 57 master's awarded. *Degree requirements:* For master's, comprehensive exam, thesis or alternative. *Entrance requirements:* For master's, GMAT, appropriate bachelor's degree, letters of reference, official transcripts, immunization records. Additional exam requirements/recommendations for international students: Required—TOEFL (minimum score 550 paper-based; 253 computer-based; 79 iBT), IELTS (minimum score 6), Pearson Test of English Academic (minimum score 56). *Application deadline:* For fall admission, 7/1 for domestic and international students; for spring admission, 11/15 for domestic students, 11/14 for international students. Applications are processed on a rolling basis. Application fee: $30 ($40 for international students). Electronic applications accepted. *Expenses:* Contact institution. *Financial support:* In 2011–12, 19 students received support. Career-related internships or fieldwork, scholarships/grants, and unspecified assistantships available. Financial award application deadline: 7/1; financial award applicants required to submit FAFSA. *Unit head:* Dr. Patricia Robertson, Chair, 870-972-2280, Fax: 870-972-3863, E-mail: probertson@astate.edu. *Application contact:* Dr. Andrew Sustich, Dean of the Graduate School, 870-972-3029, Fax: 870-972-3857, E-mail: sustich@astate.edu. Web site: http://www.astate.edu/a/business/departments/economics-finance/.

Ashland University, Dauch College of Business and Economics, Ashland, OH 44805-3702. Offers MBA. *Accreditation:* ACBSP. Part-time and evening/weekend programs available. *Faculty:* 37 full-time (13 women), 19 part-time/adjunct (5 women). *Students:* 253 full-time (116 women), 296 part-time (117 women); includes 35 minority (22 Black or African American, non-Hispanic/Latino; 5 Hispanic/Latino; 1 Native Hawaiian or other Pacific Islander, non-Hispanic/Latino; 7 Two or more races, non-Hispanic/Latino), 1 international. Average age 34. In 2011, 202 master's awarded. *Degree requirements:* For master's, thesis optional. *Entrance requirements:* For master's, 2 years of full-time work experience. Additional exam requirements/recommendations for international students: Required—TOEFL. *Application deadline:* For fall admission, 8/1 priority date for domestic students; for spring admission, 12/1 priority date for domestic students. Applications are processed on a rolling basis. Application fee: $30. Electronic applications accepted. *Expenses:* Contact institution. *Financial support:* In 2011–12, 10 students received support. Tuition waivers (partial) and unspecified assistantships available. Financial award application deadline: 4/15; financial award applicants required to submit FAFSA. *Faculty research:* Human resource management, statistical analysis, global business issues, organizational development, government and business. *Total* *annual research expenditures:* $36,410. *Unit head:* Dr. Raymond Jacobs, Associate Dean, 419-289-5931, E-mail: rjacobs@ashland.edu. *Application contact:* Stephen W. Krispinsky, Executive Director of MBA Program, 419-289-5236, Fax: 419-289-5910, E-mail: skrispin@ashland.edu. Web site: http://www.ashland.edu/mba/.

Ashworth College, Graduate Programs, Norcross, GA 30092. Offers business administration (MBA); criminal justice (MS); health care administration (MBA, MS); human resource management (MBA, MS); international business (MBA); management (MS); marketing (MBA, MS).

Aspen University, Program in Business Administration, Denver, CO 80246. Offers business administration (MBA); finance (MBA); information management (MBA); project management (MBA, Certificate). Part-time and evening/weekend programs available. Postbaccalaureate distance learning degree programs offered (no on-campus study). *Entrance requirements:* Additional exam requirements/recommendations for international students: Required—TOEFL (minimum score 530 paper-based; 71 computer-based). Electronic applications accepted.

Assumption College, Graduate Studies, Department of Business Studies, Worcester, MA 01609-1296. Offers accounting (MBA); business administration (CAGS); finance/economics (MBA); general business (MBA); human resources (MBA); international business (MBA); management (MBA); marketing (MBA); nonprofit leadership (MBA). Part-time and evening/weekend programs available. *Faculty:* 4 full-time (0 women), 16 part-time/adjunct (4 women). *Students:* 8 full-time (5 women), 133 part-time (65 women); includes 18 minority (8 Black or African American, non-Hispanic/Latino; 1 American Indian or Alaska Native, non-Hispanic/Latino; 2 Asian, non-Hispanic/Latino; 7 Hispanic/Latino), 3 international. Average age 30. 100 applicants, 75% accepted, 52 enrolled. In 2011, 53 master's, 1 other advanced degree awarded. *Degree requirements:* For master's, thesis, capstone. *Entrance requirements:* For master's and CAGS, 3 letters of recommendation, resume, essay. Additional exam requirements/recommendations for international students: Required—TOEFL (minimum score 540 paper-based; 200 computer-based; 76 iBT), IELTS (minimum score 6). *Application deadline:* For fall admission, 10/1 for domestic and international students; for winter admission, 2/1 for domestic and international students; for spring admission, 4/1 for domestic and international students. Applications are processed on a rolling basis. Application fee: $30. Electronic applications accepted. *Expenses: Tuition:* Full-time $9414; part-time $523 per credit. *Required fees:* $20 per term. Full-time tuition and fees vary according to course load and program. *Financial support:* In 2011–12, 14 students received support. Scholarships/grants, tuition waivers (partial), and unspecified assistantships available. Financial award application deadline: 5/1; financial award applicants required to submit FAFSA. *Faculty research:* Workplace diversity, dynamics of team interaction, utilization of leased employees, experiential learning project on due diligence market for prostheses. *Unit head:* Michael Lewis, Director, 508-767-7372, Fax: 508-767-7252, E-mail: milewis@assumption.edu. *Application contact:* Laura Lawrence, Graduate Programs Operations Manager, 508-767-7387, Fax: 508-767-7030, E-mail: graduate@assumption.edu. Web site: http://graduate.assumption.edu/mba/mba-assumption.

Athabasca University, Centre for Innovative Management, St. Albert, AB T8N 1B4, Canada. Offers business administration (MBA); information technology management (MBA), including policing concentration; management (GDM); project management (MBA, GDM). Part-time and evening/weekend programs available. Postbaccalaureate distance learning degree programs offered (no on-campus study). *Degree requirements:* For master's, thesis or alternative, applied project. *Entrance requirements:* For master's, 3-8 years of managerial experience, 3 years with undergraduate degree, 5 years managerial experience with professional designation, 8-10 years management experience (on exception). Electronic applications accepted. *Expenses:* Contact institution. *Faculty research:* Human resources, project management, operations research, information technology management, corporate stewardship, energy management.

Auburn University, Graduate School, College of Business, Department of Management, Auburn University, AL 36849. Offers human resource management (PhD); management (MS, PhD); management information systems (MS, PhD). *Accreditation:* AACSB. Part-time programs available. *Faculty:* 26 full-time (5 women), 1 part-time/adjunct (0 women). *Students:* 15 full-time (5 women), 14 part-time (3 women); includes 4 minority (3 Black or African American, non-Hispanic/Latino; 1 Asian, non-Hispanic/Latino), 6 international. Average age 35. 66 applicants, 24% accepted, 8 enrolled. In 2011, 2 doctorates awarded. *Degree requirements:* For master's, thesis (for some programs); for doctorate, thesis/dissertation. *Entrance requirements:* For master's, GMAT, GRE General Test (MS); for doctorate, GMAT, GRE General Test. Additional exam requirements/recommendations for international students: Required—TOEFL. *Application deadline:* For fall admission, 7/7 for domestic students; for spring admission, 11/24 for domestic students. Applications are processed on a rolling basis. Application fee: $50 ($60 for international students). Electronic applications accepted. *Expenses:* Tuition, state resident: full-time $7290; part-time $405 per credit hour. Tuition, nonresident: full-time $21,870; part-time $1215 per credit hour. *International tuition:* $22,000 full-time. *Required fees:* $1402. *Financial support:* Teaching assistantships and Federal Work-Study available. Support available to part-time students. Financial award application deadline: 3/15; financial award applicants required to submit FAFSA. *Unit head:* Dr. Christopher Shook, Head, 334-844-9565. *Application contact:* Dr. George Flowers, Dean of the Graduate School, 334-844-2125. Web site: http://business.auburn.edu/academics/departments/department-of-management/.

Auburn University, Graduate School, College of Business, Program in Business Administration, Auburn University, AL 36849. Offers MBA. *Accreditation:* AACSB. Part-time programs available. *Faculty:* 50 full-time (12 women), 5 part-time/adjunct (3 women). *Students:* 68 full-time (28 women), 333 part-time (75 women); includes 63 minority (26 Black or African American, non-Hispanic/Latino; 2 American Indian or Alaska Native, non-Hispanic/Latino; 18 Asian, non-Hispanic/Latino; 17 Hispanic/Latino), 24 international. Average age 35. 302 applicants, 63% accepted, 152 enrolled. In 2011, 158 master's awarded. *Entrance requirements:* For master's, GMAT. *Application deadline:* For fall admission, 7/7 for domestic students; for spring admission, 11/24 for domestic students. Applications are processed on a rolling basis. Application fee: $50 ($60 for international students). Electronic applications accepted. *Expenses:* Tuition, state resident: full-time $7290; part-time $405 per credit hour. Tuition, nonresident: full-time $21,870; part-time $1215 per credit hour. *International tuition:* $22,000 full-time. *Required fees:* $1402. *Financial support:* Federal Work-Study available. Support available to part-time students. Financial award application deadline: 3/15; financial award applicants required to submit FAFSA. *Unit head:* Dr. Daniel M. Gropper, Director, 334-844-4060. *Application contact:* Dr. George Flowers, Dean of the Graduate School, 334-844-2125. Web site: http://www.auburn.edu/business/mbaprog.html.

Auburn University Montgomery, School of Business, Montgomery, AL 36124-4023. Offers MBA. *Accreditation:* AACSB. Part-time and evening/weekend programs available. *Degree requirements:* For master's, comprehensive exam. *Entrance requirements:* For master's, GMAT. Additional exam requirements/recommendations for international students: Required—TOEFL. Electronic applications accepted. *Expenses:* Tuition, state resident: full-time $5076. Tuition, nonresident: full-time $15,228.

Augsburg College, Program in Business Administration, Minneapolis, MN 55454-1351. Offers MBA. Evening/weekend programs available. Electronic applications accepted.

Augusta State University, Graduate Studies, Hull College of Business, Augusta, GA 30904-2200. Offers MBA. *Accreditation:* AACSB. Part-time and evening/weekend programs available. *Faculty:* 8 full-time (2 women), 3 part-time/adjunct (1 woman). *Students:* 36 full-time (16 women), 61 part-time (24 women); includes 19 minority (7 Black or African American, non-Hispanic/Latino; 9 Asian, non-Hispanic/Latino; 3 Hispanic/Latino). Average age 30. 41 applicants, 66% accepted, 24 enrolled. In 2011, 35 master's awarded. *Entrance requirements:* For master's, GMAT. *Application deadline:* For fall admission, 7/15 priority date for domestic students, 7/1 for international students; for spring admission, 12/1 priority date for domestic students, 11/15 for international students. Applications are processed on a rolling basis. Application fee: $20. *Financial support:* Research assistantships with partial tuition reimbursements, Federal Work-Study, and institutionally sponsored loans available. Support available to part-time students. Financial award application deadline: 4/15; financial award applicants required to submit FAFSA. *Unit head:* Dr. Marc D. Miller, Dean, 706-737-1418, Fax: 706-667-4064, E-mail: mmiller@aug.edu. *Application contact:* Dr. Todd A. Schultz, Acting Associate Dean, 706-737-1562, Fax: 706-667-4064, E-mail: tschultz@aug.edu. Web site: http://www.aug.edu/coba.

Aurora University, College of Professional Studies, Dunham School of Business, Aurora, IL 60506-4892. Offers MBA. Part-time and evening/weekend programs available. *Entrance requirements:* For master's, minimum GPA of 2.75, 2 years of work experience. Additional exam requirements/recommendations for international students: Required—TOEFL (minimum score 550 paper-based; 213 computer-based). Electronic applications accepted. *Expenses:* Contact institution.

Austin Peay State University, College of Graduate Studies, College of Business, Clarksville, TN 37044. Offers management (MS). Part-time and evening/weekend programs available. Postbaccalaureate distance learning degree programs offered (no on-campus study). *Faculty:* 4 full-time (0 women). *Students:* 20 full-time (14 women), 40 part-time (22 women); includes 15 minority (9 Black or African American, non-Hispanic/Latino; 1 American Indian or Alaska Native, non-Hispanic/Latino; 1 Asian, non-Hispanic/Latino; 3 Hispanic/Latino; 1 Two or more races, non-Hispanic/Latino). Average age 36. 30 applicants, 100% accepted, 24 enrolled. In 2011, 51 master's awarded. *Degree requirements:* For master's, comprehensive exam. *Entrance requirements:* For master's, GMAT, 3 letters of recommendation. Additional exam requirements/recommendations for international students: Required—TOEFL (minimum score 500 paper-based; 173 computer-based). *Application deadline:* For fall admission, 8/1 priority date for domestic students. Applications are processed on a rolling basis. Application fee: $25. Electronic applications accepted. *Expenses:* Tuition, state resident: part-time $350 per credit hour. Tuition, nonresident: full-time $20,644; part-time $971 per credit hour. *Required fees:* $1224; $61.20 per credit hour. *Financial support:* In 2011–12, research assistantships with full tuition reimbursements (averaging $5,184 per year) were awarded; career-related internships or fieldwork, Federal Work-Study, institutionally sponsored loans, scholarships/grants, and unspecified assistantships also available. Support available to part-time students. Financial award application deadline: 3/1; financial award applicants required to submit FAFSA. *Unit head:* Dr. William Rupp, Dean, 931-221-7674, Fax: 931-221-7355, E-mail: ruppw@apsu.edu. *Application contact:* Kendra Bryant, Graduate Admissions, 800-844-2778, Fax: 931-221-6188, E-mail: admissionsweb@apsu.edu. Web site: http://www.apsu.edu/business/.

Averett University, Program in Business Administration, Danville, VA 24541-3692. Offers MBA. Part-time programs available. *Faculty:* 9 full-time (2 women). *Students:* 234 full-time (165 women), 403 part-time (241 women); includes 168 minority (149 Black or African American, non-Hispanic/Latino; 1 American Indian or Alaska Native, non-Hispanic/Latino; 9 Asian, non-Hispanic/Latino; 9 Hispanic/Latino), 1 international. Average age 37. In 2011, 152 master's awarded. *Degree requirements:* For master's, 41-credit core curriculum, minimum GPA of 3.0 throughout program, completion of degree requirements within six years from start of program. *Entrance requirements:* For master's, minimum cumulative GPA of 3.0 over the last 60 semester hours of undergraduate study toward a baccalaureate degree. Additional exam requirements/recommendations for international students: Required—TOEFL (minimum score 600 paper-based; 250 computer-based; 100 iBT). *Application deadline:* Applications are processed on a rolling basis. *Expenses: Tuition:* Full-time $8085. One-time fee: $100 full-time. Part-time tuition and fees vary according to campus/location. *Financial support:* Institutionally sponsored loans available. Support available to part-time students. *Unit head:* Dr. Eugene Steadman, Jr., Department Chair, Business Department GPS Program, 571-594-4877, E-mail: eugene.steadman@averett.edu. *Application contact:* Marietta Sanford, Director of Academic Services, 434-791-5892, E-mail: marietta.sanford@averett.edu. Web site: http://www.averett.edu/adultprograms/index.php.

Avila University, School of Business, Kansas City, MO 64145-1698. Offers accounting (MBA); finance (MBA); general management (MBA); health care administration (MBA); international business (MBA); management information systems (MBA); marketing (MBA). Part-time and evening/weekend programs available. *Faculty:* 9 full-time (3 women), 14 part-time/adjunct (5 women). *Students:* 102 full-time (49 women), 53 part-time (31 women); includes 36 minority (29 Black or African American, non-Hispanic/Latino; 1 American Indian or Alaska Native, non-Hispanic/Latino; 3 Asian, non-Hispanic/Latino; 2 Hispanic/Latino; 1 Native Hawaiian or other Pacific Islander, non-Hispanic/Latino), 33 international. Average age 32. 25 applicants, 76% accepted, 19 enrolled. In 2011, 59 master's awarded. *Degree requirements:* For master's, comprehensive exam, capstone course. *Entrance requirements:* For master's, GMAT (minimum score 420), minimum GPA of 3.0, interview. Additional exam requirements/recommendations for international students: Required—TOEFL (minimum score 550 paper-based). *Application deadline:* For fall admission, 7/30 priority date for domestic students, 7/30 for international students; for winter admission, 11/30 priority date for domestic students, 11/30 for international students; for spring admission, 2/28 priority date for domestic students, 2/28 for international students. Applications are processed on a rolling basis. Application fee: $0. Electronic applications accepted. *Expenses:* Contact institution. *Financial support:* In 2011–12, 102 students received support. Career-related internships or fieldwork and competitive merit scholarships available. Support available to part-time students. Financial award applicants required to submit FAFSA. *Faculty research:* Leadership characteristics, financial hedging, group dynamics. *Unit head:* Dr. Richard Woodall, Dean, 816-501-3720, Fax: 816-501-2463, E-mail: richard.woodall@avila.edu. *Application contact:* JoAnna Giffin, MBA Admissions Director, 816-501-3601, Fax: 816-501-2463, E-mail: joanna.giffin@avila.edu. Web site: http://www.avila.edu/mba.

Azusa Pacific University, School of Business and Management, Program in Business Administration, Azusa, CA 91702-7000. Offers MBA.

Babson College, F. W. Olin Graduate School of Business, Wellesley, Babson Park, MA 02457-0310. Offers accounting (MSA); advanced management (Certificate); business administration (MBA); global entrepreneurship (MS); technological entrepreneurship (MS). *Accreditation:* AACSB. Part-time and evening/weekend programs available. Postbaccalaureate distance learning degree programs offered (minimal on-campus study). *Entrance requirements:* For master's, GMAT, 2 years of work experience, resume, letters of recommendation. Additional exam requirements/recommendations for international students: Required—TOEFL (minimum score 100 iBT), IELTS (minimum score 6.5). Electronic applications accepted. *Faculty research:* Entrepreneurship, sustainability, global markets, process of innovation, social media and advertising.

Baker College Center for Graduate Studies - Online, Graduate Programs, Flint, MI 48507-9843. Offers accounting (MBA); business administration (DBA); finance (MBA); general business (MBA); health care management (MBA); human resources management (MBA); information management (MBA); leadership studies (MBA); management information systems (MSIS); marketing (MBA). Part-time and evening/weekend programs available. Postbaccalaureate distance learning degree programs offered. *Degree requirements:* For master's, portfolio. *Entrance requirements:* For master's, 3 years of work experience, minimum undergraduate GPA of 2.5, writing sample, 3 letters of recommendation; for doctorate, MBA or acceptable related master's degree from accredited association, 5 years work experience, minimum graduate GPA of 3.25, writing sample, 3 professional references. Additional exam requirements/recommendations for international students: Required—TOEFL (minimum score 550 paper-based; 213 computer-based). Electronic applications accepted.

Baker University, School of Professional and Graduate Studies, Programs in Business, Baldwin City, KS 66006-0065. Offers MBA, MSM. Programs also offered in Lee's Summit, MO; Overland Park, KS; Topeka, KS; and Wichita, KS. *Accreditation:* ACBSP. Part-time and evening/weekend programs available. Postbaccalaureate distance learning degree programs offered (minimal on-campus study). *Students:* 224 full-time (116 women), 353 part-time (180 women); includes 124 minority (71 Black or African American, non-Hispanic/Latino; 12 American Indian or Alaska Native, non-Hispanic/Latino; 15 Asian, non-Hispanic/Latino; 20 Hispanic/Latino; 1 Native Hawaiian or other Pacific Islander, non-Hispanic/Latino; 5 Two or more races, non-Hispanic/Latino). Average age 34. In 2011, 422 master's awarded. *Entrance requirements:* For master's, 2 years of full-time work experience. Additional exam requirements/recommendations for international students: Required—TOEFL (minimum score 600 paper-based; 250 computer-based; 100 iBT). *Application deadline:* Applications are processed on a rolling basis. Application fee: $45. *Expenses: Tuition:* Full-time $14,280; part-time $595 per credit hour. One-time fee: $105 full-time. Tuition and fees vary according to course load and program. *Financial support:* Applicants required to submit FAFSA. *Unit head:* Dr. Peggy Harris, Vice President and Dean, 785-594-8492, Fax: 785-594-8363, E-mail: peggy.harris@bakeru.edu. *Application contact:* Kelly Belk, Director of Marketing, 913-491-4432, Fax: 913-491-0470, E-mail: kbelk@bakeru.edu.

Bakke Graduate University, Programs in Pastoral Ministry and Business, Seattle, WA 98104. Offers business (MBA); global urban leadership (MA); social and civic entrepreneurship (MA); transformational leadership for the global city (D Min). Part-time programs available. Postbaccalaureate distance learning degree programs offered (minimal on-campus study). *Degree requirements:* For master's, thesis; for doctorate, thesis/dissertation. *Entrance requirements:* For master's, 2 years of ministry experience, BA in Biblical studies or theology; for doctorate, 3 years of ministry experience, M Div. Additional exam requirements/recommendations for international students: Required—TOEFL (minimum score 60 computer-based). Electronic applications accepted. *Faculty research:* Theological systems, church management, worship.

Baldwin Wallace University, Graduate Programs, Division of Business, MBA in Management - Hybrid Program, Berea, OH 44017-2088. Offers MBA. Postbaccalaureate distance learning degree programs offered (minimal on-campus study). *Students:* 12 full-time (9 women), 2 part-time (0 women); includes 1 minority (Black or African American, non-Hispanic/Latino). Average age 34. 21 applicants, 71% accepted, 9 enrolled. *Entrance requirements:* For master's, GMAT, bachelor's degree in any field, work experience. Additional exam requirements/recommendations for international students: Required—TOEFL (minimum score 213 computer-based; 79 iBT). *Expenses:* Contact institution. *Unit head:* Dale Kramer, Program Director, 440-826-3331, Fax: 440-826-3868, E-mail: dkramer@bw.edu. *Application contact:* Laura Spencer, Graduate Application Specialist, 440-826-2191, Fax: 440-826-3868, E-mail: lspencer@bw.edu. Web site: http://www.bw.edu/academics/bus/programs/mba-online/.

Baldwin Wallace University, Graduate Programs, Division of Business, Program in Business Administration - Management, Berea, OH 44017-2088. Offers MBA. Part-time and evening/weekend programs available. Postbaccalaureate distance learning degree programs offered (minimal on-campus study). *Students:* 86 full-time (46 women), 80 part-time (28 women); includes 26 minority (14 Black or African American, non-Hispanic/Latino; 5 Asian, non-Hispanic/Latino; 4 Hispanic/Latino; 3 Two or more races, non-Hispanic/Latino), 1 international. Average age 34. 46 applicants, 85% accepted, 23 enrolled. In 2011, 69 master's awarded. *Degree requirements:* For master's, minimum overall GPA of 3.0, completion of all required courses. *Entrance requirements:* For master's, GMAT, bachelor's degree in any field, work experience, minimum GPA of 3.0. Additional exam requirements/recommendations for international students: Required—TOEFL (minimum score 523 paper-based; 193 computer-based; 70 iBT). *Application deadline:* For fall admission, 7/25 priority date for domestic students, 4/30 for international students; for spring admission, 12/15 priority date for domestic students, 9/30 for international students. Applications are processed on a rolling basis. Application fee: $25. Electronic applications accepted. Application fee is waived when completed online. *Expenses:* Contact institution. *Financial support:* Career-related internships or fieldwork available. Support available to part-time students. Financial award application deadline: 5/1. *Unit head:* Dale Kramer, MBA/EMBA Director, 440-826-2392, Fax: 440-826-3868, E-mail: dkramer@bw.edu. *Application contact:* Laura Spencer, Graduate Application Specialist, 440-826-2191, Fax: 440-826-3868, E-mail: lspencer@bw.edu. Web site: http://www.bw.edu/academics/bus/programs/mba/.

Baldwin Wallace University, Graduate Programs, Division of Business, Program in Executive Management, Berea, OH 44017-2088. Offers MBA. Part-time and evening/weekend programs available. *Students:* 28 full-time (4 women), 1 part-time (0 women); includes 2 minority (1 Asian, non-Hispanic/Latino; 1 Hispanic/Latino). Average age 40. 16 applicants, 94% accepted, 12 enrolled. In 2011, 16 master's awarded. *Degree requirements:* For master's, project, minimum overall GPA of 3.0, completion of all required courses. *Entrance requirements:* For master's, interview, 10 years of work experience, current professional or managerial position, bachelor's degree in any field. Additional exam requirements/recommendations for international students: Required—TOEFL (minimum score 523 paper-based; 193 computer-based; 70 iBT). *Application deadline:* For fall admission, 7/25 priority date for domestic students, 4/30 for international students; for spring admission, 12/15 priority date for domestic students, 9/30 for international students. Applications are processed on a rolling basis. Application fee: $25. Electronic applications accepted. Application fee is waived when completed online. *Expenses:* Contact institution. *Financial support:* Career-related internships or fieldwork available. Support available to part-time students. Financial award application deadline: 5/1; financial award applicants required to submit FAFSA. *Unit head:* Dale Kramer, MBA/EMBA Director, 440-826-2392, Fax: 440-826-3868, E-mail: dkramer@bw.edu. *Application contact:* Laura Spencer, Graduate Application Specialist, 440-826-2191, Fax: 440-826-3868, E-mail: lspencer@bw.edu. Web site: http://www.bw.edu/academics/bus/programs/emba.

Ball State University, Graduate School, Miller College of Business, Interdepartmental Program in Business Administration, Muncie, IN 47306-1099. Offers MBA. *Accreditation:* AACSB. *Faculty:* 50. *Students:* 63 full-time (16 women), 191 part-time (77 women); includes 14 minority (8 Black or African American, non-Hispanic/Latino; 2 Asian, non-Hispanic/Latino; 2 Hispanic/Latino; 1 Native Hawaiian or other Pacific Islander, non-Hispanic/Latino; 1 Two or more races, non-Hispanic/Latino), 12 international. Average age 27. 166 applicants, 63% accepted, 73 enrolled. In 2011, 91 master's awarded. *Entrance requirements:* For master's, GMAT, resume. Application fee: $50. Tuition and fees vary according to program and reciprocity agreements. *Financial support:* In 2011–12, 54 students received support, including 37 teaching assistantships (averaging $9,478 per year). Financial award application deadline: 3/1. *Unit head:* Jennifer Bott, Graduate Coordinator, 765-285-1931, Fax: 765-285-8818. *Application contact:* Tamara Estep, Graduate Coordinator, 765-285-1931, Fax: 765-285-8818, E-mail: testep@bsu.edu. Web site: http://www.bsu.edu/business/mba/.

Barry University, Andreas School of Business, Graduate Certificate Programs, Miami Shores, FL 33161-6695. Offers finance (Certificate); health services administration (Certificate); international business (Certificate); management (Certificate); management information systems (Certificate); marketing (Certificate).

Barry University, Andreas School of Business, Program in Business Administration, Miami Shores, FL 33161-6695. Offers MBA, DPM/MBA, MBA/MS, MBA/MSN.

Barry University, School of Adult and Continuing Education, Division of Nursing and Andreas School of Business, Program in Nursing Administration and Business Administration, Miami Shores, FL 33161-6695. Offers MSN/MBA. *Accreditation:* AACN. Part-time and evening/weekend programs available. Electronic applications accepted. *Faculty research:* Power/empowerment, health delivery systems, managed care, employee health well-being.

Barry University, School of Adult and Continuing Education, Program in Administrative Studies, Miami Shores, FL 33161-6695. Offers MA. Part-time and evening/weekend programs available. *Entrance requirements:* For master's, GMAT, GRE or MAT, recommendations. Electronic applications accepted.

Barry University, School of Human Performance and Leisure Sciences and Andreas School of Business, Program in Sport Management and Business Administration, Miami Shores, FL 33161-6695. Offers MS/MBA. Part-time and evening/weekend programs available. Electronic applications accepted. *Faculty research:* Economic impact of professional sports, sport marketing.

Barry University, School of Podiatric Medicine, Podiatric Medicine and Surgery Program and Andreas School of Business, Podiatric Medicine/Business Administration Option, Miami Shores, FL 33161-6695. Offers DPM/MBA.

Bayamón Central University, Graduate Programs, Program in Business Administration, Bayamón, PR 00960-1725. Offers accounting (MBA); finance (MBA); general business (MBA); management (MBA); marketing (MBA). Part-time and evening/weekend programs available. *Degree requirements:* For master's, comprehensive exam (for some programs). *Entrance requirements:* For master's, EXADEP, bachelor's degree in business or related field.

Baylor University, Graduate School, Hankamer School of Business, Program in Business Administration, Waco, TX 76798. Offers MBA, JD/MBA, MBA/MSIS. *Accreditation:* AACSB. Part-time programs available. *Students:* 187 full-time (50 women), 6 part-time (0 women); includes 58 minority (15 Black or African American, non-Hispanic/Latino; 1 American Indian or Alaska Native, non-Hispanic/Latino; 16 Asian, non-Hispanic/Latino; 21 Hispanic/Latino; 5 Two or more races, non-Hispanic/Latino), 12 international. In 2011, 119 master's awarded. *Entrance requirements:* For master's, GMAT, minimum AACSB index of 1050. *Application deadline:* For fall admission, 8/1 for domestic students; for spring admission, 12/1 for domestic students. Applications are processed on a rolling basis. Application fee: $25. *Expenses:* Contact institution. *Financial support:* Research assistantships, teaching assistantships, career-related internships or fieldwork, Federal Work-Study, and institutionally sponsored loans available. *Unit head:* Dr. Gary Carini, Associate Dean, 254-710-3718, Fax: 254-710-1092, E-mail: gary_carini@baylor.edu. *Application contact:* Laurie Wilson, Director, Graduate Business Programs, 254-710-4163, Fax: 254-710-1066, E-mail: laurie_wilson@baylor.edu.

Belhaven University, School of Business, Jackson, MS 39202-1789. Offers business administration (MBA); leadership (MSL); public administration (MPA). MBA program also offered in Houston, TX, Memphis, TN and Orlando, FL. Evening/weekend programs available. *Faculty:* 16 full-time (5 women), 27 part-time/adjunct (7 women). *Students:* 415 full-time (276 women), 65 part-time (47 women); includes 341 minority (315 Black or African American, non-Hispanic/Latino; 2 American Indian or Alaska Native, non-Hispanic/Latino; 2 Asian, non-Hispanic/Latino; 19 Hispanic/Latino; 3 Two or more races, non-Hispanic/Latino). Average age 36. 389 applicants, 73% accepted, 211 enrolled. In 2011, 122 master's awarded. *Degree requirements:* For master's, comprehensive exam (for some programs), thesis (for some programs). *Entrance requirements:* For master's, GMAT, GRE General Test or MAT, minimum GPA of 2.8. *Application deadline:* Applications are processed on a rolling basis. Application fee: $25. Electronic applications accepted. *Expenses: Tuition:* Part-time $545 per contact hour. *Financial support:* Applicants required to submit FAFSA. *Unit head:* Dr. Ralph Mason, Dean, 601-968-8949, Fax: 601-968-8951, E-mail: cmason@belhaven.edu. *Application contact:* Dr. Audrey Kelleher, Vice President of Adult and Graduate Marketing and Development, 407-804-1424, Fax: 407-620-5210, E-mail: akelleher@belhaven.edu. Web site: http://www.belhaven.edu/campuses/index.htm.

Bellarmine University, W. Fielding Rubel School of Business, Louisville, KY 40205-0671. Offers EMBA, MBA. *Accreditation:* AACSB. Part-time and evening/weekend programs available. *Faculty:* 15 full-time (3 women), 6 part-time/adjunct (2 women). *Students:* 90 full-time (42 women), 104 part-time (36 women); includes 20 minority (14 Black or African American, non-Hispanic/Latino; 4 Asian, non-Hispanic/Latino; 2 Hispanic/Latino). Average age 30. In 2011, 79 master's awarded. *Degree requirements:* For master's, comprehensive exam. *Entrance requirements:* For master's, GMAT, baccalaureate degree from accredited institution. Additional exam requirements/recommendations for international students: Required—TOEFL (minimum score 550 paper-based; 213 computer-based; 80 iBT). *Application deadline:* Applications are processed on a rolling basis. Application fee: $25. Electronic applications accepted. *Expenses:* Contact institution. *Financial support:* Career-related internships or fieldwork, scholarships/grants, and unspecified assistantships available. Support available to part-time students. Financial award application deadline: 7/1. *Faculty research:* Marketing, management, small business and entrepreneurship, finance, economics. *Unit head:* Dr. Daniel L. Bauer, Dean, 800-274-4723 Ext. 8026, Fax: 502-272-8013, E-mail: dbauer@bellarmine.edu. *Application contact:* Dr. Sara Pettingill, Dean of Graduate Admission, 800-274-4723 Ext. 8258, Fax: 502-272-8002, E-mail: spettingill@bellarmine.edu. Web site: http://www.bellarmine.edu.

Bellevue University, Graduate School, College of Business, Bellevue, NE 68005-3098. Offers acquisition and contract management (MS); business administration (MBA); finance (MS); human capital management (PhD); management (MSM).

Belmont University, Jack C. Massey Graduate School of Business, Nashville, TN 37212-3757. Offers M Acc, MBA. *Accreditation:* AACSB. Part-time and evening/weekend programs available. *Faculty:* 36 full-time (12 women), 8 part-time/adjunct (4 women). *Students:* 48 full-time (23 women), 212 part-time (99 women); includes 33 minority (17 Black or African American, non-Hispanic/Latino; 7 Asian, non-Hispanic/Latino; 7 Hispanic/Latino; 2 Two or more races, non-Hispanic/Latino), 5 international. Average age 28. 128 applicants, 76% accepted, 82 enrolled. In 2011, 127 master's awarded. *Entrance requirements:* For master's, GMAT, 2 years of work experience (MBA). Additional exam requirements/recommendations for international students: Required—TOEFL (minimum score 550 paper-based; 213 computer-based). *Application deadline:* For fall admission, 7/1 for domestic and international students; for spring admission, 11/1 for domestic and international students. Applications are processed on a rolling basis. Application fee: $50. Electronic applications accepted. *Expenses:* Contact institution. *Financial support:* In 2011–12, 22 students received support. Scholarships/grants, tuition waivers (partial), and unspecified assistantships available. Financial award application deadline: 7/1; financial award applicants required to submit FAFSA. *Faculty research:* Music business, strategy, ethics, finance, accounting systems. *Unit head:* Dr. Patrick Raines, Dean, 615-460-6480, Fax: 615-460-6455, E-mail: pat.raines@belmont.edu. *Application contact:* Tonya Hollin, Admissions Assistant, 615-460-6480, Fax: 615-460-6353, E-mail: masseyadmissions@belmont.edu. Web site: http://massey.belmont.edu.

Benedictine College, Executive Master of Business Administration Program, Atchison, KS 66002-1499. Offers EMBA. Evening/weekend programs available. *Entrance requirements:* For master's, 5 years of management experience, interview. Additional exam requirements/recommendations for international students: Required—TOEFL (minimum score 533 paper-based). Electronic applications accepted. *Expenses:* Contact institution. *Faculty research:* Banking, strategic planning, ethics, leadership and entrepreneurship.

Benedictine College, Traditional Business Administration Program, Atchison, KS 66002. Offers MBA. Part-time and evening/weekend programs available. *Degree requirements:* For master's, comprehensive exam. *Entrance requirements:* For master's, GMAT. Additional exam requirements/recommendations for international students: Required—TOEFL (minimum score 533 paper-based; 200 computer-based; 72 iBT). Electronic applications accepted. *Expenses:* Contact institution.

Benedictine University, Graduate Programs, Program in Business Administration, Lisle, IL 60532-0900. Offers accounting (MBA); entrepreneurship and managing innovation (MBA); financial management (MBA); health administration (MBA); human resource management (MBA); information systems security (MBA); international business (MBA); management consulting (MBA); management information systems (MBA); marketing management (MBA); operations management and logistics (MBA); organizational leadership (MBA); MBA/MPH; MBA/MS. Part-time and evening/weekend programs available. Postbaccalaureate distance learning degree programs offered (minimal on-campus study). *Faculty:* 4 full-time (2 women), 24 part-time/adjunct (3 women). *Students:* 165 full-time (101 women), 766 part-time (381 women); includes 201 minority (118 Black or African American, non-Hispanic/Latino; 4 American Indian or Alaska Native, non-Hispanic/Latino; 37 Asian, non-Hispanic/Latino; 40 Hispanic/Latino; 2 Native Hawaiian or other Pacific Islander, non-Hispanic/Latino), 14 international. Average age 34. 313 applicants, 73% accepted, 166 enrolled. In 2011, 379 master's awarded. *Entrance requirements:* For master's, GMAT. Additional exam requirements/recommendations for international students: Required—TOEFL (minimum score 550 paper-based; 213 computer-based). *Application deadline:* For fall admission, 9/1 for domestic students; for winter admission, 12/1 for domestic students; for spring admission, 2/15 for domestic students. Applications are processed on a rolling basis. Application fee: $40. Electronic applications accepted. *Financial support:* Career-related internships or fieldwork and health care benefits available. Support available to part-time students. *Faculty research:* Strategic leadership in professional organizations, sociology of professions, organizational change, social identity theory, applications to change management. *Unit head:* Dr. Sharon Borowicz, Director, 630-829-6219, E-mail: sborowicz@ben.edu. *Application contact:* Kari Gibbons, Director, Admissions, 630-829-6200, Fax: 630-829-6584, E-mail: kgibbons@ben.edu.

Benedictine University, Graduate Programs, Program in Management and Organizational Behavior, Lisle, IL 60532-0900. Offers MS, MBA/MS, MPH/MS. Part-time and evening/weekend programs available. *Faculty:* 1 full-time (0 women), 15 part-time/adjunct (7 women). *Students:* 50 full-time (34 women), 137 part-time (104 women); includes 51 minority (38 Black or African American, non-Hispanic/Latino; 2 American Indian or Alaska Native, non-Hispanic/Latino; 5 Asian, non-Hispanic/Latino; 6 Hispanic/Latino), 5 international. Average age 40. 60 applicants, 87% accepted, 44 enrolled. In 2011, 49 master's awarded. *Entrance requirements:* For master's, GMAT. Additional exam requirements/recommendations for international students: Required—TOEFL (minimum score 550 paper-based; 213 computer-based). *Application deadline:* For fall admission, 9/1 for domestic students; for winter admission, 12/1 for domestic students; for spring admission, 2/15 for domestic students. Applications are processed on a rolling basis. Application fee: $40. Electronic applications accepted. *Financial support:* Career-related internships or fieldwork and health care benefits available. Support available to part-time students. *Faculty research:* Organizational change, transformation, development, learning organizations, career transitions for academics. *Unit head:* Dr. Peter F. Sorensen, Director, 630-829-6220, Fax: 630-960-1126, E-mail: psorensen@ben.edu. *Application contact:* Kari Gibbons, Associate Vice President, Enrollment Center, 630-829-6200, Fax: 630-829-6584, E-mail: kgibbons@ben.edu.

Benedictine University at Springfield, Program in Business Administration, Springfield, IL 62702. Offers health administration (MBA); organizational leadership (MBA). Part-time and evening/weekend programs available. *Entrance requirements:* For master's, GMAT.

Benedictine University at Springfield, Program in Management and Organizational Behavior, Springfield, IL 62702. Offers MS. Evening/weekend programs available. *Entrance requirements:* For master's, official transcripts, 2 letters of reference, essay, resume, interview.

Bentley University, McCallum Graduate School of Business, Business PhD Program, Waltham, MA 02452-4705. Offers PhD. Part-time programs available. *Degree requirements:* For doctorate, comprehensive exam, thesis/dissertation. *Entrance requirements:* For doctorate, GMAT or GRE General Test. Additional exam requirements/recommendations for international students: Required—TOEFL (minimum score 600 paper-based; 250 computer-based; 100 iBT) or IELTS (minimum score 7). Electronic applications accepted. *Faculty research:* Information systems, management (including organization behavior, strategy, entrepreneurship, business ethics), marketing, business analytics.

Bentley University, McCallum Graduate School of Business, Evening Professional MBA Program, Waltham, MA 02452-4705. Offers MBA. *Accreditation:* AACSB. Part-time and evening/weekend programs available. *Entrance requirements:* For master's, GMAT or GRE General Test. Additional exam requirements/recommendations for international students: Required—TOEFL (minimum score 600 paper-based; 250 computer-based; 100 iBT) or IELTS (minimum score 7). Electronic applications accepted. *Faculty research:* Strategy and innovation; corporate social responsibility; IT strategy; business process management; organizational change and knowledge management; discipline-specific research in accountancy, finance, information design and communication, IT, marketing and taxation.

Bentley University, McCallum Graduate School of Business, Graduate Business Certificate Program, Waltham, MA 02452-4705. Offers accounting (GBC); accounting information systems (GBC); business (GSS); business ethics (GBC); data analysis (GBC); financial planning (GBC); fraud and forensic accounting (GBC); marketing analytics (GBC); taxation (GBC). *Accreditation:* AACSB. Part-time and evening/weekend programs available. *Entrance requirements:* For degree, GMAT or GRE General Test. Additional exam requirements/recommendations for international students: Required—TOEFL (minimum score 600 paper-based; 250 computer-based; 100 iBT) or IELTS (minimum score 7). Electronic applications accepted.

Bentley University, McCallum Graduate School of Business, MBA Program, Waltham, MA 02452-4705. Offers MBA. *Accreditation:* AACSB. *Entrance requirements:* For master's, GMAT or GRE General Test. Additional exam requirements/recommendations for international students: Required—TOEFL (minimum score 600 paper-based; 250 computer-based; 100 iBT) or IELTS (minimum score 7). Electronic applications accepted. *Faculty research:* Strategy and innovation, business process management, corporate social responsibility, IT strategy, organizational change and knowledge management.

Bentley University, McCallum Graduate School of Business, MS and MBA Program, Waltham, MA 02452-4705. Offers MS/MBA. *Accreditation:* AACSB. *Entrance requirements:* Additional exam requirements/recommendations for international students: Required—TOEFL (minimum score 600 paper-based; 250 computer-based; 100 iBT) or IELTS (minimum score 7). Electronic applications accepted. *Faculty research:* Strategy and innovation, business process management, corporate social responsibility, IT strategy, organizational change and knowledge management.

Bernard M. Baruch College of the City University of New York, Zicklin School of Business, New York, NY 10010-5585. Offers MBA, MS, PhD, Certificate, JD/MBA. JD/MBA offered jointly with Brooklyn Law School and New York Law School. *Accreditation:* AACSB. Part-time and evening/weekend programs available. *Degree requirements:* For doctorate, comprehensive exam, thesis/dissertation. *Entrance requirements:* For master's, GMAT or GRE, 2 letters of recommendation, resume, 2 years of work experience; for doctorate, GMAT or GRE. Additional exam requirements/recommendations for international students: Required—TOEFL (minimum iBT score of 102) or Pearson Test of English. Electronic applications accepted.

Bernard M. Baruch College of the City University of New York, Zicklin School of Business, Zicklin Executive Programs, Executive MBA Program, New York, NY 10010-5585. Offers MBA. *Accreditation:* AACSB. *Entrance requirements:* For master's, 5 years of management-level work experience, personal interview. Additional exam requirements/recommendations for international students: Required—TOEFL. *Expenses:* Contact institution. *Faculty research:* Entrepreneurship, corporate governance, international finance, mergers and acquisitions.

Berry College, Graduate Programs, Campbell School of Business, Mount Berry, GA 30149-0159. Offers MBA. *Accreditation:* AACSB. Part-time and evening/weekend programs available. *Faculty:* 10 part-time/adjunct (4 women). *Students:* 1 (woman) full-time, 25 part-time (14 women); includes 2 minority (1 Black or African American, non-Hispanic/Latino; 1 American Indian or Alaska Native, non-Hispanic/Latino), 1 international. Average age 28. In 2011, 18 master's awarded. *Degree requirements:* For master's, thesis. *Entrance requirements:* For master's, GMAT, minimum GPA of 3.0, essay/goals statement. Additional exam requirements/recommendations for international students: Required—TOEFL (minimum score 550 paper-based; 213 computer-based). *Application deadline:* For fall admission, 7/27 for domestic students; for spring admission, 12/14 for domestic students. Applications are processed on a rolling basis. Application fee: $25 ($30 for international students). Electronic applications accepted. *Expenses:* Contact institution. *Financial support:* In 2011–12, 18 students received support, including 11 research assistantships with full tuition reimbursements available (averaging $4,871 per year); scholarships/grants, tuition waivers (partial), and unspecified assistantships also available. Support available to part-time students. Financial award application deadline: 3/1; financial award applicants required to submit FAFSA. *Faculty research:* Marketing, economics, accounting strategies, business law, entrepreneurship. *Unit head:* Dr. John Grout, Dean, 706-236-2233, Fax: 706-802-6728, E-mail: jgrout@berry.edu. *Application contact:* Brett Kennedy, Director of Admissions, 706-236-2215, Fax: 706-290-2178, E-mail: admissions@berry.edu. Web site: http://www.campbell.berry.edu/.

Bethel College, Division of Graduate Studies, Program in Business Administration, Mishawaka, IN 46545-5591. Offers MBA. Part-time and evening/weekend programs available. *Faculty:* 5 part-time/adjunct (2 women). *Students:* 5 full-time (0 women), 40 part-time (23 women); includes 8 minority (6 Black or African American, non-Hispanic/Latino; 2 Hispanic/Latino), 1 international. 36 applicants, 75% accepted, 24 enrolled. In 2011, 18 master's awarded. *Entrance requirements:* For master's, GMAT. Additional exam requirements/recommendations for international students: Required—TOEFL (minimum score 540 paper-based; 207 computer-based). *Application deadline:* For fall admission, 5/1 for international students; for spring admission, 10/1 for international students. Applications are processed on a rolling basis. Application fee: $25. Electronic applications accepted. *Financial support:* Career-related internships or fieldwork available. Financial award applicants required to submit FAFSA. *Faculty research:* Marketing. *Unit head:* Dawn Goellner, Director, 574-257-3485, E-mail: goelInd2@bethelcollege.edu. *Application contact:* Dawn Goellner, Director, 574-257-3485, Fax: 574-257-7616. Web site: http://www.bethelcollege.edu/academics/graduate/mba/.

Bethel University, Graduate Programs, McKenzie, TN 38201. Offers administration and supervision (MA Ed); business administration (MBA); conflict resolution (MA); physician assistant studies (MS). Part-time and evening/weekend programs available. *Degree requirements:* For master's, thesis (for some programs). *Entrance requirements:* For master's, GRE General Test or MAT, minimum undergraduate GPA of 2.5.

Bethel University, Graduate School, St. Paul, MN 55112-6999. Offers autism spectrum disorders (Certificate); business administration (MBA); communication (MA); counseling psychology (MA); education (M Ed); educational leadership (Ed D); gerontology (MA, Certificate); international baccalaureate education (Certificate); K-12 education (MA); literacy education (MA); nursing (MA); nursing education (Certificate); nursing leadership (Certificate); organizational leadership (MA); postsecondary teaching (Certificate); special education (MA); teaching (MA). Part-time and evening/weekend programs available. Postbaccalaureate distance learning degree programs offered (minimal on-campus study). *Faculty:* 8 full-time (3 women), 98 part-time/adjunct (46 women). *Students:* 651 full-time (419 women), 312 part-time (212 women); includes 79 minority (35 Black or African American, non-Hispanic/Latino; 2 American Indian or Alaska Native, non-Hispanic/Latino; 19 Asian, non-Hispanic/Latino; 17 Hispanic/Latino; 6 Two or more races, non-Hispanic/Latino), 6 international. Average age 36. In 2011, 245 master's, 4 doctorates, 32 other advanced degrees awarded. *Degree requirements:* For master's, comprehensive exam (for some programs), thesis (for some programs); for doctorate, comprehensive exam, thesis/dissertation. *Entrance requirements:* Additional exam requirements/recommendations for international students: Required—TOEFL (minimum score 550 paper-based; 213 computer-based; 80 iBT). *Application* accepted. Tuition and fees vary according to course load, degree level and program. *Financial support:* Applicants required to submit FAFSA. *Unit head:* Dick Crombie, Vice-President/Dean, 651-635-8000, Fax: 651-635-8004, E-mail: gs@bethel.edu. *Application contact:* Paul Ives, Director of Admissions, 651-635-8000, Fax: 651-635-8004, E-mail: gs@bethel.edu. Web site: http://gs.bethel.edu/.

Biola University, Crowell School of Business, La Mirada, CA 90639-0001. Offers MBA. *Accreditation:* ACBSP. Part-time and evening/weekend programs available. *Faculty:* 12. *Students:* 36; includes 20 minority (3 Black or African American, non-Hispanic/Latino; 9 Asian, non-Hispanic/Latino; 5 Hispanic/Latino; 3 Two or more races, non-Hispanic/Latino). In 2011, 6 master's awarded. *Entrance requirements:* For master's, GMAT, 3 years of professional experience. Additional exam requirements/recommendations for international students: Required—TOEFL (minimum score 550 paper-based; 213 computer-based). *Application deadline:* For fall admission, 4/30 priority date for domestic students. Applications are processed on a rolling basis. Application fee: $55. *Financial support:* Institutionally sponsored loans and scholarships/grants available. Support available to part-time students. Financial award applicants required to submit FAFSA. *Faculty research:* Integration of theology with business principles. *Unit head:* Dr. Larry D. Strand, Dean, 562-777-4015, Fax: 562-906-4545, E-mail: mba@biola.edu. *Application contact:* Christina Bullock, MBA Coordinator, 562-777-4015, E-mail: mba@biola.edu. Web site: http://crowell.biola.edu.

Black Hills State University, Graduate Studies, Program in Business Administration, Spearfish, SD 57799. Offers MBA. *Entrance requirements:* Additional exam requirements/recommendations for international students: Required—TOEFL (minimum score 500 paper-based; 171 computer-based; 60 iBT).

Bloomsburg University of Pennsylvania, School of Graduate Studies, College of Business, Program in Business Administration, Bloomsburg, PA 17815-1301. Offers MBA. *Accreditation:* AACSB. *Entrance requirements:* For master's, GMAT, minimum QPA of 3.0, resume, 3 letters of recommendation. Additional exam requirements/recommendations for international students: Required—TOEFL (minimum score 550 paper-based; 213 computer-based; 79 iBT). Electronic applications accepted.

Bluffton University, Programs in Business, Bluffton, OH 45817. Offers business administration (MBA); organizational management (MA). Evening/weekend programs available. *Entrance requirements:* Additional exam requirements/recommendations for international students: Required—TOEFL. Electronic applications accepted.

Bob Jones University, Graduate Programs, Greenville, SC 29614. Offers accountancy (MS); Bible (MA); Bible translation (MA); Biblical studies (Certificate); broadcast management (MS); business administration (MBA); church history (MA, PhD); church ministries (MA); church music (MM); cinema and video production (MA); counseling (MS); curriculum and instruction (Ed D); divinity (M Div); dramatic production (MA); educational leadership (MS, Ed D, Ed S); elementary education (M Ed, MAT); English (M Ed, MA, MAT); fine arts (MA); graphic design (MA); history (M Ed, MA); illustration (MA); interpretative speech (MA); mathematics (M Ed, MAT); medical missions (Certificate); ministry (MM, D Min); multi-categorical special education (M Ed, MAT); music (M Ed); New Testament interpretation (PhD); Old Testament interpretation (PhD); orchestral instrument performance (MM); organ performance (MM); pastoral studies (MA); personnel services (MS, Ed S); piano pedagogy (MM); piano performance (MM); platform arts (MA); radio and television broadcasting (MS); rhetoric and public address (MA); secondary education (M Ed); studio art (MA); teaching Bible (MA); theology (MA, PhD); voice performance (MM); youth ministries (MA); M Div/MM.

Boise State University, Graduate College, College of Business and Economics, Program in Business Administration, Boise, ID 83725-0399. Offers MBA. *Accreditation:* AACSB. Part-time programs available. *Entrance requirements:* For master's, GMAT, minimum GPA of 3.0. Additional exam requirements/recommendations for international students: Required—TOEFL. Electronic applications accepted.

Boston College, Carroll School of Management, Business Administration Program, Chestnut Hill, MA 02467-3800. Offers MBA, JD/MBA, MBA/MA, MBA/MS, MBA/MSA, MBA/MSF, MBA/MSW, MBA/PhD. *Accreditation:* AACSB. Part-time and evening/weekend programs available. *Faculty:* 59 full-time (19 women), 45 part-time/adjunct (4 women). *Students:* 200 full-time (64 women), 435 part-time (154 women); includes 81 minority (12 Black or African American, non-Hispanic/Latino; 3 American Indian or Alaska Native, non-Hispanic/Latino; 37 Asian, non-Hispanic/Latino; 20 Hispanic/Latino; 1 Native Hawaiian or other Pacific Islander, non-Hispanic/Latino; 8 Two or more races, non-Hispanic/Latino), 79 international. Average age 27. 1,095 applicants, 43% accepted, 237 enrolled. In 2011, 246 master's awarded. *Entrance requirements:* For master's, GMAT, 2 letters of recommendation, resume. Additional exam requirements/recommendations for international students: Required—TOEFL (minimum score 600 paper-based; 250 computer-based; 100 iBT). *Application deadline:* For fall admission, 4/15 for domestic and international students; for spring admission, 10/15 for domestic students. Application fee: $100. Electronic applications accepted. *Financial support:* In 2011–12, 151 fellowships, 109 research assistantships with full and partial tuition reimbursements were awarded; career-related internships or fieldwork, Federal Work-Study, scholarships/grants, tuition waivers (full and partial), and unspecified assistantships also available. Support available to part-time students. Financial award application deadline: 3/1; financial award applicants required to submit FAFSA. *Faculty research:* Investments, e-commerce, corporate finance, management of financial services, strategic management. *Unit head:* Dr. Jeffrey L. Ringuest, Associate Dean for Graduate Programs, 617-552-9100, Fax: 617-552-0514, E-mail: jeffrey.ringuest@bc.edu. *Application contact:* Shelley A. Burt, Director of Graduate Enrollment, 617-552-3920, Fax: 617-552-8078, E-mail: bcmba@bc.edu. Web site: http://www.bc.edu/mba/.

Boston University, Metropolitan College, Department of Administrative Sciences, Boston, MA 02215. Offers banking and financial management (MSM); business continuity in emergency management (MSM); economics development and tourism management (MSAS); electronic commerce, systems, and technology (MSAS); financial economics (MSAS); innovation and technology (MSAS); insurance management (MSM); international market management (MSM); multinational commerce (MSAS); project management (MSM). *Accreditation:* AACSB. Part-time and evening/weekend programs available. Postbaccalaureate distance learning degree programs offered (no on-campus study). *Faculty:* 14 full-time (2 women), 21 part-time/adjunct (2 women). *Students:* 151 full-time (75 women), 106 part-time (51 women); includes 27 minority (6 Black or African American, non-Hispanic/Latino; 14 Asian, non-Hispanic/Latino; 7 Hispanic/Latino), 173 international. Average age 28. 500 applicants, 65% accepted, 194 enrolled. In 2011, 154 master's awarded. *Degree requirements:* For master's, thesis optional. *Entrance requirements:* For master's, 1 year of work experience, minimum GPA of 3.0. Additional exam requirements/recommendations for international students: Required—TOEFL (minimum score 560 paper-based; 220 computer-based; 84 iBT). *Application deadline:* Applications are processed on a rolling basis. Application fee: $70. Electronic applications accepted. *Expenses: Tuition:* Full-time $40,848; part-time $1276 per credit hour. *Required fees:* $572; $286 per semester. *Financial support:* In 2011–12, 15 students received support, including 7 research assistantships (averaging $10,000 per year); career-related internships or fieldwork, Federal Work-Study, and unspecified assistantships also available. *Faculty research:* International business, innovative process. *Unit head:* Dr. Kip Becker, Chairman, 617-353-3016, E-mail: adminsc@bu.edu. *Application contact:* Lucille Dicker, Administrative Sciences Department, 617-353-3016, E-mail: adminsc@bu.edu. Web site: http://www.bu.edu/met/programs/.

Boston University, Metropolitan College, Program in Gastronomy, Boston, MA 02215. Offers business (MLA); communications (MLA); food policy (MLA); history and culture (MLA). Part-time and evening/weekend programs available. *Faculty:* 1 (woman) full-time, 13 part-time/adjunct (7 women). *Students:* 11 full-time (10 women), 72 part-time (61 women); includes 11 minority (2 Black or African American, non-Hispanic/Latino; 5 Asian, non-Hispanic/Latino; 3 Hispanic/Latino; 1 Two or more races, non-Hispanic/Latino), 6 international. Average age 28. 59 applicants, 53% accepted, 23 enrolled. In 2011, 9 master's awarded. *Degree requirements:* For master's, thesis optional. *Entrance requirements:* Additional exam requirements/recommendations for international students: Required—TOEFL. *Application deadline:* Applications are processed on a rolling basis. Application fee: $70. Electronic applications accepted. *Expenses: Tuition:* Full-time $40,848; part-time $1276 per credit hour. *Required fees:* $572; $286 per semester. *Financial support:* In 2011–12, 3 research assistantships (averaging $5,000 per year) were awarded; career-related internships or fieldwork, scholarships/grants, and unspecified assistantships also available. Support available to part-time students. Financial award applicants required to submit FAFSA. *Faculty research:* Food studies. *Unit head:* Dr. Rachel Black, Assistant Professor, 617-353-6291, Fax: 617-353-4130, E-mail: rblack@bu.edu. Web site: http://www.bu.edu/met/gastronomy.

Boston University, School of Management, Boston, MA 02215. Offers business administration (MBA); executive business administration (EMBA); investment management (MS); management (PhD); mathematical finance (MS, PhD); JD/MBA; MBA/MA; MBA/MPH; MBA/MS; MBA/MSIS; MD/MBA; MS/MBA. *Accreditation:* AACSB. Part-time and evening/weekend programs available. *Faculty:* 185 full-time (49 women), 60 part-time/adjunct (15 women). *Students:* 510 full-time (177 women), 736 part-time (263 women); includes 176 minority (20 Black or African American, non-Hispanic/Latino; 121 Asian, non-Hispanic/Latino; 22 Hispanic/Latino; 13 Two or more races, non-Hispanic/Latino), 250 international. Average age 30. 1,387 applicants, 28% accepted, 160 enrolled. In 2011, 557 master's, 8 doctorates awarded. *Degree requirements:* For doctorate, comprehensive exam, thesis/dissertation. *Entrance requirements:* For master's, GMAT (for MBA and MS in investment management); GMAT or GRE General Test (for MS in mathematical finance), resume, 2 letters of recommendation; for doctorate, GMAT or GRE General Test, resume, personal statement, 3 letters of recommendation, 3 essays, official transcripts. *Application deadline:* For fall admission, 1/5 for domestic and international students; for spring admission, 11/1 for domestic students. Application fee: $125. Electronic applications accepted. *Expenses: Tuition:* Full-time $40,848; part-time $1276 per credit hour. *Required fees:* $572; $286 per semester. *Financial support:* Career-related internships or fieldwork, Federal Work-Study, institutionally sponsored loans, scholarships/grants, and tuition waivers (partial) available. Financial award applicants required to submit FAFSA. *Faculty research:* Innovation policy and productivity, corporate social responsibility, risk management, information systems, entrepreneurship, clean energy, sustainability. *Unit head:* Kenneth W. Freeman, Professor/Dean, 617-353-9720, Fax: 617-353-5581, E-mail: kfreeman@bu.edu. *Application contact:* Patti Cudney, Assistant Dean, Graduate Admissions, 617-353-2670, Fax: 617-353-7368, E-mail: mba@bu.edu. Web site: http://management.bu.edu/.

Bowie State University, Graduate Programs, Program in Business Administration, Bowie, MD 20715-9465. Offers MBA. *Accreditation:* ACBSP. Part-time and evening/weekend programs available. *Faculty:* 4 full-time (0 women), 3 part-time/adjunct (0 women). *Students:* 29 full-time (11 women), 28 part-time (14 women); includes 51 minority (all Black or African American, non-Hispanic/Latino), 1 international. Average age 31. 30 applicants, 97% accepted, 17 enrolled. In 2011, 23 master's awarded. *Degree requirements:* For master's, comprehensive exam. *Entrance requirements:* For master's, GMAT, minimum undergraduate GPA of 2.5. *Application deadline:* For fall admission, 4/1 priority date for domestic students, 4/1 for international students; for spring admission, 11/1 priority date for domestic students, 11/1 for international students. Applications are processed on a rolling basis. Application fee: $40. Electronic applications accepted. *Expenses:* Tuition, state resident: full-time $4140; part-time $3105 per semester. Tuition, nonresident: full-time $7836; part-time $5877 per semester. *Required fees:* $1715; $648 per semester. *Unit head:* Dr. Falih Alsaaty, Program Coordinator, 301-860-3644, E-mail: falsaaty@bowiestate.edu. *Application contact:* Angela Issac, Information Contact, 301-860-4000.

Bowling Green State University, Graduate College, College of Business Administration, Graduate Studies in Business Program, Bowling Green, OH 43403. Offers MBA. *Accreditation:* AACSB. Part-time and evening/weekend programs available. *Degree requirements:* For master's, thesis or alternative, research project. *Entrance requirements:* For master's, GMAT. Additional exam requirements/recommendations for international students: Required—TOEFL. Electronic applications accepted. *Faculty research:* Management of change processes, supply chain management, impacts of money on society, corporate financing strategies, macro-marketing/management of sales staff and services.

Bradley University, Graduate School, Foster College of Business Administration, Executive MBA Program, Peoria, IL 61625-0002. Offers MBA. *Accreditation:* AACSB. Evening/weekend programs available. *Entrance requirements:* For master's, company sponsorship, 7 years of managerial experience, letters of recommendation. Additional exam requirements/recommendations for international students: Required—TOEFL (minimum score 550 paper-based; 213 computer-based; 79 iBT). *Expenses:* Contact institution.

Bradley University, Graduate School, Foster College of Business Administration, Program in Business Administration, Peoria, IL 61625-0002. Offers MBA. *Accreditation:* AACSB. Part-time and evening/weekend programs available. *Degree requirements:* For master's, comprehensive exam. *Entrance requirements:* For master's, GMAT, minimum undergraduate GPA of 2.75 in major, 2 letters of recommendation. Additional exam requirements/recommendations for international students: Required—TOEFL (minimum score 550 paper-based; 213 computer-based; 79 iBT).

Brandeis University, The Heller School for Social Policy and Management, Program in Nonprofit Management, Waltham, MA 02454-9110. Offers child, youth, and family management (MBA); health care management (MBA); social impact management (MBA); social policy and management (MBA); sustainable development (MBA); MBA/MA; MBA/MD. MBA/MD program offered in conjunction with Tufts University School of Medicine. *Accreditation:* AACSB. Part-time programs available. *Students:* 82 full-time (50 women), 7 part-time (5 women); includes 8 minority (2 Black or African American, non-Hispanic/Latino; 4 Asian, non-Hispanic/Latino; 2 Hispanic/Latino), 5 international. Average age 27. 130 applicants, 73% accepted, 56 enrolled. In 2011, 47 master's awarded. *Degree requirements:* For master's, team consulting project. *Entrance requirements:* For master's, GMAT (preferred) or GRE, 2 letters of recommendation, problem statement analysis, 3-5 years of professional experience. Additional exam requirements/recommendations for international students: Required—TOEFL (minimum score 600 paper-based; 250 computer-based; 100 iBT). *Application deadline:* For fall admission, 3/15 for domestic and international students. Applications are processed on a rolling basis. Application fee: $55. Electronic applications accepted. *Expenses:* Contact institution. *Financial support:* In 2011–12, 89 students received support.

Career-related internships or fieldwork, scholarships/grants, and tuition waivers (partial) available. Support available to part-time students. Financial award application deadline: 3/15; financial award applicants required to submit FAFSA. *Faculty research:* Health care; children and families; elder and disabled services; social impact management; organizations in the non-profit, for-profit, or public sector. *Unit head:* Dr. Brenda Anderson, Program Director, 781-736-8423, E-mail: banderson@brandeis.edu. *Application contact:* Shana Sconyers, Assistant Director for Admissions and Financial Aid, 781-736-4229, E-mail: sconyers@brandeis.edu. Web site: http://heller.brandeis.edu/academic/mba.html.

Brandman University, School of Business and Professional Studies, Irvine, CA 92618. Offers business administration (MBA); human resources (MS); organizational leadership (MA); public administration (MPA).

Brenau University, Sydney O. Smith Graduate School, School of Business and Mass Communication, Gainesville, GA 30501. Offers accounting (MBA); business administration (MBA); healthcare management (MBA); organizational leadership (MS); project management (MBA). Part-time and evening/weekend programs available. Postbaccalaureate distance learning degree programs offered (no on-campus study). *Degree requirements:* For master's, comprehensive exam (for some programs). *Entrance requirements:* For master's, resume, minimum undergraduate GPA of 2.5. Additional exam requirements/recommendations for international students: Required—TOEFL (minimum score 500 paper-based; 173 computer-based; 61 iBT); Recommended—IELTS (minimum score 5). Electronic applications accepted. *Expenses:* Contact institution.

Brescia University, Program in Business Administration, Owensboro, KY 42301-3023. Offers MBA. Part-time and evening/weekend programs available. *Entrance requirements:* For master's, GMAT or GRE.

Brescia University, Program in Management, Owensboro, KY 42301-3023. Offers MSM. Part-time and evening/weekend programs available. *Entrance requirements:* For master's, GMAT, minimum GPA of 2.5.

Bridgewater State University, School of Graduate Studies, School of Business, Department of Management, Bridgewater, MA 02325-0001. Offers MSM. *Entrance requirements:* For master's, GMAT.

Briercrest Seminary, Graduate Programs, Program in Leadership and Management, Caronport, SK S0H 0S0, Canada. Offers organizational leadership (MA). Part-time programs available. *Degree requirements:* For master's, comprehensive exam, thesis optional. *Entrance requirements:* Additional exam requirements/recommendations for international students: Required—TOEFL (minimum score 550 paper-based; 213 computer-based).

Brigham Young University, Graduate Studies, Marriott School of Management, Executive Master of Business Administration Program, Provo, UT 84602. Offers MBA. *Accreditation:* AACSB. Part-time and evening/weekend programs available. *Faculty:* 35 full-time (0 women). *Students:* 121 part-time (8 women); includes 5 minority (3 Asian, non-Hispanic/Latino; 1 Hispanic/Latino; 1 Native Hawaiian or other Pacific Islander, non-Hispanic/Latino), 8 international. Average age 38. 118 applicants, 58% accepted, 59 enrolled. In 2011, 60 master's awarded. *Entrance requirements:* For master's, GMAT, 5 years of management experience, minimum GPA of 3.0 in last 60 undergraduate hours. Additional exam requirements/recommendations for international students: Required—TOEFL (minimum score 590 paper-based; 240 computer-based; 94 iBT). *Application deadline:* For fall admission, 5/1 for domestic and international students. Applications are processed on a rolling basis. Application fee: $50. Electronic applications accepted. *Expenses:* Contact institution. *Financial support:* In 2011–12, 4 students received support. Application deadline: 5/1; applicants required to submit FAFSA. *Unit head:* Monte Swain, Director, 801-422-3500, Fax: 801-422-0513, E-mail: emba@byu.edu. *Application contact:* Yvette Anderson, MBA Program Admissions Director, 801-422-3500, Fax: 801-422-0513, E-mail: mba@byu.edu. Web site: http://emba.byu.edu.

Brigham Young University, Graduate Studies, Marriott School of Management, Master of Business Administration Program, Provo, UT 84602. Offers MBA, JD/MBA, MBA/MS. *Accreditation:* AACSB. *Faculty:* 78 full-time (7 women). *Students:* 312 full-time (49 women); includes 16 minority (2 Black or African American, non-Hispanic/Latino; 6 Asian, non-Hispanic/Latino; 7 Hispanic/Latino; 1 Native Hawaiian or other Pacific Islander, non-Hispanic/Latino), 44 international. Average age 29. 401 applicants, 52% accepted, 150 enrolled. In 2011, 165 master's awarded. *Entrance requirements:* For master's, GMAT, minimum GPA of 3.0 in last 60 hours. Additional exam requirements/recommendations for international students: Required—TOEFL (minimum score 590 paper-based; 240 computer-based). *Application deadline:* For fall admission, 3/1 for domestic students, 1/15 for international students. Applications are processed on a rolling basis. Application fee: $50. Electronic applications accepted. *Expenses:* Contact institution. *Financial support:* In 2011–12, 238 students received support. Teaching assistantships, career-related internships or fieldwork, institutionally sponsored loans, scholarships/grants, and unspecified assistantships available. Financial award application deadline: 3/1; financial award applicants required to submit FAFSA. *Faculty research:* Finance, organizational behavior/human relations, marketing, supply chain management, strategy. *Unit head:* Craig B. Merrill, Director, 801-422-3500, Fax: 801-422-0513, E-mail: mba@byu.edu. *Application contact:* Yvette Anderson, MBA Program Admissions Director, 801-422-3500, Fax: 801-422-0513, E-mail: mba@byu.edu. Web site: http://mba.byu.edu.

Broadview University–West Jordan, Graduate Programs, West Jordan, UT 84088. Offers business administration (MBA); health care management (MSM); information technology (MSM); managerial leadership (MSM).

Brock University, Faculty of Graduate Studies, Faculty of Business, Program in Business Administration, St. Catharines, ON L2S 3A1, Canada. Offers MBA. *Degree requirements:* For master's, thesis or alternative. *Entrance requirements:* For master's, honours degree. Additional exam requirements/recommendations for international students: Required—TOEFL (minimum score 575 paper-based; 230 computer-based; 89 iBT), IELTS (minimum score 7), TWE (minimum score 4.5). Electronic applications accepted.

Brock University, Faculty of Graduate Studies, Faculty of Business, Program in Management, St. Catharines, ON L2S 3A1, Canada. Offers M Sc. Part-time programs available. *Degree requirements:* For master's, thesis. *Entrance requirements:* For master's, GMAT, honors degree. Additional exam requirements/recommendations for international students: Required—TOEFL (minimum score 600 paper-based; 250 computer-based; 100 iBT), IELTS (minimum score 7), TWE (minimum score 4.5). Electronic applications accepted.

Bryan College, MBA Program, Dayton, TN 37321-7000. Offers MBA. *Entrance requirements:* For master's, resume, 2 letters of recommendation.

Bryant University, Graduate School of Business, Master of Business Administration Program, Smithfield, RI 02917. Offers general business (MBA). *Accreditation:* AACSB. Part-time and evening/weekend programs available. *Entrance requirements:* For master's, GMAT, transcripts, recommendation, resume, statement of objectives. Additional exam requirements/recommendations for international students: Required—TOEFL (minimum score 580 paper-based; 237 computer-based; 95 iBT). Electronic applications accepted. *Faculty research:* International business, information systems security, leadership, financial markets microstructure, commercial lending practice.

Butler University, College of Business Administration, Indianapolis, IN 46208-3485. Offers business administration (MBA); professional accounting (MP Acc). *Accreditation:* AACSB. Part-time and evening/weekend programs available. *Faculty:* 12 full-time (2 women), 4 part-time/adjunct (0 women). *Students:* 38 full-time (16 women), 172 part-time (49 women); includes 14 minority (6 Black or African American, non-Hispanic/Latino; 5 Asian, non-Hispanic/Latino; 3 Hispanic/Latino), 12 international. Average age 32. 134 applicants, 81% accepted, 44 enrolled. In 2011, 70 master's awarded. *Entrance requirements:* For master's, GMAT, minimum AACSB index of 950. *Application deadline:* For fall admission, 8/15 priority date for domestic students. Applications are processed on a rolling basis. Application fee: $35. Electronic applications accepted. *Expenses: Tuition:* Part-time $466 per credit. *Financial support:* Career-related internships or fieldwork and institutionally sponsored loans available. Support available to part-time students. Financial award application deadline: 7/15; financial award applicants required to submit FAFSA. *Faculty research:* Real estate law, international finance, total quality management, Web-based commerce, pricing policies. *Unit head:* Dr. Chuck Williams, Dean, 317-940-8491, Fax: 317-940-9455, E-mail: crwillia@butler.edu. *Application contact:* Stephanie Judge, Director of Marketing, 317-940-9886, Fax: 317-940-9455, E-mail: sjudge@butler.edu. Web site: http://www.butler.edu/cob/.

Caldwell College, Graduate Studies, Division of Business, Caldwell, NJ 07006-6195. Offers accounting (MS); business administration (MBA). *Accreditation:* ACBSP. Part-time and evening/weekend programs available. *Students:* 13 full-time (6 women), 40 part-time (25 women); includes 15 minority (8 Black or African American, non-Hispanic/Latino; 3 Asian, non-Hispanic/Latino; 4 Hispanic/Latino), 4 international. *Entrance requirements:* Additional exam requirements/recommendations for international students: Required—TOEFL (minimum score 580 paper-based; 237 computer-based). *Application deadline:* Applications are processed on a rolling basis. Application fee: $40. Electronic applications accepted. *Expenses: Tuition:* Full-time $14,400; part-time $800 per credit. *Required fees:* $200; $100 per semester. *Unit head:* Bernard O'Rourke, Division Associate Dean, 973-618-3409, Fax: 973-618-3355, E-mail: borourke@caldwell.edu. *Application contact:* Vilma Mueller, Director of Graduate Studies, 973-618-3544, E-mail: graduate@caldwell.edu. Web site: http://www.caldwell.edu/graduate.

California Baptist University, Program in Business Administration, Riverside, CA 92504-3206. Offers accounting (MBA); business administration (MBA). *Accreditation:* ACBSP. Part-time and evening/weekend programs available. *Faculty:* 12 full-time (4 women), 2 part-time/adjunct (1 woman). *Students:* 56 full-time (27 women); includes 19 minority (7 Black or African American, non-Hispanic/Latino; 2 Asian, non-Hispanic/Latino; 10 Hispanic/Latino), 9 international. Average age 30. 90 applicants, 42% accepted, 28 enrolled. In 2011, 38 master's awarded. *Degree requirements:* For master's, capstone project. *Entrance requirements:* For master's, minimum GPA of 2.5; two recommendations; comprehensive essay; resume; interview. Additional exam requirements/recommendations for international students: Required—TOEFL (minimum score 575 paper-based; 230 computer-based; 89 iBT). *Application deadline:* For fall admission, 8/1 priority date for domestic students, 7/1 for international students; for spring admission, 12/1 priority date for domestic students, 11/1 for international students. Applications are processed on a rolling basis. Application fee: $45. Electronic applications accepted. *Expenses:* Contact institution. *Financial support:* In 2011–12, 1 student received support. Federal Work-Study and institutionally sponsored loans available. Financial award applicants required to submit FAFSA. *Faculty research:* Econometrics, Biblical financial principles, strategic management and corporate performance, shared leadership models, international culture and economics. *Unit head:* Dr. Natalie Winter, Associate Dean, School of Business, 951-343-4462, Fax: 951-343-4361, E-mail: nwinter@calbaptist.edu. Web site: http://www.calbaptist.edu/mba/about/.

California Coast University, School of Administration and Management, Santa Ana, CA 92701. Offers business marketing (MBA); health care management (MBA); human resource management (MBA); management (MBA, MS). Postbaccalaureate distance learning degree programs offered (no on-campus study). Electronic applications accepted.

California Intercontinental University, School of Business, Diamond Bar, CA 91765. Offers banking and finance (MBA); entrepreneurship and business management (DBA); global business leadership (DBA); international management and marketing (MBA); organizational management and human resource management (MBA).

California International Business University, Graduate Programs, San Diego, CA 92101. Offers MBA, MSIM, DBA.

California Lutheran University, Graduate Studies, School of Management, Thousand Oaks, CA 91360-2787. Offers business (IMBA); computer science (MS); econometrics (MBA); economics (MS); entrepreneurship (MBA, Certificate); finance (MBA, Certificate); financial planning (MBA, Certificate); information systems and technology (MS); information technology management (MBA, Certificate); international business (MBA, Certificate); management and organization behavior (MBA); management and organizational behavior (Certificate); marketing (MBA, Certificate); microeconomics (MBA); nonprofit and social enterprise (MBA). Part-time and evening/weekend programs available. Postbaccalaureate distance learning degree programs offered (no on-campus study). *Entrance requirements:* For master's, GMAT, interview, minimum GPA of 3.0. *Expenses:* Contact institution.

California Miramar University, Program in Business Administration, San Diego, CA 92126. Offers MBA.

California National University for Advanced Studies, College of Business Administration, Northridge, CA 91325. Offers MBA, MHRM. Part-time programs available. Postbaccalaureate distance learning degree programs offered (no on-campus study). *Entrance requirements:* For master's, minimum GPA of 3.0. Additional exam requirements/recommendations for international students: Required—TOEFL (minimum score 213 computer-based). Electronic applications accepted.

California Polytechnic State University, San Luis Obispo, Orfalea College of Business, Graduate Programs in Business, San Luis Obispo, CA 93407. Offers business (MBA); taxation (MSA). *Faculty:* 3 full-time (1 woman), 1 (woman) part-time/adjunct. *Students:* 18 full-time (3 women), 11 part-time (2 women); includes 2 minority (1 Hispanic/Latino; 1 Two or more races, non-Hispanic/Latino). Average age 27. 85 applicants, 35% accepted, 17 enrolled. In 2011, 63 master's awarded. *Degree requirements:* For master's, comprehensive exam (for some programs), thesis or alternative. *Entrance requirements:* For master's, GMAT. Additional exam requirements/recommendations for international students: Required—TOEFL (minimum score 550 paper-based; 213 computer-based) or IELTS (minimum score 6). *Application deadline:* For fall admission, 7/1 for domestic students, 11/30 for international students. Applications are processed on a rolling basis. Application fee: $55. Electronic applications accepted. *Expenses:* Tuition, state resident: full-time $6738. Tuition, nonresident: full-time $17,898. *Required fees:* $2449. *Financial support:* Fellowships, career-related internships or fieldwork, Federal Work-Study, institutionally sponsored loans, scholarships/grants, and unspecified assistantships available. Support available to part-time students. Financial award application deadline: 3/2; financial award applicants required to submit FAFSA. *Faculty research:* International business, organizational behavior, graphic communication document systems management, commercial development of innovative technologies, effective communication skills for managers. *Unit head:* Dr. Bradford Anderson, Associate Dean/Graduate Coordinator, 805-756-5210, Fax: 805-756-0110, E-mail: bpanders@calpoly.edu. Web site: http://mba.calpoly.edu/.

California State Polytechnic University, Pomona, Academic Affairs, College of Business Administration, Master of Science in Business Administration Program, Pomona, CA 91768-2557. Offers information systems auditing (MS). *Students:* 1 (woman) full-time, 15 part-time (6 women); includes 9 minority (5 Asian, non-Hispanic/Latino; 2 Hispanic/Latino; 2 Two or more races, non-Hispanic/Latino), 1 international. Average age 32. 25 applicants, 24% accepted, 5 enrolled. In 2011, 6 master's awarded. *Application deadline:* Applications are processed on a rolling basis. Application fee: $55. Electronic applications accepted. *Expenses:* Tuition, state resident: full-time $6738. Tuition, nonresident: full-time $12,300. *Required fees:* $657. Tuition and fees vary according to course load and program. *Unit head:* Dr. Richard S. Lapidus, Dean, 909-869-2400, Fax: 909-869-6799, E-mail: rslapidus@csupomona.edu. *Application contact:* Dr. Gregory Carlton, Graduate Coordinator, 909-869-5190, E-mail: ghcarlton@csupomona.edu. Web site: http://cba.csupomona.edu/graduateprograms/.

California State Polytechnic University, Pomona, Academic Affairs, College of Business Administration, MBA Program, Pomona, CA 91768-2557. Offers MBA. *Students:* 11 full-time (3 women), 101 part-time (41 women); includes 53 minority (2 Black or African American, non-Hispanic/Latino; 27 Asian, non-Hispanic/Latino; 21 Hispanic/Latino; 3 Two or more races, non-Hispanic/Latino), 26 international. Average age 31. 143 applicants, 22% accepted, 19 enrolled. In 2011, 72 master's awarded. *Application deadline:* Applications are processed on a rolling basis. Application fee: $55. *Expenses:* Tuition, state resident: full-time $6738. Tuition, nonresident: full-time $12,300. *Required fees:* $657. Tuition and fees vary according to course load and program. *Unit head:* Dr. Richard S. Lapidus, Dean, 909-869-2400, E-mail: rslapidus@csupomona.edu. *Application contact:* Dr. Cheryl Wyrick, Graduate Coordinator, 909-869-2363, E-mail: crwyrick@csupomona.edu. Web site: http://cba.csupomona.edu/graduateprograms/.

California State University, Bakersfield, Division of Graduate Studies, Online Program in Administration, Bakersfield, CA 93311. Offers MS. *Accreditation:* AACSB. Postbaccalaureate distance learning degree programs offered. *Degree requirements:* For master's, capstone course. *Entrance requirements:* For master's, resume, 3 letters of reference. Additional exam requirements/recommendations for international students: Required—TOEFL (minimum score 550 paper-based; 213 computer-based). Application fee: $75. *Expenses: Required fees:* $1302 per unit. Part-time tuition and fees vary according to course load and program. *Unit head:* Dr. Abbas Grammy, Head, 661-654-2466, Fax: 661-664-2447, E-mail: agrammy@csub.edu. Web site: http://www.csub.edu/regional/html/msa.html.

California State University, Bakersfield, Division of Graduate Studies, School of Business and Public Administration, Program in Business Administration, Bakersfield, CA 93311. Offers MBA. *Accreditation:* AACSB. *Entrance requirements:* For master's, GMAT. *Application deadline:* Applications are processed on a rolling basis. Application fee: $55. *Expenses: Required fees:* $1302 per unit. Part-time tuition and fees vary according to course load and program. *Unit head:* Dr. Michael Bedell, MBA Program Director, 661-654-2312, E-mail: mbedell@csub.edu. *Application contact:* Kathy Carpenter, MBA Advisor, 661-654-3404, E-mail: mba@csub.edu. Web site: http://www.csub.edu/bpa/mba/.

California State University Channel Islands, Extended Education, Program in Business Administration, Camarillo, CA 93012. Offers MBA. Part-time and evening/weekend programs available. *Entrance requirements:* For master's, GMAT, 2 years work experience. Additional exam requirements/recommendations for international students: Required—TOEFL (minimum score 550 paper-based).

California State University, Chico, Office of Graduate Studies, College of Behavioral and Social Sciences, Department of Political Science, Program in Public Administration, Chico, CA 95929-0722. Offers health administration (MPA); local government management (MPA). *Accreditation:* NASPAA. Part-time programs available. *Students:* 31 full-time (18 women), 26 part-time (17 women); includes 24 minority (3 Black or African American, non-Hispanic/Latino; 1 American Indian or Alaska Native, non-Hispanic/Latino; 7 Asian, non-Hispanic/Latino; 13 Hispanic/Latino), 3 international. Average age 31. 45 applicants, 71% accepted, 18 enrolled. In 2011, 21 master's awarded. *Entrance requirements:* For master's, 2 letters of recommendation. Additional exam requirements/recommendations for international students: Required—TOEFL (minimum score 550 paper-based; 213 computer-based; 80 iBT), IELTS (minimum score 6.5). *Application deadline:* For fall admission, 3/1 priority date for domestic students, 3/1 for international students; for spring admission, 9/15 priority date for domestic students, 9/15 for international students. Applications are processed on a rolling basis. Application fee: $55. Electronic applications accepted. Tuition and fees vary according to class time, course load and degree level. *Financial support:* Fellowships and career-related internships or fieldwork available. *Unit head:* Dr. Donna Kemp, Graduate Coordinator, 530-898-5734. *Application contact:* School of Graduate, International, and Interdisciplinary Studies, 530-898-6880, Fax: 530-898-6889, E-mail: grin@csuchico.edu.

California State University, Chico, Office of Graduate Studies, College of Business, Program in Business Administration, Chico, CA 95929-0722. Offers MBA. *Accreditation:* AACSB. Part-time programs available. *Faculty:* 4 full-time (3 women). *Students:* 53 full-time (31 women), 27 part-time (13 women); includes 10 minority (7 Asian, non-Hispanic/Latino; 3 Hispanic/Latino), 39 international. Average age 27. 90 applicants, 59% accepted, 30 enrolled. In 2011, 58 master's awarded. *Degree requirements:* For master's, thesis, project, or comprehensive exam. *Entrance requirements:* For master's, GMAT or GRE, 2 letters of recommendation, statement of purpose, resume. Additional exam requirements/recommendations for international students: Required—TOEFL (minimum score 550 paper-based; 213 computer-based; 80 iBT), IELTS (minimum score 6.5), Pearson Test of English (minimum score 59). *Application deadline:* For fall admission, 3/1 for domestic and international students; for spring admission, 9/15 for domestic and international students. Application fee: $55. Electronic applications accepted. Tuition and fees vary according to class time, course load and degree level. *Financial support:* Career-related internships or fieldwork, institutionally sponsored loans, scholarships/grants, traineeships, and unspecified assistantships available. Financial award application deadline: 3/1; financial award applicants required to submit FAFSA. *Unit head:* Michael G. Ward, Interim Dean, 530-898-6272, Fax: 530-898-4584, E-mail: bus@csuchico.edu. *Application contact:* Judy L. Rice, Graduate Admissions Coordinator, 530-898-5416, Fax: 530-898-3342, E-mail: jlrice@csuchico.edu. Web site: http://catalog.csuchico.edu/viewer/BADM/BADMNONEMB.html.

California State University, Dominguez Hills, College of Business Administration and Public Policy, Program in Business Administration, Carson, CA 90747-0001. Offers MBA. *Accreditation:* ACBSP. Part-time and evening/weekend programs available. Postbaccalaureate distance learning degree programs offered (no on-campus study). *Faculty:* 71 full-time (4 women), 8 part-time/adjunct (3 women). *Students:* 55 full-time (14 women), 85 part-time (28 women); includes 54 minority (10 Black or African American, non-Hispanic/Latino; 18 Asian, non-Hispanic/Latino; 13 Hispanic/Latino; 13 Two or more races, non-Hispanic/Latino), 7 international. Average age 34. 292 applicants, 46% accepted, 83 enrolled. In 2011, 65 master's awarded. *Entrance requirements:* For master's, GMAT, minimum GPA of 2.75. Additional exam requirements/recommendations for international students: Required—TOEFL (minimum score 570 paper-based; 230 computer-based; 88 iBT). *Application deadline:* For fall admission, 4/1 for domestic and international students; for spring admission, 11/1 for domestic students, 10/1 for international students. Application fee: $55. *Faculty research:* Management. *Unit head:* Kenneth Poertner, Program Director, 310-243-2714, Fax: 310-516-4178, E-mail: kpoertner@csudh.edu. *Application contact:* Cathi Ryan, Graduate Advisor, 310-243-274, Fax: 310-516-4178, E-mail: cryan@csudh.edu. Web site: http://mbaonline.csudh.edu/index.htm.

California State University, East Bay, Office of Academic Programs and Graduate Studies, College of Business and Economics, Business Administration, MBA Program, Hayward, CA 94542-3000. Offers entrepreneurship (MBA); finance (MBA); global innovators (MBA); human resources and organizational behavior (MBA); information technology management (MBA); marketing management (MBA); operations and supply chain management (MBA); strategy and international business (MBA). Part-time and evening/weekend programs available. *Faculty:* 11 full-time (3 women). *Students:* 80 full-time (42 women), 141 part-time (61 women); includes 70 minority (5 Black or African American, non-Hispanic/Latino; 46 Asian, non-Hispanic/Latino; 13 Hispanic/Latino; 1 Native Hawaiian or other Pacific Islander, non-Hispanic/Latino; 5 Two or more races, non-Hispanic/Latino), 69 international. Average age 31. 371 applicants, 36% accepted, 79 enrolled. In 2011, 254 master's awarded. *Degree requirements:* For master's, comprehensive exam or thesis. *Entrance requirements:* For master's, GMAT (minimum 20th percentile verbal and quantitative section), bachelor's degree, minimum GPA of 2.75. Additional exam requirements/recommendations for international students: Required—TOEFL (minimum score 550 paper-based; 213 computer-based; 79 iBT). *Application deadline:* For fall admission, 6/30 for domestic and international students. Applications are processed on a rolling basis. Application fee: $55. Electronic applications accepted. *Expenses:* Contact institution. *Financial support:* Career-related internships or fieldwork, Federal Work-Study, institutionally sponsored loans, and scholarships/grants available. Support available to part-time students. Financial award application deadline: 3/2; financial award applicants required to submit FAFSA. *Unit head:* Dr. Terri Swartz, Dean, 510-885-3291, Fax: 510-885-4884, E-mail: terri.swartz@csueastbay.edu. *Application contact:* Prof. Joanna Lee, Director, CBE Graduate Programs, 510-885-3517, Fax: 510-885-2176, E-mail: joanna.lee@csueastbay.edu. Web site: http://www20.csueastbay.edu/ecat/graduate-chapters/g-buad.html#mba.

California State University, Fresno, Division of Graduate Studies, Craig School of Business, Program in Business Administration, Fresno, CA 93740-8027. Offers MBA. *Accreditation:* AACSB. Part-time programs available. *Degree requirements:* For master's, thesis or alternative. *Entrance requirements:* For master's, GMAT, minimum GPA of 2.53. Additional exam requirements/recommendations for international students: Required—TOEFL. Electronic applications accepted. *Faculty research:* International trade development, entrepreneurial outreach.

California State University, Fullerton, Graduate Studies, College of Business and Economics, Department of Information Systems and Decision Sciences, Fullerton, CA 92834-9480. Offers information systems (MS); information systems (decision sciences) (MS); information systems (e-commerce) (MS); information technology (MS); management science (MBA). Part-time programs available. *Students:* 15 full-time (2 women), 66 part-time (10 women); includes 35 minority (1 Black or African American, non-Hispanic/Latino; 23 Asian, non-Hispanic/Latino; 9 Hispanic/Latino; 2 Two or more races, non-Hispanic/Latino), 9 international. Average age 33. 82 applicants, 44% accepted, 30 enrolled. In 2011, 36 master's awarded. *Degree requirements:* For master's, project or thesis. *Entrance requirements:* For master's, GMAT, minimum AACSB index of 950. Application fee: $55. *Financial support:* Career-related internships or fieldwork, Federal Work-Study, institutionally sponsored loans, and scholarships/grants available. Support available to part-time students. Financial award application deadline: 3/1; financial award applicants required to submit FAFSA. *Unit head:* Dr. Bhushan Kapoor, Chair, 657-278-2221. *Application contact:* Admissions/Applications, 657-278-2371.

California State University, Fullerton, Graduate Studies, College of Business and Economics, Department of Management, Fullerton, CA 92834-9480. Offers entrepreneurship (MBA); management (MBA). *Accreditation:* AACSB. Part-time programs available. *Students:* 12 full-time (3 women), 51 part-time (19 women); includes 32 minority (1 Black or African American, non-Hispanic/Latino; 22 Asian, non-Hispanic/Latino; 8 Hispanic/Latino; 1 Two or more races, non-Hispanic/Latino), 5 international. Average age 28. 2 applicants, 50% accepted, 1 enrolled. In 2011, 39 master's awarded. *Degree requirements:* For master's, project or thesis. *Entrance requirements:* For master's, GMAT, minimum AACSB index of 950. Application fee: $55. *Financial support:* Career-related internships or fieldwork, Federal Work-Study, institutionally sponsored loans, and scholarships/grants available. Support available to part-time students. Financial award application deadline: 3/1; financial award applicants required to submit FAFSA. *Unit head:* Dr. Ellen Dumond, Chair, 657-278-2251. *Application contact:* Admissions/Applications, 657-278-2371.

California State University, Fullerton, Graduate Studies, College of Business and Economics, Program in Business Administration, Fullerton, CA 92834-9480. Offers e-commerce (MBA); international business (MBA). *Accreditation:* AACSB. Part-time programs available. *Students:* 63 full-time (34 women), 89 part-time (35 women); includes 57 minority (2 Black or African American, non-Hispanic/Latino; 41 Asian, non-Hispanic/Latino; 10 Hispanic/Latino; 4 Two or more races, non-Hispanic/Latino), 36 international. Average age 28. 476 applicants, 40% accepted, 60 enrolled. In 2011, 31 master's awarded. *Degree requirements:* For master's, project or thesis. *Entrance requirements:* For master's, GMAT. *Financial support:* Career-related internships or fieldwork, Federal Work-Study, institutionally sponsored loans, and scholarships/grants available. Support available to part-time students. Financial award application deadline: 3/1; financial award applicants required to submit FAFSA. *Unit head:* Dr. Anil Puri, Dean, 657-773-2592. *Application contact:* Admissions/Applications, 657-278-2371.

California State University, Long Beach, Graduate Studies, College of Business Administration, Long Beach, CA 90840. Offers MBA. *Accreditation:* AACSB. Part-time and evening/weekend programs available. *Faculty:* 19 full-time (4 women), 3 part-time/adjunct (0 women). *Students:* 64 full-time (26 women), 109 part-time (46 women); includes 61 minority (4 Black or African American, non-Hispanic/Latino; 1 American Indian or Alaska Native, non-Hispanic/Latino; 35 Asian, non-Hispanic/Latino; 13 Hispanic/Latino; 2 Native Hawaiian or other Pacific Islander, non-Hispanic/Latino; 6 Two or more races, non-Hispanic/Latino), 23 international. Average age 30. 425 applicants, 37% accepted, 37 enrolled. In 2011, 148 master's awarded. *Entrance requirements:* For master's, GMAT. *Application deadline:* For fall admission, 3/30 for domestic students. Applications are processed on a rolling basis. Application fee: $55. Electronic applications accepted. *Financial support:* Career-related internships or fieldwork and scholarships/grants available. Financial award application deadline: 3/2; financial award applicants required to submit FAFSA. *Faculty research:* Attitude formation theory, consumer motivation, gift giving, derivative and synthetic securities, financial applications of artificial intelligence. *Unit head:* Dr. Michael E. Solt, Dean, 562-985-5306, Fax: 562-985-5742, E-mail: msolt@csulb.edu. *Application contact:* Dr. H. Michael Chung, Director, Graduate Programs and Executive Education, 562-985-5565, Fax: 562-985-5742, E-mail: hmchung@csulb.edu. Web site: http://www.csulb.edu/mba.

California State University, Los Angeles, Graduate Studies, College of Business and Economics, Department of Information Systems, Los Angeles, CA 90032-8530. Offers business information systems (MBA); management (MS); management information systems (MS); office management (MBA). Part-time and evening/weekend programs available. *Faculty:* 2 full-time (1 woman), 1 part-time/adjunct (0 women). *Students:* 3 full-time (1 woman), 8 part-time (3 women); includes 4 minority (3 Asian, non-Hispanic/Latino; 1 Hispanic/Latino), 3 international. Average age 32. 20 applicants, 20% accepted, 2 enrolled. In 2011, 26 master's awarded. *Degree requirements:* For master's, comprehensive exam (MBA), thesis (MS). *Entrance requirements:* For master's, GMAT, minimum GPA of 2.5 during previous 2 years of course work. Additional exam requirements/recommendations for international students: Required—TOEFL (minimum score 550 paper-based; 213 computer-based). *Application deadline:* For fall admission, 5/1 for domestic and international students. Applications are processed on a rolling basis. Application fee: $55. Electronic applications accepted. *Expenses:* Tuition, state resident: full-time $8225. *Financial support:* Career-related internships or fieldwork and Federal Work-Study available. Support available to part-time students. Financial award application deadline: 3/1. *Unit head:* Dr. Nanda Ganesen, Chair, 323-343-2983, E-mail: nganesa@calstatela.edu. *Application contact:* Dr. Karin Brown, Acting Associate Dean of Graduate Studies, 323-343-3820, Fax: 323-343-5653, E-mail: kbrown5@calstatela.edu.

California State University, Los Angeles, Graduate Studies, College of Business and Economics, Department of Management, Los Angeles, CA 90032-8530. Offers health care management (MS); management (MBA, MS). *Accreditation:* AACSB. Part-time and evening/weekend programs available. *Faculty:* 4 part-time/adjunct (1 woman). *Students:* 10 full-time (7 women), 42 part-time (27 women); includes 31 minority (2 Black or African American, non-Hispanic/Latino; 16 Asian, non-Hispanic/Latino; 11 Hispanic/Latino; 2 Two or more races, non-Hispanic/Latino), 9 international. Average age 31. 96 applicants, 33% accepted, 14 enrolled. In 2011, 39 degrees awarded. *Entrance requirements:* For master's, GMAT, minimum GPA of 2.5 during previous 2 years of course work. Additional exam requirements/recommendations for international students: Required—TOEFL (minimum score 550 paper-based; 213 computer-based). *Application deadline:* For fall admission, 5/1 for domestic and international students. Applications are processed on a rolling basis. Application fee: $55. Electronic applications accepted. *Expenses:* Tuition, state resident: full-time $8225. *Financial support:* Application deadline: 3/1. *Unit head:* Dr. Angela Young, Chair, 323-343-2890, Fax: 323-343-6461, E-mail: ayoung3@calstatela.edu. *Application contact:* Dr. Karin Brown, Acting Associate Dean of Graduate Studies, 323-343-3820 Ext. 3827, Fax: 323-343-5653, E-mail: kbrown5@calstatela.edu. Web site: http://cbe.calstatela.edu/mgmt/.

California State University, Monterey Bay, College of Professional Studies, School of Business, Seaside, CA 93955-8001. Offers EMBA. Part-time and evening/weekend programs available. Postbaccalaureate distance learning degree programs offered (no on-campus study). *Entrance requirements:* For master's, recommendation, resume, work experience, bachelor's degree from accredited university. Additional exam requirements/recommendations for international students: Recommended—TOEFL (minimum score 550 paper-based; 213 computer-based; 79 iBT). Electronic applications accepted.

California State University, Northridge, Graduate Studies, College of Business and Economics, Northridge, CA 91330. Offers MBA. *Accreditation:* AACSB. Part-time programs available. *Degree requirements:* For master's, thesis or alternative. *Entrance requirements:* For master's, GMAT, minimum GPA of 3.0 in last 60 units. Additional exam requirements/recommendations for international students: Required—TOEFL.

California State University, Sacramento, Office of Graduate Studies, College of Business Administration, Sacramento, CA 95819-6088. Offers accountancy (MS); business administration (MBA); human resources (MBA); urban land development (MBA). *Accreditation:* AACSB. Part-time and evening/weekend programs available. *Faculty:* 61 full-time (19 women), 28 part-time/adjunct (7 women). *Students:* 39 full-time, 91 part-time; includes 40 minority (6 Black or African American, non-Hispanic/Latino; 2 American Indian or Alaska Native, non-Hispanic/Latino; 12 Asian, non-Hispanic/Latino; 11 Hispanic/Latino; 4 Native Hawaiian or other Pacific Islander, non-Hispanic/Latino; 5 Two or more races, non-Hispanic/Latino), 16 international. Average age 29. 330 applicants, 64% accepted, 54 enrolled. In 2011, 212 master's awarded. *Degree requirements:* For master's, thesis or alternative, writing proficiency exam. *Entrance requirements:* For master's, GMAT. Additional exam requirements/recommendations for international students: Required—TOEFL. *Application deadline:* For fall admission, 2/1 for domestic students, 3/1 for international students; for spring admission, 9/15 for domestic students, 9/30 for international students. Applications are processed on a rolling basis. Application fee: $55. Electronic applications accepted. *Financial support:* Research assistantships, teaching assistantships, career-related internships or fieldwork, and Federal Work-Study available. Support available to part-time students. Financial award applicants required to submit FAFSA. *Unit head:* Dr. Sanjay Varshney, Dean, 916-278-6942, Fax: 916-278-5793, E-mail: cba@csus.edu. *Application contact:* Jose Martinez, Outreach and Graduate Diversity Coordinator, 916-278-6470, Fax: 916-278-5669, E-mail: martinj@skymail.csus.edu. Web site: http://www.cba.csus.edu.

California State University, San Bernardino, Graduate Studies, College of Business and Public Administration, Master in Business Administration Program, San Bernardino, CA 92407. Offers accounting (MBA); entrepreneurship (MBA); executives (MBA); finance (MBA); global business (MBA); information assurance and security management (MBA); information management (MBA); management (MBA); marketing (MBA); professionals (MBA); supply chain management (MBA). *Accreditation:* AACSB. Part-time and evening/weekend programs available. Postbaccalaureate distance learning degree programs offered (no on-campus study). *Faculty:* 58 full-time (11 women), 26 part-time/adjunct (9 women). *Students:* 80 full-time (31 women), 137 part-time (56 women); includes 82 minority (19 Black or African American, non-Hispanic/Latino; 3 American Indian or Alaska Native, non-Hispanic/Latino; 20 Asian, non-Hispanic/Latino; 37 Hispanic/Latino; 3 Two or more races, non-Hispanic/Latino), 65 international. Average age 30. 217 applicants, 65% accepted, 79 enrolled. In 2011, 120 master's awarded. *Degree requirements:* For master's, comprehensive exam, thesis optional, portfolio, 48 units, minimum GPA of 3.0. *Entrance requirements:* For master's, GMAT, minimum GPA of 2.5. Additional exam requirements/recommendations for international students: Required—TOEFL (minimum score 550 paper-based; 213 computer-based; 79 iBT). *Application deadline:* For fall admission, 7/12 priority date for domestic students, 7/12 for international students; for winter admission, 10/26 priority date for domestic students, 10/26 for international students; for spring admission, 1/25 priority date for domestic students, 1/25 for international students. Applications are processed on a rolling basis. Application fee: $55. Electronic applications accepted. *Expenses:* Contact institution. *Financial support:* In 2011–12, 56 students received support, including 34 fellowships (averaging $3,732 per year), 18 research assistantships (averaging $2,193 per year), 4 teaching assistantships (averaging $2,606 per year); career-related internships or fieldwork, Federal Work-Study, institutionally sponsored loans, scholarships/grants, and unspecified assistantships also available. Support available to part-time students. Financial award application deadline: 3/1; financial award applicants required to submit FAFSA. *Faculty research:* Fraud, Stock Exchange, small business, logistics, job analysis. *Total annual research expenditures:* $4.8 million. *Unit head:* Dr. Lawrence C. Rose, Dean, 909-537-3703, Fax: 909-537-7026, E-mail: lrose@csusb.edu. *Application contact:* Dr. Sandra Kamusikiri, Associate Vice-President/Dean of Graduate Studies, 909-537-7058, Fax: 909-537-5078, E-mail: skamusik@csusb.edu. Web site: http://mba.csusb.edu/.

California State University, San Bernardino, Graduate Studies, College of Extended Learning, San Bernardino, CA 92407-2397. Offers executive business administration (MBA); TESOL (MA Ed). Part-time and evening/weekend programs available. *Expenses:* Tuition, state resident: full-time $7356. Tuition, nonresident: full-time $7356. *Required fees:* $1077. Tuition and fees vary according to program.

California State University, San Marcos, College of Business Administration, San Marcos, CA 92096-0001. Offers business management (MBA); government management (MBA). Evening/weekend programs available. *Degree requirements:* For master's, project. *Entrance requirements:* For master's, GMAT, minimum GPA of 3.0 in last 60 units, 3 years of full-time work experience. Additional exam requirements/recommendations for international students: Required—TOEFL (minimum score 550 paper-based; 213 computer-based). *Expenses:* Contact institution.

California State University, Stanislaus, College of Business Administration, Program in Business Administration (Executive MBA), Turlock, CA 95382. Offers EMBA. *Accreditation:* AACSB. Part-time and evening/weekend programs available. *Degree requirements:* For master's, comprehensive exam, thesis or alternative. *Entrance requirements:* For master's, GMAT or GRE, minimum GPA of 2.5, 2 letters of reference, personal statement, interview. Additional exam requirements/recommendations for international students: Required—TOEFL (minimum score 550 paper-based; 213 computer-based). *Application deadline:* For fall admission, 7/31 for domestic students. Applications are processed on a rolling basis. Application fee: $55. Electronic applications accepted. *Expenses:* Contact institution. *Unit head:* Dr. Ashour Badal, EMBA Director, 209-664-6747, Fax: 209-667-3080, E-mail: abadal@csustan.edu. *Application contact:* Extended Education, 209-667-3111, E-mail: uee@csustan.edu. Web site: http://www.extendeded.com/emba.

California State University, Stanislaus, College of Business Administration, Program in Business Administration (MBA), Turlock, CA 95382. Offers MBA. *Accreditation:* AACSB. Part-time and evening/weekend programs available. *Degree requirements:* For master's, comprehensive exam, thesis or alternative. *Entrance requirements:* For master's, GMAT or GRE, minimum GPA of 2.5, 3 letters of reference, personal statement. Additional exam requirements/recommendations for international students: Required—TOEFL (minimum score 550 paper-based; 213 computer-based). *Application deadline:* For fall admission, 4/30 for domestic students; for spring admission, 10/31 for domestic students. Application fee: $55. Electronic applications accepted. *Expenses:* Contact institution. *Financial support:* Fellowships, career-related internships or fieldwork, and Federal Work-Study available. Financial award application deadline: 3/1; financial award applicants required to submit FAFSA. *Faculty research:* Teaching creativity, graduate operations management, curricula data mining, foreign direct investment. *Unit head:* Dr. Randall Brown, MBA Director, 209-667-3280, Fax: 209-667-3080, E-mail: mbaprogram@csustan.edu. *Application contact:* Graduate School, 209-667-3129, Fax: 209-664-7025, E-mail: graduate_school@csustan.edu. Web site: http://www.csustan.edu/mba/.

California University of Pennsylvania, School of Graduate Studies and Research, Eberly College of Science and Technology, Program in Business Administration, California, PA 15419-1394. Offers MSBA. Part-time and evening/weekend programs available. *Degree requirements:* For master's, comprehensive exam. *Entrance requirements:* For master's, minimum QPA of 3.0. Additional exam requirements/recommendations for international students: Required—TOEFL (minimum score 550 paper-based; 213 computer-based). Electronic applications accepted. *Faculty research:* Economics, applied economics, consumer behavior, technology and business, impact of technology.

Cambridge College, School of Management, Cambridge, MA 02138-5304. Offers business negotiation and conflict resolution (M Mgt); general business (M Mgt); health care informatics (M Mgt); health care management (M Mgt); leadership in human and organizational dynamics (M Mgt); non-profit and public organization management (M Mgt); small business development (M Mgt); technology management (M Mgt). Part-time and evening/weekend programs available. *Degree requirements:* For master's, thesis, seminars. *Entrance requirements:* For master's, resume, 2 professional references. Additional exam requirements/recommendations for international students: Required—TOEFL (minimum score 550 paper-based; 213 computer-based; 79 iBT); Recommended—IELTS (minimum score 6). Electronic applications accepted. *Expenses:* Contact institution. *Faculty research:* Negotiation, mediation and conflict resolution; leadership; management of diverse organizations; case studies and simulation methodologies for management education, digital as a second language: social networking for digital immigrants, non-profit and public management.

Cameron University, Office of Graduate Studies, Program in Business Administration, Lawton, OK 73505-6377. Offers MBA. *Accreditation:* ACBSP. Part-time and evening/weekend programs available. Postbaccalaureate distance learning degree programs offered (no on-campus study). *Degree requirements:* For master's, comprehensive exam. *Entrance requirements:* Additional exam requirements/recommendations for international students: Required—TOEFL (minimum score 550 paper-based; 213 computer-based). Electronic applications accepted. *Faculty research:* Financial liberalization, right to work, recession, teaching evaluations, database management.

Campbellsville University, School of Business and Economics, Campbellsville, KY 42718-2799. Offers business administration (MBA); business organizational management (MAOL). Part-time and evening/weekend programs available. *Students:* 74 full-time (39 women), 34 part-time (13 women); includes 6 minority (4 Black or African American, non-Hispanic/Latino; 2 Asian, non-Hispanic/Latino), 25 international. Average age 28. In 2011, 22 master's awarded. *Entrance requirements:* For master's, GRE or GMAT. Additional exam requirements/recommendations for international students: Required—TOEFL (minimum score 550 paper-based; 213 computer-based). *Application deadline:* For fall admission, 9/14 priority date for domestic students, 9/14 for international students; for winter admission, 1/18 priority date for domestic students, 1/18 for international students; for spring admission, 4/4 priority date for domestic students, 4/4 for international students. Applications are processed on a rolling basis. Application fee: $25. Electronic applications accepted. *Expenses:* Contact institution. *Financial support:* In 2011–12, 11 students received support. Tuition waivers (full) and unspecified assistantships available. Financial award application deadline: 6/1; financial award applicants required to submit FAFSA. *Unit head:* Dr. Patricia H. Cowherd, Dean, 270-789-5553, Fax: 270-789-5066, E-mail: phcowherd@campbellsville.edu. *Application contact:* Monica Bamwine, Assistant Director of Admissions, 270-789-5221, Fax: 270-789-5071, E-mail: mkbamwine@campbellsville.edu. Web site: http://www.campbellsville.edu.

Business Administration and Management—General

Campbell University, Graduate and Professional Programs, Lundy-Fetterman School of Business, Buies Creek, NC 27506. Offers MBA, MTIM. Part-time and evening/weekend programs available. *Degree requirements:* For master's, comprehensive exam, thesis or alternative. *Entrance requirements:* For master's, GMAT, minimum GPA of 2.7, 3 letters of reference. Additional exam requirements/recommendations for international students: Required—TOEFL (minimum score 550 paper-based; 213 computer-based). *Faculty research:* Agricultural economics, investments, leadership, marketing, law and economics.

Canisius College, Graduate Division, Richard J. Wehle School of Business, Department of Management and Marketing, Buffalo, NY 14208-1098. Offers accelerated business administration (1 year) (MBA); business administration (MBA); international business (MS). *Accreditation:* AACSB. Part-time and evening/weekend programs available. *Faculty:* 35 full-time (7 women), 11 part-time/adjunct (5 women). *Students:* 102 full-time (42 women), 150 part-time (67 women); includes 29 minority (20 Black or African American, non-Hispanic/Latino; 1 American Indian or Alaska Native, non-Hispanic/Latino; 5 Asian, non-Hispanic/Latino; 1 Hispanic/Latino; 2 Two or more races, non-Hispanic/Latino), 10 international. Average age 28. 173 applicants, 66% accepted, 84 enrolled. In 2011, 97 master's awarded. *Entrance requirements:* For master's, GMAT, transcripts. Additional exam requirements/recommendations for international students: Required—TOEFL. *Application deadline:* For fall admission, 7/1 priority date for domestic students; for spring admission, 11/1 priority date for domestic students. Applications are processed on a rolling basis. Application fee: $25. Electronic applications accepted. *Financial support:* Research assistantships, career-related internships or fieldwork, Federal Work-Study, scholarships/grants, and unspecified assistantships available. Support available to part-time students. Financial award application deadline: 4/30; financial award applicants required to submit FAFSA. *Faculty research:* Global leadership effectiveness, global supply chain management, quality management. *Unit head:* Dr. Gordon W. Meyers, Chair, Management, Entrepreneurship and International Business, 716-888-2634, E-mail: meyerg@canisius.edu. *Application contact:* Jim Bagwell, Director, Graduate Programs, 716-888-2545, Fax: 716-888-3290, E-mail: bagwellj@canisius.edu. Web site: http://www.canisius.edu/academics/gradhome.asp.

Cape Breton University, Shannon School of Business, Sydney, NS B1P 6L2, Canada. Offers MBA. Part-time programs available. *Entrance requirements:* For master's, GMAT. Additional exam requirements/recommendations for international students: Required—TOEFL (minimum score 550 paper-based; 213 computer-based; 80 iBT), IELTS (minimum score 6.5). Electronic applications accepted.

Capella University, School of Business and Technology, Minneapolis, MN 55402. Offers accounting (MBA), including system design and programming; business (Certificate), including human resource management (MS, PhD, Certificate), information technology management (MS, PhD, Certificate), leadership (MBA, MS, PhD, Certificate); finance (MBA); general business (MBA); health care management (MBA); information technology (MS, Certificate), including general information technology (MS), information security, network architecture and design (MS), professional projects management (Certificate), project management and leadership (MS), system design and development (MS),); information technology management (MBA); marketing (MBA); organization and management (MBA, MS, PhD), including general business (PhD), general organization and management (MBA, MS), human resource management (MS, PhD, Certificate), information technology management (MS, PhD, Certificate), leadership (MBA, MS, PhD, Certificate); project management (MBA). Part-time and evening/weekend programs available. Postbaccalaureate distance learning degree programs offered (minimal on-campus study). Terminal master's awarded for partial completion of doctoral program. *Degree requirements:* For master's, thesis optional, integrative project; for doctorate, comprehensive exam, thesis/dissertation. *Entrance requirements:* Additional exam requirements/recommendations for international students: Required—TOEFL (minimum score 550 paper-based; 213 computer-based), TWE (minimum score 4). Electronic applications accepted. *Faculty research:* Business policies: strategic, corporate, and financial management; interplay of technological, organizational and social change.

Capital University, Law School, Program in Business Law and Taxation, Columbus, OH 43209-2394. Offers business (LL M); business and taxation (LL M); taxation (LL M); JD/LL M. Part-time and evening/weekend programs available. *Degree requirements:* For master's, thesis or alternative. *Entrance requirements:* For master's, previous course work in accounting, business law, and taxation. Additional exam requirements/recommendations for international students: Required—TOEFL (minimum score 600 paper-based; 250 computer-based). Electronic applications accepted.

Capital University, School of Management, Columbus, OH 43209-2394. Offers entrepreneurship (MBA); finance (MBA); leadership (MBA); marketing (MBA); MBA/JD; MBA/LL M; MBA/MSN; MBA/MT. *Accreditation:* ACBSP. Part-time and evening/weekend programs available. *Faculty:* 17 full-time (7 women), 23 part-time/adjunct (1 woman). *Students:* 175 part-time (75 women). Average age 31. 59 applicants, 81% accepted, 43 enrolled. In 2011, 1 degree awarded. *Degree requirements:* For master's, research project. *Entrance requirements:* For master's, GMAT, 2 years of work experience. Additional exam requirements/recommendations for international students: Required—TOEFL (minimum score 550 paper-based; 80 computer-based); Recommended—IELTS (minimum score 6.5). *Application deadline:* For fall admission, 7/1 priority date for domestic students; for winter admission, 11/1 priority date for domestic students; for spring admission, 4/1 priority date for domestic students. Applications are processed on a rolling basis. Application fee: $25. Electronic applications accepted. *Financial support:* In 2011–12, 2 fellowships (averaging $1,000 per year) were awarded; scholarships/grants and tuition waivers (full) also available. Support available to part-time students. Financial award application deadline: 8/1; financial award applicants required to submit FAFSA. *Faculty research:* Taxation, public policy, health care, management of non-profits. *Unit head:* Dr. Keirsten Moore, Assistant Dean, School of Management and Leadership, 614-236-6670, Fax: 614-296-6540, E-mail: kmoore@capital.edu. *Application contact:* Jacob Wilk, Assistant Director of Adult and Graduate Education Recruitment, 614-236-6546, Fax: 614-236-6923, E-mail: jwilk@capital.edu. Web site: http://www.capital.edu/capital-mba/.

Capitol College, Graduate Programs, Laurel, MD 20708-9759. Offers business administration (MBA); computer science (MS); electrical engineering (MS); information and telecommunications systems management (MS); information architecture (MS); network security (MS). Part-time and evening/weekend programs available. Postbaccalaureate distance learning degree programs offered (no on-campus study). *Entrance requirements:* For master's, minimum GPA of 3.0. Electronic applications accepted.

Cardinal Stritch University, College of Business and Management, Milwaukee, WI 53217-3985. Offers MBA, MSM. Programs also offered in Madison, WI and Minneapolis-St. Paul, MN. *Accreditation:* ACBSP. Part-time and evening/weekend programs available. *Degree requirements:* For master's, thesis (for some programs), case study, faculty recommendation. *Entrance requirements:* For master's, 3 years management or related experience, minimum GPA of 2.5. Additional exam requirements/recommendations for international students: Required—TOEFL. *Expenses:* Contact institution.

Carleton University, Faculty of Graduate Studies, Faculty of Business, Eric Sprott School of Business, Ottawa, ON K1S 5B6, Canada. Offers business administration (MBA); management (PhD). *Degree requirements:* For master's, thesis optional; for doctorate, comprehensive exam, thesis/dissertation. *Entrance requirements:* For master's, GMAT, honors degree; for doctorate, GMAT. Additional exam requirements/recommendations for international students: Required—TOEFL. *Faculty research:* Business information systems, finance, international business, marketing, production and operations.

Carlos Albizu University, Miami Campus, Graduate Programs, Miami, FL 33172-2209. Offers clinical psychology (Psy D); entrepreneurship (MBA); exceptional student education (MS); industrial/organizational psychology (MS); marriage and family therapy (MS); mental health counseling (MS); nonprofit management (MBA); organizational management (MBA); psychology (MS); school counseling (MS); teaching English as a second language (MS). *Accreditation:* APA. Part-time and evening/weekend programs available. *Faculty:* 19 full-time (12 women), 53 part-time/adjunct (27 women). *Students:* 524 full-time (431 women), 216 part-time (169 women); includes 563 minority (50 Black or African American, non-Hispanic/Latino; 1 American Indian or Alaska Native, non-Hispanic/Latino; 4 Asian, non-Hispanic/Latino; 492 Hispanic/Latino; 16 Native Hawaiian or other Pacific Islander, non-Hispanic/Latino), 17 international. Average age 31. 174 applicants, 67% accepted, 116 enrolled. In 2011, 157 master's, 21 doctorates awarded. Terminal master's awarded for partial completion of doctoral program. *Degree requirements:* For master's, one foreign language, comprehensive exam, integrative project (MBA), research project (exceptional student education, teaching English as a second language); for doctorate, one foreign language, comprehensive exam, internship, project. *Entrance requirements:* For master's, 3 letters of recommendation, interview, minimum GPA of 3.0, resume, statement of purpose, official transcripts; for doctorate, 3 letters of recommendation, minimum GPA of 3.0, resume, interview, statement of purpose, official transcripts. Additional exam requirements/recommendations for international students: Required—Michigan Test of English Language Proficiency. *Application deadline:* For fall admission, 4/1 priority date for domestic students, 5/1 for international students; for spring admission, 11/1 priority date for domestic students, 9/1 for international students. Applications are processed on a rolling basis. Application fee: $50. Electronic applications accepted. *Expenses: Tuition:* Full-time $9360; part-time $520 per credit. *Required fees:* $298 per term. Tuition and fees vary according to course load, degree level and program. *Financial support:* In 2011–12, 106 students received support. Federal Work-Study, scholarships/grants, and tuition discounts available. Financial award application deadline: 6/1; financial award applicants required to submit FAFSA. *Faculty research:* Psychotherapy, forensic psychology, neuropsychology, marketing strategy, entrepreneurship, special education. *Unit head:* Dr. Carmen S. Roca, Chancellor, 305-593-1223 Ext. 120, Fax: 305-629-8052, E-mail: croca@albizu.edu. *Application contact:* Vanessa Almendarez, Administrative Assistant, 305-593-1223 Ext. 137, Fax: 305-593-1854, E-mail: valmendarez@albizu.edu.

Carlow University, School of Management, MBA Program, Pittsburgh, PA 15213-3165. Offers business administration (MBA); innovation management (MBA); technology management (MBA). Part-time and evening/weekend programs available. Postbaccalaureate distance learning degree programs offered (no on-campus study). *Students:* 84 full-time (70 women), 24 part-time (17 women); includes 25 minority (22 Black or African American, non-Hispanic/Latino; 3 Hispanic/Latino). Average age 32. 138 applicants, 44% accepted, 46 enrolled. In 2011, 38 master's awarded. *Entrance requirements:* For master's, minimum undergraduate GPA of 3.0; essay; resume; transcripts; two recommendations. Additional exam requirements/recommendations for international students: Required—TOEFL (minimum score 550 paper-based; 213 computer-based). *Application deadline:* Applications are processed on a rolling basis. Application fee: $20. Electronic applications accepted. Application fee is waived when completed online. *Expenses: Tuition:* Full-time $10,290; part-time $686 per credit. Tuition and fees vary according to course load, degree level and program. *Unit head:* Dr. Enrique Mu, Director, MBA Program, 412-578-8729, Fax: 412-587-6367, E-mail: muex@carlow.edu. *Application contact:* Jo Danhires, Administrative Assistant, Admissions, 412-578-6088, Fax: 412-578-6321, E-mail: gradstudies@carlow.edu. Web site: http://gradstudies.carlow.edu/management/mba.html.

Carnegie Mellon University, Heinz College, School of Public Policy and Management, Master of Entertainment Industry Management Program, Pittsburgh, PA 15213-3891. Offers MEIM. *Accreditation:* AACSB. *Entrance requirements:* For master's, GRE or GMAT, college-level course in advanced algebra/pre-calculus; college-level courses in economics and statistics (recommended). Additional exam requirements/recommendations for international students: Required—TOEFL or IELTS.

Carnegie Mellon University, Heinz College, School of Public Policy and Management, Master of Science Program in Biotechnology and Management, Pittsburgh, PA 15213-3891. Offers MS. *Accreditation:* AACSB. *Entrance requirements:* For master's, GRE or GMAT, college-level course in advanced algebra/pre-calculus; college-level courses in economics and statistics (recommended). Additional exam requirements/recommendations for international students: Required—TOEFL or IELTS.

Carnegie Mellon University, Tepper School of Business, Pittsburgh, PA 15213-3891. Offers accounting (PhD); algorithms, combinatorics, and optimization (MS, PhD); business management and software engineering (MBMSE); civil engineering and industrial management (MS); computational finance (MSCF); economics (MS, PhD); electronic commerce (MS); environmental engineering and management (MEEM); finance (PhD); financial economics (PhD); industrial administration (MBA), including administration and public management; information systems (PhD); management of manufacturing and automation (PhD); marketing (PhD); mathematical finance (PhD); operations research (PhD); organizational behavior and theory (PhD); political economy (PhD); production and operations management (PhD); public policy and management (MS, MSED); software engineering and business management (MS); JD/MS; JD/MSIA; M Div/MS; MOM/MSIA; MSCF/MSIA. JD/MSIA offered jointly with University of Pittsburgh. Part-time programs available. Terminal master's awarded for partial completion of doctoral program. *Degree requirements:* For doctorate, thesis/dissertation. *Entrance requirements:* For master's, GMAT. Additional exam requirements/recommendations for international students: Required—TOEFL. *Expenses:* Contact institution.

Carroll University, Program in Business Administration, Waukesha, WI 53186-5593. Offers MBA. Part-time programs available. *Entrance requirements:* For master's, GRE, resume, transcripts. Additional exam requirements/recommendations for international students: Required—TOEFL. Electronic applications accepted.

Carson-Newman College, Program in Business Administration, Jefferson City, TN 37760. Offers MBA. *Faculty:* 6 full-time (3 women). *Students:* 10 full-time (5 women), 26 part-time (12 women); includes 2 minority (both Black or African American, non-Hispanic/Latino), 3 international. *Application deadline:* For fall admission, 7/15 priority date for domestic students. Application fee: $50. *Expenses: Tuition:* Full-time $6750; part-time $375 per credit hour. *Required fees:* $200. *Unit head:* Dr. Clyde Herring, Director, 865-471-3587, E-mail: ceherring@cn.edu. *Application contact:* Graduate Admissions and Services Adviser, 865-473-3468, Fax: 865-472-3475.

Case Western Reserve University, Weatherhead School of Management, Department of Operations, Management Program, Cleveland, OH 44106. Offers operations research (MSM); supply chain (MSM); MBA/MSM. *Accreditation:* AACSB. Part-time and evening/weekend programs available. *Entrance requirements:* For master's, GMAT or GRE, 3 letters of recommendation, resume. Additional exam requirements/recommendations for international students: Required—TOEFL (minimum score 600 paper-based; 250 computer-based). *Faculty research:* Supply chain management, operations management, operations/finance interface optimization, scheduling.

Case Western Reserve University, Weatherhead School of Management, Executive Doctor of Management Program, Cleveland, OH 44106. Offers management (EDM). Part-time and evening/weekend programs available. *Degree requirements:* For doctorate, thesis/dissertation. *Entrance requirements:* For doctorate, GMAT. Electronic applications accepted. *Expenses:* Contact institution. *Faculty research:* Information technology and design, emotional intelligence and leadership, entrepreneurship, governing of NP organizations, social ethics.

Case Western Reserve University, Weatherhead School of Management, Executive MBA Program, Cleveland, OH 44106. Offers EMBA. *Accreditation:* AACSB. *Entrance requirements:* For master's, GMAT (if candidate does not have an undergraduate degree from an accredited institution), work experience, interview. Electronic applications accepted. *Expenses:* Contact institution.

Case Western Reserve University, Weatherhead School of Management, Full Time MBA Program, Cleveland, OH 44106. Offers MBA, MBA/JD, MBA/M Acc, MBA/MD, MBA/MIM, MBA/MNO, MBA/MSM, MBA/MSN, MBA/MSSA. *Accreditation:* AACSB. *Entrance requirements:* For master's, GMAT, letters of recommendation, interview, work experience. Additional exam requirements/recommendations for international students: Required—TOEFL (minimum score 600 paper-based; 250 computer-based). Electronic applications accepted.

Case Western Reserve University, Weatherhead School of Management, Part-time MBA Program, Cleveland, OH 44106. Offers MBA, MBA/M Acc, MBA/MSM, MBA/MSSA. *Accreditation:* AACSB. Part-time and evening/weekend programs available. *Entrance requirements:* For master's, GMAT, interview, work experience. Additional exam requirements/recommendations for international students: Recommended—TOEFL (minimum score 600 paper-based; 250 computer-based). Electronic applications accepted.

The Catholic University of America, Metropolitan School of Professional Studies, Washington, DC 20064. Offers human resource management (MA); management (MSM). Part-time and evening/weekend programs available. *Faculty:* 45 part-time/adjunct (18 women). *Students:* 37 full-time (24 women), 129 part-time (83 women); includes 74 minority (50 Black or African American, non-Hispanic/Latino; 1 American Indian or Alaska Native, non-Hispanic/Latino; 8 Asian, non-Hispanic/Latino; 13 Hispanic/Latino; 1 Native Hawaiian or other Pacific Islander, non-Hispanic/Latino; 1 Two or more races, non-Hispanic/Latino), 15 international. Average age 36. 143 applicants, 48% accepted, 49 enrolled. In 2011, 43 degrees awarded. *Degree requirements:* For master's, minimum GPA of 3.0, capstone course. *Entrance requirements:* For master's, statement of purpose, official copies of academic transcripts, three letters of recommendation, resume. Additional exam requirements/recommendations for international students: Required—TOEFL (minimum score 237 computer-based; 93 iBT). *Application deadline:* For fall admission, 8/1 priority date for domestic students, 7/15 for international students; for spring admission, 12/1 priority date for domestic students, 10/15 for international students. Application fee: $55. *Expenses: Tuition:* Full-time $35,260; part-time $1380 per credit. *Required fees:* $80; $40 per semester hour. One-time fee: $425. *Total annual research expenditures:* $438,319. *Unit head:* Dr. Sara Thompson, Dean, 202-319-5256, Fax: 202-319-6032, E-mail: thompsons@cua.edu. *Application contact:* Andrew Woodall, Director of Graduate Admissions, 202-319-5057, Fax: 202-319-6533, E-mail: cua-admissions@cua.edu. Web site: http://metro.cua.edu/.

The Catholic University of America, School of Arts and Sciences, Department of Business and Economics, Washington, DC 20064. Offers accounting (MS); integral economic development management (MA); international political economics (MA). Part-time programs available. *Faculty:* 12 full-time (4 women), 25 part-time/adjunct (9 women). *Students:* 22 full-time (5 women), 4 part-time (2 women); includes 4 minority (2 Black or African American, non-Hispanic/Latino; 1 Asian, non-Hispanic/Latino; 1 Hispanic/Latino), 5 international. Average age 26. 55 applicants, 56% accepted, 24 enrolled. In 2011, 16 degrees awarded. *Degree requirements:* For master's, comprehensive exam. *Entrance requirements:* For master's, GRE General Test, statement of purpose, official copies of academic transcripts, three letters of recommendation. Additional exam requirements/recommendations for international students: Required—TOEFL (minimum score 580 paper-based; 237 computer-based). *Application deadline:* For fall admission, 8/1 priority date for domestic students, 7/15 for international students; for spring admission, 12/1 priority date for domestic students, 10/15 for international students. Applications are processed on a rolling basis. Application fee: $55. Electronic applications accepted. *Expenses: Tuition:* Full-time $35,260; part-time $1380 per credit. *Required fees:* $80; $40 per semester hour. One-time fee: $425. *Financial support:* Fellowships, research assistantships, teaching assistantships, Federal Work-Study, scholarships/grants, tuition waivers (full and partial), and unspecified assistantships available. Financial award application deadline: 2/1; financial award applicants required to submit FAFSA. *Faculty research:* Integrity of the marketing process, economics of energy and the environment, emerging markets, social change, international finance and economic development. *Total annual research expenditures:* $85,300. *Unit head:* Dr. Andrew V. Abela, Chair, 202-319-5235, Fax: 202-319-4426, E-mail: abela@cua.edu. *Application contact:* Andrew Woodall, Director of Graduate Admissions, 202-319-5057, Fax: 202-319-6533, E-mail: cua-admissions@cua.edu. Web site: http://economics.cua.edu/.

Centenary College, Program in Business Administration, Hackettstown, NJ 07840-2100. Offers MBA. Part-time and evening/weekend programs available. Postbaccalaureate distance learning degree programs offered (minimal on-campus study). *Entrance requirements:* For master's, GMAT.

Centenary College of Louisiana, Graduate Programs, Frost School of Business, Shreveport, LA 71104. Offers MBA. Part-time and evening/weekend programs available. *Degree requirements:* For master's, thesis. *Entrance requirements:* For master's, GMAT, minimum 5 years of professional/managerial experience. *Faculty research:* Leadership, organizational change strategy, market behavior, executive compensation.

Central European University, CEU Business School, Budapest, Hungary. Offers executive business administration (EMBA); finance (MBA); general management (MBA); information technology management (MBA); marketing (MBA); real estate management (MBA). Part-time and evening/weekend programs available. *Faculty:* 17 full-time (4 women), 12 part-time/adjunct (1 woman). *Students:* 31 full-time (12 women), 84 part-time (16 women). Average age 34. 162 applicants, 35% accepted, 31 enrolled. In 2011, 83 degrees awarded. *Degree requirements:* For master's, one foreign language. *Entrance requirements:* For master's, GMAT. Additional exam requirements/recommendations for international students: Required—TOEFL (minimum score 570 paper-based; 230 computer-based); Recommended—IELTS (minimum score 6.5). *Application deadline:* For fall admission, 5/15 priority date for domestic students, 5/22 for international students; for winter admission, 11/15 priority date for domestic students, 11/10 for international students. Applications are processed on a rolling basis. Application fee: $0. Electronic applications accepted. Tuition charges are reported in euros. *Expenses: Tuition:* Full-time 11,000 euros. *Financial support:* Tuition waivers (partial) available. *Faculty research:* Social and ethical business, marketing, international business. *Unit head:* Dr. Mel Horwitch, Dean and Managing Director, 361-887-5050, E-mail: mhorwitch@ceubusiness.com. *Application contact:* Agnes Schram, Admissions Manager, 361-887-5111, Fax: 361-887-5133, E-mail: mba@ceubusiness.com. Web site: http://www.ceubusiness.com.

Central Michigan University, Central Michigan University Global Campus, Program in Business Administration, Mount Pleasant, MI 48859. Offers enterprise resource planning (MBA, Certificate); logistics management (MBA, Certificate); value-driven organization (MBA). Part-time and evening/weekend programs available. *Entrance requirements:* For master's, GMAT. *Financial support:* Scholarships/grants available. Support available to part-time students. *Unit head:* Dr. Debasish Chakraborty, 989-774-3678, E-mail: chakt1d@cmich.edu. *Application contact:* Global Campus Student Services Call Center, 877-268-4636, E-mail: cmuglobal@cmich.edu.

Central Michigan University, College of Graduate Studies, College of Business Administration, Mount Pleasant, MI 48859. Offers accounting (MBA); business economics (MBA); business information systems (MS, Graduate Certificate), including business computing (Graduate Certificate), information systems (MS); economics (MA); finance and law (MBA), including finance; management (MBA), including consulting, general business, human resources management, international business; management information systems (MBA); management information systems/SAP (MBA); marketing and hospitality services administration (MBA), including marketing. *Accreditation:* AACSB. Part-time and evening/weekend programs available. *Degree requirements:* For master's, thesis or alternative. *Entrance requirements:* For master's, GMAT (MBA). Electronic applications accepted. *Faculty research:* Economics, enterprise software, business information systems, management, marketing.

Central Michigan University, College of Graduate Studies, Interdisciplinary Administration Programs, Mount Pleasant, MI 48859. Offers acquisitions administration (MSA, Graduate Certificate); general administration (MSA, Graduate Certificate); health services administration (MSA, Graduate Certificate); human resource administration (Graduate Certificate); human resources administration (MSA); information resource management (MSA, Graduate Certificate); international administration (MSA, Graduate Certificate); leadership (MSA, Graduate Certificate); organizational communication (MSA, Graduate Certificate); public administration (MSA, Graduate Certificate); recreation and park administration (MSA); sport administration (MSA). *Accreditation:* AACSB. Part-time and evening/weekend programs available. Postbaccalaureate distance learning degree programs offered (no on-campus study). *Degree requirements:* For master's, thesis or alternative. *Entrance requirements:* For master's, bachelor's degree with minimum GPA of 2.7. Electronic applications accepted. *Faculty research:* Interdisciplinary studies in acquisitions administration, health services administration, sport administration, recreation and park administration, and international administration.

Chadron State College, School of Professional and Graduate Studies, Department of Business and Economics, Chadron, NE 69337. Offers MBA. *Accreditation:* ACBSP. Part-time and evening/weekend programs available. Postbaccalaureate distance learning degree programs offered (minimal on-campus study). *Degree requirements:* For master's, thesis optional. *Entrance requirements:* For master's, GMAT, minimum GPA of 2.75 or 12 graduate hours at CSC with minimum GPA of 3.25. Additional exam requirements/recommendations for international students: Required—TOEFL. Electronic applications accepted.

Chaminade University of Honolulu, Graduate Services, Program in Business Administration, Honolulu, HI 96816-1578. Offers accounting (MBA); business (MBA); not-for-profit (MBA); public sector (MBA). Part-time and evening/weekend programs available. *Faculty:* 5 full-time (1 woman), 17 part-time/adjunct (6 women). *Students:* 65 full-time (37 women), 50 part-time (23 women); includes 73 minority (6 Black or African American, non-Hispanic/Latino; 37 Asian, non-Hispanic/Latino; 6 Hispanic/Latino; 17 Native Hawaiian or other Pacific Islander, non-Hispanic/Latino; 7 Two or more races, non-Hispanic/Latino), 2 international. Average age 31. 52 applicants, 79% accepted, 29 enrolled. In 2011, 45 master's awarded. *Entrance requirements:* For master's, minimum GPA of 3.0, resume. Additional exam requirements/recommendations for international students: Required—TOEFL (minimum score 650 paper-based). *Application deadline:* For fall admission, 9/1 priority date for domestic students, 9/1 for international students; for winter admission, 12/1 priority date for domestic students, 12/1 for international students; for spring admission, 3/1 priority date for domestic students, 3/1 for international students. Applications are processed on a rolling basis. Application fee: $50. Electronic applications accepted. *Expenses: Required fees:* $600 per credit hour. One-time fee: $93 part-time. *Financial support:* In 2011–12, 35 students received support. Career-related internships or fieldwork, Federal Work-Study, and institutionally sponsored loans available. Support available to part-time students. Financial award application deadline: 3/1; financial award applicants required to submit FAFSA. *Faculty research:* Total quality management, international finance, not-for-profit accounting, service-learning in business contexts. *Unit head:* Dr. Scott J. Schroeder, Dean, 808-739-4611, Fax: 808-735-4734, E-mail: sschroed@chaminade.edu. *Application contact:* 808-739-4633, Fax: 808-739-8329, E-mail: gradserv@chaminade.edu. Web site: http://www.chaminade.edu/business_communication/mba/index.php.

Champlain College, Graduate Studies, Burlington, VT 05402-0670. Offers business (MBA); digital forensic management (MS); education (M Ed); emergent media (MFA); health care management (MS); law (MS); managing innovation and information technology (MS); mediation and applied conflict studies (MS). Part-time programs available. Postbaccalaureate distance learning degree programs offered (no on-campus study). *Faculty:* 11 full-time (1 woman), 26 part-time/adjunct (11 women). *Students:* 328 full-time (213 women), 66 part-time (36 women); includes 17 minority (11 Black or African American, non-Hispanic/Latino; 1 Asian, non-Hispanic/Latino; 4 Hispanic/Latino; 1 Two or more races, non-Hispanic/Latino). Average age 37. 132 applicants, 90% accepted, 102 enrolled. In 2011, 8 master's awarded. *Degree requirements:* For master's, capstone project. *Entrance requirements:* Additional exam requirements/recommendations for international students: Required—TOEFL. *Application deadline:* For fall admission, 8/1 priority date for domestic students, 8/1 for international students; for spring admission, 1/1 priority date for domestic students, 1/1 for international students. Applications are processed on a rolling basis. Application fee: $50. Electronic applications accepted. *Expenses: Tuition:* Part-time $746 per credit. Tuition and fees vary according to program. *Financial support:* Applicants required to submit FAFSA. *Unit head:* Dr. Donald Haggerty, Associate Provost, 802-865-6403, Fax: 802-865-6447. *Application contact:* Jon Walsh, Assistant Vice President, Graduate Admission, 800-570-5858, E-mail: walsh@champlain.edu. Web site: http://www.champlain.edu/master/.

Chancellor University, College of Business, Cleveland, OH 44114-4624. Offers MBA, MMG. Part-time and evening/weekend programs available. Postbaccalaureate distance learning degree programs offered (no on-campus study). *Entrance requirements:* For master's, references, interview.

Business Administration and Management—General

Chapman University, The George L. Argyros School of Business and Economics, Orange, CA 92866. Offers business administration (Exec MBA, MBA); economic systems design (MS); JD/MBA. *Accreditation:* AACSB. Part-time and evening/weekend programs available. *Faculty:* 57 full-time (9 women), 26 part-time/adjunct (4 women). *Students:* 149 full-time (67 women), 97 part-time (34 women); includes 67 minority (6 Black or African American, non-Hispanic/Latino; 1 American Indian or Alaska Native, non-Hispanic/Latino; 24 Asian, non-Hispanic/Latino; 32 Hispanic/Latino; 1 Native Hawaiian or other Pacific Islander, non-Hispanic/Latino; 3 Two or more races, non-Hispanic/Latino), 32 international. Average age 29. 205 applicants, 67% accepted, 85 enrolled. In 2011, 151 master's awarded. *Entrance requirements:* Additional exam requirements/recommendations for international students: Required—TOEFL. Application fee: $60. Electronic applications accepted. *Expenses:* Contact institution. *Financial support:* Fellowships, Federal Work-Study, and scholarships/grants available. Financial award applicants required to submit FAFSA. *Unit head:* Dr. Arthur Kraft, Dean, 714-997-6684. *Application contact:* Debra Gonda, Associate Dean, 714-997-6894, E-mail: gonda@chapman.edu. Web site: http://www.chapman.edu/argyros.

Charleston Southern University, Program in Business, Charleston, SC 29423-8087. Offers accounting (MBA); finance (MBA); health care administration (MBA); information systems (MBA); organizational development (MBA). Part-time and evening/weekend programs available. *Degree requirements:* For master's, thesis optional. *Entrance requirements:* For master's, GMAT. Additional exam requirements/recommendations for international students: Required—TOEFL (minimum score 550 paper-based; 213 computer-based; 79 iBT).

Chatham University, Program in Business Administration, Pittsburgh, PA 15232-2826. Offers business administration (MBA); healthcare professionals (MBA); sustainability (MBA); women's leadership (MBA). Part-time and evening/weekend programs available. *Students:* 25 full-time (21 women), 53 part-time (45 women); includes 13 minority (7 Black or African American, non-Hispanic/Latino; 2 American Indian or Alaska Native, non-Hispanic/Latino; 2 Asian, non-Hispanic/Latino; 2 Hispanic/Latino), 5 international. Average age 32. 59 applicants, 64% accepted, 25 enrolled. In 2011, 21 master's awarded. *Entrance requirements:* For master's, minimum GPA of 3.0, letters of recommendation. Additional exam requirements/recommendations for international students: Required—TOEFL (minimum score 600 paper-based; 250 computer-based; 100 iBT), IELTS (minimum score 7), TWE. *Application deadline:* For fall admission, 4/1 for domestic and international students; for spring admission, 11/1 for domestic students, 10/1 for international students. Applications are processed on a rolling basis. Application fee: $45. Electronic applications accepted. Application fee is waived when completed online. *Expenses: Tuition:* Full-time $13,896. Tuition and fees vary according to program. *Financial support:* Applicants required to submit FAFSA. *Unit head:* Prof. Bruce Rosenthal, Director of Business and Entrepreneurship Program, 412-365-2433. *Application contact:* Michael May, Director of Graduate Admission, 412-365-1141, Fax: 412-365-1609, E-mail: gradadmissions@chatham.edu. Web site: http://www.chatham.edu/mba.

Christian Brothers University, School of Business, Memphis, TN 38104-5581. Offers business (MBA); financial planning (Certificate); project management (Certificate). Part-time and evening/weekend programs available. *Entrance requirements:* For master's, GMAT, GRE. Additional exam requirements/recommendations for international students: Required—TOEFL.

The Citadel, The Military College of South Carolina, Citadel Graduate College, School of Business Administration, Charleston, SC 29409. Offers MBA. *Accreditation:* AACSB. Part-time and evening/weekend programs available. *Faculty:* 18 full-time (3 women), 4 part-time/adjunct (0 women). *Students:* 38 full-time (6 women), 236 part-time (85 women); includes 23 minority (9 Black or African American, non-Hispanic/Latino; 8 Asian, non-Hispanic/Latino; 5 Hispanic/Latino; 1 Two or more races, non-Hispanic/Latino), 3 international. Average age 29. In 2011, 97 master's awarded. *Entrance requirements:* For master's, GMAT (minimum score 410), minimum undergraduate GPA of 3.0, 2 letters of reference, resume detailing previous work experience. Additional exam requirements/recommendations for international students: Required—TOEFL (minimum score 550 paper-based; 213 computer-based; 79 iBT). *Application deadline:* For fall admission, 7/20 for domestic students; for spring admission, 12/1 for domestic students. Application fee: $30. Electronic applications accepted. *Expenses: Tuition, area resident:* Part-time $501 per credit hour. Tuition, state resident: part-time $501 per credit hour. Tuition, nonresident: part-time $824 per credit hour. *Required fees:* $40 per term. One-time fee: $30. *Financial support:* Fellowships, career-related internships or fieldwork, health care benefits, and unspecified assistantships available. Support available to part-time students. Financial award application deadline: 7/1; financial award applicants required to submit FAFSA. *Faculty research:* Business statistics and regression analysis, mentoring university students, tax reform proposals, risk management data, teaching leadership, inventory costing methods, capitalism, ethics in behavioral accounting, ethics of neuro-marketing, European and Japanese business ethics, profit motives, team building, process costing, FIFO vs. weight average. *Unit head:* Dr. Ronald F. Green, Dean, 843-953-5056, Fax: 843-953-6764, E-mail: ron.green@citadel.edu. *Application contact:* Lt. Col. Kathy Jones, Director, MBA Program, 843-953-5257, Fax: 843-953-6764, E-mail: kathy.jones@citadel.edu. Web site: http://www.citadel.edu/csba/mba.html.

City University of Seattle, Graduate Division, School of Management, Bellevue, WA 98005. Offers accounting (Certificate); change leadership (MBA, Certificate); computer systems (MS); finance (Certificate); financial management (MBA); general management (MBA); general management-Europe (MBA); global marketing (MBA); human resources management (Certificate); individualized study (MBA); information security (MS); information systems (MBA); leadership (MA); marketing (MBA, Certificate); project management (MBA, MS, Certificate); sustainable business (Certificate); technology management (MBA, Certificate). Part-time and evening/weekend programs available. Postbaccalaureate distance learning degree programs offered (no on-campus study). *Faculty:* 6 full-time (2 women), 95 part-time/adjunct (33 women). *Students:* 397 full-time (193 women), 283 part-time (137 women); includes 127 minority (67 Black or African American, non-Hispanic/Latino; 5 American Indian or Alaska Native, non-Hispanic/Latino; 33 Asian, non-Hispanic/Latino; 15 Hispanic/Latino; 1 Native Hawaiian or other Pacific Islander, non-Hispanic/Latino; 6 Two or more races, non-Hispanic/Latino), 117 international. Average age 36. 151 applicants, 100% accepted, 151 enrolled. In 2011, 369 master's, 32 other advanced degrees awarded. *Degree requirements:* For master's, comprehensive exam (for some programs), thesis (for some programs). *Entrance requirements:* Additional exam requirements/recommendations for international students: Required—TOEFL (minimum score 567 paper-based; 227 computer-based; 87 iBT); Recommended—IELTS. *Application deadline:* For fall admission, 9/1 for international students; for winter admission, 12/1 for international students; for spring admission, 3/1 for international students. Applications are processed on a rolling basis. Application fee: $50. Electronic applications accepted. *Financial support:* Federal Work-Study and scholarships/grants available. Support available to part-time students. Financial award applicants required to submit FAFSA. *Unit head:* Dr. Kurt Kirstein, Dean, 425-637-1010 Ext. 5456, Fax: 425-709-5363, E-mail: kdkirstein@cityu.edu. *Application contact:* Alysa Borelli, Director, Recruiting, 888-422-4898, Fax: 425-709-5363, E-mail: info@cityu.edu. Web site: http://www.cityu.edu/programs/som/index.aspx.

Claflin University, Graduate Programs, Orangeburg, SC 29115. Offers biotechnology (MS); business administration (MBA). Part-time programs available. *Students:* 43 full-time (30 women), 25 part-time (19 women); includes 59 minority (56 Black or African American, non-Hispanic/Latino; 2 Asian, non-Hispanic/Latino; 1 Two or more races, non-Hispanic/Latino), 7 international. *Entrance requirements:* For master's, GRE, GMAT, baccalaureate degree, 3 letters of recommendation. Additional exam requirements/recommendations for international students: Recommended—TOEFL (minimum score 550 paper-based; 213 computer-based). *Application deadline:* For fall admission, 8/1 for domestic students; for spring admission, 12/1 for domestic students. Application fee: $45 ($70 for international students). *Expenses: Tuition:* Full-time $9480; part-time $395 per credit hour. *Required fees:* $310. One-time fee: $20 full-time. *Financial support:* Research assistantships and teaching assistantships available. Financial award application deadline: 4/15; financial award applicants required to submit FAFSA. *Unit head:* Michael Zeigler, Director of Admissions, 803-5355340, Fax: 803-5355385, E-mail: mike.zeigler@claflin.edu. Web site: http://www.claflin.edu.

Claremont Graduate University, Graduate Programs, Peter F. Drucker and Masatoshi Ito Graduate School of Management, Claremont, CA 91711-6160. Offers EMBA, MA, MBA, MS, PhD, Certificate, MBA/MA, MBA/PhD. Part-time programs available. *Faculty:* 12 full-time (3 women), 3 part-time/adjunct (0 women). *Students:* 135 full-time (46 women), 82 part-time (38 women); includes 95 minority (13 Black or African American, non-Hispanic/Latino; 39 Asian, non-Hispanic/Latino; 33 Hispanic/Latino; 10 Two or more races, non-Hispanic/Latino), 40 international. Average age 34. In 2011, 111 master's, 4 doctorates, 95 other advanced degrees awarded. *Entrance requirements:* For doctorate, GMAT or GRE General Test. Additional exam requirements/recommendations for international students: Required—TOEFL (minimum score 550 paper-based; 213 computer-based; 80 iBT). *Application deadline:* For fall admission, 2/15 priority date for domestic students. Applications are processed on a rolling basis. Application fee: $60. Electronic applications accepted. *Expenses:* Contact institution. *Financial support:* Fellowships, research assistantships, teaching assistantships, Federal Work-Study, institutionally sponsored loans, and scholarships/grants available. Support available to part-time students. Financial award application deadline: 2/15; financial award applicants required to submit FAFSA. *Faculty research:* Strategy and leadership, brand management, cost management and control, organizational transformation, general management. *Unit head:* Hideki Yamawaki, Dean/Professor, 909-607-9209, Fax: 909-621-8543, E-mail: hideki.yamawaki@cgu.edu. *Application contact:* Albert Ramos, Program Coordinator, 909-621-8067, Fax: 909-621-8551, E-mail: albert.ramos@cgu.edu. Web site: http://www.drucker.cgu.edu.

Claremont Graduate University, Graduate Programs, School of Politics and Economics, Program in Politics, Economics, and Business, Claremont, CA 91711-6160. Offers MA. Part-time programs available. *Students:* 9 full-time (5 women); includes 4 minority (2 Black or African American, non-Hispanic/Latino; 2 Hispanic/Latino), 3 international. Average age 26. In 2011, 6 master's awarded. *Entrance requirements:* For master's, GRE General Test. Additional exam requirements/recommendations for international students: Required—TOEFL (minimum score 550 paper-based; 213 computer-based; 80 iBT). *Application deadline:* For fall admission, 2/1 priority date for domestic students. Applications are processed on a rolling basis. Electronic applications accepted. *Expenses: Tuition:* Full-time $36,374; part-time $1581 per unit. *Required fees:* $165 per semester. *Financial support:* Federal Work-Study, institutionally sponsored loans, and scholarships/grants available. Support available to part-time students. Financial award application deadline: 2/15; financial award applicants required to submit FAFSA. *Unit head:* Jean Schroedel, Dean, 909-621-8696, Fax: 909-621-8545, E-mail: jean.schroedel@cgu.edu. *Application contact:* Lesa Hiben, Admissions Coordinator, 909-621-8699, Fax: 909-621-7545, E-mail: lesa.hiben@cga.edu. Web site: http://www.cgu.edu/pages/543.asp.

Clarion University of Pennsylvania, Office of Graduate Programs, Master of Business Administration Program, Clarion, PA 16214. Offers MBA. *Accreditation:* AACSB. Part-time and evening/weekend programs available. *Students:* 25 full-time (11 women), 70 part-time (40 women); includes 11 minority (3 Black or African American, non-Hispanic/Latino; 5 Asian, non-Hispanic/Latino; 2 Hispanic/Latino; 1 Two or more races, non-Hispanic/Latino), 6 international. Average age 32. In 2011, 25 master's awarded. *Entrance requirements:* For master's, GMAT, minimum QPA of 2.75. Additional exam requirements/recommendations for international students: Required—TOEFL (minimum score 550 paper-based; 213 computer-based). *Application deadline:* For fall admission, 8/1 priority date for domestic students, 4/15 for international students; for spring admission, 12/1 priority date for domestic students, 9/15 for international students. Applications are processed on a rolling basis. Application fee: $30. Electronic applications accepted. *Expenses:* Tuition, state resident: part-time $429 per credit. Tuition, nonresident: part-time $644 per credit. *Financial support:* Research assistantships with partial tuition reimbursements and career-related internships or fieldwork available. Support available to part-time students. Financial award application deadline: 3/1. *Unit head:* Dr. James Pesek, Interim Dean, 814-393-2600, Fax: 814-393-1910, E-mail: jpesek@clarion.edu. *Application contact:* Dr. Soga Ewedemi, MBA Director, 814-393-2605, Fax: 814-393-1910, E-mail: sewedemi@clarion.edu. Web site: http://www.clarion.edu/1077/.

Clark Atlanta University, School of Business Administration, Department of Business Administration, Atlanta, GA 30314. Offers MBA. *Accreditation:* AACSB. Part-time programs available. *Faculty:* 14 full-time (4 women). *Students:* 62 full-time (28 women), 9 part-time (5 women); includes 62 minority (59 Black or African American, non-Hispanic/Latino; 1 Asian, non-Hispanic/Latino; 2 Hispanic/Latino), 7 international. Average age 26. 79 applicants, 57% accepted, 30 enrolled. In 2011, 29 master's awarded. *Degree requirements:* For master's, thesis (for some programs). *Entrance requirements:* For master's, GMAT. Additional exam requirements/recommendations for international students: Required—TOEFL (minimum score 500 paper-based; 173 computer-based; 61 iBT). *Application deadline:* For fall admission, 4/1 for domestic and international students; for spring admission, 11/1 for domestic and international students. Applications are processed on a rolling basis. Application fee: $40 ($55 for international students). Electronic applications accepted. *Expenses: Tuition:* Full-time $13,572; part-time $754 per credit hour. *Required fees:* $806; $403 per semester. *Financial support:* Career-related internships or fieldwork, Federal Work-Study, scholarships/grants, and unspecified assistantships available. Support available to part-time students. Financial award application deadline: 4/30; financial award applicants required to submit FAFSA. *Unit head:* Dr. Kasim Alli, Chairperson, 404-880-8740, E-mail: kalli@cau.edu. *Application contact:* Michelle Clark-Davis, Graduate Program Admissions, 404-880-6605, E-mail: cauadmissions@cau.edu.

Clarke University, Program in Business Administration, Dubuque, IA 52001-3198. Offers MBA. Part-time and evening/weekend programs available. *Faculty:* 4 full-time (1 woman), 3 part-time/adjunct (2 women). *Students:* 19 full-time (13 women), 33 part-time (15 women); includes 3 minority (1 Asian, non-Hispanic/Latino; 2 Hispanic/Latino). Average age 38. In 2011, 28 master's awarded. *Entrance requirements:* For master's, GMAT, GRE General Test or MAT, minimum GPA of 3.0 in last 60 hours, previous undergraduate course work in business. *Application deadline:* Applications are processed on a rolling basis. Application fee: $25. Electronic applications accepted. *Expenses: Tuition:* Part-time $690 per credit hour. *Required fees:* $35 per credit hour. Tuition and fees vary according to program and student level. *Financial support:* Available to part-time students. Application deadline: 6/1; applicants required to submit FAFSA. *Unit head:* Wanda Ryan, Coordinator, 563-588-8143, Fax: 563-588-6789, E-mail: wanda.ryan@clarke.edu. *Application contact:* Carrie Kirk, Information Contact, 563-588-6635, Fax: 563-588-6789, E-mail: graduate@clarke.edu. Web site: http://www.clarke.edu/academics/graduate/MBA/index.htm.

Clarkson University, Graduate School, School of Business, MBA Programs, Potsdam, NY 13699. Offers MBA. *Accreditation:* AACSB. Part-time and evening/weekend programs available. Postbaccalaureate distance learning degree programs offered (minimal on-campus study). *Faculty:* 40 full-time (10 women), 1 part-time/adjunct (0 women). *Students:* 69 full-time (27 women), 26 part-time (14 women); includes 5 minority (2 Black or African American, non-Hispanic/Latino; 1 Asian, non-Hispanic/Latino; 2 Two or more races, non-Hispanic/Latino), 26 international. Average age 25. 203 applicants, 65% accepted, 71 enrolled. In 2011, 68 master's awarded. *Entrance requirements:* For master's, GMAT or GRE, transcripts of all college coursework, resume, personal statement, three letters of recommendation. Additional exam requirements/recommendations for international students: Required—TOEFL (minimum score 550 paper-based; 213 computer-based; 80 iBT), IELTS (minimum score 6.5), TSE required for some. *Application deadline:* For fall admission, 1/30 priority date for domestic students, 1/30 for international students; for spring admission, 9/1 priority date for domestic students, 9/1 for international students. Applications are processed on a rolling basis. Application fee: $25 ($35 for international students). Electronic applications accepted. *Expenses: Tuition:* Full-time $14,376; part-time $1198 per credit hour. *Required fees:* $295 per semester. *Financial support:* In 2011–12, 68 students received support. Scholarships/grants available. *Faculty research:* Industrial organization and regulated industries, end-user computing, systems analysis and design, technological marketing, leadership development. *Unit head:* Dr. Boris Jukic, Director, 315-268-6613, Fax: 315-268-3810, E-mail: bjukic@clarkson.edu. *Application contact:* Karen Fuhr, Assistant to the Graduate Director, 315-268-6613, Fax: 315-268-3810, E-mail: fuhrk@clarkson.edu. Web site: http://www.clarkson.edu/business/graduate/.

Clark University, Graduate School, Graduate School of Management, Business Administration Program, Worcester, MA 01610-1477. Offers accounting (MBA); finance (MBA); global business (MBA); health care management (MBA); management (MBA); management of information technology (MBA); marketing (MBA). *Accreditation:* AACSB. Part-time and evening/weekend programs available. *Students:* 103 full-time (47 women), 108 part-time (41 women); includes 16 minority (7 Black or African American, non-Hispanic/Latino; 5 Asian, non-Hispanic/Latino; 4 Hispanic/Latino), 69 international. Average age 30. 371 applicants, 48% accepted, 77 enrolled. In 2011, 112 master's awarded. *Degree requirements:* For master's, thesis optional. *Application deadline:* For fall admission, 6/1 priority date for domestic students; for spring admission, 12/1 priority date for domestic students. Applications are processed on a rolling basis. Application fee: $50. Electronic applications accepted. *Expenses: Tuition:* Full-time $37,000; part-time $1156 per credit hour. *Financial support:* In 2011–12, research assistantships with partial tuition reimbursements (averaging $4,800 per year), teaching assistantships with partial tuition reimbursements (averaging $4,800 per year) were awarded; fellowships, career-related internships or fieldwork, Federal Work-Study, institutionally sponsored loans, and tuition waivers (partial) also available. Support available to part-time students. Financial award application deadline: 5/31. *Faculty research:* Marketing, accounting, human resource management, management information systems, business finance. *Unit head:* Dr. Catherine Usoff, Dean, 508-793-8822, Fax: 508-793-8822, E-mail: clarkmba@clarku.edu. *Application contact:* Patrick Oroszko, Enrollment and Marketing Director, 508-793-8822, Fax: 508-793-8822, E-mail: clarkmba@clarku.edu. Web site: http://www.clarku.edu/gsom/prospective/mba/.

Clayton State University, School of Graduate Studies, Program in Business Administration, Morrow, GA 30260-0285. Offers accounting (MBA); international business (MBA); supply chain management (MBA). *Accreditation:* AACSB. Part-time and evening/weekend programs available. *Faculty:* 12 full-time (3 women). *Students:* 35 full-time (13 women), 85 part-time (25 women); includes 85 minority (78 Black or African American, non-Hispanic/Latino; 1 American Indian or Alaska Native, non-Hispanic/Latino; 3 Asian, non-Hispanic/Latino; 2 Hispanic/Latino; 1 Two or more races, non-Hispanic/Latino), 3 international. Average age 36. 62 applicants, 87% accepted, 47 enrolled. In 2011, 38 master's awarded. *Degree requirements:* For master's, thesis. *Entrance requirements:* For master's, GMAT, 3 letters of recommendation; statement of purpose; 2 official transcripts. Additional exam requirements/recommendations for international students: Required—TOEFL (minimum score 550 paper-based; 213 computer-based; 80 iBT). *Application deadline:* For fall admission, 6/15 priority date for domestic students, 5/1 for international students; for spring admission, 11/15 priority date for domestic students, 9/1 for international students. Applications are processed on a rolling basis. Application fee: $75. Electronic applications accepted. *Expenses:* Contact institution. *Financial support:* Application deadline: 7/1; applicants required to submit FAFSA. *Unit head:* Dr. Judith Ogden, Graduate Program Director, Master of Business Administration, 678-466-4509, E-mail: judithogden@clayton.edu. *Application contact:* Michelle Terrell, Program Manager, 678-466-4500, Fax: 648-466-4599, E-mail: michelleterrell@clayton.edu. Web site: http://business.clayton.edu/MBA/.

Cleary University, Online Program in Business Administration, Ann Arbor, MI 48105-2659. Offers financial planning (MBA); financial planning (Graduate Certificate); green business strategy (MBA, Graduate Certificate); management (MBA); nonprofit management (MBA, Graduate Certificate); organizational leadership (MBA); public accounting (MBA). Part-time and evening/weekend programs available. Postbaccalaureate distance learning degree programs offered (no on-campus study). *Degree requirements:* For master's, thesis. *Entrance requirements:* For master's, bachelor's degree; minimum GPA of 2.5; professional resume indicating minimum 2 years management or related experience; undergraduate degree from an accredited college or university with at least 18 quarter hours (or 12 semester hours) of accounting study (for MBA in accounting). Additional exam requirements/recommendations for international students: Required—TOEFL (minimum score 550 paper-based; 213 computer-based; 79 iBT), Michigan English Language Assessment Battery (minimum score: 75). Electronic applications accepted.

Clemson University, Graduate School, College of Architecture, Arts, and Humanities, Department of Planning and Landscape Architecture and College of Business and Behavioral Science, Program in Real Estate Development, Clemson, SC 29634. Offers MRED. *Students:* 34 full-time (7 women); includes 2 minority (1 Black or African American, non-Hispanic/Latino; 1 Hispanic/Latino), 2 international. Average age 27. 31 applicants, 81% accepted, 14 enrolled. In 2011, 19 master's awarded. *Entrance requirements:* For master's, GRE or GMAT, 3 letters of recommendation, resume, personal statement. Additional exam requirements/recommendations for international students: Required—TOEFL (minimum score 600 paper-based). *Application deadline:* For fall admission, 2/15 priority date for domestic students, 2/15 for international students. Applications are processed on a rolling basis. Application fee: $70 ($80 for international students). Electronic applications accepted. *Financial support:* In 2011–12, 5 students received support, including 1 fellowship with partial tuition reimbursement available (averaging $5,000 per year); research assistantships with partial tuition reimbursements available, teaching assistantships with partial tuition reimbursements available, career-related internships or fieldwork, scholarships/grants, health care benefits, and unspecified assistantships also available. *Faculty research:* Real estate education, real estate investment/finance, sustainability, public private partnership, historic preservation. *Unit head:* Dr. Elaine M. Worzala, Interim Director, 864-656-4258, Fax: 864-656-7519, E-mail: eworzal@clemson.edu. *Application contact:* Amy Matthews, Program Coordinator, 864-656-4257, Fax: 864-656-7519, E-mail: matthe3@clemson.edu.

Clemson University, Graduate School, College of Business and Behavioral Science, Program in Business Administration, Clemson, SC 29634. Offers entrepreneurship and innovation (MBA). *Accreditation:* AACSB. Part-time and evening/weekend programs available. *Faculty:* 30 full-time (6 women). *Students:* 83 full-time (26 women), 171 part-time (60 women); includes 30 minority (14 Black or African American, non-Hispanic/Latino; 5 Asian, non-Hispanic/Latino; 10 Hispanic/Latino; 1 Two or more races, non-Hispanic/Latino), 25 international. Average age 33. 229 applicants, 61% accepted, 94 enrolled. In 2011, 109 degrees awarded. *Entrance requirements:* For master's, GMAT. Additional exam requirements/recommendations for international students: Required—TOEFL. *Application deadline:* For fall admission, 7/1 priority date for domestic students, 4/15 for international students; for spring admission, 11/1 for international students. Applications are processed on a rolling basis. Application fee: $70 ($80 for international students). Electronic applications accepted. *Financial support:* In 2011–12, 16 students received support, including 4 fellowships with full and partial tuition reimbursements available (averaging $2,307 per year), 9 research assistantships with partial tuition reimbursements available (averaging $9,333 per year), 1 teaching assistantship with partial tuition reimbursement available (averaging $6,000 per year); institutionally sponsored loans and scholarships/grants also available. Financial award application deadline: 5/1; financial award applicants required to submit FAFSA. *Unit head:* Dr. Gregory Pickett, Director, 864-656-3975, Fax: 864-656-0947. *Application contact:* Deanna Burns, Director of Admissions, 864-656-8173, E-mail: dchambe@clemson.edu. Web site: http://www.clemson.edu/cbbs/departments/mba/.

Cleveland State University, College of Graduate Studies, Monte Ahuja College of Business, Doctor of Business Administration Program, Cleveland, OH 44115. Offers finance (DBA); global business (DBA); information systems (DBA); marketing (DBA); operations management (DBA). *Accreditation:* AACSB. Part-time and evening/weekend programs available. *Faculty:* 50 full-time (11 women). *Students:* 4 full-time (1 woman), 34 part-time (12 women); includes 3 minority (1 Black or African American, non-Hispanic/Latino; 2 Asian, non-Hispanic/Latino), 11 international. Average age 40. In 2011, 5 doctorates awarded. *Degree requirements:* For doctorate, comprehensive exam, thesis/dissertation, oral dissertation defense. *Entrance requirements:* For doctorate, GMAT, MBA or equivalent. Additional exam requirements/recommendations for international students: Required—TOEFL (minimum score 550 paper-based; 213 computer-based; 79 iBT). *Application deadline:* For spring admission, 2/28 priority date for domestic students, 2/28 for international students. Application fee: $30. Electronic applications accepted. *Expenses:* Tuition, state resident: full-time $6416; part-time $494 per credit hour. Tuition, nonresident: full-time $12,074; part-time $929 per credit hour. *Financial support:* In 2011–12, 5 research assistantships with full tuition reimbursements (averaging $12,700 per year), 4 teaching assistantships with full tuition reimbursements (averaging $12,700 per year) were awarded; tuition waivers (full) and unspecified assistantships also available. *Faculty research:* Supply chain management, international business, strategic management, risk analysis, consumer behavior. *Unit head:* Dr. Raj Shekhar G. Javalgi, Director, 216-687-3786, Fax: 216-687-9354, E-mail: r.javalgi@csuohio.edu. *Application contact:* Melinda J. Arnold, Administrative Secretary, 216-687-6952, Fax: 216-687-9257, E-mail: m.arnold@csuohio.edu. Web site: http://www.csuohio.edu/business/academics/doctoral.html.

Cleveland State University, College of Graduate Studies, Monte Ahuja College of Business, MBA Programs, Cleveland, OH 44115. Offers business administration (AMBA, MBA); executive business administration (EMBA); health care administration (MBA); off-campus programs (MBA); JD/MBA; MSN/MBA. *Accreditation:* AACSB. Part-time and evening/weekend programs available. *Faculty:* 33 full-time (9 women), 16 part-time/adjunct (2 women). *Students:* 169 full-time (72 women), 490 part-time (205 women); includes 99 minority (47 Black or African American, non-Hispanic/Latino; 33 Asian, non-Hispanic/Latino; 17 Hispanic/Latino; 2 Two or more races, non-Hispanic/Latino), 83 international. Average age 30. 716 applicants, 55% accepted, 231 enrolled. In 2011, 391 master's awarded. *Entrance requirements:* For master's, GMAT or GRE. Additional exam requirements/recommendations for international students: Required—TOEFL (minimum score 550 paper-based; 213 computer-based; 79 iBT). *Application deadline:* For fall admission, 7/15 priority date for domestic students, 5/15 for international students; for spring admission, 12/15 priority date for domestic students, 11/1 for international students. Applications are processed on a rolling basis. Application fee: $30. *Expenses:* Tuition, state resident: full-time $6416; part-time $494 per credit hour. Tuition, nonresident: full-time $12,074; part-time $929 per credit hour. *Financial support:* In 2011–12, 45 research assistantships with full and partial tuition reimbursements (averaging $6,960 per year), 1 teaching assistantship with full and partial tuition reimbursement (averaging $7,800 per year) were awarded; tuition waivers (full) and unspecified assistantships also available. Financial award application deadline: 5/15; financial award applicants required to submit FAFSA. *Total annual research expenditures:* $70,000. *Unit head:* Bruce Gottschalk, MBA Programs Administrator, 216-687-3730, Fax: 216-687-5311, E-mail: cbacsu@csuohio.edu. *Application contact:* Patricia Hite, Director, Academic Program Support, 216-687-6925, Fax: 216-687-6888, E-mail: p.hite@csuohio.edu. Web site: http://www.csuohio.edu/cba/.

Coastal Carolina University, E. Craig Wall, Sr. College of Business Administration, Conway, SC 29528-6054. Offers accounting (MBA); business (MBA). *Accreditation:* AACSB. Part-time and evening/weekend programs available. *Faculty:* 9 full-time (5 women). *Students:* 46 full-time (20 women), 28 part-time (12 women); includes 6 minority (5 Black or African American, non-Hispanic/Latino; 1 Hispanic/Latino), 11 international. Average age 27. 51 applicants, 86% accepted, 39 enrolled. In 2011, 37 master's awarded. *Entrance requirements:* For master's, GMAT, official transcripts, 2 letters of recommendation, resume, completion of prerequisites with minimum B average grade. Additional exam requirements/recommendations for international students: Required—TOEFL (minimum score 575 paper-based). *Application deadline:* For fall admission, 3/1 priority date for domestic students, 3/1 for international students; for spring admission, 11/15 priority date for domestic students, 11/15 for international students. Applications are processed on a rolling basis. Application fee: $45. Electronic applications accepted. *Expenses:* Contact institution. *Financial support:* Application deadline: 3/1; applicants required to submit FAFSA. *Unit head:* Dr. Kenneth W. Small, Director, Graduate Business Programs, 843-349-2469, Fax: 843-349-2455, E-mail: ksmall@coastal.edu. *Application contact:* Dr. James O. Luken, Associate Provost/Director of Graduate Studies, 843-349-2235, Fax: 843-349-6444, E-mail: joluken@coastal.edu. Web site: http://www.coastal.edu/business/.

College of Charleston, Graduate School, School of Business, Program in Business Administration, Charleston, SC 29424-0001. Offers MBA. *Faculty:* 5 full-time (2 women). *Students:* 32 full-time (13 women); includes 9 minority (2 Black or African American, non-Hispanic/Latino; 7 Asian, non-Hispanic/Latino). Average age 24. 95 applicants, 42% accepted, 32 enrolled. In 2011, 23 degrees awarded. *Entrance requirements:* For master's, GMAT or GRE, transcripts, recommendations, goal statement, bachelor's degree. Additional exam requirements/recommendations for international students: Required—TOEFL (minimum score 81 iBT), IELTS. *Application deadline:* For fall admission, 6/1 for domestic students. Application fee: $45. Electronic applications accepted. *Expenses:* Tuition, state resident: full-time $5455; part-time $455 per credit. Tuition, nonresident: full-time $13,917; part-time $1160 per credit. *Financial support:* Federal Work-Study, scholarships/grants, and unspecified assistantships available. Financial award application deadline: 4/1; financial award applicants required to submit FAFSA. *Unit head:* Dr. Rhonda Mack, Director, 843-953-6565, Fax: 843-953-5697, E-mail: mackr@cofc.edu. *Application contact:* Penny McKeever, Associate Director of Graduate Programs, School of Business, 843-953-8112, E-mail: mckeeverp@cofc.edu. Web site: http://sb.cofc.edu/graduate/MBA/index.php.

College of Saint Elizabeth, Department of Business Administration and Economics, Morristown, NJ 07960-6989. Offers management (MS). Part-time and evening/weekend programs available. *Faculty:* 3 full-time (1 woman), 2 part-time/adjunct (both women). *Students:* 18 full-time (16 women), 48 part-time (44 women); includes 14 minority (9 Black or African American, non-Hispanic/Latino; 5 Hispanic/Latino), 6 international. Average age 36. 40 applicants, 63% accepted, 11 enrolled. In 2011, 34 master's awarded. *Degree requirements:* For master's, capstone seminar. *Entrance requirements:* For master's, minimum GPA of 3.0, course work in principles of management. Additional exam requirements/recommendations for international students: Required—TOEFL (minimum score 550 paper-based). *Application deadline:* Applications are processed on a rolling basis. Application fee: $35. Electronic applications accepted. *Expenses: Tuition:* Part-time $899 per credit. *Required fees:* $73 per credit. *Financial support:* Career-related internships or fieldwork, tuition waivers (partial), and unspecified assistantships available. Support available to part-time students. Financial award application deadline: 3/15; financial award applicants required to submit FAFSA. *Faculty research:* American business history, business developments in Eastern Europe, MIS/programming languages, marketing strategy, strategic planning. *Unit head:* Dr. Kathleen Reddick, Director of the Graduate Program in Management, 973-290-4041, Fax: 973-290-4177, E-mail: kreddick@cse.edu. *Application contact:* Donna Tatarka, Dean of Admission, 973-290-4705, Fax: 973-290-4710, E-mail: dtatarka@cse.edu. Web site: http://www.cse.edu/academics/academic-areas/human-social-dev/business-administration/?tabID-tabGraduate&divID-progGraduate.

College of St. Joseph, Graduate Programs, Division of Business, Program in Business Administration, Rutland, VT 05701-3899. Offers MBA. Part-time and evening/weekend programs available. *Faculty:* 2 full-time (1 woman), 3 part-time/adjunct (0 women). *Students:* 19 part-time (10 women); includes 2 minority (1 Asian, non-Hispanic/Latino; 1 Hispanic/Latino). Average age 33. 14 applicants, 79% accepted, 11 enrolled. In 2011, 13 master's awarded. *Entrance requirements:* For master's, two letters of reference from academic or professional sources; official transcripts of all graduate and undergraduate study; access to computer; computer literacy. Additional exam requirements/recommendations for international students: Required—TOEFL (minimum score 550 paper-based). *Application deadline:* Applications are processed on a rolling basis. Application fee: $35. Electronic applications accepted. *Expenses:* Contact institution. *Financial support:* In 2011–12, 1 student received support, including teaching assistantships (averaging $3,000 per year). Financial award application deadline: 3/1. *Unit head:* Robert Foley, Chair, 802-773-5900 Ext. 3248, Fax: 802-776-5258, E-mail: rfoley@csj.edu. *Application contact:* Alan Young, Dean of Admissions, 802-773-5900 Ext. 3227, Fax: 802-776-5310, E-mail: alanyoung@csj.edu.

The College of Saint Rose, Graduate Studies, School of Business, Department of Business Administration, Albany, NY 12203-1419. Offers MBA, JD/MBA. JD/MBA offered jointly with Albany Law School. *Accreditation:* ACBSP. Part-time and evening/weekend programs available. *Entrance requirements:* For master's, GMAT, graduate degree, or minimum undergraduate GPA of 3.0. Additional exam requirements/recommendations for international students: Required—TOEFL (minimum score 550 paper-based; 213 computer-based). Electronic applications accepted.

The College of St. Scholastica, Graduate Studies, Department of Management, Duluth, MN 55811-4199. Offers MA, Certificate. Part-time and evening/weekend programs available. Postbaccalaureate distance learning degree programs offered (minimal on-campus study). *Faculty:* 6 full-time (0 women), 2 part-time/adjunct (1 woman). *Students:* 130 full-time (71 women), 69 part-time (44 women); includes 19 minority (5 Black or African American, non-Hispanic/Latino; 6 American Indian or Alaska Native, non-Hispanic/Latino; 2 Asian, non-Hispanic/Latino; 3 Hispanic/Latino; 3 Two or more races, non-Hispanic/Latino), 2 international. Average age 35. 125 applicants, 79% accepted, 65 enrolled. In 2011, 93 degrees awarded. *Degree requirements:* For master's, thesis. *Entrance requirements:* For master's, minimum GPA of 2.8. Additional exam requirements/recommendations for international students: Required—TOEFL (minimum score 550 paper-based; 213 computer-based; 79 iBT). *Application deadline:* For fall admission, 8/1 priority date for domestic students, 8/1 for international students; for spring admission, 11/15 priority date for domestic students, 11/15 for international students. Applications are processed on a rolling basis. Application fee: $50. Electronic applications accepted. *Expenses:* Contact institution. *Financial support:* In 2011–12, 53 students received support. Scholarships/grants available. Support available to part-time students. Financial award applicants required to submit FAFSA. *Faculty research:* Violence in higher education and workplace, screening and selection procedures in law enforcement, Internet use in criminal justice, stress management in law enforcement. *Unit head:* Randal Zimmermann, Chair, 218-625-4929, Fax: 218-723-6290, E-mail: rzimmerm@css.edu. *Application contact:* Lindsay Lahti, Director of Graduate and Extended Studies Recruitment, 218-733-2240, Fax: 218-733-2275, E-mail: gradstudies@css.edu.

College of Staten Island of the City University of New York, Graduate Programs, Program in Business Management, Staten Island, NY 10314-6600. Offers MS. Part-time and evening/weekend programs available. *Faculty:* 6 full-time (4 women). *Students:* 31 part-time (15 women). Average age 32. 54 applicants, 31% accepted, 14 enrolled. In 2011, 12 master's awarded. *Degree requirements:* For master's, minimum GPA of 3.0 in ten 3-credit courses. *Entrance requirements:* For master's, GMAT, proficiency in business fundamentals. Additional exam requirements/recommendations for international students: Required—TOEFL (minimum score 600 paper-based; 250 computer-based; 100 iBT), IELTS (minimum score 7). *Application deadline:* For fall admission, 8/1 for domestic and international students. Applications are processed on a rolling basis. Application fee: $125. Electronic applications accepted. *Expenses:* Tuition, state resident: full-time $8210; part-time $345 per credit. Tuition, nonresident: part-time $640 per credit. *Required fees:* $128 per semester. *Financial support:* Federal Work-Study and scholarships/grants available. Support available to part-time students. Financial award applicants required to submit FAFSA. *Total annual research expenditures:* $2,000. *Unit head:* Prof. Rosane Gertner, Assistant Professor of Marketing, 718-982-2964, E-mail: rosane.gertner@csi.cuny.edu. *Application contact:* Sasha Spence, Assistant Director for Graduate Admissions, 718-982-2699, Fax: 718-982-2500, E-mail: sasha.spence@csi.cuny.edu. Web site: http://www.csi.cuny.edu/catalog/graduate/business.php3.

The College of William and Mary, Mason School of Business, Williamsburg, VA 23185. Offers EMBA, M Acc, MBA, JD/MBA, MBA/MPP. *Accreditation:* AACSB. Part-time and evening/weekend programs available. *Faculty:* 59 full-time (17 women), 9 part-time/adjunct (0 women). *Students:* 337 full-time (113 women), 176 part-time (50 women); includes 61 minority (16 Black or African American, non-Hispanic/Latino; 1 American Indian or Alaska Native, non-Hispanic/Latino; 21 Asian, non-Hispanic/Latino; 15 Hispanic/Latino; 8 Two or more races, non-Hispanic/Latino), 87 international. Average age 29. 692 applicants, 57% accepted, 234 enrolled. In 2011, 301 master's awarded. *Degree requirements:* For master's, three domestic residencies and international trip (EMBA). *Entrance requirements:* For master's, GMAT or GRE. Additional exam requirements/recommendations for international students: Required—TOEFL (minimum score 600 paper-based; 250 computer-based; 100 iBT), IELTS (minimum score 6.5). *Application deadline:* For fall admission, 11/1 for domestic and international students; for winter admission, 1/10 for domestic and international students; for spring admission, 3/6 for domestic and international students. Application fee: $100. Electronic applications accepted. *Expenses:* Contact institution. *Financial support:* In 2011–12, 141 students received support, including 15 fellowships, 52 research assistantships with partial tuition reimbursements available; career-related internships or fieldwork, scholarships/grants, and unspecified assistantships also available. Financial award application deadline: 3/7; financial award applicants required to submit FAFSA. *Faculty research:* Saving and asset allocation decisions in retirement accounts, supply chain management, virtual and networked organizations, healthcare informatics, sustainable business operations. *Total annual research expenditures:* $498,867. *Unit head:* Dr. Lawrence Pulley, Dean, 757-221-2891, Fax: 757-221-2937, E-mail: larry.pulley@mason.wm.edu. *Application contact:* Amanda K. Barth, Director, Full-time MBA Admissions, 757-221-2944, Fax: 757-221-2958, E-mail: amanda.barth@mason.wm.edu. Web site: http://mason.wm.edu/.

Colorado Christian University, Program in Business Administration, Lakewood, CO 80226. Offers corporate training (MBA); information security (MA); leadership (MBA); project management (MBA). Part-time and evening/weekend programs available. Postbaccalaureate distance learning degree programs offered (minimal on-campus study). *Degree requirements:* For master's, thesis optional. *Entrance requirements:* For master's, GMAT, 2 letters of recommendation, resume. Additional exam requirements/recommendations for international students: Required—TOEFL. Electronic applications accepted. *Expenses:* Contact institution.

Colorado Mesa University, Department of Business, Grand Junction, CO 81501-3122. Offers MBA. Part-time and evening/weekend programs available. *Degree requirements:* For master's, thesis or research practicum, written comprehensive exams. *Entrance requirements:* For master's, GMAT, MAT, or GRE, minimum GPA of 3.0 for last 60 undergraduate hours, 2 letters of recommendation. Additional exam requirements/recommendations for international students: Required—TOEFL (minimum score 550 paper-based; 207 computer-based). Electronic applications accepted.

Colorado State University, Graduate School, College of Business, MBA Program, Fort Collins, CO 80523-1201. Offers MBA, MBA/DVM. *Accreditation:* AACSB. Part-time and evening/weekend programs available. *Faculty:* 16 full-time (5 women). *Students:* 282 full-time (88 women), 1,003 part-time (281 women); includes 252 minority (42 Black or African American, non-Hispanic/Latino; 8 American Indian or Alaska Native, non-Hispanic/Latino; 100 Asian, non-Hispanic/Latino; 75 Hispanic/Latino; 3 Native Hawaiian or other Pacific Islander, non-Hispanic/Latino; 24 Two or more races, non-Hispanic/Latino), 75 international. Average age 36. 552 applicants, 92% accepted, 415 enrolled. In 2011, 326 master's awarded. *Entrance requirements:* For master's, GMAT, minimum undergraduate GPA of 3.0, 4 years post-undergraduate professional work experience. Additional exam requirements/recommendations for international students: Required—TOEFL (minimum score 565 paper-based; 227 computer-based; 86 iBT); Recommended—IELTS (minimum score 6.5). *Application deadline:* For fall admission, 5/1 for domestic and international students. Application fee: $50. Electronic applications accepted. *Expenses:* Contact institution. *Financial support:* Fellowships, teaching assistantships with partial tuition reimbursements, career-related internships or fieldwork, and unspecified assistantships available. Support available to part-time students. Financial award application deadline: 6/1; financial award applicants required to submit FAFSA. *Faculty research:* E-commerce, entrepreneurship, global leadership, corporate citizenship, marketing management. *Total annual research expenditures:* $41,632. *Unit head:* Dr. John Hoxmeier, Associate Dean, 970-491-2142, Fax: 970-491-0596, E-mail: john.hoxmeier@colostate.edu. *Application contact:* Matt Leland, Admissions Coordinator, 970-491-1917, Fax: 970-491-3481, E-mail: matt.leland@colostate.edu. Web site: http://www.biz.colostate.edu/degreesCertificates/mbaPrograms/pages/default.aspx.

Colorado State University–Pueblo, Malik and Seeme Hasan School of Business, Pueblo, CO 81001-4901. Offers MBA. *Accreditation:* AACSB. Part-time and evening/weekend programs available. *Degree requirements:* For master's, thesis optional. *Entrance requirements:* For master's, GMAT, minimum GPA of 3.0. Additional exam requirements/recommendations for international students: Required—TOEFL (minimum score 550 paper-based; 217 computer-based). *Faculty research:* Total quality management, leadership, small business studies, case research and writing.

Colorado Technical University Colorado Springs, Graduate Studies, Program in Management, Colorado Springs, CO 80907-3896. Offers accounting (MBA, MSA); business administration (MBA); finance (MBA); human resources management (MBA); logistics/supply chain management (MBA); management (DM); marketing (MBA); mediation and dispute resolution (MBA); operations management (MBA); project management (MBA); technology management (MBA). Part-time and evening/weekend programs available. Postbaccalaureate distance learning degree programs offered. *Degree requirements:* For master's, thesis or alternative; for doctorate, thesis/dissertation. *Entrance requirements:* For doctorate, minimum graduate GPA of 3.0, 5 years of related work experience. *Faculty research:* Sexual harassment, performance evaluation, critical thinking.

Colorado Technical University Denver South, Programs in Business Administration and Management, Aurora, CO 80014. Offers accounting (MBA); business administration (MBA); business administration and management (EMBA); finance (MBA); human resource management (MBA); marketing (MBA); mediation and dispute resolution (MBA); operations management (MBA); project management (MBA); technology management (MBA). Part-time and evening/weekend programs available. *Degree requirements:* For master's, thesis or alternative. *Entrance requirements:* For master's, minimum undergraduate GPA of 3.0, resume.

Colorado Technical University Sioux Falls, Programs in Business Administration and Management, Sioux Falls, SD 57108. Offers business administration (MBA); business management (MSM); health science management (MSM); human resources management (MSM); information technology (MSM); organizational leadership (MSM); project management (MBA); technology management (MBA). Evening/weekend programs available. *Degree requirements:* For master's, thesis optional. *Entrance requirements:* For master's, minimum 2 years work experience, resume.

Columbia College, Master of Business Administration Program, Columbia, MO 65216-0002. Offers MBA. Evening/weekend programs available. Postbaccalaureate distance learning degree programs offered (no on-campus study). *Faculty:* 6 full-time (3 women), 47 part-time/adjunct (19 women). *Students:* 80 full-time (53 women), 406 part-time (222 women); includes 117 minority (75 Black or African American, non-Hispanic/Latino; 10 American Indian or Alaska Native, non-Hispanic/Latino; 7 Asian, non-Hispanic/Latino; 21 Hispanic/Latino; 4 Two or more races, non-Hispanic/Latino), 12 international. Average age 35. 208 applicants, 66% accepted, 124 enrolled. In 2011, 224 master's awarded. *Entrance requirements:* For master's, 3 letters of recommendation, minimum cumulative undergraduate GPA of 3.0, resume, goal statement. Additional exam requirements/recommendations for international students: Required—TOEFL (minimum score 550 paper-based; 213 computer-based; 79 iBT). *Application deadline:* For fall admission, 8/9 priority date for domestic students, 8/9 for international students; for spring admission, 12/27 priority date for domestic students, 12/27 for international students. Applications are processed on a rolling basis. Application fee: $55. Electronic applications accepted. *Expenses: Tuition:* Part-time $315 per credit hour. *Financial support:* In 2011–12, 3 students received support. Federal Work-Study and scholarships/grants available. Financial award application deadline: 3/1; financial award applicants required to submit FAFSA. *Unit head:* Dr. Diane Suhler, MBA Graduate Program Coordinator, 573-875-7640, Fax: 573-876-4493, E-mail: drsuhler@ccis.edu. *Application contact:* Samantha White, Director of Admissions, 573-875-7352, Fax: 573-875-7506, E-mail: sjwhite@ccis.edu. Web site: http://www.ccis.edu/graduate/academics/degrees.asp?MBA.

Columbia Southern University, DBA Program, Orange Beach, AL 36561. Offers DBA. Part-time and evening/weekend programs available. Postbaccalaureate distance learning degree programs offered (minimal on-campus study). *Entrance requirements:* For doctorate, 2 years professional experience, relevant academic experience. Electronic applications accepted.

Columbia Southern University, MBA Program, Orange Beach, AL 36561. Offers electronic business and technology (MBA); finance (MBA); general (MBA); healthcare management (MBA); hospitality and tourism (MBA); human resources management (MBA); international management (MBA); marketing (MBA); project management (MBA); public administration (MBA); sport management (MBA). Part-time and evening/weekend programs available. Postbaccalaureate distance learning degree programs offered (no on-campus study). *Entrance requirements:* For master's, bachelor's degree from accredited/approved institution. Additional exam requirements/recommendations for international students: Required—TOEFL. Electronic applications accepted.

Columbia University, Graduate School of Business, Berkeley-Columbia Executive MBA Program, New York, NY 10027. Offers EMBA. Offered jointly with University of California, Berkeley. Part-time programs available. *Entrance requirements:* For master's, GMAT, 2 letters of reference, interview, minimum 5 years of work experience, transcripts, resume, employee support, personal essays. Additional exam requirements/recommendations for international students: Required—TOEFL (minimum score 570 paper-based; 230 computer-based; 68 iBT). Electronic applications accepted. *Expenses:* Contact institution.

Columbia University, Graduate School of Business, Doctoral Program in Business, New York, NY 10027. Offers business (PhD), including accounting, decision, risk, and operations, finance and economics, management, marketing. *Accreditation:* AACSB. *Degree requirements:* For doctorate, comprehensive exam, thesis/dissertation, major field exam, research paper, thesis proposal. *Entrance requirements:* For doctorate, GMAT or GRE (finance), 2 letters of reference, resume. Additional exam requirements/recommendations for international students: Required—TOEFL. Electronic applications accepted. *Expenses:* Contact institution. *Faculty research:* Human decision making and behavioral research; real estate market and mortgage defaults; financial crisis and corporate governance; international business; security analysis and accounting.

Columbia University, Graduate School of Business, Executive MBA Global Program, New York, NY 10027. Offers EMBA. Program offered jointly with London Business School. *Entrance requirements:* For master's, GMAT, 2 letters of reference, interview, minimum 5 years of work experience, curriculum vitae or resume, employer support. Additional exam requirements/recommendations for international students: Recommended—TOEFL, IELTS. Electronic applications accepted. *Expenses:* Contact institution.

Columbia University, Graduate School of Business, Executive MBA Program, New York, NY 10027. Offers EMBA. *Entrance requirements:* For master's, GMAT, minimum 5 years of work experience, 2 letters of reference, interview, company sponsorship. Additional exam requirements/recommendations for international students: Recommended—TOEFL. Electronic applications accepted. *Expenses:* Contact institution. *Faculty research:* Human decision making and behavioral research; real estate market and mortgage defaults; financial crisis and corporate governance; international business; and security analysis and accounting.

Columbia University, Graduate School of Business, MBA Program, New York, NY 10027. Offers accounting (MBA); decision, risk, and operations (MBA); entrepreneurship (MBA); finance and economics (MBA); healthcare and pharmaceutical management (MBA); human resource management (MBA); international business (MBA); leadership and ethics (MBA); management (MBA); marketing (MBA); media (MBA); private equity (MBA); real estate (MBA); social enterprise (MBA); value investing (MBA); DDS/MBA; JD/MBA; MBA/MIA; MBA/MPH; MBA/MS; MD/MBA. *Entrance requirements:* For master's, GMAT, 2 letters of recommendation. Additional exam requirements/recommendations for international students: Required—TOEFL. Electronic applications accepted. *Expenses:* Contact institution. *Faculty research:* Human decision making and behavioral research; real estate market and mortgage defaults; financial crisis and corporate governance; international business; security analysis and accounting.

Columbus State University, Graduate Studies, D. Abbott Turner College of Business and Computer Science, Columbus, GA 31907-5645. Offers applied computer science (MS); business administration (MBA); modeling and simulation (Certificate); organizational leadership (MS). *Accreditation:* AACSB. *Entrance requirements:* For master's, GMAT, GRE. Additional exam requirements/recommendations for international students: Required—TOEFL (minimum score 550 paper-based; 213 computer-based; 79 iBT). Electronic applications accepted.

Concordia University, School of Business and Professional Studies, Irvine, CA 92612-3299. Offers business administration: business practice (MBA); international studies (MA). Part-time and evening/weekend programs available. *Faculty:* 9 full-time (3 women), 13 part-time/adjunct (3 women). *Students:* 104 full-time (48 women), 62 part-time (33 women); includes 56 minority (11 Black or African American, non-Hispanic/Latino; 24 Asian, non-Hispanic/Latino; 15 Hispanic/Latino; 6 Two or more races, non-Hispanic/Latino), 3 international. Average age 28. 40 applicants, 90% accepted, 34 enrolled. In 2011, 59 master's awarded. *Degree requirements:* For master's, capstone project or thesis. *Entrance requirements:* For master's, official college transcript(s), signed statement of intent, resume, two references, interview (MBA); passport photo, photocopies of valid U.S. passport, and college diploma (MAIS). Additional exam requirements/recommendations for international students: Required—TOEFL. *Application deadline:* For fall admission, 8/1 for domestic students, 6/1 for international students; for spring admission, 1/1 for domestic students, 11/1 for international students. Application fee: $50 ($125 for international students). Electronic applications accepted. *Expenses:* Contact institution. *Financial support:* In 2011–12, 14 students received support. Tuition waivers (full and partial) and unspecified assistantships available. Financial award applicants required to submit FAFSA. *Unit head:* Dr. Timothy Peters, Dean, 949-214-3363, E-mail: tim.peters@cui.edu. *Application contact:* Sherry Powers, MBA Admissions Coordinator, 949-214-3032, Fax: 949-854-6894, E-mail: sherry.powers@cui.edu. Web site: http://www.cui.edu/.

Concordia University, School of Graduate Studies, John Molson School of Business, Montréal, QC H3G 1M8, Canada. Offers administration (M Sc, Diploma); aviation management (Certificate, Diploma); business administration (MBA, UA Undergraduate Associate, PhD), including international aviation (UA Undergraduate Associate); chartered accountancy (Diploma); community organizational development (Certificate); event management and fundraising (Certificate); executive business administration (EMBA); investment management (Diploma); investment management option (MBA); management accounting (Certificate); management of healthcare organizations (Certificate); sport administration (Diploma). PhD program offered jointly with HEC Montreal, McGill University, and Université du Québec à Montréal. *Accreditation:* AACSB. Part-time and evening/weekend programs available. *Degree requirements:* For master's, one foreign language, thesis (for some programs), research project; for doctorate, one foreign language, thesis/dissertation; for other advanced degree, one foreign language. *Entrance requirements:* For master's and doctorate, GMAT. Additional exam requirements/recommendations for international students: Required—TOEFL. *Expenses:* Contact institution. *Faculty research:* General business, capital markets, international business.

Concordia University, School of Management, Portland, OR 97211-6099. Offers MBA. Evening/weekend programs available. *Degree requirements:* For master's, thesis optional. *Entrance requirements:* For master's, GMAT or professional portfolio, minimum GPA of 3.0, 2 letters of recommendation, 5 years of work experience, resume. Additional exam requirements/recommendations for international students: Required—TOEFL (minimum score 525 paper-based; 195 computer-based). *Faculty research:* Leadership characteristics in internships, marketing of MBA programs, entrepreneurship.

Concordia University Chicago, College of Graduate and Innovative Programs, Program in Business Administration, River Forest, IL 60305-1499. Offers MBA.

Concordia University, St. Paul, College of Business and Organizational Leadership, St. Paul, MN 55104-5494. Offers business and organizational leadership (MBA); criminal justice leadership (MA); health care management (MBA); human resources management (MA); leadership and management (MA). *Accreditation:* ACBSP. Evening/weekend programs available. Postbaccalaureate distance learning degree programs offered (minimal on-campus study). *Faculty:* 16 full-time (6 women), 31 part-time/adjunct (12 women). *Students:* 417 full-time (230 women), 11 part-time (5 women); includes 83 minority (40 Black or African American, non-Hispanic/Latino; 2 American Indian or Alaska Native, non-Hispanic/Latino; 25 Asian, non-Hispanic/Latino; 5 Hispanic/Latino; 1 Native Hawaiian or other Pacific Islander, non-Hispanic/Latino; 10 Two or more races, non-Hispanic/Latino), 5 international. Average age 35. 316 applicants, 74% accepted, 198 enrolled. In 2011, 204 master's awarded. *Application deadline:* Applications are processed on a rolling basis. Application fee: $50. Electronic applications accepted. *Expenses: Tuition:* Full-time $8100; part-time $435 per credit. Tuition and fees vary according to program. *Financial support:* Applicants required to submit FAFSA. *Unit head:* Dr. Bruce Corrie, Dean, 651-641-8226, Fax: 651-641-8807, E-mail: corrie@csp.edu. *Application contact:* Kimberly Craig, Director of Graduate and Cohort Admission, 651-603-6223, Fax: 651-603-6320, E-mail: craig@csp.edu.

Concordia University Wisconsin, Graduate Programs, School of Business and Legal Studies, MBA Program, Mequon, WI 53097-2402. Offers finance (MBA); health care administration (MBA); human resource management (MBA); international business (MBA); international business-bilingual English/Chinese (MBA); management (MBA); management information systems (MBA); managerial communications (MBA); marketing (MBA); public administration (MBA); risk management (MBA). Postbaccalaureate distance learning degree programs offered (minimal on-campus study). *Students:* 308 full-time (146 women), 536 part-time (288 women); includes 126 minority (76 Black or African American, non-Hispanic/Latino; 9 American Indian or Alaska Native, non-Hispanic/Latino; 15 Asian, non-Hispanic/Latino; 12 Hispanic/Latino; 14 Two or more races, non-Hispanic/Latino), 276 international. Average age 35. In 2011, 110 master's awarded. *Degree requirements:* For master's, comprehensive exam, thesis or alternative. *Entrance requirements:* Additional exam requirements/recommendations for international students: Required—TOEFL. *Application deadline:* For fall admission, 8/1 priority date for domestic students; for spring admission, 1/15 for domestic students. Applications are processed on a rolling basis. Application fee: $50. *Expenses:* Contact institution. *Financial support:* Application deadline: 8/1. *Unit head:* Dr. David Borst, Director, 262-243-4298, Fax: 262-243-4428, E-mail: david.borst@cuw.edu. *Application contact:* Mary Eberhardt, Graduate Admissions, 262-243-4551, Fax: 262-243-4428, E-mail: mary.eberhardt@cuw.edu.

Copenhagen Business School, Graduate Programs, Copenhagen, Denmark. Offers business administration (Exec MBA, MBA, PhD); business administration and information systems (M Sc); business, language and culture (M Sc); economics and business administration (M Sc); health management (MHM); international business and politics (M Sc); public administration (MPA); shipping and logistics (Exec MBA); technology, market and organization (MBA).

Corban University, Graduate School, The Corban MBA, Salem, OR 97301-9392. Offers management (MBA); non-profit management (MBA). Postbaccalaureate distance learning degree programs offered (no on-campus study).

Cornell University, Graduate School, Graduate Field of Management, Ithaca, NY 14853-0001. Offers accounting (PhD); behavioral decision theory (PhD); finance (PhD); marketing (PhD); organizational behavior (PhD); production and operations management (PhD). *Accreditation:* AACSB. *Faculty:* 53 full-time (8 women). *Students:* 39 full-time (11 women); includes 2 minority (both Asian, non-Hispanic/Latino), 23 international. Average age 29. 424 applicants, 3% accepted, 8 enrolled. In 2011, 6 doctorates awarded. *Degree requirements:* For doctorate, comprehensive exam, thesis/dissertation. *Entrance requirements:* For doctorate, GMAT or GRE General Test. Additional exam requirements/recommendations for international students: Required—TOEFL (minimum score 600 paper-based; 250 computer-based; 77 iBT). *Application deadline:* For fall admission, 1/3 for domestic students. Application fee: $95. Electronic applications accepted. *Expenses:* Contact institution. *Financial support:* In 2011–12, 38 students received support, including 4 fellowships with full tuition reimbursements available, 33 research assistantships with full tuition reimbursements available, 2 teaching assistantships with full tuition reimbursements available; institutionally sponsored loans, scholarships/grants, health care benefits, tuition waivers (full and partial), and unspecified assistantships also available. Financial award applicants required to submit FAFSA. *Faculty research:* Operations and manufacturing. *Unit head:* Director of Graduate Studies, 607-255-3669. *Application contact:* Graduate Field Assistant, 607-255-9431, E-mail: js_phd@cornell.edu. Web site: http://www.gradschool.cornell.edu/fields.php?id-91&a-2.

Cornell University, Johnson Graduate School of Management, Ithaca, NY 14853-6201. Offers EMBA, MBA, PhD, JD/MBA, M Eng/MBA, MBA/MD, MBA/MHA, MBA/MILR.

Business Administration and Management—General

Accreditation: AACSB. *Faculty:* 47 full-time (9 women), 4 part-time/adjunct (0 women). *Students:* 989 full-time (264 women); includes 163 minority (29 Black or African American, non-Hispanic/Latino; 104 Asian, non-Hispanic/Latino; 25 Hispanic/Latino; 5 Two or more races, non-Hispanic/Latino), 330 international. Average age 32. 2,283 applicants, 501 enrolled. In 2011, 468 master's awarded. *Entrance requirements:* For master's, GMAT or GRE, resume, three essays, two recommendations. Additional exam requirements/recommendations for international students: Required—TOEFL, IELTS, or Pearson Test of English. *Application deadline:* For fall admission, 3/14 for domestic students, 1/1 for international students. Application fee: $200. Electronic applications accepted. *Expenses:* Contact institution. *Financial support:* Fellowships, research assistantships, career-related internships or fieldwork, Federal Work-Study, institutionally sponsored loans, and tuition waivers (full and partial) available. Financial award application deadline: 2/15; financial award applicants required to submit FAFSA. *Unit head:* Dr. L. Joseph Thomas, Dean, 607-255-6418, E-mail: dean@johnson.cornell.edu. *Application contact:* Admissions Office, 800-847-2082, Fax: 607-255-0065, E-mail: mba@johnson.cornell.edu. Web site: http://www.johnson.cornell.edu.

Cornerstone University, Graduate Programs, Grand Rapids, MI 49525-5897. Offers business administration (MBA); education (MA Ed); management (MSM); teaching English to speakers of other languages (MA, Graduate Certificate). Programs also offered at Holland, Kalamazoo, and Troy, MI campuses. Part-time programs available. Postbaccalaureate distance learning degree programs offered. *Degree requirements:* For master's, comprehensive exam (for some programs), thesis (for some programs). *Entrance requirements:* For master's, minimum GPA of 2.5, 2 letters of reference. Additional exam requirements/recommendations for international students: Required—TOEFL (minimum score 575 paper-based; 235 computer-based). Electronic applications accepted.

Creighton University, Graduate School, Eugene C. Eppley College of Business Administration, Omaha, NE 68178-0001. Offers business administration (MBA); information technology management (MS); securities and portfolio management (MSAPM); JD/MBA; MBA/MS-ITM; MBA/MSAPM; MD/MBA; MS ITM/JD; Pharm D/MBA. *Accreditation:* AACSB. Part-time and evening/weekend programs available. Postbaccalaureate distance learning degree programs offered (minimal on-campus study). *Faculty:* 37 full-time (7 women). *Students:* 21 full-time (6 women), 280 part-time (52 women); includes 39 minority (23 Black or African American, non-Hispanic/Latino; 2 American Indian or Alaska Native, non-Hispanic/Latino; 4 Asian, non-Hispanic/Latino; 7 Hispanic/Latino; 3 Native Hawaiian or other Pacific Islander, non-Hispanic/Latino), 16 international. Average age 32. 130 applicants, 98% accepted, 120 enrolled. In 2011, 130 master's awarded. *Degree requirements:* For master's, thesis optional. *Entrance requirements:* For master's, GMAT, resume, 2 letters of recommendation. Additional exam requirements/recommendations for international students: Required—TOEFL (minimum score 550 paper-based; 213 computer-based; 80 iBT). *Application deadline:* For fall admission, 7/1 priority date for domestic students, 3/1 for international students; for winter admission, 10/1 priority date for domestic students, 7/1 for international students; for spring admission, 4/1 priority date for domestic students, 10/1 for international students. Applications are processed on a rolling basis. Application fee: $50. Electronic applications accepted. *Expenses: Tuition:* Full-time $12,672; part-time $704 per credit hour. *Required fees:* $1410; $136 per semester. Tuition and fees vary according to campus/location and reciprocity agreements. *Financial support:* In 2011–12, 10 fellowships with partial tuition reimbursements (averaging $8,448 per year) were awarded; career-related internships or fieldwork, tuition waivers (partial), and unspecified assistantships also available. Financial award application deadline: 3/1. *Faculty research:* Small business issues, economics. *Unit head:* Dr. Deborah Wells, Associate Dean for Graduate Programs, 402-280-2841, E-mail: deborahwells@creighton.edu. *Application contact:* Gail Hafer, Assistant Dean, 402-280-2829, Fax: 402-280-2172, E-mail: ghafer@creighton.edu. Web site: http://business.creighton.edu.

Cumberland University, Program in Business Administration, Lebanon, TN 37087. Offers MBA. *Accreditation:* ACBSP. Part-time and evening/weekend programs available. *Degree requirements:* For master's, comprehensive exam. *Entrance requirements:* For master's, GMAT or GRE General Test, 3 letters of recommendation. Additional exam requirements/recommendations for international students: Required—TOEFL (minimum score 500 paper-based; 173 computer-based). *Expenses:* Contact institution.

Curry College, Graduate Studies, Program in Business Administration, Milton, MA 02186-9984. Offers business administration (MBA); finance (Certificate). Part-time and evening/weekend programs available. *Degree requirements:* For master's, capstone applied project. *Entrance requirements:* For master's, resume, recommendations, interview, written statement. Additional exam requirements/recommendations for international students: Required—TOEFL (minimum score 550 paper-based; 213 computer-based; 80 iBT). *Expenses:* Contact institution.

Daemen College, Program in Executive Leadership and Change, Amherst, NY 14226-3592. Offers business (MS); health professions (MS); not-for-profit organizations (MS). Part-time and evening/weekend programs available. *Degree requirements:* For master's, thesis, cohort learning sequence (2 years for weekend cohort; 3 years for weeknight cohort). *Entrance requirements:* For master's, 2 letters of recommendation, interview, goal statement, official transcripts, resume. Additional exam requirements/recommendations for international students: Required—TOEFL (minimum score 500 paper-based; 173 computer-based; 63 iBT), IELTS (minimum score 5.5). Electronic applications accepted.

Dalhousie University, Faculty of Management, Centre for Advanced Management Education, Halifax, NS B3H 3J5, Canada. Offers financial services (MBA); information management (MIM); management (MPA); natural resources (MBA). Part-time programs available. Postbaccalaureate distance learning degree programs offered. *Entrance requirements:* For master's, GMAT, minimum GPA of 3.0, resume. Additional exam requirements/recommendations for international students: Required—TOEFL, IELTS, CANTEST, CAEL, or Michigan English Language Assessment Battery. Electronic applications accepted.

Dalhousie University, Faculty of Management, School of Business Administration, Halifax, NS B3H 3J5, Canada. Offers business administration (MBA); financial services (MBA); LL B/MBA; MBA/MLIS. Part-time programs available. *Entrance requirements:* For master's, GMAT, letter of non-financial guarantee for non-Canadian students, resume, Corporate Residency Preference Form. Additional exam requirements/recommendations for international students: Required—TOEFL, IELTS, CANTEST, CAEL, or Michigan English Language Assessment Battery. Electronic applications accepted. *Faculty research:* International business, quantitative methods, operations research, MIS, marketing, finance.

Dalhousie University, Faculty of Management, School of Public Administration, Halifax, NS B3H 3J5, Canada. Offers management (MPA); public administration (MPA, GDPA); LL B/MPA; MLIS/MPA. Part-time programs available. *Entrance requirements:* For master's, GMAT. Additional exam requirements/recommendations for international students: Required—TOEFL, IELTS, CANTEST, CAEL, or Michigan English Language Assessment Battery. Electronic applications accepted. *Expenses:* Contact institution. *Faculty research:* Municipal management, policy and program management, environmental policy, economic and social policy, business and government.

Dallas Baptist University, College of Business, Business Administration Program, Dallas, TX 75211-9299. Offers accounting (MBA); business communication (MBA); conflict resolution management (MBA); entrepreneurship (MBA); finance (MBA); health care management (MBA); international business (MBA); leading the non-profit organization (MBA); management (MBA); management information systems (MBA); marketing (MBA); project management (MBA); technology and engineering management (MBA). *Accreditation:* ACBSP. Part-time and evening/weekend programs available. *Entrance requirements:* For master's, GMAT, minimum GPA of 3.0. Additional exam requirements/recommendations for international students: Required—TOEFL, IELTS. *Application deadline:* Applications are processed on a rolling basis. Application fee: $25. Electronic applications accepted. *Expenses: Tuition:* Full-time $12,060; part-time $670 per credit hour. *Required fees:* $100; $50 per semester. *Financial support:* Federal Work-Study, institutionally sponsored loans, scholarships/grants, and tuition waivers (full and partial) available. Support available to part-time students. Financial award applicants required to submit FAFSA. *Faculty research:* Sports management, services marketing, retailing, strategic management, financial planning/investments. *Unit head:* Dr. Sandra S. Reid, Director, 214-333-5280, Fax: 214-333-5293, E-mail: graduate@dbu.edu. *Application contact:* Kit P. Montgomery, Director of Graduate Programs, 214-333-5242, Fax: 214-333-5579, E-mail: graduate@dbu.edu. Web site: http://www3.dbu.edu/graduate/mba.asp.

Dallas Baptist University, College of Business, Management Program, Dallas, TX 75211-9299. Offers conflict resolution management (MA); general management (MA); health care management (MA); human resource management (MA). Part-time and evening/weekend programs available. *Entrance requirements:* For master's, GRE General Test, minimum GPA of 3.0. Additional exam requirements/recommendations for international students: Required—TOEFL, IELTS. *Application deadline:* Applications are processed on a rolling basis. Application fee: $25. Electronic applications accepted. *Expenses: Tuition:* Full-time $12,060; part-time $670 per credit hour. *Required fees:* $100; $50 per semester. *Financial support:* Federal Work-Study, institutionally sponsored loans, scholarships/grants, and tuition waivers (full and partial) available. Support available to part-time students. Financial award applicants required to submit FAFSA. *Faculty research:* Organizational behavior, conflict personalities. *Unit head:* Joanne Hix, Director, 214-333-5280, Fax: 214-333-5293, E-mail: graduate@dbu.edu. *Application contact:* Kit P. Montgomery, Director of Graduate Programs, 214-333-5242, Fax: 214-333-5579, E-mail: graduate@dbu.edu. Web site: http://www3.dbu.edu/graduate/maom.asp.

Dallas Baptist University, Gary Cook School of Leadership, Program in Christian Education, Dallas, TX 75211-9299. Offers adult ministry (MA); business ministry (MA); Christian studies (MA); collegiate ministry (MA); communication ministry (MA); counseling ministry (MA); family ministry (MA); general ministry (MA); leading the nonprofit organization (MA); missions ministry (MA); small group ministry (MA); student ministry (MA); worship ministry (MA); MA/MA. Part-time and evening/weekend programs available. *Entrance requirements:* For master's, minimum GPA of 3.0. Additional exam requirements/recommendations for international students: Required—TOEFL. *Application deadline:* Applications are processed on a rolling basis. Application fee: $25. Electronic applications accepted. *Expenses: Tuition:* Full-time $12,060; part-time $670 per credit hour. *Required fees:* $100; $50 per semester. *Financial support:* Federal Work-Study, institutionally sponsored loans, scholarships/grants, and tuition waivers (full and partial) available. Support available to part-time students. Financial award applicants required to submit FAFSA. *Unit head:* Dr. Judy Morris, Director, 214-333-5246, Fax: 214-333-5115, E-mail: graduate@dbu.edu. *Application contact:* Kit P. Montgomery, Director of Graduate Programs, 214-333-5242, Fax: 214-333-5579, E-mail: graduate@dbu.edu. Web site: http://www3.dbu.edu/leadership/mace/.

Dallas Baptist University, Gary Cook School of Leadership, Program in Christian Education and Business Administration, Dallas, TX 75211-9299. Offers MA/MBA. Part-time and evening/weekend programs available. *Students:* 15 applicants, 80% accepted, 6 enrolled. *Entrance requirements:* Additional exam requirements/recommendations for international students: Required—TOEFL, IELTS. Application fee: $25. *Expenses: Tuition:* Full-time $12,060; part-time $670 per credit hour. *Required fees:* $100; $50 per semester. *Financial support:* Federal Work-Study, institutionally sponsored loans, scholarships/grants, and tuition waivers available. Support available to part-time students. Financial award applicants required to submit FAFSA. *Unit head:* Dr. Judy Morris, Co-Director, 214-333-5246, Fax: 214-333-5115, E-mail: graduate@dbu.edu. *Application contact:* Kit P. Montgomery, Director of Graduate Programs, 214-333-5242, Fax: 214-333-5579, E-mail: graduate@dbu.edu. Web site: http://www3.dbu.edu/leadership/dual_degrees/mace_mba.asp.

Dallas Baptist University, Professional Development Program, Dallas, TX 75211-9299. Offers accounting (MA); church leadership (MA); counseling (MA); criminal justice (MA); English as a second language (MA); finance (MA); higher education (MA); leadership studies (MA); management (MA); management information systems (MA); marketing (MA); missions (MA); professional life coaching (MA). Part-time and evening/weekend programs available. *Entrance requirements:* For master's, minimum GPA of 3.0. Additional exam requirements/recommendations for international students: Required—TOEFL, IELTS. Application fee: $25. *Expenses: Tuition:* Full-time $12,060; part-time $670 per credit hour. *Required fees:* $100; $50 per semester. *Financial support:* Federal Work-Study, institutionally sponsored loans, scholarships/grants, and tuition waivers (full and partial) available. Support available to part-time students. Financial award applicants required to submit FAFSA. *Unit head:* Angela Fogle, Acting Director, 214-333-6830, Fax: 214-333-5558, E-mail: graduate@dbu.edu. *Application contact:* Kit P. Montgomery, Director of Graduate Programs, 214-333-5242, Fax: 214-333-5579, E-mail: graduate@dbu.edu. Web site: http://www3.dbu.edu/graduate/mapd.asp.

Daniel Webster College, MBA Program, Nashua, NH 03063-1300. Offers applied management (MBA). Part-time and evening/weekend programs available. *Degree requirements:* For master's, capstone research project. *Entrance requirements:* Additional exam requirements/recommendations for international students: Required—TOEFL (minimum score 550 paper-based; 213 computer-based; 79 iBT). Electronic applications accepted.

Dartmouth College, Tuck School of Business at Dartmouth, Hanover, NH 03755. Offers MBA, MBA/MPH, MD/MBA, PhD/MBA. *Accreditation:* AACSB. *Faculty:* 45 full-time (10 women). *Students:* 547 full-time (184 women); includes 101 minority (30 Black or African American, non-Hispanic/Latino; 3 American Indian or Alaska Native, non-Hispanic/Latino; 40 Asian, non-Hispanic/Latino; 19 Hispanic/Latino; 9 Two or more races, non-Hispanic/Latino), 182 international. Average age 28. 2,744 applicants, 18% accepted, 267 enrolled. In 2011, 254 degrees awarded. *Entrance requirements:* For master's, GMAT or GRE, 2 letters of recommendation, resume/curriculum vitae. Additional exam requirements/recommendations for international students: Required—TOEFL. *Application deadline:* For fall admission, 10/1 for domestic and international students; for winter admission, 1/1 for domestic and international students; for spring admission, 4/1 for domestic and international students. Application fee: $225. Electronic applications accepted. *Expenses:* Contact institution. *Financial support:* In 2011–12, available. Financial award application deadline: 4/1; financial award applicants required to submit FAFSA. *Faculty research:* Database marketing, mutual fund investment performance, dynamic capabilities of firms, return on marketing investment, tradeoff between risk and return in international financial markets, strategic innovation in established firms. *Unit head:* Paul Danos, Dean, 603-646-2460, Fax: 603-646-1308, E-mail: tuck.public.relations@dartmouth.edu. *Application contact:* Dawna Clarke, Director of Admissions, 603-646-3162, Fax: 603-646-1441, E-mail: tuck.admissions@dartmouth.edu. Web site: http://www.tuck.dartmouth.edu/.

Davenport University, Sneden Graduate School, Grand Rapids, MI 49512. Offers accounting (MBA); business administration (EMBA); finance (MBA); health care management (MBA); human resources (MBA); information assurance (MS); public health (MPH); strategic management (MBA). Evening/weekend programs available. *Entrance requirements:* For master's, GMAT, minimum undergraduate GPA of 2.75. Additional exam requirements/recommendations for international students: Required—TOEFL. Electronic applications accepted. *Faculty research:* Leadership, management, marketing, organizational culture.

Davenport University, Sneden Graduate School, Warren, MI 48092-5209. Offers accounting (MBA); business administration (EMBA); finance (MBA); health care management (MBA); human resources management (MBA); information assurance (MS); public health (MPH); strategic management (MBA). *Entrance requirements:* For master's, minimum undergraduate GPA of 2.7.

Davenport University, Sneden Graduate School, Dearborn, MI 48126-3799. Offers accounting (MBA); business administration (EMBA); finance (MBA); health care management (MBA); human resources management (MBA); information assurance (MS); marketing (MBA); public health (MPH); strategic management (MBA). Part-time and evening/weekend programs available. Postbaccalaureate distance learning degree programs offered (no on-campus study). *Entrance requirements:* For master's, minimum GPA of 2.7, previous course work in accounting and statistics. *Faculty research:* Accounting, international accounting, social and environmental accounting, finance.

Defiance College, Program in Business Administration, Defiance, OH 43512-1610. Offers criminal justice (MBA); health care (MBA); leadership (MBA); sport management (MBA). Part-time and evening/weekend programs available. *Faculty:* 3 full-time (0 women), 2 part-time/adjunct (1 woman). *Students:* 49 part-time (21 women); includes 2 minority (both Hispanic/Latino). *Degree requirements:* For master's, thesis. *Entrance requirements:* For master's, minimum GPA of 2.5. Additional exam requirements/recommendations for international students: Recommended—TOEFL. *Application deadline:* For fall admission, 8/1 for domestic and international students. Applications are processed on a rolling basis. Application fee: $25. *Expenses: Tuition:* Full-time $10,800; part-time $450 per credit hour. *Required fees:* $95; $35 per semester. *Unit head:* Dr. Susan Wajert, Coordinator, 419-783-2372, Fax: 419-784-0426, E-mail: swajert@defiance.edu. *Application contact:* Sally Bissell, Director of Continuing Education, 419-783-2350, Fax: 419-784-0426, E-mail: sbissell@defiance.edu. Web site: http://www.defiance.edu.

Delaware State University, Graduate Programs, College of Business, Program in Business Administration, Dover, DE 19901-2277. Offers MBA. *Accreditation:* AACSB. Part-time and evening/weekend programs available. *Degree requirements:* For master's, exit exam. *Entrance requirements:* For master's, GMAT (minimum score 400), minimum GPA of 3.0 in major, 2.75 overall. Additional exam requirements/recommendations for international students: Required—TOEFL (minimum score 550 paper-based). Electronic applications accepted. *Faculty research:* Managerial economics, strategic management, qualitative effort, finance.

Delaware Valley College, MBA Program, Doylestown, PA 18901-2697. Offers accounting (MBA); food and agribusiness (MBA); general business (MBA); online global executive leadership (MBA). Part-time and evening/weekend programs available. Postbaccalaureate distance learning degree programs offered (no on-campus study). *Entrance requirements:* For master's, minimum undergraduate GPA of 3.0. *Expenses:* Contact institution.

Delta State University, Graduate Programs, College of Business, Division of Management, Marketing, and Business Administration, Cleveland, MS 38733-0001. Offers business administration (MBA). Part-time and evening/weekend programs available. *Entrance requirements:* For master's, GMAT. *Expenses:* Tuition, state resident: full-time $4702; part-time $294 per credit hour. Tuition, nonresident: full-time $12,516; part-time $760 per credit hour. *Required fees:* $586.

DePaul University, Charles H. Kellstadt Graduate School of Business, Chicago, IL 60604-2287. Offers M Acc, MA, MBA, MS, MSA, MSEPA, MSF, MSHR, MSMA, MSRE, MST, JD/MBA. *Accreditation:* AACSB. Part-time and evening/weekend programs available. *Faculty:* 148 full-time (68 women). *Students:* 1,376 full-time (519 women), 888 part-time (345 women); includes 311 minority (67 Black or African American, non-Hispanic/Latino; 159 Asian, non-Hispanic/Latino; 70 Hispanic/Latino; 4 Native Hawaiian or other Pacific Islander, non-Hispanic/Latino; 11 Two or more races, non-Hispanic/Latino), 416 international. Average age 29. 1,276 applicants, 48% accepted, 408 enrolled. In 2011, 657 master's awarded. *Entrance requirements:* For master's, GMAT, 2 letters of recommendation, resume. Additional exam requirements/recommendations for international students: Required—TOEFL (minimum score 550 paper-based; 213 computer-based; 80 iBT). *Application deadline:* For fall admission, 7/1 for domestic students, 6/1 for international students; for winter admission, 10/1 for domestic students, 9/1 for international students; for spring admission, 2/1 for domestic students, 1/1 for international students. Applications are processed on a rolling basis. Application fee: $60. Electronic applications accepted. *Expenses:* Contact institution. *Financial support:* In 2011–12, 12 research assistantships (averaging $25,768 per year) were awarded; career-related internships or fieldwork, Federal Work-Study, institutionally sponsored loans, scholarships/grants, tuition waivers (full and partial), and unspecified assistantships also available. Support available to part-time students. Financial award application deadline: 4/1. *Unit head:* Robert T. Ryan, Assistant Dean and Director, 312-362-8810, Fax: 312-362-6677, E-mail: rryan1@depaul.edu. *Application contact:* Dustin Carnwell, Director of Recruiting and Admission, 312-362-8810, Fax: 312-362-6677, E-mail: kgsb@depaul.edu. Web site: http://www.kellstadt.depaul.edu.

DeSales University, Graduate Division, MBA Program, Center Valley, PA 18034-9568. Offers accounting (MBA); computer information systems (MBA); finance (MBA); health care systems management (MBA); human resources management (MBA); management (MBA); marketing (MBA); project management (MBA); self-design (MBA). *Accreditation:* ACBSP. Part-time programs available. Postbaccalaureate distance learning degree programs offered (no on-campus study). *Entrance requirements:* For master's, GMAT, minimum GPA of 3.0, 2 years of work experience. Additional exam requirements/recommendations for international students: Required—TOEFL. *Application deadline:* Applications are processed on a rolling basis. Electronic applications accepted. Tuition and fees vary according to degree level. *Faculty research:* Quality improvement, executive development, productivity, cross-cultural managerial differences, leadership. *Unit head:* Dr. David Gilfoil, Director, 610-282-1100 Ext. 1828, Fax: 610-282-2869, E-mail: david.gilfoil@desales.edu. *Application contact:* Caryn Stopper, Director of Graduate Admissions, 610-282-1100 Ext. 1768, Fax: 610-282-0525, E-mail: caryn.stopper@desales.edu.

DeVry College of New York, Keller Graduate School of Management, New York, NY 10016-5267. Offers MAFM, MBA, MISM. *Students:* 194 full-time (96 women), 612 part-time (334 women). In 2011, 40 master's awarded.

DeVry University, Keller Graduate School of Management, Phoenix, AZ 85021-2995. Offers MAFM, MBA, MHRM, MISM, MNCM, MPA, MPM, MSA. *Students:* 27 full-time (12 women), 206 part-time (109 women). In 2011, 91 master's awarded. *Application contact:* Student Application Contact, 602-870-9222. Web site: http://www.devry.edu.

DeVry University, Keller Graduate School of Management, Fremont, CA 94555. Offers MAFM, MBA, MHRM, MISM, MNCM, MPA, MPM.

DeVry University, Keller Graduate School of Management, Long Beach, CA 90806. Offers MAFM, MBA, MHRM, MISM, MNCM, MPA, MPM.

DeVry University, Keller Graduate School of Management, Pomona, CA 91768-2642. Offers MAFM, MBA, MHRM, MISM, MNCM, MPA, MPM, MSA. *Students:* 51 full-time (18 women), 347 part-time (156 women). In 2011, 110 master's awarded. *Application contact:* Student Application Contact, 909-622-8866.

DeVry University, Keller Graduate School of Management, Palmdale, CA 93551. Offers MAFM, MBA, MHRM, MPM, Graduate Certificate.

DeVry University, Keller Graduate School of Management, Colorado Springs, CO 80920. Offers MAFM, MBA, MHRM, MISM, MNCM, MPA, MPM, Graduate Certificate.

DeVry University, Keller Graduate School of Management, Miramar, FL 33027-4150. Offers MAFM, MBA, MHRM, MISM, MNCM, MPA, MPM, MSA. *Students:* 47 full-time (23 women), 210 part-time (121 women). In 2011, 71 master's awarded. *Application contact:* Student Application Contact, 954-499-9775.

DeVry University, Keller Graduate School of Management, Orlando, FL 32839. Offers MAFM, MBA, MHRM, MISM, MNCM, MPA, MPM, MSA. *Students:* 68 full-time (31 women), 246 part-time (135 women). In 2011, 71 master's awarded. *Application contact:* Student Application Contact, 407-345-2800.

DeVry University, Keller Graduate School of Management, Alpharetta, GA 30009. Offers MAFM, MBA, MHRM, MISM, MNCM, MPA, MPM.

DeVry University, Keller Graduate School of Management, Decatur, GA 30030-2556. Offers MAFM, MBA, MHRM, MISM, MNCM, MPA, MPM, MSA. *Students:* 48 full-time (28 women), 388 part-time (249 women). In 2011, 134 master's awarded. *Application contact:* Student Application Contact, 404-270-2700.

DeVry University, Keller Graduate School of Management, Tinley Park, IL 60477. Offers MAFM, MBA, MHRM, MISM, MNCM, MPA, MPM.

DeVry University, Keller Graduate School of Management, Columbus, OH 43209-2705. Offers MAFM, MBA, MHRM, MISM, MNCM, MPA, MPM. *Students:* 39 full-time (21 women), 345 part-time (201 women). In 2011, 106 master's awarded. *Application contact:* Student Application Contact, 614-253-7291.

DeVry University, Keller Graduate School of Management, Fort Washington, PA 19034. Offers MAFM, MBA, MHRM, MISM, MNCM, MPA, MPM. *Students:* 25 full-time (14 women), 193 part-time (100 women). In 2011, 42 master's awarded. *Application contact:* Student Application Contact, 215-591-5700.

DeVry University, Keller Graduate School of Management, Irving, TX 75063-2439. Offers MAFM, MBA, MHRM, MISM, MPM. *Students:* 60 full-time (28 women), 310 part-time (158 women). In 2011, 107 master's awarded. *Application contact:* Student Application Contact, 972-929-6777.

DeVry University, Keller Graduate School of Management, Arlington, VA 22202. Offers MAFM, MBA, MHRM, MISM, MNCM, MPA, MPM. *Students:* 70 full-time (21 women), 214 part-time (88 women). In 2011, 53 master's awarded. *Application contact:* Student Application Contact, 703-414-4000. Web site: http://www.devry.edu.

DeVry University, Keller Graduate School of Management, Federal Way, WA 98001. Offers MAFM, MBA, MHRM, MISM, MNCM, MPA, MPM. *Students:* 16 full-time (8 women), 143 part-time (58 women). In 2011, 57 master's awarded. *Application contact:* Student Application Contact, 253-943-2800.

DeVry University, Keller Graduate School of Management, Mesa, AZ 85210-2011. Offers MAFM, MBA, MHRM, MISM, MNCM, MPA, MPM, Graduate Certificate.

DeVry University, Keller Graduate School of Management, Phoenix, AZ 85054. Offers MAFM, MBA, MHRM, MISM, MNCM, MPA, MPM, Graduate Certificate.

DeVry University, Keller Graduate School of Management, Irvine, CA 92602-1303. Offers MAFM, MBA, MHRM, MISM, MNCM, MPA, MPM, Graduate Certificate.

DeVry University, Keller Graduate School of Management, Elk Grove, CA 95758. Offers MAFM, MBA, MHRM, MISM, MNCM, MPA, MPM, Graduate Certificate.

DeVry University, Keller Graduate School of Management, San Diego, CA 92108-1633. Offers MAFM, MBA, MHRM, MISM, MNCM, MPA, MPM, Graduate Certificate.

DeVry University, Keller Graduate School of Management, Miami, FL 33174-2535. Offers MAFM, MBA, MHRM, MISM, MNCM, MPA, MPM, Graduate Certificate.

DeVry University, Keller Graduate School of Management, Tampa, FL 33607-5901. Offers MAFM, MBA, MHRM, MISM, MNCM, MPA, MPM, Graduate Certificate.

DeVry University, Keller Graduate School of Management, Atlanta, GA 30305-1543. Offers MAFM, MBA, MHRM, MISM, MNCM, MPA, MPM, Graduate Certificate.

DeVry University, Keller Graduate School of Management, Duluth, GA 30096-7671. Offers MAFM, MBA, MHRM, MISM, MNCM, MPA, MPM, Graduate Certificate.

DeVry University, Keller Graduate School of Management, Elgin, IL 60123. Offers MAFM, MBA, MHRM, MISM, MNCM, MPA, MPM, Graduate Certificate.

DeVry University, Keller Graduate School of Management, Lincolnshire, IL 60069-4460. Offers MAFM, MBA, MHRM, MISM, MNCM, MPA, MPM, Graduate Certificate.

DeVry University, Keller Graduate School of Management, Schaumburg, IL 60173-5009. Offers MAFM, MBA, MHRM, MISM, MNCM, MPA, MPM, Graduate Certificate.

DeVry University, Keller Graduate School of Management, Gurnee, IL 60031-9126. Offers MAFM, MBA, MHRM, MISM, MNCM, MPA, MPM, Graduate Certificate.

DeVry University, Keller Graduate School of Management, Indianapolis, IN 46240-2158. Offers MAFM, MBA, MHRM, MISM, MNCM, MPA, MPM.

DeVry University, Keller Graduate School of Management, Merrillville, IN 46410-5673. Offers MAFM, MBA, MHRM, MISM, MNCM, MPA, MPM, Graduate Certificate.

DeVry University, Keller Graduate School of Management, Bethesda, MD 20814-3304. Offers MAFM, MBA, MHRM, MISM, MNCM, MPA, MPM.

DeVry University, Keller Graduate School of Management, Kansas City, MO 64105-2112. Offers MAFM, MBA, MHRM, MISM, MNCM, MPA, MPM, Graduate Certificate.

DeVry University, Keller Graduate School of Management, St. Louis, MO 63146-4020. Offers MAFM, MBA, MHRM, MISM, MNCM, MPA, MPM, Graduate Certificate.

DeVry University, Keller Graduate School of Management, Charlotte, NC 28273-4068. Offers MAFM, MBA, MHRM, MISM, MNCM, MPA, MPM.

Business Administration and Management—General

DeVry University, Keller Graduate School of Management, Henderson, NV 89074-7120. Offers MAFM, MBA, MHRM, MISM, MNCM, MPA, MPM.

DeVry University, Keller Graduate School of Management, Seven Hills, OH 44131. Offers MAFM, MBA, MHRM, MISM, MNCM, MPA, MPM, Graduate Certificate.

DeVry University, Keller Graduate School of Management, Portland, OR 97225-6651. Offers MAFM, MBA, MHRM, MISM, MNCM, MPA, MPM.

DeVry University, Keller Graduate School of Management, Pittsburgh, PA 15222-2606. Offers MAFM, MBA, MHRM, MISM, MNCM, MPA, MPM, Graduate Certificate.

DeVry University, Keller Graduate School of Management, King of Prussia, PA 19406-2926. Offers MAFM, MBA, MHRM, MISM, MNCM, MPA, MPM, Graduate Certificate.

DeVry University, Keller Graduate School of Management, Richardson, TX 75080. Offers MBA, Graduate Certificate.

DeVry University, Keller Graduate School of Management, Houston, TX 77041. Offers MAFM, MBA, MISM, MPM. *Students:* 80 full-time (47 women), 297 part-time (171 women). In 2011, 77 master's awarded. *Application contact:* Student Application Contact, 713-973-3100.

DeVry University, Keller Graduate School of Management, Manassas, VA 20109-3173. Offers MAFM, MBA, MHRM, MISM, MNCM, MPA, MPM, Graduate Certificate.

DeVry University, Keller Graduate School of Management, Bellevue, WA 98004-5110. Offers MAFM, MBA, MHRM, MISM, MNCM, MPA, MPM, Graduate Certificate.

DeVry University, Keller Graduate School of Management, Milwaukee, WI 53202. Offers MAFM, MBA, MHRM, MISM, MNCM, MPA, MPM.

DeVry University, Keller Graduate School of Management, Waukesha, WI 53188-1157. Offers MAFM, MBA, MHRM, MISM, MNCM, MPA, MPM, Graduate Certificate.

DeVry University, Keller Graduate School of Management, Naperville, IL 60563-2361. Offers MAFM, MBA, MHRM, MISM, MNCM, MPA, MPM, Graduate Certificate.

DeVry University, Keller Graduate School of Management, Sandy, UT 84070. Offers MAFM, MBA, MHRM, MISM, MNCM, MPA, MPM.

DeVry University, Keller Graduate School of Management, North Brunswick, NJ 08902-3362. Offers MBA. *Students:* 59 full-time (29 women), 166 part-time (76 women).

DeVry University, Keller Graduate School of Management, Memphis, TN 38119. Offers MAFM, MBA, MHRM, MISM, MNCM, MPA, MPM.

DeVry University, Keller Graduate School of Management, Jacksonville, FL 32256-6040. Offers MAFM, MBA, MHRM, MISM, MNCM, MPA, MPM.

DeVry University, Keller Graduate School of Management, Anaheim, CA 92806-6136. Offers MAFM, MBA, MHRM, MISM, MNCM, MPA, MPM.

DeVry University, Keller Graduate School of Management, Paramus, NJ 07652. Offers MBA.

DeVry University, Keller Graduate School of Management, Columbus, OH 43240. Offers MAFM, MBA, MHRM, MISM, MNCM, MPA, MPM.

DeVry University, Keller Graduate School of Management, Oakland, CA 94612. Offers MAFM, MBA, MHRM, MISM, MNCM, MPA, MPM.

DeVry University, Keller Graduate School of Management, Nashville, TN 37211-4147. Offers MAFM, MBA, MHRM, MISM, MNCM, MPA, MPM.

DeVry University, Keller Graduate School of Management, Chesapeake, VA 23320-3671. Offers MAFM, MBA, MHRM, MISM, MNCM, MPA, MPM.

DeVry University, Keller Graduate School of Management, Alhambra, CA 91803. Offers MAFM, MBA, MHRM, MISM, MNCM, MPA, MPM.

DeVry University, Keller Graduate School of Management, Daly City, CA 94014-3899. Offers MAFM, MBA, MHRM, MISM, MNCM, MPA, MPM.

DeVry University, Keller Graduate School of Management, Downers Grove, IL 60515. Offers accounting and financial management (MAFM); business administration (MBA); human resources management (MHRM); information systems management (MISM); network and communications management (MNCM); project management (MPM); public administration (MPA).

DeVry University Online, Keller Graduate School of Management, Addison, IL 60101-6106. Offers M Ed, MAFM, MBA, MEE, MET, MHRM, MISM, MNCM, MPA, MPM. *Students:* 794 full-time (436 women), 5,519 part-time (3,368 women). In 2011, 1,626 master's awarded.

Doane College, Program in Management, Crete, NE 68333-2430. Offers MA. Part-time and evening/weekend programs available. *Faculty:* 2 full-time (1 woman), 21 part-time/adjunct (9 women). *Students:* 126 full-time (76 women), 15 part-time (7 women); includes 19 minority (6 Black or African American, non-Hispanic/Latino; 1 American Indian or Alaska Native, non-Hispanic/Latino; 5 Asian, non-Hispanic/Latino; 5 Hispanic/Latino; 2 Two or more races, non-Hispanic/Latino), 1 international. Average age 35. In 2011, 55 master's awarded. *Degree requirements:* For master's, thesis. *Entrance requirements:* For master's, minimum GPA of 3.0. Additional exam requirements/recommendations for international students: Required—TOEFL. *Application deadline:* Applications are processed on a rolling basis. Application fee: $25. *Expenses:* Contact institution. *Financial support:* Application deadline: 6/1; applicants required to submit FAFSA. *Unit head:* Janice Hedfield, Dean, 880-333-6263, E-mail: janice.hedfield@doane.edu. *Application contact:* Wilma Daddario, Assistant Dean, 402-466-4774, Fax: 404-466-4228, E-mail: wilma.daddario@doane.edu.

Dominican College, MBA Program, Orangeburg, NY 10962-1210. Offers MBA. Evening/weekend programs available. *Entrance requirements:* For master's, GMAT, 2 letters of recommendation. Additional exam requirements/recommendations for international students: Required—TOEFL. Electronic applications accepted. *Expenses:* Contact institution.

Dominican University, Edward A. and Lois L. Brennan School of Business, River Forest, IL 60305-1099. Offers MBA, MSA, JD/MBA, MBA/MLIS, MBA/MSW. JD/MBA offered jointly with John Marshall Law School. *Accreditation:* ACBSP. Part-time and evening/weekend programs available. Postbaccalaureate distance learning degree programs offered (no on-campus study). *Faculty:* 21 full-time (8 women), 12 part-time/adjunct (4 women). *Students:* 99 full-time (63 women), 187 part-time (94 women); includes 54 minority (22 Black or African American, non-Hispanic/Latino; 1 American Indian or Alaska Native, non-Hispanic/Latino; 15 Asian, non-Hispanic/Latino; 13 Hispanic/Latino; 3 Two or more races, non-Hispanic/Latino), 26 international. Average age 31. 70 applicants, 96% accepted, 67 enrolled. In 2011, 140 master's awarded. *Entrance requirements:* For master's, GMAT. Additional exam requirements/recommendations for international students: Required—TOEFL (minimum score 550 paper-based; 213 computer-based; 79 iBT); Recommended—IELTS (minimum score 6). *Application deadline:* Applications are processed on a rolling basis. Application fee: $25. Electronic applications accepted. *Expenses:* Contact institution. *Financial support:* Career-related internships or fieldwork, Federal Work-Study, tuition waivers (partial), and unspecified assistantships available. Support available to part-time students. Financial award applicants required to submit FAFSA. *Faculty research:* Entrepreneurship, small business finance, business ethics, marketing strategy. *Unit head:* Dr. Arvid Johnson, Dean, 708-524-6465, Fax: 708-524-6939, E-mail: ajohnson@dom.edu. *Application contact:* Matthew Quilty, Assistant Dean, Brennan School of Business, 708-524-6507, Fax: 708-524-6939, E-mail: mquilty@dom.edu. Web site: http://www.business.dom.edu.

Dominican University of California, Graduate Programs, School of Business and Leadership, MBA in Sustainable Enterprise Program, San Rafael, CA 94901-2298. Offers MBA. Part-time and evening/weekend programs available. *Students:* 36 full-time (18 women), 56 part-time (41 women); includes 21 minority (2 Black or African American, non-Hispanic/Latino; 6 Asian, non-Hispanic/Latino; 10 Hispanic/Latino; 3 Two or more races, non-Hispanic/Latino), 5 international. Average age 35. 56 applicants, 68% accepted, 26 enrolled. In 2011, 33 master's awarded. *Degree requirements:* For master's, thesis or alternative, capstone. *Entrance requirements:* For master's, minimum GPA of 3.0. Additional exam requirements/recommendations for international students: Required—TOEFL (minimum score 550 paper-based; 213 computer-based; 80 iBT), IELTS (minimum score 7). *Application deadline:* For fall admission, 6/15 priority date for domestic students, 6/15 for international students; for spring admission, 11/15 priority date for domestic students, 11/15 for international students. Applications are processed on a rolling basis. Application fee: $40. Electronic applications accepted. *Expenses: Tuition:* Full-time $15,660. *Required fees:* $300. Tuition and fees vary according to program. *Financial support:* In 2011–12, 32 students received support. Scholarships/grants available. Support available to part-time students. Financial award application deadline: 3/2; financial award applicants required to submit FAFSA. *Unit head:* Elaine McCarty, Director, 415-458-3712, Fax: 415-459-3206, E-mail: elaine.mccarty@dominican.edu.

Dowling College, School of Business, Oakdale, NY 11769-1999. Offers aviation management (MBA, Certificate); banking and finance (MBA, Certificate); corporate finance (MBA); financial planning (Certificate); health care management (MBA, Certificate); human resource management (Certificate); information systems management (MBA); management and leadership (MBA); marketing (Certificate); project management (Certificate); public management (MBA, Certificate); sport, event and entertainment management (Certificate); JD/MBA. Part-time and evening/weekend programs available. Postbaccalaureate distance learning degree programs offered (minimal on-campus study). *Faculty:* 10 full-time (4 women), 54 part-time/adjunct (6 women). *Students:* 237 full-time (99 women), 403 part-time (199 women); includes 186 minority (95 Black or African American, non-Hispanic/Latino; 62 Asian, non-Hispanic/Latino; 28 Hispanic/Latino; 1 Native Hawaiian or other Pacific Islander, non-Hispanic/Latino), 1 international. Average age 35. 345 applicants, 83% accepted, 193 enrolled. In 2011, 350 master's, 7 other advanced degrees awarded. *Degree requirements:* For master's, comprehensive exam, thesis optional. *Entrance requirements:* For master's, minimum GPA of 2.8, 2 letters of recommendation, courses or seminar in accounting and finance, resume. Additional exam requirements/recommendations for international students: Required—TOEFL (minimum score 550 paper-based). *Application deadline:* For fall admission, 9/1 priority date for domestic students; for winter admission, 1/1 priority date for domestic students; for spring admission, 2/1 priority date for domestic students. Applications are processed on a rolling basis. Application fee: $50. Electronic applications accepted. *Expenses: Tuition:* Full-time $19,162; part-time $933 per credit. *Required fees:* $1330; $700 per year. Tuition and fees vary according to course load. *Financial support:* Career-related internships or fieldwork and Federal Work-Study available. Support available to part-time students. Financial award application deadline: 6/30; financial award applicants required to submit FAFSA. *Faculty research:* International finance, computer applications, labor relations, executive development. *Unit head:* Antonia Loschiavo, Assistant Dean, 631-244-3266, Fax: 631-244-1018, E-mail: loschiat@dowling.edu. *Application contact:* Ronnie S. Macdonald, Assistant Vice President for Enrollment Services/Dean of Admissions, 631-244-3357, Fax: 631-244-1059, E-mail: macdonar@dowling.edu.

Drake University, College of Business and Public Administration, Des Moines, IA 50311-4516. Offers M Acc, MBA, MFM, MPA, JD/MBA, JD/MPA, Pharm D/MBA, Pharm D/MPA. *Accreditation:* AACSB. Part-time and evening/weekend programs available. *Faculty:* 18 full-time (4 women), 5 part-time/adjunct (0 women). *Students:* 57 full-time (27 women), 334 part-time (166 women); includes 36 minority (23 Black or African American, non-Hispanic/Latino; 2 American Indian or Alaska Native, non-Hispanic/Latino; 3 Asian, non-Hispanic/Latino; 8 Hispanic/Latino), 31 international. Average age 31. 97 applicants, 88% accepted, 77 enrolled. In 2011, 223 master's awarded. *Degree requirements:* For master's, comprehensive exam (for some programs), thesis (for some programs), internships. *Entrance requirements:* For master's, GMAT, letters of recommendation, resume. Additional exam requirements/recommendations for international students: Required—TOEFL (minimum score 550 paper-based; 213 computer-based). *Application deadline:* For fall admission, 8/15 priority date for domestic students; for winter admission, 12/20 priority date for domestic students; for spring admission, 12/1 priority date for domestic students. Applications are processed on a rolling basis. Application fee: $25. Electronic applications accepted. *Expenses:* Contact institution. *Financial support:* Fellowships with tuition reimbursements, teaching assistantships, career-related internships or fieldwork, and institutionally sponsored loans available. Support available to part-time students. Financial award application deadline: 3/1; financial award applicants required to submit FAFSA. *Faculty research:* Venture capital, online commerce, professional ethics, process improvement, project management. *Unit head:* Dr. Charles Edwards, Dean, 515-271-2871, Fax: 515-271-4518, E-mail: charles.edwards@drake.edu. *Application contact:* Danette Kenne, Director of Graduate Programs, 515-271-2188, Fax: 515-271-4518, E-mail: cbpa.gradprograms@drake.edu. Web site: http://www.cbpa.drake.edu/.

Drexel University, LeBow College of Business, Program in Business Administration, Philadelphia, PA 19104-2875. Offers business administration (MBA, PhD, APC), including accounting (MBA, PhD), decision sciences (PhD), economics (MBA, PhD), finance (MBA, PhD), legal studies (MBA), management (MBA), marketing (MBA, PhD), organizational sciences (PhD), quantitative methods (MBA), strategic management (PhD). *Accreditation:* AACSB. Part-time and evening/weekend programs available. Postbaccalaureate distance learning degree programs offered (minimal on-campus study). Terminal master's awarded for partial completion of doctoral program. *Entrance requirements:* For master's, GMAT, minimum GPA of 2.75; for doctorate, GMAT. Additional exam requirements/recommendations for international students: Required—TOEFL. Electronic applications accepted. *Faculty research:* Decision support systems, individual and group behavior, operations research, techniques and strategy.

Drury University, Breech School of Business Administration, Springfield, MO 65802. Offers MBA. *Accreditation:* AACSB; ACBSP. Part-time and evening/weekend programs available. *Entrance requirements:* For master's, GMAT. Additional exam requirements/recommendations for international students: Required—TOEFL. Electronic applications accepted. *Expenses:* Contact institution. *Faculty research:* Health care management, cross cultural management, philosophical orientation and decision making.

Duke University, The Fuqua School of Business, Cross Continent Executive MBA Program, Durham, NC 27708-0586. Offers EMBA. *Degree requirements:* For master's, one foreign language. *Expenses: Tuition:* Full-time $40,720. *Required fees:* $3107. *Financial support:* Fellowships with tuition reimbursements available. *Unit head:* John

Gallagher, Associate Dean for Executive MBA Programs, 919-660-7641, E-mail: johng@duke.edu. *Application contact:* Liz Riley Hargrove, Associate Dean for Admissions, 919-660-1956, Fax: 919-681-8026, E-mail: admissions-info@fuqua.duke.edu. Web site: http://www.fuqua.duke.edu/programs/duke_mba/cross_continent/.

Duke University, The Fuqua School of Business, Global Executive MBA Program, Durham, NC 27708-0586. Offers GEMBA. *Expenses: Tuition:* Full-time $40,720. *Required fees:* $3107. *Financial support:* Fellowships with tuition reimbursements available. *Unit head:* John Gallagher, Associate Dean for Executive MBA Programs, 919-660-7728. *Application contact:* Liz Riley Hargrove, Director of EMBA Admissions, 919-660-7705, Fax: 919-681-8026, E-mail: admissions-info@fuqua.duke.edu. Web site: http://www.fuqua.duke.edu/programs/duke_mba/global-executive/.

Duke University, The Fuqua School of Business, Weekend Executive MBA Program, Durham, NC 27708-0586. Offers WEMBA. Evening/weekend programs available. In 2011, 103 master's awarded. *Degree requirements:* For master's, one foreign language. *Expenses: Tuition:* Full-time $40,720. *Required fees:* $3107. *Unit head:* John Gallagher, Associate Dean for Executive MBA Programs, 919-660-7728, E-mail: johng@duke.edu. *Application contact:* Liz Riley Hargrove, Director of EMBA Admissions, 919-660-7705, Fax: 919-681-8026, E-mail: admissions-info@fuqua.duke.edu. Web site: http://www.fuqua.duke.edu/programs/duke_mba/weekend_executive/.

Duke University, Graduate School, Department of Business Administration, Durham, NC 27708. Offers PhD. *Faculty:* 90 full-time. *Students:* 79 full-time (26 women); includes 5 minority (1 Black or African American, non-Hispanic/Latino; 4 Asian, non-Hispanic/Latino), 49 international. 633 applicants, 4% accepted, 16 enrolled. In 2011, 12 doctorates awarded. *Degree requirements:* For doctorate, thesis/dissertation. *Entrance requirements:* For doctorate, GMAT or GRE General Test. Additional exam requirements/recommendations for international students: Required—TOEFL (minimum score 550 paper-based; 213 computer-based; 83 iBT), IELTS (minimum score 7). *Application deadline:* For fall admission, 12/8 for domestic and international students. Application fee: $75. Electronic applications accepted. *Expenses: Tuition:* Full-time $40,720. *Required fees:* $3107. *Financial support:* Fellowships with full tuition reimbursements, research assistantships, career-related internships or fieldwork, Federal Work-Study, and institutionally sponsored loans available. Financial award application deadline: 12/8; financial award applicants required to submit FAFSA. *Unit head:* James Bettman, Director of Graduate Studies, 919-660-7862, Fax: 919-681-6245, E-mail: bobbiec@mail.duke.edu. *Application contact:* Elizabeth Hutton, Director, Graduate Admissions, 919-684-3913, Fax: 919-684-2277, E-mail: grad-admissions@duke.edu. Web site: http://www.fuqua.duke.edu/programs/other_programs/phd_program/.

Duquesne University, John F. Donahue Graduate School of Business, Pittsburgh, PA 15282-0001. Offers M Acc, MBA, MS, MSISM, JD/MBA, MBA/MA, MBA/MES, MBA/MHMS, MBA/MLLS, MBA/MS, MBA/MSN, MSISM/MBA. *Accreditation:* AACSB. Part-time and evening/weekend programs available. *Faculty:* 61 full-time (16 women), 35 part-time/adjunct (11 women). *Students:* 81 full-time (34 women), 199 part-time (64 women); includes 9 minority (4 Black or African American, non-Hispanic/Latino; 3 Asian, non-Hispanic/Latino; 1 Hispanic/Latino; 1 Two or more races, non-Hispanic/Latino), 21 international. Average age 29. 324 applicants, 40% accepted, 120 enrolled. In 2011, 161 degrees awarded. *Entrance requirements:* For master's, GMAT, undergraduate transcripts, 2 letters of recommendation, current resume, personal statement. Additional exam requirements/recommendations for international students: Required—TOEFL (minimum score 577 paper-based; 233 computer-based; 90 iBT), TWE, or IELTS (minimum score 7). *Application deadline:* For fall admission, 6/1 priority date for domestic students, 5/1 for international students; for spring admission, 11/1 for domestic students, 10/1 for international students. Applications are processed on a rolling basis. Electronic applications accepted. *Expenses: Tuition:* Full-time $16,596; part-time $922 per credit. *Required fees:* $1584; $88 per credit. Tuition and fees vary according to program. *Financial support:* In 2011–12, 40 students received support, including 12 fellowships with partial tuition reimbursements available, 28 research assistantships with partial tuition reimbursements available; career-related internships or fieldwork, scholarships/grants, and unspecified assistantships also available. Financial award application deadline: 7/1; financial award applicants required to submit FAFSA. *Faculty research:* International business, investment management, business ethics, technology management, supply chain management, business strategy, finance. *Unit head:* Thomas J. Nist, Director of Graduate Programs, 412-396-6276, Fax: 412-396-1726, E-mail: nist@duq.edu. *Application contact:* Maria W. DeCrosta, Enrollment Manager, 412-396-5529, Fax: 412-396-1726, E-mail: decrostam@duq.edu. Web site: http://www.business.duq.edu/grad.

Duquesne University, School of Leadership and Professional Advancement, Pittsburgh, PA 15282-0001. Offers leadership (MS), including business ethics, community leadership, global leadership, information technology, leadership, liberal studies, professional administration, sports leadership. Part-time and evening/weekend programs available. Postbaccalaureate distance learning degree programs offered (no on-campus study). *Faculty:* 1 full-time (0 women), 88 part-time/adjunct (39 women). *Students:* 311 full-time (134 women), 151 part-time (68 women); includes 109 minority (69 Black or African American, non-Hispanic/Latino; 3 American Indian or Alaska Native, non-Hispanic/Latino; 11 Asian, non-Hispanic/Latino; 19 Hispanic/Latino; 1 Native Hawaiian or other Pacific Islander, non-Hispanic/Latino; 6 Two or more races, non-Hispanic/Latino), 9 international. Average age 35. 172 applicants, 73% accepted, 107 enrolled. In 2011, 67 degrees awarded. *Degree requirements:* For master's, capstone course. *Entrance requirements:* For master's, professional work experience, 500-word essay, resume, interview. Additional exam requirements/recommendations for international students: Required—TOEFL (minimum score 80 iBT). *Application deadline:* Applications are processed on a rolling basis. Application fee: $0. Electronic applications accepted. Application fee is waived when completed online. *Expenses: Tuition:* Full-time $16,596; part-time $922 per credit. *Required fees:* $1584; $88 per credit. Tuition and fees vary according to program. *Financial support:* Applicants required to submit FAFSA. *Unit head:* Dr. Dorothy Bassett, Dean, 412-396-2141, Fax: 412-396-4711, E-mail: bassettd@duq.edu. *Application contact:* Marianne Leister, Director of Student Services, 412-396-4933, Fax: 412-396-5072, E-mail: leister@duq.edu. Web site: http://www.duq.edu/leadership.

D'Youville College, Department of Business, Buffalo, NY 14201-1084. Offers business administration (MBA); international business (MS). Part-time and evening/weekend programs available. *Faculty:* 4 full-time (1 woman), 7 part-time/adjunct (2 women). *Students:* 54 full-time (25 women), 16 part-time (9 women); includes 16 minority (6 Black or African American, non-Hispanic/Latino; 2 Asian, non-Hispanic/Latino; 7 Hispanic/Latino; 1 Two or more races, non-Hispanic/Latino), 15 international. Average age 28. 87 applicants, 47% accepted, 26 enrolled. In 2011, 28 master's awarded. *Degree requirements:* For master's, one foreign language, project or thesis. *Entrance requirements:* For master's, minimum GPA of 3.0. Additional exam requirements/recommendations for international students: Required—TOEFL (minimum score 500 paper-based; 173 computer-based). *Application deadline:* For fall admission, 5/1 for international students; for spring admission, 9/1 for international students. Applications are processed on a rolling basis. Application fee: $25. Electronic applications accepted. *Expenses: Tuition:* Full-time $18,960; part-time $790 per credit hour. *Required fees:* $310. Tuition and fees vary according to degree level and program. *Financial support:* In 2011–12, 1 research assistantship with partial tuition reimbursement (averaging $3,000 per year) was awarded; career-related internships or fieldwork, Federal Work-Study, and scholarships/grants also available. Support available to part-time students. Financial award application deadline: 3/1; financial award applicants required to submit FAFSA. *Faculty research:* Assessment, accreditation, supply chain, online learning, adult learning. *Unit head:* Dr. Dion Daly, Chair, 716-829-8176, Fax: 716-829-7760. *Application contact:* Linda Fisher, Graduate Admissions Director, 716-829-8400, Fax: 716-829-7900, E-mail: graduateadmissions@dyc.edu. Web site: http://www.dyc.edu/academics/business/index.asp.

East Carolina University, Graduate School, College of Business, Greenville, NC 27858-4353. Offers MBA, MS. *Accreditation:* AACSB. Part-time and evening/weekend programs available. *Entrance requirements:* For master's, GMAT. Additional exam requirements/recommendations for international students: Required—TOEFL. *Application deadline:* For fall admission, 6/1 priority date for domestic students. Applications are processed on a rolling basis. Application fee: $50. *Expenses:* Tuition, state resident: full-time $3557; part-time $444.63 per semester hour. Tuition, nonresident: full-time $14,351; part-time $1793.88 per semester hour. *Required fees:* $2016; $252 per semester hour. Part-time tuition and fees vary according to course load, campus/location and program. *Financial support:* Research assistantships with partial tuition reimbursements, teaching assistantships with partial tuition reimbursements, and Federal Work-Study available. Support available to part-time students. Financial award application deadline: 6/1. *Unit head:* Dr. Stanley G. Eakins, Dean, 252-328-6966, E-mail: eakinss@ecu.edu. Web site: http://www.business.ecu.edu.

East Carolina University, Graduate School, College of Technology and Computer Science, Department of Technology Systems, Greenville, NC 27858-4353. Offers computer network professional (Certificate); industrial technology (MS), including computer networking management, digital communications, industrial distribution and logistics, information security, manufacturing, performance improvement, quality systems; information assurance (Certificate); Lean Six Sigma Black Belt (Certificate); occupational safety (MS); technology management (PhD); Website developer (Certificate). *Entrance requirements:* For master's and Certificate, GRE General Test or MAT, minimum GPA of 2.5; for doctorate, GRE General Test, related work experience. *Application deadline:* For fall admission, 6/1 priority date for domestic students. Applications are processed on a rolling basis. Application fee: $50. *Expenses:* Tuition, state resident: full-time $3557; part-time $444.63 per semester hour. Tuition, nonresident: full-time $14,351; part-time $1793.88 per semester hour. *Required fees:* $2016; $252 per semester hour. Part-time tuition and fees vary according to course load, campus/location and program. *Financial support:* Application deadline: 6/1. *Unit head:* Dr. Tijjani Mohammed, Interim Chair, 252-328-9668, E-mail: mohammedt@ecu.edu. Web site: http://www.ecu.edu/cs-tecs/techsystems/.

Eastern Illinois University, Graduate School, Lumpkin College of Business and Applied Sciences, Program in Business Administration, Charleston, IL 61920-3099. Offers accountancy (MBA, Certificate); general management (MBA). *Accreditation:* AACSB. Part-time programs available. *Entrance requirements:* For master's, GMAT. *Expenses:* Tuition, state resident: part-time $279 per credit hour. Tuition, nonresident: part-time $670 per credit hour. *Required fees:* $179.07 per credit hour. $1253 per semester.

Eastern Kentucky University, The Graduate School, College of Business and Technology, Program in Business Administration, Richmond, KY 40475-3102. Offers MBA. *Accreditation:* AACSB.

Eastern Mennonite University, Program in Business Administration, Harrisonburg, VA 22802-2462. Offers MBA. Part-time and evening/weekend programs available. *Degree requirements:* For master's, final capstone course. *Entrance requirements:* For master's, GMAT, minimum GPA of 2.5, 2 years of work experience, 2 letters of reference. Additional exam requirements/recommendations for international students: Required—TOEFL (minimum score 500 paper-based). *Expenses:* Contact institution. *Faculty research:* Information security, Anabaptist/Mennonite experiences and perspectives, limits of multi-cultural education, international development performance criteria.

Eastern Michigan University, Graduate School, College of Business, Department of Management, Ypsilanti, MI 48197. Offers human resources management and organizational development (MSHROD). Part-time and evening/weekend programs available. Postbaccalaureate distance learning degree programs offered (minimal on-campus study). *Faculty:* 19 full-time (9 women). *Students:* 30 full-time (22 women), 52 part-time (39 women); includes 18 minority (12 Black or African American, non-Hispanic/Latino; 4 Asian, non-Hispanic/Latino; 1 Hispanic/Latino; 1 Two or more races, non-Hispanic/Latino), 26 international. Average age 30. 50 applicants, 58% accepted, 10 enrolled. In 2011, 64 degrees awarded. *Degree requirements:* For master's, thesis optional. *Entrance requirements:* For master's, GMAT. Additional exam requirements/recommendations for international students: Required—TOEFL. *Application deadline:* For fall admission, 5/15 priority date for domestic students, 5/15 for international students; for winter admission, 10/15 priority date for domestic students, 10/15 for international students; for spring admission, 3/15 priority date for domestic students, 3/15 for international students. Applications are processed on a rolling basis. Application fee: $35. *Expenses:* Tuition, state resident: full-time $10,367; part-time $432 per credit hour. Tuition, nonresident: full-time $20,435; part-time $851 per credit hour. *Required fees:* $39 per credit hour. $46 per semester. One-time fee: $100. Tuition and fees vary according to course level, degree level and reciprocity agreements. *Financial support:* Fellowships, research assistantships with full tuition reimbursements, teaching assistantships with full tuition reimbursements, career-related internships or fieldwork, Federal Work-Study, institutionally sponsored loans, scholarships/grants, tuition waivers (partial), and unspecified assistantships available. Support available to part-time students. Financial award applicants required to submit FAFSA. *Unit head:* Dr. Fraya Wagner-Marsh, Department Head, 734-487-3240, Fax: 734-487-4100, E-mail: fraya.wagner@emich.edu. *Application contact:* K. Michelle Henry, Interim Director, Graduate Programs, 734-487-4444, Fax: 734-483-1316, E-mail: mhenry1@emich.edu.

Eastern Michigan University, Graduate School, College of Business, Programs in Business Administration, Ypsilanti, MI 48197. Offers business administration (MBA, Graduate Certificate); computer information systems (Graduate Certificate); e-business (MBA, Graduate Certificate); enterprise business intelligence (MBA); entrepreneurship (MBA, Graduate Certificate); finance (MBA, Graduate Certificate); human resources (MBA); human resources management (Graduate Certificate); information systems (MBA); internal auditing (MBA); international business (MBA, Graduate Certificate); marketing management (Graduate Certificate); nonprofit management (MBA); organizational development (Graduate Certificate); supply chain management (MBA, Graduate Certificate). *Accreditation:* AACSB. Part-time programs available. Postbaccalaureate distance learning degree programs offered (no on-campus study). *Students:* 79 full-time (39 women), 287 part-time (143 women); includes 55 minority (22 Black or African American, non-Hispanic/Latino; 24 Asian, non-Hispanic/Latino; 6 Hispanic/Latino; 3 Two or more races, non-Hispanic/Latino), 238 international. Average age 32. 317 applicants, 62% accepted, 89 enrolled. In 2011, 102 master's, 58 other advanced degrees awarded. *Entrance requirements:* For master's, GMAT (minimum score 450), minimum cumulative undergraduate GPA of 2.75. Additional exam requirements/recommendations for international students: Required—TOEFL. *Application deadline:* For fall admission, 5/15 for domestic students, 5/1 for international students; for winter admission, 10/15 for domestic students, 10/1 for international students; for spring admission, 3/15 for domestic students, 3/1 for international students. Applications are processed on a rolling basis. Application fee: $35. *Expenses:* Tuition, state resident: full-time $10,367; part-time $432 per credit hour. Tuition, nonresident: full-time $20,435; part-time $851 per credit hour. *Required fees:* $39 per credit hour. $46 per semester. One-time fee: $100. Tuition and fees vary according to course level, degree level and reciprocity agreements. *Financial support:* Fellowships, research assistantships with full tuition reimbursements, teaching assistantships with full tuition reimbursements, career-related internships or fieldwork, Federal Work-Study, institutionally sponsored loans, scholarships/grants, tuition waivers (partial), and unspecified assistantships available. Support available to part-time students. Financial award applicants required to submit FAFSA. *Unit head:* K. Michelle Henry, Director, Academic Services, 734-487-4444, Fax: 734-483-1316, E-mail: mhenry1@emich.edu. *Application contact:* Beste Windes, Advisor, 734-487-4444, Fax: 734-483-1316, E-mail: bwindes@emich.edu. Web site: http://www.emich.edu/public/cob/gr/grad.html.

Eastern Nazarene College, Adult and Graduate Studies, Program in Management, Quincy, MA 02170. Offers MSM.

Eastern New Mexico University, Graduate School, College of Business, Portales, NM 88130. Offers MBA. *Accreditation:* ACBSP. Part-time and evening/weekend programs available. Postbaccalaureate distance learning degree programs offered (no on-campus study). *Faculty:* 12 full-time (2 women), 1 (woman) part-time/adjunct. *Students:* 8 full-time (5 women), 87 part-time (54 women); includes 33 minority (4 Black or African American, non-Hispanic/Latino; 2 American Indian or Alaska Native, non-Hispanic/Latino; 3 Asian, non-Hispanic/Latino; 21 Hispanic/Latino; 1 Native Hawaiian or other Pacific Islander, non-Hispanic/Latino; 2 Two or more races, non-Hispanic/Latino), 9 international. Average age 33. 55 applicants, 78% accepted, 28 enrolled. In 2011, 17 degrees awarded. *Degree requirements:* For master's, comprehensive exam, comprehensive integrative project and presentation. *Entrance requirements:* For master's, GMAT (minimum score 450), minimum undergraduate GPA of 3.0. Additional exam requirements/recommendations for international students: Required—TOEFL (minimum score 550 paper-based; 213 computer-based; 79 iBT), IELTS (minimum score 6). *Application deadline:* For fall admission, 7/20 priority date for domestic students, 6/20 for international students; for spring admission, 12/15 priority date for domestic students, 11/15 for international students. Applications are processed on a rolling basis. Application fee: $10. Electronic applications accepted. *Financial support:* In 2011–12, 9 research assistantships with partial tuition reimbursements (averaging $4,250 per year) were awarded; scholarships/grants, tuition waivers (partial), and unspecified assistantships also available. Support available to part-time students. Financial award applicants required to submit FAFSA. *Unit head:* Dr. Veena Parboteeah, MBA Graduate Coordinator, 575-562-2442, Fax: 575-562-4331, E-mail: veena.parboteeah@enmu.edu. *Application contact:* Gail Crozier, Receptionist/Records Clerk, 575-562-2147, Fax: 575-562-2500, E-mail: gail.crozier@enmu.edu. Web site: http://business.enu.edu/.

Eastern Oregon University, Program in Business Administration, La Grande, OR 97850-2899. Offers MBA. Part-time programs available. Postbaccalaureate distance learning degree programs offered (minimal on-campus study). *Degree requirements:* For master's, thesis. *Entrance requirements:* For master's, GRE General Test.

Eastern University, School of Leadership and Development, St. Davids, PA 19087-3696. Offers economic development (MBA), including international development, urban development (MA, MBA); international development (MA), including global development, urban development (MA, MBA); nonprofit management (MS); organizational leadership (MA); M Div/MBA. Part-time and evening/weekend programs available. *Degree requirements:* For master's, thesis (for some programs). *Entrance requirements:* For master's, GMAT (MBA), minimum GPA of 2.5. *Expenses:* Contact institution. *Faculty research:* Micro-level economic development, China welfare and economic development, macroethics, micro- and macro-level economic development in transitional economics, organizational effectiveness.

Eastern University, School of Management Studies, St. Davids, PA 19087-3696. Offers health administration (MBA); management (MBA).

Eastern Washington University, Graduate Studies, College of Business and Public Administration, Business Administration Program, Cheney, WA 99004-2431. Offers MBA, MBA/MPA. *Accreditation:* AACSB. *Faculty:* 17 full-time (6 women). *Students:* 21 full-time (13 women), 37 part-time (7 women); includes 3 minority (1 American Indian or Alaska Native, non-Hispanic/Latino; 1 Asian, non-Hispanic/Latino; 1 Hispanic/Latino), 3 international. Average age 32. 112 applicants, 17% accepted, 19 enrolled. In 2011, 40 master's awarded. *Degree requirements:* For master's, comprehensive exam, thesis optional. *Entrance requirements:* For master's, GMAT, minimum GPA of 3.0. *Application deadline:* For fall admission, 4/1 priority date for domestic students; for spring admission, 1/15 for domestic students. Applications are processed on a rolling basis. Application fee: $50. *Financial support:* In 2011–12, 5 teaching assistantships with partial tuition reimbursements (averaging $7,000 per year) were awarded; career-related internships or fieldwork, Federal Work-Study, institutionally sponsored loans, scholarships/grants, health care benefits, tuition waivers (partial), and unspecified assistantships also available. Support available to part-time students. Financial award application deadline: 2/1. *Unit head:* Roberta Brooke, Director, 509-358-2270, Fax: 509-358-2267, E-mail: rbrooke@ewu.edu. *Application contact:* Prof. M. David Gorton, MBA Director, 509-358-2241, Fax: 509-358-2267, E-mail: mgorton@mailserver.ewu.edu. Web site: http://www.ewu.edu/cbpa.xml.

East Tennessee State University, School of Graduate Studies, College of Business and Technology, Johnson City, TN 37614. Offers M Acc, MBA, MS, Postbaccalaureate Certificate. *Accreditation:* AACSB. *Faculty:* 68 full-time (9 women), 5 part-time/adjunct (0 women). *Students:* 172 full-time (59 women), 75 part-time (22 women); includes 19 minority (4 Black or African American, non-Hispanic/Latino; 4 Asian, non-Hispanic/Latino; 7 Hispanic/Latino; 4 Two or more races, non-Hispanic/Latino), 25 international. Average age 29. In 2011, 133 master's, 7 other advanced degrees awarded. *Entrance requirements:* Additional exam requirements/recommendations for international students: Required—TOEFL (minimum score 550 paper-based; 213 computer-based; 79 iBT). Application fee: $35 ($45 for international students). *Expenses:* Tuition, state resident: full-time $7312; part-time $350 per credit hour. Tuition, nonresident: full-time $18,490; part-time $621 per credit hour. *Required fees:* $63 per credit hour. Tuition and fees vary according to course load and program. *Financial support:* In 2011–12, 119 students received support, including 54 research assistantships with full tuition reimbursements available, 16 teaching assistantships with full tuition reimbursements available. Financial award application deadline: 7/1; financial award applicants required to submit FAFSA. *Faculty research:* Artificial intelligence and accounting, profit vs. non-profit hospital comparisons, environmental compliance issues in manufacturing, international finance, case law on Americans with disabilities. *Total annual research expenditures:* $100,000. *Unit head:* Dr. Linda Garceau, Dean, 423-439-5314, Fax: 423-439-5274, E-mail: garceaul@etsu.edu. *Application contact:* School of Graduate Studies, 423-439-4221, Fax: 423-439-5624, E-mail: gradsch@etsu.edu. Web site: http://www.etsu.edu/cbat.

Edgewood College, Program in Business, Madison, WI 53711-1997. Offers accountancy (MS); accounting (MBA); business administration (MBA); finance (MBA); management (MBA); marketing (MBA); sustainability leadership (MBA). *Accreditation:* ACBSP. Part-time and evening/weekend programs available. *Students:* 24 full-time (15 women), 95 part-time (41 women); includes 9 minority (2 Black or African American, non-Hispanic/Latino; 4 Asian, non-Hispanic/Latino; 3 Hispanic/Latino), 7 international. Average age 33. In 2011, 43 master's awarded. *Entrance requirements:* For master's, GMAT (minimum score 430), minimum GPA of 2.75, 2 letters of recommendation. Additional exam requirements/recommendations for international students: Required—TOEFL (minimum score 213 computer-based). *Application deadline:* For fall admission, 8/15 for domestic students, 5/1 for international students; for spring admission, 1/8 for domestic students, 11/1 for international students. Applications are processed on a rolling basis. Application fee: $25. Electronic applications accepted. *Expenses: Tuition:* Part-time $747 per credit. Part-time tuition and fees vary according to program. *Financial support:* Career-related internships or fieldwork and scholarships/grants available. *Unit head:* Martin Preizler, Dean, 608-663-2898, Fax: 608-663-3291, E-mail: martinpreizler@edgewood.edu. *Application contact:* Joann Eastman, Admissions Counselor, 608-663-3250, Fax: 608-663-2214, E-mail: gps@edgewood.edu. Web site: http://www.edgewood.edu/Academics/Graduate.aspx.

Ellis University, MBA Program, Chicago, IL 60606-7204. Offers e-commerce (MBA); finance (MBA); general business (MBA); global management (MBA); health care administration (MBA); leadership (MBA); management of information systems (MBA); marketing (MBA); professional accounting (MBA); project management (MBA); public accounting (MBA); risk management (MBA).

Ellis University, Program in Management, Chicago, IL 60606-7204. Offers MS. *Degree requirements:* For master's, capstone course.

Elmhurst College, Graduate Programs, Program in Business Administration, Elmhurst, IL 60126-3296. Offers MBA. Part-time and evening/weekend programs available. *Faculty:* 3 full-time (1 woman), 9 part-time/adjunct (0 women). *Students:* 5 full-time (2 women), 62 part-time (23 women); includes 9 minority (5 Black or African American, non-Hispanic/Latino; 2 Asian, non-Hispanic/Latino; 2 Hispanic/Latino), 4 international. Average age 33. 51 applicants, 71% accepted, 29 enrolled. In 2011, 35 master's awarded. *Entrance requirements:* For master's, 3 recommendations, resume, statement of purpose. Additional exam requirements/recommendations for international students: Required—TOEFL (minimum score 550 paper-based; 213 computer-based). *Application deadline:* Applications are processed on a rolling basis. Application fee: $0. Electronic applications accepted. *Expenses:* Contact institution. *Financial support:* In 2011–12, 12 students received support. Federal Work-Study and scholarships/grants available. Support available to part-time students. Financial award application deadline: 6/1; financial award applicants required to submit FAFSA. *Unit head:* Elizabeth D. Kuebler, Director of Adult and Graduate Admission, 630-617-3300, Fax: 630-617-5501, E-mail: oaga@elmhurst.edu. *Application contact:* Director of Adult and Graduate Admission. Web site: http://public.elmhurst.edu/mba.

Elon University, Program in Business Administration, Elon, NC 27244-2010. Offers MBA. *Accreditation:* AACSB. Part-time and evening/weekend programs available. *Faculty:* 21 full-time (8 women). *Students:* 135 part-time (54 women). Average age 33. 100 applicants, 77% accepted, 57 enrolled. In 2011, 38 master's awarded. *Entrance requirements:* For master's, GMAT. Additional exam requirements/recommendations for international students: Required—TOEFL (minimum score 550 paper-based; 213 computer-based; 79 iBT). *Application deadline:* For fall admission, 8/1 priority date for domestic students; for spring admission, 2/1 priority date for domestic students. Applications are processed on a rolling basis. Application fee: $50. Electronic applications accepted. *Financial support:* Federal Work-Study and scholarships/grants available. Support available to part-time students. Financial award application deadline: 3/15; financial award applicants required to submit FAFSA. *Faculty research:* Business ethics, international business and global economics, sales force management, sustainable business practices, consumer behavior. *Unit head:* Dr. William Burpitt, Director, 336-278-5949, Fax: 336-278-5952, E-mail: wburpitt@elon.edu. *Application contact:* Art Fadde, Director of Graduate Admissions, 800-334-8448 Ext. 3, Fax: 336-278-7699, E-mail: afadde@elon.edu. Web site: http://www.elon.edu/mba/.

Embry-Riddle Aeronautical University–Daytona, Daytona Beach Campus Graduate Program, Department of Business Administration, Daytona Beach, FL 32114-3900. Offers MBA, MBA-AM. *Accreditation:* ACBSP. Part-time programs available. *Faculty:* 5 full-time (0 women), 5 part-time/adjunct (2 women). *Students:* 87 full-time (26 women), 43 part-time (15 women); includes 22 minority (5 Black or African American, non-Hispanic/Latino; 7 Asian, non-Hispanic/Latino; 10 Hispanic/Latino), 45 international. Average age 29. 84 applicants, 55% accepted, 32 enrolled. In 2011, 60 master's awarded. *Degree requirements:* For master's, thesis or alternative. *Entrance requirements:* For master's, GMAT, minimum GPA of 2.5. Additional exam requirements/recommendations for international students: Required—TOEFL (minimum score 550 paper-based; 213 computer-based; 79 iBT). *Application deadline:* For fall admission, 6/1 priority date for domestic students, 6/1 for international students; for spring admission, 11/1 priority date for domestic students, 10/1 for international students. Applications are processed on a rolling basis. Application fee: $50. Electronic applications accepted. *Expenses: Tuition:* Full-time $14,340; part-time $1195 per credit hour. *Financial support:* In 2011–12, 21 students received support, including 7 research assistantships with partial tuition reimbursements available (averaging $2,873 per year); teaching assistantships, career-related internships or fieldwork, Federal Work-Study, and unspecified assistantships also available. Support available to part-time students. Financial award application deadline: 4/15; financial award applicants required to submit FAFSA. *Faculty research:* Aircraft safety operations analysis, energy consumption analysis, statistical analysis of general aviation accidents, airport funding strategies, industry assessment and marketing analysis for ENAER aerospace. *Unit head:* Dr. Dawna Rhoades, MBA Program Coordinator, 386-226-7756, E-mail: dawna.rhoades@erau.edu. *Application contact:* Flavia Carreiro, Assistant Director, International and Graduate Admissions, 800-388-3728, Fax: 386-226-7070, E-mail: graduate.admissions@erau.edu. Web site: http://daytonabeach.erau.edu/cob/departments/graduate-degrees/master-business-administration/index.html.

See Display on page 659 and Close-Up on page 675.

Embry-Riddle Aeronautical University–Worldwide, Worldwide Headquarters - Graduate Degrees and Programs, Program in Business Administration for Aviation, Daytona Beach, FL 32114-3900. Offers business administration (MBAA); modeling and simulation management (Graduate Certificate). *Faculty:* 14 full-time (3 women), 102 part-time/adjunct (26 women). *Students:* 964 full-time (216 women), 882 part-time (180 women); includes 320 minority (123 Black or African American, non-Hispanic/Latino; 9 American Indian or Alaska Native, non-Hispanic/Latino; 40 Asian, non-Hispanic/Latino; 143 Hispanic/Latino; 2 Native Hawaiian or other Pacific Islander, non-Hispanic/Latino; 3 Two or more races, non-Hispanic/Latino), 20 international. Average age 37. 735 applicants, 76% accepted, 280 enrolled. In 2011, 278 master's awarded. *Degree requirements:* For master's, comprehensive exam (for some programs), thesis (for some programs). *Entrance requirements:* Additional exam requirements/recommendations for international students: Recommended—TOEFL (minimum score 550 paper-based; 213 computer-based; 79 iBT). Application fee: $50. *Expenses: Tuition:* Part-time $395 per credit hour. Tuition and fees vary according to degree level and program. *Financial support:* In 2011–12, 221 students received support. *Faculty research:* Healthcare operations management, humanitarian logistics, supply chain risk management, collaborative supply chain management, intersection of collaborative supply chain management and the learning organization, development of assessment tool measuring supply chain collaborative capacity, teaching effectiveness, teaching quality, management style effectiveness, aeronautics, small/medium-sized business leadership study, leadership factors, critical thinking, efficacy of ePortfolio. *Total annual research expenditures:* $16,331. *Unit head:* Dr. Kees Rietsema, Department Chair, 602-904-1295, E-mail: kees.rietsema@erau.edu. *Application contact:* Linda Dammer, Director of Admissions, 386-226-6396 Ext. 1, Fax: 386-226-6984, E-mail: worldwide@erau.edu.

Emmanuel College, Graduate and Professional Programs, Graduate Programs in Management, Boston, MA 02115. Offers biopharmaceutical leadership (MSM); human resource management (MSM, Graduate Certificate); management (MSM); management and leadership (Graduate Certificate); research administration (MSM, Graduate Certificate). Part-time and evening/weekend programs available. Postbaccalaureate distance learning degree programs offered (no on-campus study). *Faculty:* 60 part-time/adjunct (24 women). *Students:* 6 full-time (4 women), 216 part-time (155 women); includes 53 minority (28 Black or African American, non-Hispanic/Latino; 1 American Indian or Alaska Native, non-Hispanic/Latino; 10 Asian, non-Hispanic/Latino; 14 Hispanic/Latino). Average age 34. 61 applicants, 75% accepted, 39 enrolled. In 2011, 76 master's, 29 other advanced degrees awarded. *Degree requirements:* For master's, thesis or alternative, 36 credits, including a 6-credit capstone project. *Entrance requirements:* For master's, interview, essay, resume, 2 letters of recommendation, bachelor's degree; for Graduate Certificate, transcripts from all regionally-accredited institutions attended (showing proof of bachelor's degree completion), 2 letters of recommendation, essay, resume, interview. Additional exam requirements/recommendations for international students: Required—TOEFL (minimum score 600 paper-based; 250 computer-based; 106 iBT) or IELTS (minimum score 6.5). *Application deadline:* For fall admission, 7/31 priority date for domestic students; for spring admission, 11/30 priority date for domestic students. Applications are processed on a rolling basis. Application fee: $0. Electronic applications accepted. *Expenses: Tuition:* Part-time $2139 per course. Tuition and fees vary according to program and reciprocity agreements. *Financial support:* Applicants required to submit FAFSA. *Unit head:* Dr. Joyce DeLeo, Vice President of Academic Affairs, 617-735-9700, Fax: 617-507-0434, E-mail: gpp@emmanuel.edu. *Application contact:* Enrollment Counselor, 617-735-9700, Fax: 617-507-0434, E-mail: gpp@emmanuel.edu. Web site: http://gpp.emmanuel.edu.

Emory University, Goizueta Business School, Doctoral Program in Business, Atlanta, GA 30322-1100. Offers accounting (PhD); finance (PhD); information systems (PhD); marketing (PhD); organization and management (PhD). *Faculty:* 56 full-time (13 women). *Students:* 37 full-time (17 women); includes 21 minority (20 Asian, non-Hispanic/Latino; 1 Hispanic/Latino). Average age 29. 240 applicants, 6% accepted, 11 enrolled. In 2011, 5 doctorates awarded. *Degree requirements:* For doctorate, comprehensive exam, thesis/dissertation. *Entrance requirements:* For doctorate, GMAT (strongly preferred) or GRE. Additional exam requirements/recommendations for international students: Required—TOEFL (minimum score 250 computer-based). *Application deadline:* For fall admission, 1/3 priority date for domestic students, 1/1 for international students. Application fee: $50. Electronic applications accepted. *Expenses: Tuition:* Full-time $34,800. *Required fees:* $1300. *Financial support:* In 2011–12, 37 students received support. *Unit head:* Dr. Lawrence Benveniste, Dean, 404-727-6377, Fax: 404-727-0868, E-mail: larry_benveniste@bus.emory.edu. *Application contact:* Allison Gilmore, Director of Admissions and Student Services, 404-727-6353, Fax: 404-727-5337, E-mail: phd@bus.emory.edu.

Emory University, Goizueta Business School, Evening MBA Program, Atlanta, GA 30322-1100. Offers MBA. Part-time and evening/weekend programs available. *Faculty:* 75 full-time (19 women), 17 part-time/adjunct (2 women). *Students:* 273 part-time (65 women); includes 73 minority (20 Black or African American, non-Hispanic/Latino; 39 Asian, non-Hispanic/Latino; 13 Hispanic/Latino; 1 Two or more races, non-Hispanic/Latino), 45 international. Average age 30. 171 applicants, 71% accepted, 85 enrolled. In 2011, 112 master's awarded. *Entrance requirements:* For master's, GMAT. Additional exam requirements/recommendations for international students: Required—TOEFL; Recommended—IELTS, TWE. *Application deadline:* For fall admission, 7/20 for domestic students. Applications are processed on a rolling basis. Application fee: $150. Electronic applications accepted. *Expenses: Tuition:* Full-time $34,800. *Required fees:* $1300. *Financial support:* In 2011–12, 133 students received support. Application deadline: 6/1; applicants required to submit FAFSA. *Unit head:* Dr. Lawrence Benveniste, Dean, 404-727-6377, Fax: 404-727-0868, E-mail: larry_benveniste@bus.emory.edu. *Application contact:* Julie Barefoot, Associate Dean, 404-727-6311, Fax: 404-727-4612, E-mail: admissions@bus.emory.edu.

Emory University, Goizueta Business School, Executive MBA Program, Atlanta, GA 30322-1100. Offers MBA. Part-time and evening/weekend programs available. *Faculty:* 71 full-time (14 women), 20 part-time/adjunct (3 women). *Students:* 74 full-time (26 women); includes 23 minority (12 Black or African American, non-Hispanic/Latino; 9 Asian, non-Hispanic/Latino; 1 Hispanic/Latino; 1 Two or more races, non-Hispanic/Latino), 7 international. Average age 37. 83 applicants, 75% accepted, 33 enrolled. In 2011, 118 master's awarded. *Degree requirements:* For master's, completion of lock-step program with minimum of 54 credit hours, one elective course, global business practices with 10-day international travel component. *Entrance requirements:* For master's, GMAT. Additional exam requirements/recommendations for international students: Required—TOEFL (minimum score 600 paper-based; 250 computer-based; 100 iBT), IELTS (minimum score 7). *Application deadline:* For fall admission, 7/15 for domestic students. Applications are processed on a rolling basis. Application fee: $150. Electronic applications accepted. *Expenses: Tuition:* Full-time $34,800. *Required fees:* $1300. *Financial support:* Applicants required to submit FAFSA. *Unit head:* Jonathan Darsey, Associate Dean, 404-727-9040, Fax: 404-727-4936, E-mail: jonathan.p.darsey@emory.edu. *Application contact:* Julie Barefoot, Assistant Dean of Admissions, 404-727-6638, Fax: 404-727-4612, E-mail: julie_barefoot@bus.emory.edu.

Emory University, Goizueta Business School, Full Time MBA Program, Atlanta, GA 30322-1100. Offers MBA. *Faculty:* 79 full-time (11 women), 25 part-time/adjunct (12 women). *Students:* 313 full-time (93 women); includes 74 minority (29 Black or African American, non-Hispanic/Latino; 1 American Indian or Alaska Native, non-Hispanic/Latino; 28 Asian, non-Hispanic/Latino; 16 Hispanic/Latino), 80 international. Average age 29. 1,120 applicants, 32% accepted, 140 enrolled. In 2011, 206 master's awarded. *Entrance requirements:* For master's, GMAT. Additional exam requirements/recommendations for international students: Required—TOEFL (minimum score 600 paper-based; 100 iBT), IELTS, Pearson Test of English. *Application deadline:* For fall admission, 12/1 for domestic and international students; for winter admission, 2/1 priority date for domestic students, 2/1 for international students; for spring admission, 3/1 priority date for domestic students. Applications are processed on a rolling basis. Application fee: $150. Electronic applications accepted. *Expenses: Tuition:* Full-time $34,800. *Required fees:* $1300. *Financial support:* In 2011–12, 295 students received support. Fellowships, research assistantships, teaching assistantships, career-related internships or fieldwork, Federal Work-Study, institutionally sponsored loans, scholarships/grants, and unspecified assistantships available. Financial award application deadline: 2/1; financial award applicants required to submit FAFSA. *Unit head:* Brian Mitchell, Associate Dean, 404-727-4824, Fax: 404-712-9648, E-mail: brian.mitchell@emory.edu. *Application contact:* Julie Barefoot, Associate Dean, 404-727-6311, Fax: 404-727-4612, E-mail: admissions@emory.edu.

Emporia State University, Graduate School, School of Business, Department of Business Administration and Education, Program in Business Administration, Emporia, KS 66801-5087. Offers MBA. Part-time and evening/weekend programs available. Postbaccalaureate distance learning degree programs offered (no on-campus study). *Students:* 79 full-time (40 women), 50 part-time (26 women); includes 10 minority (1 Black or African American, non-Hispanic/Latino; 3 Asian, non-Hispanic/Latino; 4 Hispanic/Latino; 2 Two or more races, non-Hispanic/Latino), 61 international. 36 applicants, 94% accepted, 26 enrolled. In 2011, 47 master's awarded. *Entrance requirements:* For master's, GRE, 15 undergraduate credits in business, minimum undergraduate GPA of 2.7 in last 60 hours. Additional exam requirements/recommendations for international students: Required—TOEFL (minimum score 520 paper-based; 133 computer-based; 68 iBT). *Application deadline:* For fall admission, 8/15 for domestic students. Application fee: $30 ($75 for international students). *Expenses:* Tuition, state resident: full-time $2342; part-time $195 per credit hour. Tuition, nonresident: full-time $7254; part-time $605 per credit hour. *Required fees:* $66 per credit hour. Tuition and fees vary according to campus/location. *Financial support:* Career-related internships or fieldwork, health care benefits, and unspecified assistantships available. *Unit head:* Dr. Bill Barnes, Director, MBA Program, 620-341-5456, E-mail: wbarnes@emporia.edu. Web site: http://www.emporia.edu/business/programs/mba/.

Endicott College, Van Loan School of Graduate and Professional Studies, Program in Business Administration, Beverly, MA 01915-2096. Offers MBA. Part-time and evening/weekend programs available. *Faculty:* 2 full-time (1 woman), 24 part-time/adjunct (6 women). *Students:* 93 full-time (40 women), 75 part-time (36 women); includes 24 minority (11 Black or African American, non-Hispanic/Latino; 3 Asian, non-Hispanic/Latino; 10 Hispanic/Latino), 15 international. Average age 33. 100 applicants, 84% accepted, 74 enrolled. In 2011, 76 master's awarded. *Degree requirements:* For master's, thesis, project. *Entrance requirements:* For master's, letters of recommendation, resume. Additional exam requirements/recommendations for international students: Required—TOEFL. *Application deadline:* Applications are processed on a rolling basis. Application fee: $50. Electronic applications accepted. *Expenses:* Contact institution. *Financial support:* Tuition waivers (full) available. Financial award applicants required to submit FAFSA. *Faculty research:* Adult learning and development, supply chain management, marketing, ethics. *Unit head:* Richard Benedetto, Associate Dean of Graduate School, 978-232-2744, Fax: 978-232-3000, E-mail: rbenedet@endicott.edu. Web site: http://www.endicott.edu/GradProf/GPSGradMBA.aspx.

ESSEC Business School, Graduate Programs, Paris, France. Offers business administration (PhD); executive business administration (MBA); global business administration (MBA); hospitality management (MBA); international luxury brand management (MBA); management (MSM).

Everest University, Department of Business Administration, Tampa, FL 33614-5899. Offers accounting (MBA); human resources (MBA); international business (MBA). Part-time and evening/weekend programs available. *Degree requirements:* For master's, thesis optional. *Entrance requirements:* For master's, GMAT or GRE General Test, minimum GPA of 3.0.

Everest University, Division of Business Administration, Orlando, FL 32810-5674. Offers MBA. Part-time and evening/weekend programs available. *Degree requirements:* For master's, thesis or alternative.

Everest University, Graduate Programs,. Jacksonville, FL 32256. Offers business (MBA); criminal justice (MS).

Everest University, Program in Business Administration, Melbourne, FL 32935-6657. Offers MBA.

Everest University, Program in Business Administration, Tampa, FL 33619. Offers MBA. Part-time and evening/weekend programs available. Postbaccalaureate distance learning degree programs offered (minimal on-campus study). *Entrance requirements:* Additional exam requirements/recommendations for international students: Required—TOEFL (minimum score 550 paper-based; 213 computer-based).

Everest University, Program in Business Administration, Orlando, FL 32819. Offers accounting (MBA); general management (MBA); human resources (MBA); international management (MBA).

Everest University, School of Business, Pompano Beach, FL 33062. Offers MBA. Part-time and evening/weekend programs available. *Entrance requirements:* For master's, minimum GPA of 3.0. *Faculty research:* E-learning.

Everglades University, Graduate Programs, Program in Business Administration, Boca Raton, FL 33431. Offers MBA. *Entrance requirements:* Additional exam requirements/recommendations for international students: Recommended—TOEFL (minimum score 500 paper-based; 173 computer-based). Electronic applications accepted.

Excelsior College, School of Business and Technology, Albany, NY 12203-5159. Offers business administration (MBA); cybersecurity (MS); cybersecurity management (MBA, Graduate Certificate); human performance technology (MBA); information security (MBA); leadership (MBA); technology management (MBA). Part-time and evening/weekend programs available. Postbaccalaureate distance learning degree programs offered (no on-campus study).

Fairfield University, Charles F. Dolan School of Business, Fairfield, CT 06824-5195. Offers accounting (MBA, MS, CAS); accounting information systems (MBA, CAS); entrepreneurship (MBA, CAS); finance (MBA, MS, CAS); general management (MBA, CAS); human resource management (MBA, CAS); information systems and operations (MBA); information systems and operations management (CAS); international business (MBA, CAS); marketing (MBA, CAS); taxation (MBA, CAS). *Accreditation:* AACSB. Part-time and evening/weekend programs available. *Faculty:* 23 full-time (9 women), 3 part-time/adjunct (1 woman). *Students:* 87 full-time (37 women), 118 part-time (42 women); includes 13 minority (4 Black or African American, non-Hispanic/Latino; 4 Asian, non-Hispanic/Latino; 5 Hispanic/Latino), 9 international. Average age 29. 126 applicants, 47% accepted, 35 enrolled. In 2011, 90 master's awarded. *Degree requirements:* For master's, capstone course. *Entrance requirements:* For master's, GMAT (minimum score 500), 2 letters of reference, resume, minimum GPA of 3.0. Additional exam requirements/recommendations for international students: Required—TOEFL (minimum score 550 paper-based; 213 computer-bases; 80 iBT) or IELTS (minimum score 6.5). *Application deadline:* For fall admission, 5/15 for international students; for spring admission, 10/15 for international students. Applications are processed on a rolling basis. Application fee: $60. Electronic applications accepted. *Expenses:* Contact institution. *Financial support:* In 2011–12, 50 students received support, including 2 research assistantships (averaging $6,500 per year); scholarships/grants, unspecified assistantships, and merit-based one-time entrance scholarship also available. Financial award applicants required to submit FAFSA. *Faculty research:* Optimization strategies, international finance, consumer behavior, financial market volatility, Internet marketing, supply chain analysis, tax issues. *Unit head:* Dr. Donald Gibson, Dean, 203-254-4000 Ext. 4070, Fax: 203-254-4105, E-mail: dgibson@fairfield.edu. *Application contact:* Marianne Gumpper, Director of Graduate and Continuing Studies Admission, 203-254-4184, Fax: 203-254-4073, E-mail: gradadmis@fairfield.edu. Web site: http://www.fairfield.edu/dsb/dsb_grad_1.html.

Fairleigh Dickinson University, College at Florham, Anthony J. Petrocelli College of Continuing Studies, School of Administrative Science, Program in Administrative Science, Madison, NJ 07940-1099. Offers MAS.

Fairleigh Dickinson University, College at Florham, Silberman College of Business, Madison, NJ 07940-1099. Offers EMBA, MBA, MS, Certificate, MA/MBA, MBA/MA. *Accreditation:* AACSB. Part-time and evening/weekend programs available.

Fairleigh Dickinson University, College at Florham, Silberman College of Business, Departments of Management, Marketing, and Entrepreneurial Studies, Program in Management, Madison, NJ 07940-1099. Offers evolving technology (Certificate); management (MBA); MBA/MA.

Fairleigh Dickinson University, College at Florham, Silberman College of Business, Executive MBA Programs, Executive MBA Program in Management, Madison, NJ 07940-1099. Offers EMBA.

Fairleigh Dickinson University, Metropolitan Campus, Anthony J. Petrocelli College of Continuing Studies, School of Administrative Science, Program in Administrative Science, Teaneck, NJ 07666-1914. Offers MAS, Certificate.

Fairleigh Dickinson University, Metropolitan Campus, Silberman College of Business, Teaneck, NJ 07666-1914. Offers EMBA, MBA, MS, Certificate, MBA/MA. *Accreditation:* AACSB. *Entrance requirements:* For master's, GMAT.

Fairleigh Dickinson University, Metropolitan Campus, Silberman College of Business, Departments of Management, Marketing, and Entrepreneurial Studies, Program in Management, Teaneck, NJ 07666-1914. Offers management (MBA); management information systems (Certificate). *Accreditation:* AACSB.

Fairmont State University, Program in Business Administration, Fairmont, WV 26554. Offers MBA. *Accreditation:* ACBSP. Part-time and evening/weekend programs available. Postbaccalaureate distance learning degree programs offered. *Faculty:* 7 part-time/adjunct (1 woman). *Students:* 23 full-time (13 women), 35 part-time (14 women); includes 2 minority (1 Hispanic/Latino; 1 Two or more races, non-Hispanic/Latino), 4 international. Average age 30. 4 applicants, 0% accepted, 0 enrolled. *Entrance requirements:* For master's, GRE, MAT, or GMAT, minimum overall undergraduate GPA of 2.75 or 3.0 on the last 60 hours. *Application deadline:* For fall admission, 5/1 for domestic and international students. Application fee: $40. *Expenses:* Tuition, state resident: full-time $5900. Tuition, nonresident: full-time $12,596. *Unit head:* Dr. Tim Oxley, Director, 304-367-4728, Fax: - 304-367-4613, E-mail: timothy.oxley@fairmontstate.edu. Web site: http://www.fairmontstate.edu/graduatestudies/MBA_program.asp.

Fashion Institute of Technology, School of Graduate Studies, Program in Global Fashion Management, New York, NY 10001-5992. Offers MPS. Offered in collaboration with Hong Kong Polytechnic University and Institut Francais de la Mode. *Entrance requirements:* Additional exam requirements/recommendations for international students: Required—TOEFL (minimum score 550 paper-based; 213 computer-based). Electronic applications accepted.

See Display below and Close-Up on page 217.

Faulkner University, Harris College of Business and Executive Education, Montgomery, AL 36109-3398. Offers management (MSM).

Fayetteville State University, Graduate School, Program in Business Administration, Fayetteville, NC 28301-4298. Offers MBA. *Accreditation:* AACSB. *Faculty:* 15 full-time (4 women). *Students:* 20 full-time (8 women), 40 part-time (20 women); includes 33 minority (23 Black or African American, non-Hispanic/Latino; 1 American Indian or Alaska Native, non-Hispanic/Latino; 4 Asian, non-Hispanic/Latino; 4 Hispanic/Latino; 1 Native Hawaiian or other Pacific Islander, non-Hispanic/Latino), 2 international. Average age 33. 15 applicants, 100% accepted, 15 enrolled. In 2011, 15 master's awarded. *Entrance requirements:* For master's, GMAT. *Application deadline:* For fall admission, 4/15 for domestic students; for spring admission, 10/15 for domestic students. *Faculty research:* Business ethics, optimization and business simulation, consumer behavior, e-commerce and supply chain management, financial institutions. *Total annual research expenditures:* $15,000. *Unit head:* Dr. Assad Tavakoli, MBA Director/Assistant Dean, 910-672-1527, Fax: 910-672-1849, E-mail: atavakoli@uncfsu.edu. *Application contact:* Katrina Hoffman, Graduate Admissions Officer, 910-672-1374, Fax: 910-672-1470, E-mail: khoffma1@uncfsu.edu.

Felician College, Program in Business, Lodi, NJ 07644-2117. Offers innovation and entrepreneurship (MBA). Part-time and evening/weekend programs available. *Students:* 3 full-time (2 women), 80 part-time (46 women); includes 16 minority (8 Black or African American, non-Hispanic/Latino; 3 Asian, non-Hispanic/Latino; 5 Hispanic/Latino), 5 international. 28 applicants, 89% accepted, 24 enrolled. *Entrance requirements:* For master's, GMAT. *Application deadline:* Applications are processed on a rolling basis. Application fee: $40. *Expenses: Tuition:* Part-time $925 per credit. *Required fees:* $262.50 per semester. Part-time tuition and fees vary according to class time and student level. *Unit head:* Dr. Beth Castiglia, Dean, Division of Business and Management Services, 201-559-6140, E-mail: mctaggartp@felician.edu. *Application contact:* Nicole Vitale, Assistant Director of Graduate Admissions, 201-559-6077, Fax: 201-559-6138, E-mail: graduate@felician.edu. Web site: http://www.felician.edu/divisions/business-management-sciences/graduate.

See Display on next page and Close-Up on page 219.

Ferris State University, College of Business, Big Rapids, MI 49307. Offers business intelligence (MBA); design and innovation management (MBA); incident response (MBA); information security and intelligence (MS, MSISM), including business intelligence (MS), incident response (MSISM), project management (MSISM); management tools and concepts (MBA); project management (MBA). *Accreditation:* ACBSP. Part-time and evening/weekend programs available. Postbaccalaureate distance learning degree programs offered (minimal on-campus study). *Faculty:* 9 full-time (3 women), 2 part-time/adjunct (both women). *Students:* 22 full-time (7 women), 98 part-time (50 women); includes 14 minority (3 Black or African American, non-Hispanic/Latino; 4 American Indian or Alaska Native, non-Hispanic/Latino; 2 Asian, non-Hispanic/Latino; 2 Hispanic/Latino; 3 Two or more races, non-Hispanic/Latino), 3 international. Average age 34. 58 applicants, 79% accepted, 10 enrolled. In 2011, 56 master's awarded. *Degree requirements:* For master's, comprehensive exam, thesis (for MSISM). *Entrance requirements:* For master's, GRE or GMAT (waived if GPA is 3.5 or better), minimum GPA of 3.0 in junior/senior level classes, 2.75 overall; writing sample; 3 letters of reference; resume. Additional exam requirements/recommendations for international students: Required—TOEFL (minimum score 500 paper-based; 173 computer-based; 67 iBT). *Application deadline:* For fall admission, 7/1 priority date for domestic students,

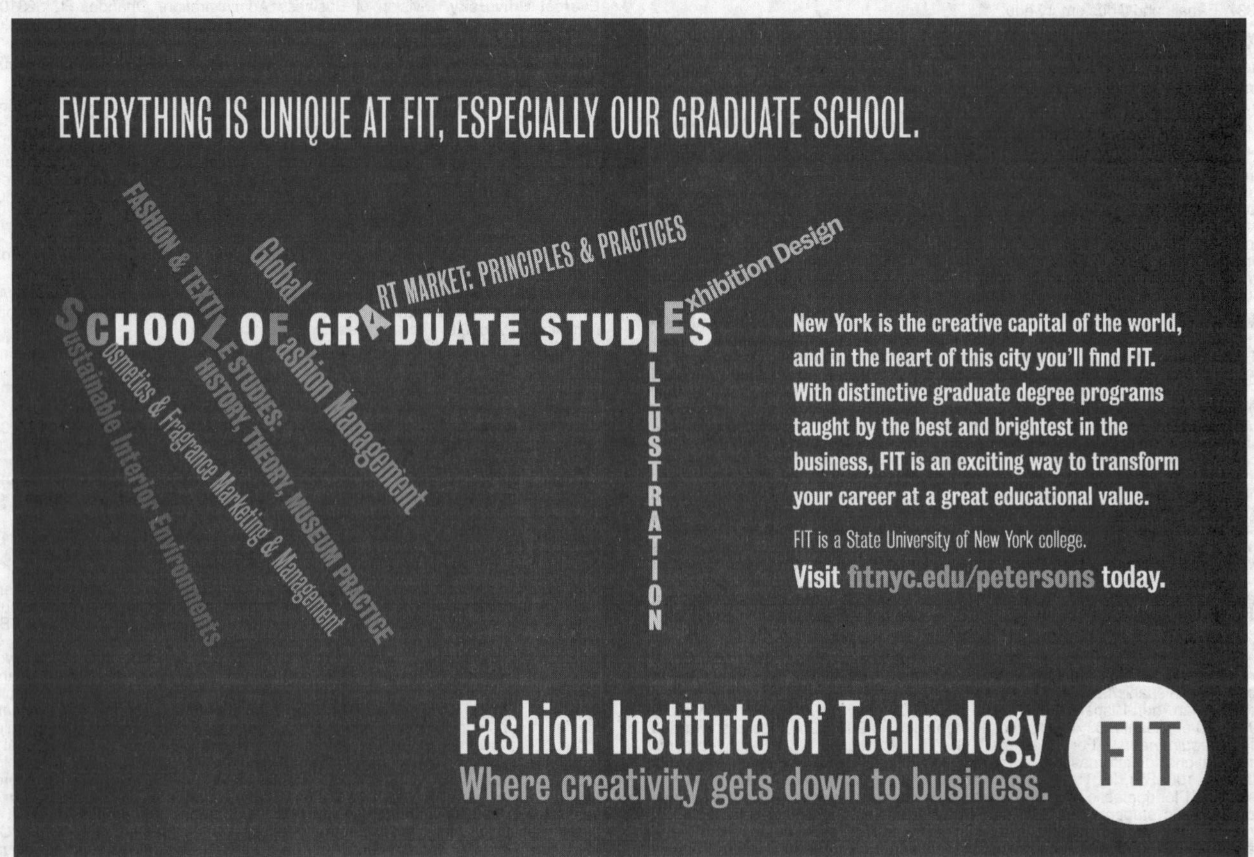

6/15 for international students; for winter admission, 11/1 priority date for domestic students, 10/15 for international students; for spring admission, 3/1 priority date for domestic students, 2/15 for international students. Applications are processed on a rolling basis. Application fee: $30. Electronic applications accepted. Application fee is waived when completed online. *Financial support:* Career-related internships or fieldwork, Federal Work-Study, scholarships/grants, and unspecified assistantships available. Support available to part-time students. Financial award application deadline: 3/15; financial award applicants required to submit FAFSA. *Faculty research:* Quality improvement, client/server end-user computing, information management and policy, security, digital forensics. *Unit head:* Dr. David Steenstra, Department Chair, 231-591-2168, Fax: 231-591-3548, E-mail: yosts@ferris.edu. *Application contact:* Shannon Yost, Department Secretary, 231-591-2168, Fax: 231-591-3548, E-mail: yosts@ferris.edu. Web site: http://cbgp.ferris.edu/.

Fitchburg State University, Division of Graduate and Continuing Education, Program in Business Administration, Fitchburg, MA 01420-2697. Offers accounting (MBA); human resource management (MBA); management (MBA). Part-time and evening/weekend programs available. Postbaccalaureate distance learning degree programs offered (no on-campus study). *Students:* 24 full-time (9 women), 57 part-time (29 women); includes 10 minority (6 Black or African American, non-Hispanic/Latino; 2 Hispanic/Latino; 2 Two or more races, non-Hispanic/Latino), 10 international. Average age 32. 32 applicants, 97% accepted, 27 enrolled. In 2011, 61 master's awarded. *Entrance requirements:* Additional exam requirements/recommendations for international students: Required—TOEFL (minimum score 550 paper-based; 213 computer-based; 79 iBT). *Application deadline:* For fall admission, 7/15 for international students; for spring admission, 12/1 for international students. Applications are processed on a rolling basis. Application fee: $25 ($50 for international students). Electronic applications accepted. *Expenses:* Tuition, state resident: full-time $2700; part-time $150 per credit. Tuition, nonresident: full-time $2700; part-time $150 per credit. *Required fees:* $2286; $127 per credit. *Financial support:* In 2011–12, research assistantships with partial tuition reimbursements (averaging $5,500 per year) were awarded; Federal Work-Study, scholarships/grants, and unspecified assistantships also available. Support available to part-time students. Financial award application deadline: 3/1; financial award applicants required to submit FAFSA. *Unit head:* Joseph McAloon, Chair, 978-665-3745, Fax: 978-665-3658, E-mail: gce@fitchburgstate.edu. *Application contact:* Kay Reynolds, Director of Admissions, 978-665-3144, Fax: 978-665-4540, E-mail: admissions@fitchburgstate.edu. Web site: http://www.fitchburgstate.edu.

Florida Agricultural and Mechanical University, Division of Graduate Studies, Research, and Continuing Education, School of Business and Industry, Tallahassee, FL 32307-3200. Offers accounting (MBA); finance (MBA); management information systems (MBA); marketing (MBA). *Degree requirements:* For master's, residency. *Entrance requirements:* For master's, GMAT, minimum GPA of 3.0.

Florida Atlantic University, College of Business, Boca Raton, FL 33431-0991. Offers Exec MBA, M Ac, M Tax, MBA, MHA, MS, PhD, Certificate. *Accreditation:* AACSB. Part-time and evening/weekend programs available. Postbaccalaureate distance learning degree programs offered (minimal on-campus study). *Faculty:* 124 full-time (44 women), 100 part-time/adjunct (25 women). *Students:* 426 full-time (185 women), 811 part-time (393 women); includes 469 minority (163 Black or African American, non-Hispanic/Latino; 1 American Indian or Alaska Native, non-Hispanic/Latino; 81 Asian, non-Hispanic/Latino; 196 Hispanic/Latino; 1 Native Hawaiian or other Pacific Islander, non-Hispanic/Latino; 27 Two or more races, non-Hispanic/Latino), 57 international. Average age 30. 1,239 applicants, 48% accepted, 222 enrolled. In 2011, 490 master's, 4 doctorates awarded. *Degree requirements:* For master's, thesis optional; for doctorate, comprehensive exam, thesis/dissertation. *Entrance requirements:* For master's, GMAT, minimum GPA of 3.0; for doctorate, GMAT, minimum graduate GPA of 3.5. Additional exam requirements/recommendations for international students: Required—TOEFL (minimum score 600 paper-based; 250 computer-based). *Application deadline:* For fall admission, 5/1 priority date for domestic students, 2/15 for international students; for spring admission, 4/1 priority date for domestic students, 1/15 for international students. Applications are processed on a rolling basis. Application fee: $30. *Expenses: Tuition, area resident:* Part-time $343.02 per credit hour. Tuition, state resident: full-time $8232. Tuition, nonresident: full-time $23,931; part-time $997.14 per credit hour. *Financial support:* Fellowships with partial tuition reimbursements, research assistantships with partial tuition reimbursements, teaching assistantships with full tuition reimbursements, career-related internships or fieldwork, Federal Work-Study, institutionally sponsored loans, tuition waivers (full and partial), and unspecified assistantships available. Support available to part-time students. Financial award application deadline: 3/1. *Faculty research:* International business, MIS, financial decision-making, marketing policy, strategy. *Unit head:* Dr. Dennis Coates, Dean, 561-297-3635, Fax: 561-297-3686, E-mail: coates@fau.edu. *Application contact:* Fredrick G. Taylor, Graduate Adviser, 561-297-3196, Fax: 561-297-1315, E-mail: ftaylor@fau.edu. Web site: http://business.fau.edu/index.aspx.

Florida Gulf Coast University, Lutgert College of Business, Master of Business Administration Program, Fort Myers, FL 33965-6565. Offers MBA. *Accreditation:* AACSB. Part-time and evening/weekend programs available. *Faculty:* 51 full-time (14 women), 11 part-time/adjunct (2 women). *Students:* 107 full-time (51 women), 45 part-time (24 women); includes 23 minority (2 Black or African American, non-Hispanic/Latino; 3 Asian, non-Hispanic/Latino; 16 Hispanic/Latino; 2 Two or more races, non-Hispanic/Latino), 6 international. Average age 29. 92 applicants, 57% accepted, 40 enrolled. In 2011, 76 master's awarded. *Entrance requirements:* For master's, GMAT, minimum GPA of 3.0. Additional exam requirements/recommendations for international students: Required—TOEFL (minimum score 550 paper-based; 213 computer-based). *Application deadline:* For fall admission, 6/1 priority date for domestic students; for spring admission, 11/1 for domestic students. Applications are processed on a rolling basis. Application fee: $30. Electronic applications accepted. *Expenses:* Tuition, state resident: full-time $8289. Tuition, nonresident: full-time $28,895. *Required fees:* $1831. One-time fee: $30 full-time. *Faculty research:* Fraud in audits, production planning in cell manufacturing systems, collaborative learning in distance courses, characteristics of minority and women-owned businesses. *Unit head:* Dr. Sandra Kauanui, Chair, Department of Management, 239-590-7433, Fax: 239-590-7330, E-mail: skauanui@fgcu.edu. *Application contact:* Marissa Ouverson, Director of Enrollment Management, 239-590-7403, Fax: 239-590-7330, E-mail: mouverso@fgcu.edu.

Florida Institute of Technology, Graduate Programs, Extended Studies Division, Melbourne, FL 32901-6975. Offers acquisition and contract management (MS); aerospace engineering (MS); business administration (MBA); computer information systems (MS); computer science (MS); electrical engineering (MS); engineering management (MS); human resources management (MS); logistics management (MS), including humanitarian and disaster relief logistics; management (MS), including acquisition and contract management, e-business, human resources management, information systems, logistics management, management, transportation management; material acquisition management (MS); mechanical engineering (MS); operations research (MS); project management (MS), including information systems, operations research; public administration (MPA); quality management (MS); software engineering (MS); space systems (MS); space systems management (MS); supply chain management (MS); systems management (MS), including information systems, operations research. Part-time and evening/weekend programs available. Postbaccalaureate distance learning degree programs offered (no on-campus study). *Faculty:* 9 full-time (2 women), 105 part-time/adjunct (24 women). *Students:* 113 full-time (52 women), 1,150 part-time (484 women); includes 496 minority (332 Black or African

American, non-Hispanic/Latino; 11 American Indian or Alaska Native, non-Hispanic/Latino; 42 Asian, non-Hispanic/Latino; 71 Hispanic/Latino; 2 Native Hawaiian or other Pacific Islander, non-Hispanic/Latino; 38 Two or more races, non-Hispanic/Latino), 11 international. Average age 35. 568 applicants, 56% accepted, 296 enrolled. In 2011, 471 master's awarded. *Degree requirements:* For master's, comprehensive exam (for some programs), capstone course. *Entrance requirements:* For master's, GMAT or resume showing 8 years of supervised experience, minimum GPA of 3.0, 2 letters of recommendation, resume. Additional exam requirements/recommendations for international students: Required—TOEFL (minimum score 550 paper-based; 213 computer-based; 79 iBT). *Application deadline:* For fall admission, 4/1 for international students; for spring admission, 9/30 for international students. Applications are processed on a rolling basis. Application fee: $0. Electronic applications accepted. *Expenses:* Contact institution. *Financial support:* Application deadline: 3/1; applicants required to submit FAFSA. *Unit head:* Dr. Theodore R. Richardson, III, Senior Associate Dean, 321-674-8123, Fax: 321-674-7597, E-mail: trichardson@fit.edu. *Application contact:* Carolyn Farrior, Director of Graduate Admissions, Online Learning and Off-Campus Programs, 321-674-7118, Fax: 321-674-8216, E-mail: cfarrior@fit.edu. Web site: http://es.fit.edu.

Florida Institute of Technology, Graduate Programs, Nathan M. Bisk College of Business, Online Programs, Melbourne, FL 32901-6975. Offers accounting (MBA); accounting and finance (MBA); business administration (MBA); finance (MBA); healthcare management (MBA); information technology (MS); information technology cybersecurity (MS); information technology management (MBA); international business (MBA); Internet marketing (MBA); management (MBA); marketing (MBA); project management (MBA). Part-time and evening/weekend programs available. Postbaccalaureate distance learning degree programs offered (no on-campus study). *Faculty:* 47 part-time/adjunct (15 women). *Students:* 8 full-time (4 women), 1,122 part-time (547 women); includes 418 minority (271 Black or African American, non-Hispanic/Latino; 5 American Indian or Alaska Native, non-Hispanic/Latino; 55 Asian, non-Hispanic/Latino; 81 Hispanic/Latino; 6 Native Hawaiian or other Pacific Islander, non-Hispanic/Latino), 23 international. Average age 36. In 2011, 329 master's awarded. *Entrance requirements:* For master's, GMAT or resume showing 8 years of supervised experience, 2 letters of recommendation, resume, competency in math past college algebra. Additional exam requirements/recommendations for international students: Required—TOEFL (minimum score 550 paper-based; 213 computer-based; 79 iBT). *Application deadline:* For fall admission, 4/1 for international students; for spring admission, 9/30 for international students. Applications are processed on a rolling basis. Electronic applications accepted. *Expenses:* Contact institution. *Financial support:* Available to part-time students. Application deadline: 3/1; applicants required to submit FAFSA. *Unit head:* Dr. Mary S. Bonhomme, Dean, Florida Tech Online/Associate Provost for Online Learning, 321-674-8202, Fax: 321-674-8216, E-mail: bonhomme@fit.edu. *Application contact:* Carolyn Farrior, Director of Graduate Admissions, Online Learning and Off-Campus Programs, 321-674-7118, Fax: 321-674-8216, E-mail: cfarrior@fit.edu. Web site: http://online.fit.edu.

Florida International University, Alvah H. Chapman, Jr. Graduate School of Business, Program in Business Administration, Miami, FL 33199. Offers EMBA, IMBA, MBA, PMBA, PhD. *Accreditation:* AACSB. Part-time and evening/weekend programs available. *Degree requirements:* For doctorate, comprehensive exam, thesis/dissertation. *Entrance requirements:* For master's, GMAT or GRE (depending on program), minimum GPA of 3.0 (upper-level coursework); for doctorate, GMAT or GRE, minimum GPA of 3.0 in post-secondary education; letter of intent; 3 letters of recommendation; resume. Additional exam requirements/recommendations for international students: Required—TOEFL (minimum score 550 paper-based; 213 computer-based; 80 iBT) or IELTS (minimum score 6.5). Electronic applications accepted. *Expenses:* Contact institution. *Faculty research:* Taxation, financial and managerial accounting, human resource management, multinational corporations, strategy, international business, auditing, artificial intelligence, international banking, investments, entrepreneurship.

Florida Memorial University, School of Business, Miami-Dade, FL 33054. Offers MBA. *Accreditation:* ACBSP. Part-time programs available. *Entrance requirements:* For master's, GMAT, 3 letters of recommendation.

Florida Southern College, Program in Business Administration, Lakeland, FL 33801-5698. Offers MBA. Part-time and evening/weekend programs available. *Entrance requirements:* For master's, GMAT or GRE General Test, 3 letters of reference, resume, personal statement. Additional exam requirements/recommendations for international students: Required—TOEFL (minimum score 550 paper-based). *Expenses:* Contact institution.

Florida State University, The Graduate School, College of Business, Tallahassee, FL 32306-1110. Offers accounting (M Acc), including accounting information services, assurance services, corporate accounting, taxation; business administration (MBA, PhD), including accounting (PhD), finance (PhD), management information systems (PhD), marketing (PhD), organizational behavior (PhD), risk management and insurance (PhD), strategic management (PhD); finance (MS); insurance (MSM); management information systems (MS); marketing (MS); JD/MBA; MSW/MBA. *Accreditation:* AACSB. Part-time programs available. Postbaccalaureate distance learning degree programs offered (no on-campus study). *Faculty:* 107 full-time (31 women). *Students:* 196 full-time (76 women), 310 part-time (109 women); includes 89 minority (27 Black or African American, non-Hispanic/Latino; 1 American Indian or Alaska Native, non-Hispanic/Latino; 31 Asian, non-Hispanic/Latino; 30 Hispanic/Latino). Average age 30. 702 applicants, 33% accepted, 205 enrolled. In 2011, 268 master's, 17 doctorates awarded. Terminal master's awarded for partial completion of doctoral program. *Degree requirements:* For doctorate, comprehensive exam, thesis/dissertation. *Entrance requirements:* For master's, GMAT, work experience (MBA, MS), minimum GPA of 3.0, letters of recommendation; for doctorate, GMAT, minimum graduate GPA of 3.5, letters of recommendation. Additional exam requirements/recommendations for international students: Required—TOEFL (minimum score 600 paper-based; 80 computer-based); Recommended—IELTS (minimum score 6.5). *Application deadline:* For fall admission, 6/1 for domestic students, 5/1 for international students; for spring admission, 10/1 for domestic students, 9/1 for international students. Applications are processed on a rolling basis. Application fee: $30. Electronic applications accepted. *Expenses:* Tuition, state resident: full-time $9474; part-time $350.88 per credit hour. Tuition, nonresident: full-time $16,236; part-time $601.34 per credit hour. *Required fees:* $630 per semester. One-time fee: $20. Tuition and fees vary according to course load and campus/location. *Financial support:* In 2011–12, 86 students received support, including 12 fellowships with full tuition reimbursements available (averaging $7,161 per year), 30 research assistantships with full tuition reimbursements available (averaging $6,000 per year), 43 teaching assistantships with full tuition reimbursements available (averaging $15,000 per year); career-related internships or fieldwork, scholarships/grants, health care benefits, tuition waivers (full and partial), and unspecified assistantships also available. Support available to part-time students. Financial award application deadline: 1/1. *Unit head:* Dr. Caryn Beck-Dudley, Dean, 850-644-3090, Fax: 850-644-0915. *Application contact:* Lisa Beverly, Director, Graduate Programs Admissions, 850-644-6458, Fax: 850-644-0588, E-mail: lbeverly@cob.fsu.edu. Web site: http://www.cob.fsu.edu/grad/.

Fontbonne University, Graduate Programs, College of Global Business and Professional Studies, Options Program in Business Administration, St. Louis, MO 63105-3098. Offers MBA. *Accreditation:* ACBSP. Evening/weekend programs available. *Degree requirements:* For master's, applied management project. *Entrance requirements:* For master's, minimum GPA of 2.5. *Expenses:* Contact institution.

Fontbonne University, Graduate Programs, College of Global Business and Professional Studies, Options Program in Management, St. Louis, MO 63105-3098. Offers MM. *Accreditation:* ACBSP. Part-time and evening/weekend programs available. Postbaccalaureate distance learning degree programs offered. *Expenses:* Contact institution.

Fontbonne University, Graduate Programs, College of Global Business and Professional Studies, Program in Business Administration, St. Louis, MO 63105-3098. Offers MBA. *Accreditation:* ACBSP. Part-time and evening/weekend programs available. *Entrance requirements:* For master's, minimum GPA of 2.5. Additional exam requirements/recommendations for international students: Required—TOEFL (minimum score 450 paper-based; 133 computer-based; 45 iBT).

Fordham University, Graduate School of Business, New York, NY 10023. Offers accounting (MBA); communications and media management (MBA); executive business administration (EMBA); finance (MBA, MS); information systems (MBA, MS); management systems (MBA); marketing (MBA); media management (MS); taxation (MS); taxation and accounting (MTA);); JD/MBA; MBA/MIM; MS/MBA. MBA/MIM offered jointly with Thunderbird School of Global Management. *Accreditation:* AACSB. Part-time and evening/weekend programs available. *Entrance requirements:* For master's, GMAT, 2 letters of recommendation, resume. Additional exam requirements/recommendations for international students: Required—TOEFL (minimum score 600 paper-based; 250 computer-based; 100 iBT). Electronic applications accepted. *Expenses:* Contact institution.

Fort Hays State University, Graduate School, College of Business and Leadership, Department of Management and Marketing, Hays, KS 67601-4099. Offers management (MBA). *Degree requirements:* For master's, thesis optional. *Entrance requirements:* For master's, GMAT. Additional exam requirements/recommendations for international students: Required—TOEFL (minimum score 550 paper-based; 213 computer-based). Electronic applications accepted. *Faculty research:* Organizational behavior and performance appraisal, data processing, international marketing.

Framingham State University, Division of Graduate and Continuing Education, Program in Business Administration, Framingham, MA 01701-9101. Offers MBA. Part-time and evening/weekend programs available. *Entrance requirements:* For master's, GMAT, GRE, or MAT.

Franciscan University of Steubenville, Graduate Programs, Department of Business, Steubenville, OH 43952-1763. Offers MBA. Part-time and evening/weekend programs available. *Degree requirements:* For master's, research paper. *Entrance requirements:* For master's, GMAT, minimum undergraduate GPA of 2.5. *Expenses:* Contact institution.

Francis Marion University, Graduate Programs, School of Business, Florence, SC 29502-0547. Offers business (MBA); health management (MBA). *Accreditation:* AACSB. Part-time and evening/weekend programs available. *Faculty:* 21 full-time (6 women). *Students:* 5 full-time (4 women), 32 part-time (25 women); includes 9 minority (7 Black or African American, non-Hispanic/Latino; 2 Asian, non-Hispanic/Latino), 1 international. Average age 30. 23 applicants, 43% accepted, 10 enrolled. In 2011, 15 master's awarded. *Degree requirements:* For master's, comprehensive exam. *Entrance requirements:* For master's, GMAT. *Application deadline:* For fall admission, 3/15 priority date for domestic students; for spring admission, 10/15 priority date for domestic students. Applications are processed on a rolling basis. Application fee: $31. *Expenses:* Tuition, state resident: full-time $8467; part-time $443.35 per credit hour. Tuition, nonresident: full-time $16,934; part-time $866.70 per credit hour. *Required fees:* $335; $12.25 per credit hour. $30 per semester. *Financial support:* Research assistantships available. Support available to part-time students. Financial award application deadline: 3/1; financial award applicants required to submit FAFSA. *Faculty research:* Ethics, directions of MBA, international business, regional economics, environmental issues. *Unit head:* Dr. M. Barry O'Brien, Dean, 843-661-1419, Fax: 843-661-1432, E-mail: mbobrien@fmarion.edu. *Application contact:* Rannie Gamble, Administrative Manager, 843-661-1286, Fax: 843-661-4688, E-mail: rgamble@fmarion.edu. Web site: http://alpha1.fmarion.edu/~mba/.

Franklin Pierce University, Graduate Studies, Rindge, NH 03461-0060. Offers curriculum and instruction (M Ed); emerging network technologies (Graduate Certificate); energy and sustainability studies (MBA); health administration (MBA, Graduate Certificate); human resource management (MBA, Graduate Certificate); information technology (MBA); information technology management (MS); leadership (MBA, DA); nursing (MS); physical therapy (DPT); physician assistant studies (MPAS); special education (M Ed); sports management (MBA). *Accreditation:* APTA. Part-time programs available. Postbaccalaureate distance learning degree programs offered (no on-campus study). *Degree requirements:* For master's, concentrated original research projects; student teaching; fieldwork and/or internship; leadership project; PRAXIS I and II (for M Ed); for doctorate, concentrated original research projects, clinical fieldwork and/or internship, leadership project. *Entrance requirements:* For master's, minimum GPA of 2.5, 3 letters of recommendation; competencies in accounting, economics, statistics, and computer skills through life experience or undergraduate coursework (for MBA); certification/e-portfolio, minimum C grade in all education courses (for M Ed); license to practice as RN (for MS in nursing); for doctorate, GRE, BA/BS, 3 letters of recommendation, personal mission statement, interview, writing sample, minimum cumulative GPA of 2.8, master's degree (for DA); 80 hours of observation/work in PT settings, completion of anatomy, chemistry, physics, and statistics, minimum GPA of 3.0 (for DPT). Additional exam requirements/recommendations for international students: Required—TOEFL (minimum score 550 paper-based; 195 computer-based; 61 iBT). Electronic applications accepted. *Faculty research:* Evidence-based practice in sports physical therapy, human resource management in economic crisis, leadership in nursing, innovation in sports facility management, differentiated learning and understanding by design.

Franklin University, MBA Program, Columbus, OH 43215-5399. Offers MBA. Part-time and evening/weekend programs available. Postbaccalaureate distance learning degree programs offered (no on-campus study). *Entrance requirements:* For master's, minimum undergraduate GPA of 2.75. Additional exam requirements/recommendations for international students: Required—TOEFL (minimum score 550 paper-based; 213 computer-based). Electronic applications accepted.

Freed-Hardeman University, Program in Business Administration, Henderson, TN 38340-2399. Offers accounting (MBA); corporate responsibility (MBA); leadership (MBA). *Accreditation:* ACBSP. Part-time and evening/weekend programs available. Postbaccalaureate distance learning degree programs offered (no on-campus study). *Entrance requirements:* For master's, GMAT. Additional exam requirements/recommendations for international students: Required—TOEFL (minimum score 500 paper-based; 173 computer-based).

Fresno Pacific University, Graduate Programs, Program in Leadership and Organizational Studies, Fresno, CA 93702-4709. Offers MA. Part-time and evening/weekend programs available. *Degree requirements:* For master's, thesis. *Entrance requirements:* For master's, MAT, GRE or GMAT, interview, 2 writing samples. Additional exam requirements/recommendations for international students: Required—TOEFL (minimum score 550 paper-based; 213 computer-based). Electronic applications accepted. *Expenses:* Contact institution. *Faculty research:* Ethics, servant leadership, communication, creative problem solving.

Friends University, Graduate School, Wichita, KS 67213. Offers accounting (MBA); business administration (MBA); business law (MBL); Christian ministry (MACM); environment science (MSES); family therapy (MSFT); global leadership and management (MA); health care leadership (MHCL); management information systems (MMIS); operations management (MSOM); organization development (MSOD); teaching (MAT). Part-time and evening/weekend programs available. Postbaccalaureate distance learning degree programs offered (no on-campus study). *Faculty:* 14 full-time (5 women), 2 part-time/adjunct (1 woman). *Students:* 158 full-time (114 women), 616 part-time (367 women); includes 159 minority (83 Black or African American, non-Hispanic/Latino; 12 American Indian or Alaska Native, non-Hispanic/Latino; 26 Asian, non-Hispanic/Latino; 22 Hispanic/Latino; 2 Native Hawaiian or other Pacific Islander, non-Hispanic/Latino; 14 Two or more races, non-Hispanic/Latino). Average age 36. 497 applicants, 68% accepted, 256 enrolled. In 2011, 341 degrees awarded. *Degree requirements:* For master's, research project. *Entrance requirements:* For master's, bachelor's degree from accredited institution, official transcripts from institution granting bachelor's degree, interview with program director, letter(s) of recommendation. Additional exam requirements/recommendations for international students: Required—TOEFL (minimum score 560 paper-based; 220 computer-based). *Application deadline:* Applications are processed on a rolling basis. Application fee: $45 ($65 for international students). Electronic applications accepted. *Expenses: Tuition:* Part-time $601 per credit hour. One-time fee: $45 full-time. Tuition and fees vary according to campus/location and program. *Financial support:* Applicants required to submit FAFSA. *Unit head:* Dr. Evelyn Hume, Dean, 800-794-6945 Ext. 5859, Fax: 316-295-5040, E-mail: evelyn_hume@friends.edu. *Application contact:* Jeanette Hanson, Executive Director of Adult Recruitment, 800-794-6945, Fax: 316-295-5050, E-mail: jeanette@friends.edu. Web site: http://www.friends.edu.

Frostburg State University, Graduate School, College of Business, Frostburg, MD 21532-1099. Offers MBA. *Accreditation:* AACSB. Part-time and evening/weekend programs available. *Entrance requirements:* For master's, GMAT. Additional exam requirements/recommendations for international students: Required—TOEFL. Electronic applications accepted. *Faculty research:* Cooperative teaching methods, strategic change processes, political marketing.

Full Sail University, Entertainment Business Master of Science Program - Online, Winter Park, FL 32792-7437. Offers MS. Postbaccalaureate distance learning degree programs offered. *Entrance requirements:* Additional exam requirements/recommendations for international students: Required—TOEFL (minimum score 550 paper-based; 213 computer-based; 79 iBT).

Gannon University, School of Graduate Studies, College of Engineering and Business, School of Business, Program in Business Administration, Erie, PA 16541-0001. Offers MBA. *Accreditation:* ACBSP. Part-time and evening/weekend programs available. Postbaccalaureate distance learning degree programs offered (no on-campus study). *Students:* 57 full-time (19 women), 61 part-time (32 women); includes 4 minority (3 Black or African American, non-Hispanic/Latino; 1 Hispanic/Latino), 15 international. Average age 26. 208 applicants, 81% accepted, 15 enrolled. In 2011, 29 master's awarded. *Degree requirements:* For master's, comprehensive exam, thesis. *Entrance requirements:* For master's, GMAT or GRE. Additional exam requirements/recommendations for international students: Required—TOEFL (minimum score 79 iBT). *Application deadline:* Applications are processed on a rolling basis. Application fee: $25. Electronic applications accepted. *Financial support:* Career-related internships or fieldwork, scholarships/grants, and administrative assistantships available. Financial award application deadline: 7/1; financial award applicants required to submit FAFSA. *Unit head:* Dr. Donna Mottilla, Director, 814-871-7780, E-mail: mottilla001@gannon.edu. *Application contact:* Kara Morgan, Director of Graduate Admissions, 814-871-5831, Fax: 814-871-5827, E-mail: graduate@gannon.edu.

Gannon University, School of Graduate Studies, College of Engineering and Business, School of Business, Program in Risk Management, Erie, PA 16541-0001. Offers Certificate. Part-time and evening/weekend programs available. *Entrance requirements:* For degree, GMAT. Additional exam requirements/recommendations for international students: Required—TOEFL (minimum score 79 iBT). *Application deadline:* Applications are processed on a rolling basis. Application fee: $25. Electronic applications accepted. *Financial support:* Application deadline: 7/1; applicants required to submit FAFSA. *Unit head:* Dr. Donna Mottilla, Director, 814-871-7780, E-mail: mottilla001@gannon.edu. *Application contact:* Kara Morgan, Director of Graduate Admissions, 814-871-5831, Fax: 814-871-5827, E-mail: graduate@gannon.edu.

Gardner-Webb University, Graduate School of Business, Boiling Springs, NC 28017. Offers IMBA, M Acc, MBA. *Accreditation:* ACBSP. Part-time and evening/weekend programs available. Postbaccalaureate distance learning degree programs offered (no on-campus study). *Students:* 30 full-time (16 women), 392 part-time (225 women); includes 119 minority (99 Black or African American, non-Hispanic/Latino; 2 American Indian or Alaska Native, non-Hispanic/Latino; 10 Asian, non-Hispanic/Latino; 8 Hispanic/Latino), 1 international. Average age 34. 317 applicants, 59% accepted, 105 enrolled. In 2011, 145 master's awarded. *Entrance requirements:* For master's, GMAT, GRE, 2 semesters of course work each in economics, statistics, and accounting. Additional exam requirements/recommendations for international students: Required—TOEFL (minimum score 500 paper-based; 173 computer-based; 61 iBT). *Application deadline:* For spring admission, 1/15 for domestic students. Applications are processed on a rolling basis. Application fee: $40. Electronic applications accepted. *Expenses:* Contact institution. *Financial support:* In 2011–12, 23 students received support. Unspecified assistantships available. Support available to part-time students. Financial award applicants required to submit FAFSA. *Unit head:* Dr. Anthony Negbenebor, Dean, 704-406-4622, E-mail: anegbenebor@gardner-webb.edu. *Application contact:* Mischia Taylor, Director of Admissions, 877-498-4723, Fax: 704-406-3895, E-mail: mataylor@gardner-webb.edu. Web site: http://www.gardner-webb.edu/admissions/graduate-studies/graduate-school-of-business/index.html.

Geneva College, Program in Business Administration, Beaver Falls, PA 15010-3599. Offers MBA. *Accreditation:* ACBSP. Part-time and evening/weekend programs available. *Faculty:* 6 full-time (1 woman). *Students:* 26 part-time (6 women). Average age 33. 5 applicants, 100% accepted, 2 enrolled. In 2011, 5 master's awarded. *Degree requirements:* For master's, 36 credit hours of course work (30 of which are required of all students). *Entrance requirements:* For master's, GMAT (if college GPA less than 2.5), undergraduate transcript, 2 letters of recommendation, resume, goals statement. Additional exam requirements/recommendations for international students: Required—TOEFL. *Application deadline:* For fall admission, 3/1 priority date for domestic students; for spring admission, 11/1 priority date for domestic students. Applications are processed on a rolling basis. Electronic applications accepted. *Expenses: Tuition:* Part-time $625 per credit hour. Tuition and fees vary according to program. *Financial support:* Application deadline: 8/1; applicants required to submit FAFSA. *Unit head:* Dr. William Pearce, Director of the MBA Program, 724-847-6881, E-mail: bpearce@geneva.edu. *Application contact:* Lori Hartge, Graduate Student Support Specialist, 724-847-6571, E-mail: mba@geneva.edu. Web site: http://www.geneva.edu/.

George Fox University, School of Business, Newberg, OR 97132-2697. Offers finance (MBA); management (DBA); management/general (MBA); marketing (DBA); organizational strategy (MBA); strategic human resource management (MBA). MBA offered part-time and full-time in Newberg, OR, and in Portland, OR. Part-time and evening/weekend programs available. Postbaccalaureate distance learning degree programs offered (minimal on-campus study). *Faculty:* 9 full-time (2 women), 6 part-time/adjunct (0 women). *Students:* 24 full-time (11 women), 239 part-time (81 women); includes 33 minority (4 Black or African American, non-Hispanic/Latino; 1 American Indian or Alaska Native, non-Hispanic/Latino; 14 Asian, non-Hispanic/Latino; 10 Hispanic/Latino; 4 Two or more races, non-Hispanic/Latino), 13 international. Average age 37. In 2011, 101 master's, 6 doctorates awarded. *Degree requirements:* For master's, capstone project; for doctorate, credit-applied research project. *Entrance requirements:* For master's, resume (5 years professional experience); 3 professional references; interview; financial e-learning course, official transcripts; for doctorate, GRE or GMAT, resume; personal mission statement; academic research writing sample; official transcript from each college/university attended; three professional references. Additional exam requirements/recommendations for international students: Required—TOEFL (minimum score 577 paper-based; 233 computer-based; 90 iBT) or IELTS (minimum score 7). *Application deadline:* For fall admission, 8/1 for domestic and international students; for spring admission, 12/1 for domestic and international students. Applications are processed on a rolling basis. Application fee: $40. Electronic applications accepted. *Expenses:* Contact institution. *Financial support:* Applicants required to submit FAFSA. *Unit head:* Dr. Dirk Barram, Professor/Dean, 800-631-0921. *Application contact:* Robin Halverson, Admissions Counselor, 800-493-4937, Fax: 503-554-6111, E-mail: mba@georgefox.edu. Web site: http://www.georgefox.edu/business/index.html.

George Mason University, School of Management, Program in Business Administration, Fairfax, VA 22030. Offers EMBA, MBA. *Accreditation:* AACSB. *Faculty:* 61 full-time (17 women), 39 part-time/adjunct (12 women). *Students:* 85 full-time (33 women), 306 part-time (100 women); includes 75 minority (18 Black or African American, non-Hispanic/Latino; 1 American Indian or Alaska Native, non-Hispanic/Latino; 41 Asian, non-Hispanic/Latino; 10 Hispanic/Latino; 1 Native Hawaiian or other Pacific Islander, non-Hispanic/Latino; 4 Two or more races, non-Hispanic/Latino), 35 international. Average age 30. 309 applicants, 59% accepted, 111 enrolled. In 2011, 147 degrees awarded. *Entrance requirements:* For master's, GMAT/GRE, resume; 2 official copies of transcripts; 2 professional letters of recommendation; personal career goals statement; professional essay; interview. Additional exam requirements/recommendations for international students: Required—TOEFL (minimum score 570 paper-based; 230 computer-based; 88 iBT), IELTS, Pearson Test of English. *Application deadline:* For fall admission, 1/15 priority date for domestic students, 2/1 for international students; for spring admission, 10/15 priority date for domestic students. Application fee: $65 ($80 for international students). Electronic applications accepted. *Expenses:* Tuition, state resident: full-time $8750; part-time $364.58 per credit. Tuition, nonresident: full-time $24,092; part-time $1003.83 per credit. *Required fees:* $2514; $104.75 per credit. *Financial support:* In 2011–12, 43 students received support, including 29 research assistantships with full and partial tuition reimbursements available (averaging $8,824 per year), 18 teaching assistantships with full and partial tuition reimbursements available (averaging $8,092 per year); career-related internships or fieldwork, Federal Work-Study, scholarships/grants, unspecified assistantships, and health care benefits (full-time research or teaching assistantship recipients) also available. Financial award application deadline: 3/1; financial award applicants required to submit FAFSA. *Faculty research:* Electronic commerce, marketing information systems, group decision-making, corporate governance, risk management. *Unit head:* Rebecca M. Diemer, Associate Director, 703-993-2216, Fax: 703-993-1778, E-mail: rdiemer@gmu.edu. *Application contact:* Nada Osman, Program Manager, 703-993-2136, Fax: 703-993-1778, E-mail: mba@gmu.edu. Web site: http://som.gmu.edu/mba-programs.

Georgetown University, Graduate School of Arts and Sciences, McDonough School of Business, Washington, DC 20057. Offers business administration (IEMBA, MBA). *Accreditation:* AACSB. *Entrance requirements:* For master's, GMAT. Additional exam requirements/recommendations for international students: Required—TOEFL. *Expenses:* Contact institution.

The George Washington University, School of Business, Washington, DC 20052. Offers M Accy, MBA, MS, MSF, MSIST, MTA, PMBA, PhD, Professional Certificate, JD/MBA, JD/MPA, MBA/MA. PMBA program also offered in Alexandria and Ashburn, VA. Part-time and evening/weekend programs available. *Faculty:* 128 full-time (40 women), 67 part-time/adjunct (16 women). *Students:* 1,039 full-time (464 women), 973 part-time (452 women); includes 539 minority (203 Black or African American, non-Hispanic/Latino; 9 American Indian or Alaska Native, non-Hispanic/Latino; 194 Asian, non-Hispanic/Latino; 114 Hispanic/Latino; 2 Native Hawaiian or other Pacific Islander, non-Hispanic/Latino; 17 Two or more races, non-Hispanic/Latino), 396 international. Average age 32. 2,743 applicants, 54% accepted, 737 enrolled. In 2011, 737 master's, 13 doctorates awarded. *Degree requirements:* For doctorate, thesis/dissertation. *Entrance requirements:* For doctorate, GMAT or GRE. Additional exam requirements/recommendations for international students: Required—TOEFL. *Application deadline:* For fall admission, 4/1 priority date for domestic students; for spring admission, 10/1 for domestic students. Applications are processed on a rolling basis. Application fee: $75. Electronic applications accepted. *Financial support:* In 2011–12, 194 students received support. Fellowships with tuition reimbursements available, teaching assistantships with tuition reimbursements available, career-related internships or fieldwork, Federal Work-Study, institutionally sponsored loans, and tuition waivers (partial) available. Financial award application deadline: 4/1. *Unit head:* Dr. Susan M. Phillips, Dean, 202-994-6380, Fax: 202-994-6382. *Application contact:* Kristin Williams, Assistant Vice President for Graduate and Special Enrollment Management, 202-994-0467, Fax: 202-994-0371, E-mail: ksw@gwu.edu. Web site: http://business.gwu.edu/grad.

Georgia College & State University, Graduate School, The J. Whitney Bunting School of Business, Milledgeville, GA 31061. Offers accountancy (MACCT); accounting (MBA); business (MBA); health services administration (MBA); information systems (MIS); management information services (MBA). *Accreditation:* AACSB. Part-time and evening/weekend programs available. Postbaccalaureate distance learning degree programs offered (no on-campus study). *Students:* 61 full-time (26 women), 134 part-time (55 women); includes 34 minority (18 Black or African American, non-Hispanic/Latino; 9 Asian, non-Hispanic/Latino; 5 Hispanic/Latino; 2 Two or more races, non-Hispanic/Latino), 17 international. Average age 30. 162 applicants, 41% accepted, 45 enrolled. In 2011, 99 master's awarded. *Entrance requirements:* For master's, GMAT or GRE. Additional exam requirements/recommendations for international students: Recommended—TOEFL (minimum score 550 paper-based; 213 computer-based; 79 iBT). *Application deadline:* For fall admission, 7/1 priority date for domestic students, 4/1 for international students; for spring admission, 11/15 priority date for domestic students, 8/1 for international students. Applications are processed on a rolling basis. Application fee: $40. Electronic applications accepted. *Expenses:* Tuition, state resident: full-time $4806; part-time $267 per credit hour. Tuition, nonresident: full-time $17,802; part-time $989 per credit hour. *Required fees:* $936 per semester. Tuition and fees vary according to course load and campus/location. *Financial support:* In 2011–12, 34 research assistantships with full tuition reimbursements were awarded; career-related internships or fieldwork and unspecified assistantships also available. Support available to part-time students. Financial award application deadline: 3/1; financial award applicants required to submit FAFSA. *Unit head:* Dr. Matthew Liao-Troth, Dean, School of Business, 478-445-5497, E-mail: matthew.liao-troth@gcsu.edu. *Application contact:* Lynn Hanson, Director of Graduate Programs, 478-445-5115, E-mail: lynn.hanson@gcsu.edu. Web site: http://www.gcsu.edu/business/graduateprograms/index.htm.

Georgia Institute of Technology, Graduate Studies and Research, College of Management, Program in Business Administration, Atlanta, GA 30332-0001. Offers accounting (MBA); e-commerce (Certificate); engineering entrepreneurship (MBA); entrepreneurship (Certificate); finance (MBA); information technology management (MBA); international business (MBA, Certificate); management of technology (Certificate); marketing (MBA); operations management (MBA); organizational behavior (MBA); strategic management (MBA). *Accreditation:* AACSB.

Georgia Institute of Technology, Graduate Studies and Research, College of Management, Program in Management, Atlanta, GA 30332-0001. Offers accounting (PhD); finance (PhD); information technology management (PhD); marketing (PhD); operations management (PhD); organizational behavior (PhD); quantitative and computational finance (MS); strategic management (PhD). *Accreditation:* AACSB. *Degree requirements:* For doctorate, comprehensive exam, thesis/dissertation, oral exams. *Entrance requirements:* For master's and doctorate, GMAT. Additional exam requirements/recommendations for international students: Required—TOEFL. *Faculty research:* MIS, management of technology, international business, entrepreneurship, operations management.

Georgian Court University, School of Business, Lakewood, NJ 08701-2697. Offers MBA. *Accreditation:* ACBSP. Part-time and evening/weekend programs available. *Faculty:* 6 full-time (4 women). *Students:* 41 full-time (28 women), 41 part-time (26 women); includes 19 minority (8 Black or African American, non-Hispanic/Latino; 5 Asian, non-Hispanic/Latino; 5 Hispanic/Latino; 1 Two or more races, non-Hispanic/Latino). Average age 32. 92 applicants, 63% accepted, 41 enrolled. In 2011, 62 master's awarded. *Entrance requirements:* For master's, GMAT or CPA exam, 3 letters of recommendation. Additional exam requirements/recommendations for international students: Required—TOEFL (minimum score 550 paper-based; 213 computer-based). *Application deadline:* For fall admission, 8/1 priority date for domestic students, 4/1 for international students; for spring admission, 1/1 priority date for domestic students, 7/1 for international students. Applications are processed on a rolling basis. Application fee: $40. Electronic applications accepted. *Expenses: Tuition:* Full-time $13,410; part-time $745 per credit. *Required fees:* $450 per year. Tuition and fees vary according to campus/location and program. *Financial support:* Scholarships/grants, health care benefits, and unspecified assistantships available. Financial award application deadline: 4/15; financial award applicants required to submit FAFSA. *Unit head:* Dr. Janice Warner, Dean, 732-987-2662, Fax: 732-987-2024, E-mail: warnerj@georgian.edu. *Application contact:* Patrick Givens, Assistant Director of Graduate Admissions, 732-987-2736, Fax: 732-987-2084, E-mail: graduateadmissions@georgian.edu. Web site: http://www.georgian.edu/business/gcu_business.htm.

Georgia Southern University, Jack N. Averitt College of Graduate Studies, College of Business Administration, The Georgia WebMBA, Statesboro, GA 30460. Offers MBA. Part-time and evening/weekend programs available. Postbaccalaureate distance learning degree programs offered. *Students:* 82 part-time (40 women); includes 20 minority (12 Black or African American, non-Hispanic/Latino; 3 Asian, non-Hispanic/Latino; 2 Hispanic/Latino; 1 Native Hawaiian or other Pacific Islander, non-Hispanic/Latino; 2 Two or more races, non-Hispanic/Latino), 3 international. Average age 32. 67 applicants, 73% accepted, 28 enrolled. In 2011, 42 master's awarded. *Entrance requirements:* For master's, GMAT. Additional exam requirements/recommendations for international students: Required—TOEFL (minimum score 550 paper-based; 213 computer-based; 80 iBT). *Application deadline:* For fall admission, 3/1 priority date for domestic students, 3/1 for international students. Applications are processed on a rolling basis. Application fee: $50. Electronic applications accepted. *Expenses:* Tuition, state resident: full-time $6300; part-time $263 per semester hour. Tuition, nonresident: full-time $25,174; part-time $1049 per semester hour. *Required fees:* $1872. *Financial support:* Application deadline: 4/15; applicants required to submit FAFSA. *Unit head:* Karen Wells, Graduate Program Director, 912-478-2357, Fax: 912-478-0292, E-mail: kwells@georgiasouthern.edu. *Application contact:* Amanda Gilliland, Coordinator for Graduate Student Recruitment, 912-478-5384, Fax: 912-478-0740, E-mail: gradadmissions@georgiasouthern.edu. Web site: http://online.georgiasouthern.edu/index.php?link=grad_MBA.

Georgia Southern University, Jack N. Averitt College of Graduate Studies, College of Business Administration, Program in Business Administration, Statesboro, GA 30460. Offers MBA. *Accreditation:* AACSB. Part-time and evening/weekend programs available. Postbaccalaureate distance learning degree programs offered. *Students:* 69 full-time (31 women), 99 part-time (36 women); includes 30 minority (17 Black or African American, non-Hispanic/Latino; 4 Asian, non-Hispanic/Latino; 8 Hispanic/Latino; 1 Two or more races, non-Hispanic/Latino), 8 international. Average age 28. 91 applicants, 74% accepted, 49 enrolled. In 2011, 75 master's awarded. *Entrance requirements:* For master's, GMAT. Additional exam requirements/recommendations for international students: Required—TOEFL (minimum score 550 paper-based; 213 computer-based; 80 iBT). *Application deadline:* For fall admission, 3/1 priority date for domestic students, 6/1 for international students; for spring admission, 10/1 priority date for domestic students, 10/1 for international students. Applications are processed on a rolling basis. Application fee: $50. Electronic applications accepted. *Expenses:* Tuition, state resident: full-time $6300; part-time $263 per semester hour. Tuition, nonresident: full-time $25,174; part-time $1049 per semester hour. *Required fees:* $1872. *Financial support:* In 2011–12, 37 students received support, including research assistantships with partial tuition reimbursements available (averaging $7,200 per year), teaching assistantships with partial tuition reimbursements available (averaging $7,200 per year); career-related internships or fieldwork, Federal Work-Study, scholarships/grants, tuition waivers (partial), and unspecified assistantships also available. Support available to part-time students. Financial award application deadline: 4/15; financial award applicants required to submit FAFSA. *Faculty research:* Applied, discipline, pedagogical theory-based, empirical-based. *Unit head:* Melissa Holland, Director, 912-478-2357, Fax: 912-478-7480, E-mail: mholland@georgiasouthern.edu. *Application contact:* Amanda Gilliland, Coordinator for Graduate Student Recruitment, 912-478-5384, Fax: 912-478-0740, E-mail: gradadmissions@georgiasouthern.edu. Web site: http://coba.georgia.southern.edu/mba/main.htm.

Georgia Southwestern State University, Graduate Studies, School of Business Administration, Americus, GA 31709-4693. Offers MBA. *Accreditation:* AACSB. *Entrance requirements:* For master's, GMAT or GRE General Test, minimum GPA of 2.5. Electronic applications accepted.

Georgia State University, J. Mack Robinson College of Business, Department of Managerial Sciences, Atlanta, GA 30302-3083. Offers business analysis (MBA, MS); decision sciences (PhD); entrepreneurship (MBA); human resources management (MBA, MS); management (MBA, PhD); operations management (MBA, MS); organization change (MS); personnel employee relations (PhD); strategic management (PhD). *Accreditation:* AACSB. Part-time and evening/weekend programs available. *Degree requirements:* For doctorate, thesis/dissertation. *Entrance requirements:* For master's and doctorate, GMAT. Additional exam requirements/recommendations for international students: Required—TOEFL (minimum score 610 paper-based; 255 computer-based; 101 iBT). Electronic applications accepted. *Faculty research:* Abusive supervision, entrepreneurship, time series and neural networks, organizational controls, inventory control systems.

Georgia State University, J. Mack Robinson College of Business, Executive Doctorate in Business Program, Atlanta, GA 30302-3083. Offers EDB. *Accreditation:* AACSB.

Georgia State University, J. Mack Robinson College of Business, Program in General Business Administration, Atlanta, GA 30302-3083. Offers accounting/information systems (MBA); economics (MBA, MS); enterprise risk management (MBA); general business (MBA); general business administration (EMBA, PMBA); information systems consulting (MBA); information systems risk management (MBA); international business and information technology (MBA); international entrepreneurship (MBA); MBA/JD. *Accreditation:* AACSB. Part-time and evening/weekend programs available. *Entrance requirements:* For master's, GMAT. Additional exam requirements/recommendations for international students: Required—TOEFL (minimum score 610 paper-based; 255 computer-based; 101 iBT). Electronic applications accepted.

Globe University–Woodbury, Minnesota School of Business, Woodbury, MN 55125. Offers business administration (MBA); health care management (MSM); information technology (MSM); managerial leadership (MSM).

Goddard College, Graduate Division, Master of Arts in Sustainable Business and Communities Program, Plainfield, VT 05667-9432. Offers MA. Postbaccalaureate distance learning degree programs offered (minimal on-campus study). *Degree requirements:* For master's, thesis. *Entrance requirements:* For master's, 3 letters of recommendation, study plan and resource list, interview.

Golden Gate University, Ageno School of Business, San Francisco, CA 94105-2968. Offers accounting (MBA); business administration (EMBA, MBA, PMBA, DBA); finance (MBA, MS, Certificate); financial planning (MS, Certificate); healthcare information systems (Certificate); human resource management (MBA, MS); human resources management (Certificate); information systems (MS); information technology (MBA); information technology management (Certificate); integrated marketing and communications (MS, Certificate); international business (MBA); management (MBA); marketing (MBA, MS, Certificate); operations supply chain management (Certificate); psychology (MA, Certificate); public administration (EMPA); public relations (MS, Certificate); technical market analysis (Certificate); JD/MBA. Part-time and evening/weekend programs available. *Faculty:* 19 full-time (6 women), 241 part-time/adjunct (72 women). *Students:* 397 full-time (230 women), 779 part-time (432 women); includes 376 minority (105 Black or African American, non-Hispanic/Latino; 5 American Indian or Alaska Native, non-Hispanic/Latino; 161 Asian, non-Hispanic/Latino; 77 Hispanic/Latino; 12 Native Hawaiian or other Pacific Islander, non-Hispanic/Latino; 16 Two or more races, non-Hispanic/Latino), 265 international. Average age 34. 871 applicants, 64% accepted, 271 enrolled. In 2011, 550 master's, 13 doctorates awarded. *Degree requirements:* For doctorate, thesis/dissertation, qualifying examination. *Entrance requirements:* For master's, GMAT (MBA), minimum GPA of 2.5 (MS). Additional exam requirements/recommendations for international students: Required—TOEFL (minimum score 550 paper-based; 213 computer-based; 79 iBT). *Application deadline:* For fall admission, 5/15 for domestic and international students; for winter admission, 1/15 for domestic and international students; for spring admission, 9/15 for domestic and international students. Applications are processed on a rolling basis. Application fee: $70 ($110 for international students). Electronic applications accepted. *Expenses:* Contact institution. *Financial support:* Career-related internships or fieldwork, Federal Work-Study, institutionally sponsored loans, and scholarships/grants available. Support available to part-time students. Financial award applicants required to submit FAFSA. *Unit head:* Dr. Paul Fouts, Dean, 415-442-7026, Fax: 415-442-6579. *Application contact:* Angela Melero, Enrollment Services, 415-442-7800, Fax: 415-442-7807, E-mail: info@ggu.edu. Web site: http://www.ggu.edu/programs/business-and-management.

Goldey-Beacom College, Graduate Program, Wilmington, DE 19808-1999. Offers business administration (MBA); finance (MS); financial management (MBA); health care management (MBA); human resource management (MBA); information technology (MBA); international business management (MBA); major finance (MBA); major taxation (MBA); management (MM); marketing management (MBA); taxation (MBA, MS). *Accreditation:* ACBSP. Part-time and evening/weekend programs available. *Faculty:* 19 full-time (7 women), 35 part-time/adjunct (12 women). *Students:* 58 full-time (32 women), 388 part-time (164 women); includes 89 minority (34 Black or African American, non-Hispanic/Latino; 2 American Indian or Alaska Native, non-Hispanic/Latino; 44 Asian, non-Hispanic/Latino; 9 Hispanic/Latino), 229 international. Average age 30. In 2011, 243 master's awarded. *Entrance requirements:* For master's, GMAT, MAT, GRE, minimum GPA of 3.0. Additional exam requirements/recommendations for international students: Required—TOEFL (minimum score 65 computer-based); Recommended—IELTS (minimum score 5). *Application deadline:* Applications are processed on a rolling basis. Application fee: $0. Electronic applications accepted. *Expenses: Tuition:* Full-time $15,750; part-time $875 per credit. *Required fees:* $10 per credit. *Financial support:* Scholarships/grants available. Support available to part-time students. Financial award application deadline: 4/1; financial award applicants required to submit FAFSA. *Unit head:* Larry W. Eby, Director of Admissions, 302-225-6289, Fax: 302-996-5408, E-mail: ebylw@gbc.edu. *Application contact:* Ashley E. Mashington, Graduate Admissions Representative, 302-225-6259, Fax: 302-996-5408, E-mail: mashina@gbc.edu. Web site: http://www.gbc.edu/programs/graduate/.

Gonzaga University, School of Business Administration, Spokane, WA 99258. Offers M Acc, MBA, JD/M Acc, JD/MBA. *Accreditation:* AACSB. Part-time and evening/weekend programs available. *Entrance requirements:* For master's, GMAT. Additional exam requirements/recommendations for international students: Required—TOEFL.

Governors State University, College of Business and Public Administration, Program in Business Administration, University Park, IL 60484. Offers MBA. *Accreditation:* ACBSP. Evening/weekend programs available. *Students:* 42 full-time (19 women), 92 part-time (41 women); includes 59 minority (46 Black or African American, non-Hispanic/Latino; 2 Asian, non-Hispanic/Latino; 11 Hispanic/Latino), 18 international. Average age 34. *Degree requirements:* For master's, thesis optional, competency exams in elementary and intermediate algebra. *Entrance requirements:* For master's, GMAT. *Application deadline:* For fall admission, 7/15 priority date for domestic students; for spring admission, 11/10 for domestic students. Applications are processed on a rolling basis. Application fee: $25. *Financial support:* Research assistantships, Federal Work-

Study, institutionally sponsored loans, scholarships/grants, and tuition waivers (full and partial) available. Support available to part-time students. Financial award application deadline: 5/1. *Unit head:* Dr. Ellen Foster-Curtis, Dean, College of Business and Public Administration, 708-534-4930, Fax: 708-534-8457, E-mail: efostercurtis@govst.edu.

Graduate School and University Center of the City University of New York, Graduate Studies, Program in Business, New York, NY 10016-4039. Offers accounting (PhD); behavioral science (PhD); finance (PhD); management planning systems (PhD). *Degree requirements:* For doctorate, thesis/dissertation. *Entrance requirements:* For doctorate, GMAT, writing sample (15 pages). Additional exam requirements/recommendations for international students: Required—TOEFL. Electronic applications accepted.

Grand Canyon University, College of Business, Phoenix, AZ 85017-1097. Offers accounting (MBA); corporate business administration (MBA); disaster preparedness and crisis management (MBA); executive fire service leadership (MS); finance (MBA); general management (MBA); government and policy (MPA); health care management (MPA); health systems management (MBA); human resource management (MBA); innovation (MBA); leadership (MBA, MS); management of information system (MBA); marketing (MBA); project-based (MBA); six sigma (MBA); strategic human resource management (MBA). *Accreditation:* ACBSP. Part-time and evening/weekend programs available. Postbaccalaureate distance learning degree programs offered (no on-campus study). *Entrance requirements:* For master's, equivalent of two years full-time professional work experience. Additional exam requirements/recommendations for international students: Required—TOEFL (minimum score 575 paper-based; 233 computer-based; 90 iBT), IELTS (minimum score 7). Electronic applications accepted.

Grand Canyon University, College of Doctoral Studies, Phoenix, AZ 85017-1097. Offers business administration (DBA); general psychology (PhD), including cognition and instruction, industrial and organizational psychology; organizational leadership (Ed D, PhD), including behavioral health (PhD), education and effective schools (PhD), higher education (PhD), instructional leadership (PhD), organizational development (Ed D). *Degree requirements:* For doctorate, comprehensive exam, thesis/dissertation. *Entrance requirements:* For doctorate, minimum GPA of 3.4 on earned advanced degree from regionally-accredited institution; transcripts; goals statement.

Grand Valley State University, Seidman College of Business, Program in Business Administration, Allendale, MI 49401-9403. Offers MBA, MSN/MBA. *Accreditation:* AACSB. Part-time and evening/weekend programs available. *Entrance requirements:* For master's, GMAT. Additional exam requirements/recommendations for international students: Required—TOEFL. Electronic applications accepted. *Faculty research:* E-commerce, continuous improvement, currency futures, manufacturing flexibility.

Grand View University, Master of Science in Innovative Leadership Program, Des Moines, IA 50316-1599. Offers business (MS); education (MS); nursing (MS). Part-time and evening/weekend programs available. *Faculty:* 7 full-time (3 women). *Students:* 31 part-time (23 women). Average age 32. In 2011, 16 master's awarded. *Degree requirements:* For master's, completion of all required coursework in common core and selected track with minimum cumulative GPA of 3.0 and no more than two grades of C. *Entrance requirements:* For master's, GRE, GMAT, or essay, minimum undergraduate GPA of 3.0, professional resume, 3 letters of recommendation, interview. Additional exam requirements/recommendations for international students: Required—TOEFL (minimum score 550 paper-based; 210 computer-based). *Application deadline:* Applications are processed on a rolling basis. Application fee: $40. Electronic applications accepted. *Expenses: Tuition:* Part-time $501 per credit. *Required fees:* $115 per semester. *Unit head:* Dr. Patricia Rinke, Dean of Graduate and Adult Programs, 515-263-2912, E-mail: prinke@grandview.edu. *Application contact:* Michael Norris, Director of Graduate Admissions, 515-263-2830, E-mail: gradadmissions@grandview.edu. Web site: http://www.grandview.edu.

Grantham University, Mark Skousen School of Business, Kansas City, MO 64153. Offers business administration (MBA); business intelligence (MS); information management (MBA); information management technology (MS); information technology (MS); performance improvement (MS); project management (MBA, MSIM). Part-time and evening/weekend programs available. Postbaccalaureate distance learning degree programs offered (no on-campus study). *Degree requirements:* For master's, capstone project. *Entrance requirements:* For master's, bachelor's degree from accredited degree-granting institution. Additional exam requirements/recommendations for international students: Required—TOEFL (minimum score 500 paper-based; 213 computer-based; 61 iBT). Electronic applications accepted.

Green Mountain College, Program in Business Administration, Poultney, VT 05764-1199. Offers MBA. Distance learning only. Postbaccalaureate distance learning degree programs offered (no on-campus study). *Entrance requirements:* For master's, GMAT or Quantitative Skills Assessment, 3 recommendations. Electronic applications accepted. *Faculty research:* Migrant farm workers and world systems theory ecosystem assessments.

Gwynedd-Mercy College, Center for Lifelong Learning, Gwynedd Valley, PA 19437-0901. Offers MSM. *Faculty:* 7 part-time/adjunct (1 woman). *Students:* 61 full-time (40 women), 56 part-time (49 women); includes 53 minority (48 Black or African American, non-Hispanic/Latino; 1 American Indian or Alaska Native, non-Hispanic/Latino; 2 Asian, non-Hispanic/Latino; 2 Hispanic/Latino). Average age 36. *Entrance requirements:* For master's, minimum GPA of 3.0. *Expenses: Tuition:* Part-time $630 per credit hour. *Unit head:* Joseph Coleman, Executive Director, 215-643-8458. *Application contact:* Information Contact, 800-342-5462, Fax: 215-641-5556. Web site: http://www.gmc.edu/workingadults/cll/contactus.php.

Hamline University, School of Business, St. Paul, MN 55104-1284. Offers business (MBA); nonprofit management (MA); public administration (MA, DPA); JD/MA; JD/MBA; LL M/MA; LL M/MBA; MA/MA; MBA/MA. Part-time and evening/weekend programs available. *Faculty:* 21 full-time (9 women), 44 part-time/adjunct (12 women). *Students:* 435 full-time (221 women), 117 part-time (63 women); includes 71 minority (44 Black or African American, non-Hispanic/Latino; 2 American Indian or Alaska Native, non-Hispanic/Latino; 17 Asian, non-Hispanic/Latino; 5 Hispanic/Latino; 3 Two or more races, non-Hispanic/Latino), 66 international. Average age 33. 316 applicants, 70% accepted, 149 enrolled. In 2011, 295 master's awarded. *Degree requirements:* For master's, thesis (for some programs); for doctorate, comprehensive exam, thesis/dissertation. *Entrance requirements:* For master's, personal statement, official transcripts, curriculum vitae, letters of recommendation, writing sample; for doctorate, personal statement, curriculum vitae, official transcripts, letters of recommendation, writing sample. Additional exam requirements/recommendations for international students: Required—TOEFL (minimum score 80 iBT). *Application deadline:* Applications are processed on a rolling basis. Application fee: $0 ($100 for international students). Electronic applications accepted. *Expenses: Tuition:* Full-time $3720; part-time $465 per credit. *Required fees:* $28 per year. Tuition and fees vary according to degree level, campus/location and program. *Financial support:* Federal Work-Study and scholarships/grants available. Support available to part-time students. Financial award applicants required to submit FAFSA. *Faculty research:* Liberal arts-based business programs, experiential learning, organizational process/politics, gender differences, social equity. *Unit head:* Dr. Anne McCarthy, Dean, 651-523-2284, Fax: 651-523-3098, E-mail: amccarthy02@gw.hamline.edu. *Application contact:* Michael Hand, Assistant Director, Graduate Admission, 651-523-2900, Fax: 651-523-3058, E-mail: mhand01@gw.hamline.edu. Web site: http://www.hamline.edu/business.

Hampton University, Graduate College, Program in Business Administration, Hampton, VA 23668. Offers MBA, PhD. Part-time and evening/weekend programs available. *Entrance requirements:* For master's, GRE General Test.

Hampton University, Hampton U Online, Hampton, VA 23668. Offers business administration (PhD); educational management (PhD); health administration (MHA); nursing (MSN, PhD).

Harding University, Paul R. Carter College of Business Administration, Searcy, AR 72149-0001. Offers health care management (MBA); information technology management (MBA); international business (MBA); leadership and organizational management (MBA). *Accreditation:* ACBSP. Part-time and evening/weekend programs available. Postbaccalaureate distance learning degree programs offered (no on-campus study). *Faculty:* 30 part-time/adjunct (6 women). *Students:* 60 full-time (25 women), 140 part-time (63 women); includes 33 minority (26 Black or African American, non-Hispanic/Latino; 1 American Indian or Alaska Native, non-Hispanic/Latino; 3 Asian, non-Hispanic/Latino; 1 Hispanic/Latino; 2 Two or more races, non-Hispanic/Latino), 24 international. Average age 30. 65 applicants, 98% accepted, 64 enrolled. In 2011, 120 master's awarded. *Degree requirements:* For master's, portfolio. *Entrance requirements:* For master's, GMAT (minimum score of 500) or GRE (minimum score of 300), minimum GPA of 3.0, 2 letters of recommendation, resume, 3 essays, all official transcripts. Additional exam requirements/recommendations for international students: Required—TOEFL (minimum score 550 paper-based; 213 computer-based; 79 iBT). *Application deadline:* For fall admission, 8/1 priority date for domestic students, 8/1 for international students; for spring admission, 12/1 priority date for domestic students, 12/1 for international students. Applications are processed on a rolling basis. Application fee: $40. *Expenses: Tuition:* Full-time $10,512; part-time $584 per credit hour. *Required fees:* $500; $25 per credit hour. Tuition and fees vary according to course load, degree level and program. *Financial support:* In 2011–12, 19 students received support. Unspecified assistantships available. Financial award application deadline: 7/30; financial award applicants required to submit FAFSA. *Unit head:* Glen Metheny, Director of Graduate Studies, 501-279-5851, Fax: 501-279-4805, E-mail: gmetheny@harding.edu. *Application contact:* Melanie Kiihnl, Recruiting Manager/Director of Marketing, 501-279-4523, Fax: 501-279-4805, E-mail: mba@harding.edu. Web site: http://www.harding.edu/mba.

Hardin-Simmons University, The Acton MBA in Entrepreneurship, Austin, TX 78701. Offers MBA. *Entrance requirements:* For master's, GMAT, letters of recommendation. Additional exam requirements/recommendations for international students: Required—TOEFL. *Application deadline:* For fall admission, 5/1 for domestic students, 2/25 for international students. Application fee: $150. *Expenses: Tuition:* Full-time $12,870; part-time $715 per credit hour. *Required fees:* $650; $110 per semester. Tuition and fees vary according to degree level. *Application contact:* Jessica Blanchard, Director of Recruiting, 512-703-1231, E-mail: jblanchard@actonmba.org. Web site: http://www.actonmba.org.

Hardin-Simmons University, Graduate School, Kelley College of Business, Abilene, TX 79698-0001. Offers MBA. *Accreditation:* ACBSP. Part-time and evening/weekend programs available. *Faculty:* 6 full-time (2 women), 1 part-time/adjunct (0 women). *Students:* 12 full-time (5 women), 16 part-time (6 women); includes 7 minority (1 Black or African American, non-Hispanic/Latino; 2 Asian, non-Hispanic/Latino; 4 Hispanic/Latino), 3 international. Average age 28. 17 applicants, 94% accepted, 12 enrolled. In 2011, 8 master's awarded. *Degree requirements:* For master's, thesis or alternative. *Entrance requirements:* For master's, GMAT, minimum GPA of 3.0 in upper-level course work, resume, interview. Additional exam requirements/recommendations for international students: Required—TOEFL (minimum score 600 paper-based; 232 computer-based; 75 iBT). *Application deadline:* For fall admission, 8/15 priority date for domestic students, 4/1 for international students; for spring admission, 1/5 priority date for domestic students, 9/1 for international students. Applications are processed on a rolling basis. Application fee: $50. *Expenses: Tuition:* Full-time $12,870; part-time $715 per credit hour. *Required fees:* $650; $110 per semester. Tuition and fees vary according to degree level. *Financial support:* In 2011–12, 26 students received support, including 20 fellowships (averaging $1,125 per year); scholarships/grants also available. Support available to part-time students. Financial award application deadline: 6/30; financial award applicants required to submit FAFSA. *Unit head:* Dr. Nancy Kucinski, Director, 325-670-1503, Fax: 325-670-1523, E-mail: kucinski@hsutx.edu. *Application contact:* Dr. Nancy Kucinski, Dean of Graduate Studies, 325-670-1298, Fax: 325-670-1564, E-mail: gradoff@hsutx.edu. Web site: http://www.hsutx.edu/academics/kelley/graduate/mba.

Harvard University, Extension School, Cambridge, MA 02138-3722. Offers applied sciences (CAS); biotechnology (ALM); educational technologies (ALM); educational technology (CET); English for graduate and professional studies (DGP); environmental management (ALM, CEM); information technology (ALM); journalism (ALM); liberal arts (ALM); management (ALM, CM); mathematics for teaching (ALM); museum studies (ALM); premedical studies (Diploma); publication and communication (CPC). Part-time and evening/weekend programs available. *Degree requirements:* For master's, thesis. *Entrance requirements:* For master's, 3 completed graduate courses with grade of B or higher. Additional exam requirements/recommendations for international students: Required—TOEFL (minimum score 600 paper-based; 250 computer-based), TWE (minimum score 5). *Expenses:* Contact institution.

Harvard University, Harvard Business School, Doctoral Programs in Management, Boston, MA 02163. Offers accounting and management (DBA); business economics (PhD); health policy management (PhD); management (DBA); marketing (DBA); organizational behavior (PhD); science, technology and management (PhD); strategy (DBA); technology and operations management (DBA). *Degree requirements:* For doctorate, comprehensive exam (for some programs), thesis/dissertation. *Entrance requirements:* For doctorate, GRE General Test or GMAT. Additional exam requirements/recommendations for international students: Required—TOEFL. *Expenses: Tuition:* Full-time $36,304. *Required fees:* $1186. Full-time tuition and fees vary according to program.

Harvard University, Harvard Business School, Master's Program in Business Administration, Boston, MA 02163. Offers MBA, JD/MBA. *Entrance requirements:* For master's, GMAT. Additional exam requirements/recommendations for international students: Required—TOEFL. *Expenses: Tuition:* Full-time $36,304. *Required fees:* $1186. Full-time tuition and fees vary according to program.

Hawai`i Pacific University, College of Business Administration, Honolulu, HI 96813. Offers accounting/CPA (MBA); e-business (MBA); economics (MBA); finance (MBA); human resource management (MA, MBA); information systems (MBA, MSIS), including knowledge management (MSIS), software engineering (MSIS), telecommunications security (MSIS); international business (MBA); management (MBA); marketing (MBA); organizational change (MA, MBA); travel industry management (MBA). Part-time and evening/weekend programs available. *Faculty:* 15 full-time (5 women), 11 part-time/adjunct (4 women). *Students:* 297 full-time (133 women), 183 part-time (87 women);

includes 282 minority (17 Black or African American, non-Hispanic/Latino; 131 Asian, non-Hispanic/Latino; 43 Hispanic/Latino; 10 Native Hawaiian or other Pacific Islander, non-Hispanic/Latino; 81 Two or more races, non-Hispanic/Latino). Average age 30. 302 applicants, 82% accepted, 160 enrolled. In 2011, 141 master's awarded. *Degree requirements:* For master's, thesis. *Entrance requirements:* For master's, GMAT. Additional exam requirements/recommendations for international students: Recommended—TOEFL (minimum score 550 paper-based; 213 computer-based; 80 iBT), TWE (minimum score 5). *Application deadline:* For fall admission, 2/15 priority date for domestic students; for spring admission, 10/15 priority date for domestic students. Applications are processed on a rolling basis. Application fee: $50. Electronic applications accepted. *Expenses: Tuition:* Full-time $13,230; part-time $735 per credit. Tuition and fees vary according to course load and program. *Financial support:* In 2011–12, 103 students received support. Research assistantships, career-related internships or fieldwork, Federal Work-Study, scholarships/grants, tuition waivers, and unspecified assistantships available. Financial award application deadline: 3/1; financial award applicants required to submit FAFSA. *Faculty research:* Statistical control process as used by management, studies in comparative cross-cultural management styles, not-for-profit management. *Unit head:* Dr. Deborah Crown, Dean, 808-544-0275, Fax: 808-544-0283, E-mail: dcrown@hpu.edu. *Application contact:* Chad Schempp, Director of Graduate Admissions, 808-543-8035, Fax: 808-544-0280, E-mail: graduate@hpu.edu. Web site: http://www.hpu.edu/mba.

See Display below and Close-Up on page 221.

HEC Montreal, School of Business Administration, Doctoral Program in Administration, Montréal, QC H3T 2A7, Canada. Offers PhD. Program offered jointly with Concordia University, McGill University, and Université du Québec à Montréal. *Accreditation:* AACSB. *Students:* 158 full-time (74 women). 125 applicants, 28% accepted, 13 enrolled. In 2011, 13 doctorates awarded. *Degree requirements:* For doctorate, one foreign language, thesis/dissertation. *Entrance requirements:* For doctorate, GMAT, GRE, master's degree in administration or related field. *Application deadline:* For fall admission, 1/15 for domestic and international students; for winter admission, 9/1 for domestic and international students. Application fee: $80. Electronic applications accepted. Application fee is waived when completed online. *Expenses:* Contact institution. *Financial support:* Research assistantships and teaching assistantships available. Financial award application deadline: 9/2. *Unit head:* Alain d'Astous, Director, 514-340-6416, Fax: 514-340-5690, E-mail: alain.dastous@hec.ca. *Application contact:* Francine Blais, Administrative Director, 514-340-6112, Fax: 514-340-6411, E-mail: virginie.lefebvre@hec.ca. Web site: http://www.hec.ca/en/programs_training/phd/index.html.

HEC Montreal, School of Business Administration, Graduate Diplomas Programs in Administration, Program in Management, Montréal, QC H3T 2A7, Canada. Offers Graduate Diploma. All courses are given in French. *Accreditation:* AACSB. Part-time programs available. *Students:* 61 full-time (35 women), 403 part-time (227 women). 229 applicants, 70% accepted, 111 enrolled. In 2011, 160 Graduate Diplomas awarded. *Degree requirements:* For Graduate Diploma, one foreign language. *Entrance requirements:* For degree, bachelor's degree (not in administration). *Application deadline:* For fall admission, 4/1 for domestic and international students; for winter admission, 9/15 for domestic and international students; for spring admission, 2/15 for domestic and international students. Application fee: $80 Canadian dollars. Electronic applications accepted. Application fee is waived when completed online. *Expenses:* Contact institution. *Financial support:* Scholarships/grants available. Financial award application deadline: 9/2. *Unit head:* Silvia Ponce, Director, 514-340-6393, Fax: 514-340-6915, E-mail: silvia.ponce@hec.ca. *Application contact:* Jo Anne Audet, Administrative Director, 514-340-1315, Fax: 514-340-6411, E-mail: joanne.audet@hec.ca. Web site: http://www.hec.ca/programmes_formations/des/dess/dess_gestion/index.html.

HEC Montreal, School of Business Administration, Graduate Diplomas Programs in Administration, Program in Management and Sustainable Development, Montréal, QC H3T 2A7, Canada. Offers Graduate Diploma. Part-time programs available. *Students:* 15 full-time (9 women), 61 part-time (37 women). 61 applicants, 72% accepted, 31 enrolled. In 2011, 32 Graduate Diplomas awarded. *Degree requirements:* For Graduate Diploma, one foreign language. *Application deadline:* For fall admission, 4/15 for domestic and international students. Application fee: $80. Electronic applications accepted. Application fee is waived when completed online. *Expenses:* Contact institution. *Financial support:* Research assistantships and teaching assistantships available. Financial award application deadline: 9/2. *Unit head:* Silvia Ponce, Director, 514-340-6393, Fax: 514-340-6915, E-mail: silvia.ponce@hec.ca. *Application contact:* Jo Anne Audet, Administrative Director, 514-340-1315, Fax: 514-340-6411, E-mail: joanne.audet@hec.ca. Web site: http://www.hec.ca/programmes_formations/des/dess/dess_gestion_developpement_durable/index.html.

HEC Montreal, School of Business Administration, Master of Science Programs in Administration, Montréal, QC H3T 2A7, Canada. Offers applied economics (M Sc); applied financial economics (M Sc); business analytics (M Sc); business intelligence (M Sc); cultural enterprises (MM); electronic commerce (M Sc); finance (M Sc); financial and strategic accounting (M Sc); financial engineering (M Sc); global supply chain management (M Sc); human resources management (M Sc); information technologies (M Sc); international business (M Sc); international logistics (M Sc); management (M Sc); management control (M Sc); marketing (M Sc); organizational development (M Sc); organizational studies (M Sc); production and operations management (M Sc); public accounting (M Sc); strategy (M Sc); taxation (LL M). *Accreditation:* AACSB. Part-time programs available. *Students:* 687 full-time (299 women), 201 part-time (107 women). 798 applicants, 55% accepted, 250 enrolled. In 2011, 249 master's awarded. *Degree requirements:* For master's, one foreign language, thesis. *Entrance requirements:* For master's, bachelor's degree in business administration or equivalent. *Application deadline:* For fall admission, 3/15 for domestic and international students; for winter admission, 9/15 for domestic and international students. Application fee: $80 Canadian dollars. Electronic applications accepted. Application fee is waived when completed online. *Expenses:* Contact institution. *Financial support:* Research assistantships, teaching assistantships, and scholarships/grants available. Financial award application deadline: 9/2. *Unit head:* Dr. Claude Laurin, Director, 514-340-6536, Fax: 514-340-6880, E-mail: claude.laurin@hec.ca. *Application contact:* Virginie Lefebvre, Administrative Director, 514-340-6112, Fax: 514-340-6411, E-mail: virginie.lefebvre@hec.ca. Web site: http://www.hec.ca/en/programs_training/msc/index.html.

HEC Montreal, School of Business Administration, Master's Program in Business Administration and Management, Montréal, QC H3T 2A7, Canada. Offers MBA. Courses are given in French or English. *Accreditation:* AACSB. Part-time programs available. *Students:* 174 full-time (56 women), 249 part-time (79 women). 507 applicants, 36% accepted, 145 enrolled. In 2011, 247 master's awarded. *Degree requirements:* For master's, one foreign language. *Entrance requirements:* For master's, GMAT, 3 years of related work experience. Additional exam requirements/recommendations for international students: Required—TOEFL (minimum score 95 iBT). *Application deadline:* For fall admission, 3/15 for domestic students, 2/1 for international students. Application fee: $80 Canadian dollars. Electronic applications accepted. Application fee is waived when completed online. *Expenses:* Contact institution. *Financial support:* Scholarships/grants available. *Unit head:* Michael Wybo, Director, 514-340-6830, Fax: 514-340-6132, E-mail: michael.wybo@hec.ca. *Application* *contact:* Julie Benoit, Administrative Director, 514-340-6137, Fax: 514-340-5640, E-mail: julie.benoit@hec.ca. Web site: http://www.hec.ca/en/programs/mba/.

Heidelberg University, Program in Business, Tiffin, OH 44883-2462. Offers MBA. Part-time and evening/weekend programs available. *Degree requirements:* For master's, thesis or alternative, internship, practicum. *Entrance requirements:* For master's, previous undergraduate course work in business, minimum GPA of 2.7. Additional exam requirements/recommendations for international students: Required—TOEFL. *Expenses:* Contact institution.

Henderson State University, Graduate Studies, School of Business Administration, Arkadelphia, AR 71999-0001. Offers MBA. *Accreditation:* AACSB. Part-time programs available. *Entrance requirements:* For master's, GMAT (minimum score 400), minimum AACSB index of 1000, minimum GPA of 2.7. Additional exam requirements/recommendations for international students: Required—TOEFL (minimum score 550 paper-based; 213 computer-based); Recommended—IELTS (minimum score 6). Electronic applications accepted.

Herzing University Online, Program in Business Administration, Milwaukee, WI 53203. Offers accounting (MBA); business administration (MBA); business management (MBA); healthcare management (MBA); human resources (MBA); marketing (MBA); project management (MBA); technology management (MBA). Postbaccalaureate distance learning degree programs offered (no on-campus study).

High Point University, Norcross Graduate School, High Point, NC 27262-3598. Offers business administration (MBA); educational leadership (M Ed); elementary education (M Ed); history (MA); nonprofit management (MA); secondary math (M Ed); special education (M Ed); strategic communication (MA); teaching elementary education k-6 (MAT); teaching secondary mathematics 9-12 (MAT). *Accreditation:* ACBSP; NCATE. Part-time and evening/weekend programs available. *Degree requirements:* For master's, comprehensive exam (for some programs), thesis (for some programs). *Entrance requirements:* For master's, GMAT (MBA), GRE, MAT, minimum GPA of 3.0. Additional exam requirements/recommendations for international students: Required—TOEFL (minimum score 550 paper-based). Electronic applications accepted.

Hodges University, Graduate Programs, Naples, FL 34119. Offers business administration (MBA); criminal justice (MS); education (MPS); information systems management (MIS); legal studies (MS); management (MSM); mental health counseling (MS); public administration (MPA). Part-time and evening/weekend programs available. Postbaccalaureate distance learning degree programs offered (no on-campus study). *Faculty:* 22 full-time (9 women), 3 part-time/adjunct (2 women). *Students:* 28 full-time (21 women), 237 part-time (156 women); includes 76 minority (35 Black or African American, non-Hispanic/Latino; 5 Asian, non-Hispanic/Latino; 36 Hispanic/Latino). Average age 36. 92 applicants, 91% accepted, 81 enrolled. *Degree requirements:* For master's, comprehensive exam (for some programs), thesis (for some programs). *Entrance requirements:* For master's, in-house entrance exam. Additional exam requirements/recommendations for international students: Recommended—TOEFL. *Application deadline:* Applications are processed on a rolling basis. Application fee: $50. Electronic applications accepted. *Expenses: Tuition:* Full-time $11,340; part-time $630 per credit hour. *Required fees:* $250 per term. *Financial support:* In 2011–12, 200 students received support. Federal Work-Study and scholarships/grants available. Financial award application deadline: 7/9; financial award applicants required to submit FAFSA. *Unit head:* Terry McMahan, President, 239-513-1122, Fax: 239-598-6253, E-mail: tmcmahan@hodges.edu. *Application contact:* Rita Lampus, Vice President of Student Enrollment Management, 239-513-1122, Fax: 239-598-6253, E-mail: rlampus@hodges.edu.

Hofstra University, Frank G. Zarb School of Business, Department of Finance, Hempstead, NY 11549. Offers banking (Advanced Certificate); business administration (MBA), including finance, real estate management (MBA, MS); corporate finance (Advanced Certificate); finance (MS), including investment analysis; investment management (Advanced Certificate); quantitative finance (MS), including real estate management (MBA, MS). Part-time and evening/weekend programs available. *Faculty:* 13 full-time (2 women), 4 part-time/adjunct (2 women). *Students:* 222 full-time (91 women), 98 part-time (23 women); includes 24 minority (6 Black or African American, non-Hispanic/Latino; 15 Asian, non-Hispanic/Latino; 3 Hispanic/Latino), 198 international. Average age 26. 666 applicants, 63% accepted, 106 enrolled. In 2011, 124 master's awarded. *Degree requirements:* For master's, capstone course (for MBA); thesis (for MS); minimum GPA of 3.0. *Entrance requirements:* For master's, GMAT/GRE, 2 letters of recommendation; resume; essay. Additional exam requirements/recommendations for international students: Required—TOEFL (minimum score 550 paper-based; 213 computer-based; 80 iBT); Recommended—IELTS (minimum score 6). *Application deadline:* Applications are processed on a rolling basis. Application fee: $70 ($75 for international students). Electronic applications accepted. *Expenses:* Contact institution. *Financial support:* In 2011–12, 32 students received support, including 26 fellowships with full and partial tuition reimbursements available (averaging $8,389 per year), 1 research assistantship with full and partial tuition reimbursement available (averaging $4,925 per year); Federal Work-Study, institutionally sponsored loans, scholarships/grants, and tuition waivers (full and partial) also available. Support available to part-time students. Financial award applicants required to submit FAFSA. *Faculty research:* International finance; investments; banking, corporate finance; real estate; derivatives. *Unit head:* Dr. K. G. Viswanathan, Chairperson, 516-463-5699, Fax: 516-463-4834, E-mail: finkgv@hofstra.edu. *Application contact:* Carol Drummer, Dean of Graduate Admissions, 516-463-4876, Fax: 516-463-4664, E-mail: gradstudent@hofstra.edu. Web site: http://www.hofstra.edu/business/.

Hofstra University, Frank G. Zarb School of Business, Department of Information Technology and Quantitative Methods, Hempstead, NY 11549. Offers business administration (MBA), including information technology, quality management; information technology (MS, Advanced Certificate). Part-time and evening/weekend programs available. *Faculty:* 9 full-time (2 women), 2 part-time/adjunct (0 women). *Students:* 16 full-time (3 women), 14 part-time (3 women); includes 6 minority (2 Black or African American, non-Hispanic/Latino; 3 Asian, non-Hispanic/Latino; 1 Hispanic/Latino), 8 international. Average age 29. 42 applicants, 76% accepted, 9 enrolled. In 2011, 4 master's awarded. *Degree requirements:* For master's, capstone course (for MBA); thesis (for MS); minimum GPA of 3.0. *Entrance requirements:* For master's, GMAT/GRE, 2 letters of recommendation; resume; essay; for Advanced Certificate, GMAT/GRE, 2 letters of recommendation; resume. Additional exam requirements/recommendations for international students: Required—TOEFL (minimum score 550 paper-based; 213 computer-based; 80 iBT); Recommended—IELTS (minimum score 6). *Application deadline:* Applications are processed on a rolling basis. Application fee: $70 ($75 for international students). Electronic applications accepted. *Expenses:* Contact institution. *Financial support:* In 2011–12, 5 students received support, including 5 fellowships with full and partial tuition reimbursements available (averaging $6,680 per year); research assistantships with full and partial tuition reimbursements available, career-related internships or fieldwork, Federal Work-Study, institutionally sponsored loans, scholarships/grants, tuition waivers (full and partial), and unspecified assistantships also available. Support available to part-time students. Financial award applicants required to submit FAFSA. *Faculty research:* IT Outsourcing, IT Strategy, SAP and enterprise systems, data mining/electronic medical records, IT and crisis management, inventory theory and modeling, forecasting. *Unit head:* Dr. Mohammed H. Tafti, Chairperson, 516-463-5720, E-mail: acsmht@hofstra.edu. *Application contact:* Carol Drummer, Dean of Graduate Admissions, 516-463-4876, Fax: 516-463-4664, E-mail: gradstudent@hofstra.edu. Web site: http://www.hofstra.edu/business/.

Hofstra University, Frank G. Zarb School of Business, Department of Management, Entrepreneurship and General Management, Hempstead, NY 11549. Offers business administration (MBA), including health services management, management, sports and entertainment management; general management (Advanced Certificate); human resource management (MS, Advanced Certificate). Part-time and evening/weekend programs available. Postbaccalaureate distance learning degree programs offered (minimal on-campus study). *Faculty:* 7 full-time (2 women), 8 part-time/adjunct (1 woman). *Students:* 92 full-time (36 women), 151 part-time (62 women); includes 58 minority (25 Black or African American, non-Hispanic/Latino; 23 Asian, non-Hispanic/Latino; 10 Hispanic/Latino), 24 international. Average age 32. 227 applicants, 72% accepted, 93 enrolled. In 2011, 74 master's awarded. *Degree requirements:* For master's, thesis optional, capstone course (for MBA); thesis (for MS); minimum GPA of 3.0. *Entrance requirements:* For master's, GMAT/GRE, 2 letters of recommendation; resume; essay. Additional exam requirements/recommendations for international students: Required—TOEFL (minimum score 550 paper-based; 213 computer-based; 80 iBT); Recommended—IELTS (minimum score 6). *Application deadline:* Applications are processed on a rolling basis. Application fee: $70 ($75 for international students). Electronic applications accepted. *Expenses:* Contact institution. *Financial support:* In 2011–12, 23 students received support, including 18 fellowships with full and partial tuition reimbursements available (averaging $5,605 per year), 1 research assistantship with full and partial tuition reimbursement available (averaging $11,370 per year); career-related internships or fieldwork, Federal Work-Study, institutionally sponsored loans, scholarships/grants, tuition waivers (full and partial), and unspecified assistantships also available. Support available to part-time students. Financial award applicants required to submit FAFSA. *Faculty research:* Business/personal ethics, sustainability, innovation, decision-making, supply chain management, learning and pedagogical issues, family business, small business, entrepreneurship. *Unit head:* Dr. Li-Lian Gao, Chairperson, 516-463-5729, Fax: 516-463-4834, E-mail: mgblzg@hofstra.edu. *Application contact:* Carol Drummer, Dean of Graduate Admissions, 516-463-4876, Fax: 516-463-4664, E-mail: gradstudent@hofstra.edu. Web site: http://www.hofstra.edu/Academics/Colleges/Zarb/MGMT/.

Hofstra University, Frank G. Zarb School of Business, Department of Marketing and International Business, Hempstead, NY 11549. Offers business administration (MBA), including international business, marketing; international business (Advanced Certificate); marketing (MS, Advanced Certificate); marketing research (MS). Part-time and evening/weekend programs available. *Faculty:* 9 full-time (0 women), 3 part-time/adjunct (0 women). *Students:* 91 full-time (54 women), 39 part-time (20 women); includes 11 minority (2 Black or African American, non-Hispanic/Latino; 3 Asian, non-Hispanic/Latino; 6 Hispanic/Latino), 73 international. Average age 27. 260 applicants, 71% accepted, 46 enrolled. In 2011, 43 master's awarded. *Degree requirements:* For master's, capstone course (MBA), thesis (MS), minimum GPA of 3.0. *Entrance requirements:* For master's, GMAT or GRE, 2 letters of recommendation, resume, essay. Additional exam requirements/recommendations for international students: Required—TOEFL (minimum score 550 paper-based; 213 computer-based; 80 iBT); Recommended—IELTS (minimum score 6). *Application deadline:* Applications are processed on a rolling basis. Application fee: $70 ($75 for international students). Electronic applications accepted. *Expenses:* Contact institution. *Financial support:* In 2011–12, 19 students received support, including 18 fellowships with full and partial tuition reimbursements available (averaging $7,371 per year); research assistantships with full and partial tuition reimbursements available, career-related internships or fieldwork, Federal Work-Study, institutionally sponsored loans, scholarships/grants, tuition waivers (full and partial), and unspecified assistantships also available. Support available to part-time students. Financial award applicants required to submit FAFSA. *Faculty research:* Outsourcing, global alliances, retailing, Web marketing, cross-cultural age research. *Unit head:* Dr. Benny Barak, Chairperson, 516-463-5707, Fax: 516-463-4834, E-mail: mktbzb@hofstra.edu. *Application contact:* Carol Drummer, Dean of Graduate Admissions, 516-463-4876, Fax: 516-463-4664, E-mail: gradstudent@hofstra.edu. Web site: http://www.hofstra.edu/business/.

Hofstra University, Frank G. Zarb School of Business, Executive Master's Program in Business Administration, Hempstead, NY 11549. Offers management (EMBA). Evening/weekend programs available. *Students:* 1 (woman) full-time, 14 part-time (4 women); includes 5 minority (1 Black or African American, non-Hispanic/Latino; 2 Asian, non-Hispanic/Latino; 2 Hispanic/Latino). Average age 35. 15 applicants, 60% accepted. In 2011, 13 master's awarded. *Degree requirements:* For master's, minimum GPA of 3.0. *Entrance requirements:* For master's, 2 letters of recommendation; minimum 7 years of management experience; resume; interview; essay. Additional exam requirements/recommendations for international students: Required—TOEFL (minimum score 550 paper-based; 213 computer-based; 80 iBT); Recommended—IELTS (minimum score 6). *Application deadline:* Applications are processed on a rolling basis. Application fee: $70 ($75 for international students). Electronic applications accepted. *Expenses:* Contact institution. *Financial support:* In 2011–12, 1 student received support, including 1 fellowship with full and partial tuition reimbursement available (averaging $3,000 per year); research assistantships with full and partial tuition reimbursements available, Federal Work-Study, institutionally sponsored loans, scholarships/grants, and tuition waivers (full and partial) also available. Support available to part-time students. Financial award applicants required to submit FAFSA. *Faculty research:* Business strategy, international business, financial management, marketing management. *Unit head:* Dr. Barry Berman, Director, 516-463-5711, E-mail: mktbxb@hofstra.edu. *Application contact:* Carol Drummer, Dean of Graduate Admissions, 516-463-4876, Fax: 516-463-4664, E-mail: gradstudent@hofstra.edu. Web site: http://www.hofstra.edu/emba.

Hofstra University, Frank G. Zarb School of Business, Programs in Accounting and Taxation, Hempstead, NY 11549. Offers accounting (MS, Advanced Certificate); business administration (MBA), including accounting, professional accountancy, taxation; taxation (MS, Advanced Certificate). Part-time and evening/weekend programs available. Postbaccalaureate distance learning degree programs offered (minimal on-campus study). *Faculty:* 13 full-time (4 women), 5 part-time/adjunct (1 woman). *Students:* 166 full-time (100 women), 70 part-time (35 women); includes 30 minority (3 Black or African American, non-Hispanic/Latino; 20 Asian, non-Hispanic/Latino; 7 Hispanic/Latino), 97 international. Average age 25. 383 applicants, 79% accepted, 113 enrolled. In 2011, 45 master's awarded. *Degree requirements:* For master's, capstone course (for MBA); thesis (for MS); minimum GPA of 3.0. *Entrance requirements:* For master's, GMAT/GRE, 2 letters of recommendation; resume; essay. Additional exam requirements/recommendations for international students: Required—TOEFL (minimum score 550 paper-based; 213 computer-based; 80 iBT); Recommended—IELTS (minimum score 6). *Application deadline:* Applications are processed on a rolling basis. Application fee: $70 ($75 for international students). Electronic applications accepted. *Expenses:* Contact institution. *Financial support:* In 2011–12, 23 students received support, including 20 fellowships with full and partial tuition reimbursements available (averaging $6,973 per year); research assistantships with full and partial tuition reimbursements available, career-related internships or fieldwork, Federal Work-Study, institutionally sponsored loans, scholarships/grants, tuition waivers (full and partial), and unspecified assistantships also available. Support available to part-time students. Financial award applicants required to submit FAFSA. *Faculty research:* Legal issues in the insurance industry, penalties regarding tax compliance and the Internal Revenue Code, agency theory and accounts of migration, plain English financial statements, learning methods for teaching XBRL. *Unit head:* Dr. Nathan S. Slavin, Chairperson, 516-463-5690, Fax: 516-463-4834, E-mail: actnzs@hofstra.edu. *Application contact:* Carol Drummer, Dean of Graduate Admissions, 516-463-4876, Fax: 516-463-4664, E-mail: gradstudent@hofstra.edu. Web site: http://www.hofstra.edu/business/.

Holy Family University, Division of Extended Learning, Philadelphia, PA 19114. Offers business administration (MBA); finance (MBA); health care administration (MBA). *Accreditation:* ACBSP. Part-time and evening/weekend programs available. *Entrance requirements:* For master's, interview, essay. Additional exam requirements/recommendations for international students: Required—TOEFL. Electronic applications accepted.

See Display below and Close-Up on page 223.

Holy Family University, Graduate School, School of Business Administration, Philadelphia, PA 19114. Offers human resources management (MS); information systems management (MS). *Accreditation:* ACBSP. Part-time and evening/weekend programs available. *Degree requirements:* For master's, comprehensive exam, thesis optional. *Entrance requirements:* For master's, GMAT, GRE, or MAT, minimum GPA of 3.0. Electronic applications accepted.

Holy Names University, Graduate Division, Department of Business, Oakland, CA 94619-1699. Offers energy and environment management (MBA); finance (MBA); management and leadership (MBA); marketing (MBA); sports management (MBA). Part-time and evening/weekend programs available. *Entrance requirements:* For master's, minimum undergraduate GPA of 2.6 overall, 3.0 in major. Additional exam requirements/recommendations for international students: Required—TOEFL (minimum score 550 paper-based; 213 computer-based; 80 iBT). *Faculty research:* Business ethics, sustainable economics, accounting models, cross-cultural management, diversity in organizations.

Hood College, Graduate School, Department of Economics and Management, Frederick, MD 21701-8575. Offers accounting (MBA); administration and management (MBA); finance (MBA); human resource management (MBA); information systems (MBA); marketing (MBA); public management (MBA). *Accreditation:* ACBSP. Part-time and evening/weekend programs available. *Degree requirements:* For master's, capstone/final research project. *Entrance requirements:* For master's, minimum GPA of 2.75, resume, letters of recommendation. Additional exam requirements/recommendations for international students: Required—TOEFL (minimum score 575 paper-based; 231 computer-based; 89 iBT). Electronic applications accepted. *Faculty research:* Corporate strategy and sustainable competitive advantages, business ethics, entrepreneurship, investments management, economic development.

Houston Baptist University, College of Business and Economics, Program in Business Administration, Houston, TX 77074-3298. Offers MBA, MSM. *Accreditation:* ACBSP. Part-time and evening/weekend programs available. *Entrance requirements:* For master's, GMAT, minimum GPA of 2.5. Additional exam requirements/recommendations for international students: Required—TOEFL (minimum score 550 paper-based; 213 computer-based). *Expenses:* Contact institution.

Howard University, School of Business, Graduate Programs in Business, Washington, DC 20059-0002. Offers accounting (MBA); entrepreneurship (MBA); finance (MBA); general management (MBA); human resources management (MBA); information systems (MBA); international business (MBA); marketing (MBA); supply chain management (MBA); JD/MBA. *Accreditation:* AACSB. Part-time and evening/weekend programs available. Postbaccalaureate distance learning degree programs offered (no on-campus study). *Entrance requirements:* For master's, GMAT, minimum 1 year post undergraduate work experience, resume, 3 letters of recommendation, advanced college algebra. Additional exam requirements/recommendations for international students: Required—TOEFL. *Faculty research:* Marketing research in multi-ethnic populations, U.S. trade policies and international relations, risk management (finance).

Hult International Business School, MBA Program, Cambridge, MA 02141. Offers MBA. *Entrance requirements:* For master's, GMAT, 3 years of management experience. Additional exam requirements/recommendations for international students: Required—TOEFL (minimum score 240 computer-based). Electronic applications accepted. *Faculty research:* Management for international development.

Hult International Business School, Program in Business Administration - Hult London Campus, London, MA WC 1B 4JP, United Kingdom. Offers entrepreneurship (MBA); international business (MBA); international finance (MBA); marketing (MBA). Part-time programs available. *Degree requirements:* For master's, comprehensive exam, thesis, internship. *Entrance requirements:* Additional exam requirements/recommendations for international students: Required—TOEFL (minimum score 580 paper-based; 237 computer-based), TWE (minimum score 5). Electronic applications accepted.

Humboldt State University, Academic Programs, College of Professional Studies, School of Business, Arcata, CA 95521-8299. Offers MBA. Part-time and evening/weekend programs available. *Students:* 9 full-time (3 women), 2 part-time (0 women); includes 1 minority (Hispanic/Latino), 3 international. Average age 29. 28 applicants, 68% accepted, 7 enrolled. In 2011, 16 master's awarded. *Degree requirements:* For master's, thesis or alternative. *Entrance requirements:* For master's, GMAT or GRE, minimum GPA of 2.5. Additional exam requirements/recommendations for international students: Required—TOEFL (minimum score 500 paper-based; 173 computer-based). *Application deadline:* For fall admission, 6/30 for domestic and international students; for spring admission, 12/15 for domestic and international students. Applications are processed on a rolling basis. Application fee: $55. *Expenses:* Contact institution. *Financial support:* Fellowships and Federal Work-Study available. Support available to part-time students. Financial award application deadline: 3/1; financial award applicants required to submit FAFSA. *Faculty research:* International business development, small town entrepreneurship, international trade: Pacific Rim. *Unit head:* Dr. Steven Hackett, Chair, 707-826-3846, Fax: 707-826-6666, E-mail: steve.hackett@humboldt.edu. *Application contact:* Dr. Carol Telesky, MBA Coordinator, 707-826-3761, Fax: 707-826-6666, E-mail: cwt5@humboldt.edu. Web site: http://www.humboldt.edu/biz/degrees/mba.html.

Husson University, School of Graduate and Professional Studies, Master of Business Administration Program, Bangor, ME 04401-2999. Offers general (corporate) (MSB); health care management (MSB); hospitality management (MSB); nonprofit management (MSB). Part-time and evening/weekend programs available. *Faculty:* 9 full-time (3 women), 12 part-time/adjunct (2 women). *Students:* 111 full-time (66 women), 60 part-time (37 women); includes 8 minority (3 Black or African American, non-Hispanic/Latino; 1 American Indian or Alaska Native, non-Hispanic/Latino; 2 Asian, non-Hispanic/Latino; 2 Hispanic/Latino). 67 applicants, 35 enrolled. In 2011, 90 master's awarded. *Degree requirements:* For master's, comprehensive exam (for some programs), thesis optional. *Entrance requirements:* For master's, GMAT or GRE, minimum GPA of 3.0. Additional exam requirements/recommendations for international students: Required—TOEFL (minimum score 550 paper-based). *Application deadline:* Applications are processed on a rolling basis. Application fee: $40. Electronic applications accepted. *Expenses:* Contact institution. *Financial support:* In 2011–12, 1 student received support. Career-related internships or fieldwork, Federal Work-Study, scholarships/grants, and unspecified assistantships available. Financial award application deadline: 4/15; financial award applicants required to submit FAFSA. *Unit head:* Dr. Ronald Nykiel, Dean, College of Business, 207-941-7111, E-mail: nykielr@husson.edu. *Application contact:* Kristen M. Card, Director of Graduate Admissions, 207-404-5660, Fax: 207-941-7935, E-mail: cardk@husson.edu. Web site: http://www.husson.edu/mba.

Idaho State University, Office of Graduate Studies, College of Business, Pocatello, ID 83209-8020. Offers business administration (MBA, Postbaccalaureate Certificate); computer information systems (MS, Postbaccalaureate Certificate). *Accreditation:* AACSB. Part-time programs available. *Degree requirements:* For master's, comprehensive exam, thesis (for some programs), oral exam; for Postbaccalaureate Certificate, comprehensive exam, thesis (for some programs), 6 hours of clerkship. *Entrance requirements:* For master's, GMAT, GRE General Test, minimum GPA of 3.0, resume outlining work experience, 2 letters of reference; for Postbaccalaureate Certificate, GMAT, GRE General Test, minimum upper-level GPA of 3.0, resume of work experience. Additional exam requirements/recommendations for international students: Required—TOEFL (minimum score 550 paper-based; 213 computer-based; 80 iBT). Electronic applications accepted. *Faculty research:* Information assurance, computer information technology, finance management, marketing.

Illinois Institute of Technology, Stuart School of Business, Program in Business Administration, Chicago, IL 60616-3793. Offers financial management (MBA); innovation and emerging enterprises (MBA); management science (MBA); marketing (MBA); sustainability (MBA); JD/MBA; M Des/MBA; MBA/MS. *Accreditation:* AACSB. Part-time and evening/weekend programs available. *Entrance requirements:* For master's, GRE (minimum score 1000) or GMAT (500). Additional exam requirements/recommendations for international students: Required—TOEFL (minimum score 600 paper-based; 85 iBT); Recommended—IELTS (minimum score 7). Electronic applications accepted. *Expenses:* Contact institution. *Faculty research:* Global management and marketing strategy, technological innovation, management science, financial management, knowledge management.

Illinois Institute of Technology, Stuart School of Business, Program in Management Science, Chicago, IL 60616-3793. Offers PhD. *Accreditation:* AACSB. Part-time programs available. *Degree requirements:* For doctorate, comprehensive exam, thesis/dissertation. *Entrance requirements:* For doctorate, GRE (minimum score 1300) or GMAT (minimum score 650). Additional exam requirements/recommendations for international students: Required—TOEFL (minimum score 600 paper-based; 85 iBT). Electronic applications accepted. *Expenses:* Contact institution. *Faculty research:* Scheduling systems, queuing systems, optimization, quality systems, foreign exchange, enterprise risk management, credit risk modeling.

Illinois State University, Graduate School, College of Business, Program in Business Administration, Normal, IL 61790-2200. Offers MBA. *Accreditation:* AACSB. Part-time programs available. *Degree requirements:* For master's, thesis optional. *Entrance requirements:* For master's, GMAT, minimum GPA of 2.75 during previous 2 years of course work. Additional exam requirements/recommendations for international students: Required—TOEFL. *Faculty research:* McLean County small business development center.

IMCA–International Management Centres Association, Programs in Business Administration, Buckingham, United Kingdom. Offers M Mgt, M Phil, MBA, MS. Postbaccalaureate distance learning degree programs offered (no on-campus study).

Independence University, Program in Business Administration, Salt Lake City, UT 84107. Offers MBA.

Indiana State University, College of Graduate and Professional Studies, College of Business, Terre Haute, IN 47809. Offers MBA. *Accreditation:* AACSB. Part-time and evening/weekend programs available. *Degree requirements:* For master's, thesis optional. *Entrance requirements:* For master's, GMAT. Electronic applications accepted. *Faculty research:* Small business and entrepreneurial sciences, production and operations management.

Indiana Tech, Program in Business Administration, Fort Wayne, IN 46803-1297. Offers accounting (MBA); health care administration (MBA); human resources (MBA); management (MBA); marketing (MBA). Part-time and evening/weekend programs available. Postbaccalaureate distance learning degree programs offered (no on-campus study). *Entrance requirements:* For master's, GMAT, minimum undergraduate GPA of 2.5, 3 letters of recommendation. Electronic applications accepted.

Indiana Tech, Program in Management, Fort Wayne, IN 46803-1297. Offers MSM. Part-time and evening/weekend programs available. *Entrance requirements:* For master's, GMAT. Electronic applications accepted.

Indiana University Bloomington, Kelley School of Business, Bloomington, IN 47405-7000. Offers MBA, MPA, MS, DBA, PhD, DBA/MIS, JD/MBA, JD/MPA, MBA/MA, PhD/MIS. PhD offered through University Graduate School. *Accreditation:* AACSB. *Faculty:* 71 full-time (10 women). *Students:* 891 full-time (261 women), 1,117 part-time (255 women); includes 361 minority (58 Black or African American, non-Hispanic/Latino; 1 American Indian or Alaska Native, non-Hispanic/Latino; 237 Asian, non-Hispanic/Latino; 47 Hispanic/Latino; 1 Native Hawaiian or other Pacific Islander, non-Hispanic/Latino; 17 Two or more races, non-Hispanic/Latino), 421 international. Average age 31. 2,748 applicants, 44% accepted, 876 enrolled. In 2011, 150 master's, 51 doctorates awarded. *Degree requirements:* For doctorate, thesis/dissertation. *Entrance requirements:* For master's, GMAT; for doctorate, GMAT, GRE General Test. Additional exam requirements/recommendations for international students: Required—TOEFL. *Application deadline:* For fall admission, 1/15 priority date for domestic students, 12/1 for international students; for winter admission, 3/1 priority date for domestic students; for spring admission, 4/15 for domestic students, 9/1 for international students. Application fee: $55 ($65 for international students). Electronic applications accepted. *Expenses:* Contact institution. *Financial support:* Fellowships with full and partial tuition reimbursements, research assistantships, teaching assistantships, career-related internships or fieldwork, Federal Work-Study, institutionally sponsored loans, tuition waivers (full and partial), and unspecified assistantships available. Support available to part-time students. Financial award application deadline: 3/1; financial award applicants required to submit FAFSA. *Total annual research expenditures:* $1.1 million. *Unit head:* Daniel Smith, Dean, 812-855-8100, Fax: 812-855-8679, E-mail: business@indiana.edu. *Application contact:* Director of Admissions and Financial Aid, 812-855-8006, Fax: 812-855-9039. Web site: http://kelley.iu.edu/.

Indiana University Kokomo, School of Business, Kokomo, IN 46904-9003. Offers business administration (MBA). *Accreditation:* AACSB. Part-time and evening/weekend programs available. *Faculty:* 14 full-time (6 women). *Students:* 10 full-time (6 women), 29 part-time (13 women); includes 5 minority (1 Black or African American, non-Hispanic/Latino; 2 American Indian or Alaska Native, non-Hispanic/Latino; 2 Asian, non-Hispanic/Latino), 1 international. Average age 35. 9 applicants, 100% accepted, 8 enrolled. In 2011, 14 master's awarded. *Degree requirements:* For master's, thesis optional, research project. *Entrance requirements:* For master's, GMAT. Additional exam requirements/recommendations for international students: Required—TOEFL (minimum score 550 paper-based; 213 computer-based). *Application deadline:* For fall admission, 8/1 priority date for domestic students, 8/1 for international students; for spring admission, 12/15 priority date for domestic students, 12/15 for international students. Applications are processed on a rolling basis. Application fee: $40 ($50 for international students). *Expenses:* Contact institution. *Financial support:* In 2011–12, 2 fellowships (averaging $500 per year) were awarded; research assistantships, teaching assistantships, career-related internships or fieldwork, and tuition waivers (partial) also available. *Faculty research:* Investments, outsourcing, technology, adoption. *Unit head:* Dr. Niranjan Pati, Dean, 756-455-9275, Fax: 756-455-9348, E-mail: npati@iuk.edu. *Application contact:* Dr. Linda Ficht, Director of MBA Program, 765-455-9275, Fax: 765-455-9348, E-mail: lficht@iuk.edu. Web site: http://www.iuk.edu/academics/majors/business/index.shtml.

Indiana University Northwest, School of Business and Economics, Gary, IN 46408-1197. Offers accountancy (M Acc); accounting (Certificate); business administration (MBA). *Accreditation:* AACSB. Part-time and evening/weekend programs available. *Faculty:* 5 full-time (0 women). *Students:* 49 full-time (10 women), 53 part-time (28 women); includes 40 minority (25 Black or African American, non-Hispanic/Latino; 8 Asian, non-Hispanic/Latino; 7 Hispanic/Latino). Average age 34. 40 applicants, 93% accepted, 26 enrolled. In 2011, 38 master's, 12 other advanced degrees awarded. *Entrance requirements:* For master's, GMAT, letter of recommendation. *Application deadline:* For fall admission, 7/15 priority date for domestic students; for spring admission, 11/15 for domestic students. Applications are processed on a rolling basis. Application fee: $25 ($45 for international students). *Expenses:* Contact institution. *Financial support:* Federal Work-Study, institutionally sponsored loans, and unspecified assistantships available. Support available to part-time students. Financial award application deadline: 7/15. *Faculty research:* International finance, wellness in the workplace, handicapped employment, MIS, regional economic forecasting. *Unit head:* Anna Rominger, Dean, 219-980-6636, Fax: 219-980-6916, E-mail: iunbiz@iun.edu. *Application contact:* John Gibson, Director of Graduate Program, 219-980-6635, Fax: 219-980-6916, E-mail: jagibson@iun.edu. Web site: http://www.iun.edu/~busnw/.

Indiana University of Pennsylvania, School of Graduate Studies and Research, Eberly College of Business and Information Technology, MBA Executive Track Program, Indiana, PA 15705-1087. Offers MBA. *Faculty:* 33 full-time (6 women). *Students:* 51 full-time (20 women), 3 part-time (1 woman); includes 13 minority (6 Black or African American, non-Hispanic/Latino; 6 Asian, non-Hispanic/Latino; 1 Two or more races, non-Hispanic/Latino). Average age 36. 51 applicants, 71% accepted, 25 enrolled. In 2011, 18 master's awarded. *Entrance requirements:* Additional exam requirements/recommendations for international students: Required—TOEFL (minimum score 540 paper-based; 207 computer-based). *Application deadline:* Applications are processed on a rolling basis. Application fee: $50. Electronic applications accepted. *Expenses:* Tuition, state resident: full-time $7488; part-time $416 per credit. Tuition, nonresident: full-time $11,232; part-time $624 per credit. *Required fees:* $2070; $192.20 per credit. $90 per semester. *Financial support:* Application deadline: 4/15; applicants required to submit FAFSA. *Unit head:* Dr. Robert Camp, Dean, 724-357-4783, E-mail: bobcamp@iup.edu. *Application contact:* Paula Stossel, Assistant Dean, 724-357-2222, Fax: 724-357-4862, E-mail: graduate-admissions@iup.edu. Web site: http://www.iup.edu/upper.aspx?id=49407.

Indiana University of Pennsylvania, School of Graduate Studies and Research, Eberly College of Business and Information Technology, Program in Business Administration, Indiana, PA 15705-1087. Offers business administration (MBA); executive business administration (MBA). *Accreditation:* AACSB. Part-time programs available. *Faculty:* 31 full-time (6 women). *Students:* 95 full-time (33 women), 70 part-time (29 women); includes 5 minority (4 Black or African American, non-Hispanic/Latino; 1 Hispanic/Latino), 124 international. Average age 24. 156 applicants, 65% accepted, 76 enrolled. In 2011, 152 master's awarded. *Degree requirements:* For master's, thesis optional. *Entrance requirements:* For master's, GMAT, 2 letters of recommendation. Additional exam requirements/recommendations for international students: Required—TOEFL (minimum score 540 paper-based; 207 computer-based). *Application deadline:* Applications are processed on a rolling basis. Application fee: $50. Electronic applications accepted. *Expenses:* Tuition, state resident: full-time $7488; part-time $416 per credit. Tuition, nonresident: full-time $11,232; part-time $624 per credit. *Required fees:* $2070; $192.20 per credit. $90 per semester. *Financial support:* In 2011–12, 29 research assistantships with full and partial tuition reimbursements (averaging $2,253 per year) were awarded; fellowships, career-related internships or fieldwork, and Federal Work-Study also available. Support available to part-time students. Financial award application deadline: 4/15; financial award applicants required to submit FAFSA. *Unit head:* Dr. Krish Krishnan, Graduate Coordinator, 724-357-2522, E-mail: krishnan@iup.edu. *Application contact:* Paula Stossel, Assistant Dean, 724-357-4511, E-mail: graduate-admissions@iup.edu. Web site: http://www.iup.edu/upper.aspx?id=49407.

Indiana University–Purdue University Fort Wayne, Doermer School of Business, Fort Wayne, IN 46805-1499. Offers business administration (MBA); business administration-accelerated (MBA). *Accreditation:* AACSB. Part-time programs available. *Faculty:* 29 full-time (11 women). *Students:* 44 full-time (16 women), 72 part-time (19 women); includes 11 minority (4 Black or African American, non-Hispanic/Latino; 4 Asian, non-Hispanic/Latino; 2 Hispanic/Latino; 1 Two or more races, non-Hispanic/Latino), 9 international. Average age 32. 85 applicants, 84% accepted, 44 enrolled. In 2011, 63 master's awarded. *Entrance requirements:* For master's, GMAT, minimum GPA of 3.0, two letters of recommendation, essay, interview. Additional exam requirements/recommendations for international students: Required—TOEFL (minimum score 600 paper-based; 250 computer-based; 100 iBT). *Application deadline:* For fall admission, 7/15 for domestic students, 5/1 for international students; for spring admission, 11/15 for domestic students, 10/1 for international students. Applications are processed on a rolling basis. Application fee: $55. *Financial support:* In 2011–12, 1 teaching assistantship with partial tuition reimbursement (averaging $12,930 per year) was awarded; scholarships/grants and unspecified assistantships also available. Support available to part-time students. Financial award application deadline: 3/1; financial award applicants required to submit FAFSA. *Faculty research:* Personal saving, enterprising communities in Eastern Europe, online purchasing. *Total annual research expenditures:* $45,738. *Unit head:* Dr. Otto Chang, Dean, 260-481-0219, Fax: 260-481-6879, E-mail: chango@ipfw.edu. *Application contact:* Dr. Lyman Lewis, MBA Program Administrator, 260-481-6474, Fax: 260-481-6879, E-mail: lewisl@ipfw.edu. Web site: http://www.ipfw.edu/business.

Indiana University–Purdue University Indianapolis, Kelley School of Business, Indianapolis, IN 46202-2896. Offers accounting (MSA); business (MBA). *Accreditation:* AACSB. Part-time and evening/weekend programs available. Postbaccalaureate distance learning degree programs offered (minimal on-campus study). *Faculty:* 20 full-time (4 women), 1 part-time/adjunct (0 women). *Students:* 114 full-time (45 women), 380 part-time (125 women); includes 79 minority (29 Black or African American, non-Hispanic/Latino; 33 Asian, non-Hispanic/Latino; 9 Hispanic/Latino; 8 Two or more races, non-Hispanic/Latino), 84 international. Average age 30. 220 applicants, 73% accepted, 123 enrolled. In 2011, 273 master's awarded. *Entrance requirements:* For master's, GMAT, previous course work in accounting, statistics. *Application deadline:* For fall admission, 4/15 priority date for domestic students, 4/15 for international students; for spring admission, 11/1 priority date for domestic students, 11/1 for international students. Applications are processed on a rolling basis. Application fee: $55 ($65 for international students). Electronic applications accepted. *Expenses:* Contact institution. *Financial support:* In 2011–12, fellowships (averaging $16,193 per year), teaching assistantships (averaging $9,000 per year) were awarded; Federal Work-Study, institutionally sponsored loans, and scholarships/grants also available. Support available to part-time students. Financial award application deadline: 3/1; financial award applicants required to submit FAFSA. *Unit head:* Phillip L. Cochran, Associate Dean, Indianapolis Programs, 317-274-4179, Fax: 317-274-2483, E-mail: busugrad@iupui.edu. *Application contact:* Julie L. Moore, Recorder/Admission Coordinator, 317-274-0885, Fax: 317-274-2483, E-mail: mbaindy@iupui.edu. Web site: http://kelley.iupui.edu/evemba.

Indiana University South Bend, School of Business and Economics, South Bend, IN 46634-7111. Offers accounting (MSA); business administration (MBA); management of information technologies (MS). Part-time and evening/weekend programs available. *Faculty:* 17 full-time (2 women), 3 part-time/adjunct (1 woman). *Students:* 78 full-time (31 women), 112 part-time (50 women); includes 17 minority (6 Black or African American, non-Hispanic/Latino; 1 American Indian or Alaska Native, non-Hispanic/Latino; 4 Asian, non-Hispanic/Latino; 5 Hispanic/Latino; 1 Two or more races, non-Hispanic/Latino), 70 international. Average age 32. 65 applicants, 74% accepted, 23 enrolled. In 2011, 37 master's awarded. *Entrance requirements:* For master's, GMAT. Additional exam requirements/recommendations for international students: Required—TOEFL (minimum score 550 paper-based; 213 computer-based). *Application deadline:* For fall admission, 7/1 priority date for domestic students, 7/1 for international students; for spring admission, 11/1 priority date for domestic students, 11/1 for international students. Applications are processed on a rolling basis. Application fee: $50 ($60 for international students). *Expenses:* Contact institution. *Financial support:* In 2011–12, 1 fellowship (averaging $3,846 per year) was awarded; Federal Work-Study and institutionally sponsored loans also available. Support available to part-time students. Financial award applicants required to submit FAFSA. *Faculty research:* Financial accounting, consumer research, capital budgeting research, business strategy research. *Unit head:* Robert H. Ducoffe, Dean, 574-520-4228, Fax: 574-520-4866. *Application contact:* Sharon Peterson, Secretary, 574-520-4138, Fax: 574-520-4866, E-mail: speterso@iusb.edu. Web site: http://www.iusb.edu/~buse/grad.

Indiana University Southeast, School of Business, New Albany, IN 47150-6405. Offers business administration (MBA); strategic finance (MS). *Accreditation:* AACSB. *Faculty:* 11 full-time (2 women). *Students:* 9 full-time (1 woman), 314 part-time (118 women); includes 24 minority (7 Black or African American, non-Hispanic/Latino; 11 Asian, non-Hispanic/Latino; 4 Native Hawaiian or other Pacific Islander, non-Hispanic/Latino; 2 Two or more races, non-Hispanic/Latino), 13 international. Average age 31. 62 applicants, 100% accepted, 50 enrolled. In 2011, 76 master's awarded. *Degree requirements:* For master's, community service. *Entrance requirements:* For master's, GMAT, work experience. Additional exam requirements/recommendations for international students: Required—TOEFL. Application fee: $35. *Expenses:* Contact institution. *Financial support:* In 2011–12, 2 teaching assistantships (averaging $4,500 per year) were awarded. *Unit head:* Dr. Jay White, Dean, 812-941-2362, Fax: 812-941-2672. *Application contact:* Admissions Counselor, 812-941-2212, Fax: 812-941-2595, E-mail: admissions@ius.edu. Web site: http://www.ius.edu/mba.

Indiana Wesleyan University, College of Adult and Professional Studies, Graduate Studies in Business, Marion, IN 46953. Offers accounting (MBA); applied management (MBA); business administration (MBA); health care (MBA); human resources (MBA); management (MS). Part-time and evening/weekend programs available. Postbaccalaureate distance learning degree programs offered (no on-campus study). *Degree requirements:* For master's, applied business or management project. *Entrance requirements:* For master's, minimum GPA of 2.5, 2 years of related work experience. Additional exam requirements/recommendations for international students: Required—TOEFL (minimum score 550 paper-based; 213 computer-based). Electronic applications accepted.

Instituto Centroamericano de Administración de Empresas, Graduate Programs, La Garita, Costa Rica. Offers agribusiness management (MIAM); business administration (EMBA); finance (MBA); real estate management (MGREM); sustainable development (MBA); technology (MBA). *Degree requirements:* For master's, comprehensive exam, essay. *Entrance requirements:* For master's, GMAT or GRE General Test, fluency in Spanish, interview, letters of recommendation, minimum 1 year of work experience. Additional exam requirements/recommendations for international students: Recommended—TOEFL. Electronic applications accepted. *Faculty research:* Competitiveness, production.

Instituto Tecnologico de Santo Domingo, Graduate School, Area of Business, Santo Domingo, Dominican Republic. Offers banking and securities markets (M Mgmt); corporate finance (M Mgmt); human resources management (M Mgmt, Certificate); international trade management (M Mgmt); marketing (M Mgmt); organizational development (M Mgmt); quality and productivity management (Certificate); tax management and planning (M Mgmt); upper management (M Mgmt).

Instituto Tecnológico y de Estudios Superiores de Monterrey, Campus Central de Veracruz, Graduate Programs, Córdoba, Mexico. Offers administration (MA); administration of information technologies (MTI); computer sciences (MCC); education (MEE); educational institution administration (MAD); educational technology (MTE); electronic commerce (MCE); finance (MAF); humanistic studies (MEH); international business for Latin America (MNL); marketing (MMT); science (MCP). Part-time and evening/weekend programs available. Postbaccalaureate distance learning degree programs offered (minimal on-campus study). *Degree requirements:* For master's, thesis (for some programs). *Entrance requirements:* For master's, PAEP College Board. Electronic applications accepted.

Instituto Tecnológico y de Estudios Superiores de Monterrey, Campus Ciudad de México, School of Business Administration, Ciudad de Mexico, Mexico. Offers business administration (EMBA, MBA, PhD); economy (MBA); finance (MBA). EMBA program offered jointly with The University of Texas at Austin. Part-time and evening/weekend programs available. Postbaccalaureate distance learning degree programs offered (minimal on-campus study). *Entrance requirements:* For master's and doctorate, Instituto entrance exam. Additional exam requirements/recommendations for international students: Required—TOEFL.

Instituto Tecnológico y de Estudios Superiores de Monterrey, Campus Ciudad Juárez, Program in Business Administration, Ciudad Juárez, Mexico. Offers MBA. Part-time programs available. Postbaccalaureate distance learning degree programs offered. *Entrance requirements:* Additional exam requirements/recommendations for international students: Required—TOEFL (minimum score 500 paper-based).

Instituto Tecnológico y de Estudios Superiores de Monterrey, Campus Ciudad Obregón, Program in Administration, Ciudad Obregón, Mexico. Offers MA.

Instituto Tecnológico y de Estudios Superiores de Monterrey, Campus Cuernavaca, Programs in Business Administration, Temixco, Mexico. Offers finance (MA); human resources management (MA); international business (MA); marketing (MA).

Instituto Tecnológico y de Estudios Superiores de Monterrey, Campus Estado de México, Professional and Graduate Division, Estado de Mexico, Mexico. Offers administration of information technologies (MITA); architecture (M Arch); business administration (GMBA, MBA); computer sciences (MCS, PhD); education (M Ed); educational institution administration (MAD); educational technology and innovation (PhD); electronic commerce (MEC); environmental systems (MS); finance (MAF); humanistic studies (MHS); information sciences and knowledge management (MISKM); information systems (MS); manufacturing systems (MS); marketing (MEM); quality systems and productivity (MS); science and materials engineering (PhD); telecommunications management (MTM). Part-time programs available. Postbaccalaureate distance learning degree programs offered (minimal on-campus study). *Degree requirements:* For master's, one foreign language, thesis (for some programs); for doctorate, one foreign language, thesis/dissertation. *Entrance requirements:* For master's, E-PAEP 500, interview; for doctorate, E-PAEP 500, research proposal. Additional exam requirements/recommendations for international students: Required—TOEFL (minimum score 550 paper-based). *Faculty research:* Surface treatments by plasmas, mechanical properties, robotics, graphical computing, mechatronics security protocols.

Instituto Tecnológico y de Estudios Superiores de Monterrey, Campus Guadalajara, Program in Business Administration, Zapopan, Mexico. Offers IEMBA, M Ad. Part-time and evening/weekend programs available. Postbaccalaureate distance learning degree programs offered. *Degree requirements:* For master's, one foreign language. *Entrance requirements:* For master's, ITESM admission test. *Faculty research:* Strategic alliances in small business, family business practice in Mexico, competitiveness under NAFTA for Mexican firms.

Instituto Tecnológico y de Estudios Superiores de Monterrey, Campus Irapuato, Graduate Programs, Irapuato, Mexico. Offers administration (MBA); administration of information technology (MAIT); administration of telecommunications (MAT); architecture (M Arch); computer science (MCS); education (M Ed); educational administration (MEA); educational innovation and technology (DEIT); educational technology (MET); electronic commerce (MBA); environmental administration and planning (MEAP); environmental systems (MES); finances (MBA); humanistic studies (MHS); international management for Latin American executives (MIMLAE); library and information science (MLIS); manufacturing quality management (MMQM); marketing research (MBA).

Instituto Tecnológico y de Estudios Superiores de Monterrey, Campus Laguna, Graduate School, Torreón, Mexico. Offers business administration (MBA); industrial engineering (MIE); management information systems (MS). Part-time programs available. *Entrance requirements:* For master's, GMAT. *Faculty research:* Computer communications from home to the university.

Instituto Tecnológico y de Estudios Superiores de Monterrey, Campus León, Program in Business Administration, León, Mexico. Offers MBA. Part-time programs available.

Instituto Tecnológico y de Estudios Superiores de Monterrey, Campus Monterrey, Graduate School of Business Administration and Leadership, Program in Business Administration, Monterrey, Mexico. Offers business administration (MA, MBA); finance (M Sc); international business (M Sc); marketing (M Sc). *Accreditation:* AACSB. Part-time programs available. *Degree requirements:* For master's, one foreign language, thesis. *Entrance requirements:* For master's, GMAT. Additional exam requirements/recommendations for international students: Required—TOEFL. *Faculty research:* Technology management, quality management, organizational theory and behavior.

Instituto Tecnológico y de Estudios Superiores de Monterrey, Campus Monterrey, Graduate School of Business Administration and Leadership, Program in Management, Monterrey, Mexico. Offers PhD. *Accreditation:* AACSB. Part-time programs available. *Degree requirements:* For doctorate, one foreign language, thesis/dissertation. *Entrance requirements:* For doctorate, GMAT. Additional exam requirements/recommendations for international students: Required—TOEFL. *Faculty research:* Quality management, manufacturing and technology management, information systems, managerial economics, business policy.

Instituto Tecnológico y de Estudios Superiores de Monterrey, Campus Querétaro, School of Business, Santiago de Querétaro, Mexico. Offers MBA. *Entrance requirements:* For master's, GRE General Test. *Faculty research:* Organizational analysis, industrial marketing, international trade.

Instituto Tecnológico y de Estudios Superiores de Monterrey, Campus Sonora Norte, Program in Business, Hermosillo, Mexico. Offers MA. *Entrance requirements:* For master's, GMAT.

Instituto Tecnológico y de Estudios Superiores de Monterrey, Campus Toluca, Graduate Programs, Toluca, Mexico. Offers MBA. Part-time and evening/weekend programs available. *Degree requirements:* For master's, one foreign language. *Faculty research:* Management in the industrial valley of Toluca.

Inter American University of Puerto Rico, Aguadilla Campus, Graduate School, Aguadilla, PR 00605. Offers accounting (MBA); counseling psychology specializing in family (MS); criminal justice (MA); educative management and leadership (MA); elementary education (M Ed); finance (MBA); human resources (MBA); industrial management (MBA); management information systems (MBA); marketing (MBA). Part-time and evening/weekend programs available. *Degree requirements:* For master's, comprehensive exam. *Entrance requirements:* For master's, EXADEP, 2 letters of recommendation, minimum GPA of 2.5. Electronic applications accepted.

Inter American University of Puerto Rico, Arecibo Campus, Program in Business Administration, Arecibo, PR 00614-4050. Offers accounting (MBA); finance (MBA); human resources (MBA).

Inter American University of Puerto Rico, Barranquitas Campus, Program in Business Administration, Barranquitas, PR 00794. Offers accounting (IMBA); finance (IMBA).

Inter American University of Puerto Rico, Guayama Campus, Department of Business Administration, Guayama, PR 00785. Offers marketing (MBA).

Inter American University of Puerto Rico, Metropolitan Campus, Graduate Programs, Program in General Business, San Juan, PR 00919-1293. Offers MBA.

Inter American University of Puerto Rico, San Germán Campus, Graduate Studies Center, Program in Business Administration, San Germán, PR 00683-5008. Offers accounting (MBA); finance (MBA); human resources (MBA, PhD); industrial relations (MBA); information sciences (MBA); management (MBA); marketing (MBA). Part-time and evening/weekend programs available. *Degree requirements:* For master's, comprehensive exam. *Entrance requirements:* For master's, GRE General Test or EXADEP, minimum GPA of 3.0. *Application deadline:* For fall admission, 4/30 priority date for domestic students; for spring admission, 11/15 for domestic students. Applications are processed on a rolling basis. Application fee: $31. *Expenses: Required fees:* $213 per semester. *Financial support:* Teaching assistantships, Federal Work-Study, and unspecified assistantships available. *Unit head:* Dr. Elba T. Irizarry, Director of Graduate Studies Center, 787-264-1912 Ext. 7357, Fax: 787-892-6350, E-mail: elbat@sg.inter.edu.

Inter American University of Puerto Rico, San Germán Campus, Graduate Studies Center, Program in Labor Relations, San Germán, PR 00683-5008. Offers PhD. Part-time and evening/weekend programs available. *Degree requirements:* For doctorate, comprehensive exam, thesis/dissertation. *Entrance requirements:* For doctorate, EXADEP or GMAT, minimum graduate GPA of 3.25. *Application deadline:* For fall admission, 4/30 priority date for domestic students; for spring admission, 11/15 for domestic students. Applications are processed on a rolling basis. Application fee: $75. *Expenses: Required fees:* $213 per semester. *Financial support:* Teaching assistantships and unspecified assistantships available. *Unit head:* Dr. Elba T. Irizarry, Director of Graduate Studies Center, 787-264-1912 Ext. 7357, Fax: 787-892-6350, E-mail: elbat@sg.inter.edu.

International College of the Cayman Islands, Graduate Program in Management, Newlands, Cayman Islands. Offers business administration (MBA); management (MS), including education, human resources. Part-time and evening/weekend programs available. *Degree requirements:* For master's, comprehensive exam. *Entrance requirements:* Additional exam requirements/recommendations for international students: Recommended—TOEFL. *Faculty research:* International human resources administration.

International Technological University, Program in Business Administration, Santa Clara, CA 95050. Offers MBA. Part-time and evening/weekend programs available. *Degree requirements:* For master's, thesis or alternative. *Entrance requirements:* For master's, 1 semester of calculus, minimum GPA of 2.5. Additional exam requirements/recommendations for international students: Required—TOEFL. *Faculty research:* High tech management, business management, international marketing.

The International University of Monaco, Graduate Programs, Monte Carlo, Monaco. Offers entrepreneurship (EMBA, MBA); financial engineering (M Sc); hedge fund and private equity (M Sc); international marketing (EMBA, MBA); international wealth management (M Sc); luxury goods and services (EMBA, M Sc, MBA); wealth and asset management (EMBA, MBA). Part-time programs available. *Degree requirements:* For master's, comprehensive exam (for some programs), applied research project. *Entrance requirements:* Additional exam requirements/recommendations for international students: Required—TOEFL (minimum score 550 paper-based; 213 computer-based), IELTS. Electronic applications accepted. *Faculty research:* Gaming, leadership, disintermediation.

Iona College, Hagan School of Business, New Rochelle, NY 10801-1890. Offers MBA, AC, PMC. *Accreditation:* AACSB. Part-time and evening/weekend programs available. *Faculty:* 29 full-time (8 women), 14 part-time/adjunct (2 women). *Students:* 99 full-time (43 women), 314 part-time (137 women); includes 66 minority (29 Black or African American, non-Hispanic/Latino; 14 Asian, non-Hispanic/Latino; 23 Hispanic/Latino), 2 international. Average age 32. 190 applicants, 71% accepted, 110 enrolled. In 2011, 190 master's, 150 other advanced degrees awarded. *Entrance requirements:* For master's, GMAT, 2 letters of recommendation. Additional exam requirements/recommendations for international students: Required—TOEFL (minimum score 550 paper-based; 213 computer-based; 80 iBT). *Application deadline:* For fall admission, 8/15 priority date for domestic students, 8/1 for international students; for winter admission, 11/15 priority date for domestic students, 11/1 for international students; for spring admission, 2/15 priority date for domestic students, 2/1 for international students. Applications are processed on a rolling basis. Application fee: $50. Electronic applications accepted. *Expenses: Tuition:* Part-time $872 per credit. *Required fees:* $225 per term. *Financial support:* Fellowships with tuition reimbursements, Federal Work-Study, scholarships/grants, tuition waivers (partial), and unspecified assistantships available. Support available to part-time students. Financial award application deadline: 4/15; financial award applicants required to submit FAFSA. *Faculty research:* Artificial intelligence, financial services, value-based management, public policy, business ethics. *Unit head:* Dr. Vincent Calluzo, Dean, 914-633-2256, E-mail: vcalluzo@iona.edu. *Application contact:* Ben Fan, Director of MBA Admissions, 914-633-2289, Fax: 914-637-2708, E-mail: sfan@iona.edu. Web site: http://www.iona.edu/hagan/.

Ithaca College, Division of Graduate and Professional Studies, School of Business, Program in Business Administration, Ithaca, NY 14850. Offers MBA. *Accreditation:* AACSB. Part-time programs available. *Faculty:* 17 full-time (5 women). *Students:* 15 full-time (5 women), 5 part-time (2 women); includes 3 minority (all Asian, non-Hispanic/Latino). Average age 25. 39 applicants, 79% accepted, 17 enrolled. In 2011, 16 master's awarded. *Degree requirements:* For master's, thesis optional. *Entrance requirements:* For master's, GMAT, minimum GPA of 3.0. Additional exam requirements/recommendations for international students: Required—TOEFL (minimum score 550 paper-based; 213 computer-based; 80 iBT). *Application deadline:* For fall admission, 3/1 for domestic and international students; for spring admission, 11/1 for domestic and international students. Applications are processed on a rolling basis. Application fee: $40. Electronic applications accepted. *Expenses:* Contact institution. *Financial support:* In 2011–12, 13 students received support, including 9 fellowships (averaging $3,323 per year), 4 teaching assistantships (averaging $5,547 per year); career-related internships or fieldwork, Federal Work-Study, and scholarships/grants also available. Support available to part-time students. Financial award application deadline: 3/1; financial award applicants required to submit CSS PROFILE or FAFSA. *Unit head:* Dr. Joanne Burress, MBA Program Director, 607-274-3143, Fax: 607-274-1263, E-mail: gps@ithaca.edu. *Application contact:* Gerard Turbide, Director, Office of Admission, 607-274-3143, Fax: 607-274-1263, E-mail: gps@ithaca.edu. Web site: http://www.ithaca.edu/business/mba.

ITT Technical Institute, Online MBA Program, Indianapolis, IN 46268-1119. Offers MBA.

Jackson State University, Graduate School, College of Business, Department of Economics, Finance and General Business, Jackson, MS 39217. Offers business administration (MBA, PhD). *Accreditation:* AACSB. Part-time and evening/weekend programs available. *Degree requirements:* For master's, comprehensive exam, thesis. *Entrance requirements:* For master's, GRE General Test, GMAT; for doctorate, MAT, GMAT. Additional exam requirements/recommendations for international students: Required—TOEFL.

Jacksonville State University, College of Graduate Studies and Continuing Education, College of Commerce and Business Administration, Jacksonville, AL 36265-1602. Offers MBA. *Accreditation:* AACSB. Part-time and evening/weekend programs available. *Degree requirements:* For master's, comprehensive exam, thesis (for some programs). *Entrance requirements:* For master's, GMAT. Additional exam requirements/recommendations for international students: Required—TOEFL (minimum score 500 paper-based; 173 computer-based; 61 iBT). Electronic applications accepted. *Expenses:* Tuition, state resident: part-time $336 per hour. Tuition, nonresident: part-time $672 per hour. Part-time tuition and fees vary according to degree level.

Jacksonville University, Davis College of Business, Accelerated Day-time MBA Program, Jacksonville, FL 32211. Offers MBA.

Jacksonville University, Davis College of Business, Executive Master of Business Administration Program, Jacksonville, FL 32211. Offers Exec MBA. *Accreditation:* AACSB. Part-time and evening/weekend programs available. *Entrance requirements:* For master's, 5 years of managerial or professional experience. Additional exam requirements/recommendations for international students: Required—TOEFL. *Faculty research:* Economic impact, vicarious learning, psychology and advertising.

Jacksonville University, Davis College of Business, Master of Business Administration Program, Jacksonville, FL 32211. Offers MBA. *Accreditation:* AACSB. Part-time and evening/weekend programs available. *Entrance requirements:* For master's, GMAT. Additional exam requirements/recommendations for international students: Required—TOEFL.

James Madison University, The Graduate School, College of Business, Program in Business Administration, Harrisonburg, VA 22807. Offers MBA. *Accreditation:* AACSB. Part-time and evening/weekend programs available. Postbaccalaureate distance learning degree programs offered (no on-campus study). *Students:* 36 full-time (13 women), 38 part-time (8 women); includes 11 minority (5 Black or African American, non-Hispanic/Latino; 5 Asian, non-Hispanic/Latino; 1 Hispanic/Latino), 2 international. Average age 27. In 2011, 18 master's awarded. *Entrance requirements:* For master's, GMAT, resume, 2 letters of recommendation. Additional exam requirements/recommendations for international students: Required—TOEFL. *Application deadline:* For fall admission, 6/1 priority date for domestic students, 5/1 for international students; for spring admission, 6/1 for domestic students, 9/1 for international students. Applications are processed on a rolling basis. Application fee: $55. Electronic applications accepted. *Expenses:* Tuition, state resident: full-time $8016; part-time $334 per credit hour. Tuition, nonresident: full-time $22,656; part-time $944 per credit hour. *Financial support:* In 2011–12, 2 students received support. Federal Work-Study and 1 athletic assistantship ($8664), 1 graduate assistantship ($7382) available. Financial award application deadline: 3/1; financial award applicants required to submit FAFSA. *Unit head:* Dr. Paul E. Bierly, Director, 540-568-3009. *Application contact:* Lynette M. Bible, Director of Graduate Admissions, 540-568-6395, Fax: 540-568-7860, E-mail: biblelm@jmu.edu.

John Brown University, Graduate Business Programs, Siloam Springs, AR 72761-2121. Offers global continuous improvement (MBA); international community development leadership (MS); leadership and ethics (MBA, MS); leadership and higher education (MS). Part-time and evening/weekend programs available. Postbaccalaureate distance learning degree programs offered (minimal on-campus study). *Faculty:* 6 full-time (2 women), 31 part-time/adjunct (7 women). *Students:* 29 full-time (13 women), 185 part-time (90 women); includes 33 minority (12 Black or African American, non-Hispanic/Latino; 3 American Indian or Alaska Native, non-Hispanic/Latino; 4 Asian, non-Hispanic/Latino; 11 Hispanic/Latino; 3 Two or more races, non-Hispanic/Latino), 7 international. 75 applicants, 88% accepted. *Entrance requirements:* For master's, MAT, GMAT or GRE if undergraduate GPA is less than 3.0, recommendation forms from three people, 200-word essay describing professional plans and reason for seeking acceptance. Additional exam requirements/recommendations for international students: Required—TOEFL (minimum score 550 paper-based; 213 computer-based; 70 iBT). *Application deadline:* Applications are processed on a rolling basis. Application fee: $35 ($100 for international students). Electronic applications accepted. *Expenses: Tuition:* Part-time $470 per credit hour. *Financial support:* Fellowships, institutionally sponsored loans, and scholarships/grants available. *Unit head:* Dr. Joe Walenciak, Program Director, 479-524-7431, E-mail: jwalenci@jbu.edu. *Application contact:* Brent Young, Graduate Business Representative, 479-524-7450, E-mail: byoung@jbu.edu. Web site: http://www.jbu.edu/grad/business/.

John Carroll University, Graduate School, John M. and Mary Jo Boler School of Business, University Heights, OH 44118-4581. Offers accountancy (MS); business (MBA). *Accreditation:* AACSB. Part-time and evening/weekend programs available. *Entrance requirements:* For master's, GMAT, minimum GPA of 2.5. Additional exam requirements/recommendations for international students: Required—TOEFL (minimum score 550 paper-based; 213 computer-based). Electronic applications accepted. *Expenses:* Contact institution. *Faculty research:* Accounting, economics and finance, management, marketing and logistics.

John F. Kennedy University, School of Management, Program in Business Administration, Pleasant Hill, CA 94523-4817. Offers business administration (MBA); organizational leadership (Certificate). Part-time and evening/weekend programs available. *Degree requirements:* For master's, thesis or alternative. *Entrance requirements:* For master's, interview. Additional exam requirements/recommendations for international students: Required—TOEFL.

The Johns Hopkins University, Carey Business School, Management Programs, Baltimore, MD 21218-2699. Offers leadership development (Certificate); organization development and human resources (MS); skilled facilitator (Certificate). Evening/weekend programs available. *Degree requirements:* For master's, 36 credits including final project. *Entrance requirements:* For master's and Certificate, minimum GPA of 3.0, resume, work experience, two letters of recommendation. Additional exam requirements/recommendations for international students: Required—TOEFL (minimum score 600 paper-based; 250 computer-based; 100 iBT). Electronic applications accepted. *Faculty research:* Agency theory and theory of the firm, technological entrepreneurship, technology policy and economic development, strategic human resources management, ethics and stakeholder theory.

The Johns Hopkins University, Carey Business School, MBA Department, Baltimore, MD 21218-2699. Offers Exec MBA, MBA, MBA/MA, MBA/MPH, MBA/MS, MBA/MSIS, MBA/MSN. Part-time and evening/weekend programs available. Postbaccalaureate distance learning degree programs offered (minimal on-campus study). *Degree requirements:* For master's, capstone project (MBA). *Entrance requirements:* For master's, GMAT or GRE, minimum GPA of 3.0, resume, work experience, two letters of recommendation. Additional exam requirements/recommendations for international students: Required—TOEFL (minimum score 600 paper-based; 250 computer-based; 100 iBT). Electronic applications accepted.

The Johns Hopkins University, School of Education, Division of Public Safety Leadership, Baltimore, MD 21218. Offers intelligence analysis (MS); management (MS). Part-time and evening/weekend programs available. *Entrance requirements:* For master's, minimum undergraduate GPA of 3.0, curriculum vitae/resume, interview, professional experience, endorsement letter (MS in management). Additional exam requirements/recommendations for international students: Required—TOEFL (minimum score 600 paper-based; 250 computer-based; 100 iBT). Electronic applications accepted. *Faculty research:* Campus and school safety, prevention and effective response to violence against women, counterterrorism training, leadership development for public safety and homeland security executives.

Jones International University, School of Business, Centennial, CO 80112. Offers accounting (MBA); business communication (MABC); entrepreneurship (MABC, MBA); finance (MBA); global enterprise management (MBA); health care management (MBA); information security management (MBA); information technology management (MBA); leadership and influence (MABC); leading the customer-driven organization (MABC); negotiation and conflict management (MBA); project management (MABC, MBA).

Business Administration and Management—General

Program only offered online. Part-time and evening/weekend programs available. Postbaccalaureate distance learning degree programs offered (no on-campus study). *Degree requirements:* For master's, capstone project. *Entrance requirements:* For master's, minimum cumulative GPA of 2.5. Additional exam requirements/recommendations for international students: Recommended—TOEFL (minimum score 550 paper-based; 213 computer-based). Electronic applications accepted.

Kansas State University, Graduate School, College of Business Administration, Program in Business Administration, Manhattan, KS 66506. Offers MBA. *Accreditation:* AACSB. Part-time programs available. *Faculty:* 1 full-time (0 women), 2 part-time/adjunct (0 women). *Students:* 45 full-time (19 women), 24 part-time (11 women); includes 4 minority (3 Asian, non-Hispanic/Latino; 1 Hispanic/Latino), 16 international. Average age 26. 82 applicants, 67% accepted, 35 enrolled. In 2011, 24 master's awarded. *Entrance requirements:* For master's, GMAT (minimum score of 500), minimum undergraduate GPA of 3.0. Additional exam requirements/recommendations for international students: Required—TOEFL (minimum score 550 paper-based; 79 iBT); Recommended—IELTS (minimum score 7). *Application deadline:* For fall admission, 2/1 priority date for domestic students, 2/1 for international students; for spring admission, 10/1 priority date for domestic students, 8/1 for international students. Applications are processed on a rolling basis. Application fee: $60. Electronic applications accepted. *Financial support:* In 2011–12, 1 research assistantship with partial tuition reimbursement (averaging $8,320 per year) was awarded; institutionally sponsored loans and scholarships/grants also available. Financial award application deadline: 3/1; financial award applicants required to submit FAFSA. *Faculty research:* Organizational citizenship behavior, service marketing, impression management, human resources management, lean manufacturing and supply chain management, financial market behavior and investment management. *Total annual research expenditures:* $204,992. *Unit head:* Ali Malekzadeh, Dean, 785-532-7227, Fax: 785-532-7216. *Application contact:* Stacy Kovar, Associate Dean for Academic Programs, 785-532-7190, Fax: 785-532-7809, E-mail: gradbusiness@ksu.edu. Web site: http://www.cba.k-state.edu/.

Kansas Wesleyan University, Program in Business Administration, Salina, KS 67401-6196. Offers business administration (MBA); sports management (MBA). Part-time and evening/weekend programs available. *Entrance requirements:* For master's, GMAT, minimum graduate GPA of 3.0 or undergraduate GPA of 3.25.

Kaplan University, Davenport Campus, School of Business, Davenport, IA 52807-2095. Offers business administration (MBA); change leadership (MS); entrepreneurship (MBA); finance (MBA); health care management (MBA, MS); human resource (MBA); international business (MBA); management (MS); marketing (MBA); project management (MBA, MS); supply chain management and logistics (MBA, MS). Part-time and evening/weekend programs available. Postbaccalaureate distance learning degree programs offered (no on-campus study). *Entrance requirements:* Additional exam requirements/recommendations for international students: Required—TOEFL (minimum score 550 paper-based; 218 computer-based; 80 iBT). Electronic applications accepted.

Kean University, Nathan Weiss Graduate College, Program in Educational Administration, Union, NJ 07083. Offers school business administration (MA); supervisors and principals (MA). *Accreditation:* NCATE. *Faculty:* 6 full-time (3 women). *Students:* 8 full-time (6 women), 201 part-time (130 women); includes 67 minority (38 Black or African American, non-Hispanic/Latino; 5 Asian, non-Hispanic/Latino; 23 Hispanic/Latino; 1 Native Hawaiian or other Pacific Islander, non-Hispanic/Latino), 1 international. Average age 36. 72 applicants, 100% accepted, 58 enrolled. In 2011, 55 master's awarded. *Degree requirements:* For master's, comprehensive exam, portfolio, field experience, research component, internship, teaching experience. *Entrance requirements:* For master's, GRE General Test or MAT, minimum GPA of 3.0, interview, 2 letters of recommendation, transcripts, personal statement, transcript. Additional exam requirements/recommendations for international students: Required—TOEFL (minimum score 79 iBT). *Application deadline:* For fall admission, 6/1 for domestic and international students; for spring admission, 12/1 for domestic and international students. Applications are processed on a rolling basis. Application fee: $75 ($150 for international students). Electronic applications accepted. *Expenses:* Tuition, state resident: full-time $11,302; part-time $550 per credit. Tuition, nonresident: full-time $15,318; part-time $674 per credit. *Required fees:* $2849; $130 per credit. Tuition and fees vary according to degree level. *Financial support:* In 2011–12, research assistantships with full tuition reimbursements (averaging $3,263 per year) were awarded; unspecified assistantships also available. Financial award applicants required to submit FAFSA. *Unit head:* Dr. Efthimia Christie, Program Coordinator, 908-737-5974, E-mail: echristi@kean.edu. *Application contact:* Ann-Marie Kay, Assistant Director of Graduate Admissions, 908-737-5922, Fax: 908-737-5925, E-mail: akay@kean.edu. Web site: http://www.kean.edu/KU/School-Business-Administrator.

Keiser University, Doctor of Business Administration Program, Fort Lauderdale, FL 33309. Offers global business (DBA); global organizational leadership (DBA); marketing (DBA).

Keiser University, Master of Business Administration Program, Fort Lauderdale, FL 33309. Offers accounting (MBA); health services management (MBA); international business (MBA); leadership for managers (MBA); marketing (MBA). Leadership for Managers and International Business concentrations also offered in Spanish. Part-time programs available. Postbaccalaureate distance learning degree programs offered (minimal on-campus study). *Entrance requirements:* For master's, minimum GPA of 2.7 from an accredited institution. Additional exam requirements/recommendations for international students: Required—TOEFL. Electronic applications accepted.

Kennesaw State University, Michael J. Coles College of Business, Doctor of Business Administration Program, Kennesaw, GA 30144-5591. Offers DBA. *Accreditation:* AACSB. Part-time programs available. *Students:* 22 full-time (10 women), 33 part-time (12 women); includes 10 minority (8 Black or African American, non-Hispanic/Latino; 2 Asian, non-Hispanic/Latino). Average age 49. *Degree requirements:* For doctorate, thesis/dissertation. *Entrance requirements:* Additional exam requirements/recommendations for international students: Required—TOEFL (minimum score 550 paper-based; 213 computer-based; 80 iBT), IELTS (minimum score 6). *Application deadline:* For spring admission, 10/1 for domestic and international students. Applications are processed on a rolling basis. Application fee: $100. Electronic applications accepted. *Expenses:* Tuition, state resident: full-time $3000; part-time $250 per semester hour. Tuition, nonresident: full-time $10,836; part-time $903 per semester hour. *Required fees:* $774 per semester. *Financial support:* Application deadline: 4/1. *Unit head:* Dr. Neal Mero, Director, 770-499-3306, E-mail: nmero@kennesaw.edu. *Application contact:* Susan Cochran, Administrative Coordinator, 678-797-2802, Fax: 770-423-6885, E-mail: scochran@kennesaw.edu.

Kennesaw State University, Michael J. Coles College of Business, Program in Business Administration, Kennesaw, GA 30144-5591. Offers MBA. *Accreditation:* AACSB. Part-time and evening/weekend programs available. Postbaccalaureate distance learning degree programs offered (no on-campus study). *Students:* 129 full-time (67 women), 326 part-time (118 women); includes 137 minority (86 Black or African American, non-Hispanic/Latino; 1 American Indian or Alaska Native, non-Hispanic/Latino; 20 Asian, non-Hispanic/Latino; 26 Hispanic/Latino; 1 Native Hawaiian or other Pacific Islander, non-Hispanic/Latino; 3 Two or more races, non-Hispanic/Latino), 30 international. Average age 34. 416 applicants, 50% accepted, 145 enrolled. In 2011, 266 master's awarded. *Entrance requirements:* For master's, GMAT (minimum score 500), minimum GPA of 2.8, 1 year of work experience. Additional exam requirements/recommendations for international students: Required—TOEFL (minimum score 550 paper-based; 213 computer-based; 80 iBT), IELTS (minimum score 6). *Application deadline:* For fall admission, 7/1 for domestic and international students; for spring admission, 12/1 for domestic and international students. Applications are processed on a rolling basis. Application fee: $60. Electronic applications accepted. *Expenses:* Tuition, state resident: full-time $3000; part-time $250 per semester hour. Tuition, nonresident: full-time $10,836; part-time $903 per semester hour. *Required fees:* $774 per semester. *Financial support:* In 2011–12, 4 research assistantships with tuition reimbursements (averaging $4,000 per year) were awarded; unspecified assistantships also available. Financial award application deadline: 4/1; financial award applicants required to submit FAFSA. *Unit head:* Dr. Sheb True, Director, 770-423-6087, E-mail: strue@kennesaw.edu. *Application contact:* Tamara Hutto, Admissions Counselor, 770-420-4377, Fax: 770-423-6885, E-mail: ksugrad@kennesaw.edu. Web site: http://www.kennesaw.edu.

Kent State University, College of Business Administration, Master's Program in Business Administration, Kent, OH 44242-0001. Offers MBA. *Accreditation:* AACSB. Part-time and evening/weekend programs available. *Faculty:* 62 full-time (21 women), 4 part-time/adjunct (0 women). *Students:* 89 full-time (46 women), 116 part-time (53 women); includes 12 minority (7 Black or African American, non-Hispanic/Latino; 4 Asian, non-Hispanic/Latino; 1 Hispanic/Latino), 37 international. Average age 27. 168 applicants, 54% accepted, 55 enrolled. In 2011, 104 master's awarded. *Entrance requirements:* For master's, GMAT, minimum GPA of 2.75. Additional exam requirements/recommendations for international students: Required—TOEFL (minimum score 550 paper-based; 213 computer-based; 79 iBT). *Application deadline:* For fall admission, 6/1 for domestic students, 4/1 for international students; for spring admission, 12/1 for domestic students. Application fee: $30 ($60 for international students). Electronic applications accepted. *Expenses:* Tuition, state resident: full-time $8136; part-time $452 per credit hour. Tuition, nonresident: full-time $14,292; part-time $794 per credit hour. *Financial support:* In 2011–12, 22 students received support, including 25 research assistantships with full tuition reimbursements available (averaging $6,700 per year); fellowships, career-related internships or fieldwork, Federal Work-Study, and unspecified assistantships also available. Financial award application deadline: 4/1; financial award applicants required to submit FAFSA. *Unit head:* Louise M. Ditchey, Administrative Director, 330-672-2282, Fax: 330-672-7303, E-mail: gradbus@kent.edu. *Application contact:* Felecia A. Urbanek, Coordinator, Graduate Programs, 330-672-2282, Fax: 330-672-7303, E-mail: gradbus@kent.edu.

Kent State University at Stark, Professional MBA Program, Canton, OH 44720-7599. Offers MBA.

Kentucky State University, College of Business and Computer Science, Frankfort, KY 40601. Offers business administration (MBA); computer science technology (MS). Part-time and evening/weekend programs available. Postbaccalaureate distance learning degree programs offered (minimal on-campus study). *Faculty:* 9 full-time (1 woman). *Students:* 24 full-time (9 women), 29 part-time (14 women); includes 26 minority (22 Black or African American, non-Hispanic/Latino; 2 Asian, non-Hispanic/Latino; 1 Hispanic/Latino; 1 Two or more races, non-Hispanic/Latino), 14 international. Average age 34. 72 applicants, 82% accepted, 15 enrolled. In 2011, 13 degrees awarded. *Degree requirements:* For master's, comprehensive exam, thesis optional. *Entrance requirements:* For master's, GMAT, GRE. Additional exam requirements/recommendations for international students: Required—TOEFL (minimum score 525 paper-based; 173 computer-based). *Application deadline:* Applications are processed on a rolling basis. Application fee: $30 ($100 for international students). Electronic applications accepted. *Expenses:* Tuition, state resident: full-time $6192; part-time $344 per credit hour. Tuition, nonresident: full-time $9522; part-time $529 per credit hour. *Required fees:* $450; $25 per credit hour. Tuition and fees vary according to course load. *Financial support:* In 2011–12, 17 students received support, including 11 research assistantships (averaging $13,449 per year); career-related internships or fieldwork, scholarships/grants, tuition waivers (partial), and unspecified assistantships also available. Financial award application deadline: 4/15; financial award applicants required to submit FAFSA. *Application contact:* Dr. Titilayo Ufomata, Acting Director of Graduate Studies, 502-597-6443, E-mail: titilayo.ufomata@kysu.edu.

Kettering University, Graduate School, Department of Business, Flint, MI 48504. Offers MBA, MS. *Accreditation:* ACBSP. Part-time and evening/weekend programs available. Postbaccalaureate distance learning degree programs offered (no on-campus study). *Faculty:* 11 full-time (3 women), 7 part-time/adjunct (0 women). *Students:* 9 full-time (1 woman), 270 part-time (83 women); includes 73 minority (46 Black or African American, non-Hispanic/Latino; 1 American Indian or Alaska Native, non-Hispanic/Latino; 7 Asian, non-Hispanic/Latino; 19 Hispanic/Latino), 20 international. Average age 33. 106 applicants, 83% accepted, 50 enrolled. In 2011, 98 master's awarded. *Entrance requirements:* Additional exam requirements/recommendations for international students: Required—TOEFL (minimum score 550 paper-based; 213 computer-based; 79 iBT). *Application deadline:* For fall admission, 9/15 for domestic students, 6/15 for international students; for winter admission, 12/15 for domestic students, 9/15 for international students; for spring admission, 3/15 for domestic students, 12/15 for international students. Applications are processed on a rolling basis. Electronic applications accepted. *Expenses: Tuition:* Full-time $11,456; part-time $716 per credit hour. *Financial support:* In 2011–12, 24 students received support, including fellowships with full tuition reimbursements available (averaging $13,000 per year), research assistantships with full tuition reimbursements available (averaging $13,000 per year), teaching assistantships with full tuition reimbursements available (averaging $13,000 per year); Federal Work-Study, scholarships/grants, and tuition waivers (partial) also available. Support available to part-time students. Financial award application deadline: 7/15. *Faculty research:* Entrepreneurship. *Total annual research expenditures:* $151,000. *Unit head:* Dr. W. L. Scheller, Department Head, 810-762-7974, Fax: 810-762-9944, E-mail: wschelle@kettering.edu. *Application contact:* Bonnie Switzer, Admissions Representative, 810-762-7953, Fax: 810-762-9935, E-mail: bswitzer@kettering.edu.

Keuka College, Program in Management, Keuka Park, NY 14478-0098. Offers MS. Evening/weekend programs available. *Degree requirements:* For master's, thesis. *Entrance requirements:* For master's, 2 letters of reference, minimum GPA of 3.0. Additional exam requirements/recommendations for international students: Required—TOEFL (minimum score 550 paper-based; 213 computer-based). *Expenses:* Contact institution. *Faculty research:* Leadership, adult education, decision making, strategic planning, business ethics.

King College, School of Business and Economics, Bristol, TN 37620-2699. Offers MBA. Part-time and evening/weekend programs available. Postbaccalaureate distance learning degree programs offered (no on-campus study). *Degree requirements:* For master's, comprehensive exam, thesis optional. *Entrance requirements:* For master's, GMAT, 2 years of work experience. Additional exam requirements/recommendations for international students: Required—TOEFL (minimum score 550 paper-based). Electronic applications accepted. *Faculty research:* Leadership, international monetary policy.

King's College, William G. McGowan School of Business, Wilkes-Barre, PA 18711-0801. Offers health care administration (MS). *Accreditation:* AACSB. Part-time programs available. *Entrance requirements:* Additional exam requirements/recommendations for international students: Required—TOEFL (minimum score 600 paper-based; 250 computer-based).

Kutztown University of Pennsylvania, College of Business, Program in Business Administration, Kutztown, PA 19530-0730. Offers MBA. Part-time and evening/weekend programs available. *Faculty:* 8 full-time (4 women), 1 part-time/adjunct (0 women). *Students:* 25 full-time (8 women), 32 part-time (17 women); includes 10 minority (1 Black or African American, non-Hispanic/Latino; 1 Asian, non-Hispanic/Latino; 8 Hispanic/Latino), 10 international. Average age 32. 57 applicants, 25% accepted, 8 enrolled. In 2011, 26 master's awarded. *Degree requirements:* For master's, comprehensive exam, thesis (for some programs). *Entrance requirements:* For master's, GMAT. Additional exam requirements/recommendations for international students: Required—TOEFL (minimum score 550 paper-based; 79 iBT). *Application deadline:* For fall admission, 8/1 for domestic and international students; for spring admission, 12/1 for domestic and international students. Applications are processed on a rolling basis. Application fee: $35. Electronic applications accepted. *Expenses:* Tuition, state resident: full-time $7488; part-time $416 per credit. Tuition, nonresident: full-time $11,232; part-time $624 per credit. *Financial support:* Career-related internships or fieldwork, Federal Work-Study, scholarships/grants, tuition waivers (partial), and unspecified assistantships available. Financial award application deadline: 3/1; financial award applicants required to submit FAFSA. *Unit head:* Dr. William Dempsey, Interim Dean, 610-683-4575, Fax: 610-683-4573, E-mail: dempsey@kutztown.edu. *Application contact:* Kelly D. Burr, Associate Director, Graduate Admissions, 610-683-4200, Fax: 610-683-1393, E-mail: graduate@kutztown.edu. Web site: http://www.kutztown.edu/academics/business/mbaprograms/.

Lake Erie College, School of Business, Painesville, OH 44077-3389. Offers general management (MBA); management healthcare administration (MBA). Part-time and evening/weekend programs available. *Faculty:* 5 full-time (3 women), 6 part-time/adjunct (1 woman). *Students:* 28 full-time (14 women), 117 part-time (57 women); includes 27 minority (15 Black or African American, non-Hispanic/Latino; 6 Asian, non-Hispanic/Latino; 2 Hispanic/Latino; 4 Two or more races, non-Hispanic/Latino), 2 international. Average age 36. 66 applicants, 71% accepted, 37 enrolled. In 2011, 86 master's awarded. *Entrance requirements:* For master's, GMAT or minimum GPA of 3.0, resume, references. Additional exam requirements/recommendations for international students: Required—TOEFL (minimum score 550 paper-based; 79 computer-based). *Application deadline:* For fall admission, 8/1 priority date for domestic students, 6/1 for international students; for spring admission, 12/15 for domestic students, 10/1 for international students. Applications are processed on a rolling basis. Application fee: $30. Electronic applications accepted. Application fee is waived when completed online. *Expenses: Tuition:* Full-time $9594; part-time $533 per credit hour. *Required fees:* $51 per credit hour. Tuition and fees vary according to program. *Financial support:* Career-related internships or fieldwork and unspecified assistantships available. Financial award applicants required to submit FAFSA. *Faculty research:* Organizational effectiveness. *Unit head:* Prof. Robert Trebar, Dean of the School of Business, 440-375-7115, Fax: 440-375-7005, E-mail: rtrebar@lec.edu. *Application contact:* Christopher Harris, Dean of Admissions and Financial Aid, 800-533-4996, Fax: 440-375-7000, E-mail: admissions@lec.edu. Web site: http://www.lec.edu/parkermba.

Lake Forest Graduate School of Management, The Leadership MBA Program (LMBA), Lake Forest, IL 60045. Offers finance (MBA); global business (MBA); healthcare management (MBA); management (MBA); marketing (MBA); organizational behavior (MBA). Part-time and evening/weekend programs available. *Faculty:* 136 part-time/adjunct (41 women). *Students:* 734 part-time (306 women); includes 161 minority (34 Black or African American, non-Hispanic/Latino; 4 American Indian or Alaska Native, non-Hispanic/Latino; 87 Asian, non-Hispanic/Latino; 14 Hispanic/Latino; 4 Native Hawaiian or other Pacific Islander, non-Hispanic/Latino; 18 Two or more races, non-Hispanic/Latino). Average age 38. In 2011, 213 master's awarded. *Entrance requirements:* For master's, 4 years of work experience in field, interview, 2 letters of recommendation. *Application deadline:* For fall admission, 7/1 for domestic students; for winter admission, 1/5 for domestic students; for spring admission, 3/1 for domestic students. Applications are processed on a rolling basis. Application fee: $75. Electronic applications accepted. *Expenses: Tuition:* Part-time $2932 per unit. *Required fees:* $50 per unit. *Financial support:* Scholarships/grants available. Support available to part-time students. Financial award applicants required to submit FAFSA. *Unit head:* Chris Multhauf, Executive Vice President of Educational Programs and Solutions, 847-574-5270, Fax: 847-295-3656, E-mail: cmulthauf@lfgsm.edu. *Application contact:* Carolyn Brune, Director of Admissions, 800-737-4MBA, Fax: 847-295-3656, E-mail: admiss@lfgsm.edu. Web site: http://www.lakeforestmba.edu/lake_forest_mba_program/LFGSM-Leadership-MBA.aspx.

Lakehead University–Orillia, MBA Program, Orillia, ON L3V 0B9, Canada. Offers MBA. Part-time programs available.

Lakeland College, Graduate Studies Division, Program in Business Administration, Sheboygan, WI 53082-0359. Offers accounting (MBA); finance (MBA); healthcare management (MBA); project management (MBA). *Entrance requirements:* For master's, GMAT. *Expenses:* Contact institution.

Lamar University, College of Graduate Studies, College of Business, Beaumont, TX 77710. Offers accounting (MBA); experiential business and entrepreneurship (MBA); financial management (MBA); healthcare administration (MBA); information systems (MBA); management (MBA). *Accreditation:* AACSB. Part-time and evening/weekend programs available. *Faculty:* 18 full-time (5 women), 5 part-time/adjunct (0 women). *Students:* 74 full-time (33 women), 72 part-time (27 women); includes 24 minority (7 Black or African American, non-Hispanic/Latino; 9 Asian, non-Hispanic/Latino; 8 Hispanic/Latino), 34 international. Average age 29. 69 applicants, 84% accepted, 16 enrolled. In 2011, 62 master's awarded. *Degree requirements:* For master's, comprehensive exam (for some programs), thesis optional. *Entrance requirements:* For master's, GMAT. Additional exam requirements/recommendations for international students: Required—TOEFL (minimum score 525 paper-based; 197 computer-based). *Application deadline:* For fall admission, 3/15 priority date for domestic students; for spring admission, 10/1 priority date for domestic students. Applications are processed on a rolling basis. Application fee: $25 ($50 for international students). *Expenses:* Tuition, state resident: full-time $5430; part-time $272 per credit hour. Tuition, nonresident: full-time $11,540; part-time $577 per credit hour. *Required fees:* $1916. *Financial support:* In 2011–12, 12 students received support, including 4 research assistantships with partial tuition reimbursements available; fellowships with tuition reimbursements available, career-related internships or fieldwork, Federal Work-Study, institutionally sponsored loans, scholarships/grants, and tuition waivers (partial) also available. Support available to part-time students. Financial award application deadline: 4/1; financial award applicants required to submit FAFSA. *Faculty research:* Marketing, finance, quantitative methods, management information systems, legal, environmental. *Unit head:* Dr. Enrique R. Venta, Dean, 409-880-8604, Fax: 409-880-8088, E-mail: henry.venta@lamar.edu. *Application contact:* Dr. Brad Mayer, Professor and Associate Dean, 409-880-2383, Fax: 409-880-8605, E-mail: bradley.mayer@lamar.edu. Web site: http://mba.lamar.edu.

La Salle University, School of Business, Philadelphia, PA 19141-1199. Offers MBA, MS, Certificate, MSN/MBA. *Accreditation:* AACSB. Part-time and evening/weekend programs available. *Entrance requirements:* For master's, GMAT; for Certificate, MBA. Additional exam requirements/recommendations for international students: Required—TOEFL. Electronic applications accepted. *Expenses:* Contact institution. *Faculty research:* Small business development, unemployment insurance costs, nonprofit business, transfer pricing, forecasting.

Lasell College, Graduate and Professional Studies in Management, Newton, MA 02466-2709. Offers elder care administration (MSM, Graduate Certificate); elder care marketing (MSM, Graduate Certificate); fundraising management (MSM, Graduate Certificate); human resource management (Graduate Certificate); human resources management (MSM); integrated marketing communication (Graduate Certificate); management (MSM, Graduate Certificate); marketing (MSM, Graduate Certificate); non-profit management (MSM, Graduate Certificate); project management (MSM, Graduate Certificate); public relations (Graduate Certificate). Part-time and evening/weekend programs available. Postbaccalaureate distance learning degree programs offered (no on-campus study). *Faculty:* 9 full-time (7 women), 20 part-time/adjunct (13 women). *Students:* 23 full-time (16 women), 92 part-time (65 women); includes 74 minority (8 Black or African American, non-Hispanic/Latino; 4 American Indian or Alaska Native, non-Hispanic/Latino; 53 Asian, non-Hispanic/Latino; 9 Hispanic/Latino), 14 international. Average age 30. 78 applicants, 67% accepted, 31 enrolled. In 2011, 49 master's, 7 other advanced degrees awarded. *Entrance requirements:* For master's and Graduate Certificate, bachelor's degree from an accredited institution. Additional exam requirements/recommendations for international students: Required—TOEFL (minimum score 550 paper-based; 213 computer-based; 79 iBT). *Application deadline:* For fall admission, 8/31 priority date for domestic students, 6/30 for international students; for spring admission, 12/31 priority date for domestic students, 10/31 for international students. Applications are processed on a rolling basis. Electronic applications accepted. *Expenses: Tuition:* Part-time $575 per credit. *Required fees:* $70 per semester. *Financial support:* Available to part-time students. Application deadline: 8/31; applicants required to submit FAFSA. *Unit head:* Dr. Joan Dolamore, Dean of Graduate and Professional Studies, 617-243-2485, Fax: 617-243-2450, E-mail: gradinfo@lasell.edu. *Application contact:* Adrienne Franciosi, Director of Graduate Admission, 617-243-2214, Fax: 617-243-2450, E-mail: gradinfo@lasell.edu. Web site: http://www.lasell.edu/Academics/Graduate-and-Professional-Studies/MS-in-Management.html.

La Sierra University, School of Business and Management, Riverside, CA 92515. Offers accounting (MBA); finance (MBA); general management (MBA); human resources management (MBA); leadership, values, and ethics for business and management (Certificate); marketing (MBA). *Degree requirements:* For master's, research project. *Entrance requirements:* For master's, GMAT, minimum GPA of 3.0. Additional exam requirements/recommendations for international students: Required—TOEFL. *Faculty research:* Financial econometrics, institutional assessment and strategic planning, legal issues in management, behavioral finance, content of financial reports.

Laurel University, School of Management, High Point, NC 27265-3197. Offers MBA.

Laurentian University, School of Graduate Studies and Research, School of Commerce and Administration, Sudbury, ON P3E 2C6, Canada. Offers MBA. Part-time and evening/weekend programs available. *Entrance requirements:* For master's, GMAT, 2 years of work experience. *Faculty research:* Small business and entrepreneurship development, mutual fund performance, donorship behavior, stress and organizations, quality programs.

Lawrence Technological University, College of Management, Southfield, MI 48075-1058. Offers business administration (MBA, DBA); business administration international (MBA); global leadership and management (MS); global operations and project management (MS); information systems (MS); information technology (DM); operations management (MS). *Accreditation:* ACBSP. Part-time and evening/weekend programs available. *Faculty:* 12 full-time (6 women), 39 part-time/adjunct (11 women). *Students:* 10 full-time (4 women), 518 part-time (228 women); includes 183 minority (123 Black or African American, non-Hispanic/Latino; 2 American Indian or Alaska Native, non-Hispanic/Latino; 44 Asian, non-Hispanic/Latino; 11 Hispanic/Latino; 3 Two or more races, non-Hispanic/Latino), 50 international. Average age 36. 420 applicants, 45% accepted, 97 enrolled. In 2011, 177 master's, 14 doctorates awarded. *Degree requirements:* For master's, thesis (for some programs). *Entrance requirements:* For master's, GMAT. Additional exam requirements/recommendations for international students: Required—TOEFL (minimum score 550 paper-based; 213 computer-based; 79 iBT). *Application deadline:* For fall admission, 7/27 priority date for domestic students, 5/23 for international students; for spring admission, 11/15 priority date for domestic students, 11/15 for international students. Applications are processed on a rolling basis. Application fee: $50. Electronic applications accepted. *Financial support:* In 2011–12, 122 students received support. Federal Work-Study and institutionally sponsored loans available. Support available to part-time students. Financial award application deadline: 4/1; financial award applicants required to submit FAFSA. *Unit head:* Dr. Alan McCord, Interim Dean, 248-204-3050, E-mail: mgtdean@ltu.edu. *Application contact:* Jane Rohrback, Director of Admissions, 248-204-3160, Fax: 248-204-2228, E-mail: admissions@ltu.edu. Web site: http://www.ltu.edu/management/index.asp.

Lebanese American University, School of Business, Beirut, Lebanon. Offers MBA.

Lebanon Valley College, Program in Business Administration, Annville, PA 17003-1400. Offers MBA. Part-time and evening/weekend programs available. *Faculty:* 3 full-time (0 women), 39 part-time/adjunct (12 women). *Students:* 177 part-time (75 women); includes 10 minority (2 Black or African American, non-Hispanic/Latino; 1 American Indian or Alaska Native, non-Hispanic/Latino; 2 Asian, non-Hispanic/Latino; 5 Hispanic/Latino). Average age 35. In 2011, 42 master's awarded. *Entrance requirements:* For master's, 3 years of work experience. *Application deadline:* Applications are processed on a rolling basis. Application fee: $30. Electronic applications accepted. *Expenses: Tuition:* Full-time $35,720; part-time $465 per credit. *Required fees:* $610. Part-time tuition and fees vary according to program. *Financial support:* Application deadline: 5/1; applicants required to submit FAFSA. *Unit head:* Jennifer Easter, Director of the MBA Program, 717-867-6335, Fax: 717-867-6018, E-mail: easter@lvc.edu. *Application contact:* Hope Witmer, Assistant Dean, Graduate Studies and Continuing Education, 717-867-6213, Fax: 717-867-6018, E-mail: witmer@lvc.edu. Web site: http://www.lvc.edu/mba.

Lehigh University, College of Business and Economics, Bethlehem, PA 18015. Offers accounting (MS), including accounting and information analysis; business administration (MBA); economics (MS, PhD); entrepreneurship (Certificate); finance (MS), including analytical finance; project management (Certificate); supply chain management (Certificate); MBA/E; MBA/M Ed. *Accreditation:* AACSB. Part-time and evening/weekend programs available. Postbaccalaureate distance learning degree programs offered (minimal on-campus study). *Faculty:* 40 full-time (10 women), 13 part-time/

adjunct (0 women). *Students:* 159 full-time (85 women), 242 part-time (85 women); includes 40 minority (5 Black or African American, non-Hispanic/Latino; 27 Asian, non-Hispanic/Latino; 7 Hispanic/Latino; 1 Native Hawaiian or other Pacific Islander, non-Hispanic/Latino), 139 international. Average age 29. 890 applicants, 40% accepted, 89 enrolled. In 2011, 166 master's, 2 doctorates awarded. Terminal master's awarded for partial completion of doctoral program. *Degree requirements:* For master's, thesis optional; for doctorate, comprehensive exam, thesis/dissertation, proposal defense. *Entrance requirements:* For master's, GMAT, GRE General Test; for doctorate, GMAT or GRE General Test. Additional exam requirements/recommendations for international students: Required—TOEFL (minimum score 600 paper-based; 250 computer-based; 94 iBT). *Application deadline:* For fall admission, 7/15 for domestic students, 5/1 for international students; for spring admission, 12/1 for domestic and international students. Applications are processed on a rolling basis. Application fee: $100. Electronic applications accepted. *Expenses:* Contact institution. *Financial support:* In 2011–12, 93 students received support, including 2 fellowships with full tuition reimbursements available (averaging $16,000 per year), 39 research assistantships with full and partial tuition reimbursements available (averaging $2,269 per year), 17 teaching assistantships with full tuition reimbursements available (averaging $13,840 per year); career-related internships or fieldwork, scholarships/grants, health care benefits, tuition waivers (full and partial), and unspecified assistantships also available. Support available to part-time students. Financial award application deadline: 1/15. *Faculty research:* Public finance, energy, investments, activity-based costing, management information systems. *Unit head:* Paul R. Brown, Dean, 610-758-6725, Fax: 610-758-4499, E-mail: prb207@lehigh.edu. *Application contact:* Corinn McBride, Director of Recruitment and Admissions, 610-758-3418, Fax: 610-758-5283, E-mail: com207@lehigh.edu. Web site: http://www.lehigh.edu/business.

Le Moyne College, Madden School of Business, Syracuse, NY 13214. Offers MBA. *Accreditation:* AACSB. Part-time and evening/weekend programs available. *Faculty:* 10 full-time (2 women), 10 part-time/adjunct (3 women). *Students:* 18 full-time (9 women), 72 part-time (29 women); includes 3 minority (2 Black or African American, non-Hispanic/Latino; 1 Asian, non-Hispanic/Latino), 1 international. Average age 29. 60 applicants, 75% accepted, 44 enrolled. In 2011, 42 master's awarded. *Degree requirements:* For master's, capstone level course. *Entrance requirements:* For master's, GMAT or GRE General Test, interview, bachelor's degree, minimum GPA of 3.0, resume, 2 letters of recommendation, personal statement, transcripts. Additional exam requirements/recommendations for international students: Required—TOEFL (minimum score 550 paper-based; 213 computer-based; 79 iBT). *Application deadline:* For fall admission, 7/1 priority date for domestic students, 7/1 for international students; for spring admission, 11/1 priority date for domestic students, 11/1 for international students. Applications are processed on a rolling basis. Application fee: $0. *Expenses: Tuition:* Full-time $12,258; part-time $681 per credit hour. *Required fees:* $25 per semester. *Financial support:* In 2011–12, 27 students received support. Career-related internships or fieldwork, scholarships/grants, health care benefits, and unspecified assistantships available. Support available to part-time students. Financial award applicants required to submit FAFSA. *Faculty research:* Performance evaluation outcomes assessment, technology outsourcing, international business, systems for Web-based information-seeking, non-profit business practices, business sustainability practices, management/leadership development, operations management optimization applications. *Unit head:* Dr. George Kulick, Associate Dean of Madden School of Business, 315-445-4786, Fax: 315-445-4787, E-mail: kulick@lemoyne.edu. *Application contact:* Kristen P. Trapasso, Director of Graduate Admission, 315-445-4265, Fax: 315-445-6027, E-mail: trapaskp@lemoyne.edu. Web site: http://www.lemoyne.edu/mba.

Lenoir-Rhyne University, Graduate Programs, Charles M. Snipes School of Business, Hickory, NC 28601. Offers accounting (MBA); entrepreneurship (MBA); global leadership (MBA); leadership development (MBA). *Accreditation:* ACBSP. Part-time and evening/weekend programs available. *Degree requirements:* For master's, capstone course. *Entrance requirements:* For master's, GMAT, minimum undergraduate GPA of 2.7, graduate 3.0. Additional exam requirements/recommendations for international students: Required—TOEFL (minimum score 600 paper-based). Electronic applications accepted. *Expenses:* Contact institution.

LeTourneau University, School of Graduate and Professional Studies, Longview, TX 75607-7001. Offers business administration (MBA); counseling (MA); education (M Ed); engineering (M Sc); health care administration (MS); psychology (MA); strategic leadership (MSL). Part-time and evening/weekend programs available. Postbaccalaureate distance learning degree programs offered (no on-campus study). *Faculty:* 19 full-time (5 women), 62 part-time/adjunct (25 women). *Students:* 12 full-time (6 women), 347 part-time (273 women); includes 191 minority (162 Black or African American, non-Hispanic/Latino; 2 American Indian or Alaska Native, non-Hispanic/Latino; 3 Asian, non-Hispanic/Latino; 20 Hispanic/Latino; 1 Native Hawaiian or other Pacific Islander, non-Hispanic/Latino; 3 Two or more races, non-Hispanic/Latino), 1 international. Average age 37. 138 applicants, 90% accepted, 120 enrolled. In 2011, 129 master's awarded. *Degree requirements:* For master's, thesis (for some programs). *Entrance requirements:* For master's, GRE (for counseling and engineering programs), minimum GPA of 2.8 (3.0 for counseling and engineering programs). Additional exam requirements/recommendations for international students: Required—TOEFL. *Application deadline:* Applications are processed on a rolling basis. Electronic applications accepted. *Expenses: Tuition:* Full-time $13,020; part-time $620 per credit hour. *Financial support:* In 2011–12, 15 students received support, including 5 research assistantships (averaging $9,600 per year); institutionally sponsored loans and unspecified assistantships also available. *Unit head:* Dr. Carol Green, Vice President, 903-233-4010, Fax: 903-233-3227, E-mail: carolgreen@letu.edu. *Application contact:* Chris Fontaine, Assistant Vice President for Enrollment Management and Marketing, 903-233-4071, Fax: 903-233-3227, E-mail: chrisfontaine@letu.edu. Web site: http://www.adults.letu.edu/.

Lewis University, College of Business, Graduate School of Management, Romeoville, IL 60446. Offers business administration (MBA), including accounting, custom elective option, e-business, finance, healthcare management, human resources management, information security, international business, management information systems, marketing, project management, technology and operations management; finance (MS); project management (MS). *Accreditation:* ACBSP. Part-time and evening/weekend programs available. Postbaccalaureate distance learning degree programs offered (no on-campus study). In 2011, 132 master's awarded. Application fee: $40. *Financial support:* Applicants required to submit FAFSA. *Unit head:* Dr. Rami Khasawneh, Dean, 800-838-0500 Ext. 5360, E-mail: khasawra@lewisu.edu. *Application contact:* Michele Ryan, Director of Admission, 815-836-5384, E-mail: gsm@lewisu.edu.

Lewis University, College of Nursing and Health Professions and College of Business, Program in Nursing/Business, Romeoville, IL 60446. Offers MSN/MBA. Part-time and evening/weekend programs available. *Students:* 5 full-time (3 women), 30 part-time (28 women); includes 19 minority (10 Black or African American, non-Hispanic/Latino; 2 Asian, non-Hispanic/Latino; 7 Hispanic/Latino). Average age 38. *Entrance requirements:* Additional exam requirements/recommendations for international students: Required—TOEFL (minimum score 550 paper-based; 213 computer-based; 80 iBT). *Application deadline:* For fall admission, 4/2 priority date for domestic students, 5/1 for international students; for spring admission, 11/15 for international students. Applications are processed on a rolling basis. Electronic applications accepted. *Financial support:* Scholarships/grants, tuition waivers (full and partial), and unspecified assistantships available. Financial award application deadline: 5/1; financial award applicants required to submit FAFSA. *Faculty research:* Cancer prevention, phenomenological methods, public policy analysis. *Total annual research expenditures:* $1,000. *Unit head:* Dr. Linda Niedringhaus, Interim Director, 815-838-0500 Ext. 5878, E-mail: niedrili@lewisu.edu. *Application contact:* Nancy Wiksten, Adult Admission Counselor, 815-838-0500 Ext. 5628, Fax: 815-836-5578, E-mail: wikstena@lewisu.edu.

Liberty University, School of Business, Lynchburg, VA 24502. Offers MA, MBA, MS. Part-time programs available. Postbaccalaureate distance learning degree programs offered (minimal on-campus study). *Students:* 959 full-time (494 women), 2,607 part-time (1,299 women); includes 771 minority (537 Black or African American, non-Hispanic/Latino; 11 American Indian or Alaska Native, non-Hispanic/Latino; 34 Asian, non-Hispanic/Latino; 119 Hispanic/Latino; 6 Native Hawaiian or other Pacific Islander, non-Hispanic/Latino; 64 Two or more races, non-Hispanic/Latino), 74 international. Average age 35. In 2011, 786 master's awarded. *Entrance requirements:* Additional exam requirements/recommendations for international students: Required—TOEFL (minimum score 600 paper-based; 250 computer-based; 100 iBT). *Application deadline:* Applications are processed on a rolling basis. Application fee: $50. Electronic applications accepted. *Expenses:* Contact institution. *Unit head:* Dr. Scott Hicks, Dean, 434-592-4808, Fax: 434-582-2366, E-mail: smhicks@liberty.edu. *Application contact:* Jay Bridge, Director of Graduate Admissions, 800-424-9595, Fax: 800-628-7977, E-mail: gradadmissions@liberty.edu. Web site: http://www.liberty.edu/academics/business/index.cfm?PID=149.

LIM College, MBA Program, New York, NY 10022-5268. Offers entrepreneurship (MBA); fashion management (MBA). *Entrance requirements:* For master's, interview. Additional exam requirements/recommendations for international students: Required—TOEFL (minimum score 550 paper-based; 213 computer-based; 80 iBT), IELTS (minimum score 6.5).

Lincoln Memorial University, School of Business, Harrogate, TN 37752-1901. Offers MBA. Part-time and evening/weekend programs available. *Degree requirements:* For master's, comprehensive exam, thesis. *Entrance requirements:* For master's, GMAT, resume, letters of recommendation, interview. Additional exam requirements/recommendations for international students: Required—TOEFL (minimum score 500 paper-based).

Lincoln University, Graduate Center, Lincoln University, PA 19352. Offers administration (MSA), including finance, human resources management; early childhood education (M Ed); elementary education (M Ed); human services (M Hum Svcs); reading (MSR). Evening/weekend programs available. *Degree requirements:* For master's, thesis. *Entrance requirements:* For master's, 5 years of work experience in human services. *Faculty research:* Gerontology/minority aging, computers in composition instruction.

Lincoln University, Graduate Studies, Oakland, CA 94612. Offers finance and investments (DBA); finance management and investment banking (MBA); general business (MBA); human resource management (MBA, DBA); international business (MBA); management information systems (MBA). Part-time and evening/weekend programs available. *Faculty:* 10 full-time (4 women), 15 part-time/adjunct (3 women). *Students:* 272 full-time (124 women), 1 part-time (0 women). *Degree requirements:* For master's, research project (thesis), internship report, or comprehensive exam; for doctorate, comprehensive exam, thesis/dissertation. *Entrance requirements:* For master's, minimum GPA of 2.7; for doctorate, GMAT (minimum score: 550), GRE (minimum score: 1000), or equivalent test results (waived for master's degree with minimum cumulative GPA of 3.3). Additional exam requirements/recommendations for international students: Required—TOEFL (minimum score 525 paper-based; 195 computer-based; 71 iBT) or IELTS (minimum score 5.5) for MBA; TOEFL (minimum score 550 paper-based; 213 computer-based; 79 iBT) or IELTS (minimum score 6) for DBA. *Application deadline:* For fall admission, 7/2 priority date for domestic students, 7/2 for international students; for spring admission, 11/25 priority date for domestic students, 11/25 for international students. Applications are processed on a rolling basis. Application fee: $75. Electronic applications accepted. *Financial support:* Teaching assistantships, career-related internships or fieldwork, and scholarships/grants available. *Unit head:* Dr. Marshall Burak, Director of Graduate Programs, 510-628-8016, Fax: 510-628-8012, E-mail: mburak@lincolnuca.edu. *Application contact:* Peggy Au, Director of Admissions and Records, 510-628-8010, Fax: 510-628-8012, E-mail: admissions@lincolnuca.edu. Web site: http://www.lincolnuca.edu/.

Lincoln University, School of Graduate Studies and Continuing Education, Jefferson City, MO 65102. Offers business administration (MBA), including accounting, entrepreneurship, management, public administration and policy; educational leadership (Ed S), including elementary leadership, secondary leadership, superintendency; guidance and counseling (M Ed), including community/agency counseling, elementary school, secondary school; history (MA); school administration and supervision (M Ed), including elementary school administration, secondary school administration, special education administration; school teaching (M Ed), including elementary school teaching, secondary school teaching; social science (MA), including history, political science, sociology; sociology (MA); sociology/criminal justice (MA). Part-time and evening/weekend programs available. *Degree requirements:* For master's and Ed S, comprehensive exam, thesis optional. *Entrance requirements:* For master's and Ed S, GRE, MAT or GMAT, minimum GPA of 2.75 in major, 2.5 overall; 3 letters of recommendation; minimum C average in English composition; personal statement of purpose. Additional exam requirements/recommendations for international students: Required—TOEFL (minimum score 500 paper-based; 173 computer-based; 61 iBT). *Faculty research:* Suicide prevention.

Lindenwood University, Graduate Programs, College of Individualized Education, St. Charles, MO 63301-1695. Offers administration (MSA); business administration (MBA); communications (MA); criminal justice and administration (MS); gerontology (MA); health management (MS); human resource management (MS); information technology (MBA, Certificate); managing information technology (MS); writing (MFA). Part-time and evening/weekend programs available. *Faculty:* 18 full-time (9 women), 128 part-time/adjunct (53 women). *Students:* 858 full-time (586 women), 69 part-time (43 women); includes 330 minority (296 Black or African American, non-Hispanic/Latino; 9 American Indian or Alaska Native, non-Hispanic/Latino; 4 Asian, non-Hispanic/Latino; 1 Hispanic/Latino; 20 Two or more races, non-Hispanic/Latino), 16 international. Average age 35. 229 applicants, 80% accepted, 172 enrolled. In 2011, 428 degrees awarded. *Degree requirements:* For master's, thesis (for some programs), 1 colloquium per term. *Entrance requirements:* For master's, interview, minimum GPA of 3.0. Additional exam requirements/recommendations for international students: Required—TOEFL (minimum score 550 paper-based; 213 computer-based; 80 iBT). *Application deadline:* For fall admission, 10/1 priority date for domestic students, 10/1 for international students; for winter admission, 1/7 priority date for domestic students, 1/7 for international students; for spring admission, 4/7 priority date for domestic students, 4/7 for international students. Applications are processed on a rolling basis. Application fee: $30 ($100 for international students). Electronic applications accepted. *Expenses: Tuition:* Full-time

$13,650; part-time $395 per credit hour. *Required fees:* $150 per semester. Tuition and fees vary according to course level and course load. *Financial support:* In 2011–12, 386 students received support. Career-related internships or fieldwork, institutionally sponsored loans, tuition waivers (partial), and unspecified assistantships available. Financial award application deadline: 6/30; financial award applicants required to submit FAFSA. *Unit head:* Dan Kemper, Dean, 636-949-4501, Fax: 636-949-4505, E-mail: dkemper@lindenwood.edu. *Application contact:* Brett Barger, Dean of Evening Admissions and Extension Campuses, 636-949-4934, Fax: 636-949-4109, E-mail: adultadmissions@lindenwood.edu.

Lindenwood University, Graduate Programs, School of Business and Entrepreneurship, St. Charles, MO 63301-1695. Offers accounting (MBA, MS); business administration (MBA); entrepreneurial studies (MBA, MS); finance (MBA, MS); human resource management (MBA); human resources (MS); international business (MBA, MS); management (MBA, MS); management information systems (MBA, MS); marketing (MBA, MS); public management (MBA, MS); sport management (MA); supply chain management (MBA). *Accreditation:* ACBSP. Part-time and evening/weekend programs available. *Faculty:* 20 full-time (8 women), 17 part-time/adjunct (5 women). *Students:* 165 full-time (66 women), 223 part-time (100 women); includes 59 minority (48 Black or African American, non-Hispanic/Latino; 4 Asian, non-Hispanic/Latino; 2 Native Hawaiian or other Pacific Islander, non-Hispanic/Latino; 5 Two or more races, non-Hispanic/Latino), 140 international. Average age 29. 156 applicants, 76% accepted, 103 enrolled. In 2011, 205 degrees awarded. *Degree requirements:* For master's, comprehensive exam (for some programs), thesis (for some programs). *Entrance requirements:* For master's, interview, minimum GPA of 3.0, letter of recommendation. Additional exam requirements/recommendations for international students: Required—TOEFL (minimum score 550 paper-based; 213 computer-based; 80 iBT). *Application deadline:* For fall admission, 8/15 priority date for domestic students, 8/15 for international students; for winter admission, 1/9 priority date for domestic students, 1/9 for international students; for spring admission, 3/12 priority date for domestic students, 3/12 for international students. Applications are processed on a rolling basis. Application fee: $30 ($100 for international students). Electronic applications accepted. *Expenses: Tuition:* Full-time $13,650; part-time $395 per credit hour. *Required fees:* $150 per semester. Tuition and fees vary according to course level and course load. *Financial support:* In 2011–12, 206 students received support. Career-related internships or fieldwork, Federal Work-Study, institutionally sponsored loans, and tuition waivers (partial) available. Financial award application deadline: 6/30; financial award applicants required to submit FAFSA. *Unit head:* Roger Ellis, Dean, 636-949-4839, E-mail: rellis@lindenwood.edu. *Application contact:* Brett Barger, Dean of Evening Admissions and Extension Campuses, 636-949-4934, Fax: 636-949-4109, E-mail: adultadmissions@lindenwood.edu. Web site: http://www.lindenwood.edu.

Lipscomb University, College of Business, Nashville, TN 37204-3951. Offers accounting (MBA); business administration (general) (MBA); conflict management (MBA); financial services (MBA); healthcare management (MBA); human resources (MHR); leadership (MBA); nonprofit management (MBA); sports management (MBA); sustainability (MBA). *Accreditation:* ACBSP. Part-time and evening/weekend programs available. *Faculty:* 13 full-time (3 women), 7 part-time/adjunct (1 woman). *Students:* 51 full-time (21 women), 83 part-time (48 women); includes 20 minority (16 Black or African American, non-Hispanic/Latino; 3 Asian, non-Hispanic/Latino; 1 Hispanic/Latino), 1 international. Average age 33. 190 applicants, 43% accepted, 54 enrolled. In 2011, 85 master's awarded. *Entrance requirements:* For master's, GMAT, interview, 2 references, resume. Additional exam requirements/recommendations for international students: Required—TOEFL (minimum score 570 paper-based; 230 computer-based). *Application deadline:* For fall admission, 6/15 for domestic students, 2/1 for international students; for winter admission, 6/1 for international students; for spring admission, 11/15 for domestic students. Applications are processed on a rolling basis. Application fee: $50 ($75 for international students). Electronic applications accepted. *Expenses:* Contact institution. *Financial support:* Career-related internships or fieldwork, scholarships/grants, tuition waivers (partial), and unspecified assistantships available. Support available to part-time students. Financial award application deadline: 7/1; financial award applicants required to submit FAFSA. *Faculty research:* Impact of spirituality on organization commitment, leadership, psychological empowerment, training. *Unit head:* Dr. Mike Kendrick, Associate Dean of Graduate Business Programs, 615-966-1833, Fax: 615-966-1818, E-mail: mikekendrick@lipscomb.edu. *Application contact:* Lisa Shacklett, Executive Director of Enrollment and Marketing, 615-966-5968, E-mail: lisa.shacklett@lipscomb.edu. Web site: http://mba.lipscomb.edu.

Long Island University–Brooklyn Campus, School of Business, Public Administration and Information Sciences, Program in Business Administration, Brooklyn, NY 11201-8423. Offers MBA. Part-time and evening/weekend programs available. *Entrance requirements:* For master's, GMAT or GRE General Test, 2 letters of recommendation. Additional exam requirements/recommendations for international students: Required—TOEFL (minimum score 500 paper-based; 173 computer-based). Electronic applications accepted.

Long Island University–C. W. Post Campus, College of Management, Department of Management, Brookville, NY 11548-1300. Offers MBA.

Long Island University–C. W. Post Campus, College of Management, School of Business, Brookville, NY 11548-1300. Offers accounting and taxation (Certificate); business administration (Certificate); finance (MBA, Certificate); general business administration (MBA); international business (MBA, Certificate); management (MBA, Certificate); management information systems (MBA, Certificate); marketing (MBA, Certificate). *Accreditation:* AACSB. Part-time and evening/weekend programs available. *Entrance requirements:* For master's, GMAT, resume, minimum GPA of 3.0, 2 letters of recommendation. Additional exam requirements/recommendations for international students: Required—TOEFL (minimum score 527 paper-based; 197 computer-based). Electronic applications accepted. *Faculty research:* Financial markets, consumer behavior.

Long Island University–Hudson at Rockland, Graduate School, Master of Business Administration Program, Orangeburg, NY 10962. Offers business administration (Post Master's Certificate); entrepreneurship (MBA); finance (MBA); healthcare sector management (MBA); management (MBA). Part-time and evening/weekend programs available. *Entrance requirements:* For master's, GMAT, college transcripts, two letters of recommendation, personal statement, resume.

Long Island University–Hudson at Westchester, Program in Business Administration, Purchase, NY 10577. Offers MBA. Part-time and evening/weekend programs available. *Entrance requirements:* For master's, GMAT. Additional exam requirements/recommendations for international students: Required—TOEFL (minimum score 500 paper-based; 173 computer-based).

Longwood University, Office of Graduate Studies, College of Business and Economics, Farmville, VA 23909. Offers retail management (MBA). *Accreditation:* AACSB. *Degree requirements:* For master's, internship. *Entrance requirements:* For master's, GMAT.

Louisiana State University and Agricultural and Mechanical College, Graduate School, E. J. Ourso College of Business, Department of Finance, Baton Rouge, LA 70803. Offers business administration (PhD), including finance; finance (MS). *Faculty:* 11 full-time (3 women), 1 part-time/adjunct (0 women). *Students:* 40 full-time (10 women), 2 part-time (0 women); includes 3 minority (2 Black or African American, non-Hispanic/Latino; 1 Two or more races, non-Hispanic/Latino), 18 international. Average age 26. 103 applicants, 31% accepted, 16 enrolled. In 2011, 15 master's, 2 doctorates awarded. *Degree requirements:* For master's, thesis or alternative; for doctorate, thesis/dissertation. *Entrance requirements:* For master's and doctorate, GMAT. Additional exam requirements/recommendations for international students: Required—TOEFL (minimum score 550 paper-based; 213 computer-based; 79 iBT) or IELTS (minimum score 6.5). *Application deadline:* For fall admission, 1/25 priority date for domestic students, 5/15 for international students; for spring admission, 10/15 for international students. Applications are processed on a rolling basis. Application fee: $50 ($70 for international students). *Financial support:* In 2011–12, 21 students received support, including 5 research assistantships with full and partial tuition reimbursements available (averaging $17,750 per year), 8 teaching assistantships with full and partial tuition reimbursements available (averaging $9,625 per year); fellowships, career-related internships or fieldwork, Federal Work-Study, scholarships/grants, health care benefits, and unspecified assistantships also available. Support available to part-time students. Financial award application deadline: 4/1; financial award applicants required to submit FAFSA. *Faculty research:* Derivatives and risk management, capital structure, asset pricing, spatial statistics, financial institutions and underwriting. *Total annual research expenditures:* $61,188. *Unit head:* Dr. Vestor Carlos Slawson, Jr., Interim Chair, 225-578-6367, Fax: 225-578-6366, E-mail: cslawson@lsu.edu. Web site: http://business.lsu.edu/finance.

Louisiana State University and Agricultural and Mechanical College, Graduate School, E. J. Ourso College of Business, Department of Management, Baton Rouge, LA 70803. Offers business administration (PhD), including management. *Accreditation:* AACSB. *Faculty:* 10 full-time (2 women). *Students:* 4 full-time (2 women); includes 1 minority (Asian, non-Hispanic/Latino), 1 international. Average age 32. *Degree requirements:* For doctorate, thesis/dissertation. *Entrance requirements:* For doctorate, GMAT. Additional exam requirements/recommendations for international students: Required—TOEFL (minimum score 550 paper-based; 213 computer-based; 79 iBT) or IELTS (minimum score 6.5). *Application deadline:* For fall admission, 1/25 priority date for domestic students, 5/15 for international students; for spring admission, 10/15 for international students. Applications are processed on a rolling basis. Application fee: $50 ($70 for international students). Electronic applications accepted. *Financial support:* In 2011–12, 4 students received support, including 2 research assistantships with full and partial tuition reimbursements available (averaging $16,500 per year), 2 teaching assistantships with full and partial tuition reimbursements available (averaging $16,500 per year); fellowships, Federal Work-Study, institutionally sponsored loans, scholarships/grants, health care benefits, and unspecified assistantships also available. Support available to part-time students. Financial award applicants required to submit FAFSA. *Faculty research:* Human resource management, organizational behavior, strategy. *Total annual research expenditures:* $34,077. *Unit head:* Dr. Timothy Chandler, Co-Chair, 225-578-6101, Fax: 225-578-6983, E-mail: mgchan@lsu.edu. *Application contact:* Dr. Hettie Richardson, Co-Chair, 225-578-6146, Fax: 225-578-6140, E-mail: hricha4@lsu.edu. Web site: http://www.business.lsu.edu/management.

Louisiana State University and Agricultural and Mechanical College, Graduate School, E. J. Ourso College of Business, Department of Marketing, Baton Rouge, LA 70803. Offers business administration (PhD), including marketing. Part-time programs available. *Faculty:* 8 full-time (1 woman). *Students:* 4 full-time (3 women), 1 (woman) part-time, 2 international. Average age 32. In 2011, 1 doctorate awarded. *Degree requirements:* For doctorate, thesis/dissertation. *Entrance requirements:* Additional exam requirements/recommendations for international students: Required—TOEFL (minimum score 550 paper-based; 213 computer-based; 79 iBT) or IELTS (minimum score 6.5). *Application deadline:* For fall admission, 1/25 priority date for domestic students, 5/15 for international students; for spring admission, 10/15 for international students. Applications are processed on a rolling basis. Application fee: $50 ($70 for international students). Electronic applications accepted. *Financial support:* In 2011–12, 4 students received support, including 4 teaching assistantships with full and partial tuition reimbursements available (averaging $18,000 per year); fellowships, research assistantships with partial tuition reimbursements available, career-related internships or fieldwork, Federal Work-Study, institutionally sponsored loans, scholarships/grants, health care benefits, and unspecified assistantships also available. Support available to part-time students. Financial award applicants required to submit FAFSA. *Faculty research:* Consumer behavior, marketing strategy, global marketing, e-commerce, branding/brand equity. *Unit head:* Dr. Alvin C. Burns, Chair, 225-578-8786, Fax: 225-578-8616, E-mail: alburns@lsu.edu. *Application contact:* Dr. Judith Garretson Folse, Graduate Adviser, 225-578-6531, Fax: 225-578-8616, E-mail: folse@lsu.edu. Web site: http://www.business.lsu.edu/marketing.

Louisiana State University and Agricultural and Mechanical College, Graduate School, E. J. Ourso College of Business, Flores MBA Program, Baton Rouge, LA 70803. Offers EMBA, MBA, PMBA. *Accreditation:* AACSB. *Students:* 234 full-time (81 women), 30 part-time (7 women); includes 31 minority (14 Black or African American, non-Hispanic/Latino; 1 American Indian or Alaska Native, non-Hispanic/Latino; 6 Asian, non-Hispanic/Latino; 8 Hispanic/Latino; 2 Two or more races, non-Hispanic/Latino), 30 international. Average age 28. 293 applicants, 49% accepted, 109 enrolled. In 2011, 151 master's awarded. *Entrance requirements:* Additional exam requirements/recommendations for international students: Required—TOEFL (minimum score 550 paper-based; 213 computer-based; 79 iBT) or IELTS (minimum score 6.5). *Application deadline:* For fall admission, 1/25 priority date for domestic students, 5/15 for international students; for spring admission, 10/15 for international students. Application fee: $50 ($70 for international students). Electronic applications accepted. *Financial support:* In 2011–12, 166 students received support, including 15 research assistantships with partial tuition reimbursements available (averaging $14,597 per year), 60 teaching assistantships with full and partial tuition reimbursements available (averaging $12,436 per year); fellowships, Federal Work-Study, institutionally sponsored loans, scholarships/grants, health care benefits, and unspecified assistantships also available. Support available to part-time students. Financial award applicants required to submit FAFSA. *Total annual research expenditures:* $126,904. *Unit head:* Dr. Ed Watson, Director, 225-578-2502, Fax: 225-578-2421, E-mail: ewatson@lsu.edu. *Application contact:* Dana Hart, Program Adviser, 225-578-8892, Fax: 225-578-2421, E-mail: dhart@lsu.edu. Web site: http://mba.lsu.edu/.

Louisiana State University in Shreveport, College of Business, Education, and Human Development, Program in Business Administration, Shreveport, LA 71115-2399. Offers MBA. *Accreditation:* ACBSP. Part-time and evening/weekend programs available. *Students:* 24 full-time (12 women), 81 part-time (37 women); includes 14 minority (12 Black or African American, non-Hispanic/Latino; 2 Hispanic/Latino), 12 international. Average age 32. 59 applicants, 95% accepted, 29 enrolled. In 2011, 34 master's awarded. *Degree requirements:* For master's, comprehensive exam. *Entrance requirements:* For master's, GMAT, minimum undergraduate GPA of 2.5, 2.75 for last 60 credits. Additional exam requirements/recommendations for international students: Required—TOEFL (minimum score 550 paper-based; 213 computer-based; 80 iBT). *Application deadline:* For fall admission, 6/30 for domestic and international students; for spring admission, 11/30 for domestic and international students. Applications are processed on a rolling basis. Application fee: $10 ($20 for international students). *Financial support:* In 2011–12, 5 research assistantships (averaging $5,000 per year) were awarded; scholarships/grants also available. *Unit head:* Dr. Bill Bigler, Program Director, 318-797-5247, Fax: 318-797-5176, E-mail: bill.bigler@lsus.edu. *Application contact:* Christianne Wojcik, Secretary, Graduate Studies, 318-797-5247, Fax: 318-798-4120, E-mail: christianne.wojcik@lsus.edu.

Louisiana Tech University, Graduate School, College of Business, Ruston, LA 71272. Offers MBA, MPA, DBA. *Accreditation:* AACSB. Part-time programs available. *Degree requirements:* For doctorate, thesis/dissertation. *Entrance requirements:* For master's and doctorate, GMAT.

Loyola Marymount University, College of Business Administration, Los Angeles, CA 90045-2659. Offers MBA, MBA/JD, MBA/MS. *Accreditation:* AACSB. *Expenses:* Contact institution. *Unit head:* Dr. Dennis Draper, Dean, 310-338-7504, E-mail: ddraper@lmu.edu. *Application contact:* Chake H. Kouyoumjian, Associate Dean of the Graduate Division, 310-338-2721, E-mail: ckouyoum@lmu.edu. Web site: http://cba.lmu.edu/.

Loyola University Chicago, Graduate School of Business, Chicago, IL 60660. Offers accountancy (MS, MSA); business administration (MBA); finance (MS); healthcare management (MBA); human resources and employee relations (MS, MSHR); information systems and operations management (MS), including information systems management; marketing (MS, MSIMC), including integrated marketing communications (MS), marketing (MSIMC); strategic financial services (MBA); JD/MBA; MBA/MSA; MSIMC/MBA; MSISM/MBA; MSN/MBA. *Accreditation:* AACSB. *Expenses: Tuition:* Full-time $15,660; part-time $870 per credit hour. *Required fees:* $125 per semester. Tuition and fees vary according to course load and program.

Loyola University Maryland, Graduate Programs, Sellinger School of Business and Management, Program in Business Administration, Baltimore, MD 21210-2699. Offers accounting (MBA); finance (MBA); general business (MBA); information systems operations management (MBA); international business (MBA); management (MBA); marketing (MBA). *Accreditation:* AACSB. Part-time and evening/weekend programs available. *Faculty:* 61 full-time (12 women), 29 part-time/adjunct (4 women). *Students:* 50 full-time (15 women), 547 part-time (210 women); includes 98 minority (39 Black or African American, non-Hispanic/Latino; 1 American Indian or Alaska Native, non-Hispanic/Latino; 28 Asian, non-Hispanic/Latino; 18 Hispanic/Latino; 2 Native Hawaiian or other Pacific Islander, non-Hispanic/Latino; 10 Two or more races, non-Hispanic/Latino), 15 international. Average age 30. In 2011, 232 master's awarded. *Entrance requirements:* For master's, GMAT (for some programs). Additional exam requirements/recommendations for international students: Required—TOEFL (minimum score 550 paper-based; 213 computer-based). *Application deadline:* For fall admission, 8/1 priority date for domestic students; for spring admission, 12/1 priority date for domestic students. Application fee: $50. Electronic applications accepted. *Financial support:* Research assistantships and unspecified assistantships available. Financial award application deadline: 4/15; financial award applicants required to submit FAFSA. *Unit head:* Dr. Karyl Leggio, Dean, 410-617-2301, E-mail: kbleggio@loyola.edu. *Application contact:* Maureen Faux, Executive Director, Graduate Admissions, 410-617-5020, Fax: 410-617-2002, E-mail: graduate@loyola.edu.

Loyola University Maryland, Graduate Programs, Sellinger School of Business and Management, Program in Executive Business Administration, Baltimore, MD 21210-2699. Offers MBA. *Accreditation:* AACSB. Evening/weekend programs available. *Faculty:* 61 full-time (12 women), 29 part-time/adjunct (4 women). *Students:* 115 full-time (30 women); includes 8 minority (5 Black or African American, non-Hispanic/Latino; 1 Asian, non-Hispanic/Latino; 2 Hispanic/Latino), 3 international. Average age 36. In 2011, 62 master's awarded. *Entrance requirements:* Additional exam requirements/recommendations for international students: Required—TOEFL (minimum score 550 paper-based; 213 computer-based). *Application deadline:* For fall admission, 8/1 priority date for domestic students. Application fee: $50. Electronic applications accepted. *Financial support:* Research assistantships and unspecified assistantships available. Financial award application deadline: 4/15; financial award applicants required to submit FAFSA. *Unit head:* Dr. Karyl Leggio, Dean, 410-617-2301, E-mail: kbleggio@loyola.edu. *Application contact:* Maureen Faux, Executive Director, Graduate Admissions, 410-617-5020, Fax: 410-617-2002, E-mail: graduate@loyola.edu.

Loyola University New Orleans, Joseph A. Butt, S.J., College of Business, Program in Business Administration, New Orleans, LA 70118-6195. Offers MBA, JD/MBA. *Accreditation:* AACSB. Part-time and evening/weekend programs available. Postbaccalaureate distance learning degree programs offered (minimal on-campus study). *Students:* 30 full-time (11 women), 43 part-time (19 women); includes 9 minority (3 Black or African American, non-Hispanic/Latino; 1 American Indian or Alaska Native, non-Hispanic/Latino; 4 Asian, non-Hispanic/Latino; 1 Hispanic/Latino), 1 international. Average age 28. 49 applicants, 80% accepted, 23 enrolled. In 2011, 32 master's awarded. *Entrance requirements:* For master's, GMAT, minimum GPA of 3.0, resume, 2 letters of recommendation, work experience in field. Additional exam requirements/recommendations for international students: Required—TOEFL (minimum score 550 paper-based; 213 computer-based). *Application deadline:* For fall admission, 6/15 priority date for domestic students, 6/15 for international students; for spring admission, 11/15 priority date for domestic students, 11/15 for international students. Applications are processed on a rolling basis. Application fee: $50. Electronic applications accepted. *Financial support:* Research assistantships, scholarships/grants, tuition waivers (partial), and unspecified assistantships available. Financial award application deadline: 5/1; financial award applicants required to submit FAFSA. *Faculty research:* Ethics, international business, entrepreneurship, quality management, risk management. *Unit head:* William B. Locander, Dean, 504-864-7979, Fax: 504-864-7970, E-mail: locander@loyno.edu. *Application contact:* Stephanie L. Mansfield, Assistant Director, Graduate Programs, 504-864-7965, Fax: 504-864-7970, E-mail: smans@loyno.edu. Web site: http://www.business.loyno.edu/mba/programs.

Lynchburg College, Graduate Studies, School of Business and Economics, Master of Business Administration Program, Lynchburg, VA 24501-3199. Offers MBA. Part-time and evening/weekend programs available. *Faculty:* 10 full-time (4 women). *Students:* 4 full-time (2 women), 45 part-time (13 women); includes 5 minority (3 Black or African American, non-Hispanic/Latino; 1 Hispanic/Latino; 1 Two or more races, non-Hispanic/Latino), 1 international. Average age 31. In 2011, 33 master's awarded. *Degree requirements:* For master's, capstone course. *Entrance requirements:* For master's, GMAT (minimum score of 400) or GRE, personal essay, 3 letters of recommendation, official transcripts (bachelor's, others as relevant), career goals statement. Additional exam requirements/recommendations for international students: Required—TOEFL (minimum score 550 paper-based; 213 computer-based; 79 iBT), IELTS (minimum score 6.5). *Application deadline:* For fall admission, 7/31 for domestic students, 6/1 for international students; for spring admission, 11/30 for domestic students, 10/15 for international students. Applications are processed on a rolling basis. Application fee: $30. Electronic applications accepted. Application fee is waived when completed online. *Expenses: Tuition:* Full-time $7740; part-time $430 per credit hour. *Financial support:* Fellowships, Federal Work-Study, scholarships/grants, health care benefits, and unspecified assistantships available. Support available to part-time students. Financial award application deadline: 7/31; financial award applicants required to submit FAFSA. *Unit head:* Dr. Atul Gupta, Professor/Director of MBA Program, 434-522-8651, E-mail: gupta@lynchburg.edu. *Application contact:* Anne Pingstock, Executive Assistant, Graduate Studies, 434-544-8383, Fax: 434-544-8483, E-mail: gradstudies@lynchburg.edu. Web site: http://www.lynchburg.edu/mba.xml.

Lynn University, College of Business and Management, Boca Raton, FL 33431-5598. Offers aviation management (MBA); financial valuation and investment management (MBA); hospitality management (MBA); international business (MBA); marketing (MBA); mass communication and media management (MBA); sports and athletics administration (MBA). Part-time and evening/weekend programs available. Postbaccalaureate distance learning degree programs offered. *Degree requirements:* For master's, project. *Entrance requirements:* For master's, GMAT or GRE, minimum undergraduate GPA of 3.0, resume, 2 letters of recommendation. Additional exam requirements/recommendations for international students: Required—TOEFL (minimum score 550 paper-based; 213 computer-based). Electronic applications accepted. *Faculty research:* Labor relations, dynamic balance in leisure-time skills, ethics in athletics, hotel development.

Maastricht School of Management, Graduate Programs, Maastricht, Netherlands. Offers business administration (MBA, DBA, PhD); facility management (Exec MBA); management (M Sc); sustainability (Exec MBA).

Madonna University, School of Business, Livonia, MI 48150-1173. Offers business administration (MBA); international business (MSBA); leadership studies (MSBA); leadership studies in criminal justice (MSBA); quality and operations management (MSBA). Part-time and evening/weekend programs available. Postbaccalaureate distance learning degree programs offered (minimal on-campus study). *Degree requirements:* For master's, thesis (for some programs), foreign language proficiency (international business). *Entrance requirements:* For master's, GMAT, GRE General Test, minimum GPA of 3.0. Electronic applications accepted. *Faculty research:* Management, women in management, future studies.

Maharishi University of Management, Graduate Studies, Program in Business Administration, Fairfield, IA 52557. Offers accounting (MBA); business administration (PhD); sustainability (MBA). Evening/weekend programs available. Postbaccalaureate distance learning degree programs offered (minimal on-campus study). *Degree requirements:* For doctorate, thesis/dissertation. *Entrance requirements:* For master's, GMAT, minimum GPA of 3.0; for doctorate, minimum GPA of 3.0. Additional exam requirements/recommendations for international students: Required—TOEFL. *Faculty research:* Leadership, effects of the group dynamics of consciousness on the economy, innovation, employee development, cooperative strategy.

Malone University, Graduate Program in Business, Canton, OH 44709. Offers MBA. *Accreditation:* ACBSP. Part-time and evening/weekend programs available. Postbaccalaureate distance learning degree programs offered (minimal on-campus study). *Faculty:* 7 full-time (2 women), 8 part-time/adjunct (2 women). *Students:* 7 full-time (3 women), 90 part-time (33 women); includes 14 minority (11 Black or African American, non-Hispanic/Latino; 3 Hispanic/Latino), 1 international. Average age 34. 56 applicants, 68% accepted, 21 enrolled. In 2011, 41 master's awarded. *Entrance requirements:* For master's, institution's own math diagnostic test, minimum GPA of 3.0. Additional exam requirements/recommendations for international students: Required—TOEFL (minimum score 550 paper-based; 213 computer-based; 79 iBT). *Application deadline:* Applications are processed on a rolling basis. *Expenses:* Contact institution. *Financial support:* Tuition waivers (partial) available. Support available to part-time students. Financial award application deadline: 6/30. *Faculty research:* Leadership, business ethics, sustainability, globalization, non-profit financial management. *Unit head:* Dr. Julia A. Frankland, Director, 330-471-8552, Fax: 330-471-8563, E-mail: jfrankland@malone.edu. *Application contact:* Mona J. McAuliffe, Graduate Recruiter, 330-471-8623, Fax: 330-471-8343, E-mail: mmcauliffe@malone.edu. Web site: http://www.malone.edu/admissions/graduate/mba/.

Marian University, Business Division, Fond du Lac, WI 54935-4699. Offers organizational leadership and quality (MS). Part-time and evening/weekend programs available. *Faculty:* 1 full-time (0 women), 14 part-time/adjunct (4 women). *Students:* 7 full-time (5 women), 94 part-time (58 women); includes 14 minority (8 Black or African American, non-Hispanic/Latino; 2 Asian, non-Hispanic/Latino; 4 Hispanic/Latino). Average age 41. 50 applicants, 94% accepted, 46 enrolled. In 2011, 44 master's awarded. *Degree requirements:* For master's, comprehensive group project. *Entrance requirements:* For master's, 3 years of managerial experience, minimum GPA of 2.75, letters of professional reference. Additional exam requirements/recommendations for international students: Required—TOEFL (minimum score 525 paper-based; 193 computer-based; 70 iBT). *Application deadline:* Applications are processed on a rolling basis. Application fee: $25. Electronic applications accepted. *Expenses:* Contact institution. *Financial support:* In 2011–12, 1 student received support. Institutionally sponsored loans available. Financial award application deadline: 3/1; financial award applicants required to submit FAFSA. *Faculty research:* Organizational values, statistical decision-making, learning organization, quality planning, customer research. *Unit head:* Dr. Jeffrey G. Reed, Dean, Marian School of Business, 920-923-8759, Fax: 920-923-7167, E-mail: jreed@marianuniversity.edu. *Application contact:* Tracy Qualman, Director of Marketing and Admission, 920-923-7159, Fax: 920-923-7167, E-mail: tqualmann@marianuniversity.edu. Web site: http://www.marianuniversity.edu/interior.aspx?id-220.

Marist College, Graduate Programs, School of Management, Business Administration Program, Poughkeepsie, NY 12601-1387. Offers business administration (MBA); executive leadership (Adv C). *Accreditation:* AACSB. Part-time and evening/weekend programs available. Postbaccalaureate distance learning degree programs offered (no on-campus study). *Entrance requirements:* For master's, GMAT, resume, 2 letters of recommendation. Additional exam requirements/recommendations for international students: Required—TOEFL (minimum score 550 paper-based; 213 computer-based; 80 iBT); Recommended—IELTS (minimum score 6.5). Electronic applications accepted. *Faculty research:* International trade law, process management, AIDS and the medical provider, mid-Hudson region economics, time quality management and organizational behavior.

Marlboro College, Graduate School, Program in Business Administration, Marlboro, VT 05344. Offers managing for sustainability (MBA). Part-time and evening/weekend programs available. Postbaccalaureate distance learning degree programs offered (minimal on-campus study). *Degree requirements:* For master's, 60 credits including capstone project. *Entrance requirements:* For master's, letter of intent, essay, transcripts, 2 letters of recommendation. Electronic applications accepted.

Marquette University, Graduate School of Management, Executive MBA Program, Milwaukee, WI 53201-1881. Offers economics (MBA); finance (MBA); human resources (MBA); international business (MBA); management information systems (MBA); marketing (MBA); operations and supply chain management (MBA); sports business (MBA). *Accreditation:* AACSB. *Students:* 50 full-time (15 women); includes 4 minority (1 Black or African American, non-Hispanic/Latino; 3 Asian, non-Hispanic/Latino), 3 international. Average age 37. 37 applicants, 81% accepted, 29 enrolled. In 2011, 36 master's awarded. *Degree requirements:* For master's, international trip. *Entrance requirements:* For master's, GMAT or GRE, two letters of recommendation, official transcripts from current and previous colleges/universities. Additional exam requirements/recommendations for international students: Required—TOEFL (minimum score 550 paper-based; 85 computer-based; 88 iBT), IELTS (minimum score 6.5), Pearson Test of English. *Application deadline:* For fall admission, 2/15 for domestic and international students. Application fee: $50. Electronic applications accepted. *Expenses:* Contact institution. *Financial support:* Application deadline: 2/15. *Faculty research:* International trade and finance, customer relationship management, consumer satisfaction, customer service . *Unit head:* Dr. Jeanne Simmons, Graduate Director, 414-288-7145, Fax: 414-288-1660, E-mail: jeanne.simmons@marquette.edu. *Application contact:* Debra Leutermann, Admissions Coordinator, 414-288-7145, Fax: 414-288-8078, E-mail: debra.leutermann@marquette.edu. Web site: http://www.busadm.mu.edu/emba/.

Marquette University, Graduate School of Management, Program in Business Administration, Milwaukee, WI 53201-1881. Offers business administration (MBA); economics (MBA); entrepreneurship (Certificate); finance (MBA); human resources (MBA); international business (MBA); management information systems (MBA); marketing (MBA); operations and supply chain management (MBA); sports business (MBA); JD/MBA; MBA/MA; MBA/MSN. *Accreditation:* AACSB. Part-time and evening/weekend programs available. *Students:* 42 full-time (14 women), 335 part-time (94 women); includes 24 minority (5 Black or African American, non-Hispanic/Latino; 1 American Indian or Alaska Native, non-Hispanic/Latino; 15 Asian, non-Hispanic/Latino; 3 Hispanic/Latino), 29 international. Average age 31. 182 applicants, 59% accepted, 103 enrolled. In 2011, 128 master's awarded. *Degree requirements:* For Certificate, business plan. *Entrance requirements:* For master's, GMAT or GRE, letters of recommendation. Additional exam requirements/recommendations for international students: Required—TOEFL (minimum score 550 paper-based; 85 computer-based; 88 iBT), IELTS (minimum score 6.5), Pearson Test of English. *Application deadline:* For fall admission, 2/15 for domestic and international students. Applications are processed on a rolling basis. Application fee: $50. Electronic applications accepted. *Expenses: Tuition:* Full-time $17,010; part-time $945 per credit hour. Tuition and fees vary according to program. *Financial support:* In 2011–12, 4 fellowships, 11 teaching assistantships were awarded; research assistantships, Federal Work-Study, institutionally sponsored loans, scholarships/grants, and tuition waivers (full and partial) also available. Support available to part-time students. Financial award application deadline: 2/15. *Faculty research:* Ethics in the professions, services marketing, technology impact on decision-making, mentoring. *Unit head:* Dr. Jeanne Simmons, Graduate Director, 414-288-7145, Fax: 414-288-1660, E-mail: jeanne.simmons@marquette.edu. *Application contact:* Debra Leutermann, Admissions Coordinator, 414-288-8064, Fax: 414-288-1902, E-mail: debra.leutermann@marquette.edu. Web site: http://business.marquette.edu/academics/mba.

Marshall University, Academic Affairs Division, College of Business, Program in Business Administration, Huntington, WV 25755. Offers EMBA, MBA. Part-time and evening/weekend programs available. *Students:* 74 full-time (22 women), 39 part-time (23 women); includes 12 minority (6 Black or African American, non-Hispanic/Latino; 1 Asian, non-Hispanic/Latino; 3 Hispanic/Latino; 1 Native Hawaiian or other Pacific Islander, non-Hispanic/Latino; 1 Two or more races, non-Hispanic/Latino), 22 international. Average age 30. In 2011, 147 master's awarded. *Degree requirements:* For master's, comprehensive assessment. *Entrance requirements:* For master's, GMAT. *Application deadline:* Applications are processed on a rolling basis. Application fee: $40. *Financial support:* Tuition waivers (full) available. Support available to part-time students. Financial award applicants required to submit FAFSA. *Unit head:* Dr. Andrew Sikula, 304-746-1956, E-mail: sikula@marshall.edu. *Application contact:* Wesley Spradlin, Information Contact, 304-746-8964, Fax: 304-746-1902, E-mail: spradlin2@marshall.edu.

Maryland Institute College of Art, Graduate Studies, The Business of Art and Design Program, Baltimore, MD 21217. Offers MPS. Part-time programs available. Postbaccalaureate distance learning degree programs offered (minimal on-campus study). *Faculty:* 15 part-time/adjunct (6 women). *Students:* 26 part-time (24 women); includes 5 minority (2 Black or African American, non-Hispanic/Latino; 1 Asian, non-Hispanic/Latino; 2 Hispanic/Latino). Average age 29. *Degree requirements:* For master's, business plan presentation. *Entrance requirements:* For master's, essay, good academic standing, resume. Additional exam requirements/recommendations for international students: Required—TOEFL (minimum score 550 paper-based; 213 computer-based; 80 iBT). *Application deadline:* For spring admission, 1/15 for domestic and international students. Application fee: $70. *Expenses:* Contact institution. *Financial support:* In 2011–12, 26 students received support, including 26 fellowships (averaging $3,400 per year); scholarships/grants also available. Financial award application deadline: 1/15; financial award applicants required to submit FAFSA. *Unit head:* Heather Bradbury, Manager, 410-225-2220, Fax: 410-225-2229, E-mail: hbradbury@mica.edu. *Application contact:* Scott G. Kelly, Associate Dean of Graduate Admission, 410-225-2256, Fax: 410-225-2408, E-mail: graduate@mica.edu. Web site: http://www.mica.edu/programs_of_study/the_business_of_art_and_design_(mps).html.

Maryland Institute College of Art, Graduate Studies, Program in Design Leadership, Baltimore, MD 21217. Offers MBA/MA. Program offered in collaboration with The Johns Hopkins University. *Entrance requirements:* Additional exam requirements/recommendations for international students: Required—TOEFL (minimum score 100 iBT) or IELTS (minimum score 7). *Application deadline:* For fall admission, 1/15 for domestic and international students. Application fee: $100. *Expenses:* Contact institution. *Unit head:* Guna Nadarajan, Vice Provost for Research/Dean, 410-225-5273, Fax: 410-225-5275, E-mail: graduate@mica.edu. *Application contact:* Scott G. Kelly, Associate Dean of Graduate Admission, 410-225-2256, Fax: 410-225-2408, E-mail: graduate@mica.edu. Web site: http://www.designleadershipmba.com/.

Marylhurst University, Department of Business Administration, Marylhurst, OR 97036-0261. Offers finance (MBA); general management (MBA); government policy and administration (MBA); green development (MBA); health care management (MBA); marketing (MBA); natural and organic resources (MBA); nonprofit management (MBA); organizational behavior (MBA); real estate (MBA); renewable energy (MBA); sustainable business (MBA). Part-time and evening/weekend programs available. Postbaccalaureate distance learning degree programs offered (no on-campus study). *Faculty:* 3 full-time (0 women), 36 part-time/adjunct (6 women). *Students:* 29 full-time (15 women), 675 part-time (373 women); includes 178 minority (59 Black or African American, non-Hispanic/Latino; 6 American Indian or Alaska Native, non-Hispanic/Latino; 34 Asian, non-Hispanic/Latino; 46 Hispanic/Latino; 4 Native Hawaiian or other Pacific Islander, non-Hispanic/Latino; 29 Two or more races, non-Hispanic/Latino), 14 international. Average age 37. 262 applicants, 91% accepted, 194 enrolled. In 2011, 352 master's awarded. *Degree requirements:* For master's, comprehensive exam, capstone course. *Entrance requirements:* For master's, GMAT (if GPA less than 3.0 and fewer than 5 years of work experience), interview, resume, 2 letters of recommendation. Additional exam requirements/recommendations for international students: Recommended—TOEFL (minimum score 550 paper-based; 213 computer-based; 80 iBT). *Application deadline:* For fall admission, 9/11 priority date for domestic students, 9/11 for international students; for winter admission, 12/15 priority date for domestic students, 12/15 for international students; for spring admission, 3/15 priority date for domestic students, 3/17 for international students. Applications are processed on a rolling basis. Application fee: $50. Electronic applications accepted. *Expenses: Tuition:* Full-time $14,796; part-time $548 per quarter hour. Tuition and fees vary according to program. *Financial support:* Scholarships/grants available. Support available to part-time students. Financial award applicants required to submit FAFSA. *Unit head:* David McNamee, Interim Chair, 503-636-8141, Fax: 503-697-5597, E-mail: mba@marylhurst.edu. *Application contact:* Maruska Lynch, Graduate Admissions Specialist, 800-634-9982 Ext. 6322, Fax: 503-699-6320, E-mail: admissions@marylhurst.edu. Web site: http://www.marylhurst.edu/.

Marymount University, Educational Partnerships Program, Arlington, VA 22207-4299. Offers business administration (MBA); health care management (MS); management studies (Certificate); organization development (Certificate). Part-time and evening/weekend programs available. *Faculty:* 1 full-time (0 women), 4 part-time/adjunct (2 women). *Students:* 1 (woman) full-time, 26 part-time (16 women); includes 11 minority (9 Black or African American, non-Hispanic/Latino; 2 Asian, non-Hispanic/Latino), 1 international. Average age 42. *Entrance requirements:* For master's, GRE General Test or GMAT, resume; for Certificate, resume. Additional exam requirements/recommendations for international students: Required—TOEFL (minimum score 600 paper-based; 250 computer-based; 96 iBT), IELTS (minimum score 6.5). *Application deadline:* For fall admission, 7/1 for international students; for spring admission, 11/15 for international students. Applications are processed on a rolling basis. Application fee: $40. Electronic applications accepted. *Expenses: Tuition:* Part-time $770 per credit hour. *Required fees:* $8 per credit hour. One-time fee: $180 full-time. *Financial support:* Career-related internships or fieldwork, Federal Work-Study, scholarships/grants, and unspecified assistantships available. Support available to part-time students. Financial award applicants required to submit FAFSA. *Unit head:* Dr. Sherri Hughes, Vice President for Academic Affairs and Provost, 703-284-1550, E-mail: sherri.hughes@marymount.edu. *Application contact:* Francesca Reed, Director, Graduate Admissions, 703-284-5901, Fax: 703-527-3815, E-mail: grad.admissions@marymount.edu.

Marymount University, School of Business Administration, Program in Business Administration, Arlington, VA 22207-4299. Offers MBA, Certificate. *Accreditation:* ACBSP. Part-time and evening/weekend programs available. *Faculty:* 11 full-time (8 women), 5 part-time/adjunct (1 woman). *Students:* 57 full-time (37 women), 95 part-time (50 women); includes 47 minority (24 Black or African American, non-Hispanic/Latino; 1 American Indian or Alaska Native, non-Hispanic/Latino; 11 Asian, non-Hispanic/Latino; 8 Hispanic/Latino; 3 Two or more races, non-Hispanic/Latino), 14 international. Average age 32. 80 applicants, 90% accepted, 53 enrolled. In 2011, 64 master's awarded. *Degree requirements:* For master's, thesis or alternative. *Entrance requirements:* For master's, GMAT or GRE General Test, resume; for Certificate, resume. Additional exam requirements/recommendations for international students: Required—TOEFL (minimum score 600 paper-based; 250 computer-based; 96 iBT), IELTS (minimum score 6.5). *Application deadline:* For fall admission, 7/1 priority date for domestic students, 7/1 for international students; for spring admission, 11/15 for domestic students, 11/16 for international students. Applications are processed on a rolling basis. Application fee: $40. Electronic applications accepted. *Expenses: Tuition:* Part-time $770 per credit hour. *Required fees:* $8 per credit hour. One-time fee: $180 full-time. *Financial support:* In 2011–12, 10 students received support. Research assistantships with full and partial tuition reimbursements available, career-related internships or fieldwork, Federal Work-Study, scholarships/grants, and unspecified assistantships available. Support available to part-time students. Financial award applicants required to submit FAFSA. *Unit head:* Dr. Terri Long, Director, 703-284-5918, E-mail: terri.long@marymount.edu. *Application contact:* Francesca Reed, Director, Graduate Admissions, 703-284-5901, Fax: 703-527-3815, E-mail: grad.admissions@marymount.edu. Web site: http://www.marymount.edu/academics/programs/businessAdminMBA.

Marymount University, School of Business Administration, Program in Management, Arlington, VA 22207-4299. Offers leadership (Certificate); management (MS); project management (Certificate). Part-time and evening/weekend programs available. *Faculty:* 8 full-time (6 women), 7 part-time/adjunct (3 women). *Students:* 2 full-time (0 women), 17 part-time (14 women); includes 6 minority (2 Black or African American, non-Hispanic/Latino; 1 Asian, non-Hispanic/Latino; 2 Hispanic/Latino; 1 Two or more races, non-Hispanic/Latino). Average age 42. 10 applicants, 40% accepted, 4 enrolled. In 2011, 11 master's, 1 other advanced degree awarded. *Degree requirements:* For master's, thesis or alternative. *Entrance requirements:* For master's, GMAT or GRE General Test, resume, at least 3 years of managerial experience, essay; for Certificate, resume, at least 3 years of managerial experience. Additional exam requirements/recommendations for international students: Required—TOEFL (minimum score 600 paper-based; 250 computer-based; 96 iBT), IELTS (minimum score 6.5). *Application deadline:* For fall admission, 7/1 priority date for domestic students, 7/1 for international students; for spring admission, 11/15 for domestic students, 11/16 for international students. Applications are processed on a rolling basis. Application fee: $40. Electronic applications accepted. *Expenses: Tuition:* Part-time $770 per credit hour. *Required fees:* $8 per credit hour. One-time fee: $180 full-time. *Financial support:* In 2011–12, 1 student received support. Research assistantships with full tuition reimbursements available, career-related internships or fieldwork, Federal Work-Study, scholarships/grants, and unspecified assistantships available. Support available to part-time students. Financial award applicants required to submit FAFSA. *Unit head:* Dr. Lorri Cooper, Director, Master's in Management Program, 703-284-5950, Fax: 703-527-3830, E-mail: lorri.cooper@marymount.edu. *Application contact:* Francesca Reed, Director, Graduate Admissions, 703-284-5901, Fax: 703-527-3815, E-mail: grad.admissions@marymount.edu.

Maryville University of Saint Louis, The John E. Simon School of Business, St. Louis, MO 63141-7299. Offers accounting (MBA, PGC); business studies (PGC); management (MBA, PGC); marketing (MBA, PGC); process and project management (MBA, PGC); sport and entertainment management (MBA, PGC). *Accreditation:* ACBSP. Part-time and evening/weekend programs available. *Faculty:* 8 full-time (3 women), 14 part-time/adjunct (5 women). *Students:* 19 full-time (10 women), 114 part-time (56 women); includes 13 minority (7 Black or African American, non-Hispanic/Latino; 3 Asian, non-Hispanic/Latino; 2 Hispanic/Latino; 1 Two or more races, non-Hispanic/Latino), 3 international. Average age 31. In 2011, 56 master's awarded. *Entrance requirements:* For master's, GMAT (unless applicant possesses undergraduate business degree with minimum cumulative GPA of 3.0, or has completed master's degree from accredited university or one early access course prior to undergraduate degree). Additional exam requirements/recommendations for international students: Required—TOEFL (minimum score 85 iBT). *Application deadline:* Applications are processed on a rolling basis. Application fee: $40 ($60 for international students). Electronic applications accepted. *Expenses: Tuition:* Full-time $21,922; part-time $675 per credit hour. *Required fees:* $233.75 per semester. *Financial support:* Career-related internships or fieldwork, Federal Work-Study, tuition waivers (partial), and campus employment available. Financial award application deadline: 3/1; financial award applicants required to submit FAFSA. *Faculty research:* International business, e-marketing, strategic planning, interpersonal management skills, financial analysis. *Unit head:* Dr. Pamela Horwitz, Dean, 314-529-9418, Fax: 314-529-9975, E-mail: horwitz@maryville.edu. *Application contact:* Kathy Dougherty, Director of MBA Programs, 314-529-9382, Fax: 314-529-9975, E-mail: business@maryville.edu. Web site: http://www.maryville.edu/academics-bu-mba.

Business Administration and Management—General

Marywood University, Academic Affairs, College of Liberal Arts and Sciences, Department of Business and Managerial Science, Scranton, PA 18509-1598. Offers finance and investments (MBA); financial information systems (MS); general management (MBA); management information systems (MBA, MS). *Accreditation:* ACBSP. *Entrance requirements:* Additional exam requirements/recommendations for international students: Required—TOEFL (minimum score 550 paper-based; 213 computer-based; 79 iBT). *Application deadline:* For fall admission, 4/1 priority date for domestic students, 3/31 for international students; for spring admission, 11/1 priority date for domestic students, 8/31 for international students. Applications are processed on a rolling basis. Application fee: $35. Electronic applications accepted. *Financial support:* Research assistantships, career-related internships or fieldwork, scholarships/grants, and unspecified assistantships available. Support available to part-time students. Financial award application deadline: 6/30; financial award applicants required to submit FAFSA. *Faculty research:* Problem formulation in ill-structured situations, corporate tax structures. *Unit head:* Dr. Arthur B. Comstock, Chair, 570-348-6211 Ext. 2449, E-mail: comstock@marywood.edu. *Application contact:* Tammy Manka, Assistant Director of Graduate Admissions, 570-348-6211 Ext. 2322, E-mail: tmanka@marywood.edu. Web site: http://www.marywood.edu/academics/gradcatalog/.

Massachusetts Institute of Technology, MIT Sloan School of Management, Cambridge, MA 02142. Offers M Fin, MBA, MS, SM, PhD. *Accreditation:* AACSB. *Degree requirements:* For master's, thesis (for some programs); for doctorate, thesis/dissertation, exams. *Entrance requirements:* For master's, GMAT, previous course work in calculus and economics; for doctorate, GMAT, GRE, previous course work in calculus and economics. Electronic applications accepted. *Expenses:* Contact institution. *Faculty research:* Financial engineering, entrepreneurship, e-business, work and employment, leaders for manufacturing .

McGill University, Faculty of Graduate and Postdoctoral Studies, Desautels Faculty of Management, Montréal, QC H3A 2T5, Canada. Offers administration (PhD); entrepreneurial studies (MBA); finance (MBA); general management (Post Master's Certificate); information systems (MBA); international business (MBA); international practicing management (MM); management (MBA); management for development (MBA); manufacturing management (MMM); marketing (MBA); operations management (MBA); public accountancy (Diploma); strategic management (MBA); MBA/LL B; MD/MBA. MMM offered jointly with Faculty of Engineering; PhD with Concordia University, HEC Montreal, Université de Montréal, Université du Québec à Montréal.

McKendree University, Graduate Programs, Master of Business Administration Program, Lebanon, IL 62254-1299. Offers business administration (MBA); human resource management (MBA); international business (MBA). Part-time and evening/weekend programs available. Postbaccalaureate distance learning degree programs offered (no on-campus study). *Entrance requirements:* For master's, official transcripts from all institutions attended, essay, minimum GPA of 3.0, three references, resume. Additional exam requirements/recommendations for international students: Required—TOEFL. Electronic applications accepted.

McMaster University, School of Graduate Studies, Faculty of Business, Hamilton, ON L8S 4M2, Canada. Offers MBA, PhD. *Accreditation:* AACSB. Part-time programs available. *Degree requirements:* For doctorate, comprehensive exam, thesis/dissertation. *Entrance requirements:* For master's, GMAT; for doctorate, GMAT or GRE, master's degree. Additional exam requirements/recommendations for international students: Required—TOEFL (minimum score 580 paper-based; 237 computer-based). *Faculty research:* Mergers, acquisitions, and restructuring; business investment; capital structure and dividend policy; employee pay/reward systems; pay and employment equity.

McNeese State University, Doré School of Graduate Studies, College of Business, Master of Business Administration Program, Lake Charles, LA 70609. Offers accounting (MBA); business administration (MBA). *Accreditation:* AACSB. Evening/weekend programs available. *Faculty:* 14 full-time (1 woman). *Students:* 45 full-time (25 women), 32 part-time (14 women); includes 8 minority (6 Black or African American, non-Hispanic/Latino; 1 American Indian or Alaska Native, non-Hispanic/Latino; 1 Hispanic/Latino), 31 international. In 2011, 34 master's awarded. *Degree requirements:* For master's, written exam. *Entrance requirements:* For master's, GMAT. *Application deadline:* For fall admission, 5/15 priority date for domestic students, 5/15 for international students; for spring admission, 10/15 priority date for domestic students, 10/15 for international students. Applications are processed on a rolling basis. Application fee: $20 ($30 for international students). *Expenses:* Tuition, state resident: part-time $519 per credit hour. Tuition and fees vary according to course load. *Financial support:* Research assistantships, teaching assistantships, and Federal Work-Study available. Support available to part-time students. Financial award application deadline: 5/1. *Faculty research:* Management development, integrating technology into the work force, union/management relations, economic development. *Unit head:* Dr. Akm Rahman, MBA Director, 337-475-5576, Fax: 337-475-5986, E-mail: mrahman@mcneese.edu. *Application contact:* Dr. Akm Rahman, MBA Director, 337-475-5576, Fax: 337-475-5986, E-mail: mrahman@mcneese.edu.

Medaille College, Program in Business Administration - Amherst, Amherst, NY 14221. Offers business administration (MBA); organizational leadership (MA). Evening/weekend programs available. *Students:* 187 full-time (106 women), 10 part-time (3 women); includes 104 minority (24 Black or African American, non-Hispanic/Latino; 21 Asian, non-Hispanic/Latino; 6 Hispanic/Latino; 53 Native Hawaiian or other Pacific Islander, non-Hispanic/Latino). Average age 34. 65 applicants, 88% accepted, 33 enrolled. In 2011, 94 master's awarded. *Degree requirements:* For master's, thesis or alternative. *Entrance requirements:* For master's, GMAT, minimum undergraduate GPA of 2.7, 3 years of work experience. Additional exam requirements/recommendations for international students: Required—TOEFL (minimum score 550 paper-based; 213 computer-based). *Application deadline:* Applications are processed on a rolling basis. Application fee: $35. Electronic applications accepted. *Expenses:* Contact institution. *Financial support:* Federal Work-Study available. Financial award applicants required to submit FAFSA. *Unit head:* Jennifer Bavifard, Associate Dean for Special Programs, 716-631-1061 Ext. 150, Fax: 716-631-1380, E-mail: jbavifar@medaille.edu. *Application contact:* Jacqueline Matheny, Executive Director of Marketing and Enrollment, 716-932-2541, Fax: 716-632-1811, E-mail: jmatheny@medaille.edu. Web site: http://www.medaille.edu/.

Medaille College, Program in Business Administration - Rochester, Rochester, NY 14623. Offers business administration (MBA); organizational leadership (MA). Evening/weekend programs available. *Students:* 17 full-time (11 women), 2 part-time (both women); includes 11 minority (5 Black or African American, non-Hispanic/Latino; 3 Asian, non-Hispanic/Latino; 1 Hispanic/Latino; 2 Native Hawaiian or other Pacific Islander, non-Hispanic/Latino). Average age 36. 31 applicants, 90% accepted, 19 enrolled. In 2011, 8 master's awarded. *Degree requirements:* For master's, thesis or alternative. *Entrance requirements:* For master's, GMAT, 3 years of work experience, minimum undergraduate GPA of 2.7. Additional exam requirements/recommendations for international students: Required—TOEFL (minimum score 550 paper-based; 213 computer-based). *Application deadline:* Applications are processed on a rolling basis. Application fee: $35. *Expenses:* Contact institution. *Financial support:* Federal Work-Study available. Financial award applicants required to submit FAFSA. *Unit head:* Jennifer Bavifard, Branch Campus Director, 716-932-2591, Fax: 716-631-1380, E-mail: jbavifard@medaille.edu. *Application contact:* Jane Rowlands, Marketing Support, 585-272-0030, Fax: 585-272-0057, E-mail: jrowlands@medaille.edu. Web site: http://www.medaille.edu/.

Melbourne Business School, Graduate Programs, Carlton, Australia. Offers business administration (Exec MBA, MBA); management (PhD); management science (PhD); marketing (PhD); social impact (Graduate Certificate); JD/MBA.

Memorial University of Newfoundland, School of Graduate Studies, Faculty of Business Administration, St. John's, NL A1C 5S7, Canada. Offers EMBA, MBA. *Accreditation:* AACSB. Part-time programs available. *Degree requirements:* For master's, thesis (for some programs). *Entrance requirements:* For master's, GMAT. Additional exam requirements/recommendations for international students: Required—TOEFL (minimum score 580 paper-based; 237 computer-based), TWE (minimum score 4). Electronic applications accepted. *Faculty research:* International business, marketing, organizational theory and behavior, management science and information systems, small business.

Mercer University, Graduate Studies, Cecil B. Day Campus, Eugene W. Stetson School of Business and Economics (Atlanta), Macon, GA 31207-0003. Offers international business (MBA); MBA/MAC; Pharm D/MBA. *Accreditation:* AACSB. Part-time and evening/weekend programs available. *Faculty:* 19 full-time (8 women), 2 part-time/adjunct (0 women). *Students:* 185 full-time (87 women), 100 part-time (51 women); includes 87 minority (67 Black or African American, non-Hispanic/Latino; 16 Asian, non-Hispanic/Latino; 4 Hispanic/Latino), 19 international. Average age 32. 169 applicants, 54% accepted, 64 enrolled. In 2011, 107 master's awarded. *Entrance requirements:* For master's, GMAT. Additional exam requirements/recommendations for international students: Required—TOEFL (minimum score 550 paper-based; 213 computer-based; 80 iBT). *Application deadline:* For fall admission, 7/1 priority date for domestic students, 7/1 for international students; for spring admission, 11/1 priority date for domestic students, 11/1 for international students. Applications are processed on a rolling basis. Application fee: $50 ($100 for international students). Electronic applications accepted. *Financial support:* Federal Work-Study available. Financial award application deadline: 5/1; financial award applicants required to submit FAFSA. *Faculty research:* Entrepreneurship, market studies, international business strategy, financial analysis. *Unit head:* Dr. Gina L. Miller, Associate Dean, 678-547-6177, Fax: 678-547-6337, E-mail: miller_gl@mercer.edu. *Application contact:* Jamie Thomas, Graduate Enrollment Associate, 678-547-6177, Fax: 678-547-6337, E-mail: atlbusadm@mercer.edu. Web site: http://www2.mercer.edu/business.

Mercer University, Graduate Studies, Macon Campus, Eugene W. Stetson School of Business and Economics (Macon), Macon, GA 31207-0003. Offers MBA. *Accreditation:* AACSB. Part-time and evening/weekend programs available. *Faculty:* 7 full-time (2 women), 1 part-time/adjunct (0 women). *Students:* 38 full-time (7 women), 28 part-time (10 women); includes 6 minority (3 Black or African American, non-Hispanic/Latino; 2 Asian, non-Hispanic/Latino; 1 Hispanic/Latino). Average age 29. 15 applicants, 93% accepted, 14 enrolled. In 2011, 29 master's awarded. *Entrance requirements:* For master's, GMAT/GRE. Additional exam requirements/recommendations for international students: Required—TOEFL (minimum score 550 paper-based; 213 computer-based). *Application deadline:* For fall admission, 8/1 for domestic students; for spring admission, 12/1 for domestic students. Applications are processed on a rolling basis. Application fee: $50 ($100 for international students). *Faculty research:* Federal Reserve System, management of nurses, sales promotion, systems for common stock selection, interest rate premiums. *Unit head:* Dr. David Scott Davis, Dean, 478-301-2990, Fax: 478-301-2635, E-mail: davis_ds@mercer.edu. *Application contact:* Robert Holland, Jr., Director/Academic Administrator, 478-301-2835, Fax: 478-301-2635, E-mail: holland_r@mercer.edu. Web site: http://www.mercer.edu/business.

Mercy College, School of Business, Program in Business Administration, Dobbs Ferry, NY 10522-1189. Offers MBA. Part-time and evening/weekend programs available. Postbaccalaureate distance learning degree programs offered (no on-campus study). *Entrance requirements:* For master's, GMAT, interview, two letters of recommendation, undergraduate transcripts. Additional exam requirements/recommendations for international students: Required—TOEFL (minimum score 600 paper-based; 250 computer-based; 100 iBT), IELTS (minimum score 8). Electronic applications accepted. *Faculty research:* Marketing systems, international business, diverse management challenges, decision making.

Meredith College, John E. Weems Graduate School, School of Business, Raleigh, NC 27607-5298. Offers business administration (MBA). *Accreditation:* AACSB. Part-time and evening/weekend programs available. *Faculty:* 10 full-time (7 women). *Students:* 4 full-time (0 women), 88 part-time (67 women); includes 25 minority (20 Black or African American, non-Hispanic/Latino; 3 Asian, non-Hispanic/Latino; 2 Hispanic/Latino). Average age 34. 47 applicants, 87% accepted, 32 enrolled. In 2011, 27 master's awarded. *Degree requirements:* For master's, thesis optional. *Entrance requirements:* For master's, GMAT, interview, minimum GPA of 2.5, letters of recommendation. Additional exam requirements/recommendations for international students: Required—TOEFL. *Application deadline:* For fall admission, 7/1 priority date for domestic students, 7/1 for international students; for spring admission, 11/1 priority date for domestic students, 11/1 for international students. Applications are processed on a rolling basis. Application fee: $50. Electronic applications accepted. *Expenses: Tuition:* Full-time $8388; part-time $466 per credit hour. *Required fees:* $120; $60 per semester. Tuition and fees vary according to program. *Financial support:* Career-related internships or fieldwork, institutionally sponsored loans, scholarships/grants, and tuition waivers (partial) available. Support available to part-time students. Financial award application deadline: 2/15; financial award applicants required to submit FAFSA. *Unit head:* Dr. Denise Rotundo, Dean, 919-760-8471, Fax: 919-760-8470. *Application contact:* Page Midyette, Coordinator, 919-760-2281, Fax: 919-760-2898, E-mail: midyette@meredith.edu.

Merrimack College, Girard School of Business and International Commerce, North Andover, MA 01845-5800. Offers management (MS). Part-time and evening/weekend programs available. *Degree requirements:* For master's, variable foreign language requirement, comprehensive exam (for some programs), thesis optional. *Entrance requirements:* Additional exam requirements/recommendations for international students: Recommended—TOEFL, IELTS. *Application deadline:* For fall admission, 8/1 priority date for domestic students, 7/15 for international students; for winter admission, 12/1 priority date for domestic students, 11/15 for international students; for spring admission, 3/1 priority date for domestic students, 2/15 for international students. *Expenses: Tuition:* Part-time $475 per credit. *Required fees:* $62.50 per semester. *Financial support:* Application deadline: 5/1; applicants required to submit FAFSA. *Unit head:* Dr. Mark Cordano, Dean, 978-837-5058, E-mail: cordanom@merrimack.edu. *Application contact:* 978-837-5073, E-mail: graduate@merrimack.edu. Web site: http://www.merrimack.edu/academics/business/graduate/msm/.

Methodist University, School of Graduate Studies, Program in Business Administration, Fayetteville, NC 28311-1498. Offers MBA. *Accreditation:* ACBSP. Part-time and evening/weekend programs available. *Entrance requirements:* For master's, GMAT or MAT. Additional exam requirements/recommendations for international students: Required—TOEFL (minimum score 500 paper-based; 173 computer-based; 60 iBT).

Metropolitan College of New York, Program in General Management, New York, NY 10013. Offers MBA. Evening/weekend programs available. *Degree requirements:* For master's, thesis, 10 day study abroad. *Entrance requirements:* For master's, GMAT. Additional exam requirements/recommendations for international students: Required—TOEFL (minimum score 600 paper-based; 220 computer-based). Electronic applications accepted. *Expenses:* Contact institution.

Metropolitan State University, College of Management, St. Paul, MN 55106-5000. Offers business administration (MBA, DBA); database administration (Graduate Certificate); healthcare information technology management (Graduate Certificate); information assurance security (Graduate Certificate); management information systems (MMIS); MIS generalist (Graduate Certificate); MIS systems analysis and design (Graduate Certificate); project management (Graduate Certificate); public and nonprofit administration (MPNA). Part-time and evening/weekend programs available. *Students:* 63 full-time (41 women), 409 part-time (192 women); includes 94 minority (38 Black or African American, non-Hispanic/Latino; 33 Asian, non-Hispanic/Latino; 14 Hispanic/Latino; 9 Two or more races, non-Hispanic/Latino), 61 international. Average age 35. *Degree requirements:* For master's, thesis optional, computer language (MMIS). *Entrance requirements:* For master's, GMAT (MBA), resume. Additional exam requirements/recommendations for international students: Required—TOEFL (minimum score 550 paper-based; 213 computer-based). *Application deadline:* For fall admission, 7/15 for international students; for winter admission, 11/15 for international students; for spring admission, 3/15 for international students. Applications are processed on a rolling basis. Application fee: $20. Electronic applications accepted. *Expenses:* Tuition, state resident: full-time $5799.06; part-time $322.17 per credit. Tuition, nonresident: full-time $11,411; part-time $633.92 per credit. Tuition and fees vary according to degree level, program and reciprocity agreements. *Financial support:* Research assistantships with partial tuition reimbursements, career-related internships or fieldwork, and Federal Work-Study available. Support available to part-time students. Financial award applicants required to submit FAFSA. *Faculty research:* Yugoslav economic system, workers' cooperatives, participative management and job enrichment, global business systems. *Unit head:* Dr. Paul Huo, Dean, 612-659-7271, Fax: 612-659-7268, E-mail: paul.huo@metrostate.edu. Web site: http://choose.metrostate.edu/comgradprograms.

Miami University, Farmer School of Business, Oxford, OH 45056. Offers accountancy (M Acc); business administration (MBA); economics (MA). *Accreditation:* AACSB. *Entrance requirements:* For master's, GMAT, minimum undergraduate GPA of 3.0 during previous 2 years or 2.75 overall. Additional exam requirements/recommendations for international students: Required—TOEFL. *Expenses:* Tuition, state resident: full-time $12,023; part-time $501 per credit hour. Tuition, nonresident: full-time $26,554; part-time $1107 per credit hour. *Required fees:* $528. *Unit head:* Dr. Roger Jenkins, Dean, 513-529-3631, Fax: 513-529-6992, E-mail: deanofbusiness@muohio.edu. *Application contact:* MBA Program Office, 513-529-6643, E-mail: miamimba@muohio.edu. Web site: http://mba.muohio.edu.

Michigan State University, The Graduate School, Eli Broad Graduate School of Management, Department of Management, East Lansing, MI 48824. Offers business administration (PhD). *Entrance requirements:* Additional exam requirements/recommendations for international students: Required—TOEFL (minimum score 550 paper-based; 213 computer-based). Electronic applications accepted.

Michigan State University, The Graduate School, Eli Broad Graduate School of Management, Department of Supply Chain Management, East Lansing, MI 48824. Offers business administration (PhD); supply chain management (MS). Part-time programs available. *Degree requirements:* For master's, field study, research project; for doctorate, comprehensive exam, thesis/dissertation, oral defense of dissertation proposal and dissertation. *Entrance requirements:* For master's, GMAT, bachelor's degree in related field, letters of recommendation, 2-3 years of work experience, minimum GPA of 3.0 in last 2 years of undergraduate course work; for doctorate, GMAT or GRE, letters of recommendation. Additional exam requirements/recommendations for international students: Required—TOEFL. Electronic applications accepted. *Expenses:* Contact institution.

Michigan State University, The Graduate School, Eli Broad Graduate School of Management, Program in Business Administration, East Lansing, MI 48824. Offers business administration (MBA, PhD); business research (MBA); corporate business administration (MBA); integrative management (MBA). Evening/weekend programs available. *Degree requirements:* For master's, enrichment experience. *Entrance requirements:* For master's, GMAT. Additional exam requirements/recommendations for international students: Required—TOEFL. Electronic applications accepted. *Expenses:* Contact institution.

Michigan Technological University, Graduate School, School of Business and Economics, Houghton, MI 49931. Offers applied natural resource economics (MS); business administration (MBA). *Accreditation:* AACSB. Part-time programs available. *Faculty:* 29 full-time (9 women), 2 part-time/adjunct (0 women). *Students:* 23 full-time (11 women), 37 part-time (15 women); includes 7 minority (1 Black or African American, non-Hispanic/Latino; 4 Asian, non-Hispanic/Latino; 1 Hispanic/Latino; 1 Two or more races, non-Hispanic/Latino), 15 international. Average age 30. 96 applicants, 46% accepted, 26 enrolled. In 2011, 26 master's awarded. *Degree requirements:* For master's, comprehensive exam (for some programs), thesis (for some programs). *Entrance requirements:* For master's, GMAT (recommended minimum score in the 50th percentile), statement of purpose, official transcripts, 2 letters of recommendation, resume/curriculum vitae, prerequisites in statistics and economics. Additional exam requirements/recommendations for international students: Required—TOEFL (minimum score 95 iBT) or IELTS. *Application deadline:* Applications are processed on a rolling basis. Electronic applications accepted. *Expenses:* Tuition, state resident: full-time $12,636; part-time $702 per credit. Tuition, nonresident: full-time $12,636; part-time $702 per credit. *Required fees:* $226; $226 per year. *Financial support:* In 2011–12, 45 students received support, including 2 fellowships with full tuition reimbursements available (averaging $6,065 per year), research assistantships with full tuition reimbursements available (averaging $6,065 per year), 3 teaching assistantships with full tuition reimbursements available (averaging $6,065 per year); career-related internships or fieldwork, Federal Work-Study, scholarships/grants, health care benefits, tuition waivers (full and partial), unspecified assistantships, and cooperative program also available. Financial award applicants required to submit FAFSA. *Total annual research expenditures:* $59,476. *Unit head:* Dr. Gene Klippel, Dean, School of Business and Economics, 906-487-2668, Fax: 906-487-1863. *Application contact:* Carol T. Wingerson, Senior Staff Assistant, 906-487-2327, Fax: 906-487-2463, E-mail: gradadms@mtu.edu. Web site: http://www.mtu.edu/business/.

Mid-America Christian University, Program in Business Administration, Oklahoma City, OK 73170-4504. Offers MBA. *Entrance requirements:* For master's, bachelor's degree from regionally-accredited college or university, minimum overall cumulative GPA of 2.75 on undergraduate course work. Additional exam requirements/recommendations for international students: Required—TOEFL (minimum score 550 paper-based; 213 computer-based).

MidAmerica Nazarene University, Graduate Studies in Management, Olathe, KS 66062-1899. Offers management (MBA); organizational administration (MA), including finance, international business, leadership, non-profit. Evening/weekend programs available. *Entrance requirements:* For master's, mathematical assessment, minimum undergraduate GPA of 3.0, letters of recommendation. Additional exam requirements/recommendations for international students: Required—TOEFL. Electronic applications accepted. *Faculty research:* Economic development, international finance, business development, employee evaluation.

Middle Tennessee State University, College of Graduate Studies, Jennings A. Jones College of Business, Department of Management and Marketing, Murfreesboro, TN 37132. Offers MBA. *Accreditation:* AACSB. Part-time and evening/weekend programs available. Postbaccalaureate distance learning degree programs offered. *Faculty:* 31 full-time (11 women), 2 part-time/adjunct (both women). *Students:* 51 full-time (20 women), 342 part-time (122 women); includes 118 minority (51 Black or African American, non-Hispanic/Latino; 2 American Indian or Alaska Native, non-Hispanic/Latino; 49 Asian, non-Hispanic/Latino; 7 Hispanic/Latino; 1 Native Hawaiian or other Pacific Islander, non-Hispanic/Latino; 8 Two or more races, non-Hispanic/Latino). Average age 30. 447 applicants, 49% accepted. In 2011, 132 master's awarded. *Degree requirements:* For master's, comprehensive exam. *Entrance requirements:* Additional exam requirements/recommendations for international students: Required—TOEFL (minimum score 525 paper-based; 195 computer-based; 71 iBT) or IELTS (minimum score 6). *Application deadline:* For fall admission, 6/1 for domestic and international students. Applications are processed on a rolling basis. Application fee: $25 ($30 for international students). Electronic applications accepted. *Expenses:* Tuition, state resident: full-time $10,008. Tuition, nonresident: full-time $25,056. *Financial support:* In 2011–12, 8 students received support. Tuition waivers available. Support available to part-time students. Financial award application deadline: 5/1; financial award applicants required to submit FAFSA. *Unit head:* Dr. Jill Austin, Chair, 615-898-2736, Fax: 615-898-5308, E-mail: jill.austin@mtsu.edu. *Application contact:* Dr. Michael D. Allen, Dean and Vice Provost for Research, 615-898-2840, Fax: 615-904-8020, E-mail: michael.allen@mtsu.edu.

Midway College, Leadership MBA Program, Midway, KY 40347-1120. Offers MBA. *Degree requirements:* For master's, capstone course. *Entrance requirements:* For master's, GMAT, bachelor's degree, minimum GPA of 3.0, 3 years of professional work experience, interview. Additional exam requirements/recommendations for international students: Required—TOEFL (minimum score 550 paper-based; 213 computer-based; 80 iBT).

Midwestern State University, Graduate Studies, College of Business Administration, Wichita Falls, TX 76308. Offers MBA. *Accreditation:* AACSB; ACBSP. Part-time and evening/weekend programs available. *Degree requirements:* For master's, comprehensive exam, thesis optional. *Entrance requirements:* For master's, GMAT. Additional exam requirements/recommendations for international students: Required—TOEFL (minimum score 550 paper-based; 213 computer-based). Electronic applications accepted. *Faculty research:* Citizenship behavior, software solutions, mediations, sales force training, stock trading volume.

Milligan College, Program in Business Administration, Milligan College, TN 37682. Offers MBA. Postbaccalaureate distance learning degree programs offered (minimal on-campus study). *Degree requirements:* For master's, comprehensive exam (for some programs), thesis or alternative. *Entrance requirements:* For master's, GMAT if undergraduate GPA less than 3.0, 2 professional recommendations, 3 years related work experience. Additional exam requirements/recommendations for international students: Required—TOEFL. Electronic applications accepted.

Millikin University, Tabor School of Business, Decatur, IL 62522-2084. Offers MBA. *Accreditation:* ACBSP. Evening/weekend programs available. *Faculty:* 5 full-time (1 woman), 8 part-time/adjunct (1 woman). *Students:* 43 full-time (13 women); includes 1 minority (Black or African American, non-Hispanic/Latino), 5 international. Average age 36. 45 applicants, 96% accepted, 43 enrolled. In 2011, 13 master's awarded. *Entrance requirements:* For master's, GMAT, resume, 3 reference letters, interview. Additional exam requirements/recommendations for international students: Required—TOEFL (minimum score 550 paper-based; 79 iBT). *Application deadline:* For spring admission, 11/1 priority date for domestic students, 8/1 for international students. Applications are processed on a rolling basis. Application fee: $0. Electronic applications accepted. *Expenses: Tuition:* Full-time $24,890; part-time $681 per credit hour. Tuition and fees vary according to program. *Financial support:* Applicants required to submit FAFSA. *Faculty research:* E-commerce, international marketing, pedagogy, total quality management, auditing. *Unit head:* Dr. James G. Dahl, Dean, 217-420-6634, Fax: 217-424-6286, E-mail: jdahl@millikin.edu. *Application contact:* Dr. Anthony Liberatore, Director of MBA Program, 217-424-6338, E-mail: aliberatore@millikin.edu. Web site: http://www.millikin.edu/ACADEMICS/TABOR/MBA/.

Millsaps College, Else School of Management, Jackson, MS 39210-0001. Offers accounting (M Acc); business administration (MBA). *Accreditation:* AACSB. Part-time programs available. *Entrance requirements:* For master's, GMAT. Additional exam requirements/recommendations for international students: Required—TOEFL. Electronic applications accepted. *Faculty research:* Ethics, audit independence, satisfaction with assurance services, political business cycles.

Mills College, Graduate Studies, Lorry I. Lokey Graduate School of Business, Oakland, CA 94613-1000. Offers management (MBA). Part-time programs available. *Faculty:* 5 full-time (3 women), 12 part-time/adjunct (7 women). *Students:* 88 full-time (82 women), 3 part-time (all women); includes 48 minority (17 Black or African American, non-Hispanic/Latino; 11 Asian, non-Hispanic/Latino; 16 Hispanic/Latino; 4 Two or more races, non-Hispanic/Latino), 4 international. Average age 31. 76 applicants, 80% accepted, 38 enrolled. In 2011, 54 master's awarded. *Entrance requirements:* For master's, 3 letters of recommendation, 2 transcripts. Additional exam requirements/recommendations for international students: Required—TOEFL (minimum score 550 paper-based; 80 iBT) or IELTS (minimum score 6). *Application deadline:* For fall admission, 2/1 priority date for domestic students, 12/15 for international students; for spring admission, 10/1 for domestic students. Applications are processed on a rolling basis. Application fee: $50. *Expenses: Tuition:* Full-time $28,280; part-time $15,640 per year. *Required fees:* $958. Tuition and fees vary according to program. *Financial support:* In 2011–12, 96 fellowships with full and partial tuition reimbursements (averaging $5,481 per year) were awarded; scholarships/grants also available. Support available to part-time students. Financial award application deadline: 2/1; financial award applicants required to submit FAFSA. *Faculty research:* Diversity and inclusion, applied econometrics, non-profit management, business communication and effective public speaking, social media and Internet marketing. *Unit head:* Dr. Deborah Merrill-Sands, Dean, 510-430-3305, Fax: 510-430-2159, E-mail: grad-studies@mills.edu. *Application contact:* Tiana Kozoil, Graduate Admission Specialist, 510-430-3305, Fax: 510-430-2159, E-mail: grad-studies@mills.edu. Web site: http://www.mills.edu/mba.

Milwaukee School of Engineering, Rader School of Business, Milwaukee, WI 53202-3109. Offers engineering management (MS); marketing and export management (MS); medical informatics (MS); new product management (MS). Part-time and evening/weekend programs available. *Faculty:* 6 full-time (2 women), 13 part-time/adjunct (3 women). *Students:* 7 full-time (2 women), 100 part-time (25 women); includes 12 minority (2 Black or African American, non-Hispanic/Latino; 6 Asian, non-Hispanic/Latino; 3 Hispanic/Latino; 1 Two or more races, non-Hispanic/Latino), 5 international. Average age 26. 51 applicants, 57% accepted, 19 enrolled. In 2011, 46 master's awarded. *Degree requirements:* For master's, thesis, thesis defense or capstone project. *Entrance requirements:* For master's, GMAT, GRE General Test, BS in engineering, science, business or related fields; 2 letters of recommendation. Additional exam requirements/recommendations for international students: Required—TOEFL (minimum score 79 iBT) or IELTS. *Application deadline:* Applications are processed on a rolling basis. Electronic applications accepted. Application fee is waived when completed online. *Expenses: Tuition:* Full-time $17,550; part-time $650 per credit hour. *Financial support:* In 2011–12, 26 students received support, including 2 research assistantships (averaging $15,000 per year); career-related internships or fieldwork also available. Support available to part-time students. Financial award applicants required to submit FAFSA. *Faculty research:* Operations, project management, quality marketing, information technology, business, databases. *Unit head:* Dr. Steven Bialek, Chairman, 414-277-7364, Fax: 414-277-7479, E-mail: bialek@msoe.edu. *Application contact:* Katie Gassenhuber, Graduate Program Associate, 800-321-6763, Fax: 414-277-7208, E-mail: gassenhuber@msoe.edu.

Minnesota State University Mankato, College of Graduate Studies, College of Business, Mankato, MN 56001. Offers MBA. *Accreditation:* AACSB. *Students:* 9 full-time (3 women), 76 part-time (22 women). *Entrance requirements:* For master's, GMAT, 2 letters of reference, resume. Additional exam requirements/recommendations for international students: Required—TOEFL. *Application deadline:* For fall admission, 7/1 for domestic students, 5/1 for international students; for spring admission, 11/1 for domestic students, 10/1 for international students. Electronic applications accepted. *Unit head:* Dr. Kevin Elliott, Graduate Coordinator, 507-389-5420. *Application contact:* 507-389-2321, E-mail: grad@mnsu.edu. Web site: http://cob.mnsu.edu/.

Minot State University, Graduate School, Program in Management, Minot, ND 58707-0002. Offers MS. *Degree requirements:* For master's, comprehensive exam (for some programs), thesis (for some programs). *Entrance requirements:* For master's, minimum GPA of 2.75. Additional exam requirements/recommendations for international students: Required—TOEFL. *Faculty research:* Distance education.

Misericordia University, College of Professional Studies and Social Sciences, Master of Business Administration Program, Dallas, PA 18612-1098. Offers MBA. Part-time and evening/weekend programs available. Postbaccalaureate distance learning degree programs offered. *Faculty:* 2 full-time (1 woman), 5 part-time/adjunct (0 women). *Students:* 75 part-time (43 women); includes 1 minority (Hispanic/Latino). Average age 32. 72 applicants, 79% accepted, 37 enrolled. In 2011, 33 master's awarded. *Entrance requirements:* For master's, GMAT, MAT, GRE (50th percentile or higher), or minimum undergraduate GPA of 2.79, interview. *Application deadline:* Applications are processed on a rolling basis. *Expenses: Tuition:* Full-time $25,700; part-time $575 per credit. *Financial support:* In 2011–12, 52 students received support. Scholarships/grants and tuition waivers available. Support available to part-time students. Financial award applicants required to submit FAFSA. *Unit head:* Dr. Fred Croop, Dean, College of Professional Studies and Social Sciences, 570-674-6327, E-mail: fcroop@misericordia.edu. *Application contact:* Larree Brown, Assistant Director of Admissions, Part-Time Undergraduate and Graduate Programs, 570-674-6451, Fax: 570-674-6232, E-mail: lbrown@misericordia.edu. Web site: http://www.misericordia.edu/mba.

Mississippi College, Graduate School, School of Business, Clinton, MS 39058. Offers accounting (Certificate); business administration (MBA), including accounting; business education (M Ed); finance (MBA, Certificate); JD/MBA. *Accreditation:* ACBSP. Part-time and evening/weekend programs available. *Degree requirements:* For master's, comprehensive exam, thesis optional. *Entrance requirements:* For master's, GMAT, minimum GPA of 2.5, 24 hours of undergraduate course work in business. Additional exam requirements/recommendations for international students: Recommended—TOEFL, IELTS. Electronic applications accepted.

Mississippi State University, College of Business, Department of Management and Information Systems, Mississippi State, MS 39762. Offers business administration (PhD), including management; information systems (MSIS). Part-time programs available. *Faculty:* 13 full-time (4 women), 1 (woman) part-time/adjunct. *Students:* 22 full-time (8 women), 9 part-time (2 women); includes 8 minority (1 Black or African American, non-Hispanic/Latino; 5 Asian, non-Hispanic/Latino; 1 Hispanic/Latino; 1 Two or more races, non-Hispanic/Latino), 5 international. Average age 31. 72 applicants, 28% accepted, 16 enrolled. In 2011, 7 master's, 1 doctorate awarded. *Degree requirements:* For master's, comprehensive exam; for doctorate, comprehensive exam, thesis/dissertation. *Entrance requirements:* For master's, GMAT, minimum GPA of 3.0 in last 60 hours of course work; for doctorate, GMAT, minimum graduate GPA of 3.25 in last 60 hours. Additional exam requirements/recommendations for international students: Required—TOEFL (minimum score 575 paper-based; 233 computer-based; 90 iBT); Recommended—IELTS (minimum score 7). *Application deadline:* For fall admission, 7/1 for domestic students, 5/1 for international students; for spring admission, 11/1 for domestic students, 9/1 for international students. Applications are processed on a rolling basis. Application fee: $40. Electronic applications accepted. *Expenses:* Tuition, state resident: full-time $5805; part-time $322.50 per credit hour. Tuition, nonresident: full-time $14,670; part-time $815 per credit hour. *Financial support:* In 2011–12, 6 teaching assistantships (averaging $12,270 per year) were awarded; Federal Work-Study and institutionally sponsored loans also available. Financial award applicants required to submit FAFSA. *Faculty research:* Electronic commerce, management of information technology. *Unit head:* Dr. Rodney Pearson, Department Head and Professor of Information Systems, 662-325-3928, Fax: 662-325-8651, E-mail: rodney.pearson@msstate.edu. *Application contact:* Dr. Barbara Spencer, Associate Dean for Research and Outreach, 662-325-1891, Fax: 662-325-8161, E-mail: bspencer@cobian.msstate.edu. Web site: http://misweb.cbi.msstate.edu/~COBI/faculty/departments/mainpage.shtml?MIS.

Mississippi State University, College of Business, Department of Marketing, Quantitative Analysis and Business Law, Mississippi State, MS 39762. Offers business administration (MBA), including marketing. Part-time and evening/weekend programs available. *Faculty:* 10 full-time (3 women). *Students:* 7 full-time (3 women); includes 1 minority (Black or African American, non-Hispanic/Latino). Average age 33. 12 applicants, 33% accepted, 4 enrolled. In 2011, 1 degree awarded. *Degree requirements:* For doctorate, comprehensive exam, thesis/dissertation. *Entrance requirements:* For doctorate, GMAT, minimum GPA of 2.75 in last 60 undergraduate hours. Additional exam requirements/recommendations for international students: Required—TOEFL (minimum score 575 paper-based; 233 computer-based; 90 iBT); Recommended—IELTS (minimum score 6.5). *Application deadline:* For fall admission, 7/1 for domestic students, 5/1 for international students; for spring admission, 11/1 for domestic students, 9/1 for international students. Applications are processed on a rolling basis. Application fee: $40. Electronic applications accepted. *Expenses:* Tuition, state resident: full-time $5805; part-time $322.50 per credit hour. Tuition, nonresident: full-time $14,670; part-time $815 per credit hour. *Financial support:* In 2011–12, 3 teaching assistantships (averaging $12,270 per year) were awarded; Federal Work-Study, institutionally sponsored loans, and scholarships/grants also available. Financial award application deadline: 4/1; financial award applicants required to submit FAFSA. *Unit head:* Dr. Jason Lueg, Associate Professor and Department Head, 662-325-3163, Fax: 662-325-7012, E-mail: jlueg@cobilan.msstate.edu. *Application contact:* Dr. Barbara Spencer, Associate Dean for Research and Outreach, 662-325-1891, Fax: 662-325-8161, E-mail: gsbi@cobilan.msstate.edu. Web site: http://business.msstate.edu/marketing/.

Mississippi State University, College of Business, Graduate Studies in Business, Mississippi State, MS 39762. Offers business administration (MBA); project management (MBA). *Accreditation:* AACSB. Part-time and evening/weekend programs available. Postbaccalaureate distance learning degree programs offered (no on-campus study). *Students:* 95 full-time (41 women), 259 part-time (84 women); includes 36 minority (13 Black or African American, non-Hispanic/Latino; 5 American Indian or Alaska Native, non-Hispanic/Latino; 3 Asian, non-Hispanic/Latino; 9 Hispanic/Latino; 1 Native Hawaiian or other Pacific Islander, non-Hispanic/Latino; 5 Two or more races, non-Hispanic/Latino), 16 international. Average age 30. 219 applicants, 58% accepted, 95 enrolled. In 2011, 170 degrees awarded. Terminal master's awarded for partial completion of doctoral program. *Degree requirements:* For master's, comprehensive exam (for some programs), thesis optional. *Entrance requirements:* For master's, GMAT, minimum GPA of 3.0 in last 60 hours of course work. Additional exam requirements/recommendations for international students: Required—TOEFL (minimum score 575 paper-based; 233 computer-based; 90 iBT); Recommended—IELTS (minimum score 6.5). *Application deadline:* For fall admission, 7/1 for domestic students, 5/1 for international students; for spring admission, 11/1 for domestic students, 9/1 for international students. Applications are processed on a rolling basis. Application fee: $40. Electronic applications accepted. *Expenses:* Tuition, state resident: full-time $5805; part-time $322.50 per credit hour. Tuition, nonresident: full-time $14,670; part-time $815 per credit hour. *Financial support:* In 2011–12, 21 research assistantships with full tuition reimbursements (averaging $11,043 per year), 28 teaching assistantships with full tuition reimbursements (averaging $9,543 per year) were awarded; Federal Work-Study, institutionally sponsored loans, scholarships/grants, and unspecified assistantships also available. Financial award application deadline: 4/1; financial award applicants required to submit FAFSA. *Unit head:* Dr. Barbara Spencer, Director, 662-325-1891, Fax: 662-325-8161, E-mail: gsbi@cobilan.msstate.edu. Web site: http://business.msstate.edu/gsb/.

Mississippi State University, College of Business, School of Accountancy, Mississippi State, MS 39762. Offers accounting (MBA); business administration (PhD); systems (MPA); taxation (MTX). MBA in accounting only offered at the Meridian campus. *Accreditation:* AACSB. *Faculty:* 8 full-time (3 women), 3 part-time/adjunct (0 women). *Students:* 46 full-time (24 women), 13 part-time (9 women); includes 4 minority (2 Black or African American, non-Hispanic/Latino; 1 Asian, non-Hispanic/Latino; 1 Two or more races, non-Hispanic/Latino), 6 international. Average age 27. 51 applicants, 47% accepted, 24 enrolled. In 2011, 56 master's awarded. *Degree requirements:* For master's, comprehensive exam. *Entrance requirements:* For master's, GMAT (minimum score of 510), minimum GPA of 2.75 overall and in upper-level accounting, 3.0 in last 60 hours of course work; for doctorate, GMAT, minimum undergraduate GPA of 3.0, both cumulative and over the last 60 hours of undergraduate work; 3.25 on all prior graduate work. Additional exam requirements/recommendations for international students: Required—TOEFL (minimum score 575 paper-based; 233 computer-based; 84 iBT); Recommended—IELTS (minimum score 7). *Application deadline:* For fall admission, 7/1 for domestic students, 5/1 for international students; for spring admission, 11/1 for domestic students, 9/1 for international students. Applications are processed on a rolling basis. Application fee: $40. Electronic applications accepted. *Expenses:* Tuition, state resident: full-time $5805; part-time $322.50 per credit hour. Tuition, nonresident: full-time $14,670; part-time $815 per credit hour. *Financial support:* Career-related internships or fieldwork, Federal Work-Study, institutionally sponsored loans, scholarships/grants, and unspecified assistantships available. Support available to part-time students. Financial award application deadline: 4/1; financial award applicants required to submit FAFSA. *Faculty research:* Income tax, financial accounting system, managerial accounting, auditing. *Unit head:* Dr. Jim Scheiner, Director, 662-325-1633, Fax: 662-325-1646, E-mail: jscheiner@cobilan.msstate.edu. *Application contact:* Dr. Barbara Spencer, Graduate Coordinator, 662-325-3710, Fax: 662-325-1646, E-mail: sac@cobilan.msstate.edu. Web site: http://www.business.msstate.edu/accounting.

Missouri Baptist University, Graduate Programs, St. Louis, MO 63141-8660. Offers business administration (MBA); Christian ministries (MACM); counseling (MAC); education (MSE); education administration (MEA); educational leadership (MSE, Ed S); teaching (MAT).

Missouri Southern State University, Program in Business Administration, Joplin, MO 64801-1595. Offers MBA. Program offered jointly with Northwest Missouri State University. *Accreditation:* ACBSP. Postbaccalaureate distance learning degree programs offered. *Degree requirements:* For master's, capstone seminar.

Missouri State University, Graduate College, College of Business Administration, Department of Computer Information Systems, Springfield, MO 65897. Offers computer information systems (MS); secondary education (MS Ed), including business. Part-time and evening/weekend programs available. Postbaccalaureate distance learning degree programs offered (no on-campus study). *Faculty:* 13 full-time (2 women), 5 part-time/adjunct (0 women). *Students:* 28 full-time (5 women), 2 part-time (1 woman); includes 2 minority (1 Asian, non-Hispanic/Latino; 1 Two or more races, non-Hispanic/Latino), 2 international. Average age 38. 20 applicants, 90% accepted, 11 enrolled. In 2011, 13 master's awarded. *Degree requirements:* For master's, thesis optional. *Entrance requirements:* For master's, GMAT, 3 years of work experience in computer information systems, minimum GPA of 2.75 (MS), 9-12 teaching certification (MS Ed). Additional exam requirements/recommendations for international students: Required—TOEFL (minimum score 550 paper-based; 213 computer-based; 79 iBT). *Application deadline:* For fall admission, 7/20 priority date for domestic students, 5/1 for international students; for spring admission, 12/20 priority date for domestic students, 9/1 for international students. Applications are processed on a rolling basis. Application fee: $35 ($50 for international students). Electronic applications accepted. *Expenses:* Contact institution. *Financial support:* Federal Work-Study, institutionally sponsored loans, scholarships/grants, and unspecified assistantships available. Support available to part-time students. Financial award application deadline: 3/31; financial award applicants required to submit FAFSA. *Faculty research:* Decision support systems, algorithms in Visual Basic, end-user satisfaction, information security. *Unit head:* Dr. Jerry Chin, Head, 417-836-4131, Fax: 417-836-6907, E-mail: jerrychin@missouristate.edu. *Application contact:* Misty Stewart, Coordinator of Graduate Admissions and Recruitment, 417-836-6079, Fax: 417-836-6200, E-mail: mistystewart@missouristate.edu. Web site: http://mscis.missouristate.edu.

Missouri State University, Graduate College, College of Business Administration, Program in Business Administration, Springfield, MO 65897. Offers MBA. *Accreditation:* AACSB. Part-time and evening/weekend programs available. *Students:* 351 full-time (148 women), 135 part-time (55 women); includes 16 minority (5 Black or African American, non-Hispanic/Latino; 2 American Indian or Alaska Native, non-Hispanic/Latino; 4 Asian, non-Hispanic/Latino; 5 Hispanic/Latino), 262 international. Average age 27. 218 applicants, 92% accepted, 141 enrolled. In 2011, 346 master's awarded. *Degree requirements:* For master's, thesis optional. *Entrance requirements:* For master's, GMAT, minimum GPA of 2.75. Additional exam requirements/ recommendations for international students: Required—TOEFL (minimum score 550 paper-based; 213 computer-based; 79 iBT). *Application deadline:* For fall admission, 7/20 priority date for domestic students, 5/1 for international students; for spring admission, 12/20 priority date for domestic students, 9/1 for international students. Applications are processed on a rolling basis. Application fee: $35 ($50 for international students). Electronic applications accepted. *Expenses:* Tuition, state resident: full-time $4086; part-time $227 per credit hour. Tuition, nonresident: full-time $8172; part-time $454 per credit hour. *Required fees:* $275 per semester. Tuition and fees vary according to course load, campus/location and program. *Financial support:* Federal Work-Study, institutionally sponsored loans, scholarships/grants, and unspecified assistantships available. Support available to part-time students. Financial award application deadline: 3/31; financial award applicants required to submit FAFSA. *Unit head:* Dr. Elizabeth Rozell, MBA Program Director, 417-836-5616, Fax: 417-836-4407, E-mail: erozell@missouristate.edu. *Application contact:* Misty Stewart, Coordinator of Graduate Admissions and Recruitment, 417-836-6079, Fax: 417-836-6200, E-mail: mistystewart@missouristate.edu. Web site: http://mba.missouristate.edu.

Molloy College, Graduate Business Program, Rockville Centre, NY 11571-5002. Offers accounting (MBA); accounting and management (MBA); management (MBA); personal financial planning and accounting (MBA); personal financial planning and management (MBA). Part-time programs available. *Faculty:* 5 full-time (0 women), 8 part-time/adjunct (2 women). *Students:* 39 full-time (18 women), 77 part-time (44 women); includes 41 minority (23 Black or African American, non-Hispanic/Latino; 1 American Indian or Alaska Native, non-Hispanic/Latino; 7 Asian, non-Hispanic/Latino; 8 Hispanic/Latino; 1 Native Hawaiian or other Pacific Islander, non-Hispanic/Latino; 1 Two or more races, non-Hispanic/Latino), 1 international. Average age 32. 57 applicants, 81% accepted, 31 enrolled. In 2011, 34 master's awarded. *Application deadline:* Applications are processed on a rolling basis. *Unit head:* Dr. Raymond Manganelli, Associate Dean and the Director Graduate Business, 516-678-5000. *Application contact:* Alina Haitz, Assistant Director of Graduate Admissions, 516-678-5000 Ext. 6399, Fax: 516-256-2247, E-mail: ahaitz@molloy.edu.

Monmouth University, The Graduate School, Leon Hess Business School, West Long Branch, NJ 07764-1898. Offers accounting (MBA, Post-Master's Certificate); business (MBA); finance (MBA); healthcare management (MBA, Post-Master's Certificate); real estate (MBA). *Accreditation:* AACSB. Part-time and evening/weekend programs available. *Faculty:* 29 full-time (10 women), 8 part-time/adjunct (2 women). *Students:* 107 full-time (44 women), 161 part-time (61 women); includes 42 minority (8 Black or African American, non-Hispanic/Latino; 19 Asian, non-Hispanic/Latino; 12 Hispanic/Latino; 3 Two or more races, non-Hispanic/Latino), 23 international. Average age 28. 193 applicants, 84% accepted, 111 enrolled. In 2011, 87 master's awarded. *Degree requirements:* For master's, capstone course. *Entrance requirements:* For master's, GMAT, minimum GPA of 3.0 in major, 2.75 overall. Additional exam requirements/ recommendations for international students: Required—TOEFL (minimum score 550 paper-based; 213 computer-based; 79 iBT), IELTS (minimum score 5), Michigan English Language Assessment Battery (minimum score 77), Cambridge A, B, C. *Application deadline:* For fall admission, 7/15 priority date for domestic students, 6/1 for international students; for spring admission, 11/15 priority date for domestic students, 11/1 for international students. Applications are processed on a rolling basis. Application fee: $50. Electronic applications accepted. *Financial support:* In 2011–12, 190 students received support, including 183 fellowships (averaging $1,638 per year), 21 research assistantships (averaging $9,311 per year); career-related internships or fieldwork, scholarships/grants, and unspecified assistantships also available. Support available to part-time students. Financial award applicants required to submit FAFSA. *Faculty research:* Information technology and marketing, behavioral research in accounting, human resources, management of technology. *Unit head:* Douglas Stives, MBA Program Director, 732-263-5894, Fax: 732-263-5517, E-mail: dstives@monmouth.edu. *Application contact:* Kevin Roane, Director, Office of Graduate Admission, 732-571-3452, Fax: 732-263-5123, E-mail: gradadm@monmouth.edu. Web site: http://www.monmouth.edu/mba.

Monroe College, King School of Business, Bronx, NY 10468-5407. Offers business management (MBA). Program also offered in New Rochelle, NY. Postbaccalaureate distance learning degree programs offered.

Montclair State University, The Graduate School, College of Humanities and Social Sciences, MA Program in Law and Governance, Montclair, NJ 07043-1624. Offers conflict management and peace studies (MA); governance, compliance and regulation (MA); intellectual property (MA); law and governance (MA); legal management (MA). Part-time and evening/weekend programs available. *Faculty:* 13 full-time (6 women), 25 part-time/adjunct (8 women). *Students:* 11 full-time (6 women), 23 part-time (13 women); includes 17 minority (8 Black or African American, non-Hispanic/Latino; 2 Asian, non-Hispanic/Latino; 5 Hispanic/Latino; 2 Two or more races, non-Hispanic/Latino), 2 international. Average age 30. 32 applicants, 44% accepted, 10 enrolled. In 2011, 16 master's awarded. *Degree requirements:* For master's, thesis or comprehensive exam. *Entrance requirements:* For master's, GRE General Test, minimum cumulative GPA of 2.75 for undergraduate work, 2 letters of recommendation, essay. Additional exam requirements/recommendations for international students: Required—TOEFL (minimum score 83 iBT) or IELTS (minimum score 6.5). *Application deadline:* Applications are processed on a rolling basis. Application fee: $60. Electronic applications accepted. *Financial support:* In 2011–12, 1 research assistantship with full tuition reimbursement (averaging $7,000 per year) was awarded; Federal Work-Study, scholarships/grants, and unspecified assistantships also available. Support available to part-time students. Financial award application deadline: 3/1; financial award applicants required to submit FAFSA. *Unit head:* Dr. William Berlin, Chair, 973-655-7576, E-mail: berlinw@mail.montclair.edu. *Application contact:* Amy Aiello, Director of Graduate Admissions and Operations, 973-655-5147, Fax: 973-655-7869, E-mail: graduate.school@montclair.edu. Web site: http://www.montclair.edu/graduate/programs-of-study/law-and-governance/.

Montclair State University, The Graduate School, School of Business, General MBA Program, Montclair, NJ 07043-1624. Offers MBA. Part-time and evening/weekend programs available. *Students:* 77 full-time (35 women), 241 part-time (103 women); includes 88 minority (21 Black or African American, non-Hispanic/Latino; 29 Asian, non-Hispanic/Latino; 35 Hispanic/Latino; 3 Two or more races, non-Hispanic/Latino), 27 international. Average age 29. 251 applicants, 42% accepted, 67 enrolled. In 2011, 126 master's awarded. *Degree requirements:* For master's, culminating experience. *Entrance requirements:* For master's, GMAT or GRE General Test, 2 letters of recommendation, resume, essay. Additional exam requirements/recommendations for international students: Required—TOEFL (minimum score 83 iBT), IELTS (minimum score 6.5). *Application deadline:* Applications are processed on a rolling basis. Application fee: $60. Electronic applications accepted. *Financial support:* In 2011–12, 14 research assistantships with full tuition reimbursements (averaging $7,000 per year), 3 teaching assistantships were awarded; Federal Work-Study, scholarships/grants, and unspecified assistantships also available. Support available to part-time students. Financial award application deadline: 3/1; financial award applicants required to submit FAFSA. *Faculty research:* Accounting, management, IOM, marketing. *Unit head:* Dr. E. LeBrent Chrite, Dean, 973-655-4304, E-mail: chritee@mail.montclair.edu. *Application contact:* Amy Aiello, Executive Director of The Graduate School, 973-655-5147, Fax: 973-655-7869, E-mail: graduate.school@montclair.edu. Web site: http://business.montclair.edu.

Montclair State University, The Graduate School, School of Business, Saturday MBA Program, Montclair, NJ 07043-1624. Offers MBA. Part-time and evening/weekend programs available. Postbaccalaureate distance learning degree programs offered (no on-campus study). *Students:* Average age 29. *Degree requirements:* For master's, culminating experience. *Entrance requirements:* For master's, GMAT or GRE General Test, 2 letters of recommendation, resume, essay. Additional exam requirements/ recommendations for international students: Required—TOEFL (minimum score 83 iBT), IELTS (minimum score 6.5). *Application deadline:* Applications are processed on a rolling basis. Application fee: $60. Electronic applications accepted. *Financial support:* Federal Work-Study, scholarships/grants, and unspecified assistantships available. Support available to part-time students. Financial award application deadline: 3/1; financial award applicants required to submit FAFSA. *Unit head:* Dr. E. LeBrent Chrite, Dean, 973-655-4304, E-mail: chritee@mail.montclair.edu. *Application contact:* Amy Aiello, Executive Director of The Graduate School, 973-655-5147, Fax: 973-655-7869, E-mail: graduate.school@montclair.edu. Web site: http://business.montclair.edu/graduate/saturday.

Monterey Institute of International Studies, Graduate School of International Policy and Management, Fisher International MBA Program, Monterey, CA 93940-2691. Offers MBA. *Accreditation:* AACSB. *Degree requirements:* For master's, one foreign language, thesis. *Entrance requirements:* For master's, GMAT, minimum GPA of 3.0, proficiency in a foreign language. Additional exam requirements/recommendations for international students: Required—TOEFL (minimum score 550 paper-based; 213 computer-based; 80 iBT). Electronic applications accepted. *Expenses: Tuition:* Full-time $32,800; part-time $1560 per credit. *Required fees:* $28 per semester. *Faculty research:* Cross-cultural consumer behavior, foreign direct investment, marketing and entrepreneurial orientation, political risk analysis and area studies, managing international human resources.

Montreat College, School of Professional and Adult Studies, Montreat, NC 28757-1267. Offers business administration (MBA); clinical mental health counseling (MA); environmental education (MS); management and leadership (MS). Evening/weekend programs available. Postbaccalaureate distance learning degree programs offered (minimal on-campus study). *Faculty:* 12 full-time (3 women), 14 part-time/adjunct (3 women). *Students:* 108 full-time (65 women), 179 part-time (111 women); includes 130 minority (116 Black or African American, non-Hispanic/Latino; 5 American Indian or Alaska Native, non-Hispanic/Latino; 2 Asian, non-Hispanic/Latino; 6 Hispanic/Latino; 1 Two or more races, non-Hispanic/Latino). Average age 34. 145 applicants, 41% accepted, 57 enrolled. In 2011, 142 master's awarded. *Degree requirements:* For master's, business consulting project (for MBA). *Entrance requirements:* For master's, GMAT. Additional exam requirements/recommendations for international students: Required—TOEFL (minimum score 550 paper-based; 213 computer-based; 80 iBT). *Application deadline:* Applications are processed on a rolling basis. *Expenses: Tuition:* Full-time $10,185; part-time $485 per credit. *Financial support:* Available to part-time students. Application deadline: 7/1; applicants required to submit FAFSA. *Unit head:* Jonathan E. Shores, Jr., Vice President for Marketing and Enrollment, 828-669-8012 Ext. 2759, Fax: 828-669-0500, E-mail: jeshores@montreat.edu. *Application contact:* Julia Pacilli, Director of Enrollment, 828-669-8012 Ext. 2756, Fax: 828-669-0500, E-mail: jpacilli@montreat.edu. Web site: http://www.montreat.edu/.

Moravian College, Moravian College Comenius Center, Business and Management Programs, Bethlehem, PA 18018-6650. Offers accounting (MBA); general management (MBA); health care management (MBA); human resource management (MBA); leadership (MSHRM); learning and performance management (MSHRM); supply chain management (MBA). Part-time and evening/weekend programs available. *Entrance requirements:* For master's, GMAT. Additional exam requirements/recommendations for international students: Required—TOEFL (minimum score 550 paper-based; 260 computer-based; 90 iBT). *Expenses:* Contact institution. *Faculty research:* Leadership, change management, human resources.

Morehead State University, Graduate Programs, College of Business and Public Affairs, Morehead, KY 40351. Offers MA, MBA, MPA, MSIS. *Accreditation:* AACSB. Part-time and evening/weekend programs available. Postbaccalaureate distance learning degree programs offered (minimal on-campus study). *Entrance requirements:* For master's, GMAT, GRE General Test, minimum GPA of 2.5 on undergraduate work. Additional exam requirements/recommendations for international students: Required—TOEFL (minimum score 525 paper-based; 173 computer-based). Electronic applications accepted. *Faculty research:* Regional economic development, accounting systems, banking market structures, macroeconomics, distance learning.

Morgan State University, School of Graduate Studies, Earl G. Graves School of Business and Management, PhD Program in Business Administration, Baltimore, MD 21251. Offers PhD. *Degree requirements:* For doctorate, thesis/dissertation. *Entrance requirements:* For doctorate, GMAT. Additional exam requirements/recommendations for international students: Required—TOEFL (minimum score 550 paper-based; 213 computer-based).

Morrison University, Graduate School, Reno, NV 89521. Offers business administration (MBA). Part-time and evening/weekend programs available. *Degree requirements:* For master's, thesis. *Entrance requirements:* For master's, GMAT, minimum 3 years minimum work experience, interview, minimum GPA of 3.0. Additional exam requirements/recommendations for international students: Recommended—TOEFL. Electronic applications accepted.

Mount Aloysius College, Masters in Business Administration Program, Cresson, PA 16630. Offers MBA. Part-time and evening/weekend programs available. *Entrance requirements:* Additional exam requirements/recommendations for international students: Recommended—TOEFL. Electronic applications accepted.

Mount Ida College, Program in Management, Newton, MA 02459-3310. Offers MSM. Part-time and evening/weekend programs available. Postbaccalaureate distance learning degree programs offered (minimal on-campus study). *Entrance requirements:* Additional exam requirements/recommendations for international students: Required—TOEFL (minimum score 550 paper-based; 220 computer-based; 79 iBT); Recommended—IELTS (minimum score 5.5). Electronic applications accepted.

Mount Marty College, Graduate Studies Division, Yankton, SD 57078-3724. Offers business administration (MBA); nurse anesthesia (MS); nursing (MSN); pastoral ministries (MPM). *Accreditation:* AANA/CANAEP (one or more programs are accredited). *Degree requirements:* For master's, thesis or alternative. *Entrance requirements:* For master's, GRE General Test, minimum GPA of 3.0. Electronic applications accepted. *Faculty research:* Clinical anesthesia, professional characteristics, motivations of applicants.

Mount Mary College, Graduate Programs, Program in Business Administration, Milwaukee, WI 53222-4597. Offers MBA. *Faculty:* 1 full-time (0 women), 5 part-time/adjunct (2 women). *Students:* 6 full-time (all women), 23 part-time (22 women); includes

13 minority (7 Black or African American, non-Hispanic/Latino; 1 Asian, non-Hispanic/Latino; 4 Hispanic/Latino; 1 Two or more races, non-Hispanic/Latino). Average age 37. 6 applicants, 67% accepted, 3 enrolled. *Degree requirements:* For master's, terminal project. *Entrance requirements:* For master's, minimum GPA of 2.75. Additional exam requirements/recommendations for international students: Required—TOEFL (minimum score 500 paper-based; 173 computer-based). *Application deadline:* For fall admission, 8/1 priority date for domestic students, 8/1 for international students; for spring admission, 12/1 priority date for domestic students, 12/1 for international students. Application fee: $45 ($100 for international students). Electronic applications accepted. *Financial support:* In 2011–12, 2 students received support. Career-related internships or fieldwork and Federal Work-Study available. Support available to part-time students. Financial award application deadline: 5/1; financial award applicants required to submit FAFSA. *Unit head:* Kristen Roche, Director, 414-258-4810, E-mail: rochek@mtmary.edu. *Application contact:* Dr. Douglas J. Mickelson, Associate Dean for Graduate and Continuing Education, 414-256-1252, Fax: 414-256-0167, E-mail: mickelsd@mtmary.edu.

Mount Mercy University, Program in Business Administration, Cedar Rapids, IA 52402-4797. Offers MBA. Evening/weekend programs available. *Entrance requirements:* For master's, minimum cumulative GPA of 3.0, 2 letters of recommendation, resume. Additional exam requirements/recommendations for international students: Required—TOEFL (minimum score 570 paper-based; 88 iBT). Electronic applications accepted.

Mount Saint Mary College, Division of Business, Newburgh, NY 12550-3494. Offers business (MBA); financial planning (MBA). Part-time and evening/weekend programs available. *Faculty:* 4 full-time (1 woman), 5 part-time/adjunct (1 woman). *Students:* 31 full-time (20 women), 39 part-time (19 women); includes 16 minority (5 Black or African American, non-Hispanic/Latino; 1 Asian, non-Hispanic/Latino; 9 Hispanic/Latino; 1 Two or more races, non-Hispanic/Latino), 9 international. Average age 32. 62 applicants, 35% accepted, 9 enrolled. In 2011, 49 master's awarded. *Degree requirements:* For master's, thesis or alternative. *Entrance requirements:* For master's, GMAT or minimum undergraduate GPA of 2.7. *Application deadline:* Applications are processed on a rolling basis. Application fee: $45. Application fee is waived when completed online. *Expenses: Tuition:* Full-time $13,356; part-time $742 per credit. *Required fees:* $70 per semester. *Financial support:* In 2011–12, 19 students received support. Unspecified assistantships available. Financial award application deadline: 4/15; financial award applicants required to submit FAFSA. *Faculty research:* Financial reform, entrepreneurship and small business development, global business relations, technology's impact on business decision-making, college-assisted business education. *Unit head:* Dr. James Gearity, Graduate Coordinator, 845-569-3121, Fax: 845-562-6762, E-mail: james.gearity@msmc.edu. *Application contact:* Courtney McDermott, Graduate Recruiter, 845-569-3402, Fax: 845-569-3450, E-mail: courtney.mcdermott@msmc.edu. Web site: http://www.msmc.edu/Academics/Graduate_Programs/master_of_business_administration.be.

Mount St. Mary's College, Graduate Division, Program in Business Administration, Los Angeles, CA 90049-1599. Offers entrepreneurship (MBA); nonprofit management (MBA); organizational leadership (MBA); project management (MBA). Evening/weekend programs available. *Entrance requirements:* Additional exam requirements/recommendations for international students: Required—TOEFL. *Application deadline:* For fall admission, 6/30 for domestic students. Electronic applications accepted. *Expenses:* Contact institution. *Financial support:* Scholarships/grants available. Financial award application deadline: 3/15; financial award applicants required to submit FAFSA. *Unit head:* Dr. Janet Robinson, Director, 310-954-4153, E-mail: jrobinson@msmc.la.edu. Web site: http://www.msmc.la.edu/graduate-programs/mba.asp.

Mount St. Mary's University, Program in Business Administration, Emmitsburg, MD 21727-7799. Offers MBA. Part-time and evening/weekend programs available. *Faculty:* 11 full-time (3 women), 6 part-time/adjunct (2 women). *Students:* 55 full-time (22 women), 196 part-time (90 women); includes 37 minority (14 Black or African American, non-Hispanic/Latino; 12 Asian, non-Hispanic/Latino; 10 Hispanic/Latino; 1 Two or more races, non-Hispanic/Latino), 10 international. Average age 31. 76 applicants, 99% accepted, 44 enrolled. In 2011, 97 master's awarded. *Degree requirements:* For master's, thesis. *Entrance requirements:* For master's, minimum undergraduate GPA of 2.75, 5 years' relevant professional business experience, or GMAT (minimum score of 500). Additional exam requirements/recommendations for international students: Required—TOEFL (minimum score 550 paper-based; 83 computer-based). *Application deadline:* Applications are processed on a rolling basis. Application fee: $35. *Expenses: Tuition:* Full-time $9000; part-time $500 per credit hour. Part-time tuition and fees vary according to program. *Financial support:* Career-related internships or fieldwork and unspecified assistantships available. Financial award applicants required to submit FAFSA. *Faculty research:* Corporate social responsibility in other countries and cultures, market research as related to healthcare and healthcare reform, pilot enforcement actions by FAA as well as aircraft ownership, taxation issues and aviation related litigation. *Unit head:* Deborah Powell, Director of Graduate and Adult Business Program, 301-447-5326, Fax: 301-447-5335, E-mail: mba@msmary.edu. *Application contact:* Director, Center for Professional and Continuing Studies. Web site: http://www.msmary.edu/School_of_business/Graduate_Programs/mba/.

Mount Vernon Nazarene University, Program in Management, Mount Vernon, OH 43050-9500. Offers MSM. *Accreditation:* ACBSP. Part-time and evening/weekend programs available.

Murray State University, College of Business and Public Affairs, MBA Program, Murray, KY 42071. Offers MBA. *Accreditation:* AACSB. Part-time and evening/weekend programs available. *Entrance requirements:* For master's, GMAT. Additional exam requirements/recommendations for international students: Required—TOEFL.

National American University, Graduate Programs, Rapid City, SD 57701. Offers MBA, MM. Programs also offered in Wichita, KS; Albuquerque, NM; Bloomington, MN; Brooklyn Center, MN; Colorado Springs, CO; Denver, CO; Independence, MO; Overland Park, KS; Rio Rancho, NM; Roseville, MN; Zona Rosa, MO. Part-time and evening/weekend programs available. Postbaccalaureate distance learning degree programs offered. *Entrance requirements:* For master's, minimum undergraduate GPA of 2.75. Additional exam requirements/recommendations for international students: Required—TOEFL, TWE. Electronic applications accepted. *Faculty research:* Tourism, finance, marketing.

National Louis University, College of Management and Business, Chicago, IL 60603. Offers business administration (MBA); human resource management and development (MS); management (MS). Part-time and evening/weekend programs available. *Students:* 71 full-time (48 women), 56 part-time (36 women); includes 80 minority (32 Black or African American, non-Hispanic/Latino; 1 American Indian or Alaska Native, non-Hispanic/Latino; 3 Asian, non-Hispanic/Latino; 42 Hispanic/Latino; 2 Two or more races, non-Hispanic/Latino). Average age 37. In 2011, 73 master's awarded. *Entrance requirements:* For master's, college-administered critical thinking and writing skills test, minimum GPA of 3.0, resume, 3 references. Additional exam requirements/recommendations for international students: Required—TOEFL (minimum score 550 paper-based; 213 computer-based; 79 iBT). *Application deadline:* Applications are processed on a rolling basis. Application fee: $40. *Financial support:* Federal Work-Study, institutionally sponsored loans, and scholarships/grants available. Support available to part-time students. Financial award applicants required to submit FAFSA. *Unit head:* Walter Roetlger, Executive Dean, 312-261-3073, Fax: 312-261-3073, E-mail: chris.multhauf@nl.edu. *Application contact:* Ken Kasprzak, Director of Admissions, 800-443-5522 Ext. 5718, Fax: 847-947-5575, E-mail: kkasprzak@nl.edu. Web site: http://www3.nl.edu/graduate/business_admin.cfm.

National University, Academic Affairs, School of Business and Management, Department of Accounting and Finance, La Jolla, CA 92037-1011. Offers accountancy (M Acc); business administration (MBA); sustainability management (MS). Part-time and evening/weekend programs available. Postbaccalaureate distance learning degree programs offered (no on-campus study). *Degree requirements:* For master's, thesis. *Entrance requirements:* For master's, interview, minimum GPA of 2.5. Additional exam requirements/recommendations for international students: Required—TOEFL (minimum score 550 paper-based; 213 computer-based; 79 iBT), IELTS (minimum score 6). *Application deadline:* Applications are processed on a rolling basis. Application fee: $60 ($65 for international students). Electronic applications accepted. *Financial support:* Career-related internships or fieldwork, institutionally sponsored loans, scholarships/grants, and tuition waivers (partial) available. Support available to part-time students. Financial award application deadline: 6/30; financial award applicants required to submit FAFSA. *Unit head:* Dr. Farhang Mossavar-Rahmani, Chair, 858-642-8409, Fax: 858-642-8726, E-mail: fmossava@nu.edu. *Application contact:* Dominick Giovanniello, Associate Regional Dean, 800-NAT-UNIV, Fax: 858-541-7792, E-mail: dgiovann@nu.edu. Web site: http://www.nu.edu/OurPrograms/SchoolOfBusinessAndManagement/AccountingAndFinance.html.

National University, Academic Affairs, School of Business and Management, Department of Management and Marketing, La Jolla, CA 92037-1011. Offers business administration (GMBA); global management (MGM). GMBA offered in Spanish. Part-time and evening/weekend programs available. Postbaccalaureate distance learning degree programs offered (no on-campus study). *Students:* 157 applicants, 100% accepted, 134 enrolled. *Degree requirements:* For master's, thesis. *Entrance requirements:* For master's, interview, minimum GPA of 2.5. Additional exam requirements/recommendations for international students: Required—TOEFL (minimum score 550 paper-based; 213 computer-based; 79 iBT), IELTS (minimum score 6). *Application deadline:* Applications are processed on a rolling basis. Application fee: $60 ($65 for international students). Electronic applications accepted. *Financial support:* Career-related internships or fieldwork, institutionally sponsored loans, scholarships/grants, and tuition waivers (partial) available. Support available to part-time students. Financial award application deadline: 6/30; financial award applicants required to submit FAFSA. *Unit head:* Dr. Ramon Corona, Chair, 858-642-8427, Fax: 858-642-8406, E-mail: rcorona@nu.edu. *Application contact:* Dominick Giovanniello, Associate Regional Dean, 800-NAT-UNIV, Fax: 858-541-7792, E-mail: dgiovann@nu.edu. Web site: http://www.nu.edu/OurPrograms/SchoolOfBusinessAndManagement/ManagementAndMarketing.html.

Naval Postgraduate School, Departments and Academic Groups, School of Business and Public Policy, Monterey, CA 93943. Offers acquisitions and contract management (MBA); business administration (EMBA, MBA); contract management (MS); defense business management (MBA); defense systems analysis (MS), including management; defense systems management (international) (MBA); executive management (MBA); financial management (MBA); information systems management (MBA); manpower systems analysis (MS); material logistics support management (MBA); program management (MS); resource planning/management for international defense (MBA); supply chain management (MBA); systems acquisition management (MBA); transportation management (MBA). Program only open to commissioned officers of the United States and friendly nations and selected United States federal civilian employees. *Accreditation:* AACSB; NASPAA. Part-time programs available. Postbaccalaureate distance learning degree programs offered (minimal on-campus study). *Faculty:* 67 full-time (15 women), 32 part-time/adjunct (12 women). *Students:* 307 full-time (29 women), 327 part-time (71 women); includes 149 minority (55 Black or African American, non-Hispanic/Latino; 5 American Indian or Alaska Native, non-Hispanic/Latino; 46 Asian, non-Hispanic/Latino; 43 Hispanic/Latino), 44 international. Average age 42. In 2011, 295 master's awarded. *Degree requirements:* For master's, thesis (for some programs), terminal project/capstone (for some programs). *Faculty research:* U. S. and European public procurement policies for small and medium-sized enterprises, examining external validity criticisms in the choice of students as subjects in accounting experiment studies, assurance of learning in contract management education, contracting for cloud computing: opportunities and risks, NPS, Apple App Store as a business model supporting U. S. Navy requirements. *Total annual research expenditures:* $9 million. *Unit head:* Raymond Franck, Department Chair, 831-656-3614, E-mail: refranck@nps.edu. *Application contact:* Acting Director of Admissions. Web site: http://www.nps.edu/Academics/Schools/GSBPP/index.html.

Nazareth College of Rochester, Graduate Studies, Department of Business, Program in Management, Rochester, NY 14618-3790. Offers MS. Part-time and evening/weekend programs available. *Entrance requirements:* For master's, minimum GPA of 3.0.

New Charter University, College of Business, Birmingham, AL 35244. Offers finance (MBA); health care management (MBA); management (MBA). Part-time and evening/weekend programs available. Postbaccalaureate distance learning degree programs offered (no on-campus study). *Entrance requirements:* For master's, course work in calculus, statistics, macroeconomics. Additional exam requirements/recommendations for international students: Required—TOEFL (minimum score 550 paper-based; 213 computer-based). Electronic applications accepted.

New England College, Program in Management, Henniker, NH 03242-3293. Offers accounting (MSA); healthcare administration (MS); international relations (MA); marketing management (MS); nonprofit leadership (MS); project management (MS); strategic leadership (MS). Part-time and evening/weekend programs available. *Degree requirements:* For master's, independent research project. Electronic applications accepted.

New Jersey City University, Graduate Studies and Continuing Education, College of Professional Studies, Department of Business Administration, Jersey City, NJ 07305-1597. Offers accounting (MS); finance (MBA, MS); marketing (MBA); organizational management and leadership (MBA). *Accreditation:* ACBSP. Part-time and evening/weekend programs available. *Students:* 11 full-time (4 women), 10 part-time (6 women); includes 7 minority (3 Black or African American, non-Hispanic/Latino; 2 Asian, non-Hispanic/Latino; 2 Hispanic/Latino), 5 international. Average age 34. In 2011, 27 master's awarded. *Entrance requirements:* Additional exam requirements/recommendations for international students: Required—TOEFL. *Application deadline:* For fall admission, 8/1 priority date for domestic students; for spring admission, 12/1 for domestic students. Applications are processed on a rolling basis. Application fee: $0. *Expenses:* Tuition, state resident: part-time $494 per credit. Tuition, nonresident: part-time $911.30 per credit. *Required fees:* $95.90 per year. *Financial support:* Career-related internships or fieldwork and unspecified assistantships available. *Unit head:* Dr. Marilyn Ettinger, Head, 201-200-3353, E-mail: mettinger@njcu.edu. *Application contact:*

Dr. William Bajor, Dean of Graduate Studies, 201-200-3409, Fax: 201-200-3411, E-mail: wbajor@njcu.edu.

New Jersey Institute of Technology, Office of Graduate Studies, College of Computing Science, Program in Information Systems, Program in Business and Information Systems, Newark, NJ 07102. Offers MS. *Students:* 19 full-time (5 women), 41 part-time (14 women); includes 31 minority (9 Black or African American, non-Hispanic/Latino; 13 Asian, non-Hispanic/Latino; 9 Hispanic/Latino), 12 international. Average age 32. 102 applicants, 62% accepted, 22 enrolled. In 2011, 28 master's awarded. *Entrance requirements:* Additional exam requirements/recommendations for international students: Required—TOEFL (minimum score 550 paper-based; 213 computer-based; 79 iBT). *Application deadline:* For fall admission, 6/1 for domestic students, 5/1 for international students; for spring admission, 11/15 for domestic and international students. Applications are processed on a rolling basis. Application fee: $65. Electronic applications accepted. *Expenses:* Tuition, state resident: full-time $7980; part-time $867 per credit. Tuition, nonresident: full-time $11,336; part-time $1196 per credit. *Required fees:* $230 per credit. *Financial support:* Application deadline: 1/15. *Unit head:* Dr. Michael P. Bieber, Associate Chair, 973-596-2681, Fax: 973-596-2986, E-mail: michael.p.bieber@njit.edu. *Application contact:* Kathryn Kelly, Director of Admissions, 973-596-3300, Fax: 973-596-3461, E-mail: admissions@njit.edu. Web site: http://is.njit.edu/academics/graduate/msbis/index.php.

New Jersey Institute of Technology, Office of Graduate Studies, School of Management, Program in Management, Newark, NJ 07102. Offers MS. Postbaccalaureate distance learning degree programs offered (no on-campus study). *Students:* 42 full-time (17 women), 25 part-time (5 women); includes 23 minority (9 Black or African American, non-Hispanic/Latino; 9 Asian, non-Hispanic/Latino; 4 Hispanic/Latino; 1 Two or more races, non-Hispanic/Latino), 35 international. Average age 30. 159 applicants, 72% accepted, 32 enrolled. In 2011, 40 master's awarded. *Entrance requirements:* Additional exam requirements/recommendations for international students: Required—TOEFL (minimum score 550 paper-based; 213 computer-based; 79 iBT). *Application deadline:* For fall admission, 6/1 priority date for domestic students, 5/1 for international students; for spring admission, 11/15 priority date for domestic students, 11/15 for international students. Applications are processed on a rolling basis. Application fee: $65. Electronic applications accepted. *Expenses:* Tuition, state resident: full-time $7980; part-time $867 per credit. Tuition, nonresident: full-time $11,336; part-time $1196 per credit. *Required fees:* $230 per credit. *Financial support:* Application deadline: 1/15. *Unit head:* Dr. Robert English, Interim Dean, 973-596-3224, Fax: 973-596-3074, E-mail: robert.english@njit.edu. *Application contact:* Kathryn Kelly, Director of Admissions, 973-596-3300, Fax: 973-596-3461, E-mail: admissions@njit.edu. Web site: http://som.njit.edu/academics/graduate/ms-management/index.php.

New Jersey Institute of Technology, Office of Graduate Studies, School of Management, Program in Management of Business Administration, Newark, NJ 07102. Offers MBA. *Accreditation:* AACSB. Part-time and evening/weekend programs available. *Students:* 90 full-time (40 women), 33 part-time (9 women); includes 63 minority (20 Black or African American, non-Hispanic/Latino; 25 Asian, non-Hispanic/Latino; 18 Hispanic/Latino), 31 international. Average age 31. 239 applicants, 65% accepted, 54 enrolled. In 2011, 63 master's awarded. *Entrance requirements:* For master's, GMAT. Additional exam requirements/recommendations for international students: Required—TOEFL (minimum score 550 paper-based; 213 computer-based; 79 iBT). *Application deadline:* For fall admission, 6/1 priority date for domestic students, 5/1 for international students; for spring admission, 11/15 priority date for domestic students, 11/15 for international students. Applications are processed on a rolling basis. Application fee: $65. Electronic applications accepted. *Expenses:* Tuition, state resident: full-time $7980; part-time $867 per credit. Tuition, nonresident: full-time $11,336; part-time $1196 per credit. *Required fees:* $230 per credit. *Financial support:* Fellowships with full and partial tuition reimbursements, research assistantships with full and partial tuition reimbursements, teaching assistantships with full and partial tuition reimbursements, career-related internships or fieldwork, Federal Work-Study, institutionally sponsored loans, and unspecified assistantships available. Financial award application deadline: 1/15. *Unit head:* Dr. Robert English, Interim Dean, 973-596-3224, Fax: 973-596-3074, E-mail: robert.english@njit.edu. *Application contact:* Kathryn Kelly, Director of Admissions, 973-596-3300, Fax: 973-596-3461, E-mail: admissions@njit.edu.

Newman University, MBA Program, Wichita, KS 67213-2097. Offers finance (MBA); international business (MBA); leadership (MBA); management (MBA); technology (MBA). Part-time programs available. *Faculty:* 4 full-time (1 woman), 7 part-time/adjunct (2 women). *Students:* 28 full-time (7 women), 83 part-time (28 women); includes 31 minority (8 Black or African American, non-Hispanic/Latino; 1 American Indian or Alaska Native, non-Hispanic/Latino; 9 Asian, non-Hispanic/Latino; 9 Hispanic/Latino; 1 Native Hawaiian or other Pacific Islander, non-Hispanic/Latino; 3 Two or more races, non-Hispanic/Latino), 23 international. Average age 31. 63 applicants, 70% accepted, 38 enrolled. In 2011, 49 master's awarded. *Degree requirements:* For master's, thesis optional. *Entrance requirements:* For master's, interview; minimum GPA of 3.0; 3 letters of recommendation; course work in algebra, statistics, macroeconomics, and financial accounting. Additional exam requirements/recommendations for international students: Required—TOEFL (minimum score 600 paper-based; 250 computer-based; 100 iBT). *Application deadline:* For fall admission, 8/1 priority date for domestic students, 7/15 for international students; for winter admission, 1/1 priority date for domestic students; for spring admission, 1/1 priority date for domestic students, 11/15 for international students. Applications are processed on a rolling basis. Application fee: $25 ($40 for international students). Electronic applications accepted. *Expenses:* Contact institution. *Financial support:* In 2011–12, 18 students received support. Federal Work-Study available. Financial award application deadline: 8/15; financial award applicants required to submit FAFSA. *Unit head:* Dr. Wendy Munday, Director of MBA Program, 316-942-4291 Ext. 2296, Fax: 316-942-4483, E-mail: mundayw@newmanu.edu. *Application contact:* Linda Kay Sabala, Director of Graduate Admissions, 316-942-4291 Ext. 2230, Fax: 316-942-4483, E-mail: sabalal@newmanu.edu. Web site: http://www.newmanu.edu.

New Mexico Highlands University, Graduate Studies, School of Business, Las Vegas, NM 87701. Offers business administration (MBA), including government nonprofit management, human resource management, international business, management, management information systems. *Accreditation:* ACBSP. *Faculty:* 20 full-time (5 women). *Students:* 63 full-time (40 women), 146 part-time (76 women); includes 131 minority (9 Black or African American, non-Hispanic/Latino; 8 American Indian or Alaska Native, non-Hispanic/Latino; 1 Asian, non-Hispanic/Latino; 110 Hispanic/Latino; 2 Native Hawaiian or other Pacific Islander, non-Hispanic/Latino; 1 Two or more races, non-Hispanic/Latino), 25 international. Average age 33. 99 applicants, 79% accepted, 49 enrolled. In 2011, 43 master's awarded. *Degree requirements:* For master's, comprehensive exam, thesis or alternative. *Entrance requirements:* For master's, minimum undergraduate GPA of 3.0. Additional exam requirements/recommendations for international students: Required—TOEFL (minimum score 540 paper-based; 207 computer-based). *Application deadline:* For fall admission, 8/1 priority date for domestic students. Applications are processed on a rolling basis. Application fee: $15. *Expenses:* Tuition, state resident: full-time $2767; part-time $146 per credit hour. Tuition, nonresident: full-time $4879; part-time $234 per credit hour. *International tuition:* $5436 full-time. *Required fees:* $737. *Financial support:* In 2011–12, 29 students received support. Career-related internships or fieldwork, Federal Work-Study, institutionally sponsored loans, scholarships/grants, tuition waivers (full and partial), and unspecified assistantships available. Support available to part-time students. Financial award application deadline: 3/1; financial award applicants required to submit FAFSA. *Faculty research:* Real estate valuation, studying expert judgments in complex accounting, decision environments, green marketing, environmentalism, marketing research methodology. *Unit head:* Dr. Margaret Young, Dean, 505-454-3522, Fax: 505-454-3354, E-mail: young_m@nmhu.edu. *Application contact:* Diane Trujillo, Administrative Assistant, Graduate Studies, 505-454-3266, Fax: 505-426-2117, E-mail: dtrujillo@nmhu.edu. Web site: http://www.nmhu.edu/business/.

New Mexico State University, Graduate School, College of Arts and Sciences, Department of Biology, Las Cruces, NM 88003-8001. Offers biology (MS, PhD); biotechnology and business (MS). Part-time programs available. *Faculty:* 21 full-time (9 women). *Students:* 71 full-time (42 women), 15 part-time (12 women); includes 26 minority (3 Black or African American, non-Hispanic/Latino; 3 American Indian or Alaska Native, non-Hispanic/Latino; 1 Asian, non-Hispanic/Latino; 18 Hispanic/Latino; 1 Two or more races, non-Hispanic/Latino), 22 international. Average age 30. 41 applicants, 44% accepted, 12 enrolled. In 2011, 11 master's, 7 doctorates awarded. *Degree requirements:* For master's, thesis (for some programs), defense or oral exam; for doctorate, comprehensive exam, thesis/dissertation, qualifying exam, defense. *Entrance requirements:* Additional exam requirements/recommendations for international students: Required—TOEFL (minimum score 550 paper-based; 0 computer-based; 79 iBT), IELTS (minimum score 6.5). *Application deadline:* For fall admission, 1/15 priority date for domestic students, 1/15 for international students; for spring admission, 10/4 priority date for domestic students, 10/4 for international students. Applications are processed on a rolling basis. Application fee: $40 ($50 for international students). Electronic applications accepted. *Expenses:* Tuition, state resident: full-time $5004; part-time $208.50 per credit. Tuition, nonresident: full-time $17,446; part-time $726.90 per credit. *Financial support:* In 2011–12, 12 fellowships (averaging $9,914 per year), 30 research assistantships (averaging $22,031 per year), 28 teaching assistantships (averaging $22,625 per year) were awarded; Federal Work-Study and health care benefits also available. Support available to part-time students. Financial award application deadline: 1/15. *Faculty research:* Microbiology, cell and organismal physiology, ecology and ethology, evolution, genetics, developmental biology. *Total annual research expenditures:* $4.4 million. *Unit head:* Dr. John Gustafson, Head, 575-646-3611, Fax: 575-646-5665, E-mail: jgustafs@nmsu.edu. *Application contact:* Gloria Valencia, Administration Assistant, 575-646-3611, Fax: 575-646-5665, E-mail: gvalenci@nmsu.edu. Web site: http://biology-web.nmsu.edu/.

New Mexico State University, Graduate School, College of Business, Department of Management, Las Cruces, NM 88003-8001. Offers PhD. *Expenses:* Tuition, state resident: full-time $5004; part-time $208.50 per credit. Tuition, nonresident: full-time $17,446; part-time $726.90 per credit. *Financial support:* In 2011–12, 10 students received support. Research assistantships, teaching assistantships, health care benefits, and unspecified assistantships available. Web site: http://business.nmsu.edu/academics/management-gb/.

New Mexico State University, Graduate School, College of Business, Program in Business Administration, Las Cruces, NM 88003-8001. Offers MBA, PhD. *Accreditation:* AACSB. Part-time and evening/weekend programs available. *Students:* 85 full-time (36 women), 117 part-time (59 women); includes 72 minority (6 Black or African American, non-Hispanic/Latino; 4 American Indian or Alaska Native, non-Hispanic/Latino; 5 Asian, non-Hispanic/Latino; 54 Hispanic/Latino; 3 Two or more races, non-Hispanic/Latino), 28 international. Average age 31. 82 applicants, 65% accepted, 36 enrolled. In 2011, 94 master's, 2 doctorates awarded. *Degree requirements:* For master's, comprehensive exam, thesis optional. *Entrance requirements:* For master's, GMAT, graduate degree, work experience. Additional exam requirements/recommendations for international students: Required—TOEFL (minimum score 530 paper-based; 197 computer-based; 79 iBT), IELTS (minimum score 6.5). *Application deadline:* For fall admission, 7/1 priority date for domestic students, 3/1 for international students; for spring admission, 11/1 priority date for domestic students, 10/1 for international students. Applications are processed on a rolling basis. Application fee: $40 ($50 for international students). Electronic applications accepted. *Expenses:* Tuition, state resident: full-time $5004; part-time $208.50 per credit. Tuition, nonresident: full-time $17,446; part-time $726.90 per credit. *Financial support:* In 2011–12, 6 fellowships (averaging $3,754 per year), 6 research assistantships with partial tuition reimbursements (averaging $12,988 per year), 40 teaching assistantships with partial tuition reimbursements (averaging $17,569 per year) were awarded; Federal Work-Study, institutionally sponsored loans, scholarships/grants, health care benefits, and unspecified assistantships also available. Financial award application deadline: 3/1. *Faculty research:* Small business/entrepreneurship, human resources, global marketing and management, supply chain management. *Unit head:* John Shonk, MBA Advisor, 575-646-8003, Fax: 575-646-7977, E-mail: mba@nmsu.edu. *Application contact:* Coordinator, 575-646-2736, Fax: 575-646-7721, E-mail: gradinfo@nmsu.edu. Web site: http://business.nmsu.edu/academics/mba/.

New York Institute of Technology, Graduate Division, School of Management, Program in Business Administration, Old Westbury, NY 11568-8000. Offers accounting (Advanced Certificate); business administration (MBA); finance (Advanced Certificate); international business (Advanced Certificate); management of information systems (Advanced Certificate); marketing (Advanced Certificate). Part-time and evening/weekend programs available. *Students:* 331 full-time (131 women), 508 part-time (211 women); includes 74 minority (26 Black or African American, non-Hispanic/Latino; 27 Asian, non-Hispanic/Latino; 15 Hispanic/Latino; 6 Two or more races, non-Hispanic/Latino), 214 international. Average age 28. In 2011, 449 degrees awarded. *Degree requirements:* For master's, thesis (for some programs). *Entrance requirements:* For master's, minimum QPA of 2.85. Additional exam requirements/recommendations for international students: Required—TOEFL (minimum score 550 paper-based; 213 computer-based). *Application deadline:* For fall admission, 7/1 priority date for domestic students; for spring admission, 12/1 priority date for domestic students. Applications are processed on a rolling basis. Application fee: $50. Electronic applications accepted. *Expenses: Tuition:* Part-time $930 per credit hour. *Financial support:* Fellowships, research assistantships with partial tuition reimbursements, institutionally sponsored loans, tuition waivers (full and partial), and unspecified assistantships available. Support available to part-time students. Financial award applicants required to submit FAFSA. *Faculty research:* Instructor performance appraisal; relationship between TOEFL, GMAT, GRE, and performance in foreign students. *Unit head:* Dr. Stephen Hartman, Director, 516-686-7691, E-mail: shartman@nyit.edu. *Application contact:* Dr. Jacquelyn Nealon, Vice President for Enrollment Services, 516-686-7925, Fax: 516-686-7597, E-mail: jnealon@nyit.edu.

New York University, Leonard N. Stern School of Business, Department of Marketing, New York, NY 10012-1019. Offers entertainment, media and technology (MBA); general marketing (MBA); marketing (PhD); product management (MBA).

Business Administration and Management—General

New York University, School of Law, New York, NY 10012-1019. Offers law (LL M, JD, JSD); law and business (Advanced Certificate); taxation (Advanced Certificate); JD/LL B; JD/LL M; JD/MA; JD/MBA; JD/MPA; JD/MPP; JD/MSW; JD/MUP; JD/PhD. *Accreditation:* ABA. Part-time programs available. *Entrance requirements:* For doctorate, LSAT (for JD). Electronic applications accepted. *Expenses:* Contact institution. *Faculty research:* International law, environmental law, corporate law, globalization of law, philosophy of law.

Niagara University, Graduate Division of Business Administration, Niagara Falls, Niagara University, NY 14109. Offers business (MBA); commerce (MBA). *Accreditation:* AACSB. Part-time and evening/weekend programs available. *Faculty:* 6 full-time (1 woman), 7 part-time/adjunct (1 woman). *Students:* 155 full-time (81 women), 71 part-time (37 women); includes 15 minority (8 Black or African American, non-Hispanic/Latino; 4 Asian, non-Hispanic/Latino; 2 Hispanic/Latino; 1 Native Hawaiian or other Pacific Islander, non-Hispanic/Latino), 43 international. Average age 33. 253 applicants, 42% accepted, 101 enrolled. In 2011, 108 master's awarded. *Entrance requirements:* For master's, GMAT. Additional exam requirements/recommendations for international students: Required—TOEFL. *Application deadline:* For fall admission, 8/1 for domestic students; for spring admission, 11/1 for domestic students. Applications are processed on a rolling basis. Application fee: $30. *Expenses: Tuition:* Full-time $13,626; part-time $757 per credit hour. *Required fees:* $50. *Financial support:* In 2011–12, 3 fellowships, 2 research assistantships were awarded; career-related internships or fieldwork and Federal Work-Study also available. Support available to part-time students. Financial award application deadline: 8/1; financial award applicants required to submit FAFSA. *Faculty research:* Capital flows, Federal Reserve policy, human resource management, public policy, issues in marketing. *Unit head:* Dr. Paul Richardson, Director, 716-286-8169, Fax: 716-286-8206, E-mail: psr@niagara.edu. *Application contact:* Carlos Tejada, Associate Dean for Graduate Recruitment, 716-286-8769, Fax: 716-286-8170. Web site: http://www.niagara.edu/mba.

Nicholls State University, Graduate Studies, College of Business Administration, Thibodaux, LA 70310. Offers MBA. *Accreditation:* AACSB. Part-time and evening/weekend programs available. *Degree requirements:* For master's, thesis optional. *Entrance requirements:* For master's, GMAT. Additional exam requirements/recommendations for international students: Required—TOEFL (minimum score 550 paper-based; 213 computer-based). Electronic applications accepted.

Nichols College, Graduate Program in Business Administration, Dudley, MA 01571-5000. Offers business administration (MBA, MOL); security management (MBA); sport management (MBA). Part-time and evening/weekend programs available. Postbaccalaureate distance learning degree programs offered (no on-campus study). *Entrance requirements:* For master's, 2 letters of recommendation. Additional exam requirements/recommendations for international students: Required—TOEFL (minimum score 500 paper-based; 213 computer-based). Electronic applications accepted.

North Carolina Central University, Division of Academic Affairs, School of Business, Durham, NC 27707-3129. Offers MBA, JD/MBA. *Accreditation:* AACSB; ACBSP. Part-time and evening/weekend programs available. *Degree requirements:* For master's, thesis. *Entrance requirements:* For master's, GMAT. Additional exam requirements/recommendations for international students: Required—TOEFL. *Faculty research:* Small business issues, research of pedagogy, African business environment.

North Carolina State University, Graduate School, Poole College of Management, Program in Business Administration, Raleigh, NC 27695. Offers biosciences management (MBA); entrepreneurship and technology commercialization (MBA); financial management (MBA); innovation management (MBA); marketing management (MBA); services management (MBA); supply chain management (MBA). *Accreditation:* AACSB. Part-time programs available. *Degree requirements:* For master's, thesis optional. *Entrance requirements:* For master's, GMAT, interview, 3 letters of recommendation. Additional exam requirements/recommendations for international students: Required—TOEFL (minimum score 600 paper-based; 250 computer-based; 100 iBT). Electronic applications accepted. *Faculty research:* Manufacturing strategy, information systems, technology commercialization, managing research and development, historical stock returns.

See Display below and Close-Up on page 225.

North Central College, Graduate and Continuing Education Programs, Department of Business, Program in Business Administration, Naperville, IL 60566-7063. Offers change management (MBA); finance (MBA); human resource management (MBA); management (MBA); marketing (MBA). Part-time and evening/weekend programs available. *Faculty:* 14 full-time (4 women), 13 part-time/adjunct (3 women). *Students:* 41 full-time (15 women), 66 part-time (31 women); includes 19 minority (2 Black or African American, non-Hispanic/Latino; 1 American Indian or Alaska Native, non-Hispanic/Latino; 12 Asian, non-Hispanic/Latino; 4 Hispanic/Latino), 1 international. Average age 30. 116 applicants, 66% accepted, 50 enrolled. In 2011, 63 master's awarded. *Degree requirements:* For master's, thesis optional, project. *Entrance requirements:* For master's, interview. Additional exam requirements/recommendations for international students: Required—TOEFL (minimum score 577 paper-based; 233 computer-based; 90 iBT). *Application deadline:* For fall admission, 8/15 for domestic students; for winter admission, 12/1 for domestic students; for spring admission, 2/1 for domestic students. Application fee: $25. *Financial support:* In 2011–12, 8 students received support. Scholarships/grants available. Support available to part-time students. *Unit head:* Dr. Jean Clifton, MBA Program Coordinator, 630-637-5244, E-mail: jmclifton@noctrl.edu. *Application contact:* Wendy Kulpinski, Director of Graduate and Continuing Education Admission, 630-637-5808, Fax: 630-637-5844, E-mail: wekulpinski@noctrl.edu.

North Central College, Graduate and Continuing Education Programs, Program in Leadership Studies, Naperville, IL 60566-7063. Offers higher education leadership (MLS); professional leadership (MLS); social entrepreneurship (MLS); sports leadership (MLS). Part-time and evening/weekend programs available. *Faculty:* 9 full-time (1 woman), 11 part-time/adjunct (5 women). *Students:* 44 full-time (28 women), 32 part-time (20 women); includes 16 minority (9 Black or African American, non-Hispanic/Latino; 6 Hispanic/Latino; 1 Two or more races, non-Hispanic/Latino), 1 international. Average age 29. 69 applicants, 74% accepted, 32 enrolled. In 2011, 20 master's awarded. *Degree requirements:* For master's, thesis optional, project. *Entrance requirements:* For master's, interview. Additional exam requirements/recommendations for international students: Required—TOEFL (minimum score 570 paper-based; 233 computer-based; 90 iBT). *Application deadline:* For fall admission, 8/15 for domestic students; for winter admission, 12/1 for domestic students; for spring admission, 2/1 for domestic students. Applications are processed on a rolling basis. Application fee: $25. *Expenses:* Contact institution. *Financial support:* In 2011–12, 1 student received support. Scholarships/grants available. Support available to part-time students. *Unit head:* Dr. Thomas Cavenagh, Program Coordinator, Leadership Studies, 630-637-5285. *Application contact:* Wendy Kulpinski, Director of Graduate and Continuing Education Admission, 630-637-5808, Fax: 630-637-5844, E-mail: wekulpinski@noctrl.edu.

Northcentral University, Graduate Studies, Prescott Valley, AZ 86314. Offers business (MBA, DBA, PhD, CAGS); education (M Ed, Ed D, PhD, CAGS); marriage and family therapy (MA, PhD); psychology (MA, PhD, CAGS). Evening/weekend programs available. Postbaccalaureate distance learning degree programs offered (no on-campus study). *Faculty:* 41 full-time (21 women), 615 part-time/adjunct (284 women). *Students:* 3,005 full-time (1,743 women), 6,198 part-time (3,248 women); includes 834 minority (577 Black or African American, non-Hispanic/Latino; 28 American Indian or Alaska Native, non-Hispanic/Latino; 81 Asian, non-Hispanic/Latino; 132 Hispanic/Latino; 16

Native Hawaiian or other Pacific Islander, non-Hispanic/Latino). Average age 44. In 2011, 367 master's, 150 doctorates, 33 other advanced degrees awarded. *Entrance requirements:* For master's, bachelor's degree from regionally-accredited institution, current resume; for doctorate and CAGS, master's degree from regionally-accredited university. Additional exam requirements/recommendations for international students: Required—TOEFL (minimum score 95 computer-based), IELTS (minimum score 7), Pearson Test of English (minimum score 60). *Application deadline:* Applications are processed on a rolling basis. Application fee: $75. *Expenses: Tuition:* Full-time $11,178. *Financial support:* Scholarships/grants available. *Unit head:* Dr. Clinton D. Gardner, President and Provost, 888-327-2877, Fax: 928-759-6381, E-mail: president@ncu.edu. *Application contact:* Marina Swedberg, Senior Director of Admissions, 480-253-3537, Fax: 928-515-5690, E-mail: swedberg@ncu.edu.

North Dakota State University, College of Graduate and Interdisciplinary Studies, College of Business, Fargo, ND 58108. Offers MBA. *Accreditation:* AACSB. Part-time and evening/weekend programs available. *Faculty:* 20 full-time (8 women). *Students:* 75 full-time (29 women), 32 part-time (11 women); includes 6 minority (2 Asian, non-Hispanic/Latino; 1 Hispanic/Latino; 3 Two or more races, non-Hispanic/Latino), 17 international. Average age 29. 56 applicants, 80% accepted, 26 enrolled. In 2011, 59 degrees awarded. *Entrance requirements:* For master's, GMAT. Additional exam requirements/recommendations for international students: Required—TOEFL (minimum score 550 paper-based; 213 computer-based; 79 iBT). *Application deadline:* For fall admission, 7/1 priority date for domestic students, 5/1 for international students; for spring admission, 11/15 for domestic students, 8/1 for international students. Applications are processed on a rolling basis. Application fee: $35. Electronic applications accepted. *Financial support:* In 2011–12, 14 students received support, including 13 research assistantships, 1 teaching assistantship; institutionally sponsored loans and tuition waivers (partial) also available. Support available to part-time students. Financial award application deadline: 5/15; financial award applicants required to submit FAFSA. *Faculty research:* Labor management, operations, international finance, agency, Internet marketing. *Unit head:* Dr. Ron Johnson, Dean, 701-231-8805. *Application contact:* Paul R. Brown, Director, 701-231-7681, Fax: 701-231-7508, E-mail: paul.brown@ndsu.edu. Web site: http://www.ndsu.nodak.edu/business/graduate_programs/.

Northeastern Illinois University, Graduate College, College of Business and Management, Chicago, IL 60625-4699. Offers accounting (MSA); finance (MBA); management (MBA); marketing (MBA). Part-time and evening/weekend programs available. *Degree requirements:* For master's, thesis optional. *Entrance requirements:* For master's, GMAT, minimum GPA of 2.75. Additional exam requirements/recommendations for international students: Required—TOEFL (minimum score 550 paper-based; 213 computer-based; 79 iBT). Electronic applications accepted. *Faculty research:* Perception of accountants and non-accountants toward future of the accounting industry, asynchronous learning outcomes, cost and efficiency of financial markets, impact of deregulation on airline industry, analysis of derivational instruments.

Northeastern State University, Graduate College, College of Business and Technology, Program in Business Administration, Tahlequah, OK 74464-2399. Offers MBA. *Accreditation:* ACBSP. Part-time and evening/weekend programs available. *Faculty:* 9 full-time (2 women). *Students:* 15 full-time (10 women), 85 part-time (41 women); includes 38 minority (7 Black or African American, non-Hispanic/Latino; 30 American Indian or Alaska Native, non-Hispanic/Latino; 1 Asian, non-Hispanic/Latino), 9 international. In 2011, 39 master's awarded. *Degree requirements:* For master's, comprehensive exam, thesis, business plan, oral exam. *Entrance requirements:* For master's, GMAT, minimum GPA of 2.5. Additional exam requirements/recommendations for international students: Required—TOEFL (minimum score 213 computer-based). *Application deadline:* For fall admission, 6/1 priority date for domestic students. Applications are processed on a rolling basis. Application fee: $0 ($25 for international students). Electronic applications accepted. *Financial support:* Teaching assistantships and Federal Work-Study available. Financial award application deadline: 3/1. *Unit head:* Dr. Sandra Edwards, Chair, 918-683-0400 Ext. 5219. *Application contact:* Margie Railey, Administrative Assistant, 918-456-5511 Ext. 2093, Fax: 918-458-2061, E-mail: railey@nsouk.edu.

Northeastern University, Graduate School of Business Administration, Boston, MA 02115-5096. Offers EMBA, MBA, MS, CAGS, JD/MBA, MBA/MSN, MS/MBA. *Accreditation:* AACSB. Part-time and evening/weekend programs available. Postbaccalaureate distance learning degree programs offered (no on-campus study). *Faculty:* 46 full-time, 5 part-time/adjunct. *Students:* 200 full-time (80 women), 483 part-time (174 women). 955 applicants, 43% accepted, 259 enrolled. In 2011, 285 master's awarded. *Entrance requirements:* For master's, GMAT, interview. Additional exam requirements/recommendations for international students: Required—TOEFL (minimum score 600 paper-based; 250 computer-based; 100 iBT). *Application deadline:* For fall admission, 11/30 for domestic and international students; for winter admission, 2/1 for domestic and international students; for spring admission, 4/15 for domestic students. Application fee: $100. Electronic applications accepted. *Expenses:* Contact institution. *Financial support:* Federal Work-Study, institutionally sponsored loans, and scholarships/grants available. Support available to part-time students. Financial award application deadline: 3/1; financial award applicants required to submit FAFSA. *Unit head:* Kate Klepper, Associate Dean, Graduate Business Programs, 617-373-5417, Fax: 617-373-8564, E-mail: k.klepper@neu.edu. *Application contact:* Evelyn Tate, Director, Graduate Admissions, 617-373-5992, Fax: 617-373-8564, E-mail: e.tate@neu.edu. Web site: http://www.cba.neu.edu/grad.

Northern Arizona University, Graduate College, NAU-Yuma, Master of Administration Program, Flagstaff , AZ 86011. Offers M Adm. Part-time programs available. Postbaccalaureate distance learning degree programs offered (no on-campus study). *Faculty:* 29 full-time (12 women). *Students:* 74 full-time (38 women), 360 part-time (192 women); includes 149 minority (20 Black or African American, non-Hispanic/Latino; 19 American Indian or Alaska Native, non-Hispanic/Latino; 10 Asian, non-Hispanic/Latino; 87 Hispanic/Latino; 2 Native Hawaiian or other Pacific Islander, non-Hispanic/Latino; 11 Two or more races, non-Hispanic/Latino), 1 international. Average age 25. 131 applicants, 95% accepted, 94 enrolled. In 2011, 156 degrees awarded. *Degree requirements:* For master's, projects. *Entrance requirements:* For master's, five years' related work experience, minimum GPA of 3.0. Additional exam requirements/recommendations for international students: Required—TOEFL (minimum score 550 paper-based; 213 computer-based; 80 iBT), IELTS (minimum score 7). *Application deadline:* For fall admission, 3/1 for international students; for spring admission, 9/15 for international students. Applications are processed on a rolling basis. Application fee: $65. Electronic applications accepted. *Expenses:* Tuition, state resident: full-time $7190; part-time $355 per credit hour. Tuition, nonresident: full-time $18,092; part-time $1005 per credit hour. *Required fees:* $818; $328 per semester. *Financial support:* Federal Work-Study and scholarships/grants available. Support available to part-time students. Financial award applicants required to submit FAFSA. *Unit head:* Dr. Alex Steenstra, Chair, 928-317-6083, E-mail: alex.steenstra@nau.edu. *Application contact:* Pam Torbico, Coordinator, 928-523-6694, E-mail: m.admin@nau.edu. Web site: http://extended.nau.edu/madmin/.

Northern Arizona University, Graduate College, The W. A. Franke College of Business, Flagstaff, AZ 86011. Offers MBA. *Accreditation:* AACSB. Part-time programs available. *Faculty:* 54 full-time (20 women). *Students:* 30 full-time (16 women), 1 (woman) part-time; includes 2 minority (1 Asian, non-Hispanic/Latino; 1 Hispanic/Latino), 1 international. Average age 32. 41 applicants, 85% accepted, 30 enrolled. In 2011, 24 degrees awarded. *Entrance requirements:* For master's, GMAT. Additional exam requirements/recommendations for international students: Required—TOEFL (minimum score 550 paper-based; 213 computer-based; 80 iBT), IELTS (minimum score 7). *Application deadline:* For fall admission, 5/15 priority date for domestic students, 3/1 for international students. Applications are processed on a rolling basis. Application fee: $65. Electronic applications accepted. *Expenses:* Contact institution. *Financial support:* In 2011–12, 6 research assistantships (averaging $9,479 per year) were awarded; Federal Work-Study, institutionally sponsored loans, scholarships/grants, health care benefits, tuition waivers (partial), and unspecified assistantships also available. Support available to part-time students. Financial award applicants required to submit FAFSA. *Faculty research:* Data processing applications for business situations and problems, accounting fraud, effects of sales tactics, self-efficacy and performance. *Unit head:* Dr. Eric Yordy, Associate Dean, 928-523-5633, Fax: 928-523-7331, E-mail: eric.yordy@nau.edu. *Application contact:* Katie Poindexter, Coordinator, 928-523-7342, Fax: 928-523-6559, E-mail: mba@nau.edu. Web site: http://www.nau.edu/franke/.

Northern Illinois University, Graduate School, College of Business, MBA Program, De Kalb, IL 60115-2854. Offers MBA. *Accreditation:* AACSB. Part-time and evening/weekend programs available. *Faculty:* 53 full-time (17 women), 3 part-time/adjunct (0 women). *Students:* 108 full-time (34 women), 460 part-time (149 women); includes 140 minority (32 Black or African American, non-Hispanic/Latino; 79 Asian, non-Hispanic/Latino; 27 Hispanic/Latino; 2 Two or more races, non-Hispanic/Latino), 28 international. Average age 31. 234 applicants, 71% accepted, 125 enrolled. In 2011, 189 master's awarded. *Degree requirements:* For master's, thesis optional, seminar. *Entrance requirements:* For master's, GMAT, minimum GPA of 2.75. Additional exam requirements/recommendations for international students: Required—TOEFL (minimum score 550 paper-based; 213 computer-based). *Application deadline:* For fall admission, 6/1 for domestic students, 5/1 for international students; for spring admission, 11/1 for domestic students, 10/1 for international students. Applications are processed on a rolling basis. Application fee: $40. Electronic applications accepted. *Financial support:* In 2011–12, 13 research assistantships with full tuition reimbursements, 1 teaching assistantship with full tuition reimbursement were awarded; fellowships with full tuition reimbursements, career-related internships or fieldwork, Federal Work-Study, scholarships/grants, tuition waivers (full), and unspecified assistantships also available. Support available to part-time students. Financial award applicants required to submit FAFSA. *Unit head:* Jeff Probhaker, Associate Dean of Graduate Affairs, 815-753-6176, E-mail: mba@niu.edu. *Application contact:* Office of Graduate Studies in Business, 815-753-6301. Web site: http://www.cob.niu.edu/mbaprograms/.

Northern Kentucky University, Office of Graduate Programs, College of Business, Program in Business Administration, Highland Heights, KY 41099. Offers business administration (MBA, Certificate); JD/MBA. *Accreditation:* AACSB. Part-time programs available. *Faculty:* 12 full-time (6 women), 3 part-time/adjunct (0 women). *Students:* 19 full-time (3 women), 121 part-time (50 women); includes 9 minority (3 Black or African American, non-Hispanic/Latino; 5 Asian, non-Hispanic/Latino; 1 Two or more races, non-Hispanic/Latino), 5 international. Average age 31. 85 applicants, 47% accepted, 28 enrolled. In 2011, 61 master's, 6 other advanced degrees awarded. *Degree requirements:* For master's, thesis optional. *Entrance requirements:* For master's, GMAT, minimum GPA of 2.5, resume, statement of purpose. Additional exam requirements/recommendations for international students: Required—TOEFL (minimum score 550 paper-based; 213 computer-based; 79 iBT); Recommended—IELTS (minimum score 6.5). *Application deadline:* For fall admission, 6/1 for domestic and international students. Applications are processed on a rolling basis. Application fee: $40. Electronic applications accepted. *Expenses:* Contact institution. *Financial support:* Unspecified assistantships available. Financial award applicants required to submit FAFSA. *Faculty research:* Strategic management, business analytics, managing and leading organizations, business ethics and culture, global business operations. *Unit head:* Dr. Doris Shaw, Associate Dean, 859-572-1321, Fax: 859-572-6177, E-mail: shawdor@nku.edu. *Application contact:* Diane Smith, Administrative Coordinator, 859-572-6657, Fax: 859-572-6177, E-mail: smithdi@nku.edu. Web site: http://cob.nku.edu/graduatedegrees/mba.html.

Northern Kentucky University, Office of Graduate Programs, College of Business, Program in Executive Leadership and Organizational Change, Highland Heights, KY 41099. Offers MS. Part-time and evening/weekend programs available. *Students:* 47 part-time (28 women); includes 6 minority (5 Black or African American, non-Hispanic/Latino; 1 Hispanic/Latino), 1 international. Average age 39. 36 applicants, 69% accepted, 25 enrolled. In 2011, 20 master's awarded. *Degree requirements:* For master's, field research project. *Entrance requirements:* For master's, minimum GPA of 2.5; essay on professional career objective; 3 letters of recommendation, 1 from a current organization; 3 years of professional or managerial work experience; full-time employment at time of entry. Additional exam requirements/recommendations for international students: Required—TOEFL (minimum score 600 paper-based; 213 computer-based; 79 iBT); Recommended—IELTS (minimum score 6.5). *Application deadline:* For fall admission, 6/15 for domestic students, 6/1 for international students. Applications are processed on a rolling basis. Application fee: $40. Electronic applications accepted. *Expenses:* Contact institution. *Financial support:* Unspecified assistantships available. Financial award applicants required to submit FAFSA. *Faculty research:* Leadership and development, organizational change, field research, team and conflict management, strategy development and systems thinking. *Unit head:* Dr. Kenneth Rhee, Program Director, 859-572-6310, Fax: 859-572-5150, E-mail: rhee@nku.edu. *Application contact:* Amberly Hurst-Nutini, Coordinator, 859-572-5947, Fax: 859-572-5150, E-mail: hurstam@nku.edu. Web site: http://cob.nku.edu/graduatedegrees/eloc.html.

North Georgia College & State University, Mike Cottrell School of Business, Dahlonega, GA 30597. Offers MBA. Part-time and evening/weekend programs available. *Faculty:* 5 full-time. *Students:* 28 part-time (5 women); includes 1 minority (Hispanic/Latino). Average age 31. 74 applicants, 20% accepted, 15 enrolled. In 2011, 22 master's awarded. *Entrance requirements:* For master's, GRE or GMAT, references, resume. Additional exam requirements/recommendations for international students: Required—TOEFL (minimum score 550 paper-based; 213 computer-based; 79 iBT), IELTS (minimum score 6.5). *Application deadline:* For fall admission, 4/1 priority date for domestic students, 4/1 for international students. Application fee: $40. Electronic applications accepted. *Expenses:* Tuition, state resident: full-time $3528; part-time $196 per credit hour. Tuition, nonresident: full-time $14,094; part-time $783 per credit hour. *Required fees:* $1718; $859 per semester. Tuition and fees vary according to course load, campus/location and program. *Financial support:* Unspecified assistantships available. Financial award applicants required to submit CSS PROFILE or FAFSA. *Faculty research:* Leadership development, psychological contract and cynicism, positive organizational behavior, service quality, economic opportunity cost, mood and likeability, proactive socialization, attitudes, perceived technology policy, task significance in teams. *Unit head:* Prof. Kelli Crickey, Program Director, 770-7816752,

Business Administration and Management—General

Fax: 770-205-5449, E-mail: kcrickey@northgeorgia.edu. *Application contact:* Susan L. Perry, Graduate Admissions Coordinator, 706-864-1543, Fax: 706-867-2795, E-mail: slperry@northgeorgia.edu. Web site: http://www.northgeorgia.edu/Graduate_Admissions/Degree_Programs/Graduate_Programs.aspx.

North Park University, School of Business and Nonprofit Management, Chicago, IL 60625-4895. Offers MBA, MHEA, MHRM, MM, MNA. Part-time and evening/weekend programs available. Postbaccalaureate distance learning degree programs offered (no on-campus study). *Entrance requirements:* For master's, GMAT, GRE. Additional exam requirements/recommendations for international students: Required—TOEFL. *Expenses:* Contact institution.

Northwest Christian University, School of Business and Management, Eugene, OR 97401-3745. Offers MBA. Part-time and evening/weekend programs available. *Degree requirements:* For master's, thesis. *Entrance requirements:* For master's, GMAT, GRE, MAT, interview, minimum undergraduate GPA of 3.0. Electronic applications accepted.

Northwestern Polytechnic University, School of Business and Information Technology, Fremont, CA 94539-7482. Offers MBA. Part-time and evening/weekend programs available. *Degree requirements:* For master's, thesis optional. *Entrance requirements:* For master's, GMAT, minimum GPA of 3.0. Additional exam requirements/recommendations for international students: Required—TOEFL (minimum score 550 paper-based; 213 computer-based; 79 iBT). *Expenses:* Contact institution. *Faculty research:* Entrepreneurship, accounting, information technology.

Northwestern University, The Graduate School, Kellogg School of Management, MBA Programs, Evanston, IL 60208. Offers MBA, JD/MBA. *Accreditation:* CAHME (one or more programs are accredited). Part-time and evening/weekend programs available. *Faculty:* 182 full-time, 103 part-time/adjunct. *Students:* 1,113 full-time, 1,065 part-time. Average age 28. 4,974 applicants, 20% accepted, 550 enrolled. In 2011, 558 master's awarded. *Entrance requirements:* For master's, GMAT, GRE, interview, 2 letters of recommendation, college transcripts, resume, essays. Additional exam requirements/recommendations for international students: Required—TOEFL. Application fee: $250. Electronic applications accepted. *Expenses:* Contact institution. *Financial support:* Fellowships, career-related internships or fieldwork, institutionally sponsored loans, and scholarships/grants available. Support available to part-time students. Financial award applicants required to submit FAFSA. *Unit head:* Sally Blount, Dean, 847-491-2840, E-mail: sallyblount@kellogg.northwestern.edu. *Application contact:* Kate Smith, Assistant Dean, Admissions and Financial Aid, 847-491-3308, Fax: 847-491-4960, E-mail: mbaadmissions@kellogg.northwestern.edu. Web site: http://www.kellogg.northwestern.edu/.

Northwestern University, McCormick School of Engineering and Applied Science, MMM Program, Evanston, IL 60208. Offers MBA/MEM. *Unit head:* Dr. Julio Ottino, Dean, 847-491-3558, Fax: 847-491-5220, E-mail: jm-ottino@northwestern.edu. *Application contact:* Dr. Bruce Alan Lindvall, Assistant Dean for Graduate Studies, 847-491-4547, Fax: 847-491-5341, E-mail: b-lindvall@northwestern.edu. Web site: http://www.mmm.northwestern.edu/.

Northwest Missouri State University, Graduate School, Melvin and Valorie Booth College of Business and Professional Studies, Program in Business Administration, Maryville, MO 64468-6001. Offers MBA. *Accreditation:* ACBSP. *Faculty:* 15 full-time (4 women). *Students:* 28 full-time (14 women), 72 part-time (36 women); includes 6 minority (1 Black or African American, non-Hispanic/Latino; 1 American Indian or Alaska Native, non-Hispanic/Latino; 2 Asian, non-Hispanic/Latino; 2 Two or more races, non-Hispanic/Latino), 4 international. 44 applicants, 93% accepted, 31 enrolled. In 2011, 73 master's awarded. *Degree requirements:* For master's, comprehensive exam. *Entrance requirements:* For master's, GMAT/GRE, minimum GPA of 2.5. Additional exam requirements/recommendations for international students: Required—TOEFL (minimum score 550 paper-based; 213 computer-based). *Application deadline:* For fall admission, 7/1 for domestic and international students; for spring admission, 12/1 for domestic students, 11/15 for international students. Applications are processed on a rolling basis. Application fee: $0 ($50 for international students). Electronic applications accepted. *Financial support:* In 2011–12, 5 research assistantships with full tuition reimbursements (averaging $6,000 per year), 6 teaching assistantships with full tuition reimbursements (averaging $6,000 per year) were awarded; unspecified assistantships also available. Financial award application deadline: 4/1; financial award applicants required to submit FAFSA. *Unit head:* Dr. Mark Jelavich, Head, 660-562-1763. *Application contact:* Dr. Gregory Haddock, Dean of Graduate School, 660-562-1145, Fax: 660-562-1096, E-mail: gradsch@nwmissouri.edu.

Northwest Nazarene University, Graduate Studies, Program in Business Administration, Nampa, ID 83686-5897. Offers business administration (MBA); business administration-health care (MBA). *Accreditation:* ACBSP. Part-time and evening/weekend programs available. Postbaccalaureate distance learning degree programs offered (no on-campus study). *Faculty:* 15 full-time (5 women), 23 part-time/adjunct (8 women). *Students:* 79 full-time (36 women), 26 part-time (11 women); includes 10 minority (3 Asian, non-Hispanic/Latino; 6 Hispanic/Latino; 1 Two or more races, non-Hispanic/Latino), 5 international. Average age 34. 13 applicants, 54% accepted, 7 enrolled. In 2011, 39 master's awarded. *Entrance requirements:* For master's, GMAT, minimum GPA of 3.0. *Application deadline:* Applications are processed on a rolling basis. Application fee: $40. Electronic applications accepted. *Expenses:* Contact institution. *Unit head:* Dr. Brenda Johnson, Director, 208-467-8415, Fax: 208-467-8440, E-mail: mba@nnu.edu. *Application contact:* Maureen Matlock, MBA Program Coordinator, 208-467-8123, Fax: 208-467-8440, E-mail: nnu-mba@nnu.edu. Web site: http://nnu.edu/mba.

Northwest University, School of Business and Management, Kirkland, WA 98033. Offers business administration (MBA); social entrepreneurship (MA). Part-time and evening/weekend programs available. *Faculty:* 6 full-time (1 woman), 7 part-time/adjunct (3 women). *Students:* 41 full-time (20 women), 3 part-time (1 woman); includes 10 minority (5 Black or African American, non-Hispanic/Latino; 3 Asian, non-Hispanic/Latino; 2 Hispanic/Latino), 9 international. Average age 34. 21 applicants, 86% accepted, 18 enrolled. In 2011, 2 master's awarded. *Degree requirements:* For master's, formalized research. *Entrance requirements:* For master's, GMAT. Additional exam requirements/recommendations for international students: Required—TOEFL (minimum score 550 paper-based; 237 computer-based; 75 iBT). *Application deadline:* For fall admission, 8/1 for domestic and international students; for spring admission, 12/1 for domestic and international students. Application fee: $75. Electronic applications accepted. *Expenses:* Contact institution. *Financial support:* Federal Work-Study, scholarships/grants, health care benefits, and tuition waivers (full and partial) available. Financial award applicants required to submit FAFSA. *Unit head:* Dr. Teresa Gillespie, Dean, 425-889-5290, E-mail: teresa.gillespie@northwestu.edu. *Application contact:* Aaron Oosterwyk, Director of Graduate and Professional Studies Enrollment, 425-889-7792, Fax: 425-803-3059, E-mail: aaron.oosterwyk@northwestu.edu. Web site: http://www.northwestu.edu/business/.

Northwood University, Michigan Campus, Richard DeVos Graduate School of Management, Midland, MI 48640-2398. Offers EMBA, MBA, MMBA. Part-time and evening/weekend programs available. *Degree requirements:* For master's, capstone project. *Entrance requirements:* For master's, GMAT, interview, letters of recommendation, resume. Additional exam requirements/recommendations for international students: Required—TOEFL (minimum score 550 paper-based; 213 computer-based). Electronic applications accepted.

Norwich University, College of Graduate and Continuing Studies, Master of Business Administration Program, Northfield, VT 05663. Offers finance (MBA); organizational leadership (MBA); project management (MBA). *Accreditation:* ACBSP. Evening/weekend programs available. *Faculty:* 19 part-time/adjunct (5 women). *Students:* 100 full-time (34 women); includes 16 minority (4 Black or African American, non-Hispanic/Latino; 1 American Indian or Alaska Native, non-Hispanic/Latino; 5 Asian, non-Hispanic/Latino; 4 Hispanic/Latino; 2 Two or more races, non-Hispanic/Latino). Average age 36. 67 applicants, 69% accepted, 46 enrolled. In 2011, 103 master's awarded. *Degree requirements:* For master's, comprehensive exam (for some programs), thesis optional. *Entrance requirements:* For master's, minimum undergraduate GPA of 2.75. Additional exam requirements/recommendations for international students: Required—TOEFL (minimum score 550 paper-based; 213 computer-based; 83 iBT). *Application deadline:* For fall admission, 8/10 for domestic and international students; for winter admission, 11/7 for domestic and international students; for spring admission, 2/6 for domestic and international students. Applications are processed on a rolling basis. Application fee: $50. Electronic applications accepted. *Expenses: Tuition:* Full-time $16,174. *Required fees:* $2130. Full-time tuition and fees vary according to program. *Financial support:* In 2011–12, 58 students received support. Scholarships/grants available. Financial award applicants required to submit FAFSA. *Unit head:* Dr. Jose Cordova, Faculty Director, 802-485-2567, Fax: 802-485-2533, E-mail: jcordova@norwich.edu. *Application contact:* Kerri Murnyack, Associate Program Director, 802-485-3304, Fax: 802-485-2533, E-mail: kmurnyuac@norwich.edu. Web site: http://mba.norwich.edu.

Notre Dame de Namur University, Division of Academic Affairs, School of Business and Management, Department of Business Administration, Belmont, CA 94002-1908. Offers business administration (MBA); finance (MBA); human resource management (MBA); marketing (MBA). Part-time and evening/weekend programs available. *Faculty:* 7 full-time (1 woman), 6 part-time/adjunct (0 women). *Students:* 42 full-time (16 women), 104 part-time (67 women); includes 56 minority (6 Black or African American, non-Hispanic/Latino; 26 Asian, non-Hispanic/Latino; 20 Hispanic/Latino; 2 Native Hawaiian or other Pacific Islander, non-Hispanic/Latino; 2 Two or more races, non-Hispanic/Latino), 23 international. Average age 34. 167 applicants, 40% accepted, 39 enrolled. In 2011, 33 degrees awarded. *Entrance requirements:* For master's, minimum GPA of 2.5. Additional exam requirements/recommendations for international students: Required—TOEFL (minimum score 550 paper-based; 213 computer-based; 79 iBT). *Application deadline:* For fall admission, 8/1 priority date for domestic students; for spring admission, 12/1 priority date for domestic students. Applications are processed on a rolling basis. Application fee: $60. Electronic applications accepted. *Expenses: Tuition:* Full-time $14,220; part-time $790 per credit. *Required fees:* $35 per semester. Tuition and fees vary according to program. *Financial support:* Available to part-time students. Applicants required to submit FAFSA. *Unit head:* Jordan Holtzman, Director, 650-508-3637, E-mail: jholtzman@ndnu.edu. *Application contact:* Candace Hallmark, Associate Director of Admissions, 650-508-3600, Fax: 650-508-3426, E-mail: grad.admit@ndnu.edu. Web site: http://www.ndnu.edu/academics/schools-programs/school-business/.

Notre Dame de Namur University, Division of Academic Affairs, School of Business and Management, Department of Management, Belmont, CA 94002-1908. Offers MSM. Part-time and evening/weekend programs available. Postbaccalaureate distance learning degree programs offered (no on-campus study). *Faculty:* 3 full-time (1 woman), 3 part-time/adjunct (1 woman). *Students:* 3 full-time (0 women), 19 part-time (10 women); includes 6 minority (1 Black or African American, non-Hispanic/Latino; 4 Asian, non-Hispanic/Latino; 1 Hispanic/Latino), 5 international. Average age 34. 16 applicants, 63% accepted, 6 enrolled. In 2011, 8 master's awarded. *Entrance requirements:* For master's, minimum GPA of 2.5. Additional exam requirements/recommendations for international students: Required—TOEFL (minimum score 550 paper-based; 213 computer-based). *Application deadline:* For fall admission, 8/1 priority date for domestic students; for spring admission, 12/1 priority date for domestic students. Applications are processed on a rolling basis. Application fee: $60. Electronic applications accepted. *Expenses: Tuition:* Full-time $14,220; part-time $790 per credit. *Required fees:* $35 per semester. Tuition and fees vary according to program. *Financial support:* Available to part-time students. Applicants required to submit FAFSA. *Unit head:* Jordan Holtzman, Director, 650-508-3637, E-mail: jholtzman@ndnu.edu. *Application contact:* Candace Hallmark, Associate Director of Admissions, 650-508-3600, Fax: 650-508-3426, E-mail: grad.admit@ndnu.edu.

Notre Dame of Maryland University, Graduate Studies, Program in Management, Baltimore, MD 21210-2476. Offers MA. Part-time and evening/weekend programs available. *Degree requirements:* For master's, thesis optional. *Entrance requirements:* For master's, minimum GPA of 3.0. Additional exam requirements/recommendations for international students: Required—TOEFL (minimum score 500 paper-based; 173 computer-based; 61 iBT). Electronic applications accepted.

Nova Southeastern University, H. Wayne Huizenga School of Business and Entrepreneurship, Fort Lauderdale, FL 33314-7796. Offers accounting (M Acc); business administration (MBA, DBA); human resource management (MSHRM); international business administration (MIBA); leadership (MS); public administration (MPA, DPA); real estate development (MS); taxation (M Tax); JD/MBA; Pharm D/MBA. Part-time and evening/weekend programs available. Postbaccalaureate distance learning degree programs offered (minimal on-campus study). *Students:* 229 full-time (112 women), 3,506 part-time (2,109 women); includes 2,506 minority (1,256 Black or African American, non-Hispanic/Latino; 8 American Indian or Alaska Native, non-Hispanic/Latino; 146 Asian, non-Hispanic/Latino; 1,058 Hispanic/Latino; 4 Native Hawaiian or other Pacific Islander, non-Hispanic/Latino; 34 Two or more races, non-Hispanic/Latino), 174 international. Average age 33. In 2011, 1,252 master's, 17 doctorates awarded. *Degree requirements:* For master's, thesis optional; for doctorate, comprehensive exam, thesis/dissertation. *Entrance requirements:* For doctorate, GMAT. Additional exam requirements/recommendations for international students: Required—TOEFL (minimum score 550 paper-based; 213 computer-based; 79 iBT), IELTS (minimum score 6). *Application deadline:* Applications are processed on a rolling basis. Application fee: $50. Electronic applications accepted. *Financial support:* In 2011–12, 2 students received support. Federal Work-Study and scholarships/grants available. Support available to part-time students. Financial award applicants required to submit FAFSA. *Faculty research:* Reputation management, call centers, international social capital, corporate earnings guidance, corporate governance. *Unit head:* Dr. D. Michael Fields, Dean, 954-262-5005, E-mail: fieldsm@nova.edu. *Application contact:* Karen Goldberg, Associate Director of Recruitment and Special Events, 954-262-5039, Fax: 954-262-3822, E-mail: karen@nova.edu. Web site: http://www.huizenga.nova.edu.

Nyack College, School of Business and Leadership, Nyack, NY 10960-3698. Offers business administration (MBA); organizational leadership (MS). Evening/weekend programs available. *Students:* 114 full-time (73 women), 60 part-time (44 women); includes 140 minority (108 Black or African American, non-Hispanic/Latino; 3 Asian, non-Hispanic/Latino; 22 Hispanic/Latino; 7 Two or more races, non-Hispanic/Latino), 9 international. Average age 40. In 2011, 75 master's awarded. *Degree requirements:* For master's, thesis (for some programs). *Entrance requirements:* For master's, GMAT (for MBA only), transcripts, personal goals statement, recommendations, resume, interview. Additional exam requirements/recommendations for international students: Required—TOEFL (minimum score 550 paper-based; 220 computer-based; 83 iBT). *Application deadline:* Applications are processed on a rolling basis. Application fee: $50. Electronic applications accepted. *Expenses:* Contact institution. *Financial support:* Applicants required to submit FAFSA. *Unit head:* Dr. Anita Underwood, Dean, 845-675-4511, Fax: 845-353-5812. *Application contact:* Traci Piescki, Director of Admissions, 800-541-6891, Fax: 845-348-3912, E-mail: admissions.grad@nyack.edu. Web site: http://www.nyack.edu/sbl.

Oakland City University, School of Business, Oakland City, IN 47660-1099. Offers MBA. Part-time and evening/weekend programs available. *Faculty:* 23 part-time/adjunct (2 women). *Students:* 40 part-time (14 women); includes 8 minority (7 Black or African American, non-Hispanic/Latino; 1 Two or more races, non-Hispanic/Latino). Average age 35. 23 applicants, 87% accepted, 18 enrolled. In 2011, 44 master's awarded. *Degree requirements:* For master's, thesis or alternative. *Entrance requirements:* For master's, GMAT, GRE, or MAT, appropriate bachelor's degree, computer literacy. Additional exam requirements/recommendations for international students: Required—TOEFL. *Application deadline:* Applications are processed on a rolling basis. Application fee: $35. *Financial support:* Institutionally sponsored loans available. Financial award application deadline: 3/10; financial award applicants required to submit FAFSA. *Faculty research:* Leadership and management styles, international business, new technologies. *Unit head:* Dr. Michael Burch, Dean, 812-749-1272, Fax: 812-749-1511, E-mail: mburch@oak.edu. *Application contact:* Kim Heldt, Director of Admissions, 812-749-1218, E-mail: kheldt@oak.edu. Web site: http://www.oak.edu/academics/school-business.php.

Oakland University, Graduate Study and Lifelong Learning, School of Business Administration, Rochester, MI 48309-4401. Offers M Acc, MBA, MS, Certificate. *Accreditation:* AACSB. Part-time and evening/weekend programs available. *Entrance requirements:* For master's, GMAT, minimum GPA of 3.0 for unconditional admission. Additional exam requirements/recommendations for international students: Required—TOEFL (minimum score 550 paper-based; 213 computer-based). Electronic applications accepted. *Expenses:* Contact institution. *Faculty research:* Rotor manufacturing induced anomaly database, Globalization Challenges project.

Oglala Lakota College, Graduate Studies, Program in Lakota Leadership and Management, Kyle, SD 57752-0490. Offers MA. Part-time and evening/weekend programs available. *Degree requirements:* For master's, thesis. *Entrance requirements:* For master's, minimum GPA of 2.5. *Faculty research:* Curriculum, values, retention of administrators, behavior, graduate follow-up.

Ohio Dominican University, Graduate Programs, Division of Business, Columbus, OH 43219-2099. Offers MBA, MS. Program also offered in Dayton, OH. *Accreditation:* ACBSP. Part-time and evening/weekend programs available. Postbaccalaureate distance learning degree programs offered (no on-campus study). *Degree requirements:* For master's, thesis or alternative. *Entrance requirements:* For master's, minimum GPA of 3.0, 3 letters of recommendation. Additional exam requirements/recommendations for international students: Required—TOEFL (minimum score 550 paper-based; 213 computer-based), IELTS (minimum score 6.5).

The Ohio State University, Graduate School, Max M. Fisher College of Business, Program in Business Administration, Columbus, OH 43210. Offers MA, MBA, PhD. *Accreditation:* AACSB. *Students:* 390 full-time (101 women), 242 part-time (60 women); includes 100 minority (22 Black or African American, non-Hispanic/Latino; 1 American Indian or Alaska Native, non-Hispanic/Latino; 57 Asian, non-Hispanic/Latino; 13 Hispanic/Latino; 7 Two or more races, non-Hispanic/Latino), 125 international. Average age 32. In 2011, 312 master's, 5 doctorates awarded. *Degree requirements:* For doctorate, thesis/dissertation. *Entrance requirements:* For master's and doctorate, GMAT. Additional exam requirements/recommendations for international students: Required—TOEFL (minimum score 600 paper-based; 250 computer-based), Michigan English Language Assessment Battery (minimum score 82). *Application deadline:* For fall admission, 8/15 priority date for domestic students, 7/1 for international students; for winter admission, 12/1 priority date for domestic students, 11/1 for international students; for spring admission, 3/1 priority date for domestic students, 2/1 for international students. Applications are processed on a rolling basis. Application fee: $40 ($50 for international students). Electronic applications accepted. *Expenses:* Tuition, state resident: full-time $11,400. Tuition, nonresident: full-time $28,125. Tuition and fees vary according to course load, degree level, campus/location and program. *Financial support:* Fellowships, research assistantships, teaching assistantships, Federal Work-Study, institutionally sponsored loans, and unspecified assistantships available. Support available to part-time students. *Unit head:* Ingrid Werner, Chair, 614-292-6460, Fax: 614-292-9006, E-mail: werner.47@osu.edu. *Application contact:* Graduate Admissions, 614-292-6031, Fax: 614-292-3656, E-mail: gradadmissions@osu.edu. Web site: http://fisher.osu.edu/ftmba.

The Ohio State University, Graduate School, Max M. Fisher College of Business, Program in Business Logistics Engineering, Columbus, OH 43210. Offers MBLE. *Faculty:* 16. *Students:* 47 full-time (22 women), 19 part-time (12 women); includes 1 minority (Asian, non-Hispanic/Latino), 63 international. Average age 24. In 2011, 29 master's awarded. *Entrance requirements:* For master's, GRE or GMAT. Additional exam requirements/recommendations for international students: Required—TOEFL (minimum score 550 paper-based; 79 iBT), Michigan English Language Assessment Battery (minimum score 82). *Application deadline:* Applications are processed on a rolling basis. Application fee: $40 ($50 for international students). Electronic applications accepted. *Expenses:* Tuition, state resident: full-time $11,400. Tuition, nonresident: full-time $28,125. Tuition and fees vary according to course load, degree level, campus/location and program. *Unit head:* Walter Zinn, Chair, 614-292-0797, E-mail: zinn.13@osu.edu. *Application contact:* Graduate Admissions, 614-292-6031, Fax: 614-292-3656, E-mail: gradadmissions@osu.edu. Web site: http://fisher.osu.edu/mble.

Ohio University, Graduate College, College of Business, Program in Business Administration, Athens, OH 45701-2979. Offers MBA. *Accreditation:* AACSB. Part-time and evening/weekend programs available. *Students:* 140 full-time (35 women), 2 part-time (1 woman); includes 21 minority (9 Black or African American, non-Hispanic/Latino; 5 Asian, non-Hispanic/Latino; 4 Hispanic/Latino; 3 Two or more races, non-Hispanic/Latino), 4 international. 125 applicants, 50% accepted, 45 enrolled. In 2011, 92 master's awarded. *Entrance requirements:* For master's, GMAT (minimum score 500), minimum GPA of 3.0. Additional exam requirements/recommendations for international students: Required—TOEFL (minimum score 600 paper-based; 250 computer-based). *Application deadline:* For fall admission, 2/1 priority date for domestic students, 1/15 for international students. Applications are processed on a rolling basis. Application fee: $50 ($55 for international students). Electronic applications accepted. *Expenses:* Contact institution. *Financial support:* In 2011–12, 20 research assistantships with full and partial tuition reimbursements (averaging $8,000 per year) were awarded; career-related internships or fieldwork and institutionally sponsored loans also available. Financial award application deadline: 2/1. *Unit head:* Dr. Hugh Sherman, Dean, 740-593-2001, Fax: 740-593-1388, E-mail: shermanh@ohio.edu. *Application contact:* Dr. Edward B. Yost, Assistant Dean, 740-593-2085, Fax: 740-593-0319, E-mail: yost@ohio.edu. Web site: http://www.cba.ohiou.edu/grad/mba.asp.

Oklahoma City University, Meinders School of Business, Program in Business Administration, Oklahoma City, OK 73106-1402. Offers finance (MBA); health administration (MBA); information technology (MBA); integrated marketing communications (MBA); international business (MBA); marketing (MBA); JD/MBA. *Accreditation:* ACBSP. Part-time and evening/weekend programs available. *Faculty:* 15 full-time (6 women), 14 part-time/adjunct (6 women). *Students:* 136 full-time (59 women), 112 part-time (34 women); includes 38 minority (14 Black or African American, non-Hispanic/Latino; 4 American Indian or Alaska Native, non-Hispanic/Latino; 11 Asian, non-Hispanic/Latino; 3 Hispanic/Latino; 6 Two or more races, non-Hispanic/Latino), 100 international. Average age 30. 252 applicants, 83% accepted, 30 enrolled. In 2011, 148 master's awarded. *Degree requirements:* For master's, comprehensive exam. *Entrance requirements:* For master's, GRE or GMAT. Additional exam requirements/recommendations for international students: Required—TOEFL (minimum score 560 paper-based; 220 computer-based; 83 iBT). *Application deadline:* Applications are processed on a rolling basis. Application fee: $50 ($70 for international students). Electronic applications accepted. *Expenses:* *Tuition:* Full-time $16,848; part-time $936 per credit hour. *Required fees:* $2070; $115 per credit hour. One-time fee: $300. *Financial support:* Career-related internships or fieldwork, Federal Work-Study, institutionally sponsored loans, and tuition waivers (partial) available. Support available to part-time students. Financial award application deadline: 6/1; financial award applicants required to submit FAFSA. *Faculty research:* Management information systems, international business strategies. *Unit head:* Dr. Steven Agee, Dean, 405-208-5130, Fax: 405-208-5098, E-mail: sagee@okcu.edu. *Application contact:* Michelle Cook, Director, Graduate Admissions, 800-633-7242, Fax: 405-208-5916, E-mail: gadmissions@okcu.edu. Web site: http://msb.okcu.edu/graduate/.

Oklahoma City University, Petree College of Arts and Sciences, Program in Liberal Arts, Oklahoma City, OK 73106-1402. Offers art (MLA); general studies (MLA); leadership/management (MLA); literature (MLA); mass communications (MLA); philosophy (MLA); writing (MLA). Part-time and evening/weekend programs available. *Faculty:* 9 full-time (5 women), 4 part-time/adjunct (0 women). *Students:* 15 full-time (6 women), 13 part-time (8 women); includes 7 minority (5 Black or African American, non-Hispanic/Latino; 1 American Indian or Alaska Native, non-Hispanic/Latino; 1 Asian, non-Hispanic/Latino), 10 international. Average age 35. 7 applicants, 86% accepted, 2 enrolled. In 2011, 22 master's awarded. *Degree requirements:* For master's, comprehensive exam, thesis optional. *Entrance requirements:* Additional exam requirements/recommendations for international students: Required—TOEFL (minimum score 550 paper-based). *Application deadline:* Applications are processed on a rolling basis. Application fee: $50 ($70 for international students). *Expenses:* *Tuition:* Full-time $16,848; part-time $936 per credit hour. *Required fees:* $2070; $115 per credit hour. One-time fee: $300. *Financial support:* Career-related internships or fieldwork and Federal Work-Study available. Support available to part-time students. Financial award application deadline: 6/1; financial award applicants required to submit FAFSA. *Unit head:* Dr. Regina Bennett, Director, 405-208-5207, Fax: 405-208-5451, E-mail: rbennett@okcu.edu. *Application contact:* Michelle Cook, Director, Admissions, 800-633-7242, Fax: 405-208-5916, E-mail: gadmissions@okcu.edu. Web site: http://www.okcu.edu/mla.

Oklahoma State University, Spears School of Business, Department of Management, Stillwater, OK 74078. Offers MBA, MS, PhD. Part-time programs available. *Faculty:* 23 full-time (7 women), 9 part-time/adjunct (5 women). *Students:* 7 full-time (2 women), 4 part-time (0 women), 5 international. Average age 31. In 2011, 1 degree awarded. *Degree requirements:* For master's, thesis or alternative; for doctorate, comprehensive exam, thesis/dissertation. *Entrance requirements:* For master's and doctorate, GRE or GMAT. Additional exam requirements/recommendations for international students: Required—TOEFL (minimum score 550 paper-based; 79 iBT). *Application deadline:* For fall admission, 3/1 for international students; for spring admission, 8/1 for international students. Applications are processed on a rolling basis. Application fee: $40 ($75 for international students). Electronic applications accepted. *Expenses:* Tuition, state resident: full-time $4044; part-time $168.50 per credit hour. Tuition, nonresident: full-time $16,008; part-time $667 per credit hour. *Required fees:* $2122; $88.45 per credit hour. One-time fee: $50. Tuition and fees vary according to course load and campus/location. *Financial support:* In 2011–12, 9 research assistantships (averaging $17,929 per year), 2 teaching assistantships (averaging $24,720 per year) were awarded; career-related internships or fieldwork, Federal Work-Study, scholarships/grants, health care benefits, tuition waivers (partial), and unspecified assistantships also available. Support available to part-time students. Financial award application deadline: 3/1; financial award applicants required to submit FAFSA. *Faculty research:* Telecommunications management, innovative decision support techniques, knowledge networking, organizational research methods, strategic planning. *Unit head:* Dr. Kenneth Eastman, Head, 405-744-5201, Fax: 405-744-5180. *Application contact:* Dr. Sheryl Emslie, Dean, 405-744-6368, Fax: 405-744-0355, E-mail: grad-i@okstate.edu. Web site: http://spears.okstate.edu/management.

Oklahoma State University, Spears School of Business, Programs in Business Administration, Stillwater, OK 74078. Offers MBA, PhD. *Accreditation:* AACSB. Part-time programs available. Postbaccalaureate distance learning degree programs offered. *Faculty:* 3 full-time (0 women). *Students:* 166 full-time (57 women), 415 part-time (101 women); includes 84 minority (10 Black or African American, non-Hispanic/Latino; 20 American Indian or Alaska Native, non-Hispanic/Latino; 12 Asian, non-Hispanic/Latino; 24 Hispanic/Latino; 18 Two or more races, non-Hispanic/Latino), 31 international. Average age 29. 737 applicants, 31% accepted, 183 enrolled. In 2011, 157 master's awarded. *Degree requirements:* For master's, thesis or alternative; for doctorate, comprehensive exam, thesis/dissertation. *Entrance requirements:* For master's and doctorate, GMAT. Additional exam requirements/recommendations for international students: Required—TOEFL (minimum score 550 paper-based; 79 iBT). *Application deadline:* For fall admission, 3/1 for international students; for spring admission, 8/1 for international students. Applications are processed on a rolling basis. Application fee: $40 ($75 for international students). Electronic applications accepted. *Expenses:* Tuition, state resident: full-time $4044; part-time $168.50 per credit hour. Tuition, nonresident: full-time $16,008; part-time $667 per credit hour. *Required fees:* $2122; $88.45 per credit hour. One-time fee: $50. Tuition and fees vary according to course load and campus/location. *Financial support:* Career-related internships or fieldwork, Federal Work-Study, scholarships/grants, health care benefits, tuition waivers, and unspecified assistantships available. Support available to part-time students. Financial award application deadline: 3/1; financial award applicants required to submit FAFSA. *Unit head:* Dr. Larry Crosby, Dean, 405-744-5075. *Application contact:* Jan Analla, Assistant Director, 405-744-2951. Web site: http://spears.okstate.edu/graduate/mba/.

Old Dominion University, College of Business and Public Administration, Doctoral Program in Business Administration, Norfolk, VA 23529. Offers finance (PhD); information technology (PhD); marketing (PhD); strategic management (PhD). *Accreditation:* AACSB. *Faculty:* 21 full-time (2 women). *Students:* 51 full-time (17 women); includes 5 minority (3 Black or African American, non-Hispanic/Latino; 1 Asian, non-Hispanic/Latino; 1 Native Hawaiian or other Pacific Islander, non-Hispanic/Latino),

29 international. Average age 35. 47 applicants, 60% accepted, 12 enrolled. In 2011, 7 doctorates awarded. *Degree requirements:* For doctorate, comprehensive exam, thesis/dissertation. *Entrance requirements:* For doctorate, GMAT. Additional exam requirements/recommendations for international students: Required—TOEFL (minimum score 550 paper-based; 213 computer-based; 79 iBT). *Application deadline:* For fall admission, 4/1 priority date for domestic students, 4/1 for international students. Application fee: $50. Electronic applications accepted. *Expenses:* Tuition, state resident: full-time $9096; part-time $379 per credit. Tuition, nonresident: full-time $23,064; part-time $961 per credit. *Required fees:* $127 per semester. One-time fee: $50. *Financial support:* In 2011–12, 27 students received support, including 2 fellowships with full tuition reimbursements available (averaging $7,500 per year), 32 research assistantships with full tuition reimbursements available (averaging $7,500 per year), 12 teaching assistantships with full tuition reimbursements available (averaging $7,500 per year); scholarships/grants and unspecified assistantships also available. Financial award application deadline: 4/1; financial award applicants required to submit FAFSA. *Faculty research:* International business, buyer behavior, financial markets, strategy, operations research. *Unit head:* Dr. John B. Ford, Graduate Program Director, 757-683-3587, Fax: 757-683-4076, E-mail: jford@odu.edu. *Application contact:* Katrina Davenport, Program Coordinator, 757-683-5138, Fax: 757-683-4076, E-mail: kdavenpo@odu.edu. Web site: http://bpa.odu.edu/bpa/academics/baphd.shtml.

Old Dominion University, College of Business and Public Administration, MBA Program, Norfolk, VA 23529. Offers business and economic forecasting (MBA); financial analysis and valuation (MBA); information technology and enterprise integration (MBA); international business (MBA); maritime and port management (MBA); public administration (MBA). *Accreditation:* AACSB. Part-time and evening/weekend programs available. *Faculty:* 66 full-time (15 women), 6 part-time/adjunct (1 woman). *Students:* 69 full-time (21 women), 230 part-time (85 women); includes 49 minority (22 Black or African American, non-Hispanic/Latino; 1 American Indian or Alaska Native, non-Hispanic/Latino; 10 Asian, non-Hispanic/Latino; 3 Hispanic/Latino; 1 Native Hawaiian or other Pacific Islander, non-Hispanic/Latino; 12 Two or more races, non-Hispanic/Latino), 19 international. Average age 31. 177 applicants, 43% accepted, 53 enrolled. In 2011, 115 master's awarded. *Entrance requirements:* For master's, GMAT, GRE, letter of reference, resume, coursework in calculus, essay. Additional exam requirements/recommendations for international students: Required—TOEFL (minimum score 550 paper-based; 213 computer-based; 80 iBT). *Application deadline:* For fall admission, 6/1 priority date for domestic students, 4/15 for international students; for spring admission, 11/1 priority date for domestic students, 10/1 for international students. Applications are processed on a rolling basis. Application fee: $75. Electronic applications accepted. *Expenses:* Tuition, state resident: full-time $9096; part-time $379 per credit. Tuition, nonresident: full-time $23,064; part-time $961 per credit. *Required fees:* $127 per semester. One-time fee: $50. *Financial support:* In 2011–12, 44 students received support, including 90 research assistantships with partial tuition reimbursements available (averaging $8,900 per year); career-related internships or fieldwork, scholarships/grants, and unspecified assistantships also available. Support available to part-time students. Financial award application deadline: 2/15; financial award applicants required to submit FAFSA. *Faculty research:* International business, buyer behavior, financial markets, strategy, operations research, maritime and transportation economics. *Unit head:* Dr. Larry Filer, Graduate Program Director, 757-683-3585, Fax: 757-683-5750, E-mail: mbainfo@odu.edu. *Application contact:* Shanna Wood, MBA Program Manager, 757-683-3585, Fax: 757-683-5750, E-mail: mbainfo@odu.edu. Web site: http://bpa.odu.edu/mba/.

Olivet Nazarene University, Graduate School, Department of Business, Bourbonnais, IL 60914. Offers business administration (MBA). Evening/weekend programs available. *Degree requirements:* For master's, thesis or alternative. *Expenses:* Contact institution.

Oral Roberts University, School of Business, Tulsa, OK 74171. Offers accounting (MBA); entrepreneurship (MBA); finance (MBA); international business (MBA); management (MBA); marketing (MBA); non-profit management (MBA); not for profit management (MNM). *Accreditation:* ACBSP. Part-time programs available. Postbaccalaureate distance learning degree programs offered (minimal on-campus study). *Degree requirements:* For master's, thesis optional. *Entrance requirements:* For master's, minimum cumulative GPA of 3.0. Additional exam requirements/recommendations for international students: Required—TOEFL (minimum score 550 paper-based; 213 computer-based; 79 iBT). Electronic applications accepted. *Faculty research:* Social media, international business and marketing.

Oregon State University, Graduate School, College of Business, Corvallis, OR 97331. Offers MAIS, MBA, Certificate. *Accreditation:* AACSB. Part-time programs available. *Degree requirements:* For master's, portfolio. *Entrance requirements:* For master's, GMAT, minimum GPA of 3.0 in last 90 hours. Additional exam requirements/recommendations for international students: Required—TOEFL. *Faculty research:* Financial and account services, market analysis and planning, innovation, family business, tourism.

Ottawa University, Graduate Studies-Arizona, Programs in Business, Ottawa, KS 66067-3399. Offers business administration (MBA); finance (MBA); human resources (MA, MBA); leadership (MBA); marketing (MBA). Programs offered in Mesa, Phoenix, Tempe and West Valley, AZ. Part-time and evening/weekend programs available. Postbaccalaureate distance learning degree programs offered. *Degree requirements:* For master's, thesis or alternative. *Entrance requirements:* For master's, minimum undergraduate GPA of 3.0. Additional exam requirements/recommendations for international students: Required—TOEFL (minimum score 550 paper-based; 213 computer-based). Electronic applications accepted.

Ottawa University, Graduate Studies-International, Ottawa, KS 66067-3399. Offers business administration (MBA). Postbaccalaureate distance learning degree programs offered (minimal on-campus study). *Degree requirements:* For master's, thesis or alternative. *Entrance requirements:* For master's, minimum undergraduate GPA of 3.0. Additional exam requirements/recommendations for international students: Required—TOEFL (minimum score 550 paper-based; 213 computer-based). Electronic applications accepted. *Expenses:* Contact institution.

Ottawa University, Graduate Studies-Kansas City, Overland Park, KS 66211. Offers business administration (MBA); human resources (MA). Part-time and evening/weekend programs available. Postbaccalaureate distance learning degree programs offered (minimal on-campus study). *Degree requirements:* For master's, thesis or alternative. *Entrance requirements:* For master's, resume, 3 letters of recommendation. Additional exam requirements/recommendations for international students: Required—TOEFL (minimum score 550 paper-based; 213 computer-based). Electronic applications accepted. *Expenses:* Contact institution.

Ottawa University, Graduate Studies-Wisconsin, Brookfield, WI 53005. Offers business administration (MBA). Part-time and evening/weekend programs available. Postbaccalaureate distance learning degree programs offered. *Degree requirements:* For master's, thesis or alternative. *Entrance requirements:* For master's, resume, 3 letters of recommendation. Additional exam requirements/recommendations for international students: Required—TOEFL (minimum score 550 paper-based; 213 computer-based). Electronic applications accepted.

Otterbein University, Department of Business, Accounting and Economics, Westerville, OH 43081. Offers MBA. Part-time and evening/weekend programs available. *Degree requirements:* For master's, consulting project team. *Entrance requirements:* For master's, GMAT, 2 reference forms, resume. Additional exam requirements/recommendations for international students: Required—TOEFL (minimum score 550 paper-based; 213 computer-based; 79 iBT). *Expenses:* Contact institution. *Faculty research:* Organizational design, dispute resolution international trade, developing economies, marketing consumer goods, human resources development.

Our Lady of the Lake University of San Antonio, School of Business and Leadership, Program in Management, San Antonio, TX 78207-4689. Offers business administration (MBA); management (MBA).

Pace University, Lubin School of Business, New York, NY 10038. Offers MBA, MS, DPS, APC. *Accreditation:* AACSB. Part-time and evening/weekend programs available. Postbaccalaureate distance learning degree programs offered (minimal on-campus study). *Students:* 238 full-time (108 women), 938 part-time (485 women); includes 200 minority (44 Black or African American, non-Hispanic/Latino; 2 American Indian or Alaska Native, non-Hispanic/Latino; 112 Asian, non-Hispanic/Latino; 36 Hispanic/Latino; 6 Two or more races, non-Hispanic/Latino), 571 international. Average age 28. 1,808 applicants, 55% accepted, 388 enrolled. In 2011, 399 master's, 6 doctorates, 1 other advanced degree awarded. *Degree requirements:* For doctorate, thesis/dissertation, oral and written exams. *Entrance requirements:* For master's, GMAT,GRE; for doctorate, GMAT, MBA or master's in business program, 10 years of experience, interview; for APC, MBA or master's in business program. Additional exam requirements/recommendations for international students: Required—TOEFL. *Application deadline:* For fall admission, 7/31 priority date for domestic students; for spring admission, 11/30 for domestic students. Applications are processed on a rolling basis. Application fee: $70. Electronic applications accepted. *Expenses:* Contact institution. *Financial support:* Research assistantships, career-related internships or fieldwork, Federal Work-Study, and tuition waivers (full and partial) available. Support available to part-time students. Financial award applicants required to submit FAFSA. *Unit head:* Neil S. Braun, Dean, 212-618-6600, E-mail: nbraun@pace.edu. *Application contact:* Susan Ford-Goldschein, Director of Graduate Admissions, 212-346-1531, Fax: 212-346-1585, E-mail: gradnyc@pace.edu. Web site: http://www.pace.edu/lubin.

Pacific Lutheran University, Division of Graduate Studies, School of Business, Tacoma, WA 98447. Offers business administration (MBA), including technology and innovation management. *Accreditation:* AACSB. Part-time and evening/weekend programs available. *Faculty:* 13 full-time (6 women), 2 part-time/adjunct (1 woman). *Students:* 37 full-time (15 women), 30 part-time (9 women); includes 12 minority (4 Black or African American, non-Hispanic/Latino; 1 American Indian or Alaska Native, non-Hispanic/Latino; 2 Asian, non-Hispanic/Latino; 1 Hispanic/Latino; 4 Two or more races, non-Hispanic/Latino), 11 international. Average age 33. In 2011, 31 master's awarded. *Entrance requirements:* For master's, GMAT. Additional exam requirements/recommendations for international students: Required—TOEFL (minimum score 550 paper-based; 213 computer-based). *Application deadline:* Applications are processed on a rolling basis. Application fee: $40. *Expenses: Tuition:* Part-time $915 per semester hour. *Financial support:* Fellowships, career-related internships or fieldwork, Federal Work-Study, scholarships/grants, and unspecified assistantships available. Financial award application deadline: 3/1. *Unit head:* Dr. James Brock, Dean, School of Business, 253-535-7251, Fax: 253-535-8723, E-mail: plumba@plu.edu. *Application contact:* Theresa Ramos, Director, MBA Program, 253-535-7330, Fax: 253-535-8723, E-mail: plumba@plu.edu. Web site: http://www.plu.edu/mba/.

Pacific States University, College of Business, Los Angeles, CA 90006. Offers accounting (MBA); finance (MBA); international business (MBA, DBA); management of information technology (MBA); real estate management (MBA). Part-time and evening/weekend programs available. Postbaccalaureate distance learning degree programs offered (no on-campus study). *Faculty:* 6 full-time (2 women), 14 part-time/adjunct (0 women). *Students:* 157 full-time (70 women); includes 13 minority (2 Black or African American, non-Hispanic/Latino; 8 Asian, non-Hispanic/Latino; 3 Native Hawaiian or other Pacific Islander, non-Hispanic/Latino), 140 international. Average age 31. 42 applicants, 83% accepted, 33 enrolled. *Degree requirements:* For doctorate, comprehensive exam, thesis/dissertation. *Entrance requirements:* For master's, minimum undergraduate GPA of 2.5 during last 90 hours of course work. Additional exam requirements/recommendations for international students: Required—TOEFL (minimum score 133 computer-based; 45 iBT), IELTS (minimum score 4.5). *Application deadline:* For fall admission, 8/15 priority date for domestic students; for winter admission, 10/15 priority date for domestic students; for spring admission, 1/15 priority date for domestic students. Applications are processed on a rolling basis. Application fee: $100. *Expenses: Tuition:* Full-time $11,040; part-time $345 per credit hour. *Required fees:* $150 per quarter. *Financial support:* Scholarships/grants available. Financial award applicants required to submit FAFSA. *Application contact:* Zolzaya Enkhbayar, Interim Registrar, 323-731-2383, Fax: 323-731-7276, E-mail: registrar@psuca.edu.

Palm Beach Atlantic University, Rinker School of Business, West Palm Beach, FL 33416-4708. Offers MBA. Part-time and evening/weekend programs available. *Faculty:* 7 full-time (2 women), 5 part-time/adjunct (1 woman). *Students:* 38 full-time (18 women), 87 part-time (43 women); includes 44 minority (25 Black or African American, non-Hispanic/Latino; 1 American Indian or Alaska Native, non-Hispanic/Latino; 4 Asian, non-Hispanic/Latino; 14 Hispanic/Latino), 16 international. Average age 32. 87 applicants, 71% accepted, 46 enrolled. In 2011, 33 master's awarded. *Entrance requirements:* For master's, GMAT, minimum GPA of 3.0. Additional exam requirements/recommendations for international students: Required—TOEFL (minimum score 550 paper-based; 213 computer-based; 79 iBT). *Application deadline:* For fall admission, 7/15 priority date for domestic students; for spring admission, 11/15 priority date for domestic students. Applications are processed on a rolling basis. Application fee: $45. Electronic applications accepted. *Expenses: Tuition:* Full-time $11,478; part-time $470 per credit hour. *Required fees:* $99 per semester. Tuition and fees vary according to course load, degree level and campus/location. *Financial support:* Applicants required to submit FAFSA. *Unit head:* Dr. Edgar Langlois, MBA Program Director, 561-803-2456, E-mail: edgar_langlois@pba.edu. *Application contact:* Graduate Admissions, 888-468-6722, Fax: 561-803-2115, E-mail: grad@pba.edu. Web site: http://www.pba.edu.

Park University, College of Graduate and Professional Studies, Kansas City, MO 54105. Offers adult education (M Ed); at-risk students (M Ed); disaster and emergency management (MPA); educational administration (M Ed); entrepreneurship (MBA); general business (MBA); general education (M Ed); government/business relations (MPA); healthcare/services management (MBA, MPA); international business (MBA); K-12 certification (MAT); management information systems (MBA); management of information systems (MPA); middle school certification (MAT); multi-cultural education (M Ed); nonprofit management (MPA); public management (MPA); school law (M Ed); secondary school certification (MAT); special education (M Ed). Part-time and evening/weekend programs available. Postbaccalaureate distance learning degree programs offered (no on-campus study). *Degree requirements:* For master's, comprehensive exam, thesis (for some programs). *Entrance requirements:* For master's, GRE, GMAT, teacher certification (M Ed). Additional exam requirements/recommendations for international students: Required—TOEFL (minimum score 550 paper-based). Electronic applications accepted. *Faculty research:* Literacy, leadership, brain based research, multicultural education, diversity.

Penn State Erie, The Behrend College, Graduate School, Erie, PA 16563-0001. Offers business administration (MBA); project management (MPM). *Accreditation:* AACSB. Part-time programs available. *Students:* 34 full-time (8 women), 57 part-time (14 women). Average age 28. 46 applicants, 63% accepted, 22 enrolled. In 2011, 86 master's awarded. *Entrance requirements:* Additional exam requirements/recommendations for international students: Required—TOEFL (minimum score 550 paper-based; 213 computer-based; 80 iBT). *Application deadline:* Applications are processed on a rolling basis. Application fee: $65. Electronic applications accepted. *Financial support:* Federal Work-Study available. Financial award application deadline: 2/15; financial award applicants required to submit FAFSA. *Unit head:* Dr. Donald L. Birx, Chancellor, 814-898-6160, Fax: 814-898-6461, E-mail: dlb69@psu.edu. *Application contact:* Ann M. Burbules, Graduate Admissions Counselor, 814-898-7255, Fax: 814-898-6044, E-mail: amb29@psu.edu. Web site: http://psbehrend.psu.edu/.

Penn State Great Valley, Graduate Studies, Management Division, Malvern, PA 19355-1488. Offers M Fin, MBA, MLD. *Accreditation:* AACSB. *Unit head:* Dr. Daniel Indro, Division Head, 610-725-5283, Fax: 610-725-5224, E-mail: dci1@psu.edu. *Application contact:* 610-648-3242, Fax: 610-889-1334. Web site: http://www.sgps.psu.edu/current/academicprograms/management/default.ashx.

Penn State Harrisburg, Graduate School, School of Business Administration, Program in Business Administration, Middletown, PA 17057-4898. Offers MBA. *Accreditation:* AACSB. *Entrance requirements:* For master's, GMAT. *Unit head:* Dr. Richard P. Young, Director, 717-948-6151, E-mail: rry100@psu.edu. *Application contact:* Robert Coffman, Director of Admissions, 717-948-6250, Fax: 717-948-6325, E-mail: ric1@psu.edu.

Penn State University Park, Graduate School, Intercollege Graduate Programs, Intercollege Graduate Program in Business Administration, State College, University Park, PA 16802-1503. Offers MBA. Offered via the PSU World Campus. Postbaccalaureate distance learning degree programs offered (no on-campus study). *Unit head:* Dr. Regina Vasilatos-Younken, Senior Associate Dean, 814-865-2516, Fax: 814-863-4627, E-mail: rxv@psu.edu. *Application contact:* Cynthia E. Nicosia, Director, Graduate Enrollment Services, 814-865-1795, Fax: 814-865-4627, E-mail: cey1@psu.edu.

Penn State University Park, Graduate School, The Mary Jean and Frank P. Smeal College of Business Administration, State College, University Park, PA 16802-1503. Offers MBA, PhD. *Accreditation:* AACSB. *Students:* 329 full-time (106 women), 4 part-time (2 women). Average age 30. 1,048 applicants, 25% accepted, 122 enrolled. In 2011, 186 master's, 11 doctorates awarded. *Entrance requirements:* Additional exam requirements/recommendations for international students: Required—TOEFL (minimum score 550 paper-based; 213 computer-based; 80 iBT). *Application deadline:* Applications are processed on a rolling basis. Application fee: $65. Electronic applications accepted. *Financial support:* Fellowships, research assistantships, and teaching assistantships available. Financial award applicants required to submit FAFSA. *Unit head:* Dr. James B. Thomas, Dean, 814-863-0448, Fax: 814-865-7064, E-mail: j2t@psu.edu. *Application contact:* Cynthia E. Nicosia, Director, Graduate Enrollment Services, 814-865-1795, Fax: 814-865-4627, E-mail: cey1@psu.edu. Web site: http://www.smeal.psu.edu/.

Pepperdine University, Graziadio School of Business and Management, Executive MBA Program, Malibu, CA 90263. Offers Exec MBA. Part-time and evening/weekend programs available. *Students:* 114 full-time (43 women), 1 part-time (0 women); includes 36 minority (11 Black or African American, non-Hispanic/Latino; 2 American Indian or Alaska Native, non-Hispanic/Latino; 19 Asian, non-Hispanic/Latino; 4 Hispanic/Latino), 2 international. 74 applicants, 91% accepted, 46 enrolled. In 2011, 104 master's awarded. *Entrance requirements:* For master's, two personal interviews; two letters of nomination; minimum of seven years professional experience, including two years at a significant level of management. *Application deadline:* For fall admission, 6/10 priority date for domestic students. Application fee: $100. *Unit head:* Dr. Linda A. Livingstone, Dean, Graziadio School of Business and Management, 310-568-5689, Fax: 310-568-5766, E-mail: linda.livingstone@pepperdine.edu. *Application contact:* Darrell Eriksen, Director of Admission and Student Accounts, Graziadio School of Business and Management, 310-568-5525, E-mail: darrell.eriksen@pepperdine.edu. Web site: http://bschool.pepperdine.edu/programs/executive/.

Pepperdine University, Graziadio School of Business and Management, Full-Time MBA Program, Malibu, CA 90263. Offers MBA. *Students:* 256 full-time (98 women), 2 part-time (1 woman); includes 54 minority (13 Black or African American, non-Hispanic/Latino; 38 Asian, non-Hispanic/Latino; 3 Hispanic/Latino), 75 international. 335 applicants, 49% accepted, 137 enrolled. In 2011, 156 master's awarded. *Entrance requirements:* For master's, GMAT or GRE, two letters of recommendation. Additional exam requirements/recommendations for international students: Required—TOEFL. *Application deadline:* For fall admission, 5/1 for domestic students, 4/1 for international students. Application fee: $75. Electronic applications accepted. *Unit head:* Dr. Linda A. Livingstone, Dean, Graziadio School of Business and Management, 310-568-5689, Fax: 310-568-5766, E-mail: linda.livingstone@pepperdine.edu. *Application contact:* Darrell Eriksen, Director of Admission and Student Accounts, Graziadio School of Business and Management, 310-568-5525, E-mail: darrell.eriksen@pepperdine.edu. Web site: http://bschool.pepperdine.edu/programs/full-time-mba/.

Pepperdine University, Graziadio School of Business and Management, Fully-Employed MBA Program, Malibu, CA 90263. Offers MBA. Part-time and evening/weekend programs available. *Students:* 190 full-time (86 women), 491 part-time (192 women); includes 210 minority (39 Black or African American, non-Hispanic/Latino; 10 American Indian or Alaska Native, non-Hispanic/Latino; 125 Asian, non-Hispanic/Latino; 32 Hispanic/Latino; 2 Native Hawaiian or other Pacific Islander, non-Hispanic/Latino; 2 Two or more races, non-Hispanic/Latino), 15 international. 227 applicants, 72% accepted, 130 enrolled. In 2011, 423 master's awarded. *Entrance requirements:* For master's, GMAT or GRE, professional recommendation. Additional exam requirements/recommendations for international students: Required—TOEFL. *Application deadline:* For fall admission, 6/25 for domestic students. Application fee: $75. Electronic applications accepted. *Unit head:* Dr. Linda A. Livingstone, Dean, Graziadio School of Business and Management, 310-568-5689, Fax: 310-568-5766, E-mail: linda.livingstone@pepperdine.edu. *Application contact:* Darrell Eriksen, Director of Admission and Student Accounts, Graziadio School of Business and Management, 310-568-5525, E-mail: darrell.eriksen@pepperdine.edu. Web site: http://bschool.pepperdine.edu/programs/mba/.

Pepperdine University, Graziadio School of Business and Management, MBA Program for Presidents and Key Executives, Malibu, CA 90263. Offers MBA. Part-time and evening/weekend programs available. *Students:* 29 full-time (6 women), 5 part-time (1 woman); includes 8 minority (2 Black or African American, non-Hispanic/Latino; 5 Asian, non-Hispanic/Latino; 1 Hispanic/Latino), 1 international. 12 applicants, 92% accepted, 8 enrolled. In 2011, 23 master's awarded. *Entrance requirements:* For master's, two letters of nomination; two personal interviews; minimum of 10 years of organizational or professional experience, including at least one year in a senior executive position. Additional exam requirements/recommendations for international students: Required—TOEFL. *Application deadline:* For fall admission, 6/15 priority date for domestic students. Application fee: $100. *Unit head:* Dr. Linda A. Livingstone, Dean, Graziadio School of Business and Management, 310-568-5689, Fax: 310-568-5766, E-mail: linda.livingstone@pepperdine.edu. *Application contact:* Darrell Eriksen, Director of Admission and Student Accounts, Graziadio School of Business and Management, 310-568-5525, E-mail: darrell.eriksen@pepperdine.edu. Web site: http://bschool.pepperdine.edu/programs/presidential-mba/.

Pepperdine University, Graziadio School of Business and Management, MS in Management and Leadership Program, Malibu, CA 90263. Offers MS. Part-time and evening/weekend programs available. *Entrance requirements:* For master's, GMAT or GRE, two letters of recommendation.

Pfeiffer University, Program in Business Administration, Misenheimer, NC 28109-0960. Offers MBA, MBA/MHA. Part-time and evening/weekend programs available. Postbaccalaureate distance learning degree programs offered (minimal on-campus study). *Entrance requirements:* For master's, GMAT, minimum GPA of 3.0.

Philadelphia University, School of Business Administration, Program in Business Administration, Philadelphia, PA 19144. Offers business administration (MBA); finance (MBA); health care management (MBA); international business (MBA); marketing (MBA); MBA/MS. Part-time and evening/weekend programs available. Postbaccalaureate distance learning degree programs offered (no on-campus study). *Entrance requirements:* For master's, GMAT. Additional exam requirements/recommendations for international students: Required—TOEFL (minimum score 550 paper-based; 213 computer-based; 79 iBT).

Phillips Theological Seminary, Programs in Theology, Tulsa, OK 74116. Offers administration of church agencies (M Div); campus ministry (M Div); church-related social work (M Div); college and seminary teaching (M Div); global mission work (M Div); institutional chaplaincy (M Div); ministerial vocations in Christian education (M Div); ministry (D Min), including parish ministry, pastoral counseling, practices of ministry; ministry and culture (MAMC), including Christian education, congregational leadership, history and practice of Christian spirituality, theology, ethics, and culture; ministry of music (M Div); pastoral care and counseling (M Div); pastoral ministry (M Div); theological studies (MTS). *Accreditation:* ATS. Part-time programs available. Postbaccalaureate distance learning degree programs offered (minimal on-campus study). *Degree requirements:* For master's, thesis (for some programs); for doctorate, thesis/dissertation. *Entrance requirements:* For master's, minimum GPA of 2.5; for doctorate, M Div, minimum GPA of 3.0. *Faculty research:* Biblical studies, historical studies, theology and culture, practical theology, theology and film.

Piedmont College, School of Business, Demorest, GA 30535-0010. Offers MBA. *Accreditation:* ACBSP. Part-time and evening/weekend programs available. *Students:* 33 full-time (16 women), 56 part-time (30 women); includes 15 minority (6 Black or African American, non-Hispanic/Latino; 1 American Indian or Alaska Native, non-Hispanic/Latino; 4 Asian, non-Hispanic/Latino; 3 Hispanic/Latino; 1 Two or more races, non-Hispanic/Latino), 1 international. Average age 32. 24 applicants, 71% accepted, 14 enrolled. In 2011, 41 degrees awarded. *Degree requirements:* For master's, capstone. *Entrance requirements:* For master's, GMAT, GRE, minimum GPA of 2.75. Additional exam requirements/recommendations for international students: Required—TOEFL (minimum score 550 paper-based; 213 computer-based). *Application deadline:* For fall admission, 7/15 for domestic students; for spring admission, 12/1 for domestic students. Applications are processed on a rolling basis. Electronic applications accepted. *Expenses: Tuition:* Part-time $407 per credit hour. Tuition and fees vary according to program. *Financial support:* Federal Work-Study and unspecified assistantships available. Financial award applicants required to submit FAFSA. *Unit head:* Dr. John Misner, Dean, 706-778-3000 Ext. 1349, Fax: 706-778-0701, E-mail: jmisner@piedmont.edu. *Application contact:* Penny Loggins, Director of Graduate Admissions, 706-778-8500 Ext. 1181, Fax: 706-778-0150, E-mail: ploggins@piedmont.edu. Web site: http://www.piedmont.edu.

Pittsburg State University, Graduate School, Kelce College of Business, Department of Management and Marketing, Pittsburg, KS 66762. Offers general administration (MBA). *Accreditation:* AACSB. *Degree requirements:* For master's, thesis or alternative. *Entrance requirements:* For master's, GMAT. *Faculty research:* Consumer behavior, productions management, forecasting interest rate swaps, strategy management.

Plymouth State University, College of Graduate Studies, Department of Graduate Studies in Business, Plymouth, NH 03264-1595. Offers MBA. *Accreditation:* ACBSP. Part-time and evening/weekend programs available. *Entrance requirements:* For master's, minimum GPA of 2.5. Additional exam requirements/recommendations for international students: Required—TOEFL (minimum score 550 paper-based). *Expenses:* Contact institution.

Point Loma Nazarene University, Program in Business Administration, San Diego, CA 92106-2899. Offers MBA. *Accreditation:* ACBSP. Part-time and evening/weekend programs available. *Entrance requirements:* For master's, GMAT, letters of recommendation.

Point Park University, School of Business, Pittsburgh, PA 15222-1984. Offers business (MBA); organizational leadership (MA). Part-time and evening/weekend programs available. *Faculty:* 11 full-time, 14 part-time/adjunct. *Students:* 110 full-time (71 women), 240 part-time (127 women); includes 87 minority (62 Black or African American, non-Hispanic/Latino; 1 American Indian or Alaska Native, non-Hispanic/Latino; 5 Asian, non-Hispanic/Latino; 9 Hispanic/Latino; 1 Native Hawaiian or other Pacific Islander, non-Hispanic/Latino; 9 Two or more races, non-Hispanic/Latino), 21 international. Average age 32. 328 applicants, 73% accepted, 146 enrolled. In 2011, 183 master's awarded. *Degree requirements:* For master's, comprehensive exam (for some programs), thesis or alternative. *Entrance requirements:* For master's, minimum QPA of 2.75; 2 letters of recommendation; resume (MA). Additional exam requirements/recommendations for international students: Required—TOEFL (minimum score 550 paper-based; 79 iBT). *Application deadline:* Applications are processed on a rolling basis. Application fee: $30. Electronic applications accepted. *Expenses: Tuition:* Full-time $13,050; part-time $725 per credit. *Required fees:* $720; $40 per credit. *Financial support:* In 2011–12, 284 students received support, including 8 teaching assistantships with full tuition reimbursements available (averaging $6,400 per year); scholarships/grants also available. Financial award application deadline: 4/15; financial award applicants required to submit FAFSA. *Faculty research:* Technology issues, foreign direct investment, multinational corporate issues, cross-cultural international organizations/administrations, regional integration issues. *Unit head:* Dr. Dimitrius Kraniou, Chair, Deptartment of Global Management and Organization, 412-392-3447, Fax: 412-392-8048, E-mail: dkraniou@pointpark.edu. *Application contact:* Michael Powell, Assistant Director, Graduate and Adult Enrollment, 412-392-3807, Fax: 412-392-6164, E-mail: mpowell@pointpark.edu. Web site: http://www.pointpark.edu.

Polytechnic Institute of New York University, Department of Technology Management, Brooklyn, NY 11201-2990. Offers construction management (Advanced Certificate); electronic business management (Advanced Certificate); entrepreneurship (Advanced Certificate); human resources management (Advanced Certificate); information management (Advanced Certificate); management (MS); management of technology (MS); organizational behavior (MS, Advanced Certificate); project management (Advanced Certificate); technology management (MBA, PhD, Advanced Certificate); telecommunications and information management (MS); telecommunications management (Advanced Certificate). Part-time and evening/weekend programs available. *Faculty:* 6 full-time (1 woman), 32 part-time/adjunct (4 women). *Students:* 185 full-time (84 women), 94 part-time (41 women); includes 56 minority (15 Black or African American, non-Hispanic/Latino; 31 Asian, non-Hispanic/Latino; 10 Hispanic/Latino), 143 international. Average age 30. 467 applicants, 48% accepted, 123 enrolled. In 2011, 174 master's, 1 doctorate awarded. *Degree requirements:* For master's, comprehensive exam (for some programs), thesis (for some programs); for doctorate, comprehensive exam, thesis/dissertation. *Entrance requirements:* For master's, GMAT, minimum B average in undergraduate course work. Additional exam requirements/recommendations for international students: Required—TOEFL (minimum score 550 paper-based; 213 computer-based; 80 iBT); Recommended—IELTS (minimum score 6.5). *Application deadline:* For fall admission, 7/31 priority date for domestic students, 4/30 for international students; for spring admission, 12/31 priority date for domestic students, 11/30 for international students. Applications are processed on a rolling basis. Application fee: $75. Electronic applications accepted. *Expenses: Tuition:* Full-time $22,464; part-time $1248 per credit. *Required fees:* $501 per semester. *Financial support:* In 2011–12, 1 fellowship (averaging $26,400 per year) was awarded; research assistantships, teaching assistantships, institutionally sponsored loans, scholarships/grants, and unspecified assistantships also available. Support available to part-time students. *Unit head:* Prof. Bharadwaj Rao, Head, 718-260-3617, Fax: 718-260-3874, E-mail: brao@poly.edu. *Application contact:* JeanCarlo Bonilla, Director of Graduate Enrollment Management, 718-260-3182, Fax: 718-260-3624, E-mail: gradinfo@poly.edu. Web site: http://www.managementdept.poly.edu.

Polytechnic Institute of NYU, Westchester Graduate Center, Graduate Programs, Department of Technology Management, Major in Management, Hawthorne, NY 10532-1507. Offers MS. Part-time and evening/weekend programs available. *Faculty:* 5 part-time/adjunct (1 woman). In 2011, 2 master's awarded. *Degree requirements:* For master's, comprehensive exam (for some programs), thesis (for some programs). *Entrance requirements:* Additional exam requirements/recommendations for international students: Required—TOEFL (minimum score 550 paper-based; 213 computer-based; 80 iBT); Recommended—IELTS (minimum score 6.5). *Application deadline:* For fall admission, 7/31 priority date for domestic students, 4/30 for international students; for spring admission, 12/31 priority date for domestic students, 11/30 for international students. Applications are processed on a rolling basis. Application fee: $75. Electronic applications accepted. *Financial support:* Institutionally sponsored loans, scholarships/grants, and unspecified assistantships available. Support available to part-time students. *Unit head:* Dr. Bharadwaj Rao, Department Head, 718-260-3617, E-mail: brao@poly.edu. *Application contact:* JeanCarlo Bonilla, Director of Graduate Enrollment Management, 718-260-3182, Fax: 718-260-3624, E-mail: gradinfo@poly.edu.

Polytechnic University of Puerto Rico, Graduate School, Hato Rey, PR 00919. Offers business administration (MBA), including computer information systems, general management, management of information systems, management of international enterprises; civil engineering (ME, MS); computer engineering (ME, MS); computer science (MCS, MS); electrical engineering (ME, MS); engineering management (MEM); environmental management (MEM); landscape architecture (M Land Arch); manufacturing competitiveness (MMC, MS); manufacturing engineering (ME, MS); mechanical engineering (M Mech E). Part-time and evening/weekend programs available. *Entrance requirements:* For master's, 3 letters of recommendation.

Polytechnic University of Puerto Rico, Miami Campus, Graduate School, Miami, FL 33166. Offers accounting (MBA); business administration (MBA); construction management (MEM); environmental management (MEM); finance (MBA); human resources management (MBA); logistics and supply chain management (MBA); management of international enterprises (MBA); manufacturing management (MEM); marketing management (MBA); project management (MBA). Part-time and evening/weekend programs available. Postbaccalaureate distance learning degree programs offered (no on-campus study). *Entrance requirements:* For master's, minimum GPA of 3.0. Electronic applications accepted.

Polytechnic University of Puerto Rico, Orlando Campus, Graduate School, Winter Park, FL 32792. Offers accounting (MBA); business administration (MBA); construction management (MEM); engineering management (MEM); environmental management (MEM); finance (MBA); human resources management (MBA); management of international enterprises (MBA); management of technology (MBA); manufacturing management (MEM). Part-time and evening/weekend programs available. Postbaccalaureate distance learning degree programs offered (no on-campus study). *Entrance requirements:* For master's, minimum GPA of 3.0. Additional exam requirements/recommendations for international students: Recommended—TOEFL. Electronic applications accepted.

Pontifical Catholic University of Puerto Rico, College of Business Administration, Ponce, PR 00717-0777. Offers MBA, DBA, PhD, Professional Certificate. Part-time and evening/weekend programs available. *Degree requirements:* For master's, thesis; for doctorate, comprehensive exam, thesis/dissertation. *Entrance requirements:* For master's, GRE, interview, minimum GPA of 2.75; for doctorate, 2 letters of recommendation, 2 years experience in a related field, interview.

Pontificia Universidad Catolica Madre y Maestra, Graduate School, Faculty of Social and Administrative Sciences, Santiago, Dominican Republic. Offers business administration (MBA), including business development, finance, international business, management skills (M Mgmt, MBA), marketing, operations, strategic cost management, strategy, tourist destination planning and management; law (LL M), including civil law, corporate business law, criminal law, international relations, real estate law; management (M Mgmt), including higher financial management, insurance program administration, management skills (M Mgmt, MBA); psychology (MA), including clinical child and adolescent psychology, forensic psychology; strategic human resources (EMBA).

Portland State University, Graduate Studies, School of Business Administration, Program in Business Administration, Portland, OR 97207-0751. Offers MBA. Part-time and evening/weekend programs available. *Degree requirements:* For master's, one foreign language, project. *Entrance requirements:* For master's, GMAT, minimum GPA of 3.0 in upper-division course work, 2 recommendations, resume, interview. Additional exam requirements/recommendations for international students: Required—TOEFL (minimum score 550 paper-based; 213 computer-based). *Faculty research:* Quality management and organizational excellence, performance measurement, customer satisfaction, values, technology management and technology transfer.

Portland State University, Graduate Studies, Systems Science Program, Portland, OR 97207-0751. Offers computational intelligence (Certificate); computer modeling and simulation (Certificate); systems science (MS); systems science/anthropology (PhD); systems science/business administration (PhD); systems science/civil engineering (PhD); systems science/economics (PhD); systems science/engineering management (PhD); systems science/general (PhD); systems science/mathematical sciences (PhD); systems science/mechanical engineering (PhD); systems science/psychology (PhD); systems science/sociology (PhD). *Degree requirements:* For doctorate, variable foreign language requirement, thesis/dissertation. *Entrance requirements:* For master's, 2 letters of recommendation; for doctorate, GMAT, GRE General Test, minimum undergraduate GPA of 3.0. Additional exam requirements/recommendations for international students: Required—TOEFL. *Faculty research:* Systems theory and methodology, artificial intelligence neural networks, information theory, nonlinear dynamics/chaos, modeling and simulation.

Post University, Program in Business Administration, Waterbury, CT 06723-2540. Offers business administration (MBA); corporate innovation (MBA); entrepreneurship (MBA); finance (MBA); leadership (MBA); marketing (MBA). Postbaccalaureate distance learning degree programs offered.

Prairie View A&M University, College of Business, Prairie View, TX 77446-0519. Offers accounting (MS); general business administration (MBA). *Accreditation:* AACSB. Part-time and evening/weekend programs available. *Entrance requirements:* For master's, GMAT, minimum GPA of 2.45. Additional exam requirements/recommendations for international students: Required—TOEFL. Electronic applications accepted. *Faculty research:* Operations, finance, marketing.

Providence College, School of Business, Providence, RI 02918. Offers accounting (MBA); entrepreneurship (MBA); finance (MBA); international business (MBA); management (MBA); marketing (MBA); not-for-profit organizations (MBA). Part-time and evening/weekend programs available. *Faculty:* 11 full-time (4 women), 6 part-time/adjunct (1 woman). *Students:* 52 full-time (21 women), 49 part-time (17 women); includes 8 minority (3 Black or African American, non-Hispanic/Latino; 2 Asian, non-Hispanic/Latino; 3 Two or more races, non-Hispanic/Latino), 6 international. Average age 26. 49 applicants, 80% accepted, 25 enrolled. In 2011, 57 master's awarded. *Degree requirements:* For master's, thesis optional. *Entrance requirements:* For master's, GMAT. Additional exam requirements/recommendations for international students: Required—TOEFL (minimum score 550 paper-based; 213 computer-based; 80 iBT). *Application deadline:* For fall admission, 8/1 priority date for domestic students, 8/1 for international students; for spring admission, 12/1 priority date for domestic students, 12/1 for international students. Applications are processed on a rolling basis. Application fee: $55. *Expenses:* Contact institution. *Financial support:* In 2011–12, 34 research assistantships with full tuition reimbursements (averaging $8,400 per year) were awarded; Federal Work-Study, institutionally sponsored loans, and unspecified assistantships also available. Support available to part-time students. Financial award application deadline: 8/1; financial award applicants required to submit FAFSA. *Unit head:* Dr. Catherine L. Pastille, Director, MBA Program, 401-865-1654, Fax: 401-865-2978, E-mail: cpastill@providence.edu. *Application contact:* Katherine A. Follett, Administrative Coordinator, 401-865-2333, Fax: 401-865-2978, E-mail: kfollett@providence.edu. Web site: http://www.providence.edu/business/Pages/default.aspx.

Purdue University, Graduate School, Krannert School of Management, Doctoral Program in Management, West Lafayette, IN 47907-2056. Offers PhD. *Students:* 60 full-time (20 women), 50 international. Average age 34. 348 applicants, 7% accepted, 14 enrolled. In 2011, 13 doctorates awarded. *Degree requirements:* For doctorate, comprehensive exam, thesis/dissertation, first-year summer paper, dissertation proposal, dissertation defense. *Entrance requirements:* For doctorate, GMAT or GRE. Additional exam requirements/recommendations for international students: Required—TOEFL (minimum score 575 paper-based; 233 computer-based); Recommended—TWE. *Application deadline:* For fall admission, 1/15 priority date for domestic students, 1/15 for international students. Application fee: $55. Electronic applications accepted. *Financial support:* In 2011–12, fellowships with full tuition reimbursements (averaging $25,000 per year), research assistantships with partial tuition reimbursements (averaging $18,000 per year), teaching assistantships with full tuition reimbursements (averaging $10,000 per year) were awarded; institutionally sponsored loans, scholarships/grants, health care benefits, tuition waivers (full and partial), unspecified assistantships, and travel funds to present at a major conference also available. Financial award application deadline: 1/15. *Faculty research:* Accounting, finance, marketing, management information systems, operations management, organizational behavior and human resource management, quantitative methods/management science, strategic management. *Unit head:* Dr. P. Christopher Earley, Dean/Professor, 765-494-4366. *Application contact:* Krannert PhD Admissions, 765-494-4375, Fax: 765-494-0136, E-mail: krannertphd@purdue.edu. Web site: http://www.krannert.purdue.edu/programs/phd/.

Purdue University, Graduate School, Krannert School of Management, Executive MBA Program, West Lafayette, IN 47907. Offers EMBA. *Faculty:* 13 full-time (1 woman), 6 part-time/adjunct (0 women). *Students:* 19 full-time (3 women); includes 4 minority (1 Black or African American, non-Hispanic/Latino; 3 Asian, non-Hispanic/Latino), 1 international. Average age 39. 19 applicants, 74% accepted, 10 enrolled. In 2011, 15 master's awarded. *Entrance requirements:* For master's, letters of recommendation, essays, transcripts, resume. *Application deadline:* For fall admission, 8/31 for domestic students, 8/15 for international students. Applications are processed on a rolling basis. Application fee: $60 ($75 for international students). Electronic applications accepted. *Financial support:* Scholarships/grants and tuition waivers (partial) available. Financial award application deadline: 6/1; financial award applicants required to submit FAFSA. *Faculty research:* Trust in organizations, regulations and supply chain impact, carbon emissions and transportation costs.. *Unit head:* Dr. Aldas P. Kriauciunas, Executive Director, 765-496-1860, Fax: 765-494-0862, E-mail: akriauci@purdue.edu. *Application contact:* JoAnn Whitford, Assistant Director of Admissions, 765-494-4580, Fax: 765-494-0862, E-mail: jwhitfor@purdue.edu. Web site: http://www.krannert.purdue.edu/programs/executive/home.asp.

Purdue University, Graduate School, Krannert School of Management, GISMA Program, Hannover, IN 30169, Germany. Offers general business (MBA). *Faculty:* 25 full-time (3 women), 5 part-time/adjunct (0 women). *Students:* 40 full-time (21 women), 35 international. Average age 30. 84 applicants, 77% accepted, 40 enrolled. In 2011, 51 master's awarded. *Entrance requirements:* For master's, GMAT, letters of recommendation. Additional exam requirements/recommendations for international students: Required—TOEFL (minimum score 550 paper-based; 213 computer-based; 77 iBT). *Application deadline:* For fall admission, 7/5 for domestic students, 8/1 for international students. Applications are processed on a rolling basis. Application fee: $55 ($60 for international students). *Expenses:* Contact institution. *Unit head:* Dr. David Schoorman, Dean/Professor of Organizational Behavior and Human Resource Management, 765-494-4391, E-mail: schoor@purdue.edu. *Application contact:* Monika Baer, Director of Admissions, 49-511 54609-36, E-mail: mbaer@gisma.com. Web site: http://www.gisma.com.

Purdue University, Graduate School, Krannert School of Management, Master of Business Administration Program, West Lafayette, IN 47907. Offers MBA. *Faculty:* 81 full-time (19 women), 2 part-time/adjunct (0 women). *Students:* 211 full-time (46 women); includes 36 minority (14 Black or African American, non-Hispanic/Latino; 17 Asian, non-Hispanic/Latino; 5 Hispanic/Latino), 114 international. Average age 27. 679 applicants, 35% accepted, 103 enrolled. In 2011, 102 master's awarded. *Entrance requirements:* For master's, GMAT, four-year baccalaureate degree, minimum GPA of

3.0, essays, recommendation letters, work/internship experience. Additional exam requirements/recommendations for international students: Required—TOEFL (minimum score 550 paper-based; 213 computer-based; 77 iBT), IELTS (minimum score 6.5), or Pearson Test of English. *Application deadline:* For fall admission, 11/1 for domestic and international students; for winter admission, 1/10 for domestic students, 2/1 for international students; for spring admission, 3/1 for domestic students. Applications are processed on a rolling basis. Application fee: $60 ($75 for international students). Electronic applications accepted. *Financial support:* Research assistantships, teaching assistantships, scholarships/grants, and unspecified assistantships available. Financial award applicants required to submit FAFSA. *Faculty research:* Capital market imperfections and the sensitivity of investment to stock prices, identifying beneficial collaboration in decentralized logistics systems, performance periods and the dynamics of the performance-risk relationship, applications of global optimization to process and molecular design. *Unit head:* Dr. P. Christopher Earley, Dean/Professor of Management, 765-494-4366. *Application contact:* Brian Precious, Director of Admissions, Marketing, Recruiting and Entrepreneurial Outreach, 765-494-0773, Fax: 765-494-9841, E-mail: krannertmasters@purdue.edu.

Purdue University, Graduate School, Krannert School of Management, Weekend Master of Business Administration Program, West Lafayette, IN 47907. Offers MBA. Part-time and evening/weekend programs available. *Faculty:* 14 full-time (2 women), 3 part-time/adjunct (0 women). *Students:* 149 part-time (35 women); includes 29 minority (12 Black or African American, non-Hispanic/Latino; 1 American Indian or Alaska Native, non-Hispanic/Latino; 12 Asian, non-Hispanic/Latino; 4 Hispanic/Latino), 39 international. 77 applicants, 94% accepted, 54 enrolled. In 2011, 50 master's awarded. *Entrance requirements:* For master's, GMAT, minimum GPA of 3.0, four-year baccalaureate degree, essays, letters of recommendation. Additional exam requirements/ recommendations for international students: Required—TOEFL (minimum score 550 paper-based; 213 computer-based; 77 iBT). *Application deadline:* For fall admission, 6/1 for domestic students; for winter admission, 9/15 for domestic students; for spring admission, 11/15 for domestic students. Applications are processed on a rolling basis. Application fee: $60 ($75 for international students). Electronic applications accepted. *Financial support:* Partial scholarships available. Financial award application deadline: 12/1; financial award applicants required to submit FAFSA. *Unit head:* Dr. P. Christopher Earley, Dean/Professor of Management, 765-494-4366. *Application contact:* Lori Stout, Admissions Coordinator, 765-494-2291, E-mail: wkndmba@purdue.edu.

Purdue University Calumet, Graduate Studies Office, School of Management, Hammond, IN 46323-2094. Offers accountancy (M Acc); business administration (MBA); business administration for executives (EMBA). Part-time and evening/weekend programs available. *Entrance requirements:* For master's, GMAT. Additional exam requirements/recommendations for international students: Required—TOEFL. Electronic applications accepted.

Queen's University at Kingston, Queens School of Business, Program in Business Administration, Kingston, ON K7L 3N6, Canada. Offers consulting and project management (MBA); finance (MBA); innovation and entrepreneurship (MBA); marketing (MBA). *Accreditation:* AACSB. *Degree requirements:* For master's, thesis optional, research project. *Entrance requirements:* For master's, GMAT, minimum B+ average. Additional exam requirements/recommendations for international students: Required—TOEFL. Electronic applications accepted. *Faculty research:* Management fundamentals, strategic thinking, global business, innovation and change, leadership.

Queens University of Charlotte, McColl School of Business, Charlotte, NC 28274-0002. Offers business administration (EMBA, MBA). *Accreditation:* AACSB; ACBSP. Part-time and evening/weekend programs available. *Degree requirements:* For master's, capstone course. *Entrance requirements:* For master's, GMAT, minimum GPA of 2.5. Additional exam requirements/recommendations for international students: Required—TOEFL. Electronic applications accepted. *Expenses:* Contact institution.

Quincy University, Program in Business Administration, Quincy, IL 62301-2699. Offers business administration (MBA); human resource management (MBA). Part-time and evening/weekend programs available. *Faculty:* 3 full-time (2 women). *Students:* 4 full-time (0 women), 22 part-time (12 women), 1 international. In 2011, 15 master's awarded. *Entrance requirements:* For master's, GMAT, previous course work in accounting, economics, finance, management or marketing, and statistics. Additional exam requirements/recommendations for international students: Required—TOEFL (minimum score 550 paper-based; 79 iBT). *Application deadline:* Applications are processed on a rolling basis. Application fee: $25. Electronic applications accepted. *Expenses:* Contact institution. *Financial support:* Applicants required to submit FAFSA. *Faculty research:* Macroeconomic forecasting, business ethics/social responsibility. *Unit head:* Dr. John Palmer, Director, 217-228-5432 Ext. 3070, E-mail: palmejo@quincy.edu. *Application contact:* Office of Admissions, 217-228-5210, Fax: 217-228-5479, E-mail: admissions@quincy.edu. Web site: http://www.quincy.edu/academics/graduate-programs/business-administation.

Quinnipiac University, School of Business, Program in Business Administration, Hamden, CT 06518-1940. Offers chartered financial analyst (MBA); finance (MBA); healthcare management (MBA); information systems management (MBA); marketing (MBA); supply chain management (MBA); JD/MBA. *Accreditation:* AACSB. Part-time and evening/weekend programs available. Postbaccalaureate distance learning degree programs offered (no on-campus study). *Faculty:* 19 full-time (4 women), 2 part-time/adjunct (1 woman). *Students:* 89 full-time (36 women), 129 part-time (50 women); includes 16 minority (5 Black or African American, non-Hispanic/Latino; 5 Asian, non-Hispanic/Latino; 6 Hispanic/Latino), 19 international. Average age 29. 206 applicants, 81% accepted, 139 enrolled. In 2011, 95 master's awarded. *Entrance requirements:* For master's, GMAT or GRE, minimum GPA of 3.0. Additional exam requirements/ recommendations for international students: Required—TOEFL (minimum score 575 paper-based; 233 computer-based; 90 iBT), IELTS (minimum score 6.5). *Application deadline:* For fall admission, 7/30 priority date for domestic students, 4/30 for international students; for spring admission, 12/15 priority date for domestic students, 9/15 for international students. Applications are processed on a rolling basis. Application fee: $45. Electronic applications accepted. *Expenses: Tuition:* Part-time $855 per credit. *Required fees:* $35 per credit. *Financial support:* In 2011–12, 23 students received support. Career-related internships or fieldwork, Federal Work-Study, scholarships/ grants, tuition waivers (partial), and unspecified assistantships available. Support available to part-time students. Financial award application deadline: 4/15; financial award applicants required to submit FAFSA. *Faculty research:* Financial markets and investments, international business, supply chain management, health care management, corporate governance. *Unit head:* Lisa Braiewa, MBA Program Director, 203-582-3710, Fax: 203-582-8664, E-mail: lisa.braiewa@quinnipiac.edu. *Application contact:* Katie Ludovico, 800-462-1944, Fax: 203-582-3443, E-mail: katie.ludovico@quinnipiac.edu. Web site: http://www.quinnipiac.edu/mba.

Radford University, College of Graduate and Professional Studies, College of Business and Economics, Program in Business Administration, Radford, VA 24142. Offers MBA. *Accreditation:* AACSB. Part-time and evening/weekend programs available. *Faculty:* 40 full-time (6 women), 2 part-time/adjunct (1 woman). *Students:* 46 full-time (16 women), 50 part-time (19 women); includes 12 minority (7 Black or African American, non-Hispanic/Latino; 1 American Indian or Alaska Native, non-Hispanic/ Latino; 4 Hispanic/Latino), 8 international. Average age 30. 40 applicants, 88% accepted, 26 enrolled. In 2011, 26 master's awarded. *Entrance requirements:* For master's, GMAT, minimum GPA of 2.75, 2 letters of reference. Additional exam requirements/recommendations for international students: Required—TOEFL (minimum score 550 paper-based; 213 computer-based; 79 iBT). *Application deadline:* For fall admission, 2/15 priority date for domestic students, 12/1 for international students; for spring admission, 7/1 for international students. Applications are processed on a rolling basis. Application fee: $50. Electronic applications accepted. *Expenses:* Tuition, state resident: full-time $6262; part-time $261 per credit hour. Tuition, nonresident: full-time $14,540; part-time $606 per credit hour. *Required fees:* $2812; $117 per credit hour. Tuition and fees vary according to program. *Financial support:* In 2011–12, 21 students received support, including 9 research assistantships (averaging $7,063 per year), 4 teaching assistantships with partial tuition reimbursements available (averaging $8,420 per year); career-related internships or fieldwork, Federal Work-Study, institutionally sponsored loans, scholarships/grants, and unspecified assistantships also available. Financial award application deadline: 3/1; financial award applicants required to submit FAFSA. *Unit head:* Chris Niles, MBA Director, 540-831-6905, E-mail: cniles@radford.edu. *Application contact:* Rebecca Conner, Graduate Admissions, 540-831-5431, Fax: 540-831-6061, E-mail: gradcollege@radford.edu. Web site: http://www.radford.edu/content/cobe/home/programs/mba.html/.

Ramapo College of New Jersey, MBA Program, Mahwah, NJ 07430-1680. Offers MBA. Part-time and evening/weekend programs available. *Entrance requirements:* For master's, GMAT or GRE (within the past five years), interview; 2 letters of reference; immunizations; official transcripts from accredited higher education institution(s) with minimum cumulative GPA of 3.0 or exceptional professional experience as determined in writing by the dean; personal statement of goals. Additional exam requirements/ recommendations for international students: Required—TOEFL (minimum score 550 paper-based; 213 computer-based; 90 iBT). Application fee: $60. Electronic applications accepted. *Expenses: Tuition, area resident:* Part-time $551.05 per credit. Tuition, nonresident: part-time $708.30 per credit. *Required fees:* $122.50 per credit. *Unit head:* Dr. Lewis M. Chakrin, Dean of the Anisfield School of Business, 201-684-7377, E-mail: lchakrin@ramapo.edu. *Application contact:* Karen L. Norton, Assistant to Dean, 201-684-6653, E-mail: knorton@ramapo.edu. Web site: http://www.ramapo.edu/mba/.

Regent's American College London, Webster Graduate School, London, United Kingdom. Offers business (MBA); finance (MS); human resources (MA); information technology management (MA); international business (MA); international non-governmental organizations (MA); international relations (MA); management and leadership (MA); marketing (MA). Part-time programs available.

Regent University, Graduate School, School of Global Leadership and Entrepreneurship, Virginia Beach, VA 23464-9800. Offers business administration (MBA), including management general; leadership (Certificate); management (MA); organizational leadership (MA, PhD), including ecclesial leadership (PhD), entrepreneurial leadership (PhD), human resource development (PhD); strategic foresight (MA); strategic leadership (DSL), including global consulting, leadership coaching, strategic foresight. Part-time and evening/weekend programs available. Postbaccalaureate distance learning degree programs offered (minimal on-campus study). *Faculty:* 13 full-time (3 women), 4 part-time/adjunct (1 woman). *Students:* 27 full-time (11 women), 589 part-time (241 women); includes 183 minority (143 Black or African American, non-Hispanic/Latino; 3 American Indian or Alaska Native, non-Hispanic/Latino; 15 Asian, non-Hispanic/Latino; 22 Hispanic/Latino), 128 international. Average age 41. 225 applicants, 57% accepted, 85 enrolled. In 2011, 80 master's, 38 doctorates awarded. *Degree requirements:* For master's, thesis or alternative, 3 credit hour culminating experience; for doctorate, thesis/dissertation. *Entrance requirements:* For master's, GRE, GMAT, minimum undergraduate GPA of 2.75, computer literacy survey, 2 recommendations, resume, transcripts, essay; for doctorate, GRE, GMAT, sample of writing, minimum 3 years of relevant experience, computer literacy survey, 2 recommendations, resume, essay, transcripts; for Certificate, writing sample, resume, transcripts. Additional exam requirements/recommendations for international students: Required—TOEFL (minimum score 577 paper-based; 233 computer-based). *Application deadline:* For fall admission, 5/1 priority date for domestic students; for spring admission, 10/1 priority date for domestic students. Applications are processed on a rolling basis. Application fee: $50. Electronic applications accepted. *Expenses:* Contact institution. *Financial support:* Career-related internships or fieldwork, scholarships/ grants, and tuition waivers (full and partial) available. Support available to part-time students. Financial award application deadline: 9/1. *Faculty research:* Servant leadership, ethics and values, telecommuting and family values, organizational communications, distance education. *Unit head:* Dr. Bruce Winston, Dean, 757-352-4306, Fax: 757-352-4634, E-mail: brucwin@regent.edu. *Application contact:* Matthew Chadwick, Director of Enrollment Support Services, 800-373-5504, Fax: 757-352-4381, E-mail: admissions@regent.edu.

Regis University, College for Professional Studies, MBA Program in Emerging Markets, Denver, CO 80221-1099. Offers MBA. Postbaccalaureate distance learning degree programs offered (no on-campus study).

Regis University, College for Professional Studies, School of Management, Denver, CO 80221-1099. Offers accounting (MS, Certificate); executive international management (Certificate); executive leadership (Certificate); executive project management (Certificate); finance and accounting (MBA); general business administration (MBA); health care management (MBA); human resource management and leadership (MSOL); information technology leadership and management (MSOL); international business (MBA); marketing (MBA); operations management (MBA); organizational leadership and management (MSOL); project leadership and management (MSOL); project management (Certificate); strategic business management (Certificate); strategic human resource management (Certificate); strategic management (MBA). Offered at Colorado Springs Campus, Northwest Denver Campus, Southeast Denver Campus, Fort Collins Campus, Broomfield Campus, Henderson (Nevada) Campus, and Summerlin (Nevada) Campus and online. Part-time and evening/weekend programs available. Postbaccalaureate distance learning degree programs offered (no on-campus study). *Degree requirements:* For master's, thesis optional, capstone project. *Entrance requirements:* For master's, GMAT or essays, interview, 2 years of full-time business work experience, resume; for Certificate, GMAT. Additional exam requirements/recommendations for international students: Required—TOEFL, TWE (minimum score 5) or university-based test. Electronic applications accepted. *Faculty research:* Impact of information technology on small business regulation of accounting, international project financing, mineral development, delivery of healthcare to rural indigenous communities.

Reinhardt University, Reinhardt Advantage MBA Program, Alpharetta, GA 30005-4442. Offers MBA. Program offered at North Fulton Center in Alpharetta, GA and at The Chambers at City Center in Woodstock, GA. Part-time and evening/weekend programs available. *Faculty:* 5 full-time (3 women). *Students:* 2 full-time (1 woman), 32 part-time (16 women); includes 6 minority (4 Black or African American, non-Hispanic/Latino; 2 Asian, non-Hispanic/Latino). Average age 38. 57 applicants, 47% accepted, 23 enrolled. In 2011, 12 degrees awarded. *Degree requirements:* For master's, comprehensive exam. *Entrance requirements:* For master's, GRE (minimum score in upper-50th percentile) or GMAT (minimum score 500), bachelor's degree with minimum GPA of 2.75, current resume, interview, 3 professional references. Additional exam requirements/recommendations for international students: Required—TOEFL. *Application deadline:* For fall admission, 5/7 for domestic and international students; for spring admission, 8/9 for domestic and international students. Applications are processed on a rolling basis. Application fee: $25. Electronic applications accepted. *Expenses: Tuition:* Full-time $7020; part-time $390 per credit hour. *Required fees:* $70 per semester hour. *Financial support:* Application deadline: 5/1; applicants required to submit FAFSA. *Unit head:* Dr. Peggy Morlier, Associate Vice President of Graduate Studies. *Application contact:* Dr. John Yelvington, MBA Coordinator and Assistant Professor of Economics, McCamish School of Business, 770-720-5637, Fax: 770-720-9236, E-mail: jsy2@reinhardt.edu. Web site: http://www.reinhardt.edu/MBA/.

Rensselaer at Hartford, Lally School of Management and Technology, Hartford, CT 06120-2991. Offers MBA, MS. Part-time and evening/weekend programs available. Postbaccalaureate distance learning degree programs offered (no on-campus study). *Degree requirements:* For master's, capstone course. *Entrance requirements:* For master's, GMAT (MBA). Additional exam requirements/recommendations for international students: Required—TOEFL (minimum score 600 paper-based; 250 computer-based; 100 iBT). Electronic applications accepted.

Rensselaer Polytechnic Institute, Graduate School, Lally School of Management and Technology, Troy, NY 12180-3590. Offers business (MBA); financial engineering and risk analysis (MS); management (MS, PhD); technology, commercialization, and entrepreneurship (MS). *Accreditation:* AACSB. Part-time and evening/weekend programs available. *Degree requirements:* For doctorate, thesis/dissertation. *Entrance requirements:* For master's, GMAT, 2 letters of recommendation, resume; for doctorate, GMAT or GRE General Test, 2 letters of recommendation. Additional exam requirements/recommendations for international students: Required—TOEFL (minimum score 600 paper-based; 250 computer-based; 100 iBT); Recommended—IELTS (minimum score 7). Electronic applications accepted. *Faculty research:* Technological entrepreneurship, operations management, new product development and marketing, finance and financial engineering and risk analytics, information systems.

Rice University, Graduate Programs, Jesse H. Jones Graduate School of Management, Houston, TX 77251-1892. Offers business administration (EMBA, MBA, PMBA); MBA/M Eng; MD/MBA. *Accreditation:* AACSB. Evening/weekend programs available. *Entrance requirements:* For master's, GMAT. Additional exam requirements/recommendations for international students: Required—TOEFL (minimum score 600 paper-based; 250 computer-based). Electronic applications accepted. *Expenses:* Contact institution. *Faculty research:* Marketing strategy, technology transfer initiatives, management accounting, leadership and change management, financial management.

The Richard Stockton College of New Jersey, School of Graduate and Continuing Studies, Program in Business Administration, Pomona, NJ 08240-0195. Offers MBA. Part-time and evening/weekend programs available. *Faculty:* 10 full-time (5 women). *Students:* 9 full-time (3 women), 36 part-time (16 women); includes 11 minority (4 Black or African American, non-Hispanic/Latino; 4 Asian, non-Hispanic/Latino; 2 Hispanic/Latino; 1 Two or more races, non-Hispanic/Latino), 1 international. Average age 28. 14 applicants, 86% accepted, 10 enrolled. In 2011, 19 master's awarded. *Degree requirements:* For master's, project. *Entrance requirements:* For master's, GMAT. Additional exam requirements/recommendations for international students: Required—TOEFL. *Application deadline:* For fall admission, 7/1 for domestic and international students; for spring admission, 12/1 for domestic and international students. Applications are processed on a rolling basis. Application fee: $50. Electronic applications accepted. *Expenses:* Tuition, state resident: full-time $13,035; part-time $543 per credit. Tuition, nonresident: full-time $20,065; part-time $836 per credit. *Required fees:* $3920; $163 per credit. Tuition and fees vary according to degree level. *Financial support:* In 2011–12, 4 students received support, including 6 research assistantships with partial tuition reimbursements available; fellowships, career-related internships or fieldwork, Federal Work-Study, scholarships/grants, and unspecified assistantships also available. Support available to part-time students. Financial award application deadline: 3/1; financial award applicants required to submit FAFSA. *Faculty research:* Business ethics, marketing channels development, event studies, total quality management. *Unit head:* Dr. Gurprit Chhatwal, Director, 609-626-3640, E-mail: mba@stockton.edu. *Application contact:* Tara Williams, Assistant Director of Graduate Enrollment Management, 609-626-3640, Fax: 609-626-6050, E-mail: gradschool@stockton.edu.

Rider University, College of Business Administration, Lawrenceville, NJ 08648-3001. Offers M Acc, MBA. *Accreditation:* AACSB. Part-time and evening/weekend programs available. *Entrance requirements:* For master's, GMAT, minimum AACSB index of 1050, resume. Additional exam requirements/recommendations for international students: Required—TOEFL (minimum score 550 paper-based; 213 computer-based). Electronic applications accepted. *Expenses:* Contact institution.

Rivier University, School of Graduate Studies, Department of Business Administration, Nashua, NH 03060. Offers MBA. Part-time and evening/weekend programs available. *Entrance requirements:* Additional exam requirements/recommendations for international students: Recommended—TOEFL.

Robert Morris University, Graduate Studies, School of Business, Moon Township, PA 15108-1189. Offers business administration (MBA); human resource management (MS); nonprofit management (MS); taxation (MS). *Accreditation:* AACSB. Part-time and evening/weekend programs available. Postbaccalaureate distance learning degree programs offered (no on-campus study). *Faculty:* 29 full-time (11 women), 3 part-time/adjunct (0 women). *Students:* 190 part-time (91 women); includes 11 minority (9 Black or African American, non-Hispanic/Latino; 1 Asian, non-Hispanic/Latino; 1 Hispanic/Latino), 4 international. *Entrance requirements:* For master's, GMAT, letters of recommendation. Additional exam requirements/recommendations for international students: Required—TOEFL (minimum score 550 paper-based; 213 computer-based; 79 iBT). *Application deadline:* For fall admission, 7/1 priority date for domestic students, 7/1 for international students; for spring admission, 11/1 priority date for domestic students, 11/1 for international students. Applications are processed on a rolling basis. Application fee: $35. Electronic applications accepted. *Expenses: Tuition:* Part-time $810 per credit. *Required fees:* $15 per course. Tuition and fees vary according to degree level. *Financial support:* Research assistantships with partial tuition reimbursements, Federal Work-Study, institutionally sponsored loans, and unspecified assistantships available. Support available to part-time students. Financial award application deadline: 5/1; financial award applicants required to submit FAFSA. *Unit head:* Dr. Patrick J. Litzinger, Interim Dean, 412-397-6383, Fax: 412-397-2217, E-mail: litzinger@rmu.edu. *Application contact:* Deborah Roach, Assistant Dean, Graduate Admissions, 412-397-5200, Fax: 412-397-2425, E-mail: graduateadmissions@rmu.edu. Web site: http://www.rmu.edu/web/cms/schools/sbus/.

Robert Morris University Illinois, Morris Graduate School of Management, Chicago, IL 60605. Offers accounting (MBA); accounting/finance (MBA); design and media (MM); health care administration (MM); higher education administration (MM); human resource management (MBA); information systems (MIS); law enforcement administration (MM); management (MBA); management/finance (MIS); management/human resource management (MBA); sports administration (MM). Part-time and evening/weekend programs available. *Faculty:* 7 full-time (1 woman), 21 part-time/adjunct (5 women). *Students:* 296 full-time (172 women), 216 part-time (136 women); includes 273 minority (160 Black or African American, non-Hispanic/Latino; 1 American Indian or Alaska Native, non-Hispanic/Latino; 32 Asian, non-Hispanic/Latino; 78 Hispanic/Latino; 2 Two or more races, non-Hispanic/Latino), 28 international. Average age 32. 247 applicants, 69% accepted, 152 enrolled. In 2011, 244 master's awarded. *Entrance requirements:* Additional exam requirements/recommendations for international students: Required—TOEFL (minimum score 550 paper-based; 173 computer-based). *Application deadline:* Applications are processed on a rolling basis. Application fee: $20 ($100 for international students). Electronic applications accepted. *Expenses: Tuition:* Full-time $13,800; part-time $2300 per course. *Financial support:* In 2011–12, 643 students received support. Federal Work-Study, scholarships/grants, tuition waivers, and leadership and athletic scholarships available. Support available to part-time students. Financial award applicants required to submit FAFSA. *Unit head:* Kayed Akkawi, Dean, 312-935-6025, Fax: 312-935-6020, E-mail: kakkawi@robertmorris.edu. *Application contact:* Fernando Villeda, Dean of Morris Graduate School of Management, 312-935-6050, Fax: 312-935-6020, E-mail: fvilleda@robertmorris.edu.

Roberts Wesleyan College, Division of Business, Rochester, NY 14624-1997. Offers nonprofit leadership (Certificate); strategic leadership (MS); strategic marketing (MS). Evening/weekend programs available. *Degree requirements:* For master's, thesis or alternative. *Entrance requirements:* For master's, GMAT, minimum GPA of 2.75, verifiable work experience. *Expenses:* Contact institution.

Rochester Institute of Technology, Graduate Enrollment Services, E. Philip Saunders College of Business, Executive MBA Program, Rochester, NY 14623-5603. Offers Exec MBA. *Accreditation:* AACSB. Part-time and evening/weekend programs available. Postbaccalaureate distance learning degree programs offered (minimal on-campus study). *Students:* 103 full-time (21 women), 2 part-time (0 women); includes 9 minority (6 Black or African American, non-Hispanic/Latino; 2 Asian, non-Hispanic/Latino; 1 Hispanic/Latino), 3 international. Average age 38. 43 applicants, 81% accepted, 17 enrolled. In 2011, 54 master's awarded. *Degree requirements:* For master's, thesis. *Entrance requirements:* For master's, GMAT, minimum 6 years of work experience. Additional exam requirements/recommendations for international students: Required—TOEFL (minimum score 580 paper-based; 237 computer-based; 92 iBT) or IELTS (minimum score 7). *Application deadline:* For fall admission, 6/30 priority date for domestic students, 2/15 for international students. Applications are processed on a rolling basis. Application fee: $50. *Expenses:* Contact institution. *Financial support:* In 2011–12, 41 students received support. Scholarships/grants available. Support available to part-time students. Financial award applicants required to submit FAFSA. *Faculty research:* Entrepreneurship, strategic growth in small business, leadership effectiveness, corporate environmental strategy and management, lean manufacturing and environmental performance. *Unit head:* Jeffrey Davis, Graduate Program Director, 585-475-4534, E-mail: jwdavis@saunders.rit.edu. *Application contact:* Diane Ellison, Assistant Vice President, Graduate Enrollment Services, 585-475-2229, Fax: 585-475-7164, E-mail: gradinfo@rit.edu. Web site: http://saunders.rit.edu/programs/executive/index.php.

Rochester Institute of Technology, Graduate Enrollment Services, E. Philip Saunders College of Business, Program in Business Administration, Rochester, NY 14623-5603. Offers MBA. *Accreditation:* AACSB. Part-time and evening/weekend programs available. *Students:* 82 full-time (29 women), 82 part-time (26 women); includes 10 minority (3 Black or African American, non-Hispanic/Latino; 5 Asian, non-Hispanic/Latino; 2 Hispanic/Latino), 47 international. Average age 29. 292 applicants, 37% accepted, 42 enrolled. In 2011, 85 degrees awarded. *Degree requirements:* For master's, comprehensive exam (for some programs), thesis (for some programs). *Entrance requirements:* For master's, GMAT, minimum GPA of 2.5. Additional exam requirements/recommendations for international students: Required—TOEFL (minimum score 580 paper-based; 237 computer-based; 92 iBT) or IELTS (minimum score 7). *Application deadline:* For fall admission, 2/15 priority date for domestic students, 2/15 for international students; for winter admission, 11/1 priority date for domestic students, 10/1 for international students; for spring admission, 2/1 priority date for domestic students, 1/1 for international students. Applications are processed on a rolling basis. Application fee: $50. *Expenses: Tuition:* Full-time $34,659; part-time $963 per credit hour. *Required fees:* $228; $76 per quarter. *Financial support:* Research assistantships with partial tuition reimbursements, teaching assistantships with partial tuition reimbursements, career-related internships or fieldwork, scholarships/grants, and unspecified assistantships available. Support available to part-time students. Financial award applicants required to submit FAFSA. *Faculty research:* Strategic use of information technology to gain a competitive advantage, developing new statistical quality control techniques and revising the existing techniques to improve their performance, corporate governance. *Unit head:* Melissa Ellison, Graduate Program Director, 585-475-6916, E-mail: mamdar@rit.edu. *Application contact:* Diane Ellison, Assistant Vice President, Graduate Enrollment Services, 585-475-2229, Fax: 585-475-7164, E-mail: gradinfo@rit.edu. Web site: http://saunders.rit.edu/.

Rockford College, Graduate Studies, Program in Business Administration, Rockford, IL 61108-2393. Offers MBA. Part-time and evening/weekend programs available. *Entrance requirements:* For master's, GMAT, 3 letters of recommendation. Additional exam requirements/recommendations for international students: Required—TOEFL (minimum score 550 paper-based; 213 computer-based; 79 iBT). *Application deadline:* Applications are processed on a rolling basis. Application fee: $50. Electronic applications accepted. *Expenses: Tuition:* Full-time $16,200; part-time $675 per credit. *Required fees:* $80; $40 per semester. Tuition and fees vary according to class time, course level, course load, degree level, campus/location and program. *Financial support:* Scholarships/grants and unspecified assistantships available. Support available to part-time students. Financial award application deadline: 3/1; financial award applicants required to submit FAFSA. *Faculty research:* Entrepreneurship, leadership, international business, services marketing, project management. *Unit head:* Prof. Jeff Fahrenwald, MBA Director, 815-226-4178, E-mail: jfahrenwald@rockford.edu. *Application contact:* Michele Mehren, Office Manager for Graduate Studies, 815-226-4041, E-mail: mmehren@rockford.edu.

Rockhurst University, Helzberg School of Management, Kansas City, MO 64110-2561. Offers MBA. *Accreditation:* AACSB. Part-time and evening/weekend programs available. *Faculty:* 21 full-time (2 women), 9 part-time/adjunct (4 women). *Students:* 110 full-time (28 women), 102 part-time (35 women); includes 20 minority (4 Black or African American, non-Hispanic/Latino; 6 Asian, non-Hispanic/Latino; 9 Hispanic/Latino; 1 Native Hawaiian or other Pacific Islander, non-Hispanic/Latino), 1 international. Average age 27. 118 applicants, 35% accepted, 38 enrolled. In 2011, 197 master's awarded. *Entrance requirements:* For master's, GMAT. Additional exam requirements/recommendations for international students: Required—TOEFL (minimum score 550 paper-based; 213 computer-based; 79 iBT). *Application deadline:* For fall admission, 7/25 priority date for domestic students; for spring admission, 12/15 priority date for domestic students. Applications are processed on a rolling basis. Application fee: $0. Electronic applications accepted. *Financial support:* Career-related internships or fieldwork available. Support available to part-time students. Financial award application deadline: 4/1; financial award applicants required to submit FAFSA. *Faculty research:* Offshoring/outsourcing, systems analysis/synthesis, work teams, multilateral trade, path dependencies/creation. *Unit head:* Dr. Cheryl McConnell, Interim Dean, 816-501-4201, Fax: 816-501-4650, E-mail: cheryl.mcconnell@rockhurst.edu. *Application contact:* Erin Reed, Director of MBA Advising, 816-501-4823, E-mail: erin.reed@rockhurst.edu. Web site: http://www.rockhurst.edu/.

Rollins College, Crummer Graduate School of Business, Winter Park, FL 32789-4499. Offers entrepreneurship (MBA); finance (MBA); international business (MBA); management (MBA); marketing (MBA); operations and technology management (MBA). *Accreditation:* AACSB. Part-time and evening/weekend programs available. Postbaccalaureate distance learning degree programs offered (minimal on-campus study). *Faculty:* 23 full-time (3 women), 6 part-time/adjunct (4 women). *Students:* 257 full-time (95 women), 121 part-time (39 women); includes 75 minority (12 Black or African American, non-Hispanic/Latino; 1 American Indian or Alaska Native, non-Hispanic/Latino; 20 Asian, non-Hispanic/Latino; 39 Hispanic/Latino; 3 Two or more races, non-Hispanic/Latino), 27 international. Average age 28. 363 applicants, 44% accepted, 100 enrolled. In 2011, 213 master's awarded. *Degree requirements:* For master's, minimum GPA of 2.85. *Entrance requirements:* For master's, GMAT or GRE, official transcripts, two letters of recommendation, essay, current resume/curriculum vitae, interview. Additional exam requirements/recommendations for international students: Required—TOEFL (minimum score 100 iBT) or IELTS (minimum score 7). *Application deadline:* Applications are processed on a rolling basis. Application fee: $50. Electronic applications accepted. *Expenses:* Contact institution. *Financial support:* In 2011–12, 258 students received support. Federal Work-Study and scholarships/grants available. Support available to part-time students. Financial award applicants required to submit FAFSA. *Faculty research:* Sustainability, world financial markets, international business, market research, strategic marketing. *Unit head:* Dr. Craig M. McAllaster, Dean, 407-646-2249, Fax: 407-646-1550, E-mail: cmcallaster@rollins.edu. *Application contact:* Eva Gauthier Oleksiw, Admissions Coordinator, 407-646-2405, Fax: 407-646-1550, E-mail: mbaadmissions@rollins.edu. Web site: http://www.rollins.edu/mba/.

Roosevelt University, Graduate Division, Walter E. Heller College of Business Administration, Program in Business Administration, Chicago, IL 60605. Offers MBA. *Accreditation:* ACBSP. Part-time and evening/weekend programs available. *Entrance requirements:* For master's, GMAT.

Roseman University of Health Sciences, MBA Program, Henderson, NV 89014. Offers MBA. Evening/weekend programs available. *Degree requirements:* For master's, comprehensive exam, entrepreneurial project, summative assessment and capstone. *Entrance requirements:* For master's, GMAT or leveling course for applicants whose overall GPA is below 3.0, bachelor's degree. Additional exam requirements/recommendations for international students: Required—TOEFL (minimum score 550 paper-based; 213 computer-based; 79 iBT). *Expenses:* Contact institution. *Faculty research:* Corporate leadership, economic development, dental practice management.

Rosemont College, Schools of Graduate and Professional Studies, Program in Business Administration and Management, Rosemont, PA 19010-1699. Offers business administration (MBA); management (MSM). Part-time and evening/weekend programs available. Postbaccalaureate distance learning degree programs offered. *Faculty:* 21 part-time/adjunct (9 women). *Students:* 22 full-time (17 women), 92 part-time (69 women); includes 47 minority (43 Black or African American, non-Hispanic/Latino; 3 Asian, non-Hispanic/Latino; 1 Hispanic/Latino), 7 international. Average age 34. 60 applicants, 70% accepted, 30 enrolled. In 2011, 33 master's awarded. *Degree requirements:* For master's, thesis (unless seeking certificate). *Application deadline:* Applications are processed on a rolling basis. Application fee: $50. Application fee is waived when completed online. *Expenses:* Contact institution. *Financial support:* Institutionally sponsored loans and unspecified assistantships available. Financial award applicants required to submit FAFSA. *Unit head:* Joan Wilder, Program Director, 610-527-0200 Ext. 3105, Fax: 610-526-2964, E-mail: jwilder@rosemont.edu. *Application contact:* Meghan Mellinger, Admissions Counselor, 610-527-0200 Ext. 2596, Fax: 610-520-4399, E-mail: gpsadmissions@rosemont.edu. Web site: http://www.rosemont.edu/.

Rowan University, Graduate School, William G. Rohrer College of Business, Glassboro, NJ 08028-1701. Offers MBA. *Accreditation:* AACSB. Part-time and evening/weekend programs available. *Degree requirements:* For master's, thesis. *Entrance requirements:* For master's, GMAT, minimum GPA of 2.8. Additional exam requirements/recommendations for international students: Required—TOEFL. Electronic applications accepted.

Royal Military College of Canada, Division of Graduate Studies and Research, Continuing Studies, Department of Business Administration, Kingston, ON K7K 7B4, Canada. Offers MBA. *Degree requirements:* For master's, thesis. *Entrance requirements:* For master's, GMAT, honours degree with second-class standing. Electronic applications accepted.

Royal Roads University, Graduate Studies, Applied Leadership and Management Program, Victoria, BC V9B 5Y2, Canada. Offers executive coaching (Graduate Certificate); health systems leadership (Graduate Certificate); project management (Graduate Certificate); public relations management (Graduate Certificate); strategic human resources management (Graduate Certificate).

Royal Roads University, Graduate Studies, Faculty of Management, Victoria, BC V9B 5Y2, Canada. Offers digital technologies management (MBA); executive management (MBA), including global aviation management, knowledge management, leadership; human resources management (MBA). Postbaccalaureate distance learning degree programs offered (minimal on-campus study). *Degree requirements:* For master's, thesis. *Entrance requirements:* For master's, 5-7 years of related work experience. Additional exam requirements/recommendations for international students: Required—TOEFL (paper-based 570; computer-based 233) or IELTS (paper-based 7) (recommended). Electronic applications accepted. *Expenses:* Contact institution. *Faculty research:* Global venture analysis standards; computer assisted venture opportunity screening; teaching philosophies, instructions and methods.

Rutgers, The State University of New Jersey, Camden, School of Business, Camden, NJ 08102-1401. Offers MBA, JD/MBA. *Accreditation:* AACSB. Part-time and evening/weekend programs available. *Entrance requirements:* For master's, GMAT, 2 letters of recommendation. Additional exam requirements/recommendations for international students: Required—TOEFL (minimum score 230 computer-based; 89 iBT). Electronic applications accepted. *Expenses:* Contact institution. *Faculty research:* Efficiency in utility industry, management information systems development, management/labor relations.

Rutgers, The State University of New Jersey, Newark, Graduate School, Program in Management, Newark, NJ 07102. Offers accounting (PhD); accounting information systems (PhD); computer information systems (PhD); finance (PhD); information technology (PhD); international business (PhD); management science (PhD); marketing (PhD); organization management (PhD). Program offered jointly with New Jersey Institute of Technology. *Accreditation:* AACSB. *Degree requirements:* For doctorate, thesis/dissertation, cumulative exams. *Entrance requirements:* For doctorate, GMAT or GRE General Test, minimum undergraduate B average. Additional exam requirements/recommendations for international students: Required—TOEFL. Electronic applications accepted. *Faculty research:* Technology management, leadership and teams, consumer behavior, financial and markets, logistics.

Rutgers, The State University of New Jersey, Newark, Rutgers Business School–Newark and New Brunswick, Newark, NJ 07102. Offers MBA, MBA/MS, MD/MBA, MPH/MBA, MS/MBA. *Accreditation:* AACSB. Part-time and evening/weekend programs available. Terminal master's awarded for partial completion of doctoral program. *Degree requirements:* For master's, 60 total credits including capstone course. *Entrance requirements:* For master's, GMAT, GRE. Additional exam requirements/recommendations for international students: Required—TOEFL (minimum score 600 paper-based; 100 computer-based). Electronic applications accepted. *Expenses:* Contact institution. *Faculty research:* Finance/economics, accounting, international business, operations research, marketing, organizational behavior, supply chain management, pharmaceutical management.

Sacred Heart University, Graduate Programs, John F. Welch College of Business, Fairfield, CT 06825-1000. Offers accounting (MBA); finance (MBA); management (MBA); marketing (MBA). *Accreditation:* AACSB. Part-time and evening/weekend programs available. Postbaccalaureate distance learning degree programs offered. *Degree requirements:* For master's, thesis or alternative. *Entrance requirements:* For master's, GMAT (preferred) or GRE General Test. Additional exam requirements/recommendations for international students: Required—TOEFL (minimum score 550 paper-based; 213 computer-based; 75 iBT). Electronic applications accepted. *Expenses:* Contact institution. *Faculty research:* Management of organizations, international business management of technology.

Sage Graduate School, School of Management, Program in Business Administration, Troy, NY 12180-4115. Offers business strategy (MBA); finance (MBA); human resources (MBA); marketing (MBA); JD/MBA. Part-time and evening/weekend programs available. *Faculty:* 2 full-time (both women), 8 part-time/adjunct (1 woman). *Students:* 20 full-time (10 women), 55 part-time (36 women); includes 10 minority (2 Black or African American, non-Hispanic/Latino; 4 Asian, non-Hispanic/Latino; 3 Hispanic/Latino; 1 Two or more races, non-Hispanic/Latino), 1 international. Average age 31. 51 applicants, 55% accepted, 19 enrolled. In 2011, 10 degrees awarded. *Entrance requirements:* For master's, minimum GPA of 2.75, resume, 2 letters of recommendation. Additional exam requirements/recommendations for international students: Required—TOEFL (minimum score 550 paper-based; 213 computer-based). *Application deadline:* Applications are processed on a rolling basis. Application fee: $40. *Expenses: Tuition:* Full-time $11,880; part-time $660 per credit hour. Tuition and fees vary according to program. *Financial support:* Fellowships, research assistantships, Federal Work-Study, scholarships/grants, and unspecified assistantships available. Support available to part-time students. Financial award application deadline: 3/1; financial award applicants required to submit FAFSA. *Unit head:* Dr. Daniel Robeson, Dean, School of Management, 518-292-8637, Fax: 518-292-1964, E-mail: robesd@sage.edu. *Application contact:* Wendy D. Diefendorf, Director of Graduate and Adult Admission, 518-244-2443, Fax: 518-244-6880, E-mail: diefew@sage.edu.

Saginaw Valley State University, College of Business and Management, Program in Business Administration, University Center, MI 48710. Offers MBA. *Accreditation:* AACSB. Part-time and evening/weekend programs available. *Faculty:* 23 full-time (4 women), 1 part-time/adjunct (0 women). *Students:* 49 full-time (18 women), 77 part-time (40 women); includes 11 minority (8 Black or African American, non-Hispanic/Latino; 1 Asian, non-Hispanic/Latino; 2 Hispanic/Latino), 53 international. Average age 28. 110 applicants, 91% accepted, 26 enrolled. In 2011, 28 master's awarded. *Entrance requirements:* Additional exam requirements/recommendations for international students: Required—TOEFL (minimum score 525 paper-based; 197 computer-based; 71 iBT). *Application deadline:* Applications are processed on a rolling basis. Application fee: $25. Electronic applications accepted. *Expenses:* Tuition, state resident: full-time $8300; part-time $5333 per year. Tuition, nonresident: full-time $15,613; part-time $10,209 per year. *International tuition:* $15,631 full-time. *Financial support:* Federal Work-Study and scholarships/grants available. Support available to part-time students. Financial award application deadline: 4/15; financial award applicants required to submit FAFSA. *Unit head:* Dr. Mark Potts, Assistant Dean of Graduate and Undergraduate Programs, 989-964-4064, E-mail: mdpotts@svsu.edu. *Application contact:* P. Laine Blasch, Graduate Recruitment Coordinator, 989-964-2182, Fax: 989-790-0180, E-mail: blasch@svsu.edu.

St. Ambrose University, College of Business, Program in Business Administration, Davenport, IA 52803-2898. Offers business administration (DBA); health care (MBA); human resources (MBA). *Accreditation:* ACBSP. Part-time and evening/weekend programs available. *Faculty:* 17 full-time (4 women), 4 part-time/adjunct (1 woman). *Students:* 44 full-time (21 women), 208 part-time (92 women); includes 23 minority (7 Black or African American, non-Hispanic/Latino; 2 American Indian or Alaska Native, non-Hispanic/Latino; 3 Asian, non-Hispanic/Latino; 11 Hispanic/Latino), 5 international. Average age 34. 133 applicants, 80% accepted, 74 enrolled. In 2011, 110 master's, 2 doctorates awarded. *Degree requirements:* For master's, comprehensive exam (for some programs), thesis or alternative, capstone seminar; for doctorate, comprehensive exam, thesis/dissertation, oral and written exams. *Entrance requirements:* For master's, GMAT; for doctorate, GMAT, master's degree. Additional exam requirements/recommendations for international students: Required—TOEFL. *Application deadline:* For fall admission, 8/15 priority date for domestic students; for winter admission, 12/15 for domestic students; for spring admission, 1/1 for domestic students. Applications are processed on a rolling basis. Application fee: $25. Electronic applications accepted. *Expenses:* Contact institution. *Financial support:* In 2011–12, 54 students received support, including 5 research assistantships with partial tuition reimbursements available (averaging $3,600 per year); career-related internships or fieldwork, scholarships/grants, tuition waivers (partial), and unspecified assistantships also available. Financial award application deadline: 3/15; financial award applicants required to submit FAFSA. *Unit head:* Dr. Linda K. Brown, MBA Director, 563-333-6343, Fax: 563-333-6243, E-mail: brownlindak@sau.edu. *Application contact:* Elizabeth Loveless, Director of Graduate Student Recruitment, 563-333-6271, Fax: 563-333-6268, E-mail: lovelesselizabethb@sau.edu. Web site: http://www.sau.edu/mba.

St. Bonaventure University, School of Graduate Studies, School of Business, St. Bonaventure, NY 14778-2284. Offers general business (MBA). *Accreditation:* AACSB. Part-time and evening/weekend programs available. *Faculty:* 20 full-time (4 women), 1 part-time/adjunct (0 women). *Students:* 71 full-time (23 women), 71 part-time (26 women); includes 4 minority (1 Black or African American, non-Hispanic/Latino; 1 American Indian or Alaska Native, non-Hispanic/Latino; 1 Asian, non-Hispanic/Latino; 1 Two or more races, non-Hispanic/Latino), 6 international. Average age 29. 85 applicants, 81% accepted, 50 enrolled. In 2011, 102 master's awarded. *Entrance requirements:* For master's, GMAT, undergraduate degree, letters of recommendation. Additional exam requirements/recommendations for international students: Required—TOEFL (minimum score 550 paper-based; 213 computer-based; 79 iBT). *Application deadline:* For fall admission, 6/15 priority date for domestic students, 2/1 for international students; for spring admission, 11/1 priority date for domestic students, 7/1 for international students. Applications are processed on a rolling basis. Application fee: $30. Electronic applications accepted. *Expenses: Tuition:* Part-time $670 per credit. *Financial support:* In 2011–12, 12 research assistantships with full and partial tuition reimbursements were awarded; career-related internships or fieldwork, Federal Work-Study, scholarships/grants, health care benefits, and unspecified assistantships also available. Support available to part-time students. Financial award application deadline: 4/15; financial award applicants required to submit FAFSA. *Unit head:* John B. Stevens, MBA Director, 716-375-7662, Fax: 716-375-2191, E-mail: jstevens@sbu.edu. *Application contact:* John B. Stevens, MBA Director, 716-375-7662, Fax: 716-375-2191, E-mail: jstevens@sbu.edu. Web site: http://www.sbu.edu/education.aspx?id-5938.

St. Cloud State University, School of Graduate Studies, G.R. Herberger College of Business, Program in Business Administration, St. Cloud, MN 56301-4498. Offers business administration (MBA); information assurance (MS). Part-time and evening/weekend programs available. *Degree requirements:* For master's, thesis or alternative. *Entrance requirements:* For master's, GMAT, minimum GPA of 2.75. Additional exam requirements/recommendations for international students: Required—Michigan English Language Assessment Battery; Recommended—TOEFL (minimum score 550 paper-based; 213 computer-based), IELTS (minimum score 6.5).

St. Edward's University, School of Management and Business, Austin, TX 78704. Offers M Ac, MA, MBA, MS, PSM, Certificate. Part-time and evening/weekend programs available. *Faculty:* 24 full-time (8 women), 35 part-time/adjunct (11 women). *Students:* 91 full-time (28 women), 359 part-time (194 women); includes 173 minority (37 Black or African American, non-Hispanic/Latino; 3 American Indian or Alaska Native, non-Hispanic/Latino; 14 Asian, non-Hispanic/Latino; 110 Hispanic/Latino; 1 Native Hawaiian or other Pacific Islander, non-Hispanic/Latino; 8 Two or more races, non-Hispanic/Latino), 18 international. Average age 33. 216 applicants, 74% accepted, 119 enrolled. In 2011, 187 master's awarded. *Degree requirements:* For master's, minimum of 24 hours in residence. *Entrance requirements:* For master's, GMAT or GRE General Test, minimum GPA of 2.75 in last 60 hours of course work. Additional exam requirements/recommendations for international students: Required—TOEFL (minimum score 550 paper-based; 213 computer-based; 79 iBT) or IELTS (minimum score 6). *Application deadline:* For fall admission, 7/1 for domestic and international students; for spring admission, 11/1 for domestic and international students. Applications are processed on a rolling basis. Application fee: $45 ($50 for international students). Electronic applications accepted. *Expenses: Tuition:* Full-time $17,550; part-time $975 per credit hour. *Required fees:* $50 per trimester. Full-time tuition and fees vary according to course load and program. *Unit head:* Marsha Kelliher, Dean, 512-448-8588, Fax: 512-448-8492, E-mail: marshak@stedwards.edu. *Application contact:* Bridget Davidson, Director, Center for Academic Progress, 512-428-1061, Fax: 512-428-1032, E-mail: bridgets@stedwards.edu. Web site: http://www.stedwards.edu.

Saint Francis University, Graduate School of Business and Human Resource Management, Loretto, PA 15940. Offers business administration (MBA); human resource management (MHRM). Part-time and evening/weekend programs available. *Faculty:* 8 full-time (2 women), 25 part-time/adjunct (12 women). *Students:* 39 full-time (17 women), 141 part-time (66 women); includes 5 minority (3 Black or African American, non-Hispanic/Latino; 2 Asian, non-Hispanic/Latino). Average age 30. 35 applicants, 86% accepted, 20 enrolled. In 2011, 66 degrees awarded. *Degree requirements:* For master's, comprehensive exam (for some programs), thesis (for some programs). *Entrance requirements:* For master's, GMAT (waived if undergraduate QPA is 3.3 or above), 2 letters of recommendation, minimum GPA of 2.75, two essays. Additional exam requirements/recommendations for international students: Required—TOEFL (minimum score 550 paper-based; 213 computer-based; 57 iBT). *Application deadline:* For fall admission, 8/15 priority date for domestic students, 8/15 for international students; for spring admission, 12/1 priority date for domestic students, 12/1 for international students. Applications are processed on a rolling basis. Application fee: $30. *Expenses:* Contact institution. *Financial support:* Fellowships with partial tuition reimbursements, career-related internships or fieldwork, and unspecified assistantships available. Financial award application deadline: 8/15. *Unit head:* Dr. Randy Frye, Director, Graduate Business Programs and Human Resource Management, 814-472-3041, Fax: 814-472-3174, E-mail: rfrye@francis.edu. *Application contact:* Nicole Marie Bauman, Coordinator, Graduate Business Programs and Human Resource Management, 814-472-3026, Fax: 814-472-3369, E-mail: nbauman@francis.edu. Web site: http://www.francis.edu.

St. John Fisher College, Ronald L. Bittner School of Business, MBA Program, Rochester, NY 14618-3597. Offers MBA. *Accreditation:* AACSB. Part-time and evening/weekend programs available. *Faculty:* 15 full-time (4 women), 4 part-time/adjunct (0 women). *Students:* 51 full-time (20 women), 93 part-time (48 women); includes 18 minority (4 Black or African American, non-Hispanic/Latino; 9 Asian, non-Hispanic/Latino; 2 Hispanic/Latino; 3 Two or more races, non-Hispanic/Latino). Average age 28. 93 applicants, 73% accepted, 44 enrolled. In 2011, 39 master's awarded. *Degree requirements:* For master's, capstone project. *Entrance requirements:* For master's, GMAT, 2 letters of recommendation, personal statement, current resume, interview. Additional exam requirements/recommendations for international students: Required—TOEFL (minimum score 575 paper-based; 233 computer-based; 80 iBT). *Application deadline:* Applications are processed on a rolling basis. Application fee: $30. Electronic applications accepted. *Expenses: Tuition:* Part-time $735 per credit. One-time fee: $50 part-time. Tuition and fees vary according to course load, degree level and program. *Financial support:* In 2011–12, 31 students received support. Scholarships/grants available. Financial award applicants required to submit FAFSA. *Faculty research:* Business strategy, consumer behavior, cross-cultural management practices, international finance, organizational trust. *Unit head:* Lori Hollenbeck, Assistant Dean of the School of Business, 585-899-3707, Fax: 585-385-8094, E-mail: lhollenbeck@sjfc.edu. *Application contact:* Jose Perales, Director of Graduate Admissions, 585-385-8067, E-mail: jperales@sjfc.edu.

St. John's University, The Peter J. Tobin College of Business, Queens, NY 11439. Offers MBA, MS, Adv C, JD/MBA, MS/JD. *Accreditation:* AACSB. Part-time and evening/weekend programs available. Postbaccalaureate distance learning degree programs offered (no on-campus study). *Faculty:* 93 full-time (23 women), 38 part-time/adjunct (8 women). *Students:* 529 full-time (278 women), 255 part-time (115 women); includes 174 minority (45 Black or African American, non-Hispanic/Latino; 2 American Indian or Alaska Native, non-Hispanic/Latino; 78 Asian, non-Hispanic/Latino; 40 Hispanic/Latino; 1 Native Hawaiian or other Pacific Islander, non-Hispanic/Latino; 8 Two or more races, non-Hispanic/Latino), 330 international. Average age 26. 838 applicants, 72% accepted, 283 enrolled. In 2011, 427 master's awarded. *Degree requirements:* For master's, comprehensive exam (for some programs), thesis optional. *Entrance requirements:* For master's, GMAT, 2 letters of recommendation, resume, statement of goals, minimum GPA of 3.0; for Adv C, GMAT, 2 letters of recommendation, resume, undergraduate and graduate transcripts, essay, MBA. Additional exam requirements/recommendations for international students: Required—TOEFL (minimum score 600 paper-based; 250 computer-based; 100 iBT), IELTS (minimum score 7). *Application deadline:* For fall admission, 5/1 priority date for domestic students, 5/1 for international students; for spring admission, 11/1 priority date for domestic students, 11/1 for international students. Applications are processed on a rolling basis. Application fee: $50. Electronic applications accepted. *Expenses:* Contact institution. *Financial support:* In 2011–12, 1 fellowship (averaging $18,180 per year), 43 research assistantships with full and partial tuition reimbursements (averaging $16,475 per year), 1 teaching assistantship (averaging $21,210 per year) were awarded; scholarships/grants and unspecified assistantships also available. Support available to part-time students. Financial award application deadline: 3/1; financial award applicants required to submit FAFSA. *Unit head:* Dr. Victoria Shoaf, Dean. *Application contact:* Carol J. Swanberg, Assistant Dean/Director of Graduate Admissions, 718-990-1345, Fax: 718-990-5242, E-mail: tobingradnyc@stjohns.edu. Web site: http://www.stjohns.edu/academics/graduate/tobin.

St. Joseph's College, Long Island Campus, Executive MBA Program, Patchogue, NY 11772-2399. Offers EMBA.

St. Joseph's College, Long Island Campus, Program in Management, Patchogue, NY 11772-2399. Offers health care (AC); health care management (MS); human resource management (AC); human resources management (MS); organizational management (MS).

St. Joseph's College, New York, Graduate Programs, Programs in Business, Brooklyn, NY 11205-3688. Offers accounting (MBA); executive business administration (EMBA); management (MS).

See Display on next page and Close-Up on page 227.

Saint Joseph's College of Maine, Master of Business Administration in Leadership Program, Standish, ME 04084. Offers leadership (MBA). Part-time programs available. Postbaccalaureate distance learning degree programs offered (no on-campus study). *Faculty:* 15 part-time/adjunct (5 women). *Students:* 68 part-time (36 women); includes 9 minority (1 Black or African American, non-Hispanic/Latino; 5 Asian, non-Hispanic/Latino; 3 Hispanic/Latino). Average age 40. 71 applicants, 93% accepted, 61 enrolled. *Entrance requirements:* For master's, two years of work experience. One-time fee: $50. *Financial support:* Applicants required to submit FAFSA. *Unit head:* Nancy Kristiansen, Director, 207-893-7841, Fax: 207-892-7423, E-mail: nkristiansen@sjcme.edu. *Application contact:* Lynne Robinson, Director of Admissions, 800-752-4723, Fax: 207-892-7480, E-mail: info@sjcme.edu. Web site: http://online.sjcme.edu/master-business-administration.php.

Saint Joseph's University, Erivan K. Haub School of Business, Philadelphia, PA 19131-1395. Offers MBA, MS, Post Master's Certificate, DO/MBA. *Accreditation:* AACSB. Part-time and evening/weekend programs available. Postbaccalaureate distance learning degree programs offered (no on-campus study). *Faculty:* 71 full-time (19 women), 55 part-time/adjunct (10 women). *Students:* 292 full-time (132 women), 886 part-time (373 women); includes 201 minority (100 Black or African American, non-Hispanic/Latino; 2 American Indian or Alaska Native, non-Hispanic/Latino; 51 Asian, non-Hispanic/Latino; 39 Hispanic/Latino; 1 Native Hawaiian or other Pacific Islander, non-Hispanic/Latino; 8 Two or more races, non-Hispanic/Latino), 160 international. Average age 32. In 2011, 462 master's awarded. *Entrance requirements:* For master's, GMAT, MAT, GRE, letters of recommendation, resume, personal statement. Additional exam requirements/recommendations for international students: Required—TOEFL (minimum score 550 paper-based; 213 computer-based; 80 iBT), IELTS (minimum score 6.5) , or Pearson Test of English (minimum score 60). *Application deadline:* For fall admission, 7/15 priority date for domestic students, 4/15 for international students; for spring admission, 11/15 priority date for domestic students, 10/15 for international students. Applications are processed on a rolling basis. Application fee: $35. Electronic applications accepted. *Expenses: Tuition:* Part-time $735 per credit hour. Tuition and fees vary according to degree level and program. *Financial support:* In 2011–12, research assistantships with full and partial tuition reimbursements (averaging $4,000 per year), teaching assistantships with full and partial tuition reimbursements (averaging $4,000 per year) were awarded; fellowships, scholarships/grants, and unspecified assistantships also available. Financial award application deadline: 5/1; financial award applicants required to submit FAFSA. *Faculty research:* Food marketing, agriculture, finance and accounting systems, advertising cues and effects. *Total annual research expenditures:* $651,955. *Unit head:* Dr. Joseph A. DiAngelo, Dean, 610-660-1645, Fax: 610-660-1649, E-mail: jodiange@sju.edu. *Application contact:* Dr. Janine N. Guerra, Associate Director, Professional MBA Program, 610-660-1695, Fax: 610-660-1599, E-mail: jguerra@sju.edu. Web site: http://www.sju.edu/hsb.

Saint Leo University, Graduate Business Studies, Saint Leo, FL 33574-6665. Offers accounting (MBA); business (MBA); health services management (MBA); human resource management (MBA); information security management (MBA); marketing (MBA); sport business (MBA). Part-time and evening/weekend programs available. Postbaccalaureate distance learning degree programs offered (no on-campus study). *Faculty:* 39 full-time (7 women), 56 part-time/adjunct (17 women). *Students:* 1,506 full-time (901 women); includes 620 minority (480 Black or African American, non-Hispanic/Latino; 5 American Indian or Alaska Native, non-Hispanic/Latino; 21 Asian, non-Hispanic/Latino; 100 Hispanic/Latino; 1 Native Hawaiian or other Pacific Islander, non-Hispanic/Latino; 13 Two or more races, non-Hispanic/Latino), 20 international. Average age 38. In 2011, 574 master's awarded. *Entrance requirements:* For master's, GMAT (minimum score 500 if applicant does not have 5 years of professional work experience), bachelor's degree with minimum GPA of 3.0 in the last 60 hours of coursework from regionally-accredited college or university; 5 years of professional work experience; resume; 2 letters of recommendation. Additional exam requirements/recommendations for international students: Required—TOEFL (minimum score 550 paper-based; 213 computer-based; 80 iBT). *Application deadline:* For fall admission, 7/1 priority date for domestic students, 7/1 for international students; for spring admission, 11/12 priority date for domestic students, 11/1 for international students. Applications are processed on a rolling basis. Application fee: $80. Electronic applications accepted. *Expenses: Tuition:* Full-time $11,340; part-time $630 per semester hour. Tuition and fees vary according to campus/location and program. *Financial support:* In 2011–12, 72 students received support. Career-related internships or fieldwork, Federal Work-Study, scholarships/grants, and health care benefits available. Financial award application deadline: 3/1; financial award applicants required to submit FAFSA. *Unit head:* Dr. Lorrie McGovern, Director, 352-588-7390, Fax: 352-588-8585, E-mail: mbaslu@saintleo.edu. *Application contact:* Jared Welling, Director of Graduate Admission, 800-707-8846, Fax: 352-588-7873, E-mail: grad.admissions@saintleo.edu. Web site: http://www.saintleo.edu/Academics/School-of-Business/Graduate-Degree-Programs.

Saint Louis University, Graduate Education, John Cook School of Business, Program in Business Administration, St. Louis, MO 63103-2097. Offers MBA. *Accreditation:* AACSB. Part-time and evening/weekend programs available. *Entrance requirements:* For master's, GMAT, letter of recommendation, resume. Additional exam requirements/recommendations for international students: Required—TOEFL (minimum score 570 paper-based; 230 computer-based; 88 iBT). Electronic applications accepted. *Expenses:* Contact institution.

Saint Martin's University, Graduate Programs, School of Business, Lacey, WA 98503. Offers MBA. Part-time and evening/weekend programs available. *Faculty:* 3 full-time (0 women), 9 part-time/adjunct (2 women). *Students:* 63 full-time (28 women), 25 part-time (13 women); includes 24 minority (7 Black or African American, non-Hispanic/Latino; 1 American Indian or Alaska Native, non-Hispanic/Latino; 9 Asian, non-Hispanic/Latino; 3 Hispanic/Latino; 4 Two or more races, non-Hispanic/Latino), 18 international. Average age 33. 31 applicants, 100% accepted, 29 enrolled. In 2011, 21 master's awarded. *Degree requirements:* For master's, thesis (for some programs). *Entrance requirements:*

For master's, GMAT. Additional exam requirements/recommendations for international students: Required—TOEFL (minimum score 525 paper-based; 197 computer-based; 71 iBT). *Application deadline:* Applications are processed on a rolling basis. Application fee: $35. *Expenses: Tuition:* Part-time $910 per credit hour. Tuition and fees vary according to course level, campus/location and program. *Financial support:* In 2011–12, 29 students received support. Career-related internships or fieldwork and scholarships/grants available. Support available to part-time students. Financial award application deadline: 3/1; financial award applicants required to submit FAFSA. *Unit head:* Dr. Heather Grob, Director, MBA Program, 360-438-4292, Fax: 360-438-4522, E-mail: hgrob@stmartin.edu. *Application contact:* Keri Olsen, Administrative Assistant, 360-438-4512, Fax: 360-438-4522, E-mail: kolsen@stmartin.edu. Web site: http://www.stmartin.edu.

Saint Mary's College of California, Graduate Business Programs, Executive MBA Program, Moraga, CA 94556. Offers MBA. Part-time and evening/weekend programs available. Postbaccalaureate distance learning degree programs offered (minimal on-campus study). *Students:* 196 full-time (75 women), 1 part-time (0 women); includes 81 minority (15 Black or African American, non-Hispanic/Latino; 1 American Indian or Alaska Native, non-Hispanic/Latino; 42 Asian, non-Hispanic/Latino; 23 Hispanic/Latino), 1 international. Average age 38. 236 applicants, 78% accepted, 138 enrolled. In 2011, 119 master's awarded. *Entrance requirements:* For master's, 5 years of management experience. Additional exam requirements/recommendations for international students: Required—TOEFL (minimum score 91 computer-based). *Application deadline:* Applications are processed on a rolling basis. Application fee: $50. *Expenses:* Contact institution. *Financial support:* Available to part-time students. Applicants required to submit FAFSA. *Unit head:* Dr. Guido Krickx, Program Director, 925-631-4514, Fax: 925-376-6521, E-mail: gak1@stmarys-ca.edu. *Application contact:* Bob Peterson, Director of Admissions, 925-631-4504, Fax: 925-376-6521, E-mail: bpeterso@stmarys-ca.edu. Web site: http://www.stmarys-ca.edu/executive-and-hybrid-executive-mba.

Saint Mary's College of California, Graduate Business Programs, Professional MBA Program, Moraga, CA 94556. Offers MBA. Part-time and evening/weekend programs available. *Students:* 86 full-time (42 women), 35 part-time (14 women); includes 40 minority (3 Black or African American, non-Hispanic/Latino; 1 American Indian or Alaska Native, non-Hispanic/Latino; 21 Asian, non-Hispanic/Latino; 14 Hispanic/Latino; 1 Two or more races, non-Hispanic/Latino), 1 international. Average age 29. 132 applicants, 70% accepted, 67 enrolled. In 2011, 45 master's awarded. *Degree requirements:* For master's, 4 half-day management practica. *Entrance requirements:* For master's, GMAT. Additional exam requirements/recommendations for international students: Required—TOEFL. *Application deadline:* Applications are processed on a rolling basis. Application fee: $50. *Expenses:* Contact institution. *Financial support:* Available to part-time students. Application deadline: 3/2; applicants required to submit FAFSA. *Unit head:* Dr. Guido Krickx, Associate Dean/Director, 925-631-4514, Fax: 925-376-6521, E-mail: gakl@stmarys-ca.edu. *Application contact:* Bob Peterson, Director of Admissions, 925-631-4505, Fax: 925-376-6521, E-mail: smcmba@stmarys-ca.edu. Web site: http://www.stmarys-ca.edu/professional-mba.

Saint Mary's College of California, School of Liberal Arts, Leadership Studies Programs, Moraga, CA 94556. Offers MA. Part-time and evening/weekend programs available. Postbaccalaureate distance learning degree programs offered (minimal on-campus study). *Students:* 15 full-time (9 women), 47 part-time (27 women); includes 40 minority (13 Black or African American, non-Hispanic/Latino; 10 Asian, non-Hispanic/Latino; 17 Hispanic/Latino), 1 international. Average age 39. In 2011, 37 master's awarded. *Degree requirements:* For master's, research project. *Entrance requirements:* For master's, letters of recommendation, interview. *Application deadline:* For fall admission, 8/1 priority date for domestic students; for winter admission, 12/1 priority date for domestic students; for spring admission, 3/31 priority date for domestic students. Applications are processed on a rolling basis. Application fee: $50. Electronic applications accepted. *Expenses:* Contact institution. *Financial support:* Available to part-time students. Applicants required to submit FAFSA. *Faculty research:* Leadership, organizational change, values, adult learning, transformative learning. *Unit head:* Kenneth Otter, Program Director, 925-631-8692, Fax: 925-631-9214, E-mail: kotter@stmarys-ca.edu. *Application contact:* Tammy Cabading, Manager, Marketing and Admissions, 925-631-4541, Fax: 925-631-9214, E-mail: tappling@stmarys-ca.edu. Web site: http://www.stmarys-ca.edu/node/6399.

Saint Mary's University, Faculty of Commerce, Halifax, NS B3H 3C3, Canada. Offers MBA, MF, PhD. *Accreditation:* AACSB. Part-time and evening/weekend programs available. *Degree requirements:* For master's, research project; for doctorate, thesis/dissertation. *Entrance requirements:* For master's, GMAT, minimum B average; for doctorate, GMAT or GRE, MBA or other master's-level degree, minimum B+ average. *Expenses:* Contact institution.

St. Mary's University, Graduate School, Bill Greehey School of Business, San Antonio, TX 78228-8507. Offers accounting (MBA); business administration (MBA), including finance, international business, management; JD/MBA. *Accreditation:* AACSB. Part-time and evening/weekend programs available. Postbaccalaureate distance learning degree programs offered (minimal on-campus study). *Degree requirements:* For master's, comprehensive exam. *Entrance requirements:* For master's, GMAT. Additional exam requirements/recommendations for international students: Required—TOEFL (minimum score 550 paper-based; 213 computer-based; 80 iBT). Electronic applications accepted. *Faculty research:* International operations, job satisfaction, total quality management, taxation, stress management.

Saint Mary's University of Minnesota, Schools of Graduate and Professional Programs, Graduate School of Business and Technology, Business Administration Program, Winona, MN 55987-1399. Offers MBA. *Unit head:* Matthew Nowakowski, Director, 612-728-5142, Fax: 612-728-5121, E-mail: mjnowa05@smumn.edu. *Application contact:* Yasin Alsaidi, Director of Admissions for Graduate and Professional Programs, 612-728-5207, Fax: 612-728-5121, E-mail: yalsaidi@smumn.edu. Web site: http://www.smumn.edu/graduate-home/areas-of-study/graduate-school-of-business-technology/master-of-business-administration-mba.

Saint Mary's University of Minnesota, Schools of Graduate and Professional Programs, Graduate School of Business and Technology, Management Program, Winona, MN 55987-1399. Offers MA. *Unit head:* Janet Dunn, Director, 612-238-4546, E-mail: jdunn@smumn.edu. *Application contact:* Yasin Alsaidi, Director of Admissions for Graduate and Professional Programs, 612-728-5207, Fax: 612-728-5121, E-mail: yalsaidi@smumn.edu. Web site: http://www.smumn.edu/graduate-home/areas-of-study/graduate-school-of-business-technology/ma-in-management.

Saint Michael's College, Graduate Programs, Program in Administration and Management, Colchester, VT 05439. Offers MSA, CAMS. Part-time and evening/weekend programs available. *Degree requirements:* For master's, portfolio. *Entrance requirements:* For master's, GMAT or GRE or 3 years of work experience, minimum undergraduate GPA of 2.8. Additional exam requirements/recommendations for international students: Required—TOEFL (minimum score 550 paper-based; 213 computer-based; 80 iBT), IELTS (minimum score 6). Electronic applications accepted. *Faculty research:* Learnership/leadership, international banking, top-quality management and organizational changes, national health care, management and ethics.

Saint Peter's University, Graduate Business Programs, MBA Program, Jersey City, NJ 07306-5997. Offers finance (MBA); health care administration (MBA); human resource management (MBA); international business (MBA); management (MBA); management information systems (MBA); marketing (MBA); risk management (MBA); MBA/MS. Part-time and evening/weekend programs available. *Entrance requirements:* Additional exam requirements/recommendations for international students: Required—TOEFL (minimum score 79 computer-based). Electronic applications accepted. *Faculty research:* Finance, health care management, human resource management, international business, management, management information systems, marketing, risk management.

St. Thomas Aquinas College, Division of Business Administration, Sparkill, NY 10976. Offers business administration (MBA); finance (MBA); management (MBA); marketing (MBA). Part-time and evening/weekend programs available. *Entrance requirements:* For master's, GMAT. Additional exam requirements/recommendations for international students: Required—TOEFL. Electronic applications accepted.

St. Thomas University, School of Business, Department of Business Administration, Miami Gardens, FL 33054-6459. Offers M Acc, MBA, Certificate. Part-time and evening/weekend programs available. *Degree requirements:* For master's, comprehensive exam. *Entrance requirements:* Additional exam requirements/recommendations for international students: Required—TOEFL (minimum score 550 paper-based; 213 computer-based; 79 iBT). Electronic applications accepted.

St. Thomas University, School of Business, Department of Management, Miami Gardens, FL 33054-6459. Offers accounting (MBA); general management (MSM, Certificate); health management (MBA, MSM, Certificate); human resource management (MBA, MSM, Certificate); international business (MBA, MIB, MSM, Certificate); justice administration (MSM, Certificate); management accounting (MSM, Certificate); public management (MSM, Certificate); sports administration (MS). Part-time and evening/weekend programs available. *Degree requirements:* For master's, comprehensive exam. *Entrance requirements:* For master's, interview, minimum GPA of 3.0 or GMAT. Additional exam requirements/recommendations for international students: Required—TOEFL (minimum score 550 paper-based; 213 computer-based; 79 iBT). Electronic applications accepted.

St. Thomas University, School of Leadership Studies, Program in Professional Studies, Miami Gardens, FL 33054-6459. Offers executive management (MPS). *Entrance requirements:* Additional exam requirements/recommendations for international students: Required—TOEFL (minimum score 550 paper-based; 213 computer-based; 79 iBT).

Saint Xavier University, Graduate Studies, Graham School of Management, Chicago, IL 60655-3105. Offers employee health benefits (Certificate); finance (MBA); financial fraud examination and management (MBA, Certificate); financial planning (MBA, Certificate); generalist/individualized (MBA); health administration (MBA); managed care (Certificate); management (MBA); marketing (MBA); project management (MBA, Certificate): MBA/MS. *Accreditation:* ACBSP. Part-time and evening/weekend programs available. *Entrance requirements:* For master's, GMAT, minimum GPA of 3.0, 2 years of work experience. *Application deadline:* For fall admission, 8/15 for domestic students. Applications are processed on a rolling basis. Application fee: $35. Electronic applications accepted. *Expenses:* Contact institution. *Financial support:* Career-related internships or fieldwork available. Support available to part-time students. Financial award applicants required to submit FAFSA. *Unit head:* Dr. John E. Eber, Dean, 773-298-3601, Fax: 773-298-3601, E-mail: eber@sxu.edu. *Application contact:* Beth Gierach, Managing Director of Admission, 773-298-3053, Fax: 773-298-3076, E-mail: gierach@sxu.edu. Web site: http://www.sxu.edu/academics/colleges_schools/gsm/.

Salem International University, School of Business, Salem, WV 26426-0500. Offers information security (MBA); international business (MBA). Part-time programs available. Postbaccalaureate distance learning degree programs offered (no on-campus study). *Entrance requirements:* For master's, minimum undergraduate GPA of 2.5, course work in business, resume. Additional exam requirements/recommendations for international students: Recommended—TOEFL (minimum score 550 paper-based; 213 computer-based), IELTS (minimum score 6.5). Electronic applications accepted. *Expenses:* Contact institution. *Faculty research:* Organizational behavior strategy, marketing services.

Salem State University, School of Graduate Studies, Program in Business Administration, Salem, MA 01970-5353. Offers MBA. Part-time and evening/weekend programs available. *Entrance requirements:* For master's, GMAT. Additional exam requirements/recommendations for international students: Required—TOEFL (minimum score 550 paper-based; 80 iBT) or IELTS (minimum score 5.5).

Salisbury University, Graduate Division, Department of Business Administration, Salisbury, MD 21801-6837. Offers accounting track (MBA); general track (MBA). *Accreditation:* AACSB. Part-time and evening/weekend programs available. *Faculty:* 9 full-time (3 women), 2 part-time/adjunct (1 woman). *Students:* 22 full-time (7 women), 25 part-time (7 women); includes 6 minority (4 Black or African American, non-Hispanic/Latino; 1 Asian, non-Hispanic/Latino; 1 Hispanic/Latino), 4 international. Average age 26. 4 applicants, 75% accepted, 3 enrolled. In 2011, 37 master's awarded. *Entrance requirements:* For master's, GMAT, resume; 2 recommendations, essay, minimum undergraduate GPA of 2.5. Additional exam requirements/recommendations for international students: Required—TOEFL (minimum score 550 paper-based; 79 iBT). *Application deadline:* For fall admission, 3/1 priority date for domestic students; for spring admission, 10/15 priority date for domestic students. Applications are processed on a rolling basis. Application fee: $45. Electronic applications accepted. *Expenses: Tuition, area resident:* Part-time $306 per credit hour. Tuition, state resident: part-time $306 per credit hour. Tuition, nonresident: part-time $595 per credit hour. *Required fees:* $68 per credit hour. *Financial support:* In 2011–12, 17 students received support. Institutionally sponsored loans, scholarships/grants, and unspecified assistantships available. Support available to part-time students. Financial award application deadline: 3/1; financial award applicants required to submit FAFSA. *Faculty research:* Chesapeake Bay Farms Feasibility Study, strategic planning retreat, shore trends survey. *Unit head:* Yvonne Downie, MBA Director, 410-548-3983, Fax: 410-546-6208, E-mail: yxdownie@salisbury.edu. *Application contact:* Aaron Basko, Assistant Vice President for Enrollment Management, 410-543-6161, Fax: 410-546-6016, E-mail: admissions@salisbury.edu. Web site: http://mba.salisbury.edu/.

Salve Regina University, Holistic Graduate Programs, Newport, RI 02840-4192. Offers holistic counseling (MA); holistic leadership (MA, CAGS); holistic leadership and change management (CAGS); holistic leadership and management (CAGS); holistic studies (CAGS); mental health counseling (CAGS); professional applications of the expressive and creative arts (CAGS). Part-time and evening/weekend programs available. *Faculty:* 2 full-time (1 woman), 13 part-time/adjunct (10 women). *Students:* 14 full-time (12 women), 75 part-time (67 women). *Degree requirements:* For master's, internship, project. *Entrance requirements:* For master's, GMAT, GRE General Test, or MAT. Additional exam requirements/recommendations for international students: Required—TOEFL (minimum score 600 paper-based; 250 computer-based; 100 iBT) or IELTS. *Application deadline:* For fall admission, 3/15 priority date for domestic students, 3/15 for international students; for spring admission, 9/15 priority date for domestic students, 9/15 for international students. Applications are processed on a rolling basis. Application fee: $60. Electronic applications accepted. *Expenses: Tuition:* Full-time $7740; part-time $430 per credit. *Required fees:* $40 per semester. Tuition and fees vary according to program. *Financial support:* Career-related internships or fieldwork and Federal Work-Study available. Support available to part-time students. Financial award application deadline: 3/1; financial award applicants required to submit FAFSA. *Unit head:* Dr. Nancy Gordon, Director, 401-341-3290, Fax: 401-341-2977, E-mail: nancy.gordon@salve.edu. *Application contact:* Kelly Alverson, Associate Director of Graduate Admissions, 401-341-2153, Fax: 401-341-2973, E-mail: kelly.alverson@salve.edu. Web site: http://www.salve.edu/academics/graduateStudies/programs/hs/.

Salve Regina University, Program in Business Administration, Newport, RI 02840-4192. Offers business administration (MBA); business studies (Certificate); human resources management (Certificate); management (Certificate); organizational development (Certificate). Part-time and evening/weekend programs available. Postbaccalaureate distance learning degree programs offered (minimal on-campus study). *Faculty:* 2 full-time (1 woman), 15 part-time/adjunct (6 women). *Students:* 35 full-time (14 women), 86 part-time (41 women); includes 10 minority (5 Black or African American, non-Hispanic/Latino; 3 Asian, non-Hispanic/Latino; 2 Hispanic/Latino), 3 international. *Entrance requirements:* For master's, GMAT, GRE General Test, or MAT, 6 undergraduate credits each in accounting, economics, quantitative analysis and calculus or statistics. Additional exam requirements/recommendations for international students: Required—TOEFL (minimum score 600 paper-based; 250 computer-based; 100 iBT) or IELTS. *Application deadline:* For fall admission, 3/15 priority date for domestic students, 3/15 for international students; for spring admission, 9/15 priority date for domestic students, 9/15 for international students. Applications are processed on a rolling basis. Application fee: $60. Electronic applications accepted. *Expenses: Tuition:* Full-time $7740; part-time $430 per credit. *Required fees:* $40 per semester. Tuition and fees vary according to program. *Financial support:* Career-related internships or fieldwork and Federal Work-Study available. Support available to part-time students. Financial award application deadline: 3/1; financial award applicants required to submit FAFSA. *Unit head:* Dr. Arlene Nicholas, Director, 401-341-3280, E-mail: arlene.nicholas@salve.edu. *Application contact:* Kelly Alverson, Associate Director of Graduate Admissions, 401-341-2153, Fax: 401-341-2973, E-mail: kelly.alverson@salve.edu. Web site: http://www.salve.edu/graduatestudies/programs/gmt/.

Salve Regina University, Program in Management, Newport, RI 02840-4192. Offers business studies (Certificate); holistic leadership and management (Certificate); human resources management (Certificate); law enforcement leadership (MS); leadership and change management (Certificate); management (Certificate); organizational development (Certificate). Part-time and evening/weekend programs available. Postbaccalaureate distance learning degree programs offered (minimal on-campus study). *Faculty:* 2 full-time (1 woman), 15 part-time/adjunct (6 women). *Students:* 9 full-time (6 women), 40 part-time (20 women); includes 2 minority (both Black or African American, non-Hispanic/Latino). *Entrance requirements:* For master's, GMAT, GRE General Test, or MAT. Additional exam requirements/recommendations for international students: Required—TOEFL (minimum score 600 paper-based; 250 computer-based; 100 iBT). *Application deadline:* For fall admission, 3/15 priority date for domestic students, 3/5 for international students; for spring admission, 3/15 priority date for domestic students, 9/15 for international students. Applications are processed on a rolling basis. Application fee: $60. Electronic applications accepted. *Expenses: Tuition:* Full-time $7740; part-time $430 per credit. *Required fees:* $40 per semester. Tuition and fees vary according to program. *Financial support:* Career-related internships or fieldwork and Federal Work-Study available. Support available to part-time students. Financial award application deadline: 3/1; financial award applicants required to submit FAFSA. *Unit head:* Dr. Arlene Nicholas, Director, 401-341-3280, E-mail: arlene.nicholas@salve.edu. *Application contact:* Kelly Alverson, Associate Director of Graduate Admissions, 401-341-2153, Fax: 401-341-2973, E-mail: kelly.alverson@salve.edu. Web site: http://www.salve.edu/graduatestudies/programs/mgt/.

Samford University, Brock School of Business, Birmingham, AL 35229. Offers M Acc, MBA, JD/M Acc, JD/MBA, MBA/M Acc. *Accreditation:* AACSB. Part-time and evening/weekend programs available. *Faculty:* 14 full-time (3 women), 1 (woman) part-time/adjunct. *Students:* 117 full-time (38 women), 18 part-time (6 women); includes 15 minority (6 Black or African American, non-Hispanic/Latino; 1 American Indian or Alaska Native, non-Hispanic/Latino; 7 Asian, non-Hispanic/Latino; 1 Hispanic/Latino), 12 international. Average age 27. 103 applicants, 83% accepted, 69 enrolled. In 2011, 71 master's awarded. *Degree requirements:* For master's, capstone course. *Entrance requirements:* For master's, GMAT. Additional exam requirements/recommendations for international students: Required—TOEFL (minimum score 80 iBT) or IELTS (minimum score 6.5). *Application deadline:* For fall admission, 7/31 priority date for domestic students, 5/1 for international students; for spring admission, 12/1 priority date for domestic students, 10/1 for international students. Applications are processed on a rolling basis. Application fee: $25. *Expenses: Tuition:* Full-time $29,934; part-time $655 per credit. *Required fees:* $705. *Financial support:* In 2011–12, 37 students received support. Career-related internships or fieldwork, institutionally sponsored loans, scholarships/grants, and tuition waivers (partial) available. Support available to part-time students. Financial award applicants required to submit FAFSA. *Faculty research:* Entrepreneurship, accounting, finance, marketing, economics. *Total annual research expenditures:* $25,000. *Unit head:* Dr. Howard Finch, Dean, 205-726-2364, Fax: 205-726-4218, E-mail: hfinch@samford.edu. *Application contact:* Rebekah DeBoer, Assistant Director of Academic Programs, 205-726-2040, Fax: 205-726-2464, E-mail: rdeboer@samford.edu. Web site: http://business.samford.edu/.

Sam Houston State University, College of Business Administration, Department of General Business and Finance, Huntsville, TX 77341. Offers banking and financial institutions (EMBA); business administration (MBA, MS); project management (MS). *Faculty:* 14 full-time (3 women). *Students:* 85 full-time (36 women), 233 part-time (103 women); includes 82 minority (31 Black or African American, non-Hispanic/Latino; 3 American Indian or Alaska Native, non-Hispanic/Latino; 11 Asian, non-Hispanic/Latino; 37 Hispanic/Latino), 11 international. Average age 31. 300 applicants, 52% accepted, 135 enrolled. In 2011, 74 master's awarded. *Entrance requirements:* For master's, GMAT. Additional exam requirements/recommendations for international students: Required—TOEFL (minimum score 550 paper-based; 213 computer-based; 79 iBT). *Application deadline:* For fall admission, 8/1 for domestic students, 6/25 for international students; for spring admission, 12/1 for domestic students, 11/12 for international students. Applications are processed on a rolling basis. Application fee: $45 ($75 for international students). Electronic applications accepted. *Expenses:* Tuition, state resident: full-time $4420; part-time $221 per credit hour. Tuition, nonresident: full-time $10,680; part-time $534 per credit hour. *Required fees:* $329 per credit hour. *Financial support:* Application deadline: 5/31; applicants required to submit FAFSA. *Unit head:* Dr. Kurt Jesswein, Chair, 936-294-4582, E-mail: kurt.jesswein@shsu.edu. *Application contact:* Dr. Leroy Ashorn, Advisor, 936-294-4040, Fax: 936-294-3612, E-mail: busgrad@shsu.edu. Web site: http://www.shsu.edu/~gba_www/.

San Diego State University, Graduate and Research Affairs, College of Business Administration, Department of Management, San Diego, CA 92182. Offers entrepreneurship (MS); human resources management (MS); management science (MS). Part-time and evening/weekend programs available. *Degree requirements:* For master's, thesis or alternative. *Entrance requirements:* For master's, GMAT, resume, letters of reference. Additional exam requirements/recommendations for international students: Required—TOEFL. Electronic applications accepted.

San Diego State University, Graduate and Research Affairs, College of Business Administration, Program in Business Administration, San Diego, CA 92182. Offers MBA. *Accreditation:* AACSB. Part-time programs available. *Degree requirements:* For master's, thesis or alternative. *Entrance requirements:* For master's, GMAT, resume, letters of reference. Additional exam requirements/recommendations for international students: Required—TOEFL. Electronic applications accepted.

San Francisco State University, Division of Graduate Studies, College of Business, San Francisco, CA 94132-1722. Offers MA, MBA, MS. *Unit head:* Dr. Caran Colvin, Dean, 415-405-3752. *Application contact:* Armaan Moattari, Assistant Director, Graduate Programs, 415-817-4314, E-mail: amoatt@sfsu.edu. Web site: http://mba.sfsu.edu.

San Jose State University, Graduate Studies and Research, Lucas Graduate School of Business, Programs in Business Administration, San Jose, CA 95192-0001. Offers MBA. *Accreditation:* AACSB. *Degree requirements:* For master's, comprehensive exam, thesis or alternative. *Entrance requirements:* For master's, GMAT, minimum GPA of 3.0. Electronic applications accepted.

Santa Clara University, Leavey School of Business, Program in Business Administration, Santa Clara, CA 95053. Offers accounting (MBA); entrepreneurship (MBA); executive business administration (EMBA); finance (MBA); food and agribusiness (MBA); international business (MBA); leading people and organizations (MBA); managing technology and innovation (MBA); marketing management (MBA); supply chain management (MBA). *Accreditation:* AACSB. Part-time and evening/weekend programs available. *Students:* 196 full-time (80 women), 669 part-time (224 women); includes 302 minority (12 Black or African American, non-Hispanic/Latino; 246 Asian, non-Hispanic/Latino; 35 Hispanic/Latino; 6 Native Hawaiian or other Pacific Islander, non-Hispanic/Latino; 3 Two or more races, non-Hispanic/Latino), 186 international. Average age 32. 365 applicants, 74% accepted, 199 enrolled. In 2011, 366 degrees awarded. *Degree requirements:* For master's, thesis or alternative. *Entrance requirements:* For master's, GMAT, GRE. Additional exam requirements/recommendations for international students: Required—TOEFL (minimum score 600 paper-based; 250 computer-based; 100 iBT). *Application deadline:* For fall admission, 6/1 for domestic and international students; for spring admission, 1/19 for domestic students, 1/17 for international students. Applications are processed on a rolling basis. Application fee: $75 ($100 for international students). Electronic applications accepted. *Expenses:* Contact institution. *Financial support:* In 2011–12, 350 students received support. Fellowships with partial tuition reimbursements available, research assistantships with partial tuition reimbursements available, career-related internships or fieldwork, Federal Work-Study, institutionally sponsored loans, scholarships/grants, health care benefits, and unspecified assistantships available. Support available to part-time students. Financial award application deadline: 6/1; financial award applicants required to submit FAFSA. *Unit head:* Elizabeth B. Ford, Senior Assistant Dean, 408-554-2752, Fax: 408-554-4571, E-mail: eford@scu.edu. *Application contact:* Tammy Fox, Assistant Director, Graduate Business Admissions, 408-554-7858, E-mail: tkfox@scu.edu.

Savannah State University, Master of Business Administration Program, Savannah, GA 31404. Offers MBA. *Accreditation:* AACSB. Part-time programs available. *Entrance requirements:* For master's, GMAT or GRE. Additional exam requirements/recommendations for international students: Required—TOEFL. Electronic applications accepted.

Schiller International University, MBA Program, Madrid, Spain, Madrid, Spain. Offers international business (MBA). Part-time programs available. *Degree requirements:* For master's, comprehensive exam, thesis optional. *Entrance requirements:* Additional exam requirements/recommendations for international students: Required—TOEFL (minimum score 550 paper-based; 213 computer-based).

Schiller International University, MBA Program Paris, France, Paris, France. Offers international business (MBA). Bilingual French/English MBA available for native French speakers. Part-time and evening/weekend programs available. Postbaccalaureate distance learning degree programs offered (no on-campus study). *Degree requirements:* For master's, comprehensive exam, thesis or alternative. *Entrance requirements:* Additional exam requirements/recommendations for international students: Required—TOEFL (minimum score 550 paper-based; 213 computer-based).

Schiller International University, MBA Programs, Florida, Largo, FL 33770. Offers financial planning (MBA); information technology (MBA); international business (MBA); international hotel and tourism management (MBA). Part-time and evening/weekend programs available. Postbaccalaureate distance learning degree programs offered (no on-campus study). *Degree requirements:* For master's, thesis optional. *Entrance requirements:* Additional exam requirements/recommendations for international students: Required—TOEFL (minimum score 550 paper-based; 213 computer-based).

Schiller International University, MBA Programs, Heidelberg, Germany, Heidelberg, Germany. Offers international business (MBA, MIM); management of information technology (MBA). Part-time and evening/weekend programs available. *Degree requirements:* For master's, thesis optional. *Entrance requirements:* Additional exam requirements/recommendations for international students: Required—TOEFL (minimum score 550 paper-based; 213 computer-based). *Faculty research:* Leadership, international economy, foreign direct investment.

Schiller International University, MBA Program, Strasbourg, France Campus, Strasbourg, France. Offers international business (MBA). Part-time and evening/weekend programs available. Postbaccalaureate distance learning degree programs offered (no on-campus study). *Degree requirements:* For master's, oral comprehensive exam or thesis. *Entrance requirements:* Additional exam requirements/recommendations for international students: Recommended—TOEFL (minimum score 550 paper-based; 213 computer-based).

Schreiner University, MBA Program, Kerrville, TX 78028-5697. Offers MBA. *Faculty:* 3 full-time (0 women). *Students:* 10 full-time (4 women). Average age 27. 22 applicants, 50% accepted, 10 enrolled. *Entrance requirements:* For master's, GMAT, 3 recommendations; personal essay; transcripts. *Application deadline:* Applications are processed on a rolling basis. Electronic applications accepted. *Expenses: Tuition:* Full-time $16,200; part-time $450 per credit hour. *Financial support:* Institutionally sponsored loans available. Financial award application deadline: 8/1. *Unit head:* Dr. Charles Torti, Director, 830-792-7255. *Application contact:* Sylvia Coday, Administrative Assistant, 830-895-7100, E-mail: scoday@schreiner.edu. Web site: http://www.schreiner.edu/mba/.

Seattle Pacific University, Master's Degree in Business Administration (MBA) Program, Seattle, WA 98119-1997. Offers MBA. *Accreditation:* AACSB. Part-time programs available. *Entrance requirements:* For master's, GMAT, minimum GPA of 3.0. Additional exam requirements/recommendations for international students: Required—TOEFL (minimum score 225 computer-based). Electronic applications accepted.

Seattle University, Albers School of Business and Economics, Master of Business Administration Program, Seattle, WA 98122-1090. Offers MBA, MIB, Certificate, JD/MBA, JD/MIB. *Accreditation:* AACSB. Part-time and evening/weekend programs available. *Faculty:* 20 full-time (5 women), 13 part-time/adjunct (5 women). *Students:* 83 full-time (38 women), 441 part-time (153 women); includes 130 minority (8 Black or African American, non-Hispanic/Latino; 1 American Indian or Alaska Native, non-Hispanic/Latino; 95 Asian, non-Hispanic/Latino; 14 Hispanic/Latino; 3 Native Hawaiian or other Pacific Islander, non-Hispanic/Latino; 9 Two or more races, non-Hispanic/Latino), 38 international. Average age 30. 257 applicants, 58% accepted, 80 enrolled. In 2011, 167 master's, 7 other advanced degrees awarded. *Entrance requirements:* For master's, GMAT, minimum GPA of 3.0, 2 years of related work experience. Additional exam requirements/recommendations for international students: Required—TOEFL (minimum score 580 paper-based; 92 iBT). *Application deadline:* For fall admission, 8/20 priority date for domestic students, 4/1 for international students; for winter admission, 11/20 priority date for domestic students, 9/1 for international students; for spring admission, 2/20 priority date for domestic students, 12/1 for international students. Applications are processed on a rolling basis. Application fee: $55. Electronic applications accepted. *Financial support:* Career-related internships or fieldwork and Federal Work-Study available. Support available to part-time students. Financial award applicants required to submit FAFSA. *Unit head:* Dr. Greg Magnan, Director, 206-296-5700, Fax: 206-296-5795, E-mail: gmagnan@seattleu.edu. *Application contact:* Janet Shandley, Director of Graduate Admissions, 206-296-5900, Fax: 206-298-5656, E-mail: grad_admissions@seattleu.edu.

Seton Hall University, Stillman School of Business, South Orange, NJ 07079-2697. Offers MBA, MS, Certificate. *Accreditation:* AACSB. Part-time and evening/weekend programs available. *Faculty:* 37 full-time (9 women), 19 part-time/adjunct (1 woman). *Students:* 166 full-time (65 women), 284 part-time (131 women); includes 113 minority (21 Black or African American, non-Hispanic/Latino; 81 Asian, non-Hispanic/Latino; 9 Hispanic/Latino; 2 Native Hawaiian or other Pacific Islander, non-Hispanic/Latino). Average age 28. 459 applicants, 59% accepted, 208 enrolled. In 2011, 210 master's awarded. *Degree requirements:* For master's, 20 hours of community service (Social Responsibility Project). *Entrance requirements:* For master's, GMAT, GRE or CPA, advanced degree from AACSB institution, MS in a business discipline, professional degree (MD, JD, PhD, DVM, DDS, etc.), minimum undergraduate GPA of 3.0. Additional exam requirements/recommendations for international students: Required—TOEFL (minimum score 102 iBT), IELTS or Pearson Test of English. *Application deadline:* For fall admission, 5/31 priority date for domestic students, 3/31 for international students; for spring admission, 10/31 priority date for domestic students, 9/30 for international students. Applications are processed on a rolling basis. Application fee: $75. Electronic applications accepted. *Expenses:* Contact institution. *Financial support:* In 2011–12, 24 students received support, including research assistantships with full tuition reimbursements available (averaging $34,404 per year); career-related internships or fieldwork, Federal Work-Study, scholarships/grants, and unspecified assistantships also available. Support available to part-time students. Financial award application deadline: 6/30; financial award applicants required to submit FAFSA. *Faculty research:* Financial, hedge funds, international business, legal issues, disclosure and branding. *Total annual research expenditures:* $500,000. *Unit head:* Dr. Joyce Strawser, Dean, 973-761-9013, Fax: 973-275-2465, E-mail: joyce.strawser@shu.edu. *Application contact:* Catherine Bianchi, Director of Graduate Admissions, 973-761-9262, Fax: 973-761-9208, E-mail: catherine.bianchi@shu.edu. Web site: http://www.shu.edu/academics/business/.

Seton Hill University, Program in Business Administration, Greensburg, PA 15601. Offers entrepreneurship (MBA, Certificate); management (MBA). Part-time and evening/weekend programs available. *Faculty:* 5 full-time (3 women), 7 part-time/adjunct (1 woman). *Students:* 30 full-time (14 women), 55 part-time (26 women); includes 4 minority (2 Black or African American, non-Hispanic/Latino; 1 American Indian or Alaska Native, non-Hispanic/Latino; 1 Hispanic/Latino), 6 international. In 2011, 35 master's awarded. *Entrance requirements:* For master's, resume, 3 letters of recommendation, personal statement, transcripts. Additional exam requirements/recommendations for international students: Required—TOEFL (minimum score 600 paper-based; 250 computer-based; 100 iBT), IELTS (minimum score 6.5). *Application deadline:* Applications are processed on a rolling basis. Application fee: $0. Electronic applications accepted. *Expenses: Tuition:* Full-time $13,446; part-time $747 per credit. *Required fees:* $700; $25 per credit. $50 per term. *Financial support:* Federal Work-Study and tuition discounts available. *Faculty research:* Entrepreneurship, leadership and strategy, knowledge management. *Unit head:* Dr. Douglas Nelson, Director, 724-830-4738, E-mail: dnelson@setonhill.edu. *Application contact:* Laurel Komarny, Program Counselor, 724-838-4209, E-mail: komarny@setonhill.edu. Web site: http://www.setonhill.edu/academics/mba/index.cfm.

Shenandoah University, Byrd School of Business, Winchester, VA 22601-5195. Offers business administration (MBA); business administration essentials (Certificate). *Accreditation:* AACSB. Part-time and evening/weekend programs available. *Faculty:* 9 full-time (1 woman), 3 part-time/adjunct (2 women). *Students:* 44 full-time (21 women), 37 part-time (20 women); includes 5 minority (2 Black or African American, non-Hispanic/Latino; 1 American Indian or Alaska Native, non-Hispanic/Latino; 2 Asian, non-Hispanic/Latino), 26 international. Average age 31. 204 applicants, 25% accepted, 24 enrolled. In 2011, 38 master's, 1 other advanced degree awarded. *Entrance requirements:* For master's, 2 letters of recommendation, resume, interview, brief narrative; for Certificate, 2 letters of recommendation, resume, interview, brief narrative, transcripts from all institutions of higher learning attended. Additional exam requirements/recommendations for international students: Required—TOEFL (minimum score 550 paper-based; 213 computer-based; 79 iBT), IELTS (minimum score 6.5), Sakae Institute of Study Abroad (minimum score 550). *Application deadline:* Applications are processed on a rolling basis. Application fee: $30. Electronic applications accepted. *Expenses: Tuition:* Full-time $17,952; part-time $748 per credit. *Required fees:* $500 per term. Tuition and fees vary according to course level, course load and program. *Financial support:* In 2011–12, 21 students received support, including 12 teaching assistantships with partial tuition reimbursements available (averaging $3,087 per year); career-related internships or fieldwork, institutionally sponsored loans, scholarships/grants, unspecified assistantships, and federal loans, alternative loans also available. Support available to part-time students. Financial award application deadline: 3/15; financial award applicants required to submit FAFSA. *Faculty research:* Supply chain management, international business, micro and macro economics, organizational behavior and theory, marketing research, general accounting. *Unit head:* Dr. Randy Boxx, Dean, 540-665-4572, Fax: 540-665-5437, E-mail: rboxx@su.edu. *Application contact:* David Anthony, Dean of Admissions, 540-665-4581, Fax: 540-665-4627, E-mail: admit@su.edu. Web site: http://www.su.edu/business/.

Shippensburg University of Pennsylvania, School of Graduate Studies, College of Arts and Sciences, Department of Sociology and Anthropology, Shippensburg, PA 17257-2299. Offers organizational development and leadership (MS), including business, communications, environmental management, higher education structure and policy, historical administration, individual and organizational development, management information systems, public organizations, social structures and organizations. Part-time and evening/weekend programs available. *Faculty:* 3 full-time (all women). *Students:* 12 full-time (6 women), 40 part-time (34 women); includes 6 minority (3 Black or African American, non-Hispanic/Latino; 2 Asian, non-Hispanic/

Latino; 1 Two or more races, non-Hispanic/Latino), 2 international. Average age 33. 52 applicants, 46% accepted, 16 enrolled. In 2011, 34 master's awarded. *Degree requirements:* For master's, capstone experience including internship. *Entrance requirements:* For master's, interview (if GPA less than 2.75), resume, personal goals statement. Additional exam requirements/recommendations for international students: Required—TOEFL (minimum score 580 paper-based; 237 computer-based); Recommended—IELTS (minimum score 6). *Application deadline:* For fall admission, 4/30 for international students; for spring admission, 9/30 for international students. Applications are processed on a rolling basis. Application fee: $30. Electronic applications accepted. *Expenses: Tuition, area resident:* Part-time $416 per credit. Tuition, state resident: part-time $416 per credit. Tuition, nonresident: part-time $624 per credit. *Required fees:* $119 per credit. *Financial support:* In 2011–12, 9 research assistantships with full tuition reimbursements (averaging $5,000 per year) were awarded; career-related internships or fieldwork, scholarships/grants, unspecified assistantships, and resident hall director and student payroll positions also available. Support available to part-time students. Financial award applicants required to submit FAFSA. *Unit head:* Dr. Barbara Denison, Program Coordinator, 717-477-1735, Fax: 717-477-4011, E-mail: bjdeni@ship.edu. *Application contact:* Jeremy R. Goshorn, Assistant Dean of Graduate Admissions, 717-477-1231, Fax: 717-477-4016, E-mail: jrgoshorn@ship.edu. Web site: http://www.ship.edu/odl/.

Shippensburg University of Pennsylvania, School of Graduate Studies, John L. Grove College of Business, Shippensburg, PA 17257-2299. Offers advanced studies in business (Certificate); business administration (MBA). *Accreditation:* AACSB. Part-time and evening/weekend programs available. Postbaccalaureate distance learning degree programs offered (minimal on-campus study). *Faculty:* 29 full-time (11 women), 1 part-time/adjunct (0 women). *Students:* 20 full-time (6 women), 110 part-time (42 women); includes 8 minority (2 Black or African American, non-Hispanic/Latino; 2 American Indian or Alaska Native, non-Hispanic/Latino; 3 Asian, non-Hispanic/Latino; 1 Hispanic/Latino), 5 international. Average age 32. 117 applicants, 50% accepted, 54 enrolled. In 2011, 44 master's awarded. *Entrance requirements:* For master's, GMAT (minimum score 450 if less than 5 years post-graduate experience, including some mid-level management), resume; relevant work/classroom experience; personal goals statement; prerequisites of quantitative analysis, computer usage, oral and written communications. Additional exam requirements/recommendations for international students: Required—TOEFL (minimum score 580 paper-based; 237 computer-based); Recommended—IELTS (minimum score 6). *Application deadline:* For fall admission, 4/30 for international students; for spring admission, 9/30 for international students. Applications are processed on a rolling basis. Application fee: $30. Electronic applications accepted. *Expenses: Tuition, area resident:* Part-time $416 per credit. Tuition, state resident: part-time $416 per credit. Tuition, nonresident: part-time $624 per credit. *Required fees:* $119 per credit. *Financial support:* In 2011–12, 8 research assistantships with full tuition reimbursements (averaging $5,000 per year) were awarded; career-related internships or fieldwork, scholarships/grants, unspecified assistantships, and resident hall director and student payroll positions also available. Support available to part-time students. Financial award application deadline: 3/1; financial award applicants required to submit FAFSA. *Unit head:* Dr. Robert D. Stephens, Director of MBA Program, 717-477-1483, Fax: 717-477-4003, E-mail: rdstep@ship.edu. *Application contact:* Jeremy R. Goshorn, Associate Dean of Graduate Admissions, 717-477-1231, Fax: 717-477-4016, E-mail: jrgoshorn@ship.edu. Web site: http://www.ship.edu/mba.

Shorter University, Professional Studies, Rome, GA 30165. Offers accountancy (MAC); business administration (MBA); curriculum and instruction (M Ed); leadership (MA). Evening/weekend programs available. *Degree requirements:* For master's, project. *Entrance requirements:* For master's, minimum undergraduate GPA of 2.75 in last 60 hours, 3 years of work experience. Additional exam requirements/recommendations for international students: Required—TOEFL (minimum score 550 paper-based; 213 computer-based; 79 iBT). *Faculty research:* Systems design, leadership, pedagogy using technology.

Silicon Valley University, Graduate Programs, San Jose, CA 95131. Offers business administration (MBA); computer engineering (MSCE); computer science (MSCS). *Degree requirements:* For master's, project (MSCS).

Silver Lake College of the Holy Family, Division of Graduate Studies, Program in Management and Organizational Behavior, Manitowoc, WI 54220-9319. Offers MS. Part-time and evening/weekend programs available. Postbaccalaureate distance learning degree programs offered (minimal on-campus study). *Degree requirements:* For master's, thesis optional. *Entrance requirements:* For master's, minimum undergraduate GPA of 3.0, statement of purpose, three letters of recommendation, professional resume. Additional exam requirements/recommendations for international students: Required—TOEFL. Electronic applications accepted.

Simmons College, School of Management, Boston, MA 02115. Offers communications management (MS); entrepreneurship (Certificate); health administration (MHA); health care administration (CAGS); management (MBA); MS/MA. *Accreditation:* AACSB. *Unit head:* Cathy Minehan, Dean. *Application contact:* 617-521-3840, Fax: 617-521-3880, E-mail: somadm@simmons.edu. Web site: http://www.simmons.edu/som.

Simon Fraser University, Graduate Studies, Faculty of Business Administration, Burnaby, BC V5A 1S6, Canada. Offers business administration (EMBA, PhD); financial management (MA); general business (MBA); global asset and wealth management (MBA); management of technology/biotechnology (MBA); MBA/MRM. *Accreditation:* AACSB. Postbaccalaureate distance learning degree programs offered. *Degree requirements:* For master's, thesis or written project. *Entrance requirements:* For master's, minimum GPA of 3.0. Additional exam requirements/recommendations for international students: Required—TOEFL. *Expenses:* Contact institution. *Faculty research:* Leadership, marketing and technology, wealth management.

SIT Graduate Institute, Graduate Programs, Master's Programs in Intercultural Service, Leadership, and Management, Brattleboro, VT 05302-0676. Offers conflict transformation (MA); intercultural service, leadership, and management (MA); international education (MA); sustainable development (MA). Postbaccalaureate distance learning degree programs offered (minimal on-campus study). *Degree requirements:* For master's, one foreign language, thesis. *Entrance requirements:* For master's, 3 letters of reference. Additional exam requirements/recommendations for international students: Required—TOEFL. *Faculty research:* Intercultural communication, conflict resolution, advising and training, world issues, international business.

Sonoma State University, School of Business and Economics, Rohnert Park, CA 94928-3609. Offers MBA. *Accreditation:* AACSB. Part-time and evening/weekend programs available. *Faculty:* 7 full-time (3 women). *Students:* 1 full-time (0 women), 37 part-time (21 women); includes 9 minority (2 American Indian or Alaska Native, non-Hispanic/Latino; 5 Hispanic/Latino; 2 Two or more races, non-Hispanic/Latino). Average age 29. 38 applicants, 32% accepted, 8 enrolled. In 2011, 39 master's awarded. *Degree requirements:* For master's, thesis or alternative. *Entrance requirements:* For master's, GMAT. Additional exam requirements/recommendations for international students: Required—TOEFL (minimum score 500 paper-based; 173 computer-based). *Application deadline:* For fall admission, 1/31 priority date for domestic students; for spring admission, 8/31 for domestic students. Applications are processed on a rolling basis. Application fee: $55. *Financial support:* Career-related internships or fieldwork, Federal Work-Study, institutionally sponsored loans, and scholarships/grants available. Support available to part-time students. Financial award application deadline: 3/2; financial award applicants required to submit FAFSA. *Unit head:* Dr. Terry Lease, Department Chair, 707-664-2377, E-mail: terry.lease@sonoma.edu. *Application contact:* Dr. Kris Wright, Associate Vice Provost, Academic Programs/Graduate Studies, 707-664-3954, E-mail: wright@sonoma.edu. Web site: http://www.sonoma.edu/busadmin/mba/.

Southeastern Louisiana University, College of Business, Hammond, LA 70402. Offers accounting (MBA); general (MBA). *Accreditation:* AACSB. *Faculty:* 18 full-time (2 women). *Students:* 85 full-time (41 women), 21 part-time (10 women); includes 11 minority (5 Black or African American, non-Hispanic/Latino; 2 Asian, non-Hispanic/Latino; 2 Hispanic/Latino; 2 Two or more races, non-Hispanic/Latino), 9 international. Average age 30. 37 applicants, 100% accepted, 23 enrolled. In 2011, 73 degrees awarded. *Entrance requirements:* For master's, GMAT (minimum score 450), minimum cumulative GPA of 2.75 for all undergraduate work attempted or 3.0 on all upper-division undergraduate coursework attempted. Additional exam requirements/recommendations for international students: Required—TOEFL (minimum score 525 paper-based; 195 computer-based; 61 iBT). *Application deadline:* For fall admission, 7/15 priority date for domestic students, 6/1 for international students; for spring admission, 12/1 priority date for domestic students, 10/1 for international students. Applications are processed on a rolling basis. Application fee: $20 ($30 for international students). Electronic applications accepted. *Expenses:* Tuition, state resident: full-time $3977; part-time $283 per semester hour. Tuition, nonresident: full-time $13,482; part-time $811 per semester hour. *Financial support:* Career-related internships or fieldwork, Federal Work-Study, institutionally sponsored loans, and scholarships/grants available. Support available to part-time students. Financial award application deadline: 5/1; financial award applicants required to submit FAFSA. *Faculty research:* Ethical decision-making in accounting, entrepreneurship and emerging information, leadership and organizational performance. *Unit head:* Dr. Randy Settoon, Dean, 985-549-2258, Fax: 985-549-5038, E-mail: rsettoon@selu.edu. *Application contact:* Sandra Meyers, Graduate Admissions Analyst, 985-549-5620, Fax: 985-549-5882, E-mail: admissions@selu.edu. Web site: http://www.selu.edu/acad_research/colleges/bus/index.html.

Southeastern Oklahoma State University, School of Business, Durant, OK 74701-0609. Offers MBA. *Accreditation:* AACSB; ACBSP. Part-time and evening/weekend programs available. *Faculty:* 13 full-time (6 women), 5 part-time/adjunct (0 women). *Students:* 7 full-time (3 women), 24 part-time (11 women); includes 7 minority (6 American Indian or Alaska Native, non-Hispanic/Latino; 1 Hispanic/Latino), 9 international. Average age 32. 15 applicants, 100% accepted, 15 enrolled. *Degree requirements:* For master's, thesis optional. *Entrance requirements:* For master's, GMAT, minimum GPA of 3.0 in last 60 hours or 2.75 overall. Additional exam requirements/recommendations for international students: Required—TOEFL (minimum score 550 paper-based; 213 computer-based; 79 iBT). *Application deadline:* For fall admission, 8/1 for domestic students, 6/1 for international students; for spring admission, 1/5 for domestic students, 11/1 for international students. Application fee: $20 ($55 for international students). Electronic applications accepted. *Expenses:* Tuition, state resident: full-time $3537; part-time $173.95 per credit hour. Tuition, nonresident: full-time $8673; part-time $459.30 per credit hour. *Required fees:* $22.55 per credit hour. *Financial support:* In 2011–12, 30 students received support, including 3 teaching assistantships with full tuition reimbursements available (averaging $5,000 per year); Federal Work-Study, institutionally sponsored loans, and tuition waivers (partial) also available. Support available to part-time students. Financial award application deadline: 6/15; financial award applicants required to submit FAFSA. *Unit head:* Dr. Lawrence Silver, MBA Coordinator, 580-745-3190, Fax: 580-745-7485, E-mail: lsilver@se.edu. *Application contact:* Carrie Williamson, Graduate Secretary, 580-745-2220, Fax: 580-745-7474, E-mail: cwilliamson@se.edu. Web site: http://www.se.edu/graduate-programs/master-of-business-administration/.

Southeastern University, College of Business and Legal Studies, Lakeland, FL 33801-6099. Offers business administration (MBA). Evening/weekend programs available. Postbaccalaureate distance learning degree programs offered. *Entrance requirements:* For master's, GMAT, minimum cumulative GPA of 3.0, writing sample. Electronic applications accepted.

Southeast Missouri State University, School of Graduate Studies, Harrison College of Business, Cape Girardeau, MO 63701-4799. Offers accounting (MBA); entrepreneurship (MBA); financial management (MBA); general management (MBA); health administration (MBA); industrial management (MBA); international business (MBA); sport management (MBA). *Accreditation:* AACSB. Part-time and evening/weekend programs available. Postbaccalaureate distance learning degree programs offered (no on-campus study). *Faculty:* 31 full-time (10 women). *Students:* 49 full-time (23 women), 77 part-time (30 women); includes 5 minority (1 Black or African American, non-Hispanic/Latino; 1 American Indian or Alaska Native, non-Hispanic/Latino; 2 Hispanic/Latino; 1 Two or more races, non-Hispanic/Latino), 35 international. Average age 27. 78 applicants, 69% accepted, 43 enrolled. In 2011, 47 master's awarded. *Degree requirements:* For master's, variable foreign language requirement, comprehensive exam, applied research project related to field. *Entrance requirements:* For master's, GMAT (minimum score of 450), minimum undergraduate GPA of 2.5, C or better in prerequisite courses. Additional exam requirements/recommendations for international students: Required—TOEFL (minimum score 550 paper-based; 213 computer-based; 79 iBT); Recommended—IELTS (minimum score 6). *Application deadline:* For fall admission, 8/1 for domestic students, 7/1 for international students; for spring admission, 11/21 for domestic students, 11/1 for international students. Applications are processed on a rolling basis. Application fee: $30 ($40 for international students). Electronic applications accepted. *Expenses:* Tuition, state resident: full-time $4896; part-time $272 per credit hour. Tuition, nonresident: full-time $8649; part-time $480.50 per credit hour. *Financial support:* In 2011–12, 46 students received support, including 12 teaching assistantships with full tuition reimbursements available (averaging $7,600 per year); career-related internships or fieldwork, Federal Work-Study, scholarships/grants, tuition waivers (full), and unspecified assistantships also available. Financial award application deadline: 6/30; financial award applicants required to submit FAFSA. *Faculty research:* Human resources, laws impacting accounting, advertising. *Unit head:* Dr. Kenneth A. Heischmidt, Director, Graduate Programs in Business, 573-651-5116, Fax: 573-651-5032, E-mail: kheischmidt@semo.edu. *Application contact:* Gail Amick, Administrative Secretary, 573-651-2049, Fax: 573-651-2001, E-mail: gamick@semo.edu. Web site: http://www.semo.edu/mba.

Southern Adventist University, School of Business and Management, Collegedale, TN 37315-0370. Offers accounting (MBA); church administration (MSA); church and nonprofit leadership (MBA); financial management (MFM); healthcare administration (MBA); management (MBA); marketing management (MBA); outdoor education (MSA). Part-time and evening/weekend programs available. Postbaccalaureate distance learning degree programs offered (no on-campus study). *Entrance requirements:* For master's, GMAT. Additional exam requirements/recommendations for international students: Required—TOEFL (minimum score 600 paper-based; 250 computer-based; 100 iBT). Electronic applications accepted.

Southern Arkansas University–Magnolia, Graduate Programs, Magnolia, AR 71754. Offers agriculture (MS); business administration (MBA); computer and information sciences (MS); education (M Ed), including counseling and development, curriculum and instruction, educational administration and supervision, elementary education, middle level, reading, secondary education, TESOL; kinesiology (M Ed); library media and information specialist (M Ed); mental health and clinical counseling (MS); public administration (MPA); school counseling (M Ed); teaching (MAT). *Accreditation:* NCATE. Part-time and evening/weekend programs available. Postbaccalaureate distance learning degree programs offered. *Faculty:* 34 full-time (15 women), 8 part-time/adjunct (5 women). *Students:* 87 full-time (62 women), 320 part-time (224 women); includes 116 minority (111 Black or African American, non-Hispanic/Latino; 2 American Indian or Alaska Native, non-Hispanic/Latino; 2 Asian, non-Hispanic/Latino; 1 Hispanic/Latino), 25 international. Average age 33. 201 applicants, 98% accepted, 156 enrolled. In 2011, 162 master's awarded. *Degree requirements:* For master's, comprehensive exam (for some programs), thesis optional. *Entrance requirements:* For master's, GRE, MAT or GMAT, minimum GPA of 2.5. Additional exam requirements/recommendations for international students: Required—TOEFL (minimum score 173 computer-based). *Application deadline:* For fall admission, 7/15 for domestic and international students; for winter admission, 12/1 for domestic and international students; for spring admission, 12/1 for domestic and international students. Applications are processed on a rolling basis. Application fee: $25 ($35 for international students). Electronic applications accepted. *Expenses:* Tuition, state resident: part-time $232 per credit. Tuition, nonresident: part-time $339 per credit. *Required fees:* $44 per credit. Part-time tuition and fees vary according to course load. *Financial support:* Career-related internships or fieldwork, Federal Work-Study, scholarships/grants, tuition waivers (full), and unspecified assistantships available. Financial award applicants required to submit FAFSA. *Faculty research:* Alternative certification for teachers, supervision of instruction, instructional leadership, counseling. *Unit head:* Dr. Kim Bloss, Dean, School of Graduate Studies, 870-235-4150, Fax: 870-235-5227, E-mail: kkbloss@saumag.edu. *Application contact:* Gaye Calhoun, Admissions Specialist, 870-235-4150, Fax: 870-235-5227, E-mail: glcalhoun@saumag.edu. Web site: http://www.saumag.edu/graduate.

Southern Connecticut State University, School of Graduate Studies, School of Business, Program in Business Administration, New Haven, CT 06515-1355. Offers MBA. Part-time and evening/weekend programs available. *Faculty:* 14 full-time (1 woman), 3 part-time/adjunct (1 woman). *Students:* 84 full-time (36 women), 81 part-time (40 women); includes 46 minority (20 Black or African American, non-Hispanic/Latino; 15 Asian, non-Hispanic/Latino; 10 Hispanic/Latino; 1 Two or more races, non-Hispanic/Latino), 10 international. 210 applicants, 24% accepted, 36 enrolled. In 2011, 70 master's awarded. *Entrance requirements:* For master's, GMAT, interview. *Application deadline:* For fall admission, 7/1 priority date for domestic students. Applications are processed on a rolling basis. Application fee: $50. Electronic applications accepted. *Expenses:* Tuition, state resident: full-time $5137; part-time $413 per credit. *Required fees:* $4008; $55 per term. *Financial support:* Application deadline: 4/15; applicants required to submit FAFSA. *Unit head:* Dr. Wafeek Abdelsayed, Director, 203-392-5873, Fax: 203-392-5988, E-mail: abdelsayedw1@southernct.edu. *Application contact:* Dr. Wafeek Abdelsayed, Director, 203-392-5873, Fax: 203-392-5988, E-mail: abdelsayedw1@southernct.edu.

Southern Illinois University Carbondale, Graduate School, College of Business and Administration, Department of Business Administration, Carbondale, IL 62901-4701. Offers MBA, PhD, JD/MBA, MBA/MA, MBA/MS. *Accreditation:* AACSB. *Faculty:* 32 full-time (3 women). *Students:* 61 full-time (19 women), 96 part-time (33 women); includes 18 minority (7 Black or African American, non-Hispanic/Latino; 9 Asian, non-Hispanic/Latino; 2 Hispanic/Latino), 35 international. Average age 26. 107 applicants, 50% accepted, 25 enrolled. In 2011, 41 master's, 16 doctorates awarded. *Degree requirements:* For doctorate, thesis/dissertation. *Entrance requirements:* For master's, GMAT, minimum GPA of 2.7; for doctorate, GMAT, minimum graduate GPA of 3.25. Additional exam requirements/recommendations for international students: Required—TOEFL. *Application deadline:* For fall admission, 6/15 priority date for domestic students. Applications are processed on a rolling basis. Application fee: $20. *Financial support:* In 2011–12, 108 students received support, including 2 fellowships with full tuition reimbursements available, 42 research assistantships with full tuition reimbursements available, 49 teaching assistantships with full tuition reimbursements available; Federal Work-Study, institutionally sponsored loans, and tuition waivers (full) also available. Support available to part-time students. *Faculty research:* Marketing, corporate finance, organizational behavior, accounting, MIS, international business. *Total annual research expenditures:* $200,000. *Unit head:* Dr. Dennis Cradit, Dean, 618-453-7960, E-mail: siu50661@siu.edu. *Application contact:* Julie Virgo, Administrative Aide, 618-453-3030, Fax: 618-453-7961, E-mail: jvirgo@siu.edu.

Southern Illinois University Edwardsville, Graduate School, School of Business, Program in Business Administration, Edwardsville, IL 62026. Offers management information systems (MBA); project management (MBA). *Accreditation:* AACSB. Part-time and evening/weekend programs available. *Students:* 17 full-time (4 women), 119 part-time (39 women); includes 10 minority (3 Black or African American, non-Hispanic/Latino; 1 Asian, non-Hispanic/Latino; 1 Hispanic/Latino; 1 Native Hawaiian or other Pacific Islander, non-Hispanic/Latino; 4 Two or more races, non-Hispanic/Latino), 8 international. 101 applicants, 40% accepted. In 2011, 69 master's awarded. *Degree requirements:* For master's, comprehensive exam. *Entrance requirements:* For master's, GMAT. Additional exam requirements/recommendations for international students: Required—TOEFL (minimum score 550 paper-based; 213 computer-based; 79 iBT), IELTS (minimum score 6.5). *Application deadline:* For fall admission, 7/22 for domestic students, 6/1 for international students; for spring admission, 12/10 for domestic students, 10/1 for international students. Applications are processed on a rolling basis. Application fee: $30. Electronic applications accepted. Tuition and fees vary according to course load and program. *Financial support:* In 2011–12, 1 fellowship with full tuition reimbursement (averaging $8,370 per year), 1 research assistantship with full tuition reimbursement (averaging $9,927 per year) were awarded; teaching assistantships with full tuition reimbursements, institutionally sponsored loans, scholarships/grants, and unspecified assistantships also available. Financial award application deadline: 3/1; financial award applicants required to submit FAFSA. *Unit head:* Dr. Janice Joplin, Director, 618-650-2485, E-mail: jjoplin@siue.edu. *Application contact:* Michelle Robinson, Coordinator of Graduate Recruitment, 618-650-2811, Fax: 618-650-3523, E-mail: michero@siue.edu. Web site: http://www.siue.edu/business/mba.

Southern Methodist University, Cox School of Business, Dallas, TX 75275. Offers accounting (MSA); business (Exec MBA); business administration (MBA), including accounting, finance, information technology and operations management, management, marketing, strategy and entrepreneurship; entrepreneurship (MS); management (MSM); JD/MBA. *Accreditation:* AACSB. Part-time and evening/weekend programs available. *Entrance requirements:* For master's, GMAT. Additional exam requirements/recommendations for international students: Required—TOEFL, Pearson Test of English. Electronic applications accepted. *Expenses:* Contact institution. *Faculty research:* Financial markets structure, international finance, accounting disclosure, corporate finance, leadership, change management, organizational behavior, entrepreneurship, strategic marketing, corporate strategy, product innovation, information systems, knowledge management, energy markets, customer relationship management.

Southern Nazarene University, Graduate College, School of Business, Bethany, OK 73008. Offers business administration (MBA); health care management (MBA); management (MS Mgt). *Accreditation:* ACBSP. Part-time and evening/weekend programs available. Postbaccalaureate distance learning degree programs offered (minimal on-campus study). *Degree requirements:* For master's, thesis optional. *Entrance requirements:* For master's, GMAT, English proficiency exam, minimum GPA of 3.0 in last 60 hours/major, 2.7 overall. *Application deadline:* For fall admission, 8/1 priority date for domestic students. Applications are processed on a rolling basis. Application fee: $25 ($35 for international students). Electronic applications accepted. *Expenses: Tuition:* Full-time $17,009; part-time $639 per credit hour. *Required fees:* $2668. *Unit head:* Dr. Thomas Herskowitz, Chair, 405-491-6358. *Application contact:* Jeff Seyfert, MBA Director, 405-491-6358, E-mail: jseyfert@snu.edu. Web site: http://snu.edu/business.

Southern New Hampshire University, School of Business, Manchester, NH 03106-1045. Offers accounting (MS); business administration (MBA, Certificate), including accounting (Certificate), business administration (MBA), finance (Certificate), forensic accounting (Certificate), human resources management (Certificate), international business (Certificate), international sport management (Certificate), leadership of not for profit organizations (Certificate), marketing (Certificate), operations management (Certificate), sport management (Certificate), taxation (Certificate); finance (MS); hospitality and tourism leadership (Certificate); information technology (MS, Certificate); information technology/international business (Certificate); integrated marketing communications (Certificate); international business (MS, DBA); marketing (MS); operations and project management (MS); organizational leadership (MS); project management (Certificate); sport management (MS); MBA/Certificate. *Accreditation:* ACBSP. Part-time and evening/weekend programs available. Postbaccalaureate distance learning degree programs offered (no on-campus study). Terminal master's awarded for partial completion of doctoral program. *Degree requirements:* For master's, one foreign language, comprehensive exam (for some programs), thesis or alternative; for doctorate, one foreign language, comprehensive exam, thesis/dissertation. *Entrance requirements:* For master's, minimum GPA of 2.5; for doctorate, GMAT. Additional exam requirements/recommendations for international students: Required—TOEFL (minimum score 500 paper-based). Electronic applications accepted.

Southern Oregon University, Graduate Studies, School of Business, Ashland, OR 97520. Offers MBA, MIM. Part-time and evening/weekend programs available. Postbaccalaureate distance learning degree programs offered (minimal on-campus study). *Faculty:* 17 full-time (2 women), 4 part-time/adjunct (2 women). *Students:* 38 full-time (20 women), 78 part-time (43 women); includes 9 minority (2 Black or African American, non-Hispanic/Latino; 3 Hispanic/Latino; 1 Native Hawaiian or other Pacific Islander, non-Hispanic/Latino; 3 Two or more races, non-Hispanic/Latino), 17 international. Average age 37. 92 applicants, 55% accepted, 40 enrolled. In 2011, 70 degrees awarded. *Degree requirements:* For master's, comprehensive exam. *Entrance requirements:* For master's, GMAT. *Application deadline:* Applications are processed on a rolling basis. Application fee: $50. Electronic applications accepted. *Expenses:* Tuition, state resident: full-time $12,600; part-time $350 per credit. Tuition, nonresident: full-time $16,200; part-time $450 per credit. *Required fees:* $1590. *Financial support:* Research assistantships with partial tuition reimbursements, career-related internships or fieldwork, Federal Work-Study, institutionally sponsored loans, scholarships/grants, and unspecified assistantships available. Support available to part-time students. *Unit head:* Rajeev Parikh, Dean, 541-552-6483, E-mail: parikhr@sou.edu. *Application contact:* Mark Bottorff, Director of Admissions, 541-552-6411, Fax: 541-552-8403, E-mail: admissions@sou.edu. Web site: http://www.sou.edu/business/graduate-programs.html.

Southern Polytechnic State University, School of Engineering Technology and Management, Department of Business Administration, Marietta, GA 30060-2896. Offers accounting (MSA); business administration (MBA, Graduate Transition Certificate). *Accreditation:* ACBSP. Part-time and evening/weekend programs available. Postbaccalaureate distance learning degree programs offered (no on-campus study). *Faculty:* 13 full-time (4 women), 7 part-time/adjunct (3 women). *Students:* 82 full-time (43 women), 142 part-time (77 women); includes 122 minority (90 Black or African American, non-Hispanic/Latino; 1 American Indian or Alaska Native, non-Hispanic/Latino; 20 Asian, non-Hispanic/Latino; 8 Hispanic/Latino; 3 Two or more races, non-Hispanic/Latino), 35 international. Average age 33. 110 applicants, 88% accepted, 72 enrolled. In 2011, 75 master's, 1 other advanced degree awarded. *Entrance requirements:* For master's, GMAT, letters of recommendation, statement of purpose, resume. Additional exam requirements/recommendations for international students: Required—TOEFL (minimum score 550 paper-based; 213 computer-based; 79 iBT), IELTS (minimum score 6.5). *Application deadline:* For fall admission, 7/1 priority date for domestic students, 5/1 for international students; for spring admission, 11/1 priority date for domestic students, 9/1 for international students. Applications are processed on a rolling basis. Application fee: $50. Electronic applications accepted. *Expenses:* Tuition, state resident: full-time $2592; part-time $216 per semester hour. Tuition, nonresident: full-time $9408; part-time $784 per semester hour. *Required fees:* $698 per term. *Financial support:* In 2011–12, 37 students received support, including 4 research assistantships with tuition reimbursements available (averaging $4,500 per year); career-related internships or fieldwork, scholarships/grants, and unspecified assistantships also available. Support available to part-time students. Financial award application deadline: 5/1; financial award applicants required to submit FAFSA. *Faculty research:* Ethics, virtual reality, sustainability, management of technology, quality management, capacity planning, human-computer interaction/interface, enterprise integration planning, economic impact of educational institutions, behavioral accounting, accounting ethics, taxation, information security, visualizational simulation, human-computer interaction. *Total annual research expenditures:* $5,000. *Unit head:* Dr. Ronny Richardson, Chair, 678-915-7440, Fax: 678-915-4967, E-mail: rrichard@spsu.edu. *Application contact:* Nikki Palamiotis, Director of Graduate Studies, 678-915-4276, Fax: 678-915-7292, E-mail: npalamio@spsu.edu. Web site: http://www.spsu.edu/business/index.htm.

Southern University and Agricultural and Mechanical College, College of Business, Baton Rouge, LA 70813. Offers MBA. *Accreditation:* AACSB. *Degree requirements:* For master's, comprehensive exam. *Entrance requirements:* For master's, GMAT. Additional exam requirements/recommendations for international students: Required—TOEFL (minimum score 525 paper-based; 193 computer-based). *Faculty research:* Accounting theory, auditing, governmental and non-profit accounting.

Southern Utah University, Program in Business Administration, Cedar City, UT 84720-2498. Offers MBA. *Accreditation:* AACSB; ACBSP. Part-time programs available. *Students:* 40 full-time (6 women), 26 part-time (3 women); includes 3 minority (1 Black or African American, non-Hispanic/Latino; 2 Asian, non-Hispanic/Latino), 7 international. 41 applicants, 80% accepted, 23 enrolled. In 2011, 63 master's awarded. *Entrance requirements:* For master's, GMAT or GRE. *Application deadline:* For fall admission, 3/1 for domestic students; for spring admission, 10/1 for domestic students. Applications are processed on a rolling basis. Application fee: $50 ($65 for international students).

Business Administration and Management—General

Electronic applications accepted. *Expenses:* Contact institution. *Financial support:* Career-related internships or fieldwork, institutionally sponsored loans, tuition waivers, and unspecified assistantships available. *Unit head:* Dr. Alan Hamlin, Chair, Management and Marketing Department, 435-586-5417, Fax: 435-586-5493, E-mail: hamlin@suu.edu. *Application contact:* Paula Alger, Advisor/Curriculum Coordinator, 435-865-8157, Fax: 435-586-5493, E-mail: alger@suu.edu. Web site: http://suu.edu/prostu/majors/business/mba.html.

Southern Wesleyan University, Program in Business Administration, Central, SC 29630-1020. Offers MBA. Evening/weekend programs available. *Degree requirements:* For master's, comprehensive exam. *Entrance requirements:* For master's, GMAT, GRE, or MAT, minimum of 3 undergraduate semester credit hours each in accounting, economics, and statistics; minimum of 18 undergraduate semester credit hours in business administration; minimum of 2 years' significant work experience. Additional exam requirements/recommendations for international students: Required—TOEFL (minimum score 500 paper-based; 173 computer-based).

Southern Wesleyan University, Program in Management, Central, SC 29630-1020. Offers MSM. Evening/weekend programs available. *Entrance requirements:* For master's, GMAT, GRE, or MAT, minimum of 18 undergraduate semester credit hours in business administration; minimum of 2 years significant work experience. Additional exam requirements/recommendations for international students: Required—TOEFL (minimum score 500 paper-based; 173 computer-based). *Expenses:* Contact institution.

South University, Graduate Programs, College of Business, Savannah, GA 31406. Offers corrections (MBA); entrepreneurship and small business (MBA); healthcare administration (MBA); hospitality management (MBA); leadership (MS); sustainability (MBA).

See Close-Up on page 241.

South University, Program in Business Administration, Atlanta, GA. Offers Accelerated MBA. Program offered by South University, Savannah Campus at Atlanta Learning Site.

See Close-Up on page 229.

South University, Program in Business Administration, Royal Palm Beach, FL 33411. Offers business administration (MBA); healthcare administration (MBA).

See Close-Up on page 247.

South University, Program in Business Administration, Montgomery, AL 36116-1120. Offers MBA.

See Close-Up on page 235.

South University, Program in Business Administration, Columbia, SC 29203. Offers MBA.

See Close-Up on page 233.

South University, Program in Business Administration, Glen Allen, VA 23060. Offers MBA.

See Close-Up on page 239.

South University, Program in Business Administration, Virginia Beach, VA 23452. Offers MBA.

See Close-Up on page 245.

South University, Program in Business Administration, Austin, TX 78681. Offers MBA.

See Close-Up on page 231.

South University, Program in Business Administration, Novi, MI 48377. Offers MBA.

See Close-Up on page 237.

South University, Program in Business Administration, Tampa, FL 33614. Offers MBA.

See Close-Up on page 243.

Southwest Baptist University, Program in Business, Bolivar, MO 65613-2597. Offers business administration (MBA); health administration (MBA). *Accreditation:* ACBSP. Part-time programs available. Postbaccalaureate distance learning degree programs offered (no on-campus study). *Degree requirements:* For master's, comprehensive exam. *Entrance requirements:* For master's, interviews, minimum GPA of 2.75. Additional exam requirements/recommendations for international students: Required—TOEFL (minimum score 550 paper-based; 213 computer-based).

Southwestern Adventist University, Business Administration Department, Keene, TX 76059. Offers accounting (MBA); finance (MBA); management/leadership (MBA). Part-time and evening/weekend programs available. *Degree requirements:* For master's, capstone course. *Entrance requirements:* For master's, GMAT, GRE General Test.

Southwestern College, Fifth-Year Graduate Programs, Winfield, KS 67156-2499. Offers leadership (MS); management (MBA); music (MA), including education, performance. Part-time programs available. *Faculty:* 3 full-time (1 woman), 12 part-time/adjunct (4 women). *Students:* 13 full-time (5 women), 8 part-time (4 women); includes 3 minority (2 Black or African American, non-Hispanic/Latino; 1 American Indian or Alaska Native, non-Hispanic/Latino), 5 international. Average age 25. 21 applicants, 90% accepted, 16 enrolled. In 2011, 8 master's awarded. *Entrance requirements:* For master's, baccalaureate degree, minimum GPA of 3.0. Additional exam requirements/recommendations for international students: Required—TOEFL (minimum score 550 paper-based; 213 computer-based). *Application deadline:* For fall admission, 4/1 priority date for domestic students; for spring admission, 12/1 priority date for domestic students. Applications are processed on a rolling basis. Electronic applications accepted. Tuition and fees vary according to program. *Financial support:* In 2011–12, 8 students received support. Federal Work-Study, tuition waivers (partial), and unspecified assistantships available. Financial award application deadline: 4/1; financial award applicants required to submit FAFSA. *Unit head:* Dr. James Sheppard, Vice President for Academic Affairs, 620-229-6227, Fax: 620-229-6224, E-mail: james.sheppard@sckans.edu. *Application contact:* Marla Sexson, Director of Admissions, 800-846-1543 Ext. 6364, Fax: 620-229-6344, E-mail: marla.sexson@sckans.edu. Web site: http://www.sckans.edu/graduate.

Southwestern College, Professional Studies Programs, Wichita, KS 67207. Offers accountancy (MA); business administration (MBA); leadership (MS); management (MS); security administration (MS); specialized ministries (MA); theological studies (MA). Part-time and evening/weekend programs available. Postbaccalaureate distance learning degree programs offered (minimal on-campus study). *Faculty:* 1 full-time (0 women), 13 part-time/adjunct (4 women). *Students:* 155 part-time (62 women); includes 36 minority (18 Black or African American, non-Hispanic/Latino; 1 American Indian or Alaska Native, non-Hispanic/Latino; 10 Hispanic/Latino; 7 Two or more races, non-Hispanic/Latino). Average age 36. 52 applicants, 44% accepted, 18 enrolled. In 2011, 89 master's awarded. *Degree requirements:* For master's, practicum/capstone project. *Entrance requirements:* For master's, baccalaureate degree; minimum GPA of 2.5 (for MA and MS), 3.0 (for MBA). Additional exam requirements/recommendations for international students: Required—TOEFL (minimum score 550 paper-based; 213 computer-based). *Application deadline:* For fall admission, 8/1 for domestic students; for spring admission, 12/1 for domestic students. Applications are processed on a rolling basis. Application fee: $0. Electronic applications accepted. Tuition and fees vary according to program. *Financial support:* In 2011–12, 8 students received support. Federal Work-Study, tuition waivers (partial), and unspecified assistantships available. Financial award application deadline: 4/1; financial award applicants required to submit FAFSA. *Unit head:* Michael Holmes, Director of Academic Affairs, 888-684-5335 Ext. 203, Fax: 316-6885218, E-mail: michael.holmes@sckans.edu. *Application contact:* Marla Sexson, Director of Admissions, 620-229-6364, Fax: 620-229-6344, E-mail: marla.sexson@sckans.edu. Web site: http://www.southwesterncollege.org.

Southwestern Oklahoma State University, College of Professional and Graduate Studies, School of Business and Technology, Weatherford, OK 73096-3098. Offers MBA. MBA distance learning degree program offered to Oklahoma residents only. Part-time and evening/weekend programs available. Postbaccalaureate distance learning degree programs offered (minimal on-campus study). *Degree requirements:* For master's, comprehensive exam. *Entrance requirements:* For master's, GMAT, minimum GPA of 2.5. Additional exam requirements/recommendations for international students: Required—TOEFL.

Southwest Minnesota State University, Department of Business and Public Affairs, Marshall, MN 56258. Offers leadership (MBA); management (MBA); marketing (MBA). Part-time and evening/weekend programs available. Postbaccalaureate distance learning degree programs offered (no on-campus study). *Degree requirements:* For master's, thesis. *Entrance requirements:* For master's, GMAT (minimum score: 450). Additional exam requirements/recommendations for international students: Recommended—TOEFL (minimum score 550 paper-based; 213 computer-based; 79 iBT), IELTS. Electronic applications accepted.

Southwest University, MBA Program, Kenner, LA 70062. Offers business administration (MBA); management (MBA); organizational management (MBA).

Southwest University, Program in Management, Kenner, LA 70062. Offers MA.

Spalding University, Graduate Studies, College of Business and Communication, Louisville, KY 40203-2188. Offers business communication (MS). Part-time and evening/weekend programs available. *Faculty:* 6 full-time (2 women), 12 part-time/adjunct (5 women). *Students:* 51 full-time (40 women), 28 part-time (26 women); includes 23 minority (21 Black or African American, non-Hispanic/Latino; 2 Asian, non-Hispanic/Latino). Average age 37. 42 applicants, 71% accepted, 27 enrolled. In 2011, 28 master's awarded. *Degree requirements:* For master's, project. *Entrance requirements:* For master's, GRE or GMAT, writing sample, interview, letters of recommendation, transcripts. Additional exam requirements/recommendations for international students: Required—TOEFL (minimum score 535 paper-based; 203 computer-based). *Application deadline:* Applications are processed on a rolling basis. Application fee: $30. *Expenses: Tuition:* Full-time $12,438. Tuition and fees vary according to course load, degree level and program. *Financial support:* In 2011–12, 26 students received support, including 1 research assistantship (averaging $1,710 per year). Financial award application deadline: 3/15; financial award applicants required to submit FAFSA. *Faculty research:* Curriculum development, consumer behavior, interdisciplinary pedagogy. *Unit head:* Dr. John Burden, Interim MSBC Director, 502-873-4443, E-mail: cbc@spalding.edu. *Application contact:* Claire Rayburn, Administrative Assistant, 502-873-7120, E-mail: crayburn@spalding.edu.

Spring Arbor University, School of Business and Management, Spring Arbor, MI 49283-9799. Offers MBA. Part-time and evening/weekend programs available. Postbaccalaureate distance learning degree programs offered. *Faculty:* 7 full-time (2 women), 9 part-time/adjunct (4 women). *Students:* 116 full-time (64 women), 7 part-time (3 women); includes 27 minority (22 Black or African American, non-Hispanic/Latino; 1 American Indian or Alaska Native, non-Hispanic/Latino; 3 Asian, non-Hispanic/Latino; 1 Hispanic/Latino), 1 international. Average age 37. In 2011, 30 master's awarded. *Degree requirements:* For master's, thesis. *Entrance requirements:* For master's, minimum overall GPA of 3.0 for all undergraduate coursework, bachelor's degree from regionally-accredited college or university, two recommendation forms from professional/academic individuals. Additional exam requirements/recommendations for international students: Required—TOEFL (minimum score 600 paper-based; 220 computer-based). *Application deadline:* Applications are processed on a rolling basis. Application fee: $40. *Expenses: Tuition:* Full-time $5500; part-time $490 per credit hour. *Required fees:* $240; $120 per term. Tuition and fees vary according to program. *Financial support:* Career-related internships or fieldwork, scholarships/grants, and tuition waivers (partial) available. Support available to part-time students. Financial award application deadline: 8/25; financial award applicants required to submit FAFSA. *Unit head:* Dr. James Coe, Dean, 517-750-1200 Ext. 1569, Fax: 517-750-6624, E-mail: jcoe@arbor.edu. *Application contact:* Greg Bentle, Coordinator of Graduate Recruitment, 517-750-6763, Fax: 517-750-6624, E-mail: gbentle@arbor.edu. Web site: http://www.arbor.edu/Master-Business-Administration/Graduate/index.aspx.

Spring Hill College, Graduate Programs, Program in Business Administration, Mobile, AL 36608-1791. Offers MBA. *Accreditation:* ACBSP. Part-time and evening/weekend programs available. *Faculty:* 4 full-time (1 woman). *Students:* 6 full-time (0 women), 17 part-time (9 women); includes 4 minority (2 Black or African American, non-Hispanic/Latino; 1 Hispanic/Latino; 1 Two or more races, non-Hispanic/Latino), 1 international. Average age 28. In 2011, 11 master's awarded. *Degree requirements:* For master's, comprehensive exam, capstone course, completion of program within 6 calendar years. *Entrance requirements:* For master's, GMAT, bachelor's degree. Additional exam requirements/recommendations for international students: Required—TOEFL (minimum score 550 paper-based; 213 computer-based; 80 iBT), IELTS (minimum score 6.5), CPE or CAE (minimum score C), Michigan English Language Assessment Battery (minimum score 90). *Application deadline:* For fall admission, 8/1 priority date for domestic students, 8/1 for international students; for spring admission, 12/1 priority date for domestic students, 12/1 for international students. Applications are processed on a rolling basis. Application fee: $25 ($35 for international students). Electronic applications accepted. *Expenses:* Contact institution. *Financial support:* Applicants required to submit FAFSA. *Unit head:* Dr. Sergio Castello, Director, 251-380-4123, Fax: 251-460-2178, E-mail: scastello@shc.edu. *Application contact:* Donna B. Tarasavage, Director of Admissions, Graduate and Continuing Studies, 251-380-3067, Fax: 251-460-2190, E-mail: dtarasavage@shc.edu. Web site: http://www.shc.edu/grad/academics/business.

Stanford University, Graduate School of Business, Stanford, CA 94305-9991. Offers MBA, PhD, JD/MBA, MBA/MS. *Accreditation:* AACSB. Terminal master's awarded for partial completion of doctoral program. *Degree requirements:* For doctorate, thesis/dissertation. *Entrance requirements:* For master's, GMAT; for doctorate, GMAT, GRE. Electronic applications accepted. *Expenses:* Contact institution.

State University of New York at Binghamton, Graduate School, School of Management, Program in Business Administration, Binghamton, NY 13902-6000. Offers business administration (MBA, PhD); health care professional executive (MBA). *Accreditation:* AACSB. *Students:* 120 full-time (47 women), 11 part-time (2 women); includes 25 minority (5 Black or African American, non-Hispanic/Latino; 9 Hispanic/Latino; 11 Native Hawaiian or other Pacific Islander, non-Hispanic/Latino), 33 international. Average age 28. 317 applicants, 48% accepted, 96 enrolled. In 2011, 89 master's, 5 doctorates awarded. *Degree requirements:* For doctorate, thesis/dissertation. *Entrance requirements:* For master's and doctorate, GMAT. Additional exam requirements/recommendations for international students: Required—TOEFL (minimum score 550 paper-based; 213 computer-based; 80 iBT). *Application deadline:* For fall admission, 3/1 priority date for domestic students, 3/1 for international students; for spring admission, 10/15 priority date for domestic students, 10/15 for international students. Applications are processed on a rolling basis. Application fee: $60. Electronic applications accepted. *Financial support:* In 2011–12, 39 students received support, including 14 fellowships with full tuition reimbursements available (averaging $17,000 per year), 13 teaching assistantships with full tuition reimbursements available (averaging $17,000 per year); research assistantships, career-related internships or fieldwork, Federal Work-Study, institutionally sponsored loans, scholarships/grants, health care benefits, tuition waivers (full and partial), and unspecified assistantships also available. Financial award application deadline: 2/15; financial award applicants required to submit FAFSA. *Unit head:* Dr. George Bobinski, Associate Dean, 607-777-2315, E-mail: gbobins@binghamton.edu. *Application contact:* Catherine Smith, Recruiting and Admissions Coordinator, 607-777-2151, Fax: 607-777-2501, E-mail: cmsmith@binghamton.edu.

State University of New York at New Paltz, Graduate School, School of Business, New Paltz, NY 12561. Offers business administration (MBA); public accountancy (MBA). Part-time and evening/weekend programs available. *Faculty:* 16 full-time (7 women). *Students:* 53 full-time (25 women), 31 part-time (15 women); includes 17 minority (5 Black or African American, non-Hispanic/Latino; 7 Asian, non-Hispanic/Latino; 5 Hispanic/Latino), 17 international. Average age 28. 65 applicants, 68% accepted, 34 enrolled. In 2011, 41 master's awarded. *Degree requirements:* For master's, internship. *Entrance requirements:* For master's, GMAT or GRE, minimum GPA of 3.0. Additional exam requirements/recommendations for international students: Required—TOEFL (minimum score 550 paper-based; 213 computer-based; 80 iBT), IELTS (minimum score 6.5). *Application deadline:* For fall admission, 5/15 priority date for domestic students, 5/15 for international students; for spring admission, 11/15 for domestic and international students. Applications are processed on a rolling basis. Application fee: $50. Electronic applications accepted. *Expenses:* Contact institution. *Financial support:* In 2011–12, 8 students received support, including 2 fellowships with partial tuition reimbursements available (averaging $6,900 per year), 6 research assistantships with partial tuition reimbursements available (averaging $5,000 per year), 1 teaching assistantship with partial tuition reimbursement available (averaging $5,000 per year); career-related internships or fieldwork, scholarships/grants, traineeships, and unspecified assistantships also available. Financial award application deadline: 8/1; financial award applicants required to submit FAFSA. *Faculty research:* Cognitive styles in management education, supporting SME e-commerce migration through e-learning, earnings management and board activity, trading future spread portfolio, global equity market correlation and volatility. *Unit head:* Dr. Hadi Salavitabar, Dean, 845-257-2930, E-mail: mba@newpaltz.edu. *Application contact:* Aaron Hines, Coordinator, 845-257-2968, E-mail: mba@newpaltz.edu. Web site: http://mba.newpaltz.edu.

State University of New York at Oswego, Graduate Studies, School of Business, Program in Business Administration, Oswego, NY 13126. Offers MBA. *Accreditation:* AACSB. Part-time and evening/weekend programs available. *Entrance requirements:* For master's, GMAT, minimum GPA of 2.6. Additional exam requirements/recommendations for international students: Required—TOEFL (minimum score 560 paper-based; 220 computer-based). *Faculty research:* Marketing, industrial finance, technology.

State University of New York College at Geneseo, Graduate Studies, School of Business, Geneseo, NY 14454-1401. Offers accounting (MS). *Accreditation:* AACSB. *Entrance requirements:* For master's, GMAT, bachelor's degree in accounting.

State University of New York Empire State College, Graduate Studies, Program in Business Administration, Saratoga Springs, NY 12866-4391. Offers MBA. Part-time programs available. Postbaccalaureate distance learning degree programs offered (minimal on-campus study). *Degree requirements:* For master's, thesis or alternative. *Entrance requirements:* For master's, previous course work in statistics, macroeconomics, microeconomics, and accounting. Additional exam requirements/recommendations for international students: Required—TOEFL (minimum score 600 paper-based; 250 computer-based). Electronic applications accepted. *Expenses:* Contact institution. *Faculty research:* Corporate strategy, managerial competencies, decision analysis, economics in transition, organizational communication.

State University of New York Empire State College, Graduate Studies, Program in Business and Policy Studies, Saratoga Springs, NY 12866-4391. Offers MA. Part-time and evening/weekend programs available. Postbaccalaureate distance learning degree programs offered (minimal on-campus study). *Degree requirements:* For master's, thesis, exam. *Entrance requirements:* For master's, proficiency in statistics. Additional exam requirements/recommendations for international students: Required—TOEFL (minimum score 600 paper-based; 280 computer-based). Electronic applications accepted. *Faculty research:* Business history, applied business statistics, labor/management relations, American social problems and business, effect of government economic policies on business.

Stephen F. Austin State University, Graduate School, College of Business, Program in Business Administration, Nacogdoches, TX 75962. Offers business (MBA); management and marketing (MBA). *Accreditation:* AACSB. Part-time and evening/weekend programs available. *Degree requirements:* For master's, comprehensive exam. *Entrance requirements:* For master's, GMAT, minimum AACSB index of 1000. Additional exam requirements/recommendations for international students: Required—TOEFL (minimum score 550 paper-based; 213 computer-based). *Faculty research:* Strategic implications, information search, multinational firms, philosophical guidance.

Stephens College, Division of Graduate and Continuing Studies, Graduate Business Programs, Columbia, MO 65215-0002. Offers MBA, MSL. Part-time programs available. Postbaccalaureate distance learning degree programs offered (minimal on-campus study). *Faculty:* 2 full-time (both women), 9 part-time/adjunct (5 women). *Students:* 65 full-time (58 women), 18 part-time (16 women); includes 15 minority (8 Black or African American, non-Hispanic/Latino; 3 Asian, non-Hispanic/Latino; 2 Hispanic/Latino; 2 Two or more races, non-Hispanic/Latino). Average age 38. 22 applicants, 68% accepted, 13 enrolled. In 2011, 43 master's awarded. *Entrance requirements:* For master's, minimum GPA of 3.0 in last 60 hours. Additional exam requirements/recommendations for international students: Required—TOEFL (minimum score 213 computer-based). *Application deadline:* For fall admission, 7/25 priority date for domestic students, 7/25 for international students; for winter admission, 12/1 priority date for domestic students, 12/1 for international students; for spring admission, 4/25 priority date for domestic students, 4/25 for international students. Applications are processed on a rolling basis. Application fee: $40. Electronic applications accepted. *Expenses: Tuition:* Full-time $2220; part-time $370 per credit hour. *Required fees:* $228; $38 per credit hour. *Financial support:* In 2011–12, 67 students received support, including 5 fellowships with full tuition reimbursements available (averaging $5,911 per year); scholarships/grants and unspecified assistantships also available. Financial award applicants required to submit FAFSA. *Unit head:* Dr. Nicole House, Director of Graduate and Continuing Studies, 800-388-7579. *Application contact:* Jennifer Deaver, Director of Recruitment, 800-388-7579, E-mail: online@stephens.edu. Web site: http://www.stephens.edu/gcs.

Stetson University, School of Business Administration, Program in Business Administration, DeLand, FL 32723. Offers MBA, JD/MBA. *Accreditation:* AACSB. Part-time and evening/weekend programs available. *Students:* 140 full-time (63 women), 61 part-time (24 women); includes 47 minority (13 Black or African American, non-Hispanic/Latino; 1 American Indian or Alaska Native, non-Hispanic/Latino; 7 Asian, non-Hispanic/Latino; 22 Hispanic/Latino; 4 Two or more races, non-Hispanic/Latino), 19 international. Average age 31. In 2011, 136 master's awarded. *Entrance requirements:* For master's, GMAT. *Application deadline:* For fall admission, 7/1 for domestic students. Application fee: $25. *Financial support:* Application deadline: 3/15. *Unit head:* Dr. Fred Augustine, Director, 386-822-7410. *Application contact:* Kathryn Hannon, Administrative Assistant, 386-822-7410, Fax: 386-822-7413, E-mail: khannon@stetson.edu.

Stevens Institute of Technology, Graduate School, Wesley J. Howe School of Technology Management, Program in Business Administration, Hoboken, NJ 07030. Offers engineering management (MBA); financial engineering (MBA); information management (MBA); information technology in financial services (MBA); information technology in the pharmaceutical industry (MBA); information technology outsourcing (MBA); pharmaceutical management (MBA); project management (MBA); technology management (MBA); telecommunications management (MBA).

Stevens Institute of Technology, Graduate School, Wesley J. Howe School of Technology Management, Program in Management, Hoboken, NJ 07030. Offers general management (MS); global innovation management (MS); human resource management (MS); information management (MS); project management (MS); technology commercialization (MS); technology management (MS). Part-time programs available. *Degree requirements:* For master's, thesis optional. *Entrance requirements:* For master's, GMAT, GRE General Test. Additional exam requirements/recommendations for international students: Required—TOEFL. Electronic applications accepted. *Faculty research:* Industrial economics.

Stony Brook University, State University of New York, Graduate School, College of Business, Program in Business Administration, Stony Brook, NY 11794. Offers finance (MBA, Certificate); health care management (MBA, Certificate); human resource management (Certificate); human resources (MBA); information systems management (MBA, Certificate); management (MBA); marketing (MBA).

Stratford University, School of Graduate Studies, Falls Church, VA 22043. Offers accounting (MS); business administration (IMBA, MBA); enterprise business management (MS); entrepreneurial management (MS); information assurance (MS); information systems (MS); software engineering (MS); telecommunications (MS). Part-time and evening/weekend programs available. Postbaccalaureate distance learning degree programs offered (no on-campus study). *Degree requirements:* For master's, comprehensive exam, capstone project. *Entrance requirements:* For master's, GRE or GMAT, baccalaureate degree. Additional exam requirements/recommendations for international students: Required—TOEFL (minimum score 213 computer-based, 79 iBT) or IELTS (6.5). Electronic applications accepted.

Strayer University, Graduate Studies, Washington, DC 20005-2603. Offers accounting (MS); acquisition (MBA); business administration (MBA); communications technology (MS); educational management (M Ed); finance (MBA); health services administration (MHSA); hospitality and tourism management (MBA); human resource management (MBA); information systems (MS), including computer security management, decision support system management, enterprise resource management, network management, software engineering management, systems development management; management (MBA); management information systems (MS); marketing (MBA); professional accounting (MS), including accounting information systems, controllership, taxation; public administration (MPA); supply chain management (MBA); technology in education (M Ed). Programs also offered at campus locations in Birmingham, AL; Chamblee, GA; Cobb County, GA; Morrow, GA; White Marsh, MD; Charleston, SC; Columbia, SC; Greensboro, NC; Greenville, SC; Lexington, KY; Louisville, KY; Nashville, TN; North Raleigh, NC; Washington, DC. Part-time and evening/weekend programs available. Postbaccalaureate distance learning degree programs offered (minimal on-campus study). *Degree requirements:* For master's, thesis. *Entrance requirements:* For master's, GMAT, GRE General Test, bachelor's degree from an accredited college or university, minimum undergraduate GPA of 2.75. Electronic applications accepted.

Suffolk University, Sawyer Business School, Master of Business Administration Program, Boston, MA 02108-2770. Offers accounting (MBA); business administration (APC); corporate financial executive track (MBA); entrepreneurship (MBA); executive business administration (EMBA); finance (MBA); global business administration (GMBA); health administration (MBA); international business (MBA); marketing (MBA); organizational behavior (MBA); strategic management (MBA); taxation (MBA); JD/MBA; MBA/GDPA; MBA/MHA; MBA/MSA; MBA/MSF; MBA/MST. *Accreditation:* AACSB. Part-time and evening/weekend programs available. Postbaccalaureate distance learning degree programs offered (no on-campus study). *Faculty:* 98 full-time (30 women), 14 part-time/adjunct (3 women). *Students:* 139 full-time (49 women), 321 part-time (138 women); includes 53 minority (17 Black or African American, non-Hispanic/Latino; 1 American Indian or Alaska Native, non-Hispanic/Latino; 21 Asian, non-Hispanic/Latino; 11 Hispanic/Latino; 1 Native Hawaiian or other Pacific Islander, non-Hispanic/Latino; 2 Two or more races, non-Hispanic/Latino), 64 international. Average age 30. 437 applicants, 61% accepted, 121 enrolled. In 2011, 283 master's awarded. *Entrance requirements:* For master's, GMAT, minimum undergraduate GPA of 2.75 (MBA), 5 years of managerial experience (EMBA). Additional exam requirements/recommendations for international students: Required—TOEFL (minimum score 550 paper-based; 213 computer-based). *Application deadline:* For fall admission, 6/15 priority date for domestic students, 6/15 for international students; for spring admission, 11/1 priority date for domestic students, 11/1 for international students. Applications are processed on a rolling basis. Application fee: $50. Electronic applications accepted. Tuition and fees vary according to program. *Financial support:* In 2011–12, 273 students received support, including 73 fellowships with full and partial tuition reimbursements available (averaging $12,415 per year); career-related internships or fieldwork, Federal Work-Study, and institutionally sponsored loans also available. Support available to part-time students. Financial award application deadline: 4/1; financial award applicants required to submit FAFSA. *Faculty research:* Foreign investments; career strategies and boundaryless careers; corporate ethics codes; interest rates, inflation, and growth options; innovation and product development performance. *Unit head:* Lillian Hallberg, Assistant Dean of Graduate Programs/Director of MBA Programs, 617-573-8306, E-mail: lhallber@suffolk.edu. *Application contact:* Ellen Driscoll, Director of Graduate Admissions, 617-573-8302, Fax: 617-305-1733, E-mail: grad.admission@suffolk.edu. Web site: http://www.suffolk.edu/mba.

Sullivan University, School of Business, Louisville, KY 40205. Offers EMBA, MBA, MPM, MSCM, MSHRL, MSM, MSMIT, PhD, Pharm D. Part-time programs available. Postbaccalaureate distance learning degree programs offered (no on-campus study). *Faculty:* 13 full-time (7 women), 11 part-time/adjunct (4 women). *Students:* 429 full-time (239 women), 322 part-time (198 women); includes 244 minority (152 Black or African American, non-Hispanic/Latino; 5 American Indian or Alaska Native, non-Hispanic/

Latino; 5 Hispanic/Latino; 56 Native Hawaiian or other Pacific Islander, non-Hispanic/Latino; 26 Two or more races, non-Hispanic/Latino), 15 international. In 2011, 171 master's awarded. *Degree requirements:* For doctorate, comprehensive exam, thesis/dissertation. *Entrance requirements:* Additional exam requirements/recommendations for international students: Required—TOEFL. *Application deadline:* Applications are processed on a rolling basis. Application fee: $100. *Unit head:* Dr. Eric S. Harter, Dean of Graduate School, 502-456-6504, Fax: 502-456-0040, E-mail: eharter@sullivan.edu. *Application contact:* Beverly Horsley, Admissions Officer, 502-456-6505, Fax: 502-456-0040, E-mail: bhorsley@sullivan.edu.

Sul Ross State University, Rio Grande College of Sul Ross State University, Alpine, TX 79832. Offers business administration (MBA); teacher education (M Ed), including bilingual education, counseling, educational diagnostics, elementary education, general education, reading, school administration, secondary education. Part-time and evening/weekend programs available. Postbaccalaureate distance learning degree programs offered (no on-campus study). *Faculty:* 11 full-time (3 women), 4 part-time/adjunct (3 women). *Students:* 45 full-time (36 women), 255 part-time (168 women); includes 218 minority (2 Black or African American, non-Hispanic/Latino; 1 American Indian or Alaska Native, non-Hispanic/Latino; 215 Hispanic/Latino), 1 international. Average age 36. In 2011, 47 master's awarded. *Degree requirements:* For master's, comprehensive exam, thesis optional, minimum GPA of 3.0. *Entrance requirements:* For master's, GMAT or GRE General Test, minimum GPA of 2.5 in last 60 hours of undergraduate work. Additional exam requirements/recommendations for international students: Required—TOEFL. *Application deadline:* Applications are processed on a rolling basis. Application fee: $0 ($50 for international students). *Financial support:* Career-related internships or fieldwork, Federal Work-Study, and institutionally sponsored loans available. Support available to part-time students. Financial award application deadline: 5/1; financial award applicants required to submit FAFSA. *Unit head:* Dr. Paul Sorrels, Associate Provost/Dean, 512-278-3339, Fax: 512-278-3330. *Application contact:* Claudia R. Wright, Director of Admissions and Records, 915-837-8050, Fax: 915-837-8431, E-mail: rcullins@sulross.edu.

Sul Ross State University, School of Professional Studies, Department of Business Administration, Alpine, TX 79832. Offers MBA. Part-time and evening/weekend programs available. *Degree requirements:* For master's, thesis optional. *Entrance requirements:* For master's, GMAT or GRE General Test, minimum GPA of 2.5 in last 60 hours of undergraduate work. *Faculty research:* Cross-cultural comparisons, U.S.-Mexico management relations.

Syracuse University, Martin J. Whitman School of Management, Syracuse, NY 13244. Offers MBA, MS, MS Acct, PhD, JD/MBA, JD/MS Acct, JD/MSF. *Accreditation:* AACSB. Part-time programs available. Postbaccalaureate distance learning degree programs offered (minimal on-campus study). *Faculty:* 69 full-time (24 women), 28 part-time/adjunct (9 women). *Students:* 312 full-time (150 women), 223 part-time (70 women); includes 95 minority (40 Black or African American, non-Hispanic/Latino; 1 American Indian or Alaska Native, non-Hispanic/Latino; 34 Asian, non-Hispanic/Latino; 14 Hispanic/Latino; 1 Native Hawaiian or other Pacific Islander, non-Hispanic/Latino; 5 Two or more races, non-Hispanic/Latino), 162 international. Average age 30. 1,810 applicants, 22% accepted, 222 enrolled. In 2011, 227 master's, 2 doctorates awarded. *Degree requirements:* For doctorate, comprehensive exam, thesis/dissertation, summer research paper. *Entrance requirements:* For master's, GMAT, 2 letters of recommendation; for doctorate, GMAT or GRE, 3 letters of recommendation. Additional exam requirements/recommendations for international students: Required—TOEFL (minimum score 600 paper-based; 250 computer-based; 100 iBT). *Application deadline:* For fall admission, 1/30 priority date for domestic students, 1/30 for international students. Applications are processed on a rolling basis. Application fee: $75. Electronic applications accepted. *Expenses:* Contact institution. *Financial support:* In 2011–12, 45 students received support. Fellowships with full tuition reimbursements available, research assistantships with partial tuition reimbursements available, teaching assistantships with partial tuition reimbursements available, career-related internships or fieldwork, scholarships/grants, tuition waivers, unspecified assistantships, and paid hourly positions available. Financial award application deadline: 1/30; financial award applicants required to submit FAFSA. *Unit head:* Dr. Melvin T. Stith, Dean, 315-443-3751. *Application contact:* Josh LaFave, Director, Graduate Enrollment, 315-443-3497, Fax: 315-443-9517, E-mail: mbainfo@syr.edu. Web site: http://whitman.syr.edu.

Tabor College, Graduate Program, Hillsboro, KS 67063. Offers accounting (MBA). Program offered at the Wichita campus only.

Tarleton State University, College of Graduate Studies, College of Business Administration, Stephenville, TX 76402. Offers MBA, MS. *Accreditation:* ACBSP. Part-time and evening/weekend programs available. Postbaccalaureate distance learning degree programs offered (minimal on-campus study). *Faculty:* 20 full-time (2 women), 10 part-time/adjunct (4 women). *Students:* 89 full-time (43 women), 380 part-time (206 women); includes 134 minority (62 Black or African American, non-Hispanic/Latino; 2 American Indian or Alaska Native, non-Hispanic/Latino; 12 Asian, non-Hispanic/Latino; 48 Hispanic/Latino; 10 Two or more races, non-Hispanic/Latino), 7 international. Average age 32. 168 applicants, 90% accepted, 124 enrolled. In 2011, 99 master's awarded. *Degree requirements:* For master's, comprehensive exam, thesis optional. *Entrance requirements:* For master's, GMAT or GRE General Test, minimum GPA of 3.0. Additional exam requirements/recommendations for international students: Required—TOEFL (minimum score 550 paper-based; 213 computer-based; 80 iBT). *Application deadline:* For fall admission, 8/5 priority date for domestic students; for spring admission, 12/1 for domestic students. Applications are processed on a rolling basis. Application fee: $30 ($130 for international students). Electronic applications accepted. *Expenses:* Tuition, state resident: full-time $3131.46; part-time $174 per credit hour. Tuition, nonresident: full-time $8225; part-time $457 per credit hour. *Required fees:* $1446. Tuition and fees vary according to course load and campus/location. *Financial support:* Research assistantships, teaching assistantships, career-related internships or fieldwork, Federal Work-Study, and institutionally sponsored loans available. Support available to part-time students. Financial award application deadline: 5/1; financial award applicants required to submit FAFSA. *Unit head:* Dr. Adolfo Benavides, Dean, 254-968-9496, Fax: 254-968-9496, E-mail: benavides@tarleton.edu. *Application contact:* Information Contact, 254-968-9104, Fax: 254-968-9670, E-mail: gradoffice@tarleton.edu. Web site: http://www.tarleton.edu.

Taylor University, Master of Business Administration Program, Upland, IN 46989-1001. Offers emerging business strategies (MBA); global leadership (MBA). Part-time programs available. *Faculty:* 1 full-time (0 women), 5 part-time/adjunct (0 women). *Students:* 42 full-time (13 women), 6 part-time (1 woman); includes 3 minority (1 Black or African American, non-Hispanic/Latino; 2 Hispanic/Latino). Average age 35. 27 applicants, 85% accepted, 22 enrolled. In 2011, 26 master's awarded. *Application deadline:* Applications are processed on a rolling basis. Application fee: $100. *Expenses: Tuition:* Full-time $9800; part-time $570 per credit hour. *Required fees:* $72 per semester. One-time fee: $100. Tuition and fees vary according to program. *Financial support:* Applicants required to submit FAFSA. *Unit head:* Dr. Evan Wood, Interim Chair, 260-627-9663, E-mail: evwood@taylor.edu. *Application contact:* Wendy Speakman, Program Director, 866-471-6062, Fax: 260-492-0452, E-mail: wnspeakman@taylor.edu. Web site: http://www.taylor.edu/mba/.

Temple University, Fox School of Business, Doctoral Programs in Business, Philadelphia, PA 19122-6096. Offers accounting (PhD); entrepreneurship (PhD); finance (PhD); international business (PhD); management information systems (PhD); marketing (PhD); risk management and insurance (PhD); statistics (PhD); strategic management (PhD); tourism and sport (PhD). *Accreditation:* AACSB. *Degree requirements:* For doctorate, thesis/dissertation. *Entrance requirements:* For doctorate, GRE General Test, GMAT, minimum GPA of 3.0, master's degree. Additional exam requirements/recommendations for international students: Required—TOEFL (minimum score 600 paper-based; 250 computer-based; 100 iBT), IELTS (minimum score 7.5). Electronic applications accepted. *Expenses:* Tuition, state resident: full-time $12,366; part-time $687 per credit hour. Tuition, nonresident: full-time $17,298; part-time $961 per credit hour. *Required fees:* $590; $213 per year.

Temple University, Fox School of Business, MBA Programs, Philadelphia, PA 19122-6096. Offers accounting (MBA); business management (MBA); financial management (MBA); healthcare and life sciences innovation (MBA); human resource management (MBA); international business (IMBA); IT management (MBA); marketing management (MBA); pharmaceutical management (MBA); strategic management (EMBA, MBA). EMBA offered in Philadelphia, PA and Tokyo, Japan. *Accreditation:* AACSB. Part-time and evening/weekend programs available. Postbaccalaureate distance learning degree programs offered (minimal on-campus study). *Entrance requirements:* For master's, GMAT, minimum undergraduate GPA of 3.0. Additional exam requirements/recommendations for international students: Required—TOEFL (minimum score 600 paper-based; 250 computer-based; 100 iBT), IELTS (minimum score 7.5). *Expenses:* Tuition, state resident: full-time $12,366; part-time $687 per credit hour. Tuition, nonresident: full-time $17,298; part-time $961 per credit hour. *Required fees:* $590; $213 per year.

Temple University, Fox School of Business, Specialized Master's Programs, Philadelphia, PA 19122-6096. Offers accountancy (MS); actuarial science (MS); finance (MS); financial engineering (MS); human resource management (MS); marketing (MS); statistics (MS). *Accreditation:* AACSB. Part-time programs available. *Entrance requirements:* For master's, GRE General Test or GMAT, minimum undergraduate GPA of 3.0. Additional exam requirements/recommendations for international students: Required—TOEFL (minimum score 600 paper-based; 250 computer-based; 100 iBT), IELTS (minimum score 7.5). *Expenses:* Tuition, state resident: full-time $12,366; part-time $687 per credit hour. Tuition, nonresident: full-time $17,298; part-time $961 per credit hour. *Required fees:* $590; $213 per year.

Tennessee State University, The School of Graduate Studies and Research, College of Business, Nashville, TN 37209-1561. Offers MBA. *Accreditation:* AACSB. Part-time and evening/weekend programs available. Postbaccalaureate distance learning degree programs offered. *Entrance requirements:* For master's, GMAT. Additional exam requirements/recommendations for international students: Required—TOEFL (minimum score 500 paper-based). Electronic applications accepted. *Faculty research:* Supply chain management, health economics, accounting, e-commerce, international business.

Tennessee Technological University, Graduate School, College of Business, Cookeville, TN 38505. Offers accounting (MBA); finance (MBA); human resource management (MBA); international business (MBA); management information systems (MBA); risk management & insurance (MBA). *Accreditation:* AACSB. Part-time and evening/weekend programs available. Postbaccalaureate distance learning degree programs offered (no on-campus study). *Faculty:* 28 full-time (5 women). *Students:* 45 full-time (19 women), 135 part-time (51 women); includes 13 minority (4 Black or African American, non-Hispanic/Latino; 5 Asian, non-Hispanic/Latino; 3 Hispanic/Latino; 1 Native Hawaiian or other Pacific Islander, non-Hispanic/Latino), 2 international. Average age 25. 193 applicants, 59% accepted, 70 enrolled. In 2011, 89 master's awarded. *Entrance requirements:* For master's, GMAT. Additional exam requirements/recommendations for international students: Required—TOEFL (minimum score 550 paper-based; 79 iBT), IELTS (minimum score 5.5), Pearson Test of English Academic. *Application deadline:* For fall admission, 8/1 for domestic students, 5/1 for international students; for spring admission, 12/1 for domestic students, 10/1 for international students. Application fee: $25 ($30 for international students). Electronic applications accepted. *Expenses:* Tuition, state resident: full-time $8094; part-time $422 per credit hour. Tuition, nonresident: full-time $20,574; part-time $1046 per credit hour. *Financial support:* In 2011–12, 5 fellowships (averaging $10,000 per year), 18 research assistantships (averaging $4,000 per year), teaching assistantships (averaging $4,000 per year) were awarded. Support available to part-time students. Financial award application deadline: 4/1. *Unit head:* Dr. Tom Timmerman, Director, 931-372-3600, Fax: 931-372-6249. *Application contact:* Shelia K. Kendrick, Coordinator of Graduate Admissions, 931-372-3808, Fax: 931-372-3497, E-mail: skendrick@tntech.edu. Web site: http://www.tntech.edu/mba.

Texas A&M International University, Office of Graduate Studies and Research, College of Business Administration, Laredo, TX 78041-1900. Offers MBA, MP Acc, MSIS. *Accreditation:* AACSB. Part-time and evening/weekend programs available. *Faculty:* 29 full-time (2 women), 2 part-time/adjunct (0 women). *Students:* 79 full-time (30 women), 216 part-time (101 women); includes 183 minority (6 Black or African American, non-Hispanic/Latino; 3 Asian, non-Hispanic/Latino; 174 Hispanic/Latino), 96 international. Average age 29. 236 applicants, 48% accepted, 84 enrolled. In 2011, 136 master's awarded. *Degree requirements:* For master's, thesis (for some programs). *Entrance requirements:* For master's, GMAT or GRE General Test. Additional exam requirements/recommendations for international students: Required—TOEFL (minimum score 550 paper-based; 213 computer-based; 79 iBT). *Application deadline:* For fall admission, 4/30 priority date for domestic students, 4/30 for international students; for spring admission, 11/30 for domestic students, 10/1 for international students. Applications are processed on a rolling basis. Application fee: $35 ($50 for international students). *Expenses:* Tuition, state resident: full-time $5063. *Financial support:* In 2011–12, 11 students received support, including 2 fellowships, 8 research assistantships, 1 teaching assistantship; Federal Work-Study, institutionally sponsored loans, and scholarships/grants also available. Support available to part-time students. Financial award application deadline: 4/1; financial award applicants required to submit FAFSA. *Unit head:* Dr. Stephen R. Sears, Dean, 956-326-2480, E-mail: steve.sears@tamiu.edu. *Application contact:* Imelda Lopez, Graduate Admissions Counselor, 956-326-2485, Fax: 956-326-2459, E-mail: lopez@tamiu.edu. Web site: http://www.tamiu.edu/ssb/.

Texas A&M University, Mays Business School, Department of Management, College Station, TX 77843. Offers human resource management (MS); management (PhD). *Faculty:* 27. *Students:* 71 full-time (46 women), 1 (woman) part-time; includes 12 minority (4 Black or African American, non-Hispanic/Latino; 5 Asian, non-Hispanic/Latino; 3 Hispanic/Latino), 6 international. Average age 31. 76 applicants, 28% accepted. In 2011, 32 master's, 2 doctorates awarded. Terminal master's awarded for partial completion of doctoral program. *Degree requirements:* For master's, comprehensive exam; for doctorate, thesis/dissertation. *Entrance requirements:* For master's, GMAT or GRE; for doctorate, GMAT or GRE General Test. Additional exam requirements/recommendations for international students: Required—TOEFL. *Application deadline:* For fall admission, 3/1 priority date for domestic students; for spring admission, 8/1 for domestic students. Applications are processed on a rolling basis. Application fee: $50 ($75 for international students). *Expenses:* Tuition, state resident: full-time $5437; part-time $226.55 per credit hour. Tuition, nonresident: full-time $12,949; part-time $539.55 per credit hour. *Required fees:* $2741. *Financial support:* In 2011–12, 25 students received support. Fellowships, research assistantships, teaching assistantships, career-related internships or fieldwork, and institutionally sponsored loans available. Financial award application deadline: 2/1. *Faculty research:* Strategic and human resource management, business and public policy, organizational behavior, organizational theory. *Unit head:* Dr. Ricky W. Griffin, Head, 979-862-3962, Fax: 979-845-9641, E-mail: rgriffin@mays.tamu.edu. *Application contact:* Kristi Mora, Senior Academic Advisor II, 979-845-6127, E-mail: kmora@mays.tamu.edu. Web site: http://mays.tamu.edu/mgmt/.

Texas A&M University–Commerce, Graduate School, College of Business, MBA Program, Commerce, TX 75429-3011. Offers MBA. *Accreditation:* AACSB. Part-time programs available. *Degree requirements:* For master's, comprehensive exam, thesis (for some programs). *Entrance requirements:* For master's, GMAT.

Texas A&M University–Commerce, Graduate School, College of Business, MS Programs, Commerce, TX 75429-3011. Offers accounting (MS); economics (MA); finance (MS); management (MS); marketing (MS). Part-time programs available. *Degree requirements:* For master's, comprehensive exam, thesis (for some programs). *Entrance requirements:* For master's, GMAT or GRE General Test. Electronic applications accepted. *Faculty research:* Economic activity, forensic economics, volatility and finance, international economics.

Texas A&M University–Corpus Christi, Graduate Studies and Research, College of Business, Corpus Christi, TX 78412-5503. Offers accounting (M Acc); health care administration (MBA); international business (MBA). *Accreditation:* AACSB. Part-time and evening/weekend programs available. *Degree requirements:* For master's, comprehensive exam, thesis (for some programs). *Entrance requirements:* For master's, GMAT. Additional exam requirements/recommendations for international students: Required—TOEFL. Electronic applications accepted.

Texas A&M University–Kingsville, College of Graduate Studies, College of Business Administration, Kingsville, TX 78363. Offers MBA, MS. *Accreditation:* ACBSP. Part-time and evening/weekend programs available. *Degree requirements:* For master's, comprehensive exam, thesis or alternative. *Entrance requirements:* For master's, GMAT, minimum GPA of 2.5. Additional exam requirements/recommendations for international students: Required—TOEFL. *Faculty research:* Capital budgeting, international trade.

Texas A&M University–San Antonio, School of Business, San Antonio, TX 78224. Offers business administration (MBA); enterprise resource planning systems (MBA); finance (MBA); healthcare management (MBA); human resources management (MBA); information assurance and security (MBA); international business (MBA); professional accounting (MPA); project management (MBA); supply chain management (MBA). Part-time and evening/weekend programs available. *Faculty:* 18 full-time (6 women), 1 part-time/adjunct (0 women). *Students:* 91 full-time (45 women), 278 part-time (150 women). Average age 33. In 2011, 20 master's awarded. *Entrance requirements:* For master's, GMAT. Additional exam requirements/recommendations for international students: Required—TOEFL (minimum score 550 paper-based; 213 computer-based; 80 iBT), IELTS (minimum score 6). *Application deadline:* For fall admission, 7/1 priority date for domestic students, 6/1 for international students; for spring admission, 11/15 priority date for domestic students, 10/1 for international students. Applications are processed on a rolling basis. Application fee: $35 ($50 for international students). Electronic applications accepted. *Expenses:* Tuition, state resident: part-time $691.11 per course. Tuition, nonresident: part-time $1621.11 per course. *Financial support:* Application deadline: 3/31; applicants required to submit FAFSA. *Unit head:* Dr. Tracy Hurley, MBA Coordinator, 210-932-6200, E-mail: tracy.hurley@tamusa.tamus.edu. *Application contact:* Melissa A. Villanueva, Graduate Admissions Specialist, 210-932-6200, Fax: 210-932-6209, E-mail: melissa.villanueva@tamusa.tamus.edu. Web site: http://www.tamusa.tamus.edu.

Texas A&M University–Texarkana, Graduate Studies and Research, College of Business, Texarkana, TX 75505-5518. Offers accounting (MSA); business administration (MBA, MS). Part-time and evening/weekend programs available. *Degree requirements:* For master's, thesis or alternative. *Entrance requirements:* For master's, minimum GPA of 2.5 in last 60 hours of bachelor's degree. Additional exam requirements/recommendations for international students: Required—TOEFL. Electronic applications accepted.

Texas Christian University, College of Science and Engineering, Department of Physics and Astronomy, Fort Worth, TX 76129-0002. Offers physics (MA, MS, PhD), including astrophysics (PhD), business (PhD), physics (PhD); PhD/MBA. *Faculty:* 7 full-time, 1 part-time/adjunct. *Students:* 3 full-time (1 woman), 13 part-time (4 women); includes 2 minority (1 Asian, non-Hispanic/Latino; 1 Hispanic/Latino), 7 international. Average age 27. 7 applicants, 71% accepted, 5 enrolled. In 2011, 1 master's, 2 doctorates awarded. Terminal master's awarded for partial completion of doctoral program. *Median time to degree:* Of those who began their doctoral program in fall 2003, 100% received their degree in 8 years or less. *Degree requirements:* For master's, comprehensive exam, thesis; for doctorate, comprehensive exam, thesis/dissertation, paper submitted to scientific journal. *Entrance requirements:* For master's and doctorate, GRE General Test, minimum GPA of 3.0. Additional exam requirements/recommendations for international students: Required—TOEFL (minimum score 600 paper-based). *Application deadline:* For fall admission, 2/1 for domestic and international students; for spring admission, 10/1 for domestic and international students. Applications are processed on a rolling basis. Application fee: $60. Electronic applications accepted. *Expenses: Tuition:* Full-time $20,250; part-time $1125 per credit hour. Part-time tuition and fees vary according to course load and program. *Financial support:* In 2011–12, 11 teaching assistantships with full tuition reimbursements (averaging $19,500 per year) were awarded; tuition waivers also available. Financial award application deadline: 2/1. *Unit head:* Dr. William R. Graham, Chairperson, 817-257-7375 Ext. 6383, Fax: 817-257-7742, E-mail: w.graham@tcu.edu. *Application contact:* Dr. Yuri Strzhemechny, Associate Professor, 817-257-7375 Ext. 5793, Fax: 817-257-7742, E-mail: y.strzhemechny@tcu.edu. Web site: http://www.phys.tcu.edu/grad_program.asp.

Texas Christian University, The Neeley School of Business at TCU, Program in Business Administration, Fort Worth, TX 76129-0002. Offers MBA. *Accreditation:* AACSB. Part-time and evening/weekend programs available. *Faculty:* 55 full-time (10 women), 1 (woman) part-time/adjunct. *Students:* 149 full-time (38 women), 127 part-time (32 women); includes 36 minority (10 Black or African American, non-Hispanic/Latino; 2 American Indian or Alaska Native, non-Hispanic/Latino; 9 Asian, non-Hispanic/Latino; 15 Hispanic/Latino), 29 international. Average age 31. 147 applicants, 95% accepted, 128 enrolled. In 2011, 118 master's awarded. *Entrance requirements:* For master's, GMAT, 3 hours of course work in college algebra. Additional exam requirements/recommendations for international students: Required—TOEFL (minimum score 600 paper-based; 250 computer-based; 100 iBT). *Application deadline:* For fall admission, 11/1 priority date for domestic students, 11/1 for international students; for winter admission, 1/15 priority date for domestic students, 1/15 for international students; for spring admission, 4/15 priority date for domestic students, 4/15 for international students. Applications are processed on a rolling basis. Application fee: $100. Electronic applications accepted. *Expenses: Tuition:* Full-time $20,250; part-time $1125 per credit hour. Part-time tuition and fees vary according to course load and program. *Financial support:* Career-related internships or fieldwork, Federal Work-Study, institutionally sponsored loans, scholarships/grants, and unspecified assistantships available. Support available to part-time students. Financial award application deadline: 5/1; financial award applicants required to submit FAFSA. *Faculty research:* Emerging financial markets, derivative trading activity, salesforce deployment, examining sales activity, litigation against tax practitioners. *Total annual research expenditures:* $2.5 million. *Unit head:* Dr. Bill Cron, Associate Dean, Graduate Programs, 817-257-7531, Fax: 817-257-6431. *Application contact:* Peggy Conway, Director, MBA Admissions, 817-257-7531, Fax: 817-257-6431, E-mail: mbainfo@tcu.edu. Web site: http://www.neeley.tcu.edu/.

Texas Southern University, Jesse H. Jones School of Business, Program in Business Administration, Houston, TX 77004-4584. Offers MBA. *Accreditation:* AACSB. Part-time and evening/weekend programs available. *Degree requirements:* For master's, comprehensive exam. *Entrance requirements:* For master's, GMAT, minimum GPA of 2.5. Electronic applications accepted.

Texas State University–San Marcos, Graduate School, Emmett and Miriam McCoy College of Business Administration, Program in Business Administration, San Marcos, TX 78666. Offers MBA. *Accreditation:* AACSB. Part-time programs available. *Faculty:* 26 full-time (9 women), 1 part-time/adjunct (0 women). *Students:* 116 full-time (49 women), 219 part-time (67 women); includes 91 minority (23 Black or African American, non-Hispanic/Latino; 1 American Indian or Alaska Native, non-Hispanic/Latino; 16 Asian, non-Hispanic/Latino; 46 Hispanic/Latino; 5 Two or more races, non-Hispanic/Latino), 17 international. Average age 30. 189 applicants, 51% accepted, 79 enrolled. In 2011, 94 master's awarded. *Degree requirements:* For master's, comprehensive exam, thesis optional. *Entrance requirements:* For master's, GMAT (minimum preferred score of 450 prior to admission decision), minimum GPA of 2.0 in last 60 hours of undergraduate work. Additional exam requirements/recommendations for international students: Required—TOEFL (minimum score 550 paper-based; 213 computer-based; 78 iBT). *Application deadline:* For fall admission, 6/1 for domestic and international students; for spring admission, 10/1 for domestic and international students. Applications are processed on a rolling basis. Application fee: $40 ($90 for international students). Electronic applications accepted. *Expenses:* Tuition, state resident: full-time $6408; part-time $3204 per semester. Tuition, nonresident: full-time $14,832; part-time $7416 per semester. *Required fees:* $1824; $912 per semester. Tuition and fees vary according to course load. *Financial support:* In 2011–12, 80 students received support, including 6 research assistantships (averaging $10,260 per year), 14 teaching assistantships (averaging $10,215 per year); Federal Work-Study, institutionally sponsored loans, scholarships/grants, health care benefits, and unspecified assistantships also available. Support available to part-time students. Financial award application deadline: 4/1; financial award applicants required to submit FAFSA. *Unit head:* Dr. Robert Davis, Associate Dean, 512-245-3591, Fax: 512-245-7973, E-mail: rd23@txstate.edu. *Application contact:* Dr. J. Michael Willoughby, Dean of Graduate School, 512-245-2581, Fax: 512-245-8365, E-mail: gradcollege@txstate.edu. Web site: http://www.business.txstate.edu/.

Texas Tech University, Graduate School, Rawls College of Business Administration, Area of Management, Lubbock, TX 79409. Offers PhD. *Accreditation:* AACSB. Part-time programs available. *Faculty:* 14 full-time (2 women). *Students:* 10 full-time (5 women); includes 1 minority (Black or African American, non-Hispanic/Latino), 4 international. Average age 32. 6 applicants, 0% accepted, 0 enrolled. In 2011, 2 degrees awarded. *Median time to degree:* Of those who began their doctoral program in fall 2003, 100% received their degree in 8 years or less. *Degree requirements:* For doctorate, comprehensive exam, thesis/dissertation, qualifying exams. *Entrance requirements:* For doctorate, GMAT, holistic profile of academic credentials. Additional exam requirements/recommendations for international students: Required—TOEFL (minimum score 550 paper-based; 213 computer-based; 79 iBT). *Application deadline:* For fall admission, 2/1 priority date for domestic students, 1/15 for international students. Applications are processed on a rolling basis. Application fee: $50 ($75 for international students). Electronic applications accepted. *Expenses:* Tuition, state resident: full-time $5899; part-time $245.80 per credit hour. Tuition, nonresident: full-time $13,411; part-time $558.80 per credit hour. *Required fees:* $2680.60; $86.50 per credit hour. $920.30 per semester. *Financial support:* In 2011–12, 5 research assistantships (averaging $14,550 per year), 4 teaching assistantships (averaging $18,000 per year) were awarded; career-related internships or fieldwork, Federal Work-Study, and scholarships/grants also available. Financial award applicants required to submit FAFSA. *Faculty research:* Entrepreneurship, leadership, health care, organization theory. *Unit head:* Dr. William Gardner, Area Coordinator, 806-742-1055, Fax: 806-742-2308, E-mail: william.gardner@ttu.edu. *Application contact:* Elizabeth Stuart, Director, Graduate Services Center, 806-742-3184, Fax: 806-742-3958, E-mail: ba_grad@ttu.edu. Web site: http://management.ba.ttu.edu.

Texas Tech University, Graduate School, Rawls College of Business Administration, Programs in Business Administration, Lubbock, TX 79409. Offers agricultural business (MBA); business administration (IMBA); business statistics (MBA); entrepreneurship and innovation (MBA); general business (MBA); health organization management (MBA); international business (MBA); management and leadership skills (MBA); management information systems (MBA); marketing (MBA); real estate (MBA); JD/MBA; MBA/M Arch; MBA/MA; MBA/MD; MBA/MS; MBA/Pharm D. Part-time and evening/weekend programs available. *Faculty:* 49 full-time (8 women), 2 part-time/adjunct (0 women). *Students:* 195 full-time (55 women), 397 part-time (101 women); includes 123 minority (27 Black or African American, non-Hispanic/Latino; 4 American Indian or Alaska Native, non-Hispanic/Latino; 31 Asian, non-Hispanic/Latino; 61 Hispanic/Latino), 38 international. Average age 31. 374 applicants, 83% accepted, 255 enrolled. In 2011, 256 degrees awarded. *Degree requirements:* For master's, capstone course. *Entrance requirements:* For master's, GMAT, holistic review of academic credentials. Additional exam requirements/recommendations for international students: Required—TOEFL (minimum score 550 paper-based; 213 computer-based; 79 iBT). *Application deadline:* For fall admission, 4/1 priority date for domestic students, 1/15 for international students; for spring admission, 9/1 priority date for domestic students, 6/15 for international students. Applications are processed on a rolling basis. Application fee: $50 ($75 for international students). Electronic applications accepted. *Expenses:* Tuition, state resident: full-time $5899; part-time $245.80 per credit hour. Tuition, nonresident: full-time $13,411; part-time $558.80 per credit hour. *Required fees:* $2680.60; $86.50 per credit hour. $920.30 per semester. *Financial support:* In 2011–12, 22 research assistantships (averaging $8,800 per year) were awarded; teaching assistantships, career-related internships or fieldwork, Federal Work-Study, scholarships/grants, health care benefits, and unspecified assistantships also available. Support available to part-time students. Financial award applicants required to submit FAFSA. *Unit head:* Dr. W. Jay Conover, Director, 806-742-1546, Fax: 806-742-3958, E-mail: jay.conover@ttu.edu. *Application contact:* Elizabeth Stuart, Director, Graduate Services Center, 806-742-3184, Fax: 806-742-3958, E-mail: ba_grad@ttu.edu. Web site: http://mba.ba.ttu.edu/.

Business Administration and Management—General

Texas Wesleyan University, Graduate Programs, Graduate Business Programs, Fort Worth, TX 76105-1536. Offers business administration (MBA); health services administration (MS); management (MiM). *Accreditation:* ACBSP. Part-time and evening/weekend programs available. *Faculty:* 16 full-time (6 women), 6 part-time/adjunct (4 women). *Students:* 7 full-time (5 women), 32 part-time (20 women); includes 8 minority (3 Black or African American, non-Hispanic/Latino; 1 Asian, non-Hispanic/Latino; 4 Hispanic/Latino), 3 international. Average age 32. 42 applicants, 24% accepted, 9 enrolled. In 2011, 25 master's awarded. *Degree requirements:* For master's, capstone course. *Entrance requirements:* For master's, GMAT, 3 letters of recommendation. *Application deadline:* For fall admission, 7/7 priority date for domestic students; for spring admission, 11/1 priority date for domestic students. Applications are processed on a rolling basis. Application fee: $50. *Expenses:* Contact institution. *Financial support:* Federal Work-Study, scholarships/grants, and tuition waivers (full and partial) available. Support available to part-time students. Financial award application deadline: 3/15; financial award applicants required to submit FAFSA. *Unit head:* Dr. Hector Quintanilla, Dean, 817-531-4840, Fax: 817-531-6585. *Application contact:* Admissions Office, 817-531-4444. Web site: http://www.txwes.edu/academics/business.

Texas Woman's University, Graduate School, College of Arts and Sciences, School of Management, Denton, TX 76201. Offers business administration (MBA); health systems management (MHSM). Part-time programs available. *Faculty:* 17 full-time (10 women), 1 part-time/adjunct (0 women). *Students:* 660 full-time (555 women), 436 part-time (364 women); includes 714 minority (465 Black or African American, non-Hispanic/Latino; 8 American Indian or Alaska Native, non-Hispanic/Latino; 116 Asian, non-Hispanic/Latino; 121 Hispanic/Latino; 4 Native Hawaiian or other Pacific Islander, non-Hispanic/Latino), 46 international. Average age 35. 428 applicants, 93% accepted, 318 enrolled. In 2011, 550 master's awarded. *Degree requirements:* For master's, thesis optional. *Entrance requirements:* For master's, 2 letters of reference, resume, 5 years relevant experience (EMBA only). Additional exam requirements/recommendations for international students: Required—TOEFL (minimum score 550 paper-based; 213 computer-based; 79 iBT). *Application deadline:* For fall admission, 8/1 priority date for domestic students, 3/1 for international students; for spring admission, 12/1 priority date for domestic students, 7/1 for international students. Applications are processed on a rolling basis. Application fee: $50 ($75 for international students). Electronic applications accepted. *Expenses:* Tuition, state resident: full-time $3834; part-time $213 per credit hour. Tuition, nonresident: full-time $9468; part-time $526 per credit hour. *Required fees:* $213 per credit hour. Tuition and fees vary according to course load. *Financial support:* In 2011–12, 254 students received support, including 15 research assistantships (averaging $11,520 per year); career-related internships or fieldwork, Federal Work-Study, institutionally sponsored loans, scholarships/grants, traineeships, health care benefits, and unspecified assistantships also available. Support available to part-time students. Financial award application deadline: 3/1; financial award applicants required to submit FAFSA. *Faculty research:* Tax research, privacy issues in Web-based marketing, multitasking, leadership, women in management, global comparative studies, corporate sustainability and responsibility. *Unit head:* Dr. P. Ann Hughes, Director, 940-898-2121, Fax: 940-898-2120, E-mail: pahughes@twu.edu. *Application contact:* Dr. Samuel Wheeler, Assistant Director of Admissions, 940-898-3188, Fax: 940-898-3081, E-mail: wheelersr@twu.edu. Web site: http://www.twu.edu/som/.

Thomas College, Graduate School, Programs in Business, Waterville, ME 04901-5097. Offers business (MBA); computer technology education (MS); education (MS); human resource management (MBA). Part-time and evening/weekend programs available. *Entrance requirements:* For master's, GMAT, GRE, MAT or minimum GPA of 3.3 in first 3 graduate-level courses. Additional exam requirements/recommendations for international students: Recommended—TOEFL.

Thomas Edison State College, School of Business and Management, Program in Management, Trenton, NJ 08608-1176. Offers MSM. Part-time programs available. Postbaccalaureate distance learning degree programs offered (minimal on-campus study). *Students:* 301 part-time (125 women); includes 100 minority (61 Black or African American, non-Hispanic/Latino; 1 American Indian or Alaska Native, non-Hispanic/Latino; 12 Asian, non-Hispanic/Latino; 25 Hispanic/Latino; 1 Two or more races, non-Hispanic/Latino), 5 international. Average age 46. In 2011, 51 master's awarded. *Degree requirements:* For master's, final capstone project. *Entrance requirements:* For master's, bachelor's degree from a regionally-accredited college or university; minimum 2 letters of recommendation; 3-5 years of related working experience; current resume. Additional exam requirements/recommendations for international students: Required—TOEFL (minimum score 550 paper-based; 213 computer-based; 79 iBT). *Application deadline:* For fall admission, 8/15 priority date for domestic students, 8/15 for international students; for winter admission, 11/15 priority date for domestic students, 11/15 for international students; for spring admission, 2/15 priority date for domestic students, 2/15 for international students. Applications are processed on a rolling basis. Application fee: $75. Electronic applications accepted. *Financial support:* Applicants required to submit FAFSA. *Unit head:* Dr. Susan Gilbert, Dean, School of Business and Management, 609-984-1130, Fax: 609-984-3898, E-mail: info@tesc.edu. *Application contact:* David Hoftiezer, Director of Admissions, 888-442-8372, Fax: 609-984-8447, E-mail: admissions@tesc.edu. Web site: http://www.tesc.edu/business/msm/index.cfm.

Thomas More College, Program in Business Administration, Crestview Hills, KY 41017-3495. Offers MBA. *Faculty:* 11 full-time (3 women), 2 part-time/adjunct (0 women). *Students:* 106 full-time (55 women); includes 7 minority (4 Black or African American, non-Hispanic/Latino; 1 Asian, non-Hispanic/Latino; 2 Hispanic/Latino). Average age 34. 26 applicants, 88% accepted, 22 enrolled. In 2011, 60 master's awarded. *Degree requirements:* For master's, comprehensive exam, final project. *Entrance requirements:* For master's, GMAT, minimum GPA of 2.7. Additional exam requirements/recommendations for international students: Required—TOEFL (minimum score 600 paper-based; 250 computer-based; 100 iBT). *Application deadline:* Applications are processed on a rolling basis. Application fee: $25. Electronic applications accepted. *Expenses: Tuition:* Full-time $13,057; part-time $570 per credit hour. Tuition and fees vary according to program. *Financial support:* In 2011–12, 10 students received support. Federal Work-Study, institutionally sponsored loans, and scholarships/grants available. Financial award application deadline: 3/15; financial award applicants required to submit FAFSA. *Faculty research:* Comparison level and consumer satisfaction, history of U. S. business development, share price reaction, quality and competition, personnel development. *Unit head:* Nathan Hartman, Director of Adult and Professional Education, 859-344-3333, Fax: 859-344-3686, E-mail: nathan.hartman@thomasmore.edu. *Application contact:* Judy Bautista, Enrollment Manager, 859-341-4554, Fax: 859-578-3589, E-mail: judy.bautista@tap.thomasmore.edu. Web site: http://www.thomasmore.edu.

Thomas University, Department of Business Administration, Thomasville, GA 31792-7499. Offers MBA. Part-time programs available. *Entrance requirements:* For master's, resume, 3 professional or academic references. Additional exam requirements/recommendations for international students: Required—TOEFL (minimum score 600 paper-based; 250 computer-based). Electronic applications accepted.

Thompson Rivers University, Program in Business Administration, Kamloops, BC V2C 5N3, Canada. Offers MBA. Part-time programs available. *Entrance requirements:* For master's, GMAT, undergraduate degree with minimum B- average in last 60 credits, personal resume. Additional exam requirements/recommendations for international students: Required—TOEFL (570 paper-based, 230 computer-based, 88 iBT), IELTS (6.5), or CAEL (70).

Thunderbird School of Global Management, Full-Time MBA Programs, Glendale, AZ 85306. Offers GMBA, MBA. Part-time and evening/weekend programs available. Postbaccalaureate distance learning degree programs offered (minimal on-campus study). *Faculty:* 48 full-time (13 women). *Students:* 509 full-time (139 women); includes 42 minority (6 Black or African American, non-Hispanic/Latino; 2 American Indian or Alaska Native, non-Hispanic/Latino; 17 Asian, non-Hispanic/Latino; 10 Hispanic/Latino; 7 Two or more races, non-Hispanic/Latino), 285 international. 440 applicants, 75% accepted, 173 enrolled. In 2011, 300 master's awarded. *Degree requirements:* For master's, one foreign language. *Entrance requirements:* For master's, GMAT, 2 years work experience. Additional exam requirements/recommendations for international students: Required—TOEFL (minimum score 600 paper-based; 250 computer-based; 100 iBT). *Application deadline:* For spring admission, 6/10 for domestic students, 4/30 for international students. Applications are processed on a rolling basis. Application fee: $125. Electronic applications accepted. *Expenses: Tuition:* Full-time $43,080; part-time $1436 per credit. *Financial support:* In 2011–12, 501 students received support. Federal Work-Study and scholarships/grants available. Support available to part-time students. Financial award application deadline: 2/15; financial award applicants required to submit FAFSA. *Faculty research:* Management, social enterprise, cross-cultural communication, finance, marketing. *Unit head:* Dr. Kay Keck, Vice President, 602-978-7077, Fax: 602-547-1356, E-mail: kay.keck@thunderbird.edu. *Application contact:* Jay Bryant, Director of Admissions, 602-978-7294, Fax: 602-439-5432, E-mail: jay.bryant@thunderbird.edu. Web site: http://www.thunderbird.edu.

Thunderbird School of Global Management, Master's Programs in Global Management, Glendale, AZ 85306. Offers global affairs and management (MA); global management (MS). *Accreditation:* AACSB. *Students:* 141 full-time (78 women); includes 12 minority (1 Black or African American, non-Hispanic/Latino; 2 Asian, non-Hispanic/Latino; 4 Hispanic/Latino; 5 Two or more races, non-Hispanic/Latino), 90 international. 132 applicants, 84% accepted, 70 enrolled. In 2011, 79 master's awarded. *Degree requirements:* For master's, one foreign language. *Entrance requirements:* For master's, GMAT/GRE. Additional exam requirements/recommendations for international students: Required—TOEFL. *Application deadline:* For fall admission, 6/10 for domestic students, 4/30 for international students. Application fee: $125. *Expenses: Tuition:* Full-time $43,080; part-time $1436 per credit. *Financial support:* Career-related internships or fieldwork, Federal Work-Study, scholarships/grants, and unspecified assistantships available. *Unit head:* Dr. Glenn Fong, Unit Head, 602-978-7156. *Application contact:* Jay Bryant, Director of Admissions, 602-978-7294, Fax: 602-439-5432, E-mail: jay.bryant@thunderbird.edu.

Tiffin University, Program in Business Administration, Tiffin, OH 44883-2161. Offers finance (MBA); general management (MBA); healthcare administration (MBA); human resources (MBA); international business (MBA); leadership (MBA); marketing (MBA); sports management (MBA). *Accreditation:* ACBSP. Part-time and evening/weekend programs available. Postbaccalaureate distance learning degree programs offered (no on-campus study). *Faculty:* 30 full-time (15 women), 22 part-time/adjunct (6 women). *Students:* 209 full-time (107 women), 340 part-time (172 women); includes 112 minority (91 Black or African American, non-Hispanic/Latino; 4 Asian, non-Hispanic/Latino; 17 Hispanic/Latino), 71 international. Average age 31. 237 applicants, 76% accepted. In 2011, 170 master's awarded. *Entrance requirements:* For master's, minimum undergraduate GPA of 2.5, work experience. Additional exam requirements/recommendations for international students: Required—TOEFL (minimum score 550 paper-based; 213 computer-based; 79 iBT). *Application deadline:* For fall admission, 8/15 for domestic students, 8/1 for international students; for spring admission, 1/9 for domestic students, 12/1 for international students. Applications are processed on a rolling basis. Electronic applications accepted. *Expenses: Tuition:* Full-time $11,200; part-time $700 per credit. Tuition and fees vary according to program. *Financial support:* Available to part-time students. Application deadline: 7/31; applicants required to submit FAFSA. *Faculty research:* Small business, executive development operations, research and statistical analysis, market research, management information systems. *Unit head:* Dr. Lillian Schumacher, Dean of the School of Business, 419-448-3053, Fax: 419-443-5002, E-mail: schumacherlb@tiffin.edu. *Application contact:* Nikki Hintze, Director of Graduate Admissions and Student Services, 800-968-6446 Ext. 3445, Fax: 419-443-5002, E-mail: hintzenm@tiffin.edu. Web site: http://www.tiffin.edu/graduateprograms/.

Trevecca Nazarene University, College of Lifelong Learning, Graduate Business Programs, Major in Business Administration, Nashville, TN 37210-2877. Offers MBA. Evening/weekend programs available. *Students:* 10 part-time (3 women); includes 3 minority (all Black or African American, non-Hispanic/Latino). In 2011, 35 master's awarded. *Entrance requirements:* For master's, GMAT, proficiency exam (quantitative skills), minimum GPA of 2.5, resume, employer letter of recommendation, 2 letters of recommendation, written business analysis. Additional exam requirements/recommendations for international students: Required—TOEFL (minimum score 550 paper-based; 213 computer-based). *Application deadline:* Applications are processed on a rolling basis. Application fee: $25. *Expenses:* Contact institution. *Financial support:* Applicants required to submit FAFSA. *Unit head:* Dr. Ed Anthony, Director of Graduate and Professional Programs (School of Business), 615-248-1529, E-mail: management@trevecca.edu. *Application contact:* Marcus Lackey, Enrollment Manager, 615-248-1427, E-mail: cll@trevecca.edu. Web site: http://www.trevecca.edu/mba.

Trident University International, College of Business Administration, Program in Business Administration, Cypress, CA 90630. Offers business administration (PhD); conflict and negotiation management (MBA); criminal justice administration (MBA); entrepreneurship (MBA); finance (MBA); general management (MBA); government accounting (MBA); human resource management (MBA); information security and digital assurance management (MBA); information technology management (MBA); international business (MBA); logistics management (MBA); marketing (MBA); project management (MBA); public management (MBA); quality management (MBA); strategic leadership (MBA). Part-time and evening/weekend programs available. Postbaccalaureate distance learning degree programs offered (no on-campus study). *Degree requirements:* For doctorate, comprehensive exam, thesis/dissertation, defense of dissertation. *Entrance requirements:* For master's, minimum GPA of 2.5 (students with GPA 3.0 or greater may transfer up to 30% of graduate level credits); for doctorate, minimum GPA of 3.4, curriculum vitae, course work in research methods or statistics. Additional exam requirements/recommendations for international students: Required—TOEFL. Electronic applications accepted.

Trinity International University, Trinity Evangelical Divinity School, Deerfield, IL 60015-1284. Offers Biblical and Near Eastern archaeology and languages (MA); Christian studies (MA, Certificate); Christian thought (MA); church history (MA, Th M); congregational ministry: pastor-teacher (M Div); congregational ministry: team ministry (M Div); counseling ministries (MA); counseling psychology (MA); cross-cultural ministry (M Div); educational studies (PhD); evangelism (MA); history of Christianity in America (MA); intercultural studies (MA, PhD); leadership and ministry management (D Min); military chaplaincy (D Min); ministry (MA); mission and evangelism (Th M); missions and evangelism (D Min); New Testament (MA, Th M); Old Testament (Th M); Old Testament and Semitic languages (MA); pastoral care (M Div); pastoral care and counseling (D Min); pastoral counseling and psychology (Th M); pastoral theology (Th M); philosophy of religion (MA); preaching (D Min); religion (MA); research ministry (M Div); systematic theology (Th M); theological studies (PhD); urban ministry (MA). *Accreditation:* ATS (one or more programs are accredited). Part-time programs available. Postbaccalaureate distance learning degree programs offered (minimal on-campus study). *Degree requirements:* For master's, comprehensive exam, thesis, fieldwork; for doctorate, comprehensive exam (for some programs), thesis/dissertation; for Certificate, comprehensive exam, integrative papers. *Entrance requirements:* For master's, GRE, MAT, minimum cumulative undergraduate GPA of 3.0; for doctorate, GRE, minimum cumulative graduate GPA of 3.2; for Certificate, GRE, MAT, minimum undergraduate GPA of 2.5. Additional exam requirements/recommendations for international students: Required—TOEFL (minimum score 580 paper-based; 237 computer-based), TWE (minimum score 4). Electronic applications accepted.

Trinity University, Department of Business Administration, San Antonio, TX 78212-7200. Offers accounting (MS). *Accreditation:* AACSB. Part-time programs available. *Entrance requirements:* For master's, GMAT, minimum GPA of 3.0, course work in accounting and business law.

Trinity Washington University, School of Professional Studies, Washington, DC 20017-1094. Offers business administration (MBA); communication (MA); international security studies (MA); organizational management (MSA), including federal program management, human resource management, nonprofit management, organizational development, public and community health. Part-time and evening/weekend programs available. *Degree requirements:* For master's, thesis (for some programs), capstone project (MSA). *Entrance requirements:* For master's, minimum GPA of 2.5. Additional exam requirements/recommendations for international students: Required—TOEFL (minimum score 550 paper-based; 213 computer-based).

Trinity Western University, School of Graduate Studies, Program in Business Administration, Langley, BC V2Y 1Y1, Canada. Offers international business (MBA); management of the growing enterprise (MBA); non-profit and charitable organization management (MBA). Part-time programs available. Postbaccalaureate distance learning degree programs offered (minimal on-campus study). *Degree requirements:* For master's, thesis or alternative, applied project. *Entrance requirements:* For master's, GMAT (minimum score of 550 recommended). Additional exam requirements/recommendations for international students: Required—TOEFL (minimum score 600 paper-based; 250 computer-based; 100 iBT), IELTS. Electronic applications accepted.

Troy University, Graduate School, College of Business, Program in Business Administration, Troy, AL 36082. Offers accounting (EMBA, MBA); criminal justice (EMBA); finance (MBA); general management (EMBA, MBA); healthcare management (EMBA); information systems (EMBA, MBA); international economic development (MBA). *Accreditation:* ACBSP. Part-time and evening/weekend programs available. *Faculty:* 50 full-time (14 women), 12 part-time/adjunct (0 women). *Students:* 326 full-time (168 women), 596 part-time (358 women); includes 524 minority (402 Black or African American, non-Hispanic/Latino; 12 American Indian or Alaska Native, non-Hispanic/Latino; 85 Asian, non-Hispanic/Latino; 21 Hispanic/Latino; 4 Two or more races, non-Hispanic/Latino). Average age 29. 644 applicants, 67% accepted, 204 enrolled. In 2011, 388 master's awarded. *Degree requirements:* For master's, minimum GPA of 3.0, capstone course, research course. *Entrance requirements:* For master's, GMAT (minimum score 500) or GRE General Test (minimum score 900), minimum GPA of 2.5; letter of recommendation, bachelor's degree. Additional exam requirements/recommendations for international students: Required—TOEFL (minimum score 523 paper-based; 193 computer-based; 70 iBT), IELTS (minimum score 6), or ACT COMPASS ESL (minimum listening, reading, and grammar score 270). *Application deadline:* Applications are processed on a rolling basis. Application fee: $50. *Expenses:* Tuition, state resident: full-time $6960; part-time $290 per credit hour. Tuition, nonresident: full-time $13,920; part-time $580 per credit hour. *Required fees:* $386 per term. *Unit head:* Dr. Edward Merkel, Director, Graduate Business Programs, 334-670-3194, Fax: 334-670-3599, E-mail: emerkel@troy.edu. *Application contact:* Brenda K. Campbell, Director of Graduate Admissions, 334-670-3178, Fax: 334-670-3733, E-mail: bcamp@troy.edu.

Troy University, Graduate School, College of Business, Program in Management, Troy, AL 36082. Offers applied management (MSM); healthcare management (MSM); human resources management (MSM); information systems (MSM); international hospitality management (MSM); international management (MSM); leadership and organizational effectiveness (MSM); public management (MS, MSM). *Accreditation:* ACBSP. Evening/weekend programs available. *Faculty:* 21 full-time (6 women), 7 part-time/adjunct (2 women). *Students:* 52 full-time (33 women), 284 part-time (183 women); includes 222 minority (186 Black or African American, non-Hispanic/Latino; 5 American Indian or Alaska Native, non-Hispanic/Latino; 11 Asian, non-Hispanic/Latino; 13 Hispanic/Latino; 1 Native Hawaiian or other Pacific Islander, non-Hispanic/Latino; 6 Two or more races, non-Hispanic/Latino). Average age 35. 157 applicants, 76% accepted, 55 enrolled. In 2011, 234 master's awarded. *Degree requirements:* For master's, Graduate Educational Testing Service Major Field Test, capstone exam, minimum GPA of 3.0. *Entrance requirements:* For master's, GMAT (minimum score 500) or GRE General Test (minimum score 900), minimum GPA of 2.5, bachelor's degree, letter of recommendation. Additional exam requirements/recommendations for international students: Required—TOEFL (minimum score 523 paper-based; 193 computer-based; 70 iBT), IELTS (minimum score 6), or ACT COMPASS ESL (minimum listening, reading, and grammar score 270). *Application deadline:* Applications are processed on a rolling basis. Application fee: $50. Electronic applications accepted. *Expenses:* Contact institution. *Unit head:* Dr. Edward Merkel, Director, Graduate Business Programs, 334-670-3194, Fax: 334-670-3599, E-mail: emerkel@troy.edu. *Application contact:* Brenda K. Campbell, Director of Graduate Admissions, 334-670-3178, Fax: 334-670-3733, E-mail: bcamp@troy.edu.

Tulane University, A. B. Freeman School of Business, New Orleans, LA 70118-5669. Offers EMBA, M Acct, M Fin, MBA, PMBA, PhD, JD/M Acct, JD/MBA, MBA/M Acc, MBA/MA, MBA/MD, MBA/ME, MBA/MPH. *Accreditation:* AACSB. Part-time and evening/weekend programs available. Terminal master's awarded for partial completion of doctoral program. *Entrance requirements:* For master's, GMAT, interview. Additional exam requirements/recommendations for international students: Required—TOEFL. Electronic applications accepted. *Expenses:* Contact institution.

Union Graduate College, School of Management, Schenectady, NY 12308-3107. Offers business administration (MBA); financial management (Certificate); general management (Certificate); health systems administration (MBA, Certificate); human resources (Certificate). *Accreditation:* AACSB. Part-time and evening/weekend programs available. *Faculty:* 18 full-time (4 women), 25 part-time/adjunct (4 women). *Students:* 122 full-time (53 women), 102 part-time (59 women); includes 47 minority (6 Black or African American, non-Hispanic/Latino; 35 Asian, non-Hispanic/Latino; 4 Hispanic/Latino; 2 Two or more races, non-Hispanic/Latino), 5 international. Average age 27. 101 applicants, 75% accepted, 68 enrolled. In 2011, 73 master's, 9 other advanced degrees awarded. *Degree requirements:* For master's, internship, capstone course. *Entrance requirements:* For master's, GMAT, GRE, minimum GPA of 3.0, 3 letters of recommendation. Additional exam requirements/recommendations for international students: Required—TOEFL (minimum score 550 paper-based; 213 computer-based). *Application deadline:* Applications are processed on a rolling basis. Application fee: $60. *Expenses: Tuition:* Full-time $22,000; part-time $775 per credit. One-time fee: $410 full-time. Tuition and fees vary according to course load and program. *Financial support:* In 2011–12, 79 students received support. Research assistantships, career-related internships or fieldwork, Federal Work-Study, scholarships/grants, health care benefits, and tuition waivers (partial) available. Support available to part-time students. Financial award applicants required to submit FAFSA. *Unit head:* Bela Musits, Dean, 518-631-9890, Fax: 518-631-9902, E-mail: musitsb@uniongraduatecollege.edu. *Application contact:* Diane Trzaskos, Admissions Coordinator, 518-631-9837, Fax: 518-631-9901, E-mail: trzaskod@uniongraduatecollege.edu. Web site: http://www.uniongraduatecollege.edu.

Union University, McAfee School of Business Administration, Jackson, TN 38305-3697. Offers MBA. Also available at Germantown campus. Evening/weekend programs available. *Entrance requirements:* For master's, GMAT, minimum GPA of 2.5. Electronic applications accepted. *Expenses:* Contact institution. *Faculty research:* Personal financial management, strategy, accounting, marketing, economics.

United States International University, School of Business Administration, Nairobi, Kenya. Offers business administration (GEMBA); entrepreneurship (MBA); finance (MBA); human resource management (MBA); information technology management (MBA); integrated studies (MBA); international business administration (MBA); management and organizational development (MS); marketing (MBA); organizational development (EMS); strategic management (MBA). Part-time and evening/weekend programs available. *Degree requirements:* For master's, thesis. *Entrance requirements:* For master's, GMAT, 2 letters of reference, resume. Additional exam requirements/recommendations for international students: Required—TOEFL (minimum score 550 paper-based; 213 computer-based). *Faculty research:* Marketing in small business enterprises, total quality management in Kenya.

United States University, School of Management, Cypress, CA 90630. Offers MBA. *Entrance requirements:* For master's, undergraduate degree from accredited institution, minimum cumulative GPA of 2.5, official transcripts.

Universidad Autonoma de Guadalajara, Graduate Programs, Guadalajara, Mexico. Offers administrative law and justice (LL M); advertising and corporate communications (MA); architecture (M Arch); business (MBA); computational science (MCC); education (Ed M, Ed D); English-Spanish translation (MA); entrepreneurship and management (MBA); integrated management of digital animation (MA); international business (MIB); international corporate law (LL M); internet technologies (MS); manufacturing systems (MMS); occupational health (MS); philosophy (MA, PhD); power electronics (MS); quality systems (MQS); renewable energy (MS); social evaluation of projects (MBA); strategic market research (MBA); tax law (MA); teaching mathematics (MA).

Universidad de las Americas, A.C., Program in Business Administration, Mexico City, Mexico. Offers finance (MBA); marketing research (MBA); production and quality (MBA).

Universidad de las Américas–Puebla, Division of Graduate Studies, School of Business and Economics, Puebla, Mexico. Offers business administration (MBA); finance (M Adm). Part-time and evening/weekend programs available. *Degree requirements:* For master's, one foreign language, thesis. *Entrance requirements:* Additional exam requirements/recommendations for international students: Required—TOEFL. *Faculty research:* System dynamics, information technology, marketing, international business, strategic planning, quality.

Universidad del Este, Graduate School, Carolina, PR 00984. Offers accounting (MBA); adult education (M Ed); agribusiness (MBA); criminal justice and criminology (MA); curriculum and instruction - early education (M Ed); curriculum and instruction - elementary (M Ed); curriculum and instruction - English (M Ed); curriculum and instruction - Spanish (M Ed); human resources (MBA); information security management (MBA); information technology and Web business development (MBA); management (MBA); public policy (MPA); social work (MA), including clinical social work; special education (M Ed); strategic leadership (MBA).

Universidad del Turabo, Graduate Programs, School in Business Administration, Program in Management, Gurabo, PR 00778-3030. Offers MBA, DBA. Part-time and evening/weekend programs available. *Students:* 42 full-time (21 women), 111 part-time (52 women); includes 140 minority (all Hispanic/Latino). Average age 36. 89 applicants, 87% accepted, 57 enrolled. In 2011, 30 master's, 6 doctorates awarded. *Entrance requirements:* For master's, GRE, EXADEP, interview. *Application deadline:* For fall admission, 8/5 for domestic students. Application fee: $25. *Unit head:* Marcelino Rivera, Dean, 787-743-7979 Ext. 4117. *Application contact:* Virginia Gonzalez, Admissions Officer, 787-746-3009.

Universidad Iberoamericana, Graduate School, Santo Domingo D.N., Dominican Republic. Offers business administration (MBA, PMBA); constitutional law (LL M); dentistry (DMD); educational management (MA); integrated marketing communication (MA); psychopedagogical intervention (M Ed); real estate law (LL M); strategic management of human talent (MM).

Universidad Metropolitana, School of Business Administration, San Juan, PR 00928-1150. Offers accounting (MBA); finance (MBA); human resources management (MBA); international business (MBA); management (MBA); management information systems (MBA); marketing (MBA). Part-time and evening/weekend programs available. *Degree requirements:* For master's, thesis or alternative. Electronic applications accepted. *Faculty research:* Latin American trade, international investments, central city business development, Hispanic consumer research, Caribbean and Asian trade cooperation.

Université de Moncton, Faculty of Administration, Moncton, NB E1A 3E9, Canada. Offers MBA, LL B/MBA. Part-time and evening/weekend programs available. Postbaccalaureate distance learning degree programs offered (no on-campus study). *Faculty:* 24 full-time (8 women), 21 part-time/adjunct (4 women). *Students:* 39 full-time (17 women), 21 international. Average age 28. 140 applicants, 45% accepted, 39 enrolled. In 2011, 20 degrees awarded. *Degree requirements:* For master's, one foreign language, thesis. *Entrance requirements:* For master's, minimum undergraduate GPA of 3.0. *Application deadline:* For fall admission, 6/1 for domestic students, 2/1 for international students; for winter admission, 11/15 for domestic students, 9/1 for international students; for spring admission, 3/31 for domestic students, 1/1 for international students. Applications are processed on a rolling basis. Application fee: $39. Electronic applications accepted. *Financial support:* In 2011–12, 7 fellowships (averaging $2,500 per year) were awarded; teaching assistantships and institutionally sponsored loans also available. Support available to part-time students. Financial award application deadline: 5/30. *Faculty research:* Service management, corporate reputation, financial management, accounting, supply chain. *Total annual research expenditures:* $150,000. *Unit head:* Dr. Nha Nguyen, Director, 506-858-4231, Fax: 506-858-4093, E-mail: nha.nguyen@umoncton.ca. *Application contact:* Natalie Allain, Admission Counselor, 506-858-4273, Fax: 506-858-4093, E-mail: natalie.allain@umoncton.ca. Web site: http://www.umoncton.ca/umcm-administration/.

Université de Sherbrooke, Faculty of Administration, Doctoral Program in Business Administration, Sherbrooke, QC J1K 2R1, Canada. Offers DBA. *Faculty:* 38 full-time (15 women). *Students:* 62 full-time (18 women). Average age 42. 47 applicants, 26%

accepted, 10 enrolled. In 2011, 4 doctorates awarded. *Degree requirements:* For doctorate, one foreign language, comprehensive exam, thesis/dissertation. *Entrance requirements:* For doctorate, 3 years of related work experience, interview, fluency in French, advanced English, good oral and written French comprehension (tested with an interview). *Application deadline:* For fall admission, 4/30 for domestic students, 1/15 for international students. Applications are processed on a rolling basis. Application fee: $70. Electronic applications accepted. *Financial support:* In 2011–12, 3 research assistantships (averaging $4,000 per year) were awarded; teaching assistantships also available. *Faculty research:* Change management, international business and finance, work organization, information technology implementation and impact on organizations, strategic management. *Unit head:* John Ingham, Program Director, 819-821-8000 Ext. 62330, Fax: 819-821-7364, E-mail: john.ingham@usherbrooke.ca. *Application contact:* Linda Pepin, Assistant Programs Director, 819-821-8000 Ext. 63427, Fax: 819-821-7364, E-mail: linda.pepin@usherbrooke.ca.

Université de Sherbrooke, Faculty of Administration, Master of Business Administration Program, Sherbrooke, QC J1K 2R1, Canada. Offers executive business administration (EMBA); general management (MBA). Part-time and evening/weekend programs available. *Faculty:* 16 full-time (2 women), 65 part-time/adjunct (21 women). *Students:* 138 full-time (50 women), 406 part-time (174 women). Average age 35. 577 applicants, 64% accepted, 247 enrolled. In 2011, 129 master's awarded. *Entrance requirements:* For master's, bachelor's degree, minimum GPA of 2.7 (on 4.3 scale), minimum of two years of work experience, letters of recommendation. *Application deadline:* For fall admission, 4/30 priority date for domestic students, 4/30 for international students. Application fee: $70. Electronic applications accepted. *Unit head:* Prof. Jean Roy, Director, 819-821-8000 Ext. 62357, Fax: 819-821-7364, E-mail: jean.roy@usherbrooke.ca. *Application contact:* Lise Custeau, Assistant Director, 819-821-8000 Ext. 63834, Fax: 819-821-7364, E-mail: lise.custeau@usherbrooke.ca. Web site: http://www.usherbrooke.ca/vers/mba.

Université de Sherbrooke, Faculty of Law, Sherbrooke, QC J1K 2R1, Canada. Offers alternative dispute resolution (LL M, Diploma); business law (Diploma); health law (LL M, Diploma); law (JD, LL D); legal management (Diploma); notarial law (DDN); transnational law (Diploma). Part-time and evening/weekend programs available. *Degree requirements:* For master's, thesis; for other advanced degree, one foreign language. *Entrance requirements:* For master's and other advanced degree, LL B. Electronic applications accepted.

Université du Québec à Chicoutimi, Graduate Programs, Program in Small and Medium-Sized Organization Management, Chicoutimi, QC G7H 2B1, Canada. Offers M Sc. Part-time programs available. *Degree requirements:* For master's, thesis. *Entrance requirements:* For master's, appropriate bachelor's degree, proficiency in French.

Université du Québec à Montréal, Graduate Programs, PhD Program in Business Administration, Montréal, QC H3C 3P8, Canada. Offers PhD. Part-time programs available. *Degree requirements:* For doctorate, thesis/dissertation. *Entrance requirements:* For doctorate, appropriate master's degree or equivalent, proficiency in French.

Université du Québec à Montréal, Graduate Programs, Program in Business Administration (Professional), Montréal, QC H3C 3P8, Canada. Offers business administration (MBA); management consultant (Diploma). Part-time programs available. *Entrance requirements:* For master's and Diploma, appropriate bachelor's degree or equivalent, proficiency in French.

Université du Québec à Montréal, Graduate Programs, Program in Business Administration (Research), Montréal, QC H3C 3P8, Canada. Offers MBA. Part-time programs available. *Entrance requirements:* For master's, appropriate bachelor's degree or equivalent and proficiency in French.

Université du Québec à Rimouski, Graduate Programs, Program in Business Administration, Rimouski, QC G5L 3A1, Canada. Offers MBA.

Université du Québec à Rimouski, Graduate Programs, Program in Management of People in Working Situation, Rimouski, QC G5L 3A1, Canada. Offers M Sc, Diploma.

Université du Québec à Trois-Rivières, Graduate Programs, Program in Business Administration, Trois-Rivières, QC G9A 5H7, Canada. Offers MBA, DBA. DBA offered jointly with Université de Sherbrooke. *Degree requirements:* For doctorate, thesis/dissertation.

Université du Québec en Abitibi-Témiscamingue, Graduate Programs, Program in Business Administration, Rouyn-Noranda, QC J9X 5E4, Canada. Offers MBA.

Université du Québec en Abitibi-Témiscamingue, Graduate Programs, Program in Organization Management, Rouyn-Noranda, QC J9X 5E4, Canada. Offers M Sc. Part-time programs available. *Degree requirements:* For master's, thesis. *Entrance requirements:* For master's, appropriate bachelor's degree, proficiency in French.

Université Laval, Faculty of Administrative Sciences, Program in Organizations Management and Development, Québec, QC G1K 7P4, Canada. Offers Diploma. Part-time programs available. *Entrance requirements:* For degree, knowledge of French. Electronic applications accepted.

Université Laval, Faculty of Administrative Sciences, Programs in Administrative Studies, Québec, QC G1K 7P4, Canada. Offers administrative studies (M Sc, PhD); financial engineering (M Sc). *Accreditation:* AACSB. Terminal master's awarded for partial completion of doctoral program. *Degree requirements:* For master's, thesis (for some programs); for doctorate, comprehensive exam, thesis/dissertation. *Entrance requirements:* For master's and doctorate, knowledge of French and English. Electronic applications accepted.

Université Laval, Faculty of Administrative Sciences, Programs in Business Administration, Québec, QC G1K 7P4, Canada. Offers accounting (MBA); agri-food management (MBA); electronic business (MBA, Diploma); factory management and logistics (MBA); finance (MBA); firm management (MBA); geomatic management (MBA); information technology management (MBA); international management (MBA); management (MBA); management accounting (MBA, Diploma); marketing (MBA); modeling and organizational decision (MBA); occupational health and safety management (MBA); pharmacy management (MBA); social and environmental responsibility (MBA); technological entrepreneurship (Diploma). *Accreditation:* AACSB. Part-time and evening/weekend programs available. Postbaccalaureate distance learning degree programs offered (no on-campus study). *Entrance requirements:* For master's and Diploma, knowledge of French and English. Electronic applications accepted.

University at Albany, State University of New York, School of Business, Albany, NY 12222-0001. Offers MBA, MS. *Accreditation:* AACSB. Part-time and evening/weekend programs available. Terminal master's awarded for partial completion of doctoral program. *Degree requirements:* For master's, project. *Entrance requirements:* For master's, GMAT. Additional exam requirements/recommendations for international students: Required—TOEFL (minimum score 550 paper-based; 213 computer-based). Electronic applications accepted.

University at Buffalo, the State University of New York, Graduate School, School of Management, Buffalo, NY 14260. Offers accounting (MS); business administration (EMBA, MBA, PMBA); finance (MS), including financial engineering, financial management; management (PhD); management information systems (MS); supply chains and operations management (MS); Au D/MBA; JD/MBA; M Arch/MBA; MA/MBA; MD/MBA; MPH/MBA; MSW/MBA; Pharm D/MBA. *Accreditation:* AACSB. Part-time and evening/weekend programs available. *Degree requirements:* For master's, thesis (for some programs); for doctorate, comprehensive exam, thesis/dissertation. *Entrance requirements:* For master's, GMAT (MBA, MS in accounting), GRE or GMAT (for all other MS concentrations); for doctorate, GMAT or GRE. Additional exam requirements/recommendations for international students: Required—TOEFL (minimum score 230 computer-based; 95 iBT). Electronic applications accepted. *Expenses:* Contact institution. *Faculty research:* Earnings management and electronic information assurance, supply chains and operations management, corporate financing and asset pricing, consumer behavior and quantitative modeling of marketing behavior, leadership and politics in organizations.

The University of Akron, Graduate School, College of Business Administration, Department of Management, Akron, OH 44325. Offers electronic business (MBA); entrepreneurship (MBA); health services administration (MSM); human resources (MSM); information systems management (MSM); management (MBA); management of technology (MBA); supply chain management (MSM); JD/MBA; JD/MSM. *Accreditation:* AACSB. Part-time and evening/weekend programs available. *Faculty:* 19 full-time (3 women), 13 part-time/adjunct (3 women). *Students:* 69 full-time (26 women), 126 part-time (41 women); includes 16 minority (10 Black or African American, non-Hispanic/Latino; 2 Asian, non-Hispanic/Latino; 1 Hispanic/Latino; 3 Two or more races, non-Hispanic/Latino), 37 international. Average age 30. 154 applicants, 56% accepted, 66 enrolled. In 2011, 68 master's awarded. *Entrance requirements:* For master's, GMAT, minimum GPA of 2.75, two letters of recommendation, statement of purpose, resume. Additional exam requirements/recommendations for international students: Required—TOEFL (minimum score 550 paper-based; 213 computer-based; 79 iBT). *Application deadline:* For fall admission, 7/15 for domestic and international students; for spring admission, 11/15 for domestic and international students. Application fee: $30 ($40 for international students). Electronic applications accepted. *Expenses:* Tuition, state resident: full-time $7038; part-time $391 per credit hour. Tuition, nonresident: full-time $12,051; part-time $670 per credit hour. *Required fees:* $1274; $34 per credit hour. *Financial support:* In 2011–12, 1 research assistantship with full tuition reimbursement, 24 teaching assistantships with full tuition reimbursements were awarded; career-related internships or fieldwork and Federal Work-Study also available. *Faculty research:* Human resource management, innovation, entrepreneurship, technology management and technology transfer, artificial intelligence and belief functions. *Total annual research expenditures:* $48,868. *Unit head:* Dr. Steve Ash, Interim Chair, 330-972-6086, Fax: 330-972-6588, E-mail: ash@uakron.edu. *Application contact:* Dr. Susan Hanlon, Director of Graduate Business Programs, 330-972-7043, Fax: 330-972-6588, E-mail: shanlon@uakron.edu. Web site: http://www.uakron.edu/cba/cba-home/dept-cent-inst/management/index.dot.

The University of Alabama, Graduate School, Manderson Graduate School of Business, Department of Management and Marketing, Program in Management, Tuscaloosa, AL 35487. Offers MA, MS, PhD. *Accreditation:* AACSB. Part-time and evening/weekend programs available. Postbaccalaureate distance learning degree programs offered (no on-campus study). *Faculty:* 20 full-time (5 women). *Students:* 24 full-time (9 women), 29 part-time (10 women); includes 6 minority (3 Black or African American, non-Hispanic/Latino; 1 Asian, non-Hispanic/Latino; 1 Hispanic/Latino; 1 Two or more races, non-Hispanic/Latino), 17 international. Average age 31. 56 applicants, 41% accepted, 16 enrolled. In 2011, 15 master's, 5 doctorates awarded. Terminal master's awarded for partial completion of doctoral program. *Degree requirements:* For master's, comprehensive exam (for some programs), thesis (for some programs), formal project paper; for doctorate, comprehensive exam, thesis/dissertation. *Entrance requirements:* For master's and doctorate, GMAT or GRE, minimum GPA of 3.0. Additional exam requirements/recommendations for international students: Required—TOEFL (minimum score 600 paper-based) or IELTS (minimum score 6.5). *Application deadline:* For fall admission, 6/30 priority date for domestic students, 1/31 for international students; for spring admission, 10/30 for domestic students. Applications are processed on a rolling basis. Application fee: $50 ($60 for international students). *Expenses:* Tuition, state resident: full-time $8600. Tuition, nonresident: full-time $21,900. *Financial support:* In 2011–12, 5 fellowships with full and partial tuition reimbursements (averaging $15,000 per year), 2 research assistantships (averaging $18,444 per year), 2 teaching assistantships (averaging $16,200 per year) were awarded; scholarships/grants, health care benefits, and unspecified assistantships also available. *Faculty research:* Leadership, entrepreneurship, health care management, organizational behavior, strategy. *Unit head:* Dr. Robert M. Morgan, Department Head, 205-348-6183, Fax: 205-348-6695, E-mail: rmorgan@cba.ua.edu. *Application contact:* Courtney Cox, Office Associate II, 205-348-6183, Fax: 205-348-6695, E-mail: crhodes@cba.ua.edu. Web site: http://cba.ua.edu/mgt.

The University of Alabama, Graduate School, Manderson Graduate School of Business, Program in General Commerce and Business, Tuscaloosa, AL 35487. Offers EMBA, MBA. *Accreditation:* AACSB. Part-time programs available. *Students:* 235 full-time (64 women), 4 part-time (1 woman); includes 33 minority (13 Black or African American, non-Hispanic/Latino; 9 Asian, non-Hispanic/Latino; 6 Hispanic/Latino; 1 Native Hawaiian or other Pacific Islander, non-Hispanic/Latino; 4 Two or more races, non-Hispanic/Latino), 15 international. Average age 28. 230 applicants, 52% accepted, 91 enrolled. In 2011, 117 degrees awarded. *Entrance requirements:* For master's, GMAT or GRE. Additional exam requirements/recommendations for international students: Required—TOEFL (minimum score 550 paper-based). *Application deadline:* For winter admission, 1/2 priority date for domestic students, 1/1 for international students; for spring admission, 4/15 for domestic and international students. Applications are processed on a rolling basis. Application fee: $50 ($60 for international students). Electronic applications accepted. *Expenses:* Tuition, state resident: full-time $8600. Tuition, nonresident: full-time $21,900. *Financial support:* In 2011–12, 26 students received support, including 22 research assistantships (averaging $5,400 per year), 4 teaching assistantships; health care benefits also available. Financial award application deadline: 4/15. *Unit head:* Susan C. West, Assistant Dean and Director of MBA Programs, 205-348-0954, Fax: 205-348-0479, E-mail: swest@cba.ua.edu. *Application contact:* Blake Bedsole, Coordinator of Graduate Recruiting and Admissions, 205-348-9122, Fax: 205-348-4504, E-mail: bbedsole@cba.ua.edu.

The University of Alabama at Birmingham, School of Business, Birmingham, AL 35294. Offers M Acct, MBA. *Accreditation:* AACSB. *Entrance requirements:* For master's, GMAT. *Application deadline:* Applications are processed on a rolling basis. Electronic applications accepted. *Expenses:* Tuition, state resident: full-time $5922; part-time $309 per hour. Tuition, nonresident: full-time $13,428; part-time $726 per hour. Tuition and fees vary according to program. *Financial support:* Fellowships and career-related internships or fieldwork available. *Unit head:* Dr. David R. Klock, Dean, 205-934-8800, Fax: 205-934-8886, E-mail: dklock@uab.edu. *Application contact:* Director, 205-934-8817. Web site: http://www.uab.edu/business/.

The University of Alabama in Huntsville, School of Graduate Studies, College of Business Administration, Department of Management and Marketing, Huntsville, AL 35899. Offers federal contract procurement (Certificate); management (MBA), including acquisition management, entrepreneurship, federal contract accounting, finance, human resource management, logistics and supply chain management, marketing, project management; supply chain management (Certificate); technology and innovation management (Certificate). *Accreditation:* AACSB. Part-time and evening/weekend programs available. *Faculty:* 11 full-time (2 women), 3 part-time/adjunct (0 women). *Students:* 52 full-time (25 women), 145 part-time (68 women); includes 28 minority (14 Black or African American, non-Hispanic/Latino; 4 American Indian or Alaska Native, non-Hispanic/Latino; 7 Asian, non-Hispanic/Latino; 2 Hispanic/Latino; 1 Two or more races, non-Hispanic/Latino), 15 international. Average age 31. 103 applicants, 73% accepted, 65 enrolled. In 2011, 76 master's awarded. *Degree requirements:* For master's, comprehensive exam, thesis or alternative. *Entrance requirements:* For master's, GMAT (minimum score 500), minimum AACSB index of 1080. Additional exam requirements/recommendations for international students: Required—TOEFL (minimum score 550 paper-based; 213 computer-based; 62 iBT). *Application deadline:* For fall admission, 8/1 for domestic students, 4/1 for international students; for spring admission, 12/1 for domestic students, 9/1 for international students. Applications are processed on a rolling basis. Application fee: $40 ($50 for international students). Electronic applications accepted. *Expenses:* Tuition, state resident: full-time $7830; part-time $473.50 per credit. Tuition, nonresident: full-time $18,748; part-time $1128.33 per credit. Tuition and fees vary according to course load and program. *Financial support:* In 2011–12, 12 students received support, including 7 research assistantships with full tuition reimbursements available (averaging $9,829 per year), 4 teaching assistantships with full tuition reimbursements available (averaging $8,000 per year); career-related internships or fieldwork, Federal Work-Study, institutionally sponsored loans, scholarships/grants, health care benefits, and unspecified assistantships also available. Support available to part-time students. Financial award application deadline: 4/1; financial award applicants required to submit FAFSA. *Faculty research:* Strategic human resources, corporate governance, cross-function integration and the management of research and development, determinants of team performance. *Total annual research expenditures:* $3.4 million. *Unit head:* Dr. Cynthia Gramm, Chair, 256-824-6913, Fax: 256-824-6328, E-mail: cynthia.gramm@uah.edu. *Application contact:* Jennifer Pettitt, Director of Graduate Programs, 256-824-6681, Fax: 256-824-7571, E-mail: jennifer.pettitt@uah.edu.

University of Alaska Anchorage, College of Business and Public Policy, Program in Business Administration, Anchorage, AK 99508. Offers MBA. *Accreditation:* AACSB. Part-time programs available. *Degree requirements:* For master's, comprehensive exam, thesis (for some programs), capstone projects. *Entrance requirements:* Additional exam requirements/recommendations for international students: Required—TOEFL (minimum score 550 paper-based; 213 computer-based). *Faculty research:* Complex global environments.

University of Alaska Fairbanks, School of Management, Department of Business Administration, Fairbanks, AK 99775-6080. Offers capital markets (MBA); general management (MBA). *Accreditation:* AACSB. Part-time programs available. *Faculty:* 12 full-time (4 women), 1 part-time/adjunct (0 women). *Students:* 32 full-time (19 women), 27 part-time (18 women); includes 13 minority (3 Black or African American, non-Hispanic/Latino; 4 American Indian or Alaska Native, non-Hispanic/Latino; 3 Asian, non-Hispanic/Latino; 1 Native Hawaiian or other Pacific Islander, non-Hispanic/Latino; 2 Two or more races, non-Hispanic/Latino), 8 international. Average age 31. 43 applicants, 63% accepted, 24 enrolled. In 2011, 23 master's awarded. *Degree requirements:* For master's, comprehensive exam, thesis or alternative. *Entrance requirements:* For master's, GMAT. Additional exam requirements/recommendations for international students: Required—TOEFL (minimum score 550 paper-based; 213 computer-based; 80 iBT). *Application deadline:* For fall admission, 6/1 priority date for domestic students, 2/1 for international students; for spring admission, 10/15 priority date for domestic students, 9/1 for international students. Applications are processed on a rolling basis. Application fee: $60. Electronic applications accepted. *Expenses:* Tuition, state resident: full-time $6696; part-time $372 per credit. Tuition, nonresident: full-time $13,680; part-time $760 per credit. Tuition and fees vary according to course load and reciprocity agreements. *Financial support:* In 2011–12, 3 research assistantships with tuition reimbursements (averaging $4,896 per year), 4 teaching assistantships with tuition reimbursements (averaging $14,245 per year) were awarded; fellowships with tuition reimbursements, career-related internships or fieldwork, Federal Work-Study, scholarships/grants, health care benefits, and unspecified assistantships also available. Support available to part-time students. Financial award application deadline: 2/15; financial award applicants required to submit FAFSA. *Faculty research:* Consumer behavior, marketing, international finance and business, strategic risk, organization theory. *Total annual research expenditures:* $1,000. *Unit head:* Dr. Ping Lan, Director, MBA Program, 907-474-7688, Fax: 907-474-5219, E-mail: plan@alaska.edu. *Application contact:* Mike Earnest, Director of Admissions, 907-474-7500, Fax: 907-474-5379, E-mail: admissions@uaf.edu. Web site: http://www.uaf.edu/som/programs/mba/.

University of Alaska Southeast, Graduate Programs, Program in Business Administration, Juneau, AK 99801. Offers MBA. Part-time and evening/weekend programs available. Postbaccalaureate distance learning degree programs offered (minimal on-campus study). *Degree requirements:* For master's, residential seminar. *Entrance requirements:* For master's, curriculum vitae, letters of reference, minimum GPA of 3.0. Additional exam requirements/recommendations for international students: Recommended—TOEFL. Electronic applications accepted. *Faculty research:* Services marketing; marketing and technology issues: social capital and entrepreneurship; motivation and managerial tactics.

University of Alberta, Faculty of Graduate Studies and Research, Doctoral Program in Business, Edmonton, AB T6G 2E1, Canada. Offers accounting (PhD); finance (PhD); human resources/industrial relations (PhD); management science (PhD); marketing (PhD); organizational analysis (PhD); MBA/PhD. *Accreditation:* AACSB. Part-time programs available. *Degree requirements:* For doctorate, comprehensive exam, thesis/dissertation. *Entrance requirements:* For doctorate, GMAT. Additional exam requirements/recommendations for international students: Required—TOEFL (minimum score 550 paper-based; 213 computer-based). Electronic applications accepted. *Faculty research:* Accounting, capital markets and corporate finance, organizational change and human resource management, marketing, strategic management.

University of Alberta, Faculty of Graduate Studies and Research, Executive MBA Program, Edmonton, AB T6G 2E1, Canada. Offers business administration (Exec MBA). Program offered jointly with University of Calgary. *Accreditation:* AACSB. *Entrance requirements:* For master's, GMAT. Additional exam requirements/recommendations for international students: Required—TOEFL. Electronic applications accepted. *Expenses:* Contact institution.

University of Alberta, Faculty of Graduate Studies and Research, Program in Business Administration, Edmonton, AB T6G 2E1, Canada. Offers international business (MBA); leisure and sport management (MBA); natural resources and energy (MBA); technology commercialization (MBA); MBA/LL B; MBA/M Ag; MBA/M Eng; MBA/MF; MBA/PhD. *Accreditation:* AACSB. Part-time and evening/weekend programs available. *Degree requirements:* For master's, thesis or alternative. *Entrance requirements:* For master's, GMAT. Additional exam requirements/recommendations for international students: Required—TOEFL (minimum score 600 paper-based; 250 computer-based). Electronic applications accepted. *Faculty research:* Natural resources and energy/management and policy/family enterprise/international business/healthcare research management.

The University of Arizona, Eller College of Management, Tucson, AZ 85721. Offers M Ac, MA, MBA, MPA, MS, PhD, JD/MA, JD/MBA, JD/PhD. *Accreditation:* AACSB. Evening/weekend programs available. *Faculty:* 72 full-time (19 women), 3 part-time/adjunct (0 women). *Students:* 660 full-time (237 women), 66 part-time (35 women); includes 125 minority (14 Black or African American, non-Hispanic/Latino; 6 American Indian or Alaska Native, non-Hispanic/Latino; 24 Asian, non-Hispanic/Latino; 56 Hispanic/Latino; 1 Native Hawaiian or other Pacific Islander, non-Hispanic/Latino; 24 Two or more races, non-Hispanic/Latino), 266 international. Average age 30. 1,656 applicants, 46% accepted, 294 enrolled. In 2011, 407 master's, 23 doctorates awarded. *Degree requirements:* For doctorate, thesis/dissertation. *Entrance requirements:* Additional exam requirements/recommendations for international students: Required—TOEFL (minimum score 550 paper-based; 213 computer-based; 79 iBT). *Application deadline:* Applications are processed on a rolling basis. Application fee: $75. Electronic applications accepted. *Expenses:* Contact institution. *Financial support:* In 2011–12, 56 research assistantships with full tuition reimbursements (averaging $22,861 per year), 155 teaching assistantships with full tuition reimbursements (averaging $23,106 per year) were awarded; career-related internships or fieldwork, Federal Work-Study, scholarships/grants, health care benefits, tuition waivers (partial), and unspecified assistantships also available. Financial award application deadline: 3/15. *Total annual research expenditures:* $6.5 million. *Unit head:* Dr. Len Jessup, Dean, 520-621-2125, Fax: 520-621-8105, E-mail: pportney@email.arizona.edu. *Application contact:* Information Contact, 520-621-2165, Fax: 520-621-8105, E-mail: mbaadmissions@eller.arizona.edu. Web site: http://www.eller.arizona.edu/.

University of Arkansas, Graduate School, Sam M. Walton College of Business Administration, Program in Business Administration, Fayetteville, AR 72701-1201. Offers MBA, PhD. *Accreditation:* AACSB. Part-time and evening/weekend programs available. Postbaccalaureate distance learning degree programs offered (minimal on-campus study). *Students:* 35 full-time (13 women), 113 part-time (31 women); includes 13 minority (4 Black or African American, non-Hispanic/Latino; 3 Asian, non-Hispanic/Latino; 2 Hispanic/Latino; 4 Two or more races, non-Hispanic/Latino), 12 international. In 2011, 65 master's awarded. *Degree requirements:* For doctorate, thesis/dissertation. *Entrance requirements:* For master's and doctorate, GMAT. Application fee: $40 ($50 for international students). *Financial support:* In 2011–12, 23 research assistantships were awarded; fellowships with tuition reimbursements, teaching assistantships, career-related internships or fieldwork, and Federal Work-Study also available. Support available to part-time students. Financial award application deadline: 4/1; financial award applicants required to submit FAFSA. *Unit head:* Dr. Moez Limayem, MBA Director, 479-575-2851, E-mail: mlimayem@uark.edu. *Application contact:* Rebel Smith, Assistant Director of Marketing and Recruiting, 479-575-6123, E-mail: gsb@walton.uark.edu. Web site: http://gsb.uark.edu/.

University of Arkansas at Little Rock, Graduate School, College of Business Administration, Little Rock, AR 72204-1099. Offers accountancy (M Acc, Graduate Certificate); business administration (MBA); construction management (Graduate Certificate); management (Graduate Certificate); management information system (MIS); management information systems (Graduate Certificate); management information systems leadership (Graduate Certificate); taxation (MS, Graduate Certificate). *Accreditation:* AACSB. Part-time and evening/weekend programs available. *Entrance requirements:* For master's, GMAT, minimum undergraduate GPA of 2.7. Additional exam requirements/recommendations for international students: Required—TOEFL (minimum score 525 paper-based; 195 computer-based).

University of Atlanta, Graduate Programs, Atlanta, GA 30360. Offers business (MS); business administration (Exec MBA, MBA); computer science (MS); educational leadership (MS, Ed D); healthcare administration (MS, D Sc, Graduate Certificate); information technology for management (Graduate Certificate); international project management (Graduate Certificate); law (JD); managerial science (DBA); project management (Graduate Certificate); social science (MS). Postbaccalaureate distance learning degree programs offered. *Entrance requirements:* For master's, minimum cumulative GPA of 2.5.

University of Baltimore, Graduate School, Merrick School of Business, Baltimore, MD 21201-5779. Offers MBA, MS, Graduate Certificate, JD/MBA, MBA/MSN, MBA/Pharm D. *Accreditation:* AACSB. Part-time and evening/weekend programs available. Postbaccalaureate distance learning degree programs offered (no on-campus study). *Entrance requirements:* For master's, GMAT. Additional exam requirements/recommendations for international students: Required—TOEFL (minimum score 550 paper-based; 213 computer-based). Electronic applications accepted. *Faculty research:* Finance, economics, accounting, health care, management information systems.

University of Baltimore, Joint University of Baltimore/Towson University (UB/Towson) MBA Program, Baltimore, MD 21201-5779. Offers MBA, JD/MBA, MBA/MSN, MBA/Pharm D. MBA/MSN, MBA/PhamrD offered jointly with University of Maryland, Baltimore. *Accreditation:* AACSB. Part-time and evening/weekend programs available. Postbaccalaureate distance learning degree programs offered (no on-campus study). *Entrance requirements:* For master's, GMAT. Additional exam requirements/recommendations for international students: Required—TOEFL (minimum score 550 paper-based; 213 computer-based).

University of Bridgeport, School of Business, Bridgeport, CT 06604. Offers accounting (MBA); finance (MBA); general business (MBA); global financial services (MBA); human resource management (MBA); information systems and knowledge management (MBA); international business (MBA); management (MBA); marketing (MBA); operations management (MBA); small business and entrepreneurship (MBA); specialized business (MBA). Part-time and evening/weekend programs available. *Faculty:* 11 full-time (2 women), 39 part-time/adjunct (8 women). *Students:* 198 full-time (105 women), 94 part-time (47 women); includes 38 minority (16 Black or African American, non-Hispanic/Latino; 9 Asian, non-Hispanic/Latino; 10 Hispanic/Latino; 3 Two or more races, non-Hispanic/Latino), 227 international. Average age 28. 835 applicants, 56% accepted, 57 enrolled. In 2011, 155 master's awarded. *Degree requirements:* For master's, thesis optional. *Entrance requirements:* For master's, GMAT. Additional exam requirements/recommendations for international students: Recommended—TOEFL (minimum score 550 paper-based; 213 computer-based; 80 iBT), IELTS (minimum score 6.5). *Application deadline:* For fall admission, 8/1 priority date for domestic students, 8/1 for international students; for spring admission, 12/1 priority date for domestic students, 12/1 for international students. Applications are processed on a rolling basis. Application fee: $50. Electronic applications accepted. *Expenses:* Contact institution. *Financial support:* In 2011–12, 69 students received support. Fellowships, research assistantships, teaching assistantships, career-related internships or fieldwork, Federal Work-Study, institutionally sponsored loans, and tuition waivers (partial) available. Support available to part-time students. Financial award application deadline: 6/1; financial award applicants required to submit FAFSA. *Unit head:* Dr. Robert Gilmore, Dean, 203-576-4384, Fax: 203-576-4388, E-mail: rgilmore@bridgeport.edu. *Application* *contact:* Karissa Peckham, Dean of Admissions, 203-576-4552, Fax: 203-576-4941, E-mail: mba@bridgeport.edu. Web site: http://www.bridgeport.edu.

The University of British Columbia, Sauder School of Business, Doctoral Program in Commerce and Business Administration, Vancouver, BC V6T 1Z1, Canada. Offers accounting (PhD); finance (PhD); international business (PhD); management information systems (PhD); management science (PhD); marketing (PhD); organizational behavior (PhD); strategy and business economics (PhD); transportation and logistics (PhD); urban land economics (PhD). *Degree requirements:* For doctorate, comprehensive exam, thesis/dissertation. *Entrance requirements:* For doctorate, GMAT or GRE. Additional exam requirements/recommendations for international students: Required—TOEFL (minimum score 600 paper-based; 250 computer-based; 100 iBT). Electronic applications accepted.

The University of British Columbia, Sauder School of Business, MBA Program, Vancouver, BC V6T 1Z1, Canada. Offers IMBA, MBA. *Accreditation:* AACSB. Part-time and evening/weekend programs available. Postbaccalaureate distance learning degree programs offered (minimal on-campus study). *Entrance requirements:* For master's, GMAT, minimum B average in undergraduate course work. Additional exam requirements/recommendations for international students: Required—TOEFL, IELTS or Michigan English Language Assessment Battery. Electronic applications accepted. *Expenses:* Contact institution. *Faculty research:* Financial economics and reporting, human resources, information systems, management science, marketing.

University of Calgary, Faculty of Graduate Studies, Haskayne School of Business, Alberta/Haskayne Executive MBA Program, Calgary, AB T2N 1N4, Canada. Offers EMBA. Program offered with School of Business at The University of Alberta. *Accreditation:* AACSB. Part-time programs available. *Entrance requirements:* For master's, GMAT, minimum GPA of 3.0, minimum 7 years of work experience, 3 letters of reference. Additional exam requirements/recommendations for international students: Required—TOEFL (minimum score 600 paper-based; 250 computer-based; 100 iBT). *Expenses:* Contact institution. *Faculty research:* Accounting, data analysis and modeling, strategy, entrepreneurship, negotiations.

University of Calgary, Faculty of Graduate Studies, Haskayne School of Business, Program in Business Administration, Calgary, AB T2N 1N4, Canada. Offers MBA, MBA/LL B, MBA/MBT, MBA/MD, MBA/MSW. *Accreditation:* AACSB. Part-time and evening/weekend programs available. *Degree requirements:* For master's, comprehensive exam, thesis optional. *Entrance requirements:* For master's, GMAT (minimum score 550), minimum GPA of 3.0, resume, 3 years of work experience, 3 letters of reference, 4 year bachelor degree. Additional exam requirements/recommendations for international students: Required—TOEFL (minimum score 600 paper-based; 250 computer-based). Electronic applications accepted. *Expenses:* Contact institution. *Faculty research:* Entrepreneurship, ethics, strategy, finance energy management and sustainability.

University of Calgary, Faculty of Graduate Studies, Haskayne School of Business, Program in Management, Calgary, AB T2N 1N4, Canada. Offers MBA, PhD. *Accreditation:* AACSB. Terminal master's awarded for partial completion of doctoral program. *Degree requirements:* For master's, one foreign language, comprehensive exam, thesis; for doctorate, one foreign language, comprehensive exam, thesis/dissertation, written and oral exams. *Entrance requirements:* For master's, GMAT, GRE, minimum GPA of 3.3 in last 2 years of course work, 2 letters of ref.; for doctorate, GMAT, GRE, minimum GPA of 3.5 in last 2 years of course work, 2 letters of reference. Additional exam requirements/recommendations for international students: Required—TOEFL (minimum score 600 paper-based; 250 computer-based; 100 iBT), IELTS (minimum score 7). Electronic applications accepted. *Faculty research:* Operations management, international business, management information systems, accounting, finance, sustainable development.

University of California, Berkeley, Graduate Division, Haas School of Business and School of Law, Concurrent JD/MBA Program, Berkeley, CA 94720-1500. Offers JD/MBA. *Accreditation:* AACSB; ABA. *Faculty:* 77 full-time (18 women), 152 part-time/adjunct (24 women). *Students:* 2 full-time (0 women). *Entrance requirements:* Additional exam requirements/recommendations for international students: Required—TOEFL. Application fee: $200. Electronic applications accepted. *Financial support:* Application deadline: 3/1; applicants required to submit FAFSA. *Unit head:* Julia Hwang, Director, MBA Program, 510-642-1405, Fax: 510-643-6659, E-mail: julia_hwang@haas.berkeley.edu. *Application contact:* Office of Admissions, 510-642-1405, Fax: 510-643-6659, E-mail: admissions@boalt.berkeley.edu. Web site: http://mba.haas.berkeley.edu/academics/concurrentdegrees.html.

University of California, Berkeley, Graduate Division, Haas School of Business and School of Public Health, Concurrent MBA/MPH Program, Berkeley, CA 94720-1500. Offers MBA/MPH. *Accreditation:* AACSB; CEPH. *Faculty:* 77 full-time (18 women), 152 part-time/adjunct (24 women). *Students:* 37 full-time (23 women); includes 15 minority (13 Asian, non-Hispanic/Latino; 1 Hispanic/Latino; 1 Two or more races, non-Hispanic/Latino), 9 international. Average age 28. *Entrance requirements:* Additional exam requirements/recommendations for international students: Required—TOEFL. Application fee: $200. Electronic applications accepted. *Financial support:* Fellowships with tuition reimbursements, teaching assistantships with tuition reimbursements, career-related internships or fieldwork, scholarships/grants, and unspecified assistantships available. Financial award applicants required to submit FAFSA. *Unit head:* Prof. Kristi Raube, Director, Health Services Management Program, 510-642-5023, Fax: 510-643-6659, E-mail: raube@haas.berkeley.edu. *Application contact:* Lee Forgue, Student Affairs Officer, 510-642-5023, Fax: 510-643-6659, E-mail: eilis@haas.berkeley.edu. Web site: http://www.haas.berkeley.edu/.

University of California, Berkeley, Graduate Division, Haas School of Business, Evening and Weekend MBA Program, Berkeley, CA 94720-1500. Offers MBA. *Accreditation:* AACSB. Part-time and evening/weekend programs available. *Faculty:* 77 full-time (18 women), 152 part-time/adjunct (24 women). *Students:* 804 part-time (204 women); includes 190 minority (7 Black or African American, non-Hispanic/Latino; 1 American Indian or Alaska Native, non-Hispanic/Latino; 148 Asian, non-Hispanic/Latino; 15 Hispanic/Latino; 19 Two or more races, non-Hispanic/Latino), 345 international. Average age 34. 677 applicants. In 2011, 312 master's awarded. *Degree requirements:* For master's, academic retreat, experiential learning course. *Entrance requirements:* For master's, GMAT or GRE, BA or BS. Additional exam requirements/recommendations for international students: Required—TOEFL (minimum score 570 paper-based; 230 computer-based; 68 iBT). *Application deadline:* For fall admission, 11/15 for domestic students; for winter admission, 1/18 for domestic students; for spring admission, 3/15 for domestic students. Application fee: $200. Electronic applications accepted. *Expenses:* Contact institution. *Financial support:* In 2011–12, 291 students received support, including 21 fellowships (averaging $10,000 per year); research assistantships, teaching assistantships, scholarships/grants, and unspecified assistantships also available. Support available to part-time students. Financial award application deadline: 6/6; financial award applicants required to submit FAFSA. *Faculty research:* Accounting, business and public policy, economic analysis and public policy, finance, management of organizations, marketing, operations and information technology management, real estate. *Unit head:* Jonathan Kaplan, Executive Director, 510-643-0434, Fax: 510-643-5902, E-mail: ewmbaadm@haas.berkeley.edu. *Application contact:* Evening and Weekend MBA Admissions Office, 510-642-0292, Fax: 510-643-5902, E-mail: ewmbaadm@haas.berkeley.edu. Web site: http://ewmba.haas.berkeley.edu/.

University of California, Berkeley, Graduate Division, Haas School of Business, Full-Time MBA Program, Berkeley, CA 94720-1902. Offers MBA. *Accreditation:* AACSB. *Faculty:* 77 full-time (18 women), 152 part-time/adjunct (24 women). *Students:* 492 full-time (154 women); includes 124 minority (7 Black or African American, non-Hispanic/Latino; 1 American Indian or Alaska Native, non-Hispanic/Latino; 74 Asian, non-Hispanic/Latino; 27 Hispanic/Latino; 15 Two or more races, non-Hispanic/Latino), 184 international. Average age 29. 3,444 applicants, 12% accepted, 236 enrolled. In 2011, 237 master's awarded. *Degree requirements:* For master's, 51 units, one Innovative Leader Curriculum experiential learning course. *Entrance requirements:* For master's, GMAT, BA/BS. Additional exam requirements/recommendations for international students: Required—TOEFL (minimum score 570 paper-based; 230 computer-based; 68 iBT), IELTS. *Application deadline:* For fall admission, 10/12 for domestic and international students; for winter admission, 12/1 for domestic and international students; for spring admission, 3/7 for domestic and international students. Application fee: $200. Electronic applications accepted. *Expenses:* Contact institution. *Financial support:* In 2011–12, 336 students received support, including 217 fellowships with full and partial tuition reimbursements available (averaging $24,810 per year), 160 teaching assistantships with partial tuition reimbursements available (averaging $8,654 per year); research assistantships with partial tuition reimbursements available, career-related internships or fieldwork, institutionally sponsored loans, and scholarships/grants also available. Financial award application deadline: 5/22; financial award applicants required to submit FAFSA. *Faculty research:* Accounting, business and public policy, finance, management of organizations, marketing, operations and information technology management, real estate. *Unit head:* Julia Hwang, Executive Director, 510-642-1407, Fax: 510-643-6659, E-mail: julia_hwang@haas.berkeley.edu. *Application contact:* Stephanie Fujii, Executive Director, Full-Time MBA Admissions, 510-642-1405, Fax: 510-643-6659, E-mail: mbaadm@haas.berkeley.edu. Web site: http://mba.haas.berkeley.edu/.

University of California, Berkeley, Graduate Division, Haas School of Business and Program in International and Area Studies, MBA/MA Program in International and Area Studies, Berkeley, CA 94720-1500. Offers MBA/MA. *Accreditation:* AACSB. *Entrance requirements:* Additional exam requirements/recommendations for international students: Required—TOEFL. Application fee: $200. *Financial support:* Fellowships with full tuition reimbursements, research assistantships, teaching assistantships with partial tuition reimbursements, career-related internships or fieldwork, scholarships/grants, and unspecified assistantships available. Financial award application deadline: 6/6; financial award applicants required to submit FAFSA. *Unit head:* Julia Hwang, Director, MBA Program, 510-642-1405, Fax: 510-643-6659, E-mail: julia_hwang@haas.berkeley.edu. *Application contact:* 510-642-1405, Fax: 510-643-6659.

University of California, Berkeley, Graduate Division, Haas School of Business, PhD in Business Administration Program, Berkeley, CA 94720-1500. Offers accounting (PhD); business and public policy (PhD); finance (PhD); management of organizations (PhD); marketing (PhD); operations management (PhD); real estate (PhD). *Accreditation:* AACSB. *Faculty:* 77 full-time (18 women), 152 part-time/adjunct (24 women). *Students:* 79 full-time (25 women); includes 13 minority (12 Asian, non-Hispanic/Latino; 1 Hispanic/Latino), 34 international. Average age 30. 547 applicants, 5% accepted, 15 enrolled. In 2011, 14 doctorates awarded. *Degree requirements:* For doctorate, comprehensive exam, thesis/dissertation, written preliminary exams, oral qualifying exam. *Entrance requirements:* For doctorate, GMAT or GRE, minimum GPA of 3.0 in undergraduate and graduate coursework. Additional exam requirements/recommendations for international students: Required—TOEFL (minimum score 570 paper-based; 230 computer-based; 70 iBT), IELTS (minimum score 7). *Application deadline:* For fall admission, 12/10 for domestic and international students. Application fee: $80 ($100 for international students). Electronic applications accepted. *Financial support:* In 2011–12, 66 students received support, including 58 fellowships with full and partial tuition reimbursements available (averaging $29,000 per year), 77 teaching assistantships with full and partial tuition reimbursements available; research assistantships with full and partial tuition reimbursements available, scholarships/grants, health care benefits, tuition waivers (full), unspecified assistantships, and transit pass, travel grants also available. Financial award application deadline: 12/10; financial award applicants required to submit FAFSA. *Faculty research:* Accounting, business and public policy, finance, management of organizations, marketing, operations and information technology management, real estate. *Unit head:* Dr. Sunil Dutta, Director, 510-642-1229, Fax: 510-643-4255, E-mail: kimg@haas.berkeley.edu. *Application contact:* Kim Guilfoyle, Director, Student Affairs, 510-642-3944, Fax: 510-643-4255, E-mail: kimg@haas.berkeley.edu. Web site: http://www.haas.berkeley.edu/Phd/.

University of California, Berkeley, UC Berkeley Extension, Certificate Programs in Business, Berkeley, CA 94720-1500. Offers accounting (Certificate); business administration (Certificate); finance (Certificate); human resource management (Certificate); management (Certificate); marketing (Certificate); project management (Certificate). *Accreditation:* AACSB. Postbaccalaureate distance learning degree programs offered.

University of California, Berkeley, UC Berkeley Extension, International Diploma Programs, Berkeley, CA 94720-1500. Offers business administration (Certificate); finance (Certificate); global business management (Certificate); marketing (Certificate); project management (Certificate). *Accreditation:* AACSB.

University of California, Davis, Graduate School of Management, Daytime MBA Program, Davis, CA 95616. Offers MBA, JD/MBA, M Engr/MBA, MBA/MPH, MBA/MS, MD/MBA, MSN/MBA. *Faculty:* 31 full-time (13 women), 26 part-time/adjunct (0 women). *Students:* 109 full-time (35 women); includes 27 minority (19 Asian, non-Hispanic/Latino; 5 Hispanic/Latino; 3 Two or more races, non-Hispanic/Latino), 28 international. Average age 28. 340 applicants, 24% accepted, 53 enrolled. In 2011, 60 master's awarded. *Entrance requirements:* For master's, GMAT or GRE, letters of recommendation, resume, essays, equivalent of a 4-year U.S. undergraduate degree. Additional exam requirements/recommendations for international students: Required—TOEFL (minimum score 600 paper-based; 250 computer-based; 100 iBT), IELTS (minimum score 7), Pearson Test of English (minimum score 68). *Application deadline:* For fall admission, 3/6 priority date for domestic students, 3/6 for international students. Applications are processed on a rolling basis. Application fee: $125. Electronic applications accepted. *Financial support:* In 2011–12, 99 students received support. Research assistantships with partial tuition reimbursements available, teaching assistantships with partial tuition reimbursements available, career-related internships or fieldwork, Federal Work-Study, institutionally sponsored loans, scholarships/grants, tuition waivers (partial), and unspecified assistantships available. Financial award application deadline: 3/1; financial award applicants required to submit FAFSA. *Faculty research:* Technology management, finance, marketing, corporate governance and investor welfare, organizational behavior. *Unit head:* James Stevens, Assistant Dean of Student Affairs, 530-752-7658, Fax: 530-754-9355, E-mail: admissions@gsm.ucdavis.edu. *Application contact:* Bill Sandefer, Director, Admissions, 530-752-7658, Fax: 530-754-9355, E-mail: admissions@gsm.ucdavis.edu. Web site: http://www.gsm.ucdavis.edu.

University of California, Davis, Graduate School of Management, MBA Programs in Sacramento and San Francisco Bay Area, Davis, CA 95616. Offers MBA. Part-time and evening/weekend programs available. *Faculty:* 31 full-time (13 women), 26 part-time/adjunct (0 women). *Students:* 448 part-time (136 women); includes 191 minority (9 Black or African American, non-Hispanic/Latino; 2 American Indian or Alaska Native, non-Hispanic/Latino; 138 Asian, non-Hispanic/Latino; 37 Hispanic/Latino; 2 Native Hawaiian or other Pacific Islander, non-Hispanic/Latino; 3 Two or more races, non-Hispanic/Latino), 43 international. Average age 31. 237 applicants, 67% accepted, 111 enrolled. In 2011, 143 master's awarded. *Entrance requirements:* For master's, GMAT or GRE, letters of recommendation, resume, equivalent of a 4 year undergraduate degree. Additional exam requirements/recommendations for international students: Required—TOEFL (minimum score 600 paper-based; 250 computer-based; 100 iBT), IELTS (minimum score 7), Pearson Test of English (minimum score 68). *Application deadline:* For fall admission, 3/6 priority date for domestic students, 3/6 for international students. Applications are processed on a rolling basis. Application fee: $125. Electronic applications accepted. *Expenses:* Contact institution. *Financial support:* In 2011–12, 35 students received support. Scholarships/grants available. Financial award application deadline: 3/31; financial award applicants required to submit FAFSA. *Faculty research:* Technology management, finance, marketing, corporate governance and investor welfare, organizational behavior. *Unit head:* James Stevens, Assistant Dean of Student Affairs, 530-752-7658, Fax: 530-754-9355, E-mail: admissions@gsm.ucdavis.edu. *Application contact:* Bill Sandefer, Director, Admissions, 530-752-7658, Fax: 530-754-9355, E-mail: admissions@gsm.ucdavis.edu. Web site: http://www.gsm.ucdavis.edu.

University of California, Irvine, The Paul Merage School of Business, Doctoral Program in Management, Irvine, CA 92697. Offers PhD. *Students:* 49 full-time (18 women); includes 7 minority (6 Asian, non-Hispanic/Latino; 1 Hispanic/Latino), 21 international. Average age 32. 230 applicants, 3% accepted, 6 enrolled. In 2011, 7 doctorates awarded. Application fee: $80 ($100 for international students). *Unit head:* Dr. Robin Keller, Director, 949-824-6348, Fax: 949-824-2835, E-mail: lrkeller@uci.edu. *Application contact:* Noelia Negrete, Assistant Director, 949-824-8318, Fax: 949-824-1592, E-mail: nnegrete@uci.edu. Web site: http://merage.uci.edu/PhD/Default.aspx.

University of California, Irvine, The Paul Merage School of Business, Executive MBA Program, Irvine, CA 92697. Offers EMBA. *Students:* 41 full-time (12 women), 31 part-time (6 women); includes 25 minority (2 Black or African American, non-Hispanic/Latino; 19 Asian, non-Hispanic/Latino; 4 Hispanic/Latino), 3 international. Average age 39. 68 applicants, 65% accepted, 35 enrolled. In 2011, 40 master's awarded. Application fee: $80 ($100 for international students). *Unit head:* Anthony Hansford, Assistant Dean, 949-824-3801, E-mail: hansfora@uci.edu. *Application contact:* Sofia Trinidad Dang, Associate Director, Student Affairs, 949-824-5374, Fax: 949-824-0522, E-mail: sofia.dang@uci.edu. Web site: http://merage.uci.edu/ExecutiveMBA/.

University of California, Irvine, The Paul Merage School of Business, Full-Time MBA Program, Irvine, CA 92697. Offers MBA. *Students:* 179 full-time (48 women), 16 part-time (2 women); includes 45 minority (3 Black or African American, non-Hispanic/Latino; 1 American Indian or Alaska Native, non-Hispanic/Latino; 34 Asian, non-Hispanic/Latino; 6 Hispanic/Latino; 1 Native Hawaiian or other Pacific Islander, non-Hispanic/Latino), 68 international. Average age 28. 845 applicants, 31% accepted, 112 enrolled. In 2011, 93 master's awarded. Application fee: $80 ($100 for international students). *Unit head:* Gary Lindblad, Assistant Dean and Director, 949-824-9654, Fax: 949-824-2235, E-mail: lindblad@uci.edu. *Application contact:* Sarah Ramsey, Director of Recruitment and Admission, 949-824-0462, Fax: 949-824-2235, E-mail: seramsey@uci.edu. Web site: http://merage.uci.edu/FullTimeMBA/default.aspx.

University of California, Irvine, The Paul Merage School of Business, Fully Employed MBA Program, Irvine, CA 92697. Offers MBA. Part-time programs available. *Students:* 145 full-time (36 women), 293 part-time (97 women); includes 174 minority (5 Black or African American, non-Hispanic/Latino; 1 American Indian or Alaska Native, non-Hispanic/Latino; 141 Asian, non-Hispanic/Latino; 25 Hispanic/Latino; 2 Native Hawaiian or other Pacific Islander, non-Hispanic/Latino), 26 international. Average age 30. 213 applicants, 80% accepted, 116 enrolled. In 2011, 180 master's awarded. *Application deadline:* For fall admission, 7/11 for domestic students. Application fee: $80 ($100 for international students). *Unit head:* Mary Clark, Assistant Dean, 949-824-4207, Fax: 949-824-2235, E-mail: mary.clark@uci.edu. *Application contact:* Mae Jennifer Shores, Director of Recruitment and Admissions, 949-824-1276, E-mail: mshores@exchange.uci.edu. Web site: http://merage.uci.edu/FullyEmployedMBA/default.aspx.

University of California, Los Angeles, Graduate Division, UCLA Anderson School of Management, Los Angeles, CA 90095-1481. Offers accounting (PhD); Asia Pacific (EMBA); business administration (EMBA, MBA); decisions, operations and technology management (PhD); finance (PhD); financial engineering (MFE); global economics and management (PhD); Latin America (EMBA); management and organizations (PhD); marketing (PhD); strategy (PhD); DDS/MBA; MBA/JD; MBA/MD; MBA/MLAS; MBA/MLIS; MBA/MPH; MBA/MPP; MBA/MSCS; MBA/MSN; MBA/MUP. *Accreditation:* AACSB. Part-time programs available. *Faculty:* 90 full-time (14 women), 62 part-time/adjunct (14 women). *Students:* 1,103 full-time (312 women), 842 part-time (223 women); includes 663 minority (18 Black or African American, non-Hispanic/Latino; 510 Asian, non-Hispanic/Latino; 46 Hispanic/Latino; 2 Native Hawaiian or other Pacific Islander, non-Hispanic/Latino; 87 Two or more races, non-Hispanic/Latino), 469 international. 4,737 applicants, 32% accepted, 875 enrolled. In 2011, 759 master's, 6 doctorates awarded. *Degree requirements:* For master's, comprehensive exam, field study consulting project (for MBA); thesis/dissertation (for MFE); for doctorate, comprehensive exam, thesis/dissertation, oral and written qualifying exams. *Entrance requirements:* For master's, GMAT (for MBA); GMAT or GRE General Test (for MFE), 4-year bachelor's degree or equivalent; for doctorate, GMAT or GRE General Test, 4-year bachelor's degree from regionally-accredited institution; minimum GPA of 3.0. Additional exam requirements/recommendations for international students: Required—TOEFL (minimum score 560 paper-based; 220 computer-based; 87 iBT), IELTS (minimum score 7). *Application deadline:* For fall admission, 10/26 for domestic and international students; for winter admission, 1/11 for domestic and international students; for spring admission, 4/18 for domestic and international students. Application fee: $200. Electronic applications accepted. *Expenses:* Contact institution. *Financial support:* In 2011–12, 600 students received support. Fellowships, research assistantships, teaching assistantships, career-related internships or fieldwork, institutionally sponsored loans, scholarships/grants, health care benefits, and tuition waivers (partial) available. Financial award application deadline: 4/15; financial award applicants required to submit FAFSA. *Unit head:* Judy D. Olian, Dean, 310-825-7982, Fax: 310-206-2073, E-mail: judy.olian@anderson.ucla.edu. *Application contact:* Robert Weiler, Assistant Dean, Director of MBA Admissions and Financial Aid, 310-825-6944, Fax: 310-825-8582, E-mail: mba.admissions@anderson.ucla.edu. Web site: http://www.anderson.ucla.edu/.

See Display on this page and Close-Up on page 249.

University of California, Riverside, Graduate Division, A. Gary Anderson Graduate School of Management, Riverside, CA 92521-0102. Offers MBA. *Accreditation:* AACSB. Part-time and evening/weekend programs available. *Faculty:* 24 full-time (4 women), 27 part-time/adjunct (5 women). *Students:* 178 full-time (90 women), 5 part-time (1 woman); includes 48 minority (4 Black or African American, non-Hispanic/Latino; 37 Asian, non-

Business Administration and Management—General

Hispanic/Latino; 7 Hispanic/Latino), 107 international. Average age 27. 439 applicants, 49% accepted, 98 enrolled. In 2011, 88 master's awarded. *Degree requirements:* For master's, thesis optional. *Entrance requirements:* For master's, GMAT or GRE, minimum GPA of 3.2. Additional exam requirements/recommendations for international students: Required—TOEFL (minimum score 550 paper-based; 213 computer-based; 80 iBT), IELTS. *Application deadline:* For fall admission, 9/1 for domestic students, 5/1 for international students; for winter admission, 12/1 for domestic students, 9/1 for international students; for spring admission, 3/1 for domestic students, 10/1 for international students. Applications are processed on a rolling basis. Application fee: $100 ($125 for international students). *Expenses:* Contact institution. *Financial support:* In 2011–12, 44 students received support, including 55 fellowships with partial tuition reimbursements available (averaging $21,354 per year), 1 research assistantship with full tuition reimbursement available (averaging $48,120 per year), 45 teaching assistantships with partial tuition reimbursements available (averaging $20,000 per year); career-related internships or fieldwork, institutionally sponsored loans, scholarships/grants, and tuition waivers (full) also available. Financial award application deadline: 5/1; financial award applicants required to submit FAFSA. *Faculty research:* Option pricing, marketing, decision modeling, new technologies in cost accounting, supply chain management, operations, production and inventory systems, entrepreneurial finance, e-commerce. *Unit head:* Dr. Yunzeng Wang, Interim Dean, 951-827-6329, Fax: 951-827-3970, E-mail: mba@ucr.edu. *Application contact:* Dr. Rami Zwick, Associate Dean/Graduate Adviser, 951-827-7766, Fax: 951-827-3970, E-mail: mba@ucr.edu. Web site: http://agsm.ucr.edu/.

University of California, San Diego, Office of Graduate Studies, Rady School of Management, La Jolla, CA 92093. Offers MBA.

University of Central Arkansas, Graduate School, College of Business Administration, Program in Business Administration, Conway, AR 72035-0001. Offers MBA. *Accreditation:* AACSB. Part-time and evening/weekend programs available. *Students:* 21 full-time (5 women), 20 part-time (8 women); includes 6 minority (4 Black or African American, non-Hispanic/Latino; 1 American Indian or Alaska Native, non-Hispanic/Latino; 1 Native Hawaiian or other Pacific Islander, non-Hispanic/Latino), 4 international. Average age 27. 18 applicants, 89% accepted, 13 enrolled. In 2011, 23 master's awarded. *Entrance requirements:* For master's, GMAT, minimum GPA of 2.7. Additional exam requirements/recommendations for international students: Required—TOEFL (minimum score 550 paper-based; 213 computer-based). *Application deadline:* For fall admission, 3/1 priority date for domestic students, 3/1 for international students; for spring admission, 10/1 priority date for domestic students, 10/1 for international students. Applications are processed on a rolling basis. Application fee: $25 ($50 for international students). *Expenses:* Tuition, state resident: full-time $4834; part-time $398.35 per credit hour. Tuition, nonresident: full-time $8686. *Financial support:* In 2011–12, 4 research assistantships with partial tuition reimbursements (averaging $5,000 per year) were awarded; career-related internships or fieldwork, Federal Work-Study, scholarships/grants, tuition waivers (partial), and unspecified assistantships also available. Support available to part-time students. Financial award application deadline: 2/15. *Unit head:* Dr. Michael Rubach, MBA Director, 501-450-5316, Fax: 501-450-5302, E-mail: mrubach@uca.edu. *Application contact:* Sandy Burks, Administrative Specialist, 501-450-3124, Fax: 501-450-5678, E-mail: slburks@uca..edu.

University of Central Florida, College of Business Administration, Department of Management, Orlando, FL 32816. Offers entrepreneurship (Graduate Certificate); management (MSM); technology ventures (Graduate Certificate). *Accreditation:* AACSB. *Faculty:* 27 full-time (8 women), 4 part-time/adjunct (2 women). *Students:* 6 part-time (3 women); includes 1 minority (Hispanic/Latino), 2 international. Average age 29. 20 applicants, 80% accepted, 6 enrolled. In 2011, 1 master's, 8 other advanced degrees awarded. *Entrance requirements:* For master's, GMAT, minimum GPA of 3.0 in last 60 hours. *Application deadline:* For fall admission, 2/1 priority date for domestic students; for spring admission, 11/1 priority date for domestic students. Application fee: $30. Electronic applications accepted. *Expenses:* Tuition, state resident: part-time $277.08 per credit hour. Tuition, nonresident: part-time $277.08 per credit hour. Part-time tuition and fees vary according to degree level and program. *Financial support:* Fellowships, research assistantships, and teaching assistantships available. *Unit head:* Dr. Stephen Goodman, Chair, 407-823-2675, Fax: 407-823-3725, E-mail: sgoodman@bus.ucf.edu. *Application contact:* Judy Ryder, Director, Graduate Admissions, 407-823-2364, Fax: 407-823-0219, E-mail: jryder@bus.ucf.edu. Web site: http://www.graduatecatalog.ucf.edu/programs/program.aspx?id=1080&program=Management MS.

University of Central Florida, College of Business Administration, Program in Business Administration, Orlando, FL 32816. Offers MBA, PhD. *Accreditation:* AACSB. Part-time and evening/weekend programs available. *Students:* 288 full-time (122 women), 247 part-time (102 women); includes 115 minority (36 Black or African American, non-Hispanic/Latino; 2 American Indian or Alaska Native, non-Hispanic/Latino; 27 Asian, non-Hispanic/Latino; 45 Hispanic/Latino; 1 Native Hawaiian or other Pacific Islander, non-Hispanic/Latino; 4 Two or more races, non-Hispanic/Latino), 41 international. Average age 30. 334 applicants, 60% accepted, 163 enrolled. In 2011, 286 master's, 7 doctorates awarded. *Degree requirements:* For master's, exam; for doctorate, thesis/dissertation, departmental candidacy exam. *Entrance requirements:* For master's and doctorate, GMAT, minimum GPA of 3.0 in last 60 hours. Additional exam requirements/recommendations for international students: Required—TOEFL. *Application deadline:* For fall admission, 2/1 priority date for domestic students; for spring admission, 11/1 priority date for domestic students. Application fee: $30. Electronic applications accepted. *Expenses:* Tuition, state resident: part-time $277.08 per credit hour. Tuition, nonresident: part-time $277.08 per credit hour. Part-time tuition and fees vary according to degree level and program. *Financial support:* In 2011–12, 58 students received support, including 11 fellowships with partial tuition reimbursements available (averaging $8,700 per year), 5 research assistantships with partial tuition reimbursements available (averaging $8,500 per year), 48 teaching assistantships with partial tuition reimbursements available (averaging $12,300 per year); career-related internships or fieldwork, Federal Work-Study, institutionally sponsored loans, tuition waivers (partial), and unspecified assistantships also available. Financial award application deadline: 3/1; financial award applicants required to submit FAFSA. *Unit head:* Dr. Foard L. Jones, Interim Dean, 407-823-2183, E-mail: foard.jones@bus.ucf.edu. *Application contact:* Judy Ryder, Director, Graduate Admissions, 407-823-2364, Fax: 407-823-0219, E-mail: judy.ryder@bus.ucf.edu. Web site: http://web.bus.ucf.edu/academics/graduate_office/.

University of Central Missouri, The Graduate School, Harmon College of Business Administration, Warrensburg, MO 64093. Offers accountancy (MA); accounting (MBA); ethical strategic leadership (MBA); finance (MBA); general business (MBA); information systems (MBA); information technology (MS); marketing (MBA). Part-time programs available. Postbaccalaureate distance learning degree programs offered. *Entrance requirements:* Additional exam requirements/recommendations for international students: Required—TOEFL (minimum score 550 paper-based; 79 computer-based). Electronic applications accepted.

University of Charleston, Executive Master of Business Administration Program, Charleston, WV 25304-1099. Offers EMBA. Part-time and evening/weekend programs available. *Degree requirements:* For master's, practicum paper, minimum cumulative GPA of 3.0. *Entrance requirements:* For master's, GMAT, undergraduate degree from regionally-accredited institution; minimum GPA of 3.0 in undergraduate work (recommended); three years of work experience since receiving the undergraduate degree (recommended); minimum of two professional recommendations, one from current employer, addressing career potential and ability to do graduate work. Additional exam requirements/recommendations for international students: Required—TOEFL, IELTS. *Application deadline:* Applications are processed on a rolling basis. Electronic applications accepted. *Financial support:* In 2011–12, 3 students received support. Scholarships/grants available. Support available to part-time students. Financial award application deadline: 3/1; financial award applicants required to submit FAFSA. *Unit head:* 304-357-4373, Fax: 304-357-4877. *Application contact:* Sandy Dolin, Application Coordinator, 304-357-4752, E-mail: sandradolin@ucwv.edu. Web site: http://www.ucwv.edu/business/emba/.

University of Charleston, Master of Business Administration and Leadership Program, Charleston, WV 25301. Offers MBA. *Degree requirements:* For master's, thesis, professional portfolio, minimum cumulative GPA of 3.0. *Entrance requirements:* For master's, official transcripts for all undergraduate work; minimum GPA of 3.0; personal interview. Additional exam requirements/recommendations for international students: Required—TOEFL, IELTS. *Application deadline:* Applications are processed on a rolling basis. Electronic applications accepted. *Financial support:* Career-related internships or fieldwork and scholarships/grants available. Financial award application deadline: 3/1; financial award applicants required to submit FAFSA. *Unit head:* 304-357-4373. *Application contact:* Cheryl Fout, Administrative Assistant to the Dean, 304-357-4373, E-mail: cherylfout@ucwv.edu. Web site: http://www.ucwv.edu/business/mbal/.

University of Chicago, Booth School of Business, Doctoral Program in Business, Chicago, IL 60637-1513. Offers PhD. *Accreditation:* AACSB. *Degree requirements:* For doctorate, thesis/dissertation, workshops, curriculum paper. *Entrance requirements:* For doctorate, GMAT or GRE, resume, transcripts, letters of referral, essay, interview. Additional exam requirements/recommendations for international students: Required—TOEFL, IELTS. Electronic applications accepted. *Faculty research:* Accounting, finance, marketing, economics, econometrics and statistics.

University of Chicago, Booth School of Business, Full-Time MBA Program, Chicago, IL 60637. Offers accounting (MBA); analytic finance (MBA); analytic management (MBA); business administration (PhD); econometrics and statistics (MBA); economics (MBA); entrepreneurship (MBA); finance (MBA); general management (MBA); health administration and policy (Certificate); human resource management (MBA); international business (IMBA, MBA); managerial and organizational behavior (MBA); marketing management (MBA); operations management (MBA); strategic management (MBA); MBA/AM; MBA/JD; MBA/MA; MBA/MD; MBA/MPP. *Accreditation:* AACSB. Part-time and evening/weekend programs available. *Faculty:* 166 full-time, 32 part-time/adjunct. *Students:* 1,160 full-time (412 women); includes 316 minority (61 Black or African American, non-Hispanic/Latino; 173 Asian, non-Hispanic/Latino; 63 Hispanic/Latino; 19 Two or more races, non-Hispanic/Latino), 378 international. Average age 28. 4,169 applicants, 575 enrolled. In 2011, 1,423 master's, 19 doctorates awarded. Terminal master's awarded for partial completion of doctoral program. *Entrance requirements:* For master's, GMAT, 2 letters of recommendation, 3 essays, resume, interview. Additional exam requirements/recommendations for international students: Required—TOEFL (minimum score 600 paper-based; 250 computer-based; 104 iBT), IELTS. *Application deadline:* For fall admission, 10/12 priority date for domestic students, 10/12 for international students; for winter admission, 1/4 for domestic and international students; for spring admission, 4/4 for domestic and international students. Application fee: $200. Electronic applications accepted. *Expenses:* Contact institution. *Financial support:* Fellowships available. Financial award applicants required to submit FAFSA. *Faculty research:* Finance, marketing, economics, entrepreneurship, strategy, management. *Unit head:* Stacey Kole, Deputy Dean, 773-702-7121. *Application contact:* Kurt Ahlm, Associate Dean of Student Recruitment and Admissions, 773-702-7369, Fax: 773-702-9085, E-mail: admissions@chicagobooth.edu. Web site: http://chicagobooth.edu/.

University of Chicago, Booth School of Business, Part-Time Evening MBA Program, Chicago, IL 60611. Offers MBA. *Accreditation:* AACSB. Part-time and evening/weekend programs available. *Entrance requirements:* For master's, GMAT, 2 letters of recommendation, interview. Additional exam requirements/recommendations for international students: Required—TOEFL (minimum score 600 paper-based; 250 computer-based), IELTS. Electronic applications accepted. *Expenses:* Contact institution. *Faculty research:* Finance, entrepreneurship, strategy, marketing, international business.

University of Chicago, Booth School of Business, Part-Time Weekend MBA Program, Chicago, IL 60611. Offers MBA. *Accreditation:* AACSB. Part-time and evening/weekend programs available. *Entrance requirements:* For master's, GMAT, 2 letters of recommendation, interview, resume. Additional exam requirements/recommendations for international students: Required—TOEFL or IELTS. *Faculty research:* Finance, marketing, international business, strategy, entrepreneurship.

University of Cincinnati, Graduate School, Carl H. Lindner College of Business, MBA Program, Cincinnati, OH 45221. Offers MBA. Part-time and evening/weekend programs available. *Faculty:* 79 full-time (22 women), 71 part-time/adjunct (24 women). *Students:* 138 full-time (45 women), 95 part-time (39 women); includes 28 minority (10 Black or African American, non-Hispanic/Latino; 10 Asian, non-Hispanic/Latino; 6 Hispanic/Latino; 1 Native Hawaiian or other Pacific Islander, non-Hispanic/Latino; 1 Two or more races, non-Hispanic/Latino), 66 international. Average age 25. 217 applicants, 90% accepted, 143 enrolled. In 2011, 116 degrees awarded. *Degree requirements:* For master's, capstone project. *Entrance requirements:* For master's, GMAT, resume, letters of recommendation, essays, official transcripts. Additional exam requirements/recommendations for international students: Required—TOEFL (minimum score 600 paper-based; 250 computer-based; 100 iBT). *Application deadline:* For fall admission, 1/15 priority date for domestic students, 4/1 for international students. Application fee: $65 ($70 for international students). Electronic applications accepted. *Expenses:* Contact institution. *Financial support:* In 2011–12, 110 students received support. Scholarships/grants, tuition waivers (full and partial), and unspecified assistantships available. Financial award application deadline: 2/1; financial award applicants required to submit FAFSA. *Unit head:* Dr. Robert Dwyer, Academic Program Director, 513-556-7103, E-mail: robert.dwyer@uc.edu. *Application contact:* Dona Clary, Director, Graduate Programs Office, 513-556-3546, Fax: 513-558-7006, E-mail: dona.clary@uc.edu. Web site: http://www.business.uc.edu/mba.

University of Cincinnati, Graduate School, Carl H. Lindner College of Business, PhD Programs, Cincinnati, OH 45221. Offers accounting (PhD); finance (PhD); information systems (PhD); management (PhD); marketing (PhD); quantitative analysis and operations management (PhD). *Faculty:* 56 full-time (13 women). *Students:* 34 full-time (12 women), 12 part-time (4 women); includes 2 minority (1 Asian, non-Hispanic/Latino; 1 Hispanic/Latino), 25 international. Average age 29. 120 applicants, 13% accepted, 10 enrolled. In 2011, 8 degrees awarded. *Median time to degree:* Of those who began their doctoral program in fall 2003, 65% received their degree in 8 years or less. *Degree requirements:* For doctorate, comprehensive exam, thesis/dissertation. *Entrance* *requirements:* For doctorate, GMAT, GRE, transcripts, essays, resume, letters of recommendation. Additional exam requirements/recommendations for international students: Required—TOEFL (minimum score 600 paper-based; 250 computer-based; 100 iBT). *Application deadline:* For fall admission, 2/1 for domestic and international students. Application fee: $65 ($70 for international students). Electronic applications accepted. *Expenses:* Contact institution. *Financial support:* In 2011–12, 39 students received support, including 30 research assistantships with full and partial tuition reimbursements available (averaging $14,640 per year); scholarships/grants, tuition waivers (full and partial), and unspecified assistantships also available. Financial award application deadline: 2/1; financial award applicants required to submit FAFSA. *Unit head:* Dr. Suzanne Masterson, Director, 513-556-7125, Fax: 513-556-5499, E-mail: suzanne.masterson@uc.edu. *Application contact:* Deborah Schildknecht, Assistant Director, 513-556-7190, Fax: 513-558-7006, E-mail: deborah.schildknecht@uc.edu. Web site: http://www.business.uc.edu/phd.

University of Colorado at Colorado Springs, Graduate School of Business Administration, Colorado Springs, CO 80933-7150. Offers MBA. *Accreditation:* AACSB. Part-time and evening/weekend programs available. *Faculty:* 30 full-time (10 women), 7 part-time/adjunct (3 women). *Students:* 271 full-time (107 women), 150 part-time (48 women); includes 58 minority (9 Black or African American, non-Hispanic/Latino; 21 Asian, non-Hispanic/Latino; 26 Hispanic/Latino; 2 Two or more races, non-Hispanic/Latino), 15 international. Average age 32. 119 applicants, 76% accepted, 43 enrolled. In 2011, 140 master's awarded. *Entrance requirements:* For master's, GMAT or GRE. Additional exam requirements/recommendations for international students: Recommended—TOEFL. *Application deadline:* For fall admission, 6/1 for domestic and international students; for spring admission, 11/1 for domestic and international students. Application fee: $60 ($75 for international students). *Expenses:* Contact institution. *Financial support:* In 2011–12, 20 students received support. Career-related internships or fieldwork, Federal Work-Study, and scholarships/grants available. Support available to part-time students. Financial award application deadline: 3/1; financial award applicants required to submit FAFSA. *Faculty research:* Quality financial reporting, investments and corporate governance, group support systems, environmental and project management, customer relationship management. *Unit head:* Dr. Venkateshwar Reddy, Dean, 719-255-3113, Fax: 719-255-3100, E-mail: vreddy@uccs.edu. *Application contact:* Windy Haddad, MBA Program Director, 719-255-3401, Fax: 719-255-3100, E-mail: whaddad@uccs.edu. Web site: http://www.uccs.edu/mba.

University of Colorado Boulder, Leeds School of Business, Master of Business Administration Program, Boulder, CO 80309. Offers MBA. *Accreditation:* AACSB. *Students:* 325 full-time (101 women), 10 part-time (3 women); includes 25 minority (2 Black or African American, non-Hispanic/Latino; 3 American Indian or Alaska Native, non-Hispanic/Latino; 15 Asian, non-Hispanic/Latino; 5 Hispanic/Latino), 27 international. Average age 30. 191 applicants, 99% accepted, 99 enrolled. In 2011, 148 master's awarded. *Entrance requirements:* For master's, GMAT, minimum undergraduate GPA of 2.75. *Application deadline:* Applications are processed on a rolling basis. Application fee: $50 ($60 for international students). Electronic applications accepted. *Financial support:* In 2011–12, 184 students received support, including 150 fellowships (averaging $4,091 per year), 1 research assistantship with full and partial tuition reimbursement available (averaging $28,116 per year), 2 teaching assistantships with full and partial tuition reimbursements available (averaging $13,421 per year); institutionally sponsored loans, scholarships/grants, health care benefits, and unspecified assistantships also available. Financial award applicants required to submit FAFSA. *Application contact:* E-mail: leedsms@colorado.edu. Web site: http://leeds.colorado.edu/mba.

University of Colorado Denver, Business School, Master of Business Administration Program, Denver, CO 80217. Offers business intelligence (MBA); business strategy (MBA); business to business marketing (MBA); business to consumer marketing (MBA); change management (MBA); corporate financial management (MBA); enterprise technology management (MBA); entrepreneurship (MBA); health administration (MBA), including financial management, health administration, health information technologies, international health management and policy; human resources management (MBA); investment management (MBA); managing for sustainability (MBA); services management (MBA); sports and entertainment management (MBA). *Accreditation:* AACSB. Part-time and evening/weekend programs available. Postbaccalaureate distance learning degree programs offered (no on-campus study). *Students:* 784 full-time (306 women), 203 part-time (81 women); includes 135 minority (18 Black or African American, non-Hispanic/Latino; 5 American Indian or Alaska Native, non-Hispanic/Latino; 50 Asian, non-Hispanic/Latino; 58 Hispanic/Latino; 4 Two or more races, non-Hispanic/Latino), 38 international. Average age 31. 433 applicants, 76% accepted, 212 enrolled. In 2011, 326 master's awarded. *Degree requirements:* For master's, 48 semester hours, including 30 of core courses, 3 in international business, and 15 in electives from over 50 other graduate business courses. *Entrance requirements:* For master's, GMAT, resume, official transcripts, essay, two letters of recommendation, financial statements (for international applicants). Additional exam requirements/recommendations for international students: Required—TOEFL (minimum score 560 paper-based; 197 computer-based; 83 iBT). *Application deadline:* For fall admission, 4/15 priority date for domestic students, 3/15 for international students; for spring admission, 10/15 priority date for domestic students, 10/1 for international students. Applications are processed on a rolling basis. Application fee: $50 ($75 for international students). Electronic applications accepted. *Expenses:* Contact institution. *Financial support:* Scholarships/grants available. Support available to part-time students. Financial award application deadline: 4/1; financial award applicants required to submit FAFSA. *Faculty research:* Marketing, management, entrepreneurship, finance, health administration. *Unit head:* Elizabeth Cooperman, Professor of Finance and Managing for Sustainability/MBA Program Director, 303-315-8422, E-mail: elizabeth.cooperman@ucdenver.edu. *Application contact:* Shelly Townley, Admissions Director, Graduate Programs, 303-315-8202, E-mail: shelly.townley@ucdenver.edu. Web site: http://www.ucdenver.edu/academics/colleges/business/degrees/ms/accounting/Pages/Accounting.aspx.

University of Colorado Denver, Business School, Program in Management and Organization, Denver, CO 80217. Offers communications management (MS); entrepreneurship and innovation (MS); global management (MS); human resources management (MS); leadership and management (MS); sports and entertainment management (MS). *Accreditation:* AACSB. Part-time and evening/weekend programs available. Postbaccalaureate distance learning degree programs offered (no on-campus study). *Students:* 29 full-time (14 women), 14 part-time (10 women); includes 3 minority (2 Asian, non-Hispanic/Latino; 1 Hispanic/Latino), 5 international. Average age 31. 32 applicants, 63% accepted, 14 enrolled. In 2011, 22 master's awarded. *Degree requirements:* For master's, 30 semester hours (12 of required courses, 12 of management electives, and 6 of free electives). *Entrance requirements:* For master's, GMAT, resume, two letters of recommendation, essay, financial statements (for international applicants). Additional exam requirements/recommendations for international students: Required—TOEFL (minimum score 525 paper-based; 197 computer-based; 71 iBT). *Application deadline:* For fall admission, 4/15 priority date for domestic students, 3/15 for international students; for spring admission, 10/15 priority date for domestic students, 10/1 for international students. Applications are processed on a rolling basis. Application fee: $50 ($75 for international students). Electronic applications accepted. *Expenses:* Contact institution. *Financial support:* Federal Work-Study and scholarships/grants available. Support available to part-time students. Financial award application deadline: 4/1; financial award applicants required to submit FAFSA. *Faculty research:* Human resource management, management of catastrophe, turnaround strategies. *Unit head:* Dr. Kenneth Bettenhausen, Associate Professor/Director of MS in Management, 303-315-8425, E-mail: kenneth.bettenhausen@ucdenver.edu. *Application contact:* Shelly Townley, Admissions Director, Graduate Programs, 303-315-8202, E-mail: shelly.townley@ucdenver.edu. Web site: http://www.ucdenver.edu/academics/colleges/business/degrees/ms/management/Pages/Management.aspx.

University of Connecticut, Graduate School, School of Business, Storrs, CT 06269. Offers accounting (MS, PhD); business administration (Exec MBA, MBA, PhD); finance (PhD); health care management and insurance studies (MBA); management (PhD); management consulting (MBA); marketing (PhD); marketing intelligence (MBA); MA/MBA; MBA/MSW. *Accreditation:* AACSB. *Degree requirements:* For master's, comprehensive exam; for doctorate, thesis/dissertation. *Entrance requirements:* For master's and doctorate, GMAT. Additional exam requirements/recommendations for international students: Required—TOEFL (minimum score 550 paper-based; 213 computer-based). Electronic applications accepted.

See Display on next page and Close-Up on page 251.

University of Dallas, Graduate School of Management, Irving, TX 75062-4736. Offers accounting (MBA, MM, MS); business management (MBA, MM); corporate finance (MBA, MM); financial services (MBA); global business (MBA, MM); health services management (MBA, MM); human resource management (MBA, MM); information assurance (MBA, MM, MS); information technology (MBA, MM, MS); information technology service management (MBA, MM, MS); marketing management (MBA, MM); organization development (MBA, MM); project management (MBA, MM); sports and entertainment management (MBA, MM); strategic leadership (MBA, MM); supply chain management (MBA); supply chain management and market logistics (MM). *Accreditation:* ACBSP. Part-time and evening/weekend programs available. Postbaccalaureate distance learning degree programs offered (no on-campus study). *Entrance requirements:* Additional exam requirements/recommendations for international students: Required—TOEFL. Electronic applications accepted. *Expenses:* Contact institution.

University of Dayton, School of Business Administration, Dayton, OH 45469-1300. Offers accounting (MBA); cyber security (MBA); finance (MBA); marketing (MBA); JD/MBA. *Accreditation:* AACSB. Part-time and evening/weekend programs available. *Faculty:* 23 full-time (6 women), 13 part-time/adjunct (2 women). *Students:* 170 full-time (72 women), 117 part-time (43 women); includes 26 minority (16 Black or African American, non-Hispanic/Latino; 6 Asian, non-Hispanic/Latino; 3 Hispanic/Latino; 1 Two or more races, non-Hispanic/Latino), 49 international. Average age 28. 366 applicants, 72% accepted, 126 enrolled. In 2011, 147 master's awarded. *Entrance requirements:* For master's, GMAT or GRE. Additional exam requirements/recommendations for international students: Required—TOEFL (minimum score 550 paper-based; 213 computer-based; 80 iBT); Recommended—IELTS (minimum score 6.5). *Application deadline:* For fall admission, 3/1 for international students; for winter admission, 7/1 for international students; for spring admission, 1/1 for international students. Applications are processed on a rolling basis. Application fee: $0 ($50 for international students). Electronic applications accepted. *Expenses:* Contact institution. *Financial support:* In 2011–12, 12 research assistantships with full and partial tuition reimbursements (averaging $7,020 per year) were awarded; career-related internships or fieldwork, institutionally sponsored loans, scholarships/grants, health care benefits, and unspecified assistantships also available. Support available to part-time students. Financial award application deadline: 3/15; financial award applicants required to submit FAFSA. *Faculty research:* Management information systems, economics, finance, entrepreneurship, marketing, accounting and cyber security. *Unit head:* Janice M. Glynn, Director, MBA Program, 937-229-3733, Fax: 937-229-3882, E-mail: glynn@udayton.edu. *Application contact:* Jeffrey Carter, Assistant Director, MBA Program, 937-229-3733, Fax: 937-229-3882, E-mail: jeff.carter@notes.udayton.edu. Web site: http://business.udayton.edu/mba/.

University of Delaware, Alfred Lerner College of Business and Economics, Program in Business Administration, Newark, DE 19716. Offers MBA, MA/MBA, MBA/MIB, MBA/MS. *Accreditation:* AACSB. Part-time and evening/weekend programs available. *Entrance requirements:* For master's, GMAT, 2 letters of recommendation, resume. Additional exam requirements/recommendations for international students: Required—TOEFL (minimum score 600 paper-based; 260 computer-based; 79 iBT). Electronic applications accepted. *Expenses:* Contact institution. *Faculty research:* Finance, corporate governance, information systems, leadership, marketing.

University of Delaware, College of Agriculture and Natural Resources, Department of Entomology and Wildlife Ecology, Newark, DE 19716. Offers entomology and applied ecology (MS, PhD), including avian ecology, evolution and taxonomy, insect biological control, insect ecology and behavior (MS), insect genetics, pest management, plant-insect interactions, wildlife ecology and management. Part-time programs available. *Degree requirements:* For master's, comprehensive exam, thesis, oral exam, seminar; for doctorate, comprehensive exam, thesis/dissertation, qualifying exam, seminar. *Entrance requirements:* For master's, GRE General Test, minimum GPA of 3.0 in field, 2.8 overall; for doctorate, GRE General Test, GRE Subject Test (biology), minimum GPA of 3.0 in field, 2.8 overall. Additional exam requirements/recommendations for international students: Required—TOEFL. Electronic applications accepted. *Faculty research:* Ecology and evolution of plant-insect interactions, ecology of wildlife conservation management, habitat restoration, biological control, applied ecosystem management.

University of Denver, Daniels College of Business, Denver, CO 80208. Offers IMBA, M Acc, MBA, MS. *Accreditation:* AACSB. Part-time and evening/weekend programs available. *Faculty:* 103 full-time (29 women), 66 part-time/adjunct (12 women). *Students:* 549 full-time (215 women), 461 part-time (191 women); includes 97 minority (15 Black or African American, non-Hispanic/Latino; 6 American Indian or Alaska Native, non-Hispanic/Latino; 31 Asian, non-Hispanic/Latino; 36 Hispanic/Latino; 9 Two or more races, non-Hispanic/Latino), 309 international. Average age 29. 2,214 applicants, 49% accepted, 458 enrolled. In 2011, 610 degrees awarded. *Entrance requirements:* For master's, GMAT or GRE General Test. Additional exam requirements/recommendations for international students: Required—TOEFL (minimum score 570 paper-based; 88 iBT). *Application deadline:* For fall admission, 1/15 priority date for domestic students. Applications are processed on a rolling basis. Application fee: $60. Electronic applications accepted. *Financial support:* In 2011–12, 343 students received support, including 84 teaching assistantships with full and partial tuition reimbursements available (averaging $1,869 per year); career-related internships or fieldwork, Federal Work-Study, institutionally sponsored loans, scholarships/grants, and unspecified assistantships also available. Support available to part-time students. Financial award application deadline: 2/15; financial award applicants required to submit FAFSA. *Unit head:* Dr. Chris Riordan, Dean, 303-871-4324, E-mail: christine.riordan@du.edu.

Business Administration and Management—General

Application contact: Admissions, 303-871-3416, Fax: 303-871-4466, E-mail: daniels@du.edu. Web site: http://www.daniels.du.edu.

University of Detroit Mercy, College of Business Administration, Program in Business Administration, Detroit, MI 48221. Offers MBA, JD/MBA. *Accreditation:* AACSB. Part-time and evening/weekend programs available. *Degree requirements:* For master's, thesis or alternative. *Entrance requirements:* For master's, GMAT, minimum GPA of 2.75.

University of Detroit Mercy, College of Business Administration, Program in Business Turnaround Management, Detroit, MI 48221. Offers MS, Certificate.

University of Detroit Mercy, College of Business Administration, Program in Executive MBA, Detroit, MI 48221. Offers EMBA.

University of Dubuque, Program in Business Administration, Dubuque, IA 52001-5099. Offers MBA. Part-time and evening/weekend programs available. *Entrance requirements:* For master's, 2 letters of recommendation. Electronic applications accepted.

University of Evansville, Schroeder Family School of Business Administration, Evansville, IN 47722. Offers executive business administration (MBA). *Accreditation:* AACSB. Part-time and evening/weekend programs available. *Entrance requirements:* For master's, GMAT or GRE (upon request), minimum 5 years professional experience, 2 letters of recommendation. Additional exam requirements/recommendations for international students: Required—TOEFL (minimum score 577 paper-based; 90 iBT). *Expenses:* Contact institution.

The University of Findlay, Graduate and Professional Studies, College of Business, Findlay, OH 45840-3653. Offers health care management (MBA); hospitality management (MBA); organizational leadership (MBA); public management (MBA). Part-time and evening/weekend programs available. Postbaccalaureate distance learning degree programs offered (no on-campus study). *Faculty:* 18 full-time (5 women), 1 part-time/adjunct (0 women). *Students:* 25 full-time (15 women), 184 part-time (100 women); includes 13 minority (3 Black or African American, non-Hispanic/Latino; 7 Asian, non-Hispanic/Latino; 3 Hispanic/Latino), 78 international. Average age 25. 72 applicants, 82% accepted, 24 enrolled. In 2011, 168 master's awarded. *Degree requirements:* For master's, thesis, cumulative project. *Entrance requirements:* For master's, GMAT or GRE, bachelor's degree from accredited institution, minimum undergraduate GPA of 3.0. Additional exam requirements/recommendations for international students: Required—TOEFL (minimum score 550 paper-based; 213 computer-based; 80 iBT). *Application deadline:* Applications are processed on a rolling basis. Application fee: $25. Electronic applications accepted. *Expenses:* Contact institution. *Financial support:* In 2011–12, 5 research assistantships with full and partial tuition reimbursements (averaging $4,200 per year) were awarded; career-related internships or fieldwork, Federal Work-Study, health care benefits, and unspecified assistantships also available. Financial award application deadline: 4/1; financial award applicants required to submit FAFSA. *Faculty research:* Health care management, operations and logistics management. *Unit head:* Dr. Paul Sears, Dean, 419-434-4704, Fax: 419-434-4822. *Application contact:* Heather Riffle, Assistant Director, Graduate and Professional Studies, 419-434-4640, Fax: 419-434-5517, E-mail: riffle@findlay.edu. Web site: http://www.findlay.edu/.

University of Florida, Graduate School, Warrington College of Business Administration, Hough Graduate School of Business, Department of Management, Gainesville, FL 32611. Offers geriatric care management (MSM); health care risk management (MSM); international business (MAIB); management (MSM, PhD). *Accreditation:* AACSB. Postbaccalaureate distance learning degree programs offered. *Faculty:* 11 full-time (2 women). *Students:* 235 full-time (122 women), 75 part-time (44 women); includes 85 minority (18 Black or African American, non-Hispanic/Latino; 19 Asian, non-Hispanic/Latino; 48 Hispanic/Latino), 60 international. Average age 25. 58 applicants, 78% accepted, 40 enrolled. In 2011, 239 master's, 2 doctorates awarded. *Degree requirements:* For master's, comprehensive exam, thesis; for doctorate, comprehensive exam, thesis/dissertation. *Entrance requirements:* For master's and doctorate, GMAT or GRE General Test, minimum GPA of 3.0. Additional exam requirements/recommendations for international students: Required—TOEFL (minimum score 550 paper-based; 213 computer-based; 80 iBT), IELTS (minimum score 6). *Application deadline:* For fall admission, 1/1 for domestic and international students. Applications are processed on a rolling basis. Application fee: $30. Electronic applications accepted. *Financial support:* Fellowships, research assistantships, teaching assistantships, and unspecified assistantships available. Financial award applicants required to submit FAFSA. *Faculty research:* Job attitudes, personality and individual differences, organizational entry and exit, knowledge management, competitive dynamics. *Unit head:* Dr. Robert E. Thomas, Chair, 352-392-0136, Fax: 352-392-6020, E-mail: rethomas@ufl.edu. *Application contact:* Dr. Jason A. Colquitt, Graduate Coordinator, 352-846-0507, Fax: 352-392-6020, E-mail: colquitt@ufl.edu. Web site: http://www.cba.ufl.edu/mang/.

University of Florida, Graduate School, Warrington College of Business Administration, Hough Graduate School of Business, Programs in Business Administration, Gainesville, FL 32611. Offers accounting (MBA); arts administration (MBA); business strategy and public policy (MBA); competitive strategy (MBA); decision and information sciences (MBA); electronic commerce (MBA); finance (MBA); general business (MBA); global management (MBA); Graham-Buffett security analysis (MBA); health administration (MBA); human resources management (MBA); international studies (MBA); Latin American business (MBA); management (MBA); marketing (MBA); sports administration (MBA); JD/MBA; MBA/MS; MBA/PhD; MBA/Pharm D; MD/MBA. *Accreditation:* AACSB. Part-time and evening/weekend programs available. *Faculty:* 71 full-time (10 women). *Students:* 412 full-time (111 women), 467 part-time (135 women); includes 235 minority (39 Black or African American, non-Hispanic/Latino; 7 American Indian or Alaska Native, non-Hispanic/Latino; 79 Asian, non-Hispanic/Latino; 109 Hispanic/Latino; 1 Native Hawaiian or other Pacific Islander, non-Hispanic/Latino), 44 international. Average age 32. 589 applicants, 52% accepted, 247 enrolled. In 2011, 505 master's awarded. *Degree requirements:* For master's, capstone course. *Entrance requirements:* For master's, GMAT, minimum GPA of 3.0, interview. Additional exam requirements/recommendations for international students: Required—TOEFL (minimum score 550 paper-based; 213 computer-based; 80 iBT), IELTS (minimum score 6). *Application deadline:* For fall admission, 7/1 for domestic students, 1/1 for international students; for spring admission, 12/1 for domestic and international students. Applications are processed on a rolling basis. Application fee: $30. Electronic applications accepted. *Financial support:* Teaching assistantships, career-related internships or fieldwork, scholarships/grants, and unspecified assistantships available. Support available to part-time students. Financial award applicants required to submit FAFSA. *Faculty research:* Accounting, finance, insurance, management, real estate, urban analysis marketing. *Unit head:* Prof. Alexander D. Sevilla, Assistant Dean/Director, 352-273-3252 Ext. 1206, E-mail: alex.sevilla@warrington.ufl.edu. *Application contact:* Prof. Kelli Gust, Associate Director, 352-273-3255, Fax: 352-392-8791, E-mail: kelly.gust@warrington.ufl.edu. Web site: http://www.floridamba.ufl.edu/.

University of Georgia, Terry College of Business, Program in Business Administration, Athens, GA 30602. Offers MA, MBA, PhD, JD/MBA. *Accreditation:* AACSB. *Faculty:* 57 full-time (13 women). *Students:* 437 full-time (155 women), 10 part-time (3 women); includes 78 minority (46 Black or African American, non-Hispanic/Latino; 24 Asian, non-Hispanic/Latino; 8 Two or more races, non-Hispanic/Latino), 37 international. Average age 31. 641 applicants, 41% accepted, 197 enrolled. In 2011, 258 master's, 13 doctorates awarded. *Degree requirements:* For master's, thesis (MA); for doctorate, thesis/dissertation. *Entrance requirements:* For master's, GMAT (MBA), GRE General Test (MA); for doctorate, GMAT or GRE General Test. *Application deadline:* For fall admission, 7/1 priority date for domestic students; for spring admission, 11/15 for domestic students. Application fee: $50. Electronic applications accepted. *Financial support:* Fellowships, research assistantships, teaching assistantships, and unspecified assistantships available. *Unit head:* Dr. Richard L. Daniels, Director, 404-842-4862, Fax: 706-542-5351, E-mail: rdaniels@terry.uga.edu. *Application contact:* Interim Associate Dean. Web site: http://mba.terry.uga.edu/.

University of Guam, Office of Graduate Studies, School of Business and Public Administration, Business Administration Program, Mangilao, GU 96923. Offers PMBA. *Entrance requirements:* For master's, GMAT. Additional exam requirements/recommendations for international students: Required—TOEFL.

University of Guelph, Graduate Studies, College of Management and Economics, Guelph, ON N1G 2W1, Canada. Offers M Sc, MA, MBA, PhD.

University of Hartford, Barney School of Business, Program in Business Administration, West Hartford, CT 06117-1599. Offers MBA, MBA/M Eng. *Accreditation:* AACSB. Part-time and evening/weekend programs available. *Entrance requirements:* For master's, GMAT, 2 letters of recommendation, resume. Additional exam requirements/recommendations for international students: Required—TOEFL (minimum score 550 paper-based; 213 computer-based). Electronic applications accepted.

University of Hartford, College of Education, Nursing, and Health Professions, Program in Nursing, West Hartford, CT 06117-1599. Offers community/public health nursing (MSN); nursing education (MSN); nursing management (MSN). *Accreditation:* AACN. Part-time and evening/weekend programs available. *Degree requirements:* For master's, research project. *Entrance requirements:* For master's, BSN, Connecticut RN license. Additional exam requirements/recommendations for international students: Required—TOEFL (minimum score 550 paper-based; 213 computer-based). Electronic applications accepted. *Expenses:* Contact institution. *Faculty research:* Child development, women in doctoral study, applying feminist theory in teaching methods, near death experience, grandmothers as primary care providers.

University of Hawaii at Manoa, Graduate Division, Shidler College of Business, Executive MBA Programs, Honolulu, HI 96822. Offers executive business administration (EMBA); Vietnam focused business administration (EMBA). *Accreditation:* AACSB. Part-time programs available. *Entrance requirements:* For master's, GMAT, minimum GPA of 3.0.

University of Hawaii at Manoa, Graduate Division, Shidler College of Business, Program in Business Administration, Honolulu, HI 96822. Offers Asian business studies (MBA); Chinese business studies (MBA); decision sciences (MBA); entrepreneurship (MBA); finance (MBA); finance and banking (MBA); human resources management (MBA); information management (MBA); information technology (MBA); international business (MBA); Japanese business studies (MBA); marketing (MBA); organizational behavior (MBA); organizational management (MBA); real estate (MBA); student-designed track (MBA). *Accreditation:* AACSB. Part-time and evening/weekend programs available. *Degree requirements:* For master's, thesis optional. *Entrance requirements:* For master's, GMAT, minimum GPA of 3.0. Additional exam requirements/recommendations for international students: Required—TOEFL (minimum score 600 paper-based; 250 computer-based; 100 iBT), IELTS (minimum score 7). *Expenses:* Contact institution.

University of Houston, Bauer College of Business, Houston, TX 77204. Offers MBA, MS, MS Accy, PhD. *Accreditation:* AACSB. Part-time and evening/weekend programs available. *Degree requirements:* For master's, 30 hours completed in residence, minimum cumulative GPA of 3.0 at UH, no more than 11 semester hours of 'C' grades or below in graduate courses taken at UH; for doctorate, comprehensive exam, thesis/dissertation, minimum GPA of 3.25, continuous full time enrollment, dissertation defense within 6 years of entering the program. *Entrance requirements:* For master's, GMAT or GRE (MBA), official transcripts from all higher education institutions attended, resume, letters of recommendation, self appraisal and goal statement (MBA); for doctorate, GMAT or GRE, letter of financial backing, statement of understanding, reference letters, statement of academic and research interests. Additional exam requirements/recommendations for international students: Required—TOEFL (minimum score 603 paper-based; 250 computer-based; 100 iBT), IELTS (minimum score 6.5), Pearson Test of English (minimum score: 70). Electronic applications accepted. *Faculty research:* Accountancy and taxation, finance, international business, management.

University of Houston–Clear Lake, School of Business, Program in Business Administration, Houston, TX 77058-1098. Offers MBA. *Accreditation:* AACSB. Part-time and evening/weekend programs available. *Degree requirements:* For master's, thesis optional. *Entrance requirements:* For master's, GMAT. Additional exam requirements/recommendations for international students: Required—TOEFL (minimum score 550 paper-based; 213 computer-based). Electronic applications accepted.

University of Houston–Downtown, College of Business, Houston, TX 77002. Offers MBA. Evening/weekend programs available. *Entrance requirements:* For master's, GMAT, personal statement, resume, 2 professional references. Additional exam requirements/recommendations for international students: Required—TOEFL. *Application deadline:* For fall admission, 7/15 for domestic and international students. Applications are processed on a rolling basis. Application fee: $35 ($60 for international students). Electronic applications accepted. *Expenses:* Contact institution. *Financial support:* Applicants required to submit FAFSA. *Faculty research:* Corporate finance, sustainability, recruitment and selection, international strategic management, gender and race discrimination. *Unit head:* Dr. Don Bates, Dean, College of Business, 713-221-8017, Fax: 713-221-8675. *Application contact:* Traneshia Parker, Associate Director of International Student Services and Graduate Admissions, 713-221-8093, Fax: 713-221-8658, E-mail: parkert@uhd.edu. Web site: http://www.uhd.edu/academic/colleges/business/mba/index.html.

University of Houston–Victoria, School of Business Administration, Victoria, TX 77901-4450. Offers accounting (MBA); economic development and entrepreneurship (MS); finance (GMBA, MBA); general business (MBA); international business (MBA); management (GMBA, MBA); marketing (MBA). *Accreditation:* AACSB. Part-time and evening/weekend programs available. Postbaccalaureate distance learning degree programs offered (minimal on-campus study). *Entrance requirements:* For master's, GMAT. Additional exam requirements/recommendations for international students: Required—TOEFL (minimum score 550 paper-based; 213 computer-based). Electronic applications accepted. *Faculty research:* Economic development, marketing, finance.

University of Idaho, College of Graduate Studies, College of Business and Economics, Department of Business and Economics, Moscow, ID 83844-3161. Offers economics (MS); general management (MBA). *Faculty:* 9 full-time, 1 part-time/adjunct. *Students:* 15 full-time, 10 part-time. Average age 39. In 2011, 9 master's awarded. *Application deadline:* For fall admission, 8/1 for domestic students; for spring admission, 12/15 for domestic students. Applications are processed on a rolling basis. Application fee: $60. Electronic applications accepted. *Expenses:* Tuition, state resident: full-time $3874; part-time $334 per credit hour. Tuition, nonresident: full-time $16,394; part-time $861 per credit hour. *Required fees:* $2808; $99 per credit hour. Tuition and fees vary according to program. *Financial support:* Applicants required to submit FAFSA. *Unit head:* Dr. Jeffrey Bailey, Interim Associate Dean, 208-885-6478, E-mail: cbe@uidaho.edu. *Application contact:* Erick Larson, Director of Graduate Admissions, 208-885-4723, E-mail: gadms@uidaho.edu. Web site: http://www.uidaho.edu/cbe/business.

University of Illinois at Chicago, Graduate College, Liautaud Graduate School of Business, Program in Business Administration, Chicago, IL 60607-7128. Offers MBA, PhD, MBA/MA, MBA/MD, MBA/MPH, MBA/MS. *Accreditation:* AACSB. Part-time programs available. *Entrance requirements:* For master's, GMAT, minimum GPA of 2.75; for doctorate, GMAT. Additional exam requirements/recommendations for international students: Required—TOEFL. Electronic applications accepted.

University of Illinois at Springfield, Graduate Programs, College of Business and Management, Program in Business Administration, Springfield, IL 62703-5407. Offers MBA. *Accreditation:* AACSB. Part-time and evening/weekend programs available. *Faculty:* 4 full-time (0 women), 2 part-time/adjunct (0 women). *Students:* 68 full-time (19 women), 85 part-time (36 women); includes 20 minority (7 Black or African American, non-Hispanic/Latino; 1 American Indian or Alaska Native, non-Hispanic/Latino; 9 Asian, non-Hispanic/Latino; 3 Hispanic/Latino), 8 international. Average age 32. 121 applicants, 69% accepted, 53 enrolled. In 2011, 68 master's awarded. *Degree requirements:* For master's, closure course. *Entrance requirements:* For master's, GMAT or substantial supervisory experience and managerial responsibility, minimum cumulative GPA of 2.5; 3 letters of reference; resume; single-spaced essay, no more than two pages, discussing career goals and/or professional aspirations. Additional exam requirements/recommendations for international students: Required—TOEFL (minimum score 550 paper-based; 176 computer-based; 61 iBT). *Application deadline:* Applications are processed on a rolling basis. Application fee: $50 ($60 for international students). Electronic applications accepted. *Expenses:* Tuition, state resident: full-time $6978; part-time $290.75 per credit hour. Tuition, nonresident: full-time $15,282; part-time $636.75 per credit hour. *Required fees:* $2106; $87.75 per credit hour. *Financial support:* In 2011–12, fellowships with full tuition reimbursements (averaging $8,550 per year), research assistantships with full tuition reimbursements (averaging $8,550 per year), teaching assistantships with full tuition reimbursements (averaging $8,550 per year) were awarded; career-related internships or fieldwork, Federal Work-Study, scholarships/grants, health care benefits, and unspecified assistantships also available. Support available to part-time students. Financial award application deadline: 11/15; financial award applicants required to submit FAFSA. *Unit head:* Dr. Mark Puclik, Program Administrator, 217-206-6781, Fax: 217-206-7543, E-mail: puclik.mark@uis.edu. *Application contact:* Dr. Lynn Pardie, Office of Graduate Studies, 800-252-8533, Fax: 217-206-7623, E-mail: lpard1@uis.edu. Web site: http://www.uis.edu/mba/.

University of Illinois at Urbana–Champaign, Graduate College, College of Business, Department of Business Administration, Champaign, IL 61820. Offers business administration (MS, PhD); technology management (MS). *Accreditation:* AACSB. *Faculty:* 42 full-time (6 women), 8 part-time/adjunct (3 women). *Students:* 117 full-time (42 women), 7 part-time (1 woman); includes 6 minority (2 Black or African American, non-Hispanic/Latino; 3 Asian, non-Hispanic/Latino; 1 Two or more races, non-Hispanic/Latino), 99 international. 391 applicants, 31% accepted, 74 enrolled. In 2011, 49 master's, 8 doctorates awarded. *Entrance requirements:* For master's, minimum GPA of 3.0; for doctorate, GMAT or GRE, minimum GPA of 3.0. Additional exam requirements/recommendations for international students: Required—TOEFL (minimum score 550 paper-based; 231 computer-based; 79 iBT) or IELTS (6.5). *Application deadline:* Applications are processed on a rolling basis. Application fee: $75 ($90 for international students). Electronic applications accepted. *Expenses:* Contact institution. *Financial support:* In 2011–12, 28 fellowships, 34 research assistantships, 12 teaching assistantships were awarded; tuition waivers (full and partial) also available. *Unit head:* William J. Qualls, Interim Head, 217-265-0794, Fax: 217-244-7969, E-mail: wqualls@illinois.edu. *Application contact:* J. E. Miller, Coordinator of Graduate Programs, 217-244-8002, Fax: 217-244-7969, E-mail: j-miller@illinois.edu. Web site: http://www.business.illinois.edu/ba/.

University of Illinois at Urbana–Champaign, Graduate College, College of Business, Program in Business Administration, Champaign, IL 61820. Offers MBA, Ed M/MBA, JD/MBA, M Arch/MBA, MCS/MBA, MHRIR/MBA, MS/MBA, PhD/MBA. *Accreditation:* AACSB. Part-time programs available. *Students:* 338 full-time (92 women), 7 part-time (1 woman); includes 74 minority (22 Black or African American, non-Hispanic/Latino; 2 American Indian or Alaska Native, non-Hispanic/Latino; 34 Asian, non-Hispanic/Latino; 10 Hispanic/Latino; 1 Native Hawaiian or other Pacific Islander, non-Hispanic/Latino; 5 Two or more races, non-Hispanic/Latino), 98 international. 882 applicants, 22% accepted, 135 enrolled. In 2011, 203 master's awarded. *Entrance requirements:* For master's, GMAT. Additional exam requirements/recommendations for international students: Required—TOEFL. Application fee: $75 ($90 for international students). Electronic applications accepted. *Financial support:* In 2011–12, 1 fellowship, 4 teaching assistantships were awarded; research assistantships also available. *Unit head:* Stig Lanneskog, Interim Associate Dean, 217-244-8019, Fax: 217-333-1156, E-mail: slanessk@illinois.edu. *Application contact:* Jackie Wilson, Admissions Director, 217-244-2953, Fax: 217-333-1156, E-mail: jjwilson@illinois.edu. Web site: http://www.mba.uiuc.edu/M/.

University of Indianapolis, Graduate Programs, School of Business, Indianapolis, IN 46227-3697. Offers EMBA, MBA, Graduate Certificate. *Accreditation:* ACBSP. Part-time and evening/weekend programs available. *Faculty:* 2 full-time (0 women), 4 part-time/adjunct (1 woman). *Students:* 25 full-time (7 women), 97 part-time (56 women); includes 14 minority (6 Black or African American, non-Hispanic/Latino; 5 Asian, non-Hispanic/Latino; 2 Hispanic/Latino; 1 Two or more races, non-Hispanic/Latino), 13 international. Average age 30. In 2011, 77 master's awarded. *Entrance requirements:* For master's, GMAT, interview, minimum GPA of 2.8, 2 letters of recommendation, resume. Additional exam requirements/recommendations for international students: Required—TOEFL (minimum score 550 paper-based; 213 computer-based). *Application deadline:* Applications are processed on a rolling basis. Application fee: $50. Tuition and fees vary according to degree level and program. *Financial support:* Tuition waivers (full and partial) and unspecified assistantships available. Support available to part-time students. Financial award application deadline: 5/1; financial award applicants required to submit FAFSA. *Unit head:* Dr. Sheela Yadav, Dean, 317-788-3232, E-mail: syadav@uindy.edu. *Application contact:* Stephen A. Tokar, Sr., Director of Graduate Business Programs, 317-788-4905, E-mail: tokarsa@uindy.edu. Web site: http://gradbus.uindy.edu/.

The University of Iowa, Henry B. Tippie College of Business, Department of Finance, Iowa City, IA 52242-1316. Offers PhD. *Faculty:* 22 full-time (4 women), 8 part-time/adjunct (2 women). *Students:* 14 full-time (7 women), 11 international. Average age 31. 88 applicants, 6% accepted, 3 enrolled. In 2011, 3 doctorates awarded. *Degree requirements:* For doctorate, comprehensive exam, thesis/dissertation, thesis defense. *Entrance requirements:* For doctorate, GMAT or GRE. Additional exam requirements/recommendations for international students: Required—TOEFL (minimum score 600 paper-based; 250 computer-based; 100 iBT). *Application deadline:* For fall admission, 1/15 for domestic and international students. Applications are processed on a rolling basis. Application fee: $60 ($100 for international students). Electronic applications accepted. *Financial support:* In 2011–12, 14 students received support, including 14 fellowships with full tuition reimbursements available (averaging $6,000 per year), 14 teaching assistantships with full tuition reimbursements available (averaging $16,575 per year); institutionally sponsored loans, scholarships/grants, health care benefits, and unspecified assistantships also available. Financial award application deadline: 1/15. *Faculty research:* International finance, real estate finance, theoretical and empirical corporate finance, theoretical and empirical asset pricing bond pricing and derivatives. *Unit head:* Prof. Erik Lie, Department Executive Officer, 319-335-0929, Fax: 319-335-3690, E-mail: erik-lie@uiowa.edu. *Application contact:* Renea L. Jay, PhD Program Coordinator, 319-335-0830, Fax: 319-335-1956, E-mail: renea-jay@uiowa.edu. Web site: http://tippie.uiowa.edu/finance/.

The University of Iowa, Henry B. Tippie College of Business, Department of Management and Organizations, Iowa City, IA 52242-1316. Offers PhD. *Accreditation:* AACSB. *Faculty:* 21 full-time (7 women), 29 part-time/adjunct (8 women). *Students:* 14 full-time (4 women); includes 2 minority (both Hispanic/Latino), 1 international. Average age 32. 51 applicants, 8% accepted, 3 enrolled. In 2011, 3 doctorates awarded. *Degree requirements:* For doctorate, comprehensive exam, thesis/dissertation, thesis defense. *Entrance requirements:* For doctorate, GMAT or GRE. Additional exam requirements/recommendations for international students: Required—TOEFL (minimum score 600 paper-based; 250 computer-based; 100 iBT). *Application deadline:* For fall admission, 1/15 for domestic and international students. Applications are processed on a rolling basis. Application fee: $60 ($100 for international students). Electronic applications accepted. *Financial support:* In 2011–12, 14 students received support, including 3 fellowships with full tuition reimbursements available (averaging $16,908 per year), 11 teaching assistantships with full tuition reimbursements available (averaging $16,908 per year); institutionally sponsored loans, scholarships/grants, health care benefits, and unspecified assistantships also available. Financial award application deadline: 1/15; financial award applicants required to submit FAFSA. *Faculty research:* Decision-making, human resources, personal selection, organizational behavior, training. *Unit head:* Prof. Jay Christensen-Szalanski, Department Executive Officer, 319-335-0927, Fax: 319-335-1956, E-mail: jay-christensen-szalanski@uiowa.edu. *Application contact:* Renea L. Jay, PhD Program Coordinator, 319-335-0830, Fax: 319-335-1956, E-mail: renea-jay@uiowa.edu. Web site: http://tippie.uiowa.edu/management-organizations/.

The University of Iowa, Henry B. Tippie College of Business, Department of Management Sciences, Iowa City, IA 52242-1316. Offers business administration (PhD), including management sciences. *Accreditation:* AACSB. *Faculty:* 18 full-time (3 women), 9 part-time/adjunct (1 woman). *Students:* 15 full-time (6 women), 1 (woman) part-time; includes 1 minority (Asian, non-Hispanic/Latino), 13 international. Average age 29. 22 applicants, 18% accepted, 4 enrolled. In 2011, 1 doctorate awarded. *Degree requirements:* For doctorate, comprehensive exam, thesis/dissertation, thesis defense. *Entrance requirements:* For doctorate, GRE General Test or GMAT. Additional exam requirements/recommendations for international students: Required—TOEFL (minimum score 600 paper-based; 250 computer-based; 100 iBT). *Application deadline:* For fall admission, 2/1 for domestic and international students. Applications are processed on a rolling basis. Application fee: $60 ($100 for international students). Electronic applications accepted. *Financial support:* In 2011–12, 15 students received support, including 2 research assistantships with full tuition reimbursements available (averaging $16,908 per year), 13 teaching assistantships with full tuition reimbursements available (averaging $16,908 per year); institutionally sponsored loans, scholarships/grants, health care benefits, and unspecified assistantships also available. Financial award application deadline: 2/1. *Faculty research:* Optimization, supply chain management, data mining, logistics, database management. *Unit head:* Prof. Kurt Anstreicher, Department Executive Officer, 319-335-0858, Fax: 319-335-1956, E-mail: kurt-anstreicher@uiowa.edu. *Application contact:* Renea L. Jay, PhD Program Coordinator, 319-335-0830, Fax: 319-335-1956, E-mail: renea-jay@uiowa.edu. Web site: http://tippie.uiowa.edu/management-sciences/.

The University of Iowa, Henry B. Tippie College of Business, Henry B. Tippie School of Management, Iowa City, IA 52242-1316. Offers finance (MBA); investment management (MBA); marketing (MBA); process and operations excellence (MBA); strategic innovation (MBA); JD/MBA; MBA/MA; MBA/MD; MBA/MHA; MBA/MSN. *Accreditation:* AACSB. Part-time and evening/weekend programs available. *Faculty:* 62 full-time (19 women), 26 part-time/adjunct (6 women). *Students:* 153 full-time (34 women), 876 part-time (288 women); includes 87 minority (16 Black or African American, non-Hispanic/Latino; 4 American Indian or Alaska Native, non-Hispanic/Latino; 43 Asian, non-Hispanic/Latino; 24 Hispanic/Latino), 130 international. Average age 32. 697 applicants, 66% accepted, 362 enrolled. In 2011, 361 master's awarded. *Degree requirements:* For master's, minimum GPA of 2.75. *Entrance requirements:* For master's, GMAT, quality work experience and leadership as shown through resume, references, and essays. Additional exam requirements/recommendations for international students: Required—TOEFL (minimum score 600 paper-based; 250 computer-based; 100 iBT), IELTS (minimum score 7). *Application deadline:* For fall admission, 7/30 for domestic students, 4/15 for international students; for spring admission, 12/15 for domestic and international students. Applications are processed on a rolling basis. Application fee: $60 ($100 for international students). Electronic applications accepted. *Expenses:* Contact institution. *Financial support:* In 2011–12, 110 students received support, including 110 fellowships (averaging $9,059 per year), 82 research assistantships with partial tuition reimbursements available (averaging $8,609 per year), 16 teaching assistantships with partial tuition reimbursements available (averaging $14,530 per year); career-related internships or fieldwork, scholarships/grants, health care benefits, and unspecified assistantships also available. Financial award application deadline: 4/15; financial award applicants required to submit FAFSA. *Faculty research:* Capital markets, econometrics, optimization, investments and empirical corporate finance, Iowa electronic markets. *Unit head:* Prof. Jarjisu Sa-Aadu, Associate Dean, MBA Programs, 800-622-4692, Fax: 319-335-3604, E-mail: jsa-aadu@uiowa.edu. *Application contact:* Jodi Schafer, Director of Admissions and Financial Aid, 319-335-0864, Fax: 319-335-3604, E-mail: jodi-schafer@uiowa.edu. Web site: http://tippie.uiowa.edu/mba.

The University of Kansas, Graduate Studies, School of Business, Program in Business, Lawrence, KS 66045. Offers PhD. *Accreditation:* AACSB. *Faculty:* 60 full-time (11 women), 54 part-time/adjunct (16 women). *Students:* 81 full-time (23 women), 1 part-time (0 women); includes 9 minority (2 Black or African American, non-Hispanic/Latino; 1 American Indian or Alaska Native, non-Hispanic/Latino; 5 Asian, non-Hispanic/Latino; 1 Two or more races, non-Hispanic/Latino), 25 international. Average age 35. 261 applicants, 27% accepted, 45 enrolled. In 2011, 3 doctorates awarded. *Degree requirements:* For doctorate, comprehensive exam, thesis/dissertation, departmental qualifying exam. *Entrance requirements:* For doctorate, GMAT or GRE. Additional exam requirements/recommendations for international students: Required—TOEFL (minimum score 600 paper-based; 250 computer-based; 100 iBT). *Application deadline:* For fall admission, 1/10 for domestic and international students. Applications are processed on a rolling basis. Application fee: $65. Electronic applications accepted. Tuition and fees vary according to course load, campus/location, program and reciprocity agreements. *Financial support:* Fellowships with full tuition reimbursements, research assistantships with full tuition reimbursements, teaching assistantships with full tuition reimbursements, scholarships/grants, health care benefits, tuition waivers (full), and unspecified assistantships available. *Faculty research:* Tax, mergers and acquisitions, risk analysis personality and work outcomes, services, marketing, business ethics, corporate turnarounds. *Unit head:* Charly Edmonds, Director, 785-864-3841, Fax: 785-864-5376, E-mail: bschoolphd@ku.edu. *Application contact:* Charly Edmonds, Director, 785-864-3841, E-mail: bschoolphd@ku.edu. Web site: http://www.business.ku.edu/.

The University of Kansas, Graduate Studies, School of Business, Program in Business Administration and Management, Lawrence, KS 66045. Offers finance (MBA); human resources management (MBA); information systems (MBA); international business (MBA); management (MBA); marketing (MBA); strategic management (MBA); JD/MBA; MBA/MA; MBA/MM; MBA/MS; MBA/Pharm D. *Accreditation:* AACSB. Part-time programs available. *Faculty:* 57 full-time (12 women), 20 part-time/adjunct (13 women). *Students:* 159 full-time (51 women), 233 part-time (69 women); includes 58 minority (15 Black or African American, non-Hispanic/Latino; 3 American Indian or Alaska Native, non-Hispanic/Latino; 23 Asian, non-Hispanic/Latino; 11 Hispanic/Latino; 6 Two or more races, non-Hispanic/Latino), 41 international. Average age 30. 173 applicants, 72% accepted, 91 enrolled. In 2011, 135 degrees awarded. *Degree requirements:* For master's, comprehensive exam (for some programs), thesis optional. *Entrance requirements:* For master's, GMAT, 2 years of professional work experience. Additional exam requirements/recommendations for international students: Required—TOEFL (minimum score 53 paper-based; 20 computer-based); Recommended—IELTS (minimum score 6). *Application deadline:* For fall admission, 6/1 priority date for domestic students, 5/1 for international students; for spring admission, 11/1 priority date for domestic students, 10/1 for international students. Applications are processed on a rolling basis. Application fee: $65. Electronic applications accepted. Tuition and fees vary according to course load, campus/location, program and reciprocity agreements. *Financial support:* Research assistantships, career-related internships or fieldwork, Federal Work-Study, institutionally sponsored loans, scholarships/grants, and unspecified assistantships available. Financial award application deadline: 6/1; financial award applicants required to submit FAFSA. *Faculty research:* Advanced audit technologies, real options and asset pricing, corporate governance, foreign direct investment, CEO characteristics and organizational innovation. *Unit head:* Dr. Cathy Shenoy, Director of MBA Programs, 785-864-7519, E-mail: cshenoy@ku.edu. *Application contact:* Dee Steinle, Administrative Director of Master's Programs, 785-864-7596, Fax: 785-864-5376, E-mail: dsteinle@ku.edu. Web site: http://www.business.ku.edu/.

University of Kentucky, Graduate School, Gatton College of Business and Economics, Program in Business Administration, Lexington, KY 40506-0032. Offers MBA, PhD. *Accreditation:* AACSB. *Degree requirements:* For master's, comprehensive exam; for doctorate, comprehensive exam, thesis/dissertation. *Entrance requirements:* For master's, GMAT, minimum undergraduate GPA of 2.75; for doctorate, GMAT, minimum undergraduate GPA of 3.0. Additional exam requirements/recommendations for international students: Required—TOEFL (minimum score 550 paper-based; 213 computer-based). Electronic applications accepted. *Faculty research:* Expert systems in manufacturing, knowledge acquisition and management, financial institutions, market in service organizations, strategic planning.

University of La Verne, College of Business and Public Management, Graduate Programs in Business Administration, La Verne, CA 91750-4443. Offers accounting (MBA); executive management (MBA-EP); finance (MBA, MBA-EP); health services management (MBA); information technology (MBA, MBA-EP); international business (MBA, MBA-EP); leadership (MBA-EP); managed care (MBA); management (MBA, MBA-EP); marketing (MBA, MBA-EP). Part-time and evening/weekend programs available. *Faculty:* 34 full-time (15 women), 38 part-time/adjunct (13 women). *Students:* 525 full-time (243 women), 231 part-time (114 women); includes 199 minority (27 Black or African American, non-Hispanic/Latino; 1 American Indian or Alaska Native, non-Hispanic/Latino; 55 Asian, non-Hispanic/Latino; 113 Hispanic/Latino; 3 Two or more races, non-Hispanic/Latino), 436 international. Average age 28. In 2011, 403 master's awarded. *Entrance requirements:* For master's, minimum undergraduate GPA of 3.0, 2 letters of recommendation, resume. Additional exam requirements/recommendations for international students: Required—TOEFL (minimum score 550 paper-based; 213 computer-based). *Application deadline:* Applications are processed on a rolling basis. Application fee: $50. *Expenses:* Contact institution. *Financial support:* Career-related internships or fieldwork, institutionally sponsored loans, and scholarships/grants available. Financial award application deadline: 3/2; financial award applicants required to submit FAFSA. *Unit head:* Dr. Abe Helou, Chairperson, 909-593-3511 Ext. 4211, Fax: 909-392-2704, E-mail: ihelou@laverne.edu. *Application contact:* Rina Lazarian, Program and Admission Specialist, 909-593-3511 Ext. 4819, Fax: 909-392-2704, E-mail: cbpm@ulv.edu.

University of La Verne, College of Business and Public Management, Program in Organizational Management and Leadership, La Verne, CA 91750-4443. Offers nonprofit management (Certificate); organizational leadership (Certificate); organizational management and leadership (MS). Part-time programs available. *Faculty:* 34 full-time (15 women), 38 part-time/adjunct (13 women). *Students:* 87 full-time (44 women), 78 part-time (56 women); includes 70 minority (13 Black or African American, non-Hispanic/Latino; 12 Asian, non-Hispanic/Latino; 43 Hispanic/Latino; 2 Two or more races, non-Hispanic/Latino), 48 international. Average age 33. In 2011, 138 master's awarded. *Degree requirements:* For master's, thesis or research project. *Entrance requirements:* For master's, minimum undergraduate GPA of 2.75, 2 letters of recommendation, interview, resume. Additional exam requirements/recommendations for international students: Required—TOEFL (minimum score 550 paper-based; 213 computer-based). *Application deadline:* Applications are processed on a rolling basis. Application fee: $50. *Expenses:* Contact institution. *Financial support:* Institutionally sponsored loans available. Financial award application deadline: 3/2; financial award applicants required to submit FAFSA. *Unit head:* Dr. Kathy Duncan, Program Director, 909-593-3511 Ext. 4415, E-mail: kduncan2@laverne.edu. *Application contact:* Program and Admissions Specialist, 909-593-3511 Ext. 4819, Fax: 909-392-2761, E-mail: cbpm@laverne.edu. Web site: http://laverne.edu/catalog/program/ms-leadership-and-management/.

University of La Verne, Regional Campus Administration, Graduate Programs, Central Coast/Vandenberg Air Force Base Campuses, La Verne, CA 91750-4443. Offers business (MBA-EP), including health services management, information technology; health administration (MHA); leadership and management (MS). *Entrance requirements:* For master's, 2 letters of recommendation, resume. *Expenses:* Contact institution.

University of La Verne, Regional Campus Administration, Graduate Programs, High Desert Campus, Victorville, CA 92392. Offers business (MBA). *Entrance requirements:* For master's, 2 letters of recommendation, resume. *Expenses:* Contact institution.

University of La Verne, Regional Campus Administration, Graduate Programs, Inland Empire Campus, Rancho Cucamonga, CA 91730. Offers business (MBA-EP), including health services management, information technology, management, marketing; leadership and management (MS). *Entrance requirements:* For master's, 2 letters of recommendation, resume. *Expenses:* Contact institution.

University of La Verne, Regional Campus Administration, Graduate Programs, Kern County Campus, Bakersfield, CA 93301. Offers business (MBA-EP); health administration (MHA); leadership and management (MS). *Entrance requirements:* For master's, 2 letters of recommendation, resume. *Expenses:* Contact institution.

University of La Verne, Regional Campus Administration, Graduate Programs, Orange County Campus, Garden Grove, CA 92840. Offers business (MBA); health administration (MHA); leadership and management (MS). *Entrance requirements:* For master's, 2 letters of recommendation, resume. *Expenses:* Contact institution.

University of La Verne, Regional Campus Administration, Graduate Programs, San Fernando Valley Campus, Burbank, CA 91505. Offers business (MBA-EP); leadership and management (MS). *Entrance requirements:* For master's, 2 letters of recommendation, resume. *Expenses:* Contact institution.

University of La Verne, Regional Campus Administration, Graduate Programs, Ventura County/Point Mugu Naval Air Station Campuses, La Verne, CA 91750-4443. Offers leadership and management (MS). *Entrance requirements:* For master's, 2 letters of recommendation, resume. *Expenses:* Contact institution.

University of La Verne, Regional Campus Administration, Graduate Program, ULV Online, La Verne, CA 91750-4443. Offers business administration (MBA). *Entrance requirements:* For master's, resume, 2 letters of recommendation. *Expenses: Tuition:* Part-time $645 per credit hour.

University of Lethbridge, School of Graduate Studies, Lethbridge, AB T1K 3M4, Canada. Offers accounting (MScM); addictions counseling (M Sc); agricultural biotechnology (M Sc); agricultural studies (M Sc, MA); anthropology (MA); archaeology (MA); art (MA, MFA); biochemistry (M Sc); biological sciences (M Sc); biomolecular science (PhD); biosystems and biodiversity (PhD); Canadian studies (MA); chemistry (M Sc); computer science (M Sc); computer science and geographical information science (M Sc); counseling psychology (M Ed); dramatic arts (MA); earth, space, and physical science (PhD); economics (MA); educational leadership (M Ed); English (MA); environmental science (M Sc); evolution and behavior (PhD); exercise science (M Sc); finance (MScM); French (MA); French/German (MA); French/Spanish (MA); general education (M Ed); general management (MScM); geography (M Sc, MA); German (MA); health science (M Sc); history (MA); human resource management and labour relations (MScM); individualized multidisciplinary (M Sc, MA); information systems (MScM); international management (MScM); kinesiology (M Sc, MA); management (M Sc, MA); marketing (MScM); mathematics (M Sc); music (M Mus, MA); Native American studies (MA); neuroscience (M Sc, PhD); new media (MA); nursing (M Sc); philosophy (MA); physics (M Sc); policy and strategy (MScM); political science (MA); psychology (M Sc, MA); religious studies (MA); social sciences (MA); sociology (MA); theatre and dramatic arts (MFA); theoretical and computational science (PhD); urban and regional studies (MA); women's studies (MA). Part-time and evening/weekend programs available. *Degree requirements:* For doctorate, comprehensive exam, thesis/dissertation. *Entrance requirements:* For master's, GMAT (M Sc in management), bachelor's degree in related field, minimum GPA of 3.0 during previous 20 graded semester courses, 2 years teaching or related experience (M Ed); for doctorate, master's degree, minimum graduate GPA of 3.5. Additional exam requirements/recommendations for international students: Required—TOEFL. *Faculty research:* Movement and brain plasticity, gibberellin physiology, photosynthesis, carbon cycling, molecular properties of main-group ring components.

University of Louisiana at Lafayette, BI Moody III College of Business Administration MBA Program, Lafayette, LA 70504. Offers MBA. *Accreditation:* AACSB. Part-time and evening/weekend programs available. *Entrance requirements:* For master's, GRE General Test. Additional exam requirements/recommendations for international students: Required—TOEFL (minimum score 550 paper-based; 213 computer-based).

University of Louisiana at Monroe, Graduate School, College of Business Administration, Monroe, LA 71209-0001. Offers MBA. *Accreditation:* AACSB. Part-time and evening/weekend programs available. *Faculty:* 8 full-time (2 women). *Students:* 27 full-time (11 women), 53 part-time (17 women); includes 11 minority (9 Black or African American, non-Hispanic/Latino; 2 Asian, non-Hispanic/Latino), 19 international. Average age 28. 19 applicants, 79% accepted, 14 enrolled. In 2011, 29 master's awarded. *Degree requirements:* For master's, comprehensive exam. *Entrance requirements:* For master's, GMAT, minimum GPA of 2.5, minimum AACSB index of 950. Additional exam requirements/recommendations for international students: Required—TOEFL (minimum score 500 paper-based; 61 computer-based). *Application deadline:* For fall admission, 8/24 for domestic students, 7/1 for international students; for winter admission, 12/14 for domestic students; for spring admission, 1/19 for domestic students, 11/1 for international students. Applications are processed on a rolling basis. Application fee: $20 ($30 for international students). Electronic applications accepted. *Expenses:* Tuition, state resident: full-time $3436; part-time $240 per credit hour. Tuition, nonresident: full-time $3436; part-time $240 per credit hour. *International tuition:* $10,733 full-time. *Required fees:* $1460.90. *Financial support:* In 2011–12, 17 research assistantships with full tuition reimbursements (averaging $2,500 per year) were awarded; career-related internships or fieldwork, Federal Work-Study, and unspecified assistantships also available. Financial award application deadline: 4/1; financial award applicants required to submit FAFSA. *Faculty research:* Information assurance framework, TPB in e-learning, bias in balanced scorecard. *Unit head:* Dr. Ronald Berry, Dean, 318-342-1100, Fax: 318-342-1101, E-mail: rberry@ulm.edu. *Application contact:* Dr. Donna Walton Luse, Program Chair, 318-342-1106, Fax: 318-342-1101, E-mail: luse@ulm.edu. Web site: http://www.ulm.edu/mba/.

University of Louisville, Graduate School, College of Business, MBA Programs, Louisville, KY 40292-0001. Offers entrepreneurship (MBA); global business (MBA); health sector management (weekend format) (MBA). *Accreditation:* AACSB. Part-time and evening/weekend programs available. *Faculty:* 28 full-time (8 women), 3 part-time/adjunct (1 woman). *Students:* 111 full-time (35 women), 112 part-time (33 women); includes 19 minority (4 Black or African American, non-Hispanic/Latino; 1 American Indian or Alaska Native, non-Hispanic/Latino; 7 Asian, non-Hispanic/Latino; 3 Hispanic/Latino; 4 Two or more races, non-Hispanic/Latino), 12 international. Average age 29. 223 applicants, 53% accepted, 94 enrolled. In 2011, 119 degrees awarded. *Degree requirements:* For master's, international learning experience. *Entrance requirements:* For master's, GMAT, 2 letters of reference, personal interview, resume, personal statement, college transcript(s). Additional exam requirements/recommendations for international students: Required—TOEFL (minimum score 83 iBT). *Application deadline:* For fall admission, 7/1 for domestic students; for spring admission, 12/1 for domestic students. Applications are processed on a rolling basis. Application fee: $50. *Expenses:* Tuition, state resident: full-time $9692; part-time $539 per credit hour. Tuition, nonresident: full-time $20,168; part-time $1121 per credit hour. Tuition and fees vary according to program and reciprocity agreements. *Financial support:* In 2011–12, 16 students received support, including 3 fellowships with full tuition reimbursements available (averaging $15,500 per year), 10 research assistantships with full tuition reimbursements available (averaging $12,000 per year); health care benefits and unspecified assistantships also available. Financial award application deadline: 3/31; financial award applicants required to submit FAFSA. *Faculty research:* Entrepreneurship, venture capital, retailing/franchising, corporate governance and leadership, supply chain management. *Unit head:* Dr. R. Charles Moyer, Dean, 502-852-6443, Fax: 502-852-7557, E-mail: charlie.moyer@louisville.edu. *Application contact:* L. Eddie Smith, Director of IT and Master's Programs Admissions/Recruiting Manager, 502-852-7257, Fax: 502-852-4901, E-mail: eddie.smith@louisville.edu. Web site: http://business.louisville.edu/mba.

University of Maine, Graduate School, College of Business, Public Policy and Health, The Maine Business School, Orono, ME 04469. Offers accounting (MBA); business and sustainability (MBA); finance (MBA); management (MBA). *Accreditation:* AACSB. Part-time and evening/weekend programs available. *Faculty:* 20 full-time (8 women), 6 part-time/adjunct (2 women). *Students:* 47 full-time (19 women), 15 part-time (2 women); includes 5 minority (1 American Indian or Alaska Native, non-Hispanic/Latino; 2 Asian, non-Hispanic/Latino; 2 Hispanic/Latino), 5 international. Average age 29. 41 applicants, 71% accepted, 24 enrolled. In 2011, 28 master's awarded. *Entrance requirements:* For master's, GMAT. Additional exam requirements/recommendations for international students: Required—TOEFL (minimum score 550 paper-based; 213 computer-based). *Application deadline:* For fall admission, 6/1 priority date for domestic students, 6/1 for international students; for spring admission, 11/1 priority date for domestic students, 11/1 for international students. Applications are processed on a rolling basis. Application fee: $65. Electronic applications accepted. *Expenses:* Contact institution. *Financial support:* In 2011–12, 16 students received support, including 3 teaching assistantships with full tuition reimbursements available (averaging $13,600 per year); career-related internships or fieldwork, Federal Work-Study, institutionally sponsored loans, scholarships/grants, tuition waivers (full and partial), and unspecified assistantships also available. Financial award application deadline: 3/1. *Faculty research:* Entrepreneurship, investment management, international markets, decision support systems, strategic planning. *Unit head:* Dr. Nory Jones, Director of Graduate Programs, 207-581-1971, Fax: 207-581-1930, E-mail: mba@maine.edu. *Application contact:* Scott G. Delcourt, Associate Dean of the Graduate School, 207-581-3291, Fax: 207-581-3232, E-mail: graduate@maine.edu. Web site: http://www.umaine.edu/business/.

University of Management and Technology, Program in Business Administration, Arlington, VA 22209. Offers acquisition management (DBA); general management (MBA, DBA); project management (MBA, DBA). Part-time and evening/weekend programs available. Postbaccalaureate distance learning degree programs offered (no on-campus study). *Degree requirements:* For master's, comprehensive exam. *Entrance requirements:* For master's, 3 recommendations, resume. Additional exam requirements/recommendations for international students: Required—TOEFL (minimum score 550 paper-based; 213 computer-based). Electronic applications accepted.

University of Management and Technology, Program in Management, Arlington, VA 22209. Offers acquisition management (MS, AC); general management (MS); project management (MS, AC); public administration (MPA, MS, AC). Part-time and evening/weekend programs available. Postbaccalaureate distance learning degree programs offered (no on-campus study). *Entrance requirements:* For master's, 3 recommendations, resume. Additional exam requirements/recommendations for international students: Required—TOEFL (minimum score 550 paper-based; 213 computer-based). Electronic applications accepted.

The University of Manchester, Manchester Business School, Manchester, United Kingdom. Offers accounting (M Phil, PhD); business (M Ent, D Ent); business and management (M Phil); business management (PhD).

University of Manitoba, Faculty of Graduate Studies, Asper School of Business, Winnipeg, MB R3T 2N2, Canada. Offers M Sc, MBA, PhD. *Accreditation:* AACSB.

University of Mary, Gary Tharaldson School of Business, Bismarck, ND 58504-9652. Offers accountancy (MBA); business administration (MBA); health care (MBA); human resource management (MBA); management (MBA); project management (MPM); strategic leadership (MSSL). Part-time and evening/weekend programs available. *Faculty:* 8 full-time (5 women), 66 part-time/adjunct (22 women). *Students:* 340 full-time (190 women), 189 part-time (91 women); includes 69 minority (28 Black or African American, non-Hispanic/Latino; 25 American Indian or Alaska Native, non-Hispanic/Latino; 7 Asian, non-Hispanic/Latino; 7 Hispanic/Latino; 1 Native Hawaiian or other Pacific Islander, non-Hispanic/Latino; 1 Two or more races, non-Hispanic/Latino), 14 international. Average age 35. 207 applicants, 95% accepted, 148 enrolled. In 2011, 265 master's awarded. *Degree requirements:* For master's, strategic planning seminar. *Entrance requirements:* For master's, minimum GPA of 2.5. Additional exam requirements/recommendations for international students: Required—TOEFL (minimum score 500 paper-based; 197 computer-based; 71 iBT). *Application deadline:* Applications are processed on a rolling basis. Application fee: $40. *Financial support:* Application deadline: 8/1; applicants required to submit FAFSA. *Unit head:* Dr. Shanda Traiser, Director of the School of Accelerated and Distance Education, 701-355-8160, Fax: 701-255-7687, E-mail: straiser@umary.edu. *Application contact:* Wayne G. Maruska, Graduate Program Advisor, 701-355-8134, Fax: 701-255-7687, E-mail: wmaruska@umary.edu.

University of Mary Hardin-Baylor, Graduate Studies in Business Administration, Belton, TX 76513. Offers accounting (MBA); information systems management (MBA); management (MBA). Part-time and evening/weekend programs available. *Faculty:* 11 full-time (4 women), 5 part-time/adjunct (3 women). *Students:* 48 full-time (26 women), 23 part-time (12 women); includes 19 minority (7 Black or African American, non-Hispanic/Latino; 1 Asian, non-Hispanic/Latino; 11 Hispanic/Latino), 29 international. Average age 29. 102 applicants, 69% accepted, 25 enrolled. In 2011, 11 master's awarded. *Degree requirements:* For master's, comprehensive exam. *Entrance requirements:* For master's, GMAT, minimum GPA of 3.0, work experience, interview. *Application deadline:* For fall admission, 6/1 priority date for domestic students; for spring admission, 11/1 for domestic students. Applications are processed on a rolling basis. Application fee: $35 ($135 for international students). Electronic applications accepted. *Expenses: Tuition:* Full-time $12,780. *Required fees:* $2350. *Financial support:* Federal Work-Study and scholarships (for some active duty military personnel only) available. Financial award applicants required to submit FAFSA. *Unit head:* Dr. Terry Fox, Program Director, 254-295-5406, E-mail: terry.fox@umhb.edu. *Application contact:* Melissa Ford, Director of Graduate Admissions, 254-295-4020, Fax: 254-295-5301, E-mail: mford@umhb.edu.

University of Maryland, College Park, Academic Affairs, Joint Program in Business and Management/Public Policy, College Park, MD 20742. Offers MBA/MPM. *Accreditation:* AACSB. *Students:* 18 full-time (7 women); includes 3 minority (2 Black or African American, non-Hispanic/Latino; 1 Two or more races, non-Hispanic/Latino), 1 international. 53 applicants, 32% accepted, 11 enrolled. *Application deadline:* For fall admission, 4/1 for domestic students, 2/1 for international students; for spring admission, 10/15 for domestic students, 6/1 for international students. Applications are processed on a rolling basis. Application fee: $75. Electronic applications accepted. *Expenses: Tuition, area resident:* Part-time $525 per credit hour. Tuition, state resident: part-time $525 per credit hour. Tuition, nonresident: part-time $1131 per credit hour. *Required fees:* $386.31 per term. Tuition and fees vary according to program. *Financial support:* In 2011–12, 2 fellowships with full tuition reimbursements (averaging $29,929 per year), 1 research assistantship (averaging $20,094 per year), 11 teaching assistantships (averaging $15,540 per year) were awarded. Financial award applicants required to submit FAFSA. *Unit head:* Dr. Charles Caramello, Dean of the Graduate School, 301-405-0358, Fax: 301-314-9305. *Application contact:* Dean of Graduate School, 301-405-0358, Fax: 301-314-9305.

University of Maryland, College Park, Academic Affairs, Robert H. Smith School of Business, Combined MSW/MBA Program, College Park, MD 20742. Offers MSW/MBA.

Business Administration and Management—General

Accreditation: AACSB. *Students:* 1 (woman) full-time, all international. 3 applicants, 33% accepted, 0 enrolled. *Entrance requirements:* Additional exam requirements/recommendations for international students: Required—TOEFL. *Application deadline:* For fall admission, 5/1 priority date for domestic students, 2/1 for international students; for spring admission, 11/30 for domestic students, 6/1 for international students. Application fee: $75. *Expenses: Tuition, area resident:* Part-time $525 per credit hour. Tuition, state resident: part-time $525 per credit hour. Tuition, nonresident: part-time $1131 per credit hour. *Required fees:* $386.31 per term. Tuition and fees vary according to program. *Financial support:* In 2011–12, 1 teaching assistantship (averaging $14,772 per year) was awarded; fellowships and research assistantships also available. *Unit head:* Dr. Anand Anandalingam, Dean, 301-405-0582, E-mail: ganand@umd.edu. *Application contact:* Dr. Charles A. Caramello, Dean of Graduate School, 301-405-0358, Fax: 301-314-9305.

University of Maryland, College Park, Academic Affairs, Robert H. Smith School of Business, Executive MBA Program, College Park, MD 20742. Offers EMBA. *Accreditation:* AACSB. *Students:* 80 full-time (18 women), 1 part-time (0 women); includes 25 minority (16 Black or African American, non-Hispanic/Latino; 8 Asian, non-Hispanic/Latino; 1 Two or more races, non-Hispanic/Latino), 1 international. 24 applicants, 96% accepted, 23 enrolled. In 2011, 21 master's awarded. *Entrance requirements:* For master's, minimum GPA of 3.0, 7-12 years professional experience. Additional exam requirements/recommendations for international students: Required—TOEFL. *Application deadline:* For fall admission, 5/1 priority date for domestic students, 2/1 for international students; for spring admission, 11/30 for domestic students, 6/1 for international students. Application fee: $75. *Expenses: Tuition, area resident:* Part-time $525 per credit hour. Tuition, state resident: part-time $525 per credit hour. Tuition, nonresident: part-time $1131 per credit hour. *Required fees:* $386.31 per term. Tuition and fees vary according to program. *Financial support:* In 2011–12, 11 fellowships with full and partial tuition reimbursements (averaging $12,545 per year) were awarded. *Unit head:* Anand Anandalingam, Dean, 301-405-5082, E-mail: ganand@umd.edu. *Application contact:* Dr. Charles A. Caramello, Dean of Graduate School, 301-405-0358, Fax: 301-314-9305, E-mail: ccaramel@umd.edu.

University of Maryland, College Park, Academic Affairs, Robert H. Smith School of Business, Joint Program in Business and Management, College Park, MD 20742. Offers MBA/MS. *Accreditation:* AACSB. *Students:* 5 full-time (1 woman), 12 part-time (3 women); includes 6 minority (1 American Indian or Alaska Native, non-Hispanic/Latino; 3 Asian, non-Hispanic/Latino; 2 Hispanic/Latino), 3 international. 15 applicants, 40% accepted, 3 enrolled. *Entrance requirements:* Additional exam requirements/recommendations for international students: Required—TOEFL. *Application deadline:* For fall admission, 5/1 for domestic students, 2/1 for international students; for spring admission, 11/30 for domestic students, 6/1 for international students. Applications are processed on a rolling basis. Application fee: $75. Electronic applications accepted. *Expenses: Tuition, area resident:* Part-time $525 per credit hour. Tuition, state resident: part-time $525 per credit hour. Tuition, nonresident: part-time $1131 per credit hour. *Required fees:* $386.31 per term. Tuition and fees vary according to program. *Financial support:* In 2011–12, 1 fellowship with full tuition reimbursement (averaging $39,858 per year), 1 teaching assistantship (averaging $14,772 per year) were awarded. *Unit head:* Dr. Anand Anandalingam, Dean, 301-405-0582, E-mail: ganand@umd.edu. *Application contact:* Dr. Charles A. Caramello, Dean of Graduate School, 301-405-0358, Fax: 301-314-9305.

University of Maryland, College Park, Academic Affairs, Robert H. Smith School of Business, Program in Business Administration, College Park, MD 20742. Offers MBA. *Accreditation:* AACSB. Part-time and evening/weekend programs available. Postbaccalaureate distance learning degree programs offered. *Students:* 793 full-time (234 women), 374 part-time (125 women); includes 324 minority (103 Black or African American, non-Hispanic/Latino; 174 Asian, non-Hispanic/Latino; 34 Hispanic/Latino; 1 Native Hawaiian or other Pacific Islander, non-Hispanic/Latino; 12 Two or more races, non-Hispanic/Latino), 170 international. 1,215 applicants, 53% accepted, 396 enrolled. In 2011, 480 master's awarded. *Entrance requirements:* For master's, GMAT, minimum GPA of 3.0, resume, 3 letters of recommendation. Additional exam requirements/recommendations for international students: Required—TOEFL. *Application deadline:* For fall admission, 5/1 for domestic students, 2/1 for international students; for spring admission, 11/30 for domestic students, 6/1 for international students. Applications are processed on a rolling basis. Application fee: $75. Electronic applications accepted. *Expenses: Tuition, area resident:* Part-time $525 per credit hour. Tuition, state resident: part-time $525 per credit hour. Tuition, nonresident: part-time $1131 per credit hour. *Required fees:* $386.31 per term. Tuition and fees vary according to program. *Financial support:* In 2011–12, 33 fellowships with full and partial tuition reimbursements (averaging $28,929 per year), 114 teaching assistantships (averaging $14,914 per year) were awarded. Financial award applicants required to submit FAFSA. *Faculty research:* Accounting, entrepreneurship, finance management and organization, management server and statistical information systems. *Unit head:* Dr. Anand Anandalingam, Dean, 301-405-0582, E-mail: ganand@umd.edu. *Application contact:* Dr. Charles A. Caramello, Dean of Graduate School, 301-405-0358, Fax: 301-314-9305.

University of Maryland, College Park, Academic Affairs, Robert H. Smith School of Business, Program in Business and Management, College Park, MD 20742. Offers MS, PhD. *Accreditation:* AACSB. Part-time programs available. *Students:* 444 full-time (253 women), 89 part-time (49 women); includes 78 minority (39 Black or African American, non-Hispanic/Latino; 36 Asian, non-Hispanic/Latino; 3 Hispanic/Latino), 377 international. 2,183 applicants, 31% accepted, 332 enrolled. In 2011, 86 master's, 17 doctorates awarded. *Degree requirements:* For master's, thesis optional; for doctorate, comprehensive exam, thesis/dissertation. *Entrance requirements:* For master's, GMAT, minimum GPA of 3.0, resume, 2 letters of recommendation; for doctorate, GMAT or GRE General Test, minimum GPA of 3.0, resume, 2 letters of recommendation. Additional exam requirements/recommendations for international students: Required—TOEFL. *Application deadline:* For fall admission, 12/15 for domestic and international students. Applications are processed on a rolling basis. Application fee: $75. Electronic applications accepted. *Expenses: Tuition, area resident:* Part-time $525 per credit hour. Tuition, state resident: part-time $525 per credit hour. Tuition, nonresident: part-time $1131 per credit hour. *Required fees:* $386.31 per term. Tuition and fees vary according to program. *Financial support:* In 2011–12, 9 fellowships with full and partial tuition reimbursements (averaging $14,444 per year), 2 research assistantships with tuition reimbursements (averaging $20,526 per year), 87 teaching assistantships with tuition reimbursements (averaging $22,122 per year) were awarded. Financial award applicants required to submit FAFSA. *Unit head:* Anand Anandallngam, Dean, 301-405-0582, E-mail: ganand@umd.edu. *Application contact:* Dr. Charles A. Caramello, Dean of Graduate School, 301-405-0358, Fax: 301-314-9305.

University of Maryland, College Park, Academic Affairs, Robert H. Smith School of Business, Program in Business Management/Law, College Park, MD 20742. Offers JD/MBA. *Accreditation:* AACSB. *Students:* 1 full-time (0 women), 3 part-time (2 women); includes 1 minority (Asian, non-Hispanic/Latino). 2 applicants, 50% accepted, 1 enrolled. *Entrance requirements:* Additional exam requirements/recommendations for international students: Required—TOEFL. *Application deadline:* For fall admission, 5/1 for domestic students, 2/1 for international students; for spring admission, 11/30 for domestic students, 6/1 for international students. Applications are processed on a rolling basis. Application fee: $75. *Expenses: Tuition, area resident:* Part-time $525 per credit hour. Tuition, state resident: part-time $525 per credit hour. Tuition, nonresident: part-time $1131 per credit hour. *Required fees:* $386.31 per term. Tuition and fees vary according to program. *Financial support:* Applicants required to submit FAFSA. *Unit head:* Dr. Anand Anandalingam, Dean, 301-405-0582, E-mail: ganand@umd.edu. *Application contact:* Dr. Charles A. Caramello, Dean of Graduate School, 301-405-0358, Fax: 301-314-9305.

University of Maryland University College, Graduate School of Management and Technology, Doctoral Program in Management, Adelphi, MD 20783. Offers DM. *Accreditation:* AACSB. Part-time programs available. *Students:* 1 full-time (0 women), 260 part-time (124 women); includes 109 minority (87 Black or African American, non-Hispanic/Latino; 9 Asian, non-Hispanic/Latino; 11 Hispanic/Latino; 2 Two or more races, non-Hispanic/Latino), 14 international. Average age 46. 107 applicants, 100% accepted, 5 enrolled. In 2011, 56 doctorates awarded. *Degree requirements:* For doctorate, comprehensive exam, thesis/dissertation. *Application deadline:* Applications are processed on a rolling basis. Application fee: $100. Electronic applications accepted. *Financial support:* Federal Work-Study and scholarships/grants available. Support available to part-time students. Financial award application deadline: 6/1; financial award applicants required to submit FAFSA. *Unit head:* Dr. Bryan Booth, Executive Director, 240-684-2400, Fax: 240-684-2401, E-mail: bbooth@umuc.edu. *Application contact:* Admissions Coordinator, 800-888-8682, Fax: 240-684-2151, E-mail: newgrad@umuc.edu. Web site: http://www.umuc.edu/grad/dm/dm_home.shtml.

University of Maryland University College, Graduate School of Management and Technology, Program in Business Administration, Adelphi, MD 20783. Offers MBA, Certificate. *Accreditation:* AACSB. Part-time and evening/weekend programs available. Postbaccalaureate distance learning degree programs offered (no on-campus study). *Students:* 12 full-time (6 women), 2,762 part-time (1,594 women); includes 1,632 minority (1,235 Black or African American, non-Hispanic/Latino; 7 American Indian or Alaska Native, non-Hispanic/Latino; 171 Asian, non-Hispanic/Latino; 160 Hispanic/Latino; 4 Native Hawaiian or other Pacific Islander, non-Hispanic/Latino; 55 Two or more races, non-Hispanic/Latino), 57 international. Average age 34. 844 applicants, 100% accepted, 611 enrolled. In 2011, 1100 degrees awarded. *Degree requirements:* For master's, thesis or alternative, capstone course. *Application deadline:* Applications are processed on a rolling basis. Application fee: $50. Electronic applications accepted. *Financial support:* Federal Work-Study and scholarships/grants available. Support available to part-time students. Financial award application deadline: 6/1; financial award applicants required to submit FAFSA. *Unit head:* Anna Andriasova, Associate Chair, MBA Program, 240-684-2400, Fax: 240-684-2401, E-mail: anna.andriasova@umuc.edu. *Application contact:* Coordinator, Graduate Admissions, 800-888-8682, Fax: 240-684-2151, E-mail: newgrad@umuc.edu. Web site: http://www.umuc.edu/grad/mba.

University of Maryland University College, Graduate School of Management and Technology, Program in Management, Adelphi, MD 20783. Offers MS, Certificate. Offered evenings and weekends only. Part-time and evening/weekend programs available. Postbaccalaureate distance learning degree programs offered (no on-campus study). *Students:* 99 full-time (64 women), 3,893 part-time (2,682 women); includes 2,404 minority (1,932 Black or African American, non-Hispanic/Latino; 10 American Indian or Alaska Native, non-Hispanic/Latino; 165 Asian, non-Hispanic/Latino; 218 Hispanic/Latino; 8 Native Hawaiian or other Pacific Islander, non-Hispanic/Latino; 71 Two or more races, non-Hispanic/Latino), 60 international. Average age 35. 1,307 applicants, 100% accepted, 758 enrolled. In 2011, 724 master's, 188 other advanced degrees awarded. *Degree requirements:* For master's, thesis or alternative. *Application deadline:* Applications are processed on a rolling basis. Application fee: $50. Electronic applications accepted. *Financial support:* Federal Work-Study and scholarships/grants available. Support available to part-time students. Financial award application deadline: 6/1; financial award applicants required to submit FAFSA. *Unit head:* Dr. Alan Sutherland, Director, 240-684-2400, Fax: 240-684-2401, E-mail: asutherland@umuc.edu. *Application contact:* Coordinator, Graduate Admissions, 888-888-8682, Fax: 240-684-2151, E-mail: newgrad@umuc.edu. Web site: http://www.umuc.edu/grad/msm/msm_home.shtml.

University of Mary Washington, College of Business, Fredericksburg, VA 22401-5358. Offers business administration (MBA); management information systems (MSMIS). Part-time and evening/weekend programs available. *Faculty:* 11 full-time (4 women), 9 part-time/adjunct (1 woman). *Students:* 107 full-time (57 women), 253 part-time (123 women); includes 100 minority (78 Black or African American, non-Hispanic/Latino; 1 American Indian or Alaska Native, non-Hispanic/Latino; 8 Asian, non-Hispanic/Latino; 13 Hispanic/Latino), 5 international. Average age 36. 82 applicants, 61% accepted, 34 enrolled. In 2011, 85 master's awarded. *Entrance requirements:* For master's, GMAT or GRE, minimum GPA of 3.0. Additional exam requirements/recommendations for international students: Required—TOEFL (minimum score 570 paper-based; 230 computer-based; 88 iBT), IELTS (minimum score 6.5). *Application deadline:* For fall admission, 6/1 priority date for domestic students, 6/1 for international students; for spring admission, 10/1 for domestic and international students. Application fee: $50. Electronic applications accepted. *Financial support:* Available to part-time students. Application deadline: 3/15; applicants required to submit FAFSA. *Faculty research:* Management of IT offshoring, boundary theory and co-creation matrix: hermeneutics perspectives, text and image mining, queuing theory and supply chain, organizational learning. *Unit head:* Dr. Lynne D. Richardson, Dean, 540-654-2470, Fax: 540-654-2430, E-mail: lynne.richardson@umw.edu. *Application contact:* Matthew E. Mejia, Associate Dean of Admissions, 540-286-8088, Fax: 540-286-8085, E-mail: mmejia@umw.edu. Web site: http://business.umw.edu/.

University of Massachusetts Amherst, Graduate School, Interdisciplinary Programs, Dual Degree Program in Business Administration and Civil Engineering, Amherst, MA 01003. Offers MSCE/MBA. Part-time programs available. *Entrance requirements:* Additional exam requirements/recommendations for international students: Required—TOEFL (minimum score 600 paper-based; 250 computer-based; 100 iBT), IELTS (minimum score 7). *Application deadline:* For fall admission, 2/1 for domestic and international students. Applications are processed on a rolling basis. Application fee: $50 ($65 for international students). Electronic applications accepted. Tuition and fees vary according to course load, campus/location and program. *Financial support:* Career-related internships or fieldwork, Federal Work-Study, scholarships/grants, traineeships, health care benefits, tuition waivers (full), and unspecified assistantships available. Support available to part-time students. Financial award application deadline: 2/1; financial award applicants required to submit FAFSA. *Unit head:* Dr. Sanjay Arwade, Graduate Program Director, 413-545-0686, Fax: 413-545-2840, E-mail: muriel@ecs.umass.edu. *Application contact:* Lindsay DeSantis, Interim Supervisor of Admissions, 413-545-0722, Fax: 413-577-0010, E-mail: gradadm@grad.umass.edu. Web site: http://www-new.ecs.umass.edu/degrees#MBA.

University of Massachusetts Amherst, Graduate School, Interdisciplinary Programs, Dual Degree Program in Business Administration and Public Policy and Administration, Amherst, MA 01003. Offers MPPA/MBA. *Accreditation:* AACSB. Part-time programs available. *Students:* 12 full-time (8 women); includes 2 minority (1 Asian, non-Hispanic/Latino; 1 Two or more races, non-Hispanic/Latino), 1 international. Average age 30. 16

applicants, 75% accepted, 8 enrolled. *Entrance requirements:* Additional exam requirements/recommendations for international students: Required—TOEFL (minimum score 600 paper-based; 250 computer-based; 100 iBT), IELTS (minimum score 7). *Application deadline:* For fall admission, 2/1 for domestic and international students. Applications are processed on a rolling basis. Application fee: $50 ($65 for international students). Electronic applications accepted. Tuition and fees vary according to course load, campus/location and program. *Financial support:* Career-related internships or fieldwork, Federal Work-Study, scholarships/grants, traineeships, health care benefits, tuition waivers (full), and unspecified assistantships available. Support available to part-time students. Financial award application deadline: 2/1; financial award applicants required to submit FAFSA. *Unit head:* Dr. M. V. Lee Badgett, Graduate Program Director, 413-545-3956, Fax: 413-545-1108. *Application contact:* Lindsay DeSantis, Interim Supervisor of Admissions, 413-545-0722, Fax: 413-577-0010, E-mail: gradadm@grad.umass.edu. Web site: http://www.masspolicy.org/acad_mppa_mba.html.

University of Massachusetts Amherst, Graduate School, Interdisciplinary Programs, Dual Degree Program in Business Administration and Sport Management, Amherst, MA 01003. Offers MBA/MS. Part-time programs available. *Students:* 18 full-time (7 women); includes 2 minority (1 Asian, non-Hispanic/Latino; 1 Hispanic/Latino), 2 international. Average age 27. 83 applicants, 22% accepted, 10 enrolled. *Entrance requirements:* Additional exam requirements/recommendations for international students: Required—TOEFL (minimum score 600 paper-based; 250 computer-based; 100 iBT), IELTS (minimum score 7). *Application deadline:* For fall admission, 2/1 for domestic and international students; for spring admission, 10/1 for domestic and international students. Applications are processed on a rolling basis. Application fee: $50 ($65 for international students). Electronic applications accepted. Tuition and fees vary according to course load, campus/location and program. *Financial support:* Career-related internships or fieldwork, Federal Work-Study, scholarships/grants, traineeships, health care benefits, tuition waivers (full), and unspecified assistantships available. Support available to part-time students. Financial award application deadline: 2/1; financial award applicants required to submit FAFSA. *Unit head:* Dr. Stephen M. McKelvey, Graduate Program Director, 413-545-0471, Fax: 413-545-0642. *Application contact:* Lindsay DeSantis, Interim Supervisor of Admissions, 413-545-0722, Fax: 413-577-0010, E-mail: gradadm@grad.umass.edu. Web site: http://www.isenberg.umass.edu/MBA/Full-Time_MBA/Dual_Degree_Programs/.

University of Massachusetts Amherst, Graduate School, Isenberg School of Management, Part-time Master of Business Administration Program, Amherst, MA 01003. Offers MBA. *Accreditation:* AACSB. Part-time and evening/weekend programs available. Postbaccalaureate distance learning degree programs offered (no on-campus study). *Students:* 42 full-time (17 women), 1,019 part-time (285 women); includes 197 minority (28 Black or African American, non-Hispanic/Latino; 2 American Indian or Alaska Native, non-Hispanic/Latino; 113 Asian, non-Hispanic/Latino; 37 Hispanic/Latino; 3 Native Hawaiian or other Pacific Islander, non-Hispanic/Latino; 14 Two or more races, non-Hispanic/Latino), 66 international. Average age 36. 338 applicants, 87% accepted, 220 enrolled. In 2011, 377 master's awarded. *Entrance requirements:* For master's, GMAT or GRE. Additional exam requirements/recommendations for international students: Required—TOEFL (minimum score 600 paper-based; 250 computer-based; 100 iBT), IELTS (minimum score 7). *Application deadline:* For fall admission, 7/1 for domestic and international students; for spring admission, 10/1 for domestic and international students. Applications are processed on a rolling basis. Application fee: $50 ($65 for international students). Electronic applications accepted. Tuition and fees vary according to course load, campus/location and program. *Unit head:* Dr. John Wells, Graduate Program Director, 413-545-5608, Fax: 413-577-2234, E-mail: gradprog@som.umass.edu. *Application contact:* Lindsay DeSantis, Interim Supervisor of Admissions, 415-545-0722, Fax: 413-577-0010, E-mail: gradadm@grad.umass.edu. Web site: http://www.isenberg.umass.edu/MBA/Part-Time_Online_MBAs/.

University of Massachusetts Amherst, Graduate School, Isenberg School of Management, Program in Management, Amherst, MA 01003. Offers accounting (PhD); business administration (MBA); business administration/sport management (MBA/MS); finance (PhD); hospitality and tourism management (PhD); management science (PhD); marketing (PhD); organization studies (PhD); sport management (PhD); strategic management (PhD); MBA/MS; MPH/MPPA. *Accreditation:* AACSB. Part-time programs available. *Faculty:* 61 full-time (14 women). *Students:* 92 full-time (34 women), 9 part-time (3 women); includes 8 minority (1 Black or African American, non-Hispanic/Latino; 4 Asian, non-Hispanic/Latino; 3 Hispanic/Latino), 47 international. Average age 33. 340 applicants, 15% accepted, 29 enrolled. In 2011, 31 master's, 13 doctorates awarded. Terminal master's awarded for partial completion of doctoral program. *Degree requirements:* For doctorate, comprehensive exam, thesis/dissertation. *Entrance requirements:* For master's and doctorate, GMAT. Additional exam requirements/recommendations for international students: Required—TOEFL (minimum score 550 paper-based; 213 computer-based; 80 iBT), IELTS (minimum score 6.5). *Application deadline:* For fall admission, 1/20 for domestic and international students. Applications are processed on a rolling basis. Application fee: $50 ($65 for international students). Electronic applications accepted. Tuition and fees vary according to course load, campus/location and program. *Financial support:* Fellowships with full and partial tuition reimbursements, research assistantships with full and partial tuition reimbursements, teaching assistantships with full and partial tuition reimbursements, career-related internships or fieldwork, Federal Work-Study, scholarships/grants, traineeships, health care benefits, tuition waivers (full and partial), and unspecified assistantships available. Support available to part-time students. Financial award application deadline: 1/20. *Unit head:* Dr. William Woodridge, Chair, 413-545-5675, Fax: 413-577-2234. *Application contact:* Lindsay DeSantis, Interim Supervisor of Admissions, 413-545-0722, Fax: 413-577-0010, E-mail: gradadm@grad.umass.edu. Web site: http://www.isenberg.umass.edu/.

University of Massachusetts Boston, Office of Graduate Studies, College of Management, Program in Business Administration, Boston, MA 02125-3393. Offers MBA, MS/MBA. *Accreditation:* AACSB. Part-time and evening/weekend programs available. *Degree requirements:* For master's, capstone project. *Entrance requirements:* For master's, GMAT, minimum GPA of 3.0. *Faculty research:* International finance, human resource management, management information systems, investment and corporate finance, international marketing.

University of Massachusetts Dartmouth, Graduate School, Charlton College of Business, Program in Business Administration, North Dartmouth, MA 02747-2300. Offers accounting (Postbaccalaureate Certificate); business administration (MBA); business foundation (online) (Graduate Certificate); finance (PMC); international business (online) (Graduate Certificate); leadership (online) (Graduate Certificate); management (Postbaccalaureate Certificate); marketing (Postbaccalaureate Certificate); supply chain management (PMC). *Accreditation:* AACSB. Part-time programs available. *Faculty:* 35 full-time (11 women), 26 part-time/adjunct (7 women). *Students:* 81 full-time (29 women), 119 part-time (56 women); includes 17 minority (6 Black or African American, non-Hispanic/Latino; 1 American Indian or Alaska Native, non-Hispanic/Latino; 3 Asian, non-Hispanic/Latino; 5 Hispanic/Latino; 2 Two or more races, non-Hispanic/Latino), 42 international. Average age 31. 132 applicants, 92% accepted, 68 enrolled. In 2011, 91 master's, 18 other advanced degrees awarded. *Entrance requirements:* For master's, GMAT, statement of intent, resume, 3 letters of recommendation; for other advanced degree, statement of intent, resume, 3 letters of recommendation. Additional exam requirements/recommendations for international students: Required—TOEFL (minimum score 500 paper-based; 200 computer-based; 72 iBT). *Application deadline:* For fall admission, 3/1 for domestic students, 2/1 for international students; for spring admission, 11/1 for domestic students, 10/15 for international students. Application fee: $40 ($60 for international students). Electronic applications accepted. *Expenses:* Tuition, state resident: full-time $2071; part-time $86.29 per credit. Tuition, nonresident: full-time $8099; part-time $337.46 per credit. *Required fees:* $438.58 per credit. Part-time tuition and fees vary according to class time, course load, degree level and reciprocity agreements. *Financial support:* Research assistantships, teaching assistantships, Federal Work-Study, and unspecified assistantships available. Support available to part-time students. Financial award application deadline: 3/1; financial award applicants required to submit FAFSA. *Faculty research:* Global business environment, e-commerce, managing diversity, agile manufacturing, green business. *Total annual research expenditures:* $8,653. *Unit head:* Stephanie Jacobsen, Program Coordinator, 508-999-8543, Fax: 508-999-8646, E-mail: s.jacobsen@umassd.edu. *Application contact:* Elan Turcotte-Shamski, Graduate Admissions Officer, 508-999-8604, Fax: 508-999-8183, E-mail: graduate@umassd.edu. Web site: http://www.umassd.edu/charlton/.

University of Massachusetts Lowell, College of Management, Lowell, MA 01854-2881. Offers business administration (MBA); foundations of business (Graduate Certificate); new venture creation (Graduate Certificate). *Accreditation:* AACSB. Part-time and evening/weekend programs available. *Entrance requirements:* For master's, GMAT.

University of Memphis, Graduate School, Fogelman College of Business and Economics, Program in Business Administration, Memphis, TN 38152. Offers accounting (MBA, PhD); economics (MBA, PhD); executive business administration (MBA); finance (PhD); finance, insurance, and real estate (MBA, MS); international business administration (IMBA); management (MBA, MS, PhD); management information systems (MBA, MS, PhD); management science (MBA); marketing (MBA, MS); marketing and supply chain management (PhD); real estate development (MS); JD/MBA. *Accreditation:* AACSB. *Degree requirements:* For master's, comprehensive exam; for doctorate, comprehensive exam, thesis/dissertation. *Entrance requirements:* For master's, GMAT, resume; for doctorate, GMAT, interview, minimum GPA of 3.4, resume, letter of recommendation. Additional exam requirements/recommendations for international students: Required—TOEFL (minimum score 550 paper-based; 220 computer-based). *Faculty research:* Competitive business strategy, finance microstructures, supply chain management innovations, health care economics, litigation risks and corporate audits.

University of Miami, Graduate School, School of Business Administration, Program in Business Administration, Coral Gables, FL 33124. Offers accounting (MBA); computer information systems (MBA); executive and professional (MBA), including international business, management; finance (MBA); international business (MBA); management (MBA); management science (MBA); marketing (MBA); professional management (MSPM); JD/MBA; MBA/MSIE. *Accreditation:* AACSB. Evening/weekend programs available. *Degree requirements:* For master's, comprehensive exam. *Entrance requirements:* For master's, GMAT. Additional exam requirements/recommendations for international students: Required—TOEFL (minimum score 550 paper-based; 213 computer-based; 59 iBT). Electronic applications accepted. *Faculty research:* Leadership, e-commerce, supply chain management.

University of Michigan, Ross School of Business, Doctoral Program in Business Administration, Ann Arbor, MI 48109-1234. Offers PhD. Offered through the Horace H. Rackham School of Graduate Studies. *Accreditation:* AACSB. *Degree requirements:* For doctorate, comprehensive exam, thesis/dissertation, oral defense of dissertation, preliminary exam. *Entrance requirements:* For doctorate, GMAT or GRE. Additional exam requirements/recommendations for international students: Required—TOEFL (paper-based 600, computer-based 250, iBT 106) or IELTS (7). Electronic applications accepted. *Faculty research:* Accounting; business information technology; finance; international business/business economics; management and organizations; marketing; operations and management science; strategy.

University of Michigan–Dearborn, College of Business, Dearborn, MI 48128-1491. Offers accounting (MBA, MS); business analytics (MS); finance (MBA, MS); information systems (MS); international business (MBA); management (MBA); management information systems (MBA); marketing (MBA); supply chain management (MBA, MS); MBA/MHSA; MBA/MSE; MBA/MSF; MBA/MSIS; MSF/MSA. *Accreditation:* AACSB. Part-time and evening/weekend programs available. Postbaccalaureate distance learning degree programs offered (no on-campus study). *Faculty:* 50 full-time (6 women), 32 part-time/adjunct (18 women). *Students:* 65 full-time (29 women), 356 part-time (121 women); includes 79 minority (19 Black or African American, non-Hispanic/Latino; 36 American Indian or Alaska Native, non-Hispanic/Latino; 15 Hispanic/Latino; 1 Native Hawaiian or other Pacific Islander, non-Hispanic/Latino; 8 Two or more races, non-Hispanic/Latino), 80 international. Average age 28. 175 applicants, 53% accepted, 68 enrolled. In 2011, 173 master's awarded. *Entrance requirements:* For master's, GMAT or GRE, 2 years of work experience (MBA); course work in computer applications, statistics, and pre-calculus or finite mathematics; 18 credits of accounting course work beyond introductory courses (MS in accounting). Additional exam requirements/recommendations for international students: Required—TOEFL (minimum score 560 paper-based; 220 computer-based; 84 iBT), IELTS. *Application deadline:* For fall admission, 8/1 priority date for domestic students, 6/1 for international students; for winter admission, 12/1 priority date for domestic students, 10/1 for international students; for spring admission, 4/1 priority date for domestic students, 2/1 for international students. Applications are processed on a rolling basis. Application fee: $60. Electronic applications accepted. *Expenses:* Contact institution. *Financial support:* Career-related internships or fieldwork, Federal Work-Study, and scholarships/grants available. Support available to part-time students. Financial award application deadline: 9/1; financial award applicants required to submit FAFSA. *Faculty research:* Cultural diversity, buyer-supplier relations, error detection in data, economic evolution. *Unit head:* Dr. Lee Redding, Interim Dean, 313-593-5248, Fax: 313-271-9835, E-mail: lredding@umd.umich.edu. *Application contact:* Joan Doherty, Academic Advisor/Counselor, 313-593-5460, Fax: 313-271-9838, E-mail: gradbusiness@umd.umich.edu. Web site: http://www.cob.umd.umich.edu.

University of Michigan–Flint, School of Management, Flint, MI 48502-1950. Offers MBA. *Accreditation:* AACSB. Part-time programs available. Postbaccalaureate distance learning degree programs offered (minimal on-campus study). *Degree requirements:* For master's, thesis or alternative. *Entrance requirements:* For master's, GMAT, 2 years of work experience, minimum GPA of 3.0, 1 year college course work in mathematics. Additional exam requirements/recommendations for international students: Required—TOEFL (minimum score 560 paper-based; 220 computer-based; 84 iBT), IELTS (minimum score 6.5). Electronic applications accepted. *Faculty research:* Business performance evaluations, consumer satisfaction, mergers and acquisitions success.

Business Administration and Management—General

University of Minnesota, Duluth, Graduate School, Labovitz School of Business and Economics, Program in Business Administration, Duluth, MN 55812-2496. Offers MBA. *Accreditation:* AACSB. Part-time and evening/weekend programs available. *Entrance requirements:* For master's, GMAT, minimum GPA of 3.0; course work in accounting, business administration, and economics. Additional exam requirements/ recommendations for international students: Required—TOEFL (minimum score 550 paper-based; 213 computer-based; 79 iBT). *Expenses:* Contact institution. *Faculty research:* Regional economic analysis, marketing, management, human resources, organizational behavior.

University of Minnesota, Twin Cities Campus, Carlson School of Management, Minneapolis, MN 55455. Offers EMBA, M Acc, MA, MBA, MBT, PhD, JD/MBA, MBA/ MPP, MD/MBA, MHA/MBA, Pharm D/MBA. *Accreditation:* AACSB. Part-time and evening/weekend programs available. *Faculty:* 135 full-time (38 women), 26 part-time/ adjunct (8 women). *Students:* 446 full-time (205 women), 1,584 part-time (554 women); includes 194 minority (26 Black or African American, non-Hispanic/Latino; 4 American Indian or Alaska Native, non-Hispanic/Latino; 140 Asian, non-Hispanic/Latino; 20 Hispanic/Latino; 4 Two or more races, non-Hispanic/Latino), 221 international. Average age 28. In 2011, 754 master's, 13 doctorates awarded. Terminal master's awarded for partial completion of doctoral program. *Degree requirements:* For doctorate, comprehensive exam, thesis/dissertation. Electronic applications accepted. *Expenses:* Contact institution. *Financial support:* Fellowships with full and partial tuition reimbursements, research assistantships with full tuition reimbursements, teaching assistantships with full and partial tuition reimbursements, career-related internships or fieldwork, Federal Work-Study, institutionally sponsored loans, scholarships/grants, health care benefits, tuition waivers (full and partial), and unspecified assistantships available. Support available to part-time students. Financial award application deadline: 4/1; financial award applicants required to submit FAFSA. *Faculty research:* Finance and accounting: financial reporting, asset pricing models and corporate finance; information and decision sciences: on-line auctions, information transparency and recommender systems; marketing: psychological influences on consumer behavior, brand equity, pricing and marketing channels; operations: lean manufacturing, quality management and global supply chains; strategic management and organization: global strategy, networks, entrepreneurship and innovation, sustainability. *Unit head:* Prof. Sri Zaheer, Dean, 612-626-9636, Fax: 612-624-6374, E-mail: csdean@umn.edu. Web site: http://www.carlsonschool.umn.edu.

University of Mississippi, Graduate School, School of Business Administration, Oxford, University, MS 38677. Offers business administration (MBA, PhD); systems management (MS); JD/MBA. *Accreditation:* AACSB. *Students:* 75 full-time (20 women), 58 part-time (19 women); includes 11 minority (8 Black or African American, non-Hispanic/Latino; 1 Hispanic/Latino; 2 Two or more races, non-Hispanic/Latino), 10 international. *Degree requirements:* For doctorate, thesis/dissertation. *Entrance requirements:* For master's, GMAT, minimum GPA of 3.0; for doctorate, GMAT. Additional exam requirements/recommendations for international students: Required—TOEFL. *Application deadline:* For fall admission, 2/1 for domestic students; for spring admission, 10/1 for domestic students. Applications are processed on a rolling basis. Application fee: $25. Electronic applications accepted. *Financial support:* Fellowships, career-related internships or fieldwork, scholarships/grants, tuition waivers (full), and unspecified assistantships available. Financial award application deadline: 3/1; financial award applicants required to submit FAFSA. *Unit head:* Dr. Ken Cyree, Dean, 662-915-5820, Fax: 662-915-5821, E-mail: info@bus.olemiss.edu. *Application contact:* Dr. Christy M. Wyandt, Associate Dean, 662-915-7474, Fax: 662-915-7577, E-mail: cwyandt@olemiss.edu. Web site: http://www.olemissbusiness.com/.

University of Missouri, Graduate School, Robert J. Trulaske, Sr. College of Business, Program in Business Administration, Columbia, MO 65211. Offers MBA, PhD. *Accreditation:* AACSB. *Faculty:* 42 full-time (9 women), 4 part-time/adjunct (2 women). *Students:* 182 full-time (61 women), 17 part-time (9 women); includes 12 minority (2 Black or African American, non-Hispanic/Latino; 7 Asian, non-Hispanic/Latino; 3 Two or more races, non-Hispanic/Latino), 71 international. Average age 26. 399 applicants, 27% accepted, 79 enrolled. In 2011, 103 master's, 2 doctorates awarded. *Degree requirements:* For doctorate, thesis/dissertation. *Entrance requirements:* For master's and doctorate, GMAT, minimum GPA of 3.0. Additional exam requirements/ recommendations for international students: Required—TOEFL (minimum score 500 paper-based; 173 computer-based; 61 iBT). *Application deadline:* For fall admission, 2/1 priority date for domestic students. Applications are processed on a rolling basis. Application fee: $55 ($75 for international students). *Expenses:* Tuition, state resident: full-time $5881. Tuition, nonresident: full-time $15,183. *Required fees:* $952. Tuition and fees vary according to campus/location and program. *Financial support:* Research assistantships, teaching assistantships, and institutionally sponsored loans available. *Unit head:* Dr. Bruce J. Walker, Dean, E-mail: walkerb@missouri.edu. *Application contact:* Jan Curry, 573-882-2750, E-mail: curryja@missouri.edu. Web site: http:// business.missouri.edu/.

University of Missouri–Kansas City, Henry W. Bloch School of Management, Kansas City, MO 64110-2499. Offers accounting (MS); business administration (MBA); entrepreneurial real estate (MERE); entrepreneurship and innovation (PhD); finance (MS); public affairs (MPA, PhD); JD/MBA; LL M/MPA. PhD (interdisciplinary) offered through the School of Graduate Studies. *Accreditation:* AACSB; NASPAA. Part-time and evening/weekend programs available. *Faculty:* 51 full-time (14 women), 29 part-time/ adjunct (9 women). *Students:* 272 full-time (126 women), 407 part-time (180 women); includes 91 minority (43 Black or African American, non-Hispanic/Latino; 20 Asian, non-Hispanic/Latino; 19 Hispanic/Latino; 9 Two or more races, non-Hispanic/Latino), 49 international. Average age 30. 397 applicants, 63% accepted, 202 enrolled. In 2011, 257 master's awarded. Terminal master's awarded for partial completion of doctoral program. *Entrance requirements:* For master's, GMAT, GRE, 2 writing essays, 2 references; support of employer; for doctorate, GRE, minimum GPA of 3.0. Additional exam requirements/recommendations for international students: Required—TOEFL (minimum score 550 paper-based; 213 computer-based; 80 iBT). *Application deadline:* For fall admission, 5/1 priority date for domestic students, 5/1 for international students; for spring admission, 10/1 priority date for domestic students, 10/1 for international students. Applications are processed on a rolling basis. Application fee: $45 ($50 for international students). Electronic applications accepted. *Expenses:* Tuition, state resident: full-time $5798; part-time $322.10 per credit hour. Tuition, nonresident: full-time $14,969; part-time $831.60 per credit hour. *Required fees:* $93.51 per credit hour. *Financial support:* In 2011–12, 29 research assistantships with partial tuition reimbursements (averaging $11,490 per year), 3 teaching assistantships with partial tuition reimbursements (averaging $11,600 per year) were awarded; career-related internships or fieldwork, Federal Work-Study, institutionally sponsored loans, scholarships/grants, tuition waivers (full and partial), and unspecified assistantships also available. Support available to part-time students. Financial award application deadline: 3/1; financial award applicants required to submit FAFSA. *Faculty research:* Entrepreneurship, finance, non-profit, risk management. *Unit head:* Dr. Teng-Kee Tan, Dean, 816-235-2215, Fax: 816-235-2206. *Application contact:* 816-235-1111, E-mail: admit@umkc.edu. Web site: http://www.bloch.umkc.edu.

University of Missouri–St. Louis, College of Business Administration, Program in Business Administration, St. Louis, MO 63121. Offers accounting (MBA); business administration (Certificate); finance (MBA); human resource management (Certificate); information systems (MBA); logistics and supply chain management (MBA, Certificate); marketing (MBA); marketing management (Certificate); operations management (MBA). *Accreditation:* AACSB. Part-time and evening/weekend programs available. *Faculty:* 32 full-time (7 women), 10 part-time/adjunct (2 women). *Students:* 126 full-time (48 women), 305 part-time (141 women); includes 61 minority (25 Black or African American, non-Hispanic/Latino; 23 Asian, non-Hispanic/Latino; 9 Hispanic/Latino; 1 Native Hawaiian or other Pacific Islander, non-Hispanic/Latino; 3 Two or more races, non-Hispanic/Latino), 47 international. Average age 30. 241 applicants, 70% accepted, 134 enrolled. In 2011, 150 master's, 1 doctorate, 19 other advanced degrees awarded. *Entrance requirements:* For master's, GMAT, 2 letters of recommendation. Additional exam requirements/recommendations for international students: Required—TOEFL (minimum score 550 paper-based; 213 computer-based). *Application deadline:* For fall admission, 7/1 for domestic and international students; for spring admission, 12/1 for domestic and international students. Applications are processed on a rolling basis. Application fee: $35 ($40 for international students). Electronic applications accepted. *Expenses:* Tuition, state resident: full-time $6273; part-time $3866 per year. Tuition, nonresident: full-time $14,969; part-time $9980 per year. *Required fees:* $315 per year. *Financial support:* In 2011–12, 32 research assistantships with full and partial tuition reimbursements (averaging $6,000 per year), 6 teaching assistantships with full and partial tuition reimbursements (averaging $12,276 per year) were awarded; career-related internships or fieldwork, Federal Work-Study, and institutionally sponsored loans also available. Support available to part-time students. Financial award application deadline: 4/1; financial award applicants required to submit FAFSA. *Faculty research:* Human resources, strategic management, marketing strategy, consumer behavior product development, advertising. *Unit head:* Karl Kottemann, Assistant Director, 314-516-5885, Fax: 314-516-6420, E-mail: mba@umsl.edu. *Application contact:* 314-516-5458, Fax: 314-516-6996, E-mail: gradadm@umsl.edu. Web site: http://www.umsl.edu/ divisions/business/mbaonline/mbaprog.htm.

University of Missouri–St. Louis, Graduate School, Program in Public Policy Administration, St. Louis, MO 63121. Offers health policy (MPPA); local government management (MPPA, Certificate); managing human resources and organization (MPPA); nonprofit organization management (MPPA); nonprofit organization management and leadership (Certificate); policy research and analysis (MPPA). *Accreditation:* NASPAA. Part-time and evening/weekend programs available. *Faculty:* 10 full-time (5 women), 9 part-time/adjunct (4 women). *Students:* 33 full-time (17 women), 76 part-time (48 women); includes 30 minority (25 Black or African American, non-Hispanic/Latino; 2 American Indian or Alaska Native, non-Hispanic/Latino; 1 Asian, non-Hispanic/Latino; 2 Hispanic/Latino), 9 international. Average age 32. 68 applicants, 50% accepted, 27 enrolled. In 2011, 23 master's, 22 Certificates awarded. *Entrance requirements:* For master's, 3 letters of recommendation. Additional exam requirements/ recommendations for international students: Required—TOEFL (minimum score 550 paper-based; 213 computer-based). *Application deadline:* For fall admission, 7/1 priority date for domestic students, 7/1 for international students; for spring admission, 12/1 priority date for domestic students, 12/1 for international students. Applications are processed on a rolling basis. Application fee: $35 ($40 for international students). Electronic applications accepted. *Expenses:* Tuition, state resident: full-time $6273; part-time $3866 per year. Tuition, nonresident: full-time $14,969; part-time $9980 per year. *Required fees:* $315 per year. *Financial support:* In 2011–12, 2 research assistantships with full and partial tuition reimbursements (averaging $12,000 per year) were awarded; career-related internships or fieldwork also available. Financial award application deadline: 4/1; financial award applicants required to submit FAFSA. *Faculty research:* Urban policy, public finance, evaluation. *Unit head:* Dr. Deborah Balser, Director, 314-516-5145, Fax: 314-516-5210, E-mail: balserd@msx.umsl.edu. *Application contact:* 314-516-5458, Fax: 314-516-6996, E-mail: gradadm@umsl.edu. Web site: http://www.umsl.edu/divisions/graduate/mppa/.

University of Mobile, Graduate Programs, Program in Business Administration, Mobile, AL 36613. Offers MBA. *Accreditation:* ACBSP. Part-time and evening/weekend programs available. *Faculty:* 3 full-time (all women), 2 part-time/adjunct (0 women). *Students:* 8 full-time (3 women), 30 part-time (22 women); includes 18 minority (all Black or African American, non-Hispanic/Latino), 5 international. Average age 35. 16 applicants, 100% accepted, 11 enrolled. In 2011, 8 master's awarded. *Degree requirements:* For master's, comprehensive exam. *Entrance requirements:* For master's, GMAT. Additional exam requirements/recommendations for international students: Required—TOEFL (minimum score 550 paper-based; 213 computer-based; 80 iBT). *Application deadline:* For fall admission, 8/3 priority date for domestic students; for spring admission, 12/23 for domestic students. Applications are processed on a rolling basis. Application fee: $40 ($50 for international students). *Expenses: Tuition:* Full-time $8262; part-time $459 per credit hour. *Required fees:* $110 per term. *Financial support:* Application deadline: 8/1. *Faculty research:* Management, personnel management, small business, diversity. *Unit head:* Dr. Jane Finley, Dean, School of Business, 251-442-2219, Fax: 251-442-2523, E-mail: jfinley@umobile.edu. *Application contact:* Tammy C. Eubanks, Administrative Assistant to Dean of Graduate Programs, 251-442-2270, Fax: 251-442-2523, E-mail: teubanks@umobile.edu. Web site: http:// www.umobile.edu/.

The University of Montana, Graduate School, School of Business Administration, MBA Professional Program, Missoula, MT 59812-0002. Offers MBA, JD/MBA, MBA/Pharm D. *Accreditation:* AACSB. Part-time and evening/weekend programs available. Postbaccalaureate distance learning degree programs offered (minimal on-campus study). *Degree requirements:* For master's, thesis optional. *Entrance requirements:* For master's, GMAT. Additional exam requirements/recommendations for international students: Required—TOEFL. *Faculty research:* Information systems, research methods, international business, human resource management, marketing.

University of Montevallo, Stephens College of Business, Montevallo, AL 35115. Offers MBA. *Accreditation:* AACSB. Part-time and evening/weekend programs available. *Students:* 11 full-time (4 women), 18 part-time (11 women); includes 12 minority (8 Black or African American, non-Hispanic/Latino; 3 Hispanic/Latino; 1 Two or more races, non-Hispanic/Latino), 1 international. *Degree requirements:* For master's, comprehensive exam. *Entrance requirements:* Additional exam requirements/recommendations for international students: Required—TOEFL (minimum score 550 paper-based). *Application deadline:* For fall admission, 7/15 for domestic students; for spring admission, 11/15 for domestic students. Application fee: $25. *Unit head:* Dr. Stephen H. Craft, Dean, 205-665-6540. *Application contact:* Rebecca Hartley, Coordinator for Graduate Studies, 205-665-6350, Fax: 205-665-6353, E-mail: hartleyrs@ montevallo.edu. Web site: http://www.montevallo.edu/scob/.

University of Nebraska at Kearney, Graduate Studies, College of Business and Technology, Department of Business, Kearney, NE 68849-0001. Offers business administration (MBA). *Accreditation:* AACSB. Part-time and evening/weekend programs available. *Degree requirements:* For master's, thesis optional. *Entrance requirements:* For master's, GMAT. Additional exam requirements/recommendations for international students: Required—TOEFL (minimum score 550 paper-based; 213 computer-based).

Electronic applications accepted. *Faculty research:* Small business financial management, employment law, expert systems, international trade and marketing, environmental economics.

University of Nebraska at Omaha, Graduate Studies, College of Business Administration, Program in Business Administration, Omaha, NE 68182. Offers EMBA, MBA. *Accreditation:* AACSB. Part-time and evening/weekend programs available. *Faculty:* 24 full-time (8 women). *Students:* 83 full-time (34 women), 230 part-time (68 women); includes 30 minority (7 Black or African American, non-Hispanic/Latino; 13 Asian, non-Hispanic/Latino; 7 Hispanic/Latino; 3 Two or more races, non-Hispanic/Latino), 20 international. Average age 30. 162 applicants, 61% accepted, 94 enrolled. In 2011, 122 master's awarded. *Degree requirements:* For master's, thesis (for some programs), capstone course. *Entrance requirements:* For master's, GMAT, minimum AACSB index of 1040, minimum GPA of 3.0, resume. Additional exam requirements/recommendations for international students: Required—TOEFL (minimum score 550 paper-based; 213 computer-based; 80 iBT). *Application deadline:* For fall admission, 7/1 for domestic students; for spring admission, 11/1 for domestic students. Applications are processed on a rolling basis. Application fee: $45. Electronic applications accepted. *Financial support:* In 2011–12, 24 students received support, including 13 research assistantships with tuition reimbursements available; Federal Work-Study, institutionally sponsored loans, scholarships/grants, tuition waivers (partial), and unspecified assistantships also available. Support available to part-time students. Financial award application deadline: 3/1; financial award applicants required to submit FAFSA. *Unit head:* Dr. Lynn Harland, Associate Dean, 402-554-2303. *Application contact:* Lex Kaczmarek, Director, 402-554-2303.

University of Nebraska–Lincoln, Graduate College, College of Business Administration, Interdepartmental Area of Business, Lincoln, NE 68588. Offers accountancy (PhD); business (MBA); finance (MA, PhD), including business; management (MA, PhD), including business; marketing (MA, PhD), including business; JD/MBA; M Arch/MBA. *Accreditation:* AACSB. Part-time programs available. Postbaccalaureate distance learning degree programs offered. *Degree requirements:* For doctorate, comprehensive exam, thesis/dissertation. *Entrance requirements:* For master's and doctorate, GMAT. Additional exam requirements/recommendations for international students: Required—TOEFL (minimum score 550 paper-based; 213 computer-based). Electronic applications accepted.

University of Nevada, Las Vegas, Graduate College, College of Business, Program in Business Administration, Las Vegas, NV 89154-6031. Offers Exec MBA, MBA, DMD/MBA, MBA/JD, MBA/MS. *Accreditation:* AACSB. Part-time and evening/weekend programs available. *Faculty:* 28 full-time (4 women), 1 (woman) part-time/adjunct. *Students:* 131 full-time (39 women), 79 part-time (27 women); includes 40 minority (6 Black or African American, non-Hispanic/Latino; 21 Asian, non-Hispanic/Latino; 7 Hispanic/Latino; 6 Two or more races, non-Hispanic/Latino), 23 international. Average age 31. 102 applicants, 70% accepted, 50 enrolled. In 2011, 90 master's awarded. *Entrance requirements:* For master's, GMAT. Additional exam requirements/recommendations for international students: Required—TOEFL (minimum score 550 paper-based; 213 computer-based; 80 iBT), IELTS (minimum score 7). *Application deadline:* For fall admission, 5/1 priority date for domestic students, 5/1 for international students; for spring admission, 10/1 priority date for domestic students, 10/1 for international students. Applications are processed on a rolling basis. Application fee: $60 ($95 for international students). Electronic applications accepted. *Financial support:* In 2011–12, 20 students received support, including 5 research assistantships with partial tuition reimbursements available (averaging $7,625 per year), 15 teaching assistantships with partial tuition reimbursements available (averaging $9,543 per year); institutionally sponsored loans, scholarships/grants, health care benefits, and unspecified assistantships also available. Financial award application deadline: 3/1. *Faculty research:* Economic effects on wages, benefits and economic effects of risk, uncertainty; asymmetric information: adverse selection, moral hazard; business processes. *Total annual research expenditures:* $713. *Unit head:* Dr. Reza Torkzadeh, Department Chair/Professor/Associate Dean, 702-895-1832, Fax: 702-895-3655, E-mail: reza.torkzadeh@unlv.edu. *Application contact:* Graduate College Admissions Evaluator, 702-895-3320, Fax: 702-895-4180, E-mail: gradcollege@unlv.edu. Web site: http://business.unlv.edu/mba/content.asp?content=78.

University of Nevada, Reno, Graduate School, College of Business Administration, Department of Business Administration, Reno, NV 89557. Offers MBA. *Accreditation:* AACSB. Part-time and evening/weekend programs available. Postbaccalaureate distance learning degree programs offered. *Entrance requirements:* For master's, GMAT, minimum GPA of 2.75. Additional exam requirements/recommendations for international students: Required—TOEFL (minimum score 500 paper-based; 173 computer-based; 61 iBT), IELTS (minimum score 6). Electronic applications accepted.

University of New Brunswick Fredericton, School of Graduate Studies, Faculty of Business Administration, Fredericton, NB E3B 5A3, Canada. Offers business administration (MBA); engineering management (MBA); entrepreneurship (MBA); sports and recreation management (MBA); MBA/LL B. Part-time programs available. *Faculty:* 23 full-time (3 women), 5 part-time/adjunct (2 women). *Students:* 50 full-time (10 women), 27 part-time (12 women). In 2011, 46 master's awarded. *Degree requirements:* For master's, thesis optional. *Entrance requirements:* For master's, GMAT (minimum score 550), minimum GPA of 3.0; 3-5 years work experience. Additional exam requirements/recommendations for international students: Required—TOEFL (minimum score 580 paper-based; 92 iBT) or IELTS (minimum score 7). *Application deadline:* For fall admission, 3/1 priority date for domestic students. Applications are processed on a rolling basis. Application fee: $50 Canadian dollars. *Financial support:* In 2011–12, 7 fellowships, 1 research assistantship (averaging $4,500 per year), 17 teaching assistantships (averaging $2,250 per year) were awarded. *Faculty research:* Accounting and auditing practices, human resource management, the non-profit sector, marketing, strategic management, entrepreneurship, investment practices, supply chain management, operations management. *Unit head:* Judy Roy, Director of Graduate Studies, 506-458-7307, Fax: 506-453-3561, E-mail: jroy@unb.ca. *Application contact:* Marilyn Davis, Acting Graduate Secretary, 506-453-4766, Fax: 506-453-3561, E-mail: mbacontact@unb.ca. Web site: http://www.business.unbf.ca.

University of New Brunswick Saint John, MBA Program, Saint John, NB E2L 4L5, Canada. Offers administration (MBA); electronic commerce (MBA); international business (MBA); natural resource management (MBA). Part-time programs available. *Faculty:* 19 full-time (4 women), 14 part-time/adjunct (8 women). *Students:* 58 full-time (24 women), 130 part-time (46 women). 93 applicants, 78% accepted, 25 enrolled. In 2011, 36 master's awarded. *Entrance requirements:* For master's, GMAT, minimum GPA of 3.0. Additional exam requirements/recommendations for international students: Required—TOEFL (minimum score 580 paper-based; 237 computer-based), IELTS (minimum score 7), TWE (minimum score 4.5). *Application deadline:* For fall admission, 5/15 for domestic and international students. Applications are processed on a rolling basis. Application fee: $100. Electronic applications accepted. *Expenses:* Contact institution. *Financial support:* In 2011–12, 4 students received support. Career-related internships or fieldwork and scholarships/grants available. *Faculty research:* Business use of weblogs and podcasts to communicate, corporate governance, high-involvement work systems, international competitiveness, supply chain management and logistics. *Unit head:* Henryk Sterniczuk, Director of Graduate Studies, 506-648-5573, Fax: 506-648-5574, E-mail: sternicz@unbsj.ca. *Application contact:* Tammy Morin, Secretary, 506-648-5746, Fax: 506-648-5574, E-mail: tmorin@unbsj.ca. Web site: http://www.mba.unbsj.ca.

University of New Hampshire, Graduate School Manchester Campus, Manchester, NH 03101. Offers business administration (MBA); counseling (M Ed); education (M Ed, MAT); educational administration and supervision (M Ed, Ed S); information technology (MS); management of technology (MS); public administration (MPA); public health (MPH, Certificate); social work (MSW); software systems engineering (Certificate). Part-time and evening/weekend programs available. *Students:* 78 full-time (50 women), 130 part-time (65 women); includes 62 minority (2 Black or African American, non-Hispanic/Latino; 56 Asian, non-Hispanic/Latino; 4 Hispanic/Latino), 4 international. Average age 34. 132 applicants, 55% accepted, 57 enrolled. In 2011, 66 master's, 9 other advanced degrees awarded. *Degree requirements:* For master's, thesis or alternative. *Entrance requirements:* Additional exam requirements/recommendations for international students: Required—TOEFL (minimum score 550 paper-based; 213 computer-based; 80 iBT). *Application deadline:* For fall admission, 6/1 for domestic students, 4/1 for international students; for spring admission, 12/1 for domestic students. Applications are processed on a rolling basis. Application fee: $65. Electronic applications accepted. *Expenses:* Tuition, state resident: full-time $12,360; part-time $687 per credit hour. Tuition, nonresident: full-time $25,680; part-time $1058 per credit hour. *International tuition:* $29,550 full-time. *Required fees:* $1666; $833 per course. $416.50 per semester. Tuition and fees vary according to course load and degree level. *Financial support:* In 2011–12, 11 students received support, including 2 teaching assistantships; fellowships, research assistantships, Federal Work-Study, scholarships/grants, health care benefits, and unspecified assistantships also available. Support available to part-time students. Financial award application deadline: 3/1; financial award applicants required to submit FAFSA. *Unit head:* Candice Brown, Director, 603-641-4313, E-mail: unhm.gradcenter@unh.edu. *Application contact:* Graduate Admissions Office, 603-862-3000, Fax: 603-862-0275, E-mail: grad.school@unh.edu. Web site: http://www.gradschool.unh.edu/manchester/.

University of New Hampshire, Graduate School, Whittemore School of Business and Economics, Department of Business Administration, Durham, NH 03824. Offers business administration (MBA); executive business administration (MBA); health management (MBA); management of technology (MS). *Accreditation:* AACSB. Part-time and evening/weekend programs available. *Faculty:* 24 full-time (4 women). *Students:* 103 full-time (31 women), 79 part-time (22 women); includes 8 minority (2 Black or African American, non-Hispanic/Latino; 3 Asian, non-Hispanic/Latino; 3 Hispanic/Latino), 11 international. Average age 34. 165 applicants, 58% accepted, 69 enrolled. In 2011, 73 master's awarded. *Entrance requirements:* For master's, GMAT. Additional exam requirements/recommendations for international students: Required—TOEFL (minimum score 550 paper-based; 213 computer-based; 80 iBT). *Application deadline:* For fall admission, 7/1 priority date for domestic students, 4/1 for international students; for spring admission, 11/1 for domestic students. Applications are processed on a rolling basis. Application fee: $65. *Expenses:* Contact institution. *Financial support:* In 2011–12, 27 students received support. Fellowships, research assistantships, teaching assistantships, career-related internships or fieldwork, Federal Work-Study, scholarships/grants, and tuition waivers (full and partial) available. Financial award application deadline: 2/15. *Unit head:* Christine Shea, Chairperson, 603-862-3316. *Application contact:* Wendy Harris, Administrative Assistant, 603-862-3326, E-mail: wsbe.grad@unh.edu. Web site: http://www.mba.unh.edu/.

University of New Haven, Graduate School, School of Business, Executive Program in Business Administration, West Haven, CT 06516-1916. Offers EMBA. Part-time and evening/weekend programs available. *Students:* 5 full-time (0 women), 2 part-time (both women); includes 1 minority (Black or African American, non-Hispanic/Latino), 1 international. Average age 45. In 2011, 3 master's awarded. *Entrance requirements:* Additional exam requirements/recommendations for international students: Required—TOEFL (minimum score 520 paper-based; 190 computer-based; 70 iBT), IELTS (minimum score 5.5). *Application deadline:* For fall admission, 5/31 for international students; for winter admission, 10/15 for international students; for spring admission, 1/15 for international students. Applications are processed on a rolling basis. Application fee: $50. Electronic applications accepted. *Expenses:* Contact institution. *Financial support:* Research assistantships with partial tuition reimbursements, teaching assistantships with partial tuition reimbursements, career-related internships or fieldwork, Federal Work-Study, health care benefits, and unspecified assistantships available. Financial award application deadline: 5/1; financial award applicants required to submit FAFSA. *Unit head:* Lawrence Flanagan, Executive Dean, 203-932-7402. *Application contact:* Eloise Gormley, Director of Graduate Admissions, 203-932-7449, Fax: 203-932-7137, E-mail: gradinfo@newhaven.edu. Web site: http://www.newhaven.edu/6465/.

University of New Haven, Graduate School, School of Business, Program in Business Administration, West Haven, CT 06516-1916. Offers accounting (MBA, Certificate), including CPA (MBA); business management (Certificate); business policy and strategy (MBA); finance (MBA), including CFA; global marketing (MBA); human resource management (Certificate); human resources management (MBA); international business (Certificate); marketing (Certificate); sports management (MBA); telecommunications management (Certificate); MBA/MPA. Part-time and evening/weekend programs available. *Students:* 215 full-time (106 women), 182 part-time (87 women); includes 73 minority (38 Black or African American, non-Hispanic/Latino; 2 American Indian or Alaska Native, non-Hispanic/Latino; 22 Asian, non-Hispanic/Latino; 11 Hispanic/Latino), 129 international. 179 applicants, 97% accepted, 93 enrolled. In 2011, 197 master's, 28 other advanced degrees awarded. *Degree requirements:* For master's, thesis or alternative. *Entrance requirements:* For master's, GMAT. Additional exam requirements/recommendations for international students: Required—TOEFL (minimum score 520 paper-based; 190 computer-based; 70 iBT), IELTS (minimum score 5.5). *Application deadline:* For fall admission, 5/31 for international students; for winter admission, 10/15 for international students; for spring admission, 1/15 for international students. Applications are processed on a rolling basis. Application fee: $50. Electronic applications accepted. *Expenses:* Contact institution. *Financial support:* Research assistantships with partial tuition reimbursements, teaching assistantships with partial tuition reimbursements, Federal Work-Study, scholarships/grants, health care benefits, tuition waivers, and unspecified assistantships available. Support available to part-time students. Financial award applicants required to submit FAFSA. *Unit head:* Charles Coleman, Chairman, 203-932-7375. *Application contact:* Eloise Gormley, Director of Graduate Admissions, 203-932-7449, Fax: 203-932-7137, E-mail: gradinfo@newhaven.edu. Web site: http://www.newhaven.edu/7433/.

University of New Mexico, Robert O. Anderson Graduate School of Management, Albuquerque, NM 87131. Offers EMBA, M Acct, MBA, JD/M Acct, JD/MBA, MBA/MA, MBA/MEME. *Accreditation:* AACSB. Part-time and evening/weekend programs available. *Faculty:* 53 full-time (17 women), 47 part-time/adjunct (22 women). *Students:* 334 full-time (163 women), 347 part-time (170 women); includes 305 minority (12 Black or African American, non-Hispanic/Latino; 16 American Indian or Alaska Native, non-Hispanic/Latino; 33 Asian, non-Hispanic/Latino; 242 Hispanic/Latino; 2 Two or more races, non-Hispanic/Latino), 36 international. Average age 30. 331 applicants, 65% accepted, 175 enrolled. In 2011, 283 master's awarded. *Degree requirements:* For master's, minimum GPA of 3.0. *Entrance requirements:* For master's, GMAT or GRE. Additional exam requirements/recommendations for international students: Required—TOEFL (minimum score 550 paper-based; 213 computer-based; 79 iBT). *Application deadline:* For fall admission, 4/1 priority date for domestic students, 4/1 for international students; for spring admission, 10/1 priority date for domestic students, 10/1 for international students. Applications are processed on a rolling basis. Application fee: $50. Electronic applications accepted. *Financial support:* In 2011–12, 62 students received support, including 62 fellowships (averaging $3,400 per year), 50 research assistantships with partial tuition reimbursements available (averaging $6,000 per year); career-related internships or fieldwork, Federal Work-Study, scholarships/grants, and unspecified assistantships also available. Support available to part-time students. Financial award application deadline: 6/1. *Faculty research:* Organizational and social aspects of accounting, international management of technology and entrepreneurship, business ethics and corporate social responsibility, marketing, information assurance and fraud. *Unit head:* Douglas M. Brown, Dean, 505-277-6471, Fax: 505-277-0344, E-mail: browndm@mgt.unm.edu. *Application contact:* Megan Conner, Director, Student Services, 505-277-3290, Fax: 505-277-8436, E-mail: mconner@mgt.unm.edu. Web site: http://www.mgt.unm.edu.

University of New Orleans, Graduate School, College of Business Administration, Program in Business Administration, New Orleans, LA 70148. Offers MBA. *Accreditation:* AACSB. *Degree requirements:* For master's, thesis optional. *Entrance requirements:* For master's, GMAT. Additional exam requirements/recommendations for international students: Required—TOEFL (minimum score 550 paper-based; 213 computer-based; 79 iBT). Electronic applications accepted.

University of North Alabama, College of Business, Florence, AL 35632-0001. Offers MBA. *Accreditation:* ACBSP. Part-time and evening/weekend programs available. *Faculty:* 3 full-time (0 women), 21 part-time/adjunct (3 women). *Students:* 113 full-time (57 women), 404 part-time (182 women); includes 249 minority (42 Black or African American, non-Hispanic/Latino; 3 American Indian or Alaska Native, non-Hispanic/Latino; 193 Asian, non-Hispanic/Latino; 3 Hispanic/Latino; 8 Two or more races, non-Hispanic/Latino), 46 international. Average age 35. In 2011, 163 master's awarded. *Entrance requirements:* For master's, GMAT, minimum GPA of 2.75 in last 60 hours, 2.5 overall on a 3.0 scale; 27 hours of course work in business and economics. *Application deadline:* For fall admission, 7/1 priority date for domestic students; for spring admission, 12/1 for domestic students. Applications are processed on a rolling basis. Application fee: $25. Electronic applications accepted. *Financial support:* Federal Work-Study available. Support available to part-time students. Financial award application deadline: 4/1. *Unit head:* Dr. Kerry Gatlin, Dean, 256-765-4261, Fax: 256-765-4170, E-mail: kpgatlin@una.edu. *Application contact:* Kim Mauldin, Director of Admissions, 256-765-4608, Fax: 256-765-4960, E-mail: komauldin@una.edu. Web site: http://www.una.edu/business/.

The University of North Carolina at Chapel Hill, Kenan-Flagler Business School, Doctoral Program in Business Administration, Chapel Hill, NC 27599. Offers accounting (PhD); finance (PhD); marketing (PhD); operations management (PhD); organizational behavior (PhD); strategy (PhD). *Accreditation:* AACSB. *Degree requirements:* For doctorate, thesis/dissertation. *Entrance requirements:* For doctorate, GMAT or GRE General Test. Electronic applications accepted. *Expenses:* Contact institution.

The University of North Carolina at Chapel Hill, Kenan-Flagler Business School, Executive MBA Programs, Chapel Hill, NC 27599. Offers MBA. *Accreditation:* AACSB. Evening/weekend programs available. Postbaccalaureate distance learning degree programs offered (minimal on-campus study). *Degree requirements:* For master's, exams, project. *Entrance requirements:* For master's, GMAT, 5 years of full-time work experience, interview. Electronic applications accepted. *Expenses:* Contact institution.

The University of North Carolina at Chapel Hill, Kenan-Flagler Business School, MBA Program, Chapel Hill, NC 27599. Offers MBA, MBA/JD, MBA/MHA, MBA/MRP, MBA/MSIS. *Accreditation:* AACSB. *Degree requirements:* For master's, exams, practicum. *Entrance requirements:* For master's, GMAT, interview, minimum 2 years of work experience. Additional exam requirements/recommendations for international students: Required—TOEFL. Electronic applications accepted.

The University of North Carolina at Charlotte, Graduate School, Belk College of Business, Department of Management, Charlotte, NC 28223-0001. Offers business administration (MBA); real estate finance and development (Certificate). *Faculty:* 13 full-time (4 women). *Students:* 148 full-time (59 women), 280 part-time (87 women); includes 60 minority (24 Black or African American, non-Hispanic/Latino; 3 American Indian or Alaska Native, non-Hispanic/Latino; 20 Asian, non-Hispanic/Latino; 8 Hispanic/Latino; 5 Two or more races, non-Hispanic/Latino), 145 international. Average age 30. 289 applicants, 68% accepted, 127 enrolled. In 2011, 198 master's, 3 other advanced degrees awarded. *Degree requirements:* For master's, thesis or alternative. *Entrance requirements:* Additional exam requirements/recommendations for international students: Required—TOEFL (minimum score 557 paper-based; 220 computer-based; 83 iBT). Application fee: $65 ($75 for international students). *Expenses:* Tuition, state resident: full-time $3689. Tuition, nonresident: full-time $15,226. *Required fees:* $2198. Tuition and fees vary according to course load and program. *Financial support:* In 2011–12, 66 teaching assistantships (averaging $12,286 per year) were awarded; career-related internships or fieldwork, institutionally sponsored loans, and scholarships/grants also available. Financial award application deadline: 4/1. *Unit head:* Dr. Joe Mazzola, Interim Dean, 704-687-7577, Fax: 704-687-4014, E-mail: jmazzola@uncc.edu. *Application contact:* Kathy B. Giddings, Director of Graduate Admissions, 704-687-5503, Fax: 704-687-3279, E-mail: gradadm@uncc.edu. Web site: http://belkcollege.uncc.edu/about-college/departments/management.

The University of North Carolina at Greensboro, Graduate School, Bryan School of Business and Economics, Department of Business Administration, Greensboro, NC 27412-5001. Offers MBA, PMC, Postbaccalaureate Certificate, MS/MBA, MSN/MBA. *Accreditation:* AACSB. *Entrance requirements:* For master's, GMAT, GRE General Test, managerial experience. Additional exam requirements/recommendations for international students: Required—TOEFL. Electronic applications accepted.

The University of North Carolina at Pembroke, Graduate Studies, School of Business, Program in Business Administration, Pembroke, NC 28372-1510. Offers MBA. Part-time and evening/weekend programs available. *Degree requirements:* For master's, thesis optional. *Entrance requirements:* For master's, GMAT, minimum GPA of 3.0 in major or 2.5 overall. Additional exam requirements/recommendations for international students: Required—TOEFL.

The University of North Carolina Wilmington, School of Business, Program in Business Administration, Wilmington, NC 28403-3297. Offers MBA. *Accreditation:* AACSB. Part-time and evening/weekend programs available. *Degree requirements:* For master's, comprehensive exam, thesis (for some programs), final project. *Entrance requirements:* For master's, GMAT, 1 year of appropriate work experience. Additional exam requirements/recommendations for international students: Required—TOEFL (minimum score 550 paper-based; 217 computer-based; 79 iBT), IELTS (minimum score 6.5).

University of North Dakota, Graduate School, College of Business and Public Administration, Business Administration Program, Grand Forks, ND 58202. Offers MBA. *Accreditation:* AACSB. Part-time and evening/weekend programs available. Postbaccalaureate distance learning degree programs offered (minimal on-campus study). *Degree requirements:* For master's, comprehensive exam, thesis or alternative, project. *Entrance requirements:* For master's, GMAT, minimum GPA of 3.25. Additional exam requirements/recommendations for international students: Required—TOEFL (minimum score 550 paper-based; 213 computer-based; 79 iBT), IELTS (minimum score 6.5). Electronic applications accepted.

University of Northern Iowa, Graduate College, College of Business Administration, Program in Business Administration, Cedar Falls, IA 50614. Offers MBA. *Accreditation:* AACSB. Part-time and evening/weekend programs available. *Students:* 20 full-time (9 women), 32 part-time (13 women); includes 2 minority (1 Black or African American, non-Hispanic/Latino; 1 Asian, non-Hispanic/Latino), 28 international. 52 applicants, 38% accepted, 14 enrolled. In 2011, 31 master's awarded. *Entrance requirements:* For master's, GMAT (minimum score 500), minimum GPA of 3.0. Additional exam requirements/recommendations for international students: Required—TOEFL (minimum score 500 paper-based; 180 computer-based; 61 iBT). *Application deadline:* For fall admission, 8/1 priority date for domestic students. Applications are processed on a rolling basis. Application fee: $50 ($70 for international students). Electronic applications accepted. *Expenses:* Tuition, state resident: full-time $7476. Tuition, nonresident: full-time $16,410. *Required fees:* $942. *Financial support:* Career-related internships or fieldwork, Federal Work-Study, scholarships/grants, and tuition waivers (full and partial) available. Support available to part-time students. Financial award application deadline: 2/1. *Unit head:* Dr. Leslie K. Wilson, Acting Associate Dean, 319-273-6240, Fax: 319-273-2922, E-mail: leslie.wilson@uni.edu. *Application contact:* Laurie S. Russell, Record Analyst, 319-273-2623, Fax: 319-273-2885, E-mail: laurie.russell@uni.edu. Web site: http://www.cba.uni.edu/mba/.

University of North Florida, Coggin College of Business, MBA Program, Jacksonville, FL 32224. Offers accounting (MBA); construction management (MBA); e-commerce (MBA); economics (MBA); finance (MBA); human resource management (MBA); international business (MBA); logistics (MBA); management applications (MBA). *Accreditation:* AACSB. Part-time and evening/weekend programs available. *Faculty:* 19 full-time (6 women), 1 part-time/adjunct (0 women). *Students:* 145 full-time (57 women), 277 part-time (108 women); includes 67 minority (19 Black or African American, non-Hispanic/Latino; 21 Asian, non-Hispanic/Latino; 20 Hispanic/Latino; 7 Two or more races, non-Hispanic/Latino), 34 international. Average age 29. 200 applicants, 48% accepted, 70 enrolled. In 2011, 153 master's awarded. *Entrance requirements:* For master's, GMAT or GRE, U.S. bachelor's degree from regionally-accredited university or equivalent foreign degree. Additional exam requirements/recommendations for international students: Required—TOEFL (minimum score 550 paper-based; 213 computer-based; 79 iBT). *Application deadline:* For fall admission, 7/1 priority date for domestic students, 5/1 for international students; for spring admission, 11/1 priority date for domestic students, 10/1 for international students. Applications are processed on a rolling basis. Application fee: $30. *Expenses:* Tuition, state resident: full-time $8793; part-time $366.38 per credit hour. Tuition, nonresident: full-time $23,502; part-time $979.24 per credit hour. *Required fees:* $1384; $57.66 per credit hour. Tuition and fees vary according to course load and program. *Financial support:* In 2011–12, 55 students received support, including 1 teaching assistantship (averaging $5,333 per year); research assistantships, Federal Work-Study, and tuition waivers (partial) also available. Support available to part-time students. Financial award application deadline: 4/1; financial award applicants required to submit FAFSA. *Faculty research:* Performance measures, costing, and inventory issues in logistics and supply chain management; inter-organizational systems; international management and marketing practices; e-commerce; organizational learning and socialization processes. *Total annual research expenditures:* $7,686. *Unit head:* Dr. C. Bruce Kavan, Chair, 904-620-2780, Fax: 904-620-2832. *Application contact:* Cheryl Campbell, Graduate Advisor, 904-620-2575, Fax: 904-620-2832, E-mail: ccampbell@unf.edu. Web site: http://www.unf.edu/coggin/academics/graduate/mba.aspx.

University of North Texas, Toulouse Graduate School, College of Business, Denton, TX 76203. Offers MBA, MS, PhD. *Accreditation:* AACSB. Part-time and evening/weekend programs available. *Degree requirements:* For master's, thesis or alternative; for doctorate, thesis/dissertation. *Entrance requirements:* For master's, GMAT or GRE General Test, resume, 3 letters of recommendation; for doctorate, GMAT or GRE General Test, statement of purpose, resume, 3 letters of recommendation. Additional exam requirements/recommendations for international students: Recommended—TOEFL (minimum score 550 paper-based; 213 computer-based; 79 iBT). Electronic applications accepted. *Expenses:* Tuition, state resident: part-time $100 per credit hour. Tuition, nonresident: part-time $413 per credit hour. *Faculty research:* Oil and gas accounting, expert systems, stock returns, occupational safety, service marketing.

University of Notre Dame, Mendoza College of Business, Executive Master of Business Administration Program, Notre Dame, IN 46556. Offers MBA. Program also offered at Notre Dame Chicago Commons in downtown Chicago, IL. *Accreditation:* AACSB. *Faculty:* 21 full-time (1 woman), 8 part-time/adjunct (2 women). *Students:* 241 full-time (47 women); includes 52 minority (15 Black or African American, non-Hispanic/Latino; 1 American Indian or Alaska Native, non-Hispanic/Latino; 16 Asian, non-Hispanic/Latino; 9 Hispanic/Latino; 11 Two or more races, non-Hispanic/Latino), 7 international. Average age 37. 267 applicants, 62% accepted, 113 enrolled. In 2011, 112 master's awarded. *Entrance requirements:* For master's, 5 years of work experience in management. *Application deadline:* For fall admission, 6/1 for domestic students; for winter admission, 11/1 for domestic students. Applications are processed on a rolling basis. Application fee: $100. Electronic applications accepted. *Expenses:* Contact institution. *Financial support:* In 2011–12, 12 students received support, including 12 fellowships (averaging $7,500 per year). Financial award application deadline: 6/1; financial award applicants required to submit FAFSA. *Faculty research:* Exchange rates, compensation, market microstructure or volatility in foreign currency, ethical negotiation/decision-making. *Unit head:* Paul C. Velasco, Director of Degree Programs, 574-631-8876, Fax: 574-631-6783, E-mail: pcvelasco@nd.edu. *Application contact:* Dr. Barry J. VanDyck, Director of Admissions and Recruiting, Executive MBA Program, 574-631-8351, Fax: 574-631-6783, E-mail: bvandyck@nd.edu. Web site: http://emba.nd.edu.

University of Notre Dame, Mendoza College of Business, Master of Business Administration Program, Notre Dame, IN 46556. Offers MBA. *Accreditation:* AACSB. *Faculty:* 71 full-time (10 women), 15 part-time/adjunct (2 women). *Students:* 326 full-time (77 women); includes 25 minority (5 Black or African American, non-Hispanic/Latino; 1 American Indian or Alaska Native, non-Hispanic/Latino; 5 Hispanic/Latino; 14 Native Hawaiian or other Pacific Islander, non-Hispanic/Latino), 53 international. Average age 27. 798 applicants, 37% accepted, 130 enrolled. In 2011, 203 master's awarded. *Entrance requirements:* For master's, GMAT, GRE, work experience. Additional exam requirements/recommendations for international students: Required—TOEFL (minimum score 600 paper-based; 250 computer-based). *Application deadline:* For fall admission, 10/31 priority date for domestic students, 10/31 for international students; for winter admission, 1/9 priority date for domestic students, 1/9 for international students; for spring admission, 4/2 for domestic students, 4/23 for international students. Applications are processed on a rolling basis. Application fee: $175. Electronic applications accepted. *Financial support:* In 2011–12, 212 students received support, including fellowships with full and partial tuition reimbursements available (averaging $25,000 per year), research assistantships (averaging $3,000 per year), teaching assistantships (averaging $3,000 per year); career-related internships or fieldwork, Federal Work-Study, institutionally sponsored loans, scholarships/grants, and unspecified assistantships also available. Financial award application deadline: 4/2; financial award applicants required to submit FAFSA. *Faculty research:* Market micro-structure, marketing and public policy, corporate finance and accounting, corporate governance and ethical behavior, high performing organizations. *Unit head:* Dr. Edward J. Conlon, Associate Dean, Graduate Programs, 574-631-9295, Fax: 574-631-4825, E-mail: econlon@nd.edu. *Application contact:* Brian T. Lohr, Director of MBA Admissions, 574-631-8488, Fax: 574-631-8800, E-mail: blohr@nd.edu. Web site: http://business.nd.edu/mba/.

University of Oklahoma, Michael F. Price College of Business, Program in Business Administration, Norman, OK 73019. Offers MBA, PhD, JD/MBA, MBA/MS. *Accreditation:* AACSB. Part-time and evening/weekend programs available. *Students:* 129 full-time (38 women), 151 part-time (29 women); includes 33 minority (7 Black or African American, non-Hispanic/Latino; 6 American Indian or Alaska Native, non-Hispanic/Latino; 7 Asian, non-Hispanic/Latino; 8 Hispanic/Latino; 5 Two or more races, non-Hispanic/Latino), 35 international. Average age 29. 314 applicants, 45% accepted, 104 enrolled. In 2011, 82 master's, 5 doctorates awarded. Terminal master's awarded for partial completion of doctoral program. *Degree requirements:* For master's, comprehensive exam (for some programs); for doctorate, thesis/dissertation. *Entrance requirements:* For master's, minimum GPA of 3.2; for doctorate, GMAT. Additional exam requirements/recommendations for international students: Required—TOEFL (minimum score 550 paper-based; 79 iBT). *Application deadline:* For fall admission, 6/1 for domestic students, 3/1 for international students; for spring admission, 11/1 for domestic students, 9/1 for international students. Applications are processed on a rolling basis. Application fee: $40 ($90 for international students). Electronic applications accepted. *Expenses:* Tuition, state resident: full-time $4087; part-time $170.30 per credit hour. Tuition, nonresident: full-time $14,875; part-time $619.80 per credit hour. *Required fees:* $2659; $100.25 per credit hour. Tuition and fees vary according to course load and degree level. *Financial support:* In 2011–12, 161 students received support, including 12 fellowships with full tuition reimbursements available (averaging $5,300 per year); career-related internships or fieldwork, scholarships/grants, health care benefits, unspecified assistantships, and summer internships also available. Financial award applicants required to submit FAFSA. *Faculty research:* Corporate finance issues (capital structure, dividend policy and privatization), IT and organizational behavior, entrepreneurship and venture capital, corporate governance and risk management, earning management, behavior of intermediaries in real markets, strategy and firm performance, liquidity risk in financial markets, energy assets. *Unit head:* Dr. Kenneth Evans, Dean, 405-325-0100, Fax: 405-325-3421, E-mail: evansk@ou.edu. *Application contact:* Amber Hasbrook, Academic Counselor, 405-325-4107, Fax: 405-325-7753, E-mail: amber.hasbrook@ou.edu. Web site: http://price.ou.edu.

See Display below and Close-Up on page 253.

University of Oregon, Graduate School, Charles H. Lundquist College of Business, Department of Management, Eugene, OR 97403. Offers PhD. *Accreditation:* AACSB. Part-time programs available. Terminal master's awarded for partial completion of doctoral program. *Degree requirements:* For doctorate, thesis/dissertation, 2 comprehensive exams. *Entrance requirements:* For doctorate, GMAT. Additional exam requirements/recommendations for international students: Required—TOEFL.

University of Oregon, Graduate School, Charles H. Lundquist College of Business, Department of Management: General Business, Eugene, OR 97403. Offers MBA. *Accreditation:* AACSB. *Entrance requirements:* For master's, GMAT. Additional exam requirements/recommendations for international students: Required—TOEFL.

University of Ottawa, Faculty of Graduate and Postdoctoral Studies, Telfer School of Management, Executive Business Administration Program, Ottawa, ON K1N 6N5, Canada. Offers EMBA. *Accreditation:* AACSB. Evening/weekend programs available. *Entrance requirements:* For master's, bachelor's degree or equivalent, minimum B average, business experience. Additional exam requirements/recommendations for international students: Recommended—TOEFL (minimum score 237 computer-based). Electronic applications accepted. *Expenses:* Contact institution.

University of Ottawa, Faculty of Graduate and Postdoctoral Studies, Telfer School of Management, MBA Program, Ottawa, ON K1N 6N5, Canada. Offers MBA. *Accreditation:* AACSB. Part-time and evening/weekend programs available. *Degree requirements:* For master's, thesis optional. *Entrance requirements:* For master's, GMAT, bachelor's degree or equivalent, minimum B average, minimum 2 years of work experience. Additional exam requirements/recommendations for international students: Recommended—TOEFL (minimum score 237 computer-based). Electronic applications accepted.

See Display on next page and Close-Up on page 255.

University of Pennsylvania, Wharton School, Management Department, Philadelphia, PA 19104. Offers MBA, PhD. *Accreditation:* AACSB. *Entrance requirements:* For master's, GMAT; for doctorate, GMAT or GRE. *Expenses: Tuition:* Full-time $26,660; part-time $4944 per course. *Required fees:* $2318; $291 per course. Tuition and fees vary according to course load, degree level and program. *Faculty research:* Cross-cultural leadership, international technology transfers, human resource management, financial services.

University of Pennsylvania, Wharton School, Wharton Doctoral Programs, Philadelphia, PA 19104. Offers accounting (PhD); applied economics (PhD); ethics and legal studies (PhD); finance (PhD); health care management and economics (PhD); management (PhD); marketing (PhD); operations and information management (PhD); statistics (PhD). *Accreditation:* AACSB. *Degree requirements:* For doctorate, thesis/dissertation. *Entrance requirements:* For doctorate, GMAT or GRE, letters of recommendation. Additional exam requirements/recommendations for international students: Required—TOEFL, TWE. Electronic applications accepted. *Expenses: Tuition:* Full-time $26,660; part-time $4944 per course. *Required fees:* $2318; $291 per course. Tuition and fees vary according to course load, degree level and program.

University of Pennsylvania, Wharton School, The Wharton MBA Program, Philadelphia, PA 19104. Offers MBA, DMD/MBA, JD/MBA, MBA/MA, MBA/MS, MBA/MSN, MBA/MSW, MBA/PhD, MD/MBA, VMD/MBA. *Accreditation:* AACSB. *Entrance requirements:* For master's, GMAT, interview, 2 letters of recommendation, resume/curriculum vitae. Additional exam requirements/recommendations for international students: Required—TOEFL. Electronic applications accepted. *Expenses: Tuition:* Full-time $26,660; part-time $4944 per course. *Required fees:* $2318; $291 per course. Tuition and fees vary according to course load, degree level and program. *Faculty research:* Entrepreneurial studies, finance, management of technology.

University of Pennsylvania, Wharton School, The Wharton MBA Program for Executives, Wharton Executive MBA East, Philadelphia, PA 19104. Offers MBA. *Accreditation:* AACSB. Evening/weekend programs available. *Entrance requirements:* For master's, GMAT. Additional exam requirements/recommendations for international students: Recommended—TOEFL. *Expenses: Tuition:* Full-time $26,660; part-time $4944 per course. *Required fees:* $2318; $291 per course. Tuition and fees vary according to course load, degree level and program.

Business Administration and Management—General

University of Pennsylvania, Wharton School, The Wharton MBA Program for Executives, Wharton Executive MBA West, Philadelphia, PA 19104. Offers MBA. *Accreditation:* AACSB. Evening/weekend programs available. *Entrance requirements:* For master's, GMAT. Additional exam requirements/recommendations for international students: Recommended—TOEFL. *Expenses: Tuition:* Full-time $26,660; part-time $4944 per course. *Required fees:* $2318; $291 per course. Tuition and fees vary according to course load, degree level and program.

University of Phoenix–Atlanta Campus, School of Business, Sandy Springs, GA 30350-4153. Offers accounting (MBA); business administration (MBA); global management (MBA); human resources management (MBA, MM); management (MM); marketing (MBA); public administration (MM). Evening/weekend programs available. Postbaccalaureate distance learning degree programs offered. *Degree requirements:* For master's, thesis (for some programs). *Entrance requirements:* For master's, minimum undergraduate GPA of 3.0, 3 years of work experience. Additional exam requirements/recommendations for international students: Required—TOEFL (minimum score 550 paper-based; 213 computer-based; 79 iBT).

University of Phoenix–Augusta Campus, School of Business, Augusta, GA 30909-4583. Offers accounting (MBA); business administration (MBA); business and management (MBA, MM); global management (MBA); human resources management (MBA, MM); management (MM); marketing (MBA); public administration (MBA, MM). Postbaccalaureate distance learning degree programs offered.

University of Phoenix–Austin Campus, School of Business, Austin, TX 78759. Offers accounting (MBA); business administration (MBA); business and management (MBA); e-business (MBA); global management (MBA); human resources management (MBA, MM); management (MM); marketing (MBA); public administration (MBA). Postbaccalaureate distance learning degree programs offered.

University of Phoenix–Bay Area Campus, School of Business, San Jose, CA 95134-1805. Offers accountancy (MS); accounting (MBA); business administration (MBA, DBA); energy management (MBA); global management (MBA); health care management (MBA); human resource management (MBA); human resources management (MM); management (MM); marketing (MBA); organizational leadership (DM); project management (MBA); public administration (MPA); technology management (MBA). Evening/weekend programs available. Postbaccalaureate distance learning degree programs offered (no on-campus study). *Degree requirements:* For master's, thesis (for some programs). *Entrance requirements:* For master's, minimum undergraduate GPA of 3.0, 3 years of work experience. Additional exam requirements/recommendations for international students: Required—TOEFL (minimum score 550 paper-based; 213 computer-based; 79 iBT). Electronic applications accepted.

University of Phoenix–Birmingham Campus, College of Graduate Business and Management, Birmingham, AL 35244. Offers accounting (MBA); business administration (MBA); global management (MBA); human resources management (MBA, MM); management (MM); marketing (MBA); public administration (MM).

University of Phoenix–Boston Campus, School of Business, Braintree, MA 02184-4949. Offers administration (MBA); global management (MBA). Evening/weekend programs available. *Degree requirements:* For master's, thesis (for some programs). *Entrance requirements:* For master's, 3 years of work experience, minimum undergraduate GPA of 3.0. Additional exam requirements/recommendations for international students: Required—TOEFL (minimum score 550 paper-based; 213 computer-based; 79 iBT).

University of Phoenix–Central Florida Campus, College of Information Systems and Technology, Maitland, FL 32751-7057. Offers management (MIS); technology management (MBA). Evening/weekend programs available. *Degree requirements:* For master's, thesis (for some programs). *Entrance requirements:* For master's, minimum undergraduate GPA of 3.0, 3 years work experience. Additional exam requirements/recommendations for international students: Required—TOEFL (minimum score 550 paper-based; 213 computer-based; 79 iBT). Electronic applications accepted.

University of Phoenix–Central Florida Campus, School of Business, Maitland, FL 32751-7057. Offers accounting (MBA); business administration (MBA); business and management (MM); global management (MBA); human resources management (MBA, MM); management (MM); marketing (MBA); public administration (MBA, MM). Evening/weekend programs available. *Degree requirements:* For master's, thesis (for some programs). *Entrance requirements:* For master's, minimum undergraduate GPA of 3.0, 3 years work experience. Additional exam requirements/recommendations for international students: Required—TOEFL (minimum score 550 paper-based; 213 computer-based; 79 iBT). Electronic applications accepted.

University of Phoenix–Central Massachusetts Campus, School of Business, Westborough, MA 01581-3906. Offers business administration (MBA); global management (MBA). Evening/weekend programs available. *Degree requirements:* For master's, thesis (for some programs). *Entrance requirements:* For master's, minimum undergraduate GPA of 3.0, 3 years of work experience. Additional exam requirements/recommendations for international students: Required—TOEFL (minimum score 550 paper-based; 213 computer-based; 79 iBT). Electronic applications accepted.

University of Phoenix–Central Valley Campus, School of Business, Fresno, CA 93720-1562. Offers accounting (MBA); business administration (MBA); global management (MBA); human resources management (MBA, MM); management (MM); marketing (MBA); public administration (MBA, MM).

University of Phoenix–Charlotte Campus, School of Business, Charlotte, NC 28273-3409. Offers accounting (MBA); business administration (MBA); global management (MBA). Evening/weekend programs available. *Degree requirements:* For master's, thesis (for some programs). *Entrance requirements:* For master's, minimum undergraduate GPA of 3.0, 3 years work experience. Additional exam requirements/recommendations for international students: Required—TOEFL (minimum score 550 paper-based; 213 computer-based; 79 iBT). Electronic applications accepted.

University of Phoenix–Chattanooga Campus, School of Business, Chattanooga, TN 37421-3707. Offers accounting (MBA); business administration (MBA); business and management (MBA); global management (MBA); human resources management (MBA, MM); management (MM); marketing (MBA); public administration (MBA, MM). Postbaccalaureate distance learning degree programs offered.

University of Phoenix–Cheyenne Campus, School of Business, Cheyenne, WY 82009. Offers global management (MBA); human resources management (MBA, MM); management (MM); marketing (MBA); public administration (MBA, MM). Postbaccalaureate distance learning degree programs offered.

University of Phoenix–Chicago Campus, School of Business, Schaumburg, IL 60173-4399. Offers business administration (MBA); global management (MBA); human resources management (MBA); information systems (MIS); management (MM). Evening/weekend programs available. *Degree requirements:* For master's, thesis (for some programs). *Entrance requirements:* For master's, minimum undergraduate GPA of 3.0, 3 years of work experience. Additional exam requirements/recommendations for international students: Required—TOEFL (minimum score 550 paper-based; 213 computer-based; 79 iBT). Electronic applications accepted.

University of Phoenix–Cincinnati Campus, School of Business, West Chester, OH 45069-4875. Offers accounting (MBA); business administration (MBA); global management (MBA); human resources management (MBA, MM); management (MM); marketing (MBA); public administration (MM). Evening/weekend programs available.

Degree requirements: For master's, thesis (for some programs). *Entrance requirements:* For master's, minimum undergraduate GPA of 3.0, 3 years of work experience. Additional exam requirements/recommendations for international students: Required—TOEFL (minimum score 550 paper-based; 213 computer-based; 79 iBT). Electronic applications accepted.

University of Phoenix–Cleveland Campus, School of Business, Independence, OH 44131-2194. Offers accounting (MBA); business administration (MBA); global management (MBA); human resources management (MBA, MM); management (MM); marketing (MBA); public administration (MBA, MM). Evening/weekend programs available. Postbaccalaureate distance learning degree programs offered (no on-campus study). *Degree requirements:* For master's, thesis (for some programs). *Entrance requirements:* For master's, minimum undergraduate GPA of 3.0, 3 years of work experience. Additional exam requirements/recommendations for international students: Required—TOEFL (minimum score 550 paper-based; 213 computer-based; 79 iBT). Electronic applications accepted.

University of Phoenix–Columbia Campus, School of Business, Columbia, SC 29223. Offers MBA. Postbaccalaureate distance learning degree programs offered.

University of Phoenix–Columbus Georgia Campus, School of Business, Columbus, GA 31904-6321. Offers accounting (MBA); business administration (MBA); global management (MBA); human resources management (MBA, MM); management (MM); marketing (MBA); public administration (MBA). Evening/weekend programs available. *Degree requirements:* For master's, thesis (for some programs). *Entrance requirements:* For master's, minimum undergraduate GPA of 3.0, 3 years of work experience. Additional exam requirements/recommendations for international students: Required—TOEFL (minimum score 550 paper-based; 213 computer-based; 79 iBT). Electronic applications accepted.

University of Phoenix–Columbus Ohio Campus, School of Business, Columbus, OH 43240-4032. Offers accounting (MBA); business administration (MBA); global management (MBA); human resources management (MBA, MM); management (MM); marketing (MBA); public administration (MM). Evening/weekend programs available. Postbaccalaureate distance learning degree programs offered. *Degree requirements:* For master's, thesis (for some programs). *Entrance requirements:* For master's, minimum undergraduate GPA of 3.0, 3 years of work experience. Additional exam requirements/recommendations for international students: Required—TOEFL (minimum score 550 paper-based; 213 computer-based; 79 iBT). Electronic applications accepted.

University of Phoenix–Dallas Campus, School of Business, Dallas, TX 75251-2009. Offers accounting (MBA); business administration (MBA); global management (MBA); human resources management (MBA, MM); management (MM); marketing (MBA); public administration (MBA, MM). Evening/weekend programs available. Postbaccalaureate distance learning degree programs offered. *Degree requirements:* For master's, thesis (for some programs). *Entrance requirements:* For master's, 3 years of work experience, minimum undergraduate GPA of 3.0. Additional exam requirements/recommendations for international students: Required—TOEFL (minimum score 550 paper-based; 213 computer-based; 79 iBT). Electronic applications accepted.

University of Phoenix–Denver Campus, College of Information Systems and Technology, Lone Tree, CO 80124-5453. Offers e-business (MBA); management (MIS); technology management (MBA). Evening/weekend programs available. Postbaccalaureate distance learning degree programs offered. *Degree requirements:* For master's, thesis (for some programs). *Entrance requirements:* For master's, minimum undergraduate GPA of 3.0, 3 years of work experience. Additional exam requirements/recommendations for international students: Required—TOEFL (minimum score 550 paper-based; 213 computer-based; 79 iBT). Electronic applications accepted.

University of Phoenix–Denver Campus, School of Business, Lone Tree, CO 80124-5453. Offers accountancy (MSA); accounting (MBA); business administration (MBA); e-business (MBA); global management (MBA); human resources management (MBA, MM); management (MM); marketing (MBA); public administration (MBA, MM). Evening/weekend programs available. Postbaccalaureate distance learning degree programs offered. *Degree requirements:* For master's, thesis (for some programs). *Entrance requirements:* For master's, minimum undergraduate GPA of 3.0, 3 years work experience. Additional exam requirements/recommendations for international students: Required—TOEFL (minimum score 550 paper-based; 213 computer-based; 79 iBT). Electronic applications accepted.

University of Phoenix–Des Moines Campus, School of Business, Des Moines, IA 50266. Offers accounting (MBA); business administration (MBA); global management (MBA); human resources management (MBA, MM); management (MM); marketing (MBA); public administration (MBA, MM). Postbaccalaureate distance learning degree programs offered.

University of Phoenix–Eastern Washington Campus, School of Business, Spokane Valley, WA 99212-2531. Offers accounting (MBA); business administration (MBA); human resources management (MBA); marketing (MBA); public administration (MBA). Evening/weekend programs available. *Degree requirements:* For master's, thesis (for some programs). *Entrance requirements:* For master's, minimum undergraduate GPA of 3.0, 3 years of work experience. Additional exam requirements/recommendations for international students: Required—TOEFL (minimum score 550 paper-based; 213 computer-based; 79 iBT). Electronic applications accepted.

University of Phoenix–Fairfield County Campus, School of Business, Norwalk, CT 06854-1799. Offers MBA.

University of Phoenix–Harrisburg Campus, School of Business, Harrisburg, PA 17112. Offers accounting (MBA); business administration (MBA); business and management (MBA); global management (MBA); human resources management (MBA, MM); management (MM); marketing (MBA); public administration (MBA, MM). Postbaccalaureate distance learning degree programs offered.

University of Phoenix–Hawaii Campus, School of Business, Honolulu, HI 96813-4317. Offers accounting (MBA); business administration (MBA); global management (MBA); human resources management (MBA, MM); management (MM); marketing (MBA); public administration (MBA, MM). Evening/weekend programs available. *Degree requirements:* For master's, thesis (for some programs). *Entrance requirements:* For master's, minimum undergraduate GPA of 3.0, 3 years work experience. Additional exam requirements/recommendations for international students: Required—TOEFL (minimum score 550 paper-based; 213 computer-based; 79 iBT). Electronic applications accepted.

University of Phoenix–Houston Campus, School of Business, Houston, TX 77079-2004. Offers accounting (MBA); business administration (MBA); global management (MBA); human resources management (MBA, MM); management (MM); marketing (MBA); public administration (MBA, MM). Evening/weekend programs available. Postbaccalaureate distance learning degree programs offered. *Degree requirements:* For master's, thesis (for some programs). *Entrance requirements:* For master's, 3 years of work experience, minimum undergraduate GPA of 3.0. Additional exam requirements/recommendations for international students: Required—TOEFL (minimum score 550 paper-based; 213 computer-based; 79 iBT). Electronic applications accepted.

University of Phoenix–Idaho Campus, School of Business, Meridian, ID 83642-5114. Offers accounting (MBA); administration (MBA); global management (MBA); human resources management (MBA, MM); management (MM); marketing (MBA); public administration (MM). Evening/weekend programs available. Postbaccalaureate distance learning degree programs offered. *Degree requirements:* For master's, thesis (for some programs). *Entrance requirements:* For master's, 3 years of work experience, minimum undergraduate GPA of 3.0. Additional exam requirements/recommendations for international students: Required—TOEFL (minimum score 550 paper-based; 213 computer-based). Electronic applications accepted.

University of Phoenix–Indianapolis Campus, School of Business, Indianapolis, IN 46250-932. Offers accounting (MBA); business administration (MBA); global management (MBA); human resources management (MBA, MM); management (MM); marketing (MBA); public administration (MM). Evening/weekend programs available. *Degree requirements:* For master's, thesis (for some programs). *Entrance requirements:* For master's, minimum undergraduate GPA of 3.0, 3 years of work experience. Additional exam requirements/recommendations for international students: Required—TOEFL (minimum score 550 paper-based; 213 computer-based). Electronic applications accepted.

University of Phoenix–Jersey City Campus, School of Business, Jersey City, NJ 07310. Offers accounting (MBA); business administration (MBA); global management (MBA); human resources management (MBA, MM); management (MM); marketing (MBA); public administration (MBA, MM).

University of Phoenix–Kansas City Campus, School of Business, Kansas City, MO 64131-4517. Offers accounting (MBA); business administration (MBA); global management (MBA); human resources management (MBA, MM); management (MM); marketing (MBA); public administration (MBA). Evening/weekend programs available. *Degree requirements:* For master's, thesis (for some programs). *Entrance requirements:* For master's, minimum undergraduate GPA of 3.0, 3 years of work experience. Additional exam requirements/recommendations for international students: Required—TOEFL (minimum score 550 paper-based; 213 computer-based). Electronic applications accepted.

University of Phoenix–Las Vegas Campus, School of Business, Las Vegas, NV 89128. Offers accounting (MBA); business administration (MBA); global management (MBA); human resources management (MBA, MM); management (MM); marketing (MBA); public administration (MM). Evening/weekend programs available. Postbaccalaureate distance learning degree programs offered (no on-campus study). *Degree requirements:* For master's, thesis (for some programs). *Entrance requirements:* For master's, minimum undergraduate GPA of 3.0, 3 years of work experience. Additional exam requirements/recommendations for international students: Required—TOEFL (minimum score 550 paper-based; 213 computer-based; 79 iBT). Electronic applications accepted.

University of Phoenix–Little Rock Campus, School of Business, Little Rock, AR 72211-3500. Offers MBA, MM. Evening/weekend programs available. *Degree requirements:* For master's, thesis (for some programs). *Entrance requirements:* For master's, minimum undergraduate GPA of 3.0, 3 years of work experience. Additional exam requirements/recommendations for international students: Required—TOEFL (minimum score 550 paper-based; 213 computer-based). Electronic applications accepted.

University of Phoenix–Louisiana Campus, School of Business, Metairie, LA 70001-2082. Offers accounting (MBA); business administration (MBA); global management (MBA); human resources management (MBA, MM); management (MM); marketing (MBA); public administration (MBA). Evening/weekend programs available. *Degree requirements:* For master's, thesis (for some programs). *Entrance requirements:* For master's, minimum undergraduate GPA of 3.0, 3 years work experience. Additional exam requirements/recommendations for international students: Required—TOEFL (minimum score 550 paper-based; 213 computer-based; 79 iBT). Electronic applications accepted.

University of Phoenix–Louisville Campus, School of Business, Louisville, KY 40223-3839. Offers MBA. Evening/weekend programs available. Postbaccalaureate distance learning degree programs offered. *Students:* 27 full-time (16 women); includes 9 minority (all Black or African American, non-Hispanic/Latino). Average age 40. *Entrance requirements:* Additional exam requirements/recommendations for international students: Required—TOEFL, TOEIC (Test of English as an International Communication), Berlitz Online English Proficiency Exam, Pearson Test of English, or IELTS. *Application deadline:* Applications are processed on a rolling basis. Application fee: $45. Electronic applications accepted. *Expenses: Tuition:* Full-time $12,854. *Required fees:* $915. One-time fee: $45 full-time. Full-time tuition and fees vary according to course load, campus/location and program. *Financial support:* Scholarships/grants available. Financial award applicants required to submit FAFSA. *Application contact:* 866-766-0766. Web site: http://www.phoenix.edu/colleges_divisions/business.html.

University of Phoenix–Madison Campus, School of Business, Madison, WI 53718-2416. Offers accounting (MBA); business and management (MBA); e-business (MBA); global management (MBA); human resources management (MBA, MM); management (MM); marketing (MBA); public administration (MBA).

University of Phoenix–Maryland Campus, School of Business, Columbia, MD 21045-5424. Offers global management (MBA); technology management (MBA). Evening/weekend programs available. Postbaccalaureate distance learning degree programs offered. *Students:* 121 full-time (58 women); includes 65 minority (59 Black or African American, non-Hispanic/Latino; 3 Asian, non-Hispanic/Latino; 1 Hispanic/Latino; 2 Two or more races, non-Hispanic/Latino), 3 international. Average age 41. *Entrance requirements:* Additional exam requirements/recommendations for international students: Required—TOEFL, TOEIC (Test of English as an International Communication), Berlitz Online English Proficiency Exam, PTE (Pearson Test of English), or IELTS. *Application deadline:* Applications are processed on a rolling basis. Application fee: $45. Electronic applications accepted. *Expenses: Tuition:* Full-time $17,098. *Required fees:* $915. One-time fee: $45 full-time. Full-time tuition and fees vary according to course load, campus/location and program. *Financial support:* Scholarships/grants available. Financial award applicants required to submit FAFSA. *Application contact:* 866-766-0766. Web site: http://www.phoenix.edu/colleges_divisions/business.html.

University of Phoenix–Memphis Campus, School of Business, Cordova, TN 38018. Offers accounting (MBA); business and management (MBA); e-business (MBA); global management (MBA); human resources management (MBA, MM); management (MM); marketing (MBA); public administration (MBA, MM).

University of Phoenix–Milwaukee Campus, School of Business, Milwaukee, WI 53045. Offers accounting (MS); business administration (MBA, DBA); human resources management (MM); management (MM); organizational leadership (DM); public administration (MPA).

University of Phoenix–Minneapolis/St. Louis Park Campus, School of Business, St. Louis Park, MN 55426. Offers accounting (MBA); business administration (MBA); global management (MBA); human resources management (MBA); management (MM); marketing (MBA); public administration (MBA).

University of Phoenix–Nashville Campus, School of Business, Nashville, TN 37214-5048. Offers business administration (MBA); human resources management (MBA); management (MM). Evening/weekend programs available. *Degree requirements:* For master's, thesis (for some programs). *Entrance requirements:* For master's, minimum undergraduate GPA of 3.0, 3 years of work experience. Additional exam requirements/recommendations for international students: Required—TOEFL (minimum score 550 paper-based; 213 computer-based; 79 iBT). Electronic applications accepted.

University of Phoenix–New Mexico Campus, School of Business, Albuquerque, NM 87113-1570. Offers accounting (MBA); business administration (MBA); global management (MBA); human resources management (MBA, MM); management (MM); marketing (MBA). Evening/weekend programs available. *Degree requirements:* For master's, thesis (for some programs). *Entrance requirements:* For master's, 3 years of work experience, minimum undergraduate GPA of 3.0. Additional exam requirements/recommendations for international students: Required—TOEFL (minimum score 550 paper-based; 213 computer-based; 79 iBT). Electronic applications accepted.

University of Phoenix–Northern Nevada Campus, School of Business, Reno, NV 89521-5862. Offers accounting (MBA); business administration (MBA); global management (MBA); human resources management (MBA, MM); management (MM); marketing (MBA); public administration (MBA, MM).

University of Phoenix–Northern Virginia Campus, School of Business, Reston, VA 20190. Offers business administration (MBA); public accounting (MPA). Evening/weekend programs available. Postbaccalaureate distance learning degree programs offered. *Entrance requirements:* For master's, minimum undergraduate GPA of 2.5 from accredited university, 3 years of work experience, citizen of the United States or valid visa. Additional exam requirements/recommendations for international students: Required—TOEFL (minimum score 79 iBT), TOEFL (minimum score 213 paper, 79 iBT), TOEIC, IELTS or Berlitz. Electronic applications accepted.

University of Phoenix–North Florida Campus, College of Information Systems and Technology, Jacksonville, FL 32216-0959. Offers information systems (MIS); management (MIS). Evening/weekend programs available. *Degree requirements:* For master's, thesis (for some programs). *Entrance requirements:* For master's, minimum undergraduate GPA of 3.0, 3 years work experience. Additional exam requirements/recommendations for international students: Required—TOEFL (minimum score 550 paper-based; 213 computer-based; 79 iBT). Electronic applications accepted.

University of Phoenix–North Florida Campus, School of Business, Jacksonville, FL 32216-0959. Offers accounting (MBA); business administration (MBA); global management (MBA); human resources management (MBA, MM); management (MM); marketing (MBA); public administration (MBA, MM). Evening/weekend programs available. *Degree requirements:* For master's, thesis (for some programs). *Entrance requirements:* For master's, minimum undergraduate GPA of 3.0, 3 years work experience. Additional exam requirements/recommendations for international students: Required—TOEFL (minimum score 550 paper-based; 213 computer-based; 79 iBT). Electronic applications accepted.

University of Phoenix–Northwest Arkansas Campus, School of Business, Rogers, AR 72756-9615. Offers accounting (MBA); business and management (MBA); global management (MBA); human resources management (MBA, MM); management (MM); marketing (MBA); public administration (MBA, MM).

University of Phoenix–Oklahoma City Campus, School of Business, Oklahoma City, OK 73116-8244. Offers accounting (MBA); business administration (MBA); global management (MBA); human resource management (MBA); management (MM); marketing (MBA). Evening/weekend programs available. *Degree requirements:* For master's, thesis (for some programs). *Entrance requirements:* For master's, minimum undergraduate GPA of 3.0, 3 years of work experience. Additional exam requirements/recommendations for international students: Required—TOEFL (minimum score 550 paper-based; 213 computer-based; 79 iBT). Electronic applications accepted.

University of Phoenix–Omaha Campus, School of Business, Omaha, NE 68154-5240. Offers accounting (MBA); business and management (MBA); global management (MBA); human resources management (MBA, MM); management (MM); marketing (MBA); public administration (MBA, MM).

University of Phoenix–Online Campus, School of Advanced Studies, Phoenix, AZ 85034-7209. Offers business administration (DBA); education (Ed S); educational leadership (Ed D), including curriculum and instruction, education technology, educational leadership; health administration (DHA); higher education administration (PhD); industrial/organizational psychology (PhD); nursing (PhD); organizational leadership (DM), including information systems and technology, organizational leadership. Evening/weekend programs available. Postbaccalaureate distance learning degree programs offered. *Students:* 7,581 full-time (5,042 women); includes 3,199 minority (2,505 Black or African American, non-Hispanic/Latino; 68 American Indian or Alaska Native, non-Hispanic/Latino; 158 Asian, non-Hispanic/Latino; 395 Hispanic/Latino; 46 Native Hawaiian or other Pacific Islander, non-Hispanic/Latino; 27 Two or more races, non-Hispanic/Latino), 397 international. Average age 44. *Degree requirements:* For doctorate, thesis/dissertation. *Entrance requirements:* Additional exam requirements/recommendations for international students: Required—TOEFL, TOEIC (Test of English as an International Communication), Berlitz Online English Proficiency Exam, Pearson Test of English, or IELTS. *Application deadline:* Applications are processed on a rolling basis. Application fee: $45. Electronic applications accepted. *Expenses:* Contact institution. *Financial support:* Scholarships/grants available. Financial award applicants required to submit FAFSA. *Unit head:* Dr. Jeremy Moreland, Executive Dean. *Application contact:* 866-766-0766. Web site: http://www.phoenix.edu/colleges_divisions/doctoral.html.

University of Phoenix–Online Campus, School of Business, Phoenix, AZ 85034-7209. Offers accountancy (MS); accounting (MBA); business administration (MBA); energy management (MBA); global management (MBA); health care management (MBA); human resource management (MBA); human resources management (MM); international (MM); management (MM); marketing (MBA, Graduate Certificate); organizational management (MA); project management (MBA, Graduate Certificate); public administration (MBA, MM, MPA); technology management (MBA). Evening/weekend programs available. Postbaccalaureate distance learning degree programs offered. *Students:* 18,883 full-time (11,868 women); includes 6,302 minority (4,182 Black or African American, non-Hispanic/Latino; 121 American Indian or Alaska Native, non-Hispanic/Latino; 478 Asian, non-Hispanic/Latino; 1,252 Hispanic/Latino; 121 Native Hawaiian or other Pacific Islander, non-Hispanic/Latino; 148 Two or more races, non-Hispanic/Latino), 1,000 international. Average age 37. *Entrance requirements:* Additional exam requirements/recommendations for international students: Required—TOEFL, TOEIC (Test of English as an International Communication), Berlitz Online English Proficiency Exam, Pearson Test of English, or IELTS. *Application deadline:* Applications are processed on a rolling basis. Application fee: $45. Electronic applications accepted. *Expenses: Tuition:* Full-time $17,160. *Required fees:* $920. One-time fee: $45 full-time. Full-time tuition and fees vary according to course load, degree level, campus/location and program. *Financial support:* Scholarships/grants available. Financial award applicants required to submit FAFSA. *Application contact:* 866-766-0766. Web site: http://www.phoenix.edu/colleges_divisions/business.html.

University of Phoenix–Oregon Campus, School of Business, Tigard, OR 97223. Offers accounting (MBA); business administration (MBA); global management (MBA); human resource management (MM); human resources management (MBA); management (MM); marketing (MBA); public administration (MM). Evening/weekend programs available. *Degree requirements:* For master's, thesis (for some programs). *Entrance requirements:* For master's, minimum undergraduate GPA of 3.0, 3 years of work experience. Additional exam requirements/recommendations for international students: Required—TOEFL (minimum score 550 paper-based; 213 computer-based; 79 iBT). Electronic applications accepted.

University of Phoenix–Philadelphia Campus, School of Business, Wayne, PA 19087-2121. Offers accounting (MBA); business administration (MBA); global management (MBA); human resources management (MBA, MM); management (MM); marketing (MBA); public administration (MM). Evening/weekend programs available. *Degree requirements:* For master's, thesis (for some programs). *Entrance requirements:* For master's, minimum undergraduate GPA of 3.0, 3 years work experience. Additional exam requirements/recommendations for international students: Required—TOEFL (minimum score 550 paper-based; 213 computer-based; 79 iBT). Electronic applications accepted.

University of Phoenix–Phoenix Main Campus, School of Business, Tempe, AZ 85282-2371. Offers accounting (MBA, MS); business administration (MBA); energy management (MBA); global management (MBA); health care management (MBA); human resource management (MBA); management (MM); marketing (MBA); project management (MBA); public administration (MPA); technology management (MBA). Evening/weekend programs available. Postbaccalaureate distance learning degree programs offered. *Students:* 1,151 full-time (531 women); includes 310 minority (99 Black or African American, non-Hispanic/Latino; 10 American Indian or Alaska Native, non-Hispanic/Latino; 39 Asian, non-Hispanic/Latino; 130 Hispanic/Latino; 15 Native Hawaiian or other Pacific Islander, non-Hispanic/Latino; 17 Two or more races, non-Hispanic/Latino), 63 international. Average age 34. *Entrance requirements:* Additional exam requirements/recommendations for international students: Required—TOEFL, TOEIC (Test of English as an International Communication), Berlitz Online English Proficiency Exam, Pearson Test of English, or IELTS. *Application deadline:* Applications are processed on a rolling basis. Application fee: $45. Electronic applications accepted. *Expenses:* Contact institution. *Financial support:* Scholarships/grants available. Financial award applicants required to submit FAFSA. *Application contact:* 866-766-0766. Web site: http://www.phoenix.edu/colleges_divisions/business.html.

University of Phoenix–Pittsburgh Campus, School of Business, Pittsburgh, PA 15276. Offers accounting (MBA); business administration (MBA); global management (MBA); human resources management (MBA, MM); management (MM); marketing (MBA); public administration (MBA, MM). Evening/weekend programs available. *Degree requirements:* For master's, thesis (for some programs). *Entrance requirements:* For master's, minimum undergraduate GPA of 3.0, 3 years work experience. Additional exam requirements/recommendations for international students: Required—TOEFL (minimum score 550 paper-based; 213 computer-based; 79 iBT). Electronic applications accepted.

University of Phoenix–Puerto Rico Campus, School of Business, Guaynabo, PR 00968. Offers accounting (MBA); energy management (MBA); global management (MBA); human resource management (MBA); marketing (MBA); project management (MBA); small business administration (MBA). Evening/weekend programs available. *Degree requirements:* For master's, thesis (for some programs). *Entrance requirements:* For master's, minimum undergraduate GPA of 3.0, 3 years work experience. Additional exam requirements/recommendations for international students: Required—TOEFL (minimum score 550 paper-based; 213 computer-based; 79 iBT). Electronic applications accepted.

University of Phoenix–Raleigh Campus, College of Information Systems and Technology, Raleigh, NC 27606. Offers information systems and technology (MIS); management (MIS); technology management (MBA).

University of Phoenix–Raleigh Campus, School of Business, Raleigh, NC 27606. Offers accounting (MBA); business administration (MBA); e-business (MBA); global management (MBA); human resources management (MBA); marketing (MBA).

University of Phoenix–Richmond Campus, School of Business, Richmond, VA 23230. Offers accounting (MBA); business administration (MBA); global management (MBA); human resources management (MBA, MM); management (MM); marketing (MBA); public administration (MBA, MM). Evening/weekend programs available. *Degree requirements:* For master's, thesis (for some programs). *Entrance requirements:* For master's, minimum undergraduate GPA of 3.0, 3 years work experience. Additional exam requirements/recommendations for international students: Required—TOEFL (minimum score 550 paper-based; 213 computer-based; 79 iBT). Electronic applications accepted.

University of Phoenix–Sacramento Valley Campus, College of Information Systems and Technology, Sacramento, CA 95833-3632. Offers management (MIS); technology management (MBA). Evening/weekend programs available. *Degree requirements:* For master's, thesis (for some programs). *Entrance requirements:* For master's, minimum undergraduate GPA of 3.0, 3 years work experience. Additional exam requirements/recommendations for international students: Required—TOEFL (minimum score 550 paper-based; 213 computer-based; 79 iBT). Electronic applications accepted.

University of Phoenix–Sacramento Valley Campus, School of Business, Sacramento, CA 95833-3632. Offers accounting (MBA); business administration (MBA); global management (MBA); human resources management (MBA, MM); management (MM); marketing (MBA); public administration (MBA, MM). Evening/weekend programs available. *Degree requirements:* For master's, thesis (for some programs). *Entrance requirements:* For master's, minimum undergraduate GPA of 3.0, 3 years work experience. Additional exam requirements/recommendations for international students: Required—TOEFL (minimum score 550 paper-based; 213 computer-based; 79 iBT). Electronic applications accepted.

University of Phoenix–St. Louis Campus, School of Business, St. Louis, MO 63043-4828. Offers accounting (MBA); business administration (MBA); global management (MBA); human resources management (MBA, MM); management (MM); marketing (MBA); public administration (MM). Evening/weekend programs available. *Degree requirements:* For master's, thesis (for some programs). *Entrance requirements:* For master's, 3 years of work experience, minimum undergraduate GPA of 3.0. Additional exam requirements/recommendations for international students: Required—TOEFL (minimum score 550 paper-based; 213 computer-based; 79 iBT). Electronic applications accepted.

University of Phoenix–San Antonio Campus, School of Business, San Antonio, TX 78230. Offers accounting (MBA); business administration (MBA); e-business (MBA); global management (MBA); human resources management (MBA, MM); management (MM); marketing (MBA); public administration (MBA, MM).

University of Phoenix–San Diego Campus, College of Information Systems and Technology, San Diego, CA 92123. Offers management (MIS); technology management (MBA). Evening/weekend programs available. *Degree requirements:* For master's, thesis (for some programs). *Entrance requirements:* For master's, minimum undergraduate GPA of 3.0, 3 years work experience. Additional exam requirements/recommendations for international students: Required—TOEFL (minimum score 550 paper-based; 213 computer-based; 79 iBT). Electronic applications accepted.

University of Phoenix–San Diego Campus, School of Business, San Diego, CA 92123. Offers accounting (MBA); business administration (MBA); global management (MBA); human resources management (MBA, MM); management (MM); marketing (MBA); public administration (MBA). Evening/weekend programs available. *Degree requirements:* For master's, thesis (for some programs). *Entrance requirements:* For master's, 3 years of work experience, minimum undergraduate GPA of 3.0. Additional exam requirements/recommendations for international students: Required—TOEFL (minimum score 550 paper-based; 213 computer-based; 79 iBT). Electronic applications accepted.

University of Phoenix–Savannah Campus, School of Business, Savannah, GA 31405-7400. Offers accounting (MBA); business administration (MBA); global management (MBA); human resources management (MBA, MM); management (MM); marketing (MBA); public administration (MBA, MM).

University of Phoenix–Southern Arizona Campus, School of Business, Tucson, AZ 85711. Offers accountancy (MS); accounting (MBA); business administration (MBA); global management (MBA); human resources management (MBA); management (MM); marketing (MBA). Evening/weekend programs available. *Degree requirements:* For master's, thesis (for some programs). *Entrance requirements:* For master's, minimum undergraduate GPA of 3.0, 3 years of work experience. Additional exam requirements/recommendations for international students: Required—TOEFL (minimum score 550 paper-based; 213 computer-based; 79 iBT). Electronic applications accepted.

University of Phoenix–Southern California Campus, School of Business, Costa Mesa, CA 92626. Offers accounting (MIS); business administration (MBA); energy management (MBA); global management (MBA); health care management (MBA); human resource management (MBA); management (MM); marketing (MBA); project management (MBA); public administration (MPA); technology management (MBA). Evening/weekend programs available. Postbaccalaureate distance learning degree programs offered. *Students:* 699 full-time (341 women); includes 318 minority (124 Black or African American, non-Hispanic/Latino; 4 American Indian or Alaska Native, non-Hispanic/Latino; 44 Asian, non-Hispanic/Latino; 124 Hispanic/Latino; 15 Native Hawaiian or other Pacific Islander, non-Hispanic/Latino; 7 Two or more races, non-Hispanic/Latino), 29 international. Average age 38. *Entrance requirements:* Additional exam requirements/recommendations for international students: Required—TOEFL, TOEIC (Test of English as an International Communication), Berlitz Online English Proficiency Exam, Pearson Test of English, or IELTS. *Application deadline:* Applications are processed on a rolling basis. Application fee: $45. Electronic applications accepted. *Expenses:* Contact institution. *Financial support:* Scholarships/grants available. Financial award applicants required to submit FAFSA. *Application contact:* 866-766-0766. Web site: http://www.phoenix.edu/colleges_divisions/business.html.

University of Phoenix–Southern Colorado Campus, School of Business, Colorado Springs, CO 80919-2335. Offers accounting (MBA); business administration (MBA); global management (MBA); human resources management (MBA, MM); management (MM); marketing (MBA); public administration (MM). Evening/weekend programs available. *Degree requirements:* For master's, thesis (for some programs). *Entrance requirements:* For master's, minimum undergraduate GPA of 3.0, 3 years of work experience. Additional exam requirements/recommendations for international students: Required—TOEFL (minimum score 550 paper-based; 213 computer-based; 79 iBT). Electronic applications accepted.

University of Phoenix–South Florida Campus, College of Information Systems and Technology, Fort Lauderdale, FL 33309. Offers management (MIS); technology management (MBA). Evening/weekend programs available. *Degree requirements:* For master's, thesis (for some programs). *Entrance requirements:* For master's, minimum undergraduate GPA of 3.0, 3 years of work experience. Additional exam requirements/recommendations for international students: Required—TOEFL (minimum score 550 paper-based; 213 computer-based; 79 iBT). Electronic applications accepted.

University of Phoenix–South Florida Campus, School of Business, Fort Lauderdale, FL 33309. Offers accounting (MBA); business administration (MBA); global management (MBA); human resource management (MBA); human resources management (MM); management (MM); marketing (MBA); public administration (MBA, MM). Evening/weekend programs available. *Degree requirements:* For master's, thesis (for some programs). *Entrance requirements:* For master's, minimum undergraduate GPA of 3.0, 3 years work experience. Additional exam requirements/recommendations for international students: Required—TOEFL (minimum score 550 paper-based; 213 computer-based; 79 iBT). Electronic applications accepted.

University of Phoenix–Springfield Campus, School of Business, Springfield, MO 65804-7211. Offers accounting (MBA); business administration (MBA); global management (MBA); human resources management (MBA, MM); management (MM); marketing (MBA); public administration (MBA, MM).

University of Phoenix–Tulsa Campus, School of Business, Tulsa, OK 74134-1412. Offers accounting (MBA); business (MM); business administration (MBA); global management (MBA); human resources management (MBA); marketing (MBA). Evening/weekend programs available. *Degree requirements:* For master's, thesis (for some programs). *Entrance requirements:* For master's, minimum undergraduate GPA of 3.0, 3 years work experience. Additional exam requirements/recommendations for international students: Required—TOEFL (minimum score 550 paper-based; 213 computer-based; 79 iBT).

University of Phoenix–Utah Campus, School of Business, Salt Lake City, UT 84123-4617. Offers accounting (MBA); business administration (MBA); global management (MBA); human resource management (MBA, MM); management (MM); marketing (MBA); technology management (MBA). Evening/weekend programs available. *Degree requirements:* For master's, thesis (for some programs). *Entrance requirements:* For master's, minimum undergraduate GPA of 3.0, 3 years of work experience. Additional exam requirements/recommendations for international students: Required—TOEFL (minimum score 550 paper-based; 213 computer-based; 79 iBT). Electronic applications accepted.

University of Phoenix–Vancouver Campus, John Sperling School of Business, College of Graduate Business and Management, Burnaby, BC V5C 6G9, Canada. Offers accounting (MBA); business administration (MBA); global management (MBA); human resources management (MBA, MM); marketing (MBA). Evening/weekend programs available. *Degree requirements:* For master's, thesis (for some programs). *Entrance requirements:* For master's, minimum undergraduate GPA of 3.0, 3 years of work experience. Additional exam requirements/recommendations for international students: Required—TOEFL (minimum score 550 paper-based; 213 computer-based; 79 iBT). Electronic applications accepted.

University of Phoenix–Washington Campus, School of Business, Seattle, WA 98188-7500. Offers MBA. Evening/weekend programs available. *Degree requirements:* For master's, thesis (for some programs). *Entrance requirements:* For master's, minimum undergraduate GPA of 3.0, 3 years of work experience. Additional exam requirements/recommendations for international students: Required—TOEFL (minimum score 550 paper-based; 213 computer-based; 79 iBT). Electronic applications accepted.

University of Phoenix–Washington D.C. Campus, School of Business, Washington, DC 20001. Offers accountancy (MS); business administration (MBA, DBA); human resources management (MM); management (MM); organizational leadership (DM); public administration (MPA).

University of Phoenix–West Florida Campus, School of Business, Temple Terrace, FL 33637. Offers accounting (MBA); business administration (MBA); global management (MBA); human resources management (MBA, MM); management (MM); marketing (MBA); public administration (MBA, MM). Evening/weekend programs available. *Degree requirements:* For master's, thesis (for some programs). *Entrance requirements:* For master's, 3 years of work experience, minimum undergraduate GPA of 3.0. Additional exam requirements/recommendations for international students: Required—TOEFL (minimum score 550 paper-based; 213 computer-based; 79 iBT). Electronic applications accepted.

University of Phoenix–West Michigan Campus, School of Business, Walker, MI 49544. Offers MBA, MSA. Evening/weekend programs available. *Degree requirements:* For master's, thesis (for some programs). *Entrance requirements:* For master's, 3 years of work experience, minimum undergraduate GPA of 3.0. Additional exam requirements/recommendations for international students: Required—TOEFL (minimum score 550 paper-based; 213 computer-based; 79 iBT). Electronic applications accepted.

University of Phoenix–Wichita Campus, School of Business, Wichita, KS 67226-4011. Offers MBA. Evening/weekend programs available. *Degree requirements:* For master's, thesis (for some programs). *Entrance requirements:* For master's, minimum undergraduate GPA of 3.0, 3 years of work experience. Additional exam requirements/recommendations for international students: Required—TOEFL (minimum score 550 paper-based; 213 computer-based; 79 iBT). Electronic applications accepted.

University of Pittsburgh, Graduate School of Public and International Affairs, Public Policy and Management Program for Mid-Career Professionals, Pittsburgh, PA 15260. Offers development planning (MPPM); international development (MPPM); international political economy (MPPM); international security studies (MPPM); management of non profit organizations (MPPM); metropolitan management and regional development (MPPM); policy analysis and evaluation (MPPM). Part-time programs available. *Faculty:* 26 full-time (12 women), 47 part-time/adjunct (19 women). *Students:* 18 full-time (5 women), 29 part-time (12 women); includes 7 minority (3 Black or African American, non-Hispanic/Latino; 1 Hispanic/Latino; 3 Two or more races, non-Hispanic/Latino), 12 international. Average age 38. 43 applicants, 51% accepted, 19 enrolled. In 2011, 26 master's awarded. *Degree requirements:* For master's, thesis optional, capstone seminar. *Entrance requirements:* For master's, 2 letters of recommendation, resume, 5 years of supervisory or budgetary experience. Additional exam requirements/recommendations for international students: Required—TOEFL (minimum score 600 paper-based; 250 computer-based; 100 iBT), TWE (minimum score 4); Recommended—IELTS (minimum score 7). *Application deadline:* For fall admission, 6/1 priority date for domestic students, 2/15 for international students; for spring admission, 1/1 priority date for domestic students, 8/1 for international students. Applications are processed on a rolling basis. Application fee: $50. Electronic applications accepted. *Expenses:* Tuition, state resident: full-time $18,774; part-time $760 per credit. Tuition, nonresident: full-time $30,736; part-time $1258 per credit. *Required fees:* $740; $200 per term. Tuition and fees vary according to program. *Financial support:* In 2011–12, 14 students received support. Scholarships/grants and tuition waivers (partial) available. Support available to part-time students. Financial award application deadline: 2/1. *Faculty research:* Nonprofit management, urban and regional affairs, policy analysis and evaluation, security and intelligence studies, global political economy, nongovernmental organizations, civil society, development planning and environmental sustainability, human security. *Total annual research expenditures:* $892,349. *Unit head:* Dr. George Dougherty, Jr., Director, Executive Education, 412-648-7603, Fax: 412-648-2605, E-mail: gwdjr@pitt.edu. *Application contact:* Michael T. Rizzi, Associate Director of Student Services, 412-648-7640, Fax: 412-648-7641, E-mail: rizzim@pitt.edu. Web site: http://www.gspia.pitt.edu/.

University of Pittsburgh, Katz Graduate School of Business, Doctoral Program in Business Administration, Pittsburgh, PA 15260. Offers accounting (PhD); finance (PhD); information systems (PhD); marketing (PhD); operations/decision sciences/artificial intelligence (PhD); organizational behavior and human resource management (PhD); strategic planning (PhD). *Accreditation:* AACSB. *Faculty:* 54 full-time (16 women). *Students:* 51 full-time (21 women); includes 9 minority (4 Black or African American, non-Hispanic/Latino; 4 Asian, non-Hispanic/Latino; 1 Hispanic/Latino), 23 international. 373 applicants, 7% accepted, 10 enrolled. In 2011, 6 doctorates awarded. *Degree requirements:* For doctorate, comprehensive exam, thesis/dissertation. *Entrance requirements:* For doctorate, GMAT or GRE. Additional exam requirements/recommendations for international students: Required—TOEFL. *Application deadline:* For fall admission, 2/1 priority date for domestic students, 2/1 for international students. Applications are processed on a rolling basis. Application fee: $50. Electronic applications accepted. *Expenses:* Tuition, state resident: full-time $18,774; part-time $760 per credit. Tuition, nonresident: full-time $30,736; part-time $1258 per credit. *Required fees:* $740; $200 per term. Tuition and fees vary according to program. *Financial support:* In 2011–12, 38 students received support, including 29 research assistantships with full tuition reimbursements available (averaging $19,400 per year), 10 teaching assistantships with full tuition reimbursements available (averaging $24,700 per year); fellowships, Federal Work-Study, scholarships/grants, health care benefits, and unspecified assistantships also available. Financial award application deadline: 2/1. *Faculty research:* Accounting statements and reporting, corporate finance, information systems processes, structures and decision-making, consumer behavior and marketing models. *Total annual research expenditures:* $254,031. *Unit head:* Dr. Dennis Galletta, Director, 412-648-1699, Fax: 412-624-3633, E-mail: galletta@katz.pitt.edu. *Application contact:* Carrie Woods, Assistant Director, 412-648-1525, Fax: 412-624-3633, E-mail: cawoods@katz.pitt.edu. Web site: http://www.business.pitt.edu/katz/phd/.

University of Pittsburgh, Katz Graduate School of Business, Executive MBA Program, Pittsburgh, PA 15260. Offers EMBA. *Accreditation:* AACSB. Evening/weekend programs available. *Faculty:* 30 full-time (6 women), 6 part-time/adjunct (2 women). *Students:* 60 full-time (11 women); includes 19 minority (1 Black or African American, non-Hispanic/Latino; 4 Asian, non-Hispanic/Latino; 14 Hispanic/Latino). Average age 36. 98 applicants, 76% accepted, 60 enrolled. In 2011, 62 master's awarded. *Entrance requirements:* For master's, GMAT (for candidates with less than 10 years experience, GPA less than 3.0, or limited quantitative background), 3 credits of course work in college-level calculus, minimum 5 years management experience, references, interview, bachelor's degree. Additional exam requirements/recommendations for international students: Required—TOEFL or IELTS. *Application deadline:* For winter admission, 12/1 priority date for domestic students, 3/1 for international students. Applications are processed on a rolling basis. Application fee: $0. Electronic applications accepted.

Business Administration and Management—General

Expenses: Contact institution. *Financial support:* Scholarships/grants, tuition waivers (partial), and unspecified assistantships available. Financial award application deadline: 12/1. *Faculty research:* Accounting statements and reporting, corporate finance, information systems processes, structures and decision-making, consumer behavior and marketing models. *Unit head:* Dr. Laurie J. Kirsch, Senior Associate Dean, Professional Programs, 412-648-1565, Fax: 412-648-1552, E-mail: lkirsch@katz.pitt.edu. *Application contact:* Nicholas Hamilton-Archer, Director of Operations, 412-648-1607, Fax: 412-648-1787, E-mail: embaprogram@katz.pitt.edu. Web site: http://www.business.pitt.edu/katz/emba/.

University of Pittsburgh, Katz Graduate School of Business, Master of Business Administration Programs, Pittsburgh , PA 15260. Offers finance (MBA); information systems (MBA); marketing (MBA); operations management (MBA); organizational behavior and human resource management (MBA); organizational leadership (Certificate); strategy, environment and organizations (MBA); technology, innovation and entrepreneurship (Certificate); MBA/JD; MBA/MIB; MBA/MPIA; MBA/MSE; MBA/MSIS; MID/MBA. *Accreditation:* AACSB. Part-time and evening/weekend programs available. *Faculty:* 62 full-time (17 women), 21 part-time/adjunct (4 women). *Students:* 179 full-time (63 women), 572 part-time (373 women); includes 69 minority (29 Black or African American, non-Hispanic/Latino; 24 Asian, non-Hispanic/Latino; 16 Hispanic/Latino), 83 international. Average age 29. 391 applicants, 42% accepted, 78 enrolled. *Degree requirements:* For master's, minimum GPA of 3.0. *Entrance requirements:* For master's, GMAT, recommendations, undergraduate transcripts, essay, resume, interview, bachelor's degree. Additional exam requirements/recommendations for international students: Required—TOEFL (minimum score 600 paper, 250 computer, 100 iBT) or IELTS. *Application deadline:* For fall admission, 4/1 priority date for domestic students, 2/1 for international students. Application fee: $50. Electronic applications accepted. *Expenses:* Tuition, state resident: full-time $18,774; part-time $760 per credit. Tuition, nonresident: full-time $30,736; part-time $1258 per credit. *Required fees:* $740; $200 per term. Tuition and fees vary according to program. *Financial support:* In 2011–12, 58 students received support. Career-related internships or fieldwork and scholarships/grants available. Financial award application deadline: 3/1; financial award applicants required to submit FAFSA. *Faculty research:* Accounting statements and reporting, corporate finance, information systems processes, structures and decision-making, consumer behavior and marketing models. *Unit head:* William T. Valenta, Assistant Dean/Director, 412-648-1610, Fax: 412-648-1659, E-mail: wtvalenta@katz.pitt.edu. *Application contact:* Thomas Keller, Director of MBA Admissions, 412-648-1700, Fax: 412-648-1659, E-mail: mba@katz.pitt.edu. Web site: http://www.business.pitt.edu/katz/mba/.

University of Pittsburgh, Katz Graduate School of Business, MBA/Juris Doctor Program, Pittsburgh, PA 15260. Offers MBA/JD. *Faculty:* 62 full-time (17 women), 21 part-time/adjunct (4 women). *Students:* 13 full-time (5 women); includes 2 minority (1 Black or African American, non-Hispanic/Latino; 1 Hispanic/Latino). Average age 28. 19 applicants, 95% accepted, 7 enrolled. *Entrance requirements:* Additional exam requirements/recommendations for international students: Required—TOEFL (minimum score 600 paper, 250 computer, 100 iBT) or IELTS. *Application deadline:* For fall admission, 4/1 priority date for domestic students, 2/1 for international students. Application fee: $50. Electronic applications accepted. *Expenses:* Tuition, state resident: full-time $18,774; part-time $760 per credit. Tuition, nonresident: full-time $30,736; part-time $1258 per credit. *Required fees:* $740; $200 per term. Tuition and fees vary according to program. *Financial support:* In 2011–12, 5 students received support. Career-related internships or fieldwork and scholarships/grants available. Financial award application deadline: 3/1; financial award applicants required to submit FAFSA. *Faculty research:* Accounting statements and reporting, corporate finance, information systems processes, structures and decision-making, consumer behavior and marketing models. *Unit head:* William T. Valenta, Assistant Dean/Director, 412-648-1610, Fax: 412-648-1659, E-mail: wtvalenta@katz.pitt.edu. *Application contact:* Thomas Keller, Director of MBA Admissions, 412-648-1700, Fax: 412-648-1659, E-mail: mba@katz.pitt.edu. Web site: http://www.business.pitt.edu/katz/mba/academics/programs/mba-jd.php.

University of Pittsburgh, Katz Graduate School of Business, MBA/Master of International Business Dual Degree Program, Pittsburgh, PA 15260. Offers MBA/MIB. Part-time and evening/weekend programs available. *Faculty:* 62 full-time (17 women), 21 part-time/adjunct (4 women). *Students:* 1 full-time (0 women), 6 part-time (5 women); includes 1 minority (Hispanic/Latino). Average age 29. 25 applicants, 28% accepted, 5 enrolled. *Entrance requirements:* Additional exam requirements/recommendations for international students: Required—TOEFL (minimum score 600 paper-based; 250 computer-based; 100 iBT) or IELTS. *Application deadline:* For fall admission, 4/1 priority date for domestic students, 2/1 for international students. Application fee: $50. Electronic applications accepted. *Expenses:* Tuition, state resident: full-time $18,774; part-time $760 per credit. Tuition, nonresident: full-time $30,736; part-time $1258 per credit. *Required fees:* $740; $200 per term. Tuition and fees vary according to program. *Financial support:* In 2011–12, 5 students received support. Career-related internships or fieldwork and scholarships/grants available. Financial award application deadline: 3/1; financial award applicants required to submit FAFSA. *Faculty research:* Transitional economies, incentives and governance; corporate finance, mergers and acquisitions; global information systems and structures; consumer behavior and marketing models; entrepreneurship and globalization. *Unit head:* William T. Valenta, Assistant Dean/Director, 412-648-1610, Fax: 412-648-1659, E-mail: wtvalenta@katz.pitt.edu. *Application contact:* Thomas Keller, Director of MBA Admissions, 412-648-1700, Fax: 412-648-1659, E-mail: mba@katz.pitt.edu. Web site: http://www.business.pitt.edu/katz/mba/academics/programs/mba-mib.php.

University of Pittsburgh, Katz Graduate School of Business, MBA/Master of International Development Joint Degree Program, Pittsburgh, PA 15260. Offers MID/MBA. *Accreditation:* AACSB. Part-time and evening/weekend programs available. *Faculty:* 62 full-time (17 women), 21 part-time/adjunct (4 women). *Students:* 1 (woman) full-time. Average age 25. 2 applicants, 50% accepted, 1 enrolled. *Entrance requirements:* Additional exam requirements/recommendations for international students: Required—TOEFL (minimum score 600 paper, 250 computer, 100 iBT) or IELTS. *Application deadline:* For fall admission, 4/1 priority date for domestic students, 2/1 for international students. Application fee: $50. Electronic applications accepted. *Expenses:* Tuition, state resident: full-time $18,774; part-time $760 per credit. Tuition, nonresident: full-time $30,736; part-time $1258 per credit. *Required fees:* $740; $200 per term. Tuition and fees vary according to program. *Financial support:* Career-related internships or fieldwork and scholarships/grants available. Financial award application deadline: 3/1; financial award applicants required to submit FAFSA. *Faculty research:* Accounting statements and reporting, corporate finance, information systems processes, structures and decision-making, consumer behavior and marketing models. *Unit head:* Wiliam T. Valenta, Assistant Dean/Director, 412-648-1610, Fax: 412-648-1659, E-mail: wtvalenta@katz.pitt.edu. *Application contact:* Thomas Keller, Director of MBA Admissions, 412-648-1700, Fax: 412-648-1659, E-mail: mba@katz.pitt.edu. Web site: http://www.business.pitt.edu/katz/mba/academics/programs/mba-mid.php.

University of Pittsburgh, Katz Graduate School of Business, MBA/Master of Public and International Affairs Dual-Degree Program, Pittsburgh, PA 15260. Offers MBA/MPIA. *Accreditation:* AACSB. Part-time and evening/weekend programs available. *Faculty:* 62 full-time (17 women), 21 part-time/adjunct (4 women). *Students:* 1 full-time. Average age 24. 6 applicants, 83% accepted, 1 enrolled. *Entrance requirements:* Additional exam requirements/recommendations for international students: Required—TOEFL (minimum score 600 paper, 250 computer, 100 iBT) or IELTS. *Application deadline:* For fall admission, 4/1 priority date for domestic students, 2/1 for international students. Application fee: $50. Electronic applications accepted. *Expenses:* Tuition, state resident: full-time $18,774; part-time $760 per credit. Tuition, nonresident: full-time $30,736; part-time $1258 per credit. *Required fees:* $740; $200 per term. Tuition and fees vary according to program. *Financial support:* In 2011–12, 1 student received support. Career-related internships or fieldwork and scholarships/grants available. Financial award application deadline: 3/1; financial award applicants required to submit FAFSA. *Faculty research:* Transitional economies; incentives and governance; corporate finance, mergers and acquisitions; global information systems and structures, consumer behavior and marketing models, entrepreneurship and globalization. *Unit head:* William T. Valenta, Assistant Dean/Director, 412-648-1610, Fax: 412-648-1659, E-mail: wtvalenta@katz.pitt.edu. *Application contact:* Thomas Keller, Director of MBA Admissions, 412-648-1700, Fax: 412-648-1659, E-mail: mba@katz.pitt.edu.

University of Pittsburgh, Katz Graduate School of Business, MBA/Master of Science in Engineering Joint Degree Program, Pittsburgh, PA 15260. Offers MBA/MSE. *Accreditation:* AACSB. Part-time and evening/weekend programs available. *Faculty:* 62 full-time (17 women), 21 part-time/adjunct (4 women). *Students:* 11 full-time (1 woman), 33 part-time (7 women); includes 6 minority (2 Black or African American, non-Hispanic/Latino; 3 Asian, non-Hispanic/Latino; 1 Hispanic/Latino), 2 international. Average age 28. 13 applicants, 69% accepted, 4 enrolled. *Entrance requirements:* Additional exam requirements/recommendations for international students: Required—TOEFL (minimum score 600 paper, 250 computer, 100 iBT) or IELTS. *Application deadline:* For fall admission, 4/1 for domestic students, 2/1 for international students. Application fee: $50. Electronic applications accepted. *Expenses:* Tuition, state resident: full-time $18,774; part-time $760 per credit. Tuition, nonresident: full-time $30,736; part-time $1258 per credit. *Required fees:* $740; $200 per term. Tuition and fees vary according to program. *Financial support:* In 2011–12, 4 students received support. Career-related internships or fieldwork and scholarships/grants available. Financial award application deadline: 3/1; financial award applicants required to submit FAFSA. *Faculty research:* Accounting statements and reporting, corporate finance, information systems processes, structures and decision-making, consumer behavior and marketing models. *Unit head:* William T. Valenta, Assistant Dean/Director, 412-648-1610, Fax: 412-648-1659, E-mail: wtvalenta@katz.pitt.edu. *Application contact:* Thomas Keller, Director of MBA Admissions, 412-648-1700, Fax: 412-648-1659, E-mail: mba@katz.pitt.edu. Web site: http://www.business.pitt.edu/katz/mba/academics/programs/mba-msengineering.php.

University of Portland, Dr. Robert B. Pamplin, Jr. School of Business, Portland, OR 97203-5798. Offers business administration (MBA); entrepreneurship (MBA); finance (MBA, MS); health care management (MBA); marketing (MBA); nonprofit management (EMBA); operations and technology management (MBA); sustainability (MBA). *Accreditation:* AACSB. Part-time and evening/weekend programs available. *Faculty:* 13 full-time (1 woman), 8 part-time/adjunct (1 woman). *Students:* 50 full-time (13 women), 90 part-time (41 women); includes 19 minority (1 Black or African American, non-Hispanic/Latino; 1 American Indian or Alaska Native, non-Hispanic/Latino; 8 Asian, non-Hispanic/Latino; 5 Hispanic/Latino; 2 Native Hawaiian or other Pacific Islander, non-Hispanic/Latino; 2 Two or more races, non-Hispanic/Latino), 18 international. Average age 31. In 2011, 54 master's awarded. *Entrance requirements:* For master's, GMAT, minimum GPA of 3.0, resume, 2 letters of recommendation. Additional exam requirements/recommendations for international students: Required—TOEFL (minimum score 570 paper-based; 89 iBT), IELTS (minimum score 7). *Application deadline:* For fall admission, 7/15 priority date for domestic students, 7/15 for international students; for spring admission, 12/15 priority date for domestic students, 12/15 for international students. Applications are processed on a rolling basis. Application fee: $50. *Expenses:* Contact institution. *Financial support:* Federal Work-Study, scholarships/grants, and tuition waivers (partial) available. Support available to part-time students. Financial award application deadline: 3/1; financial award applicants required to submit FAFSA. *Unit head:* Dr. Howard Feldman, Associate Dean, 503-943-7224, E-mail: feldman@up.edu. *Application contact:* Melissa McCarthy, Academic Specialist, 503-943-7225, E-mail: mccarthy@up.edu. Web site: http://business.up.edu/.

University of Puerto Rico, Mayagüez Campus, Graduate Studies, College of Business Administration, Mayagüez, PR 00681-9000. Offers business administration (MBA); finance (MBA); human resources (MBA); industrial management (MBA). Part-time and evening/weekend programs available. *Students:* 46 full-time (30 women), 16 part-time (9 women); includes 59 minority (all Hispanic/Latino), 3 international. 18 applicants, 44% accepted, 5 enrolled. In 2011, 14 master's awarded. *Degree requirements:* For master's, comprehensive exam. *Entrance requirements:* For master's, GMAT or EXADEP, bachelor's degree with courses in calculus, microeconomics, accounting and statistics. Additional exam requirements/recommendations for international students: Required—TOEFL (minimum score 500 paper-based; 173 computer-based). *Application deadline:* For fall admission, 2/15 for domestic and international students; for spring admission, 9/15 for domestic and international students. Applications are processed on a rolling basis. Application fee: $25. Tuition and fees vary according to course level and course load. *Financial support:* In 2011–12, 4 students received support, including 4 teaching assistantships (averaging $8,500 per year); Federal Work-Study and institutionally sponsored loans also available. *Faculty research:* Organizational studies, management, accounting. *Total annual research expenditures:* $20,000. *Unit head:* Dr. Rosario Ortiz, Graduate Student Coordinator, 787-265-3800, Fax: 787-832-5320, E-mail: rosario.ortiz@upr.edu. *Application contact:* Milagros Soto, Student Administrator, 787-265-3887, Fax: 787-832-5320, E-mail: milagros.soto1@upr.edu. Web site: http://enterprise.uprm.edu/.

University of Puerto Rico, Río Piedras, College of Business Administration, San Juan, PR 00931-3300. Offers accounting (MBA); finance (MBA, PhD); general business (MBA); human resources management (MBA); international trade and business (MBA, PhD); marketing (MBA); operations management (MBA); quantitative methods (MBA). *Accreditation:* ACBSP. Part-time programs available. *Degree requirements:* For master's, comprehensive exam, thesis or alternative, research project. *Entrance requirements:* For master's, GMAT or PAEG, minimum GPA of 3.0, letter of recommendation; for doctorate, GMAT, PAEG, minimum GPA of 3.0, master degree. *Faculty research:* Management.

University of Redlands, School of Business, Redlands, CA 92373-0999. Offers business (MBA); information technology (MS); management (MA). Evening/weekend programs available. *Entrance requirements:* For master's, minimum GPA of 3.0, 2 letters of recommendation. *Faculty research:* Human resources management, educational leadership, humanities, teacher education.

University of Regina, Faculty of Graduate Studies and Research, Kenneth Levene Graduate School of Business, Regina, SK S4S 0A2, Canada. Offers M Admin, MBA, MHRM, Master's Certificate. Part-time and evening/weekend programs available. *Faculty:* 32 full-time (12 women), 10 part-time/adjunct (0 women). *Students:* 95 full-time (37 women), 66 part-time (37 women). 161 applicants, 67% accepted. In 2011, 69 master's awarded. *Degree requirements:* For master's, project. *Entrance requirements:* For master's, GMAT, two years relevant work experience. Additional exam requirements/recommendations for international students: Required—TOEFL (minimum score 580 paper-based; 80 iBT), IELTS (minimum score 6.5). *Application deadline:* Applications are processed on a rolling basis. Application fee: $100. Electronic applications accepted. *Expenses:* Contact institution. *Financial support:* In 2011–12, 6 fellowships (averaging $6,000 per year), 13 teaching assistantships (averaging $2,298 per year) were awarded; research assistantships and scholarships/grants also available. Financial award application deadline: 6/15. *Faculty research:* Management of public and private sector organizations. *Unit head:* Dr. Morina Rennie, Dean, 306-585-4162, Fax: 306-585-4805, E-mail: morina.rennie@uregina.ca. *Application contact:* Dr. Ronald Camp, Graduate Program Coordinator/Associate Graduate Dean, 306-337-2387, Fax: 306-585-5361, E-mail: ronald.camp@uregina.ca. Web site: http://www.uregina.ca/admin/academic/graduate_school/index.htm.

University of Rhode Island, Graduate School, College of Business Administration, Kingston, RI 02881. Offers accounting (MS); business administration (MBA, PhD), including finance and insurance (PhD), management (PhD), marketing (PhD), operations and supply chain management (MBA); finance (MBA); general business (MBA); management (MBA); marketing (MBA); supply chain management (MBA). *Accreditation:* AACSB. Part-time and evening/weekend programs available. *Faculty:* 56 full-time (15 women), 8 part-time/adjunct (4 women). *Students:* 93 full-time (40 women), 226 part-time (90 women); includes 35 minority (7 Black or African American, non-Hispanic/Latino; 1 American Indian or Alaska Native, non-Hispanic/Latino; 15 Asian, non-Hispanic/Latino; 11 Hispanic/Latino; 1 Two or more races, non-Hispanic/Latino), 24 international. In 2011, 78 master's, 3 doctorates awarded. *Degree requirements:* For master's, comprehensive exam (for some programs), thesis optional; for doctorate, comprehensive exam, thesis/dissertation. *Entrance requirements:* For master's, GMAT or GRE, 2 letters of recommendation, resume; for doctorate, GMAT or GRE, 3 letters of recommendation, resume. Additional exam requirements/recommendations for international students: Required—TOEFL (minimum score 575 paper-based; 233 computer-based; 91 iBT). Application fee: $65. Electronic applications accepted. *Expenses:* Tuition, state resident: full-time $10,432; part-time $580 per credit hour. Tuition, nonresident: full-time $23,130; part-time $1285 per credit hour. *Required fees:* $1362; $36 per credit hour. $35 per semester. One-time fee: $130. *Financial support:* In 2011–12, 13 teaching assistantships with full and partial tuition reimbursements (averaging $13,020 per year) were awarded. Financial award applicants required to submit FAFSA. *Unit head:* Dr. Mark Higgins, Dean, 401-874-4244, Fax: 401-874-4312, E-mail: markhiggins@uri.edu. *Application contact:* Lisa Lancellotta, Coordinator, MBA Programs, 401-874-4241, Fax: 401-874-4312, E-mail: mba@uri.edu. Web site: http://www.cba.uri.edu/.

University of Richmond, Robins School of Business, Richmond, VA 23173. Offers MBA, JD/MBA. *Accreditation:* AACSB. Part-time and evening/weekend programs available. *Faculty:* 28 full-time (7 women), 5 part-time/adjunct (1 woman). *Students:* 26 full-time (11 women), 95 part-time (25 women); includes 16 minority (5 Black or African American, non-Hispanic/Latino; 6 Asian, non-Hispanic/Latino; 5 Hispanic/Latino), 4 international. Average age 27. 57 applicants, 79% accepted, 37 enrolled. In 2011, 42 degrees awarded. *Degree requirements:* For master's, capstone project. *Entrance requirements:* For master's, GMAT, 2 years of work experience. Additional exam requirements/recommendations for international students: Required—TOEFL (minimum score 600 paper-based; 250 computer-based; 100 iBT). *Application deadline:* For fall admission, 5/1 for domestic and international students; for spring admission, 12/15 for domestic and international students. Application fee: $50. Electronic applications accepted. *Financial support:* In 2011–12, 75 students received support, including 4 research assistantships with full tuition reimbursements available (averaging $36,610 per year); unspecified assistantships also available. Support available to part-time students. Financial award applicants required to submit FAFSA. *Faculty research:* Entrepreneurship, investments, auditing, consumer behavior, strategic management. *Unit head:* Dr. Nancy Bagranoff, Dean, Robins School of Business, 804-289-8549, Fax: 804-287-6544, E-mail: nbagrano@richmond.edu. *Application contact:* Dr. Richard S. Coughlan, Senior Associate Dean/MBA Program Director, 804-289-8553, Fax: 804-287-1228, E-mail: rcoughla@richmond.edu. Web site: http://robins.richmond.edu/.

University of Rochester, William E. Simon Graduate School of Business Administration, Doctoral Program in Business Administration, Rochester, NY 14627. Offers PhD. *Accreditation:* AACSB. *Degree requirements:* For doctorate, comprehensive exam, thesis/dissertation, qualifying exam. *Entrance requirements:* For doctorate, GMAT or GRE, previous course work in calculus. Additional exam requirements/recommendations for international students: Required—TOEFL. *Expenses:* Contact institution.

University of Rochester, William E. Simon Graduate School of Business Administration, Master's Program in Business Administration, Rochester, NY 14627. Offers MBA. *Accreditation:* AACSB. Part-time and evening/weekend programs available. *Entrance requirements:* For master's, GMAT, previous course work in calculus. Additional exam requirements/recommendations for international students: Required—TOEFL. *Expenses: Tuition:* Full-time $41,040.

University of St. Francis, College of Business and Health Administration, School of Business, Joliet, IL 60435-6169. Offers MBA, MSM. Part-time and evening/weekend programs available. Postbaccalaureate distance learning degree programs offered (no on-campus study). *Faculty:* 8 full-time (2 women), 8 part-time/adjunct (2 women). *Students:* 29 full-time (17 women), 129 part-time (75 women); includes 38 minority (22 Black or African American, non-Hispanic/Latino; 6 Asian, non-Hispanic/Latino; 8 Hispanic/Latino; 2 Two or more races, non-Hispanic/Latino), 4 international. Average age 38. 94 applicants, 60% accepted, 39 enrolled. In 2011, 60 degrees awarded. *Entrance requirements:* For master's, GMAT or 2 years of managerial experience, minimum GPA of 2.75, 2 letters recommendation, personal essay, computer proficiency. Additional exam requirements/recommendations for international students: Required—TOEFL (minimum score 550 paper-based; 213 computer-based). *Application deadline:* Applications are processed on a rolling basis. Application fee: $30. Electronic applications accepted. *Expenses: Tuition:* Part-time $656 per credit hour. Part-time tuition and fees vary according to degree level, campus/location and program. *Financial support:* In 2011–12, 38 students received support. Scholarships/grants, tuition waivers (partial), and unspecified assistantships available. Support available to part-time students. Financial award applicants required to submit FAFSA. *Unit head:* Dr. Christopher Clott, Dean, 815-740-3395, Fax: 815-774-2920, E-mail: cclott@stfrancis.edu. *Application contact:* Sandra Sloka, Director of Admissions for Graduate and Degree Completion Programs, 800-735-7500, Fax: 815-740-5032, E-mail: ssloka@stfrancis.edu.

University of Saint Francis, Graduate School, Department of Business Administration, Fort Wayne, IN 46808-3994. Offers business administration (MBA); healthcare administration (MHA). Part-time and evening/weekend programs available. Postbaccalaureate distance learning degree programs offered (no on-campus study). *Faculty:* 8 full-time (5 women), 2 part-time/adjunct (0 women). *Students:* 5 full-time (1 woman), 16 part-time (11 women); includes 1 minority (Hispanic/Latino). In 2011, 11 master's awarded. *Entrance requirements:* For master's, GMAT, minimum AACSB index of 900, minimum GPA of 2.5. *Application deadline:* For fall admission, 7/1 priority date for domestic students; for spring admission, 11/1 priority date for domestic students. Applications are processed on a rolling basis. Application fee: $20. Application fee is waived when completed online. *Financial support:* Federal Work-Study, scholarships/grants, tuition waivers (full and partial), and unspecified assistantships available. Financial award applicants required to submit FAFSA. *Unit head:* Karen Palumbo, Director of Graduate Programs, 260-399-7700 Ext. 8312, Fax: 260-399-8174, E-mail: kpalumbo@st.edu. *Application contact:* James Cashdollar, Admissions Counselor, 260-399-7700 Ext. 6302, Fax: 260-399-8152, E-mail: jcashdollar@sf.edu. Web site: http://www.sf.edu.

University of Saint Joseph, Department of Business, West Hartford, CT 06117-2700. Offers management (MS). Part-time and evening/weekend programs available. *Students:* 18 full-time (15 women), 32 part-time (23 women); includes 9 minority (6 Black or African American, non-Hispanic/Latino; 2 Asian, non-Hispanic/Latino; 1 Hispanic/Latino), 1 international. Average age 33. *Entrance requirements:* For master's, 2 letters of recommendation. *Application deadline:* Applications are processed on a rolling basis. Application fee: $50. Electronic applications accepted. Application fee is waived when completed online. *Expenses: Tuition:* Part-time $670 per credit. *Required fees:* $40 per credit. Tuition and fees vary according to course load, degree level, campus/location and program. *Financial support:* Career-related internships or fieldwork and unspecified assistantships available. Support available to part-time students. Financial award applicants required to submit FAFSA. *Application contact:* Graduate Admissions Assistant, 860-231-5261, E-mail: graduate@usj.edu.

University of Saint Mary, Graduate Programs, Program in Business Administration, Leavenworth, KS 66048-5082. Offers MBA. Part-time and evening/weekend programs available. *Degree requirements:* For master's, thesis. *Entrance requirements:* For master's, minimum undergraduate GPA of 2.75.

University of Saint Mary, Graduate Programs, Program in Management, Leavenworth, KS 66048-5082. Offers MS. Part-time and evening/weekend programs available. *Degree requirements:* For master's, thesis, oral or written exam. *Entrance requirements:* For master's, minimum undergraduate GPA of 2.75.

University of St. Thomas, Cameron School of Business, Houston, TX 77006-4696. Offers MBA, MSA. *Accreditation:* ACBSP. Part-time and evening/weekend programs available. *Faculty:* 25 full-time (10 women), 3 part-time/adjunct (0 women). *Students:* 140 full-time (67 women), 260 part-time (139 women); includes 163 minority (42 Black or African American, non-Hispanic/Latino; 31 Asian, non-Hispanic/Latino; 85 Hispanic/Latino; 1 Native Hawaiian or other Pacific Islander, non-Hispanic/Latino; 4 Two or more races, non-Hispanic/Latino), 111 international. Average age 30. 156 applicants, 98% accepted, 116 enrolled. In 2011, 156 master's awarded. *Degree requirements:* For master's, capstone (for some programs), additional course requirements for those sitting for state accountancy exam. *Entrance requirements:* For master's, GMAT or GRE, minimum GPA of 2.5, 3 letters of recommendation. Additional exam requirements/recommendations for international students: Required—TOEFL (minimum score 550 paper-based; 213 computer-based; 79 iBT), IELTS (minimum score 6.5). *Application deadline:* Applications are processed on a rolling basis. Application fee: $35. Electronic applications accepted. *Expenses: Tuition:* Full-time $16,920; part-time $940 per credit hour. *Required fees:* $236; $83 per term. One-time fee: $100. Tuition and fees vary according to course load, campus/location and program. *Financial support:* In 2011–12, 21 students received support. Federal Work-Study, scholarships/grants, unspecified assistantships, and state work-study, institutional employment available. Support available to part-time students. Financial award application deadline: 4/15; financial award applicants required to submit FAFSA. *Unit head:* Dr. Bahman Mirshab, Dean, 713-525-2100, Fax: 713-525-2110, E-mail: cameron@stthom.edu. *Application contact:* Juletta Palyan, Assistant Director, 713-525-2100, Fax: 713-525-2110, E-mail: cameron@stthom.edu. Web site: http://www.stthom.edu/Schools_Centers_of_Excellence/Schools_of_Study/Cameron_School_of_Business/Index.aqf.

University of St. Thomas, Graduate Studies, Opus College of Business, Evening UST MBA Program, Minneapolis, MN 55403. Offers MBA. Part-time and evening/weekend programs available. *Faculty:* 68 full-time (45 women), 29 part-time/adjunct (19 women). *Students:* 947 part-time (380 women); includes 104 minority (20 Black or African American, non-Hispanic/Latino; 3 American Indian or Alaska Native, non-Hispanic/Latino; 53 Asian, non-Hispanic/Latino; 19 Hispanic/Latino; 2 Native Hawaiian or other Pacific Islander, non-Hispanic/Latino; 7 Two or more races, non-Hispanic/Latino), 25 international. Average age 32. 138 applicants, 99% accepted, 112 enrolled. In 2011, 274 master's awarded. *Entrance requirements:* For master's, GMAT. Additional exam requirements/recommendations for international students: Required—TOEFL (minimum score 80 iBT), IELTS, or Michigan Language Assessment Battery. *Application deadline:* For fall admission, 5/1 priority date for domestic students; for spring admission, 11/1 priority date for domestic students. Applications are processed on a rolling basis. Application fee: $60. Electronic applications accepted. *Financial support:* In 2011–12, 61 students received support. Scholarships/grants available. Financial award application deadline: 6/1. *Unit head:* Corey Eakins, Program Director, 651-962-4200, Fax: 651-962-4129, E-mail: eveningmba@stthomas.edu. *Application contact:* Shanna Davis, Director of Recruiting and Admissions, 651-962-4200, Fax: 651-962-4129, E-mail: eveningmba@stthomas.edu. Web site: http://www.stthomas.edu/eveningmba.

University of St. Thomas, Graduate Studies, Opus College of Business, Executive UST MBA Program, Minneapolis, MN 55403. Offers MBA. Part-time programs available. *Students:* 37 part-time (13 women); includes 3 minority (2 Black or African American, non-Hispanic/Latino; 1 Asian, non-Hispanic/Latino), 1 international. Average age 42. 22 applicants, 100% accepted, 19 enrolled. In 2011, 24 master's awarded. *Entrance requirements:* For master's, five years of significant management or leadership experience. *Application deadline:* For fall admission, 10/7 for domestic and international students. Applications are processed on a rolling basis. Application fee: $100. Electronic applications accepted. *Expenses:* Contact institution. *Unit head:* Dr. Jack Militello, Director, 651-962-4230, Fax: 651-962-4235, E-mail: execmba@stthomas.edu. *Application contact:* Katherine Johnson, Manager, 651-962-4230, Fax: 651-962-4235, E-mail: execmba@stthomas.edu. Web site: http://www.stthomas.edu/execmba.

University of St. Thomas, Graduate Studies, Opus College of Business, Full-time UST MBA Program, Minneapolis, MN 55403. Offers MBA. *Faculty:* 20 full-time (14 women), 5 part-time/adjunct (3 women). *Students:* 90 full-time (33 women); includes 16 minority (4 Black or African American, non-Hispanic/Latino; 8 Asian, non-Hispanic/Latino; 3 Hispanic/Latino; 1 Two or more races, non-Hispanic/Latino), 11 international. Average age 28. 65 applicants, 89% accepted, 40 enrolled. In 2011, 62 master's awarded. *Entrance requirements:* For master's, GMAT. Additional exam requirements/recommendations for international students: Required—TOEFL (minimum score 80 iBT), IELTS (minimum score 7), or Michigan English Language Assessment Battery. *Application deadline:* For fall admission, 6/15 for domestic and international students. Applications are processed on a rolling basis. Application fee: $60. Electronic applications accepted. *Financial support:* In 2011–12, 50 students received support. Scholarships/grants, tuition waivers (full and partial), and unspecified assistantships available. Financial award application deadline: 4/15. *Unit head:* Deb Basarich-Cownie, Program Director, 651-962-8800, Fax: 651-962-4129, E-mail: ustmba@stthomas.edu.

Business Administration and Management—General

Application contact: Shanna Davis, Director of Recruiting and Admissions, 651-962-8800, Fax: 651-962-4129, E-mail: ustmba@stthomas.edu. Web site: http://www.stthomas.edu/mba.

University of San Diego, School of Business Administration, Masters in Business Administration (MBA) Program, San Diego, CA 92110-2492. Offers MBA, JD/MBA. Part-time and evening/weekend programs available. *Students:* 75 full-time (18 women), 116 part-time (40 women); includes 30 minority (3 Black or African American, non-Hispanic/Latino; 1 American Indian or Alaska Native, non-Hispanic/Latino; 10 Asian, non-Hispanic/Latino; 13 Hispanic/Latino; 1 Native Hawaiian or other Pacific Islander, non-Hispanic/Latino; 2 Two or more races, non-Hispanic/Latino), 19 international. Average age 29. In 2011, 79 master's awarded. *Degree requirements:* For master's, community service, capstone project. *Entrance requirements:* For master's, GMAT, minimum GPA of 3.0, minimum 2 years of full-time work experience. Additional exam requirements/recommendations for international students: Required—TOEFL, TWE. *Application deadline:* For fall admission, 4/1 priority date for domestic students. Applications are processed on a rolling basis. Application fee: $80. Electronic applications accepted. *Expenses: Tuition:* Full-time $22,482; part-time $1249 per unit. *Required fees:* $224. Full-time tuition and fees vary according to course load and degree level. *Financial support:* In 2011–12, 135 students received support. Career-related internships or fieldwork, Federal Work-Study, institutionally sponsored loans, scholarships/grants, and unspecified assistantships available. Support available to part-time students. Financial award application deadline: 4/1; financial award applicants required to submit FAFSA. *Faculty research:* Exchange rate forecasting, corporate governance, performance of private equity funds, economic geography, food banking. *Unit head:* Dr. Manzur Rahman, Academic Director, MBA Programs, 619-260-2388, E-mail: mba@sandiego.edu. *Application contact:* Monica Mahon, Associate Director of Graduate Admissions, 619-260-4524, Fax: 619-260-4158, E-mail: grads@sandiego.edu. Web site: http://www.sandiego.edu/MBA.

University of San Diego, School of Business Administration, Program in Executive Leadership, San Diego, CA 92110-2492. Offers MS. Evening/weekend programs available. *Students:* 44 full-time (13 women); includes 9 minority (1 American Indian or Alaska Native, non-Hispanic/Latino; 2 Asian, non-Hispanic/Latino; 5 Hispanic/Latino; 1 Two or more races, non-Hispanic/Latino). Average age 43. In 2011, 20 master's awarded. *Entrance requirements:* For master's, GMAT, 15 or more years of professional experience, minimum GPA of 3.0. Additional exam requirements/recommendations for international students: Required—TOEFL (minimum score 580 paper-based; 237 computer-based; 92 iBT), TWE. Application fee: $80. *Expenses: Tuition:* Full-time $22,482; part-time $1249 per unit. *Required fees:* $224. Full-time tuition and fees vary according to course load and degree level. *Financial support:* In 2011–12, 17 students received support. Scholarships/grants available. Financial award application deadline: 4/1; financial award applicants required to submit FAFSA. *Unit head:* Christina De Vaca, Director, MS in Executive Leadership, 619-260-7821, Fax: 619-260-4891, E-mail: msel@sandiego.edu. *Application contact:* Monica Mahon, Associate Director of Graduate Admissions, 619-260-4524, Fax: 619-260-4158, E-mail: grads@sandiego.edu. Web site: http://www.sandiego.edu/business/programs/graduate/leadership/executive_leadership/.

University of San Francisco, School of Management, Masagung Graduate School of Management, MBA for Executives Program, San Francisco, CA 94117-1080. Offers MBA. *Accreditation:* AACSB. *Faculty:* 4 full-time (0 women), 9 part-time/adjunct (2 women). *Students:* 46 full-time (20 women), 1 (woman) part-time; includes 23 minority (7 Black or African American, non-Hispanic/Latino; 9 Asian, non-Hispanic/Latino; 4 Hispanic/Latino; 3 Two or more races, non-Hispanic/Latino), 3 international. Average age 38. 20 applicants, 85% accepted, 16 enrolled. In 2011, 38 master's awarded. Application fee: $50. *Expenses:* Contact institution. *Financial support:* In 2011–12, 15 students received support. Applicants required to submit FAFSA. *Unit head:* Dr. Karl Boedecker, Director, 415-422-2511, Fax: 415-422-6315. *Application contact:* Kelly Tarry, Secretary, 415-422-2525, E-mail: mbae@usfca.edu.

University of San Francisco, School of Management, Masagung Graduate School of Management, Program in Business Administration, San Francisco, CA 94117-1080. Offers business economics (MBA); e-business (MBA); entrepreneurship (MBA); finance (MBA); international business (MBA); management (MBA); marketing (MBA); telecommunications management and policy (MBA); JD/MBA; MSN/MBA. *Accreditation:* AACSB. *Faculty:* 18 full-time (4 women), 18 part-time/adjunct (9 women). *Students:* 247 full-time (122 women), 9 part-time (3 women); includes 85 minority (5 Black or African American, non-Hispanic/Latino; 55 Asian, non-Hispanic/Latino; 16 Hispanic/Latino; 1 Native Hawaiian or other Pacific Islander, non-Hispanic/Latino; 8 Two or more races, non-Hispanic/Latino), 38 international. Average age 29. 552 applicants, 55% accepted, 99 enrolled. In 2011, 173 master's awarded. *Entrance requirements:* For master's, GMAT, minimum undergraduate GPA of 3.2. Additional exam requirements/recommendations for international students: Required—TOEFL. *Application deadline:* For fall admission, 7/1 priority date for domestic students; for spring admission, 11/30 for domestic students. Applications are processed on a rolling basis. Application fee: $55 ($65 for international students). *Expenses: Tuition:* Full-time $20,070; part-time $1115 per unit. Tuition and fees vary according to course load, campus/location and program. *Financial support:* In 2011–12, 33 students received support. Fellowships available. Financial award application deadline: 3/2; financial award applicants required to submit FAFSA. *Faculty research:* International financial markets, technology transfer licensing, international marketing, strategic planning. *Total annual research expenditures:* $50,000. *Unit head:* Kelly Brookes, Director, 415-422-2221, Fax: 415-422-6315. *Application contact:* Director, MBA Program, 415-422-2221, Fax: 415-422-6315, E-mail: mba@usfca.edu.

University of Saskatchewan, College of Graduate Studies and Research, Edwards School of Business, Saskatoon, SK S7N 5A2, Canada. Offers M Sc, MBA, MP Acc. Part-time programs available. *Degree requirements:* For master's, thesis (for some programs). *Entrance requirements:* For master's, GMAT. Additional exam requirements/recommendations for international students: Required—TOEFL.

The University of Scranton, College of Graduate and Continuing Education, Program in Business Administration, Scranton, PA 18510. Offers accounting (MBA); finance (MBA); general business administration (MBA); health care management (MBA); international business (MBA); management information systems (MBA); marketing (MBA); operations management (MBA). *Accreditation:* AACSB. Part-time and evening/weekend programs available. Postbaccalaureate distance learning degree programs offered (no on-campus study). *Faculty:* 34 full-time (8 women). *Students:* 276 full-time (94 women), 243 part-time (88 women); includes 14 minority (10 Black or African American, non-Hispanic/Latino; 3 Asian, non-Hispanic/Latino; 1 Hispanic/Latino), 49 international. Average age 33. 358 applicants, 80% accepted. In 2011, 101 master's awarded. *Degree requirements:* For master's, capstone experience. *Entrance requirements:* For master's, GMAT, minimum GPA of 2.75. Additional exam requirements/recommendations for international students: Required—TOEFL (minimum score 500 paper-based; 173 computer-based), IELTS (minimum score 5.5). *Application deadline:* Applications are processed on a rolling basis. Application fee: $0. *Financial support:* In 2011–12, 12 students received support, including 12 teaching assistantships with full and partial tuition reimbursements available (averaging $8,433 per year); fellowships, career-related internships or fieldwork, Federal Work-Study, and unspecified assistantships also available. Support available to part-time students. Financial award application deadline: 3/1. *Faculty research:* Financial markets, strategic impact of total quality management, internal accounting controls, consumer preference, information systems and the Internet. *Unit head:* Dr. Murli Rajan, Director, 570-941-4043, Fax: 570-941-4342. *Application contact:* Joseph M. Roback, Director of Admissions, 570-941-4385, Fax: 570-941-5928, E-mail: robackj2@scranton.edu. Web site: http://www.academic.scranton.edu/department/mba/.

University of Sioux Falls, Vucurevich School of Business, Sioux Falls, SD 57105-1699. Offers entrepreneurial leadership (MBA); general management (MBA); health care management (MBA); marketing (MBA). Part-time and evening/weekend programs available. *Faculty:* 8 full-time (3 women), 7 part-time/adjunct (2 women). *Students:* 119 part-time (60 women); includes 2 minority (1 Black or African American, non-Hispanic/Latino; 1 Asian, non-Hispanic/Latino). 50 applicants, 90% accepted, 45 enrolled. *Degree requirements:* For master's, project. *Entrance requirements:* For master's, minimum GPA of 3.0. Additional exam requirements/recommendations for international students: Required—TOEFL. Application fee: $25. *Expenses:* Contact institution. *Financial support:* Institutionally sponsored loans, scholarships/grants, and tuition waivers (full) available. Financial award applicants required to submit FAFSA. *Unit head:* Rebecca T. Murdock, MBA Director, 605-575-2068, E-mail: mba@usiouxfalls.edu. *Application contact:* Student Contact, 605-331-6680. Web site: http://www.usiouxfalls.edu/mba.

University of South Africa, College of Economic and Management Sciences, Pretoria, South Africa. Offers accounting (D Admin, D Com); accounting science (DA); auditing (D Admin, D Com); business administration (M Tech); business economics (D Admin); business leadership (DBL); business management (D Admin, D Com); economic management analysis (M Tech); economics (D Admin, D Com, PhD); human resource development (M Tech); industrial psychology (D Admin, D Com, PhD); logistics (D Com); marketing (M Tech); public administration (D Admin, D Com, DPA, PhD); public management (M Tech); quantitative management (D Admin, D Com); real estate (M Tech); statistics (D Admin, PhD); tourism management (D Admin, D Com); transport economics (D Admin, D Com).

University of South Africa, Graduate School of Business Leadership, Pretoria, South Africa. Offers MBA, MBL, DBL.

University of South Alabama, Graduate School, Mitchell College of Business, Program in Business Management, Mobile, AL 36688-0002. Offers general management (MBA). *Accreditation:* AACSB. Part-time and evening/weekend programs available. *Faculty:* 18 full-time (6 women). *Students:* 66 full-time (29 women), 4 part-time (2 women); includes 9 minority (4 Black or African American, non-Hispanic/Latino; 1 American Indian or Alaska Native, non-Hispanic/Latino; 2 Asian, non-Hispanic/Latino; 2 Hispanic/Latino), 8 international. 88 applicants, 41% accepted, 28 enrolled. In 2011, 26 master's awarded. *Degree requirements:* For master's, comprehensive exam. *Entrance requirements:* For master's, GMAT, minimum undergraduate GPA of 3.0. *Application deadline:* For fall admission, 7/15 priority date for domestic students, 6/15 for international students; for spring admission, 12/1 priority date for domestic students, 11/1 for international students. Applications are processed on a rolling basis. Application fee: $35. *Expenses:* Tuition, state resident: full-time $7968; part-time $332 per credit hour. Tuition, nonresident: full-time $15,936; part-time $664 per credit hour. *Financial support:* Research assistantships available. Support available to part-time students. Financial award application deadline: 4/1. *Unit head:* Dr. John Gamble, Director of Graduate Studies, 251-460-6418. *Application contact:* Dr. B. Keith Harrison, Dean of the Graduate School, 251-460-6310, Fax: 251-461-1513, E-mail: kharriso@usouthal.edu.

University of South Carolina, The Graduate School, Darla Moore School of Business, Columbia, SC 29208. Offers accountancy (M Acc), including business measurement and assurance; business administration (MBA, PhD); economics (MA, PhD); human resources (MHR); international business administration (IMBA); JD/M Acc; JD/MA; JD/MHR. *Accreditation:* AACSB. Part-time and evening/weekend programs available. Postbaccalaureate distance learning degree programs offered (minimal on-campus study). *Degree requirements:* For doctorate, one foreign language, thesis/dissertation. *Entrance requirements:* For master's, GMAT, GRE, minimum GPA of 3.0; for doctorate, GMAT or GRE. Additional exam requirements/recommendations for international students: Required—TOEFL (minimum score 600 paper-based; 250 computer-based). Electronic applications accepted. *Expenses:* Contact institution. *Faculty research:* Finance, marketing, strategic management, international management, operations.

The University of South Dakota, Graduate School, Beacom School of Business, Department of Business Administration, Vermillion, SD 57069-2390. Offers MBA, JD/MBA. *Accreditation:* AACSB. Part-time and evening/weekend programs available. Postbaccalaureate distance learning degree programs offered (no on-campus study). *Degree requirements:* For master's, thesis or alternative. *Entrance requirements:* For master's, GMAT, minimum GPA of 2.7, resume. Additional exam requirements/recommendations for international students: Required—TOEFL (minimum score 550 paper-based; 213 computer-based; 79 iBT). Electronic applications accepted. *Expenses:* Contact institution.

The University of South Dakota, Graduate School, Program in Administrative Studies, Vermillion, SD 57069-2390. Offers MS. Part-time and evening/weekend programs available. Postbaccalaureate distance learning degree programs offered (no on-campus study). *Degree requirements:* For master's, thesis or alternative. *Entrance requirements:* For master's, 3 years of work or experience, minimum GPA of 2.7, resume. Additional exam requirements/recommendations for international students: Required—TOEFL (minimum score 550 paper-based; 213 computer-based; 79 iBT). Electronic applications accepted. *Expenses:* Tuition, state resident: full-time $3118.50; part-time $173.25 per credit hour. Tuition, nonresident: full-time $6601; part-time $366.70 per credit hour. *Required fees:* $2268; $126 per credit hour. Tuition and fees vary according to program.

University of Southern California, Graduate School, Marshall School of Business, Los Angeles, CA 90089. Offers M Acc, MBA, MBT, MMM, MS, PhD, DDS/MBA, JD/MBT, MBA/Ed D, MBA/M Pl, MBA/MD, MBA/MRED, MBA/MS, MBA/MSW, MBA/Pharm D. *Accreditation:* AACSB. *Degree requirements:* For doctorate, thesis/dissertation. *Entrance requirements:* For master's, GMAT and/or CPA Exam; for doctorate, GMAT or GRE. Additional exam requirements/recommendations for international students: Required—TOEFL. Electronic applications accepted.

University of Southern Indiana, Graduate Studies, College of Business, Program in Business Administration, Evansville, IN 47712-3590. Offers MBA. *Accreditation:* AACSB. Part-time and evening/weekend programs available. *Faculty:* 15 full-time (0 women). *Students:* 6 full-time (1 woman), 74 part-time (25 women); includes 1 minority (Asian, non-Hispanic/Latino), 8 international. Average age 30. 37 applicants, 78% accepted, 19 enrolled. In 2011, 31 master's awarded. *Entrance requirements:* For master's, GMAT, minimum GPA of 2.5, resume. Additional exam requirements/recommendations for international students: Required—TOEFL (minimum score 550 paper-based; 213 computer-based; 79 iBT), IELTS (minimum score 6). *Application deadline:* For fall admission, 8/15 for domestic students, 3/1 for international students. Applications are processed on a rolling basis. Application fee: $35. Electronic applications accepted. *Expenses:* Tuition, state resident: full-time $5044; part-time $280.21 per credit hour. Tuition, nonresident: full-time $9949; part-time $552.71 per credit hour. *Required fees:* $240; $22.75 per term. Tuition and fees vary according to course load and reciprocity agreements. *Financial support:* In 2011–12, 2 students received support. Federal Work-Study, scholarships/grants, tuition waivers (full and partial), and unspecified assistantships available. Financial award application deadline: 3/1; financial award applicants required to submit FAFSA. *Unit head:* Dr. Brian L. McGuire, Program Director, 812-465-7031, E-mail: bmcguire@usi.edu. *Application contact:* Information Contact, 812-464-1803. Web site: http://business.usi.edu/mba/.

University of Southern Maine, Lewiston-Auburn College, Program in Leadership Studies, Portland, ME 04104-9300. Offers MLS. Part-time programs available. Postbaccalaureate distance learning degree programs offered (minimal on-campus study).

University of Southern Maine, School of Business, Portland, ME 04104-9300. Offers accounting (MBA); business administration (MBA); finance (MBA); health management and policy (MBA); sustainability (MBA); JD/MBA; MBA/MSA; MBA/MSN; MS/MBA. *Accreditation:* AACSB. Part-time and evening/weekend programs available. *Faculty:* 20 full-time (5 women), 2 part-time/adjunct (1 woman). *Students:* 28 full-time (9 women), 91 part-time (39 women), 1 international. Average age 33. 64 applicants, 72% accepted, 33 enrolled. *Entrance requirements:* For master's, GMAT, minimum AACSB index of 1100. Additional exam requirements/recommendations for international students: Required—TOEFL (minimum score 550 paper-based; 213 computer-based; 79 iBT). *Application deadline:* For fall admission, 8/1 priority date for domestic students, 5/1 for international students; for spring admission, 12/1 priority date for domestic students, 9/1 for international students. Applications are processed on a rolling basis. Application fee: $65. Electronic applications accepted. *Financial support:* In 2011–12, 3 research assistantships with partial tuition reimbursements (averaging $9,000 per year), 3 teaching assistantships with partial tuition reimbursements (averaging $9,000 per year) were awarded; career-related internships or fieldwork, Federal Work-Study, scholarships/grants, tuition waivers (full and partial), and unspecified assistantships also available. Support available to part-time students. Financial award application deadline: 2/15; financial award applicants required to submit FAFSA. *Faculty research:* Economic development, management information systems, real options, system dynamics, simulation. *Unit head:* John Voyer, Director, 207-780-4020, Fax: 207-780-4665, E-mail: voyer@usm.maine.edu. *Application contact:* Alice B. Cash, Assistant Director for Student Affairs, 207-780-4184, Fax: 207-780-4662, E-mail: acash@usm.maine.edu. Web site: http://www.usm.maine.edu/sb.

University of Southern Mississippi, Graduate School, College of Business, Department of Management and Marketing, Hattiesburg, MS 39406-0001. Offers business administration (MBA). *Accreditation:* AACSB. Part-time and evening/weekend programs available. *Faculty:* 61 full-time (27 women). *Students:* 21 full-time (10 women), 22 part-time (11 women); includes 7 minority (6 Black or African American, non-Hispanic/Latino; 1 Native Hawaiian or other Pacific Islander, non-Hispanic/Latino), 4 international. Average age 29. 38 applicants, 61% accepted, 18 enrolled. In 2011, 47 degrees awarded. *Degree requirements:* For master's, comprehensive exam. *Entrance requirements:* For master's, GMAT, minimum GPA of 2.75 on last 60 hours. Additional exam requirements/recommendations for international students: Required—TOEFL, IELTS. *Application deadline:* For fall admission, 7/15 priority date for domestic students, 7/15 for international students; for spring admission, 11/15 priority date for domestic students, 11/15 for international students. Application fee: $50. Electronic applications accepted. *Financial support:* In 2011–12, 14 research assistantships with full and partial tuition reimbursements (averaging $7,200 per year), 1 teaching assistantship with full tuition reimbursement (averaging $7,200 per year) were awarded; Federal Work-Study, institutionally sponsored loans, scholarships/grants, health care benefits, and unspecified assistantships also available. Support available to part-time students. Financial award application deadline: 3/15; financial award applicants required to submit FAFSA. *Faculty research:* Inflation accounting, self-esteem training, international trade policy, health care marketing, ethics in strategic planning. *Unit head:* Dr. Joseph Peyrefitte, Chair, 601-266-4659. *Application contact:* Dr. Joseph Peyrefitte, Associate Dean, 601-266-4659, Fax: 601-266-5814. Web site: http://www.usm.edu/graduateschool/table.php.

University of South Florida, Graduate School, College of Business, Department of Business Administration, Tampa, FL 33620-9951. Offers entrepreneurship (MBA); information systems (PhD); leadership and organizational effectiveness (MSM); management and organization (MBA); management information systems (MS); marketing (PhD). *Accreditation:* AACSB. Part-time and evening/weekend programs available. *Faculty:* 4 full-time (2 women), 1 part-time/adjunct (0 women). *Students:* 139 full-time (47 women), 156 part-time (55 women); includes 60 minority (11 Black or African American, non-Hispanic/Latino; 1 American Indian or Alaska Native, non-Hispanic/Latino; 22 Asian, non-Hispanic/Latino; 25 Hispanic/Latino; 1 Two or more races, non-Hispanic/Latino), 68 international. Average age 30. 300 applicants, 44% accepted, 92 enrolled. In 2011, 120 master's awarded. *Degree requirements:* For master's, comprehensive exam, thesis (for some programs); for doctorate, comprehensive exam, thesis/dissertation, 90 credit hours, minimum GPA of 3.0. *Entrance requirements:* For master's, GMAT (preferred) or GRE, minimum GPA of 3.0 in last 60 hours of course work, at least two letters of recommendation, statement of purpose, two years of significant professional work experience, resume; for doctorate, GMAT (preferred) or GRE, minimum GPA of 3.0 in last 60 hours of course work, at least two letters of recommendation, personal statement, interview. Additional exam requirements/recommendations for international students: Required—TOEFL (minimum score 550 paper-based; 213 computer-based; 79 iBT) or IELTS (minimum score 6.5). *Application deadline:* For fall admission, 6/1 for domestic students, 1/2 for international students; for spring admission, 10/15 for domestic students, 6/1 for international students. Application fee: $30. *Financial support:* Scholarships/grants, health care benefits, and unspecified assistantships available. Financial award applicants required to submit FAFSA. *Unit head:* Dr. Jacqueline Reck, Associate Dean, 813-974-6721, Fax: 813-974-4518, E-mail: jreck@usf.edu. *Application contact:* Irene Hurst, Assistant Director, Graduate Studies, 813-974-3335, Fax: 813-974-4518, E-mail: hurst@usf.edu. Web site: http://www.coba.usf.edu.

University of South Florida, Graduate School, College of Business, Department of Management and Organization, Tampa, FL 33620-9951. Offers management (MS). *Accreditation:* AACSB. Part-time programs available. Postbaccalaureate distance learning degree programs offered (minimal on-campus study). *Faculty:* 10 full-time (2 women), 7 part-time/adjunct (1 woman). *Students:* 5 full-time (2 women), 10 part-time (9 women); includes 2 minority (both Black or African American, non-Hispanic/Latino), 5 international. Average age 30. 23 applicants, 43% accepted, 7 enrolled. In 2011, 14 master's awarded. Terminal master's awarded for partial completion of doctoral program. *Degree requirements:* For master's, comprehensive exam. *Entrance requirements:* For master's, GMAT (minimum score of 500), minimum GPA of 3.0 in last 60 hours of coursework, personal statement, five years of managerial experience. Additional exam requirements/recommendations for international students: Required—TOEFL (minimum score 550 paper-based; 213 computer-based; 79 iBT) or IELTS (minimum score 6.5). *Application deadline:* For fall admission, 6/1 for domestic students, 1/2 for international students. Application fee: $30. Electronic applications accepted. *Financial support:* In 2011–12, 4 students received support, including 1 research assistantship with tuition reimbursement available (averaging $9,002 per year), 3 teaching assistantships with tuition reimbursements available (averaging $9,002 per year); tuition waivers also available. Financial award applicants required to submit FAFSA. *Total annual research expenditures:* $313,162. *Unit head:* Dr. Sally R. Fuller, Chair, 813-974-1766, E-mail: sfuller@usf.edu. *Application contact:* Diane Striepling, Assistant to the Department Chair, 813-974-3156, Fax: 813-974-4518, E-mail: dstriepl@usf.edu.

University of South Florida, Graduate School, College of Business, Executive Program in Business Administration, Tampa, FL 33620-9951. Offers MBA. *Accreditation:* AACSB. Evening/weekend programs available. *Students:* Average age 31. In 2011, 23 master's awarded. *Degree requirements:* For master's, thesis or alternative. *Entrance requirements:* For master's, GMAT, minimum 5 years of management/professional experience, minimum GPA of 3.0, interview, letters of recommendation, statement of corporate approval. Additional exam requirements/recommendations for international students: Required—TOEFL (minimum score 550 paper-based; 213 computer-based; 79 iBT) or IELTS (minimum score 6.5). *Application deadline:* For fall admission, 5/31 for domestic students, 1/2 for international students. Applications are processed on a rolling basis. Application fee: $30. *Expenses:* Contact institution. *Unit head:* Irene Hurst, Program Director, 813-974-3335, Fax: 813-974-4518, E-mail: ihurst@usf.edu. *Application contact:* Chris Williams, Program Administrator, 813-974-4876, Fax: 813-974-4518, E-mail: cmwilliams@usf.edu. Web site: http://www.emba.usf.edu/.

University of South Florida–Polytechnic, College of Technology and Innovation, Lakeland, FL 33803. Offers business administration (MBA); information technology (MSIT).

University of South Florida–St. Petersburg Campus, College of Business, St. Petersburg, FL 33701. Offers MBA. Part-time programs available. *Students:* 33 full-time (16 women), 88 part-time (41 women); includes 21 minority (2 Black or African American, non-Hispanic/Latino; 10 Asian, non-Hispanic/Latino; 6 Hispanic/Latino; 3 Two or more races, non-Hispanic/Latino), 2 international. Average age 29. 150 applicants, 37% accepted, 30 enrolled. In 2011, 48 master's awarded. *Entrance requirements:* For master's, GMAT (minimum score of 500), bachelor's degree with minimum GPA of 3.0 overall or in upper two years from regionally-accredited institution; resume. Additional exam requirements/recommendations for international students: Required—TOEFL (minimum score 550 paper-based; 79 iBT); Recommended—IELTS. *Application deadline:* For fall admission, 7/1 for domestic students, 5/1 for international students; for spring admission, 10/15 for domestic students, 7/1 for international students. Applications are processed on a rolling basis. Application fee: $30. Electronic applications accepted. *Expenses:* Tuition, state resident: full-time $8847. Tuition, nonresident: full-time $18,423. One-time fee: $35 full-time. Full-time tuition and fees vary according to course load and program. *Financial support:* Applicants required to submit FAFSA. *Unit head:* Dr. Maling Ebrahimpour, Dean, 727-873-4154, Fax: 727-873-4192, E-mail: bizdean@stpete.usf.edu. *Application contact:* Eric Douthirt, Enrollment Management Specialist, 727-873-4567, Fax: 727-873-4889, E-mail: douthirt@usfsp.edu. Web site: http://www.usfsp.edu/cob/.

University of South Florida Sarasota-Manatee, College of Business, Sarasota, FL 34243. Offers MBA. Part-time and evening/weekend programs available. *Faculty:* 6 full-time (1 woman). *Students:* 19 full-time (10 women), 27 part-time (10 women); includes 6 minority (2 Black or African American, non-Hispanic/Latino; 1 Asian, non-Hispanic/Latino; 3 Hispanic/Latino), 1 international. Average age 33. 59 applicants, 32% accepted, 14 enrolled. In 2011, 18 master's awarded. *Entrance requirements:* For master's, GRE or GMAT. Additional exam requirements/recommendations for international students: Required—TOEFL (minimum score 213 computer-based; 79 iBT) or IELTS. *Application deadline:* For fall admission, 2/15 for domestic students, 1/2 for international students; for spring admission, 10/15 for domestic students, 6/1 for international students. Applications are processed on a rolling basis. Application fee: $30. Electronic applications accepted. *Expenses:* Tuition, state resident: full-time $9301; part-time $387.55 per credit hour. Tuition, nonresident: full-time $19,412; part-time $808.85 per credit hour. *Required fees:* $15; $5 per semester. One-time fee: $30. *Financial support:* Federal Work-Study, scholarships/grants, health care benefits, and unspecified assistantships available. Support available to part-time students. Financial award application deadline: 3/1; financial award applicants required to submit FAFSA. *Faculty research:* Mergers and acquisitions, customer loyalty, employment discrimination, measurement of quality, efficiency of markets. *Unit head:* Dr. Robert L. Anderson, Dean, 941-359-4274, Fax: 941-359-4367, E-mail: randerson@sar.usf.edu. *Application contact:* Aaron Reecher, MBA Academic Program Specialist, 941-359-4333, E-mail: areecher@sar.usf.edu. Web site: http://www.sarasota.usf.edu/Academics/COB/.

The University of Tampa, John H. Sykes College of Business, Tampa, FL 33606-1490. Offers accounting (MS); entrepreneurship (MBA); finance (MBA, MS); information systems management (MBA); innovation management (MBA); international business (MBA); marketing (MBA, MS); nonprofit management (MBA). *Accreditation:* AACSB. Part-time and evening/weekend programs available. *Faculty:* 38 full-time (14 women), 5 part-time/adjunct (1 woman). *Students:* 161 full-time (65 women), 193 part-time (82 women); includes 65 minority (11 Black or African American, non-Hispanic/Latino; 1 American Indian or Alaska Native, non-Hispanic/Latino; 8 Asian, non-Hispanic/Latino; 39 Hispanic/Latino; 2 Native Hawaiian or other Pacific Islander, non-Hispanic/Latino; 4 Two or more races, non-Hispanic/Latino), 58 international. Average age 29. 837 applicants, 41% accepted, 196 enrolled. In 2011, 259 degrees awarded. *Degree requirements:* For master's, capstone. *Entrance requirements:* For master's, GMAT or GRE, 4-year undergraduate degree, minimum GPA of 3.0, professional experience (for Executive MBA). Additional exam requirements/recommendations for international students: Required—TOEFL (minimum score 577 paper-based; 230 computer-based; 90 iBT); Recommended—IELTS (minimum score 7.5). *Application deadline:* Applications are processed on a rolling basis. Application fee: $40. Electronic applications accepted. *Expenses: Tuition:* Full-time $8320; part-time $520 per credit hour. *Required fees:* $40 per semester. Tuition and fees vary according to program. *Financial support:* In 2011–12, 124 students received support. Career-related internships or fieldwork, scholarships/grants, unspecified assistantships, and grants available. Financial award applicants required to submit FAFSA. *Faculty research:* Job market signaling, on-line shopping behaviors and social media, the Tampa Bay economy, digital literacy, entrepreneurship in small businesses. *Unit head:* Dennis Nostrand, Vice President, Enrollment/Admissions, 813-257-1808, E-mail: dnostrand@ut.edu. *Application contact:* Charlene Tobie, Associate Director of Admissions, 813-257-3566, E-mail: ctobie@ut.edu. Web site: http://ut.edu/graduate.

The University of Tennessee, Graduate School, College of Business Administration, Program in Business Administration, Knoxville, TN 37996. Offers accounting (PhD); finance (MBA, PhD); logistics and transportation (MBA, PhD); management (PhD); marketing (MBA, PhD); operations management (MBA); professional business administration (MBA); statistics (PhD); JD/MBA; MS/MBA; Pharm D/MBA. Pharm D/MBA offered jointly with The University of Tennessee Health Science Center. *Accreditation:* AACSB. Postbaccalaureate distance learning degree programs offered. *Degree requirements:* For master's, thesis or alternative; for doctorate, thesis/dissertation. *Entrance requirements:* For master's and doctorate, GMAT, minimum GPA of 2.7. Additional exam requirements/recommendations for international students: Required—TOEFL. Electronic applications accepted. *Expenses:* Tuition, state resident: full-time $8332; part-time $464 per credit hour. Tuition, nonresident: full-time $25,174; part-time $1400 per credit hour. *Required fees:* $1162; $56 per credit hour. Tuition and fees vary according to program.

The University of Tennessee, Graduate School, College of Business Administration, Program in Management Science, Knoxville, TN 37996. Offers MS, PhD. *Accreditation:* AACSB. *Degree requirements:* For master's, thesis or alternative; for doctorate, thesis/dissertation. *Entrance requirements:* For master's and doctorate, GMAT or GRE General Test, minimum GPA of 2.7. Additional exam requirements/recommendations for international students: Required—TOEFL. Electronic applications accepted. *Expenses:* Tuition, state resident: full-time $8332; part-time $464 per credit hour. Tuition, nonresident: full-time $25,174; part-time $1400 per credit hour. *Required fees:* $1162; $56 per credit hour. Tuition and fees vary according to program.

The University of Tennessee at Chattanooga, Graduate School, College of Business, Program in Business Administration, Chattanooga, TN 37403. Offers EMBA, MBA. *Accreditation:* AACSB. Part-time and evening/weekend programs available. *Faculty:* 11 full-time (3 women), 1 part-time/adjunct (0 women). *Students:* 98 full-time (36 women), 155 part-time (62 women); includes 45 minority (22 Black or African American, non-Hispanic/Latino; 13 Asian, non-Hispanic/Latino; 7 Hispanic/Latino; 3 Two or more races, non-Hispanic/Latino). Average age 29. 123 applicants, 89% accepted, 55 enrolled. In 2011, 102 master's awarded. *Entrance requirements:* For master's, GMAT (minimum score 450) or GRE General Test (minimum score 1000). Additional exam requirements/recommendations for international students: Required—TOEFL (minimum score 550 paper-based; 213 computer-based; 79 iBT), IELTS (minimum score 6). *Application deadline:* For fall admission, 8/1 priority date for domestic students, 6/1 for international students; for spring admission, 12/1 priority date for domestic students, 10/1 for international students. Applications are processed on a rolling basis. Application fee: $35. Electronic applications accepted. *Expenses:* Tuition, state resident: full-time $6472; part-time $359 per credit hour. Tuition, nonresident: full-time $20,006; part-time $1111 per credit hour. *Required fees:* $1320; $160 per credit hour. *Financial support:* Career-related internships or fieldwork, scholarships/grants, tuition waivers (partial), and unspecified assistantships available. Support available to part-time students. *Faculty research:* Diversity, operations/production management, entrepreneurial processes, customer satisfaction and retention, branding. *Unit head:* Lawrence Ettkin, Department Head, 423-425-4403, Fax: 423-425-5255, E-mail: lawrence-ettkin@utc.edu. *Application contact:* Dr. Jerald Ainsworth, Dean of Graduate Studies, 423-425-4478, Fax: 423-425-5223, E-mail: jerald-ainsworth@utc.edu. Web site: http://www.utc.edu/Academic/BusinessGraduatePrograms/MBA.php.

The University of Tennessee at Martin, Graduate Programs, College of Business and Global Affairs, Program in Business, Martin, TN 38238-1000. Offers MBA. *Accreditation:* AACSB. Part-time programs available. Postbaccalaureate distance learning degree programs offered (no on-campus study). *Faculty:* 28. *Students:* 66 (19 women); includes 6 minority (4 Black or African American, non-Hispanic/Latino; 2 Asian, non-Hispanic/Latino), 8 international. 41 applicants, 46% accepted, 16 enrolled. In 2011, 43 master's awarded. *Degree requirements:* For master's, comprehensive exam. *Entrance requirements:* For master's, GMAT, minimum GPA of 2.5, resume. Additional exam requirements/recommendations for international students: Required—TOEFL (minimum score 525 paper-based; 197 computer-based; 71 iBT). *Application deadline:* For fall admission, 8/1 priority date for domestic students, 8/1 for international students; for spring admission, 1/1 priority date for domestic students, 1/1 for international students. Applications are processed on a rolling basis. Application fee: $30 ($50 for international students). Electronic applications accepted. *Expenses:* Tuition, state resident: full-time $6726; part-time $374 per credit hour. Tuition, nonresident: full-time $19,136; part-time $1064 per credit hour. *Required fees:* $61 per credit hour. *Financial support:* In 2011–12, 11 students received support, including 9 research assistantships with full tuition reimbursements available (averaging $6,919 per year), 2 teaching assistantships (averaging $6,911 per year); career-related internships or fieldwork, scholarships/grants, and unspecified assistantships also available. Support available to part-time students. Financial award application deadline: 3/1. *Unit head:* Dr. Kevin Hammond, Coordinator, 731-881-7236, Fax: 731-881-7241, E-mail: bagrad@utm.edu. *Application contact:* Linda S. Arant, Student Services Specialist, 731-881-7012, Fax: 731-881-7499, E-mail: larant@utm.edu.

The University of Texas at Arlington, Graduate School, College of Business, Program in Business Administration, Arlington, TX 76019. Offers accounting (PhD); business statistics (PhD); finance (MBA, PhD); information systems (MBA, PhD); management (MBA, PhD); marketing (MBA, PhD); operations management (MBA, PhD); real estate (MBA). *Accreditation:* AACSB. Part-time and evening/weekend programs available. *Students:* 505 full-time (189 women), 369 part-time (140 women); includes 199 minority (58 Black or African American, non-Hispanic/Latino; 2 American Indian or Alaska Native, non-Hispanic/Latino; 70 Asian, non-Hispanic/Latino; 56 Hispanic/Latino; 1 Native Hawaiian or other Pacific Islander, non-Hispanic/Latino; 12 Two or more races, non-Hispanic/Latino), 306 international. 416 applicants, 81% accepted, 234 enrolled. In 2011, 495 master's, 3 doctorates awarded. *Degree requirements:* For master's, thesis optional; for doctorate, comprehensive exam, thesis/dissertation. *Entrance requirements:* For master's, GMAT or GRE; for doctorate, GMAT, minimum GPA of 3.0 (undergraduate), 3.4 (graduate); 30 hours of graduate course work. Additional exam requirements/recommendations for international students: Required—TOEFL (minimum score 550 paper-based; 213 computer-based; 79 iBT). *Application deadline:* For fall admission, 6/1 for domestic students, 4/1 for international students; for spring admission, 10/15 for domestic students, 9/15 for international students. Applications are processed on a rolling basis. Application fee: $40 ($70 for international students). Electronic applications accepted. *Financial support:* Career-related internships or fieldwork, scholarships/grants, and unspecified assistantships available. Support available to part-time students. Financial award application deadline: 6/1; financial award applicants required to submit FAFSA. *Unit head:* Dr. Edmund Prater, Director of PhD Programs, 817-272-2131, Fax: 817-272-5799. *Application contact:* Melanie McGee, Director of MBA Program, 817-272-3005, Fax: 817-272-5799, E-mail: mwmcgee@uta.edu.

The University of Texas at Austin, Graduate School, McCombs School of Business, Department of Management, Austin, TX 78712-1111. Offers PhD. *Accreditation:* AACSB. *Degree requirements:* For doctorate, thesis/dissertation. *Entrance requirements:* For doctorate, GMAT or GRE. *Application deadline:* For fall admission, 2/1 for domestic students. Application fee: $50 ($75 for international students). Electronic applications accepted. *Financial support:* Fellowships, research assistantships, and teaching assistantships available. Financial award application deadline: 2/1. *Unit head:* Dr. James Fedrickson, Chair, 512-471-5694, E-mail: james.fredrickson@mccombs.utexas.edu. *Application contact:* Dr. Janet Dukerich, Graduate Adviser, 512-471-7876, E-mail: janet.dukerich@mccombs.utexas.edu. Web site: http://www.mccombs.utexas.edu/dept/management/.

The University of Texas at Austin, Graduate School, McCombs School of Business, Executive MBA Program at Mexico City, Austin, TX 78712-1111. Offers MBA. Program offered jointly with Instituto Tecnológico y de Estudios Superiores de Monterrey, Campus Ciudad de México. *Accreditation:* AACSB. *Entrance requirements:* For master's, GMAT, 5 years of work experience. Additional exam requirements/recommendations for international students: Required—TOEFL. *Application deadline:* For fall admission, 5/31 for domestic students. Application fee: $125. *Unit head:* Dr. Genaro Gutierrez, Director, 512-471-5296, E-mail: genaro@austin.utexas.edu. *Application contact:* Carolyn M. Rathbun, Assistant Director, 512-232-7664, E-mail:

mackenzie.snyder@mccombs.utexas.edu. Web site: http://www.mccombs.utexas.edu/MBA/MBA-Mexico.aspx.

The University of Texas at Austin, Graduate School, McCombs School of Business, Programs in MBA, Austin, TX 78712-1111. Offers MBA, JD/MBA, MBA/MA, MBA/MP Aff, MBA/MSN. *Accreditation:* AACSB. Part-time programs available. *Entrance requirements:* For master's, GMAT, minimum 2 years of full-time work experience. Additional exam requirements/recommendations for international students: Required—TOEFL. *Application deadline:* For fall admission, 4/15 priority date for domestic students. Applications are processed on a rolling basis. Application fee: $125. Electronic applications accepted. *Financial support:* Fellowships with partial tuition reimbursements, research assistantships, teaching assistantships, career-related internships or fieldwork, scholarships/grants, and tuition waivers (partial) available. Financial award application deadline: 3/31; financial award applicants required to submit FAFSA. *Unit head:* Thomas W. Gilligan, Dean, 512-471-5058, E-mail: dean.gilligan@mccombs.utexas.edu. *Application contact:* Matt Turner, Director of Admissions, 512-232-6723, E-mail: matt.turner@mccombs.utexas.edu. Web site: http://mba.mccombs.utexas.edu.

The University of Texas at Brownsville, Graduate Studies, School of Business, Brownsville, TX 78520-4991. Offers MBA. Part-time and evening/weekend programs available. Postbaccalaureate distance learning degree programs offered (minimal on-campus study). *Degree requirements:* For master's, capstone courses. *Entrance requirements:* For master's, GRE General Test. Additional exam requirements/recommendations for international students: Required—TOEFL. *Faculty research:* Binational and international business.

The University of Texas at Dallas, Naveen Jindal School of Management, Richardson, TX 75080. Offers EMBA, MBA, MS, PhD, MSEE/MBA. Part-time and evening/weekend programs available. Postbaccalaureate distance learning degree programs offered. *Faculty:* 88 full-time (16 women), 52 part-time/adjunct (13 women). *Students:* 1,707 full-time (827 women), 1,491 part-time (627 women); includes 604 minority (91 Black or African American, non-Hispanic/Latino; 6 American Indian or Alaska Native, non-Hispanic/Latino; 343 Asian, non-Hispanic/Latino; 130 Hispanic/Latino; 1 Native Hawaiian or other Pacific Islander, non-Hispanic/Latino; 33 Two or more races, non-Hispanic/Latino), 1,457 international. Average age 30. 3,900 applicants, 54% accepted, 1170 enrolled. In 2011, 1,103 master's, 11 doctorates awarded. *Degree requirements:* For doctorate, thesis/dissertation. *Entrance requirements:* For master's and doctorate, GMAT. Additional exam requirements/recommendations for international students: Required—TOEFL (minimum score 550 paper-based; 215 computer-based). *Application deadline:* For fall admission, 7/15 for domestic students, 5/1 for international students; for spring admission, 11/15 for domestic students, 9/1 for international students. Applications are processed on a rolling basis. Application fee: $50 ($100 for international students). Electronic applications accepted. *Expenses:* Tuition, state resident: full-time $11,170; part-time $620.56 per credit hour. Tuition, nonresident: full-time $20,212; part-time $1122.89 per credit hour. *Financial support:* In 2011–12, 965 students received support, including 6 research assistantships with partial tuition reimbursements available (averaging $19,105 per year), 123 teaching assistantships with partial tuition reimbursements available (averaging $14,676 per year); career-related internships or fieldwork, Federal Work-Study, institutionally sponsored loans, scholarships/grants, and unspecified assistantships also available. Support available to part-time students. Financial award application deadline: 4/30; financial award applicants required to submit FAFSA. *Faculty research:* Finance, marketing and organization, strategy, management education for physicians. *Total annual research expenditures:* $2.4 million. *Unit head:* Dr. Hasan Pirkul, Dean, 972-883-2705, Fax: 972-883-2799, E-mail: hpirkul@utdallas.edu. *Application contact:* David B. Ritchey, Director of Advising, 972-883-2750, Fax: 972-883-6425, E-mail: davidr@utdallas.edu. Web site: http://jindal.utdallas.edu/.

See Display on page 162 and Close-Up on page 257.

The University of Texas at El Paso, Graduate School, College of Business Administration, Programs in Business Administration, El Paso, TX 79968-0001. Offers business administration (MBA, Certificate); international business (PhD). *Accreditation:* AACSB. Part-time and evening/weekend programs available. Postbaccalaureate distance learning degree programs offered (no on-campus study). *Students:* 345 (147 women); includes 200 minority (5 Black or African American, non-Hispanic/Latino; 7 Asian, non-Hispanic/Latino; 188 Hispanic/Latino), 95 international. Average age 34. 135 applicants, 67% accepted, 73 enrolled. In 2011, 42 master's awarded. *Entrance requirements:* For master's, GMAT, minimum GPA of 2.7. Additional exam requirements/recommendations for international students: Required—TOEFL. *Application deadline:* For fall admission, 7/1 priority date for domestic students, 3/1 for international students; for spring admission, 11/1 priority date for domestic students, 9/1 for international students. Applications are processed on a rolling basis. Application fee: $15 ($65 for international students). Electronic applications accepted. *Financial support:* In 2011–12, research assistantships with partial tuition reimbursements (averaging $18,750 per year), teaching assistantships with partial tuition reimbursements (averaging $15,000 per year) were awarded; Federal Work-Study, institutionally sponsored loans, and tuition waivers (partial) also available. Financial award application deadline: 3/15; financial award applicants required to submit FAFSA. *Unit head:* Laura M. Uribarri, Director, 915-747-5379, Fax: 915-747-5147, E-mail: mba@utep.edu. *Application contact:* Dr. Benjamin Flores, Interim Dean of the Graduate School, 915-747-5491, Fax: 915-747-5788, E-mail: bflores@utep.edu.

See Display below and Close-Up on page 259.

The University of Texas at San Antonio, College of Business, Department of Information Systems and Cyber Security, San Antonio, TX 78249-0617. Offers business (MBA); business administration (PhD); information technology (MSIT); management of technology (MSMOT). Part-time and evening/weekend programs available. *Faculty:* 11 full-time (3 women), 5 part-time/adjunct (1 woman). *Students:* 23 full-time (7 women), 73 part-time (13 women); includes 41 minority (3 Black or African American, non-Hispanic/Latino; 5 Asian, non-Hispanic/Latino; 30 Hispanic/Latino; 1 Native Hawaiian or other Pacific Islander, non-Hispanic/Latino; 2 Two or more races, non-Hispanic/Latino), 4 international. Average age 31. 50 applicants, 40% accepted, 13 enrolled. In 2011, 41 master's awarded. *Degree requirements:* For master's, thesis or alternative; for doctorate, comprehensive exam, thesis/dissertation. *Entrance requirements:* For master's, GMAT, bachelor's degree with 18 credit hours in the field of study or another appropriate field of study, statement of purpose; for doctorate, GMAT or GRE, resume or curriculum vitae, three letters of recommendation from academic or professional sources familiar with the applicant's background. Additional exam requirements/recommendations for international students: Required—TOEFL (minimum score 500 paper-based; 61 iBT), IELTS (minimum score 5). *Application deadline:* For fall admission, 7/1 for domestic students, 4/1 for international students; for spring admission, 11/1 for domestic students, 9/1 for international students. Applications are processed on a rolling basis. Application fee: $45 ($85 for international students). Electronic applications accepted. *Expenses:* Tuition, state resident: full-time $3148; part-time $2176 per semester. Tuition, nonresident: full-time $8782; part-time $5932 per semester. *Required fees:* $719 per semester. *Financial support:* In 2011–12, 23 students received support, including 10 fellowships (averaging $22,000 per year), research assistantships (averaging $10,000 per year), teaching assistantships (averaging $10,000 per year); scholarships/grants, health care benefits, and unspecified assistantships also available. *Faculty research:* economics of information systems, information security, digital forensics, information systems strategy, adoption and diffusion. *Total annual research expenditures:* $300,000. *Unit head:* Dr. Jan Clark, Chair, 210-458-5244, Fax: 210-458-6305, E-mail: jan.clark@utsa.edu. *Application contact:* Katherine Pope, Graduate Advisor of Record, 210-458-7316, Fax: 210-458-4398, E-mail: katherine.pope@utsa.edu.

The University of Texas at San Antonio, College of Business, Department of Management Science and Statistics, San Antonio, TX 78249-0617. Offers applied statistics (MS, PhD); management science (MBA). *Accreditation:* AACSB. Part-time and evening/weekend programs available. *Faculty:* 11 full-time (2 women), 4 part-time/adjunct (3 women). *Students:* 36 full-time (12 women), 23 part-time (8 women); includes 16 minority (3 Black or African American, non-Hispanic/Latino; 5 Asian, non-Hispanic/Latino; 8 Hispanic/Latino), 21 international. Average age 31. 47 applicants, 60% accepted, 21 enrolled. In 2011, 8 master's, 4 doctorates awarded. *Degree requirements:* For master's, comprehensive exam (for some programs), thesis or alternative; for doctorate, comprehensive exam, thesis/dissertation. *Entrance requirements:* For master's, GMAT, minimum of 36 semester credit hours of coursework beyond any hours acquired in the MBA-leveling courses; statement of purpose; for doctorate, GRE, minimum cumulative GPA of 3.3 in the last 60 hours of coursework; transcripts from all colleges and universities attended; curriculum vitae; statement of academic work experiences, interests, and goals; three letters of recommendation; BA, BS, or MS in mathematics, statistics, or closely-related field. Additional exam requirements/recommendations for international students: Required—TOEFL (minimum score 500 paper-based; 61 iBT), IELTS (minimum score 5). *Application deadline:* For fall admission, 7/1 for domestic students, 4/1 for international students; for spring admission, 11/1 for domestic students, 9/1 for international students. Applications are processed on a rolling basis. Application fee: $45 ($85 for international students). Electronic applications accepted. *Expenses:* Tuition, state resident: full-time $3148; part-time $2176 per semester. Tuition, nonresident: full-time $8782; part-time $5932 per semester. *Required fees:* $719 per semester. *Financial support:* In 2011–12, fellowships (averaging $22,000 per year), research assistantships (averaging $10,000 per year), teaching assistantships (averaging $10,000 per year) were awarded; scholarships/grants, health care benefits, and unspecified assistantships also available. *Faculty research:* Statistical signal processing, reliability and life-testing experiments, modeling decompression sickness using survival analysis. *Unit head:* Dr. Raydel Tullous, Chair, 210-458-6345, Fax: 210-458-6350, E-mail: raydel.tullous@utsa.edu. *Application contact:* Katherine Pope, Graduate Assistant of Record, 210-458-7316, Fax: 210-458-4398, E-mail: katherine.pope@utsa.edu.

The University of Texas at San Antonio, College of Business, General Business Program, San Antonio, TX 78249-0617. Offers business (MBA); business administration (PhD), including accounting, business administration, finance, information technology, management and organization studies, marketing; information systems (MBA); international business (MBA); management accounting (MBA); management of technology (MBA); marketing management (MBA); taxation (MBA). *Students:* 170 full-time (52 women), 120 part-time (49 women); includes 90 minority (14 Black or African American, non-Hispanic/Latino; 2 American Indian or Alaska Native, non-Hispanic/Latino; 15 Asian, non-Hispanic/Latino; 55 Hispanic/Latino; 1 Native Hawaiian or other Pacific Islander, non-Hispanic/Latino; 3 Two or more races, non-Hispanic/Latino), 37 international. Average age 32. 395 applicants, 45% accepted, 133 enrolled. In 2011, 95 master's, 8 doctorates awarded. *Entrance requirements:* Additional exam requirements/recommendations for international students: Required—TOEFL (minimum score 500 paper-based; 61 iBT), IELTS (minimum score 5). *Application deadline:* For fall admission, 7/1 for domestic students, 4/1 for international students; for spring admission, 11/1 for domestic students, 9/1 for international students. Application fee: $45 ($85 for international students). *Expenses:* Tuition, state resident: full-time $3148; part-time $2176 per semester. Tuition, nonresident: full-time $8782; part-time $5932 per semester. *Required fees:* $719 per semester. *Financial support:* In 2011–12, fellowships (averaging $22,000 per year), research assistantships (averaging $10,000 per year), teaching assistantships (averaging $10,000 per year) were awarded. *Unit head:* Dr. Lynda Y. de la Vinna, Dean, 210-458-4317, Fax: 210-458-4308, E-mail: lynda.delavina@utsa.edu. *Application contact:* Katherine Pope, Director of Graduate Student Services, 210-458-7316, Fax: 210-458-4398, E-mail: katherine.pope@utsa.edu. Web site: http://business.utsa.edu.

The University of Texas at Tyler, College of Business and Technology, School of Business Administration, Tyler, TX 75799-0001. Offers business administration (MBA); general management (MBA); health care (MBA). Part-time programs available. Postbaccalaureate distance learning degree programs offered (no on-campus study). *Entrance requirements:* Additional exam requirements/recommendations for international students: Required—TOEFL (minimum score 550 paper-based; 79 computer-based). *Faculty research:* General business, inventory control, institutional markets, service marketing, product distribution, accounting fraud, financial reporting and recognition.

The University of Texas of the Permian Basin, Office of Graduate Studies, School of Business, Program in Management, Odessa, TX 79762-0001. Offers MBA. *Accreditation:* AACSB. *Entrance requirements:* For master's, GMAT. Additional exam requirements/recommendations for international students: Required—TOEFL (minimum score 550 paper-based; 213 computer-based).

The University of Texas–Pan American, College of Business Administration, Edinburg, TX 78539. Offers M Acc, MBA, MS, PhD. *Accreditation:* AACSB. Part-time and evening/weekend programs available. *Degree requirements:* For master's, thesis optional; for doctorate, one foreign language, thesis/dissertation, internship. *Entrance requirements:* For master's, GMAT, minimum AACSB index of 1000 (based on last 60 semester hours); for doctorate, GMAT. Additional exam requirements/recommendations for international students: Required—TOEFL. Application fee: $0. Tuition and fees vary according to course load, program and student level. *Financial support:* Fellowships, research assistantships, teaching assistantships, career-related internships or fieldwork, and Federal Work-Study available. Support available to part-time students. Financial award application deadline: 9/5. *Unit head:* Dr. Teofilo Ozuna, Jr., Dean, 956-665-3315, E-mail: ozuna@utpa.edu. Web site: http://portal.utpa.edu/utpa_main/daa_home/coba_home/coba_mba.

University of the Cumberlands, Hutton School of Business, Williamsburg, KY 40769-1372. Offers MBA. Part-time programs available. Postbaccalaureate distance learning degree programs offered (no on-campus study). *Entrance requirements:* For master's, GMAT, GRE. Additional exam requirements/recommendations for international students: Required—TOEFL. Electronic applications accepted.

University of the District of Columbia, School of Business and Public Administration, Program in Business Administration, Washington, DC 20008-1175. Offers MBA. *Accreditation:* ACBSP. *Degree requirements:* For master's, comprehensive exam, thesis optional. *Entrance requirements:* For master's, GMAT, writing proficiency exam. *Expenses: Tuition, area resident:* Full-time $7580; part-time $421 per credit hour. Tuition, state resident: full-time $8580; part-time $477 per credit hour. Tuition, nonresident: full-time $14,580; part-time $810 per credit hour. *Required fees:* $620; $30 per credit hour. $310 per semester.

University of the Incarnate Word, Extended Academic Programs, Program in Administration, San Antonio, TX 78209-6397. Offers MA. *Faculty:* 12 part-time/adjunct (2 women). *Students:* 19 full-time (9 women), 197 part-time (114 women); includes 114 minority (23 Black or African American, non-Hispanic/Latino; 2 American Indian or Alaska Native, non-Hispanic/Latino; 6 Asian, non-Hispanic/Latino; 82 Hispanic/Latino; 1 Native Hawaiian or other Pacific Islander, non-Hispanic/Latino). Average age 37. 96 applicants, 100% accepted, 68 enrolled. In 2011, 53 master's awarded. *Degree requirements:* For master's, capstone experience. *Expenses: Tuition:* Part-time $725 per credit hour. Tuition and fees vary according to degree level. *Unit head:* Dr. Cyndi Porter, Vice President, 877-603-1130, E-mail: porter@uiwtx.edu. *Application contact:* Julie Weber, Director of Marketing and Recruitment, 210-832-2100, Fax: 210-829-2756, E-mail: eapadmission@uiwtx.edu. Web site: http://adcap.uiw.edu/academics/graduate_degrees/ma_administration.

University of the Incarnate Word, Extended Academic Programs, Program in Business Administration, San Antonio, TX 78209-6397. Offers MBA. *Faculty:* 3 full-time (0 women), 20 part-time/adjunct (8 women). *Students:* 13 full-time (4 women), 168 part-time (88 women); includes 110 minority (19 Black or African American, non-Hispanic/Latino; 5 Asian, non-Hispanic/Latino; 85 Hispanic/Latino; 1 Native Hawaiian or other Pacific Islander, non-Hispanic/Latino). Average age 36. 53 applicants, 100% accepted, 40 enrolled. In 2011, 67 master's awarded. *Expenses: Tuition:* Part-time $725 per credit hour. Tuition and fees vary according to degree level. *Unit head:* Dr. Cyndi Porter, Vice President, 877-603-1130, E-mail: porter@uiwtx.edu. *Application contact:* Julie Weber, Director of Marketing and Recruitment, 210-832-2100, Fax: 210-829-2756, E-mail: eapadmission@uiwtx.edu. Web site: http://adcap.uiw.edu/academics/graduate_degrees/mba.

University of the Incarnate Word, School of Graduate Studies and Research, H-E-B School of Business and Administration, Programs in Administration, San Antonio, TX 78209-6397. Offers adult education (MAA); applied administration (MAA); communication arts (MAA); healthcare administration (MAA); instructional technology (MAA); international business (Certificate); nutrition (MAA); organizational development (MAA, Certificate); project management (Certificate); sports management (MAA). Part-time and evening/weekend programs available. Postbaccalaureate distance learning degree programs offered (no on-campus study). *Faculty:* 23 full-time (10 women), 26 part-time/adjunct (12 women). *Students:* 25 full-time (18 women), 54 part-time (33 women); includes 50 minority (10 Black or African American, non-Hispanic/Latino; 40 Hispanic/Latino), 5 international. Average age 34. 35 applicants, 94% accepted, 19 enrolled. In 2011, 38 master's awarded. *Degree requirements:* For master's, capstone. *Entrance requirements:* For master's, GRE, GMAT, undergraduate degree, minimum GPA of 2.5. Additional exam requirements/recommendations for international students: Required—TOEFL (minimum score 560 paper-based; 220 computer-based; 83 iBT). *Application deadline:* Applications are processed on a rolling basis. Application fee: $20. Electronic applications accepted. *Expenses: Tuition:* Part-time $725 per credit hour. Tuition and fees vary according to degree level. *Financial support:* Federal Work-Study and scholarships/grants available. Financial award applicants required to submit FAFSA. *Unit head:* Dr. Mark Teachout, MAA Programs Director, 210-829-3177, Fax: 210-805-3564, E-mail: teachout@uiwtx.edu. *Application contact:* Andrea Cyterski-Acosta, Dean of Enrollment, 210-829-6005, Fax: 210-829-3921, E-mail: admis@uiwtx.edu. Web site: http://www.uiw.edu/maa/index.htm and http://www.uiw.edu/maa/admissions.html.

University of the Incarnate Word, School of Graduate Studies and Research, H-E-B School of Business and Administration, Programs in Business Administration, San Antonio, TX 78209-6397. Offers general business (MBA); international business (MBA); international business strategy (MBA); sports management (MBA). *Accreditation:* ACBSP. Part-time and evening/weekend programs available. Postbaccalaureate distance learning degree programs offered. *Faculty:* 23 full-time (10 women), 26 part-time/adjunct (12 women). *Students:* 78 full-time (38 women), 93 part-time (46 women); includes 85 minority (11 Black or African American, non-Hispanic/Latino; 5 Asian, non-Hispanic/Latino; 68 Hispanic/Latino; 1 Native Hawaiian or other Pacific Islander, non-Hispanic/Latino), 42 international. Average age 28. 114 applicants, 96% accepted, 40 enrolled. In 2011, 83 master's awarded. *Degree requirements:* For master's, capstone. *Entrance requirements:* For master's, GMAT (minimum score 450), undergraduate degree with minimum overall GPA of 2.5. Additional exam requirements/recommendations for international students: Required—TOEFL (minimum score 560 paper-based; 220 computer-based; 83 iBT). *Application deadline:* Applications are processed on a rolling basis. Application fee: $20. Electronic applications accepted. *Expenses: Tuition:* Part-time $725 per credit hour. Tuition and fees vary according to degree level. *Financial support:* Federal Work-Study and scholarships/grants available. Financial award applicants required to submit FAFSA. *Unit head:* Dr. Jeannie Scott, Acting Dean, 210-283-5002, Fax: 210-805-3564, E-mail: scott@uiwtx.edu. *Application contact:* Andrea Cyterski-Acosta, Dean of Enrollment, 210-829-6005, Fax: 210-829-3921, E-mail: admis@uiwtx.edu. Web site: http://www.uiw.edu/mba/index.htm and http://www.uiw.edu/mba/admission.html.

University of the Pacific, Eberhardt School of Business, Stockton, CA 95211-0197. Offers MBA, JD/MBA. *Accreditation:* AACSB. Part-time programs available. *Faculty:* 25 full-time (8 women), 3 part-time/adjunct (0 women). *Students:* 37 full-time (16 women); includes 10 minority (1 Black or African American, non-Hispanic/Latino; 1 American Indian or Alaska Native, non-Hispanic/Latino; 8 Asian, non-Hispanic/Latino), 14 international. Average age 24. 66 applicants, 45% accepted, 15 enrolled. In 2011, 28 master's awarded. *Entrance requirements:* For master's, GMAT. Additional exam requirements/recommendations for international students: Required—TOEFL (minimum score 475 paper-based; 150 computer-based). *Application deadline:* For fall admission, 7/31 priority date for domestic students; for spring admission, 11/30 for domestic students. Applications are processed on a rolling basis. Application fee: $75. *Expenses: Tuition:* Full-time $18,900; part-time $1181 per unit. *Required fees:* $949. *Financial support:* Fellowships, research assistantships, Federal Work-Study, and institutionally sponsored loans available. Support available to part-time students. Financial award application deadline: 3/1; financial award applicants required to submit FAFSA. *Unit head:* Dr. Richard Flaherty, Dean, 209-946-2466, Fax: 209-946-2586. *Application contact:* Dr. Chris Lozano, MBA Recruiting Director, 209-946-2597, Fax: 209-946-2586, E-mail: clozano@pacific.edu. Web site: http://www.pacific.edu/mba/.

University of the Sacred Heart, Graduate Programs, Department of Business Administration, San Juan, PR 00914-0383. Offers human resource management (MBA); information systems auditing (MS); information technology (Certificate); international marketing (MBA); management information systems (MBA); production and marketing of special events (Certificate); taxation (MBA). Part-time and evening/weekend programs available. *Degree requirements:* For master's, thesis. *Entrance requirements:* For master's, EXADEP, minimum undergraduate GPA of 2.75, interview.

University of the Southwest, Graduate Programs, Hobbs, NM 88240-9129. Offers business administration (MBA); curriculum and instruction (MSE); curriculum and instruction: bilingual (MSE); curriculum and instruction: TESOL (MSE); early childhood education (MSE); educational administration (MSE); mental health counseling (MSE); school counseling (MSE); special education (MSE); sports management (MBA). Part-time and evening/weekend programs available. Postbaccalaureate distance learning degree programs offered (no on-campus study). *Faculty:* 13 full-time (6 women), 28 part-time/adjunct (17 women). *Students:* 76 full-time (63 women), 229 part-time (194 women); includes 104 minority (50 Black or African American, non-Hispanic/Latino; 2 American Indian or Alaska Native, non-Hispanic/Latino; 8 Asian, non-Hispanic/Latino; 44 Hispanic/Latino). Average age 38. 173 applicants, 71% accepted, 101 enrolled. In 2011, 75 master's awarded. *Degree requirements:* For master's, comprehensive exam, thesis (for some programs). *Entrance requirements:* Additional exam requirements/recommendations for international students: Recommended—TOEFL. *Application deadline:* Applications are processed on a rolling basis. Application fee: $50. Electronic applications accepted. *Expenses: Tuition:* Full-time $12,288; part-time $512 per credit hour. One-time fee: $50. Tuition and fees vary according to course load. *Financial support:* In 2011–12, 47 students received support. Federal Work-Study available. Financial award application deadline: 4/1; financial award applicants required to submit FAFSA. *Unit head:* Dr. Mary Harris, Dean of Education, 575-492-2162, Fax: 575-392-6006, E-mail: mharris@usw.edu. *Application contact:* Melissa Mitchell, Senior Online Program Advisor, 575-492-2142, Fax: 575-392-6006, E-mail: mmitchell@usw.edu. Web site: http://www.usw.edu/admissions/graduate_admission/graduate_admissions.

University of the Virgin Islands, Graduate Programs, Division of Business Administration, Saint Thomas, VI 00802-9990. Offers MBA. Part-time and evening/weekend programs available. *Degree requirements:* For master's, comprehensive exam or thesis. *Entrance requirements:* For master's, GMAT, minimum GPA of 2.5. Additional exam requirements/recommendations for international students: Required—TOEFL (minimum score 550 paper-based; 213 computer-based). *Faculty research:* Management information systems.

University of the West, Department of Business Administration, Rosemead, CA 91770. Offers business administration (EMBA); finance (MBA); information technology and management (MBA); international business (MBA); nonprofit organization management (MBA). Part-time and evening/weekend programs available. *Entrance requirements:* Additional exam requirements/recommendations for international students: Required—TOEFL.

The University of Toledo, College of Graduate Studies, College of Business and Innovation, Toledo, OH 43606-3390. Offers EMBA, MBA, MSA, PhD, Certificate, JD/MBA, MD/MBA. *Accreditation:* AACSB. Part-time and evening/weekend programs available. *Faculty:* 39. *Students:* 128 full-time (49 women), 289 part-time (112 women); includes 44 minority (28 Black or African American, non-Hispanic/Latino; 1 American Indian or Alaska Native, non-Hispanic/Latino; 7 Asian, non-Hispanic/Latino; 6 Hispanic/Latino; 2 Two or more races, non-Hispanic/Latino), 161 international. Average age 27. 254 applicants, 67% accepted, 124 enrolled. In 2011, 261 master's, 5 doctorates awarded. *Degree requirements:* For doctorate, thesis/dissertation. *Entrance requirements:* For master's, doctorate, and Certificate, GMAT, minimum GPA of 2.7 for all prior academic work, three letters of recommendation, statement of purpose, transcripts from all prior institutions attended. Additional exam requirements/recommendations for international students: Required—TOEFL (minimum score 550 paper-based; 213 computer-based; 80 iBT), IELTS (minimum score 6.5). *Application deadline:* For fall admission, 1/15 priority date for domestic students, 1/15 for international students. Applications are processed on a rolling basis. Application fee: $45 ($75 for international students). Electronic applications accepted. *Financial support:* In 2011–12, 92 research assistantships with full and partial tuition reimbursements (averaging $6,372 per year) were awarded; career-related internships or fieldwork, Federal Work-Study, institutionally sponsored loans, scholarships/grants, tuition waivers (full and partial), unspecified assistantships, and administrative assistantships also available. Support available to part-time students. *Unit head:* Dr. Thomas G. Gutteridge, Dean, 419-530-4612, E-mail: cobusiness@utoledo.edu. *Application contact:* Graduate School Office, 419-530-4723, Fax: 419-530-4724, E-mail: grdsch@utnet.utoledo.edu. Web site: http://www.utoledo.edu/business/index.html.

University of Toronto, School of Graduate Studies, Rotman School of Management, Toronto, ON M5S 1A1, Canada. Offers MBA, MF, PhD, JD/MBA. *Accreditation:* AACSB. Part-time and evening/weekend programs available. *Degree requirements:* For doctorate, thesis/dissertation. *Entrance requirements:* For master's, GMAT (MBA), minimum mid-B average in final undergraduate year; minimum 2 years of full-time work experience; 2-3 letters of reference; for doctorate, GMAT or GRE, minimum B+ average, master's degree in business administration, 2-3 letters of reference. *Expenses:* Contact institution. *Faculty research:* Natural resources, organizational behavior, finance, marketing, strategic management.

University of Tulsa, Graduate School, Collins College of Business, Business Administration/Computer Science Program, Tulsa, OK 74104-3189. Offers MBA/MS. Part-time programs available. *Students:* 1 full-time (0 women). Average age 24. 1 applicant, 0% accepted, 0 enrolled. *Entrance requirements:* Additional exam requirements/recommendations for international students: Required—TOEFL (minimum score 577 paper-based; 233 computer-based; 91 iBT), IELTS (minimum score 6.5). *Application deadline:* Applications are processed on a rolling basis. Application fee: $40. Electronic applications accepted. *Expenses: Tuition:* Full-time $17,748; part-time $986 per hour. *Required fees:* $5 per contact hour. $75 per semester. Tuition and fees vary according to program. *Financial support:* In 2011–12, 1 student received support, including 1 teaching assistantship with full and partial tuition reimbursement available (averaging $6,061 per year); fellowships with full and partial tuition reimbursements available, research assistantships with full and partial tuition reimbursements available, career-related internships or fieldwork, Federal Work-Study, institutionally sponsored loans, scholarships/grants, health care benefits, tuition waivers, and unspecified assistantships also available. Support available to part-time students. Financial award application deadline: 2/1; financial award applicants required to submit FAFSA. *Unit head:* Dr. Linda Nichols, Associate Dean, 918-631-2242, Fax: 918-631-2142, E-mail: linda-nichols@utulsa.edu. *Application contact:* Information Contact, 918-631-2242, E-mail: graduate-business@utulsa.edu.

University of Tulsa, Graduate School, Collins College of Business, Master of Business Administration Program, Tulsa, OK 74104-3189. Offers accounting (MBA); business administration (MBA); energy management (MBA); finance (MBA); international business (MBA); management information systems (MBA); taxation (MBA); JD/MBA; MBA/MSCS; MBA/MSF. *Accreditation:* AACSB. Part-time and evening/weekend programs available. *Faculty:* 32 full-time (6 women). *Students:* 56 full-time (29 women), 28 part-time (7 women); includes 7 minority (1 Black or African American, non-Hispanic/Latino; 2 American Indian or Alaska Native, non-Hispanic/Latino; 2 Asian, non-Hispanic/Latino; 2 Hispanic/Latino), 16 international. Average age 26. 70 applicants, 67% accepted, 29 enrolled. In 2011, 35 master's awarded. *Entrance requirements:* For master's, GMAT. Additional exam requirements/recommendations for international students: Required—TOEFL (minimum score 577 paper-based; 233 computer-based; 91 iBT), IELTS (minimum score 6.5). *Application deadline:* Applications are processed on a rolling basis. Application fee: $40. Electronic applications accepted. *Expenses: Tuition:* Full-time $17,748; part-time $986 per hour. *Required fees:* $5 per contact hour. $75 per semester. Tuition and fees vary according to program. *Financial support:* In 2011–12, 30 students received support, including 30 teaching assistantships (averaging $11,044 per year); fellowships, research assistantships, career-related internships or fieldwork, institutionally sponsored loans, scholarships/grants, health care benefits, tuition waivers (full and partial), and unspecified assistantships also available. Support available to part-time students. Financial award application deadline: 2/1; financial award applicants required to submit FAFSA. *Faculty research:* Accounting, energy management, finance, international business, management information systems, taxation. *Unit head:* Dr. Linda Nichols, Associate Dean of the Collins College of Business, 918-631-2242, Fax: 918-631-2142, E-mail: linda-nichols@utulsa.edu. *Application contact:* Information Contact, 918-631-2242, E-mail: graduate-business@utulsa.edu. Web site: http://www.cba.utulsa.edu/.

University of Utah, Graduate School, David Eccles School of Business, Salt Lake City, UT 84112. Offers EMBA, M Acc, M Stat, MBA, MHA, MRED, MS, PMBA, PhD. *Accreditation:* AACSB. Part-time and evening/weekend programs available. *Faculty:* 75 full-time (26 women), 2 part-time/adjunct (0 women). *Students:* 705 full-time (149 women), 185 part-time (39 women); includes 76 minority (3 Black or African American, non-Hispanic/Latino; 2 American Indian or Alaska Native, non-Hispanic/Latino; 30 Asian, non-Hispanic/Latino; 25 Hispanic/Latino; 2 Native Hawaiian or other Pacific Islander, non-Hispanic/Latino; 14 Two or more races, non-Hispanic/Latino), 85 international. Average age 31. 1,189 applicants, 43% accepted, 426 enrolled. In 2011, 388 master's, 6 doctorates awarded. *Median time to degree:* Of those who began their doctoral program in fall 2003, 100% received their degree in 8 years or less. *Degree requirements:* For doctorate, comprehensive exam, thesis/dissertation, oral and written qualifying exams. *Entrance requirements:* For master's, GMAT, GRE (for some programs), minimum undergraduate GPA of 3.0; for doctorate, GMAT, GRE. Additional exam requirements/recommendations for international students: Required—TOEFL (minimum score 600 paper-based; 250 computer-based; 100 iBT), IELTS (minimum score 7). Application fee: $55 ($65 for international students). Electronic applications accepted. *Expenses:* Contact institution. *Financial support:* In 2011–12, 50 students received support, including 8 fellowships with partial tuition reimbursements available, 13 teaching assistantships with partial tuition reimbursements available; career-related internships or fieldwork and health care benefits also available. Financial award applicants required to submit FAFSA. *Faculty research:* Information systems, investment, financial accounting, international strategy. *Total annual research expenditures:* $533,504. *Unit head:* Dr. Taylor Randall, Dean, 801-587-3860, Fax: 801-581-3074, E-mail: dean@business.utah.edu. *Application contact:* Andrea Chmelik, Program Coordinator, 801-581-7785, Fax: 801-581-3666, E-mail: andrea.chmelik@business.utah.edu. Web site: http://www.business.utah.edu/.

University of Vermont, Graduate College, School of Business Administration, Burlington, VT 05405. Offers M Acc, MBA. *Accreditation:* AACSB. Part-time programs available. *Faculty:* 25. *Students:* 56 (24 women); includes 3 minority (2 Asian, non-Hispanic/Latino; 1 Hispanic/Latino), 6 international. 61 applicants, 56% accepted, 18 enrolled. In 2011, 25 master's awarded. *Entrance requirements:* For master's, GMAT, resume. Additional exam requirements/recommendations for international students: Required—TOEFL (minimum score 550 paper-based; 213 computer-based; 80 iBT). *Application deadline:* For fall admission, 4/1 priority date for domestic students, 4/1 for international students. Applications are processed on a rolling basis. Application fee: $40. Electronic applications accepted. *Financial support:* Fellowships, teaching assistantships, and Federal Work-Study available. Financial award application deadline: 3/1. *Unit head:* Dr. Michael Gurdon, Dean, 802-656-4015. *Application contact:* Dr. Michael Gurdon, Coordinator, 802-656-4015.

University of Victoria, Faculty of Graduate Studies, Faculty of Business, Victoria, BC V8W 2Y2, Canada. Offers MBA, MBA/LL B. *Accreditation:* AACSB. Part-time programs available. *Entrance requirements:* For master's, GMAT, minimum B average. Additional exam requirements/recommendations for international students: Required—TOEFL (minimum score 575 paper-based; 233 computer-based), IELTS (minimum score 7). Electronic applications accepted. *Expenses:* Contact institution. *Faculty research:* Organizational design and analysis, negotiation and conflict management, human resources management, entrepreneurship, international marketing and tourism.

University of Virginia, Darden Graduate School of Business Administration, Charlottesville, VA 22903. Offers MBA, PhD, MBA/JD, MBA/MA, MBA/MD, MBA/ME, MBA/MSN. *Accreditation:* AACSB. *Faculty:* 64 full-time (15 women), 4 part-time/adjunct (2 women). *Students:* 797 full-time (221 women); includes 126 minority (30 Black or African American, non-Hispanic/Latino; 48 Asian, non-Hispanic/Latino; 34 Hispanic/Latino; 1 Native Hawaiian or other Pacific Islander, non-Hispanic/Latino; 13 Two or more races, non-Hispanic/Latino), 185 international. Average age 29. 2,330 applicants, 29% accepted, 399 enrolled. In 2011, 365 master's, 2 doctorates awarded. *Degree requirements:* For doctorate, thesis/dissertation. *Entrance requirements:* For master's, GMAT, resume; 2 letters of recommendation; interview; for doctorate, GMAT, resume; essay; 2 letters of recommendation; interview. Additional exam requirements/recommendations for international students: Required—TOEFL. *Application deadline:* For fall admission, 3/1 for domestic students, 3/2 for international students. Applications are processed on a rolling basis. Application fee: $200. Electronic applications accepted. *Expenses:* Contact institution. *Financial support:* Career-related internships or fieldwork available. Financial award applicants required to submit FAFSA. *Unit head:* Robert F. Bruner, Dean, 434-924-3900, E-mail: darden@virginia.edu. *Application contact:* Sara Neher, Assistant Dean of MBA Admissions, 434-924-3900, E-mail: darden@virginia.edu. Web site: http://www.darden.virginia.edu/html/default.aspx.

University of Virginia, McIntire School of Commerce, Charlottesville, VA 22903. Offers accounting (MS); commerce (MSC), including financial services, marketing and management; management of information technology (MS). *Accreditation:* AACSB. *Faculty:* 62 full-time (20 women), 2 part-time/adjunct (1 woman). *Students:* 166 full-time (76 women), 70 part-time (17 women); includes 45 minority (3 Black or African American, non-Hispanic/Latino; 29 Asian, non-Hispanic/Latino; 10 Hispanic/Latino; 3 Two or more races, non-Hispanic/Latino), 29 international. Average age 27. 434 applicants, 61% accepted, 166 enrolled. In 2011, 263 master's awarded. *Entrance requirements:* For master's, GMAT, 2 letters of recommendation. Additional exam requirements/recommendations for international students: Required—TOEFL (minimum score 600 paper-based; 250 computer-based; 100 iBT), IELTS (minimum score 7). *Application deadline:* Applications are processed on a rolling basis. Application fee: $75. Electronic applications accepted. *Expenses:* Contact institution. *Financial support:* Fellowships, research assistantships, teaching assistantships, career-related internships or fieldwork, and Federal Work-Study available. Financial award applicants required to submit FAFSA. *Unit head:* Carl Zeithaml, Dean, 434-924-3110, Fax: 434-924-7074, E-mail: mcs@virginia.edu. *Application contact:* Emma Candalier, Associate Director of Graduate Recruiting, 434-243-4992, Fax: 434-924-4511, E-mail: ecandalier@virginia.edu. Web site: http://www.commerce.virginia.edu/.

University of Washington, Graduate School, Michael G. Foster School of Business, Seattle, WA 98195-3233. Offers auditing and assurance (MP Acc); business (PhD); business administration (evening) (MBA); business administration (full-time) (MBA); executive business administration (MBA); global business administration (MBA); global executive business administration (MBA); taxation (MP Acc); technology management (MBA); JD/MBA; MBA/MAIS; MBA/MHA. *Accreditation:* AACSB. Part-time programs available. *Faculty:* 100 full-time (28 women), 55 part-time/adjunct (22 women). *Students:* 385 full-time (116 women), 483 part-time (118 women); includes 183 minority (16 Black or African American, non-Hispanic/Latino; 2 American Indian or Alaska Native, non-

Hispanic/Latino; 133 Asian, non-Hispanic/Latino; 25 Hispanic/Latino; 2 Native Hawaiian or other Pacific Islander, non-Hispanic/Latino; 5 Two or more races, non-Hispanic/Latino), 178 international. Average age 32. 1,367 applicants, 76% accepted, 868 enrolled. In 2011, 458 master's, 12 doctorates awarded. Terminal master's awarded for partial completion of doctoral program. *Degree requirements:* For doctorate, comprehensive exam, thesis/dissertation. *Entrance requirements:* For master's, GMAT; for doctorate, GMAT, GRE. Additional exam requirements/recommendations for international students: Required—TOEFL (minimum score 600 paper-based; 250 computer-based; 100 iBT). *Application deadline:* For fall admission, 3/15 for domestic students, 1/20 for international students. Application fee: $75. Electronic applications accepted. *Expenses:* Contact institution. *Financial support:* Fellowships with partial tuition reimbursements, research assistantships with partial tuition reimbursements, teaching assistantships with partial tuition reimbursements, Federal Work-Study, institutionally sponsored loans, and scholarships/grants available. Financial award application deadline: 2/28; financial award applicants required to submit FAFSA. *Faculty research:* Finance, marketing, organizational behavior, information technology, strategy. *Unit head:* Dr. James Jiambalvo, Dean, 206-543-4750. *Application contact:* Erin Ernst, Assistant Director of Admissions, 206-543-4661, Fax: 206-616-7351, E-mail: mba@u.washington.edu. Web site: http://www.foster.washington.edu/mba.

University of Washington, Bothell, School of Business, Bothell, WA 98011-8246. Offers leadership (MBA); technology (MBA). Part-time and evening/weekend programs available. *Faculty:* 22 full-time (5 women), 4 part-time/adjunct (1 woman). *Students:* 121 full-time (41 women), 1 part-time (0 women); includes 36 minority (2 Black or African American, non-Hispanic/Latino; 26 Asian, non-Hispanic/Latino; 5 Hispanic/Latino; 3 Two or more races, non-Hispanic/Latino), 5 international. Average age 33. 136 applicants, 62% accepted, 68 enrolled. In 2011, 66 master's awarded. *Degree requirements:* For master's, 72 credits, minimum cumulative GPA of 3.0. *Entrance requirements:* For master's, GMAT or GRE General Test. Additional exam requirements/recommendations for international students: Required—TOEFL (minimum score 580 paper-based; 237 computer-based; 92 iBT), IELTS (minimum score 7). *Application deadline:* For fall admission, 4/16 priority date for domestic students, 4/16 for international students. Application fee: $75. Electronic applications accepted. *Expenses:* Contact institution. *Financial support:* Federal Work-Study and scholarships/grants available. Financial award application deadline: 2/28; financial award applicants required to submit FAFSA. *Faculty research:* Leadership, supply chain management, entrepreneurship, game theory, corporate finance, marketing innovation. *Unit head:* Prof. Sandeep Krishnamurthy, Director, 425-352-5229, Fax: 425-352-5277, E-mail: sandeep@uw.edu. *Application contact:* Kathryn Chester, MBA Admissions Coordinator, 425-352-3275, Fax: 425-352-5277, E-mail: kchester@uwb.edu. Web site: http://www.uwb.edu/mba.

University of Washington, Tacoma, Graduate Programs, MBA Programs, Tacoma, WA 98402-3100. Offers accounting (MBA); business administration (MBA); certified financial analyst (MBA). Part-time and evening/weekend programs available. *Entrance requirements:* For master's, GMAT, minimum GPA of 3.0 in final graded 90 quarter credits or 60 graded semester credits; at least 2 years of professional/management work experience. Additional exam requirements/recommendations for international students: Required—TOEFL (minimum score 580 paper-based; 237 computer-based; 92 iBT). Electronic applications accepted. *Expenses:* Contact institution. *Faculty research:* International accounting, marketing, change management, investments, corporate social responsibility.

University of Waterloo, Graduate Studies, Centre for Business, Entrepreneurship and Technology, Waterloo, ON N2L 3G1, Canada. Offers MBET. *Entrance requirements:* For master's, honors degree. Additional exam requirements/recommendations for international students: Required—TOEFL (minimum score 550 paper-based; 213 computer-based), TWE. Electronic applications accepted.

The University of Western Ontario, Richard Ivey School of Business, London, ON N6A 3K7, Canada. Offers business (EMBA, PhD); corporate strategy and leadership elective (MBA); entrepreneurship elective (MBA); finance elective (MBA); health sector stream (MBA); international management elective (MBA); marketing elective (MBA); JD/MBA. *Degree requirements:* For master's, thesis (for some programs); for doctorate, thesis/dissertation. *Entrance requirements:* For master's, GMAT, 2 years of full-time work experience, interview. Additional exam requirements/recommendations for international students: Required—TOEFL (minimum score 100 computer; 100 iBT) or IELTS (minimium score 6). Electronic applications accepted. *Faculty research:* Strategy, organizational behavior, international business, finance, operations management.

University of West Florida, College of Business, Program in Business Administration, Pensacola, FL 32514-5750. Offers MBA. *Accreditation:* AACSB. Part-time and evening/weekend programs available. *Faculty:* 13 full-time (5 women), 3 part-time/adjunct (2 women). *Students:* 19 full-time (13 women), 89 part-time (31 women); includes 19 minority (8 Black or African American, non-Hispanic/Latino; 1 American Indian or Alaska Native, non-Hispanic/Latino; 2 Asian, non-Hispanic/Latino; 6 Hispanic/Latino; 2 Two or more races, non-Hispanic/Latino), 15 international. Average age 29. 58 applicants, 69% accepted, 28 enrolled. In 2011, 36 master's awarded. *Degree requirements:* For master's, industry portfolio project based on information from five of the core MBA courses. *Entrance requirements:* For master's, GMAT or GRE, official transcripts; minimum undergraduate GPA of 3.0; bachelor's degree; business course academic preparation; graduate-level motivation and writing abilities as noted in essay responses; two letters of recommendation; appropriate employment at increasing levels of responsibility via resume. Additional exam requirements/recommendations for international students: Required—TOEFL (minimum score 550 paper-based; 213 computer-based). *Application deadline:* For fall admission, 6/30 for domestic students, 6/1 for international students; for spring admission, 10/1 for domestic and international students. Applications are processed on a rolling basis. Application fee: $30. *Expenses:* Tuition, state resident: full-time $5729; part-time $302 per credit hour. Tuition, nonresident: full-time $20,059; part-time $961 per credit hour. *Required fees:* $1509; $63 per credit hour. *Financial support:* In 2011–12, 29 fellowships (averaging $465 per year), 42 research assistantships with partial tuition reimbursements (averaging $2,150 per year) were awarded; unspecified assistantships also available. Financial award application deadline: 4/15; financial award applicants required to submit FAFSA. *Faculty research:* Robotics, corporate behavior, international trade, franchising, counterfeiting. *Unit head:* Dr. W. Timothy O'Keefe, Associate Dean and Director, 850-474-2348. *Application contact:* Cheryl Powell, Academic Advisor, 850-474-2348. Web site: http://uwf.edu/mba/gradprograms.cfm.

University of West Florida, College of Professional Studies, Department of Applied Science, Technology and Administration, Program in Administration, Pensacola, FL 32514-5750. Offers acquisition and contract administration (MSA); biomedical/pharmaceutical (MSA); criminal justice administration (MSA); database administration (MSA); education leadership (MSA); healthcare administration (MSA); human performance technology (MSA); leadership (MSA); nursing administration (MSA); public administration (MSA); software engineering administration (MSA). Part-time and evening/weekend programs available. Postbaccalaureate distance learning degree programs offered (no on-campus study). *Students:* 36 full-time (28 women), 158 part-time (95 women); includes 61 minority (31 Black or African American, non-Hispanic/Latino; 4 American Indian or Alaska Native, non-Hispanic/Latino; 4 Asian, non-Hispanic/Latino; 17 Hispanic/Latino; 2 Native Hawaiian or other Pacific Islander, non-Hispanic/Latino; 3 Two or more races, non-Hispanic/Latino), 1 international. Average age 34. 102 applicants, 59% accepted, 40 enrolled. In 2011, 62 master's awarded. *Entrance requirements:* For master's, GRE General Test, letter of intent, names of references. Additional exam requirements/recommendations for international students: Required—TOEFL (minimum score 550 paper-based; 213 computer-based). *Application deadline:* For fall admission, 6/1 for domestic and international students; for spring admission, 10/1 for domestic and international students. Applications are processed on a rolling basis. Application fee: $30. *Expenses:* Tuition, state resident: full-time $5729; part-time $302 per credit hour. Tuition, nonresident: full-time $20,059; part-time $961 per credit hour. *Required fees:* $1509; $63 per credit hour. *Financial support:* Unspecified assistantships available. Financial award application deadline: 4/15; financial award applicants required to submit FAFSA. *Unit head:* Dr. Karen Rasmussen, Chairperson, 850-474-2301, Fax: 850-474-2804, E-mail: krasmuss@uwf.edu. *Application contact:* Terry McCray, Assistant Director of Graduate Admissions, 850-473-7718, Fax: 850-473-7714, E-mail: gradadmissions@uwf.edu. Web site: http://uwf.edu/msaprogram/.

University of West Florida, College of Professional Studies, Department of Research and Applied Studies, Pensacola, FL 32514-5750. Offers administration (MSA), including acquisition and contract administration, biomedical/pharmaceutical, criminal justice administration, database administration, education leadership, healthcare administration, human performance technology, leadership, nursing administration, public administration, software engineering and administration; college student personnel administration (M Ed), including college personnel administration, guidance and counseling; curriculum and instruction (M Ed, Ed S); educational leadership (M Ed); middle and secondary level education and ESOL (M Ed). Part-time and evening/weekend programs available. *Faculty:* 2 full-time (both women), 3 part-time/adjunct (2 women). *Students:* 26 full-time (15 women), 13 part-time (9 women); includes 8 minority (4 Black or African American, non-Hispanic/Latino; 2 American Indian or Alaska Native, non-Hispanic/Latino; 1 Hispanic/Latino; 1 Two or more races, non-Hispanic/Latino), 1 international. Average age 26. 51 applicants, 51% accepted, 16 enrolled. In 2011, 17 master's, 49 Ed Ss awarded. *Entrance requirements:* For master's, GRE or MAT, official transcripts; minimum undergraduate GPA of 3.0; letter of intent; three letters of recommendation; resume. Additional exam requirements/recommendations for international students: Required—TOEFL (minimum score 550 paper-based; 213 computer-based). *Application deadline:* For fall admission, 6/1 for domestic and international students; for spring admission, 10/1 for domestic and international students. Applications are processed on a rolling basis. Application fee: $30. *Expenses:* Tuition, state resident: full-time $5729; part-time $302 per credit hour. Tuition, nonresident: full-time $20,059; part-time $961 per credit hour. *Required fees:* $1509; $63 per credit hour. *Financial support:* In 2011–12, 33 fellowships (averaging $860 per year), 10 research assistantships (averaging $3,280 per year), 2 teaching assistantships (averaging $3,760 per year) were awarded; unspecified assistantships also available. Financial award application deadline: 4/15; financial award applicants required to submit FAFSA. *Unit head:* Dr. Joyce Nichols, Chairperson, 850-857-6042, E-mail: jcoleman0@uwf.edu. *Application contact:* Terry McCray, Assistant Director of Graduate Admissions, 850-473-7718, Fax: 850-473-7714, E-mail: gradadmissions@uwf.edu. Web site: http://uwf.edu/pcl/.

University of West Georgia, Richards College of Business, Program of Business Administration, Carrollton, GA 30118. Offers MBA. *Accreditation:* AACSB. Part-time and evening/weekend programs available. Postbaccalaureate distance learning degree programs offered (no on-campus study). *Faculty:* 7 full-time (2 women). *Students:* 30 full-time (14 women), 65 part-time (34 women); includes 23 minority (17 Black or African American, non-Hispanic/Latino; 6 Hispanic/Latino), 12 international. Average age 30. 74 applicants, 55% accepted, 16 enrolled. In 2011, 87 master's awarded. *Degree requirements:* For master's, comprehensive exam. *Entrance requirements:* For master's, GMAT, minimum GPA of 2.5. Additional exam requirements/recommendations for international students: Required—TOEFL (minimum score 550 paper-based; 213 computer-based; 79 iBT); Recommended—IELTS (minimum score 6.5). *Application deadline:* For fall admission, 7/15 for domestic students, 6/1 for international students; for spring admission, 11/15 for domestic students, 10/15 for international students. Applications are processed on a rolling basis. Application fee: $30. Electronic applications accepted. *Expenses:* Contact institution. *Financial support:* In 2011–12, 8 research assistantships with full tuition reimbursements (averaging $8,000 per year) were awarded; career-related internships or fieldwork, tuition waivers (partial), and unspecified assistantships also available. Support available to part-time students. Financial award application deadline: 7/1; financial award applicants required to submit FAFSA. *Faculty research:* Distance learning, small business development, e-commerce, computer self-efficacy. *Unit head:* Dr. Blaise J. Bergiel, Associate Dean/Interim MBA Director, 678-839-5252, E-mail: bbergiel@westga.edu. *Application contact:* Dr. Hope Udombon, Administrative Director of Graduate Business Programs, 678-839-5355, Fax: 678-839-5040, E-mail: udombon@westga.edu. Web site: http://www.westga.edu/rcob.

University of Windsor, Faculty of Graduate Studies, Odette School of Business, Windsor, ON N9B 3P4, Canada. Offers MBA, MM, MBA/LL B. Evening/weekend programs available. *Degree requirements:* For master's, thesis or alternative. *Entrance requirements:* For master's, GMAT, minimum B average. Additional exam requirements/recommendations for international students: Required—TOEFL (minimum score 600 paper-based; 250 computer-based). Electronic applications accepted. *Faculty research:* Accounting, administrative studies, finance, marketing, business policy and strategy.

University of Wisconsin–Eau Claire, College of Business, Program in Business Administration, Eau Claire, WI 54702-4004. Offers MBA. *Accreditation:* AACSB. Part-time and evening/weekend programs available. Postbaccalaureate distance learning degree programs offered (no on-campus study). *Faculty:* 31 full-time (11 women). *Students:* 10 full-time (6 women), 235 part-time (108 women); includes 29 minority (8 Black or African American, non-Hispanic/Latino; 1 American Indian or Alaska Native, non-Hispanic/Latino; 13 Asian, non-Hispanic/Latino; 5 Hispanic/Latino; 2 Two or more races, non-Hispanic/Latino), 2 international. Average age 33. 154 applicants, 82% accepted, 72 enrolled. In 2011, 70 master's awarded. Terminal master's awarded for partial completion of doctoral program. *Degree requirements:* For master's, thesis optional, applied field project. *Entrance requirements:* For master's, GMAT or GRE, minimum GPA of 2.75 overall. Additional exam requirements/recommendations for international students: Required—TOEFL (minimum score 550 paper-based; 213 computer-based; 79 iBT); Recommended—IELTS (minimum score 7). *Application deadline:* For fall admission, 7/1 priority date for domestic students, 6/1 for international students; for spring admission, 12/1 priority date for domestic students, 11/1 for international students. Applications are processed on a rolling basis. Application fee: $56. *Expenses:* Tuition, state resident: full-time $7312; part-time $406 per credit. Tuition, nonresident: full-time $16,771; part-time $932 per credit. *Required fees:* $1101; $61 per credit. *Financial support:* In 2011–12, 34 students received support. Federal Work-Study and unspecified assistantships available. Financial award application deadline: 3/1; financial award applicants required to submit FAFSA. *Unit head:* Dr. Robert Erffmeyer, Director, 715-836-5509, Fax: 715-836-4014, E-mail: erffmerc@uwec.edu. *Application contact:* Nancy Amdahl, Graduate Dean Assistant, 715-836-2721, Fax: 715-836-2902, E-mail: graduate@uwec.edu. Web site: http://www.uwec.edu/cob/graduate/index.htm.

University of Wisconsin–Green Bay, Graduate Studies, Program in Management, Green Bay, WI 54311-7001. Offers MS. Part-time programs available. *Faculty:* 6 full-time (1 woman), 1 part-time/adjunct (0 women). *Students:* 5 full-time (4 women), 16 part-time (7 women); includes 1 minority (Black or African American, non-Hispanic/Latino), 2 international. Average age 30. 8 applicants, 88% accepted, 6 enrolled. In 2011, 15 master's awarded. *Degree requirements:* For master's, thesis or alternative. *Entrance requirements:* For master's, GMAT or GRE General Test, minimum GPA of 3.0. *Application deadline:* For fall admission, 8/1 for domestic students; for spring admission, 11/1 for domestic students. Applications are processed on a rolling basis. Application fee: $56. Electronic applications accepted. *Expenses:* Tuition, state resident: full-time $7312; part-time $406 per credit. Tuition, nonresident: full-time $16,771; part-time $932 per credit. *Required fees:* $1312; $55 per credit. Tuition and fees vary according to reciprocity agreements. *Financial support:* Career-related internships or fieldwork, Federal Work-Study, and institutionally sponsored loans available. Financial award application deadline: 7/15; financial award applicants required to submit FAFSA. *Faculty research:* Planning methods, budgeting, decision-making, organizational behavior and theory, management. *Unit head:* Dr. Meir Russ, Chair, 920-465-2757, E-mail: russm@uwgb.edu. *Application contact:* Inga Zile, Graduate Studies Coordinator, 920-465-2123, Fax: 920-465-2043, E-mail: zilei@uwgb.edu. Web site: http://www.uwgb.edu/management/.

University of Wisconsin–La Crosse, Office of University Graduate Studies, College of Business Administration, La Crosse, WI 54601-3742. Offers MBA. *Accreditation:* AACSB. Part-time and evening/weekend programs available. *Faculty:* 32 full-time (10 women). *Students:* 30 full-time (16 women), 31 part-time (10 women); includes 3 minority (1 Asian, non-Hispanic/Latino; 1 Hispanic/Latino; 1 Two or more races, non-Hispanic/Latino), 27 international. Average age 29. 90 applicants, 40% accepted, 24 enrolled. In 2011, 31 master's awarded. *Degree requirements:* For master's, thesis optional. *Entrance requirements:* For master's, GMAT. Additional exam requirements/recommendations for international students: Required—TOEFL (minimum score 550 paper-based; 213 computer-based; 79 iBT). *Application deadline:* For fall admission, 6/15 priority date for domestic students, 6/15 for international students; for spring admission, 11/15 priority date for domestic students, 11/15 for international students. Applications are processed on a rolling basis. Application fee: $56. Electronic applications accepted. *Expenses:* Contact institution. *Financial support:* In 2011–12, 7 research assistantships with partial tuition reimbursements (averaging $5,756 per year) were awarded; Federal Work-Study, scholarships/grants, health care benefits, and tuition waivers (partial) also available. Support available to part-time students. Financial award application deadline: 3/15; financial award applicants required to submit FAFSA. *Faculty research:* Tax regulation, accounting standards, public sector information technology, corporate social responsibility, economics of sports. *Unit head:* Dr. Bruce May, Associate Dean, 608-785-8095, Fax: 608-785-6700, E-mail: may.bruce@uwlax.edu. *Application contact:* Martina Skobic, Director of MBA and International Programs, 608-785-8371, Fax: 608-785-6700, E-mail: mskobic@uwlax.edu. Web site: http://www.uwlax.edu/ba/graduate/gradstudents.htm.

University of Wisconsin–Madison, Graduate School, Wisconsin School of Business, Wisconsin Evening MBA Program, Madison, WI 53706-1380. Offers general management (MBA). Part-time and evening/weekend programs available. *Faculty:* 10 full-time (1 woman), 11 part-time/adjunct (3 women). *Students:* 161 part-time (41 women); includes 24 minority (5 Black or African American, non-Hispanic/Latino; 1 American Indian or Alaska Native, non-Hispanic/Latino; 16 Asian, non-Hispanic/Latino; 2 Hispanic/Latino), 2 international. Average age 31. 65 applicants, 89% accepted, 47 enrolled. In 2011, 58 master's awarded. *Entrance requirements:* For master's, GMAT, bachelor's degree, 2 years work experience. Additional exam requirements/recommendations for international students: Required—TOEFL (minimum score 600 paper-based; 250 computer-based; 100 iBT). *Application deadline:* For fall admission, 5/1 priority date for domestic students, 5/1 for international students. Applications are processed on a rolling basis. Application fee: $56. Electronic applications accepted. *Expenses:* Contact institution. *Financial support:* Scholarships/grants available. Support available to part-time students. Financial award application deadline: 5/1; financial award applicants required to submit FAFSA. *Faculty research:* Regulation, housing economy, environmental issues on supply chain management, marketing strategy, cost management. *Unit head:* Linda Uitvlugt, Assistant Dean for Wisconsin MBA Programs, 608-263-1169, Fax: 608-262-3607, E-mail: emba@bus.wisc.edu. *Application contact:* Mary Schey, Director of Admissions, 608-263-1169, Fax: 608-262-3607, E-mail: emba@bus.wisc.edu. Web site: http://www.bus.wisc.edu/evemba/.

University of Wisconsin–Madison, Graduate School, Wisconsin School of Business, Wisconsin Executive MBA Program, Madison, WI 53706-1380. Offers general management (MBA). Part-time and evening/weekend programs available. *Faculty:* 12 full-time (1 woman), 7 part-time/adjunct (1 woman). *Students:* 76 part-time (25 women); includes 11 minority (5 Black or African American, non-Hispanic/Latino; 5 Asian, non-Hispanic/Latino; 1 Hispanic/Latino), 6 international. Average age 43. 51 applicants, 92% accepted, 39 enrolled. In 2011, 27 master's awarded. *Entrance requirements:* For master's, 8 years professional work experience, 5 years leadership experience, minimum GPA of 3.0. Additional exam requirements/recommendations for international students: Recommended—TOEFL. *Application deadline:* For fall admission, 5/1 priority date for domestic students, 5/1 for international students. Applications are processed on a rolling basis. Application fee: $56. Electronic applications accepted. *Expenses:* Tuition, state resident: full-time $10,296; part-time $643.51 per credit. Tuition, nonresident: full-time $24,054; part-time $1503.40 per credit. *Required fees:* $70.06 per credit. Tuition and fees vary according to course load, campus/location, program and reciprocity agreements. *Financial support:* Scholarships/grants available. Support available to part-time students. Financial award application deadline: 5/1; financial award applicants required to submit FAFSA. *Faculty research:* Marketing strategy, housing markets, corporate governance, healthcare fiscal management, management in cross-cultural boundaries. *Unit head:* Linda Uitvlugt, Assistant Dean, 608-263-1169, Fax: 608-262-3607, E-mail: emba@bus.wisc.edu. *Application contact:* Mary Schey, Director of Admissions, 608-263-1169, Fax: 608-262-3607, E-mail: emba@bus.wisc.edu. Web site: http://www.bus.wisc.edu/execmba/.

University of Wisconsin–Madison, Graduate School, Wisconsin School of Business, Wisconsin Full-Time MBA Program, Madison, WI 53706-1380. Offers applied security analysis (MBA); arts administration (MBA); brand and product management (MBA); corporate finance and investment banking (MBA); marketing research (MBA); operations and technology management (MBA); real estate (MBA); risk management and insurance (MBA); strategic human resource management (MBA); supply chain management (MBA). *Faculty:* 32 full-time (6 women), 27 part-time/adjunct (7 women). *Students:* 228 full-time (75 women); includes 53 minority (16 Black or African American, non-Hispanic/Latino; 25 Asian, non-Hispanic/Latino; 10 Hispanic/Latino; 2 Native Hawaiian or other Pacific Islander, non-Hispanic/Latino), 28 international. Average age 28. 509 applicants, 30% accepted, 111 enrolled. In 2011, 120 master's awarded. *Degree requirements:* For master's, thesis (for arts administration). *Entrance requirements:* For master's, GMAT, bachelor's or equivalent degree, 2 years of work experience, letters of recommendation. Additional exam requirements/recommendations for international students: Required—TOEFL (minimum score 600 paper-based; 250 computer-based; 100 iBT), IELTS. *Application deadline:* For fall admission, 11/4 for domestic and international students; for winter admission, 2/3 for domestic and international students; for spring admission, 4/27 for domestic and international students. Applications are processed on a rolling basis. Application fee: $56. Electronic applications accepted. *Expenses:* Tuition, state resident: full-time $10,296; part-time $643.51 per credit. Tuition, nonresident: full-time $24,054; part-time $1503.40 per credit. *Required fees:* $70.06 per credit. Tuition and fees vary according to course load, campus/location, program and reciprocity agreements. *Financial support:* In 2011–12, 176 students received support, including 20 fellowships with full and partial tuition reimbursements available (averaging $18,756 per year), 128 research assistantships with full tuition reimbursements available (averaging $25,185 per year), 28 teaching assistantships with full tuition reimbursements available (averaging $25,097 per year); scholarships/grants, health care benefits, and unspecified assistantships also available. Financial award application deadline: 4/27; financial award applicants required to submit FAFSA. *Faculty research:* Market consequences of International Financial Reporting Standards (IFRS), inter-firm relationships and strategic partnerships, application of Bayesian statistical methods and applied probability models to understanding individuals' behaviors in the context of customer relationship management (CRM) applications, liquidity provision and the structure of financial markets, strategic management of global startups. *Unit head:* Dr. Larry "Chip" W. Hunter, Associate Dean of Master's Programs, 608-265-3494, Fax: 608-265-4192, E-mail: lhunter@bus.wisc.edu. *Application contact:* Maria Reis, Assistant Director of MBA Marketing and Recruiting, 608-262-4000, Fax: 608-265-4192, E-mail: mreis@bus.wisc.edu. Web site: http://www.bus.wisc.edu/mba.

University of Wisconsin–Milwaukee, Graduate School, Sheldon B. Lubar School of Business, Milwaukee, WI 53201. Offers business administration (MBA); enterprise resource planning (Certificate); investment management (Certificate); management science (MS, PhD); nonprofit management and leadership (MS, Certificate); state and local taxation (Certificate); MS/MBA. *Accreditation:* AACSB. Part-time and evening/weekend programs available. *Faculty:* 50 full-time (11 women), 4 part-time/adjunct (2 women). *Students:* 293 full-time (100 women), 343 part-time (127 women); includes 73 minority (21 Black or African American, non-Hispanic/Latino; 2 American Indian or Alaska Native, non-Hispanic/Latino; 28 Asian, non-Hispanic/Latino; 3 Hispanic/Latino; 19 Two or more races, non-Hispanic/Latino), 66 international. Average age 32. 370 applicants, 46% accepted, 104 enrolled. In 2011, 255 master's, 9 doctorates awarded. *Degree requirements:* For master's, comprehensive exam (for some programs); for doctorate, comprehensive exam, thesis/dissertation. *Entrance requirements:* For master's and doctorate, GMAT or GRE General Test. Additional exam requirements/recommendations for international students: Required—TOEFL (minimum score 550 paper-based; 79 iBT), IELTS (minimum score 6.5). *Application deadline:* For fall admission, 1/1 priority date for domestic students; for spring admission, 9/1 for domestic students. Applications are processed on a rolling basis. Application fee: $56 ($96 for international students). Electronic applications accepted. *Expenses:* Contact institution. *Financial support:* In 2011–12, 5 fellowships with full tuition reimbursements, 2 research assistantships with full tuition reimbursements, 41 teaching assistantships with full tuition reimbursements were awarded; career-related internships or fieldwork, Federal Work-Study, health care benefits, unspecified assistantships, and project assistantships also available. Support available to part-time students. Financial award application deadline: 4/15; financial award applicants required to submit FAFSA. *Faculty research:* Applied management research in finance, MIS, marketing, operations research, organizational sciences. *Total annual research expenditures:* $620,657. *Unit head:* Timothy L. Smunt, Dean, 414-229-6256, Fax: 414-229-2372, E-mail: tsmunt@uwm.edu. *Application contact:* Matthew Jensen, 414-229-5403, E-mail: mba-ms@uwm.edu. Web site: http://www4.uwm.edu/business.

University of Wisconsin–Oshkosh, Graduate Studies, College of Business, Program in Business Administration, Oshkosh, WI 54901. Offers MBA. *Accreditation:* AACSB. Part-time programs available. *Degree requirements:* For master's, integrative seminar. *Entrance requirements:* For master's, GMAT, GRE, minimum undergraduate GPA of 2.75. Additional exam requirements/recommendations for international students: Required—TOEFL (minimum score 550 paper-based; 213 computer-based; 79 iBT). Electronic applications accepted.

University of Wisconsin–Parkside, School of Business and Technology, Kenosha, WI 53141-2000. Offers MBA, MSCIS. *Accreditation:* AACSB. Part-time and evening/weekend programs available. *Entrance requirements:* For master's, GMAT. Additional exam requirements/recommendations for international students: Required—TOEFL (minimum score 550 paper-based; 216 computer-based; 79 iBT). Electronic applications accepted. *Expenses:* Contact institution. *Faculty research:* Business strategy, ethics in accounting and finance, mutual funds, decision analysis and neural networks, management skills.

University of Wisconsin–River Falls, Outreach and Graduate Studies, College of Business and Economics, River Falls, WI 54022. Offers MBA, MM. *Accreditation:* AACSB. *Degree requirements:* For master's, thesis or alternative. *Entrance requirements:* Additional exam requirements/recommendations for international students: Required—TOEFL (minimum score 550 paper-based; 79 iBT). Electronic applications accepted.

University of Wisconsin–Stevens Point, College of Letters and Science, Division of Business and Economics, Stevens Point, WI 54481-3897. Offers MBA. Program offered jointly with University of Wisconsin–Oshkosh.

University of Wisconsin–Whitewater, School of Graduate Studies, College of Business and Economics, Program in Business Administration, Whitewater, WI 53190-1790. Offers finance (MBA); human resource management (MBA); information technology management (MBA); international business (MBA); management (MBA); marketing (MBA); operations and supply chain management (MBA). *Accreditation:* AACSB. Part-time and evening/weekend programs available. Postbaccalaureate distance learning degree programs offered (no on-campus study). *Students:* 170 full-time (53 women), 538 part-time (213 women); includes 130 minority (28 Black or African American, non-Hispanic/Latino; 87 Asian, non-Hispanic/Latino; 15 Hispanic/Latino). Average age 31. 448 applicants, 33% accepted, 120 enrolled. In 2011, 304 master's awarded. *Entrance requirements:* For master's, GMAT or GRE, minimum AACSB index of 1000, minimum GPA of 2.75. Additional exam requirements/recommendations for international students: Required—TOEFL (minimum score 550 paper-based; 213 computer-based; 80 iBT), IELTS (minimum score 6). *Application deadline:* For fall admission, 7/15 for domestic and international students; for spring admission, 12/1 for domestic and international students. Applications are processed on a rolling basis. Application fee: $56. Electronic applications accepted. *Expenses:* Tuition, state resident: full-time $4088. Tuition, nonresident: full-time $8817. Tuition and fees vary according to program. *Financial support:* In 2011–12, research assistantships (averaging $7,245 per year) were awarded; Federal Work-Study, unspecified assistantships, and out-of-state fee waivers also available. Support available to part-time students. Financial award application deadline: 3/15; financial award applicants required to submit FAFSA. *Faculty research:* Interface between social institutions and individual behavior, technology and innovation management, occupational mental health, workplace deviance and workplace romance. *Unit head:* Dr. John Chenoweth, Associate Dean, 262-472-1945, Fax: 262-472-4863, E-mail: chenowej@uww.edu.

Business Administration and Management—General

University of Wyoming, College of Business, Program in Business Administration, Laramie, WY 82070. Offers MBA. *Accreditation:* AACSB. Part-time and evening/weekend programs available. Postbaccalaureate distance learning degree programs offered (minimal on-campus study). *Degree requirements:* For master's, comprehensive exam, thesis or alternative. *Entrance requirements:* For master's, GMAT, GRE General Test, minimum GPA of 3.0. Additional exam requirements/recommendations for international students: Required—TOEFL (minimum score 550 paper-based; 210 computer-based; 80 iBT). Electronic applications accepted. *Faculty research:* Natural resource marketing and product development, work place violence.

Upper Iowa University, Online Master's Programs, Fayette, IA 52142-1857. Offers accounting (MBA); corporate financial management (MBA); global business (MBA); health and human services (MPA); higher education administration (MHEA); homeland security (MPA); human resources management (MBA); justice administration (MPA); organizational development (MBA); public personnel management (MPA); quality management (MBA). MBA also available at Madison, WI campus. Part-time programs available. Postbaccalaureate distance learning degree programs offered (no on-campus study). *Degree requirements:* For master's, research project. *Entrance requirements:* For master's, GMAT, GRE, or minimum GPA of 2.7 during last 60 hours. Additional exam requirements/recommendations for international students: Required—TOEFL (minimum score 570 paper-based; 230 computer-based). Electronic applications accepted. *Faculty research:* Total quality management, CQI, teams, organization culture and climate, management.

Urbana University, Division of Business Administration, Urbana, OH 43078-2091. Offers MBA. Part-time and evening/weekend programs available. *Degree requirements:* For master's, comprehensive exam, thesis or alternative. *Entrance requirements:* For master's, GMAT, minimum GPA of 2.7, BS in business, 3 letters of recommendation, work experience. Additional exam requirements/recommendations for international students: Required—TOEFL (minimum score 550 paper-based; 213 computer-based). *Faculty research:* Organizational behavior, taxation, segmentation, information systems, retail gravitation.

Ursuline College, School of Graduate Studies, Program in Business Administration, Pepper Pike, OH 44124-4398. Offers MBA. *Faculty:* 2 part-time/adjunct (0 women). *Students:* 86 full-time (58 women), 12 part-time (11 women); includes 36 minority (30 Black or African American, non-Hispanic/Latino; 1 American Indian or Alaska Native, non-Hispanic/Latino; 1 Asian, non-Hispanic/Latino; 1 Hispanic/Latino; 1 Native Hawaiian or other Pacific Islander, non-Hispanic/Latino; 2 Two or more races, non-Hispanic/Latino). Average age 38. 83 applicants, 93% accepted, 70 enrolled. In 2011, 15 master's awarded. *Expenses: Tuition:* Part-time $875 per credit hour. *Required fees:* $170 per semester. *Unit head:* Nancy Brown, Assistant Program Coordinator, 440-684-6038, Fax: 440-684-6088, E-mail: nbrown@ursuline.edu. *Application contact:* Melanie Steele, Graduate Admission Assistant, 440-646-8119, Fax: 440-684-6088, E-mail: graduateadmissions@ursuline.edu.

Utah State University, School of Graduate Studies, College of Business, Program in Business Administration, Logan, UT 84322. Offers MBA. *Accreditation:* AACSB. Part-time and evening/weekend programs available. Postbaccalaureate distance learning degree programs offered (minimal on-campus study). *Degree requirements:* For master's, comprehensive exam. *Entrance requirements:* For master's, GMAT or GRE, minimum GPA of 3.0. Additional exam requirements/recommendations for international students: Required—TOEFL. Electronic applications accepted. *Faculty research:* Marketing strategy, technology and innovation, public utility finance, international competitiveness.

Utah Valley University, MBA Program, Orem, UT 84058-5999. Offers accounting (MBA); management (MBA). Evening/weekend programs available. *Application contact:* Eric Wilding, Intermediate Research Analyst, 801-863-7923, E-mail: eric.wilding@uvu.edu. Web site: http://www.uvu.edu/mba/.

Valdosta State University, Program in Business Administration, Valdosta, GA 31698. Offers MBA. *Accreditation:* AACSB. Part-time and evening/weekend programs available. Postbaccalaureate distance learning degree programs offered (no on-campus study). *Faculty:* 6 full-time (1 woman). *Students:* 15 full-time (8 women), 37 part-time (22 women); includes 14 minority (10 Black or African American, non-Hispanic/Latino; 2 American Indian or Alaska Native, non-Hispanic/Latino; 2 Native Hawaiian or other Pacific Islander, non-Hispanic/Latino). Average age 26. 59 applicants, 49% accepted, 12 enrolled. In 2011, 24 master's awarded. *Degree requirements:* For master's, comprehensive written and/or oral exams. *Entrance requirements:* For master's, GMAT, minimum GPA of 2.75. Additional exam requirements/recommendations for international students: Required—TOEFL (minimum score 523 paper-based; 193 computer-based). *Application deadline:* For fall admission, 7/1 for domestic and international students; for spring admission, 11/1 for domestic students. Applications are processed on a rolling basis. Application fee: $35. Electronic applications accepted. *Expenses:* Tuition, state resident: full-time $7098; part-time $217 per hour. Tuition, nonresident: full-time $20,630; part-time $780 per hour. *Financial support:* In 2011–12, 5 students received support, including 5 research assistantships with full tuition reimbursements available (averaging $3,652 per year); institutionally sponsored loans and scholarships/grants also available. Support available to part-time students. Financial award application deadline: 7/1; financial award applicants required to submit FAFSA. *Unit head:* Dr. Mel Schnake, Director, 229-245-2233, Fax: 229-245-2795, E-mail: mschnake@valdosta.edu. *Application contact:* Jessica DeVane, Coordinator of Graduate Admissions, 229-333-5694, Fax: 229-245-3853, E-mail: jldevane@valdosta.edu.

Valparaiso University, Graduate School, College of Business Administration, Valparaiso, IN 46383. Offers business administration (MBA); engineering management (MEM); management (Certificate); JD/MBA; MSN/MBA. *Accreditation:* AACSB. Part-time and evening/weekend programs available. Postbaccalaureate distance learning degree programs offered (minimal on-campus study). *Faculty:* 18 part-time/adjunct (6 women). *Students:* 14 full-time (3 women), 49 part-time (22 women); includes 11 minority (5 Black or African American, non-Hispanic/Latino; 1 Asian, non-Hispanic/Latino; 2 Hispanic/Latino; 3 Two or more races, non-Hispanic/Latino), 4 international. Average age 34. In 2011, 31 master's, 5 other advanced degrees awarded. *Entrance requirements:* For master's, GMAT, GRE, minimum GPA of 3.0. Additional exam requirements/recommendations for international students: Required—TOEFL (minimum score 550 paper-based; 213 computer-based; 80 iBT). *Application deadline:* Applications are processed on a rolling basis. Application fee: $30 ($50 for international students). Electronic applications accepted. *Expenses:* Contact institution. *Financial support:* Available to part-time students. Applicants required to submit FAFSA. *Unit head:* Bruce MacLean, Director of Graduate Programs in Management, 219-465-7952, Fax: 219-464-5789, E-mail: bruce.maclean@valpo.edu. *Application contact:* Cindy Scanlan, Assistant Director of Graduate Programs in Management, 219-465-7952, Fax: 219-464-5789, E-mail: cindy.scanlan@valpo.edu. Web site: http://valpo.edu/mba.

Vancouver Island University, Master of Business Administration Program, Nanaimo, BC V9R 5S5, Canada. Offers international business (MBA), including finance, marketing. Program offered jointly with University of Hertfordshire. *Accreditation:* ACBSP. Part-time programs available. *Faculty:* 23 full-time (3 women), 3 part-time/adjunct (2 women). *Students:* 135 full-time (59 women), 2 part-time (0 women); includes 9 minority (1 Black or African American, non-Hispanic/Latino; 2 American Indian or Alaska Native, non-Hispanic/Latino; 5 Asian, non-Hispanic/Latino; 1 Hispanic/Latino), 102 international. Average age 27. 632 applicants, 46% accepted, 135 enrolled. In 2011, 145 master's awarded. *Degree requirements:* For master's, thesis. *Entrance requirements:* Additional exam requirements/recommendations for international students: Required—TOEFL (minimum score 550 paper-based; 213 computer-based). *Application deadline:* For fall admission, 2/28 priority date for domestic students, 2/28 for international students; for winter admission, 4/30 for domestic and international students. Applications are processed on a rolling basis. Application fee: $150. Electronic applications accepted. *Financial support:* In 2011–12, 8 students received support. Scholarships/grants available. *Faculty research:* Tourism development, entrepreneurship, organizational development, strategic planning, international business strategy, intercultural team work. *Unit head:* Brock Dykeman, Director, 250-740-6178, Fax: 250-740-6551, E-mail: brock.dykeman@viu.ca. *Application contact:* Jane Kelly, International Admissions Manager, 250-740-6384, Fax: 250-740-6471, E-mail: kellyj@mala.bc.ca. Web site: http://www.viu.ca/mba/index.asp.

Vanderbilt University, Owen Graduate School of Management, Executive MBA and Americas MBA Program, Nashville, TN 37240-1001. Offers Americas business administration for executives (EMBA); executive business administration (EMBA). *Accreditation:* AACSB. Evening/weekend programs available. *Faculty:* 17 full-time (1 woman), 6 part-time/adjunct (1 woman). *Students:* 104 full-time (26 women); includes 16 minority (6 Black or African American, non-Hispanic/Latino; 10 Asian, non-Hispanic/Latino), 4 international. Average age 36. 80 applicants, 74% accepted, 55 enrolled. In 2011, 50 master's awarded. *Entrance requirements:* For master's, GMAT, minimum of 5 years of professional work experience. *Application deadline:* For fall admission, 6/1 for domestic and international students. Applications are processed on a rolling basis. Application fee: $150. Electronic applications accepted. *Expenses:* Contact institution. *Financial support:* In 2011–12, 1 student received support. Scholarships/grants available. Financial award application deadline: 3/31; financial award applicants required to submit FAFSA. *Unit head:* Juli Bennett, Executive Director, 615-322-3120, Fax: 615-343-2293, E-mail: juli.bennett@owen.vanderbilt.edu. *Application contact:* Sarah Fairbank, Director, 615-322-0745, Fax: 615-343-2293, E-mail: sarah.fairbank@owen.vanderbilt.edu. Web site: http://www.owen.vanderbilt.edu.

Vanderbilt University, Owen Graduate School of Management, Full Time MBA Program, Nashville, TN 37203. Offers MBA, JD/MBA, MBA/M Div, MBA/MA, MBA/MD. *Accreditation:* AACSB. *Faculty:* 39 full-time (5 women). *Students:* 347 full-time (104 women); includes 53 minority (11 Black or African American, non-Hispanic/Latino; 1 American Indian or Alaska Native, non-Hispanic/Latino; 19 Asian, non-Hispanic/Latino; 17 Hispanic/Latino; 5 Two or more races, non-Hispanic/Latino), 7 international. Average age 28. 1,103 applicants, 32% accepted, 161 enrolled. In 2011, 183 master's awarded. *Entrance requirements:* For master's, GMAT, GRE, 2 years of work experience (recommended). Additional exam requirements/recommendations for international students: Required—TOEFL. *Application deadline:* For fall admission, 11/28 priority date for domestic students, 11/28 for international students; for winter admission, 1/16 priority date for domestic students, 1/16 for international students; for spring admission, 3/5 priority date for domestic students, 3/5 for international students. Applications are processed on a rolling basis. Application fee: $0. Electronic applications accepted. *Financial support:* In 2011–12, 200 students received support. Scholarships/grants and tuition waivers (full and partial) available. Financial award application deadline: 5/1; financial award applicants required to submit FAFSA. *Faculty research:* Financial markets, services marketing, operations, organization studies, health care. *Unit head:* Consuela Knox, Senior Associate Director, 615-322-6469, Fax: 615-343-1175, E-mail: admissions@owen.vanderbilt.edu. *Application contact:* Cori Washington, Communications Assistant, 615-322-6469, Fax: 615-343-1175, E-mail: admissions@owen.vanderbilt.edu. Web site: http://www.owen.vanderbilt.edu.

Vanguard University of Southern California, Graduate Program in Business, Costa Mesa, CA 92626-9601. Offers MBA. Part-time and evening/weekend programs available. *Entrance requirements:* For master's, MAT or GMAT, minimum GPA of 3.0. Additional exam requirements/recommendations for international students: Required—TOEFL (minimum score 550 paper-based; 213 computer-based; 79 iBT). Electronic applications accepted. *Expenses:* Contact institution.

Villanova University, Villanova School of Business, Executive MBA Program, Villanova, PA 19085. Offers EMBA. *Accreditation:* AACSB. Evening/weekend programs available. *Faculty:* 101 full-time (32 women), 38 part-time/adjunct (8 women). *Students:* 53 part-time (7 women); includes 5 minority (3 Black or African American, non-Hispanic/Latino; 1 Hispanic/Latino; 1 Native Hawaiian or other Pacific Islander, non-Hispanic/Latino), 1 international. Average age 37. In 2011, 26 master's awarded. *Degree requirements:* For master's, minimum cumulative GPA of 3.0, only two missed classes per module. *Entrance requirements:* For master's, significant managerial or executive work experience, employer approval. Additional exam requirements/recommendations for international students: Required—TOEFL (minimum score 550 paper-based; 213 computer-based; 80 iBT). *Application deadline:* For fall admission, 6/30 for domestic and international students. Applications are processed on a rolling basis. Application fee: $50. Electronic applications accepted. *Expenses:* Contact institution. *Financial support:* Scholarships/grants available. Financial award application deadline: 6/30; financial award applicants required to submit FAFSA. *Faculty research:* Business analytics; creativity, innovation and entrepreneurship; global leadership; marketing and public policy; real estate; church management. *Unit head:* Kristy Irwin, Director of Recruitment and Marketing, 610-519-6288, Fax: 610-519-6273, E-mail: kristy.irwin@villanova.edu. *Application contact:* Kristy Irwin, Director of Recruitment and Marketing, 610-519-6288, Fax: 610-519-6273, E-mail: kristy.irwin@villanova.edu. Web site: http://www.emba.villanova.edu/.

Villanova University, Villanova School of Business, MBA - The Fast Track Program, Villanova, PA 19085. Offers finance (MBA); health care management (MBA); international business (MBA); management information systems (MBA); marketing (MBA); real estate (MBA); strategic management (MBA). *Accreditation:* AACSB. Part-time and evening/weekend programs available. *Faculty:* 101 full-time (32 women), 38 part-time/adjunct (8 women). *Students:* 123 part-time (46 women); includes 14 minority (1 Black or African American, non-Hispanic/Latino; 3 American Indian or Alaska Native, non-Hispanic/Latino; 5 Asian, non-Hispanic/Latino; 1 Hispanic/Latino; 4 Two or more races, non-Hispanic/Latino). Average age 29. In 2011, 53 master's awarded. *Degree requirements:* For master's, minimum GPA of 3.0. *Entrance requirements:* For master's, GMAT, work experience. Additional exam requirements/recommendations for international students: Required—TOEFL (minimum score 550 paper-based; 213 computer-based; 80 iBT). *Application deadline:* For fall admission, 6/30 for domestic and international students. Application fee: $50. Electronic applications accepted. *Expenses: Tuition:* Part-time $675 per credit. Part-time tuition and fees vary according to degree level and program. *Financial support:* Scholarships/grants available. Financial award application deadline: 6/30; financial award applicants required to submit FAFSA. *Faculty research:* Business analytics; creativity, innovation and entrepreneurship; global leadership; marketing and public policy; real estate; church management. *Unit head:* Kristy Irwin, Director of Recruitment and Marketing, 610-519-6288, Fax: 610-519-6273, E-mail: kristy.irwin@villanova.edu. *Application contact:* Meredith L. Lockyer, Assistant

Director, 610-519-7016, Fax: 610-519-6273, E-mail: meredith.lockyer@villanova.edu. Web site: http://www.mba.villanova.edu.

Villanova University, Villanova School of Business, MBA - The Flex Track Program, Villanova, PA 19085. Offers finance (MBA); health care management (MBA); international business (MBA); management information systems (MBA); marketing (MBA); real estate (MBA); strategic management (MBA); JD/MBA. *Accreditation:* AACSB. Part-time and evening/weekend programs available. Postbaccalaureate distance learning degree programs offered (minimal on-campus study). *Faculty:* 101 full-time (32 women), 38 part-time/adjunct (8 women). *Students:* 18 full-time (9 women), 412 part-time (127 women); includes 45 minority (7 Black or African American, non-Hispanic/ Latino; 1 American Indian or Alaska Native, non-Hispanic/Latino; 25 Asian, non-Hispanic/Latino; 4 Hispanic/Latino; 1 Native Hawaiian or other Pacific Islander, non-Hispanic/Latino; 7 Two or more races, non-Hispanic/Latino). Average age 30. In 2011, 150 master's awarded. *Degree requirements:* For master's, minimum GPA of 3.0. *Entrance requirements:* For master's, GMAT, work experience. Additional exam requirements/recommendations for international students: Required—TOEFL (minimum score 550 paper-based; 213 computer-based; 80 iBT). *Application deadline:* For fall admission, 6/30 for domestic and international students; for winter admission, 11/15 for domestic and international students; for spring admission, 3/30 for domestic students, 3/ 31 for international students. Applications are processed on a rolling basis. Application fee: $50. Electronic applications accepted. *Expenses: Tuition:* Part-time $675 per credit. Part-time tuition and fees vary according to degree level and program. *Financial support:* In 2011–12, 18 research assistantships with full tuition reimbursements (averaging $13,100 per year) were awarded; scholarships/grants and unspecified assistantships also available. Financial award application deadline: 6/30; financial award applicants required to submit FAFSA. *Faculty research:* Business analytics; creativity, innovation and entrepreneurship; global leadership; marketing and public policy; real estate; church management. *Unit head:* Kristy Irwin, Director of Recruitment and Marketing, 610-610-6288, Fax: 610-519-6273, E-mail: kristy.irwin@villanova.edu. *Application contact:* Meredity L. Lockyer, Assistant Director, 610-519-7016, Fax: 610-519-6273, E-mail: meredith.lockyer@villanova.edu. Web site: http://www.mba.villanova.edu.

Virginia College at Birmingham, Program in Business Administration, Birmingham, AL 35209. Offers healthcare (MBA); management (MBA). Part-time and evening/weekend programs available. Postbaccalaureate distance learning degree programs offered (no on-campus study). In 2011, 3 master's awarded. *Entrance requirements:* For master's, bachelor's degree in related academic area. *Financial support:* Career-related internships or fieldwork, Federal Work-Study, institutionally sponsored loans, scholarships/grants, and military educational benefits available. Support available to part-time students. Financial award applicants required to submit FAFSA. *Unit head:* Lisa Bacon, Unit Head, 877-812-8428, E-mail: admissions@vc.edu. *Application contact:* Angela Beck, Director of Admissions, 205-802-1200, E-mail: admissions@vc.edu. Web site: http://www.vc.edu/site/program.cfm?programID-7.

Virginia College at Birmingham, Virginia College Online, Birmingham, AL 35209. Offers business administration (MBA); criminal justice (MCJ); cybersecurity (MC). Part-time and evening/weekend programs available. Postbaccalaureate distance learning degree programs offered (no on-campus study). *Financial support:* Military educational benefits available. Financial award applicants required to submit FAFSA. *Unit head:* Stan Banks, President, 877-207-1933, E-mail: vcoadm@vc.edu. *Application contact:* Christina Eschelman, Director of Admissions, 877-207-1933, E-mail: vcoadm@vc.edu. Web site: http://www.vconline.edu/.

Virginia Commonwealth University, Graduate School, School of Business, Program in Business Administration, Richmond, VA 23284-9005. Offers MBA, Postbaccalaureate Certificate. *Students:* 121 full-time (41 women), 213 part-time (72 women); includes 72 minority (31 Black or African American, non-Hispanic/Latino; 1 American Indian or Alaska Native, non-Hispanic/Latino; 22 Asian, non-Hispanic/Latino; 11 Hispanic/Latino; 1 Native Hawaiian or other Pacific Islander, non-Hispanic/Latino; 6 Two or more races, non-Hispanic/Latino), 26 international. 203 applicants, 71% accepted, 120 enrolled. In 2011, 119 master's, 6 other advanced degrees awarded. *Entrance requirements:* For master's, GMAT. Additional exam requirements/recommendations for international students: Required—TOEFL (minimum score 600 paper-based; 250 computer-based; 100 iBT). *Application deadline:* For fall admission, 7/1 for domestic students; for spring admission, 11/1 for domestic students. Applications are processed on a rolling basis. Application fee: $50. Electronic applications accepted. *Expenses:* Tuition, state resident: full-time $9133; part-time $507 per credit. Tuition, nonresident: full-time $18,777; part-time $1043 per credit. *Required fees:* $77 per credit. Tuition and fees vary according to degree level, campus/location, program and student level. *Financial support:* Fellowships, research assistantships, teaching assistantships, Federal Work-Study, institutionally sponsored loans, and tuition waivers (full and partial) available. Financial award application deadline: 3/15; financial award applicants required to submit FAFSA. *Unit head:* Dr. E. G. Miller, Interim Chair, 804-827-7404, Fax: 804-828-8884, E-mail: egmiller@vcu.edu. *Application contact:* Jana P. McQuaid, Assistant Dean, Master's Programs, 804-828-4622, Fax: 804-828-7174, E-mail: jpmcquaid@vcu.edu. Web site: http://www.business.vcu.edu/graduate.html.

Virginia Commonwealth University, Graduate School, School of Business, Program in Management, Richmond, VA 23284-9005. Offers Certificate. *Expenses:* Tuition, state resident: full-time $9133; part-time $507 per credit. Tuition, nonresident: full-time $18,777; part-time $1043 per credit. *Required fees:* $77 per credit. Tuition and fees vary according to degree level, campus/location, program and student level.

Virginia International University, School of Business, Fairfax, VA 22030. Offers accounting (MBA); executive management (Graduate Certificate); global logistics (MBA); health care management (MBA); human resources management (MBA); international business management (MBA); international finance (MBA); marketing management (MBA). Part-time programs available. *Entrance requirements:* For master's and Graduate Certificate, bachelor's degree. Additional exam requirements/ recommendations for international students: Required—TOEFL (minimum score 550 paper-based; 213 computer-based; 80 iBT), IELTS (minimum score 6). Electronic applications accepted.

Virginia Polytechnic Institute and State University, Graduate School, College of Science, Program in Biomedical Technology Development and Management, Blacksburg, VA 24061. Offers MS. *Degree requirements:* For master's, comprehensive exam (for some programs), thesis (for some programs). *Entrance requirements:* For master's, GRE. Additional exam requirements/recommendations for international students: Required—TOEFL (minimum score 550 paper-based; 213 computer-based). *Application deadline:* For fall admission, 7/1 for domestic and international students; for spring admission, 12/1 for domestic and international students. Applications are processed on a rolling basis. Application fee: $65. Electronic applications accepted. *Expenses:* Tuition, state resident: full-time $10,048; part-time $558.25 per credit hour. Tuition, nonresident: full-time $19,497; part-time $1083.25 per credit hour. *Required fees:* $405 per semester. Tuition and fees vary according to course load, campus/ location and program. *Financial support:* Career-related internships or fieldwork, Federal Work-Study, scholarships/grants, health care benefits, and unspecified assistantships available. *Unit head:* Dr. Kenneth H. Wong, Unit Head, 571-858-3203, Fax: 540-231-7511, E-mail: khwong@vt.edu. *Application contact:* Jennifer LeFurgy, Information Contact, 571-858-3200, Fax: 540-231-7511, E-mail: jlefurgy@vt.edu.

Virginia Polytechnic Institute and State University, Graduate School, Pamplin College of Business, Department of Management, Blacksburg, VA 24061. Offers PhD. *Accreditation:* AACSB. *Degree requirements:* For doctorate, comprehensive exam (for some programs), thesis/dissertation (for some programs). *Entrance requirements:* For doctorate, GRE. Additional exam requirements/recommendations for international students: Required—TOEFL (minimum score 550 paper-based; 213 computer-based). *Application deadline:* For fall admission, 7/1 for domestic and international students; for spring admission, 11/1 for domestic and international students. Applications are processed on a rolling basis. Application fee: $65. Electronic applications accepted. *Expenses:* Tuition, state resident: full-time $10,048; part-time $558.25 per credit hour. Tuition, nonresident: full-time $19,497; part-time $1083.25 per credit hour. *Required fees:* $405 per semester. Tuition and fees vary according to course load, campus/ location and program. *Financial support:* In 2011–12, 7 teaching assistantships with full tuition reimbursements (averaging $14,758 per year) were awarded; career-related internships or fieldwork, Federal Work-Study, scholarships/grants, health care benefits, and unspecified assistantships also available. Financial award application deadline: 1/ 15. *Faculty research:* Compensation, organization effectiveness, selection, strategic planning, labor/management relations. *Unit head:* Dr. Anju Seth, Unit Head, 540-231-6353, Fax: 540-231-4487, E-mail: aseth@vt.edu. *Application contact:* Kevin Carlson, Information Contact, 540-231-4990, Fax: 540-231-4487, E-mail: kevinc@vt.edu. Web site: http://www.management.pamplin.vt.edu/academics/phd/index.html.

Virginia Polytechnic Institute and State University, Graduate School, Pamplin College of Business, Program in Business Administration, Blacksburg, VA 24061. Offers MBA. *Accreditation:* AACSB. *Degree requirements:* For master's, comprehensive exam (for some programs), thesis (for some programs). *Entrance requirements:* For master's, GRE. Additional exam requirements/recommendations for international students: Required—TOEFL (minimum score 550 paper-based; 213 computer-based). *Application deadline:* For fall admission, 7/1 for domestic and international students; for spring admission, 12/1 for domestic and international students. Applications are processed on a rolling basis. Application fee: $65. Electronic applications accepted. *Expenses:* Tuition, state resident: full-time $10,048; part-time $558.25 per credit hour. Tuition, nonresident: full-time $19,497; part-time $1083.25 per credit hour. *Required fees:* $405 per semester. Tuition and fees vary according to course load, campus/location and program. *Financial support:* Teaching assistantships with full tuition reimbursements, career-related internships or fieldwork, Federal Work-Study, scholarships/grants, health care benefits, and unspecified assistantships available. Financial award application deadline: 1/15. *Unit head:* Dr. Stephen J. Skripak, Unit Head, 540-231-6152, Fax: 540-231-4487, E-mail: sskripak@vt.edu. Web site: http://www.cob.vt.edu/.

Viterbo University, Graduate Program in Business, La Crosse, WI 54601-4797. Offers MBA. *Accreditation:* ACBSP.

Wagner College, Division of Graduate Studies, Department of Business Administration, Staten Island, NY 10301-4495. Offers accelerated business administration (MBA); accounting (MS); finance (MBA); health care administration (MBA); international business (MBA); management (Exec MBA, MBA); marketing (MBA). *Accreditation:* ACBSP. Part-time and evening/weekend programs available. *Faculty:* 8 full-time (3 women), 20 part-time/adjunct (2 women). *Students:* 112 full-time (42 women), 41 part-time (15 women); includes 44 minority (12 Black or African American, non-Hispanic/ Latino; 1 American Indian or Alaska Native, non-Hispanic/Latino; 8 Asian, non-Hispanic/ Latino; 20 Hispanic/Latino; 3 Two or more races, non-Hispanic/Latino), 2 international. Average age 30. 97 applicants, 99% accepted, 79 enrolled. In 2011, 69 master's awarded. *Degree requirements:* For master's, thesis optional. *Entrance requirements:* For master's, GMAT, minimum GPA of 2.75, proficiency in computers and math. Additional exam requirements/recommendations for international students: Required—TOEFL (minimum score 550 paper-based; 217 computer-based; 79 iBT). *Application deadline:* For fall admission, 5/1 priority date for domestic students, 3/1 for international students; for spring admission, 12/1 for domestic students, 11/1 for international students. Applications are processed on a rolling basis. Application fee: $50 ($85 for international students). *Expenses: Tuition:* Full-time $16,200; part-time $890 per credit. *Financial support:* Career-related internships or fieldwork, unspecified assistantships, and alumni fellowship grant available. Financial award applicants required to submit FAFSA. *Unit head:* Prof. Mary LoRe, Director, 718-420-4127, Fax: 718-420-4274, E-mail: mlore@wagner.edu. *Application contact:* Patricia Clancy, Administrative Assistant, 718-420-4464, Fax: 718-390-3105, E-mail: patricia.clancy@wagner.edu. Web site: http://www.wagner.edu/departments/mba/main.

Wake Forest University, Schools of Business, Charlotte Evening MBA Program, Charlotte, NC 28202. Offers MBA. *Accreditation:* AACSB. Evening/weekend programs available. *Faculty:* 62 full-time (16 women), 41 part-time/adjunct (14 women). *Students:* 98 full-time (27 women); includes 18 minority (9 Black or African American, non-Hispanic/Latino; 3 Asian, non-Hispanic/Latino; 6 Hispanic/Latino), 5 international. Average age 31. In 2011, 52 master's awarded. *Degree requirements:* For master's, 54 total credit hours. *Entrance requirements:* For master's, GMAT or GRE, letters of recommendation, official transcripts, current resume or curriculum vitae, three years of work experience. Additional exam requirements/recommendations for international students: Required—TOEFL (minimum score 600 paper-based; 250 computer-based; 100 iBT), Pearson Test of English. *Application deadline:* For fall admission, 6/1 for domestic and international students. Applications are processed on a rolling basis. Application fee: $100. Electronic applications accepted. *Expenses:* Contact institution. *Financial support:* In 2011–12, 42 students received support. Scholarships/grants available. Financial award application deadline: 4/1; financial award applicants required to submit FAFSA. *Faculty research:* The influence of personal relationships on business decision-making and management of change; drivers of perceived value and consumer behavior; impact of accounting on auditing, financial, managerial, systems and taxation stakeholders; corporate governance and executive compensation; impact of operations strategies on competitiveness. *Unit head:* Melenie Lankau, Senior Associate Dean of Graduate Programs and Diversity, 704-365-1717, Fax: 704-365-3511, E-mail: cltbusadmissions@wfu.edu. *Application contact:* Judi Affeldt, Administrative Assistant, 704-365-1717, Fax: 704-365-3511, E-mail: cltbusadmissions@wfu.edu. Web site: http:// www.uptownmba.com/about-us/programs/.

Wake Forest University, Schools of Business, Evening MBA Program–Winston-Salem, Winston-Salem, NC 27106. Offers MBA, PhD/MBA. *Accreditation:* AACSB. Evening/ weekend programs available. *Faculty:* 62 full-time (16 women), 41 part-time/adjunct (14 women). *Students:* 72 full-time (22 women); includes 12 minority (4 Black or African American, non-Hispanic/Latino; 1 American Indian or Alaska Native, non-Hispanic/ Latino; 5 Asian, non-Hispanic/Latino; 1 Hispanic/Latino; 1 Two or more races, non-Hispanic/Latino), 2 international. Average age 32. In 2011, 38 master's awarded. *Degree requirements:* For master's, 54 total credit hours. *Entrance requirements:* For master's, GMAT or GRE, letters of recommendation, official transcripts, current resume or curriculum vitae, three years of work experience. Additional exam requirements/ recommendations for international students: Required—TOEFL (minimum score 600 paper-based; 250 computer-based; 100 iBT), Pearson Test of English. *Application deadline:* For fall admission, 7/15 for domestic and international students. Applications are processed on a rolling basis. Application fee: $100. Electronic applications accepted. *Expenses:* Contact institution. *Financial support:* In 2011–12, 24 students received support. Scholarships/grants available. Financial award applicants required to submit FAFSA. *Faculty research:* The influence of personal relationships on business decision-making and management of change; drivers of perceived value and consumer behavior; impact of accounting on auditing, financial, managerial, systems and taxation stakeholders; corporate governance and executive compensation; impact of operations strategies on competitiveness. *Unit head:* Bill Davis, Academic Director of Winston-Salem Evening MBA Program, 336-758-5422, Fax: 336-758-5830, E-mail: busadmissions@wfu.edu. *Application contact:* Tamara Paquee, Administrative Assistant, 336-758-5422, Fax: 336-758-5830, E-mail: busadmissions@wfu.edu. Web site: http://www.business.wfu.edu/.

Wake Forest University, Schools of Business, Full-time MBA Program, Winston-Salem, NC 27106. Offers consulting/general management (MBA); entrepreneurship (MBA); finance (MBA); health (MBA); marketing (MBA); operations management (MBA); JD/MBA; MD/MBA; MSA/MBA. *Accreditation:* AACSB. *Faculty:* 62 full-time (16 women), 41 part-time/adjunct (14 women). *Students:* 120 full-time (28 women); includes 14 minority (8 Black or African American, non-Hispanic/Latino; 4 Asian, non-Hispanic/Latino; 1 Hispanic/Latino; 1 Two or more races, non-Hispanic/Latino), 28 international. Average age 28. In 2011, 62 master's awarded. *Degree requirements:* For master's, 65.5 credit hours. *Entrance requirements:* For master's, GMAT or GRE, letters of recommendation, official transcripts, current resume or curriculum vitae, 2 years of work experience. Additional exam requirements/recommendations for international students: Required—TOEFL (minimum score 600 paper-based; 250 computer-based; 100 iBT), Pearson Test of English. *Application deadline:* For fall admission, 4/15 for domestic and international students. Applications are processed on a rolling basis. Application fee: $100. Electronic applications accepted. *Expenses:* Contact institution. *Financial support:* In 2011–12, 84 students received support. Career-related internships or fieldwork, scholarships/grants, and unspecified assistantships available. Financial award application deadline: 2/15; financial award applicants required to submit FAFSA. *Faculty research:* The influence of personal relationships on business decision-making and management of change; drivers of perceived value and consumer behavior; impact of accounting on auditing, financial, managerial, systems and taxation stakeholders; corporate governance and executive compensation; impact of operations strategies on competitiveness. *Unit head:* Jon Duchac, Director, Full-time MBA Program, 336-758-5422, Fax: 336-758-5830, E-mail: busadmissions@wfu.edu. *Application contact:* Tamara Paquee, Administrative Assistant, 336-758-5422, Fax: 336-758-5830, E-mail: busadmissions@wfu.edu. Web site: http://www.business.wfu.edu/.

Wake Forest University, Schools of Business, MA in Management Program, Winston-Salem, NC 27106. Offers MA. *Faculty:* 62 full-time (16 women), 41 part-time/adjunct (14 women). *Students:* 96 full-time (39 women); includes 38 minority (26 Black or African American, non-Hispanic/Latino; 2 American Indian or Alaska Native, non-Hispanic/Latino; 3 Asian, non-Hispanic/Latino; 5 Hispanic/Latino; 2 Two or more races, non-Hispanic/Latino), 7 international. Average age 23. In 2011, 84 master's awarded. *Degree requirements:* For master's, 41.5 credit hours. *Entrance requirements:* For master's, GMAT or GRE, letters of recommendation, official transcripts, current resume or curriculum vitae. Additional exam requirements/recommendations for international students: Required—TOEFL (minimum score 600 paper-based; 250 computer-based; 100 iBT), Pearson Test of English. *Application deadline:* For fall admission, 6/15 for domestic and international students. Applications are processed on a rolling basis. Application fee: $100. Electronic applications accepted. *Financial support:* In 2011–12, 65 students received support. Scholarships/grants available. Financial award application deadline: 4/1; financial award applicants required to submit FAFSA. *Faculty research:* The influence of personal relationships on business decision-making and management of change; drivers of perceived value and consumer behavior; impact of accounting on auditing, financial, managerial, systems and taxation stakeholders; corporate governance and executive compensation; impact of operations strategies on competitiveness. *Unit head:* Derrick Boone, Director, MA in Management Program, 336-758-5422, Fax: 336-758-5830, E-mail: busadmissions@wfu.edu. *Application contact:* Tamara Paquee, Administrative Assistant, 336-758-5422, Fax: 336-758-5830, E-mail: busadmissions@wfu.edu. Web site: http://www.business.wfu.edu/.

Wake Forest University, Schools of Business, Saturday MBA Program–Charlotte, Charlotte, NC 28202. Offers MBA. *Accreditation:* AACSB. Evening/weekend programs available. *Faculty:* 62 full-time (16 women), 41 part-time/adjunct (14 women). *Students:* 66 full-time (17 women); includes 19 minority (8 Black or African American, non-Hispanic/Latino; 6 Asian, non-Hispanic/Latino; 3 Hispanic/Latino; 2 Two or more races, non-Hispanic/Latino), 1 international. Average age 33. In 2011, 40 master's awarded. *Degree requirements:* For master's, 54 total credit hours. *Entrance requirements:* For master's, GMAT or GRE, letters of recommendation, official transcripts, current resume or curriculum vitae, three years of work experience. Additional exam requirements/recommendations for international students: Required—TOEFL (minimum score 600 paper-based; 250 computer-based; 100 iBT), Pearson Test of English. *Application deadline:* For spring admission, 11/1 for domestic and international students. Applications are processed on a rolling basis. Application fee: $100. Electronic applications accepted. *Expenses:* Contact institution. *Financial support:* In 2011–12, 14 students received support. Scholarships/grants available. Financial award application deadline: 9/1; financial award applicants required to submit FAFSA. *Faculty research:* The influence of personal relationships on business decision-making and management of change; drivers of perceived value and consumer behavior; impact of accounting on auditing, financial, managerial, systems and taxation stakeholders; corporate governance and executive compensation; impact of operations strategies on competitiveness. *Unit head:* Melenie Lankau, Senior Associate Dean of Graduate Programs and Diversity, 704-365-1717, Fax: 704-365-3511, E-mail: cltbusadmissions@wfu.edu. *Application contact:* Judi Affeldt, Administrative Assistant, 704-365-1717, Fax: 704-365-3511, E-mail: cltbusadmissions@wfu.edu. Web site: http://www.mba.wfu.edu/.

Walden University, Graduate Programs, School of Management, Minneapolis, MN 55401. Offers accounting (MS, DBA), including accounting for the professional (MS), CPA (MS), self-designed (MS); accounting and management (MS), including accounting for strategic managers, self-designed; accounting for managers (MBA); advanced project management (Post-Graduate Certificate); applied project management (Post-Graduate Certificate); corporate finance (MBA); entrepreneurship (MBA, DBA); finance (DBA); global management (MS); global supply chain management (DBA); healthcare management (MBA, DBA); healthcare system improvement (MBA); human resource management (MBA, MS, PhD), including functional human resource management (MS), integrating functional and strategic human resource management (MS), organizational strategy (MS); information systems management (DBA); international business (MBA, DBA); leadership (MBA, MS, DBA), including entrepreneurship (MS), general management (MS), human resources leadership (MS), innovation and technology (MS), leader development (MS), leading sustainability (MS), project management (MS), self-designed (MS); management (MS), including healthcare management; managers as leaders (MS); marketing (MBA, DBA); project management (MBA, MS, DBA); research strategies (MS); risk management (MBA); self-designed (MBA, DBA, PhD); social impact management (DBA); strategies for sustainability (MBA); strategy and operations (MS); sustainable management (MS); technology (MBA); technology entrepreneurship (DBA); technology management (MS). Part-time and evening/weekend programs available. Postbaccalaureate distance learning degree programs offered (minimal on-campus study). *Faculty:* 32 full-time (14 women), 275 part-time/adjunct (98 women). *Students:* 3,962 full-time (2,095 women), 1,557 part-time (959 women); includes 3,003 minority (2,510 Black or African American, non-Hispanic/Latino; 25 American Indian or Alaska Native, non-Hispanic/Latino; 140 Asian, non-Hispanic/Latino; 240 Hispanic/Latino; 9 Native Hawaiian or other Pacific Islander, non-Hispanic/Latino; 79 Two or more races, non-Hispanic/Latino), 395 international. Average age 41. In 2011, 586 master's, 87 doctorates, 4 other advanced degrees awarded. *Degree requirements:* For doctorate, thesis/dissertation (for some programs), residency. *Entrance requirements:* For master's, bachelor's degree or equivalent in related field; minimum GPA of 2.5; official transcripts; goal statement; access to computer and Internet; for doctorate, master's degree or equivalent in related field; minimum GPA of 3.0; 3 years of related professional/academic experience (preferred). Additional exam requirements/recommendations for international students: Required—TOEFL (minimum score 550 paper-based; 213 computer-based), IELTS (minimum score 6.5), Michigan English Language Assessment Battery (minimum score 82). *Application deadline:* Applications are processed on a rolling basis. Application fee: $50. Electronic applications accepted. *Financial support:* Federal Work-Study, scholarships/grants, unspecified assistantships, and family tuition reduction, active duty/veteran tuition reduction, group tuition reduction, interest-free payment plans, employee tuition reduction available. Support available to part-time students. Financial award applicants required to submit FAFSA. *Unit head:* Dr. William Schulz, III, Associate Dean, 800-925-3368. *Application contact:* Jennifer Hall, Vice President of Enrollment Management, 866-4-WALDEN, E-mail: info@waldenu.edu. Web site: http://www.waldenu.edu/Colleges-and-Schools/College-of-Management-and-Technology.htm.

Walden University, Graduate Programs, School of Public Policy and Administration, Minneapolis, MN 55401. Offers criminal justice (MPA, MPP, MS), including emergency management (MS, PhD), homeland security policy (MS, PhD), homeland security policy and coordination (MS, PhD), law and public policy (MS, PhD), policy analysis (MS, PhD), public management and leadership (MS, PhD), self-designed (MS), terrorism, mediation, and peace (MS, PhD); criminal justice leadership and executive management (MS), including emergency management (MS, PhD), homeland security policy (MS, PhD), homeland security policy and coordination (MS, PhD), law and public policy (MS, PhD), policy analysis (MS, PhD), public management and leadership (MS, PhD), self-designed, terrorism, mediation, and peace (MS, PhD); emergency management (MPA, MPP, MS), including criminal justice (MS, PhD), homeland security (MS), public management and leadership (MS, PhD), terrorism and emergency management (MS); government management (Postbaccalaureate Certificate); health policy (MPA); homeland security policy (MPA, MPP); homeland security policy and coordination (MPA, MPP); interdisciplinary policy studies (MPA, MPP); international nongovernmental organizations (MPA, MPP); law and public policy (MPA, MPP); local government management for sustainable communities (MPA, MPP); nonprofit management (Postbaccalaureate Certificate); nonprofit management and leadership (MPA, MPP, MS); policy analysis (MPA); public management and leadership (MPA, MPP); public policy and administration (PhD), including criminal justice (MS, PhD), emergency management (MS, PhD), health policy, homeland security policy (MS, PhD), homeland security policy and coordination (MS, PhD), interdisciplinary policy studies, international nongovernmental organizations, law and public policy (MS, PhD), local government management for sustainable communities, nonprofit management and leadership, policy analysis (MS, PhD), public management and leadership (MS, PhD), terrorism, mediation, and peace (MS, PhD); terrorism, mediation, and peace (MPA, MPP). Part-time and evening/weekend programs available. Postbaccalaureate distance learning degree programs offered (minimal on-campus study). *Faculty:* 9 full-time (3 women), 90 part-time/adjunct (41 women). *Students:* 1,396 full-time (886 women), 902 part-time (581 women); includes 1,392 minority (1,205 Black or African American, non-Hispanic/Latino; 11 American Indian or Alaska Native, non-Hispanic/Latino; 35 Asian, non-Hispanic/Latino; 95 Hispanic/Latino; 2 Native Hawaiian or other Pacific Islander, non-Hispanic/Latino; 44 Two or more races, non-Hispanic/Latino), 82 international. Average age 41. In 2011, 265 master's, 34 doctorates, 13 other advanced degrees awarded. *Degree requirements:* For doctorate, thesis/dissertation, residency. *Entrance requirements:* For master's, bachelor's degree or equivalent in related field, minimum GPA of 2.5; for doctorate, master's degree or equivalent in related field; minimum GPA of 3.0; official transcripts; three years of related professional/academic experience (preferred); access to computer and Internet. Additional exam requirements/recommendations for international students: Required—TOEFL (minimum score 550 paper-based; 213 computer-based), IELTS (minimum score 6.5), or Michigan English Language Assessment Battery (minimum score 82). *Application deadline:* Applications are processed on a rolling basis. Application fee: $50. Electronic applications accepted. *Financial support:* Federal Work-Study, scholarships/grants, unspecified assistantships, and family tuition reduction, active duty/veteran tuition reduction, group tuition reduction, interest-free payment plans, employee tuition reduction available. Support available to part-time students. Financial award applicants required to submit FAFSA. *Unit head:* Dr. Mark Gordon, Associate Dean, 800-925-3368. *Application contact:* Jennifer Hall, Vice President of Enrollment Management, 866-4-WALDEN, E-mail: info@waldenu.edu. Web site: http://www.waldenu.edu/Colleges-and-Schools/College-of-Social-and-Behavioral-Sciences/School-of-Public-Policy-and-Administration.htm.

Walsh College of Accountancy and Business Administration, Graduate Programs, Program in Business Administration, Troy, MI 48007-7006. Offers MBA. *Accreditation:* ACBSP. *Entrance requirements:* For master's, GMAT, minimum GPA of 2.75, previous course work in business. Additional exam requirements/recommendations for international students: Required—TOEFL. Electronic applications accepted.

Walsh College of Accountancy and Business Administration, Graduate Programs, Program in Management, Troy, MI 48007-7006. Offers MSIB, MSSL. Part-time and evening/weekend programs available. *Entrance requirements:* For master's, minimum GPA of 2.75, previous course work in business. Additional exam requirements/recommendations for international students: Required—TOEFL. Electronic applications accepted.

Walsh University, Graduate Studies, MBA Program, North Canton, OH 44720-3396. Offers health care management (MBA); integrated marketing communications (MBA); management (MBA). Part-time and evening/weekend programs available. *Faculty:* 7 full-time (2 women), 24 part-time/adjunct (7 women). *Students:* 21 full-time (11 women), 151 part-time (74 women); includes 13 minority (8 Black or African American, non-Hispanic/Latino; 2 American Indian or Alaska Native, non-Hispanic/Latino; 3 Hispanic/Latino). Average age 34. 62 applicants, 81% accepted, 45 enrolled. In 2011, 57 master's awarded. *Entrance requirements:* For master's, GMAT, minimum GPA of 3.0. Additional exam requirements/recommendations for international students: Required—TOEFL (minimum score 500 paper-based; 173 computer-based; 61 iBT). *Application deadline:* For fall admission, 7/15 priority date for domestic students. Applications are processed on a rolling basis. Application fee: $25. Electronic applications accepted. *Expenses:* *Tuition:* Full-time $10,170; part-time $565 per credit hour. *Financial support:* In 2011–12, 106 students received support, including 10 research assistantships with partial tuition reimbursements available (averaging $5,674 per year), 4 teaching assistantships (averaging $5,763 per year); tuition waivers (partial), unspecified assistantships, and tuition discounts also available. Support available to part-time students. Financial award application deadline: 12/31; financial award applicants required to submit FAFSA. *Faculty research:* Patient and physician satisfaction, advancing and improving learning with information technology, consumer-driven healthcare, branding and the service industry, service provider training and customer satisfaction. *Unit head:* Dr. Michael A. Petrochuk, Director of the MBA Program and Assistant Professor, 330-244-4764, Fax: 330-490-7359, E-mail: mpetrochuk@walsh.edu. *Application contact:* Audra Dice, Graduate and Transfer Admissions Counselor, 330-490-7181, Fax: 330-244-4925, E-mail: adice@walsh.edu. Web site: http://www.walsh.edu/mba-program.

Warner Pacific College, Graduate Programs, Portland, OR 97215-4099. Offers biblical and theological studies (MA); biblical studies (M Rel); education (M Ed); management/organizational leadership (MS); pastoral ministries (M Rel); religion and ethics (M Rel); teaching (MA); theology (M Rel). Part-time programs available. *Degree requirements:* For master's, thesis or alternative, presentation of defense. *Entrance requirements:* For master's, interview, minimum GPA of 2.5, letters of recommendations. *Faculty research:* New Testament studies, nineteenth-century Wesleyan theology, preaching and church growth, Christian ethics.

Warner University, School of Business, Lake Wales, FL 33859. Offers MBA. Part-time and evening/weekend programs available. *Degree requirements:* For master's, comprehensive exam. *Entrance requirements:* For master's, GMAT, minimum GPA of 3.0, letters of recommendation (2). Additional exam requirements/recommendations for international students: Required—TOEFL. Electronic applications accepted.

Warner University, School of Professional Studies, Lake Wales, FL 33859. Offers management (MSM). Part-time and evening/weekend programs available. Postbaccalaureate distance learning degree programs offered. *Entrance requirements:* For master's, MAT, minimum GPA of 3.0; letters of recommendation (2). Additional exam requirements/recommendations for international students: Required—TOEFL (minimum score 550 paper-based). Electronic applications accepted.

Washburn University, School of Business, Topeka, KS 66621. Offers MBA. *Accreditation:* AACSB. Part-time and evening/weekend programs available. *Entrance requirements:* For master's, GMAT, minimum GPA of 2.75. Additional exam requirements/recommendations for international students: Required—TOEFL (minimum score 550 paper-based; 213 computer-based; 80 iBT); Recommended—IELTS (minimum score 6.5). Electronic applications accepted. *Expenses:* Tuition, state resident: full-time $5346; part-time $297 per credit hour. Tuition, nonresident: full-time $10,908; part-time $606 per credit hour. *Required fees:* $86; $43 per semester. *Faculty research:* Ethics in information technology, forecasting for shareholder value creation, model for measuring expected losses from litigation contingencies, business vs. family commitment in family businesses, calculated intangible value and brand recognition.

Washington Adventist University, MBA Program, Takoma Park, MD 20912. Offers MBA. Part-time programs available. Postbaccalaureate distance learning degree programs offered (no on-campus study). *Faculty:* 15 part-time/adjunct. *Students:* 7 full-time (1 woman), 34 part-time (26 women); includes 28 minority (27 Black or African American, non-Hispanic/Latino; 1 Hispanic/Latino). Average age 31. In 2011, 32 master's awarded. *Entrance requirements:* For master's, minimum undergraduate GPA of 2.75, curriculum vitae, interview, essay, personal statement. Additional exam requirements/recommendations for international students: Required—TOEFL (minimum score 550 paper-based; 213 computer-based), IELTS (minimum score 5). *Application deadline:* Applications are processed on a rolling basis. Application fee: $50. *Expenses: Tuition:* Part-time $560 per credit hour. *Financial support:* Institutionally sponsored loans available. Support available to part-time students. Financial award applicants required to submit FAFSA. *Unit head:* Dr. Jude Edwards, Dean, School of Graduate and Professional Studies, 301-891-4092. *Application contact:* Rahneeka Hazelton, 301-891-4092, Fax: 301-891-4023, E-mail: rhazelto@wau.edu. Web site: http://www.wau.edu/index.php?option=com_content&view=article&id=406&Itemid=963.

Washington State University, Graduate School, College of Business, Business Administration Programs, Pullman, WA 99164. Offers business administration (MBA, PhD), including accounting (PhD), finance (PhD), management and operations (PhD), management information systems (PhD), marketing (PhD). *Accreditation:* AACSB. *Faculty:* 47. *Students:* 93 full-time (35 women), 94 part-time (32 women); includes 25 minority (4 Black or African American, non-Hispanic/Latino; 2 American Indian or Alaska Native, non-Hispanic/Latino; 11 Asian, non-Hispanic/Latino; 7 Hispanic/Latino; 1 Two or more races, non-Hispanic/Latino), 33 international. Average age 31. 310 applicants, 31% accepted, 67 enrolled. In 2011, 15 doctorates awarded. *Degree requirements:* For master's, comprehensive exam (for some programs), thesis (for some programs), final presentation; for doctorate, comprehensive exam, thesis/dissertation, oral and written exams. *Entrance requirements:* For master's and doctorate, GMAT, minimum GPA of 3.0, 3 letters of recommendation. Additional exam requirements/recommendations for international students: Required—TOEFL. *Application deadline:* For fall admission, 3/1 priority date for domestic students, 3/1 for international students; for spring admission, 6/1 priority date for domestic students, 6/1 for international students. Applications are processed on a rolling basis. Application fee: $75. Electronic applications accepted. *Financial support:* In 2011–12, 102 students received support, including 36 teaching assistantships with full and partial tuition reimbursements available (averaging $18,204 per year); career-related internships or fieldwork, Federal Work-Study, institutionally sponsored loans, health care benefits, tuition waivers (partial), unspecified assistantships, and teaching associateships also available. Financial award application deadline: 4/1. *Total annual research expenditures:* $344,000. *Unit head:* Dr. Eric Spangenberg, Dean, 509-335-8150, E-mail: ers@wsu.edu. *Application contact:* Graduate School Admissions, 800-GRADWSU, Fax: 509-335-1949, E-mail: gradsch@wsu.edu.

Washington State University Tri-Cities, Graduate Programs, College of Business, Richland, WA 99352-1671. Offers business management (MBA). Part-time and evening/weekend programs available. *Faculty:* 56. *Students:* 37 full-time (9 women), 15 part-time (6 women); includes 11 minority (1 American Indian or Alaska Native, non-Hispanic/Latino; 5 Asian, non-Hispanic/Latino; 5 Hispanic/Latino), 1 international. Average age 30. 38 applicants, 58% accepted, 17 enrolled. In 2011, 13 master's awarded. *Degree requirements:* For master's, thesis (for some programs), oral presentation exam. *Entrance requirements:* For master's, GMAT, minimum GPA of 3.0, 3 letters of recommendation. Additional exam requirements/recommendations for international students: Required—TOEFL (minimum score 550 paper-based; 213 computer-based). *Application deadline:* For fall admission, 1/10 priority date for domestic students, 1/10 for international students; for spring admission, 7/1 priority date for domestic students, 7/1 for international students. Application fee: $75. *Financial support:* In 2011–12, 17 students received support. *Faculty research:* Strategy, organizational transformation, technology and instructional effectiveness, market research effects of type (fonts), optimization of price structure, accounting ethic. *Unit head:* Dr. John Thornton, Director, 509-372-7246, Fax: 509-372-7354, E-mail: jthornt@tricity.wsu.edu. *Application contact:* Graduate School Admissions, 800-GRADWSU, Fax: 509-335-1949, E-mail: gradsch@wsu.edu. Web site: http://www.tricity.wsu.edu/business/.

Washington State University Vancouver, Graduate Programs, Program in Business Administration, Vancouver, WA 98686. Offers MBA. *Faculty:* 14. *Students:* 2 full-time (0 women), 30 part-time (12 women); includes 5 minority (4 Asian, non-Hispanic/Latino; 1 Hispanic/Latino). Average age 36. 20 applicants, 30% accepted, 4 enrolled. In 2011, 20 master's awarded. *Degree requirements:* For master's, comprehensive exam (for some programs), thesis (for some programs), final presentation, portfolio. *Entrance requirements:* For master's, GMAT, minimum GPA of 3.0, 3 letters of recommendation, resume. Additional exam requirements/recommendations for international students: Required—TOEFL. *Application deadline:* For fall admission, 1/10 priority date for domestic students; for spring admission, 7/1 priority date for domestic students, 7/1 for international students. Application fee: $75. *Financial support:* In 2011–12, research assistantships (averaging $14,634 per year), teaching assistantships with full tuition reimbursements (averaging $13,383 per year) were awarded. Financial award application deadline: 2/15. *Faculty research:* Liquidity, cost of capital and firm value, business ethics, corporate governance, finance and nonfinancial performance measurement, negotiations, project management. *Unit head:* Dr. Jane Cote, Academic Director, 360-546-9756, E-mail: cotej@vancouver.wsu.edu. *Application contact:* Graduate School Admissions, 800-GRADWSU, Fax: 509-335-1949, E-mail: gradsch@wsu.edu. Web site: http://www.vancouver.wsu.edu/programs/bus/mba3.html.

Washington University in St. Louis, Olin Business School, St. Louis, MO 63130-4899. Offers EMBA, M Acc, MBA, MS, PhD, JD/MBA, M Arch/MBA, M Eng/MBA, MBA/MA, MBA/MSW. *Accreditation:* AACSB. *Faculty:* 88 full-time (29 women), 47 part-time/adjunct (10 women). *Students:* 490 full-time (169 women), 531 part-time (133 women); includes 137 minority (25 Black or African American, non-Hispanic/Latino; 1 American Indian or Alaska Native, non-Hispanic/Latino; 77 Asian, non-Hispanic/Latino; 8 Hispanic/Latino; 1 Native Hawaiian or other Pacific Islander, non-Hispanic/Latino; 25 Two or more races, non-Hispanic/Latino), 316 international. *Entrance requirements:* Additional exam requirements/recommendations for international students: Required—TOEFL. Electronic applications accepted. *Unit head:* Dr. Mahendra Gupta, Dean, 314-935-6344. *Application contact:* Information Contact, 314-935-6880, Fax: 314-935-4887, E-mail: graduateschool@artsci.wustl.edu. Web site: http://www.olin.wustl.edu/.

Wayland Baptist University, Graduate Programs, Programs in Business Administration/Management, Plainview, TX 79072-6998. Offers general business (MBA); health care administration (MBA); human resource management (MBA); international management (MBA); management (MA, MBA), including health care administration (MA), human resource management (MA), organization management (MA); management information systems (MBA). Part-time and evening/weekend programs available. Postbaccalaureate distance learning degree programs offered (no on-campus study). *Degree requirements:* For master's, capstone course. *Entrance requirements:* For master's, GMAT, GRE or MAT. Additional exam requirements/recommendations for international students: Required—TOEFL (minimum score 500 paper-based; 173 computer-based; 61 iBT). Electronic applications accepted.

Waynesburg University, Graduate and Professional Studies, Waynesburg, PA 15370-1222. Offers business (MBA), including finance, health systems, human resources, leadership, market development; counseling (MA), including addictions counseling, clinical mental health; education (MAT); nursing (MSN), including administration, education, informatics, palliative care; nursing practice (DNP); special education (M Ed); technology (M Ed); MSN/MBA. *Accreditation:* AACN. Part-time and evening/weekend programs available. *Degree requirements:* For doctorate, thesis/dissertation. *Entrance requirements:* Additional exam requirements/recommendations for international students: Required—TOEFL. Electronic applications accepted.

Wayne State College, School of Business and Technology, Wayne, NE 68787. Offers MBA. Part-time and evening/weekend programs available. Postbaccalaureate distance learning degree programs offered (minimal on-campus study). *Entrance requirements:* For master's, GMAT, minimum overall GPA of 3.0. Additional exam requirements/recommendations for international students: Required—TOEFL (minimum score 550 paper-based; 213 computer-based).

Wayne State University, School of Business Administration, Detroit, MI 48202. Offers accounting (MBA, MS); industrial relations (MBA); taxation (MST); JD/MBA. *Accreditation:* AACSB. Part-time and evening/weekend programs available. Postbaccalaureate distance learning degree programs offered. *Students:* 182 full-time (68 women), 731 part-time (305 women); includes 256 minority (144 Black or African American, non-Hispanic/Latino; 2 American Indian or Alaska Native, non-Hispanic/Latino; 85 Asian, non-Hispanic/Latino; 12 Hispanic/Latino; 13 Two or more races, non-Hispanic/Latino), 76 international. Average age 30. 675 applicants, 39% accepted, 181 enrolled. In 2011, 325 master's awarded. *Degree requirements:* For doctorate, thesis/dissertation. *Entrance requirements:* For master's, GMAT; for doctorate, GMAT (minimum score of 600), minimum undergraduate GPA 3.0, 3.5 upper-division or graduate; three letters of recommendation; brief essay. Additional exam requirements/recommendations for international students: Required—TOEFL (minimum score 550 paper-based; 213 computer-based); Recommended—TWE (minimum score 6). *Application deadline:* For fall admission, 6/1 priority date for domestic students, 5/1 for international students; for winter admission, 10/1 for domestic students, 9/1 for international students; for spring admission, 2/1 for domestic students, 1/1 for international students. Applications are processed on a rolling basis. Application fee: $50. Electronic applications accepted. *Expenses:* Tuition, state resident: part-time $512.85 per credit. Tuition, nonresident: part-time $1132.65 per credit. *Required fees:* $26.60 per credit. $199.65 per semester. Tuition and fees vary according to course load and program. *Financial support:* In 2011–12, 116 students received support, including 2 fellowships with tuition reimbursements available (averaging $18,000 per year), 2 teaching assistantships with tuition reimbursements available (averaging $1,800 per year); scholarships/grants, health care benefits, and unspecified assistantships also available. Support available to part-time students. Financial award applicants required to submit FAFSA. *Faculty research:* Corporate financial valuation, strategic advertising, information technology effectiveness, financial accounting and taxation, organizational performance and effectiveness. *Total annual research expenditures:* $257,637. *Unit head:* Dr. Margaret Williams, Interim Dean, 313-577-4501, Fax: 313-577-4557, E-mail: margaret.l.williams@wayne.edu. *Application contact:* Linda Zaddach, Assistant Dean, 313-577-4510, E-mail: l.s.zaddach@wayne.edu. Web site: http://business.wayne.edu/.

See Display on next page and Close-Up on page 261.

Webber International University, Graduate School of Business, Babson Park, FL 33827-0096. Offers accounting (MBA); management (MBA); security management (MBA); sports management (MBA). Part-time and evening/weekend programs available. *Degree requirements:* For master's, thesis or alternative. *Entrance requirements:* For master's, previous course work in financial and managerial accounting. Additional exam requirements/recommendations for international students: Required—TOEFL. *Faculty research:* Finance strategy, market research, investments, intranet.

Weber State University, John B. Goddard School of Business and Economics, Program in Business Administration, Ogden, UT 84408-1001. Offers MBA. *Accreditation:* AACSB. Part-time and evening/weekend programs available. *Entrance requirements:* For master's, GMAT, resume, letters of recommendation. Additional exam requirements/recommendations for international students: Required—TOEFL (minimum score 550 paper-based; 213 computer-based). Electronic applications accepted.

Business Administration and Management—General

Webster University, George Herbert Walker School of Business and Technology, Department of Business, St. Louis, MO 63119-3194. Offers business (MA); business and organizational security management (MBA); computer resources and information management (MBA); environmental management (MBA); finance (MA, MBA); health services management (MBA); human resources development (MBA); human resources management (MBA); international business (MA, MBA); management and leadership (MBA); marketing (MBA); procurement and acquisitions management (MBA); telecommunications management (MBA). *Accreditation:* ACBSP. Part-time and evening/weekend programs available. Postbaccalaureate distance learning degree programs offered (no on-campus study). *Degree requirements:* For master's, comprehensive exam (for some programs), thesis (for some programs). *Entrance requirements:* Additional exam requirements/recommendations for international students: Required—TOEFL. *Expenses: Tuition:* Full-time $10,890; part-time $605 per credit hour. Tuition and fees vary according to campus/location and program.

Webster University, George Herbert Walker School of Business and Technology, Department of Management, St. Louis, MO 63119-3194. Offers business and organizational security management (MA); computer resources and information management (MA); environmental management (MS); government contracting (Certificate); health care management (MA); health services management (MA); human resources development (MA); human resources management (MA); management (DM); management and leadership (MA); marketing (MA); nonprofit management (Certificate); procurement and acquisitions management (MA); public administration (MA); quality management (MA); space systems operations management (MS); telecommunications management (MA). *Accreditation:* ACBSP. Part-time and evening/weekend programs available. Postbaccalaureate distance learning degree programs offered (no on-campus study). *Degree requirements:* For master's, thesis (for some programs); for doctorate, thesis/dissertation, written exam. *Entrance requirements:* For doctorate, GMAT, 3 years of work experience, MBA. Additional exam requirements/recommendations for international students: Required—TOEFL. *Expenses: Tuition:* Full-time $10,890; part-time $605 per credit hour. Tuition and fees vary according to campus/location and program.

Wesleyan College, Department of Business and Economics, EMBA Program, Macon, GA 31210-4462. Offers EMBA. Evening/weekend programs available. *Entrance requirements:* For master's, GMAT, LSAT, GRE or MAT, 5 years of work experience, 5 years of management experience. Additional exam requirements/recommendations for international students: Required—TOEFL (minimum score 550 paper-based). Electronic applications accepted.

Wesley College, Business Program, Dover, DE 19901-3875. Offers environmental management (MBA); executive leadership (MBA); management (MBA). Executive leadership concentration also offered at New Castle, DE location. Part-time and evening/weekend programs available. *Entrance requirements:* For master's, GMAT or GRE, minimum undergraduate GPA of 2.75.

West Chester University of Pennsylvania, College of Business and Public Affairs, The School of Business, West Chester, PA 19383. Offers business (Certificate); business administration: technology/electronic (MBA); economics and finance (MBA); general business (MBA). *Accreditation:* AACSB. Part-time and evening/weekend programs available. Postbaccalaureate distance learning degree programs offered (minimal on-campus study). *Faculty:* 8 part-time/adjunct (4 women). *Students:* 2 full-time (both women), 78 part-time (23 women); includes 12 minority (5 Black or African American, non-Hispanic/Latino; 7 Asian, non-Hispanic/Latino), 3 international. Average age 34. 66 applicants, 47% accepted, 19 enrolled. In 2011, 9 master's, 1 other advanced degree awarded. *Degree requirements:* For master's, minimum GPA of 3.0. *Entrance requirements:* For master's, GMAT, statement of professional goals, resume, two letters of recommendation, transcripts. Additional exam requirements/recommendations for international students: Required—TOEFL (minimum score 550 paper-based; 213 computer-based; 80 iBT). *Application deadline:* For fall admission, 4/15 priority date for domestic students, 3/15 for international students; for spring admission, 10/15 priority date for domestic students, 9/1 for international students. Applications are processed on a rolling basis. Application fee: $45. Electronic applications accepted. *Expenses:* Tuition, state resident: full-time $7488; part-time $416 per credit. Tuition, nonresident: full-time $11,232; part-time $624 per credit. *Required fees:* $1784.64; $67.59 per credit. Tuition and fees vary according to program. *Financial support:* Unspecified assistantships available. Support available to part-time students. Financial award application deadline: 2/15; financial award applicants required to submit FAFSA. *Unit head:* Dr. Paul Christ, MBA Director and Graduate Coordinator, 610-425-5000, E-mail: mba@wcupa.edu. *Application contact:* Office of Graduate Studies, 610-436-2943, Fax: 610-436-2763, E-mail: gradstudy@wcupa.edu. Web site: http://www.wcumba.org/.

Western Carolina University, Graduate School, College of Business, Program in Business Administration, Cullowhee, NC 28723. Offers MBA. *Accreditation:* AACSB. Part-time and evening/weekend programs available. *Students:* 33 full-time (12 women), 65 part-time (26 women); includes 8 minority (1 Black or African American, non-Hispanic/Latino; 1 American Indian or Alaska Native, non-Hispanic/Latino; 1 Asian, non-Hispanic/Latino; 4 Hispanic/Latino; 1 Two or more races, non-Hispanic/Latino), 4 international. Average age 31. 50 applicants, 78% accepted, 30 enrolled. In 2011, 36 master's awarded. *Entrance requirements:* For master's, GMAT, appropriate undergraduate degree, 3 letters of recommendation. Additional exam requirements/recommendations for international students: Required—TOEFL (minimum score 550 paper-based; 270 computer-based; 79 iBT). *Application deadline:* For fall admission, 5/1 priority date for domestic students; for spring admission, 9/1 priority date for domestic students. Applications are processed on a rolling basis. Application fee: $50. *Expenses:* Tuition, state resident: full-time $3348. Tuition, nonresident: full-time $12,933. *Required fees:* $3155. *Financial support:* Fellowships, research assistantships with full and partial tuition reimbursements, teaching assistantships with full and partial tuition reimbursements, career-related internships or fieldwork, institutionally sponsored loans, traineeships, and unspecified assistantships available. Financial award application deadline: 3/31; financial award applicants required to submit FAFSA. *Faculty research:* Marketing strategy, biotechnology, executive education, business statistics, supply chain management, innovation. *Unit head:* A.J. Grube, Department Head, 828-227-3028, Fax: 828-227-7414, E-mail: agrube@email.wcu.edu. *Application contact:* Admissions Specialist for Business Administration, 828-227-7398, Fax: 828-227-7480, E-mail: gradsch@email.wcu.edu. Web site: http://www.wcu.edu/cob/mba/index.htm.

Western Connecticut State University, Division of Graduate Studies, Ancell School of Business, Program in Business Administration, Danbury, CT 06810-6885. Offers accounting (MBA); business administration (MBA). Part-time programs available. *Faculty:* 6 full-time (3 women), 1 part-time/adjunct (0 women). *Students:* 7 full-time (1 woman), 45 part-time (18 women); includes 10 minority (1 Black or African American, non-Hispanic/Latino; 4 Asian, non-Hispanic/Latino; 5 Hispanic/Latino). Average age 33. In 2011, 25 degrees awarded. *Degree requirements:* For master's, comprehensive exam, completion of program within 8 years. *Entrance requirements:* For master's, GMAT. Additional exam requirements/recommendations for international students: Recommended—TOEFL (minimum score 550 paper-based; 213 computer-based; 79 iBT), IELTS (minimum score 6). *Application deadline:* For fall admission, 8/5 priority date for domestic students; for spring admission, 1/5 priority date for domestic students. Applications are processed on a rolling basis. Application fee: $50. Tuition and fees vary according to course level, course load, degree level and program. *Financial support:* Application deadline: 5/1; applicants required to submit FAFSA. *Faculty research:* Global strategic marketing planning, project management and team coordination; email, discussion boards that act as blogs and videoconferencing. *Unit head:* Dr. Fred Tesch, MBA Coordinator, 203-837-8654, Fax: 203-837-8527. *Application contact:* Chris Shankle, Associate Director of Graduate Studies, 203-837-9005, Fax: 203-837-8326, E-mail: shanklec@wcsu.edu.

Western Governors University, College of Business, Salt Lake City, UT 84107. Offers information technology management (MBA); management and strategy (MBA); strategic leadership (MBA). Evening/weekend programs available. *Students:* 1,665 full-time (684 women); includes 430 minority (202 Black or African American, non-Hispanic/Latino; 18 American Indian or Alaska Native, non-Hispanic/Latino; 72 Asian, non-Hispanic/Latino; 97 Hispanic/Latino; 2 Native Hawaiian or other Pacific Islander, non-Hispanic/Latino; 39 Two or more races, non-Hispanic/Latino), 31 international. Average age 38. In 2011, 388 master's awarded. *Degree requirements:* For master's, capstone project. *Entrance requirements:* For master's, Readiness Assessment, commitment counseling discussion, transcript submissions, completion of orientation. Additional exam requirements/recommendations for international students: Required—TOEFL (minimum score 450 paper-based; 80 iBT). *Application deadline:* Applications are processed on a rolling basis. Application fee: $65. Electronic applications accepted. *Expenses: Tuition:* Full-time $6500. Full-time tuition and fees vary according to program. *Financial support:* Scholarships/grants and tuition waivers (partial) available. Financial award applicants required to submit FAFSA. *Application contact:* Enrollment Department, 866-225-5948, Fax: 801-274-3306, E-mail: info@wgu.edu.

Western Illinois University, School of Graduate Studies, College of Business and Technology, Program in Business Administration, Macomb, IL 61455-1390. Offers MBA. *Accreditation:* AACSB. Part-time programs available. *Students:* 50 full-time (18 women), 54 part-time (23 women); includes 4 minority (2 Black or African American, non-Hispanic/Latino; 1 Hispanic/Latino; 1 Two or more races, non-Hispanic/Latino), 12 international. Average age 30. 46 applicants, 57% accepted. In 2011, 48 master's awarded. *Degree requirements:* For master's, thesis or alternative. *Entrance requirements:* For master's, GMAT. Additional exam requirements/recommendations for international students: Required—TOEFL (minimum score 550 paper-based; 213 computer-based; 80 iBT). *Application deadline:* Applications are processed on a rolling basis. Application fee: $30. Electronic applications accepted. *Expenses:* Tuition, state resident: part-time $281.16 per credit hour. Tuition, nonresident: part-time $562.32 per credit hour. Part-time tuition and fees vary according to campus/location and reciprocity agreements. *Financial support:* In 2011–12, 29 students received support, including 29 research assistantships with full tuition reimbursements available (averaging $7,360 per year). Financial award applicants required to submit FAFSA. *Unit head:* Dr. John Drea, Associate Dean, 309-298-2442. *Application contact:* Dr. Nancy Parsons, Interim Associate Provost and Director of Graduate Studies, 309-298-1806, Fax: 309-298-2345, E-mail: grad-office@wiu.edu. Web site: http://wiu.edu/cbt.

Western International University, Graduate Programs in Business, Master of Business Administration Program, Phoenix, AZ 85021-2718. Offers MBA. Part-time and evening/weekend programs available. Postbaccalaureate distance learning degree programs offered (no on-campus study). *Entrance requirements:* For master's, minimum GPA of 2.75. Additional exam requirements/recommendations for international students: Required—TOEFL (minimum score 550 paper-based; 213 computer-based; 79 iBT), TWE (minimum score 5), or IELTS (minimum score 6.5). Electronic applications accepted.

Western International University, Graduate Programs in Business, Master of Business Administration Program in Management, Phoenix, AZ 85021-2718. Offers MBA. Part-time and evening/weekend programs available. Postbaccalaureate distance learning degree programs offered (no on-campus study). *Entrance requirements:* For master's, minimum GPA of 2.75. Additional exam requirements/recommendations for international students: Required—TOEFL (minimum score 550 paper-based; 213 computer-based; 79 iBT), TWE (minimum score 5), or IELTS (minimum score 6.5). Electronic applications accepted.

Western Kentucky University, Graduate Studies, Gordon Ford College of Business, MBA Program, Bowling Green, KY 42101. Offers MBA. *Accreditation:* AACSB. Part-time and evening/weekend programs available. *Degree requirements:* For master's, comprehensive exam, thesis optional. *Entrance requirements:* For master's, GMAT, minimum GPA of 2.5. Additional exam requirements/recommendations for international students: Required—TOEFL (minimum score 555 paper-based; 213 computer-based; 79 iBT). *Faculty research:* Business and international education, web page development, management training, international studies, globalization.

Western Michigan University, Graduate College, Haworth College of Business, Department of Finance and Commercial Law, Kalamazoo, MI 49008. Offers finance (MBA). *Accreditation:* AACSB. *Entrance requirements:* For master's, GMAT.

Western New England University, College of Business, Program in Business Administration (General), Springfield, MA 01119. Offers general business (MBA); sport management (MBA). *Accreditation:* AACSB. Part-time and evening/weekend programs available. *Students:* 111 part-time (51 women); includes 12 minority (6 Black or African American, non-Hispanic/Latino; 1 Asian, non-Hispanic/Latino; 3 Hispanic/Latino; 2 Two or more races, non-Hispanic/Latino), 1 international. *Entrance requirements:* For master's, GMAT, 2 letters of reference, resume. *Application deadline:* Applications are processed on a rolling basis. Application fee: $30. *Financial support:* Available to part-time students. Applicants required to submit FAFSA. *Unit head:* Dr. Julie Siciliano, Jr., Dean, 413-782-1231. *Application contact:* Matt Fox, Director of Recruiting and Marketing for Adult Learners, 413-782-1249, Fax: 413-782-1779, E-mail: learn@wne.edu. Web site: http://www1.wne.edu/business/index.cfm?selection-doc.1279.

Western New Mexico University, Graduate Division, Department of Business Administration and Criminal Justice, Silver City, NM 88062-0680. Offers business administration (MBA). *Accreditation:* ACBSP. Part-time and evening/weekend programs available. *Entrance requirements:* For master's, GMAT. Additional exam requirements/recommendations for international students: Required—TOEFL (minimum score 550 paper-based; 213 computer-based). Electronic applications accepted.

Western Washington University, Graduate School, College of Business and Economics, Bellingham, WA 98225-5996. Offers MBA, MP Acc. *Accreditation:* AACSB. Part-time and evening/weekend programs available. *Degree requirements:* For master's, comprehensive exam. *Entrance requirements:* For master's, GMAT, minimum GPA of 3.0 in last 60 semester hours or last 90 quarter hours. Additional exam requirements/recommendations for international students: Required—TOEFL (minimum score 567 paper-based; 227 computer-based). Electronic applications accepted. *Faculty research:* Enterprise strategy/corporate social performance, sustainability/environmental management/nonprofit marketing, managerial/environmental accounting, organizational applications of collaborative technology, environmental and resource economics.

Westminster College, The Bill and Vieve Gore School of Business, Salt Lake City, UT 84105-3697. Offers accountancy (M Acc); business administration (MBA, Certificate); technology management (MBATM). *Accreditation:* ACBSP. Part-time and evening/weekend programs available. Postbaccalaureate distance learning degree programs offered (minimal on-campus study). *Faculty:* 24 full-time (7 women), 19 part-time/adjunct (3 women). *Students:* 153 full-time (45 women), 241 part-time (79 women); includes 27 minority (1 Black or African American, non-Hispanic/Latino; 16 Asian, non-Hispanic/Latino; 10 Hispanic/Latino), 1 international. Average age 33. 502 applicants, 38% accepted, 111 enrolled. In 2011, 182 master's, 37 other advanced degrees awarded. *Degree requirements:* For master's, international trip, minimum grade of C in all classes. *Entrance requirements:* For master's, GMAT, 2 professional recommendations, employer letter of support, personal resume, essay questions, official transcripts. Additional exam requirements/recommendations for international students: Required—TOEFL (minimum score 600 paper-based; 250 computer-based; 100 iBT), IELTS (minimum score 7). *Application deadline:* Applications are processed on a rolling basis. Application fee: $50. Electronic applications accepted. *Expenses:* Contact institution. *Financial support:* In 2011–12, 22 students received support. Career-related internships or fieldwork and tuition reimbursement, tuition remission available. Support available to part-time students. Financial award applicants required to submit FAFSA. *Faculty research:* Innovation and entrepreneurship, business strategy and change, financial analysis and capital budgeting, leadership development, knowledge management. *Unit head:* Dr. Jin Wang, Dean, Gore School of Business, 801-832-2600, Fax: 801-832-3106, E-mail: jwang@westminstercollege.edu. *Application contact:* Dr. Gary Daynes, Vice President for Strategic Outreach and Enrollment, 801-832-2200, Fax: 801-832-3101, E-mail: admission@westminstercollege.edu. Web site: http://www.westminstercollege.edu/mba/.

West Texas A&M University, College of Business, Department of Management, Marketing, and General Business, Canyon, TX 79016-0001. Offers business administration (MBA). Part-time and evening/weekend programs available. Postbaccalaureate distance learning degree programs offered (minimal on-campus study). *Entrance requirements:* For master's, GMAT. Additional exam requirements/recommendations for international students: Required—TOEFL (minimum score 550 paper-based). Electronic applications accepted. *Faculty research:* Human resources, international business, southern Asian markets, global strategies, international trade composition.

West Virginia University, College of Business and Economics, Program in Business Administration, Morgantown, WV 26506. Offers MBA, JD/MBA. *Accreditation:* AACSB. Part-time and evening/weekend programs available. *Entrance requirements:* For master's, GMAT. Additional exam requirements/recommendations for international students: Required—TOEFL. Electronic applications accepted. *Faculty research:* Financial management, managerial accounting, marketing, planning, corporate finance.

West Virginia Wesleyan College, MBA Program, Buckhannon, WV 26201. Offers MBA. Part-time and evening/weekend programs available. *Degree requirements:* For master's, exit evaluation. *Entrance requirements:* For master's, GMAT. Additional exam requirements/recommendations for international students: Required—TOEFL.

Wheeling Jesuit University, Department of Business, Wheeling, WV 26003-6295. Offers accounting (MS); business administration (MBA). *Accreditation:* ACBSP. Part-time and evening/weekend programs available. *Faculty:* 6 full-time (1 woman), 4 part-time/adjunct (1 woman). *Students:* 23 full-time (5 women), 37 part-time (20 women); includes 5 minority (1 Black or African American, non-Hispanic/Latino; 1 Asian, non-Hispanic/Latino; 3 Hispanic/Latino), 1 international. Average age 30. 39 applicants, 97% accepted, 17 enrolled. In 2011, 19 master's awarded. *Entrance requirements:* For master's, GMAT, minimum undergraduate GPA of 2.8. Additional exam requirements/recommendations for international students: Required—TOEFL (minimum score 600 paper-based; 250 computer-based; 100 iBT). *Application deadline:* For fall admission, 8/1 priority date for domestic students, 8/1 for international students; for spring admission, 12/15 priority date for domestic students, 12/1 for international students. Applications are processed on a rolling basis. Application fee: $25. Electronic applications accepted. *Expenses: Tuition:* Full-time $9720; part-time $540 per credit hour. *Required fees:* $250. *Financial support:* In 2011–12, 13 students received support. Career-related internships or fieldwork and unspecified assistantships available. Financial award application deadline: 8/1; financial award applicants required to submit FAFSA. *Faculty research:* Forensic economics, philosophic economics, consumer behavior, international business, economic development. *Unit head:* Dr. Edward W. Younkins, Director of Graduate Business Programs, 304-243-2255, Fax: 304-243-8703, E-mail: younkins@wju.edu. *Application contact:* Melissa Rataiczak, Associate Director of Enrollment for Leadership Programs, 304-243-2236, Fax: 304-243-2397, E-mail: mrataiczak@wju.edu. Web site: http://www.wju.edu/academics/bus/gradprog.asp.

WHU - Otto Beisheim School of Management, Graduate Programs, Vallendar, Germany. Offers EMBA, MBA, MS. EMBA offered jointly with Kellogg School of Management.

Wichita State University, Graduate School, W. Frank Barton School of Business, Department of Business, Wichita, KS 67260. Offers EMBA, MBA, MSN/MBA. *Accreditation:* AACSB. Part-time and evening/weekend programs available. *Expenses:* Tuition, state resident: full-time $4746; part-time $263.65 per credit. Tuition, nonresident: full-time $11,669; part-time $648.30 per credit. *Unit head:* Angela Jones, Director, 316-978-3230, E-mail: angela.jones@wichita.edu. *Application contact:* Carrie C. Henderson, Admissions Coordinator, 316-978-3095, Fax: 316-978-3253, E-mail: carrie.henderson@wichita.edu. Web site: http://www.wichita.edu/.

Widener University, School of Business Administration, Chester, PA 19013-5792. Offers MBA, MHA, MHR, MS, JD/MBA, MD/MBA, MD/MHA, ME/MBA, Psy D/MBA, Psy D/MHA, Psy D/MHR. *Accreditation:* AACSB. Part-time and evening/weekend programs available. *Entrance requirements:* For master's, minimum GPA of 2.5. Electronic applications accepted. *Expenses:* Contact institution. *Faculty research:* Cost containment in health care, human resource management, productivity, globalization.

Wilfrid Laurier University, Faculty of Graduate and Postdoctoral Studies, School of Business and Economics, Business Administration Program, Waterloo, ON N2L 3C5, Canada. Offers co-op (MBA); full-time (MBA); part-time (MBA). *Accreditation:* AACSB. Part-time and evening/weekend programs available. *Degree requirements:* For master's, thesis. *Entrance requirements:* For master's, GMAT, minimum 2 years of business experience (for 12-month or part-time MBA formats), minimum B average in 4-year BA program. Additional exam requirements/recommendations for international students: Required—TOEFL (minimum score 89 iBT). Electronic applications accepted.

Wilfrid Laurier University, Faculty of Graduate and Postdoctoral Studies, School of Business and Economics, Department of Business, Waterloo, ON N2L 3C5, Canada. Offers accounting (PhD); finance (M Fin); financial economics (PhD); marketing (PhD); operations and supply chain management (PhD); organizational behavior and human resource management (M Sc); organizational behaviour and human resource management (PhD); supply chain management (M Sc); technology management (EMTM). Part-time and evening/weekend programs available. *Degree requirements:* For master's, thesis optional; for doctorate, comprehensive exam, thesis/dissertation. *Entrance requirements:* For master's, GMAT, 4-year honors degree with minimum B+ average; for doctorate, GMAT, master's degree, minimum B+ average. Additional exam requirements/recommendations for international students: Required—TOEFL (minimum score 89 iBT). Electronic applications accepted. *Faculty research:* Financial economics, management and organizational behavior, operations and supply chain management.

Wilkes University, College of Graduate and Professional Studies, Jay S. Sidhu School of Business and Leadership, Wilkes-Barre, PA 18766-0002. Offers accounting (MBA); entrepreneurship (MBA); finance (MBA); health care administration (MBA); human resource management (MBA); international business (MBA); marketing (MBA); operations management (MBA); organizational leadership and development (MBA). *Accreditation:* ACBSP. Part-time and evening/weekend programs available. *Students:* 48 full-time (20 women), 134 part-time (62 women); includes 12 minority (2 Black or African American, non-Hispanic/Latino; 5 Asian, non-Hispanic/Latino; 2 Hispanic/Latino; 3 Two or more races, non-Hispanic/Latino), 9 international. Average age 30. In 2011, 69 master's awarded. *Entrance requirements:* For master's, GMAT. Additional exam requirements/recommendations for international students: Required—TOEFL (minimum score 550 paper-based; 213 computer-based; 79 iBT). *Application deadline:* Applications are processed on a rolling basis. Application fee: $45 ($65 for international students). Electronic applications accepted. *Expenses:* Contact institution. *Financial support:* Federal Work-Study and unspecified assistantships available. Financial award application deadline: 3/1; financial award applicants required to submit FAFSA. *Unit head:* Dr. Jeffrey Alves, Dean, 570-408-4702, Fax: 570-408-7846, E-mail: jeffrey.alves@wilkes.edu. *Application contact:* Erin Sutzko, Director of Extended Learning, 570-408-4253, Fax: 570-408-7846, E-mail: erin.sutzko@wilkes.edu. Web site: http://www.wilkes.edu/pages/457.asp.

Willamette University, George H. Atkinson Graduate School of Management, Salem, OR 97301-3931. Offers MBA, JD/MBA. *Accreditation:* AACSB; NASPAA. Part-time and evening/weekend programs available. *Faculty:* 19 full-time (5 women), 25 part-time/adjunct (7 women). *Students:* 203 full-time (91 women), 110 part-time (54 women); includes 43 minority (10 Black or African American, non-Hispanic/Latino; 3 American Indian or Alaska Native, non-Hispanic/Latino; 19 Asian, non-Hispanic/Latino; 7 Hispanic/Latino; 3 Native Hawaiian or other Pacific Islander, non-Hispanic/Latino; 1 Two or more races, non-Hispanic/Latino), 66 international. Average age 28. 278 applicants, 86% accepted, 137 enrolled. In 2011, 146 master's awarded. *Degree requirements:* For master's, minimum cumulative GPA of 3.0. *Entrance requirements:* For master's, GMAT or GRE, essays, transcripts, references, resume, interview. Additional exam requirements/recommendations for international students: Required—TOEFL (minimum score 570 paper-based; 230 computer-based; 88 iBT), IELTS (minimum score 6.5). *Application deadline:* For fall admission, 1/10 priority date for domestic students, 1/10 for international students; for winter admission, 3/1 priority date for domestic students, 3/1 for international students; for spring admission, 5/1 priority date for domestic students, 5/1 for international students. Applications are processed on a rolling basis. Application fee: $100. Electronic applications accepted. Application fee is waived when completed online. *Expenses:* Contact institution. *Financial support:* In 2011–12, 172 students received support, including 12 research assistantships with tuition reimbursements available (averaging $2,000 per year); career-related internships or fieldwork, Federal Work-Study, scholarships/grants, unspecified assistantships, and merit-based scholarships also available. Financial award application deadline: 5/1; financial award applicants required to submit FAFSA. *Faculty research:* Entrepreneurship, organizational behavior, social networks, general management, finance, marketing, public management, human resources, social networks, angel investing, public budgeting, operations. *Unit head:* Dr. Debra J. Ringold, Dean/Professor of Free Enterprise, 503-370-6440, Fax: 503-370-3011, E-mail: dringold@willamette.edu. *Application contact:* Aimee Akimoff, Director of Recruitment, 503-370-6167, Fax: 503-370-3011, E-mail: aakimoff@willamette.edu. Web site: http://www.willamette.edu/mba/.

William Carey University, School of Business, Hattiesburg, MS 39401-5499. Offers MBA. Part-time programs available. *Entrance requirements:* For master's, GMAT. Additional exam requirements/recommendations for international students: Required—TOEFL (minimum score 500 paper-based; 213 computer-based).

William Paterson University of New Jersey, Christos M. Cotsakos College of Business, Wayne, NJ 07470-8420. Offers MBA. *Accreditation:* AACSB. Part-time and evening/weekend programs available. *Entrance requirements:* For master's, GMAT, minimum AACSB index of 1000. Electronic applications accepted. *Faculty research:* Appropriate marketing variables for international food retail chains, racial attitudes among corporate managers in northern New Jersey.

Wilmington University, College of Business, New Castle, DE 19720-6491. Offers accounting (MBA, MS); business administration (MBA, DBA); environmental stewardship (MBA); finance (MBA); health care administration (MBA, MSM); homeland security (MBA, MSM); human resource management (MSM); management information systems (MBA, MSN); marketing (MSM); marketing management (MBA); military leadership (MSM); organizational leadership (MBA, MSM); public administration (MSM). Part-time and evening/weekend programs available. *Faculty:* 4 full-time (0 women). *Students:* 266 full-time (121 women), 700 part-time (505 women). Average age 34. *Entrance requirements:* Additional exam requirements/recommendations for international students: Required—TOEFL (minimum score 500 paper-based; 173 computer-based). *Application deadline:* Applications are processed on a rolling basis. Application fee: $35. Electronic applications accepted. *Expenses: Tuition:* Part-time $534 per credit hour. *Required fees:* $25 per term. *Financial support:* Applicants required to submit FAFSA. *Unit head:* Dr. Donald W. Durandetta, Dean, 302-356-6780, E-mail: donald.w.durandetta@wilmu.edu. *Application contact:* Chris Ferguson, Director of Admissions, 302-356-4636 Ext. 256, Fax: 302-328-5164, E-mail: inquire@wilmcoll.edu. Web site: http://www.wilmu.edu/business/.

Wingate University, Byrum School of Business, Wingate, NC 28174-0159. Offers MAC, MBA. *Accreditation:* ACBSP. Part-time and evening/weekend programs available. *Faculty:* 8 full-time (0 women), 4 part-time/adjunct (0 women). *Students:* 13 full-time (5 women), 100 part-time (48 women); includes 7 minority (5 Black or African American, non-Hispanic/Latino; 1 Asian, non-Hispanic/Latino; 1 Hispanic/Latino), 3 international. Average age 29. In 2011, 20 master's awarded. *Entrance requirements:* For master's, GMAT, work experience, 2 letters of recommendation. *Application deadline:* For fall admission, 8/15 priority date for domestic students; for spring admission, 12/15 priority date for domestic students. Applications are processed on a rolling basis. Application fee: $50. Electronic applications accepted. *Expenses:* Contact institution. *Financial support:* In 2011–12, 9 students received support. Federal Work-Study and scholarships/grants available. Support available to part-time students. Financial award application deadline: 8/1; financial award applicants required to submit FAFSA. *Faculty research:* Stochastic processes, business ethics, regional economic development, municipal finance, consumer behavior. *Unit head:* Joseph M. Graham, Dean, 704-233-8148, Fax: 704-233-8146, E-mail: graham@wingate.edu. *Application contact:* Mary May, MBA Coordinator, 704-233-8148, Fax: 704-233-8146. Web site: http://www.wingate.edu/academics/school-of-business.

Winston-Salem State University, Program in Business Administration, Winston-Salem, NC 27110-0003. Offers MBA. *Accreditation:* AACSB. Part-time and evening/weekend programs available. Postbaccalaureate distance learning degree programs offered (minimal on-campus study). *Entrance requirements:* For master's, GMAT, resume, 3 letters of recommendation. Electronic applications accepted. *Faculty research:* Innovative entrepreneurship and customer service, econometrics and operations research.

Winthrop University, College of Business Administration, Program in Business Administration, Rock Hill, SC 29733. Offers MBA. *Accreditation:* AACSB. *Entrance requirements:* For master's, GMAT.

Woodbury University, School of Business and Management, Burbank, CA 91504-1099. Offers business administration (MBA); organizational leadership (MA). *Accreditation:* ACBSP. Part-time and evening/weekend programs available. *Faculty:* 9 full-time (4 women), 8 part-time/adjunct (0 women). *Students:* 105 full-time (63 women), 30 part-time (16 women); includes 46 minority (10 Black or African American, non-Hispanic/Latino; 1 American Indian or Alaska Native, non-Hispanic/Latino; 10 Asian, non-Hispanic/Latino; 22 Hispanic/Latino; 3 Native Hawaiian or other Pacific Islander, non-Hispanic/Latino), 27 international. Average age 30. 66 applicants, 33% accepted, 17 enrolled. In 2011, 101 master's awarded. *Entrance requirements:* For master's, GMAT, transcripts, resume. Additional exam requirements/recommendations for international students: Required—TOEFL (minimum score 550 paper-based; 220 computer-based; 83 iBT), IELTS (minimum score 6.5). *Application deadline:* For fall admission, 8/1 priority date for domestic students; for spring admission, 12/1 for domestic and international students. Applications are processed on a rolling basis. Application fee: $35 ($50 for international students). *Expenses: Tuition:* Full-time $24,921; part-time $923 per unit. *Required fees:* $8 per unit. $50 per term. One-time fee: $110. Tuition and fees vary according to program. *Financial support:* In 2011–12, 14 students received support. Scholarships/grants available. *Faculty research:* Total quality management, leadership. *Unit head:* Dr. Andre Van Niekerk, Dean, 818-767-0888 Ext. 264, Fax: 818-767-0032. *Application contact:* Ani Khukoyan, Assistant Director, Graduate Admissions, 818-767-0888 Ext. 224, Fax: 818-767-7520, E-mail: ani.khukoyan@woodbury.edu. Web site: http://www.woodburyu.edu.

Worcester Polytechnic Institute, Graduate Studies and Research, School of Business, Worcester, MA 01609-2280. Offers information technology (MS), including information security management; management (Graduate Certificate); marketing and technological innovation (MS); operations design and leadership (MS); technology (MBA, MS). *Accreditation:* AACSB. Part-time and evening/weekend programs available. Postbaccalaureate distance learning degree programs offered (minimal on-campus study). *Faculty:* 12 full-time (7 women), 12 part-time/adjunct (2 women). *Students:* 108 full-time (64 women), 206 part-time (55 women); includes 27 minority (4 Black or African American, non-Hispanic/Latino; 12 Asian, non-Hispanic/Latino; 4 Hispanic/Latino; 7 Two or more races, non-Hispanic/Latino), 131 international. 596 applicants, 48% accepted, 131 enrolled. In 2011, 75 master's awarded. *Degree requirements:* For master's, thesis optional. *Entrance requirements:* For master's, GMAT (MBA), GMAT or GRE General Test (MS), resume; for Graduate Certificate, GMAT or GRE General Test, statement of purpose, 3 letters of recommendation. Additional exam requirements/recommendations for international students: Required—TOEFL (minimum score 563 paper-based; 223 computer-based; 84 iBT), IELTS (minimum score 7). *Application deadline:* For fall admission, 6/1 priority date for domestic students, 6/1 for international students; for spring admission, 11/1 priority date for domestic students, 10/1 for international students. Applications are processed on a rolling basis. Application fee: $70. Electronic applications accepted. *Financial support:* Career-related internships or fieldwork, institutionally sponsored loans, scholarships/grants, and unspecified assistantships available. Financial award application deadline: 6/1; financial award applicants required to submit FAFSA. *Faculty research:* Organizational aesthetics, resistance in organizations, dynamics of product innovation, economic approaches to productivity, corporate earnings forecasts and value relevance, ERP implementation, improving Web accessibility, information quality assessment, measuring strategic and transactional IT, website quality, service operations modeling, healthcare operations and performance analysis, entrepreneurship, leadership and change. *Unit head:* Dr. Mark Rice, Dean, 508-831-4665, Fax: 508-831-5218, E-mail: rice@wpi.edu. *Application contact:* Peggy Caisse, Recruiting Operations Coordinator, 508-831-4665, Fax: 508-831-5720, E-mail: mcaisse@wpi.edu. Web site: http://www.biz.wpi.edu/Graduate/.

Worcester State University, Graduate Studies, Program in Management, Worcester, MA 01602-2597. Offers accounting (MS); managerial leadership (MS). Part-time and evening/weekend programs available. *Faculty:* 1 full-time (0 women), 2 part-time/adjunct (1 woman). *Students:* 10 full-time (5 women), 18 part-time (7 women); includes 6 minority (2 Black or African American, non-Hispanic/Latino; 1 Asian, non-Hispanic/Latino; 2 Hispanic/Latino; 1 Two or more races, non-Hispanic/Latino), 3 international. Average age 31. 26 applicants, 62% accepted, 8 enrolled. In 2011, 5 master's awarded. *Degree requirements:* For master's, comprehensive exam (for some programs), thesis optional. *Entrance requirements:* For master's, GMAT. Additional exam requirements/recommendations for international students: Required—TOEFL (minimum score 500 paper-based; 61 iBT). *Application deadline:* For fall admission, 6/15 for domestic and international students; for spring admission, 4/1 for domestic and international students. Applications are processed on a rolling basis. Application fee: $40. Electronic applications accepted. *Expenses:* Tuition, state resident: full-time $2700; part-time $150 per credit. Tuition, nonresident: full-time $2700; part-time $150 per credit. *Required fees:* $2016; $112 per credit. *Financial support:* In 2011–12, 3 students received support, including 3 research assistantships with full tuition reimbursements available (averaging $4,800 per year); career-related internships or fieldwork, scholarships/grants, and unspecified assistantships also available. Financial award application deadline: 3/1; financial award applicants required to submit FAFSA. *Unit head:* Dr. Laurie Dahlin, Coordinator, 508-929-8084, Fax: 508-929-8048, E-mail: ldahlin@worcester.edu. *Application contact:* Sara Grady, Assistant Dean of Continuing Education, 508-929-8787, Fax: 508-929-8100, E-mail: sara.grady@worcester.edu.

Wright State University, School of Graduate Studies, Raj Soin College of Business, Program in Business Administration, Dayton, OH 45435. Offers MBA.

Xavier University, Williams College of Business, Master of Business Administration Program, Cincinnati, OH 45207. Offers business administration (Exec MBA, MBA); business intelligence (MBA); finance (MBA); health industry (MBA); international business (MBA); management information systems (MBA); marketing (MBA); MBA/MHSA; MSN/MBA. *Accreditation:* AACSB. Part-time and evening/weekend programs available. *Faculty:* 45 full-time (17 women), 13 part-time/adjunct (4 women). *Students:* 188 full-time (63 women), 630 part-time (206 women); includes 112 minority (36 Black or African American, non-Hispanic/Latino; 3 American Indian or Alaska Native, non-Hispanic/Latino; 52 Asian, non-Hispanic/Latino; 17 Hispanic/Latino; 1 Native Hawaiian or other Pacific Islander, non-Hispanic/Latino; 3 Two or more races, non-Hispanic/Latino), 45 international. Average age 30. 319 applicants, 63% accepted, 149 enrolled. In 2011, 403 master's awarded. *Degree requirements:* For master's, capstone course. *Entrance requirements:* For master's, GMAT or GRE. Additional exam requirements/recommendations for international students: Required—TOEFL (minimum score 550 paper-based; 213 computer-based; 80 iBT). *Application deadline:* For fall admission, 8/1 priority date for domestic students, 5/1 for international students; for spring admission, 12/1 priority date for domestic students, 9/1 for international students. Applications are processed on a rolling basis. Application fee: $0. Electronic applications accepted. *Expenses:* Contact institution. *Financial support:* In 2011–12, 176 students received support. Scholarships/grants, tuition waivers (partial), and unspecified assistantships available. Financial award application deadline: 3/1; financial award applicants required to submit FAFSA. *Unit head:* Dr. Hema Krishnan, Associate Dean, 513-745-3420, Fax: 513-745-3455, E-mail: krishnan@xavier.edu. *Application contact:* Anna Marie Whelan, Assistant Director, MBA Programs, 513-745-3525, Fax: 513-745-2929, E-mail: whelana@xavier.edu. Web site: http://www.xavier.edu/williams/mba/.

Yale University, Yale School of Management and Graduate School of Arts and Sciences, Doctoral Program in Management, New Haven, CT 06520. Offers accounting (PhD); financial economics (PhD); marketing (PhD); organizations and management (PhD). *Accreditation:* AACSB. *Faculty:* 42 full-time (8 women). *Students:* 33 full-time (9 women); includes 4 minority (all Asian, non-Hispanic/Latino), 16 international. 439 applicants, 3% accepted, 4 enrolled. In 2011, 2 doctorates awarded. *Degree requirements:* For doctorate, comprehensive exam, thesis/dissertation. *Entrance requirements:* For doctorate, GMAT or GRE General Test. Additional exam requirements/recommendations for international students: Required—TOEFL or IELTS. *Application deadline:* For fall admission, 1/2 for domestic and international students. Application fee: $100. Electronic applications accepted. *Expenses:* Contact institution. *Financial support:* In 2011–12, 31 students received support, including 31 fellowships with full tuition reimbursements available, 31 research assistantships with full tuition reimbursements available, 31 teaching assistantships with full tuition reimbursements available; institutionally sponsored loans, scholarships/grants, and health care benefits also available. Financial award application deadline: 1/2. *Faculty research:* Pricing of options and futures, term structure of interest rates, use of accounting numbers in debt contracts, product differentiation, e-commerce and marketing, behavioral finance. *Unit head:* Carla Mills, Registrar, 203-432-3955, Fax: 203-432-0342.

Yale University, Yale School of Management, Program in Business Administration, New Haven, CT 06520. Offers MBA, PhD, MBA/JD, MBA/M Arch, MBA/M Div, MBA/MA, MBA/MEM, MBA/MF, MBA/MFA, MBA/MPH, MBA/PhD, MD/MBA. *Accreditation:* AACSB. *Faculty:* 68 full-time (13 women), 27 part-time/adjunct (6 women). *Students:* 475 full-time (170 women). Average age 28. 2,823 applicants, 19% accepted, 227 enrolled. In 2011, 220 master's, 2 doctorates awarded. Terminal master's awarded for partial completion of doctoral program. *Degree requirements:* For master's, international experience; for doctorate, comprehensive exam, thesis/dissertation. *Entrance requirements:* For master's, GMAT or GRE; for doctorate, GMAT or GRE General Test (preferred). Additional exam requirements/recommendations for international students: Required—TOEFL, Pearson Test of English, or IELTS. *Application deadline:* For fall admission, 10/6 priority date for domestic students, 10/6 for international students; for winter admission, 1/5 priority date for domestic students, 1/5 for international students; for spring admission, 4/12 priority date for domestic students, 4/12 for international students. Application fee: $225. Electronic applications accepted. *Expenses:* Contact institution. *Financial support:* Career-related internships or fieldwork, Federal Work-Study, institutionally sponsored loans, and scholarships/grants available. Financial award applicants required to submit FAFSA. *Faculty research:* Finance, strategy, marketing, leadership, operations. *Unit head:* Edward A. Snyder, Dean, 203-432-6035, Fax: 203-432-5092. *Application contact:* Bruce DelMonico, Director of Admissions, 203-432-5635, Fax: 203-432-7004, E-mail: mba.admissions@yale.edu. Web site: http://www.mba.yale.edu/.

York College of Pennsylvania, Donald Graham School of Business, York, PA 17405-7199. Offers accounting (MBA); continuous improvement (MBA); finance (MBA); management (MBA); marketing (MBA); self-designed (MBA). *Accreditation:* ACBSP. Part-time and evening/weekend programs available. *Faculty:* 14 full-time (3 women), 1 part-time/adjunct (0 women). *Students:* 11 full-time (5 women), 99 part-time (40 women); includes 10 minority (5 Black or African American, non-Hispanic/Latino; 1 Asian, non-Hispanic/Latino; 3 Hispanic/Latino; 1 Two or more races, non-Hispanic/Latino), 1 international. Average age 29. 49 applicants, 80% accepted, 26 enrolled. In 2011, 33 master's awarded. *Entrance requirements:* For master's, GMAT. Additional exam requirements/recommendations for international students: Required—TOEFL (minimum score 530 paper-based; 200 computer-based; 72 iBT). *Application deadline:* For fall admission, 7/15 priority date for domestic students; for spring admission, 12/15 priority date for domestic students. Applications are processed on a rolling basis. Application fee: $50. Electronic applications accepted. *Expenses: Tuition:* Full-time $12,060; part-time $670 per credit hour. *Required fees:* $340 per semester. Tuition and fees vary according to degree level. *Financial support:* In 2011–12, 3 students received support. Scholarships/grants available. Financial award application deadline: 4/15; financial award applicants required to submit FAFSA. *Unit head:* Dr. David Greisler, MBA Director, 717-815-6410, Fax: 717-600-3999, E-mail: dgreisle@ycp.edu. *Application contact:* Brenda Adams, Assistant Director, MBA Program, 717-815-1749, Fax: 717-600-3999, E-mail: badams@ycp.edu. Web site: http://www.ycp.edu/mba.

Yorktown University, School of Business, Denver, CO 80246. Offers entrepreneurship (MBA); sport management (MBA).

York University, Faculty of Graduate Studies, Schulich School of Business, Toronto, ON M3J 1P3, Canada. Offers administration (PhD); business (MBA); finance (MF); international business (IMBA); public administration (MPA); MBA/JD; MBA/MA; MBA/MFA. Part-time and evening/weekend programs available. *Faculty:* 112 full-time (35 women), 191 part-time/adjunct (61 women). *Students:* 706 full-time (240 women), 401 part-time (136 women). Average age 28. 1,621 applicants, 46% accepted, 439 enrolled. In 2011, 528 master's, 10 doctorates awarded. *Degree requirements:* For master's, advanced proficiency in a second language, work term (IMBA); for doctorate, comprehensive exam, thesis/dissertation. *Entrance requirements:* For master's, GMAT (GRE acceptable for MF), minimum GPA of 3.0 (3.3 for MF); for doctorate, GMAT or GRE, minimum GPA of 3.3. Additional exam requirements/recommendations for international students: Required—TOEFL (minimum score 600 paper-based; 100 iBT), IELTS (minimum score 7), York English Language Test (minimum score 1). *Application deadline:* For fall admission, 5/1 for domestic students, 2/1 for international students; for winter admission, 10/1 for domestic students, 9/1 for international students. Applications are processed on a rolling basis. Application fee: $150. Electronic applications accepted. *Financial support:* In 2011–12, 800 students received support, including fellowships (averaging $5,000 per year), research assistantships (averaging $3,000 per year), teaching assistantships (averaging $7,000 per year); career-related internships or fieldwork, scholarships/grants, and bursaries for part-time students also available. Financial award application deadline: 2/1. *Faculty research:* Accounting, finance, marketing, operations management and information systems, organizational studies, strategic management. *Unit head:* Dezso Horvath, Dean, 416-736-5070, E-mail: dhorvath@schulich.yorku.ca. *Application contact:* Graduate Admissions, 416-736-5060, Fax: 416-650-8174, E-mail: admissions@schulich.yorku.ca. Web site: http://www.schulich.yorku.ca.

See Display below and Close-Up on page 263.

Youngstown State University, Graduate School, Williamson College of Business Administration, Youngstown, OH 44555-0001. Offers MBA, Certificate. *Accreditation:* AACSB. Part-time and evening/weekend programs available. *Degree requirements:* For master's, thesis optional. *Entrance requirements:* For master's, GMAT, minimum GPA of 2.7. Additional exam requirements/recommendations for international students: Required—TOEFL. *Faculty research:* Taxation and compliance, business ethics, operations management, organizational behavior, gender issues.

ADELPHI UNIVERSITY

Robert B. Willumstad School of Business

Programs of Study

Adelphi University's Robert B. Willumstad School of Business creates managers, leaders, and entrepreneurs who can flourish amidst unprecedented change. The School believes that the best business leaders are those who enjoy an intellectual challenge, have a deep appreciation of the theoretical and the practical, understand today's realities and tomorrow's possibilities, and see the link between the skills they learn and the character they display.

Adelphi's M.B.A. program requires a minimum of 33 credits and a maximum of 66, accommodating students with varied academic backgrounds. It meets state, regional, and national accreditation standards and serves middle-level professionals seeking advancement in management careers. The curriculum integrates contemporary management issues and business fundamentals, enabling students to perform with distinction in the global environment. Its mission is to produce intellectually well-rounded, effective communicators who are aware of societal issues and responsibilities, and have a thorough understanding of the legal, environmental, technological, and social issues that affect an organization's operation. Candidates are required to fulfill or waive graduate prerequisites in financial accounting, computer applications, and mathematics for managers.

The curriculum begins with a 24-credit foundation core consisting of studies in the legal and ethical environment, macroeconomics, microeconomics, corporate finance, management theory, marketing management, management information systems, and statistical methods. The 21-credit advanced core includes accounting for managerial analysis, entrepreneurship/intrapreneurship, communication and negotiations, building shareholder value, leadership and innovation, technology management, and total quality management. Specializations are available in accounting, finance, health services administration, human resources management, management information systems, marketing, and sport management.

Students with four years' managerial experience may elect the GOAL M.B.A. program. This accelerated program requires fourteen courses; students take two courses per term over seven 8-week terms. Courses are held on Saturdays only. A post-master's certificate in human resource management is open to students with master's degrees in any field.

Most graduate students in the Willumstad School of Business attend part time and are working full time. To accommodate their busy schedules and make it easier for them to complete their degrees, courses are offered at both the main Garden City campus and the Hauppauge Center. Courses for all graduate degree and certificate programs are scheduled Monday through Thursday evenings and Saturday mornings in Garden City. Each course meets once a week. Qualified students may also select the fast-track GOAL M.B.A. program option.

Research Facilities

The University's primary research holdings are at Swirbul Library and include 600,000 volumes (including bound periodicals and government publications), 806,000 items in microformats, 33,000 audiovisual items, and online access to more than 61,000 electronic journal titles and 221 research databases.

Financial Aid

Financial aid counseling is available. Students may qualify for federal and state aid programs, scholarships, and fellowship programs, including a limited number of graduate assistantships.

Cost of Study

The 2012–13 tuition rate is $965 per credit hour. University fees range from about $315 to $550 per semester. Students should also plan for expenditures associated with books, travel, and personal items.

Living and Housing Costs

The University assists single and married students in finding suitable accommodations whenever possible. The cost of living depends on the location and number of rooms rented.

Student Group

The School's 410 graduate students form a diverse and vibrant community. They come from across the United States and 40 percent come from other countries. Undergraduate majors range from anthropology and economics to nursing and fine arts, and students' professional backgrounds range from bank officers and senior accountants to government officials and entrepreneurs. There are 137 part-time students. Students' average age is 31, and 48 percent are women. Guest speakers, internship opportunities, and the Distinguished Executive Lecture Series further enhance the learning environment. Professional clubs and organizations provide forums to exchange ideas. The School has been granted a charter for the Beta Xi chapter of Delta Mu Delta, one of the oldest national honor societies in business administration. Delta Mu Delta is a member of the Association of College Honor Societies.

Location

Located in historic Garden City, New York, 45 minutes from Manhattan and 20 minutes from Queens, Adelphi's 75-acre suburban campus is known for the beauty of its landscape and architecture. The campus is a short walk from the Long Island Railroad and convenient to New York's major airports and several major highways. Off-campus centers are located in Manhattan, Hauppauge, and Poughkeepsie. Students enjoy the benefits of being close to the financial, medical, and technological centers and cultural and sporting facilities of Manhattan and Long Island. The campus is close to fine restaurants and shopping, and only 15 minutes from Long Island's beautiful beaches.

The University

Founded in 1896, Adelphi is a fully accredited, private university with nearly 8,000 undergraduate, graduate, and returning-adult students in the arts and sciences, business, clinical psychology, education, nursing, and social work. Students come from forty-three states and forty-five countries. The Princeton Review named Adelphi University a Best College in the Northeastern Region, and the *Fiske Guide to Colleges* recognized Adelphi as a Best Buy in higher education for the sixth year in a row. The University is one of only twenty-five private institutions in the nation to earn this recognition.

Applying

Applicants must have a bachelor's degree from an accredited college or university and provide official academic transcripts, an essay, GMAT scores, and two letters of recommendation from academic or professional sources. Additional requirements for international students may be found online at http://admissions.adelphi.edu/international.

The Robert B. Willumstad School of Business accepts applicants on a rolling basis. The application deadlines for international students are May 1 for the fall semester and November 1 for the spring semester.

Correspondence and Information

Adelphi University
One South Avenue
Garden City, New York 11530
United States
Phone: 516-877-4600 (Robert B. Willumstad School of Business)
516-877-3050 (Office of University Admissions)
800-ADELPHI (toll-free for Office of University Admissions)
E-mail: admissions@adelphi.edu
Web site: http://www.adelphi.edu

THE FACULTY AND THEIR RESEARCH

There are 40 full-time faculty members in the Robert B. Willumstad School of Business, all with advanced degrees. The faculty is known for its teaching excellence. Over the past few years, the School has hired a number of new faculty members with specialties in management, marketing, and decision sciences; accounting and law; and finance and economics. Students should visit http://business.adelphi.edu/faculty for complete faculty information.

Adelphi's campus is located in historic Garden City, Long Island, New York.

A registered arboretum, Adelphi is truly a green campus.

ARGOSY UNIVERSITY, ATLANTA

College of Business

Programs of Study

Argosy University, Atlanta, offers the Master of Business Administration (M.B.A.) degree, the Master of Science in Management (M.S.M.) degree, the Master of Public Administration (M.P.A.) degree, the Doctor of Education (Ed.D.) degree in Organizational Leadership, and the Doctor of Business Administration (D.B.A.) degree. The business programs are designed to serve the needs of talented students, regardless of their undergraduate degrees. The College of Business welcomes and encourages students from diverse academic backgrounds.

The Master of Business Administration (M.B.A.) program develops action-oriented managers and leaders who focus on leading themselves and others to solutions that serve their organizations. Students acquire skills to identify challenges and opportunities, draw on the latest technology and information, use advanced analytical and planning approaches, and execute plans for leading positive change. Students develop these competencies through focusing on critical thinking, persuasive communications, technical knowledge, and a deep understanding of the human side of business. The program is designed to build upon the talents of students, independent of their undergraduate field of study. The program consists of eight core courses (24 credit hours) and four concentration courses (12 credit hours), scheduled to enable busy professionals to balance the demands of career, family, and school. In addition to the core requirements, students can select concentrations in corporate compliance, finance, healthcare administration, information systems management (limited availability, Program Chair approval needed to enter), international business, management, and marketing. A student may also select four courses (12 credit hours) to create a customized concentration that better fits their specific career goals, with approval of their program chair. The M.B.A. program culminates in an applied capstone project in which all students have the opportunity to integrate the core business competencies with their concentration specialty.

The Master of Science in Management (M.S.M.) program is designed to improve and extend the interpersonal and problem-solving skills necessary for employment in the private, nonprofit, and public sectors. The program focuses on situation diagnostics, opportunity and problem evaluation, and implementation of an action plan.

The Master of Public Administration (M.P.A.) program is designed to develop action-oriented problem-solving managers for the public sector, especially at the state and local levels of government. Students develop the competencies required to execute the duties and responsibilities of public sector managers, including evaluation and supervision of employees, reinforcement of the organizational mission, and effective management of organizational resources.

The Doctor of Education (Ed.D.) in Organizational Leadership program is designed to meet the special requirements of working professionals who wish to develop their knowledge and skills to handle the changing needs of modern organizations. Based on the belief that success for an organization is directly and substantially linked to leaders within the organization, Argosy University seeks to inform, enhance, challenge, and support the development of organizational leaders ready to face the complex issues present in an ever-changing world. The program focuses on the qualities of transformational leadership, not just managerial attributes. This approach prepares students to lead complex organizations faced with strategic challenges, such as increasing globalization, changing economies, societal shifts, and individual organizational relationships. Some assignments will require applying principles in live situations. Students should be aware that they will at times need access to an organization—whether their employer or another organization—to maximize the opportunity to develop their competencies.

In the Doctor of Business Administration (D.B.A.) program, industry and academic professionals have the opportunity to build upon master's-level competencies, skills, and knowledge to prepare themselves to perform more effectively in existing professional roles, to qualify for roles with increasing responsibility, and/or develop capabilities for a second career in teaching at the college level. The program requires students to develop applied research inquiry and analytical skills and helps them develop competencies in understanding and performing applied research which can then be used to foster innovation and lead organizational change. The D.B.A. program consists of five research foundation courses, six core courses, four concentration courses, one elective course, and 12 credit hours in dissertation study. Students must also successfully complete the comprehensive written examination during or after their final semester of coursework in order to move into the dissertation process. D.B.A. concentrations are offered in accounting,, information systems (limited availability, Program Chair approval needed to enter), international business, management, and marketing. In addition, with approval of the student's program chair, a student may select four courses (12 credit hours) to create a customized concentration that better fits their specific career goals. The program is structured to enable busy professionals to balance the demands of career, family, and school. Courses are offered in a variety of formats including condensed weekend classes, regular weekly sessions, or a combination of class settings and online activities.

Research Facilities

Argosy University libraries provide curriculum support and educational resources, including current text materials, diagnostic training documents, reference materials and databases, journals and dissertations, and major and current titles in program areas. There is an online public-access catalog of library resources available throughout the Argosy University system. Students have remote access to the campus library database, enabling them to study and conduct research at home. Academic databases offer dissertation abstracts, academic journals, and professional periodicals. All library computers are Internet accessible. Software applications include Word, Excel, PowerPoint, SPSS, and various test-scoring programs.

Argosy University, Atlanta

Financial Aid

Financial aid is available to those who qualify. Argosy University, Atlanta, offers access to federal and state aid programs, merit-based awards, grants, loans, and a work-study program. As a first step, students should complete the Free Application for Federal Student Aid (FAFSA). Prospective students can apply electronically at http://www.fafsa.ed.gov or at the campus.

Cost of Study

Tuition varies by program. Students should contact Argosy University, Atlanta, for tuition information.

Living and Housing Costs

Students typically live in apartments in the metropolitan Atlanta area. Living expenses vary according to each student's preferred standard of living, housing, and transportation. The University does not offer or operate student housing. Most students are full-time working professionals who live within driving distance of the campus. Several nearby hotels offer special rates for those who commute from long distances. The Admissions Department also maintains a list of housing options, including contact information, for University students who wish to share housing. For more information, students should contact the Admissions Department.

Student Group

Admission to Argosy University, Atlanta, is selective to ensure a dynamic and engaged student body. It encourages diversity in academic and employment backgrounds and promotes integration of the student body into professional life through established connections with local and national professional associations. Argosy University offers a professionally oriented education with rich opportunities to gain practical experience in class, field placements, and internships. Full-time students and working professionals gain the extensive knowledge and range of skills necessary for effective performance in their chosen fields.

Student Outcomes

Students can register with the University's online career-services system and use select services from a distance, such as degree-specific career e-mail lists, national job posts, and virtual job fairs. Students should contact the University for more information.

Location

Argosy University, Atlanta, is housed in a modern building in Sandy Springs, a northern suburb of Atlanta. The campus features a café and an outdoor lake side terrace. Beyond the University, students find a wide selection of affordable housing options. This major metropolitan area offers many social and recreational opportunities, from clubs and concerts to galleries and museums, from a growing restaurant scene to Braves baseball games and in-line skating in Piedmont Park.

Many businesses in the area provide varied opportunities for student training. Atlanta's business environment includes technology companies such as EarthLink and Macquarium as well as corporate giants such as the Coca-Cola Company, CNN, Delta Air Lines, AT&T, and Georgia Pacific.

The University

Argosy University is a private institution with nineteen locations across the nation. Argosy University, Atlanta, provides students with a career resources office, an academic resources center, and extensive information access for research. It offers the resources of a large university, plus the friendliness and personal attention of a small campus.

The innovative programs feature dynamic, relevant, and practical curricula delivered in flexible class formats. Students enjoy scheduling options that make it easier to fit school into their busy lives, choosing from day and evening courses, on campus or online. Many students find a combination of class formats to be an ideal way of continuing their education while meeting family and professional demands.

Argosy University is accredited by the Accrediting Commission for Senior Colleges and Universities of the Western Association of Schools and Colleges (985 Atlantic Avenue, Suite 100, Alameda, California, 94501, http://www.wascsenior.org).

Applying

Argosy University, Atlanta, accepts students year-round on a rolling admissions basis, depending on availability of required courses. Applications for admission are available online or by contacting the campus.

Correspondence and Information

Argosy University, Atlanta
980 Hammond Drive, Suite 100
Atlanta, Georgia 30328
United States
Phone: 770-671-1200
888-671-4777 (toll-free)
Fax: 770-671-9055
E-mail: auadmissions@argosy.edu
Web site: http://www.argosy.edu/atlanta

THE FACULTY

The Argosy University faculty comprises working professionals who are eager to help students succeed. Members bring real-world experience and the latest practice innovations to the academic setting. The diverse faculty members of the College of Business are widely recognized for contributions to the field. Many are published scholars, and most hold doctoral degrees. They are committed to providing a substantive education that combines comprehensive knowledge with critical skills and practical workplace relevance. Above all, faculty members are committed to their students' personal and professional growth.

ARGOSY UNIVERSITY, CHICAGO

College of Business

Programs of Study

Argosy University, Chicago, offers the Master of Business Administration (M.B.A.), the Master of Science in Management (M.S.M.), and the Doctor of Business Administration (D.B.A.) degrees. The business programs are designed to serve the needs of talented students, regardless of their undergraduate degrees. The College of Business welcomes and encourages students from diverse academic backgrounds.

The Master of Business Administration (M.B.A.) program is designed to develop action-oriented managers and leaders who focus on leading themselves and others to solutions that serve their organizations. Students acquire skills to identify challenges and opportunities, draw on the latest technology and information, use advanced analytical and planning approaches, and execute plans for leading positive change. Competencies are developed through focusing on critical thinking, persuasive communications, technical knowledge, and a deep understanding of the human side of business. By focusing on competencies in this manner, the program builds upon the talents of students, Independent of their undergraduate field of study. Students from diverse academic and professional backgrounds are welcomed and encouraged. In addition to completing the core course requirements, students develop expertise and specific insights in one of the following concentrations: Corporate Compliance, Finance, Fraud Examination, Healthcare Administration, Information Systems Management (availability of this concentration is limited; Program Chair approval is necessary), International Business, Management, Marketing, Public Administration, or Sustainable Management. In addition, with approval of the student's program chair, a student may select four courses (12 credit hours) to create a customized concentration that better fits their specific career goals. For all students, the MBA program culminates in an applied Capstone Project in which they integrate the core business competencies with their concentration specialty.

The Master of Science (M.S.) in Management program is designed to improve and extend the interpersonal and problem solving skills necessary for successful leaders in the private, nonprofit, and public sectors. The program focuses on situation diagnostics, opportunity and problem evaluation, and implementation of an action plan.

The Master of Public Administration (M.P.A.) program is designed to develop action-oriented problem-solving managers for the public sector, especially at the state and local levels of government. Students develop the competencies required to execute the duties and responsibilities of public sector managers, including evaluation and supervision of employees, reinforcement of the organizational mission, and effective management of organizational resources.

The Doctor of Business Administration (D.B.A.) program enables industry and academic professionals to build upon master's-level competencies, skills, and knowledge, preparing themselves to perform more effectively in existing professional roles, to qualify for roles with increasing responsibility, and/or develop capabilities for a second career in teaching at the college level. The program requires students to develop applied research inquiry and analytical skills. The DBA program is designed to help students develop competencies in understanding and performing applied research, which can then be used to foster innovation and lead organizational change. Students must choose a concentration in accounting, global business sustainability, information systems (availability of this concentration is limited; Program Chair approval is necessary), international business, management, or marketing. In addition, with approval of the student's program chair, a student may select four courses (12 credit hours) to create a customized concentration that better fits their specific career goals.

Research Facilities

Argosy University libraries provide curriculum support and educational resources, including current text materials, diagnostic training documents, reference materials and databases, journals and dissertations, and major and current titles in program areas. There is an online public-access catalog of library resources available throughout the Argosy University system. Students have full remote access to the campus library database, enabling them to study and conduct research at home. Academic databases offer dissertation abstracts, academic journals, and professional periodicals. All library computers are Internet accessible. Software applications include Word, Excel, PowerPoint, SPSS, and various test-scoring programs.

Financial Aid

Financial aid is available to those who qualify. Argosy University, Chicago, offers access to federal and state aid programs, merit-based awards, grants, loans, and a work-study program. As a first step, students should complete the Free Application for Federal Student Aid (FAFSA). Prospective students can apply electronically at http://www.fafsa.ed.gov or at the campus.

Cost of Study

Tuition varies by program. Students should contact Argosy University, Chicago, for tuition information.

Living and Housing Costs

Students typically live in apartments in the metropolitan Chicago area. Living expenses vary according to each student's preferred standard of living, housing, and transportation. The University does not offer or operate student housing. Most of the students are full-time working professionals who live within driving distance of the campus. Several nearby hotels offer special rates for those who commute from long distances. The Admissions Department also maintains a list of housing options, including contact information for university students who wish to share housing. For more information, students should contact the Admissions Department.

Argosy University, Chicago

Student Group

Admission to Argosy University, Chicago, is selective to ensure a highly qualified student body. It encourages diversity in academic and employment backgrounds and promotes integration of the student body into professional life through established connections with local and national professional associations. Argosy University offers a professionally oriented education with rich opportunities to gain practical experience in class, field placements, and internships. Full-time students and working professionals gain the extensive knowledge and range of skills necessary for effective performance in their chosen fields.

Student Outcomes

Students can register with the University's online career-services system and use select services from a distance, such as degree-specific career e-mail lists, national job posts, and virtual job fairs. Students should contact the University for more information.

Location

Chicago is a city of world-class status and beauty, drawing visitors from around the globe. Argosy University, Chicago, sits in the heart of The Loop, the city's business and entertainment center. Located on the shores of Lake Michigan, Chicago is home to world-champion sports teams, an internationally acclaimed symphony orchestra, renowned architecture, and a variety of history and art museums. Recreational opportunities include hiking and cycling on miles of lakefront trails, golfing, and shopping. Many businesses in the area provide excellent opportunities for student training. Chicago's thriving business environment includes a broad array of companies including Boeing and Pepsi America. The commercial banking headquarters of JP Morgan Chase is also located in Chicago.

The University

Argosy University is a private institution with nineteen locations across the nation. Argosy University, Chicago, provides students with an academic resources center and extensive information access for research. It offers the resources of a large university plus the friendliness and personal attention of a small campus. Argosy University, Chicago, is closely associated with Argosy University, Schaumburg, located 45 minutes from downtown Chicago.

The innovative programs feature dynamic, relevant, and practical curricula delivered in flexible class formats. Students enjoy scheduling options that make it easier to fit school into their busy lives, choosing from day and evening courses, on campus or online. Many students find a combination of class formats to be an ideal way of continuing their education while meeting family and professional demands.

Argosy University is accredited by the Accrediting Commission for Senior Colleges and Universities of the Western Association for Schools and Colleges (985 Atlantic Avenue, Suite 100, Alameda, California, 94501, http://www.wascsenior.org).

Applying

Argosy University, Chicago, accepts students year-round on a rolling admissions basis, depending on availability of required courses. Applications for admission are available online or by contacting the campus.

Correspondence and Information

Argosy University, Chicago
225 North Michigan Avenue, Suite 1300
Chicago, Illinois 60601
United States
Phone: 312-777-7600
800-626-4123 (toll-free)
Fax: 312-777-7748
E-mail: auadmissions@argosy.edu
Web site: http://www.argosy.edu/chicago

THE FACULTY

The Argosy University faculty comprises working professionals who are eager to help students succeed. Members bring real-world experience and the latest practice innovations to the academic setting. The diverse faculty members of the College of Business are widely recognized for contributions to their fields. Many are published scholars, and most hold doctoral degrees. They provide a substantive education that combines comprehensive knowledge with critical skills and practical workplace relevance. Above all, faculty members are committed to their students' personal and professional development.

ARGOSY UNIVERSITY, DALLAS

College of Business

Programs of Study

Argosy University, Dallas, offers the Master of Business Administration (M.B.A.) degree; the Master of Public Administration (M.P.A.) degree; Master of Science degrees in Human Resource Management, Non-Profit Management, Organizational Leadership, and Service Sector Management; the Doctor of Business Administration (D.B.A.) degree; and the Doctor of Education (Ed.D.) in Organizational Leadership degree. The programs are designed to serve the needs of talented students, regardless of their undergraduate degrees. The College of Business welcomes and encourages students from diverse academic and professional backgrounds.

The Master of Business Administration (M.B.A.) program develops action-oriented managers and leaders who focus on leading themselves and others to solutions that serve their organizations. Students acquire skills to identify challenges and opportunities, draw on the latest technology and information, use advanced analytical and planning approaches, and execute plans for leading positive change. Students develop these competencies through focusing on critical thinking, persuasive communications, technical knowledge, and a deep understanding of the human side of business. The program is designed to build upon the talents of students, independent of their undergraduate field of study. The program consists of eight core courses (24 credit hours) and four concentration courses (12 credit hours), scheduled to enable busy professionals to balance the demands of career, family, and school. In addition to the core requirements, students can select concentrations in corporate compliance, finance, fraud examination, healthcare administration, information systems management (limited availability, Program Chair approval needed to enter), international business, management, marketing, public administration, and sustainable management. A student may also select four courses (12 credit hours) to create a customized concentration that better fits their specific career goals, with approval of their program chair. The M.B.A. program culminates in an applied capstone project in which all students have the opportunity to integrate the core business competencies with their concentration specialty.

The Master of Public Administration (M.P.A.) program is designed to develop action-oriented problem-solving managers for the public sector, especially at the state and local levels of government. Students develop the competencies required to execute the duties and responsibilities of public sector managers, including evaluation and supervision of employees, reinforcement of the organizational mission, and effective management of organizational resources.

The Master of Science (M.S.) sequence of programs focuses on the immediate need for management/leadership/interpersonal skills to enhance a student's career potential within an organization or field, or to accelerate their career within a given area of interest. The programs address the needs of individuals whose near-term career responsibilities include managing and leading employees and interacting with customers, clients, and stakeholders. In many cases, these individuals have much of the technical knowledge they need but lack both the language of business and the breadth of leadership and interpersonal skills to maximize their career potential. Examples range from accountants who want to manage a small accounting partnership, to engineers asked to lead a department, to department managers in retail firms who want to progress to store management roles. Also included would be managers in local or regional nonprofit organizations, small-firm management or technical consultants, human resource professionals, and a range of service sector managers from the hospitality industry to transportation to event planning professionals. The degree programs offered are Master of Science in Human Resource Management, Master of Science in Non-Profit Management, Master of Science in Organizational Leadership, and Master of Science in Service Sector Management.

In the Doctor of Business Administration (D.B.A.) program, industry and academic professionals have the opportunity to build upon master's-level competencies, skills, and knowledge to prepare themselves to perform more effectively in existing professional roles, to qualify for roles with increasing responsibility, and/or develop capabilities for a second career in teaching at the college level. The program requires students to develop applied research inquiry and analytical skills and helps them develop competencies in understanding and performing applied research which can then be used to foster innovation and lead organizational change. The D.B.A. program consists of five research foundation courses, six core courses, four concentration courses, one elective course, and 12 credit hours in dissertation study. Students must also successfully complete the comprehensive written examination during or after their final semester of coursework in order to move into the dissertation process. D.B.A. concentrations are offered in accounting, global business sustainability, information systems (limited availability, Program Chair approval needed to enter), international business, management, and marketing. In addition, with approval of the student's program chair, a student may select four courses (12 credit hours) to create a customized concentration that better fits their specific career goals. The program is structured to enable busy professionals to balance the demands of career, family, and school. Courses are offered in a variety of formats including condensed weekend classes, regular weekly sessions, or a combination of class settings and online activities.

The Doctor of Education (Ed.D.) in Organizational Leadership program is designed to meet the special requirements of working professionals who wish to develop their knowledge and skills to handle the changing needs of modern organizations. Based on the belief that success for an organization is directly and substantially linked to leaders within the organization, Argosy University seeks to inform, enhance, challenge, and support the development of organizational leaders ready to face the complex issues present in an ever-changing world. The program focuses on the qualities of transformational leadership, not just managerial attributes. This approach prepares students to lead complex organizations faced with strategic challenges, such as increasing globalization, changing economies, societal shifts, and individual organizational relationships. Some assignments will require applying principles in live situations. Students should be aware that they will at times need access to an organization—whether their employer or another organization—to maximize the opportunity to develop their competencies.

Research Facilities

Argosy University libraries provide curriculum support and educational resources, including current text materials, diagnostic training documents, reference materials and databases, journals and dissertations, and major and current titles in program areas. There is an online public-access catalog of library resources available throughout the Argosy University system. Students have remote access to the campus library database, enabling them to study and conduct research at home. Academic databases offer dissertation abstracts, academic journals, and professional periodicals. All library computers are Internet accessible. Software applications include Word, Excel, PowerPoint, SPSS, and various test-scoring programs.

Financial Aid

Financial aid is available to those who qualify. Argosy University, Dallas, offers access to federal and state aid programs, merit-based awards, grants, loans, and a work-study program. As a first step, students should complete the Free Application for Federal Student Aid (FAFSA). Prospective students can apply electronically at http://www.fafsa.ed.gov or at the campus.

Cost of Study

Tuition varies by program. Students should contact Argosy University, Dallas, for tuition information.

Living and Housing Costs

Students typically live in apartments in the metropolitan Dallas area. Living expenses vary according to each student's preferred standard of living, housing, and transportation. The University does not offer or operate student housing. Most of the students are full-time working professionals who live within driving distance of the campus. Several nearby hotels offer special rates for those who commute from long distances. The Admissions Department also maintains a list of housing options, including contact information, for University students who wish to share housing. For more information, students should contact the Admissions Department.

Student Group

Admission to Argosy University, Dallas, is selective to ensure a dynamic and engaged student body. It encourages diversity in academic and employment backgrounds and promotes integration of the student body into professional life through established connections with local and national professional associations. Argosy University offers a professionally oriented education with rich opportunities to gain practical experience in class, field placements, and internships. Full-time students and working professionals gain the extensive knowledge and range of skills necessary for effective performance in their chosen fields.

Student Outcomes

Students can register with the University's online career-services system and use select services from a distance, such as degree-specific career e-mail lists, national job posts, and virtual job fairs. Students should contact the University for more information.

Location

Argosy University, Dallas, offers a north-central location in Dallas, with easy access to freeways, neighboring colleges and universities, libraries, shops, restaurants, theaters, art museums, and other tourist attractions. Many businesses in the metropolitan area offer excellent training facilities for students. The city is home to a broad array of companies, including Lockheed Martin Corporation, Baylor University Medical System, and Southwest Airlines.

The University

Argosy University is a private institution with nineteen locations across the nation. Argosy University, Dallas, provides students with a career resources office, an academic resources center, and extensive information access for research. It offers the resources of a large university, plus the friendliness and personal attention of a small campus.

Argosy University, Dallas, offers the opportunity to take one class at a time, with each class lasting for one month. Students are never required to study for multiple exams at the same time. New classes start each month. This flexible format lets students begin working on a graduate degree without waiting for the traditional semester to start.

Argosy University is accredited by the Accrediting Commission for Senior Colleges and Universities of the Western Association for Schools and Colleges (985 Atlantic Avenue, Suite 100, Alameda, California, 94501, http://www.wascsenior.org).

Applying

Argosy University, Dallas, accepts students year-round on a rolling admissions basis, depending on availability of required courses. Applications for admission are available online or by contacting the campus.

Correspondence and Information

Argosy University, Dallas
5001 Lyndon B. Johnson Freeway
Heritage Square
Farmers Branch, Texas 75244
United States
Phone: 214-890-9900
866-954-9900 (toll-free)
Fax: 214-378-8555
E-mail: auadmissions@argosy.edu
Web site: http://www.argosy.edu/dallas

THE FACULTY

The Argosy University faculty comprises working professionals who are eager to help students succeed. Members bring real-world experience and the latest practice innovations to the academic setting. The diverse faculty members of the College of Business are widely recognized for contributions to the field. Many are published scholars, and most hold doctoral degrees. They are committed to providing a substantive education that combines comprehensive knowledge with critical skills and practical workplace relevance. Above all, faculty members are committed to their students' personal and professional development.

ARGOSY UNIVERSITY, DENVER

College of Business

Programs of Study

Argosy University, Denver, offers the Master of Business Administration (M.B.A.) degree; the Master of Public Administration (M.P.A.) degree; Master of Science degrees in Human Resource Management, Non-Profit Management, Organizational Leadership, and Service Sector Management; the Doctor of Business Administration (D.B.A.) degree; and the Doctor of Education (Ed.D.) in Organizational Leadership degree. The business programs are designed to serve the needs of talented students, regardless of their undergraduate degrees. The College of Business welcomes and encourages students from diverse academic backgrounds.

The Master of Business Administration (M.B.A.) program develops action-oriented managers and leaders who focus on leading themselves and others to solutions that serve their organizations. Students acquire skills to identify challenges and opportunities, draw on the latest technology and information, use advanced analytical and planning approaches, and execute plans for leading positive change. Students develop these competencies through focusing on critical thinking, persuasive communications, technical knowledge, and a deep understanding of the human side of business. The program is designed to build upon the talents of students, independent of their undergraduate field of study. The program consists of eight core courses (24 credit hours) and four concentration courses (12 credit hours), scheduled to enable busy professionals to balance the demands of career, family, and school. In addition to the core requirements, students can select concentrations in corporate compliance, finance, fraud examination, healthcare administration, information systems management (limited availability, Program Chair approval needed to enter), international business, management, marketing, public administration, and sustainable management. A student may also select four courses (12 credit hours) to create a customized concentration that better fits their specific career goals, with approval of their program chair. The M.B.A. program culminates in an applied capstone project in which all students have the opportunity to integrate the core business competencies with their concentration specialty.

The Master of Public Administration (M.P.A.) program is designed to develop action-oriented problem-solving managers for the public sector, especially at the state and local levels of government. Students develop the competencies required to execute the duties and responsibilities of public sector managers, including evaluation and supervision of employees, reinforcement of the organizational mission, and effective management of organizational resources.

The Master of Science (M.S.) sequence of programs focuses on the immediate need for management/leadership/interpersonal skills to enhance a student's career potential within an organization or field, or to accelerate their career within a given area of interest. The programs address the needs of individuals whose near-term career responsibilities include managing and leading employees and interacting with customers, clients, and stakeholders. In many cases, these individuals have much of the technical knowledge they need but lack both the language of business and the breadth of leadership and interpersonal skills to maximize their career potential. Examples range from accountants who want to manage a small accounting partnership, to engineers asked to lead a department, to department managers in retail firms who want to progress to store management roles. Also included would be managers in local or regional nonprofit organizations, small-firm management or technical consultants, human resource professionals, and a range of service sector managers from the hospitality industry to transportation to event planning professionals. The degree programs offered are Master of Science in Human Resource Management, Master of Science in Non-Profit Management, Master of Science in Organizational Leadership, and Master of Science in Service Sector Management.

In the Doctor of Business Administration (D.B.A.) program, industry and academic professionals have the opportunity to build upon master's-level competencies, skills, and knowledge to prepare themselves to perform more effectively in existing professional roles, to qualify for roles with increasing responsibility, and/or develop capabilities for a second career in teaching at the college level. The program requires students to develop applied research inquiry and analytical skills and helps them develop competencies in understanding and performing applied research which can then be used to foster innovation and lead organizational change. The D.B.A. program consists of five research foundation courses, six core courses, four concentration courses, one elective course, and 12 credit hours in dissertation study. Students must also successfully complete the comprehensive written examination during or after their final semester of coursework in order to move into the dissertation process. D.B.A. concentrations are offered in accounting, global business sustainability, information systems (limited availability, Program Chair approval needed to enter), international business, management, and marketing. In addition, with approval of the student's program chair, a student may select four courses (12 credit hours) to create a customized concentration that better fits their specific career goals. The program is structured to enable busy professionals to balance the demands of career, family, and school. Courses are offered in a variety of formats including condensed weekend classes, regular weekly sessions, or a combination of class settings and online activities.

The Doctor of Education (Ed.D.) in Organizational Leadership program is designed to meet the special requirements of working professionals who wish to develop their knowledge and skills to handle the changing needs of modern organizations. Based on the belief that success for an organization is directly and substantially linked to leaders within the organization, Argosy University seeks to inform, enhance, challenge, and support the development of organizational leaders ready to face the complex issues present in an ever-changing world. The program focuses on the qualities of transformational leadership, not just managerial attributes. This approach prepares students to lead complex organizations faced with strategic challenges, such as increasing globalization, changing economies, societal shifts, and individual organizational relationships. Some assignments will require applying principles in live situations. Students should be aware that they will at times need access to an organization—whether their employer or another organization—to maximize the opportunity to develop their competencies.

Research Facilities

Argosy University libraries provide curriculum support and educational resources, including current text materials, diagnostic training documents, reference materials and databases, journals and dissertations, and major and current titles in program areas. There is an online public-access catalog of library resources available throughout the Argosy University system. Students have remote access to the campus library database, enabling them to study and conduct research at home. Academic databases offer dissertation abstracts, academic journals, and professional periodicals. All library computers are Internet accessible. Software applications include Word, Excel, PowerPoint, SPSS, and various test-scoring programs.

Argosy University, Denver

Financial Aid

Financial aid is available to those who qualify. Argosy University, Denver, offers access to federal and state aid programs, merit-based awards, grants, loans, and a work-study program. As a first step, students should complete the Free Application for Federal Student Aid (FAFSA). Prospective students can apply electronically at http://www.fafsa.ed.gov or at the campus.

Cost of Study

Tuition varies by program. Students should contact Argosy University, Denver, for tuition information.

Living and Housing Costs

Students typically live in apartments in the metropolitan Denver area. Living expenses vary according to each student's preferred standard of living, housing, and transportation. The University does not offer or operate student housing. Most of the students are full-time working professionals who live within driving distance of the campus. Several nearby hotels offer special rates for those who commute from long distances. The Admissions Department also maintains a list of housing options, including contact information for University students who wish to share housing. For more information, students should contact the Admissions Department.

Student Group

Admission to Argosy University, Denver, is selective to ensure a dynamic and engaged student body. It encourages diversity in academic and employment backgrounds and promotes integration of the student body into professional life through established connections with local and national professional associations. Argosy University offers a professionally oriented education with rich opportunities to gain practical experience in class, field placements, and internships. Full-time students and working professionals gain the extensive knowledge and range of skills necessary for effective performance in their chosen fields.

Student Outcomes

Students can register with the University's online career-services system and use select services from a distance, such as degree-specific career e-mail lists, national job posts, and virtual job fairs. Students should contact the University for more information.

Location

Argosy University, Denver, is conveniently located at 7600 East Eastman Avenue in Denver, Colorado. The campus is close to a variety of local libraries, shops, restaurants, theaters, and art museums. Denver's thriving professional organizations, major corporations, high-tech companies, hospitals, schools, clinics, and social service agencies can also provide varied training opportunities for students.

The University

Argosy University is a private institution with nineteen locations across the nation. Argosy University, Denver, provides students with a career resources office, an academic resources center, and extensive information access for research. It offers the resources of a large university, plus the friendliness and personal attention of a small campus.

The innovative programs feature dynamic, relevant, and practical curricula delivered in flexible class formats. Students enjoy scheduling options that make it easier to fit school into their busy lives, choosing from day and evening courses, on campus or online. Many students find a combination of class formats to be an ideal way of continuing their education while meeting family and professional demands.

Argosy University is accredited by the Accrediting Commission for Senior Colleges and Universities of the Western Association for Schools and Colleges (985 Atlantic Avenue, Suite 100, Alameda, California, 94501, http://www.wascsenior.org)..

Applying

Argosy University, Denver, accepts students year-round on a rolling admissions basis, depending on availability of required courses. Applications for admission are available online or by contacting the campus.

Correspondence and Information

Argosy University, Denver
7600 East Eastman Avenue
Denver, Colorado 80231
United States
Phone: 303-923-4110
866-431-5981 (toll-free)
Fax: 303-923-4111
E-mail: auadmissions@argosy.edu
Web site: http://www.argosy.edu/denver

THE FACULTY

The Argosy University faculty comprises working professionals who are eager to help students succeed. Members bring real-world experience and the latest practice innovations to the academic setting. The diverse faculty members of the College of Business are widely recognized for contributions to the field. Many are published scholars, and most hold doctoral degrees. They are committed to providing a substantive education that combines comprehensive knowledge with critical skills and practical workplace relevance. Above all, faculty members are committed to their students' personal and professional development.

ARGOSY UNIVERSITY, HAWAI'I

College of Business

Programs of Study

Argosy University, Hawai'i, offers the Master of Business Administration (M.B.A.) degree; the Master of Public Administration (M.P.A) degree; Master of Science (M.S.) degrees in Human Resource Management, Non-Profit Management, Organizational Leadership, and Service Sector Management; the Doctor of Business Administration (D.B.A.) degree; and the Doctor of Education (Ed.D.) degree in Organizational Leadership. The business programs are designed to serve the needs of talented students, regardless of their undergraduate degrees. The College of Business welcomes and encourages students from diverse academic backgrounds.

The Master of Business Administration (M.B.A.) program develops action-oriented managers and leaders who focus on leading themselves and others to solutions that serve their organizations. Students acquire skills to identify challenges and opportunities, draw on the latest technology and information, use advanced analytical and planning approaches, and execute plans for leading positive change. Students develop these competencies through focusing on critical thinking, persuasive communications, technical knowledge, and a deep understanding of the human side of business. The program is designed to build upon the talents of students, independent of their undergraduate field of study. The program consists of eight core courses (24 credit hours) and four concentration courses (12 credit hours), scheduled to enable busy professionals to balance the demands of career, family, and school. In addition to the core requirements, students can select concentrations in corporate compliance, finance, fraud examination, healthcare administration, information systems management (limited availability, Program Chair approval needed to enter), international business, management, marketing, public administration, and sustainable management. A student may also select four courses (12 credit hours) to create a customized concentration that better fits their specific career goals, with approval of their program chair. The M.B.A. program culminates in an applied capstone project in which all students have the opportunity to integrate the core business competencies with their concentration specialty.

The Master of Public Administration (M.P.A.) program is designed to develop action-oriented problem-solving managers for the public sector, especially at the state and local levels of government. Students develop the competencies required to execute the duties and responsibilities of public sector managers, including evaluation and supervision of employees, reinforcement of the organizational mission, and effective management of organizational resources.

The Master of Science (M.S.) programs focus on the immediate need for management/leadership/interpersonal skills to enhance a student's career potential within an organization or field, or to accelerate their career within a given area of interest. The programs address the needs of individuals whose near-term career responsibilities include managing and leading employees and interacting with customers, clients, and stakeholders. In many cases, these individuals have much of the technical knowledge they need but lack both the language of business and the breadth of leadership and interpersonal skills to maximize their career potential. Examples range from accountants who want to manage a small accounting partnership, to engineers asked to lead a department, to department managers in retail firms who want to progress to store management roles. Also included would be managers in local or regional nonprofit organizations, small-firm management or technical consultants, human resource professionals, and a range of service sector managers from the hospitality industry to transportation to event planning professionals. The degree programs offered are Master of Science in Human Resource Management, Master of Science in Non-Profit Management, Master of Science in Organizational Leadership, and Master of Science in Service Sector Management.

In the Doctor of Business Administration (D.B.A.) program, industry and academic professionals have the opportunity to build upon master's-level competencies, skills, and knowledge to prepare themselves to perform more effectively in existing professional roles, to qualify for roles with increasing responsibility, and/or develop capabilities for a second career in teaching at the college level. The program requires students to develop applied research inquiry and analytical skills and helps them develop competencies in understanding and performing applied research which can then be used to foster innovation and lead organizational change. The D.B.A. program consists of five research foundation courses, six core courses, four concentration courses, one elective course, and 12 credit hours in dissertation study. Students must also successfully complete the comprehensive written examination during or after their final semester of coursework in order to move into the dissertation process. D.B.A. concentrations are offered in accounting, global business sustainability, information systems (limited availability, Program Chair approval needed to enter), international business, management, and marketing. In addition, with approval of the student's program chair, a student may select four courses (12 credit hours) to create a customized concentration that better fits their specific career goals. The program is structured to enable busy professionals to balance the demands of career, family, and school. Courses are offered in a variety of formats including condensed weekend classes, regular weekly sessions, or a combination of class settings and online activities.

The Doctor of Education (Ed.D.) in Organizational Leadership program is designed to meet the special requirements of working professionals who wish to develop their knowledge and skills to handle the changing needs of modern organizations. Based on the belief that success for an organization is directly and substantially linked to leaders within the organization, Argosy University seeks to inform, enhance, challenge, and support the development of organizational leaders ready to face the complex issues present in an ever-changing world. The program focuses on the qualities of transformational leadership, not just managerial attributes. This approach prepares students to lead complex organizations faced with strategic challenges, such as increasing globalization, changing economies, societal shifts, and individual organizational relationships. Some assignments will require applying principles in live situations. Students should be aware that they will at times need access to an organization—whether their employer or another organization—to maximize the opportunity to develop their competencies.

Research Facilities

Argosy University libraries provide curriculum support and educational resources, including current text materials, diagnostic training documents, reference materials and databases, journals and dissertations, and major and current titles in program areas. There is an online public-access catalog of library resources available throughout the Argosy University system. Students have remote access to the campus library database, enabling them to study and conduct research at home. Academic databases offer dissertation abstracts, academic journals, and professional periodicals. All library

computers are Internet accessible. Software applications include Word, Excel, PowerPoint, SPSS, and various test-scoring programs.

Financial Aid

Financial aid is available to those who qualify. Argosy University, Hawai'i, offers access to federal and state aid programs, merit-based awards, grants, loans, and a work-study program. As a first step, students should complete the Free Application for Federal Student Aid (FAFSA). Prospective students can apply electronically at http://www.fafsa.ed.gov or at the campus.

Cost of Study

Tuition varies by program. Students should contact Argosy University, Hawai'i, for tuition information.

Living and Housing Costs

Students typically live in apartments in the metropolitan Honolulu area. Living expenses vary according to each student's preferred standard of living, housing, and transportation. The University does not offer or operate student housing. Most of the students are full-time working professionals who live within driving distance of the campus. Several nearby hotels offer special rates for those who commute from long distances. The Admissions Department also maintains a list of housing options, including contact information for University students who wish to share housing. For more information, students should contact the Admissions Department.

Student Group

Admission to Argosy University, Hawai'i, is selective to ensure a dynamic and engaged student body. The University encourages diversity in academic and employment backgrounds and promotes integration of the student body into professional life through established connections with local and national professional associations. Argosy University offers a professionally oriented education with rich opportunities to gain practical experience in class, field placements, and internships. Full-time students and working professionals gain the extensive knowledge and range of skills necessary for effective performance in their chosen fields.

Student Outcomes

Students can register with the University's online career-services system and use select services from a distance, such as degree-specific career e-mail lists, national job posts, and virtual job fairs. Students should contact the University for more information.

Location

Argosy University, Hawai'i, is located in downtown Honolulu on Oahu. Additional satellite locations on Maui and in Hilo on the Island of Hawaii offer programs to communities on the neighboring islands. These locations connect the campus to Hawaii and to the local and native communities of the Pacific Islands and the Pacific Rim. Students enjoy the cultural and recreational opportunities that these locations provide. University faculty and staff members often work in cooperation with the Hawaii community to create an educational focus on social issues, human diversity, and programs that make a difference to underserved populations.

Honolulu's business environment includes a broad array of companies. The area's largest employers include Bank of Hawaii, Queens Medical Center, and the U.S. government. Many businesses in the metropolitan area provide varied opportunities for student training.

The University

Argosy University is a private institution with nineteen locations across the nation. Argosy University, Hawai'i, provides students with a career resources office, an academic resources center, and extensive information access for research. It offers the resources of a large university, plus the friendliness and personal attention of a small campus. The innovative programs feature dynamic, relevant, and practical curricula delivered in flexible class formats. Students enjoy scheduling options that make it easier to fit school into their busy lives, choosing from day and evening courses, on campus or online. Many students find a combination of class formats to be an ideal way of continuing their education while meeting family and professional demands.

Argosy University is accredited by the Accrediting Commission for Senior Colleges and Universities of the Western Association for Schools and Colleges (985 Atlantic Avenue, Suite 100, Alameda, California, 94501, http://www.wascsenior.org).

Applying

Argosy University, Hawai'i, accepts students year-round on a rolling admissions basis, depending on availability of required courses. Applications for admission are available online or by contacting the campus.

Correspondence and Information

Argosy University, Hawai'i
1001 Bishop Street, Suite 400
Honolulu, Hawaii 96813
United States
Phone: 808-536-5555
888-323-2777 (toll-free)
Fax: 808-536-5505
E-mail: auadmissions@argosy.edu
Web site: http://www.argosy.edu/hawaii

THE FACULTY

The Argosy University faculty comprises working professionals who are eager to help students succeed. Members bring real-world experience and the latest practice innovations to the academic setting. The diverse faculty members of the College of Business are widely recognized for contributions to the field. Many are published scholars, and most hold doctoral degrees. They are committed to providing a substantive education that combines comprehensive knowledge with critical skills and practical workplace relevance. Above all, faculty members are committed to their students' personal and professional development.

ARGOSY UNIVERSITY, INLAND EMPIRE

College of Business

Programs of Study

Argosy University, Inland Empire, offers the Master of Business Administration (M.B.A.) degree; the Master of Public Administration (M.P.A.) degree; Master of Science (M.S.) degrees in Human Resource Management, Non-Profit Management, Organizational Leadership, and Service Sector Management; the Doctor of Education (Ed.D.) degree in Organizational Leadership; and the Doctor of Business Administration (D.B.A.) degree. The business programs are designed to serve the needs of talented students, regardless of their undergraduate degrees. The College of Business welcomes and encourages students from diverse academic backgrounds.

The Master of Business Administration (M.B.A.) program develops action-oriented managers and leaders who focus on leading themselves and others to solutions that serve their organizations. Students acquire skills to identify challenges and opportunities, draw on the latest technology and information, use advanced analytical and planning approaches, and execute plans for leading positive change. Students develop these competencies through focusing on critical thinking, persuasive communications, technical knowledge, and a deep understanding of the human side of business. The program is designed to build upon the talents of students, independent of their undergraduate field of study. The program consists of eight core courses (24 credit hours) and four concentration courses (12 credit hours), scheduled to enable busy professionals to balance the demands of career, family, and school. In addition to the core requirements, students can select concentrations in corporate compliance, finance, fraud examination, healthcare administration, information systems management (limited availability, Program Chair approval needed to enter), international business, management, marketing, public administration, and sustainable management. A student may also select four courses (12 credit hours) to create a customized concentration that better fits their specific career goals, with approval of their program chair. The M.B.A. program culminates in an applied capstone project in which all students have the opportunity to integrate the core business competencies with their concentration specialty.

The Master of Public Administration (M.P.A.) program is designed to develop action-oriented problem-solving managers for the public sector, especially at the state and local levels of government. Students develop the competencies required to execute the duties and responsibilities of public sector managers, including evaluation and supervision of employees, reinforcement of the organizational mission, and effective management of organizational resources.

The Master of Science (M.S.) programs focus on the immediate need for management/leadership/interpersonal skills to enhance a student's career potential within an organization or field, or to accelerate their career within a given area of interest. The programs address the needs of individuals whose near-term career responsibilities include managing and leading employees and interacting with customers, clients, and stakeholders. In many cases, these individuals have much of the technical knowledge they need but lack both the language of business and the breadth of leadership and interpersonal skills to maximize their career potential. Examples range from accountants who want to manage a small accounting partnership, to engineers asked to lead a department, to department managers in retail firms who want to progress to store management roles. Also included would be managers in local or regional nonprofit organizations, small-firm management or technical consultants, human resource professionals, and a range of service sector managers from the hospitality industry to transportation to event planning professionals. The degree programs offered are Master of Science in Human Resource Management, Master of Science in Non-Profit Management, Master of Science in Organizational Leadership, and Master of Science in Service Sector Management.

The Doctor of Education (Ed.D.) in Organizational Leadership program is designed to meet the special requirements of working professionals who wish to develop their knowledge and skills to handle the changing needs of modern organizations. Based on the belief that success for an organization is directly and substantially linked to leaders within the organization, Argosy University seeks to inform, enhance, challenge, and support the development of organizational leaders ready to face the complex issues present in an ever-changing world. The program focuses on the qualities of transformational leadership, not just managerial attributes. This approach prepares students to lead complex organizations faced with strategic challenges, such as increasing globalization, changing economies, societal shifts, and individual organizational relationships. Some assignments will require applying principles in live situations. Students should be aware that they will at times need access to an organization—whether their employer or another organization—to maximize the opportunity to develop their competencies.

In the Doctor of Business Administration (D.B.A.) program, industry and academic professionals have the opportunity to build upon master's-level competencies, skills, and knowledge to prepare themselves to perform more effectively in existing professional roles, to qualify for roles with increasing responsibility, and/or develop capabilities for a second career in teaching at the college level. The program requires students to develop applied research inquiry and analytical skills and helps them develop competencies in understanding and performing applied research which can then be used to foster innovation and lead organizational change. The D.B.A. program consists of five research foundation courses, six core courses, four concentration courses, one elective course, and 12 credit hours in dissertation study. Students must also successfully complete the comprehensive written examination during or after their final semester of coursework in order to move into the dissertation process. D.B.A. concentrations are offered in accounting, global business sustainability, information systems (limited availability, Program Chair approval needed to enter), international business, management, and marketing. In addition, with approval of the student's program chair, a student may select four courses (12 credit hours) to create a customized concentration that better fits their specific career goals. The program is structured to enable busy professionals to balance the demands of career, family, and school. Courses are offered in a variety of formats including condensed weekend classes, regular weekly sessions, or a combination of class settings and online activities.

Research Facilities

Argosy University libraries provide curriculum support and educational resources, including current text materials, diagnostic training documents, reference materials and databases, journals and dissertations, and major and current titles in program areas. There is an online public-access catalog of library resources available throughout the Argosy University system. Students have remote access to the campus library database, enabling them to study and conduct research at home. Academic databases offer dissertation abstracts, academic journals, and professional periodicals. All library

computers are Internet accessible. Software applications include Word, Excel, PowerPoint, SPSS, and various test-scoring programs.

Financial Aid

Financial aid is available to those who qualify. Argosy University, Inland Empire, offers access to federal and state aid programs, merit-based awards, grants, loans, and a work-study program. As a first step, students should complete the Free Application for Federal Student Aid (FAFSA). Prospective students can apply electronically at http://www.fafsa.ed.gov or at the campus.

Cost of Study

Tuition varies by program. Students should contact Argosy University, Inland Empire, for tuition information.

Living and Housing Costs

Students typically live in apartments in the metropolitan San Bernardino area. Living expenses vary according to each student's preferred standard of living, housing, and transportation. The University does not offer or operate student housing. Most of the students are full-time working professionals who live within driving distance of the campus. Several nearby hotels offer special rates for those who commute from long distances. The Admissions Department also maintains a list of housing options, including contact information for university students who wish to share housing. For more information, students should contact the Admissions Department.

Student Group

Admission to Argosy University, Inland Empire, is selective to ensure a dynamic and engaged student body. The University encourages diversity in academic and employment backgrounds and promotes integration of the student body into professional life through established connections with local and national professional associations. Argosy University offers a professionally oriented education with rich opportunities to gain practical experience in class, field placements, and internships. Full-time students and working professionals gain the extensive knowledge and range of skills necessary for effective performance in their chosen fields.

Student Outcomes

Students can register with the University's online career-services system and use select services from a distance, such as degree-specific career e-mail lists, national job posts, and virtual job fairs. Students should contact the University for more information.

Location

Argosy University's Inland Empire facility features classrooms, computer labs, a resource center with Internet access, student lounge, staff and faculty offices, and proximity to the region's many cultural and recreational attractions. The University provides a supportive educational environment with convenient class options that enable students to earn a degree while fulfilling other life responsibilities. All of the programs are thoroughly oriented to the real working world with a focus on developing technical proficiency in each student's field as well as an overall professional career approach. Many businesses in the area provide varied opportunities for student training.

The University

Argosy University is a private institution with nineteen locations across the nation. Argosy University, Inland Empire, provides students with a career resources office, an academic resources center, and extensive information access for research. It offers the resources of a large university plus the friendliness and personal attention of a small campus.

The innovative programs feature dynamic, relevant, and practical curricula delivered in flexible class formats. Students enjoy scheduling options that make it easier to fit school into their busy lives, choosing from day and evening courses, on campus or online. Many students find a combination of class formats to be an ideal way of continuing their education while meeting family and professional demands.

Argosy University is accredited by the Accrediting Commission for Senior Colleges and Universities of the Western Association for Schools and Colleges (985 Atlantic Avenue, Suite 100, Alameda, California, 94501, http://www.wascsenior.org).

Applying

Argosy University, Inland Empire, accepts students year-round on a rolling admissions basis, depending on availability of required courses. Applications for admission are available online or by contacting the campus.

Correspondence and Information

Argosy University, Inland Empire
3401 Centre Lake Drive, Suite 200
Ontario, California 91761
United States
Phone: 909-472-0800
866-217-9075 (toll-free)
Fax: 909-472-0801
E-mail: auadmissions@argosy.edu
Web site: http://www.argosy.edu/inlandempire

THE FACULTY

The Argosy University faculty comprises working professionals who are eager to help students succeed. Members bring real-world experience and the latest practice innovations to the academic setting. The diverse faculty members of the College of Business are widely recognized for contributions to the field. Many are published scholars, and most hold doctoral degrees. They are committed to providing a substantive education that combines comprehensive knowledge with critical skills and practical workplace relevance. Above all, faculty members are committed to their students' personal and professional development.

ARGOSY UNIVERSITY, LOS ANGELES

College of Business

ARGOSY UNIVERSITY
tradition | passion | excellence

Programs of Study

Argosy University, Los Angeles, offers the Master of Business Administration (M.B.A.) degree; the Master of Public Administration (M.P.A.) degree; Master of Science (M.S.) degrees in Human Resource Management, Non-Profit Management, Organizational Leadership, and Service Sector Management; the Doctor of Education (Ed.D.) degree in Organizational Leadership; and the Doctor of Business Administration (D.B.A.) degree. The business programs are designed to serve the needs of talented students, regardless of their undergraduate degrees. The College of Business welcomes and encourages students from diverse academic backgrounds.

The Master of Business Administration (M.B.A.) program develops action-oriented managers and leaders who focus on leading themselves and others to solutions that serve their organizations. Students acquire skills to identify challenges and opportunities, draw on the latest technology and information, use advanced analytical and planning approaches, and execute plans for leading positive change. Students develop these competencies through focusing on critical thinking, persuasive communications, technical knowledge, and a deep understanding of the human side of business. The program is designed to build upon the talents of students, independent of their undergraduate field of study. The program consists of eight core courses (24 credit hours) and four concentration courses (12 credit hours), scheduled to enable busy professionals to balance the demands of career, family, and school. In addition to the core requirements, students can select concentrations in corporate compliance, finance, fraud examination, healthcare administration, information systems management (limited availability, Program Chair approval needed to enter), international business, management, marketing, public administration, and sustainable management. A student may also select four courses (12 credit hours) to create a customized concentration that better fits their specific career goals, with approval of their program chair. The M.B.A. program culminates in an applied capstone project in which all students have the opportunity to integrate the core business competencies with their concentration specialty.

The Master of Public Administration (M.P.A.) program is designed to develop action-oriented problem-solving managers for the public sector, especially at the state and local levels of government. Students develop the competencies required to execute the duties and responsibilities of public sector managers, including evaluation and supervision of employees, reinforcement of the organizational mission, and effective management of organizational resources.

The Master of Science (M.S.) programs focus on the immediate need for management/leadership/interpersonal skills to enhance a student's career potential within an organization or field, or to accelerate their career within a given area of interest. The programs address the needs of individuals whose near-term career responsibilities include managing and leading employees and interacting with customers, clients, and stakeholders. In many cases, these individuals have much of the technical knowledge they need but lack both the language of business and the breadth of leadership and interpersonal skills to maximize their career potential. Examples range from accountants who want to manage a small accounting partnership, to engineers asked to lead a department, to department managers in retail firms who want to progress to store management roles. Also included would be managers in local or regional nonprofit organizations, small-firm management or technical consultants, human resource professionals, and a range of service sector managers from the hospitality industry to transportation to event planning professionals. The degree programs offered are Master of Science in Human Resource Management, Master of Science in Non-Profit Management, Master of Science in Organizational Leadership, and Master of Science in Service Sector Management.

The Doctor of Education (Ed.D.) in Organizational Leadership program is designed to meet the special requirements of working professionals who wish to develop their knowledge and skills to handle the changing needs of modern organizations. Based on the belief that success for an organization is directly and substantially linked to leaders within the organization, Argosy University seeks to inform, enhance, challenge, and support the development of organizational leaders ready to face the complex issues present in an ever-changing world. The program focuses on the qualities of transformational leadership, not just managerial attributes. This approach prepares students to lead complex organizations faced with strategic challenges, such as increasing globalization, changing economies, societal shifts, and individual organizational relationships. Some assignments will require applying principles in live situations. Students should be aware that they will at times need access to an organization—whether their employer or another organization—to maximize the opportunity to develop their competencies.

In the Doctor of Business Administration (D.B.A.) program, industry and academic professionals have the opportunity to build upon master's-level competencies, skills, and knowledge to prepare themselves to perform more effectively in existing professional roles, to qualify for roles with increasing responsibility, and/or develop capabilities for a second career in teaching at the college level. The program requires students to develop applied research inquiry and analytical skills and helps them develop competencies in understanding and performing applied research which can then be used to foster innovation and lead organizational change. The D.B.A. program consists of five research foundation courses, six core courses, four concentration courses, one elective course, and 12 credit hours in dissertation study. Students must also successfully complete the comprehensive written examination during or after their final semester of coursework in order to move into the dissertation process. D.B.A. concentrations are offered in accounting, global business sustainability, information systems (limited availability, Program Chair approval needed to enter), international business, management, and marketing. In addition, with approval of the student's program chair, a student may select four courses (12 credit hours) to create a customized concentration that better fits their specific career goals. The program is structured to enable busy professionals to balance the demands of career, family, and school. Courses are offered in a variety of formats including condensed weekend classes, regular weekly sessions, or a combination of class settings and online activities.

Research Facilities

Argosy University libraries provide curriculum support and educational resources, including current text materials, diagnostic training documents, reference materials and databases, journals and dissertations, and major and current titles in program areas. There is an online public-access catalog of library resources available throughout the Argosy University system. Students have remote access to the campus library database, enabling them to study and conduct research at home. Academic databases offer dissertation abstracts, academic journals, and professional periodicals. All library

Argosy University, Los Angeles

computers are Internet accessible. Software applications include Word, Excel, PowerPoint, SPSS, and various test-scoring programs.

Financial Aid

Financial aid is available to those who qualify. Argosy University, Los Angeles, offers access to federal and state aid programs, merit-based awards, grants, loans, and a work-study program. As a first step, students should complete the Free Application for Federal Student Aid (FAFSA). Prospective students can apply electronically at http://www.fafsa.ed.gov or at the campus.

Cost of Study

Tuition varies by program. Students should contact Argosy University, Los Angeles, for tuition information.

Living and Housing Costs

Students typically live in apartments in the metropolitan Santa Monica area. Living expenses vary according to each student's preferred standard of living, housing, and transportation. The University does not offer or operate student housing. Most of the students are full-time working professionals who live within driving distance of the campus. Several nearby hotels offer special rates for those who commute from long distances. The Admissions Department also maintains a list of housing options, including contact information for university students who wish to share housing. For more information, students should contact the Admissions Department.

Student Group

Admission to Argosy University, Los Angeles, is selective to ensure a dynamic and engaged student body. The University encourages diversity in academic and employment backgrounds and promotes integration of the student body into professional life through established connections with local and national professional associations. Argosy University offers a professionally oriented education with rich opportunities to gain practical experience in class, field placements, and internships. Full-time students and working professionals gain the extensive knowledge and range of skills necessary for effective performance in their chosen fields.

Student Outcomes

Students can register with the University's online career-services system and use select services from a distance, such as degree-specific career e-mail lists, national job posts, and virtual job fairs. Students should contact the University for more information.

Location

Argosy University, Los Angeles, is only minutes away from Los Angeles International Airport and the Pacific coast, and is conveniently located near the interchange between I-405 and I-105.

The business environment in the Los Angeles metropolitan area includes a broad array of companies, including a proliferation of entertainment, technology, and software firms. Among the principal employers in the area are Yahoo!, MTV Networks, RAND Corporation, and Symantec Corporation. The many businesses in the area provide varied opportunities for student training.

The University

Argosy University is a private institution with nineteen locations across the nation. Argosy University, Los Angeles, provides students with a career resources office, an academic resources center, and extensive information access for research. It offers the resources of a large university plus the friendliness and personal attention of a small campus.

The innovative programs feature dynamic, relevant, and practical curricula delivered in flexible class formats. Students enjoy scheduling options that make it easier to fit school into their busy lives, choosing from day and evening courses, on campus or online. Many students find a combination of class formats to be an ideal way of continuing their education while meeting family and professional demands.

Argosy University is accredited by the Accrediting Commission for Senior Colleges and Universities of the Western Association for Schools and Colleges (985 Atlantic Avenue, Suite 100, Alameda, California, 94501, http://www.wascsenior.org).

Applying

Argosy University, Los Angeles, accepts students year-round on a rolling admissions basis, depending on availability of required courses. Applications for admission are available online or by contacting the campus.

Correspondence and Information

Argosy University, Los Angeles
5230 Pacific Concourse, Suite 200
Los Angeles, California 90045
United States
Phone: 310-531-9700
866-505-0332 (toll-free)
Fax: 310-531-9801
E-mail: auadmissions@argosy.edu
Web site: http://www.argosy.edu/losangeles

THE FACULTY

The Argosy University faculty comprises working professionals who are eager to help students succeed. Members bring real-world experience and the latest practice innovations to the academic setting. The diverse faculty members of the College of Business are widely recognized for contributions to the field. Many are published scholars, and most hold doctoral degrees. They are committed to providing a substantive education that combines comprehensive knowledge with critical skills and practical workplace relevance. Above all, faculty members are committed to their students' personal and professional development.

ARGOSY UNIVERSITY, NASHVILLE

College of Business

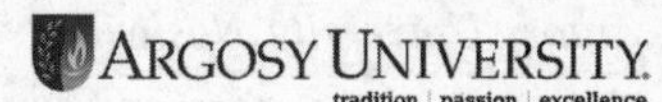

Programs of Study

Argosy University, Nashville, offers the Master of Business Administration (M.B.A.) degree; the Master of Public Administration (M.P.A.) degree; the Master of Science in Management (M.S.M.) degree; Master of Science (M.S.) degrees in Human Resource Management, Non-Profit Management, Organizational Leadership, and Service Sector Management; the Doctor of Education (Ed.D.) degree in Organizational Leadership; and the Doctor of Business Administration (D.B.A.) degree. The business programs are designed to serve the needs of talented students, regardless of their undergraduate degrees. The College of Business welcomes and encourages students from diverse academic backgrounds.

The Master of Business Administration (M.B.A.) program develops action-oriented managers and leaders who focus on leading themselves and others to solutions that serve their organizations. Students acquire skills to identify challenges and opportunities, draw on the latest technology and information, use advanced analytical and planning approaches, and execute plans for leading positive change. Students develop these competencies through focusing on critical thinking, persuasive communications, technical knowledge, and a deep understanding of the human side of business. The program is designed to build upon the talents of students, independent of their undergraduate field of study. The program consists of eight core courses (24 credit hours) and four concentration courses (12 credit hours), scheduled to enable busy professionals to balance the demands of career, family, and school. In addition to the core requirements, students can select concentrations in corporate compliance, finance, fraud examination, healthcare administration, information systems management (limited availability, Program Chair approval needed to enter), international business, management, marketing, public administration, and sustainable management. A student may also select four courses (12 credit hours) to create a customized concentration that better fits their specific career goals, with approval of their program chair. The M.B.A. program culminates in an applied capstone project in which all students have the opportunity to integrate the core business competencies with their concentration specialty.

The Master of Public Administration (M.P.A.) program is designed to develop action-oriented problem-solving managers for the public sector, especially at the state and local levels of government. Students develop the competencies required to execute the duties and responsibilities of public sector managers, including evaluation and supervision of employees, reinforcement of the organizational mission, and effective management of organizational resources.

The Master of Science in Management (M.S.M.) degree program is designed to improve and extend the interpersonal and problem-solving skills necessary for employment in the private, nonprofit, and public sectors. The program focuses on situation diagnostics, opportunity and problem evaluation, and implementation of an action plan.

The Master of Science (M.S.) programs focus on the immediate need for management/leadership/interpersonal skills to enhance a student's career potential within an organization or field, or to accelerate their career within a given area of interest. The programs address the needs of individuals whose near-term career responsibilities include managing and leading employees and interacting with customers, clients, and stakeholders. In many cases, these individuals have much of the technical knowledge they need but lack both the language of business and the breadth of leadership and interpersonal skills to maximize their career potential. Examples range from accountants who want to manage a small accounting partnership, to engineers asked to lead a department, to department managers in retail firms who want to progress to store management roles. Also included would be managers in local or regional nonprofit organizations, small-firm management or technical consultants, human resource professionals, and a range of service sector managers from the hospitality industry to transportation to event planning professionals. The degree programs offered are Master of Science in Human Resource Management, Master of Science in Non-Profit Management, Master of Science in Organizational Leadership, and Master of Science in Service Sector Management.

The Doctor of Education (Ed.D.) in Organizational Leadership program is designed to meet the special requirements of working professionals who wish to develop their knowledge and skills to handle the changing needs of modern organizations. Based on the belief that success for an organization is directly and substantially linked to leaders within the organization, Argosy University seeks to inform, enhance, challenge, and support the development of organizational leaders ready to face the complex issues present in an ever-changing world. The program focuses on the qualities of transformational leadership, not just managerial attributes. This approach prepares students to lead complex organizations faced with strategic challenges, such as increasing globalization, changing economies, societal shifts, and individual organizational relationships. Some assignments will require applying principles in live situations. Students should be aware that they will at times need access to an organization—whether their employer or another organization—to maximize the opportunity to develop their competencies.

In the Doctor of Business Administration (D.B.A.) program, industry and academic professionals have the opportunity to build upon master's-level competencies, skills, and knowledge to prepare themselves to perform more effectively in existing professional roles, to qualify for roles with increasing responsibility, and/or develop capabilities for a second career in teaching at the college level. The program requires students to develop applied research inquiry and analytical skills and helps them develop competencies in understanding and performing applied research which can then be used to foster innovation and lead organizational change. The D.B.A. program consists of five research foundation courses, six core courses, four concentration courses, one elective course, and 12 credit hours in dissertation study. Students must also successfully complete the comprehensive written examination during or after their final semester of coursework in order to move into the dissertation process. D.B.A. concentrations are offered in accounting, global business sustainability, information systems (limited availability, Program Chair approval needed to enter), international business, management, and marketing. In addition, with approval of the student's program chair, a student may select four courses (12 credit hours) to create a customized concentration that better fits their specific career goals. The program is structured to enable busy professionals to balance the demands of career, family, and school. Courses are offered in a variety of formats including condensed weekend classes, regular weekly sessions, or a combination of class settings and online activities.

Research Facilities

Argosy University libraries provide curriculum support and educational resources, including current text materials, diagnostic training documents, reference materials and databases, journals and dissertations, and major and current titles in program areas. There is an online public-access catalog of library resources available throughout the Argosy University system. Students have remote access to the campus library database, enabling them to study and conduct research at home. Academic databases offer dissertation abstracts, academic journals, and professional periodicals. All library computers are Internet accessible. Software applications include Word, Excel, PowerPoint, SPSS, and various test-scoring programs.

Financial Aid

Financial aid is available to those who qualify. Argosy University, Nashville, offers access to federal and state aid programs, merit-based awards, grants, loans, and a work-study program. As a first step, students should complete the Free Application for Federal Student Aid (FAFSA). Prospective students can apply electronically at http://www.fafsa.ed.gov or at the campus.

Cost of Study

Tuition varies by program. Students should contact Argosy University, Nashville, for tuition information.

Living and Housing Costs

Students typically live in apartments in the metropolitan Nashville area. Living expenses vary according to each student's preferred standard of living, housing, and transportation. The University does not offer or operate student housing. Most of the students are full-time working professionals who live within driving distance of the campus. Several nearby hotels offer special rates for those who commute from long distances. The Admissions Department also maintains a list of housing options, including contact information, for University students who wish to share housing. For more information, students should contact the Admissions Department.

Student Group

Admission to Argosy University, Nashville, is selective to ensure a dynamic and engaged student body. It encourages diversity in academic and employment backgrounds and promotes integration of the student body into professional life through established connections with local and national professional associations. Argosy University offers a professionally oriented education with rich opportunities to gain practical experience in class, field placements, and internships. Full-time students and working professionals gain the extensive knowledge and range of skills necessary for effective performance in their chosen fields.

Student Outcomes

Students can register with the University's online career-services system and use select services from a distance, such as degree-specific career e-mail lists, national job posts, and virtual job fairs. Students should contact the University for more information.

Location

Argosy University, Nashville, is located at 100 Centerview Drive in Nashville, Tennessee. This growing city offers a variety of recreational activities, including the ballet and symphony, the newly established Frist Museum of Art, and professional sports. Nashville is known as Music City, USA, and is home to the Country Music Hall of Fame. The business environment includes companies such as Moses Cone Health Systems, Inc., and Novant Health, Inc.

The University

Argosy University is a private institution with nineteen locations across the nation. Argosy University, Nashville, provides students with a career resources office, an academic resources center, and extensive information access for research. It offers the resources of a large university, plus the friendliness and personal attention of a small campus.

The innovative programs feature dynamic, relevant, and practical curricula delivered in flexible class formats. Students enjoy scheduling options that make it easier to fit school into their busy lives, choosing from day and evening courses, on campus or online. Many students find a combination of class formats to be an ideal way of continuing their education while meeting family and professional demands.

Argosy University is accredited by the Accrediting Commission for Senior Colleges and Universities of the Western Association for Schools and Colleges (985 Atlantic Avenue, Suite 100, Alameda, California, 94501, http://www.wascsenior.org).

Applying

Argosy University, Nashville, accepts students year-round on a rolling admissions basis, depending on availability of required courses. Applications for admission are available online or by contacting the campus.

Correspondence and Information

Argosy University, Nashville
100 Centerview Drive, Suite 225
Nashville, Tennessee 37214
United States
Phone: 615-525-2800
866-833-6598 (toll-free)
Fax: 615-525-2900
E-mail: auadmissions@argosy.edu
Web site: http://www.argosy.edu/nashville

THE FACULTY

The Argosy University faculty comprises working professionals who are eager to help students succeed. Members bring real-world experience and the latest practice innovations to the academic setting. The diverse faculty members of the College of Business are widely recognized for contributions to the field. Most hold doctoral degrees. They are committed to providing a substantive education that combines comprehensive knowledge with critical skills and practical workplace relevance. Above all, faculty members are committed to their students' personal and professional development.

ARGOSY UNIVERSITY, ORANGE COUNTY

College of Business

Programs of Study

Argosy University, Orange County, offers the Master of Business Administration (M.B.A.) degree; the Master of Public Administration (M.P.A.) degree; Master of Science (M.S.) degrees in Human Resource Management, Non-Profit Management, Organizational Leadership, and Service Sector Management; the Doctor of Education (Ed.D.) degree in Organizational Leadership, and the Doctor of Business Administration (D.B.A.) degree. The business programs are designed to serve the needs of talented students, regardless of their undergraduate degrees. The College of Business welcomes and encourages students from diverse academic backgrounds.

The Master of Business Administration (M.B.A.) program develops action-oriented managers and leaders who focus on leading themselves and others to solutions that serve their organizations. Students acquire skills to identify challenges and opportunities, draw on the latest technology and information, use advanced analytical and planning approaches, and execute plans for leading positive change. Students develop these competencies through focusing on critical thinking, persuasive communications, technical knowledge, and a deep understanding of the human side of business. The program is designed to build upon the talents of students, independent of their undergraduate field of study. The program consists of eight core courses (24 credit hours) and four concentration courses (12 credit hours), scheduled to enable busy professionals to balance the demands of career, family, and school. In addition to the core requirements, students can select concentrations in corporate compliance, finance, fraud examination, healthcare administration, information systems management (limited availability, Program Chair approval needed to enter), international business, management, marketing, public administration, and sustainable management. A student may also select four courses (12 credit hours) to create a customized concentration that better fits their specific career goals, with approval of their program chair. The M.B.A. program culminates in an applied capstone project in which all students have the opportunity to integrate the core business competencies with their concentration specialty.

The Master of Public Administration (M.P.A.) program is designed to develop action-oriented problem-solving managers for the public sector, especially at the state and local levels of government. Students develop the competencies required to execute the duties and responsibilities of public sector managers, including evaluation and supervision of employees, reinforcement of the organizational mission, and effective management of organizational resources.

The Master of Science (M.S.) programs focus on the immediate need for management/leadership/interpersonal skills to enhance a student's career potential within an organization or field, or to accelerate their career within a given area of interest. The programs address the needs of individuals whose near-term career responsibilities include managing and leading employees and interacting with customers, clients, and stakeholders. In many cases, these individuals have much of the technical knowledge they need but lack both the language of business and the breadth of leadership and interpersonal skills to maximize their career potential. Examples range from accountants who want to manage a small accounting partnership, to engineers asked to lead a department, to department managers in retail firms who want to progress to store management roles. Also included would be managers in local or regional nonprofit organizations, small-firm management or technical consultants, human resource professionals, and a range of service sector managers from the hospitality industry to transportation to event planning professionals. The degree programs offered are Master of Science in Human Resource Management, Master of Science in Non-Profit Management, Master of Science in Organizational Leadership, and Master of Science in Service Sector Management.

The Doctor of Education (Ed.D.) in Organizational Leadership program is designed to meet the special requirements of working professionals who wish to develop their knowledge and skills to handle the changing needs of modern organizations. Based on the belief that success for an organization is directly and substantially linked to leaders within the organization, Argosy University seeks to inform, enhance, challenge, and support the development of organizational leaders ready to face the complex issues present in an ever-changing world. The program focuses on the qualities of transformational leadership, not just managerial attributes. This approach prepares students to lead complex organizations faced with strategic challenges, such as increasing globalization, changing economies, societal shifts, and individual organizational relationships. Some assignments will require applying principles in live situations. Students should be aware that they will at times need access to an organization—whether their employer or another organization—to maximize the opportunity to develop their competencies.

In the Doctor of Business Administration (D.B.A.) program, industry and academic professionals have the opportunity to build upon master's-level competencies, skills, and knowledge to prepare themselves to perform more effectively in existing professional roles, to qualify for roles with increasing responsibility, and/or develop capabilities for a second career in teaching at the college level. The program requires students to develop applied research inquiry and analytical skills and helps them develop competencies in understanding and performing applied research which can then be used to foster innovation and lead organizational change. The D.B.A. program consists of five research foundation courses, six core courses, four concentration courses, one elective course, and 12 credit hours in dissertation study. Students must also successfully complete the comprehensive written examination during or after their final semester of coursework in order to move into the dissertation process. D.B.A. concentrations are offered in accounting, global business sustainability, information systems (limited availability, Program Chair approval needed to enter), international business, management, and marketing. In addition, with approval of the student's program chair, a student may select four courses (12 credit hours) to create a customized concentration that better fits their specific career goals. The program is structured to enable busy professionals to balance the demands of career, family, and school. Courses are offered in a variety of formats including condensed weekend classes, regular weekly sessions, or a combination of class settings and online activities.

Research Facilities

Argosy University libraries provide curriculum support and educational resources, including current text materials, diagnostic training documents, reference materials and databases, journals and dissertations, and major and current titles in program areas. There is an online public-access catalog of library resources available throughout the Argosy University system. Students have remote access to the campus library database, enabling them to study and conduct research at home. Academic databases offer dissertation abstracts, academic journals, and professional periodicals. All library

computers are Internet accessible. Software applications include Word, Excel, PowerPoint, SPSS, and various test-scoring programs.

Financial Aid

Financial aid is available to those who qualify. Argosy University, Orange County, offers access to federal and state aid programs, merit-based awards, grants, loans, and a work-study program. As a first step, students should complete the Free Application for Federal Student Aid (FAFSA). Prospective students can apply electronically at http://www.fafsa.ed.gov or at the campus.

Cost of Study

Tuition varies by program. Students should contact Argosy University, Orange County, for tuition information.

Living and Housing Costs

Students typically live in apartments in the Santa Ana metropolitan area. Living expenses vary according to each student's preferred standard of living, housing, and transportation. The University does not offer or operate student housing. Most of the students are full-time working professionals who live within driving distance of the campus. Several nearby hotels offer special rates for those who commute from long distances. The Admissions Department also maintains a list of housing options, including contact information, for University students who wish to share housing. For more information, students should contact the Admissions Department.

Student Group

Admission to Argosy University, Orange County, is selective to ensure a dynamic and engaged student body. It encourages diversity in academic and employment backgrounds and promotes integration of the student body into professional life through established connections with local and national professional associations. Argosy University offers a professionally oriented education with rich opportunities to gain practical experience in class, field placements, and internships. Full-time students and working professionals gain the extensive knowledge and range of skills necessary for effective performance in their chosen fields.

Student Outcomes

Students can register with the University's online career-services system and use select services from a distance, such as degree-specific career e-mail lists, national job posts, and virtual job fairs. Students should contact the University for more information.

Location

Argosy University, Orange County, attracts students from Southern California as well as around the country and the world. Orange County features a temperate climate, sunny beaches, and a host of cultural and entertainment options. The campus is located approximately 30 miles south of downtown Los Angeles, 90 miles north of San Diego, and just minutes from one of the many freeways that connect the Southern California basin. Regional parks and preserved lands provide opportunities for hiking, biking, riding, and other recreational activities. Whether it is ultrachic Newport Beach, artsy Laguna Beach, or unspoiled Catalina Island, Orange County's oceanside personalities are as varied as the people who visit the area.

Many businesses in the area provide excellent opportunities for student training. Orange County's business environment includes a broad array of companies. The area's largest employers include Ingram Micro Inc., the ITT Industries, and OneSource.

The University

Argosy University is a private institution with nineteen locations across the nation. Argosy University, Orange County, provides students with a career resources office, an academic resources center, and extensive information access for research. It offers the resources of a large university plus the friendliness and personal attention of a small campus.

The innovative programs feature dynamic, relevant, and practical curricula delivered in flexible class formats. Students enjoy scheduling options that make it easier to fit school into their busy lives, choosing from day and evening courses, on campus or online. Many students find a combination of class formats to be an ideal way of continuing their education while meeting family and professional demands.

Argosy University is accredited by the Accrediting Commission for Senior Colleges and Universities of the Western Association for Schools and Colleges (985 Atlantic Avenue, Suite 100, Alameda, California, 94501, http://www.wascsenior.org).

Applying

Argosy University, Orange County, accepts students year-round on a rolling admissions basis, depending on availability of required courses. Applications for admission are available online or by contacting the campus.

Correspondence and Information

Argosy University, Orange County
601 South Lewis Street
Orange, California 92868
United States
Phone: 714-620-3700
800-716-9598 (toll-free)
Fax: 714-620-3800
E-mail: auadmissions@argosy.edu
Web site: http://www.argosy.edu/orangecounty/

THE FACULTY

The Argosy University faculty comprises working professionals who are eager to help students succeed. Members bring real-world experience and the latest practice innovations to the academic setting. The diverse faculty members of the College of Business are widely recognized for contributions to the field. Many are published scholars, and most hold doctoral degrees. They are committed to providing a substantive education that combines comprehensive knowledge with critical skills and practical workplace relevance. Above all, faculty members are committed to their students' personal and professional development.

ARGOSY UNIVERSITY, PHOENIX

College of Business

Programs of Study

Argosy University, Phoenix, offers the Master of Business Administration (M.B.A.) degree; the Master of Public Administration (M.P.A.) degree; Master of Science (M.S.) degrees in Human Resource Management, Non-Profit Management, Organizational Leadership, and Service Sector Management; and the Doctor of Business Administration (D.B.A.) degree. The business programs are designed to serve the needs of talented students regardless of their undergraduate degrees. The College of Business welcomes and encourages students from diverse academic backgrounds.

The Master of Business Administration (M.B.A.) program develops action-oriented managers and leaders who focus on leading themselves and others to solutions that serve their organizations. Students acquire skills to identify challenges and opportunities, draw on the latest technology and information, use advanced analytical and planning approaches, and execute plans for leading positive change. Students develop these competencies through focusing on critical thinking, persuasive communications, technical knowledge, and a deep understanding of the human side of business. The program is designed to build upon the talents of students, independent of their undergraduate field of study. The program consists of eight core courses (24 credit hours) and four concentration courses (12 credit hours), scheduled to enable busy professionals to balance the demands of career, family, and school. In addition to the core requirements, students can select concentrations in corporate compliance, finance, fraud examination, healthcare administration, information systems management (limited availability, Program Chair approval needed to enter), international business, management, marketing, public administration, and sustainable management. A student may also select four courses (12 credit hours) to create a customized concentration that better fits their specific career goals, with approval of their program chair. The M.B.A. program culminates in an applied capstone project in which all students have the opportunity to integrate the core business competencies with their concentration specialty.

The Master of Public Administration (M.P.A.) program is designed to develop action-oriented problem-solving managers for the public sector, especially at the state and local levels of government. Students develop the competencies required to execute the duties and responsibilities of public sector managers, including evaluation and supervision of employees, reinforcement of the organizational mission, and effective management of organizational resources.

The Master of Science (M.S.) programs focus on the immediate need for management/leadership/interpersonal skills to enhance a student's career potential within an organization or field, or to accelerate their career within a given area of interest. The programs address the needs of individuals whose near-term career responsibilities include managing and leading employees and interacting with customers, clients, and stakeholders. In many cases, these individuals have much of the technical knowledge they need but lack both the language of business and the breadth of leadership and interpersonal skills to maximize their career potential. Examples range from accountants who want to manage a small accounting partnership, to engineers asked to lead a department, to department managers in retail firms who want to progress to store management roles. Also included would be managers in local or regional nonprofit organizations, small-firm management or technical consultants, human resource professionals, and a range of service sector managers from the hospitality industry to transportation to event planning professionals. The degree programs offered are Master of Science in Human Resource Management, Master of Science in Non-Profit Management, Master of Science in Organizational Leadership, and Master of Science in Service Sector Management.

In the Doctor of Business Administration (D.B.A.) program, industry and academic professionals have the opportunity to build upon master's-level competencies, skills, and knowledge to prepare themselves to perform more effectively in existing professional roles, to qualify for roles with increasing responsibility, and/or develop capabilities for a second career in teaching at the college level. The program requires students to develop applied research inquiry and analytical skills and helps them develop competencies in understanding and performing applied research which can then be used to foster innovation and lead organizational change. The D.B.A. program consists of five research foundation courses, six core courses, four concentration courses, one elective course, and 12 credit hours in dissertation study. Students must also successfully complete the comprehensive written examination during or after their final semester of coursework in order to move into the dissertation process. D.B.A. concentrations are offered in accounting, global business sustainability, information systems (limited availability, Program Chair approval needed to enter), international business, management, and marketing. In addition, with approval of the student's program chair, a student may select four courses (12 credit hours) to create a customized concentration that better fits their specific career goals. The program is structured to enable busy professionals to balance the demands of career, family, and school. Courses are offered in a variety of formats including condensed weekend classes, regular weekly sessions, or a combination of class settings and online activities.

Research Facilities

Argosy University libraries provide curriculum support and educational resources, including current text materials, diagnostic training documents, reference materials and databases, journals and dissertations, and major and current titles in program areas. There is an online public-access catalog of library resources available throughout the Argosy University system. Students have remote access to the campus library database, enabling them to study and conduct research at home. Academic databases offer dissertation abstracts, academic journals, and professional periodicals. All library computers are Internet accessible. Software applications include Word, Excel, PowerPoint, SPSS, and various test-scoring programs.

Argosy University, Phoenix

Financial Aid

Financial aid is available to those who qualify. Argosy University, Phoenix, offers access to federal and state aid programs, merit-based awards, grants, loans, and a work-study program. As a first step, students should complete the Free Application for Federal Student Aid (FAFSA). Prospective students can apply electronically at http://www.fafsa.ed.gov or at the campus.

Cost of Study

Tuition varies by program. Students should contact Argosy University, Phoenix, for tuition information.

Living and Housing Costs

Students typically live in apartments in the metropolitan Phoenix area. Living expenses vary according to each student's preferred standard of living, housing, and transportation. The University does not offer or operate student housing. Most of the students are full-time working professionals who live within driving distance of the campus. Several nearby hotels offer special rates for those who commute from long distances. The Admissions Department also maintains a list of housing options, including contact information for University students who wish to share housing. For more information, students should contact the Admissions Department.

Student Group

Admission to Argosy University, Phoenix, is selective to ensure a dynamic and engaged student body. It encourages diversity in academic and employment backgrounds and promotes integration of the student body into professional life through established connections with local and national professional associations. Argosy University offers a professionally oriented education with rich opportunities to gain practical experience in class, field placements, and internships. Full-time students and working professionals gain the extensive knowledge and range of skills necessary for effective performance in their chosen fields.

Student Outcomes

Students can register with the University's online career-services system and use select services from a distance, such as degree-specific career e-mail lists, national job posts, and virtual job fairs. Students should contact the University for more information.

Location

Argosy University, Phoenix offers classes in an intimate, small-group setting. The campus is conveniently located near I-17, close to shops, restaurants, and recreational areas. Phoenix is home to several major league sports teams, and the city offers an array of cultural activities ranging from opera and theater to science museums. The multicultural environment of Arizona, coupled with Argosy University's professional training affiliations throughout the state, creates an exciting opportunity for students to work with urban, rural, and culturally diverse populations.

Many businesses in the area provide varied opportunities for student training. The business environment in Phoenix includes a wide variety of companies such as Intel and Go Daddy Group, an Internet company. Wells Fargo, Home Depot, Lowe's, and Wal-Mart also represent some of the area's largest employers.

The University

Argosy University is a private institution with nineteen locations across the nation. Argosy University, Phoenix, provides students with a career resources office, an academic resources center, and extensive information access for research. It offers the resources of a large university, plus the friendliness and personal attention of a small campus. The innovative programs feature dynamic, relevant, and practical curricula delivered in flexible class formats. Students enjoy scheduling options that make it easier to fit school into their busy lives, choosing from day and evening courses, on campus or online. Many students find a combination of class formats to be an ideal way of continuing their education while meeting family and professional demands.

Argosy University is accredited by the Accrediting Commission for Senior Colleges and Universities of the Western Association for Schools and Colleges (985 Atlantic Avenue, Suite 100, Alameda, California, 94501, http://www.wascsenior.org).

Applying

Argosy University, Phoenix, accepts students year-round on a rolling admissions basis, depending on availability of required courses. Applications for admission are available online or by contacting the campus.

Correspondence and Information

Argosy University, Phoenix
2233 West Dunlap Avenue
Phoenix, Arizona 85021
United States
Phone: 602-216-2600
866-216-2777 (toll-free)
Fax: 602-216-3151
E-mail: auadmissions@argosy.edu
Web site: http://www.argosy.edu/phoenix/

THE FACULTY

The Argosy University faculty comprises working professionals who are eager to help students succeed. Members bring real-world experience and the latest practice innovations to the academic setting. The diverse faculty members of the College of Business are widely recognized for contributions to the field. Many are published scholars, and most hold doctoral degrees. They are committed to providing a substantive education that combines comprehensive knowledge with critical skills and practical workplace relevance. Above all, faculty members are committed to their students' personal and professional development.

ARGOSY UNIVERSITY, SALT LAKE CITY

College of Business

Programs of Study

Argosy University, Salt Lake City, offers the Master of Business Administration (M.B.A.) degree; the Master of Public Administration (M.P.A.) degree; Master of Science (M.S.) degrees in Human Resource Management, Non-Profit Management, Organizational Leadership, and Service Sector Management; the Doctor of Education (Ed.D.) in Organizational Leadership; and the Doctor of Business Administration (D.B.A.) degree. The business programs are designed to serve the needs of talented students, regardless of their undergraduate degrees. The College of Business welcomes and encourages students from diverse academic backgrounds.

The Master of Business Administration (M.B.A.) program is designed to develop action-oriented managers and leaders who focus on leading themselves and others to solutions that serve their organizations. Students acquire skills to identify challenges and opportunities, draw on the latest technology and information, use advanced analytical and planning approaches, and execute plans for leading positive change. Competencies are developed through focusing on critical thinking, persuasive communications, technical knowledge, and a deep understanding of the human side of business. By focusing on competencies in this manner, the program builds upon the talents of students, independent of their undergraduate field of study. Students from diverse academic and professional backgrounds are welcomed and encouraged. In addition to completing the core course requirements, students develop expertise and specific insights in one of the following concentrations: corporate compliance, finance, fraud examination, health-care administration, information systems management (availability of this concentration is limited; program chair approval is necessary to enter), international business, management, marketing, public administration, or sustainable management. In addition, with approval of the student's program chair, a student may select four courses (12 credit hours) to create a customized concentration that better fits their specific career goals. For all students, the M.B.A. program culminates in an applied capstone project in which they integrate the core business competencies with their concentration specialty.

The Master of Public Administration (M.P.A.) program is designed to develop action-oriented problem-solving managers for the public sector, especially at the state and local levels of government. Students develop the competencies required to execute the duties and responsibilities of public sector managers, including evaluation and supervision of employees, reinforcement of the organizational mission, and effective management of organizational resources.

The Master of Science (M.S.) programs focus on the immediate need for management/leadership/interpersonal skills to enhance a student's career potential within an organization or field, or to accelerate their career within a given area of interest. The programs address the needs of individuals whose near-term career responsibilities include managing and leading employees and interacting with customers, clients, and stakeholders. In many cases, these individuals have much of the technical knowledge they need but lack both the language of business and the breadth of leadership and interpersonal skills to maximize their career potential. Examples range from accountants who want to manage a small accounting partnership, to engineers asked to lead a department, to department managers in retail firms who want to progress to store management roles. Also included would be managers in local or regional nonprofit organizations, small-firm management or technical consultants, human resource professionals, and a range of service sector managers from the hospitality industry to transportation to event planning professionals. The degree programs offered are Master of Science in Human Resource Management, Master of Science in Non-Profit Management, Master of Science in Organizational Leadership, and Master of Science in Service Sector Management.

The Doctor of Education (Ed.D.) in Organizational Leadership program is designed to meet the special requirements of working professionals who wish to develop their knowledge and skills to handle the changing needs of modern organizations. Based on the belief that success for an organization is directly and substantially linked to leaders within the organization, Argosy University seeks to inform, enhance, challenge, and support the development of organizational leaders ready to face the complex issues present in an ever-changing world. The program focuses on the qualities of transformational leadership, not just managerial attributes. This approach prepares students to lead complex organizations faced with strategic challenges, such as increasing globalization, changing economies, societal shifts, and individual organizational relationships. Some assignments will require applying principles in live situations. Students should be aware that they will at times need access to an organization—whether their employer or another organization—to maximize the opportunity to develop their competencies.

The Doctor of Business Administration program enables industry and academic professionals to build upon master's-level competencies, skills, and knowledge, preparing themselves to perform more effectively in existing professional roles, to qualify for roles with increasing responsibility, and/or develop capabilities for a second career in teaching at the college level. The program requires students to develop applied research inquiry and analytical skills. The D.B.A. program is designed to help students develop competencies in understanding and performing applied research, which can then be used to foster innovation and lead organizational change. Students must choose a concentration in accounting, global business sustainability, information systems (availability of this concentration is limited; program chair approval is necessary to enter), international business, management, or marketing. In addition, with approval of the student's program chair, a student may select four courses (12 credit hours) to create a customized concentration that better fits their specific career goals.

Research Facilities

Argosy University libraries provide curriculum support and educational resources, including current text materials, diagnostic training documents, reference materials and databases, journals and dissertations, and major and current titles in program areas. There is an online public-access catalog of library resources available throughout the Argosy University system. Students have remote access to the campus library database, enabling them to study and conduct research at home. Academic databases offer dissertation abstracts, academic journals, and professional periodicals. All library computers are Internet accessible. Software applications include Word, Excel, PowerPoint, SPSS, and various test-scoring programs.

Financial Aid

Financial aid is available to those who qualify. Argosy University, Salt Lake City, offers access to federal and state aid programs, merit-based awards, grants, loans, and a work-study program. As a first step, students should complete the Free Application for Federal Student Aid (FAFSA). Prospective students can apply electronically at http://www.fafsa.ed.gov or at the campus.

Cost of Study

Tuition varies by program. Students should contact Argosy University, Salt Lake City, for tuition information.

Living and Housing Costs

Students typically live in apartments in the metropolitan Salt Lake City area. Living expenses vary according to each student's preferred standard of living, housing, and transportation. The University does not offer or operate student housing. Most of the students are full-time working professionals who live within driving distance of the campus. Several nearby hotels offer special rates for those who commute from long distances. The Admissions Department also maintains a list of housing options, including contact information for University students who wish to share housing. For more information, students should contact the Admissions Department.

Student Group

Admission to Argosy University, Salt Lake City, is selective to ensure a dynamic and engaged student body. It encourages diversity in academic and employment backgrounds and promotes integration of the student body into professional life through established connections with local and national professional associations. Argosy University offers a professionally oriented education with rich opportunities to gain practical experience in class, field placements, and internships. Full-time students and working professionals gain the extensive knowledge and range of skills necessary for effective performance in their chosen fields.

Student Outcomes

Students can register with the University's online career-services system and use select services from a distance, such as degree-specific career e-mail lists, national job posts, and virtual job fairs. Students should contact the University for more information.

Location

Argosy University, Salt Lake City, offers a supportive, engaging learning environment in an intimate, small-group setting. Argosy University, Salt Lake City, is conveniently located in Draper, Utah, nestled in the Wasatch Mountains about 20 miles south of Salt Lake City. The area's business climate and numerous hospitals, schools, clinics, and social service agencies can provide many training opportunities for students.

The University

Argosy University is a private institution with nineteen locations across the nation. Argosy University, Salt Lake City, provides students with a career resources office, an academic resources center, and extensive information access for research. It offers the resources of a large university, plus the friendliness and personal attention of a small campus. The innovative programs feature dynamic, relevant, and practical curricula delivered in flexible class formats. Students enjoy scheduling options that make it easier to fit school into their busy lives, choosing from day and evening courses, on campus or online. Many students find a combination of class formats to be an ideal way of continuing their education while meeting family and professional demands.

Argosy University is accredited by the Accrediting Commission for Senior Colleges and Universities of the Western Association for Schools and Colleges (985 Atlantic Avenue, Suite 100, Alameda, California, 94501, http://www.wascsenior.org).

Applying

Argosy University, Salt Lake City, accepts students year-round on a rolling admissions basis, depending on availability of required courses. Applications for admission are available online or by contacting the campus.

Correspondence and Information

Argosy University, Salt Lake City
121 Election Road, Suite 300
Draper, Utah 84020
United States
Phone: 801-601-5000
888-639-4756 (toll-free)
Fax: 801-601-4990
E-mail: auadmissions@argosy.edu
Web site: http://www.argosy.edu/saltlakecity

THE FACULTY

The Argosy University faculty comprises working professionals who are eager to help students succeed. Members bring real-world experience and the latest practice innovations to the academic setting. The diverse faculty members of the College of Business are widely recognized for contributions to the field. Many are published scholars, and most hold doctoral degrees. They are committed to providing a substantive education that combines comprehensive knowledge with critical skills and practical workplace relevance. Above all, faculty members are committed to their students' personal and professional development.

ARGOSY UNIVERSITY, SAN DIEGO

College of Business

Programs of Study

Argosy University, San Diego, offers the Master of Business Administration (M.B.A.) degree; Master of Science (M.S.) degrees in Human Resource Management, Non-Profit Management, Organizational Leadership, and Service Sector Management; the Master of Public Administration (M.P.A) degree; the Doctor of Business Administration (D.B.A.) degree; and the Doctor of Education (Ed.D.) degree in Organizational Leadership. The business programs are designed to serve the needs of talented students, regardless of their undergraduate degrees. The College of Business welcomes and encourages students from diverse academic backgrounds.

The Master of Business Administration (M.B.A.) program is designed to develop action-oriented managers and leaders who focus on leading themselves and others to solutions that serve their organizations. Students acquire skills to identify challenges and opportunities, draw on the latest technology and information, use advanced analytical and planning approaches, and execute plans for leading positive change. Competencies are developed through focusing on critical thinking, persuasive communications, technical knowledge, and a deep understanding of the human side of business. By focusing on competencies in this manner, the program builds upon the talents of students, independent of their undergraduate field of study. Students from diverse academic and professional backgrounds are welcomed and encouraged. In addition to completing the core course requirements, students develop expertise and specific insights in one of the following concentrations: corporate compliance, finance, fraud examination, health-care administration, information systems management (availability of this concentration is limited; program chair approval is necessary to enter), international business, management, marketing, public administration, or sustainable management. In addition, with approval of the student's program chair, a student may select four courses (12 credit hours) to create a customized concentration that better fits their specific career goals. For all students, the M.B.A. program culminates in an applied capstone project in which they integrate the core business competencies with their concentration specialty.

The Master of Science (M.S.) programs focus on the immediate need for management/leadership/interpersonal skills to enhance a student's career potential within an organization or field, or to accelerate their career within a given area of interest. The programs address the needs of individuals whose near-term career responsibilities include managing and leading employees and interacting with customers, clients, and stakeholders. In many cases, these individuals have much of the technical knowledge they need but lack both the language of business and the breadth of leadership and interpersonal skills to maximize their career potential. Examples range from accountants who want to manage a small accounting partnership, to engineers asked to lead a department, to department managers in retail firms who want to progress to store management roles. Also included would be managers in local or regional nonprofit organizations, small-firm management or technical consultants, human resource professionals, and a range of service sector managers from the hospitality industry to transportation to event planning professionals. The degree programs offered are Master of Science in Human Resource Management, Master of Science in Non-Profit Management, Master of Science in Organizational Leadership, and Master of Science in Service Sector Management.

The Master of Public Administration (M.P.A.) program is designed to develop action-oriented problem-solving managers for the public sector, especially at the state and local levels of government. Students develop the competencies required to execute the duties and responsibilities of public sector managers, including evaluation and supervision of employees, reinforcement of the organizational mission, and effective management of organizational resources.

The Doctor of Business Administration (D.B.A.) program enables industry and academic professionals to build upon master's-level competencies, skills, and knowledge, preparing themselves to perform more effectively in existing professional roles, to qualify for roles with increasing responsibility, and/or develop capabilities for a second career in teaching at the college level. The program requires students to develop applied research inquiry and analytical skills. The D.B.A. program is designed to help students develop competencies in understanding and performing applied research, which can then be used to foster innovation and lead organizational change. Students must choose a concentration in accounting, global business sustainability, information systems (availability of this concentration is limited; program chair approval is necessary to enter), international business, management, or marketing. In addition, with approval of the student's program chair, a student may select four courses (12 credit hours) to create a customized concentration that better fits their specific career goals.

The Doctor of Education (Ed.D.) in Organizational Leadership program is designed for working professionals who wish to develop the knowledge and skills required to hold leadership positions in complex organizations. The program focuses on transformational leadership skills in addition to managerial attributes. This approach prepares students for such strategic challenges as increasing globalization, changing economies, societal shifts, and individual-organizational relationships.

Research Facilities

Argosy University libraries provide curriculum support and educational resources, including current text materials, diagnostic training documents, reference materials and databases, journals and dissertations, and major and current titles in program areas. There is an online public-access catalog of library resources available throughout the Argosy University system. Students have remote access to the campus library database, enabling them to study and conduct research at home. Academic databases offer dissertation abstracts, academic journals, and professional periodicals. All library computers are Internet accessible. Software applications include Word, Excel, PowerPoint, SPSS, and various test-scoring programs.

Financial Aid

Financial aid is available to those who qualify. Argosy University, San Diego, offers access to federal and state aid programs, merit-based awards, grants, loans, and a work-study program. As a first step, students should complete the Free Application for Federal Student Aid (FAFSA). Prospective students can apply electronically at http://www.fafsa.ed.gov or at the campus.

Cost of Study

Tuition varies by program. Students should contact Argosy University, San Diego, for tuition information.

Living and Housing Costs

Students typically live in apartments in the metropolitan San Diego area. Living expenses vary according to each student's preferred standard of living, housing, and transportation. The University does not offer or operate student housing. Most of the students are full-time working professionals who live within driving distance of the campus. Several nearby hotels offer special rates for those who commute from long distances. The Admissions Department also maintains a list of housing options, including contact information, for University students who wish to share housing. For more information, students should contact the Admissions Department.

Student Group

Admission to Argosy University, San Diego, is selective to ensure a dynamic and engaged student body. It encourages diversity in academic and employment backgrounds and promotes integration of the student body into professional life through established connections with local and national professional associations. Argosy University offers a professionally oriented education with rich opportunities to gain practical experience in class, field placements, and internships. Full-time students and working professionals gain the extensive knowledge and range of skills necessary for effective performance in their chosen fields.

Student Outcomes

Students can register with the University's online career-services system and use select services from a distance, such as degree-specific career e-mail lists, national job posts, and virtual job fairs. Students should contact the University for more information.

Location

San Diego, southern California's second-largest city, offers an ideal climate year-round, 70 miles of beautiful beaches, colorful neighborhoods, and a dynamic downtown district. Argosy University, San Diego, offers classrooms, a library resource center, a student lounge, staff and faculty offices, and other amenities. The area offers numerous attractions, including the famous San Diego Zoo and Wild Animal Park and Sea World. Many businesses in the area provide varied opportunities for student training. San Diego's business environment includes several Fortune 500 companies such as QUALCOMM and Pfizer, Inc., and a concentration of technology companies.

The University

Argosy University is a private institution with nineteen locations across the nation. Argosy University, San Diego, provides students with a career resources office, an academic resources center, and extensive information access for research. It offers the resources of a large university, plus the friendliness and personal attention of a small campus.

The innovative programs feature dynamic, relevant, and practical curricula delivered in flexible class formats. Students enjoy scheduling options that make it easier to fit school into their busy lives, choosing from day and evening courses, on campus or online. Many students find a combination of class formats to be an ideal way of continuing their education while meeting family and professional demands.

Argosy University is accredited by the Accrediting Commission for Senior Colleges and Universities of the Western Association for Schools and Colleges (985 Atlantic Avenue, Suite 100, Alameda, California, 94501, http://www.wascsenior.org).

Applying

Argosy University, San Diego, accepts students year-round on a rolling admissions basis, depending on availability of required courses. Applications for admission are available online or by contacting the campus.

Correspondence and Information

Argosy University, San Diego
1615 Murray Canyon Road, Suite 100
San Diego, California 92108
United States
Phone: 619-321-3000
866-505-0333 (toll-free)
Fax: 619-321-3005
E-mail: auadmissions@argosy.edu
Web site: http://www.argosy.edu/sandiego/

THE FACULTY

The Argosy University faculty comprises working professionals who are eager to help students succeed. Members bring real-world experience and the latest practice innovations to the academic setting. The diverse faculty members of the College of Business are widely recognized for contributions to the field. Many are published scholars, and most hold doctoral degrees. They are committed to providing a substantive education that combines comprehensive knowledge with critical skills and practical workplace relevance. Above all, faculty members are committed to their students' personal and professional development.

ARGOSY UNIVERSITY, SAN FRANCISCO BAY AREA

College of Business

Programs of Study

Argosy University, San Francisco Bay Area, offers the Master of Business Administration (M.B.A.) degree; Master of Science (M.S.) degrees in Human Resource Management, Non-Profit Management, Organizational Leadership, and Service Sector Management; the Master of Public Administration (M.P.A) degree; the Doctor of Business Administration (D.B.A.) degree; and the Doctor of Education (Ed.D.) degree in Organizational Leadership. The business programs are designed to serve the needs of talented students, regardless of their undergraduate degrees. The College of Business welcomes and encourages students from diverse academic backgrounds.

The Master of Business Administration (M.B.A.) program is designed to develop action-oriented managers and leaders who focus on leading themselves and others to solutions that serve their organizations. Students acquire skills to identify challenges and opportunities, draw on the latest technology and information, use advanced analytical and planning approaches, and execute plans for leading positive change. Competencies are developed through focusing on critical thinking, persuasive communications, technical knowledge, and a deep understanding of the human side of business. By focusing on competencies in this manner, the program builds upon the talents of students, independent of their undergraduate field of study. Students from diverse academic and professional backgrounds are welcomed and encouraged. In addition to completing the core course requirements, students develop expertise and specific insights in one of the following concentrations: corporate compliance, finance, fraud examination, health-care administration, information systems management (availability of this concentration is limited; program chair approval is necessary to enter), international business, management, marketing, public administration, or sustainable management. In addition, with approval of the student's program chair, a student may select four courses (12 credit hours) to create a customized concentration that better fits their specific career goals. For all students, the M.B.A. program culminates in an applied capstone project in which they integrate the core business competencies with their concentration specialty.

The Master of Science (M.S.) programs focus on the immediate need for management/leadership/interpersonal skills to enhance a student's career potential within an organization or field, or to accelerate their career within a given area of interest. The programs address the needs of individuals whose near-term career responsibilities include managing and leading employees and interacting with customers, clients, and stakeholders. In many cases, these individuals have much of the technical knowledge they need but lack both the language of business and the breadth of leadership and interpersonal skills to maximize their career potential. Examples range from accountants who want to manage a small accounting partnership, to engineers asked to lead a department, to department managers in retail firms who want to progress to store management roles. Also included would be managers in local or regional nonprofit organizations, small-firm management or technical consultants, human resource professionals, and a range of service sector managers from the hospitality industry to transportation to event planning professionals. The degree programs offered are Master of Science in Human Resource Management, Master of Science in Non-Profit Management, Master of Science in Organizational Leadership, and Master of Science in Service Sector Management.

The Master of Public Administration (M.P.A.) program is designed to develop action-oriented problem-solving managers for the public sector, especially at the state and local levels of government. Students develop the competencies required to execute the duties and responsibilities of public sector managers, including evaluation and supervision of employees, reinforcement of the organizational mission, and effective management of organizational resources.

The Doctor of Business Administration (D.B.A.) program enables industry and academic professionals to build upon master's-level competencies, skills, and knowledge, preparing themselves to perform more effectively in existing professional roles, to qualify for roles with increasing responsibility, and/or develop capabilities for a second career in teaching at the college level. The program requires students to develop applied research inquiry and analytical skills. The D.B.A. program is designed to help students develop competencies in understanding and performing applied research, which can then be used to foster innovation and lead organizational change. Students must choose a concentration in accounting, global business sustainability, information systems (availability of this concentration is limited; program chair approval is necessary to enter), international business, management, or marketing. In addition, with approval of the student's program chair, a student may select four courses (12 credit hours) to create a customized concentration that better fits their specific career goals.

The Doctor of Education (D.Ed.) in Organizational Leadership program is designed for working professionals who wish to develop the knowledge and skills required to hold leadership positions in complex organizations. The program focuses on transformational leadership skills in addition to managerial attributes. This approach prepares students for such strategic challenges as increasing globalization, changing economies, societal shifts, and individual-organizational relationships.

Research Facilities

Argosy University libraries provide curriculum support and educational resources, including current text materials, diagnostic training documents, reference materials and databases, journals and dissertations, and major and current titles in program areas. There is an online public-access catalog of library resources available throughout the Argosy University system. Students have remote access to the campus library database, enabling them to study and conduct research at home. Academic databases offer dissertation abstracts, academic journals, and professional periodicals. All library computers are Internet accessible. Software applications include Word, Excel, PowerPoint, SPSS, and various test-scoring programs.

Argosy University, San Francisco Bay Area

Financial Aid

Financial aid is available to those who qualify. Argosy University, San Francisco Bay Area, offers access to federal and state aid programs, merit-based awards, grants, loans, and a work-study program. As a first step, students should complete the Free Application for Federal Student Aid (FAFSA). Prospective students can apply electronically at http://www.fafsa.ed.gov or at the campus.

Cost of Study

Tuition varies by program. Students should contact Argosy University, San Francisco Bay Area, for tuition information.

Living and Housing Costs

Students typically live in apartments in the metropolitan San Francisco area. Living expenses vary according to each student's preferred standard of living, housing, and transportation. The University does not offer or operate student housing. Most of the students are full-time working professionals who live within driving distance of the campus. Several nearby hotels offer special rates for those who commute from long distances. The Admissions Department also maintains a list of housing options, including contact information for University students who wish to share housing. For more information, students should contact the Admissions Department.

Student Group

Admission to Argosy University, San Francisco Bay Area, is selective to ensure a dynamic and engaged student body. The University encourages diversity in academic and employment backgrounds and promotes integration of the student body into professional life through established connections with local and national professional associations. Argosy University offers a professionally oriented education with rich opportunities to gain practical experience in class, field placements, and internships. Full-time students and working professionals gain the extensive knowledge and range of skills necessary for effective performance in their chosen fields.

Student Outcomes

Students can register with the University's online career-services system and use select services from a distance, such as degree-specific career e-mail lists, national job posts, and virtual job fairs. Students should contact the University for more information.

Location

Located in northern California, Argosy University, San Francisco Bay Area, attracts students from the immediate area as well as from around the country and the world. In July 2007, the San Francisco Bay Area campus moved to its new location at 1005 Atlantic Avenue in Alameda. The energy in San Francisco is contagious. Numerous surveys rank San Francisco as the most wired city in the world, thanks to its high concentration of computer-savvy citizens and businesses.

Many businesses in the area provide varied opportunities for student training. The Bay Area and nearby Silicon Valley are home to leading new media companies such as Pixar, ILM, and Sega. A who's who of technology companies call the Bay Area home, including Apple, Cisco, Hewlett-Packard, Intel, Oracle, and Sun Microsystems. San Francisco also is the home of traditional companies such as BankAmerica, Chevron, Levi-Strauss, Safeway, and Wells Fargo.

The University

Argosy University is a private institution with nineteen locations across the nation. Argosy University, San Francisco Bay Area, provides students with a career resources office, an academic resources center, and extensive information access for research. It offers the resources of a large university plus the friendliness and personal attention of a small campus.

The innovative programs feature dynamic, relevant, and practical curricula delivered in flexible class formats. Students enjoy scheduling options that make it easier to fit school into their busy lives, choosing from day and evening courses, on campus or online. Many students find a combination of class formats to be an ideal way of continuing their education while meeting family and professional demands.

Argosy University is accredited by the Accrediting Commission for Senior Colleges and Universities of the Western Association for Schools and Colleges (985 Atlantic Avenue, Suite 100, Alameda, California, 94501, http://www.wascsenior.org).

Applying

Argosy University, San Francisco Bay Area, accepts students year-round on a rolling admissions basis, depending on availability of required courses. Applications for admission are available online or by contacting the campus.

Correspondence and Information

Argosy University, San Francisco Bay Area
1005 Atlantic Avenue
Alameda, California 94501
United States
Phone: 510-217-4700
866-215-2777 (toll-free)
Fax: 510-217-4806
E-mail: auadmissions@argosy.edu
Web site: http://www.argosy.edu/sanfrancisco

THE FACULTY

The Argosy University faculty comprises working professionals who are eager to help students succeed. Members bring real-world experience and the latest practice innovations to the academic setting. The diverse faculty members of the College of Business are widely recognized for contributions to the field. Many are published scholars, and most hold doctoral degrees. They committed to providing a substantive education that combines comprehensive knowledge with critical skills and practical workplace relevance. Above all, faculty members are committed to their students' personal and professional development.

ARGOSY UNIVERSITY, SARASOTA

College of Business

Programs of Study

Argosy University, Sarasota, offers the Master of Business Administration (M.B.A.) degree; the Master of Public Administration (M.P.A.) degree; Master of Science (M.S.) degrees in Human Resource Management, Non-Profit Management, Organizational Leadership, and Service Sector Management; the Doctor of Business Administration (D.B.A.) degree; and the Doctor of Education (Ed.D.) degree in Organizational Leadership. The business programs are designed to serve the needs of talented students, regardless of their undergraduate degrees. The College of Business welcomes and encourages students from diverse academic backgrounds.

The Master of Business Administration (M.B.A.) program is designed to develop action-oriented managers and leaders who focus on leading themselves and others to solutions that serve their organizations. Students acquire skills to identify challenges and opportunities, draw on the latest technology and information, use advanced analytical and planning approaches, and execute plans for leading positive change. Competencies are developed through focusing on critical thinking, persuasive communications, technical knowledge, and a deep understanding of the human side of business. By focusing on competencies in this manner, the program builds upon the talents of students, independent of their undergraduate field of study. Students from diverse academic and professional backgrounds are welcomed and encouraged. In addition to completing the core course requirements, students develop expertise and specific insights in one of the following concentrations: corporate compliance, finance, fraud examination, health-care administration, information systems management (availability of this concentration is limited; program chair approval is necessary to enter), international business, management, marketing, public administration, or sustainable management. In addition, with approval of the student's program chair, a student may select four courses (12 credit hours) to create a customized concentration that better fits their specific career goals. For all students, the M.B.A. program culminates in an applied capstone project in which they integrate the core business competencies with their concentration specialty.

The Master of Public Administration (M.P.A.) program is designed to develop action-oriented problem-solving managers for the public sector, especially at the state and local levels of government. Students develop the competencies required to execute the duties and responsibilities of public sector managers, including evaluation and supervision of employees, reinforcement of the organizational mission, and effective management of organizational resources.

The Master of Science (M.S.) programs focus on the immediate need for management/leadership/interpersonal skills to enhance a student's career potential within an organization or field, or to accelerate their career within a given area of interest. The programs address the needs of individuals whose near-term career responsibilities include managing and leading employees and interacting with customers, clients, and stakeholders. In many cases, these individuals have much of the technical knowledge they need but lack both the language of business and the breadth of leadership and interpersonal skills to maximize their career potential. Examples range from accountants who want to manage a small accounting partnership, to engineers asked to lead a department, to department managers in retail firms who want to progress to store management roles. Also included would be managers in local or regional nonprofit organizations, small-firm management or technical consultants, human resource professionals, and a range of service sector managers from the hospitality industry to transportation to event planning professionals. The degree programs offered are Master of Science in Human Resource Management, Master of Science in Non-Profit Management, Master of Science in Organizational Leadership, and Master of Science in Service Sector Management.

The Doctor of Business Administration (D.B.A.) program enables industry and academic professionals to build upon master's-level competencies, skills, and knowledge, preparing themselves to perform more effectively in existing professional roles, to qualify for roles with increasing responsibility, and/or develop capabilities for a second career in teaching at the college level. The program requires students to develop applied research inquiry and analytical skills. The D.B.A. program is designed to help students develop competencies in understanding and performing applied research, which can then be used to foster innovation and lead organizational change. Students must choose a concentration in accounting, global business sustainability, information systems (availability of this concentration is limited; program chair approval is necessary to enter), international business, management, or marketing. In addition, with approval of the student's program chair, a student may select four courses (12 credit hours) to create a customized concentration that better fits their specific career goals.

The Doctor of Education (Ed.D.) in Organizational Leadership program is designed for working professionals who wish to develop the knowledge and skills required to hold leadership positions in complex organizations. The program focuses on transformational leadership skills in addition to managerial attributes. This approach prepares students for such strategic challenges as increasing globalization, changing economies, societal shifts, and individual-organizational relationships.

Research Facilities

Argosy University libraries provide curriculum support and educational resources, including current text materials, diagnostic training documents, reference materials and databases, journals and dissertations, and major and current titles in program areas. There is an online public-access catalog of library resources available throughout the Argosy University system. Students have remote access to the campus library database, enabling them to study and conduct research at home. Academic databases offer dissertation abstracts, academic journals, and professional periodicals. All library computers are Internet accessible. Software applications include Word, Excel, PowerPoint, SPSS, and various test-scoring programs.

Financial Aid

Financial aid is available to those who qualify. Argosy University, Sarasota, offers access to federal and state aid programs, merit-based awards, grants, loans, and a work-study program. As a first step, students should complete the Free Application for Federal Student Aid (FAFSA). Prospective students can apply electronically at http://www.fafsa.ed.gov or at the campus.

Cost of Study

Tuition varies by program. Students should contact Argosy University, Sarasota, for tuition information.

Argosy University, Sarasota

Living and Housing Costs

Students typically live in apartments in the metropolitan Sarasota area. Living expenses vary according to each student's preferred standard of living, housing, and transportation. The University does not offer or operate student housing. Most of the students are full-time working professionals who live within driving distance of the campus. Several nearby hotels offer special rates for those who commute from long distances. The Admissions Department also maintains a list of housing options, including contact information for University students who wish to share housing. For more information, students should contact the Admissions Department.

Student Group

Admission to Argosy University, Sarasota, is selective to ensure a dynamic and engaged student body. It encourages diversity in academic and employment backgrounds and promotes integration of the student body into professional life through established connections with local and national professional associations. Argosy University offers a professionally oriented education with rich opportunities to gain practical experience in class, field placements, and internships. Full-time students and working professionals gain the extensive knowledge and range of skills necessary for effective performance in their chosen fields.

Student Outcomes

Students can register with the University's online career-services system and use select services from a distance, such as degree-specific career e-mail lists, national job posts, and virtual job fairs. Students should contact the University for more information.

Location

Located in northeast Sarasota, the campus is specifically designed for postsecondary and graduate-level instruction through a unique combination of in-residence course work, tutorials, and online study courses. Several of the programs are off-site tutorials and intensive one-week classroom sessions. Students may also complete up to 49 percent of the work of some degree programs via online courses that allow interaction with faculty members and classmates from any Internet connection.

Sarasota is recognized as Florida's cultural center and is home to a professional symphony, ballet, and opera as well as dozens of theaters and art galleries. Well-known vacation attractions such as Disney World, Busch Gardens–Tampa, and the city of Miami are within a few hours' drive. The area enjoys mild winters and endless summer beauty.

The growing business sector in the Gulf Coast community helps make it one of the top 20 places to live and work. ASO Corporation, Nelson Publishing, and Select Technology Group are among the numerous companies headquartered in Sarasota County. The area's top employers include Sarasota Memorial Hospital and Publix Supermarkets. Many businesses in the area provide varied opportunities for student training.

The University

Argosy University is a private institution with nineteen locations across the nation. Argosy University, Sarasota, provides students with a career resources office, an academic resources center, and extensive information access for research. It offers the resources of a large university plus the friendliness and personal attention of a small campus. The innovative programs feature dynamic, relevant, and practical curricula delivered in flexible class formats.

Students enjoy scheduling options that make it easier to fit school into their busy lives, choosing from day and evening courses, on campus or online. Many students find a combination of class formats to be an ideal way of continuing their education while meeting family and professional demands.

Argosy University is accredited by the Accrediting Commission for Senior Colleges and Universities of the Western Association for Schools and Colleges (985 Atlantic Avenue, Suite 100, Alameda, California, 94501, http://www.wascsenior.org).

Applying

Argosy University, Sarasota, accepts students year-round on a rolling admissions basis, depending on availability of required courses. Applications for admission are available online or by contacting the campus.

Correspondence and Information

Argosy University, Sarasota
5250 17th Street
Sarasota, Florida 34235
United States
Phone: 941-379-0404
800-331-5995 (toll-free)
Fax: 941-379-5976
E-mail: auadmissions@argosy.edu
Web site: http://www.argosy.edu/sarasota

THE FACULTY

The Argosy University faculty comprises working professionals who are eager to help students succeed. Members bring real-world experience and the latest practice innovations to the academic setting. The diverse faculty members of the College of Business are widely recognized for contributions to the field. Many are published scholars, and most hold doctoral degrees. They are committed to providing a substantive education that combines comprehensive knowledge with critical skills and practical workplace relevance. Above all, faculty members are committed to their students' personal and professional development.

ARGOSY UNIVERSITY, SCHAUMBURG

College of Business

Programs of Study

Argosy University, Schaumburg, offers the Master of Business Administration (M.B.A.) degree, the Master of Public Administration (M.P.A.) degree, the Master of Science in Management (M.S.M.) degree, the Doctor of Education (Ed.D.) degree in Organizational Leadership, and the Doctor of Business Administration (D.B.A.) degree. The business programs are designed to serve the needs of talented students, regardless of their undergraduate degrees. The College of Business welcomes and encourages students from diverse academic backgrounds.

The Master of Business Administration (M.B.A.) program is designed to develop action-oriented managers and leaders who focus on leading themselves and others to solutions that serve their organizations. Students acquire skills to identify challenges and opportunities, draw on the latest technology and information, use advanced analytical and planning approaches, and execute plans for leading positive change. Competencies are developed through focusing on critical thinking, persuasive communications, technical knowledge, and a deep understanding of the human side of business. By focusing on competencies in this manner, the program builds upon the talents of students, independent of their undergraduate field of study. Students from diverse academic and professional backgrounds are welcomed and encouraged. In addition to completing the core course requirements, students develop expertise and specific insights in one of the following concentrations: corporate compliance, finance, fraud examination, health-care administration, information systems management (availability of this concentration is limited; program chair approval is necessary to enter), international business, management, marketing, public administration, or sustainable management. In addition, with approval of the student's program chair, a student may select four courses (12 credit hours) to create a customized concentration that better fits their specific career goals. For all students, the M.B.A. program culminates in an applied capstone project in which they integrate the core business competencies with their concentration specialty.

The Master of Public Administration (M.P.A.) program is designed to develop action-oriented problem-solving managers for the public sector, especially at the state and local levels of government. Students develop the competencies required to execute the duties and responsibilities of public sector managers, including evaluation and supervision of employees, reinforcement of the organizational mission, and effective management of organizational resources.

The Master of Science in Management (M.S.M.) program is designed to improve and extend the interpersonal and problem-solving skills necessary for successful leaders in the private, non-profit, and public sectors. The program focuses on situation diagnostics, opportunity and problem evaluation, and implementation of an action plan.

The Doctor of Education (Ed. D.) in Organizational Leadership program is designed for working professionals who wish to develop the knowledge and skills required to hold leadership positions in complex organizations. The program focuses on transformational leadership skills in addition to managerial attributes. This approach prepares students for such strategic challenges as increasing globalization, changing economies, societal shifts, and individual-organizational relationships.

The Doctor of Business Administration (D.B.A.) program enables industry and academic professionals to build upon master's-level competencies, skills, and knowledge, preparing themselves to perform more effectively in existing professional roles, to qualify for roles with increasing responsibility, and/or develop capabilities for a second career in teaching at the college level. The program requires students to develop applied research inquiry and analytical skills. The D.B.A. program is designed to help students develop competencies in understanding and performing applied research, which can then be used to foster innovation and lead organizational change. Students must choose a concentration in accounting, global business sustainability, information systems (availability of this concentration is limited; program chair approval is necessary to enter), international business, management, or marketing. In addition, with approval of the student's program chair, a student may select four courses (12 credit hours) to create a customized concentration that better fits their specific career goals.

Research Facilities

Argosy University libraries provide curriculum support and educational resources, including current text materials, diagnostic training documents, reference materials and databases, journals and dissertations, and major and current titles in program areas. There is an online public-access catalog of library resources available throughout the Argosy University system. Students have remote access to the campus library database, enabling them to study and conduct research at home. Academic databases offer dissertation abstracts, academic journals, and professional periodicals. All library computers are Internet accessible. Software applications include Word, Excel, PowerPoint, SPSS, and various test-scoring programs.

Financial Aid

Financial aid is available to those who qualify. Argosy University, Schaumburg, offers access to federal and state aid programs, merit-based awards, grants, loans, and a work-study program. As a first step, students should complete the Free Application for Federal Student Aid (FAFSA). Prospective students can apply electronically at http://www.fafsa.ed.gov or at the campus.

Cost of Study

Tuition varies by program. Students should contact Argosy University, Schaumburg, for tuition information.

Living and Housing Costs

Students typically live in apartments in the metropolitan Schaumburg area. Living expenses vary according to each student's preferred standard of living, housing, and transportation. The University does not offer or operate student housing. Most of the students are full-time working professionals who live within driving distance of the campus. Several nearby hotels offer special rates for those who commute from long distances. The Admissions Department also maintains a list of housing options, including contact information for University students who wish to share housing. For more information, students should contact the Admissions Department.

Student Group

Admission to Argosy University, Schaumburg, is selective to ensure a dynamic and engaged student body. The University encourages diversity in academic and employment backgrounds and promotes integration of the student body into professional life through established connections with local and national professional associations. Argosy University offers a professionally oriented education with rich opportunities to gain practical experience in class, field placements, and internships. Full-time students and working professionals gain the extensive knowledge and range of skills necessary for effective performance in their chosen fields.

Student Outcomes

Students can register with the University's online career-services system and use select services from a distance, such as degree-specific career e-mail lists, national job posts, and virtual job fairs. Students should contact the University for more information.

Location

Argosy University, Schaumburg, is located in the northwest suburban area, approximately 45 minutes from downtown Chicago. The campus's small size allows it to offer a highly personal atmosphere and flexible programs tailored to students' needs. Visitors to Chicago experience a range of attractions to stimulate both intellectual and recreational pursuits. Located on the shores of Lake Michigan in the Midwest, Chicago is home to world-champion sports teams, an internationally acclaimed symphony orchestra, renowned architecture, and nearly 3 million residents. Among the variety of history and art museums in the city, the Chicago Cultural Center offers more than 600 art programs and exhibits each year. Recreational opportunities include hiking and cycling on miles of lakefront trails, golfing, and shopping.

Many businesses in the area provide varied opportunities for student training. Schaumburg's thriving business environment includes 5,000 businesses that employ 80,000 people. The area's largest employers are Motorola, Experian, Cingular, and IBM.

The University

Argosy University is a private institution with nineteen locations across the nation. Argosy University, Schaumburg, provides students with a career resources office, an academic resources center, and extensive information access for research. It offers the resources of a large university plus the friendliness and personal attention of a small campus. Argosy University, Schaumburg, is closely associated with Argosy University's Chicago campus.

The innovative programs feature dynamic, relevant, and practical curricula delivered in flexible class formats. Students enjoy scheduling options that make it easier to fit school into their busy lives, choosing from day and evening courses, on campus or online. Many students find a combination of class formats to be an ideal way of continuing their education while meeting family and professional demands.

Argosy University is accredited by the Accrediting Commission for Senior Colleges and Universities of the Western Association for Schools and Colleges (985 Atlantic Avenue, Suite 100, Alameda, California, 94501, http://www.wascsenior.org).

Applying

Argosy University, Schaumburg, accepts students year-round on a rolling admissions basis, depending on availability of required courses. Applications for admission are available online or by contacting the campus.

Correspondence and Information

Argosy University, Schaumburg
999 North Plaza Drive, Suite 111
Schaumburg, Illinois 60173-5403
United States
Phone: 847-969-4900
866-290-2777 (toll-free)
Fax: 847-969-4999
E-mail: auadmissions@argosy.edu
Web site: http://www.argosy.edu/schaumburg

THE FACULTY

The Argosy University faculty comprises working professionals who are eager to help students succeed. Members bring real-world experience and the latest practice innovations to the academic setting. The diverse faculty members of the College of Business are widely recognized for contributions to their fields. Many are published scholars, and most hold doctoral degrees. They are committed to providing a substantive education that combines comprehensive knowledge with critical skills and practical workplace relevance. Above all, faculty members are committed to their students' personal and professional development.

ARGOSY UNIVERSITY, SEATTLE

College of Business

Programs of Study

Argosy University, Seattle, offers the Master of Business Administration (M.B.A.) degree; the Master of Public Administration (M.P.A.) degree; Master of Science (M.S.) degrees in Human Resource Management, Non-Profit Management, Organizational Leadership, and Service Sector Management; the Doctor of Business Administration (D.B.A.) degree; and the Doctor of Education (Ed.D.) degree in Organizational Leadership. The business programs are designed to serve the needs of talented students, regardless of their undergraduate degrees. The College of Business welcomes and encourages students from diverse academic backgrounds.

The Master of Business Administration (M.B.A.) program is designed to develop action-oriented managers and leaders who focus on leading themselves and others to solutions that serve their organizations. Students acquire skills to identify challenges and opportunities, draw on the latest technology and information, use advanced analytical and planning approaches, and execute plans for leading positive change. Competencies are developed through focusing on critical thinking, persuasive communications, technical knowledge, and a deep understanding of the human side of business. By focusing on competencies in this manner, the program builds upon the talents of students, independent of their undergraduate field of study. Students from diverse academic and professional backgrounds are welcomed and encouraged. In addition to completing the core course requirements, students develop expertise and specific insights in one of the following concentrations: corporate compliance, finance, fraud examination, health-care administration, information systems management (availability of this concentration is limited; program chair approval is necessary to enter), international business, management, marketing, public administration, or sustainable management. In addition, with approval of the student's program chair, a student may select four courses (12 credit hours) to create a customized concentration that better fits their specific career goals. For all students, the M.B.A. program culminates in an applied capstone project in which they integrate the core business competencies with their concentration specialty.

The Master of Public Administration (M.P.A.) program is designed to develop action-oriented problem-solving managers for the public sector, especially at the state and local levels of government. Students develop the competencies required to execute the duties and responsibilities of public sector managers, including evaluation and supervision of employees, reinforcement of the organizational mission, and effective management of organizational resources.

The Master of Science (M.S.) programs focus on the immediate need for management/leadership/interpersonal skills to enhance a student's career potential within an organization or field, or to accelerate their career within a given area of interest. The programs address the needs of individuals whose near-term career responsibilities include managing and leading employees and interacting with customers, clients, and stakeholders. In many cases, these individuals have much of the technical knowledge they need but lack both the language of business and the breadth of leadership and interpersonal skills to maximize their career potential. Examples range from accountants who want to manage a small accounting partnership, to engineers asked to lead a department, to department managers in retail firms who want to progress to store management roles. Also included would be managers in local or regional nonprofit organizations, small-firm management or technical consultants, human resource professionals, and a range of service sector managers from the hospitality industry to transportation to event planning professionals. The degree programs offered are Master of Science in Human Resource Management, Master of Science in Non-Profit Management, Master of Science in Organizational Leadership, and Master of Science in Service Sector Management.

The Doctor of Business Administration (D.B.A.) program enables industry and academic professionals to build upon master's-level competencies, skills, and knowledge, preparing themselves to perform more effectively in existing professional roles, to qualify for roles with increasing responsibility, and/or develop capabilities for a second career in teaching at the college level. The program requires students to develop applied research inquiry and analytical skills. The D.B.A. program is designed to help students develop competencies in understanding and performing applied research, which can then be used to foster innovation and lead organizational change. Students must choose a concentration in accounting, global business sustainability, information systems (availability of this concentration is limited; program chair approval is necessary to enter), international business, management, or marketing. In addition, with approval of the student's program chair, a student may select four courses (12 credit hours) to create a customized concentration that better fits their specific career goals.

The Doctor of Education (Ed.D.) in Organizational Leadership program is designed for working professionals who wish to develop the knowledge and skills required to hold leadership positions in complex organizations. The program focuses on transformational leadership skills in addition to managerial attributes. This approach prepares students for such strategic challenges as increasing globalization, changing economies, societal shifts, and individual-organizational relationships.

Research Facilities

Argosy University libraries provide curriculum support and educational resources, including current text materials, diagnostic training documents, reference materials and databases, journals and dissertations, and major and current titles in program areas. There is an online public-access catalog of library resources available throughout the Argosy University system. Students have remote access to the campus library database, enabling them to study and conduct research at home. Academic databases offer dissertation abstracts, academic journals, and professional periodicals. All library computers are Internet accessible. Software applications include Word, Excel, PowerPoint, SPSS, and various test-scoring programs.

Argosy University, Seattle

Financial Aid

Financial aid is available to those who qualify. Argosy University, Seattle, offers access to federal and state aid programs, merit-based awards, grants, loans, and a work-study program. As a first step, students should complete the Free Application for Federal Student Aid (FAFSA). Prospective students can apply electronically at http://www.fafsa.ed.gov or at the campus.

Cost of Study

Tuition varies by program. Students should contact Argosy University, Seattle, for tuition information.

Living and Housing Costs

Students typically live in apartments in the metropolitan Seattle area. Living expenses vary according to each student's preferred standard of living, housing, and transportation. The University does not offer or operate student housing. Most of the students are full-time working professionals who live within driving distance of the campus. Several nearby hotels offer special rates for those who commute from long distances. The Admissions Department also maintains a list of housing options, including contact information for university students who wish to share housing. For more information, students should contact the Admissions Department.

Student Group

Admission to Argosy University, Seattle, is selective to ensure a dynamic and engaged student body. It encourages diversity in academic and employment backgrounds and promotes integration of the student body into professional life through established connections with local and national professional associations. Argosy University offers a professionally oriented education with rich opportunities to gain practical experience in class, field placements, and internships. Full-time students and working professionals gain the extensive knowledge and range of skills necessary for effective performance in their chosen fields.

Student Outcomes

Students can register with the University's online career-services system and use select services from a distance, such as degree-specific career e-mail lists, national job posts, and virtual job fairs. Students should contact the University for more information.

Location

The faculty and staff members at Argosy University, Seattle, aspire to provide a supportive, collaborative, engaging, yet challenging learning environment. Easily reached through the King County Public Transportation System, the campus offers convenient access to local libraries, shops, and restaurants. Seattle offers numerous historical and multicultural museums, a symphony, ballet, and many theater companies. Seattle is home to several major league sports teams, and offers a myriad of outdoor recreational opportunities, such as camping, hiking, fishing, skiing, and rock-climbing.

Many businesses in the area provide varied opportunities for student training. Seattle's business environment encompasses a wide range of industries and features such giants as Microsoft, Boeing, and Alaska Air Group. The Port of Seattle and University of Washington are also among the area's largest employers.

The University

Argosy University is a private institution with nineteen locations across the nation. Argosy University, Seattle, provides students with a career resources office, an academic resources center, and extensive information access for research. It offers the resources of a large university plus the friendliness and personal attention of a small campus.

The innovative programs feature dynamic, relevant, and practical curricula delivered in flexible class formats. Students enjoy scheduling options that make it easier to fit school into their busy lives, choosing from day and evening courses, on campus or online. Many students find a combination of class formats to be an ideal way of continuing their education while meeting family and professional demands.

Argosy University is accredited by the Accrediting Commission for Senior Colleges and Universities of the Western Association for Schools and Colleges (985 Atlantic Avenue, Suite 100, Alameda, California, 94501, http://www.wascsenior.org).

Applying

Argosy University, Seattle, accepts students year-round on a rolling admissions basis, depending on availability of required courses. Applications for admission are available online or by contacting the campus.

Correspondence and Information

Argosy University, Seattle
2601-A Elliott Avenue
Seattle, Washington 98121
United States
Phone: 206-283-4500
866-283-2777 (toll-free)
Fax: 206-393-3592
E-mail: auadmissions@argosy.edu
Web site: http://www.argosy.edu/seattle

THE FACULTY

The Argosy University faculty comprises working professionals who are eager to help students succeed. Members bring real-world experience and the latest practice innovations to the academic setting. The diverse faculty members of the College of Business are widely recognized for contributions to their field. Many are published scholars, and most hold doctoral degrees. They are committed to providing a substantive education that combines comprehensive knowledge with critical skills and practical workplace relevance. Above all, faculty members are committed to their students' personal and professional development.

ARGOSY UNIVERSITY, TAMPA

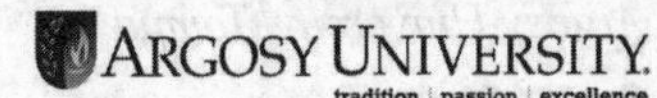

College of Business

Programs of Study

Argosy University, Tampa, offers the Master of Business Administration (M.B.A.) degree; the Master of Public Administration (M.P.A.) degree; the Master of Science in Management (M.S.M.); Master of Science (M.S.) degrees in Human Resource Management, Non-Profit Management, Organizational Leadership, and Service Sector Management; the Doctor of Business Administration (D.B.A.) degree; and the Doctor of Education (Ed.D.) degree in Organizational Leadership. The business programs are designed to serve the needs of talented students, regardless of their undergraduate degrees. The College of Business welcomes and encourages students from diverse academic backgrounds.

The Master of Business Administration (M.B.A.) program develops action-oriented managers and leaders who focus on leading themselves and others to solutions that serve their organizations. Students acquire skills to identify challenges and opportunities, draw on the latest technology and information, use advanced analytical and planning approaches, and execute plans for leading positive change. Students develop these competencies through focusing on critical thinking, persuasive communications, technical knowledge, and a deep understanding of the human side of business. The program is designed to build upon the talents of students, independent of their undergraduate field of study. The program consists of eight core courses (24 credit hours) and four concentration courses (12 credit hours), scheduled to enable busy professionals to balance the demands of career, family, and school. In addition to the core requirements, students can select concentrations in corporate compliance, finance, fraud examination, healthcare administration, information systems management (limited availability, Program Chair approval needed to enter), international business, management, marketing, public administration, and sustainable management. A student may also select four courses (12 credit hours) to create a customized concentration that better fits their specific career goals, with approval of their program chair. The M.B.A. program culminates in an applied capstone project in which all students have the opportunity to integrate the core business competencies with their concentration specialty.

The Master of Public Administration (M.P.A.) program is designed to develop action-oriented problem-solving managers for the public sector, especially at the state and local levels of government. Students develop the competencies required to execute the duties and responsibilities of public sector managers, including evaluation and supervision of employees, reinforcement of the organizational mission, and effective management of organizational resources.

The Master of Science in Management (M.S.M.) program is designed to improve and extend the interpersonal and problem-solving skills necessary for employment in the private, nonprofit, and public sectors. The program focuses on situation diagnostics, opportunity and problem evaluation, and implementation of an action plan.

The Master of Science (M.S.) programs focus on the immediate need for management/leadership/interpersonal skills to enhance a student's career potential within an organization or field, or to accelerate their career within a given area of interest. The programs address the needs of individuals whose near-term career responsibilities include managing and leading employees and interacting with customers, clients, and stakeholders. In many cases, these individuals have much of the technical knowledge they need but lack both the language of business and the breadth of leadership and interpersonal skills to maximize their career potential. Examples range from accountants who want to manage a small accounting partnership, to engineers asked to lead a department, to department managers in retail firms who want to progress to store management roles. Also included would be managers in local or regional nonprofit organizations, small-firm management or technical consultants, human resource professionals, and a range of service sector managers from the hospitality industry to transportation to event planning professionals. The degree programs offered are Master of Science in Human Resource Management, Master of Science in Non-Profit Management, Master of Science in Organizational Leadership, and Master of Science in Service Sector Management.

The Doctor of Business Administration (D.B.A.) program enables industry and academic professionals to build upon master's-level competencies, skills, and knowledge, preparing themselves to perform more effectively in existing professional roles, to qualify for roles with increasing responsibility, and/or develop capabilities for a second career in teaching at the college level. The program requires students to develop applied research inquiry and analytical skills. The D.B.A. program is designed to help students develop competencies in understanding and performing applied research, which can then be used to foster innovation and lead organizational change. Students must choose a concentration in accounting, global business sustainability, information systems (availability of this concentration is limited; program chair approval is necessary to enter), international business, management, or marketing. In addition, with approval of the student's program chair, a student may select four courses (12 credit hours) to create a customized concentration that better fits their specific career goals.

The Doctor of Education (Ed.D.) in Organizational Leadership program is designed for working professionals who wish to develop the knowledge and skills required to hold leadership positions in complex organizations. The program focuses on transformational leadership skills in addition to managerial attributes. This approach prepares students for such strategic challenges as increasing globalization, changing economies, societal shifts, and individual-organizational relationships.

Research Facilities

Argosy University libraries provide curriculum support and educational resources, including current text materials, diagnostic training documents, reference materials and databases, journals and dissertations, and major and current titles in program areas. There is an online public-access catalog of library resources available throughout the Argosy University system. Students have remote access to the campus library database, enabling them to study and conduct research at home. Academic databases offer dissertation abstracts, academic journals, and professional periodicals. All library computers are Internet accessible. Software applications include Word, Excel, PowerPoint, SPSS, and various test-scoring programs.

Financial Aid

Financial aid is available to those who qualify. Argosy University, Tampa, offers access to federal and state aid programs, merit-based awards, grants, loans, and a work-study program. As a first step, students should complete the Free Application for Federal Student Aid (FAFSA). Prospective students can apply electronically at http://www.fafsa.ed.gov or on the campus.

Argosy University, Tampa

Cost of Study

Tuition varies by program. Students should contact Argosy University, Tampa, for tuition information.

Living and Housing Costs

Students typically live in apartments in the metropolitan Tampa area. Living expenses vary according to each student's preferred standard of living, housing, and transportation. The University does not offer or operate student housing. Most of the students are full-time working professionals who live within driving distance of the campus. Several nearby hotels offer special rates for those who commute from long distances. The Admissions Department also maintains a list of housing options, including contact information for University students who wish to share housing. For more information, students should contact the Admissions Department.

Student Group

Admission to Argosy University, Tampa, is selective to ensure a dynamic and engaged student body. It encourages diversity in academic and employment backgrounds and promotes integration of the student body into professional life through established connections with local and national professional associations. Argosy University offers a professionally oriented education with rich opportunities to gain practical experience in class, field placements, and internships. Full-time students and working professionals gain the extensive knowledge and range of skills necessary for effective performance in their chosen fields.

Student Outcomes

Students can register with the University's online career-services system and use select services from a distance, such as degree-specific career e-mail lists, national job posts, and virtual job fairs. Students should contact the University for more information.

Location

Located in sunny Florida, Argosy University, Tampa, attracts a diverse student population from throughout the United States, the Caribbean, Europe, Africa, and Asia. Tampa's central location affords students the opportunity to work for major corporations and hear speakers of international acclaim. The school offers rigorous programs of study in a supportive, collaborative environment. The campus sits within an hour's drive of some of the most popular tourist destinations in the world, including the Disney theme parks, Busch Gardens, and the Florida Gulf Coast beaches. Major-league sporting events, concerts, theaters, world-renowned restaurants, recreational facilities, and a cosmopolitan social scene are all within easy reach. Tampa combines the opportunities of a large city with the friendliness of a small town with a strong sense of community.

The Tampa-St. Petersburg-Clearwater metropolitan area offers a diversified economic base fueled by a broad array of companies, including Verizon Communications and JP Morgan Chase. In addition, Tampa serves as headquarters for three Fortune 100 companies—OSI Restaurant Partners; TECO, an energy provider; and Raymond Jones Financial. Many businesses in the area provide varied opportunities for student training.

The University

Argosy University is a private institution with nineteen locations across the nation. Argosy University, Tampa, provides students with a career resources office, an academic resources center, and extensive information access for research. It offers the resources of a large university plus the friendliness and personal attention of a small campus.

The innovative programs feature dynamic, relevant, and practical curricula delivered in flexible class formats. Students enjoy scheduling options that make it easier to fit school into their busy lives, choosing from day and evening courses, on campus or online. Many students find a combination to be an ideal way of continuing their education while meeting family and professional demands.

Argosy University is accredited by the Accrediting Commission for Senior Colleges and Universities of the Western Association for Schools and Colleges (985 Atlantic Avenue, Suite 100, Alameda, California, 94501, http://www.wascsenior.org). Licensed by the Commission for Independent Education, License No. 2610.

Applying

Argosy University, Tampa, accepts students on a rolling admissions basis year-round, depending on availability of required courses. Applications for admission are available online or by contacting the campus.

Correspondence and Information

Argosy University, Tampa
1403 North Howard Avenue
Tampa, Florida 33607
United States
Phone: 813-393-5290
800-850-6488 (toll-free)
Fax: 813-874-1989
E-mail: auadmissions@argosy.edu
Web site: http://www.argosy.edu/tampa

THE FACULTY

The Argosy University faculty comprises working professionals who are eager to help students succeed. Members bring real-world experience and the latest practice innovations to the academic setting. The diverse faculty members of the College of Business are widely recognized for contributions to the field. Many are published scholars, and most hold doctoral degrees. They are committed to providing a substantive education that combines comprehensive knowledge with critical skills and practical workplace relevance. Above all, faculty members are committed to their students' personal and professional development.

ARGOSY UNIVERSITY, TWIN CITIES

College of Business

Programs of Study

Argosy University, Twin Cities, offers the Master of Business Administration (M.B.A.) degree; the Master of Public Administration (M.P.A.) degree; Master of Science (M.S.) degrees in Human Resource Management, Non-Profit Management, Organizational Leadership, and Service Sector Management; the Doctor of Education (Ed.D.) degree in Organizational Leadership; and the Doctor of Business Administration (D.B.A.) degree. The business programs are designed to serve the needs of talented students, regardless of their undergraduate degrees. The College of Business welcomes and encourages students from diverse academic backgrounds.

The Master of Business Administration (M.B.A.) program develops action-oriented managers and leaders who focus on leading themselves and others to solutions that serve their organizations. Students acquire skills to identify challenges and opportunities, draw on the latest technology and information, use advanced analytical and planning approaches, and execute plans for leading positive change. Students develop these competencies through focusing on critical thinking, persuasive communications, technical knowledge, and a deep understanding of the human side of business. The program is designed to build upon the talents of students, independent of their undergraduate field of study. The program consists of eight core courses (24 credit hours) and four concentration courses (12 credit hours), scheduled to enable busy professionals to balance the demands of career, family, and school. In addition to the core requirements, students can select concentrations in corporate compliance, finance, fraud examination, healthcare administration, information systems management (limited availability, Program Chair approval needed to enter), international business, management, marketing, public administration, and sustainable management. A student may also select four courses (12 credit hours) to create a customized concentration that better fits their specific career goals, with approval of their program chair. The M.B.A. program culminates in an applied capstone project in which all students have the opportunity to integrate the core business competencies with their concentration specialty.

The Master of Public Administration (M.P.A.) program is designed to develop action-oriented problem-solving managers for the public sector, especially at the state and local levels of government. Students develop the competencies required to execute the duties and responsibilities of public sector managers, including evaluation and supervision of employees, reinforcement of the organizational mission, and effective management of organizational resources.

The Master of Science (M.S.) programs focus on the immediate need for management/leadership/interpersonal skills to enhance a student's career potential within an organization or field, or to accelerate their career within a given area of interest. The programs address the needs of individuals whose near-term career responsibilities include managing and leading employees and interacting with customers, clients, and stakeholders. In many cases, these individuals have much of the technical knowledge they need but lack both the language of business and the breadth of leadership and interpersonal skills to maximize their career potential. Examples range from accountants who want to manage a small accounting partnership, to engineers asked to lead a department, to department managers in retail firms who want to progress to store management roles. Also included would be managers in local or regional nonprofit organizations, small-firm management or technical consultants, human resource professionals, and a range of service sector managers from the hospitality industry to transportation to event planning professionals. The degree programs offered are Master of Science in Human Resource Management, Master of Science in Non-Profit Management, Master of Science in Organizational Leadership, and Master of Science in Service Sector Management.

The Doctor of Education in Organizational Leadership program is designed for working professionals who wish to develop the knowledge and skills required to hold leadership positions in complex organizations. The program focuses on transformational leadership skills in addition to managerial attributes. This approach prepares students for such strategic challenges as increasing globalization, changing economies, societal shifts, and individual-organizational relationships.

The Doctor of Business Administration program enables industry and academic professionals to build upon master's-level competencies, skills, and knowledge, preparing themselves to perform more effectively in existing professional roles, to qualify for roles with increasing responsibility, and/or develop capabilities for a second career in teaching at the college level. The program requires students to develop applied research inquiry and analytical skills. The D.B.A. program is designed to help students develop competencies in understanding and performing applied research, which can then be used to foster innovation and lead organizational change. Students must choose a concentration in accounting, global business sustainability, information systems (availability of this concentration is limited; program chair approval is necessary to enter), international business, management, or marketing. In addition, with approval of the student's program chair, a student may select four courses (12 credit hours) to create a customized concentration that better fits their specific career goals.

Research Facilities

Argosy University libraries provide curriculum support and educational resources, including current text materials, diagnostic training documents, reference materials and databases, journals and dissertations, and major and current titles in program areas. There is an online public-access catalog of library resources available throughout the Argosy University system. Students have remote access to the campus library database, enabling them to study and conduct research at home. Academic databases offer dissertation abstracts, academic journals, and professional periodicals. All library computers are Internet accessible. Software applications include Word, Excel, PowerPoint, SPSS, and various test-scoring programs.

Argosy University, Twin Cities

Financial Aid

Financial aid is available to those who qualify. Argosy University, Twin Cities, offers access to federal and state aid programs, merit-based awards, grants, loans, and a work-study program. As a first step, students should complete the Free Application for Federal Student Aid (FAFSA). Prospective students can apply electronically at http://www.fafsa.ed.gov or at the campus.

Cost of Study

Tuition varies by program. Students should contact Argosy University, Twin Cities, for tuition information.

Living and Housing Costs

Students typically live in apartments in the metropolitan Eagan area. Living expenses vary according to each student's preferred standard of living, housing, and transportation. The University does not offer or operate student housing. Most of the students are full-time working professionals who live within driving distance of the campus. Several nearby hotels offer special rates for those who commute from long distances. The Admissions Department also maintains a list of housing options, including contact information for university students who wish to share housing. For more information, students should contact the Admissions Department.

Student Group

Admission to Argosy University, Twin Cities, is selective to ensure a dynamic and engaged student body. The University encourages diversity in academic and employment backgrounds and promotes integration of the student body into professional life through established connections with local and national professional associations. Argosy University offers a professionally oriented education with rich opportunities to gain practical experience in class, field placements, and internships. Full-time students and working professionals gain the extensive knowledge and range of skills necessary for effective performance in their chosen fields.

Student Outcomes

Students can register with the University's online career-services system and use select services from a distance, such as degree-specific career e-mail lists, national job posts, and virtual job fairs. Students should contact the University for more information.

Location

Argosy University, Twin Cities, offers challenging academics in a supportive environment. The campus is nestled in a parklike suburban setting within 10 miles of the airport and the Mall of America. Students enjoy the convenience of nearby shops, restaurants, and housing and easy freeway access. The neighboring Eagan Community Center offers many amenities, including walking paths, a fitness center, meeting rooms, and an outdoor amphitheater. The Twin Cities of Minneapolis and St. Paul have been rated by popular magazines as one of the most livable metropolitan areas in the country. With a population of 2.5 million, the area offers an abundance of recreational activities. Year-round outdoor activities, nationally acclaimed venues for theater art and music, and professional sports teams attract residents and visitors alike.

Many businesses in the area provide varied opportunities for student training. The Minneapolis-St. Paul metropolitan area offers a diversified economic base fueled by a broad array of companies. Among the numerous publicly traded companies headquartered in the area are Target, UnitedHealth Group, 3M, General Mills, and U.S. Bancorp.

The University

Argosy University is a private institution with nineteen locations across the nation. Argosy University, Twin Cities, provides students with a career resources office, an academic resources center, and extensive information access for research. It offers the resources of a large university plus the friendliness and personal attention of a small campus.

The innovative programs feature dynamic, relevant, and practical curricula delivered in flexible class formats. Students enjoy scheduling options that make it easier to fit school into their busy lives, choosing from day and evening courses, on campus or online. Many students find a combination of class formats to be an ideal way of continuing their education while meeting family and professional demands.

Argosy University is accredited by the Accrediting Commission for Senior Colleges and Universities of the Western Association for Schools and Colleges (985 Atlantic Avenue, Suite 100, Alameda, California, 94501, http://www.wascsenior.org).

Applying

Argosy University, Twin Cities, accepts students year-round on a rolling admissions basis, depending on availability of required courses. Applications for admission are available online or by contacting the campus.

Correspondence and Information

Argosy University, Twin Cities
1515 Central Parkway
Eagan, Minnesota 55121
United States
Phone: 651-846-2882
888-844-2004 (toll-free)
Fax: 651-994-7956
E-mail: auadmissions@argosy.edu
Web site: http://www.argosy.edu/twincities

THE FACULTY

The Argosy University faculty comprises working professionals who are eager to help students succeed. Members bring real-world experience and the latest practice innovations to the academic setting. The diverse faculty members of the College of Business are widely recognized for contributions to the field. Many are published scholars, and most hold doctoral degrees. They are committed to providing a substantive education that combines comprehensive knowledge with critical skills and practical workplace relevance. Above all, faculty members are committed to their students' personal and professional development.

ARGOSY UNIVERSITY, WASHINGTON DC

College of Business

Programs of Study

Argosy University, Washington DC, offers the Master of Business Administration (M.B.A.) degree; the Master of Public Administration (M.P.A.) degree; the Master of Science in Management (M.S.M.) degree; Master of Science (M.S.) degrees in Human Resource Management, Non-Profit Management, Organizational Leadership, and Service Sector Management; the Doctor of Business Administration (D.B.A.) degree; and the Doctor of Education (Ed.D.) in Organizational Leadership degree. The business programs are designed to serve the needs of talented students, regardless of their undergraduate degrees. The College of Business welcomes and encourages students from diverse academic backgrounds.

The Master of Business Administration (M.B.A.) program is designed to develop action-oriented managers and leaders who focus on leading themselves and others to solutions that serve their organizations. Students acquire skills to identify challenges and opportunities, draw on the latest technology and information, use advanced analytical and planning approaches, and execute plans for leading positive change. Competencies are developed through focusing on critical thinking, persuasive communications, technical knowledge, and a deep understanding of the human side of business. By focusing on competencies in this manner, the program builds upon the talents of students, independent of their undergraduate field of study. Students from diverse academic and professional backgrounds are welcomed and encouraged. In addition to completing the core course requirements, students develop expertise and specific insights in one of the following concentrations: corporate compliance, finance, fraud examination, health-care administration, information systems management (availability of this concentration is limited; program chair approval is necessary to enter), international business, management, marketing, public administration, or sustainable management. In addition, with approval of the student's program chair, a student may select four courses (12 credit hours) to create a customized concentration that better fits their specific career goals. For all students, the M.B.A. program culminates in an applied capstone project in which they integrate the core business competencies with their concentration specialty.

The Master of Public Administration (M.P.A.) program is designed to develop action-oriented problem-solving managers for the public sector, especially at the state and local levels of government. Students develop the competencies required to execute the duties and responsibilities of public sector managers, including evaluation and supervision of employees, reinforcement of the organizational mission, and effective management of organizational resources.

The Master of Science in Management (M.S.M.) program is designed to improve and extend the interpersonal and problem-solving skills necessary for successful leaders in the private, nonprofit, and public sectors. The program focuses on situation diagnostics, opportunity and problem evaluation, and implementation of an action plan.

The Master of Science (M.S.) programs focus on the immediate need for management/leadership/interpersonal skills to enhance a student's career potential within an organization or field, or to accelerate their career within a given area of interest. The programs address the needs of individuals whose near-term career responsibilities include managing and leading employees and interacting with customers, clients, and stakeholders. In many cases, these individuals have much of the technical knowledge they need but lack both the language of business and the breadth of leadership and interpersonal skills to maximize their career potential. Examples range from accountants who want to manage a small accounting partnership, to engineers asked to lead a department, to department managers in retail firms who want to progress to store management roles. Also included would be managers in local or regional nonprofit organizations, small-firm management or technical consultants, human resource professionals, and a range of service sector managers from the hospitality industry to transportation to event planning professionals. The degree programs offered are Master of Science in Human Resource Management, Master of Science in Non-Profit Management, Master of Science in Organizational Leadership, and Master of Science in Service Sector Management.

The Doctor of Business Administration program enables industry and academic professionals to build upon master's-level competencies, skills, and knowledge, preparing themselves to perform more effectively in existing professional roles, to qualify for roles with increasing responsibility, and/or develop capabilities for a second career in teaching at the college level. The program requires students to develop applied research inquiry and analytical skills. The D.B.A. program is designed to help students develop competencies in understanding and performing applied research, which can then be used to foster innovation and lead organizational change. Students must choose a concentration in accounting, global business sustainability, information systems (availability of this concentration is limited; program chair approval is necessary to enter), international business, management, or marketing. In addition, with approval of the student's program chair, a student may select four courses (12 credit hours) to create a customized concentration that better fits their specific career goals.

The Doctor of Education in Organizational Leadership program is designed for working professionals who wish to develop the knowledge and skills required to hold leadership positions in complex organizations. The program focuses on transformational leadership skills in addition to managerial attributes. This approach prepares students for such strategic challenges as increasing globalization, changing economies, societal shifts, and individual-organizational relationships.

Research Facilities

Argosy University libraries provide curriculum support and educational resources, including current text materials, diagnostic training documents, reference materials and databases, journals and dissertations, and major and current titles in program areas. There is an online public-access catalog of library resources available throughout the Argosy University system. Students have remote access to the campus library database, enabling them to study and conduct research at home. Academic databases offer dissertation abstracts, academic journals, and professional periodicals. All library computers are Internet accessible. Software applications include Word, Excel, PowerPoint, SPSS, and various test-scoring programs.

Financial Aid

Financial aid is available to those who qualify. Argosy University, Washington DC, offers access to federal and state aid programs, merit-based awards, grants, loans, and a work-study program. As a first step, students should complete the Free Application for Federal

Argosy University, Washington DC

Student Aid (FAFSA). Prospective students can apply electronically at http://www.fafsa.ed.gov or at the campus.

Cost of Study

Tuition varies by program. Students should contact Argosy University, Washington DC, for tuition information.

Living and Housing Costs

Students typically live in apartments in the metropolitan Arlington, Virginia, area. Living expenses vary according to each student's preferred standard of living, housing, and transportation. The University does not offer or operate student housing. Most of the students are full-time working professionals who live within driving distance of the campus. Several nearby hotels offer special rates for those who commute from long distances. The Admissions Department also maintains a list of housing options, including contact information for University students who wish to share housing. For more information, students should contact the Admissions Department.

Student Group

Admission to Argosy University, Washington DC, is selective to ensure a dynamic and engaged student body. It encourages diversity in academic and employment backgrounds and promotes integration of the student body into professional life through established connections with local and national professional associations. Argosy University offers a professionally oriented education with rich opportunities to gain practical experience in class, field placements, and internships. Full-time students and working professionals gain the extensive knowledge and range of skills necessary for effective performance in their chosen fields.

Student Outcomes

Students can register with the University's online career-services system and use select services from a distance, such as degree-specific career e-mail lists, national job posts, and virtual job fairs. Students should contact the University for more information.

Location

Argosy University, Washington DC, is located in suburban Arlington, Virginia. The University is conveniently situated to provide access to most major highways in the area and is easily accessible by public transportation. In proximity to Georgetown, students enjoy access to the many diverse attractions of the D.C. area. Additional campus space is located at The Art Institute of Washington Building (1820 Fort Myer Drive). The University houses administrative offices and seven classrooms at this location. Perhaps best known as the home of the Pentagon and Arlington National Cemetery, Arlington, Virginia, is one of the most highly educated areas in the nation. It is also one of the most diverse.

Many businesses in the area provide varied opportunities for student training. Major employers in the region include MCI Telecommunications Corporation; Bell Atlantic Network Services, Inc.; and Gannett/USA Today Company, Inc.

Argosy University, Washington DC, is certified to operate by the State Council of Higher Education for Virginia (James Monroe Building, 101 North 14th Street, Richmond, Virginia 23219; 804-225-2600).

The University

Argosy University is a private institution with nineteen locations across the nation. Argosy University, Washington DC, provides students with a career resources office, an academic resources center, and extensive information access for research. It offers the resources of a large university, plus the friendliness and personal attention of a small campus. The innovative programs feature dynamic, relevant, and practical curricula delivered in flexible class formats. Students enjoy scheduling options that make it easier to fit school into their busy lives, choosing from day and evening courses, on campus or online. Many students find a combination of class formats to be an ideal way of continuing their education while meeting family and professional demands.

Argosy University is accredited by the Accrediting Commission for Senior Colleges and Universities of the Western Association for Schools and Colleges (985 Atlantic Avenue, Suite 100, Alameda, California, 94501, http://www.wascsenior.org).

Applying

Argosy University, Washington DC, accepts students year-round on a rolling admissions basis, depending on availability of required courses. Applications for admission are available online or by contacting the campus.

Correspondence and Information

Argosy University, Washington DC
1550 Wilson Boulevard, Suite 600
Arlington, Virginia 22209
United States
Phone: 703-526-5800
866-703-2777 (toll-free)
Fax: 703-526-5850
E-mail: auadmissions@argosy.edu
Web site: http://www.argosy.edu/washingtondc

THE FACULTY

The Argosy University faculty comprises working professionals who are eager to help students succeed. Members bring real-world experience and the latest practice innovations to the academic setting. The diverse faculty members of the College of Business are widely recognized for contributions to the field. Many are published scholars, and most hold doctoral degrees. They are committed to providing a substantive education that combines comprehensive knowledge with critical skills and practical workplace relevance. Above all, faculty members are committed to their students' personal and professional development.

FASHION INSTITUTE OF TECHNOLOGY

State University of New York

M.P.S. in Global Fashion Management

Programs of Study

The Fashion Institute of Technology (FIT), a State University of New York (SUNY) college of art and design, business, and technology, is home to a mix of innovative achievers, creative thinkers, and industry pioneers. FIT fosters interdisciplinary initiatives, advances research, and provides access to an international network of professionals. With a reputation for excellence, FIT offers its diverse student body access to world-class faculty, dynamic and relevant curricula, and a superior education at an affordable cost. It offers seven programs of graduate study. The programs in Art Market: Principles and Practices; Exhibition Design; Fashion and Textile Studies: History, Theory, Museum Practice; and Sustainable Interior Environments lead to the Master of Arts (M.A.) degree. The Illustration program leads to the Master of Fine Arts (M.F.A.) degree. The Master of Professional Studies (M.P.S.) degree programs are Cosmetics and Fragrance Marketing and Management, and Global Fashion Management.

Global Fashion Management is a 36-credit, full-time M.P.S. program offered in collaboration with Hong Kong Polytechnic University, in Hong Kong, and the Institut Français de la Mode, in Paris. The program is designed to prepare current fashion executives for senior managerial positions. The course of study is completed in three semesters and brings students from all three institutions together for intensive seminars held at each of the three participating institutions, thus providing a unique international experience for those involved. The curriculum includes courses in production management and the supply chain, global marketing and fashion brand management, current technologies in the fashion industry, international team management, international culture and business, challenges to profitability, and politics and world trade.

Research Facilities

The School of Graduate Studies is primarily located in the campus's Shirley Goodman Resource Center, which also houses the Gladys Marcus Library and The Museum at FIT. School of Graduate Studies facilities include conference rooms; a fully equipped conservation laboratory; a multipurpose laboratory for conservation projects and the dressing of mannequins; storage facilities for costume and textile materials; a graduate student lounge with computer and printer access; a graduate student library reading room with computers, reference materials, and copies of past classes' qualifying and thesis papers; specialized wireless classrooms; traditional and digital illustration studios; and classrooms equipped with model stands, easels, and drafting tables.

The Gladys Marcus Library houses more than 300,000 volumes of print, nonprint, and digital resources. Specialized holdings include industry reference materials, manufacturers' catalogues, original fashion sketches and scrapbooks, photographs, portfolios of plates, and sample books. The FIT Digital Library provides access to over 90 searchable online databases.

The Museum at FIT houses one of the world's most important collections of clothing and textiles and is the only museum in New York City dedicated to the art of fashion. The permanent collection encompasses more than 50,000 garments and accessories dating from the eighteenth century to the present, with particular strength in twentieth-century fashion, as well as 30,000 textiles and 100,000 textile swatches. Each year, nearly 100,000 visitors are drawn to the museum's award-winning exhibitions and public programs.

Financial Aid

FIT directly administers its institutional grants, scholarships, and loans. Federal funding administered by the college may include Federal Perkins Loans, federally subsidized and unsubsidized Direct Loans for students, Grad PLUS loans, and the Federal Work-Study Program. Priority for institutionally administered funds is given to students enrolled and designated as full-time.

Cost of Study

Tuition for New York State residents is $4599 per semester, or $383 per credit. Out-of-state residents' tuition is $8352 per semester, or $696 per credit. Tuition and fees are subject to change at the discretion of FIT's Board of Trustees. Additional expenses—for class materials, textbooks, and travel—may apply and vary per program.

Living and Housing Costs

On-campus housing is available to graduate students. Traditional residence hall accommodations (including meal plan) cost from $6119 to $6299 per semester. Apartment-style housing options (not including meal plan) cost from $5241 to $9521 per semester.

Student Group

Enrollment in the School of Graduate Studies is approximately 200 students per academic year, allowing considerable individualized advisement. Students come to FIT from throughout the country and around the world.

Student Outcomes

Students in the Global Fashion Management program maintain full-time employment in the industry while working toward their degree, which provides the basis for advancement to positions of upper-level managerial responsibility.

Location

FIT is located in Manhattan's Chelsea neighborhood, at the heart of the advertising, visual arts, marketing, fashion, business, design, and communications industries. Students are connected to New York City and gain unparalleled exposure to their field through guest lectures, field trips, internships, and sponsored competitions. The location provides access to major museums, galleries, and auction houses as well as dining, entertainment, and shopping options. The campus is near subway, bus, and commuter rail lines.

Applying

Applicants to all School of Graduate Studies programs must hold a baccalaureate degree in an appropriate major from a college or university, with a cumulative GPA of 3.0 or higher. International students from non-English-speaking countries are required to submit minimum TOEFL scores of 550 on the written test, 213 on the computer test, or 80 on the Internet test. Students applying to the Global Fashion Management program must submit GRE scores. Each major has additional, specialized prerequisites for admission; for detailed information, students should visit the School of Graduate Studies on FIT's Web site.

Fashion Institute of Technology

Domestic and international students use the same application when seeking admission. The deadline for completed applications with transcripts and supplemental materials is February 15 for the Global Fashion Management program. After the deadline date, applicants are considered on a rolling admissions basis. Candidates may apply online at fitnyc.edu/gradstudies.

Correspondence and Information

School of Graduate Studies
Shirley Goodman Resource Center, Room E315
Fashion Institute of Technology
227 West 27 Street
New York, New York 10001-5992
Phone: 212-217-4300
Fax: 212-217-4301
E-mail: gradinfo@fitnyc.edu
Web site: http://www.fitnyc.edu/gradstudies
http://www.fitnyc.edu/GFM

THE FACULTY

The faculty members listed below constitute a partial listing. Guest lecturers are not included.

Pamela Ellsworth, Associate Chairperson; M.P.S., Fashion Institute of Technology.
Brooke Carlson, Sc.D., New Haven.
Praveen K. Chaudhry, Ph.D., Pennsylvania.
Robert Day, M.A., Berkeley.
Robin Lewis, B.S., Northwestern.
Tom Nastos, B.S., Fashion Institute of Technology.
Jeanette Nostra, B.S., Goddard.
Judith Ryba, Ph.D., Paris Dauphine (France).

FELICIAN COLLEGE

Division of Business and Management Science

Programs of Study

The Division of Business and Management Science is a shining example of Felician College's high-quality programs and academic excellence. The Division of Business has a unique and entrepreneurial spirit—it is innovative, dynamic, visionary, on the cutting edge, and highly responsive to the needs of students, corporations, and the workforce. This spirit is quickly earning Felician a reputation as a leader in business education in New Jersey. The Division offers two strong master's degree programs, an M.B.A. in Innovation and Entrepreneurial Leadership and a Master of Science in Healthcare Administration.

Felician College's **M.B.A. in Innovation and Entrepreneurial Leadership** has an approach unlike other M.B.A. programs, focusing on the development of competencies through the delivery of academic content. This nurtures students' growth as competent, ethical, articulate, and creative leaders. The program uses a unique combination of classroom and online learning combined with hands-on practical application. The goal of the program is to create visionary thinking and innovative leadership for individuals who wish to start their own businesses or be agents of change within their corporations.

Specially tailored to meet the needs of working adults, the program meets only one night a week, from 6 to 10 p.m., and allows students to complete the 36-credit degree in less than two years. The program is conveniently located at the Felician College campuses in Lodi and Rutherford and several branch campuses across the state.

The cohort-based program allows students to progress with a cohesive learning team so they can grow and benefit from teamwork and the support and guidance of an academic learning community. The curriculum prepares students with both the technical knowledge they need for solving complex problems and the core competencies that will equip them with the survival skills necessary for the competitive business world. The Felician M.B.A. core competencies, which are a part of the content in every course, include critical reasoning, effective communication, emotional intelligence, teamwork, ethical decision-making, and creativity.

The **Master of Science in Healthcare Administration** combines business acumen with a solid base in healthcare administration and management skills, preparing graduates to fill the growing need for healthcare professionals and administrators at all levels. The program explores the changing demands of a global healthcare system and includes courses in health policy, ethics, financial management, and healthcare resource allocation.

Students enter the 39-credit program as part of a cohort learning team, completing one evening course every eight weeks. Courses are delivered by a diverse panel of faculty experts that includes both Felician professors and experienced practitioners from within the business and health-care fields. Students also complete a unique executive residency with a mentor at a mid- to executive-management level within the health-care field. The program offers a blended approach, combining online course work with in-person faculty interaction to maximize flexibility and support.

Research Facilities

The College Library is a two-story building that serves the needs of students, faculty and staff members, and alumni with more than 110,000 books and over 800 periodical subscriptions. This collection is enhanced by large holdings of materials in microform, which can be used on the library's reader/printer equipment. With its computers linked to information services such as Dialog and OCLC, and as a member of the New Jersey Library Network and VALE, the library locates and obtains information, journal articles, and books not available in its collection from sources all over the country. Computerized databases can also be accessed directly by users through the online FirstSearch workstation, where up-to-date information on 40 million books and an index of 15,000 periodicals is available. The library is also connected to the Internet and has several CD-ROM workstations. Through EBSCOhost, Bell & Howell's ProQuest, CINAHL, and other services, students and faculty and staff members have access to numerous online journal indexes—as well as articles from thousands of periodicals—from anywhere on the campus computer network or from their home computers. An experienced staff of professional librarians is available to assist users.

The College's computer facilities include an academic and administrative network, four computerized labs, a computerized learning center, and two computer centers that are available for students, with about 200 computers available for student/faculty member use. All classrooms, offices, and facilities are wired for Internet and e-mail.

Financial Aid

To qualify for financial aid, a student must complete the Free Application for Federal Student Aid (FAFSA).

Cost of Study

In 2012–13, graduate tuition was $925 per credit. Fees are additional. Scholarships, fellowships, work-study programs, and loans are available.

Living and Housing Costs

Students are housed in two residence halls on the Rutherford campus, Milton Court and Elliott Terrace. Both buildings have housing organized around student suites with semiprivate baths. On-campus room and board is approximately $11,400 per year. On-campus housing is not available to married students.

Student Group

Felician College enrolls approximately 2,300 students. In fall 2011, there were approximately 350 students enrolled in graduate programs. A close-knit community, business students participate in clubs and activities that build relationships and networks for the future. For example, Students in Free Enterprise (SIFE) is an innovative group that helps students develop skills by learning and putting into proactive practice the principles of free enterprise. Working in teams, students undertake projects that use free market economic principles, entrepreneurial strategies, and management skills to achieve stated objectives and goals. Felician's SIFE group recently placed second in competition with other such groups from colleges and universities around the country.

Location

Felician College's Lodi campus is located on the banks of the Saddle River on a beautifully landscaped campus of 27 acres and offers a collegiate setting in suburban Bergen County, within easy driving distance of New York City. The Felician College Rutherford Campus is set on 10.5 beautifully landscaped acres in the heart of the historic community of Rutherford, New Jersey. Only 15 minutes from the Lodi campus, the Rutherford complex contains student residences, classroom buildings, a student center, and a gymnasium. The campus is a short distance from downtown Rutherford, where there are many shops and businesses of interest to students. Regular shuttle bus service between the two campuses is a quick 10-minute ride that turns two campuses into a one-campus home for the students.

The College

Felician College, a coeducational liberal arts college, is a Catholic, private, independent institution for students representing diverse religious, racial, and ethnic backgrounds. The College operates on two campuses in Lodi and Rutherford, New Jersey. The College is one of the institutions of higher learning conducted by the Felician Sisters in the United States. Its mission is to provide a values-oriented education based in the liberal arts while it prepares students for meaningful lives and careers in contemporary society. To meet the needs of students and to provide personal enrichment courses to matriculated and nonmatriculated students, Felician College offers day, evening, and weekend programs. The College is accredited by the Middle States Association of Colleges and Schools and carries program accreditation from the Commission on Collegiate Nursing Education, the International Assembly for Collegiate Business Education, and the Teacher Education Accreditation Council.

Applying

Admission to Felician College is as personalized as the College's educational programs. Each application is holistically reviewed, including careful consideration of the applicant's academic achievement, work history, motivation, and suitability. Students must submit the completed application, the $40 nonrefundable application fee, official transcripts, GMAT scores, a resume, and a personal statement. Upon the discretion of the division admission committee, the GMAT requirement may be waived for those students with significant and progressive postgraduate professional experience. Applications are processed on a rolling basis.

Correspondence and Information

Office of Graduate Admission
Felician College
262 South Main Street
Lodi, New Jersey 07644-2117
United States
Phone: 201-559-6077 (Admissions)
E-mail: graduate@felician.edu
Web site: http://www.felician.edu/business/index.asp

THE FACULTY

All courses are taught by fully qualified faculty members with advanced degrees, who are dedicated to teaching, advising, and continued involvement in their disciplines. The student-faculty ratio of 12:1 facilitates close working relationships and the development of individualized programs of instruction. The faculty is composed of both lay and religious men and women who are committed to the intellectual and spiritual growth of every student.

Specific information regarding the faculty of Felician College is available on the College's Web site at http://www.felician.edu.

HAWAI'I PACIFIC UNIVERSITY

College of Business Administration

Programs of Study

Hawai'i Pacific University (HPU), an established institution with leading programs in business administration, information systems, and management, offers a comprehensive Master of Business Administration (M.B.A.) degree program. This program is noted for several distinct features. First, it is pragmatic, emphasizing real-world applications, case studies, and specific skills and competencies needed in contemporary business. Second, most courses include both an entrepreneurial and an international perspective. Third, computer applications are integrated into many of the M.B.A. courses. Fourth, interpersonal and communication skills are stressed throughout the curriculum. Lastly, as a major partner in the downtown business community, Hawai'i Pacific University coordinates a large internship program that provides part-time and full-time managerial, technical, and professional positions in leading business firms. Through this internship program, M.B.A. candidates have the opportunity to supplement their income while earning academic credit.

The M.B.A. program at Hawai'i Pacific University requires 42 semester hours of graduate work. Prerequisite courses in business subjects may be required. The curriculum is organized into eight core courses (24 semester hours), three College of Business seminars (3 semester hours), three elective courses (9 semester hours), and two capstone courses (6 semester hours). Students may concentrate in any one of twelve business areas, including accounting, e-business, economics, finance, health-care management, human resource management, information systems, international business, management, marketing, organizational change, and travel industry management. The M.B.A. program is also available completely online, with the same high quality curriculum as the classroom format. There is a complete set of online courses for five of the twelve M.B.A. concentrations. For more information, prospective students may visit http://online.hpu.edu.

The University also offers joint M.B.A. programs. An **M.B.A./M.A. in Global Leadership and Sustainable Development** is designed for the exceptional student whose background, education, and worldview have inspired an interest in assuming leadership positions in the global community. In addition, the joint **M.B.A./M.A. in Organizational Change** examines the models and strategies for leading change, continuous improvement, and performance management. The **M.B.A./M.A. in Human Resource Management** is designed for students interested in human resources, but who also desire expertise in business and management. The **M.B.A./M.S. in Information Systems** is designed to provide leading managers with the technical skills needed in the arena of information systems. The **M.B.A./M.S. in Nursing** is designed for professional nurses who seek preparation for management positions in the health-care industry. Lastly, the **M.B.A./M.A. in Communication** will prepare students for careers that integrate employee communication, media, public relations, promotions, and marketing.

Research Facilities

To support graduate studies, HPU's Meader and Atherton libraries offer over 110,000 bound volumes, 350,000 microfiche items, and periodical subscriptions to 1,500 print titles and 30,000 electronic journals. Databases of public and state university libraries, legislative information, and business-oriented statistical data are also available in the library or online. Students can access HPU's library databases, course information, their academic information, and an e-mail account through Pipeline, the University's internal Web site for students. The University's accessible on-campus computer center houses more than 420 computers with specialized software to support graduate academic programs. HPU also provides free Wi-Fi so students have wireless access to Pipeline resources anywhere on campus. A significant number of online courses are available as well.

Financial Aid

The University participates in all federal financial aid programs designated for graduate students. These programs provide aid in the form of subsidized (need-based) and unsubsidized (non-need-based) Federal Stafford Student Loans. Through these loans, funds may be available to cover a student's entire cost of education. To apply for aid, students must submit the Free Application for Federal Student Aid (FAFSA) beginning January 1.

The University also offers several types of institutional graduate scholarships to new full-time, degree-seeking students. U.S. citizens, permanent residents, and international students who have a demonstrated financial need may apply. HPU's graduate scholarships include the Graduate Trustee Scholarship of $6000 ($3000 for two semesters), the Graduate Dean Scholarship of $4000 ($2000 for two semesters), and the Graduate Kokua Scholarship of $2000 ($1000 for two semesters). Factors that may be considered when evaluating requests are previous academic record, community involvement and service, and professional work experience and achievement.

In order to be eligible for the best award package, students should apply by HPU's priority deadline of March 1. Applications received after the priority deadline will be awarded on a funds-available basis. Mailing of student award letters usually begins by the end of March. Applicants will be notified by mail as decisions are made.

Cost of Study

Tuition for graduate students enrolled in fall and spring semesters is determined on a per-credit basis; full-time status for a graduate student is 9 credits. Tuition for the optional winter and summer sessions is also determined on a per-credit basis. For the 2012–13 academic year (excluding winter and summer sessions), full-time tuition is $13,770 for the M.B.A. program. Other expenses, including books, personal expenses, fees, and a student bus pass are estimated at $3285.

Living and Housing Costs

The University has off-campus housing for graduate students and an apartment referral service. The cost of living in off-campus housing is approximately $12,482 for a double-occupancy room. Additional graduate housing information is available online at www.hpu.edu/housing.

Hawai'i Pacific University

Student Group

University enrollment currently stands at more than 8,200. HPU is one of the most culturally diverse universities in America, with students from all fifty U.S. states and more than 100 countries.

Location

Hawai'i Pacific University combines the excitement of an urban, downtown campus with the serenity of a residential campus. The urban campus is ideally located in downtown Honolulu, the business and financial center of the Pacific. The downtown campus is composed of seven buildings in the center of Honolulu's business district and is home to the College of Business Administration and the College of Humanities and Social Sciences.

Eight miles away, situated on 135 acres in Kaneohe, the windward Hawai'i Loa campus is the site of the College of Nursing and Health Sciences and the College of Natural and Computational Sciences. The Hawai'i Loa campus has residence halls; dining commons; the Educational Technology Center; a student center; and outdoor recreational facilities including a soccer field, tennis courts, a softball field, and an exercise room.

HPU is affiliated with the Oceanic Institute, an aquaculture research facility located on a 56-acre site at Makapu'u Point on the windward coast of Oahu, Hawaii. All three sites are linked by HPU shuttle and also easily accessible by public transportation.

Notably, the downtown campus location is within walking distance of shopping and dining. Iolani Palace, the only royal palace in the United States, is a few blocks away, as are the State Capitol, City Hall, and the Blaisdell Concert Hall. The Honolulu Academy of Arts, Museum of Contemporary Art, Waikiki Aquarium, Honolulu Zoo, and many other cultural attractions are located nearby.

The University

HPU is a private, nonprofit university with approximately 8,200 students. Founded in 1965, HPU prides itself on maintaining strong academic programs, small class sizes, individual attention to students, and a diverse faculty and student population. Students may choose from more than fifty acclaimed undergraduate programs and fourteen distinguished graduate programs.

HPU is recognized as a Best in the West college by The Princeton Review and *U.S. News & World Report* and a Best Buy by *Barron's* business magazine.

HPU boasts more than 500 full- and part-time faculty members from around the world with outstanding academic and professional credentials. HPU's student-centered approach and low student-to-faculty ratio of 15:1 results in personal attention and one-on-one guidance. The average class size is under 25.

A wide range of counseling and other student support services are available. There are more than fifty student organizations on campus, including the Graduate Student Organization.

Applying

Hawai'i Pacific University seeks students with academic promise, outstanding career potential, and high motivation. Applicants seeking an M.B.A. should complete and forward a graduate admissions application form, send in the $50 nonrefundable application fee, have official transcripts sent from all colleges or universities previously attended, have two letters of recommendation forwarded, and submit a resume and GMAT results. International applicants should submit scores from a recognized English proficiency test such as TOEFL. Admissions decisions are made on a rolling basis and applicants are notified between one and two weeks after all documents have been submitted. Applicants to Hawai'i Pacific University's graduate program are encouraged to submit applications online at http://www.hpu.edu/hpumba.

Correspondence and Information

Graduate Admissions
Hawai'i Pacific University
1164 Bishop Street, #911
Honolulu, Hawaii 96813
Phone: 808-544-1135
866-GRAD-HPU (toll-free)
Fax: 808-544-0280
E-mail: graduate@hpu.edu
Web site: http://www.hpu.edu/hpumba

THE FACULTY AND THEIR RESEARCH

Leinaala Ahu-Isa, Assistant Professor of Management; Ph.D., Hawaii at Manoa.
Michelle Alarcon-Catt, Assistant Professor of Management; M.B.A., Pepperdine.
Eric Drabkin, Affiliate Associate Professor of Economics; Ph.D., UCLA.
Susan Fox-Wolfgramm, Professor of Management; Ph.D., Texas Tech.
Joseph Ha, Professor of Marketing; Ph.D., Rutgers.
Mark Lane, Associate Professor of Finance; Ph.D., Missouri–Columbia.
Leroy Laney, Professor of Finance and Economics; Ph.D., Colorado at Boulder.
Aytun Ozturk, Associate Professor of Quantitative Methods; Ph.D., Pittsburgh.
Joseph D. Patoskie, Associate Professor of Travel Industry Management; Ph.D., Texas Tech.
Lawrence Rowland, Department Chair/Assistant Professor of Information Systems; Ed.D., USC.
Niti Villinger, Associate Professor of Management; Ph.D., Cambridge.
Warren Wee, Associate Dean/Associate Professor of Accounting; Ph.D., Hawaii at Manoa.

HOLY FAMILY UNIVERSITY

Division of Extended Learning Accelerated M.B.A. Program

Programs of Study

Holy Family University's accelerated M.B.A. program is different from most others. It's the University's belief that learning should be more than imitation. Courses for adult students are intended to be not only educational and interesting, but also relevant.

Offered by the Division of Extended Learning, Holy Family's Master of Business Administration degree is designed to meet the needs of working adults. The program requires students to combine their work experience with textbook learning. Holy Family students and their employers have found this approach extraordinarily beneficial, with class assignments and projects implemented in the workplace and published in professional journals.

The Master of Business Administration program comprises ten courses and 30 credits, covering the necessary content areas expected of the M.B.A. graduate, and may be completed within twenty months. Students may choose to add a concentration—three 3-credit courses—in finance, health-care administration, or human resource administration.

The program is open to those currently working in business, with at least three years of progressive managerial experience. Holy Family also offers a New Professionals M.B.A. Program for those with less than three years of managerial experience. It comprises twelve courses and 36 credits, and can be completed within two years.

Each eight-week course in the regular program meets once a week. Students enrolled in hybrid courses meet in the classroom one Saturday per month, with all other course work completed online.

Research Facilities

Accelerated programs are housed at Holy Family University–Woodhaven, which is a short drive from the Northeast Philadelphia campus. There, the University library currently houses more than 124,000 items, including more than 4,000 DVDs and videos selected to support the learning, teaching, and informational needs of the University community. The library offers print and online access to the full text of over 13,000 journals and periodicals. Over two dozen full-text databases are available on and off campus, including Academic Search Premier, WilsonWeb OmniFile, CINAHL, and PsycARTICLES. In addition, the library has over 8,500 electronic books available from home or campus via NetLibrary and other interfaces.

Financial Aid

Holy Family is committed to helping adults further their education by consistently maintaining competitive tuition rates. Most graduate students are eligible for Federal Stafford Loans when attending with a half-time enrollment status (6 graduate credits) or greater. For more information, potential students may contact the Financial Aid Office via e-mail at finaid@holyfamily.edu or by phone at 267-341-3233.

Cost of Study

Tuition for Holy Family's accelerated M.B.A. programs is $675 per credit hour.

Living and Housing Costs

Holy Family University does not provide graduate student housing; however, there are numerous housing options available in the nearby area.

Student Group

Approximately 110 students, all of them studying part-time, are enrolled in the accelerated M.B.A. programs. These students are working professionals, and Holy Family's educational philosophy acknowledges their work and life experience as contributions they bring to the classroom.

Student Outcomes

Because the students in this program are also working professionals, the emphasis on case studies allows students to apply their learning immediately and provides a basis for advancement in the workplace.

Location

Holy Family University's Woodhaven campus occupies 4.76 acres on Bristol Pike, in Bensalem, Pennsylvania. It is situated next to the Woodhaven Road exit of I-95. Woodhaven, opened in fall 2003, is home to the Division of Extended Learning. The 27,000-square-foot building houses both academics and administration; convenient parking for 300 vehicles is available. Woodhaven offers academic classrooms, administrative and faculty offices, a conference room, a large meeting/seminar room, a computer lab, and a lounge with vending machines. The campus also has the capacity for large group sessions.

The University

Holy Family University prides itself on programs that offer students real-world experience. This focus on preparedness and student outcomes is designed to help graduates stand out, with distinction.

Respect for the individual, the dignity of the human person—these values are taught, lived, and form the foundation of Holy Family University. Concern for moral values and social justice guides the University's programs and enriches the student's education and experience.

Applying

Application requirements for the accelerated M.B.A. programs include a bachelor's degree from a regionally accredited four-year institution; a minimum 3.0 grade point average on a 4.0 scale (applicants with a grade point average under 3.0 may be required to take the GMAT); an application form and $50 nonrefundable fee, made payable to Holy

Family University; a current resume showing three years of managerial experience (managing people or projects); two professional recommendations, one from a supervisor; a statement of professional goals; official transcripts from all universities previously attended; and demonstrated competency through undergraduate course work, related work experiences, standardized tests, or other proof of knowledge, in financial and managerial accounting, finance, economics, business statistics, and marketing. At the discretion of the M.B.A. Admissions Committee, candidates may be invited for a personal interview.

Correspondence and Information

Division of Extended Learning
Holy Family University–Woodhaven
1311 Bristol Pike
Bensalem, Pennsylvania 19020
United States
Phone: 267-341-5030
Fax: 215-633-0558
E-mail: acclearn@holyfamily.edu
Web site: http://accelerated.holyfamily.edu/accelerated-programs/holy-family-university-mba-program/

THE FACULTY

Faculty members in the Division of Extended Learning (DEL) bring their extensive business experience into the classroom, enabling M.B.A. students to learn what is being practiced in today's workplace. DEL facilitators come from a variety of industries and disciplines, so students are exposed to exactly the kinds of diverse viewpoints and backgrounds that comprise contemporary decision makers.

NORTH CAROLINA STATE UNIVERSITY

Jenkins Graduate School of Management
Program in Business Administration

Programs of Study

The Master of Business Administration (M.B.A.) at North Carolina State University (NC State) emphasizes the management of innovation and technology. Students take an integrated core curriculum, with a focus on technology, business processes, and practical applications, in a collaborative learning environment. Through simulations, case studies, and projects, students learn from real-world examples and experiences. Full-time students take a course in managerial effectiveness, which emphasizes communication skills, networking, negotiations, team skills, ethics, and social responsibility.

Students begin the program by taking core courses. Students in the full- and part-time programs then choose a concentration from biosciences management, entrepreneurship, financial management, marketing management, product innovation management, services management, and supply chain management. Full-time students complete the program in twenty-one months; part-time students complete the program in thirty-three months, and online students complete the program in twenty-four months.

Biosciences management is an exciting area of specialization at NC State. Life sciences is one of today's fastest-growing business sectors, offering new opportunities for those who can provide managerial leadership in a technology-focused environment. This concentration was designed and is taught by faculty members with extensive experience in biotechnology and pharmaceuticals, working closely with industry leaders located in the Research Triangle Park.

Services management is another area of concentration. Services are dominating the economy, providing about three fourths of all jobs—a rising share of which are highly skilled and technology-intensive. This fuels a growing need for managers skilled in outsourcing, consulting, and process re-engineering. NC State's management and engineering faculties are at the forefront of curriculum development and research in the evolving discipline of services science, management, and engineering (SSME), working with IBM and a growing list of other company partners.

The entrepreneurship concentration within the M.B.A. teaches students how to turn technologies into business, using real technologies as live case studies. Supported by the National Science Foundation, the Kenan Institute, and several other organizations, graduate students and faculty members in the College of Management work closely in teams with their counterparts in the science and engineering disciplines to identify, evaluate, and commercialize promising technologies. The TEC curriculum follows the complete product-development cycle. Students gain evaluation skills for commercializing new technologies, along with an understanding of what it takes to start and run a high-technology business. Students also interact with business experts and entrepreneurs from outside the University.

Research Facilities

The Poole College of Management is headquartered in Nelson Hall, which houses classrooms, computer labs, and the offices of the faculty members and students. Classrooms feature tiered seating, laptop connections, a wireless network, and complete multimedia facilities. The Poole College of Management's computer lab houses 100 microcomputers connected to a campuswide network. Students have access to a wide range of spreadsheet, word processing, database, statistical, and econometric software, along with several large databases.

D. H. Hill Library, which is located near the center of the campus, offers access to millions of volumes of books and journals and an extensive and growing collection of CD-ROM and electronic databases. Graduate students also have borrowing privileges at Duke University, North Carolina Central University, and the University of North Carolina at Chapel Hill.

Financial Aid

Graduate assistantships and scholarships are available to full-time students through the M.B.A. program. Grants and loan programs are available through the Graduate School and the University's Financial Aid Office.

Cost of Study

For full-time students who are North Carolina residents, tuition and fees in 2012–13 are $9329 per semester; the estimated total for living expenses, including tuition and fees, books, medical insurance, housing, food, clothing, transportation, and other miscellaneous items is $15,000 per semester. Tuition and fees for full-time nonresidents are $15,595 per semester. Part-time students on the main campus who are North Carolina residents pay $6911 per semester for tuition and fees only; nonresidents pay $11,601. Part-time students on the Research Triangle Park campus or in the online program who are North Carolina residents pay $4998; nonresidents pay $7158.

Living and Housing Costs

On-campus dormitory facilities are provided for unmarried graduate students. In 2012–13, the rent for double-occupancy rooms starts at $2700 per semester. Accommodations in Wolf Village, the newest residence hall for graduate students, cost $2755 per semester. Apartments for married students in King Village rent for $560 per month for a studio, $620 for a one-bedroom apartment, and $715 for a two-bedroom apartment.

Student Group

Almost all M.B.A. students have professional work experience, many in high-technology industries, such as telecommunications or software, and others in industries such as health care or financial services, in which technology is the key to a competitive advantage. A technical background is not essential for the M.B.A., but all students must be willing to learn about technology and the management challenges it creates. More than 75 percent of M.B.A. students have undergraduate degrees in business, computer science, sciences, or engineering. The rest come from a variety of fields, including the social sciences and humanities.

The average full-time M.B.A. student has four years of work experience. The average part-time student has seven years of professional experience. Women compose approximately 30 percent of each entering full-time class; members of minority groups account for approximately 15 percent; international students account for approximately 33 percent of the full-time class.

Student Outcomes

The placement and promotion of graduates is the strongest testament to the value of the NC State M.B.A. program. The program's alumni include managers, entrepreneurs, and innovators in all fields and in all sizes of companies. Recent employers include SAS Institute, IBM, Progress Energy, Red Hat, John Deere, GlaxoSmithKline, Cisco Systems, and several local start-up ventures.

Location

Raleigh, the state capital, has a population of 405,791. Nearby is the Research Triangle Park, one of the largest and fastest-growing research institutions of its type in the country. The Raleigh metro area population is 1,742,816. The University's concert series has more subscribers than any other in the United States. Excellent sports and recreational facilities are also available.

The University

NC State was founded in 1889 as a land-grant institution. Within 100 years, it became one of the nation's leading research universities. Located in the Research Triangle, a world-renowned center of research, industry, technology, and education, the College of Management is housed on the 623-acre main campus of NC State, which lies just west of downtown Raleigh, the state capital. NC State comprises eleven colleges and schools serving a total student population of more than 30,000. More than 5,000 of those students are in graduate programs.

Applying

M.B.A. students must have a baccalaureate degree from an accredited college or university and are strongly encouraged to have had courses in calculus, statistics, accounting, and economics. Calculus or statistics must be completed prior to enrollment, with a grade of C or better. Admissions decisions are based on previous academic performance, GMAT or GRE scores, essays, letters of reference, and previous work and volunteer experience. Applicants whose native language is not English, regardless of citizenship, must also submit TOEFL scores of at least 250 (computer-based) or an IELTS score of 7.5; applicants to the part-time programs may apply for a TOEFL waiver. Interviews are by invitation.

The NC State M.B.A. program accepts applications for the fall semester only for the full-time program, with application deadlines of October 15, January 15, and March 1. Part-time students may enter the program in either fall or spring, with application deadlines of October 15 for spring entry and February 15 and April 8 for fall entry. Online students may enter the program in the fall only, with application deadlines of October 15, February 15, and April 8. Once an application has been received and is complete, it is reviewed for admission. This rolling admission process allows an applicant to receive an admission decision within six weeks of receipt of a completed application.

Correspondence and Information

Ms. Pam Bostic, Director
M.B.A. Program
North Carolina State University
Box 8114
Raleigh, North Carolina 27695
United States
Phone: 919-515-5584
Fax: 919-515-5073
E-mail: mba@ncsu.edu
Web site: http://www.mba.ncsu.edu

THE FACULTY AND THEIR RESEARCH

The graduate faculty members of the M.B.A. program are outstanding teachers and researchers. In recent years, faculty members have been selected for the University of North Carolina Board of Governors' Award, Alumni Distinguished Professorships, and the NC State Academy of Outstanding Teachers. They match their teaching methods to the subject material, using case discussions, group projects, lectures, class discussions, and guest speakers as appropriate. Several faculty members serve on the editorial boards of journals in accounting, finance, marketing, operations, project management, and strategy. They have been ranked in the top twenty nationally for publishing in the top economics and finance journals.

Many faculty members held positions in management before receiving their doctoral degrees and stay in touch with today's business world through consulting and executive education.

Group work is an important part of the M.B.A. experience.

Classes are offered on the main campus and in the Research Triangle Park (RTP).

ST. JOSEPH'S COLLEGE, NEW YORK

Programs in Business

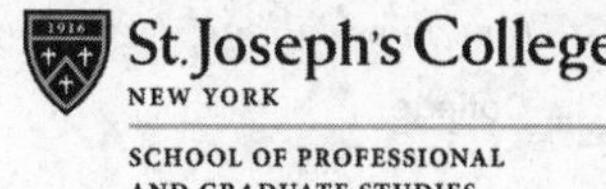

Programs of Study

The Graduate Management Programs at St. Joseph's College (SJC) were designed around two interrelated concepts—developing specific abilities needed for success in the workplace and relating theoretical knowledge to the real world. Consonant with the values espoused in the mission and goals of the College, the programs support ethical behavior and social responsibility as a foundation of managerial practice. The curricula encourage a proactive perspective relative to the challenges and opportunities inherent in promoting diversity in the workplace.

Designed for working adults holding leadership positions in the public service, private, and nonprofit sectors, the graduate management programs promote managerial effectiveness and the enhancement of human performance in organizations. Students select from degree options and specialties that bolster their marketability in their chosen field. Choices include an Executive Master of Business Administration (E.M.B.A.), which is also available online; an M.B.A. in accounting; an M.B.A. in health-care management including a new concentration in health information technology; or a Master of Science in Management with a specialization in organizational management, health-care management, or human resources management. Each program is solidly rooted in groundbreaking research—that is, innovative scholarly investigation into the key distinctions between superior leaders and average performers in the workplace. Based on this research, the programs help students strengthen a variety of abilities, including goal and action management, people management, and analytic reasoning. Students create an individualized plan to target those abilities they wish to develop.

The Self-Directed Managerial Applications Component of each course addresses an appropriate issue, problem, or task within an actual organizational environment. Students learn to apply classroom knowledge and develop one or more managerial-effectiveness abilities. Students are also required to complete a minimum of two projects as participants in management teams.

Certificates in health-care management and human resources management are also offered. These 15-credit programs are designed to provide practitioners with advanced study of current health-care or human resources trends and practices and the latest leadership and management tools necessary to advance their careers.

Research Facilities

The Callahan Library at the Long Island Campus is a modern, 25,000-square-foot, freestanding facility with seating for more than 300 readers. A curriculum library, seminar rooms, administrative offices, and two classrooms are housed in this building. Holdings include more than 105,000 volumes and 307 periodical titles, and they are supplemented by videos and other instructional aids. Patrons have access to the Internet and to several online academic databases. A fully automated library system, Endeavor, ensures the efficient retrieval and management of all library resources. Other resources include the library at St. Joseph's Brooklyn Campus, with more than 109,000 volumes, and membership in the Long Island Library Resources Council, which facilitates cooperative associations with the academic and special libraries on Long Island. Internet access, subscriptions to several online full-text databases, and membership in the international bibliographic utility, OCLC, allow almost limitless access to available information.

McEntegart Hall is a fully air-conditioned five-level structure. Three spacious reading areas with a capacity for 300 readers, including individual study carrels and shelf space for 200,000 volumes, provide an excellent environment for research. In addition, McEntegart Hall houses the college archives, a curriculum library, three computer laboratories, a nursing education laboratory, and a videoconference room. There are eight classrooms, a chapel, cafeteria, and faculty and student lounges.

A high-speed fiber-optic intracampus network connects all offices, instructional facilities, computer laboratories, and libraries on both the Brooklyn and Long Island campuses. The network provides Internet access to all students and faculty and staff members. An integrated online library system enables students to search for and check out books at either campus. Online databases and other electronic resources are available to students from either campus or from their home computers. Two wireless laptop classrooms with "smart classroom" features provide flexible instruction spaces with the latest technologies. Videoconferencing facilities connect the two campuses, allowing for real-time distance learning in a small-group setting.

Financial Aid

Financial aid is available in the form of federal and private loans and scholarships. Students should contact the Financial Aid Office for more information (Brooklyn Campus, telephone: 718-940-5700; Long Island Campus, telephone: 631-687-2600).

Cost of Study

In 2012–13, tuition is $19,500 or $715 per credit for graduate programs. Per semester, the college and technology fees for 12 or more credits totaled $200.

Living and Housing Costs

Off-campus housing is available at the St. George Hotel for Brooklyn campus students. New York's number-one resource for student housing and St. Joseph's College have partnered to offer off-campus housing. Accommodations include cable TV, high-speed access, a completely furnished bedroom, a full bath, a closet, a kitchen on each floor, and 24-hour security. Housing applications are available online.

Student Group

The total enrollment for all graduate programs on both campuses is 740.

Location

St. Joseph's College has two campuses—the main campus in the residential Clinton Hill section of Brooklyn and the campus in Patchogue, New York. The main campus offers easy access to all transit lines; to the Long Island Expressway; to all bridges in Brooklyn, Manhattan, and Queens; and to the Verrazano-Narrows Bridge to Staten Island. Within the space of half an hour, students leaving St. Joseph's College may find themselves in the Metropolitan Museum of Art, the 42nd Street Library, Carnegie Hall and Lincoln Center, the Broadway theater district, Madison Square Garden, or Shea Stadium. The College itself stands in the center of one of the nation's most diversified academic communities, consisting of six colleges and universities within a 2-mile radius of each other. The 27-acre Long Island campus, adjacent to Great Patchogue Lake, is an ideal setting for studying, socializing, and partaking in extracurricular activities. Just off Sunrise Highway, the College is easily accessible from all parts of Long Island.

St. Joseph's College, New York

The College

St. Joseph's College is a fully accredited institution that has been dedicated to providing a diverse population of students in the New York metropolitan area with an affordable education rooted in the liberal arts tradition since 1916. Independent and coeducational, the College provides a strong academic and value-oriented education at the undergraduate and graduate levels. For over a decade, the College has consistently ranked among America's best colleges by *U.S. News & World Report* and *Forbes*.

Applying

All applicants must have a baccalaureate degree from an accredited institution of higher education with an undergraduate grade point average of at least 3.0. In addition, applicants typically are required to be employed in a full-time position and to have substantial work experience involving supervision, program development, specialized training, considerable responsibility, and/or independent judgment. When an applicant's experiential qualifications fall short of the aforementioned criteria, the GMAT is required. Students must submit the completed application; the application fee; official transcripts; a current chronological resume; a completed verification of employment form, with a verification letter outlining designated duties from the current (or previous) employer; and two letters of recommendation. An interview is required.

Correspondence and Information

Brooklyn Campus
St. Joseph's College
245 Clinton Avenue
Brooklyn, New York 11205
Phone: 718-940-5800
E-mail: brooklynap@sjcny.edu
Web site: http://www.sjcny.edu/Academics/Graduate-Programs/260

Long Island Campus
St. Joseph's College
155 West Roe Boulevard
Patchogue, New York 11772
Phone: 631-687-4501
E-mail: suffolkap@sjcny.edu

THE FACULTY

FULL-TIME FACULTY

James J. Barkocy, Assistant Professor of Business; M.B.A., NYU.
Mary Chance, Assistant Professor of Business and Director of Graduate Management Studies; M.S.T., Long Island; CPA.
Stanley Chu, Accounting; M.B.A., St. John's (New York).
Stanley F. Fox, Associate Professor of Business; Ph.D., Walden.
Eileen White Jahn, Associate Professor of Business; Ph.D., CUNY, Baruch.
William Cotesworth Keller, Associate Professor of Business; Ph.D., Walden.
Robert A. Marose, Associate Professor of Business; Ph.D., Polytechnic.
Robert J. Nobile, Assistant Professor of Business; J.D., St. John's (New York).
Charles J. Pendola, Assistant Professor of Business; J.D., Touro; CPA.
Lauren Grace Pete, Associate Professor of Health Administration; J.D., Yeshiva; Ph.D., CUNY Graduate Center.
Diane Pfadenhauer, Assistant Professor of Business; J.D., St. John's (New York).
John Sardelis, Assistant Professor of Health Administration; Dr.P.H., Columbia.
Robert Seperson, Assistant Professor of Business; M.B.A., Dowling.
John J. Skinnon, Assistant Professor of Accounting; M.S.T., Long Island; CPA.
Richard Torz, Associate Professor of Economics; Ph.D., CUNY Graduate Center.

PRECEPTORS

Sharon Didier, Business; Ph.D., Capella.
Charles Dyon, Business; M.B.A., NYU.
Thomas Horan, Business; M.S., Long Island; CPA.
Marie Losquadro, Associate Dean of the Suffolk Campus, Business; M.S., NYIT.
Jay Zuckerman, Health Administration; M.P.A., SUNY at Albany; M.S., SUNY at Stony Brook.

LECTURERS

Ivo Antoniazzi, Business; Ed.D., Columbia.
Hsien-hung Chiu, Economics; M.A., Fu-Jen Catholic; M.A., SUNY at Stony Brook.
John Furnari, Business; M.A., CUNY, Queens.
Brenda Gill, Business; J.D., Fordham.
Heidi Hayden, Business; M.S., St. Joseph's (New York).
Steven Jarmon, Business; M.A., Denver.
Linda Lombardi, Health Administration; Ph.D., CUNY Graduate Center.
Verina Mathis-Crawford, Business; M.B.A., Pace.
Arthur Rescigno, Business; M.S., Columbia.
M. Par Rostom, Business; M.A, Temple.
Alan Vitters, Business; Ph.D., Utah.
Gail Whelan, Business; M.S., NYIT.

SOUTH UNIVERSITY

Atlanta Learning Site
Accelerated Business Administration Program

Program of Study

The Accelerated Master of Business Administration degree (A.M.B.A) program at South University is designed for professionals working in a variety of organizations who seek to have a greater understanding of the concepts, organizational structures, and strategies driving today's complex organization environment. This is an intensive program presented from a management perspective and designed to be completed in one year. The delivery structure of the program gives students the ability to balance the rigors of work and home while pursuing their master's degree.

Classes are held 24 Saturdays per year and are supplemented with Internet-mediated course work and synchronous meetings via conference calls and web-based meetings.

Financial Aid

A range of financial aid options is available to students who qualify. South University offers access to federal and state programs, including grants, loans, and work-study programs. Eligible students may apply for veterans' educational benefits and are encouraged to investigate the availability of grants and scholarships through community resources. As a first step, students should complete the Free Application for Federal Student Aid (FAFSA). Students may apply electronically at http://www.fafsa.ed.gov or through the program.

Cost of Study

Tuition information for the Accelerated Master of Business Administration program may be obtained by contacting the Admissions Department or through the University's website, www.southuniversity.edu/amba.

Living and Housing Costs

South University does not offer or operate student housing. Students who commute from long distances can arrange to stay at nearby hotels that offer long-term rates. More information is available by contacting the Admissions Department.

Student Outcomes

The South University Career Services Department has been established to assist currently enrolled students in developing their career plans and reaching their employment goals. Career services include, but are not limited to, one-on-one career counseling, special career-related workshops and programs, coaching for resume and cover letter development, and resume referral to employers.

Location

The Art Institute of Atlanta, located at 6600 Peachtree Dunwoody Road, Atlanta, Georgia, is approved as a teaching site (off-campus) for the offering of South University's Accelerated Master of Business Administration (AMBA) and the Accelerated Master of Healthcare Administration (AMBA) programs.

The University

South University is accredited by the Southern Association of Colleges and Schools Commission on Colleges to award associate, baccalaureate, masters, and doctorate degrees. Contact the Commission on Colleges at 1866 Southern Lane, Decatur, Georgia 30033-4097 or call 404-679-4500 for questions about the accreditation of South University.

Applying

Students are accepted into the Accelerated Master of Business Administration degree program on a monthly basis, with the exception of December. Entrance into the program is gained through a formal application review and interview process. Acceptance is competitive and based on the admission committee's evaluation of the applicant's academic background and personal motivation. Application packets are available by contacting the South University Admissions Department (800-952-4491, toll-free) or visiting the University's website (http://www.southuniversity.edu/amba).

Correspondence and Information

Applications for admission to the South University Accelerated Master of Business Administration program are available by contacting:

Accelerated Master of Business Administration Program
Brock Hass, Director, Off-Campus Programs
South University
709 Mall Boulevard
Savannah, Georgia 31406
United States
Phone: 800-952-4491(toll-free)
E-mail: bhass@southuniversity.edu
Website: http://www.southuniversity.edu/

See suprograms.info for program duration; tuition, fees, and other costs; median debt; federal salary data; alumni success; and other important info. (http://www.southuniversity.edu/programs-info/form/)

THE FACULTY

One of the most outstanding aspects of South University's Accelerated Business Administration Program is the dedication of the faculty members and their ability to cultivate a supportive learning environment. Faculty members are committed to their roles as mentors, teachers, and co-learners. They are also dedicated to the training of students who can assume positions of leadership within the business administration field. A current list of program faculty members appears in the South University catalog, which is available on the South University website (http://www.southuniversity.edu).

For students who have a bachelor's degree, an M.B.A. degree could be just one year away with the Accelerated Master of Business Administration program from South University.

SOUTH UNIVERSITY

Austin Campus
Business Administration Program

Program of Study

The Master of Business Administration (M.B.A.) degree program at South University is designed to provide students with a process-based curriculum versus the standard functional-based curriculum. Students may choose one of eight specializations or mix courses for a general M.B.A. degree. The delivery structure of the program gives students the ability to balance the rigors of work and home while pursuing their master's degree. Students can complete one or two courses each term, with each quarter lasting ten weeks.

The curriculum for the program includes foundation courses in economics, decision-making, behavioral sciences, and strategic environment. The core of the program presents a functional approach to the long- and short-run decisions that must be made to deliver goods and services to constituents.

Research Facilities

Along with classrooms and offices, the campus includes a bookstore, student lounge, and career services center. The South University Library provides in-library and remote access to electronic databases so that students may retrieve periodicals in paper or electronic form. Internet access is available on all computers throughout the campus. South University recommends that students in the M.B.A. degree program own a laptop computer for use with the program's multimedia classroom, business research, and electronic communication.

Financial Aid

A range of financial aid options is available to students who qualify. The Austin campus of South University offers access to federal and state programs, including grants, loans, and work-study programs. Eligible students may apply for veterans' educational benefits and are encouraged to investigate the availability of grants and scholarships through community resources. As a first step, students should complete the Free Application for Federal Student Aid (FAFSA). Students may apply electronically at http://www.fafsa.ed.gov or through the program.

Cost of Study

Tuition information for the Business Administration program may be obtained by contacting the Admissions Department at South University's Austin campus.

Living and Housing Costs

South University, Austin does not offer or operate student housing. Business Administration program students typically live in apartments in the Austin area. Students who commute from long distances can arrange to stay at nearby hotels that offer long-term rates. More information is available by contacting the Admissions Department.

Student Group

The Austin campus of South University has a diverse student body enrolled in both day and evening classes. Students are primarily commuters who live within 50 miles of the city.

Student Outcomes

The South University Career Services Department has been established to assist currently enrolled students in developing their career plans and reaching their employment goals. Career services include, but are not limited to, one-on-one career counseling, special career-related workshops and programs, coaching for resume and cover letter development, and resume referral to employers.

Location

The South University, Austin campus is conveniently located just off of West Parmer Lane near Round Rock just north of Austin. Students attending the Austin campus gain a well-rounded educational and cultural experience as a result of the free-spirited, eclectic culture of this musically focused community. The Austin-Round Rock area is also considered a major center for high-tech advancement while also emerging as a hub for pharmaceutical and biotechnology companies.

The University

South University is accredited by the Southern Association of Colleges and Schools Commission on Colleges to award associate, baccalaureate, masters, and doctorate degrees. Contact the Commission on Colleges at 1866 Southern Lane, Decatur, Georgia 30033-4097 or call 404-679-4500 for questions about the accreditation of South University.

Applying

Students are accepted into the Master of Business Administration degree program every academic quarter. Entrance into the program is gained through a formal application review and interview process. Acceptance is competitive and based on the admission committee's evaluation of the applicant's academic background and personal motivation. Application packets are available by calling the South University Admissions Department (877-659-5706, toll-free) or visiting the University's website (http://www.southuniversity.edu).

Correspondence and Information

Applications for admission to the South University Master of Business Administration program are available by contacting:

M.B.A. Program
Suzanne Melton, Senior Director of Admissions
South University
7700 West Parmer Lane, Building A, Suite A100
Austin, Texas 78729
Phone: 512-516-8800
877-659-5706 (toll-free)
Fax: 512-516-8680
E-mail: suausadm@southuniversity.edu
Website: http://www.southuniversity.edu/Austin

South University

See suprograms.info for program duration, tuition, fees, and other costs, median debt, federal salary data, alumni success, and other important information.
http://www.southuniversity.edu/programs-info/form/

South University in Austin, Texas, has a diverse student body enrolled in day, evening, weekend, and online classes.

THE FACULTY

One of the most outstanding aspects of South University's Business Administration program is the dedication of the faculty members and their ability to cultivate a supportive learning environment. Faculty members are committed to their roles as mentors, teachers, and co-learners. They are also dedicated to the training of students who can assume positions of leadership within the business administration field. A current list of program faculty members appears in the South University catalog, which is available on the South University website (http://www.southuniversity.edu).

SOUTH UNIVERSITY

Columbia Campus
Business Administration Program M.B.A., Accelerated M.B.A., and Healthcare Administration M.B.A. Programs

Program of Study

The Master of Business Administration (M.B.A.) degree program at South University is designed to provide students with a process-based curriculum versus the standard functional-based curriculum. Students may choose one of eight specializations or mix courses for a general M.B.A. degree. The delivery structure of the program gives students the ability to balance the rigors of work and home while pursuing their master's degree. Students can complete one or two courses each term, with each quarter lasting ten weeks. The curriculum for the program includes foundation courses in economics, decision-making, behavioral sciences, and strategic environment. The core of the program presents a functional approach to the long- and short-run decisions that must be made to deliver goods and services to constituents.

The Accelerated Master of Business Administration (A.M.B.A.) degree program at South University is designed for professionals working in a variety of organizations who seek to have a greater understanding of the concepts, organizational structures, and strategies driving today's complex organization environment. The Accelerated Master of Business Administration in Healthcare Administration degree program is designed to prepare students for a leadership role within the healthcare industry. Both are intensive programs presented from a management perspective and designed to be completed in one year. The delivery structure of the programs gives students the ability to balance the rigors of work and home while pursuing their master's degree.

Classes are held 24 Saturdays per year and are supplemented with Internet-mediated course work and synchronous meetings via conference calls and web-based meetings.

Research Facilities

Along with classrooms and offices, the campus includes a bookstore, student lounge, and career services center. The South University Library provides in-library and remote access to electronic databases so that students may retrieve periodicals in paper or electronic form. Internet access is available on all computers throughout the campus. South University recommends that students in the M.B.A. and A.M.B.A. degree programs own a laptop computer for use with the program's multimedia classroom, business research, and electronic communication.

Financial Aid

A range of financial aid options is available to students who qualify. The Columbia campus of South University offers access to federal and state programs, including grants, loans, and work-study programs. Eligible students may apply for veterans' educational benefits and are encouraged to investigate the availability of grants and scholarships through community resources. As a first step, students should complete the Free Application for Federal Student Aid (FAFSA). Students may apply electronically at http://www.fafsa.ed.gov or through the program.

Cost of Study

Tuition information for the M.B.A. and A.M.B.A. programs may be obtained by contacting the Admissions Department.

Living and Housing Costs

South University does not offer or operate student housing. M.B.A. and A.M.B.A. program students typically live in apartments in the Columbia area. Students who commute from long distances can arrange to stay at nearby hotels that offer long-term rates. More information is available by contacting the Admissions Department.

Student Group

The Columbia campus of South University has a diverse student body enrolled in both day and evening classes. Students are primarily commuters who live within 50 miles of the city.

Student Outcomes

The South University Career Services Department has been established to assist currently enrolled students in developing their career plans and reaching their employment goals. Career services include, but are not limited to, one-on-one career counseling, special career-related workshops and programs, coaching for resume and cover letter development, and resume referral to employers.

Location

South University's Columbia campus is located in the Carolina Research Park in northeast Columbia. The campus features spacious classrooms, multiple computer labs, a fully equipped medical lab, and a student lounge. The campus is located just minutes from downtown off I-77 at Farrow Road and Park Lane.

The campus surroundings are highlighted by a natural wooded landscape and vast green space featuring a tranquil campus courtyard. Convenient to malls, shopping, and the growing east side of Columbia, the new campus location provides easier access to students throughout the greater Columbia area

The University

South University is accredited by the Southern Association of Colleges and Schools Commission on Colleges to award associate, baccalaureate, masters, and doctorate degrees. Contact the Commission on Colleges at 1866 Southern Lane, Decatur, Georgia 30033-4097 or call 404-679-4500 for questions about the accreditation of South University.

Applying

Students are accepted into the Master of Business Administration degree program every academic quarter. Students are accepted into the Accelerated Master of Business Administration and Healthcare Administration degree programs on a monthly basis, with the exception of the month of

December. Entrance into the program is gained through a formal application review and interview process. Acceptance is competitive and based on the admission committee's evaluation of the applicant's academic background and personal motivation. Application packets for the M.B.A. degree program are available by contacting the South University Admissions Department (866-629-3031, toll-free) or visiting the University's website (http://www.southuniversity.edu). Application packets for the A.M.B.A. programs are available by calling the South University Admissions Department (800-952-4491, toll-free) or visiting the University's website (http://www.southuniversity.edu/amba).

Correspondence and Information

Applications for admission to the South University Master of Business Administration program are available by contacting:

M.B.A. Program
South University
9 Science Court
Columbia, South Carolina 29203
United States
Phone: 803-799-9082
866-629-3031 (toll-free)
Fax: 803-935-4382
E-mail: coladmis@southuniversity.edu
Website: http://www.southuniversity.edu

See suprograms.info for program duration; tuition, fees, and other costs; median debt; federal salary data; alumni success; and other important information. http://www.southuniversity.edu/programs-info/form/

Applications for admission to the South University Accelerated Master of Business Administration and Accelerated M.B.A. Healthcare Administration programs are available by contacting:

A.M.B.A./A.M.B.A. Healthcare Administration Programs
Brock Haas, Director, Off-Campus Programs
South University
709 Mall Boulevard
Savannah, Georgia 31406
United States
Phone: 800-952-4491 (toll-free)
Fax: 803-935-4382
E-mail: bhaas@southuniversity.edu
Website: http://www.southuniversity.edu/amba

See suprograms.info for program duration; tuition, fees, and other costs; median debt; federal salary data; alumni success; and other important information. http://www.southuniversity.edu/programs-info/form/

THE FACULTY

One of the most outstanding aspects of South University's M.B.A. and A.M.B.A. programs is the dedication of the faculty members and their ability to cultivate a supportive learning environment. Faculty members are committed to their roles as mentors, teachers, and co-learners. They are also dedicated to the training of students who can assume positions of leadership within their respective fields. A current list of program faculty members appears in the South University catalog, which is available on the South University website (http://www.southuniversity.edu).

South University's campus is on the growing east side of Columbia, just minutes from downtown.

SOUTH UNIVERSITY

Montgomery Campus Business Administration Program

Program of Study

The Master of Business Administration (M.B.A.) degree program at South University is designed to provide students with a process-based curriculum versus the standard functional-based curriculum. Students may choose one of eight specializations or mix courses for a general M.B.A. degree. The delivery structure of the program gives students the ability to balance the rigors of work and home while pursuing their master's degree. Students can complete one or two courses each term, with each quarter lasting ten weeks.

The curriculum for the program includes foundation courses in economics, decision-making, behavioral sciences, and strategic environment. The core of the program presents a functional approach to the long- and short-run decisions that must be made to deliver goods and services to constituents.

Research Facilities

Along with classrooms and offices, the campus includes a bookstore, student lounge, and career services center. The South University Library provides in-library and remote access to electronic databases so that students may retrieve periodicals in paper or electronic form. Internet access is available on all computers throughout the campus. South University recommends that students in the M.B.A. degree program own a laptop computer for use with the program's multimedia classroom, business research, and electronic communication.

Financial Aid

A range of financial aid options is available to students who qualify. The Montgomery campus of South University offers access to federal and state programs, including grants, loans, and work-study programs. Eligible students may apply for veterans' educational benefits and are encouraged to investigate the availability of grants and scholarships through community resources. As a first step, students should complete the Free Application for Federal Student Aid (FAFSA). Students may apply electronically at http://www.fafsa.ed.gov or through the program.

Cost of Study

Tuition information for the business administration program may be obtained by contacting the Admissions Department at South University's Montgomery campus.

Living and Housing Costs

South University offers school-sponsored student housing at its Montgomery, Alabama, campus in conjunction with a local apartment complex. Students who commute from long distances can arrange to stay at nearby hotels that offer long-term rates. More information may be obtained by contacting the University toll free at 866-629-2962.

Student Group

The Montgomery campus of South University has a diverse student body enrolled in both day and evening classes. Students are primarily commuters who live within 50 miles of the city.

Student Outcomes

The South University Career Services Department has been established to assist currently enrolled students in developing their career plans and reaching their employment goals. Career services include, but are not limited to, one-on-one career counseling, special career-related workshops and programs, coaching for resume and cover letter development, and resume referral to employers.

Location

South University, Montgomery is located on the rapidly growing east side of Alabama's capital city. As the state capital, Montgomery is a hub of government, banking, and law as well as a state center for culture and entertainment. Montgomery is situated in the middle of the southeastern U.S. and is less than a 3-hour drive from Atlanta, Georgia, and the Gulf of Mexico.

The University

South University is accredited by the Southern Association of Colleges and Schools Commission on Colleges to award associate, baccalaureate, masters, and doctorate degrees. Contact the Commission on Colleges at 1866 Southern Lane, Decatur, Georgia 30033-4097 or call 404-679-4500 for questions about the accreditation of South University.

Applying

Students are accepted into the Master of Business Administration degree program every academic quarter. Entrance into the program is gained through a formal application review and interview process. Acceptance is competitive and based on the admission committee's evaluation of the applicant's academic background and personal motivation. Application packets are available by calling the South University Admissions Department (866-629-2962, toll-free) or visiting the University's website (http://www.southuniversity.edu).

Correspondence and Information

Applications for admission to the South University Master of Business Administration program are available by contacting:

M.B.A. Program
South University
5355 Vaughn Road
Montgomery, Alabama 36116
United States
Phone: 334-395-8800
866-629-2962 (toll-free)
Fax: 334-395-8859
E-mail: mtgadmis@southuniversity.edu
Website: http://www.southuniversity.edu/Montgomery

See suprograms.info for program duration; tuition, fees, and other costs; median debt; federal salary data; alumni success; and other important information. http://www.southuniversity.edu/programs-info/form/

THE FACULTY

One of the most outstanding aspects of South University's Business Administration program is the dedication of the faculty members and their ability to cultivate a supportive learning environment. Faculty members are committed to their roles as mentors, teachers, and co-learners. They are also dedicated to the training of students who can assume positions of leadership within the business administration field. A current list of program faculty members appears in the South University catalog, which is available on the South University website (http://www.southuniversity.edu).

South University's Montgomery campus has a diverse student body enrolled in both day and evening classes.

SOUTH UNIVERSITY

Novi Campus
Business Administration Program

Program of Study

The Master of Business Administration (M.B.A.) degree program at South University is designed to provide students with a process-based curriculum versus the standard functional-based curriculum. Students may choose one of eight specializations or mix courses for a general M.B.A. degree. The delivery structure of the program gives students the ability to balance the rigors of work and home while pursuing their master's degree. Students can complete one or two courses each term, with each quarter lasting ten weeks.

The curriculum for the program includes foundation courses in economics, decision-making, behavioral sciences, and strategic environment. The core of the program presents a functional approach to the long- and short-run decisions that must be made to deliver goods and services to constituents.

Research Facilities

Along with classrooms and offices, the campus includes a bookstore, student lounge, and career services center. The South University Library provides in-library and remote access to electronic databases so that students may retrieve periodicals in paper or electronic form. Internet access is available on all computers throughout the campus. South University recommends that students in the M.B.A. degree program own a laptop computer for use with the program's multimedia classroom, business research, and electronic communication.

Financial Aid

A range of financial aid options is available to students who qualify. The Novi campus of South University offers access to federal and state programs, including grants, loans, and work-study programs. Eligible students may apply for veterans' educational benefits and are encouraged to investigate the availability of grants and scholarships through community resources. As a first step, students should complete the Free Application for Federal Student Aid (FAFSA). Students may apply electronically at http://www.fafsa.ed.gov or through the program.

Cost of Study

Tuition information for the Business Administration program may be obtained by contacting the Admissions Department at South University's Novi campus.

Living and Housing Costs

South University, Novi does not offer or operate student housing. Business Administration program students typically live in apartments in the Novi area. Students who commute from long distances can arrange to stay at nearby hotels that offer long-term rates. More information is available by contacting the Admissions Department.

Student Group

The Novi campus of South University has a diverse student body enrolled in both day and evening classes. Students are primarily commuters who live within 50 miles of the city.

Student Outcomes

The South University Career Services Department has been established to assist currently enrolled students in developing their career plans and reaching their employment goals. Career services include, but are not limited to, one-on-one career counseling, special career-related workshops and programs, coaching for resume and cover letter development, and resume referral to employers.

Location

South University's Novi campus occupies more than 30,000 square feet of a new building located at 41555 Twelve Mile Road, in Novi, Michigan. The campus features spacious classrooms, a computer lab, nursing lab, health science lab, and physical therapy lab. The campus is located northwest of Detroit near Ann Arbor, Michigan.

The University

South University is accredited by the Southern Association of Colleges and Schools Commission on Colleges to award associate, baccalaureate, masters, and doctorate degrees. Contact the Commission on Colleges at 1866 Southern Lane, Decatur, Georgia 30033-4097 or call 404-679-4500 for questions about the accreditation of South University.

South University, Novi is licensed under the laws of the Michigan Department of Energy, Labor, and Economic Growth to award baccalaureate and master's degrees.

Applying

Students are accepted into the Master of Business Administration degree program every academic quarter. Entrance into the program is gained through a formal application review and interview process. Acceptance is competitive and based on the admission committee's evaluation of the applicant's academic background and personal motivation. Application packets are available by calling the South University Admissions Department (877-693-2085, toll-free) or visiting the University's website (http://www.southuniversity.edu).

South University

Correspondence and Information

Applications for admission to the South University Master of Business Administration program are available by contacting:

M.B.A. Program
South University
41555 Twelve Mile Road
Novi, Michigan 48377
United States
Phone: 248-675-0200
877-693-2085 (toll-free)
Fax: 248-675-0190
E-mail: sunovadmis@southuniversity.edu
Website: http://www.southuniversity.edu/Novi

See suprograms.info for program duration; tuition, fees, and other costs; median debt; federal salary data; alumni success; and other important information. http://www.southuniversity.edu/programs-info/form/

THE FACULTY

One of the most outstanding aspects of South University's Business Administration program is the dedication of the faculty members and their ability to cultivate a supportive learning environment. Faculty members are committed to their roles as mentors, teachers, and co-learners. They are also dedicated to the training of students who can assume positions of leadership within their respective fields. A current list of program faculty members appears in the South University catalog, which is available on the South University website (http://www.southuniversity.edu).

South University's Novi campus is located northwest of Detroit near Ann Arbor, Michigan.

SOUTH UNIVERSITY

Richmond Campus
Business Administration Program

Program of Study

The Master of Business Administration (M.B.A.) degree program at South University is designed to provide students with a process-based curriculum versus the standard functional-based curriculum. Students may choose one of eight specializations or mix courses for a general M.B.A. degree. The delivery structure of the program gives students the ability to balance the rigors of work and home while pursuing their master's degree. Students can complete one or two courses each term, with each quarter lasting ten weeks.

The curriculum for the program includes foundation courses in economics, decision-making, behavioral sciences, and strategic environment. The core of the program presents a functional approach to the long- and short-run decisions that must be made to deliver goods and services to constituents.

Research Facilities

Along with classrooms and offices, the campus includes a bookstore, student lounge, and career services center. The South University Library provides in-library and remote access to electronic databases so that students may retrieve periodicals in paper or electronic form. Internet access is available on all computers throughout the campus. South University recommends that students in the M.B.A. degree program own a laptop computer for use with the program's multimedia classroom, business research, and electronic communication.

Financial Aid

A range of financial aid options is available to students who qualify. The Richmond campus of South University offers access to federal and state programs, including grants, loans, and work-study programs. Eligible students may apply for veterans' educational benefits and are encouraged to investigate the availability of grants and scholarships through community resources. As a first step, students should complete the Free Application for Federal Student Aid (FAFSA). Students may apply electronically at http://www.fafsa.ed.gov or through the program.

Cost of Study

Tuition information for the Business Administration program may be obtained by contacting the Admissions Department at South University's Richmond campus.

Living and Housing Costs

South University, Richmond does not offer or operate student housing. Business Administration program students typically live in apartments in the Richmond area. Students who commute from long distances can arrange to stay at nearby hotels that offer long-term rates. More information is available by contacting the Admissions Department.

Student Group

The Richmond campus of South University has a diverse student body enrolled in both day and evening classes. Students are primarily commuters who live within 50 miles of the city.

Student Outcomes

The South University Career Services Department has been established to assist currently enrolled students in developing their career plans and reaching their employment goals. Career services include, but are not limited to, one-on-one career counseling, special career-related workshops and programs, coaching for resume and cover letter development, and resume referral to employers.

Location

South University, Richmond is located in the West Broad Village on a 115-acre tract of land, which is mixed use containing retail, office, apartments, and condominiums, in the Short Pump Area northwest of Richmond. It is one of South University's newest campus locations and occupies approximately 30,000 square feet of classroom, computer lab, library, and office space in Glen Allen, Virginia.

The University

South University is accredited by the Southern Association of Colleges and Schools Commission on Colleges to award associate, baccalaureate, masters, and doctorate degrees. Contact the Commission on Colleges at 1866 Southern Lane, Decatur, Georgia 30033-4097 or call 404-679-4500 for questions about the accreditation of South University.

South University's Richmond campus is certified by The State Council for Higher Education in Virginia (James Monroe Building, 101 North Fourteenth Street, Richmond, Virginia 23219; 804-225-2600) to operate in Virginia.

Applying

Students are accepted into the Master of Business Administration degree program every academic quarter. Entrance into the program is gained through a formal application review and interview process. Acceptance is competitive and based on the admission committee's evaluation of the applicant's academic background and personal motivation. Application packets are available by calling the South University Admissions Department (888-422-6790, toll-free) or visiting the University's website (http://www.southuniversity.edu).

South University

Correspondence and Information

Applications for admission to the South University Master of Business Administration program are available by contacting:

M.B.A. Program
South University
2151 Old Brick Road
Glen Allen, Virginia 23060
United States
Phone: 804-727-6800
888-422-6790 (toll-free)
Fax: 804-727-6790
E-mail: suriadm@southuniversity.edu
Website: http://www.southuniversity.edu/richmond

See suprograms.info for program duration, tuition, fees, and other costs, median debt, federal salary data, alumni success, and other important information. http://www.southuniversity.edu/programs-info/form/

THE FACULTY

One of the most outstanding aspects of South University's Business Administration program is the dedication of the faculty members and their ability to cultivate a supportive learning environment. Faculty members are committed to their roles as mentors, teachers, and co-learners. They are also dedicated to the training of students who can assume positions of leadership within the business administration field. A current list of program faculty members appears in the South University catalog, which is available on the South University website (http://www.southuniversity.edu).

South University Richmond is located in the West Broad Development in Glen Allen, Virginia, minutes from downtown Richmond and the area's cultural activities.

SOUTH UNIVERSITY

Savannah Campus

Accelerated M.B.A. and Healthcare Administration M.B.A. Programs

Program of Study

The Accelerated Master of Business Administration (A.M.B.A.) degree program at South University is designed for professionals working in a variety of organizations who seek to have a greater understanding of the concepts, organizational structures, and strategies driving today's complex organization environment. The Accelerated Master of Business Administration in Healthcare Administration degree program is designed to prepare students for a leadership role within the healthcare industry. Both are intensive programs presented from a management perspective and designed to be completed in one year. The delivery structure of the programs gives students the ability to balance the rigors of work and home while pursuing their master's degree.

Classes are held 24 Saturdays per year and are supplemented with Internet-mediated course work and synchronous meetings via conference calls and web-based meetings.

Research Facilities

Along with classrooms and offices, the campus includes a bookstore, student lounge, and career services center. The South University Library provides in-library and remote access to electronic databases so that students may retrieve periodicals in paper or electronic form. Internet access is available on all computers throughout the campus. South University recommends that students in the A.M.B.A. degree programs own a laptop computer for use with the program's multimedia classroom, business research, and electronic communication.

Financial Aid

A range of financial aid options is available to students who qualify. The Savannah campus of South University offers access to federal and state programs, including grants, loans, and work-study programs. Eligible students may apply for veterans' educational benefits and are encouraged to investigate the availability of grants and scholarships through community resources. As a first step, students should complete the Free Application for Federal Student Aid (FAFSA). Students may apply electronically at http://www.fafsa.ed.gov or through the program.

Cost of Study

Tuition information for the Accelerated Master of Business Administration and Healthcare Administration M.B.A. programs may be obtained by contacting the Admissions Department.

Living and Housing Costs

South University offers school-sponsored student housing at its Savannah, Georgia, campus in conjunction with a local apartment complex. Students who commute from long distances can arrange to stay at nearby hotels that offer long-term rates. More information may be obtained by contacting the Director of Student Housing at 912-201-8000.

Student Group

The Savannah campus of South University has a diverse student body enrolled in both day and evening classes. Students are primarily commuters who live within 50 miles of the city.

Student Outcomes

The South University Career Services Department has been established to assist currently enrolled students in developing their career plans and reaching their employment goals. Career services include, but are not limited to, one-on-one career counseling, special career-related workshops and programs, coaching for resume and cover letter development, and resume referral to employers.

Location

Located on the south side of the historic city of Savannah, the campus is situated on 9 acres of land. It is convenient to the city's bustling midtown section and a full range of educational and cultural activities. The Atlantic Ocean and recreational amenities of Tybee Island, including beaches and numerous outdoor activities, are just a short drive away. In addition, the campus is located just a short drive from Hilton Head Island and Charleston, South Carolina.

The University

South University is accredited by the Southern Association of Colleges and Schools Commission on Colleges to award associate, baccalaureate, masters, and doctorate degrees. Contact the Commission on Colleges at 1866 Southern Lane, Decatur, Georgia 30033-4097 or call 404-679-4500 for questions about the accreditation of South University.

Applying

Students are accepted into the Accelerated Master of Business Administration and Healthcare Administration degree programs on a monthly basis, with the exception of the month of December. Entrance into the program is gained through a formal application review and interview process. Acceptance is competitive and based on the admission committee's evaluation of the applicant's academic background and personal motivation. Application packets are available by calling the South University Admissions Department (800-952-4491, toll-free) or visiting the University's website (http://www.southuniversity.edu/amba).

Correspondence and Information

Applications for admission to the South University Accelerated Master of Business Administration and Accelerated Healthcare Administration M.B.A. programs are available by contacting:

Accelerated M.B.A./Accelerated Healthcare M.B.A. Programs
Brock Haas, Director, Off-Campus Programs
South University
709 Mall Boulevard
Savannah, Georgia 31406
United States
Phone: 800-952-4491(toll-free)
Fax: 803-935-4382
E-mail: bhaas@southuniversity.edu
Website: http://www.southuniversity.edu/Savannah

See suprograms.info for program duration; tuition, fees, and other costs; median debt; federal salary data; alumni success; and other important information. http://www.southuniversity.edu/programs-info/form/

THE FACULTY

One of the most outstanding aspects of South University's Accelerated Business Administration and Healthcare Administration programs is the dedication of the faculty members and their ability to cultivate a supportive learning environment. Faculty members are committed to their roles as mentors, teachers, and co-learners. They are also dedicated to the training of students who can assume positions of leadership within their respective fields. A current list of program faculty members appears in the South University catalog, which is available on the South University website (http://www.southuniversity.edu).

South University's Savannah campus is located on the south side of the historic city of Savannah, convenient to the city's bustling midtown section and a full range of educational and cultural activities.

SOUTH UNIVERSITY

Tampa Campus
Business Administration Program

Program of Study

The Master of Business Administration (M.B.A.) degree program at South University is designed to provide students with a process-based curriculum versus the standard functional-based curriculum. Students may choose one of eight specializations or mix courses for a general M.B.A. degree. The delivery structure of the program gives students the ability to balance the rigors of work and home while pursuing their master's degree. Students can complete one or two courses each term, with each quarter lasting ten weeks.

The curriculum for the program includes foundation courses in economics, decision-making, behavioral sciences, and strategic environment. The core of the program presents a functional approach to the long- and short-run decisions that must be made to deliver goods and services to constituents.

Research Facilities

Along with classrooms and offices, the campus includes a bookstore, student lounge, and career services center. The South University Library provides in-library and remote access to electronic databases so that students may retrieve periodicals in paper or electronic form. Internet access is available on all computers throughout the campus. South University recommends that students in the M.B.A. degree program own a laptop computer for use with the program's multimedia classroom, business research, and electronic communication.

Financial Aid

A range of financial aid options is available to students who qualify. The Tampa campus of South University offers access to federal and state programs, including grants, loans, and work-study programs. Eligible students may apply for veterans' educational benefits and are encouraged to investigate the availability of grants and scholarships through community resources. As a first step, students should complete the Free Application for Federal Student Aid (FAFSA). Students may apply electronically at http://www.fafsa.ed.gov or through the program.

Cost of Study

Tuition information for the Business Administration program may be obtained by contacting the Admissions Department at South University's Tampa campus.

Living and Housing Costs

South University, Tampa does not offer or operate student housing. Business Administration program students typically live in apartments in the Tampa area. Students who commute from long distances can arrange to stay at nearby hotels that offer long-term rates. More information is available by contacting the Admissions Department.

Student Group

The Tampa campus of South University has a diverse student body enrolled in both day and evening classes. Students are primarily commuters who live within 50 miles of the city.

Student Outcomes

The South University Career Services Department has been established to assist currently enrolled students in developing their career plans and reaching their employment goals. Career services include, but are not limited to, one-on-one career counseling, special career-related workshops and programs, coaching for resume and cover letter development, and resume referral to employers.

Location

Located on North Himes Avenue, South University's Tampa campus affords students the opportunity to enjoy all the culture and excitement a large city has to offer. Major-league sporting events, major concerts, theater, world-renowned restaurants, and a cosmopolitan social scene are all within easy reach.

The University

South University is accredited by the Southern Association of Colleges and Schools Commission on Colleges to award associate, baccalaureate, masters, and doctorate degrees. Contact the Commission on Colleges at 1866 Southern Lane, Decatur, Georgia 30033-4097 or call 404-679-4500 for questions about the accreditation of South University.

South University, Tampa is licensed by the Florida commission for Independent Education, License No. 2987.

Applying

Students are accepted into the Master of Business Administration degree program every academic quarter. Entrance into the program is gained through a formal application review and interview process. Acceptance is competitive and based on the admission committee's evaluation of the applicant's academic background and personal motivation. Application packets are available by calling the South University Admissions Department (800-846-1472, toll-free) or visiting the University's website (http://www.southuniversity.edu).

South University

Correspondence and Information

Applications for admission to the South University Master of Business Administration program are available by contacting:

M.B.A. Program
Michele D'Alessio, Director of Admissions
South University
4401 North Himes Avenue, Suite 175
Tampa, Florida 33614-7095
United States
Phone: 813-393-3800
800-846-1472 (toll-free)
Fax: 813-393-3814
E-mail: sutaadm@southuniversity.edu
Website: http://www.southuniversity.edu/tampa

See suprograms.info for program duration, tuition, fees, and other costs, median debt, federal salary data, alumni success, and other important information. http://www.southuniversity.edu/programs-info/form/

THE FACULTY

One of the most outstanding aspects of South University's Business Administration program is the dedication of the faculty members and their ability to cultivate a supportive learning environment. Faculty members are committed to their roles as mentors, teachers, and co-learners. They are also dedicated to the training of students who can assume positions of leadership within the business administration field. A current list of program faculty members appears in the South University catalog, which is available on the South University website (http://www.southuniversity.edu).

South University's Tampa campus provides ample classroom and student service areas and features several smart classrooms with audiovisual technology.

SOUTH UNIVERSITY

Virginia Beach Campus
Business Administration Program

Program of Study

The Master of Business Administration (M.B.A.) degree program at South University is designed to provide students with a process-based curriculum versus the standard functional-based curriculum. Students may choose one of eight specializations or mix courses for a general M.B.A. degree. The delivery structure of the program gives students the ability to balance the rigors of work and home while pursuing their master's degree. Students can complete one or two courses each term, with each quarter lasting ten weeks.

The curriculum for the program includes foundation courses in economics, decision-making, behavioral sciences, and strategic environment. The core of the program presents a functional approach to the long- and short-run decisions that must be made to deliver goods and services to constituents.

Research Facilities

Along with classrooms and offices, the campus includes a bookstore, student lounge, and career services center. The South University Library provides in-library and remote access to electronic databases so that students may retrieve periodicals in paper or electronic form. Internet access is available on all computers throughout the campus. South University recommends that students in the M.B.A. degree program own a laptop computer for use with the program's multimedia classroom, business research, and electronic communication.

Financial Aid

A range of financial aid options is available to students who qualify. The Virginia Beach campus of South University offers access to federal and state programs, including grants, loans, and work-study programs. Eligible students may apply for veterans' educational benefits and are encouraged to investigate the availability of grants and scholarships through community resources. As a first step, students should complete the Free Application for Federal Student Aid (FAFSA). Students may apply electronically at http://www.fafsa.ed.gov or through the program.

Cost of Study

Tuition information for the business administration program may be obtained by contacting the Admissions Department at South University's Virginia Beach campus.

Living and Housing Costs

South University does not offer or operate student housing. Business Administration program students typically live in apartments in the Virginia Beach area. Students who commute from long distances can arrange to stay at nearby hotels that offer long-term rates. More information is available by contacting the Admissions Department.

Student Group

The Virginia Beach campus of South University has a diverse student body enrolled in both day and evening classes. Students are primarily commuters who live within 50 miles of the city.

Student Outcomes

The South University Career Services Department has been established to assist currently enrolled students in developing their career plans and reaching their employment goals. Career services include, but are not limited to, one-on-one career counseling, special career-related workshops and programs, coaching for resume and cover letter development, and resume referral to employers.

Location

South University's Virginia Beach campus is located in 32,600 square feet of space in the attractive and convenient Convergence Center in Virginia Beach's popular Central Business District. The Virginia Beach campus features a distance-learning center, a library, bookstore, on-site security, student and faculty lounges, as well as health-science labs.

The University

South University is accredited by the Southern Association of Colleges and Schools Commission on Colleges to award associate, baccalaureate, masters, and doctorate degrees. Contact the Commission on Colleges at 1866 Southern Lane, Decatur, Georgia 30033-4097 or call 404-679-4500 for questions about the accreditation of South University.

South University's Virginia Beach campus is certified by The State Council for Higher Education in Virginia (James Monroe Building, 101 North Fourteenth Street, Richmond, Virginia 23219; 804-225-2600) to operate in Virginia.

Applying

Students are accepted into the Master of Business Administration degree program every academic quarter. Entrance into the program is gained through a formal application review and interview process. Acceptance is competitive and based on the admission committee's evaluation of the applicant's academic background and personal motivation. Application packets are available by calling the South University Admissions Department (877-206-1845, toll-free) or visiting the University's website (http://www.southuniversity.edu).

South University

Correspondence and Information

Applications for admission to the South University Master of Business Administration program are available by contacting:

M.B.A. Program
South University
301 Bendix Road, Suite 100
Virginia Beach, Virginia 23452
United States
Phone: 757-493-6900
877-206-1845 (toll-free)
Fax: 757-493-6990
E-mail: suvbabm@southuniversity.edu
Website: http://www.southuniversity.edu/virginia-beach

See suprograms.info for program duration; tuition, fees, and other costs; median debt; federal salary data; alumni success; and other important information. http://www.southuniversity.edu/programs-info/form/

THE FACULTY

One of the most outstanding aspects of South University's Business Administration program is the dedication of the faculty members and their ability to cultivate a supportive learning environment. Faculty members are committed to their roles as mentors, teachers, and co-learners. They are also dedicated to the training of students who can assume positions of leadership within the business administration field. A current list of program faculty members appears in the South University catalog, which is available on the South University website (http://www.southuniversity.edu).

South University's Virginia Beach campus is located in the popular Central Business District.

SOUTH UNIVERSITY

West Palm Beach Campus
Business Administration Program
M.B.A., Accelerated M.B.A., and Healthcare Administration M.B.A. Programs

Program of Study

The Master of Business Administration (M.B.A.) degree program at South University is designed to provide students with a process-based curriculum versus the standard functional-based curriculum. Students may choose one of eight specializations or mix courses for a general M.B.A. degree. The delivery structure of the program gives students the ability to balance the rigors of work and home while pursuing their master's degree. Students can complete one or two courses each term, with each quarter lasting ten weeks. The curriculum for the program includes foundation courses in economics, decision-making, behavioral sciences, and strategic environment. The core of the program presents a functional approach to the long- and short-run decisions that must be made to deliver goods and services to constituents.

The Accelerated Master of Business Administration (A.M.B.A.) degree program at South University is designed for professionals working in a variety of organizations who seek to have a greater understanding of the concepts, organizational structures, and strategies driving today's complex organization environment. The Accelerated Master of Business Administration in Healthcare Administration degree program is designed to prepare students for a leadership role within the healthcare industry. Both are intensive programs presented from a management perspective and designed to be completed in one year. The delivery structure of the program gives students the ability to balance the rigors of work and home while pursuing their master's degree.

Classes are held 24 Saturdays per year and are supplemented with Internet-mediated course work and synchronous meetings via conference calls and Web-based meetings.

Research Facilities

Along with classrooms and offices, the campus includes a bookstore, student lounge, and career services center. The South University Library provides in-library and remote access to electronic databases so that students may retrieve periodicals in paper or electronic form. Internet access is available on all computers throughout the campus. South University recommends that students in the M.B.A. and A.M.B.A. degree programs own a laptop computer for use with the program's multimedia classroom, business research, and electronic communication.

Financial Aid

A range of financial aid options is available to students who qualify. The West Palm Beach campus of South University offers access to federal and state programs, including grants, loans, and work-study programs. Eligible students may apply for veterans' educational benefits and are encouraged to investigate the availability of grants and scholarships through community resources. As a first step, students should complete the Free Application for Federal Student Aid (FAFSA). Students may apply electronically at http://www.fafsa.ed.gov or through the program.

Cost of Study

Tuition information for the M.B.A. and A.M.B.A. programs may be obtained by contacting the Admissions Department.

Living and Housing Costs

South University does not offer or operate student housing. M.B.A. and A.M.B.A. program students typically live in apartments in the West Palm Beach area. Students who commute from long distances can arrange to stay at nearby hotels that offer long-term rates. More information is available by contacting the Admissions Department.

Student Group

The West Palm Beach campus of South University has a diverse student body enrolled in both day and evening classes. Students are primarily commuters who live within 50 miles of the city.

Student Outcomes

The South University Career Services Department has been established to assist currently enrolled students in developing their career plans and reaching their employment goals. Career services include, but are not limited to, one-on-one career counseling, special career-related workshops and programs, coaching for resume and cover letter development, and resume referral to employers.

Location

South University, West Palm Beach is centrally located near the heart of Palm Beach County, close to the South Florida beaches. It has been in its current location since 2010 when it moved into its brand-new facility specifically built to support the growing population of the campus. The 32,000-square-foot, three-building campus is in the hub of cultural, economic, and government activity in West Palm Beach

The University

South University is accredited by the Southern Association of Colleges and Schools Commission on Colleges to award associate, baccalaureate, masters, and doctorate degrees. Contact the Commission on Colleges at 1866 Southern Lane, Decatur, Georgia 30033-4097 or call 404-679-4500 for questions about the accreditation of South University.

Licensed by the Florida Commission for Independent Education, License No. 2987.

Applying

Students are accepted into the Master of Business Administration degree program every academic quarter. Students are accepted into the Accelerated Master of Business Administration and Healthcare Administration degree programs on a monthly basis, with the exception of the month of December. Entrance into the program is gained through a formal application review and interview process. Acceptance is competitive and based on the admission committee's evaluation of the applicant's academic background and personal motivation. Application packets for the M.B.A. degree program are available by calling the South University Admissions Department (866-629-2902, toll-free) or visiting the University's website (http://www.southuniversity.edu). Application packets for the A.M.B.A. programs are available by calling the South University Admissions Department (800-952-4491, toll-free) or visiting the University's website (http://www.southuniversity.edu/amba).

Correspondence and Information

Applications for admission to the South University Master of Business Administration program are available by contacting:

M.B.A. Program
South University
University Centre
9801 Belvedere Road
Royal Palm Beach, Florida 33411
United States
Phone: 561-273-6500
866-629-2902 (toll-free)
Fax: 561-273-6420
E-mail: suwpbadmis@edmc.edu
Website: http://www.southuniversity.edu

See suprograms.info for program duration; tuition, fees, and other costs; median debt; federal salary data; alumni success; and other important information. http://www.southuniversity.edu/programs-info/form/

Applications for admission to the South University Accelerated Master of Business Administration and Accelerated Healthcare Administration M.B.A. programs are available by contacting:

Accelerated M.B.A./ Accelerated Healthcare M.B.A. Programs
Brock Haas, Director, Off-Campus Programs
South University
709 Mall Boulevard
Savannah, Georgia 31406
United States
Phone: 800-952-4491 (toll-free)
Fax: 803-935-4382
E-mail: bhaas@southuniversity.edu
Website: http://www.southuniversity.edu/amba

See suprograms.info for program duration; tuition, fees, and other costs; median debt; federal salary data; alumni success; and other important information. http://www.southuniversity.edu/programs-info/form/

THE FACULTY

One of the most outstanding aspects of South University's M.B.A. and A.M.B.A. programs is the dedication of the faculty members and their ability to cultivate a supportive learning environment. Faculty members are committed to their roles as mentors, teachers, and co-learners. They are also dedicated to the training of students who can assume positions of leadership within their respective fields. A current list of program faculty members appears in the South University catalog, which is available on the South University website (http://www.southuniversity.edu).

South University's West Palm Beach facility features a hurricane-resistant infrastructure, with several large labs, lecture halls, a library, and seminar rooms.

UNIVERSITY OF CALIFORNIA, LOS ANGELES

UCLAAnderson
School of Management

UCLA Anderson School of Management
Master of Business Administration Program

Programs of Study

UCLA Anderson School of Management recently implemented fundamental changes to its curriculum to better prepare M.B.A. students to succeed in the marketplace. This new curriculum is focused on four key components designed to help students quickly build the knowledge and skills necessary to realize their career goals.

Through Leadership Foundations and the Management Communications Program, UCLA Anderson works with students to build crucial leadership and communication skills. The School offers a customized core that aligns each student's academic experience with their career aspirations and helps students build depth of expertise in their chosen area through the pursuit of tracks and specializations. Students can choose to pursue a marketing, finance, consulting, or custom track. If they wish to dive even deeper, specializations are available in areas such as real estate, health-care management, entertainment, and entrepreneurship.

The capstone Applied Management Research Program, a twenty-week experiential learning process in which students work as a team, allows students to apply the knowledge they've gained in the classroom to solving the challenges of a real-world client. This sharpens both their teamwork and their written and verbal communication skills via the final report and presentation to the client.

Research Facilities

UCLA Anderson's Rosenfeld Library is ranked among the top U.S. business school libraries. Rosenfeld Library provides access to over 100 specialized databases, as well as to an expanding array of electronic journals and texts supporting all areas of business and management, such as accounting, business economics, strategy and policy, finance, human resources, marketing, and organizational behavior. It also delivers robust reference, consultation, course outreach, course reserves, facilities management, document delivery, and information fluency programs. The library's print collections support the UCLA Anderson curriculum in all areas of business and management and comprise 180,600 volumes, 2,900 currently received serial subscriptions, 633,000 microforms, and over 269,000 historical corporate reports. While the Rosenfeld Library's information sources are of particular value to the M.B.A. curriculum; Rosenfeld Library is one of twelve UCLA campus libraries whose vast resources are also available to the M.B.A. student. In addition, UCLA students, including Anderson M.B.A.'s, are part of the University of California (UC) Library system and have access to those information resources through a variety of programs ranging from licensed databases to interlibrary loan to borrowing print materials. The Rosenfeld Library also participates in an international interlibrary loan program that allows it to borrow materials M.B.A. students may need from libraries beyond the UC system.

Research programs and study centers associated with the School and its faculty include the Harold and Pauline Price Center for Entrepreneurial Studies, the Center for Global Management, the Richard S. Ziman Center for Real Estate, the UCLA Anderson Forecast, the Laurence D. and Lori W. Fink Center for Finance & Investments, and the Center for Management of Enterprise in Media, Entertainment, & Sports.

Financial Aid

Merit fellowships, donor fellowships, and need-based grants are available. Private education loans are available for international students who do not have a U.S. cosigner. A limited number of research and teaching assistantship positions are also available.

Cost of Study

For 2012–13, tuition and fees per academic year total $49,564 for California residents and $56,063 for nonresidents. These costs are subject to change.

Living and Housing Costs

Room and board for the 2012–13 academic year are estimated to be $14,040. Books and supplies will be $4900 (including a $2500 laptop computer allowance). These costs are for students living off campus in shared housing. Additional costs may include support of dependents and medical expenses. Married students should budget additional costs from personal resources as financial aid only covers the student's costs.

Student Group

UCLA Anderson has a vibrant student body whose extraordinary intellectual, cultural, social, and athletic energies spill out of the classroom into a plethora of nonacademic activities. The average age of the most recent entering class for the Full-Time M.B.A. Program (class of 2013) is 28 and the average number of years postgraduate work experience is five years. Of this class, 33 percent are female and 33 percent are international.

Location

Los Angeles is among the world's most vibrant and exciting cities. In addition to being the entertainment capital of the world, businesses in Los Angeles create four times the gross domestic product and diversity of the Silicon Valley. The city is home to Fortune 500 companies and major industries, ranging from financial services and health care to manufacturing and aerospace. The city hosts even more small businesses, which are a significant source of U.S. economic growth. From its location in Southern California, Los Angeles serves as a gateway to both Asia and Latin America.

UCLA Anderson students enjoy access to extensive cultural and recreational opportunities with museums, sporting events, theaters, and countless other activities offered both on campus and throughout the city. Because the location is such a cultural crossroads, there are always opportunities to engage with people from various backgrounds and points of view. Students benefit from this interaction both professionally and personally, learning as they share cultural traditions with each other.

The School

UCLA Anderson's management education complex is a testament to the School's vision for superior management education. Continuing the School's reputation as a national leader in the use of technology in M.B.A. instruction, the eleven specially designed case study rooms have power, wireless, and wired network data ports at each seat, as well as a custom teaching lectern with state-of-the-art audiovisual and instructional technologies that support, enhance, and extend the School's active learning environment.

The Rosenfeld Library houses three computer labs for M.B.A. students, one of which includes twenty-three desktop computers and two networked printers. The other two collaborative labs also provide wired and wireless network access and printing and can seat up to fifteen teams of 5 students. The library also houses a professional audiovisual presentation facility, known as the Boardroom, as well as twenty-four additional collaborative pods for teamwork.

Applying

Applicants may apply for fall 2013 admission starting August 1, 2012. More information and updates are available online at www.mba.anderson.ucla.edu.

Correspondence and Information

Rob Weiler
Associate Dean, Full-Time M.B.A. Program
UCLA Anderson School of Management
110 Westwood Plaza, Suite C201
Los Angeles, California 90095-1481
United States
Phone: 310-825-3325
E-mail: mba.admissions@anderson.ucla.edu
Web site: http://www.anderson.ucla.edu/programs/mba/

THE FACULTY

Judy D. Olian, Dean and John E. Anderson Chair in Management, UCLA Anderson School of Management; Ph.D. (industrial relations), Wisconsin–Madison.

Accounting

David Aboody, Professor and Area Chair; Ph.D., Berkeley. Shlomo Benartzi, Professor and Co-Chair of the Behavioral Decision-Making Group; Ph.D., Cornell. Maria Boss, Lecturer; J.D., California, Hastings Law. Gonzalo Freixes, Lecturer and Associate Dean; J.D., Loyola Law School. Jane Guerin, Lecturer; J.D., Denver. Carla Hayn, Professor and Senior Associate Dean; Ph.D., Michigan. John S. Hughes, Ernst and Young Chair in Accounting; Ph.D., Purdue. Gordon Klein, Lecturer; J.D., Michigan. Danny Litt, Lecturer; M.B.A., UCLA. Bruce Miller, Professor Emeritus; Ph.D., Stanford. Bugra Ozel, Assistant Professor; Ph.D., Columbia. Richard Saouma, Assistant Professor; Ph.D., Stanford. Eric Sussman, Senior Lecturer; M.B.A., Stanford. Brett Trueman, Professor; Ph.D., Columbia.

University of California, Los Angeles

Decisions, Operations, and Technology Management
Reza Ahmadi, Professor; Ph.D., Texas at Austin. Christiane Barz, Assistant Professor; Dr. rer. pol., Karlsruhe (Germany). Sushil Bikhchandani, Professor and Faculty Vice Chairman; Ph.D., Stanford. Felipe Caro, Assistant Professor; Ph.D., MIT. Charles J. Corbett, Professor; Ph.D., INSEAD. Donald Erlenkotter, Professor Emeritus; Ph.D., Stanford. Bob Foster, Adjunct Professor; M.B.A., UCLA. Arthur Geoffrion, James A. Collins Chair in Management Emeritus; Ph.D., Stanford. F. A. Hagigi, Adjunct Professor and Director, Global Health Initiatives; Ph.D., UCLA. Arielle Herman, Senior Lecturer; Ph.D., Paris. Uday S. Karmarkar, Distinguished Professor and L. A. Times Chair in Technology and Strategy; Ph.D., MIT. John W. Mamer, Professor; Ph.D., Berkeley. Kevin McCardle, Professor; Ph.D., UCLA. Donald Morrison, Professor Emeritus; Ph.D., Stanford. William Pierskalla, Distinguished Professor Emeritus and Dean Emeritus; Ph.D., Stanford. Kumar Rajaram, Professor; Ph.D., Pennsylvania (Wharton). Guillaume Roels, Assistant Professor; Ph.D., MIT. Rakesh Sarin, Paine Chair in Management; Ph.D., UCLA. Christopher S. Tang, Distinguished Professor and Edward W. Carter Chair in Business Administration; Ph.D., Yale.

Finance
Daniel Andrei, Assistant Professor; Ph.D., Lausanne (Switzerland). Antonio Bernardo, Robert D. Beyer '83 Term Chair in Management; Ph.D., Stanford. Michael Brennan, Professor Emeritus; Ph.D., MIT. Bruce I. Carlin, Associate Professor; Ph.D., Duke. Bhagwan Chowdhry, Professor; Ph.D., Chicago. William Cockrum, Adjunct Professor; M.B.A., Harvard. Andrea Eisfeldt, Associate Professor; Ph.D., Chicago. Stuart Gabriel, Arden Realty Chair and Director, Richard S. Ziman Center for Real Estate at UCLA; Ph.D., Berkeley. Mark J. Garmaise, Associate Professor; Ph.D., Stanford. Robert Geske, Associate Professor; Ph.D., Berkeley. Mark Grinblatt, Japan Alumni Chair in International Finance; Ph.D., Yale. Jason Hsu, Adjunct Professor; Ph.D., UCLA. Francis Longstaff, Allstate Professor of Insurance and Finance; Ph.D., Chicago. Hanno Lustig, Associate Professor; Ph.D., Stanford. Richard Roll, Distinguished Professor and Joel Fried Chair in Applied Finance; Ph.D., Chicago. Eduardo Schwartz, California Chair in Real Estate and Land Economics; Ph.D., British Columbia. Avanidhar (Subra) Subrahmanyam, Goldyne and Irwin Hearsh Chair in Money and Banking; Ph.D., UCLA. Walter Torous, Professor Emeritus; Ph.D., Pennsylvania. Ivo Welch, Distinguished Professor and J. Fred Weston Professor of Finance; Ph.D., Chicago.

Global Economics and Management
Antonio Bernardo, Robert D. Beyer '83 Term Chair in Management; Ph.D., Stanford. Leonardo Bursztyn, Assistant Professor; Ph.D., Harvard. Christian Dippel, Assistant Professor; Ph.D., Toronto. Sebastian Edwards, Henry Ford II Chair in International Management; Ph.D., Chicago. Mark J. Garmaise, Associate Professor; Ph.D., Stanford. Paola Giuliano, Assistant Professor; Ph.D., Berkeley. Jonathan Greenblatt, Lecturer; M.B.A., Northwestern. Edward Leamer, Distinguished Professor, Chauncey J. Medberry Chair in Management and Director, UCLA Anderson Forecast; Ph.D., Michigan. Hanno Lustig, Associate Professor; Ph.D., Stanford. Daniel Nathanson, EMBA Faculty Advisor; Ph.D., Pennsylvania (Wharton). Alfred Osborne, Professor and Senior Associate Dean; Ph.D., Stanford. Hans Schollhammer, Professor; D.B.A., Indiana. Robert Spich, Senior Lecturer; Ph.D., Washington (Seattle). Victor Tabbush, Adjunct Professor Emeritus; Ph.D., UCLA. Nico Voigtlander, Assistant Professor; Ph.D., Pompeu Fabra (Spain). Romain Wacziarg, Professor of Economics; Ph.D., Harvard.

Management and Organizationals
Corinne Bendersky, Assistant Professor; Ph.D., MIT. Samuel Culbert, Professor; Ph.D., UCLA. Christopher Erickson, Professor; Ph.D., MIT. Iris Firstenberg, Adjunct Associate Professor; Ph.D., UCLA. Eric Flamholtz, Professor Emeritus; Ph.D., Michigan. Noah Goldstein, Associate Professor; Ph.D., Arizona State. Sanford M. Jacoby, Howard Noble Distinguished Professor; Ph.D., Berkeley. Keyvan Kashkooli, Assistant Professor; Ph.D., Berkeley. Barbara S. Lawrence, Professor; Ph.D., MIT. David Lewin, Neil H. Jacoby Chair in Management; Ph.D., UCLA. Robert M. McCann, Associate Dean of Global Initiatives; Ph.D., California, Santa Barbara. Daniel J. B. Mitchell, Professor Emeritus; Ph.D., MIT. Judy D. Olian, Dean and John E. Anderson Chair in Management; Ph.D., Wisconsin–Madison. William G. Ouchi, Distinguished Professor and Sanford and Betty Sigoloff Chair in Corporate Renewal; Ph.D., Chicago. Anthony Raia, Professor Emeritus; Ph.D., UCLA. Jenessa Shapiro, Assistant Professor of Management and Organizations; Ph.D., Arizona State. Margaret Shih, Associate Professor and Area Chair; Ph.D., Harvard. John Ullmen, Lecturer; Ph.D., UCLA. Miguel M. Unzueta, Associate Professor; Ph.D., Stanford. Maia Young, Associate; Ph.D., Stanford.

Information Systems
George Geis, Adjunct Professor; Ph.D., USC. Bennet P. Lientz, Professor Emeritus; Ph.D., Washington (Seattle). E. B. Swanson, Professor and Area Chair; Ph.D., Berkeley.

Marketing
Andrew Ainslie, Associate Professor; Ph.D., Chicago. Anke Audenaert, Adjunct Assistant Professor; M.A., Catholic University Leuven, (Belgium). Anand V. Bodapati, Associate Professor; Ph.D., Stanford. Randolph E. Bucklin, Peter W. Mullin Professor and Faculty Chairman; Ph.D., Stanford. Lee Cooper, Professor Emeritus; Ph.D., Illinois. Aimee Drolet Rossi, Professor; Ph.D., Stanford. Dominique Hanssens, Bud Knapp Professor of Marketing; Ph.D., Purdue. Sanjog Misra, Professor; Ph.D., Buffalo, SUNY. Danny Oppenheimer, Associate Professor; Ph.D., Stanford. Peter Rossi, Distinguished Professor and James Collins Professor of Marketing, Statistics and Economics; Ph.D., Chicago. Carol Scott, Professor Emeritus; Ph.D., Northwestern. Suzanne Shu, Assistant Professor; Ph.D., Chicago. Sanjay Sood, Associate Professor; Ph.D., Stanford. Stephen Spiller, Assistant Professor; Ph.D., Duke. Jim Stengel, Adjunct Professor; M.B.A., Penn State. Andres Terech, Adjunct Assistant Professor; Ph.D., UCLA. Raphael Thomadsen, Assistant Professor; Ph.D., Stanford. Robert Zeithammer, Assistant Professor; Ph.D., MIT. Shi (shir) Zhang, Associate Professor; Ph.D., Columbia.

Strategy
Sushil Bikhchandani, Professor and Faculty Vice Chairman; Ph.D., Stanford. Michael Darby, Warren C. Cordner Professor of Money and Financial Markets; Ph.D., Chicago. Florian Ederer, Assistant Professor; Ph.D., MIT. Craig Fox, Ho-Su Wu Term Chair in Management; Ph.D., Stanford. Phillip Leslie, Associate Professor; Ph.D., Yale. Marvin Lieberman, Professor of Policy; Ph.D., Harvard. Steven Lippman, George W. Robbins Chair in Management; Ph.D., Stanford. John McDonough, Professor Emeritus; D.B.A., Harvard. Subramaniam Ramanarayanan, Assistant Professor; Ph.D., Northwestern. Richard P. Rumelt, Harry and Elsa Kunin Chair in Business and Society; D.B.A., Harvard. Mariko Sakakibara, Professor of Policy; Ph.D., Harvard. Jason Snyder, Assistant Professor; Ph.D., Berkeley.

Photograph of UCLA Anderson School of Management Complex by Peden+Munk.

UNIVERSITY OF CONNECTICUT

School of Business

M.B.A. Program

Program of Study

Educating leaders for over 130 years, the University of Connecticut (UConn) has been ranked among the top 5 percent of business schools worldwide by *Bloomberg Businessweek, Forbes,* and *U.S. News & World Report.*

UConn's flagship full-time M.B.A. program offers students a practical, comprehensive, and individualized business education that integrates basic business fundamentals, innovative experiential learning, and personal interests. This carefully blended curriculum differentiates UConn M.B.A. graduates and uniquely positions them for career success.

Essential to UConn's M.B.A. curriculum is the incorporation of innovative experiential learning accelerators, such as the SS&C Technologies Financial Accelerator, Innovation Accelerator, Student Managed Fund, Sustainable Community Outreach and Public Engagement (SCOPE) program, and the Stamford Learning Accelerator. These unique practice-based initiatives integrate traditional teaching and classroom experience with high-profile business partnering to close the gap between theory and practice.

The UConn M.B.A. program also offers a number of international learning opportunities that allow students to participate in a variety of international electives abroad. These one- to two-week courses are typically held in January, May, and during other break periods to minimize conflict with regular semester course work.

Year One of the program follows a lockstep format in which all students go through the core curriculum together—no exceptions. This ensures the same foundation of knowledge for every UConn M.B.A. student. The first-year core curriculum covers fundamentals across all business disciplines including preterm work on business law and ethics; a multisemester project, the Application of Core Teaching (ACT), the first formal exposure to experiential and integrated learning; and a non-credit seminar series focused on enhancing personal, team, and communication skills for the workplace.

In the spring of Year One, M.B.A. students develop an individualized plan of study in consultation with an advisory committee comprised of business school faculty, career counselors, and alumni/experts in the field. A student's individualized plan of study consists of eight courses (24 credits) including a primary area of emphasis, one to two courses (3–6 credits) of experiential learning, and carefully selected electives. Ultimately, the approved plan is a strategic bundle of courses and experiences that best aligns with each student's personal career goals and objectives.

After fulfilling the summer Internship Milestone, M.B.A. students continue with Year Two, pursuing the customized plan of study developed and approved in Year One. Most, if not all, second-year course offerings will be delivered in Hartford, Stamford, and/or Waterbury to best coordinate with the experiential learning centers where students will be participating.

The integration of business fundamentals and experiential learning helps provide the real-world experience that today's global businesses demand.

Research Facilities

UConn M.B.A. students study in state-of-the-art research and learning facilities. Classrooms and meeting spaces are outfitted with broad multimedia capability reflecting the School's commitment to meet the demands of the information era.

UConn's accelerator labs also serve as advanced business solution centers in which M.B.A. students, research faculty, and corporate managers jointly investigate and develop solutions to real-world, real-time, complex challenges facing business today.

The School's various centers—Connecticut Center for Entrepreneurship and Innovation, Center for Real Estate and Urban Economic Studies, Center for International Business Education and Research (CIBER), GE Global Learning Center, and the ING Center for Financial Services—provide specialized resources for students at the University of Connecticut.

The University of Connecticut libraries form the largest public research collection in the state. The collection contains some 3.6 million volumes; 51,000 currently received print and electronic periodicals; 4.3 million units of microform; 15,000 reference sources; 232,000 maps; sound and video recordings; musical scores; and a growing array of electronic resources, including e-books, e-sound recordings, and image databases.

Financial Aid

Although the cost of a UConn M.B.A. is among the most affordable, candidates often need financial assistance. Financial aid is available in the form of loans and scholarships. Most financial aid is awarded on the basis of established need, primarily determined through an analysis of an applicant's Free Application for Federal Student Aid (FAFSA). The School of Business also offers a limited number of merit-based graduate teaching assistantships. Out-of-state candidates who have demonstrated a high likelihood of success can also benefit from the Tuition Assistance Program. In this program, out-of-state students receive the benefit of paying in-state tuition fees. There are a limited number of these awards, so work experience and GMAT scores are important determinants. For more information, contact the University of Connecticut financial aid office at 860-486-2819 or visit the Web site at http://www.financialaid.uconn.edu.

Cost of Study

Tuition and fees for the 2011–12 academic year (two semesters) for the full-time M.B.A. program at UConn were $12,130 for Connecticut residents and $28,438 for nonresidents. Additional costs, including required health insurance, textbooks, mobile computer, laundry, and incidentals, can add up to an estimated $7500. Fees are subject to change without notice.

Living and Housing Costs

For a nine-month academic year, the approximate cost of living, in addition to tuition and fees, is estimated to be $12,104. Most M.B.A. students choose to live off campus, however some opt for graduate housing on campus. Specific information is available by contacting the Department of Residential Life at http://www.reslife.uconn.edu. A wide variety of off-campus housing is available to students. A visit to the area is recommended for all students interested in finding off-campus housing.

Student Group

UConn M.B.A. students come from a wide variety of undergraduate institutions, both domestic and international. Their undergraduate degrees represent majors in many diverse areas—from engineering and English, sciences and fine arts, to business to economics. In a typical class of students, 35 percent are women, the average age is 28, and approximately 30 percent are international students. Friendliness and familiarity characterize student life at the main campus. Social and professional organizations, including the Graduate Business Association (GBA), offer a variety of activities to satisfy the needs of students.

Student Outcomes

UConn's career-planning activities begin during orientation and continue throughout the M.B.A. Primary recruiters include General Electric, CIGNA, Aetna, IBM, United Technologies Corp., Wachovia, Hartford Financial Services, PricewaterhouseCoopers, Gerber Technologies, ESPN, and UBS. For the class of 2010, the mean base salary was $90,313.

Location

The University's span of more than 4,300 acres includes ten schools and colleges at its main campus in Storrs, separate schools of law and social work in Hartford, five regional campuses throughout the state, and schools of medicine and dental medicine at the UConn Health Center in Farmington. Right in the middle of Fortune 500 territory, the state capital and metropolitan area of Hartford is 30 minutes away, Boston is a 90-minute drive, and New York City is a 3-hour drive.

The University and The School

UConn has grown in recent years from a strong regional school to a prominent national academic institution with over 29,000 students and 190,000 alumni. The UConn School of Business is nationally accredited by AACSB International and is a member of the Graduate Management Admissions Council (GMAC) and the European Foundation for Management Development (EFMD). UConn is also accredited by the New England Association of Schools and Colleges (NEASC).

Applying

Admission to UConn's M.B.A. program is very competitive. The minimum requirements for admission include two years of postgraduate professional work experience; a minimum 3.0 GPA on a 4.0 scale, or the equivalent, from a four-year accredited institution; and a total GMAT score of at least 560. For international students whose native language is not English, a TOEFL score of at least 233 (computer-based) is required. The application deadline for international applicants is February 1. For domestic applicants the deadline is March 1.

Program of Study

Correspondence and Information

For the master's program:

Full-Time M.B.A. Director, Storrs
School of Business
University of Connecticut
2100 Hillside Road, Unit 1041
Storrs, Connecticut 06269-1041
Phone: 860-486-2872
Fax: 860-486-5222
E-mail: UConnMBA@business.uconn.edu
Web site: http://mba.uconn.edu

For the Ph.D. program:

Ph.D. Director
School of Business
University of Connecticut
2100 Hillside Road, Unit 1041
Storrs, Connecticut 06269-1041
Phone: 860-486-5822
Fax: 860-486-0270
E-mail: phdmail@business.uconn.edu
Web site: http://www.business.uconn.edu

The University of Connecticut's $27-million School of Business facility opened its doors in 2001.

THE FACULTY

Accounting
Stanley Biggs, Ph.D., Minnesota.
Joseph Bittner, M.B.A., Connecticut.
Wayne Bragg, M.B.A., Connecticut.
Amy Dunbar, Ph.D., Texas at Austin.
Larry Gramling, Ph.D., Maryland.
Robert Hoskin, Ph.D., Cornell.
Richard Hurley, Ph.D., Connecticut.
Mohamed E. Hussein, Ph.D., Pittsburgh.
Alfred Zhu Liu, Ph.D., California, Irvine.
Brent McCallum, M.S., American.
Cliff Nelson, D.B.A., Illinois.
Jose Oaks, M.B.A., NYU.
David Papandria, B.S., Marian (Indianapolis); CPA.
John Phillips, Ph.D., Iowa.
George Plesko, Ph.D., Wisconsin–Madison.
Paul A. Ramunni, M.S.A., LIU.
Michael Redemske, M.S., DePaul.
Sarah Rice, Ph.D., Ohio State.
Andrew Rosman, Ph.D., North Carolina at Chapel Hill.
Gim Seow, Ph.D., Oregon.
David Weber, Ph.D., Colorado at Boulder.
Michael Willenborg, Ph.D., Penn State.

Finance
Kathleen Bailey, J.D., Connecticut.
Walter Dolde, Ph.D., Yale.
Assaf Eisdorfer, Ph.D., Rochester.
Chinmoy Ghosh, Ph.D., Penn State.
Carmelo Giaccotto, Ph.D., Kentucky.
Joseph Golec, Ph.D., Washington (St. Louis).
Shantaram P. Hegde, Ph.D., Massachusetts.
Paul Hsu, Ph.D., Columbia.
Linda S. Klein, Ph.D., Florida State.
John Knopf, Ph.D., NYU.
Jeffrey Kramer, Ph.D., Connecticut.
Norman Moore, Ph.D., Florida State.
Thomas O'Brien, Ph.D., Florida.
Katherine Pancak, J.D., Boston College.
James Sfiridis, Ph.D., Connecticut.
Rexford Santerre, Ph.D., Connecticut.

Management
T. Lane Barrow, M.A., Harvard.
Qing Cao, Ph.D., Maryland.
Dimo Dimov, Ph.D., London.
Richard Dino, Ph.D., SUNY at Buffalo.
Lucy Gilson, Ph.D., Georgia Tech.
Jodi Goodman, Ph.D., Georgia Tech.
David Lavoie, Ph.D., Wisconsin.
Michael Lubatkin, D.B.A., Tennessee.
Nora Madjar-Nanovska, Ph.D., Illinois.
John Mathieu, Ph.D., Old Dominion.
Elaine Mosakowski, Ph.D., Berkeley.
Gary Powell, Ph.D., Massachusetts.
Gregory Reilly, Ph.D., Wisconsin.
Jeffrey Roberts, Ph.D., Connecticut.
Eugene Salorio, D.B.A., Harvard.
Zeki Simsek, Ph.D., Connecticut.
David Souder, Ph.D., Minnesota.
Henry Ulrich, Ph.D., Rhode Island.
John F. Veiga, D.B.A., Kent State.

Marketing and Business Law
Robert Bird, J.D., Boston University.
Mary Caravella, D.B.A., Harvard.
Vincent Carrafiello, J.D., Connecticut.
Robin Coulter, Ph.D., Pittsburgh.
Mark DeAngelis, J.D., Suffolk.
Karla Fox, J.D., Duke.
Wynd Harris, Ph.D., Oklahoma.
Subhash C. Jain, Ph.D., Oregon.
Hongju Liu, Ph.D., Chicago.
Kevin McEvoy, M.B.A., Boston College.
Joseph Pancras, Ph.D., NYU.
Girish Punj, Ph.D., Carnegie Mellon.
Samuel Schrager, J.D., Miami.
Murphy Sewall, Ph.D., Washington (St. Louis).
Susan Spiggle, Ph.D., Connecticut.
Mark Spurling, J.D., Western New England.
Narasimhan Srinivasan, Ph.D., SUNY at Buffalo.

Operations and Information Management
Sulin Ba, Ph.D., Texas at Austin.
Xue Bai, Ph.D., Carnegie Mellon.
S. Bhattacharjee, Ph.D., SUNY at Buffalo.
Fidan Boylu, Ph.D., Florida.
Hsuan-Wei Michelle Chen, Ph.D., Texas at Austin.
John Clapp, Ph.D., Columbia.
Jose Cruz, Ph.D., Massachusetts Amherst.
Robert Day, Ph.D., Maryland, College Park.
Moustapha Diaby, Ph.D., SUNY at Buffalo.
Timothy Dowding, Ph.D., Connecticut.
Robert Garfinkel, Ph.D., Johns Hopkins.
Ram Gopal, Ph.D., SUNY at Buffalo.
John Harding, Ph.D., Berkeley.
Wei-Kuang Huang, Ph.D., Rutgers.
Robert Johnson, Ph.D., Rochester.
Ray Kehrahn, M.B.A., Connecticut.
Cuihong Li, Ph.D., Carnegie Mellon.
Xinxin Li, Ph.D., Pennsylvania.
James Marsden, Ph.D., Purdue.
Suresh Nair, Ph.D., Northwestern.
Manuel Nunez, Ph.D., MIT.
Ramesh Sankaranarayanan, Ph.D., NYU.
Jan Stallaert, Ph.D., UCLA.
Lakshman Thakur, Eng.Sc.D., Columbia.
Yung-Chin (Alex) Tung, Ph.D., Kentucky.
Zhongju Zhang, Ph.D., Washington (Seattle).
Dmitry Zhdanov, Ph.D., Minnesota, Twin Cities.

UConn provides state-of-the-art experiential learning opportunities through such collaborative initiatives as the SS&C Technologies Financial Accelerator (above).

UNIVERSITY OF OKLAHOMA

Price College of Business

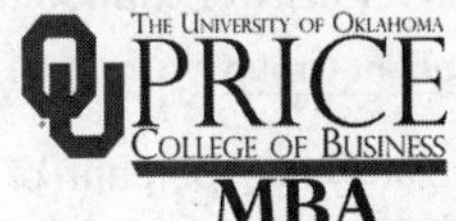

Programs of Study

The Price College of Business at the University of Oklahoma (OU) offers the following graduate programs: the Master of Business Administration (M.B.A.), the Master of Accountancy (M.Acc.), the Master of Science in Management Information Systems (M.S. in MIS), and the Doctor of Philosophy (Ph.D.). Dual-degree programs offered include the M.B.A./M.S. in MIS, M.B.A./J.D., M.B.A./M.Acc., M.Acc./M.S. in MIS, and generic dual degrees, which combine any other graduate program available at OU with the M.B.A. For the dual-degree programs, applicants must apply and be admitted to each program separately. Programs in the Price College of Business are fully accredited by AACSB International–The Association to Advance Collegiate Schools of Business.

The full-time M.B.A. is a 47-credit hour, sixteen-month program, with all courses taken at the graduate level. The full-time program facilitates the development of professional skills and broad business perspectives through opportunities such as unique summer internships in New York (Price Scholars), London (Dunham Scholars), Houston (Energy Scholars), and Dallas (Corporate Scholars) along with other domestic and international internships, case competitions, and working in teams on real-life cases. Interacting with excellent faculty members keeps OU M.B.A. students on the cutting edge of knowledge. A customized program in one of five specializations—finance, risk management, energy, entrepreneurship, or MIS—allows personal attention for each student. Students specializing in energy can spend a spring semester abroad, study at the Institute of French Petroleum, and receive an M.S. in Energy Economics, in addition to their OU M.B.A. Low tuition costs plus significant scholarship and assistantship opportunities make the OU M.B.A. an outstanding program for those looking to improve their professional opportunities and create a pathway to business leadership.

The professional part-time M.B.A. requires 47 credit hours, with all courses taken at the graduate level. Designed for the working professional, all courses are offered in the evening and are based in downtown Oklahoma City.

Both M.B.A. programs require that the student become familiar with the functional areas of business, the necessary tools for management decision making, and the environment in which business firms operate. Students from all undergraduate majors are encouraged to apply.

The M.Acc. is a full-time 33-hour program for students with an undergraduate degree in accounting from a program accredited by AACSB International. Other students may enter this program, but they must take a minimum of 24 hours of undergraduate accounting courses as well as other undergraduate business courses. The M.Acc. program is designed to prepare students not only to pass the CPA exam, but for positions of responsibility in the accounting profession. It combines a broad-based business curriculum with in-depth accounting training, affording students the opportunity to specialize in chosen areas of accounting practice (e.g., assurance services, financial reporting, and taxation).

The M.S. in MIS is a 32-hour program designed for people with an undergraduate degree in a discipline other than MIS who wish to embark on a career as an information system analyst or designer. The program combines a solid base of business and organizational knowledge with in-depth exposure to information systems technologies. The curriculum contains 15 hours of graduate business courses and 17 hours of graduate MIS courses. In addition, candidates must demonstrate competency in two programming languages. The M.S. in MIS program admits a small number of highly qualified students.

The full-time Ph.D. program is small and research-oriented. The program requires a minimum of 90 graduate hours past a bachelor's degree. Eighteen hours of course work are stipulated; most degree requirements and major, in addition to supporting fields, are determined on an individual basis. Close association with faculty members, as well as early research involvement, is standard. Doctoral students normally receive financial aid. Doctoral majors are available in accounting, finance, management and entrepreneurship, management information systems, and marketing/supply chain management. A master's degree is not required to enter the doctoral program.

Research Facilities

Research facilities that are available to graduate students include an extensive university library, the Amoco Business Resource Information Center, a graduate computer lab, the Bass Business History Collection, the Oklahoma University Research Institute, the Center for Economic and Management Research, and extensive computer facilities including a new trading floor lab.

Financial Aid

Graduate assistantships of up to $18,700 a year, special instructorships, fellowships and scholarships, and tuition-waiver scholarships are available for qualified graduate students. Graduate assistantships may include a full waiver of resident and nonresident tuition.

Cost of Study

Tuition in 2012–13 for full-time state residents is $325 per credit hour; nonresident students pay $803 per credit hour. Books and supplies are estimated at $1000 per academic year; other fees vary by program.

Living and Housing Costs

Many graduate students live on campus in one of the university's three apartment complexes or in the residence halls. Prices for apartments vary from $475 to $1000 per month. Room and board rates for the residence halls are approximately $4191 for one semester. For more information, students can call 405-325-2511 or visit the Web site at http://www.housing.ou.edu.

University of Oklahoma

Student Group

Typically, 45 percent of an M.B.A. class consists of business majors, 24 percent engineering majors, and the remainder science and humanities majors. More than 40 percent have two years or more of work experience. The average age is 27 and approximately 30 percent are women. There are generally 300 to 350 graduate students in the College.

Location

Although part of the Oklahoma City metropolitan area, Norman began as and continues to be an independent community with a permanent population of approximately 113,000. It has extensive parks and recreation programs, a 10,000-acre lake and park area, a community theater, an art center and art league, and other amenities of a university town. Norman is minutes from downtown Oklahoma City and 3 hours from Dallas. Summers are hot with high humidity, and winters are mild to cold.

The University

The University of Oklahoma, which was founded in 1890, is a doctoral degree-granting research university. The Norman campus serves as home to all of the University's academic programs, except health-related fields. Both the Norman and Health Sciences Center colleges offer programs at the Schusterman Center, the site of OU-Tulsa. OU enrolls more than 31,000 students, has more than 2,400 full-time faculty members, and has twenty colleges offering 163 majors at the baccalaureate level, 166 majors at the master's level, eighty-one majors at the doctoral level, twenty-seven majors at the first-professional level, and twenty-six graduate certificates.

Applying

There is a nonrefundable application processing fee of $40 for U.S. citizens and permanent residents and $90 for international applicants. Admission is open to qualified individuals holding a bachelor's degree from an accredited college or university who show high promise of success in graduate study. Applicants need not have undergraduate backgrounds in business. All applicants must submit satisfactory scores on the Graduate Management Admission Test (GMAT) or Graduate Records Examination (GRE). International applicants must submit satisfactory scores on the Test of English as a Foreign Language (TOEFL) or the Cambridge IELTS. In addition, the Test of Spoken English (TSE) is required of international applicants to the Ph.D. program. Letters of recommendation are required for all applicants.

Students may enter the M.Acc. program in the fall semester beginning in late August, the spring semester beginning in early January, or the eight-week summer session beginning in early June. Students may enter the M.B.A. program, M.S. in MIS program, and doctoral program in the fall semester only.

Correspondence and Information

Graduate Programs Office
Price College of Business
1003 Asp Avenue, Suite 1040
University of Oklahoma
Norman, Oklahoma 73019-4302
United States
Phone: 405-325-4107
Fax: 405-325-7753
E-mail: oklahomamba@ou.edu
Web site: http://price.ou.edu/mba/

THE FACULTY AND THEIR RESEARCH

Faculty members in the Price College of Business are dedicated to students. As researchers in their respective fields, they bring real-world knowledge and experience to the classroom. Recognized nationally and internationally, Oklahoma M.B.A. faculty members demonstrate extensive knowledge in their diverse teaching and research interests.

More information about the faculty of the Price College of Business can be found at http://www.ou.edu/content/price/left/faculty_research.html.

UNIVERSITY OF OTTAWA

Telfer School of Management
Master of Business Administration

Programs of Study

The Telfer School of Management at the University of Ottawa is uniquely positioned to link with and learn from Canada's leaders. With some 3,600 graduate and undergraduate students, 200 full- and part-time faculty members, and 22,000 alumni, the Telfer School of Management is a diverse and vibrant environment in which students, faculty, researchers, and alumni can forge rewarding lifelong relationships. The Telfer School is among the 1 percent of business schools in the world to have achieved the triple crown of accreditations (AACSB, AMBA, and EQUIS).

The Telfer School believes that an M.B.A. education should prepare managers and leaders to focus on results, value, and outcomes with discipline and adaptability. To that end, it offers an intensive and integrated program that features small classes, high levels of interaction, and peer learning, all conducted in world-class facilities. All business schools face the challenge of integrating curriculum in a way that is relevant and practical; Telfer's utilization of leadership from high-performance organizations provides an integration theme that has several unique advantages.

The Telfer M.B.A.'s integrated curriculum trains ambitious managers to lead people, take charge of organizations, allocate resources effectively, and articulate strategic vision—all fundamental skills of high performance managers.

In addition, the Telfer M.B.A. provides students with opportunities to work directly with business-intelligence tools and closely examine methods and processes used by organizations to create integrated performance management systems. The curriculum covers the fundamental skills needed by leaders to achieve high performance in any industry or sector.

Using the extensive network within the local business community and the public sector, students must complete a major project under the supervision of a faculty member, the mentorship of a Certified Management Consultant from the Canadian Association of Management (CAMC), and the direction of an executive from the host organization. While completing the project, students apply their newly acquired knowledge and skills, balance theory and practice, and gain valuable management experience. Students have completed projects for numerous firms, including Adobe, Alcatel Lucent, Bank of Canada, Canada Post, Cirque du Soleil, Foreign Affairs Canada, International Trade Canada, Live Work Learn Play LLP, Lumenera Corporation, March Networks, National Research Council (NRC), PAI Medical Group, Pricewaterhouse Coopers, Ottawa Senators, RBC, SNC-Lavalin, the *Ottawa Citizen,* and Volvo Cars of Canada.

Program delivery is flexible. Full- and part-time study options allow students to complete the degree requirements in as little as twelve months or as long as sixty months. Courses are offered in a variety of formats ranging from day or evening classes spread over twelve weeks, to half-courses delivered intensively over a weekend.

The Telfer M.B.A. draws students from around the world, from a variety of educational backgrounds and diverse professional experiences. The program is designed to build on the diversity and wealth of its students' profiles. A cohort environment allows students to work and learn together, benefiting from each other's strengths, capabilities, and experiences. Students participate in national and international case competitions annually. The strong performance of the Telfer School's M.B.A. teams over the years is a clear reflection of its talented students and the high quality of the program.

Other graduate management programs offered at the Telfer School include the Executive M.B.A. (EMBA), a twenty-one month program with classes one day a week; the Master of Health Administration (M.H.A.), a sixteen-month program that includes a four-month administrative residency; the Master of Science in management (M.Sc.); the Master of Science in Health Systems (M.Sc.); and e-commerce and e-business graduate certificates.

Research Facilities

The Telfer School fosters the development of the students' high-tech skills by providing them with state-of-the-art computing and teaching facilities. From private rooms to multimedia labs and teaching rooms, students can prepare their assignments using common and specialized software, advanced financial and accounting databases, the Internet, electronic mail, and the computerized libraries of the University.

A dedicated Management Library ensures that students can access—directly and easily—indispensable learning materials, such as the latest academic journals and trade publications and the increasing number of online databases and electronic resources applied to management

The Telfer School of Management proudly promotes its Career Centre, which is dedicated exclusively to management students. The Career Centre provides a wide array of first-class services, programs, events, and resources to help students and alumni chart successful courses for the future. It also cultivates strong relationships with employers in all business and government sectors, creating employment opportunities, enhancing student value, and facilitating employer recruitment.

The University also offers a variety of services and resources that contribute to the student's professional development and success in achieving career goals.

Financial Aid

The Telfer School of Management's goal is to attract top quality candidates to its M.B.A. program. Numerous scholarships are awarded, which reflects the Telfer School's ongoing commitment to reward exceptional students for their academic successes and achievements. Students can visit the Web site at http://www.telfer.uOttawa.ca/mba to learn more about scholarships and awards.

Canadian citizens and permanent residents in need of financial aid can apply for government assistance. The Telfer School of Management provides funds for teaching assistants and research assistants. The University also offers various awards primarily for Canadian citizens or permanent residents who intend to pursue or are pursuing full-time graduate studies.

Cost of Study

In 2012–13, tuition for a full-time M.B.A. program (three semesters) is Can$23,394 for Canadian students and Can$34,085 for international students. For part-time students, tuition is Can$377 per credit, with 54 credits needed.

Living and Housing Costs

Other estimated costs for the academic year include housing (off campus), Can$7500; food, Can$4800; books, Can$1500; and for non-Canadians, health insurance, Can$750.

Location

Located in the heart of the nation's capital, the Telfer School of Management at the University of Ottawa is at the center of an extensive group of government and private organizations that drive most of Canada's business and trade nationally and internationally. The main campus is located in the downtown core and is within walking distance of shopping malls, restaurants, cinemas, and museums.

The University and The Telfer School

The University of Ottawa is a cosmopolitan campus where more than 40,000 students from a variety of cultural heritages live and learn in an atmosphere of tolerance and understanding. International students benefit from the University's long tradition of excellence in teaching and research while learning about the multicultural Canadian social mosaic. The Telfer School of Management provides a rich educational experience—both inside and outside the classroom—that prepares students to be leaders in the new global, knowledge-based economy. The Telfer School's graduates are in demand by high-technology companies, leading consulting firms, financial institutions, and public-sector organizations in Canada and abroad. The Telfer School of Management at the University of Ottawa received accreditation from AACSB International in 2003, AMBA in 2005, and EQUIS in 2009. It is one of only two Canadian business schools to be recognized by these prestigious international organizations.

Applying

Admission to the Telfer M.B.A. program is competitive and granted to candidates who clearly demonstrate high promise of success. The admission requirements are: a baccalaureate degree with at least a B or a 70 percent overall standing, at least three years of full-time work experience, and at least a 50th percentile score on the GMAT. The most recent average score was 615 and the range was 550–780. Application deadlines are February 1 for international students and April 1 for students from the United States and Canada. Students should allow four to six weeks for notification. Preference is given to candidates who have greater work experience, particularly where there is evidence of career progression.

University of Ottawa

Correspondence and Information
M.B.A. Program
University of Ottawa Telfer School of Management
55 Laurier Avenue East, Room 4160
Ottawa, Ontario K1N 6N5
Canada
Phone: 613-562-5884
800-965-5512 (toll-free)
Fax: 613-562-5912
E-mail: mba@telfer.uOttawa.ca
Web site: http://www.telfer.uOttawa.ca/mba

THE FACULTY

Many of the Telfer School's faculty members serve as consultants to major corporations and government organizations around the world. Holders of numerous teaching and research awards, the professors combine excellence in teaching with outstanding scholarship.

Administration

Dean: François Julien, Associate Professor; Ph.D., Waterloo.
Vice-Dean and Associate Dean (Programs): Jacques Barrette, Full Professor; Ph.D., Montréal.
Associate Dean (Academic) and Secretary: Martine Spence, Full Professor; M.B.A., Concordia (Montréal); Ph.D., Middlesex.
Accreditation Team Leader, Associate Professor: Michel Nedzela, Associate Professor; M.S., Stanford.
Director of the Master of Business Administration (M.B.A.) Program: Michael Miles, Assistant Professor; Ph.D., Fielding Institute.
Director of the Executive M.B.A. (EMBA) Program: Sophia Leong; M.B.A., Ottawa.
Director of the Master of Health Administration (M.H.A.) Program: Brian Malcolmson; M.H.A., Ottawa.
Director of the Master of Science in Health Systems (M.Sc.): Craig Kuziemsky; Associate Professor; Ph.D., Victoria (British Columbia).
Director of the Master of Science in Management (M.Sc.): Mark Freel, Full Professor; Ph.D., Aberdeen.
Director, Undergraduate Program: Julie Beauchamp, Associate Professor, Ph.D., McGill.

Professors

Fodil Adjaoud, Full Professor; M.B.A., Ph.D., Laval.
Sadrudin Ahmed, Professor Emeritus; M.B.A., Ph.D., Western Ontario.
Douglas Angus, Full Professor; M.A., Ottawa.
Jacques Barrette, Vice Dean and Associate Dean (Programs), Full Professor; Ph.D., Montréal.
Julie Beauchamp, Undergraduate Program Director, Assistant Professor; Ph.D., McGill.
Walid Ben Amar, Assistant Professor; Ph.D., HEC Montréal.
Sarah Ben Amor, Assistant Professor; Ph.D., Laval.
Morad Benyoucef, Associate Professor; Ph.D., Montréal.
Silvia Bonaccio, Associate Professor; Ph.D., Purdue.
Ameur Boujenoui, Assistant Professor; Ph.D., HEC Montréal.
James E. Bowen, Adjunct Professor; Ph.D., Carleton.
Richard Bozec, Full Professor; Ph.D., Montréal.
Kevin Brand, Associate Professor; S.M., Sc.D., Harvard.
Tom Brzustowski, Full Professor; Ph.D., Princeton.
Jonathan Calof, Associate Professor; M.B.A., Ph.D., Western Ontario.
Denis H. J. Caro, Full Professor; M.B.A., Ph.D., Minnesota.
Jules Carrière, Associate Professor; Ph.D., Montréal.
Tyler Chamberlin, Assistant Professor; Ph.D., Manchester.
Imed Eddine Chkir, Associate Professor; Ph.D., Laval.
Samia Chreim, Associate Professor; Ph.D., HEC Montréal.
Robert Collier, Lecturer; B.A., Carleton; CMA.
Brian Conheady, Assistant Professor; M.B.A., McGill; CMA.
Jean Couillard, Associate Professor; M.B.A., Ph.D., Laval.
Margaret Dalziel, Associate Professor; M.B.A., McGill; Ph.D., Montréal.
David H. J. Delcorde, Lecturer; M.B.A., Heriot-Watt (Edinburgh); Ph.D., London South Bank (UK).
Shujun Ding, Associate Professor; Ph.D, Calgary.
Anna Dodonova, Associate Professor; Ph.D., Michigan.
David Doloreux, Full Professor; Ph.D., Waterloo.
Sylvain Durocher, Associate Professor; Ph.D., Quebec at Montréal.
Ronald Eden, Associate Professor; M.B.A., Dalhousie; Ph.D., NYU; CA.
Leila Hamzaoui Essoussi, Associate Professor; D.E.A., Doctorat en Gestion, Aix en Provence.
Dominique J. Ferrand, Associate Professor; Ph.D., Laval.
Bruce M. Firestone, Entrepreneur-in-Residence; Ph.D., Australian National.
Mark Freel, Director, MSc in Management Program, Full Professor; Ph.D., Aberdeen.
Devinder Gandhi, Full Professor; Ph.D., Pennsylvania.
Swee Goh, Professor Emeritus; M.B.A., Ph.D., Toronto.
Chen Guo, Associate Professor; M.B.A., Ph.D., Queen's at Kingston.
Michael Guolla, Teaching Associate; Ph.D., Michigan.
Mirou Jaana, Associate Professor; Ph.D., Iowa.
Yuri Khoroshilov, Associate Professor; Ph.D., Michigan.
Gurprit S. Kindra, Full Professor; M.B.A., Northwest Missouri State; Ph.D., Iowa.
Kaouthar Lajili-Kobeissi, Associate Professor; Ph.D., Illinois.
Nathalie Lam, Adjunct Professor; Ph.D., California.
Daniel E. Lane, Full Professor; Ph.D., British Columbia.
Laurent Lapierre, Associate Professor; Ph.D., McMaster.
David Large, Assistant Professor; M.B.A., Ph.D., Western Ontario.
Joanne Leck, Full Professor; M.B.A., Ph.D., McGill.
Sharon Leiba-O'Sullivan, Associate Professor; M.B.A., McGill; Ph.D., Toronto.
Jonathan Linton, Full Professor; Ph.D., York.
Judith Madill, Full Professor; Ph.D., Western Ontario.
Michael Maingot, Full Professor; Ph.D., Queen's (Belfast).
Pranlal Manga, Full Professor; Ph.D., Toronto.
Philip McIlkenny, Associate Professor; Ph.D., Essex.
Cheryl McWatters, Full Professor; M.B.A., Ph.D., Queens.
Wojtek Michalowski, Full Professor; Ph.D., Warsaw.
Muriel Mignerat, Assistant Professor; Ph.D., HEC Montréal.
Michael Miles, Director, M.B.A. Program, Assistant Professor; Ph.D., Fielding Institute.
Michael Mulvey, Assistant Professor; Ph.D., Penn State.
John Nash, Adjunct Professor; D.Phil., Oxford.
Alan O'Sullivan, Assistant Professor; M.B.A., Dublin; Ph.D., McGill.
Sharon O'Sullivan, Associate Professor; M.B.A., McGill; Ph.D. Toronto.
Barbara Orser, Full Professor; Ph.D., Bradford.
Gilles Paquet, Full Professor; doctoral studies, Queens.
Jonathan Patrick, Assistant Professor; Ph.D., British Columbia.
Kathryn Pedwell, Assistant Professor; M.B.A., Ph.D., Calgary.
Ajax Persaud, Associate Professor, Ph.D., Carleton.
Rhonda Pyper, Assistant Professor; M.B.A., Laurentian; CMA.
Tony Quon, Associate Professor; Ph.D., Princeton.
Bijan Raajemi, Associate Professor; Ph.D., Waterloo.
Abdul Rahman, Full Professor; Ph.D., Concordia (Montréal).
William Rentz, Associate Professor; Ph.D., Rochester.
Greg Richards, Professor of Performance Management; M.B.A., Ottawa; Ph.D., Carleton (Ottawa).
Allan Riding, Full Professor; Ph.D., McGill.
Umar Ruhi, Assistant Professor; M.B.A., Ph.D., McMaster.
Jeffrey Sidney, Full Professor; Ph.D., Michigan.
Martine Spence, Associate Dean (Academic) and Secretary, Full Professor; M.B.A., Concordia; Ph.D., Middlesex.
Patrick Woodcock, Assistant Professor; M.B.A., Ph.D., Western Ontario.
David J. Wright, Full Professor; Ph.D., Cambridge.
Mehdi Zahaf, Associate Professor; Ph.D., HEC Montréal.
Daniel Zeghal, Full Professor; M.B.A., Ph.D., Laval; CGA.

THE UNIVERSITY OF TEXAS AT DALLAS

Naveen Jindal School of Management

NAVEEN JINDAL
SCHOOL OF MANAGEMENT

Programs of Study

The Naveen Jindal School of Management's ten dynamic master's programs answer the challenges facing today's business leaders. The curriculum for each of these degrees is built around a strong core of classes with detailed study addressing specific industry issues. These master's programs—accounting, finance, healthcare management, information technology and management, innovation and entrepreneurship, international management studies, management and administrative sciences, marketing, supply chain management, and systems engineering and management—also prepare students to take national certification exams, including CPA, CFA, CFP, Certified Internal Auditor, and others.

Master's degrees require 36 credit hours for completion. Jindal School of Management classes are offered year-round, with a full schedule of courses offered in the evening to accommodate working professionals. Full-time graduate students could complete a master's degree in three semesters; most graduate students complete their degree programs within three calendar years by taking a blend of on-campus and online programs. Several master's degrees, including accounting, information technology and management, and supply chain management may be earned either fully or almost completely with online classes.

The Jindal School also offers eight M.B.A. programs with concentrations in accounting, finance, healthcare administration, healthcare management for physicians, information systems, innovation and entrepreneurship, internal audit, international management, leadership in organizations, marketing, operations management, product lifecycle and supply chain management, project management, strategic management, and supply chain management. Employers particularly like the strong analytical skills University of Texas at Dallas (UT Dallas) students develop during their M.B.A. studies, and students may focus their course work to match their individual career goals.

These programs are nationally recognized and offer a terrific tuition value for in-state students. Several of these 53-hour programs include an international study trip, most offer opportunities to take classes online, and all develop cross-disciplinary skills sought by the most competitive employers in the nation and around the world.

Representatives from many corporations—ranging from retail to transportation to banking, finance, health care and communications—partner with the Jindal School of Management. These industry executives sit on various advisory panels, provide financial and research support, and serve as mentors to undergraduate and graduate students. Faculty members seek these outside professionals as classroom speakers, adding real-life perspective to textbook learning.

Research Facilities

The Jindal School of Management faculty has been recognized globally for its research productivity. The faculty ranks fifteenth in North America and sixteenth globally based on research contributions to major journals, according to *The UTD Top 100 Business School Research Rankings,* and ranks twenty-second worldwide according to *Financial Times.* Research by the information systems faculty and operations management faculty ranks in the top 5 nationally in those respective fields. The Jindal School also hosts twelve Centers of Excellence where faculty and students join to tackle real-world issues faced by local businesses. Students also have the opportunity to apply for internships with these centers and participate in the meetings and lectures they sponsor for industry professionals.

Financial Aid

The Naveen Jindal School of Management Scholarship Committee makes awards each fall based on merit, need, or a combination of the two. The annual Scholarship Breakfast most recently generated more than $100,000 in scholarships specifically for Jindal School students at all levels. Students may also apply for the Dean's Excellence Scholarships, several of which are awarded each year. Full-time M.B.A. students with strong academic potential are eligible for significant scholarship and grant assistance. Last year, the Jindal School awarded more than $430,000 in scholarships to graduate students. Applications are available from the UT Dallas Office of Financial Aid. The University participates in most federal and state aid programs. Short-term loans are also available. Prospective students should visit the Jindal School of Management's Web site at http://jindal.utdallas.edu for more information.

Cost of Study

Tuition for in-state full-time graduate students (9 hours) for fall 2012 is $5970. For graduate students attending school part-time, tuition is $2654 for 3 hours and $4238 for 6 hours. These prices exclude fees and other charges. The cost of obtaining a master's degree depends upon how many hours a student completes each semester. The Full-Time M.B.A. costs about $28,000 for students entering in fall 2012, although generous scholarships are available to well-qualified students.

Living and Housing Costs

UT Dallas offers on-campus apartments, Waterview Park, which are operated by a private company. These apartments offer a variety of floorplans, are competitively priced, and fill quickly. Interested students should visit http://www.utdallas.edu for on-campus housing information.

The surrounding metropolitan area offers off-campus housing options in a wide range of prices and amenities. An array of shopping and dining establishments, representing everything from large chains to small, single proprietor–run shops, are within bicycling distance of campus.

The Comet Cruiser, a Dallas Area Rapid Transit bus route, connects the University campus with nearby shopping, apartment complexes, and the DART light rail line that goes to downtown Dallas for additional easy-access housing, shopping, and entertainment options. The Comet Cruiser runs Monday through Saturday and is free to students.

Student Groups

About 60 percent of Naveen Jindal School of Management graduate students are working professionals seeking an advanced degree; they often take classes online, in the evening, and during the summer semester. The Jindal School's environment is both challenging and naturally diverse. About a third of the graduate students take 9 or more hours a semester. With about 6,700 students, Naveen Jindal School of Management is the largest of the seven schools of UT Dallas. Jindal School students are equally split between undergraduate and graduate studies.

Most graduate students have at least five years of work experience. Women make up about 40 percent of master's students, and minorities represent almost 30 percent of the student population. About 30 percent of the students are from another country. Students range in age from 20 to more than 70; the average age is 30.

Location

The University of Texas at Dallas campus is in Richardson, a close suburb to the vibrant and diverse city of Dallas. The median age in the Dallas-Fort Worth area is about 33, younger than the national average of almost 37. The region is home to five professional sports teams: the Dallas Cowboys, Dallas Stars, FC Dallas, the two-time American League pennant-winning Texas Rangers, and the 2011 NBA champion Dallas Mavericks. Dallas is the only city is the world with buildings designed by four Prizker Prize–winning architects in one block and is also home to the nation's largest state fair—the Texas State Fair—which runs from late September through October. Dallas and Fort Worth both have a wide spectrum of cultural activities, from world-class museums and opera to internationally recognized symphony performances and the best in pop, folk, and country music.

Because of Dallas' central location in the U.S., air travel to either coast is as short as three hours and many major cities in Europe and the Far East are a nonstop flight away. The campus, about 18 miles north of downtown Dallas, is convenient to the George Bush Turnpike, U.S. Highway 75 and the Dallas North Tollway.

The University and The School

The University of Texas at Dallas was established in 1969 by the Texas Legislature as a response to the developing high-tech industry in North Texas. Originally conceived by Cecil Green, J. Erik Jonsson, and Eugene McDermott—founders of Texas Instruments—the University initially offered only master's degrees in engineering and science. More than 40 years later, the University has about 19,000 students in undergraduate, graduate, and doctoral programs.

The two largest alumni gifts in University history, with a combined value of $30 million, were made in October 2011 to the newly named Naveen Jindal School of Management. Gifts from Naveen Jindal (M.B.A. '92) and Charles (M.S. '80) and Nancy (B.S. '80) Davidson endow professorial chairs, provide scholarships, and fund research.

Construction is slated to begin in 2013 on the Jindal School's 120,000-square-foot addition to provide space for the growing faculty (currently more than 200) and student populations. The Jindal School is fully accredited by AACSB International–The Association to Advance Collegiate Schools of Business and currently occupies a 204,000-square-foot building that opened in 2003.

The twelve research centers at the Jindal School seek graduate students to run studies for corporate clients, offering students a high level of interaction with real-life business issues during their time in school.

Applying

Prerequisites for all graduate admissions include a bachelor's degree from an accredited institution, as well as calculus and spreadsheet proficiency. Undergraduate work in business-related courses is not required. Additional requirements include GMAT or GRE scores, a complete application, an essay of educational intent, and three recent letters of reference. A TOEFL score is required from those for whom English is not the native language. Applicants are evaluated on personal qualities and academic backgrounds, following admission formula guidelines of the International Association for Management Education. Personal interviews are not required. Admission deadlines vary by program and according to the applicant's citizenship status. Application requirements and deadlines are available on the School's Web site at http://jindal.utdallas.edu.

Master's programs in healthcare management, international management studies, innovation and entrepreneurship, and marketing do not require calculus. Applicants who do not meet the calculus requirement may be admitted but must make up the deficiency in the first semester at UT Dallas.

Most programs enroll students in the next semester after acceptance. Certain programs, including the Full-Time M.B.A. and Executive M.B.A., admit students only once each year.

Correspondence and Information

Jennifer Lasagna, Adviser
Naveen Jindal School of Management, SM40
The University of Texas at Dallas
800 West Campbell Road
Richardson, Texas 75080
Phone: 972-883-5828
Fax: 972-883-4095
E-mail: lasagna@utdallas.edu
Web site: http://jindal.utdallas.edu

THE FACULTY

Faculty research at the Naveen Jindal School of Management covers a range of topics, from findings of corruption in Asia to developing models for predicting the timing and frequency of future patient re-admissions related to congestive heart failure. Jindal School faculty members are well-represented in professional associations and publications and speak at events worldwide. A complete list of faculty members and their research publications is available online at jindal.utdallas.edu/faculty.

Hans-Joachim Adler, Senior Lecturer of Information Systems and Operations Management; Ph.D., Lyon (France).
Arthur Agulnek, Senior Lecturer of Accounting; B.S., Brooklyn State.
Shawn Alborz, Senior Lecturer of Information Systems and Operations Management; Ph.D., Melbourne (Australia).
Ashiq Ali, Davidson Distinguished Professor of Accounting; Ph.D., Columbia.
Frank Anderson, Senior Lecturer of Finance and Managerial Economics; M.B.A., SMU.
Nina Baranchuk, Assistant Professor of Finance and Managerial Economics; Ph.D., Washington (St. Louis).

The University of Texas at Dallas

John Barden, Senior Lecturer of Accounting; M.B.A., Manhattan.
Indranil Bardhan, Associate Professor of Accounting and Management Information Systems; Ph.D., Texas at Austin.
Alain Bensoussan, Distinguished Research Professor of Risk Management, Operations Management; Ph.D., Paris.
Abhijit Biswas, Senior Lecturer of Marketing; Ph.D. candidate, Purdue.
Ron Blair, Senior Lecturer of Accounting; M.B.A., Oklahoma.
Daniel Bochsler, Director, Executive MBA; M.B.A., Houston.
Tiffany Bortz, Senior Lecturer of Accounting; M.S., Texas A&M.
Judd Bradbury, Senior Lecturer of Information Systems and Operations Management; M.S., Purdue.
Norris Bruce, Associate Professor of Marketing; Ph.D., Duke.
Metin Cakanyildirim, Associate Professor of Information Management and Operations Management; Ph.D., Cornell.
Huseyin Cavusoglu, Associate Professor in Information Systems and Operations Management; Ph.D., Texas at Dallas.
Bobby Chang, Senior Lecturer and Director of Global Leadership Executive M.B.A.; M.B.A., USC.
Daniel Cohen, Associate Professor Accounting; Ph.D., Northwestern.
David Cordell, Clinical Professor of Finance and Managerial Economics; Ph.D., Texas at Austin.
William Cready, Ashbel Smith Professor of Accounting; Ph.D., Ohio State.
Rachel Croson, Professor of Organizations, Strategy, and International Management and Professor of Economics; Ph.D., Harvard.
Zhonglan (Di) Dai, Assistant Professor of Accounting; Ph.D., North Carolina at Chapel Hill.
Tevfik Dalgic, Clinical Professor of Organizations, Strategy, and International Management; Ph.D., Gazi (Turkey).
Milind Dawande, Professor of Information Systems and Operations Management; Ph.D., Carnegie Mellon.
Ted Day, Professor of Finance and Managerial Economics; Ph.D., Stanford.
Gene Deluke, Senior Lecturer of Information Systems and Operations Management; M.S., SMU.
Greg Dess, Andrew R. Cecil Endowed Chair in Applied Ethics; Ph.D., Washington (Seattle).
Alexander Edsel, Senior Lecturer of Marketing; J.D., Buenos Aires (Argentina).
Amal El-Ashmawi, Senior Lecturer of Finance and Managerial Economics; M.S., Texas at Dallas.
Adolf Enthoven, Professor of Accounting; Ph.D., Rotterdam.
Rebecca Files, Assistant Professor of Accounting; Ph.D., Texas A&M.
Forney Fleming, Clinical Professor of Healthcare Management; M.D., Texas Medical Branch.
David Ford, Jr., Professor of Organizations, Strategy, and International Management; Ph.D., Wisconsin–Madison.
Bernhard Ganglmair, Assistant Professor of Finance and Managerial Economics; Ph.D., Zurich (Switzerland).
Xianjun Geng, Assistant Professor of Information Systems and Operations Management; Ph.D., Texas at Austin.
Mary Beth Goodrich, Senior Lecturer of Accounting; M.B.A., LSU.
Umit Gurun, Assistant Professor of Accounting; Ph.D., Michigan State.
Richard Harrison, Associate Professor of International Management Studies; Ph.D., Stanford.
Ernan Haruvy, Associate Professor of Marketing; Ph.D., Texas at Austin.
Maria Hasenhuttl, Senior Lecturer of Organizations, Strategy, and International Management; Ph.D., Texas at Dallas.
Julie Haworth, Senior Lecturer of Marketing; M.B.A., Texas at Austin.
Charlie Hazzard, Clinical Professor of Organizations, Strategy, and International Management; M.B.A. Pennsylvania.
Robert Hicks, Clinical Professor in Organizational Behavior; Ph.D., USC.
Gerald Hoag, Associate Dean for Executive Education and Director of Leadership Center at UT Dallas; M.B.A., Stanford.
Varghese Jacob, Ashbel Smith Professor of Information Systems and Operations Management and Senior Associate Dean; Ph.D., Purdue.
Ganesh Janakiraman, Associate Professor of Information Systems and Operations Management; Ph.D., Cornell.
Surya Janakiraman, Associate Professor of Accounting; Ph.D., Pennsylvania.
Jennifer Johnson, Senior Lecturer of Accounting; M.S., Texas A&M.
Marilyn Kaplan, Undergraduate Dean; Ph.D., Texas at Dallas.
Robert Kieschnick, Associate Professor of Finance and Managerial Economics; Ph.D., Texas at Austin.
Jackie Kimzey, Senior Lecturer of Organizations, Strategy, and International Management; M.B.A., Dallas.
Constantine Konstans, Professor of Accounting; Ph.D., Michigan State.
Todd Kravet, Assistant Professor of Accounting; Ph.D., Washington (Seattle).
Nanda Kumar, Associate Professor of Marketing; Ph.D., Chicago.
Seung-Hyun Lee, Associate Professor of Organizations, Strategy, and International Management; Ph.D., Ohio State.
Peter Lewin, Clinical Professor of Finance and Managerial Economics; Ph.D., Chicago.
Stan Liebowitz, Ashbel Smith Professor of Finance and Managerial Economics; Ph.D., UCLA.
Elizabeth Lim, Assistant Professor of Organizations, Strategy, and International Management; Ph.D., Connecticut.
Zhiang (John) Lin, Professor of Organizations, Strategy, and International Management; Ph.D., Carnegie Mellon.
Chris Linsteadt, Senior Lecturer of Accounting; M.S., M.B.A., Texas at Dallas.
Sumit Majumdar, Professor of Information Systems and Operations Management; Ph.D., Minnesota.
Livia Markoczy, Associate Professor of Organizations, Strategy, and International Management; Ph.D., Cambridge.
Stanimir Markov, Associate Professor of Accounting; Ph.D., Rochester.
John McCracken, Clinical Professor of Medical Management; Ph.D., Pennsylvania (Wharton).
Dennis McCuistion, Clinical Professor of Corporate Governance; M.L.A., SMU.
Diane McNulty, Associate Dean for External Affairs and Senior Lecturer of Business Policy; Ph.D., Texas at Dallas.
Syam Menon, Associate Professor of Information Systems and Operations Management; Ph.D., Chicago.
Radha Mookerjee, Senior Lecturer of Information Systems and Operations Management; Ph.D., Purdue.
Vijay Mookerjee, Professor of Information Systems and Operations Management; Ph.D., Purdue.
B. P. S. Murthi, Associate Professor of Marketing; Ph.D., Carnegie Mellon.
Volkan Muslu, Assistant Professor of Accounting; Ph.D., MIT.
Kumar Nair, Senior Lecturer of Strategy, Organizational Performance, and Leadership; Ph.D., Twente (Netherlands).
Ramachandran Natarajan, Associate Professor of Accounting; Ph.D., Pennsylvania (Wharton).
Shun-Chen Niu, Professor of Information Systems and Operations Management; Ph.D., Berkeley.
Ozalp Ozer, Associate Professor of Information Systems and Operations Management; Ph.D. Columbia.
Arzu Ozoguz, Assistant Professor of Finance and Managerial Economics; Ph.D., INSEAD.
Madison Pedigo, Senior Lecturer of Organizations, Strategy, and International Management; M.B.A., Ohio State.
Mike Peng, Provost's Distinguished Professor of Global Strategy, Organizations, Strategy, and International Management; Ph.D., Washington (Seattle).
Joseph Picken, Clinical Professor of Organizations, Strategy, and International Management; Ph.D., Texas at Arlington.
Hasan Pirkul, Dean and Caruth Chair Professor of Decision Sciences; Ph.D., Rochester.
Nataliya Polkovnichenko, Senior Lecturer of Finance and Managerial Economics; M.S., Minnesota.
Valery Polkovnichenko, Assistant Professor of Finance and Managerial Economics; Ph.D., Northwestern.
Matt Polze, Senior Lecturer of Accounting; J.D., M.P.A., Texas.
Ashutosh Prasad, Associate Professor of Marketing; Ph.D., Texas at Austin.
Suresh Radhakrishnan, Professor of Accounting; Ph.D., NYU.
Srinivasan Raghunathan, Professor of Information Systems and Operations Management; Ph.D., Pittsburgh.
Roberto Ragozzino, Assistant Professor of Organizations, Strategy, and International Management; Ph.D., Ohio State.
Divakar Rajamani, Clinical Professor of Information Systems and Operations Management; Ph.D., Windsor.
Kannan Ramanathan, Senior Lecturer of Information Systems and Operations Management; Ph.D., Illinois at Urbana-Champaign.
Ram Rao, Founders Professor of Marketing; Ph.D., Carnegie Mellon.
Brian Ratchford, Davidson Distinguished Professor of Marketing; Ph.D., Rochester.
Michael Rebello, Professor of Finance and Managerial Economics; Ph.D., Texas at Austin.
Carolyn Reichert, Senior Lecturer of Finance and Managerial Economics; Ph.D., Penn State.
Orlando Richard, Associate Professor of Organizations, Strategy, and International Management; Ph.D., Kentucky.
Robert Robb, Senior Lecturer of Organizations, Strategy, and International Management; M.S., Utah.
Young Ryu, Associate Professor of Information Systems and Operations Management; Ph.D., Texas at Dallas.
Mark Salamasick, Senior Lecturer of Accounting; M.B.A., Central Michigan.
Jane Salk, Associate Professor of Organizations, Strategy, and International Management; Ph.D., MIT.
Sumit Sarkar, Ashbel Smith Professor of Information Systems and Operations Management; Ph.D., Rochester.
Michael Savoie, Director of Center for Information Technology and Management; Ph.D., North Texas.
Avanti Sethi, Senior Lecturer of Information Systems and Operations Management; Ph.D., Carnegie Mellon.
Suresh Sethi, Ashbel Smith Professor of Operations Management and Fellow of the Royal Society of Canada and the New York Academy; Ph.D., Carnegie Mellon.
Rajiv Shah, Clinical Professor of Organizations, Strategy, and International Management; Ph.D., Rice.
Harpreet Singh, Assistant Professor of Information Systems and Operations Management; Ph.D., Connecticut.
Jeanne Sluder, Senior Lecturer of Organizations, Strategy, and International Management; Ph.D., Texas Woman's.
Gonca Soysal, Assistant Professor of Marketing; Ph.D., Northwestern.
David Springate, Associate Professor of Finance and Managerial Economics; D.B.A., Harvard.
Kathryn Stecke, Ashbel Smith Professor of Information Systems and Operations Management; Ph.D., Purdue.
Andrei Strijnev, Assistant Professor of Marketing; Ph.D., Washington (St. Louis).
Upender Subramanian, Assistant Professor Marketing; Ph.D., Pennsylvania.
Jim Szot, Senior Lecturer and Interim Director, Executive Education Project Management Program; M.B.A., Dallas.
Lou Thompson, Senior Lecturer of Information Systems and Operations Management; M.S., DePaul.
Mark Thouin, Senior Lecturer of Information Systems and Operations Management; Ph.D., Texas Tech.
Amy Troutman, Assistant Director of Accounting Programs and Senior Lecturer; M.P.A., Texas at Austin.
Eric Tsang, Associate Professor of Organizations, Strategy, and International Management; Ph.D., Cambridge.
Yu Wang, Assistant Professor of Marketing; Ph.D., Michigan.
McClain (John) Watson, Senior Lecturer of Organizations, Strategy, and International Management; Ph.D., Iowa
Kelsey Wei, Assistant Professor of Finance and Managerial Economics; Ph.D., Texas.
Joe Wells, Clinical Professor of Finance and Managerial Economics; Ph.D., Cornell.
John Wiorkowski, Professor of Information Systems and Operations Management; Ph.D., Chicago.
Habte Woldu, Senior Lecturer of Organizations, Strategy, and International Management; Ph.D., Poznan (Poland).
Fang Wu, Clinical Professor of Marketing; Ph.D., Texas at Austin.
Yexiao Xu, Associate Professor of Finance and Managerial Economics; Ph.D., Princeton.
Yuanping Ying, Assistant Professor of Marketing; Ph.D., Michigan.
Alejandro Zentner, Assistant Professor of Finance and Managerial Economics; Ph.D., Chicago.
Harold Zhang, Professor of Finance and Managerial Economics; Ph.D., Duke.
Jun Zhang, Assistant Professor of Information Systems and Operations Management; Ph.D., Carnegie Mellon.
Feng Zhao, Assistant Professor of Finance and Managerial Economics; Ph.D., Cornell.
Zhiqiang (Eric) Zheng; Associate Professor of Information Systems and Operations Management; Ph.D., Pennsylvania.
Yibin Zhou, Assistant Professor of Accounting; Ph.D., Toronto.
Laurie Ziegler, Senior Lecturer of Organizations, Strategy, and International Management; Ph.D., Texas at Arlington.

The strong North Texas economy provides many job opportunities in fields such as health care, finance, transportation, and information technology for graduates of the Naveen Jindal School of Management Full-Time M.B.A. program.

THE UNIVERSITY OF TEXAS AT EL PASO

College of Business Administration
Master of Business Administration Program

Programs of Study

The Master of Business Administration (M.B.A.) program at The University of Texas at El Paso (UTEP) is designed for students from a wide range of backgrounds who are seeking a graduate business education with a dynamic international focus. By offering a menu of flexible schedules and class formats, the program meets the needs of both full-time students and working professionals. Students bring professional perspectives to the classroom from a range of industries: cross-border business, health care, engineering, education, and more.

The program awards the Master of Business Administration degree. The course of study offers concentrations in computer information systems, economics, finance, international business, management, supply chain management, and health systems. Students are enrolled in the program for 48 credit hours, which can be completed in the following three formats.

Full-Time M.B.A.: The 22-month full-time M.B.A. offers students courses in a traditional semester format. Students participate in corporate engagement projects with multinational companies, nonprofits, and start-up businesses, which bring an experiential learning component to their classroom education. Language workshops in Spanish and Mandarin are features of this format.

Accelerated M.B.A.: The 24-month Accelerated M.B.A. is a cohort format that is designed for working professionals. The courses are taken in six-week modules during evenings and weekends, year-round.

Executive M.B.A.: The 18-month Executive M.B.A. is a cohort format for business, government, and nonprofit leaders with at least eight years of management experience. The classes meet for two weekends (Friday and Saturday) a month. Courses are taken in topical modules with two courses completed every five sessions. Executive M.B.A. electives are specifically designed to augment and develop critical leadership skills.

Ph.D. in International Business, Master of Science in Economics, and Master of Accounting: These degrees are also available within the College of Business.

Research Facilities

UTEP M.B.A. students enjoy exclusive access to a state-of-the-art downtown Graduate Business Center (GBC). In addition to the M.B.A. classrooms and student collaboration rooms, the GBC houses several of the College's applied research centers including the Center for Hispanic Entrepreneurship; the Centers for Entrepreneurial Development, Advancement, and Research and Support; and the M.B.A. Corporate Engagement Projects. The College of Business Administration is also home to the Center for Multicultural Management and Ethics and the Border Region Modeling Project.

Financial Aid

The M.B.A. program offers assistantship positions to more than half of the full-time M.B.A. students. Full-time M.B.A. applicants who meet certain qualifications are guaranteed a fellowship. In addition, domestic students have access to financial aid. Scholarship opportunities are available.

Cost of Study

In-state tuition and fees for the full-time and accelerated M.B.A. programs are approximately $1377 per course or $22,032 for the degree program. Tuition and fees for international students are approximately $2455 per course and $39,280 for the degree program. International students who receive an assistantship or University fellowship are eligible for in-state tuition and fees.

Executive M.B.A. program costs, which include tuition, fees, books/course materials, and international travel research course lodging and ground transportation, are $36,000 for in-state and international students.

Living and Housing Costs

On-campus housing is available. Most students commute from their established residences or find rental housing in the El Paso area.

Student Group

The UTEP M.B.A. program serves a diverse population of over 350 students from more than twenty countries. Many M.B.A. students are involved with the UTEP M.B.A. Student Association and the local chapter of the National Society of Hispanic MBAs. Through these organizations, students take part in networking events, national conferences and career expos, community service projects, and other social activities.

Student Outcomes

UTEP M.B.A. graduates are employed by multinational corporations all over the world including JP Morgan Chase, Boeing, KPMG, Phillips, Lockheed Martin, Procter & Gamble, Amazon, ADP, Helen of Troy, and many others. Given the entrepreneurial spirit of the region, many UTEP M.B.A. graduates launch their own businesses as well.

Location

El Paso is located in West Texas. It borders New Mexico and Mexico and has a population of more than 650,000. The University offers a picturesque campus within the shadows of the towering Franklin Mountains, from the top of which it is possible to see two countries and three states, all within a stone's throw of each other. This Paso del Norte region is one of the largest international communities in the world with a population of over 2.2 million and access via airports, interstate highways, and international crossings. Along with its ruggedly beautiful environment, the city is home to many creative international artists, hiking/biking trails, world-class rock climbing, athletic events, great weather, and a host of entertainment opportunities.

The University and The College

The University of Texas at El Paso provides a living, breathing laboratory for critical research in areas such as national security, international business, epidemiology, desalination, and engineering. UTEP is the second-oldest academic component of the University of Texas system. It was founded by the Texas legislature in 1914 as the State School of Mines and Metallurgy, a name that reflected the scope of education offered at that time. UTEP's present

The University of Texas at El Paso

366-acre site features distinctive Bhutanese-style architecture. UTEP has become an internationally recognized research and doctoral university, with more than 21,000 students and 100,000 alumni. UTEP offers 181 bachelor's, master's, and doctoral degrees, all of which reflect a quality of education that has led major magazines to praise the University for the success of its business, engineering, and health sciences programs.

The College of Business Administration is accredited by the Association to Advance Collegiate Schools of Business International (AACSB)—the only school in the El Paso metropolitan area to be awarded this distinction. AACSB accreditation represents the highest standard of achievement for business schools worldwide. Fewer than 5 percent of the world's 13,000 business programs have earned AACSB accreditation. The UTEP M.B.A. program was ranked number 1 by *Hispanic Business* magazine 2010, 2011, and 2012. The program was also selected as the 2012 example of *Excelencia* in Education for graduate programs, recognizing success in academic achievement for Hispanics.

Applying

Applicants should submit the following in order to be considered for admission to the M.B.A. program: online application for admission into a graduate degree program (accessible at mba.utep.edu), official transcript from an accredited institution demonstrating completion of a four-year bachelor's degree or equivalent and official transcripts from all colleges or universities attended, a one-page statement of purpose, resume, two letters of reference, GMAT score (for full-time and accelerated M.B.A. programs), and TOEFL score of at least 250/600 (for international students). Applicants to the Accelerated M.B.A. program must have at least one year of professional work experience; Executive M.B.A. applicants must demonstrate at least eight years of managerial experience. Additional details are available online at http://mba.utep.edu.

All the materials listed above must be submitted before an admission decision can be made. Application deadlines vary by program; specific dates are available online at http://mba.utep.edu.

Correspondence and Information

Laura M. Uribarri, Assistant Dean for M.B.A. Programs
The University of Texas at El Paso
Graduate Business Center
El Paso, Texas 79968-0587
United States
Phone: 915-747-7727
Fax: 915-532-8213
E-mail: mba@utep.edu
Web site: http://www.business.utep.edu
http://mba.utep.edu

THE FACULTY

Full-time faculty members in the UTEP M.B.A. program hold doctoral degrees from top institutions worldwide. They bring to the classroom a global perspective and conduct research important to the global marketplace. Faculty members have recently been cited for high research productivity in the area of international business, leading their disciplines in creating relevant knowledge. Adjunct professors bring their vast industry experience to the M.B.A. learning experience as well.

Dr. José Humberto Ablanedo Rosas, Assistant Professor of Operations and Supply Chain Management; Mississippi.

Dr. Kallol Bagchi, Associate Professor of ISDS; Florida Atlantic.

Dr. Gary Braun, Associate Professor of Accounting; Arizona.

Dr. Chung Wenming, Assistant Professor of Operations and Supply Chain Management; Michigan State.

Dr. Erik Devos, Associate Professor of Finance; SUNY at Binghamton.

Dr. William Elliott, Associate Professor of Finance; Arizona.

Dr. Rick Francis, Assistant Professor of Accounting; Oklahoma.

Dr. Leo Gemoets, Associate Professor of ISDS; Spartan Health Sciences University (Saint Lucia).

Dr. Sid Glandon, Associate Professor of Accounting; Louisiana Tech.

Dr. Terry Glandon, Associate Professor of Accounting; Texas at Arlington.

Dr. Laura Guerrero, Assistant Professor of Management; Western Ontario.

Dr. John Hadjimarcou, Department Chair, Associate Professor of Marketing; Kent State.

Dr. Laura Hall, Associate Professor of Information and Decision Sciences; Florida State.

Dr. Esperanza Huerta, Assistant Professor of Accounting; Claremont.

Dr. Santiago Ibarreche, Professor of Management; Colorado.

Dr. Fernando R. Jiménez Arévalo, Assistant Professor of Marketing; Oklahoma State.

Dr. Steve Johnson, Associate Dean for Academic Affairs; Alabama.

Dr. Peeter Kirs, Associate Professor of CIS; Buffalo, SUNY.

Dr. Adam Mahmood, Professor of CIS; Texas Tech.

Dr. Donald Michie, Professor of Marketing; Wisconsin–Madison.

Dr. Somnath Mukhopadhyay, Associate Professor of ISDS; Arizona State.

Dr. Joseph O'Connor, Assistant Professor of Management; Wisconsin–Milwaukee.

Dr. Richard Posthuma, Professor of Management; Purdue.

Dr. Karl Putnam, Associate Professor of Accounting; Oklahoma State.

Dr. Edward Ramirez, Assistant Professor of Marketing; Florida State.

Dr. Miguel Ramos, Assistant Professor of Management; Minnesota.

Dr. Tim Roth, Department Chair and Professor of Economics, Texas A&M.

Dr. Stephen Salter, Professor of Accounting; South Carolina.

Dr. Godwin Udo, Professor of ISDS; Clemson.

Dr. James Upson, Assistant Professor of Finance; Memphis.

Dr. Oscar Varela, Professor of Finance; Alabama.

Dr. Fernanda Wagstaff, Associate Professor of Management; Texas A&M.

Dr. Zuobao (Eddie) Wei, Associate Professor of Finance; New Orleans.

Dr. Feixue (Faith) Xie, Associate Professor of Finance; Pittsburg.

M.B.A. students attend classes in the state-of-the-art UTEP Graduate Center located in downtown El Paso.

WAYNE STATE UNIVERSITY

School of Business Administration

School of Business Administration

Programs of Study

Wayne State University (WSU) offers several graduate programs in business: the Graduate Certificate in Business, Master of Business Administration (M.B.A.), Master of Science in Accounting (M.S.A.), Master of Science in Taxation (M.S.T.), Doctor of Philosophy (Ph.D.) in business administration, and the joint J.D./M.B.A. degree. One of the nation's most diverse campuses with students representing all fifty states and more than seventy countries, WSU offers many perspectives in the study of global business. Wayne State's graduate business programs are accredited by AACSB International—The Association to Advance Collegiate Schools of Business. This organization holds the highest standards of achievement for business schools worldwide. Member institutions confirm their commitment to quality and continuous improvement through a rigorous and comprehensive peer review.

The **Graduate Certificate in Business** program is a flexible, fast-paced program that provides non-business degree holders with business knowledge pertaining to the daily operations of corporate, nonprofit, and entrepreneurial settings. Students will develop skills in accounting, finance, management, and marketing, as well as have the opportunity to further their knowledge through elective course work. The six-course, 13-credit-hour program can be completed in as little as one semester, or as long as three years.

The **Master of Business Administration (M.B.A.)** program at WSU emphasizes practical and conceptual knowledge to prepare individuals for successful careers in business, government, nonprofit, and other organizations. The program is designed to meet the demands of the ever-changing workplace. The flexible, generalized program includes online courses. There are three phases of course work required: foundation, core, and electives or concentrations. Depending on the student's academic background, there may be no or as many as eight foundation courses required. Often, applicants with prior business education are able to waive all or some of these foundation courses. Once foundation requirements are fulfilled, students take six core courses and six course electives which can be used as part of a general curriculum or applied toward the completion of one or more of the twelve concentrations offered. Elective options cover a wide range of disciplines including accounting, business administration, finance, global supply chain management, marketing, management, information systems management, and marketing. Concentrations are available in accounting systems, auditing, corporate governance, finance, financial accounting, global supply chain, information systems management, internal audit, international business, management, marketing, and taxation.

The **Master of Science in Accounting (M.S.A.)** program prepares individuals for professional careers in public accounting. The primary objective of the program is to prepare students for public accounting careers rather than entry-level jobs, while meeting the 150-hour education requirement for licensure as a certified public accountant (CPA) in the state of Michigan. A secondary objective is to better prepare students for professional examinations, especially the CPA exam. Students with undergraduate degrees in accounting who are pursuing careers in private industry, financial institutions, government, and nonprofit organizations will benefit from the expanded study in accounting and business.

The **Master of Science in Taxation (M.S.T.)** program trains students for entry into professional tax practice in both the public and private sectors. Through the interdisciplinary nature of the program, students learn the accounting, legal, and public policy aspects of taxation. Students with a bachelor's degree in accounting usually meet all of the program's foundation requirements. Applicants with a bachelor's degree in a field other than accounting may have to complete foundation courses in the areas of accounting, business law, information systems management, and statistics.

The **Doctor of Philosophy (Ph.D.)** in business administration prepares students to become faculty members at major research universities. The program places a heavy emphasis on global perspectives and focuses on quantitative skills, which enables students to engage in research projects with faculty members. Currently, tracks are available in finance, marketing, and management. Assistantships, scholarships, and fellowships are available to doctoral students on a competitive basis.

Through WSU's **J.D./M.B.A. program,** qualified applicants may elect to complete both a law degree and the M.B.A. degree. The program allows students to fulfill the requirements of both programs concurrently. Students will need to complete all the requirements for both degrees, but Wayne State University Law School courses may count for up to 6 elective credits toward the M.B.A. degree. Students are granted five or six years to complete the requirements for both degrees, depending on whether the student entered as a part- or full-time student. The first year of the program is spent in the Law School. Students must be admitted to the Law School and to the M.B.A. program in the School of Business Administration and must obtain the separate approval of both units in order to participate. Students must take both the GMAT and the LSAT and meet all other admission requirements for both programs. More information about the WSU Law School can be found at http://www.law.wayne.edu.

Semesters begin in September, January, and May. The academic year has two 15-week semesters in fall and winter. For those interested in taking classes year-round, Wayne State schedules some spring and summer courses in separate eight-week sessions and others in a thirteen-week combined spring/summer semester. A full schedule of graduate courses is offered each term.

Research Facilities

Wayne State University School of Business Administration offers a wide range of computing resources to students. The School has a dedicated computer laboratory exclusively for business school students. It is equipped with the latest PC workstations, network printers, and business software. Software products allow faculty members to record lectures that students can view from any computer with Internet access. Many M.B.A. courses are available online. High-speed wireless Internet is accessible to registered students in all campus buildings.

The University Library System provides access to many business resources, including electronic indexes with abstracts and full text, and subject guides that focus on specific areas of research. Many of these resources are accessible online. The library system provides open-access computer labs for the campus community; there are more than 800 computers with a variety of applications in support of student learning. A 24-hour Extended Study Center is open in the Undergraduate Library during the fall and winter semesters.

Financial Aid

The Office of Scholarships and Financial Aid provides students with information regarding sources of funds. The University awards graduate and professional scholarships to both full- and part-time graduate students. The School of Business Administration also grants private scholarships to business students. The School's academic departments provide graduate teaching and research assistantships. Stipends for assistantships average $15,713 plus tuition and benefits for nine-month appointments.

Cost of Study

Effective fall 2011, tuition is $595 per credit hour for Michigan residents and $1215 per credit hour for non-residents. For current tuition and fee information, visit http://reg.wayne.edu/.

Living and Housing Costs

WSU Housing offers a number of options for students including residence halls, modern apartment buildings with views of the city, and historic apartments on campus. The University's residence halls, located in the heart of the campus, are just steps from the 24-hour Undergraduate Library, the Recreation and Fitness Center, the Student Center, and classes. Apartment costs range from $668 per month for an efficiency apartment to $1440 per month for a three-bedroom apartment. Residence halls range from $3952 to $7200 for the academic year. For more specific information, visit http://www.housing.wayne.edu.

Student Group

The School of Business Administration enrolls approximately 240 full-time and 800 part-time graduate students. Women form 44 percent of current graduate enrollment and more than 7 percent is international students. The average age of an M.B.A. student is 28 years, although the age range is 17 to 58. A typical class size is about 30 students. Typically, M.B.A. students have five years of work experience, and approximately 93 percent are employed either full- or part-time, with more than half holding supervisory positions.

Student Outcomes

Most students pursuing a master's degree in business administration, accounting, or taxation have already made impressive starts to their careers. An advanced degree can be a vehicle to broaden expertise, enhance opportunities for advancement, and increase earning potential. The School of Business Administration has a Career Planning and Placement Office dedicated only to business students and regularly assists students in finding permanent positions locally, nationally, and internationally.

Location

Located in Detroit, an international gateway connecting the United States and Canada, Wayne State University provides a unique setting for learning business. The main campus is located in Midtown Detroit, which is home to renowned museums, galleries, and theaters, most within walking distance. It encompasses 203 acres of landscaped walkways and gathering spots, linking 100 buildings. Downtown Detroit is just a few miles away, with restaurants, professional sports venues, and many other entertainment and business activities.

In addition, Wayne State operates a number of extension centers in metropolitan Detroit. Business courses are offered at WSU's Oakland Center in Farmington Hills.

The University

Wayne State University is Michigan's only urban research university, filling a unique niche by providing access to a world-class education at a great value. Wayne State's thirteen schools and colleges offer more than 400 academic programs to nearly 32,000 graduate and undergraduate students.

Applying

The M.B.A., M.S.A., and M.S.T. programs are open to students who hold a bachelor's degree from a regionally accredited institution and who demonstrate promise of success in pursuing graduate study. The online application for graduate admission (http://www.gradapply.wayne.edu), an application fee, official transcripts from all collegiate institutions attended, and GMAT results are required. Admission is granted each semester. The application and other required documents are due by June 1 for fall semester admission, October 1 for winter semester admission, and February 1 for spring-summer semester admission. International students must provide required materials six months prior to the beginning of the term in which they want to begin their studies.

Applicants to the Ph.D. program may be admitted with a bachelor's or a master's degree and are expected to have sufficient competence in math, computing, and statistics to satisfy prerequisites for the quantitative courses in the Ph.D. curriculum. Students who have not completed macroeconomics, microeconomics, and calculus prerequisites prior to admission must enroll in these courses during the first year of the doctoral program. Minimum requirements include a 3.0 undergraduate GPA (or 3.0 upper-division GPA), 3.5 graduate GPA, and a minimum 600 GMAT score. International applicants must meet the University requirements for TOEFL scores. Three letters of recommendation and an essay on career objectives must be included with applications for admission to the Ph.D. program.

Correspondence and Information

Graduate Programs Office
School of Business Administration
Wayne State University
Detroit, Michigan 48202
United States
Phone: 313-577-4511
Fax: 313-577-9442
E-mail: gradbusiness@wayne.edu
Web site: http://www.business.wayne.edu

THE FACULTY

Angela Andrews, Assistant Professor of Accounting; Ph.D., Michigan State.

Mark E. Bayless, Associate Professor of Finance; Ph.D., Washington (St. Louis).

Richard F. Beltramini, Professor of Marketing; Ph.D., Texas at Austin.

B. Anthony Billings, Professor of Tax; Ph.D., Texas A&M.

Abhijit Biswas, Professor of Marketing and Kmart Endowed Chair; Ph.D., Houston.

William Burrell, Lecturer in Global Supply Chain Management; M.B.A., Wayne State.

Timothy W. Butler, Associate Professor of Global Supply Chain Management; Ph.D., South Carolina.

Hugh M. Cannon, Adcraft/Simons-Michelson Professor of Advertising; Ph.D., NYU.

Brett Crawford, Senior Lecturer of Management; Ph.D., Copenhagen Business School.

Sudip Datta, Professor of Finance and T. Norris Hitchman Chair; Ph.D., SUNY.

Ranjan D'Mello, Associate Professor of Finance; Ph.D., Ohio State.

Sujay Dutta, Assistant Professor of Marketing; Ph.D., LSU.

Abhijit Guha, Assistant Professor of Marketing; Ph.D., Duke.

Jia Hao, Assistant Professor of Finance; Ph.D., Utah.

Elisia Hopkins, Lecturer in Management; M.A., Kentucky.

David Huff, Senior Lecturer in Global Supply Chain Management; Ph.D., Wayne State.

Atif Ikram, Assistant Professor of Finance; Ph.D., Arizona State.

Mai Iskandar-Datta, Professor of Finance; Ph.D., Missouri–Columbia.

Xiaowen Jiang, Assistant Professor of Accounting; Ph.D., Boston University.

Deborah Jones, Senior Lecturer of Accounting and Taxation; Ph.D., Kent State.

Scott Julian, Associate Professor of Management; Ph.D., LSU.

Pyung Kang, Assistant Professor of Accounting; Ph.D., Rutgers.

Frank LaMarra, Lecturer in Accounting; M.B.A., Wayne State; CPA.

Cheol Lee, Assistant Professor of Accounting; Ph.D., SUNY at Buffalo.

Jaegul Lee, Assistant Professor of Management; Ph.D., Carnegie Mellon.

Ariel Levi, Senior Lecturer in Management; Ph.D., Yale.

Kun Liu, Assistant Professor in Management; Ph.D., Utah.

David Lucas, Senior Lecturer in Management; Ph.D., Wayne State.

Natalia Lorinkova, Assistant Professor of Management; Ph.D., Maryland, College Park.

James E. Martin, Professor of Management and Industrial Relations; Ph.D., Washington (St. Louis).

Marick Masters, Professor of Management; Ph.D., Illinois.

Santanu Mitra, Associate Professor of Accounting and Interim Chair of Accounting Department; Ph.D., LSU.

Fred Morgan, Professor of Marketing; Ph.D., Michigan State.

Mbodja Mougoué, Associate Professor of Finance; Ph.D., New Orleans.

Thomas J. Naughton, Associate Professor of Management; Ph.D., SUNY at Buffalo.

Sheri Perelli, Senior Lecturer in Management; Ph.D., Case Western Reserve.

Kelly R. Price, Associate Professor of Finance; Ph.D., Michigan.

Arik Ragowsky, Associate Professor of Information Systems Management and Director, Manufacturing Information Systems Center; Ph.D., Tel Aviv.

Paul Reagan, Senior Lecturer in Management; Ph.D., Michigan State.

Irvin D. Reid, Professor of Management; Ph.D., Pennsylvania.

Alan Reinstein, George Husband Endowed Professor of Accounting; D.B.A., Kentucky; CPA.

Celia Livermore Romm, Professor of Information Systems Management; Ph.D., Toronto.

Mark Savitskie, Lecturer in Accounting; M.B.A., Wayne State.

Pamela Schmidt, Assistant Professor of Accounting; Ph.D., Arkansas.

Margaret Smoller, Associate Professor of Finance and Interim Associate Dean for Undergraduate Programs; Ph.D., Florida.

Toni M. Somers, Professor of Information Systems Management and Interim Chair of Management and Information Systems Management Department; Ph.D., Toledo.

Albert D. Spalding Jr., Associate Professor of Business Law and Taxation; J.D., M.B.A., George Washington; CPA.

Myles S. Stern, Associate Professor of Accounting; Ph.D., Michigan State.

Jeffrey J. Stoltman, Associate Professor of Marketing; Ph.D., Syracuse.

Andrea Tangari, Assistant Professor of Marketing; Ph.D., Arkansas.

John Taylor, Associate Professor of Global Supply Chain Management and Chair of Marketing and Global Supply Chain Management Department; Ph.D., Michigan State.

Amanuel G. Tekleab, Associate Professor of Management; Ph.D., Maryland.

Harish L. Verma, Associate Professor of Global Supply Chain Management; Ph.D., Michigan State.

William H. Volz, Professor of Business Law; J.D., Wayne State; M.B.A., Harvard.

John D. Wagster, Associate Professor of Finance; Ph.D., Texas A&M.

Tina Walsh, Senior Lecturer in Accounting; LL.M., Florida.

Daniel Weimer, Lecturer in Accounting; M.A., Michigan; CPA.

David L. Williams, Associate Professor of Marketing; Ph.D., Wayne State.

Larry Williams, Professor of Management and Psychology; Ph.D., Indiana.

Margaret Williams, Professor of Management and Interim Dean; Ph.D., Indiana.

Maef Woods, Assistant Professor of Accounting; Ph.D., Cincinnati.

Tingting Yan, Assistant Professor of Global Supply Chain Management; Ph.D., Arizona State.

Attila Yaprak, Professor of Marketing; Ph.D., Georgia State.

YORK UNIVERSITY

Schulich School of Business

Programs of Study

The Schulich School of Business at York University is known as Canada's Global Business School™. Since its inception in 1966, Schulich has built a strong reputation worldwide due to its global reach, innovative programs, and diverse perspectives on management and leadership. Through the graduate management programs offered by Schulich, students examine business issues in a global environment and learn how to manage complexity, ambiguity, and change.

Schulich's innovative master's-level programs emphasize relevance to real-world contexts. The School's broad range of degrees lets students choose the program of study that fits their needs and career direction. Programs include the Master of Business Administration (M.B.A.), International M.B.A. (I.M.B.A.), Executive M.B.A., Master of Accounting (M.Acc.), Master of Finance (M.F.), Master of Science in business analytics (M.S.), Master of Public Administration (M.P.A.), and the M.B.A./J.D., M.B.A./M.F.A. or M.B.A./M.A. joint programs which combine business with law, fine arts, or arts respectively. For those considering a career in academia, the Ph.D. in administration is offered.

The Schulich M.B.A. offers an integrated approach to general management fundamentals. It balances qualitative and quantitative skills and combines classroom learning with hands-on experience through a six-month strategic consulting project. The sixteen-month program offers multiple start dates, the ability to switch between full- and part-time study, and the option to specialize in one or more areas.

Schulich's I.M.B.A. is an ideal choice for those interested in launching a global career or growing an existing one. Building upon the M.B.A. curriculum, students master a second language, gain specialized knowledge of two global trading regions, and complete an internationally focused strategic consulting project.

The Kellogg-Schulich Executive M.B.A., in conjunction with Northwestern University, is an eighteen-month program that emphasizes U.S., Canadian, and international perspectives on global leadership and strategic management. The E.M.B.A. includes three residence weeks, alternating study weekends, and international study seminars abroad.

The Ph.D. in administration prepares students for a stimulating career in academic teaching and research. Graduates from this rigorous program of study contribute to the global practice and knowledge of business. Students are exposed to quantitative and qualitative research methods and techniques through core and elective courses. Students can tailor specializations to their individual needs in either management functions or thematic issues such as international business and change management.

Schulich's practical management education is complemented by over 160 electives and nineteen specializations. Students can choose to focus on a management function (accounting, economics, finance, marketing, strategic management, operations management, or organizational behavior), an industry sector (arts and media, global mining management, health industry management, or not-for-profit management), or special business topics (business and sustainability, entrepreneurship, or international business). Depending on the program of study, there may be additional opportunities to deepen and broaden specialized knowledge using diploma and professional designation programs.

Research Facilities

York University offerss five libraries with considerable resources, including a book collection of more than 2.5 million volumes and more than 205,000 serials (periodicals, magazines, reports and digests, collections of microfiche, maps, videos, films, sound recordings, compact discs, and databases). In addition, the Peter Bronfman Business Library at Schulich houses one of the best business reference collections in metropolitan Toronto.

Financial Aid

A range of financial support is available to students of the Schulich School of Business. Scholarships, awards, and bursaries are awarded based on achievement or financial need. Full-time applicants are automatically considered for entrance scholarships based on admissions information. The School's entrance scholarships and awards are among the highest value offered to M.B.A. students in Canada and recognize excellence in academics and community involvement.

In addition to these funding opportunities, Schulich students may apply for support through private and government student loan programs. On-campus jobs, research, and teaching assistantships are also available.

Cost of Study

Students pay fees each semester according to whether they are enrolled on a full- or part-time basis. The 2012–13 full-time tuition is approximately $14,950 per term for Canadian residents and $17,500 per term for non-residents. Tuition for the entire two-year Executive M.B.A. is $112,000 for both Canadian and international students. All costs are in Canadian dollars.

Living and Housing Costs

On-campus housing is available at reasonable rates. Housing, travel, course materials, and personal expenses vary with each student but range from $6500 to $8000 per term. All costs are in Canadian dollars.

Student Group

Schulich attracts a diverse student population. Approximately 50 percent of the student body is international, 37 percent are women, and almost 70 percent come from an undergraduate program other than business. The average age of an incoming M.B.A. student is 29 years; students possess an average of five years of work experience.

For many students, involvement in the Schulich community is critical to their experience. Student groups, clubs, social functions, and recruiting events provide countless opportunities to enrich formal in-class learning with extracurricular activities. Schulich alumni often say their involvement outside of the classroom helped to build lifelong friendships and create treasured memories that enhanced the value of their Schulich experience.

Student Outcomes

At Schulich, career management is a lifetime investment and helping students to transition into a new post-M.B.A. career is a top priority. Whether moving into a new function or switching industries, the Career Development Centre (CDC) works closely with students to identify career choices and objectives, develop a proactive career plan, and hone skill sets. Students can take advantage of training, counseling expertise, and networking opportunities. This support has helped over 85 percent of Schulich graduates land their first job offer within three months of graduation.

Graduates join Schulich's network of more than 23,000 alumni living in over ninety countries around the world. Schulich alumni are among award recipients in the Caldwell Partner's national program that honours Canadians under the age of 40 who have reached a significant level of success. Graduates are recruited by leading companies such as Bombardier, CIBC, Deloitte, Ernst & Young, Canadian government agencies, Kraft, Labatt/AB InBev, Procter and Gamble, RBC, Starbucks, Sick Kids Hospital, Telus, and Walmart Canada.

Location

Located in Toronto, the financial and cultural centre of Canada and one of the world's greatest multicultural cities, Schulich has built strong ties to the corporate community. The School has access to the head offices of many organizations. Close to 200 distinguished CEOs, leading academics, and senior government representatives act as advisers on Schulich's boards, teach in its classrooms, and provide guidance and counsel to students through the Schulich mentorship program.

The University and The School

Founded in 1959, York University has earned an international reputation for excellence in teaching, research, and scholarship in both undergraduate and graduate studies. Today, York is the third-largest university in Canada and home to the Schulich School of Business.

The Schulich M.B.A. is ranked in the world's top tier of business schools by the Economist Intelligence Unit (first in Canada, ninth in the world); *Forbes* (first in Canada, tenth best non–U.S. school); the Aspen Institute, a U.S. think tank (second in the world in social and environmental stewardship); and *Expansión* (first in Canada, twentieth in the world) in their most recent global surveys.

The School's continued success can be attributed its cutting-edge programs; challenging classes; and focus on teaching students to examine business from multiple perspectives, implement effective strategies, and excel in team environments.

Applying

In order to be considered for admission to the M.B.A. or I.M.B.A., students must have an honours undergraduate degree from a recognized university, with a minimum B average in the last two years of full-time study; acceptable scores on all GMAT measures; and at least two years of full-time work (post-undergraduate degree). Schulich also looks for leadership qualities, communication skills, creativity, and innovation in supplemental essays. Interviews may be required on a select basis.

In some instances, nonbaccalaureate candidates may be considered for admission. These candidates must have at least eight years of high-quality management experience and must have demonstrated a strong upward progression in their careers in addition to the other admission requirements.

Application deadlines for the M.B.A., I.M.B.A., and master's programs vary. Students should refer to the Schulich Web site for current deadline information and start dates. For scholarship consideration, applications should be submitted by the early deadline stated on the Web site. The application deadline for the Ph.D. program is December 1.

Correspondence and Information

Division of Student Services and International Relations
Schulich School of Business
York University
4700 Keele Street
Toronto, Ontario M3J 1P3
Canada
Phone: 416-736-5060
Fax: 416-650-8174
E-mail: admissions@schulich.yorku.ca
Web site: http://www.schulich.yorku.ca
Facebook: Schulich MBA/IMBA/MF Admissions
Twitter: http://twitter.com/#!/Schulich_MBA

THE FACULTY

Schulich faculty members are leading scholars from the world's top universities, passionate about their chosen fields, dedicated to their students, and committed to award-winning research. As pioneers in areas such as risk management, business and sustainability, global marketing, and entrepreneurism, they draw on their research findings to enrich every class. Many professors are also working practitioners and believe that a combination of active and interactive learning leads to the most effective teaching process. Schulich faculty members draw on a range of pedagogical approaches, including lectures, group work, case studies, simulations, and real-world projects.

Dezsö J. Horváth, Dean, Tanna H. Schulich Chair in Strategic Management, and Professor of Policy; Ph.D., Umeå (Sweden).

Accounting

Marcia Annisette, Associate Professor; Ph.D., Manchester (England).
Thomas H. Beechy, Professor Emeritus; D.B.A., Washington (St. Louis); CPA.
Kathryn Bewley, Associate Professor; Ph.D., Waterloo; CA.
Janne Chung, Associate Professor; Ph.D., Edith Cowan (Australia).
Cameron Graham, Associate Professor; Ph.D., Calgary.
Sylvia Hsingwen Hsu, Assistant Professor; Ph.D., Wisconsin–Madison.
Amin Mawani, Associate Professor; Ph.D., Waterloo.
Dean Neu, Professor; Ph.D., Queen's at Kingston; CA.
Sandy Qian Qu, Assistant Professor; Ph.D., Alberta.
Alan J. Richardson, Professor; Ph.D., Queen's at Kingston; CGA, FCGA.
Linda Thorne, Associate Professor; Ph.D., McGill; CA.
Viswanath Umashanker Trivedi, Associate Professor; Ph.D., Arizona.

Economics

A. Bhanich Supapol, Associate Professor; Ph.D., Carleton (Ottawa).
Irene Henriques, Associate Professor; Ph.D., Queen's at Kingston.
Fred Lazar, Associate Professor; Ph.D., Harvard.
Perry A. Sadorsky, Associate Professor; Ph.D., Queen's at Kingston.
John N. Smithin, Professor; Ph.D., McMaster.
Bernard M. Wolf, Professor Emeritus; Ph.D., Yale.

Finance

Kee-Hong Bae, Professor; Ph.D., Ohio State.
Melanie Cao, Associate Professor; Ph.D., Toronto.
Archishman Chakraborty, Associate Professor; Ph.D., Princeton.
Ming Dong, Associate Professor; Ph.D., Ohio.
Mark Kamstra, Associate Professor; Ph.D., California, San Diego.
Nadia Massoud, Associate Professor; Ph.D., Queen's at Kingston.
Elizabeth M. Maynes, Associate Professor; Ph.D., Queen's at Kingston.
Moshe Arye Milevsky, Associate Professor; Ph.D., York.
Debarshi Nandy, Assistant Professor; Ph.D., Boston College.
Eliezer Prisman, Professor and Nigel Martin Chair in Finance; D.Sc., Technion (Israel).
Gordon S. Roberts, Professor and CIBC Professor of Financial Services; Ph.D., Boston College.
Pauline M. Shum, Associate Professor; Ph.D., Toronto.
Yisong Sam Tian, Associate Professor; Ph.D., York.

Marketing

Russell Belk, Professor and Kraft Foods Canada Chair in Marketing; Ph.D., Minnesota.
Samuel K. Bonsu, Associate Professor; Ph.D., Rhode Island.
Alexandra Campbell, Associate Professor; Ph.D., Toronto.
Peter Darke, Associate Professor; Ph.D., Toronto.
Eileen Fischer, Professor and Anne and Max Tanenbaum Chair in Entrepreneurship and Family Enterprise; Ph.D., Queen's at Kingston.
Brenda Gainer, Associate Professor and Royal Bank Professor of Nonprofit Management; Ph.D., York.
Markus Giesler, Assistant Professor; Ph.D., Witten/Herdecke (Germany).
Ashwin Joshi, Associate Professor; Ph.D., Queen's at Kingston.
Robert Kozinets, Associate Professor; Ph.D., Queen's at Kingston.
Alan Middleton, Assistant Professor; Ph.D., York.
Yigang Pan, Professor; Ph.D., Columbia.
Marshall D. Rice, Associate Professor; Ph.D., Illinois.
Ajay K. Sirsi, Associate Professor; Ph.D., Arizona.
Donald N. Thompson, Professor Emeritus; Ph.D., Berkeley.
Detlev Zwick, Associate Professor; Ph.D., Rhode Island.

Operations Management and Information Systems

Markus Biehl, Associate Professor; Ph.D., Georgia Tech.
John Buzacott, Professor Emeritus; Ph.D., Birmingham (England).
Wade D. Cook, Professor and Gordon Charlton Shaw Professor of Management Science; Ph.D., Dalhousie.
Richard H. Irving, Associate Professor; Ph.D., Waterloo.
David Johnston, Associate Professor; Ph.D., Western Ontario.
Henry Kim, Associate Professor; Ph.D., Toronto.
Mehmet Murat Kristal, Assistant Professor; Ph.D., North Carolina.
Moran Levesque, Associate Professor; Ph.D., British Columbia.
Ronald J. McClean, Assistant Professor; Ph.D., Waterloo.
Dorit Nevo, Associate Professor; Ph.D., British Columbia.
Mark Pagell, Associate Professor; Ph.D., Michigan.
Danièle Thomassin-Singh, Assistant Professor; Ph.D., Case Western Reserve.
Peter Tryfos, Professor Emeritus; Ph.D., Berkeley.
Michael Wade, Associate Professor; Ph.D., Western Ontario.
J. Scott Yeomans, Associate Professor; Ph.D., McMaster.

Organizational Behavior and Industrial Relations

Chris Bell, Associate Professor; Ph.D., Duke.
Patricia Bradshaw, Associate Professor; Ph.D., York.
Ronald J. Burke, Professor Emeritus; Ph.D., Michigan.
André deCarufel, Associate Professor; Ph.D., North Carolina.
David E. Dimick, Associate Professor and Associate Dean, Academic; Ph.D., Minnesota.
Ingo Holzinger, Assistant Professor; Ph.D., Wisconsin–Madison.
Rekha Karambayya, Associate Professor; Ph.D., Northwestern.
Gareth Morgan, Distinguished Research Professor; Ph.D., Lancaster (England).
Christine Oliver, Professor and Henry J. Knowles Chair in Organizational Strategy; Ph.D., Toronto.
Hazel Rosin, Associate Professor; Ph.D., Yale.
Mary Waller, Associate Professor; Ph.D., Texas at Austin.
Eleanor Westney, Professor and Scotiabank Professor in International Business; Ph.D., Princeton.
Lorna Wright, Associate Professor; Ph.D., Western Ontario.

Policy/Strategic Management

Jean Adams, Assistant Professor; Ph.D., York.
Preet Aulakh, Professor and Pierre Lassonde Chair in International Business; Ph.D., Texas at Austin.
Ellen Auster, Professor; Ph.D., Cornell.
Wesley Cragg, Professor Emeritus; D.Phil., Oxford.
Andrew Crane, Professor and George R. Gardiner Professor of Business Ethics; Ph.D., Nottingham (England).
James L. Darroch, Associate Professor; Ph.D., York.
Yuval Deutsch, Associate Professor; Ph.D., British Columbia.
Burkard Eberlein, Assistant Professor; Ph.D., Konstanz (Germany).
Moshe Farjoun, Associate Professor; Ph.D., Northwestern.
James M. Gillies, Professor Emeritus; Ph.D., Indiana.
Dezsö J. Horváth, Dean and Tanna H. Schulich Chair in Strategic Management; Ph.D., Umeå (Sweden).
Bryan Husted, Professor and Erivan K. Haub Chair in Business and Sustainability; Ph.D., Berkeley.
Matthias Kipping, Professor; D.Phil., München (Germany).
Stan Li, Associate Professor; Ph.D., Toronto.
H. Ian Macdonald, Professor Emeritus and President Emeritus; B.Phil., Oxford.
Anoop Madhok, Professor; Ph.D., McGill.
Dirk Matten, Professor and Hewlett-Packard Chair in Corporate Social Responsibility; Dr.rer.pol., Dr.habil., Düsseldorf (Germany).
Charles J. McMillan, Professor; Ph.D., Bradford (England).
Theodore Peridis, Associate Professor; Ph.D., NYU.
Willow Sheremata, Associate Professor; Ph.D., NYU.
Justin Tan, Professor and Newmont Mining Chair in Business Strategy; Ph.D., Virginia Tech.
Stephen Weiss, Associate Professor; Ph.D., Pennsylvania.
Tom Wesson, Associate Professor; Ph.D., Harvard.
Brenda J. Zimmerman, Associate Professor; Ph.D., York; CA, Ontario.

The Schulich School of Business and Executive Learning Centre.

Section 2
Accounting and Finance

his section contains a directory of institutions offering graduate work in accounting and finance. Additional information about programs listed in the directory but not augmented by an in-depth entry may be obtained by writing directly to the dean of a graduate school or chair of a department at the address given in the directory.

For programs offering related work, see also in this book *Business Administration and Management, International Business,* and *Nonprofit Management.* In the other guides in this series:

Graduate Programs in the Humanities, Arts & Social Sciences
See *Economics* and *Family and Consumer Sciences (Consumer Economics)*

Graduate Programs in the Physical Sciences, Mathematics, Agricultural Sciences, the Environment & Natural Resources
See *Mathematical Sciences*

Graduate Programs in Engineering & Applied Sciences
See *Computer Science and Information Technology*

CONTENTS

Program Directories

Displays and Close-Ups

See:

Accounting

Abilene Christian University, Graduate School, College of Business Administration, Abilene, TX 79699-9100. Offers M Acc. *Accreditation:* AACSB. Part-time programs available. *Faculty:* 7 part-time/adjunct (0 women). *Students:* 26 full-time (10 women), 3 part-time (2 women); includes 1 minority (Hispanic/Latino), 7 international. 28 applicants, 61% accepted, 16 enrolled. In 2011, 25 master's awarded. *Entrance requirements:* For master's, GMAT. Additional exam requirements/recommendations for international students: Required—TOEFL (minimum score 550 paper-based; 213 computer-based; 80 iBT), IELTS (minimum score 6). *Application deadline:* For fall admission, 4/1 priority date for domestic students; for spring admission, 11/1 for domestic students. Applications are processed on a rolling basis. Application fee: $50. Electronic applications accepted. *Expenses: Tuition:* Full-time $14,168; part-time $787 per hour. *Required fees:* $82 per hour. $10 per term. *Financial support:* In 2011–12, 15 students received support. Federal Work-Study and scholarships/grants available. Support available to part-time students. Financial award application deadline: 4/1; financial award applicants required to submit FAFSA. *Faculty research:* Organizational structure, financial management, cost accounting, unit analysis management. *Unit head:* Bill Fowler, Department Chair, 325-674-2080, Fax: 325-674-2564, E-mail: bill.fowler@coba.acu.edu. *Application contact:* David Pittman, Graduate Admissions Counselor, 325-674-2656, Fax: 325-674-6717, E-mail: gradinfo@acu.edu. Web site: http://www.acu.edu/academics/coba/index.html.

Adelphi University, Robert B. Willumstad School of Business, Graduate Opportunity for Accelerated Learning MBA Program, Garden City, NY 11530-0701. Offers accounting (MBA); finance (MBA). *Accreditation:* AACSB. Part-time and evening/weekend programs available. *Students:* 13 full-time (7 women), 23 part-time (7 women); includes 17 minority (7 Black or African American, non-Hispanic/Latino; 6 Asian, non-Hispanic/Latino; 4 Hispanic/Latino), 2 international. Average age 41. In 2011, 14 master's awarded. *Entrance requirements:* For master's, GMAT, 2 letters of recommendation, four years managerial experience, letter of sponsorship from current place of employment, resume. Additional exam requirements/recommendations for international students: Required—TOEFL (minimum score 550 paper-based; 213 computer-based; 80 iBT). *Application deadline:* For fall admission, 4/1 for international students; for spring admission, 11/1 for international students. Applications are processed on a rolling basis. Application fee: $50. Electronic applications accepted. *Expenses: Tuition:* Full-time $29,600; part-time $930 per credit. *Required fees:* $1100. *Financial support:* Research assistantships with full and partial tuition reimbursements, career-related internships or fieldwork, Federal Work-Study, institutionally sponsored loans, scholarships/grants, and unspecified assistantships available. Financial award application deadline: 3/1; financial award applicants required to submit FAFSA. *Faculty research:* Capital market, executive compensation, business ethics, classical value theory, labor economics. *Unit head:* Rakesh Gupta, Chairperson, 516-877-4670, Fax: 516-877-4607, E-mail: gradbusinquiries@adelphi.edu. *Application contact:* Christine Murphy, Director of Admissions, 516-877-3050, Fax: 516-877-3039, E-mail: graduateadmissions@adelphi.edu.

Alabama State University, Department of Accounting and Finance, Montgomery, AL 36101-0271. Offers accountancy (M Acc). *Faculty:* 3 full-time (1 woman). *Students:* 9 full-time (6 women), 10 part-time (6 women); includes 17 minority (16 Black or African American, non-Hispanic/Latino; 1 Two or more races, non-Hispanic/Latino), 2 international. Average age 26. 20 applicants, 35% accepted, 3 enrolled. In 2011, 8 master's awarded. *Entrance requirements:* For master's, GMAT, graduate writing competency test. Additional exam requirements/recommendations for international students: Required—TOEFL (minimum score 500 paper-based; 173 computer-based). *Application deadline:* For fall admission, 7/15 for domestic students; for spring admission, 12/15 for domestic students. Applications are processed on a rolling basis. Application fee: $10. *Financial support:* In 2011–12, 2 research assistantships (averaging $9,450 per year) were awarded. *Unit head:* Dr. Jean Crawford, Chair, 334-229-4134, Fax: 334-229-4870, E-mail: jcrawford@asunet.alasu.edu. *Application contact:* Dr. Doris Screws, Dean of Graduate Studies, 334-229-4274, Fax: 334-229-4928, E-mail: dscrews@alasu.edu. Web site: http://www.alasu.edu/academics/colleges—departments/college-of-business-administration/college-of-business-academics/accounting—finance/index.aspx.

Albany State University, College of Business, Albany, GA 31705-2717. Offers accounting (MBA); general (MBA); healthcare (MBA). *Accreditation:* ACBSP. Part-time and evening/weekend programs available. *Faculty:* 3 full-time (0 women), 1 part-time/adjunct (0 women). *Students:* 4 full-time (2 women), 22 part-time (16 women); includes 24 minority (all Black or African American, non-Hispanic/Latino), 1 international. Average age 33. 22 applicants, 77% accepted, 9 enrolled. In 2011, 5 master's awarded. *Degree requirements:* For master's, comprehensive exam, internship, 3 hours of physical education. *Entrance requirements:* For master's, GMAT (minimum score of 450)/GRE (minimum score of 800) for those without earned master's degree or higher, minimum undergraduate GPA of 2.5, 2 letters of reference, official transcript, pre-entrance medical record and certificate of immunization. *Application deadline:* For fall admission, 6/1 for domestic students, 5/1 for international students; for spring admission, 11/1 for domestic students, 10/1 for international students. Applications are processed on a rolling basis. Application fee: $20. Electronic applications accepted. *Expenses:* Tuition, state resident: full-time $3204; part-time $178 per credit hour. Tuition, nonresident: full-time $12,816; part-time $712 per credit hour. *Required fees:* $379 per semester. *Financial support:* Application deadline: 4/15; applicants required to submit FAFSA. *Faculty research:* Diversity issues, ancestry, understanding finance through use of technology. *Unit head:* Dr. Fidelis Ikem, Interim Dean, 229-430-7009, Fax: 229-430-5119, E-mail: fidelis.ikem@asurams.edu. *Application contact:* Jeffrey Pierce, II, Graduate Counselor, 229-430-4646, Fax: 229-430-4105, E-mail: jeffrey.pierce@asurams.edu. Web site: http://asu-sacs.asurams.edu/ASUCatalog/Graduate/index.html.

American InterContinental University Buckhead Campus, Program in Business Administration, Atlanta, GA 30326-1016. Offers accounting and finance (MBA); management (MBA); marketing (MBA). Evening/weekend programs available. Postbaccalaureate distance learning degree programs offered. *Entrance requirements:* For master's, minimum cumulative undergraduate GPA of 2.0. Additional exam requirements/recommendations for international students: Required—TOEFL (minimum score 530 paper-based; 230 computer-based). Electronic applications accepted. *Faculty research:* Leadership management, international advertising.

American InterContinental University Online, Program in Business Administration, Hoffman Estates, IL 60192. Offers accounting and finance (MBA); finance (MBA); healthcare management (MBA); human resource management (MBA); international business (MBA); management (MBA); marketing (MBA); operations management (MBA); organizational psychology and development (MBA); project management (MBA). Evening/weekend programs available. Postbaccalaureate distance learning degree programs offered (no on-campus study). *Entrance requirements:* Additional exam requirements/recommendations for international students: Required—TOEFL (minimum score 550 paper-based; 213 computer-based). Electronic applications accepted.

American InterContinental University South Florida, Program in International Business, Weston, FL 33326. Offers accounting and finance (MBA); human resource management (MBA); management (MBA); marketing (MBA). Part-time and evening/weekend programs available. Postbaccalaureate distance learning degree programs offered. Electronic applications accepted.

American International College, School of Business Administration, MBA Program, Springfield, MA 01109-3189. Offers accounting (MBA); corporate/public communication (MBA); finance (MBA); general business (MBA); hospitality, hotel and service management (MBA); international business (MBA); international business practice (MBA); management (MBA); management information systems (MBA); marketing (MBA). International business practice program developed in cooperation with the Mountbatten Institute.

American International College, School of Business Administration, Program in Accounting and Taxation, Springfield, MA 01109-3189. Offers MSAT.

American Public University System, AMU/APU Graduate Programs, Charles Town, WV 25414. Offers accounting (MBA, MS); administration and supervision (M Ed); criminal justice (MA); emergency and disaster management (MA); entrepreneurship (MBA); environmental policy and management (MS), including environmental planning, environmental sustainability, fish and wildlife management, general (MA, MS), global environmental management; finance (MBA); general (MBA); global business management (MBA); guidance and counseling (M Ed); history (MA), including American history, ancient and classical history, European history, global history, military and diplomatic history, public history; homeland security (MA); homeland security resource allocation (MBA); humanities (MA); information technology (MS), including digital forensics, enterprise software development, information assurance and security, IT project management; information technology management (MBA); intelligence studies (MA), including criminal intelligence, general (MA, MS), homeland security, intelligence analysis, intelligence collection, intelligence operations, terrorism studies; international relations and conflict resolution (MA), including comparative and security issues, conflict resolution, international and transnational security issues, peacekeeping; legal studies (MA); management (MA), including defense management, general (MA, MS), human resource management, organizational leadership, public administration, reverse logistics, strategic consulting; marketing (MBA); military history (MA), including American military history, American revolution, civil war, war since 1946, World War II; military studies (MA), including air warfare, asymmetrical warfare, joint warfare, land warfare, naval warfare, strategic leadership; national security studies (MA), including general (MA, MS), homeland security, regional security studies, security and intelligence analysis, terrorism studies; nonprofit management (MBA); political science (MA), including American politics and government, comparative government and development, public policy; psychology (MA); public administration (MA, MPA), including disaster management (MPA), environmental policy (MA), health policy (MPA), human resources (MPA), national security (MPA), organizational management (MPA), security management (MPA); public health (MA, MPH), including emergency management (MPH), environmental health (MPH), public administration (MA); reverse logistics management (MA); security management (MA); space studies (MS), including aerospace science, planetary science; sports and health sciences (MS); sports management (MS), including coaching theory and strategy, sports administration; teaching (M Ed), including curriculum and instruction for elementary teachers, elementary, elementary reading, English language learners, instructional leadership, online learning, secondary social sciences, special education; transportation and logistics management (MA), including maritime engineering management. Programs offered via distance learning only. Part-time and evening/weekend programs available. Postbaccalaureate distance learning degree programs offered (no on-campus study). *Faculty:* 445 full-time (241 women), 1,360 part-time/adjunct (617 women). *Students:* 688 full-time (338 women), 10,168 part-time (3,706 women); includes 3,130 minority (1,007 Black or African American, non-Hispanic/Latino; 103 American Indian or Alaska Native, non-Hispanic/Latino; 825 Asian, non-Hispanic/Latino; 810 Hispanic/Latino; 51 Native Hawaiian or other Pacific Islander, non-Hispanic/Latino; 334 Two or more races, non-Hispanic/Latino), 134 international. Average age 35. In 2011, 2,386 master's awarded. *Degree requirements:* For master's, comprehensive exam or practicum. *Entrance requirements:* For master's, official transcript showing earned bachelor's degree from institution accredited by recognized accrediting body. Additional exam requirements/recommendations for international students: Required—TOEFL (minimum score 550 paper-based; 213 computer-based), IELTS (minimum score 6.5). *Application deadline:* Applications are processed on a rolling basis. Application fee: $0. Electronic applications accepted. *Expenses: Tuition:* Part-time $325 per credit hour. *Financial support:* Applicants required to submit FAFSA. *Faculty research:* Military history, criminal justice, management performance, national security. *Unit head:* Dr. Karan Powell, Executive Vice President and Provost, 877-468-6268, Fax: 304-724-3780. *Application contact:* Terry Grant, Vice President of Enrollment Management, 877-468-6268, Fax: 304-724-3780, E-mail: info@apus.edu. Web site: http://www.apus.edu.

American University, Kogod School of Business, Department of Accounting, Program in Accounting, Washington, DC 20016-8044. Offers MS. Part-time and evening/weekend programs available. *Students:* 34 full-time (19 women), 39 part-time (14 women); includes 23 minority (8 Black or African American, non-Hispanic/Latino; 11 Asian, non-Hispanic/Latino; 4 Hispanic/Latino), 21 international. Average age 28. 153 applicants, 46% accepted, 32 enrolled. In 2011, 45 master's awarded. *Entrance requirements:* For master's, GMAT, resume, personal statement, interview. Additional exam requirements/recommendations for international students: Required—TOEFL. *Application deadline:* For fall admission, 2/1 priority date for domestic students; for spring admission, 10/1 priority date for domestic students. Applications are processed on a rolling basis. Application fee: $100. *Expenses:* Contact institution. *Financial support:* Fellowships, research assistantships, career-related internships or fieldwork, Federal Work-Study, and institutionally sponsored loans available. Support available to part-time students. Financial award application deadline: 2/1. *Unit head:* Dr. Ajay Adhikari, Chair, 202-885-1993, Fax: 202-885-1992, E-mail: aadhika@american.edu. *Application contact:* Shannon Demko, Associate Director of Graduate Admissions, 202-885-1994, Fax: 202-885-1108, E-mail: demko@american.edu. Web site: http://www.american.edu/kogod/.

American University, Kogod School of Business, Master of Business Administration Program, Washington, DC 20016-8044. Offers accounting (MBA); consulting (MBA), including business systems consulting, management consulting; entrepreneurship (MBA); entrepreneurship (Certificate); finance (MBA); global emerging markets (MBA); leadership and strategic human capital management (MBA); marketing (MBA); real estate (MBA); MBA/JD; MBA/LL M; MBA/MA. Part-time and evening/weekend programs available. *Faculty:* 13 full-time (6 women). *Students:* 96 full-time (43 women), 104 part-time (35 women); includes 49 minority (14 Black or African American, non-Hispanic/Latino; 16 Asian, non-Hispanic/Latino; 16 Hispanic/Latino; 1 Native Hawaiian or other Pacific Islander, non-Hispanic/Latino; 2 Two or more races, non-Hispanic/Latino), 22 international. Average age 29. 340 applicants, 52% accepted, 52 enrolled. In 2011, 124 master's awarded. *Entrance requirements:* For master's, GMAT, resume, personal statement, interview. Additional exam requirements/recommendations for international students: Required—TOEFL. *Application deadline:* For fall admission, 2/1 priority date for domestic students; for spring admission, 10/1 priority date for domestic students. Applications are processed on a rolling basis. Application fee: $100. *Expenses:* Contact institution. *Financial support:* In 2011–12, 19 students received support. Fellowships, research assistantships with partial tuition reimbursements available, career-related internships or fieldwork, Federal Work-Study, and institutionally sponsored loans available. Support available to part-time students. Financial award application deadline: 2/1. *Faculty research:* Information technology, decision-aiding methodology, negotiation. *Unit head:* Dr. Stevan R. Holmberg, Chair, 202-885-1921, Fax: 202-885-1916, E-mail: sholmbe@american.edu. *Application contact:* Shannon Demko, Director of Admissions, 202-885-1968, Fax: 202-885-1078, E-mail: demko@american.edu. Web site: http://www.american.edu/kogod/.

Anderson University, Falls School of Business, Anderson, IN 46012-3495. Offers accountancy (MA); business administration (MBA, DBA). *Accreditation:* ACBSP.

Andrews University, School of Graduate Studies, School of Business, Graduate Programs in Business, Berrien Springs, MI 49104. Offers MBA, MSA. *Students:* 12 full-time (2 women), 18 part-time (8 women); includes 8 minority (5 Black or African American, non-Hispanic/Latino; 1 Asian, non-Hispanic/Latino; 2 Hispanic/Latino), 10 international. Average age 30. 71 applicants, 41% accepted, 14 enrolled. In 2011, 6 master's awarded. *Entrance requirements:* For master's, GMAT. Additional exam requirements/recommendations for international students: Required—TOEFL (minimum score 550 paper-based). Application fee: $40. *Unit head:* Dr. Leonard K. Gashugi, Chair, 769-471-3429, E-mail: gashugi@andrews.edu. *Application contact:* Carolyn Hurst, Supervisor of Graduate Admission, 800-253-2874, Fax: 269-471-6321, E-mail: graduate@andrews.edu.

Angelo State University, College of Graduate Studies, College of Business, Department of Accounting, Economics, and Finance, San Angelo, TX 76909. Offers accounting (MBA); professional accountancy (MPAC). Part-time and evening/weekend programs available. *Faculty:* 4 full-time (0 women), 1 part-time/adjunct (0 women). *Students:* 11 full-time (7 women), 6 part-time (4 women); includes 3 minority (all Hispanic/Latino). Average age 24. 9 applicants, 33% accepted, 3 enrolled. In 2011, 11 master's awarded. *Entrance requirements:* For master's, GMAT or GRE. Additional exam requirements/recommendations for international students: Required—TOEFL or IELTS. *Application deadline:* For fall admission, 7/15 priority date for domestic students, 6/10 for international students; for spring admission, 12/1 priority date for domestic students, 11/1 for international students. Applications are processed on a rolling basis. Application fee: $40 ($50 for international students). Electronic applications accepted. *Financial support:* In 2011–12, 15 students received support. Career-related internships or fieldwork, Federal Work-Study, and scholarships/grants available. Support available to part-time students. Financial award application deadline: 3/1; financial award applicants required to submit FAFSA. *Unit head:* Dr. Thomas A. Bankston, Department Head, 325-942-2046 Ext. 248, Fax: 325-942-2285, E-mail: thomas.bankston@angelo.edu. *Application contact:* Dr. Norman A. Sunderman, Graduate Advisor, 325-942-2046 Ext. 245, E-mail: norman.sunderman@angelo.edu. Web site: http://www.angelo.edu/dept/aef/.

Appalachian State University, Cratis D. Williams Graduate School, Department of Accounting, Boone, NC 28608. Offers taxation (MS). Part-time programs available. *Faculty:* 10 full-time (4 women), 1 (woman) part-time/adjunct. *Students:* 53 full-time (20 women), 9 part-time (7 women); includes 2 minority (both Asian, non-Hispanic/Latino), 2 international. 79 applicants, 84% accepted, 41 enrolled. In 2011, 52 master's awarded. *Degree requirements:* For master's, comprehensive exam, thesis optional. *Entrance requirements:* For master's, GMAT, 3 letters of recommendation. Additional exam requirements/recommendations for international students: Required—TOEFL (minimum score 550 paper-based; 230 computer-based; 79 iBT), IELTS (minimum score 6.5). *Application deadline:* For fall admission, 3/15 priority date for domestic students, 2/1 for international students; for spring admission, 11/1 for domestic students, 7/1 for international students. Applications are processed on a rolling basis. Application fee: $55. Electronic applications accepted. *Expenses:* Tuition, state resident: full-time $4040; part-time $180 per semester hour. Tuition, nonresident: full-time $15,900; part-time $760 per semester hour. *Required fees:* $2500; $20 per semester hour. Tuition and fees vary according to campus/location. *Financial support:* In 2011–12, 17 research assistantships (averaging $4,000 per year) were awarded; fellowships, teaching assistantships, Federal Work-Study, scholarships/grants, and unspecified assistantships also available. Financial award application deadline: 4/1; financial award applicants required to submit FAFSA. *Faculty research:* Audit assurance risk, state taxation, financial accounting inconsistencies, management information systems, charitable contribution taxation. *Unit head:* Dr. Timothy Forsyth, Chairman, 828-262-2036, Fax: 828-262-6640. *Application contact:* Dr. William Pollard, Director, 828-262-6232, Fax: 828-262-6640, E-mail: pollardwb@appstate.edu. Web site: http://www.acc.appstate.edu.

Argosy University, Atlanta, College of Business, Atlanta, GA 30328. Offers accounting (DBA); corporate compliance (MBA); customized professional concentration (MBA, DBA); finance (MBA); healthcare administration (MBA); information systems (DBA); information systems management (MBA); international business (MBA, DBA); management (MBA, MSM, DBA); marketing (MBA, DBA).

See Close-Up on page 179.

Argosy University, Chicago, College of Business, Chicago, IL 60601. Offers accounting (DBA); customized professional concentration (MBA, DBA); finance (MBA); fraud examination (MBA); global business sustainability (DBA); healthcare administration (MBA); information systems (DBA); information systems management (MBA); international business (MBA, DBA); management (MBA, MSM, DBA); marketing (MBA, DBA); organizational leadership (Ed D); public administration (MBA); sustainable management (MBA). Postbaccalaureate distance learning degree programs offered (minimal on-campus study).

See Close-Up on page 181.

Argosy University, Dallas, College of Business, Farmers Branch, TX 75244. Offers accounting (DBA, AGC); corporate compliance (MBA, Graduate Certificate); customized professional concentration (MBA); finance (MBA, Graduate Certificate); fraud examination (MBA, Graduate Certificate); global business sustainability (DBA, AGC); healthcare administration (Graduate Certificate); healthcare management (MBA); information systems (MBA, DBA, AGC); information systems management (Graduate Certificate); international business (MBA, DBA, AGC, Graduate Certificate); management (MBA, DBA, AGC, Graduate Certificate); marketing (MBA, DBA, AGC, Graduate Certificate); public administration (MBA, Graduate Certificate); sustainable management (MBA, Graduate Certificate).

See Close-Up on page 183.

Argosy University, Denver, College of Business, Denver, CO 80231. Offers accounting (DBA); corporate compliance (MBA); customized professional concentration (MBA, DBA); finance (MBA); fraud examination (MBA); global business sustainability (DBA); healthcare administration (MBA); information systems (DBA); information systems management (MBA); international business (MBA, DBA); management (MBA, MSM, DBA); marketing (MBA, DBA); organizational leadership (Ed D); public administration (MBA); sustainable management (MBA).

See Close-Up on page 185.

Argosy University, Hawai`i, College of Business, Honolulu, HI 96813. Offers accounting (DBA); corporate compliance (MBA); customized professional concentration (MBA, DBA); finance (MBA, Certificate); fraud examination (MBA); global business sustainability (DBA); healthcare administration (MBA, Certificate); information systems (DBA); information systems management (MBA, Certificate); international business (MBA, DBA, Certificate); management (MBA, MSM, DBA); marketing (MBA, DBA, Certificate); organizational leadership (Ed D); public administration (MBA); sustainable management (MBA).

See Close-Up on page 187.

Argosy University, Inland Empire, College of Business, San Bernardino, CA 92408. Offers accounting (DBA); corporate compliance (MBA); customized professional concentration (MBA, DBA); finance (MBA); fraud examination (MBA); global business sustainability (DBA); healthcare administration (MBA); information systems (DBA); information systems management (MBA); international business (MBA, DBA); management (MBA, MSM, DBA); marketing (MBA, DBA); organizational leadership (Ed D); public administration (MBA); sustainable management (MBA).

See Close-Up on page 189.

Argosy University, Los Angeles, College of Business, Santa Monica, CA 90045. Offers accounting (DBA); corporate compliance (MBA); customized professional concentration (MBA, DBA); finance (MBA); fraud examination (MBA); global business sustainability (DBA); healthcare administration (MBA); information systems (DBA); information systems management (MBA); international business (MBA, DBA); management (MBA, MSM, DBA); marketing (MBA, DBA); organizational leadership (Ed D); public administration (MBA); sustainable management (MBA).

See Close-Up on page 191.

Argosy University, Nashville, College of Business, Nashville, TN 37214. Offers accounting (DBA); customized professional concentration (MBA, DBA); finance (MBA); healthcare administration (MBA); information systems (MBA, DBA); international business (MBA, DBA); management (MBA, MSM, DBA); marketing (MBA, DBA).

See Close-Up on page 193.

Argosy University, Orange County, College of Business, Orange, CA 92868. Offers accounting (DBA, Adv C); corporate compliance (MBA); customized professional concentration (MBA, DBA); finance (MBA, Certificate); fraud examination (MBA); global business sustainability (DBA); healthcare administration (MBA, Certificate); information systems (DBA, Adv C, Certificate); information systems management (MBA); international business (MBA, DBA, Adv C, Certificate); management (MBA, MSM, DBA, Adv C); marketing (MBA, DBA, Adv C, Certificate); organizational leadership (Ed D); public administration (MBA, Certificate); sustainable management (MBA).

See Close-Up on page 195.

Argosy University, Phoenix, College of Business, Phoenix, AZ 85021. Offers accounting (DBA); corporate compliance (MBA); customized professional concentration (MBA, DBA); finance (MBA); fraud examination (MBA); global business sustainability (DBA); healthcare administration (MBA); information systems (DBA); information systems management (MBA); international business (MBA, DBA); management (MBA, DBA); marketing (MBA, DBA); public administration (MBA); sustainable management (MBA).

See Close-Up on page 197.

Argosy University, Salt Lake City, College of Business, Draper, UT 84020. Offers accounting (DBA); corporate compliance (MBA); customized professional concentration (MBA, DBA); finance (MBA); fraud examination (MBA); global business sustainability (DBA); healthcare administration (MBA); information systems (DBA); information systems management (MBA); international business (MBA, DBA); management (MBA, DBA); marketing (MBA, DBA); public administration (MBA); sustainable management (MBA).

See Close-Up on page 199.

Argosy University, San Diego, College of Business, San Diego, CA 92108. Offers accounting (DBA); corporate compliance (MBA); customized professional concentration (MBA, DBA); finance (MBA); fraud examination (MBA); global business sustainability (DBA); information systems (DBA); information systems management (MBA); international business (MBA, DBA); management (MBA, MSM, DBA); marketing (MBA, DBA); organizational leadership (Ed D); public administration (MBA).

See Close-Up on page 201.

Argosy University, San Francisco Bay Area, College of Business, Alameda, CA 94501. Offers accounting (DBA); corporate compliance (MBA); customized professional concentration (MBA, DBA); finance (MBA); fraud examination (MBA); global business sustainability (DBA); healthcare administration (MBA); information systems (DBA); information systems management (MBA); international business (MBA, DBA); management (MBA, MSM, DBA); marketing (MBA, DBA); organizational leadership (Ed D); public administration (MBA); sustainable management (MBA).

See Close-Up on page 203.

Argosy University, Sarasota, College of Business, Sarasota, FL 34235. Offers accounting (DBA, Adv C); corporate compliance (MBA, DBA, Certificate); customized professional concentration (MBA, DBA); finance (MBA, Certificate); fraud examination (MBA, Certificate); global business sustainability (DBA, Adv C); healthcare administration (MBA, Certificate); information systems (DBA, Adv C, Certificate); information systems management (MBA); international business (MBA, DBA, Adv C, Certificate); management (MBA, MSM, DBA, Adv C, Certificate); marketing (MBA, DBA, Adv C, Certificate); organizational leadership (Ed D); public administration (MBA, Certificate); sustainable management (MBA, Certificate).

See Close-Up on page 205.

Argosy University, Schaumburg, College of Business, Schaumburg, IL 60173-5403. Offers accounting (DBA, Adv C); customized professional concentration (MBA, DBA); finance (MBA, Certificate); fraud examination (MBA); global business sustainability (DBA); healthcare administration (MBA, Certificate); information systems (DBA, Adv C,

Certificate); information systems management (MBA); international business (MBA, DBA, Adv C, Certificate); management (MBA, MSM, DBA, Adv C, Certificate); marketing (MBA, DBA, Adv C, Certificate); organizational leadership (Ed D); public administration (MBA); sustainable management (MBA).

See Close-Up on page 207.

Argosy University, Seattle, College of Business, Seattle, WA 98121. Offers accounting (DBA); corporate compliance (MBA); customized professional concentration (MBA, DBA); finance (MBA); fraud examination (MBA); global business sustainability (DBA); healthcare administration (MBA); information systems (DBA); information systems management (MBA); international business (MBA, DBA); management (MBA, MSM, DBA); marketing (MBA, DBA); organizational leadership (Ed D); public administration (MBA); sustainable management (MBA).

See Close-Up on page 209.

Argosy University, Tampa, College of Business, Tampa, FL 33607. Offers accounting (DBA); corporate compliance (MBA); customized professional concentration (MBA, DBA); finance (MBA); fraud examination (MBA); global business sustainability (DBA); healthcare administration (MBA); information systems (DBA); information systems management (MBA); international business (MBA, DBA); management (MBA, MSM, DBA); marketing (MBA, DBA); organizational leadership (Ed D); public administration (MBA); sustainable management (MBA).

See Close-Up on page 211.

Argosy University, Twin Cities, College of Business, Eagan, MN 55121. Offers accounting (DBA); customized professional concentration (MBA, DBA); finance (MBA); fraud examination (MBA); global business sustainability (DBA); healthcare administration (MBA); information systems (DBA); information systems management (MBA); international business (MBA, DBA); management (MBA, MSM, DBA); marketing (MBA, DBA); organizational leadership (Ed D); public administration (MBA); sustainable management (MBA).

See Close-Up on page 213.

Argosy University, Washington DC, College of Business, Arlington, VA 22209. Offers accounting (DBA); customized professional concentration (MBA, DBA); finance (MBA); fraud examination (MBA); global business sustainability (DBA); healthcare administration (MBA); information systems (DBA); information systems management (MBA); international business (MBA, DBA, Certificate); management (MBA, MSM, DBA); marketing (MBA, DBA, Certificate); organizational leadership (Ed D); public administration (MBA); sustainable management (MBA).

See Close-Up on page 215.

Arizona State University, W. P. Carey School of Business, Program in Business Administration, Tempe, AZ 85287-4906. Offers accountancy (PhD); agribusiness (PhD); business administration (MBA); finance (PhD); financial management and markets (MBA); information management (MBA); information systems (PhD); management (PhD); marketing (PhD); strategic marketing and services leadership (MBA); supply chain financial management (MBA); supply chain management (MBA, PhD); JD/MBA; MBA/M Acc; MBA/M Arch. *Accreditation:* AACSB. Part-time and evening/weekend programs available. Postbaccalaureate distance learning degree programs offered (minimal on-campus study). Terminal master's awarded for partial completion of doctoral program. *Degree requirements:* For master's, thesis or alternative, internship, interactive Program of Study (iPOS) submitted before completing 50 percent of required credit hours; for doctorate, comprehensive exam, thesis/dissertation, interactive Program of Study (iPOS) submitted before completing 50 percent of required credit hours. *Entrance requirements:* For master's, GMAT, minimum GPA of 3.0 in last 2 years of work leading to bachelor's degree, 2 letters of recommendation, professional resume, official transcripts, 3 essays; for doctorate, GMAT or GRE, minimum GPA of 3.0 in last 2 years of work leading to bachelor's degree, 3 letters of recommendation, resume, personal statement/essay. Additional exam requirements/recommendations for international students: Required—TOEFL (minimum score 550 paper-based; 213 computer-based; 80 iBT), IELTS (minimum score 6.5). Electronic applications accepted. *Expenses:* Contact institution.

Arizona State University, W. P. Carey School of Business, School of Accountancy, Tempe, AZ 85287-3606. Offers accountancy (M Acc, M Tax); business administration (accountancy) (PhD). *Accreditation:* AACSB. Part-time and evening/weekend programs available. *Degree requirements:* For master's, thesis optional, interactive Program of Study (iPOS) submitted before completing 50 percent of required credit hours. *Entrance requirements:* For master's, GMAT (waivers may apply for ASU accountancy undergraduates), minimum GPA of 3.0 in last 2 years of work leading to bachelor's degree, 2 letters of recommendation, professional resume, official transcripts, responses to 3 essay questions. Additional exam requirements/recommendations for international students: Required—TOEFL (minimum score 550 paper-based; 213 computer-based; 80 iBT), IELTS (minimum score 6.5). Electronic applications accepted. *Expenses:* Contact institution.

Arkansas State University, Graduate School, College of Business, Department of Accounting, Jonesboro, State University, AR 72467. Offers accountancy (M Acc). Part-time programs available. *Faculty:* 6 full-time (2 women). *Students:* 22 full-time (16 women), 11 part-time (6 women); includes 1 minority (Native Hawaiian or other Pacific Islander, non-Hispanic/Latino), 20 international. Average age 27. 22 applicants, 82% accepted, 11 enrolled. In 2011, 13 master's awarded. *Degree requirements:* For master's, comprehensive exam, thesis or alternative. *Entrance requirements:* For master's, GMAT, appropriate bachelor's degree, letters of reference, official transcript, immunization records. Additional exam requirements/recommendations for international students: Required—TOEFL (minimum score 550 paper-based; 253 computer-based; 79 iBT), IELTS (minimum score 6), Pearson Test of English Academic (minimum score 56). *Application deadline:* For fall admission, 7/1 for domestic and international students; for spring admission, 11/15 for domestic students, 11/14 for international students. Applications are processed on a rolling basis. Application fee: $30 ($40 for international students). Electronic applications accepted. *Expenses:* Contact institution. *Financial support:* In 2011–12, 3 students received support. Career-related internships or fieldwork, scholarships/grants, and unspecified assistantships available. Financial award application deadline: 7/1; financial award applicants required to submit FAFSA. *Unit head:* Dr. John Robertson, Chair, 870-972-3038, Fax: 870-972-3868, E-mail: jfrobert@astate.edu. *Application contact:* Dr. Andrew Sustich, Dean of the Graduate School, 870-972-3029, Fax: 870-972-3857, E-mail: sustich@astate.edu. Web site: http://www.astate.edu/a/business/departments/accounting/.

Assumption College, Graduate Studies, Department of Business Studies, Worcester, MA 01609-1296. Offers accounting (MBA); business administration (CAGS); finance/economics (MBA); general business (MBA); human resources (MBA); international business (MBA); management (MBA); marketing (MBA); nonprofit leadership (MBA). Part-time and evening/weekend programs available. *Faculty:* 4 full-time (0 women), 16 part-time/adjunct (4 women). *Students:* 8 full-time (5 women), 133 part-time (65 women); includes 18 minority (8 Black or African American, non-Hispanic/Latino; 1 American Indian or Alaska Native, non-Hispanic/Latino; 2 Asian, non-Hispanic/Latino; 7 Hispanic/Latino), 3 international. Average age 30. 100 applicants, 75% accepted, 52 enrolled. In 2011, 53 master's, 1 other advanced degree awarded. *Degree requirements:* For master's, thesis, capstone. *Entrance requirements:* For master's and CAGS, 3 letters of recommendation, resume, essay. Additional exam requirements/recommendations for international students: Required—TOEFL (minimum score 540 paper-based; 200 computer-based; 76 iBT), IELTS (minimum score 6). *Application deadline:* For fall admission, 10/1 for domestic and international students; for winter admission, 2/1 for domestic and international students; for spring admission, 4/1 for domestic and international students. Applications are processed on a rolling basis. Application fee: $30. Electronic applications accepted. *Expenses: Tuition:* Full-time $9414; part-time $523 per credit. *Required fees:* $20 per term. Full-time tuition and fees vary according to course load and program. *Financial support:* In 2011–12, 14 students received support. Scholarships/grants, tuition waivers (partial), and unspecified assistantships available. Financial award application deadline: 5/1; financial award applicants required to submit FAFSA. *Faculty research:* Workplace diversity, dynamics of team interaction, utilization of leased employees, experiential learning project on due diligence market for prostheses. *Unit head:* Michael Lewis, Director, 508-767-7372, Fax: 508-767-7252, E-mail: milewis@assumption.edu. *Application contact:* Laura Lawrence, Graduate Programs Operations Manager, 508-767-7387, Fax: 508-767-7030, E-mail: graduate@assumption.edu. Web site: http://graduate.assumption.edu/mba/mba-assumption.

Auburn University, Graduate School, College of Business, School of Accountancy, Auburn University, AL 36849. Offers M Acc. *Accreditation:* AACSB. Part-time programs available. *Faculty:* 13 full-time (4 women), 3 part-time/adjunct (2 women). *Students:* 49 full-time (24 women), 47 part-time (29 women); includes 3 minority (1 Black or African American, non-Hispanic/Latino; 2 Hispanic/Latino), 1 international. Average age 27. 136 applicants, 60% accepted, 62 enrolled. In 2011, 65 master's awarded. *Entrance requirements:* For master's, GMAT, GRE General Test. Additional exam requirements/recommendations for international students: Required—TOEFL. *Application deadline:* For fall admission, 7/7 for domestic students; for spring admission, 11/24 for domestic students. Applications are processed on a rolling basis. Application fee: $50 ($60 for international students). Electronic applications accepted. *Expenses:* Tuition, state resident: full-time $7290; part-time $405 per credit hour. Tuition, nonresident: full-time $21,870; part-time $1215 per credit hour. *International tuition:* $22,000 full-time. *Required fees:* $1402. *Financial support:* Teaching assistantships and Federal Work-Study available. Support available to part-time students. Financial award application deadline: 3/15; financial award applicants required to submit FAFSA. *Unit head:* Dewayne Searcy, Director, 334-844-5827. *Application contact:* Dr. George Flowers, Dean of the Graduate School, 334-844-2125. Web site: http://business.auburn.edu/academics/departments/school-of-accountancy.

Avila University, School of Business, Kansas City, MO 64145-1698. Offers accounting (MBA); finance (MBA); general management (MBA); health care administration (MBA); international business (MBA); management information systems (MBA); marketing (MBA). Part-time and evening/weekend programs available. *Faculty:* 9 full-time (3 women), 14 part-time/adjunct (5 women). *Students:* 102 full-time (49 women), 53 part-time (31 women); includes 36 minority (29 Black or African American, non-Hispanic/Latino; 1 American Indian or Alaska Native, non-Hispanic/Latino; 3 Asian, non-Hispanic/Latino; 2 Hispanic/Latino; 1 Native Hawaiian or other Pacific Islander, non-Hispanic/Latino), 33 international. Average age 32. 25 applicants, 76% accepted, 19 enrolled. In 2011, 59 master's awarded. *Degree requirements:* For master's, comprehensive exam, capstone course. *Entrance requirements:* For master's, GMAT (minimum score 420), minimum GPA of 3.0, interview. Additional exam requirements/recommendations for international students: Required—TOEFL (minimum score 550 paper-based). *Application deadline:* For fall admission, 7/30 priority date for domestic students, 7/30 for international students; for winter admission, 11/30 priority date for domestic students, 11/30 for international students; for spring admission, 2/28 priority date for domestic students, 2/28 for international students. Applications are processed on a rolling basis. Application fee: $0. Electronic applications accepted. *Expenses:* Contact institution. *Financial support:* In 2011–12, 102 students received support. Career-related internships or fieldwork and competitive merit scholarships available. Support available to part-time students. Financial award applicants required to submit FAFSA. *Faculty research:* Leadership characteristics, financial hedging, group dynamics. *Unit head:* Dr. Richard Woodall, Dean, 816-501-3720, Fax: 816-501-2463, E-mail: richard.woodall@avila.edu. *Application contact:* JoAnna Giffin, MBA Admissions Director, 816-501-3601, Fax: 816-501-2463, E-mail: joanna.giffin@avila.edu. Web site: http://www.avila.edu/mba.

Babson College, F. W. Olin Graduate School of Business, Wellesley, Babson Park, MA 02457-0310. Offers accounting (MSA); advanced management (Certificate); business administration (MBA); global entrepreneurship (MS); technological entrepreneurship (MS). *Accreditation:* AACSB. Part-time and evening/weekend programs available. Postbaccalaureate distance learning degree programs offered (minimal on-campus study). *Entrance requirements:* For master's, GMAT, 2 years of work experience, resume, letters of recommendation. Additional exam requirements/recommendations for international students: Required—TOEFL (minimum score 100 iBT), IELTS (minimum score 6.5). Electronic applications accepted. *Faculty research:* Entrepreneurship, sustainability, global markets, process of innovation, social media and advertising.

Baker College Center for Graduate Studies - Online, Graduate Programs, Flint, MI 48507-9843. Offers accounting (MBA); business administration (DBA); finance (MBA); general business (MBA); health care management (MBA); human resources management (MBA); information management (MBA); leadership studies (MBA); management information systems (MSIS); marketing (MBA). Part-time and evening/weekend programs available. Postbaccalaureate distance learning degree programs offered. *Degree requirements:* For master's, portfolio. *Entrance requirements:* For master's, 3 years of work experience, minimum undergraduate GPA of 2.5, writing sample, 3 letters of recommendation; for doctorate, MBA or acceptable related master's degree from accredited association, 5 years work experience, minimum graduate GPA of 3.25, writing sample, 3 professional references. Additional exam requirements/recommendations for international students: Required—TOEFL (minimum score 550 paper-based; 213 computer-based). Electronic applications accepted.

Baldwin Wallace University, Graduate Programs, Division of Business, Program in Accounting, Berea, OH 44017-2088. Offers MBA. Part-time and evening/weekend programs available. *Students:* 31 full-time (19 women), 20 part-time (10 women); includes 7 minority (3 Black or African American, non-Hispanic/Latino; 1 Asian, non-Hispanic/Latino; 2 Hispanic/Latino; 1 Two or more races, non-Hispanic/Latino). Average age 35. 16 applicants, 63% accepted, 6 enrolled. In 2011, 24 master's awarded. *Degree requirements:* For master's, minimum overall GPA of 3.0, completion of all required courses. *Entrance requirements:* For master's, GMAT, minimum GPA of 3.0, work experience, bachelor's degree in any field, undergraduate accounting coursework. Additional exam requirements/recommendations for international students: Required—TOEFL (minimum score 523 paper-based; 193 computer-based; 70 iBT). *Application deadline:* For fall admission, 7/25 priority date for domestic students, 4/30 for international students; for spring admission, 12/15 priority date for domestic students, 9/30 for international students. Applications are processed on a rolling basis. Application fee: $25. Electronic applications accepted. Application fee is waived when completed online. *Expenses:* Contact institution. *Financial support:* Career-related internships or fieldwork available. Support available to part-time students. Financial award application deadline: 5/1. *Unit head:* Thomas Garvey, Director, 440-826-2438, Fax: 440-826-3868, E-mail: tgarvey@bw.edu. *Application contact:* Laura Spencer, Graduate Application Specialist, 440-826-2191, Fax: 440-826-3868, E-mail: lspencer@bw.edu. Web site: http://www.bw.edu/academics/bus/programs/amba/.

Ball State University, Graduate School, Miller College of Business, Department of Accounting, Muncie, IN 47306-1099. Offers MS. *Accreditation:* AACSB. *Faculty:* 8 full-time (2 women). *Students:* 24 full-time (8 women), 4 part-time (2 women); includes 3 minority (2 Black or African American, non-Hispanic/Latino; 1 Asian, non-Hispanic/Latino), 12 international. Average age 25. 39 applicants, 77% accepted, 12 enrolled. In 2011, 25 master's awarded. Application fee: $50. Tuition and fees vary according to program and reciprocity agreements. *Financial support:* In 2011–12, 13 students received support, including 9 teaching assistantships with full tuition reimbursements available (averaging $13,928 per year). Financial award application deadline: 3/1. *Unit head:* Dr. Lucinda Van Alst, Head, 765-285-5100, E-mail: lvanalst@bsu.edu. *Application contact:* Dr. Mark Myring, Information Contact, 765-285-5100, Fax: 765-285-8024. Web site: http://cms.bsu.edu/Academics/CollegesandDepartments/MCOB/Programs/Depts/Accounting.aspx.

Barry University, Andreas School of Business, Program in Accounting, Miami Shores, FL 33161-6695. Offers MSA.

Bayamón Central University, Graduate Programs, Program in Business Administration, Bayamón, PR 00960-1725. Offers accounting (MBA); finance (MBA); general business (MBA); management (MBA); marketing (MBA). Part-time and evening/weekend programs available. *Degree requirements:* For master's, comprehensive exam (for some programs). *Entrance requirements:* For master's, EXADEP, bachelor's degree in business or related field.

Baylor University, Graduate School, Hankamer School of Business, Department of Accounting and Business Law, Waco, TX 76798. Offers M Acc, MT, JD/M Acc, JD/MT. *Accreditation:* AACSB. Part-time programs available. *Faculty:* 11 full-time (2 women). *Students:* 56 full-time (22 women), 8 part-time (5 women); includes 11 minority (1 Black or African American, non-Hispanic/Latino; 10 Hispanic/Latino), 2 international. In 2011, 61 master's awarded. *Entrance requirements:* For master's, GMAT. *Application deadline:* For fall admission, 8/1 for domestic students; for spring admission, 12/1 for domestic students. Applications are processed on a rolling basis. Application fee: $25. *Financial support:* Research assistantships, career-related internships or fieldwork, Federal Work-Study, and institutionally sponsored loans available. *Faculty research:* Continuing professional education (CPE), accounting education, retirement plans. *Unit head:* Dr. Jane Baldwin, Adviser, 254-710-3536, Fax: 254-710-2421, E-mail: jane_baldwin@baylor.edu. *Application contact:* Vicky Todd, Administrative Assistant, 254-710-3718, Fax: 254-710-1066, E-mail: mba@hsb.baylor.edu.

Benedictine University, Graduate Programs, Program in Accountancy, Lisle, IL 60532-0900. Offers MS. Evening/weekend programs available. *Students:* 6 full-time (5 women), 40 part-time (25 women); includes 15 minority (5 Black or African American, non-Hispanic/Latino; 6 Asian, non-Hispanic/Latino; 4 Hispanic/Latino), 7 international. 23 applicants, 78% accepted, 16 enrolled. In 2011, 13 degrees awarded. *Entrance requirements:* For master's, official transcripts, 2 letters of reference, resume. Additional exam requirements/recommendations for international students: Required—TOEFL. *Application deadline:* Applications are processed on a rolling basis. Electronic applications accepted. *Unit head:* Dr. Sharon Borowicz, Director, 630-829-6219, E-mail: sborowicz@ben.edu. *Application contact:* Kari Gibbons, Associate Vice President, Enrollment Center, 630-829-6200, Fax: 630-829-6584, E-mail: kgibbons@ben.edu.

Benedictine University, Graduate Programs, Program in Business Administration, Lisle, IL 60532-0900. Offers accounting (MBA); entrepreneurship and managing innovation (MBA); financial management (MBA); health administration (MBA); human resource management (MBA); information systems security (MBA); international business (MBA); management consulting (MBA); management information systems (MBA); marketing management (MBA); operations management and logistics (MBA); organizational leadership (MBA); MBA/MPH; MBA/MS. Part-time and evening/weekend programs available. Postbaccalaureate distance learning degree programs offered (minimal on-campus study). *Faculty:* 4 full-time (2 women), 24 part-time/adjunct (3 women). *Students:* 165 full-time (101 women), 766 part-time (381 women); includes 201 minority (118 Black or African American, non-Hispanic/Latino; 4 American Indian or Alaska Native, non-Hispanic/Latino; 37 Asian, non-Hispanic/Latino; 40 Hispanic/Latino; 2 Native Hawaiian or other Pacific Islander, non-Hispanic/Latino), 14 international. Average age 34. 313 applicants, 73% accepted, 166 enrolled. In 2011, 379 master's awarded. *Entrance requirements:* For master's, GMAT. Additional exam requirements/recommendations for international students: Required—TOEFL (minimum score 550 paper-based; 213 computer-based). *Application deadline:* For fall admission, 9/1 for domestic students; for winter admission, 12/1 for domestic students; for spring admission, 2/15 for domestic students. Applications are processed on a rolling basis. Application fee: $40. Electronic applications accepted. *Financial support:* Career-related internships or fieldwork and health care benefits available. Support available to part-time students. *Faculty research:* Strategic leadership in professional organizations, sociology of professions, organizational change, social identity theory, applications to change management. *Unit head:* Dr. Sharon Borowicz, Director, 630-829-6219, E-mail: sborowicz@ben.edu. *Application contact:* Kari Gibbons, Director, Admissions, 630-829-6200, Fax: 630-829-6584, E-mail: kgibbons@ben.edu.

Bentley University, McCallum Graduate School of Business, Accountancy PhD Program, Waltham, MA 02452-4705. Offers PhD. Part-time programs available. *Degree requirements:* For doctorate, comprehensive exam, thesis/dissertation. *Entrance requirements:* For doctorate, GMAT or GRE General Test. Additional exam requirements/recommendations for international students: Required—TOEFL (minimum score 650 paper-based; 250 computer-based; 100 iBT) or IELTS (minimum score 7). Electronic applications accepted. *Faculty research:* Accounting information systems, financial fraud, forensic accounting, enterprise risks and controls, managerial incentive systems, earnings management, auditor ethos and independence, audit team brainstorming, auditor-client negotiations, information technology auditing, corporate ethics and internal controls, corporate governance.

Bentley University, McCallum Graduate School of Business, Master's Program in Accounting, Waltham, MA 02452-4705. Offers MSA. *Accreditation:* AACSB. Part-time and evening/weekend programs available. *Entrance requirements:* For master's, GMAT or GRE General Test. Additional exam requirements/recommendations for international students: Required—TOEFL (minimum score 600 paper-based; 250 computer-based; 100 iBT) or IELTS (minimum score 7). Electronic applications accepted. *Faculty research:* Audit risk assessment, ethics in accounting, corporate governance, accounting information systems and management control, tax policy, forensic accounting.

Bernard M. Baruch College of the City University of New York, Zicklin School of Business, Department of Accounting, Program in Accounting, New York, NY 10010-5585. Offers MBA, MS, PhD. PhD offered jointly with Graduate School and University Center of the City University of New York. *Accreditation:* AACSB. Part-time and evening/weekend programs available. *Degree requirements:* For doctorate, comprehensive exam, thesis/dissertation. *Entrance requirements:* For master's, GMAT, 2 letters of recommendation, resume, 2 years of work experience; for doctorate, GMAT. Additional exam requirements/recommendations for international students: Required—TOEFL (minimum score 590 paper-based; 243 computer-based), TWE (minimum score 5).

Bloomsburg University of Pennsylvania, School of Graduate Studies, College of Business, Department of Accounting, Bloomsburg, PA 17815-1301. Offers M Acc, MBA.

Bob Jones University, Graduate Programs, Greenville, SC 29614. Offers accountancy (MS); Bible (MA); Bible translation (MA); Biblical studies (Certificate); broadcast management (MS); business administration (MBA); church history (MA, PhD); church ministries (MA); church music (MM); cinema and video production (MA); counseling (MS); curriculum and instruction (Ed D); divinity (M Div); dramatic production (MA); educational leadership (MS, Ed D, Ed S); elementary education (M Ed, MAT); English (M Ed, MA, MAT); fine arts (MA); graphic design (MA); history (M Ed, MA); illustration (MA); interpretative speech (MA); mathematics (M Ed, MAT); medical missions (Certificate); ministry (MM, D Min); multi-categorical special education (M Ed, MAT); music (M Ed); New Testament interpretation (PhD); Old Testament interpretation (PhD); orchestral instrument performance (MM); organ performance (MM); pastoral studies (MA); personnel services (MS, Ed S); piano pedagogy (MM); piano performance (MM); platform arts (MA); radio and television broadcasting (MS); rhetoric and public address (MA); secondary education (M Ed); studio art (MA); teaching Bible (MA); theology (MA, PhD); voice performance (MM); youth ministries (MA); M Div/MM.

Boise State University, Graduate College, College of Business and Economics, Program in Accountancy, Boise, ID 83725-0399. Offers accountancy (MSA); taxation (MSA). *Accreditation:* AACSB. Part-time programs available. *Entrance requirements:* For master's, GMAT, minimum GPA of 3.0. Additional exam requirements/recommendations for international students: Required—TOEFL. Electronic applications accepted.

Boston College, Carroll School of Management, Programs in Accounting, Chestnut Hill, MA 02467-3800. Offers MSA. *Faculty:* 11 full-time (2 women), 8 part-time/adjunct (0 women). *Students:* 80 full-time (37 women); includes 10 minority (9 Asian, non-Hispanic/Latino; 1 Hispanic/Latino), 33 international. Average age 26. 533 applicants, 38% accepted, 80 enrolled. In 2011, 76 master's awarded. *Entrance requirements:* For master's, GMAT, recommendations, resume. Additional exam requirements/recommendations for international students: Required—TOEFL (minimum score 600 paper-based; 250 computer-based; 100 iBT). *Application deadline:* For fall admission, 3/15 for domestic and international students; for spring admission, 2/15 for domestic and international students. Application fee: $100. Electronic applications accepted. *Financial support:* In 2011–12, 45 fellowships, 45 research assistantships were awarded; tuition waivers (partial) also available. *Faculty research:* Financial reporting, auditing, tax planning, financial statement analysis. *Unit head:* Dr. Jeffrey L. Ringuest, Associate Dean, Graduate Programs, 617-552-9100, Fax: 617-552-0514, E-mail: gsomdean@bc.edu. *Application contact:* Shelley A. Burt, Director of Graduate Enrollment, 617-552-3920, Fax: 617-552-8078, E-mail: bcmba@bc.edu. Web site: http://www.bc.edu/msa/.

Bowling Green State University, Graduate College, College of Business Administration, Program in Accountancy, Bowling Green, OH 43403. Offers M Acc. *Accreditation:* AACSB. Part-time programs available. *Degree requirements:* For master's, thesis or alternative. *Entrance requirements:* For master's, GMAT. Additional exam requirements/recommendations for international students: Required—TOEFL. Electronic applications accepted. *Faculty research:* Financial reporting and auditing, accounting information systems, taxation.

Bradley University, Graduate School, Foster College of Business Administration, Program in Accounting, Peoria, IL 61625-0002. Offers MSA. *Accreditation:* AACSB. Part-time and evening/weekend programs available. *Degree requirements:* For master's, comprehensive exam. *Entrance requirements:* For master's, GMAT, minimum undergraduate GPA of 2.75 in major, 2 letters of recommendation. Additional exam requirements/recommendations for international students: Required—TOEFL (minimum score 550 paper-based; 213 computer-based; 79 iBT).

Brenau University, Sydney O. Smith Graduate School, School of Business and Mass Communication, Gainesville, GA 30501. Offers accounting (MBA); business administration (MBA); healthcare management (MBA); organizational leadership (MS); project management (MBA). Part-time and evening/weekend programs available. Postbaccalaureate distance learning degree programs offered (no on-campus study). *Degree requirements:* For master's, comprehensive exam (for some programs). *Entrance requirements:* For master's, resume, minimum undergraduate GPA of 2.5. Additional exam requirements/recommendations for international students: Required—TOEFL (minimum score 500 paper-based; 173 computer-based; 61 iBT); Recommended—IELTS (minimum score 5). Electronic applications accepted. *Expenses:* Contact institution.

Bridgewater State University, School of Graduate Studies, School of Business, Department of Accounting and Finance, Bridgewater, MA 02325-0001. Offers MSM. Part-time and evening/weekend programs available. *Entrance requirements:* For master's, GMAT.

Brigham Young University, Graduate Studies, Marriott School of Management, Master of Accountancy Program, Provo, UT 84602. Offers M Acc, JD/M Acc. *Accreditation:* AACSB. *Faculty:* 26 full-time (2 women), 10 part-time/adjunct (3 women). *Students:* 158 full-time (31 women); includes 8 minority (1 Black or African American, non-Hispanic/Latino; 2 Asian, non-Hispanic/Latino; 4 Hispanic/Latino; 1 Native Hawaiian or other Pacific Islander, non-Hispanic/Latino), 13 international. Average age 23. 255 applicants, 70% accepted, 158 enrolled. In 2011, 156 master's awarded. *Entrance requirements:* For master's, GMAT, minimum GPA of 3.0 in last 60 hours. Additional exam requirements/recommendations for international students: Required—TOEFL (minimum score 580 paper-based; 230 computer-based). *Application deadline:* For fall admission, 3/1 for domestic and international students. Application fee: $50. Electronic applications accepted. *Expenses:* Contact institution. *Financial support:* In 2011–12, 116 students received support. Application deadline: 3/1; applicants required to submit FAFSA. *Unit head:* Dr. Steve Glover, Director, 801-422-6080, Fax: 801-422-0621, E-mail: sg@byu.edu. *Application contact:* Julie Averett, Academic Advisor, 801-422-3951, Fax: 801-422-0621, E-mail: soa@byu.edu. Web site: http://marriottschool.byu.edu/macc.

Brock University, Faculty of Graduate Studies, Faculty of Business, Program in Accountancy, St. Catharines, ON L2S 3A1, Canada. Offers M Acc. *Degree requirements:* For master's, thesis or alternative. *Entrance requirements:* For master's, honours degree. Additional exam requirements/recommendations for international students: Required—TOEFL (minimum score 550 paper-based; 213 computer-based; 80 iBT), IELTS (minimum score 6.5), TWE (minimum score 4.5). Electronic applications accepted.

Brooklyn College of the City University of New York, Division of Graduate Studies, Department of Economics, Brooklyn, NY 11210-2889. Offers accounting (MS); business economics (MS), including economic analysis, global business and finance; economics (MA). Part-time and evening/weekend programs available. *Degree requirements:* For master's, comprehensive exam, thesis or alternative. *Entrance requirements:* For master's, GMAT (for MS), 2 letters of recommendation. Additional exam requirements/recommendations for international students: Required—TOEFL (minimum score 550 paper-based; 213 computer-based; 79 iBT). Electronic applications accepted. *Faculty research:* Econometrics, environmental economics, microeconomics, macroeconomics, taxation.

Bryant University, Graduate School of Business, Master of Professional Accountancy Program, Smithfield, RI 02917. Offers MPAC. Part-time programs available. *Entrance requirements:* For master's, GMAT, transcripts, resume, recommendation, personal statement. Additional exam requirements/recommendations for international students: Required—TOEFL (minimum score 580 paper-based; 237 computer-based; 95 iBT). Electronic applications accepted. *Faculty research:* Director compensation, public sector auditing, employee stock options, financial disclosure, XBRL.

Butler University, College of Business Administration, Indianapolis, IN 46208-3485. Offers business administration (MBA); professional accounting (MP Acc). *Accreditation:* AACSB. Part-time and evening/weekend programs available. *Faculty:* 12 full-time (2 women), 4 part-time/adjunct (0 women). *Students:* 38 full-time (16 women), 172 part-time (49 women); includes 14 minority (6 Black or African American, non-Hispanic/Latino; 5 Asian, non-Hispanic/Latino; 3 Hispanic/Latino), 12 international. Average age 32. 134 applicants, 81% accepted, 44 enrolled. In 2011, 70 master's awarded. *Entrance requirements:* For master's, GMAT, minimum AACSB index of 950. *Application deadline:* For fall admission, 8/15 priority date for domestic students. Applications are processed on a rolling basis. Application fee: $35. Electronic applications accepted. *Expenses: Tuition:* Part-time $466 per credit. *Financial support:* Career-related internships or fieldwork and institutionally sponsored loans available. Support available to part-time students. Financial award application deadline: 7/15; financial award applicants required to submit FAFSA. *Faculty research:* Real estate law, international finance, total quality management, Web-based commerce, pricing policies. *Unit head:* Dr. Chuck Williams, Dean, 317-940-8491, Fax: 317-940-9455, E-mail: crwillia@butler.edu. *Application contact:* Stephanie Judge, Director of Marketing, 317-940-9886, Fax: 317-940-9455, E-mail: sjudge@butler.edu. Web site: http://www.butler.edu/cob/.

Caldwell College, Graduate Studies, Division of Business, Caldwell, NJ 07006-6195. Offers accounting (MS); business administration (MBA). *Accreditation:* ACBSP. Part-time and evening/weekend programs available. *Students:* 13 full-time (6 women), 40 part-time (25 women); includes 15 minority (8 Black or African American, non-Hispanic/Latino; 3 Asian, non-Hispanic/Latino; 4 Hispanic/Latino), 4 international. *Entrance requirements:* Additional exam requirements/recommendations for international students: Required—TOEFL (minimum score 580 paper-based; 237 computer-based). *Application deadline:* Applications are processed on a rolling basis. Application fee: $40. Electronic applications accepted. *Expenses: Tuition:* Full-time $14,400; part-time $800 per credit. *Required fees:* $200; $100 per semester. *Unit head:* Bernard O'Rourke, Division Associate Dean, 973-618-3409, Fax: 973-618-3355, E-mail: borourke@caldwell.edu. *Application contact:* Vilma Mueller, Director of Graduate Studies, 973-618-3544, E-mail: graduate@caldwell.edu. Web site: http://www.caldwell.edu/graduate.

California Baptist University, Program in Business Administration, Riverside, CA 92504-3206. Offers accounting (MBA); business administration (MBA). *Accreditation:* ACBSP. Part-time and evening/weekend programs available. *Faculty:* 12 full-time (4 women), 2 part-time/adjunct (1 woman). *Students:* 56 full-time (27 women); includes 19 minority (7 Black or African American, non-Hispanic/Latino; 2 Asian, non-Hispanic/Latino; 10 Hispanic/Latino), 9 international. Average age 30. 90 applicants, 42% accepted, 28 enrolled. In 2011, 38 master's awarded. *Degree requirements:* For master's, capstone project. *Entrance requirements:* For master's, minimum GPA of 2.5; two recommendations; comprehensive essay; resume; interview. Additional exam requirements/recommendations for international students: Required—TOEFL (minimum score 575 paper-based; 230 computer-based; 89 iBT). *Application deadline:* For fall admission, 8/1 priority date for domestic students, 7/1 for international students; for spring admission, 12/1 priority date for domestic students, 11/1 for international students. Applications are processed on a rolling basis. Application fee: $45. Electronic applications accepted. *Expenses:* Contact institution. *Financial support:* In 2011–12, 1 student received support. Federal Work-Study and institutionally sponsored loans available. Financial award applicants required to submit FAFSA. *Faculty research:* Econometrics, Biblical financial principles, strategic management and corporate performance, shared leadership models, international culture and economics. *Unit head:* Dr. Natalie Winter, Associate Dean, School of Business, 951-343-4462, Fax: 951-343-4361, E-mail: nwinter@calbaptist.edu. Web site: http://www.calbaptist.edu/mba/about/.

California State Polytechnic University, Pomona, Academic Affairs, College of Business Administration, Master of Science in Business Administration Program, Pomona, CA 91768-2557. Offers information systems auditing (MS). *Students:* 1 (woman) full-time, 15 part-time (6 women); includes 9 minority (5 Asian, non-Hispanic/Latino; 2 Hispanic/Latino; 2 Two or more races, non-Hispanic/Latino), 1 international. Average age 32. 25 applicants, 24% accepted, 5 enrolled. In 2011, 6 master's awarded. *Application deadline:* Applications are processed on a rolling basis. Application fee: $55. Electronic applications accepted. *Expenses:* Tuition, state resident: full-time $6738. Tuition, nonresident: full-time $12,300. *Required fees:* $657. Tuition and fees vary according to course load and program. *Unit head:* Dr. Richard S. Lapidus, Dean, 909-869-2400, Fax: 909-869-6799, E-mail: rslapidus@csupomona.edu. *Application contact:* Dr. Gregory Carlton, Graduate Coordinator, 909-869-5190, E-mail: ghcarlton@csupomona.edu. Web site: http://cba.csupomona.edu/graduateprograms/.

California State Polytechnic University, Pomona, Academic Affairs, College of Business Administration, Program in Accountancy, Pomona, CA 91768-2557. Offers MS. *Students:* 3 full-time (2 women), 1 (woman) part-time, all international. Average age 32. *Application deadline:* Applications are processed on a rolling basis. Application fee: $55. Electronic applications accepted. *Expenses:* Tuition, state resident: full-time $6738. Tuition, nonresident: full-time $12,300. *Required fees:* $657. Tuition and fees vary according to course load and program. *Unit head:* Dr. Richard S. Lapidus, Dean, 909-869-2363, E-mail: rslapidus@csupomona.edu. *Application contact:* Dr. Steven Curl, Associate Dean, 909-869-4244, E-mail: scurl@csupomona.edu. Web site: http://cba.csupomona.edu/cba/news/.

California State University, East Bay, Office of Academic Programs and Graduate Studies, College of Business and Economics, Department of Accounting and Finance, Option in Accounting/Finance, Hayward, CA 94542-3000. Offers MBA. *Degree requirements:* For master's, comprehensive exam or thesis. *Entrance requirements:* For master's, GMAT, minimum GPA of 2.75. Additional exam requirements/recommendations for international students: Required—TOEFL (minimum score 550 paper-based; 213 computer-based). *Application deadline:* For fall admission, 6/30 for domestic and international students. Applications are processed on a rolling basis. Application fee: $55. Electronic applications accepted. *Expenses:* Tuition, state resident: full-time $6738; part-time $1302 per quarter. Tuition, nonresident: full-time $12,690; part-time $2294 per quarter. *Required fees:* $449 per quarter. Tuition and fees vary according to degree level, program and reciprocity agreements. *Financial support:* Career-related internships or fieldwork, Federal Work-Study, and institutionally sponsored loans available. Support available to part-time students. Financial award application deadline: 3/1; financial award applicants required to submit FAFSA. *Unit head:* Prof. Micah Frankel, Graduate Adviser, 510-885-3397, Fax: 510-885-4796, E-mail: micah.frankel@csueastbay.edu. *Application contact:* Donna Wiley, Interim Associate Director, 510-885-2928, Fax: 510-885-4777, E-mail: donna.wiley@csueastbay.edu. Web site: http://www.cbe.csueastbay.edu/acct/.

California State University, Fresno, Division of Graduate Studies, Craig School of Business, Department of Accountancy, Fresno, CA 93740-8027. Offers MS. Part-time programs available. *Degree requirements:* For master's, comprehensive exam. *Entrance requirements:* For master's, GMAT, minimum GPA of 2.75. Additional exam requirements/recommendations for international students: Required—TOEFL. Electronic applications accepted.

California State University, Fullerton, Graduate Studies, College of Business and Economics, Department of Accounting, Fullerton, CA 92834-9480. Offers accounting (MBA, MS); taxation (MS). *Accreditation:* AACSB. Part-time programs available. *Students:* 136 full-time (78 women), 70 part-time (44 women); includes 96 minority (2 Black or African American, non-Hispanic/Latino; 79 Asian, non-Hispanic/Latino; 12 Hispanic/Latino; 3 Two or more races, non-Hispanic/Latino), 57 international. Average age 28. 228 applicants, 55% accepted, 49 enrolled. In 2011, 68 master's awarded. *Degree requirements:* For master's, thesis or alternative, project. *Entrance requirements:* For master's, GMAT, minimum AACSB index of 950. *Application deadline:* Applications are processed on a rolling basis. Application fee: $55. Electronic applications accepted. *Financial support:* Career-related internships or fieldwork, Federal Work-Study, institutionally sponsored loans, and scholarships/grants available. Support available to part-time students. Financial award application deadline: 3/1; financial award applicants required to submit FAFSA. *Unit head:* Dr. Betty Chavis, Chair, 657-278-2225. *Application contact:* Admissions/Applications, 657-278-2371.

California State University, Los Angeles, Graduate Studies, College of Business and Economics, Department of Accounting, Los Angeles, CA 90032-8530. Offers accountancy (MS), including business taxation, financial accounting, information systems, management accounting; accounting (MBA). Part-time and evening/weekend programs available. *Faculty:* 6 full-time (1 woman), 1 part-time/adjunct (0 women). *Students:* 50 full-time (29 women), 34 part-time (15 women); includes 44 minority (1 Black or African American, non-Hispanic/Latino; 32 Asian, non-Hispanic/Latino; 10 Hispanic/Latino; 1 Two or more races, non-Hispanic/Latino), 28 international. Average age 31. 137 applicants, 37% accepted, 20 enrolled. In 2011, 56 master's awarded. *Degree requirements:* For master's, comprehensive exam (MBA), thesis (MS). *Entrance requirements:* For master's, GMAT, minimum GPA of 2.5 during previous 2 years of course work. Additional exam requirements/recommendations for international students: Required—TOEFL (minimum score 550 paper-based; 213 computer-based). *Application deadline:* For fall admission, 5/1 for domestic and international students. Applications are processed on a rolling basis. Application fee: $55. Electronic applications accepted. *Expenses:* Tuition, state resident: full-time $8225. *Financial support:* Career-related internships or fieldwork and Federal Work-Study available. Support available to part-time students. Financial award application deadline: 3/1. *Unit head:* Dr. Kathryn Hansen, Chair, 323-343-2830, Fax: 323-343-6439, E-mail: khansen3@calstatela.edu. *Application contact:* Dr. Karin Brown, Acting Associate Dean of Graduate Studies, 323-343-3820, Fax: 323-343-5653, E-mail: kbrown5@calstatela.edu. Web site: http://cbe.calstatela.edu/acct/.

California State University, Sacramento, Office of Graduate Studies, College of Business Administration, Sacramento, CA 95819-6088. Offers accountancy (MS); business administration (MBA); human resources (MBA); urban land development (MBA). *Accreditation:* AACSB. Part-time and evening/weekend programs available. *Faculty:* 61 full-time (19 women), 28 part-time/adjunct (7 women). *Students:* 39 full-time, 91 part-time; includes 40 minority (6 Black or African American, non-Hispanic/Latino; 2 American Indian or Alaska Native, non-Hispanic/Latino; 12 Asian, non-Hispanic/Latino; 11 Hispanic/Latino; 4 Native Hawaiian or other Pacific Islander, non-Hispanic/Latino; 5 Two or more races, non-Hispanic/Latino), 16 international. Average age 29. 330 applicants, 64% accepted, 54 enrolled. In 2011, 212 master's awarded. *Degree requirements:* For master's, thesis or alternative, writing proficiency exam. *Entrance requirements:* For master's, GMAT. Additional exam requirements/recommendations for international students: Required—TOEFL. *Application deadline:* For fall admission, 2/1 for domestic students, 3/1 for international students; for spring admission, 9/15 for domestic students, 9/30 for international students. Applications are processed on a rolling basis. Application fee: $55. Electronic applications accepted. *Financial support:* Research assistantships, teaching assistantships, career-related internships or fieldwork, and Federal Work-Study available. Support available to part-time students. Financial award applicants required to submit FAFSA. *Unit head:* Dr. Sanjay Varshney, Dean, 916-278-6942, Fax: 916-278-5793, E-mail: cba@csus.edu. *Application contact:* Jose Martinez, Outreach and Graduate Diversity Coordinator, 916-278-6470, Fax: 916-278-5669, E-mail: martinj@skymail.csus.edu. Web site: http://www.cba.csus.edu.

California State University, San Bernardino, Graduate Studies, College of Business and Public Administration, Master in Business Administration Program, San Bernardino, CA 92407. Offers accounting (MBA); entrepreneurship (MBA); executives (MBA); finance (MBA); global business (MBA); information assurance and security management (MBA); information management (MBA); management (MBA); marketing (MBA); professionals (MBA); supply chain management (MBA). *Accreditation:* AACSB. Part-time and evening/weekend programs available. Postbaccalaureate distance learning degree programs offered (no on-campus study). *Faculty:* 58 full-time (11 women), 26 part-time/adjunct (9 women). *Students:* 80 full-time (31 women), 137 part-time (56 women); includes 82 minority (19 Black or African American, non-Hispanic/Latino; 3 American Indian or Alaska Native, non-Hispanic/Latino; 20 Asian, non-Hispanic/Latino; 37 Hispanic/Latino; 3 Two or more races, non-Hispanic/Latino), 65 international. Average age 30. 217 applicants, 65% accepted, 79 enrolled. In 2011, 120 master's awarded. *Degree requirements:* For master's, comprehensive exam, thesis optional, portfolio, 48 units, minimum GPA of 3.0. *Entrance requirements:* For master's, GMAT, minimum GPA of 2.5. Additional exam requirements/recommendations for international students: Required—TOEFL (minimum score 550 paper-based; 213 computer-based; 79 iBT). *Application deadline:* For fall admission, 7/12 priority date for domestic students, 7/12 for international students; for winter admission, 10/26 priority date for domestic students, 10/26 for international students; for spring admission, 1/25 priority date for domestic students, 1/25 for international students. Applications are processed on a rolling basis. Application fee: $55. Electronic applications also accepted. *Expenses:* Contact institution. *Financial support:* In 2011–12, 56 students received support, including 34 fellowships (averaging $3,732 per year), 18 research assistantships (averaging $2,193 per year), 4 teaching assistantships (averaging $2,606 per year); career-related internships or fieldwork, Federal Work-Study, institutionally sponsored loans, scholarships/grants, and unspecified assistantships also available. Support available to part-time students. Financial award application deadline: 3/1; financial award applicants required to submit FAFSA. *Faculty research:* Fraud, Stock Exchange, small business, logistics, job analysis. *Total annual research expenditures:* $4.8 million. *Unit head:* Dr. Lawrence C. Rose, Dean, 909-537-3703, Fax: 909-537-7026, E-mail: lrose@csusb.edu. *Application contact:* Dr. Sandra Kamusikiri, Associate Vice-President/Dean of Graduate Studies, 909-537-7058, Fax: 909-537-5078, E-mail: skamusik@csusb.edu. Web site: http://mba.csusb.edu/.

California Western School of Law, Graduate and Professional Programs, San Diego, CA 92101-3090. Offers law (LL M, JD); JD/MBA; JD/MSW; JD/PhD; MCL/LL M. JD/MSW and JD/MBA offered jointly with San Diego State University; JD/PhD with University of California, San Diego. *Accreditation:* ABA. Part-time programs available. *Entrance requirements:* For doctorate, LSAT. Additional exam requirements/recommendations for international students: Required—TOEFL. Electronic applications accepted. *Faculty research:* Biotechnology, child and family law, international law, labor and employment law, sports law.

Canisius College, Graduate Division, Richard J. Wehle School of Business, Department of Accounting, Buffalo, NY 14208-1098. Offers accounting (MBA); forensic accounting (MS); professional accounting (MBA). Part-time and evening/weekend programs available. *Faculty:* 8 full-time (2 women). *Students:* 55 full-time (27 women), 27 part-time (15 women); includes 12 minority (3 Black or African American, non-Hispanic/Latino; 7 Asian, non-Hispanic/Latino; 2 Hispanic/Latino), 7 international. Average age 28. 67 applicants, 75% accepted, 25 enrolled. In 2011, 22 master's awarded. *Entrance requirements:* For master's, GMAT, transcripts. Additional exam requirements/recommendations for international students: Required—TOEFL. *Application deadline:* For fall admission, 7/1 priority date for domestic students; for spring admission, 11/1 priority date for domestic students. Applications are processed on a rolling basis. Application fee: $25. Electronic applications accepted. *Financial support:* Career-related internships or fieldwork, Federal Work-Study, scholarships/grants, tuition waivers (partial), and unspecified assistantships available. Support available to part-time students. Financial award application deadline: 4/30; financial award applicants required to submit FAFSA. *Faculty research:* Auditing (process and operational factors), fraud from a global perspective, managing risk in software development, valuation of intellectual property. *Unit head:* Dr. Joseph B. O'Donnell, Chair/Professor, 716-888-2868, E-mail: odonnelj@canisius.edu. *Application contact:* Jim Bagwell, Director, Graduate Admissions, 716-888-2545, Fax: 716-888-3290, E-mail: bagwellj@canisius.edu. Web site: http://www.canisius.edu/academics/gradhome.asp.

Capella University, School of Business and Technology, Minneapolis, MN 55402. Offers accounting (MBA), including system design and programming; business (Certificate), including human resource management (MS, PhD, Certificate), information technology management (MS, PhD, Certificate), leadership (MBA, MS, PhD, Certificate); finance (MBA); general business (MBA); health care management (MBA); information technology (MS, Certificate), including general information technology (MS), information security, network architecture and design (MS), professional projects management (Certificate), project management and leadership (MS), system design and development (MS),); information technology management (MBA); marketing (MBA); organization and management (MBA, MS, PhD), including general business (PhD), general organization and management (MBA, MS), human resource management (MS, PhD, Certificate), information technology management (MS, PhD, Certificate), leadership (MBA, MS, PhD, Certificate); project management (MBA). Part-time and evening/weekend programs available. Postbaccalaureate distance learning degree programs offered (minimal on-campus study). Terminal master's awarded for partial completion of doctoral program. *Degree requirements:* For master's, thesis optional, integrative project; for doctorate, comprehensive exam, thesis/dissertation. *Entrance requirements:* Additional exam requirements/recommendations for international students: Required—TOEFL (minimum score 550 paper-based; 213 computer-based), TWE (minimum score 4). Electronic applications accepted. *Faculty research:* Business policies: strategic, corporate, and financial management; interplay of technological, organizational and social change.

Carnegie Mellon University, Tepper School of Business, Program in Accounting, Pittsburgh, PA 15213-3891. Offers PhD. *Accreditation:* AACSB. *Degree requirements:* For doctorate, thesis/dissertation. *Entrance requirements:* For doctorate, GRE.

Case Western Reserve University, Weatherhead School of Management, Department of Accountancy, Cleveland, OH 44106. Offers M Acc, PhD, MBA/M Acc. *Accreditation:* AACSB. Evening/weekend programs available. *Degree requirements:* For doctorate, thesis/dissertation. *Entrance requirements:* For master's and doctorate, GMAT. *Faculty research:* Auditing, regulation, financial reporting, public interest, efficient markets.

The Catholic University of America, School of Arts and Sciences, Department of Business and Economics, Washington, DC 20064. Offers accounting (MS); integral economic development management (MA); international political economics (MA). Part-time programs available. *Faculty:* 12 full-time (4 women), 25 part-time/adjunct (9 women). *Students:* 22 full-time (5 women), 4 part-time (2 women); includes 4 minority (2 Black or African American, non-Hispanic/Latino; 1 Asian, non-Hispanic/Latino; 1 Hispanic/Latino), 5 international. Average age 26. 55 applicants, 56% accepted, 24 enrolled. In 2011, 16 degrees awarded. *Degree requirements:* For master's, comprehensive exam. *Entrance requirements:* For master's, GRE General Test, statement of purpose, official copies of academic transcripts, three letters of recommendation. Additional exam requirements/recommendations for international students: Required—TOEFL (minimum score 580 paper-based; 237 computer-based). *Application deadline:* For fall admission, 8/1 priority date for domestic students, 7/15 for international students; for spring admission, 12/1 priority date for domestic students, 10/15 for international students. Applications are processed on a rolling basis. Application fee: $55. Electronic applications accepted. *Expenses: Tuition:* Full-time $35,260; part-time $1380 per credit. *Required fees:* $80; $40 per semester hour. One-time fee: $425. *Financial support:* Fellowships, research assistantships, teaching assistantships, Federal Work-Study, scholarships/grants, tuition waivers (full and partial), and unspecified assistantships available. Financial award application deadline: 2/1; financial award applicants required to submit FAFSA. *Faculty research:* Integrity of the marketing process, economics of energy and the environment, emerging markets, social change, international finance and economic development. *Total annual research expenditures:* $85,300. *Unit head:* Dr. Andrew V. Abela, Chair, 202-319-5235, Fax: 202-319-4426, E-mail: abela@cua.edu. *Application contact:* Andrew Woodall, Director of Graduate Admissions, 202-319-5057, Fax: 202-319-6533, E-mail: cua-admissions@cua.edu. Web site: http://economics.cua.edu.

Centenary College, Program in Professional Accounting, Hackettstown, NJ 07840-2100. Offers MS. Part-time and evening/weekend programs available. Postbaccalaureate distance learning degree programs offered (minimal on-campus study).

Central Michigan University, College of Graduate Studies, College of Business Administration, School of Accounting, Mount Pleasant, MI 48859. Offers MBA. *Accreditation:* AACSB. Part-time and evening/weekend programs available. *Degree requirements:* For master's, comprehensive exam (for some programs), thesis (for some programs). *Entrance requirements:* For master's, GMAT. Electronic applications accepted. *Faculty research:* Accounting and financial reporting for local government, tax accounting for partnerships and small corporations, accounting for employee stock ownership plans.

Central Washington University, Graduate Studies and Research, College of Business, Department of Accounting, Ellensburg, WA 98926. Offers MPA. *Accreditation:* AACSB. Part-time programs available. *Faculty:* 11 full-time (2 women). *Students:* 26 full-time (16 women), 8 part-time (6 women); includes 13 minority (1 American Indian or Alaska Native, non-Hispanic/Latino; 10 Asian, non-Hispanic/Latino; 1 Hispanic/Latino; 1 Native Hawaiian or other Pacific Islander, non-Hispanic/Latino). 55 applicants, 82% accepted, 34 enrolled. In 2011, 22 master's awarded. *Degree requirements:* For master's, comprehensive exam. *Entrance requirements:* For master's, GMAT, minimum GPA of 3.0. Additional exam requirements/recommendations for international students: Required—TOEFL (minimum score 550 paper-based; 213 computer-based; 79 iBT), IELTS (minimum score 6.5). *Application deadline:* For fall admission, 2/1 priority date for domestic students; for winter admission, 10/1 for domestic students; for spring admission, 1/1 for domestic students. Applications are processed on a rolling basis. Application fee: $50. Electronic applications accepted. *Expenses:* Tuition, state resident: full-time $8112; part-time $270 per credit. Tuition, nonresident: full-time $18,069; part-time $602 per credit. *Required fees:* $924. *Financial support:* In 2011–12, research assistantships with full and partial tuition reimbursements (averaging $9,234 per year), 3 teaching assistantships with full and partial tuition reimbursements (averaging $9,234 per year) were awarded; Federal Work-Study, health care benefits, and unspecified assistantships also available. *Unit head:* Dr. Ronald Tidd, Program Director, 509-963-3340, Fax: 509-963-2875, E-mail: tiddr@cwu.edu. *Application contact:* Justine Eason, Admissions Program Coordinator, 509-963-3103, Fax: 509-963-1799, E-mail: masters@cwu.edu.

Chaminade University of Honolulu, Graduate Services, Program in Business Administration, Honolulu, HI 96816-1578. Offers accounting (MBA); business (MBA); not-for-profit (MBA); public sector (MBA). Part-time and evening/weekend programs available. *Faculty:* 5 full-time (1 woman), 17 part-time/adjunct (6 women). *Students:* 65 full-time (37 women), 50 part-time (23 women); includes 73 minority (6 Black or African American, non-Hispanic/Latino; 37 Asian, non-Hispanic/Latino; 6 Hispanic/Latino; 17 Native Hawaiian or other Pacific Islander, non-Hispanic/Latino; 7 Two or more races, non-Hispanic/Latino), 2 international. Average age 31. 52 applicants, 79% accepted, 29 enrolled. In 2011, 45 master's awarded. *Entrance requirements:* For master's, minimum GPA of 3.0, resume. Additional exam requirements/recommendations for international students: Required—TOEFL (minimum score 650 paper-based). *Application deadline:* For fall admission, 9/1 priority date for domestic students, 9/1 for international students; for winter admission, 12/1 priority date for domestic students, 12/1 for international students; for spring admission, 3/1 priority date for domestic students, 3/1 for international students. Applications are processed on a rolling basis. Application fee: $50. Electronic applications accepted. *Expenses: Required fees:* $600 per credit hour. One-time fee: $93 part-time. *Financial support:* In 2011–12, 35 students received support. Career-related internships or fieldwork, Federal Work-Study, and institutionally sponsored loans available. Support available to part-time students. Financial award application deadline: 3/1; financial award applicants required to submit FAFSA. *Faculty research:* Total quality management, international finance, not-for-profit accounting, service-learning in business contexts. *Unit head:* Dr. Scott J. Schroeder, Dean, 808-739-4611, Fax: 808-735-4734, E-mail: sschroed@chaminade.edu. *Application contact:* 808-739-4633, Fax: 808-739-8329, E-mail: gradserv@chaminade.edu. Web site: http://www.chaminade.edu/business_communication/mba/index.php.

Charleston Southern University, Program in Business, Charleston, SC 29423-8087. Offers accounting (MBA); finance (MBA); health care administration (MBA); information systems (MBA); organizational development (MBA). Part-time and evening/weekend programs available. *Degree requirements:* For master's, thesis optional. *Entrance requirements:* For master's, GMAT. Additional exam requirements/recommendations for international students: Required—TOEFL (minimum score 550 paper-based; 213 computer-based; 79 iBT).

Chatham University, Program in Accounting, Pittsburgh, PA 15232-2826. Offers M Acc, MAC. Part-time and evening/weekend programs available. *Students:* 18 full-time (11 women), 15 part-time (9 women); includes 5 minority (3 Black or African American, non-Hispanic/Latino; 2 Asian, non-Hispanic/Latino), 4 international. Average age 32. 24 applicants, 67% accepted, 13 enrolled. *Entrance requirements:* Additional exam requirements/recommendations for international students: Required—TOEFL (minimum score 600 paper-based; 250 computer-based; 100 iBT), IELTS (minimum score 7), TWE. *Application deadline:* For fall admission, 4/1 for domestic and international students; for spring admission, 11/1 for domestic students, 10/1 for international students. Applications are processed on a rolling basis. Application fee: $45. Electronic applications accepted. Application fee is waived when completed online. *Expenses: Tuition:* Full-time $13,896. Tuition and fees vary according to program. *Financial support:* Applicants required to submit FAFSA. *Unit head:* Prof. Bruce Rosenthal, Director of Business and Entrepreneurship Program, 412-365-2433. *Application contact:* Michael May, Director of Graduate Admission, 412-365-1141, Fax: 412-365-1609, E-mail: gradadmissions@chatham.edu. Web site: http://www.chatham.edu/macc.

City University of Seattle, Graduate Division, School of Management, Bellevue, WA 98005. Offers accounting (Certificate); change leadership (MBA, Certificate); computer systems (MS); finance (Certificate); financial management (MBA); general management (MBA); general management-Europe (MBA); global marketing (MBA); human resources management (Certificate); individualized study (MBA); information security (MS); information systems (MBA); leadership (MA); marketing (MBA, Certificate); project management (MBA, MS, Certificate); sustainable business (Certificate); technology management (MBA, Certificate). Part-time and evening/weekend programs available. Postbaccalaureate distance learning degree programs offered (no on-campus study). *Faculty:* 6 full-time (2 women), 95 part-time/adjunct (33 women). *Students:* 397 full-time (193 women), 283 part-time (137 women); includes 127 minority (67 Black or African American, non-Hispanic/Latino; 5 American Indian or Alaska Native, non-Hispanic/Latino; 33 Asian, non-Hispanic/Latino; 15 Hispanic/Latino; 1 Native Hawaiian or other Pacific Islander, non-Hispanic/Latino; 6 Two or more races, non-Hispanic/Latino), 117 international. Average age 36. 151 applicants, 100% accepted, 151 enrolled. In 2011, 369 master's, 32 other advanced degrees awarded. *Degree requirements:* For master's, comprehensive exam (for some programs), thesis (for some programs). *Entrance requirements:* Additional exam requirements/recommendations for international students: Required—TOEFL (minimum score 567 paper-based; 227 computer-based; 87 iBT); Recommended—IELTS. *Application deadline:* For fall admission, 9/1 for international students; for winter admission, 12/1 for international students; for spring admission, 3/1 for international students. Applications are processed on a rolling basis. Application fee: $50. Electronic applications accepted. *Financial support:* Federal Work-Study and scholarships/grants available. Support available to part-time students. Financial award applicants required to submit FAFSA. *Unit head:* Dr. Kurt Kirstein, Dean, 425-637-1010 Ext. 5456, Fax: 425-709-5363, E-mail: kdkirstein@cityu.edu. *Application contact:* Alysa Borelli, Director, Recruiting, 888-422-4898, Fax: 425-709-5363, E-mail: info@cityu.edu. Web site: http://www.cityu.edu/programs/som/index.aspx.

Clark Atlanta University, School of Business Administration, Department of Accounting, Atlanta, GA 30314. Offers MA. Part-time programs available. *Faculty:* 2 full-time (both women). *Students:* 6 full-time (5 women); all minorities (all Black or African American, non-Hispanic/Latino). Average age 23. 13 applicants, 69% accepted, 1 enrolled. In 2011, 15 master's awarded. *Entrance requirements:* For master's, GMAT, minimum undergraduate GPA of 2.5. Additional exam requirements/recommendations for international students: Required—TOEFL (minimum score 500 paper-based; 173

computer-based; 61 iBT). *Application deadline:* For fall admission, 4/1 for domestic and international students; for spring admission, 11/1 for domestic and international students. Applications are processed on a rolling basis. Application fee: $40 ($55 for international students). Electronic applications accepted. *Expenses: Tuition:* Full-time $13,572; part-time $754 per credit hour. *Required fees:* $806; $403 per semester. *Financial support:* Career-related internships or fieldwork, Federal Work-Study, scholarships/grants, and unspecified assistantships available. Support available to part-time students. Financial award application deadline: 4/30; financial award applicants required to submit FAFSA. *Unit head:* Dr. Kasim Alli, Chairperson, 404-880-8740, E-mail: kalli@cau.edu. *Application contact:* Michelle Clark-Davis, Graduate Program Admissions, 404-880-6605, E-mail: cauadmissions@cau.edu.

Clark University, Graduate School, Graduate School of Management, Business Administration Program, Worcester, MA 01610-1477. Offers accounting (MBA); finance (MBA); global business (MBA); health care management (MBA); management (MBA); management of information technology (MBA); marketing (MBA). *Accreditation:* AACSB. Part-time and evening/weekend programs available. *Students:* 103 full-time (47 women), 108 part-time (41 women); includes 16 minority (7 Black or African American, non-Hispanic/Latino; 5 Asian, non-Hispanic/Latino; 4 Hispanic/Latino), 69 international. Average age 30. 371 applicants, 48% accepted, 77 enrolled. In 2011, 112 master's awarded. *Degree requirements:* For master's, thesis optional. *Application deadline:* For fall admission, 6/1 priority date for domestic students; for spring admission, 12/1 priority date for domestic students. Applications are processed on a rolling basis. Application fee: $50. Electronic applications accepted. *Expenses: Tuition:* Full-time $37,000; part-time $1156 per credit hour. *Financial support:* In 2011–12, research assistantships with partial tuition reimbursements (averaging $4,800 per year), teaching assistantships with partial tuition reimbursements (averaging $4,800 per year) were awarded; fellowships, career-related internships or fieldwork, Federal Work-Study, institutionally sponsored loans, and tuition waivers (partial) also available. Support available to part-time students. Financial award application deadline: 5/31. *Faculty research:* Marketing, accounting, human resource management, management information systems, business finance. *Unit head:* Dr. Catherine Usoff, Dean, 508-793-8822, Fax: 508-793-8822, E-mail: clarkmba@clarku.edu. *Application contact:* Patrick Oroszko, Enrollment and Marketing Director, 508-793-8822, Fax: 508-793-8822, E-mail: clarkmba@clarku.edu. Web site: http://www.clarku.edu/gsom/prospective/mba/.

Clayton State University, School of Graduate Studies, Program in Business Administration, Morrow, GA 30260-0285. Offers accounting (MBA); international business (MBA); supply chain management (MBA). *Accreditation:* AACSB. Part-time and evening/weekend programs available. *Faculty:* 12 full-time (3 women). *Students:* 35 full-time (13 women), 85 part-time (25 women); includes 85 minority (78 Black or African American, non-Hispanic/Latino; 1 American Indian or Alaska Native, non-Hispanic/Latino; 3 Asian, non-Hispanic/Latino; 2 Hispanic/Latino; 1 Two or more races, non-Hispanic/Latino), 3 international. Average age 36. 62 applicants, 87% accepted, 47 enrolled. In 2011, 38 master's awarded. *Degree requirements:* For master's, thesis. *Entrance requirements:* For master's, GMAT, 3 letters of recommendation; statement of purpose; 2 official transcripts. Additional exam requirements/recommendations for international students: Required—TOEFL (minimum score 550 paper-based; 213 computer-based; 80 iBT). *Application deadline:* For fall admission, 6/15 priority date for domestic students, 5/1 for international students; for spring admission, 11/15 priority date for domestic students, 9/1 for international students. Applications are processed on a rolling basis. Application fee: $75. Electronic applications accepted. *Expenses:* Contact institution. *Financial support:* Application deadline: 7/1; applicants required to submit FAFSA. *Unit head:* Dr. Judith Ogden, Graduate Program Director, Master of Business Administration, 678-466-4509, E-mail: judithogden@clayton.edu. *Application contact:* Michelle Terrell, Program Manager, 678-466-4500, Fax: 648-466-4599, E-mail: michelleterrell@clayton.edu. Web site: http://business.clayton.edu/MBA/.

Cleary University, Online Program in Business Administration, Ann Arbor, MI 48105-2659. Offers financial planning (MBA); financial planning (Graduate Certificate); green business strategy (MBA, Graduate Certificate); management (MBA); nonprofit management (MBA, Graduate Certificate); organizational leadership (MBA); public accounting (MBA). Part-time and evening/weekend programs available. Postbaccalaureate distance learning degree programs offered (no on-campus study). *Degree requirements:* For master's, thesis. *Entrance requirements:* For master's, bachelor's degree; minimum GPA of 2.5; professional resume indicating minimum 2 years management or related experience; undergraduate degree from an accredited college or university with at least 18 quarter hours (or 12 semester hours) of accounting study (for MBA in accounting). Additional exam requirements/recommendations for international students: Required—TOEFL (minimum score 550 paper-based; 213 computer-based; 79 iBT), Michigan English Language Assessment Battery (minimum score: 75). Electronic applications accepted.

Clemson University, Graduate School, College of Business and Behavioral Science, School of Accountancy and Finance, Clemson, SC 29634. Offers MP Acc. *Accreditation:* AACSB. Part-time programs available. *Faculty:* 23 full-time (8 women), 1 (woman) part-time/adjunct. *Students:* 48 full-time (25 women), 2 part-time (1 woman); includes 2 minority (1 Black or African American, non-Hispanic/Latino; 1 Asian, non-Hispanic/Latino), 10 international. Average age 24. 137 applicants, 39% accepted, 42 enrolled. In 2011, 32 master's awarded. *Degree requirements:* For master's, oral final exam. *Entrance requirements:* For master's, GMAT, BS in accounting or equivalent, minimum GPA of 3.0. Additional exam requirements/recommendations for international students: Required—TOEFL. *Application deadline:* For fall admission, 5/1 priority date for domestic students, 4/15 for international students; for spring admission, 10/1 for domestic students, 9/15 for international students. Applications are processed on a rolling basis. Application fee: $70 ($80 for international students). Electronic applications accepted. *Financial support:* In 2011–12, 17 students received support, including 14 teaching assistantships with partial tuition reimbursements available (averaging $5,704 per year); fellowships with full and partial tuition reimbursements available, research assistantships with partial tuition reimbursements available, career-related internships or fieldwork, institutionally sponsored loans, scholarships/grants, health care benefits, and unspecified assistantships also available. Support available to part-time students. Financial award applicants required to submit FAFSA. *Unit head:* Dr. Ralph E. Welton, Jr., Director, 864-656-4881, Fax: 864-656-4892, E-mail: edwlsur@clemson.edu. *Application contact:* Dr. Thomas L. Dickens, Jr., Program Coordinator, 864-656-4890, Fax: 864-656-4892, E-mail: dickent@clemson.edu. Web site: http://business.clemson.edu/departments/acct/acct_about.htm.

Cleveland State University, College of Graduate Studies, Monte Ahuja College of Business, Department of Accounting, Cleveland, OH 44115. Offers financial accounting/audit (M Acc); taxation (M Acc). *Accreditation:* AACSB. Part-time and evening/weekend programs available. *Faculty:* 13 full-time (3 women), 11 part-time/adjunct (3 women). *Students:* 111 full-time (52 women), 156 part-time (86 women); includes 37 minority (22 Black or African American, non-Hispanic/Latino; 9 Asian, non-Hispanic/Latino; 3 Hispanic/Latino; 3 Two or more races, non-Hispanic/Latino), 71 international. Average age 29. 253 applicants, 69% accepted, 84 enrolled. In 2011, 66 master's awarded. *Entrance requirements:* For master's, GMAT, minimum GPA of 2.75. Additional exam requirements/recommendations for international students: Required—TOEFL (minimum score 525 paper-based; 197 computer-based). *Application deadline:* For fall admission, 7/15 priority date for domestic students; for spring admission, 12/15 priority date for domestic students. Applications are processed on a rolling basis. Application fee: $30. *Expenses:* Tuition, state resident: full-time $6416; part-time $494 per credit hour. Tuition, nonresident: full-time $12,074; part-time $929 per credit hour. *Financial support:* In 2011–12, 3 research assistantships with full and partial tuition reimbursements (averaging $6,960 per year) were awarded; career-related internships or fieldwork, Federal Work-Study, scholarships/grants, and unspecified assistantships also available. Financial award applicants required to submit FAFSA. *Faculty research:* Internal auditing, computer auditing, accounting education, managerial accounting. *Unit head:* Bruce W. McClain, Chair, 216-687-3652, Fax: 216-687-9212, E-mail: b.mcclain@csuohio.edu. *Application contact:* Bruce Gottschalk, MBA Programs Administrator, 216-687-3730, Fax: 216-687-5311, E-mail: cbacsu@csuohio.edu. Web site: http://www.csuohio.edu/business/academics/act/macc.html.

Coastal Carolina University, E. Craig Wall, Sr. College of Business Administration, Conway, SC 29528-6054. Offers accounting (MBA); business (MBA). *Accreditation:* AACSB. Part-time and evening/weekend programs available. *Faculty:* 9 full-time (5 women). *Students:* 46 full-time (20 women), 28 part-time (12 women); includes 6 minority (5 Black or African American, non-Hispanic/Latino; 1 Hispanic/Latino), 11 international. Average age 27. 51 applicants, 86% accepted, 39 enrolled. In 2011, 37 master's awarded. *Entrance requirements:* For master's, GMAT, official transcripts, 2 letters of recommendation, resume, completion of prerequisites with minimum B average grade. Additional exam requirements/recommendations for international students: Required—TOEFL (minimum score 575 paper-based). *Application deadline:* For fall admission, 3/1 priority date for domestic students, 3/1 for international students; for spring admission, 11/15 priority date for domestic students, 11/15 for international students. Applications are processed on a rolling basis. Application fee: $45. Electronic applications accepted. *Expenses:* Contact institution. *Financial support:* Application deadline: 3/1; applicants required to submit FAFSA. *Unit head:* Dr. Kenneth W. Small, Director, Graduate Business Programs, 843-349-2469, Fax: 843-349-2455, E-mail: ksmall@coastal.edu. *Application contact:* Dr. James O. Luken, Associate Provost/Director of Graduate Studies, 843-349-2235, Fax: 843-349-6444, E-mail: joluken@coastal.edu. Web site: http://www.coastal.edu/business/.

The College at Brockport, State University of New York, School of Business Administration and Economics, Brockport, NY 14420-2997. Offers forensic accounting (MS). Part-time programs available. *Students:* 15 full-time (6 women), 13 part-time (9 women); includes 4 minority (2 Black or African American, non-Hispanic/Latino; 1 Asian, non-Hispanic/Latino; 1 Hispanic/Latino). 31 applicants, 61% accepted, 14 enrolled. In 2011, 11 master's awarded. *Entrance requirements:* For master's, GMAT or GRE General Test. Additional exam requirements/recommendations for international students: Required—TOEFL (minimum score 550 paper-based; 213 computer-based; 79 iBT). *Application deadline:* For fall admission, 7/1 priority date for domestic students, 7/1 for international students; for spring admission, 12/1 priority date for domestic students, 12/1 for international students. Application fee: $50. Electronic applications accepted. *Financial support:* Career-related internships or fieldwork, Federal Work-Study, scholarships/grants, and unspecified assistantships available. Financial award application deadline: 3/15; financial award applicants required to submit FAFSA. *Unit head:* Dr. Daniel Petree, Dean, 585-395-2623, Fax: 585-395-2542. *Application contact:* Dr. Donald A. Kent, Graduate Admissions Counselor, 585-395-5521, Fax: 585-395-2515, E-mail: dkent@brockport.edu. Web site: http://www.brockport.edu/bus-econ/.

College of Charleston, Graduate School, School of Business, Program in Accountancy, Charleston, SC 29424-0001. Offers MS. *Accreditation:* AACSB. Evening/weekend programs available. *Faculty:* 10 full-time (4 women). *Students:* 28 full-time (13 women), 4 part-time (all women), 3 international. Average age 25. 64 applicants, 44% accepted, 25 enrolled. In 2011, 24 degrees awarded. *Entrance requirements:* For master's, GMAT, minimum GPA of 3.0 in last 60 hours of undergraduate course work, 24 hours of course work in accounting, 2 letters of reference. Additional exam requirements/recommendations for international students: Required—TOEFL (minimum score 81 iBT). *Application deadline:* For fall admission, 7/1 for domestic students. Applications are processed on a rolling basis. Application fee: $45. Electronic applications accepted. *Expenses:* Tuition, state resident: full-time $5455; part-time $455 per credit. Tuition, nonresident: full-time $13,917; part-time $1160 per credit. *Financial support:* In 2011–12, research assistantships (averaging $6,200 per year) were awarded; Federal Work-Study, institutionally sponsored loans, scholarships/grants, and unspecified assistantships also available. Support available to part-time students. Financial award application deadline: 3/1; financial award applicants required to submit FAFSA. *Unit head:* Dr. Roger B. Daniels, Director, 843-953-8041, E-mail: danielsr@cofc.edu. Web site: http://sb.cofc.edu/graduate/accountancy/index.php.

The College of Saint Rose, Graduate Studies, School of Business, Department of Accounting, Albany, NY 12203-1419. Offers MS. Part-time and evening/weekend programs available. *Entrance requirements:* For master's, GMAT, graduate degree, or minimum undergraduate GPA of 3.0. Additional exam requirements/recommendations for international students: Required—TOEFL (minimum score 550 paper-based; 213 computer-based). Electronic applications accepted.

The College of William and Mary, Mason School of Business, Master of Accounting Program, Williamsburg, VA 23185. Offers M Acc. *Accreditation:* AACSB. *Faculty:* 13 full-time (4 women), 4 part-time/adjunct (1 woman). *Students:* 84 full-time (43 women); includes 10 minority (1 Black or African American, non-Hispanic/Latino; 4 Asian, non-Hispanic/Latino; 4 Hispanic/Latino; 1 Two or more races, non-Hispanic/Latino), 19 international. Average age 24. 296 applicants, 52% accepted, 83 enrolled. In 2011, 91 master's awarded. *Entrance requirements:* For master's, GMAT, 2 written recommendations, interview. Additional exam requirements/recommendations for international students: Required—TOEFL (minimum score 620 paper-based; 260 computer-based; 102 IBT) or IELTS (minimum score 7). *Application deadline:* Applications are processed on a rolling basis. Application fee: $80. Electronic applications accepted. *Expenses:* Contact institution. *Financial support:* In 2011–12, 75 students received support, including 12 research assistantships (averaging $4,000 per year); fellowships, scholarships/grants, and unspecified assistantships also available. Financial award application deadline: 3/15; financial award applicants required to submit FAFSA. *Faculty research:* Valuation, voluntary disclosure, auditing, taxation, executive compensation. *Unit head:* Linda Espahbodi, Director, 757-221-2953, Fax: 757-221-7862, E-mail: linda.espahbodi@mason.wm.edu. *Application contact:* Martha Howard, Associate Director, 757-221-2875, Fax: 757-221-7862, E-mail: martha.howard@mason.wm.edu. Web site: http://mason.wm.edu/programs/macc/index.php.

Colorado State University, Graduate School, College of Business, Department of Accounting, Fort Collins, CO 80523-1271. Offers M Acc. Part-time programs available. *Faculty:* 10 full-time (3 women). *Students:* 49 full-time (30 women), 27 part-time (18 women); includes 9 minority (2 Black or African American, non-Hispanic/Latino; 3 Asian, non-Hispanic/Latino; 4 Hispanic/Latino), 8 international. Average age 31. 80 applicants, 81% accepted, 46 enrolled. In 2011, 37 master's awarded. *Degree requirements:* For master's, thesis or alternative. *Entrance requirements:* For master's, GMAT, minimum GPA of 3.0; BA/BS. Additional exam requirements/recommendations for international students: Required—TOEFL (minimum score 565 paper-based; 227 computer-based;

86 iBT). *Application deadline:* For fall admission, 7/15 for domestic students, 6/1 for international students; for spring admission, 11/15 for domestic students, 11/1 for international students. Applications are processed on a rolling basis. Application fee: $50. Electronic applications accepted. *Expenses:* Tuition, state resident: full-time $7992. Tuition, nonresident: full-time $19,592. *Required fees:* $1735; $58 per credit. *Financial support:* Fellowships with partial tuition reimbursements, research assistantships with partial tuition reimbursements, and unspecified assistantships available. Financial award application deadline: 3/1; financial award applicants required to submit FAFSA. *Faculty research:* Financial accounting and reporting, managerial accounting, earnings management, stock options, corporate social responsibility. *Unit head:* Dr. Bill Rankin, Department Head, 970-491-4244, Fax: 970-491-2676, E-mail: bill.rankin@business.colostate.edu. *Application contact:* Janet Estes, Graduate Contact, 970-491-4612, Fax: 970-491-2676, E-mail: janet.estes@colostate.edu. Web site: http://www.biz.colostate.edu/accounting/Pages/default.aspx.

Colorado Technical University Colorado Springs, Graduate Studies, Program in Management, Colorado Springs, CO 80907-3896. Offers accounting (MBA, MSA); business administration (MBA); finance (MBA); human resources management (MBA); logistics/supply chain management (MBA); management (DM); marketing (MBA); mediation and dispute resolution (MBA); operations management (MBA); project management (MBA); technology management (MBA). Part-time and evening/weekend programs available. Postbaccalaureate distance learning degree programs offered. *Degree requirements:* For master's, thesis or alternative; for doctorate, thesis/dissertation. *Entrance requirements:* For doctorate, minimum graduate GPA of 3.0, 5 years of related work experience. *Faculty research:* Sexual harassment, performance evaluation, critical thinking.

Colorado Technical University Denver South, Programs in Business Administration and Management, Aurora, CO 80014. Offers accounting (MBA); business administration (MBA); business administration and management (EMBA); finance (MBA); human resource management (MBA); marketing (MBA); mediation and dispute resolution (MBA); operations management (MBA); project management (MBA); technology management (MBA). Part-time and evening/weekend programs available. *Degree requirements:* For master's, thesis or alternative. *Entrance requirements:* For master's, minimum undergraduate GPA of 3.0, resume.

Columbia University, Graduate School of Business, Doctoral Program in Business, New York, NY 10027. Offers business (PhD), including accounting, decision, risk, and operations, finance and economics, management, marketing. *Accreditation:* AACSB. *Degree requirements:* For doctorate, comprehensive exam, thesis/dissertation, major field exam, research paper, thesis proposal. *Entrance requirements:* For doctorate, GMAT or GRE (finance), 2 letters of reference, resume. Additional exam requirements/recommendations for international students: Required—TOEFL. Electronic applications accepted. *Expenses:* Contact institution. *Faculty research:* Human decision making and behavioral research; real estate market and mortgage defaults; financial crisis and corporate governance; international business; security analysis and accounting.

Columbia University, Graduate School of Business, MBA Program, New York, NY 10027. Offers accounting (MBA); decision, risk, and operations (MBA); entrepreneurship (MBA); finance and economics (MBA); healthcare and pharmaceutical management (MBA); human resource management (MBA); international business (MBA); leadership and ethics (MBA); management (MBA); marketing (MBA); media (MBA); private equity (MBA); real estate (MBA); social enterprise (MBA); value investing (MBA); DDS/MBA; JD/MBA; MBA/MIA; MBA/MPH; MBA/MS; MD/MBA. *Entrance requirements:* For master's, GMAT, 2 letters of recommendation. Additional exam requirements/recommendations for international students: Required—TOEFL. Electronic applications accepted. *Expenses:* Contact institution. *Faculty research:* Human decision making and behavioral research; real estate market and mortgage defaults; financial crisis and corporate governance; international business; security analysis and accounting.

Concordia University, School of Graduate Studies, John Molson School of Business, Montréal, QC H3G 1M8, Canada. Offers administration (M Sc, Diploma); aviation management (Certificate, Diploma); business administration (MBA, UA Undergraduate Associate, PhD), including international aviation (UA Undergraduate Associate); chartered accountancy (Diploma); community organizational development (Certificate); event management and fundraising (Certificate); executive business administration (EMBA); investment management (Diploma); investment management option (MBA); management accounting (Certificate); management of healthcare organizations (Certificate); sport administration (Diploma). PhD program offered jointly with HEC Montreal, McGill University, and Université du Québec à Montréal. *Accreditation:* AACSB. Part-time and evening/weekend programs available. *Degree requirements:* For master's, one foreign language, thesis (for some programs), research project; for doctorate, one foreign language, thesis/dissertation; for other advanced degree, one foreign language. *Entrance requirements:* For master's and doctorate, GMAT. Additional exam requirements/recommendations for international students: Required—TOEFL. *Expenses:* Contact institution. *Faculty research:* General business, capital markets, international business.

Cornell University, Graduate School, Graduate Field of Management, Ithaca, NY 14853-0001. Offers accounting (PhD); behavioral decision theory (PhD); finance (PhD); marketing (PhD); organizational behavior (PhD); production and operations management (PhD). *Accreditation:* AACSB. *Faculty:* 53 full-time (8 women). *Students:* 39 full-time (11 women); includes 2 minority (both Asian, non-Hispanic/Latino), 23 international. Average age 29. 424 applicants, 3% accepted, 8 enrolled. In 2011, 6 doctorates awarded. *Degree requirements:* For doctorate, comprehensive exam, thesis/dissertation. *Entrance requirements:* For doctorate, GMAT or GRE General Test. Additional exam requirements/recommendations for international students: Required—TOEFL (minimum score 600 paper-based; 250 computer-based; 77 iBT). *Application deadline:* For fall admission, 1/3 for domestic students. Application fee: $95. Electronic applications accepted. *Expenses:* Contact institution. *Financial support:* In 2011–12, 38 students received support, including 4 fellowships with full tuition reimbursements available, 33 research assistantships with full tuition reimbursements available, 2 teaching assistantships with full tuition reimbursements available; institutionally sponsored loans, scholarships/grants, health care benefits, tuition waivers (full and partial), and unspecified assistantships also available. Financial award applicants required to submit FAFSA. *Faculty research:* Operations and manufacturing. *Unit head:* Director of Graduate Studies, 607-255-3669. *Application contact:* Graduate Field Assistant, 607-255-9431, E-mail: js_phd@cornell.edu. Web site: http://www.gradschool.cornell.edu/fields.php?id-91&a-2.

Daemen College, Department of Accounting/Information Systems, Amherst, NY 14226-3592. Offers global business (MS), including accounting, global business, management information systems, marketing. Part-time and evening/weekend programs available. *Degree requirements:* For master's, minimum GPA of 3.0. *Entrance requirements:* For master's, GMAT if undergraduate GPA is less than 3.0, 2 letters of recommendation; goal statement; transcripts; demonstration of satisfactory oral and written English. Additional exam requirements/recommendations for international students: Required—TOEFL (minimum score 500 paper-based; 173 computer-based; 63 iBT), IELTS (minimum score 5.5). Electronic applications accepted. *Faculty research:* Internationalization of small business, cultural influences on business practices, international human resource practices.

Dallas Baptist University, College of Business, Business Administration Program, Dallas, TX 75211-9299. Offers accounting (MBA); business communication (MBA); conflict resolution management (MBA); entrepreneurship (MBA); finance (MBA); health care management (MBA); international business (MBA); leading the non-profit organization (MBA); management (MBA); management information systems (MBA); marketing (MBA); project management (MBA); technology and engineering management (MBA). *Accreditation:* ACBSP. Part-time and evening/weekend programs available. *Entrance requirements:* For master's, GMAT, minimum GPA of 3.0. Additional exam requirements/recommendations for international students: Required—TOEFL, IELTS. *Application deadline:* Applications are processed on a rolling basis. Application fee: $25. Electronic applications accepted. *Expenses: Tuition:* Full-time $12,060; part-time $670 per credit hour. *Required fees:* $100; $50 per semester. *Financial support:* Federal Work-Study, institutionally sponsored loans, scholarships/grants, and tuition waivers (full and partial) available. Support available to part-time students. Financial award applicants required to submit FAFSA. *Faculty research:* Sports management, services marketing, retailing, strategic management, financial planning/investments. *Unit head:* Dr. Sandra S. Reid, Director, 214-333-5280, Fax: 214-333-5293, E-mail: graduate@dbu.edu. *Application contact:* Kit P. Montgomery, Director of Graduate Programs, 214-333-5242, Fax: 214-333-5579, E-mail: graduate@dbu.edu. Web site: http://www3.dbu.edu/graduate/mba.asp.

Dallas Baptist University, Professional Development Program, Dallas, TX 75211-9299. Offers accounting (MA); church leadership (MA); counseling (MA); criminal justice (MA); English as a second language (MA); finance (MA); higher education (MA); leadership studies (MA); management (MA); management information systems (MA); marketing (MA); missions (MA); professional life coaching (MA). Part-time and evening/weekend programs available. *Entrance requirements:* For master's, minimum GPA of 3.0. Additional exam requirements/recommendations for international students: Required—TOEFL, IELTS. Application fee: $25. *Expenses: Tuition:* Full-time $12,060; part-time $670 per credit hour. *Required fees:* $100; $50 per semester. *Financial support:* Federal Work-Study, institutionally sponsored loans, scholarships/grants, and tuition waivers (full and partial) available. Support available to part-time students. Financial award applicants required to submit FAFSA. *Unit head:* Angela Fogle, Acting Director, 214-333-6830, Fax: 214-333-5558, E-mail: graduate@dbu.edu. *Application contact:* Kit P. Montgomery, Director of Graduate Programs, 214-333-5242, Fax: 214-333-5579, E-mail: graduate@dbu.edu. Web site: http://www3.dbu.edu/graduate/mapd.asp.

Davenport University, Sneden Graduate School, Grand Rapids, MI 49512. Offers accounting (MBA); business administration (EMBA); finance (MBA); health care management (MBA); human resources (MBA); information assurance (MS); public health (MPH); strategic management (MBA). Evening/weekend programs available. *Entrance requirements:* For master's, GMAT, minimum undergraduate GPA of 2.75. Additional exam requirements/recommendations for international students: Required—TOEFL. Electronic applications accepted. *Faculty research:* Leadership, management, marketing, organizational culture.

Davenport University, Sneden Graduate School, Warren, MI 48092-5209. Offers accounting (MBA); business administration (EMBA); finance (MBA); health care management (MBA); human resources management (MBA); information assurance (MS); public health (MPH); strategic management (MBA). *Entrance requirements:* For master's, minimum undergraduate GPA of 2.7.

Davenport University, Sneden Graduate School, Dearborn, MI 48126-3799. Offers accounting (MBA); business administration (EMBA); finance (MBA); health care management (MBA); human resources management (MBA); information assurance (MS); marketing (MBA); public health (MPH); strategic management (MBA). Part-time and evening/weekend programs available. Postbaccalaureate distance learning degree programs offered (no on-campus study). *Entrance requirements:* For master's, minimum GPA of 2.7, previous course work in accounting and statistics. *Faculty research:* Accounting, international accounting, social and environmental accounting, finance.

Delaware Valley College, MBA Program, Doylestown, PA 18901-2697. Offers accounting (MBA); food and agribusiness (MBA); general business (MBA); online global executive leadership (MBA). Part-time and evening/weekend programs available. Postbaccalaureate distance learning degree programs offered (no on-campus study). *Entrance requirements:* For master's, minimum undergraduate GPA of 3.0. *Expenses:* Contact institution.

Delta State University, Graduate Programs, College of Business, Division of Accounting, Computer Information Systems, and Finance, Cleveland, MS 38733-0001. Offers accountancy (MPA). *Expenses:* Tuition, state resident: full-time $4702; part-time $294 per credit hour. Tuition, nonresident: full-time $12,516; part-time $760 per credit hour. *Required fees:* $586.

DePaul University, Charles H. Kellstadt Graduate School of Business, School of Accountancy and Management Information Systems, Chicago, IL 60604-2287. Offers accountancy (M Acc, MSA); business information technology (MS); e-business (MBA, MS); financial management and control (MBA); management accounting (MBA); management information systems (MBA); taxation (MST). Part-time and evening/weekend programs available. *Faculty:* 30 full-time (9 women), 54 part-time/adjunct (7 women). *Students:* 44 full-time (13 women), 22 part-time (4 women); includes 8 minority (2 Black or African American, non-Hispanic/Latino; 3 Asian, non-Hispanic/Latino; 2 Hispanic/Latino; 1 Two or more races, non-Hispanic/Latino), 4 international. Average age 29. In 2011, 141 master's awarded. *Entrance requirements:* For master's, GMAT, 2 letters of recommendation, resume. Additional exam requirements/recommendations for international students: Required—TOEFL (minimum score 550 paper-based; 213 computer-based). *Application deadline:* For fall admission, 7/1 for domestic students; for winter admission, 10/1 for domestic students; for spring admission, 2/1 for domestic students. Applications are processed on a rolling basis. Application fee: $60. *Financial support:* In 2011–12, 7 research assistantships with full tuition reimbursements (averaging $4,100 per year) were awarded; institutionally sponsored loans also available. Financial award application deadline: 4/2. *Faculty research:* Tax policy, property transactions, stock options as compensation, standards setting, activity-based costing in health care. *Unit head:* Kevin Stevens, Director, 312-362-6989, E-mail: kstevens@depaul.edu. *Application contact:* Christopher E. Kinsella, Director of Cohort MBA Programs, 312-362-8810, Fax: 312-362-6677, E-mail: kgsb@depaul.edu. Web site: http://accountancy.depaul.edu/.

DeSales University, Graduate Division, MBA Program, Center Valley, PA 18034-9568. Offers accounting (MBA); computer information systems (MBA); finance (MBA); health care systems management (MBA); human resources management (MBA); management (MBA); marketing (MBA); project management (MBA); self-design (MBA). *Accreditation:* ACBSP. Part-time programs available. Postbaccalaureate distance learning degree programs offered (no on-campus study). *Entrance requirements:* For master's, GMAT, minimum GPA of 3.0, 2 years of work experience. Additional exam requirements/recommendations for international students: Required—TOEFL. *Application deadline:* Applications are processed on a rolling basis. Electronic applications accepted. Tuition and fees vary according to degree level. *Faculty research:* Quality improvement, executive development, productivity, cross-cultural managerial differences, leadership. *Unit head:* Dr. David Gilfoil, Director, 610-282-1100 Ext. 1828, Fax: 610-282-2869, E-mail: david.gilfoil@desales.edu. *Application contact:* Caryn Stopper, Director of Graduate Admissions, 610-282-1100 Ext. 1768, Fax: 610-282-0525, E-mail: caryn.stopper@desales.edu.

DeVry University, Keller Graduate School of Management, Downers Grove, IL 60515. Offers accounting and financial management (MAFM); business administration (MBA); human resources management (MHRM); information systems management (MISM); network and communications management (MNCM); project management (MPM); public administration (MPA).

Dominican University, Edward A. and Lois L. Brennan School of Business, River Forest, IL 60305-1099. Offers MBA, MSA, JD/MBA, MBA/MLIS, MBA/MSW. JD/MBA offered jointly with John Marshall Law School. *Accreditation:* ACBSP. Part-time and evening/weekend programs available. Postbaccalaureate distance learning degree programs offered (no on-campus study). *Faculty:* 21 full-time (8 women), 12 part-time/adjunct (4 women). *Students:* 99 full-time (63 women), 187 part-time (94 women); includes 54 minority (22 Black or African American, non-Hispanic/Latino; 1 American Indian or Alaska Native, non-Hispanic/Latino; 15 Asian, non-Hispanic/Latino; 13 Hispanic/Latino; 3 Two or more races, non-Hispanic/Latino), 26 international. Average age 31. 70 applicants, 96% accepted, 67 enrolled. In 2011, 140 master's awarded. *Entrance requirements:* For master's, GMAT. Additional exam requirements/recommendations for international students: Required—TOEFL (minimum score 550 paper-based; 213 computer-based; 79 iBT); Recommended—IELTS (minimum score 6). *Application deadline:* Applications are processed on a rolling basis. Application fee: $25. Electronic applications accepted. *Expenses:* Contact institution. *Financial support:* Career-related internships or fieldwork, Federal Work-Study, tuition waivers (partial), and unspecified assistantships available. Support available to part-time students. Financial award applicants required to submit FAFSA. *Faculty research:* Entrepreneurship, small business finance, business ethics, marketing strategy. *Unit head:* Dr. Arvid Johnson, Dean, 708-524-6465, Fax: 708-524-6939, E-mail: ajohnson@dom.edu. *Application contact:* Matthew Quilty, Assistant Dean, Brennan School of Business, 708-524-6507, Fax: 708-524-6939, E-mail: mquilty@dom.edu. Web site: http://www.business.dom.edu.

Drexel University, LeBow College of Business, Department of Accounting, Program in Accounting, Philadelphia, PA 19104-2875. Offers MS. *Entrance requirements:* For master's, GMAT, minimum GPA of 2.75. Additional exam requirements/recommendations for international students: Required—TOEFL. Electronic applications accepted.

Drexel University, LeBow College of Business, Program in Business Administration, Philadelphia, PA 19104-2875. Offers business administration (MBA, PhD, APC), including accounting (MBA, PhD), decision sciences (PhD), economics (MBA, PhD), finance (MBA, PhD), legal studies (MBA), management (MBA), marketing (MBA, PhD), organizational sciences (PhD), quantitative methods (MBA), strategic management (PhD). *Accreditation:* AACSB. Part-time and evening/weekend programs available. Postbaccalaureate distance learning degree programs offered (minimal on-campus study). Terminal master's awarded for partial completion of doctoral program. *Entrance requirements:* For master's, GMAT, minimum GPA of 2.75; for doctorate, GMAT. Additional exam requirements/recommendations for international students: Required—TOEFL. Electronic applications accepted. *Faculty research:* Decision support systems, individual and group behavior, operations research, techniques and strategy.

East Carolina University, Graduate School, College of Business, Department of Accounting, Greenville, NC 27858-4353. Offers MS. *Expenses:* Tuition, state resident: full-time $3557; part-time $444.63 per semester hour. Tuition, nonresident: full-time $14,351; part-time $1793.88 per semester hour. *Required fees:* $2016; $252 per semester hour. Part-time tuition and fees vary according to course load, campus/location and program. *Unit head:* Dr. Dan L. Schisler, Chair, 252-328-6055, E-mail: schislerd@ecu.edu.

Eastern Illinois University, Graduate School, Lumpkin College of Business and Applied Sciences, Program in Business Administration, Charleston, IL 61920-3099. Offers accountancy (MBA, Certificate); general management (MBA). *Accreditation:* AACSB. Part-time programs available. *Entrance requirements:* For master's, GMAT. *Expenses:* Tuition, state resident: part-time $279 per credit hour. Tuition, nonresident: part-time $670 per credit hour. *Required fees:* $179.07 per credit hour. $1253 per semester.

Eastern Michigan University, Graduate School, College of Business, Department of Accounting and Finance, Ypsilanti, MI 48197. Offers accounting (MS); accounting information systems (MS). Part-time and evening/weekend programs available. Postbaccalaureate distance learning degree programs offered (minimal on-campus study). *Faculty:* 25 full-time (8 women). *Students:* 57 full-time (31 women), 45 part-time (25 women); includes 14 minority (4 Black or African American, non-Hispanic/Latino; 10 Asian, non-Hispanic/Latino), 23 international. Average age 29. 66 applicants, 61% accepted, 23 enrolled. In 2011, 47 degrees awarded. *Entrance requirements:* For master's, GMAT. Additional exam requirements/recommendations for international students: Required—TOEFL. *Application deadline:* Applications are processed on a rolling basis. Application fee: $35. *Expenses:* Tuition, state resident: full-time $10,367; part-time $432 per credit hour. Tuition, nonresident: full-time $20,435; part-time $851 per credit hour. *Required fees:* $39 per credit hour. $46 per semester. One-time fee: $100. Tuition and fees vary according to course level, degree level and reciprocity agreements. *Financial support:* Fellowships, research assistantships with full tuition reimbursements, teaching assistantships with full tuition reimbursements, career-related internships or fieldwork, Federal Work-Study, institutionally sponsored loans, scholarships/grants, tuition waivers (partial), and unspecified assistantships available. Support available to part-time students. Financial award applicants required to submit FAFSA. *Unit head:* Dr. Zafar Khan, Interim Department Head, 734-487-3320, Fax: 734-487-0806, E-mail: zafar.khan@emich.edu. *Application contact:* Dr. Phil Lewis, Advisor, 734-487-6817, Fax: 734-482-0806, E-mail: plewis4@emich.edu. Web site: http://www.accfin.emich.edu.

East Tennessee State University, School of Graduate Studies, College of Business and Technology, Department of Accountancy, Johnson City, TN 37614. Offers M Acc. *Accreditation:* AACSB. Part-time and evening/weekend programs available. *Faculty:* 6 full-time (0 women), 1 part-time/adjunct (0 women). *Students:* 44 full-time (26 women), 11 part-time (4 women); includes 1 minority (Asian, non-Hispanic/Latino), 8 international. Average age 25. 56 applicants, 64% accepted, 24 enrolled. In 2011, 21 master's awarded. *Degree requirements:* For master's, comprehensive exam, capstone, professional accounting experience. *Entrance requirements:* For master's, GMAT, minimum GPA of 2.5. Additional exam requirements/recommendations for international students: Required—TOEFL (minimum score 550 paper-based; 213 computer-based; 79 iBT). *Application deadline:* For fall admission, 6/1 for domestic students, 4/30 for international students; for spring admission, 11/1 for domestic students, 9/30 for international students. Application fee: $35 ($45 for international students). Electronic applications accepted. *Expenses:* Tuition, state resident: full-time $7312; part-time $350 per credit hour. Tuition, nonresident: full-time $18,490; part-time $621 per credit hour. *Required fees:* $63 per credit hour. Tuition and fees vary according to course load and program. *Financial support:* In 2011–12, 36 students received support, including 16 research assistantships with full tuition reimbursements available (averaging $6,000 per year); career-related internships or fieldwork, institutionally sponsored loans, scholarships/grants, and unspecified assistantships also available. Financial award application deadline: 7/1; financial award applicants required to submit FAFSA. *Faculty research:* Financial accounting, taxation, auditing, management accounting. *Unit head:* Dr. Gary Burkette, Chair, 423-439-4432, Fax: 423-439-8659, E-mail: burkette@etsu.edu. *Application contact:* Cindy Hill, Graduate Specialist, 423-439-6590, Fax: 423-439-5624, E-mail: hillcc@etsu.edu.

Edgewood College, Program in Business, Madison, WI 53711-1997. Offers accountancy (MS); accounting (MBA); business administration (MBA); finance (MBA); management (MBA); marketing (MBA); sustainability leadership (MBA). *Accreditation:* ACBSP. Part-time and evening/weekend programs available. *Students:* 24 full-time (15 women), 95 part-time (41 women); includes 9 minority (2 Black or African American, non-Hispanic/Latino; 4 Asian, non-Hispanic/Latino; 3 Hispanic/Latino), 7 international. Average age 33. In 2011, 43 master's awarded. *Entrance requirements:* For master's, GMAT (minimum score 430), minimum GPA of 2.75, 2 letters of recommendation. Additional exam requirements/recommendations for international students: Required—TOEFL (minimum score 213 computer-based). *Application deadline:* For fall admission, 8/15 for domestic students, 5/1 for international students; for spring admission, 1/8 for domestic students, 11/1 for international students. Applications are processed on a rolling basis. Application fee: $25. Electronic applications accepted. *Expenses: Tuition:* Part-time $747 per credit. Part-time tuition and fees vary according to program. *Financial support:* Career-related internships or fieldwork and scholarships/grants available. *Unit head:* Martin Preizler, Dean, 608-663-2898, Fax: 608-663-3291, E-mail: martinpreizler@edgewood.edu. *Application contact:* Joann Eastman, Admissions Counselor, 608-663-3250, Fax: 608-663-2214, E-mail: gps@edgewood.edu. Web site: http://www.edgewood.edu/Academics/Graduate.aspx.

Ellis University, MBA Program, Chicago, IL 60606-7204. Offers e-commerce (MBA); finance (MBA); general business (MBA); global management (MBA); health care administration (MBA); leadership (MBA); management of information systems (MBA); marketing (MBA); professional accounting (MBA); project management (MBA); public accounting (MBA); risk management (MBA).

Elmhurst College, Graduate Programs, Program in Professional Accountancy, Elmhurst, IL 60126-3296. Offers MPA. Part-time and evening/weekend programs available. *Faculty:* 2 full-time (0 women), 1 part-time/adjunct (0 women). *Students:* 2 full-time (1 woman), 17 part-time (7 women); includes 4 minority (1 Black or African American, non-Hispanic/Latino; 3 Hispanic/Latino). Average age 30. 21 applicants, 57% accepted, 9 enrolled. In 2011, 8 master's awarded. *Entrance requirements:* For master's, 3 recommendations, resume, statement of purpose. Additional exam requirements/recommendations for international students: Required—TOEFL (minimum score 550 paper-based; 213 computer-based). *Application deadline:* Applications are processed on a rolling basis. Application fee: $0. Electronic applications accepted. *Expenses:* Contact institution. *Financial support:* In 2011–12, 5 students received support. Federal Work-Study and scholarships/grants available. Support available to part-time students. Financial award application deadline: 6/1; financial award applicants required to submit FAFSA. *Unit head:* Elizabeth D. Kuebler, Director of Adult and Graduate Admission, 630-617-3300, Fax: 630-617-5501, E-mail: oaga@elmhurst.edu. *Application contact:* Elizabeth D. Kuebler, Director of Adult and Graduate Admission, 630-617-3300, Fax: 630-617-5501, E-mail: oaga@elmhurst.edu.

Emory University, Goizueta Business School, Doctoral Program in Business, Atlanta, GA 30322-1100. Offers accounting (PhD); finance (PhD); information systems (PhD); marketing (PhD); organization and management (PhD). *Faculty:* 56 full-time (13 women). *Students:* 37 full-time (17 women); includes 21 minority (20 Asian, non-Hispanic/Latino; 1 Hispanic/Latino). Average age 29. 240 applicants, 6% accepted, 11 enrolled. In 2011, 5 doctorates awarded. *Degree requirements:* For doctorate, comprehensive exam, thesis/dissertation. *Entrance requirements:* For doctorate, GMAT (strongly preferred) or GRE. Additional exam requirements/recommendations for international students: Required—TOEFL (minimum score 250 computer-based). *Application deadline:* For fall admission, 1/3 priority date for domestic students, 1/1 for international students. Application fee: $50. Electronic applications accepted. *Expenses: Tuition:* Full-time $34,800. *Required fees:* $1300. *Financial support:* In 2011–12, 37 students received support. *Unit head:* Dr. Lawrence Benveniste, Dean, 404-727-6377, Fax: 404-727-0868, E-mail: larry_benveniste@bus.emory.edu. *Application contact:* Allison Gilmore, Director of Admissions and Student Services, 404-727-6353, Fax: 404-727-5337, E-mail: phd@bus.emory.edu.

Everest University, Department of Business Administration, Tampa, FL 33614-5899. Offers accounting (MBA); human resources (MBA); international business (MBA). Part-time and evening/weekend programs available. *Degree requirements:* For master's, thesis optional. *Entrance requirements:* For master's, GMAT or GRE General Test, minimum GPA of 3.0.

Everest University, Program in Business Administration, Orlando, FL 32819. Offers accounting (MBA); general management (MBA); human resources (MBA); international management (MBA).

Fairfield University, Charles F. Dolan School of Business, Fairfield, CT 06824-5195. Offers accounting (MBA, MS, CAS); accounting information systems (MBA, CAS); entrepreneurship (MBA, CAS); finance (MBA, MS, CAS); general management (MBA, CAS); human resource management (MBA, CAS); information systems and operations (MBA); information systems and operations management (CAS); international business (MBA, CAS); marketing (MBA, CAS); taxation (MBA, CAS). *Accreditation:* AACSB. Part-time and evening/weekend programs available. *Faculty:* 23 full-time (9 women), 3 part-time/adjunct (1 woman). *Students:* 87 full-time (37 women), 118 part-time (42 women); includes 13 minority (4 Black or African American, non-Hispanic/Latino; 4 Asian, non-Hispanic/Latino; 5 Hispanic/Latino), 9 international. Average age 29. 126 applicants, 47% accepted, 35 enrolled. In 2011, 90 master's awarded. *Degree requirements:* For master's, capstone course. *Entrance requirements:* For master's, GMAT (minimum score 500), 2 letters of reference, resume, minimum GPA of 3.0. Additional exam requirements/recommendations for international students: Required—TOEFL (minimum score 550 paper-based; 213 computer-bases; 80 iBT) or IELTS (minimum score 6.5). *Application deadline:* For fall admission, 5/15 for international students; for spring admission, 10/15 for international students. Applications are processed on a rolling basis. Application fee: $60. Electronic applications accepted. *Expenses:* Contact institution. *Financial support:* In 2011–12, 50 students received support, including 2 research assistantships (averaging $6,500 per year); scholarships/grants, unspecified assistantships, and merit-based one-time entrance scholarship also available. Financial award applicants required to submit FAFSA. *Faculty research:* Optimization strategies, international finance, consumer behavior, financial market volatility, Internet marketing, supply chain analysis, tax issues. *Unit head:* Dr. Donald Gibson, Dean, 203-254-4000 Ext. 4070, Fax: 203-254-4105, E-mail: dgibson@fairfield.edu. *Application contact:* Marianne Gumpper, Director of Graduate and Continuing Studies Admission, 203-254-

4184, Fax: 203-254-4073, E-mail: gradadmis@fairfield.edu. Web site: http://www.fairfield.edu/dsb/dsb_grad_1.html.

Fairleigh Dickinson University, College at Florham, Silberman College of Business, Department of Accounting, Law, and Tax, Program in Accounting, Madison, NJ 07940-1099. Offers MS. *Entrance requirements:* For master's, GMAT.

Fairleigh Dickinson University, Metropolitan Campus, Silberman College of Business, Department of Accounting, Law, and Tax, Program in Accounting, Teaneck, NJ 07666-1914. Offers MBA, MS, Certificate. *Faculty research:* Corporate accounting, legal issues.

Fitchburg State University, Division of Graduate and Continuing Education, Program in Business Administration, Fitchburg, MA 01420-2697. Offers accounting (MBA); human resource management (MBA); management (MBA). Part-time and evening/weekend programs available. Postbaccalaureate distance learning degree programs offered (no on-campus study). *Students:* 24 full-time (9 women), 57 part-time (29 women); includes 10 minority (6 Black or African American, non-Hispanic/Latino; 2 Hispanic/Latino; 2 Two or more races, non-Hispanic/Latino), 10 international. Average age 32. 32 applicants, 97% accepted, 27 enrolled. In 2011, 61 master's awarded. *Entrance requirements:* Additional exam requirements/recommendations for international students: Required—TOEFL (minimum score 550 paper-based; 213 computer-based; 79 iBT). *Application deadline:* For fall admission, 7/15 for international students; for spring admission, 12/1 for international students. Applications are processed on a rolling basis. Application fee: $25 ($50 for international students). Electronic applications accepted. *Expenses:* Tuition, state resident: full-time $2700; part-time $150 per credit. Tuition, nonresident: full-time $2700; part-time $150 per credit. *Required fees:* $2286; $127 per credit. *Financial support:* In 2011–12, research assistantships with partial tuition reimbursements (averaging $5,500 per year) were awarded; Federal Work-Study, scholarships/grants, and unspecified assistantships also available. Support available to part-time students. Financial award application deadline: 3/1; financial award applicants required to submit FAFSA. *Unit head:* Joseph McAloon, Chair, 978-665-3745, Fax: 978-665-3658, E-mail: gce@fitchburgstate.edu. *Application contact:* Kay Reynolds, Director of Admissions, 978-665-3144, Fax: 978-665-4540, E-mail: admissions@fitchburgstate.edu. Web site: http://www.fitchburgstate.edu.

Florida Agricultural and Mechanical University, Division of Graduate Studies, Research, and Continuing Education, School of Business and Industry, Tallahassee, FL 32307-3200. Offers accounting (MBA); finance (MBA); management information systems (MBA); marketing (MBA). *Degree requirements:* For master's, residency. *Entrance requirements:* For master's, GMAT, minimum GPA of 3.0.

Florida Atlantic University, College of Business, School of Accounting, Boca Raton, FL 33431-0991. Offers M Ac, M Tax, PhD. *Accreditation:* AACSB. Part-time and evening/weekend programs available. Postbaccalaureate distance learning degree programs offered (minimal on-campus study). *Faculty:* 26 full-time (12 women), 28 part-time/adjunct (9 women). *Students:* 65 full-time (32 women), 284 part-time (165 women); includes 113 minority (38 Black or African American, non-Hispanic/Latino; 24 Asian, non-Hispanic/Latino; 45 Hispanic/Latino; 6 Two or more races, non-Hispanic/Latino), 6 international. Average age 32. 349 applicants, 42% accepted, 61 enrolled. In 2011, 187 master's awarded. *Degree requirements:* For master's, comprehensive exam, thesis optional. *Entrance requirements:* For master's, GMAT, BS in accounting or equivalent, minimum GPA of 3.0 in accounting. Additional exam requirements/recommendations for international students: Required—TOEFL (minimum score 600 paper-based; 250 computer-based). *Application deadline:* For fall admission, 7/1 priority date for domestic students, 2/15 for international students; for spring admission, 11/1 priority date for domestic students, 7/15 for international students. Applications are processed on a rolling basis. Application fee: $30. *Expenses: Tuition, area resident:* Part-time $343.02 per credit hour. Tuition, state resident: full-time $8232. Tuition, nonresident: full-time $23,931; part-time $997.14 per credit hour. *Financial support:* Fellowships, research assistantships with partial tuition reimbursements, teaching assistantships, career-related internships or fieldwork, Federal Work-Study, institutionally sponsored loans, scholarships/grants, and tuition waivers (partial) available. Support available to part-time students. Financial award application deadline: 3/1. *Faculty research:* Systems and computer applications, accounting theory, information systems. *Unit head:* Dr. Kimberly Dunn, Director, 561-297-3638, Fax: 561-297-7023, E-mail: kdunn@fau.edu. Web site: http://business.fau.edu/departments/accounting/index.aspx.

Florida Gulf Coast University, Lutgert College of Business, Program in Accounting and Taxation, Fort Myers, FL 33965-6565. Offers MS. Part-time and evening/weekend programs available. *Faculty:* 51 full-time (14 women), 11 part-time/adjunct (2 women). *Students:* 38 full-time (20 women), 19 part-time (11 women); includes 15 minority (3 Black or African American, non-Hispanic/Latino; 2 Asian, non-Hispanic/Latino; 8 Hispanic/Latino; 2 Two or more races, non-Hispanic/Latino), 2 international. Average age 29. 34 applicants, 71% accepted, 19 enrolled. In 2011, 33 master's awarded. *Degree requirements:* For master's, thesis or alternative. *Entrance requirements:* For master's, GMAT, minimum GPA of 3.0. Additional exam requirements/recommendations for international students: Required—TOEFL (minimum score 550 paper-based; 213 computer-based). *Application deadline:* For fall admission, 6/1 priority date for domestic students; for spring admission, 11/1 for domestic students. Applications are processed on a rolling basis. Application fee: $30. Electronic applications accepted. *Expenses:* Tuition, state resident: full-time $8289. Tuition, nonresident: full-time $28,895. *Required fees:* $1831. One-time fee: $30 full-time. *Faculty research:* Stock petitions, mergers and acquisitions, deferred taxes, fraud and accounting regulations, graphical reporting practices. *Unit head:* Dr. Ara Volkan, Chair, 239-590-7380, Fax: 239-590-7330, E-mail: avolkan@fgcu.edu. *Application contact:* Marisa Ouverson, Director of Enrollment Management, 239-590-7403, Fax: 239-590-7330, E-mail: mouverso@fgcu.edu.

Florida Institute of Technology, Graduate Programs, Nathan M. Bisk College of Business, Online Programs, Melbourne, FL 32901-6975. Offers accounting (MBA); accounting and finance (MBA); business administration (MBA); finance (MBA); healthcare management (MBA); information technology (MS); information technology cybersecurity (MS); information technology management (MBA); international business (MBA); Internet marketing (MBA); management (MBA); marketing (MBA); project management (MBA). Part-time and evening/weekend programs available. Postbaccalaureate distance learning degree programs offered (no on-campus study). *Faculty:* 47 part-time/adjunct (15 women). *Students:* 8 full-time (4 women), 1,122 part-time (547 women); includes 418 minority (271 Black or African American, non-Hispanic/Latino; 5 American Indian or Alaska Native, non-Hispanic/Latino; 55 Asian, non-Hispanic/Latino; 81 Hispanic/Latino; 6 Native Hawaiian or other Pacific Islander, non-Hispanic/Latino), 23 international. Average age 36. In 2011, 329 master's awarded. *Entrance requirements:* For master's, GMAT or resume showing 8 years of supervised experience, 2 letters of recommendation, resume, competency in math past college algebra. Additional exam requirements/recommendations for international students: Required—TOEFL (minimum score 550 paper-based; 213 computer-based; 79 iBT). *Application deadline:* For fall admission, 4/1 for international students; for spring admission, 9/30 for international students. Applications are processed on a rolling basis. Electronic applications accepted. *Expenses:* Contact institution. *Financial support:* Available to part-time students. Application deadline: 3/1; applicants required to submit FAFSA. *Unit head:* Dr. Mary S. Bonhomme, Dean, Florida Tech Online/Associate Provost for Online Learning, 321-674-8202, Fax: 321-674-8216, E-mail: bonhomme@fit.edu. *Application contact:* Carolyn Farrior, Director of Graduate Admissions, Online Learning and Off-Campus Programs, 321-674-7118, Fax: 321-674-8216, E-mail: cfarrior@fit.edu. Web site: http://online.fit.edu.

Florida International University, Alvah H. Chapman, Jr. Graduate School of Business, School of Accounting, Program in Accounting, Miami, FL 33199. Offers M Acc. *Accreditation:* AACSB. Part-time and evening/weekend programs available. *Entrance requirements:* For master's, GMAT or GRE, minimum GPA of 3.0 (upper-level coursework); resume. Additional exam requirements/recommendations for international students: Required—TOEFL (minimum score 550 paper-based; 213 computer-based; 80 iBT) or IELTS (minimum score 6.5). Electronic applications accepted. *Expenses:* Contact institution. *Faculty research:* Financial and managerial accounting.

Florida State University, The Graduate School, College of Business, Tallahassee, FL 32306-1110. Offers accounting (M Acc), including accounting information services, assurance services, corporate accounting, taxation; business administration (MBA, PhD), including accounting (PhD), finance (PhD), management information systems (PhD), marketing (PhD), organizational behavior (PhD), risk management and insurance (PhD), strategic management (PhD); finance (MS); insurance (MSM); management information systems (MS); marketing (MS); JD/MBA; MSW/MBA. *Accreditation:* AACSB. Part-time programs available. Postbaccalaureate distance learning degree programs offered (no on-campus study). *Faculty:* 107 full-time (31 women). *Students:* 196 full-time (76 women), 310 part-time (109 women); includes 89 minority (27 Black or African American, non-Hispanic/Latino; 1 American Indian or Alaska Native, non-Hispanic/Latino; 31 Asian, non-Hispanic/Latino; 30 Hispanic/Latino). Average age 30. 702 applicants, 33% accepted, 205 enrolled. In 2011, 268 master's, 17 doctorates awarded. Terminal master's awarded for partial completion of doctoral program. *Degree requirements:* For doctorate, comprehensive exam, thesis/dissertation. *Entrance requirements:* For master's, GMAT, work experience (MBA, MS), minimum GPA of 3.0, letters of recommendation; for doctorate, GMAT, minimum graduate GPA of 3.5, letters of recommendation. Additional exam requirements/recommendations for international students: Required—TOEFL (minimum score 600 paper-based; 80 computer-based); Recommended—IELTS (minimum score 6.5). *Application deadline:* For fall admission, 6/1 for domestic students, 5/1 for international students; for spring admission, 10/1 for domestic students, 9/1 for international students. Applications are processed on a rolling basis. Application fee: $30. Electronic applications accepted. *Expenses:* Tuition, state resident: full-time $9474; part-time $350.88 per credit hour. Tuition, nonresident: full-time $16,236; part-time $601.34 per credit hour. *Required fees:* $630 per semester. One-time fee: $20. Tuition and fees vary according to course load and campus/location. *Financial support:* In 2011–12, 86 students received support, including 12 fellowships with full tuition reimbursements available (averaging $7,161 per year), 30 research assistantships with full tuition reimbursements available (averaging $6,000 per year), 43 teaching assistantships with full tuition reimbursements available (averaging $15,000 per year); career-related internships or fieldwork, scholarships/grants, health care benefits, tuition waivers (full and partial), and unspecified assistantships also available. Support available to part-time students. Financial award application deadline: 1/1. *Unit head:* Dr. Caryn Beck-Dudley, Dean, 850-644-3090, Fax: 850-644-0915. *Application contact:* Lisa Beverly, Director, Graduate Programs Admissions, 850-644-6458, Fax: 850-644-0588, E-mail: lbeverly@cob.fsu.edu. Web site: http://www.cob.fsu.edu/grad/.

Fontbonne University, Graduate Programs, College of Global Business and Professional Studies, Program in Accounting, St. Louis, MO 63105-3098. Offers MS. Part-time programs available. *Entrance requirements:* For master's, GMAT. Additional exam requirements/recommendations for international students: Required—TOEFL (minimum score 197 computer-based; 71 iBT).

Fordham University, Graduate School of Business, New York, NY 10023. Offers accounting (MBA); communications and media management (MBA); executive business administration (EMBA); finance (MBA, MS); information systems (MBA, MS); management systems (MBA); marketing (MBA); media management (MS); taxation (MS); taxation and accounting (MTA);); JD/MBA; MBA/MIM; MS/MBA. MBA/MIM offered jointly with Thunderbird School of Global Management. *Accreditation:* AACSB. Part-time and evening/weekend programs available. *Entrance requirements:* For master's, GMAT, 2 letters of recommendation, resume. Additional exam requirements/recommendations for international students: Required—TOEFL (minimum score 600 paper-based; 250 computer-based; 100 iBT). Electronic applications accepted. *Expenses:* Contact institution.

Franklin University, Accounting Program, Columbus, OH 43215-5399. Offers MSA. Postbaccalaureate distance learning degree programs offered (minimal on-campus study).

Freed-Hardeman University, Program in Business Administration, Henderson, TN 38340-2399. Offers accounting (MBA); corporate responsibility (MBA); leadership (MBA). *Accreditation:* ACBSP. Part-time and evening/weekend programs available. Postbaccalaureate distance learning degree programs offered (no on-campus study). *Entrance requirements:* For master's, GMAT. Additional exam requirements/recommendations for international students: Required—TOEFL (minimum score 500 paper-based; 173 computer-based).

Friends University, Graduate School, Wichita, KS 67213. Offers accounting (MBA); business administration (MBA); business law (MBL); Christian ministry (MACM); environment science (MSES); family therapy (MSFT); global leadership and management (MA); health care leadership (MHCL); management information systems (MMIS); operations management (MSOM); organization development (MSOD); teaching (MAT). Part-time and evening/weekend programs available. Postbaccalaureate distance learning degree programs offered (no on-campus study). *Faculty:* 14 full-time (5 women), 2 part-time/adjunct (1 woman). *Students:* 158 full-time (114 women), 616 part-time (367 women); includes 159 minority (83 Black or African American, non-Hispanic/Latino; 12 American Indian or Alaska Native, non-Hispanic/Latino; 26 Asian, non-Hispanic/Latino; 22 Hispanic/Latino; 2 Native Hawaiian or other Pacific Islander, non-Hispanic/Latino; 14 Two or more races, non-Hispanic/Latino). Average age 36. 497 applicants, 68% accepted, 256 enrolled. In 2011, 341 degrees awarded. *Degree requirements:* For master's, research project. *Entrance requirements:* For master's, bachelor's degree from accredited institution, official transcripts from institution granting bachelor's degree, interview with program director, letter(s) of recommendation. Additional exam requirements/recommendations for international students: Required—TOEFL (minimum score 560 paper-based; 220 computer-based). *Application deadline:* Applications are processed on a rolling basis. Application fee: $45 ($65 for international students). Electronic applications accepted. *Expenses: Tuition:* Part-time $601 per credit hour. One-time fee: $45 full-time. Tuition and fees vary according to campus/location and program. *Financial support:* Applicants required to submit FAFSA. *Unit head:* Dr. Evelyn Hume, Dean, 800-794-6945 Ext. 5859, Fax: 316-295-5040, E-mail: evelyn_hume@friends.edu. *Application contact:* Jeanette Hanson, Executive Director of Adult Recruitment, 800-794-6945, Fax: 316-295-5050, E-mail: jeanette@friends.edu. Web site: http://www.friends.edu.

Gannon University, School of Graduate Studies, College of Engineering and Business, School of Business, Program in Accounting, Erie, PA 16541-0001. Offers Certificate.

Part-time and evening/weekend programs available. *Entrance requirements:* For degree, GMAT. Additional exam requirements/recommendations for international students: Required—TOEFL (minimum score 79 iBT). *Application deadline:* Applications are processed on a rolling basis. Application fee: $25. Electronic applications accepted. *Financial support:* Application deadline: 7/1; applicants required to submit FAFSA. *Unit head:* Dr. Donna Mottilla, Director, 814-871-7780, E-mail: mottilla001@gannon.edu. *Application contact:* Kara Morgan, Director of Graduate Admissions, 814-871-5831, Fax: 814-871-5827, E-mail: graduate@gannon.edu.

George Mason University, School of Management, Program in Accounting, Fairfax, VA 22030. Offers MS. *Accreditation:* AACSB. *Faculty:* 19 full-time (9 women), 10 part-time/adjunct (2 women). *Students:* 26 full-time (15 women), 18 part-time (7 women); includes 15 minority (2 Black or African American, non-Hispanic/Latino; 10 Asian, non-Hispanic/Latino; 3 Hispanic/Latino), 9 international. Average age 24. 65 applicants, 43% accepted, 19 enrolled. In 2011, 24 degrees awarded. *Entrance requirements:* For master's, GMAT/GRE, resume; official transcripts; 2 letters of recommendation; personal statement; professional essay; interview. Additional exam requirements/recommendations for international students: Required—TOEFL (minimum score 570 paper-based; 230 computer-based; 88 iBT), IELTS, Pearson Test of English. *Application deadline:* For fall admission, 1/14 priority date for domestic students; for spring admission, 10/15 priority date for domestic students, 10/1 for international students. Application fee: $65 ($80 for international students). Electronic applications accepted. *Expenses:* Tuition, state resident: full-time $8750; part-time $364.58 per credit. Tuition, nonresident: full-time $24,092; part-time $1003.83 per credit. *Required fees:* $2514; $104.75 per credit. *Financial support:* In 2011–12, 6 students received support, including 5 research assistantships with full and partial tuition reimbursements available (averaging $10,035 per year), 1 teaching assistantship with full and partial tuition reimbursement available (averaging $11,150 per year); career-related internships or fieldwork, Federal Work-Study, scholarships/grants, unspecified assistantships, and health care benefits (full-time research or teaching assistantship recipients) also available. Financial award application deadline: 3/1; financial award applicants required to submit FAFSA. *Faculty research:* Current leading global business issues, including offshore outsourcing, international financial risk, and comparative systems of innovation; business management/practices; emerging technology and generating new business. *Unit head:* Dr. Edward Douthett, Acting Area Chair, 703-993-4234, Fax: 703-993-1809, E-mail: edouthet@gmu.edu. *Application contact:* Janine Ford, Accounting Administrative Associate, 703-993-4199, Fax: 703-993-1809, E-mail: jford12@gmu.edu. Web site: http://som.gmu.edu/msa.

The George Washington University, School of Business, Department of Accountancy, Washington, DC 20052. Offers M Accy, MBA, PhD. *Accreditation:* AACSB. Part-time and evening/weekend programs available. *Faculty:* 19 full-time (8 women), 13 part-time/adjunct (2 women). *Students:* 93 full-time (65 women), 58 part-time (28 women); includes 19 minority (5 Black or African American, non-Hispanic/Latino; 1 American Indian or Alaska Native, non-Hispanic/Latino; 8 Asian, non-Hispanic/Latino; 4 Hispanic/Latino; 1 Two or more races, non-Hispanic/Latino), 76 international. Average age 26. 341 applicants, 52% accepted, 77 enrolled. In 2011, 111 master's, 1 doctorate awarded. *Degree requirements:* For doctorate, thesis/dissertation. *Entrance requirements:* For master's, GMAT; for doctorate, GMAT or GRE. Additional exam requirements/recommendations for international students: Required—TOEFL. *Application deadline:* For fall admission, 4/1 priority date for domestic students; for spring admission, 10/1 for domestic students. Applications are processed on a rolling basis. Application fee: $75. *Financial support:* In 2011–12, 50 students received support. Fellowships, teaching assistantships, career-related internships or fieldwork, Federal Work-Study, and institutionally sponsored loans available. Financial award application deadline: 4/1. *Faculty research:* Management accounting and capital markets, financial accounting and the analytic hierarchy process, ethics and accounting, accounting information systems. *Unit head:* Dr. Keith Smith, Chair, 202-994-7461, E-mail: kes@gwu.edu. *Application contact:* Louba Hatoum, Program Director, 202-994-4450, E-mail: lhatoum@gwu.edu. Web site: http://www.gwu.edu/~accy/.

Georgia College & State University, Graduate School, The J. Whitney Bunting School of Business, Milledgeville, GA 31061. Offers accountancy (MACCT); accounting (MBA); business (MBA); health services administration (MBA); information systems (MIS); management information services (MBA). *Accreditation:* AACSB. Part-time and evening/weekend programs available. Postbaccalaureate distance learning degree programs offered (no on-campus study). *Students:* 61 full-time (26 women), 134 part-time (55 women); includes 34 minority (18 Black or African American, non-Hispanic/Latino; 9 Asian, non-Hispanic/Latino; 5 Hispanic/Latino; 2 Two or more races, non-Hispanic/Latino), 17 international. Average age 30. 162 applicants, 41% accepted, 45 enrolled. In 2011, 99 master's awarded. *Entrance requirements:* For master's, GMAT or GRE. Additional exam requirements/recommendations for international students: Recommended—TOEFL (minimum score 550 paper-based; 213 computer-based; 79 iBT). *Application deadline:* For fall admission, 7/1 priority date for domestic students, 4/1 for international students; for spring admission, 11/15 priority date for domestic students, 8/1 for international students. Applications are processed on a rolling basis. Application fee: $40. Electronic applications accepted. *Expenses:* Tuition, state resident: full-time $4806; part-time $267 per credit hour. Tuition, nonresident: full-time $17,802; part-time $989 per credit hour. *Required fees:* $936 per semester. Tuition and fees vary according to course load and campus/location. *Financial support:* In 2011–12, 34 research assistantships with full tuition reimbursements were awarded; career-related internships or fieldwork and unspecified assistantships also available. Support available to part-time students. Financial award application deadline: 3/1; financial award applicants required to submit FAFSA. *Unit head:* Dr. Matthew Liao-Troth, Dean, School of Business, 478-445-5497, E-mail: matthew.liao-troth@gcsu.edu. *Application contact:* Lynn Hanson, Director of Graduate Programs, 478-445-5115, E-mail: lynn.hanson@gcsu.edu. Web site: http://www.gcsu.edu/business/graduateprograms/index.htm.

Georgia Institute of Technology, Graduate Studies and Research, College of Management, Program in Business Administration, Atlanta, GA 30332-0001. Offers accounting (MBA); e-commerce (Certificate); engineering entrepreneurship (MBA); entrepreneurship (Certificate); finance (MBA); information technology management (MBA); international business (MBA, Certificate); management of technology (Certificate); marketing (MBA); operations management (MBA); organizational behavior (MBA); strategic management (MBA). *Accreditation:* AACSB.

Georgia Institute of Technology, Graduate Studies and Research, College of Management, Program in Management, Atlanta, GA 30332-0001. Offers accounting (PhD); finance (PhD); information technology management (PhD); marketing (PhD); operations management (PhD); organizational behavior (PhD); quantitative and computational finance (MS); strategic management (PhD). *Accreditation:* AACSB. *Degree requirements:* For doctorate, comprehensive exam, thesis/dissertation, oral exams. *Entrance requirements:* For master's and doctorate, GMAT. Additional exam requirements/recommendations for international students: Required—TOEFL. *Faculty research:* MIS, management of technology, international business, entrepreneurship, operations management.

Georgia Southern University, Jack N. Averitt College of Graduate Studies, College of Business Administration, School of Accountancy, Statesboro, GA 30460. Offers accounting (M Acc). *Accreditation:* AACSB. Part-time and evening/weekend programs available. *Students:* 79 full-time (37 women), 20 part-time (6 women); includes 18 minority (14 Black or African American, non-Hispanic/Latino; 2 Asian, non-Hispanic/Latino; 2 Two or more races, non-Hispanic/Latino), 13 international. Average age 25. 48 applicants, 83% accepted, 28 enrolled. In 2011, 47 master's awarded. *Entrance requirements:* For master's, GMAT. Additional exam requirements/recommendations for international students: Required—TOEFL (minimum score 550 paper-based; 213 computer-based; 80 iBT). *Application deadline:* For fall admission, 3/1 priority date for domestic students, 3/1 for international students; for spring admission, 10/1 priority date for domestic students, 10/1 for international students. Applications are processed on a rolling basis. Application fee: $50. Electronic applications accepted. *Expenses:* Contact institution. *Financial support:* In 2011–12, 34 students received support, including research assistantships with partial tuition reimbursements available (averaging $7,200 per year), teaching assistantships with partial tuition reimbursements available (averaging $7,200 per year); career-related internships or fieldwork, Federal Work-Study, scholarships/grants, tuition waivers (partial), and unspecified assistantships also available. Support available to part-time students. Financial award application deadline: 4/15; financial award applicants required to submit FAFSA. *Faculty research:* Consolidation of fraud in the financial statement, reasons why firms switch auditions for the financial audit, internalization of accounting standards, pedagogy issues in accounting and law courses. *Unit head:* Dr. Mary Jill Lockwood, Director, 912-478-2228, Fax: 912-478-0105, E-mail: mjl@georgiasouthern.edu. *Application contact:* Amanda Gilliland, Coordinator for Graduate Student Recruitment, 912-478-5384, Fax: 912-478-0740, E-mail: gradadmissions@georgiasouthern.edu. Web site: http://www.coba.georgiasouthern.edu/depts/acc/.

Georgia State University, J. Mack Robinson College of Business, Program in General Business Administration, Atlanta, GA 30302-3083. Offers accounting/information systems (MBA); economics (MBA, MS); enterprise risk management (MBA); general business (MBA); general business administration (EMBA, PMBA); information systems consulting (MBA); information systems risk management (MBA); international business and information technology (MBA); international entrepreneurship (MBA); MBA/JD. *Accreditation:* AACSB. Part-time and evening/weekend programs available. *Entrance requirements:* For master's, GMAT. Additional exam requirements/recommendations for international students: Required—TOEFL (minimum score 610 paper-based; 255 computer-based; 101 iBT). Electronic applications accepted.

Georgia State University, J. Mack Robinson College of Business, School of Accountancy, School of Accountancy, Atlanta, AB 30303. Offers MBA, MPA, PhD, Certificate. *Accreditation:* AACSB. Part-time programs available. *Degree requirements:* For doctorate, thesis/dissertation. *Entrance requirements:* For master's and doctorate, GMAT. Additional exam requirements/recommendations for international students: Required—TOEFL (minimum score 610 paper-based; 255 computer-based; 101 iBT). Electronic applications accepted.

Golden Gate University, Ageno School of Business, San Francisco, CA 94105-2968. Offers accounting (MBA); business administration (EMBA, MBA, PMBA, DBA); finance (MBA, MS, Certificate); financial planning (MS, Certificate); healthcare information systems (Certificate); human resource management (MBA, MS); human resources management (Certificate); information systems (MS); information technology (MBA); information technology management (Certificate); integrated marketing and communications (MS, Certificate); international business (MBA); management (MBA); marketing (MBA, MS, Certificate); operations supply chain management (Certificate); psychology (MA, Certificate); public administration (EMPA); public relations (MS, Certificate); technical market analysis (Certificate); JD/MBA. Part-time and evening/weekend programs available. *Faculty:* 19 full-time (6 women), 241 part-time/adjunct (72 women). *Students:* 397 full-time (230 women), 779 part-time (432 women); includes 376 minority (105 Black or African American, non-Hispanic/Latino; 5 American Indian or Alaska Native, non-Hispanic/Latino; 161 Asian, non-Hispanic/Latino; 77 Hispanic/Latino; 12 Native Hawaiian or other Pacific Islander, non-Hispanic/Latino; 16 Two or more races, non-Hispanic/Latino), 265 international. Average age 34. 871 applicants, 64% accepted, 271 enrolled. In 2011, 550 master's, 13 doctorates awarded. *Degree requirements:* For doctorate, thesis/dissertation, qualifying examination. *Entrance requirements:* For master's, GMAT (MBA), minimum GPA of 2.5 (MS). Additional exam requirements/recommendations for international students: Required—TOEFL (minimum score 550 paper-based; 213 computer-based; 79 iBT). *Application deadline:* For fall admission, 5/15 for domestic and international students; for winter admission, 1/15 for domestic and international students; for spring admission, 9/15 for domestic and international students. Applications are processed on a rolling basis. Application fee: $70 ($110 for international students). Electronic applications accepted. *Expenses:* Contact institution. *Financial support:* Career-related internships or fieldwork, Federal Work-Study, institutionally sponsored loans, and scholarships/grants available. Support available to part-time students. Financial award applicants required to submit FAFSA. *Unit head:* Dr. Paul Fouts, Dean, 415-442-7026, Fax: 415-442-6579. *Application contact:* Angela Melero, Enrollment Services, 415-442-7800, Fax: 415-442-7807, E-mail: info@ggu.edu. Web site: http://www.ggu.edu/programs/business-and-management.

Golden Gate University, School of Accounting, San Francisco, CA 94105-2968. Offers accounting (M Ac, Graduate Certificate); forensic (M Ac); forensic accounting (Graduate Certificate); taxation (M Ac). Part-time and evening/weekend programs available. *Faculty:* 6 full-time (2 women), 55 part-time/adjunct (16 women). *Students:* 112 full-time (70 women), 157 part-time (99 women); includes 76 minority (1 American Indian or Alaska Native, non-Hispanic/Latino; 52 Asian, non-Hispanic/Latino; 17 Hispanic/Latino; 4 Native Hawaiian or other Pacific Islander, non-Hispanic/Latino; 2 Two or more races, non-Hispanic/Latino), 81 international. Average age 31. 149 applicants, 64% accepted, 53 enrolled. In 2011, 114 master's awarded. *Entrance requirements:* For master's, minimum GPA of 3.0. Additional exam requirements/recommendations for international students: Required—TOEFL. *Application deadline:* For fall admission, 5/15 for international students; for winter admission, 1/15 for international students; for spring admission, 9/15 for international students. Applications are processed on a rolling basis. Application fee: $70 ($110 for international students). Electronic applications accepted. *Financial support:* Career-related internships or fieldwork, Federal Work-Study, institutionally sponsored loans, and scholarships/grants available. Support available to part-time students. Financial award applicants required to submit FAFSA. *Faculty research:* Forensic accounting, audit, tax, CPA exam. *Unit head:* Mary Canning, 415-442-7885, Fax: 415-543-2607. *Application contact:* Angela Melero, Enrollment Services, 415-442-7800, Fax: 415-442-7807, E-mail: info@ggu.edu.

Gonzaga University, School of Business Administration, Spokane, WA 99258. Offers M Acc, MBA, JD/M Acc, JD/MBA. *Accreditation:* AACSB. Part-time and evening/weekend programs available. *Entrance requirements:* For master's, GMAT. Additional exam requirements/recommendations for international students: Required—TOEFL.

Governors State University, College of Business and Public Administration, Program in Accounting, University Park, IL 60484. Offers MS. *Students:* 15 full-time (11 women), 34 part-time (23 women); includes 17 minority (14 Black or African American, non-Hispanic/Latino; 3 Asian, non-Hispanic/Latino), 5 international. Average age 31. *Entrance requirements:* For master's, GMAT. *Application deadline:* For fall admission, 7/

15 priority date for domestic students; for spring admission, 11/10 for domestic students. Applications are processed on a rolling basis. Application fee: $25. *Financial support:* Application deadline: 5/1. *Unit head:* Dr. Ellen Foster-Curtis, Dean, College of Business and Public Administration, 708-534-4930, Fax: 708-534-8457, E-mail: efostercurtis@govst.edu.

Graduate School and University Center of the City University of New York, Graduate Studies, Program in Business, New York, NY 10016-4039. Offers accounting (PhD); behavioral science (PhD); finance (PhD); management planning systems (PhD). *Degree requirements:* For doctorate, thesis/dissertation. *Entrance requirements:* For doctorate, GMAT, writing sample (15 pages). Additional exam requirements/recommendations for international students: Required—TOEFL. Electronic applications accepted.

Grand Canyon University, College of Business, Phoenix, AZ 85017-1097. Offers accounting (MBA); corporate business administration (MBA); disaster preparedness and crisis management (MBA); executive fire service leadership (MS); finance (MBA); general management (MBA); government and policy (MPA); health care management (MPA); health systems management (MBA); human resource management (MBA); innovation (MBA); leadership (MBA, MS); management of information system (MBA); marketing (MBA); project-based (MBA); six sigma (MBA); strategic human resource management (MBA). *Accreditation:* ACBSP. Part-time and evening/weekend programs available. Postbaccalaureate distance learning degree programs offered (no on-campus study). *Entrance requirements:* For master's, equivalent of two years full-time professional work experience. Additional exam requirements/recommendations for international students: Required—TOEFL (minimum score 575 paper-based; 233 computer-based; 90 iBT), IELTS (minimum score 7). Electronic applications accepted.

Grand Valley State University, Seidman College of Business, Program in Accounting, Allendale, MI 49401-9403. Offers MSA. *Accreditation:* AACSB. Part-time and evening/weekend programs available. *Degree requirements:* For master's, comprehensive exam. *Entrance requirements:* For master's, GMAT. Additional exam requirements/recommendations for international students: Required—TOEFL. *Faculty research:* Public trust, capacity measurement, theoretical capacity, economic order quantity.

Harvard University, Harvard Business School, Doctoral Programs in Management, Boston, MA 02163. Offers accounting and management (DBA); business economics (PhD); health policy management (PhD); management (DBA); marketing (DBA); organizational behavior (PhD); science, technology and management (PhD); strategy (DBA); technology and operations management (DBA). *Degree requirements:* For doctorate, comprehensive exam (for some programs), thesis/dissertation. *Entrance requirements:* For doctorate, GRE General Test or GMAT. Additional exam requirements/recommendations for international students: Required—TOEFL. *Expenses: Tuition:* Full-time $36,304. *Required fees:* $1186. Full-time tuition and fees vary according to program.

Hawai`i Pacific University, College of Business Administration, Honolulu, HI 96813. Offers accounting/CPA (MBA); e-business (MBA); economics (MBA); finance (MBA); human resource management (MA, MBA); information systems (MBA, MSIS), including knowledge management (MSIS), software engineering (MSIS), telecommunications security (MSIS); international business (MBA); management (MBA); marketing (MBA); organizational change (MA, MBA); travel industry management (MBA). Part-time and evening/weekend programs available. *Faculty:* 15 full-time (5 women), 11 part-time/adjunct (4 women). *Students:* 297 full-time (133 women), 183 part-time (87 women); includes 282 minority (17 Black or African American, non-Hispanic/Latino; 131 Asian, non-Hispanic/Latino; 43 Hispanic/Latino; 10 Native Hawaiian or other Pacific Islander, non-Hispanic/Latino; 81 Two or more races, non-Hispanic/Latino). Average age 30. 302 applicants, 82% accepted, 160 enrolled. In 2011, 141 master's awarded. *Degree requirements:* For master's, thesis. *Entrance requirements:* For master's, GMAT. Additional exam requirements/recommendations for international students: Recommended—TOEFL (minimum score 550 paper-based; 213 computer-based; 80 iBT), TWE (minimum score 5). *Application deadline:* For fall admission, 2/15 priority date for domestic students; for spring admission, 10/15 priority date for domestic students. Applications are processed on a rolling basis. Application fee: $50. Electronic applications accepted. *Expenses: Tuition:* Full-time $13,230; part-time $735 per credit. Tuition and fees vary according to course load and program. *Financial support:* In 2011–12, 103 students received support. Research assistantships, career-related internships or fieldwork, Federal Work-Study, scholarships/grants, tuition waivers, and unspecified assistantships available. Financial award application deadline: 3/1; financial award applicants required to submit FAFSA. *Faculty research:* Statistical control process as used by management, studies in comparative cross-cultural management styles, not-for-profit management. *Unit head:* Dr. Deborah Crown, Dean, 808-544-0275, Fax: 808-544-0283, E-mail: dcrown@hpu.edu. *Application contact:* Chad Schempp, Director of Graduate Admissions, 808-543-8035, Fax: 808-544-0280, E-mail: graduate@hpu.edu. Web site: http://www.hpu.edu/mba.

See Display on page 98 and Close-Up on page 221.

HEC Montreal, School of Business Administration, Graduate Diplomas Programs in Administration, Program in Public Accounting, Montréal, QC H3T 2A7, Canada. Offers Graduate Diploma. All courses are given in French. Part-time programs available. *Students:* 183 full-time (111 women), 32 part-time (19 women). 257 applicants, 81% accepted, 187 enrolled. In 2011, 156 Graduate Diplomas awarded. *Degree requirements:* For Graduate Diploma, one foreign language. *Entrance requirements:* For degree, bachelor's degree in accounting. *Application deadline:* For spring admission, 2/15 for domestic and international students. Application fee: $80 Canadian dollars. Electronic applications accepted. Application fee is waived when completed online. *Expenses:* Contact institution. *Financial support:* Research assistantships, teaching assistantships, and scholarships/grants available. Financial award application deadline: 9/2. *Unit head:* Silvia Ponce, Director, 514-340-6393, Fax: 514-340-6915, E-mail: silvia.ponce@hec.ca. *Application contact:* Jo Anne Audet, Administrative Director, 514-340-1315, Fax: 514-340-6411, E-mail: joanne.audet@hec.ca. Web site: http://www.hec.ca/programmes_formations/des/dess/dess_comptabilite_publique/index.html.

HEC Montreal, School of Business Administration, Master of Science Programs in Administration, Program in Financial and Strategic Accounting, Montréal, QC H3T 2A7, Canada. Offers M Sc. Part-time programs available. *Students:* 6 full-time (2 women), 3 part-time (0 women). 17 applicants, 53% accepted, 6 enrolled. In 2011, 5 master's awarded. *Degree requirements:* For master's, one foreign language, thesis. *Entrance requirements:* For master's, Test de francais international (TFI) with minimum score of 850 (for those who have never studied in French), BBA, undergraduate degree in another field, degree deemed equivalent by program director and minimum GPA of 3.0 on 4.3 scale. *Application deadline:* For fall admission, 3/15 for domestic and international students; for winter admission, 9/15 for domestic and international students. Application fee: $80. Electronic applications accepted. Application fee is waived when completed online. *Expenses:* Contact institution. *Financial support:* Research assistantships, teaching assistantships, and scholarships/grants available. Financial award application deadline: 9/2. *Unit head:* Claude Laurin, Director, 514-340-6847, Fax: 514-340-6880, E-mail: claude.laurin@hec.ca. *Application contact:* Virginie Lefebvre, Administrative Director, 514-340-6112, Fax: 514-340-6411, E-mail: virginie.lefebvre@hec.ca. Web site: http://www.hec.ca/en/programs_training/msc/options/financial_strategic_accounting/index.html.

HEC Montreal, School of Business Administration, Master of Science Programs in Administration, Program in Management Control, Montréal, QC H3T 2A7, Canada. Offers M Sc. Part-time programs available. *Students:* 27 full-time (13 women), 7 part-time (2 women). 30 applicants, 50% accepted, 10 enrolled. In 2011, 10 master's awarded. *Degree requirements:* For master's, one foreign language, thesis. *Entrance requirements:* For master's, Test de francais international (TFI) with minimum score of 850 (for those who have never studied in French), BBA, undergraduate degree in another field, degree deemed equivalent by program director and minimum GPA of 3.0 on 4.3 scale. *Application deadline:* For fall admission, 3/15 for domestic and international students; for winter admission, 9/15 for domestic and international students. Application fee: $80 Canadian dollars. Electronic applications accepted. Application fee is waived when completed online. *Expenses:* Contact institution. *Financial support:* Fellowships, research assistantships, teaching assistantships, and scholarships/grants available. Financial award application deadline: 9/2. *Unit head:* Dr. Claude Laurin, Director, 514-340-6485, Fax: 514-340-6880, E-mail: claude.laurin@hec.ca. *Application contact:* Virginie Lefebvre, Administrative Director, 514-340-6112, Fax: 514-340-6411, E-mail: virginie.lefebvre@hec.ca. Web site: http://www.hec.ca/en/programs_training/msc/options/management_control/index.html.

HEC Montreal, School of Business Administration, Master of Science Programs in Administration, Program in Public Accounting, Montréal, QC H3T 2A7, Canada. Offers M Sc. All courses are given in French. Part-time programs available. *Students:* 6 full-time (1 woman), 32 part-time (18 women). 38 applicants, 97% accepted, 15 enrolled. In 2011, 13 master's awarded. *Degree requirements:* For master's, one foreign language, thesis. *Entrance requirements:* For master's, Test de francais international (TFI) with minimum score of 850 (for those who have never studied in French), BBA, undergraduate degree in another field, degree deemed equivalent by program director and minimum GPA of 3.0 on 4.3 scale. *Application deadline:* For fall admission, 3/15 for domestic and international students; for winter admission, 9/15 for domestic and international students; for spring admission, 4/15 for domestic and international students. Application fee: $80. Electronic applications accepted. Application fee is waived when completed online. *Expenses:* Contact institution. *Financial support:* Research assistantships, teaching assistantships, and scholarships/grants available. Financial award application deadline: 9/2. *Unit head:* Claude Laurin, Director, 514-340-6485, Fax: 514-340-6880, E-mail: claude.laurin@hec.ca. *Application contact:* Virginie Lefebvre, Administrative Director, 514-340-6112, Fax: 514-340-6411, E-mail: virginie.lefebvre@hec.ca. Web site: http://www.hec.ca/programmes_formations/des/microprogrammes/microprogramme_expertise_comptable/index.html.

Hendrix College, Program in Accounting, Conway, AR 72032-3080. Offers MA. Part-time programs available. *Entrance requirements:* For master's, GMAT. Additional exam requirements/recommendations for international students: Required—TOEFL. *Faculty research:* Meta-analysis, utility regulatory entities.

Herzing University Online, Program in Business Administration, Milwaukee, WI 53203. Offers accounting (MBA); business administration (MBA); business management (MBA); healthcare management (MBA); human resources (MBA); marketing (MBA); project management (MBA); technology management (MBA). Postbaccalaureate distance learning degree programs offered (no on-campus study).

Hofstra University, Frank G. Zarb School of Business, Programs in Accounting and Taxation, Hempstead, NY 11549. Offers accounting (MS, Advanced Certificate); business administration (MBA), including accounting, professional accountancy, taxation; taxation (MS, Advanced Certificate). Part-time and evening/weekend programs available. Postbaccalaureate distance learning degree programs offered (minimal on-campus study). *Faculty:* 13 full-time (4 women), 5 part-time/adjunct (1 woman). *Students:* 166 full-time (100 women), 70 part-time (35 women); includes 30 minority (3 Black or African American, non-Hispanic/Latino; 20 Asian, non-Hispanic/Latino; 7 Hispanic/Latino), 97 international. Average age 25. 383 applicants, 79% accepted, 113 enrolled. In 2011, 45 master's awarded. *Degree requirements:* For master's, capstone course (for MBA); thesis (for MS); minimum GPA of 3.0. *Entrance requirements:* For master's, GMAT/GRE, 2 letters of recommendation; resume; essay. Additional exam requirements/recommendations for international students: Required—TOEFL (minimum score 550 paper-based; 213 computer-based; 80 iBT); Recommended—IELTS (minimum score 6). *Application deadline:* Applications are processed on a rolling basis. Application fee: $70 ($75 for international students). Electronic applications accepted. *Expenses:* Contact institution. *Financial support:* In 2011–12, 23 students received support, including 20 fellowships with full and partial tuition reimbursements available (averaging $6,973 per year); research assistantships with full and partial tuition reimbursements available, career-related internships or fieldwork, Federal Work-Study, institutionally sponsored loans, scholarships/grants, tuition waivers (full and partial), and unspecified assistantships also available. Support available to part-time students. Financial award applicants required to submit FAFSA. *Faculty research:* Legal issues in the insurance industry, penalties regarding tax compliance and the Internal Revenue Code, agency theory and accounts of migration, plain English financial statements, learning methods for teaching XBRL. *Unit head:* Dr. Nathan S. Slavin, Chairperson, 516-463-5690, Fax: 516-463-4834, E-mail: actnzs@hofstra.edu. *Application contact:* Carol Drummer, Dean of Graduate Admissions, 516-463-4876, Fax: 516-463-4664, E-mail: gradstudent@hofstra.edu. Web site: http://www.hofstra.edu/business/.

Hood College, Graduate School, Department of Economics and Management, Frederick, MD 21701-8575. Offers accounting (MBA); administration and management (MBA); finance (MBA); human resource management (MBA); information systems (MBA); marketing (MBA); public management (MBA). *Accreditation:* ACBSP. Part-time and evening/weekend programs available. *Degree requirements:* For master's, capstone/final research project. *Entrance requirements:* For master's, minimum GPA of 2.75, resume, letters of recommendation. Additional exam requirements/recommendations for international students: Required—TOEFL (minimum score 575 paper-based; 231 computer-based; 89 iBT). Electronic applications accepted. *Faculty research:* Corporate strategy and sustainable competitive advantages, business ethics, entrepreneurship, investments management, economic development.

Houston Baptist University, College of Business and Economics, Program in Accounting, Houston, TX 77074-3298. Offers MACCT. *Entrance requirements:* For master's, GMAT. Additional exam requirements/recommendations for international students: Required—TOEFL (minimum score 550 paper-based; 213 computer-based).

Howard University, School of Business, Graduate Programs in Business, Washington, DC 20059-0002. Offers accounting (MBA); entrepreneurship (MBA); finance (MBA); general management (MBA); human resources management (MBA); information systems (MBA); international business (MBA); marketing (MBA); supply chain management (MBA); JD/MBA. *Accreditation:* AACSB. Part-time and evening/weekend programs available. Postbaccalaureate distance learning degree programs offered (no on-campus study). *Entrance requirements:* For master's, GMAT, minimum 1 year post undergraduate work experience, resume, 3 letters of recommendation, advanced college algebra. Additional exam requirements/recommendations for international students: Required—TOEFL. *Faculty research:* Marketing research in multi-ethnic populations, U.S. trade policies and international relations, risk management (finance).

Hunter College of the City University of New York, Graduate School, School of Arts and Sciences, Department of Economics, Program in Accounting, New York, NY 10021-5085. Offers MS. *Faculty:* 6 full-time (1 woman), 6 part-time/adjunct (2 women). *Students:* 17 full-time (7 women), 42 part-time (26 women); includes 26 minority (5 Black or African American, non-Hispanic/Latino; 13 Asian, non-Hispanic/Latino; 8 Hispanic/Latino), 13 international. Average age 28. 70 applicants, 73% accepted, 26 enrolled. In 2011, 21 master's awarded. *Application deadline:* For fall admission, 4/1 for domestic students, 2/1 for international students; for spring admission, 11/1 for domestic students, 9/1 for international students. Application fee: $125. *Expenses:* Tuition, state resident: full-time $8210; part-time $345 per credit. Tuition, nonresident: full-time $15,360; part-time $640 per credit. *Required fees:* $280 per semester. One-time fee: $125. Tuition and fees vary according to class time, campus/location and program. *Unit head:* Dr. Marjorie P. Honig, Chairperson, 212-772-5400, Fax: 212-772-5398, E-mail: mhonig@hunter.cuny.edu. *Application contact:* Dr. Tashiaki Mitsudome, Graduate Advisor, 212-772-5430, E-mail: tashiaki.mitsudome@hunter.cuny.edu.

Illinois State University, Graduate School, College of Business, Department of Accounting, Normal, IL 61790-2200. Offers MPA, MS. *Accreditation:* AACSB. *Degree requirements:* For master's, comprehensive exam. *Entrance requirements:* For master's, GMAT, minimum GPA of 2.75 in last 60 hours of course work. Additional exam requirements/recommendations for international students: Required—TOEFL.

Indiana Tech, Program in Business Administration, Fort Wayne, IN 46803-1297. Offers accounting (MBA); health care administration (MBA); human resources (MBA); management (MBA); marketing (MBA). Part-time and evening/weekend programs available. Postbaccalaureate distance learning degree programs offered (no on-campus study). *Entrance requirements:* For master's, GMAT, minimum undergraduate GPA of 2.5, 3 letters of recommendation. Electronic applications accepted.

Indiana University Northwest, School of Business and Economics, Gary, IN 46408-1197. Offers accountancy (M Acc); accounting (Certificate); business administration (MBA). *Accreditation:* AACSB. Part-time and evening/weekend programs available. *Faculty:* 5 full-time (0 women). *Students:* 49 full-time (10 women), 53 part-time (28 women); includes 40 minority (25 Black or African American, non-Hispanic/Latino; 8 Asian, non-Hispanic/Latino; 7 Hispanic/Latino). Average age 34. 40 applicants, 93% accepted, 26 enrolled. In 2011, 38 master's, 12 other advanced degrees awarded. *Entrance requirements:* For master's, GMAT, letter of recommendation. *Application deadline:* For fall admission, 7/15 priority date for domestic students; for spring admission, 11/15 for domestic students. Applications are processed on a rolling basis. Application fee: $25 ($45 for international students). *Expenses:* Contact institution. *Financial support:* Federal Work-Study, institutionally sponsored loans, and unspecified assistantships available. Support available to part-time students. Financial award application deadline: 7/15. *Faculty research:* International finance, wellness in the workplace, handicapped employment, MIS, regional economic forecasting. *Unit head:* Anna Rominger, Dean, 219-980-6636, Fax: 219-980-6916, E-mail: iunbiz@iun.edu. *Application contact:* John Gibson, Director of Graduate Program, 219-980-6635, Fax: 219-980-6916, E-mail: jagibson@iun.edu. Web site: http://www.iun.edu/~busnw/.

Indiana University–Purdue University Indianapolis, Kelley School of Business, Indianapolis, IN 46202-2896. Offers accounting (MSA); business (MBA). *Accreditation:* AACSB. Part-time and evening/weekend programs available. Postbaccalaureate distance learning degree programs offered (minimal on-campus study). *Faculty:* 20 full-time (4 women), 1 part-time/adjunct (0 women). *Students:* 114 full-time (45 women), 380 part-time (125 women); includes 79 minority (29 Black or African American, non-Hispanic/Latino; 33 Asian, non-Hispanic/Latino; 9 Hispanic/Latino; 8 Two or more races, non-Hispanic/Latino), 84 international. Average age 30. 220 applicants, 73% accepted, 123 enrolled. In 2011, 273 master's awarded. *Entrance requirements:* For master's, GMAT, previous course work in accounting, statistics. *Application deadline:* For fall admission, 4/15 priority date for domestic students, 4/15 for international students; for spring admission, 11/1 priority date for domestic students, 11/1 for international students. Applications are processed on a rolling basis. Application fee: $55 ($65 for international students). Electronic applications accepted. *Expenses:* Contact institution. *Financial support:* In 2011–12, fellowships (averaging $16,193 per year), teaching assistantships (averaging $9,000 per year) were awarded; Federal Work-Study, institutionally sponsored loans, and scholarships/grants also available. Support available to part-time students. Financial award application deadline: 3/1; financial award applicants required to submit FAFSA. *Unit head:* Phillip L. Cochran, Associate Dean, Indianapolis Programs, 317-274-4179, Fax: 317-274-2483, E-mail: busugrad@iupui.edu. *Application contact:* Julie L. Moore, Recorder/Admission Coordinator, 317-274-0885, Fax: 317-274-2483, E-mail: mbaindy@iupui.edu. Web site: http://kelley.iupui.edu/evemba.

Indiana University South Bend, School of Business and Economics, South Bend, IN 46634-7111. Offers accounting (MSA); business administration (MBA); management of information technologies (MS). Part-time and evening/weekend programs available. *Faculty:* 17 full-time (2 women), 3 part-time/adjunct (1 woman). *Students:* 78 full-time (31 women), 112 part-time (50 women); includes 17 minority (6 Black or African American, non-Hispanic/Latino; 1 American Indian or Alaska Native, non-Hispanic/Latino; 4 Asian, non-Hispanic/Latino; 5 Hispanic/Latino; 1 Two or more races, non-Hispanic/Latino), 70 international. Average age 32. 65 applicants, 74% accepted, 23 enrolled. In 2011, 37 master's awarded. *Entrance requirements:* For master's, GMAT. Additional exam requirements/recommendations for international students: Required—TOEFL (minimum score 550 paper-based; 213 computer-based). *Application deadline:* For fall admission, 7/1 priority date for domestic students, 7/1 for international students; for spring admission, 11/1 priority date for domestic students, 11/1 for international students. Applications are processed on a rolling basis. Application fee: $50 ($60 for international students). *Expenses:* Contact institution. *Financial support:* In 2011–12, 1 fellowship (averaging $3,846 per year) was awarded; Federal Work-Study and institutionally sponsored loans also available. Support available to part-time students. Financial award applicants required to submit FAFSA. *Faculty research:* Financial accounting, consumer research, capital budgeting research, business strategy research. *Unit head:* Robert H. Ducoffe, Dean, 574-520-4228, Fax: 574-520-4866. *Application contact:* Sharon Peterson, Secretary, 574-520-4138, Fax: 574-520-4866, E-mail: speterso@iusb.edu. Web site: http://www.iusb.edu/~buse/grad.

Indiana Wesleyan University, College of Adult and Professional Studies, Graduate Studies in Business, Marion, IN 46953. Offers accounting (MBA); applied management (MBA); business administration (MBA); health care (MBA); human resources (MBA); management (MS). Part-time and evening/weekend programs available. Postbaccalaureate distance learning degree programs offered (no on-campus study). *Degree requirements:* For master's, applied business or management project. *Entrance requirements:* For master's, minimum GPA of 2.5, 2 years of related work experience. Additional exam requirements/recommendations for international students: Required—TOEFL (minimum score 550 paper-based; 213 computer-based). Electronic applications accepted.

Instituto Tecnologico de Santo Domingo, Graduate School, Area of Humanities and Social Sciences, Santo Domingo, Dominican Republic. Offers accounting (Certificate); adult education (Certificate); applied linguistics (MA); economics (MA); education (M Ed); educational psychology (MA, Certificate); gender and development (MA, Certificate); humanistic studies (MA); international marketing management (Certificate); international relations in the Caribbean basin (Certificate); intervention systems in family therapy (MA); linguistic and literary communication (Certificate); pedagogical support (MA); social science education (M Ed); sustainable human development (MA); terminal illness and death psychology (Certificate); youth and adult education (M Ed).

Inter American University of Puerto Rico, Aguadilla Campus, Graduate School, Aguadilla, PR 00605. Offers accounting (MBA); counseling psychology specializing in family (MS); criminal justice (MA); educative management and leadership (MA); elementary education (M Ed); finance (MBA); human resources (MBA); industrial management (MBA); management information systems (MBA); marketing (MBA). Part-time and evening/weekend programs available. *Degree requirements:* For master's, comprehensive exam. *Entrance requirements:* For master's, EXADEP, 2 letters of recommendation, minimum GPA of 2.5. Electronic applications accepted.

Inter American University of Puerto Rico, Arecibo Campus, Program in Business Administration, Arecibo, PR 00614-4050. Offers accounting (MBA); finance (MBA); human resources (MBA).

Inter American University of Puerto Rico, Barranquitas Campus, Program in Business Administration, Barranquitas, PR 00794. Offers accounting (IMBA); finance (IMBA).

Inter American University of Puerto Rico, Metropolitan Campus, Graduate Programs, Program in Accounting, San Juan, PR 00919-1293. Offers MBA. *Degree requirements:* For master's, comprehensive exam. *Entrance requirements:* For master's, GRE or EXADEP, interview. Electronic applications accepted.

Inter American University of Puerto Rico, Ponce Campus, Graduate School, Mercedita, PR 00715-1602. Offers accounting (MBA); biology (M Ed); chemistry (M Ed); criminal justice (MA); elementary education (M Ed); English as a Second Language (M Ed); finance (MBA); history (M Ed); human resources (MBA); marketing (MBA); mathematics (M Ed); Spanish (M Ed). *Entrance requirements:* For master's, minimum GPA of 2.5.

Inter American University of Puerto Rico, San Germán Campus, Graduate Studies Center, Program in Business Administration, San Germán, PR 00683-5008. Offers accounting (MBA); finance (MBA); human resources (MBA, PhD); industrial relations (MBA); information sciences (MBA); management (MBA); marketing (MBA). Part-time and evening/weekend programs available. *Degree requirements:* For master's, comprehensive exam. *Entrance requirements:* For master's, GRE General Test or EXADEP, minimum GPA of 3.0. *Application deadline:* For fall admission, 4/30 priority date for domestic students; for spring admission, 11/15 for domestic students. Applications are processed on a rolling basis. Application fee: $31. *Expenses: Required fees:* $213 per semester. *Financial support:* Teaching assistantships, Federal Work-Study, and unspecified assistantships available. *Unit head:* Dr. Elba T. Irizarry, Director of Graduate Studies Center, 787-264-1912 Ext. 7357, Fax: 787-892-6350, E-mail: elbat@sg.inter.edu.

Iona College, Hagan School of Business, Department of Accounting, New Rochelle, NY 10801-1890. Offers general accounting (MBA, PMC); public accounting (MBA, PMC). Part-time and evening/weekend programs available. *Faculty:* 4 full-time (1 woman), 1 part-time/adjunct (0 women). *Students:* 17 full-time (10 women), 44 part-time (12 women); includes 9 minority (4 Black or African American, non-Hispanic/Latino; 5 Hispanic/Latino). Average age 27. 33 applicants, 70% accepted, 14 enrolled. In 2011, 22 master's, 5 other advanced degrees awarded. *Entrance requirements:* For master's, GMAT, two letters of recommendation; for PMC, GMAT. Additional exam requirements/recommendations for international students: Required—TOEFL (minimum score 550 paper-based; 213 computer-based; 80 iBT). *Application deadline:* For fall admission, 8/15 priority date for domestic students, 8/1 for international students; for winter admission, 11/15 priority date for domestic students, 11/1 for international students; for spring admission, 2/15 priority date for domestic students, 2/1 for international students. Applications are processed on a rolling basis. Application fee: $50. Electronic applications accepted. *Expenses: Tuition:* Part-time $872 per credit. *Required fees:* $225 per term. *Financial support:* Scholarships/grants, tuition waivers (partial), and unspecified assistantships available. Support available to part-time students. Financial award application deadline: 4/15; financial award applicants required to submit FAFSA. *Unit head:* Dr. Jeffry Haber, Chair, 914-633-2244, E-mail: jhaber@iona.edu. *Application contact:* Ben Fan, Director of MBA Admissions, 914-633-2289, Fax: 914-637-2708, E-mail: sfan@iona.edu.

Iowa State University of Science and Technology, Department of Accounting, Ames, IA 50011-1350. Offers M Acc. *Accreditation:* AACSB. *Degree requirements:* For master's, thesis or alternative. *Entrance requirements:* For master's, GMAT, resume. Additional exam requirements/recommendations for international students: Recommended—TOEFL (minimum score 600 paper-based; 100 iBT), IELTS (minimum score 7). *Application deadline:* For fall admission, 5/15 priority date for domestic students, 5/15 for international students; for spring admission, 11/1 priority date for domestic students, 11/1 for international students. Application fee: $50 ($90 for international students). Electronic applications accepted. *Unit head:* Dr. Anne Clem, Director of Graduate Education, 515-294-8118, Fax: 515-294-2446, E-mail: busgrad@iastate.edu. *Application contact:* Debbie Johnson, Information Contact, 515-294-8118, Fax: 515-294-2446, E-mail: busgrad@iastate.edu. Web site: http://www.business.iastate.edu/masters/macc.

Ithaca College, Division of Graduate and Professional Studies, School of Business, Program in Professional Accountancy, Ithaca, NY 14850. Offers MBA. Part-time programs available. *Faculty:* 4 full-time (2 women). *Students:* 9 full-time (4 women), 3 part-time (2 women); includes 1 minority (Asian, non-Hispanic/Latino), 1 international. Average age 25. 19 applicants, 79% accepted, 7 enrolled. In 2011, 26 master's awarded. *Degree requirements:* For master's, thesis optional. *Entrance requirements:* For master's, GMAT, minimum GPA of 3.0. Additional exam requirements/recommendations for international students: Required—TOEFL (minimum score 550 paper-based; 213 computer-based; 80 iBT). *Application deadline:* For fall admission, 3/1 for domestic and international students; for spring admission, 11/1 for domestic and international students. Applications are processed on a rolling basis. Application fee: $40. Electronic applications accepted. *Expenses:* Contact institution. *Financial support:* In 2011–12, 9 students received support, including 9 fellowships (averaging $5,200 per year); career-related internships or fieldwork, Federal Work-Study, and scholarships/grants also available. Support available to part-time students. Financial award application deadline: 3/1; financial award applicants required to submit CSS PROFILE or FAFSA. *Unit head:* Dr. Joanne Burress, MBA Program Director, 607-274-3143, Fax: 607-274-1263, E-mail: gps@ithaca.edu. *Application contact:* Gerard Turbide, Director, Office of Admission, 607-274-3143, Fax: 607-274-1263, E-mail: gps@ithaca.edu. Web site: http://www.ithaca.edu/business/mba.

Jackson State University, Graduate School, College of Business, Department of Accounting, Jackson, MS 39217. Offers MPA. *Accreditation:* AACSB. Part-time and evening/weekend programs available. *Degree requirements:* For master's, comprehensive exam. *Entrance requirements:* For master's, GRE General Test, GMAT. Additional exam requirements/recommendations for international students: Required—TOEFL (minimum score 520 paper-based; 195 computer-based; 67 iBT).

James Madison University, The Graduate School, College of Business, Program in Accounting, Harrisonburg, VA 22807. Offers MS. *Accreditation:* AACSB. Part-time and evening/weekend programs available. *Students:* 59 full-time (17 women), 6 part-time (2 women); includes 6 minority (4 Asian, non-Hispanic/Latino; 2 Hispanic/Latino). Average age 27. In 2011, 61 master's awarded. *Entrance requirements:* For master's, GMAT or CPA exam. Additional exam requirements/recommendations for international students: Required—TOEFL. *Application deadline:* For fall admission, 5/1 priority date for domestic students, 5/1 for international students; for spring admission, 9/1 priority date for domestic students, 9/1 for international students. Applications are processed on a rolling basis. Application fee: $55. Electronic applications accepted. *Expenses:* Tuition, state resident: full-time $8016; part-time $334 per credit hour. Tuition, nonresident: full-time $22,656; part-time $944 per credit hour. *Financial support:* In 2011–12, 20 students received support. Federal Work-Study and 20 graduate assistantships ($7382) available. Financial award application deadline: 3/1; financial award applicants required to submit FAFSA. *Faculty research:* Controllership, government accounting. *Unit head:* Dr. Paul A. Copley, Academic Unit Head, 540-568-3081. *Application contact:* Dr. Nancy Nichols, Program Director, 540-568-3081.

John Carroll University, Graduate School, John M. and Mary Jo Boler School of Business, University Heights, OH 44118-4581. Offers accountancy (MS); business (MBA). *Accreditation:* AACSB. Part-time and evening/weekend programs available. *Entrance requirements:* For master's, GMAT, minimum GPA of 2.5. Additional exam requirements/recommendations for international students: Required—TOEFL (minimum score 550 paper-based; 213 computer-based). Electronic applications accepted. *Expenses:* Contact institution. *Faculty research:* Accounting, economics and finance, management, marketing and logistics.

Johnson & Wales University, The Alan Shawn Feinstein Graduate School, MBA Program in Global Business Leadership, Providence, RI 02903-3703. Offers accounting (MBA); enhanced accounting (MBA); hospitality (MBA). Part-time programs available. *Entrance requirements:* For master's, minimum GPA of 2.75. Additional exam requirements/recommendations for international students: Required—TOEFL (minimum score 550 paper-based; 210 computer-based) or IELTS (recommended); Recommended—TWE. *Faculty research:* International banking, global economy, international trade, cultural differences.

Jones International University, School of Business, Centennial, CO 80112. Offers accounting (MBA); business communication (MABC); entrepreneurship (MABC, MBA); finance (MBA); global enterprise management (MBA); health care management (MBA); information security management (MBA); information technology management (MBA); leadership and influence (MABC); leading the customer-driven organization (MABC); negotiation and conflict management (MBA); project management (MABC, MBA). Program only offered online. Part-time and evening/weekend programs available. Postbaccalaureate distance learning degree programs offered (no on-campus study). *Degree requirements:* For master's, capstone project. *Entrance requirements:* For master's, minimum cumulative GPA of 2.5. Additional exam requirements/recommendations for international students: Recommended—TOEFL (minimum score 550 paper-based; 213 computer-based). Electronic applications accepted.

Kansas State University, Graduate School, College of Business Administration, Department of Accounting, Manhattan, KS 66506. Offers M Acc. *Accreditation:* AACSB. *Faculty:* 8 full-time (2 women). *Students:* 46 full-time (28 women), 5 part-time (4 women); includes 1 minority (Hispanic/Latino), 11 international. Average age 23. 64 applicants, 81% accepted, 37 enrolled. In 2011, 49 master's awarded. *Entrance requirements:* For master's, GMAT (minimum score of 500), minimum undergraduate GPA of 3.0. Additional exam requirements/recommendations for international students: Required—TOEFL (minimum score 550 paper-based; 79 iBT); Recommended—IELTS (minimum score 7). *Application deadline:* For fall admission, 2/1 priority date for domestic students, 2/1 for international students; for spring admission, 10/1 priority date for domestic students, 8/1 for international students. Applications are processed on a rolling basis. Application fee: $60. Electronic applications accepted. *Financial support:* In 2011–12, 2 research assistantships with partial tuition reimbursements (averaging $9,360 per year), 5 teaching assistantships with full and partial tuition reimbursements (averaging $9,472 per year) were awarded; institutionally sponsored loans and scholarships/grants also available. Support available to part-time students. Financial award application deadline: 3/1; financial award applicants required to submit FAFSA. *Faculty research:* Accounting education, accounting ethics, capital markets (empirical/archival), research in tax and financial reporting, behavioral research in accounting. *Total annual research expenditures:* $65,765. *Unit head:* Richard Ott, Head, 785-532-6184, Fax: 785-532-5959. *Application contact:* Stacy Kovar, Associate Dean for Academic Programs, 785-532-7190, Fax: 785-532-7809, E-mail: gradbusiness@ksu.edu.

Kean University, College of Business and Public Management, Program in Accounting, Union, NJ 07083. Offers MS. *Faculty:* 13 full-time (3 women). *Students:* 20 full-time (12 women), 39 part-time (18 women); includes 24 minority (7 Black or African American, non-Hispanic/Latino; 3 Asian, non-Hispanic/Latino; 14 Hispanic/Latino), 8 international. Average age 30. 47 applicants, 83% accepted, 24 enrolled. In 2011, 37 master's awarded. *Entrance requirements:* For master's, GMAT, 2 letters of recommendation, interview, minimum GPA of 3.0. Additional exam requirements/recommendations for international students: Required—TOEFL (minimum score 79 iBT). *Application deadline:* For fall admission, 6/1 for domestic and international students; for spring admission, 12/1 for domestic and international students. Applications are processed on a rolling basis. Application fee: $75 ($150 for international students). Electronic applications accepted. *Expenses:* Tuition, state resident: full-time $11,302; part-time $550 per credit. Tuition, nonresident: full-time $15,318; part-time $674 per credit. *Required fees:* $2849; $130 per credit. Tuition and fees vary according to degree level. *Financial support:* In 2011–12, 2 research assistantships with full tuition reimbursements (averaging $3,263 per year) were awarded; unspecified assistantships also available. Financial award applicants required to submit FAFSA. *Unit head:* Prof. James Capone, Program Coordinator, 908-737-4110, E-mail: jcapone@kean.edu. *Application contact:* Reenat Hasan, Admissions Counselor, 908-737-5923, Fax: 908-737-5925, E-mail: rhasan@exchange.kean.edu. Web site: http://www.kean.edu/KU/Accounting.

Keiser University, Master of Business Administration Program, Fort Lauderdale, FL 33309. Offers accounting (MBA); health services management (MBA); international business (MBA); leadership for managers (MBA); marketing (MBA). Leadership for Managers and International Business concentrations also offered in Spanish. Part-time programs available. Postbaccalaureate distance learning degree programs offered (minimal on-campus study). *Entrance requirements:* For master's, minimum GPA of 2.7 from an accredited institution. Additional exam requirements/recommendations for international students: Required—TOEFL. Electronic applications accepted.

Kennesaw State University, Michael J. Coles College of Business, Program in Accounting, Kennesaw, GA 30144-5591. Offers M Acc. *Accreditation:* AACSB. Part-time and evening/weekend programs available. *Students:* 62 full-time (33 women), 9 part-time (5 women); includes 17 minority (11 Black or African American, non-Hispanic/Latino; 5 Asian, non-Hispanic/Latino; 1 Hispanic/Latino), 13 international. Average age 31. 120 applicants, 72% accepted, 55 enrolled. In 2011, 85 master's awarded. *Entrance requirements:* For master's, GMAT, minimum GPA of 2.8. Additional exam requirements/recommendations for international students: Required—TOEFL (minimum score 550 paper-based; 213 computer-based; 80 iBT), IELTS (minimum score 6). *Application deadline:* For fall admission, 4/1 for domestic and international students. Applications are processed on a rolling basis. Application fee: $60. Electronic applications accepted. *Expenses:* Tuition, state resident: full-time $3000; part-time $250 per semester hour. Tuition, nonresident: full-time $10,836; part-time $903 per semester hour. *Required fees:* $774 per semester. *Financial support:* In 2011–12, 4 research assistantships with tuition reimbursements (averaging $4,000 per year) were awarded; unspecified assistantships also available. Financial award application deadline: 4/1. *Unit head:* Dr. Kathyrn Epps, Director, 770-423-6085, E-mail: kepps@kennesaw.edu. *Application contact:* Tamara Hutto, Admissions Counselor, 770-420-4377, Fax: 770-423-6885. Web site: http://www.kennesaw.edu.

Kent State University, College of Business Administration, Doctoral Program in Accounting, Kent, OH 44242-0001. Offers PhD. *Faculty:* 11 full-time (4 women). *Students:* 8 full-time (2 women), 2 international. Average age 30. 32 applicants, 16% accepted, 4 enrolled. In 2011, 1 doctorate awarded. *Degree requirements:* For doctorate, comprehensive exam, thesis/dissertation, oral defense. *Entrance requirements:* For doctorate, GMAT. Additional exam requirements/recommendations for international students: Required—TOEFL (minimum score 600 paper-based; 250 computer-based; 100 iBT). *Application deadline:* For fall admission, 2/1 for domestic students, 1/1 for international students. Application fee: $30 ($60 for international students). Electronic applications accepted. *Expenses:* Tuition, state resident: full-time $8136; part-time $452 per credit hour. Tuition, nonresident: full-time $14,292; part-time $794 per credit hour. *Financial support:* In 2011–12, 3 students received support, including 6 teaching assistantships with full tuition reimbursements available (averaging $17,000 per year); Federal Work-Study also available. Financial award application deadline: 2/1; financial award applicants required to submit FAFSA. *Faculty research:* Information economics, capital management, use of accounting information, curriculum design. *Unit head:* Dr. Linda Zucca, Chair and Associate Professor, 330-672-2545, Fax: 330-672-2548, E-mail: lzucca@kent.edu. *Application contact:* Felecia A. Urbanek, Coordinator, Graduate Programs, 330-672-2282, Fax: 330-672-7303, E-mail: gradbus@kent.edu. Web site: http://www.kent.edu/business/Grad/phd/index.cfm.

Kent State University, College of Business Administration, Master's Program in Accounting, Kent, OH 44242-0001. Offers MS. Part-time programs available. *Faculty:* 10 full-time (4 women), 2 part-time/adjunct (0 women). *Students:* 41 full-time (20 women), 12 part-time (6 women); includes 2 minority (1 Black or African American, non-Hispanic/Latino; 1 Asian, non-Hispanic/Latino), 26 international. Average age 26. 47 applicants, 85% accepted, 18 enrolled. In 2011, 22 master's awarded. *Degree requirements:* For master's, internship. *Entrance requirements:* For master's, GMAT, minimum GPA of 2.75. Additional exam requirements/recommendations for international students: Required—TOEFL (minimum score 550 paper-based; 213 computer-based; 79 iBT). *Application deadline:* For fall admission, 4/1 priority date for domestic students, 4/1 for international students; for spring admission, 12/1 for domestic students. Applications are processed on a rolling basis. Application fee: $30 ($60 for international students). Electronic applications accepted. *Expenses:* Tuition, state resident: full-time $8136; part-time $452 per credit hour. Tuition, nonresident: full-time $14,292; part-time $794 per credit hour. *Financial support:* In 2011–12, 8 students received support, including 8 research assistantships with full tuition reimbursements available (averaging $3,350 per year); Federal Work-Study also available. Financial award application deadline: 4/1; financial award applicants required to submit FAFSA. *Faculty research:* Financial accounting, managerial accounting, auditing, systems, nonprofit. *Unit head:* Dr. Linda Zucca, Chair and Associate Professor, 330-672-2545, Fax: 330-672-2548, E-mail: lzucca@kent.edu. *Application contact:* Louise M. Ditchey, Administrative Director, 330-672-2282, Fax: 330-672-7303, E-mail: gradbus@kent.edu. Web site: http://www.kent.edu/business/Grad/msa/index.cfm.

Lakeland College, Graduate Studies Division, Program in Business Administration, Sheboygan, WI 53082-0359. Offers accounting (MBA); finance (MBA); healthcare management (MBA); project management (MBA). *Entrance requirements:* For master's, GMAT. *Expenses:* Contact institution.

Lamar University, College of Graduate Studies, College of Business, Beaumont, TX 77710. Offers accounting (MBA); experiential business and entrepreneurship (MBA); financial management (MBA); healthcare administration (MBA); information systems (MBA); management (MBA). *Accreditation:* AACSB. Part-time and evening/weekend programs available. *Faculty:* 18 full-time (5 women), 5 part-time/adjunct (0 women). *Students:* 74 full-time (33 women), 72 part-time (27 women); includes 24 minority (7 Black or African American, non-Hispanic/Latino; 9 Asian, non-Hispanic/Latino; 8 Hispanic/Latino), 34 international. Average age 29. 69 applicants, 84% accepted, 16 enrolled. In 2011, 62 master's awarded. *Degree requirements:* For master's, comprehensive exam (for some programs), thesis optional. *Entrance requirements:* For master's, GMAT. Additional exam requirements/recommendations for international students: Required—TOEFL (minimum score 525 paper-based; 197 computer-based). *Application deadline:* For fall admission, 3/15 priority date for domestic students; for spring admission, 10/1 priority date for domestic students. Applications are processed on a rolling basis. Application fee: $25 ($50 for international students). *Expenses:* Tuition, state resident: full-time $5430; part-time $272 per credit hour. Tuition, nonresident: full-time $11,540; part-time $577 per credit hour. *Required fees:* $1916. *Financial support:* In 2011–12, 12 students received support, including 4 research assistantships with partial tuition reimbursements available; fellowships with tuition reimbursements available, career-related internships or fieldwork, Federal Work-Study, institutionally sponsored loans, scholarships/grants, and tuition waivers (partial) also available. Support available to part-time students. Financial award application deadline: 4/1; financial award applicants required to submit FAFSA. *Faculty research:* Marketing, finance, quantitative methods, management information systems, legal, environmental. *Unit head:* Dr. Enrique R. Venta, Dean, 409-880-8604, Fax: 409-880-8088, E-mail: henry.venta@lamar.edu. *Application contact:* Dr. Brad Mayer, Professor and Associate Dean, 409-880-2383, Fax: 409-880-8605, E-mail: bradley.mayer@lamar.edu. Web site: http://mba.lamar.edu.

La Sierra University, School of Business and Management, Riverside, CA 92515. Offers accounting (MBA); finance (MBA); general management (MBA); human resources management (MBA); leadership, values, and ethics for business and management (Certificate); marketing (MBA). *Degree requirements:* For master's, research project. *Entrance requirements:* For master's, GMAT, minimum GPA of 3.0. Additional exam requirements/recommendations for international students: Required—TOEFL. *Faculty research:* Financial econometrics, institutional assessment and strategic planning, legal issues in management, behavioral finance, content of financial reports.

Lehigh University, College of Business and Economics, Department of Accounting, Bethlehem, PA 18015. Offers accounting and information analysis (MS). *Accreditation:*

AACSB. *Faculty:* 6 full-time (0 women). *Students:* 43 full-time (29 women), 17 part-time (14 women); includes 1 minority (Hispanic/Latino), 46 international. Average age 23. 149 applicants, 68% accepted, 19 enrolled. In 2011, 23 master's awarded. *Entrance requirements:* For master's, GMAT. Additional exam requirements/recommendations for international students: Required—TOEFL (minimum score 105 iBT). *Application deadline:* For fall admission, 5/1 for domestic and international students. Applications are processed on a rolling basis. Application fee: $100. Electronic applications accepted. *Expenses:* Contact institution. *Financial support:* In 2011–12, 6 research assistantships with partial tuition reimbursements (averaging $2,500 per year) were awarded; scholarships/grants and tuition waivers (partial) also available. Financial award application deadline: 1/15. *Faculty research:* Behavioral accounting, internal control, information systems, supply chain management, financial accounting. *Unit head:* Dr. Heibatollah Sami, Director, 610-758-3407, Fax: 610-758-6429, E-mail: hes205@lehigh.edu. *Application contact:* Corinn McBride, Director of Recruitment and Admissions, 610-758-3418, Fax: 610-758-5283, E-mail: com207@lehigh.edu. Web site: http://www4.lehigh.edu/business/academics/depts/accounting.

Lehman College of the City University of New York, Division of Natural and Social Sciences, Department of Economics and Accounting, Bronx, NY 10468-1589. Offers accounting (MS). *Entrance requirements:* For master's, GMAT.

Lenoir-Rhyne University, Graduate Programs, Charles M. Snipes School of Business, Hickory, NC 28601. Offers accounting (MBA); entrepreneurship (MBA); global leadership (MBA); leadership development (MBA). *Accreditation:* ACBSP. Part-time and evening/weekend programs available. *Degree requirements:* For master's, capstone course. *Entrance requirements:* For master's, GMAT, minimum undergraduate GPA of 2.7, graduate 3.0. Additional exam requirements/recommendations for international students: Required—TOEFL (minimum score 600 paper-based). Electronic applications accepted. *Expenses:* Contact institution.

Lewis University, College of Business, Graduate School of Management, Program in Business Administration, Romeoville, IL 60446. Offers accounting (MBA); custom elective option (MBA); e-business (MBA); finance (MBA); healthcare management (MBA); human resources management (MBA); information security (MBA); international business (MBA); management information systems (MBA); marketing (MBA); project management (MBA); technology and operations management (MBA). Part-time and evening/weekend programs available. *Students:* 112 full-time (60 women), 232 part-time (118 women); includes 104 minority (62 Black or African American, non-Hispanic/Latino; 1 American Indian or Alaska Native, non-Hispanic/Latino; 7 Asian, non-Hispanic/Latino; 33 Hispanic/Latino; 1 Native Hawaiian or other Pacific Islander, non-Hispanic/Latino), 9 international. Average age 28. In 2011, 99 master's awarded. *Entrance requirements:* For master's, interview, bachelor's degree, resume, 2 recommendations. Additional exam requirements/recommendations for international students: Required—TOEFL (minimum score 550 paper-based; 213 computer-based). *Application deadline:* For fall admission, 8/15 priority date for domestic students, 5/1 for international students; for spring admission, 11/15 for international students. Applications are processed on a rolling basis. Application fee: $40. Electronic applications accepted. *Financial support:* Career-related internships or fieldwork, Federal Work-Study, scholarships/grants, and unspecified assistantships available. Financial award application deadline: 5/1; financial award applicants required to submit FAFSA. *Unit head:* Dr. Maureen Culleeney, Academic Program Director, 815-838-0500 Ext. 5631, E-mail: culleema@lewisu.edu. *Application contact:* Michele Ryan, Director of Admission, 815-838-0500 Ext. 5384, E-mail: gsm@lewisu.edu.

Lincoln University, School of Graduate Studies and Continuing Education, Jefferson City, MO 65102. Offers business administration (MBA), including accounting, entrepreneurship, management, public administration and policy; educational leadership (Ed S), including elementary leadership, secondary leadership, superintendency; guidance and counseling (M Ed), including community/agency counseling, elementary school, secondary school; history (MA); school administration and supervision (M Ed), including elementary school administration, secondary school administration, special education administration; school teaching (M Ed), including elementary school teaching, secondary school teaching; social science (MA), including history, political science, sociology; sociology (MA); sociology/criminal justice (MA). Part-time and evening/weekend programs available. *Degree requirements:* For master's and Ed S, comprehensive exam, thesis optional. *Entrance requirements:* For master's and Ed S, GRE, MAT or GMAT, minimum GPA of 2.75 in major, 2.5 overall; 3 letters of recommendation; minimum C average in English composition; personal statement of purpose. Additional exam requirements/recommendations for international students: Required—TOEFL (minimum score 500 paper-based; 173 computer-based; 61 iBT). *Faculty research:* Suicide prevention.

Lindenwood University, Graduate Programs, School of Business and Entrepreneurship, St. Charles, MO 63301-1695. Offers accounting (MBA, MS); business administration (MBA); entrepreneurial studies (MBA, MS); finance (MBA, MS); human resource management (MBA); human resources (MS); international business (MBA, MS); management (MBA, MS); management information systems (MBA, MS); marketing (MBA, MS); public management (MBA, MS); sport management (MA); supply chain management (MBA). *Accreditation:* ACBSP. Part-time and evening/weekend programs available. *Faculty:* 20 full-time (8 women), 17 part-time/adjunct (5 women). *Students:* 165 full-time (66 women), 223 part-time (100 women); includes 59 minority (48 Black or African American, non-Hispanic/Latino; 4 Asian, non-Hispanic/Latino; 2 Native Hawaiian or other Pacific Islander, non-Hispanic/Latino; 5 Two or more races, non-Hispanic/Latino), 140 international. Average age 29. 156 applicants, 76% accepted, 103 enrolled. In 2011, 205 degrees awarded. *Degree requirements:* For master's, comprehensive exam (for some programs), thesis (for some programs). *Entrance requirements:* For master's, interview, minimum GPA of 3.0, letter of recommendation. Additional exam requirements/recommendations for international students: Required—TOEFL (minimum score 550 paper-based; 213 computer-based; 80 iBT). *Application deadline:* For fall admission, 8/15 priority date for domestic students, 8/15 for international students; for winter admission, 1/9 priority date for domestic students, 1/9 for international students; for spring admission, 3/12 priority date for domestic students, 3/12 for international students. Applications are processed on a rolling basis. Application fee: $30 ($100 for international students). Electronic applications accepted. *Expenses: Tuition:* Full-time $13,650; part-time $395 per credit hour. *Required fees:* $150 per semester. Tuition and fees vary according to course level and course load. *Financial support:* In 2011–12, 206 students received support. Career-related internships or fieldwork, Federal Work-Study, institutionally sponsored loans, and tuition waivers (partial) available. Financial award application deadline: 6/30; financial award applicants required to submit FAFSA. *Unit head:* Roger Ellis, Dean, 636-949-4839, E-mail: rellis@lindenwood.edu. *Application contact:* Brett Barger, Dean of Evening Admissions and Extension Campuses, 636-949-4934, Fax: 636-949-4109, E-mail: adultadmissions@lindenwood.edu. Web site: http://www.lindenwood.edu.

Lipscomb University, College of Business, Nashville, TN 37204-3951. Offers accounting (MBA); business administration (general) (MBA); conflict management (MBA); financial services (MBA); healthcare management (MBA); human resources (MHR); leadership (MBA); nonprofit management (MBA); sports management (MBA); sustainability (MBA). *Accreditation:* ACBSP. Part-time and evening/weekend programs available. *Faculty:* 13 full-time (3 women), 7 part-time/adjunct (1 woman). *Students:* 51 full-time (21 women), 83 part-time (48 women); includes 20 minority (16 Black or African American, non-Hispanic/Latino; 3 Asian, non-Hispanic/Latino; 1 Hispanic/Latino), 1 international. Average age 33. 190 applicants, 43% accepted, 54 enrolled. In 2011, 85 master's awarded. *Entrance requirements:* For master's, GMAT, interview, 2 references, resume. Additional exam requirements/recommendations for international students: Required—TOEFL (minimum score 570 paper-based; 230 computer-based). *Application deadline:* For fall admission, 6/15 for domestic students, 2/1 for international students; for winter admission, 6/1 for international students; for spring admission, 11/15 for domestic students. Applications are processed on a rolling basis. Application fee: $50 ($75 for international students). Electronic applications accepted. *Expenses:* Contact institution. *Financial support:* Career-related internships or fieldwork, scholarships/grants, tuition waivers (partial), and unspecified assistantships available. Support available to part-time students. Financial award application deadline: 7/1; financial award applicants required to submit FAFSA. *Faculty research:* Impact of spirituality on organization commitment, leadership, psychological empowerment, training. *Unit head:* Dr. Mike Kendrick, Associate Dean of Graduate Business Programs, 615-966-1833, Fax: 615-966-1818, E-mail: mikekendrick@lipscomb.edu. *Application contact:* Lisa Shacklett, Executive Director of Enrollment and Marketing, 615-966-5968, E-mail: lisa.shacklett@lipscomb.edu. Web site: http://mba.lipscomb.edu.

Lipscomb University, Program in Accountancy, Nashville, TN 37204-3951. Offers M Acc. Part-time and evening/weekend programs available. *Faculty:* 1 full-time (0 women), 3 part-time/adjunct (1 woman). *Students:* 7 full-time (5 women), 9 part-time (5 women). Average age 28. 15 applicants, 60% accepted, 5 enrolled. In 2011, 34 master's awarded. *Degree requirements:* For master's, internship. *Entrance requirements:* For master's, GMAT, 2 references, interview. Additional exam requirements/recommendations for international students: Required—TOEFL (minimum score 570 paper-based; 230 computer-based). *Application deadline:* For fall admission, 6/15 for domestic students; for spring admission, 11/15 for domestic students. Applications are processed on a rolling basis. Application fee: $50 ($75 for international students). Electronic applications accepted. *Expenses:* Contact institution. *Financial support:* Career-related internships or fieldwork, Federal Work-Study, scholarships/grants, tuition waivers (partial), and unspecified assistantships available. Support available to part-time students. Financial award application deadline: 7/1. *Faculty research:* Internal auditing, ethics and fraud. *Unit head:* Dr. Perry Moore, Director, 615-966-5795, Fax: 615-966-1818, E-mail: perry.moore@lipscomb.edu. *Application contact:* Lisa Shacklett, Executive Director of Enrollment and Marketing, 615-966-5968, Fax: 615-966-1818, E-mail: lisa.shacklett@lipscomb.edu. Web site: http://macc.lipscomb.edu.

Long Island University–Brooklyn Campus, School of Business, Public Administration and Information Sciences, Program in Accountancy, Taxation and Law, Brooklyn, NY 11201-8423. Offers accounting (MS); taxation (MS). Part-time and evening/weekend programs available. *Entrance requirements:* For master's, GMAT or GRE General Test, 2 letters of recommendation. Additional exam requirements/recommendations for international students: Required—TOEFL (minimum score 500 paper-based; 173 computer-based). Electronic applications accepted.

Long Island University–C. W. Post Campus, College of Management, School of Business, Brookville, NY 11548-1300. Offers accounting and taxation (Certificate); business administration (Certificate); finance (MBA, Certificate); general business administration (MBA); international business (MBA, Certificate); management (MBA, Certificate); management information systems (MBA, Certificate); marketing (MBA, Certificate). *Accreditation:* AACSB. Part-time and evening/weekend programs available. *Entrance requirements:* For master's, GMAT, resume, minimum GPA of 3.0, 2 letters of recommendation. Additional exam requirements/recommendations for international students: Required—TOEFL (minimum score 527 paper-based; 197 computer-based). Electronic applications accepted. *Faculty research:* Financial markets, consumer behavior.

Long Island University–C. W. Post Campus, College of Management, School of Professional Accountancy, Brookville, NY 11548-1300. Offers accounting (MS); taxation (MS). Part-time and evening/weekend programs available. *Entrance requirements:* For master's, GMAT, minimum GPA of 2.5, BS in accounting from accredited college or university. Electronic applications accepted. *Faculty research:* International taxation.

Louisiana State University and Agricultural and Mechanical College, Graduate School, E. J. Ourso College of Business, Department of Accounting, Baton Rouge, LA 70803. Offers MS, PhD. *Faculty:* 10 full-time (4 women). *Students:* 93 full-time (48 women), 9 part-time (4 women); includes 10 minority (3 Black or African American, non-Hispanic/Latino; 4 Asian, non-Hispanic/Latino; 3 Hispanic/Latino), 18 international. Average age 25. 125 applicants, 42% accepted, 50 enrolled. In 2011, 65 master's, 1 doctorate awarded. *Degree requirements:* For doctorate, thesis/dissertation. *Entrance requirements:* For master's, GMAT, minimum GPA of 3.2; for doctorate, GMAT, minimum GPA of 3.4. Additional exam requirements/recommendations for international students: Required—TOEFL (minimum score 550 paper-based; 213 computer-based; 79 iBT) or IELTS (minimum score 6.5). *Application deadline:* For fall admission, 1/25 priority date for domestic students, 5/15 for international students; for spring admission, 10/15 for international students. Applications are processed on a rolling basis. Application fee: $50 ($70 for international students). Electronic applications accepted. *Financial support:* In 2011–12, 52 students received support, including 8 research assistantships with full and partial tuition reimbursements available (averaging $18,625 per year), 17 teaching assistantships with full and partial tuition reimbursements available (averaging $10,582 per year); fellowships, Federal Work-Study, scholarships/grants, health care benefits, tuition waivers (full and partial), and unspecified assistantships also available. Support available to part-time students. Financial award application deadline: 4/15; financial award applicants required to submit FAFSA. *Faculty research:* Financial accounting, auditing fraud. *Total annual research expenditures:* $34,360. *Unit head:* Dr. Sam Tiras, Chair, 225-578-6202, Fax: 225-578-6201, E-mail: tiras@lsu.edu. *Application contact:* Dr. Jacquelyn Moffit, MS Program Advisor, 225-578-6219, Fax: 225-578-6201, E-mail: jsmoff22@lsu.edu. Web site: http://business.lsu.edu/Accounting/Pages/About-Us.aspx.

Louisiana Tech University, Graduate School, College of Business, School of Professional Accountancy, Ruston, LA 71272. Offers MBA, MPA, DBA. *Accreditation:* AACSB. Part-time programs available. *Degree requirements:* For doctorate, thesis/dissertation. *Entrance requirements:* For master's and doctorate, GMAT.

Loyola University Chicago, Graduate School of Business, Accountancy Department, Chicago, IL 60660. Offers MS, MSA. *Accreditation:* AACSB. Part-time and evening/weekend programs available. *Entrance requirements:* For master's, GMAT, letters of recommendation. Additional exam requirements/recommendations for international students: Required—TOEFL (minimum score 550 paper-based; 213 computer-based; 80 iBT). Electronic applications accepted. *Expenses: Tuition:* Full-time $15,660; part-time $870 per credit hour. *Required fees:* $125 per semester. Tuition and fees vary according to course load and program. *Faculty research:* Financial disclosure, web-based accounting issues, activities-based costing.

Loyola University Maryland, Graduate Programs, Sellinger School of Business and Management, Program in Business Administration, Baltimore, MD 21210-2699. Offers accounting (MBA); finance (MBA); general business (MBA); information systems operations management (MBA); international business (MBA); management (MBA); marketing (MBA). *Accreditation:* AACSB. Part-time and evening/weekend programs available. *Faculty:* 61 full-time (12 women), 29 part-time/adjunct (4 women). *Students:* 50 full-time (15 women), 547 part-time (210 women); includes 98 minority (39 Black or African American, non-Hispanic/Latino; 1 American Indian or Alaska Native, non-Hispanic/Latino; 28 Asian, non-Hispanic/Latino; 18 Hispanic/Latino; 2 Native Hawaiian or other Pacific Islander, non-Hispanic/Latino; 10 Two or more races, non-Hispanic/Latino), 15 international. Average age 30. In 2011, 232 master's awarded. *Entrance requirements:* For master's, GMAT (for some programs). Additional exam requirements/recommendations for international students: Required—TOEFL (minimum score 550 paper-based; 213 computer-based). *Application deadline:* For fall admission, 8/1 priority date for domestic students; for spring admission, 12/1 priority date for domestic students. Application fee: $50. Electronic applications accepted. *Financial support:* Research assistantships and unspecified assistantships available. Financial award application deadline: 4/15; financial award applicants required to submit FAFSA. *Unit head:* Dr. Karyl Leggio, Dean, 410-617-2301, E-mail: kbleggio@loyola.edu. *Application contact:* Maureen Faux, Executive Director, Graduate Admissions, 410-617-5020, Fax: 410-617-2002, E-mail: graduate@loyola.edu.

Maharishi University of Management, Graduate Studies, Program in Business Administration, Fairfield, IA 52557. Offers accounting (MBA); business administration (PhD); sustainability (MBA). Evening/weekend programs available. Postbaccalaureate distance learning degree programs offered (minimal on-campus study). *Degree requirements:* For doctorate, thesis/dissertation. *Entrance requirements:* For master's, GMAT, minimum GPA of 3.0; for doctorate, minimum GPA of 3.0. Additional exam requirements/recommendations for international students: Required—TOEFL. *Faculty research:* Leadership, effects of the group dynamics of consciousness on the economy, innovation, employee development, cooperative strategy.

Marquette University, Graduate School of Management, Program in Accounting, Milwaukee, WI 53201-1881. Offers MSA. *Accreditation:* AACSB. Part-time and evening/weekend programs available. *Faculty:* 11 full-time (4 women), 3 part-time/adjunct (1 woman). *Students:* 67 full-time (41 women), 13 part-time (9 women); includes 4 minority (3 Asian, non-Hispanic/Latino; 1 Hispanic/Latino), 50 international. Average age 23. 215 applicants, 45% accepted, 28 enrolled. In 2011, 24 master's awarded. *Entrance requirements:* For master's, GMAT or GRE, letters of recommendation (if applying for financial aid). Additional exam requirements/recommendations for international students: Required—TOEFL (minimum score 550 paper-based; 85 computer-based; 88 iBT), IELTS (minimum score 6.5), Pearson Test of English. *Application deadline:* For fall admission, 2/15 for domestic and international students. Applications are processed on a rolling basis. Application fee: $50. Electronic applications accepted. *Expenses: Tuition:* Full-time $17,010; part-time $945 per credit hour. Tuition and fees vary according to program. *Financial support:* In 2011–12, 2 teaching assistantships were awarded; fellowships and research assistantships also available. Financial award application deadline: 2/15. *Faculty research:* Financial (accounting) literacy, international perception of corruption, effect of carbon credits on accounting and tax transactions, targeted tax breaks. *Unit head:* Dr. Michael Akers, Chair, 414-288-1453. *Application contact:* Debra Leutermann, Admissions Coordinator, 414-288-8064, E-mail: debra.leutermann@marquette.edu. Web site: http://www.busadm.mu.edu/graduate/.

Marshall University, Academic Affairs Division, College of Business, Program in Accountancy, Huntington, WV 25755. Offers MS. *Students:* 29 full-time (18 women), 7 part-time (4 women), 14 international. Average age 26. In 2011, 9 master's awarded. *Entrance requirements:* For master's, undergraduate degree in accounting with minimum GPA of 3.0 or GMAT. *Unit head:* Dr. Jeffrey Archambault, Director, 304-696-2655. *Application contact:* Wesley Spradlin, Information Contact, 304-746-8964, Fax: 304-746-1902, E-mail: spradlin2@marshall.edu. Web site: http://www.marshall.edu/wpmu/cob/graduate/m-s-in-accounting/.

Maryville University of Saint Louis, The John E. Simon School of Business, St. Louis, MO 63141-7299. Offers accounting (MBA, PGC); business studies (PGC); management (MBA, PGC); marketing (MBA, PGC); process and project management (MBA, PGC); sport and entertainment management (MBA, PGC). *Accreditation:* ACBSP. Part-time and evening/weekend programs available. *Faculty:* 8 full-time (3 women), 14 part-time/adjunct (5 women). *Students:* 19 full-time (10 women), 114 part-time (56 women); includes 13 minority (7 Black or African American, non-Hispanic/Latino; 3 Asian, non-Hispanic/Latino; 2 Hispanic/Latino; 1 Two or more races, non-Hispanic/Latino), 3 international. Average age 31. In 2011, 56 master's awarded. *Entrance requirements:* For master's, GMAT (unless applicant possesses undergraduate business degree with minimum cumulative GPA of 3.0, or has completed master's degree from accredited university or one early access course prior to undergraduate degree). Additional exam requirements/recommendations for international students: Required—TOEFL (minimum score 85 iBT). *Application deadline:* Applications are processed on a rolling basis. Application fee: $40 ($60 for international students). Electronic applications accepted. *Expenses: Tuition:* Full-time $21,922; part-time $675 per credit hour. *Required fees:* $233.75 per semester. *Financial support:* Career-related internships or fieldwork, Federal Work-Study, tuition waivers (partial), and campus employment available. Financial award application deadline: 3/1; financial award applicants required to submit FAFSA. *Faculty research:* International business, e-marketing, strategic planning, interpersonal management skills, financial analysis. *Unit head:* Dr. Pamela Horwitz, Dean, 314-529-9418, Fax: 314-529-9975, E-mail: horwitz@maryville.edu. *Application contact:* Kathy Dougherty, Director of MBA Programs, 314-529-9382, Fax: 314-529-9975, E-mail: business@maryville.edu. Web site: http://www.maryville.edu/academics-bu-mba.

McGill University, Faculty of Graduate and Postdoctoral Studies, Desautels Faculty of Management, Montréal, QC H3A 2T5, Canada. Offers administration (PhD); entrepreneurial studies (MBA); finance (MBA); general management (Post Master's Certificate); information systems (MBA); international business (MBA); international practicing management (MM); management (MBA); management for development (MBA); manufacturing management (MMM); marketing (MBA); operations management (MBA); public accountancy (Diploma); strategic management (MBA); MBA/LL B; MD/MBA. MMM offered jointly with Faculty of Engineering; PhD with Concordia University, HEC Montreal, Université de Montréal, Université du Québec à Montréal.

McNeese State University, Doré School of Graduate Studies, College of Business, Master of Business Administration Program, Lake Charles, LA 70609. Offers accounting (MBA); business administration (MBA). *Accreditation:* AACSB. Evening/weekend programs available. *Faculty:* 14 full-time (1 woman). *Students:* 45 full-time (25 women), 32 part-time (14 women); includes 8 minority (6 Black or African American, non-Hispanic/Latino; 1 American Indian or Alaska Native, non-Hispanic/Latino; 1 Hispanic/Latino), 31 international. In 2011, 34 master's awarded. *Degree requirements:* For master's, written exam. *Entrance requirements:* For master's, GMAT. *Application deadline:* For fall admission, 5/15 priority date for domestic students, 5/15 for international students; for spring admission, 10/15 priority date for domestic students, 10/15 for international students. Applications are processed on a rolling basis. Application fee: $20 ($30 for international students). *Expenses:* Tuition, state resident: part-time $519 per credit hour. Tuition and fees vary according to course load. *Financial support:* Research assistantships, teaching assistantships, and Federal Work-Study available. Support available to part-time students. Financial award application deadline: 5/1. *Faculty research:* Management development, integrating technology into the work force, union/management relations, economic development. *Unit head:* Dr. Akm Rahman, MBA Director, 337-475-5576, Fax: 337-475-5986, E-mail: mrahman@mcneese.edu. *Application contact:* Dr. Akm Rahman, MBA Director, 337-475-5576, Fax: 337-475-5986, E-mail: mrahman@mcneese.edu.

Mercer University, Graduate Studies, Cecil B. Day Campus, Eugene W. Stetson School of Business and Economics (Atlanta), Macon, GA 31207-0003. Offers international business (MBA); MBA/MAC; Pharm D/MBA. *Accreditation:* AACSB. Part-time and evening/weekend programs available. *Faculty:* 19 full-time (8 women), 2 part-time/adjunct (0 women). *Students:* 185 full-time (87 women), 100 part-time (51 women); includes 87 minority (67 Black or African American, non-Hispanic/Latino; 16 Asian, non-Hispanic/Latino; 4 Hispanic/Latino), 19 international. Average age 32. 169 applicants, 54% accepted, 64 enrolled. In 2011, 107 master's awarded. *Entrance requirements:* For master's, GMAT. Additional exam requirements/recommendations for international students: Required—TOEFL (minimum score 550 paper-based; 213 computer-based; 80 iBT). *Application deadline:* For fall admission, 7/1 priority date for domestic students, 7/1 for international students; for spring admission, 11/1 priority date for domestic students, 11/1 for international students. Applications are processed on a rolling basis. Application fee: $50 ($100 for international students). Electronic applications accepted. *Financial support:* Federal Work-Study available. Financial award application deadline: 5/1; financial award applicants required to submit FAFSA. *Faculty research:* Entrepreneurship, market studies, international business strategy, financial analysis. *Unit head:* Dr. Gina L. Miller, Associate Dean, 678-547-6177, Fax: 678-547-6337, E-mail: miller_gl@mercer.edu. *Application contact:* Jamie Thomas, Graduate Enrollment Associate, 678-547-6177, Fax: 678-547-6337, E-mail: atlbusadm@mercer.edu. Web site: http://www2.mercer.edu/business.

Mercy College, School of Business, Program in Public Accounting, Dobbs Ferry, NY 10522-1189. Offers MS. Part-time and evening/weekend programs available. *Entrance requirements:* For master's, GMAT, two page written professional goals statement, resume, two letters of reference, interview, undergraduate transcripts. Additional exam requirements/recommendations for international students: Required—TOEFL (minimum score 600 paper-based; 250 computer-based; 100 iBT), IELTS (minimum score 8). Electronic applications accepted. *Expenses:* Contact institution. *Faculty research:* Auditing, taxation, financial statements.

Mercyhurst College, Graduate Studies, Program in Organizational Leadership, Erie, PA 16546. Offers accounting (MS); entrepreneurship (MS); higher education administration (MS); human resources (MS); nonprofit management (MS); organizational leadership (Certificate); sports leadership (MS). Part-time and evening/weekend programs available. *Faculty:* 1 full-time (0 women), 11 part-time/adjunct (4 women). *Students:* 42 full-time (16 women), 22 part-time (15 women); includes 5 minority (3 Black or African American, non-Hispanic/Latino; 1 American Indian or Alaska Native, non-Hispanic/Latino; 1 Hispanic/Latino), 9 international. Average age 30. 60 applicants, 62% accepted, 25 enrolled. In 2011, 27 master's, 2 other advanced degrees awarded. *Degree requirements:* For master's, thesis. *Entrance requirements:* For master's, GRE General Test or MAT, interview, resume, essay, three professional references, transcripts. Additional exam requirements/recommendations for international students: Required—TOEFL. *Application deadline:* For fall admission, 8/1 priority date for domestic students, 7/1 for international students; for winter admission, 11/1 for domestic students, 10/1 for international students; for spring admission, 2/1 for domestic students, 1/1 for international students. Applications are processed on a rolling basis. Application fee: $35. Electronic applications accepted. *Expenses: Tuition:* Part-time $570 per credit. *Required fees:* $90 per term. Tuition and fees vary according to program. *Financial support:* In 2011–12, 16 students received support, including 112 research assistantships with full and partial tuition reimbursements available (averaging $6,000 per year); career-related internships or fieldwork and unspecified assistantships also available. Support available to part-time students. Financial award application deadline: 5/1; financial award applicants required to submit FAFSA. *Faculty research:* Leadership training, organizational communication, leadership pedagogy. *Unit head:* Dr. Gilbert Jacobs, Director, 814-824-2390, E-mail: gjacobs@mercyhurst.edu. *Application contact:* Sarah Murphy, Academic Coordinator, 814-824-2297, Fax: 814-824-2055, E-mail: smurphy@mercyhurst.edu.

Miami University, Farmer School of Business, Department of Accountancy, Oxford, OH 45056. Offers M Acc. *Accreditation:* AACSB. *Students:* 28 full-time (9 women); includes 1 minority (Black or African American, non-Hispanic/Latino), 4 international. Average age 24. In 2011, 58 master's awarded. *Entrance requirements:* For master's, GMAT, minimum cumulative undergraduate GPA of 3.0. Additional exam requirements/recommendations for international students: Required—TOEFL. *Application deadline:* For fall admission, 1/1 priority date for domestic students, 11/15 for international students. Application fee: $50. *Expenses:* Tuition, state resident: full-time $12,023; part-time $501 per credit hour. Tuition, nonresident: full-time $26,554; part-time $1107 per credit hour. *Required fees:* $528. *Financial support:* Fellowships with full tuition reimbursements, research assistantships, Federal Work-Study, health care benefits, tuition waivers (full), and unspecified assistantships available. Financial award application deadline: 3/1; financial award applicants required to submit FAFSA. *Unit head:* Marc Rubin, Chair, 513-529-6200, Fax: 513-529-4740, E-mail: rubinma@muohio.edu. *Application contact:* Gretchen Radler, Academic Program Director, 513-529-3372, E-mail: miamiacc@muohio.edu. Web site: http://www.fsb.muohio.edu/departments/accountancy/macc.

Michigan State University, The Graduate School, Eli Broad Graduate School of Management, Department of Accounting and Information Systems, East Lansing, MI 48824. Offers accounting (MS); business administration (PhD). *Accreditation:* AACSB. *Entrance requirements:* Additional exam requirements/recommendations for international students: Required—TOEFL. Electronic applications accepted.

Middle Tennessee State University, College of Graduate Studies, Jennings A. Jones College of Business, Department of Accounting, Murfreesboro, TN 37132. Offers MS. *Accreditation:* AACSB. Part-time and evening/weekend programs available. Postbaccalaureate distance learning degree programs offered. *Faculty:* 9 full-time (5 women), 1 part-time/adjunct (0 women). *Students:* 15 full-time (8 women), 86 part-time (44 women); includes 33 minority (13 Black or African American, non-Hispanic/Latino; 1 American Indian or Alaska Native, non-Hispanic/Latino; 16 Asian, non-Hispanic/Latino; 2 Hispanic/Latino; 1 Two or more races, non-Hispanic/Latino). Average age 28. 97 applicants, 64% accepted. In 2011, 40 master's awarded. *Entrance requirements:* Additional exam requirements/recommendations for international students: Required—TOEFL (minimum score 525 paper-based; 195 computer-based; 71 iBT) or IELTS (minimum score 6). *Application deadline:* For fall admission, 6/1 for domestic and international students. Applications are processed on a rolling basis. Application fee: $25 ($30 for international students). Electronic applications accepted. *Expenses:* Tuition, state resident: full-time $10,008. Tuition, nonresident: full-time $25,056. *Financial support:* In 2011–12, 10 students received support. Tuition waivers available. Support available to part-time students. Financial award application deadline: 5/1; financial award applicants required to submit FAFSA. *Faculty research:* Forensic accounting, healthcare applications. *Unit head:* Dr. G. Robert Smith, Jr., Interim Chair, 615-898-2558, Fax: 615-898-5839, E-mail: robert.smith@mtsu.edu. *Application contact:* Dr. Michael D. Allen, Dean and Vice Provost for Research, 615-898-2840, Fax: 615-904-8020, E-mail: michael.allen@mtsu.edu.

Millsaps College, Else School of Management, Jackson, MS 39210-0001. Offers accounting (M Acc); business administration (MBA). *Accreditation:* AACSB. Part-time programs available. *Entrance requirements:* For master's, GMAT. Additional exam requirements/recommendations for international students: Required—TOEFL. Electronic applications accepted. *Faculty research:* Ethics, audit independence, satisfaction with assurance services, political business cycles.

Mississippi College, Graduate School, School of Business, Clinton, MS 39058. Offers accounting (Certificate); business administration (MBA), including accounting; business education (M Ed); finance (MBA, Certificate); JD/MBA. *Accreditation:* ACBSP. Part-time and evening/weekend programs available. *Degree requirements:* For master's, comprehensive exam, thesis optional. *Entrance requirements:* For master's, GMAT, minimum GPA of 2.5, 24 hours of undergraduate course work in business. Additional exam requirements/recommendations for international students: Recommended—TOEFL, IELTS. Electronic applications accepted.

Mississippi State University, College of Business, School of Accountancy, Mississippi State, MS 39762. Offers accounting (MBA); business administration (PhD); systems (MPA); taxation (MTX). MBA in accounting only offered at the Meridian campus. *Accreditation:* AACSB. *Faculty:* 8 full-time (3 women), 3 part-time/adjunct (0 women). *Students:* 46 full-time (24 women), 13 part-time (9 women); includes 4 minority (2 Black or African American, non-Hispanic/Latino; 1 Asian, non-Hispanic/Latino; 1 Two or more races, non-Hispanic/Latino), 6 international. Average age 27. 51 applicants, 47% accepted, 24 enrolled. In 2011, 56 master's awarded. *Degree requirements:* For master's, comprehensive exam. *Entrance requirements:* For master's, GMAT (minimum score of 510), minimum GPA of 2.75 overall and in upper-level accounting, 3.0 in last 60 hours of course work; for doctorate, GMAT, minimum undergraduate GPA of 3.0, both cumulative and over the last 60 hours of undergraduate work; 3.25 on all prior graduate work. Additional exam requirements/recommendations for international students: Required—TOEFL (minimum score 575 paper-based; 233 computer-based; 84 iBT); Recommended—IELTS (minimum score 7). *Application deadline:* For fall admission, 7/1 for domestic students, 5/1 for international students; for spring admission, 11/1 for domestic students, 9/1 for international students. Applications are processed on a rolling basis. Application fee: $40. Electronic applications accepted. *Expenses:* Tuition, state resident: full-time $5805; part-time $322.50 per credit hour. Tuition, nonresident: full-time $14,670; part-time $815 per credit hour. *Financial support:* Career-related internships or fieldwork, Federal Work-Study, institutionally sponsored loans, scholarships/grants, and unspecified assistantships available. Support available to part-time students. Financial award application deadline: 4/1; financial award applicants required to submit FAFSA. *Faculty research:* Income tax, financial accounting system, managerial accounting, auditing. *Unit head:* Dr. Jim Scheiner, Director, 662-325-1633, Fax: 662-325-1646, E-mail: jscheiner@cobilan.msstate.edu. *Application contact:* Dr. Barbara Spencer, Graduate Coordinator, 662-325-3710, Fax: 662-325-1646, E-mail: sac@cobilan.msstate.edu. Web site: http://www.business.msstate.edu/accounting.

Missouri State University, Graduate College, College of Business Administration, School of Accountancy, Springfield, MO 65897. Offers M Acc. *Accreditation:* AACSB. Part-time and evening/weekend programs available. *Faculty:* 16 full-time (3 women). *Students:* 80 full-time (48 women), 37 part-time (21 women); includes 2 minority (1 Asian, non-Hispanic/Latino; 1 Two or more races, non-Hispanic/Latino), 50 international. Average age 28. 61 applicants, 77% accepted, 26 enrolled. In 2011, 65 master's awarded. *Entrance requirements:* For master's, GMAT, minimum GPA of 2.75. Additional exam requirements/recommendations for international students: Required—TOEFL (minimum score 550 paper-based; 213 computer-based; 79 iBT). *Application deadline:* For fall admission, 7/20 priority date for domestic students, 5/1 for international students; for spring admission, 12/20 priority date for domestic students, 9/1 for international students. Applications are processed on a rolling basis. Application fee: $35 ($50 for international students). Electronic applications accepted. *Expenses:* Tuition, state resident: full-time $4086; part-time $227 per credit hour. Tuition, nonresident: full-time $8172; part-time $454 per credit hour. *Required fees:* $275 per semester. Tuition and fees vary according to course load, campus/location and program. *Financial support:* Career-related internships or fieldwork, Federal Work-Study, institutionally sponsored loans, scholarships/grants, tuition waivers (partial), and unspecified assistantships available. Support available to part-time students. Financial award application deadline: 3/31; financial award applicants required to submit FAFSA. *Faculty research:* Forensic accounting, international accounting standards, accounting education, tax compliance. *Unit head:* Dr. John R. Williams, Director, 417-836-5414, Fax: 417-836-6337, E-mail: accountancy@missouristate.edu. *Application contact:* Misty Stewart, Coordinator for Graduate Admissions and Recruitment, 417-836-6079, Fax: 417-836-6200, E-mail: mistystewart@missouristate.edu. Web site: http://www.missouristate.edu/soa/.

Molloy College, Graduate Business Program, Rockville Centre, NY 11571-5002. Offers accounting (MBA); accounting and management (MBA); management (MBA); personal financial planning and accounting (MBA); personal financial planning and management (MBA). Part-time programs available. *Faculty:* 5 full-time (0 women), 8 part-time/adjunct (2 women). *Students:* 39 full-time (18 women), 77 part-time (44 women); includes 41 minority (23 Black or African American, non-Hispanic/Latino; 1 American Indian or Alaska Native, non-Hispanic/Latino; 7 Asian, non-Hispanic/Latino; 8 Hispanic/Latino; 1 Native Hawaiian or other Pacific Islander, non-Hispanic/Latino; 1 Two or more races, non-Hispanic/Latino), 1 international. Average age 32. 57 applicants, 81% accepted, 31 enrolled. In 2011, 34 master's awarded. *Application deadline:* Applications are processed on a rolling basis. *Unit head:* Dr. Raymond Manganelli, Associate Dean and the Director Graduate Business, 516-678-5000. *Application contact:* Alina Haitz, Assistant Director of Graduate Admissions, 516-678-5000 Ext. 6399, Fax: 516-256-2247, E-mail: ahaitz@molloy.edu.

Monmouth University, The Graduate School, Leon Hess Business School, West Long Branch, NJ 07764-1898. Offers accounting (MBA, Post-Master's Certificate); business (MBA); finance (MBA); healthcare management (MBA, Post-Master's Certificate); real estate (MBA). *Accreditation:* AACSB. Part-time and evening/weekend programs available. *Faculty:* 29 full-time (10 women), 8 part-time/adjunct (2 women). *Students:* 107 full-time (44 women), 161 part-time (61 women); includes 42 minority (8 Black or African American, non-Hispanic/Latino; 19 Asian, non-Hispanic/Latino; 12 Hispanic/Latino; 3 Two or more races, non-Hispanic/Latino), 23 international. Average age 28. 193 applicants, 84% accepted, 111 enrolled. In 2011, 87 master's awarded. *Degree requirements:* For master's, capstone course. *Entrance requirements:* For master's, GMAT, minimum GPA of 3.0 in major, 2.75 overall. Additional exam requirements/recommendations for international students: Required—TOEFL (minimum score 550 paper-based; 213 computer-based; 79 iBT), IELTS (minimum score 5), Michigan English Language Assessment Battery (minimum score 77), Cambridge A, B, C. *Application deadline:* For fall admission, 7/15 priority date for domestic students, 6/1 for international students; for spring admission, 11/15 priority date for domestic students, 11/1 for international students. Applications are processed on a rolling basis. Application fee: $50. Electronic applications accepted. *Financial support:* In 2011–12, 190 students received support, including 183 fellowships (averaging $1,638 per year), 21 research assistantships (averaging $9,311 per year); career-related internships or fieldwork, scholarships/grants, and unspecified assistantships also available. Support available to part-time students. Financial award applicants required to submit FAFSA. *Faculty research:* Information technology and marketing, behavioral research in accounting, human resources, management of technology. *Unit head:* Douglas Stives, MBA Program Director, 732-263-5894, Fax: 732-263-5517, E-mail: dstives@monmouth.edu. *Application contact:* Kevin Roane, Director, Office of Graduate Admission, 732-571-3452, Fax: 732-263-5123, E-mail: gradadm@monmouth.edu. Web site: http://www.monmouth.edu/mba.

Montana State University, College of Graduate Studies, College of Business, Bozeman, MT 59717. Offers professional accountancy (MP Ac). *Accreditation:* AACSB. Part-time programs available. *Degree requirements:* For master's, comprehensive exam. *Entrance requirements:* For master's, GRE General Test, GMAT, minimum undergraduate GPA of 3.1 (preferred). Additional exam requirements/recommendations for international students: Required—TOEFL (minimum score 550 paper-based; 213 computer-based). Electronic applications accepted. *Faculty research:* Tax research, accounting education, fraud issues, CPA exams.

Montclair State University, The Graduate School, School of Business, Department of Accounting, Law and Taxation, Post Master's Certificate Program in Accounting, Montclair, NJ 07043-1624. Offers Post Master's Certificate. Part-time and evening/weekend programs available. *Students:* 1 (woman) full-time, 3 part-time; includes 2 minority (1 Black or African American, non-Hispanic/Latino; 1 Asian, non-Hispanic/Latino). Average age 30. 7 applicants, 57% accepted, 1 enrolled. In 2011, 3 Post Master's Certificates awarded. *Entrance requirements:* For degree, 2 letters of recommendation, essay. Additional exam requirements/recommendations for international students: Required—TOEFL (minimum score 83 iBT), IELTS (minimum score 6.5). *Application deadline:* Applications are processed on a rolling basis. Application fee: $60. Electronic applications accepted. *Financial support:* Federal Work-Study, scholarships/grants, and unspecified assistantships available. Support available to part-time students. Financial award application deadline: 3/1; financial award applicants required to submit FAFSA. *Faculty research:* Costs and benefits (to the economy) of tax incentive programs, sustainability and financial accounting, auditors' (expanded) role post-great recession, revising rules for restructuring charges, aggressive accounting and ethical behavior. *Unit head:* Prof. Frank Aquilino, Head, 973-655-4174. *Application contact:* Amy Aiello, Executive Director of The Graduate School, 973-655-5147, Fax: 973-655-7869, E-mail: graduate.school@montclair.edu. Web site: http://business.montclair.edu/alt.

Montclair State University, The Graduate School, School of Business, Department of Accounting, Law and Taxation, Program in Accounting, Montclair, NJ 07043-1624. Offers MS. Part-time and evening/weekend programs available. *Students:* 18 full-time (11 women), 14 part-time (5 women); includes 5 minority (1 Black or African American, non-Hispanic/Latino; 1 Asian, non-Hispanic/Latino; 3 Hispanic/Latino), 5 international. Average age 30. 48 applicants, 44% accepted, 15 enrolled. In 2011, 8 degrees awarded. *Degree requirements:* For master's, culminating experience. *Entrance requirements:* For master's, GMAT, 2 letters of recommendation, resume, essay. Additional exam requirements/recommendations for international students: Required—TOEFL (minimum score 83 iBT), IELTS (minimum score 6.5). *Application deadline:* Applications are processed on a rolling basis. Application fee: $60. Electronic applications accepted. *Financial support:* Federal Work-Study, scholarships/grants, and unspecified assistantships available. Support available to part-time students. Financial award application deadline: 3/1; financial award applicants required to submit FAFSA. *Faculty research:* Costs and benefits (to the economy) of tax incentive programs, sustainability and financial accounting, auditors' (expanded) role post-Great Recession, revising rules for restructuring charges, aggressive accounting and ethical behavior. *Unit head:* Prof. Frank Aquilino, Head, 973-655-4174. *Application contact:* Amy Aiello, Executive Director of The Graduate School, 973-655-5147, Fax: 973-655-7869, E-mail: graduate.school@montclair.edu. Web site: http://business.montclair.edu/graduate/msaccounting.

Moravian College, Moravian College Comenius Center, Business and Management Programs, Bethlehem, PA 18018-6650. Offers accounting (MBA); general management (MBA); health care management (MBA); human resource management (MBA); leadership (MSHRM); learning and performance management (MSHRM); supply chain management (MBA). Part-time and evening/weekend programs available. *Entrance requirements:* For master's, GMAT. Additional exam requirements/recommendations for international students: Required—TOEFL (minimum score 550 paper-based; 260 computer-based; 90 iBT). *Expenses:* Contact institution. *Faculty research:* Leadership, change management, human resources.

Murray State University, College of Business and Public Affairs, Master of Professional Accountancy (MPAC) Program, Murray, KY 42071. Offers MPAC. Part-time programs available. *Degree requirements:* For master's, thesis. *Entrance requirements:* For master's, GMAT or GRE. Additional exam requirements/recommendations for international students: Required—TOEFL (minimum score 525 paper-based; 197 computer-based). *Faculty research:* Corporate governance, information systems innovations, public finances, accounting education.

National University, Academic Affairs, School of Business and Management, Department of Accounting and Finance, La Jolla, CA 92037-1011. Offers accountancy (M Acc); business administration (MBA); sustainability management (MS). Part-time and evening/weekend programs available. Postbaccalaureate distance learning degree programs offered (no on-campus study). *Degree requirements:* For master's, thesis. *Entrance requirements:* For master's, interview, minimum GPA of 2.5. Additional exam requirements/recommendations for international students: Required—TOEFL (minimum score 550 paper-based; 213 computer-based; 79 iBT), IELTS (minimum score 6). *Application deadline:* Applications are processed on a rolling basis. Application fee: $60 ($65 for international students). Electronic applications accepted. *Financial support:* Career-related internships or fieldwork, institutionally sponsored loans, scholarships/grants, and tuition waivers (partial) available. Support available to part-time students. Financial award application deadline: 6/30; financial award applicants required to submit FAFSA. *Unit head:* Dr. Farhang Mossavar-Rahmani, Chair, 858-642-8409, Fax: 858-642-8726, E-mail: fmossava@nu.edu. *Application contact:* Dominick Giovanniello, Associate Regional Dean, 800-NAT-UNIV, Fax: 858-541-7792, E-mail: dgiovann@nu.edu. Web site: http://www.nu.edu/OurPrograms/SchoolOfBusinessAndManagement/AccountingAndFinance.html.

New England College, Program in Management, Henniker, NH 03242-3293. Offers accounting (MSA); healthcare administration (MS); international relations (MA); marketing management (MS); nonprofit leadership (MS); project management (MS); strategic leadership (MS). Part-time and evening/weekend programs available. *Degree requirements:* For master's, independent research project. Electronic applications accepted.

New Jersey City University, Graduate Studies and Continuing Education, College of Professional Studies, Department of Business Administration, Program in Accounting, Jersey City, NJ 07305-1597. Offers MS. Part-time and evening/weekend programs available. *Students:* 23 full-time (15 women), 22 part-time (12 women); includes 19 minority (4 Black or African American, non-Hispanic/Latino; 11 Asian, non-Hispanic/Latino; 4 Hispanic/Latino), 13 international. In 2011, 15 master's awarded. *Entrance requirements:* Additional exam requirements/recommendations for international students: Required—TOEFL. *Expenses:* Tuition, state resident: part-time $494 per credit. Tuition, nonresident: part-time $911.30 per credit. *Required fees:* $95.90 per year. *Unit head:* Robert J. Matthews, Graduate Coordinator, 201-200-3353, E-mail: rmatthews@njcu.edu. *Application contact:* Dr. William Bajor, Dean of Graduate Studies, 201-200-3409, Fax: 201-200-3411, E-mail: wbajor@njcu.edu.

New Mexico State University, Graduate School, College of Business, Department of Accounting and Information Systems, Las Cruces, NM 88003-8001. Offers M Acct. *Accreditation:* AACSB. Part-time programs available. *Faculty:* 11 full-time (4 women). *Students:* 29 full-time (13 women), 22 part-time (17 women); includes 13 minority (3 Asian, non-Hispanic/Latino; 9 Hispanic/Latino; 1 Two or more races, non-Hispanic/Latino), 6 international. Average age 30. 26 applicants, 69% accepted, 12 enrolled. In 2011, 31 degrees awarded. *Degree requirements:* For master's, comprehensive exam, thesis optional. *Entrance requirements:* For master's, GMAT, minimum undergraduate accounting GPA of 3.0 (upper-division). Additional exam requirements/recommendations for international students: Required—TOEFL (minimum score 530 paper-based; 197 computer-based; 79 iBT), IELTS (minimum score 6.5). *Application deadline:* For fall admission, 7/1 priority date for domestic students, 3/1 for international students; for spring admission, 11/1 priority date for domestic students. Applications are processed on a rolling basis. Application fee: $40 ($50 for international students). Electronic applications accepted. *Expenses:* Tuition, state resident: full-time $5004; part-time $208.50 per credit. Tuition, nonresident: full-time $17,446; part-time $726.90 per credit. *Financial support:* In 2011–12, 16 teaching assistantships (averaging $11,331 per year) were awarded; research assistantships, career-related internships or fieldwork, Federal Work-Study, scholarships/grants, traineeships, health care benefits, and unspecified assistantships also available. Support available to part-time students. Financial award application deadline: 3/1. *Faculty research:* Taxation, financial accounting, managerial accounting, accounting systems, accounting education. *Unit head:* Dr. Ed Scribner, Department Head, 575-646-4901, Fax: 575-646-1552, E-mail: escribne@nmsu.edu. *Application contact:* Dr. Cindy L. Seipel, Master of Accountancy Director, 575-646-5206, Fax: 575-646-1552, E-mail: cseipel@nmsu.edu. Web site: http://business.nmsu.edu/academics/accounting-is/.

New York Institute of Technology, Graduate Division, School of Management, Program in Business Administration, Old Westbury, NY 11568-8000. Offers accounting (Advanced Certificate); business administration (MBA); finance (Advanced Certificate); international business (Advanced Certificate); management of information systems (Advanced Certificate); marketing (Advanced Certificate). Part-time and evening/weekend programs available. *Students:* 331 full-time (131 women), 508 part-time (211 women); includes 74 minority (26 Black or African American, non-Hispanic/Latino; 27 Asian, non-Hispanic/Latino; 15 Hispanic/Latino; 6 Two or more races, non-Hispanic/Latino), 214 international. Average age 28. In 2011, 449 degrees awarded. *Degree requirements:* For master's, thesis (for some programs). *Entrance requirements:* For master's, minimum QPA of 2.85. Additional exam requirements/recommendations for international students: Required—TOEFL (minimum score 550 paper-based; 213 computer-based). *Application deadline:* For fall admission, 7/1 priority date for domestic students; for spring admission, 12/1 priority date for domestic students. Applications are processed on a rolling basis. Application fee: $50. Electronic applications accepted. *Expenses: Tuition:* Part-time $930 per credit hour. *Financial support:* Fellowships, research assistantships with partial tuition reimbursements, institutionally sponsored loans, tuition waivers (full and partial), and unspecified assistantships available. Support available to part-time students. Financial award applicants required to submit FAFSA. *Faculty research:* Instructor performance appraisal; relationship between TOEFL, GMAT, GRE, and performance in foreign students. *Unit head:* Dr. Stephen Hartman, Director, 516-686-7691, E-mail: shartman@nyit.edu. *Application contact:* Dr. Jacquelyn Nealon, Vice President for Enrollment Services, 516-686-7925, Fax: 516-686-7597, E-mail: jnealon@nyit.edu.

New York University, Leonard N. Stern School of Business, Department of Accounting, New York, NY 10012-1019. Offers MBA, PhD. *Faculty research:* Earnings management and financial analysis effectiveness and accounting policy, value-relevance of financial reporting, intangibles-related reporting and analysis, equity.

North Carolina State University, Graduate School, Poole College of Management, Program in Accounting, Raleigh, NC 27695. Offers MAC. Part-time programs available. *Degree requirements:* For master's, thesis optional. *Entrance requirements:* For master's, GMAT, interview. Additional exam requirements/recommendations for international students: Required—TOEFL. Electronic applications accepted. *Faculty research:* Financial reporting issues using positive economic models and empirical studies of human behavior related to accounting decisions.

Northeastern Illinois University, Graduate College, College of Business and Management, Chicago, IL 60625-4699. Offers accounting (MSA); finance (MBA); management (MBA); marketing (MBA). Part-time and evening/weekend programs available. *Degree requirements:* For master's, thesis optional. *Entrance requirements:* For master's, GMAT, minimum GPA of 2.75. Additional exam requirements/recommendations for international students: Required—TOEFL (minimum score 550 paper-based; 213 computer-based; 79 iBT). Electronic applications accepted. *Faculty research:* Perception of accountants and non-accountants toward future of the accounting industry, asynchronous learning outcomes, cost and efficiency of financial markets, impact of deregulation on airline industry, analysis of derivational instruments.

Northeastern State University, Graduate College, College of Business and Technology, Program in Accounting and Financial Analysis, Tahlequah, OK 74464-2399. Offers MS. Part-time and evening/weekend programs available. *Students:* 17 full-time (8 women), 51 part-time (33 women); includes 12 minority (3 Black or African American, non-Hispanic/Latino; 4 American Indian or Alaska Native, non-Hispanic/Latino; 2 Asian, non-Hispanic/Latino; 3 Hispanic/Latino), 2 international. In 2011, 16 master's awarded. *Entrance requirements:* For master's, GMAT. Additional exam requirements/recommendations for international students: Required—TOEFL (minimum score 213 computer-based). *Application deadline:* For fall admission, 6/1 priority date for domestic students. Applications are processed on a rolling basis. Application fee: $25. Electronic applications accepted. *Unit head:* Dr. Gary Freeman, Coordinator, 918-449-6524, E-mail: freemandg@nsuok.edu. *Application contact:* Margie Railey, Administrative Assistant, 918-456-5511 Ext. 2093, Fax: 918-458-2061, E-mail: railey@nsouk.edu.

Northeastern University, Graduate School of Professional Accounting, Boston, MA 02115-5096. Offers MS, MST, MS/MBA. Postbaccalaureate distance learning degree programs offered (no on-campus study). *Faculty:* 8 full-time, 6 part-time/adjunct. *Students:* 100 full-time (47 women), 77 part-time (31 women). Average age 26. 284 applicants, 58% accepted, 116 enrolled. In 2011, 127 master's awarded. *Entrance requirements:* For master's, GMAT, interview. Additional exam requirements/recommendations for international students: Required—TOEFL (minimum score 600 paper-based; 250 computer-based; 100 iBT). *Application deadline:* For fall admission, 8/1 for domestic students, 2/1 for international students; for winter admission, 11/15 for domestic and international students; for spring admission, 3/15 for domestic students. Application fee: $100. Electronic applications accepted. *Expenses:* Contact institution. *Financial support:* In 2011–12, 58 fellowships (averaging $8,295 per year) were awarded; career-related internships or fieldwork, Federal Work-Study, institutionally sponsored loans, and scholarships/grants also available. Support available to part-time students. Financial award application deadline: 3/1; financial award applicants required to submit FAFSA. *Unit head:* Kate Klepper, Associate Dean, Graduate Business Programs, 617-373-5417, Fax: 617-373-8564, E-mail: k.klepper@neu.edu. *Application contact:* Annarita Meeker, Director, Graduate Accounting and Tax Programs, 617-373-4621, Fax: 617-373-8564, E-mail: a.meeker@neu.edu. Web site: http://www.cba.neu.edu/grad.

Northern Illinois University, Graduate School, College of Business, Department of Accountancy, De Kalb, IL 60115-2854. Offers MAS, MST. *Accreditation:* AACSB. Part-time and evening/weekend programs available. *Faculty:* 14 full-time (4 women). *Students:* 127 full-time (54 women), 76 part-time (40 women); includes 35 minority (4 Black or African American, non-Hispanic/Latino; 19 Asian, non-Hispanic/Latino; 11 Hispanic/Latino; 1 Two or more races, non-Hispanic/Latino), 28 international. Average age 27. 168 applicants, 51% accepted, 55 enrolled. In 2011, 138 master's awarded. *Degree requirements:* For master's, thesis optional. *Entrance requirements:* For master's, GMAT, minimum GPA of 2.75. Additional exam requirements/recommendations for international students: Required—TOEFL (minimum score 550 paper-based; 213 computer-based). *Application deadline:* For fall admission, 4/1 priority date for domestic students, 5/1 for international students; for spring admission, 9/15 priority date for domestic students, 10/1 for international students. Applications are processed on a rolling basis. Application fee: $40. Electronic applications accepted. *Financial support:* In 2011–12, 26 research assistantships with full tuition reimbursements, 11 teaching assistantships with full tuition reimbursements were awarded; fellowships with full tuition reimbursements, career-related internships or fieldwork, Federal Work-Study, scholarships/grants, tuition waivers (full), and unspecified assistantships also available. Support available to part-time students. Financial award applicants required to submit FAFSA. *Faculty research:* Accounting fraud, governmental accounting, corporate income tax planning, auditing, ethics. *Unit head:* Dr. James C. Young, Chair, 815-753-1250, Fax: 815-753-8515. *Application contact:* Dr. Rowene Linden, Graduate Adviser, 815-753-6200. Web site: http://www.cob.niu.edu/accy/.

Northern Kentucky University, Office of Graduate Programs, College of Business, Program in Accountancy, Highland Heights, KY 41099. Offers accountancy (M Acc); advanced taxation (Certificate). Part-time and evening/weekend programs available. *Faculty:* 7 full-time (1 woman), 3 part-time/adjunct (0 women). *Students:* 11 full-time (2 women), 66 part-time (26 women); includes 5 minority (2 Black or African American, non-Hispanic/Latino; 1 Asian, non-Hispanic/Latino; 2 Hispanic/Latino). Average age 30. 85 applicants, 56% accepted, 43 enrolled. In 2011, 32 degrees awarded. *Degree requirements:* For master's, capstone course. *Entrance requirements:* For master's, GMAT (minimum score 450), minimum GPA of 2.5. Additional exam requirements/recommendations for international students: Required—TOEFL (minimum score 550 paper-based; 213 computer-based; 79 iBT); Recommended—IELTS (minimum score 6.5). *Application deadline:* For fall admission, 7/1 priority date for domestic students, 6/1 for international students; for spring admission, 12/1 priority date for domestic students, 10/1 for international students. Applications are processed on a rolling basis. Application fee: $40. Electronic applications accepted. *Expenses:* Tuition, state resident: full-time $7614; part-time $423 per credit hour. Tuition, nonresident: full-time $13,104; part-time $728 per credit hour. Tuition and fees vary according to degree level and reciprocity agreements. *Financial support:* Unspecified assistantships available. Financial award applicants required to submit FAFSA. *Faculty research:* Behavioral influences on accounting decisions, historical development of accounting, auditing and accounting failures. *Unit head:* Robert Salyer, Director, 859-572-7695, Fax: 859-572-7694, E-mail: salyerb@nku.edu. *Application contact:* Dr. Peg Griffin, Director of Graduate Programs, 859-572-6934, Fax: 859-572-6670, E-mail: griffinp@nku.edu. Web site: http://cob.nku.edu/departments/accountancy/graduate/macc/index.php.

Northwestern University, The Graduate School, Kellogg School of Management, Department of Accounting Information and Management, Evanston, IL 60208. Offers accounting (PhD). Admissions and degree offered through The Graduate School. *Degree requirements:* For doctorate, comprehensive exam, thesis/dissertation. *Entrance requirements:* For doctorate, GMAT or GRE General Test. Additional exam requirements/recommendations for international students: Required—TOEFL. Electronic applications accepted. *Faculty research:* Managerial and financial accounting theory, financial accounting/theory, managerial accounting and performance measurement, international accounting, joint cost allocation.

Nova Southeastern University, H. Wayne Huizenga School of Business and Entrepreneurship, Fort Lauderdale, FL 33314-7796. Offers accounting (M Acc); business administration (MBA, DBA); human resource management (MSHRM); international business administration (MIBA); leadership (MS); public administration (MPA, DPA); real estate development (MS); taxation (M Tax); JD/MBA; Pharm D/MBA. Part-time and evening/weekend programs available. Postbaccalaureate distance learning degree programs offered (minimal on-campus study). *Students:* 229 full-time (112 women), 3,506 part-time (2,109 women); includes 2,506 minority (1,256 Black or African American, non-Hispanic/Latino; 8 American Indian or Alaska Native, non-Hispanic/Latino; 146 Asian, non-Hispanic/Latino; 1,058 Hispanic/Latino; 4 Native Hawaiian or other Pacific Islander, non-Hispanic/Latino; 34 Two or more races, non-Hispanic/Latino), 174 international. Average age 33. In 2011, 1,252 master's, 17 doctorates awarded. *Degree requirements:* For master's, thesis optional; for doctorate, comprehensive exam, thesis/dissertation. *Entrance requirements:* For doctorate, GMAT. Additional exam requirements/recommendations for international students: Required—TOEFL (minimum score 550 paper-based; 213 computer-based; 79 iBT), IELTS (minimum score 6). *Application deadline:* Applications are processed on a rolling basis. Application fee: $50. Electronic applications accepted. *Financial support:* In 2011–12, 2 students received support. Federal Work-Study and scholarships/grants available. Support available to part-time students. Financial award applicants required to submit FAFSA. *Faculty research:* Reputation management, call centers, international social capital, corporate earnings guidance, corporate governance. *Unit head:* Dr. D. Michael Fields, Dean, 954-262-5005, E-mail: fieldsm@nova.edu. *Application contact:* Karen Goldberg, Associate Director of Recruitment and Special Events, 954-262-5039, Fax: 954-262-3822, E-mail: karen@nova.edu. Web site: http://www.huizenga.nova.edu.

Oakland University, Graduate Study and Lifelong Learning, School of Business Administration, Department of Accounting and Finance, Rochester, MI 48309-4401. Offers accounting (M Acc, Certificate); finance (Certificate).

The Ohio State University, Graduate School, Max M. Fisher College of Business, Department of Accounting and Management Information Systems, Columbus, OH 43210. Offers M Acc, MA, MS, PhD. *Accreditation:* AACSB. *Faculty:* 18. *Students:* 81 full-time (51 women), 8 part-time (2 women); includes 7 minority (2 Black or African American, non-Hispanic/Latino; 2 Asian, non-Hispanic/Latino; 2 Hispanic/Latino; 1 Two or more races, non-Hispanic/Latino), 35 international. Average age 25. In 2011, 89 master's awarded. Terminal master's awarded for partial completion of doctoral program. *Degree requirements:* For doctorate, thesis/dissertation. *Entrance* *requirements:* For master's and doctorate, GMAT (preferred) or GRE. Additional exam requirements/recommendations for international students: Required—TOEFL (minimum score 600 paper-based; 250 computer-based), Michigan English Language Assessment Battery (minimum score 82). *Application deadline:* For fall admission, 8/15 priority date for domestic students, 7/1 for international students; for winter admission, 12/1 priority date for domestic students, 11/1 for international students; for spring admission, 3/1 priority date for domestic students, 2/1 for international students. Applications are processed on a rolling basis. Application fee: $40 ($50 for international students). Electronic applications accepted. *Expenses:* Tuition, state resident: full-time $11,400. Tuition, nonresident: full-time $28,125. Tuition and fees vary according to course load, degree level, campus/location and program. *Financial support:* Fellowships, research assistantships, teaching assistantships, career-related internships or fieldwork, Federal Work-Study, and institutionally sponsored loans available. Support available to part-time students. *Faculty research:* Artificial intelligence, protocol analysis, database design in decision-supporting systems. *Unit head:* J. Richard Dietrich, Chair, 614-247-6299, Fax: 614-292-2118, E-mail: dietrich.59@osu.edu. *Application contact:* Graduate Admissions, 614-292-6031, Fax: 614-292-3656, E-mail: gradadmissions@osu.edu. Web site: http://fisher.osu.edu/departments/accounting-and-mis/.

The Ohio State University, Graduate School, Max M. Fisher College of Business, Program in Accounting, Columbus, OH 43210. Offers M Acc, MA, MS. *Faculty:* 18. *Students:* 81 full-time (51 women), 8 part-time (2 women); includes 7 minority (2 Black or African American, non-Hispanic/Latino; 2 Asian, non-Hispanic/Latino; 2 Hispanic/Latino; 1 Two or more races, non-Hispanic/Latino), 35 international. Average age 25. In 2011, 89 master's awarded. *Entrance requirements:* Additional exam requirements/recommendations for international students: Required—TOEFL (minimum score 550 paper-based; 79 iBT), Michigan English Language Assessment Battery (minimum score 82). *Application deadline:* Applications are processed on a rolling basis. Application fee: $40 ($50 for international students). Electronic applications accepted. *Expenses:* Tuition, state resident: full-time $11,400. Tuition, nonresident: full-time $28,125. Tuition and fees vary according to course load, degree level, campus/location and program. *Unit head:* Annette Beatty, Chair, 614-292-2081, Fax: 614-292-2118, E-mail: beatty.86@osu.edu. *Application contact:* Graduate Admissions, 614-292-6031, Fax: 614-292-3656, E-mail: gradadmissions@osu.edu. Web site: http://www.cob.ohio-state.edu/macc.

Oklahoma City University, Meinders School of Business, Program in Accounting, Oklahoma City, OK 73106-1402. Offers MSA. Part-time and evening/weekend programs available. *Faculty:* 5 full-time (4 women), 2 part-time/adjunct (0 women). *Students:* 20 full-time (6 women), 20 part-time (12 women); includes 4 minority (2 Asian, non-Hispanic/Latino; 1 Hispanic/Latino; 1 Two or more races, non-Hispanic/Latino), 12 international. Average age 31. 18 applicants, 89% accepted, 8 enrolled. In 2011, 8 master's awarded. *Entrance requirements:* Additional exam requirements/recommendations for international students: Required—TOEFL (minimum score 570 paper-based; 230 computer-based; 88 iBT). *Application deadline:* Applications are processed on a rolling basis. Application fee: $50 ($70 for international students). Electronic applications accepted. *Expenses: Tuition:* Full-time $16,848; part-time $936 per credit hour. *Required fees:* $2070; $115 per credit hour. One-time fee: $300. *Financial support:* Career-related internships or fieldwork, Federal Work-Study, and institutionally sponsored loans available. Support available to part-time students. Financial award application deadline: 8/1; financial award applicants required to submit FAFSA. *Faculty research:* Financial accounting, auditing, tax. *Unit head:* Dr. Jacci Rodgers, Chair, Accounting and Information Technology, 405-208-5824, Fax: 405-208-5356, E-mail: jrodgers@okcu.edu. *Application contact:* Michelle Cook, Director, Admissions, 800-633-7242, Fax: 405-208-5916, E-mail: gadmissions@okcu.edu. Web site: http://www.okcu.edu/business/graduate/degree%20programs/msa.aspx.

Oklahoma State University, Spears School of Business, School of Accounting, Stillwater, OK 74078. Offers MS, PhD. *Accreditation:* AACSB. Part-time programs available. *Faculty:* 15 full-time (5 women), 3 part-time/adjunct (0 women). *Students:* 55 full-time (18 women), 35 part-time (13 women); includes 9 minority (1 Black or African American, non-Hispanic/Latino; 2 American Indian or Alaska Native, non-Hispanic/Latino; 1 Hispanic/Latino; 5 Two or more races, non-Hispanic/Latino), 10 international. Average age 27. 77 applicants, 36% accepted, 10 enrolled. In 2011, 61 master's, 1 doctorate awarded. *Degree requirements:* For master's, thesis or alternative; for doctorate, comprehensive exam, thesis/dissertation. *Entrance requirements:* For master's and doctorate, GRE or GMAT. Additional exam requirements/recommendations for international students: Required—TOEFL (minimum score 550 paper-based; 79 iBT). *Application deadline:* For fall admission, 3/1 for international students; for spring admission, 8/1 for international students. Applications are processed on a rolling basis. Application fee: $40 ($75 for international students). Electronic applications accepted. *Expenses:* Tuition, state resident: full-time $4044; part-time $168.50 per credit hour. Tuition, nonresident: full-time $16,008; part-time $667 per credit hour. *Required fees:* $2122; $88.45 per credit hour. One-time fee: $50. Tuition and fees vary according to course load and campus/location. *Financial support:* In 2011–12, 5 research assistantships (averaging $18,984 per year), 26 teaching assistantships (averaging $10,050 per year) were awarded; career-related internships or fieldwork, Federal Work-Study, scholarships/grants, health care benefits, tuition waivers (partial), and unspecified assistantships also available. Support available to part-time students. Financial award application deadline: 3/1; financial award applicants required to submit FAFSA. *Faculty research:* International accounting, accounting education, cost-management, taxation, oil and gas. *Unit head:* Dr. Bud Lacy, Head, 405-744-5123, Fax: 405-744-1680. *Application contact:* Dr. Sheryl Tucker, Dean, 405-744-7099, Fax: 405-744-0355, E-mail: grad-i@okstate.edu. Web site: http://spears.okstate.edu/accounting.

Old Dominion University, College of Business and Public Administration, Program in Accounting, Norfolk, VA 23529. Offers MS. *Accreditation:* AACSB. Part-time and evening/weekend programs available. *Faculty:* 12 full-time (4 women), 4 part-time/adjunct (2 women). *Students:* 18 full-time (10 women), 30 part-time (12 women); includes 8 minority (4 Black or African American, non-Hispanic/Latino; 2 Asian, non-Hispanic/Latino; 1 Hispanic/Latino; 1 Native Hawaiian or other Pacific Islander, non-Hispanic/Latino), 9 international. Average age 31. 37 applicants, 68% accepted, 22 enrolled. In 2011, 27 master's awarded. *Degree requirements:* For master's, comprehensive exam. *Entrance requirements:* For master's, GMAT, minimum GPA of 3.0. Additional exam requirements/recommendations for international students: Required—TOEFL (minimum score 550 paper-based). *Application deadline:* For fall admission, 7/1 priority date for domestic students, 4/15 for international students; for spring admission, 11/1 priority date for domestic students, 10/1 for international students. Applications are processed on a rolling basis. Application fee: $50. *Expenses:* Tuition, state resident: full-time $9096; part-time $379 per credit. Tuition, nonresident: full-time $23,064; part-time $961 per credit. *Required fees:* $127 per semester. One-time fee: $50. *Financial support:* In 2011–12, 4 students received support, including 8 research assistantships with partial tuition reimbursements available (averaging $6,400 per year); career-related internships or fieldwork and unspecified assistantships also available. Financial award application deadline: 2/15; financial award applicants required to submit FAFSA. *Faculty research:* Assurance services, international accounting, strategic costing, business valuation. *Unit head:* Dr. Yin Xu, Graduate Program Director, 757-683-3554, Fax: 757-683-5639, E-mail: yxu@odu.edu. Web site: http://bpa.odu.edu/bpa/academics/msa.shtml.

Oral Roberts University, School of Business, Tulsa, OK 74171. Offers accounting (MBA); entrepreneurship (MBA); finance (MBA); international business (MBA); management (MBA); marketing (MBA); non-profit management (MBA); not for profit management (MNM). *Accreditation:* ACBSP. Part-time programs available. Postbaccalaureate distance learning degree programs offered (minimal on-campus study). *Degree requirements:* For master's, thesis optional. *Entrance requirements:* For master's, minimum cumulative GPA of 3.0. Additional exam requirements/recommendations for international students: Required—TOEFL (minimum score 550 paper-based; 213 computer-based; 79 iBT). Electronic applications accepted. *Faculty research:* Social media, international business and marketing.

Our Lady of the Lake University of San Antonio, School of Business and Leadership, Program in Accounting/Finance, San Antonio, TX 78207-4689. Offers MBA. Part-time and evening/weekend programs available.

Pace University, Lubin School of Business, Accounting Program, New York, NY 10038. Offers managerial accounting (MBA); public accounting (MBA, MS). *Accreditation:* AACSB. Part-time and evening/weekend programs available. *Students:* 62 full-time (33 women), 227 part-time (149 women); includes 42 minority (2 Black or African American, non-Hispanic/Latino; 1 American Indian or Alaska Native, non-Hispanic/Latino; 33 Asian, non-Hispanic/Latino; 6 Hispanic/Latino), 159 international. Average age 28. 530 applicants, 68% accepted, 123 enrolled. In 2011, 114 master's awarded. *Entrance requirements:* For master's, GMAT, GRE. Additional exam requirements/recommendations for international students: Required—TOEFL. *Application deadline:* For fall admission, 7/31 priority date for domestic students; for spring admission, 11/30 for domestic students. Applications are processed on a rolling basis. Application fee: $70. Electronic applications accepted. *Expenses: Tuition:* Part-time $990 per credit. *Required fees:* $168 per semester. Tuition and fees vary according to course load and degree level. *Financial support:* Research assistantships, career-related internships or fieldwork, and Federal Work-Study available. Support available to part-time students. Financial award applicants required to submit FAFSA. *Unit head:* Dr. Rudolph A. Jacob, Chairperson, 212-618-6420, E-mail: rjacob@pace.edu. *Application contact:* Susan Ford-Goldschein, Director of Graduate Admissions, 212-346-1531, Fax: 212-346-1585, E-mail: gradnyc@pace.edu. Web site: http://www.pace.edu/.

Pacific States University, College of Business, Los Angeles, CA 90006. Offers accounting (MBA); finance (MBA); international business (MBA, DBA); management of information technology (MBA); real estate management (MBA). Part-time and evening/weekend programs available. Postbaccalaureate distance learning degree programs offered (no on-campus study). *Faculty:* 6 full-time (2 women), 14 part-time/adjunct (0 women). *Students:* 157 full-time (70 women); includes 13 minority (2 Black or African American, non-Hispanic/Latino; 8 Asian, non-Hispanic/Latino; 3 Native Hawaiian or other Pacific Islander, non-Hispanic/Latino), 140 international. Average age 31. 42 applicants, 83% accepted, 33 enrolled. *Degree requirements:* For doctorate, comprehensive exam, thesis/dissertation. *Entrance requirements:* For master's, minimum undergraduate GPA of 2.5 during last 90 hours of course work. Additional exam requirements/recommendations for international students: Required—TOEFL (minimum score 133 computer-based; 45 iBT), IELTS (minimum score 4.5). *Application deadline:* For fall admission, 8/15 priority date for domestic students; for winter admission, 10/15 priority date for domestic students; for spring admission, 1/15 priority date for domestic students. Applications are processed on a rolling basis. Application fee: $100. *Expenses: Tuition:* Full-time $11,040; part-time $345 per credit hour. *Required fees:* $150 per quarter. *Financial support:* Scholarships/grants available. Financial award applicants required to submit FAFSA. *Application contact:* Zolzaya Enkhbayar, Interim Registrar, 323-731-2383, Fax: 323-731-7276, E-mail: registrar@psuca.edu.

Pittsburg State University, Graduate School, Kelce College of Business, Department of Accounting, Pittsburg, KS 66762. Offers MBA. *Degree requirements:* For master's, thesis or alternative. *Entrance requirements:* For master's, GMAT. *Faculty research:* Accountant's legal liability, computer audit.

Polytechnic University of Puerto Rico, Miami Campus, Graduate School, Miami, FL 33166. Offers accounting (MBA); business administration (MBA); construction management (MEM); environmental management (MEM); finance (MBA); human resources management (MBA); logistics and supply chain management (MBA); management of international enterprises (MBA); manufacturing management (MEM); marketing management (MBA); project management (MBA). Part-time and evening/weekend programs available. Postbaccalaureate distance learning degree programs offered (no on-campus study). *Entrance requirements:* For master's, minimum GPA of 3.0. Electronic applications accepted.

Polytechnic University of Puerto Rico, Orlando Campus, Graduate School, Winter Park, FL 32792. Offers accounting (MBA); business administration (MBA); construction management (MEM); engineering management (MEM); environmental management (MEM); finance (MBA); human resources management (MBA); management of international enterprises (MBA); management of technology (MBA); manufacturing management (MEM). Part-time and evening/weekend programs available. Postbaccalaureate distance learning degree programs offered (no on-campus study). *Entrance requirements:* For master's, minimum GPA of 3.0. Additional exam requirements/recommendations for international students: Recommended—TOEFL. Electronic applications accepted.

Pontifical Catholic University of Puerto Rico, College of Business Administration, Program in Accounting, Ponce, PR 00717-0777. Offers MBA. Part-time and evening/weekend programs available. *Degree requirements:* For master's, thesis. *Entrance requirements:* For master's, GRE, interview, minimum GPA of 2.75.

Pontifical Catholic University of Puerto Rico, College of Business Administration, Program in Management and Accounting, Ponce, PR 00717-0777. Offers Professional Certificate.

Prairie View A&M University, College of Business, Prairie View, TX 77446-0519. Offers accounting (MS); general business administration (MBA). *Accreditation:* AACSB. Part-time and evening/weekend programs available. *Entrance requirements:* For master's, GMAT, minimum GPA of 2.45. Additional exam requirements/recommendations for international students: Required—TOEFL. Electronic applications accepted. *Faculty research:* Operations, finance, marketing.

Providence College, School of Business, Providence, RI 02918. Offers accounting (MBA); entrepreneurship (MBA); finance (MBA); international business (MBA); management (MBA); marketing (MBA); not-for-profit organizations (MBA). Part-time and evening/weekend programs available. *Faculty:* 11 full-time (4 women), 6 part-time/adjunct (1 woman). *Students:* 52 full-time (21 women), 49 part-time (17 women); includes 8 minority (3 Black or African American, non-Hispanic/Latino; 2 Asian, non-Hispanic/Latino; 3 Two or more races, non-Hispanic/Latino), 6 international. Average age 26. 49 applicants, 80% accepted, 25 enrolled. In 2011, 57 master's awarded. *Degree requirements:* For master's, thesis optional. *Entrance requirements:* For master's, GMAT. Additional exam requirements/recommendations for international students: Required—TOEFL (minimum score 550 paper-based; 213 computer-based; 80 iBT). *Application deadline:* For fall admission, 8/1 priority date for domestic students, 8/1 for international students; for spring admission, 12/1 priority date for domestic students, 12/1 for international students. Applications are processed on a rolling basis. Application fee: $55. *Expenses:* Contact institution. *Financial support:* In 2011–12, 34 research assistantships with full tuition reimbursements (averaging $8,400 per year) were awarded; Federal Work-Study, institutionally sponsored loans, and unspecified assistantships also available. Support available to part-time students. Financial award application deadline: 8/1; financial award applicants required to submit FAFSA. *Unit head:* Dr. Catherine L. Pastille, Director, MBA Program, 401-865-1654, Fax: 401-865-2978, E-mail: cpastill@providence.edu. *Application contact:* Katherine A. Follett, Administrative Coordinator, 401-865-2333, Fax: 401-865-2978, E-mail: kfollett@providence.edu. Web site: http://www.providence.edu/business/Pages/default.aspx.

Purdue University Calumet, Graduate Studies Office, School of Management, Hammond, IN 46323-2094. Offers accountancy (M Acc); business administration (MBA); business administration for executives (EMBA). Part-time and evening/weekend programs available. *Entrance requirements:* For master's, GMAT. Additional exam requirements/recommendations for international students: Required—TOEFL. Electronic applications accepted.

Queens College of the City University of New York, Division of Graduate Studies, Social Science Division, Department of Accounting, Flushing, NY 11367-1597. Offers MS. *Faculty:* 19 full-time (1 woman). *Students:* 29 full-time (16 women), 292 part-time (160 women); includes 165 minority (21 Black or African American, non-Hispanic/Latino; 119 Asian, non-Hispanic/Latino; 25 Hispanic/Latino), 39 international. 215 applicants, 57% accepted, 80 enrolled. In 2011, 83 master's awarded. Application fee: $125. *Expenses:* Tuition, state resident: part-time $345 per credit. Tuition, nonresident: part-time $640 per credit. *Required fees:* $145.25 per semester. *Unit head:* Dr. Israel Blumenfrucht, Chairperson, 718-997-5070, E-mail: israel_blumenfrucht@qc.edu. *Application contact:* Mario Caruso, Director of Graduate Admissions, 718-997-5200, Fax: 718-997-5193, E-mail: graduate_admissions@qc.edu.

Regis University, College for Professional Studies, School of Management, Denver, CO 80221-1099. Offers accounting (MS, Certificate); executive international management (Certificate); executive leadership (Certificate); executive project management (Certificate); finance and accounting (MBA); general business administration (MBA); health care management (MBA); human resource management and leadership (MSOL); information technology leadership and management (MSOL); international business (MBA); marketing (MBA); operations management (MBA); organizational leadership and management (MSOL); project leadership and management (MSOL); project management (Certificate); strategic business management (Certificate); strategic human resource management (Certificate); strategic management (MBA). Offered at Colorado Springs Campus, Northwest Denver Campus, Southeast Denver Campus, Fort Collins Campus, Broomfield Campus, Henderson (Nevada) Campus, and Summerlin (Nevada) Campus and online. Part-time and evening/weekend programs available. Postbaccalaureate distance learning degree programs offered (no on-campus study). *Degree requirements:* For master's, thesis optional, capstone project. *Entrance requirements:* For master's, GMAT or essays, interview, 2 years of full-time business work experience, resume; for Certificate, GMAT. Additional exam requirements/recommendations for international students: Required—TOEFL, TWE (minimum score 5) or university-based test. Electronic applications accepted. *Faculty research:* Impact of information technology on small business regulation of accounting, international project financing, mineral development, delivery of healthcare to rural indigenous communities.

Rhode Island College, School of Graduate Studies, School of Management, Department of Accounting and Computer Information Systems, Providence, RI 02908-1991. Offers accounting (MP Ac); financial planning (CGS). Part-time and evening/weekend programs available. *Faculty:* 1 (woman) full-time, 1 (woman) part-time/adjunct. *Students:* 4 full-time (2 women), 17 part-time (12 women); includes 1 minority (Black or African American, non-Hispanic/Latino). Average age 29. In 2011, 4 master's awarded. *Entrance requirements:* For master's, GMAT (unless applicant is a CPA or has passed a state bar exam); for CGS, GMAT, bachelor's degree from an accredited college or university, official transcripts of all undergraduate and graduate records. Additional exam requirements/recommendations for international students: Recommended—TOEFL (minimum score 550 paper-based; 213 computer-based; 79 iBT). *Application deadline:* For fall admission, 3/1 for domestic students. Applications are processed on a rolling basis. Application fee: $50. *Expenses:* Tuition, state resident: full-time $8592; part-time $358 per credit hour. Tuition, nonresident: full-time $16,800; part-time $700 per credit hour. *Required fees:* $602; $22 per credit. $72 per term. *Financial support:* Federal Work-Study, scholarships/grants, and health care benefits available. Support available to part-time students. Financial award application deadline: 5/15; financial award applicants required to submit FAFSA. *Unit head:* Prof. Jane Przybyla, Chair, 401-456-8036. *Application contact:* Graduate Studies, 401-456-8700. Web site: http://www.ric.edu/accountingComputerInformationSystems/.

Rhodes College, Department of Commerce and Business, Memphis, TN 38112-1690. Offers accounting (MS). Part-time programs available. *Faculty:* 5 full-time (3 women), 2 part-time/adjunct (0 women). *Students:* 10 full-time (1 woman). Average age 22. In 2011, 13 master's awarded. *Entrance requirements:* For master's, GMAT. Additional exam requirements/recommendations for international students: Required—TOEFL (minimum score 550 paper-based). *Application deadline:* For fall admission, 3/1 for domestic students. Application fee: $25. *Expenses: Tuition:* Full-time $36,154; part-time $1520 per credit. *Required fees:* $310. *Financial support:* Career-related internships or fieldwork and scholarships/grants available. Financial award application deadline: 3/1; financial award applicants required to submit FAFSA. *Unit head:* Dr. Pamela H. Church, Program Director, 901-843-3863, Fax: 901-843-3798, E-mail: church@rhodes.edu. *Application contact:* Dr. Pamela H. Church, Program Director, 901-843-3863, Fax: 901-843-3798, E-mail: church@rhodes.edu. Web site: http://www.rhodes.edu.

Rider University, College of Business Administration, Program in Accountancy, Lawrenceville, NJ 08648-3001. Offers M Acc. *Accreditation:* AACSB. *Entrance requirements:* For master's, GMAT, resume. Additional exam requirements/recommendations for international students: Required—TOEFL (minimum score 550 paper-based; 213 computer-based). Electronic applications accepted. *Expenses: Tuition:* Full-time $32,820; part-time $710 per credit. *Required fees:* $350; $35 per course. Tuition and fees vary according to campus/location and program. *Faculty research:* Financial reporting, corporate governance, information technology, ethics, pedagogy.

Robert Morris University Illinois, Morris Graduate School of Management, Chicago, IL 60605. Offers accounting (MBA); accounting/finance (MBA); design and media (MM); health care administration (MM); higher education administration (MM); human resource management (MBA); information systems (MIS); law enforcement administration (MM); management (MBA); management/finance (MIS); management/human resource management (MBA); sports administration (MM). Part-time and evening/weekend programs available. *Faculty:* 7 full-time (1 woman), 21 part-time/adjunct (5 women). *Students:* 296 full-time (172 women), 216 part-time (136 women); includes 273 minority (160 Black or African American, non-Hispanic/Latino; 1 American Indian or Alaska Native, non-Hispanic/Latino; 32 Asian, non-Hispanic/Latino; 78 Hispanic/Latino; 2 Two or more races, non-Hispanic/Latino), 28 international. Average age 32. 247 applicants, 69% accepted, 152 enrolled. In 2011, 244 master's awarded. *Entrance requirements:* Additional exam requirements/recommendations for international students: Required—TOEFL (minimum score 550 paper-based; 173 computer-based). *Application deadline:* Applications are processed on a rolling basis. Application fee: $20 ($100 for international students). Electronic applications accepted. *Expenses: Tuition:* Full-time $13,800; part-time $2300 per course. *Financial support:* In 2011–12, 643 students received support. Federal Work-Study, scholarships/grants, tuition waivers, and leadership and athletic scholarships available. Support available to part-time students. Financial award applicants required to submit FAFSA. *Unit head:* Kayed Akkawi, Dean, 312-935-6025, Fax: 312-935-6020, E-mail: kakkawi@robertmorris.edu. *Application contact:* Fernando Villeda, Dean of Morris Graduate School of Management, 312-935-6050, Fax: 312-935-6020, E-mail: fvilleda@robertmorris.edu.

Rochester Institute of Technology, Graduate Enrollment Services, E. Philip Saunders College of Business, Program in Accounting, Rochester, NY 14623-5603. Offers MBA. Part-time and evening/weekend programs available. *Students:* 17 full-time (10 women), 7 part-time (3 women); includes 2 minority (1 Black or African American, non-Hispanic/Latino; 1 Asian, non-Hispanic/Latino), 5 international. Average age 28. 48 applicants, 52% accepted, 14 enrolled. In 2011, 17 degrees awarded. *Entrance requirements:* For master's, GMAT, minimum GPA of 2.5. Additional exam requirements/recommendations for international students: Required—TOEFL (minimum score 580 paper-based; 237 computer-based; 92 iBT) or IELTS (minimum score 7). *Application deadline:* For fall admission, 2/15 priority date for domestic students, 2/15 for international students; for winter admission, 11/1 priority date for domestic students; for spring admission, 2/1 priority date for domestic students. Applications are processed on a rolling basis. Application fee: $50. *Expenses: Tuition:* Full-time $34,659; part-time $963 per credit hour. *Required fees:* $228; $76 per quarter. *Financial support:* Research assistantships with partial tuition reimbursements, teaching assistantships with partial tuition reimbursements, career-related internships or fieldwork, scholarships/grants, and unspecified assistantships available. Support available to part-time students. Financial award applicants required to submit FAFSA. *Faculty research:* Formation and taxation of business entities, auditor independence: the conundrum of tax services, ethics in accounting and business or the lack thereof, accounting crisis: a curricular response. *Unit head:* Melissa Ellison, Graduate Program Director, 585-475-6916, E-mail: mamdar@rit.edu. *Application contact:* Diane Ellison, Assistant Vice President, Graduate Enrollment Services, 585-475-2229, Fax: 585-475-7164, E-mail: gradinfo@rit.edu. Web site: http://saunders.rit.edu/graduate/index.php.

Rocky Mountain College, Program in Accountancy, Billings, MT 59102-1796. Offers M Acc. Part-time programs available. *Faculty:* 2 full-time (1 woman), 1 part-time/adjunct (0 women). *Students:* 7 full-time (4 women), 1 international. In 2011, 3 master's awarded. *Entrance requirements:* Additional exam requirements/recommendations for international students: Required—TOEFL (minimum score 570 paper-based; 230 computer-based; 88 iBT), IELTS (minimum score 6.5). *Application deadline:* Applications are processed on a rolling basis. Application fee: $35 ($40 for international students). Electronic applications accepted. *Financial support:* Federal Work-Study and scholarships/grants available. Financial award applicants required to submit FAFSA. *Unit head:* Anthony Piltz, Academic Vice President, 406-657-1020, Fax: 406-259-9751, E-mail: piltza@rocky.edu. *Application contact:* Kelly Edwards, Director of Admissions, 406-657-1026, Fax: 406-657-1189, E-mail: admissions@rocky.edu. Web site: http://www.rocky.edu/academics/academic-programs/undergraduate-majors/accountancy/index.php.

Roosevelt University, Graduate Division, Walter E. Heller College of Business Administration, Program in Accounting, Chicago, IL 60605. Offers MSA. Part-time and evening/weekend programs available. *Entrance requirements:* For master's, GMAT.

Rowan University, Graduate School, William G. Rohrer College of Business, Department of Accounting and Finance, Program in Accounting, Glassboro, NJ 08028-1701. Offers MBA. Part-time and evening/weekend programs available. *Degree requirements:* For master's, comprehensive exam, thesis. *Entrance requirements:* For master's, GRE General Test. Additional exam requirements/recommendations for international students: Required—TOEFL. Electronic applications accepted.

Rutgers, The State University of New Jersey, Newark, Graduate School, Program in Management, Newark, NJ 07102. Offers accounting (PhD); accounting information systems (PhD); computer information systems (PhD); finance (PhD); information technology (PhD); international business (PhD); management science (PhD); marketing (PhD); organization management (PhD). Program offered jointly with New Jersey Institute of Technology. *Accreditation:* AACSB. *Degree requirements:* For doctorate, thesis/dissertation, cumulative exams. *Entrance requirements:* For doctorate, GMAT or GRE General Test, minimum undergraduate B average. Additional exam requirements/recommendations for international students: Required—TOEFL. Electronic applications accepted. *Faculty research:* Technology management, leadership and teams, consumer behavior, financial and markets, logistics.

Rutgers, The State University of New Jersey, Newark, Rutgers Business School–Newark and New Brunswick, Doctoral Programs in Management, Newark, NJ 07102. Offers accounting (PhD); accounting information systems (PhD); economics (PhD); finance (PhD); individualized study (PhD); information technology (PhD); international business (PhD); management science (PhD); marketing science (PhD); organizational management (PhD); science, technology and management (PhD); supply chain management (PhD). *Degree requirements:* For doctorate, comprehensive exam, thesis/dissertation. *Entrance requirements:* For doctorate, GRE or GMAT. Additional exam requirements/recommendations for international students: Required—TOEFL (minimum score 550 paper-based; 213 computer-based; 79 iBT). Electronic applications accepted.

Sacred Heart University, Graduate Programs, John F. Welch College of Business, Fairfield, CT 06825-1000. Offers accounting (MBA); finance (MBA); management (MBA); marketing (MBA). *Accreditation:* AACSB. Part-time and evening/weekend programs available. Postbaccalaureate distance learning degree programs offered. *Degree requirements:* For master's, thesis or alternative. *Entrance requirements:* For master's, GMAT (preferred) or GRE General Test. Additional exam requirements/recommendations for international students: Required—TOEFL (minimum score 550 paper-based; 213 computer-based; 75 iBT). Electronic applications accepted. *Expenses:* Contact institution. *Faculty research:* Management of organizations, international business management of technology.

St. Ambrose University, College of Business, Program in Accounting, Davenport, IA 52803-2898. Offers MAC. Part-time and evening/weekend programs available. *Faculty:* 4 full-time (3 women), 2 part-time/adjunct (1 woman). *Students:* 14 full-time (8 women), 12 part-time (4 women); includes 1 minority (Hispanic/Latino), 3 international. Average age 27. 21 applicants, 81% accepted, 12 enrolled. In 2011, 25 master's awarded. *Degree requirements:* For master's, comprehensive exam (for some programs), thesis or alternative, capstone seminar. *Entrance requirements:* For master's, GMAT. *Application deadline:* For fall admission, 8/15 priority date for domestic students; for winter admission, 12/15 priority date for domestic students; for spring admission, 1/1 priority date for domestic students. Applications are processed on a rolling basis.

Application fee: $25. Electronic applications accepted. *Expenses: Tuition:* Full-time $13,770; part-time $765 per credit hour. *Required fees:* $60 per semester. Tuition and fees vary according to degree level, program and reciprocity agreements. *Financial support:* In 2011–12, 23 students received support, including 1 research assistantship with partial tuition reimbursement available (averaging $3,600 per year); career-related internships or fieldwork, scholarships/grants, tuition waivers (partial), and unspecified assistantships also available. Financial award application deadline: 3/15; financial award applicants required to submit FAFSA. *Unit head:* Lewis Marx, Director, 563-333-6186, Fax: 563-333-6243, E-mail: marxlewisd@sau.edu. *Application contact:* Deborah K. Bennett, Administrative Assistant, 563-333-6266, Fax: 563-333-6268, E-mail: bennettdeborahk@sau.edu. Web site: http://web.sau.edu/accounting/masterofaccounting/.

St. Edward's University, School of Management and Business, Area of Business Administration, Austin, TX 78704. Offers accounting (MBA); business management (MBA); finance (Certificate); global entrepreneurship (MBA); marketing (MBA, Certificate). Part-time and evening/weekend programs available. *Students:* 35 full-time (14 women), 218 part-time (114 women); includes 102 minority (22 Black or African American, non-Hispanic/Latino; 1 American Indian or Alaska Native, non-Hispanic/Latino; 11 Asian, non-Hispanic/Latino; 62 Hispanic/Latino; 1 Native Hawaiian or other Pacific Islander, non-Hispanic/Latino; 5 Two or more races, non-Hispanic/Latino), 14 international. Average age 32. 94 applicants, 71% accepted, 48 enrolled. In 2011, 104 master's awarded. *Degree requirements:* For master's, minimum of 24 resident hours. *Entrance requirements:* For master's, GMAT or GRE General Test, minimum GPA of 2.75 in last 60 hours of course work. Additional exam requirements/recommendations for international students: Required—TOEFL (minimum score 550 paper-based; 213 computer-based; 79 iBT) or IELTS (minimum score 6). *Application deadline:* For fall admission, 7/1 for domestic and international students; for spring admission, 11/1 for domestic and international students. Applications are processed on a rolling basis. Application fee: $45 ($50 for international students). Electronic applications accepted. *Expenses: Tuition:* Full-time $17,550; part-time $975 per credit hour. *Required fees:* $50 per trimester. Full-time tuition and fees vary according to course load and program. *Unit head:* Dr. Stan Horner, Director, 512-428-1279, Fax: 512-448-8492, E-mail: stanleyh@stedwards.edu. *Application contact:* Sarah Hennes, Graduate Admissions Coordinator, 512-448-8600, Fax: 512-428-1032, E-mail: sarahhe@stedwards.edu. Web site: http://www.stedwards.edu.

St. Edward's University, School of Management and Business, Program in Accounting, Austin, TX 78704. Offers M Ac. Part-time and evening/weekend programs available. *Students:* 4 full-time (1 woman), 43 part-time (33 women); includes 12 minority (3 Black or African American, non-Hispanic/Latino; 1 Asian, non-Hispanic/Latino; 7 Hispanic/Latino; 1 Two or more races, non-Hispanic/Latino), 1 international. Average age 32. 26 applicants, 85% accepted, 15 enrolled. In 2011, 10 master's awarded. *Degree requirements:* For master's, minimum of 24 resident hours. *Entrance requirements:* For master's, GMAT or GRE General Test, minimum GPA of 2.75 in last 60 hours of course work and in accounting. Additional exam requirements/recommendations for international students: Required—TOEFL (minimum score 550 paper-based; 213 computer-based; 79 iBT) or IELTS (minimum score 6). *Application deadline:* For fall admission, 7/1 for domestic and international students; for spring admission, 11/1 for domestic and international students. Applications are processed on a rolling basis. Application fee: $45 ($50 for international students). Electronic applications accepted. *Expenses: Tuition:* Full-time $17,550; part-time $975 per credit hour. *Required fees:* $50 per trimester. Full-time tuition and fees vary according to course load and program. *Unit head:* Dr. Louise E. Single, Director, 512-492-3114, Fax: 512-448-8492, E-mail: louises@stedwards.edu. *Application contact:* Gloria Candelaria, Graduate Admissions Coordinator, 512-448-8600, Fax: 512-428-1032, E-mail: gloriaca@stedwards.edu. Web site: http://www.stedwards.edu.

St. Francis College, Program in Professional Accountancy, Brooklyn Heights, NY 11201-4398. Offers MS.

St. John's University, The Peter J. Tobin College of Business, Department of Accounting and Taxation, Program in Accounting, Queens, NY 11439. Offers accounting (MBA); controllership (MBA, Adv C). *Accreditation:* AACSB. Part-time and evening/weekend programs available. Postbaccalaureate distance learning degree programs offered (no on-campus study). *Students:* 237 full-time (139 women), 66 part-time (39 women); includes 54 minority (10 Black or African American, non-Hispanic/Latino; 1 American Indian or Alaska Native, non-Hispanic/Latino; 29 Asian, non-Hispanic/Latino; 11 Hispanic/Latino; 1 Native Hawaiian or other Pacific Islander, non-Hispanic/Latino; 2 Two or more races, non-Hispanic/Latino), 148 international. Average age 25. 377 applicants, 72% accepted, 128 enrolled. In 2011, 178 master's awarded. *Degree requirements:* For master's, comprehensive exam (for some programs), thesis optional. *Entrance requirements:* For master's, GMAT, 2 letters of recommendation, resume, transcripts, statement of goals, bachelor's degree in business; for Adv C, GMAT, 2 letters of recommendation, resume, undergraduate and graduate transcript, essay, MBA. Additional exam requirements/recommendations for international students: Required—TOEFL (minimum score 600 paper-based; 250 computer-based; 100 iBT), IELTS (minimum score 7). *Application deadline:* For fall admission, 5/1 priority date for domestic students, 5/1 for international students; for spring admission, 11/1 priority date for domestic students, 11/1 for international students. Applications are processed on a rolling basis. Application fee: $50. Electronic applications accepted. *Expenses:* Contact institution. *Financial support:* Research assistantships, scholarships/grants, and unspecified assistantships available. Support available to part-time students. Financial award application deadline: 3/1; financial award applicants required to submit FAFSA. *Unit head:* Dr. Ardian Fitzsimons, Chair, 718-990-1345, E-mail: fitzsima@stjohns.edu. *Application contact:* Carol J. Swanberg, Assistant Dean/Director of Graduate Admissions, 718-990-1345, Fax: 718-990-5242, E-mail: tobingradnyc@stjohns.edu.

St. Joseph's College, Long Island Campus, Program in Accounting, Patchogue, NY 11772-2399. Offers MBA.

St. Joseph's College, New York, Graduate Programs, Programs in Business, Field of Accounting, Brooklyn, NY 11205-3688. Offers MBA.

Saint Joseph's College of Maine, Master of Accountancy Program, Standish, ME 04084. Offers M Acc. Part-time programs available. Postbaccalaureate distance learning degree programs offered (no on-campus study). *Faculty:* 29 part-time/adjunct (10 women). *Students:* 40 part-time (22 women); includes 4 minority (1 Black or African American, non-Hispanic/Latino; 1 Asian, non-Hispanic/Latino; 2 Hispanic/Latino). *Entrance requirements:* For master's, baccalaureate degree with minimum cumulative GPA of 2.5; successful completion of each of the following prior to program enrollment: financial accounting, managerial accounting, introduction of finance/business finance and macroeconomics. *Application deadline:* Applications are processed on a rolling basis. Application fee: $50. Electronic applications accepted. One-time fee: $50. *Financial support:* Applicants required to submit FAFSA. *Unit head:* Nancy Kristiansen, Director, 207-893-7841, Fax: 207-893-7423, E-mail: nkristiansen@sjcme.edu. *Application contact:* Lynne Robinson, Admissions Department/Graduate and Professional Studies, 800-752-4723, Fax: 207-892-7480, E-mail: info@sjcme.edu. Web site: http://online.sjcme.edu/online-master-of-accountancy.php.

Saint Joseph's University, Erivan K. Haub School of Business, Professional MBA Program, Philadelphia, PA 19131-1395. Offers accounting (MBA); finance (MBA), including finance; general business (MBA); health and medical services administration (MBA); human resource management (MBA); international business (MBA); international marketing (MBA); management (MBA); marketing (MBA); DO/MBA. DO/MBA offered jointly with Philadelphia College of Osteopathic Medicine. Part-time and evening/weekend programs available. Postbaccalaureate distance learning degree programs offered (no on-campus study). *Students:* 98 full-time (42 women), 528 part-time (208 women); includes 102 minority (47 Black or African American, non-Hispanic/Latino; 1 American Indian or Alaska Native, non-Hispanic/Latino; 28 Asian, non-Hispanic/Latino; 20 Hispanic/Latino; 1 Native Hawaiian or other Pacific Islander, non-Hispanic/Latino; 5 Two or more races, non-Hispanic/Latino), 45 international. Average age 31. In 2011, 290 master's awarded. *Entrance requirements:* For master's, GMAT or GRE, 2 letters of recommendation, resume, personal statement. Additional exam requirements/recommendations for international students: Required—TOEFL (minimum score 550 paper-based; 213 computer-based; 80 iBT), IELTS (minimum score 6.5), or Pearson Test of English (minimum score 60). *Application deadline:* For fall admission, 7/15 priority date for domestic students, 4/15 for international students; for spring admission, 11/15 priority date for domestic students, 10/15 for international students. Applications are processed on a rolling basis. Application fee: $35. Electronic applications accepted. *Expenses: Tuition:* Part-time $735 per credit hour. Tuition and fees vary according to degree level and program. *Financial support:* Scholarships/grants and unspecified assistantships available. Financial award application deadline: 5/1; financial award applicants required to submit FAFSA. *Unit head:* Adele C. Foley, Associate Dean/Director, Graduate Business Programs, 610-660-1691, Fax: 610-660-1599, E-mail: afoley@sju.edu. *Application contact:* Dr. Janine N. Guerra, Associate Director, Professional MBA Program, 610-660-1695, Fax: 610-660-1599, E-mail: jguerra@sju.edu. Web site: http://www.sju.edu/mba.

Saint Leo University, Graduate Business Studies, Saint Leo, FL 33574-6665. Offers accounting (MBA); business (MBA); health services management (MBA); human resource management (MBA); information security management (MBA); marketing (MBA); sport business (MBA). Part-time and evening/weekend programs available. Postbaccalaureate distance learning degree programs offered (no on-campus study). *Faculty:* 39 full-time (7 women), 56 part-time/adjunct (17 women). *Students:* 1,506 full-time (901 women); includes 620 minority (480 Black or African American, non-Hispanic/Latino; 5 American Indian or Alaska Native, non-Hispanic/Latino; 21 Asian, non-Hispanic/Latino; 100 Hispanic/Latino; 1 Native Hawaiian or other Pacific Islander, non-Hispanic/Latino; 13 Two or more races, non-Hispanic/Latino), 20 international. Average age 38. In 2011, 574 master's awarded. *Entrance requirements:* For master's, GMAT (minimum score 500 if applicant does not have 5 years of professional work experience), bachelor's degree with minimum GPA of 3.0 in the last 60 hours of coursework from regionally-accredited college or university; 5 years of professional work experience; resume; 2 letters of recommendation. Additional exam requirements/recommendations for international students: Required—TOEFL (minimum score 550 paper-based; 213 computer-based; 80 iBT). *Application deadline:* For fall admission, 7/1 priority date for domestic students, 7/1 for international students; for spring admission, 11/12 priority date for domestic students, 11/1 for international students. Applications are processed on a rolling basis. Application fee: $80. Electronic applications accepted. *Expenses: Tuition:* Full-time $11,340; part-time $630 per semester hour. Tuition and fees vary according to campus/location and program. *Financial support:* In 2011–12, 72 students received support. Career-related internships or fieldwork, Federal Work-Study, scholarships/grants, and health care benefits available. Financial award application deadline: 3/1; financial award applicants required to submit FAFSA. *Unit head:* Dr. Lorrie McGovern, Director, 352-588-7390, Fax: 352-588-8585, E-mail: mbaslu@saintleo.edu. *Application contact:* Jared Welling, Director of Graduate Admission, 800-707-8846, Fax: 352-588-7873, E-mail: grad.admissions@saintleo.edu. Web site: http://www.saintleo.edu/Academics/School-of-Business/Graduate-Degree-Programs.

Saint Louis University, Graduate Education, John Cook School of Business, Department of Accounting, St. Louis, MO 63103-2097. Offers M Acct, MBA. Part-time and evening/weekend programs available. *Entrance requirements:* For master's, GMAT. Additional exam requirements/recommendations for international students: Required—TOEFL (minimum score 570 paper-based; 230 computer-based; 88 iBT). Electronic applications accepted. *Expenses:* Contact institution. *Faculty research:* Tax policy, market valuation/corporate governance, foreign currency translation, accounting for income taxes, earnings quality.

St. Mary's University, Graduate School, Bill Greehey School of Business, Program in Accounting, San Antonio, TX 78228-8507. Offers MBA. Part-time programs available. Postbaccalaureate distance learning degree programs offered (minimal on-campus study). *Degree requirements:* For master's, comprehensive exam. *Entrance requirements:* For master's, GMAT. Additional exam requirements/recommendations for international students: Required—TOEFL (minimum score 550 paper-based; 213 computer-based; 80 iBT). Electronic applications accepted.

Saint Peter's University, Graduate Business Programs, Program in Accountancy, Jersey City, NJ 07306-5997. Offers MS, MBA/MS. Part-time and evening/weekend programs available. *Entrance requirements:* Additional exam requirements/recommendations for international students: Required—TOEFL (minimum score 79 computer-based). Electronic applications accepted.

St. Thomas University, School of Business, Department of Management, Miami Gardens, FL 33054-6459. Offers accounting (MBA); general management (MSM, Certificate); health management (MBA, MSM, Certificate); human resource management (MBA, MSM, Certificate); international business (MBA, MIB, MSM, Certificate); justice administration (MSM, Certificate); management accounting (MSM, Certificate); public management (MSM, Certificate); sports administration (MS). Part-time and evening/weekend programs available. *Degree requirements:* For master's, comprehensive exam. *Entrance requirements:* For master's, interview, minimum GPA of 3.0 or GMAT. Additional exam requirements/recommendations for international students: Required—TOEFL (minimum score 550 paper-based; 213 computer-based; 79 iBT). Electronic applications accepted.

Salisbury University, Graduate Division, Department of Business Administration, Salisbury, MD 21801-6837. Offers accounting track (MBA); general track (MBA). *Accreditation:* AACSB. Part-time and evening/weekend programs available. *Faculty:* 9 full-time (3 women), 2 part-time/adjunct (1 woman). *Students:* 22 full-time (7 women), 25 part-time (7 women); includes 6 minority (4 Black or African American, non-Hispanic/Latino; 1 Asian, non-Hispanic/Latino; 1 Hispanic/Latino), 4 international. Average age 26. 4 applicants, 75% accepted, 3 enrolled. In 2011, 37 master's awarded. *Entrance requirements:* For master's, GMAT, resume; 2 recommendations, essay, minimum undergraduate GPA of 2.5. Additional exam requirements/recommendations for international students: Required—TOEFL (minimum score 550 paper-based; 79 iBT). *Application deadline:* For fall admission, 3/1 priority date for domestic students; for spring admission, 10/15 priority date for domestic students. Applications are processed on a rolling basis. Application fee: $45. Electronic applications accepted. *Expenses: Tuition, area resident:* Part-time $306 per credit hour. Tuition, state resident: part-time $306 per credit hour. Tuition, nonresident: part-time $595 per credit hour. *Required* *fees:* $68 per credit hour. *Financial support:* In 2011–12, 17 students received support. Institutionally sponsored loans, scholarships/grants, and unspecified assistantships available. Support available to part-time students. Financial award application deadline: 3/1; financial award applicants required to submit FAFSA. *Faculty research:* Chesapeake Bay Farms Feasibility Study, strategic planning retreat, shore trends survey. *Unit head:* Yvonne Downie, MBA Director, 410-548-3983, Fax: 410-546-6208, E-mail: yxdownie@salisbury.edu. *Application contact:* Aaron Basko, Assistant Vice President for Enrollment Management, 410-543-6161, Fax: 410-546-6016, E-mail: admissions@salisbury.edu. Web site: http://mba.salisbury.edu/.

Sam Houston State University, College of Business Administration, Department of Accounting, Huntsville, TX 77341. Offers MS. Part-time programs available. *Faculty:* 10 full-time (4 women). *Students:* 45 full-time (22 women), 14 part-time (6 women); includes 8 minority (2 Black or African American, non-Hispanic/Latino; 1 Asian, non-Hispanic/Latino; 5 Hispanic/Latino), 4 international. Average age 27. 47 applicants, 72% accepted, 34 enrolled. In 2011, 27 master's awarded. *Entrance requirements:* For master's, GMAT. Additional exam requirements/recommendations for international students: Required—TOEFL (minimum score 550 paper-based; 213 computer-based; 79 iBT). *Application deadline:* For fall admission, 8/1 for domestic students, 6/25 for international students; for spring admission, 12/1 for domestic students, 11/12 for international students. Applications are processed on a rolling basis. Application fee: $45 ($75 for international students). Electronic applications accepted. *Expenses:* Tuition, state resident: full-time $4420; part-time $221 per credit hour. Tuition, nonresident: full-time $10,680; part-time $534 per credit hour. *Required fees:* $329 per credit hour. *Financial support:* Application deadline: 5/31; applicants required to submit FAFSA. *Unit head:* Dr. Philip Morris, Chair, 936-294-1258, E-mail: morris@shsu.edu. *Application contact:* Dr. Leroy Ashorn, Advisor, 936-294-1246, Fax: 936-294-3612, E-mail: busgrad@shsu.edu.

San Diego State University, Graduate and Research Affairs, College of Business Administration, Charles W. Lamden School of Accountancy, San Diego, CA 92182. Offers MS. *Accreditation:* AACSB. *Degree requirements:* For master's, thesis or alternative. *Entrance requirements:* For master's, GMAT, resume, letters of reference. Additional exam requirements/recommendations for international students: Required—TOEFL. Electronic applications accepted.

San Francisco State University, Division of Graduate Studies, College of Business, Program in Accountancy, San Francisco, CA 94132-1722. Offers MS. Part-time programs available. *Entrance requirements:* For master's, GMAT, copy of transcripts, written statement of purpose, resume, two letters of reference. Additional exam requirements/recommendations for international students: Required—TOEFL or IELTS. Electronic applications accepted. *Unit head:* Dr. Joanne Duke, Interim Associate Dean, 415-817-4351. *Application contact:* Armaan Moattari, Assistant Director, Graduate Programs, 415-817-4314, E-mail: amoatt@sfsu.edu. Web site: http://cob.sfsu.edu/cob/graduate-programs/msa.cfm.

San Jose State University, Graduate Studies and Research, Lucas Graduate School of Business, Program in Accounting, San Jose, CA 95192-0001. Offers MS. *Degree requirements:* For master's, comprehensive exam, thesis or alternative. *Entrance requirements:* For master's, GMAT, minimum GPA of 3.0. Electronic applications accepted.

Santa Clara University, Leavey School of Business, Program in Business Administration, Santa Clara, CA 95053. Offers accounting (MBA); entrepreneurship (MBA); executive business administration (EMBA); finance (MBA); food and agribusiness (MBA); international business (MBA); leading people and organizations (MBA); managing technology and innovation (MBA); marketing management (MBA); supply chain management (MBA). *Accreditation:* AACSB. Part-time and evening/weekend programs available. *Students:* 196 full-time (80 women), 669 part-time (224 women); includes 302 minority (12 Black or African American, non-Hispanic/Latino; 246 Asian, non-Hispanic/Latino; 35 Hispanic/Latino; 6 Native Hawaiian or other Pacific Islander, non-Hispanic/Latino; 3 Two or more races, non-Hispanic/Latino), 186 international. Average age 32. 365 applicants, 74% accepted, 199 enrolled. In 2011, 366 degrees awarded. *Degree requirements:* For master's, thesis or alternative. *Entrance requirements:* For master's, GMAT, GRE. Additional exam requirements/recommendations for international students: Required—TOEFL (minimum score 600 paper-based; 250 computer-based; 100 iBT). *Application deadline:* For fall admission, 6/1 for domestic and international students; for spring admission, 1/19 for domestic students, 1/17 for international students. Applications are processed on a rolling basis. Application fee: $75 ($100 for international students). Electronic applications accepted. *Expenses:* Contact institution. *Financial support:* In 2011–12, 350 students received support. Fellowships with partial tuition reimbursements available, research assistantships with partial tuition reimbursements available, career-related internships or fieldwork, Federal Work-Study, institutionally sponsored loans, scholarships/grants, health care benefits, and unspecified assistantships available. Support available to part-time students. Financial award application deadline: 6/1; financial award applicants required to submit FAFSA. *Unit head:* Elizabeth B. Ford, Senior Assistant Dean, 408-554-2752, Fax: 408-554-4571, E-mail: eford@scu.edu. *Application contact:* Tammy Fox, Assistant Director, Graduate Business Admissions, 408-554-7858, E-mail: tkfox@scu.edu.

Seattle University, Albers School of Business and Economics, Master of Professional Accounting Program, Seattle, WA 98122-1090. Offers MPAC. Part-time and evening/weekend programs available. *Faculty:* 8 full-time (2 women), 1 part-time/adjunct (0 women). *Students:* 50 full-time (31 women), 36 part-time (22 women); includes 32 minority (1 Black or African American, non-Hispanic/Latino; 23 Asian, non-Hispanic/Latino; 3 Hispanic/Latino; 2 Native Hawaiian or other Pacific Islander, non-Hispanic/Latino; 3 Two or more races, non-Hispanic/Latino), 25 international. Average age 31. 110 applicants, 55% accepted, 21 enrolled. In 2011, 1 master's awarded. *Entrance requirements:* For master's, GMAT, minimum GPA of 3.0. Additional exam requirements/recommendations for international students: Required—TOEFL (minimum score 580 paper-based; 92 iBT). *Application deadline:* For fall admission, 5/1 priority date for domestic students, 4/1 for international students; for winter admission, 11/20 priority date for domestic students, 9/1 for international students; for spring admission, 2/20 priority date for domestic students, 12/1 for international students. Applications are processed on a rolling basis. Application fee: $55. Electronic applications accepted. *Financial support:* Career-related internships or fieldwork and Federal Work-Study available. Support available to part-time students. Financial award applicants required to submit FAFSA. *Unit head:* Dr. Bruce Koch, Program Director, 206-296-5700, Fax: 206-296-5795, E-mail: kochb@seattleu.edu. *Application contact:* Janet Shandley, Director of Graduate Admissions, 206-296-5900, Fax: 206-298-5656, E-mail: grad_admissions@seattleu.edu.

Seton Hall University, Stillman School of Business, Department of Accounting, South Orange, NJ 07079-2697. Offers accounting (MS); professional accounting (MS); taxation (Certificate). Part-time and evening/weekend programs available. *Faculty:* 7 full-time (1 woman), 1 part-time/adjunct (0 women). *Students:* 41 full-time (27 women), 82 part-time (22 women); includes 56 minority (5 Black or African American, non-Hispanic/Latino; 46 Asian, non-Hispanic/Latino; 3 Hispanic/Latino; 2 Two or more races, non-Hispanic/Latino). Average age 28. 166 applicants, 80% accepted, 77 enrolled. In 2011, 40 master's awarded. *Entrance requirements:* For master's, GMAT, GRE or CPA, advanced degree from AACSB institution, MS in a business discipline, professional degree (MD, JD, PhD, DVM, DDS, etc.), minimum undergraduate GPA of 3.0. Additional exam requirements/recommendations for international students: Required—TOEFL (minimum score 102 iBT), IELTS or Pearson Test of English. *Application deadline:* For fall admission, 5/31 priority date for domestic students, 3/31 for international students; for spring admission, 10/31 for domestic students, 9/30 for international students. Applications are processed on a rolling basis. Application fee: $75. Electronic applications accepted. *Expenses: Tuition:* Part-time $1033 per credit hour. *Required fees:* $85 per semester. *Financial support:* In 2011–12, 2 students received support, including research assistantships with full tuition reimbursements available (averaging $35,610 per year); career-related internships or fieldwork, scholarships/grants, and unspecified assistantships also available. Support available to part-time students. Financial award application deadline: 6/30; financial award applicants required to submit FAFSA. *Faculty research:* Voluntary disclosure, international accounting, pension and retirement accounting, ethics in financial reporting, executive compensation. *Unit head:* Dr. Mark Holtzman, Chair, 973-761-9133, Fax: 973-761-9217, E-mail: mark.holtzman@shu.edu. *Application contact:* Catherine Bianchi, Director of Graduate Admissions, 973-761-9262, Fax: 973-761-9208, E-mail: catherine.bianchi@shu.edu. Web site: http://www.shu.edu/academics/business/ms-programs.cfm.

Seton Hall University, Stillman School of Business, Programs in Business Administration, South Orange, NJ 07079-2697. Offers accounting (MBA); finance (MBA); information technology management (MBA); international business (MBA); management (MBA); marketing (MBA); sport management (MBA); supply chain management (MBA). Part-time and evening/weekend programs available. *Faculty:* 37 full-time (9 women), 19 part-time/adjunct (1 woman). *Students:* 166 full-time (65 women), 284 part-time (131 women); includes 113 minority (21 Black or African American, non-Hispanic/Latino; 81 Asian, non-Hispanic/Latino; 9 Hispanic/Latino; 2 Native Hawaiian or other Pacific Islander, non-Hispanic/Latino). Average age 29. 459 applicants, 59% accepted, 208 enrolled. In 2011, 210 master's awarded. *Degree requirements:* For master's, 20 hours of community service (Social Responsibility Project). *Entrance requirements:* For master's, GMAT, GRE or CPA, advanced degree from AACSB institution, MS in a business discipline, professional degree (MD, JD, PhD, DVM, DDS, etc.), minimum undergraduate GPA of 3.0. Additional exam requirements/recommendations for international students: Required—TOEFL (minimum score 102 iBT), IELTS or Pearson Test of English. *Application deadline:* For fall admission, 5/31 priority date for domestic students, 3/31 for international students; for spring admission, 10/31 priority date for domestic students, 9/30 for international students. Applications are processed on a rolling basis. Application fee: $75. Electronic applications accepted. *Expenses: Tuition:* Part-time $1033 per credit hour. *Required fees:* $85 per semester. *Financial support:* In 2011–12, research assistantships with full tuition reimbursements (averaging $35,610 per year) were awarded; career-related internships or fieldwork, Federal Work-Study, scholarships/grants, and unspecified assistantships also available. Support available to part-time students. Financial award application deadline: 6/30; financial award applicants required to submit FAFSA. *Faculty research:* Financial, hedge funds, international business, legal issues, disclosure and branding. *Unit head:* Dr. Joyce A. Strawser, Dean, 973-761-9013, Fax: 973-761-9217, E-mail: joyce.strawser@shu.edu. *Application contact:* Catherine Bianchi, Director of Graduate Admissions, 973-761-9262, Fax: 973-761-9208, E-mail: catherine.bianchi@shu.edu. Web site: http://www.shu.edu/academics/business.

Shorter University, Professional Studies, Rome, GA 30165. Offers accountancy (MAC); business administration (MBA); curriculum and instruction (M Ed); leadership (MA). Evening/weekend programs available. *Degree requirements:* For master's, project. *Entrance requirements:* For master's, minimum undergraduate GPA of 2.75 in last 60 hours, 3 years of work experience. Additional exam requirements/recommendations for international students: Required—TOEFL (minimum score 550 paper-based; 213 computer-based; 79 iBT). *Faculty research:* Systems design, leadership, pedagogy using technology.

Southeastern Louisiana University, College of Business, Hammond, LA 70402. Offers accounting (MBA); general (MBA). *Accreditation:* AACSB. *Faculty:* 18 full-time (2 women). *Students:* 85 full-time (41 women), 21 part-time (10 women); includes 11 minority (5 Black or African American, non-Hispanic/Latino; 2 Asian, non-Hispanic/Latino; 2 Hispanic/Latino; 2 Two or more races, non-Hispanic/Latino), 9 international. Average age 30. 37 applicants, 100% accepted, 23 enrolled. In 2011, 73 degrees awarded. *Entrance requirements:* For master's, GMAT (minimum score 450), minimum cumulative GPA of 2.75 for all undergraduate work attempted or 3.0 on all upper-division undergraduate coursework attempted. Additional exam requirements/recommendations for international students: Required—TOEFL (minimum score 525 paper-based; 195 computer-based; 61 iBT). *Application deadline:* For fall admission, 7/15 priority date for domestic students, 6/1 for international students; for spring admission, 12/1 priority date for domestic students, 10/1 for international students. Applications are processed on a rolling basis. Application fee: $20 ($30 for international students). Electronic applications accepted. *Expenses:* Tuition, state resident: full-time $3977; part-time $283 per semester hour. Tuition, nonresident: full-time $13,482; part-time $811 per semester hour. *Financial support:* Career-related internships or fieldwork, Federal Work-Study, institutionally sponsored loans, and scholarships/grants available. Support available to part-time students. Financial award application deadline: 5/1; financial award applicants required to submit FAFSA. *Faculty research:* Ethical decision-making in accounting, entrepreneurship and emerging information, leadership and organizational performance. *Unit head:* Dr. Randy Settoon, Dean, 985-549-2258, Fax: 985-549-5038, E-mail: rsettoon@selu.edu. *Application contact:* Sandra Meyers, Graduate Admissions Analyst, 985-549-5620, Fax: 985-549-5882, E-mail: admissions@selu.edu. Web site: http://www.selu.edu/acad_research/colleges/bus/index.html.

Southeast Missouri State University, School of Graduate Studies, Harrison College of Business, Cape Girardeau, MO 63701-4799. Offers accounting (MBA); entrepreneurship (MBA); financial management (MBA); general management (MBA); health administration (MBA); industrial management (MBA); international business (MBA); sport management (MBA). *Accreditation:* AACSB. Part-time and evening/weekend programs available. Postbaccalaureate distance learning degree programs offered (no on-campus study). *Faculty:* 31 full-time (10 women). *Students:* 49 full-time (23 women), 77 part-time (30 women); includes 5 minority (1 Black or African American, non-Hispanic/Latino; 1 American Indian or Alaska Native, non-Hispanic/Latino; 2 Hispanic/Latino; 1 Two or more races, non-Hispanic/Latino), 35 international. Average age 27. 78 applicants, 69% accepted, 43 enrolled. In 2011, 47 master's awarded. *Degree requirements:* For master's, variable foreign language requirement, comprehensive exam, applied research project related to field. *Entrance requirements:* For master's, GMAT (minimum score of 450), minimum undergraduate GPA of 2.5, C or better in prerequisite courses. Additional exam requirements/recommendations for international students: Required—TOEFL (minimum score 550 paper-based; 213 computer-based; 79 iBT); Recommended—IELTS (minimum score 6). *Application deadline:* For fall admission, 8/1 for domestic students, 7/1 for international students; for spring admission, 11/21 for domestic students, 11/1 for international students. Applications are processed on a rolling basis. Application fee: $30 ($40 for international students). Electronic applications accepted. *Expenses:* Tuition, state resident: full-time

$4896; part-time $272 per credit hour. Tuition, nonresident: full-time $8649; part-time $480.50 per credit hour. *Financial support:* In 2011–12, 46 students received support, including 12 teaching assistantships with full tuition reimbursements available (averaging $7,600 per year); career-related internships or fieldwork, Federal Work-Study, scholarships/grants, tuition waivers (full), and unspecified assistantships also available. Financial award application deadline: 6/30; financial award applicants required to submit FAFSA. *Faculty research:* Human resources, laws impacting accounting, advertising. *Unit head:* Dr. Kenneth A. Heischmidt, Director, Graduate Programs in Business, 573-651-5116, Fax: 573-651-5032, E-mail: kheischmidt@semo.edu. *Application contact:* Gail Amick, Administrative Secretary, 573-651-2049, Fax: 573-651-2001, E-mail: gamick@semo.edu. Web site: http://www.semo.edu/mba.

Southern Adventist University, School of Business and Management, Collegedale, TN 37315-0370. Offers accounting (MBA); church administration (MSA); church and nonprofit leadership (MBA); financial management (MFM); healthcare administration (MBA); management (MBA); marketing management (MBA); outdoor education (MSA). Part-time and evening/weekend programs available. Postbaccalaureate distance learning degree programs offered (no on-campus study). *Entrance requirements:* For master's, GMAT. Additional exam requirements/recommendations for international students: Required—TOEFL (minimum score 600 paper-based; 250 computer-based; 100 iBT). Electronic applications accepted.

Southern Illinois University Carbondale, Graduate School, College of Business and Administration, School of Accountancy, Carbondale, IL 62901-4701. Offers M Acc, PhD, JD/M Acc. *Accreditation:* AACSB. Part-time programs available. *Faculty:* 10 full-time (1 woman). *Students:* 54 full-time (29 women), 16 part-time (9 women); includes 8 minority (4 Black or African American, non-Hispanic/Latino; 1 American Indian or Alaska Native, non-Hispanic/Latino; 1 Asian, non-Hispanic/Latino; 2 Hispanic/Latino), 24 international. 56 applicants, 63% accepted, 21 enrolled. In 2011, 40 master's awarded. *Degree requirements:* For doctorate, thesis/dissertation. *Entrance requirements:* For master's, GMAT, minimum GPA of 2.7; for doctorate, GMAT, minimum graduate GPA of 3.25. Additional exam requirements/recommendations for international students: Required—TOEFL. *Application deadline:* For fall admission, 6/15 priority date for domestic students. Applications are processed on a rolling basis. Application fee: $20. *Financial support:* In 2011–12, 15 students received support, including 6 research assistantships with full tuition reimbursements available, 6 teaching assistantships with full tuition reimbursements available; fellowships with full tuition reimbursements available, Federal Work-Study, and institutionally sponsored loans also available. Support available to part-time students. Financial award application deadline: 4/1. *Faculty research:* Not-for-profit accounting, SEC regulations, computers and accounting education, taxation. *Unit head:* Dr. Marcus Odom, Director, 618-453-2289, E-mail: modom@cba.siu.edu. *Application contact:* Jeri Novara, Administrative Clerk, 618-453-1400, E-mail: jnovara@cba.siu.edu.

Southern Illinois University Edwardsville, Graduate School, School of Business, Department of Accounting, Edwardsville, IL 62026. Offers accountancy (MSA); taxation (MSA). *Accreditation:* AACSB. Part-time and evening/weekend programs available. *Faculty:* 5 full-time (1 woman). *Students:* 18 full-time (8 women), 21 part-time (12 women); includes 3 minority (1 Asian, non-Hispanic/Latino; 1 Hispanic/Latino; 1 Two or more races, non-Hispanic/Latino), 2 international. 54 applicants, 43% accepted. In 2011, 22 master's awarded. *Degree requirements:* For master's, thesis or alternative, final exam. *Entrance requirements:* For master's, GMAT. Additional exam requirements/recommendations for international students: Required—TOEFL (minimum score 550 paper-based; 213 computer-based; 79 iBT), IELTS (minimum score 6.5). *Application deadline:* For fall admission, 7/22 for domestic students, 6/1 for international students; for spring admission, 12/10 for domestic students, 10/1 for international students. Applications are processed on a rolling basis. Application fee: $30. Electronic applications accepted. Tuition and fees vary according to course load and program. *Financial support:* In 2011–12, 1 fellowship with full tuition reimbursement (averaging $8,370 per year) was awarded; research assistantships with full tuition reimbursements, teaching assistantships with full tuition reimbursements, institutionally sponsored loans, scholarships/grants, and unspecified assistantships also available. Financial award application deadline: 3/1; financial award applicants required to submit FAFSA. *Unit head:* Dr. Michael Costigan, Chair, 618-650-2633, E-mail: mcostig@siue.edu. *Application contact:* Michelle Robinson, Coordinator of Graduate Recruitment, 618-650-2811, Fax: 618-650-3523, E-mail: michero@siue.edu. Web site: http://www.siue.edu/business/accounting/.

Southern Methodist University, Cox School of Business, MBA Program, Dallas, TX 75275. Offers accounting (MBA); finance (MBA); financial consulting (MBA); general business (MBA); information technology and operations management (MBA); management (MBA); marketing (MBA); real estate (MBA); strategy and entrepreneurship (MBA). Part-time and evening/weekend programs available. *Entrance requirements:* For master's, GMAT. Additional exam requirements/recommendations for international students: Required—TOEFL. Electronic applications accepted. *Expenses:* Contact institution. *Faculty research:* Corporate finance, financial reporting, modeling consumer decision-making, competition between national brands and store brands, institutional determinants of firms' strategy.

Southern Methodist University, Cox School of Business, Program in Accounting, Dallas, TX 75275. Offers MSA. Part-time programs available. *Entrance requirements:* For master's, GMAT. Additional exam requirements/recommendations for international students: Required—TOEFL. *Expenses:* Contact institution. *Faculty research:* Capital markets, taxation, business combinations, intangibles accounting, accounting history.

Southern New Hampshire University, School of Business, Manchester, NH 03106-1045. Offers accounting (MS); business administration (MBA, Certificate), including accounting (Certificate), business administration (MBA), finance (Certificate), forensic accounting (Certificate), human resources management (Certificate), international business (Certificate), international sport management (Certificate), leadership of not for profit organizations (Certificate), marketing (Certificate), operations management (Certificate), sport management (Certificate), taxation (Certificate); finance (MS); hospitality and tourism leadership (Certificate); information technology (MS, Certificate); information technology/international business (Certificate); integrated marketing communications (Certificate); international business (MS, DBA); marketing (MS); operations and project management (MS); organizational leadership (MS); project management (Certificate); sport management (MS); MBA/Certificate. *Accreditation:* ACBSP. Part-time and evening/weekend programs available. Postbaccalaureate distance learning degree programs offered (no on-campus study). Terminal master's awarded for partial completion of doctoral program. *Degree requirements:* For master's, one foreign language, comprehensive exam (for some programs), thesis or alternative; for doctorate, one foreign language, comprehensive exam, thesis/dissertation. *Entrance requirements:* For master's, minimum GPA of 2.5; for doctorate, GMAT. Additional exam requirements/recommendations for international students: Required—TOEFL (minimum score 500 paper-based). Electronic applications accepted.

Southern Polytechnic State University, School of Engineering Technology and Management, Department of Business Administration, Marietta, GA 30060-2896. Offers accounting (MSA); business administration (MBA, Graduate Transition Certificate). *Accreditation:* ACBSP. Part-time and evening/weekend programs available. Postbaccalaureate distance learning degree programs offered (no on-campus study). *Faculty:* 13 full-time (4 women), 7 part-time/adjunct (3 women). *Students:* 82 full-time (43 women), 142 part-time (77 women); includes 122 minority (90 Black or African American, non-Hispanic/Latino; 1 American Indian or Alaska Native, non-Hispanic/Latino; 20 Asian, non-Hispanic/Latino; 8 Hispanic/Latino; 3 Two or more races, non-Hispanic/Latino), 35 international. Average age 33. 110 applicants, 88% accepted, 72 enrolled. In 2011, 75 master's, 1 other advanced degree awarded. *Entrance requirements:* For master's, GMAT, letters of recommendation, statement of purpose, resume. Additional exam requirements/recommendations for international students: Required—TOEFL (minimum score 550 paper-based; 213 computer-based; 79 iBT), IELTS (minimum score 6.5). *Application deadline:* For fall admission, 7/1 priority date for domestic students, 5/1 for international students; for spring admission, 11/1 priority date for domestic students, 9/1 for international students. Applications are processed on a rolling basis. Application fee: $50. Electronic applications accepted. *Expenses:* Tuition, state resident: full-time $2592; part-time $216 per semester hour. Tuition, nonresident: full-time $9408; part-time $784 per semester hour. *Required fees:* $698 per term. *Financial support:* In 2011–12, 37 students received support, including 4 research assistantships with tuition reimbursements available (averaging $4,500 per year); career-related internships or fieldwork, scholarships/grants, and unspecified assistantships also available. Support available to part-time students. Financial award application deadline: 5/1; financial award applicants required to submit FAFSA. *Faculty research:* Ethics, virtual reality, sustainability, management of technology, quality management, capacity planning, human-computer interaction/interface, enterprise integration planning, economic impact of educational institutions, behavioral accounting, accounting ethics, taxation, information security, visualizational simulation, human-computer interaction. *Total annual research expenditures:* $5,000. *Unit head:* Dr. Ronny Richardson, Chair, 678-915-7440, Fax: 678-915-4967, E-mail: rrichard@spsu.edu. *Application contact:* Nikki Palamiotis, Director of Graduate Studies, 678-915-4276, Fax: 678-915-7292, E-mail: npalamio@spsu.edu. Web site: http://www.spsu.edu/business/index.htm.

Southern Utah University, Program in Accounting, Cedar City, UT 84720-2498. Offers M Acc. Part-time programs available. *Students:* 40 full-time (7 women), 19 part-time (10 women); includes 3 minority (2 Asian, non-Hispanic/Latino; 1 Hispanic/Latino). Average age 28. 35 applicants, 83% accepted, 18 enrolled. In 2011, 45 master's awarded. *Entrance requirements:* For master's, GMAT or GRE. *Application deadline:* For fall admission, 3/1 for domestic students; for spring admission, 10/1 for domestic students. Applications are processed on a rolling basis. Application fee: $50 ($65 for international students). Electronic applications accepted. *Expenses:* Contact institution. *Faculty research:* Cost accounting, intermediate accounting text, GAAP policy, statements on Standards for Accounting and Review Services (SSARS). *Unit head:* Dr. David Christensen, Chair, Accounting Department, 435-865-8058, Fax: 435-586-5493, E-mail: christensen@suu.edu. *Application contact:* Paula Alger, Advisor/Curriculum Coordinator, 435-865-8157, Fax: 435-586-5493, E-mail: alger@suu.edu.

Southwestern Adventist University, Business Administration Department, Keene, TX 76059. Offers accounting (MBA); finance (MBA); management/leadership (MBA). Part-time and evening/weekend programs available. *Degree requirements:* For master's, capstone course. *Entrance requirements:* For master's, GMAT, GRE General Test.

Southwestern College, Professional Studies Programs, Wichita, KS 67207. Offers accountancy (MA); business administration (MBA); leadership (MS); management (MS); security administration (MS); specialized ministries (MA); theological studies (MA). Part-time and evening/weekend programs available. Postbaccalaureate distance learning degree programs offered (minimal on-campus study). *Faculty:* 1 full-time (0 women), 13 part-time/adjunct (4 women). *Students:* 155 part-time (62 women); includes 36 minority (18 Black or African American, non-Hispanic/Latino; 1 American Indian or Alaska Native, non-Hispanic/Latino; 10 Hispanic/Latino; 7 Two or more races, non-Hispanic/Latino). Average age 36. 52 applicants, 44% accepted, 18 enrolled. In 2011, 89 master's awarded. *Degree requirements:* For master's, practicum/capstone project. *Entrance requirements:* For master's, baccalaureate degree; minimum GPA of 2.5 (for MA and MS), 3.0 (for MBA). Additional exam requirements/recommendations for international students: Required—TOEFL (minimum score 550 paper-based; 213 computer-based). *Application deadline:* For fall admission, 8/1 for domestic students; for spring admission, 12/1 for domestic students. Applications are processed on a rolling basis. Application fee: $0. Electronic applications accepted. Tuition and fees vary according to program. *Financial support:* In 2011–12, 8 students received support. Federal Work-Study, tuition waivers (partial), and unspecified assistantships available. Financial award application deadline: 4/1; financial award applicants required to submit FAFSA. *Unit head:* Michael Holmes, Director of Academic Affairs, 888-684-5335 Ext. 203, Fax: 316-6885218, E-mail: michael.holmes@sckans.edu. *Application contact:* Marla Sexson, Director of Admissions, 620-229-6364, Fax: 620-229-6344, E-mail: marla.sexson@sckans.edu. Web site: http://www.southwesterncollege.org.

State University of New York at Binghamton, Graduate School, School of Management, Program in Accounting, Binghamton, NY 13902-6000. Offers MS, PhD. Evening/weekend programs available. *Students:* 135 full-time (55 women), 22 part-time (10 women); includes 38 minority (1 Black or African American, non-Hispanic/Latino; 4 Hispanic/Latino; 33 Native Hawaiian or other Pacific Islander, non-Hispanic/Latino), 53 international. Average age 24. 432 applicants, 34% accepted, 115 enrolled. In 2011, 159 master's awarded. *Degree requirements:* For doctorate, thesis/dissertation. *Entrance requirements:* For master's and doctorate, GMAT. Additional exam requirements/recommendations for international students: Required—TOEFL (minimum score 550 paper-based; 213 computer-based; 80 iBT). *Application deadline:* For fall admission, 3/1 priority date for domestic students, 3/1 for international students; for spring admission, 10/15 priority date for domestic students, 10/15 for international students. Applications are processed on a rolling basis. Application fee: $60. Electronic applications accepted. *Financial support:* In 2011–12, 12 students received support, including 2 research assistantships with full tuition reimbursements available (averaging $6,000 per year), teaching assistantships with full tuition reimbursements available (averaging $17,000 per year); career-related internships or fieldwork, Federal Work-Study, institutionally sponsored loans, scholarships/grants, health care benefits, and unspecified assistantships also available. Financial award application deadline: 2/15; financial award applicants required to submit FAFSA. *Unit head:* Dr. Upinder Dhillon, Dean of School of Management, 607-777-2314, E-mail: dhillon@binghamton.edu. *Application contact:* Catherine Smith, Recruiting and Admissions Coordinator, 607-777-2151, Fax: 607-777-2501, E-mail: cmsmith@binghamton.edu.

State University of New York at New Paltz, Graduate School, School of Business, New Paltz, NY 12561. Offers business administration (MBA); public accountancy (MBA). Part-time and evening/weekend programs available. *Faculty:* 16 full-time (7 women). *Students:* 53 full-time (25 women), 31 part-time (15 women); includes 17 minority (5 Black or African American, non-Hispanic/Latino; 7 Asian, non-Hispanic/Latino; 5 Hispanic/Latino), 17 international. Average age 28. 65 applicants, 68% accepted, 34 enrolled. In 2011, 41 master's awarded. *Degree requirements:* For master's, internship. *Entrance requirements:* For master's, GMAT or GRE, minimum GPA of 3.0. Additional exam requirements/recommendations for international students: Required—TOEFL (minimum score 550 paper-based; 213 computer-based; 80 iBT), IELTS (minimum score 6.5). *Application deadline:* For fall admission, 5/15 priority date for domestic students, 5/15 for international students; for spring admission, 11/15 for domestic and international students. Applications are processed on a rolling basis. Application fee: $50. Electronic applications accepted. *Expenses:* Contact institution. *Financial support:* In 2011–12, 8 students received support, including 2 fellowships with partial tuition reimbursements available (averaging $6,900 per year), 6 research assistantships with partial tuition reimbursements available (averaging $5,000 per year), 1 teaching assistantship with partial tuition reimbursement available (averaging $5,000 per year); career-related internships or fieldwork, scholarships/grants, traineeships, and unspecified assistantships also available. Financial award application deadline: 8/1; financial award applicants required to submit FAFSA. *Faculty research:* Cognitive styles in management education, supporting SME e-commerce migration through e-learning, earnings management and board activity, trading future spread portfolio, global equity market correlation and volatility. *Unit head:* Dr. Hadi Salavitabar, Dean, 845-257-2930, E-mail: mba@newpaltz.edu. *Application contact:* Aaron Hines, Coordinator, 845-257-2968, E-mail: mba@newpaltz.edu. Web site: http://mba.newpaltz.edu.

State University of New York College at Geneseo, Graduate Studies, School of Business, Geneseo, NY 14454-1401. Offers accounting (MS). *Accreditation:* AACSB. *Entrance requirements:* For master's, GMAT, bachelor's degree in accounting.

State University of New York College at Old Westbury, Program in Accounting, Old Westbury, NY 11568-0210. Offers MS. Part-time and evening/weekend programs available. *Entrance requirements:* For master's, GMAT, 2 letters of recommendation. Additional exam requirements/recommendations for international students: Required—TOEFL (minimum score 550 paper-based; 213 computer-based). Electronic applications accepted. *Faculty research:* Corporate governance, asset pricing, corporate finance, hedge funds, taxation.

State University of New York Institute of Technology, Program in Accountancy, Utica, NY 13504-3050. Offers MS. *Accreditation:* AACSB. Part-time and evening/weekend programs available. Postbaccalaureate distance learning degree programs offered (no on-campus study). *Degree requirements:* For master's, capstone courses. *Entrance requirements:* For master's, GMAT, minimum GPA of 3.0, letters of recommendation. Additional exam requirements/recommendations for international students: Required—TOEFL (minimum score 550 paper-based; 213 computer-based). *Faculty research:* Cash flows, accounting earnings, stock price analysis.

Stephen F. Austin State University, Graduate School, College of Business, Program in Professional Accountancy, Nacogdoches, TX 75962. Offers MPAC. Students admitted at the undergraduate level. *Degree requirements:* For master's, comprehensive exam. *Entrance requirements:* For master's, GMAT. Additional exam requirements/recommendations for international students: Required—TOEFL.

Stetson University, School of Business Administration, Program in Accounting, DeLand, FL 32723. Offers M Acc. *Accreditation:* AACSB. Part-time programs available. *Students:* 41 full-time (22 women), 9 part-time (4 women); includes 13 minority (5 Black or African American, non-Hispanic/Latino; 1 American Indian or Alaska Native, non-Hispanic/Latino; 3 Asian, non-Hispanic/Latino; 4 Hispanic/Latino), 3 international. Average age 36. In 2011, 54 master's awarded. *Entrance requirements:* For master's, GMAT. *Application deadline:* For fall admission, 7/1 for domestic students. Application fee: $25. *Financial support:* In 2011–12, 3 research assistantships were awarded; Federal Work-Study and institutionally sponsored loans also available. Support available to part-time students. Financial award application deadline: 3/15. *Unit head:* Dr. Michael E. Bitter, Director, 386-822-7410. *Application contact:* Kathryn Hannon, Assistant Director of Graduate Business Programs, 386-822-7410, Fax: 386-822-7413, E-mail: khannon@stetson.edu.

Stratford University, School of Graduate Studies, Falls Church, VA 22043. Offers accounting (MS); business administration (IMBA, MBA); enterprise business management (MS); entrepreneurial management (MS); information assurance (MS); information systems (MS); software engineering (MS); telecommunications (MS). Part-time and evening/weekend programs available. Postbaccalaureate distance learning degree programs offered (no on-campus study). *Degree requirements:* For master's, comprehensive exam, capstone project. *Entrance requirements:* For master's, GRE or GMAT, baccalaureate degree. Additional exam requirements/recommendations for international students: Required—TOEFL (minimum score 213 computer-based, 79 iBT) or IELTS (6.5). Electronic applications accepted.

Strayer University, Graduate Studies, Washington, DC 20005-2603. Offers accounting (MS); acquisition (MBA); business administration (MBA); communications technology (MS); educational management (M Ed); finance (MBA); health services administration (MHSA); hospitality and tourism management (MBA); human resource management (MBA); information systems (MS), including computer security management, decision support system management, enterprise resource management, network management, software engineering management, systems development management; management (MBA); management information systems (MS); marketing (MBA); professional accounting (MS), including accounting information systems, controllership, taxation; public administration (MPA); supply chain management (MBA); technology in education (M Ed). Programs also offered at campus locations in Birmingham, AL; Chamblee, GA; Cobb County, GA; Morrow, GA; White Marsh, MD; Charleston, SC; Columbia, SC; Greensboro, NC; Greenville, SC; Lexington, KY; Louisville, KY; Nashville, TN; North Raleigh, NC; Washington, DC. Part-time and evening/weekend programs available. Postbaccalaureate distance learning degree programs offered (minimal on-campus study). *Degree requirements:* For master's, thesis. *Entrance requirements:* For master's, GMAT, GRE General Test, bachelor's degree from an accredited college or university, minimum undergraduate GPA of 2.75. Electronic applications accepted.

Suffolk University, Sawyer Business School, Department of Accounting, Boston, MA 02108-2770. Offers accounting (MSA, GDPA); taxation (MST); GDPA/MST; MBA/GDPA; MBA/MSA; MBA/MST. *Accreditation:* AACSB. Part-time and evening/weekend programs available. *Faculty:* 11 full-time (5 women), 7 part-time/adjunct (4 women). *Students:* 113 full-time (83 women), 142 part-time (72 women); includes 26 minority (6 Black or African American, non-Hispanic/Latino; 1 American Indian or Alaska Native, non-Hispanic/Latino; 15 Asian, non-Hispanic/Latino; 3 Hispanic/Latino; 1 Two or more races, non-Hispanic/Latino), 97 international. Average age 29. 519 applicants, 76% accepted, 106 enrolled. In 2011, 93 master's, 6 GDPAs awarded. *Entrance requirements:* For master's, GMAT. Additional exam requirements/recommendations for international students: Required—TOEFL (minimum score 550 paper-based; 213 computer-based; 80 iBT). *Application deadline:* For fall admission, 6/15 priority date for domestic students, 6/15 for international students; for spring admission, 11/1 priority date for domestic students, 11/1 for international students. Applications are processed on a rolling basis. Application fee: $50. Electronic applications accepted. Tuition and fees vary according to program. *Financial support:* In 2011–12, 94 students received support, including 43 fellowships with full and partial tuition reimbursements available (averaging $23,365 per year); career-related internships or fieldwork, Federal Work-Study, and institutionally sponsored loans also available. Support available to part-time students. Financial award application deadline: 4/1; financial award applicants required to submit CSS PROFILE. *Faculty research:* Tax policy, tax research, decision-making in accounting, accounting information systems, capital markets and strategic planning. *Unit head:* Lewis Shaw, Chair, 617-573-8615, Fax: 617-994-4260, E-mail: lshaw@suffolk.edu. *Application contact:* Ellen Driscoll, Director of Graduate Admissions, 617-573-8302, Fax: 617-305-1733, E-mail: grad.admission@suffolk.edu. Web site: http://www.suffolk.edu/msa.

Suffolk University, Sawyer Business School, Master of Business Administration Program, Boston, MA 02108-2770. Offers accounting (MBA); business administration (APC); corporate financial executive track (MBA); entrepreneurship (MBA); executive business administration (EMBA); finance (MBA); global business administration (GMBA); health administration (MBA); international business (MBA); marketing (MBA); organizational behavior (MBA); strategic management (MBA); taxation (MBA); JD/MBA; MBA/GDPA; MBA/MHA; MBA/MSA; MBA/MSF; MBA/MST. *Accreditation:* AACSB. Part-time and evening/weekend programs available. Postbaccalaureate distance learning degree programs offered (no on-campus study). *Faculty:* 98 full-time (30 women), 14 part-time/adjunct (3 women). *Students:* 139 full-time (49 women), 321 part-time (138 women); includes 53 minority (17 Black or African American, non-Hispanic/Latino; 1 American Indian or Alaska Native, non-Hispanic/Latino; 21 Asian, non-Hispanic/Latino; 11 Hispanic/Latino; 1 Native Hawaiian or other Pacific Islander, non-Hispanic/Latino; 2 Two or more races, non-Hispanic/Latino), 64 international. Average age 30. 437 applicants, 61% accepted, 121 enrolled. In 2011, 283 master's awarded. *Entrance requirements:* For master's, GMAT, minimum undergraduate GPA of 2.75 (MBA), 5 years of managerial experience (EMBA). Additional exam requirements/recommendations for international students: Required—TOEFL (minimum score 550 paper-based; 213 computer-based). *Application deadline:* For fall admission, 6/15 priority date for domestic students, 6/15 for international students; for spring admission, 11/1 priority date for domestic students, 11/1 for international students. Applications are processed on a rolling basis. Application fee: $50. Electronic applications accepted. Tuition and fees vary according to program. *Financial support:* In 2011–12, 273 students received support, including 73 fellowships with full and partial tuition reimbursements available (averaging $12,415 per year); career-related internships or fieldwork, Federal Work-Study, and institutionally sponsored loans also available. Support available to part-time students. Financial award application deadline: 4/1; financial award applicants required to submit FAFSA. *Faculty research:* Foreign investments; career strategies and boundaryless careers; corporate ethics codes; interest rates, inflation, and growth options; innovation and product development performance. *Unit head:* Lillian Hallberg, Assistant Dean of Graduate Programs/Director of MBA Programs, 617-573-8306, E-mail: lhallber@suffolk.edu. *Application contact:* Ellen Driscoll, Director of Graduate Admissions, 617-573-8302, Fax: 617-305-1733, E-mail: grad.admission@suffolk.edu. Web site: http://www.suffolk.edu/mba.

Syracuse University, Martin J. Whitman School of Management, PhD Program in Business Administration, Syracuse, NY 13244. Offers accounting (PhD); finance (PhD); management information systems (PhD); managerial statistics (PhD); marketing (PhD); operations management (PhD); organizational behavior (PhD); strategy and human resources (PhD); supply chain management (PhD). *Faculty:* 79 full-time (20 women), 25 part-time/adjunct (6 women). *Students:* 32 full-time (10 women); includes 6 minority (3 Black or African American, non-Hispanic/Latino; 2 Asian, non-Hispanic/Latino; 1 Hispanic/Latino), 18 international. Average age 32. 260 applicants, 8% accepted, 12 enrolled. In 2011, 2 doctorates awarded. *Degree requirements:* For doctorate, comprehensive exam, thesis/dissertation, summer research paper. *Entrance requirements:* For doctorate, GMAT or GRE General Test, 3 recommendations. Additional exam requirements/recommendations for international students: Required—TOEFL (minimum score 600 paper-based; 250 computer-based; 100 iBT). *Application deadline:* For fall admission, 2/15 priority date for domestic students, 2/15 for international students. Applications are processed on a rolling basis. Application fee: $65. Electronic applications accepted. *Expenses: Tuition:* Part-time $1206 per credit. *Financial support:* In 2011–12, 1 fellowship with full tuition reimbursement (averaging $19,570 per year), 30 teaching assistantships with full tuition reimbursements (averaging $17,000 per year) were awarded; research assistantships with full tuition reimbursements, health care benefits, and unspecified assistantships also available. Financial award application deadline: 1/30. *Faculty research:* Marketing models, market microstructure, supply chain, auditing, corporate governance. *Unit head:* Dr. Eunkyu Lee, Director of the PhD Program, 315-443-3429, E-mail: elee06@syr.edu. *Application contact:* Carol Hilleges, Administrative Specialist, 315-443-9601, Fax: 315-443-3671, E-mail: clhilleg@syr.edu. Web site: http://whitman.syr.edu/phd/.

Syracuse University, Martin J. Whitman School of Management, Program in Accounting, Syracuse, NY 13244. Offers MS Acct, JD/MS Acct. Postbaccalaureate distance learning degree programs offered (minimal on-campus study). *Faculty:* 79 full-time (20 women), 25 part-time/adjunct (6 women). *Students:* 79 full-time (37 women), 2 part-time (1 woman); includes 21 minority (4 Black or African American, non-Hispanic/Latino; 16 Asian, non-Hispanic/Latino; 1 Hispanic/Latino), 27 international. Average age 23. 320 applicants, 36% accepted, 60 enrolled. In 2011, 48 master's awarded. *Entrance requirements:* For master's, GMAT, 2 letters of recommendation, bachelor's degree in accounting. Additional exam requirements/recommendations for international students: Required—TOEFL (minimum score 600 paper-based; 250 computer-based; 100 iBT). *Application deadline:* For fall admission, 1/15 priority date for domestic students, 1/15 for international students; for winter admission, 11/1 for domestic and international students. Applications are processed on a rolling basis. Application fee: $75. Electronic applications accepted. *Expenses: Tuition:* Part-time $1206 per credit. *Financial support:* In 2011–12, 5 students received support. Fellowships with full tuition reimbursements available, teaching assistantships with partial tuition reimbursements available, career-related internships or fieldwork, scholarships/grants, and tuition waivers (partial) available. Financial award application deadline: 3/1. *Unit head:* Prof. Randall Elder, Senior Associate Dean, 315-443-3359, Fax: 315-443-9517, E-mail: rjelder@syr.edu. *Application contact:* Josh LaFave, Director of Graduate Enrollment, 315-443-3497, Fax: 315-443-9517, E-mail: mbainfo@syr.edu. Web site: http://whitman.syr.edu/msacc/.

Syracuse University, Martin J. Whitman School of Management, Program in Business Administration, Syracuse, NY 13244. Offers accounting (MBA); entrepreneurship (MBA); finance (MBA); marketing (MBA); supply chain management (MBA). Postbaccalaureate distance learning degree programs offered (minimal on-campus study). *Faculty:* 79 full-time (20 women), 25 part-time/adjunct (6 women). *Students:* 116 full-time (43 women), 188 part-time (58 women); includes 62 minority (33 Black or African American, non-Hispanic/Latino; 1 American Indian or Alaska Native, non-Hispanic/Latino; 13 Asian, non-Hispanic/Latino; 9 Hispanic/Latino; 1 Native Hawaiian or other Pacific Islander, non-Hispanic/Latino; 5 Two or more races, non-Hispanic/Latino), 44 international. Average age 33. 276 applicants, 49% accepted, 77 enrolled. In 2011, 132 master's awarded. *Entrance requirements:* For master's, GMAT, 2 letters of recommendation. Additional exam requirements/recommendations for international students: Required—TOEFL (minimum score 600 paper-based; 250 computer-based; 100 iBT). *Application deadline:* For fall admission, 1/15 priority date for domestic students, 1/15 for international students. Applications are processed on a rolling basis. Application fee: $75. Electronic applications accepted. *Expenses: Tuition:* Part-time $1206 per credit. *Financial support:* In 2011–12, 17 students received support. Fellowships with full and partial tuition reimbursements available, teaching assistantships with partial tuition reimbursements available, career-related internships or fieldwork, scholarships/grants, tuition waivers (partial), unspecified assistantships, and paid hourly positions available. Support available to part-time students. Financial award application deadline: 3/1. *Unit head:* Prof. Dennis Gillen, Chair and Associate Professor of Management, 315-443-3432, Fax: 315-443-9517, E-mail: dgillen@syr.edu. *Application contact:* Josh LaFave, Director, Graduate Enrollment, 315-443-3497, Fax: 315-443-9517, E-mail: mbainfo@syr.edu. Web site: http://whitman.syr.edu/ftmba/.

Syracuse University, Martin J. Whitman School of Management, Program in Professional Accounting, Syracuse, NY 13244. Offers MS. *Students:* 4 part-time (3 women); includes 1 minority (Asian, non-Hispanic/Latino). Average age 29. 3 applicants, 67% accepted, 0 enrolled. In 2011, 1 master's awarded. *Expenses: Tuition:* Part-time $1206 per credit. *Unit head:* Dr. Melvin T. Stith, Dean, 315-443-3751. *Application contact:* Carol J. Swanberg, Director of Graduate Admissions and Financial Aid, 315-443-9214, Fax: 315-443-9517, E-mail: mbainfo@syr.edu.

Tabor College, Graduate Program, Hillsboro, KS 67063. Offers accounting (MBA). Program offered at the Wichita campus only.

Tarleton State University, College of Graduate Studies, College of Business Administration, Department of Accounting, Finance and Economics, Stephenville, TX 76402. Offers business administration (MBA). Part-time and evening/weekend programs available. *Faculty:* 6 full-time (0 women), 2 part-time/adjunct (0 women). *Students:* 48 full-time (25 women), 192 part-time (101 women); includes 74 minority (30 Black or African American, non-Hispanic/Latino; 1 American Indian or Alaska Native, non-Hispanic/Latino; 7 Asian, non-Hispanic/Latino; 29 Hispanic/Latino; 7 Two or more races, non-Hispanic/Latino), 1 international. Average age 31. 99 applicants, 92% accepted, 74 enrolled. In 2011, 50 master's awarded. *Degree requirements:* For master's, comprehensive exam. *Entrance requirements:* For master's, GRE or GMAT, minimum GPA of 3.0. Additional exam requirements/recommendations for international students: Required—TOEFL (minimum score 550 paper-based; 213 computer-based; 80 iBT). *Application deadline:* For fall admission, 8/5 priority date for domestic students; for spring admission, 12/1 for domestic students. Applications are processed on a rolling basis. Application fee: $30 ($130 for international students). Electronic applications accepted. *Expenses:* Tuition, state resident: full-time $3131.46; part-time $174 per credit hour. Tuition, nonresident: full-time $8225; part-time $457 per credit hour. *Required fees:* $1446. Tuition and fees vary according to course load and campus/location. *Financial support:* Research assistantships and teaching assistantships available. Financial award application deadline: 5/1; financial award applicants required to submit FAFSA. *Unit head:* Dr. Steve Steed, Interim Department Head, 254-968-9645, Fax: 254-968-9665, E-mail: ssteed@tarleton.edu. *Application contact:* Information Contact, 254-968-9104, Fax: 254-968-9670, E-mail: gradoffice@tarleton.edu. Web site: http://www.tarleton.edu/~afe/.

Temple University, Fox School of Business, Doctoral Programs in Business, Philadelphia, PA 19122-6096. Offers accounting (PhD); entrepreneurship (PhD); finance (PhD); international business (PhD); management information systems (PhD); marketing (PhD); risk management and insurance (PhD); statistics (PhD); strategic management (PhD); tourism and sport (PhD). *Accreditation:* AACSB. *Degree requirements:* For doctorate, thesis/dissertation. *Entrance requirements:* For doctorate, GRE General Test, GMAT, minimum GPA of 3.0, master's degree. Additional exam requirements/recommendations for international students: Required—TOEFL (minimum score 600 paper-based; 250 computer-based; 100 iBT), IELTS (minimum score 7.5). Electronic applications accepted. *Expenses:* Tuition, state resident: full-time $12,366; part-time $687 per credit hour. Tuition, nonresident: full-time $17,298; part-time $961 per credit hour. *Required fees:* $590; $213 per year.

Temple University, Fox School of Business, MBA Programs, Philadelphia, PA 19122-6096. Offers accounting (MBA); business management (MBA); financial management (MBA); healthcare and life sciences innovation (MBA); human resource management (MBA); international business (IMBA); IT management (MBA); marketing management (MBA); pharmaceutical management (MBA); strategic management (EMBA, MBA). EMBA offered in Philadelphia, PA and Tokyo, Japan. *Accreditation:* AACSB. Part-time and evening/weekend programs available. Postbaccalaureate distance learning degree programs offered (minimal on-campus study). *Entrance requirements:* For master's, GMAT, minimum undergraduate GPA of 3.0. Additional exam requirements/recommendations for international students: Required—TOEFL (minimum score 600 paper-based; 250 computer-based; 100 iBT), IELTS (minimum score 7.5). *Expenses:* Tuition, state resident: full-time $12,366; part-time $687 per credit hour. Tuition, nonresident: full-time $17,298; part-time $961 per credit hour. *Required fees:* $590; $213 per year.

Temple University, Fox School of Business, Specialized Master's Programs, Philadelphia, PA 19122-6096. Offers accountancy (MS); actuarial science (MS); finance (MS); financial engineering (MS); human resource management (MS); marketing (MS); statistics (MS). *Accreditation:* AACSB. Part-time programs available. *Entrance requirements:* For master's, GRE General Test or GMAT, minimum undergraduate GPA of 3.0. Additional exam requirements/recommendations for international students: Required—TOEFL (minimum score 600 paper-based; 250 computer-based; 100 iBT), IELTS (minimum score 7.5). *Expenses:* Tuition, state resident: full-time $12,366; part-time $687 per credit hour. Tuition, nonresident: full-time $17,298; part-time $961 per credit hour. *Required fees:* $590; $213 per year.

Tennessee Technological University, Graduate School, College of Business, Cookeville, TN 38505. Offers accounting (MBA); finance (MBA); human resource management (MBA); international business (MBA); management information systems (MBA); risk management & insurance (MBA). *Accreditation:* AACSB. Part-time and evening/weekend programs available. Postbaccalaureate distance learning degree programs offered (no on-campus study). *Faculty:* 28 full-time (5 women). *Students:* 45 full-time (19 women), 135 part-time (51 women); includes 13 minority (4 Black or African American, non-Hispanic/Latino; 5 Asian, non-Hispanic/Latino; 3 Hispanic/Latino; 1 Native Hawaiian or other Pacific Islander, non-Hispanic/Latino), 2 international. Average age 25. 193 applicants, 59% accepted, 70 enrolled. In 2011, 89 master's awarded. *Entrance requirements:* For master's, GMAT. Additional exam requirements/recommendations for international students: Required—TOEFL (minimum score 550 paper-based; 79 iBT), IELTS (minimum score 5.5), Pearson Test of English Academic. *Application deadline:* For fall admission, 8/1 for domestic students, 5/1 for international students; for spring admission, 12/1 for domestic students, 10/1 for international students. Application fee: $25 ($30 for international students). Electronic applications accepted. *Expenses:* Tuition, state resident: full-time $8094; part-time $422 per credit hour. Tuition, nonresident: full-time $20,574; part-time $1046 per credit hour. *Financial support:* In 2011–12, 5 fellowships (averaging $10,000 per year), 18 research assistantships (averaging $4,000 per year), teaching assistantships (averaging $4,000 per year) were awarded. Support available to part-time students. Financial award application deadline: 4/1. *Unit head:* Dr. Tom Timmerman, Director, 931-372-3600, Fax: 931-372-6249. *Application contact:* Shelia K. Kendrick, Coordinator of Graduate Admissions, 931-372-3808, Fax: 931-372-3497, E-mail: skendrick@tntech.edu. Web site: http://www.tntech.edu/mba.

Texas A&M International University, Office of Graduate Studies and Research, College of Business Administration, Division of International Banking and Finance Studies, Laredo, TX 78041-1900. Offers accounting (MP Acc); international banking (MBA). *Faculty:* 13 full-time (2 women). *Students:* 49 full-time (21 women), 195 part-time (95 women); includes 171 minority (3 Black or African American, non-Hispanic/Latino; 1 Asian, non-Hispanic/Latino; 167 Hispanic/Latino), 63 international. Average age 30. 122 applicants, 75% accepted, 80 enrolled. In 2011, 121 master's awarded. *Entrance requirements:* For master's, GMAT or GRE General Test. Additional exam requirements/recommendations for international students: Required—TOEFL (minimum score 550 paper-based; 213 computer-based; 79 iBT). *Application deadline:* For fall admission, 4/30 priority date for domestic students, 4/30 for international students; for spring admission, 11/30 for domestic students, 10/1 for international students. Applications are processed on a rolling basis. Application fee: $35 ($50 for international students). *Expenses:* Tuition, state resident: full-time $5063. *Financial support:* In 2011–12, 3 students received support, including 3 research assistantships. *Unit head:* Dr. Ken Hung, Chair, 956-326-2541, Fax: 956-326-2481, E-mail: ken.hung@tamiu.edu. *Application contact:* Imelda Lopez, Graduate Admissions Counselor, 956-326-2485, Fax: 956-326-2459, E-mail: lopez@tamiu.edu. Web site: http://www.tamiu.edu/ssb/divisions.php?optN-210.

Texas A&M University, Mays Business School, Department of Accounting, College Station, TX 77843. Offers MS, PhD. *Accreditation:* AACSB. *Faculty:* 15. *Students:* 131 full-time (67 women), 5 part-time (2 women); includes 18 minority (4 Black or African American, non-Hispanic/Latino; 9 Asian, non-Hispanic/Latino; 4 Hispanic/Latino; 1 Two or more races, non-Hispanic/Latino), 9 international. Average age 27. In 2011, 111 master's, 4 doctorates awarded. Terminal master's awarded for partial completion of doctoral program. *Degree requirements:* For master's, comprehensive exam; for doctorate, thesis/dissertation. *Entrance requirements:* For master's, GMAT; for doctorate, GMAT or GRE General Test. Additional exam requirements/recommendations for international students: Required—TOEFL. *Application deadline:* For fall admission, 3/1 priority date for domestic students; for spring admission, 8/1 for domestic students. Applications are processed on a rolling basis. Application fee: $50 ($75 for international students). *Expenses:* Tuition, state resident: full-time $5437; part-time $226.55 per credit hour. Tuition, nonresident: full-time $12,949; part-time $539.55 per credit hour. *Required fees:* $2741. *Financial support:* In 2011–12, 100 students received support. Fellowships, research assistantships, teaching assistantships, career-related internships or fieldwork, and institutionally sponsored loans available. Financial award application deadline: 2/1. *Faculty research:* Financial reporting, taxation management, decision-making, accounting information systems, government accounting. *Unit head:* Dr. James J. Benjamin, Head, 979-845-0356, E-mail: jbenjamin@mays.tamu.edu. *Application contact:* 979-845-5017, Fax: 979-862-2393, E-mail: maysmba@tamu.edu. Web site: http://mays.tamu.edu/acct/.

Texas A&M University–Commerce, Graduate School, College of Business, MS Programs, Commerce, TX 75429-3011. Offers accounting (MS); economics (MA); finance (MS); management (MS); marketing (MS). Part-time programs available. *Degree requirements:* For master's, comprehensive exam, thesis (for some programs). *Entrance requirements:* For master's, GMAT or GRE General Test. Electronic applications accepted. *Faculty research:* Economic activity, forensic economics, volatility and finance, international economics.

Texas A&M University–Corpus Christi, Graduate Studies and Research, College of Business, Corpus Christi, TX 78412-5503. Offers accounting (M Acc); health care administration (MBA); international business (MBA). *Accreditation:* AACSB. Part-time and evening/weekend programs available. *Degree requirements:* For master's, comprehensive exam, thesis (for some programs). *Entrance requirements:* For master's, GMAT. Additional exam requirements/recommendations for international students: Required—TOEFL. Electronic applications accepted.

Texas A&M University–San Antonio, School of Business, San Antonio, TX 78224. Offers business administration (MBA); enterprise resource planning systems (MBA); finance (MBA); healthcare management (MBA); human resources management (MBA); information assurance and security (MBA); international business (MBA); professional accounting (MPA); project management (MBA); supply chain management (MBA). Part-time and evening/weekend programs available. *Faculty:* 18 full-time (6 women), 1 part-time/adjunct (0 women). *Students:* 91 full-time (45 women), 278 part-time (150 women). Average age 33. In 2011, 20 master's awarded. *Entrance requirements:* For master's, GMAT. Additional exam requirements/recommendations for international students: Required—TOEFL (minimum score 550 paper-based; 213 computer-based; 80 iBT), IELTS (minimum score 6). *Application deadline:* For fall admission, 7/1 priority date for domestic students, 6/1 for international students; for spring admission, 11/15 priority date for domestic students, 10/1 for international students. Applications are processed on a rolling basis. Application fee: $35 ($50 for international students). Electronic applications accepted. *Expenses:* Tuition, state resident: part-time $691.11 per course. Tuition, nonresident: part-time $1621.11 per course. *Financial support:* Application deadline: 3/31; applicants required to submit FAFSA. *Unit head:* Dr. Tracy Hurley, MBA Coordinator, 210-932-6200, E-mail: tracy.hurley@tamusa.tamus.edu. *Application contact:* Melissa A. Villanueva, Graduate Admissions Specialist, 210-932-6200, Fax: 210-932-6209, E-mail: melissa.villanueva@tamusa.tamus.edu. Web site: http://www.tamusa.tamus.edu.

Texas A&M University–Texarkana, Graduate Studies and Research, College of Business, Texarkana, TX 75505-5518. Offers accounting (MSA); business administration (MBA, MS). Part-time and evening/weekend programs available. *Degree requirements:* For master's, thesis or alternative. *Entrance requirements:* For master's, minimum GPA of 2.5 in last 60 hours of bachelor's degree. Additional exam requirements/recommendations for international students: Required—TOEFL. Electronic applications accepted.

Texas Christian University, The Neeley School of Business at TCU, Master of Accounting Program, Fort Worth, TX 76129-0002. Offers M Ac. *Accreditation:* AACSB. *Faculty:* 12 full-time (4 women). *Students:* 47 full-time (20 women); includes 2 minority (1 Asian, non-Hispanic/Latino; 1 Hispanic/Latino), 6 international. Average age 22. 74 applicants, 59% accepted, 42 enrolled. In 2011, 46 master's awarded. *Entrance requirements:* For master's, GMAT, undergraduate degree in accounting from U.S.-accredited university. Additional exam requirements/recommendations for international students: Required—TOEFL (minimum score 600 paper-based; 250 computer-based; 100 iBT). *Application deadline:* For fall admission, 2/15 priority date for domestic students, 2/15 for international students; for spring admission, 9/15 priority date for domestic students, 9/15 for international students. Applications are processed on a rolling basis. Electronic applications accepted. *Expenses: Tuition:* Full-time $20,250; part-time $1125 per credit hour. Part-time tuition and fees vary according to course load and program. *Financial support:* Tuition waivers (partial) and unspecified assistantships available. Financial award application deadline: 2/15; financial award applicants required to submit FAFSA. *Unit head:* Dr. Patricia Walters, Director, 817-257-7223, E-mail: p.walters1@tcu.edu. Web site: http://www.neeley.tcu.edu/Academics/Master_of_Accounting/MAc.aspx.

Texas State University–San Marcos, Graduate School, Emmett and Miriam McCoy College of Business Administration, Program in Accounting, San Marcos, TX 78666. Offers M Acy. Part-time programs available. *Faculty:* 10 full-time (7 women), 1 part-time/adjunct (0 women). *Students:* 81 full-time (44 women), 40 part-time (20 women); includes 25 minority (3 Black or African American, non-Hispanic/Latino; 13 Asian, non-

Hispanic/Latino; 9 Hispanic/Latino), 6 international. Average age 28. 66 applicants, 52% accepted, 20 enrolled. In 2011, 55 master's awarded. *Degree requirements:* For master's, comprehensive exam. *Entrance requirements:* For master's, GMAT (minimum preferred score of 450 prior to admission decision), minimum GPA of 2.0 in last 60 hours of undergraduate work. Additional exam requirements/recommendations for international students: Required—TOEFL (minimum score 550 paper-based; 213 computer-based; 78 iBT). *Application deadline:* For fall admission, 6/1 for domestic and international students; for spring admission, 10/1 for domestic and international students. Applications are processed on a rolling basis. Application fee: $40 ($90 for international students). Electronic applications accepted. *Expenses:* Tuition, state resident: full-time $6408; part-time $3204 per semester. Tuition, nonresident: full-time $14,832; part-time $7416 per semester. *Required fees:* $1824; $912 per semester. Tuition and fees vary according to course load. *Financial support:* In 2011–12, 58 students received support, including 1 research assistantship (averaging $10,152 per year), 4 teaching assistantships (averaging $10,152 per year); Federal Work-Study, institutionally sponsored loans, scholarships/grants, health care benefits, and unspecified assistantships also available. Support available to part-time students. Financial award application deadline: 4/1; financial award applicants required to submit FAFSA. *Unit head:* Dr. Robert Davis, Associate Dean, 512-245-3591, Fax: 512-245-7973, E-mail: rd23@txstate.edu. *Application contact:* Dr. J. Michael Willoughby, Dean of Graduate School, 512-245-2581, Fax: 512-245-8365, E-mail: gradcollege@txstate.edu. Web site: http://www.business.txstate.edu/accounting.

Texas State University–San Marcos, Graduate School, Emmett and Miriam McCoy College of Business Administration, Program in Accounting and Information Technology, San Marcos, TX 78666. Offers MS. *Faculty:* 7 full-time (2 women). *Students:* 6 full-time (2 women), 11 part-time (4 women); includes 2 minority (both Asian, non-Hispanic/Latino), 3 international. Average age 33. 11 applicants, 82% accepted, 3 enrolled. In 2011, 7 master's awarded. *Degree requirements:* For master's, comprehensive exam. *Entrance requirements:* For master's, GMAT, official transcript from each college or university attended, 2 letters of recommendation, resume. Additional exam requirements/recommendations for international students: Required—TOEFL (minimum score 550 paper-based; 213 computer-based; 78 iBT). *Application deadline:* For fall admission, 6/1 for domestic and international students; for spring admission, 10/1 for domestic and international students. Application fee: $40 ($90 for international students). *Expenses:* Tuition, state resident: full-time $6408; part-time $3204 per semester. Tuition, nonresident: full-time $14,832; part-time $7416 per semester. *Required fees:* $1824; $912 per semester. Tuition and fees vary according to course load. *Financial support:* In 2011–12, 8 students received support, including 2 teaching assistantships (averaging $10,283 per year); research assistantships, Federal Work-Study, institutionally sponsored loans, scholarships/grants, health care benefits, and unspecified assistantships also available. Support available to part-time students. *Unit head:* Dr. Robert Davis, Associate Dean, 512-245-3591, Fax: 512-245-7973, E-mail: rd23@txstate.edu. *Application contact:* Dr. J. Michael Willoughby, Dean of Graduate School, 512-245-2581, Fax: 512-245-8365, E-mail: gradcollege@txstate.edu.

Texas Tech University, Graduate School, Rawls College of Business Administration, Area of Accounting, Lubbock, TX 79409. Offers accounting (PhD); audit/financial reporting (MSA); taxation (MSA); JD/MSA. *Accreditation:* AACSB. Part-time programs available. *Faculty:* 14 full-time (2 women). *Students:* 190 full-time (100 women), 19 part-time (8 women); includes 24 minority (5 Black or African American, non-Hispanic/Latino; 2 American Indian or Alaska Native, non-Hispanic/Latino; 8 Asian, non-Hispanic/Latino; 9 Hispanic/Latino), 7 international. Average age 24. 178 applicants, 73% accepted, 121 enrolled. In 2011, 61 degrees awarded. Terminal master's awarded for partial completion of doctoral program. *Degree requirements:* For master's, capstone course; for doctorate, comprehensive exam, thesis/dissertation, qualifying exams. *Entrance requirements:* For master's and doctorate, GMAT, holistic profile of academic credentials. Additional exam requirements/recommendations for international students: Required—TOEFL (minimum score 550 paper-based; 213 computer-based; 79 iBT). *Application deadline:* For fall admission, 2/1 for domestic students, 1/15 for international students. Applications are processed on a rolling basis. Application fee: $50 ($75 for international students). Electronic applications accepted. *Expenses:* Tuition, state resident: full-time $5899; part-time $245.80 per credit hour. Tuition, nonresident: full-time $13,411; part-time $558.80 per credit hour. *Required fees:* $2680.60; $86.50 per credit hour. $920.30 per semester. *Financial support:* In 2011–12, 9 research assistantships (averaging $14,933 per year), 2 teaching assistantships (averaging $18,000 per year) were awarded; fellowships, career-related internships or fieldwork, Federal Work-Study, scholarships/grants, health care benefits, and unspecified assistantships also available. Financial award applicants required to submit FAFSA. *Faculty research:* Governmental and nonprofit accounting, managerial and financial accounting. *Unit head:* Dr. Robert Ricketts, Area Coordinator, 806-742-3180, Fax: 806-742-3182, E-mail: robert.ricketts@ttu.edu. *Application contact:* Elizabeth Stuart, 806-742-3184, Fax: 806-742-3958, E-mail: ba_grad@ttu.edu. Web site: http://accounting.ba.ttu.edu.

Towson University, Joint Program in Accounting and Business Advisory Services, Towson, MD 21252-0001. Offers MS. Program offered jointly with University of Baltimore. *Accreditation:* AACSB. Part-time and evening/weekend programs available. *Students:* 29 full-time (20 women), 44 part-time (24 women); includes 21 minority (11 Black or African American, non-Hispanic/Latino; 1 American Indian or Alaska Native, non-Hispanic/Latino; 9 Asian, non-Hispanic/Latino), 18 international. *Entrance requirements:* For master's, GMAT, GRE General Test, minimum GPA of 3.0. *Application deadline:* Applications are processed on a rolling basis. Application fee: $50. Electronic applications accepted. *Expenses:* Tuition, state resident: part-time $337 per credit. Tuition, nonresident: part-time $709 per credit. *Required fees:* $99 per credit. *Unit head:* Martin Freedman, Graduate Program Director, 410-704-4143, E-mail: mfreedman@towson.edu. *Application contact:* Carol Abraham, The Graduate School, 410-704-6163, Fax: 401-704-4675, E-mail: grads@towson.edu.

Trinity University, Department of Business Administration, San Antonio, TX 78212-7200. Offers accounting (MS). *Accreditation:* AACSB. Part-time programs available. *Entrance requirements:* For master's, GMAT, minimum GPA of 3.0, course work in accounting and business law.

Troy University, Graduate School, College of Business, Program in Business Administration, Troy, AL 36082. Offers accounting (EMBA, MBA); criminal justice (EMBA); finance (MBA); general management (EMBA, MBA); healthcare management (EMBA); information systems (EMBA, MBA); international economic development (MBA). *Accreditation:* ACBSP. Part-time and evening/weekend programs available. *Faculty:* 50 full-time (14 women), 12 part-time/adjunct (0 women). *Students:* 326 full-time (168 women), 596 part-time (358 women); includes 524 minority (402 Black or African American, non-Hispanic/Latino; 12 American Indian or Alaska Native, non-Hispanic/Latino; 85 Asian, non-Hispanic/Latino; 21 Hispanic/Latino; 4 Two or more races, non-Hispanic/Latino). Average age 29. 644 applicants, 67% accepted, 204 enrolled. In 2011, 388 master's awarded. *Degree requirements:* For master's, minimum GPA of 3.0, capstone course, research course. *Entrance requirements:* For master's, GMAT (minimum score 500) or GRE General Test (minimum score 900), minimum GPA of 2.5; letter of recommendation, bachelor's degree. Additional exam requirements/recommendations for international students: Required—TOEFL (minimum score 523 paper-based; 193 computer-based; 70 iBT), IELTS (minimum score 6), or ACT COMPASS ESL (minimum listening, reading, and grammar score 270). *Application deadline:* Applications are processed on a rolling basis. Application fee: $50. *Expenses:* Tuition, state resident: full-time $6960; part-time $290 per credit hour. Tuition, nonresident: full-time $13,920; part-time $580 per credit hour. *Required fees:* $386 per term. *Unit head:* Dr. Edward Merkel, Director, Graduate Business Programs, 334-670-3194, Fax: 334-670-3599, E-mail: emerkel@troy.edu. *Application contact:* Brenda K. Campbell, Director of Graduate Admissions, 334-670-3178, Fax: 334-670-3733, E-mail: bcamp@troy.edu.

Truman State University, Graduate School, School of Business, Program in Accounting, Kirksville, MO 63501-4221. Offers M Ac. *Accreditation:* AACSB. *Degree requirements:* For master's, comprehensive exam. *Entrance requirements:* For master's, GMAT, minimum GPA of 3.0. Additional exam requirements/recommendations for international students: Required—TOEFL (minimum score 550 paper-based; 213 computer-based). Electronic applications accepted.

Universidad del Este, Graduate School, Carolina, PR 00984. Offers accounting (MBA); adult education (M Ed); agribusiness (MBA); criminal justice and criminology (MA); curriculum and instruction - early education (M Ed); curriculum and instruction - elementary (M Ed); curriculum and instruction - English (M Ed); curriculum and instruction - Spanish (M Ed); human resources (MBA); information security management (MBA); information technology and Web business development (MBA); management (MBA); public policy (MPA); social work (MA), including clinical social work; special education (M Ed); strategic leadership (MBA).

Universidad del Turabo, Graduate Programs, School in Business Administration, Program in Accounting, Gurabo, PR 00778-3030. Offers MBA. Part-time and evening/weekend programs available. *Students:* 18 full-time (9 women), 28 part-time (23 women); includes 44 minority (all Hispanic/Latino). Average age 32. 19 applicants, 100% accepted, 16 enrolled. In 2011, 24 master's awarded. *Entrance requirements:* For master's, GRE, EXADEP, interview. *Application deadline:* For fall admission, 8/5 for domestic students. Application fee: $25. *Unit head:* Marcelino Rivera, Dean, 787-743-7979 Ext. 4117. *Application contact:* Virginia Gonzalez, Admissions Officer, 787-746-3009.

Universidad Metropolitana, School of Business Administration, Program in Accounting, San Juan, PR 00928-1150. Offers MBA. Part-time programs available. *Degree requirements:* For master's, thesis or alternative. *Entrance requirements:* For master's, GMAT, PAEG, interview. Electronic applications accepted.

Université de Sherbrooke, Faculty of Administration, Program in Accounting, Sherbrooke, QC J1K 2R1, Canada. Offers M Sc. *Faculty:* 11 full-time (9 women), 9 part-time/adjunct (7 women). *Students:* 18 full-time (12 women), 11 part-time (2 women). Average age 26. 34 applicants, 68% accepted, 11 enrolled. In 2011, 15 master's awarded. *Degree requirements:* For master's, one foreign language, thesis. *Entrance requirements:* For master's, bachelor's degree in related field, minimum GPA of 3.0 (on 4.3 scale). *Application deadline:* For fall admission, 4/30 for domestic students, 1/15 for international students. Applications are processed on a rolling basis. Application fee: $70. Electronic applications accepted. *Faculty research:* Financial analysis, management accounting, certification, system and control. *Unit head:* Prof. Julien Bilodeau, Director, Graduate Programs in Business, 819-821-8000 Ext. 62355, E-mail: julien.bilodeau@usherbrooke.ca. *Application contact:* Marie-Claude Drouin, Programs Assistant Director, 819-821-8000 Ext. 63301.

Université du Québec à Montréal, Graduate Programs, Program in Accounting, Montréal, QC H3C 3P8, Canada. Offers M Sc, MPA, Diploma. Part-time programs available. *Degree requirements:* For master's, thesis (for some programs). *Entrance requirements:* For master's, appropriate bachelor's degree or equivalent and proficiency in French.

Université du Québec à Trois-Rivières, Graduate Programs, Program in Accounting Science, Trois-Rivières, QC G9A 5H7, Canada. Offers MBA.

Université du Québec en Outaouais, Graduate Programs, Program in Accounting, Gatineau, QC J8X 3X7, Canada. Offers MA, DESS, Diploma. Part-time and evening/weekend programs available. *Students:* 19 full-time, 85 part-time. *Application deadline:* For fall admission, 6/1 for domestic students, 3/1 for international students; for winter admission, 11/1 for domestic students, 10/1 for international students. Application fee: $30 Canadian dollars. *Unit head:* Denis Gendron, Director, 819-595-3900 Ext. 2655, Fax: 818-773-1760, E-mail: denis.gendron@uqo.ca. *Application contact:* Registrar's Office, 819-773-1850, Fax: 819-773-1835, E-mail: registraire@uqo.ca.

Université du Québec en Outaouais, Graduate Programs, Program in Executive Certified Management Accounting, Gatineau, QC J8X 3X7, Canada. Offers MBA, DESS. Part-time and evening/weekend programs available. *Students:* 30 full-time, 38 part-time. *Degree requirements:* For master's, thesis (for some programs). *Application deadline:* For fall admission, 6/1 priority date for domestic students, 3/1 for international students; for winter admission, 11/1 priority date for domestic students, 10/1 for international students. Application fee: $30. *Unit head:* Denis Gendron, Director, 819-595-3900 Ext. 2655, Fax: 819-773-1760, E-mail: denis.gendron@uqo.ca. *Application contact:* Registrar's Office, 819-773-1850, Fax: 819-773-1835, E-mail: registraire@uqo.ca.

Université Laval, Faculty of Administrative Sciences, Programs in Business Administration, Québec, QC G1K 7P4, Canada. Offers accounting (MBA); agri-food management (MBA); electronic business (MBA, Diploma); factory management and logistics (MBA); finance (MBA); firm management (MBA); geomatic management (MBA); information technology management (MBA); international management (MBA); management (MBA); management accounting (MBA, Diploma); marketing (MBA); modeling and organizational decision (MBA); occupational health and safety management (MBA); pharmacy management (MBA); social and environmental responsibility (MBA); technological entrepreneurship (Diploma). *Accreditation:* AACSB. Part-time and evening/weekend programs available. Postbaccalaureate distance learning degree programs offered (no on-campus study). *Entrance requirements:* For master's and Diploma, knowledge of French and English. Electronic applications accepted.

Université Laval, Faculty of Administrative Sciences, Programs in Public Accountancy, Québec, QC G1K 7P4, Canada. Offers MBA, Diploma. Part-time programs available. *Entrance requirements:* For master's and Diploma, knowledge of French and English. Electronic applications accepted.

University at Albany, State University of New York, School of Business, Department of Accounting and Law, Albany, NY 12222-0001. Offers accounting (MS); taxation (MS). *Accreditation:* AACSB. *Degree requirements:* For master's, research project. *Entrance requirements:* For master's, GMAT. Additional exam requirements/recommendations for international students: Required—TOEFL (minimum score 550 paper-based; 213 computer-based). Electronic applications accepted. *Faculty research:* Professional ethics, statistical analysis, cost management systems, accounting theory.

University at Buffalo, the State University of New York, Graduate School, School of Management, Buffalo, NY 14260. Offers accounting (MS); business administration

(EMBA, MBA, PMBA); finance (MS), including financial engineering, financial management; management (PhD); management information systems (MS); supply chains and operations management (MS); Au D/MBA; JD/MBA; M Arch/MBA; MA/MBA; MD/MBA; MPH/MBA; MSW/MBA; Pharm D/MBA. *Accreditation:* AACSB. Part-time and evening/weekend programs available. *Degree requirements:* For master's, thesis (for some programs); for doctorate, comprehensive exam, thesis/dissertation. *Entrance requirements:* For master's, GMAT (MBA, MS in accounting), GRE or GMAT (for all other MS concentrations); for doctorate, GMAT or GRE. Additional exam requirements/recommendations for international students: Required—TOEFL (minimum score 230 computer-based; 95 iBT). Electronic applications accepted. *Expenses:* Contact institution. *Faculty research:* Earnings management and electronic information assurance, supply chains and operations management, corporate financing and asset pricing, consumer behavior and quantitative modeling of marketing behavior, leadership and politics in organizations.

The University of Akron, Graduate School, College of Business Administration, School of Accountancy, Akron, OH 44325. Offers accountancy (MS); accounting-information systems (MS); taxation (MT); JD/MT. *Accreditation:* AACSB. Part-time and evening/weekend programs available. *Faculty:* 7 full-time (1 woman), 15 part-time/adjunct (3 women). *Students:* 92 full-time (39 women), 62 part-time (26 women); includes 9 minority (4 Black or African American, non-Hispanic/Latino; 4 Asian, non-Hispanic/Latino; 1 Hispanic/Latino), 23 international. Average age 27. 75 applicants, 73% accepted, 40 enrolled. In 2011, 44 master's awarded. *Entrance requirements:* For master's, GMAT, minimum GPA of 2.75, two letters of recommendation, resume, statement of purpose. Additional exam requirements/recommendations for international students: Required—TOEFL (minimum score 550 paper-based; 213 computer-based; 79 iBT). *Application deadline:* For fall admission, 7/15 for domestic and international students; for spring admission, 11/15 for domestic and international students. Applications are processed on a rolling basis. Application fee: $30 ($40 for international students). Electronic applications accepted. *Expenses:* Tuition, state resident: full-time $7038; part-time $391 per credit hour. Tuition, nonresident: full-time $12,051; part-time $670 per credit hour. *Required fees:* $1274; $34 per credit hour. *Financial support:* In 2011–12, 1 research assistantship with full tuition reimbursement, 30 teaching assistantships with full tuition reimbursements were awarded. *Faculty research:* Financial reporting and management accounting auditing and assurance of financial information, business and information systems risk and security management, corporate governance and ethics, accounting education. *Total annual research expenditures:* $21,546. *Unit head:* Dr. Thomas Calderon, Chair, 330-972-6099, E-mail: tcalderon@uakron.edu. *Application contact:* Dr. Susan Hanlon, Director of Graduate Business Programs, 330-972-7043, Fax: 330-972-6588, E-mail: shanlon@uakron.edu. Web site: http://www.uakron.edu/cba/cba-home/dept-cent-inst/accountancy/.

The University of Alabama, Graduate School, Manderson Graduate School of Business, Culverhouse School of Accountancy, Tuscaloosa, AL 35487. Offers accounting (M Acc, PhD); tax accounting (MTA). *Accreditation:* AACSB. *Faculty:* 18 full-time (5 women). *Students:* 117 full-time (57 women), 1 (woman) part-time; includes 7 minority (3 Black or African American, non-Hispanic/Latino; 2 Asian, non-Hispanic/Latino; 2 Hispanic/Latino), 1 international. Average age 24. 236 applicants, 56% accepted, 95 enrolled. In 2011, 94 degrees awarded. *Degree requirements:* For doctorate, thesis/dissertation. *Entrance requirements:* For master's and doctorate, GMAT, minimum GPA of 3.0. Additional exam requirements/recommendations for international students: Required—TOEFL. *Application deadline:* For fall admission, 7/1 priority date for domestic students, 6/1 for international students; for spring admission, 11/1 priority date for domestic students, 9/1 for international students. Applications are processed on a rolling basis. Application fee: $50 ($60 for international students). Electronic applications accepted. *Expenses:* Tuition, state resident: full-time $8600. Tuition, nonresident: full-time $21,900. *Financial support:* In 2011–12, 79 students received support, including 4 fellowships with full tuition reimbursements available (averaging $15,000 per year), 21 research assistantships with full and partial tuition reimbursements available (averaging $6,367 per year), 17 teaching assistantships with full and partial tuition reimbursements available (averaging $6,367 per year); career-related internships or fieldwork, Federal Work-Study, institutionally sponsored loans, scholarships/grants, health care benefits, and unspecified assistantships also available. Financial award application deadline: 3/31. *Faculty research:* Corporate governance, audit decision-making, earning management, valuation, executive compensation, not-for-profit. *Unit head:* Dr. Mary S. Stone, Director, 205-348-2915, Fax: 205-348-8453, E-mail: mstone@cba.ua.edu. *Application contact:* Sandy D. Davidson, Advisor, 205-348-6131, Fax: 205-348-8453, E-mail: sdavidso@cba.ua.edu. Web site: http://www.cba.ua.edu/accounting/.

The University of Alabama at Birmingham, School of Business, Program in Accounting, Birmingham, AL 35294. Offers M Acct. *Accreditation:* AACSB. *Expenses:* Tuition, state resident: full-time $5922; part-time $309 per hour. Tuition, nonresident: full-time $13,428; part-time $726 per hour. Tuition and fees vary according to program. *Unit head:* Dr. Jenice Prather-Kinsey, Director, 205-934-8880. *Application contact:* Director, 205-934-8817. Web site: http://www.uab.edu/business/degrees-certificates/master-of-accounting.

The University of Alabama in Huntsville, School of Graduate Studies, College of Business Administration, Department of Accounting and Finance, Huntsville, AL 35899. Offers accounting (M Acc), including CPA preparatory with an emphasis in taxation, CPA preparatory with emphasis in assurance and financial reporting, general accounting, information systems audit and control (ISAC). *Accreditation:* AACSB. Part-time and evening/weekend programs available. *Faculty:* 7 full-time (2 women), 4 part-time/adjunct (1 woman). *Students:* 21 full-time (14 women), 28 part-time (13 women); includes 8 minority (6 Black or African American, non-Hispanic/Latino; 1 American Indian or Alaska Native, non-Hispanic/Latino; 1 Asian, non-Hispanic/Latino), 4 international. Average age 33. 30 applicants, 70% accepted, 19 enrolled. In 2011, 24 master's awarded. *Degree requirements:* For master's, comprehensive exam, thesis or alternative. *Entrance requirements:* For master's, GMAT (minimum score 500), minimum AACSB index of 1080. Additional exam requirements/recommendations for international students: Required—TOEFL (minimum score 550 paper-based; 213 computer-based; 62 iBT). *Application deadline:* For fall admission, 8/1 for domestic students, 4/1 for international students; for spring admission, 12/1 for domestic students, 9/1 for international students. Applications are processed on a rolling basis. Application fee: $40 ($50 for international students). Electronic applications accepted. *Expenses:* Tuition, state resident: full-time $7830; part-time $473.50 per credit. Tuition, nonresident: full-time $18,748; part-time $1128.33 per credit. Tuition and fees vary according to course load and program. *Financial support:* In 2011–12, 5 students received support, including 1 research assistantship with full tuition reimbursement available (averaging $14,400 per year), 2 teaching assistantships with full tuition reimbursements available (averaging $5,000 per year); career-related internships or fieldwork, Federal Work-Study, institutionally sponsored loans, scholarships/grants, health care benefits, and unspecified assistantships also available. Support available to part-time students. Financial award application deadline: 4/1; financial award applicants required to submit FAFSA. *Faculty research:* Accounting information systems, emerging technologies in accounting, behavioral accounting, state and local taxation, financial accounting. *Total annual research expenditures:* $66,318. *Unit head:* Dr. John Burnett, Interim Chair, 256-824-2923, Fax: 256-824-2929, E-mail: burnettj@uah.edu. *Application contact:* Jennifer Pettitt, Director of Graduate Programs, 256-824-6681, Fax: 256-824-7571, E-mail: jennifer.pettitt@uah.edu.

The University of Alabama in Huntsville, School of Graduate Studies, College of Business Administration, Department of Management and Marketing, Huntsville, AL 35899. Offers federal contract procurement (Certificate); management (MBA), including acquisition management, entrepreneurship, federal contract accounting, finance, human resource management, logistics and supply chain management, marketing, project management; supply chain management (Certificate); technology and innovation management (Certificate). *Accreditation:* AACSB. Part-time and evening/weekend programs available. *Faculty:* 11 full-time (2 women), 3 part-time/adjunct (0 women). *Students:* 52 full-time (25 women), 145 part-time (68 women); includes 28 minority (14 Black or African American, non-Hispanic/Latino; 4 American Indian or Alaska Native, non-Hispanic/Latino; 7 Asian, non-Hispanic/Latino; 2 Hispanic/Latino; 1 Two or more races, non-Hispanic/Latino), 15 international. Average age 31. 103 applicants, 73% accepted, 65 enrolled. In 2011, 76 master's awarded. *Degree requirements:* For master's, comprehensive exam, thesis or alternative. *Entrance requirements:* For master's, GMAT (minimum score 500), minimum AACSB index of 1080. Additional exam requirements/recommendations for international students: Required—TOEFL (minimum score 550 paper-based; 213 computer-based; 62 iBT). *Application deadline:* For fall admission, 8/1 for domestic students, 4/1 for international students; for spring admission, 12/1 for domestic students, 9/1 for international students. Applications are processed on a rolling basis. Application fee: $40 ($50 for international students). Electronic applications accepted. *Expenses:* Tuition, state resident: full-time $7830; part-time $473.50 per credit. Tuition, nonresident: full-time $18,748; part-time $1128.33 per credit. Tuition and fees vary according to course load and program. *Financial support:* In 2011–12, 12 students received support, including 7 research assistantships with full tuition reimbursements available (averaging $9,829 per year), 4 teaching assistantships with full tuition reimbursements available (averaging $8,000 per year); career-related internships or fieldwork, Federal Work-Study, institutionally sponsored loans, scholarships/grants, health care benefits, and unspecified assistantships also available. Support available to part-time students. Financial award application deadline: 4/1; financial award applicants required to submit FAFSA. *Faculty research:* Strategic human resources, corporate governance, cross-function integration and the management of research and development, determinants of team performance. *Total annual research expenditures:* $3.4 million. *Unit head:* Dr. Cynthia Gramm, Chair, 256-824-6913, Fax: 256-824-6328, E-mail: cynthia.gramm@uah.edu. *Application contact:* Jennifer Pettitt, Director of Graduate Programs, 256-824-6681, Fax: 256-824-7571, E-mail: jennifer.pettitt@uah.edu.

University of Alberta, Faculty of Graduate Studies and Research, Doctoral Program in Business, Edmonton, AB T6G 2E1, Canada. Offers accounting (PhD); finance (PhD); human resources/industrial relations (PhD); management science (PhD); marketing (PhD); organizational analysis (PhD); MBA/PhD. *Accreditation:* AACSB. Part-time programs available. *Degree requirements:* For doctorate, comprehensive exam, thesis/dissertation. *Entrance requirements:* For doctorate, GMAT. Additional exam requirements/recommendations for international students: Required—TOEFL (minimum score 550 paper-based; 213 computer-based). Electronic applications accepted. *Faculty research:* Accounting, capital markets and corporate finance, organizational change and human resource management, marketing, strategic management.

The University of Arizona, Eller College of Management, Department of Accounting, Tucson, AZ 85721. Offers M Ac. *Accreditation:* AACSB. Part-time programs available. *Faculty:* 9 full-time (4 women). *Students:* 45 full-time (25 women), 7 part-time (4 women); includes 13 minority (1 American Indian or Alaska Native, non-Hispanic/Latino; 2 Asian, non-Hispanic/Latino; 9 Hispanic/Latino; 1 Two or more races, non-Hispanic/Latino), 4 international. Average age 26. 168 applicants, 39% accepted, 36 enrolled. In 2011, 62 master's awarded. *Degree requirements:* For master's, comprehensive exam, 1-year residency. *Entrance requirements:* For master's, GMAT (minimum score 550), 2 letters of recommendation, 3 writing samples, resume. Additional exam requirements/recommendations for international students: Required—TOEFL (minimum score 600 paper-based; 250 computer-based; 100 iBT). *Application deadline:* For fall admission, 3/1 priority date for domestic students, 3/1 for international students; for spring admission, 10/1 priority date for domestic students, 10/1 for international students. Applications are processed on a rolling basis. Application fee: $75. Electronic applications accepted. *Expenses:* Contact institution. *Financial support:* In 2011–12, 31 teaching assistantships with full tuition reimbursements (averaging $26,048 per year) were awarded; career-related internships or fieldwork, Federal Work-Study, scholarships/grants, health care benefits, tuition waivers (partial), and unspecified assistantships also available. Financial award application deadline: 3/15. *Faculty research:* Auditing, financial reporting and financial markets, taxation policy and markets, behavioral research in accounting. *Unit head:* Dr. Dan S. Dhaliwal, Head, 520-621-2146, Fax: 520-621-3742, E-mail: dhaliwal@eller.arizona.edu. *Application contact:* Carol Plagman, Programs Coordinator, 520-621-3712, Fax: 520-621-3742, E-mail: accounting@eller.arizona.edu. Web site: http://accounting.eller.arizona.edu/.

University of Arkansas, Graduate School, Sam M. Walton College of Business Administration, Department of Accounting, Fayetteville, AR 72701-1201. Offers M Acc. *Accreditation:* AACSB. *Students:* 47 full-time (21 women), 6 part-time (1 woman); includes 4 minority (2 Black or African American, non-Hispanic/Latino; 1 Asian, non-Hispanic/Latino; 1 Two or more races, non-Hispanic/Latino), 9 international. In 2011, 25 master's awarded. *Entrance requirements:* For master's, GMAT. Application fee: $40 ($50 for international students). *Financial support:* In 2011–12, 18 research assistantships, 2 teaching assistantships were awarded; fellowships with tuition reimbursements, career-related internships or fieldwork, and Federal Work-Study also available. Support available to part-time students. Financial award application deadline: 4/1; financial award applicants required to submit FAFSA. *Unit head:* Dr. Vernon Richardson, Chair, 479-575-4051, Fax: 479-575-2863, E-mail: vrichardson@walton.uark.edu. *Application contact:* Dr. Gary Peters, Graduate Coordinator, 479-575-4117, Fax: 479-575-2863, E-mail: peters@uark.edu. Web site: http://gsb.uark.edu/.

University of Arkansas at Little Rock, Graduate School, College of Business Administration, Little Rock, AR 72204-1099. Offers accountancy (M Acc, Graduate Certificate); business administration (MBA); construction management (Graduate Certificate); management (Graduate Certificate); management information system (MIS); management information systems (Graduate Certificate); management information systems leadership (Graduate Certificate); taxation (MS, Graduate Certificate). *Accreditation:* AACSB. Part-time and evening/weekend programs available. *Entrance requirements:* For master's, GMAT, minimum undergraduate GPA of 2.7. Additional exam requirements/recommendations for international students: Required—TOEFL (minimum score 525 paper-based; 195 computer-based).

University of Baltimore, Graduate School, Merrick School of Business, Department of Accounting and Management Information Systems, Baltimore, MD 21201-5779. Offers accounting and business advisory services (MS); accounting fundamentals (Graduate Certificate); forensic accounting (Graduate Certificate). Part-time and evening/weekend programs available. *Entrance requirements:* For master's, GMAT. Additional exam requirements/recommendations for international students: Required—TOEFL (minimum score 550 paper-based; 213 computer-based). Electronic applications accepted. *Faculty research:* Health care, accounting and administration, managerial accounting, financial accounting theory, accounting information.

University of Bridgeport, School of Business, Bridgeport, CT 06604. Offers accounting (MBA); finance (MBA); general business (MBA); global financial services (MBA); human resource management (MBA); information systems and knowledge management (MBA); international business (MBA); management (MBA); marketing (MBA); operations management (MBA); small business and entrepreneurship (MBA); specialized business (MBA). Part-time and evening/weekend programs available. *Faculty:* 11 full-time (2 women), 39 part-time/adjunct (8 women). *Students:* 198 full-time (105 women), 94 part-time (47 women); includes 38 minority (16 Black or African American, non-Hispanic/Latino; 9 Asian, non-Hispanic/Latino; 10 Hispanic/Latino; 3 Two or more races, non-Hispanic/Latino), 227 international. Average age 28. 835 applicants, 56% accepted, 57 enrolled. In 2011, 155 master's awarded. *Degree requirements:* For master's, thesis optional. *Entrance requirements:* For master's, GMAT. Additional exam requirements/recommendations for international students: Recommended—TOEFL (minimum score 550 paper-based; 213 computer-based; 80 iBT), IELTS (minimum score 6.5). *Application deadline:* For fall admission, 8/1 priority date for domestic students, 8/1 for international students; for spring admission, 12/1 priority date for domestic students, 12/1 for international students. Applications are processed on a rolling basis. Application fee: $50. Electronic applications accepted. *Expenses:* Contact institution. *Financial support:* In 2011–12, 69 students received support. Fellowships, research assistantships, teaching assistantships, career-related internships or fieldwork, Federal Work-Study, institutionally sponsored loans, and tuition waivers (partial) available. Support available to part-time students. Financial award application deadline: 6/1; financial award applicants required to submit FAFSA. *Unit head:* Dr. Robert Gilmore, Dean, 203-576-4384, Fax: 203-576-4388, E-mail: rgilmore@bridgeport.edu. *Application contact:* Karissa Peckham, Dean of Admissions, 203-576-4552, Fax: 203-576-4941, E-mail: mba@bridgeport.edu. Web site: http://www.bridgeport.edu.

The University of British Columbia, Sauder School of Business, Doctoral Program in Commerce and Business Administration, Vancouver, BC V6T 1Z1, Canada. Offers accounting (PhD); finance (PhD); international business (PhD); management information systems (PhD); management science (PhD); marketing (PhD); organizational behavior (PhD); strategy and business economics (PhD); transportation and logistics (PhD); urban land economics (PhD). *Degree requirements:* For doctorate, comprehensive exam, thesis/dissertation. *Entrance requirements:* For doctorate, GMAT or GRE. Additional exam requirements/recommendations for international students: Required—TOEFL (minimum score 600 paper-based; 250 computer-based; 100 iBT). Electronic applications accepted.

University of California, Berkeley, Graduate Division, Haas School of Business, PhD in Business Administration Program, Berkeley, CA 94720-1500. Offers accounting (PhD); business and public policy (PhD); finance (PhD); management of organizations (PhD); marketing (PhD); operations management (PhD); real estate (PhD). *Accreditation:* AACSB. *Faculty:* 77 full-time (18 women), 152 part-time/adjunct (24 women). *Students:* 79 full-time (25 women); includes 13 minority (12 Asian, non-Hispanic/Latino; 1 Hispanic/Latino), 34 international. Average age 30. 547 applicants, 5% accepted, 15 enrolled. In 2011, 14 doctorates awarded. *Degree requirements:* For doctorate, comprehensive exam, thesis/dissertation, written preliminary exams, oral qualifying exam. *Entrance requirements:* For doctorate, GMAT or GRE, minimum GPA of 3.0 in undergraduate and graduate coursework. Additional exam requirements/recommendations for international students: Required—TOEFL (minimum score 570 paper-based; 230 computer-based; 70 iBT), IELTS (minimum score 7). *Application deadline:* For fall admission, 12/10 for domestic and international students. Application fee: $80 ($100 for international students). Electronic applications accepted. *Financial support:* In 2011–12, 66 students received support, including 58 fellowships with full and partial tuition reimbursements available (averaging $29,000 per year), 77 teaching assistantships with full and partial tuition reimbursements available; research assistantships with full and partial tuition reimbursements available, scholarships/grants, health care benefits, tuition waivers (full), unspecified assistantships, and transit pass, travel grants also available. Financial award application deadline: 12/10; financial award applicants required to submit FAFSA. *Faculty research:* Accounting, business and public policy, finance, management of organizations, marketing, operations and information technology management, real estate. *Unit head:* Dr. Sunil Dutta, Director, 510-642-1229, Fax: 510-643-4255, E-mail: kimg@haas.berkeley.edu. *Application contact:* Kim Guilfoyle, Director, Student Affairs, 510-642-3944, Fax: 510-643-4255, E-mail: kimg@haas.berkeley.edu. Web site: http://www.haas.berkeley.edu/Phd/.

University of California, Berkeley, UC Berkeley Extension, Certificate Programs in Business, Berkeley, CA 94720-1500. Offers accounting (Certificate); business administration (Certificate); finance (Certificate); human resource management (Certificate); management (Certificate); marketing (Certificate); project management (Certificate). *Accreditation:* AACSB. Postbaccalaureate distance learning degree programs offered.

University of California, Los Angeles, Graduate Division, UCLA Anderson School of Management, Los Angeles, CA 90095-1481. Offers accounting (PhD); Asia Pacific (EMBA); business administration (EMBA, MBA); decisions, operations and technology management (PhD); finance (PhD); financial engineering (MFE); global economics and management (PhD); Latin America (EMBA); management and organizations (PhD); marketing (PhD); strategy (PhD); DDS/MBA; MBA/JD; MBA/MD; MBA/MLAS; MBA/MLIS; MBA/MPH; MBA/MPP; MBA/MSCS; MBA/MSN; MBA/MUP. *Accreditation:* AACSB. Part-time programs available. *Faculty:* 90 full-time (14 women), 62 part-time/adjunct (14 women). *Students:* 1,103 full-time (312 women), 842 part-time (223 women); includes 663 minority (18 Black or African American, non-Hispanic/Latino; 510 Asian, non-Hispanic/Latino; 46 Hispanic/Latino; 2 Native Hawaiian or other Pacific Islander, non-Hispanic/Latino; 87 Two or more races, non-Hispanic/Latino), 469 international. 4,737 applicants, 32% accepted, 875 enrolled. In 2011, 759 master's, 6 doctorates awarded. *Degree requirements:* For master's, comprehensive exam, field study consulting project (for MBA); thesis/dissertation (for MFE); for doctorate, comprehensive exam, thesis/dissertation, oral and written qualifying exams. *Entrance requirements:* For master's, GMAT (for MBA); GMAT or GRE General Test (for MFE), 4-year bachelor's degree or equivalent; for doctorate, GMAT or GRE General Test, 4-year bachelor's degree from regionally-accredited institution; minimum GPA of 3.0. Additional exam requirements/recommendations for international students: Required—TOEFL (minimum score 560 paper-based; 220 computer-based; 87 iBT), IELTS (minimum score 7). *Application deadline:* For fall admission, 10/26 for domestic and international students; for winter admission, 1/11 for domestic and international students; for spring admission, 4/18 for domestic and international students. Application fee: $200. Electronic applications accepted. *Expenses:* Contact institution. *Financial support:* In 2011–12, 600 students received support. Fellowships, research assistantships, teaching assistantships, career-related internships or fieldwork, institutionally sponsored loans, scholarships/grants, health care benefits, and tuition waivers (partial) available. Financial award application deadline: 4/15; financial award applicants required to submit FAFSA. *Unit head:* Judy D. Olian, Dean, 310-825-7982, Fax: 310-206-2073, E-mail: judy.olian@anderson.ucla.edu. *Application contact:* Robert Weiler, Assistant Dean, Director of MBA Admissions and Financial Aid, 310-825-6944, Fax: 310-825-8582, E-mail: mba.admissions@anderson.ucla.edu. Web site: http://www.anderson.ucla.edu/.

See Display on page 141 and Close-Up on page 249.

University of Central Arkansas, Graduate School, College of Business Administration, Program in Accounting, Conway, AR 72035-0001. Offers M Acc. Part-time programs available. *Students:* 19 full-time (9 women), 1 (woman) part-time; includes 5 minority (1 American Indian or Alaska Native, non-Hispanic/Latino; 4 Two or more races, non-Hispanic/Latino), 3 international. Average age 25. 11 applicants, 91% accepted, 8 enrolled. In 2011, 15 master's awarded. *Degree requirements:* For master's, capstone course. *Entrance requirements:* For master's, GMAT, minimum GPA of 2.7. Additional exam requirements/recommendations for international students: Required—TOEFL (minimum score 550 paper-based; 213 computer-based). *Application deadline:* For fall admission, 3/1 for domestic and international students; for spring admission, 10/1 for domestic and international students. Applications are processed on a rolling basis. Application fee: $25 ($50 for international students). *Expenses:* Tuition, state resident: full-time $4834; part-time $398.35 per credit hour. Tuition, nonresident: full-time $8686. *Financial support:* In 2011–12, 4 research assistantships with partial tuition reimbursements (averaging $5,000 per year) were awarded; career-related internships or fieldwork, Federal Work-Study, scholarships/grants, tuition waivers (partial), and unspecified assistantships also available. Support available to part-time students. Financial award application deadline: 2/15. *Unit head:* Dr. Tom Oxner, Interim Chair, 501-450-5333, Fax: 501-450-5302. *Application contact:* Sandy Burks, Administrative Specialist, 501-450-3124, Fax: 501-450-5678, E-mail: slburks@uca.edu.

University of Central Florida, College of Business Administration, Kenneth G. Dixon School of Accounting, Orlando, FL 32816. Offers MSA, MST. *Accreditation:* AACSB. Part-time and evening/weekend programs available. *Faculty:* 23 full-time (11 women), 1 (woman) part-time/adjunct. *Students:* 116 full-time (60 women), 123 part-time (62 women); includes 58 minority (9 Black or African American, non-Hispanic/Latino; 24 Asian, non-Hispanic/Latino; 20 Hispanic/Latino; 2 Native Hawaiian or other Pacific Islander, non-Hispanic/Latino; 3 Two or more races, non-Hispanic/Latino), 12 international. Average age 29. 141 applicants, 60% accepted, 66 enrolled. In 2011, 104 master's awarded. *Degree requirements:* For master's, comprehensive exam. *Entrance requirements:* For master's, GMAT, minimum GPA of 3.0 in last 60 hours. Additional exam requirements/recommendations for international students: Required—TOEFL. *Application deadline:* For fall admission, 6/15 priority date for domestic students; for spring admission, 11/1 priority date for domestic students. Electronic applications accepted. *Expenses:* Tuition, state resident: part-time $277.08 per credit hour. Tuition, nonresident: part-time $277.08 per credit hour. Part-time tuition and fees vary according to degree level and program. *Financial support:* In 2011–12, 11 students received support, including 1 fellowship (averaging $10,000 per year), 2 research assistantships (averaging $6,500 per year), 9 teaching assistantships with partial tuition reimbursements available (averaging $6,900 per year); career-related internships or fieldwork, Federal Work-Study, institutionally sponsored loans, tuition waivers (partial), and unspecified assistantships also available. Financial award application deadline: 3/1; financial award applicants required to submit FAFSA. *Unit head:* Dr. Sean Robb, Director, 407-823-2871, Fax: 407-823-3881, E-mail: srobb@bus.ucf.edu. *Application contact:* Judy Ryder, Director, Graduate Admissions, 407-823-2364, Fax: 407-823-0219, E-mail: jryder@bus.ucf.edu. Web site: http://web.bus.ucf.edu/accounting/.

University of Central Missouri, The Graduate School, Harmon College of Business Administration, Warrensburg, MO 64093. Offers accountancy (MA); accounting (MBA); ethical strategic leadership (MBA); finance (MBA); general business (MBA); information systems (MBA); information technology (MS); marketing (MBA). Part-time programs available. Postbaccalaureate distance learning degree programs offered. *Entrance requirements:* Additional exam requirements/recommendations for international students: Required—TOEFL (minimum score 550 paper-based; 79 computer-based). Electronic applications accepted.

University of Charleston, Executive Master of Forensic Accounting Program, Charleston, WV 25304-1099. Offers EMFA. Part-time and evening/weekend programs available. *Entrance requirements:* For master's, undergraduate degree from regionally-accredited institution; minimum GPA of 3.0 in undergraduate work (recommended); three years of work experience since receiving undergraduate degree (recommended); minimum of two professional recommendations, one from current employer, addressing career potential and ability to do graduate work. Additional exam requirements/recommendations for international students: Required—TOEFL. *Application deadline:* Applications are processed on a rolling basis. Electronic applications accepted. *Financial support:* In 2011–12, 1 student received support. Applicants required to submit FAFSA. *Application contact:* Linda Anderson, Administrative Assistant, 304-357-4870, Fax: 304-357-4872, E-mail: lindaanderson@ucwv.edu. Web site: http://www.ucwv.edu/Forensic-Accounting/.

University of Chicago, Booth School of Business, Full-Time MBA Program, Chicago, IL 60637. Offers accounting (MBA); analytic finance (MBA); analytic management (MBA); business administration (PhD); econometrics and statistics (MBA); economics (MBA); entrepreneurship (MBA); finance (MBA); general management (MBA); health administration and policy (Certificate); human resource management (MBA); international business (IMBA, MBA); managerial and organizational behavior (MBA); marketing management (MBA); operations management (MBA); strategic management (MBA); MBA/AM; MBA/JD; MBA/MA; MBA/MD; MBA/MPP. *Accreditation:* AACSB. Part-time and evening/weekend programs available. *Faculty:* 166 full-time, 32 part-time/adjunct. *Students:* 1,160 full-time (412 women); includes 316 minority (61 Black or African American, non-Hispanic/Latino; 173 Asian, non-Hispanic/Latino; 63 Hispanic/Latino; 19 Two or more races, non-Hispanic/Latino), 378 international. Average age 28. 4,169 applicants, 575 enrolled. In 2011, 1,423 master's, 19 doctorates awarded. Terminal master's awarded for partial completion of doctoral program. *Entrance requirements:* For master's, GMAT, 2 letters of recommendation, 3 essays, resume, interview. Additional exam requirements/recommendations for international students: Required—TOEFL (minimum score 600 paper-based; 250 computer-based; 104 iBT), IELTS. *Application deadline:* For fall admission, 10/12 priority date for domestic students, 10/12 for international students; for winter admission, 1/4 for domestic and international students; for spring admission, 4/4 for domestic and international students. Application fee: $200. Electronic applications accepted. *Expenses:* Contact institution. *Financial support:* Fellowships available. Financial award applicants required to submit FAFSA. *Faculty research:* Finance, marketing, economics, entrepreneurship, strategy, management. *Unit head:* Stacey Kole, Deputy Dean, 773-702-7121. *Application contact:* Kurt Ahlm, Associate Dean of Student Recruitment and Admissions, 773-702-7369, Fax: 773-702-9085, E-mail: admissions@chicagobooth.edu. Web site: http://chicagobooth.edu/.

University of Cincinnati, Graduate School, Carl H. Lindner College of Business, MS Program, Cincinnati, OH 45221. Offers accounting (MS); information systems (MS); marketing (MS); quantitative analysis (MS). Part-time and evening/weekend programs available. *Faculty:* 79 full-time (22 women), 71 part-time/adjunct (24 women). *Students:* 171 full-time (75 women), 106 part-time (46 women); includes 19 minority (6 Black or African American, non-Hispanic/Latino; 1 American Indian or Alaska Native, non-

Hispanic/Latino; 7 Asian, non-Hispanic/Latino; 2 Hispanic/Latino; 3 Two or more races, non-Hispanic/Latino), 114 international. 404 applicants, 77% accepted, 125 enrolled. *Degree requirements:* For master's, thesis (for some programs). *Entrance requirements:* For master's, GMAT, GRE, resume, transcripts, essays, letters of recommendation. Additional exam requirements/recommendations for international students: Required—TOEFL (minimum score 600 paper-based; 250 computer-based; 100 iBT). *Application deadline:* For fall admission, 1/15 priority date for domestic students, 4/1 for international students. Applications are processed on a rolling basis. Application fee: $65 ($70 for international students). Electronic applications accepted. *Expenses:* Contact institution. *Financial support:* In 2011–12, 10 teaching assistantships with full and partial tuition reimbursements (averaging $5,400 per year) were awarded; scholarships/grants, tuition waivers (full and partial), and unspecified assistantships also available. Financial award application deadline: 2/1; financial award applicants required to submit FAFSA. *Unit head:* Dr. David Szymanski, Dean, 513-556-7001, Fax: 513-556-4891, E-mail: will.mcintosh@uc.edu. *Application contact:* Dona Clary, Director, Graduate Programs Office, 513-556-3546, Fax: 513-558-7006, E-mail: dona.clary@uc.edu.

University of Cincinnati, Graduate School, Carl H. Lindner College of Business, PhD Programs, Cincinnati, OH 45221. Offers accounting (PhD); finance (PhD); information systems (PhD); management (PhD); marketing (PhD); quantitative analysis and operations management (PhD). *Faculty:* 56 full-time (13 women). *Students:* 34 full-time (12 women), 12 part-time (4 women); includes 2 minority (1 Asian, non-Hispanic/Latino; 1 Hispanic/Latino), 25 international. Average age 29. 120 applicants, 13% accepted, 10 enrolled. In 2011, 8 degrees awarded. *Median time to degree:* Of those who began their doctoral program in fall 2003, 65% received their degree in 8 years or less. *Degree requirements:* For doctorate, comprehensive exam, thesis/dissertation. *Entrance requirements:* For doctorate, GMAT, GRE, transcripts, essays, resume, letters of recommendation. Additional exam requirements/recommendations for international students: Required—TOEFL (minimum score 600 paper-based; 250 computer-based; 100 iBT). *Application deadline:* For fall admission, 2/1 for domestic and international students. Application fee: $65 ($70 for international students). Electronic applications accepted. *Expenses:* Contact institution. *Financial support:* In 2011–12, 39 students received support, including 30 research assistantships with full and partial tuition reimbursements available (averaging $14,640 per year); scholarships/grants, tuition waivers (full and partial), and unspecified assistantships also available. Financial award application deadline: 2/1; financial award applicants required to submit FAFSA. *Unit head:* Dr. Suzanne Masterson, Director, 513-556-7125, Fax: 513-556-5499, E-mail: suzanne.masterson@uc.edu. *Application contact:* Deborah Schildknecht, Assistant Director, 513-556-7190, Fax: 513-558-7006, E-mail: deborah.schildknecht@uc.edu. Web site: http://www.business.uc.edu/phd.

University of Colorado Boulder, Leeds School of Business, Division of Business Administration, Boulder, CO 80309. Offers accounting (MS, PhD); finance (PhD); information systems (PhD); marketing (PhD); operations (PhD); strategic, organizational, and entrepreneurial studies (PhD). *Students:* 129 full-time (65 women), 6 part-time (0 women); includes 15 minority (1 Black or African American, non-Hispanic/Latino; 8 Asian, non-Hispanic/Latino; 5 Hispanic/Latino; 1 Two or more races, non-Hispanic/Latino), 21 international. Average age 27. 332 applicants, 9% accepted, 13 enrolled. In 2011, 53 master's, 6 doctorates awarded. *Entrance requirements:* For master's, GMAT, minimum undergraduate GPA of 3.0. *Application deadline:* For fall admission, 3/31 for domestic and international students; for spring admission, 10/31 for domestic and international students. Application fee: $50 ($60 for international students). Electronic applications accepted. *Financial support:* In 2011–12, 61 students received support, including 24 fellowships (averaging $3,398 per year), 19 research assistantships with full and partial tuition reimbursements available (averaging $27,830 per year), 15 teaching assistantships with full and partial tuition reimbursements available (averaging $25,615 per year); institutionally sponsored loans, scholarships/grants, health care benefits, and unspecified assistantships also available. Financial award applicants required to submit FAFSA. *Application contact:* E-mail: leedsphd@colorado.edu. Web site: http://leeds.colorado.edu/phdprog.

University of Colorado Denver, Business School, Program in Accounting, Denver, CO 80217. Offers auditing and forensic accounting (MS); financial accounting (MS); information systems audit control (MS); taxation (MS). *Accreditation:* AACSB. Part-time and evening/weekend programs available. *Students:* 133 full-time (76 women), 32 part-time (16 women); includes 28 minority (6 Black or African American, non-Hispanic/Latino; 1 American Indian or Alaska Native, non-Hispanic/Latino; 15 Asian, non-Hispanic/Latino; 5 Hispanic/Latino; 1 Two or more races, non-Hispanic/Latino), 19 international. Average age 30. 92 applicants, 54% accepted, 30 enrolled. In 2011, 57 master's awarded. *Degree requirements:* For master's, 30 semester hours. *Entrance requirements:* For master's, GMAT, essay, resume, two letters of recommendation; financial statements (for international students). Additional exam requirements/recommendations for international students: Required—TOEFL (minimum score 525 paper-based; 197 computer-based; 71 iBT), IELTS (minimum score 6). *Application deadline:* For fall admission, 4/15 priority date for domestic students, 3/15 for international students; for spring admission, 10/15 for domestic students, 10/1 for international students. Applications are processed on a rolling basis. Application fee: $50 ($75 for international students). Electronic applications accepted. *Expenses:* Contact institution. *Financial support:* Federal Work-Study and scholarships/grants available. Support available to part-time students. Financial award application deadline: 4/1; financial award applicants required to submit FAFSA. *Faculty research:* Transfer pricing, behavioral accounting, environmental accounting, health services, international auditing. *Unit head:* Bruce Neumann, Professor, 303-315-8473, E-mail: bruce.neumann@ucdenver.edu. *Application contact:* Shelly Townley, Admissions Director, Graduate Programs, 303-315-8202, E-mail: shelly.townley@ucdenver.edu. Web site: http://www.ucdenver.edu/academics/colleges/business/degrees/ms/accounting/Pages/Accounting.aspx.

University of Connecticut, Graduate School, School of Business, Field of Accounting, Storrs, CT 06269. Offers MS, PhD. *Accreditation:* AACSB. *Entrance requirements:* Additional exam requirements/recommendations for international students: Required—TOEFL (minimum score 550 paper-based; 213 computer-based). Electronic applications accepted.

University of Dallas, Graduate School of Management, Irving, TX 75062-4736. Offers accounting (MBA, MM, MS); business management (MBA, MM); corporate finance (MBA, MM); financial services (MBA); global business (MBA, MM); health services management (MBA, MM); human resource management (MBA, MM); information assurance (MBA, MM, MS); information technology (MBA, MM, MS); information technology service management (MBA, MM, MS); marketing management (MBA, MM); organization development (MBA, MM); project management (MBA, MM); sports and entertainment management (MBA, MM); strategic leadership (MBA, MM); supply chain management (MBA); supply chain management and market logistics (MM). *Accreditation:* ACBSP. Part-time and evening/weekend programs available. Postbaccalaureate distance learning degree programs offered (no on-campus study). *Entrance requirements:* Additional exam requirements/recommendations for international students: Required—TOEFL. Electronic applications accepted. *Expenses:* Contact institution.

University of Dayton, School of Business Administration, Dayton, OH 45469-1300. Offers accounting (MBA); cyber security (MBA); finance (MBA); marketing (MBA); JD/MBA. *Accreditation:* AACSB. Part-time and evening/weekend programs available. *Faculty:* 23 full-time (6 women), 13 part-time/adjunct (2 women). *Students:* 170 full-time (72 women), 117 part-time (43 women); includes 26 minority (16 Black or African American, non-Hispanic/Latino; 6 Asian, non-Hispanic/Latino; 3 Hispanic/Latino; 1 Two or more races, non-Hispanic/Latino), 49 international. Average age 28. 366 applicants, 72% accepted, 126 enrolled. In 2011, 147 master's awarded. *Entrance requirements:* For master's, GMAT or GRE. Additional exam requirements/recommendations for international students: Required—TOEFL (minimum score 550 paper-based; 213 computer-based; 80 iBT); Recommended—IELTS (minimum score 6.5). *Application deadline:* For fall admission, 3/1 for international students; for winter admission, 7/1 for international students; for spring admission, 1/1 for international students. Applications are processed on a rolling basis. Application fee: $0 ($50 for international students). Electronic applications accepted. *Expenses:* Contact institution. *Financial support:* In 2011–12, 12 research assistantships with full and partial tuition reimbursements (averaging $7,020 per year) were awarded; career-related internships or fieldwork, institutionally sponsored loans, scholarships/grants, health care benefits, and unspecified assistantships also available. Support available to part-time students. Financial award application deadline: 3/15; financial award applicants required to submit FAFSA. *Faculty research:* Management information systems, economics, finance, entrepreneurship, marketing, accounting and cyber security. *Unit head:* Janice M. Glynn, Director, MBA Program, 937-229-3733, Fax: 937-229-3882, E-mail: glynn@udayton.edu. *Application contact:* Jeffrey Carter, Assistant Director, MBA Program, 937-229-3733, Fax: 937-229-3882, E-mail: jeff.carter@notes.udayton.edu. Web site: http://business.udayton.edu/mba/.

University of Delaware, Alfred Lerner College of Business and Economics, Department of Accounting and Management Information Systems, Newark, DE 19716. Offers accounting (MS); information systems and technology management (MS). *Accreditation:* AACSB. Part-time and evening/weekend programs available. *Degree requirements:* For master's, thesis optional. *Entrance requirements:* For master's, GMAT. Additional exam requirements/recommendations for international students: Required—TOEFL (minimum score 550 paper-based; 213 computer-based). Electronic applications accepted. *Faculty research:* External reporting, managerial accounting, auditing information systems, taxation.

University of Denver, Daniels College of Business, School of Accountancy, Denver, CO 80208. Offers accountancy (M Acc); accounting (MBA). *Accreditation:* AACSB. Part-time and evening/weekend programs available. *Faculty:* 15 full-time (6 women), 4 part-time/adjunct (2 women). *Students:* 36 full-time (22 women), 77 part-time (52 women); includes 9 minority (3 Asian, non-Hispanic/Latino; 6 Hispanic/Latino), 58 international. Average age 26. 468 applicants, 46% accepted, 90 enrolled. In 2011, 75 degrees awarded. *Entrance requirements:* For master's, GRE General Test or GMAT, essay, two letters of recommendation. Additional exam requirements/recommendations for international students: Required—TOEFL (minimum score 570 paper-based; 88 iBT). *Application deadline:* For fall admission, 11/15 priority date for domestic students; for spring admission, 10/15 priority date for domestic students. Applications are processed on a rolling basis. Application fee: $100. Electronic applications accepted. *Financial support:* In 2011–12, 36 students received support, including 6 teaching assistantships with full and partial tuition reimbursements available (averaging $1,766 per year); career-related internships or fieldwork, Federal Work-Study, institutionally sponsored loans, scholarships/grants, and unspecified assistantships also available. Support available to part-time students. Financial award application deadline: 3/15; financial award applicants required to submit FAFSA. *Faculty research:* Management accounting, activity-based management, benchmarking, financial management and human services, derivatives. *Unit head:* Dr. Sharon Lassar, Director, 303-871-2032, E-mail: slassar@du.edu. *Application contact:* Victoria Chen, Graduate Admissions Director, 303-871-2032, E-mail: victoria.chen@du.edu. Web site: http://www.daniels.du.edu/schoolsdepartments/accountancy/.

University of Florida, Graduate School, Warrington College of Business Administration, Fisher School of Accounting, Gainesville, FL 32611-7166. Offers M Acc, PhD, JD/M Acc. *Accreditation:* AACSB. Part-time programs available. *Faculty:* 9 full-time (2 women). *Students:* 211 full-time (93 women), 10 part-time (6 women); includes 47 minority (4 Black or African American, non-Hispanic/Latino; 1 American Indian or Alaska Native, non-Hispanic/Latino; 25 Asian, non-Hispanic/Latino; 17 Hispanic/Latino), 15 international. Average age 24. 288 applicants, 38% accepted, 84 enrolled. In 2011, 118 master's, 1 doctorate awarded. *Degree requirements:* For master's, comprehensive exam, thesis optional; for doctorate, comprehensive exam, thesis/dissertation. *Entrance requirements:* For master's, GRE General Test (minimum combined score 1100, 550 verbal, 550 quantitative), GMAT, minimum GPA of 3.0; for doctorate, GRE (minimum scores: verbal 550, quantitative 550), GMAT (taken within last 3 years), minimum GPA of 3.0, BS. Additional exam requirements/recommendations for international students: Required—TOEFL (minimum score 80 iBT), IELTS (minimum score 6). *Application deadline:* Applications are processed on a rolling basis. Application fee: $30. Electronic applications accepted. *Financial support:* Research assistantships, Federal Work-Study, and unspecified assistantships available. Support available to part-time students. Financial award application deadline: 1/15; financial award applicants required to submit FAFSA. *Faculty research:* Financial reporting, managerial accounting, auditing, taxation. *Unit head:* Dr. Gary McGill, Director and Associate Dean, 352-273-0219, Fax: 352-392-7962, E-mail: mcgill@ufl.edu. *Application contact:* Dominique A. DeSantiago, Associate Director, 352-273-0200, Fax: 352-392-7962, E-mail: dom.desantiago@cba.ufl.edu. Web site: http://www.cba.ufl.edu/fsoa/.

University of Florida, Graduate School, Warrington College of Business Administration, Hough Graduate School of Business, Programs in Business Administration, Gainesville, FL 32611. Offers accounting (MBA); arts administration (MBA); business strategy and public policy (MBA); competitive strategy (MBA); decision and information sciences (MBA); electronic commerce (MBA); finance (MBA); general business (MBA); global management (MBA); Graham-Buffett security analysis (MBA); health administration (MBA); human resources management (MBA); international studies (MBA); Latin American business (MBA); management (MBA); marketing (MBA); sports administration (MBA); JD/MBA; MBA/MS; MBA/PhD; MBA/Pharm D; MD/MBA. *Accreditation:* AACSB. Part-time and evening/weekend programs available. *Faculty:* 71 full-time (10 women). *Students:* 412 full-time (111 women), 467 part-time (135 women); includes 235 minority (39 Black or African American, non-Hispanic/Latino; 7 American Indian or Alaska Native, non-Hispanic/Latino; 79 Asian, non-Hispanic/Latino; 109 Hispanic/Latino; 1 Native Hawaiian or other Pacific Islander, non-Hispanic/Latino), 44 international. Average age 32. 589 applicants, 52% accepted, 247 enrolled. In 2011, 505 master's awarded. *Degree requirements:* For master's, capstone course. *Entrance requirements:* For master's, GMAT, minimum GPA of 3.0, interview. Additional exam requirements/recommendations for international students: Required—TOEFL (minimum score 550 paper-based; 213 computer-based; 80 iBT), IELTS (minimum score 6). *Application deadline:* For fall admission, 7/1 for domestic students, 1/1 for international students; for spring admission, 12/1 for domestic and international students. Applications are processed on a rolling basis. Application fee: $30. Electronic applications accepted. *Financial support:* Teaching assistantships, career-related internships or fieldwork, scholarships/grants, and unspecified assistantships available. Support available to part-time students. Financial award applicants required to submit FAFSA. *Faculty research:* Accounting, finance, insurance, management, real estate, urban analysis marketing. *Unit head:* Prof. Alexander D. Sevilla, Assistant Dean/ Director, 352-273-3252 Ext. 1206, E-mail: alex.sevilla@warrington.ufl.edu. *Application contact:* Prof. Kelli Gust, Associate Director, 352-273-3255, Fax: 352-392-8791, E-mail: kelly.gust@warrington.ufl.edu. Web site: http://www.floridamba.ufl.edu/.

University of Georgia, Terry College of Business, J. M. Tull School of Accounting, Athens, GA 30602. Offers M Acc, JD/M Acc. *Accreditation:* AACSB. *Faculty:* 17 full-time (7 women). *Students:* 152 full-time (81 women), 8 part-time (6 women); includes 21 minority (6 Black or African American, non-Hispanic/Latino; 7 Asian, non-Hispanic/ Latino; 6 Hispanic/Latino; 2 Two or more races, non-Hispanic/Latino), 4 international. Average age 23. 274 applicants, 31% accepted, 68 enrolled. In 2011, 121 master's awarded. *Entrance requirements:* For master's, GMAT. *Application deadline:* For fall admission, 7/1 priority date for domestic students; for spring admission, 11/15 for domestic students. Application fee: $50. Electronic applications accepted. *Financial support:* Fellowships, research assistantships, teaching assistantships, and unspecified assistantships available. *Unit head:* Dr. Benjamin C. Ayers, Director, 706-542-1616, Fax: 706-542-3630, E-mail: bayers@terry.uga.edu. *Application contact:* Dr. E. Michael Bamber, Graduate Coordinator, 706-542-3601, E-mail: mbamber@terry.uga.edu. Web site: http://www.terry.uga.edu/accounting/.

University of Hartford, Barney School of Business, Department of Accounting and Taxation, West Hartford, CT 06117-1599. Offers professional accounting (Certificate); taxation (MSAT). Part-time and evening/weekend programs available. *Entrance requirements:* For master's, GMAT, 2 letters of recommendation, resume. Additional exam requirements/recommendations for international students: Required—TOEFL (minimum score 550 paper-based; 213 computer-based). Electronic applications accepted.

University of Hawaii at Manoa, Graduate Division, Shidler College of Business, Program in Accounting, Honolulu, HI 96822. Offers accounting (M Acc); accounting law (M Acc); information systems (M Acc); taxation (M Acc). Part-time programs available. *Entrance requirements:* For master's, GMAT, bachelor's degree in accounting, minimum GPA of 3.0. Additional exam requirements/recommendations for international students: Required—TOEFL (minimum score 550 paper-based; 213 computer-based; 79 iBT), IELTS (minimum score 5). *Faculty research:* International accounting, current tax topics, insurance industry financial reporting, behavioral accounting, auditing.

University of Hawaii at Manoa, Graduate Division, Shidler College of Business, Program in International Management, Honolulu, HI 96822. Offers Asian finance (PhD); global information technology management (PhD); international accounting (PhD); international marketing (PhD); international organization and strategy (PhD). Part-time programs available. *Degree requirements:* For doctorate, comprehensive exam, thesis/ dissertation. *Entrance requirements:* For doctorate, GMAT or GRE General Test, minimum GPA of 3.0. Additional exam requirements/recommendations for international students: Required—TOEFL (minimum score 600 paper-based; 250 computer-based; 100 iBT), IELTS (minimum score 7). *Expenses:* Contact institution.

University of Houston, Bauer College of Business, Accountancy and Taxation Program, Houston, TX 77204. Offers accountancy (MS Accy); accountancy and taxation (PhD). *Accreditation:* AACSB. Part-time and evening/weekend programs available. *Degree requirements:* For master's, 30 hours completed in residence, minimum cumulative GPA of 3.0 at UH, no more than 11 semester hours of 'C' grades or below in graduate courses taken at UH; for doctorate, continuous full time enrollment, dissertation defense within 6 years of entering the program. *Entrance requirements:* For master's, GMAT, official transcripts from all higher education institutions attended, letters of recommendation, resume, goals statement; for doctorate, GMAT or GRE, letter of financial backing, statement of understanding, reference letters, statement of academic and research interests. Additional exam requirements/recommendations for international students: Required—TOEFL (minimum score 550 paper-based; 213 computer-based; 79 iBT), IELTS (minimum score 6.5), Pearson Test of English (minimum score: 70). Electronic applications accepted. *Faculty research:* Accountancy and taxation, finance, international business, management.

University of Houston–Clear Lake, School of Business, Program in Accounting, Houston, TX 77058-1098. Offers accounting (MS); professional accounting (MS). *Accreditation:* AACSB. Part-time and evening/weekend programs available. *Degree requirements:* For master's, thesis optional. *Entrance requirements:* For master's, GMAT. Additional exam requirements/recommendations for international students: Required—TOEFL (minimum score 550 paper-based; 213 computer-based). Electronic applications accepted.

University of Houston–Victoria, School of Business Administration, Victoria, TX 77901-4450. Offers accounting (MBA); economic development and entrepreneurship (MS); finance (GMBA, MBA); general business (MBA); international business (MBA); management (GMBA, MBA); marketing (MBA). *Accreditation:* AACSB. Part-time and evening/weekend programs available. Postbaccalaureate distance learning degree programs offered (minimal on-campus study). *Entrance requirements:* For master's, GMAT. Additional exam requirements/recommendations for international students: Required—TOEFL (minimum score 550 paper-based; 213 computer-based). Electronic applications accepted. *Faculty research:* Economic development, marketing, finance.

University of Idaho, College of Graduate Studies, College of Business and Economics, Department of Accounting, Moscow, ID 83844-3161. Offers accountancy (M Acct). *Accreditation:* AACSB. *Faculty:* 3 full-time. *Students:* 24 full-time, 7 part-time. Average age 25. In 2011, 24 master's awarded. *Degree requirements:* For master's, comprehensive exam. *Entrance requirements:* For master's, minimum GPA of 3.0. *Application deadline:* For fall admission, 8/1 for domestic students; for spring admission, 12/15 for domestic students. Applications are processed on a rolling basis. Application fee: $60. Electronic applications accepted. *Expenses:* Tuition, state resident: full-time $3874; part-time $334 per credit hour. Tuition, nonresident: full-time $16,394; part-time $861 per credit hour. *Required fees:* $2808; $99 per credit hour. Tuition and fees vary according to program. *Financial support:* Research assistantships and teaching assistantships available. Financial award applicants required to submit FAFSA. *Unit head:* Dr. Marla Kraut, Head, 208-885-6453, Fax: 208-885-6296, E-mail: amberg@ uidaho.edu. *Application contact:* Erick Larson, Director of Graduate Admissions, 208-885-4723, E-mail: gadms@uidaho.edu. Web site: http://www.uidaho.edu/cbe/ accounting/.

University of Illinois at Chicago, Graduate College, Liautaud Graduate School of Business, Department of Accounting, Chicago, IL 60607-7128. Offers MS, MBA/MS. *Accreditation:* AACSB. Part-time programs available. *Entrance requirements:* For master's, GMAT, minimum GPA of 2.75. Additional exam requirements/ recommendations for international students: Required—TOEFL. Electronic applications accepted. *Faculty research:* Governmental accounting, managerial accounting, auditing.

University of Illinois at Springfield, Graduate Programs, College of Business and Management, Program in Accountancy, Springfield, IL 62703-5407. Offers MA. Part-time and evening/weekend programs available. *Faculty:* 6 full-time (2 women), 2 part-time/adjunct (1 woman). *Students:* 42 full-time (21 women), 77 part-time (44 women); includes 13 minority (8 Black or African American, non-Hispanic/Latino; 5 Asian, non-Hispanic/Latino), 14 international. Average age 29. 72 applicants, 65% accepted, 37 enrolled. In 2011, 34 master's awarded. *Degree requirements:* For master's, capstone course. *Entrance requirements:* For master's, minimum undergraduate GPA of 2.5 in prerequisite coursework, introductory course in financial and managerial accounting, college math through business calculus, principles of economics (micro and macro), statistics, computer applications. Additional exam requirements/recommendations for international students: Required—TOEFL (minimum score 550 paper-based). *Application deadline:* Applications are processed on a rolling basis. Application fee: $50 ($60 for international students). Electronic applications accepted. *Expenses:* Tuition, state resident: full-time $6978; part-time $290.75 per credit hour. Tuition, nonresident: full-time $15,282; part-time $636.75 per credit hour. *Required fees:* $2106; $87.75 per credit hour. *Financial support:* In 2011–12, fellowships with full tuition reimbursements (averaging $8,550 per year), research assistantships with full tuition reimbursements (averaging $8,550 per year), teaching assistantships with full tuition reimbursements (averaging $8,550 per year) were awarded; career-related internships or fieldwork, Federal Work-Study, scholarships/grants, health care benefits, and unspecified assistantships also available. Support available to part-time students. Financial award application deadline: 11/15; financial award applicants required to submit FAFSA. *Unit head:* Dr. Leonard Branson, Program Administrator, 217-206-6299, Fax: 217-206-7543, E-mail: lbran1@uis.edu. *Application contact:* Dr. Lynn Pardie, Office of Graduate Studies, 800-252-8533, Fax: 217-206-7623, E-mail: lpardie1@uis.edu. Web site: http:// www.uis.edu/accountancy.

University of Illinois at Urbana–Champaign, Graduate College, College of Business, Department of Accountancy, Champaign, IL 61820. Offers accountancy (MAS, MS, PhD); taxation (MS); MAS/JD. *Accreditation:* AACSB. *Faculty:* 26 full-time (8 women), 6 part-time/adjunct (2 women). *Students:* 369 full-time (220 women), 7 part-time (5 women); includes 65 minority (3 Black or African American, non-Hispanic/Latino; 47 Asian, non-Hispanic/Latino; 12 Hispanic/Latino; 3 Two or more races, non-Hispanic/ Latino), 182 international. 1,040 applicants, 42% accepted, 346 enrolled. In 2011, 378 master's, 2 doctorates awarded. *Entrance requirements:* For master's, GMAT (for MAS), minimum GPA of 3.0; for doctorate, GMAT, minimum GPA of 3.0. Additional exam requirements/recommendations for international students: Required—TOEFL. *Application deadline:* Applications are processed on a rolling basis. Application fee: $75 ($90 for international students). Electronic applications accepted. *Financial support:* In 2011–12, 22 fellowships, 14 research assistantships, 81 teaching assistantships were awarded; tuition waivers (full and partial) also available. *Unit head:* Theodore Sougiannis, Head, 217-244-0555, Fax: 217-244-0902, E-mail: sougiani@illinois.edu. *Application contact:* Cindy Wood, Administrative Aide, 217-333-4572, Fax: 217-244-0902, E-mail: ckwood@illinois.edu. Web site: http://www.business.illinois.edu/ accountancy.

The University of Iowa, Henry B. Tippie College of Business, M Ac Program in Accountancy, Iowa City, IA 52242-1316. Offers M Ac, JD/M Ac. Part-time programs available. *Students:* 48 full-time (20 women), 2 part-time (1 woman); includes 3 minority (1 Black or African American, non-Hispanic/Latino; 1 Asian, non-Hispanic/Latino; 1 Hispanic/Latino), 10 international. Average age 25. 188 applicants, 20% accepted, 35 enrolled. In 2011, 33 master's awarded. *Entrance requirements:* Additional exam requirements/recommendations for international students: Required—TOEFL, IELTS. *Application deadline:* For fall admission, 7/15 for domestic students, 4/15 for international students; for spring admission, 12/1 for domestic students, 10/1 for international students. Application fee: $60 ($100 for international students). Electronic applications accepted. *Unit head:* Prof. Douglas V. DeJong, Dean, 319-335-0910, Fax: 319-335-1956, E-mail: douglas-dejong@uiowa.edu. *Application contact:* Prof. Thomas J. Carroll, Director, Admissions and Financial Aid, 319-335-2727, Fax: 319-335-3604, E-mail: thomas-carroll@uiowa.edu. Web site: http://tippie.uiowa.edu/accounting/mac/.

The University of Iowa, Henry B. Tippie College of Business, PhD Program in Accounting, Iowa City, IA 52242-1316. Offers PhD. *Accreditation:* AACSB. *Faculty:* 15 full-time (3 women), 6 part-time/adjunct (1 woman). *Students:* 13 full-time (4 women); includes 1 minority (Asian, non-Hispanic/Latino), 5 international. Average age 30. 62 applicants, 10% accepted, 2 enrolled. In 2011, 1 doctorate awarded. *Degree requirements:* For doctorate, comprehensive exam, thesis/dissertation, thesis defense. *Entrance requirements:* For doctorate, GMAT. Additional exam requirements/ recommendations for international students: Required—TOEFL (minimum score 600 paper-based; 250 computer-based; 100 iBT) or IELTS (minimum score 7). *Application deadline:* For fall admission, 1/15 priority date for domestic students, 1/15 for international students. Applications are processed on a rolling basis. Application fee: $60 ($100 for international students). Electronic applications accepted. *Financial support:* In 2011–12, 9 students received support, including 9 fellowships (averaging $9,592 per year), 2 research assistantships with full tuition reimbursements available (averaging $16,908 per year), 44 teaching assistantships with full tuition reimbursements available (averaging $16,277 per year); institutionally sponsored loans, scholarships/grants, health care benefits, and unspecified assistantships also available. Financial award application deadline: 1/15. *Faculty research:* Corporate financial reporting issues; financial statement information and capital markets; cost structure: analysis, estimation, and management; experimental and prediction economics; income taxes and interaction of financial and tax reporting systems. *Unit head:* Prof. Douglas V. DeJong, Department Executive Officer, 319-335-0910, Fax: 319-335-1956, E-mail: douglas-dejong@uiowa.edu. *Application contact:* Renea L. Jay, PhD Coordinator, 319-335-0830, Fax: 319-335-1956, E-mail: renea-jay@uiowa.edu. Web site: http:// tippie.uiowa.edu/accounting/.

The University of Kansas, Graduate Studies, School of Business, Master of Accounting (MAcc) Program, Lawrence, KS 66045-7585. Offers M Acc. *Accreditation:* AACSB. Part-time programs available. *Faculty:* 20. *Students:* 123 full-time (52 women), 15 part-time (9 women); includes 18 minority (2 Black or African American, non-Hispanic/Latino; 1 American Indian or Alaska Native, non-Hispanic/Latino; 8 Asian, non-Hispanic/Latino; 1 Hispanic/Latino; 6 Two or more races, non-Hispanic/Latino), 7 international. Average age 23. 137 applicants, 69% accepted, 88 enrolled. In 2011, 123 master's awarded. *Degree requirements:* For master's, 30 credits. *Entrance requirements:* For master's, GMAT. Additional exam requirements/recommendations for international students: Required—TOEFL (minimum score 53 paper-based; 20 computer-based); Recommended—IELTS (minimum score 6). *Application deadline:* For fall admission, 3/1 priority date for domestic students, 2/15 for international students; for spring admission, 11/1 for domestic students, 10/1 for international students. Applications are processed on a rolling basis. Application fee: $65. Electronic applications accepted. Tuition and fees vary according to course load, campus/location, program and reciprocity agreements. *Financial support:* Fellowships, research assistantships, teaching assistantships, career-related internships or fieldwork, Federal Work-Study, institutionally sponsored loans, and scholarships/grants available. Financial award application deadline: 6/1; financial award applicants required to submit FAFSA. *Faculty research:* Audit; artificial intelligence; agency theory; compensation; production, regulation, and use of accounting information. *Unit head:* Dr. John T. Sweeney, Director, 785-864-4500, Fax: 785-864-5328, E-mail: jtsweeney@ku.edu. *Application contact:* Karen Heintzen, Assistant Director, 785-864-7558, Fax: 785-864-5376, E-mail: heintzen@ku.edu. Web site: http://www.business.ku.edu/.

Accounting

University of Kentucky, Graduate School, Gatton College of Business and Economics, Program in Accounting, Lexington, KY 40506-0032. Offers MSACC. *Accreditation:* AACSB. *Degree requirements:* For master's, comprehensive exam. *Entrance requirements:* For master's, GRE General Test, minimum undergraduate GPA of 2.75. Additional exam requirements/recommendations for international students: Required—TOEFL (minimum score 550 paper-based; 213 computer-based). Electronic applications accepted. *Faculty research:* Taxation, financial accounting and auditing, managerial accounting, not-for-profit accounting.

University of La Verne, College of Business and Public Management, Graduate Programs in Business Administration, La Verne, CA 91750-4443. Offers accounting (MBA); executive management (MBA-EP); finance (MBA, MBA-EP); health services management (MBA); information technology (MBA, MBA-EP); international business (MBA, MBA-EP); leadership (MBA-EP); managed care (MBA); management (MBA, MBA-EP); marketing (MBA, MBA-EP). Part-time and evening/weekend programs available. *Faculty:* 34 full-time (15 women), 38 part-time/adjunct (13 women). *Students:* 525 full-time (243 women), 231 part-time (114 women); includes 199 minority (27 Black or African American, non-Hispanic/Latino; 1 American Indian or Alaska Native, non-Hispanic/Latino; 55 Asian, non-Hispanic/Latino; 113 Hispanic/Latino; 3 Two or more races, non-Hispanic/Latino), 436 international. Average age 28. In 2011, 403 master's awarded. *Entrance requirements:* For master's, minimum undergraduate GPA of 3.0, 2 letters of recommendation, resume. Additional exam requirements/recommendations for international students: Required—TOEFL (minimum score 550 paper-based; 213 computer-based). *Application deadline:* Applications are processed on a rolling basis. Application fee: $50. *Expenses:* Contact institution. *Financial support:* Career-related internships or fieldwork, institutionally sponsored loans, and scholarships/grants available. Financial award application deadline: 3/2; financial award applicants required to submit FAFSA. *Unit head:* Dr. Abe Helou, Chairperson, 909-593-3511 Ext. 4211, Fax: 909-392-2704, E-mail: ihelou@laverne.edu. *Application contact:* Rina Lazarian, Program and Admission Specialist, 909-593-3511 Ext. 4819, Fax: 909-392-2704, E-mail: cbpm@ulv.edu.

University of Lethbridge, School of Graduate Studies, Lethbridge, AB T1K 3M4, Canada. Offers accounting (MScM); addictions counseling (M Sc); agricultural biotechnology (M Sc); agricultural studies (M Sc, MA); anthropology (MA); archaeology (MA); art (MA, MFA); biochemistry (M Sc); biological sciences (M Sc); biomolecular science (PhD); biosystems and biodiversity (PhD); Canadian studies (MA); chemistry (M Sc); computer science (M Sc); computer science and geographical information science (M Sc); counseling psychology (M Ed); dramatic arts (MA); earth, space, and physical science (PhD); economics (MA); educational leadership (M Ed); English (MA); environmental science (M Sc); evolution and behavior (PhD); exercise science (M Sc); finance (MScM); French (MA); French/German (MA); French/Spanish (MA); general education (M Ed); general management (MScM); geography (M Sc, MA); German (MA); health science (M Sc); history (MA); human resource management and labour relations (MScM); individualized multidisciplinary (M Sc, MA); information systems (MScM); international management (MScM); kinesiology (M Sc, MA); management (M Sc, MA); marketing (MScM); mathematics (M Sc); music (M Mus, MA); Native American studies (MA); neuroscience (M Sc, PhD); new media (MA); nursing (M Sc); philosophy (MA); physics (M Sc); policy and strategy (MScM); political science (MA); psychology (M Sc, MA); religious studies (MA); social sciences (MA); sociology (MA); theatre and dramatic arts (MFA); theoretical and computational science (PhD); urban and regional studies (MA); women's studies (MA). Part-time and evening/weekend programs available. *Degree requirements:* For doctorate, comprehensive exam, thesis/dissertation. *Entrance requirements:* For master's, GMAT (M Sc in management), bachelor's degree in related field, minimum GPA of 3.0 during previous 20 graded semester courses, 2 years teaching or related experience (M Ed); for doctorate, master's degree, minimum graduate GPA of 3.5. Additional exam requirements/recommendations for international students: Required—TOEFL. *Faculty research:* Movement and brain plasticity, gibberellin physiology, photosynthesis, carbon cycling, molecular properties of main-group ring components.

University of Louisville, Graduate School, College of Business, School of Accountancy, Louisville, KY 40292-0001. Offers MAC, MBA/MAC. *Accreditation:* AACSB. Part-time and evening/weekend programs available. *Faculty:* 7 full-time (1 woman). *Students:* 16 full-time (9 women), 7 part-time (3 women); includes 2 minority (both Black or African American, non-Hispanic/Latino), 3 international. Average age 28. 33 applicants, 73% accepted, 11 enrolled. In 2011, 23 master's awarded. *Entrance requirements:* For master's, GMAT, 2 letters of reference, resume, personal statement, personal interview, transcript. Additional exam requirements/recommendations for international students: Required—TOEFL (minimum score 83 iBT). *Application deadline:* For fall admission, 5/15 priority date for domestic students. Applications are processed on a rolling basis. Application fee: $50. *Expenses:* Tuition, state resident: full-time $9692; part-time $539 per credit hour. Tuition, nonresident: full-time $20,168; part-time $1121 per credit hour. Tuition and fees vary according to program and reciprocity agreements. *Financial support:* In 2011–12, 3 students received support, including 2 research assistantships with full tuition reimbursements available (averaging $12,000 per year); health care benefits and unspecified assistantships also available. Financial award application deadline: 3/15; financial award applicants required to submit FAFSA. *Faculty research:* Audit judgment and decision-making, information systems, taxation, cost and managerial accounting. *Total annual research expenditures:* $146,460. *Unit head:* Dr. Charles Moyer, Dean, 502-852-6443, Fax: 502-852-7557, E-mail: charlie.moyer@louisville.edu. *Application contact:* L. Eddie Smith, Director of IT and Master's Programs Admissions/Recruiting Manager, 502-852-7257, Fax: 502-852-4901, E-mail: eddie.smith@louisville.edu. Web site: http://business.louisville.edu/masterofaccountancy.

University of Maine, Graduate School, College of Business, Public Policy and Health, The Maine Business School, Orono, ME 04469. Offers accounting (MBA); business and sustainability (MBA); finance (MBA); management (MBA). *Accreditation:* AACSB. Part-time and evening/weekend programs available. *Faculty:* 20 full-time (8 women), 6 part-time/adjunct (2 women). *Students:* 47 full-time (19 women), 15 part-time (2 women); includes 5 minority (1 American Indian or Alaska Native, non-Hispanic/Latino; 2 Asian, non-Hispanic/Latino; 2 Hispanic/Latino), 5 international. Average age 29. 41 applicants, 71% accepted, 24 enrolled. In 2011, 28 master's awarded. *Entrance requirements:* For master's, GMAT. Additional exam requirements/recommendations for international students: Required—TOEFL (minimum score 550 paper-based; 213 computer-based). *Application deadline:* For fall admission, 6/1 priority date for domestic students, 6/1 for international students; for spring admission, 11/1 priority date for domestic students, 11/1 for international students. Applications are processed on a rolling basis. Application fee: $65. Electronic applications accepted. *Expenses:* Contact institution. *Financial support:* In 2011–12, 16 students received support, including 3 teaching assistantships with full tuition reimbursements available (averaging $13,600 per year); career-related internships or fieldwork, Federal Work-Study, institutionally sponsored loans, scholarships/grants, tuition waivers (full and partial), and unspecified assistantships also available. Financial award application deadline: 3/1. *Faculty research:* Entrepreneurship, investment management, international markets, decision support systems, strategic planning. *Unit head:* Dr. Nory Jones, Director of Graduate Programs, 207-581-1971, Fax: 207-581-1930, E-mail: mba@maine.edu. *Application contact:* Scott G. Delcourt, Associate Dean of the Graduate School, 207-581-3291, Fax: 207-581-3232, E-mail: graduate@maine.edu. Web site: http://www.umaine.edu/business/.

The University of Manchester, Manchester Business School, Manchester, United Kingdom. Offers accounting (M Phil, PhD); business (M Ent, D Ent); business and management (M Phil); business management (PhD).

University of Mary, Gary Tharaldson School of Business, Bismarck, ND 58504-9652. Offers accountancy (MBA); business administration (MBA); health care (MBA); human resource management (MBA); management (MBA); project management (MPM); strategic leadership (MSSL). Part-time and evening/weekend programs available. *Faculty:* 8 full-time (5 women), 66 part-time/adjunct (22 women). *Students:* 340 full-time (190 women), 189 part-time (91 women); includes 69 minority (28 Black or African American, non-Hispanic/Latino; 25 American Indian or Alaska Native, non-Hispanic/Latino; 7 Asian, non-Hispanic/Latino; 7 Hispanic/Latino; 1 Native Hawaiian or other Pacific Islander, non-Hispanic/Latino; 1 Two or more races, non-Hispanic/Latino), 14 international. Average age 35. 207 applicants, 95% accepted, 148 enrolled. In 2011, 265 master's awarded. *Degree requirements:* For master's, strategic planning seminar. *Entrance requirements:* For master's, minimum GPA of 2.5. Additional exam requirements/recommendations for international students: Required—TOEFL (minimum score 500 paper-based; 197 computer-based; 71 iBT). *Application deadline:* Applications are processed on a rolling basis. Application fee: $40. *Financial support:* Application deadline: 8/1; applicants required to submit FAFSA. *Unit head:* Dr. Shanda Traiser, Director of the School of Accelerated and Distance Education, 701-355-8160, Fax: 701-255-7687, E-mail: straiser@umary.edu. *Application contact:* Wayne G. Maruska, Graduate Program Advisor, 701-355-8134, Fax: 701-255-7687, E-mail: wmaruska@umary.edu.

University of Mary Hardin-Baylor, Graduate Studies in Business Administration, Belton, TX 76513. Offers accounting (MBA); information systems management (MBA); management (MBA). Part-time and evening/weekend programs available. *Faculty:* 11 full-time (4 women), 5 part-time/adjunct (3 women). *Students:* 48 full-time (26 women), 23 part-time (12 women); includes 19 minority (7 Black or African American, non-Hispanic/Latino; 1 Asian, non-Hispanic/Latino; 11 Hispanic/Latino), 29 international. Average age 29. 102 applicants, 69% accepted, 25 enrolled. In 2011, 11 master's awarded. *Degree requirements:* For master's, comprehensive exam. *Entrance requirements:* For master's, GMAT, minimum GPA of 3.0, work experience, interview. *Application deadline:* For fall admission, 6/1 priority date for domestic students; for spring admission, 11/1 for domestic students. Applications are processed on a rolling basis. Application fee: $35 ($135 for international students). Electronic applications accepted. *Expenses: Tuition:* Full-time $12,780. *Required fees:* $2350. *Financial support:* Federal Work-Study and scholarships (for some active duty military personnel only) available. Financial award applicants required to submit FAFSA. *Unit head:* Dr. Terry Fox, Program Director, 254-295-5406, E-mail: terry.fox@umhb.edu. *Application contact:* Melissa Ford, Director of Graduate Admissions, 254-295-4020, Fax: 254-295-5301, E-mail: mford@umhb.edu.

University of Maryland University College, Graduate School of Management and Technology, Program in Accounting and Financial Management, Adelphi, MD 20783. Offers MS, Certificate. *Accreditation:* AACSB. Part-time and evening/weekend programs available. Postbaccalaureate distance learning degree programs offered (no on-campus study). *Students:* 9 full-time (5 women), 532 part-time (336 women); includes 289 minority (205 Black or African American, non-Hispanic/Latino; 48 Asian, non-Hispanic/Latino; 30 Hispanic/Latino; 1 Native Hawaiian or other Pacific Islander, non-Hispanic/Latino; 5 Two or more races, non-Hispanic/Latino), 24 international. Average age 35. 151 applicants, 100% accepted, 92 enrolled. In 2011, 118 degrees awarded. *Degree requirements:* For master's, thesis or alternative, capstone course. *Application deadline:* Applications are processed on a rolling basis. Application fee: $50. Electronic applications accepted. *Financial support:* Federal Work-Study and scholarships/grants available. Support available to part-time students. Financial award application deadline: 6/1; financial award applicants required to submit FAFSA. *Unit head:* Dr. James Howard, Director, 240-684-2400, Fax: 240-684-2401, E-mail: jhoward@umuc.edu. *Application contact:* Coordinator, Graduate Admissions, 800-888-8682, Fax: 240-684-2151, E-mail: newgrad@umuc.edu. Web site: http://www.umuc.edu/grad/msaf.html.

University of Maryland University College, Graduate School of Management and Technology, Program in Accounting and Information Technology, Adelphi, MD 20783. Offers MS, Certificate. *Accreditation:* AACSB. Part-time and evening/weekend programs available. Postbaccalaureate distance learning degree programs offered (no on-campus study). *Students:* 2 full-time (both women), 216 part-time (137 women); includes 137 minority (111 Black or African American, non-Hispanic/Latino; 14 Asian, non-Hispanic/Latino; 11 Hispanic/Latino; 1 Two or more races, non-Hispanic/Latino), 3 international. Average age 36. 62 applicants, 100% accepted, 39 enrolled. In 2011, 34 master's, 6 other advanced degrees awarded. *Degree requirements:* For master's, thesis or alternative, capstone course. *Application deadline:* Applications are processed on a rolling basis. Application fee: $50. Electronic applications accepted. *Financial support:* Federal Work-Study and scholarships/grants available. Support available to part-time students. Financial award application deadline: 6/1; financial award applicants required to submit FAFSA. *Unit head:* Dr. Kathryn Klose, Director, 240-684-2400, Fax: 240-684-2401, E-mail: kklose@umuc.edu. *Application contact:* Coordinator, Graduate Admissions, 800-888-8682, Fax: 240-684-2151, E-mail: newgrad@umuc.edu.

University of Massachusetts Amherst, Graduate School, Isenberg School of Management, Department of Accounting, Amherst, MA 01003. Offers MSA. *Accreditation:* AACSB. Part-time programs available. *Students:* 27 full-time (7 women), 10 part-time (3 women); includes 9 minority (1 Black or African American, non-Hispanic/Latino; 5 Asian, non-Hispanic/Latino; 3 Hispanic/Latino). Average age 23. 63 applicants, 90% accepted, 37 enrolled. In 2011, 46 master's awarded. *Entrance requirements:* For master's, GMAT. Additional exam requirements/recommendations for international students: Required—TOEFL (minimum score 550 paper-based; 213 computer-based; 80 iBT), IELTS (minimum score 6.5). *Application deadline:* For fall admission, 2/1 for domestic and international students. Applications are processed on a rolling basis. Application fee: $50 ($65 for international students). Electronic applications accepted. Tuition and fees vary according to course load, campus/location and program. *Unit head:* Dr. James F. Smith, Graduate Program Director, 413-545-5645, Fax: 413-545-3858. *Application contact:* Lindsay DeSantis, Interim Supervisor of Admissions, 413-545-0722, Fax: 413-577-0010, E-mail: gradadm@grad.umass.edu. Web site: http://www.isenberg.umass.edu/accounting/Graduate/MSA/.

University of Massachusetts Amherst, Graduate School, Isenberg School of Management, Program in Management, Amherst, MA 01003. Offers accounting (PhD); business administration (MBA); business administration/sport management (MBA/MS); finance (PhD); hospitality and tourism management (PhD); management science (PhD); marketing (PhD); organization studies (PhD); sport management (PhD); strategic management (PhD); MBA/MS; MPH/MPPA. *Accreditation:* AACSB. Part-time programs available. *Faculty:* 61 full-time (14 women). *Students:* 92 full-time (34 women), 9 part-time (3 women); includes 8 minority (1 Black or African American, non-Hispanic/Latino; 4 Asian, non-Hispanic/Latino; 3 Hispanic/Latino), 47 international. Average age 33. 340 applicants, 15% accepted, 29 enrolled. In 2011, 31 master's, 13 doctorates awarded. Terminal master's awarded for partial completion of doctoral program. *Degree* *requirements:* For doctorate, comprehensive exam, thesis/dissertation. *Entrance requirements:* For master's and doctorate, GMAT. Additional exam requirements/recommendations for international students: Required—TOEFL (minimum score 550 paper-based; 213 computer-based; 80 iBT), IELTS (minimum score 6.5). *Application deadline:* For fall admission, 1/20 for domestic and international students. Applications are processed on a rolling basis. Application fee: $50 ($65 for international students). Electronic applications accepted. Tuition and fees vary according to course load, campus/location and program. *Financial support:* Fellowships with full and partial tuition reimbursements, research assistantships with full and partial tuition reimbursements, teaching assistantships with full and partial tuition reimbursements, career-related internships or fieldwork, Federal Work-Study, scholarships/grants, traineeships, health care benefits, tuition waivers (full and partial), and unspecified assistantships available. Support available to part-time students. Financial award application deadline: 1/20. *Unit head:* Dr. William Woodridge, Chair, 413-545-5675, Fax: 413-577-2234. *Application contact:* Lindsay DeSantis, Interim Supervisor of Admissions, 413-545-0722, Fax: 413-577-0010, E-mail: gradadm@grad.umass.edu. Web site: http://www.isenberg.umass.edu/.

University of Massachusetts Dartmouth, Graduate School, Charlton College of Business, Program in Business Administration, North Dartmouth, MA 02747-2300. Offers accounting (Postbaccalaureate Certificate); business administration (MBA); business foundation (online) (Graduate Certificate); finance (PMC); international business (online) (Graduate Certificate); leadership (online) (Graduate Certificate); management (Postbaccalaureate Certificate); marketing (Postbaccalaureate Certificate); supply chain management (PMC). *Accreditation:* AACSB. Part-time programs available. *Faculty:* 35 full-time (11 women), 26 part-time/adjunct (7 women). *Students:* 81 full-time (29 women), 119 part-time (56 women); includes 17 minority (6 Black or African American, non-Hispanic/Latino; 1 American Indian or Alaska Native, non-Hispanic/Latino; 3 Asian, non-Hispanic/Latino; 5 Hispanic/Latino; 2 Two or more races, non-Hispanic/Latino), 42 international. Average age 31. 132 applicants, 92% accepted, 68 enrolled. In 2011, 91 master's, 18 other advanced degrees awarded. *Entrance requirements:* For master's, GMAT, statement of intent, resume, 3 letters of recommendation; for other advanced degree, statement of intent, resume, 3 letters of recommendation. Additional exam requirements/recommendations for international students: Required—TOEFL (minimum score 500 paper-based; 200 computer-based; 72 iBT). *Application deadline:* For fall admission, 3/1 for domestic students, 2/1 for international students; for spring admission, 11/1 for domestic students, 10/15 for international students. Application fee: $40 ($60 for international students). Electronic applications accepted. *Expenses:* Tuition, state resident: full-time $2071; part-time $86.29 per credit. Tuition, nonresident: full-time $8099; part-time $337.46 per credit. *Required fees:* $438.58 per credit. Part-time tuition and fees vary according to class time, course load, degree level and reciprocity agreements. *Financial support:* Research assistantships, teaching assistantships, Federal Work-Study, and unspecified assistantships available. Support available to part-time students. Financial award application deadline: 3/1; financial award applicants required to submit FAFSA. *Faculty research:* Global business environment, e-commerce, managing diversity, agile manufacturing, green business. *Total annual research expenditures:* $8,653. *Unit head:* Stephanie Jacobsen, Program Coordinator, 508-999-8543, Fax: 508-999-8646, E-mail: s.jacobsen@umassd.edu. *Application contact:* Elan Turcotte-Shamski, Graduate Admissions Officer, 508-999-8604, Fax: 508-999-8183, E-mail: graduate@umassd.edu. Web site: http://www.umassd.edu/charlton/.

University of Memphis, Graduate School, Fogelman College of Business and Economics, Program in Business Administration, Memphis, TN 38152. Offers accounting (MBA, PhD); economics (MBA, PhD); executive business administration (MBA); finance (PhD); finance, insurance, and real estate (MBA, MS); international business administration (IMBA); management (MBA, MS, PhD); management information systems (MBA, MS, PhD); management science (MBA); marketing (MBA, MS); marketing and supply chain management (PhD); real estate development (MS); JD/MBA. *Accreditation:* AACSB. *Degree requirements:* For master's, comprehensive exam; for doctorate, comprehensive exam, thesis/dissertation. *Entrance requirements:* For master's, GMAT, resume; for doctorate, GMAT, interview, minimum GPA of 3.4, resume, letter of recommendation. Additional exam requirements/recommendations for international students: Required—TOEFL (minimum score 550 paper-based; 220 computer-based). *Faculty research:* Competitive business strategy, finance microstructures, supply chain management innovations, health care economics, litigation risks and corporate audits.

University of Memphis, Graduate School, Fogelman College of Business and Economics, School of Accountancy, Memphis, TN 38152. Offers accounting (MS); accounting systems (MS); taxation (MS). *Accreditation:* AACSB. *Degree requirements:* For master's, comprehensive exam. *Entrance requirements:* For master's, GMAT. *Faculty research:* Financial accounting, corporate governance, EDP auditing, evolution of system analysis, investor behavior and investment decisions.

University of Miami, Graduate School, School of Business Administration, Department of Accounting, Coral Gables, FL 33124. Offers professional accounting (MP Acc); taxation (MS Tax). *Accreditation:* AACSB. Part-time and evening/weekend programs available. *Entrance requirements:* For master's, GMAT or CPA exam. Additional exam requirements/recommendations for international students: Required—TOEFL. Electronic applications accepted. *Faculty research:* Financial reporting, audit risk, public policy and taxation issues, government accounting and public choice, corporate governance.

University of Miami, Graduate School, School of Business Administration, Program in Business Administration, Coral Gables, FL 33124. Offers accounting (MBA); computer information systems (MBA); executive and professional (MBA), including international business, management; finance (MBA); international business (MBA); management (MBA); management science (MBA); marketing (MBA); professional management (MSPM); JD/MBA; MBA/MSIE. *Accreditation:* AACSB. Evening/weekend programs available. *Degree requirements:* For master's, comprehensive exam. *Entrance requirements:* For master's, GMAT. Additional exam requirements/recommendations for international students: Required—TOEFL (minimum score 550 paper-based; 213 computer-based; 59 iBT). Electronic applications accepted. *Faculty research:* Leadership, e-commerce, supply chain management.

University of Michigan–Dearborn, College of Business, Dearborn, MI 48128-1491. Offers accounting (MBA, MS); business analytics (MS); finance (MBA, MS); information systems (MS); international business (MBA); management (MBA); management information systems (MBA); marketing (MBA); supply chain management (MBA, MS); MBA/MHSA; MBA/MSE; MBA/MSF; MBA/MSIS; MSF/MSA. *Accreditation:* AACSB. Part-time and evening/weekend programs available. Postbaccalaureate distance learning degree programs offered (no on-campus study). *Faculty:* 50 full-time (6 women), 32 part-time/adjunct (18 women). *Students:* 65 full-time (29 women), 356 part-time (121 women); includes 79 minority (19 Black or African American, non-Hispanic/Latino; 36 American Indian or Alaska Native, non-Hispanic/Latino; 15 Hispanic/Latino; 1 Native Hawaiian or other Pacific Islander, non-Hispanic/Latino; 8 Two or more races, non-Hispanic/Latino), 80 international. Average age 28. 175 applicants, 53% accepted, 68 enrolled. In 2011, 173 master's awarded. *Entrance requirements:* For master's, GMAT or GRE, 2 years of work experience (MBA); course work in computer applications, statistics, and pre-calculus or finite mathematics; 18 credits of accounting course work beyond introductory courses (MS in accounting). Additional exam requirements/recommendations for international students: Required—TOEFL (minimum score 560 paper-based; 220 computer-based; 84 iBT), IELTS. *Application deadline:* For fall admission, 8/1 priority date for domestic students, 6/1 for international students; for winter admission, 12/1 priority date for domestic students, 10/1 for international students; for spring admission, 4/1 priority date for domestic students, 2/1 for international students. Applications are processed on a rolling basis. Application fee: $60. Electronic applications accepted. *Expenses:* Contact institution. *Financial support:* Career-related internships or fieldwork, Federal Work-Study, and scholarships/grants available. Support available to part-time students. Financial award application deadline: 9/1; financial award applicants required to submit FAFSA. *Faculty research:* Cultural diversity, buyer-supplier relations, error detection in data, economic evolution. *Unit head:* Dr. Lee Redding, Interim Dean, 313-593-5248, Fax: 313-271-9835, E-mail: lredding@umd.umich.edu. *Application contact:* Joan Doherty, Academic Advisor/Counselor, 313-593-5460, Fax: 313-271-9838, E-mail: gradbusiness@umd.umich.edu. Web site: http://www.cob.umd.umich.edu.

University of Minnesota, Twin Cities Campus, Carlson School of Management, Doctoral Program in Business Administration, Minneapolis, MN 55455-0213. Offers accounting (PhD); finance (PhD); information and decision sciences (PhD); marketing (PhD); operations and management science (PhD); strategic management and organization (PhD). *Faculty:* 104 full-time (30 women). *Students:* 74 full-time (30 women); includes 8 minority (5 Asian, non-Hispanic/Latino; 3 Hispanic/Latino), 50 international. Average age 30. 320 applicants, 8% accepted, 15 enrolled. In 2011, 13 doctorates awarded. *Degree requirements:* For doctorate, comprehensive exam, thesis/dissertation, written and oral preliminary exams, proposal defense, final defense. *Entrance requirements:* For doctorate, GMAT, GRE General Test. Additional exam requirements/recommendations for international students: Required—TOEFL (minimum score 600 paper-based; 250 computer-based; 100 iBT); Recommended—IELTS (minimum score 7.5). *Application deadline:* For fall admission, 12/31 for domestic and international students. Applications are processed on a rolling basis. Application fee: $75 ($95 for international students). Electronic applications accepted. *Expenses:* Contact institution. *Financial support:* In 2011–12, 66 students received support, including 112 fellowships with full tuition reimbursements available (averaging $6,700 per year), 55 research assistantships with full tuition reimbursements available (averaging $6,750 per year), 54 teaching assistantships with full tuition reimbursements available (averaging $6,750 per year); institutionally sponsored loans, scholarships/grants, health care benefits, and unspecified assistantships also available. Financial award application deadline: 12/31. *Faculty research:* Corporate strategy, finance, entrepreneurship, marketing, information and decision science, operations, accounting, quality management. *Unit head:* Dr. Shawn P. Curley, Director, 612-624-6546, Fax: 612-624-8221, E-mail: curley@umn.edu. *Application contact:* Earlene K. Bronson, Assistant Director, 612-624-0875, Fax: 612-624-8221, E-mail: brons003@umn.edu. Web site: http://www.csom.umn.edu/phd-BA/.

University of Minnesota, Twin Cities Campus, Carlson School of Management, Master's Program in Accountancy, Minneapolis, MN 55455-0213. Offers M Acc. *Accreditation:* AACSB. Part-time and evening/weekend programs available. *Faculty:* 15 full-time (3 women), 5 part-time/adjunct (1 woman). *Students:* 26 full-time (14 women), 7 part-time (5 women); includes 20 minority (all Asian, non-Hispanic/Latino), 5 international. Average age 23. 334 applicants, 7% accepted, 22 enrolled. In 2011, 45 master's awarded. *Entrance requirements:* For master's, GMAT, letters of recommendation. Additional exam requirements/recommendations for international students: Required—TOEFL (minimum score 550 paper-based; 213 computer-based; 79 iBT), IELTS (minimum score 6.5). *Application deadline:* For fall admission, 4/30 priority date for domestic students, 2/28 for international students; for spring admission, 10/15 priority date for domestic students, 10/15 for international students. Applications are processed on a rolling basis. Application fee: $75 ($95 for international students). Electronic applications accepted. *Expenses:* Contact institution. *Financial support:* In 2011–12, 6 students received support, including 6 fellowships (averaging $2,750 per year), 9 teaching assistantships with partial tuition reimbursements available (averaging $4,541 per year); institutionally sponsored loans also available. Financial award application deadline: 7/15; financial award applicants required to submit FAFSA. *Faculty research:* Capitol market-based accounting, cognitive skill acquisition in auditing, incentives and control in organizations, economic consequences of securities regulation, earnings management. *Unit head:* Larry Kallio, Director of Graduate Studies, 612-624-9818, Fax: 612-626-7795, E-mail: kalli008@umn.edu. *Application contact:* Information Contact, 612-625-3014, Fax: 612-625-6002, E-mail: gsquest@umn.edu. Web site: http://www.carlsonschool.umn.edu/macc.

University of Mississippi, Graduate School, School of Accountancy, Oxford, University, MS 38677. Offers accountancy (M Acc, PhD); taxation accounting (M Tax). *Accreditation:* AACSB. *Students:* 94 full-time (39 women), 23 part-time (13 women); includes 15 minority (7 Black or African American, non-Hispanic/Latino; 1 American Indian or Alaska Native, non-Hispanic/Latino; 5 Asian, non-Hispanic/Latino; 1 Hispanic/Latino; 1 Two or more races, non-Hispanic/Latino), 8 international. *Degree requirements:* For doctorate, thesis/dissertation. *Entrance requirements:* For master's, GMAT, minimum GPA of 3.0; for doctorate, GMAT. Additional exam requirements/recommendations for international students: Required—TOEFL. *Application deadline:* For fall admission, 4/1 for domestic students; for spring admission, 10/1 for domestic students. Applications are processed on a rolling basis. *Financial support:* Scholarships/grants available. Financial award application deadline: 3/1; financial award applicants required to submit FAFSA. *Unit head:* Dr. Mark Wilder, Interim Dean, 662-915-7468, Fax: 662-915-7483, E-mail: umaccy@olemiss.edu. *Application contact:* Dr. Christy M. Wyandt, Associate Dean, 662-915-7474, Fax: 662-915-7577, E-mail: cwyandt@olemiss.edu.

University of Missouri, Graduate School, Robert J. Trulaske, Sr. College of Business, School of Accountancy, Columbia, MO 65211. Offers M Acc, PhD. *Accreditation:* AACSB. Part-time programs available. *Faculty:* 15 full-time (7 women). *Students:* 137 full-time (56 women); includes 8 minority (2 Black or African American, non-Hispanic/Latino; 6 Asian, non-Hispanic/Latino), 6 international. Average age 23. 161 applicants, 58% accepted, 93 enrolled. In 2011, 117 master's, 4 doctorates awarded. *Degree requirements:* For master's, thesis or alternative; for doctorate, thesis/dissertation. *Entrance requirements:* For master's and doctorate, GMAT, minimum GPA of 3.0. Additional exam requirements/recommendations for international students: Required—TOEFL (minimum score 600 paper-based; 250 computer-based; 100 iBT). *Application deadline:* For fall admission, 2/1 priority date for domestic students. Applications are processed on a rolling basis. Application fee: $55 ($75 for international students). *Expenses:* Tuition, state resident: full-time $5881. Tuition, nonresident: full-time $15,183. *Required fees:* $952. Tuition and fees vary according to campus/location and program. *Financial support:* Fellowships, research assistantships, teaching assistantships, and institutionally sponsored loans available. *Unit head:* Dr. Jere Francis, Department Chair, 573-882-5156, E-mail: francis@missouri.edu. *Application contact:* Karen Staggs, 573-882-4463, E-mail: staggsk@missouri.edu. Web site: http://business.missouri.edu/43/default.aspx.

Accounting

University of Missouri–Kansas City, Henry W. Bloch School of Management, Kansas City, MO 64110-2499. Offers accounting (MS); business administration (MBA); entrepreneurial real estate (MERE); entrepreneurship and innovation (PhD); finance (MS); public affairs (MPA, PhD); JD/MBA; LL M/MPA. PhD (interdisciplinary) offered through the School of Graduate Studies. *Accreditation:* AACSB; NASPAA. Part-time and evening/weekend programs available. *Faculty:* 51 full-time (14 women), 29 part-time/adjunct (9 women). *Students:* 272 full-time (126 women), 407 part-time (180 women); includes 91 minority (43 Black or African American, non-Hispanic/Latino; 20 Asian, non-Hispanic/Latino; 19 Hispanic/Latino; 9 Two or more races, non-Hispanic/Latino), 49 international. Average age 30. 397 applicants, 63% accepted, 202 enrolled. In 2011, 257 master's awarded. Terminal master's awarded for partial completion of doctoral program. *Entrance requirements:* For master's, GMAT, GRE, 2 writing essays, 2 references; support of employer; for doctorate, GRE, minimum GPA of 3.0. Additional exam requirements/recommendations for international students: Required—TOEFL (minimum score 550 paper-based; 213 computer-based; 80 iBT). *Application deadline:* For fall admission, 5/1 priority date for domestic students, 5/1 for international students; for spring admission, 10/1 priority date for domestic students, 10/1 for international students. Applications are processed on a rolling basis. Application fee: $45 ($50 for international students). Electronic applications accepted. *Expenses:* Tuition, state resident: full-time $5798; part-time $322.10 per credit hour. Tuition, nonresident: full-time $14,969; part-time $831.60 per credit hour. *Required fees:* $93.51 per credit hour. *Financial support:* In 2011–12, 29 research assistantships with partial tuition reimbursements (averaging $11,490 per year), 3 teaching assistantships with partial tuition reimbursements (averaging $11,600 per year) were awarded; career-related internships or fieldwork, Federal Work-Study, institutionally sponsored loans, scholarships/grants, tuition waivers (full and partial), and unspecified assistantships also available. Support available to part-time students. Financial award application deadline: 3/1; financial award applicants required to submit FAFSA. *Faculty research:* Entrepreneurship, finance, non-profit, risk management. *Unit head:* Dr. Teng-Kee Tan, Dean, 816-235-2215, Fax: 816-235-2206. *Application contact:* 816-235-1111, E-mail: admit@umkc.edu. Web site: http://www.bloch.umkc.edu.

University of Missouri–St. Louis, College of Business Administration, Program in Accounting, St. Louis, MO 63121. Offers M Acc. *Accreditation:* AACSB. Part-time and evening/weekend programs available. *Faculty:* 9 full-time (4 women). *Students:* 62 full-time (36 women), 40 part-time (25 women); includes 14 minority (5 Black or African American, non-Hispanic/Latino; 1 American Indian or Alaska Native, non-Hispanic/Latino; 8 Asian, non-Hispanic/Latino), 15 international. Average age 27. 78 applicants, 40% accepted, 18 enrolled. In 2011, 40 master's awarded. *Entrance requirements:* For master's, GMAT, 2 letters of recommendation. Additional exam requirements/recommendations for international students: Required—TOEFL (minimum score 550 paper-based; 213 computer-based). *Application deadline:* For fall admission, 3/15 for domestic and international students; for spring admission, 10/15 for domestic and international students. Application fee: $35 ($40 for international students). Electronic applications accepted. *Expenses:* Tuition, state resident: full-time $6273; part-time $3866 per year. Tuition, nonresident: full-time $14,969; part-time $9980 per year. *Required fees:* $315 per year. *Financial support:* Career-related internships or fieldwork, Federal Work-Study, and institutionally sponsored loans available. Support available to part-time students. Financial award application deadline: 4/1; financial award applicants required to submit FAFSA. *Faculty research:* Accounting information in contracts, financial reporting issues, empirical valuation issues. *Unit head:* Karl Kottemann, Assistant Director, 314-516-5885, Fax: 314-516-6420, E-mail: mba@umsl.edu. *Application contact:* 314-516-5458, Fax: 314-516-6996, E-mail: gradadm@umsl.edu. Web site: http://www.umsl.edu/academics/PDFS/program_guide_business.pdf.

University of Missouri–St. Louis, College of Business Administration, Program in Business Administration, St. Louis, MO 63121. Offers accounting (MBA); business administration (Certificate); finance (MBA); human resource management (Certificate); information systems (MBA); logistics and supply chain management (MBA, Certificate); marketing (MBA); marketing management (Certificate); operations management (MBA). *Accreditation:* AACSB. Part-time and evening/weekend programs available. *Faculty:* 32 full-time (7 women), 10 part-time/adjunct (2 women). *Students:* 126 full-time (48 women), 305 part-time (141 women); includes 61 minority (25 Black or African American, non-Hispanic/Latino; 23 Asian, non-Hispanic/Latino; 9 Hispanic/Latino; 1 Native Hawaiian or other Pacific Islander, non-Hispanic/Latino; 3 Two or more races, non-Hispanic/Latino), 47 international. Average age 30. 241 applicants, 70% accepted, 134 enrolled. In 2011, 150 master's, 1 doctorate, 19 other advanced degrees awarded. *Entrance requirements:* For master's, GMAT, 2 letters of recommendation. Additional exam requirements/recommendations for international students: Required—TOEFL (minimum score 550 paper-based; 213 computer-based). *Application deadline:* For fall admission, 7/1 for domestic and international students; for spring admission, 12/1 for domestic and international students. Applications are processed on a rolling basis. Application fee: $35 ($40 for international students). Electronic applications accepted. *Expenses:* Tuition, state resident: full-time $6273; part-time $3866 per year. Tuition, nonresident: full-time $14,969; part-time $9980 per year. *Required fees:* $315 per year. *Financial support:* In 2011–12, 32 research assistantships with full and partial tuition reimbursements (averaging $6,000 per year), 6 teaching assistantships with full and partial tuition reimbursements (averaging $12,276 per year) were awarded; career-related internships or fieldwork, Federal Work-Study, and institutionally sponsored loans also available. Support available to part-time students. Financial award application deadline: 4/1; financial award applicants required to submit FAFSA. *Faculty research:* Human resources, strategic management, marketing strategy, consumer behavior product development, advertising. *Unit head:* Karl Kottemann, Assistant Director, 314-516-5885, Fax: 314-516-6420, E-mail: mba@umsl.edu. *Application contact:* 314-516-5458, Fax: 314-516-6996, E-mail: gradadm@umsl.edu. Web site: http://www.umsl.edu/divisions/business/mbaonline/mbaprog.htm.

The University of Montana, Graduate School, School of Business Administration, Department of Accounting and Finance, Missoula, MT 59812-0002. Offers accounting (M Acct). *Accreditation:* AACSB. *Degree requirements:* For master's, thesis optional. *Entrance requirements:* For master's, GMAT. Additional exam requirements/recommendations for international students: Required—TOEFL (minimum score 580 paper-based; 237 computer-based). *Faculty research:* Income tax, financial markets, nonprofit accounting, accounting information systems, auditing.

University of Nebraska at Omaha, Graduate Studies, College of Business Administration, Department of Accounting, Omaha, NE 68182. Offers M Acc. Part-time and evening/weekend programs available. *Faculty:* 9 full-time (4 women). *Students:* 21 full-time (12 women), 25 part-time (13 women); includes 4 minority (2 Asian, non-Hispanic/Latino; 1 Hispanic/Latino; 1 Two or more races, non-Hispanic/Latino), 4 international. Average age 27. 31 applicants, 32% accepted, 8 enrolled. In 2011, 6 master's awarded. *Degree requirements:* For master's, comprehensive exam (for some programs), thesis (for some programs). *Entrance requirements:* For master's, GMAT, minimum GPA of 3.0. Additional exam requirements/recommendations for international students: Required—TOEFL (minimum score 600 paper-based; 250 computer-based; 100 iBT). *Application deadline:* For fall admission, 5/1 priority date for domestic students; for spring admission, 12/1 priority date for domestic students. Applications are processed on a rolling basis. Application fee: $45. Electronic applications accepted. *Financial support:* In 2011–12, 5 students received support, including 3 research assistantships with tuition reimbursements available; Federal Work-Study, institutionally sponsored loans, scholarships/grants, tuition waivers (partial), and unspecified assistantships also available. Support available to part-time students. Financial award application deadline: 3/1; financial award applicants required to submit FAFSA. *Unit head:* Dr. Susan Eldridge, Chairperson, 402-554-3650. *Application contact:* Burch Kealey.

University of Nebraska–Lincoln, Graduate College, College of Business Administration, Interdepartmental Area of Business, Lincoln, NE 68588. Offers accountancy (PhD); business (MBA); finance (MA, PhD), including business; management (MA, PhD), including business; marketing (MA, PhD), including business; JD/MBA; M Arch/MBA. *Accreditation:* AACSB. Part-time programs available. Postbaccalaureate distance learning degree programs offered. *Degree requirements:* For doctorate, comprehensive exam, thesis/dissertation. *Entrance requirements:* For master's and doctorate, GMAT. Additional exam requirements/recommendations for international students: Required—TOEFL (minimum score 550 paper-based; 213 computer-based). Electronic applications accepted.

University of Nebraska–Lincoln, Graduate College, College of Business Administration, School of Accountancy, Lincoln, NE 68588. Offers MPA, PhD, JD/MPA. *Accreditation:* AACSB. *Entrance requirements:* For master's, GMAT. Additional exam requirements/recommendations for international students: Required—TOEFL (minimum score 550 paper-based; 213 computer-based). Electronic applications accepted. *Faculty research:* Auditing, financial accounting, managerial accounting, capital markets, tax accounting.

University of Nevada, Las Vegas, Graduate College, College of Business, Department of Accounting, Las Vegas, NV 89154-6003. Offers MS, Advanced Certificate, Certificate. *Accreditation:* AACSB. Part-time and evening/weekend programs available. *Faculty:* 10 full-time (3 women), 6 part-time/adjunct (0 women). *Students:* 49 full-time (22 women), 51 part-time (28 women); includes 25 minority (12 Asian, non-Hispanic/Latino; 3 Hispanic/Latino; 10 Two or more races, non-Hispanic/Latino), 12 international. Average age 30. 49 applicants, 76% accepted, 22 enrolled. In 2011, 55 master's awarded. *Entrance requirements:* For master's, GMAT. Additional exam requirements/recommendations for international students: Required—TOEFL (minimum score 550 paper-based; 213 computer-based; 80 iBT), IELTS (minimum score 7). *Application deadline:* For fall admission, 8/1 priority date for domestic students, 5/1 for international students; for spring admission, 12/1 priority date for domestic students, 10/1 for international students. Applications are processed on a rolling basis. Application fee: $60 ($95 for international students). Electronic applications accepted. *Financial support:* In 2011–12, 5 students received support, including 5 teaching assistantships (averaging $10,000 per year); institutionally sponsored loans, scholarships/grants, health care benefits, and unspecified assistantships also available. Financial award application deadline: 3/1. *Faculty research:* The study of auditor's judgments and judgment biases, the study of business processes, risk-based auditing, performance measurement, information presentation and decision-making. *Unit head:* Dr. Paulette Tandy, Chair/Associate Professor, 702-895-1559, Fax: 702-895-4306, E-mail: paulette.tandy@unlv.edu. *Application contact:* Graduate College Admissions Evaluator, 702-895-3320, Fax: 702-895-4180, E-mail: gradcollege@unlv.edu. Web site: http://business.unlv.edu/accounting/.

University of Nevada, Reno, Graduate School, College of Business Administration, Department of Accounting and Information Systems, Reno, NV 89557. Offers M Acc. *Accreditation:* AACSB. *Entrance requirements:* For master's, GMAT or GRE (if undergraduate degree is not from an AACSB-accredited business school with minimum GPA of 3.5), minimum GPA of 2.75. Additional exam requirements/recommendations for international students: Required—TOEFL (minimum score 500 paper-based; 173 computer-based; 61 iBT), IELTS (minimum score 6). Electronic applications accepted. *Faculty research:* Financial reporting/auditing, taxation.

University of New Hampshire, Graduate School, Whittemore School of Business and Economics, Department of Accounting and Finance, Durham, NH 03824. Offers accounting (MS). Part-time programs available. *Faculty:* 8 full-time (2 women). *Students:* 9 full-time (4 women), 14 part-time (10 women); includes 8 minority (6 Black or African American, non-Hispanic/Latino; 1 Asian, non-Hispanic/Latino; 1 Hispanic/Latino), 2 international. Average age 34. 3 applicants, 0% accepted, 0 enrolled. In 2011, 13 master's awarded. *Entrance requirements:* For master's, GMAT. Additional exam requirements/recommendations for international students: Required—TOEFL (minimum score 550 paper-based; 213 computer-based; 80 iBT). *Application deadline:* For fall admission, 5/1 priority date for domestic students, 4/1 for international students; for spring admission, 12/1 for domestic students. Applications are processed on a rolling basis. Application fee: $65. *Expenses:* Tuition, state resident: full-time $12,360; part-time $687 per credit hour. Tuition, nonresident: full-time $25,680; part-time $1058 per credit hour. *International tuition:* $29,550 full-time. *Required fees:* $1666; $833 per course. $416.50 per semester. Tuition and fees vary according to course load and degree level. *Financial support:* In 2011–12, 9 students received support, including 1 fellowship; research assistantships and teaching assistantships also available. Financial award application deadline: 2/15. *Unit head:* Dr. Ahmad Etebari, Chairperson, 603-862-3359, E-mail: ahmad.etebari@unh.edu. *Application contact:* Wendy Harris, Administrative Assistant, 603-862-3326, E-mail: wsbe.grad@unh.edu. Web site: http://wsbe.unh.edu/Accounting_and_Finance.

University of New Haven, Graduate School, School of Business, Program in Accounting, West Haven, CT 06516-1916. Offers financial accounting (MS); managerial accounting (MS). *Students:* 19 full-time (14 women), 22 part-time (13 women); includes 6 minority (4 Black or African American, non-Hispanic/Latino; 1 Asian, non-Hispanic/Latino; 1 Hispanic/Latino), 13 international. 12 applicants, 100% accepted, 9 enrolled. In 2011, 22 master's awarded. *Degree requirements:* For master's, thesis. *Application deadline:* Applications are processed on a rolling basis. Application fee: $50. *Expenses:* *Tuition:* Part-time $750 per credit. *Financial support:* Research assistantships with partial tuition reimbursements, teaching assistantships with partial tuition reimbursements, and Federal Work-Study available. Support available to part-time students. Financial award application deadline: 5/1; financial award applicants required to submit FAFSA. *Unit head:* Robert Wnek, Coordinator, 203-932-7111. *Application contact:* Eloise Gormley, Director of Graduate Admissions, 203-932-7449, Fax: 203-932-7137, E-mail: gradinfo@newhaven.edu.

University of New Haven, Graduate School, School of Business, Program in Business Administration, West Haven, CT 06516-1916. Offers accounting (MBA, Certificate), including CPA (MBA); business management (Certificate); business policy and strategy (MBA); finance (MBA), including CFA; global marketing (MBA); human resource management (Certificate); human resources management (MBA); international business (Certificate); marketing (Certificate); sports management (MBA); telecommunications management (Certificate); MBA/MPA. Part-time and evening/weekend programs available. *Students:* 215 full-time (106 women), 182 part-time (87 women); includes 73 minority (38 Black or African American, non-Hispanic/Latino; 2 American Indian or Alaska Native, non-Hispanic/Latino; 22 Asian, non-Hispanic/Latino; 11 Hispanic/Latino), 129 international. 179 applicants, 97% accepted, 93 enrolled. In 2011, 197 master's, 28 other advanced degrees awarded. *Degree requirements:* For master's, thesis or alternative. *Entrance requirements:* For master's, GMAT. Additional exam requirements/ recommendations for international students: Required—TOEFL (minimum score 520 paper-based; 190 computer-based; 70 iBT), IELTS (minimum score 5.5). *Application deadline:* For fall admission, 5/31 for international students; for winter admission, 10/15 for international students; for spring admission, 1/15 for international students. Applications are processed on a rolling basis. Application fee: $50. Electronic applications accepted. *Expenses:* Contact institution. *Financial support:* Research assistantships with partial tuition reimbursements, teaching assistantships with partial tuition reimbursements, Federal Work-Study, scholarships/grants, health care benefits, tuition waivers, and unspecified assistantships available. Support available to part-time students. Financial award applicants required to submit FAFSA. *Unit head:* Charles Coleman, Chairman, 203-932-7375. *Application contact:* Eloise Gormley, Director of Graduate Admissions, 203-932-7449, Fax: 203-932-7137, E-mail: gradinfo@newhaven.edu. Web site: http://www.newhaven.edu/7433/.

University of New Mexico, Robert O. Anderson Graduate School of Management, Department of Accounting, Albuquerque, NM 87131. Offers accounting (MBA); advanced accounting (M Acct); professional accounting (M Acct); tax accounting (M Acct); JD/M Acct. *Accreditation:* AACSB. Part-time and evening/weekend programs available. *Faculty:* 13 full-time (4 women), 3 part-time/adjunct (all women). In 2011, 72 master's awarded. *Degree requirements:* For master's, minimum GPA of 3.0. *Entrance requirements:* For master's, GMAT or GRE. Additional exam requirements/ recommendations for international students: Required—TOEFL (minimum score 550 paper-based; 213 computer-based; 79 iBT). *Application deadline:* For fall admission, 4/1 priority date for domestic students, 4/1 for international students; for spring admission, 10/1 priority date for domestic students, 10/1 for international students. Applications are processed on a rolling basis. Application fee: $50. Electronic applications accepted. *Financial support:* Fellowships, research assistantships, career-related internships or fieldwork, Federal Work-Study, scholarships/grants, and unspecified assistantships available. Support available to part-time students. *Faculty research:* Critical accounting, accounting pedagogy, theory, taxation, information fraud. *Unit head:* Dr. Craig White, Chair, 505-277-6471, Fax: 505-277-7108, E-mail: white@mgt.unm.edu. *Application contact:* Tina Armijo, Office Administrator, 505-277-6471, Fax: 505-277-7108, E-mail: profmacct@mgt.unm.edu. Web site: http://accounting.mgt.unm.edu.

University of New Orleans, Graduate School, College of Business Administration, Department of Accounting, Program in Accounting, New Orleans, LA 70148. Offers MS. *Accreditation:* AACSB. Part-time and evening/weekend programs available. *Degree requirements:* For master's, thesis optional. *Entrance requirements:* For master's, GMAT. Additional exam requirements/recommendations for international students: Required—TOEFL (minimum score 550 paper-based; 213 computer-based; 79 iBT). Electronic applications accepted.

The University of North Carolina at Chapel Hill, Kenan-Flagler Business School, Accounting Program, Chapel Hill, NC 27599. Offers MAC. *Entrance requirements:* For master's, GMAT. Additional exam requirements/recommendations for international students: Required—TOEFL. *Expenses:* Contact institution. *Faculty research:* Corporate taxation, international taxation, financial accounting, corporate governance, strategy.

The University of North Carolina at Chapel Hill, Kenan-Flagler Business School, Doctoral Program in Business Administration, Chapel Hill, NC 27599. Offers accounting (PhD); finance (PhD); marketing (PhD); operations management (PhD); organizational behavior (PhD); strategy (PhD). *Accreditation:* AACSB. *Degree requirements:* For doctorate, thesis/dissertation. *Entrance requirements:* For doctorate, GMAT or GRE General Test. Electronic applications accepted. *Expenses:* Contact institution.

The University of North Carolina at Charlotte, Graduate School, Belk College of Business, Department of Accounting, Charlotte, NC 28223-0001. Offers M Acc. *Accreditation:* AACSB. Part-time and evening/weekend programs available. *Faculty:* 10 full-time (2 women), 2 part-time/adjunct (0 women). *Students:* 70 full-time (35 women), 69 part-time (33 women); includes 27 minority (11 Black or African American, non-Hispanic/Latino; 7 Asian, non-Hispanic/Latino; 7 Hispanic/Latino; 2 Two or more races, non-Hispanic/Latino), 15 international. Average age 29. 171 applicants, 70% accepted, 74 enrolled. In 2011, 74 degrees awarded. *Degree requirements:* For master's, thesis or alternative. *Entrance requirements:* For master's, GMAT, minimum GPA of 3.0 in undergraduate major, 2.8 overall. Additional exam requirements/recommendations for international students: Required—TOEFL (minimum score 557 paper-based; 220 computer-based; 83 iBT). *Application deadline:* For fall admission, 7/15 for domestic students, 5/1 for international students; for spring admission, 11/15 for domestic students, 10/1 for international students. Applications are processed on a rolling basis. Application fee: $65 ($75 for international students). Electronic applications accepted. *Expenses:* Tuition, state resident: full-time $3689. Tuition, nonresident: full-time $15,226. *Required fees:* $2198. Tuition and fees vary according to course load and program. *Financial support:* Career-related internships or fieldwork, institutionally sponsored loans, scholarships/grants, and unspecified assistantships available. Support available to part-time students. Financial award application deadline: 4/1; financial award applicants required to submit FAFSA. *Faculty research:* Corporate financial reporting trends, use of latest software for accounting and business applications, latest developments in federal and international taxation. *Unit head:* Dr. Jack Cathey, Interim Department Chair, 704-687-7690, Fax: 704-687-6938, E-mail: jmcathey@uncc.edu. *Application contact:* Kathy B. Giddings, Director of Graduate Admissions, 704-687-5503, Fax: 704-687-3279, E-mail: gradadm@uncc.edu. Web site: http://belkcollege.uncc.edu/about-college/departments/accounting.

The University of North Carolina at Greensboro, Graduate School, Bryan School of Business and Economics, Department of Accounting and Finance, Greensboro, NC 27412-5001. Offers accounting (MS); accounting systems (MS); financial accounting and reporting (MS); financial analysis (PMC); tax concentration (MS). *Accreditation:* AACSB. *Entrance requirements:* For master's, GMAT, GRE General Test, previous course work in accounting and business. Additional exam requirements/ recommendations for international students: Required—TOEFL. Electronic applications accepted.

The University of North Carolina Wilmington, School of Business, Program in Accountancy, Wilmington, NC 28403-3297. Offers MSA. *Degree requirements:* For master's, thesis or alternative, portfolio project. *Entrance requirements:* For master's, GMAT. Additional exam requirements/recommendations for international students: Required—TOEFL (minimum score 550 paper-based; 217 computer-based; 79 iBT), IELTS (minimum score 6.5).

University of North Dakota, Graduate School, College of Business and Public Administration, Department of Accountancy, Grand Forks, ND 58202. Offers M Acc. Part-time programs available. *Degree requirements:* For master's, comprehensive exam, thesis or alternative, final exam. *Entrance requirements:* For master's, GMAT, minimum GPA of 3.0. Additional exam requirements/recommendations for international students: Required—TOEFL (minimum score 550 paper-based; 213 computer-based; 79 iBT), IELTS (minimum score 6.5). Electronic applications accepted.

University of Northern Colorado, Graduate School, Monfort College of Business, Greeley, CO 80639. Offers accounting (MA).

University of Northern Iowa, Graduate College, College of Business Administration, Program in Accounting, Cedar Falls, IA 50614. Offers M Acc. *Students:* 30 full-time (16 women), 1 part-time (0 women); includes 2 minority (1 Black or African American, non-Hispanic/Latino; 1 Asian, non-Hispanic/Latino). 61 applicants, 46% accepted, 21 enrolled. In 2011, 21 master's awarded. *Degree requirements:* For master's, thesis or alternative. *Entrance requirements:* For master's, GMAT. Additional exam requirements/ recommendations for international students: Required—TOEFL (minimum score 575 paper-based; 230 computer-based; 89 iBT). *Application deadline:* For fall admission, 8/1 priority date for domestic students. Applications are processed on a rolling basis. Application fee: $50 ($70 for international students). *Expenses:* Tuition, state resident: full-time $7476. Tuition, nonresident: full-time $16,410. *Required fees:* $942. *Financial support:* Application deadline: 2/1. *Unit head:* Dr. Martha Wartick, Head, 319-273-7754, Fax: 319-273-2922, E-mail: marty.wartick@uni.edu. *Application contact:* Laurie S. Russell, Record Analyst, 319-273-2623, Fax: 319-273-2885, E-mail: laurie.russell@uni.edu. Web site: http://www.cba.uni.edu/accounting/.

University of North Florida, Coggin College of Business, MACC Program, Jacksonville, FL 32224. Offers M Acc. *Accreditation:* AACSB. Part-time and evening/ weekend programs available. *Faculty:* 14 full-time (1 woman), 1 part-time/adjunct (0 women). *Students:* 24 full-time (11 women), 24 part-time (13 women); includes 4 minority (1 Black or African American, non-Hispanic/Latino; 2 Asian, non-Hispanic/Latino; 1 Two or more races, non-Hispanic/Latino), 1 international. Average age 28. 36 applicants, 61% accepted, 13 enrolled. In 2011, 25 master's awarded. *Entrance requirements:* For master's, GMAT or GRE, U.S. bachelor's degree from regionally-accredited university or equivalent foreign degree. Additional exam requirements/ recommendations for international students: Required—TOEFL (minimum score 550 paper-based; 213 computer-based; 79 iBT). *Application deadline:* For fall admission, 7/1 priority date for domestic students, 5/1 for international students; for spring admission, 11/1 priority date for domestic students, 10/1 for international students. Applications are processed on a rolling basis. Application fee: $30. Electronic applications accepted. *Expenses:* Tuition, state resident: full-time $8793; part-time $366.38 per credit hour. Tuition, nonresident: full-time $23,502; part-time $979.24 per credit hour. *Required fees:* $1384; $57.66 per credit hour. Tuition and fees vary according to course load and program. *Financial support:* In 2011–12, 12 students received support. Teaching assistantships, career-related internships or fieldwork, Federal Work-Study, and tuition waivers (partial) available. Financial award application deadline: 4/1; financial award applicants required to submit FAFSA. *Faculty research:* Enterprise-wide risk management, accounting input in the strategic planning process, accounting information systems, taxation issues in lawsuits and damage awards, database design. *Total annual research expenditures:* $21,539. *Unit head:* Dr. Charles Calhoun, Chair, 904-620-2630, Fax: 904-620-3861, E-mail: ccalhoun@unf.edu. *Application contact:* Lillith Richardson, Assistant Director, The Graduate School, 904-620-1360, Fax: 904-620-1362, E-mail: graduateschool@unf.edu. Web site: http://www.unf.edu/coggin/academics/graduate/macc.aspx.

University of North Florida, Coggin College of Business, MBA Program, Jacksonville, FL 32224. Offers accounting (MBA); construction management (MBA); e-commerce (MBA); economics (MBA); finance (MBA); human resource management (MBA); international business (MBA); logistics (MBA); management applications (MBA). *Accreditation:* AACSB. Part-time and evening/weekend programs available. *Faculty:* 19 full-time (6 women), 1 part-time/adjunct (0 women). *Students:* 145 full-time (57 women), 277 part-time (108 women); includes 67 minority (19 Black or African American, non-Hispanic/Latino; 21 Asian, non-Hispanic/Latino; 20 Hispanic/Latino; 7 Two or more races, non-Hispanic/Latino), 34 international. Average age 29. 200 applicants, 48% accepted, 70 enrolled. In 2011, 153 master's awarded. *Entrance requirements:* For master's, GMAT or GRE, U.S. bachelor's degree from regionally-accredited university or equivalent foreign degree. Additional exam requirements/recommendations for international students: Required—TOEFL (minimum score 550 paper-based; 213 computer-based; 79 iBT). *Application deadline:* For fall admission, 7/1 priority date for domestic students, 5/1 for international students; for spring admission, 11/1 priority date for domestic students, 10/1 for international students. Applications are processed on a rolling basis. Application fee: $30. *Expenses:* Tuition, state resident: full-time $8793; part-time $366.38 per credit hour. Tuition, nonresident: full-time $23,502; part-time $979.24 per credit hour. *Required fees:* $1384; $57.66 per credit hour. Tuition and fees vary according to course load and program. *Financial support:* In 2011–12, 55 students received support, including 1 teaching assistantship (averaging $5,333 per year); research assistantships, Federal Work-Study, and tuition waivers (partial) also available. Support available to part-time students. Financial award application deadline: 4/1; financial award applicants required to submit FAFSA. *Faculty research:* Performance measures, costing, and inventory issues in logistics and supply chain management; inter-organizational systems; international management and marketing practices; e-commerce; organizational learning and socialization processes. *Total annual research expenditures:* $7,686. *Unit head:* Dr. C. Bruce Kavan, Chair, 904-620-2780, Fax: 904-620-2832. *Application contact:* Cheryl Campbell, Graduate Advisor, 904-620-2575, Fax: 904-620-2832, E-mail: ccampbell@unf.edu. Web site: http://www.unf.edu/coggin/academics/graduate/mba.aspx.

University of North Texas, Toulouse Graduate School, College of Business, Department of Accounting, Denton, TX 76203. Offers accounting (MS, PhD); taxation (MS). *Accreditation:* AACSB. Part-time programs available. *Degree requirements:* For master's, comprehensive exam; for doctorate, thesis/dissertation. *Entrance requirements:* For master's, GMAT or GRE General Test, essay, 3 letters of recommendation, resume; for doctorate, GMAT or GRE General Test, statement of purpose, resume, 3 letters of recommendation. Additional exam requirements/ recommendations for international students: Recommended—TOEFL (minimum score 550 paper-based; 213 computer-based). Electronic applications accepted. *Expenses:* Tuition, state resident: part-time $100 per credit hour. Tuition, nonresident: part-time $413 per credit hour. *Faculty research:* Empirical tax research issues, empirical financial accounting issues, problems and issues in public interest areas, historical perspective for accounting issues, behavioral issues in auditing and accounting systems.

University of Notre Dame, Mendoza College of Business, Program in Accountancy, Notre Dame, IN 46556. Offers financial reporting and assurance services (MS); tax services (MS). *Accreditation:* AACSB. *Faculty:* 36 full-time (4 women), 15 part-time/ adjunct (0 women). *Students:* 81 full-time (38 women); includes 9 minority (2 Black or African American, non-Hispanic/Latino; 4 Asian, non-Hispanic/Latino; 3 Hispanic/ Latino), 16 international. Average age 22. 307 applicants, 35% accepted, 81 enrolled. In 2011, 102 master's awarded. *Entrance requirements:* For master's, GMAT. Additional exam requirements/recommendations for international students: Required—TOEFL (minimum score 630 paper-based; 267 computer-based; 109 iBT). *Application deadline:* For fall admission, 10/31 for domestic and international students; for spring admission, 5/1 for domestic and international students. Applications are processed on a rolling basis. Application fee: $50 ($100 for international students). Electronic applications accepted. *Financial support:* In 2011–12, 79 students received support, including 79 fellowships (averaging $16,082 per year); scholarships/grants and unspecified assistantships also available. Financial award application deadline: 2/28; financial award applicants required to submit FAFSA. *Faculty research:* Stock valuation, accounting information in decision-making, choice of accounting method, taxes cost on capital. *Unit* *head:* Dr. Michael H. Morris, Director, 574-631-9732, Fax: 574-631-5300, E-mail: msacct.1@nd.edu. *Application contact:* Helen High, Assistant Director of Admissions and Student Services, 574-631-6499, Fax: 574-631-5300, E-mail: msacct.1@nd.edu. Web site: http://business.nd.edu/msa.

University of Oklahoma, Michael F. Price College of Business, School of Accounting, Norman, OK 73019. Offers M Acc. *Accreditation:* AACSB. Part-time programs available. *Faculty:* 11 full-time (4 women), 1 part-time/adjunct (0 women). *Students:* 28 full-time (16 women), 4 part-time (2 women); includes 7 minority (2 American Indian or Alaska Native, non-Hispanic/Latino; 4 Asian, non-Hispanic/Latino; 1 Two or more races, non-Hispanic/Latino), 8 international. Average age 26. 33 applicants, 64% accepted, 15 enrolled. In 2011, 40 degrees awarded. *Degree requirements:* For master's, comprehensive exam. *Entrance requirements:* For master's, GMAT, minimum GPA of 3.0 in last 60 hours. Additional exam requirements/recommendations for international students: Required—TOEFL (minimum score 550 paper-based; 79 iBT). *Application deadline:* For fall admission, 6/15 for domestic students, 3/1 for international students; for spring admission, 11/15 for domestic students, 9/1 for international students. Applications are processed on a rolling basis. Application fee: $40 ($90 for international students). Electronic applications accepted. *Expenses:* Tuition, state resident: full-time $4087; part-time $170.30 per credit hour. Tuition, nonresident: full-time $14,875; part-time $619.80 per credit hour. *Required fees:* $2659; $100.25 per credit hour. Tuition and fees vary according to course load and degree level. *Financial support:* In 2011–12, 6 research assistantships with partial tuition reimbursements (averaging $13,247 per year), 5 teaching assistantships with partial tuition reimbursements (averaging $12,155 per year) were awarded; career-related internships or fieldwork, scholarships/grants, and unspecified assistantships also available. Financial award applicants required to submit FAFSA. *Faculty research:* Auditing, capital markets, corporate valuation, ethics, financial accounting. *Unit head:* Dr. Frances L. Ayres, Director, 405-325-4221, Fax: 405-325-2096, E-mail: fayres@ou.edu. *Application contact:* Amber Hasbrook, Academic Counselor, 405-325-4107, Fax: 405-325-7753, E-mail: amber.hasbrook@ou.edu. Web site: http://price.ou.edu/accounting.

See Display on page 153 and Close-Up on page 253.

University of Oregon, Graduate School, Charles H. Lundquist College of Business, Department of Accounting, Eugene, OR 97403. Offers M Actg, PhD. *Accreditation:* AACSB. Part-time programs available. *Degree requirements:* For doctorate, thesis/dissertation, 2 comprehensive exams. *Entrance requirements:* For master's, GMAT, minimum GPA of 3.0, bachelor's degree in accounting or equivalent; for doctorate, GMAT. Additional exam requirements/recommendations for international students: Required—TOEFL. *Faculty research:* Empirical financial accounting, effects of regulation on accounting standards, use of protocol analysis as a research methodology in accounting.

University of Pennsylvania, Wharton School, Accounting Department, Philadelphia, PA 19104. Offers MBA, PhD. *Accreditation:* AACSB. Terminal master's awarded for partial completion of doctoral program. *Degree requirements:* For doctorate, thesis/dissertation. *Entrance requirements:* For master's, GMAT; for doctorate, GMAT or GRE. *Expenses: Tuition:* Full-time $26,660; part-time $4944 per course. *Required fees:* $2318; $291 per course. Tuition and fees vary according to course load, degree level and program. *Faculty research:* Financial reporting, information disclosure, performance measurement, executive compensation, corporate governance.

University of Phoenix–Atlanta Campus, School of Business, Sandy Springs, GA 30350-4153. Offers accounting (MBA); business administration (MBA); global management (MBA); human resources management (MBA, MM); management (MM); marketing (MBA); public administration (MM). Evening/weekend programs available. Postbaccalaureate distance learning degree programs offered. *Degree requirements:* For master's, thesis (for some programs). *Entrance requirements:* For master's, minimum undergraduate GPA of 3.0, 3 years of work experience. Additional exam requirements/recommendations for international students: Required—TOEFL (minimum score 550 paper-based; 213 computer-based; 79 iBT).

University of Phoenix–Augusta Campus, School of Business, Augusta, GA 30909-4583. Offers accounting (MBA); business administration (MBA); business and management (MBA, MM); global management (MBA); human resources management (MBA, MM); management (MM); marketing (MBA); public administration (MBA, MM). Postbaccalaureate distance learning degree programs offered.

University of Phoenix–Austin Campus, School of Business, Austin, TX 78759. Offers accounting (MBA); business administration (MBA); business and management (MBA); e-business (MBA); global management (MBA); human resources management (MBA, MM); management (MM); marketing (MBA); public administration (MBA). Postbaccalaureate distance learning degree programs offered.

University of Phoenix–Bay Area Campus, School of Business, San Jose, CA 95134-1805. Offers accountancy (MS); accounting (MBA); business administration (MBA, DBA); energy management (MBA); global management (MBA); health care management (MBA); human resource management (MBA); human resources management (MM); management (MM); marketing (MBA); organizational leadership (DM); project management (MBA); public administration (MPA); technology management (MBA). Evening/weekend programs available. Postbaccalaureate distance learning degree programs offered (no on-campus study). *Degree requirements:* For master's, thesis (for some programs). *Entrance requirements:* For master's, minimum undergraduate GPA of 3.0, 3 years of work experience. Additional exam requirements/recommendations for international students: Required—TOEFL (minimum score 550 paper-based; 213 computer-based; 79 iBT). Electronic applications accepted.

University of Phoenix–Birmingham Campus, College of Graduate Business and Management, Birmingham, AL 35244. Offers accounting (MBA); business administration (MBA); global management (MBA); human resources management (MBA, MM); management (MM); marketing (MBA); public administration (MM).

University of Phoenix–Central Florida Campus, School of Business, Maitland, FL 32751-7057. Offers accounting (MBA); business administration (MBA); business and management (MM); global management (MBA); human resources management (MBA, MM); management (MM); marketing (MBA); public administration (MBA, MM). Evening/weekend programs available. *Degree requirements:* For master's, thesis (for some programs). *Entrance requirements:* For master's, minimum undergraduate GPA of 3.0, 3 years work experience. Additional exam requirements/recommendations for international students: Required—TOEFL (minimum score 550 paper-based; 213 computer-based; 79 iBT). Electronic applications accepted.

University of Phoenix–Central Valley Campus, School of Business, Fresno, CA 93720-1562. Offers accounting (MBA); business administration (MBA); global management (MBA); human resources management (MBA, MM); management (MM); marketing (MBA); public administration (MBA, MM).

University of Phoenix–Charlotte Campus, School of Business, Charlotte, NC 28273-3409. Offers accounting (MBA); business administration (MBA); global management (MBA). Evening/weekend programs available. *Degree requirements:* For master's, thesis (for some programs). *Entrance requirements:* For master's, minimum undergraduate GPA of 3.0, 3 years work experience. Additional exam requirements/recommendations for international students: Required—TOEFL (minimum score 550 paper-based; 213 computer-based; 79 iBT). Electronic applications accepted.

University of Phoenix–Chattanooga Campus, School of Business, Chattanooga, TN 37421-3707. Offers accounting (MBA); business administration (MBA); business and management (MBA); global management (MBA); human resources management (MBA, MM); management (MM); marketing (MBA); public administration (MBA, MM). Postbaccalaureate distance learning degree programs offered.

University of Phoenix–Cincinnati Campus, School of Business, West Chester, OH 45069-4875. Offers accounting (MBA); business administration (MBA); global management (MBA); human resources management (MBA, MM); management (MM); marketing (MBA); public administration (MM). Evening/weekend programs available. *Degree requirements:* For master's, thesis (for some programs). *Entrance requirements:* For master's, minimum undergraduate GPA of 3.0, 3 years of work experience. Additional exam requirements/recommendations for international students: Required—TOEFL (minimum score 550 paper-based; 213 computer-based; 79 iBT). Electronic applications accepted.

University of Phoenix–Cleveland Campus, School of Business, Independence, OH 44131-2194. Offers accounting (MBA); business administration (MBA); global management (MBA); human resources management (MBA, MM); management (MM); marketing (MBA); public administration (MBA, MM). Evening/weekend programs available. Postbaccalaureate distance learning degree programs offered (no on-campus study). *Degree requirements:* For master's, thesis (for some programs). *Entrance requirements:* For master's, minimum undergraduate GPA of 3.0, 3 years of work experience. Additional exam requirements/recommendations for international students: Required—TOEFL (minimum score 550 paper-based; 213 computer-based; 79 iBT). Electronic applications accepted.

University of Phoenix–Columbus Georgia Campus, School of Business, Columbus, GA 31904-6321. Offers accounting (MBA); business administration (MBA); global management (MBA); human resources management (MBA, MM); management (MM); marketing (MBA); public administration (MBA). Evening/weekend programs available. *Degree requirements:* For master's, thesis (for some programs). *Entrance requirements:* For master's, minimum undergraduate GPA of 3.0, 3 years of work experience. Additional exam requirements/recommendations for international students: Required—TOEFL (minimum score 550 paper-based; 213 computer-based; 79 iBT). Electronic applications accepted.

University of Phoenix–Columbus Ohio Campus, School of Business, Columbus, OH 43240-4032. Offers accounting (MBA); business administration (MBA); global management (MBA); human resources management (MBA, MM); management (MM); marketing (MBA); public administration (MM). Evening/weekend programs available. Postbaccalaureate distance learning degree programs offered. *Degree requirements:* For master's, thesis (for some programs). *Entrance requirements:* For master's, minimum undergraduate GPA of 3.0, 3 years of work experience. Additional exam requirements/recommendations for international students: Required—TOEFL (minimum score 550 paper-based; 213 computer-based; 79 iBT). Electronic applications accepted.

University of Phoenix–Dallas Campus, School of Business, Dallas, TX 75251-2009. Offers accounting (MBA); business administration (MBA); global management (MBA); human resources management (MBA, MM); management (MM); marketing (MBA); public administration (MBA, MM). Evening/weekend programs available. Postbaccalaureate distance learning degree programs offered. *Degree requirements:* For master's, thesis (for some programs). *Entrance requirements:* For master's, 3 years of work experience, minimum undergraduate GPA of 3.0. Additional exam requirements/recommendations for international students: Required—TOEFL (minimum score 550 paper-based; 213 computer-based; 79 iBT). Electronic applications accepted.

University of Phoenix–Denver Campus, School of Business, Lone Tree, CO 80124-5453. Offers accountancy (MSA); accounting (MBA); business administration (MBA); e-business (MBA); global management (MBA); human resources management (MBA, MM); management (MM); marketing (MBA); public administration (MBA, MM). Evening/weekend programs available. Postbaccalaureate distance learning degree programs offered. *Degree requirements:* For master's, thesis (for some programs). *Entrance requirements:* For master's, minimum undergraduate GPA of 3.0, 3 years work experience. Additional exam requirements/recommendations for international students: Required—TOEFL (minimum score 550 paper-based; 213 computer-based; 79 iBT). Electronic applications accepted.

University of Phoenix–Des Moines Campus, School of Business, Des Moines, IA 50266. Offers accounting (MBA); business administration (MBA); global management (MBA); human resources management (MBA, MM); management (MM); marketing (MBA); public administration (MBA, MM). Postbaccalaureate distance learning degree programs offered.

University of Phoenix–Eastern Washington Campus, School of Business, Spokane Valley, WA 99212-2531. Offers accounting (MBA); business administration (MBA); human resources management (MBA); marketing (MBA); public administration (MBA). Evening/weekend programs available. *Degree requirements:* For master's, thesis (for some programs). *Entrance requirements:* For master's, minimum undergraduate GPA of 3.0, 3 years of work experience. Additional exam requirements/recommendations for international students: Required—TOEFL (minimum score 550 paper-based; 213 computer-based; 79 iBT). Electronic applications accepted.

University of Phoenix–Harrisburg Campus, School of Business, Harrisburg, PA 17112. Offers accounting (MBA); business administration (MBA); business and management (MBA); global management (MBA); human resources management (MBA, MM); management (MM); marketing (MBA); public administration (MBA, MM). Postbaccalaureate distance learning degree programs offered.

University of Phoenix–Hawaii Campus, School of Business, Honolulu, HI 96813-4317. Offers accounting (MBA); business administration (MBA); global management (MBA); human resources management (MBA, MM); management (MM); marketing (MBA); public administration (MBA, MM). Evening/weekend programs available. *Degree requirements:* For master's, thesis (for some programs). *Entrance requirements:* For master's, minimum undergraduate GPA of 3.0, 3 years of work experience. Additional exam requirements/recommendations for international students: Required—TOEFL (minimum score 550 paper-based; 213 computer-based; 79 iBT). Electronic applications accepted.

University of Phoenix–Houston Campus, School of Business, Houston, TX 77079-2004. Offers accounting (MBA); business administration (MBA); global management (MBA); human resources management (MBA, MM); management (MM); marketing (MBA); public administration (MBA, MM). Evening/weekend programs available. Postbaccalaureate distance learning degree programs offered. *Degree requirements:* For master's, thesis (for some programs). *Entrance requirements:* For master's, 3 years of work experience, minimum undergraduate GPA of 3.0. Additional exam requirements/recommendations for international students: Required—TOEFL (minimum score 550 paper-based; 213 computer-based; 79 iBT). Electronic applications accepted.

University of Phoenix–Idaho Campus, School of Business, Meridian, ID 83642-5114. Offers accounting (MBA); administration (MBA); global management (MBA); human resources management (MBA, MM); management (MM); marketing (MBA); public administration (MM). Evening/weekend programs available. Postbaccalaureate distance learning degree programs offered. *Degree requirements:* For master's, thesis (for some programs). *Entrance requirements:* For master's, 3 years of work experience, minimum undergraduate GPA of 3.0. Additional exam requirements/recommendations for international students: Required—TOEFL (minimum score 550 paper-based; 213 computer-based). Electronic applications accepted.

University of Phoenix–Indianapolis Campus, School of Business, Indianapolis, IN 46250-932. Offers accounting (MBA); business administration (MBA); global management (MBA); human resources management (MBA, MM); management (MM); marketing (MBA); public administration (MM). Evening/weekend programs available. *Degree requirements:* For master's, thesis (for some programs). *Entrance requirements:* For master's, minimum undergraduate GPA of 3.0, 3 years of work experience. Additional exam requirements/recommendations for international students: Required—TOEFL (minimum score 550 paper-based; 213 computer-based). Electronic applications accepted.

University of Phoenix–Jersey City Campus, School of Business, Jersey City, NJ 07310. Offers accounting (MBA); business administration (MBA); global management (MBA); human resources management (MBA, MM); management (MM); marketing (MBA); public administration (MBA, MM).

University of Phoenix–Kansas City Campus, School of Business, Kansas City, MO 64131-4517. Offers accounting (MBA); business administration (MBA); global management (MBA); human resources management (MBA, MM); management (MM); marketing (MBA); public administration (MBA). Evening/weekend programs available. *Degree requirements:* For master's, thesis (for some programs). *Entrance requirements:* For master's, minimum undergraduate GPA of 3.0, 3 years of work experience. Additional exam requirements/recommendations for international students: Required—TOEFL (minimum score 550 paper-based; 213 computer-based). Electronic applications accepted.

University of Phoenix–Las Vegas Campus, School of Business, Las Vegas, NV 89128. Offers accounting (MBA); business administration (MBA); global management (MBA); human resources management (MBA, MM); management (MM); marketing (MBA); public administration (MM). Evening/weekend programs available. Postbaccalaureate distance learning degree programs offered (no on-campus study). *Degree requirements:* For master's, thesis (for some programs). *Entrance requirements:* For master's, minimum undergraduate GPA of 3.0, 3 years of work experience. Additional exam requirements/recommendations for international students: Required—TOEFL (minimum score 550 paper-based; 213 computer-based; 79 iBT). Electronic applications accepted.

University of Phoenix–Louisiana Campus, School of Business, Metairie, LA 70001-2082. Offers accounting (MBA); business administration (MBA); global management (MBA); human resources management (MBA, MM); management (MM); marketing (MBA); public administration (MBA). Evening/weekend programs available. *Degree requirements:* For master's, thesis (for some programs). *Entrance requirements:* For master's, minimum undergraduate GPA of 3.0, 3 years work experience. Additional exam requirements/recommendations for international students: Required—TOEFL (minimum score 550 paper-based; 213 computer-based; 79 iBT). Electronic applications accepted.

University of Phoenix–Madison Campus, School of Business, Madison, WI 53718-2416. Offers accounting (MBA); business and management (MBA); e-business (MBA); global management (MBA); human resources management (MBA, MM); management (MM); marketing (MBA); public administration (MBA).

University of Phoenix–Memphis Campus, School of Business, Cordova, TN 38018. Offers accounting (MBA); business and management (MBA); e-business (MBA); global management (MBA); human resources management (MBA, MM); management (MM); marketing (MBA); public administration (MBA, MM).

University of Phoenix–Milwaukee Campus, School of Business, Milwaukee, WI 53045. Offers accounting (MS); business administration (MBA, DBA); human resources management (MM); management (MM); organizational leadership (DM); public administration (MPA).

University of Phoenix–Minneapolis/St. Louis Park Campus, School of Business, St. Louis Park, MN 55426. Offers accounting (MBA); business administration (MBA); global management (MBA); human resources management (MBA); management (MM); marketing (MBA); public administration (MBA).

University of Phoenix–New Mexico Campus, School of Business, Albuquerque, NM 87113-1570. Offers accounting (MBA); business administration (MBA); global management (MBA); human resources management (MBA, MM); management (MM); marketing (MBA). Evening/weekend programs available. *Degree requirements:* For master's, thesis (for some programs). *Entrance requirements:* For master's, 3 years of work experience, minimum undergraduate GPA of 3.0. Additional exam requirements/recommendations for international students: Required—TOEFL (minimum score 550 paper-based; 213 computer-based; 79 iBT). Electronic applications accepted.

University of Phoenix–Northern Nevada Campus, School of Business, Reno, NV 89521-5862. Offers accounting (MBA); business administration (MBA); global management (MBA); human resources management (MBA, MM); management (MM); marketing (MBA); public administration (MBA, MM).

University of Phoenix–Northern Virginia Campus, School of Business, Reston, VA 20190. Offers business administration (MBA); public accounting (MPA). Evening/weekend programs available. Postbaccalaureate distance learning degree programs offered. *Entrance requirements:* For master's, minimum undergraduate GPA of 2.5 from accredited university, 3 years of work experience, citizen of the United States or valid visa. Additional exam requirements/recommendations for international students: Required—TOEFL (minimum score 79 iBT), TOEFL (minimum score 213 paper, 79 iBT), TOEIC, IELTS or Berlitz. Electronic applications accepted.

University of Phoenix–North Florida Campus, School of Business, Jacksonville, FL 32216-0959. Offers accounting (MBA); business administration (MBA); global management (MBA); human resources management (MBA, MM); management (MM); marketing (MBA); public administration (MBA, MM). Evening/weekend programs available. *Degree requirements:* For master's, thesis (for some programs). *Entrance requirements:* For master's, minimum undergraduate GPA of 3.0, 3 years work experience. Additional exam requirements/recommendations for international students: Required—TOEFL (minimum score 550 paper-based; 213 computer-based; 79 iBT). Electronic applications accepted.

University of Phoenix–Northwest Arkansas Campus, School of Business, Rogers, AR 72756-9615. Offers accounting (MBA); business and management (MBA); global management (MBA); human resources management (MBA, MM); management (MM); marketing (MBA); public administration (MBA, MM).

University of Phoenix–Oklahoma City Campus, School of Business, Oklahoma City, OK 73116-8244. Offers accounting (MBA); business administration (MBA); global management (MBA); human resource management (MBA); management (MM); marketing (MBA). Evening/weekend programs available. *Degree requirements:* For master's, thesis (for some programs). *Entrance requirements:* For master's, minimum undergraduate GPA of 3.0, 3 years of work experience. Additional exam requirements/recommendations for international students: Required—TOEFL (minimum score 550 paper-based; 213 computer-based; 79 iBT). Electronic applications accepted.

University of Phoenix–Omaha Campus, School of Business, Omaha, NE 68154-5240. Offers accounting (MBA); business and management (MBA); global management (MBA); human resources management (MBA, MM); management (MM); marketing (MBA); public administration (MBA, MM).

University of Phoenix–Online Campus, School of Business, Phoenix, AZ 85034-7209. Offers accountancy (MS); accounting (MBA); business administration (MBA); energy management (MBA); global management (MBA); health care management (MBA); human resource management (MBA); human resources management (MM); international (MM); management (MM); marketing (MBA, Graduate Certificate); organizational management (MA); project management (MBA, Graduate Certificate); public administration (MBA, MM, MPA); technology management (MBA). Evening/weekend programs available. Postbaccalaureate distance learning degree programs offered. *Students:* 18,883 full-time (11,868 women); includes 6,302 minority (4,182 Black or African American, non-Hispanic/Latino; 121 American Indian or Alaska Native, non-Hispanic/Latino; 478 Asian, non-Hispanic/Latino; 1,252 Hispanic/Latino; 121 Native Hawaiian or other Pacific Islander, non-Hispanic/Latino; 148 Two or more races, non-Hispanic/Latino), 1,000 international. Average age 37. *Entrance requirements:* Additional exam requirements/recommendations for international students: Required—TOEFL, TOEIC (Test of English as an International Communication), Berlitz Online English Proficiency Exam, Pearson Test of English, or IELTS. *Application deadline:* Applications are processed on a rolling basis. Application fee: $45. Electronic applications accepted. *Expenses: Tuition:* Full-time $17,160. *Required fees:* $920. One-time fee: $45 full-time. Full-time tuition and fees vary according to course load, degree level, campus/location and program. *Financial support:* Scholarships/grants available. Financial award applicants required to submit FAFSA. *Application contact:* 866-766-0766. Web site: http://www.phoenix.edu/colleges_divisions/business.html.

University of Phoenix–Oregon Campus, School of Business, Tigard, OR 97223. Offers accounting (MBA); business administration (MBA); global management (MBA); human resource management (MM); human resources management (MBA); management (MM); marketing (MBA); public administration (MM). Evening/weekend programs available. *Degree requirements:* For master's, thesis (for some programs). *Entrance requirements:* For master's, minimum undergraduate GPA of 3.0, 3 years of work experience. Additional exam requirements/recommendations for international students: Required—TOEFL (minimum score 550 paper-based; 213 computer-based; 79 iBT). Electronic applications accepted.

University of Phoenix–Philadelphia Campus, School of Business, Wayne, PA 19087-2121. Offers accounting (MBA); business administration (MBA); global management (MBA); human resources management (MBA, MM); management (MM); marketing (MBA); public administration (MM). Evening/weekend programs available. *Degree requirements:* For master's, thesis (for some programs). *Entrance requirements:* For master's, minimum undergraduate GPA of 3.0, 3 years work experience. Additional exam requirements/recommendations for international students: Required—TOEFL (minimum score 550 paper-based; 213 computer-based; 79 iBT). Electronic applications accepted.

University of Phoenix–Phoenix Main Campus, School of Business, Tempe, AZ 85282-2371. Offers accounting (MBA, MS); business administration (MBA); energy management (MBA); global management (MBA); health care management (MBA); human resource management (MBA); management (MM); marketing (MBA); project management (MBA); public administration (MPA); technology management (MBA). Evening/weekend programs available. Postbaccalaureate distance learning degree programs offered. *Students:* 1,151 full-time (531 women); includes 310 minority (99 Black or African American, non-Hispanic/Latino; 10 American Indian or Alaska Native, non-Hispanic/Latino; 39 Asian, non-Hispanic/Latino; 130 Hispanic/Latino; 15 Native Hawaiian or other Pacific Islander, non-Hispanic/Latino; 17 Two or more races, non-Hispanic/Latino), 63 international. Average age 34. *Entrance requirements:* Additional exam requirements/recommendations for international students: Required—TOEFL, TOEIC (Test of English as an International Communication), Berlitz Online English Proficiency Exam, Pearson Test of English, or IELTS. *Application deadline:* Applications are processed on a rolling basis. Application fee: $45. Electronic applications accepted. *Expenses:* Contact institution. *Financial support:* Scholarships/grants available. Financial award applicants required to submit FAFSA. *Application contact:* 866-766-0766. Web site: http://www.phoenix.edu/colleges_divisions/business.html.

University of Phoenix–Pittsburgh Campus, School of Business, Pittsburgh, PA 15276. Offers accounting (MBA); business administration (MBA); global management (MBA); human resources management (MBA, MM); management (MM); marketing (MBA); public administration (MBA, MM). Evening/weekend programs available. *Degree requirements:* For master's, thesis (for some programs). *Entrance requirements:* For master's, minimum undergraduate GPA of 3.0, 3 years work experience. Additional exam requirements/recommendations for international students: Required—TOEFL (minimum score 550 paper-based; 213 computer-based; 79 iBT). Electronic applications accepted.

University of Phoenix–Puerto Rico Campus, School of Business, Guaynabo, PR 00968. Offers accounting (MBA); energy management (MBA); global management (MBA); human resource management (MBA); marketing (MBA); project management (MBA); small business administration (MBA). Evening/weekend programs available. *Degree requirements:* For master's, thesis (for some programs). *Entrance requirements:* For master's, minimum undergraduate GPA of 3.0, 3 years work experience. Additional exam requirements/recommendations for international students: Required—TOEFL (minimum score 550 paper-based; 213 computer-based; 79 iBT). Electronic applications accepted.

University of Phoenix–Raleigh Campus, School of Business, Raleigh, NC 27606. Offers accounting (MBA); business administration (MBA); e-business (MBA); global management (MBA); human resources management (MBA); marketing (MBA).

University of Phoenix–Richmond Campus, School of Business, Richmond, VA 23230. Offers accounting (MBA); business administration (MBA); global management (MBA); human resources management (MBA, MM); management (MM); marketing (MBA); public administration (MBA, MM). Evening/weekend programs available. *Degree requirements:* For master's, thesis (for some programs). *Entrance requirements:* For master's, minimum undergraduate GPA of 3.0, 3 years work experience. Additional exam requirements/recommendations for international students: Required—TOEFL (minimum score 550 paper-based; 213 computer-based; 79 iBT). Electronic applications accepted.

University of Phoenix–Sacramento Valley Campus, School of Business, Sacramento, CA 95833-3632. Offers accounting (MBA); business administration (MBA); global management (MBA); human resources management (MBA, MM); management (MM); marketing (MBA); public administration (MBA, MM). Evening/weekend programs available. *Degree requirements:* For master's, thesis (for some programs). *Entrance* *requirements:* For master's, minimum undergraduate GPA of 3.0, 3 years work experience. Additional exam requirements/recommendations for international students: Required—TOEFL (minimum score 550 paper-based; 213 computer-based; 79 iBT). Electronic applications accepted.

University of Phoenix–St. Louis Campus, School of Business, St. Louis, MO 63043-4828. Offers accounting (MBA); business administration (MBA); global management (MBA); human resources management (MBA, MM); management (MM); marketing (MBA); public administration (MM). Evening/weekend programs available. *Degree requirements:* For master's, thesis (for some programs). *Entrance requirements:* For master's, 3 years of work experience, minimum undergraduate GPA of 3.0. Additional exam requirements/recommendations for international students: Required—TOEFL (minimum score 550 paper-based; 213 computer-based; 79 iBT). Electronic applications accepted.

University of Phoenix–San Antonio Campus, School of Business, San Antonio, TX 78230. Offers accounting (MBA); business administration (MBA); e-business (MBA); global management (MBA); human resources management (MBA, MM); management (MM); marketing (MBA); public administration (MBA, MM).

University of Phoenix–San Diego Campus, School of Business, San Diego, CA 92123. Offers accounting (MBA); business administration (MBA); global management (MBA); human resources management (MBA, MM); management (MM); marketing (MBA); public administration (MBA). Evening/weekend programs available. *Degree requirements:* For master's, thesis (for some programs). *Entrance requirements:* For master's, 3 years of work experience, minimum undergraduate GPA of 3.0. Additional exam requirements/recommendations for international students: Required—TOEFL (minimum score 550 paper-based; 213 computer-based; 79 iBT). Electronic applications accepted.

University of Phoenix–Savannah Campus, School of Business, Savannah, GA 31405-7400. Offers accounting (MBA); business administration (MBA); global management (MBA); human resources management (MBA, MM); management (MM); marketing (MBA); public administration (MBA, MM).

University of Phoenix–Southern Arizona Campus, School of Business, Tucson, AZ 85711. Offers accountancy (MS); accounting (MBA); business administration (MBA); global management (MBA); human resources management (MBA); management (MM); marketing (MBA). Evening/weekend programs available. *Degree requirements:* For master's, thesis (for some programs). *Entrance requirements:* For master's, minimum undergraduate GPA of 3.0, 3 years of work experience. Additional exam requirements/recommendations for international students: Required—TOEFL (minimum score 550 paper-based; 213 computer-based; 79 iBT). Electronic applications accepted.

University of Phoenix–Southern California Campus, School of Business, Costa Mesa, CA 92626. Offers accounting (MIS); business administration (MBA); energy management (MBA); global management (MBA); health care management (MBA); human resource management (MBA); management (MM); marketing (MBA); project management (MBA); public administration (MPA); technology management (MBA). Evening/weekend programs available. Postbaccalaureate distance learning degree programs offered. *Students:* 699 full-time (341 women); includes 318 minority (124 Black or African American, non-Hispanic/Latino; 4 American Indian or Alaska Native, non-Hispanic/Latino; 44 Asian, non-Hispanic/Latino; 124 Hispanic/Latino; 15 Native Hawaiian or other Pacific Islander, non-Hispanic/Latino; 7 Two or more races, non-Hispanic/Latino), 29 international. Average age 38. *Entrance requirements:* Additional exam requirements/recommendations for international students: Required—TOEFL, TOEIC (Test of English as an International Communication), Berlitz Online English Proficiency Exam, Pearson Test of English, or IELTS. *Application deadline:* Applications are processed on a rolling basis. Application fee: $45. Electronic applications accepted. *Expenses:* Contact institution. *Financial support:* Scholarships/grants available. Financial award applicants required to submit FAFSA. *Application contact:* 866-766-0766. Web site: http://www.phoenix.edu/colleges_divisions/business.html.

University of Phoenix–Southern Colorado Campus, School of Business, Colorado Springs, CO 80919-2335. Offers accounting (MBA); business administration (MBA); global management (MBA); human resources management (MBA, MM); management (MM); marketing (MBA); public administration (MM). Evening/weekend programs available. *Degree requirements:* For master's, thesis (for some programs). *Entrance requirements:* For master's, minimum undergraduate GPA of 3.0, 3 years of work experience. Additional exam requirements/recommendations for international students: Required—TOEFL (minimum score 550 paper-based; 213 computer-based; 79 iBT). Electronic applications accepted.

University of Phoenix–South Florida Campus, School of Business, Fort Lauderdale, FL 33309. Offers accounting (MBA); business administration (MBA); global management (MBA); human resource management (MBA); human resources management (MM); management (MM); marketing (MBA); public administration (MBA, MM). Evening/weekend programs available. *Degree requirements:* For master's, thesis (for some programs). *Entrance requirements:* For master's, minimum undergraduate GPA of 3.0, 3 years work experience. Additional exam requirements/recommendations for international students: Required—TOEFL (minimum score 550 paper-based; 213 computer-based; 79 iBT). Electronic applications accepted.

University of Phoenix–Springfield Campus, School of Business, Springfield, MO 65804-7211. Offers accounting (MBA); business administration (MBA); global management (MBA); human resources management (MBA, MM); management (MM); marketing (MBA); public administration (MBA, MM).

University of Phoenix–Tulsa Campus, School of Business, Tulsa, OK 74134-1412. Offers accounting (MBA); business (MM); business administration (MBA); global management (MBA); human resources management (MBA); marketing (MBA). Evening/weekend programs available. *Degree requirements:* For master's, thesis (for some programs). *Entrance requirements:* For master's, minimum undergraduate GPA of 3.0, 3 years work experience. Additional exam requirements/recommendations for international students: Required—TOEFL (minimum score 550 paper-based; 213 computer-based; 79 iBT).

University of Phoenix–Utah Campus, School of Business, Salt Lake City, UT 84123-4617. Offers accounting (MBA); business administration (MBA); global management (MBA); human resource management (MBA, MM); management (MM); marketing (MBA); technology management (MBA). Evening/weekend programs available. *Degree requirements:* For master's, thesis (for some programs). *Entrance requirements:* For master's, minimum undergraduate GPA of 3.0, 3 years of work experience. Additional exam requirements/recommendations for international students: Required—TOEFL (minimum score 550 paper-based; 213 computer-based; 79 iBT). Electronic applications accepted.

University of Phoenix–Vancouver Campus, John Sperling School of Business, College of Graduate Business and Management, Burnaby, BC V5C 6G9, Canada. Offers accounting (MBA); business administration (MBA); global management (MBA); human resources management (MBA, MM); marketing (MBA). Evening/weekend programs available. *Degree requirements:* For master's, thesis (for some programs). *Entrance requirements:* For master's, minimum undergraduate GPA of 3.0, 3 years of work experience. Additional exam requirements/recommendations for international students: Required—TOEFL (minimum score 550 paper-based; 213 computer-based; 79 iBT). Electronic applications accepted.

University of Phoenix–Washington D.C. Campus, School of Business, Washington, DC 20001. Offers accountancy (MS); business administration (MBA, DBA); human resources management (MM); management (MM); organizational leadership (DM); public administration (MPA).

University of Phoenix–West Florida Campus, School of Business, Temple Terrace, FL 33637. Offers accounting (MBA); business administration (MBA); global management (MBA); human resources management (MBA, MM); management (MM); marketing (MBA); public administration (MBA, MM). Evening/weekend programs available. *Degree requirements:* For master's, thesis (for some programs). *Entrance requirements:* For master's, 3 years of work experience, minimum undergraduate GPA of 3.0. Additional exam requirements/recommendations for international students: Required—TOEFL (minimum score 550 paper-based; 213 computer-based; 79 iBT). Electronic applications accepted.

University of Pittsburgh, Katz Graduate School of Business, Doctoral Program in Business Administration, Pittsburgh, PA 15260. Offers accounting (PhD); finance (PhD); information systems (PhD); marketing (PhD); operations/decision sciences/artificial intelligence (PhD); organizational behavior and human resource management (PhD); strategic planning (PhD). *Accreditation:* AACSB. *Faculty:* 54 full-time (16 women). *Students:* 51 full-time (21 women); includes 9 minority (4 Black or African American, non-Hispanic/Latino; 4 Asian, non-Hispanic/Latino; 1 Hispanic/Latino), 23 international. 373 applicants, 7% accepted, 10 enrolled. In 2011, 6 doctorates awarded. *Degree requirements:* For doctorate, comprehensive exam, thesis/dissertation. *Entrance requirements:* For doctorate, GMAT or GRE. Additional exam requirements/recommendations for international students: Required—TOEFL. *Application deadline:* For fall admission, 2/1 priority date for domestic students, 2/1 for international students. Applications are processed on a rolling basis. Application fee: $50. Electronic applications accepted. *Expenses:* Tuition, state resident: full-time $18,774; part-time $760 per credit. Tuition, nonresident: full-time $30,736; part-time $1258 per credit. *Required fees:* $740; $200 per term. Tuition and fees vary according to program. *Financial support:* In 2011–12, 38 students received support, including 29 research assistantships with full tuition reimbursements available (averaging $19,400 per year), 10 teaching assistantships with full tuition reimbursements available (averaging $24,700 per year); fellowships, Federal Work-Study, scholarships/grants, health care benefits, and unspecified assistantships also available. Financial award application deadline: 2/1. *Faculty research:* Accounting statements and reporting, corporate finance, information systems processes, structures and decision-making, consumer behavior and marketing models. *Total annual research expenditures:* $254,031. *Unit head:* Dr. Dennis Galletta, Director, 412-648-1699, Fax: 412-624-3633, E-mail: galletta@katz.pitt.edu. *Application contact:* Carrie Woods, Assistant Director, 412-648-1525, Fax: 412-624-3633, E-mail: cawoods@katz.pitt.edu. Web site: http://www.business.pitt.edu/katz/phd/.

University of Pittsburgh, Katz Graduate School of Business, Master of Science in Accounting Program, Pittsburgh, PA 15260. Offers MS. Part-time programs available. *Faculty:* 16 full-time (7 women), 4 part-time/adjunct (2 women). *Students:* 48 full-time (27 women), 5 part-time (3 women); includes 5 minority (4 Asian, non-Hispanic/Latino; 1 Two or more races, non-Hispanic/Latino), 20 international. Average age 24. 334 applicants, 22% accepted, 30 enrolled. *Degree requirements:* For master's, minimum GPA of 3.0. *Entrance requirements:* For master's, GMAT, references, work experience relevant for program, interview, recommendations, essays, resume, transcripts. Additional exam requirements/recommendations for international students: Required—TOEFL or IELTS. *Application deadline:* For fall admission, 4/1 priority date for domestic students, 2/1 for international students. Applications are processed on a rolling basis. Application fee: $50. Electronic applications accepted. *Expenses:* Contact institution. *Financial support:* In 2011–12, 19 students received support. Scholarships/grants available. *Faculty research:* Accounting statements and reporting, corporate finance, information systems processes, structures and decision-making, consumer behavior and marketing models. *Total annual research expenditures:* $11,398. *Unit head:* Dr. Karen Shastri, 412-648-1533, Fax: 412-624-5198, E-mail: kshastri@katz.pitt.edu. *Application contact:* Jessica Fick, Administrative Assistant, 412-624-0147, Fax: 412-624-5198, E-mail: macc@katz.pitt.edu. Web site: http://www.business.pitt.edu/katz/macc/.

University of Puerto Rico, Río Piedras, College of Business Administration, San Juan, PR 00931-3300. Offers accounting (MBA); finance (MBA, PhD); general business (MBA); human resources management (MBA); international trade and business (MBA, PhD); marketing (MBA); operations management (MBA); quantitative methods (MBA). *Accreditation:* ACBSP. Part-time programs available. *Degree requirements:* For master's, comprehensive exam, thesis or alternative, research project. *Entrance requirements:* For master's, GMAT or PAEG, minimum GPA of 3.0, letter of recommendation; for doctorate, GMAT, PAEG, minimum GPA of 3.0, master degree. *Faculty research:* Management.

University of Rhode Island, Graduate School, College of Business Administration, Kingston, RI 02881. Offers accounting (MS); business administration (MBA, PhD), including finance and insurance (PhD), management (PhD), marketing (PhD), operations and supply chain management (MBA); finance (MBA); general business (MBA); management (MBA); marketing (MBA); supply chain management (MBA). *Accreditation:* AACSB. Part-time and evening/weekend programs available. *Faculty:* 56 full-time (15 women), 8 part-time/adjunct (4 women). *Students:* 93 full-time (40 women), 226 part-time (90 women); includes 35 minority (7 Black or African American, non-Hispanic/Latino; 1 American Indian or Alaska Native, non-Hispanic/Latino; 15 Asian, non-Hispanic/Latino; 11 Hispanic/Latino; 1 Two or more races, non-Hispanic/Latino), 24 international. In 2011, 78 master's, 3 doctorates awarded. *Degree requirements:* For master's, comprehensive exam (for some programs), thesis optional; for doctorate, comprehensive exam, thesis/dissertation. *Entrance requirements:* For master's, GMAT or GRE, 2 letters of recommendation, resume; for doctorate, GMAT or GRE, 3 letters of recommendation, resume. Additional exam requirements/recommendations for international students: Required—TOEFL (minimum score 575 paper-based; 233 computer-based; 91 iBT). Application fee: $65. Electronic applications accepted. *Expenses:* Tuition, state resident: full-time $10,432; part-time $580 per credit hour. Tuition, nonresident: full-time $23,130; part-time $1285 per credit hour. *Required fees:* $1362; $36 per credit hour. $35 per semester. One-time fee: $130. *Financial support:* In 2011–12, 13 teaching assistantships with full and partial tuition reimbursements (averaging $13,020 per year) were awarded. Financial award applicants required to submit FAFSA. *Unit head:* Dr. Mark Higgins, Dean, 401-874-4244, Fax: 401-874-4312, E-mail: markhiggins@uri.edu. *Application contact:* Lisa Lancellotta, Coordinator, MBA Programs, 401-874-4241, Fax: 401-874-4312, E-mail: mba@uri.edu. Web site: http://www.cba.uri.edu/.

University of Rochester, William E. Simon Graduate School of Business Administration, Master's Program in Accountancy, Rochester, NY 14627. Offers MS. *Expenses: Tuition:* Full-time $41,040.

University of St. Thomas, Graduate Studies, Opus College of Business, Master of Science in Accountancy Program, Minneapolis, MN 55403. Offers MS. *Students:* 21 full-time (6 women); includes 2 minority (1 Asian, non-Hispanic/Latino; 1 Hispanic/Latino), 2 international. Average age 23. 39 applicants, 74% accepted, 19 enrolled. In 2011, 25 master's awarded. *Entrance requirements:* For master's, GMAT. Additional exam requirements/recommendations for international students: Required—TOEFL (minimum score 94 iBT), IELTS (minimum score 7). *Application deadline:* For spring admission, 5/4 for domestic students, 1/13 for international students. Applications are processed on a rolling basis. Application fee: $60. Electronic applications accepted. *Financial support:* Career-related internships or fieldwork and scholarships/grants available. *Unit head:* Kristine Sharockman, Director, 651-962-4110, Fax: 651-962-4141, E-mail: msacct@stthomas.edu. *Application contact:* Cathy Davis, Program Manager, 651-962-4110, Fax: 651-962-4141, E-mail: msacct@stthomas.edu. Web site: http://www.stthomas.edu/accountancy.

University of San Diego, School of Business Administration, Programs in Accountancy and Taxation, San Diego, CA 92110-2492. Offers accountancy (MS); taxation (MS). Part-time and evening/weekend programs available. *Students:* 20 full-time (16 women), 6 part-time (4 women); includes 10 minority (4 Asian, non-Hispanic/Latino; 6 Hispanic/Latino), 9 international. Average age 23. In 2011, 22 master's awarded. *Entrance requirements:* For master's, GMAT (minimum score 550), minimum GPA of 3.0. Additional exam requirements/recommendations for international students: Required—TOEFL (minimum score 580 paper-based; 237 computer-based; 92 iBT), TWE. *Expenses: Tuition:* Full-time $22,482; part-time $1249 per unit. *Required fees:* $224. Full-time tuition and fees vary according to course load and degree level. *Financial support:* In 2011–12, 10 students received support. Career-related internships or fieldwork, Federal Work-Study, institutionally sponsored loans, scholarships/grants, and unspecified assistantships available. Support available to part-time students. Financial award application deadline: 4/1; financial award applicants required to submit FAFSA. *Faculty research:* Accounting, financial report, taxation, and Sarbanes-Oxley. *Unit head:* Dr. Diane Pattison, Academic Director, Accountancy Programs, 619-260-4850, E-mail: pattison@sandiego.edu. *Application contact:* Monica Mahon, Associate Director of Graduate Admissions, 619-260-4524, Fax: 619-260-4158, E-mail: grads@sandiego.edu. Web site: http://www.sandiego.edu/business/centers/accountancy/.

University of Saskatchewan, College of Graduate Studies and Research, Edwards School of Business, Department of Accounting, Saskatoon, SK S7N 5A2, Canada. Offers M Sc, MP Acc. Part-time programs available. *Degree requirements:* For master's, thesis (for some programs). *Entrance requirements:* For master's, GMAT. Additional exam requirements/recommendations for international students: Required—TOEFL.

The University of Scranton, College of Graduate and Continuing Education, Program in Business Administration, Scranton, PA 18510. Offers accounting (MBA); finance (MBA); general business administration (MBA); health care management (MBA); international business (MBA); management information systems (MBA); marketing (MBA); operations management (MBA). *Accreditation:* AACSB. Part-time and evening/weekend programs available. Postbaccalaureate distance learning degree programs offered (no on-campus study). *Faculty:* 34 full-time (8 women). *Students:* 276 full-time (94 women), 243 part-time (88 women); includes 14 minority (10 Black or African American, non-Hispanic/Latino; 3 Asian, non-Hispanic/Latino; 1 Hispanic/Latino), 49 international. Average age 33. 358 applicants, 80% accepted. In 2011, 101 master's awarded. *Degree requirements:* For master's, capstone experience. *Entrance requirements:* For master's, GMAT, minimum GPA of 2.75. Additional exam requirements/recommendations for international students: Required—TOEFL (minimum score 500 paper-based; 173 computer-based), IELTS (minimum score 5.5). *Application deadline:* Applications are processed on a rolling basis. Application fee: $0. *Financial support:* In 2011–12, 12 students received support, including 12 teaching assistantships with full and partial tuition reimbursements available (averaging $8,433 per year); fellowships, career-related internships or fieldwork, Federal Work-Study, and unspecified assistantships also available. Support available to part-time students. Financial award application deadline: 3/1. *Faculty research:* Financial markets, strategic impact of total quality management, internal accounting controls, consumer preference, information systems and the Internet. *Unit head:* Dr. Murli Rajan, Director, 570-941-4043, Fax: 570-941-4342. *Application contact:* Joseph M. Roback, Director of Admissions, 570-941-4385, Fax: 570-941-5928, E-mail: robackj2@scranton.edu. Web site: http://www.academic.scranton.edu/department/mba/.

University of South Africa, College of Economic and Management Sciences, Pretoria, South Africa. Offers accounting (D Admin, D Com); accounting science (DA); auditing (D Admin, D Com); business administration (M Tech); business economics (D Admin); business leadership (DBL); business management (D Admin, D Com); economic management analysis (M Tech); economics (D Admin, D Com, PhD); human resource development (M Tech); industrial psychology (D Admin, D Com, PhD); logistics (D Com); marketing (M Tech); public administration (D Admin, D Com, DPA, PhD); public management (M Tech); quantitative management (D Admin, D Com); real estate (M Tech); statistics (D Admin, PhD); tourism management (D Admin, D Com); transport economics (D Admin, D Com).

University of South Alabama, Graduate School, Mitchell College of Business, Program in Accounting, Mobile, AL 36688-0002. Offers M Acc. Part-time and evening/weekend programs available. *Faculty:* 4 full-time (1 woman). *Students:* 26 full-time (8 women), 5 part-time (4 women); includes 3 minority (2 Black or African American, non-Hispanic/Latino; 1 Two or more races, non-Hispanic/Latino), 6 international. In 2011, 9 master's awarded. *Degree requirements:* For master's, comprehensive exam. *Entrance requirements:* For master's, GMAT, minimum undergraduate GPA of 3.0. *Application deadline:* For fall admission, 7/15 priority date for domestic students, 6/15 for international students; for spring admission, 12/1 priority date for domestic students, 11/1 for international students. Applications are processed on a rolling basis. Application fee: $35. *Expenses:* Tuition, state resident: full-time $7968; part-time $332 per credit hour. Tuition, nonresident: full-time $15,936; part-time $664 per credit hour. *Financial support:* Available to part-time students. Application deadline: 4/1. *Unit head:* Dr. John Gamble, Dean, Mitchell College of Business, 251-460-6180, Fax: 251-460-6529. *Application contact:* Dr. B. Keith Harrison, Dean of the Graduate School, 251-460-6310, Fax: 251-461-1513, E-mail: kharriso@usouthal.edu. Web site: http://www.southalabama.edu/mcob/accounting.html.

University of South Carolina, The Graduate School, Darla Moore School of Business, Master of Accountancy Program, Columbia, SC 29208. Offers business measurement and assurance (M Acc); JD/M Acc. *Accreditation:* AACSB. Part-time programs available. *Degree requirements:* For master's, comprehensive exam. *Entrance requirements:* For master's, GMAT. Additional exam requirements/recommendations for international students: Required—TOEFL (minimum score 250 computer-based; 100 iBT); Recommended—IELTS. Electronic applications accepted. *Faculty research:* Judgment modeling, international accounting, accounting information systems, behavioral accounting, cost/management accounting.

The University of South Dakota, Graduate School, Beacom School of Business, Department of Accounting, Vermillion, SD 57069-2390. Offers professional accountancy (MP Acc); JD/MP Acc. Part-time programs available. Postbaccalaureate distance learning degree programs offered. *Degree requirements:* For master's, comprehensive exam. *Entrance requirements:* For master's, GMAT, minimum GPA of 2.7, resume. Additional exam requirements/recommendations for international students: Required—TOEFL (minimum score 550 paper-based; 213 computer-based; 79 iBT). Electronic applications accepted. *Expenses:* Tuition, state resident: full-time $3118.50; part-time $173.25 per credit hour. Tuition, nonresident: full-time $6601; part-time $366.70 per credit hour. *Required fees:* $2268; $126 per credit hour. Tuition and fees vary according to program.

University of Southern California, Graduate School, Marshall School of Business, Leventhal School of Accounting, Los Angeles, CA 90089. Offers accounting (M Acc); business taxation (MBT); JD/MBT. Part-time programs available. *Degree requirements:* For master's, 30-48 units of study. *Entrance requirements:* For master's, GMAT, undergraduate degree, communication skills. Additional exam requirements/recommendations for international students: Required—TOEFL (minimum score 100 computer-based). Electronic applications accepted. *Faculty research:* State and local taxation, Securities and Exchange Commission, governance, auditing fees, financial accounting, enterprise zones, women in business.

University of Southern Maine, School of Business, Portland, ME 04104-9300. Offers accounting (MBA); business administration (MBA); finance (MBA); health management and policy (MBA); sustainability (MBA); JD/MBA; MBA/MSA; MBA/MSN; MS/MBA. *Accreditation:* AACSB. Part-time and evening/weekend programs available. *Faculty:* 20 full-time (5 women), 2 part-time/adjunct (1 woman). *Students:* 28 full-time (9 women), 91 part-time (39 women), 1 international. Average age 33. 64 applicants, 72% accepted, 33 enrolled. *Entrance requirements:* For master's, GMAT, minimum AACSB index of 1100. Additional exam requirements/recommendations for international students: Required—TOEFL (minimum score 550 paper-based; 213 computer-based; 79 iBT). *Application deadline:* For fall admission, 8/1 priority date for domestic students, 5/1 for international students; for spring admission, 12/1 priority date for domestic students, 9/1 for international students. Applications are processed on a rolling basis. Application fee: $65. Electronic applications accepted. *Financial support:* In 2011–12, 3 research assistantships with partial tuition reimbursements (averaging $9,000 per year), 3 teaching assistantships with partial tuition reimbursements (averaging $9,000 per year) were awarded; career-related internships or fieldwork, Federal Work-Study, scholarships/grants, tuition waivers (full and partial), and unspecified assistantships also available. Support available to part-time students. Financial award application deadline: 2/15; financial award applicants required to submit FAFSA. *Faculty research:* Economic development, management information systems, real options, system dynamics, simulation. *Unit head:* John Voyer, Director, 207-780-4020, Fax: 207-780-4665, E-mail: voyer@usm.maine.edu. *Application contact:* Alice B. Cash, Assistant Director for Student Affairs, 207-780-4184, Fax: 207-780-4662, E-mail: acash@usm.maine.edu. Web site: http://www.usm.maine.edu/sb.

University of Southern Mississippi, Graduate School, College of Business, School of Accountancy and Information Systems, Hattiesburg, MS 39406-0001. Offers accountancy (MPA). *Accreditation:* AACSB. Part-time and evening/weekend programs available. *Faculty:* 7 full-time (4 women), 2 part-time/adjunct (both women). *Students:* 26 full-time (18 women), 6 part-time (5 women); includes 2 minority (1 Black or African American, non-Hispanic/Latino; 1 Hispanic/Latino). Average age 26. 23 applicants, 78% accepted, 16 enrolled. In 2011, 14 degrees awarded. *Degree requirements:* For master's, comprehensive exam. *Entrance requirements:* For master's, GMAT, minimum GPA of 2.75 on last 60 hours. Additional exam requirements/recommendations for international students: Required—TOEFL, IELTS. *Application deadline:* For fall admission, 7/15 priority date for domestic students, 7/15 for international students; for spring admission, 11/15 priority date for domestic students, 11/15 for international students. Applications are processed on a rolling basis. Application fee: $50. Electronic applications accepted. *Financial support:* In 2011–12, 7 research assistantships with full tuition reimbursements (averaging $7,200 per year) were awarded; Federal Work-Study, institutionally sponsored loans, scholarships/grants, health care benefits, and unspecified assistantships also available. Support available to part-time students. Financial award application deadline: 3/15; financial award applicants required to submit FAFSA. *Faculty research:* Bank liquidity, subchapter S corporations, internal auditing, governmental accounting, inflation accounting. *Unit head:* Dr. Skip Hughes, Director, 601-266-4322, Fax: 601-266-4639. *Application contact:* Dr. Michael Dugan, Director of Graduate Studies, 601-266-4641, Fax: 601-266-5814. Web site: http://www.usm.edu/graduateschool/table.php.

University of South Florida, Graduate School, College of Business, School of Accounting, Tampa, FL 33620-9951. Offers accounting (M Acc); business administration (PhD), including accounting. *Accreditation:* AACSB. Part-time and evening/weekend programs available. *Faculty:* 12 full-time (6 women), 7 part-time/adjunct (1 woman). *Students:* 52 full-time (32 women), 44 part-time (24 women); includes 20 minority (2 Black or African American, non-Hispanic/Latino; 1 American Indian or Alaska Native, non-Hispanic/Latino; 6 Asian, non-Hispanic/Latino; 11 Hispanic/Latino). Average age 28. 100 applicants, 52% accepted, 37 enrolled. In 2011, 41 master's, 1 doctorate awarded. Terminal master's awarded for partial completion of doctoral program. *Degree requirements:* For master's, thesis or alternative, 30 credits, minimum GPA of 3.0; for doctorate, comprehensive exam, thesis/dissertation. *Entrance requirements:* For master's, GMAT, minimum of 21 hours with minimum GPA of 3.0 at a USAACSB-accredited program within the last five years; for doctorate, GMAT or GRE, minimum GPA of 3.0 in last 60 hours, at least two letters of recommendation, statement of purpose, interview. Additional exam requirements/recommendations for international students: Required—TOEFL (minimum score 550 paper-based; 213 computer-based; 79 iBT) or IELTS (minimum score 6.5). *Application deadline:* For fall admission, 6/1 for domestic students, 1/2 for international students; for spring admission, 10/15 for domestic students, 6/1 for international students. Application fee: $30. Electronic applications accepted. *Financial support:* In 2011–12, 18 students received support, including 18 teaching assistantships with tuition reimbursements available (averaging $12,273 per year); scholarships/grants, health care benefits, and unspecified assistantships also available. Financial award applicants required to submit FAFSA. *Faculty research:* Auditor independence, audit committee decisions, fraud detection and reporting, disclosure effects, effects of information technology on accounting, governmental accounting/auditing, accounting information systems, the reporting and use of financial information, fair value accounting issues, corporate governance and financial reporting quality. *Total annual research expenditures:* $294,891. *Unit head:* Dr. Stephanie Bryant, Chairperson, 813-974-4186, Fax: 813-974-6528, E-mail: sbryant2@usf.edu. *Application contact:* Christy Ward, Advisor, 813-974-4290, Fax: 813-974-2797, E-mail: cward@coba.usf.edu. Web site: http://www.usfaccounting.com.

The University of Tampa, John H. Sykes College of Business, Tampa, FL 33606-1490. Offers accounting (MS); entrepreneurship (MBA); finance (MBA, MS); information systems management (MBA); innovation management (MBA); international business (MBA); marketing (MBA, MS); nonprofit management (MBA). *Accreditation:* AACSB. Part-time and evening/weekend programs available. *Faculty:* 38 full-time (14 women), 5 part-time/adjunct (1 woman). *Students:* 161 full-time (65 women), 193 part-time (82 women); includes 65 minority (11 Black or African American, non-Hispanic/Latino; 1 American Indian or Alaska Native, non-Hispanic/Latino; 8 Asian, non-Hispanic/Latino; 39 Hispanic/Latino; 2 Native Hawaiian or other Pacific Islander, non-Hispanic/Latino; 4

Two or more races, non-Hispanic/Latino), 58 international. Average age 29. 837 applicants, 41% accepted, 196 enrolled. In 2011, 259 degrees awarded. *Degree requirements:* For master's, capstone. *Entrance requirements:* For master's, GMAT or GRE, 4-year undergraduate degree, minimum GPA of 3.0, professional experience (for Executive MBA). Additional exam requirements/recommendations for international students: Required—TOEFL (minimum score 577 paper-based; 230 computer-based; 90 iBT); Recommended—IELTS (minimum score 7.5). *Application deadline:* Applications are processed on a rolling basis. Application fee: $40. Electronic applications accepted. *Expenses: Tuition:* Full-time $8320; part-time $520 per credit hour. *Required fees:* $40 per semester. Tuition and fees vary according to program. *Financial support:* In 2011–12, 124 students received support. Career-related internships or fieldwork, scholarships/grants, unspecified assistantships, and grants available. Financial award applicants required to submit FAFSA. *Faculty research:* Job market signaling, on-line shopping behaviors and social media, the Tampa Bay economy, digital literacy, entrepreneurship in small businesses. *Unit head:* Dennis Nostrand, Vice President, Enrollment/Admissions, 813-257-1808, E-mail: dnostrand@ut.edu. *Application contact:* Charlene Tobie, Associate Director of Admissions, 813-257-3566, E-mail: ctobie@ut.edu. Web site: http://ut.edu/graduate.

The University of Tennessee, Graduate School, College of Business Administration, Department of Accounting, Knoxville, TN 37996. Offers accounting (M Acc), including assurance; systems (M Acc); taxation. (M Acc). *Accreditation:* AACSB. *Degree requirements:* For master's, thesis or alternative. *Entrance requirements:* For master's, GMAT, minimum GPA of 2.7. Additional exam requirements/recommendations for international students: Required—TOEFL. Electronic applications accepted. *Expenses:* Tuition, state resident: full-time $8332; part-time $464 per credit hour. Tuition, nonresident: full-time $25,174; part-time $1400 per credit hour. *Required fees:* $1162; $56 per credit hour. Tuition and fees vary according to program.

The University of Tennessee, Graduate School, College of Business Administration, Program in Business Administration, Knoxville, TN 37996. Offers accounting (PhD); finance (MBA, PhD); logistics and transportation (MBA, PhD); management (PhD); marketing (MBA, PhD); operations management (MBA); professional business administration (MBA); statistics (PhD); JD/MBA; MS/MBA; Pharm D/MBA. Pharm D/MBA offered jointly with The University of Tennessee Health Science Center. *Accreditation:* AACSB. Postbaccalaureate distance learning degree programs offered. *Degree requirements:* For master's, thesis or alternative; for doctorate, thesis/dissertation. *Entrance requirements:* For master's and doctorate, GMAT, minimum GPA of 2.7. Additional exam requirements/recommendations for international students: Required—TOEFL. Electronic applications accepted. *Expenses:* Tuition, state resident: full-time $8332; part-time $464 per credit hour. Tuition, nonresident: full-time $25,174; part-time $1400 per credit hour. *Required fees:* $1162; $56 per credit hour. Tuition and fees vary according to program.

The University of Tennessee at Chattanooga, Graduate School, College of Business, Program in Accountancy, Chattanooga, TN 37403. Offers M Acc. *Accreditation:* AACSB. Part-time and evening/weekend programs available. *Faculty:* 7 full-time (1 woman), 1 (woman) part-time/adjunct. *Students:* 18 full-time (9 women), 29 part-time (18 women); includes 7 minority (3 Black or African American, non-Hispanic/Latino; 3 Asian, non-Hispanic/Latino; 1 Hispanic/Latino). Average age 28. 22 applicants, 73% accepted, 9 enrolled. In 2011, 12 master's awarded. *Entrance requirements:* For master's, GMAT (minimum score 450). Additional exam requirements/recommendations for international students: Required—TOEFL (minimum score 550 paper-based; 213 computer-based; 79 iBT), IELTS (minimum score 6). *Application deadline:* For fall admission, 8/1 priority date for domestic students, 6/1 for international students; for spring admission, 12/1 priority date for domestic students, 10/1 for international students. Applications are processed on a rolling basis. Application fee: $35. Electronic applications accepted. *Expenses:* Tuition, state resident: full-time $6472; part-time $359 per credit hour. Tuition, nonresident: full-time $20,006; part-time $1111 per credit hour. *Required fees:* $1320; $160 per credit hour. *Financial support:* Research assistantships, career-related internships or fieldwork, scholarships/grants, and unspecified assistantships available. Support available to part-time students. Financial award applicants required to submit FAFSA. *Faculty research:* Performance measurement, auditing, income taxation, corporate efficiency, portfolio management and performance. *Unit head:* Dr. Stan Davis, Head, 423-425-4152, Fax: 423-425-5255, E-mail: stan-davis@utc.edu. *Application contact:* Dr. Jerald Ainsworth, Dean of Graduate Studies, 423-425-4478, Fax: 423-425-5223, E-mail: jerald-ainsworth@utc.edu. Web site: http://www.utc.edu/Academic/BusinessGraduatePrograms/MAcc.php.

The University of Texas at Arlington, Graduate School, College of Business, Accounting Department, Arlington, TX 76019. Offers accounting (MP Acc, MS, PhD); taxation (MS). *Accreditation:* AACSB. Part-time and evening/weekend programs available. *Faculty:* 13 full-time (3 women). *Students:* 93 full-time (53 women), 129 part-time (59 women); includes 50 minority (11 Black or African American, non-Hispanic/Latino; 1 American Indian or Alaska Native, non-Hispanic/Latino; 21 Asian, non-Hispanic/Latino; 15 Hispanic/Latino; 2 Two or more races, non-Hispanic/Latino), 33 international. 169 applicants, 62% accepted, 55 enrolled. In 2011, 64 master's, 1 doctorate awarded. *Degree requirements:* For master's, thesis optional; for doctorate, comprehensive exam, thesis/dissertation. *Entrance requirements:* For master's and doctorate, GMAT. Additional exam requirements/recommendations for international students: Required—TOEFL (minimum score 550 paper-based; 213 computer-based; 79 iBT). *Application deadline:* For fall admission, 6/1 for domestic students, 4/1 for international students; for spring admission, 10/15 for domestic students, 9/15 for international students. Applications are processed on a rolling basis. Application fee: $40 ($70 for international students). *Financial support:* In 2011–12, 100 students received support, including 10 teaching assistantships (averaging $13,590 per year); fellowships, research assistantships, career-related internships or fieldwork, scholarships/grants, and unspecified assistantships also available. Financial award application deadline: 6/1; financial award applicants required to submit FAFSA. *Unit head:* Dr. Chandra Subramaniam, Chair, 817-272-7029, Fax: 817-282-5793, E-mail: subramaniam@uta.edu. *Application contact:* Carly S. Andrews, Graduate Advisor, 817-272-3047, Fax: 817-272-5793, E-mail: graduate.accounting.advisor@uta.edu. Web site: http://www2.uta.edu/accounting/.

The University of Texas at Arlington, Graduate School, College of Business, Program in Business Administration, Arlington, TX 76019. Offers accounting (PhD); business statistics (PhD); finance (MBA, PhD); information systems (MBA, PhD); management (MBA, PhD); marketing (MBA, PhD); operations management (MBA, PhD); real estate (MBA). *Accreditation:* AACSB. Part-time and evening/weekend programs available. *Students:* 505 full-time (189 women), 369 part-time (140 women); includes 199 minority (58 Black or African American, non-Hispanic/Latino; 2 American Indian or Alaska Native, non-Hispanic/Latino; 70 Asian, non-Hispanic/Latino; 56 Hispanic/Latino; 1 Native Hawaiian or other Pacific Islander, non-Hispanic/Latino; 12 Two or more races, non-Hispanic/Latino), 306 international. 416 applicants, 81% accepted, 234 enrolled. In 2011, 495 master's, 3 doctorates awarded. *Degree requirements:* For master's, thesis optional; for doctorate, comprehensive exam, thesis/dissertation. *Entrance requirements:* For master's, GMAT or GRE; for doctorate, GMAT, minimum GPA of 3.0 (undergraduate), 3.4 (graduate); 30 hours of graduate course work. Additional exam requirements/recommendations for international students: Required—TOEFL (minimum score 550 paper-based; 213 computer-based; 79 iBT). *Application deadline:* For fall admission, 6/1 for domestic students, 4/1 for international students; for spring admission, 10/15 for domestic students, 9/15 for international students. Applications are processed on a rolling basis. Application fee: $40 ($70 for international students). Electronic applications accepted. *Financial support:* Career-related internships or fieldwork, scholarships/grants, and unspecified assistantships available. Support available to part-time students. Financial award application deadline: 6/1; financial award applicants required to submit FAFSA. *Unit head:* Dr. Edmund Prater, Director of PhD Programs, 817-272-2131, Fax: 817-272-5799. *Application contact:* Melanie McGee, Director of MBA Program, 817-272-3005, Fax: 817-272-5799, E-mail: mwmcgee@uta.edu.

The University of Texas at Austin, Graduate School, McCombs School of Business, Department of Accounting, Austin, TX 78712-1111. Offers MPA, PhD. *Accreditation:* AACSB. *Degree requirements:* For doctorate, comprehensive exam, thesis/dissertation. *Entrance requirements:* For master's and doctorate, GMAT. Additional exam requirements/recommendations for international students: Required—TOEFL. *Application deadline:* For fall admission, 4/15 priority date for domestic students. Applications are processed on a rolling basis. Application fee: $80 ($100 for international students). Electronic applications accepted. *Financial support:* Fellowships, research assistantships, teaching assistantships, career-related internships or fieldwork, and scholarships/grants available. Financial award application deadline: 2/1. *Unit head:* Lillian Mills, Chair, 512-471-1251, Fax: 512-471-4607, E-mail: lillian.mills@mccombs@utexas.edu. *Application contact:* Ross Jennings, Graduate Adviser, 512-471-5340, E-mail: ross.jennings@mccombs.utexas.edu. Web site: http://www.mccombs.utexas.edu/departments/accounting/.

The University of Texas at Dallas, Naveen Jindal School of Management, Program in Accounting, Richardson, TX 75080. Offers assurance services (MS); corporate accounting (MS); internal audit (MS); taxation (MS). *Accreditation:* AACSB. *Faculty:* 16 full-time (4 women), 11 part-time/adjunct (5 women). *Students:* 398 full-time (258 women), 402 part-time (238 women); includes 136 minority (18 Black or African American, non-Hispanic/Latino; 1 American Indian or Alaska Native, non-Hispanic/Latino; 79 Asian, non-Hispanic/Latino; 28 Hispanic/Latino; 10 Two or more races, non-Hispanic/Latino), 411 international. Average age 28. 825 applicants, 59% accepted, 308 enrolled. In 2011, 314 master's awarded. *Entrance requirements:* For master's, GMAT, minimum GPA of 3.0 in upper-level course work in field. Additional exam requirements/recommendations for international students: Required—TOEFL (minimum score 550 paper-based; 215 computer-based). *Application deadline:* For fall admission, 7/15 for domestic students, 5/1 for international students; for spring admission, 11/15 for domestic students, 9/1 for international students. Applications are processed on a rolling basis. Application fee: $50 ($100 for international students). Electronic applications accepted. *Expenses:* Tuition, state resident: full-time $11,170; part-time $620.56 per credit hour. Tuition, nonresident: full-time $20,212; part-time $1122.89 per credit hour. *Financial support:* In 2011–12, 257 students received support, including 5 teaching assistantships with partial tuition reimbursements available (averaging $10,050 per year); research assistantships with partial tuition reimbursements available, career-related internships or fieldwork, Federal Work-Study, institutionally sponsored loans, scholarships/grants, and unspecified assistantships also available. Support available to part-time students. Financial award application deadline: 4/30; financial award applicants required to submit FAFSA. *Faculty research:* Privatization and accounting/auditing, corporate performance and executive compensation, risk management, information technology in accounting. *Unit head:* Amy Troutman, Associate Area Coordinator, 972-883-6719, Fax: 972-883-6823, E-mail: amybass@utdallas.edu. *Application contact:* Jennifer Johnson, Director, Graduate Accounting Programs, 972-883-5912, E-mail: jennifer.johnson@utdallas.edu. Web site: http://jindal.utdallas.edu/academic-areas/accounting/.

The University of Texas at Dallas, Naveen Jindal School of Management, Programs in Management Science, Richardson, TX 75080. Offers accounting (PhD); finance (PhD); information systems (PhD); marketing (PhD); operations management (PhD). *Accreditation:* AACSB. Part-time and evening/weekend programs available. *Faculty:* 14 full-time (4 women). *Students:* 75 full-time (30 women), 8 part-time (4 women); includes 5 minority (4 Asian, non-Hispanic/Latino; 1 Two or more races, non-Hispanic/Latino), 71 international. Average age 31. 224 applicants, 11% accepted, 20 enrolled. In 2011, 10 doctorates awarded. *Degree requirements:* For doctorate, thesis/dissertation. *Entrance requirements:* For doctorate, GMAT, minimum GPA of 3.0. Additional exam requirements/recommendations for international students: Required—TOEFL (minimum score 550 paper-based; 215 computer-based). *Application deadline:* For fall admission, 7/15 for domestic students, 5/1 for international students; for spring admission, 11/15 for domestic students, 9/1 for international students. Applications are processed on a rolling basis. Application fee: $50 ($100 for international students). Electronic applications accepted. *Expenses:* Tuition, state resident: full-time $11,170; part-time $620.56 per credit hour. Tuition, nonresident: full-time $20,212; part-time $1122.89 per credit hour. *Financial support:* In 2011–12, 76 students received support, including 3 research assistantships with partial tuition reimbursements available (averaging $21,600 per year), 68 teaching assistantships with partial tuition reimbursements available (averaging $16,162 per year); career-related internships or fieldwork, Federal Work-Study, institutionally sponsored loans, scholarships/grants, and unspecified assistantships also available. Support available to part-time students. Financial award application deadline: 4/30; financial award applicants required to submit FAFSA. *Faculty research:* Empirical generalizations in marketing, diffusion of generations of technology, stochastic brand-choice theory, acceptance of trade deals by supermarkets, nonparametric estimations of market share response. *Unit head:* Dr. Sumit Sarkar, Program Director, 972-883-2745, Fax: 972-883-5977, E-mail: som_phd.@utdallas.edu. *Application contact:* LeeAnne Sloane, Coordinator, 972-883-2745, Fax: 972-883-5977, E-mail: som_phd@utdallas.edu. Web site: http://jindal.utdallas.edu/academic-programs/phd-programs/management-science/.

The University of Texas at El Paso, Graduate School, College of Business Administration, Department of Accounting, El Paso, TX 79968-0001. Offers M Acc. *Accreditation:* AACSB. Part-time and evening/weekend programs available. *Students:* 23 (13 women); includes 16 minority (1 Black or African American, non-Hispanic/Latino; 15 Hispanic/Latino). Average age 34. In 2011, 2 master's awarded. *Entrance requirements:* For master's, GMAT, minimum GPA of 3.0. Additional exam requirements/recommendations for international students: Required—TOEFL; Recommended—IELTS. *Application deadline:* For fall admission, 8/1 priority date for domestic students, 3/1 for international students; for spring admission, 11/1 priority date for domestic students, 9/1 for international students. Applications are processed on a rolling basis. Application fee: $45 ($80 for international students). Electronic applications accepted. *Financial support:* In 2011–12, research assistantships with partial tuition reimbursements (averaging $18,750 per year), teaching assistantships with partial tuition reimbursements (averaging $15,000 per year) were awarded; fellowships with partial tuition reimbursements, institutionally sponsored loans, scholarships/grants, health care benefits, tuition waivers (partial), and unspecified assistantships also available. Support available to part-time students. Financial award application deadline: 3/15; financial award applicants required to submit FAFSA. *Faculty research:*

International accounting, tax, not-for-profit accounting. *Unit head:* Dr. Ray Zimmerman, Chair, 915-747-5192, Fax: 915-747-8618, E-mail: rzimmer@utep.edu. *Application contact:* Dr. Benjamin Flores, Interim Dean of the Graduate School, 915-747-5491, Fax: 915-747-5788, E-mail: bflores@utep.edu. Web site: http://business.utep.edu/Accounting/.

The University of Texas at San Antonio, College of Business, Department of Accounting, San Antonio, TX 78249-0617. Offers M Acy. *Accreditation:* AACSB. Part-time and evening/weekend programs available. *Faculty:* 12 full-time (4 women), 4 part-time/adjunct (2 women). *Students:* 61 full-time (30 women), 51 part-time (18 women); includes 40 minority (4 Black or African American, non-Hispanic/Latino; 6 Asian, non-Hispanic/Latino; 29 Hispanic/Latino; 1 Two or more races, non-Hispanic/Latino), 16 international. Average age 29. 83 applicants, 48% accepted, 31 enrolled. In 2011, 45 master's awarded. *Degree requirements:* For master's, thesis or alternative. *Entrance requirements:* For master's, GMAT, bachelor's degree with 18 hour credit hours in field of study, transcripts, statement of purpose. Additional exam requirements/recommendations for international students: Required—TOEFL (minimum score 500 paper-based; 61 iBT), IELTS (minimum score 5). *Application deadline:* For fall admission, 7/1 for domestic students, 4/1 for international students; for spring admission, 11/1 for domestic students, 9/1 for international students. Application fee: $45 ($85 for international students). *Expenses:* Tuition, state resident: full-time $3148; part-time $2176 per semester. Tuition, nonresident: full-time $8782; part-time $5932 per semester. *Required fees:* $719 per semester. *Financial support:* In 2011–12, research assistantships (averaging $10,000 per year), teaching assistantships (averaging $10,000 per year) were awarded; Federal Work-Study and scholarships/grants also available. *Faculty research:* Capital markets, corporate governance, auditing, health care accounting, fraud. *Unit head:* Dr. James E. Groff, Chair, 210-458-5239, Fax: 210-458-4322, E-mail: james.groff@utsa.edu. *Application contact:* Dr. Jeff Boone, Advisor of Record Accounting Doctoral Programs, 210-458-7091, E-mail: jeff.boone@utsa.edu.

The University of Texas at San Antonio, College of Business, General Business Program, San Antonio, TX 78249-0617. Offers business (MBA); business administration (PhD), including accounting, business administration, finance, information technology, management and organization studies, marketing; information systems (MBA); international business (MBA); management accounting (MBA); management of technology (MBA); marketing management (MBA); taxation (MBA). *Students:* 170 full-time (52 women), 120 part-time (49 women); includes 90 minority (14 Black or African American, non-Hispanic/Latino; 2 American Indian or Alaska Native, non-Hispanic/Latino; 15 Asian, non-Hispanic/Latino; 55 Hispanic/Latino; 1 Native Hawaiian or other Pacific Islander, non-Hispanic/Latino; 3 Two or more races, non-Hispanic/Latino), 37 international. Average age 32. 395 applicants, 45% accepted, 133 enrolled. In 2011, 95 master's, 8 doctorates awarded. *Entrance requirements:* Additional exam requirements/recommendations for international students: Required—TOEFL (minimum score 500 paper-based; 61 iBT), IELTS (minimum score 5). *Application deadline:* For fall admission, 7/1 for domestic students, 4/1 for international students; for spring admission, 11/1 for domestic students, 9/1 for international students. Application fee: $45 ($85 for international students). *Expenses:* Tuition, state resident: full-time $3148; part-time $2176 per semester. Tuition, nonresident: full-time $8782; part-time $5932 per semester. *Required fees:* $719 per semester. *Financial support:* In 2011–12, fellowships (averaging $22,000 per year), research assistantships (averaging $10,000 per year), teaching assistantships (averaging $10,000 per year) were awarded. *Unit head:* Dr. Lynda Y. de la Vinna, Dean, 210-458-4317, Fax: 210-458-4308, E-mail: lynda.delavina@utsa.edu. *Application contact:* Katherine Pope, Director of Graduate Student Services, 210-458-7316, Fax: 210-458-4398, E-mail: katherine.pope@utsa.edu. Web site: http://business.utsa.edu.

The University of Texas of the Permian Basin, Office of Graduate Studies, School of Business, Program in Accountancy, Odessa, TX 79762-0001. Offers MPA. *Entrance requirements:* For master's, GMAT. Additional exam requirements/recommendations for international students: Required—TOEFL (minimum score 550 paper-based; 213 computer-based).

The University of Texas–Pan American, College of Business Administration, Program in Accounting, Edinburg, TX 78539. Offers M Acc, MS. Part-time and evening/weekend programs available. *Entrance requirements:* For master's, GMAT. Additional exam requirements/recommendations for international students: Required—TOEFL (minimum score 500 paper-based). *Application deadline:* For fall admission, 7/25 priority date for domestic students, 7/1 for international students; for spring admission, 12/15 priority date for domestic students, 11/1 for international students. Applications are processed on a rolling basis. Application fee: $35. Electronic applications accepted. Tuition and fees vary according to course load, program and student level. *Financial support:* Career-related internships or fieldwork, scholarships/grants, and unspecified assistantships available. *Faculty research:* Financial and managerial accounting, international accounting, taxation, ethics. *Unit head:* Dr. Jan M. Smolarski, Chair, 956-665-3384, E-mail: jmsmolarski@utpa.edu.

University of the Incarnate Word, School of Graduate Studies and Research, H-E-B School of Business and Administration, Programs in Accounting, San Antonio, TX 78209-6397. Offers MS. Part-time and evening/weekend programs available. *Faculty:* 23 full-time (10 women), 26 part-time/adjunct (12 women). *Students:* 30 full-time (12 women), 42 part-time (31 women); includes 39 minority (1 Black or African American, non-Hispanic/Latino; 38 Hispanic/Latino), 8 international. Average age 30. 41 applicants, 85% accepted, 23 enrolled. In 2011, 38 master's awarded. *Entrance requirements:* For master's, GMAT. Additional exam requirements/recommendations for international students: Required—TOEFL (minimum score 560 paper-based; 220 computer-based; 83 iBT). *Application deadline:* Applications are processed on a rolling basis. Application fee: $20. Electronic applications accepted. *Expenses: Tuition:* Part-time $725 per credit hour. Tuition and fees vary according to degree level. *Financial support:* Federal Work-Study and scholarships/grants available. Financial award applicants required to submit FAFSA. *Unit head:* Dr. Henry Elrod, 210-829-3184, Fax: 210-805-3564, E-mail: elrod@uiwtx.edu. *Application contact:* Andrea Cyterski-Acosta, Dean of Enrollment, 210-829-6005, Fax: 210-829-3921, E-mail: admis@uiwtx.edu. Web site: http://www.uiw.edu/gradstudies/documents/msaccounting.pdf.

University of the Sacred Heart, Graduate Programs, Department of Business Administration, San Juan, PR 00914-0383. Offers human resource management (MBA); information systems auditing (MS); information technology (Certificate); international marketing (MBA); management information systems (MBA); production and marketing of special events (Certificate); taxation (MBA). Part-time and evening/weekend programs available. *Degree requirements:* For master's, thesis. *Entrance requirements:* For master's, EXADEP, minimum undergraduate GPA of 2.75, interview.

The University of Toledo, College of Graduate Studies, College of Business and Innovation, Department of Accounting, Toledo, OH 43606-3390. Offers MSA. Part-time and evening/weekend programs available. *Faculty:* 8. *Students:* 8 full-time (6 women), 31 part-time (21 women); includes 2 minority (1 Black or African American, non-Hispanic/Latino; 1 Hispanic/Latino), 11 international. Average age 28. 49 applicants, 71% accepted, 21 enrolled. In 2011, 28 master's awarded. *Entrance requirements:* For master's, GMAT, minimum GPA of 2.7 for all prior academic work, three letters of recommendation, statement of purpose, transcripts from all prior institutions attended. Additional exam requirements/recommendations for international students: Required—TOEFL (minimum score 550 paper-based; 213 computer-based; 80 iBT), IELTS (minimum score 6.5). *Application deadline:* For fall admission, 8/1 for domestic students, 5/1 for international students; for spring admission, 11/15 for domestic students, 10/1 for international students. Applications are processed on a rolling basis. Application fee: $45 ($75 for international students). Electronic applications accepted. *Financial support:* In 2011–12, 6 research assistantships with full and partial tuition reimbursements (averaging $5,250 per year) were awarded; career-related internships or fieldwork, Federal Work-Study, institutionally sponsored loans, scholarships/grants, tuition waivers (full and partial), and unspecified assistantships also available. Support available to part-time students. *Faculty research:* Estate gift tax, audit and legal liability, corporate tax, accounting information systems. *Unit head:* Dr. Donald Saftner, Chair, 419-530-2327. *Application contact:* Graduate School Office, 419-530-4723, Fax: 419-530-4724, E-mail: grdsch@utnet.utoledo.edu.

University of Tulsa, Graduate School, Collins College of Business, Master of Business Administration Program, Tulsa, OK 74104-3189. Offers accounting (MBA); business administration (MBA); energy management (MBA); finance (MBA); international business (MBA); management information systems (MBA); taxation (MBA); JD/MBA; MBA/MSCS; MBA/MSF. *Accreditation:* AACSB. Part-time and evening/weekend programs available. *Faculty:* 32 full-time (6 women). *Students:* 56 full-time (29 women), 28 part-time (7 women); includes 7 minority (1 Black or African American, non-Hispanic/Latino; 2 American Indian or Alaska Native, non-Hispanic/Latino; 2 Asian, non-Hispanic/Latino; 2 Hispanic/Latino), 16 international. Average age 26. 70 applicants, 67% accepted, 29 enrolled. In 2011, 35 master's awarded. *Entrance requirements:* For master's, GMAT. Additional exam requirements/recommendations for international students: Required—TOEFL (minimum score 577 paper-based; 233 computer-based; 91 iBT), IELTS (minimum score 6.5). *Application deadline:* Applications are processed on a rolling basis. Application fee: $40. Electronic applications accepted. *Expenses: Tuition:* Full-time $17,748; part-time $986 per hour. *Required fees:* $5 per contact hour. $75 per semester. Tuition and fees vary according to program. *Financial support:* In 2011–12, 30 students received support, including 30 teaching assistantships (averaging $11,044 per year); fellowships, research assistantships, career-related internships or fieldwork, institutionally sponsored loans, scholarships/grants, health care benefits, tuition waivers (full and partial), and unspecified assistantships also available. Support available to part-time students. Financial award application deadline: 2/1; financial award applicants required to submit FAFSA. *Faculty research:* Accounting, energy management, finance, international business, management information systems, taxation. *Unit head:* Dr. Linda Nichols, Associate Dean of the Collins College of Business, 918-631-2242, Fax: 918-631-2142, E-mail: linda-nichols@utulsa.edu. *Application contact:* Information Contact, 918-631-2242, E-mail: graduate-business@utulsa.edu. Web site: http://www.cba.utulsa.edu/.

University of Utah, Graduate School, David Eccles School of Business, School of Accounting, Salt Lake City, UT 84112. Offers M Acc, PhD. *Accreditation:* AACSB. Part-time and evening/weekend programs available. *Faculty:* 17 full-time (7 women). *Students:* 84 full-time (26 women), 27 part-time (11 women); includes 12 minority (1 American Indian or Alaska Native, non-Hispanic/Latino; 7 Asian, non-Hispanic/Latino; 3 Hispanic/Latino; 1 Two or more races, non-Hispanic/Latino), 8 international. Average age 29. 170 applicants, 50% accepted, 77 enrolled. In 2011, 103 degrees awarded. *Degree requirements:* For doctorate, thesis/dissertation, oral qualifying exams, written qualifying exams. *Entrance requirements:* For master's, GMAT, minimum undergraduate GPA of 3.0; for doctorate, GMAT. Additional exam requirements/recommendations for international students: Required—TOEFL (minimum score 600 paper-based; 250 computer-based; 100 iBT), IELTS (minimum score 7). *Application deadline:* For fall admission, 3/1 priority date for domestic students, 3/1 for international students; for spring admission, 11/1 for domestic and international students. Applications are processed on a rolling basis. Application fee: $55 ($65 for international students). Electronic applications accepted. *Expenses:* Contact institution. *Financial support:* In 2011–12, 15 students received support, including 8 fellowships with partial tuition reimbursements available (averaging $5,500 per year), 6 teaching assistantships with partial tuition reimbursements available (averaging $1,100 per year); research assistantships, Federal Work-Study, tuition waivers (full), and unspecified assistantships also available. Financial award application deadline: 4/1; financial award applicants required to submit FAFSA. *Faculty research:* Auditing, taxation, information systems, financial accounting, accounting theory, international accounting . *Total annual research expenditures:* $91,427. *Unit head:* Dr. Martha Eining, Chair, 801-581-7673, Fax: 801-581-3581, E-mail: martha.eining@utah.edu. *Application contact:* Andrea Chmelik, Admissions Coordinator, 801-585-1719, Fax: 801-581-3666, E-mail: andrea.chmelik@business.utah.edu. Web site: http://www.business.utah.edu/accounting/.

University of Vermont, Graduate College, School of Business Administration, Program in Accounting, Burlington, VT 05405. Offers M Acc. *Students:* 25 (15 women); includes 5 minority (1 Black or African American, non-Hispanic/Latino; 3 Asian, non-Hispanic/Latino; 1 Hispanic/Latino), 8 international. 82 applicants, 65% accepted, 22 enrolled. In 2011, 11 master's awarded. *Entrance requirements:* For master's, GMAT, GRE. Additional exam requirements/recommendations for international students: Required—TOEFL (minimum score 550 paper-based; 213 computer-based; 80 iBT). *Application deadline:* For fall admission, 4/1 for domestic and international students; for spring admission, 12/1 for domestic and international students. Applications are processed on a rolling basis. Application fee: $40. Electronic applications accepted. *Unit head:* Dr. Michael Gurdon, Coordinator, 802-656-3177. *Application contact:* Dr. M. Gurdon, Coordinator, 802-656-0513.

University of Virginia, McIntire School of Commerce, Program in Accounting, Charlottesville, VA 22903. Offers MS. *Accreditation:* AACSB. *Students:* 72 full-time (35 women); includes 11 minority (1 Black or African American, non-Hispanic/Latino; 6 Asian, non-Hispanic/Latino; 3 Hispanic/Latino; 1 Two or more races, non-Hispanic/Latino), 10 international. Average age 23. 193 applicants, 64% accepted, 72 enrolled. In 2011, 123 master's awarded. *Entrance requirements:* For master's, GMAT, 2 letters of recommendation, 12 hours of accounting courses. Additional exam requirements/recommendations for international students: Required—TOEFL (minimum score 600 paper-based; 250 computer-based; 100 iBT), IELTS (minimum score 7). *Application deadline:* For fall admission, 9/1 priority date for domestic students, 12/1 for international students. Applications are processed on a rolling basis. Application fee: $75. Electronic applications accepted. *Expenses:* Contact institution. *Financial support:* Fellowships and Federal Work-Study available. Financial award applicants required to submit FAFSA. *Unit head:* Roger Martin, Director, 434-982-2182, Fax: 434-924-4511, E-mail: rdm3h@virginia.edu. *Application contact:* Emma Candalier, Associate Director of Graduate Recruiting, 434-243-4992, Fax: 434-924-4511, E-mail: ecandalier@virginia.edu.

University of Washington, Graduate School, Michael G. Foster School of Business, Seattle, WA 98195-3233. Offers auditing and assurance (MP Acc); business (PhD); business administration (evening) (MBA); business administration (full-time) (MBA); executive business administration (MBA); global business administration (MBA); global executive business administration (MBA); taxation (MP Acc); technology management (MBA); JD/MBA; MBA/MAIS; MBA/MHA. *Accreditation:* AACSB. Part-time programs available. *Faculty:* 100 full-time (28 women), 55 part-time/adjunct (22 women). *Students:* 385 full-time (116 women), 483 part-time (118 women); includes 183 minority (16 Black or African American, non-Hispanic/Latino; 2 American Indian or Alaska Native, non-Hispanic/Latino; 133 Asian, non-Hispanic/Latino; 25 Hispanic/Latino; 2 Native Hawaiian or other Pacific Islander, non-Hispanic/Latino; 5 Two or more races, non-Hispanic/Latino), 178 international. Average age 32. 1,367 applicants, 76% accepted, 868 enrolled. In 2011, 458 master's, 12 doctorates awarded. Terminal master's awarded for partial completion of doctoral program. *Degree requirements:* For doctorate, comprehensive exam, thesis/dissertation. *Entrance requirements:* For master's, GMAT; for doctorate, GMAT, GRE. Additional exam requirements/recommendations for international students: Required—TOEFL (minimum score 600 paper-based; 250 computer-based; 100 iBT). *Application deadline:* For fall admission, 3/15 for domestic students, 1/20 for international students. Application fee: $75. Electronic applications accepted. *Expenses:* Contact institution. *Financial support:* Fellowships with partial tuition reimbursements, research assistantships with partial tuition reimbursements, teaching assistantships with partial tuition reimbursements, Federal Work-Study, institutionally sponsored loans, and scholarships/grants available. Financial award application deadline: 2/28; financial award applicants required to submit FAFSA. *Faculty research:* Finance, marketing, organizational behavior, information technology, strategy. *Unit head:* Dr. James Jiambalvo, Dean, 206-543-4750. *Application contact:* Erin Ernst, Assistant Director of Admissions, 206-543-4661, Fax: 206-616-7351, E-mail: mba@u.washington.edu. Web site: http://www.foster.washington.edu/mba.

University of Washington, Tacoma, Graduate Programs, MBA Programs, Tacoma, WA 98402-3100. Offers accounting (MBA); business administration (MBA); certified financial analyst (MBA). Part-time and evening/weekend programs available. *Entrance requirements:* For master's, GMAT, minimum GPA of 3.0 in final graded 90 quarter credits or 60 graded semester credits; at least 2 years of professional/management work experience. Additional exam requirements/recommendations for international students: Required—TOEFL (minimum score 580 paper-based; 237 computer-based; 92 iBT). Electronic applications accepted. *Expenses:* Contact institution. *Faculty research:* International accounting, marketing, change management, investments, corporate social responsibility.

University of Waterloo, Graduate Studies, Faculty of Arts, School of Accounting and Finance, Waterloo, ON N2L 3G1, Canada. Offers accounting (M Acc, PhD); finance (M Acc); taxation (M Tax). *Degree requirements:* For master's, thesis or alternative; for doctorate, thesis/dissertation. *Entrance requirements:* For master's, honors degree, minimum B average, resumé; for doctorate, GMAT, master's degree, minimum A-average, resume. Additional exam requirements/recommendations for international students: Required—TOEFL, TWE. Electronic applications accepted. *Expenses:* Contact institution. *Faculty research:* Auditing, management accounting.

University of West Florida, College of Business, Department of Accounting, Pensacola, FL 32514-5750. Offers M Acc. Part-time and evening/weekend programs available. *Faculty:* 10 full-time (1 woman), 3 part-time/adjunct (0 women). *Students:* 20 full-time (11 women), 49 part-time (28 women); includes 14 minority (4 Black or African American, non-Hispanic/Latino; 4 Asian, non-Hispanic/Latino; 3 Hispanic/Latino; 3 Two or more races, non-Hispanic/Latino), 2 international. Average age 31. 30 applicants, 87% accepted, 18 enrolled. In 2011, 22 master's awarded. *Entrance requirements:* For master's, GMAT (minimum score 450) or equivalent GRE score, official transcripts; bachelor's degree; two letters of recommendation; letter of intent. Additional exam requirements/recommendations for international students: Required—TOEFL (minimum score 550 paper-based; 213 computer-based). *Application deadline:* For fall admission, 6/30 priority date for domestic students, 6/1 for international students; for spring admission, 10/1 for domestic and international students. Application fee: $30. *Expenses:* Tuition, state resident: full-time $5729; part-time $302 per credit hour. Tuition, nonresident: full-time $20,059; part-time $961 per credit hour. *Required fees:* $1509; $63 per credit hour. *Financial support:* In 2011–12, 17 fellowships (averaging $475 per year), 9 research assistantships with partial tuition reimbursements (averaging $2,156 per year) were awarded; unspecified assistantships also available. Financial award application deadline: 4/15; financial award applicants required to submit FAFSA. *Faculty research:* Audit risk, tax legislation, product costing, bank core deposit intangibles, financial reporting. *Unit head:* Dr. Doug Waggle, Chairperson, 850-474-2719, E-mail: dwaggle@uwf.edu. *Application contact:* Terry McCray, Assistant Director of Graduate Admissions, 850-473-7718, Fax: 850-473-7714, E-mail: gradadmissions@uwf.edu. Web site: http://uwf.edu/account/gradprograms.cfm.

University of West Georgia, Richards College of Business, Department of Accounting and Finance, Carrollton, GA 30118. Offers MP Acc. *Accreditation:* AACSB. Part-time and evening/weekend programs available. *Faculty:* 8 full-time (2 women). *Students:* 15 full-time (5 women), 10 part-time (6 women); includes 8 minority (6 Black or African American, non-Hispanic/Latino; 2 Asian, non-Hispanic/Latino), 3 international. Average age 32. 17 applicants, 59% accepted, 1 enrolled. In 2011, 19 master's awarded. *Degree requirements:* For master's, comprehensive exam. *Entrance requirements:* For master's, GMAT, minimum GPA of 2.5. Additional exam requirements/recommendations for international students: Required—TOEFL (minimum score 550 paper-based; 213 computer-based; 79 iBT); Recommended—IELTS (minimum score 6.5). *Application deadline:* For fall admission, 7/15 for domestic students, 6/1 for international students; for spring admission, 11/15 for domestic students, 10/15 for international students. Applications are processed on a rolling basis. Application fee: $30. Electronic applications accepted. *Expenses:* Contact institution. *Financial support:* In 2011–12, 1 student received support, including 1 research assistantship with full tuition reimbursement available (averaging $4,500 per year); tuition waivers (partial) also available. Financial award application deadline: 7/1; financial award applicants required to submit FAFSA. *Faculty research:* Taxpayer insolvency, non-gap financial measures, deferred taxes, financial accounting issues. *Total annual research expenditures:* $40,000. *Unit head:* Dr. James R. Colley, Chair, 678-839-6469, Fax: 678-839-5041, E-mail: jcolley@westga.edu. *Application contact:* Dr. Hope Udombon, Administrative Director of Graduate Business Programs, 678-839-5355, Fax: 678-839-5040, E-mail: hudombon@westga.edu. Web site: http://www.westga.edu/accfin/.

University of Wisconsin–Madison, Graduate School, Wisconsin School of Business, Doctoral Program in Accounting and Information Systems, Madison, WI 53706-1380. Offers PhD. *Accreditation:* AACSB. *Faculty:* 10 full-time (3 women), 5 part-time/adjunct (2 women). *Students:* 12 full-time (8 women); includes 1 minority (American Indian or Alaska Native, non-Hispanic/Latino), 2 international. Average age 29. 64 applicants, 8% accepted, 3 enrolled. In 2011, 2 doctorates awarded. *Degree requirements:* For doctorate, comprehensive exam, thesis/dissertation. *Entrance requirements:* For doctorate, GMAT or GRE. Additional exam requirements/recommendations for international students: Required—Pearson Test of English (minimum score 73; written 80); Recommended—TOEFL (minimum score 623 paper-based; 263 computer-based; 106 iBT), IELTS (minimum score 7.5). *Application deadline:* For fall admission, 12/15 priority date for domestic students, 12/15 for international students. Application fee: $56. Electronic applications accepted. *Expenses:* Contact institution. *Financial support:* In 2011–12, 12 students received support, including 1 fellowship with full tuition reimbursement available (averaging $18,756 per year), research assistantships with full tuition reimbursements available (averaging $16,506 per year), 11 teaching assistantships with full tuition reimbursements available (averaging $14,088 per year); Federal Work-Study, institutionally sponsored loans, scholarships/grants, health care benefits, and unspecified assistantships also available. Financial award application deadline: 2/1. *Faculty research:* Auditing, financial reporting, economic theory, strategy, computer models. *Unit head:* Prof. Jon Davis, Chair, 608-263-4264. *Application contact:* Belle Heberling, Assistant Director for Research Programs, 608-262-3749, Fax: 608-890-0180, E-mail: phd@bus.wisc.edu. Web site: http://www.bus.wisc.edu/phd.

University of Wisconsin–Madison, Graduate School, Wisconsin School of Business, Master of Accountancy Program, Madison, WI 53706-1380. Offers accountancy (M Acc); tax (M Acc). *Faculty:* 13 full-time (5 women). *Students:* 112 full-time (46 women); includes 9 minority (2 Black or African American, non-Hispanic/Latino; 5 Asian, non-Hispanic/Latino; 2 Hispanic/Latino), 13 international. Average age 22. 245 applicants, 43% accepted, 103 enrolled. In 2011, 87 degrees awarded. *Degree requirements:* For master's, minimum GPA of 3.0. *Entrance requirements:* For master's, GMAT, essays. Additional exam requirements/recommendations for international students: Required—TOEFL (minimum score 100 computer-based), Pearson Test of English. *Application deadline:* For fall admission, 9/15 for domestic and international students; for winter admission, 1/7 for domestic and international students. Application fee: $56. Electronic applications accepted. *Expenses:* Tuition, state resident: full-time $10,296; part-time $643.51 per credit. Tuition, nonresident: full-time $24,054; part-time $1503.40 per credit. *Required fees:* $70.06 per credit. Tuition and fees vary according to course load, campus/location, program and reciprocity agreements. *Financial support:* In 2011–12, 84 students received support, including 5 research assistantships with full tuition reimbursements available (averaging $4,695 per year), 32 teaching assistantships with full tuition reimbursements available (averaging $6,691 per year); career-related internships or fieldwork, scholarships/grants, and unspecified assistantships also available. Financial award application deadline: 5/1; financial award applicants required to submit FAFSA. *Faculty research:* Internal control deficiencies, impairment recognition, accounting misstatements, earnings restatements, voluntary disclosure. *Unit head:* Terry Warfield, Professor/Chair of Accounting and Information Systems, 608-262-1028, E-mail: twarfield@bus.wisc.edu. *Application contact:* Kristen Ann Fuhremann, Director, 608-262-0316, Fax: 608-263-0477, E-mail: kfuhremann@bus.wisc.edu. Web site: http://bus.wisc.edu/degrees-programs/msmacc.

University of Wisconsin–Whitewater, School of Graduate Studies, College of Business and Economics, Department of Accounting, Whitewater, WI 53190-1790. Offers MPA. Part-time and evening/weekend programs available. Postbaccalaureate distance learning degree programs offered (no on-campus study). *Students:* 126 full-time (54 women), 33 part-time (12 women); includes 19 minority (7 Black or African American, non-Hispanic/Latino; 10 Asian, non-Hispanic/Latino; 2 Hispanic/Latino). Average age 25. 51 applicants, 71% accepted, 28 enrolled. In 2011, 98 master's awarded. *Degree requirements:* For master's, thesis or alternative. *Entrance requirements:* For master's, GMAT, minimum AACSB index of 1000, minimum GPA of 2.75. Additional exam requirements/recommendations for international students: Required—TOEFL (minimum score 550 paper-based; 213 computer-based; 80 iBT), IELTS (minimum score 6). *Application deadline:* For fall admission, 7/15 priority date for domestic students, 7/15 for international students; for spring admission, 12/1 priority date for domestic students, 12/1 for international students. Applications are processed on a rolling basis. Application fee: $56. Electronic applications accepted. *Expenses:* Tuition, state resident: full-time $4088. Tuition, nonresident: full-time $8817. Tuition and fees vary according to program. *Financial support:* In 2011–12, 1 research assistantship (averaging $7,245 per year) was awarded; Federal Work-Study, unspecified assistantships, and out of state fee waiver also available. Support available to part-time students. Financial award application deadline: 3/15; financial award applicants required to submit FAFSA. *Faculty research:* Laws/economy/quality of life; tax, accounting and public policy. *Unit head:* Dr. Robert Gruber, Professor and Program Coordinator, 262-472-1945, Fax: 262-172-4863, E-mail: gruberr@uww.edu. *Application contact:* Dr. John Chenoweth, Associate Dean, 262-472-1945, Fax: 262-472-4863, E-mail: chenowej@uww.edu.

University of Wyoming, College of Business, Program in Accounting, Laramie, WY 82070. Offers MS. *Degree requirements:* For master's, thesis optional. *Entrance requirements:* For master's, GMAT or GRE, minimum GPA of 3.0. Additional exam requirements/recommendations for international students: Required—TOEFL (minimum score 540 paper-based; 207 computer-based; 76 iBT). Electronic applications accepted. *Faculty research:* Taxation, accounting education, assessment, not-for-profit accounting, fraud examination, ethics, management accounting.

Upper Iowa University, Online Master's Programs, Fayette, IA 52142-1857. Offers accounting (MBA); corporate financial management (MBA); global business (MBA); health and human services (MPA); higher education administration (MHEA); homeland security (MPA); human resources management (MBA); justice administration (MPA); organizational development (MBA); public personnel management (MPA); quality management (MBA). MBA also available at Madison, WI campus. Part-time programs available. Postbaccalaureate distance learning degree programs offered (no on-campus study). *Degree requirements:* For master's, research project. *Entrance requirements:* For master's, GMAT, GRE, or minimum GPA of 2.7 during last 60 hours. Additional exam requirements/recommendations for international students: Required—TOEFL (minimum score 570 paper-based; 230 computer-based). Electronic applications accepted. *Faculty research:* Total quality management, CQI, teams, organization culture and climate, management.

Utah State University, School of Graduate Studies, College of Business, School of Accountancy, Logan, UT 84322. Offers M Acc. *Accreditation:* AACSB. Part-time programs available. *Entrance requirements:* For master's, GMAT, minimum GPA of 3.0, 3 recommendation letters. Additional exam requirements/recommendations for international students: Required—TOEFL. *Faculty research:* Relationship theory, enterprise systems, just in time/loan, reported earnings measures, accounting education.

Utah Valley University, MBA Program, Orem, UT 84058-5999. Offers accounting (MBA); management (MBA). Evening/weekend programs available. *Application contact:* Eric Wilding, Intermediate Research Analyst, 801-863-7923, E-mail: eric.wilding@uvu.edu. Web site: http://www.uvu.edu/mba/.

Utica College, Program in Accountancy, Utica, NY 13502-4892. Offers MBA. Part-time and evening/weekend programs available. Postbaccalaureate distance learning degree programs offered. *Entrance requirements:* For master's, BS, minimum GPA of 3.0. Additional exam requirements/recommendations for international students: Required—TOEFL (minimum score 525 paper-based; 195 computer-based). Electronic applications accepted. *Expenses:* Contact institution.

Vanderbilt University, Owen Graduate School of Management and Graduate School, Master of Accountancy Program, Nashville, TN 37240-1001. Offers M Acc. *Accreditation:* AACSB. *Faculty:* 39 full-time (5 women). *Students:* 26 full-time (11 women); includes 2 minority (1 American Indian or Alaska Native, non-Hispanic/Latino; 1 Asian, non-Hispanic/Latino). Average age 23. 185 applicants, 21% accepted, 26 enrolled. In 2011, 28 master's awarded. *Entrance requirements:* For master's, GMAT or GRE. Additional exam requirements/recommendations for international students:

Required—TOEFL, IELTS. *Application deadline:* For fall admission, 10/7 priority date for domestic students, 10/10 for international students; for winter admission, 1/9 for domestic and international students; for spring admission, 3/5 for domestic students. Application fee: $50. Electronic applications accepted. *Expenses:* Contact institution. *Financial support:* Scholarships/grants and tuition waivers available. Financial award application deadline: 5/1; financial award applicants required to submit FAFSA. *Faculty research:* Financial marketing, operations, human resources. *Unit head:* Dr. Karl Hackbrack, Faculty, 615-322-3641, E-mail: karl.hackenbrack@owen.vanderbilt.edu. *Application contact:* Amy Johnson, Program Director, 615-322-6509, Fax: 615-343-1175, E-mail: ajohnson@owen.vanderbilt.edu. Web site: http://www.owen.vanderbilt.edu/vanderbilt/programs/master-of-accountancy/index.cfm.

Villanova University, Villanova School of Business, Master of Accountancy Program, Villanova, PA 19085. Offers MAC. *Accreditation:* AACSB. *Faculty:* 101 full-time (32 women), 38 part-time/adjunct (8 women). *Students:* 31 part-time (13 women); includes 4 minority (1 Black or African American, non-Hispanic/Latino; 1 Asian, non-Hispanic/Latino; 2 Two or more races, non-Hispanic/Latino). Average age 24. In 2011, 32 master's awarded. *Degree requirements:* For master's, minimum cumulative GPA of 3.0. *Entrance requirements:* For master's, undergraduate accounting major or the following pre-requisite courses: intermediate accounting I and II, federal income tax and auditing. Additional exam requirements/recommendations for international students: Required—TOEFL (minimum score 550 paper-based; 213 computer-based; 80 iBT). *Application deadline:* For spring admission, 3/15 for domestic and international students. Applications are processed on a rolling basis. Application fee: $50. Electronic applications accepted. *Expenses: Tuition:* Part-time $675 per credit. Part-time tuition and fees vary according to degree level and program. *Financial support:* Scholarships/grants available. Financial award application deadline: 6/30; financial award applicants required to submit FAFSA. *Faculty research:* Business analytics; creativity, innovation and entrepreneurship; global leadership; marketing and public policy; real estate; church management. *Unit head:* Kristy Irwin, Director of Recruitment and Marketing, 610-519-6288, Fax: 610-519-6273, E-mail: kristy.irwin@villanova.edu. *Application contact:* Meredith L. Lockyer, Assistant Director, 610-519-7016, Fax: 610-519-6273, E-mail: meredith.lockyer@villanova.edu. Web site: http://www.gradbusiness.villanova.edu.

Virginia Commonwealth University, Graduate School, School of Business, Program in Accounting, Richmond, VA 23284-9005. Offers M Acc, MBA, PhD. *Accreditation:* AACSB. *Students:* 35 full-time (27 women), 24 part-time (14 women); includes 18 minority (10 Black or African American, non-Hispanic/Latino; 2 Asian, non-Hispanic/Latino; 1 Hispanic/Latino; 5 Two or more races, non-Hispanic/Latino), 9 international. 54 applicants, 59% accepted, 19 enrolled. In 2011, 30 master's awarded. *Degree requirements:* For doctorate, thesis/dissertation. *Entrance requirements:* For master's, GMAT; for doctorate, GMAT, relevant work experience. Additional exam requirements/recommendations for international students: Required—TOEFL (minimum score 600 paper-based; 250 computer-based; 100 iBT). *Application deadline:* For fall admission, 7/1 for domestic students; for spring admission, 11/1 for domestic students. Applications are processed on a rolling basis. Application fee: $50. Electronic applications accepted. *Expenses:* Tuition, state resident: full-time $9133; part-time $507 per credit. Tuition, nonresident: full-time $18,777; part-time $1043 per credit. *Required fees:* $77 per credit. Tuition and fees vary according to degree level, campus/location, program and student level. *Financial support:* Fellowships, research assistantships, teaching assistantships, Federal Work-Study, institutionally sponsored loans, and tuition waivers (full and partial) available. Financial award application deadline: 3/15; financial award applicants required to submit FAFSA. *Unit head:* Dr. Carolyn S. Norman, Professor/Interim Chair, 804-828-3160, E-mail: castrand@vcu.edu. *Application contact:* Jana P. McQuaid, Assistant Dean, Master's Programs, 804-828-4622, Fax: 804-828-7174, E-mail: jpmcquaid@vcu.edu.

Virginia International University, School of Business, Fairfax, VA 22030. Offers accounting (MBA); executive management (Graduate Certificate); global logistics (MBA); health care management (MBA); human resources management (MBA); international business management (MBA); international finance (MBA); marketing management (MBA). Part-time programs available. *Entrance requirements:* For master's and Graduate Certificate, bachelor's degree. Additional exam requirements/recommendations for international students: Required—TOEFL (minimum score 550 paper-based; 213 computer-based; 80 iBT), IELTS (minimum score 6). Electronic applications accepted.

Virginia Polytechnic Institute and State University, Graduate School, Pamplin College of Business, Department of Accounting and Information Systems, Blacksburg, VA 24061. Offers MACIS, PhD. *Accreditation:* AACSB. *Degree requirements:* For master's, comprehensive exam (for some programs), thesis (for some programs); for doctorate, comprehensive exam (for some programs), thesis/dissertation (for some programs). *Entrance requirements:* For master's and doctorate, GRE. Additional exam requirements/recommendations for international students: Required—TOEFL (minimum score 550 paper-based; 213 computer-based). *Application deadline:* For fall admission, 7/1 for domestic and international students; for spring admission, 12/1 for domestic and international students. Applications are processed on a rolling basis. Application fee: $65. Electronic applications accepted. *Expenses:* Tuition, state resident: full-time $10,048; part-time $558.25 per credit hour. Tuition, nonresident: full-time $19,497; part-time $1083.25 per credit hour. *Required fees:* $405 per semester. Tuition and fees vary according to course load, campus/location and program. *Financial support:* Fellowships with full tuition reimbursements, teaching assistantships with full tuition reimbursements, career-related internships or fieldwork, Federal Work-Study, scholarships/grants, health care benefits, and unspecified assistantships available. Financial award application deadline: 1/15. *Faculty research:* Financial accounting, international accounting, management accounting. *Unit head:* Dr. Robert M. Brown, Unit Head, 540-231-5869, Fax: 540-231-2511, E-mail: moren@vt.edu. *Application contact:* Linda Wallace, Information Contact, 540-231-6328, Fax: 540-231-2511, E-mail: wallacel@vt.edu. Web site: http://www.cob.vt.edu/acis/.

Wagner College, Division of Graduate Studies, Department of Business Administration, Program in Accounting, Staten Island, NY 10301-4495. Offers MS. Part-time programs available. *Faculty:* 3 full-time (all women), 1 part-time/adjunct (0 women). *Students:* 24 full-time (9 women), 9 part-time (4 women); includes 5 minority (1 Black or African American, non-Hispanic/Latino; 1 Asian, non-Hispanic/Latino; 2 Hispanic/Latino; 1 Two or more races, non-Hispanic/Latino). Average age 23. 29 applicants, 100% accepted, 24 enrolled. In 2011, 20 master's awarded. *Degree requirements:* For master's, thesis. *Entrance requirements:* For master's, bachelor's degree in accounting or business with a concentration in accounting. Additional exam requirements/recommendations for international students: Required—TOEFL (minimum score 550 paper-based; 217 computer-based; 79 iBT). *Application deadline:* For fall admission, 5/1 priority date for domestic students, 3/1 for international students; for spring admission, 12/1 priority date for domestic students, 10/1 for international students. Applications are processed on a rolling basis. Application fee: $50 ($85 for international students). *Expenses: Tuition:* Full-time $16,200; part-time $890 per credit. *Financial support:* Career-related internships or fieldwork, unspecified assistantships, and alumni fellowship grant available. Financial award applicants required to submit FAFSA. *Unit head:* Prof. Margaret Horan, Director, 718-390-3437, E-mail: phoran@wagner.edu. *Application contact:* Patricia Clancy, Administrative Assistant, Admissions, 718-420-4464, Fax: 718-390-3105, E-mail: patricia.clancy@wagner.edu.

Wake Forest University, Graduate School of Arts and Sciences, Department of Accountancy, Winston-Salem, NC 27109. Offers MSA. *Accreditation:* AACSB. *Entrance requirements:* For master's, GMAT. Additional exam requirements/recommendations for international students: Required—TOEFL (minimum score 213 computer-based). Electronic applications accepted.

Wake Forest University, Schools of Business, MS in Accountancy Program, Winston-Salem, NC 27106. Offers assurance services (MSA); tax consulting (MSA); transaction services (MSA). *Faculty:* 62 full-time (16 women), 41 part-time/adjunct (14 women). *Students:* 183 full-time (86 women); includes 33 minority (17 Black or African American, non-Hispanic/Latino; 1 American Indian or Alaska Native, non-Hispanic/Latino; 6 Asian, non-Hispanic/Latino; 9 Hispanic/Latino), 19 international. Average age 23. In 2011, 82 master's awarded. *Degree requirements:* For master's, 30 credit hours. *Entrance requirements:* For master's, GMAT, letters of recommendation, official transcripts, current resume or curriculum vitae. Additional exam requirements/recommendations for international students: Required—TOEFL (minimum score 600 paper-based; 250 computer-based; 100 iBT), Pearson Test of English. *Application deadline:* For fall admission, 6/1 for domestic and international students. Applications are processed on a rolling basis. Application fee: $100. Electronic applications accepted. *Financial support:* In 2011–12, 152 students received support. Career-related internships or fieldwork and scholarships/grants available. Financial award application deadline: 2/15; financial award applicants required to submit FAFSA. *Faculty research:* The influence of personal relationships on business decision-making and management of change; drivers of perceived value and consumer behavior; impact of accounting on auditing, financial, managerial, systems and taxation stakeholders; corporate governance and executive compensation; impact of operations strategies on competitiveness. *Unit head:* Jack Wilkerson, Senior Associate Dean of Accounting Programs, 336-758-5422, Fax: 336-758-5830, E-mail: busadmissions@wfu.edu. *Application contact:* Tamara Paquee, Administrative Assistant, 336-758-5422, Fax: 336-758-5830, E-mail: busadmissions@wfu.edu. Web site: http://www.business.wfu.edu/.

Walden University, Graduate Programs, School of Management, Minneapolis, MN 55401. Offers accounting (MS, DBA), including accounting for the professional (MS), CPA (MS), self-designed (MS); accounting and management (MS), including accounting for strategic managers, self-designed; accounting for managers (MBA); advanced project management (Post-Graduate Certificate); applied project management (Post-Graduate Certificate); corporate finance (MBA); entrepreneurship (MBA, DBA); finance (DBA); global management (MS); global supply chain management (DBA); healthcare management (MBA, DBA); healthcare system improvement (MBA); human resource management (MBA, MS, PhD), including functional human resource management (MS), integrating functional and strategic human resource management (MS), organizational strategy (MS); information systems management (DBA); international business (MBA, DBA); leadership (MBA, MS, DBA), including entrepreneurship (MS), general management (MS), human resources leadership (MS), innovation and technology (MS), leader development (MS), leading sustainability (MS), project management (MS), self-designed (MS); management (MS), including healthcare management; managers as leaders (MS); marketing (MBA, DBA); project management (MBA, MS, DBA); research strategies (MS); risk management (MBA); self-designed (MBA, DBA, PhD); social impact management (DBA); strategies for sustainability (MBA); strategy and operations (MS); sustainable management (MS); technology (MBA); technology entrepreneurship (DBA); technology management (MS). Part-time and evening/weekend programs available. Postbaccalaureate distance learning degree programs offered (minimal on-campus study). *Faculty:* 32 full-time (14 women), 275 part-time/adjunct (98 women). *Students:* 3,962 full-time (2,095 women), 1,557 part-time (959 women); includes 3,003 minority (2,510 Black or African American, non-Hispanic/Latino; 25 American Indian or Alaska Native, non-Hispanic/Latino; 140 Asian, non-Hispanic/Latino; 240 Hispanic/Latino; 9 Native Hawaiian or other Pacific Islander, non-Hispanic/Latino; 79 Two or more races, non-Hispanic/Latino), 395 international. Average age 41. In 2011, 586 master's, 87 doctorates, 4 other advanced degrees awarded. *Degree requirements:* For doctorate, thesis/dissertation (for some programs), residency. *Entrance requirements:* For master's, bachelor's degree or equivalent in related field; minimum GPA of 2.5; official transcripts; goal statement; access to computer and Internet; for doctorate, master's degree or equivalent in related field; minimum GPA of 3.0; 3 years of related professional/academic experience (preferred). Additional exam requirements/recommendations for international students: Required—TOEFL (minimum score 550 paper-based; 213 computer-based), IELTS (minimum score 6.5), Michigan English Language Assessment Battery (minimum score 82). *Application deadline:* Applications are processed on a rolling basis. Application fee: $50. Electronic applications accepted. *Financial support:* Federal Work-Study, scholarships/grants, unspecified assistantships, and family tuition reduction, active duty/veteran tuition reduction, group tuition reduction, interest-free payment plans, employee tuition reduction available. Support available to part-time students. Financial award applicants required to submit FAFSA. *Unit head:* Dr. William Schulz, III, Associate Dean, 800-925-3368. *Application contact:* Jennifer Hall, Vice President of Enrollment Management, 866-4-WALDEN, E-mail: info@waldenu.edu. Web site: http://www.waldenu.edu/Colleges-and-Schools/College-of-Management-and-Technology.htm.

Walsh College of Accountancy and Business Administration, Graduate Programs, Program in Accountancy, Troy, MI 48007-7006. Offers MSPA. Part-time and evening/weekend programs available. *Degree requirements:* For master's, thesis optional. *Entrance requirements:* For master's, minimum GPA of 2.75, previous course work in business. Additional exam requirements/recommendations for international students: Required—TOEFL. Electronic applications accepted.

Washington State University, Graduate School, College of Business, Business Administration Programs, Pullman, WA 99164. Offers business administration (MBA, PhD), including accounting (PhD), finance (PhD), management and operations (PhD), management information systems (PhD), marketing (PhD). *Accreditation:* AACSB. *Faculty:* 47. *Students:* 93 full-time (35 women), 94 part-time (32 women); includes 25 minority (4 Black or African American, non-Hispanic/Latino; 2 American Indian or Alaska Native, non-Hispanic/Latino; 11 Asian, non-Hispanic/Latino; 7 Hispanic/Latino; 1 Two or more races, non-Hispanic/Latino), 33 international. Average age 31. 310 applicants, 31% accepted, 67 enrolled. In 2011, 15 doctorates awarded. *Degree requirements:* For master's, comprehensive exam (for some programs), thesis (for some programs), final presentation; for doctorate, comprehensive exam, thesis/dissertation, oral and written exams. *Entrance requirements:* For master's and doctorate, GMAT, minimum GPA of 3.0, 3 letters of recommendation. Additional exam requirements/recommendations for international students: Required—TOEFL. *Application deadline:* For fall admission, 3/1 priority date for domestic students, 3/1 for international students; for spring admission, 6/1 priority date for domestic students, 6/1 for international students. Applications are processed on a rolling basis. Application fee: $75. Electronic applications accepted. *Financial support:* In 2011–12, 102 students received support, including 36 teaching assistantships with full and partial tuition reimbursements available (averaging $18,204 per year); career-related internships or fieldwork, Federal Work-Study, institutionally sponsored loans, health care benefits, tuition waivers (partial), unspecified assistantships, and teaching associateships also available. Financial award application deadline: 4/1. *Total annual research expenditures:* $344,000. *Unit head:* Dr. Eric Spangenberg, Dean, 509-335-8150, E-mail: ers@wsu.edu. *Application contact:* Graduate School Admissions, 800-GRADWSU, Fax: 509-335-1949, E-mail: gradsch@wsu.edu.

Washington State University, Graduate School, College of Business, Department of Accounting, Pullman, WA 99164. Offers accounting and information systems (M Acc); accounting and taxation (M Acc). *Accreditation:* AACSB. *Faculty:* 9. *Students:* 53 full-time (31 women), 16 part-time (7 women); includes 57 minority (1 Black or African American, non-Hispanic/Latino; 54 Asian, non-Hispanic/Latino; 2 Hispanic/Latino), 21 international. Average age 24. 127 applicants, 39% accepted, 36 enrolled. In 2011, 25 master's awarded. *Degree requirements:* For master's, comprehensive exam (for some programs), thesis (for some programs), oral exam, research paper. *Entrance requirements:* For master's, GMAT (minimum score of 600), resume; statement of purpose identifying area of interest, experiences, and intended research focus; minimum GPA of 3.25. Additional exam requirements/recommendations for international students: Required—TOEFL (minimum score 580 paper-based; 237 computer-based), IELTS. *Application deadline:* For fall admission, 1/10 priority date for domestic students, 1/10 for international students. Applications are processed on a rolling basis. Application fee: $75. Electronic applications accepted. *Financial support:* In 2011–12, research assistantships (averaging $13,917 per year), 7 teaching assistantships with tuition reimbursements (averaging $18,204 per year) were awarded; Federal Work-Study, institutionally sponsored loans, tuition waivers (partial), and teaching associateships also available. Financial award application deadline: 3/1. *Faculty research:* Ethics, taxation, auditing. *Unit head:* Dr. John Sweeney, Chair, 509-335-8541, Fax: 509-335-4275, E-mail: jtsweeney@wsu.edu. *Application contact:* Graduate School Admissions, 800-GRADWSU, Fax: 509-335-1949, E-mail: gradsch@wsu.edu. Web site: http://www.business.wsu.edu/academics/Accounting/.

Washington University in St. Louis, Olin Business School, Program in Accounting, St. Louis, MO 63130-4899. Offers MS. Part-time programs available. *Faculty:* 88 full-time (29 women), 47 part-time/adjunct (10 women). *Students:* 71 full-time (52 women), 1 (woman) part-time; includes 2 minority (1 Asian, non-Hispanic/Latino; 1 Two or more races, non-Hispanic/Latino), 52 international. Average age 24. 403 applicants, 23% accepted, 49 enrolled. In 2011, 38 master's awarded. *Entrance requirements:* For master's, GMAT or GRE. Additional exam requirements/recommendations for international students: Required—TOEFL. *Application deadline:* For fall admission, 11/8 for domestic and international students; for winter admission, 2/7 for domestic and international students; for spring admission, 3/7 for domestic students. Application fee: $100. Electronic applications accepted. *Financial support:* Applicants required to submit FAFSA. *Unit head:* Joseph Peter Fox, Associate Dean and Director of MBA Programs, 314-935-6322, Fax: 314-935-4464, E-mail: fox@wustl.edu. *Application contact:* Dr. Gary Hochberg, Director, Specialized Master's Programs, 314-935-6380, Fax: 314-935-4464, E-mail: hochberg@wustl.edu.

Wayne State University, School of Business Administration, Detroit, MI 48202. Offers accounting (MBA, MS); industrial relations (MBA); taxation (MST); JD/MBA. *Accreditation:* AACSB. Part-time and evening/weekend programs available. Postbaccalaureate distance learning degree programs offered. *Students:* 182 full-time (68 women), 731 part-time (305 women); includes 256 minority (144 Black or African American, non-Hispanic/Latino; 2 American Indian or Alaska Native, non-Hispanic/Latino; 85 Asian, non-Hispanic/Latino; 12 Hispanic/Latino; 13 Two or more races, non-Hispanic/Latino), 76 international. Average age 30. 675 applicants, 39% accepted, 181 enrolled. In 2011, 325 master's awarded. *Degree requirements:* For doctorate, thesis/dissertation. *Entrance requirements:* For master's, GMAT; for doctorate, GMAT (minimum score of 600), minimum undergraduate GPA 3.0, 3.5 upper-division or graduate; three letters of recommendation; brief essay. Additional exam requirements/recommendations for international students: Required—TOEFL (minimum score 550 paper-based; 213 computer-based); Recommended—TWE (minimum score 6). *Application deadline:* For fall admission, 6/1 priority date for domestic students, 5/1 for international students; for winter admission, 10/1 for domestic students, 9/1 for international students; for spring admission, 2/1 for domestic students, 1/1 for international students. Applications are processed on a rolling basis. Application fee: $50. Electronic applications accepted. *Expenses:* Tuition, state resident: part-time $512.85 per credit. Tuition, nonresident: part-time $1132.65 per credit. *Required fees:* $26.60 per credit. $199.65 per semester. Tuition and fees vary according to course load and program. *Financial support:* In 2011–12, 116 students received support, including 2 fellowships with tuition reimbursements available (averaging $18,000 per year), 2 teaching assistantships with tuition reimbursements available (averaging $1,800 per year); scholarships/grants, health care benefits, and unspecified assistantships also available. Support available to part-time students. Financial award applicants required to submit FAFSA. *Faculty research:* Corporate financial valuation, strategic advertising, information technology effectiveness, financial accounting and taxation, organizational performance and effectiveness. *Total annual research expenditures:* $257,637. *Unit head:* Dr. Margaret Williams, Interim Dean, 313-577-4501, Fax: 313-577-4557, E-mail: margaret.l.williams@wayne.edu. *Application contact:* Linda Zaddach, Assistant Dean, 313-577-4510, E-mail: l.s.zaddach@wayne.edu. Web site: http://business.wayne.edu/.

See Display on page 172 and Close-Up on page 261.

Webber International University, Graduate School of Business, Babson Park, FL 33827-0096. Offers accounting (MBA); management (MBA); security management (MBA); sports management (MBA). Part-time and evening/weekend programs available. *Degree requirements:* For master's, thesis or alternative. *Entrance requirements:* For master's, previous course work in financial and managerial accounting. Additional exam requirements/recommendations for international students: Required—TOEFL. *Faculty research:* Finance strategy, market research, investments, intranet.

Weber State University, John B. Goddard School of Business and Economics, School of Accountancy, Ogden, UT 84408-1001. Offers accounting (M Acc); taxation (M Tax). *Accreditation:* AACSB. Part-time programs available. *Entrance requirements:* For master's, GMAT. *Faculty research:* Taxation, financial accounting, auditing, managerial accounting, accounting education.

Western Carolina University, Graduate School, College of Business, Program in Accountancy, Cullowhee, NC 28723. Offers M Ac. Part-time and evening/weekend programs available. *Students:* 13 full-time (8 women), 21 part-time (13 women); includes 2 minority (1 Asian, non-Hispanic/Latino; 1 Hispanic/Latino), 1 international. Average age 30. 25 applicants, 92% accepted, 20 enrolled. In 2011, 26 master's awarded. *Entrance requirements:* For master's, GMAT, appropriate undergraduate degree, 3 letters of recommendation. Additional exam requirements/recommendations for international students: Required—TOEFL (minimum score 550 paper-based; 270 computer-based; 79 iBT). *Application deadline:* For fall admission, 5/1 priority date for domestic students; for spring admission, 9/1 priority date for domestic students. Applications are processed on a rolling basis. Application fee: $50. *Expenses:* Tuition, state resident: full-time $3348. Tuition, nonresident: full-time $12,933. *Required fees:* $3155. *Financial support:* Fellowships, research assistantships with full and partial tuition reimbursements, teaching assistantships with full and partial tuition reimbursements, career-related internships or fieldwork, institutionally sponsored loans, scholarships/grants, and unspecified assistantships available. Financial award application deadline: 3/31; financial award applicants required to submit FAFSA. *Unit head:* Dr. Susan Swanger, Director, 828-227-3525, Fax: 828-227-7414, E-mail: swanger@email.wcu.edu. *Application contact:* Admissions Specialist for Accountancy, 828-227-7398, Fax: 828-227-7480, E-mail: gradsch@email.wcu.edu. Web site: http://www.wcu.edu/3935.asp.

Western Connecticut State University, Division of Graduate Studies, Ancell School of Business, Program in Business Administration, Danbury, CT 06810-6885. Offers accounting (MBA); business administration (MBA). Part-time programs available. *Faculty:* 6 full-time (3 women), 1 part-time/adjunct (0 women). *Students:* 7 full-time (1 woman), 45 part-time (18 women); includes 10 minority (1 Black or African American, non-Hispanic/Latino; 4 Asian, non-Hispanic/Latino; 5 Hispanic/Latino). Average age 33. In 2011, 25 degrees awarded. *Degree requirements:* For master's, comprehensive exam, completion of program within 8 years. *Entrance requirements:* For master's, GMAT. Additional exam requirements/recommendations for international students: Recommended—TOEFL (minimum score 550 paper-based; 213 computer-based; 79 iBT), IELTS (minimum score 6). *Application deadline:* For fall admission, 8/5 priority date for domestic students; for spring admission, 1/5 priority date for domestic students. Applications are processed on a rolling basis. Application fee: $50. Tuition and fees vary according to course level, course load, degree level and program. *Financial support:* Application deadline: 5/1; applicants required to submit FAFSA. *Faculty research:* Global strategic marketing planning, project management and team coordination; email, discussion boards that act as blogs and videoconferencing. *Unit head:* Dr. Fred Tesch, MBA Coordinator, 203-837-8654, Fax: 203-837-8527. *Application contact:* Chris Shankle, Associate Director of Graduate Studies, 203-837-9005, Fax: 203-837-8326, E-mail: shanklec@wcsu.edu.

Western Illinois University, School of Graduate Studies, College of Business and Technology, Department of Accountancy, Macomb, IL 61455-1390. Offers M Acct. *Accreditation:* AACSB. Part-time programs available. *Students:* 15 full-time (10 women), 3 part-time (all women); includes 2 minority (both Black or African American, non-Hispanic/Latino), 1 international. Average age 26. 12 applicants, 67% accepted. In 2011, 13 master's awarded. *Degree requirements:* For master's, thesis or alternative. *Entrance requirements:* For master's, GMAT. Additional exam requirements/recommendations for international students: Required—TOEFL (minimum score 550 paper-based; 213 computer-based; 80 iBT). *Application deadline:* Applications are processed on a rolling basis. Application fee: $30. Electronic applications accepted. *Expenses:* Tuition, state resident: part-time $281.16 per credit hour. Tuition, nonresident: part-time $562.32 per credit hour. Part-time tuition and fees vary according to campus/location and reciprocity agreements. *Financial support:* In 2011–12, 8 students received support, including 8 research assistantships with full tuition reimbursements available (averaging $7,360 per year). Financial award applicants required to submit FAFSA. *Unit head:* Dr. John Elfrink, Chairperson, 309-298-1152. *Application contact:* Dr. Nancy Parsons, Assistant Director of Graduate Studies, 309-298-1806, Fax: 309-298-2345, E-mail: grad-office@wiu.edu. Web site: http://wiu.edu/accountancy.

Western Michigan University, Graduate College, Haworth College of Business, Department of Accountancy, Kalamazoo, MI 49008. Offers MSA. *Accreditation:* AACSB. *Entrance requirements:* For master's, GMAT.

Western New England University, College of Business, Program in Accounting, Springfield, MA 01119. Offers MSA. Part-time and evening/weekend programs available. *Students:* 52 part-time (28 women); includes 1 minority (Hispanic/Latino), 2 international. *Entrance requirements:* For master's, GMAT, 2 letters of reference, resume. *Application deadline:* Applications are processed on a rolling basis. Application fee: $30. *Financial support:* Available to part-time students. Application deadline: 4/1; applicants required to submit FAFSA. *Unit head:* Dr. William Bosworth, Chair, Accounting and Finance, 413-782-1231, E-mail: wboswort@wne.edu. *Application contact:* Matt Fox, Director of Recruiting and Marketing for Adult Learners, 413-782-1249, Fax: 413-782-1779, E-mail: learn@wne.edu. Web site: http://www1.wne.edu/business/index.cfm?selection-doc.1280.

Westminster College, The Bill and Vieve Gore School of Business, Salt Lake City, UT 84105-3697. Offers accountancy (M Acc); business administration (MBA, Certificate); technology management (MBATM). *Accreditation:* ACBSP. Part-time and evening/weekend programs available. Postbaccalaureate distance learning degree programs offered (minimal on-campus study). *Faculty:* 24 full-time (7 women), 19 part-time/adjunct (3 women). *Students:* 153 full-time (45 women), 241 part-time (79 women); includes 27 minority (1 Black or African American, non-Hispanic/Latino; 16 Asian, non-Hispanic/Latino; 10 Hispanic/Latino), 1 international. Average age 33. 502 applicants, 38% accepted, 111 enrolled. In 2011, 182 master's, 37 other advanced degrees awarded. *Degree requirements:* For master's, international trip, minimum grade of C in all classes. *Entrance requirements:* For master's, GMAT, 2 professional recommendations, employer letter of support, personal resume, essay questions, official transcripts. Additional exam requirements/recommendations for international students: Required—TOEFL (minimum score 600 paper-based; 250 computer-based; 100 iBT), IELTS (minimum score 7). *Application deadline:* Applications are processed on a rolling basis. Application fee: $50. Electronic applications accepted. *Expenses:* Contact institution. *Financial support:* In 2011–12, 22 students received support. Career-related internships or fieldwork and tuition reimbursement, tuition remission available. Support available to part-time students. Financial award applicants required to submit FAFSA. *Faculty research:* Innovation and entrepreneurship, business strategy and change, financial analysis and capital budgeting, leadership development, knowledge management. *Unit head:* Dr. Jin Wang, Dean, Gore School of Business, 801-832-2600, Fax: 801-832-3106, E-mail: jwang@westminstercollege.edu. *Application contact:* Dr. Gary Daynes, Vice President for Strategic Outreach and Enrollment, 801-832-2200, Fax: 801-832-3101, E-mail: admission@westminstercollege.edu. Web site: http://www.westminstercollege.edu/mba/.

West Texas A&M University, College of Business, Department of Accounting, Economics, and Finance, Program in Accounting, Canyon, TX 79016-0001. Offers MP Acc. Part-time and evening/weekend programs available. Postbaccalaureate distance learning degree programs offered (minimal on-campus study). *Degree requirements:* For master's, comprehensive exam, thesis optional. *Entrance requirements:* For master's, GMAT. Additional exam requirements/recommendations for international students: Required—TOEFL (minimum score 550 paper-based). Electronic applications accepted. *Faculty research:* Texas economy, service learnings, small business, entrepreneurship, corporation conversion.

West Texas A&M University, College of Business, Department of Accounting, Economics, and Finance, Program in Accounting/Business Administration, Canyon, TX 79016-0001. Offers professional accounting (MPA). Integrated program that allows students to enter program as undergraduates; after bachelor's degree in business administration is earned they progress into graduate accounting phase. Part-time programs available. Postbaccalaureate distance learning degree programs offered (minimal on-campus study). *Entrance requirements:* For master's, GMAT. Additional exam requirements/recommendations for international students: Required—TOEFL (minimum score 550 paper-based). Electronic applications accepted.

West Virginia University, College of Business and Economics, Division of Accounting, Morgantown, WV 26506. Offers MPA. *Accreditation:* AACSB. Part-time and evening/weekend programs available. *Entrance requirements:* For master's, GMAT (minimum 50th percentile), BS in accounting or equivalent, minimum GPA of 3.0. Additional exam requirements/recommendations for international students: Required—TOEFL. Electronic applications accepted. *Faculty research:* Financial reporting, government/not-for-profit accounting, information systems/technology, forensic accounting, internal control.

Wheeling Jesuit University, Department of Business, Wheeling, WV 26003-6295. Offers accounting (MS); business administration (MBA). *Accreditation:* ACBSP. Part-time and evening/weekend programs available. *Faculty:* 6 full-time (1 woman), 4 part-time/adjunct (1 woman). *Students:* 23 full-time (5 women), 37 part-time (20 women); includes 5 minority (1 Black or African American, non-Hispanic/Latino; 1 Asian, non-Hispanic/Latino; 3 Hispanic/Latino), 1 international. Average age 30. 39 applicants, 97% accepted, 17 enrolled. In 2011, 19 master's awarded. *Entrance requirements:* For master's, GMAT, minimum undergraduate GPA of 2.8. Additional exam requirements/recommendations for international students: Required—TOEFL (minimum score 600 paper-based; 250 computer-based; 100 iBT). *Application deadline:* For fall admission, 8/1 priority date for domestic students, 8/1 for international students; for spring admission, 12/15 priority date for domestic students, 12/1 for international students. Applications are processed on a rolling basis. Application fee: $25. Electronic applications accepted. *Expenses: Tuition:* Full-time $9720; part-time $540 per credit hour. *Required fees:* $250. *Financial support:* In 2011–12, 13 students received support. Career-related internships or fieldwork and unspecified assistantships available. Financial award application deadline: 8/1; financial award applicants required to submit FAFSA. *Faculty research:* Forensic economics, philosophic economics, consumer behavior, international business, economic development. *Unit head:* Dr. Edward W. Younkins, Director of Graduate Business Programs, 304-243-2255, Fax: 304-243-8703, E-mail: younkins@wju.edu. *Application contact:* Melissa Rataiczak, Associate Director of Enrollment for Leadership Programs, 304-243-2236, Fax: 304-243-2397, E-mail: mrataiczak@wju.edu. Web site: http://www.wju.edu/academics/bus/gradprog.asp.

Wichita State University, Graduate School, W. Frank Barton School of Business, School of Accountancy, Wichita, KS 67260. Offers M Acc. *Accreditation:* AACSB. Part-time and evening/weekend programs available. *Expenses:* Tuition, state resident: full-time $4746; part-time $263.65 per credit. Tuition, nonresident: full-time $11,669; part-time $648.30 per credit. *Unit head:* Dr. Paul D. Harrison, Director, 316-978-3215, Fax: 316-978-3660, E-mail: paul.harrison@wichita.edu. *Application contact:* Michael B. Flores, Assistant Director and Graduate Advisor, 316-978-3724, E-mail: michael.flores@wichita.edu. Web site: http://www.wichita.edu/.

Widener University, School of Business Administration, Program in Accounting Information Systems, Chester, PA 19013-5792. Offers MS. Part-time and evening/weekend programs available. *Entrance requirements:* For master's, Certified Management Accountant Exam, Certified Public Accountant Exam, or GMAT, minimum GPA of 2.5. Electronic applications accepted.

Wilfrid Laurier University, Faculty of Graduate and Postdoctoral Studies, School of Business and Economics, Department of Business, Waterloo, ON N2L 3C5, Canada. Offers accounting (PhD); finance (M Fin); financial economics (PhD); marketing (PhD); operations and supply chain management (PhD); organizational behavior and human resource management (M Sc); organizational behaviour and human resource management (PhD); supply chain management (M Sc); technology management (EMTM). Part-time and evening/weekend programs available. *Degree requirements:* For master's, thesis optional; for doctorate, comprehensive exam, thesis/dissertation. *Entrance requirements:* For master's, GMAT, 4-year honors degree with minimum B+ average; for doctorate, GMAT, master's degree, minimum B+ average. Additional exam requirements/recommendations for international students: Required—TOEFL (minimum score 89 iBT). Electronic applications accepted. *Faculty research:* Financial economics, management and organizational behavior, operations and supply chain management.

Wilkes University, College of Graduate and Professional Studies, Jay S. Sidhu School of Business and Leadership, Wilkes-Barre, PA 18766-0002. Offers accounting (MBA); entrepreneurship (MBA); finance (MBA); health care administration (MBA); human resource management (MBA); international business (MBA); marketing (MBA); operations management (MBA); organizational leadership and development (MBA). *Accreditation:* ACBSP. Part-time and evening/weekend programs available. *Students:* 48 full-time (20 women), 134 part-time (62 women); includes 12 minority (2 Black or African American, non-Hispanic/Latino; 5 Asian, non-Hispanic/Latino; 2 Hispanic/Latino; 3 Two or more races, non-Hispanic/Latino), 9 international. Average age 30. In 2011, 69 master's awarded. *Entrance requirements:* For master's, GMAT. Additional exam requirements/recommendations for international students: Required—TOEFL (minimum score 550 paper-based; 213 computer-based; 79 iBT). *Application deadline:* Applications are processed on a rolling basis. Application fee: $45 ($65 for international students). Electronic applications accepted. *Expenses:* Contact institution. *Financial support:* Federal Work-Study and unspecified assistantships available. Financial award application deadline: 3/1; financial award applicants required to submit FAFSA. *Unit head:* Dr. Jeffrey Alves, Dean, 570-408-4702, Fax: 570-408-7846, E-mail: jeffrey.alves@wilkes.edu. *Application contact:* Erin Sutzko, Director of Extended Learning, 570-408-4253, Fax: 570-408-7846, E-mail: erin.sutzko@wilkes.edu. Web site: http://www.wilkes.edu/pages/457.asp.

Wilmington University, College of Business, New Castle, DE 19720-6491. Offers accounting (MBA, MS); business administration (MBA, DBA); environmental stewardship (MBA); finance (MBA); health care administration (MBA, MSM); homeland security (MBA, MSM); human resource management (MSM); management information systems (MBA, MSN); marketing (MSM); marketing management (MBA); military leadership (MSM); organizational leadership (MBA, MSM); public administration (MSM). Part-time and evening/weekend programs available. *Faculty:* 4 full-time (0 women). *Students:* 266 full-time (121 women), 700 part-time (505 women). Average age 34. *Entrance requirements:* Additional exam requirements/recommendations for international students: Required—TOEFL (minimum score 500 paper-based; 173 computer-based). *Application deadline:* Applications are processed on a rolling basis. Application fee: $35. Electronic applications accepted. *Expenses: Tuition:* Part-time $534 per credit hour. *Required fees:* $25 per term. *Financial support:* Applicants required to submit FAFSA. *Unit head:* Dr. Donald W. Durandetta, Dean, 302-356-6780, E-mail: donald.w.durandetta@wilmu.edu. *Application contact:* Chris Ferguson, Director of Admissions, 302-356-4636 Ext. 256, Fax: 302-328-5164, E-mail: inquire@wilmcoll.edu. Web site: http://www.wilmu.edu/business/.

Worcester State University, Graduate Studies, Program in Management, Worcester, MA 01602-2597. Offers accounting (MS); managerial leadership (MS). Part-time and evening/weekend programs available. *Faculty:* 1 full-time (0 women), 2 part-time/adjunct (1 woman). *Students:* 10 full-time (5 women), 18 part-time (7 women); includes 6 minority (2 Black or African American, non-Hispanic/Latino; 1 Asian, non-Hispanic/Latino; 2 Hispanic/Latino; 1 Two or more races, non-Hispanic/Latino), 3 international. Average age 31. 26 applicants, 62% accepted, 8 enrolled. In 2011, 5 master's awarded. *Degree requirements:* For master's, comprehensive exam (for some programs), thesis optional. *Entrance requirements:* For master's, GMAT. Additional exam requirements/recommendations for international students: Required—TOEFL (minimum score 500 paper-based; 61 iBT). *Application deadline:* For fall admission, 6/15 for domestic and international students; for spring admission, 4/1 for domestic and international students. Applications are processed on a rolling basis. Application fee: $40. Electronic applications accepted. *Expenses:* Tuition, state resident: full-time $2700; part-time $150 per credit. Tuition, nonresident: full-time $2700; part-time $150 per credit. *Required fees:* $2016; $112 per credit. *Financial support:* In 2011–12, 3 students received support, including 3 research assistantships with full tuition reimbursements available (averaging $4,800 per year); career-related internships or fieldwork, scholarships/grants, and unspecified assistantships also available. Financial award application deadline: 3/1; financial award applicants required to submit FAFSA. *Unit head:* Dr. Laurie Dahlin, Coordinator, 508-929-8084, Fax: 508-929-8048, E-mail: ldahlin@worcester.edu. *Application contact:* Sara Grady, Assistant Dean of Continuing Education, 508-929-8787, Fax: 508-929-8100, E-mail: sara.grady@worcester.edu.

Wright State University, School of Graduate Studies, Raj Soin College of Business, Department of Accountancy, Accountancy Program, Dayton, OH 45435. Offers M Acc.

Yale University, Yale School of Management and Graduate School of Arts and Sciences, Doctoral Program in Management, New Haven, CT 06520. Offers accounting (PhD); financial economics (PhD); marketing (PhD); organizations and management (PhD). *Accreditation:* AACSB. *Faculty:* 42 full-time (8 women). *Students:* 33 full-time (9 women); includes 4 minority (all Asian, non-Hispanic/Latino), 16 international. 439 applicants, 3% accepted, 4 enrolled. In 2011, 2 doctorates awarded. *Degree requirements:* For doctorate, comprehensive exam, thesis/dissertation. *Entrance requirements:* For doctorate, GMAT or GRE General Test. Additional exam requirements/recommendations for international students: Required—TOEFL or IELTS. *Application deadline:* For fall admission, 1/2 for domestic and international students. Application fee: $100. Electronic applications accepted. *Expenses:* Contact institution. *Financial support:* In 2011–12, 31 students received support, including 31 fellowships with full tuition reimbursements available, 31 research assistantships with full tuition reimbursements available, 31 teaching assistantships with full tuition reimbursements available; institutionally sponsored loans, scholarships/grants, and health care benefits also available. Financial award application deadline: 1/2. *Faculty research:* Pricing of options and futures, term structure of interest rates, use of accounting numbers in debt contracts, product differentiation, e-commerce and marketing, behavioral finance. *Unit head:* Carla Mills, Registrar, 203-432-3955, Fax: 203-432-0342.

Yeshiva University, Sy Syms School of Business, New York, NY 10016. Offers accounting (MS). Part-time programs available. *Entrance requirements:* For master's, minimum GPA of 3.5 or GMAT.

York College of Pennsylvania, Donald Graham School of Business, York, PA 17405-7199. Offers accounting (MBA); continuous improvement (MBA); finance (MBA); management (MBA); marketing (MBA); self-designed (MBA). *Accreditation:* ACBSP. Part-time and evening/weekend programs available. *Faculty:* 14 full-time (3 women), 1 part-time/adjunct (0 women). *Students:* 11 full-time (5 women), 99 part-time (40 women); includes 10 minority (5 Black or African American, non-Hispanic/Latino; 1 Asian, non-Hispanic/Latino; 3 Hispanic/Latino; 1 Two or more races, non-Hispanic/Latino), 1 international. Average age 29. 49 applicants, 80% accepted, 26 enrolled. In 2011, 33 master's awarded. *Entrance requirements:* For master's, GMAT. Additional exam requirements/recommendations for international students: Required—TOEFL (minimum score 530 paper-based; 200 computer-based; 72 iBT). *Application deadline:* For fall admission, 7/15 priority date for domestic students; for spring admission, 12/15 priority date for domestic students. Applications are processed on a rolling basis. Application fee: $50. Electronic applications accepted. *Expenses: Tuition:* Full-time $12,060; part-time $670 per credit hour. *Required fees:* $340 per semester. Tuition and fees vary according to degree level. *Financial support:* In 2011–12, 3 students received support. Scholarships/grants available. Financial award application deadline: 4/15; financial award applicants required to submit FAFSA. *Unit head:* Dr. David Greisler, MBA Director, 717-815-6410, Fax: 717-600-3999, E-mail: dgreisle@ycp.edu. *Application contact:* Brenda Adams, Assistant Director, MBA Program, 717-815-1749, Fax: 717-600-3999, E-mail: badams@ycp.edu. Web site: http://www.ycp.edu/mba.

Youngstown State University, Graduate School, Williamson College of Business Administration, Department of Accounting and Finance, Youngstown, OH 44555-0001. Offers accounting (MBA). *Accreditation:* AACSB. Part-time and evening/weekend programs available. *Degree requirements:* For master's, thesis optional. *Entrance requirements:* For master's, GMAT, minimum GPA of 2.7. Additional exam requirements/recommendations for international students: Required—TOEFL. *Faculty research:* Taxation and compliance, capital markets, accounting information systems, accounting theory, tax and government accounting.

Finance and Banking

Adelphi University, Robert B. Willumstad School of Business, Graduate Opportunity for Accelerated Learning MBA Program, Garden City, NY 11530-0701. Offers accounting (MBA); finance (MBA). *Accreditation:* AACSB. Part-time and evening/weekend programs available. *Students:* 13 full-time (7 women), 23 part-time (7 women); includes 17 minority (7 Black or African American, non-Hispanic/Latino; 6 Asian, non-Hispanic/Latino; 4 Hispanic/Latino), 2 international. Average age 41. In 2011, 14 master's awarded. *Entrance requirements:* For master's, GMAT, 2 letters of recommendation, four years managerial experience, letter of sponsorship from current place of employment, resume. Additional exam requirements/recommendations for international students: Required—TOEFL (minimum score 550 paper-based; 213 computer-based; 80 iBT). *Application deadline:* For fall admission, 4/1 for international students; for spring admission, 11/1 for international students. Applications are processed on a rolling basis. Application fee: $50. Electronic applications accepted. *Expenses: Tuition:* Full-time $29,600; part-time $930 per credit. *Required fees:* $1100. *Financial support:* Research assistantships with full and partial tuition reimbursements, career-related internships or fieldwork, Federal Work-Study, institutionally sponsored loans, scholarships/grants, and unspecified assistantships available. Financial award application deadline: 3/1; financial award applicants required to submit FAFSA. *Faculty research:* Capital market, executive compensation, business ethics, classical value theory, labor economics. *Unit head:* Rakesh Gupta, Chairperson, 516-877-4670, Fax: 516-877-4607, E-mail: gradbusinquiries@adelphi.edu. *Application contact:* Christine Murphy, Director of Admissions, 516-877-3050, Fax: 516-877-3039, E-mail: graduateadmissions@adelphi.edu.

Adelphi University, Robert B. Willumstad School of Business, MBA Program, Garden City, NY 11530-0701. Offers finance (MBA); management information systems (MBA); management/human resource management (MBA); marketing/e-commerce (MBA). *Accreditation:* AACSB. Part-time and evening/weekend programs available. *Students:* 258 full-time (121 women), 111 part-time (58 women); includes 67 minority (22 Black or African American, non-Hispanic/Latino; 18 Asian, non-Hispanic/Latino; 24 Hispanic/Latino; 3 Two or more races, non-Hispanic/Latino), 172 international. Average age 28. In 2011, 111 master's awarded. *Degree requirements:* For master's, capstone course. *Entrance requirements:* For master's, GMAT, 2 letters of recommendation. Additional exam requirements/recommendations for international students: Required—TOEFL (minimum score 550 paper-based; 213 computer-based; 80 iBT). *Application deadline:* For fall admission, 4/1 for international students; for spring admission, 11/1 for international students. Applications are processed on a rolling basis. Application fee: $50. Electronic applications accepted. *Expenses: Tuition:* Full-time $29,600; part-time $930 per credit. *Required fees:* $1100. *Financial support:* Research assistantships with full and partial tuition reimbursements, career-related internships or fieldwork, Federal Work-Study, institutionally sponsored loans, scholarships/grants, and unspecified assistantships available. Financial award application deadline: 3/1; financial award applicants required to submit FAFSA. *Faculty research:* Supply chain management, distribution channels, productivity benchmark analysis, data envelopment analysis, financial portfolio analysis. *Unit head:* Rakesh Gupta, 516-877-4670, Fax: 516-877-4607, E-mail: gradbusinquiries@adelphi.edu. *Application contact:* Christine Murphy, Director of Admissions, 516-877-3050, Fax: 516-877-3039, E-mail: graduateadmissions@adelphi.edu. Web site: http://business.adelphi.edu/degree-programs/graduate-degree-programs/m-b-a/.

See Display on page 68 and Close-Up on page 177.

The American College, Graduate Programs, Bryn Mawr, PA 19010-2105. Offers financial services (MSFS); leadership (MSM). Part-time and evening/weekend programs available. Postbaccalaureate distance learning degree programs offered (minimal on-campus study). Electronic applications accepted. *Faculty research:* Retirement counseling, social security, aging, family composition, inflation.

American College of Thessaloniki, Department of Business Administration, Pylea, Greece. Offers banking and finance (MBA); entrepreneurship (MBA, Certificate); finance (Certificate); management (MBA, Certificate); marketing (MBA, Certificate). Part-time and evening/weekend programs available. *Degree requirements:* For master's, thesis. *Entrance requirements:* For master's, bachelor's degree. Additional exam requirements/recommendations for international students: Recommended—TOEFL. Electronic applications accepted.

American InterContinental University Buckhead Campus, Program in Business Administration, Atlanta, GA 30326-1016. Offers accounting and finance (MBA); management (MBA); marketing (MBA). Evening/weekend programs available. Postbaccalaureate distance learning degree programs offered. *Entrance requirements:* For master's, minimum cumulative undergraduate GPA of 2.0. Additional exam requirements/recommendations for international students: Required—TOEFL (minimum score 530 paper-based; 230 computer-based). Electronic applications accepted. *Faculty research:* Leadership management, international advertising.

American InterContinental University Online, Program in Business Administration, Hoffman Estates, IL 60192. Offers accounting and finance (MBA); finance (MBA); healthcare management (MBA); human resource management (MBA); international business (MBA); management (MBA); marketing (MBA); operations management (MBA); organizational psychology and development (MBA); project management (MBA). Evening/weekend programs available. Postbaccalaureate distance learning degree programs offered (no on-campus study). *Entrance requirements:* Additional exam requirements/recommendations for international students: Required—TOEFL (minimum score 550 paper-based; 213 computer-based). Electronic applications accepted.

American InterContinental University South Florida, Program in International Business, Weston, FL 33326. Offers accounting and finance (MBA); human resource management (MBA); management (MBA); marketing (MBA). Part-time and evening/weekend programs available. Postbaccalaureate distance learning degree programs offered. Electronic applications accepted.

American International College, School of Business Administration, MBA Program, Springfield, MA 01109-3189. Offers accounting (MBA); corporate/public communication (MBA); finance (MBA); general business (MBA); hospitality, hotel and service management (MBA); international business (MBA); international business practice (MBA); management (MBA); management information systems (MBA); marketing (MBA). International business practice program developed in cooperation with the Mountbatten Institute.

American Public University System, AMU/APU Graduate Programs, Charles Town, WV 25414. Offers accounting (MBA, MS); administration and supervision (M Ed); criminal justice (MA); emergency and disaster management (MA); entrepreneurship (MBA); environmental policy and management (MS), including environmental planning, environmental sustainability, fish and wildlife management, general (MA, MS), global environmental management; finance (MBA); general (MBA); global business management (MBA); guidance and counseling (M Ed); history (MA), including American history, ancient and classical history, European history, global history, military and diplomatic history, public history; homeland security (MA); homeland security resource allocation (MBA); humanities (MA); information technology (MS), including digital forensics, enterprise software development, information assurance and security, IT project management; information technology management (MBA); intelligence studies (MA), including criminal intelligence, general (MA, MS), homeland security, intelligence analysis, intelligence collection, intelligence operations, terrorism studies; international relations and conflict resolution (MA), including comparative and security issues, conflict resolution, international and transnational security issues, peacekeeping; legal studies (MA); management (MA), including defense management, general (MA, MS), human resource management, organizational leadership, public administration, reverse logistics, strategic consulting; marketing (MBA); military history (MA), including American military history, American revolution, civil war, war since 1946, World War II; military studies (MA), including air warfare, asymmetrical warfare, joint warfare, land warfare, naval warfare, strategic leadership; national security studies (MA), including general (MA, MS), homeland security, regional security studies, security and intelligence analysis, terrorism studies; nonprofit management (MBA); political science (MA), including American politics and government, comparative government and development, public policy; psychology (MA); public administration (MA, MPA), including disaster management (MPA), environmental policy (MA), health policy (MPA), human resources (MPA), national security (MPA), organizational management (MPA), security management (MPA); public health (MA, MPH), including emergency management (MPH), environmental health (MPH), public administration (MA); reverse logistics management (MA); security management (MA); space studies (MS), including aerospace science, planetary science; sports and health sciences (MS); sports management (MS), including coaching theory and strategy, sports administration; teaching (M Ed), including curriculum and instruction for elementary teachers, elementary, elementary reading, English language learners, instructional leadership, online learning, secondary social sciences, special education; transportation and logistics management (MA), including maritime engineering management. Programs offered via distance learning only. Part-time and evening/weekend programs available. Postbaccalaureate distance learning degree programs offered (no on-campus study). *Faculty:* 445 full-time (241 women), 1,360 part-time/adjunct (617 women). *Students:* 688 full-time (338 women), 10,168 part-time (3,706 women); includes 3,130 minority (1,007 Black or African American, non-Hispanic/Latino; 103 American Indian or Alaska Native, non-Hispanic/Latino; 825 Asian, non-Hispanic/Latino; 810 Hispanic/Latino; 51 Native Hawaiian or other Pacific Islander, non-Hispanic/Latino; 334 Two or more races, non-Hispanic/Latino), 134 international. Average age 35. In 2011, 2,386 master's awarded. *Degree requirements:* For master's, comprehensive exam or practicum. *Entrance requirements:* For master's, official transcript showing earned bachelor's degree from institution accredited by recognized accrediting body. Additional exam requirements/recommendations for international students: Required—TOEFL (minimum score 550 paper-based; 213 computer-based), IELTS (minimum score 6.5). *Application deadline:* Applications are processed on a rolling basis. Application fee: $0. Electronic applications accepted. *Expenses: Tuition:* Part-time $325 per credit hour. *Financial support:* Applicants required to submit FAFSA. *Faculty research:* Military history, criminal justice, management performance, national security. *Unit head:* Dr. Karan Powell, Executive Vice President and Provost, 877-468-6268, Fax: 304-724-3780. *Application contact:* Terry Grant, Vice President of Enrollment Management, 877-468-6268, Fax: 304-724-3780, E-mail: info@apus.edu. Web site: http://www.apus.edu.

American University, Kogod School of Business, Department of Finance, Program in Finance, Washington, DC 20016-8044. Offers MS. Part-time and evening/weekend programs available. *Students:* 30 full-time (12 women), 54 part-time (23 women); includes 13 minority (4 Black or African American, non-Hispanic/Latino; 6 Asian, non-Hispanic/Latino; 3 Hispanic/Latino), 35 international. Average age 29. 389 applicants, 20% accepted, 21 enrolled. In 2011, 24 master's awarded. *Entrance requirements:* For master's, GMAT, resume, personal statement, interview. Additional exam requirements/recommendations for international students: Required—TOEFL. *Application deadline:* For fall admission, 2/1 priority date for domestic students; for spring admission, 10/1 priority date for domestic students. Applications are processed on a rolling basis. Application fee: $100. *Expenses: Tuition:* Full-time $24,264; part-time $1348 per credit hour. *Required fees:* $430. Tuition and fees vary according to course load and program. *Financial support:* In 2011–12, 15 students received support. Fellowships, research assistantships with partial tuition reimbursements available, career-related internships or fieldwork, Federal Work-Study, institutionally sponsored loans, and tuition waivers (partial) available. Support available to part-time students. Financial award application deadline: 2/1. *Faculty research:* Development finance, market microstructure, international investment, real estate finance, quantitative modeling. *Unit head:* Dr. Ronald Anderson, Chair, 202-885-2199, Fax: 202-885-1946, E-mail: randers@american.edu. *Application contact:* Shannon Demko, Director of Admissions, 202-885-1968, Fax: 202-885-1078, E-mail: demko@american.edu. Web site: http://www.american.edu/kogod/.

American University, Kogod School of Business, Master of Business Administration Program, Washington, DC 20016-8044. Offers accounting (MBA); consulting (MBA), including business systems consulting, management consulting; entrepreneurship (MBA); entrepreneurship (Certificate); finance (MBA); global emerging markets (MBA); leadership and strategic human capital management (MBA); marketing (MBA); real estate (MBA); MBA/JD; MBA/LL M; MBA/MA. Part-time and evening/weekend programs available. *Faculty:* 13 full-time (6 women). *Students:* 96 full-time (43 women), 104 part-time (35 women); includes 49 minority (14 Black or African American, non-Hispanic/Latino; 16 Asian, non-Hispanic/Latino; 16 Hispanic/Latino; 1 Native Hawaiian or other Pacific Islander, non-Hispanic/Latino; 2 Two or more races, non-Hispanic/Latino), 22 international. Average age 29. 340 applicants, 52% accepted, 52 enrolled. In 2011, 124 master's awarded. *Entrance requirements:* For master's, GMAT, resume, personal statement, interview. Additional exam requirements/recommendations for international students: Required—TOEFL. *Application deadline:* For fall admission, 2/1 priority date for domestic students; for spring admission, 10/1 priority date for domestic students. Applications are processed on a rolling basis. Application fee: $100. *Expenses:* Contact institution. *Financial support:* In 2011–12, 19 students received support. Fellowships, research assistantships with partial tuition reimbursements available, career-related internships or fieldwork, Federal Work-Study, and institutionally sponsored loans available. Support available to part-time students. Financial award application deadline: 2/1. *Faculty research:* Information technology, decision-aiding methodology, negotiation. *Unit head:* Dr. Stevan R. Holmberg, Chair, 202-885-1921, Fax: 202-885-1916, E-mail: sholmbe@american.edu. *Application contact:* Shannon Demko, Director of Admissions, 202-885-1968, Fax: 202-885-1078, E-mail: demko@american.edu. Web site: http://www.american.edu/kogod/.

American University, School of Public Affairs, Department of Public Administration, Washington, DC 20016-8070. Offers key executive leadership (MPA); leadership for organizational change (Certificate); non-profit management (Certificate); organization development (MSOD); public administration (MPA, PhD); public financial management (Certificate); public management (Certificate); public policy (MPP, Certificate), including public policy (MPP), public policy analysis (Certificate); public policy analysis (Certificate); LL M/MPA; MPA/JD; MPP/JD; MPP/LL M. Part-time and evening/weekend programs available. *Faculty:* 28 full-time (13 women), 14 part-time/adjunct (4 women). *Students:* 232 full-time (145 women), 240 part-time (145 women); includes 111 minority (62 Black or African American, non-Hispanic/Latino; 6 American Indian or Alaska Native, non-Hispanic/Latino; 21 Asian, non-Hispanic/Latino; 15 Hispanic/Latino; 7 Two or more races, non-Hispanic/Latino), 42 international. Average age 30. 809 applicants, 69% accepted, 172 enrolled. In 2011, 171 master's, 4 doctorates, 14 other advanced degrees awarded. *Degree requirements:* For master's, comprehensive exam; for doctorate, comprehensive exam, thesis/dissertation. *Entrance requirements:* For master's, GRE, statement of purpose; 2 recommendations, resume; for doctorate, GRE, 3 recommendations, statement of purpose, resume, writing sample; for Certificate, bachelor's degree. Additional exam requirements/recommendations for international students: Required—TOEFL. *Application deadline:* For fall admission, 2/1 for domestic students; for spring admission, 11/1 for domestic students. Application fee: $55. *Expenses: Tuition:* Full-time $24,264; part-time $1348 per credit hour. *Required fees:* $430. Tuition and fees vary according to course load and program. *Financial support:* Fellowships, research assistantships, teaching assistantships, career-related internships or fieldwork, Federal Work-Study, and institutionally sponsored loans available. Financial award application deadline: 2/1. *Faculty research:* Urban management, conservation politics, state and local budgeting, tax policy. *Unit head:* Dr. Jocelyn Johnston, Chair, 202-885-2608, Fax: 202-885-2347, E-mail: johnston@american.edu. *Application contact:* Brenda Manley, Admissions and Financial Aid Manager, 202-885-6202, Fax: 202-885-2355, E-mail: bmanley@american.edu. Web site: http://www.american.edu/spa/dpap/.

The American University in Dubai, Master in Business Administration Program, Dubai, United Arab Emirates. Offers general (MBA); healthcare management (MBA); international finance (MBA); international marketing (MBA); management of construction enterprises (MBA). Part-time and evening/weekend programs available. *Degree requirements:* For master's, thesis optional. *Entrance requirements:* For master's, GMAT, Interview. Additional exam requirements/recommendations for international students: Required—TOEFL (minimum score 550 paper-based; 213 computer-based; 79 iBT). Electronic applications accepted.

Andrews University, School of Graduate Studies, School of Business, Graduate Programs in Business, Berrien Springs, MI 49104. Offers MBA, MSA. *Students:* 12 full-time (2 women), 18 part-time (8 women); includes 8 minority (5 Black or African American, non-Hispanic/Latino; 1 Asian, non-Hispanic/Latino; 2 Hispanic/Latino), 10 international. Average age 30. 71 applicants, 41% accepted, 14 enrolled. In 2011, 6 master's awarded. *Entrance requirements:* For master's, GMAT. Additional exam requirements/recommendations for international students: Required—TOEFL (minimum score 550 paper-based). Application fee: $40. *Unit head:* Dr. Leonard K. Gashugi, Chair, 769-471-3429, E-mail: gashugi@andrews.edu. *Application contact:* Carolyn Hurst, Supervisor of Graduate Admission, 800-253-2874, Fax: 269-471-6321, E-mail: graduate@andrews.edu.

Argosy University, Atlanta, College of Business, Atlanta, GA 30328. Offers accounting (DBA); corporate compliance (MBA); customized professional concentration (MBA, DBA); finance (MBA); healthcare administration (MBA); information systems (DBA); information systems management (MBA); international business (MBA, DBA); management (MBA, MSM, DBA); marketing (MBA, DBA).

See Close-Up on page 179.

Argosy University, Chicago, College of Business, Chicago, IL 60601. Offers accounting (DBA); customized professional concentration (MBA, DBA); finance (MBA); fraud examination (MBA); global business sustainability (DBA); healthcare administration (MBA); information systems (DBA); information systems management (MBA); international business (MBA, DBA); management (MBA, MSM, DBA); marketing (MBA, DBA); organizational leadership (Ed D); public administration (MBA); sustainable management (MBA). Postbaccalaureate distance learning degree programs offered (minimal on-campus study).

See Close-Up on page 181.

Argosy University, Dallas, College of Business, Farmers Branch, TX 75244. Offers accounting (DBA, AGC); corporate compliance (MBA, Graduate Certificate); customized professional concentration (MBA); finance (MBA, Graduate Certificate); fraud examination (MBA, Graduate Certificate); global business sustainability (DBA, AGC); healthcare administration (Graduate Certificate); healthcare management (MBA); information systems (MBA, DBA, AGC); information systems management (Graduate Certificate); international business (MBA, DBA, AGC, Graduate Certificate); management (MBA, DBA, AGC, Graduate Certificate); marketing (MBA, DBA, AGC, Graduate Certificate); public administration (MBA, Graduate Certificate); sustainable management (MBA, Graduate Certificate).

See Close-Up on page 183.

Argosy University, Denver, College of Business, Denver, CO 80231. Offers accounting (DBA); corporate compliance (MBA); customized professional concentration (MBA, DBA); finance (MBA); fraud examination (MBA); global business sustainability (DBA); healthcare administration (MBA); information systems (DBA); information systems management (MBA); international business (MBA, DBA); management (MBA, MSM, DBA); marketing (MBA, DBA); organizational leadership (Ed D); public administration (MBA); sustainable management (MBA).

See Close-Up on page 185.

Argosy University, Hawai`i, College of Business, Honolulu, HI 96813. Offers accounting (DBA); corporate compliance (MBA); customized professional concentration (MBA, DBA); finance (MBA, Certificate); fraud examination (MBA); global business sustainability (DBA); healthcare administration (MBA, Certificate); information systems (DBA); information systems management (MBA, Certificate); international business (MBA, DBA, Certificate); management (MBA, MSM, DBA); marketing (MBA, DBA, Certificate); organizational leadership (Ed D); public administration (MBA); sustainable management (MBA).

See Close-Up on page 187.

Argosy University, Inland Empire, College of Business, San Bernardino, CA 92408. Offers accounting (DBA); corporate compliance (MBA); customized professional concentration (MBA, DBA); finance (MBA); fraud examination (MBA); global business sustainability (DBA); healthcare administration (MBA); information systems (DBA); information systems management (MBA); international business (MBA, DBA); management (MBA, MSM, DBA); marketing (MBA, DBA); organizational leadership (Ed D); public administration (MBA); sustainable management (MBA).

See Close-Up on page 189.

Argosy University, Los Angeles, College of Business, Santa Monica, CA 90045. Offers accounting (DBA); corporate compliance (MBA); customized professional concentration (MBA, DBA); finance (MBA); fraud examination (MBA); global business sustainability (DBA); healthcare administration (MBA); information systems (DBA); information systems management (MBA); international business (MBA, DBA); management (MBA, MSM, DBA); marketing (MBA, DBA); organizational leadership (Ed D); public administration (MBA); sustainable management (MBA).

See Close-Up on page 191.

Argosy University, Nashville, College of Business, Nashville, TN 37214. Offers accounting (DBA); customized professional concentration (MBA, DBA); finance (MBA); healthcare administration (MBA); information systems (MBA, DBA); international business (MBA, DBA); management (MBA, MSM, DBA); marketing (MBA, DBA).

See Close-Up on page 193.

Argosy University, Orange County, College of Business, Orange, CA 92868. Offers accounting (DBA, Adv C); corporate compliance (MBA); customized professional concentration (MBA, DBA); finance (MBA, Certificate); fraud examination (MBA); global business sustainability (DBA); healthcare administration (MBA, Certificate); information systems (DBA, Adv C, Certificate); information systems management (MBA); international business (MBA, DBA, Adv C, Certificate); management (MBA, MSM, DBA, Adv C); marketing (MBA, DBA, Adv C, Certificate); organizational leadership (Ed D); public administration (MBA, Certificate); sustainable management (MBA).

See Close-Up on page 195.

Argosy University, Phoenix, College of Business, Phoenix, AZ 85021. Offers accounting (DBA); corporate compliance (MBA); customized professional concentration (MBA, DBA); finance (MBA); fraud examination (MBA); global business sustainability (DBA); healthcare administration (MBA); information systems (DBA); information systems management (MBA); international business (MBA, DBA); management (MBA, DBA); marketing (MBA, DBA); public administration (MBA); sustainable management (MBA).

See Close-Up on page 197.

Argosy University, Salt Lake City, College of Business, Draper, UT 84020. Offers accounting (DBA); corporate compliance (MBA); customized professional concentration (MBA, DBA); finance (MBA); fraud examination (MBA); global business sustainability (DBA); healthcare administration (MBA); information systems (DBA); information systems management (MBA); international business (MBA, DBA); management (MBA, DBA); marketing (MBA, DBA); public administration (MBA); sustainable management (MBA).

See Close-Up on page 199.

Argosy University, San Diego, College of Business, San Diego, CA 92108. Offers accounting (DBA); corporate compliance (MBA); customized professional concentration (MBA, DBA); finance (MBA); fraud examination (MBA); global business sustainability (DBA); information systems (DBA); information systems management (MBA); international business (MBA, DBA); management (MBA, MSM, DBA); marketing (MBA, DBA); organizational leadership (Ed D); public administration (MBA).

See Close-Up on page 201.

Argosy University, San Francisco Bay Area, College of Business, Alameda, CA 94501. Offers accounting (DBA); corporate compliance (MBA); customized professional concentration (MBA, DBA); finance (MBA); fraud examination (MBA); global business sustainability (DBA); healthcare administration (MBA); information systems (DBA); information systems management (MBA); international business (MBA, DBA); management (MBA, MSM, DBA); marketing (MBA, DBA); organizational leadership (Ed D); public administration (MBA); sustainable management (MBA).

See Close-Up on page 203.

Argosy University, Sarasota, College of Business, Sarasota, FL 34235. Offers accounting (DBA, Adv C); corporate compliance (MBA, DBA, Certificate); customized professional concentration (MBA, DBA); finance (MBA, Certificate); fraud examination (MBA, Certificate); global business sustainability (DBA, Adv C); healthcare administration (MBA, Certificate); information systems (DBA, Adv C, Certificate); information systems management (MBA); international business (MBA, DBA, Adv C, Certificate); management (MBA, MSM, DBA, Adv C, Certificate); marketing (MBA, DBA, Adv C, Certificate); organizational leadership (Ed D); public administration (MBA, Certificate); sustainable management (MBA, Certificate).

See Close-Up on page 205.

Argosy University, Schaumburg, College of Business, Schaumburg, IL 60173-5403. Offers accounting (DBA, Adv C); customized professional concentration (MBA, DBA); finance (MBA, Certificate); fraud examination (MBA); global business sustainability (DBA); healthcare administration (MBA, Certificate); information systems (DBA, Adv C, Certificate); information systems management (MBA); international business (MBA, DBA, Adv C, Certificate); management (MBA, MSM, DBA, Adv C, Certificate); marketing (MBA, DBA, Adv C, Certificate); organizational leadership (Ed D); public administration (MBA); sustainable management (MBA).

See Close-Up on page 207.

Argosy University, Seattle, College of Business, Seattle, WA 98121. Offers accounting (DBA); corporate compliance (MBA); customized professional concentration (MBA, DBA); finance (MBA); fraud examination (MBA); global business sustainability (DBA); healthcare administration (MBA); information systems (DBA); information systems management (MBA); international business (MBA, DBA); management (MBA, MSM, DBA); marketing (MBA, DBA); organizational leadership (Ed D); public administration (MBA); sustainable management (MBA).

See Close-Up on page 209.

Argosy University, Tampa, College of Business, Tampa, FL 33607. Offers accounting (DBA); corporate compliance (MBA); customized professional concentration (MBA, DBA); finance (MBA); fraud examination (MBA); global business sustainability (DBA); healthcare administration (MBA); information systems (DBA); information systems management (MBA); international business (MBA, DBA); management (MBA, MSM, DBA); marketing (MBA, DBA); organizational leadership (Ed D); public administration (MBA); sustainable management (MBA).

See Close-Up on page 211.

Argosy University, Twin Cities, College of Business, Eagan, MN 55121. Offers accounting (DBA); customized professional concentration (MBA, DBA); finance (MBA); fraud examination (MBA); global business sustainability (DBA); healthcare administration (MBA); information systems (DBA); information systems management (MBA); international business (MBA, DBA); management (MBA, MSM, DBA); marketing (MBA, DBA); organizational leadership (Ed D); public administration (MBA); sustainable management (MBA).

See Close-Up on page 213.

Argosy University, Washington DC, College of Business, Arlington, VA 22209. Offers accounting (DBA); customized professional concentration (MBA, DBA); finance (MBA); fraud examination (MBA); global business sustainability (DBA); healthcare administration (MBA); information systems (DBA); information systems management (MBA); international business (MBA, DBA, Certificate); management (MBA, MSM, DBA); marketing (MBA, DBA, Certificate); organizational leadership (Ed D); public administration (MBA); sustainable management (MBA).

See Close-Up on page 215.

Arizona State University, W. P. Carey School of Business, Program in Business Administration, Tempe, AZ 85287-4906. Offers accountancy (PhD); agribusiness (PhD); business administration (MBA); finance (PhD); financial management and markets (MBA); information management (MBA); information systems (PhD); management (PhD); marketing (PhD); strategic marketing and services leadership (MBA); supply chain financial management (MBA); supply chain management (MBA, PhD); JD/MBA; MBA/M Acc; MBA/M Arch. *Accreditation:* AACSB. Part-time and evening/weekend programs available. Postbaccalaureate distance learning degree programs offered (minimal on-campus study). Terminal master's awarded for partial completion of doctoral program. *Degree requirements:* For master's, thesis or alternative, internship, interactive Program of Study (iPOS) submitted before completing 50 percent of required credit hours; for doctorate, comprehensive exam, thesis/dissertation, interactive Program of Study (iPOS) submitted before completing 50 percent of required credit hours. *Entrance requirements:* For master's, GMAT, minimum GPA of 3.0 in last 2 years of work leading to bachelor's degree, 2 letters of recommendation, professional resume, official transcripts, 3 essays; for doctorate, GMAT or GRE, minimum GPA of 3.0 in last 2 years of work leading to bachelor's degree, 3 letters of recommendation, resume, personal statement/essay. Additional exam requirements/recommendations for international students: Required—TOEFL (minimum score 550 paper-based; 213 computer-based; 80 iBT), IELTS (minimum score 6.5). Electronic applications accepted. *Expenses:* Contact institution.

Aspen University, Program in Business Administration, Denver, CO 80246. Offers business administration (MBA); finance (MBA); information management (MBA); project management (MBA, Certificate). Part-time and evening/weekend programs available. Postbaccalaureate distance learning degree programs offered (no on-campus study). *Entrance requirements:* Additional exam requirements/recommendations for international students: Required—TOEFL (minimum score 530 paper-based; 71 computer-based). Electronic applications accepted.

Assumption College, Graduate Studies, Department of Business Studies, Worcester, MA 01609-1296. Offers accounting (MBA); business administration (CAGS); finance/economics (MBA); general business (MBA); human resources (MBA); international business (MBA); management (MBA); marketing (MBA); nonprofit leadership (MBA). Part-time and evening/weekend programs available. *Faculty:* 4 full-time (0 women), 16 part-time/adjunct (4 women). *Students:* 8 full-time (5 women), 133 part-time (65 women); includes 18 minority (8 Black or African American, non-Hispanic/Latino; 1 American Indian or Alaska Native, non-Hispanic/Latino; 2 Asian, non-Hispanic/Latino; 7 Hispanic/Latino), 3 international. Average age 30. 100 applicants, 75% accepted, 52 enrolled. In 2011, 53 master's, 1 other advanced degree awarded. *Degree requirements:* For master's, thesis, capstone. *Entrance requirements:* For master's and CAGS, 3 letters of recommendation, resume, essay. Additional exam requirements/recommendations for international students: Required—TOEFL (minimum score 540 paper-based; 200 computer-based; 76 iBT), IELTS (minimum score 6). *Application deadline:* For fall admission, 10/1 for domestic and international students; for winter admission, 2/1 for domestic and international students; for spring admission, 4/1 for domestic and international students. Applications are processed on a rolling basis. Application fee: $30. Electronic applications accepted. *Expenses: Tuition:* Full-time $9414; part-time $523 per credit. *Required fees:* $20 per term. Full-time tuition and fees vary according to course load and program. *Financial support:* In 2011–12, 14 students received support. Scholarships/grants, tuition waivers (partial), and unspecified assistantships available. Financial award application deadline: 5/1; financial award applicants required to submit FAFSA. *Faculty research:* Workplace diversity, dynamics of team interaction, utilization of leased employees, experiential learning project on due diligence market for prostheses. *Unit head:* Michael Lewis, Director, 508-767-7372, Fax: 508-767-7252, E-mail: milewis@assumption.edu. *Application contact:* Laura Lawrence, Graduate Programs Operations Manager, 508-767-7387, Fax: 508-767-7030, E-mail: graduate@assumption.edu. Web site: http://graduate.assumption.edu/mba/mba-assumption.

Auburn University, Graduate School, College of Business, Department of Finance, Auburn University, AL 36849. Offers MS. *Faculty:* 8 full-time (2 women). *Students:* 20 full-time (6 women), 5 part-time (2 women), 10 international. Average age 26. 147 applicants, 40% accepted, 10 enrolled. In 2011, 17 master's awarded. Application fee: $50 ($60 for international students). *Expenses:* Tuition, state resident: full-time $7290; part-time $405 per credit hour. Tuition, nonresident: full-time $21,870; part-time $1215 per credit hour. *International tuition:* $22,000 full-time. *Required fees:* $1402. *Financial support:* Applicants required to submit FAFSA. *Unit head:* Dr. John S. Jahera, Jr., Head, 334-844-5344. *Application contact:* Dr. George Flowers, Dean of the Graduate School, 334-844-2125.

Avila University, School of Business, Kansas City, MO 64145-1698. Offers accounting (MBA); finance (MBA); general management (MBA); health care administration (MBA); international business (MBA); management information systems (MBA); marketing (MBA). Part-time and evening/weekend programs available. *Faculty:* 9 full-time (3 women), 14 part-time/adjunct (5 women). *Students:* 102 full-time (49 women), 53 part-time (31 women); includes 36 minority (29 Black or African American, non-Hispanic/Latino; 1 American Indian or Alaska Native, non-Hispanic/Latino; 3 Asian, non-Hispanic/Latino; 2 Hispanic/Latino; 1 Native Hawaiian or other Pacific Islander, non-Hispanic/Latino), 33 international. Average age 32. 25 applicants, 76% accepted, 19 enrolled. In 2011, 59 master's awarded. *Degree requirements:* For master's, comprehensive exam, capstone course. *Entrance requirements:* For master's, GMAT (minimum score 420), minimum GPA of 3.0, interview. Additional exam requirements/recommendations for international students: Required—TOEFL (minimum score 550 paper-based). *Application deadline:* For fall admission, 7/30 priority date for domestic students, 7/30 for international students; for winter admission, 11/30 priority date for domestic students, 11/30 for international students; for spring admission, 2/28 priority date for domestic students, 2/28 for international students. Applications are processed on a rolling basis. Application fee: $0. Electronic applications accepted. *Expenses:* Contact institution. *Financial support:* In 2011–12, 102 students received support. Career-related internships or fieldwork and competitive merit scholarships available. Support available to part-time students. Financial award applicants required to submit FAFSA. *Faculty research:* Leadership characteristics, financial hedging, group dynamics. *Unit head:* Dr. Richard Woodall, Dean, 816-501-3720, Fax: 816-501-2463, E-mail: richard.woodall@avila.edu. *Application contact:* JoAnna Giffin, MBA Admissions Director, 816-501-3601, Fax: 816-501-2463, E-mail: joanna.giffin@avila.edu. Web site: http://www.avila.edu/mba.

Azusa Pacific University, School of Business and Management, Azusa, CA 91702-7000. Offers business administration (MBA); diversity for strategic advantage (MA); entrepreneurship (MBA); finance (MBA); human and organizational development (MA); human resources and organizational development (MBA); human resources management (MA); international business (MBA); marketing (MBA); non-profit management (MA); organizational development and change (MA); performance improvement (MA); public administration (MA); strategic management (MBA). Part-time and evening/weekend programs available. *Degree requirements:* For master's, thesis (for some programs), final project. *Entrance requirements:* For master's, GMAT, minimum GPA of 3.0. Additional exam requirements/recommendations for international students: Required—TOEFL (minimum score 600 paper-based). *Expenses:* Contact institution. *Faculty research:* Gender issues, financial risk, leadership and ethics, marketing strategy.

Baker College Center for Graduate Studies - Online, Graduate Programs, Flint, MI 48507-9843. Offers accounting (MBA); business administration (DBA); finance (MBA); general business (MBA); health care management (MBA); human resources management (MBA); information management (MBA); leadership studies (MBA); management information systems (MSIS); marketing (MBA). Part-time and evening/weekend programs available. Postbaccalaureate distance learning degree programs offered. *Degree requirements:* For master's, portfolio. *Entrance requirements:* For master's, 3 years of work experience, minimum undergraduate GPA of 2.5, writing sample, 3 letters of recommendation; for doctorate, MBA or acceptable related master's degree from accredited association, 5 years work experience, minimum graduate GPA of 3.25, writing sample, 3 professional references. Additional exam requirements/recommendations for international students: Required—TOEFL (minimum score 550 paper-based; 213 computer-based). Electronic applications accepted.

Barry University, Andreas School of Business, Graduate Certificate Programs, Miami Shores, FL 33161-6695. Offers finance (Certificate); health services administration (Certificate); international business (Certificate); management (Certificate); management information systems (Certificate); marketing (Certificate).

Bayamón Central University, Graduate Programs, Program in Business Administration, Bayamón, PR 00960-1725. Offers accounting (MBA); finance (MBA); general business (MBA); management (MBA); marketing (MBA). Part-time and evening/weekend programs available. *Degree requirements:* For master's, comprehensive exam (for some programs). *Entrance requirements:* For master's, EXADEP, bachelor's degree in business or related field.

Bellevue University, Graduate School, College of Business, Bellevue, NE 68005-3098. Offers acquisition and contract management (MS); business administration (MBA); finance (MS); human capital management (PhD); management (MSM).

Benedictine University, Graduate Programs, Program in Business Administration, Lisle, IL 60532-0900. Offers accounting (MBA); entrepreneurship and managing innovation (MBA); financial management (MBA); health administration (MBA); human resource management (MBA); information systems security (MBA); international business (MBA); management consulting (MBA); management information systems (MBA); marketing management (MBA); operations management and logistics (MBA); organizational leadership (MBA); MBA/MPH; MBA/MS. Part-time and evening/weekend programs available. Postbaccalaureate distance learning degree programs offered (minimal on-campus study). *Faculty:* 4 full-time (2 women), 24 part-time/adjunct (3 women). *Students:* 165 full-time (101 women), 766 part-time (381 women); includes 201 minority (118 Black or African American, non-Hispanic/Latino; 4 American Indian or Alaska Native, non-Hispanic/Latino; 37 Asian, non-Hispanic/Latino; 40 Hispanic/Latino; 2 Native Hawaiian or other Pacific Islander, non-Hispanic/Latino), 14 international. Average age 34. 313 applicants, 73% accepted, 166 enrolled. In 2011, 379 master's awarded. *Entrance requirements:* For master's, GMAT. Additional exam requirements/recommendations for international students: Required—TOEFL (minimum score 550 paper-based; 213 computer-based). *Application deadline:* For fall admission, 9/1 for domestic students; for winter admission, 12/1 for domestic students; for spring admission, 2/15 for domestic students. Applications are processed on a rolling basis. Application fee: $40. Electronic applications accepted. *Financial support:* Career-related internships or fieldwork and health care benefits available. Support available to part-time students. *Faculty research:* Strategic leadership in professional organizations, sociology of professions, organizational change, social identity theory, applications to change management. *Unit head:* Dr. Sharon Borowicz, Director, 630-829-6219, E-mail: sborowicz@ben.edu. *Application contact:* Kari Gibbons, Director, Admissions, 630-829-6200, Fax: 630-829-6584, E-mail: kgibbons@ben.edu.

Bentley University, McCallum Graduate School of Business, Master's Program in Financial Planning, Waltham, MA 02452-4705. Offers MSFP. Part-time and evening/weekend programs available. Postbaccalaureate distance learning degree programs offered (no on-campus study). *Entrance requirements:* For master's, GMAT or GRE General Test. Additional exam requirements/recommendations for international students: Required—TOEFL (minimum score 600 paper-based; 250 computer-based; 100 iBT) or IELTS (minimum score 7). Electronic applications accepted. *Faculty research:* International financial planning, compensation and benefits, retirement planning.

Bentley University, McCallum Graduate School of Business, Program in Finance, Waltham, MA 02452-4705. Offers MSF. Part-time and evening/weekend programs available. *Entrance requirements:* For master's, GMAT or GRE General Test. Additional exam requirements/recommendations for international students: Required—TOEFL (minimum score 600 paper-based; 250 computer-based; 100 iBT) or IELTS (minimum score 7). Electronic applications accepted. *Faculty research:* Management of financial institutions; corporate governance and executive compensation; asset valuation; international mergers and acquisitions; hedging, risk management and derivatives.

Bernard M. Baruch College of the City University of New York, Zicklin School of Business, Department of Economics and Finance, Program in Finance, New York, NY 10010-5585. Offers MBA, MS, PhD. PhD offered jointly with Graduate School and University Center of the City University of New York. Part-time and evening/weekend programs available. *Degree requirements:* For doctorate, comprehensive exam, thesis/dissertation. *Entrance requirements:* For master's, GMAT, 2 letters of recommendation, resume, 2 years of work experience; for doctorate, GMAT. Additional exam requirements/recommendations for international students: Required—TOEFL (minimum score 590 paper-based; 243 computer-based), TWE (minimum score 5).

Bernard M. Baruch College of the City University of New York, Zicklin School of Business, Zicklin Executive Programs, Executive Program in Finance, New York, NY 10010-5585. Offers MS. Evening/weekend programs available. *Entrance requirements:* For master's, personal interview, work experience. *Expenses:* Contact institution. *Faculty research:* Corporate finance, investments, options, securities, system risk.

Boston College, Carroll School of Management, Graduate Finance Programs, Chestnut Hill, MA 02467-3800. Offers MSF, PhD, MBA/MSF. Part-time programs available. *Faculty:* 15 full-time (2 women), 6 part-time/adjunct (0 women). *Students:* 57 full-time (15 women), 45 part-time (8 women); includes 14 minority (1 Black or African American, non-Hispanic/Latino; 8 Asian, non-Hispanic/Latino; 4 Hispanic/Latino; 1 Two or more races, non-Hispanic/Latino), 40 international. Average age 26. 978 applicants, 8% accepted, 44 enrolled. In 2011, 84 master's, 13 doctorates awarded. *Degree requirements:* For doctorate, thesis/dissertation. *Entrance requirements:* For master's, GMAT, resume, recommendations; for doctorate, GMAT or GRE, curriculum vitae, recommendations. Additional exam requirements/recommendations for international students: Required—TOEFL (minimum score 600 paper-based; 250 computer-based; 100 iBT). *Application deadline:* For fall admission, 3/15 for domestic and international students; for spring admission, 10/15 for domestic and international students. Application fee: $100. Electronic applications accepted. *Financial support:* In 2011–12, 45 fellowships with partial tuition reimbursements, 39 research assistantships with tuition reimbursements were awarded; teaching assistantships with tuition reimbursements, Federal Work-Study, scholarships/grants, and unspecified assistantships also available. Financial award application deadline: 3/1; financial award applicants required to submit FAFSA. *Faculty research:* Security and derivative markets, financial institutions, corporate finance and capital markets, market macrostructure, investments, portfolio analysis. *Unit head:* Dr. Jeffrey L. Ringuest, Associate Dean for Graduate Programs, 617-552-9100, Fax: 617-552-0541, E-mail: gsomdean@bc.edu. *Application contact:* Shelley A. Burt, Director of Graduate Enrollment, 617-552-3920, Fax: 617-552-8078, E-mail: bcmba@bc.edu.

Boston University, Metropolitan College, Department of Administrative Sciences, Boston, MA 02215. Offers banking and financial management (MSM); business continuity in emergency management (MSM); economics development and tourism management (MSAS); electronic commerce, systems, and technology (MSAS); financial economics (MSAS); innovation and technology (MSAS); insurance management (MSM); international market management (MSM); multinational commerce (MSAS); project management (MSM). *Accreditation:* AACSB. Part-time and evening/weekend programs available. Postbaccalaureate distance learning degree programs offered (no on-campus study). *Faculty:* 14 full-time (2 women), 21 part-time/adjunct (2 women). *Students:* 151 full-time (75 women), 106 part-time (51 women); includes 27 minority (6 Black or African American, non-Hispanic/Latino; 14 Asian, non-Hispanic/Latino; 7 Hispanic/Latino), 173 international. Average age 28. 500 applicants, 65% accepted, 194 enrolled. In 2011, 154 master's awarded. *Degree requirements:* For master's, thesis optional. *Entrance requirements:* For master's, 1 year of work experience, minimum GPA of 3.0. Additional exam requirements/recommendations for international students: Required—TOEFL (minimum score 560 paper-based; 220 computer-based; 84 iBT). *Application deadline:* Applications are processed on a rolling basis. Application fee: $70. Electronic applications accepted. *Expenses: Tuition:* Full-time $40,848; part-time $1276 per credit hour. *Required fees:* $572; $286 per semester. *Financial support:* In 2011–12, 15 students received support, including 7 research assistantships (averaging $10,000 per year); career-related internships or fieldwork, Federal Work-Study, and unspecified assistantships also available. *Faculty research:* International business, innovative process. *Unit head:* Dr. Kip Becker, Chairman, 617-353-3016, E-mail: adminsc@bu.edu. *Application contact:* Lucille Dicker, Administrative Sciences Department, 617-353-3016, E-mail: adminsc@bu.edu. Web site: http://www.bu.edu/met/programs/.

Boston University, School of Law, Boston, MA 02215. Offers American law (LL M); banking (LL M); intellectual property law (LL M); law (JD); taxation (LL M); JD/LL M; JD/MA; JD/MBA; JD/MPH; JD/MS. *Accreditation:* ABA. *Faculty:* 55 full-time (26 women), 88 part-time/adjunct (25 women). *Students:* 971 full-time (496 women), 62 part-time (27 women); includes 224 minority (38 Black or African American, non-Hispanic/Latino; 2 American Indian or Alaska Native, non-Hispanic/Latino; 85 Asian, non-Hispanic/Latino; 72 Hispanic/Latino; 27 Two or more races, non-Hispanic/Latino), 156 international. Average age 26. 7,073 applicants, 20% accepted, 242 enrolled. In 2011, 169 master's, 271 doctorates awarded. *Degree requirements:* For master's, thesis (for some programs); for doctorate, thesis/dissertation, research project resulting in a paper. *Entrance requirements:* For master's, JD; for doctorate, LSAT. Additional exam requirements/recommendations for international students: Required—TOEFL (minimum score 600 paper-based; 250 computer-based; 100 iBT). *Application deadline:* For fall admission, 3/1 for domestic and international students. Applications are processed on a rolling basis. Application fee: $75. Electronic applications accepted. *Expenses: Tuition:* Full-time $40,848; part-time $1276 per credit hour. *Required fees:* $572; $286 per semester. *Financial support:* In 2011–12, 533 students received support. Career-related internships or fieldwork, Federal Work-Study, institutionally sponsored loans, and scholarships/grants available. Financial award application deadline: 3/1; financial award applicants required to submit FAFSA. *Faculty research:* Litigation and dispute resolution, intellectual property law, business organizations and finance law, international law, health law. *Unit head:* Maureen A. O'Rourke, Dean, 617-353-3112, Fax: 617-353-7400, E-mail: lawdean@bu.edu. *Application contact:* Alissa Leonard, Director of Admissions and Financial Aid, 617-353-3100, Fax: 617-353-0578, E-mail: bulawadm@bu.edu. Web site: http://www.bu.edu/law/.

Brandeis University, International Business School, Program in International Economics and Finance, Waltham, MA 02454-9110. Offers MA. *Entrance requirements:* For master's, GRE.

Bridgewater State University, School of Graduate Studies, School of Business, Department of Accounting and Finance, Bridgewater, MA 02325-0001. Offers MSM. Part-time and evening/weekend programs available. *Entrance requirements:* For master's, GMAT.

Brigham Young University, Graduate Studies, Marriott School of Management, Master of Public Administration Program, Provo, UT 84602. Offers finance (MPA); human resources (MPA); local government (MPA); nonprofit management (MPA); JD/MPA. *Faculty:* 17 full-time (2 women), 14 part-time/adjunct (4 women). *Students:* 119 full-time (61 women); includes 16 minority (1 American Indian or Alaska Native, non-Hispanic/Latino; 6 Asian, non-Hispanic/Latino; 5 Hispanic/Latino; 4 Native Hawaiian or other Pacific Islander, non-Hispanic/Latino), 13 international. Average age 27. 132 applicants, 57% accepted, 61 enrolled. In 2011, 57 master's awarded. *Entrance requirements:* For master's, GRE or GMAT, minimum GPA of 3.0. Additional exam requirements/recommendations for international students: Required—TOEFL (minimum score 580 paper-based; 85 iBT), IELTS (minimum score 7). *Application deadline:* For fall admission, 1/15 for domestic and international students. Application fee: $50. Electronic applications accepted. *Expenses: Tuition:* Full-time $5760; part-time $320 per credit. Tuition and fees vary according to student's religious affiliation. *Financial support:* In 2011–12, 93 students received support. Career-related internships or fieldwork and scholarships/grants available. Financial award application deadline: 3/1; financial award applicants required to submit FAFSA. *Faculty research:* Taxes, budgeting, nonprofit, ethics, decision modeling, work balance, organizational behavior. *Unit head:* Dr. David W. Hart, Director, 801-422-4221, Fax: 801-422-0311, E-mail: mpa@byu.edu. *Application contact:* Catherine Cooper, Associate Director, 801-422-4221, E-mail: mpa@byu.edu. Web site: http://marriottschool.byu.edu/mpa.

Brooklyn College of the City University of New York, Division of Graduate Studies, Department of Economics, Brooklyn, NY 11210-2889. Offers accounting (MS); business economics (MS), including economic analysis, global business and finance; economics (MA). Part-time and evening/weekend programs available. *Degree requirements:* For master's, comprehensive exam, thesis or alternative. *Entrance requirements:* For master's, GMAT (for MS), 2 letters of recommendation. Additional exam requirements/recommendations for international students: Required—TOEFL (minimum score 550 paper-based; 213 computer-based; 79 iBT). Electronic applications accepted. *Faculty research:* Econometrics, environmental economics, microeconomics, macroeconomics, taxation.

California College of the Arts, Graduate Programs, Program in Design Strategy, San Francisco, CA 94107. Offers MBA. *Accreditation:* NASAD. *Degree requirements:* For master's, thesis. *Entrance requirements:* Additional exam requirements/recommendations for international students: Required—TOEFL (minimum score 600 paper-based; 250 computer-based; 100 iBT).

California Intercontinental University, School of Business, Diamond Bar, CA 91765. Offers banking and finance (MBA); entrepreneurship and business management (DBA); global business leadership (DBA); international management and marketing (MBA); organizational management and human resource management (MBA).

California Lutheran University, Graduate Studies, School of Management, Thousand Oaks, CA 91360-2787. Offers business (IMBA); computer science (MS); econometrics (MBA); economics (MS); entrepreneurship (MBA, Certificate); finance (MBA, Certificate); financial planning (MBA, Certificate); information systems and technology (MS); information technology management (MBA, Certificate); international business (MBA, Certificate); management and organization behavior (MBA); management and organizational behavior (Certificate); marketing (MBA, Certificate); microeconomics (MBA); nonprofit and social enterprise (MBA). Part-time and evening/weekend programs available. Postbaccalaureate distance learning degree programs offered (no on-campus study). *Entrance requirements:* For master's, GMAT, interview, minimum GPA of 3.0. *Expenses:* Contact institution.

California State University, East Bay, Office of Academic Programs and Graduate Studies, College of Business and Economics, Business Administration, MBA Program, Hayward, CA 94542-3000. Offers entrepreneurship (MBA); finance (MBA); global innovators (MBA); human resources and organizational behavior (MBA); information technology management (MBA); marketing management (MBA); operations and supply chain management (MBA); strategy and international business (MBA). Part-time and evening/weekend programs available. *Faculty:* 11 full-time (3 women). *Students:* 80 full-time (42 women), 141 part-time (61 women); includes 70 minority (5 Black or African American, non-Hispanic/Latino; 46 Asian, non-Hispanic/Latino; 13 Hispanic/Latino; 1 Native Hawaiian or other Pacific Islander, non-Hispanic/Latino; 5 Two or more races, non-Hispanic/Latino), 69 international. Average age 31. 371 applicants, 36% accepted, 79 enrolled. In 2011, 254 master's awarded. *Degree requirements:* For master's, comprehensive exam or thesis. *Entrance requirements:* For master's, GMAT (minimum 20th percentile verbal and quantitative section), bachelor's degree, minimum GPA of 2.75. Additional exam requirements/recommendations for international students: Required—TOEFL (minimum score 550 paper-based; 213 computer-based; 79 iBT). *Application deadline:* For fall admission, 6/30 for domestic and international students. Applications are processed on a rolling basis. Application fee: $55. Electronic applications accepted. *Expenses:* Contact institution. *Financial support:* Career-related internships or fieldwork, Federal Work-Study, institutionally sponsored loans, and scholarships/grants available. Support available to part-time students. Financial award application deadline: 3/2; financial award applicants required to submit FAFSA. *Unit head:* Dr. Terri Swartz, Dean, 510-885-3291, Fax: 510-885-4884, E-mail: terri.swartz@csueastbay.edu. *Application contact:* Prof. Joanna Lee, Director, CBE Graduate Programs, 510-885-3517, Fax: 510-885-2176, E-mail: joanna.lee@csueastbay.edu. Web site: http://www20.csueastbay.edu/ecat/graduate-chapters/g-buad.html#mba.

California State University, East Bay, Office of Academic Programs and Graduate Studies, College of Business and Economics, Department of Accounting and Finance, Option in Accounting/Finance, Hayward, CA 94542-3000. Offers MBA. *Degree requirements:* For master's, comprehensive exam or thesis. *Entrance requirements:* For master's, GMAT, minimum GPA of 2.75. Additional exam requirements/recommendations for international students: Required—TOEFL (minimum score 550 paper-based; 213 computer-based). *Application deadline:* For fall admission, 6/30 for domestic and international students. Applications are processed on a rolling basis. Application fee: $55. Electronic applications accepted. *Expenses:* Tuition, state resident: full-time $6738; part-time $1302 per quarter. Tuition, nonresident: full-time $12,690; part-time $2294 per quarter. *Required fees:* $449 per quarter. Tuition and fees vary according to degree level, program and reciprocity agreements. *Financial support:* Career-related internships or fieldwork, Federal Work-Study, and institutionally sponsored loans available. Support available to part-time students. Financial award application deadline: 3/1; financial award applicants required to submit FAFSA. *Unit head:* Prof. Micah Frankel, Graduate Adviser, 510-885-3397, Fax: 510-885-4796, E-mail: micah.frankel@csueastbay.edu. *Application contact:* Donna Wiley, Interim Associate Director, 510-885-2928, Fax: 510-885-4777, E-mail: donna.wiley@csueastbay.edu. Web site: http://www.cbe.csueastbay.edu/acct/.

California State University, Fullerton, Graduate Studies, College of Business and Economics, Department of Finance, Fullerton, CA 92834-9480. Offers MBA. Part-time programs available. *Students:* 27 full-time (5 women), 55 part-time (16 women); includes 30 minority (1 Black or African American, non-Hispanic/Latino; 21 Asian, non-Hispanic/Latino; 7 Hispanic/Latino; 1 Two or more races, non-Hispanic/Latino), 25 international. Average age 29. 4 applicants, 100% accepted, 3 enrolled. In 2011, 52 master's awarded. *Degree requirements:* For master's, project or thesis. *Entrance requirements:* For master's, GMAT, minimum AACSB index of 950. Application fee: $55. *Financial support:* Career-related internships or fieldwork, Federal Work-Study, institutionally sponsored loans, and scholarships/grants available. Support available to part-time students. Financial award application deadline: 3/1; financial award applicants required to submit FAFSA. *Unit head:* Dr. John Erickson, Chair, 657-278-2217. *Application contact:* Admissions/Applications, 657-278-2371.

California State University, Los Angeles, Graduate Studies, College of Business and Economics, Department of Finance and Law, Los Angeles, CA 90032-8530. Offers finance and banking (MBA, MS). Part-time and evening/weekend programs available. *Faculty:* 3 full-time (0 women). *Students:* 6 full-time (3 women), 12 part-time (5 women); includes 8 minority (1 Black or African American, non-Hispanic/Latino; 6 Asian, non-Hispanic/Latino; 1 Hispanic/Latino), 9 international. Average age 27. 40 applicants, 30% accepted, 6 enrolled. In 2011, 19 master's awarded. *Degree requirements:* For master's, comprehensive exam (MBA), thesis (MS). *Entrance requirements:* For master's, GMAT, minimum GPA of 2.5 during previous 2 years of course work. Additional exam requirements/recommendations for international students: Required—TOEFL (minimum score 550 paper-based; 213 computer-based). *Application deadline:* For fall admission, 5/1 for domestic and international students. Applications are processed on a rolling basis. Application fee: $55. Electronic applications accepted. *Expenses:* Tuition, state resident: full-time $8225. *Financial support:* Career-related internships or fieldwork and Federal Work-Study available. Support available to part-time students. Financial award application deadline: 3/1. *Unit head:* Dr. Hsing Fang, Chair, 323-343-2870, Fax: 323-343-2885, E-mail: hfang@calstatela.edu. *Application contact:* Dr. Karin Brown, Acting Associate Dean of Graduate Studies, 323-343-3820, Fax: 323-343-5653, E-mail: kbrown5@calstatela.edu. Web site: http://cbe.calstatela.edu/fin/.

California State University, San Bernardino, Graduate Studies, College of Business and Public Administration, Master in Business Administration Program, San Bernardino, CA 92407. Offers accounting (MBA); entrepreneurship (MBA); executives (MBA); finance (MBA); global business (MBA); information assurance and security management (MBA); information management (MBA); management (MBA); marketing (MBA); professionals (MBA); supply chain management (MBA). *Accreditation:* AACSB. Part-time and evening/weekend programs available. Postbaccalaureate distance learning degree programs offered (no on-campus study). *Faculty:* 58 full-time (11 women), 26 part-time/adjunct (9 women). *Students:* 80 full-time (31 women), 137 part-time (56 women); includes 82 minority (19 Black or African American, non-Hispanic/Latino; 3 American Indian or Alaska Native, non-Hispanic/Latino; 20 Asian, non-Hispanic/Latino; 37 Hispanic/Latino; 3 Two or more races, non-Hispanic/Latino), 65 international. Average age 30. 217 applicants, 65% accepted, 79 enrolled. In 2011, 120 master's awarded. *Degree requirements:* For master's, comprehensive exam, thesis optional, portfolio, 48 units, minimum GPA of 3.0. *Entrance requirements:* For master's, GMAT, minimum GPA of 2.5. Additional exam requirements/recommendations for international students: Required—TOEFL (minimum score 550 paper-based; 213 computer-based; 79 iBT). *Application deadline:* For fall admission, 7/12 priority date for domestic students, 7/12 for international students; for winter admission, 10/26 priority date for domestic students, 10/26 for international students; for spring admission, 1/25 priority date for domestic students, 1/25 for international students. Applications are processed on a rolling basis. Application fee: $55. Electronic applications accepted. *Expenses:* Contact institution. *Financial support:* In 2011–12, 56 students received support, including 34 fellowships (averaging $3,732 per year), 18 research assistantships (averaging $2,193 per year), 4 teaching assistantships (averaging $2,606 per year); career-related internships or fieldwork, Federal Work-Study, institutionally sponsored loans, scholarships/grants, and unspecified assistantships also available. Support available to part-time students. Financial award application deadline: 3/1; financial award applicants required to submit FAFSA. *Faculty research:* Fraud, Stock Exchange, small business, logistics, job analysis. *Total annual research expenditures:* $4.8 million. *Unit head:* Dr. Lawrence C. Rose, Dean, 909-537-3703, Fax: 909-537-7026, E-mail: lrose@csusb.edu. *Application contact:* Dr. Sandra Kamusikiri, Associate Vice-President/ Dean of Graduate Studies, 909-537-7058, Fax: 909-537-5078, E-mail: skamusik@ csusb.edu. Web site: http://mba.csusb.edu/.

Capella University, School of Business and Technology, Minneapolis, MN 55402. Offers accounting (MBA), including system design and programming; business (Certificate), including human resource management (MS, PhD, Certificate), information technology management (MS, PhD, Certificate), leadership (MBA, MS, PhD, Certificate); finance (MBA); general business (MBA); health care management (MBA); information technology (MS, Certificate), including general information technology (MS), information security, network architecture and design (MS), professional projects management (Certificate), project management and leadership (MS), system design and development (MS),); information technology management (MBA); marketing (MBA); organization and management (MBA, MS, PhD), including general business (PhD), general organization and management (MBA, MS), human resource management (MS, PhD, Certificate), information technology management (MS, PhD, Certificate), leadership (MBA, MS, PhD, Certificate); project management (MBA). Part-time and evening/weekend programs available. Postbaccalaureate distance learning degree programs offered (minimal on-campus study). Terminal master's awarded for partial completion of doctoral program. *Degree requirements:* For master's, thesis optional, integrative project; for doctorate, comprehensive exam, thesis/dissertation. *Entrance requirements:* Additional exam requirements/recommendations for international students: Required—TOEFL (minimum score 550 paper-based; 213 computer-based), TWE (minimum score 4). Electronic applications accepted. *Faculty research:* Business policies: strategic, corporate, and financial management; interplay of technological, organizational and social change.

Capital University, School of Management, Columbus, OH 43209-2394. Offers entrepreneurship (MBA); finance (MBA); leadership (MBA); marketing (MBA); MBA/JD; MBA/LL M; MBA/MSN; MBA/MT. *Accreditation:* ACBSP. Part-time and evening/ weekend programs available. *Faculty:* 17 full-time (7 women), 23 part-time/adjunct (1 woman). *Students:* 175 part-time (75 women). Average age 31. 59 applicants, 81% accepted, 43 enrolled. In 2011, 1 degree awarded. *Degree requirements:* For master's, research project. *Entrance requirements:* For master's, GMAT, 2 years of work experience. Additional exam requirements/recommendations for international students: Required—TOEFL (minimum score 550 paper-based; 80 computer-based); Recommended—IELTS (minimum score 6.5). *Application deadline:* For fall admission, 7/1 priority date for domestic students; for winter admission, 11/1 priority date for domestic students; for spring admission, 4/1 priority date for domestic students. Applications are processed on a rolling basis. Application fee: $25. Electronic applications accepted. *Financial support:* In 2011–12, 2 fellowships (averaging $1,000 per year) were awarded; scholarships/grants and tuition waivers (full) also available. Support available to part-time students. Financial award application deadline: 8/1; financial award applicants required to submit FAFSA. *Faculty research:* Taxation, public policy, health care, management of non-profits. *Unit head:* Dr. Keirsten Moore, Assistant Dean, School of Management and Leadership, 614-236-6670, Fax: 614-296-6540, E-mail: kmoore@capital.edu. *Application contact:* Jacob Wilk, Assistant Director of Adult and Graduate Education Recruitment, 614-236-6546, Fax: 614-236-6923, E-mail: jwilk@capital.edu. Web site: http://www.capital.edu/capital-mba/.

Carnegie Mellon University, Tepper School of Business, Program in Financial Economics, Pittsburgh, PA 15213-3891. Offers PhD. *Degree requirements:* For doctorate, thesis/dissertation. *Entrance requirements:* For doctorate, GRE General Test.

Case Western Reserve University, Weatherhead School of Management, Department of Banking and Finance, Cleveland, OH 44106. Offers MBA. *Entrance requirements:* For master's, GMAT. *Faculty research:* Monetary and fiscal policy, corporate finance, future markets, derivative pricing, capital market efficiency.

Case Western Reserve University, Weatherhead School of Management, Department of Operations, Cleveland, OH 44106. Offers management (MS, MSM), including finance (MS), information systems (MS), marketing (MS), operations research, quality management (MS), supply chain (MSM); management for liberal arts graduates (MSM); operations research (PhD); MBA/MSM. Part-time programs available. *Degree requirements:* For doctorate, thesis/dissertation. *Entrance requirements:* For master's, GRE General Test; for doctorate, GMAT, GRE General Test. *Faculty research:* Mathematical finance, mathematical programming, scheduling, stochastic optimization, environmental/energy models.

Central European University, CEU Business School, Budapest, Hungary. Offers executive business administration (EMBA); finance (MBA); general management (MBA); information technology management (MBA); marketing (MBA); real estate management (MBA). Part-time and evening/weekend programs available. *Faculty:* 17 full-time (4 women), 12 part-time/adjunct (1 woman). *Students:* 31 full-time (12 women), 84 part-time (16 women). Average age 34. 162 applicants, 35% accepted, 31 enrolled. In 2011, 83 degrees awarded. *Degree requirements:* For master's, one foreign language. *Entrance requirements:* For master's, GMAT. Additional exam requirements/ recommendations for international students: Required—TOEFL (minimum score 570 paper-based; 230 computer-based); Recommended—IELTS (minimum score 6.5). *Application deadline:* For fall admission, 5/15 priority date for domestic students, 5/22 for international students; for winter admission, 11/15 priority date for domestic students, 11/10 for international students. Applications are processed on a rolling basis. Application fee: $0. Electronic applications accepted. Tuition charges are reported in euros. *Expenses: Tuition:* Full-time 11,000 euros. *Financial support:* Tuition waivers (partial) available. *Faculty research:* Social and ethical business, marketing, international business. *Unit head:* Dr. Mel Horwitch, Dean and Managing Director, 361-887-5050, E-mail: mhorwitch@ceubusiness.com. *Application contact:* Agnes Schram, Admissions Manager, 361-887-5111, Fax: 361-887-5133, E-mail: mba@ ceubusiness.com. Web site: http://www.ceubusiness.com.

Central Michigan University, College of Graduate Studies, College of Business Administration, Department of Finance and Law, Mount Pleasant, MI 48859. Offers finance (MBA). Part-time and evening/weekend programs available. *Degree requirements:* For master's, thesis or alternative. *Entrance requirements:* For master's, GMAT. Electronic applications accepted. *Faculty research:* Investments, commercial banking, financial management.

Charleston Southern University, Program in Business, Charleston, SC 29423-8087. Offers accounting (MBA); finance (MBA); health care administration (MBA); information systems (MBA); organizational development (MBA). Part-time and evening/weekend programs available. *Degree requirements:* For master's, thesis optional. *Entrance requirements:* For master's, GMAT. Additional exam requirements/recommendations for international students: Required—TOEFL (minimum score 550 paper-based; 213 computer-based; 79 iBT).

Christian Brothers University, School of Business, Memphis, TN 38104-5581. Offers business (MBA); financial planning (Certificate); project management (Certificate). Part-time and evening/weekend programs available. *Entrance requirements:* For master's, GMAT, GRE. Additional exam requirements/recommendations for international students: Required—TOEFL.

City University of Seattle, Graduate Division, School of Management, Bellevue, WA 98005. Offers accounting (Certificate); change leadership (MBA, Certificate); computer systems (MS); finance (Certificate); financial management (MBA); general management (MBA); general management-Europe (MBA); global marketing (MBA); human resources management (Certificate); individualized study (MBA); information security (MS); information systems (MBA); leadership (MA); marketing (MBA, Certificate); project management (MBA, MS, Certificate); sustainable business (Certificate); technology management (MBA, Certificate). Part-time and evening/weekend programs available. Postbaccalaureate distance learning degree programs offered (no on-campus study). *Faculty:* 6 full-time (2 women), 95 part-time/adjunct (33 women). *Students:* 397 full-time (193 women), 283 part-time (137 women); includes 127 minority (67 Black or African American, non-Hispanic/Latino; 5 American Indian or Alaska Native, non-Hispanic/ Latino; 33 Asian, non-Hispanic/Latino; 15 Hispanic/Latino; 1 Native Hawaiian or other Pacific Islander, non-Hispanic/Latino; 6 Two or more races, non-Hispanic/Latino), 117 international. Average age 36. 151 applicants, 100% accepted, 151 enrolled. In 2011, 369 master's, 32 other advanced degrees awarded. *Degree requirements:* For master's, comprehensive exam (for some programs), thesis (for some programs). *Entrance requirements:* Additional exam requirements/recommendations for international students: Required—TOEFL (minimum score 567 paper-based; 227 computer-based; 87 iBT); Recommended—IELTS. *Application deadline:* For fall admission, 9/1 for international students; for winter admission, 12/1 for international students; for spring admission, 3/1 for international students. Applications are processed on a rolling basis. Application fee: $50. Electronic applications accepted. *Financial support:* Federal Work-Study and scholarships/grants available. Support available to part-time students. Financial award applicants required to submit FAFSA. *Unit head:* Dr. Kurt Kirstein, Dean, 425-637-1010 Ext. 5456, Fax: 425-709-5363, E-mail: kdkirstein@cityu.edu. *Application contact:* Alysa Borelli, Director, Recruiting, 888-422-4898, Fax: 425-709-5363, E-mail: info@cityu.edu. Web site: http://www.cityu.edu/programs/som/ index.aspx.

Claremont McKenna College, Robert Day School of Economics and Finance, Claremont, CA 91711. Offers finance (MA). *Students:* 20 full-time (7 women); includes 4 minority (3 Asian, non-Hispanic/Latino; 1 Hispanic/Latino), 7 international. Average age 23. 296 applicants, 11% accepted, 20 enrolled. In 2011, 17 master's awarded. *Entrance requirements:* For master's, GMAT or GRE, 2 letters of recommendation, resume, interview. Additional exam requirements/recommendations for international students: Required—TOEFL. *Application deadline:* For fall admission, 11/2 for domestic and international students; for winter admission, 1/15 for domestic students; for spring admission, 3/9 for domestic students, 2/10 for international students. Application fee: $70. Electronic applications accepted. *Financial support:* In 2011–12, 20 students received support, including 20 fellowships with full and partial tuition reimbursements available. Financial award applicants required to submit FAFSA. *Unit head:* Brock Blomberg, Dean, 909-607-9597, E-mail: bblomberg@cmc.edu. *Application contact:* Kevin Arnold, Director of Graduate Admission, 909-607-3347, E-mail: karnold@ cmc.edu. Web site: http://www.claremontmckenna.edu/rdschool/.

Clark University, Graduate School, Graduate School of Management, Business Administration Program, Worcester, MA 01610-1477. Offers accounting (MBA); finance (MBA); global business (MBA); health care management (MBA); management (MBA); management of information technology (MBA); marketing (MBA). *Accreditation:* AACSB. Part-time and evening/weekend programs available. *Students:* 103 full-time (47 women), 108 part-time (41 women); includes 16 minority (7 Black or African American, non-Hispanic/Latino; 5 Asian, non-Hispanic/Latino; 4 Hispanic/Latino), 69 international. Average age 30. 371 applicants, 48% accepted, 77 enrolled. In 2011, 112 master's awarded. *Degree requirements:* For master's, thesis optional. *Application deadline:* For fall admission, 6/1 priority date for domestic students; for spring admission, 12/1 priority date for domestic students. Applications are processed on a rolling basis. Application fee: $50. Electronic applications accepted. *Expenses: Tuition:* Full-time $37,000; part-time $1156 per credit hour. *Financial support:* In 2011–12, research assistantships with partial tuition reimbursements (averaging $4,800 per year), teaching assistantships with partial tuition reimbursements (averaging $4,800 per year) were awarded; fellowships, career-related internships or fieldwork, Federal Work-Study, institutionally sponsored loans, and tuition waivers (partial) also available. Support available to part-time students. Financial award application deadline: 5/31. *Faculty research:* Marketing, accounting, human resource management, management information systems, business finance. *Unit head:* Dr. Catherine Usoff, Dean, 508-793-8822, Fax: 508-793-8822, E-mail: clarkmba@clarku.edu. *Application contact:* Patrick Oroszko, Enrollment and Marketing Director, 508-793-8822, Fax: 508-793-8822, E-mail: clarkmba@clarku.edu. Web site: http://www.clarku.edu/gsom/prospective/mba/.

Clark University, Graduate School, Graduate School of Management, Program in Finance, Worcester, MA 01610-1477. Offers MSF. *Students:* 213 full-time (127 women), 1 part-time (0 women); includes 1 minority (Asian, non-Hispanic/Latino), 210 international. Average age 23. 1,275 applicants, 43% accepted, 96 enrolled. In 2011, 98 master's awarded. *Degree requirements:* For master's, thesis optional. *Application deadline:* For fall admission, 6/1 priority date for domestic students; for spring admission, 12/1 priority date for domestic students. Applications are processed on a rolling basis. Application fee: $50. Electronic applications accepted. *Expenses: Tuition:* Full-time $37,000; part-time $1156 per credit hour. *Financial support:* In 2011–12, research assistantships with partial tuition reimbursements (averaging $4,800 per year), teaching assistantships with partial tuition reimbursements (averaging $4,800 per year) were awarded; fellowships and tuition waivers (partial) also available. Financial award application deadline: 5/31. *Faculty research:* Marketing, accounting, human resource management, management information systems, business finance. *Unit head:* Dr. Catherine Usoff, Dean, 508-793-8822, Fax: 508-793-8822, E-mail: clarkmba@ clarku.edu. *Application contact:* Patrick Oroszko, Enrollment and Marketing Director, 508-793-8822, Fax: 508-793-8822, E-mail: clarkmba@clarku.edu. Web site: http:// www.clarku.edu/gsom/prospective/msf/.

Cleary University, Online Program in Business Administration, Ann Arbor, MI 48105-2659. Offers financial planning (MBA); financial planning (Graduate Certificate); green business strategy (MBA, Graduate Certificate); management (MBA); nonprofit management (MBA, Graduate Certificate); organizational leadership (MBA); public accounting (MBA). Part-time and evening/weekend programs available. Postbaccalaureate distance learning degree programs offered (no on-campus study). *Degree requirements:* For master's, thesis. *Entrance requirements:* For master's, bachelor's degree; minimum GPA of 2.5; professional resume indicating minimum 2 years management or related experience; undergraduate degree from an accredited college or university with at least 18 quarter hours (or 12 semester hours) of accounting study (for MBA in accounting). Additional exam requirements/recommendations for international students: Required—TOEFL (minimum score 550 paper-based; 213 computer-based; 79 iBT), Michigan English Language Assessment Battery (minimum score: 75). Electronic applications accepted.

Cleveland State University, College of Graduate Studies, Maxine Goodman Levin College of Urban Affairs, Program in Environmental Studies, Cleveland, OH 44115. Offers environmental nonprofit management (MAES); environmental planning (MAES); geographic information systems (Certificate); policy and administration (MAES); sustainable economic development (MAES); urban economic development (Certificate); urban real estate development and finance (Certificate); JD/MAES. Part-time and evening/weekend programs available. *Faculty:* 26 full-time (10 women), 3 part-time/adjunct (0 women). *Students:* 12 full-time (5 women), 23 part-time (12 women); includes 1 minority (Asian, non-Hispanic/Latino), 4 international. 18 applicants, 61% accepted, 6 enrolled. In 2011, 9 master's awarded. *Degree requirements:* For master's, thesis or alternative, exit project. *Entrance requirements:* For master's, GRE General Test (minimum score: verbal and quantitative in 40th percentile, analytical writing 4.0), minimum GPA of 3.0. Additional exam requirements/recommendations for international students: Required—TOEFL (minimum score 525 paper-based; 197 computer-based; 65 iBT). *Application deadline:* For fall admission, 7/15 priority date for domestic students, 5/15 for international students; for spring admission, 11/1 for international students. Applications are processed on a rolling basis. Application fee: $30. Electronic applications accepted. *Expenses:* Tuition, state resident: full-time $6416; part-time $494 per credit hour. Tuition, nonresident: full-time $12,074; part-time $929 per credit hour. *Financial support:* In 2011–12, 6 students received support, including 2 research assistantships with full and partial tuition reimbursements available (averaging $7,200 per year), 4 teaching assistantships with full and partial tuition reimbursements available (averaging $2,400 per year); career-related internships or fieldwork, scholarships/grants, traineeships, and unspecified assistantships also available. Support available to part-time students. Financial award application deadline: 3/1; financial award applicants required to submit FAFSA. *Faculty research:* Environmental policy and administration, environmental planning, geographic information systems (GIS), urban sustainability planning and management, energy policy, land re-use. *Unit head:* Dr. Sanda Kaufman, Director, 216-687-2367, Fax: 216-687-9342, E-mail: s.kaufman@csuohio.edu. *Application contact:* Joan Demko, Graduate Academic Program Specialist, 216-523-7522, Fax: 216-687-5398, E-mail: urbanprograms@csuohio.edu. Web site: http://urban.csuohio.edu/academics/graduate/maes/.

Cleveland State University, College of Graduate Studies, Maxine Goodman Levin College of Urban Affairs, Program in Public Administration, Cleveland, OH 44115. Offers city management (MPA); economic development (MPA); healthcare administration (MPA); local and urban management (Certificate); non-profit management (Certificate); public financial management (MPA); public management (MPA); urban economic development (Certificate); JD/MPA. *Accreditation:* NASPAA. Part-time and evening/weekend programs available. *Faculty:* 26 full-time (10 women), 14 part-time/adjunct (8 women). *Students:* 36 full-time (22 women), 70 part-time (41 women); includes 31 minority (26 Black or African American, non-Hispanic/Latino; 1 American Indian or Alaska Native, non-Hispanic/Latino; 1 Asian, non-Hispanic/Latino; 2 Hispanic/Latino; 1 Two or more races, non-Hispanic/Latino), 4 international. Average age 36. 122 applicants, 52% accepted, 41 enrolled. In 2011, 45 master's awarded. *Degree requirements:* For master's, thesis or alternative, capstone course. *Entrance requirements:* For master's, GRE General Test (minimum scores in 40th percentile verbal and quantitative, 4.0 writing), minimum GPA of 3.0. Additional exam requirements/recommendations for international students: Required—TOEFL (minimum score 525 paper-based; 197 computer-based; 65 iBT). *Application deadline:* For fall admission, 7/15 priority date for domestic students, 5/15 for international students; for spring admission, 11/1 for international students. Applications are processed on a rolling basis. Application fee: $30. Electronic applications accepted. *Expenses:* Tuition, state resident: full-time $6416; part-time $494 per credit hour. Tuition, nonresident: full-time $12,074; part-time $929 per credit hour. *Financial support:* In 2011–12, 9 students received support, including 6 research assistantships with full and partial tuition reimbursements available (averaging $7,200 per year), 3 teaching assistantships with full and partial tuition reimbursements available (averaging $4,800 per year); career-related internships or fieldwork, scholarships/grants, traineeships, and unspecified assistantships also available. Support available to part-time students. Financial award application deadline: 3/1; financial award applicants required to submit FAFSA. *Faculty research:* Health care administration, public management, economic development, city management, nonprofit management. *Unit head:* Dr. Nancy Meyer-Emerick, Director, 216-687-2261, Fax: 216-687-9342, E-mail: n.meyeremerick@csuohio.edu. *Application contact:* Joan Demko, Graduate Academic Programs Specialist, 216-523-7522, Fax: 216-687-5398, E-mail: urbanprograms@csuohio.edu. Web site: http://urban.csuohio.edu/academics/graduate/mpa/.

Cleveland State University, College of Graduate Studies, Maxine Goodman Levin College of Urban Affairs, Program in Urban Planning, Design, and Development, Cleveland, OH 44115. Offers economic development (MUPDD); environmental sustainability (MUPDD); geographic information systems (Certificate); historic preservation (MUPDD); housing and neighborhood development (MUPDD); urban economic development (Certificate); urban real estate development and finance (MUPDD, Certificate); JD/MUPDD. *Accreditation:* ACSP. Part-time and evening/weekend programs available. *Faculty:* 32 full-time (19 women), 8 part-time/adjunct (4 women). *Students:* 30 full-time (10 women), 28 part-time (17 women); includes 9 minority (6 Black or African American, non-Hispanic/Latino; 3 Hispanic/Latino), 5 international. Average age 38. 91 applicants, 45% accepted, 21 enrolled. In 2011, 24 master's awarded. *Degree requirements:* For master's, thesis or alternative, capstone seminar. *Entrance requirements:* For master's, GRE General Test (minimum score in 50th percentile verbal and quantitative, 4.0 analytical writing), minimum GPA of 3.0. Additional exam requirements/recommendations for international students: Required—TOEFL (minimum score 525 paper-based; 197 computer-based; 65 iBT). *Application deadline:* For fall admission, 7/15 priority date for domestic students, 5/15 for international students; for spring admission, 11/1 for international students. Applications are processed on a rolling basis. Application fee: $30. Electronic applications accepted. *Expenses:* Tuition, state resident: full-time $6416; part-time $494 per credit hour. Tuition, nonresident: full-time $12,074; part-time $929 per credit hour. *Financial support:* In 2011–12, 15 students received support, including 10 research assistantships with full and partial tuition reimbursements available (averaging $6,960 per year), 5 teaching assistantships with full and partial tuition reimbursements available (averaging $6,960 per year); career-related internships or fieldwork, Federal Work-Study, scholarships/grants, tuition waivers, and unspecified assistantships also available. Support available to part-time students. Financial award application deadline: 3/1; financial award applicants required to submit FAFSA. *Faculty research:* Housing and neighborhood development, urban housing policy, environmental sustainability, economic development, GIS and planning decision support. *Unit head:* Dr. William Dennis Keating, Director, 216-687-2298, Fax: 216-687-2013, E-mail: w.keating@csuohio.edu. *Application contact:* Joan Demko, Graduate Program Coordinator, 216-523-7522, Fax: 216-687-5398, E-mail: urbanprograms@csuohio.edu. Web site: http://urban.csuohio.edu/academics/graduate/mupdd/.

Cleveland State University, College of Graduate Studies, Maxine Goodman Levin College of Urban Affairs, Program in Urban Studies, Cleveland, OH 44115. Offers law and public policy (MS); public finance (MS); urban economic development (Certificate); urban policy analysis (MS); urban real estate development (MS); urban real estate development and finance (Certificate). PhD program offered jointly with The University of Akron. Part-time and evening/weekend programs available. *Faculty:* 26 full-time (10 women), 20 part-time/adjunct (11 women). *Students:* 16 full-time (10 women), 35 part-time (18 women); includes 7 minority (all Black or African American, non-Hispanic/Latino), 17 international. Average age 37. 63 applicants, 49% accepted, 18 enrolled. In 2011, 7 master's, 5 doctorates, 6 other advanced degrees awarded. *Degree requirements:* For master's, thesis or alternative, exit project; for doctorate, comprehensive exam, thesis/dissertation. *Entrance requirements:* For master's, GRE General Test, minimum GPA of 3.0; for doctorate, GRE General Test, minimum GPA of 3.5. Additional exam requirements/recommendations for international students: Required—TOEFL (minimum score 525 paper-based; 197 computer-based; 65 iBT). *Application deadline:* For fall admission, 1/15 priority date for domestic students, 1/15 for international students. Applications are processed on a rolling basis. Application fee: $30. Electronic applications accepted. *Expenses:* Tuition, state resident: full-time $6416; part-time $494 per credit hour. Tuition, nonresident: full-time $12,074; part-time $929 per credit hour. *Financial support:* In 2011–12, 15 students received support, including 8 research assistantships with full and partial tuition reimbursements available (averaging $9,000 per year), 7 teaching assistantships with full and partial tuition reimbursements available (averaging $2,400 per year); career-related internships or fieldwork, scholarships/grants, traineeships, and unspecified assistantships also available. Support available to part-time students. Financial award application deadline: 3/1; financial award applicants required to submit FAFSA. *Faculty research:* Environmental issues, economic development, urban and public policy, public management. *Unit head:* Dr. Mittie Davis Jones, Director, 216-687-3861, Fax: 216-687-9342, E-mail: m.d.jones97@csuohio.edu. *Application contact:* Joan Demko, Graduate Academic Program Specialist, 216-523-7522, Fax: 216-687-5398, E-mail: urbanprograms@csuohio.edu. Web site: http://urban.csuohio.edu/academics/graduate/msus/.

Cleveland State University, College of Graduate Studies, Monte Ahuja College of Business, Doctor of Business Administration Program, Cleveland, OH 44115. Offers finance (DBA); global business (DBA); information systems (DBA); marketing (DBA); operations management (DBA). *Accreditation:* AACSB. Part-time and evening/weekend programs available. *Faculty:* 50 full-time (11 women). *Students:* 4 full-time (1 woman), 34 part-time (12 women); includes 3 minority (1 Black or African American, non-Hispanic/Latino; 2 Asian, non-Hispanic/Latino), 11 international. Average age 40. In 2011, 5 doctorates awarded. *Degree requirements:* For doctorate, comprehensive exam, thesis/dissertation, oral dissertation defense. *Entrance requirements:* For doctorate, GMAT, MBA or equivalent. Additional exam requirements/recommendations for international students: Required—TOEFL (minimum score 550 paper-based; 213 computer-based; 79 iBT). *Application deadline:* For spring admission, 2/28 priority date for domestic students, 2/28 for international students. Application fee: $30. Electronic applications accepted. *Expenses:* Tuition, state resident: full-time $6416; part-time $494 per credit hour. Tuition, nonresident: full-time $12,074; part-time $929 per credit hour. *Financial support:* In 2011–12, 5 research assistantships with full tuition reimbursements (averaging $12,700 per year), 4 teaching assistantships with full tuition reimbursements (averaging $12,700 per year) were awarded; tuition waivers (full) and unspecified assistantships also available. *Faculty research:* Supply chain management, international business, strategic management, risk analysis, consumer behavior. *Unit head:* Dr. Raj Shekhar G. Javalgi, Director, 216-687-3786, Fax: 216-687-9354, E-mail: r.javalgi@csuohio.edu. *Application contact:* Melinda J. Arnold, Administrative Secretary, 216-687-6952, Fax: 216-687-9257, E-mail: m.arnold@csuohio.edu. Web site: http://www.csuohio.edu/business/academics/doctoral.html.

College for Financial Planning, Graduate Programs, Greenwood Village, CO 80111. Offers finance (MSF); financial analysis (MSF); personal financial planning (MS). Part-time and evening/weekend programs available. Postbaccalaureate distance learning degree programs offered (no on-campus study). *Degree requirements:* For master's, capstone course or thesis. *Entrance requirements:* Additional exam requirements/recommendations for international students: Required—TOEFL (minimum score 550 paper-based; 213 computer-based). *Application deadline:* Applications are processed on a rolling basis. Electronic applications accepted. *Financial support:* In 2011–12, 5 students received support. *Application contact:* Brett Sanborn, Director of Enrollment, 303-220-4951, Fax: 303-220-1810, E-mail: brett.sanborn@cffp.edu. Web site: http://www.cffp.edu.

Colorado State University, Graduate School, College of Business, Program in Financial Risk Management, Fort Collins, CO 80523-0015. Offers MSBA. *Entrance requirements:* For master's, GMAT or GRE, undergraduate degree with minimum GPA of 3.0; coursework in business finance, probability and statistics, and differential equations; academic experience with computer programming; current resume; 3 letters of recommendation. Additional exam requirements/recommendations for international students: Required—TOEFL (minimum score 565 paper-based; 227 computer-based; 86 iBT) or IELTS (minimum score 6.5). *Application deadline:* For fall admission, 7/1 for domestic students, 6/1 for international students. Application fee: $50. Electronic applications accepted. *Expenses:* Tuition, state resident: full-time $7992. Tuition, nonresident: full-time $19,592. *Required fees:* $1735; $58 per credit. *Unit head:* Dr. John Hoxmeier, Associate Dean, 970-491-2142, Fax: 970-491-0596, E-mail: john.hoxmeier@colostate.edu. *Application contact:* Rachel Stoll, Admissions Coordinator, 970-491-3704, Fax: 970-491-3481, E-mail: rachel.stoll@colostate.edu.

Colorado Technical University Colorado Springs, Graduate Studies, Program in Management, Colorado Springs, CO 80907-3896. Offers accounting (MBA, MSA); business administration (MBA); finance (MBA); human resources management (MBA); logistics/supply chain management (MBA); management (DM); marketing (MBA); mediation and dispute resolution (MBA); operations management (MBA); project management (MBA); technology management (MBA). Part-time and evening/weekend programs available. Postbaccalaureate distance learning degree programs offered. *Degree requirements:* For master's, thesis or alternative; for doctorate, thesis/dissertation. *Entrance requirements:* For doctorate, minimum graduate GPA of 3.0, 5 years of related work experience. *Faculty research:* Sexual harassment, performance evaluation, critical thinking.

Colorado Technical University Denver South, Programs in Business Administration and Management, Aurora, CO 80014. Offers accounting (MBA); business administration (MBA); business administration and management (EMBA); finance (MBA); human resource management (MBA); marketing (MBA); mediation and dispute resolution (MBA); operations management (MBA); project management (MBA); technology management (MBA). Part-time and evening/weekend programs available. *Degree requirements:* For master's, thesis or alternative. *Entrance requirements:* For master's, minimum undergraduate GPA of 3.0, resume.

Columbia Southern University, MBA Program, Orange Beach, AL 36561. Offers electronic business and technology (MBA); finance (MBA); general (MBA); healthcare management (MBA); hospitality and tourism (MBA); human resources management

(MBA); international management (MBA); marketing (MBA); project management (MBA); public administration (MBA); sport management (MBA). Part-time and evening/ weekend programs available. Postbaccalaureate distance learning degree programs offered (no on-campus study). *Entrance requirements:* For master's, bachelor's degree from accredited/approved institution. Additional exam requirements/recommendations for international students: Required—TOEFL. Electronic applications accepted.

Columbia University, Graduate School of Business, Doctoral Program in Business, New York, NY 10027. Offers business (PhD), including accounting, decision, risk, and operations, finance and economics, management, marketing. *Accreditation:* AACSB. *Degree requirements:* For doctorate, comprehensive exam, thesis/dissertation, major field exam, research paper, thesis proposal. *Entrance requirements:* For doctorate, GMAT or GRE (finance), 2 letters of reference, resume. Additional exam requirements/ recommendations for international students: Required—TOEFL. Electronic applications accepted. *Expenses:* Contact institution. *Faculty research:* Human decision making and behavioral research; real estate market and mortgage defaults; financial crisis and corporate governance; international business; security analysis and accounting.

Columbia University, Graduate School of Business, MBA Program, New York, NY 10027. Offers accounting (MBA); decision, risk, and operations (MBA); entrepreneurship (MBA); finance and economics (MBA); healthcare and pharmaceutical management (MBA); human resource management (MBA); international business (MBA); leadership and ethics (MBA); management (MBA); marketing (MBA); media (MBA); private equity (MBA); real estate (MBA); social enterprise (MBA); value investing (MBA); DDS/MBA; JD/MBA; MBA/MIA; MBA/MPH; MBA/MS; MD/MBA. *Entrance requirements:* For master's, GMAT, 2 letters of recommendation. Additional exam requirements/ recommendations for international students: Required—TOEFL. Electronic applications accepted. *Expenses:* Contact institution. *Faculty research:* Human decision making and behavioral research; real estate market and mortgage defaults; financial crisis and corporate governance; international business; security analysis and accounting.

Concordia University Wisconsin, Graduate Programs, School of Business and Legal Studies, MBA Program, Mequon, WI 53097-2402. Offers finance (MBA); health care administration (MBA); human resource management (MBA); international business (MBA); international business-bilingual English/Chinese (MBA); management (MBA); management information systems (MBA); managerial communications (MBA); marketing (MBA); public administration (MBA); risk management (MBA). Postbaccalaureate distance learning degree programs offered (minimal on-campus study). *Students:* 308 full-time (146 women), 536 part-time (288 women); includes 126 minority (76 Black or African American, non-Hispanic/Latino; 9 American Indian or Alaska Native, non-Hispanic/Latino; 15 Asian, non-Hispanic/Latino; 12 Hispanic/Latino; 14 Two or more races, non-Hispanic/Latino), 276 international. Average age 35. In 2011, 110 master's awarded. *Degree requirements:* For master's, comprehensive exam, thesis or alternative. *Entrance requirements:* Additional exam requirements/ recommendations for international students: Required—TOEFL. *Application deadline:* For fall admission, 8/1 priority date for domestic students; for spring admission, 1/15 for domestic students. Applications are processed on a rolling basis. Application fee: $50. *Expenses:* Contact institution. *Financial support:* Application deadline: 8/1. *Unit head:* Dr. David Borst, Director, 262-243-4298, Fax: 262-243-4428, E-mail: david.borst@ cuw.edu. *Application contact:* Mary Eberhardt, Graduate Admissions, 262-243-4551, Fax: 262-243-4428, E-mail: mary.eberhardt@cuw.edu.

Cornell University, Graduate School, Graduate Field of Management, Ithaca, NY 14853-0001. Offers accounting (PhD); behavioral decision theory (PhD); finance (PhD); marketing (PhD); organizational behavior (PhD); production and operations management (PhD). *Accreditation:* AACSB. *Faculty:* 53 full-time (8 women). *Students:* 39 full-time (11 women); includes 2 minority (both Asian, non-Hispanic/Latino), 23 international. Average age 29. 424 applicants, 3% accepted, 8 enrolled. In 2011, 6 doctorates awarded. *Degree requirements:* For doctorate, comprehensive exam, thesis/ dissertation. *Entrance requirements:* For doctorate, GMAT or GRE General Test. Additional exam requirements/recommendations for international students: Required—TOEFL (minimum score 600 paper-based; 250 computer-based; 77 iBT). *Application deadline:* For fall admission, 1/3 for domestic students. Application fee: $95. Electronic applications accepted. *Expenses:* Contact institution. *Financial support:* In 2011–12, 38 students received support, including 4 fellowships with full tuition reimbursements available, 33 research assistantships with full tuition reimbursements available, 2 teaching assistantships with full tuition reimbursements available; institutionally sponsored loans, scholarships/grants, health care benefits, tuition waivers (full and partial), and unspecified assistantships also available. Financial award applicants required to submit FAFSA. *Faculty research:* Operations and manufacturing. *Unit head:* Director of Graduate Studies, 607-255-3669. *Application contact:* Graduate Field Assistant, 607-255-9431, E-mail: js_phd@cornell.edu. Web site: http://www.gradschool.cornell.edu/fields.php?id-91&a-2.

Cornell University, Graduate School, Graduate Fields of Arts and Sciences, Field of Economics, Ithaca, NY 14853-0001. Offers applied economics (PhD); basic analytical economics (PhD); econometrics and economic statistics (PhD); economic development and planning (PhD); economic theory (PhD); industrial organization and control (PhD); international economics (PhD); labor economics (PhD); monetary and macroeconomics (PhD); public finance (PhD). *Faculty:* 83 full-time (10 women). *Students:* 104 full-time (40 women); includes 6 minority (1 Black or African American, non-Hispanic/Latino; 4 Asian, non-Hispanic/Latino; 1 Hispanic/Latino), 62 international. Average age 28. 718 applicants, 16% accepted, 32 enrolled. In 2011, 19 doctorates awarded. *Degree requirements:* For doctorate, comprehensive exam, thesis/dissertation. *Entrance requirements:* For doctorate, GRE General Test, 3 letters of recommendation. Additional exam requirements/recommendations for international students: Required—TOEFL (minimum score 550 paper-based; 213 computer-based; 77 iBT). *Application deadline:* For fall admission, 1/15 priority date for domestic students. Application fee: $95. Electronic applications accepted. *Financial support:* In 2011–12, 28 fellowships with full tuition reimbursements, 17 research assistantships with full tuition reimbursements, 43 teaching assistantships with full tuition reimbursements were awarded; institutionally sponsored loans, scholarships/grants, health care benefits, tuition waivers (full and partial), and unspecified assistantships also available. Financial award applicants required to submit FAFSA. *Faculty research:* Learning and games, economics of education, political economy, transfer payments, time series and nonparametrics. *Unit head:* Director of Graduate Studies, 607-255-4893, Fax: 607-255-2818. *Application contact:* Graduate Field Assistant, 607-255-4893, Fax: 607-255-2818, E-mail: econ_phd@cornell.edu. Web site: http://www.gradschool.cornell.edu/fields.php?id-79&a-2.

Curry College, Graduate Studies, Program in Business Administration, Milton, MA 02186-9984. Offers business administration (MBA); finance (Certificate). Part-time and evening/weekend programs available. *Degree requirements:* For master's, capstone applied project. *Entrance requirements:* For master's, resume, recommendations, interview, written statement. Additional exam requirements/recommendations for international students: Required—TOEFL (minimum score 550 paper-based; 213 computer-based; 80 iBT). *Expenses:* Contact institution.

Dalhousie University, Faculty of Management, Centre for Advanced Management Education, Halifax, NS B3H 3J5, Canada. Offers financial services (MBA); information management (MIM); management (MPA); natural resources (MBA). Part-time programs available. Postbaccalaureate distance learning degree programs offered. *Entrance requirements:* For master's, GMAT, minimum GPA of 3.0, resume. Additional exam requirements/recommendations for international students: Required—TOEFL, IELTS, CANTEST, CAEL, or Michigan English Language Assessment Battery. Electronic applications accepted.

Dalhousie University, Faculty of Management, School of Business Administration, Halifax, NS B3H 3J5, Canada. Offers business administration (MBA); financial services (MBA); LL B/MBA; MBA/MLIS. Part-time programs available. *Entrance requirements:* For master's, GMAT, letter of non-financial guarantee for non-Canadian students, resume, Corporate Residency Preference Form. Additional exam requirements/ recommendations for international students: Required—TOEFL, IELTS, CANTEST, CAEL, or Michigan English Language Assessment Battery. Electronic applications accepted. *Faculty research:* International business, quantitative methods, operations research, MIS, marketing, finance.

Dallas Baptist University, College of Business, Business Administration Program, Dallas, TX 75211-9299. Offers accounting (MBA); business communication (MBA); conflict resolution management (MBA); entrepreneurship (MBA); finance (MBA); health care management (MBA); international business (MBA); leading the non-profit organization (MBA); management (MBA); management information systems (MBA); marketing (MBA); project management (MBA); technology and engineering management (MBA). *Accreditation:* ACBSP. Part-time and evening/weekend programs available. *Entrance requirements:* For master's, GMAT, minimum GPA of 3.0. Additional exam requirements/recommendations for international students: Required—TOEFL, IELTS. *Application deadline:* Applications are processed on a rolling basis. Application fee: $25. Electronic applications accepted. *Expenses: Tuition:* Full-time $12,060; part-time $670 per credit hour. *Required fees:* $100; $50 per semester. *Financial support:* Federal Work-Study, institutionally sponsored loans, scholarships/grants, and tuition waivers (full and partial) available. Support available to part-time students. Financial award applicants required to submit FAFSA. *Faculty research:* Sports management, services marketing, retailing, strategic management, financial planning/investments. *Unit head:* Dr. Sandra S. Reid, Director, 214-333-5280, Fax: 214-333-5293, E-mail: graduate@dbu.edu. *Application contact:* Kit P. Montgomery, Director of Graduate Programs, 214-333-5242, Fax: 214-333-5579, E-mail: graduate@dbu.edu. Web site: http://www3.dbu.edu/graduate/mba.asp.

Dallas Baptist University, Professional Development Program, Dallas, TX 75211-9299. Offers accounting (MA); church leadership (MA); counseling (MA); criminal justice (MA); English as a second language (MA); finance (MA); higher education (MA); leadership studies (MA); management (MA); management information systems (MA); marketing (MA); missions (MA); professional life coaching (MA). Part-time and evening/ weekend programs available. *Entrance requirements:* For master's, minimum GPA of 3.0. Additional exam requirements/recommendations for international students: Required—TOEFL, IELTS. Application fee: $25. *Expenses: Tuition:* Full-time $12,060; part-time $670 per credit hour. *Required fees:* $100; $50 per semester. *Financial support:* Federal Work-Study, institutionally sponsored loans, scholarships/grants, and tuition waivers (full and partial) available. Support available to part-time students. Financial award applicants required to submit FAFSA. *Unit head:* Angela Fogle, Acting Director, 214-333-6830, Fax: 214-333-5558, E-mail: graduate@dbu.edu. *Application contact:* Kit P. Montgomery, Director of Graduate Programs, 214-333-5242, Fax: 214-333-5579, E-mail: graduate@dbu.edu. Web site: http://www3.dbu.edu/graduate/ mapd.asp.

Davenport University, Sneden Graduate School, Grand Rapids, MI 49512. Offers accounting (MBA); business administration (EMBA); finance (MBA); health care management (MBA); human resources (MBA); information assurance (MS); public health (MPH); strategic management (MBA). Evening/weekend programs available. *Entrance requirements:* For master's, GMAT, minimum undergraduate GPA of 2.75. Additional exam requirements/recommendations for international students: Required—TOEFL. Electronic applications accepted. *Faculty research:* Leadership, management, marketing, organizational culture.

Davenport University, Sneden Graduate School, Warren, MI 48092-5209. Offers accounting (MBA); business administration (EMBA); finance (MBA); health care management (MBA); human resources management (MBA); information assurance (MS); public health (MPH); strategic management (MBA). *Entrance requirements:* For master's, minimum undergraduate GPA of 2.7.

Davenport University, Sneden Graduate School, Dearborn, MI 48126-3799. Offers accounting (MBA); business administration (EMBA); finance (MBA); health care management (MBA); human resources management (MBA); information assurance (MS); marketing (MBA); public health (MPH); strategic management (MBA). Part-time and evening/weekend programs available. Postbaccalaureate distance learning degree programs offered (no on-campus study). *Entrance requirements:* For master's, minimum GPA of 2.7, previous course work in accounting and statistics. *Faculty research:* Accounting, international accounting, social and environmental accounting, finance.

DePaul University, Charles H. Kellstadt Graduate School of Business, Department of Finance, Chicago, IL 60604-2287. Offers behavioral finance (MBA); computational finance (MS); finance (MBA, MSF); financial analysis (MBA); financial management and control (MBA); international marketing and finance (MBA); managerial finance (MBA); real estate (MS); real estate finance and investment (MBA); strategy, execution and valuation (MBA). Part-time and evening/weekend programs available. *Faculty:* 26 full-time (5 women), 31 part-time/adjunct (4 women). *Students:* 454 full-time (138 women), 190 part-time (41 women); includes 85 minority (13 Black or African American, non-Hispanic/Latino; 53 Asian, non-Hispanic/Latino; 17 Hispanic/Latino; 2 Two or more races, non-Hispanic/Latino), 129 international. In 2011, 239 master's awarded. *Entrance requirements:* For master's, GMAT, 2 letters of recommendation, resume. Additional exam requirements/recommendations for international students: Required—TOEFL (minimum score 550 paper-based; 213 computer-based; 80 iBT). *Application deadline:* For fall admission, 7/1 for domestic students, 6/1 for international students; for winter admission, 10/1 for domestic students, 9/1 for international students; for spring admission, 2/1 for domestic students, 1/1 for international students. Applications are processed on a rolling basis. Application fee: $60. Electronic applications accepted. *Financial support:* In 2011–12, 10 students received support, including 10 research assistantships (averaging $15,120 per year); scholarships/grants and unspecified assistantships also available. Financial award application deadline: 6/1; financial award applicants required to submit FAFSA. *Faculty research:* Derivatives, valuation, international finance, real estate, corporate finance, behavioral finance. *Unit head:* Ali M. Fatemi, Professor and Chair, 312-362-8826, Fax: 312-362-6566, E-mail: afatemi@ depaul.edu. *Application contact:* Melissa Booth, Director of Admission and Recruitment, 312-362-6353, Fax: 312-362-6677, E-mail: kgsb@depaul.edu. Web site: http:// www.fin.depaul.edu/.

DePaul University, Charles H. Kellstadt Graduate School of Business, School of Accountancy and Management Information Systems, Chicago, IL 60604-2287. Offers accountancy (M Acc, MSA); business information technology (MS); e-business (MBA, MS); financial management and control (MBA); management accounting (MBA);

management information systems (MBA); taxation (MST). Part-time and evening/weekend programs available. *Faculty:* 30 full-time (9 women), 54 part-time/adjunct (7 women). *Students:* 44 full-time (13 women), 22 part-time (4 women); includes 8 minority (2 Black or African American, non-Hispanic/Latino; 3 Asian, non-Hispanic/Latino; 2 Hispanic/Latino; 1 Two or more races, non-Hispanic/Latino), 4 international. Average age 29. In 2011, 141 master's awarded. *Entrance requirements:* For master's, GMAT, 2 letters of recommendation, resume. Additional exam requirements/recommendations for international students: Required—TOEFL (minimum score 550 paper-based; 213 computer-based). *Application deadline:* For fall admission, 7/1 for domestic students; for winter admission, 10/1 for domestic students; for spring admission, 2/1 for domestic students. Applications are processed on a rolling basis. Application fee: $60. *Financial support:* In 2011–12, 7 research assistantships with full tuition reimbursements (averaging $4,100 per year) were awarded; institutionally sponsored loans also available. Financial award application deadline: 4/2. *Faculty research:* Tax policy, property transactions, stock options as compensation, standards setting, activity-based costing in health care. *Unit head:* Kevin Stevens, Director, 312-362-6989, E-mail: kstevens@depaul.edu. *Application contact:* Christopher E. Kinsella, Director of Cohort MBA Programs, 312-362-8810, Fax: 312-362-6677, E-mail: kgsb@depaul.edu. Web site: http://accountancy.depaul.edu/.

DePaul University, School of Public Service, Chicago, IL 60604. Offers administrative foundations (Certificate); community development (Certificate); financial administration management (Certificate); health administration (Certificate); health law and policy (MS); international public services (MS); leadership and policy studies (MS); metropolitan planning (Certificate); nonprofit leadership (Certificate); nonprofit management (MNM); public administration (MPA); public service management (MS), including association management, fundraising and philanthropy, healthcare administration, higher education administration, metropolitan planning; public services (Certificate); JD/MS. Part-time and evening/weekend programs available. Postbaccalaureate distance learning degree programs offered (minimal on-campus study). *Faculty:* 14 full-time (3 women), 43 part-time/adjunct (24 women). *Students:* 366 full-time (266 women), 316 part-time (216 women); includes 283 minority (143 Black or African American, non-Hispanic/Latino; 1 American Indian or Alaska Native, non-Hispanic/Latino; 35 Asian, non-Hispanic/Latino; 88 Hispanic/Latino; 16 Two or more races, non-Hispanic/Latino), 13 international. Average age 29. 162 applicants, 100% accepted, 94 enrolled. In 2011, 108 master's awarded. *Degree requirements:* For master's, thesis or integrative seminar. *Entrance requirements:* For master's, minimum GPA of 2.7. Additional exam requirements/recommendations for international students: Required—TOEFL (minimum score 550 paper-based; 213 computer-based; 80 iBT), IELTS (minimum score 6.5). *Application deadline:* Applications are processed on a rolling basis. Application fee: $40. Electronic applications accepted. *Financial support:* In 2011–12, 60 students received support, including 3 research assistantships with full tuition reimbursements available (averaging $7,000 per year); career-related internships or fieldwork, Federal Work-Study, institutionally sponsored loans, scholarships/grants, tuition waivers (partial), and unspecified assistantships also available. Support available to part-time students. Financial award application deadline: 7/1; financial award applicants required to submit FAFSA. *Faculty research:* Government financing, transportation, leadership, health care, volunteerism and organizational behavior, non-profit organizations. *Total annual research expenditures:* $20,000. *Unit head:* Dr. J. Patrick Murphy, Director, 312-362-5608, Fax: 312-362-5506, E-mail: jpmurphy@depaul.edu. *Application contact:* Megan B. Balderston, Director of Admissions and Marketing, 312-362-5565, Fax: 312-362-5506, E-mail: pubserv@depaul.edu. Web site: http://las.depaul.edu/sps/.

DeSales University, Graduate Division, MBA Program, Center Valley, PA 18034-9568. Offers accounting (MBA); computer information systems (MBA); finance (MBA); health care systems management (MBA); human resources management (MBA); management (MBA); marketing (MBA); project management (MBA); self-design (MBA). *Accreditation:* ACBSP. Part-time programs available. Postbaccalaureate distance learning degree programs offered (no on-campus study). *Entrance requirements:* For master's, GMAT, minimum GPA of 3.0, 2 years of work experience. Additional exam requirements/recommendations for international students: Required—TOEFL. *Application deadline:* Applications are processed on a rolling basis. Electronic applications accepted. Tuition and fees vary according to degree level. *Faculty research:* Quality improvement, executive development, productivity, cross-cultural managerial differences, leadership. *Unit head:* Dr. David Gilfoil, Director, 610-282-1100 Ext. 1828, Fax: 610-282-2869, E-mail: david.gilfoil@desales.edu. *Application contact:* Caryn Stopper, Director of Graduate Admissions, 610-282-1100 Ext. 1768, Fax: 610-282-0525, E-mail: caryn.stopper@desales.edu.

DeVry University, Keller Graduate School of Management, Downers Grove, IL 60515. Offers accounting and financial management (MAFM); business administration (MBA); human resources management (MHRM); information systems management (MISM); network and communications management (MNCM); project management (MPM); public administration (MPA).

Dowling College, School of Business, Oakdale, NY 11769-1999. Offers aviation management (MBA, Certificate); banking and finance (MBA, Certificate); corporate finance (MBA); financial planning (Certificate); health care management (MBA, Certificate); human resource management (Certificate); information systems management (MBA); management and leadership (MBA); marketing (Certificate); project management (Certificate); public management (MBA, Certificate); sport, event and entertainment management (Certificate); JD/MBA. Part-time and evening/weekend programs available. Postbaccalaureate distance learning degree programs offered (minimal on-campus study). *Faculty:* 10 full-time (4 women), 54 part-time/adjunct (6 women). *Students:* 237 full-time (99 women), 403 part-time (199 women); includes 186 minority (95 Black or African American, non-Hispanic/Latino; 62 Asian, non-Hispanic/Latino; 28 Hispanic/Latino; 1 Native Hawaiian or other Pacific Islander, non-Hispanic/Latino), 1 international. Average age 35. 345 applicants, 83% accepted, 193 enrolled. In 2011, 350 master's, 7 other advanced degrees awarded. *Degree requirements:* For master's, comprehensive exam, thesis optional. *Entrance requirements:* For master's, minimum GPA of 2.8, 2 letters of recommendation, courses or seminar in accounting and finance, resume. Additional exam requirements/recommendations for international students: Required—TOEFL (minimum score 550 paper-based). *Application deadline:* For fall admission, 9/1 priority date for domestic students; for winter admission, 1/1 priority date for domestic students; for spring admission, 2/1 priority date for domestic students. Applications are processed on a rolling basis. Application fee: $50. Electronic applications accepted. *Expenses: Tuition:* Full-time $19,162; part-time $933 per credit. *Required fees:* $1330; $700 per year. Tuition and fees vary according to course load. *Financial support:* Career-related internships or fieldwork and Federal Work-Study available. Support available to part-time students. Financial award application deadline: 6/30; financial award applicants required to submit FAFSA. *Faculty research:* International finance, computer applications, labor relations, executive development. *Unit head:* Antonia Loschiavo, Assistant Dean, 631-244-3266, Fax: 631-244-1018, E-mail: loschiat@dowling.edu. *Application contact:* Ronnie S. Macdonald, Assistant Vice President for Enrollment Services/Dean of Admissions, 631-244-3357, Fax: 631-244-1059, E-mail: macdonar@dowling.edu.

Drexel University, LeBow College of Business, Department of Finance, Philadelphia, PA 19104-2875. Offers MS. *Degree requirements:* For master's, seminar paper. *Entrance requirements:* For master's, GMAT, minimum GPA of 2.75. Additional exam requirements/recommendations for international students: Required—TOEFL. Electronic applications accepted. *Faculty research:* Investment analysis, portfolio mix, capital budgeting, banking and financial institutions, international finance.

Drexel University, LeBow College of Business, Program in Business Administration, Philadelphia, PA 19104-2875. Offers business administration (MBA, PhD, APC), including accounting (MBA, PhD), decision sciences (PhD), economics (MBA, PhD), finance (MBA, PhD), legal studies (MBA), management (MBA), marketing (MBA, PhD), organizational sciences (PhD), quantitative methods (MBA), strategic management (PhD). *Accreditation:* AACSB. Part-time and evening/weekend programs available. Postbaccalaureate distance learning degree programs offered (minimal on-campus study). Terminal master's awarded for partial completion of doctoral program. *Entrance requirements:* For master's, GMAT, minimum GPA of 2.75; for doctorate, GMAT. Additional exam requirements/recommendations for international students: Required—TOEFL. Electronic applications accepted. *Faculty research:* Decision support systems, individual and group behavior, operations research, techniques and strategy.

Eastern Michigan University, Graduate School, College of Business, Programs in Business Administration, Ypsilanti, MI 48197. Offers business administration (MBA, Graduate Certificate); computer information systems (Graduate Certificate); e-business (MBA, Graduate Certificate); enterprise business intelligence (MBA); entrepreneurship (MBA, Graduate Certificate); finance (MBA, Graduate Certificate); human resources (MBA); human resources management (Graduate Certificate); information systems (MBA); internal auditing (MBA); international business (MBA, Graduate Certificate); marketing management (Graduate Certificate); nonprofit management (MBA); organizational development (Graduate Certificate); supply chain management (MBA, Graduate Certificate). *Accreditation:* AACSB. Part-time programs available. Postbaccalaureate distance learning degree programs offered (no on-campus study). *Students:* 79 full-time (39 women), 287 part-time (143 women); includes 55 minority (22 Black or African American, non-Hispanic/Latino; 24 Asian, non-Hispanic/Latino; 6 Hispanic/Latino; 3 Two or more races, non-Hispanic/Latino), 238 international. Average age 32. 317 applicants, 62% accepted, 89 enrolled. In 2011, 102 master's, 58 other advanced degrees awarded. *Entrance requirements:* For master's, GMAT (minimum score 450), minimum cumulative undergraduate GPA of 2.75. Additional exam requirements/recommendations for international students: Required—TOEFL. *Application deadline:* For fall admission, 5/15 for domestic students, 5/1 for international students; for winter admission, 10/15 for domestic students, 10/1 for international students; for spring admission, 3/15 for domestic students, 3/1 for international students. Applications are processed on a rolling basis. Application fee: $35. *Expenses:* Tuition, state resident: full-time $10,367; part-time $432 per credit hour. Tuition, nonresident: full-time $20,435; part-time $851 per credit hour. *Required fees:* $39 per credit hour. $46 per semester. One-time fee: $100. Tuition and fees vary according to course level, degree level and reciprocity agreements. *Financial support:* Fellowships, research assistantships with full tuition reimbursements, teaching assistantships with full tuition reimbursements, career-related internships or fieldwork, Federal Work-Study, institutionally sponsored loans, scholarships/grants, tuition waivers (partial), and unspecified assistantships available. Support available to part-time students. Financial award applicants required to submit FAFSA. *Unit head:* K. Michelle Henry, Director, Academic Services, 734-487-4444, Fax: 734-483-1316, E-mail: mhenry1@emich.edu. *Application contact:* Beste Windes, Advisor, 734-487-4444, Fax: 734-483-1316, E-mail: bwindes@emich.edu. Web site: http://www.emich.edu/public/cob/gr/grad.html.

East Tennessee State University, School of Graduate Studies, College of Arts and Sciences, Department of Political Science, International Affairs and Public Administration, Johnson City, TN 37614. Offers city management (MCM); economic development (Postbaccalaureate Certificate); not-for-profit administration (MPA); planning and development (MPA); public financial management (MPA); urban planning (Postbaccalaureate Certificate). Part-time programs available. *Faculty:* 7 full-time (2 women), 1 part-time/adjunct (0 women). *Students:* 27 full-time (12 women), 12 part-time (4 women); includes 9 minority (5 Black or African American, non-Hispanic/Latino; 1 American Indian or Alaska Native, non-Hispanic/Latino; 3 Hispanic/Latino), 4 international. Average age 29. 32 applicants, 63% accepted, 15 enrolled. In 2011, 12 degrees awarded. *Degree requirements:* For master's, internship. *Entrance requirements:* For master's, GRE General Test, three letters of recommendation; for Postbaccalaureate Certificate, GRE General Test. Additional exam requirements/recommendations for international students: Required—TOEFL (minimum score 550 paper-based; 213 computer-based; 79 iBT). *Application deadline:* For fall admission, 6/1 for domestic students, 4/29 for international students; for spring admission, 11/1 for domestic students, 9/30 for international students. Application fee: $35 ($45 for international students). Electronic applications accepted. *Expenses:* Tuition, state resident: full-time $7312; part-time $350 per credit hour. Tuition, nonresident: full-time $18,490; part-time $621 per credit hour. *Required fees:* $63 per credit hour. Tuition and fees vary according to course load and program. *Financial support:* In 2011–12, 18 students received support, including 7 research assistantships with full tuition reimbursements available (averaging $6,000 per year); career-related internships or fieldwork, institutionally sponsored loans, scholarships/grants, and unspecified assistantships also available. Financial award application deadline: 7/1; financial award applicants required to submit FAFSA. *Faculty research:* American politics, comparative politics, international relations, public administration, public law. *Unit head:* Dr. Weixing Chen, Chair, 423-439-4217, Fax: 423-439-4348, E-mail: chen@etsu.edu. *Application contact:* Gail Powers, Graduate Specialist, 423-439-4703, Fax: 423-439-5624, E-mail: pwersg@etsu.edu.

Edgewood College, Program in Business, Madison, WI 53711-1997. Offers accountancy (MS); accounting (MBA); business administration (MBA); finance (MBA); management (MBA); marketing (MBA); sustainability leadership (MBA). *Accreditation:* ACBSP. Part-time and evening/weekend programs available. *Students:* 24 full-time (15 women), 95 part-time (41 women); includes 9 minority (2 Black or African American, non-Hispanic/Latino; 4 Asian, non-Hispanic/Latino; 3 Hispanic/Latino), 7 international. Average age 33. In 2011, 43 master's awarded. *Entrance requirements:* For master's, GMAT (minimum score 430), minimum GPA of 2.75, 2 letters of recommendation. Additional exam requirements/recommendations for international students: Required—TOEFL (minimum score 213 computer-based). *Application deadline:* For fall admission, 8/15 for domestic students, 5/1 for international students; for spring admission, 1/8 for domestic students, 11/1 for international students. Applications are processed on a rolling basis. Application fee: $25. Electronic applications accepted. *Expenses: Tuition:* Part-time $747 per credit. Part-time tuition and fees vary according to program. *Financial support:* Career-related internships or fieldwork and scholarships/grants available. *Unit head:* Martin Preizler, Dean, 608-663-2898, Fax: 608-663-3291, E-mail: martinpreizler@edgewood.edu. *Application contact:* Joann Eastman, Admissions Counselor, 608-663-3250, Fax: 608-663-2214, E-mail: gps@edgewood.edu. Web site: http://www.edgewood.edu/Academics/Graduate.aspx.

Ellis University, MBA Program, Chicago, IL 60606-7204. Offers e-commerce (MBA); finance (MBA); general business (MBA); global management (MBA); health care administration (MBA); leadership (MBA); management of information systems (MBA); marketing (MBA); professional accounting (MBA); project management (MBA); public accounting (MBA); risk management (MBA).

Emory University, Goizueta Business School, Doctoral Program in Business, Atlanta, GA 30322-1100. Offers accounting (PhD); finance (PhD); information systems (PhD); marketing (PhD); organization and management (PhD). *Faculty:* 56 full-time (13 women). *Students:* 37 full-time (17 women); includes 21 minority (20 Asian, non-Hispanic/Latino; 1 Hispanic/Latino). Average age 29. 240 applicants, 6% accepted, 11 enrolled. In 2011, 5 doctorates awarded. *Degree requirements:* For doctorate, comprehensive exam, thesis/dissertation. *Entrance requirements:* For doctorate, GMAT (strongly preferred) or GRE. Additional exam requirements/recommendations for international students: Required—TOEFL (minimum score 250 computer-based). *Application deadline:* For fall admission, 1/3 priority date for domestic students, 1/1 for international students. Application fee: $50. Electronic applications accepted. *Expenses: Tuition:* Full-time $34,800. *Required fees:* $1300. *Financial support:* In 2011–12, 37 students received support. *Unit head:* Dr. Lawrence Benveniste, Dean, 404-727-6377, Fax: 404-727-0868, E-mail: larry_benveniste@bus.emory.edu. *Application contact:* Allison Gilmore, Director of Admissions and Student Services, 404-727-6353, Fax: 404-727-5337, E-mail: phd@bus.emory.edu.

Fairfield University, Charles F. Dolan School of Business, Fairfield, CT 06824-5195. Offers accounting (MBA, MS, CAS); accounting information systems (MBA, CAS); entrepreneurship (MBA, CAS); finance (MBA, MS, CAS); general management (MBA, CAS); human resource management (MBA, CAS); information systems and operations (MBA); information systems and operations management (CAS); international business (MBA, CAS); marketing (MBA, CAS); taxation (MBA, CAS). *Accreditation:* AACSB. Part-time and evening/weekend programs available. *Faculty:* 23 full-time (9 women), 3 part-time/adjunct (1 woman). *Students:* 87 full-time (37 women), 118 part-time (42 women); includes 13 minority (4 Black or African American, non-Hispanic/Latino; 4 Asian, non-Hispanic/Latino; 5 Hispanic/Latino), 9 international. Average age 29. 126 applicants, 47% accepted, 35 enrolled. In 2011, 90 master's awarded. *Degree requirements:* For master's, capstone course. *Entrance requirements:* For master's, GMAT (minimum score 500), 2 letters of reference, resume, minimum GPA of 3.0. Additional exam requirements/recommendations for international students: Required—TOEFL (minimum score 550 paper-based; 213 computer-bases; 80 iBT) or IELTS (minimum score 6.5). *Application deadline:* For fall admission, 5/15 for international students; for spring admission, 10/15 for international students. Applications are processed on a rolling basis. Application fee: $60. Electronic applications accepted. *Expenses:* Contact institution. *Financial support:* In 2011–12, 50 students received support, including 2 research assistantships (averaging $6,500 per year); scholarships/grants, unspecified assistantships, and merit-based one-time entrance scholarship also available. Financial award applicants required to submit FAFSA. *Faculty research:* Optimization strategies, international finance, consumer behavior, financial market volatility, Internet marketing, supply chain analysis, tax issues. *Unit head:* Dr. Donald Gibson, Dean, 203-254-4000 Ext. 4070, Fax: 203-254-4105, E-mail: dgibson@fairfield.edu. *Application contact:* Marianne Gumpper, Director of Graduate and Continuing Studies Admission, 203-254-4184, Fax: 203-254-4073, E-mail: gradadmis@fairfield.edu. Web site: http://www.fairfield.edu/dsb/dsb_grad_1.html.

Fairleigh Dickinson University, College at Florham, Silberman College of Business, Department of Economics, Finance, and International Business, Program in Finance, Madison, NJ 07940-1099. Offers MBA, Certificate.

Fairleigh Dickinson University, Metropolitan Campus, Silberman College of Business, Department of Economics, Finance and International Business, Program in Finance, Teaneck, NJ 07666-1914. Offers MBA, Certificate.

Florida Agricultural and Mechanical University, Division of Graduate Studies, Research, and Continuing Education, School of Business and Industry, Tallahassee, FL 32307-3200. Offers accounting (MBA); finance (MBA); management information systems (MBA); marketing (MBA). *Degree requirements:* For master's, residency. *Entrance requirements:* For master's, GMAT, minimum GPA of 3.0.

Florida Institute of Technology, Graduate Programs, Nathan M. Bisk College of Business, Online Programs, Melbourne, FL 32901-6975. Offers accounting (MBA); accounting and finance (MBA); business administration (MBA); finance (MBA); healthcare management (MBA); information technology (MS); information technology cybersecurity (MS); information technology management (MBA); international business (MBA); Internet marketing (MBA); management (MBA); marketing (MBA); project management (MBA). Part-time and evening/weekend programs available. Postbaccalaureate distance learning degree programs offered (no on-campus study). *Faculty:* 47 part-time/adjunct (15 women). *Students:* 8 full-time (4 women), 1,122 part-time (547 women); includes 418 minority (271 Black or African American, non-Hispanic/Latino; 5 American Indian or Alaska Native, non-Hispanic/Latino; 55 Asian, non-Hispanic/Latino; 81 Hispanic/Latino; 6 Native Hawaiian or other Pacific Islander, non-Hispanic/Latino), 23 international. Average age 36. In 2011, 329 master's awarded. *Entrance requirements:* For master's, GMAT or resume showing 8 years of supervised experience, 2 letters of recommendation, resume, competency in math past college algebra. Additional exam requirements/recommendations for international students: Required—TOEFL (minimum score 550 paper-based; 213 computer-based; 79 iBT). *Application deadline:* For fall admission, 4/1 for international students; for spring admission, 9/30 for international students. Applications are processed on a rolling basis. Electronic applications accepted. *Expenses:* Contact institution. *Financial support:* Available to part-time students. Application deadline: 3/1; applicants required to submit FAFSA. *Unit head:* Dr. Mary S. Bonhomme, Dean, Florida Tech Online/Associate Provost for Online Learning, 321-674-8202, Fax: 321-674-8216, E-mail: bonhomme@fit.edu. *Application contact:* Carolyn Farrior, Director of Graduate Admissions, Online Learning and Off-Campus Programs, 321-674-7118, Fax: 321-674-8216, E-mail: cfarrior@fit.edu. Web site: http://online.fit.edu.

Florida International University, Alvah H. Chapman, Jr. Graduate School of Business, Department of Finance and Real Estate, Miami, FL 33199. Offers finance (MSF); international real estate (MS); real estate (MS). Part-time and evening/weekend programs available. *Entrance requirements:* For master's, GMAT or GRE, minimum GPA of 3.0 (upper-level coursework); letter of intent; resume. Additional exam requirements/recommendations for international students: Required—TOEFL (minimum score 550 paper-based; 213 computer-based; 80 iBT) or IELTS (minimum score 6.5). Electronic applications accepted. *Expenses:* Contact institution. *Faculty research:* Investment, corporate and international finance, commercial real estate.

Florida State University, The Graduate School, College of Business, Tallahassee, FL 32306-1110. Offers accounting (M Acc), including accounting information services, assurance services, corporate accounting, taxation; business administration (MBA, PhD), including accounting (PhD), finance (PhD), management information systems (PhD), marketing (PhD), organizational behavior (PhD), risk management and insurance (PhD), strategic management (PhD); finance (MS); insurance (MSM); management information systems (MS); marketing (MS); JD/MBA; MSW/MBA. *Accreditation:* AACSB. Part-time programs available. Postbaccalaureate distance learning degree programs offered (no on-campus study). *Faculty:* 107 full-time (31 women). *Students:* 196 full-time (76 women), 310 part-time (109 women); includes 89 minority (27 Black or African American, non-Hispanic/Latino; 1 American Indian or Alaska Native, non-Hispanic/Latino; 31 Asian, non-Hispanic/Latino; 30 Hispanic/Latino). Average age 30. 702 applicants, 33% accepted, 205 enrolled. In 2011, 268 master's, 17 doctorates awarded. Terminal master's awarded for partial completion of doctoral program. *Degree requirements:* For doctorate, comprehensive exam, thesis/dissertation. *Entrance requirements:* For master's, GMAT, work experience (MBA, MS), minimum GPA of 3.0, letters of recommendation; for doctorate, GMAT, minimum graduate GPA of 3.5, letters of recommendation. Additional exam requirements/recommendations for international students: Required—TOEFL (minimum score 600 paper-based; 80 computer-based); Recommended—IELTS (minimum score 6.5). *Application deadline:* For fall admission, 6/1 for domestic students, 5/1 for international students; for spring admission, 10/1 for domestic students, 9/1 for international students. Applications are processed on a rolling basis. Application fee: $30. Electronic applications accepted. *Expenses:* Tuition, state resident: full-time $9474; part-time $350.88 per credit hour. Tuition, nonresident: full-time $16,236; part-time $601.34 per credit hour. *Required fees:* $630 per semester. One-time fee: $20. Tuition and fees vary according to course load and campus/location. *Financial support:* In 2011–12, 86 students received support, including 12 fellowships with full tuition reimbursements available (averaging $7,161 per year), 30 research assistantships with full tuition reimbursements available (averaging $6,000 per year), 43 teaching assistantships with full tuition reimbursements available (averaging $15,000 per year); career-related internships or fieldwork, scholarships/grants, health care benefits, tuition waivers (full and partial), and unspecified assistantships also available. Support available to part-time students. Financial award application deadline: 1/1. *Unit head:* Dr. Caryn Beck-Dudley, Dean, 850-644-3090, Fax: 850-644-0915. *Application contact:* Lisa Beverly, Director, Graduate Programs Admissions, 850-644-6458, Fax: 850-644-0588, E-mail: lbeverly@cob.fsu.edu. Web site: http://www.cob.fsu.edu/grad/.

Fordham University, Graduate School of Business, New York, NY 10023. Offers accounting (MBA); communications and media management (MBA); executive business administration (EMBA); finance (MBA, MS); information systems (MBA, MS); management systems (MBA); marketing (MBA); media management (MS); taxation (MS); taxation and accounting (MTA);); JD/MBA; MBA/MIM; MS/MBA. MBA/MIM offered jointly with Thunderbird School of Global Management. *Accreditation:* AACSB. Part-time and evening/weekend programs available. *Entrance requirements:* For master's, GMAT, 2 letters of recommendation, resume. Additional exam requirements/recommendations for international students: Required—TOEFL (minimum score 600 paper-based; 250 computer-based; 100 iBT). Electronic applications accepted. *Expenses:* Contact institution.

Gannon University, School of Graduate Studies, College of Engineering and Business, School of Business, Program in Finance, Erie, PA 16541-0001. Offers Certificate. Part-time and evening/weekend programs available. *Students:* 1 full-time (0 women); minority (Black or African American, non-Hispanic/Latino). Average age 29. 2 applicants, 50% accepted, 1 enrolled. *Entrance requirements:* For degree, GMAT. Additional exam requirements/recommendations for international students: Required—TOEFL (minimum score 79 iBT). *Application deadline:* Applications are processed on a rolling basis. Application fee: $25. Electronic applications accepted. *Financial support:* Application deadline: 7/1; applicants required to submit FAFSA. *Unit head:* Dr. Donna Mottilla, Director, 814-871-7780, E-mail: mottilla001@gannon.edu. *Application contact:* Kara Morgan, Director of Graduate Admissions, 814-871-5831, Fax: 814-871-5827, E-mail: graduate@gannon.edu.

George Fox University, School of Business, Newberg, OR 97132-2697. Offers finance (MBA); management (DBA); management/general (MBA); marketing (DBA); organizational strategy (MBA); strategic human resource management (MBA). MBA offered part-time and full-time in Newberg, OR, and in Portland, OR. Part-time and evening/weekend programs available. Postbaccalaureate distance learning degree programs offered (minimal on-campus study). *Faculty:* 9 full-time (2 women), 6 part-time/adjunct (0 women). *Students:* 24 full-time (11 women), 239 part-time (81 women); includes 33 minority (4 Black or African American, non-Hispanic/Latino; 1 American Indian or Alaska Native, non-Hispanic/Latino; 14 Asian, non-Hispanic/Latino; 10 Hispanic/Latino; 4 Two or more races, non-Hispanic/Latino), 13 international. Average age 37. In 2011, 101 master's, 6 doctorates awarded. *Degree requirements:* For master's, capstone project; for doctorate, credit-applied research project. *Entrance requirements:* For master's, resume (5 years professional experience); 3 professional references; interview; financial e-learning course, official transcripts; for doctorate, GRE or GMAT, resume; personal mission statement; academic research writing sample; official transcript from each college/university attended; three professional references. Additional exam requirements/recommendations for international students: Required—TOEFL (minimum score 577 paper-based; 233 computer-based; 90 iBT) or IELTS (minimum score 7). *Application deadline:* For fall admission, 8/1 for domestic and international students; for spring admission, 12/1 for domestic and international students. Applications are processed on a rolling basis. Application fee: $40. Electronic applications accepted. *Expenses:* Contact institution. *Financial support:* Applicants required to submit FAFSA. *Unit head:* Dr. Dirk Barram, Professor/Dean, 800-631-0921. *Application contact:* Robin Halverson, Admissions Counselor, 800-493-4937, Fax: 503-554-6111, E-mail: mba@georgefox.edu. Web site: http://www.georgefox.edu/business/index.html.

Georgetown University, Graduate School of Arts and Sciences, Department of Economics, Washington, DC 20057. Offers econometrics (PhD); economic development (PhD); economic theory (PhD); industrial organization (PhD); international macro and finance (PhD); international trade (PhD); labor economics (PhD); macroeconomics (PhD); public economics and political economics (PhD); MA/PhD; MS/MA. *Degree requirements:* For doctorate, comprehensive exam, thesis/dissertation. *Entrance requirements:* For doctorate, GRE General Test. Additional exam requirements/recommendations for international students: Required—TOEFL. *Faculty research:* International economics, economic development.

The George Washington University, School of Business, Department of Finance, Washington, DC 20052. Offers finance (MSF, PhD); finance and investments (MBA); real estate and urban development (MBA). Part-time and evening/weekend programs available. *Faculty:* 17 full-time (4 women), 4 part-time/adjunct (1 woman). *Students:* 106 full-time (41 women), 45 part-time (11 women); includes 33 minority (7 Black or African American, non-Hispanic/Latino; 11 Asian, non-Hispanic/Latino; 10 Hispanic/Latino; 5 Two or more races, non-Hispanic/Latino), 87 international. Average age 29. 728 applicants, 25% accepted, 93 enrolled. In 2011, 48 master's awarded. *Degree requirements:* For doctorate, thesis/dissertation. *Entrance requirements:* For master's, GMAT; for doctorate, GMAT or GRE. Additional exam requirements/recommendations for international students: Required—TOEFL. *Application deadline:* For fall admission, 4/1 priority date for domestic students; for spring admission, 10/1 for domestic students. Applications are processed on a rolling basis. Application fee: $75. *Financial support:* In 2011–12, 38 students received support. Fellowships, teaching assistantships, career-related internships or fieldwork, Federal Work-Study, and institutionally sponsored loans available. Financial award application deadline: 4/1. *Unit head:* Mark S. Klock, Chair, 202-994-5996, E-mail: klock@gwu.edu. *Application contact:* Kristin Williams, Assistant

Vice President for Graduate and Special Enrollment Management, 202-994-0467, Fax: 202-994-0371, E-mail: ksw@gwu.edu.

Georgia Institute of Technology, Graduate Studies and Research, College of Management, Program in Business Administration, Atlanta, GA 30332-0001. Offers accounting (MBA); e-commerce (Certificate); engineering entrepreneurship (MBA); entrepreneurship (Certificate); finance (MBA); information technology management (MBA); international business (MBA, Certificate); management of technology (Certificate); marketing (MBA); operations management (MBA); organizational behavior (MBA); strategic management (MBA). *Accreditation:* AACSB.

Georgia Institute of Technology, Graduate Studies and Research, College of Management, Program in Management, Atlanta, GA 30332-0001. Offers accounting (PhD); finance (PhD); information technology management (PhD); marketing (PhD); operations management (PhD); organizational behavior (PhD); quantitative and computational finance (MS); strategic management (PhD). *Accreditation:* AACSB. *Degree requirements:* For doctorate, comprehensive exam, thesis/dissertation, oral exams. *Entrance requirements:* For master's and doctorate, GMAT. Additional exam requirements/recommendations for international students: Required—TOEFL. *Faculty research:* MIS, management of technology, international business, entrepreneurship, operations management.

Georgia State University, Andrew Young School of Policy Studies, Department of Public Management and Policy, Atlanta, GA 30303. Offers disaster management (Certificate); non-profit management (Certificate); planning and economic development (Certificate); public administration (MPA), including criminal justice, management and finance, nonprofit management, planning and economic development, policy analysis and evaluation, public health; public policy (MPP, PhD), including disaster policy (MPP), nonprofit policy (MPP), planning and economic development policy (MPP), public finance policy (MPP), social policy (MPP); JD/MPA. *Accreditation:* NASPAA (one or more programs are accredited). Part-time and evening/weekend programs available. Terminal master's awarded for partial completion of doctoral program. *Degree requirements:* For master's, thesis optional; for doctorate, comprehensive exam, thesis/dissertation. *Entrance requirements:* For master's and doctorate, GRE General Test. Additional exam requirements/recommendations for international students: Required—TOEFL. Electronic applications accepted. *Faculty research:* Public management, policy analysis, public finance, planning and economic development, nonprofit leadership and policy.

Georgia State University, J. Mack Robinson College of Business, Department of Finance, Atlanta, GA 30302-3083. Offers MBA, MS, PhD. Part-time and evening/weekend programs available. Terminal master's awarded for partial completion of doctoral program. *Degree requirements:* For doctorate, comprehensive exam, thesis/dissertation. *Entrance requirements:* For master's and doctorate, GMAT. Additional exam requirements/recommendations for international students: Required—TOEFL (minimum score 610 paper-based; 253 computer-based; 101 iBT). Electronic applications accepted.

Georgia State University, J. Mack Robinson College of Business, Department of Risk Management and Insurance, Program in Personal Financial Planning, Atlanta, GA 30302-3083. Offers MBA, MS, Certificate. Part-time and evening/weekend programs available. *Entrance requirements:* For master's, GMAT, GRE. Additional exam requirements/recommendations for international students: Required—TOEFL (minimum score 610 paper-based; 255 computer-based; 101 iBT). Electronic applications accepted.

Golden Gate University, Ageno School of Business, San Francisco, CA 94105-2968. Offers accounting (MBA); business administration (EMBA, MBA, PMBA, DBA); finance (MBA, MS, Certificate); financial planning (MS, Certificate); healthcare information systems (Certificate); human resource management (MBA, MS); human resources management (Certificate); information systems (MS); information technology (MBA); information technology management (Certificate); integrated marketing and communications (MS, Certificate); international business (MBA); management (MBA); marketing (MBA, MS, Certificate); operations supply chain management (Certificate); psychology (MA, Certificate); public administration (EMPA); public relations (MS, Certificate); technical market analysis (Certificate); JD/MBA. Part-time and evening/weekend programs available. *Faculty:* 19 full-time (6 women), 241 part-time/adjunct (72 women). *Students:* 397 full-time (230 women), 779 part-time (432 women); includes 376 minority (105 Black or African American, non-Hispanic/Latino; 5 American Indian or Alaska Native, non-Hispanic/Latino; 161 Asian, non-Hispanic/Latino; 77 Hispanic/Latino; 12 Native Hawaiian or other Pacific Islander, non-Hispanic/Latino; 16 Two or more races, non-Hispanic/Latino), 265 international. Average age 34. 871 applicants, 64% accepted, 271 enrolled. In 2011, 550 master's, 13 doctorates awarded. *Degree requirements:* For doctorate, thesis/dissertation, qualifying examination. *Entrance requirements:* For master's, GMAT (MBA), minimum GPA of 2.5 (MS). Additional exam requirements/recommendations for international students: Required—TOEFL (minimum score 550 paper-based; 213 computer-based; 79 iBT). *Application deadline:* For fall admission, 5/15 for domestic and international students; for winter admission, 1/15 for domestic and international students; for spring admission, 9/15 for domestic and international students. Applications are processed on a rolling basis. Application fee: $70 ($110 for international students). Electronic applications accepted. *Expenses:* Contact institution. *Financial support:* Career-related internships or fieldwork, Federal Work-Study, institutionally sponsored loans, and scholarships/grants available. Support available to part-time students. Financial award applicants required to submit FAFSA. *Unit head:* Dr. Paul Fouts, Dean, 415-442-7026, Fax: 415-442-6579. *Application contact:* Angela Melero, Enrollment Services, 415-442-7800, Fax: 415-442-7807, E-mail: info@ggu.edu. Web site: http://www.ggu.edu/programs/business-and-management.

Goldey-Beacom College, Graduate Program, Wilmington, DE 19808-1999. Offers business administration (MBA); finance (MS); financial management (MBA); health care management (MBA); human resource management (MBA); information technology (MBA); international business management (MBA); major finance (MBA); major taxation (MBA); management (MM); marketing management (MBA); taxation (MBA, MS). *Accreditation:* ACBSP. Part-time and evening/weekend programs available. *Faculty:* 19 full-time (7 women), 35 part-time/adjunct (12 women). *Students:* 58 full-time (32 women), 388 part-time (164 women); includes 89 minority (34 Black or African American, non-Hispanic/Latino; 2 American Indian or Alaska Native, non-Hispanic/Latino; 44 Asian, non-Hispanic/Latino; 9 Hispanic/Latino), 229 international. Average age 30. In 2011, 243 master's awarded. *Entrance requirements:* For master's, GMAT, MAT, GRE, minimum GPA of 3.0. Additional exam requirements/recommendations for international students: Required—TOEFL (minimum score 65 computer-based); Recommended—IELTS (minimum score 5). *Application deadline:* Applications are processed on a rolling basis. Application fee: $0. Electronic applications accepted. *Expenses: Tuition:* Full-time $15,750; part-time $875 per credit. *Required fees:* $10 per credit. *Financial support:* Scholarships/grants available. Support available to part-time students. Financial award application deadline: 4/1; financial award applicants required to submit FAFSA. *Unit head:* Larry W. Eby, Director of Admissions, 302-225-6289, Fax: 302-996-5408, E-mail: ebylw@gbc.edu. *Application contact:* Ashley E. Mashington, Graduate Admissions Representative, 302-225-6259, Fax: 302-996-5408, E-mail: mashina@gbc.edu. Web site: http://www.gbc.edu/programs/graduate/.

Graduate School and University Center of the City University of New York, Graduate Studies, Program in Business, New York, NY 10016-4039. Offers accounting (PhD); behavioral science (PhD); finance (PhD); management planning systems (PhD). *Degree requirements:* For doctorate, thesis/dissertation. *Entrance requirements:* For doctorate, GMAT, writing sample (15 pages). Additional exam requirements/recommendations for international students: Required—TOEFL. Electronic applications accepted.

Grand Canyon University, College of Business, Phoenix, AZ 85017-1097. Offers accounting (MBA); corporate business administration (MBA); disaster preparedness and crisis management (MBA); executive fire service leadership (MS); finance (MBA); general management (MBA); government and policy (MPA); health care management (MPA); health systems management (MBA); human resource management (MBA); innovation (MBA); leadership (MBA, MS); management of information system (MBA); marketing (MBA); project-based (MBA); six sigma (MBA); strategic human resource management (MBA). *Accreditation:* ACBSP. Part-time and evening/weekend programs available. Postbaccalaureate distance learning degree programs offered (no on-campus study). *Entrance requirements:* For master's, equivalent of two years full-time professional work experience. Additional exam requirements/recommendations for international students: Required—TOEFL (minimum score 575 paper-based; 233 computer-based; 90 iBT), IELTS (minimum score 7). Electronic applications accepted.

Hawai`i Pacific University, College of Business Administration, Honolulu, HI 96813. Offers accounting/CPA (MBA); e-business (MBA); economics (MBA); finance (MBA); human resource management (MA, MBA); information systems (MBA, MSIS), including knowledge management (MSIS), software engineering (MSIS), telecommunications security (MSIS); international business (MBA); management (MBA); marketing (MBA); organizational change (MA, MBA); travel industry management (MBA). Part-time and evening/weekend programs available. *Faculty:* 15 full-time (5 women), 11 part-time/adjunct (4 women). *Students:* 297 full-time (133 women), 183 part-time (87 women); includes 282 minority (17 Black or African American, non-Hispanic/Latino; 131 Asian, non-Hispanic/Latino; 43 Hispanic/Latino; 10 Native Hawaiian or other Pacific Islander, non-Hispanic/Latino; 81 Two or more races, non-Hispanic/Latino). Average age 30. 302 applicants, 82% accepted, 160 enrolled. In 2011, 141 master's awarded. *Degree requirements:* For master's, thesis. *Entrance requirements:* For master's, GMAT. Additional exam requirements/recommendations for international students: Recommended—TOEFL (minimum score 550 paper-based; 213 computer-based; 80 iBT), TWE (minimum score 5). *Application deadline:* For fall admission, 2/15 priority date for domestic students; for spring admission, 10/15 priority date for domestic students. Applications are processed on a rolling basis. Application fee: $50. Electronic applications accepted. *Expenses: Tuition:* Full-time $13,230; part-time $735 per credit. Tuition and fees vary according to course load and program. *Financial support:* In 2011–12, 103 students received support. Research assistantships, career-related internships or fieldwork, Federal Work-Study, scholarships/grants, tuition waivers, and unspecified assistantships available. Financial award application deadline: 3/1; financial award applicants required to submit FAFSA. *Faculty research:* Statistical control process as used by management, studies in comparative cross-cultural management styles, not-for-profit management. *Unit head:* Dr. Deborah Crown, Dean, 808-544-0275, Fax: 808-544-0283, E-mail: dcrown@hpu.edu. *Application contact:* Chad Schempp, Director of Graduate Admissions, 808-543-8035, Fax: 808-544-0280, E-mail: graduate@hpu.edu. Web site: http://www.hpu.edu/mba.

See Display on page 98 and Close-Up on page 221.

HEC Montreal, School of Business Administration, Graduate Diplomas Programs in Administration, Program in Financial Professions, Montréal, QC H3T 2A7, Canada. Offers Graduate Diploma. All courses are given in French. Part-time programs available. *Students:* 33 full-time (8 women), 1 part-time (0 women). 104 applicants, 60% accepted, 34 enrolled. In 2011, 21 Graduate Diplomas awarded. *Entrance requirements:* For degree, bachelor's degree in administration (for finance option). *Application deadline:* For fall admission, 4/15 for domestic and international students. Application fee: $80. Electronic applications accepted. Application fee is waived when completed online. *Expenses:* Contact institution. *Financial support:* Research assistantships, teaching assistantships, and scholarships/grants available. Financial award application deadline: 9/2. *Unit head:* Silvia Ponce, Academic Supervisor, 514-340-6393, Fax: 514-340-6915, E-mail: silvia.ponce@hec.ca. *Application contact:* Jo Anne Audet, Administrative Director, 514-340-1315, Fax: 514-340-6411, E-mail: joanne.audet@hec.ca. Web site: http://www.hec.ca/programmes_formations/des/dess/dess_professions_financieres/index.html.

HEC Montreal, School of Business Administration, Master of Science Programs in Administration, Program in Applied Financial Economics, Montréal, QC H3T 2A7, Canada. Offers M Sc. Part-time programs available. *Students:* 21 full-time (7 women), 1 part-time (0 women). 16 applicants, 56% accepted, 5 enrolled. In 2011, 5 master's awarded. *Degree requirements:* For master's, one foreign language, thesis. *Entrance requirements:* For master's, Test de francais international (TFI) with minimum score of 850 (for those who have never studied in French), BBA, undergraduate degree in another field, degree deemed equivalent by program director and minimum GPA of 3.0 on 4.3 scale. *Application deadline:* For fall admission, 3/15 for domestic and international students; for winter admission, 9/15 for domestic and international students. Application fee: $80 Canadian dollars. Electronic applications accepted. Application fee is waived when completed online. *Expenses:* Contact institution. *Financial support:* Fellowships, research assistantships, teaching assistantships, and scholarships/grants available. Financial award application deadline: 9/2. *Unit head:* Dr. Claude Laurin, Director, 514-340-6485, Fax: 514-340-6880, E-mail: claude.laurin@hec.ca. *Application contact:* Virginie Lefebvre, Administrative Director, 514-340-6112, Fax: 514-340-6411, E-mail: virginie.lefebvre@hec.ca. Web site: http://www.hec.ca/en/programs_training/msc/options/finance/applied_financial_economics/index.html.

HEC Montreal, School of Business Administration, Master of Science Programs in Administration, Program in Finance, Montréal, QC H3T 2A7, Canada. Offers M Sc. Part-time programs available. *Students:* 80 full-time (19 women), 12 part-time (5 women). 132 applicants, 47% accepted, 30 enrolled. In 2011, 34 master's awarded. *Degree requirements:* For master's, one foreign language. *Entrance requirements:* For master's, Test de francais international (TFI) with minimum score of 850 (for those who have never studied in French), BBA, undergraduate degree in another field, degree deemed equivalent by program director and minimum GPA of 3.0 on 4.3 scale. *Application deadline:* For fall admission, 3/15 for domestic and international students; for winter admission, 9/15 for domestic and international students. Application fee: $80 Canadian dollars. Electronic applications accepted. Application fee is waived when completed online. *Expenses:* Contact institution. *Financial support:* Fellowships, research assistantships, teaching assistantships, and scholarships/grants available. Financial award application deadline: 9/2. *Unit head:* Dr. Claude Laurin, Director, 514-340-6485, Fax: 514-340-6880, E-mail: claude.laurin@hec.ca. *Application contact:* Virginie Lefebvre, Administrative Director, 514-340-6112, Fax: 514-340-6411, E-mail:

virginie.lefebvre@hec.ca. Web site: http://www.hec.ca/en/programs_training/msc/options/finance/finance/index.html.

Hofstra University, Frank G. Zarb School of Business, Department of Finance, Hempstead, NY 11549. Offers banking (Advanced Certificate); business administration (MBA), including finance, real estate management (MBA, MS); corporate finance (Advanced Certificate); finance (MS), including investment analysis; investment management (Advanced Certificate); quantitative finance (MS), including real estate management (MBA, MS). Part-time and evening/weekend programs available. *Faculty:* 13 full-time (2 women), 4 part-time/adjunct (2 women). *Students:* 222 full-time (91 women), 98 part-time (23 women); includes 24 minority (6 Black or African American, non-Hispanic/Latino; 15 Asian, non-Hispanic/Latino; 3 Hispanic/Latino), 198 international. Average age 26. 666 applicants, 63% accepted, 106 enrolled. In 2011, 124 master's awarded. *Degree requirements:* For master's, capstone course (for MBA); thesis (for MS); minimum GPA of 3.0. *Entrance requirements:* For master's, GMAT/GRE, 2 letters of recommendation; resume; essay. Additional exam requirements/recommendations for international students: Required—TOEFL (minimum score 550 paper-based; 213 computer-based; 80 iBT); Recommended—IELTS (minimum score 6). *Application deadline:* Applications are processed on a rolling basis. Application fee: $70 ($75 for international students). Electronic applications accepted. *Expenses:* Contact institution. *Financial support:* In 2011–12, 32 students received support, including 26 fellowships with full and partial tuition reimbursements available (averaging $8,389 per year), 1 research assistantship with full and partial tuition reimbursement available (averaging $4,925 per year); Federal Work-Study, institutionally sponsored loans, scholarships/grants, and tuition waivers (full and partial) also available. Support available to part-time students. Financial award applicants required to submit FAFSA. *Faculty research:* International finance; investments; banking, corporate finance; real estate; derivatives. *Unit head:* Dr. K. G. Viswanathan, Chairperson, 516-463-5699, Fax: 516-463-4834, E-mail: finkgv@hofstra.edu. *Application contact:* Carol Drummer, Dean of Graduate Admissions, 516-463-4876, Fax: 516-463-4664, E-mail: gradstudent@hofstra.edu. Web site: http://www.hofstra.edu/business/.

Holy Family University, Division of Extended Learning, Philadelphia, PA 19114. Offers business administration (MBA); finance (MBA); health care administration (MBA). *Accreditation:* ACBSP. Part-time and evening/weekend programs available. *Entrance requirements:* For master's, interview, essay. Additional exam requirements/recommendations for international students: Required—TOEFL. Electronic applications accepted.

See Display on page 100 and Close-Up on page 223.

Holy Names University, Graduate Division, Department of Business, Oakland, CA 94619-1699. Offers energy and environment management (MBA); finance (MBA); management and leadership (MBA); marketing (MBA); sports management (MBA). Part-time and evening/weekend programs available. *Entrance requirements:* For master's, minimum undergraduate GPA of 2.6 overall, 3.0 in major. Additional exam requirements/recommendations for international students: Required—TOEFL (minimum score 550 paper-based; 213 computer-based; 80 iBT). *Faculty research:* Business ethics, sustainable economics, accounting models, cross-cultural management, diversity in organizations.

Hood College, Graduate School, Department of Economics and Management, Frederick, MD 21701-8575. Offers accounting (MBA); administration and management (MBA); finance (MBA); human resource management (MBA); information systems (MBA); marketing (MBA); public management (MBA). *Accreditation:* ACBSP. Part-time and evening/weekend programs available. *Degree requirements:* For master's, capstone/final research project. *Entrance requirements:* For master's, minimum GPA of 2.75, resume, letters of recommendation. Additional exam requirements/recommendations for international students: Required—TOEFL (minimum score 575 paper-based; 231 computer-based; 89 iBT). Electronic applications accepted. *Faculty research:* Corporate strategy and sustainable competitive advantages, business ethics, entrepreneurship, investments management, economic development.

Howard University, School of Business, Graduate Programs in Business, Washington, DC 20059-0002. Offers accounting (MBA); entrepreneurship (MBA); finance (MBA); general management (MBA); human resources management (MBA); information systems (MBA); international business (MBA); marketing (MBA); supply chain management (MBA); JD/MBA. *Accreditation:* AACSB. Part-time and evening/weekend programs available. Postbaccalaureate distance learning degree programs offered (no on-campus study). *Entrance requirements:* For master's, GMAT, minimum 1 year post undergraduate work experience, resume, 3 letters of recommendation, advanced college algebra. Additional exam requirements/recommendations for international students: Required—TOEFL. *Faculty research:* Marketing research in multi-ethnic populations, U.S. trade policies and international relations, risk management (finance).

Hult International Business School, Program in Business Administration - Hult London Campus, London, MA WC 1B 4JP, United Kingdom. Offers entrepreneurship (MBA); international business (MBA); international finance (MBA); marketing (MBA). Part-time programs available. *Degree requirements:* For master's, comprehensive exam, thesis, internship. *Entrance requirements:* Additional exam requirements/recommendations for international students: Required—TOEFL (minimum score 580 paper-based; 237 computer-based), TWE (minimum score 5). Electronic applications accepted.

Hult International Business School, Program in Finance, Cambridge, MA 02141. Offers MF.

Hult International Business School, Program in Finance - Hult Dubai Campus, Dubai, MA 02141, United Arab Emirates. Offers MF.

Hult International Business School, Program in Finance - Hult London Campus, London, MA WC 1B 4JP, United Kingdom. Offers MF. *Entrance requirements:* Additional exam requirements/recommendations for international students: Required—TOEFL (minimum score 580 paper-based; 237 computer-based), TWE (minimum score 5). Electronic applications accepted.

Illinois Institute of Technology, Chicago-Kent College of Law, Chicago, IL 60661-3691. Offers family law (LL M); financial services (LL M); international intellectual property (LL M); international law (LL M); law (JD); taxation (LL M); JD/LL M; JD/MBA; JD/MPA; JD/MPH; JD/MS. *Accreditation:* ABA. Part-time and evening/weekend programs available. *Entrance requirements:* For doctorate, LSAT, LSDAS. Additional exam requirements/recommendations for international students: Required—TOEFL (minimum score 600 paper-based; 250 computer-based; 100 iBT); Recommended—IELTS (minimum score 7). Electronic applications accepted. *Expenses:* Contact institution. *Faculty research:* Constitutional law, bioethics, environmental law.

Illinois Institute of Technology, Stuart School of Business, Program in Business Administration, Chicago, IL 60616-3793. Offers financial management (MBA); innovation and emerging enterprises (MBA); management science (MBA); marketing (MBA); sustainability (MBA); JD/MBA; M Des/MBA; MBA/MS. *Accreditation:* AACSB. Part-time and evening/weekend programs available. *Entrance requirements:* For master's, GRE (minimum score 1000) or GMAT (500). Additional exam requirements/recommendations for international students: Required—TOEFL (minimum score 600 paper-based; 85 iBT); Recommended—IELTS (minimum score 7). Electronic applications accepted. *Expenses:* Contact institution. *Faculty research:* Global management and marketing strategy, technological innovation, management science, financial management, knowledge management.

Illinois Institute of Technology, Stuart School of Business, Program in Finance, Chicago, IL 60616-3793. Offers MS, JD/MS, MBA/MS. Part-time and evening/weekend programs available. *Entrance requirements:* For master's, GRE (minimum score 1200) or GMAT (600). Additional exam requirements/recommendations for international students: Required—TOEFL (minimum score 600 paper-based; 85 iBT); Recommended—IELTS (minimum score 7). Electronic applications accepted. *Expenses:* Contact institution. *Faculty research:* Factor models for investment management, credit rating and credit risk management, hedge fund performance analysis, option trading and risk management, global asset allocation strategies.

Indiana University Bloomington, School of Public and Environmental Affairs, Public Affairs Programs, Bloomington, IN 47405. Offers comparative and international affairs (MPA); economic development (MPA); energy (MPA); environmental policy (PhD); environmental policy and natural resource management (MPA); hazardous materials management (Certificate); information systems (MPA); international development (MPA); local government management (MPA); nonprofit management (MPA, Certificate); policy analysis (MPA); public budgeting and financial management (Certificate); public finance (PhD); public financial administration (MPA); public management (MPA, PhD, Certificate); public policy analysis (PhD); social entrepreneurship (Certificate); specialized public affairs (MPA); sustainability and sustainable development (MPA); JD/MPA; MPA/MA; MPA/MIS; MPA/MLS; MSES/MPA. *Accreditation:* NASPAA (one or more programs are accredited). Part-time programs available. *Faculty:* 80 full-time (30 women), 102 part-time/adjunct (43 women). *Students:* 338 full-time, 30 part-time; includes 27 minority (7 Black or African American, non-Hispanic/Latino; 2 American Indian or Alaska Native, non-Hispanic/Latino; 10 Asian, non-Hispanic/Latino; 8 Hispanic/Latino), 56 international. Average age 24. 501 applicants, 148 enrolled. In 2011, 172 master's, 7 doctorates awarded. *Degree requirements:* For master's, core classes, capstone, internship; for doctorate, comprehensive exam, thesis/dissertation. *Entrance requirements:* For master's, GRE General Test or GMAT, official transcripts, 3 letters of recommendation, resume, personal statement; for doctorate, GRE General Test or LSAT, official transcripts, 3 letters of recommendation, resume or curriculum vitae, statement of purpose. Additional exam requirements/recommendations for international students: Required—TOEFL (minimum score 600 paper-based; 96 iBT); Recommended—IELTS (minimum score 7). *Application deadline:* For fall admission, 2/1 priority date for domestic students, 12/1 for international students. Applications are processed on a rolling basis. Application fee: $55 ($65 for international students). Electronic applications accepted. *Financial support:* Fellowships with partial tuition reimbursements, research assistantships with partial tuition reimbursements, teaching assistantships with partial tuition reimbursements, career-related internships or fieldwork, Federal Work-Study, scholarships/grants, health care benefits, unspecified assistantships, and Service Corps programs available. Financial award application deadline: 2/1; financial award applicants required to submit FAFSA. *Faculty research:* Comparative and international affairs, environmental policy and resource management, policy analysis, public finance, public management, urban management, nonprofit management, energy policy, social policy, public finance. *Unit head:* Jennifer Forney, Director of Graduate Student Services, 812-855-9485, Fax: 812-856-3665, E-mail: speampo@indiana.edu. *Application contact:* Admissions Assistant, 812-855-2840, E-mail: speaapps@indiana.edu. Web site: http://www.indiana.edu/~spea/prospective_students/masters/.

Indiana University Southeast, School of Business, New Albany, IN 47150-6405. Offers business administration (MBA); strategic finance (MS). *Accreditation:* AACSB. *Faculty:* 11 full-time (2 women). *Students:* 9 full-time (1 woman), 314 part-time (118 women); includes 24 minority (7 Black or African American, non-Hispanic/Latino; 11 Asian, non-Hispanic/Latino; 4 Native Hawaiian or other Pacific Islander, non-Hispanic/Latino; 2 Two or more races, non-Hispanic/Latino), 13 international. Average age 31. 62 applicants, 100% accepted, 50 enrolled. In 2011, 76 master's awarded. *Degree requirements:* For master's, community service. *Entrance requirements:* For master's, GMAT, work experience. Additional exam requirements/recommendations for international students: Required—TOEFL. Application fee: $35. *Expenses:* Contact institution. *Financial support:* In 2011–12, 2 teaching assistantships (averaging $4,500 per year) were awarded. *Unit head:* Dr. Jay White, Dean, 812-941-2362, Fax: 812-941-2672. *Application contact:* Admissions Counselor, 812-941-2212, Fax: 812-941-2595, E-mail: admissions@ius.edu. Web site: http://www.ius.edu/mba.

Instituto Centroamericano de Administración de Empresas, Graduate Programs, La Garita, Costa Rica. Offers agribusiness management (MIAM); business administration (EMBA); finance (MBA); real estate management (MGREM); sustainable development (MBA); technology (MBA). *Degree requirements:* For master's, comprehensive exam, essay. *Entrance requirements:* For master's, GMAT or GRE General Test, fluency in Spanish, interview, letters of recommendation, minimum 1 year of work experience. Additional exam requirements/recommendations for international students: Recommended—TOEFL. Electronic applications accepted. *Faculty research:* Competitiveness, production.

Instituto Tecnologico de Santo Domingo, Graduate School, Area of Business, Santo Domingo, Dominican Republic. Offers banking and securities markets (M Mgmt); corporate finance (M Mgmt); human resources management (M Mgmt, Certificate); international trade management (M Mgmt); marketing (M Mgmt); organizational development (M Mgmt); quality and productivity management (Certificate); tax management and planning (M Mgmt); upper management (M Mgmt).

Instituto Tecnológico y de Estudios Superiores de Monterrey, Campus Central de Veracruz, Graduate Programs, Córdoba, Mexico. Offers administration (MA); administration of information technologies (MTI); computer sciences (MCC); education (MEE); educational institution administration (MAD); educational technology (MTE); electronic commerce (MCE); finance (MAF); humanistic studies (MEH); international business for Latin America (MNL); marketing (MMT); science (MCP). Part-time and evening/weekend programs available. Postbaccalaureate distance learning degree programs offered (minimal on-campus study). *Degree requirements:* For master's, thesis (for some programs). *Entrance requirements:* For master's, PAEP College Board. Electronic applications accepted.

Instituto Tecnológico y de Estudios Superiores de Monterrey, Campus Ciudad de México, School of Business Administration, Ciudad de Mexico, Mexico. Offers business administration (EMBA, MBA, PhD); economy (MBA); finance (MBA). EMBA program offered jointly with The University of Texas at Austin. Part-time and evening/weekend programs available. Postbaccalaureate distance learning degree programs offered (minimal on-campus study). *Entrance requirements:* For master's and doctorate, Instituto entrance exam. Additional exam requirements/recommendations for international students: Required—TOEFL.

Instituto Tecnológico y de Estudios Superiores de Monterrey, Campus Ciudad Obregón, Program in Finance, Ciudad Obregón, Mexico. Offers MF.

Instituto Tecnológico y de Estudios Superiores de Monterrey, Campus Cuernavaca, Programs in Business Administration, Temixco, Mexico. Offers finance (MA); human resources management (MA); international business (MA); marketing (MA).

Instituto Tecnológico y de Estudios Superiores de Monterrey, Campus Estado de México, Professional and Graduate Division, Estado de Mexico, Mexico. Offers administration of information technologies (MITA); architecture (M Arch); business administration (GMBA, MBA); computer sciences (MCS, PhD); education (M Ed); educational institution administration (MAD); educational technology and innovation (PhD); electronic commerce (MEC); environmental systems (MS); finance (MAF); humanistic studies (MHS); information sciences and knowledge management (MISKM); information systems (MS); manufacturing systems (MS); marketing (MEM); quality systems and productivity (MS); science and materials engineering (PhD); telecommunications management (MTM). Part-time programs available. Postbaccalaureate distance learning degree programs offered (minimal on-campus study). *Degree requirements:* For master's, one foreign language, thesis (for some programs); for doctorate, one foreign language, thesis/dissertation. *Entrance requirements:* For master's, E-PAEP 500, interview; for doctorate, E-PAEP 500, research proposal. Additional exam requirements/recommendations for international students: Required—TOEFL (minimum score 550 paper-based). *Faculty research:* Surface treatments by plasmas, mechanical properties, robotics, graphical computing, mechatronics security protocols.

Instituto Tecnológico y de Estudios Superiores de Monterrey, Campus Guadalajara, Program in Finance, Zapopan, Mexico. Offers MF. *Degree requirements:* For master's, one foreign language, thesis. *Entrance requirements:* For master's, ITESM admission test.

Instituto Tecnológico y de Estudios Superiores de Monterrey, Campus Irapuato, Graduate Programs, Irapuato, Mexico. Offers administration (MBA); administration of information technology (MAIT); administration of telecommunications (MAT); architecture (M Arch); computer science (MCS); education (M Ed); educational administration (MEA); educational innovation and technology (DEIT); educational technology (MET); electronic commerce (MBA); environmental administration and planning (MEAP); environmental systems (MES); finances (MBA); humanistic studies (MHS); international management for Latin American executives (MIMLAE); library and information science (MLIS); manufacturing quality management (MMQM); marketing research (MBA).

Instituto Tecnológico y de Estudios Superiores de Monterrey, Campus Monterrey, Graduate School of Business Administration and Leadership, Program in Business Administration, Monterrey, Mexico. Offers business administration (MA, MBA); finance (M Sc); international business (M Sc); marketing (M Sc). *Accreditation:* AACSB. Part-time programs available. *Degree requirements:* For master's, one foreign language, thesis. *Entrance requirements:* For master's, GMAT. Additional exam requirements/ recommendations for international students: Required—TOEFL. *Faculty research:* Technology management, quality management, organizational theory and behavior.

Inter American University of Puerto Rico, Aguadilla Campus, Graduate School, Aguadilla, PR 00605. Offers accounting (MBA); counseling psychology specializing in family (MS); criminal justice (MA); educative management and leadership (MA); elementary education (M Ed); finance (MBA); human resources (MBA); industrial management (MBA); management information systems (MBA); marketing (MBA). Part-time and evening/weekend programs available. *Degree requirements:* For master's, comprehensive exam. *Entrance requirements:* For master's, EXADEP, 2 letters of recommendation, minimum GPA of 2.5. Electronic applications accepted.

Inter American University of Puerto Rico, Arecibo Campus, Program in Business Administration, Arecibo, PR 00614-4050. Offers accounting (MBA); finance (MBA); human resources (MBA).

Inter American University of Puerto Rico, Barranquitas Campus, Program in Business Administration, Barranquitas, PR 00794. Offers accounting (IMBA); finance (IMBA).

Inter American University of Puerto Rico, Metropolitan Campus, Graduate Programs, Program in Finance, San Juan, PR 00919-1293. Offers MBA. *Degree requirements:* For master's, comprehensive exam. *Entrance requirements:* For master's, GRE or EXADEP, interview. Electronic applications accepted.

Inter American University of Puerto Rico, Ponce Campus, Graduate School, Mercedita, PR 00715-1602. Offers accounting (MBA); biology (M Ed); chemistry (M Ed); criminal justice (MA); elementary education (M Ed); English as a Second Language (M Ed); finance (MBA); history (M Ed); human resources (MBA); marketing (MBA); mathematics (M Ed); Spanish (M Ed). *Entrance requirements:* For master's, minimum GPA of 2.5.

Inter American University of Puerto Rico, San Germán Campus, Graduate Studies Center, Program in Business Administration, San Germán, PR 00683-5008. Offers accounting (MBA); finance (MBA); human resources (MBA, PhD); industrial relations (MBA); information sciences (MBA); management (MBA); marketing (MBA). Part-time and evening/weekend programs available. *Degree requirements:* For master's, comprehensive exam. *Entrance requirements:* For master's, GRE General Test or EXADEP, minimum GPA of 3.0. *Application deadline:* For fall admission, 4/30 priority date for domestic students; for spring admission, 11/15 for domestic students. Applications are processed on a rolling basis. Application fee: $31. *Expenses: Required fees:* $213 per semester. *Financial support:* Teaching assistantships, Federal Work-Study, and unspecified assistantships available. *Unit head:* Dr. Elba T. Irizarry, Director of Graduate Studies Center, 787-264-1912 Ext. 7357, Fax: 787-892-6350, E-mail: elbat@sg.inter.edu.

The International University of Monaco, Graduate Programs, Monte Carlo, Monaco. Offers entrepreneurship (EMBA, MBA); financial engineering (M Sc); hedge fund and private equity (M Sc); international marketing (EMBA, MBA); international wealth management (M Sc); luxury goods and services (EMBA, M Sc, MBA); wealth and asset management (EMBA, MBA). Part-time programs available. *Degree requirements:* For master's, comprehensive exam (for some programs), applied research project. *Entrance requirements:* Additional exam requirements/recommendations for international students: Required—TOEFL (minimum score 550 paper-based; 213 computer-based), IELTS. Electronic applications accepted. *Faculty research:* Gaming, leadership, disintermediation.

Iona College, Hagan School of Business, Department of Finance, Business Economics and Legal Studies, New Rochelle, NY 10801-1890. Offers financial management (MBA, PMC). Part-time and evening/weekend programs available. *Faculty:* 10 full-time (3 women), 3 part-time/adjunct (1 woman). *Students:* 31 full-time (11 women), 86 part-time (33 women); includes 14 minority (6 Black or African American, non-Hispanic/Latino; 4 Asian, non-Hispanic/Latino; 4 Hispanic/Latino), 2 international. Average age 29. 44 applicants, 75% accepted, 33 enrolled. In 2011, 68 master's awarded. *Entrance requirements:* For master's, GMAT, 2 letters of recommendation. Additional exam requirements/recommendations for international students: Required—TOEFL (minimum score 550 paper-based; 213 computer-based; 80 iBT). *Application deadline:* For fall admission, 8/15 priority date for domestic students, 8/1 for international students; for winter admission, 11/15 priority date for domestic students, 11/1 for international students; for spring admission, 2/15 priority date for domestic students, 2/1 for international students. Applications are processed on a rolling basis. Application fee: $50. Electronic applications accepted. *Expenses:* Contact institution. *Financial support:* Scholarships/grants, tuition waivers (partial), and unspecified assistantships available. Support available to part-time students. Financial award application deadline: 4/15; financial award applicants required to submit FAFSA. *Faculty research:* Options, insurance financing, asset depreciation ranges, international finance, emerging markets. *Unit head:* Dr. Anand Shetty, Chairman, 914-633-2284, E-mail: ashetty@iona.edu. *Application contact:* Ben Fan, Director of MBA Admissions, 914-633-2289, Fax: 914-637-2708, E-mail: sfan@iona.edu. Web site: http://www.iona.edu/hagan/.

The Johns Hopkins University, Carey Business School, Finance Programs, Baltimore, MD 21218-2699. Offers finance (MS); financial management (Certificate); investments (Certificate). Part-time and evening/weekend programs available. *Degree requirements:* For master's, 36 credits including final project. *Entrance requirements:* For master's, GMAT or GRE (recommended), minimum GPA of 3.0, resume, work experience, two letters of recommendation; for Certificate, minimum GPA of 3.0, resume, work experience, two letters of recommendation. Additional exam requirements/ recommendations for international students: Required—TOEFL (minimum score 600 paper-based; 250 computer-based; 100 iBT). Electronic applications accepted. *Faculty research:* Financial econometrics, high frequency data modeling, corporate finance.

Jones International University, School of Business, Centennial, CO 80112. Offers accounting (MBA); business communication (MABC); entrepreneurship (MABC, MBA); finance (MBA); global enterprise management (MBA); health care management (MBA); information security management (MBA); information technology management (MBA); leadership and influence (MABC); leading the customer-driven organization (MABC); negotiation and conflict management (MBA); project management (MABC, MBA). Program only offered online. Part-time and evening/weekend programs available. Postbaccalaureate distance learning degree programs offered (no on-campus study). *Degree requirements:* For master's, capstone project. *Entrance requirements:* For master's, minimum cumulative GPA of 2.5. Additional exam requirements/ recommendations for international students: Recommended—TOEFL (minimum score 550 paper-based; 213 computer-based). Electronic applications accepted.

Kaplan University, Davenport Campus, School of Business, Davenport, IA 52807-2095. Offers business administration (MBA); change leadership (MS); entrepreneurship (MBA); finance (MBA); health care management (MBA, MS); human resource (MBA); international business (MBA); management (MS); marketing (MBA); project management (MBA, MS); supply chain management and logistics (MBA, MS). Part-time and evening/weekend programs available. Postbaccalaureate distance learning degree programs offered (no on-campus study). *Entrance requirements:* Additional exam requirements/recommendations for international students: Required—TOEFL (minimum score 550 paper-based; 218 computer-based; 80 iBT). Electronic applications accepted.

Kent State University, College of Business Administration, Doctoral Program in Finance, Kent, OH 44242-0001. Offers PhD. *Faculty:* 11 full-time (4 women). *Students:* 18 full-time (8 women); includes 1 minority (Black or African American, non-Hispanic/ Latino), 6 international. Average age 36. 20 applicants, 15% accepted, 3 enrolled. In 2011, 1 doctorate awarded. *Degree requirements:* For doctorate, comprehensive exam, thesis/dissertation, oral defense. *Entrance requirements:* For doctorate, GMAT or GRE. Additional exam requirements/recommendations for international students: Required—TOEFL (minimum score 600 paper-based; 250 computer-based; 100 iBT). *Application deadline:* For fall admission, 2/1 for domestic students, 1/1 for international students. Application fee: $30 ($60 for international students). Electronic applications accepted. *Expenses:* Tuition, state resident: full-time $8136; part-time $452 per credit hour. Tuition, nonresident: full-time $14,292; part-time $794 per credit hour. *Financial support:* In 2011–12, 12 students received support, including 12 teaching assistantships with full tuition reimbursements available (averaging $17,000 per year); Federal Work-Study also available. Financial award application deadline: 2/1; financial award applicants required to submit FAFSA. *Faculty research:* Corporate finance, investments, international finance, futures and options, risk and insurance. *Unit head:* Dr. John Thornton, Chair and Associate Professor, 330-672-2426, Fax: 330-672-9806, E-mail: jthornt5@kent.edu. *Application contact:* Felecia A. Urbanek, Coordinator, Graduate Programs, 330-672-2282, Fax: 330-672-7303, E-mail: gradbus@kent.edu. Web site: http://business.kent.edu/grad.

Lake Forest Graduate School of Management, The Leadership MBA Program (LMBA), Lake Forest, IL 60045. Offers finance (MBA); global business (MBA); healthcare management (MBA); management (MBA); marketing (MBA); organizational behavior (MBA). Part-time and evening/weekend programs available. *Faculty:* 136 part-time/adjunct (41 women). *Students:* 734 part-time (306 women); includes 161 minority (34 Black or African American, non-Hispanic/Latino; 4 American Indian or Alaska Native, non-Hispanic/Latino; 87 Asian, non-Hispanic/Latino; 14 Hispanic/Latino; 4 Native Hawaiian or other Pacific Islander, non-Hispanic/Latino; 18 Two or more races, non-Hispanic/Latino). Average age 38. In 2011, 213 master's awarded. *Entrance requirements:* For master's, 4 years of work experience in field, interview, 2 letters of recommendation. *Application deadline:* For fall admission, 7/1 for domestic students; for winter admission, 1/5 for domestic students; for spring admission, 3/1 for domestic students. Applications are processed on a rolling basis. Application fee: $75. Electronic applications accepted. *Expenses: Tuition:* Part-time $2932 per unit. *Required fees:* $50 per unit. *Financial support:* Scholarships/grants available. Support available to part-time students. Financial award applicants required to submit FAFSA. *Unit head:* Chris Multhauf, Executive Vice President of Educational Programs and Solutions, 847-574-5270, Fax: 847-295-3656, E-mail: cmulthauf@lfgsm.edu. *Application contact:* Carolyn Brune, Director of Admissions, 800-737-4MBA, Fax: 847-295-3656, E-mail: admiss@lfgsm.edu. Web site: http://www.lakeforestmba.edu/lake_forest_mba_program/LFGSM-Leadership-MBA.aspx.

Lakeland College, Graduate Studies Division, Program in Business Administration, Sheboygan, WI 53082-0359. Offers accounting (MBA); finance (MBA); healthcare management (MBA); project management (MBA). *Entrance requirements:* For master's, GMAT. *Expenses:* Contact institution.

Lamar University, College of Graduate Studies, College of Business, Beaumont, TX 77710. Offers accounting (MBA); experiential business and entrepreneurship (MBA); financial management (MBA); healthcare administration (MBA); information systems (MBA); management (MBA). *Accreditation:* AACSB. Part-time and evening/weekend programs available. *Faculty:* 18 full-time (5 women), 5 part-time/adjunct (0 women). *Students:* 74 full-time (33 women), 72 part-time (27 women); includes 24 minority (7 Black or African American, non-Hispanic/Latino; 9 Asian, non-Hispanic/Latino; 8 Hispanic/Latino), 34 international. Average age 29. 69 applicants, 84% accepted, 16 enrolled. In 2011, 62 master's awarded. *Degree requirements:* For master's, comprehensive exam (for some programs), thesis optional. *Entrance requirements:* For master's, GMAT. Additional exam requirements/recommendations for international students: Required—TOEFL (minimum score 525 paper-based; 197 computer-based). *Application deadline:* For fall admission, 3/15 priority date for domestic students; for spring admission, 10/1 priority date for domestic students. Applications are processed on a rolling basis. Application fee: $25 ($50 for international students). *Expenses:* Tuition, state resident: full-time $5430; part-time $272 per credit hour. Tuition, nonresident: full-time $11,540; part-time $577 per credit hour. *Required fees:* $1916. *Financial support:* In 2011–12, 12 students received support, including 4 research assistantships with partial tuition reimbursements available; fellowships with tuition reimbursements available, career-related internships or fieldwork, Federal Work-Study, institutionally sponsored loans, scholarships/grants, and tuition waivers (partial) also available. Support available to part-time students. Financial award application deadline: 4/1; financial award applicants required to submit FAFSA. *Faculty research:* Marketing, finance, quantitative methods, management information systems, legal, environmental. *Unit head:* Dr. Enrique R. Venta, Dean, 409-880-8604, Fax: 409-880-8088, E-mail: henry.venta@lamar.edu. *Application contact:* Dr. Brad Mayer, Professor and Associate Dean, 409-880-2383, Fax: 409-880-8605, E-mail: bradley.mayer@lamar.edu. Web site: http://mba.lamar.edu.

La Sierra University, School of Business and Management, Riverside, CA 92515. Offers accounting (MBA); finance (MBA); general management (MBA); human resources management (MBA); leadership, values, and ethics for business and management (Certificate); marketing (MBA). *Degree requirements:* For master's, research project. *Entrance requirements:* For master's, GMAT, minimum GPA of 3.0. Additional exam requirements/recommendations for international students: Required—TOEFL. *Faculty research:* Financial econometrics, institutional assessment and strategic planning, legal issues in management, behavioral finance, content of financial reports.

Lehigh University, College of Business and Economics, Department of Finance, Bethlehem, PA 18015. Offers analytical finance (MS). *Faculty:* 6 full-time (1 woman), 1 part-time/adjunct (0 women). *Students:* 56 full-time (31 women), 33 part-time (10 women); includes 9 minority (6 Asian, non-Hispanic/Latino; 2 Hispanic/Latino; 1 Native Hawaiian or other Pacific Islander, non-Hispanic/Latino), 51 international. Average age 26. 508 applicants, 22% accepted, 37 enrolled. In 2011, 55 master's awarded. *Degree requirements:* For master's, capstone project. *Entrance requirements:* For master's, GMAT or GRE, bachelor's degree from a mathematically rigorous program, minimum GPA of 3.0. Additional exam requirements/recommendations for international students: Required—TOEFL (minimum score 600 paper-based; 250 computer-based; 94 iBT). *Application deadline:* For fall admission, 7/15 for domestic students, 2/15 for international students. Applications are processed on a rolling basis. Application fee: $100. Electronic applications accepted. *Expenses:* Contact institution. *Unit head:* Richard Kish, Department Chair, 610-758-4205, E-mail: rjk7@lehigh.edu. *Application contact:* Corinn McBride, Director of Recruitment and Admissions, 610-758-3418, Fax: 610-758-5283, E-mail: com207@lehigh.edu. Web site: http://www4.lehigh.edu/business/academics/depts/finance.

Lewis University, College of Business, Graduate School of Management, Program in Business Administration, Romeoville, IL 60446. Offers accounting (MBA); custom elective option (MBA); e-business (MBA); finance (MBA); healthcare management (MBA); human resources management (MBA); information security (MBA); international business (MBA); management information systems (MBA); marketing (MBA); project management (MBA); technology and operations management (MBA). Part-time and evening/weekend programs available. *Students:* 112 full-time (60 women), 232 part-time (118 women); includes 104 minority (62 Black or African American, non-Hispanic/Latino; 1 American Indian or Alaska Native, non-Hispanic/Latino; 7 Asian, non-Hispanic/Latino; 33 Hispanic/Latino; 1 Native Hawaiian or other Pacific Islander, non-Hispanic/Latino), 9 international. Average age 28. In 2011, 99 master's awarded. *Entrance requirements:* For master's, interview, bachelor's degree, resume, 2 recommendations. Additional exam requirements/recommendations for international students: Required—TOEFL (minimum score 550 paper-based; 213 computer-based). *Application deadline:* For fall admission, 8/15 priority date for domestic students, 5/1 for international students; for spring admission, 11/15 for international students. Applications are processed on a rolling basis. Application fee: $40. Electronic applications accepted. *Financial support:* Career-related internships or fieldwork, Federal Work-Study, scholarships/grants, and unspecified assistantships available. Financial award application deadline: 5/1; financial award applicants required to submit FAFSA. *Unit head:* Dr. Maureen Culleeney, Academic Program Director, 815-838-0500 Ext. 5631, E-mail: culleema@lewisu.edu. *Application contact:* Michele Ryan, Director of Admission, 815-838-0500 Ext. 5384, E-mail: gsm@lewisu.edu.

Lewis University, College of Business, Graduate School of Management, Program in Finance, Romeoville, IL 60446. Offers MS. Part-time and evening/weekend programs available. *Students:* 16 full-time (5 women), 15 part-time (11 women); includes 5 minority (4 Black or African American, non-Hispanic/Latino; 1 Hispanic/Latino), 3 international. Average age 29. In 2011, 11 master's awarded. *Entrance requirements:* For master's, bachelor's degree, interview, resume, 2 recommendations, minimum GPA of 2.75. Additional exam requirements/recommendations for international students: Required—TOEFL (minimum score 550 paper-based; 213 computer-based; 80 iBT). *Application deadline:* For fall admission, 5/1 for international students; for spring admission, 11/15 for international students. Applications are processed on a rolling basis. Application fee: $40. Electronic applications accepted. *Financial support:* Career-related internships or fieldwork, Federal Work-Study, scholarships/grants, and unspecified assistantships available. Support available to part-time students. Financial award application deadline: 5/1; financial award applicants required to submit FAFSA. *Unit head:* Dr. Robert Atra, Academic Program Director, 815-838-0500 Ext. 5804, E-mail: atraro@lewisu.edu. *Application contact:* Michele Ryan, Director of Admission, 815-838-0500 Ext. 5384, E-mail: gsm@lewisu.edu.

Lincoln University, Graduate Center, Lincoln University, PA 19352. Offers administration (MSA), including finance, human resources management; early childhood education (M Ed); elementary education (M Ed); human services (M Hum Svcs); reading (MSR). Evening/weekend programs available. *Degree requirements:* For master's, thesis. *Entrance requirements:* For master's, 5 years of work experience in human services. *Faculty research:* Gerontology/minority aging, computers in composition instruction.

Lincoln University, Graduate Studies, Oakland, CA 94612. Offers finance and investments (DBA); finance management and investment banking (MBA); general business (MBA); human resource management (MBA, DBA); international business (MBA); management information systems (MBA). Part-time and evening/weekend programs available. *Faculty:* 10 full-time (4 women), 15 part-time/adjunct (3 women). *Students:* 272 full-time (124 women), 1 part-time (0 women). *Degree requirements:* For master's, research project (thesis), internship report, or comprehensive exam; for doctorate, comprehensive exam, thesis/dissertation. *Entrance requirements:* For master's, minimum GPA of 2.7; for doctorate, GMAT (minimum score: 550), GRE (minimum score: 1000), or equivalent test results (waived for master's degree with minimum cumulative GPA of 3.3). Additional exam requirements/recommendations for international students: Required—TOEFL (minimum score 525 paper-based; 195 computer-based; 71 iBT) or IELTS (minimum score 5.5) for MBA; TOEFL (minimum score 550 paper-based; 213 computer-based; 79 iBT) or IELTS (minimum score 6) for DBA. *Application deadline:* For fall admission, 7/2 priority date for domestic students, 7/2 for international students; for spring admission, 11/25 priority date for domestic students, 11/25 for international students. Applications are processed on a rolling basis. Application fee: $75. Electronic applications accepted. *Financial support:* Teaching assistantships, career-related internships or fieldwork, and scholarships/grants available. *Unit head:* Dr. Marshall Burak, Director of Graduate Programs, 510-628-8016, Fax: 510-628-8012, E-mail: mburak@lincolnuca.edu. *Application contact:* Peggy Au, Director of Admissions and Records, 510-628-8010, Fax: 510-628-8012, E-mail: admissions@lincolnuca.edu. Web site: http://www.lincolnuca.edu/.

Lindenwood University, Graduate Programs, School of Business and Entrepreneurship, St. Charles, MO 63301-1695. Offers accounting (MBA, MS); business administration (MBA); entrepreneurial studies (MBA, MS); finance (MBA, MS); human resource management (MBA); human resources (MS); international business (MBA, MS); management (MBA, MS); management information systems (MBA, MS); marketing (MBA, MS); public management (MBA, MS); sport management (MA); supply chain management (MBA). *Accreditation:* ACBSP. Part-time and evening/weekend programs available. *Faculty:* 20 full-time (8 women), 17 part-time/adjunct (5 women). *Students:* 165 full-time (66 women), 223 part-time (100 women); includes 59 minority (48 Black or African American, non-Hispanic/Latino; 4 Asian, non-Hispanic/Latino; 2 Native Hawaiian or other Pacific Islander, non-Hispanic/Latino; 5 Two or more races, non-Hispanic/Latino), 140 international. Average age 29. 156 applicants, 76% accepted, 103 enrolled. In 2011, 205 degrees awarded. *Degree requirements:* For master's, comprehensive exam (for some programs), thesis (for some programs). *Entrance requirements:* For master's, interview, minimum GPA of 3.0, letter of recommendation. Additional exam requirements/recommendations for international students: Required—TOEFL (minimum score 550 paper-based; 213 computer-based; 80 iBT). *Application deadline:* For fall admission, 8/15 priority date for domestic students, 8/15 for international students; for winter admission, 1/9 priority date for domestic students, 1/9 for international students; for spring admission, 3/12 priority date for domestic students, 3/12 for international students. Applications are processed on a rolling basis. Application fee: $30 ($100 for international students). Electronic applications accepted. *Expenses: Tuition:* Full-time $13,650; part-time $395 per credit hour. *Required fees:* $150 per semester. Tuition and fees vary according to course level and course load. *Financial support:* In 2011–12, 206 students received support. Career-related internships or fieldwork, Federal Work-Study, institutionally sponsored loans, and tuition waivers (partial) available. Financial award application deadline: 6/30; financial award applicants required to submit FAFSA. *Unit head:* Roger Ellis, Dean, 636-949-4839, E-mail: rellis@lindenwood.edu. *Application contact:* Brett Barger, Dean of Evening Admissions and Extension Campuses, 636-949-4934, Fax: 636-949-4109, E-mail: adultadmissions@lindenwood.edu. Web site: http://www.lindenwood.edu.

Lipscomb University, College of Business, Nashville, TN 37204-3951. Offers accounting (MBA); business administration (general) (MBA); conflict management (MBA); financial services (MBA); healthcare management (MBA); human resources (MHR); leadership (MBA); nonprofit management (MBA); sports management (MBA); sustainability (MBA). *Accreditation:* ACBSP. Part-time and evening/weekend programs available. *Faculty:* 13 full-time (3 women), 7 part-time/adjunct (1 woman). *Students:* 51 full-time (21 women), 83 part-time (48 women); includes 20 minority (16 Black or African American, non-Hispanic/Latino; 3 Asian, non-Hispanic/Latino; 1 Hispanic/Latino), 1 international. Average age 33. 190 applicants, 43% accepted, 54 enrolled. In 2011, 85 master's awarded. *Entrance requirements:* For master's, GMAT, interview, 2 references, resume. Additional exam requirements/recommendations for international students: Required—TOEFL (minimum score 570 paper-based; 230 computer-based). *Application deadline:* For fall admission, 6/15 for domestic students, 2/1 for international students; for winter admission, 6/1 for international students; for spring admission, 11/15 for domestic students. Applications are processed on a rolling basis. Application fee: $50 ($75 for international students). Electronic applications accepted. *Expenses:* Contact institution. *Financial support:* Career-related internships or fieldwork, scholarships/grants, tuition waivers (partial), and unspecified assistantships available. Support available to part-time students. Financial award application deadline: 7/1; financial award applicants required to submit FAFSA. *Faculty research:* Impact of spirituality on organization commitment, leadership, psychological empowerment, training. *Unit head:* Dr. Mike Kendrick, Associate Dean of Graduate Business Programs, 615-966-1833, Fax: 615-966-1818, E-mail: mikekendrick@lipscomb.edu. *Application contact:* Lisa Shacklett, Executive Director of Enrollment and Marketing, 615-966-5968, E-mail: lisa.shacklett@lipscomb.edu. Web site: http://mba.lipscomb.edu.

Long Island University–C. W. Post Campus, College of Management, School of Business, Brookville, NY 11548-1300. Offers accounting and taxation (Certificate); business administration (Certificate); finance (MBA, Certificate); general business administration (MBA); international business (MBA, Certificate); management (MBA, Certificate); management information systems (MBA, Certificate); marketing (MBA, Certificate). *Accreditation:* AACSB. Part-time and evening/weekend programs available. *Entrance requirements:* For master's, GMAT, resume, minimum GPA of 3.0, 2 letters of recommendation. Additional exam requirements/recommendations for international students: Required—TOEFL (minimum score 527 paper-based; 197 computer-based). Electronic applications accepted. *Faculty research:* Financial markets, consumer behavior.

Long Island University–Hudson at Rockland, Graduate School, Master of Business Administration Program, Orangeburg, NY 10962. Offers business administration (Post Master's Certificate); entrepreneurship (MBA); finance (MBA); healthcare sector management (MBA); management (MBA). Part-time and evening/weekend programs available. *Entrance requirements:* For master's, GMAT, college transcripts, two letters of recommendation, personal statement, resume.

Louisiana State University and Agricultural and Mechanical College, Graduate School, E. J. Ourso College of Business, Department of Finance, Baton Rouge, LA 70803. Offers business administration (PhD), including finance; finance (MS). *Faculty:* 11 full-time (3 women), 1 part-time/adjunct (0 women). *Students:* 40 full-time (10 women), 2 part-time (0 women); includes 3 minority (2 Black or African American, non-Hispanic/Latino; 1 Two or more races, non-Hispanic/Latino), 18 international. Average age 26. 103 applicants, 31% accepted, 16 enrolled. In 2011, 15 master's, 2 doctorates awarded. *Degree requirements:* For master's, thesis or alternative; for doctorate, thesis/dissertation. *Entrance requirements:* For master's and doctorate, GMAT. Additional exam requirements/recommendations for international students: Required—TOEFL (minimum score 550 paper-based; 213 computer-based; 79 iBT) or IELTS (minimum score 6.5). *Application deadline:* For fall admission, 1/25 priority date for domestic students, 5/15 for international students; for spring admission, 10/15 for international students. Applications are processed on a rolling basis. Application fee: $50 ($70 for international students). *Financial support:* In 2011–12, 21 students received support, including 5 research assistantships with full and partial tuition reimbursements available (averaging $17,750 per year), 8 teaching assistantships with full and partial tuition reimbursements available (averaging $9,625 per year); fellowships, career-related internships or fieldwork, Federal Work-Study, scholarships/grants, health care benefits, and unspecified assistantships also available. Support available to part-time students. Financial award application deadline: 4/1; financial award applicants required to submit FAFSA. *Faculty research:* Derivatives and risk management, capital structure, asset pricing, spatial statistics, financial institutions and underwriting. *Total annual research* *expenditures:* $61,188. *Unit head:* Dr. Vestor Carlos Slawson, Jr., Interim Chair, 225-578-6367, Fax: 225-578-6366, E-mail: cslawson@lsu.edu. Web site: http://business.lsu.edu/finance.

Louisiana Tech University, Graduate School, College of Business, Department of Finance and Economics, Ruston, LA 71272. Offers business economics (MBA, DBA); finance (MBA, DBA). Part-time programs available. *Degree requirements:* For doctorate, thesis/dissertation. *Entrance requirements:* For master's and doctorate, GMAT.

Loyola University Chicago, Graduate School of Business, Chicago, IL 60660. Offers accountancy (MS, MSA); business administration (MBA); finance (MS); healthcare management (MBA); human resources and employee relations (MS, MSHR); information systems and operations management (MS), including information systems management; marketing (MS, MSIMC), including integrated marketing communications (MS), marketing (MSIMC); strategic financial services (MBA); JD/MBA; MBA/MSA; MSIMC/MBA; MSISM/MBA; MSN/MBA. *Accreditation:* AACSB. *Expenses: Tuition:* Full-time $15,660; part-time $870 per credit hour. *Required fees:* $125 per semester. Tuition and fees vary according to course load and program.

Loyola University Maryland, Graduate Programs, Sellinger School of Business and Management, Program in Business Administration, Baltimore, MD 21210-2699. Offers accounting (MBA); finance (MBA); general business (MBA); information systems operations management (MBA); international business (MBA); management (MBA); marketing (MBA). *Accreditation:* AACSB. Part-time and evening/weekend programs available. *Faculty:* 61 full-time (12 women), 29 part-time/adjunct (4 women). *Students:* 50 full-time (15 women), 547 part-time (210 women); includes 98 minority (39 Black or African American, non-Hispanic/Latino; 1 American Indian or Alaska Native, non-Hispanic/Latino; 28 Asian, non-Hispanic/Latino; 18 Hispanic/Latino; 2 Native Hawaiian or other Pacific Islander, non-Hispanic/Latino; 10 Two or more races, non-Hispanic/Latino), 15 international. Average age 30. In 2011, 232 master's awarded. *Entrance requirements:* For master's, GMAT (for some programs). Additional exam requirements/recommendations for international students: Required—TOEFL (minimum score 550 paper-based; 213 computer-based). *Application deadline:* For fall admission, 8/1 priority date for domestic students; for spring admission, 12/1 priority date for domestic students. Application fee: $50. Electronic applications accepted. *Financial support:* Research assistantships and unspecified assistantships available. Financial award application deadline: 4/15; financial award applicants required to submit FAFSA. *Unit head:* Dr. Karyl Leggio, Dean, 410-617-2301, E-mail: kbleggio@loyola.edu. *Application contact:* Maureen Faux, Executive Director, Graduate Admissions, 410-617-5020, Fax: 410-617-2002, E-mail: graduate@loyola.edu.

Loyola University Maryland, Graduate Programs, Sellinger School of Business and Management, Program in Finance, Baltimore, MD 21210-2699. Offers MSF. Part-time and evening/weekend programs available. *Faculty:* 61 full-time (12 women), 29 part-time/adjunct (4 women). *Students:* 1 full-time (0 women), 42 part-time (5 women); includes 9 minority (3 Black or African American, non-Hispanic/Latino; 5 Asian, non-Hispanic/Latino; 1 Hispanic/Latino). Average age 33. In 2011, 16 master's awarded. *Entrance requirements:* Additional exam requirements/recommendations for international students: Required—TOEFL (minimum score 550 paper-based; 213 computer-based). *Application deadline:* For fall admission, 8/1 priority date for domestic students; for spring admission, 12/1 priority date for domestic students. Application fee: $50. Electronic applications accepted. *Financial support:* Research assistantships and unspecified assistantships available. Financial award application deadline: 4/15; financial award applicants required to submit FAFSA. *Unit head:* Dr. Karyl Leggio, Dean, 410-617-2301. *Application contact:* Maureen Faux, Executive Director, Graduate Admissions, 410-617-5020, Fax: 410-617-2002, E-mail: graduate@loyola.edu.

Manhattanville College, Graduate Studies, Humanities and Social Sciences Programs, Program in Finance, Purchase, NY 10577-2132. Offers MS. Part-time and evening/weekend programs available. *Entrance requirements:* Additional exam requirements/recommendations for international students: Required—TOEFL. Electronic applications accepted.

Marquette University, Graduate School of Management, Executive MBA Program, Milwaukee, WI 53201-1881. Offers economics (MBA); finance (MBA); human resources (MBA); international business (MBA); management information systems (MBA); marketing (MBA); operations and supply chain management (MBA); sports business (MBA). *Accreditation:* AACSB. *Students:* 50 full-time (15 women); includes 4 minority (1 Black or African American, non-Hispanic/Latino; 3 Asian, non-Hispanic/Latino), 3 international. Average age 37. 37 applicants, 81% accepted, 29 enrolled. In 2011, 36 master's awarded. *Degree requirements:* For master's, international trip. *Entrance requirements:* For master's, GMAT or GRE, two letters of recommendation, official transcripts from current and previous colleges/universities. Additional exam requirements/recommendations for international students: Required—TOEFL (minimum score 550 paper-based; 85 computer-based; 88 iBT), IELTS (minimum score 6.5), Pearson Test of English. *Application deadline:* For fall admission, 2/15 for domestic and international students. Application fee: $50. Electronic applications accepted. *Expenses:* Contact institution. *Financial support:* Application deadline: 2/15. *Faculty research:* International trade and finance, customer relationship management, consumer satisfaction, customer service . *Unit head:* Dr. Jeanne Simmons, Graduate Director, 414-288-7145, Fax: 414-288-1660, E-mail: jeanne.simmons@marquette.edu. *Application contact:* Debra Leutermann, Admissions Coordinator, 414-288-7145, Fax: 414-288-8078, E-mail: debra.leutermann@marquette.edu. Web site: http://www.busadm.mu.edu/emba/.

Marquette University, Graduate School of Management, Program in Business Administration, Milwaukee, WI 53201-1881. Offers business administration (MBA); economics (MBA); entrepreneurship (Certificate); finance (MBA); human resources (MBA); international business (MBA); management information systems (MBA); marketing (MBA); operations and supply chain management (MBA); sports business (MBA); JD/MBA; MBA/MA; MBA/MSN. *Accreditation:* AACSB. Part-time and evening/weekend programs available. *Students:* 42 full-time (14 women), 335 part-time (94 women); includes 24 minority (5 Black or African American, non-Hispanic/Latino; 1 American Indian or Alaska Native, non-Hispanic/Latino; 15 Asian, non-Hispanic/Latino; 3 Hispanic/Latino), 29 international. Average age 31. 182 applicants, 59% accepted, 103 enrolled. In 2011, 128 master's awarded. *Degree requirements:* For Certificate, business plan. *Entrance requirements:* For master's, GMAT or GRE, letters of recommendation. Additional exam requirements/recommendations for international students: Required—TOEFL (minimum score 550 paper-based; 85 computer-based; 88 iBT), IELTS (minimum score 6.5), Pearson Test of English. *Application deadline:* For fall admission, 2/15 for domestic and international students. Applications are processed on a rolling basis. Application fee: $50. Electronic applications accepted. *Expenses: Tuition:* Full-time $17,010; part-time $945 per credit hour. Tuition and fees vary according to program. *Financial support:* In 2011–12, 4 fellowships, 11 teaching assistantships were awarded; research assistantships, Federal Work-Study, institutionally sponsored loans, scholarships/grants, and tuition waivers (full and partial) also available. Support available to part-time students. Financial award application deadline: 2/15. *Faculty research:* Ethics in the professions, services marketing, technology impact on decision-making, mentoring. *Unit head:* Dr. Jeanne Simmons, Graduate Director, 414-288-7145, Fax: 414-288-1660, E-mail: jeanne.simmons@marquette.edu. *Application contact:* Debra Leutermann, Admissions Coordinator, 414-288-8064, Fax: 414-288-1902, E-mail: debra.leutermann@marquette.edu. Web site: http://business.marquette.edu/academics/mba.

Marylhurst University, Department of Business Administration, Marylhurst, OR 97036-0261. Offers finance (MBA); general management (MBA); government policy and administration (MBA); green development (MBA); health care management (MBA); marketing (MBA); natural and organic resources (MBA); nonprofit management (MBA); organizational behavior (MBA); real estate (MBA); renewable energy (MBA); sustainable business (MBA). Part-time and evening/weekend programs available. Postbaccalaureate distance learning degree programs offered (no on-campus study). *Faculty:* 3 full-time (0 women), 36 part-time/adjunct (6 women). *Students:* 29 full-time (15 women), 675 part-time (373 women); includes 178 minority (59 Black or African American, non-Hispanic/Latino; 6 American Indian or Alaska Native, non-Hispanic/Latino; 34 Asian, non-Hispanic/Latino; 46 Hispanic/Latino; 4 Native Hawaiian or other Pacific Islander, non-Hispanic/Latino; 29 Two or more races, non-Hispanic/Latino), 14 international. Average age 37. 262 applicants, 91% accepted, 194 enrolled. In 2011, 352 master's awarded. *Degree requirements:* For master's, comprehensive exam, capstone course. *Entrance requirements:* For master's, GMAT (if GPA less than 3.0 and fewer than 5 years of work experience), interview, resume, 2 letters of recommendation. Additional exam requirements/recommendations for international students: Recommended—TOEFL (minimum score 550 paper-based; 213 computer-based; 80 iBT). *Application deadline:* For fall admission, 9/11 priority date for domestic students, 9/11 for international students; for winter admission, 12/15 priority date for domestic students, 12/15 for international students; for spring admission, 3/15 priority date for domestic students, 3/17 for international students. Applications are processed on a rolling basis. Application fee: $50. Electronic applications accepted. *Expenses: Tuition:* Full-time $14,796; part-time $548 per quarter hour. Tuition and fees vary according to program. *Financial support:* Scholarships/grants available. Support available to part-time students. Financial award applicants required to submit FAFSA. *Unit head:* David McNamee, Interim Chair, 503-636-8141, Fax: 503-697-5597, E-mail: mba@marylhurst.edu. *Application contact:* Maruska Lynch, Graduate Admissions Specialist, 800-634-9982 Ext. 6322, Fax: 503-699-6320, E-mail: admissions@marylhurst.edu. Web site: http://www.marylhurst.edu/.

Marywood University, Academic Affairs, College of Liberal Arts and Sciences, Department of Business and Managerial Science, Emphasis in Finance and Investments, Scranton, PA 18509-1598. Offers MBA. *Entrance requirements:* For master's, GMAT. Additional exam requirements/recommendations for international students: Required—TOEFL (minimum score 550 paper-based; 213 computer-based; 79 iBT). *Application deadline:* For fall admission, 4/1 priority date for domestic students, 3/31 for international students; for spring admission, 11/1 priority date for domestic students, 8/31 for international students. Applications are processed on a rolling basis. Application fee: $35. Electronic applications accepted. *Financial support:* Career-related internships or fieldwork, scholarships/grants, and unspecified assistantships available. Support available to part-time students. Financial award application deadline: 6/30; financial award applicants required to submit FAFSA. *Faculty research:* Accountant/auditor liability, corporate finance acquisitions and mergers, corporate bankruptcy. *Unit head:* Dr. Arthur Comstock, Chair, 570-348-6211 Ext. 2449, E-mail: comstock@marywood.edu. *Application contact:* Tammy Manka, Assistant Director of Graduate Admissions, 570-348-6211 Ext. 2322, E-mail: tmanka@marywood.edu. Web site: http://www.marywood.edu/academics/gradcatalog/.

McGill University, Faculty of Graduate and Postdoctoral Studies, Desautels Faculty of Management, Montréal, QC H3A 2T5, Canada. Offers administration (PhD); entrepreneurial studies (MBA); finance (MBA); general management (Post Master's Certificate); information systems (MBA); international business (MBA); international practicing management (MM); management (MBA); management for development (MBA); manufacturing management (MMM); marketing (MBA); operations management (MBA); public accountancy (Diploma); strategic management (MBA); MBA/LL B; MD/MBA. MMM offered jointly with Faculty of Engineering; PhD with Concordia University, HEC Montreal, Université de Montréal, Université du Québec à Montréal.

Michigan State University, The Graduate School, Eli Broad Graduate School of Management, Department of Finance, East Lansing, MI 48824. Offers business administration (PhD); finance (MS). *Entrance requirements:* Additional exam requirements/recommendations for international students: Required—TOEFL. Electronic applications accepted.

MidAmerica Nazarene University, Graduate Studies in Management, Olathe, KS 66062-1899. Offers management (MBA); organizational administration (MA), including finance, international business, leadership, non-profit. Evening/weekend programs available. *Entrance requirements:* For master's, mathematical assessment, minimum undergraduate GPA of 3.0, letters of recommendation. Additional exam requirements/recommendations for international students: Required—TOEFL. Electronic applications accepted. *Faculty research:* Economic development, international finance, business development, employee evaluation.

Mississippi College, Graduate School, School of Business, Clinton, MS 39058. Offers accounting (Certificate); business administration (MBA), including accounting; business education (M Ed); finance (MBA, Certificate); JD/MBA. *Accreditation:* ACBSP. Part-time and evening/weekend programs available. *Degree requirements:* For master's, comprehensive exam, thesis optional. *Entrance requirements:* For master's, GMAT, minimum GPA of 2.5, 24 hours of undergraduate course work in business. Additional exam requirements/recommendations for international students: Recommended—TOEFL, IELTS. Electronic applications accepted.

Mississippi State University, College of Business, Department of Finance and Economics, Mississippi State, MS 39762. Offers applied economics (PhD); business administration (PhD), including finance; economics (MA); finance (MSBA). Part-time programs available. *Faculty:* 7 full-time (2 women). *Students:* 10 full-time (2 women), 4 part-time (2 women); includes 1 minority (Black or African American, non-Hispanic/Latino), 8 international. Average age 31. 16 applicants, 13% accepted, 0 enrolled. In 2011, 4 degrees awarded. Terminal master's awarded for partial completion of doctoral program. *Median time to degree:* Of those who began their doctoral program in fall 2003, 100% received their degree in 8 years or less. *Degree requirements:* For master's, comprehensive exam, thesis optional; for doctorate, comprehensive exam, thesis/dissertation. *Entrance requirements:* For master's and doctorate, GMAT, GRE General Test. Additional exam requirements/recommendations for international students: Required—TOEFL (minimum score 575 paper-based; 233 computer-based; 90 iBT); Recommended—IELTS (minimum score 6.5). *Application deadline:* For fall admission, 7/1 for domestic students, 5/1 for international students; for spring admission, 11/1 for domestic students, 10/1 for international students. Applications are processed on a rolling basis. Application fee: $40. Electronic applications accepted. *Expenses:* Tuition, state resident: full-time $5805; part-time $322.50 per credit hour. Tuition, nonresident: full-time $14,670; part-time $815 per credit hour. *Financial support:* In 2011–12, 9 teaching assistantships with tuition reimbursements (averaging $12,719 per year) were awarded; Federal Work-Study, scholarships/grants, health care benefits, and unspecified assistantships also available. Financial award application deadline: 4/1; financial award applicants required to submit FAFSA. *Faculty research:* Economics development, mergers, event studies, economic education, bank performance. *Total annual research expenditures:* $1.9 million. *Unit head:* Dr. Mike Highfield, Department Head, 662-325-1984, Fax: 662-325-1977, E-mail: m.highfield@msstate.edu. *Application contact:* Dr. Benjamin F. Blair, Associate Professor/Graduate Coordinator, 662-325-1980, Fax: 662-325-1977, E-mail: bblair@cobilan.msstate.edu. Web site: http://www.business.msstate.edu/finance_and_economics/.

Molloy College, Graduate Business Program, Rockville Centre, NY 11571-5002. Offers accounting (MBA); accounting and management (MBA); management (MBA); personal financial planning and accounting (MBA); personal financial planning and management (MBA). Part-time programs available. *Faculty:* 5 full-time (0 women), 8 part-time/adjunct (2 women). *Students:* 39 full-time (18 women), 77 part-time (44 women); includes 41 minority (23 Black or African American, non-Hispanic/Latino; 1 American Indian or Alaska Native, non-Hispanic/Latino; 7 Asian, non-Hispanic/Latino; 8 Hispanic/Latino; 1 Native Hawaiian or other Pacific Islander, non-Hispanic/Latino; 1 Two or more races, non-Hispanic/Latino), 1 international. Average age 32. 57 applicants, 81% accepted, 31 enrolled. In 2011, 34 master's awarded. *Application deadline:* Applications are processed on a rolling basis. *Unit head:* Dr. Raymond Manganelli, Associate Dean and the Director Graduate Business, 516-678-5000. *Application contact:* Alina Haitz, Assistant Director of Graduate Admissions, 516-678-5000 Ext. 6399, Fax: 516-256-2247, E-mail: ahaitz@molloy.edu.

Monmouth University, The Graduate School, Leon Hess Business School, West Long Branch, NJ 07764-1898. Offers accounting (MBA, Post-Master's Certificate); business (MBA); finance (MBA); healthcare management (MBA, Post-Master's Certificate); real estate (MBA). *Accreditation:* AACSB. Part-time and evening/weekend programs available. *Faculty:* 29 full-time (10 women), 8 part-time/adjunct (2 women). *Students:* 107 full-time (44 women), 161 part-time (61 women); includes 42 minority (8 Black or African American, non-Hispanic/Latino; 19 Asian, non-Hispanic/Latino; 12 Hispanic/Latino; 3 Two or more races, non-Hispanic/Latino), 23 international. Average age 28. 193 applicants, 84% accepted, 111 enrolled. In 2011, 87 master's awarded. *Degree requirements:* For master's, capstone course. *Entrance requirements:* For master's, GMAT, minimum GPA of 3.0 in major, 2.75 overall. Additional exam requirements/recommendations for international students: Required—TOEFL (minimum score 550 paper-based; 213 computer-based; 79 iBT), IELTS (minimum score 5), Michigan English Language Assessment Battery (minimum score 77), Cambridge A, B, C. *Application deadline:* For fall admission, 7/15 priority date for domestic students, 6/1 for international students; for spring admission, 11/15 priority date for domestic students, 11/1 for international students. Applications are processed on a rolling basis. Application fee: $50. Electronic applications accepted. *Financial support:* In 2011–12, 190 students received support, including 183 fellowships (averaging $1,638 per year), 21 research assistantships (averaging $9,311 per year); career-related internships or fieldwork, scholarships/grants, and unspecified assistantships also available. Support available to part-time students. Financial award applicants required to submit FAFSA. *Faculty research:* Information technology and marketing, behavioral research in accounting, human resources, management of technology. *Unit head:* Douglas Stives, MBA Program Director, 732-263-5894, Fax: 732-263-5517, E-mail: dstives@monmouth.edu. *Application contact:* Kevin Roane, Director, Office of Graduate Admission, 732-571-3452, Fax: 732-263-5123, E-mail: gradadm@monmouth.edu. Web site: http://www.monmouth.edu/mba.

Montclair State University, The Graduate School, School of Business, Post Master's Certificate Program in Finance, Montclair, NJ 07043-1624. Offers MBA, Certificate, Post Master's Certificate. Part-time and evening/weekend programs available. *Students:* 1 part-time; minority (Hispanic/Latino). Average age 30. 1 applicant, 100% accepted, 1 enrolled. *Entrance requirements:* For degree, essay. Additional exam requirements/recommendations for international students: Required—TOEFL (minimum score 83 iBT) or IELTS (minimum score 6.5). *Application deadline:* For fall admission, 6/1 for international students; for spring admission, 10/1 for international students. Applications are processed on a rolling basis. Application fee: $60. Electronic applications accepted. *Financial support:* Federal Work-Study, scholarships/grants, and unspecified assistantships available. Support available to part-time students. Financial award application deadline: 3/1; financial award applicants required to submit FAFSA. *Faculty research:* Foreign direct investment, central banking and inflation, African economic development, intraday trade, working capital management. *Unit head:* Dr. Richard Lord, Chair, 973-655-5255. *Application contact:* Amy Aiello, Executive Director of The Graduate School, 973-655-5147, Fax: 973-655-7869, E-mail: graduate.school@montclair.edu.

Mount Saint Mary College, Division of Business, Newburgh, NY 12550-3494. Offers business (MBA); financial planning (MBA). Part-time and evening/weekend programs available. *Faculty:* 4 full-time (1 woman), 5 part-time/adjunct (1 woman). *Students:* 31 full-time (20 women), 39 part-time (19 women); includes 16 minority (5 Black or African American, non-Hispanic/Latino; 1 Asian, non-Hispanic/Latino; 9 Hispanic/Latino; 1 Two or more races, non-Hispanic/Latino), 9 international. Average age 32. 62 applicants, 35% accepted, 9 enrolled. In 2011, 49 master's awarded. *Degree requirements:* For master's, thesis or alternative. *Entrance requirements:* For master's, GMAT or minimum undergraduate GPA of 2.7. *Application deadline:* Applications are processed on a rolling basis. Application fee: $45. Application fee is waived when completed online. *Expenses: Tuition:* Full-time $13,356; part-time $742 per credit. *Required fees:* $70 per semester. *Financial support:* In 2011–12, 19 students received support. Unspecified assistantships available. Financial award application deadline: 4/15; financial award applicants required to submit FAFSA. *Faculty research:* Financial reform, entrepreneurship and small business development, global business relations, technology's impact on business decision-making, college-assisted business education. *Unit head:* Dr. James Gearity, Graduate Coordinator, 845-569-3121, Fax: 845-562-6762, E-mail: james.gearity@msmc.edu. *Application contact:* Courtney McDermott, Graduate Recruiter, 845-569-3402, Fax: 845-569-3450, E-mail: courtney.mcdermott@msmc.edu. Web site: http://www.msmc.edu/Academics/Graduate_Programs/master_of_business_administration.be.

National University, Academic Affairs, College of Letters and Sciences, Department of Professional Studies, La Jolla, CA 92037-1011. Offers alternative dispute resolution (Certificate); criminal justice (MCJ); professional screen writing (MFA); public administration (MPA), including public finance, social transformation and community development. Part-time and evening/weekend programs available. Postbaccalaureate distance learning degree programs offered (no on-campus study). *Degree requirements:* For master's, thesis. *Entrance requirements:* For master's, interview, minimum GPA of 2.5. Additional exam requirements/recommendations for international students: Required—TOEFL (minimum score 550 paper-based; 213 computer-based; 79 iBT), IELTS (minimum score 6). *Application deadline:* Applications are processed on a rolling basis. Application fee: $60 ($65 for international students). Electronic applications accepted. *Financial support:* Career-related internships or fieldwork, institutionally sponsored loans, scholarships/grants, and tuition waivers (partial) available. Support available to part-time students. Financial award application deadline: 6/30; financial award applicants required to submit FAFSA. *Unit head:* James G. Larsen, Associate Professor and Chair, 858-642-8418, Fax: 858-642-8715, E-mail: jlarson@nu.edu. *Application contact:* Dominick Giovanniello, Associate Regional Dean, 800-NAT-UNIV, Fax: 858-541-7792, E-mail: dgiovann@nu.edu. Web site: http://www.nu.edu/OurPrograms/CollegeOfLettersAndSciences/ProfessionalStudies.html.

National University, Academic Affairs, School of Business and Management, Department of Accounting and Finance, La Jolla, CA 92037-1011. Offers accountancy (M Acc); business administration (MBA); sustainability management (MS). Part-time and evening/weekend programs available. Postbaccalaureate distance learning degree programs offered (no on-campus study). *Degree requirements:* For master's, thesis. *Entrance requirements:* For master's, interview, minimum GPA of 2.5. Additional exam requirements/recommendations for international students: Required—TOEFL (minimum score 550 paper-based; 213 computer-based; 79 iBT), IELTS (minimum score 6). *Application deadline:* Applications are processed on a rolling basis. Application fee: $60 ($65 for international students). Electronic applications accepted. *Financial support:* Career-related internships or fieldwork, institutionally sponsored loans, scholarships/grants, and tuition waivers (partial) available. Support available to part-time students. Financial award application deadline: 6/30; financial award applicants required to submit FAFSA. *Unit head:* Dr. Farhang Mossavar-Rahmani, Chair, 858-642-8409, Fax: 858-642-8726, E-mail: fmossava@nu.edu. *Application contact:* Dominick Giovanniello, Associate Regional Dean, 800-NAT-UNIV, Fax: 858-541-7792, E-mail: dgiovann@nu.edu. Web site: http://www.nu.edu/OurPrograms/SchoolOfBusinessAndManagement/AccountingAndFinance.html.

Naval Postgraduate School, Departments and Academic Groups, Department of Defense Analysis, Monterey, CA 93943. Offers command and control (MS); communications (MS); defense analysis (MS), including astronautics; financial management (MS); information operations (MS); irregular warfare (MS); national security affairs (MS); operations analysis (MS); special operations (MA, MS), including command and control (MS), communications (MS), financial management (MS), information operations (MS), irregular warfare (MS), national security affairs, operations analysis (MS), tactile missiles (MS), terrorist operations and financing (MS); tactile missiles (MS); terrorist operations and financing (MS). Program only open to commissioned officers of the United States and friendly nations and selected United States federal civilian employees. Part-time programs available. *Faculty:* 26 full-time (10 women), 2 part-time/adjunct (both women). *Students:* 182 full-time (5 women); includes 18 minority (5 Black or African American, non-Hispanic/Latino; 1 American Indian or Alaska Native, non-Hispanic/Latino; 5 Asian, non-Hispanic/Latino; 7 Hispanic/Latino), 36 international. Average age 38. In 2011, 98 master's awarded. *Degree requirements:* For master's, thesis. *Faculty research:* CTF Global Ecco Project, long-term strategy seminar: SOF 2030, Afghanistan endgames, core lab Philippines project, DMDC data vulnerability. *Total annual research expenditures:* $3.4 million. *Unit head:* Prof. John Arquilla, Department Chair, 831-656-3540, E-mail: jarquilla@nps.edu. Web site: http://nps.edu/Academics/Schools/GSOIS/Departments/DA/index.html.

Naval Postgraduate School, Departments and Academic Groups, School of Business and Public Policy, Monterey, CA 93943. Offers acquisitions and contract management (MBA); business administration (EMBA, MBA); contract management (MS); defense business management (MBA); defense systems analysis (MS), including management; defense systems management (international) (MBA); executive management (MBA); financial management (MBA); information systems management (MBA); manpower systems analysis (MS); material logistics support management (MBA); program management (MS); resource planning/management for international defense (MBA); supply chain management (MBA); systems acquisition management (MBA); transportation management (MBA). Program only open to commissioned officers of the United States and friendly nations and selected United States federal civilian employees. *Accreditation:* AACSB; NASPAA. Part-time programs available. Postbaccalaureate distance learning degree programs offered (minimal on-campus study). *Faculty:* 67 full-time (15 women), 32 part-time/adjunct (12 women). *Students:* 307 full-time (29 women), 327 part-time (71 women); includes 149 minority (55 Black or African American, non-Hispanic/Latino; 5 American Indian or Alaska Native, non-Hispanic/Latino; 46 Asian, non-Hispanic/Latino; 43 Hispanic/Latino), 44 international. Average age 42. In 2011, 295 master's awarded. *Degree requirements:* For master's, thesis (for some programs), terminal project/capstone (for some programs). *Faculty research:* U. S. and European public procurement policies for small and medium-sized enterprises, examining external validity criticisms in the choice of students as subjects in accounting experiment studies, assurance of learning in contract management education, contracting for cloud computing: opportunities and risks, NPS, Apple App Store as a business model supporting U. S. Navy requirements. *Total annual research expenditures:* $9 million. *Unit head:* Raymond Franck, Department Chair, 831-656-3614, E-mail: refranck@nps.edu. *Application contact:* Acting Director of Admissions. Web site: http://www.nps.edu/Academics/Schools/GSBPP/index.html.

New Charter University, College of Business, Birmingham, AL 35244. Offers finance (MBA); health care management (MBA); management (MBA). Part-time and evening/weekend programs available. Postbaccalaureate distance learning degree programs offered (no on-campus study). *Entrance requirements:* For master's, course work in calculus, statistics, macroeconomics. Additional exam requirements/recommendations for international students: Required—TOEFL (minimum score 550 paper-based; 213 computer-based). Electronic applications accepted.

New England College of Business and Finance, Program in Finance, Boston, MA 02111-2645. Offers MSF. Postbaccalaureate distance learning degree programs offered (no on-campus study).

New Jersey City University, Graduate Studies and Continuing Education, College of Professional Studies, Department of Business Administration, Program in Finance, Jersey City, NJ 07305-1597. Offers MS. Part-time and evening/weekend programs available. *Students:* 19 full-time (10 women), 12 part-time (6 women); includes 8 minority (6 Asian, non-Hispanic/Latino; 2 Hispanic/Latino), 20 international. In 2011, 8 master's awarded. *Degree requirements:* For master's, thesis. *Entrance requirements:* Additional exam requirements/recommendations for international students: Required—TOEFL. *Expenses:* Tuition, state resident: part-time $494 per credit. Tuition, nonresident: part-time $911.30 per credit. *Required fees:* $95.90 per year. *Unit head:* Rosilyn Overton, Graduate Coordinator, 201-200-3353, E-mail: roverton@njcu.edu. *Application contact:* Dr. William Bajor, Dean of Graduate Studies, 201-200-3409, Fax: 201-200-3411, E-mail: wbajor@njcu.edu.

Newman University, MBA Program, Wichita, KS 67213-2097. Offers finance (MBA); international business (MBA); leadership (MBA); management (MBA); technology (MBA). Part-time programs available. *Faculty:* 4 full-time (1 woman), 7 part-time/adjunct (2 women). *Students:* 28 full-time (7 women), 83 part-time (28 women); includes 31 minority (8 Black or African American, non-Hispanic/Latino; 1 American Indian or Alaska Native, non-Hispanic/Latino; 9 Asian, non-Hispanic/Latino; 9 Hispanic/Latino; 1 Native Hawaiian or other Pacific Islander, non-Hispanic/Latino; 3 Two or more races, non-Hispanic/Latino), 23 international. Average age 31. 63 applicants, 70% accepted, 38 enrolled. In 2011, 49 master's awarded. *Degree requirements:* For master's, thesis optional. *Entrance requirements:* For master's, interview; minimum GPA of 3.0; 3 letters of recommendation; course work in algebra, statistics, macroeconomics, and financial accounting. Additional exam requirements/recommendations for international students: Required—TOEFL (minimum score 600 paper-based; 250 computer-based; 100 iBT). *Application deadline:* For fall admission, 8/1 priority date for domestic students, 7/15 for international students; for winter admission, 1/1 priority date for domestic students; for spring admission, 1/1 priority date for domestic students, 11/15 for international students. Applications are processed on a rolling basis. Application fee: $25 ($40 for international students). Electronic applications accepted. *Expenses:* Contact institution. *Financial support:* In 2011–12, 18 students received support. Federal Work-Study available. Financial award application deadline: 8/15; financial award applicants required to submit FAFSA. *Unit head:* Dr. Wendy Munday, Director of MBA Program, 316-942-4291 Ext. 2296, Fax: 316-942-4483, E-mail: mundayw@newmanu.edu. *Application contact:* Linda Kay Sabala, Director of Graduate Admissions, 316-942-4291 Ext. 2230, Fax: 316-942-4483, E-mail: sabalal@newmanu.edu. Web site: http://www.newmanu.edu.

New Mexico State University, Graduate School, College of Business, Department of Finance, Las Cruces, NM 88003-8001. Offers Graduate Certificate. *Faculty:* 10 full-time (4 women). *Students:* 1 (woman) full-time; minority (Hispanic/Latino). Average age 47. 1 applicant, 0% accepted, 0 enrolled. In 2011, 1 Graduate Certificate awarded. *Entrance requirements:* Additional exam requirements/recommendations for international students: Required—TOEFL (minimum score 550 paper-based; 79 iBT), IELTS (minimum score 6.5). Application fee: $40 ($50 for international students). *Expenses:* Tuition, state resident: full-time $5004; part-time $208.50 per credit. Tuition, nonresident: full-time $17,446; part-time $726.90 per credit. *Unit head:* Dr. Lizbeth Ellis, Head, 575-646-3201, Fax: 575-646-2820, E-mail: lellis@nmsu.edu. *Application contact:* Coordinator, 575-646-2736, Fax: 575-646-7721, E-mail: gradinfo@nmsu.edu. Web site: http://business.nmsu.edu/academics/finance/.

The New School, The New School for Social Research, Department of Economics, New York, NY 10003. Offers economics (M Phil, MA, MS, DS Sc, PhD); global finance (MS); global political economy and finance (MA). Part-time and evening/weekend programs available. Terminal master's awarded for partial completion of doctoral program. *Degree requirements:* For master's, exam; for doctorate, one foreign language, thesis/dissertation, qualifying exam. *Entrance requirements:* For master's, GRE General Test; for doctorate, GRE General Test, MA. Additional exam requirements/recommendations for international students: Required—TOEFL (minimum score 600 paper-based; 250 computer-based; 100 iBT). Electronic applications accepted. *Faculty research:* Heterodox, history of economic thought, post-Keynesian, global political economy and finance.

New York Institute of Technology, Graduate Division, School of Management, Program in Business Administration, Old Westbury, NY 11568-8000. Offers accounting (Advanced Certificate); business administration (MBA); finance (Advanced Certificate); international business (Advanced Certificate); management of information systems (Advanced Certificate); marketing (Advanced Certificate). Part-time and evening/weekend programs available. *Students:* 331 full-time (131 women), 508 part-time (211 women); includes 74 minority (26 Black or African American, non-Hispanic/Latino; 27 Asian, non-Hispanic/Latino; 15 Hispanic/Latino; 6 Two or more races, non-Hispanic/Latino), 214 international. Average age 28. In 2011, 449 degrees awarded. *Degree requirements:* For master's, thesis (for some programs). *Entrance requirements:* For master's, minimum QPA of 2.85. Additional exam requirements/recommendations for international students: Required—TOEFL (minimum score 550 paper-based; 213 computer-based). *Application deadline:* For fall admission, 7/1 priority date for domestic students; for spring admission, 12/1 priority date for domestic students. Applications are processed on a rolling basis. Application fee: $50. Electronic applications accepted. *Expenses: Tuition:* Part-time $930 per credit hour. *Financial support:* Fellowships, research assistantships with partial tuition reimbursements, institutionally sponsored loans, tuition waivers (full and partial), and unspecified assistantships available. Support available to part-time students. Financial award applicants required to submit FAFSA. *Faculty research:* Instructor performance appraisal; relationship between TOEFL, GMAT, GRE, and performance in foreign students. *Unit head:* Dr. Stephen Hartman, Director, 516-686-7691, E-mail: shartman@nyit.edu. *Application contact:* Dr. Jacquelyn Nealon, Vice President for Enrollment Services, 516-686-7925, Fax: 516-686-7597, E-mail: jnealon@nyit.edu.

New York Law School, Graduate Programs, New York, NY 10013. Offers financial services (LL M); law (JD); mental disability law (MA); real estate (LL M); taxation (LL M); JD/MA; JD/MBA. JD/MBA offered jointly with Bernard M. Baruch College of the City University of New York; JD/MA in forensic psychology offered jointly with John Jay College of Criminal Justice of the City University of New York. *Accreditation:* ABA. Part-time and evening/weekend programs available. Postbaccalaureate distance learning degree programs offered (minimal on-campus study). *Faculty:* 103 full-time (45 women), 118 part-time/adjunct (42 women). *Students:* 1,416 full-time (760 women), 456 part-time (204 women); includes 476 minority (134 Black or African American, non-Hispanic/Latino; 5 American Indian or Alaska Native, non-Hispanic/Latino; 74 Asian, non-Hispanic/Latino; 243 Hispanic/Latino; 1 Native Hawaiian or other Pacific Islander, non-Hispanic/Latino; 19 Two or more races, non-Hispanic/Latino). Average age 27. 6,058 applicants, 44% accepted, 519 enrolled. In 2011, 37 master's, 515 doctorates awarded. *Entrance requirements:* For master's, JD (for LL M ; for doctorate, LSAT, letters of recommendation, resume. Additional exam requirements/recommendations for international students: Recommended—TOEFL (minimum score 600 paper-based; 250 computer-based; 100 iBT). *Application deadline:* For fall admission, 4/1 priority date for domestic students, 4/1 for international students. Applications are processed on a rolling basis. Application fee: $0. Electronic applications accepted. *Expenses: Tuition:* Full-time $46,200; part-time $35,600 per year. *Required fees:* $1600; $1300 per year. Tuition and fees vary according to degree level and student level. *Financial support:* In 2011–12, 588 students received support, including 34 fellowships (averaging $3,010 per year), 229 research assistantships (averaging $4,322 per year), 17 teaching assistantships (averaging $4,278 per year); career-related internships or fieldwork, Federal Work-Study, institutionally sponsored loans, and scholarships/grants also available. Support available to part-time students. Financial award application deadline: 4/1; financial award applicants required to submit FAFSA. *Unit head:* Carol A. Buckler, Interim Dean, 212-431-2840, Fax: 212-219-3752, E-mail: cbuckler@nyls.edu. *Application contact:* Susan W. Gross, Senior Director of Admissions and Financial Aid, 212-431-2888, Fax: 212-966-1522, E-mail: sgross@nyls.edu. Web site: http://www.nyls.edu.

See Display on page 1606 and Close-Up on page 1627.

New York University, Leonard N. Stern School of Business, Department of Finance, New York, NY 10012-1019. Offers MBA, PhD. *Faculty research:* Derivative securities, pricing of assets, credit risk, portfolio management, international finance.

New York University, Robert F. Wagner Graduate School of Public Service, Program in Public Administration, New York, NY 10012. Offers public administration (PhD); public and nonprofit management and policy (MPA, Advanced Certificate), including developmental administration (Advanced Certificate), financial management and public finance, human resources management (Advanced Certificate), international administration (Advanced Certificate), management (MPA), management for public and nonprofit organizations (Advanced Certificate), public policy analysis, quantitative analysis and computer applications (Advanced Certificate), urban public policy (Advanced Certificate); JD/MPA; MBA/MPA; MPA/MA. *Accreditation:* NASPAA (one or more programs are accredited). Part-time programs available. *Faculty:* 32 full-time (13 women), 41 part-time/adjunct (22 women). *Students:* 431 full-time (323 women), 131 part-time (98 women); includes 148 minority (35 Black or African American, non-Hispanic/Latino; 53 Asian, non-Hispanic/Latino; 38 Hispanic/Latino; 1 Native Hawaiian or other Pacific Islander, non-Hispanic/Latino; 21 Two or more races, non-Hispanic/Latino), 62 international. Average age 28. 1,063 applicants, 58% accepted, 205 enrolled. In 2011, 213 master's, 8 doctorates awarded. *Degree requirements:* For master's, thesis or alternative, capstone end event; for doctorate, one foreign language, thesis/dissertation. *Entrance requirements:* Additional exam requirements/recommendations for international students: Required—TOEFL, IELTS, TWE. *Application deadline:* For fall admission, 1/15 for domestic students, 1/5 for international students; for spring admission, 10/15 for domestic students, 9/15 for international students. Application fee: $85. Electronic applications accepted. *Expenses:* Contact institution. *Financial support:* In 2011–12, 118 students received support, including 117 fellowships (averaging $13,500 per year); career-related internships or fieldwork, Federal Work-Study, scholarships/grants, health care benefits, and unspecified assistantships also available. Support available to part-time students. Financial award application deadline: 1/5; financial award applicants required to submit FAFSA. *Unit head:* Katty Jones, Director, Program Services, 212-998-7411, Fax: 212-995-4164, E-mail: katty.jones@nyu.edu. *Application contact:* Christopher Alexander, Communications Coordinator, 212-998-7414, Fax: 212-995-4611, E-mail: wagner.admissions@nyu.edu. Web site: http://www.nyu.edu.wagner/.

New York University, School of Continuing and Professional Studies, The Preston Robert Tisch Center for Hospitality, Tourism, and Sports Management, Program in Hospitality Industry Studies, New York, NY 10012-1019. Offers brand strategy (MS); hospitality industry studies (Advanced Certificate); hotel finance (MS). Part-time and evening/weekend programs available. *Faculty:* 13 full-time (5 women), 20 part-time/adjunct (4 women). *Students:* 22 full-time (14 women), 30 part-time (16 women); includes 11 minority (3 Black or African American, non-Hispanic/Latino; 4 Asian, non-Hispanic/Latino; 4 Hispanic/Latino), 14 international. Average age 29. 83 applicants, 58% accepted, 20 enrolled. In 2011, 17 master's, 4 other advanced degrees awarded. *Degree requirements:* For master's, thesis. *Entrance requirements:* For master's, GRE/GMAT only upon request, relevant professional work, internship or volunteer experience. Additional exam requirements/recommendations for international students: Required—TOEFL (minimum score 600 paper-based; 250 computer-based; 100 iBT), IELTS (minimum score 7). *Application deadline:* For fall admission, 2/1 priority date for domestic students, 2/1 for international students; for spring admission, 10/15 priority date for domestic students, 8/15 for international students. Applications are processed on a rolling basis. Application fee: $150. Electronic applications accepted. *Financial support:* In 2011–12, 51 students received support, including 35 fellowships (averaging $3,034 per year); scholarships/grants also available. Support available to part-time students. Financial award application deadline: 2/15; financial award applicants required to submit FAFSA. *Application contact:* Admissions Office, 212-998-7100, E-mail: scps.gradadmissions@nyu.edu. Web site: http://www.scps.nyu.edu/areas-of-study/tisch/graduate-programs/ms-hospitality-industry-studies/.

New York University, School of Continuing and Professional Studies, Schack Institute of Real Estate, Program in Real Estate, New York, NY 10012-1019. Offers real estate (MS, Advanced Certificate), including finance and investment (MS), strategic real estate management (MS); real estate development (MS, Advanced Certificate), including business of development (MS), community development (MS), global real estate (MS), sustainable development (MS). Part-time and evening/weekend programs available. *Faculty:* 10 full-time (3 women), 94 part-time/adjunct (17 women). *Students:* 111 full-time (36 women), 352 part-time (75 women); includes 37 minority (9 Black or African American, non-Hispanic/Latino; 1 American Indian or Alaska Native, non-Hispanic/Latino; 21 Asian, non-Hispanic/Latino; 6 Hispanic/Latino), 50 international. Average age 31. 279 applicants, 63% accepted, 99 enrolled. In 2011, 186 master's, 28 other advanced degrees awarded. *Degree requirements:* For master's, thesis, capstone. *Entrance requirements:* For master's, GRE/GMAT only upon request, relevant professional work, internship or volunteer experience. Additional exam requirements/recommendations for international students: Required—TOEFL (minimum score 600 paper-based; 250 computer-based; 100 iBT), IELTS (minimum score 7). *Application deadline:* For fall admission, 2/1 priority date for domestic students, 2/1 for international students; for spring admission, 10/15 priority date for domestic students, 8/15 for international students. Applications are processed on a rolling basis. Application fee: $150. Electronic applications accepted. *Financial support:* In 2011–12, 225 students received support, including 201 fellowships (averaging $2,349 per year); scholarships/grants also available. Support available to part-time students. Financial award application deadline: 3/2. *Faculty research:* Economics and market cycles, international property rights, comparative metropolitan economies, current market trends. *Unit head:* Rosemary Scanlon, Divisional Dean. *Application contact:* Office of Admissions, 212-998-7100, E-mail: scps.gradadmissions@nyu.edu. Web site: http://www.scps.nyu.edu/areas-of-study/real-estate/graduate-programs/.

North Central College, Graduate and Continuing Education Programs, Department of Business, Program in Business Administration, Naperville, IL 60566-7063. Offers change management (MBA); finance (MBA); human resource management (MBA); management (MBA); marketing (MBA). Part-time and evening/weekend programs available. *Faculty:* 14 full-time (4 women), 13 part-time/adjunct (3 women). *Students:* 41 full-time (15 women), 66 part-time (31 women); includes 19 minority (2 Black or African American, non-Hispanic/Latino; 1 American Indian or Alaska Native, non-Hispanic/Latino; 12 Asian, non-Hispanic/Latino; 4 Hispanic/Latino), 1 international. Average age 30. 116 applicants, 66% accepted, 50 enrolled. In 2011, 63 master's awarded. *Degree requirements:* For master's, thesis optional, project. *Entrance requirements:* For master's, interview. Additional exam requirements/recommendations for international students: Required—TOEFL (minimum score 577 paper-based; 233 computer-based; 90 iBT). *Application deadline:* For fall admission, 8/15 for domestic students; for winter admission, 12/1 for domestic students; for spring admission, 2/1 for domestic students. Application fee: $25. *Financial support:* In 2011–12, 8 students received support. Scholarships/grants available. Support available to part-time students. *Unit head:* Dr. Jean Clifton, MBA Program Coordinator, 630-637-5244, E-mail: jmclifton@noctrl.edu. *Application contact:* Wendy Kulpinski, Director of Graduate and Continuing Education Admission, 630-637-5808, Fax: 630-637-5844, E-mail: wekulpinski@noctrl.edu.

Northeastern Illinois University, Graduate College, College of Business and Management, Chicago, IL 60625-4699. Offers accounting (MSA); finance (MBA); management (MBA); marketing (MBA). Part-time and evening/weekend programs available. *Degree requirements:* For master's, thesis optional. *Entrance requirements:* For master's, GMAT, minimum GPA of 2.75. Additional exam requirements/recommendations for international students: Required—TOEFL (minimum score 550 paper-based; 213 computer-based; 79 iBT). Electronic applications accepted. *Faculty research:* Perception of accountants and non-accountants toward future of the accounting industry, asynchronous learning outcomes, cost and efficiency of financial markets, impact of deregulation on airline industry, analysis of derivational instruments.

Northeastern State University, Graduate College, College of Business and Technology, Program in Accounting and Financial Analysis, Tahlequah, OK 74464-2399. Offers MS. Part-time and evening/weekend programs available. *Students:* 17 full-time (8 women), 51 part-time (33 women); includes 12 minority (3 Black or African American, non-Hispanic/Latino; 4 American Indian or Alaska Native, non-Hispanic/Latino; 2 Asian, non-Hispanic/Latino; 3 Hispanic/Latino), 2 international. In 2011, 16 master's awarded. *Entrance requirements:* For master's, GMAT. Additional exam requirements/recommendations for international students: Required—TOEFL (minimum score 213 computer-based). *Application deadline:* For fall admission, 6/1 priority date for domestic students. Applications are processed on a rolling basis. Application fee: $25. Electronic applications accepted. *Unit head:* Dr. Gary Freeman, Coordinator, 918-449-6524, E-mail: freemandg@nsuok.edu. *Application contact:* Margie Railey, Administrative Assistant, 918-456-5511 Ext. 2093, Fax: 918-458-2061, E-mail: railey@nsuok.edu.

North Greenville University, T. Walter Brashier Graduate School, Greer, SC 29651. Offers Christian ministry (MCM, D Min); education (M Ed); financial planning (MBA); human resources (MBA). Part-time and evening/weekend programs available. Postbaccalaureate distance learning degree programs offered (no on-campus study). *Faculty:* 8 full-time (3 women), 15 part-time/adjunct (0 women). *Students:* 55 full-time (33 women), 148 part-time (53 women); includes 48 minority (37 Black or African American, non-Hispanic/Latino; 1 American Indian or Alaska Native, non-Hispanic/Latino; 3 Asian, non-Hispanic/Latino; 5 Hispanic/Latino; 2 Two or more races, non-Hispanic/Latino). Average age 32. 180 applicants, 98% accepted, 170 enrolled. In 2011, 58 master's awarded. *Degree requirements:* For master's, comprehensive exam (for some programs), thesis or alternative, capstone course. *Entrance requirements:* For master's, minimum GPA of 2.25 overall, 2.5 in major; for doctorate, MAT. Additional exam requirements/recommendations for international students: Required—TOEFL (minimum score 550 paper-based; 213 computer-based). *Application deadline:* For fall admission, 8/1 for domestic students, 6/1 for international students; for winter admission, 1/1 for domestic students, 10/1 for international students; for spring admission, 3/1 for domestic students, 1/1 for international students. Applications are processed on a rolling basis. Application fee: $30. Electronic applications accepted. *Financial support:* In 2011–12, 112 students received support, including 1 research assistantship (averaging $2,000 per year); Federal Work-Study, institutionally sponsored loans, scholarships/grants, tuition waivers (partial), and unspecified assistantships also available. Support available to part-time students. Financial award applicants required to submit FAFSA. *Faculty research:* Organizational behavior, church growth, homiletics, human resources, business strategy. *Unit head:* Dr. Joseph Samuel Isgett, Jr., Vice President for Graduate Studies, 864-877-3052, Fax: 864-877-1653, E-mail: sisgett@ngu.edu. *Application contact:* Tawana P. Scott, Dean of Graduate Enrollment, 864-877-1598, Fax: 864-877-1653, E-mail: tscott@ngu.edu. Web site: http://www.ngu.edu/gradschool.php.

Northwestern University, The Graduate School, Kellogg School of Management, Department of Finance, Evanston, IL 60208. Offers PhD. Admissions and degree offered through The Graduate School. *Degree requirements:* For doctorate, comprehensive exam, thesis/dissertation. *Entrance requirements:* For doctorate, GMAT or GRE General Test, 2 years of undergraduate course work in mathematics. Additional exam requirements/recommendations for international students: Required—TOEFL. Electronic applications accepted. *Faculty research:* Corporate finance, asset pricing, international finance, micro-structure, empirical finance.

Norwich University, College of Graduate and Continuing Studies, Master of Business Administration Program, Northfield, VT 05663. Offers finance (MBA); organizational leadership (MBA); project management (MBA). *Accreditation:* ACBSP. Evening/weekend programs available. *Faculty:* 19 part-time/adjunct (5 women). *Students:* 100 full-time (34 women); includes 16 minority (4 Black or African American, non-Hispanic/Latino; 1 American Indian or Alaska Native, non-Hispanic/Latino; 5 Asian, non-Hispanic/Latino; 4 Hispanic/Latino; 2 Two or more races, non-Hispanic/Latino). Average age 36. 67 applicants, 69% accepted, 46 enrolled. In 2011, 103 master's awarded. *Degree requirements:* For master's, comprehensive exam (for some programs), thesis optional. *Entrance requirements:* For master's, minimum undergraduate GPA of 2.75. Additional exam requirements/recommendations for international students: Required—TOEFL (minimum score 550 paper-based; 213 computer-based; 83 iBT). *Application deadline:* For fall admission, 8/10 for domestic and international students; for winter admission, 11/7 for domestic and international students; for spring admission, 2/6 for domestic and international students. Applications are processed on a rolling basis. Application fee: $50. Electronic applications accepted. *Expenses: Tuition:* Full-time $16,174. *Required fees:* $2130. Full-time tuition and fees vary according to program. *Financial support:* In 2011–12, 58 students received support. Scholarships/grants available. Financial award applicants required to submit FAFSA. *Unit head:* Dr. Jose Cordova, Faculty Director, 802-485-2567, Fax: 802-485-2533, E-mail: jcordova@norwich.edu. *Application contact:* Kerri Murnyack, Associate Program Director, 802-485-3304, Fax: 802-485-2533, E-mail: kmurnyuac@norwich.edu. Web site: http://mba.norwich.edu.

Notre Dame de Namur University, Division of Academic Affairs, School of Business and Management, Department of Business Administration, Belmont, CA 94002-1908. Offers business administration (MBA); finance (MBA); human resource management (MBA); marketing (MBA). Part-time and evening/weekend programs available. *Faculty:* 7 full-time (1 woman), 6 part-time/adjunct (0 women). *Students:* 42 full-time (16 women), 104 part-time (67 women); includes 56 minority (6 Black or African American, non-Hispanic/Latino; 26 Asian, non-Hispanic/Latino; 20 Hispanic/Latino; 2 Native Hawaiian or other Pacific Islander, non-Hispanic/Latino; 2 Two or more races, non-Hispanic/Latino), 23 international. Average age 34. 167 applicants, 40% accepted, 39 enrolled. In 2011, 33 degrees awarded. *Entrance requirements:* For master's, minimum GPA of 2.5. Additional exam requirements/recommendations for international students: Required—TOEFL (minimum score 550 paper-based; 213 computer-based; 79 iBT). *Application deadline:* For fall admission, 8/1 priority date for domestic students; for spring admission, 12/1 priority date for domestic students. Applications are processed on a rolling basis. Application fee: $60. Electronic applications accepted. *Expenses: Tuition:* Full-time $14,220; part-time $790 per credit. *Required fees:* $35 per semester. Tuition and fees vary according to program. *Financial support:* Available to part-time students. Applicants required to submit FAFSA. *Unit head:* Jordan Holtzman, Director, 650-508-3637, E-mail: jholtzman@ndnu.edu. *Application contact:* Candace Hallmark, Associate Director of Admissions, 650-508-3600, Fax: 650-508-3426, E-mail: grad.admit@ndnu.edu. Web site: http://www.ndnu.edu/academics/schools-programs/school-business/.

Oakland University, Graduate Study and Lifelong Learning, School of Business Administration, Department of Accounting and Finance, Rochester, MI 48309-4401. Offers accounting (M Acc, Certificate); finance (Certificate).

Ohio University, Graduate College, College of Arts and Sciences, Department of Economics, Athens, OH 45701-2979. Offers applied economics (MA); financial economics (MFE). Part-time and evening/weekend programs available. *Students:* 53 full-time (19 women), 34 part-time (14 women); includes 7 minority (5 Black or African American, non-Hispanic/Latino; 1 Asian, non-Hispanic/Latino; 1 Hispanic/Latino), 47 international. 66 applicants, 52% accepted, 12 enrolled. In 2011, 48 master's awarded. *Degree requirements:* For master's, thesis or alternative. *Entrance requirements:* For master's, GRE or GMAT (recommended), minimum GPA of 3.0. Additional exam requirements/recommendations for international students: Required—TOEFL (minimum score 550 paper-based; 80 iBT) or IELTS (minimum score 6.5). *Application deadline:* For fall admission, 2/15 priority date for domestic students, 2/15 for international students; for winter admission, 12/1 for domestic students, 10/1 for international students. Application fee: $50 ($55 for international students). Electronic applications accepted. *Financial support:* Research assistantships with full and partial tuition reimbursements, Federal Work-Study, tuition waivers (partial), and unspecified assistantships available. Financial award application deadline: 2/15. *Faculty research:* Macroeconomics, public finance, international economics and finance, monetary theory, healthcare economics. *Unit head:* Dr. Rosmary Rossiter, Chair, 740-593-2040, E-mail: rossiter@ohio.edu. *Application contact:* Dr. K. Doroodian, Graduate Chair, 740-593-2046, E-mail: doroodia@ohio.edu. Web site: http://www.ohiou.edu/economics/.

Oklahoma City University, Meinders School of Business, Program in Business Administration, Oklahoma City, OK 73106-1402. Offers finance (MBA); health administration (MBA); information technology (MBA); integrated marketing communications (MBA); international business (MBA); marketing (MBA); JD/MBA. *Accreditation:* ACBSP. Part-time and evening/weekend programs available. *Faculty:* 15 full-time (6 women), 14 part-time/adjunct (6 women). *Students:* 136 full-time (59 women), 112 part-time (34 women); includes 38 minority (14 Black or African American, non-Hispanic/Latino; 4 American Indian or Alaska Native, non-Hispanic/Latino; 11 Asian, non-Hispanic/Latino; 3 Hispanic/Latino; 6 Two or more races, non-Hispanic/Latino), 100 international. Average age 30. 252 applicants, 83% accepted, 30 enrolled. In 2011, 148 master's awarded. *Degree requirements:* For master's, comprehensive exam. *Entrance requirements:* For master's, GRE or GMAT. Additional exam requirements/recommendations for international students: Required—TOEFL (minimum score 560 paper-based; 220 computer-based; 83 iBT). *Application deadline:* Applications are processed on a rolling basis. Application fee: $50 ($70 for international students). Electronic applications accepted. *Expenses: Tuition:* Full-time $16,848; part-time $936 per credit hour. *Required fees:* $2070; $115 per credit hour. One-time fee: $300. *Financial support:* Career-related internships or fieldwork, Federal Work-Study, institutionally sponsored loans, and tuition waivers (partial) available. Support available to part-time students. Financial award application deadline: 6/1; financial award applicants required to submit FAFSA. *Faculty research:* Management information systems, international business strategies. *Unit head:* Dr. Steven Agee, Dean, 405-208-5130, Fax: 405-208-5098, E-mail: sagee@okcu.edu. *Application contact:* Michelle Cook, Director, Graduate Admissions, 800-633-7242, Fax: 405-208-5916, E-mail: gadmissions@okcu.edu. Web site: http://msb.okcu.edu/graduate/.

Oklahoma State University, Spears School of Business, Department of Finance, Stillwater, OK 74078. Offers finance (PhD); quantitative financial economics (MS). Part-time programs available. *Faculty:* 13 full-time (1 woman), 5 part-time/adjunct (0 women). *Students:* 19 full-time (9 women), 9 part-time (3 women); includes 2 minority (1 Black or African American, non-Hispanic/Latino; 1 Asian, non-Hispanic/Latino), 12 international. Average age 29. 47 applicants, 13% accepted, 4 enrolled. In 2011, 9 master's, 2 doctorates awarded. *Degree requirements:* For master's, thesis or alternative; for doctorate, comprehensive exam, thesis/dissertation. *Entrance requirements:* For master's and doctorate, GRE or GMAT. Additional exam requirements/recommendations for international students: Required—TOEFL (minimum score 550 paper-based; 79 iBT). *Application deadline:* For fall admission, 3/1 for international students; for spring admission, 8/1 for international students. Applications are processed on a rolling basis. Application fee: $40 ($75 for international students). Electronic applications accepted. *Expenses:* Tuition, state resident: full-time $4044; part-time $168.50 per credit hour. Tuition, nonresident: full-time $16,008; part-time $667 per credit hour. *Required fees:* $2122; $88.45 per credit hour. One-time fee: $50. Tuition and fees vary according to course load and campus/location. *Financial support:* In 2011–12, 12 research assistantships (averaging $10,710 per year), 5 teaching assistantships (averaging $24,252 per year) were awarded; career-related internships or fieldwork, Federal Work-Study, scholarships/grants, health care benefits, tuition waivers (partial), and unspecified assistantships also available. Support available to part-time students. Financial award application deadline: 3/1; financial award applicants required to submit FAFSA. *Faculty research:* Corporate risk management, derivatives banking, investments and securities issuance, corporate governance, banking. *Unit head:* Dr. John Polonchek, Head, 405-744-5199, Fax: 405-744-5180. *Application contact:* Dr. Sheryl Tucker, Dean, 405-744-6368, Fax: 405-744-0355, E-mail: grad-i@okstate.edu. Web site: http://spears.okstate.edu/finance/.

Old Dominion University, College of Business and Public Administration, Doctoral Program in Business Administration, Norfolk, VA 23529. Offers finance (PhD); information technology (PhD); marketing (PhD); strategic management (PhD). *Accreditation:* AACSB. *Faculty:* 21 full-time (2 women). *Students:* 51 full-time (17 women); includes 5 minority (3 Black or African American, non-Hispanic/Latino; 1 Asian, non-Hispanic/Latino; 1 Native Hawaiian or other Pacific Islander, non-Hispanic/Latino), 29 international. Average age 35. 47 applicants, 60% accepted, 12 enrolled. In 2011, 7 doctorates awarded. *Degree requirements:* For doctorate, comprehensive exam, thesis/dissertation. *Entrance requirements:* For doctorate, GMAT. Additional exam requirements/recommendations for international students: Required—TOEFL (minimum score 550 paper-based; 213 computer-based; 79 iBT). *Application deadline:* For fall admission, 4/1 priority date for domestic students, 4/1 for international students. Application fee: $50. Electronic applications accepted. *Expenses:* Tuition, state resident: full-time $9096; part-time $379 per credit. Tuition, nonresident: full-time $23,064; part-time $961 per credit. *Required fees:* $127 per semester. One-time fee: $50. *Financial support:* In 2011–12, 27 students received support, including 2 fellowships with full tuition reimbursements available (averaging $7,500 per year), 32 research assistantships with full tuition reimbursements available (averaging $7,500 per year), 12 teaching assistantships with full tuition reimbursements available (averaging $7,500 per year); scholarships/grants and unspecified assistantships also available. Financial award application deadline: 4/1; financial award applicants required to submit FAFSA. *Faculty research:* International business, buyer behavior, financial markets, strategy, operations research. *Unit head:* Dr. John B. Ford, Graduate Program Director, 757-683-3587, Fax: 757-683-4076, E-mail: jford@odu.edu. *Application contact:* Katrina Davenport, Program Coordinator, 757-683-5138, Fax: 757-683-4076, E-mail: kdavenpo@odu.edu. Web site: http://bpa.odu.edu/bpa/academics/baphd.shtml.

Old Dominion University, College of Business and Public Administration, MBA Program, Norfolk, VA 23529. Offers business and economic forecasting (MBA); financial analysis and valuation (MBA); information technology and enterprise integration (MBA); international business (MBA); maritime and port management (MBA); public administration (MBA). *Accreditation:* AACSB. Part-time and evening/weekend programs available. *Faculty:* 66 full-time (15 women), 6 part-time/adjunct (1 woman). *Students:* 69 full-time (21 women), 230 part-time (85 women); includes 49 minority (22 Black or African American, non-Hispanic/Latino; 1 American Indian or Alaska Native, non-Hispanic/Latino; 10 Asian, non-Hispanic/Latino; 3 Hispanic/Latino; 1 Native Hawaiian or other Pacific Islander, non-Hispanic/Latino; 12 Two or more races, non-Hispanic/Latino), 19 international. Average age 31. 177 applicants, 43% accepted, 53 enrolled. In 2011, 115 master's awarded. *Entrance requirements:* For master's, GMAT, GRE, letter of reference, resume, coursework in calculus, essay. Additional exam requirements/recommendations for international students: Required—TOEFL (minimum score 550 paper-based; 213 computer-based; 80 iBT). *Application deadline:* For fall admission, 6/1 priority date for domestic students, 4/15 for international students; for spring admission, 11/1 priority date for domestic students, 10/1 for international students. Applications are processed on a rolling basis. Application fee: $75. Electronic applications accepted. *Expenses:* Tuition, state resident: full-time $9096; part-time $379 per credit. Tuition, nonresident: full-time $23,064; part-time $961 per credit. *Required fees:* $127 per semester. One-time fee: $50. *Financial support:* In 2011–12, 44 students received support, including 90 research assistantships with partial tuition reimbursements available (averaging $8,900 per year); career-related internships or fieldwork, scholarships/grants, and unspecified assistantships also available. Support available to part-time students. Financial award application deadline: 2/15; financial award applicants required to submit FAFSA. *Faculty research:* International business, buyer behavior, financial markets, strategy, operations research, maritime and transportation economics. *Unit head:* Dr. Larry Filer, Graduate Program Director, 757-683-3585, Fax: 757-683-5750, E-mail: mbainfo@odu.edu. *Application contact:* Shanna Wood, MBA Program Manager, 757-683-3585, Fax: 757-683-5750, E-mail: mbainfo@odu.edu. Web site: http://bpa.odu.edu/mba/.

Oral Roberts University, School of Business, Tulsa, OK 74171. Offers accounting (MBA); entrepreneurship (MBA); finance (MBA); international business (MBA); management (MBA); marketing (MBA); non-profit management (MBA); not for profit management (MNM). *Accreditation:* ACBSP. Part-time programs available. Postbaccalaureate distance learning degree programs offered (minimal on-campus study). *Degree requirements:* For master's, thesis optional. *Entrance requirements:* For master's, minimum cumulative GPA of 3.0. Additional exam requirements/recommendations for international students: Required—TOEFL (minimum score 550 paper-based; 213 computer-based; 79 iBT). Electronic applications accepted. *Faculty research:* Social media, international business and marketing.

Ottawa University, Graduate Studies-Arizona, Programs in Business, Ottawa, KS 66067-3399. Offers business administration (MBA); finance (MBA); human resources (MA, MBA); leadership (MBA); marketing (MBA). Programs offered in Mesa, Phoenix, Tempe and West Valley, AZ. Part-time and evening/weekend programs available. Postbaccalaureate distance learning degree programs offered. *Degree requirements:* For master's, thesis or alternative. *Entrance requirements:* For master's, minimum undergraduate GPA of 3.0. Additional exam requirements/recommendations for international students: Required—TOEFL (minimum score 550 paper-based; 213 computer-based). Electronic applications accepted.

Our Lady of the Lake University of San Antonio, School of Business and Leadership, Program in Accounting/Finance, San Antonio, TX 78207-4689. Offers MBA. Part-time and evening/weekend programs available.

Pace University, Lubin School of Business, Financial Management Program, New York, NY 10038. Offers banking and finance (MBA); corporate financial management (MBA); financial management (MBA); investment management (MBA, MS). Part-time and evening/weekend programs available. *Students:* 92 full-time (38 women), 386 part-time (178 women); includes 67 minority (18 Black or African American, non-Hispanic/Latino; 35 Asian, non-Hispanic/Latino; 11 Hispanic/Latino; 3 Two or more races, non-Hispanic/Latino), 306 international. Average age 28. 891 applicants, 64% accepted, 154 enrolled. In 2011, 173 master's awarded. *Entrance requirements:* For master's, GMAT, GRE. Additional exam requirements/recommendations for international students: Required—TOEFL. *Application deadline:* For fall admission, 7/31 priority date for domestic students; for spring admission, 11/30 for domestic students. Applications are processed on a rolling basis. Application fee: $70. Electronic applications accepted. *Expenses: Tuition:* Part-time $990 per credit. *Required fees:* $168 per semester. Tuition and fees vary according to course load and degree level. *Financial support:* Research assistantships, career-related internships or fieldwork, Federal Work-Study, and tuition waivers (full and partial) available. Support available to part-time students. Financial award application deadline: 8/15; financial award applicants required to submit FAFSA. *Unit head:* Dr. P. V. Viswanath, Chairperson, 212-618-6518, E-mail: pviswanath@pace.edu. *Application contact:* Susan Ford-Goldschein, Director of Graduate Admissions, 212-346-1531, Fax: 212-346-1585, E-mail: gradnyc@pace.edu. Web site: http://www.pace.edu/.

Pacific States University, College of Business, Los Angeles, CA 90006. Offers accounting (MBA); finance (MBA); international business (MBA, DBA); management of information technology (MBA); real estate management (MBA). Part-time and evening/weekend programs available. Postbaccalaureate distance learning degree programs offered (no on-campus study). *Faculty:* 6 full-time (2 women), 14 part-time/adjunct (0 women). *Students:* 157 full-time (70 women); includes 13 minority (2 Black or African American, non-Hispanic/Latino; 8 Asian, non-Hispanic/Latino; 3 Native Hawaiian or other Pacific Islander, non-Hispanic/Latino), 140 international. Average age 31. 42 applicants, 83% accepted, 33 enrolled. *Degree requirements:* For doctorate, comprehensive exam, thesis/dissertation. *Entrance requirements:* For master's, minimum undergraduate GPA of 2.5 during last 90 hours of course work. Additional exam requirements/recommendations for international students: Required—TOEFL (minimum score 133 computer-based; 45 iBT), IELTS (minimum score 4.5). *Application deadline:* For fall admission, 8/15 priority date for domestic students; for winter admission, 10/15 priority date for domestic students; for spring admission, 1/15 priority date for domestic students. Applications are processed on a rolling basis. Application fee: $100. *Expenses: Tuition:* Full-time $11,040; part-time $345 per credit hour. *Required fees:* $150 per quarter. *Financial support:* Scholarships/grants available. Financial award applicants required to submit FAFSA. *Application contact:* Zolzaya Enkhbayar, Interim Registrar, 323-731-2383, Fax: 323-731-7276, E-mail: registrar@psuca.edu.

Penn State Great Valley, Graduate Studies, Management Division, Malvern, PA 19355-1488. Offers M Fin, MBA, MLD. *Accreditation:* AACSB. *Unit head:* Dr. Daniel Indro, Division Head, 610-725-5283, Fax: 610-725-5224, E-mail: dci1@psu.edu. *Application contact:* 610-648-3242, Fax: 610-889-1334. Web site: http://www.sgps.psu.edu/current/academicprograms/management/default.ashx.

Pepperdine University, Graziadio School of Business and Management, MS in Applied Finance Program, Malibu, CA 90263. Offers MS. *Students:* 72 full-time (45 women), all international. 376 applicants, 46% accepted, 47 enrolled. In 2011, 18 master's awarded. *Entrance requirements:* For master's, GMAT or GRE, two letters of recommendation. Additional exam requirements/recommendations for international students: Required—TOEFL. *Application deadline:* For fall admission, 1/10 for domestic students. Application fee: $100. *Unit head:* Dr. Linda A. Livingstone, Dean, Graziadio School of Business and Management, 310-568-5689, Fax: 310-568-5766, E-mail: linda.livingstone@pepperdine.edu. *Application contact:* Darrell Eriksen, Director of Admission and Student Accounts, Graziadio School of Business and Management, 310-568-5525, E-mail: darrell.eriksen@pepperdine.edu. Web site: http://bschool.pepperdine.edu/programs/masters-finance/.

Philadelphia University, School of Business Administration, Program in Business Administration, Philadelphia, PA 19144. Offers business administration (MBA); finance (MBA); health care management (MBA); international business (MBA); marketing (MBA); MBA/MS. Part-time and evening/weekend programs available. Postbaccalaureate distance learning degree programs offered (no on-campus study). *Entrance requirements:* For master's, GMAT. Additional exam requirements/recommendations for international students: Required—TOEFL (minimum score 550 paper-based; 213 computer-based; 79 iBT).

Polytechnic Institute of New York University, Department of Finance and Risk Engineering, Brooklyn, NY 11201-2990. Offers financial engineering (MS, Advanced Certificate), including capital markets (MS), computational finance (MS), financial technology (MS); financial technology management (Advanced Certificate); organizational behavior (Advanced Certificate); risk management (Advanced Certificate); technology management (Advanced Certificate). Part-time and evening/weekend programs available. *Faculty:* 6 full-time (2 women), 23 part-time/adjunct (5 women). *Students:* 149 full-time (49 women), 44 part-time (8 women); includes 30 minority (6 Black or African American, non-Hispanic/Latino; 22 Asian, non-Hispanic/Latino; 2 Hispanic/Latino), 135 international. Average age 27. 515 applicants, 36% accepted, 102 enrolled. In 2011, 95 degrees awarded. *Degree requirements:* For master's, comprehensive exam (for some programs), thesis (for some programs). *Entrance requirements:* For master's, GMAT, minimum B average in undergraduate course work. Additional exam requirements/recommendations for international students: Required—TOEFL (minimum score 550 paper-based; 213 computer-based; 80 iBT); Recommended—IELTS (minimum score 6.5). *Application deadline:* For fall admission, 7/31 priority date for domestic students, 4/30 for international students; for spring admission, 12/31 priority date for domestic students, 11/30 for international students. Applications are processed on a rolling basis. Application fee: $75. Electronic applications accepted. *Expenses: Tuition:* Full-time $22,464; part-time $1248 per credit. *Required fees:* $501 per semester. *Financial support:* Institutionally sponsored loans, scholarships/grants, and unspecified assistantships available. Support available to part-time students. Financial award applicants required to submit FAFSA. *Unit head:* Prof. Charles S. Tapiero, Academic Director, 718-260-3653, Fax: 718-260-3874, E-mail: ctapiero@poly.edu. *Application contact:* JeanCarlo Bonilla, Director, Graduate Enrollment Management, 718-260-3182, Fax: 718-260-3624.

Polytechnic University of Puerto Rico, Miami Campus, Graduate School, Miami, FL 33166. Offers accounting (MBA); business administration (MBA); construction management (MEM); environmental management (MEM); finance (MBA); human resources management (MBA); logistics and supply chain management (MBA); management of international enterprises (MBA); manufacturing management (MEM); marketing management (MBA); project management (MBA). Part-time and evening/weekend programs available. Postbaccalaureate distance learning degree programs offered (no on-campus study). *Entrance requirements:* For master's, minimum GPA of 3.0. Electronic applications accepted.

Polytechnic University of Puerto Rico, Orlando Campus, Graduate School, Winter Park, FL 32792. Offers accounting (MBA); business administration (MBA); construction management (MEM); engineering management (MEM); environmental management (MEM); finance (MBA); human resources management (MBA); management of international enterprises (MBA); management of technology (MBA); manufacturing management (MEM). Part-time and evening/weekend programs available. Postbaccalaureate distance learning degree programs offered (no on-campus study). *Entrance requirements:* For master's, minimum GPA of 3.0. Additional exam requirements/recommendations for international students: Recommended—TOEFL. Electronic applications accepted.

Pontifical Catholic University of Puerto Rico, College of Business Administration, Program in Finance, Ponce, PR 00717-0777. Offers MBA. Part-time and evening/weekend programs available. *Degree requirements:* For master's, thesis. *Entrance requirements:* For master's, GRE, interview, minimum GPA of 2.75.

Pontificia Universidad Catolica Madre y Maestra, Graduate School, Faculty of Social and Administrative Sciences, Santiago, Dominican Republic. Offers business administration (MBA), including business development, finance, international business, management skills (M Mgmt, MBA), marketing, operations, strategic cost management, strategy, tourist destination planning and management; law (LL M), including civil law, corporate business law, criminal law, international relations, real estate law; management (M Mgmt), including higher financial management, insurance program administration, management skills (M Mgmt, MBA); psychology (MA), including clinical child and adolescent psychology, forensic psychology; strategic human resources (EMBA).

Portland State University, Graduate Studies, School of Business Administration, Master of Science in Financial Analysis Program, Portland, OR 97207-0751. Offers MSFA. Part-time and evening/weekend programs available. *Entrance requirements:* For master's, GMAT, minimum GPA of 2.75, 2 recommendations, resume, interview. Additional exam requirements/recommendations for international students: Required—TOEFL (minimum score 550 paper-based; 213 computer-based).

Post University, Program in Business Administration, Waterbury, CT 06723-2540. Offers business administration (MBA); corporate innovation (MBA); entrepreneurship (MBA); finance (MBA); leadership (MBA); marketing (MBA). Postbaccalaureate distance learning degree programs offered.

Princeton University, Graduate School, Bendheim Center for Finance, Princeton, NJ 08544-1019. Offers M Fin. *Entrance requirements:* For master's, GRE General Test. Additional exam requirements/recommendations for international students: Required—TOEFL (minimum score 600 paper-based; 250 computer-based). Electronic applications accepted.

Providence College, School of Business, Providence, RI 02918. Offers accounting (MBA); entrepreneurship (MBA); finance (MBA); international business (MBA); management (MBA); marketing (MBA); not-for-profit organizations (MBA). Part-time and evening/weekend programs available. *Faculty:* 11 full-time (4 women), 6 part-time/adjunct (1 woman). *Students:* 52 full-time (21 women), 49 part-time (17 women); includes 8 minority (3 Black or African American, non-Hispanic/Latino; 2 Asian, non-Hispanic/Latino; 3 Two or more races, non-Hispanic/Latino), 6 international. Average age 26. 49 applicants, 80% accepted, 25 enrolled. In 2011, 57 master's awarded. *Degree requirements:* For master's, thesis optional. *Entrance requirements:* For master's, GMAT. Additional exam requirements/recommendations for international students: Required—TOEFL (minimum score 550 paper-based; 213 computer-based; 80 iBT). *Application deadline:* For fall admission, 8/1 priority date for domestic students, 8/1 for international students; for spring admission, 12/1 priority date for domestic students, 12/1 for international students. Applications are processed on a rolling basis. Application fee: $55. *Expenses:* Contact institution. *Financial support:* In 2011–12, 34 research assistantships with full tuition reimbursements (averaging $8,400 per year) were awarded; Federal Work-Study, institutionally sponsored loans, and unspecified assistantships also available. Support available to part-time students. Financial award application deadline: 8/1; financial award applicants required to submit FAFSA. *Unit head:* Dr. Catherine L. Pastille, Director, MBA Program, 401-865-1654, Fax: 401-865-2978, E-mail: cpastill@providence.edu. *Application contact:* Katherine A. Follett, Administrative Coordinator, 401-865-2333, Fax: 401-865-2978, E-mail: kfollett@providence.edu. Web site: http://www.providence.edu/business/Pages/default.aspx.

Purdue University, Graduate School, Krannert School of Management, Master of Science in Finance Program, West Lafayette, IN 47907. Offers MSF. *Faculty:* 81 full-time (19 women), 2 part-time/adjunct (0 women). *Students:* 27 full-time (14 women);

includes 6 minority (5 Asian, non-Hispanic/Latino; 1 Hispanic/Latino), 18 international. Average age 26. 717 applicants, 8% accepted, 27 enrolled. In 2011, 30 master's awarded. *Entrance requirements:* For master's, GMAT or GRE, minimum GPA of 3.0, four-year baccalaureate degree, essays, letters of recommendation. Additional exam requirements/recommendations for international students: Required—TOEFL (minimum score 550 paper-based; 213 computer-based; 77 iBT). *Application deadline:* For fall admission, 11/1 priority date for domestic students, 11/1 for international students; for winter admission, 1/15 for domestic and international students; for spring admission, 3/1 for domestic students. Applications are processed on a rolling basis. Application fee: $60 ($75 for international students). Electronic applications accepted. *Expenses:* Contact institution. *Financial support:* Application deadline: 3/1; applicants required to submit FAFSA. *Unit head:* Dr. P. Christopher Earley, Dean/Professor of Management, 765-494-4366. *Application contact:* Brian Precious, Director of Admissions, Marketing, Recruiting and Entrepreneurial Outreach, 765-494-0773, Fax: 765-494-9841, E-mail: krannertmasters@purdue.edu. Web site: http://www.krannert.purdue.edu/programs/masters/Degree_Programs/Full_Time/MSF/home.asp.

Queen's University at Kingston, Queens School of Business, Program in Business Administration, Kingston, ON K7L 3N6, Canada. Offers consulting and project management (MBA); finance (MBA); innovation and entrepreneurship (MBA); marketing (MBA). *Accreditation:* AACSB. *Degree requirements:* For master's, thesis optional, research project. *Entrance requirements:* For master's, GMAT, minimum B+ average. Additional exam requirements/recommendations for international students: Required—TOEFL. Electronic applications accepted. *Faculty research:* Management fundamentals, strategic thinking, global business, innovation and change, leadership.

Quinnipiac University, School of Business, Program in Business Administration, Hamden, CT 06518-1940. Offers chartered financial analyst (MBA); finance (MBA); healthcare management (MBA); information systems management (MBA); marketing (MBA); supply chain management (MBA); JD/MBA. *Accreditation:* AACSB. Part-time and evening/weekend programs available. Postbaccalaureate distance learning degree programs offered (no on-campus study). *Faculty:* 19 full-time (4 women), 2 part-time/adjunct (1 woman). *Students:* 89 full-time (36 women), 129 part-time (50 women); includes 16 minority (5 Black or African American, non-Hispanic/Latino; 5 Asian, non-Hispanic/Latino; 6 Hispanic/Latino), 19 international. Average age 29. 206 applicants, 81% accepted, 139 enrolled. In 2011, 95 master's awarded. *Entrance requirements:* For master's, GMAT or GRE, minimum GPA of 3.0. Additional exam requirements/recommendations for international students: Required—TOEFL (minimum score 575 paper-based; 233 computer-based; 90 iBT), IELTS (minimum score 6.5). *Application deadline:* For fall admission, 7/30 priority date for domestic students, 4/30 for international students; for spring admission, 12/15 priority date for domestic students, 9/15 for international students. Applications are processed on a rolling basis. Application fee: $45. Electronic applications accepted. *Expenses: Tuition:* Part-time $855 per credit. *Required fees:* $35 per credit. *Financial support:* In 2011–12, 23 students received support. Career-related internships or fieldwork, Federal Work-Study, scholarships/grants, tuition waivers (partial), and unspecified assistantships available. Support available to part-time students. Financial award application deadline: 4/15; financial award applicants required to submit FAFSA. *Faculty research:* Financial markets and investments, international business, supply chain management, health care management, corporate governance. *Unit head:* Lisa Braiewa, MBA Program Director, 203-582-3710, Fax: 203-582-8664, E-mail: lisa.braiewa@quinnipiac.edu. *Application contact:* Katie Ludovico, 800-462-1944, Fax: 203-582-3443, E-mail: katie.ludovico@quinnipiac.edu. Web site: http://www.quinnipiac.edu/mba.

Regent's American College London, Webster Graduate School, London, United Kingdom. Offers business (MBA); finance (MS); human resources (MA); information technology management (MA); international business (MA); international non-governmental organizations (MA); international relations (MA); management and leadership (MA); marketing (MA). Part-time programs available.

Regis University, College for Professional Studies, School of Management, Denver, CO 80221-1099. Offers accounting (MS, Certificate); executive international management (Certificate); executive leadership (Certificate); executive project management (Certificate); finance and accounting (MBA); general business administration (MBA); health care management (MBA); human resource management and leadership (MSOL); information technology leadership and management (MSOL); international business (MBA); marketing (MBA); operations management (MBA); organizational leadership and management (MSOL); project leadership and management (MSOL); project management (Certificate); strategic business management (Certificate); strategic human resource management (Certificate); strategic management (MBA). Offered at Colorado Springs Campus, Northwest Denver Campus, Southeast Denver Campus, Fort Collins Campus, Broomfield Campus, Henderson (Nevada) Campus, and Summerlin (Nevada) Campus and online. Part-time and evening/weekend programs available. Postbaccalaureate distance learning degree programs offered (no on-campus study). *Degree requirements:* For master's, thesis optional, capstone project. *Entrance requirements:* For master's, GMAT or essays, interview, 2 years of full-time business work experience, resume; for Certificate, GMAT. Additional exam requirements/recommendations for international students: Required—TOEFL, TWE (minimum score 5) or university-based test. Electronic applications accepted. *Faculty research:* Impact of information technology on small business regulation of accounting, international project financing, mineral development, delivery of healthcare to rural indigenous communities.

Rhode Island College, School of Graduate Studies, School of Management, Department of Accounting and Computer Information Systems, Providence, RI 02908-1991. Offers accounting (MP Ac); financial planning (CGS). Part-time and evening/weekend programs available. *Faculty:* 1 (woman) full-time, 1 (woman) part-time/adjunct. *Students:* 4 full-time (2 women), 17 part-time (12 women); includes 1 minority (Black or African American, non-Hispanic/Latino). Average age 29. In 2011, 4 master's awarded. *Entrance requirements:* For master's, GMAT (unless applicant is a CPA or has passed a state bar exam); for CGS, GMAT, bachelor's degree from an accredited college or university, official transcripts of all undergraduate and graduate records. Additional exam requirements/recommendations for international students: Recommended—TOEFL (minimum score 550 paper-based; 213 computer-based; 79 iBT). *Application deadline:* For fall admission, 3/1 for domestic students. Applications are processed on a rolling basis. Application fee: $50. *Expenses:* Tuition, state resident: full-time $8592; part-time $358 per credit hour. Tuition, nonresident: full-time $16,800; part-time $700 per credit hour. *Required fees:* $602; $22 per credit. $72 per term. *Financial support:* Federal Work-Study, scholarships/grants, and health care benefits available. Support available to part-time students. Financial award application deadline: 5/15; financial award applicants required to submit FAFSA. *Unit head:* Prof. Jane Przybyla, Chair, 401-456-8036. *Application contact:* Graduate Studies, 401-456-8700. Web site: http://www.ric.edu/accountingComputerInformationSystems/.

Robert Morris University Illinois, Morris Graduate School of Management, Chicago, IL 60605. Offers accounting (MBA); accounting/finance (MBA); design and media (MM); health care administration (MM); higher education administration (MM); human resource management (MBA); information systems (MIS); law enforcement administration (MM); management (MBA); management/finance (MIS); management/human resource management (MBA); sports administration (MM). Part-time and evening/weekend programs available. *Faculty:* 7 full-time (1 woman), 21 part-time/adjunct (5 women). *Students:* 296 full-time (172 women), 216 part-time (136 women); includes 273 minority (160 Black or African American, non-Hispanic/Latino; 1 American Indian or Alaska Native, non-Hispanic/Latino; 32 Asian, non-Hispanic/Latino; 78 Hispanic/Latino; 2 Two or more races, non-Hispanic/Latino), 28 international. Average age 32. 247 applicants, 69% accepted, 152 enrolled. In 2011, 244 master's awarded. *Entrance requirements:* Additional exam requirements/recommendations for international students: Required—TOEFL (minimum score 550 paper-based; 173 computer-based). *Application deadline:* Applications are processed on a rolling basis. Application fee: $20 ($100 for international students). Electronic applications accepted. *Expenses: Tuition:* Full-time $13,800; part-time $2300 per course. *Financial support:* In 2011–12, 643 students received support. Federal Work-Study, scholarships/grants, tuition waivers, and leadership and athletic scholarships available. Support available to part-time students. Financial award applicants required to submit FAFSA. *Unit head:* Kayed Akkawi, Dean, 312-935-6025, Fax: 312-935-6020, E-mail: kakkawi@robertmorris.edu. *Application contact:* Fernando Villeda, Dean of Morris Graduate School of Management, 312-935-6050, Fax: 312-935-6020, E-mail: fvilleda@robertmorris.edu.

Rochester Institute of Technology, Graduate Enrollment Services, E. Philip Saunders College of Business, Program in Finance, Rochester, NY 14623-5603. Offers MS. Part-time and evening/weekend programs available. *Students:* 34 full-time (16 women), 4 part-time (0 women); includes 1 minority (Black or African American, non-Hispanic/Latino), 31 international. Average age 25. 191 applicants, 37% accepted, 22 enrolled. In 2011, 26 degrees awarded. *Degree requirements:* For master's, comprehensive exam (for some programs), thesis (for some programs). *Entrance requirements:* For master's, GMAT, minimum GPA of 2.5. Additional exam requirements/recommendations for international students: Required—TOEFL (minimum score 580 paper-based; 237 computer-based; 92 iBT) or IELTS (minimum score 7). *Application deadline:* For fall admission, 2/15 priority date for domestic students, 2/15 for international students; for winter admission, 11/1 priority date for domestic students; for spring admission, 2/1 priority date for domestic students. Applications are processed on a rolling basis. Application fee: $50. Electronic applications accepted. *Expenses: Tuition:* Full-time $34,659; part-time $963 per credit hour. *Required fees:* $228; $76 per quarter. *Financial support:* Research assistantships with partial tuition reimbursements, teaching assistantships with partial tuition reimbursements, career-related internships or fieldwork, scholarships/grants, and unspecified assistantships available. Support available to part-time students. Financial award applicants required to submit FAFSA. *Faculty research:* Formation and taxation of business entities, modeling demand, production and cost functions in computerized business and economic simulations, economic games and educational software. *Unit head:* Melissa Ellison, Graduate Program Director, 585-475-2354, E-mail: maescb@rit.edu. *Application contact:* Diane Ellison, Assistant Vice President, Graduate Enrollment Services, 585-475-2229, Fax: 585-475-7164, E-mail: gradinfo@rit.edu. Web site: http://saunders.rit.edu/graduate/index.php.

Rollins College, Crummer Graduate School of Business, Winter Park, FL 32789-4499. Offers entrepreneurship (MBA); finance (MBA); international business (MBA); management (MBA); marketing (MBA); operations and technology management (MBA). *Accreditation:* AACSB. Part-time and evening/weekend programs available. Postbaccalaureate distance learning degree programs offered (minimal on-campus study). *Faculty:* 23 full-time (3 women), 6 part-time/adjunct (4 women). *Students:* 257 full-time (95 women), 121 part-time (39 women); includes 75 minority (12 Black or African American, non-Hispanic/Latino; 1 American Indian or Alaska Native, non-Hispanic/Latino; 20 Asian, non-Hispanic/Latino; 39 Hispanic/Latino; 3 Two or more races, non-Hispanic/Latino), 27 international. Average age 28. 363 applicants, 44% accepted, 100 enrolled. In 2011, 213 master's awarded. *Degree requirements:* For master's, minimum GPA of 2.85. *Entrance requirements:* For master's, GMAT or GRE, official transcripts, two letters of recommendation, essay, current resume/curriculum vitae, interview. Additional exam requirements/recommendations for international students: Required—TOEFL (minimum score 100 iBT) or IELTS (minimum score 7). *Application deadline:* Applications are processed on a rolling basis. Application fee: $50. Electronic applications accepted. *Expenses:* Contact institution. *Financial support:* In 2011–12, 258 students received support. Federal Work-Study and scholarships/grants available. Support available to part-time students. Financial award applicants required to submit FAFSA. *Faculty research:* Sustainability, world financial markets, international business, market research, strategic marketing. *Unit head:* Dr. Craig M. McAllaster, Dean, 407-646-2249, Fax: 407-646-1550, E-mail: cmcallaster@rollins.edu. *Application contact:* Eva Gauthier Oleksiw, Admissions Coordinator, 407-646-2405, Fax: 407-646-1550, E-mail: mbaadmissions@rollins.edu. Web site: http://www.rollins.edu/mba/.

Rowan University, Graduate School, William G. Rohrer College of Business, Department of Accounting and Finance, Program in Finance, Glassboro, NJ 08028-1701. Offers MBA. Part-time and evening/weekend programs available. *Degree requirements:* For master's, comprehensive exam, thesis. *Entrance requirements:* For master's, GRE General Test. Additional exam requirements/recommendations for international students: Required—TOEFL. Electronic applications accepted.

Rutgers, The State University of New Jersey, Newark, Graduate School, Program in Management, Newark, NJ 07102. Offers accounting (PhD); accounting information systems (PhD); computer information systems (PhD); finance (PhD); information technology (PhD); international business (PhD); management science (PhD); marketing (PhD); organization management (PhD). Program offered jointly with New Jersey Institute of Technology. *Accreditation:* AACSB. *Degree requirements:* For doctorate, thesis/dissertation, cumulative exams. *Entrance requirements:* For doctorate, GMAT or GRE General Test, minimum undergraduate B average. Additional exam requirements/recommendations for international students: Required—TOEFL. Electronic applications accepted. *Faculty research:* Technology management, leadership and teams, consumer behavior, financial and markets, logistics.

Rutgers, The State University of New Jersey, Newark, Rutgers Business School–Newark and New Brunswick, Doctoral Programs in Management, Newark, NJ 07102. Offers accounting (PhD); accounting information systems (PhD); economics (PhD); finance (PhD); individualized study (PhD); information technology (PhD); international business (PhD); management science (PhD); marketing science (PhD); organizational management (PhD); science, technology and management (PhD); supply chain management (PhD). *Degree requirements:* For doctorate, comprehensive exam, thesis/dissertation. *Entrance requirements:* For doctorate, GRE or GMAT. Additional exam requirements/recommendations for international students: Required—TOEFL (minimum score 550 paper-based; 213 computer-based; 79 iBT). Electronic applications accepted.

Sacred Heart University, Graduate Programs, John F. Welch College of Business, Fairfield, CT 06825-1000. Offers accounting (MBA); finance (MBA); management (MBA); marketing (MBA). *Accreditation:* AACSB. Part-time and evening/weekend programs available. Postbaccalaureate distance learning degree programs offered. *Degree requirements:* For master's, thesis or alternative. *Entrance requirements:* For master's, GMAT (preferred) or GRE General Test. Additional exam requirements/recommendations for international students: Required—TOEFL (minimum score 550 paper-based; 213 computer-based; 75 iBT). Electronic applications accepted.

Expenses: Contact institution. *Faculty research:* Management of organizations, international business management of technology.

Sage Graduate School, School of Management, Program in Business Administration, Troy, NY 12180-4115. Offers business strategy (MBA); finance (MBA); human resources (MBA); marketing (MBA); JD/MBA. Part-time and evening/weekend programs available. *Faculty:* 2 full-time (both women), 8 part-time/adjunct (1 woman). *Students:* 20 full-time (10 women), 55 part-time (36 women); includes 10 minority (2 Black or African American, non-Hispanic/Latino; 4 Asian, non-Hispanic/Latino; 3 Hispanic/Latino; 1 Two or more races, non-Hispanic/Latino), 1 international. Average age 31. 51 applicants, 55% accepted, 19 enrolled. In 2011, 10 degrees awarded. *Entrance requirements:* For master's, minimum GPA of 2.75, resume, 2 letters of recommendation. Additional exam requirements/recommendations for international students: Required—TOEFL (minimum score 550 paper-based; 213 computer-based). *Application deadline:* Applications are processed on a rolling basis. Application fee: $40. *Expenses: Tuition:* Full-time $11,880; part-time $660 per credit hour. Tuition and fees vary according to program. *Financial support:* Fellowships, research assistantships, Federal Work-Study, scholarships/ grants, and unspecified assistantships available. Support available to part-time students. Financial award application deadline: 3/1; financial award applicants required to submit FAFSA. *Unit head:* Dr. Daniel Robeson, Dean, School of Management, 518-292-8637, Fax: 518-292-1964, E-mail: robesd@sage.edu. *Application contact:* Wendy D. Diefendorf, Director of Graduate and Adult Admission, 518-244-2443, Fax: 518-244-6880, E-mail: diefew@sage.edu.

St. Edward's University, School of Management and Business, Area of Business Administration, Austin, TX 78704. Offers accounting (MBA); business management (MBA); finance (Certificate); global entrepreneurship (MBA); marketing (MBA, Certificate). Part-time and evening/weekend programs available. *Students:* 35 full-time (14 women), 218 part-time (114 women); includes 102 minority (22 Black or African American, non-Hispanic/Latino; 1 American Indian or Alaska Native, non-Hispanic/ Latino; 11 Asian, non-Hispanic/Latino; 62 Hispanic/Latino; 1 Native Hawaiian or other Pacific Islander, non-Hispanic/Latino; 5 Two or more races, non-Hispanic/Latino), 14 international. Average age 32. 94 applicants, 71% accepted, 48 enrolled. In 2011, 104 master's awarded. *Degree requirements:* For master's, minimum of 24 resident hours. *Entrance requirements:* For master's, GMAT or GRE General Test, minimum GPA of 2.75 in last 60 hours of course work. Additional exam requirements/recommendations for international students: Required—TOEFL (minimum score 550 paper-based; 213 computer-based; 79 iBT) or IELTS (minimum score 6). *Application deadline:* For fall admission, 7/1 for domestic and international students; for spring admission, 11/1 for domestic and international students. Applications are processed on a rolling basis. Application fee: $45 ($50 for international students). Electronic applications accepted. *Expenses: Tuition:* Full-time $17,550; part-time $975 per credit hour. *Required fees:* $50 per trimester. Full-time tuition and fees vary according to course load and program. *Unit head:* Dr. Stan Horner, Director, 512-428-1279, Fax: 512-448-8492, E-mail: stanleyh@stedwards.edu. *Application contact:* Sarah Hennes, Graduate Admissions Coordinator, 512-448-8600, Fax: 512-428-1032, E-mail: sarahhe@stedwards.edu. Web site: http://www.stedwards.edu.

St. John's University, The Peter J. Tobin College of Business, Department of Economics and Finance, Program in Finance, Queens, NY 11439. Offers finance (MBA, Adv C); investment management (MS). Part-time and evening/weekend programs available. *Students:* 92 full-time (42 women), 73 part-time (29 women); includes 38 minority (11 Black or African American, non-Hispanic/Latino; 1 American Indian or Alaska Native, non-Hispanic/Latino; 15 Asian, non-Hispanic/Latino; 9 Hispanic/Latino; 2 Two or more races, non-Hispanic/Latino), 72 international. Average age 27. 126 applicants, 72% accepted, 41 enrolled. In 2011, 77 master's awarded. *Degree requirements:* For master's, comprehensive exam (for some programs), thesis optional. *Entrance requirements:* For master's, GMAT, 2 letters of recommendation, resume, transcripts, essay; for Adv C, GMAT, 2 letters of recommendation, resume, undergraduate and graduate transcripts, essay, MBA. Additional exam requirements/ recommendations for international students: Required—TOEFL (minimum score 600 paper-based; 250 computer-based; 100 iBT), IELTS (minimum score 7). *Application deadline:* For fall admission, 5/1 priority date for domestic students, 5/1 for international students; for spring admission, 11/1 priority date for domestic students, 11/1 for international students. Applications are processed on a rolling basis. Application fee: $50. Electronic applications accepted. *Expenses:* Contact institution. *Financial support:* Research assistantships, scholarships/grants, and unspecified assistantships available. Support available to part-time students. Financial award application deadline: 3/1; financial award applicants required to submit FAFSA. *Unit head:* Dr. Vipul K. Bansal, Chair, 718-990-6419, E-mail: bansalv@stjohns.edu. *Application contact:* Carol J. Swanberg, Assistant Dean/Director of Graduate Admissions, 718-990-1345, Fax: 718-990-5242, E-mail: tobingradnyc@stjohns.edu.

Saint Joseph's University, Erivan K. Haub School of Business, MS in Financial Services Program, Philadelphia, PA 19131-1395. Offers MS. Part-time and evening/ weekend programs available. Postbaccalaureate distance learning degree programs offered (no on-campus study). *Students:* 51 full-time (25 women), 50 part-time (18 women); includes 5 minority (2 Black or African American, non-Hispanic/Latino; 2 Asian, non-Hispanic/Latino; 1 Hispanic/Latino), 51 international. Average age 28. In 2011, 32 master's awarded. *Entrance requirements:* For master's, GMAT or GRE, 2 letters of recommendation, resume, personal statement. Additional exam requirements/ recommendations for international students: Required—TOEFL (minimum score 550 paper-based; 213 computer-based; 80 iBT), IELTS (minimum score 6.5), or Pearson Test of English (minimum score 60). *Application deadline:* For fall admission, 7/15 priority date for domestic students, 5/15 for international students; for spring admission, 11/15 priority date for domestic students, 10/15 for international students. Applications are processed on a rolling basis. Application fee: $35. Electronic applications accepted. *Expenses: Tuition:* Part-time $735 per credit hour. Tuition and fees vary according to degree level and program. *Financial support:* Research assistantships, scholarships/ grants, and unspecified assistantships available. Financial award applicants required to submit FAFSA. *Unit head:* David Benglian, Director, 610-660-1626, Fax: 610-660-1599, E-mail: david.benglian@sju.edu. *Application contact:* Karena Whitmore, Administrative Assistant, MS Programs, 610-660-3211, Fax: 610-660-1599, E-mail: kwhitmor@sju.edu. Web site: http://www.sju.edu/hsb/fsp.

Saint Joseph's University, Erivan K. Haub School of Business, Professional MBA Program, Philadelphia, PA 19131-1395. Offers accounting (MBA); finance (MBA), including finance; general business (MBA); health and medical services administration (MBA); human resource management (MBA); international business (MBA); international marketing (MBA); management (MBA); marketing (MBA); DO/MBA. DO/ MBA offered jointly with Philadelphia College of Osteopathic Medicine. Part-time and evening/weekend programs available. Postbaccalaureate distance learning degree programs offered (no on-campus study). *Students:* 98 full-time (42 women), 528 part-time (208 women); includes 102 minority (47 Black or African American, non-Hispanic/ Latino; 1 American Indian or Alaska Native, non-Hispanic/Latino; 28 Asian, non-Hispanic/Latino; 20 Hispanic/Latino; 1 Native Hawaiian or other Pacific Islander, non-Hispanic/Latino; 5 Two or more races, non-Hispanic/Latino), 45 international. Average age 31. In 2011, 290 master's awarded. *Entrance requirements:* For master's, GMAT or GRE, 2 letters of recommendation, resume, personal statement. Additional exam requirements/recommendations for international students: Required—TOEFL (minimum score 550 paper-based; 213 computer-based; 80 iBT), IELTS (minimum score 6.5), or Pearson Test of English (minimum score 60). *Application deadline:* For fall admission, 7/ 15 priority date for domestic students, 4/15 for international students; for spring admission, 11/15 priority date for domestic students, 10/15 for international students. Applications are processed on a rolling basis. Application fee: $35. Electronic applications accepted. *Expenses: Tuition:* Part-time $735 per credit hour. Tuition and fees vary according to degree level and program. *Financial support:* Scholarships/ grants and unspecified assistantships available. Financial award application deadline: 5/ 1; financial award applicants required to submit FAFSA. *Unit head:* Adele C. Foley, Associate Dean/Director, Graduate Business Programs, 610-660-1691, Fax: 610-660-1599, E-mail: afoley@sju.edu. *Application contact:* Dr. Janine N. Guerra, Associate Director, Professional MBA Program, 610-660-1695, Fax: 610-660-1599, E-mail: jguerra@sju.edu. Web site: http://www.sju.edu/mba.

Saint Louis University, Graduate Education, John Cook School of Business, Department of Finance, St. Louis, MO 63103-2097. Offers MBA, MSF. Part-time and evening/weekend programs available. *Degree requirements:* For master's, thesis. *Entrance requirements:* For master's, GMAT or GRE General Test, letters of recommendation, resume. Additional exam requirements/recommendations for international students: Required—TOEFL (minimum score 570 paper-based; 230 computer-based; 88 iBT). Electronic applications accepted. *Expenses:* Contact institution. *Faculty research:* Market microstructure, corporate governance, banking, portfolio performance and asset allocation.

Saint Mary's College of California, Graduate Business Programs, MS in Financial Analysis and Investment Management Program, Moraga, CA 94556. Offers MS. *Students:* 26 full-time (10 women), 1 part-time; includes 14 minority (1 Black or African American, non-Hispanic/Latino; 11 Asian, non-Hispanic/Latino; 2 Hispanic/Latino), 1 international. Average age 31. In 2011, 27 master's awarded. Tuition and fees vary according to course load, degree level and program. *Unit head:* Dr. Guido Krickx, Associate Dean/Director, 925-631-4514, Fax: 925-376-6521, E-mail: gakl@stmarys-ca.edu. *Application contact:* Bob Peterson, Director of Admissions, 925-631-4505, Fax: 925-376-6521, E-mail: bpeterso@stmarys-ca.edu. Web site: http://www.stmarys-ca.edu/ms-in-financial-analysis-and-investment-management-ms-faim.

St. Mary's University, Graduate School, Bill Greehey School of Business, MBA Program, San Antonio, TX 78228-8507. Offers finance (MBA); international business (MBA); management (MBA). Part-time and evening/weekend programs available. Postbaccalaureate distance learning degree programs offered (minimal on-campus study). *Degree requirements:* For master's, comprehensive exam. *Entrance requirements:* For master's, GMAT. Additional exam requirements/recommendations for international students: Required—TOEFL (minimum score 570 paper-based; 230 computer-based; 80 iBT).

Saint Peter's University, Graduate Business Programs, MBA Program, Jersey City, NJ 07306-5997. Offers finance (MBA); health care administration (MBA); human resource management (MBA); international business (MBA); management (MBA); management information systems (MBA); marketing (MBA); risk management (MBA); MBA/MS. Part-time and evening/weekend programs available. *Entrance requirements:* Additional exam requirements/recommendations for international students: Required—TOEFL (minimum score 79 computer-based). Electronic applications accepted. *Faculty research:* Finance, health care management, human resource management, international business, management, management information systems, marketing, risk management.

St. Thomas Aquinas College, Division of Business Administration, Sparkill, NY 10976. Offers business administration (MBA); finance (MBA); management (MBA); marketing (MBA). Part-time and evening/weekend programs available. *Entrance requirements:* For master's, GMAT. Additional exam requirements/recommendations for international students: Required—TOEFL. Electronic applications accepted.

Saint Xavier University, Graduate Studies, Graham School of Management, Chicago, IL 60655-3105. Offers employee health benefits (Certificate); finance (MBA); financial fraud examination and management (MBA, Certificate); financial planning (MBA, Certificate); generalist/individualized (MBA); health administration (MBA); managed care (Certificate); management (MBA); marketing (MBA); project management (MBA, Certificate); MBA/MS. *Accreditation:* ACBSP. Part-time and evening/weekend programs available. *Entrance requirements:* For master's, GMAT, minimum GPA of 3.0, 2 years of work experience. *Application deadline:* For fall admission, 8/15 for domestic students. Applications are processed on a rolling basis. Application fee: $35. Electronic applications accepted. *Expenses:* Contact institution. *Financial support:* Career-related internships or fieldwork available. Support available to part-time students. Financial award applicants required to submit FAFSA. *Unit head:* Dr. John E. Eber, Dean, 773-298-3601, Fax: 773-298-3601, E-mail: eber@sxu.edu. *Application contact:* Beth Gierach, Managing Director of Admission, 773-298-3053, Fax: 773-298-3076, E-mail: gierach@sxu.edu. Web site: http://www.sxu.edu/academics/colleges_schools/gsm/.

Sam Houston State University, College of Business Administration, Department of General Business and Finance, Huntsville, TX 77341. Offers banking and financial institutions (EMBA); business administration (MBA, MS); project management (MS). *Faculty:* 14 full-time (3 women). *Students:* 85 full-time (36 women), 233 part-time (103 women); includes 82 minority (31 Black or African American, non-Hispanic/Latino; 3 American Indian or Alaska Native, non-Hispanic/Latino; 11 Asian, non-Hispanic/Latino; 37 Hispanic/Latino), 11 international. Average age 31. 300 applicants, 52% accepted, 135 enrolled. In 2011, 74 master's awarded. *Entrance requirements:* For master's, GMAT. Additional exam requirements/recommendations for international students: Required—TOEFL (minimum score 550 paper-based; 213 computer-based; 79 iBT). *Application deadline:* For fall admission, 8/1 for domestic students, 6/25 for international students; for spring admission, 12/1 for domestic students, 11/12 for international students. Applications are processed on a rolling basis. Application fee: $45 ($75 for international students). Electronic applications accepted. *Expenses:* Tuition, state resident: full-time $4420; part-time $221 per credit hour. Tuition, nonresident: full-time $10,680; part-time $534 per credit hour. *Required fees:* $329 per credit hour. *Financial support:* Application deadline: 5/31; applicants required to submit FAFSA. *Unit head:* Dr. Kurt Jesswein, Chair, 936-294-4582, E-mail: kurt.jesswein@shsu.edu. *Application contact:* Dr. Leroy Ashorn, Advisor, 936-294-4040, Fax: 936-294-3612, E-mail: busgrad@shsu.edu. Web site: http://www.shsu.edu/~gba_www/.

San Diego State University, Graduate and Research Affairs, College of Business Administration, Department of Finance, San Diego, CA 92182. Offers MS. Part-time and evening/weekend programs available. *Degree requirements:* For master's, thesis or alternative. *Entrance requirements:* For master's, GMAT, resume, letters of reference. Additional exam requirements/recommendations for international students: Required—TOEFL. Electronic applications accepted.

Santa Clara University, Leavey School of Business, Program in Business Administration, Santa Clara, CA 95053. Offers accounting (MBA); entrepreneurship (MBA); executive business administration (EMBA); finance (MBA); food and agribusiness (MBA); international business (MBA); leading people and organizations

(MBA); managing technology and innovation (MBA); marketing management (MBA); supply chain management (MBA). *Accreditation:* AACSB. Part-time and evening/weekend programs available. *Students:* 196 full-time (80 women), 669 part-time (224 women); includes 302 minority (12 Black or African American, non-Hispanic/Latino; 246 Asian, non-Hispanic/Latino; 35 Hispanic/Latino; 6 Native Hawaiian or other Pacific Islander, non-Hispanic/Latino; 3 Two or more races, non-Hispanic/Latino), 186 international. Average age 32. 365 applicants, 74% accepted, 199 enrolled. In 2011, 366 degrees awarded. *Degree requirements:* For master's, thesis or alternative. *Entrance requirements:* For master's, GMAT, GRE. Additional exam requirements/recommendations for international students: Required—TOEFL (minimum score 600 paper-based; 250 computer-based; 100 iBT). *Application deadline:* For fall admission, 6/1 for domestic and international students; for spring admission, 1/19 for domestic students, 1/17 for international students. Applications are processed on a rolling basis. Application fee: $75 ($100 for international students). Electronic applications accepted. *Expenses:* Contact institution. *Financial support:* In 2011–12, 350 students received support. Fellowships with partial tuition reimbursements available, research assistantships with partial tuition reimbursements available, career-related internships or fieldwork, Federal Work-Study, institutionally sponsored loans, scholarships/grants, health care benefits, and unspecified assistantships available. Support available to part-time students. Financial award application deadline: 6/1; financial award applicants required to submit FAFSA. *Unit head:* Elizabeth B. Ford, Senior Assistant Dean, 408-554-2752, Fax: 408-554-4571, E-mail: eford@scu.edu. *Application contact:* Tammy Fox, Assistant Director, Graduate Business Admissions, 408-554-7858, E-mail: tkfox@scu.edu.

Schiller International University, MBA Programs, Florida, Largo, FL 33770. Offers financial planning (MBA); information technology (MBA); international business (MBA); international hotel and tourism management (MBA). Part-time and evening/weekend programs available. Postbaccalaureate distance learning degree programs offered (no on-campus study). *Degree requirements:* For master's, thesis optional. *Entrance requirements:* Additional exam requirements/recommendations for international students: Required—TOEFL (minimum score 550 paper-based; 213 computer-based).

Seattle University, Albers School of Business and Economics, Master of Science in Finance Program, Seattle, WA 98122-1090. Offers MSF, Certificate, JD/MSF. Part-time and evening/weekend programs available. *Faculty:* 22 full-time (8 women), 1 (woman) part-time/adjunct. *Students:* 16 full-time (6 women), 50 part-time (14 women); includes 16 minority (3 Black or African American, non-Hispanic/Latino; 8 Asian, non-Hispanic/Latino; 3 Hispanic/Latino; 1 Native Hawaiian or other Pacific Islander, non-Hispanic/Latino; 1 Two or more races, non-Hispanic/Latino), 10 international. Average age 31. 48 applicants, 29% accepted, 9 enrolled. In 2011, 19 master's awarded. *Entrance requirements:* For master's, GMAT, minimum GPA of 3.0, 2 years of related work experience. Additional exam requirements/recommendations for international students: Required—TOEFL (minimum score 580 paper-based; 92 iBT). *Application deadline:* For fall admission, 8/20 priority date for domestic students, 4/1 for international students; for winter admission, 11/20 priority date for domestic students, 9/1 for international students; for spring admission, 2/20 priority date for domestic students, 12/1 for international students. Applications are processed on a rolling basis. Application fee: $55. Electronic applications accepted. *Financial support:* Career-related internships or fieldwork and Federal Work-Study available. Support available to part-time students. Financial award applicants required to submit FAFSA. *Unit head:* Dr. Fiona Robertson, Chair, 206-296-5791, Fax: 206-296-5795, E-mail: robertsf@seattleu.edu. *Application contact:* Janet Shandley, Director of Graduate Admissions, 206-296-5900, Fax: 206-298-5656, E-mail: grad_admissions@seattleu.edu.

Seton Hall University, Stillman School of Business, Programs in Business Administration, South Orange, NJ 07079-2697. Offers accounting (MBA); finance (MBA); information technology management (MBA); international business (MBA); management (MBA); marketing (MBA); sport management (MBA); supply chain management (MBA). Part-time and evening/weekend programs available. *Faculty:* 37 full-time (9 women), 19 part-time/adjunct (1 woman). *Students:* 166 full-time (65 women), 284 part-time (131 women); includes 113 minority (21 Black or African American, non-Hispanic/Latino; 81 Asian, non-Hispanic/Latino; 9 Hispanic/Latino; 2 Native Hawaiian or other Pacific Islander, non-Hispanic/Latino). Average age 29. 459 applicants, 59% accepted, 208 enrolled. In 2011, 210 master's awarded. *Degree requirements:* For master's, 20 hours of community service (Social Responsibility Project). *Entrance requirements:* For master's, GMAT, GRE or CPA, advanced degree from AACSB institution, MS in a business discipline, professional degree (MD, JD, PhD, DVM, DDS, etc.), minimum undergraduate GPA of 3.0. Additional exam requirements/recommendations for international students: Required—TOEFL (minimum score 102 iBT), IELTS or Pearson Test of English. *Application deadline:* For fall admission, 5/31 priority date for domestic students, 3/31 for international students; for spring admission, 10/31 priority date for domestic students, 9/30 for international students. Applications are processed on a rolling basis. Application fee: $75. Electronic applications accepted. *Expenses: Tuition:* Part-time $1033 per credit hour. *Required fees:* $85 per semester. *Financial support:* In 2011–12, research assistantships with full tuition reimbursements (averaging $35,610 per year) were awarded; career-related internships or fieldwork, Federal Work-Study, scholarships/grants, and unspecified assistantships also available. Support available to part-time students. Financial award application deadline: 6/30; financial award applicants required to submit FAFSA. *Faculty research:* Financial, hedge funds, international business, legal issues, disclosure and branding. *Unit head:* Dr. Joyce A. Strawser, Dean, 973-761-9013, Fax: 973-761-9217, E-mail: joyce.strawser@shu.edu. *Application contact:* Catherine Bianchi, Director of Graduate Admissions, 973-761-9262, Fax: 973-761-9208, E-mail: catherine.bianchi@shu.edu. Web site: http://www.shu.edu/academics/business.

Simon Fraser University, Graduate Studies, Faculty of Business Administration, Burnaby, BC V5A 1S6, Canada. Offers business administration (EMBA, PhD); financial management (MA); general business (MBA); global asset and wealth management (MBA); management of technology/biotechnology (MBA); MBA/MRM. *Accreditation:* AACSB. Postbaccalaureate distance learning degree programs offered. *Degree requirements:* For master's, thesis or written project. *Entrance requirements:* For master's, minimum GPA of 3.0. Additional exam requirements/recommendations for international students: Required—TOEFL. *Expenses:* Contact institution. *Faculty research:* Leadership, marketing and technology, wealth management.

Southeast Missouri State University, School of Graduate Studies, Harrison College of Business, Cape Girardeau, MO 63701-4799. Offers accounting (MBA); entrepreneurship (MBA); financial management (MBA); general management (MBA); health administration (MBA); industrial management (MBA); international business (MBA); sport management (MBA). *Accreditation:* AACSB. Part-time and evening/weekend programs available. Postbaccalaureate distance learning degree programs offered (no on-campus study). *Faculty:* 31 full-time (10 women). *Students:* 49 full-time (23 women), 77 part-time (30 women); includes 5 minority (1 Black or African American, non-Hispanic/Latino; 1 American Indian or Alaska Native, non-Hispanic/Latino; 2 Hispanic/Latino; 1 Two or more races, non-Hispanic/Latino), 35 international. Average age 27. 78 applicants, 69% accepted, 43 enrolled. In 2011, 47 master's awarded. *Degree requirements:* For master's, variable foreign language requirement, comprehensive exam, applied research project related to field. *Entrance requirements:* For master's, GMAT (minimum score of 450), minimum undergraduate GPA of 2.5, C or better in prerequisite courses. Additional exam requirements/recommendations for international students: Required—TOEFL (minimum score 550 paper-based; 213 computer-based; 79 iBT); Recommended—IELTS (minimum score 6). *Application deadline:* For fall admission, 8/1 for domestic students, 7/1 for international students; for spring admission, 11/21 for domestic students, 11/1 for international students. Applications are processed on a rolling basis. Application fee: $30 ($40 for international students). Electronic applications accepted. *Expenses:* Tuition, state resident: full-time $4896; part-time $272 per credit hour. Tuition, nonresident: full-time $8649; part-time $480.50 per credit hour. *Financial support:* In 2011–12, 46 students received support, including 12 teaching assistantships with full tuition reimbursements available (averaging $7,600 per year); career-related internships or fieldwork, Federal Work-Study, scholarships/grants, tuition waivers (full), and unspecified assistantships also available. Financial award application deadline: 6/30; financial award applicants required to submit FAFSA. *Faculty research:* Human resources, laws impacting accounting, advertising. *Unit head:* Dr. Kenneth A. Heischmidt, Director, Graduate Programs in Business, 573-651-5116, Fax: 573-651-5032, E-mail: kheischmidt@semo.edu. *Application contact:* Gail Amick, Administrative Secretary, 573-651-2049, Fax: 573-651-2001, E-mail: gamick@semo.edu. Web site: http://www.semo.edu/mba.

Southern Adventist University, School of Business and Management, Collegedale, TN 37315-0370. Offers accounting (MBA); church administration (MSA); church and nonprofit leadership (MBA); financial management (MFM); healthcare administration (MBA); management (MBA); marketing management (MBA); outdoor education (MSA). Part-time and evening/weekend programs available. Postbaccalaureate distance learning degree programs offered (no on-campus study). *Entrance requirements:* For master's, GMAT. Additional exam requirements/recommendations for international students: Required—TOEFL (minimum score 600 paper-based; 250 computer-based; 100 iBT). Electronic applications accepted.

Southern Illinois University Edwardsville, Graduate School, School of Business, Department of Economics and Finance, Edwardsville, IL 62026. Offers MA, MS. Part-time and evening/weekend programs available. *Faculty:* 13 full-time (2 women). *Students:* 17 full-time (3 women), 14 part-time (6 women); includes 4 minority (3 Black or African American, non-Hispanic/Latino; 1 Asian, non-Hispanic/Latino), 8 international. 49 applicants, 45% accepted. In 2011, 19 master's awarded. *Degree requirements:* For master's, thesis or alternative, final exam, portfolio. *Entrance requirements:* For master's, GMAT or GRE. Additional exam requirements/recommendations for international students: Required—TOEFL (minimum score 550 paper-based; 213 computer-based; 79 iBT), IELTS (minimum score 6.5). *Application deadline:* For fall admission, 7/22 for domestic students, 6/1 for international students; for spring admission, 12/10 for domestic students, 10/1 for international students. Applications are processed on a rolling basis. Application fee: $30. Electronic applications accepted. Tuition and fees vary according to course load and program. *Financial support:* In 2011–12, 1 fellowship with full tuition reimbursement (averaging $8,370 per year), 4 research assistantships with full tuition reimbursements (averaging $9,927 per year), 1 teaching assistantship with full tuition reimbursement (averaging $9,927 per year) were awarded; institutionally sponsored loans, scholarships/grants, and unspecified assistantships also available. Financial award application deadline: 3/1; financial award applicants required to submit FAFSA. *Unit head:* Dr. Rik Hafer, Chair, 618-650-2542, E-mail: rhafer@siue.edu. *Application contact:* Dr. Ali Kutan, Director, 618-650-3473, E-mail: akutan@siue.edu. Web site: http://www.siue.edu/business/econfin/.

Southern Methodist University, Cox School of Business, MBA Program, Dallas, TX 75275. Offers accounting (MBA); finance (MBA); financial consulting (MBA); general business (MBA); information technology and operations management (MBA); management (MBA); marketing (MBA); real estate (MBA); strategy and entrepreneurship (MBA). Part-time and evening/weekend programs available. *Entrance requirements:* For master's, GMAT. Additional exam requirements/recommendations for international students: Required—TOEFL. Electronic applications accepted. *Expenses:* Contact institution. *Faculty research:* Corporate finance, financial reporting, modeling consumer decision-making, competition between national brands and store brands, institutional determinants of firms' strategy.

Southern New Hampshire University, School of Business, Manchester, NH 03106-1045. Offers accounting (MS); business administration (MBA, Certificate), including accounting (Certificate), business administration (MBA), finance (Certificate), forensic accounting (Certificate), human resources management (Certificate), international business (Certificate), international sport management (Certificate), leadership of not for profit organizations (Certificate), marketing (Certificate), operations management (Certificate), sport management (Certificate), taxation (Certificate); finance (MS); hospitality and tourism leadership (Certificate); information technology (MS, Certificate); information technology/international business (Certificate); integrated marketing communications (Certificate); international business (MS, DBA); marketing (MS); operations and project management (MS); organizational leadership (MS); project management (Certificate); sport management (MS); MBA/Certificate. *Accreditation:* ACBSP. Part-time and evening/weekend programs available. Postbaccalaureate distance learning degree programs offered (no on-campus study). Terminal master's awarded for partial completion of doctoral program. *Degree requirements:* For master's, one foreign language, comprehensive exam (for some programs), thesis or alternative; for doctorate, one foreign language, comprehensive exam, thesis/dissertation. *Entrance requirements:* For master's, minimum GPA of 2.5; for doctorate, GMAT. Additional exam requirements/recommendations for international students: Required—TOEFL (minimum score 500 paper-based). Electronic applications accepted.

Southwestern Adventist University, Business Administration Department, Keene, TX 76059. Offers accounting (MBA); finance (MBA); management/leadership (MBA). Part-time and evening/weekend programs available. *Degree requirements:* For master's, capstone course. *Entrance requirements:* For master's, GMAT, GRE General Test.

State University of New York at Binghamton, Graduate School, School of Arts and Sciences, Department of Economics, Binghamton, NY 13902-6000. Offers economics (MA, PhD); economics and finance (MA, PhD). *Faculty:* 21 full-time (6 women), 4 part-time/adjunct (2 women). *Students:* 43 full-time (18 women), 28 part-time (13 women); includes 5 minority (1 Black or African American, non-Hispanic/Latino; 2 Asian, non-Hispanic/Latino; 2 Hispanic/Latino), 56 international. Average age 28. 150 applicants, 33% accepted, 14 enrolled. In 2011, 22 master's, 8 doctorates awarded. Terminal master's awarded for partial completion of doctoral program. *Degree requirements:* For doctorate, thesis/dissertation. *Entrance requirements:* For master's and doctorate, GRE General Test. Additional exam requirements/recommendations for international students: Required—TOEFL (minimum score 550 paper-based; 213 computer-based; 80 iBT). *Application deadline:* For fall admission, 8/1 priority date for domestic students, 8/1 for international students. Applications are processed on a rolling basis. Application fee: $60. Electronic applications accepted. *Financial support:* In 2011–12, 28 students received support, including 1 fellowship with full tuition reimbursement available (averaging $14,500 per year), 24 teaching assistantships with full tuition reimbursements available (averaging $14,500 per year); career-related internships or fieldwork, Federal Work-Study, institutionally sponsored loans, scholarships/grants, health care benefits, tuition waivers (full and partial), and unspecified assistantships also available. Financial award application deadline: 2/15; financial award applicants required to submit FAFSA. *Unit head:* Dr. Susan Wolcott, Chairperson, 607-777-2339, E-mail: swolcott@binghamton.edu. *Application contact:* Catherine Smith, Recruiting and Admissions Coordinator, 607-777-2151, Fax: 607-777-2501, E-mail: cmsmith@binghamton.edu.

Stevens Institute of Technology, Graduate School, Wesley J. Howe School of Technology Management, Program in Business Administration, Hoboken, NJ 07030. Offers engineering management (MBA); financial engineering (MBA); information management (MBA); information technology in financial services (MBA); information technology in the pharmaceutical industry (MBA); information technology outsourcing (MBA); pharmaceutical management (MBA); project management (MBA); technology management (MBA); telecommunications management (MBA).

Stony Brook University, State University of New York, Graduate School, College of Business, Program in Business Administration, Stony Brook, NY 11794. Offers finance (MBA, Certificate); health care management (MBA, Certificate); human resource management (Certificate); human resources (MBA); information systems management (MBA, Certificate); management (MBA); marketing (MBA).

Strayer University, Graduate Studies, Washington, DC 20005-2603. Offers accounting (MS); acquisition (MBA); business administration (MBA); communications technology (MS); educational management (M Ed); finance (MBA); health services administration (MHSA); hospitality and tourism management (MBA); human resource management (MBA); information systems (MS), including computer security management, decision support system management, enterprise resource management, network management, software engineering management, systems development management; management (MBA); management information systems (MS); marketing (MBA); professional accounting (MS), including accounting information systems, controllership, taxation; public administration (MPA); supply chain management (MBA); technology in education (M Ed). Programs also offered at campus locations in Birmingham, AL; Chamblee, GA; Cobb County, GA; Morrow, GA; White Marsh, MD; Charleston, SC; Columbia, SC; Greensboro, NC; Greenville, SC; Lexington, KY; Louisville, KY; Nashville, TN; North Raleigh, NC; Washington, DC. Part-time and evening/weekend programs available. Postbaccalaureate distance learning degree programs offered (minimal on-campus study). *Degree requirements:* For master's, thesis. *Entrance requirements:* For master's, GMAT, GRE General Test, bachelor's degree from an accredited college or university, minimum undergraduate GPA of 2.75. Electronic applications accepted.

Suffolk University, Sawyer Business School, Master of Business Administration Program, Boston, MA 02108-2770. Offers accounting (MBA); business administration (APC); corporate financial executive track (MBA); entrepreneurship (MBA); executive business administration (EMBA); finance (MBA); global business administration (GMBA); health administration (MBA); international business (MBA); marketing (MBA); organizational behavior (MBA); strategic management (MBA); taxation (MBA); JD/MBA; MBA/GDPA; MBA/MHA; MBA/MSA; MBA/MSF; MBA/MST. *Accreditation:* AACSB. Part-time and evening/weekend programs available. Postbaccalaureate distance learning degree programs offered (no on-campus study). *Faculty:* 98 full-time (30 women), 14 part-time/adjunct (3 women). *Students:* 139 full-time (49 women), 321 part-time (138 women); includes 53 minority (17 Black or African American, non-Hispanic/Latino; 1 American Indian or Alaska Native, non-Hispanic/Latino; 21 Asian, non-Hispanic/Latino; 11 Hispanic/Latino; 1 Native Hawaiian or other Pacific Islander, non-Hispanic/Latino; 2 Two or more races, non-Hispanic/Latino), 64 international. Average age 30. 437 applicants, 61% accepted, 121 enrolled. In 2011, 283 master's awarded. *Entrance requirements:* For master's, GMAT, minimum undergraduate GPA of 2.75 (MBA), 5 years of managerial experience (EMBA). Additional exam requirements/recommendations for international students: Required—TOEFL (minimum score 550 paper-based; 213 computer-based). *Application deadline:* For fall admission, 6/15 priority date for domestic students, 6/15 for international students; for spring admission, 11/1 priority date for domestic students, 11/1 for international students. Applications are processed on a rolling basis. Application fee: $50. Electronic applications accepted. Tuition and fees vary according to program. *Financial support:* In 2011–12, 273 students received support, including 73 fellowships with full and partial tuition reimbursements available (averaging $12,415 per year); career-related internships or fieldwork, Federal Work-Study, and institutionally sponsored loans also available. Support available to part-time students. Financial award application deadline: 4/1; financial award applicants required to submit FAFSA. *Faculty research:* Foreign investments; career strategies and boundaryless careers; corporate ethics codes; interest rates, inflation, and growth options; innovation and product development performance. *Unit head:* Lillian Hallberg, Assistant Dean of Graduate Programs/Director of MBA Programs, 617-573-8306, E-mail: lhallber@suffolk.edu. *Application contact:* Ellen Driscoll, Director of Graduate Admissions, 617-573-8302, Fax: 617-305-1733, E-mail: grad.admission@suffolk.edu. Web site: http://www.suffolk.edu/mba.

Suffolk University, Sawyer Business School, Programs in Finance, Boston, MA 02108-2770. Offers MSF, MSFSB, CPASF, JD/MSF. *Accreditation:* AACSB. Part-time and evening/weekend programs available. *Faculty:* 16 full-time (2 women). *Students:* 61 part-time (26 women); includes 6 minority (2 Black or African American, non-Hispanic/Latino; 3 Asian, non-Hispanic/Latino; 1 Two or more races, non-Hispanic/Latino), 21 international. Average age 28. 306 applicants, 20% accepted, 22 enrolled. In 2011, 24 master's awarded. *Entrance requirements:* For master's, GMAT, interview. Additional exam requirements/recommendations for international students: Required—TOEFL (minimum score 550 paper-based; 213 computer-based; 80 iBT). *Application deadline:* For fall admission, 6/15 priority date for domestic students, 6/15 for international students; for spring admission, 11/1 priority date for domestic students, 11/1 for international students. Applications are processed on a rolling basis. Application fee: $50. Electronic applications accepted. *Expenses:* Contact institution. *Financial support:* In 2011–12, 40 students received support, including 18 fellowships (averaging $20,057 per year); career-related internships or fieldwork, Federal Work-Study, and institutionally sponsored loans also available. Support available to part-time students. Financial award application deadline: 4/1; financial award applicants required to submit FAFSA. *Faculty research:* Financial institutions, corporate finance, ownership structure, dividend policy, corporate restructuring. *Unit head:* Dr. Ki Han, Director, 617-573-8641, E-mail: msf@suffolk.edu. *Application contact:* Ellen Driscoll, Director of Graduate Admissions, 617-573-8302, Fax: 617-305-1733, E-mail: grad.admission@suffolk.edu. Web site: http://www.suffolk.edu/msf.

Syracuse University, Martin J. Whitman School of Management, PhD Program in Business Administration, Syracuse, NY 13244. Offers accounting (PhD); finance (PhD); management information systems (PhD); managerial statistics (PhD); marketing (PhD); operations management (PhD); organizational behavior (PhD); strategy and human resources (PhD); supply chain management (PhD). *Faculty:* 79 full-time (20 women), 25 part-time/adjunct (6 women). *Students:* 32 full-time (10 women); includes 6 minority (3 Black or African American, non-Hispanic/Latino; 2 Asian, non-Hispanic/Latino; 1 Hispanic/Latino), 18 international. Average age 32. 260 applicants, 8% accepted, 12 enrolled. In 2011, 2 doctorates awarded. *Degree requirements:* For doctorate, comprehensive exam, thesis/dissertation, summer research paper. *Entrance requirements:* For doctorate, GMAT or GRE General Test, 3 recommendations. Additional exam requirements/recommendations for international students: Required—TOEFL (minimum score 600 paper-based; 250 computer-based; 100 iBT). *Application deadline:* For fall admission, 2/15 priority date for domestic students, 2/15 for international students. Applications are processed on a rolling basis. Application fee: $65. Electronic applications accepted. *Expenses: Tuition:* Part-time $1206 per credit. *Financial support:* In 2011–12, 1 fellowship with full tuition reimbursement (averaging $19,570 per year), 30 teaching assistantships with full tuition reimbursements (averaging $17,000 per year) were awarded; research assistantships with full tuition reimbursements, health care benefits, and unspecified assistantships also available. Financial award application deadline: 1/30. *Faculty research:* Marketing models, market microstructure, supply chain, auditing, corporate governance. *Unit head:* Dr. Eunkyu Lee, Director of the PhD Program, 315-443-3429, E-mail: elee06@syr.edu. *Application contact:* Carol Hilleges, Administrative Specialist, 315-443-9601, Fax: 315-443-3671, E-mail: clhilleg@syr.edu. Web site: http://whitman.syr.edu/phd/.

Syracuse University, Martin J. Whitman School of Management, Program in Business Administration, Syracuse, NY 13244. Offers accounting (MBA); entrepreneurship (MBA); finance (MBA); marketing (MBA); supply chain management (MBA). Postbaccalaureate distance learning degree programs offered (minimal on-campus study). *Faculty:* 79 full-time (20 women), 25 part-time/adjunct (6 women). *Students:* 116 full-time (43 women), 188 part-time (58 women); includes 62 minority (33 Black or African American, non-Hispanic/Latino; 1 American Indian or Alaska Native, non-Hispanic/Latino; 13 Asian, non-Hispanic/Latino; 9 Hispanic/Latino; 1 Native Hawaiian or other Pacific Islander, non-Hispanic/Latino; 5 Two or more races, non-Hispanic/Latino), 44 international. Average age 33. 276 applicants, 49% accepted, 77 enrolled. In 2011, 132 master's awarded. *Entrance requirements:* For master's, GMAT, 2 letters of recommendation. Additional exam requirements/recommendations for international students: Required—TOEFL (minimum score 600 paper-based; 250 computer-based; 100 iBT). *Application deadline:* For fall admission, 1/15 priority date for domestic students, 1/15 for international students. Applications are processed on a rolling basis. Application fee: $75. Electronic applications accepted. *Expenses: Tuition:* Part-time $1206 per credit. *Financial support:* In 2011–12, 17 students received support. Fellowships with full and partial tuition reimbursements available, teaching assistantships with partial tuition reimbursements available, career-related internships or fieldwork, scholarships/grants, tuition waivers (partial), unspecified assistantships, and paid hourly positions available. Support available to part-time students. Financial award application deadline: 3/1. *Unit head:* Prof. Dennis Gillen, Chair and Associate Professor of Management, 315-443-3432, Fax: 315-443-9517, E-mail: dgillen@syr.edu. *Application contact:* Josh LaFave, Director, Graduate Enrollment, 315-443-3497, Fax: 315-443-9517, E-mail: mbainfo@syr.edu. Web site: http://whitman.syr.edu/ftmba/.

Syracuse University, Martin J. Whitman School of Management, Program in Finance, Syracuse, NY 13244. Offers MS, JD/MSF. *Faculty:* 79 full-time (20 women), 25 part-time/adjunct (6 women). *Students:* 78 full-time (57 women), 1 part-time (0 women); includes 2 minority (both Asian, non-Hispanic/Latino), 73 international. Average age 23. 903 applicants, 12% accepted, 53 enrolled. In 2011, 45 master's awarded. *Entrance requirements:* For master's, GMAT, 2 letters of recommendation, bachelor's degree in finance or economics. Additional exam requirements/recommendations for international students: Required—TOEFL (minimum score 600 paper-based; 250 computer-based; 100 iBT). *Application deadline:* For fall admission, 1/15 priority date for domestic students, 1/15 for international students; for winter admission, 11/1 for domestic and international students. Applications are processed on a rolling basis. Application fee: $75. Electronic applications accepted. *Expenses: Tuition:* Part-time $1206 per credit. *Financial support:* Career-related internships or fieldwork available. Financial award application deadline: 3/1. *Unit head:* Don Harter, Associate Dean of Graduate Programs, 315-4 443-3963, Fax: 315-443-9517, E-mail: dharter@syr.edu. *Application contact:* Josh LaFave, Director of Graduate Enrollment, 315-443-3497, Fax: 315-443-9517, E-mail: mbainfo@syr.edu. Web site: http://whitman.syr.edu/msfin/.

Tarleton State University, College of Graduate Studies, College of Business Administration, Department of Accounting, Finance and Economics, Stephenville, TX 76402. Offers business administration (MBA). Part-time and evening/weekend programs available. *Faculty:* 6 full-time (0 women), 2 part-time/adjunct (0 women). *Students:* 48 full-time (25 women), 192 part-time (101 women); includes 74 minority (30 Black or African American, non-Hispanic/Latino; 1 American Indian or Alaska Native, non-Hispanic/Latino; 7 Asian, non-Hispanic/Latino; 29 Hispanic/Latino; 7 Two or more races, non-Hispanic/Latino), 1 international. Average age 31. 99 applicants, 92% accepted, 74 enrolled. In 2011, 50 master's awarded. *Degree requirements:* For master's, comprehensive exam. *Entrance requirements:* For master's, GRE or GMAT, minimum GPA of 3.0. Additional exam requirements/recommendations for international students: Required—TOEFL (minimum score 550 paper-based; 213 computer-based; 80 iBT). *Application deadline:* For fall admission, 8/5 priority date for domestic students; for spring admission, 12/1 for domestic students. Applications are processed on a rolling basis. Application fee: $30 ($130 for international students). Electronic applications accepted. *Expenses:* Tuition, state resident: full-time $3131.46; part-time $174 per credit hour. Tuition, nonresident: full-time $8225; part-time $457 per credit hour. *Required fees:* $1446. Tuition and fees vary according to course load and campus/location. *Financial support:* Research assistantships and teaching assistantships available. Financial award application deadline: 5/1; financial award applicants required to submit FAFSA. *Unit head:* Dr. Steve Steed, Interim Department Head, 254-968-9645, Fax: 254-968-9665, E-mail: ssteed@tarleton.edu. *Application contact:* Information Contact, 254-968-9104, Fax: 254-968-9670, E-mail: gradoffice@tarleton.edu. Web site: http://www.tarleton.edu/~afe/.

Télé-université, Graduate Programs, Québec, QC G1K 9H5, Canada. Offers computer science (PhD); corporate finance (MS); distance learning (MS). Part-time programs available.

Temple University, Fox School of Business, Doctoral Programs in Business, Philadelphia, PA 19122-6096. Offers accounting (PhD); entrepreneurship (PhD); finance (PhD); international business (PhD); management information systems (PhD); marketing (PhD); risk management and insurance (PhD); statistics (PhD); strategic management (PhD); tourism and sport (PhD). *Accreditation:* AACSB. *Degree requirements:* For doctorate, thesis/dissertation. *Entrance requirements:* For doctorate, GRE General Test, GMAT, minimum GPA of 3.0, master's degree. Additional exam requirements/recommendations for international students: Required—TOEFL (minimum score 600 paper-based; 250 computer-based; 100 iBT), IELTS (minimum score 7.5). Electronic applications accepted. *Expenses:* Tuition, state resident: full-time $12,366; part-time $687 per credit hour. Tuition, nonresident: full-time $17,298; part-time $961 per credit hour. *Required fees:* $590; $213 per year.

Temple University, Fox School of Business, Specialized Master's Programs, Philadelphia, PA 19122-6096. Offers accountancy (MS); actuarial science (MS); finance (MS); financial engineering (MS); human resource management (MS); marketing (MS); statistics (MS). *Accreditation:* AACSB. Part-time programs available. *Entrance requirements:* For master's, GRE General Test or GMAT, minimum undergraduate GPA of 3.0. Additional exam requirements/recommendations for international students: Required—TOEFL (minimum score 600 paper-based; 250 computer-based; 100 iBT), IELTS (minimum score 7.5). *Expenses:* Tuition, state resident: full-time $12,366; part-time $687 per credit hour. Tuition, nonresident: full-time $17,298; part-time $961 per credit hour. *Required fees:* $590; $213 per year.

Tennessee Technological University, Graduate School, College of Business, Cookeville, TN 38505. Offers accounting (MBA); finance (MBA); human resource management (MBA); international business (MBA); management information systems (MBA); risk management & insurance (MBA). *Accreditation:* AACSB. Part-time and evening/weekend programs available. Postbaccalaureate distance learning degree programs offered (no on-campus study). *Faculty:* 28 full-time (5 women). *Students:* 45 full-time (19 women), 135 part-time (51 women); includes 13 minority (4 Black or African American, non-Hispanic/Latino; 5 Asian, non-Hispanic/Latino; 3 Hispanic/Latino; 1 Native Hawaiian or other Pacific Islander, non-Hispanic/Latino), 2 international. Average age 25. 193 applicants, 59% accepted, 70 enrolled. In 2011, 89 master's awarded. *Entrance requirements:* For master's, GMAT. Additional exam requirements/recommendations for international students: Required—TOEFL (minimum score 550 paper-based; 79 iBT), IELTS (minimum score 5.5), Pearson Test of English Academic. *Application deadline:* For fall admission, 8/1 for domestic students, 5/1 for international students; for spring admission, 12/1 for domestic students, 10/1 for international students. Application fee: $25 ($30 for international students). Electronic applications accepted. *Expenses:* Tuition, state resident: full-time $8094; part-time $422 per credit hour. Tuition, nonresident: full-time $20,574; part-time $1046 per credit hour. *Financial support:* In 2011–12, 5 fellowships (averaging $10,000 per year), 18 research assistantships (averaging $4,000 per year), teaching assistantships (averaging $4,000 per year) were awarded. Support available to part-time students. Financial award application deadline: 4/1. *Unit head:* Dr. Tom Timmerman, Director, 931-372-3600, Fax: 931-372-6249. *Application contact:* Shelia K. Kendrick, Coordinator of Graduate Admissions, 931-372-3808, Fax: 931-372-3497, E-mail: skendrick@tntech.edu. Web site: http://www.tntech.edu/mba.

Texas A&M International University, Office of Graduate Studies and Research, College of Business Administration, Division of International Banking and Finance Studies, Laredo, TX 78041-1900. Offers accounting (MP Acc); international banking (MBA). *Faculty:* 13 full-time (2 women). *Students:* 49 full-time (21 women), 195 part-time (95 women); includes 171 minority (3 Black or African American, non-Hispanic/Latino; 1 Asian, non-Hispanic/Latino; 167 Hispanic/Latino), 63 international. Average age 30. 122 applicants, 75% accepted, 80 enrolled. In 2011, 121 master's awarded. *Entrance requirements:* For master's, GMAT or GRE General Test. Additional exam requirements/recommendations for international students: Required—TOEFL (minimum score 550 paper-based; 213 computer-based; 79 iBT). *Application deadline:* For fall admission, 4/30 priority date for domestic students, 4/30 for international students; for spring admission, 11/30 for domestic students, 10/1 for international students. Applications are processed on a rolling basis. Application fee: $35 ($50 for international students). *Expenses:* Tuition, state resident: full-time $5063. *Financial support:* In 2011–12, 3 students received support, including 3 research assistantships. *Unit head:* Dr. Ken Hung, Chair, 956-326-2541, Fax: 956-326-2481, E-mail: ken.hung@tamiu.edu. *Application contact:* Imelda Lopez, Graduate Admissions Counselor, 956-326-2485, Fax: 956-326-2459, E-mail: lopez@tamiu.edu. Web site: http://www.tamiu.edu/ssb/divisions.php?optN-210.

Texas A&M University, Mays Business School, Department of Finance, College Station, TX 77843. Offers MS, PhD. *Faculty:* 15. *Students:* 163 full-time (48 women), 4 part-time (2 women); includes 25 minority (2 Black or African American, non-Hispanic/Latino; 1 American Indian or Alaska Native, non-Hispanic/Latino; 10 Asian, non-Hispanic/Latino; 12 Hispanic/Latino), 8 international. Average age 27. 110 applicants, 33% accepted. In 2011, 120 master's, 6 doctorates awarded. Terminal master's awarded for partial completion of doctoral program. *Degree requirements:* For master's, comprehensive exam; for doctorate, thesis/dissertation. *Entrance requirements:* For master's, GMAT; for doctorate, GMAT or GRE General Test. Additional exam requirements/recommendations for international students: Required—TOEFL. *Application deadline:* For fall admission, 3/1 priority date for domestic students; for spring admission, 8/1 for domestic students. Applications are processed on a rolling basis. Application fee: $50 ($75 for international students). *Expenses:* Tuition, state resident: full-time $5437; part-time $226.55 per credit hour. Tuition, nonresident: full-time $12,949; part-time $539.55 per credit hour. *Required fees:* $2741. *Financial support:* In 2011–12, 30 students received support. Fellowships, research assistantships, teaching assistantships, career-related internships or fieldwork, and institutionally sponsored loans available. Financial award application deadline: 2/1. *Unit head:* Sorin Sorescu, Head, 979-458-0380, Fax: 979-845-3884, E-mail: smsorescu@mays.tamu.edu. *Application contact:* Timothy Dye, Assistant Head, 979-845-3446, E-mail: tdye@mays.tamu.edu. Web site: http://mays.tamu.edu/finc/.

Texas A&M University–Commerce, Graduate School, College of Business, MS Programs, Commerce, TX 75429-3011. Offers accounting (MS); economics (MA); finance (MS); management (MS); marketing (MS). Part-time programs available. *Degree requirements:* For master's, comprehensive exam, thesis (for some programs). *Entrance requirements:* For master's, GMAT or GRE General Test. Electronic applications accepted. *Faculty research:* Economic activity, forensic economics, volatility and finance, international economics.

Texas A&M University–San Antonio, School of Business, San Antonio, TX 78224. Offers business administration (MBA); enterprise resource planning systems (MBA); finance (MBA); healthcare management (MBA); human resources management (MBA); information assurance and security (MBA); international business (MBA); professional accounting (MPA); project management (MBA); supply chain management (MBA). Part-time and evening/weekend programs available. *Faculty:* 18 full-time (6 women), 1 part-time/adjunct (0 women). *Students:* 91 full-time (45 women), 278 part-time (150 women). Average age 33. In 2011, 20 master's awarded. *Entrance requirements:* For master's, GMAT. Additional exam requirements/recommendations for international students: Required—TOEFL (minimum score 550 paper-based; 213 computer-based; 80 iBT), IELTS (minimum score 6). *Application deadline:* For fall admission, 7/1 priority date for domestic students, 6/1 for international students; for spring admission, 11/15 priority date for domestic students, 10/1 for international students. Applications are processed on a rolling basis. Application fee: $35 ($50 for international students). Electronic applications accepted. *Expenses:* Tuition, state resident: part-time $691.11 per course. Tuition, nonresident: part-time $1621.11 per course. *Financial support:* Application deadline: 3/31; applicants required to submit FAFSA. *Unit head:* Dr. Tracy Hurley, MBA Coordinator, 210-932-6200, E-mail: tracy.hurley@tamusa.tamus.edu. *Application contact:* Melissa A. Villanueva, Graduate Admissions Specialist, 210-932-6200, Fax: 210-932-6209, E-mail: melissa.villanueva@tamusa.tamus.edu. Web site: http://www.tamusa.tamus.edu.

Texas Tech University, Graduate School, Rawls College of Business Administration, Area of Finance, Lubbock, TX 79409. Offers MS, PhD. Part-time programs available. *Faculty:* 13 full-time (1 woman). *Students:* 38 full-time (6 women), 13 part-time (5 women); includes 8 minority (2 American Indian or Alaska Native, non-Hispanic/Latino; 2 Asian, non-Hispanic/Latino; 4 Hispanic/Latino), 19 international. Average age 29. 69 applicants, 45% accepted, 26 enrolled. In 2011, 15 master's, 1 doctorate awarded. Terminal master's awarded for partial completion of doctoral program. *Degree requirements:* For master's, capstone course; for doctorate, comprehensive exam, thesis/dissertation, qualifying exams. *Entrance requirements:* For master's and doctorate, GMAT, holistic review of academic credentials. Additional exam requirements/recommendations for international students: Required—TOEFL (minimum score 550 paper-based; 213 computer-based; 79 iBT). *Application deadline:* For fall admission, 4/1 priority date for domestic students, 1/15 for international students; for spring admission, 9/1 priority date for domestic students, 6/15 for international students. Applications are processed on a rolling basis. Application fee: $50 ($75 for international students). Electronic applications accepted. *Expenses:* Tuition, state resident: full-time $5899; part-time $245.80 per credit hour. Tuition, nonresident: full-time $13,411; part-time $558.80 per credit hour. *Required fees:* $2680.60; $86.50 per credit hour. $920.30 per semester. *Financial support:* In 2011–12, 8 research assistantships (averaging $15,700 per year), 3 teaching assistantships (averaging $18,000 per year) were awarded; Federal Work-Study and scholarships/grants also available. Support available to part-time students. Financial award applicants required to submit FAFSA. *Faculty research:* Portfolio theory, banking and financial institutions, corporate finance, securities and options futures. *Unit head:* Dr. Drew Winters, Area Coordinator, 806-742-3350, Fax: 806-742-2099, E-mail: drew.winters@ttu.edu. *Application contact:* Elizabeth Stuart, Director, Graduate Services Center, 806-742-3184, Fax: 806-742-3958, E-mail: ba_grad@ttu.edu. Web site: http://finance.ba.ttu.edu.

Thomas M. Cooley Law School, JD and LL M Programs, Lansing, MI 48901-3038. Offers administrative law (public law) (JD); business transactions (JD); Canadian law (JD); Constitutional law and civil rights (public law) (JD); corporate law and finance (LL M); environmental law (public law) (JD); general practice (JD); insurance (LL M); intellectual property (LL M, JD); international law (JD); litigation (JD); self-directed (LL M, JD); taxation (LL M, JD); U.S. law for foreign attorneys (LL M); JD/MBA; JD/MPA; JD/MSW. *Accreditation:* ABA. Part-time and evening/weekend programs available. Postbaccalaureate distance learning degree programs offered (no on-campus study). *Faculty:* 131 full-time (55 women), 286 part-time/adjunct (93 women). *Students:* 781 full-time (368 women), 2,964 part-time (1,450 women); includes 1,055 minority (543 Black or African American, non-Hispanic/Latino; 19 American Indian or Alaska Native, non-Hispanic/Latino; 179 Asian, non-Hispanic/Latino; 205 Hispanic/Latino; 9 Native Hawaiian or other Pacific Islander, non-Hispanic/Latino; 100 Two or more races, non-Hispanic/Latino), 220 international. Average age 30. 4,032 applicants, 80% accepted, 1161 enrolled. In 2011, 40 master's, 999 doctorates awarded. *Degree requirements:* For master's, thesis optional; for doctorate, minimum of 3 credits of clinical experience. *Entrance requirements:* For master's, JD or LL B; for doctorate, LSAT. Additional exam requirements/recommendations for international students: Required—TOEFL. *Application deadline:* For fall admission, 9/1 for domestic and international students; for winter admission, 1/1 for domestic and international students; for spring admission, 5/1 for domestic and international students. Applications are processed on a rolling basis. Electronic applications accepted. *Expenses: Tuition:* Full-time $34,300; part-time $1225 per credit hour. *Required fees:* $40; $40 per year. Tuition and fees vary according to degree level and student level. *Financial support:* In 2011–12, 2,324 students received support. Career-related internships or fieldwork, Federal Work-Study, scholarships/grants, traineeships, and unspecified assistantships available. Support available to part-time students. Financial award applicants required to submit FAFSA. *Faculty research:* Wrongful convictions, civil rights, environmental law, litigation techniques, data mining, intellectual property, practical and skills-based legal education. *Unit head:* Don LeDuc, President and Dean, 517-371-5140 Ext. 2009, Fax: 517-334-5152. *Application contact:* Dr. Paul Zelenski, Associate Dean of Enrollment and Student Services, 517-371-5140 Ext. 2244, Fax: 517-334-5718, E-mail: admissions@cooley.edu. Web site: http://www.cooley.edu/.

Tiffin University, Program in Business Administration, Tiffin, OH 44883-2161. Offers finance (MBA); general management (MBA); healthcare administration (MBA); human resources (MBA); international business (MBA); leadership (MBA); marketing (MBA); sports management (MBA). *Accreditation:* ACBSP. Part-time and evening/weekend programs available. Postbaccalaureate distance learning degree programs offered (no on-campus study). *Faculty:* 30 full-time (15 women), 22 part-time/adjunct (6 women). *Students:* 209 full-time (107 women), 340 part-time (172 women); includes 112 minority (91 Black or African American, non-Hispanic/Latino; 4 Asian, non-Hispanic/Latino; 17 Hispanic/Latino), 71 international. Average age 31. 237 applicants, 76% accepted. In 2011, 170 master's awarded. *Entrance requirements:* For master's, minimum undergraduate GPA of 2.5, work experience. Additional exam requirements/recommendations for international students: Required—TOEFL (minimum score 550 paper-based; 213 computer-based; 79 iBT). *Application deadline:* For fall admission, 8/15 for domestic students, 8/1 for international students; for spring admission, 1/9 for domestic students, 12/1 for international students. Applications are processed on a rolling basis. Electronic applications accepted. *Expenses: Tuition:* Full-time $11,200; part-time $700 per credit. Tuition and fees vary according to program. *Financial support:* Available to part-time students. Application deadline: 7/31; applicants required to submit FAFSA. *Faculty research:* Small business, executive development operations, research and statistical analysis, market research, management information systems. *Unit head:* Dr. Lillian Schumacher, Dean of the School of Business, 419-448-3053, Fax: 419-443-5002, E-mail: schumacherlb@tiffin.edu. *Application contact:* Nikki Hintze, Director of Graduate Admissions and Student Services, 800-968-6446 Ext. 3445, Fax: 419-443-5002, E-mail: hintzenm@tiffin.edu. Web site: http://www.tiffin.edu/graduateprograms/.

Trident University International, College of Business Administration, Program in Business Administration, Cypress, CA 90630. Offers business administration (PhD); conflict and negotiation management (MBA); criminal justice administration (MBA); entrepreneurship (MBA); finance (MBA); general management (MBA); government accounting (MBA); human resource management (MBA); information security and digital assurance management (MBA); information technology management (MBA); international business (MBA); logistics management (MBA); marketing (MBA); project management (MBA); public management (MBA); quality management (MBA); strategic leadership (MBA). Part-time and evening/weekend programs available. Postbaccalaureate distance learning degree programs offered (no on-campus study). *Degree requirements:* For doctorate, comprehensive exam, thesis/dissertation, defense of dissertation. *Entrance requirements:* For master's, minimum GPA of 2.5 (students with GPA 3.0 or greater may transfer up to 30% of graduate level credits); for doctorate, minimum GPA of 3.4, curriculum vitae, course work in research methods or statistics. Additional exam requirements/recommendations for international students: Required—TOEFL. Electronic applications accepted.

Troy University, Graduate School, College of Business, Program in Business Administration, Troy, AL 36082. Offers accounting (EMBA, MBA); criminal justice (EMBA); finance (MBA); general management (EMBA, MBA); healthcare management (EMBA); information systems (EMBA, MBA); international economic development (MBA). *Accreditation:* ACBSP. Part-time and evening/weekend programs available. *Faculty:* 50 full-time (14 women), 12 part-time/adjunct (0 women). *Students:* 326 full-time (168 women), 596 part-time (358 women); includes 524 minority (402 Black or African American, non-Hispanic/Latino; 12 American Indian or Alaska Native, non-Hispanic/Latino; 85 Asian, non-Hispanic/Latino; 21 Hispanic/Latino; 4 Two or more races, non-Hispanic/Latino). Average age 29. 644 applicants, 67% accepted, 204 enrolled. In 2011, 388 master's awarded. *Degree requirements:* For master's, minimum GPA of 3.0, capstone course, research course. *Entrance requirements:* For master's, GMAT (minimum score 500) or GRE General Test (minimum score 900), minimum GPA of 2.5; letter of recommendation, bachelor's degree. Additional exam requirements/recommendations for international students: Required—TOEFL (minimum score 523 paper-based; 193 computer-based; 70 iBT), IELTS (minimum score 6), or ACT COMPASS ESL (minimum listening, reading, and grammar score 270). *Application deadline:* Applications are processed on a rolling basis. Application fee: $50. *Expenses:* Tuition, state resident: full-time $6960; part-time $290 per credit hour. Tuition, nonresident: full-time $13,920; part-time $580 per credit hour. *Required fees:* $386 per term. *Unit head:* Dr. Edward Merkel, Director, Graduate Business Programs, 334-670-3194, Fax: 334-670-3599, E-mail: emerkel@troy.edu. *Application contact:* Brenda K. Campbell, Director of Graduate Admissions, 334-670-3178, Fax: 334-670-3733, E-mail: bcamp@troy.edu.

Union Graduate College, School of Management, Schenectady, NY 12308-3107. Offers business administration (MBA); financial management (Certificate); general management (Certificate); health systems administration (MBA, Certificate); human resources (Certificate). *Accreditation:* AACSB. Part-time and evening/weekend programs available. *Faculty:* 18 full-time (4 women), 25 part-time/adjunct (4 women). *Students:* 122 full-time (53 women), 102 part-time (59 women); includes 47 minority (6 Black or African American, non-Hispanic/Latino; 35 Asian, non-Hispanic/Latino; 4 Hispanic/Latino; 2 Two or more races, non-Hispanic/Latino), 5 international. Average age 27. 101 applicants, 75% accepted, 68 enrolled. In 2011, 73 master's, 9 other advanced degrees awarded. *Degree requirements:* For master's, internship, capstone course. *Entrance requirements:* For master's, GMAT, GRE, minimum GPA of 3.0, 3 letters of recommendation. Additional exam requirements/recommendations for international students: Required—TOEFL (minimum score 550 paper-based; 213 computer-based). *Application deadline:* Applications are processed on a rolling basis. Application fee: $60. *Expenses: Tuition:* Full-time $22,000; part-time $775 per credit. One-time fee: $410 full-time. Tuition and fees vary according to course load and program. *Financial support:* In 2011–12, 79 students received support. Research assistantships, career-related internships or fieldwork, Federal Work-Study, scholarships/grants, health care benefits, and tuition waivers (partial) available. Support available to part-time students. Financial award applicants required to submit FAFSA. *Unit head:* Bela Musits, Dean, 518-631-9890, Fax: 518-631-9902, E-mail: musitsb@uniongraduatecollege.edu. *Application contact:* Diane Trzaskos, Admissions Coordinator, 518-631-9837, Fax: 518-631-9901, E-mail: trzaskod@uniongraduatecollege.edu. Web site: http://www.uniongraduatecollege.edu.

United States International University, School of Business Administration, Nairobi, Kenya. Offers business administration (GEMBA); entrepreneurship (MBA); finance (MBA); human resource management (MBA); information technology management (MBA); integrated studies (MBA); international business administration (MBA); management and organizational development (MS); marketing (MBA); organizational development (EMS); strategic management (MBA). Part-time and evening/weekend programs available. *Degree requirements:* For master's, thesis. *Entrance requirements:* For master's, GMAT, 2 letters of reference, resume. Additional exam requirements/recommendations for international students: Required—TOEFL (minimum score 550 paper-based; 213 computer-based). *Faculty research:* Marketing in small business enterprises, total quality management in Kenya.

Universidad Central del Este, Graduate School, San Pedro de Macoris, Dominican Republic. Offers environmental engineering (ME); financial management (M Ad); higher education (M Ed), including higher education management, higher education pedagogy; human resources (M Ad). *Entrance requirements:* For master's, letters of recommendation.

Universidad de las Americas, A.C., Program in Business Administration, Mexico City, Mexico. Offers finance (MBA); marketing research (MBA); production and quality (MBA).

Universidad de las Américas–Puebla, Division of Graduate Studies, School of Business and Economics, Puebla, Mexico. Offers business administration (MBA); finance (M Adm). Part-time and evening/weekend programs available. *Degree requirements:* For master's, one foreign language, thesis. *Entrance requirements:* Additional exam requirements/recommendations for international students: Required—TOEFL. *Faculty research:* System dynamics, information technology, marketing, international business, strategic planning, quality.

Universidad de las Américas–Puebla, Division of Graduate Studies, School of Social Sciences, Program in Economics, Puebla, Mexico. Offers economics (MA); finance (M Adm). Part-time and evening/weekend programs available. *Degree requirements:* For master's, one foreign language, thesis. *Faculty research:* Economic models (mathematics), industrial organization, assets and values market.

Universidad Metropolitana, School of Business Administration, Program in Finance, San Juan, PR 00928-1150. Offers MBA.

Université de Sherbrooke, Faculty of Administration, Program in Finance, Sherbrooke, QC J1K 2R1, Canada. Offers M Sc. *Faculty:* 6 full-time (1 woman), 9 part-time/adjunct (1 woman). *Students:* 100 full-time (19 women), 24 part-time (4 women). Average age 25. 229 applicants, 49% accepted, 56 enrolled. In 2011, 39 master's awarded. *Degree requirements:* For master's, one foreign language, thesis. *Entrance requirements:* For master's, bachelor's degree in related field, minimum GPA of 3.0 (on 4.3 scale). *Application deadline:* For fall admission, 4/30 for domestic students, 1/15 for international students. Applications are processed on a rolling basis. Application fee: $70. Electronic applications accepted. *Faculty research:* Public projects analysis, financial econometrics, risk management, portfolio management. *Unit head:* Prof. Julien Bilodeau, Director, Graduate Programs in Business, 819-821-8000 Ext. 62355. *Application contact:* Marie-Claude Drouin, Assistant Programs Director, 819-821-8000 Ext. 63301.

Université du Québec à Montréal, Graduate Programs, Program in Finance, Montréal, QC H3C 3P8, Canada. Offers Diploma. Part-time programs available. *Entrance requirements:* For degree, appropriate bachelor's degree or equivalent, proficiency in French.

Université du Québec à Trois-Rivières, Graduate Programs, Program in Finance, Trois-Rivières, QC G9A 5H7, Canada. Offers DESS.

Université du Québec en Outaouais, Graduate Programs, Program in Financial Services, Gatineau, QC J8X 3X7, Canada. Offers MBA, DESS, Diploma. Part-time and evening/weekend programs available. *Students:* 48 full-time, 46 part-time. *Degree requirements:* For master's, thesis (for some programs). *Application deadline:* For fall admission, 6/1 priority date for domestic students, 3/1 for international students; for winter admission, 11/1 priority date for domestic students, 10/1 for international students. Application fee: $30. *Unit head:* Denis Gendron, Director, 819-595-3900 Ext. 2655, Fax: 819-773-1760, E-mail: denis.gendron@uqo.ca. *Application contact:* Registrar's Office, 819-773-1850, Fax: 819-773-1835, E-mail: registraire@ugo.ca. Web site: http://www.uqo.ca/programmes-etudes/programmes/3457.htm.

Université Laval, Faculty of Administrative Sciences, Programs in Business Administration, Québec, QC G1K 7P4, Canada. Offers accounting (MBA); agri-food management (MBA); electronic business (MBA, Diploma); factory management and logistics (MBA); finance (MBA); firm management (MBA); geomatic management (MBA); information technology management (MBA); international management (MBA); management (MBA); management accounting (MBA, Diploma); marketing (MBA); modeling and organizational decision (MBA); occupational health and safety management (MBA); pharmacy management (MBA); social and environmental responsibility (MBA); technological entrepreneurship (Diploma). *Accreditation:* AACSB. Part-time and evening/weekend programs available. Postbaccalaureate distance learning degree programs offered (no on-campus study). *Entrance requirements:* For master's and Diploma, knowledge of French and English. Electronic applications accepted.

University at Albany, State University of New York, School of Business, Department of Finance, Albany, NY 12222-0001. Offers MBA. *Degree requirements:* For master's, field study project. *Entrance requirements:* For master's, GMAT. Additional exam requirements/recommendations for international students: Required—TOEFL (minimum score 550 paper-based; 213 computer-based). Electronic applications accepted. *Faculty research:* Tax-exempt securities, public finance, financial engineering, international finance, investments management.

University at Buffalo, the State University of New York, Graduate School, School of Management, Buffalo, NY 14260. Offers accounting (MS); business administration (EMBA, MBA, PMBA); finance (MS), including financial engineering, financial management; management (PhD); management information systems (MS); supply chains and operations management (MS); Au D/MBA; JD/MBA; M Arch/MBA; MA/MBA; MD/MBA; MPH/MBA; MSW/MBA; Pharm D/MBA. *Accreditation:* AACSB. Part-time and evening/weekend programs available. *Degree requirements:* For master's, thesis (for some programs); for doctorate, comprehensive exam, thesis/dissertation. *Entrance requirements:* For master's, GMAT (MBA, MS in accounting), GRE or GMAT (for all other MS concentrations); for doctorate, GMAT or GRE. Additional exam requirements/recommendations for international students: Required—TOEFL (minimum score 230 computer-based; 95 iBT). Electronic applications accepted. *Expenses:* Contact institution. *Faculty research:* Earnings management and electronic information assurance, supply chains and operations management, corporate financing and asset pricing, consumer behavior and quantitative modeling of marketing behavior, leadership and politics in organizations.

The University of Akron, Graduate School, College of Business Administration, Department of Finance, Akron, OH 44325. Offers MBA, JD/MBA. Part-time and evening/weekend programs available. *Faculty:* 10 full-time (4 women), 4 part-time/adjunct (0 women). *Students:* 33 full-time (7 women), 29 part-time (6 women); includes 3 minority (1 Black or African American, non-Hispanic/Latino; 1 Hispanic/Latino; 1 Two or more races, non-Hispanic/Latino), 17 international. Average age 28. 51 applicants, 61% accepted, 16 enrolled. In 2011, 37 master's awarded. *Entrance requirements:* For master's, GMAT, minimum GPA of 2.75, two letters of recommendation, statement of purpose, resume. Additional exam requirements/recommendations for international students: Required—TOEFL (minimum score 550 paper-based; 213 computer-based; 79 iBT). *Application deadline:* For fall admission, 7/15 for domestic and international students; for spring admission, 11/15 for domestic and international students. Application fee: $30 ($40 for international students). Electronic applications accepted. *Expenses:* Tuition, state resident: full-time $7038; part-time $391 per credit hour. Tuition, nonresident: full-time $12,051; part-time $670 per credit hour. *Required fees:* $1274; $34 per credit hour. *Financial support:* In 2011–12, 1 research assistantship with full tuition reimbursement, 12 teaching assistantships with full tuition reimbursements were awarded. *Faculty research:* Corporate finance, financial markets and institutions, investment and equity market analysis, personal financial planning, real estate. *Unit head:* David A. Redle, Chair, 330-972-6329, E-mail: dredle@uakron.edu. *Application contact:* Dr. Susan Hanlon, Director of Graduate Business Programs, 330-972-7043, Fax: 330-972-6588, E-mail: shanlon@uakron.edu. Web site: http://www.uakron.edu/cba/cba-home/dept-cent-inst/finance/.

The University of Alabama, Graduate School, College of Human Environmental Sciences, Program in Human Environmental Science, Tuscaloosa, AL 35487. Offers family financial planning and counseling (MS); interactive technology (MS); quality management (MS); restaurant and meeting management (MS); rural community health (MS); sport management (MS). *Faculty:* 1 full-time (0 women). *Students:* 80 full-time (53 women), 93 part-time (55 women); includes 51 minority (42 Black or African American, non-Hispanic/Latino; 3 American Indian or Alaska Native, non-Hispanic/Latino; 3 Hispanic/Latino; 3 Two or more races, non-Hispanic/Latino), 1 international. Average age 33. 118 applicants, 79% accepted, 75 enrolled. In 2011, 83 degrees awarded. *Degree requirements:* For master's, comprehensive exam. *Entrance requirements:* For master's, GRE (for some specializations), minimum GPA of 3.0. Additional exam requirements/recommendations for international students: Required—TOEFL. *Application deadline:* Applications are processed on a rolling basis. Application fee: $50 ($60 for international students). Electronic applications accepted. *Expenses:* Tuition, state resident: full-time $8600. Tuition, nonresident: full-time $21,900. *Faculty research:* Hospitality management, sports medicine education, technology and education. *Unit head:* Dr. Milla D. Boschung, Dean, 205-348-6250, Fax: 205-348-1786, E-mail: mboschun@ches.ua.edu. *Application contact:* Dr. Stuart Usdan, Associate Dean, 205-348-6150, Fax: 205-348-3789, E-mail: susdan@ches.ua.edu.

The University of Alabama, Graduate School, Manderson Graduate School of Business, Economics, Finance and Legal Studies Department, Tuscaloosa, AL 35487. Offers economics (MA, PhD); finance (MS, PhD). *Faculty:* 29 full-time (3 women). *Students:* 90 full-time (27 women), 5 part-time (0 women); includes 12 minority (8 Black or African American, non-Hispanic/Latino; 3 Asian, non-Hispanic/Latino; 1 Hispanic/Latino), 18 international. Average age 27. 304 applicants, 27% accepted, 30 enrolled. In 2011, 45 master's, 5 doctorates awarded. Terminal master's awarded for partial completion of doctoral program. *Median time to degree:* Of those who began their doctoral program in fall 2003, 99% received their degree in 8 years or less. *Degree requirements:* For master's, comprehensive exam (MA), thesis (MS); for doctorate, comprehensive exam, thesis/dissertation. *Entrance requirements:* For master's, GMAT, GRE; for doctorate, GRE or GMAT. Additional exam requirements/recommendations for international students: Required—TOEFL (minimum score 550 paper-based; 213 computer-based). *Application deadline:* For fall admission, 7/1 priority date for domestic students, 1/15 for international students; for spring admission, 11/1 priority date for domestic students, 6/1 for international students. Applications are processed on a rolling basis. Application fee: $50 ($60 for international students). Electronic applications accepted. *Expenses:* Tuition, state resident: full-time $8600. Tuition, nonresident: full-time $21,900. *Financial support:* In 2011–12, 37 students received support, including 2 fellowships (averaging $10,000 per year), 22 research assistantships with full and partial tuition reimbursements available (averaging $15,000 per year), 18 teaching assistantships with full and partial tuition reimbursements available (averaging $12,000 per year); Federal Work-Study, institutionally sponsored loans, and unspecified assistantships also available. Financial award application deadline: 1/15. *Faculty research:* Taxation, futures market, monetary theory and policy, income distribution. *Unit head:* Prof. Billy P. Helms, Head, 205-348-8067, E-mail: bhelms@cba.ua.edu. *Application contact:* Debra F. Wheatley, 205-348-6683, Fax: 205-348-0590, E-mail: dwheatle@cba.ua.edu. Web site: http://www.cba.ua.edu/.

Finance and Banking

The University of Alabama in Huntsville, School of Graduate Studies, College of Business Administration, Department of Accounting and Finance, Huntsville, AL 35899. Offers accounting (M Acc), including CPA preparatory with an emphasis in taxation, CPA preparatory with emphasis in assurance and financial reporting, general accounting, information systems audit and control (ISAC). *Accreditation:* AACSB. Part-time and evening/weekend programs available. *Faculty:* 7 full-time (2 women), 4 part-time/adjunct (1 woman). *Students:* 21 full-time (14 women), 28 part-time (13 women); includes 8 minority (6 Black or African American, non-Hispanic/Latino; 1 American Indian or Alaska Native, non-Hispanic/Latino; 1 Asian, non-Hispanic/Latino), 4 international. Average age 33. 30 applicants, 70% accepted, 19 enrolled. In 2011, 24 master's awarded. *Degree requirements:* For master's, comprehensive exam, thesis or alternative. *Entrance requirements:* For master's, GMAT (minimum score 500), minimum AACSB index of 1080. Additional exam requirements/recommendations for international students: Required—TOEFL (minimum score 550 paper-based; 213 computer-based; 62 iBT). *Application deadline:* For fall admission, 8/1 for domestic students, 4/1 for international students; for spring admission, 12/1 for domestic students, 9/1 for international students. Applications are processed on a rolling basis. Application fee: $40 ($50 for international students). Electronic applications accepted. *Expenses:* Tuition, state resident: full-time $7830; part-time $473.50 per credit. Tuition, nonresident: full-time $18,748; part-time $1128.33 per credit. Tuition and fees vary according to course load and program. *Financial support:* In 2011–12, 5 students received support, including 1 research assistantship with full tuition reimbursement available (averaging $14,400 per year), 2 teaching assistantships with full tuition reimbursements available (averaging $5,000 per year); career-related internships or fieldwork, Federal Work-Study, institutionally sponsored loans, scholarships/grants, health care benefits, and unspecified assistantships also available. Support available to part-time students. Financial award application deadline: 4/1; financial award applicants required to submit FAFSA. *Faculty research:* Accounting information systems, emerging technologies in accounting, behavioral accounting, state and local taxation, financial accounting. *Total annual research expenditures:* $66,318. *Unit head:* Dr. John Burnett, Interim Chair, 256-824-2923, Fax: 256-824-2929, E-mail: burnettj@uah.edu. *Application contact:* Jennifer Pettitt, Director of Graduate Programs, 256-824-6681, Fax: 256-824-7571, E-mail: jennifer.pettitt@uah.edu.

The University of Alabama in Huntsville, School of Graduate Studies, College of Business Administration, Department of Management and Marketing, Huntsville, AL 35899. Offers federal contract procurement (Certificate); management (MBA), including acquisition management, entrepreneurship, federal contract accounting, finance, human resource management, logistics and supply chain management, marketing, project management; supply chain management (Certificate); technology and innovation management (Certificate). *Accreditation:* AACSB. Part-time and evening/weekend programs available. *Faculty:* 11 full-time (2 women), 3 part-time/adjunct (0 women). *Students:* 52 full-time (25 women), 145 part-time (68 women); includes 28 minority (14 Black or African American, non-Hispanic/Latino; 4 American Indian or Alaska Native, non-Hispanic/Latino; 7 Asian, non-Hispanic/Latino; 2 Hispanic/Latino; 1 Two or more races, non-Hispanic/Latino), 15 international. Average age 31. 103 applicants, 73% accepted, 65 enrolled. In 2011, 76 master's awarded. *Degree requirements:* For master's, comprehensive exam, thesis or alternative. *Entrance requirements:* For master's, GMAT (minimum score 500), minimum AACSB index of 1080. Additional exam requirements/recommendations for international students: Required—TOEFL (minimum score 550 paper-based; 213 computer-based; 62 iBT). *Application deadline:* For fall admission, 8/1 for domestic students, 4/1 for international students; for spring admission, 12/1 for domestic students, 9/1 for international students. Applications are processed on a rolling basis. Application fee: $40 ($50 for international students). Electronic applications accepted. *Expenses:* Tuition, state resident: full-time $7830; part-time $473.50 per credit. Tuition, nonresident: full-time $18,748; part-time $1128.33 per credit. Tuition and fees vary according to course load and program. *Financial support:* In 2011–12, 12 students received support, including 7 research assistantships with full tuition reimbursements available (averaging $9,829 per year), 4 teaching assistantships with full tuition reimbursements available (averaging $8,000 per year); career-related internships or fieldwork, Federal Work-Study, institutionally sponsored loans, scholarships/grants, health care benefits, and unspecified assistantships also available. Support available to part-time students. Financial award application deadline: 4/1; financial award applicants required to submit FAFSA. *Faculty research:* Strategic human resources, corporate governance, cross-function integration and the management of research and development, determinants of team performance. *Total annual research expenditures:* $3.4 million. *Unit head:* Dr. Cynthia Gramm, Chair, 256-824-6913, Fax: 256-824-6328, E-mail: cynthia.gramm@uah.edu. *Application contact:* Jennifer Pettitt, Director of Graduate Programs, 256-824-6681, Fax: 256-824-7571, E-mail: jennifer.pettitt@uah.edu.

University of Alaska Fairbanks, School of Management, Department of Business Administration, Fairbanks, AK 99775-6080. Offers capital markets (MBA); general management (MBA). *Accreditation:* AACSB. Part-time programs available. *Faculty:* 12 full-time (4 women), 1 part-time/adjunct (0 women). *Students:* 32 full-time (19 women), 27 part-time (18 women); includes 13 minority (3 Black or African American, non-Hispanic/Latino; 4 American Indian or Alaska Native, non-Hispanic/Latino; 3 Asian, non-Hispanic/Latino; 1 Native Hawaiian or other Pacific Islander, non-Hispanic/Latino; 2 Two or more races, non-Hispanic/Latino), 8 international. Average age 31. 43 applicants, 63% accepted, 24 enrolled. In 2011, 23 master's awarded. *Degree requirements:* For master's, comprehensive exam, thesis or alternative. *Entrance requirements:* For master's, GMAT. Additional exam requirements/recommendations for international students: Required—TOEFL (minimum score 550 paper-based; 213 computer-based; 80 iBT). *Application deadline:* For fall admission, 6/1 priority date for domestic students, 2/1 for international students; for spring admission, 10/15 priority date for domestic students, 9/1 for international students. Applications are processed on a rolling basis. Application fee: $60. Electronic applications accepted. *Expenses:* Tuition, state resident: full-time $6696; part-time $372 per credit. Tuition, nonresident: full-time $13,680; part-time $760 per credit. Tuition and fees vary according to course load and reciprocity agreements. *Financial support:* In 2011–12, 3 research assistantships with tuition reimbursements (averaging $4,896 per year), 4 teaching assistantships with tuition reimbursements (averaging $14,245 per year) were awarded; fellowships with tuition reimbursements, career-related internships or fieldwork, Federal Work-Study, scholarships/grants, health care benefits, and unspecified assistantships also available. Support available to part-time students. Financial award application deadline: 2/15; financial award applicants required to submit FAFSA. *Faculty research:* Consumer behavior, marketing, international finance and business, strategic risk, organization theory. *Total annual research expenditures:* $1,000. *Unit head:* Dr. Ping Lan, Director, MBA Program, 907-474-7688, Fax: 907-474-5219, E-mail: plan@alaska.edu. *Application contact:* Mike Earnest, Director of Admissions, 907-474-7500, Fax: 907-474-5379, E-mail: admissions@uaf.edu. Web site: http://www.uaf.edu/som/programs/mba/.

University of Alberta, Faculty of Graduate Studies and Research, Department of Economics, Edmonton, AB T6G 2E1, Canada. Offers economics (MA, PhD); economics and finance (MA); environmental and natural resource economics (PhD). Part-time programs available. *Degree requirements:* For doctorate, thesis/dissertation. *Entrance requirements:* For master's and doctorate, GRE. Additional exam requirements/recommendations for international students: Required—TOEFL. *Faculty research:* Public finance, international trade, industrial organization, Pacific Rim economics, monetary economics.

University of Alberta, Faculty of Graduate Studies and Research, Doctoral Program in Business, Edmonton, AB T6G 2E1, Canada. Offers accounting (PhD); finance (PhD); human resources/industrial relations (PhD); management science (PhD); marketing (PhD); organizational analysis (PhD); MBA/PhD. *Accreditation:* AACSB. Part-time programs available. *Degree requirements:* For doctorate, comprehensive exam, thesis/dissertation. *Entrance requirements:* For doctorate, GMAT. Additional exam requirements/recommendations for international students: Required—TOEFL (minimum score 550 paper-based; 213 computer-based). Electronic applications accepted. *Faculty research:* Accounting, capital markets and corporate finance, organizational change and human resource management, marketing, strategic management.

The University of Arizona, Eller College of Management, Department of Finance, Tucson, AZ 85721. Offers MS, PhD. Part-time programs available. *Faculty:* 8 full-time (2 women), 1 part-time/adjunct. Terminal master's awarded for partial completion of doctoral program. *Degree requirements:* For master's, project; for doctorate, comprehensive exam, thesis/dissertation. *Entrance requirements:* Additional exam requirements/recommendations for international students: Required—TOEFL (minimum score 550 paper-based; 213 computer-based; 79 iBT). *Application deadline:* For fall admission, 2/15 for domestic and international students. Applications are processed on a rolling basis. Application fee: $75. Electronic applications accepted. *Expenses:* Contact institution. *Financial support:* In 2011–12, 3 research assistantships with full tuition reimbursements (averaging $25,599 per year), 8 teaching assistantships with full tuition reimbursements (averaging $25,665 per year) were awarded; health care benefits, tuition waivers (partial), and unspecified assistantships also available. Financial award application deadline: 3/15. *Faculty research:* Corporate finance, banking, investments, stock market. *Unit head:* Dr. Chris Lamoureux, Head, 520-621-7488, Fax: 520-621-1261, E-mail: lamoureu@lamfin.eller.arizona.edu. *Application contact:* Kay Ross, Program Coordinator, 520-621-1520, Fax: 520-621-1261, E-mail: kross@eller.arizona.edu. Web site: http://www.finance.eller.arizona.edu/.

University of Baltimore, Graduate School, Merrick School of Business, Department of Economics, Finance, and Management Science, Baltimore, MD 21201-5779. Offers business/finance (MS). Part-time and evening/weekend programs available. *Entrance requirements:* For master's, GMAT. Additional exam requirements/recommendations for international students: Required—TOEFL (minimum score 550 paper-based; 213 computer-based). Electronic applications accepted. *Faculty research:* International finance, corporate finance, health care, regional economics, small business.

University of Bridgeport, School of Business, Bridgeport, CT 06604. Offers accounting (MBA); finance (MBA); general business (MBA); global financial services (MBA); human resource management (MBA); information systems and knowledge management (MBA); international business (MBA); management (MBA); marketing (MBA); operations management (MBA); small business and entrepreneurship (MBA); specialized business (MBA). Part-time and evening/weekend programs available. *Faculty:* 11 full-time (2 women), 39 part-time/adjunct (8 women). *Students:* 198 full-time (105 women), 94 part-time (47 women); includes 38 minority (16 Black or African American, non-Hispanic/Latino; 9 Asian, non-Hispanic/Latino; 10 Hispanic/Latino; 3 Two or more races, non-Hispanic/Latino), 227 international. Average age 28. 835 applicants, 56% accepted, 57 enrolled. In 2011, 155 master's awarded. *Degree requirements:* For master's, thesis optional. *Entrance requirements:* For master's, GMAT. Additional exam requirements/recommendations for international students: Recommended—TOEFL (minimum score 550 paper-based; 213 computer-based; 80 iBT), IELTS (minimum score 6.5). *Application deadline:* For fall admission, 8/1 priority date for domestic students, 8/1 for international students; for spring admission, 12/1 priority date for domestic students, 12/1 for international students. Applications are processed on a rolling basis. Application fee: $50. Electronic applications accepted. *Expenses:* Contact institution. *Financial support:* In 2011–12, 69 students received support. Fellowships, research assistantships, teaching assistantships, career-related internships or fieldwork, Federal Work-Study, institutionally sponsored loans, and tuition waivers (partial) available. Support available to part-time students. Financial award application deadline: 6/1; financial award applicants required to submit FAFSA. *Unit head:* Dr. Robert Gilmore, Dean, 203-576-4384, Fax: 203-576-4388, E-mail: rgilmore@bridgeport.edu. *Application contact:* Karissa Peckham, Dean of Admissions, 203-576-4552, Fax: 203-576-4941, E-mail: mba@bridgeport.edu. Web site: http://www.bridgeport.edu.

The University of British Columbia, Sauder School of Business, Doctoral Program in Commerce and Business Administration, Vancouver, BC V6T 1Z1, Canada. Offers accounting (PhD); finance (PhD); international business (PhD); management information systems (PhD); management science (PhD); marketing (PhD); organizational behavior (PhD); strategy and business economics (PhD); transportation and logistics (PhD); urban land economics (PhD). *Degree requirements:* For doctorate, comprehensive exam, thesis/dissertation. *Entrance requirements:* For doctorate, GMAT or GRE. Additional exam requirements/recommendations for international students: Required—TOEFL (minimum score 600 paper-based; 250 computer-based; 100 iBT). Electronic applications accepted.

University of California, Berkeley, Graduate Division, Haas School of Business, PhD in Business Administration Program, Berkeley, CA 94720-1500. Offers accounting (PhD); business and public policy (PhD); finance (PhD); management of organizations (PhD); marketing (PhD); operations management (PhD); real estate (PhD). *Accreditation:* AACSB. *Faculty:* 77 full-time (18 women), 152 part-time/adjunct (24 women). *Students:* 79 full-time (25 women); includes 13 minority (12 Asian, non-Hispanic/Latino; 1 Hispanic/Latino), 34 international. Average age 30. 547 applicants, 5% accepted, 15 enrolled. In 2011, 14 doctorates awarded. *Degree requirements:* For doctorate, comprehensive exam, thesis/dissertation, written preliminary exams, oral qualifying exam. *Entrance requirements:* For doctorate, GMAT or GRE, minimum GPA of 3.0 in undergraduate and graduate coursework. Additional exam requirements/recommendations for international students: Required—TOEFL (minimum score 570 paper-based; 230 computer-based; 70 iBT), IELTS (minimum score 7). *Application deadline:* For fall admission, 12/10 for domestic and international students. Application fee: $80 ($100 for international students). Electronic applications accepted. *Financial support:* In 2011–12, 66 students received support, including 58 fellowships with full and partial tuition reimbursements available (averaging $29,000 per year), 77 teaching assistantships with full and partial tuition reimbursements available; research assistantships with full and partial tuition reimbursements available, scholarships/grants, health care benefits, tuition waivers (full), unspecified assistantships, and transit pass, travel grants also available. Financial award application deadline: 12/10; financial award applicants required to submit FAFSA. *Faculty research:* Accounting, business and public policy, finance, management of organizations, marketing, operations and information technology management, real estate. *Unit head:* Dr. Sunil Dutta, Director, 510-642-1229, Fax: 510-643-4255, E-mail: kimg@haas.berkeley.edu. *Application contact:* Kim Guilfoyle, Director, Student Affairs, 510-642-3944, Fax: 510-643-4255, E-mail: kimg@haas.berkeley.edu. Web site: http://www.haas.berkeley.edu/Phd/.

University of California, Berkeley, UC Berkeley Extension, Certificate Programs in Business, Berkeley, CA 94720-1500. Offers accounting (Certificate); business administration (Certificate); finance (Certificate); human resource management (Certificate); management (Certificate); marketing (Certificate); project management (Certificate). *Accreditation:* AACSB. Postbaccalaureate distance learning degree programs offered.

University of California, Berkeley, UC Berkeley Extension, International Diploma Programs, Berkeley, CA 94720-1500. Offers business administration (Certificate); finance (Certificate); global business management (Certificate); marketing (Certificate); project management (Certificate). *Accreditation:* AACSB.

University of California, Los Angeles, Graduate Division, UCLA Anderson School of Management, Los Angeles, CA 90095-1481. Offers accounting (PhD); Asia Pacific (EMBA); business administration (EMBA, MBA); decisions, operations and technology management (PhD); finance (PhD); financial engineering (MFE); global economics and management (PhD); Latin America (EMBA); management and organizations (PhD); marketing (PhD); strategy (PhD); DDS/MBA; MBA/JD; MBA/MD; MBA/MLAS; MBA/MLIS; MBA/MPH; MBA/MPP; MBA/MSCS; MBA/MSN; MBA/MUP. *Accreditation:* AACSB. Part-time programs available. *Faculty:* 90 full-time (14 women), 62 part-time/adjunct (14 women). *Students:* 1,103 full-time (312 women), 842 part-time (223 women); includes 663 minority (18 Black or African American, non-Hispanic/Latino; 510 Asian, non-Hispanic/Latino; 46 Hispanic/Latino; 2 Native Hawaiian or other Pacific Islander, non-Hispanic/Latino; 87 Two or more races, non-Hispanic/Latino), 469 international. 4,737 applicants, 32% accepted, 875 enrolled. In 2011, 759 master's, 6 doctorates awarded. *Degree requirements:* For master's, comprehensive exam, field study consulting project (for MBA); thesis/dissertation (for MFE); for doctorate, comprehensive exam, thesis/dissertation, oral and written qualifying exams. *Entrance requirements:* For master's, GMAT (for MBA); GMAT or GRE General Test (for MFE), 4-year bachelor's degree or equivalent; for doctorate, GMAT or GRE General Test, 4-year bachelor's degree from regionally-accredited institution; minimum GPA of 3.0. Additional exam requirements/recommendations for international students: Required—TOEFL (minimum score 560 paper-based; 220 computer-based; 87 iBT), IELTS (minimum score 7). *Application deadline:* For fall admission, 10/26 for domestic and international students; for winter admission, 1/11 for domestic and international students; for spring admission, 4/18 for domestic and international students. Application fee: $200. Electronic applications accepted. *Expenses:* Contact institution. *Financial support:* In 2011–12, 600 students received support. Fellowships, research assistantships, teaching assistantships, career-related internships or fieldwork, institutionally sponsored loans, scholarships/grants, health care benefits, and tuition waivers (partial) available. Financial award application deadline: 4/15; financial award applicants required to submit FAFSA. *Unit head:* Judy D. Olian, Dean, 310-825-7982, Fax: 310-206-2073, E-mail: judy.olian@anderson.ucla.edu. *Application contact:* Robert Weiler, Assistant Dean, Director of MBA Admissions and Financial Aid, 310-825-6944, Fax: 310-825-8582, E-mail: mba.admissions@anderson.ucla.edu. Web site: http://www.anderson.ucla.edu/.

See Display on page 141 and Close-Up on page 249.

University of California, Santa Cruz, Division of Graduate Studies, Division of Social Sciences, Program in Applied Economics and Finance, Santa Cruz, CA 95064. Offers MS. *Degree requirements:* For master's, thesis or alternative, project. *Entrance requirements:* For master's, GRE General Test, GRE Subject Test. Additional exam requirements/recommendations for international students: Required—TOEFL (minimum score 550 paper-based; 220 computer-based; 83 iBT); Recommended—IELTS (minimum score 8). Electronic applications accepted. *Faculty research:* Economic decision-making skills for the design and operation of complex institutional systems.

University of Central Missouri, The Graduate School, Harmon College of Business Administration, Warrensburg, MO 64093. Offers accountancy (MA); accounting (MBA); ethical strategic leadership (MBA); finance (MBA); general business (MBA); information systems (MBA); information technology (MS); marketing (MBA). Part-time programs available. Postbaccalaureate distance learning degree programs offered. *Entrance requirements:* Additional exam requirements/recommendations for international students: Required—TOEFL (minimum score 550 paper-based; 79 computer-based). Electronic applications accepted.

University of Chicago, Booth School of Business, Full-Time MBA Program, Chicago, IL 60637. Offers accounting (MBA); analytic finance (MBA); analytic management (MBA); business administration (PhD); econometrics and statistics (MBA); economics (MBA); entrepreneurship (MBA); finance (MBA); general management (MBA); health administration and policy (Certificate); human resource management (MBA); international business (IMBA, MBA); managerial and organizational behavior (MBA); marketing management (MBA); operations management (MBA); strategic management (MBA); MBA/AM; MBA/JD; MBA/MA; MBA/MD; MBA/MPP. *Accreditation:* AACSB. Part-time and evening/weekend programs available. *Faculty:* 166 full-time, 32 part-time/adjunct. *Students:* 1,160 full-time (412 women); includes 316 minority (61 Black or African American, non-Hispanic/Latino; 173 Asian, non-Hispanic/Latino; 63 Hispanic/Latino; 19 Two or more races, non-Hispanic/Latino), 378 international. Average age 28. 4,169 applicants, 575 enrolled. In 2011, 1,423 master's, 19 doctorates awarded. Terminal master's awarded for partial completion of doctoral program. *Entrance requirements:* For master's, GMAT, 2 letters of recommendation, 3 essays, resume, interview. Additional exam requirements/recommendations for international students: Required—TOEFL (minimum score 600 paper-based; 250 computer-based; 104 iBT), IELTS. *Application deadline:* For fall admission, 10/12 priority date for domestic students, 10/12 for international students; for winter admission, 1/4 for domestic and international students; for spring admission, 4/4 for domestic and international students. Application fee: $200. Electronic applications accepted. *Expenses:* Contact institution. *Financial support:* Fellowships available. Financial award applicants required to submit FAFSA. *Faculty research:* Finance, marketing, economics, entrepreneurship, strategy, management. *Unit head:* Stacey Kole, Deputy Dean, 773-702-7121. *Application contact:* Kurt Ahlm, Associate Dean of Student Recruitment and Admissions, 773-702-7369, Fax: 773-702-9085, E-mail: admissions@chicagobooth.edu. Web site: http://chicagobooth.edu/.

University of Cincinnati, Graduate School, Carl H. Lindner College of Business, PhD Programs, Cincinnati, OH 45221. Offers accounting (PhD); finance (PhD); information systems (PhD); management (PhD); marketing (PhD); quantitative analysis and operations management (PhD). *Faculty:* 56 full-time (13 women). *Students:* 34 full-time (12 women), 12 part-time (4 women); includes 2 minority (1 Asian, non-Hispanic/Latino; 1 Hispanic/Latino), 25 international. Average age 29. 120 applicants, 13% accepted, 10 enrolled. In 2011, 8 degrees awarded. *Median time to degree:* Of those who began their doctoral program in fall 2003, 65% received their degree in 8 years or less. *Degree requirements:* For doctorate, comprehensive exam, thesis/dissertation. *Entrance requirements:* For doctorate, GMAT, GRE, transcripts, essays, resume, letters of recommendation. Additional exam requirements/recommendations for international students: Required—TOEFL (minimum score 600 paper-based; 250 computer-based; 100 iBT). *Application deadline:* For fall admission, 2/1 for domestic and international students. Application fee: $65 ($70 for international students). Electronic applications accepted. *Expenses:* Contact institution. *Financial support:* In 2011–12, 39 students received support, including 30 research assistantships with full and partial tuition reimbursements available (averaging $14,640 per year); scholarships/grants, tuition waivers (full and partial), and unspecified assistantships also available. Financial award application deadline: 2/1; financial award applicants required to submit FAFSA. *Unit head:* Dr. Suzanne Masterson, Director, 513-556-7125, Fax: 513-556-5499, E-mail: suzanne.masterson@uc.edu. *Application contact:* Deborah Schildknecht, Assistant Director, 513-556-7190, Fax: 513-558-7006, E-mail: deborah.schildknecht@uc.edu. Web site: http://www.business.uc.edu/phd.

University of Colorado Boulder, Leeds School of Business, Division of Business Administration, Boulder, CO 80309. Offers accounting (MS, PhD); finance (PhD); information systems (PhD); marketing (PhD); operations (PhD); strategic, organizational, and entrepreneurial studies (PhD). *Students:* 129 full-time (65 women), 6 part-time (0 women); includes 15 minority (1 Black or African American, non-Hispanic/Latino; 8 Asian, non-Hispanic/Latino; 5 Hispanic/Latino; 1 Two or more races, non-Hispanic/Latino), 21 international. Average age 27. 332 applicants, 9% accepted, 13 enrolled. In 2011, 53 master's, 6 doctorates awarded. *Entrance requirements:* For master's, GMAT, minimum undergraduate GPA of 3.0. *Application deadline:* For fall admission, 3/31 for domestic and international students; for spring admission, 10/31 for domestic and international students. Application fee: $50 ($60 for international students). Electronic applications accepted. *Financial support:* In 2011–12, 61 students received support, including 24 fellowships (averaging $3,398 per year), 19 research assistantships with full and partial tuition reimbursements available (averaging $27,830 per year), 15 teaching assistantships with full and partial tuition reimbursements available (averaging $25,615 per year); institutionally sponsored loans, scholarships/grants, health care benefits, and unspecified assistantships also available. Financial award applicants required to submit FAFSA. *Application contact:* E-mail: leedsphd@colorado.edu. Web site: http://leeds.colorado.edu/phdprog.

University of Colorado Denver, Business School, Master of Business Administration Program, Denver, CO 80217. Offers business intelligence (MBA); business strategy (MBA); business to business marketing (MBA); business to consumer marketing (MBA); change management (MBA); corporate financial management (MBA); enterprise technology management (MBA); entrepreneurship (MBA); health administration (MBA), including financial management, health administration, health information technologies, international health management and policy; human resources management (MBA); investment management (MBA); managing for sustainability (MBA); services management (MBA); sports and entertainment management (MBA). *Accreditation:* AACSB. Part-time and evening/weekend programs available. Postbaccalaureate distance learning degree programs offered (no on-campus study). *Students:* 784 full-time (306 women), 203 part-time (81 women); includes 135 minority (18 Black or African American, non-Hispanic/Latino; 5 American Indian or Alaska Native, non-Hispanic/Latino; 50 Asian, non-Hispanic/Latino; 58 Hispanic/Latino; 4 Two or more races, non-Hispanic/Latino), 38 international. Average age 31. 433 applicants, 76% accepted, 212 enrolled. In 2011, 326 master's awarded. *Degree requirements:* For master's, 48 semester hours, including 30 of core courses, 3 in international business, and 15 in electives from over 50 other graduate business courses. *Entrance requirements:* For master's, GMAT, resume, official transcripts, essay, two letters of recommendation, financial statements (for international applicants). Additional exam requirements/recommendations for international students: Required—TOEFL (minimum score 560 paper-based; 197 computer-based; 83 iBT). *Application deadline:* For fall admission, 4/15 priority date for domestic students, 3/15 for international students; for spring admission, 10/15 priority date for domestic students, 10/1 for international students. Applications are processed on a rolling basis. Application fee: $50 ($75 for international students). Electronic applications accepted. *Expenses:* Contact institution. *Financial support:* Scholarships/grants available. Support available to part-time students. Financial award application deadline: 4/1; financial award applicants required to submit FAFSA. *Faculty research:* Marketing, management, entrepreneurship, finance, health administration. *Unit head:* Elizabeth Cooperman, Professor of Finance and Managing for Sustainability/MBA Program Director, 303-315-8422, E-mail: elizabeth.cooperman@ucdenver.edu. *Application contact:* Shelly Townley, Admissions Director, Graduate Programs, 303-315-8202, E-mail: shelly.townley@ucdenver.edu. Web site: http://www.ucdenver.edu/academics/colleges/business/degrees/ms/accounting/Pages/Accounting.aspx.

University of Colorado Denver, Business School, Program in Finance, Denver, CO 80217. Offers economics (MS); finance (MS); financial analysis and management (MS); financial and commodities risk management (MS); risk management and insurance (MS); MS/MBA. Part-time and evening/weekend programs available. *Students:* 60 full-time (19 women), 33 part-time (11 women); includes 9 minority (5 Asian, non-Hispanic/Latino; 3 Hispanic/Latino; 1 Two or more races, non-Hispanic/Latino), 27 international. Average age 30. 83 applicants, 59% accepted, 24 enrolled. In 2011, 45 master's awarded. *Degree requirements:* For master's, 30 semester hours (18 of required core courses, 9 of finance electives, and 3 of free elective). *Entrance requirements:* For master's, GMAT, essay, resume, two letters of recommendation, financial statements (for international students). Additional exam requirements/recommendations for international students: Required—TOEFL (minimum score 525 paper-based; 197 computer-based; 70 iBT), IELTS (minimum score 6). *Application deadline:* For fall admission, 4/15 priority date for domestic students, 3/15 for international students; for spring admission, 10/15 priority date for domestic students, 10/1 for international students. Applications are processed on a rolling basis. Application fee: $50 ($75 for international students). Electronic applications accepted. *Expenses:* Contact institution. *Financial support:* Federal Work-Study and scholarships/grants available. Support available to part-time students. Financial award application deadline: 4/1; financial award applicants required to submit FAFSA. *Faculty research:* Corporate governance, debt maturity policies, regulation and financial markets, option management strategies. *Unit head:* Dr. Ajeyo Banerjee, Associate Professor/Director of MS in Finance Program, 303-315-8456, E-mail: ajeyo.banerjee@ucdenver.edu. *Application contact:* Shelly Townley, Admissions Director, Graduate Programs, 303-315-8202, E-mail: shelly.townley@ucdenver.edu. Web site: http://www.ucdenver.edu/academics/colleges/business/degrees/ms/finance/Pages/Finance.aspx.

University of Connecticut, Graduate School, College of Liberal Arts and Sciences, Department of Public Policy, Field of Public Administration, Storrs, CT 06269. Offers nonprofit management (Graduate Certificate); public administration (MPA); public financial management (Graduate Certificate); JD/MPA; MPA/MSW. *Accreditation:* NASPAA. *Degree requirements:* For master's, comprehensive exam, internship. *Entrance requirements:* For master's, GRE General Test. Additional exam requirements/recommendations for international students: Required—TOEFL (minimum score 550 paper-based; 213 computer-based). Electronic applications accepted.

University of Connecticut, Graduate School, School of Business, Storrs, CT 06269. Offers accounting (MS, PhD); business administration (Exec MBA, MBA, PhD); finance (PhD); health care management and insurance studies (MBA); management (PhD); management consulting (MBA); marketing (PhD); marketing intelligence (MBA); MA/MBA; MBA/MSW. *Accreditation:* AACSB. *Degree requirements:* For master's, comprehensive exam; for doctorate, thesis/dissertation. *Entrance requirements:* For master's and doctorate, GMAT. Additional exam requirements/recommendations for

international students: Required—TOEFL (minimum score 550 paper-based; 213 computer-based). Electronic applications accepted.

See Display on page 144 and Close-Up on page 251.

University of Dallas, Graduate School of Management, Irving, TX 75062-4736. Offers accounting (MBA, MM, MS); business management (MBA, MM); corporate finance (MBA, MM); financial services (MBA); global business (MBA, MM); health services management (MBA, MM); human resource management (MBA, MM); information assurance (MBA, MM, MS); information technology (MBA, MM, MS); information technology service management (MBA, MM, MS); marketing management (MBA, MM); organization development (MBA, MM); project management (MBA, MM); sports and entertainment management (MBA, MM); strategic leadership (MBA, MM); supply chain management (MBA); supply chain management and market logistics (MM). *Accreditation:* ACBSP. Part-time and evening/weekend programs available. Postbaccalaureate distance learning degree programs offered (no on-campus study). *Entrance requirements:* Additional exam requirements/recommendations for international students: Required—TOEFL. Electronic applications accepted. *Expenses:* Contact institution.

University of Dayton, School of Business Administration, Dayton, OH 45469-1300. Offers accounting (MBA); cyber security (MBA); finance (MBA); marketing (MBA); JD/MBA. *Accreditation:* AACSB. Part-time and evening/weekend programs available. *Faculty:* 23 full-time (6 women), 13 part-time/adjunct (2 women). *Students:* 170 full-time (72 women), 117 part-time (43 women); includes 26 minority (16 Black or African American, non-Hispanic/Latino; 6 Asian, non-Hispanic/Latino; 3 Hispanic/Latino; 1 Two or more races, non-Hispanic/Latino), 49 international. Average age 28. 366 applicants, 72% accepted, 126 enrolled. In 2011, 147 master's awarded. *Entrance requirements:* For master's, GMAT or GRE. Additional exam requirements/recommendations for international students: Required—TOEFL (minimum score 550 paper-based; 213 computer-based; 80 iBT); Recommended—IELTS (minimum score 6.5). *Application deadline:* For fall admission, 3/1 for international students; for winter admission, 7/1 for international students; for spring admission, 1/1 for international students. Applications are processed on a rolling basis. Application fee: $0 ($50 for international students). Electronic applications accepted. *Expenses:* Contact institution. *Financial support:* In 2011–12, 12 research assistantships with full and partial tuition reimbursements (averaging $7,020 per year) were awarded; career-related internships or fieldwork, institutionally sponsored loans, scholarships/grants, health care benefits, and unspecified assistantships also available. Support available to part-time students. Financial award application deadline: 3/15; financial award applicants required to submit FAFSA. *Faculty research:* Management information systems, economics, finance, entrepreneurship, marketing, accounting and cyber security. *Unit head:* Janice M. Glynn, Director, MBA Program, 937-229-3733, Fax: 937-229-3882, E-mail: glynn@udayton.edu. *Application contact:* Jeffrey Carter, Assistant Director, MBA Program, 937-229-3733, Fax: 937-229-3882, E-mail: jeff.carter@notes.udayton.edu. Web site: http://business.udayton.edu/mba/.

University of Delaware, Alfred Lerner College of Business and Economics, Department of Finance, Newark, DE 19716. Offers MS.

University of Denver, Daniels College of Business, Reiman School of Finance, Denver, CO 80208. Offers IMBA, MBA, MS. Part-time and evening/weekend programs available. *Faculty:* 17 full-time (4 women), 4 part-time/adjunct (0 women). *Students:* 79 full-time (37 women), 52 part-time (16 women); includes 5 minority (1 Black or African American, non-Hispanic/Latino; 3 Asian, non-Hispanic/Latino; 1 Hispanic/Latino), 97 international. Average age 25. 715 applicants, 27% accepted, 75 enrolled. In 2011, 76 degrees awarded. *Entrance requirements:* For master's, GRE General Test or GMAT, essay, two letters of recommendation. Additional exam requirements/recommendations for international students: Required—TOEFL (minimum score 570 paper-based; 88 iBT). *Application deadline:* For fall admission, 11/15 priority date for domestic students; for spring admission, 10/15 priority date for domestic students. Applications are processed on a rolling basis. Application fee: $100. Electronic applications accepted. *Financial support:* In 2011–12, 22 students received support, including 12 teaching assistantships with partial tuition reimbursements available (averaging $1,656 per year); career-related internships or fieldwork, Federal Work-Study, institutionally sponsored loans, scholarships/grants, and unspecified assistantships also available. Support available to part-time students. Financial award application deadline: 2/15; financial award applicants required to submit FAFSA. *Unit head:* Dr. Thomas Cook, Co-Director, 303-871-2012, E-mail: thomas.cook@du.edu. *Application contact:* Tara Stenbakken, Graduate Admissions Counselor, 303-871-4211, E-mail: tara.stenbakken@du.edu. Web site: http://daniels.du.edu/schoolsdepartments/finance/.

University of Florida, Graduate School, Warrington College of Business Administration, Hough Graduate School of Business, Department of Finance, Insurance and Real Estate, Gainesville, FL 32611. Offers finance (MS, PhD); financial services (Certificate); insurance (PhD); real estate and urban analysis (MS, PhD); JD/MBA. *Faculty:* 13 full-time (0 women). *Students:* 107 full-time (28 women), 10 part-time (2 women); includes 20 minority (6 Black or African American, non-Hispanic/Latino; 8 Asian, non-Hispanic/Latino; 6 Hispanic/Latino), 31 international. Average age 26. 245 applicants, 2% accepted, 3 enrolled. In 2011, 103 master's, 2 doctorates awarded. Terminal master's awarded for partial completion of doctoral program. *Degree requirements:* For master's, comprehensive exam, thesis; for doctorate, comprehensive exam, thesis/dissertation. *Entrance requirements:* For master's, GMAT or GRE General Test, minimum GPA of 3.0 for last 60 hours of undergraduate degree, work experience (preferred); for doctorate, GMAT or GRE General Test, minimum GPA of 3.0. Additional exam requirements/recommendations for international students: Required—TOEFL (minimum score 550 paper-based; 213 computer-based; 80 iBT), IELTS (minimum score 6). *Application deadline:* For fall admission, 1/15 priority date for domestic students, 1/15 for international students. Applications are processed on a rolling basis. Application fee: $30. Electronic applications accepted. *Financial support:* Fellowships, research assistantships, teaching assistantships, career-related internships or fieldwork, scholarships/grants, and unspecified assistantships available. Financial award application deadline: 1/15; financial award applicants required to submit FAFSA. *Faculty research:* Banking, empirical corporate finance, hedge funds. *Unit head:* Dr. Mahendrarajah Nimalendran, Chair, 352-392-9526, Fax: 352-392-0301, E-mail: nimal@ufl.edu. *Application contact:* Mark J. Flannery, Graduate Coordinator, 352-392-3184, Fax: 352-392-0301, E-mail: flannery@ufl.edu. Web site: http://www.cba.ufl.edu/fire/.

University of Florida, Graduate School, Warrington College of Business Administration, Hough Graduate School of Business, Programs in Business Administration, Gainesville, FL 32611. Offers accounting (MBA); arts administration (MBA); business strategy and public policy (MBA); competitive strategy (MBA); decision and information sciences (MBA); electronic commerce (MBA); finance (MBA); general business (MBA); global management (MBA); Graham-Buffett security analysis (MBA); health administration (MBA); human resources management (MBA); international studies (MBA); Latin American business (MBA); management (MBA); marketing (MBA); sports administration (MBA); JD/MBA; MBA/MS; MBA/PhD; MBA/Pharm D; MD/MBA. *Accreditation:* AACSB. Part-time and evening/weekend programs available. *Faculty:* 71 full-time (10 women). *Students:* 412 full-time (111 women), 467 part-time (135 women); includes 235 minority (39 Black or African American, non-Hispanic/Latino; 7 American Indian or Alaska Native, non-Hispanic/Latino; 79 Asian, non-Hispanic/Latino; 109 Hispanic/Latino; 1 Native Hawaiian or other Pacific Islander, non-Hispanic/Latino), 44 international. Average age 32. 589 applicants, 52% accepted, 247 enrolled. In 2011, 505 master's awarded. *Degree requirements:* For master's, capstone course. *Entrance requirements:* For master's, GMAT, minimum GPA of 3.0, interview. Additional exam requirements/recommendations for international students: Required—TOEFL (minimum score 550 paper-based; 213 computer-based; 80 iBT), IELTS (minimum score 6). *Application deadline:* For fall admission, 7/1 for domestic students, 1/1 for international students; for spring admission, 12/1 for domestic and international students. Applications are processed on a rolling basis. Application fee: $30. Electronic applications accepted. *Financial support:* Teaching assistantships, career-related internships or fieldwork, scholarships/grants, and unspecified assistantships available. Support available to part-time students. Financial award applicants required to submit FAFSA. *Faculty research:* Accounting, finance, insurance, management, real estate, urban analysis marketing. *Unit head:* Prof. Alexander D. Sevilla, Assistant Dean/Director, 352-273-3252 Ext. 1206, E-mail: alex.sevilla@warrington.ufl.edu. *Application contact:* Prof. Kelli Gust, Associate Director, 352-273-3255, Fax: 352-392-8791, E-mail: kelly.gust@warrington.ufl.edu. Web site: http://www.floridamba.ufl.edu/.

University of Hawaii at Manoa, Graduate Division, Shidler College of Business, Program in Business Administration, Honolulu, HI 96822. Offers Asian business studies (MBA); Chinese business studies (MBA); decision sciences (MBA); entrepreneurship (MBA); finance (MBA); finance and banking (MBA); human resources management (MBA); information management (MBA); information technology (MBA); international business (MBA); Japanese business studies (MBA); marketing (MBA); organizational behavior (MBA); organizational management (MBA); real estate (MBA); student-designed track (MBA). *Accreditation:* AACSB. Part-time and evening/weekend programs available. *Degree requirements:* For master's, thesis optional. *Entrance requirements:* For master's, GMAT, minimum GPA of 3.0. Additional exam requirements/recommendations for international students: Required—TOEFL (minimum score 600 paper-based; 250 computer-based; 100 iBT), IELTS (minimum score 7). *Expenses:* Contact institution.

University of Hawaii at Manoa, Graduate Division, Shidler College of Business, Program in International Management, Honolulu, HI 96822. Offers Asian finance (PhD); global information technology management (PhD); international accounting (PhD); international marketing (PhD); international organization and strategy (PhD). Part-time programs available. *Degree requirements:* For doctorate, comprehensive exam, thesis/dissertation. *Entrance requirements:* For doctorate, GMAT or GRE General Test, minimum GPA of 3.0. Additional exam requirements/recommendations for international students: Required—TOEFL (minimum score 600 paper-based; 250 computer-based; 100 iBT), IELTS (minimum score 7). *Expenses:* Contact institution.

University of Houston, Bauer College of Business, Finance Program, Houston, TX 77204. Offers MS. Part-time and evening/weekend programs available. *Degree requirements:* For master's, 30 hours completed in residence, minimum cumulative GPA of 3.0 at UH, no more than 11 semester hours of 'C' grades or below in graduate courses taken at UH. *Entrance requirements:* For master's, GMAT or GRE, official transcripts from all higher education institutions attended, resume, goal statement, letters of recommendation. Additional exam requirements/recommendations for international students: Required—TOEFL (minimum score 620 paper-based; 260 computer-based; 105 iBT), IELTS (minimum score 7.5). Electronic applications accepted. *Faculty research:* Accountancy and taxation, finance, international business, management.

University of Houston–Clear Lake, School of Business, Program in Finance, Houston, TX 77058-1098. Offers MS. Part-time and evening/weekend programs available. *Degree requirements:* For master's, thesis optional. *Entrance requirements:* For master's, GMAT. Additional exam requirements/recommendations for international students: Required—TOEFL (minimum score 550 paper-based; 213 computer-based). Electronic applications accepted.

University of Houston–Victoria, School of Business Administration, Victoria, TX 77901-4450. Offers accounting (MBA); economic development and entrepreneurship (MS); finance (GMBA, MBA); general business (MBA); international business (MBA); management (GMBA, MBA); marketing (MBA). *Accreditation:* AACSB. Part-time and evening/weekend programs available. Postbaccalaureate distance learning degree programs offered (minimal on-campus study). *Entrance requirements:* For master's, GMAT. Additional exam requirements/recommendations for international students: Required—TOEFL (minimum score 550 paper-based; 213 computer-based). Electronic applications accepted. *Faculty research:* Economic development, marketing, finance.

University of Illinois at Urbana–Champaign, Graduate College, College of Business, Department of Finance, Champaign, IL 61820. Offers MS, PhD. *Faculty:* 17 full-time (1 woman), 3 part-time/adjunct (0 women). *Students:* 161 full-time (79 women), 9 part-time (1 woman); includes 7 minority (5 Asian, non-Hispanic/Latino; 1 Hispanic/Latino; 1 Two or more races, non-Hispanic/Latino), 151 international. 1,298 applicants, 17% accepted, 137 enrolled. In 2011, 115 master's, 4 doctorates awarded. *Entrance requirements:* For master's and doctorate, GMAT or GRE, minimum GPA of 3.0. Additional exam requirements/recommendations for international students: Required—TOEFL. *Application deadline:* Applications are processed on a rolling basis. Application fee: $75 ($90 for international students). Electronic applications accepted. *Financial support:* In 2011–12, 7 fellowships, 21 research assistantships, 5 teaching assistantships were awarded; tuition waivers (full and partial) also available. *Unit head:* Charles M. Kahn, Chair, 217-333-2813, Fax: 217-244-3102, E-mail: c-kahn@illinois.edu. *Application contact:* Denise Madden, Office Support Associate, 217-244-2371, Fax: 217-244-9867, E-mail: djmadden@illinois.edu. Web site: http://www.business.illinois.edu/finance.

The University of Iowa, Henry B. Tippie College of Business, Department of Finance, Iowa City, IA 52242-1316. Offers PhD. *Faculty:* 22 full-time (4 women), 8 part-time/adjunct (2 women). *Students:* 14 full-time (7 women), 11 international. Average age 31. 88 applicants, 6% accepted, 3 enrolled. In 2011, 3 doctorates awarded. *Degree requirements:* For doctorate, comprehensive exam, thesis/dissertation, thesis defense. *Entrance requirements:* For doctorate, GMAT or GRE. Additional exam requirements/recommendations for international students: Required—TOEFL (minimum score 600 paper-based; 250 computer-based; 100 iBT). *Application deadline:* For fall admission, 1/15 for domestic and international students. Applications are processed on a rolling basis. Application fee: $60 ($100 for international students). Electronic applications accepted. *Financial support:* In 2011–12, 14 students received support, including 14 fellowships with full tuition reimbursements available (averaging $6,000 per year), 14 teaching assistantships with full tuition reimbursements available (averaging $16,575 per year); institutionally sponsored loans, scholarships/grants, health care benefits, and unspecified assistantships also available. Financial award application deadline: 1/15. *Faculty research:* International finance, real estate finance, theoretical and empirical corporate finance, theoretical and empirical asset pricing bond pricing and derivatives. *Unit head:* Prof. Erik Lie, Department Executive Officer, 319-335-0929, Fax: 319-335-3690, E-mail: erik-lie@uiowa.edu. *Application contact:* Renea L. Jay, PhD Program Coordinator, 319-335-0830, Fax: 319-335-1956, E-mail: renea-jay@uiowa.edu. Web site: http://tippie.uiowa.edu/finance/.

The University of Iowa, Henry B. Tippie College of Business, Henry B. Tippie School of Management, Iowa City, IA 52242-1316. Offers finance (MBA); investment management (MBA); marketing (MBA); process and operations excellence (MBA); strategic innovation (MBA); JD/MBA; MBA/MA; MBA/MD; MBA/MHA; MBA/MSN. *Accreditation:* AACSB. Part-time and evening/weekend programs available. *Faculty:* 62 full-time (19 women), 26 part-time/adjunct (6 women). *Students:* 153 full-time (34 women), 876 part-time (288 women); includes 87 minority (16 Black or African American, non-Hispanic/Latino; 4 American Indian or Alaska Native, non-Hispanic/Latino; 43 Asian, non-Hispanic/Latino; 24 Hispanic/Latino), 130 international. Average age 32. 697 applicants, 66% accepted, 362 enrolled. In 2011, 361 master's awarded. *Degree requirements:* For master's, minimum GPA of 2.75. *Entrance requirements:* For master's, GMAT, quality work experience and leadership as shown through resume, references, and essays. Additional exam requirements/recommendations for international students: Required—TOEFL (minimum score 600 paper-based; 250 computer-based; 100 iBT), IELTS (minimum score 7). *Application deadline:* For fall admission, 7/30 for domestic students, 4/15 for international students; for spring admission, 12/15 for domestic and international students. Applications are processed on a rolling basis. Application fee: $60 ($100 for international students). Electronic applications accepted. *Expenses:* Contact institution. *Financial support:* In 2011–12, 110 students received support, including 110 fellowships (averaging $9,059 per year), 82 research assistantships with partial tuition reimbursements available (averaging $8,609 per year), 16 teaching assistantships with partial tuition reimbursements available (averaging $14,530 per year); career-related internships or fieldwork, scholarships/grants, health care benefits, and unspecified assistantships also available. Financial award application deadline: 4/15; financial award applicants required to submit FAFSA. *Faculty research:* Capital markets, econometrics, optimization, investments and empirical corporate finance, Iowa electronic markets. *Unit head:* Prof. Jarjisu Sa-Aadu, Associate Dean, MBA Programs, 800-622-4692, Fax: 319-335-3604, E-mail: jsa-aadu@uiowa.edu. *Application contact:* Jodi Schafer, Director of Admissions and Financial Aid, 319-335-0864, Fax: 319-335-3604, E-mail: jodi-schafer@uiowa.edu. Web site: http://tippie.uiowa.edu/mba.

University of La Verne, College of Business and Public Management, Graduate Programs in Business Administration, La Verne, CA 91750-4443. Offers accounting (MBA); executive management (MBA-EP); finance (MBA, MBA-EP); health services management (MBA); information technology (MBA, MBA-EP); international business (MBA, MBA-EP); leadership (MBA-EP); managed care (MBA); management (MBA, MBA-EP); marketing (MBA, MBA-EP). Part-time and evening/weekend programs available. *Faculty:* 34 full-time (15 women), 38 part-time/adjunct (13 women). *Students:* 525 full-time (243 women), 231 part-time (114 women); includes 199 minority (27 Black or African American, non-Hispanic/Latino; 1 American Indian or Alaska Native, non-Hispanic/Latino; 55 Asian, non-Hispanic/Latino; 113 Hispanic/Latino; 3 Two or more races, non-Hispanic/Latino), 436 international. Average age 28. In 2011, 403 master's awarded. *Entrance requirements:* For master's, minimum undergraduate GPA of 3.0, 2 letters of recommendation, resume. Additional exam requirements/recommendations for international students: Required—TOEFL (minimum score 550 paper-based; 213 computer-based). *Application deadline:* Applications are processed on a rolling basis. Application fee: $50. *Expenses:* Contact institution. *Financial support:* Career-related internships or fieldwork, institutionally sponsored loans, and scholarships/grants available. Financial award application deadline: 3/2; financial award applicants required to submit FAFSA. *Unit head:* Dr. Abe Helou, Chairperson, 909-593-3511 Ext. 4211, Fax: 909-392-2704, E-mail: ihelou@laverne.edu. *Application contact:* Rina Lazarian, Program and Admission Specialist, 909-593-3511 Ext. 4819, Fax: 909-392-2704, E-mail: cbpm@ulv.edu.

University of Lethbridge, School of Graduate Studies, Lethbridge, AB T1K 3M4, Canada. Offers accounting (MScM); addictions counseling (M Sc); agricultural biotechnology (M Sc); agricultural studies (M Sc, MA); anthropology (MA); archaeology (MA); art (MA, MFA); biochemistry (M Sc); biological sciences (M Sc); biomolecular science (PhD); biosystems and biodiversity (PhD); Canadian studies (MA); chemistry (M Sc); computer science (M Sc); computer science and geographical information science (M Sc); counseling psychology (M Ed); dramatic arts (MA); earth, space, and physical science (PhD); economics (MA); educational leadership (M Ed); English (MA); environmental science (M Sc); evolution and behavior (PhD); exercise science (M Sc); finance (MScM); French (MA); French/German (MA); French/Spanish (MA); general education (M Ed); general management (MScM); geography (M Sc, MA); German (MA); health science (M Sc); history (MA); human resource management and labour relations (MScM); individualized multidisciplinary (M Sc, MA); information systems (MScM); international management (MScM); kinesiology (M Sc, MA); management (M Sc, MA); marketing (MScM); mathematics (M Sc); music (M Mus, MA); Native American studies (MA); neuroscience (M Sc, PhD); new media (MA); nursing (M Sc); philosophy (MA); physics (M Sc); policy and strategy (MScM); political science (MA); psychology (M Sc, MA); religious studies (MA); social sciences (MA); sociology (MA); theatre and dramatic arts (MFA); theoretical and computational science (PhD); urban and regional studies (MA); women's studies (MA). Part-time and evening/weekend programs available. *Degree requirements:* For doctorate, comprehensive exam, thesis/dissertation. *Entrance requirements:* For master's, GMAT (M Sc in management), bachelor's degree in related field, minimum GPA of 3.0 during previous 20 graded semester courses, 2 years teaching or related experience (M Ed); for doctorate, master's degree, minimum graduate GPA of 3.5. Additional exam requirements/recommendations for international students: Required—TOEFL. *Faculty research:* Movement and brain plasticity, gibberellin physiology, photosynthesis, carbon cycling, molecular properties of main-group ring components.

University of Maine, Graduate School, College of Business, Public Policy and Health, The Maine Business School, Orono, ME 04469. Offers accounting (MBA); business and sustainability (MBA); finance (MBA); management (MBA). *Accreditation:* AACSB. Part-time and evening/weekend programs available. *Faculty:* 20 full-time (8 women), 6 part-time/adjunct (2 women). *Students:* 47 full-time (19 women), 15 part-time (2 women); includes 5 minority (1 American Indian or Alaska Native, non-Hispanic/Latino; 2 Asian, non-Hispanic/Latino; 2 Hispanic/Latino), 5 international. Average age 29. 41 applicants, 71% accepted, 24 enrolled. In 2011, 28 master's awarded. *Entrance requirements:* For master's, GMAT. Additional exam requirements/recommendations for international students: Required—TOEFL (minimum score 550 paper-based; 213 computer-based). *Application deadline:* For fall admission, 6/1 priority date for domestic students, 6/1 for international students; for spring admission, 11/1 priority date for domestic students, 11/1 for international students. Applications are processed on a rolling basis. Application fee: $65. Electronic applications accepted. *Expenses:* Contact institution. *Financial support:* In 2011–12, 16 students received support, including 3 teaching assistantships with full tuition reimbursements available (averaging $13,600 per year); career-related internships or fieldwork, Federal Work-Study, institutionally sponsored loans, scholarships/grants, tuition waivers (full and partial), and unspecified assistantships also available. Financial award application deadline: 3/1. *Faculty research:* Entrepreneurship, investment management, international markets, decision support systems, strategic planning. *Unit head:* Dr. Nory Jones, Director of Graduate Programs, 207-581-1971, Fax: 207-581-1930, E-mail: mba@maine.edu. *Application contact:* Scott G. Delcourt, Associate Dean of the Graduate School, 207-581-3291, Fax: 207-581-3232, E-mail: graduate@maine.edu. Web site: http://www.umaine.edu/business/.

University of Maryland University College, Graduate School of Management and Technology, Program in Accounting and Financial Management, Adelphi, MD 20783. Offers MS, Certificate. *Accreditation:* AACSB. Part-time and evening/weekend programs available. Postbaccalaureate distance learning degree programs offered (no on-campus study). *Students:* 9 full-time (5 women), 532 part-time (336 women); includes 289 minority (205 Black or African American, non-Hispanic/Latino; 48 Asian, non-Hispanic/Latino; 30 Hispanic/Latino; 1 Native Hawaiian or other Pacific Islander, non-Hispanic/Latino; 5 Two or more races, non-Hispanic/Latino), 24 international. Average age 35. 151 applicants, 100% accepted, 92 enrolled. In 2011, 118 degrees awarded. *Degree requirements:* For master's, thesis or alternative, capstone course. *Application deadline:* Applications are processed on a rolling basis. Application fee: $50. Electronic applications accepted. *Financial support:* Federal Work-Study and scholarships/grants available. Support available to part-time students. Financial award application deadline: 6/1; financial award applicants required to submit FAFSA. *Unit head:* Dr. James Howard, Director, 240-684-2400, Fax: 240-684-2401, E-mail: jhoward@umuc.edu. *Application contact:* Coordinator, Graduate Admissions, 800-888-8682, Fax: 240-684-2151, E-mail: newgrad@umuc.edu. Web site: http://www.umuc.edu/grad/msaf.html.

University of Maryland University College, Graduate School of Management and Technology, Program in Financial Management and Information Systems, Adelphi, MD 20783. Offers MS, Certificate. Part-time and evening/weekend programs available. Postbaccalaureate distance learning degree programs offered (no on-campus study). *Students:* 4 full-time (2 women), 169 part-time (80 women); includes 107 minority (80 Black or African American, non-Hispanic/Latino; 15 Asian, non-Hispanic/Latino; 9 Hispanic/Latino; 3 Two or more races, non-Hispanic/Latino), 4 international. Average age 34. 63 applicants, 100% accepted, 25 enrolled. In 2011, 39 degrees awarded. *Degree requirements:* For master's, thesis or alternative. *Application deadline:* Applications are processed on a rolling basis. Application fee: $50. Electronic applications accepted. *Financial support:* Federal Work-Study and scholarships/grants available. Support available to part-time students. Financial award application deadline: 6/1; financial award applicants required to submit FAFSA. *Unit head:* Dr. Jayanta Sen, Director, 240-684-2400, Fax: 240-684-2401, E-mail: jsen@umuc.edu. *Application contact:* Coordinator, Graduate Admissions, 800-888-8682, Fax: 240-684-2151, E-mail: newgrad@umuc.edu. Web site: http://www.umuc.edu/programs/grad/fmis/.

University of Massachusetts Amherst, Graduate School, Isenberg School of Management, Program in Management, Amherst, MA 01003. Offers accounting (PhD); business administration (MBA); business administration/sport management (MBA/MS); finance (PhD); hospitality and tourism management (PhD); management science (PhD); marketing (PhD); organization studies (PhD); sport management (PhD); strategic management (PhD); MBA/MS; MPH/MPPA. *Accreditation:* AACSB. Part-time programs available. *Faculty:* 61 full-time (14 women). *Students:* 92 full-time (34 women), 9 part-time (3 women); includes 8 minority (1 Black or African American, non-Hispanic/Latino; 4 Asian, non-Hispanic/Latino; 3 Hispanic/Latino), 47 international. Average age 33. 340 applicants, 15% accepted, 29 enrolled. In 2011, 31 master's, 13 doctorates awarded. Terminal master's awarded for partial completion of doctoral program. *Degree requirements:* For doctorate, comprehensive exam, thesis/dissertation. *Entrance requirements:* For master's and doctorate, GMAT. Additional exam requirements/recommendations for international students: Required—TOEFL (minimum score 550 paper-based; 213 computer-based; 80 iBT), IELTS (minimum score 6.5). *Application deadline:* For fall admission, 1/20 for domestic and international students. Applications are processed on a rolling basis. Application fee: $50 ($65 for international students). Electronic applications accepted. Tuition and fees vary according to course load, campus/location and program. *Financial support:* Fellowships with full and partial tuition reimbursements, research assistantships with full and partial tuition reimbursements, teaching assistantships with full and partial tuition reimbursements, career-related internships or fieldwork, Federal Work-Study, scholarships/grants, traineeships, health care benefits, tuition waivers (full and partial), and unspecified assistantships available. Support available to part-time students. Financial award application deadline: 1/20. *Unit head:* Dr. William Woodridge, Chair, 413-545-5675, Fax: 413-577-2234. *Application contact:* Lindsay DeSantis, Interim Supervisor of Admissions, 413-545-0722, Fax: 413-577-0010, E-mail: gradadm@grad.umass.edu. Web site: http://www.isenberg.umass.edu/.

University of Massachusetts Dartmouth, Graduate School, Charlton College of Business, Program in Business Administration, North Dartmouth, MA 02747-2300. Offers accounting (Postbaccalaureate Certificate); business administration (MBA); business foundation (online) (Graduate Certificate); finance (PMC); international business (online) (Graduate Certificate); leadership (online) (Graduate Certificate); management (Postbaccalaureate Certificate); marketing (Postbaccalaureate Certificate); supply chain management (PMC). *Accreditation:* AACSB. Part-time programs available. *Faculty:* 35 full-time (11 women), 26 part-time/adjunct (7 women). *Students:* 81 full-time (29 women), 119 part-time (56 women); includes 17 minority (6 Black or African American, non-Hispanic/Latino; 1 American Indian or Alaska Native, non-Hispanic/Latino; 3 Asian, non-Hispanic/Latino; 5 Hispanic/Latino; 2 Two or more races, non-Hispanic/Latino), 42 international. Average age 31. 132 applicants, 92% accepted, 68 enrolled. In 2011, 91 master's, 18 other advanced degrees awarded. *Entrance requirements:* For master's, GMAT, statement of intent, resume, 3 letters of recommendation; for other advanced degree, statement of intent, resume, 3 letters of recommendation. Additional exam requirements/recommendations for international students: Required—TOEFL (minimum score 500 paper-based; 200 computer-based; 72 iBT). *Application deadline:* For fall admission, 3/1 for domestic students, 2/1 for international students; for spring admission, 11/1 for domestic students, 10/15 for international students. Application fee: $40 ($60 for international students). Electronic applications accepted. *Expenses:* Tuition, state resident: full-time $2071; part-time $86.29 per credit. Tuition, nonresident: full-time $8099; part-time $337.46 per credit. *Required fees:* $438.58 per credit. Part-time tuition and fees vary according to class time, course load, degree level and reciprocity agreements. *Financial support:* Research assistantships, teaching assistantships, Federal Work-Study, and unspecified assistantships available. Support available to part-time students. Financial award application deadline: 3/1; financial award applicants required to submit FAFSA. *Faculty research:* Global business environment, e-commerce, managing diversity, agile manufacturing, green business. *Total annual research expenditures:* $8,653. *Unit head:* Stephanie Jacobsen, Program Coordinator, 508-999-8543, Fax: 508-999-8646, E-mail: s.jacobsen@umassd.edu. *Application contact:* Elan Turcotte-Shamski, Graduate Admissions Officer, 508-999-8604, Fax: 508-999-8183, E-mail: graduate@umassd.edu. Web site: http://www.umassd.edu/charlton/.

University of Memphis, Graduate School, Fogelman College of Business and Economics, Program in Business Administration, Memphis, TN 38152. Offers accounting (MBA, PhD); economics (MBA, PhD); executive business administration (MBA); finance (PhD); finance, insurance, and real estate (MBA, MS); international business administration (IMBA); management (MBA, MS, PhD); management information systems (MBA, MS, PhD); management science (MBA); marketing (MBA, MS); marketing and supply chain management (PhD); real estate development (MS); JD/MBA. *Accreditation:* AACSB. *Degree requirements:* For master's, comprehensive exam; for doctorate, comprehensive exam, thesis/dissertation. *Entrance requirements:* For master's, GMAT, resume; for doctorate, GMAT, interview, minimum GPA of 3.4, resume, letter of recommendation. Additional exam requirements/recommendations for international students: Required—TOEFL (minimum score 550 paper-based; 220 computer-based). *Faculty research:* Competitive business strategy, finance microstructures, supply chain management innovations, health care economics, litigation risks and corporate audits.

University of Miami, Graduate School, School of Business Administration, Program in Business Administration, Coral Gables, FL 33124. Offers accounting (MBA); computer information systems (MBA); executive and professional (MBA), including international business, management; finance (MBA); international business (MBA); management (MBA); management science (MBA); marketing (MBA); professional management (MSPM); JD/MBA; MBA/MSIE. *Accreditation:* AACSB. Evening/weekend programs available. *Degree requirements:* For master's, comprehensive exam. *Entrance requirements:* For master's, GMAT. Additional exam requirements/recommendations for international students: Required—TOEFL (minimum score 550 paper-based; 213 computer-based; 59 iBT). Electronic applications accepted. *Faculty research:* Leadership, e-commerce, supply chain management.

University of Michigan–Dearborn, College of Business, Dearborn, MI 48128-1491. Offers accounting (MBA, MS); business analytics (MS); finance (MBA, MS); information systems (MS); international business (MBA); management (MBA); management information systems (MBA); marketing (MBA); supply chain management (MBA, MS); MBA/MHSA; MBA/MSE; MBA/MSF; MBA/MSIS; MSF/MSA. *Accreditation:* AACSB. Part-time and evening/weekend programs available. Postbaccalaureate distance learning degree programs offered (no on-campus study). *Faculty:* 50 full-time (6 women), 32 part-time/adjunct (18 women). *Students:* 65 full-time (29 women), 356 part-time (121 women); includes 79 minority (19 Black or African American, non-Hispanic/Latino; 36 American Indian or Alaska Native, non-Hispanic/Latino; 15 Hispanic/Latino; 1 Native Hawaiian or other Pacific Islander, non-Hispanic/Latino; 8 Two or more races, non-Hispanic/Latino), 80 international. Average age 28. 175 applicants, 53% accepted, 68 enrolled. In 2011, 173 master's awarded. *Entrance requirements:* For master's, GMAT or GRE, 2 years of work experience (MBA); course work in computer applications, statistics, and pre-calculus or finite mathematics; 18 credits of accounting course work beyond introductory courses (MS in accounting). Additional exam requirements/recommendations for international students: Required—TOEFL (minimum score 560 paper-based; 220 computer-based; 84 iBT), IELTS. *Application deadline:* For fall admission, 8/1 priority date for domestic students, 6/1 for international students; for winter admission, 12/1 priority date for domestic students, 10/1 for international students; for spring admission, 4/1 priority date for domestic students, 2/1 for international students. Applications are processed on a rolling basis. Application fee: $60. Electronic applications accepted. *Expenses:* Contact institution. *Financial support:* Career-related internships or fieldwork, Federal Work-Study, and scholarships/grants available. Support available to part-time students. Financial award application deadline: 9/1; financial award applicants required to submit FAFSA. *Faculty research:* Cultural diversity, buyer-supplier relations, error detection in data, economic evolution. *Unit head:* Dr. Lee Redding, Interim Dean, 313-593-5248, Fax: 313-271-9835, E-mail: lredding@umd.umich.edu. *Application contact:* Joan Doherty, Academic Advisor/Counselor, 313-593-5460, Fax: 313-271-9838, E-mail: gradbusiness@umd.umich.edu. Web site: http://www.cob.umd.umich.edu.

University of Minnesota, Twin Cities Campus, Carlson School of Management, Carlson Full-Time MBA Program, Minneapolis, MN 55455. Offers finance (MBA); information technology (MBA); management (MBA); marketing (MBA); medical industry orientation (MBA); supply chain and operations (MBA); JD/MBA; MBA/MPP; MD/MBA; MHA/MBA; Pharm D/MBA. *Accreditation:* AACSB. *Faculty:* 58 full-time (17 women), 23 part-time/adjunct (5 women). *Students:* 172 full-time (54 women); includes 16 minority (4 Black or African American, non-Hispanic/Latino; 10 Asian, non-Hispanic/Latino; 2 Two or more races, non-Hispanic/Latino), 41 international. Average age 28. 538 applicants, 41% accepted, 99 enrolled. In 2011, 97 master's awarded. *Entrance requirements:* For master's, GMAT or GRE. Additional exam requirements/recommendations for international students: Required—TOEFL (minimum score 580 paper-based; 240 computer-based; 84 iBT), IELTS (minimum score 7), or Pearson Test of English. *Application deadline:* For fall admission, 4/1 for domestic students, 2/1 for international students. Application fee: $60 ($90 for international students). Electronic applications accepted. *Expenses:* Contact institution. *Financial support:* In 2011–12, 116 students received support, including 116 fellowships with full and partial tuition reimbursements available (averaging $18,702 per year); research assistantships with partial tuition reimbursements available, teaching assistantships with partial tuition reimbursements available, career-related internships or fieldwork, Federal Work-Study, institutionally sponsored loans, scholarships/grants, health care benefits, and unspecified assistantships also available. Financial award application deadline: 4/1; financial award applicants required to submit FAFSA. *Faculty research:* Finance and accounting: financial reporting, asset pricing models and corporate finance; information and decision sciences: on-line auctions, information transparency and recommender systems; marketing: psychological influences on consumer behavior, brand equity, pricing and marketing channels; operations: lean manufacturing, quality management and global supply chains; strategic management and organization: global strategy, networks, entrepreneurship and innovation, sustainability. *Unit head:* Philip J. Miller, Assistant Dean, MBA Programs and Graduate Business Career Center, 612-625-5555, Fax: 612-625-1012, E-mail: mba@umn.edu. *Application contact:* Linh Gilles, Director of Admissions and Recruiting, 612-625-5555, Fax: 612-625-1012, E-mail: ftmba@umn.edu. Web site: http://www.csom.umn.edu/MBA/full-time/.

University of Minnesota, Twin Cities Campus, Carlson School of Management, Carlson Part-Time MBA Program, Minneapolis, MN 55455. Offers finance (MBA); information technology (MBA); management (MBA); marketing (MBA); supply chain and operations (MBA). Part-time and evening/weekend programs available. *Faculty:* 63 full-time (16 women), 27 part-time/adjunct (4 women). *Students:* 1,459 part-time (463 women); includes 94 minority (11 Black or African American, non-Hispanic/Latino; 3 American Indian or Alaska Native, non-Hispanic/Latino; 68 Asian, non-Hispanic/Latino; 10 Hispanic/Latino; 2 Two or more races, non-Hispanic/Latino), 72 international. Average age 28. 336 applicants, 86% accepted, 256 enrolled. In 2011, 479 master's awarded. *Entrance requirements:* For master's, GMAT or GRE. Additional exam requirements/recommendations for international students: Required—TOEFL (minimum score 580 paper-based; 240 computer-based; 84 iBT), IELTS (minimum score 7), or Pearson Test of English. *Application deadline:* For fall admission, 5/1 priority date for domestic students, 5/1 for international students; for spring admission, 10/1 priority date for domestic students, 10/1 for international students. Applications are processed on a rolling basis. Application fee: $60 ($90 for international students). Electronic applications accepted. *Expenses:* Contact institution. *Financial support:* Applicants required to submit FAFSA. *Faculty research:* Finance and accounting: financial reporting, asset pricing models and corporate finance; information and decision sciences: on-line auctions, information transparency and recommender systems; marketing: psychological influences on consumer behavior, brand equity, pricing and marketing channels; operations: lean manufacturing, quality management and global supply chains; strategic management and organization: global strategy, networks, entrepreneurship and innovation, sustainability. *Unit head:* Philip J. Miller, Assistant Dean, MBA Programs and Graduate Business Career Center, 612-624-2039, Fax: 612-625-1012, E-mail: mba@umn.edu. *Application contact:* Linh Gilles, Director of Admissions and Recruiting, 612-625-5555, Fax: 612-625-1012, E-mail: ptmba@umn.edu. Web site: http://www.carlsonschool.umn.edu/ptmba.

University of Minnesota, Twin Cities Campus, Carlson School of Management, Doctoral Program in Business Administration, Minneapolis, MN 55455-0213. Offers accounting (PhD); finance (PhD); information and decision sciences (PhD); marketing (PhD); operations and management science (PhD); strategic management and organization (PhD). *Faculty:* 104 full-time (30 women). *Students:* 74 full-time (30 women); includes 8 minority (5 Asian, non-Hispanic/Latino; 3 Hispanic/Latino), 50 international. Average age 30. 320 applicants, 8% accepted, 15 enrolled. In 2011, 13 doctorates awarded. *Degree requirements:* For doctorate, comprehensive exam, thesis/dissertation, written and oral preliminary exams, proposal defense, final defense. *Entrance requirements:* For doctorate, GMAT, GRE General Test. Additional exam requirements/recommendations for international students: Required—TOEFL (minimum score 600 paper-based; 250 computer-based; 100 iBT); Recommended—IELTS (minimum score 7.5). *Application deadline:* For fall admission, 12/31 for domestic and international students. Applications are processed on a rolling basis. Application fee: $75 ($95 for international students). Electronic applications accepted. *Expenses:* Contact institution. *Financial support:* In 2011–12, 66 students received support, including 112 fellowships with full tuition reimbursements available (averaging $6,700 per year), 55 research assistantships with full tuition reimbursements available (averaging $6,750 per year), 54 teaching assistantships with full tuition reimbursements available (averaging $6,750 per year); institutionally sponsored loans, scholarships/grants, health care benefits, and unspecified assistantships also available. Financial award application deadline: 12/31. *Faculty research:* Corporate strategy, finance, entrepreneurship, marketing, information and decision science, operations, accounting, quality management. *Unit head:* Dr. Shawn P. Curley, Director, 612-624-6546, Fax: 612-624-8221, E-mail: curley@umn.edu. *Application contact:* Earlene K. Bronson, Assistant Director, 612-624-0875, Fax: 612-624-8221, E-mail: brons003@umn.edu. Web site: http://www.csom.umn.edu/phd-BA/.

University of Missouri–Kansas City, Henry W. Bloch School of Management, Kansas City, MO 64110-2499. Offers accounting (MS); business administration (MBA); entrepreneurial real estate (MERE); entrepreneurship and innovation (PhD); finance (MS); public affairs (MPA, PhD); JD/MBA; LL M/MPA. PhD (interdisciplinary) offered through the School of Graduate Studies. *Accreditation:* AACSB; NASPAA. Part-time and evening/weekend programs available. *Faculty:* 51 full-time (14 women), 29 part-time/adjunct (9 women). *Students:* 272 full-time (126 women), 407 part-time (180 women); includes 91 minority (43 Black or African American, non-Hispanic/Latino; 20 Asian, non-Hispanic/Latino; 19 Hispanic/Latino; 9 Two or more races, non-Hispanic/Latino), 49 international. Average age 30. 397 applicants, 63% accepted, 202 enrolled. In 2011, 257 master's awarded. Terminal master's awarded for partial completion of doctoral program. *Entrance requirements:* For master's, GMAT, GRE, 2 writing essays, 2 references; support of employer; for doctorate, GRE, minimum GPA of 3.0. Additional exam requirements/recommendations for international students: Required—TOEFL (minimum score 550 paper-based; 213 computer-based; 80 iBT). *Application deadline:* For fall admission, 5/1 priority date for domestic students, 5/1 for international students; for spring admission, 10/1 priority date for domestic students, 10/1 for international students. Applications are processed on a rolling basis. Application fee: $45 ($50 for international students). Electronic applications accepted. *Expenses:* Tuition, state resident: full-time $5798; part-time $322.10 per credit hour. Tuition, nonresident: full-time $14,969; part-time $831.60 per credit hour. *Required fees:* $93.51 per credit hour. *Financial support:* In 2011–12, 29 research assistantships with partial tuition reimbursements (averaging $11,490 per year), 3 teaching assistantships with partial tuition reimbursements (averaging $11,600 per year) were awarded; career-related internships or fieldwork, Federal Work-Study, institutionally sponsored loans, scholarships/grants, tuition waivers (full and partial), and unspecified assistantships also available. Support available to part-time students. Financial award application deadline: 3/1; financial award applicants required to submit FAFSA. *Faculty research:* Entrepreneurship, finance, non-profit, risk management. *Unit head:* Dr. Teng-Kee Tan, Dean, 816-235-2215, Fax: 816-235-2206. *Application contact:* 816-235-1111, E-mail: admit@umkc.edu. Web site: http://www.bloch.umkc.edu.

University of Missouri–St. Louis, College of Business Administration, Program in Business Administration, St. Louis, MO 63121. Offers accounting (MBA); business administration (Certificate); finance (MBA); human resource management (Certificate); information systems (MBA); logistics and supply chain management (MBA, Certificate); marketing (MBA); marketing management (Certificate); operations management (MBA). *Accreditation:* AACSB. Part-time and evening/weekend programs available. *Faculty:* 32 full-time (7 women), 10 part-time/adjunct (2 women). *Students:* 126 full-time (48 women), 305 part-time (141 women); includes 61 minority (25 Black or African American, non-Hispanic/Latino; 23 Asian, non-Hispanic/Latino; 9 Hispanic/Latino; 1 Native Hawaiian or other Pacific Islander, non-Hispanic/Latino; 3 Two or more races, non-Hispanic/Latino), 47 international. Average age 30. 241 applicants, 70% accepted, 134 enrolled. In 2011, 150 master's, 1 doctorate, 19 other advanced degrees awarded. *Entrance requirements:* For master's, GMAT, 2 letters of recommendation. Additional exam requirements/recommendations for international students: Required—TOEFL (minimum score 550 paper-based; 213 computer-based). *Application deadline:* For fall admission, 7/1 for domestic and international students; for spring admission, 12/1 for domestic and international students. Applications are processed on a rolling basis. Application fee: $35 ($40 for international students). Electronic applications accepted. *Expenses:* Tuition, state resident: full-time $6273; part-time $3866 per year. Tuition, nonresident: full-time $14,969; part-time $9980 per year. *Required fees:* $315 per year. *Financial support:* In 2011–12, 32 research assistantships with full and partial tuition reimbursements (averaging $6,000 per year), 6 teaching assistantships with full and partial tuition reimbursements (averaging $12,276 per year) were awarded; career-related internships or fieldwork, Federal Work-Study, and institutionally sponsored loans also available. Support available to part-time students. Financial award application deadline: 4/1; financial award applicants required to submit FAFSA. *Faculty research:* Human resources, strategic management, marketing strategy, consumer behavior product development, advertising. *Unit head:* Karl Kottemann, Assistant Director, 314-516-5885, Fax: 314-516-6420, E-mail: mba@umsl.edu. *Application contact:* 314-516-5458, Fax: 314-516-6996, E-mail: gradadm@umsl.edu. Web site: http://www.umsl.edu/divisions/business/mbaonline/mbaprog.htm.

University of Nebraska–Lincoln, Graduate College, College of Business Administration, Interdepartmental Area of Business, Department of Finance, Lincoln, NE 68588. Offers business (MA, PhD). *Degree requirements:* For doctorate, comprehensive exam, thesis/dissertation. *Entrance requirements:* For master's and doctorate, GMAT. Additional exam requirements/recommendations for international students: Required—TOEFL (minimum score 100 iBT). Electronic applications accepted. *Faculty research:* Banking, investments, international finance, insurance, corporate finance.

University of Nevada, Las Vegas, Graduate College, College of Business, Department of Finance, Las Vegas, NV 89154. Offers Certificate. *Faculty:* 12 full-time (0 women). *Students:* 2 part-time (0 women); includes 1 minority (Black or African American, non-Hispanic/Latino). Average age 31. 2 applicants, 100% accepted, 1 enrolled. *Application* *deadline:* For fall admission, 5/1 for international students; for spring admission, 10/1 for international students. Electronic applications accepted. *Faculty research:* Financial markets, preferred stock, and stock re-purchases; hospitality industry finance and corporate finance; mergers and acquisitions; real estate; executive compensation. *Unit head:* Dr. Paul Thistle, Chair/Professor, 702-895-3856, E-mail: paul.thistle@unlv.edu. *Application contact:* Graduate College Admissions Evaluator, 702-895-3320, Fax: 702-895-4180, E-mail: gradcollege@unlv.edu. Web site: http://business.unlv.edu/finance/.

University of Nevada, Reno, Graduate School, College of Business Administration, Department of Finance, Reno, NV 89557. Offers MS. Part-time programs available. *Degree requirements:* For master's, thesis optional. *Entrance requirements:* For master's, GMAT or GRE, minimum GPA of 2.75. Additional exam requirements/recommendations for international students: Required—TOEFL (minimum score 500 paper-based; 173 computer-based; 61 iBT), IELTS (minimum score 6). Electronic applications accepted. *Faculty research:* Financial business problems, economic theory, financial concepts theory.

University of New Haven, Graduate School, School of Business, Program in Business Administration, West Haven, CT 06516-1916. Offers accounting (MBA, Certificate), including CPA (MBA); business management (Certificate); business policy and strategy (MBA); finance (MBA), including CFA; global marketing (MBA); human resource management (Certificate); human resources management (MBA); international business (Certificate); marketing (Certificate); sports management (MBA); telecommunications management (Certificate); MBA/MPA. Part-time and evening/weekend programs available. *Students:* 215 full-time (106 women), 182 part-time (87 women); includes 73 minority (38 Black or African American, non-Hispanic/Latino; 2 American Indian or Alaska Native, non-Hispanic/Latino; 22 Asian, non-Hispanic/Latino; 11 Hispanic/Latino), 129 international. 179 applicants, 97% accepted, 93 enrolled. In 2011, 197 master's, 28 other advanced degrees awarded. *Degree requirements:* For master's, thesis or alternative. *Entrance requirements:* For master's, GMAT. Additional exam requirements/recommendations for international students: Required—TOEFL (minimum score 520 paper-based; 190 computer-based; 70 iBT), IELTS (minimum score 5.5). *Application deadline:* For fall admission, 5/31 for international students; for winter admission, 10/15 for international students; for spring admission, 1/15 for international students. Applications are processed on a rolling basis. Application fee: $50. Electronic applications accepted. *Expenses:* Contact institution. *Financial support:* Research assistantships with partial tuition reimbursements, teaching assistantships with partial tuition reimbursements, Federal Work-Study, scholarships/grants, health care benefits, tuition waivers, and unspecified assistantships available. Support available to part-time students. Financial award applicants required to submit FAFSA. *Unit head:* Charles Coleman, Chairman, 203-932-7375. *Application contact:* Eloise Gormley, Director of Graduate Admissions, 203-932-7449, Fax: 203-932-7137, E-mail: gradinfo@newhaven.edu. Web site: http://www.newhaven.edu/7433/.

University of New Haven, Graduate School, School of Business, Program in Finance and Financial Services, West Haven, CT 06516-1916. Offers finance (Certificate); finance and financial services (MS). *Students:* 30 full-time (16 women), 18 part-time (12 women); includes 6 minority (4 Black or African American, non-Hispanic/Latino; 1 Asian, non-Hispanic/Latino; 1 Hispanic/Latino), 37 international. Average age 28. 20 applicants, 95% accepted, 11 enrolled. In 2011, 23 master's, 1 other advanced degree awarded. *Application deadline:* Applications are processed on a rolling basis. Application fee: $50. *Expenses: Tuition:* Part-time $750 per credit. *Financial support:* Research assistantships with partial tuition reimbursements, teaching assistantships with partial tuition reimbursements, career-related internships or fieldwork, and Federal Work-Study available. Financial award application deadline: 5/1; financial award applicants required to submit FAFSA. *Unit head:* Dr. Charles Coleman, Coordinator, 203-932-7375. *Application contact:* Eloise Gormley, Director of Graduate Admissions, 203-932-7449, Fax: 203-932-7137, E-mail: gradinfo@newhaven.edu.

University of New Mexico, Graduate School, College of Arts and Sciences, Department of Economics, Albuquerque, NM 87131-2039. Offers environmental/natural resources (MA, PhD); international/development (MA, PhD); labor/human resources (MA, PhD); public finance (MA, PhD). Part-time programs available. *Faculty:* 14 full-time (7 women), 8 part-time/adjunct (1 woman). *Students:* 37 full-time (9 women), 25 part-time (6 women); includes 10 minority (3 Asian, non-Hispanic/Latino; 6 Hispanic/Latino; 1 Two or more races, non-Hispanic/Latino), 17 international. Average age 35. 61 applicants, 49% accepted, 14 enrolled. In 2011, 10 master's, 3 doctorates awarded. Terminal master's awarded for partial completion of doctoral program. *Degree requirements:* For master's, comprehensive exam, thesis (for some programs); for doctorate, comprehensive exam, thesis/dissertation. *Entrance requirements:* For master's and doctorate, GRE General Test, 3 letters of recommendation, letter of intent, curriculum vitae. Additional exam requirements/recommendations for international students: Required—TOEFL (minimum score 520 paper-based; 190 computer-based; 68 iBT). *Application deadline:* For fall admission, 3/1 priority date for domestic students, 3/1 for international students. Applications are processed on a rolling basis. Application fee: $50. Electronic applications accepted. *Financial support:* In 2011–12, 47 students received support, including 3 fellowships with tuition reimbursements available (averaging $3,611 per year), 14 research assistantships with tuition reimbursements available (averaging $7,791 per year), 15 teaching assistantships with tuition reimbursements available (averaging $7,467 per year); career-related internships or fieldwork, Federal Work-Study, scholarships/grants, health care benefits, and unspecified assistantships also available. Support available to part-time students. Financial award application deadline: 3/1; financial award applicants required to submit FAFSA. *Faculty research:* Core theory, econometrics, public finance, international/development economics, labor/human resource economics, environmental/natural resource economics. *Total annual research expenditures:* $1.8 million. *Unit head:* Dr. Robert Berrens, Chair, 505-277-5304, Fax: 505-277-9445, E-mail: rberrens@unm.edu. *Application contact:* Rikk Murphy, Academic Advisor, 505-277-3056, Fax: 505-277-9445, E-mail: rikk@unm.edu. Web site: http://econ.unm.edu.

University of New Mexico, Robert O. Anderson Graduate School of Management, Department of Finance, International, Technology and Entrepreneurship, Albuquerque, NM 87131-1221. Offers finance (MBA); international management (MBA); international management in Latin America (MBA); management of technology (MBA). Part-time and evening/weekend programs available. *Faculty:* 14 full-time (2 women), 17 part-time/adjunct (4 women). In 2011, 53 master's awarded. *Degree requirements:* For master's, minimum GPA of 3.0. *Entrance requirements:* For master's, GMAT or GRE. Additional exam requirements/recommendations for international students: Required—TOEFL (minimum score 550 paper-based; 213 computer-based; 79 iBT). *Application deadline:* For fall admission, 4/1 priority date for domestic students, 4/1 for international students; for spring admission, 10/1 priority date for domestic students, 10/1 for international students. Applications are processed on a rolling basis. Application fee: $50. Electronic applications accepted. *Financial support:* Fellowships, research assistantships, career-related internships or fieldwork, Federal Work-Study, scholarships/grants, and unspecified assistantships available. Support available to part-time students. Financial award application deadline: 6/1. *Faculty research:* Corporate finance, investments, management in Latin America, management of technology, entrepreneurship. *Unit head:* Dr. Leslie Boni, Chair, 505-277-6471, Fax: 505-277-7108. *Application contact:* Megan Conner, Director, Student Services, 505-277-3290, Fax: 505-277-8436, E-mail: mconner@mgt.unm.edu.

University of New Orleans, Graduate School, College of Business Administration, Department of Economics and Finance, New Orleans, LA 70148. Offers economics and finance (MS); financial economics (PhD). *Accreditation:* AACSB. Terminal master's awarded for partial completion of doctoral program. *Degree requirements:* For master's, thesis optional; for doctorate, one foreign language, comprehensive exam, thesis/dissertation, general exams. *Entrance requirements:* For doctorate, GRE General Test, minimum GPA of 3.0. Additional exam requirements/recommendations for international students: Required—TOEFL (minimum score 550 paper-based; 213 computer-based; 79 iBT). *Faculty research:* Monetary economics, international economics, urban economics, real estate.

The University of North Carolina at Chapel Hill, Kenan-Flagler Business School, Doctoral Program in Business Administration, Chapel Hill, NC 27599. Offers accounting (PhD); finance (PhD); marketing (PhD); operations management (PhD); organizational behavior (PhD); strategy (PhD). *Accreditation:* AACSB. *Degree requirements:* For doctorate, thesis/dissertation. *Entrance requirements:* For doctorate, GMAT or GRE General Test. Electronic applications accepted. *Expenses:* Contact institution.

The University of North Carolina at Charlotte, Graduate School, College of Liberal Arts and Sciences, Department of Political Science, Charlotte, NC 28223-0001. Offers emergency management (Certificate); non-profit management (Certificate); public administration (MPA), including arts administration, emergency management, non-profit management, public finance; public finance (Certificate); urban management and policy (Certificate). *Accreditation:* NASPAA. Part-time and evening/weekend programs available. *Faculty:* 19 full-time (8 women), 2 part-time/adjunct (1 woman). *Students:* 25 full-time (12 women), 71 part-time (50 women); includes 29 minority (26 Black or African American, non-Hispanic/Latino; 1 Asian, non-Hispanic/Latino; 1 Hispanic/Latino; 1 Two or more races, non-Hispanic/Latino), 2 international. Average age 29. 53 applicants, 77% accepted, 22 enrolled. In 2011, 20 master's, 6 other advanced degrees awarded. Terminal master's awarded for partial completion of doctoral program. *Degree requirements:* For master's, thesis or alternative. *Entrance requirements:* For master's, GRE General Test or MAT, minimum GPA of 3.0 in undergraduate major, 2.75 overall. Additional exam requirements/recommendations for international students: Required—TOEFL (minimum score 557 paper-based; 220 computer-based; 83 iBT). *Application deadline:* For fall admission, 7/1 for domestic students, 5/1 for international students; for spring admission, 11/1 for domestic students, 10/1 for international students. Applications are processed on a rolling basis. Application fee: $65 ($75 for international students). Electronic applications accepted. *Expenses:* Tuition, state resident: full-time $3689. Tuition, nonresident: full-time $15,226. *Required fees:* $2198. Tuition and fees vary according to course load and program. *Financial support:* In 2011–12, 6 students received support, including 6 research assistantships (averaging $9,167 per year); career-related internships or fieldwork, Federal Work-Study, institutionally sponsored loans, scholarships/grants, and unspecified assistantships also available. Support available to part-time students. Financial award application deadline: 4/1; financial award applicants required to submit FAFSA. *Faculty research:* Terrorism, public administration, nonprofit and arts administration, educational policy, social policy. *Total annual research expenditures:* $168,058. *Unit head:* Dr. Theodore S. Arrington, Chair, 704-687-2571, Fax: 704-687-3497, E-mail: tarrngtn@uncc.edu. *Application contact:* Kathy B. Giddings, Director of Graduate Admissions, 704-687-5503, Fax: 704-687-3279, E-mail: gradadm@uncc.edu. Web site: http://www.politicalscience.uncc.edu/mpa_handbook.html.

The University of North Carolina at Greensboro, Graduate School, Bryan School of Business and Economics, Department of Accounting and Finance, Greensboro, NC 27412-5001. Offers accounting (MS); accounting systems (MS); financial accounting and reporting (MS); financial analysis (PMC); tax concentration (MS). *Accreditation:* AACSB. *Entrance requirements:* For master's, GMAT, GRE General Test, previous course work in accounting and business. Additional exam requirements/recommendations for international students: Required—TOEFL. Electronic applications accepted.

University of North Florida, Coggin College of Business, MBA Program, Jacksonville, FL 32224. Offers accounting (MBA); construction management (MBA); e-commerce (MBA); economics (MBA); finance (MBA); human resource management (MBA); international business (MBA); logistics (MBA); management applications (MBA). *Accreditation:* AACSB. Part-time and evening/weekend programs available. *Faculty:* 19 full-time (6 women), 1 part-time/adjunct (0 women). *Students:* 145 full-time (57 women), 277 part-time (108 women); includes 67 minority (19 Black or African American, non-Hispanic/Latino; 21 Asian, non-Hispanic/Latino; 20 Hispanic/Latino; 7 Two or more races, non-Hispanic/Latino), 34 international. Average age 29. 200 applicants, 48% accepted, 70 enrolled. In 2011, 153 master's awarded. *Entrance requirements:* For master's, GMAT or GRE, U.S. bachelor's degree from regionally-accredited university or equivalent foreign degree. Additional exam requirements/recommendations for international students: Required—TOEFL (minimum score 550 paper-based; 213 computer-based; 79 iBT). *Application deadline:* For fall admission, 7/1 priority date for domestic students, 5/1 for international students; for spring admission, 11/1 priority date for domestic students, 10/1 for international students. Applications are processed on a rolling basis. Application fee: $30. *Expenses:* Tuition, state resident: full-time $8793; part-time $366.38 per credit hour. Tuition, nonresident: full-time $23,502; part-time $979.24 per credit hour. *Required fees:* $1384; $57.66 per credit hour. Tuition and fees vary according to course load and program. *Financial support:* In 2011–12, 55 students received support, including 1 teaching assistantship (averaging $5,333 per year); research assistantships, Federal Work-Study, and tuition waivers (partial) also available. Support available to part-time students. Financial award application deadline: 4/1; financial award applicants required to submit FAFSA. *Faculty research:* Performance measures, costing, and inventory issues in logistics and supply chain management; inter-organizational systems; international management and marketing practices; e-commerce; organizational learning and socialization processes. *Total annual research expenditures:* $7,686. *Unit head:* Dr. C. Bruce Kavan, Chair, 904-620-2780, Fax: 904-620-2832. *Application contact:* Cheryl Campbell, Graduate Advisor, 904-620-2575, Fax: 904-620-2832, E-mail: ccampbell@unf.edu. Web site: http://www.unf.edu/coggin/academics/graduate/mba.aspx.

University of North Texas, Toulouse Graduate School, College of Business, Department of Finance, Insurance, Real Estate, and Law, Denton, TX 76203. Offers finance (PhD); finance, insurance, real estate, and law (MS); real estate (MS). Part-time programs available. *Degree requirements:* For master's, thesis optional; for doctorate, comprehensive exam, thesis/dissertation. *Entrance requirements:* For master's, GMAT; for doctorate, GMAT or GRE General Test. Additional exam requirements/recommendations for international students: Recommended—TOEFL (minimum score 550 paper-based; 213 computer-based; 79 iBT). *Expenses:* Tuition, state resident: part-time $100 per credit hour. Tuition, nonresident: part-time $413 per credit hour. *Faculty research:* Financial impact of regulation, risk management, taxes and valuation, bankruptcy, real financial options.

University of Oregon, Graduate School, Charles H. Lundquist College of Business, Department of Finance, Eugene, OR 97403. Offers PhD. Part-time programs available.

Terminal master's awarded for partial completion of doctoral program. *Degree requirements:* For doctorate, thesis/dissertation, 2 comprehensive exams. *Entrance requirements:* For doctorate, GMAT. Additional exam requirements/recommendations for international students: Required—TOEFL. *Faculty research:* Changes in firm value in response to corporate takeovers and defenses, capital structure, regulatory changes, financial intermediaries.

University of Ottawa, Faculty of Graduate and Postdoctoral Studies, Interdisciplinary Programs, Ottawa, ON K1N 6N5, Canada. Offers e-business (Certificate); e-commerce (Certificate); finance (Certificate); health services and policies research (Diploma); population health (PhD); population health risk assessment and management (Certificate); public management and governance (Certificate); systems science (Certificate).

University of Pennsylvania, Wharton School, Finance Department, Philadelphia, PA 19104. Offers MBA, PhD. *Degree requirements:* For doctorate, thesis/dissertation. *Entrance requirements:* For doctorate, GMAT or GRE. *Expenses: Tuition:* Full-time $26,660; part-time $4944 per course. *Required fees:* $2318; $291 per course. Tuition and fees vary according to course load, degree level and program. *Faculty research:* Corporate finance, investments, macroeconomics, international finance.

University of Pittsburgh, Katz Graduate School of Business, Doctoral Program in Business Administration, Pittsburgh, PA 15260. Offers accounting (PhD); finance (PhD); information systems (PhD); marketing (PhD); operations/decision sciences/artificial intelligence (PhD); organizational behavior and human resource management (PhD); strategic planning (PhD). *Accreditation:* AACSB. *Faculty:* 54 full-time (16 women). *Students:* 51 full-time (21 women); includes 9 minority (4 Black or African American, non-Hispanic/Latino; 4 Asian, non-Hispanic/Latino; 1 Hispanic/Latino), 23 international. 373 applicants, 7% accepted, 10 enrolled. In 2011, 6 doctorates awarded. *Degree requirements:* For doctorate, comprehensive exam, thesis/dissertation. *Entrance requirements:* For doctorate, GMAT or GRE. Additional exam requirements/ recommendations for international students: Required—TOEFL. *Application deadline:* For fall admission, 2/1 priority date for domestic students, 2/1 for international students. Applications are processed on a rolling basis. Application fee: $50. Electronic applications accepted. *Expenses:* Tuition, state resident: full-time $18,774; part-time $760 per credit. Tuition, nonresident: full-time $30,736; part-time $1258 per credit. *Required fees:* $740; $200 per term. Tuition and fees vary according to program. *Financial support:* In 2011–12, 38 students received support, including 29 research assistantships with full tuition reimbursements available (averaging $19,400 per year), 10 teaching assistantships with full tuition reimbursements available (averaging $24,700 per year); fellowships, Federal Work-Study, scholarships/grants, health care benefits, and unspecified assistantships also available. Financial award application deadline: 2/1. *Faculty research:* Accounting statements and reporting, corporate finance, information systems processes, structures and decision-making, consumer behavior and marketing models. *Total annual research expenditures:* $254,031. *Unit head:* Dr. Dennis Galletta, Director, 412-648-1699, Fax: 412-624-3633, E-mail: galletta@katz.pitt.edu. *Application contact:* Carrie Woods, Assistant Director, 412-648-1525, Fax: 412-624-3633, E-mail: cawoods@katz.pitt.edu. Web site: http://www.business.pitt.edu/katz/phd/.

University of Pittsburgh, Katz Graduate School of Business, Master of Business Administration Programs, Pittsburgh , PA 15260. Offers finance (MBA); information systems (MBA); marketing (MBA); operations management (MBA); organizational behavior and human resource management (MBA); organizational leadership (Certificate); strategy, environment and organizations (MBA); technology, innovation and entrepreneurship (Certificate); MBA/JD; MBA/MIB; MBA/MPIA; MBA/MSE; MBA/ MSIS; MID/MBA. *Accreditation:* AACSB. Part-time and evening/weekend programs available. *Faculty:* 62 full-time (17 women), 21 part-time/adjunct (4 women). *Students:* 179 full-time (63 women), 572 part-time (373 women); includes 69 minority (29 Black or African American, non-Hispanic/Latino; 24 Asian, non-Hispanic/Latino; 16 Hispanic/ Latino), 83 international. Average age 29. 391 applicants, 42% accepted, 78 enrolled. *Degree requirements:* For master's, minimum GPA of 3.0. *Entrance requirements:* For master's, GMAT, recommendations, undergraduate transcripts, essay, resume, interview, bachelor's degree. Additional exam requirements/recommendations for international students: Required—TOEFL (minimum score 600 paper, 250 computer, 100 iBT) or IELTS. *Application deadline:* For fall admission, 4/1 priority date for domestic students, 2/1 for international students. Application fee: $50. Electronic applications accepted. *Expenses:* Tuition, state resident: full-time $18,774; part-time $760 per credit. Tuition, nonresident: full-time $30,736; part-time $1258 per credit. *Required fees:* $740; $200 per term. Tuition and fees vary according to program. *Financial support:* In 2011–12, 58 students received support. Career-related internships or fieldwork and scholarships/grants available. Financial award application deadline: 3/1; financial award applicants required to submit FAFSA. *Faculty research:* Accounting statements and reporting, corporate finance, information systems processes, structures and decision-making, consumer behavior and marketing models. *Unit head:* William T. Valenta, Assistant Dean/Director, 412-648-1610, Fax: 412-648-1659, E-mail: wtvalenta@katz.pitt.edu. *Application contact:* Thomas Keller, Director of MBA Admissions, 412-648-1700, Fax: 412-648-1659, E-mail: mba@katz.pitt.edu. Web site: http://www.business.pitt.edu/katz/mba/.

University of Portland, Dr. Robert B. Pamplin, Jr. School of Business, Portland, OR 97203-5798. Offers business administration (MBA); entrepreneurship (MBA); finance (MBA, MS); health care management (MBA); marketing (MBA); nonprofit management (EMBA); operations and technology management (MBA); sustainability (MBA). *Accreditation:* AACSB. Part-time and evening/weekend programs available. *Faculty:* 13 full-time (1 woman), 8 part-time/adjunct (1 woman). *Students:* 50 full-time (13 women), 90 part-time (41 women); includes 19 minority (1 Black or African American, non-Hispanic/Latino; 1 American Indian or Alaska Native, non-Hispanic/Latino; 8 Asian, non-Hispanic/Latino; 5 Hispanic/Latino; 2 Native Hawaiian or other Pacific Islander, non-Hispanic/Latino; 2 Two or more races, non-Hispanic/Latino), 18 international. Average age 31. In 2011, 54 master's awarded. *Entrance requirements:* For master's, GMAT, minimum GPA of 3.0, resume, 2 letters of recommendation. Additional exam requirements/recommendations for international students: Required—TOEFL (minimum score 570 paper-based; 89 iBT), IELTS (minimum score 7). *Application deadline:* For fall admission, 7/15 priority date for domestic students, 7/15 for international students; for spring admission, 12/15 priority date for domestic students, 12/15 for international students. Applications are processed on a rolling basis. Application fee: $50. *Expenses:* Contact institution. *Financial support:* Federal Work-Study, scholarships/grants, and tuition waivers (partial) available. Support available to part-time students. Financial award application deadline: 3/1; financial award applicants required to submit FAFSA. *Unit head:* Dr. Howard Feldman, Associate Dean, 503-943-7224, E-mail: feldman@up.edu. *Application contact:* Melissa McCarthy, Academic Specialist, 503-943-7225, E-mail: mccarthy@up.edu. Web site: http://business.up.edu/.

University of Puerto Rico, Mayagüez Campus, Graduate Studies, College of Business Administration, Mayagüez, PR 00681-9000. Offers business administration (MBA); finance (MBA); human resources (MBA); industrial management (MBA). Part-time and evening/weekend programs available. *Students:* 46 full-time (30 women), 16 part-time (9 women); includes 59 minority (all Hispanic/Latino), 3 international. 18 applicants, 44% accepted, 5 enrolled. In 2011, 14 master's awarded. *Degree requirements:* For master's, comprehensive exam. *Entrance requirements:* For master's, GMAT or EXADEP, bachelor's degree with courses in calculus, microeconomics, accounting and statistics. Additional exam requirements/ recommendations for international students: Required—TOEFL (minimum score 500 paper-based; 173 computer-based). *Application deadline:* For fall admission, 2/15 for domestic and international students; for spring admission, 9/15 for domestic and international students. Applications are processed on a rolling basis. Application fee: $25. Tuition and fees vary according to course level and course load. *Financial support:* In 2011–12, 4 students received support, including 4 teaching assistantships (averaging $8,500 per year); Federal Work-Study and institutionally sponsored loans also available. *Faculty research:* Organizational studies, management, accounting. *Total annual research expenditures:* $20,000. *Unit head:* Dr. Rosario Ortiz, Graduate Student Coordinator, 787-265-3800, Fax: 787-832-5320, E-mail: rosario.ortiz@upr.edu. *Application contact:* Milagros Soto, Student Administrator, 787-265-3887, Fax: 787-832-5320, E-mail: milagros.soto1@upr.edu. Web site: http://enterprise.uprm.edu/.

University of Puerto Rico, Río Piedras, College of Business Administration, San Juan, PR 00931-3300. Offers accounting (MBA); finance (MBA, PhD); general business (MBA); human resources management (MBA); international trade and business (MBA, PhD); marketing (MBA); operations management (MBA); quantitative methods (MBA). *Accreditation:* ACBSP. Part-time programs available. *Degree requirements:* For master's, comprehensive exam, thesis or alternative, research project. *Entrance requirements:* For master's, GMAT or PAEG, minimum GPA of 3.0, letter of recommendation; for doctorate, GMAT, PAEG, minimum GPA of 3.0, master degree. *Faculty research:* Management.

University of Rhode Island, Graduate School, College of Business Administration, Kingston, RI 02881. Offers accounting (MS); business administration (MBA, PhD), including finance and insurance (PhD), management (PhD), marketing (PhD), operations and supply chain management (MBA); finance (MBA); general business (MBA); management (MBA); marketing (MBA); supply chain management (MBA). *Accreditation:* AACSB. Part-time and evening/weekend programs available. *Faculty:* 56 full-time (15 women), 8 part-time/adjunct (4 women). *Students:* 93 full-time (40 women), 226 part-time (90 women); includes 35 minority (7 Black or African American, non-Hispanic/Latino; 1 American Indian or Alaska Native, non-Hispanic/Latino; 15 Asian, non-Hispanic/Latino; 11 Hispanic/Latino; 1 Two or more races, non-Hispanic/Latino), 24 international. In 2011, 78 master's, 3 doctorates awarded. *Degree requirements:* For master's, comprehensive exam (for some programs), thesis optional; for doctorate, comprehensive exam, thesis/dissertation. *Entrance requirements:* For master's, GMAT or GRE, 2 letters of recommendation, resume; for doctorate, GMAT or GRE, 3 letters of recommendation, resume. Additional exam requirements/recommendations for international students: Required—TOEFL (minimum score 575 paper-based; 233 computer-based; 91 iBT). Application fee: $65. Electronic applications accepted. *Expenses:* Tuition, state resident: full-time $10,432; part-time $580 per credit hour. Tuition, nonresident: full-time $23,130; part-time $1285 per credit hour. *Required fees:* $1362; $36 per credit hour. $35 per semester. One-time fee: $130. *Financial support:* In 2011–12, 13 teaching assistantships with full and partial tuition reimbursements (averaging $13,020 per year) were awarded. Financial award applicants required to submit FAFSA. *Unit head:* Dr. Mark Higgins, Dean, 401-874-4244, Fax: 401-874-4312, E-mail: markhiggins@uri.edu. *Application contact:* Lisa Lancellotta, Coordinator, MBA Programs, 401-874-4241, Fax: 401-874-4312, E-mail: mba@uri.edu. Web site: http://www.cba.uri.edu/.

University of San Francisco, School of Management, Masagung Graduate School of Management, Investor Relations Program, San Francisco, CA 94117-1080. Offers MA. *Faculty:* 3 full-time (1 woman). *Students:* 7 full-time (4 women), 5 international. Average age 25. 21 applicants, 62% accepted, 6 enrolled. In 2011, 5 master's awarded. *Expenses: Tuition:* Full-time $20,070; part-time $1115 per unit. Tuition and fees vary according to course load, campus/location and program. *Financial support:* In 2011–12, 3 students received support. *Unit head:* John Veitch, Chair, 415-422-6784, Fax: 415-422-5784. *Application contact:* Information Contact, 415-422-2221, Fax: 415-422-2217, E-mail: management@usfca.edu. Web site: http://www.usfca.edu/management/mair/.

University of San Francisco, School of Management, Masagung Graduate School of Management, Program in Business Administration, San Francisco, CA 94117-1080. Offers business economics (MBA); e-business (MBA); entrepreneurship (MBA); finance (MBA); international business (MBA); management (MBA); marketing (MBA); telecommunications management and policy (MBA); JD/MBA; MSN/MBA. *Accreditation:* AACSB. *Faculty:* 18 full-time (4 women), 18 part-time/adjunct (9 women). *Students:* 247 full-time (122 women), 9 part-time (3 women); includes 85 minority (5 Black or African American, non-Hispanic/Latino; 55 Asian, non-Hispanic/Latino; 16 Hispanic/Latino; 1 Native Hawaiian or other Pacific Islander, non-Hispanic/Latino; 8 Two or more races, non-Hispanic/Latino), 38 international. Average age 29. 552 applicants, 55% accepted, 99 enrolled. In 2011, 173 master's awarded. *Entrance requirements:* For master's, GMAT, minimum undergraduate GPA of 3.2. Additional exam requirements/ recommendations for international students: Required—TOEFL. *Application deadline:* For fall admission, 7/1 priority date for domestic students; for spring admission, 11/30 for domestic students. Applications are processed on a rolling basis. Application fee: $55 ($65 for international students). *Expenses: Tuition:* Full-time $20,070; part-time $1115 per unit. Tuition and fees vary according to course load, campus/location and program. *Financial support:* In 2011–12, 33 students received support. Fellowships available. Financial award application deadline: 3/2; financial award applicants required to submit FAFSA. *Faculty research:* International financial markets, technology transfer licensing, international marketing, strategic planning. *Total annual research expenditures:* $50,000. *Unit head:* Kelly Brookes, Director, 415-422-2221, Fax: 415-422-6315. *Application contact:* Director, MBA Program, 415-422-2221, Fax: 415-422-6315, E-mail: mba@usfca.edu.

University of San Francisco, School of Management, Masagung Graduate School of Management, Program in Financial Analysis, San Francisco, CA 94117-1080. Offers MS, MS/MBA. *Faculty:* 4 full-time (0 women), 9 part-time/adjunct (2 women). *Students:* 124 full-time (59 women), 5 part-time (3 women); includes 28 minority (21 Asian, non-Hispanic/Latino; 7 Hispanic/Latino), 71 international. Average age 27. 445 applicants, 32% accepted, 70 enrolled. In 2011, 93 master's awarded. *Expenses: Tuition:* Full-time $20,070; part-time $1115 per unit. Tuition and fees vary according to course load, campus/location and program. *Financial support:* In 2011–12, 38 students received support. *Unit head:* Dr. John Veitch. *Application contact:* Information Contact, 415-422-2221, Fax: 415-422-6983, E-mail: management@usfca.edu. Web site: http://www.usfca.edu/management/msfa/.

University of Saskatchewan, College of Graduate Studies and Research, Edwards School of Business, Department of Finance and Management Science, Saskatoon, SK S7N 5A2, Canada. Offers finance (M Sc). Part-time programs available. *Degree requirements:* For master's, thesis. *Entrance requirements:* For master's, GMAT. Additional exam requirements/recommendations for international students: Required—TOEFL.

The University of Scranton, College of Graduate and Continuing Education, Program in Business Administration, Scranton, PA 18510. Offers accounting (MBA); finance (MBA); general business administration (MBA); health care management (MBA);

international business (MBA); management information systems (MBA); marketing (MBA); operations management (MBA). *Accreditation:* AACSB. Part-time and evening/weekend programs available. Postbaccalaureate distance learning degree programs offered (no on-campus study). *Faculty:* 34 full-time (8 women). *Students:* 276 full-time (94 women), 243 part-time (88 women); includes 14 minority (10 Black or African American, non-Hispanic/Latino; 3 Asian, non-Hispanic/Latino; 1 Hispanic/Latino), 49 international. Average age 33. 358 applicants, 80% accepted. In 2011, 101 master's awarded. *Degree requirements:* For master's, capstone experience. *Entrance requirements:* For master's, GMAT, minimum GPA of 2.75. Additional exam requirements/recommendations for international students: Required—TOEFL (minimum score 500 paper-based; 173 computer-based), IELTS (minimum score 5.5). *Application deadline:* Applications are processed on a rolling basis. Application fee: $0. *Financial support:* In 2011–12, 12 students received support, including 12 teaching assistantships with full and partial tuition reimbursements available (averaging $8,433 per year); fellowships, career-related internships or fieldwork, Federal Work-Study, and unspecified assistantships also available. Support available to part-time students. Financial award application deadline: 3/1. *Faculty research:* Financial markets, strategic impact of total quality management, internal accounting controls, consumer preference, information systems and the Internet. *Unit head:* Dr. Murli Rajan, Director, 570-941-4043, Fax: 570-941-4342. *Application contact:* Joseph M. Roback, Director of Admissions, 570-941-4385, Fax: 570-941-5928, E-mail: robackj2@scranton.edu. Web site: http://www.academic.scranton.edu/department/mba/.

University of Southern Maine, School of Business, Portland, ME 04104-9300. Offers accounting (MBA); business administration (MBA); finance (MBA); health management and policy (MBA); sustainability (MBA); JD/MBA; MBA/MSA; MBA/MSN; MS/MBA. *Accreditation:* AACSB. Part-time and evening/weekend programs available. *Faculty:* 20 full-time (5 women), 2 part-time/adjunct (1 woman). *Students:* 28 full-time (9 women), 91 part-time (39 women), 1 international. Average age 33. 64 applicants, 72% accepted, 33 enrolled. *Entrance requirements:* For master's, GMAT, minimum AACSB index of 1100. Additional exam requirements/recommendations for international students: Required—TOEFL (minimum score 550 paper-based; 213 computer-based; 79 iBT). *Application deadline:* For fall admission, 8/1 priority date for domestic students, 5/1 for international students; for spring admission, 12/1 priority date for domestic students, 9/1 for international students. Applications are processed on a rolling basis. Application fee: $65. Electronic applications accepted. *Financial support:* In 2011–12, 3 research assistantships with partial tuition reimbursements (averaging $9,000 per year), 3 teaching assistantships with partial tuition reimbursements (averaging $9,000 per year) were awarded; career-related internships or fieldwork, Federal Work-Study, scholarships/grants, tuition waivers (full and partial), and unspecified assistantships also available. Support available to part-time students. Financial award application deadline: 2/15; financial award applicants required to submit FAFSA. *Faculty research:* Economic development, management information systems, real options, system dynamics, simulation. *Unit head:* John Voyer, Director, 207-780-4020, Fax: 207-780-4665, E-mail: voyer@usm.maine.edu. *Application contact:* Alice B. Cash, Assistant Director for Student Affairs, 207-780-4184, Fax: 207-780-4662, E-mail: acash@usm.maine.edu. Web site: http://www.usm.maine.edu/sb.

University of South Florida, Graduate School, College of Business, Department of Finance, Tampa, FL 33620-9951. Offers finance (MS, PhD); real estate (MSRE). Part-time and evening/weekend programs available. *Faculty:* 14 full-time (3 women), 11 part-time/adjunct (2 women). *Students:* 48 full-time (16 women), 11 part-time (2 women); includes 6 minority (2 Black or African American, non-Hispanic/Latino; 3 Asian, non-Hispanic/Latino; 1 Hispanic/Latino), 28 international. Average age 26. 102 applicants, 53% accepted, 28 enrolled. In 2011, 14 master's, 1 doctorate awarded. Terminal master's awarded for partial completion of doctoral program. *Degree requirements:* For master's, thesis or alternative; for doctorate, comprehensive exam, thesis/dissertation. *Entrance requirements:* For master's, GMAT (minimum score of 550), minimum GPA of 3.0 in last 30 hours; for doctorate, GMAT or GRE, at least two letters of recommendation, personal statement, interview. Additional exam requirements/recommendations for international students: Required—TOEFL (minimum score 550 paper-based; 213 computer-based; 79 iBT) or IELTS (minimum score 6.5). *Application deadline:* For fall admission, 6/1 for domestic students, 1/2 for international students; for spring admission, 10/15 for domestic students, 6/1 for international students. Application fee: $30. Electronic applications accepted. *Financial support:* In 2011–12, 17 students received support, including 8 research assistantships (averaging $14,357 per year), 9 teaching assistantships with tuition reimbursements available (averaging $11,972 per year); scholarships/grants, health care benefits, and unspecified assistantships also available. Financial award application deadline: 6/30. *Faculty research:* Corporate governance, international finance, asset pricing models, risk management, market efficiency. *Total annual research expenditures:* $332,885. *Unit head:* Dr. Scott Besley, Chairperson, 813-974-2081, Fax: 813-974-3084, E-mail: sbesley@coba.usf.edu. *Application contact:* Wendy Baker, Assistant Director, Graduate Studies, 813-974-3335, Fax: 813-974-4518, E-mail: wbaker@usf.edu.

The University of Tampa, John H. Sykes College of Business, Tampa, FL 33606-1490. Offers accounting (MS); entrepreneurship (MBA); finance (MBA, MS); information systems management (MBA); innovation management (MBA); international business (MBA); marketing (MBA, MS); nonprofit management (MBA). *Accreditation:* AACSB. Part-time and evening/weekend programs available. *Faculty:* 38 full-time (14 women), 5 part-time/adjunct (1 woman). *Students:* 161 full-time (65 women), 193 part-time (82 women); includes 65 minority (11 Black or African American, non-Hispanic/Latino; 1 American Indian or Alaska Native, non-Hispanic/Latino; 8 Asian, non-Hispanic/Latino; 39 Hispanic/Latino; 2 Native Hawaiian or other Pacific Islander, non-Hispanic/Latino; 4 Two or more races, non-Hispanic/Latino), 58 international. Average age 29. 837 applicants, 41% accepted, 196 enrolled. In 2011, 259 degrees awarded. *Degree requirements:* For master's, capstone. *Entrance requirements:* For master's, GMAT or GRE, 4-year undergraduate degree, minimum GPA of 3.0, professional experience (for Executive MBA). Additional exam requirements/recommendations for international students: Required—TOEFL (minimum score 577 paper-based; 230 computer-based; 90 iBT); Recommended—IELTS (minimum score 7.5). *Application deadline:* Applications are processed on a rolling basis. Application fee: $40. Electronic applications accepted. *Expenses: Tuition:* Full-time $8320; part-time $520 per credit hour. *Required fees:* $40 per semester. Tuition and fees vary according to program. *Financial support:* In 2011–12, 124 students received support. Career-related internships or fieldwork, scholarships/grants, unspecified assistantships, and grants available. Financial award applicants required to submit FAFSA. *Faculty research:* Job market signaling, on-line shopping behaviors and social media, the Tampa Bay economy, digital literacy, entrepreneurship in small businesses. *Unit head:* Dennis Nostrand, Vice President, Enrollment/Admissions, 813-257-1808, E-mail: dnostrand@ut.edu. *Application contact:* Charlene Tobie, Associate Director of Admissions, 813-257-3566, E-mail: ctobie@ut.edu. Web site: http://ut.edu/graduate.

The University of Tennessee, Graduate School, College of Business Administration, Program in Business Administration, Knoxville, TN 37996. Offers accounting (PhD); finance (MBA, PhD); logistics and transportation (MBA, PhD); management (PhD); marketing (MBA, PhD); operations management (MBA); professional business administration (MBA); statistics (PhD); JD/MBA; MS/MBA; Pharm D/MBA. Pharm D/MBA offered jointly with The University of Tennessee Health Science Center. *Accreditation:* AACSB. Postbaccalaureate distance learning degree programs offered. *Degree requirements:* For master's, thesis or alternative; for doctorate, thesis/dissertation. *Entrance requirements:* For master's and doctorate, GMAT, minimum GPA of 2.7. Additional exam requirements/recommendations for international students: Required—TOEFL. Electronic applications accepted. *Expenses:* Tuition, state resident: full-time $8332; part-time $464 per credit hour. Tuition, nonresident: full-time $25,174; part-time $1400 per credit hour. *Required fees:* $1162; $56 per credit hour. Tuition and fees vary according to program.

The University of Texas at Arlington, Graduate School, College of Business, Department of Finance and Real Estate, Arlington, TX 76019. Offers finance (PhD); quantitative finance (MS); real estate (MS). Part-time and evening/weekend programs available. *Faculty:* 7 full-time (0 women), 1 (woman) part-time/adjunct. *Students:* 23 full-time (8 women), 40 part-time (11 women); includes 19 minority (5 Black or African American, non-Hispanic/Latino; 7 Asian, non-Hispanic/Latino; 6 Hispanic/Latino; 1 Two or more races, non-Hispanic/Latino), 15 international. 47 applicants, 57% accepted, 13 enrolled. In 2011, 42 degrees awarded. *Degree requirements:* For master's, thesis optional; for doctorate, comprehensive exam, thesis/dissertation. *Entrance requirements:* For master's, GMAT/GRE, minimum GPA of 3.0; for doctorate, GMAT/GRE. Additional exam requirements/recommendations for international students: Required—TOEFL (minimum score 550 paper-based; 213 computer-based; 79 iBT). *Application deadline:* For fall admission, 6/1 priority date for domestic students, 4/1 for international students; for spring admission, 10/15 for domestic students, 9/15 for international students. Applications are processed on a rolling basis. Application fee: $40 ($70 for international students). *Financial support:* In 2011–12, 7 teaching assistantships (averaging $16,857 per year) were awarded; career-related internships or fieldwork, Federal Work-Study, institutionally sponsored loans, and unspecified assistantships also available. Financial award application deadline: 6/1; financial award applicants required to submit FAFSA. *Unit head:* Dr. David Diltz, Chair, 817-272-3705, Fax: 817-272-2252, E-mail: diltz@uta.edu. *Application contact:* Dr. Fred Forgey, Graduate Advisor, 817-272-0359, Fax: 817-272-2252, E-mail: realestate@uta.edu. Web site: http://wweb.uta.edu/finance/.

The University of Texas at Arlington, Graduate School, College of Business, Program in Business Administration, Arlington, TX 76019. Offers accounting (PhD); business statistics (PhD); finance (MBA, PhD); information systems (MBA, PhD); management (MBA, PhD); marketing (MBA, PhD); operations management (MBA, PhD); real estate (MBA). *Accreditation:* AACSB. Part-time and evening/weekend programs available. *Students:* 505 full-time (189 women), 369 part-time (140 women); includes 199 minority (58 Black or African American, non-Hispanic/Latino; 2 American Indian or Alaska Native, non-Hispanic/Latino; 70 Asian, non-Hispanic/Latino; 56 Hispanic/Latino; 1 Native Hawaiian or other Pacific Islander, non-Hispanic/Latino; 12 Two or more races, non-Hispanic/Latino), 306 international. 416 applicants, 81% accepted, 234 enrolled. In 2011, 495 master's, 3 doctorates awarded. *Degree requirements:* For master's, thesis optional; for doctorate, comprehensive exam, thesis/dissertation. *Entrance requirements:* For master's, GMAT or GRE; for doctorate, GMAT, minimum GPA of 3.0 (undergraduate), 3.4 (graduate); 30 hours of graduate course work. Additional exam requirements/recommendations for international students: Required—TOEFL (minimum score 550 paper-based; 213 computer-based; 79 iBT). *Application deadline:* For fall admission, 6/1 for domestic students, 4/1 for international students; for spring admission, 10/15 for domestic students, 9/15 for international students. Applications are processed on a rolling basis. Application fee: $40 ($70 for international students). Electronic applications accepted. *Financial support:* Career-related internships or fieldwork, scholarships/grants, and unspecified assistantships available. Support available to part-time students. Financial award application deadline: 6/1; financial award applicants required to submit FAFSA. *Unit head:* Dr. Edmund Prater, Director of PhD Programs, 817-272-2131, Fax: 817-272-5799. *Application contact:* Melanie McGee, Director of MBA Program, 817-272-3005, Fax: 817-272-5799, E-mail: mwmcgee@uta.edu.

The University of Texas at Austin, Graduate School, McCombs School of Business, Department of Finance, Austin, TX 78712-1111. Offers MSF, PhD. *Entrance requirements:* For doctorate, GMAT or GRE. *Application deadline:* For fall admission, 1/15 priority date for domestic students. Applications are processed on a rolling basis. Application fee: $50 ($75 for international students). Electronic applications accepted. *Financial support:* Fellowships with full tuition reimbursements, research assistantships with partial tuition reimbursements, and teaching assistantships with partial tuition reimbursements available. Financial award application deadline: 2/1. *Unit head:* Jay Hartzell, Chair, 512-471-6779, E-mail: jay.hartzell@mccombs.utexas.edu. *Application contact:* Andres Almazan, Graduate Advisor, 521-471-5856, E-mail: andres.almazan@mccombs.utexas.edu. Web site: http://www.mccombs.utexas.edu/dept/finance/.

The University of Texas at Dallas, Naveen Jindal School of Management, Program in Finance, Richardson, TX 75080. Offers finance (MS); financial analysis (MS); financial engineering and risk management (MS); investment management (MS). Part-time and evening/weekend programs available. *Faculty:* 18 full-time (3 women), 8 part-time/adjunct (1 woman). *Students:* 358 full-time (187 women), 81 part-time (19 women); includes 34 minority (1 Black or African American, non-Hispanic/Latino; 24 Asian, non-Hispanic/Latino; 6 Hispanic/Latino; 3 Two or more races, non-Hispanic/Latino), 352 international. Average age 25. 864 applicants, 56% accepted, 235 enrolled. In 2011, 93 master's awarded. *Entrance requirements:* For master's, GMAT. Additional exam requirements/recommendations for international students: Required—TOEFL (minimum score 550 paper-based; 215 computer-based). *Application deadline:* For fall admission, 7/15 for domestic students, 5/1 for international students; for spring admission, 11/15 for domestic students, 9/1 for international students. Applications are processed on a rolling basis. Application fee: $50 ($100 for international students). Electronic applications accepted. *Expenses:* Tuition, state resident: full-time $11,170; part-time $620.56 per credit hour. Tuition, nonresident: full-time $20,212; part-time $1122.89 per credit hour. *Financial support:* In 2011–12, 161 students received support. Research assistantships with partial tuition reimbursements available, teaching assistantships with partial tuition reimbursements available, career-related internships or fieldwork, Federal Work-Study, institutionally sponsored loans, scholarships/grants, and unspecified assistantships available. Support available to part-time students. Financial award application deadline: 4/30; financial award applicants required to submit FAFSA. *Faculty research:* Econometrics, industrial organization, auction theory, file-sharing copyrights and bundling, international financial management, entrepreneurial finance. *Unit head:* Dr. Robert Kieschnick, Area Coordinator, 972-883-6273, E-mail: rkiesch@utdallas.edu. *Application contact:* James Parker, Assistant Director, 972-883-5842, E-mail: jparker@utdallas.edu. Web site: http://jindal.utdallas.edu/academic-areas/finance-and-managerial-economics/.

The University of Texas at Dallas, Naveen Jindal School of Management, Program in Management and Administrative Sciences, Richardson, TX 75080. Offers electronic commerce (MS); finance (MS); healthcare administration (MS); information systems (MS); innovation and entrepreneurship (MS); international management (MS); leadership in organizations (MS); marketing (MS); operations (MS); organizations (MS); real estate (MS); strategy (MS). *Accreditation:* AACSB. Part-time and evening/weekend programs available. *Faculty:* 26 full-time (6 women), 9 part-time/adjunct (2 women). *Students:* 128 full-time (69 women), 169 part-time (95 women); includes 76 minority (18 Black or African American, non-Hispanic/Latino; 1 American Indian or Alaska Native, non-Hispanic/Latino; 37 Asian, non-Hispanic/Latino; 15 Hispanic/Latino; 1 Native Hawaiian or other Pacific Islander, non-Hispanic/Latino; 4 Two or more races, non-Hispanic/Latino), 77 international. Average age 34. 220 applicants, 63% accepted, 68 enrolled. In 2011, 58 master's awarded. *Degree requirements:* For master's, thesis optional. *Entrance requirements:* For master's, GMAT. Additional exam requirements/recommendations for international students: Required—TOEFL (minimum score 550 paper-based; 215 computer-based). *Application deadline:* For fall admission, 7/15 for domestic students, 5/1 for international students; for spring admission, 11/15 for domestic students, 9/1 for international students. Applications are processed on a rolling basis. Application fee: $50 ($100 for international students). Electronic applications accepted. *Expenses:* Tuition, state resident: full-time $11,170; part-time $620.56 per credit hour. Tuition, nonresident: full-time $20,212; part-time $1122.89 per credit hour. *Financial support:* In 2011–12, 68 students received support, including 7 teaching assistantships with partial tuition reimbursements available (averaging $16,200 per year); research assistantships with partial tuition reimbursements available, career-related internships or fieldwork, Federal Work-Study, institutionally sponsored loans, scholarships/grants, and unspecified assistantships also available. Support available to part-time students. Financial award application deadline: 4/30; financial award applicants required to submit FAFSA. *Faculty research:* Integrated and detailed knowledge of functional areas of management, analytical tools for effective appraisal and decision-making. *Unit head:* Dr. Gregory Dess, Area Coordinator, 972-883-4439, E-mail: gdess@utdallas.edu. *Application contact:* James Parker, Assistant Director, 972-883-5842, E-mail: jparker@utdallas.edu. Web site: http://jindal.utdallas.edu/academic-areas/organizations-strategy-and-international-management/.

The University of Texas at Dallas, Naveen Jindal School of Management, Programs in Management Science, Richardson, TX 75080. Offers accounting (PhD); finance (PhD); information systems (PhD); marketing (PhD); operations management (PhD). *Accreditation:* AACSB. Part-time and evening/weekend programs available. *Faculty:* 14 full-time (4 women). *Students:* 75 full-time (30 women), 8 part-time (4 women); includes 5 minority (4 Asian, non-Hispanic/Latino; 1 Two or more races, non-Hispanic/Latino), 71 international. Average age 31. 224 applicants, 11% accepted, 20 enrolled. In 2011, 10 doctorates awarded. *Degree requirements:* For doctorate, thesis/dissertation. *Entrance requirements:* For doctorate, GMAT, minimum GPA of 3.0. Additional exam requirements/recommendations for international students: Required—TOEFL (minimum score 550 paper-based; 215 computer-based). *Application deadline:* For fall admission, 7/15 for domestic students, 5/1 for international students; for spring admission, 11/15 for domestic students, 9/1 for international students. Applications are processed on a rolling basis. Application fee: $50 ($100 for international students). Electronic applications accepted. *Expenses:* Tuition, state resident: full-time $11,170; part-time $620.56 per credit hour. Tuition, nonresident: full-time $20,212; part-time $1122.89 per credit hour. *Financial support:* In 2011–12, 76 students received support, including 3 research assistantships with partial tuition reimbursements available (averaging $21,600 per year), 68 teaching assistantships with partial tuition reimbursements available (averaging $16,162 per year); career-related internships or fieldwork, Federal Work-Study, institutionally sponsored loans, scholarships/grants, and unspecified assistantships also available. Support available to part-time students. Financial award application deadline: 4/30; financial award applicants required to submit FAFSA. *Faculty research:* Empirical generalizations in marketing, diffusion of generations of technology, stochastic brand-choice theory, acceptance of trade deals by supermarkets, nonparametric estimations of market share response. *Unit head:* Dr. Sumit Sarkar, Program Director, 972-883-2745, Fax: 972-883-5977, E-mail: som_phd.@utdallas.edu. *Application contact:* LeeAnne Sloane, Coordinator, 972-883-2745, Fax: 972-883-5977, E-mail: som_phd@utdallas.edu. Web site: http://jindal.utdallas.edu/academic-programs/phd-programs/management-science/.

The University of Texas at San Antonio, College of Business, Department of Finance, San Antonio, TX 78249-0617. Offers business (MBA), including finance; construction science and management (MS); finance (MS). Part-time and evening/weekend programs available. *Faculty:* 8 full-time (1 woman), 1 part-time/adjunct (0 women). *Students:* 37 full-time (16 women), 48 part-time (7 women); includes 27 minority (4 Black or African American, non-Hispanic/Latino; 3 Asian, non-Hispanic/Latino; 19 Hispanic/Latino; 1 Two or more races, non-Hispanic/Latino), 15 international. Average age 28. 77 applicants, 51% accepted, 23 enrolled. In 2011, 20 master's awarded. *Degree requirements:* For master's, comprehensive exam, thesis or alternative, 33 semester credit hours. *Entrance requirements:* For master's, GMAT or GRE. Additional exam requirements/recommendations for international students: Required—TOEFL (minimum score 500 paper-based; 61 iBT), IELTS (minimum score 5). *Application deadline:* For fall admission, 7/1 for domestic students, 4/1 for international students; for spring admission, 11/1 for domestic students, 9/1 for international students. Applications are processed on a rolling basis. Application fee: $45 ($85 for international students). Electronic applications accepted. *Expenses:* Tuition, state resident: full-time $3148; part-time $2176 per semester. Tuition, nonresident: full-time $8782; part-time $5932 per semester. *Required fees:* $719 per semester. *Financial support:* In 2011–12, 12 students received support, including research assistantships (averaging $10,000 per year), teaching assistantships (averaging $10,000 per year). *Faculty research:* Corporate finance, governance, capital structure, compensations, venture capital, restructuring, bankruptcy, international finance, market interrelationships, pricing, options and futures, micro-structure, comparative corporate studies, interest rate, instruments and strategies. *Total annual research expenditures:* $5,000. *Unit head:* Dr. Lalatendu Misra, Chair, 210-458-6315, Fax: 210-458-6320, E-mail: kfairchild@utsa.edu. *Application contact:* Katherine Pope, Graduate Advisor of Record, 210-458-7316, Fax: 210-458-7316, E-mail: katherine.pope@utsa.edu.

The University of Texas at San Antonio, College of Business, General Business Program, San Antonio, TX 78249-0617. Offers business (MBA); business administration (PhD), including accounting, business administration, finance, information technology, management and organization studies, marketing; information systems (MBA); international business (MBA); management accounting (MBA); management of technology (MBA); marketing management (MBA); taxation (MBA). *Students:* 170 full-time (52 women), 120 part-time (49 women); includes 90 minority (14 Black or African American, non-Hispanic/Latino; 2 American Indian or Alaska Native, non-Hispanic/Latino; 15 Asian, non-Hispanic/Latino; 55 Hispanic/Latino; 1 Native Hawaiian or other Pacific Islander, non-Hispanic/Latino; 3 Two or more races, non-Hispanic/Latino), 37 international. Average age 32. 395 applicants, 45% accepted, 133 enrolled. In 2011, 95 master's, 8 doctorates awarded. *Entrance requirements:* Additional exam requirements/recommendations for international students: Required—TOEFL (minimum score 500 paper-based; 61 iBT), IELTS (minimum score 5). *Application deadline:* For fall admission, 7/1 for domestic students, 4/1 for international students; for spring admission, 11/1 for domestic students, 9/1 for international students. Application fee: $45 ($85 for international students). *Expenses:* Tuition, state resident: full-time $3148; part-time $2176 per semester. Tuition, nonresident: full-time $8782; part-time $5932 per semester. *Required fees:* $719 per semester. *Financial support:* In 2011–12, fellowships (averaging $22,000 per year), research assistantships (averaging $10,000 per year), teaching assistantships (averaging $10,000 per year) were awarded. *Unit head:* Dr. Lynda Y. de la Vinna, Dean, 210-458-4317, Fax: 210-458-4308, E-mail: lynda.delavina@utsa.edu. *Application contact:* Katherine Pope, Director of Graduate Student Services, 210-458-7316, Fax: 210-458-4398, E-mail: katherine.pope@utsa.edu. Web site: http://business.utsa.edu.

The University of Texas–Pan American, College of Business Administration, Program in Business Administration, Edinburg, TX 78539. Offers business administration (MBA); finance (PhD); management (PhD); marketing (PhD). Part-time and evening/weekend programs available. Postbaccalaureate distance learning degree programs offered (no on-campus study). *Degree requirements:* For master's, thesis optional. *Entrance requirements:* For master's, GMAT, minimum GPA of 3.0. Additional exam requirements/recommendations for international students: Required—TOEFL (minimum score 500 paper-based). *Application deadline:* For fall admission, 7/25 priority date for domestic students, 7/1 for international students; for spring admission, 12/15 priority date for domestic students, 11/1 for international students. Applications are processed on a rolling basis. Application fee: $35. Electronic applications accepted. Tuition and fees vary according to course load, program and student level. *Financial support:* Research assistantships with partial tuition reimbursements, scholarships/grants, and unspecified assistantships available. *Faculty research:* Human resources, border region, entrepreneurship, marketing. *Unit head:* Business Administration Building, 956-665-3313, E-mail: mbaprog@utpa.edu. Web site: http://portal.utpa.edu/utpa_main/daa_home/coba_new_home/coba_degrees/coba_graduate.

University of the West, Department of Business Administration, Rosemead, CA 91770. Offers business administration (EMBA); finance (MBA); information technology and management (MBA); international business (MBA); nonprofit organization management (MBA). Part-time and evening/weekend programs available. *Entrance requirements:* Additional exam requirements/recommendations for international students: Required—TOEFL.

The University of Toledo, College of Graduate Studies, College of Business and Innovation, Department of Finance, Toledo, OH 43606-3390. Offers MBA. Part-time and evening/weekend programs available. *Faculty:* 4. *Students:* 23 full-time (6 women), 41 part-time (13 women); includes 8 minority (6 Black or African American, non-Hispanic/Latino; 1 Asian, non-Hispanic/Latino; 1 Hispanic/Latino), 23 international. Average age 27. 47 applicants, 68% accepted, 21 enrolled. In 2011, 78 master's awarded. *Entrance requirements:* For master's, GMAT, minimum GPA of 2.7 for all prior academic work, three letters of recommendation, statement of purpose, transcripts from all prior institutions attended. Additional exam requirements/recommendations for international students: Required—TOEFL (minimum score 550 paper-based; 213 computer-based; 80 iBT), IELTS (minimum score 6.5). *Application deadline:* For fall admission, 1/15 priority date for domestic students, 1/15 for international students. Applications are processed on a rolling basis. Application fee: $45 ($75 for international students). Electronic applications accepted. *Financial support:* In 2011–12, 13 research assistantships with full and partial tuition reimbursements (averaging $4,204 per year) were awarded; career-related internships or fieldwork, Federal Work-Study, institutionally sponsored loans, scholarships/grants, tuition waivers (full and partial), unspecified assistantships, and administrative assistantships also available. Support available to part-time students. *Faculty research:* Financial management, banking, international finance, investments. *Unit head:* Dr. Mark Vonderembse, Chair, 419-530-4319. *Application contact:* Graduate School Office, 419-530-4723, Fax: 419-530-4724, E-mail: grdsch@utnet.utoledo.edu. Web site: http://www.utoledo.edu/business/index.html.

University of Toronto, School of Graduate Studies, Faculty of Arts and Science, Department of Economics, Program in Financial Economics, Toronto, ON M5S 1A1, Canada. Offers MFE. *Entrance requirements:* Additional exam requirements/recommendations for international students: Required—TOEFL (minimum score 102 iBT), TWE. Electronic applications accepted.

University of Tulsa, Graduate School, Collins College of Business, Finance/Applied Mathematics Program, Tulsa, OK 74104-3189. Offers MS/MS. Part-time and evening/weekend programs available. *Students:* 1 (woman) full-time. Average age 26. 3 applicants, 67% accepted, 0 enrolled. *Entrance requirements:* Additional exam requirements/recommendations for international students: Required—TOEFL (minimum score 577 paper-based; 233 computer-based; 91 iBT), IELTS (minimum score 6.5). *Application deadline:* Applications are processed on a rolling basis. Application fee: $40. Electronic applications accepted. *Expenses: Tuition:* Full-time $17,748; part-time $986 per hour. *Required fees:* $5 per contact hour. $75 per semester. Tuition and fees vary according to program. *Financial support:* In 2011–12, 1 student received support, including 1 teaching assistantship (averaging $6,061 per year); fellowships, career-related internships or fieldwork, Federal Work-Study, institutionally sponsored loans, scholarships/grants, health care benefits, tuition waivers (full and partial), and unspecified assistantships also available. Support available to part-time students. Financial award application deadline: 2/1; financial award applicants required to submit FAFSA. *Unit head:* Linda Nichols, Associate Dean, 918-631-2242, Fax: 918-631-2142, E-mail: linda-nichols@utulsa.edu. *Application contact:* Information Contact, 918-631-2242, E-mail: graduate-business@utulsa.edu.

University of Tulsa, Graduate School, Collins College of Business, Master of Business Administration Program, Tulsa, OK 74104-3189. Offers accounting (MBA); business administration (MBA); energy management (MBA); finance (MBA); international business (MBA); management information systems (MBA); taxation (MBA); JD/MBA; MBA/MSCS; MBA/MSF. *Accreditation:* AACSB. Part-time and evening/weekend programs available. *Faculty:* 32 full-time (6 women). *Students:* 56 full-time (29 women), 28 part-time (7 women); includes 7 minority (1 Black or African American, non-Hispanic/Latino; 2 American Indian or Alaska Native, non-Hispanic/Latino; 2 Asian, non-Hispanic/Latino; 2 Hispanic/Latino), 16 international. Average age 26. 70 applicants, 67% accepted, 29 enrolled. In 2011, 35 master's awarded. *Entrance requirements:* For master's, GMAT. Additional exam requirements/recommendations for international students: Required—TOEFL (minimum score 577 paper-based; 233 computer-based; 91 iBT), IELTS (minimum score 6.5). *Application deadline:* Applications are processed on a rolling basis. Application fee: $40. Electronic applications accepted. *Expenses: Tuition:* Full-time $17,748; part-time $986 per hour. *Required fees:* $5 per contact hour. $75 per semester. Tuition and fees vary according to program. *Financial support:* In 2011–12, 30 students received support, including 30 teaching assistantships (averaging $11,044 per year); fellowships, research assistantships, career-related internships or fieldwork, institutionally sponsored loans, scholarships/grants, health care benefits, tuition waivers (full and partial), and unspecified assistantships also available. Support available to part-time students. Financial award application deadline: 2/1; financial award applicants required to submit FAFSA. *Faculty research:* Accounting, energy management, finance, international business, management information systems, taxation. *Unit head:* Dr. Linda Nichols, Associate Dean of the Collins College of Business, 918-631-2242, Fax: 918-631-2142, E-mail: linda-nichols@utulsa.edu. *Application contact:* Information Contact, 918-631-2242, E-mail: graduate-business@utulsa.edu. Web site: http://www.cba.utulsa.edu/.

University of Tulsa, Graduate School, Collins College of Business, MBA/MS Program in Finance, Tulsa, OK 74104-3189. Offers MBA/MS. Part-time and evening/weekend programs available. *Students:* 2 full-time (0 women), 5 part-time (1 woman); includes 1 minority (American Indian or Alaska Native, non-Hispanic/Latino), 1 international. Average age 29. 1 applicant, 100% accepted, 1 enrolled. *Entrance requirements:* Additional exam requirements/recommendations for international students: Required—TOEFL (minimum score 577 paper-based; 233 computer-based; 91 iBT), IELTS (minimum score 6.5). *Application deadline:* Applications are processed on a rolling basis. Application fee: $40. Electronic applications accepted. *Expenses: Tuition:* Full-time $17,748; part-time $986 per hour. *Required fees:* $5 per contact hour. $75 per semester. Tuition and fees vary according to program. *Financial support:* In 2011–12, 4 students received support, including 4 teaching assistantships (averaging $9,480 per year); fellowships, career-related internships or fieldwork, Federal Work-Study, institutionally sponsored loans, scholarships/grants, health care benefits, tuition waivers, and unspecified assistantships also available. Support available to part-time students. Financial award application deadline: 2/1. *Unit head:* Linda Nichols, Associate Dean, 918-631-2242, Fax: 918-631-2142, E-mail: linda-nichols@utulsa.edu. *Application contact:* Information Contact, 918-631-2242, E-mail: graduate-business@utulsa.edu. Web site: http://www.utulsa.edu/academics/colleges/collins-college-of-business/bus-dept-schools/graduate-business-programs/degree-programs/MS-in-Finance-Program.

University of Tulsa, Graduate School, Collins College of Business, Program in Finance, Tulsa, OK 74104-3189. Offers corporate finance (MS); investments and portfolio management (MS); risk management (MS); JD/MSF; MBA/MSF; MSF/MSAM. Part-time and evening/weekend programs available. *Faculty:* 10 full-time (1 woman). *Students:* 33 full-time (14 women), 2 part-time (0 women), 25 international. Average age 24. 121 applicants, 59% accepted, 21 enrolled. In 2011, 12 master's awarded. *Degree requirements:* For master's, thesis optional. *Entrance requirements:* For master's, GMAT. Additional exam requirements/recommendations for international students: Required—TOEFL (minimum score 577 paper-based; 233 computer-based; 91 iBT), IELTS (minimum score 6.5). *Application deadline:* Applications are processed on a rolling basis. Application fee: $40. Electronic applications accepted. *Expenses: Tuition:* Full-time $17,748; part-time $986 per hour. *Required fees:* $5 per contact hour. $75 per semester. Tuition and fees vary according to program. *Financial support:* In 2011–12, 4 students received support, including 4 teaching assistantships with full and partial tuition reimbursements available (averaging $12,355 per year); fellowships with full and partial tuition reimbursements available, research assistantships with full and partial tuition reimbursements available, career-related internships or fieldwork, Federal Work-Study, institutionally sponsored loans, scholarships/grants, health care benefits, tuition waivers (full and partial), and unspecified assistantships also available. Support available to part-time students. Financial award application deadline: 2/1; financial award applicants required to submit FAFSA. *Unit head:* Dr. Linda Nichols, Associate Dean, 918-631-2242, Fax: 918-631-2142, E-mail: linda-nichols@utulsa.edu. *Application contact:* Information Contact, 918-631-2242, E-mail: graduate-business@utulsa.edu. Web site: http://www.utulsa.edu/academics/colleges/collins-college-of-business/bus-dept-schools/School-of-Finance-Operations-Management-and-International-Busine.

University of Utah, Graduate School, David Eccles School of Business, Department of Finance, Salt Lake City, UT 84112. Offers MS, PhD. *Faculty:* 17 full-time (4 women), 2 part-time/adjunct (0 women). *Students:* 47 full-time (18 women), 20 part-time (3 women); includes 8 minority (1 Black or African American, non-Hispanic/Latino; 3 Asian, non-Hispanic/Latino; 2 Hispanic/Latino; 2 Two or more races, non-Hispanic/Latino), 25 international. Average age 28. 116 applicants, 39% accepted, 37 enrolled. In 2011, 43 degrees awarded. Terminal master's awarded for partial completion of doctoral program. *Degree requirements:* For master's, comprehensive exam; for doctorate, thesis/dissertation, oral qualifying exams, written qualifying exams, research paper. *Entrance requirements:* For master's, GMAT, minimum undergraduate GPA of 3.0; for doctorate, GMAT/GRE. Additional exam requirements/recommendations for international students: Required—TOEFL (minimum score 600 paper-based; 250 computer-based; 100 iBT), IELTS (minimum score 7). *Application deadline:* For fall admission, 3/1 priority date for domestic students, 3/1 for international students. Applications are processed on a rolling basis. Application fee: $55 ($65 for international students). Electronic applications accepted. *Financial support:* In 2011–12, 11 students received support, including 7 teaching assistantships (averaging $7,950 per year); fellowships, research assistantships, tuition waivers (full and partial), and unspecified assistantships also available. Financial award application deadline: 4/1; financial award applicants required to submit FAFSA. *Faculty research:* Investment, managerial finance, corporate finance, capital budgeting, risk management. *Total annual research expenditures:* $194,872. *Unit head:* Dr. Uri Loewenstein, Chair, 801-581-4419, Fax: 801-581-3956, E-mail: uri.lowenstein@business.utah.edu. *Application contact:* Andrea Chmelik, Admissions and Program Coordinator, 801-585-1719, Fax: 801-581-3666, E-mail: andrea.chmelik@business.utah.edu. Web site: http://www.business.utah.edu/finance/.

University of Virginia, McIntire School of Commerce, Program in Commerce, Charlottesville, VA 22903. Offers financial services (MSC); marketing and management (MSC). *Students:* 93 full-time (40 women); includes 14 minority (8 Asian, non-Hispanic/Latino; 5 Hispanic/Latino; 1 Two or more races, non-Hispanic/Latino), 16 international. Average age 22. 241 applicants, 59% accepted, 93 enrolled. In 2011, 72 master's awarded. *Entrance requirements:* For master's, GMAT, 2 letters of recommendation; prerequisite course work in financial accounting, microeconomics, and introduction to business. Additional exam requirements/recommendations for international students: Required—TOEFL (minimum score 600 paper-based; 250 computer-based; 100 iBT), IELTS (minimum score 7). *Application deadline:* For fall admission, 9/15 priority date for domestic students, 1/15 for international students. Applications are processed on a rolling basis. Application fee: $75. Electronic applications accepted. *Expenses:* Contact institution. *Financial support:* Scholarships/grants available. Financial award application deadline: 3/1; financial award applicants required to submit CSS PROFILE or FAFSA. *Unit head:* Ira C. Harris, Head, 434-924-8816, Fax: 434-924-7074, E-mail: ich3x@comm.virginia.edu. *Application contact:* Emma Candalier, Associate Director of Graduate Recruiting, 434-243-4992, Fax: 434-924-4511, E-mail: ecandalier@virginia.edu. Web site: http://www.commerce.virginia.edu/academic_programs/MSCommerce/Pages/index.aspx.

University of Washington, Graduate School, School of Public Health, Department of Health Services, Seattle, WA 98195. Offers bioinformatics (PhD); cancer prevention and control (PhD); clinical research (MS); community-oriented public health practice (MPH); economics or finance (PhD); evaluation sciences (PhD); health behavior and health promotion (PhD); health policy research (PhD); health services (MS, PhD); health services administration (EMHA, MHA); health systems policy (MPH); maternal and child health (MPH, PhD); occupational health (PhD); population health and social determinants (PhD); social and behavioral sciences (MPH); sociology and demography (PhD); JD/MHA; MHA/MBA; MHA/MD; MHA/MPA; MPH/JD; MPH/MD; MPH/MN; MPH/MPA; MPH/MS; MPH/MSD; MPH/MSW; MPH/PhD. Part-time and evening/weekend programs available. Postbaccalaureate distance learning degree programs offered (minimal on-campus study). *Faculty:* 40 full-time (23 women), 62 part-time/adjunct (25 women). *Students:* 98 full-time (78 women), 86 part-time (64 women); includes 49 minority (7 Black or African American, non-Hispanic/Latino; 3 American Indian or Alaska Native, non-Hispanic/Latino; 28 Asian, non-Hispanic/Latino; 11 Hispanic/Latino), 3 international. Average age 32. 374 applicants, 49% accepted, 104 enrolled. In 2011, 43 master's, 5 doctorates awarded. Terminal master's awarded for partial completion of doctoral program. *Degree requirements:* For master's, thesis (for some programs), practicum (MPH); for doctorate, comprehensive exam, thesis/dissertation. *Entrance requirements:* For master's and doctorate, GRE General Test, minimum GPA of 3.0. Additional exam requirements/recommendations for international students: Required—TOEFL (minimum score 580 paper-based; 237 computer-based; 92 iBT), IELTS (minimum score 7). *Application deadline:* For fall admission, 1/1 for domestic students, 11/1 for international students. Application fee: 75 Albanian leks. Electronic applications accepted. *Financial support:* In 2011–12, 47 students received support, including 10 fellowships with full and partial tuition reimbursements available (averaging $22,000 per year), 10 research assistantships with full and partial tuition reimbursements available (averaging $18,700 per year), 3 teaching assistantships with full and partial tuition reimbursements available (averaging $4,575 per year); institutionally sponsored loans, traineeships, and health care benefits also available. Financial award application deadline: 2/28; financial award applicants required to submit FAFSA. *Faculty research:* Public health practice, health promotion and disease prevention, maternal and child health, organizational behavior and culture, health policy. *Unit head:* Dr. Larry Kessler, Chair, 206-543-2930. *Application contact:* Kitty A. Andert, MPH/MS/PhD Programs Manager, 206-616-2926, Fax: 206-543-3964, E-mail: kitander@u.washington.edu. Web site: http://depts.washington.edu/hserv/.

University of Washington, Tacoma, Graduate Programs, MBA Programs, Tacoma, WA 98402-3100. Offers accounting (MBA); business administration (MBA); certified financial analyst (MBA). Part-time and evening/weekend programs available. *Entrance requirements:* For master's, GMAT, minimum GPA of 3.0 in final graded 90 quarter credits or 60 graded semester credits; at least 2 years of professional/management work experience. Additional exam requirements/recommendations for international students: Required—TOEFL (minimum score 580 paper-based; 237 computer-based; 92 iBT). Electronic applications accepted. *Expenses:* Contact institution. *Faculty research:* International accounting, marketing, change management, investments, corporate social responsibility.

University of Waterloo, Graduate Studies, Faculty of Arts, School of Accounting and Finance, Waterloo, ON N2L 3G1, Canada. Offers accounting (M Acc, PhD); finance (M Acc); taxation (M Tax). *Degree requirements:* For master's, thesis or alternative; for doctorate, thesis/dissertation. *Entrance requirements:* For master's, honors degree, minimum B average, resumé; for doctorate, GMAT, master's degree, minimum A-average, resume. Additional exam requirements/recommendations for international students: Required—TOEFL, TWE. Electronic applications accepted. *Expenses:* Contact institution. *Faculty research:* Auditing, management accounting.

The University of Western Ontario, Richard Ivey School of Business, London, ON N6A 3K7, Canada. Offers business (EMBA, PhD); corporate strategy and leadership elective (MBA); entrepreneurship elective (MBA); finance elective (MBA); health sector stream (MBA); international management elective (MBA); marketing elective (MBA); JD/MBA. *Degree requirements:* For master's, thesis (for some programs); for doctorate, thesis/dissertation. *Entrance requirements:* For master's, GMAT, 2 years of full-time work experience, interview. Additional exam requirements/recommendations for international students: Required—TOEFL (minimum score 100 computer; 100 iBT) or IELTS (minimium score 6). Electronic applications accepted. *Faculty research:* Strategy, organizational behavior, international business, finance, operations management.

University of Wisconsin–Madison, Graduate School, Wisconsin School of Business, Doctoral Program in Finance, Investment and Banking, Madison, WI 53706-1380. Offers PhD. *Faculty:* 16 full-time (1 woman), 7 part-time/adjunct (3 women). *Students:* 10 full-time (2 women), 9 international. Average age 28. 89 applicants, 3% accepted, 2 enrolled. In 2011, 2 doctorates awarded. *Degree requirements:* For doctorate, comprehensive exam, thesis/dissertation. *Entrance requirements:* For doctorate, GMAT or GRE. Additional exam requirements/recommendations for international students: Required—Pearson Test of English (minimum score 73; written 80); Recommended—TOEFL (minimum score 623 paper-based; 263 computer-based; 106 iBT), IELTS (minimum score 7.5). *Application deadline:* For fall admission, 12/15 priority date for domestic students, 12/15 for international students. Application fee: $56. Electronic applications accepted. *Expenses:* Contact institution. *Financial support:* In 2011–12, 10 students received support, including fellowships with full tuition reimbursements available (averaging $18,756 per year), research assistantships with full tuition reimbursements available (averaging $16,506 per year), 10 teaching assistantships with full tuition reimbursements available (averaging $14,088 per year); Federal Work-Study, institutionally sponsored loans, scholarships/grants, health care benefits, and unspecified assistantships also available. Financial award application deadline: 2/1; financial award applicants required to submit FAFSA. *Faculty research:* Banking and financial institutions, business cycles, investments, derivatives, corporate finance. *Unit head:* Prof. James Hodder, Chair, 608-262-8774, Fax: 608-265-4195, E-mail: rkrainer@bus.wisc.edu. *Application contact:* Belle Heberling, Assistant Director for Research Programs, 608-262-3749, Fax: 608-890-0180, E-mail: phd@bus.wisc.edu. Web site: http://www.bus.wisc.edu/phd.

University of Wisconsin–Madison, Graduate School, Wisconsin School of Business, MS Program in Quantitative Finance, Madison, WI 53706-1380. Offers MS. *Faculty:* 1 full-time (0 women). *Students:* 6 full-time (2 women), all international. Average age 26. 142 applicants, 3% accepted, 4 enrolled. In 2011, 1 master's awarded. *Entrance requirements:* For master's, GMAT or GRE. Additional exam requirements/recommendations for international students: Required—Pearson Test of English (minimum score 73; written 80); Recommended—TOEFL (minimum score 623 paper-based; 263 computer-based; 106 iBT), IELTS. *Application deadline:* For fall admission, 3/15 for domestic and international students. Application fee: $56. Electronic applications accepted. *Expenses:* Contact institution. *Financial support:* In 2011–12, 4 students received support, including 4 teaching assistantships with full tuition reimbursements available (averaging $9,392 per year); career-related internships or fieldwork, Federal Work-Study, institutionally sponsored loans, scholarships/grants, health care benefits, and unspecified assistantships also available. Financial award application deadline: 3/15; financial award applicants required to submit FAFSA. *Faculty research:* Capital markets, derivatives, financial markets, liquidity constraints. *Unit head:* Prof. David Brown, Director, 608-265-5281, Fax: 608-265-4195, E-mail: dbrown@bus.wisc.edu. *Application contact:* Belle Heberling, Assistant Director for Research Programs, 608-262-3749, Fax: 608-890-0180, E-mail: ms@bus.wisc.edu. Web site: http://www.bus.wisc.edu/ms.

University of Wisconsin–Madison, Graduate School, Wisconsin School of Business, Wisconsin Full-Time MBA Program, Madison, WI 53706-1380. Offers applied security analysis (MBA); arts administration (MBA); brand and product management (MBA); corporate finance and investment banking (MBA); marketing research (MBA); operations and technology management (MBA); real estate (MBA); risk management and insurance (MBA); strategic human resource management (MBA); supply chain management (MBA). *Faculty:* 32 full-time (6 women), 27 part-time/adjunct (7 women). *Students:* 228 full-time (75 women); includes 53 minority (16 Black or African American, non-Hispanic/Latino; 25 Asian, non-Hispanic/Latino; 10 Hispanic/Latino; 2 Native Hawaiian or other Pacific Islander, non-Hispanic/Latino), 28 international. Average age 28. 509 applicants, 30% accepted, 111 enrolled. In 2011, 120 master's awarded.

Degree requirements: For master's, thesis (for arts administration). *Entrance requirements:* For master's, GMAT, bachelor's or equivalent degree, 2 years of work experience, letters of recommendation. Additional exam requirements/recommendations for international students: Required—TOEFL (minimum score 600 paper-based; 250 computer-based; 100 iBT), IELTS. *Application deadline:* For fall admission, 11/4 for domestic and international students; for winter admission, 2/3 for domestic and international students; for spring admission, 4/27 for domestic and international students. Applications are processed on a rolling basis. Application fee: $56. Electronic applications accepted. *Expenses:* Tuition, state resident: full-time $10,296; part-time $643.51 per credit. Tuition, nonresident: full-time $24,054; part-time $1503.40 per credit. *Required fees:* $70.06 per credit. Tuition and fees vary according to course load, campus/location, program and reciprocity agreements. *Financial support:* In 2011–12, 176 students received support, including 20 fellowships with full and partial tuition reimbursements available (averaging $18,756 per year), 128 research assistantships with full tuition reimbursements available (averaging $25,185 per year), 28 teaching assistantships with full tuition reimbursements available (averaging $25,097 per year); scholarships/grants, health care benefits, and unspecified assistantships also available. Financial award application deadline: 4/27; financial award applicants required to submit FAFSA. *Faculty research:* Market consequences of International Financial Reporting Standards (IFRS), inter-firm relationships and strategic partnerships, application of Bayesian statistical methods and applied probability models to understanding individuals' behaviors in the context of customer relationship management (CRM) applications, liquidity provision and the structure of financial markets, strategic management of global startups. *Unit head:* Dr. Larry "Chip" W. Hunter, Associate Dean of Master's Programs, 608-265-3494, Fax: 608-265-4192, E-mail: lhunter@bus.wisc.edu. *Application contact:* Maria Reis, Assistant Director of MBA Marketing and Recruiting, 608-262-4000, Fax: 608-265-4192, E-mail: mreis@bus.wisc.edu. Web site: http://www.bus.wisc.edu/mba.

University of Wisconsin–Whitewater, School of Graduate Studies, College of Business and Economics, Program in Business Administration, Whitewater, WI 53190-1790. Offers finance (MBA); human resource management (MBA); information technology management (MBA); international business (MBA); management (MBA); marketing (MBA); operations and supply chain management (MBA). *Accreditation:* AACSB. Part-time and evening/weekend programs available. Postbaccalaureate distance learning degree programs offered (no on-campus study). *Students:* 170 full-time (53 women), 538 part-time (213 women); includes 130 minority (28 Black or African American, non-Hispanic/Latino; 87 Asian, non-Hispanic/Latino; 15 Hispanic/Latino). Average age 31. 448 applicants, 33% accepted, 120 enrolled. In 2011, 304 master's awarded. *Entrance requirements:* For master's, GMAT or GRE, minimum AACSB index of 1000, minimum GPA of 2.75. Additional exam requirements/recommendations for international students: Required—TOEFL (minimum score 550 paper-based; 213 computer-based; 80 iBT), IELTS (minimum score 6). *Application deadline:* For fall admission, 7/15 for domestic and international students; for spring admission, 12/1 for domestic and international students. Applications are processed on a rolling basis. Application fee: $56. Electronic applications accepted. *Expenses:* Tuition, state resident: full-time $4088. Tuition, nonresident: full-time $8817. Tuition and fees vary according to program. *Financial support:* In 2011–12, research assistantships (averaging $7,245 per year) were awarded; Federal Work-Study, unspecified assistantships, and out-of-state fee waivers also available. Support available to part-time students. Financial award application deadline: 3/15; financial award applicants required to submit FAFSA. *Faculty research:* Interface between social institutions and individual behavior, technology and innovation management, occupational mental health, workplace deviance and workplace romance. *Unit head:* Dr. John Chenoweth, Associate Dean, 262-472-1945, Fax: 262-472-4863, E-mail: chenowej@uww.edu.

University of Wyoming, College of Business, Department of Economics and Finance, Program in Economics and Finance, Laramie, WY 82070. Offers MS. *Degree requirements:* For master's, thesis. *Entrance requirements:* For master's, GRE, minimum GPA of 3.0. Additional exam requirements/recommendations for international students: Required—TOEFL (minimum score 540 paper-based; 207 computer-based; 76 iBT). *Faculty research:* Financial economics.

University of Wyoming, College of Business, Department of Economics and Finance, Program in Finance, Laramie, WY 82070. Offers MS. Part-time programs available. *Degree requirements:* For master's, thesis. *Entrance requirements:* For master's, GMAT, GRE, minimum GPA of 3.0. Additional exam requirements/recommendations for international students: Required—TOEFL (minimum score 540 paper-based; 207 computer-based; 76 iBT). *Faculty research:* Banking.

Upper Iowa University, Online Master's Programs, Fayette, IA 52142-1857. Offers accounting (MBA); corporate financial management (MBA); global business (MBA); health and human services (MPA); higher education administration (MHEA); homeland security (MPA); human resources management (MBA); justice administration (MPA); organizational development (MBA); public personnel management (MPA); quality management (MBA). MBA also available at Madison, WI campus. Part-time programs available. Postbaccalaureate distance learning degree programs offered (no on-campus study). *Degree requirements:* For master's, research project. *Entrance requirements:* For master's, GMAT, GRE, or minimum GPA of 2.7 during last 60 hours. Additional exam requirements/recommendations for international students: Required—TOEFL (minimum score 570 paper-based; 230 computer-based). Electronic applications accepted. *Faculty research:* Total quality management, CQI, teams, organization culture and climate, management.

Valparaiso University, Graduate School, Program in International Economics and Finance, Valparaiso, IN 46383. Offers MS. Part-time and evening/weekend programs available. *Students:* 27 full-time (8 women), 13 part-time (5 women); includes 1 minority (Asian, non-Hispanic/Latino), 35 international. Average age 24. In 2011, 23 master's awarded. *Entrance requirements:* For master's, 1 semester of college level calculus; 1 statistics or quantitative methods class; 2 semesters of introductory economics; 1 introductory accounting course; minimum undergraduate GPA of 3.0; 2 letters of recommendation. Additional exam requirements/recommendations for international students: Required—TOEFL (minimum score 550 paper-based; 213 computer-based; 80 iBT). Application fee: $30 ($50 for international students). *Expenses: Tuition:* Part-time $560 per credit hour. Tuition and fees vary according to course load and program. *Financial support:* Available to part-time students. Applicants required to submit FAFSA. *Unit head:* Dr. David L. Rowland, Dean, Graduate School and Continuing Education/Associate Provost, 219-464-5313, Fax: 219-464-5381, E-mail: david.rowland@valpo.edu. *Application contact:* Dustin Jesch, Coordinator, U.S. Student Engagement, 219-464-5313, Fax: 219-464-5381, E-mail: dustin.jesch@valpo.edu. Web site: http://valpo.edu/grad/ief/.

Vancouver Island University, Master of Business Administration Program, Nanaimo, BC V9R 5S5, Canada. Offers international business (MBA), including finance, marketing. Program offered jointly with University of Hertfordshire. *Accreditation:* ACBSP. Part-time programs available. *Faculty:* 23 full-time (3 women), 3 part-time/adjunct (2 women). *Students:* 135 full-time (59 women), 2 part-time (0 women); includes 9 minority (1 Black or African American, non-Hispanic/Latino; 2 American Indian or Alaska Native, non-Hispanic/Latino; 5 Asian, non-Hispanic/Latino; 1 Hispanic/Latino), 102 international. Average age 27. 632 applicants, 46% accepted, 135 enrolled. In 2011, 145 master's awarded. *Degree requirements:* For master's, thesis. *Entrance requirements:* Additional exam requirements/recommendations for international students: Required—TOEFL (minimum score 550 paper-based; 213 computer-based). *Application deadline:* For fall admission, 2/28 priority date for domestic students, 2/28 for international students; for winter admission, 4/30 for domestic and international students. Applications are processed on a rolling basis. Application fee: $150. Electronic applications accepted. *Financial support:* In 2011–12, 8 students received support. Scholarships/grants available. *Faculty research:* Tourism development, entrepreneurship, organizational development, strategic planning, international business strategy, intercultural team work. *Unit head:* Brock Dykeman, Director, 250-740-6178, Fax: 250-740-6551, E-mail: brock.dykeman@viu.ca. *Application contact:* Jane Kelly, International Admissions Manager, 250-740-6384, Fax: 250-740-6471, E-mail: kellyj@mala.bc.ca. Web site: http://www.viu.ca/mba/index.asp.

Vanderbilt University, Owen Graduate School of Management, MS in Finance Program, Nashville, TN 37240-1001. Offers MSF. *Faculty:* 34 full-time (6 women). *Students:* 41 full-time (12 women); includes 21 minority (1 Black or African American, non-Hispanic/Latino; 19 Asian, non-Hispanic/Latino; 1 Two or more races, non-Hispanic/Latino), 22 international. Average age 26. 902 applicants, 9% accepted, 41 enrolled. In 2011, 38 master's awarded. *Entrance requirements:* For master's, GMAT and/or GRE. Additional exam requirements/recommendations for international students: Required—TOEFL (minimum score 640 paper-based; 105 computer-based). *Application deadline:* For fall admission, 11/29 priority date for domestic students, 11/29 for international students; for winter admission, 1/31 priority date for domestic students, 1/31 for international students; for spring admission, 3/14 priority date for domestic students, 3/14 for international students. Electronic applications accepted. *Financial support:* Scholarships/grants available. Financial award applicants required to submit FAFSA. *Unit head:* Dr. Kate Barraclough, Director, 615-343-8108, E-mail: kate.barraclough@owen.vanderbilt.edu. *Application contact:* Cori Washington, Communications Assistant, 615-322-6469, Fax: 615-343-1175, E-mail: admissions@owen.vanderbilt.edu. Web site: http://www.owen.vanderbilt.edu.

Villanova University, Villanova School of Business, Master of Science in Finance Program, Villanova, PA 19085. Offers MSF. *Faculty:* 101 full-time (32 women), 38 part-time/adjunct (8 women). *Students:* 29 full-time (5 women); includes 7 minority (1 Black or African American, non-Hispanic/Latino; 5 Asian, non-Hispanic/Latino; 1 Two or more races, non-Hispanic/Latino), 6 international. Average age 24. In 2011, 28 master's awarded. *Degree requirements:* For master's, minimum cumulative GPA of 3.0. *Entrance requirements:* For master's, GMAT, prerequisite course in principles of finance. Additional exam requirements/recommendations for international students: Required—TOEFL (minimum score 550 paper-based; 213 computer-based; 80 iBT). *Application deadline:* For spring admission, 3/15 for domestic and international students. Applications are processed on a rolling basis. Application fee: $50. Electronic applications accepted. *Expenses: Tuition:* Part-time $675 per credit. Part-time tuition and fees vary according to degree level and program. *Financial support:* In 2011–12, 4 research assistantships (averaging $6,550 per year) were awarded; scholarships/grants and unspecified assistantships also available. Financial award application deadline: 6/30; financial award applicants required to submit FAFSA. *Faculty research:* Business analytics; creativity, innovation and entrepreneurship; global leadership; marketing and public policy; real estate; church management. *Unit head:* Kristy Irwin, Director of Recruitment and Marketing, 610-519-6288, Fax: 610-519-6273, E-mail: kristy.irwin@villanova.edu. *Application contact:* Meredith L. Lockyer, Assistant Director, 610-519-7016, Fax: 610-519-6273, E-mail: meredith.lockyer@villanova.edu. Web site: http://www.gradbusiness.villanova.edu.

Villanova University, Villanova School of Business, MBA - The Fast Track Program, Villanova, PA 19085. Offers finance (MBA); health care management (MBA); international business (MBA); management information systems (MBA); marketing (MBA); real estate (MBA); strategic management (MBA). *Accreditation:* AACSB. Part-time and evening/weekend programs available. *Faculty:* 101 full-time (32 women), 38 part-time/adjunct (8 women). *Students:* 123 part-time (46 women); includes 14 minority (1 Black or African American, non-Hispanic/Latino; 3 American Indian or Alaska Native, non-Hispanic/Latino; 5 Asian, non-Hispanic/Latino; 1 Hispanic/Latino; 4 Two or more races, non-Hispanic/Latino). Average age 29. In 2011, 53 master's awarded. *Degree requirements:* For master's, minimum GPA of 3.0. *Entrance requirements:* For master's, GMAT, work experience. Additional exam requirements/recommendations for international students: Required—TOEFL (minimum score 550 paper-based; 213 computer-based; 80 iBT). *Application deadline:* For fall admission, 6/30 for domestic and international students. Application fee: $50. Electronic applications accepted. *Expenses: Tuition:* Part-time $675 per credit. Part-time tuition and fees vary according to degree level and program. *Financial support:* Scholarships/grants available. Financial award application deadline: 6/30; financial award applicants required to submit FAFSA. *Faculty research:* Business analytics; creativity, innovation and entrepreneurship; global leadership; marketing and public policy; real estate; church management. *Unit head:* Kristy Irwin, Director of Recruitment and Marketing, 610-519-6288, Fax: 610-519-6273, E-mail: kristy.irwin@villanova.edu. *Application contact:* Meredith L. Lockyer, Assistant Director, 610-519-7016, Fax: 610-519-6273, E-mail: meredith.lockyer@villanova.edu. Web site: http://www.mba.villanova.edu.

Villanova University, Villanova School of Business, MBA - The Flex Track Program, Villanova, PA 19085. Offers finance (MBA); health care management (MBA); international business (MBA); management information systems (MBA); marketing (MBA); real estate (MBA); strategic management (MBA); JD/MBA. *Accreditation:* AACSB. Part-time and evening/weekend programs available. Postbaccalaureate distance learning degree programs offered (minimal on-campus study). *Faculty:* 101 full-time (32 women), 38 part-time/adjunct (8 women). *Students:* 18 full-time (9 women), 412 part-time (127 women); includes 45 minority (7 Black or African American, non-Hispanic/Latino; 1 American Indian or Alaska Native, non-Hispanic/Latino; 25 Asian, non-Hispanic/Latino; 4 Hispanic/Latino; 1 Native Hawaiian or other Pacific Islander, non-Hispanic/Latino; 7 Two or more races, non-Hispanic/Latino). Average age 30. In 2011, 150 master's awarded. *Degree requirements:* For master's, minimum GPA of 3.0. *Entrance requirements:* For master's, GMAT, work experience. Additional exam requirements/recommendations for international students: Required—TOEFL (minimum score 550 paper-based; 213 computer-based; 80 iBT). *Application deadline:* For fall admission, 6/30 for domestic and international students; for winter admission, 11/15 for domestic and international students; for spring admission, 3/30 for domestic students, 3/31 for international students. Applications are processed on a rolling basis. Application fee: $50. Electronic applications accepted. *Expenses: Tuition:* Part-time $675 per credit. Part-time tuition and fees vary according to degree level and program. *Financial support:* In 2011–12, 18 research assistantships with full tuition reimbursements (averaging $13,100 per year) were awarded; scholarships/grants and unspecified assistantships also available. Financial award application deadline: 6/30; financial award applicants required to submit FAFSA. *Faculty research:* Business analytics; creativity, innovation and entrepreneurship; global leadership; marketing and public policy; real estate; church management. *Unit head:* Kristy Irwin, Director of Recruitment and Marketing, 610-610-6288, Fax: 610-519-6273, E-mail: kristy.irwin@villanova.edu. *Application contact:*

Meredity L. Lockyer, Assistant Director, 610-519-7016, Fax: 610-519-6273, E-mail: meredith.lockyer@villanova.edu. Web site: http://www.mba.villanova.edu.

Virginia Commonwealth University, Graduate School, School of Business, Program in Finance, Insurance, and Real Estate, Richmond, VA 23284-9005. Offers MS. *Faculty:* 11 full-time (0 women). *Entrance requirements:* For master's, GMAT. Additional exam requirements/recommendations for international students: Required—TOEFL (minimum score 600 paper-based; 250 computer-based; 100 iBT); Recommended—IELTS (minimum score 6.5). *Application deadline:* For fall admission, 6/1 for domestic students; for spring admission, 11/1 for domestic students. Applications are processed on a rolling basis. Application fee: $50. Electronic applications accepted. *Expenses:* Tuition, state resident: full-time $9133; part-time $507 per credit. Tuition, nonresident: full-time $18,777; part-time $1043 per credit. *Required fees:* $77 per credit. Tuition and fees vary according to degree level, campus/location, program and student level. *Financial support:* Fellowships, research assistantships, teaching assistantships, Federal Work-Study, institutionally sponsored loans, and tuition waivers (full and partial) available. Financial award application deadline: 3/15; financial award applicants required to submit FAFSA. *Unit head:* Dr. Nanda Rangan, Chair, 804-828-6002, Fax: 804-828-7174, E-mail: nkrangan@vcu.edu. *Application contact:* Jana P. McQuaid, Assistant Dean, Master's Programs, 804-828-4622, Fax: 804-828-7174, E-mail: jpmcquaid@vcu.edu. Web site: http://www.business.vcu.edu/graduate.html.

Virginia International University, School of Business, Fairfax, VA 22030. Offers accounting (MBA); executive management (Graduate Certificate); global logistics (MBA); health care management (MBA); human resources management (MBA); international business management (MBA); international finance (MBA); marketing management (MBA). Part-time programs available. *Entrance requirements:* For master's and Graduate Certificate, bachelor's degree. Additional exam requirements/ recommendations for international students: Required—TOEFL (minimum score 550 paper-based; 213 computer-based; 80 iBT), IELTS (minimum score 6). Electronic applications accepted.

Virginia Polytechnic Institute and State University, Graduate School, Pamplin College of Business, Department of Finance, Blacksburg, VA 24061. Offers MS, PhD. *Degree requirements:* For master's, comprehensive exam (for some programs), thesis (for some programs); for doctorate, comprehensive exam (for some programs), thesis/ dissertation (for some programs). *Entrance requirements:* For master's and doctorate, GRE. Additional exam requirements/recommendations for international students: Required—TOEFL (minimum score 550 paper-based; 213 computer-based). *Application deadline:* For fall admission, 7/1 for domestic and international students; for spring admission, 12/1 for domestic and international students. Applications are processed on a rolling basis. Application fee: $65. Electronic applications accepted. *Expenses:* Tuition, state resident: full-time $10,048; part-time $558.25 per credit hour. Tuition, nonresident: full-time $19,497; part-time $1083.25 per credit hour. *Required fees:* $405 per semester. Tuition and fees vary according to course load, campus/location and program. *Financial support:* Teaching assistantships with full tuition reimbursements, career-related internships or fieldwork, Federal Work-Study, scholarships/grants, health care benefits, and unspecified assistantships available. Financial award application deadline: 1/15. *Faculty research:* Capital markets, corporate finance, investment banking, derivatives, international finance. *Unit head:* Dr. Raman Kumar, Unit Head, 540-231-5700, Fax: 540-231-4487, E-mail: raman.kumar@vt.edu. *Application contact:* Dilip Shome, Information Contact, 540-231-3607, Fax: 540-231-4487, E-mail: dilip@ vt.edu. Web site: http://www.finance.pamplin.vt.edu/.

Wagner College, Division of Graduate Studies, Department of Business Administration, Program in Finance, Staten Island, NY 10301-4495. Offers MBA. Part-time and evening/ weekend programs available. *Faculty:* 4 full-time (3 women), 2 part-time/adjunct (1 woman). *Students:* 21 full-time (3 women), 10 part-time (3 women); includes 3 minority (1 Hispanic/Latino; 2 Two or more races, non-Hispanic/Latino), 1 international. Average age 24. 18 applicants, 100% accepted, 17 enrolled. In 2011, 5 master's awarded. *Degree requirements:* For master's, thesis optional. *Entrance requirements:* For master's, GMAT, minimum GPA of 2.6, computer and math proficiency. Additional exam requirements/recommendations for international students: Required—TOEFL (minimum score 550 paper-based; 217 computer-based; 79 iBT). *Application deadline:* For fall admission, 4/1 priority date for domestic students, 3/1 for international students; for spring admission, 12/1 priority date for domestic students, 10/1 for international students. Applications are processed on a rolling basis. Application fee: $50 ($85 for international students). *Expenses: Tuition:* Full-time $16,200; part-time $890 per credit. *Financial support:* Career-related internships or fieldwork, unspecified assistantships, and alumni fellowship grant available. Financial award applicants required to submit FAFSA. *Unit head:* Dr. Cathyann Tully, 718-390-3439, Fax: 718-420-4274, E-mail: cathyann.tully@wagner.edu. *Application contact:* Patricia Clancy, Administrative Assistant, Admissions, 718-420-4464, Fax: 718-390-3105, E-mail: patricia.clancy@ wagner.edu.

Wake Forest University, Schools of Business, Full-time MBA Program, Winston-Salem, NC 27106. Offers consulting/general management (MBA); entrepreneurship (MBA); finance (MBA); health (MBA); marketing (MBA); operations management (MBA); JD/MBA; MD/MBA; MSA/MBA. *Accreditation:* AACSB. *Faculty:* 62 full-time (16 women), 41 part-time/adjunct (14 women). *Students:* 120 full-time (28 women); includes 14 minority (8 Black or African American, non-Hispanic/Latino; 4 Asian, non-Hispanic/ Latino; 1 Hispanic/Latino; 1 Two or more races, non-Hispanic/Latino), 28 international. Average age 28. In 2011, 62 master's awarded. *Degree requirements:* For master's, 65.5 credit hours. *Entrance requirements:* For master's, GMAT or GRE, letters of recommendation, official transcripts, current resume or curriculum vitae, 2 years of work experience. Additional exam requirements/recommendations for international students: Required—TOEFL (minimum score 600 paper-based; 250 computer-based; 100 iBT), Pearson Test of English. *Application deadline:* For fall admission, 4/15 for domestic and international students. Applications are processed on a rolling basis. Application fee: $100. Electronic applications accepted. *Expenses:* Contact institution. *Financial support:* In 2011–12, 84 students received support. Career-related internships or fieldwork, scholarships/grants, and unspecified assistantships available. Financial award application deadline: 2/15; financial award applicants required to submit FAFSA. *Faculty research:* The influence of personal relationships on business decision-making and management of change; drivers of perceived value and consumer behavior; impact of accounting on auditing, financial, managerial, systems and taxation stakeholders; corporate governance and executive compensation; impact of operations strategies on competitiveness. *Unit head:* Jon Duchac, Director, Full-time MBA Program, 336-758-5422, Fax: 336-758-5830, E-mail: busadmissions@wfu.edu. *Application contact:* Tamara Paquee, Administrative Assistant, 336-758-5422, Fax: 336-758-5830, E-mail: busadmissions@wfu.edu. Web site: http://www.business.wfu.edu/.

Walden University, Graduate Programs, School of Management, Minneapolis, MN 55401. Offers accounting (MS, DBA), including accounting for the professional (MS), CPA (MS), self-designed (MS); accounting and management (MS), including accounting for strategic managers, self-designed; accounting for managers (MBA); advanced project management (Post-Graduate Certificate); applied project management (Post-Graduate Certificate); corporate finance (MBA); entrepreneurship (MBA, DBA); finance (DBA); global management (MS); global supply chain management (DBA); healthcare management (MBA, DBA); healthcare system improvement (MBA); human resource management (MBA, MS, PhD), including functional human resource management (MS), integrating functional and strategic human resource management (MS), organizational strategy (MS); information systems management (DBA); international business (MBA, DBA); leadership (MBA, MS, DBA), including entrepreneurship (MS), general management (MS), human resources leadership (MS), innovation and technology (MS), leader development (MS), leading sustainability (MS), project management (MS), self-designed (MS); management (MS), including healthcare management; managers as leaders (MS); marketing (MBA, DBA); project management (MBA, MS, DBA); research strategies (MS); risk management (MBA); self-designed (MBA, DBA, PhD); social impact management (DBA); strategies for sustainability (MBA); strategy and operations (MS); sustainable management (MS); technology (MBA); technology entrepreneurship (DBA); technology management (MS). Part-time and evening/weekend programs available. Postbaccalaureate distance learning degree programs offered (minimal on-campus study). *Faculty:* 32 full-time (14 women), 275 part-time/adjunct (98 women). *Students:* 3,962 full-time (2,095 women), 1,557 part-time (959 women); includes 3,003 minority (2,510 Black or African American, non-Hispanic/Latino; 25 American Indian or Alaska Native, non-Hispanic/Latino; 140 Asian, non-Hispanic/Latino; 240 Hispanic/ Latino; 9 Native Hawaiian or other Pacific Islander, non-Hispanic/Latino; 79 Two or more races, non-Hispanic/Latino), 395 international. Average age 41. In 2011, 586 master's, 87 doctorates, 4 other advanced degrees awarded. *Degree requirements:* For doctorate, thesis/dissertation (for some programs), residency. *Entrance requirements:* For master's, bachelor's degree or equivalent in related field; minimum GPA of 2.5; official transcripts; goal statement; access to computer and Internet; for doctorate, master's degree or equivalent in related field; minimum GPA of 3.0; 3 years of related professional/academic experience (preferred). Additional exam requirements/ recommendations for international students: Required—TOEFL (minimum score 550 paper-based; 213 computer-based), IELTS (minimum score 6.5), Michigan English Language Assessment Battery (minimum score 82). *Application deadline:* Applications are processed on a rolling basis. Application fee: $50. Electronic applications accepted. *Financial support:* Federal Work-Study, scholarships/grants, unspecified assistantships, and family tuition reduction, active duty/veteran tuition reduction, group tuition reduction, interest-free payment plans, employee tuition reduction available. Support available to part-time students. Financial award applicants required to submit FAFSA. *Unit head:* Dr. William Schulz, III, Associate Dean, 800-925-3368. *Application contact:* Jennifer Hall, Vice President of Enrollment Management, 866-4-WALDEN, E-mail: info@waldenu.edu. Web site: http://www.waldenu.edu/Colleges-and-Schools/College-of-Management-and-Technology.htm.

Walsh College of Accountancy and Business Administration, Graduate Programs, Program in Finance, Troy, MI 48007-7006. Offers MSF. Part-time and evening/weekend programs available. *Entrance requirements:* For master's, minimum GPA of 2.75, previous course work in business. Additional exam requirements/recommendations for international students: Required—TOEFL. Electronic applications accepted.

Washington State University, Graduate School, College of Business, Business Administration Programs, Pullman, WA 99164. Offers business administration (MBA, PhD), including accounting (PhD), finance (PhD), management and operations (PhD), management information systems (PhD), marketing (PhD). *Accreditation:* AACSB. *Faculty:* 47. *Students:* 93 full-time (35 women), 94 part-time (32 women); includes 25 minority (4 Black or African American, non-Hispanic/Latino; 2 American Indian or Alaska Native, non-Hispanic/Latino; 11 Asian, non-Hispanic/Latino; 7 Hispanic/Latino; 1 Two or more races, non-Hispanic/Latino), 33 international. Average age 31. 310 applicants, 31% accepted, 67 enrolled. In 2011, 15 doctorates awarded. *Degree requirements:* For master's, comprehensive exam (for some programs), thesis (for some programs), final presentation; for doctorate, comprehensive exam, thesis/dissertation, oral and written exams. *Entrance requirements:* For master's and doctorate, GMAT, minimum GPA of 3.0, 3 letters of recommendation. Additional exam requirements/recommendations for international students: Required—TOEFL. *Application deadline:* For fall admission, 3/1 priority date for domestic students, 3/1 for international students; for spring admission, 6/ 1 priority date for domestic students, 6/1 for international students. Applications are processed on a rolling basis. Application fee: $75. Electronic applications accepted. *Financial support:* In 2011–12, 102 students received support, including 36 teaching assistantships with full and partial tuition reimbursements available (averaging $18,204 per year); career-related internships or fieldwork, Federal Work-Study, institutionally sponsored loans, health care benefits, tuition waivers (partial), unspecified assistantships, and teaching associateships also available. Financial award application deadline: 4/1. *Total annual research expenditures:* $344,000. *Unit head:* Dr. Eric Spangenberg, Dean, 509-335-8150, E-mail: ers@wsu.edu. *Application contact:* Graduate School Admissions, 800-GRADWSU, Fax: 509-335-1949, E-mail: gradsch@ wsu.edu.

Washington University in St. Louis, Olin Business School, Program in Finance, St. Louis, MO 63130-4899. Offers MS. Part-time programs available. *Faculty:* 88 full-time (29 women), 47 part-time/adjunct (10 women). *Students:* 80 full-time (24 women), 5 part-time (0 women); includes 2 minority (both Asian, non-Hispanic/Latino), 46 international. Average age 24. 1,338 applicants, 8% accepted, 54 enrolled. In 2011, 67 master's awarded. *Entrance requirements:* For master's, GMAT or GRE. Additional exam requirements/recommendations for international students: Required—TOEFL. *Application deadline:* For fall admission, 11/15 for domestic and international students; for winter admission, 2/15 for domestic students, 2/14 for international students; for spring admission, 3/21 for domestic students. Application fee: $100. Electronic applications accepted. *Expenses:* Contact institution. *Financial support:* Applicants required to submit FAFSA. *Unit head:* Joseph Peter Fox, Associate Dean and Director of MBA Programs, 314-935-6322, Fax: 314-935-4464, E-mail: fox@wustl.edu. *Application contact:* Dr. Gary Hochberg, Director, Specialized Master's Programs, 314-935-6380, Fax: 314-935-4464, E-mail: hochberg@wustl.edu. Web site: http://www.olin.wustl.edu/ prospective/.

Waynesburg University, Graduate and Professional Studies, Waynesburg, PA 15370-1222. Offers business (MBA), including finance, health systems, human resources, leadership, market development; counseling (MA), including addictions counseling, clinical mental health; education (MAT); nursing (MSN), including administration, education, informatics, palliative care; nursing practice (DNP); special education (M Ed); technology (M Ed); MSN/MBA. *Accreditation:* AACN. Part-time and evening/weekend programs available. *Degree requirements:* For doctorate, thesis/dissertation. *Entrance requirements:* Additional exam requirements/recommendations for international students: Required—TOEFL. Electronic applications accepted.

Wayne State University, College of Liberal Arts and Sciences, Department of Political Science, Program in Public Administration, Detroit, MI 48202. Offers aging policy and management (MPA); criminal justice policy and management (MPA); economic development policy and management (MPA); health services policy and management (MPA); human resources management (MPA); information technology management (MPA); non-profit management (MPA); organizational behavior and management (MPA); public budgeting and financial management (MPA); public policy analysis and program evaluation (MPA); social welfare policy and management (MPA); urban policy and management (MPA). *Accreditation:* NASPAA. Evening/weekend programs available. *Students:* 22 full-time (17 women), 45 part-time (33 women); includes 19 minority (16 Black or African American, non-Hispanic/Latino; 1 American Indian or Alaska Native, non-Hispanic/Latino; 2 Hispanic/Latino), 1 international. Average age 31. 75 applicants, 28% accepted, 11 enrolled. In 2011, 20 master's awarded. *Degree requirements:* For master's, comprehensive exam. *Entrance requirements:* For master's, GRE General Test. Additional exam requirements/recommendations for international students: Required—TOEFL (minimum score 550 paper-based; 213 computer-based); Recommended—TWE (minimum score 5.5). *Application deadline:* For fall admission, 6/1 priority date for domestic students, 5/1 for international students; for winter admission, 10/1 priority date for domestic students, 9/1 for international students; for spring admission, 2/1 priority date for domestic students, 1/1 for international students. Applications are processed on a rolling basis. Application fee: $50. Electronic applications accepted. *Expenses:* Tuition, state resident: part-time $512.85 per credit. Tuition, nonresident: part-time $1132.65 per credit. *Required fees:* $26.60 per credit. $199.65 per semester. Tuition and fees vary according to course load and program. *Financial support:* In 2011–12, 7 students received support. Scholarships/grants available. *Faculty research:* Urban politics, urban education, state administration. *Unit head:* Dr. Brady Baybeck, Director, 313-577-2630, E-mail: mpa@wayne.edu. Web site: http://clasweb.clas.wayne.edu/mapa.

Wayne State University, Law School, Detroit, MI 48202. Offers corporate and finance law (LL M); labor and employment law (LL M); law (JD, PhD); taxation (LL M); United States law (LL M); JD/MA; JD/MADR; JD/MBA. *Accreditation:* ABA. Part-time and evening/weekend programs available. *Faculty:* 40 full-time (16 women), 21 part-time/adjunct (4 women). *Students:* 504 full-time (212 women), 96 part-time (45 women); includes 94 minority (36 Black or African American, non-Hispanic/Latino; 3 American Indian or Alaska Native, non-Hispanic/Latino; 38 Asian, non-Hispanic/Latino; 17 Hispanic/Latino), 14 international. Average age 27. 1,164 applicants, 45% accepted, 196 enrolled. In 2011, 17 master's, 198 doctorates awarded. *Degree requirements:* For master's, essay. *Entrance requirements:* For master's, JD; for doctorate, LSAT, LDAS report with LSAT scores, bachelor's degree from accredited institution, personal statement, transcripts from all U.S. undergraduate schools attended and an analysis and summary of the transcripts; letter of recommendation (up to two are accepted). Additional exam requirements/recommendations for international students: Required—TOEFL (minimum score 600 paper-based); Recommended—TWE. *Application deadline:* For fall admission, 3/15 priority date for domestic students, 3/15 for international students. Applications are processed on a rolling basis. Application fee: $50. Electronic applications accepted. *Expenses:* Contact institution. *Financial support:* Federal Work-Study and scholarships/grants available. Support available to part-time students. Financial award application deadline: 3/15; financial award applicants required to submit FAFSA. *Faculty research:* Constitutional law, intellectual property, commercial law, health law, tax law. *Total annual research expenditures:* $160,129. *Unit head:* Robert Ackerman, Dean, 313-577-9016, E-mail: ackerman@wayne.edu. *Application contact:* Erica M. Jackson, Assistant Dean of Admissions, 313-577-3937, E-mail: lawinquire@wayne.edu. Web site: http://www.law.wayne.edu/.

Webster University, George Herbert Walker School of Business and Technology, Department of Business, St. Louis, MO 63119-3194. Offers business (MA); business and organizational security management (MBA); computer resources and information management (MBA); environmental management (MBA); finance (MA, MBA); health services management (MBA); human resources development (MBA); human resources management (MBA); international business (MA, MBA); management and leadership (MBA); marketing (MBA); procurement and acquisitions management (MBA); telecommunications management (MBA). *Accreditation:* ACBSP. Part-time and evening/weekend programs available. Postbaccalaureate distance learning degree programs offered (no on-campus study). *Degree requirements:* For master's, comprehensive exam (for some programs), thesis (for some programs). *Entrance requirements:* Additional exam requirements/recommendations for international students: Required—TOEFL. *Expenses: Tuition:* Full-time $10,890; part-time $605 per credit hour. Tuition and fees vary according to campus/location and program.

West Chester University of Pennsylvania, College of Business and Public Affairs, The School of Business, West Chester, PA 19383. Offers business (Certificate); business administration: technology/electronic (MBA); economics and finance (MBA); general business (MBA). *Accreditation:* AACSB. Part-time and evening/weekend programs available. Postbaccalaureate distance learning degree programs offered (minimal on-campus study). *Faculty:* 8 part-time/adjunct (4 women). *Students:* 2 full-time (both women), 78 part-time (23 women); includes 12 minority (5 Black or African American, non-Hispanic/Latino; 7 Asian, non-Hispanic/Latino), 3 international. Average age 34. 66 applicants, 47% accepted, 19 enrolled. In 2011, 9 master's, 1 other advanced degree awarded. *Degree requirements:* For master's, minimum GPA of 3.0. *Entrance requirements:* For master's, GMAT, statement of professional goals, resume, two letters of recommendation, transcripts. Additional exam requirements/recommendations for international students: Required—TOEFL (minimum score 550 paper-based; 213 computer-based; 80 iBT). *Application deadline:* For fall admission, 4/15 priority date for domestic students, 3/15 for international students; for spring admission, 10/15 priority date for domestic students, 9/1 for international students. Applications are processed on a rolling basis. Application fee: $45. Electronic applications accepted. *Expenses:* Tuition, state resident: full-time $7488; part-time $416 per credit. Tuition, nonresident: full-time $11,232; part-time $624 per credit. *Required fees:* $1784.64; $67.59 per credit. Tuition and fees vary according to program. *Financial support:* Unspecified assistantships available. Support available to part-time students. Financial award application deadline: 2/15; financial award applicants required to submit FAFSA. *Unit head:* Dr. Paul Christ, MBA Director and Graduate Coordinator, 610-425-5000, E-mail: mba@wcupa.edu. *Application contact:* Office of Graduate Studies, 610-436-2943, Fax: 610-436-2763, E-mail: gradstudy@wcupa.edu. Web site: http://www.wcumba.org/.

Western International University, Graduate Programs in Business, Master of Business Administration Program in Finance, Phoenix, AZ 85021-2718. Offers MBA. Part-time and evening/weekend programs available. Postbaccalaureate distance learning degree programs offered (no on-campus study). *Entrance requirements:* For master's, minimum GPA of 2.75. Additional exam requirements/recommendations for international students: Required—TOEFL (minimum score 550 paper-based; 213 computer-based; 79 iBT), TWE (minimum score 5), or IELTS (minimum score 6.5). Electronic applications accepted.

Western Michigan University, Graduate College, Haworth College of Business, Department of Finance and Commercial Law, Kalamazoo, MI 49008. Offers finance (MBA). *Accreditation:* AACSB. *Entrance requirements:* For master's, GMAT.

West Texas A&M University, College of Business, Department of Accounting, Economics, and Finance, Program in Finance and Economics, Canyon, TX 79016-0001. Offers MS. Part-time and evening/weekend programs available. Postbaccalaureate distance learning degree programs offered (minimal on-campus study). *Degree requirements:* For master's, comprehensive exam, thesis optional. *Entrance requirements:* For master's, GMAT. Additional exam requirements/recommendations for international students: Required—TOEFL (minimum score 550 paper-based). Electronic applications accepted. *Faculty research:* International trade composition, cycle of poverty, trade effects in Asian countries, structural problems in Japanese economy, reform and the US sugar program-Nebraska.

Wilfrid Laurier University, Faculty of Graduate and Postdoctoral Studies, School of Business and Economics, Department of Business, Waterloo, ON N2L 3C5, Canada. Offers accounting (PhD); finance (M Fin); financial economics (PhD); marketing (PhD); operations and supply chain management (PhD); organizational behavior and human resource management (M Sc); organizational behaviour and human resource management (PhD); supply chain management (M Sc); technology management (EMTM). Part-time and evening/weekend programs available. *Degree requirements:* For master's, thesis optional; for doctorate, comprehensive exam, thesis/dissertation. *Entrance requirements:* For master's, GMAT, 4-year honors degree with minimum B+ average; for doctorate, GMAT, master's degree, minimum B+ average. Additional exam requirements/recommendations for international students: Required—TOEFL (minimum score 89 iBT). Electronic applications accepted. *Faculty research:* Financial economics, management and organizational behavior, operations and supply chain management.

Wilkes University, College of Graduate and Professional Studies, Jay S. Sidhu School of Business and Leadership, Wilkes-Barre, PA 18766-0002. Offers accounting (MBA); entrepreneurship (MBA); finance (MBA); health care administration (MBA); human resource management (MBA); international business (MBA); marketing (MBA); operations management (MBA); organizational leadership and development (MBA). *Accreditation:* ACBSP. Part-time and evening/weekend programs available. *Students:* 48 full-time (20 women), 134 part-time (62 women); includes 12 minority (2 Black or African American, non-Hispanic/Latino; 5 Asian, non-Hispanic/Latino; 2 Hispanic/Latino; 3 Two or more races, non-Hispanic/Latino), 9 international. Average age 30. In 2011, 69 master's awarded. *Entrance requirements:* For master's, GMAT. Additional exam requirements/recommendations for international students: Required—TOEFL (minimum score 550 paper-based; 213 computer-based; 79 iBT). *Application deadline:* Applications are processed on a rolling basis. Application fee: $45 ($65 for international students). Electronic applications accepted. *Expenses:* Contact institution. *Financial support:* Federal Work-Study and unspecified assistantships available. Financial award application deadline: 3/1; financial award applicants required to submit FAFSA. *Unit head:* Dr. Jeffrey Alves, Dean, 570-408-4702, Fax: 570-408-7846, E-mail: jeffrey.alves@wilkes.edu. *Application contact:* Erin Sutzko, Director of Extended Learning, 570-408-4253, Fax: 570-408-7846, E-mail: erin.sutzko@wilkes.edu. Web site: http://www.wilkes.edu/pages/457.asp.

Wilmington University, College of Business, New Castle, DE 19720-6491. Offers accounting (MBA, MS); business administration (MBA, DBA); environmental stewardship (MBA); finance (MBA); health care administration (MBA, MSM); homeland security (MBA, MSM); human resource management (MSM); management information systems (MBA, MSN); marketing (MSM); marketing management (MBA); military leadership (MSM); organizational leadership (MBA, MSM); public administration (MSM). Part-time and evening/weekend programs available. *Faculty:* 4 full-time (0 women). *Students:* 266 full-time (121 women), 700 part-time (505 women). Average age 34. *Entrance requirements:* Additional exam requirements/recommendations for international students: Required—TOEFL (minimum score 500 paper-based; 173 computer-based). *Application deadline:* Applications are processed on a rolling basis. Application fee: $35. Electronic applications accepted. *Expenses: Tuition:* Part-time $534 per credit hour. *Required fees:* $25 per term. *Financial support:* Applicants required to submit FAFSA. *Unit head:* Dr. Donald W. Durandetta, Dean, 302-356-6780, E-mail: donald.w.durandetta@wilmu.edu. *Application contact:* Chris Ferguson, Director of Admissions, 302-356-4636 Ext. 256, Fax: 302-328-5164, E-mail: inquire@wilmcoll.edu. Web site: http://www.wilmu.edu/business/.

Wright State University, School of Graduate Studies, Raj Soin College of Business, Department of Finance and Financial Services, Dayton, OH 45435. Offers finance (MBA); MBA/MS. *Entrance requirements:* For master's, GMAT, minimum AACSB index of 1000. Additional exam requirements/recommendations for international students: Required—TOEFL.

Xavier University, Williams College of Business, Master of Business Administration Program, Cincinnati, OH 45207. Offers business administration (Exec MBA, MBA); business intelligence (MBA); finance (MBA); health industry (MBA); international business (MBA); management information systems (MBA); marketing (MBA); MBA/MHSA; MSN/MBA. *Accreditation:* AACSB. Part-time and evening/weekend programs available. *Faculty:* 45 full-time (17 women), 13 part-time/adjunct (4 women). *Students:* 188 full-time (63 women), 630 part-time (206 women); includes 112 minority (36 Black or African American, non-Hispanic/Latino; 3 American Indian or Alaska Native, non-Hispanic/Latino; 52 Asian, non-Hispanic/Latino; 17 Hispanic/Latino; 1 Native Hawaiian or other Pacific Islander, non-Hispanic/Latino; 3 Two or more races, non-Hispanic/Latino), 45 international. Average age 30. 319 applicants, 63% accepted, 149 enrolled. In 2011, 403 master's awarded. *Degree requirements:* For master's, capstone course. *Entrance requirements:* For master's, GMAT or GRE. Additional exam requirements/recommendations for international students: Required—TOEFL (minimum score 550 paper-based; 213 computer-based; 80 iBT). *Application deadline:* For fall admission, 8/1 priority date for domestic students, 5/1 for international students; for spring admission, 12/1 priority date for domestic students, 9/1 for international students. Applications are processed on a rolling basis. Application fee: $0. Electronic applications accepted. *Expenses:* Contact institution. *Financial support:* In 2011–12, 176 students received support. Scholarships/grants, tuition waivers (partial), and unspecified assistantships available. Financial award application deadline: 3/1; financial award applicants required to submit FAFSA. *Unit head:* Dr. Hema Krishnan, Associate Dean, 513-745-3420, Fax: 513-745-3455, E-mail: krishnan@xavier.edu. *Application contact:* Anna Marie Whelan, Assistant Director, MBA Programs, 513-745-3525, Fax: 513-745-2929, E-mail: whelana@xavier.edu. Web site: http://www.xavier.edu/williams/mba/.

Yale University, Yale School of Management and Graduate School of Arts and Sciences, Doctoral Program in Management, New Haven, CT 06520. Offers accounting (PhD); financial economics (PhD); marketing (PhD); organizations and management (PhD). *Accreditation:* AACSB. *Faculty:* 42 full-time (8 women). *Students:* 33 full-time (9 women); includes 4 minority (all Asian, non-Hispanic/Latino), 16 international. 439 applicants, 3% accepted, 4 enrolled. In 2011, 2 doctorates awarded. *Degree requirements:* For doctorate, comprehensive exam, thesis/dissertation. *Entrance requirements:* For doctorate, GMAT or GRE General Test. Additional exam requirements/recommendations for international students: Required—TOEFL or IELTS. *Application deadline:* For fall admission, 1/2 for domestic and international students. Application fee: $100. Electronic applications accepted. *Expenses:* Contact institution. *Financial support:* In 2011–12, 31 students received support, including 31 fellowships with full tuition reimbursements available, 31 research assistantships with full tuition reimbursements available, 31 teaching assistantships with full tuition reimbursements available; institutionally sponsored loans, scholarships/grants, and health care benefits also available. Financial award application deadline: 1/2. *Faculty research:* Pricing of options and futures, term structure of interest rates, use of accounting numbers in debt contracts, product differentiation, e-commerce and marketing, behavioral finance. *Unit head:* Carla Mills, Registrar, 203-432-3955, Fax: 203-432-0342.

York College of Pennsylvania, Donald Graham School of Business, York, PA 17405-7199. Offers accounting (MBA); continuous improvement (MBA); finance (MBA);

management (MBA); marketing (MBA); self-designed (MBA). *Accreditation:* ACBSP. Part-time and evening/weekend programs available. *Faculty:* 14 full-time (3 women), 1 part-time/adjunct (0 women). *Students:* 11 full-time (5 women), 99 part-time (40 women); includes 10 minority (5 Black or African American, non-Hispanic/Latino; 1 Asian, non-Hispanic/Latino; 3 Hispanic/Latino; 1 Two or more races, non-Hispanic/Latino), 1 international. Average age 29. 49 applicants, 80% accepted, 26 enrolled. In 2011, 33 master's awarded. *Entrance requirements:* For master's, GMAT. Additional exam requirements/recommendations for international students: Required—TOEFL (minimum score 530 paper-based; 200 computer-based; 72 iBT). *Application deadline:* For fall admission, 7/15 priority date for domestic students; for spring admission, 12/15 priority date for domestic students. Applications are processed on a rolling basis. Application fee: $50. Electronic applications accepted. *Expenses: Tuition:* Full-time $12,060; part-time $670 per credit hour. *Required fees:* $340 per semester. Tuition and fees vary according to degree level. *Financial support:* In 2011–12, 3 students received support. Scholarships/grants available. Financial award application deadline: 4/15; financial award applicants required to submit FAFSA. *Unit head:* Dr. David Greisler, MBA Director, 717-815-6410, Fax: 717-600-3999, E-mail: dgreisle@ycp.edu. *Application contact:* Brenda Adams, Assistant Director, MBA Program, 717-815-1749, Fax: 717-600-3999, E-mail: badams@ycp.edu. Web site: http://www.ycp.edu/mba.

York University, Faculty of Graduate Studies, Schulich School of Business, Toronto, ON M3J 1P3, Canada. Offers administration (PhD); business (MBA); finance (MF); international business (IMBA); public administration (MPA); MBA/JD; MBA/MA; MBA/MFA. Part-time and evening/weekend programs available. *Faculty:* 112 full-time (35 women), 191 part-time/adjunct (61 women). *Students:* 706 full-time (240 women), 401 part-time (136 women). Average age 28. 1,621 applicants, 46% accepted, 439 enrolled. In 2011, 528 master's, 10 doctorates awarded. *Degree requirements:* For master's, advanced proficiency in a second language, work term (IMBA); for doctorate, comprehensive exam, thesis/dissertation. *Entrance requirements:* For master's, GMAT (GRE acceptable for MF), minimum GPA of 3.0 (3.3 for MF); for doctorate, GMAT or GRE, minimum GPA of 3.3. Additional exam requirements/recommendations for international students: Required—TOEFL (minimum score 600 paper-based; 100 iBT), IELTS (minimum score 7), York English Language Test (minimum score 1). *Application deadline:* For fall admission, 5/1 for domestic students, 2/1 for international students; for winter admission, 10/1 for domestic students, 9/1 for international students. Applications are processed on a rolling basis. Application fee: $150. Electronic applications accepted. *Financial support:* In 2011–12, 800 students received support, including fellowships (averaging $5,000 per year), research assistantships (averaging $3,000 per year), teaching assistantships (averaging $7,000 per year); career-related internships or fieldwork, scholarships/grants, and bursaries for part-time students also available. Financial award application deadline: 2/1. *Faculty research:* Accounting, finance, marketing, operations management and information systems, organizational studies, strategic management. *Unit head:* Dezso Horvath, Dean, 416-736-5070, E-mail: dhorvath@schulich.yorku.ca. *Application contact:* Graduate Admissions, 416-736-5060, Fax: 416-650-8174, E-mail: admissions@schulich.yorku.ca. Web site: http://www.schulich.yorku.ca.

See Display on page 175 and Close-Up on page 263.

Youngstown State University, Graduate School, College of Liberal Arts and Social Sciences, Department of Economics, Youngstown, OH 44555-0001. Offers economics (MA); financial economics (MA). Part-time programs available. *Degree requirements:* For master's, comprehensive exam, thesis optional. *Entrance requirements:* For master's, minimum GPA of 2.7, 21 hours in economics. Additional exam requirements/recommendations for international students: Required—TOEFL. *Faculty research:* Forecasting, applied econometrics, labor economics, applied macroeconomics, industrial organization.

Youngstown State University, Graduate School, Williamson College of Business Administration, Department of Accounting and Finance, Youngstown, OH 44555-0001. Offers accounting (MBA). *Accreditation:* AACSB. Part-time and evening/weekend programs available. *Degree requirements:* For master's, thesis optional. *Entrance requirements:* For master's, GMAT, minimum GPA of 2.7. Additional exam requirements/recommendations for international students: Required—TOEFL. *Faculty research:* Taxation and compliance, capital markets, accounting information systems, accounting theory, tax and government accounting.

Investment Management

Alaska Pacific University, Graduate Programs, Business Administration Department, Anchorage, AK 99508-4672. Offers business administration (MBA), including business administration, health services administration; information and communication technology (MBAICT); investment (CGS). Part-time and evening/weekend programs available. *Degree requirements:* For master's, capstone course. *Entrance requirements:* For master's, GMAT or GRE General Test, minimum GPA of 3.0. Additional exam requirements/recommendations for international students: Required—TOEFL (minimum score 550 paper-based; 79 computer-based).

Boston University, School of Management, Boston, MA 02215. Offers business administration (MBA); executive business administration (EMBA); investment management (MS); management (PhD); mathematical finance (MS, PhD); JD/MBA; MBA/MA; MBA/MPH; MBA/MS; MBA/MSIS; MD/MBA; MS/MBA. *Accreditation:* AACSB. Part-time and evening/weekend programs available. *Faculty:* 185 full-time (49 women), 60 part-time/adjunct (15 women). *Students:* 510 full-time (177 women), 736 part-time (263 women); includes 176 minority (20 Black or African American, non-Hispanic/Latino; 121 Asian, non-Hispanic/Latino; 22 Hispanic/Latino; 13 Two or more races, non-Hispanic/Latino), 250 international. Average age 30. 1,387 applicants, 28% accepted, 160 enrolled. In 2011, 557 master's, 8 doctorates awarded. *Degree requirements:* For doctorate, comprehensive exam, thesis/dissertation. *Entrance requirements:* For master's, GMAT (for MBA and MS in investment management); GMAT or GRE General Test (for MS in mathematical finance), resume, 2 letters of recommendation; for doctorate, GMAT or GRE General Test, resume, personal statement, 3 letters of recommendation, 3 essays, official transcripts. *Application deadline:* For fall admission, 1/5 for domestic and international students; for spring admission, 11/1 for domestic students. Application fee: $125. Electronic applications accepted. *Expenses: Tuition:* Full-time $40,848; part-time $1276 per credit hour. *Required fees:* $572; $286 per semester. *Financial support:* Career-related internships or fieldwork, Federal Work-Study, institutionally sponsored loans, scholarships/grants, and tuition waivers (partial) available. Financial award applicants required to submit FAFSA. *Faculty research:* Innovation policy and productivity, corporate social responsibility, risk management, information systems, entrepreneurship, clean energy, sustainability. *Unit head:* Kenneth W. Freeman, Professor/Dean, 617-353-9720, Fax: 617-353-5581, E-mail: kfreeman@bu.edu. *Application contact:* Patti Cudney, Assistant Dean, Graduate Admissions, 617-353-2670, Fax: 617-353-7368, E-mail: mba@bu.edu. Web site: http://management.bu.edu/.

Concordia University, School of Graduate Studies, John Molson School of Business, Montréal, QC H3G 1M8, Canada. Offers administration (M Sc, Diploma); aviation management (Certificate, Diploma); business administration (MBA, UA Undergraduate Associate, PhD), including international aviation (UA Undergraduate Associate); chartered accountancy (Diploma); community organizational development (Certificate); event management and fundraising (Certificate); executive business administration (EMBA); investment management (Diploma); investment management option (MBA); management accounting (Certificate); management of healthcare organizations (Certificate); sport administration (Diploma). PhD program offered jointly with HEC Montreal, McGill University, and Université du Québec à Montréal. *Accreditation:* AACSB. Part-time and evening/weekend programs available. *Degree requirements:* For master's, one foreign language, thesis (for some programs), research project; for doctorate, one foreign language, thesis/dissertation; for other advanced degree, one foreign language. *Entrance requirements:* For master's and doctorate, GMAT. Additional exam requirements/recommendations for international students: Required—TOEFL. *Expenses:* Contact institution. *Faculty research:* General business, capital markets, international business.

Gannon University, School of Graduate Studies, College of Engineering and Business, School of Business, Program in Investments, Erie, PA 16541-0001. Offers Certificate. Part-time and evening/weekend programs available. *Students:* 1 part-time (0 women), all international. Average age 30. *Entrance requirements:* For degree, GMAT. Additional exam requirements/recommendations for international students: Required—TOEFL (minimum score 79 iBT). *Application deadline:* Applications are processed on a rolling basis. Application fee: $25. Electronic applications accepted. *Financial support:* Application deadline: 7/1; applicants required to submit FAFSA. *Unit head:* Dr. Donna Mottilla, Director, 814-871-7780, E-mail: mottilla001@gannon.edu. *Application contact:* Kara Morgan, Director of Graduate Admissions, 814-871-5831, Fax: 814-871-5827, E-mail: graduate@gannon.edu.

The George Washington University, School of Business, Department of Finance, Washington, DC 20052. Offers finance (MSF, PhD); finance and investments (MBA); real estate and urban development (MBA). Part-time and evening/weekend programs available. *Faculty:* 17 full-time (4 women), 4 part-time/adjunct (1 woman). *Students:* 106 full-time (41 women), 45 part-time (11 women); includes 33 minority (7 Black or African American, non-Hispanic/Latino; 11 Asian, non-Hispanic/Latino; 10 Hispanic/Latino; 5 Two or more races, non-Hispanic/Latino), 87 international. Average age 29. 728 applicants, 25% accepted, 93 enrolled. In 2011, 48 master's awarded. *Degree requirements:* For doctorate, thesis/dissertation. *Entrance requirements:* For master's, GMAT; for doctorate, GMAT or GRE. Additional exam requirements/recommendations for international students: Required—TOEFL. *Application deadline:* For fall admission, 4/1 priority date for domestic students; for spring admission, 10/1 for domestic students. Applications are processed on a rolling basis. Application fee: $75. *Financial support:* In 2011–12, 38 students received support. Fellowships, teaching assistantships, career-related internships or fieldwork, Federal Work-Study, and institutionally sponsored loans available. Financial award application deadline: 4/1. *Unit head:* Mark S. Klock, Chair, 202-994-5996, E-mail: klock@gwu.edu. *Application contact:* Kristin Williams, Assistant Vice President for Graduate and Special Enrollment Management, 202-994-0467, Fax: 202-994-0371, E-mail: ksw@gwu.edu.

Hofstra University, Frank G. Zarb School of Business, Department of Finance, Hempstead, NY 11549. Offers banking (Advanced Certificate); business administration (MBA), including finance, real estate management (MBA, MS); corporate finance (Advanced Certificate); finance (MS), including investment analysis; investment management (Advanced Certificate); quantitative finance (MS), including real estate management (MBA, MS). Part-time and evening/weekend programs available. *Faculty:* 13 full-time (2 women), 4 part-time/adjunct (2 women). *Students:* 222 full-time (91 women), 98 part-time (23 women); includes 24 minority (6 Black or African American, non-Hispanic/Latino; 15 Asian, non-Hispanic/Latino; 3 Hispanic/Latino), 198 international. Average age 26. 666 applicants, 63% accepted, 106 enrolled. In 2011, 124 master's awarded. *Degree requirements:* For master's, capstone course (for MBA); thesis (for MS); minimum GPA of 3.0. *Entrance requirements:* For master's, GMAT/GRE, 2 letters of recommendation; resume; essay. Additional exam requirements/recommendations for international students: Required—TOEFL (minimum score 550 paper-based; 213 computer-based; 80 iBT); Recommended—IELTS (minimum score 6). *Application deadline:* Applications are processed on a rolling basis. Application fee: $70 ($75 for international students). Electronic applications accepted. *Expenses:* Contact institution. *Financial support:* In 2011–12, 32 students received support, including 26 fellowships with full and partial tuition reimbursements available (averaging $8,389 per year), 1 research assistantship with full and partial tuition reimbursement available (averaging $4,925 per year); Federal Work-Study, institutionally sponsored loans, scholarships/grants, and tuition waivers (full and partial) also available. Support available to part-time students. Financial award applicants required to submit FAFSA. *Faculty research:* International finance; investments; banking, corporate finance; real estate; derivatives. *Unit head:* Dr. K. G. Viswanathan, Chairperson, 516-463-5699, Fax: 516-463-4834, E-mail: finkgv@hofstra.edu. *Application contact:* Carol Drummer, Dean of Graduate Admissions, 516-463-4876, Fax: 516-463-4664, E-mail: gradstudent@hofstra.edu. Web site: http://www.hofstra.edu/business/.

The Johns Hopkins University, Carey Business School, Finance Programs, Baltimore, MD 21218-2699. Offers finance (MS); financial management (Certificate); investments (Certificate). Part-time and evening/weekend programs available. *Degree requirements:* For master's, 36 credits including final project. *Entrance requirements:* For master's, GMAT or GRE (recommended), minimum GPA of 3.0, resume, work experience, two letters of recommendation; for Certificate, minimum GPA of 3.0, resume, work experience, two letters of recommendation. Additional exam requirements/recommendations for international students: Required—TOEFL (minimum score 600 paper-based; 250 computer-based; 100 iBT). Electronic applications accepted. *Faculty research:* Financial econometrics, high frequency data modeling, corporate finance.

Lincoln University, Graduate Studies, Oakland, CA 94612. Offers finance and investments (DBA); finance management and investment banking (MBA); general business (MBA); human resource management (MBA, DBA); international business (MBA); management information systems (MBA). Part-time and evening/weekend programs available. *Faculty:* 10 full-time (4 women), 15 part-time/adjunct (3 women). *Students:* 272 full-time (124 women), 1 part-time (0 women). *Degree requirements:* For master's, research project (thesis), internship report, or comprehensive exam; for doctorate, comprehensive exam, thesis/dissertation. *Entrance requirements:* For master's, minimum GPA of 2.7; for doctorate, GMAT (minimum score: 550), GRE (minimum score: 1000), or equivalent test results (waived for master's degree with minimum cumulative GPA of 3.3). Additional exam requirements/recommendations for international students: Required—TOEFL (minimum score 525 paper-based; 195 computer-based; 71 iBT) or IELTS (minimum score 5.5) for MBA; TOEFL (minimum score 550 paper-based; 213 computer-based; 79 iBT) or IELTS (minimum score 6) for DBA. *Application deadline:* For fall admission, 7/2 priority date for domestic students, 7/2 for international students; for spring admission, 11/25 priority date for domestic students, 11/25 for international students. Applications are processed on a rolling basis. Application fee: $75. Electronic applications accepted. *Financial support:* Teaching assistantships, career-related internships or fieldwork, and scholarships/grants available. *Unit head:* Dr. Marshall Burak, Director of Graduate Programs, 510-628-8016, Fax: 510-628-8012, E-mail: mburak@lincolnuca.edu. *Application contact:* Peggy Au, Director of Admissions and Records, 510-628-8010, Fax: 510-628-8012, E-mail: admissions@lincolnuca.edu. Web site: http://www.lincolnuca.edu/.

Lynn University, College of Business and Management, Boca Raton, FL 33431-5598. Offers aviation management (MBA); financial valuation and investment management (MBA); hospitality management (MBA); international business (MBA); marketing (MBA); mass communication and media management (MBA); sports and athletics administration (MBA). Part-time and evening/weekend programs available. Postbaccalaureate distance learning degree programs offered. *Degree requirements:* For master's, project. *Entrance requirements:* For master's, GMAT or GRE, minimum undergraduate GPA of 3.0, resume, 2 letters of recommendation. Additional exam requirements/recommendations for international students: Required—TOEFL (minimum score 550 paper-based; 213 computer-based). Electronic applications accepted. *Faculty research:* Labor relations, dynamic balance in leisure-time skills, ethics in athletics, hotel development.

Marywood University, Academic Affairs, College of Liberal Arts and Sciences, Department of Business and Managerial Science, Emphasis in Finance and Investments, Scranton, PA 18509-1598. Offers MBA. *Entrance requirements:* For master's, GMAT. Additional exam requirements/recommendations for international students: Required—TOEFL (minimum score 550 paper-based; 213 computer-based; 79 iBT). *Application deadline:* For fall admission, 4/1 priority date for domestic students, 3/31 for international students; for spring admission, 11/1 priority date for domestic students, 8/31 for international students. Applications are processed on a rolling basis. Application fee: $35. Electronic applications accepted. *Financial support:* Career-related internships or fieldwork, scholarships/grants, and unspecified assistantships available. Support available to part-time students. Financial award application deadline: 6/30; financial award applicants required to submit FAFSA. *Faculty research:* Accountant/auditor liability, corporate finance acquisitions and mergers, corporate bankruptcy. *Unit head:* Dr. Arthur Comstock, Chair, 570-348-6211 Ext. 2449, E-mail: comstock@marywood.edu. *Application contact:* Tammy Manka, Assistant Director of Graduate Admissions, 570-348-6211 Ext. 2322, E-mail: tmanka@marywood.edu. Web site: http://www.marywood.edu/academics/gradcatalog/.

Pace University, Lubin School of Business, Financial Management Program, New York, NY 10038. Offers banking and finance (MBA); corporate financial management (MBA); financial management (MBA); investment management (MBA, MS). Part-time and evening/weekend programs available. *Students:* 92 full-time (38 women), 386 part-time (178 women); includes 67 minority (18 Black or African American, non-Hispanic/Latino; 35 Asian, non-Hispanic/Latino; 11 Hispanic/Latino; 3 Two or more races, non-Hispanic/Latino), 306 international. Average age 28. 891 applicants, 64% accepted, 154 enrolled. In 2011, 173 master's awarded. *Entrance requirements:* For master's, GMAT, GRE. Additional exam requirements/recommendations for international students: Required—TOEFL. *Application deadline:* For fall admission, 7/31 priority date for domestic students; for spring admission, 11/30 for domestic students. Applications are processed on a rolling basis. Application fee: $70. Electronic applications accepted. *Expenses: Tuition:* Part-time $990 per credit. *Required fees:* $168 per semester. Tuition and fees vary according to course load and degree level. *Financial support:* Research assistantships, career-related internships or fieldwork, Federal Work-Study, and tuition waivers (full and partial) available. Support available to part-time students. Financial award application deadline: 8/15; financial award applicants required to submit FAFSA. *Unit head:* Dr. P. V. Viswanath, Chairperson, 212-618-6518, E-mail: pviswanath@pace.edu. *Application contact:* Susan Ford-Goldschein, Director of Graduate Admissions, 212-346-1531, Fax: 212-346-1585, E-mail: gradnyc@pace.edu. Web site: http://www.pace.edu/.

Quinnipiac University, School of Business, Program in Business Administration, Hamden, CT 06518-1940. Offers chartered financial analyst (MBA); finance (MBA); healthcare management (MBA); information systems management (MBA); marketing (MBA); supply chain management (MBA); JD/MBA. *Accreditation:* AACSB. Part-time and evening/weekend programs available. Postbaccalaureate distance learning degree programs offered (no on-campus study). *Faculty:* 19 full-time (4 women), 2 part-time/adjunct (1 woman). *Students:* 89 full-time (36 women), 129 part-time (50 women); includes 16 minority (5 Black or African American, non-Hispanic/Latino; 5 Asian, non-Hispanic/Latino; 6 Hispanic/Latino), 19 international. Average age 29. 206 applicants, 81% accepted, 139 enrolled. In 2011, 95 master's awarded. *Entrance requirements:* For master's, GMAT or GRE, minimum GPA of 3.0. Additional exam requirements/recommendations for international students: Required—TOEFL (minimum score 575 paper-based; 233 computer-based; 90 iBT), IELTS (minimum score 6.5). *Application deadline:* For fall admission, 7/30 priority date for domestic students, 4/30 for international students; for spring admission, 12/15 priority date for domestic students, 9/15 for international students. Applications are processed on a rolling basis. Application fee: $45. Electronic applications accepted. *Expenses: Tuition:* Part-time $855 per credit. *Required fees:* $35 per credit. *Financial support:* In 2011–12, 23 students received support. Career-related internships or fieldwork, Federal Work-Study, scholarships/grants, tuition waivers (partial), and unspecified assistantships available. Support available to part-time students. Financial award application deadline: 4/15; financial award applicants required to submit FAFSA. *Faculty research:* Financial markets and investments, international business, supply chain management, health care management, corporate governance. *Unit head:* Lisa Braiewa, MBA Program Director, 203-582-3710, Fax: 203-582-8664, E-mail: lisa.braiewa@quinnipiac.edu. *Application contact:* Katie Ludovico, 800-462-1944, Fax: 203-582-3443, E-mail: katie.ludovico@quinnipiac.edu. Web site: http://www.quinnipiac.edu/mba.

St. John's University, The Peter J. Tobin College of Business, Department of Economics and Finance, Program in Finance, Queens, NY 11439. Offers finance (MBA, Adv C); investment management (MS). Part-time and evening/weekend programs available. *Students:* 92 full-time (42 women), 73 part-time (29 women); includes 38 minority (11 Black or African American, non-Hispanic/Latino; 1 American Indian or Alaska Native, non-Hispanic/Latino; 15 Asian, non-Hispanic/Latino; 9 Hispanic/Latino; 2 Two or more races, non-Hispanic/Latino), 72 international. Average age 27. 126 applicants, 72% accepted, 41 enrolled. In 2011, 77 master's awarded. *Degree requirements:* For master's, comprehensive exam (for some programs), thesis optional. *Entrance requirements:* For master's, GMAT, 2 letters of recommendation, resume, transcripts, essay; for Adv C, GMAT, 2 letters of recommendation, resume, undergraduate and graduate transcripts, essay, MBA. Additional exam requirements/recommendations for international students: Required—TOEFL (minimum score 600 paper-based; 250 computer-based; 100 iBT), IELTS (minimum score 7). *Application deadline:* For fall admission, 5/1 priority date for domestic students, 5/1 for international students; for spring admission, 11/1 priority date for domestic students, 11/1 for international students. Applications are processed on a rolling basis. Application fee: $50. Electronic applications accepted. *Expenses:* Contact institution. *Financial support:* Research assistantships, scholarships/grants, and unspecified assistantships available. Support available to part-time students. Financial award application deadline: 3/1; financial award applicants required to submit FAFSA. *Unit head:* Dr. Vipul K. Bansal, Chair, 718-990-6419, E-mail: bansalv@stjohns.edu. *Application contact:* Carol J. Swanberg, Assistant Dean/Director of Graduate Admissions, 718-990-1345, Fax: 718-990-5242, E-mail: tobingradnyc@stjohns.edu.

Saint Mary's College of California, Graduate Business Programs, MS in Financial Analysis and Investment Management Program, Moraga, CA 94556. Offers MS. *Students:* 26 full-time (10 women), 1 part-time; includes 14 minority (1 Black or African American, non-Hispanic/Latino; 11 Asian, non-Hispanic/Latino; 2 Hispanic/Latino), 1 international. Average age 31. In 2011, 27 master's awarded. Tuition and fees vary according to course load, degree level and program. *Unit head:* Dr. Guido Krickx, Associate Dean/Director, 925-631-4514, Fax: 925-376-6521, E-mail: gakl@stmarys-ca.edu. *Application contact:* Bob Peterson, Director of Admissions, 925-631-4505, Fax: 925-376-6521, E-mail: bpeterso@stmarys-ca.edu. Web site: http://www.stmarys-ca.edu/ms-in-financial-analysis-and-investment-management-ms-faim.

University of Colorado Denver, Business School, Master of Business Administration Program, Denver, CO 80217. Offers business intelligence (MBA); business strategy (MBA); business to business marketing (MBA); business to consumer marketing (MBA); change management (MBA); corporate financial management (MBA); enterprise technology management (MBA); entrepreneurship (MBA); health administration (MBA), including financial management, health administration, health information technologies, international health management and policy; human resources management (MBA); investment management (MBA); managing for sustainability (MBA); services management (MBA); sports and entertainment management (MBA). *Accreditation:* AACSB. Part-time and evening/weekend programs available. Postbaccalaureate distance learning degree programs offered (no on-campus study). *Students:* 784 full-time (306 women), 203 part-time (81 women); includes 135 minority (18 Black or African American, non-Hispanic/Latino; 5 American Indian or Alaska Native, non-Hispanic/Latino; 50 Asian, non-Hispanic/Latino; 58 Hispanic/Latino; 4 Two or more races, non-Hispanic/Latino), 38 international. Average age 31. 433 applicants, 76% accepted, 212 enrolled. In 2011, 326 master's awarded. *Degree requirements:* For master's, 48 semester hours, including 30 of core courses, 3 in international business, and 15 in electives from over 50 other graduate business courses. *Entrance requirements:* For master's, GMAT, resume, official transcripts, essay, two letters of recommendation, financial statements (for international applicants). Additional exam requirements/recommendations for international students: Required—TOEFL (minimum score 560 paper-based; 197 computer-based; 83 iBT). *Application deadline:* For fall admission, 4/15 priority date for domestic students, 3/15 for international students; for spring admission, 10/15 priority date for domestic students, 10/1 for international students. Applications are processed on a rolling basis. Application fee: $50 ($75 for international students). Electronic applications accepted. *Expenses:* Contact institution. *Financial support:* Scholarships/grants available. Support available to part-time students. Financial award application deadline: 4/1; financial award applicants required to submit FAFSA. *Faculty research:* Marketing, management, entrepreneurship, finance, health administration. *Unit head:* Elizabeth Cooperman, Professor of Finance and Managing for Sustainability/MBA Program Director, 303-315-8422, E-mail: elizabeth.cooperman@ucdenver.edu. *Application contact:* Shelly Townley, Admissions Director, Graduate Programs, 303-315-8202, E-mail: shelly.townley@ucdenver.edu. Web site: http://www.ucdenver.edu/academics/colleges/business/degrees/ms/accounting/Pages/Accounting.aspx.

The University of Iowa, Henry B. Tippie College of Business, Henry B. Tippie School of Management, Iowa City, IA 52242-1316. Offers finance (MBA); investment management (MBA); marketing (MBA); process and operations excellence (MBA); strategic innovation (MBA); JD/MBA; MBA/MA; MBA/MD; MBA/MHA; MBA/MSN. *Accreditation:* AACSB. Part-time and evening/weekend programs available. *Faculty:* 62 full-time (19 women), 26 part-time/adjunct (6 women). *Students:* 153 full-time (34 women), 876 part-time (288 women); includes 87 minority (16 Black or African American, non-Hispanic/Latino; 4 American Indian or Alaska Native, non-Hispanic/Latino; 43 Asian, non-Hispanic/Latino; 24 Hispanic/Latino), 130 international. Average age 32. 697 applicants, 66% accepted, 362 enrolled. In 2011, 361 master's awarded. *Degree requirements:* For master's, minimum GPA of 2.75. *Entrance requirements:* For master's, GMAT, quality work experience and leadership as shown through resume, references, and essays. Additional exam requirements/recommendations for international students: Required—TOEFL (minimum score 600 paper-based; 250 computer-based; 100 iBT), IELTS (minimum score 7). *Application deadline:* For fall admission, 7/30 for domestic students, 4/15 for international students; for spring admission, 12/15 for domestic and international students. Applications are processed on a rolling basis. Application fee: $60 ($100 for international students). Electronic applications accepted. *Expenses:* Contact institution. *Financial support:* In 2011–12, 110 students received support, including 110 fellowships (averaging $9,059 per year), 82 research assistantships with partial tuition reimbursements available (averaging $8,609 per year), 16 teaching assistantships with partial tuition reimbursements available (averaging $14,530 per year); career-related internships or fieldwork, scholarships/grants, health care benefits, and unspecified assistantships also available. Financial award application deadline: 4/15; financial award applicants required to submit FAFSA. *Faculty research:* Capital markets, econometrics, optimization, investments and empirical corporate finance, Iowa electronic markets. *Unit head:* Prof. Jarjisu Sa-Aadu, Associate Dean, MBA Programs, 800-622-4692, Fax: 319-335-3604, E-mail: jsa-aadu@uiowa.edu. *Application contact:* Jodi Schafer, Director of Admissions and Financial Aid, 319-335-0864, Fax: 319-335-3604, E-mail: jodi-schafer@uiowa.edu. Web site: http://tippie.uiowa.edu/mba.

University of San Francisco, School of Management, Masagung Graduate School of Management, Risk Management Graduate Program, San Francisco, CA 94117-1080. Offers MS. *Expenses: Tuition:* Full-time $20,070; part-time $1115 per unit. Tuition and fees vary according to course load, campus/location and program. *Unit head:* John Veitch, Director, 415-422-5555, Fax: 415-422-5784. *Application contact:* Kelly Brookes, Director, MBA Program, 415-422-2221, Fax: 415-422-6315, E-mail: mba@usfca.edu. Web site: http://www.usfca.edu/management/msrm/.

The University of Texas at Dallas, Naveen Jindal School of Management, Program in Finance, Richardson, TX 75080. Offers finance (MS); financial analysis (MS); financial engineering and risk management (MS); investment management (MS). Part-time and evening/weekend programs available. *Faculty:* 18 full-time (3 women), 8 part-time/adjunct (1 woman). *Students:* 358 full-time (187 women), 81 part-time (19 women); includes 34 minority (1 Black or African American, non-Hispanic/Latino; 24 Asian, non-Hispanic/Latino; 6 Hispanic/Latino; 3 Two or more races, non-Hispanic/Latino), 352 international. Average age 25. 864 applicants, 56% accepted, 235 enrolled. In 2011, 93 master's awarded. *Entrance requirements:* For master's, GMAT. Additional exam requirements/recommendations for international students: Required—TOEFL (minimum score 550 paper-based; 215 computer-based). *Application deadline:* For fall admission, 7/15 for domestic students, 5/1 for international students; for spring admission, 11/15 for domestic students, 9/1 for international students. Applications are processed on a rolling basis. Application fee: $50 ($100 for international students). Electronic applications accepted. *Expenses:* Tuition, state resident: full-time $11,170; part-time $620.56 per credit hour. Tuition, nonresident: full-time $20,212; part-time $1122.89 per credit hour. *Financial support:* In 2011–12, 161 students received support. Research assistantships with partial tuition reimbursements available, teaching assistantships with partial tuition reimbursements available, career-related internships or fieldwork, Federal Work-Study, institutionally sponsored loans, scholarships/grants, and unspecified assistantships available. Support available to part-time students. Financial award application deadline: 4/30; financial award applicants required to submit FAFSA. *Faculty research:* Econometrics, industrial organization, auction theory, file-sharing copyrights and bundling, international financial management, entrepreneurial finance. *Unit head:* Dr. Robert Kieschnick, Area Coordinator, 972-883-6273, E-mail: rkiesch@utdallas.edu. *Application contact:* James Parker, Assistant Director, 972-883-5842, E-mail: jparker@utdallas.edu. Web site: http://jindal.utdallas.edu/academic-areas/finance-and-managerial-economics/.

University of Tulsa, Graduate School, Collins College of Business, Program in Finance, Tulsa, OK 74104-3189. Offers corporate finance (MS); investments and portfolio management (MS); risk management (MS); JD/MSF; MBA/MSF; MSF/MSAM. Part-time and evening/weekend programs available. *Faculty:* 10 full-time (1 woman). *Students:* 33 full-time (14 women), 2 part-time (0 women), 25 international. Average age 24. 121 applicants, 59% accepted, 21 enrolled. In 2011, 12 master's awarded. *Degree requirements:* For master's, thesis optional. *Entrance requirements:* For master's, GMAT. Additional exam requirements/recommendations for international students: Required—TOEFL (minimum score 577 paper-based; 233 computer-based; 91 iBT), IELTS (minimum score 6.5). *Application deadline:* Applications are processed on a rolling basis. Application fee: $40. Electronic applications accepted. *Expenses: Tuition:* Full-time $17,748; part-time $986 per hour. *Required fees:* $5 per contact hour. $75 per semester. Tuition and fees vary according to program. *Financial support:* In 2011–12, 4 students received support, including 4 teaching assistantships with full and partial tuition reimbursements available (averaging $12,355 per year); fellowships with full and partial tuition reimbursements available, research assistantships with full and partial tuition reimbursements available, career-related internships or fieldwork, Federal Work-Study, institutionally sponsored loans, scholarships/grants, health care benefits, tuition waivers (full and partial), and unspecified assistantships also available. Support available to part-time students. Financial award application deadline: 2/1; financial award applicants required to submit FAFSA. *Unit head:* Dr. Linda Nichols, Associate Dean, 918-631-2242, Fax: 918-631-2142, E-mail: linda-nichols@utulsa.edu. *Application contact:* Information Contact, 918-631-2242, E-mail: graduate-business@utulsa.edu. Web site: http://www.utulsa.edu/academics/colleges/collins-college-of-business/bus-dept-schools/School-of-Finance-Operations-Management-and-International-Busine.

University of Wisconsin–Madison, Graduate School, Wisconsin School of Business, Doctoral Program in Finance, Investment and Banking, Madison, WI 53706-1380. Offers PhD. *Faculty:* 16 full-time (1 woman), 7 part-time/adjunct (3 women). *Students:* 10 full-time (2 women), 9 international. Average age 28. 89 applicants, 3% accepted, 2 enrolled. In 2011, 2 doctorates awarded. *Degree requirements:* For doctorate, comprehensive exam, thesis/dissertation. *Entrance requirements:* For doctorate, GMAT or GRE. Additional exam requirements/recommendations for international students: Required—Pearson Test of English (minimum score 73; written 80); Recommended—TOEFL (minimum score 623 paper-based; 263 computer-based; 106 iBT), IELTS (minimum score 7.5). *Application deadline:* For fall admission, 12/15 priority date for domestic students, 12/15 for international students. Application fee: $56. Electronic applications accepted. *Expenses:* Contact institution. *Financial support:* In 2011–12, 10 students received support, including fellowships with full tuition reimbursements available (averaging $18,756 per year), research assistantships with full tuition reimbursements available (averaging $16,506 per year), 10 teaching assistantships with full tuition reimbursements available (averaging $14,088 per year); Federal Work-Study, institutionally sponsored loans, scholarships/grants, health care benefits, and unspecified assistantships also available. Financial award application deadline: 2/1; financial award applicants required to submit FAFSA. *Faculty research:* Banking and financial institutions, business cycles, investments, derivatives, corporate finance. *Unit head:* Prof. James Hodder, Chair, 608-262-8774, Fax: 608-265-4195, E-mail: rkrainer@bus.wisc.edu. *Application contact:* Belle Heberling, Assistant Director for Research Programs, 608-262-3749, Fax: 608-890-0180, E-mail: phd@bus.wisc.edu. Web site: http://www.bus.wisc.edu/phd.

University of Wisconsin–Milwaukee, Graduate School, Sheldon B. Lubar School of Business, Milwaukee, WI 53201. Offers business administration (MBA); enterprise resource planning (Certificate); investment management (Certificate); management science (MS, PhD); nonprofit management and leadership (MS, Certificate); state and local taxation (Certificate); MS/MBA. *Accreditation:* AACSB. Part-time and evening/weekend programs available. *Faculty:* 50 full-time (11 women), 4 part-time/adjunct (2 women). *Students:* 293 full-time (100 women), 343 part-time (127 women); includes 73 minority (21 Black or African American, non-Hispanic/Latino; 2 American Indian or Alaska Native, non-Hispanic/Latino; 28 Asian, non-Hispanic/Latino; 3 Hispanic/Latino; 19 Two or more races, non-Hispanic/Latino), 66 international. Average age 32. 370 applicants, 46% accepted, 104 enrolled. In 2011, 255 master's, 9 doctorates awarded. *Degree requirements:* For master's, comprehensive exam (for some programs); for doctorate, comprehensive exam, thesis/dissertation. *Entrance requirements:* For master's and doctorate, GMAT or GRE General Test. Additional exam requirements/recommendations for international students: Required—TOEFL (minimum score 550 paper-based; 79 iBT), IELTS (minimum score 6.5). *Application deadline:* For fall admission, 1/1 priority date for domestic students; for spring admission, 9/1 for domestic students. Applications are processed on a rolling basis. Application fee: $56 ($96 for international students). Electronic applications accepted. *Expenses:* Contact institution. *Financial support:* In 2011–12, 5 fellowships with full tuition reimbursements, 2 research assistantships with full tuition reimbursements, 41 teaching assistantships with full tuition reimbursements were awarded; career-related internships or fieldwork, Federal Work-Study, health care benefits, unspecified assistantships, and project assistantships also available. Support available to part-time students. Financial award application deadline: 4/15; financial award applicants required to submit FAFSA. *Faculty research:* Applied management research in finance, MIS, marketing, operations research, organizational sciences. *Total annual research expenditures:* $620,657. *Unit head:* Timothy L. Smunt, Dean, 414-229-6256, Fax: 414-229-2372, E-mail: tsmunt@uwm.edu. *Application contact:* Matthew Jensen, 414-229-5403, E-mail: mba-ms@uwm.edu. Web site: http://www4.uwm.edu/business.

Taxation

American International College, School of Business Administration, Program in Accounting and Taxation, Springfield, MA 01109-3189. Offers MSAT.

American University, Kogod School of Business, Department of Accounting, Program in Taxation, Washington, DC 20016-8044. Offers MS, Certificate. Part-time and evening/weekend programs available. *Students:* 7 full-time (3 women), 86 part-time (39 women); includes 34 minority (13 Black or African American, non-Hispanic/Latino; 16 Asian, non-Hispanic/Latino; 4 Hispanic/Latino; 1 Two or more races, non-Hispanic/Latino), 8 international. Average age 32. 51 applicants, 84% accepted, 33 enrolled. In 2011, 30 master's awarded. *Entrance requirements:* For master's, GMAT or CPA exam, resume, personal statement, interview; for Certificate, bachelor's degree. Additional exam requirements/recommendations for international students: Required—TOEFL. *Application deadline:* For fall admission, 2/1 priority date for domestic students; for spring admission, 10/1 priority date for domestic students. Applications are processed on a rolling basis. Application fee: $100. *Expenses:* Contact institution. *Financial support:* Fellowships, career-related internships or fieldwork, Federal Work-Study, and institutionally sponsored loans available. Support available to part-time students. Financial award application deadline: 2/1. *Faculty research:* International transactions, corporate partnership, taxation, real estate, estate gift planning. *Unit head:* Dr. Ajay Adhikari, Chair, 202-885-1993, Fax: 202-885-1892, E-mail: aadhika@american.edu. *Application contact:* Shannon Demko, Director of Admissions, 202-885-1968, Fax: 202-885-1078, E-mail: demko@american.edu. Web site: http://www.american.edu/kogod/.

Appalachian State University, Cratis D. Williams Graduate School, Department of Accounting, Boone, NC 28608. Offers taxation (MS). Part-time programs available. *Faculty:* 10 full-time (4 women), 1 (woman) part-time/adjunct. *Students:* 53 full-time (20 women), 9 part-time (7 women); includes 2 minority (both Asian, non-Hispanic/Latino), 2 international. 79 applicants, 84% accepted, 41 enrolled. In 2011, 52 master's awarded. *Degree requirements:* For master's, comprehensive exam, thesis optional. *Entrance requirements:* For master's, GMAT, 3 letters of recommendation. Additional exam requirements/recommendations for international students: Required—TOEFL (minimum score 550 paper-based; 230 computer-based; 79 iBT), IELTS (minimum score 6.5). *Application deadline:* For fall admission, 3/15 priority date for domestic students, 2/1 for international students; for spring admission, 11/1 for domestic students, 7/1 for international students. Applications are processed on a rolling basis. Application fee: $55. Electronic applications accepted. *Expenses:* Tuition, state resident: full-time $4040; part-time $180 per semester hour. Tuition, nonresident: full-time $15,900; part-time $760 per semester hour. *Required fees:* $2500; $20 per semester hour. Tuition and fees vary according to campus/location. *Financial support:* In 2011–12, 17 research assistantships (averaging $4,000 per year) were awarded; fellowships, teaching assistantships, Federal Work-Study, scholarships/grants, and unspecified assistantships also available. Financial award application deadline: 4/1; financial award applicants required to submit FAFSA. *Faculty research:* Audit assurance risk, state taxation, financial accounting inconsistencies, management information systems, charitable contribution taxation. *Unit head:* Dr. Timothy Forsyth, Chairman, 828-262-2036, Fax: 828-262-6640. *Application contact:* Dr. William Pollard, Director, 828-262-6232, Fax: 828-262-6640, E-mail: pollardwb@appstate.edu. Web site: http://www.acc.appstate.edu.

Bentley University, McCallum Graduate School of Business, Master's Program in Taxation, Waltham, MA 02452-4705. Offers MST. Part-time and evening/weekend programs available. Postbaccalaureate distance learning degree programs offered (no on-campus study). *Entrance requirements:* For master's, GMAT or GRE General Test. Additional exam requirements/recommendations for international students: Required—TOEFL (minimum score 600 paper-based; 250 computer-based; 100 iBT) or IELTS (minimum score 7). Electronic applications accepted. *Faculty research:* Taxation of intellectual property, tax dispute resolution, corporate tax planning and advocacy, estate and financial planning.

Bernard M. Baruch College of the City University of New York, Zicklin School of Business, Department of Accounting, Program in Taxation, New York, NY 10010-5585. Offers MBA, MS. Part-time and evening/weekend programs available. *Entrance requirements:* For master's, GMAT, 2 letters of recommendation, resume, 2 years of work experience. Additional exam requirements/recommendations for international students: Required—TOEFL (minimum score 590 paper-based; 243 computer-based), TWE.

Boise State University, Graduate College, College of Business and Economics, Program in Accountancy, Boise, ID 83725-0399. Offers accountancy (MSA); taxation (MSA). *Accreditation:* AACSB. Part-time programs available. *Entrance requirements:* For master's, GMAT, minimum GPA of 3.0. Additional exam requirements/recommendations for international students: Required—TOEFL. Electronic applications accepted.

Boston University, School of Law, Boston, MA 02215. Offers American law (LL M); banking (LL M); intellectual property law (LL M); law (JD); taxation (LL M); JD/LL M; JD/MA; JD/MBA; JD/MPH; JD/MS. *Accreditation:* ABA. *Faculty:* 55 full-time (26 women), 88 part-time/adjunct (25 women). *Students:* 971 full-time (496 women), 62 part-time (27 women); includes 224 minority (38 Black or African American, non-Hispanic/Latino; 2 American Indian or Alaska Native, non-Hispanic/Latino; 85 Asian, non-Hispanic/Latino; 72 Hispanic/Latino; 27 Two or more races, non-Hispanic/Latino), 156 international. Average age 26. 7,073 applicants, 20% accepted, 242 enrolled. In 2011, 169 master's, 271 doctorates awarded. *Degree requirements:* For master's, thesis (for some programs); for doctorate, thesis/dissertation, research project resulting in a paper. *Entrance requirements:* For master's, JD; for doctorate, LSAT. Additional exam requirements/recommendations for international students: Required—TOEFL (minimum score 600 paper-based; 250 computer-based; 100 iBT). *Application deadline:* For fall admission, 3/1 for domestic and international students. Applications are processed on a rolling basis. Application fee: $75. Electronic applications accepted. *Expenses: Tuition:* Full-time $40,848; part-time $1276 per credit hour. *Required fees:* $572; $286 per semester. *Financial support:* In 2011–12, 533 students received support. Career-related internships or fieldwork, Federal Work-Study, institutionally sponsored loans, and scholarships/grants available. Financial award application deadline: 3/1; financial award applicants required to submit FAFSA. *Faculty research:* Litigation and dispute resolution, intellectual property law, business organizations and finance law, international law, health law. *Unit head:* Maureen A. O'Rourke, Dean, 617-353-3112, Fax: 617-353-7400, E-mail: lawdean@bu.edu. *Application contact:* Alissa Leonard, Director of Admissions and Financial Aid, 617-353-3100, Fax: 617-353-0578, E-mail: bulawadm@bu.edu. Web site: http://www.bu.edu/law/.

Bryant University, Graduate School of Business, Master of Science in Taxation Program, Smithfield, RI 02917. Offers MST. Part-time and evening/weekend programs available. *Entrance requirements:* For master's, GMAT, recommendation, resume. Additional exam requirements/recommendations for international students: Required—TOEFL (minimum score 580 paper-based; 237 computer-based; 95 iBT). Electronic applications accepted. *Expenses:* Contact institution. *Faculty research:* Tax efficiencies of mutual funds, cost segregation studies, taxation of partnerships, property transactions.

California Miramar University, Program in Taxation and Trade for Executives, San Diego, CA 92126. Offers MT.

California Polytechnic State University, San Luis Obispo, Orfalea College of Business, Graduate Programs in Business, San Luis Obispo, CA 93407. Offers business (MBA); taxation (MSA). *Faculty:* 3 full-time (1 woman), 1 (woman) part-time/adjunct. *Students:* 18 full-time (3 women), 11 part-time (2 women); includes 2 minority (1 Hispanic/Latino; 1 Two or more races, non-Hispanic/Latino). Average age 27. 85 applicants, 35% accepted, 17 enrolled. In 2011, 63 master's awarded. *Degree requirements:* For master's, comprehensive exam (for some programs), thesis or alternative. *Entrance requirements:* For master's, GMAT. Additional exam requirements/recommendations for international students: Required—TOEFL (minimum score 550 paper-based; 213 computer-based) or IELTS (minimum score 6). *Application deadline:* For fall admission, 7/1 for domestic students, 11/30 for international students. Applications are processed on a rolling basis. Application fee: $55. Electronic applications accepted. *Expenses:* Tuition, state resident: full-time $6738. Tuition, nonresident: full-time $17,898. *Required fees:* $2449. *Financial support:* Fellowships, career-related internships or fieldwork, Federal Work-Study, institutionally sponsored loans, scholarships/grants, and unspecified assistantships available. Support available to part-time students. Financial award application deadline: 3/2; financial award applicants required to submit FAFSA. *Faculty research:* International business, organizational behavior, graphic communication document systems management, commercial development of innovative technologies, effective communication skills for managers. *Unit head:* Dr. Bradford Anderson, Associate Dean/Graduate Coordinator, 805-756-5210, Fax: 805-756-0110, E-mail: bpanders@calpoly.edu. Web site: http://mba.calpoly.edu/.

California State University, East Bay, Office of Academic Programs and Graduate Studies, College of Business and Economics, Department of Accounting and Finance, Taxation Program, Hayward, CA 94542-3000. Offers MS. Part-time and evening/weekend programs available. Postbaccalaureate distance learning degree programs offered. *Faculty:* 2 full-time (0 women). *Students:* 3 full-time (1 woman), 41 part-time (24 women); includes 20 minority (4 Black or African American, non-Hispanic/Latino; 15 Asian, non-Hispanic/Latino; 1 Hispanic/Latino), 1 international. Average age 37. 39 applicants, 72% accepted, 15 enrolled. In 2011, 12 master's awarded. *Degree requirements:* For master's, final project. *Entrance requirements:* For master's, GMAT, U.S. CPA exam or Enrolled Agents Exam, minimum GPA of 2.75. Additional exam requirements/recommendations for international students: Required—TOEFL (minimum score 550 paper-based; 213 computer-based). *Application deadline:* For fall admission, 6/30 for domestic and international students. Applications are processed on a rolling basis. Application fee: $55. Electronic applications accepted. *Expenses:* Tuition, state resident: full-time $6738; part-time $1302 per quarter. Tuition, nonresident: full-time $12,690; part-time $2294 per quarter. *Required fees:* $449 per quarter. Tuition and fees vary according to degree level, program and reciprocity agreements. *Financial support:* Career-related internships or fieldwork, Federal Work-Study, and institutionally sponsored loans available. Support available to part-time students. Financial award application deadline: 3/2; financial award applicants required to submit FAFSA. *Unit head:* Dr. Micah Frankel, Chair, Accounting and Finance, 510-885-3397, Fax: 510-885-7175, E-mail: micah.frankel@csueastbay.edu. *Application contact:* Dr. Gary McBride, Graduate Advisor, 510-885-2922, Fax: 510-885-7175, E-mail: gary.mcbride@csueastbay.edu. Web site: http://www.cbe.csueastbay.edu/acct/taxation.htm.

California State University, Fullerton, Graduate Studies, College of Business and Economics, Department of Accounting, Fullerton, CA 92834-9480. Offers accounting (MBA, MS); taxation (MS). *Accreditation:* AACSB. Part-time programs available. *Students:* 136 full-time (78 women), 70 part-time (44 women); includes 96 minority (2 Black or African American, non-Hispanic/Latino; 79 Asian, non-Hispanic/Latino; 12 Hispanic/Latino; 3 Two or more races, non-Hispanic/Latino), 57 international. Average age 28. 228 applicants, 55% accepted, 49 enrolled. In 2011, 68 master's awarded. *Degree requirements:* For master's, thesis or alternative, project. *Entrance requirements:* For master's, GMAT, minimum AACSB index of 950. *Application deadline:* Applications are processed on a rolling basis. Application fee: $55. Electronic applications accepted. *Financial support:* Career-related internships or fieldwork, Federal Work-Study, institutionally sponsored loans, and scholarships/grants available. Support available to part-time students. Financial award application deadline: 3/1; financial award applicants required to submit FAFSA. *Unit head:* Dr. Betty Chavis, Chair, 657-278-2225. *Application contact:* Admissions/Applications, 657-278-2371.

California State University, Los Angeles, Graduate Studies, College of Business and Economics, Department of Accounting, Los Angeles, CA 90032-8530. Offers accountancy (MS), including business taxation, financial accounting, information systems, management accounting; accounting (MBA). Part-time and evening/weekend programs available. *Faculty:* 6 full-time (1 woman), 1 part-time/adjunct (0 women). *Students:* 50 full-time (29 women), 34 part-time (15 women); includes 44 minority (1 Black or African American, non-Hispanic/Latino; 32 Asian, non-Hispanic/Latino; 10 Hispanic/Latino; 1 Two or more races, non-Hispanic/Latino), 28 international. Average age 31. 137 applicants, 37% accepted, 20 enrolled. In 2011, 56 master's awarded. *Degree requirements:* For master's, comprehensive exam (MBA), thesis (MS). *Entrance requirements:* For master's, GMAT, minimum GPA of 2.5 during previous 2 years of course work. Additional exam requirements/recommendations for international students: Required—TOEFL (minimum score 550 paper-based; 213 computer-based). *Application deadline:* For fall admission, 5/1 for domestic and international students. Applications are processed on a rolling basis. Application fee: $55. Electronic applications accepted. *Expenses:* Tuition, state resident: full-time $8225. *Financial support:* Career-related internships or fieldwork and Federal Work-Study available. Support available to part-time students. Financial award application deadline: 3/1. *Unit head:* Dr. Kathryn Hansen, Chair, 323-343-2830, Fax: 323-343-6439, E-mail: khansen3@calstatela.edu. *Application contact:* Dr. Karin Brown, Acting Associate Dean of Graduate Studies, 323-343-3820, Fax: 323-343-5653, E-mail: kbrown5@calstatela.edu. Web site: http://cbe.calstatela.edu/acct/.

California State University, Northridge, Graduate Studies, The Tseng College of Extended Learning, Northridge, CA 91330. Offers knowledge management (MKM); public administration (MPA); taxation (MS). *Entrance requirements:* For master's, GRE (if cumulative undergraduate GPA less than 3.0).

Capital University, Law School, Program in Business Law and Taxation, Columbus, OH 43209-2394. Offers business (LL M); business and taxation (LL M); taxation (LL M); JD/LL M. Part-time and evening/weekend programs available. *Degree requirements:* For master's, thesis or alternative. *Entrance requirements:* For master's, previous course work in accounting, business law, and taxation. Additional exam requirements/recommendations for international students: Required—TOEFL (minimum score 600 paper-based; 250 computer-based). Electronic applications accepted.

Capital University, Law School, Program in Taxation, Columbus, OH 43209-2394. Offers taxation (MT). Part-time and evening/weekend programs available. *Degree requirements:* For master's, thesis or alternative. *Entrance requirements:* For master's, previous course work in accounting, business law, and taxation. Additional exam requirements/recommendations for international students: Required—TOEFL (minimum score 600 paper-based; 250 computer-based). Electronic applications accepted. *Expenses:* Contact institution.

Chapman University, School of Law, Orange, CA 92866. Offers advocacy and dispute resolution (JD); entertainment and media law (LL M); entertainment law (JD); environmental, land use, and real estate (JD); international law (JD); law (JD); prosecutorial science (LL M); tax law (JD); taxation (LL M); trial advocacy (LL M); JD/MBA; JD/MFA. *Accreditation:* ABA. Part-time and evening/weekend programs available. *Faculty:* 49 full-time (20 women), 26 part-time/adjunct (6 women). *Students:* 526 full-time (265 women), 58 part-time (25 women); includes 139 minority (4 Black or African American, non-Hispanic/Latino; 2 American Indian or Alaska Native, non-Hispanic/Latino; 68 Asian, non-Hispanic/Latino; 45 Hispanic/Latino; 2 Native Hawaiian or other Pacific Islander, non-Hispanic/Latino; 18 Two or more races, non-Hispanic/Latino), 11 international. Average age 26. 2,823 applicants, 34% accepted, 160 enrolled. In 2011, 43 master's, 177 doctorates awarded. *Entrance requirements:* For doctorate, LSAT, minimum undergraduate GPA of 2.75. Additional exam requirements/recommendations for international students: Required—TOEFL (minimum score 600 paper-based; 213 computer-based; 80 iBT). *Application deadline:* For fall admission, 4/15 priority date for domestic students. Applications are processed on a rolling basis. Application fee: $65. Electronic applications accepted. *Expenses:* Contact institution. *Financial support:* Fellowships, Federal Work-Study, and scholarships/grants available. Financial award applicants required to submit FAFSA. *Unit head:* Dr. Tom Campbell, Dean, 714-628-2500. *Application contact:* Marissa Vargas, Assistant Director of Admission and Financial Aid, 877-CHAPLAW, E-mail: mvargas@chapman.edu. Web site: http://www.chapman.edu/law/.

Cleveland State University, College of Graduate Studies, Monte Ahuja College of Business, Department of Accounting, Cleveland, OH 44115. Offers financial accounting/audit (M Acc); taxation (M Acc). *Accreditation:* AACSB. Part-time and evening/weekend programs available. *Faculty:* 13 full-time (3 women), 11 part-time/adjunct (3 women). *Students:* 111 full-time (52 women), 156 part-time (86 women); includes 37 minority (22 Black or African American, non-Hispanic/Latino; 9 Asian, non-Hispanic/Latino; 3 Hispanic/Latino; 3 Two or more races, non-Hispanic/Latino), 71 international. Average age 29. 253 applicants, 69% accepted, 84 enrolled. In 2011, 66 master's awarded. *Entrance requirements:* For master's, GMAT, minimum GPA of 2.75. Additional exam requirements/recommendations for international students: Required—TOEFL (minimum score 525 paper-based; 197 computer-based). *Application deadline:* For fall admission, 7/15 priority date for domestic students; for spring admission, 12/15 priority date for domestic students. Applications are processed on a rolling basis. Application fee: $30. *Expenses:* Tuition, state resident: full-time $6416; part-time $494 per credit hour. Tuition, nonresident: full-time $12,074; part-time $929 per credit hour. *Financial support:* In 2011–12, 3 research assistantships with full and partial tuition reimbursements (averaging $6,960 per year) were awarded; career-related internships or fieldwork, Federal Work-Study, scholarships/grants, and unspecified assistantships also available. Financial award applicants required to submit FAFSA. *Faculty research:* Internal auditing, computer auditing, accounting education, managerial accounting. *Unit head:* Bruce W. McClain, Chair, 216-687-3652, Fax: 216-687-9212, E-mail: b.mcclain@csuohio.edu. *Application contact:* Bruce Gottschalk, MBA Programs Administrator, 216-687-3730, Fax: 216-687-5311, E-mail: cbacsu@csuohio.edu. Web site: http://www.csuohio.edu/business/academics/act/macc.html.

DePaul University, Charles H. Kellstadt Graduate School of Business, School of Accountancy and Management Information Systems, Chicago, IL 60604-2287. Offers accountancy (M Acc, MSA); business information technology (MS); e-business (MBA, MS); financial management and control (MBA); management accounting (MBA); management information systems (MBA); taxation (MST). Part-time and evening/weekend programs available. *Faculty:* 30 full-time (9 women), 54 part-time/adjunct (7 women). *Students:* 44 full-time (13 women), 22 part-time (4 women); includes 8 minority (2 Black or African American, non-Hispanic/Latino; 3 Asian, non-Hispanic/Latino; 2 Hispanic/Latino; 1 Two or more races, non-Hispanic/Latino), 4 international. Average age 29. In 2011, 141 master's awarded. *Entrance requirements:* For master's, GMAT, 2 letters of recommendation, resume. Additional exam requirements/recommendations for international students: Required—TOEFL (minimum score 550 paper-based; 213 computer-based). *Application deadline:* For fall admission, 7/1 for domestic students; for winter admission, 10/1 for domestic students; for spring admission, 2/1 for domestic students. Applications are processed on a rolling basis. Application fee: $60. *Financial support:* In 2011–12, 7 research assistantships with full tuition reimbursements (averaging $4,100 per year) were awarded; institutionally sponsored loans also available. Financial award application deadline: 4/2. *Faculty research:* Tax policy, property transactions, stock options as compensation, standards setting, activity-based costing in health care. *Unit head:* Kevin Stevens, Director, 312-362-6989, E-mail: kstevens@depaul.edu. *Application contact:* Christopher E. Kinsella, Director of Cohort MBA Programs, 312-362-8810, Fax: 312-362-6677, E-mail: kgsb@depaul.edu. Web site: http://accountancy.depaul.edu/.

Fairfield University, Charles F. Dolan School of Business, Fairfield, CT 06824-5195. Offers accounting (MBA, MS, CAS); accounting information systems (MBA, CAS); entrepreneurship (MBA, CAS); finance (MBA, MS, CAS); general management (MBA, CAS); human resource management (MBA, CAS); information systems and operations (MBA); information systems and operations management (CAS); international business (MBA, CAS); marketing (MBA, CAS); taxation (MBA, CAS). *Accreditation:* AACSB. Part-time and evening/weekend programs available. *Faculty:* 23 full-time (9 women), 3 part-time/adjunct (1 woman). *Students:* 87 full-time (37 women), 118 part-time (42 women); includes 13 minority (4 Black or African American, non-Hispanic/Latino; 4 Asian, non-Hispanic/Latino; 5 Hispanic/Latino), 9 international. Average age 29. 126 applicants, 47% accepted, 35 enrolled. In 2011, 90 master's awarded. *Degree requirements:* For master's, capstone course. *Entrance requirements:* For master's, GMAT (minimum score 500), 2 letters of reference, resume, minimum GPA of 3.0. Additional exam requirements/recommendations for international students: Required—TOEFL (minimum score 550 paper-based; 213 computer-bases; 80 iBT) or IELTS (minimum score 6.5). *Application deadline:* For fall admission, 5/15 for international students; for spring admission, 10/15 for international students. Applications are processed on a rolling basis. Application fee: $60. Electronic applications accepted. *Expenses:* Contact institution. *Financial support:* In 2011–12, 50 students received support, including 2 research assistantships (averaging $6,500 per year); scholarships/grants, unspecified assistantships, and merit-based one-time entrance scholarship also available. Financial award applicants required to submit FAFSA. *Faculty research:* Optimization strategies, international finance, consumer behavior, financial market volatility, Internet marketing, supply chain analysis, tax issues. *Unit head:* Dr. Donald Gibson, Dean, 203-254-4000 Ext. 4070, Fax: 203-254-4105, E-mail: dgibson@fairfield.edu. *Application contact:* Marianne Gumpper, Director of Graduate and Continuing Studies Admission, 203-254-4184, Fax: 203-254-4073, E-mail: gradadmis@fairfield.edu. Web site: http://www.fairfield.edu/dsb/dsb_grad_1.html.

Fairleigh Dickinson University, College at Florham, Silberman College of Business, Department of Accounting, Law, and Tax, Program in Taxation, Madison, NJ 07940-1099. Offers MS, Certificate.

Fairleigh Dickinson University, Metropolitan Campus, Silberman College of Business, Department of Accounting, Law, and Tax, Program in Taxation, Teaneck, NJ 07666-1914. Offers MS.

Florida Atlantic University, College of Business, School of Accounting, Program in Taxation, Boca Raton, FL 33431-0991. Offers M Tax. Part-time and evening/weekend programs available. Postbaccalaureate distance learning degree programs offered (minimal on-campus study). *Faculty:* 26 full-time (12 women), 28 part-time/adjunct (9 women). *Students:* 5 full-time (1 woman), 18 part-time (10 women); includes 7 minority (1 Black or African American, non-Hispanic/Latino; 4 Hispanic/Latino; 2 Two or more races, non-Hispanic/Latino), 1 international. Average age 29. 39 applicants, 41% accepted, 7 enrolled. In 2011, 16 master's awarded. *Degree requirements:* For master's, comprehensive exam, thesis optional. *Entrance requirements:* For master's, GMAT, minimum GPA of 3.0. Additional exam requirements/recommendations for international students: Required—TOEFL (minimum score 600 paper-based; 250 computer-based). *Application deadline:* For fall admission, 7/1 priority date for domestic students, 2/15 for international students; for spring admission, 11/1 priority date for domestic students, 7/15 for international students. Applications are processed on a rolling basis. Application fee: $30. *Expenses: Tuition, area resident:* Part-time $343.02 per credit hour. Tuition, state resident: full-time $8232. Tuition, nonresident: full-time $23,931; part-time $997.14 per credit hour. *Financial support:* Career-related internships or fieldwork, Federal Work-Study, institutionally sponsored loans, scholarships/grants, tuition waivers (full and partial), and unspecified assistantships available. Support available to part-time students. Financial award application deadline: 3/1. *Unit head:* Dr. Somnath Bhattacharya, Director, 561-297-3638, Fax: 561-297-7023, E-mail: sbhatt@fau.edu. *Application contact:* Fredrick G. Taylor, Graduate Adviser, 561-297-3196, Fax: 561-297-1315, E-mail: ftaylor@fau.edu.

Florida Gulf Coast University, Lutgert College of Business, Program in Accounting and Taxation, Fort Myers, FL 33965-6565. Offers MS. Part-time and evening/weekend programs available. *Faculty:* 51 full-time (14 women), 11 part-time/adjunct (2 women). *Students:* 38 full-time (20 women), 19 part-time (11 women); includes 15 minority (3 Black or African American, non-Hispanic/Latino; 2 Asian, non-Hispanic/Latino; 8 Hispanic/Latino; 2 Two or more races, non-Hispanic/Latino), 2 international. Average age 29. 34 applicants, 71% accepted, 19 enrolled. In 2011, 33 master's awarded. *Degree requirements:* For master's, thesis or alternative. *Entrance requirements:* For master's, GMAT, minimum GPA of 3.0. Additional exam requirements/recommendations for international students: Required—TOEFL (minimum score 550 paper-based; 213 computer-based). *Application deadline:* For fall admission, 6/1 priority date for domestic students; for spring admission, 11/1 for domestic students. Applications are processed on a rolling basis. Application fee: $30. Electronic applications accepted. *Expenses:* Tuition, state resident: full-time $8289. Tuition, nonresident: full-time $28,895. *Required fees:* $1831. One-time fee: $30 full-time. *Faculty research:* Stock petitions, mergers and acquisitions, deferred taxes, fraud and accounting regulations, graphical reporting practices. *Unit head:* Dr. Ara Volkan, Chair, 239-590-7380, Fax: 239-590-7330, E-mail: avolkan@fgcu.edu. *Application contact:* Marisa Ouverson, Director of Enrollment Management, 239-590-7403, Fax: 239-590-7330, E-mail: mouverso@fgcu.edu.

Florida International University, Alvah H. Chapman, Jr. Graduate School of Business, School of Accounting, Program in Taxation, Miami, FL 33199. Offers MST. Part-time and evening/weekend programs available. *Entrance requirements:* For master's, GMAT or GRE, minimum GPA of 3.0; resume. Additional exam requirements/recommendations for international students: Required—TOEFL (minimum score 550 paper-based; 213 computer-based; 80 iBT) or IELTS (minimum score 6.5). Electronic applications accepted. *Expenses:* Contact institution. *Faculty research:* Corporate taxation, small business taxation.

Florida State University, The Graduate School, College of Business, Tallahassee, FL 32306-1110. Offers accounting (M Acc), including accounting information services, assurance services, corporate accounting, taxation; business administration (MBA, PhD), including accounting (PhD), finance (PhD), management information systems (PhD), marketing (PhD), organizational behavior (PhD), risk management and insurance (PhD), strategic management (PhD); finance (MS); insurance (MSM); management information systems (MS); marketing (MS); JD/MBA; MSW/MBA. *Accreditation:* AACSB. Part-time programs available. Postbaccalaureate distance learning degree programs offered (no on-campus study). *Faculty:* 107 full-time (31 women). *Students:* 196 full-time (76 women), 310 part-time (109 women); includes 89 minority (27 Black or African American, non-Hispanic/Latino; 1 American Indian or Alaska Native, non-Hispanic/Latino; 31 Asian, non-Hispanic/Latino; 30 Hispanic/Latino). Average age 30. 702 applicants, 33% accepted, 205 enrolled. In 2011, 268 master's, 17 doctorates awarded. Terminal master's awarded for partial completion of doctoral program. *Degree requirements:* For doctorate, comprehensive exam, thesis/dissertation. *Entrance requirements:* For master's, GMAT, work experience (MBA, MS), minimum GPA of 3.0, letters of recommendation; for doctorate, GMAT, minimum graduate GPA of 3.5, letters of recommendation. Additional exam requirements/recommendations for international students: Required—TOEFL (minimum score 600 paper-based; 80 computer-based); Recommended—IELTS (minimum score 6.5). *Application deadline:* For fall admission, 6/1 for domestic students, 5/1 for international students; for spring admission, 10/1 for domestic students, 9/1 for international students. Applications are processed on a rolling basis. Application fee: $30. Electronic applications accepted. *Expenses:* Tuition, state resident: full-time $9474; part-time $350.88 per credit hour. Tuition, nonresident: full-time $16,236; part-time $601.34 per credit hour. *Required fees:* $630 per semester. One-time fee: $20. Tuition and fees vary according to course load and campus/location. *Financial support:* In 2011–12, 86 students received support, including 12 fellowships with full tuition reimbursements available (averaging $7,161 per year), 30 research assistantships with full tuition reimbursements available (averaging $6,000 per year), 43 teaching assistantships with full tuition reimbursements available (averaging $15,000 per year); career-related internships or fieldwork, scholarships/grants, health care benefits, tuition waivers (full and partial), and unspecified assistantships also available. Support available to part-time students. Financial award application deadline: 1/1. *Unit head:* Dr. Caryn Beck-Dudley, Dean, 850-644-3090, Fax: 850-644-0915. *Application contact:* Lisa Beverly, Director, Graduate Programs Admissions, 850-644-6458, Fax: 850-644-0588, E-mail: lbeverly@cob.fsu.edu. Web site: http://www.cob.fsu.edu/grad/.

Fontbonne University, Graduate Programs, College of Global Business and Professional Studies, Program in Taxation, St. Louis, MO 63105-3098. Offers MST. Part-time and evening/weekend programs available. *Entrance requirements:* For master's, minimum GPA of 2.5. Additional exam requirements/recommendations for international students: Required—TOEFL (minimum score 197 computer-based; 71 iBT).

Fordham University, Graduate School of Business, New York, NY 10023. Offers accounting (MBA); communications and media management (MBA); executive business administration (EMBA); finance (MBA, MS); information systems (MBA, MS); management systems (MBA); marketing (MBA); media management (MS); taxation (MS); taxation and accounting (MTA);); JD/MBA; MBA/MIM; MS/MBA. MBA/MIM offered jointly with Thunderbird School of Global Management. *Accreditation:* AACSB. Part-time and evening/weekend programs available. *Entrance requirements:* For master's, GMAT, 2 letters of recommendation, resume. Additional exam requirements/recommendations for international students: Required—TOEFL (minimum score 600 paper-based; 250 computer-based; 100 iBT). Electronic applications accepted. *Expenses:* Contact institution.

Georgetown University, Law Center, Washington, DC 20001. Offers global health law (LL M); individualized study (LL M); international business and economic law (LL M); law (JD, SJD); national security law (LL M); securities and financial regulation (LL M); taxation (LL M); JD/LL M; JD/MA; JD/MBA; JD/MPH; JD/PhD. *Accreditation:* ABA. Part-time and evening/weekend programs available. *Degree requirements:* For master's, thesis; for doctorate, thesis/dissertation (for some programs). *Entrance requirements:* For master's, JD, LL B, or first law degree earned in country of origin; for doctorate, LSAT (for JD). Additional exam requirements/recommendations for international students: Required—TOEFL. *Expenses:* Contact institution. *Faculty research:* Constitutional law, legal history, jurisprudence.

Georgia State University, J. Mack Robinson College of Business, School of Accountancy, Program in Taxation, Atlanta, GA 30303. Offers MTX. Part-time and evening/weekend programs available. *Entrance requirements:* For master's, GMAT, GRE General Test or LSAT. Additional exam requirements/recommendations for international students: Required—TOEFL (minimum score 610 paper-based; 255 computer-based; 101 iBT). Electronic applications accepted.

Golden Gate University, School of Accounting, San Francisco, CA 94105-2968. Offers accounting (M Ac, Graduate Certificate); forensic (M Ac); forensic accounting (Graduate Certificate); taxation (M Ac). Part-time and evening/weekend programs available. *Faculty:* 6 full-time (2 women), 55 part-time/adjunct (16 women). *Students:* 112 full-time (70 women), 157 part-time (99 women); includes 76 minority (1 American Indian or Alaska Native, non-Hispanic/Latino; 52 Asian, non-Hispanic/Latino; 17 Hispanic/Latino; 4 Native Hawaiian or other Pacific Islander, non-Hispanic/Latino; 2 Two or more races, non-Hispanic/Latino), 81 international. Average age 31. 149 applicants, 64% accepted, 53 enrolled. In 2011, 114 master's awarded. *Entrance requirements:* For master's, minimum GPA of 3.0. Additional exam requirements/recommendations for international students: Required—TOEFL. *Application deadline:* For fall admission, 5/15 for international students; for winter admission, 1/15 for international students; for spring admission, 9/15 for international students. Applications are processed on a rolling basis. Application fee: $70 ($110 for international students). Electronic applications accepted. *Financial support:* Career-related internships or fieldwork, Federal Work-Study, institutionally sponsored loans, and scholarships/grants available. Support available to part-time students. Financial award applicants required to submit FAFSA. *Faculty research:* Forensic accounting, audit, tax, CPA exam. *Unit head:* Mary Canning, 415-442-7885, Fax: 415-543-2607. *Application contact:* Angela Melero, Enrollment Services, 415-442-7800, Fax: 415-442-7807, E-mail: info@ggu.edu.

Golden Gate University, School of Law, San Francisco, CA 94105-2968. Offers environmental law (LL M); intellectual property law (LL M); international legal studies (LL M, SJD); law (JD); taxation (LL M); U. S. legal studies (LL M); JD/MBA; JD/PhD. *Accreditation:* ABA. Part-time and evening/weekend programs available. *Degree requirements:* For doctorate, thesis/dissertation (for some programs). *Entrance requirements:* For doctorate, LSAT (for JD). Additional exam requirements/recommendations for international students: Required—TOEFL (minimum score 600 paper-based; 250 computer-based). Electronic applications accepted. *Expenses:* Contact institution. *Faculty research:* International law, intellectual property law, environmental law, real estate, civil rights.

Golden Gate University, School of Taxation, San Francisco, CA 94105-2968. Offers advanced studies in taxation (Certificate); estate planning (Certificate); international tax (Certificate); tax (Certificate); taxation (MS). Part-time and evening/weekend programs available. *Faculty:* 6 full-time (1 woman), 82 part-time/adjunct (21 women). *Students:* 65 full-time (42 women), 607 part-time (328 women); includes 191 minority (16 Black or African American, non-Hispanic/Latino; 124 Asian, non-Hispanic/Latino; 32 Hispanic/Latino; 15 Native Hawaiian or other Pacific Islander, non-Hispanic/Latino; 4 Two or more races, non-Hispanic/Latino), 31 international. Average age 37. 300 applicants, 86% accepted, 140 enrolled. In 2011, 216 master's awarded. *Entrance requirements:* For master's, minimum GPA of 3.0. Additional exam requirements/recommendations for international students: Required—TOEFL. *Application deadline:* For fall admission, 5/15 for international students; for winter admission, 1/15 for international students; for spring admission, 9/15 for international students. Applications are processed on a rolling basis. Application fee: $70 ($110 for international students). Electronic applications accepted. *Expenses:* Contact institution. *Financial support:* Career-related internships or fieldwork, Federal Work-Study, institutionally sponsored loans, and scholarships/grants available. Support available to part-time students. Financial award applicants required to submit FAFSA. *Unit head:* Mary Canning, Dean, 415-442-7885, Fax: 415-442-7807. *Application contact:* Angela Melero, Enrollment Services, 415-442-7800, Fax: 415-442-7807, E-mail: info@ggu.edu. Web site: http://www.ggu.edu/programs/taxation/master-of-science-in-taxation.

Goldey-Beacom College, Graduate Program, Wilmington, DE 19808-1999. Offers business administration (MBA); finance (MS); financial management (MBA); health care management (MBA); human resource management (MBA); information technology (MBA); international business management (MBA); major finance (MBA); major taxation (MBA); management (MM); marketing management (MBA); taxation (MBA, MS). *Accreditation:* ACBSP. Part-time and evening/weekend programs available. *Faculty:* 19 full-time (7 women), 35 part-time/adjunct (12 women). *Students:* 58 full-time (32 women), 388 part-time (164 women); includes 89 minority (34 Black or African American, non-Hispanic/Latino; 2 American Indian or Alaska Native, non-Hispanic/Latino; 44 Asian, non-Hispanic/Latino; 9 Hispanic/Latino), 229 international. Average age 30. In 2011, 243 master's awarded. *Entrance requirements:* For master's, GMAT, MAT, GRE, minimum GPA of 3.0. Additional exam requirements/recommendations for international students: Required—TOEFL (minimum score 65 computer-based);

Taxation

Recommended—IELTS (minimum score 5). *Application deadline:* Applications are processed on a rolling basis. Application fee: $0. Electronic applications accepted. *Expenses: Tuition:* Full-time $15,750; part-time $875 per credit. *Required fees:* $10 per credit. *Financial support:* Scholarships/grants available. Support available to part-time students. Financial award application deadline: 4/1; financial award applicants required to submit FAFSA. *Unit head:* Larry W. Eby, Director of Admissions, 302-225-6289, Fax: 302-996-5408, E-mail: ebylw@gbc.edu. *Application contact:* Ashley E. Mashington, Graduate Admissions Representative, 302-225-6259, Fax: 302-996-5408, E-mail: mashina@gbc.edu. Web site: http://www.gbc.edu/programs/graduate/.

Grand Valley State University, Seidman College of Business, Program in Taxation, Allendale, MI 49401-9403. Offers MST. Part-time and evening/weekend programs available. *Entrance requirements:* For master's, GMAT. Additional exam requirements/recommendations for international students: Required—TOEFL. Electronic applications accepted. *Faculty research:* Individual income taxation, state taxation, pass-through entities, estate and gift taxation, sale-leasebacks.

HEC Montreal, School of Business Administration, Graduate Diplomas Programs in Administration, Program in Taxation, Montréal, QC H3T 2A7, Canada. Offers Graduate Diploma. All courses are given in French. Part-time programs available. *Students:* 35 full-time (18 women), 68 part-time (28 women). 89 applicants, 47% accepted, 33 enrolled. In 2011, 16 Graduate Diplomas awarded. *Degree requirements:* For Graduate Diploma, one foreign language. *Entrance requirements:* For degree, diploma in law, accounting, or economics. *Application deadline:* For fall admission, 4/1 for domestic and international students; for winter admission, 9/15 for domestic and international students. Application fee: $80 Canadian dollars. Electronic applications accepted. Application fee is waived when completed online. *Expenses:* Tuition, state resident: full-time $2601.36. Tuition, nonresident: full-time $7030. *International tuition:* $17,474.04 full-time. *Required fees:* $1381.77. Tuition and fees vary according to degree level and program. *Financial support:* Research assistantships, teaching assistantships, and scholarships/grants available. Financial award application deadline: 9/2. *Unit head:* Silvia Ponce, Director, 514-340-6393, Fax: 514-340-6915, E-mail: silvia.ponce@hec.ca. *Application contact:* Jo Anne Audet, Administrative Director, 514-340-1315, Fax: 514-340-6411, E-mail: joanne.audet@hec.ca. Web site: http://www.hec.ca/programmes_formations/des/dess/dess_fiscalite/index.html.

HEC Montreal, School of Business Administration, Master of Science Programs in Administration, LL M Program in Taxation, Montréal, QC H3T 2A7, Canada. Offers LL M. Program offered in French only. Part-time programs available. *Students:* 5 full-time (4 women), 33 part-time (17 women). 9 applicants, 100% accepted, 3 enrolled. In 2011, 26 master's awarded. *Degree requirements:* For master's, one foreign language. *Entrance requirements:* For master's, bachelor's degree in taxation. *Application deadline:* For fall admission, 4/1 for domestic and international students. Application fee: $80. Electronic applications accepted. Application fee is waived when completed online. *Expenses:* Tuition, state resident: full-time $2601.36. Tuition, nonresident: full-time $7030. *International tuition:* $17,474.04 full-time. *Required fees:* $1381.77. Tuition and fees vary according to degree level and program. *Financial support:* Research assistantships and teaching assistantships available. Financial award application deadline: 9/2. *Unit head:* Silvia Ponce, Director, 514-340-6393, Fax: 514-340-6915, E-mail: silvia.ponce@hec.ca. *Application contact:* Jo Anne Audet, Administrative Director, 514-340-1315, Fax: 514-340-6411, E-mail: joanne.audet@hec.ca. Web site: http://www.hec.ca/programmes_formations/des/maitrises_professionnelles/llm/index.html.

Hofstra University, Frank G. Zarb School of Business, Programs in Accounting and Taxation, Hempstead, NY 11549. Offers accounting (MS, Advanced Certificate); business administration (MBA), including accounting, professional accountancy, taxation; taxation (MS, Advanced Certificate). Part-time and evening/weekend programs available. Postbaccalaureate distance learning degree programs offered (minimal on-campus study). *Faculty:* 13 full-time (4 women), 5 part-time/adjunct (1 woman). *Students:* 166 full-time (100 women), 70 part-time (35 women); includes 30 minority (3 Black or African American, non-Hispanic/Latino; 20 Asian, non-Hispanic/Latino; 7 Hispanic/Latino), 97 international. Average age 25. 383 applicants, 79% accepted, 113 enrolled. In 2011, 45 master's awarded. *Degree requirements:* For master's, capstone course (for MBA); thesis (for MS); minimum GPA of 3.0. *Entrance requirements:* For master's, GMAT/GRE, 2 letters of recommendation; resume; essay. Additional exam requirements/recommendations for international students: Required—TOEFL (minimum score 550 paper-based; 213 computer-based; 80 iBT); Recommended—IELTS (minimum score 6). *Application deadline:* Applications are processed on a rolling basis. Application fee: $70 ($75 for international students). Electronic applications accepted. *Expenses:* Contact institution. *Financial support:* In 2011–12, 23 students received support, including 20 fellowships with full and partial tuition reimbursements available (averaging $6,973 per year); research assistantships with full and partial tuition reimbursements available, career-related internships or fieldwork, Federal Work-Study, institutionally sponsored loans, scholarships/grants, tuition waivers (full and partial), and unspecified assistantships also available. Support available to part-time students. Financial award applicants required to submit FAFSA. *Faculty research:* Legal issues in the insurance industry, penalties regarding tax compliance and the Internal Revenue Code, agency theory and accounts of migration, plain English financial statements, learning methods for teaching XBRL. *Unit head:* Dr. Nathan S. Slavin, Chairperson, 516-463-5690, Fax: 516-463-4834, E-mail: actnzs@hofstra.edu. *Application contact:* Carol Drummer, Dean of Graduate Admissions, 516-463-4876, Fax: 516-463-4664, E-mail: gradstudent@hofstra.edu. Web site: http://www.hofstra.edu/business/.

Illinois Institute of Technology, Chicago-Kent College of Law, Chicago, IL 60661-3691. Offers family law (LL M); financial services (LL M); international intellectual property (LL M); international law (LL M); law (JD); taxation (LL M); JD/LL M; JD/MBA; JD/MPA; JD/MPH; JD/MS. *Accreditation:* ABA. Part-time and evening/weekend programs available. *Entrance requirements:* For doctorate, LSAT, LSDAS. Additional exam requirements/recommendations for international students: Required—TOEFL (minimum score 600 paper-based; 250 computer-based; 100 iBT); Recommended—IELTS (minimum score 7). Electronic applications accepted. *Expenses:* Contact institution. *Faculty research:* Constitutional law, bioethics, environmental law.

Instituto Tecnologico de Santo Domingo, Graduate School, Area of Business, Santo Domingo, Dominican Republic. Offers banking and securities markets (M Mgmt); corporate finance (M Mgmt); human resources management (M Mgmt, Certificate); international trade management (M Mgmt); marketing (M Mgmt); organizational development (M Mgmt); quality and productivity management (Certificate); tax management and planning (M Mgmt); upper management (M Mgmt).

John Marshall Law School, Graduate and Professional Programs, Chicago, IL 60604-3968. Offers employee benefits (LL M, MS); global legal studies (LL M); information technology (MS); information technology and privacy law (LL M); intellectual property (LL M, MS); international business and trade (LL M); law (JD); real estate (LL M, MS); taxation (LL M, MS); trial advocacy (LL M); JD/LL M; JD/MA; JD/MBA; JD/MPA. JD/MBA offered jointly with Dominican University; JD/MA and JD/MPA with Roosevelt University. *Accreditation:* ABA. Part-time and evening/weekend programs available. *Faculty:* 69 full-time (22 women), 133 part-time/adjunct (40 women). *Students:* 1,305 full-time (598 women), 368 part-time (180 women); includes 385 minority (148 Black or African American, non-Hispanic/Latino; 15 American Indian or Alaska Native, non-Hispanic/Latino; 108 Asian, non-Hispanic/Latino; 110 Hispanic/Latino; 2 Native Hawaiian or other Pacific Islander, non-Hispanic/Latino; 2 Two or more races, non-Hispanic/Latino), 40 international. Average age 27. 3,513 applicants, 48% accepted, 365 enrolled. In 2011, 86 master's, 403 doctorates awarded. *Degree requirements:* For master's, 24 credits; for doctorate, 90 credits. *Entrance requirements:* For master's, JD; for doctorate, LSAT. Additional exam requirements/recommendations for international students: Required—TOEFL. *Application deadline:* For fall admission, 3/1 priority date for domestic students, 3/1 for international students; for spring admission, 10/15 priority date for domestic students, 10/15 for international students. Applications are processed on a rolling basis. Application fee: $0. Electronic applications accepted. *Expenses:* Contact institution. *Financial support:* In 2011–12, 1,350 students received support. Scholarships/grants and tuition waivers (full and partial) available. Support available to part-time students. Financial award application deadline: 6/1; financial award applicants required to submit FAFSA. *Unit head:* John Corkery, Dean, 312-427-2737. *Application contact:* William B. Powers, Associate Dean of Admission and Student Affairs, 800-537-4280, Fax: 312-427-5136, E-mail: admission@jmls.edu.

Long Island University–Brooklyn Campus, School of Business, Public Administration and Information Sciences, Program in Accountancy, Taxation and Law, Brooklyn, NY 11201-8423. Offers accounting (MS); taxation (MS). Part-time and evening/weekend programs available. *Entrance requirements:* For master's, GMAT or GRE General Test, 2 letters of recommendation. Additional exam requirements/recommendations for international students: Required—TOEFL (minimum score 500 paper-based; 173 computer-based). Electronic applications accepted.

Long Island University–C. W. Post Campus, College of Management, School of Business, Brookville, NY 11548-1300. Offers accounting and taxation (Certificate); business administration (Certificate); finance (MBA, Certificate); general business administration (MBA); international business (MBA, Certificate); management (MBA, Certificate); management information systems (MBA, Certificate); marketing (MBA, Certificate). *Accreditation:* AACSB. Part-time and evening/weekend programs available. *Entrance requirements:* For master's, GMAT, resume, minimum GPA of 3.0, 2 letters of recommendation. Additional exam requirements/recommendations for international students: Required—TOEFL (minimum score 527 paper-based; 197 computer-based). Electronic applications accepted. *Faculty research:* Financial markets, consumer behavior.

Long Island University–C. W. Post Campus, College of Management, School of Professional Accountancy, Brookville, NY 11548-1300. Offers accounting (MS); taxation (MS). Part-time and evening/weekend programs available. *Entrance requirements:* For master's, GMAT, minimum GPA of 2.5, BS in accounting from accredited college or university. Electronic applications accepted. *Faculty research:* International taxation.

Loyola Marymount University, Loyola Law School Los Angeles, Los Angeles, CA 90015. Offers law (JD); taxation (LL M); JD/LL M; JD/MBA. *Accreditation:* ABA. Part-time and evening/weekend programs available. *Faculty:* 74 full-time (35 women), 55 part-time/adjunct (13 women). *Students:* 1,021 full-time (533 women), 258 part-time (106 women); includes 953 minority (51 Black or African American, non-Hispanic/Latino; 8 American Indian or Alaska Native, non-Hispanic/Latino; 259 Asian, non-Hispanic/Latino; 163 Hispanic/Latino; 4 Native Hawaiian or other Pacific Islander, non-Hispanic/Latino; 468 Two or more races, non-Hispanic/Latino). Average age 26. 6,781 applicants, 24% accepted, 391 enrolled. In 2011, 23 master's, 403 doctorates awarded. *Entrance requirements:* For master's, JD; for doctorate, LSAT. *Application deadline:* For fall admission, 2/1 for domestic and international students. Applications are processed on a rolling basis. Application fee: $65. Electronic applications accepted. *Financial support:* Research assistantships, Federal Work-Study, and scholarships/grants available. Financial award application deadline: 3/11; financial award applicants required to submit FAFSA. *Unit head:* Victor Gold, Dean, 213-736-1062, Fax: 213-487-6736, E-mail: victor.gold@lls.edu. *Application contact:* Jannell Lundy Roberts, Assistant Dean, Admissions, 213-736-1074, Fax: 213-736-6523, E-mail: admissions@lls.edu. Web site: http://www.lls.edu/.

Loyola University Chicago, School of Law, Chicago, IL 60611. Offers advocacy (LL M); business and corporate governance law (MJ); business law (LL M, MJ); child and family law (LL M); children's law and policy (MJ); health law (LL M, MJ); health law and policy (D Law, SJD); international law (LL M); law (JD); rule of law development (LL M); tax law (LL M); U. S. law for foreign lawyers (LL M); JD/MA; JD/MBA; JD/MSW; MJ/MSW. *Accreditation:* ABA. Part-time and evening/weekend programs available. Postbaccalaureate distance learning degree programs offered (minimal on-campus study). *Faculty:* 48 full-time (17 women), 129 part-time/adjunct (60 women). *Students:* 857 full-time (434 women), 9 part-time (3 women); includes 201 minority (77 Black or African American, non-Hispanic/Latino; 1 American Indian or Alaska Native, non-Hispanic/Latino; 40 Asian, non-Hispanic/Latino; 63 Hispanic/Latino; 20 Two or more races, non-Hispanic/Latino), 11 international. Average age 25. 5,040 applicants, 34% accepted, 271 enrolled. *Entrance requirements:* Additional exam requirements/recommendations for international students: Required—TOEFL (minimum score 550 paper-based; 79 iBT), IELTS (minimum score 6.5). *Application deadline:* For fall admission, 3/1 for domestic students. Applications are processed on a rolling basis. Application fee: $0. Electronic applications accepted. *Expenses: Tuition:* Full-time $15,660; part-time $870 per credit hour. *Required fees:* $125 per semester. Tuition and fees vary according to course load and program. *Unit head:* Pamela Bloomquist, Assistant Dean for Admission and Financial Assistance, Law School, 312-915-7170, Fax: 312-915-7906, E-mail: ploom@luc.edu. *Application contact:* Ronald P. Martin, Associate Director, Graduate and Professional Enrollment Management Operations, 312-915-8951, E-mail: rmarti7@luc.edu. Web site: http://www.luc.edu/law/.

Mississippi State University, College of Business, School of Accountancy, Mississippi State, MS 39762. Offers accounting (MBA); business administration (PhD); systems (MPA); taxation (MTX). MBA in accounting only offered at the Meridian campus. *Accreditation:* AACSB. *Faculty:* 8 full-time (3 women), 3 part-time/adjunct (0 women). *Students:* 46 full-time (24 women), 13 part-time (9 women); includes 4 minority (2 Black or African American, non-Hispanic/Latino; 1 Asian, non-Hispanic/Latino; 1 Two or more races, non-Hispanic/Latino), 6 international. Average age 27. 51 applicants, 47% accepted, 24 enrolled. In 2011, 56 master's awarded. *Degree requirements:* For master's, comprehensive exam. *Entrance requirements:* For master's, GMAT (minimum score of 510), minimum GPA of 2.75 overall and in upper-level accounting, 3.0 in last 60 hours of course work; for doctorate, GMAT, minimum undergraduate GPA of 3.0, both cumulative and over the last 60 hours of undergraduate work; 3.25 on all prior graduate work. Additional exam requirements/recommendations for international students: Required—TOEFL (minimum score 575 paper-based; 233 computer-based; 84 iBT); Recommended—IELTS (minimum score 7). *Application deadline:* For fall admission, 7/1 for domestic students, 5/1 for international students; for spring admission, 11/1 for domestic students, 9/1 for international students. Applications are processed on a rolling basis. Application fee: $40. Electronic applications accepted. *Expenses:* Tuition, state resident: full-time $5805; part-time $322.50 per credit hour. Tuition, nonresident: full-time $14,670; part-time $815 per credit hour. *Financial support:* Career-related internships or fieldwork, Federal Work-Study, institutionally sponsored loans, scholarships/grants, and unspecified assistantships available. Support available to part-time students. Financial award application deadline: 4/1; financial award applicants required to submit FAFSA. *Faculty research:* Income tax, financial accounting system, managerial accounting, auditing. *Unit head:* Dr. Jim Scheiner, Director, 662-325-1633, Fax: 662-325-1646, E-mail: jscheiner@cobilan.msstate.edu. *Application contact:* Dr. Barbara Spencer, Graduate Coordinator, 662-325-3710, Fax: 662-325-1646, E-mail: sac@cobilan.msstate.edu. Web site: http://www.business.msstate.edu/accounting.

New York Law School, Graduate Programs, New York, NY 10013. Offers financial services (LL M); law (JD); mental disability law (MA); real estate (LL M); taxation (LL M); JD/MA; JD/MBA. JD/MBA offered jointly with Bernard M. Baruch College of the City University of New York; JD/MA in forensic psychology offered jointly with John Jay College of Criminal Justice of the City University of New York. *Accreditation:* ABA. Part-time and evening/weekend programs available. Postbaccalaureate distance learning degree programs offered (minimal on-campus study). *Faculty:* 103 full-time (45 women), 118 part-time/adjunct (42 women). *Students:* 1,416 full-time (760 women), 456 part-time (204 women); includes 476 minority (134 Black or African American, non-Hispanic/Latino; 5 American Indian or Alaska Native, non-Hispanic/Latino; 74 Asian, non-Hispanic/Latino; 243 Hispanic/Latino; 1 Native Hawaiian or other Pacific Islander, non-Hispanic/Latino; 19 Two or more races, non-Hispanic/Latino). Average age 27. 6,058 applicants, 44% accepted, 519 enrolled. In 2011, 37 master's, 515 doctorates awarded. *Entrance requirements:* For master's, JD (for LL M ; for doctorate, LSAT, letters of recommendation, resume. Additional exam requirements/recommendations for international students: Recommended—TOEFL (minimum score 600 paper-based; 250 computer-based; 100 iBT). *Application deadline:* For fall admission, 4/1 priority date for domestic students, 4/1 for international students. Applications are processed on a rolling basis. Application fee: $0. Electronic applications accepted. *Expenses: Tuition:* Full-time $46,200; part-time $35,600 per year. *Required fees:* $1600; $1300 per year. Tuition and fees vary according to degree level and student level. *Financial support:* In 2011–12, 588 students received support, including 34 fellowships (averaging $3,010 per year), 229 research assistantships (averaging $4,322 per year), 17 teaching assistantships (averaging $4,278 per year); career-related internships or fieldwork, Federal Work-Study, institutionally sponsored loans, and scholarships/grants also available. Support available to part-time students. Financial award application deadline: 4/1; financial award applicants required to submit FAFSA. *Unit head:* Carol A. Buckler, Interim Dean, 212-431-2840, Fax: 212-219-3752, E-mail: cbuckler@nyls.edu. *Application contact:* Susan W. Gross, Senior Director of Admissions and Financial Aid, 212-431-2888, Fax: 212-966-1522, E-mail: sgross@nyls.edu. Web site: http://www.nyls.edu.

See Display on page 1606 and Close-Up on page 1627.

New York University, School of Law, New York, NY 10012-1019. Offers law (LL M, JD, JSD); law and business (Advanced Certificate); taxation (Advanced Certificate); JD/LL B; JD/LL M; JD/MA; JD/MBA; JD/MPA; JD/MPP; JD/MSW; JD/MUP; JD/PhD. *Accreditation:* ABA. Part-time programs available. *Entrance requirements:* For doctorate, LSAT (for JD). Electronic applications accepted. *Expenses:* Contact institution. *Faculty research:* International law, environmental law, corporate law, globalization of law, philosophy of law.

Northern Illinois University, Graduate School, College of Business, Department of Accountancy, De Kalb, IL 60115-2854. Offers MAS, MST. *Accreditation:* AACSB. Part-time and evening/weekend programs available. *Faculty:* 14 full-time (4 women). *Students:* 127 full-time (54 women), 76 part-time (40 women); includes 35 minority (4 Black or African American, non-Hispanic/Latino; 19 Asian, non-Hispanic/Latino; 11 Hispanic/Latino; 1 Two or more races, non-Hispanic/Latino), 28 international. Average age 27. 168 applicants, 51% accepted, 55 enrolled. In 2011, 138 master's awarded. *Degree requirements:* For master's, thesis optional. *Entrance requirements:* For master's, GMAT, minimum GPA of 2.75. Additional exam requirements/recommendations for international students: Required—TOEFL (minimum score 550 paper-based; 213 computer-based). *Application deadline:* For fall admission, 4/1 priority date for domestic students, 5/1 for international students; for spring admission, 9/15 priority date for domestic students, 10/1 for international students. Applications are processed on a rolling basis. Application fee: $40. Electronic applications accepted. *Financial support:* In 2011–12, 26 research assistantships with full tuition reimbursements, 11 teaching assistantships with full tuition reimbursements were awarded; fellowships with full tuition reimbursements, career-related internships or fieldwork, Federal Work-Study, scholarships/grants, tuition waivers (full), and unspecified assistantships also available. Support available to part-time students. Financial award applicants required to submit FAFSA. *Faculty research:* Accounting fraud, governmental accounting, corporate income tax planning, auditing, ethics. *Unit head:* Dr. James C. Young, Chair, 815-753-1250, Fax: 815-753-8515. *Application contact:* Dr. Rowene Linden, Graduate Adviser, 815-753-6200. Web site: http://www.cob.niu.edu/accy/.

Northern Kentucky University, Office of Graduate Programs, College of Business, Program in Accountancy, Highland Heights, KY 41099. Offers accountancy (M Acc); advanced taxation (Certificate). Part-time and evening/weekend programs available. *Faculty:* 7 full-time (1 woman), 3 part-time/adjunct (0 women). *Students:* 11 full-time (2 women), 66 part-time (26 women); includes 5 minority (2 Black or African American, non-Hispanic/Latino; 1 Asian, non-Hispanic/Latino; 2 Hispanic/Latino). Average age 30. 85 applicants, 56% accepted, 43 enrolled. In 2011, 32 degrees awarded. *Degree requirements:* For master's, capstone course. *Entrance requirements:* For master's, GMAT (minimum score 450), minimum GPA of 2.5. Additional exam requirements/recommendations for international students: Required—TOEFL (minimum score 550 paper-based; 213 computer-based; 79 iBT); Recommended—IELTS (minimum score 6.5). *Application deadline:* For fall admission, 7/1 priority date for domestic students, 6/1 for international students; for spring admission, 12/1 priority date for domestic students, 10/1 for international students. Applications are processed on a rolling basis. Application fee: $40. Electronic applications accepted. *Expenses:* Tuition, state resident: full-time $7614; part-time $423 per credit hour. Tuition, nonresident: full-time $13,104; part-time $728 per credit hour. Tuition and fees vary according to degree level and reciprocity agreements. *Financial support:* Unspecified assistantships available. Financial award applicants required to submit FAFSA. *Faculty research:* Behavioral influences on accounting decisions, historical development of accounting, auditing and accounting failures. *Unit head:* Robert Salyer, Director, 859-572-7695, Fax: 859-572-7694, E-mail: salyerb@nku.edu. *Application contact:* Dr. Peg Griffin, Director of Graduate Programs, 859-572-6934, Fax: 859-572-6670, E-mail: griffinp@nku.edu. Web site: http://cob.nku.edu/departments/accountancy/graduate/macc/index.php.

Northwestern University, Law School, Chicago, IL 60611-3069. Offers international human rights (LL M); law (JD); law and business (LL M); tax (LL M in Tax); JD/LL M; JD/MBA; JD/PhD; LL M/Certificate. Executive LL M programs offered in Madrid (Spain), Seoul (South Korea), and Tel Aviv (Israel). *Accreditation:* ABA. *Entrance requirements:* For master's, law degree or equivalent, letter of recommendation, resume; for doctorate, LSAT, 1 letter of recommendation, resume. Additional exam requirements/recommendations for international students: Required—TOEFL. Electronic applications accepted. *Expenses:* Contact institution. *Faculty research:* Constitutional law, corporate law, international law, law and social policy, ethical studies.

Nova Southeastern University, H. Wayne Huizenga School of Business and Entrepreneurship, Fort Lauderdale, FL 33314-7796. Offers accounting (M Acc); business administration (MBA, DBA); human resource management (MSHRM); international business administration (MIBA); leadership (MS); public administration (MPA, DPA); real estate development (MS); taxation (M Tax); JD/MBA; Pharm D/MBA. Part-time and evening/weekend programs available. Postbaccalaureate distance learning degree programs offered (minimal on-campus study). *Students:* 229 full-time (112 women), 3,506 part-time (2,109 women); includes 2,506 minority (1,256 Black or African American, non-Hispanic/Latino; 8 American Indian or Alaska Native, non-Hispanic/Latino; 146 Asian, non-Hispanic/Latino; 1,058 Hispanic/Latino; 4 Native Hawaiian or other Pacific Islander, non-Hispanic/Latino; 34 Two or more races, non-Hispanic/Latino), 174 international. Average age 33. In 2011, 1,252 master's, 17 doctorates awarded. *Degree requirements:* For master's, thesis optional; for doctorate, comprehensive exam, thesis/dissertation. *Entrance requirements:* For doctorate, GMAT. Additional exam requirements/recommendations for international students: Required—TOEFL (minimum score 550 paper-based; 213 computer-based; 79 iBT), IELTS (minimum score 6). *Application deadline:* Applications are processed on a rolling basis. Application fee: $50. Electronic applications accepted. *Financial support:* In 2011–12, 2 students received support. Federal Work-Study and scholarships/grants available. Support available to part-time students. Financial award applicants required to submit FAFSA. *Faculty research:* Reputation management, call centers, international social capital, corporate earnings guidance, corporate governance. *Unit head:* Dr. D. Michael Fields, Dean, 954-262-5005, E-mail: fieldsm@nova.edu. *Application contact:* Karen Goldberg, Associate Director of Recruitment and Special Events, 954-262-5039, Fax: 954-262-3822, E-mail: karen@nova.edu. Web site: http://www.huizenga.nova.edu.

Pace University, Lubin School of Business, Taxation Program, New York, NY 10038. Offers MBA, MS. Part-time and evening/weekend programs available. *Students:* 6 full-time (1 woman), 52 part-time (28 women); includes 11 minority (3 Black or African American, non-Hispanic/Latino; 6 Asian, non-Hispanic/Latino; 2 Hispanic/Latino), 12 international. Average age 29. 46 applicants, 74% accepted, 13 enrolled. In 2011, 27 master's awarded. *Entrance requirements:* For master's, GMAT or GRE. Additional exam requirements/recommendations for international students: Required—TOEFL. *Application deadline:* For fall admission, 7/31 priority date for domestic students; for spring admission, 11/30 for domestic students. Applications are processed on a rolling basis. Application fee: $70. Electronic applications accepted. *Expenses: Tuition:* Part-time $990 per credit. *Required fees:* $168 per semester. Tuition and fees vary according to course load and degree level. *Financial support:* Research assistantships, career-related internships or fieldwork, and Federal Work-Study available. Support available to part-time students. Financial award applicants required to submit FAFSA. *Unit head:* Dr. Richard Kraus, Chairperson, Legal Studies and Taxation Department, 212-618-6476, E-mail: rkraus@pace.edu. *Application contact:* Susan Ford-Goldschein, Director of Graduate Admissions, 212-346-1531, Fax: 212-346-1585, E-mail: gradnyc@pace.edu. Web site: http://www.pace.edu/.

Philadelphia University, School of Business Administration, Program in Taxation, Philadelphia, PA 19144. Offers MS. Part-time and evening/weekend programs available. *Entrance requirements:* For master's, GMAT. Additional exam requirements/recommendations for international students: Required—TOEFL (minimum score 550 paper-based; 213 computer-based; 79 iBT). Electronic applications accepted.

Robert Morris University, Graduate Studies, School of Business, Moon Township, PA 15108-1189. Offers business administration (MBA); human resource management (MS); nonprofit management (MS); taxation (MS). *Accreditation:* AACSB. Part-time and evening/weekend programs available. Postbaccalaureate distance learning degree programs offered (no on-campus study). *Faculty:* 29 full-time (11 women), 3 part-time/adjunct (0 women). *Students:* 190 part-time (91 women); includes 11 minority (9 Black or African American, non-Hispanic/Latino; 1 Asian, non-Hispanic/Latino; 1 Hispanic/Latino), 4 international. *Entrance requirements:* For master's, GMAT, letters of recommendation. Additional exam requirements/recommendations for international students: Required—TOEFL (minimum score 550 paper-based; 213 computer-based; 79 iBT). *Application deadline:* For fall admission, 7/1 priority date for domestic students, 7/1 for international students; for spring admission, 11/1 priority date for domestic students, 11/1 for international students. Applications are processed on a rolling basis. Application fee: $35. Electronic applications accepted. *Expenses: Tuition:* Part-time $810 per credit. *Required fees:* $15 per course. Tuition and fees vary according to degree level. *Financial support:* Research assistantships with partial tuition reimbursements, Federal Work-Study, institutionally sponsored loans, and unspecified assistantships available. Support available to part-time students. Financial award application deadline: 5/1; financial award applicants required to submit FAFSA. *Unit head:* Dr. Patrick J. Litzinger, Interim Dean, 412-397-6383, Fax: 412-397-2217, E-mail: litzinger@rmu.edu. *Application contact:* Deborah Roach, Assistant Dean, Graduate Admissions, 412-397-5200, Fax: 412-397-2425, E-mail: graduateadmissions@rmu.edu. Web site: http://www.rmu.edu/web/cms/schools/sbus/.

St. John's University, The Peter J. Tobin College of Business, Department of Accounting and Taxation, Program in Taxation, Queens, NY 11439. Offers MBA, MS, Adv C. Part-time and evening/weekend programs available. Postbaccalaureate distance learning degree programs offered (no on-campus study). *Students:* 35 full-time (18 women), 31 part-time (10 women); includes 39 minority (10 Black or African American, non-Hispanic/Latino; 18 Asian, non-Hispanic/Latino; 9 Hispanic/Latino; 2 Two or more races, non-Hispanic/Latino), 3 international. Average age 27. 117 applicants, 73% accepted, 42 enrolled. In 2011, 65 master's awarded. *Degree requirements:* For master's, comprehensive exam (for some programs), thesis optional. *Entrance requirements:* For master's, GMAT (waived for MS applicants who have successfully completed the CPA exam), 2 letters of recommendation, resume, transcripts, statement of goals, bachelor's degree in accounting; for Adv C, GMAT, 2 letters of recommendation, resume, undergraduate and graduate transcripts, essay, MBA in accounting. Additional exam requirements/recommendations for international students: Required—TOEFL (minimum score 600 paper-based; 250 computer-based; 100 iBT), IELTS (minimum score 7). *Application deadline:* For fall admission, 5/1 priority date for domestic students, 5/1 for international students; for spring admission, 11/1 priority date for domestic students, 11/1 for international students. Applications are processed on a rolling basis. Application fee: $50. Electronic applications accepted. *Expenses:* Contact institution. *Financial support:* Research assistantships, scholarships/grants, and unspecified assistantships available. Support available to part-time students. Financial award application deadline: 3/1; financial award applicants required to submit FAFSA. *Unit head:* Dr. Adrian Fitzsimons, Chair, 718-990-1345, E-mail: fitzsima@stjohns.edu. *Application contact:* Carol J. Swanberg, Assistant Dean/Director of Graduate Admissions, 718-990-1345, Fax: 718-990-5242, E-mail: tobingradnyc@stjohns.edu.

St. Thomas University, School of Law, Miami Gardens, FL 33054-6459. Offers international human rights (LL M); international taxation (LL M); law (JD); JD/MBA; JD/MS. *Accreditation:* ABA. Postbaccalaureate distance learning degree programs offered (no on-campus study). *Degree requirements:* For master's, thesis (international taxation). *Entrance requirements:* For doctorate, LSAT. Electronic applications accepted. *Expenses:* Contact institution.

Taxation

San Jose State University, Graduate Studies and Research, Lucas Graduate School of Business, Program in Taxation, San Jose, CA 95192-0001. Offers MS. *Degree requirements:* For master's, comprehensive exam, thesis or alternative. *Entrance requirements:* For master's, GMAT, minimum GPA of 3.0. Electronic applications accepted.

Seton Hall University, Stillman School of Business, Department of Accounting, South Orange, NJ 07079-2697. Offers accounting (MS); professional accounting (MS); taxation (Certificate). Part-time and evening/weekend programs available. *Faculty:* 7 full-time (1 woman), 1 part-time/adjunct (0 women). *Students:* 41 full-time (27 women), 82 part-time (22 women); includes 56 minority (5 Black or African American, non-Hispanic/Latino; 46 Asian, non-Hispanic/Latino; 3 Hispanic/Latino; 2 Two or more races, non-Hispanic/Latino). Average age 28. 166 applicants, 80% accepted, 77 enrolled. In 2011, 40 master's awarded. *Entrance requirements:* For master's, GMAT, GRE or CPA, advanced degree from AACSB institution, MS in a business discipline, professional degree (MD, JD, PhD, DVM, DDS, etc.), minimum undergraduate GPA of 3.0. Additional exam requirements/recommendations for international students: Required—TOEFL (minimum score 102 iBT), IELTS or Pearson Test of English. *Application deadline:* For fall admission, 5/31 priority date for domestic students, 3/31 for international students; for spring admission, 10/31 for domestic students, 9/30 for international students. Applications are processed on a rolling basis. Application fee: $75. Electronic applications accepted. *Expenses: Tuition:* Part-time $1033 per credit hour. *Required fees:* $85 per semester. *Financial support:* In 2011–12, 2 students received support, including research assistantships with full tuition reimbursements available (averaging $35,610 per year); career-related internships or fieldwork, scholarships/grants, and unspecified assistantships also available. Support available to part-time students. Financial award application deadline: 6/30; financial award applicants required to submit FAFSA. *Faculty research:* Voluntary disclosure, international accounting, pension and retirement accounting, ethics in financial reporting, executive compensation. *Unit head:* Dr. Mark Holtzman, Chair, 973-761-9133, Fax: 973-761-9217, E-mail: mark.holtzman@shu.edu. *Application contact:* Catherine Bianchi, Director of Graduate Admissions, 973-761-9262, Fax: 973-761-9208, E-mail: catherine.bianchi@shu.edu. Web site: http://www.shu.edu/academics/business/ms-programs.cfm.

Seton Hall University, Stillman School of Business, Department of Taxation, South Orange, NJ 07079-2697. Offers MS. Part-time and evening/weekend programs available. *Faculty:* 1 full-time (0 women), 3 part-time/adjunct (0 women). *Students:* 5 part-time (1 woman); includes 1 minority (Asian, non-Hispanic/Latino). Average age 37. In 2011, 7 master's awarded. *Entrance requirements:* For master's, GMAT, GRE or CPA, advanced degree from AACSB institution, MS in a business discipline, professional degree (MD, JD, PhD, DVM, DDS, etc.), minimum undergraduate GPA of 3.0. Additional exam requirements/recommendations for international students: Required—TOEFL (minimum score 102 iBT), IELTS or Pearson Test of English. *Application deadline:* For fall admission, 6/1 priority date for domestic students, 4/11 for international students; for spring admission, 11/1 priority date for domestic students, 10/1 for international students. Application fee: $75. Electronic applications accepted. *Expenses:* Contact institution. *Financial support:* In 2011–12, 1 student received support, including research assistantships with full tuition reimbursements available (averaging $35,610 per year); career-related internships or fieldwork, scholarships/grants, and unspecified assistantships also available. Support available to part-time students. Financial award application deadline: 6/1; financial award applicants required to submit FAFSA. *Faculty research:* Issues affecting cost capitalization, estate valuation discounts, qualified terminable interest property elections, eastern European tax initiatives, realigning the capital structure of closely-held business enterprises. *Unit head:* Dr. Mark Holtzman, Department Chair, 973-761-9133, Fax: 973-761-9217, E-mail: eastonre@shu.edu. *Application contact:* Catherine Bianchi, Director of Graduate Admissions, 973-761-9220, Fax: 973-761-9208, E-mail: catherine.bianchi@shu.edu. Web site: http://www.shu.edu/academics/business/mba/.

Southern Illinois University Edwardsville, Graduate School, School of Business, Department of Accounting, Edwardsville, IL 62026. Offers accountancy (MSA); taxation (MSA). *Accreditation:* AACSB. Part-time and evening/weekend programs available. *Faculty:* 5 full-time (1 woman). *Students:* 18 full-time (8 women), 21 part-time (12 women); includes 3 minority (1 Asian, non-Hispanic/Latino; 1 Hispanic/Latino; 1 Two or more races, non-Hispanic/Latino), 2 international. 54 applicants, 43% accepted. In 2011, 22 master's awarded. *Degree requirements:* For master's, thesis or alternative, final exam. *Entrance requirements:* For master's, GMAT. Additional exam requirements/recommendations for international students: Required—TOEFL (minimum score 550 paper-based; 213 computer-based; 79 iBT), IELTS (minimum score 6.5). *Application deadline:* For fall admission, 7/22 for domestic students, 6/1 for international students; for spring admission, 12/10 for domestic students, 10/1 for international students. Applications are processed on a rolling basis. Application fee: $30. Electronic applications accepted. Tuition and fees vary according to course load and program. *Financial support:* In 2011–12, 1 fellowship with full tuition reimbursement (averaging $8,370 per year) was awarded; research assistantships with full tuition reimbursements, teaching assistantships with full tuition reimbursements, institutionally sponsored loans, scholarships/grants, and unspecified assistantships also available. Financial award application deadline: 3/1; financial award applicants required to submit FAFSA. *Unit head:* Dr. Michael Costigan, Chair, 618-650-2633, E-mail: mcostig@siue.edu. *Application contact:* Michelle Robinson, Coordinator of Graduate Recruitment, 618-650-2811, Fax: 618-650-3523, E-mail: michero@siue.edu. Web site: http://www.siue.edu/business/accounting/.

Southern Methodist University, Dedman School of Law, Dallas, TX 75275-0110. Offers foreign law school graduates (LL M); law (JD, SJD); law-general (LL M); taxation (LL M); JD/MA; JD/MBA. *Accreditation:* ABA. Part-time and evening/weekend programs available. *Degree requirements:* For master's, thesis optional; for doctorate, thesis/dissertation (for some programs), 30 hours of public service (for JD). *Entrance requirements:* For master's, JD; for doctorate, LSAT (for JD). Additional exam requirements/recommendations for international students: Required—TOEFL (minimum score 575 paper-based; 233 computer-based; 91 iBT). Electronic applications accepted. *Expenses:* Contact institution. *Faculty research:* Corporate law, intellectual property, international law, commercial law, dispute resolution.

Southern New Hampshire University, School of Business, Manchester, NH 03106-1045. Offers accounting (MS); business administration (MBA, Certificate), including accounting (Certificate), business administration (MBA), finance (Certificate), forensic accounting (Certificate), human resources management (Certificate), international business (Certificate), international sport management (Certificate), leadership of not for profit organizations (Certificate), marketing (Certificate), operations management (Certificate), sport management (Certificate), taxation (Certificate); finance (MS); hospitality and tourism leadership (Certificate); information technology (MS, Certificate); information technology/international business (Certificate); integrated marketing communications (Certificate); international business (MS, DBA); marketing (MS); operations and project management (MS); organizational leadership (MS); project management (Certificate); sport management (MS); MBA/Certificate. *Accreditation:* ACBSP. Part-time and evening/weekend programs available. Postbaccalaureate distance learning degree programs offered (no on-campus study). Terminal master's awarded for partial completion of doctoral program. *Degree requirements:* For master's, one foreign language, comprehensive exam (for some programs), thesis or alternative; for doctorate, one foreign language, comprehensive exam, thesis/dissertation. *Entrance requirements:* For master's, minimum GPA of 2.5; for doctorate, GMAT. Additional exam requirements/recommendations for international students: Required—TOEFL (minimum score 500 paper-based). Electronic applications accepted.

Strayer University, Graduate Studies, Washington, DC 20005-2603. Offers accounting (MS); acquisition (MBA); business administration (MBA); communications technology (MS); educational management (M Ed); finance (MBA); health services administration (MHSA); hospitality and tourism management (MBA); human resource management (MBA); information systems (MS), including computer security management, decision support system management, enterprise resource management, network management, software engineering management, systems development management; management (MBA); management information systems (MS); marketing (MBA); professional accounting (MS), including accounting information systems, controllership, taxation; public administration (MPA); supply chain management (MBA); technology in education (M Ed). Programs also offered at campus locations in Birmingham, AL; Chamblee, GA; Cobb County, GA; Morrow, GA; White Marsh, MD; Charleston, SC; Columbia, SC; Greensboro, NC; Greenville, SC; Lexington, KY; Louisville, KY; Nashville, TN; North Raleigh, NC; Washington, DC. Part-time and evening/weekend programs available. Postbaccalaureate distance learning degree programs offered (minimal on-campus study). *Degree requirements:* For master's, thesis. *Entrance requirements:* For master's, GMAT, GRE General Test, bachelor's degree from an accredited college or university, minimum undergraduate GPA of 2.75. Electronic applications accepted.

Suffolk University, Sawyer Business School, Department of Accounting, Boston, MA 02108-2770. Offers accounting (MSA, GDPA); taxation (MST); GDPA/MST; MBA/GDPA; MBA/MSA; MBA/MST. *Accreditation:* AACSB. Part-time and evening/weekend programs available. *Faculty:* 11 full-time (5 women), 7 part-time/adjunct (4 women). *Students:* 113 full-time (83 women), 142 part-time (72 women); includes 26 minority (6 Black or African American, non-Hispanic/Latino; 1 American Indian or Alaska Native, non-Hispanic/Latino; 15 Asian, non-Hispanic/Latino; 3 Hispanic/Latino; 1 Two or more races, non-Hispanic/Latino), 97 international. Average age 29. 519 applicants, 76% accepted, 106 enrolled. In 2011, 93 master's, 6 GDPAs awarded. *Entrance requirements:* For master's, GMAT. Additional exam requirements/recommendations for international students: Required—TOEFL (minimum score 550 paper-based; 213 computer-based; 80 iBT). *Application deadline:* For fall admission, 6/15 priority date for domestic students, 6/15 for international students; for spring admission, 11/1 priority date for domestic students, 11/1 for international students. Applications are processed on a rolling basis. Application fee: $50. Electronic applications accepted. Tuition and fees vary according to program. *Financial support:* In 2011–12, 94 students received support, including 43 fellowships with full and partial tuition reimbursements available (averaging $23,365 per year); career-related internships or fieldwork, Federal Work-Study, and institutionally sponsored loans also available. Support available to part-time students. Financial award application deadline: 4/1; financial award applicants required to submit CSS PROFILE. *Faculty research:* Tax policy, tax research, decision-making in accounting, accounting information systems, capital markets and strategic planning. *Unit head:* Lewis Shaw, Chair, 617-573-8615, Fax: 617-994-4260, E-mail: lshaw@suffolk.edu. *Application contact:* Ellen Driscoll, Director of Graduate Admissions, 617-573-8302, Fax: 617-305-1733, E-mail: grad.admission@suffolk.edu. Web site: http://www.suffolk.edu/msa.

Suffolk University, Sawyer Business School, Master of Business Administration Program, Boston, MA 02108-2770. Offers accounting (MBA); business administration (APC); corporate financial executive track (MBA); entrepreneurship (MBA); executive business administration (EMBA); finance (MBA); global business administration (GMBA); health administration (MBA); international business (MBA); marketing (MBA); organizational behavior (MBA); strategic management (MBA); taxation (MBA); JD/MBA; MBA/GDPA; MBA/MHA; MBA/MSA; MBA/MSF; MBA/MST. *Accreditation:* AACSB. Part-time and evening/weekend programs available. Postbaccalaureate distance learning degree programs offered (no on-campus study). *Faculty:* 98 full-time (30 women), 14 part-time/adjunct (3 women). *Students:* 139 full-time (49 women), 321 part-time (138 women); includes 53 minority (17 Black or African American, non-Hispanic/Latino; 1 American Indian or Alaska Native, non-Hispanic/Latino; 21 Asian, non-Hispanic/Latino; 11 Hispanic/Latino; 1 Native Hawaiian or other Pacific Islander, non-Hispanic/Latino; 2 Two or more races, non-Hispanic/Latino), 64 international. Average age 30. 437 applicants, 61% accepted, 121 enrolled. In 2011, 283 master's awarded. *Entrance requirements:* For master's, GMAT, minimum undergraduate GPA of 2.75 (MBA), 5 years of managerial experience (EMBA). Additional exam requirements/recommendations for international students: Required—TOEFL (minimum score 550 paper-based; 213 computer-based). *Application deadline:* For fall admission, 6/15 priority date for domestic students, 6/15 for international students; for spring admission, 11/1 priority date for domestic students, 11/1 for international students. Applications are processed on a rolling basis. Application fee: $50. Electronic applications accepted. Tuition and fees vary according to program. *Financial support:* In 2011–12, 273 students received support, including 73 fellowships with full and partial tuition reimbursements available (averaging $12,415 per year); career-related internships or fieldwork, Federal Work-Study, and institutionally sponsored loans also available. Support available to part-time students. Financial award application deadline: 4/1; financial award applicants required to submit FAFSA. *Faculty research:* Foreign investments; career strategies and boundaryless careers; corporate ethics codes; interest rates, inflation, and growth options; innovation and product development performance. *Unit head:* Lillian Hallberg, Assistant Dean of Graduate Programs/Director of MBA Programs, 617-573-8306, E-mail: lhallber@suffolk.edu. *Application contact:* Ellen Driscoll, Director of Graduate Admissions, 617-573-8302, Fax: 617-305-1733, E-mail: grad.admission@suffolk.edu. Web site: http://www.suffolk.edu/mba.

Taft Law School, Graduate Programs, Santa Ana, CA 92704-6954. Offers American jurisprudence (LL M); law (JD); taxation (LL M).

Temple University, James E. Beasley School of Law, Philadelphia, PA 19122. Offers law (JD); legal education (SJD); taxation (LL M); transnational law (LL M); trial advocacy (LL M); JD/LL M; JD/MBA. *Accreditation:* ABA. Part-time and evening/weekend programs available. *Entrance requirements:* For doctorate, LSAT (for JD). Additional exam requirements/recommendations for international students: Recommended—TOEFL. Electronic applications accepted. *Expenses:* Contact institution. *Faculty research:* Evidence, gender issues, health care law, immigration law, and intellectual property law .

Texas Tech University, Graduate School, Rawls College of Business Administration, Area of Accounting, Lubbock, TX 79409. Offers accounting (PhD); audit/financial reporting (MSA); taxation (MSA); JD/MSA. *Accreditation:* AACSB. Part-time programs available. *Faculty:* 14 full-time (2 women). *Students:* 190 full-time (100 women), 19 part-time (8 women); includes 24 minority (5 Black or African American, non-Hispanic/Latino; 2 American Indian or Alaska Native, non-Hispanic/Latino; 8 Asian, non-Hispanic/Latino; 9 Hispanic/Latino), 7 international. Average age 24. 178 applicants, 73% accepted, 121 enrolled. In 2011, 61 degrees awarded. Terminal master's awarded for partial completion of doctoral program. *Degree requirements:* For master's, capstone course;

for doctorate, comprehensive exam, thesis/dissertation, qualifying exams. *Entrance requirements:* For master's and doctorate, GMAT, holistic profile of academic credentials. Additional exam requirements/recommendations for international students: Required—TOEFL (minimum score 550 paper-based; 213 computer-based; 79 iBT). *Application deadline:* For fall admission, 2/1 for domestic students, 1/15 for international students. Applications are processed on a rolling basis. Application fee: $50 ($75 for international students). Electronic applications accepted. *Expenses:* Tuition, state resident: full-time $5899; part-time $245.80 per credit hour. Tuition, nonresident: full-time $13,411; part-time $558.80 per credit hour. *Required fees:* $2680.60; $86.50 per credit hour. $920.30 per semester. *Financial support:* In 2011–12, 9 research assistantships (averaging $14,933 per year), 2 teaching assistantships (averaging $18,000 per year) were awarded; fellowships, career-related internships or fieldwork, Federal Work-Study, scholarships/grants, health care benefits, and unspecified assistantships also available. Financial award applicants required to submit FAFSA. *Faculty research:* Governmental and nonprofit accounting, managerial and financial accounting. *Unit head:* Dr. Robert Ricketts, Area Coordinator, 806-742-3180, Fax: 806-742-3182, E-mail: robert.ricketts@ttu.edu. *Application contact:* Elizabeth Stuart, 806-742-3184, Fax: 806-742-3958, E-mail: ba_grad@ttu.edu. Web site: http://accounting.ba.ttu.edu.

Thomas M. Cooley Law School, JD and LL M Programs, Lansing, MI 48901-3038. Offers administrative law (public law) (JD); business transactions (JD); Canadian law (JD); Constitutional law and civil rights (public law) (JD); corporate law and finance (LL M); environmental law (public law) (JD); general practice (JD); insurance (LL M); intellectual property (LL M, JD); international law (JD); litigation (JD); self-directed (LL M, JD); taxation (LL M, JD); U.S. law for foreign attorneys (LL M); JD/MBA; JD/MPA; JD/MSW. *Accreditation:* ABA. Part-time and evening/weekend programs available. Postbaccalaureate distance learning degree programs offered (no on-campus study). *Faculty:* 131 full-time (55 women), 286 part-time/adjunct (93 women). *Students:* 781 full-time (368 women), 2,964 part-time (1,450 women); includes 1,055 minority (543 Black or African American, non-Hispanic/Latino; 19 American Indian or Alaska Native, non-Hispanic/Latino; 179 Asian, non-Hispanic/Latino; 205 Hispanic/Latino; 9 Native Hawaiian or other Pacific Islander, non-Hispanic/Latino; 100 Two or more races, non-Hispanic/Latino), 220 international. Average age 30. 4,032 applicants, 80% accepted, 1161 enrolled. In 2011, 40 master's, 999 doctorates awarded. *Degree requirements:* For master's, thesis optional; for doctorate, minimum of 3 credits of clinical experience. *Entrance requirements:* For master's, JD or LL B; for doctorate, LSAT. Additional exam requirements/recommendations for international students: Required—TOEFL. *Application deadline:* For fall admission, 9/1 for domestic and international students; for winter admission, 1/1 for domestic and international students; for spring admission, 5/1 for domestic and international students. Applications are processed on a rolling basis. Electronic applications accepted. *Expenses: Tuition:* Full-time $34,300; part-time $1225 per credit hour. *Required fees:* $40; $40 per year. Tuition and fees vary according to degree level and student level. *Financial support:* In 2011–12, 2,324 students received support. Career-related internships or fieldwork, Federal Work-Study, scholarships/grants, traineeships, and unspecified assistantships available. Support available to part-time students. Financial award applicants required to submit FAFSA. *Faculty research:* Wrongful convictions, civil rights, environmental law, litigation techniques, data mining, intellectual property, practical and skills-based legal education. *Unit head:* Don LeDuc, President and Dean, 517-371-5140 Ext. 2009, Fax: 517-334-5152. *Application contact:* Dr. Paul Zelenski, Associate Dean of Enrollment and Student Services, 517-371-5140 Ext. 2244, Fax: 517-334-5718, E-mail: admissions@cooley.edu. Web site: http://www.cooley.edu/.

Troy University, Graduate School, College of Business, Program in Taxation, Troy, AL 36082. Offers MTX, Certificate. Part-time and evening/weekend programs available. *Faculty:* 3 full-time (1 woman). *Students:* 2 full-time (1 woman), 17 part-time (13 women); includes 11 minority (10 Black or African American, non-Hispanic/Latino; 1 Two or more races, non-Hispanic/Latino). Average age 32. 31 applicants, 65% accepted, 8 enrolled. *Degree requirements:* For master's, minimum GPA of 3.0, research paper, capstone course. *Entrance requirements:* For master's, GMAT (minimum score of 500), minimum GPA of 2.5; letter of recommendation; bachelor's degree, CPA, or CFP. Additional exam requirements/recommendations for international students: Required—TOEFL (minimum score 523 paper-based; 193 computer-based; 70 iBT), IELTS (minimum score 6), or ACT COMPASS ESL (minimum listening, reading, and grammar score 270). *Application deadline:* Applications are processed on a rolling basis. Application fee: $50. Electronic applications accepted. *Expenses:* Tuition, state resident: full-time $6960; part-time $290 per credit hour. Tuition, nonresident: full-time $13,920; part-time $580 per credit hour. *Required fees:* $386 per term. *Unit head:* Dr. Kay Sheridan, Director, 334-670-3143, Fax: 334-670-3708, E-mail: ksheridan@troy.edu. *Application contact:* Brenda K. Campbell, Director of Graduate Admissions, 334-670-3178, Fax: 334-670-3733, E-mail: bcamp@troy.edu.

Université de Montréal, Faculty of Law, Montréal, QC H3C 3J7, Canada. Offers business law (DESS); common law (North America) (JD); international law (DESS); law (LL M, LL D, DDN, DESS, LL B); tax law (LL M). Part-time programs available. *Degree requirements:* For master's, thesis; for doctorate, thesis/dissertation, project; for other advanced degree, thesis (for some programs). Electronic applications accepted. *Faculty research:* Legal theory; constitutional, private, and public law.

Université de Sherbrooke, Faculty of Administration, Program in Taxation, Sherbrooke, QC J1K 2R1, Canada. Offers M Tax, Diploma. Part-time and evening/weekend programs available. *Faculty:* 12 full-time (2 women), 68 part-time/adjunct (26 women). *Students:* 90 full-time (38 women), 113 part-time (58 women). Average age 32. 187 applicants, 68% accepted, 91 enrolled. In 2011, 47 master's awarded. *Degree requirements:* For master's, one foreign language, thesis. *Entrance requirements:* For master's, bachelor's degree in business, law or economics; basic knowledge of Canadian taxation (2 courses). *Application deadline:* For fall admission, 4/30 priority date for domestic students, 4/5 for international students; for winter admission, 10/15 priority date for domestic students, 10/15 for international students. Applications are processed on a rolling basis. Application fee: $70. Electronic applications accepted. *Faculty research:* Taxation research, public finances. *Unit head:* Chantal Amiot, Director, 819-821-8000 Ext. 63731, Fax: 819-821-7364, E-mail: chantal.amiot@usherbrooke.ca. *Application contact:* Linda Pepin, Assistant to the Director, 819-821-8000 Ext. 63427, Fax: 819-821-7364, E-mail: linda.pepin@usherbrooke.ca.

University at Albany, State University of New York, School of Business, Department of Accounting and Law, Albany, NY 12222-0001. Offers accounting (MS); taxation (MS). *Accreditation:* AACSB. *Degree requirements:* For master's, research project. *Entrance requirements:* For master's, GMAT. Additional exam requirements/recommendations for international students: Required—TOEFL (minimum score 550 paper-based; 213 computer-based). Electronic applications accepted. *Faculty research:* Professional ethics, statistical analysis, cost management systems, accounting theory.

The University of Akron, Graduate School, College of Business Administration, School of Accountancy, Program in Taxation, Akron, OH 44325. Offers MT. *Students:* 15 full-time (4 women), 34 part-time (14 women); includes 5 minority (2 Black or African American, non-Hispanic/Latino; 2 Asian, non-Hispanic/Latino; 1 Hispanic/Latino), 1 international. Average age 31. 26 applicants, 81% accepted, 19 enrolled. In 2011, 23 master's awarded. *Entrance requirements:* For master's, GMAT, minimum GPA of 2.75, two letters of recommendation, resume, statement of purpose. Additional exam requirements/recommendations for international students: Required—TOEFL (minimum score 550 paper-based; 213 computer-based; 79 iBT). *Application deadline:* For fall admission, 7/15 for domestic and international students; for spring admission, 11/15 for domestic and international students. Application fee: $30 ($40 for international students). Electronic applications accepted. *Expenses:* Tuition, state resident: full-time $7038; part-time $391 per credit hour. Tuition, nonresident: full-time $12,051; part-time $670 per credit hour. *Required fees:* $1274; $34 per credit hour. *Unit head:* Coordinator. *Application contact:* Dr. Susan Hanlon, Director of Graduate Business Programs, 330-972-7043, Fax: 330-972-6588, E-mail: shanlon@uakron.edu.

The University of Alabama, Graduate School, Manderson Graduate School of Business, Culverhouse School of Accountancy, Tuscaloosa, AL 35487. Offers accounting (M Acc, PhD); tax accounting (MTA). *Accreditation:* AACSB. *Faculty:* 18 full-time (5 women). *Students:* 117 full-time (57 women), 1 (woman) part-time; includes 7 minority (3 Black or African American, non-Hispanic/Latino; 2 Asian, non-Hispanic/Latino; 2 Hispanic/Latino), 1 international. Average age 24. 236 applicants, 56% accepted, 95 enrolled. In 2011, 94 degrees awarded. *Degree requirements:* For doctorate, thesis/dissertation. *Entrance requirements:* For master's and doctorate, GMAT, minimum GPA of 3.0. Additional exam requirements/recommendations for international students: Required—TOEFL. *Application deadline:* For fall admission, 7/1 priority date for domestic students, 6/1 for international students; for spring admission, 11/1 priority date for domestic students, 9/1 for international students. Applications are processed on a rolling basis. Application fee: $50 ($60 for international students). Electronic applications accepted. *Expenses:* Tuition, state resident: full-time $8600. Tuition, nonresident: full-time $21,900. *Financial support:* In 2011–12, 79 students received support, including 4 fellowships with full tuition reimbursements available (averaging $15,000 per year), 21 research assistantships with full and partial tuition reimbursements available (averaging $6,367 per year), 17 teaching assistantships with full and partial tuition reimbursements available (averaging $6,367 per year); career-related internships or fieldwork, Federal Work-Study, institutionally sponsored loans, scholarships/grants, health care benefits, and unspecified assistantships also available. Financial award application deadline: 3/31. *Faculty research:* Corporate governance, audit decision-making, earning management, valuation, executive compensation, not-for-profit. *Unit head:* Dr. Mary S. Stone, Director, 205-348-2915, Fax: 205-348-8453, E-mail: mstone@cba.ua.edu. *Application contact:* Sandy D. Davidson, Advisor, 205-348-6131, Fax: 205-348-8453, E-mail: sdavidso@cba.ua.edu. Web site: http://www.cba.ua.edu/accounting/.

The University of Alabama in Huntsville, School of Graduate Studies, College of Business Administration, Department of Accounting and Finance, Huntsville, AL 35899. Offers accounting (M Acc), including CPA preparatory with an emphasis in taxation, CPA preparatory with emphasis in assurance and financial reporting, general accounting, information systems audit and control (ISAC). *Accreditation:* AACSB. Part-time and evening/weekend programs available. *Faculty:* 7 full-time (2 women), 4 part-time/adjunct (1 woman). *Students:* 21 full-time (14 women), 28 part-time (13 women); includes 8 minority (6 Black or African American, non-Hispanic/Latino; 1 American Indian or Alaska Native, non-Hispanic/Latino; 1 Asian, non-Hispanic/Latino), 4 international. Average age 33. 30 applicants, 70% accepted, 19 enrolled. In 2011, 24 master's awarded. *Degree requirements:* For master's, comprehensive exam, thesis or alternative. *Entrance requirements:* For master's, GMAT (minimum score 500), minimum AACSB index of 1080. Additional exam requirements/recommendations for international students: Required—TOEFL (minimum score 550 paper-based; 213 computer-based; 62 iBT). *Application deadline:* For fall admission, 8/1 for domestic students, 4/1 for international students; for spring admission, 12/1 for domestic students, 9/1 for international students. Applications are processed on a rolling basis. Application fee: $40 ($50 for international students). Electronic applications accepted. *Expenses:* Tuition, state resident: full-time $7830; part-time $473.50 per credit. Tuition, nonresident: full-time $18,748; part-time $1128.33 per credit. Tuition and fees vary according to course load and program. *Financial support:* In 2011–12, 5 students received support, including 1 research assistantship with full tuition reimbursement available (averaging $14,400 per year), 2 teaching assistantships with full tuition reimbursements available (averaging $5,000 per year); career-related internships or fieldwork, Federal Work-Study, institutionally sponsored loans, scholarships/grants, health care benefits, and unspecified assistantships also available. Support available to part-time students. Financial award application deadline: 4/1; financial award applicants required to submit FAFSA. *Faculty research:* Accounting information systems, emerging technologies in accounting, behavioral accounting, state and local taxation, financial accounting. *Total annual research expenditures:* $66,318. *Unit head:* Dr. John Burnett, Interim Chair, 256-824-2923, Fax: 256-824-2929, E-mail: burnettj@uah.edu. *Application contact:* Jennifer Pettitt, Director of Graduate Programs, 256-824-6681, Fax: 256-824-7571, E-mail: jennifer.pettitt@uah.edu.

University of Arkansas at Little Rock, Graduate School, College of Business Administration, Little Rock, AR 72204-1099. Offers accountancy (M Acc, Graduate Certificate); business administration (MBA); construction management (Graduate Certificate); management (Graduate Certificate); management information system (MIS); management information systems (Graduate Certificate); management information systems leadership (Graduate Certificate); taxation (MS, Graduate Certificate). *Accreditation:* AACSB. Part-time and evening/weekend programs available. *Entrance requirements:* For master's, GMAT, minimum undergraduate GPA of 2.7. Additional exam requirements/recommendations for international students: Required—TOEFL (minimum score 525 paper-based; 195 computer-based).

University of Baltimore, Graduate School, Merrick School of Business, Program in Taxation, Baltimore, MD 21201-5779. Offers MS. Part-time and evening/weekend programs available. *Entrance requirements:* For master's, GMAT, minimum GPA of 3.0. Additional exam requirements/recommendations for international students: Required—TOEFL (minimum score 550 paper-based; 213 computer-based). *Expenses:* Contact institution. *Faculty research:* Taxation of not-for-profit entities.

University of Baltimore, School of Law, Baltimore, MD 21201-5779. Offers law (JD); law of the United States (LL M); taxation (LL M); JD/LL M; JD/MBA; JD/MPA; JD/MS; JD/PhD. JD/MS offered jointly with Division of Criminology, Criminal Justice, and Social Policy; JD/PhD with University of Maryland, Baltimore. *Accreditation:* ABA. Part-time and evening/weekend programs available. *Faculty:* 76 full-time (36 women), 102 part-time/adjunct (31 women). *Students:* 738 full-time (370 women), 360 part-time (172 women); includes 203 minority (89 Black or African American, non-Hispanic/Latino; 1 American Indian or Alaska Native, non-Hispanic/Latino; 56 Asian, non-Hispanic/Latino; 39 Hispanic/Latino; 1 Native Hawaiian or other Pacific Islander, non-Hispanic/Latino; 17 Two or more races, non-Hispanic/Latino), 2 international. Average age 27. 2,105 applicants, 41% accepted, 328 enrolled. In 2011, 297 degrees awarded. *Entrance requirements:* For doctorate, LSAT. *Application deadline:* For fall admission, 4/1 priority date for domestic students, 4/1 for international students. Applications are processed on a rolling basis. Application fee: $60. Electronic applications accepted. *Expenses:* Contact institution. *Financial support:* In 2011–12, 192 students received support. Research assistantships, teaching assistantships, career-related internships or fieldwork, Federal Work-Study, institutionally sponsored loans, and scholarships/grants available. Support available to part-time students. Financial award application deadline: 4/1; financial award applicants required to submit FAFSA. *Faculty research:* Plain view doctrine, statute of limitations, bankruptcy, family law, international and comparative law, Constitutional law. *Unit head:* Ronald Weich, Dean, 410-837-4458. *Application contact:* Jeffrey L. Zavrotny, Assistant Dean for Admissions, 410-837-5809, Fax: 410-837-4188, E-mail: jzavrotny@ubalt.edu. Web site: http://law.ubalt.edu/.

University of Central Florida, College of Business Administration, Kenneth G. Dixon School of Accounting, Program in Taxation, Orlando, FL 32816. Offers MST. Part-time and evening/weekend programs available. *Students:* 28 full-time (14 women), 17 part-time (9 women); includes 10 minority (2 Black or African American, non-Hispanic/Latino; 3 Asian, non-Hispanic/Latino; 5 Hispanic/Latino), 2 international. Average age 28. 19 applicants, 68% accepted, 12 enrolled. In 2011, 26 master's awarded. *Degree requirements:* For master's, comprehensive exam. *Entrance requirements:* For master's, GMAT, minimum GPA of 3.0 in last 60 hours of course work. Additional exam requirements/recommendations for international students: Required—TOEFL. *Application deadline:* For fall admission, 2/1 priority date for domestic students; for spring admission, 11/1 priority date for domestic students. Application fee: $30. Electronic applications accepted. *Expenses:* Tuition, state resident: part-time $277.08 per credit hour. Tuition, nonresident: part-time $277.08 per credit hour. Part-time tuition and fees vary according to degree level and program. *Financial support:* In 2011–12, 3 students received support, including 1 fellowship (averaging $10,000 per year), 1 research assistantship (averaging $6,500 per year), 2 teaching assistantships with partial tuition reimbursements available (averaging $6,900 per year); career-related internships or fieldwork, Federal Work-Study, institutionally sponsored loans, tuition waivers (partial), and unspecified assistantships also available. Financial award application deadline: 3/1; financial award applicants required to submit FAFSA. *Unit head:* Dr. Sean Robb, Director, 407-823-2876. *Application contact:* Judy Ryder, Director, Graduate Admissions, 407-823-2364, Fax: 407-823-0219, E-mail: jryder@bus.ucf.edu. Web site: http://web.bus.ucf.edu/accounting/?page=1265.

University of Denver, College of Law, Graduate Tax Program, Denver, CO 80208. Offers LL M, MT. Part-time and evening/weekend programs available. *Faculty:* 10 full-time (2 women), 10 part-time/adjunct (0 women). *Students:* 53 full-time (22 women), 102 part-time (38 women); includes 24 minority (6 Black or African American, non-Hispanic/Latino; 1 American Indian or Alaska Native, non-Hispanic/Latino; 8 Asian, non-Hispanic/Latino; 6 Hispanic/Latino; 3 Two or more races, non-Hispanic/Latino), 6 international. Average age 31. In 2011, 81 degrees awarded. *Entrance requirements:* For master's, LSAT (for LL M), GMAT (for MT), JD from ABA-approved institution (for LL M). Additional exam requirements/recommendations for international students: Required—TOEFL (minimum score 550 paper-based; 80 iBT)or IELTS (minimum score 6). *Application deadline:* Applications are processed on a rolling basis. Application fee: $30. *Expenses:* Contact institution. *Financial support:* In 2011–12, 55 students received support. Federal Work-Study, institutionally sponsored loans, scholarships/grants, and tuition waivers (full and partial) available. Support available to part-time students. Financial award application deadline: 6/30; financial award applicants required to submit FAFSA. *Faculty research:* All areas of tax, including individual, estate and gift, state and local, qualified plans, partnerships, C corporations and S corporations, procedural and ethical aspects of the practice of tax. *Unit head:* Prof. Mark A. Vogel, Director, 303-871-6239, Fax: 303-871-6358, E-mail: mvogel@du.edu. *Application contact:* Information Contact, 303-871-6239, Fax: 303-871-6358, E-mail: gtp@du.edu. Web site: http://www.du.edu/tax/.

University of Florida, Levin College of Law, Gainesville, FL 32611. Offers comparative law (LL M); environmental law (LL M); international taxation (LL M); law (JD); taxation (LL M, SJD). *Accreditation:* ABA. *Faculty:* 77 full-time (37 women), 36 part-time/adjunct (10 women). *Students:* 1,111 full-time (476 women); includes 257 minority (68 Black or African American, non-Hispanic/Latino; 14 American Indian or Alaska Native, non-Hispanic/Latino; 57 Asian, non-Hispanic/Latino; 118 Hispanic/Latino), 45 international. Average age 24. 3,024 applicants, 29% accepted, 295 enrolled. In 2011, 406 doctorates awarded. *Entrance requirements:* For doctorate, LSAT (for JD). Additional exam requirements/recommendations for international students: Required—TOEFL (minimum score 250 computer-based; 100 iBT). *Application deadline:* For fall admission, 3/15 for domestic and international students. Applications are processed on a rolling basis. Application fee: $30. Electronic applications accepted. *Financial support:* In 2011–12, 291 students received support, including 34 research assistantships (averaging $9,867 per year); Federal Work-Study, institutionally sponsored loans, scholarships/grants, health care benefits, and unspecified assistantships also available. Financial award application deadline: 4/15; financial award applicants required to submit FAFSA. *Faculty research:* Environmental and land use law, taxation, dispute resolution, family law, Constitutional law. *Unit head:* Robert Jerry, Dean, 352-273-0600, Fax: 352-392-8727, E-mail: jerryr@law.ufl.edu. *Application contact:* Michelle Adorno, Assistant Dean for Admissions, 352-273-0890, Fax: 352-392-4087, E-mail: madorno@law.ufl.edu. Web site: http://www.law.ufl.edu/.

University of Hartford, Barney School of Business, Department of Accounting and Taxation, West Hartford, CT 06117-1599. Offers professional accounting (Certificate); taxation (MSAT). Part-time and evening/weekend programs available. *Entrance requirements:* For master's, GMAT, 2 letters of recommendation, resume. Additional exam requirements/recommendations for international students: Required—TOEFL (minimum score 550 paper-based; 213 computer-based). Electronic applications accepted.

University of Hawaii at Manoa, Graduate Division, Shidler College of Business, Program in Accounting, Honolulu, HI 96822. Offers accounting (M Acc); accounting law (M Acc); information systems (M Acc); taxation (M Acc). Part-time programs available. *Entrance requirements:* For master's, GMAT, bachelor's degree in accounting, minimum GPA of 3.0. Additional exam requirements/recommendations for international students: Required—TOEFL (minimum score 550 paper-based; 213 computer-based; 79 iBT), IELTS (minimum score 5). *Faculty research:* International accounting, current tax topics, insurance industry financial reporting, behavioral accounting, auditing.

University of Houston, Law Center, Houston, TX 77204-6060. Offers energy, environment, and natural resources (LL M); health law (LL M); intellectual property and information law (LL M); international law (LL M); law (LL M, JD); tax law (LL M). *Accreditation:* ABA. Part-time and evening/weekend programs available. *Entrance requirements:* For doctorate, LSAT. Additional exam requirements/recommendations for international students: Required—TOEFL (minimum score 600 paper-based; 100 iBT). Electronic applications accepted. *Expenses:* Contact institution. *Faculty research:* Health law, international, tax, environmental/energy, information law/intellectual property.

University of Illinois at Urbana–Champaign, Graduate College, College of Business, Department of Accountancy, Champaign, IL 61820. Offers accountancy (MAS, MS, PhD); taxation (MS); MAS/JD. *Accreditation:* AACSB. *Faculty:* 26 full-time (8 women), 6 part-time/adjunct (2 women). *Students:* 369 full-time (220 women), 7 part-time (5 women); includes 65 minority (3 Black or African American, non-Hispanic/Latino; 47 Asian, non-Hispanic/Latino; 12 Hispanic/Latino; 3 Two or more races, non-Hispanic/Latino), 182 international. 1,040 applicants, 42% accepted, 346 enrolled. In 2011, 378 master's, 2 doctorates awarded. *Entrance requirements:* For master's, GMAT (for MAS), minimum GPA of 3.0; for doctorate, GMAT, minimum GPA of 3.0. Additional exam requirements/recommendations for international students: Required—TOEFL. *Application deadline:* Applications are processed on a rolling basis. Application fee: $75 ($90 for international students). Electronic applications accepted. *Financial support:* In 2011–12, 22 fellowships, 14 research assistantships, 81 teaching assistantships were awarded; tuition waivers (full and partial) also available. *Unit head:* Theodore Sougiannis, Head, 217-244-0555, Fax: 217-244-0902, E-mail: sougiani@illinois.edu. *Application contact:* Cindy Wood, Administrative Aide, 217-333-4572, Fax: 217-244-0902, E-mail: ckwood@illinois.edu. Web site: http://www.business.illinois.edu/accountancy.

University of Memphis, Graduate School, Fogelman College of Business and Economics, School of Accountancy, Memphis, TN 38152. Offers accounting (MS); accounting systems (MS); taxation (MS). *Accreditation:* AACSB. *Degree requirements:* For master's, comprehensive exam. *Entrance requirements:* For master's, GMAT. *Faculty research:* Financial accounting, corporate governance, EDP auditing, evolution of system analysis, investor behavior and investment decisions.

University of Miami, Graduate School, School of Business Administration, Department of Accounting, Coral Gables, FL 33124. Offers professional accounting (MP Acc); taxation (MS Tax). *Accreditation:* AACSB. Part-time and evening/weekend programs available. *Entrance requirements:* For master's, GMAT or CPA exam. Additional exam requirements/recommendations for international students: Required—TOEFL. Electronic applications accepted. *Faculty research:* Financial reporting, audit risk, public policy and taxation issues, government accounting and public choice, corporate governance.

University of Miami, Graduate School, School of Law, Coral Gables, FL 33124-8087. Offers business and financial law (Certificate); employment, labor and immigration law (JD); estate planning (LL M); international law (LL M), including general international law, inter-American law, international arbitration, U.S. transnational law for foreign lawyers; law (JD); ocean and coastal law (LL M); real property development (real estate) (LL M); taxation (LL M); JD/LL M; JD/LL M/MBA; JD/MA; JD/MBA; JD/MD; JD/MM; JD/MPH; JD/MPS. *Accreditation:* ABA. *Faculty:* 82 full-time (37 women), 107 part-time/adjunct (41 women). *Students:* 1,348 full-time (588 women), 135 part-time (58 women); includes 395 minority (90 Black or African American, non-Hispanic/Latino; 9 American Indian or Alaska Native, non-Hispanic/Latino; 49 Asian, non-Hispanic/Latino; 236 Hispanic/Latino; 1 Native Hawaiian or other Pacific Islander, non-Hispanic/Latino; 10 Two or more races, non-Hispanic/Latino), 56 international. Average age 24. 4,729 applicants, 46% accepted, 447 enrolled. In 2011, 96 master's, 385 doctorates awarded. *Entrance requirements:* For doctorate, LSAT, 2 letters of recommendation. Additional exam requirements/recommendations for international students: Required—TOEFL (minimum score 580 paper-based; 237 computer-based; 92 iBT). *Application deadline:* For fall admission, 1/6 priority date for domestic students, 1/6 for international students. Applications are processed on a rolling basis. Application fee: $60. Electronic applications accepted. *Expenses:* Contact institution. *Financial support:* Fellowships, research assistantships, career-related internships or fieldwork, Federal Work-Study, institutionally sponsored loans, scholarships/grants, and unspecified assistantships available. Financial award application deadline: 3/1; financial award applicants required to submit FAFSA. *Faculty research:* National security law, international finance, Internet law/law of electronic commerce, law of the seas, art law/cultural heritage law. *Unit head:* Michael Goodnight, Associate Dean of Admissions and Enrollment Management, 305-284-2527, Fax: 305-284-3084, E-mail: mgoodnig@law.miami.edu. *Application contact:* Therese Lambert, Director of Student Recruitment, 305-284-6746, Fax: 305-284-3084, E-mail: tlambert@law.miami.edu. Web site: http://www.law.miami.edu/.

University of Michigan, Law School, Ann Arbor, MI 48109-1215. Offers comparative law (MCL); international tax (LL M); law (LL M, JD, SJD); JD/MA; JD/MBA; JD/MHSA; JD/MPH; JD/MPP; JD/MS; JD/MSI; JD/MSW; JD/MUP; JD/PhD. *Accreditation:* ABA. *Faculty:* 94 full-time (33 women), 36 part-time/adjunct (10 women). *Students:* 1,149 full-time (534 women); includes 242 minority (42 Black or African American, non-Hispanic/Latino; 17 American Indian or Alaska Native, non-Hispanic/Latino; 129 Asian, non-Hispanic/Latino; 53 Hispanic/Latino; 1 Native Hawaiian or other Pacific Islander, non-Hispanic/Latino), 30 international. 5,424 applicants, 21% accepted, 359 enrolled. In 2011, 36 master's, 383 doctorates awarded. *Entrance requirements:* For master's and doctorate, LSAT. Additional exam requirements/recommendations for international students: Required—TOEFL. *Application deadline:* For fall admission, 2/15 for domestic students. Applications are processed on a rolling basis. Application fee: $75. Electronic applications accepted. *Expenses:* Contact institution. *Financial support:* In 2011–12, 838 students received support. Career-related internships or fieldwork, Federal Work-Study, institutionally sponsored loans, and scholarships/grants available. Financial award applicants required to submit FAFSA. *Unit head:* Evan H. Caminker, Dean, 734-764-1358. *Application contact:* Sarah C. Zearfoss, Assistant Dean and Director of Admissions, 734-764-0537, Fax: 734-647-3218, E-mail: law.jd.admissions@umich.edu. Web site: http://www.law.umich.edu/.

University of Minnesota, Twin Cities Campus, Carlson School of Management, Master's Program in Business Taxation, Minneapolis, MN 55455-0213. Offers MBT. Part-time and evening/weekend programs available. *Faculty:* 2 full-time (1 woman), 14 part-time/adjunct (4 women). *Students:* 29 full-time (17 women), 59 part-time (36 women); includes 27 minority (3 Black or African American, non-Hispanic/Latino; 22 Asian, non-Hispanic/Latino; 2 Hispanic/Latino), 7 international. Average age 32. 35 applicants, 100% accepted, 32 enrolled. In 2011, 43 master's awarded. *Entrance requirements:* For master's, GMAT or LSAT. Additional exam requirements/recommendations for international students: Required—TOEFL (minimum score 550 paper-based; 213 computer-based; 79 iBT), IELTS (minimum score 6.5). *Application deadline:* For fall admission, 6/15 priority date for domestic students, 6/15 for international students; for spring admission, 10/15 priority date for domestic students, 10/15 for international students. Applications are processed on a rolling basis. Application fee: $75 ($95 for international students). Electronic applications accepted. *Expenses:* Contact institution. *Financial support:* In 2011–12, 14 students received support, including 9 fellowships (averaging $1,750 per year); teaching assistantships, career-related internships or fieldwork, and institutionally sponsored loans also available. Financial award application deadline: 8/1; financial award applicants required to submit FAFSA. *Faculty research:* Partnership taxation, tax theory, corporate taxation. *Unit head:* Frank Gigler, Director of Graduate Studies, 612-624-7641, Fax: 612-626-7795, E-mail: gigle003@umn.edu. *Application contact:* Information Contact, 612-626-7511, E-mail: gsguest@umn.edu. Web site: http://www.carlson.umn.edu/master-business-taxation/.

University of Mississippi, Graduate School, School of Accountancy, Oxford, University, MS 38677. Offers accountancy (M Acc, PhD); taxation accounting (M Tax). *Accreditation:* AACSB. *Students:* 94 full-time (39 women), 23 part-time (13 women); includes 15 minority (7 Black or African American, non-Hispanic/Latino; 1 American Indian or Alaska Native, non-Hispanic/Latino; 5 Asian, non-Hispanic/Latino; 1 Hispanic/Latino; 1 Two or more races, non-Hispanic/Latino), 8 international. *Degree requirements:* For doctorate, thesis/dissertation. *Entrance requirements:* For master's, GMAT, minimum GPA of 3.0; for doctorate, GMAT. Additional exam requirements/

recommendations for international students: Required—TOEFL. *Application deadline:* For fall admission, 4/1 for domestic students; for spring admission, 10/1 for domestic students. Applications are processed on a rolling basis. *Financial support:* Scholarships/grants available. Financial award application deadline: 3/1; financial award applicants required to submit FAFSA. *Unit head:* Dr. Mark Wilder, Interim Dean, 662-915-7468, Fax: 662-915-7483, E-mail: umaccy@olemiss.edu. *Application contact:* Dr. Christy M. Wyandt, Associate Dean, 662-915-7474, Fax: 662-915-7577, E-mail: cwyandt@olemiss.edu.

University of Missouri–Kansas City, School of Law, Kansas City, MO 64110-2499. Offers law (LL M, JD), including general (LL M), taxation (LL M); JD/LL M; JD/MBA; JD/MPA; LL M/MPA. *Accreditation:* ABA. Part-time programs available. *Faculty:* 32 full-time (13 women), 7 part-time/adjunct (3 women). *Students:* 452 full-time (162 women), 55 part-time (24 women); includes 56 minority (22 Black or African American, non-Hispanic/Latino; 3 American Indian or Alaska Native, non-Hispanic/Latino; 14 Asian, non-Hispanic/Latino; 16 Hispanic/Latino; 1 Two or more races, non-Hispanic/Latino), 25 international. Average age 28. 929 applicants, 21% accepted, 172 enrolled. In 2011, 30 master's, 156 doctorates awarded. *Degree requirements:* For master's, thesis (for general). *Entrance requirements:* For master's, LSAT, minimum GPA of 3.0 (for general), 2.7 (for taxation); for doctorate, LSAT. Additional exam requirements/recommendations for international students: Required—TOEFL (minimum score 550 paper-based; 213 computer-based; 80 iBT). *Application deadline:* For fall admission, 3/1 priority date for domestic students, 3/1 for international students. Applications are processed on a rolling basis. Application fee: $50. Electronic applications accepted. *Expenses:* Contact institution. *Financial support:* In 2011–12, 40 teaching assistantships with partial tuition reimbursements (averaging $2,327 per year) were awarded; career-related internships or fieldwork, Federal Work-Study, institutionally sponsored loans, scholarships/grants, and tuition waivers (full and partial) also available. Support available to part-time students. Financial award application deadline: 3/1; financial award applicants required to submit FAFSA. *Faculty research:* Family and children's issues, litigation, estate planning, urban law, business, tax entrepreneurial law. *Unit head:* Ellen Y. Suni, Dean, 816-235-1007, Fax: 816-235-5276, E-mail: sunie@umkc.edu. *Application contact:* Debbie Brooks, Director of Admissions, 816-235-1672, Fax: 816-235-5276, E-mail: brooksdv@umkc.edu. Web site: http://www.law.umkc.edu/.

University of New Haven, Graduate School, School of Business, Program in Taxation, West Haven, CT 06516-1916. Offers MS, Certificate. Part-time and evening/weekend programs available. *Students:* 3 full-time (all women), 38 part-time (25 women); includes 17 minority (13 Black or African American, non-Hispanic/Latino; 1 Asian, non-Hispanic/Latino; 2 Hispanic/Latino; 1 Two or more races, non-Hispanic/Latino), 1 international. Average age 37. 14 applicants, 100% accepted, 10 enrolled. In 2011, 9 master's, 1 other advanced degree awarded. *Degree requirements:* For master's, thesis or alternative. *Entrance requirements:* For master's, GMAT. Additional exam requirements/recommendations for international students: Required—TOEFL (minimum score 520 paper-based; 190 computer-based; 70 iBT); Recommended—IELTS (minimum score 5.5). *Application deadline:* For fall admission, 5/31 for international students; for winter admission, 10/15 for international students; for spring admission, 1/15 for international students. Applications are processed on a rolling basis. Application fee: $50. Electronic applications accepted. *Expenses:* Contact institution. *Financial support:* Research assistantships with partial tuition reimbursements, teaching assistantships with partial tuition reimbursements, career-related internships or fieldwork, Federal Work-Study, scholarships/grants, tuition waivers, and unspecified assistantships available. Support available to part-time students. Financial award application deadline: 5/1; financial award applicants required to submit FAFSA. *Unit head:* Prof. Robert Wnek, Coordinator, 203-932-7111. *Application contact:* Eloise Gormley, Director of Graduate Admissions, 203-932-7449, Fax: 203-932-7137, E-mail: gradinfo@newhaven.edu. Web site: http://www.newhaven.edu/6856/.

University of New Mexico, Robert O. Anderson Graduate School of Management, Department of Accounting, Albuquerque, NM 87131. Offers accounting (MBA); advanced accounting (M Acct); professional accounting (M Acct); tax accounting (M Acct); JD/M Acct. *Accreditation:* AACSB. Part-time and evening/weekend programs available. *Faculty:* 13 full-time (4 women), 3 part-time/adjunct (all women). In 2011, 72 master's awarded. *Degree requirements:* For master's, minimum GPA of 3.0. *Entrance requirements:* For master's, GMAT or GRE. Additional exam requirements/recommendations for international students: Required—TOEFL (minimum score 550 paper-based; 213 computer-based; 79 iBT). *Application deadline:* For fall admission, 4/1 priority date for domestic students, 4/1 for international students; for spring admission, 10/1 priority date for domestic students, 10/1 for international students. Applications are processed on a rolling basis. Application fee: $50. Electronic applications accepted. *Financial support:* Fellowships, research assistantships, career-related internships or fieldwork, Federal Work-Study, scholarships/grants, and unspecified assistantships available. Support available to part-time students. *Faculty research:* Critical accounting, accounting pedagogy, theory, taxation, information fraud. *Unit head:* Dr. Craig White, Chair, 505-277-6471, Fax: 505-277-7108, E-mail: white@mgt.unm.edu. *Application contact:* Tina Armijo, Office Administrator, 505-277-6471, Fax: 505-277-7108, E-mail: profmacct@mgt.unm.edu. Web site: http://accounting.mgt.unm.edu.

University of New Orleans, Graduate School, College of Business Administration, Department of Accounting, Program in Taxation, New Orleans, LA 70148. Offers MS. Part-time and evening/weekend programs available. *Degree requirements:* For master's, thesis optional. *Entrance requirements:* For master's, GMAT. Additional exam requirements/recommendations for international students: Required—TOEFL (minimum score 550 paper-based; 213 computer-based; 79 iBT). Electronic applications accepted.

The University of North Carolina at Greensboro, Graduate School, Bryan School of Business and Economics, Department of Accounting and Finance, Greensboro, NC 27412-5001. Offers accounting (MS); accounting systems (MS); financial accounting and reporting (MS); financial analysis (PMC); tax concentration (MS). *Accreditation:* AACSB. *Entrance requirements:* For master's, GMAT, GRE General Test, previous course work in accounting and business. Additional exam requirements/recommendations for international students: Required—TOEFL. Electronic applications accepted.

University of North Texas, Toulouse Graduate School, College of Business, Department of Accounting, Denton, TX 76203. Offers accounting (MS, PhD); taxation (MS). *Accreditation:* AACSB. Part-time programs available. *Degree requirements:* For master's, comprehensive exam; for doctorate, thesis/dissertation. *Entrance requirements:* For master's, GMAT or GRE General Test, essay, 3 letters of recommendation, resume; for doctorate, GMAT or GRE General Test, statement of purpose, resume, 3 letters of recommendation. Additional exam requirements/recommendations for international students: Recommended—TOEFL (minimum score 550 paper-based; 213 computer-based). Electronic applications accepted. *Expenses:* Tuition, state resident: part-time $100 per credit hour. Tuition, nonresident: part-time $413 per credit hour. *Faculty research:* Empirical tax research issues, empirical financial accounting issues, problems and issues in public interest areas, historical perspective for accounting issues, behavioral issues in auditing and accounting systems.

University of Notre Dame, Mendoza College of Business, Program in Accountancy, Notre Dame, IN 46556. Offers financial reporting and assurance services (MS); tax services (MS). *Accreditation:* AACSB. *Faculty:* 36 full-time (4 women), 15 part-time/adjunct (0 women). *Students:* 81 full-time (38 women); includes 9 minority (2 Black or African American, non-Hispanic/Latino; 4 Asian, non-Hispanic/Latino; 3 Hispanic/Latino), 16 international. Average age 22. 307 applicants, 35% accepted, 81 enrolled. In 2011, 102 master's awarded. *Entrance requirements:* For master's, GMAT. Additional exam requirements/recommendations for international students: Required—TOEFL (minimum score 630 paper-based; 267 computer-based; 109 iBT). *Application deadline:* For fall admission, 10/31 for domestic and international students; for spring admission, 5/1 for domestic and international students. Applications are processed on a rolling basis. Application fee: $50 ($100 for international students). Electronic applications accepted. *Financial support:* In 2011–12, 79 students received support, including 79 fellowships (averaging $16,082 per year); scholarships/grants and unspecified assistantships also available. Financial award application deadline: 2/28; financial award applicants required to submit FAFSA. *Faculty research:* Stock valuation, accounting information in decision-making, choice of accounting method, taxes cost on capital. *Unit head:* Dr. Michael H. Morris, Director, 574-631-9732, Fax: 574-631-5300, E-mail: msacct.1@nd.edu. *Application contact:* Helen High, Assistant Director of Admissions and Student Services, 574-631-6499, Fax: 574-631-5300, E-mail: msacct.1@nd.edu. Web site: http://business.nd.edu/msa.

University of San Diego, School of Business Administration, Program in Taxation, San Diego, CA 92110-2492. Offers MS. *Entrance requirements:* For master's, GMAT (minimum score of 550), official transcripts for all prior undergraduate and graduate work, minimum accounting and overall GPA of 3.0. Application fee: $80. *Expenses: Tuition:* Full-time $22,482; part-time $1249 per unit. *Required fees:* $224. Full-time tuition and fees vary according to course load and degree level. *Unit head:* Dr. David Pyke, Dean, 619-260-4886, E-mail: davidpyke@sandiego.edu. *Application contact:* Stephen Pultz, Director of Admissions and Enrollment, 619-260-4506, Fax: 619-260-6836, E-mail: admissions@sandiego.edu.

University of San Diego, School of Business Administration, Programs in Accountancy and Taxation, San Diego, CA 92110-2492. Offers accountancy (MS); taxation (MS). Part-time and evening/weekend programs available. *Students:* 20 full-time (16 women), 6 part-time (4 women); includes 10 minority (4 Asian, non-Hispanic/Latino; 6 Hispanic/Latino), 9 international. Average age 23. In 2011, 22 master's awarded. *Entrance requirements:* For master's, GMAT (minimum score 550), minimum GPA of 3.0. Additional exam requirements/recommendations for international students: Required—TOEFL (minimum score 580 paper-based; 237 computer-based; 92 iBT), TWE. *Expenses: Tuition:* Full-time $22,482; part-time $1249 per unit. *Required fees:* $224. Full-time tuition and fees vary according to course load and degree level. *Financial support:* In 2011–12, 10 students received support. Career-related internships or fieldwork, Federal Work-Study, institutionally sponsored loans, scholarships/grants, and unspecified assistantships available. Support available to part-time students. Financial award application deadline: 4/1; financial award applicants required to submit FAFSA. *Faculty research:* Accounting, financial report, taxation, and Sarbanes-Oxley. *Unit head:* Dr. Diane Pattison, Academic Director, Accountancy Programs, 619-260-4850, E-mail: pattison@sandiego.edu. *Application contact:* Monica Mahon, Associate Director of Graduate Admissions, 619-260-4524, Fax: 619-260-4158, E-mail: grads@sandiego.edu. Web site: http://www.sandiego.edu/business/centers/accountancy/.

University of San Diego, School of Law, San Diego, CA 92110-2492. Offers business and corporate law (LL M); comparative law (LL M); general studies (LL M); international law (LL M); law (JD); taxation (LL M, Diploma); JD/IMBA; JD/MA; JD/MBA. *Accreditation:* ABA. Part-time and evening/weekend programs available. *Faculty:* 55 full-time (19 women), 71 part-time/adjunct (21 women). *Students:* 896 full-time (445 women), 177 part-time (79 women); includes 341 minority (15 Black or African American, non-Hispanic/Latino; 4 American Indian or Alaska Native, non-Hispanic/Latino; 159 Asian, non-Hispanic/Latino; 114 Hispanic/Latino; 2 Native Hawaiian or other Pacific Islander, non-Hispanic/Latino; 47 Two or more races, non-Hispanic/Latino), 31 international. Average age 36. 4,314 applicants, 38% accepted, 300 enrolled. In 2011, 71 master's, 322 doctorates awarded. *Entrance requirements:* For master's, JD, LL B or equivalent from an ABA-accredited law school; for doctorate, LSAT, bachelor's degree. Additional exam requirements/recommendations for international students: Required—TOEFL (minimum score 600 paper-based; 250 computer-based; 98 iBT). *Application deadline:* For fall admission, 2/1 priority date for domestic students. Applications are processed on a rolling basis. Application fee: $50. Electronic applications accepted. *Expenses:* Contact institution. *Financial support:* In 2011–12, 627 students received support. Career-related internships or fieldwork, Federal Work-Study, institutionally sponsored loans, and scholarships/grants available. Support available to part-time students. Financial award application deadline: 3/1; financial award applicants required to submit FAFSA. *Unit head:* Dr. Stephen C. Ferruolo, Dean, 619-260-2330, Fax: 619-260-2218. *Application contact:* Jorge Garcia, Director of Admissions and Financial Aid, 619-260-4528, Fax: 619-260-2218, E-mail: jdinfo@sandiego.edu. Web site: http://www.sandiego.edu/usdlaw/.

University of Southern California, Graduate School, Marshall School of Business, Leventhal School of Accounting, Los Angeles, CA 90089. Offers accounting (M Acc); business taxation (MBT); JD/MBT. Part-time programs available. *Degree requirements:* For master's, 30-48 units of study. *Entrance requirements:* For master's, GMAT, undergraduate degree, communication skills. Additional exam requirements/recommendations for international students: Required—TOEFL (minimum score 100 computer-based). Electronic applications accepted. *Faculty research:* State and local taxation, Securities and Exchange Commission, governance, auditing fees, financial accounting, enterprise zones, women in business.

The University of Texas at Arlington, Graduate School, College of Business, Accounting Department, Arlington, TX 76019. Offers accounting (MP Acc, MS, PhD); taxation (MS). *Accreditation:* AACSB. Part-time and evening/weekend programs available. *Faculty:* 13 full-time (3 women). *Students:* 93 full-time (53 women), 129 part-time (59 women); includes 50 minority (11 Black or African American, non-Hispanic/Latino; 1 American Indian or Alaska Native, non-Hispanic/Latino; 21 Asian, non-Hispanic/Latino; 15 Hispanic/Latino; 2 Two or more races, non-Hispanic/Latino), 33 international. 169 applicants, 62% accepted, 55 enrolled. In 2011, 64 master's, 1 doctorate awarded. *Degree requirements:* For master's, thesis optional; for doctorate, comprehensive exam, thesis/dissertation. *Entrance requirements:* For master's and doctorate, GMAT. Additional exam requirements/recommendations for international students: Required—TOEFL (minimum score 550 paper-based; 213 computer-based; 79 iBT). *Application deadline:* For fall admission, 6/1 for domestic students, 4/1 for international students; for spring admission, 10/15 for domestic students, 9/15 for international students. Applications are processed on a rolling basis. Application fee: $40 ($70 for international students). *Financial support:* In 2011–12, 100 students received support, including 10 teaching assistantships (averaging $13,590 per year); fellowships, research assistantships, career-related internships or fieldwork, scholarships/grants, and unspecified assistantships also available. Financial award application deadline: 6/1; financial award applicants required to submit FAFSA. *Unit head:* Dr. Chandra Subramaniam, Chair, 817-272-7029, Fax: 817-282-5793, E-mail: subramaniam@uta.edu. *Application contact:* Carly S. Andrews, Graduate Advisor, 817-

272-3047, Fax: 817-272-5793, E-mail: graduate.accounting.advisor@uta.edu. Web site: http://www2.uta.edu/accounting/.

The University of Texas at Dallas, Naveen Jindal School of Management, Program in Accounting, Richardson, TX 75080. Offers assurance services (MS); corporate accounting (MS); internal audit (MS); taxation (MS). *Accreditation:* AACSB. *Faculty:* 16 full-time (4 women), 11 part-time/adjunct (5 women). *Students:* 398 full-time (258 women), 402 part-time (238 women); includes 136 minority (18 Black or African American, non-Hispanic/Latino; 1 American Indian or Alaska Native, non-Hispanic/Latino; 79 Asian, non-Hispanic/Latino; 28 Hispanic/Latino; 10 Two or more races, non-Hispanic/Latino), 411 international. Average age 28. 825 applicants, 59% accepted, 308 enrolled. In 2011, 314 master's awarded. *Entrance requirements:* For master's, GMAT, minimum GPA of 3.0 in upper-level course work in field. Additional exam requirements/recommendations for international students: Required—TOEFL (minimum score 550 paper-based; 215 computer-based). *Application deadline:* For fall admission, 7/15 for domestic students, 5/1 for international students; for spring admission, 11/15 for domestic students, 9/1 for international students. Applications are processed on a rolling basis. Application fee: $50 ($100 for international students). Electronic applications accepted. *Expenses:* Tuition, state resident: full-time $11,170; part-time $620.56 per credit hour. Tuition, nonresident: full-time $20,212; part-time $1122.89 per credit hour. *Financial support:* In 2011–12, 257 students received support, including 5 teaching assistantships with partial tuition reimbursements available (averaging $10,050 per year); research assistantships with partial tuition reimbursements available, career-related internships or fieldwork, Federal Work-Study, institutionally sponsored loans, scholarships/grants, and unspecified assistantships also available. Support available to part-time students. Financial award application deadline: 4/30; financial award applicants required to submit FAFSA. *Faculty research:* Privatization and accounting/auditing, corporate performance and executive compensation, risk management, information technology in accounting. *Unit head:* Amy Troutman, Associate Area Coordinator, 972-883-6719, Fax: 972-883-6823, E-mail: amybass@utdallas.edu. *Application contact:* Jennifer Johnson, Director, Graduate Accounting Programs, 972-883-5912, E-mail: jennifer.johnson@utdallas.edu. Web site: http://jindal.utdallas.edu/academic-areas/accounting/.

The University of Texas at San Antonio, College of Business, General Business Program, San Antonio, TX 78249-0617. Offers business (MBA); business administration (PhD), including accounting, business administration, finance, information technology, management and organization studies, marketing; information systems (MBA); international business (MBA); management accounting (MBA); management of technology (MBA); marketing management (MBA); taxation (MBA). *Students:* 170 full-time (52 women), 120 part-time (49 women); includes 90 minority (14 Black or African American, non-Hispanic/Latino; 2 American Indian or Alaska Native, non-Hispanic/Latino; 15 Asian, non-Hispanic/Latino; 55 Hispanic/Latino; 1 Native Hawaiian or other Pacific Islander, non-Hispanic/Latino; 3 Two or more races, non-Hispanic/Latino), 37 international. Average age 32. 395 applicants, 45% accepted, 133 enrolled. In 2011, 95 master's, 8 doctorates awarded. *Entrance requirements:* Additional exam requirements/recommendations for international students: Required—TOEFL (minimum score 500 paper-based; 61 iBT), IELTS (minimum score 5). *Application deadline:* For fall admission, 7/1 for domestic students, 4/1 for international students; for spring admission, 11/1 for domestic students, 9/1 for international students. Application fee: $45 ($85 for international students). *Expenses:* Tuition, state resident: full-time $3148; part-time $2176 per semester. Tuition, nonresident: full-time $8782; part-time $5932 per semester. *Required fees:* $719 per semester. *Financial support:* In 2011–12, fellowships (averaging $22,000 per year), research assistantships (averaging $10,000 per year), teaching assistantships (averaging $10,000 per year) were awarded. *Unit head:* Dr. Lynda Y. de la Vinna, Dean, 210-458-4317, Fax: 210-458-4308, E-mail: lynda.delavina@utsa.edu. *Application contact:* Katherine Pope, Director of Graduate Student Services, 210-458-7316, Fax: 210-458-4398, E-mail: katherine.pope@utsa.edu. Web site: http://business.utsa.edu.

University of the Pacific, McGeorge School of Law, Sacramento, CA 95817. Offers advocacy (JD); criminal justice (JD); experiential law teaching (LL M); intellectual property (JD); international legal studies (JD); international water resources law (LL M, JSD); law (JD); public law and policy (JD); public policy and law (LL M); tax (JD); transnational business practice (LL M); JD/MBA; JD/MPPA. *Accreditation:* ABA. Part-time and evening/weekend programs available. *Faculty:* 48 full-time (20 women), 59 part-time/adjunct (18 women). *Students:* 704 full-time (325 women), 255 part-time (122 women); includes 254 minority (19 Black or African American, non-Hispanic/Latino; 19 American Indian or Alaska Native, non-Hispanic/Latino; 151 Asian, non-Hispanic/Latino; 65 Hispanic/Latino), 41 international. Average age 27. 3,564 applicants, 38% accepted, 228 enrolled. In 2011, 36 master's, 307 doctorates awarded. *Degree requirements:* For master's, thesis (for some programs); for doctorate, thesis/dissertation (for some programs). *Entrance requirements:* For master's, JD; for doctorate, LSAT (for JD), LL M (for JSD). Additional exam requirements/recommendations for international students: Required—TOEFL (minimum score 600 paper-based; 250 computer-based; 100 iBT). *Application deadline:* For fall admission, 3/15 priority date for domestic students. Applications are processed on a rolling basis. Application fee: $50. Electronic applications accepted. *Expenses:* Contact institution. *Financial support:* Fellowships, research assistantships, teaching assistantships, career-related internships or fieldwork, Federal Work-Study, institutionally sponsored loans, and scholarships/grants available. Support available to part-time students. Financial award applicants required to submit FAFSA. *Faculty research:* International legal studies, public policy and law, advocacy, intellectual property law, taxation, criminal law. *Unit head:* Elizabeth Rindskopf Parker, Dean, 916-739-7151, E-mail: elizabeth@pacific.edu. *Application contact:* 916-739-7105, Fax: 916-739-7301, E-mail: mcgeorge@pacific.edu. Web site: http://www.mcgeorge.edu/.

University of the Sacred Heart, Graduate Programs, Department of Business Administration, Program in Taxation, San Juan, PR 00914-0383. Offers MBA. Part-time and evening/weekend programs available. *Degree requirements:* For master's, thesis. *Entrance requirements:* For master's, EXADEP, minimum undergraduate GPA of 2.75, interview.

University of Tulsa, Graduate School, Collins College of Business, Master of Business Administration Program, Tulsa, OK 74104-3189. Offers accounting (MBA); business administration (MBA); energy management (MBA); finance (MBA); international business (MBA); management information systems (MBA); taxation (MBA); JD/MBA; MBA/MSCS; MBA/MSF. *Accreditation:* AACSB. Part-time and evening/weekend programs available. *Faculty:* 32 full-time (6 women). *Students:* 56 full-time (29 women), 28 part-time (7 women); includes 7 minority (1 Black or African American, non-Hispanic/Latino; 2 American Indian or Alaska Native, non-Hispanic/Latino; 2 Asian, non-Hispanic/Latino; 2 Hispanic/Latino), 16 international. Average age 26. 70 applicants, 67% accepted, 29 enrolled. In 2011, 35 master's awarded. *Entrance requirements:* For master's, GMAT. Additional exam requirements/recommendations for international students: Required—TOEFL (minimum score 577 paper-based; 233 computer-based; 91 iBT), IELTS (minimum score 6.5). *Application deadline:* Applications are processed on a rolling basis. Application fee: $40. Electronic applications accepted. *Expenses: Tuition:* Full-time $17,748; part-time $986 per hour. *Required fees:* $5 per contact hour. $75 per semester. Tuition and fees vary according to program. *Financial support:* In 2011–12, 30 students received support, including 30 teaching assistantships (averaging $11,044 per year); fellowships, research assistantships, career-related internships or fieldwork, institutionally sponsored loans, scholarships/grants, health care benefits, tuition waivers (full and partial), and unspecified assistantships also available. Support available to part-time students. Financial award application deadline: 2/1; financial award applicants required to submit FAFSA. *Faculty research:* Accounting, energy management, finance, international business, management information systems, taxation. *Unit head:* Dr. Linda Nichols, Associate Dean of the Collins College of Business, 918-631-2242, Fax: 918-631-2142, E-mail: linda-nichols@utulsa.edu. *Application contact:* Information Contact, 918-631-2242, E-mail: graduate-business@utulsa.edu. Web site: http://www.cba.utulsa.edu/.

University of Tulsa, Graduate School, Collins College of Business, Online Program in Taxation, Tulsa, OK 74104-3189. Offers M Tax, JD/M Tax. Part-time and evening/weekend programs available. Postbaccalaureate distance learning degree programs offered (no on-campus study). *Faculty:* 4 full-time (2 women), 1 part-time/adjunct (0 women). *Students:* 3 full-time (all women), 31 part-time (16 women); includes 2 minority (1 Black or African American, non-Hispanic/Latino; 1 Asian, non-Hispanic/Latino). Average age 37. 21 applicants, 52% accepted, 8 enrolled. In 2011, 11 master's awarded. *Entrance requirements:* For master's, GMAT or LSAT. Additional exam requirements/recommendations for international students: Required—TOEFL (minimum score 577 paper-based; 233 computer-based; 91 iBT), IELTS (minimum score 6.5). *Application deadline:* Applications are processed on a rolling basis. Application fee: $40. Electronic applications accepted. *Expenses: Tuition:* Full-time $17,748; part-time $986 per hour. *Required fees:* $5 per contact hour. $75 per semester. Tuition and fees vary according to program. *Financial support:* Fellowships, research assistantships, teaching assistantships with partial tuition reimbursements, career-related internships or fieldwork, Federal Work-Study, institutionally sponsored loans, scholarships/grants, health care benefits, tuition waivers (full and partial), and unspecified assistantships available. Support available to part-time students. Financial award application deadline: 2/1; financial award applicants required to submit FAFSA. *Unit head:* Dr. Linda Nichols, Associate Dean of the Collins College of Business, 918-631-2242, Fax: 918-631-2142, E-mail: linda-nichols@utulsa.edu. *Application contact:* Information Contact, 918-631-2242, E-mail: graduate-business@utulsa.edu.

University of Washington, Graduate School, Michael G. Foster School of Business, Seattle, WA 98195-3233. Offers auditing and assurance (MP Acc); business (PhD); business administration (evening) (MBA); business administration (full-time) (MBA); executive business administration (MBA); global business administration (MBA); global executive business administration (MBA); taxation (MP Acc); technology management (MBA); JD/MBA; MBA/MAIS; MBA/MHA. *Accreditation:* AACSB. Part-time programs available. *Faculty:* 100 full-time (28 women), 55 part-time/adjunct (22 women). *Students:* 385 full-time (116 women), 483 part-time (118 women); includes 183 minority (16 Black or African American, non-Hispanic/Latino; 2 American Indian or Alaska Native, non-Hispanic/Latino; 133 Asian, non-Hispanic/Latino; 25 Hispanic/Latino; 2 Native Hawaiian or other Pacific Islander, non-Hispanic/Latino; 5 Two or more races, non-Hispanic/Latino), 178 international. Average age 32. 1,367 applicants, 76% accepted, 868 enrolled. In 2011, 458 master's, 12 doctorates awarded. Terminal master's awarded for partial completion of doctoral program. *Degree requirements:* For doctorate, comprehensive exam, thesis/dissertation. *Entrance requirements:* For master's, GMAT; for doctorate, GMAT, GRE. Additional exam requirements/recommendations for international students: Required—TOEFL (minimum score 600 paper-based; 250 computer-based; 100 iBT). *Application deadline:* For fall admission, 3/15 for domestic students, 1/20 for international students. Application fee: $75. Electronic applications accepted. *Expenses:* Contact institution. *Financial support:* Fellowships with partial tuition reimbursements, research assistantships with partial tuition reimbursements, teaching assistantships with partial tuition reimbursements, Federal Work-Study, institutionally sponsored loans, and scholarships/grants available. Financial award application deadline: 2/28; financial award applicants required to submit FAFSA. *Faculty research:* Finance, marketing, organizational behavior, information technology, strategy. *Unit head:* Dr. James Jiambalvo, Dean, 206-543-4750. *Application contact:* Erin Ernst, Assistant Director of Admissions, 206-543-4661, Fax: 206-616-7351, E-mail: mba@u.washington.edu. Web site: http://www.foster.washington.edu/mba.

University of Washington, Graduate School, School of Law, Seattle, WA 98195-3020. Offers Asian law (LL M, PhD); intellectual property law and policy (LL M); law (JD); law of sustainable international development (LL M); taxation (LL M); JD/LL M; JD/MA; JD/MAIS; JD/MBA; JD/MPA; JD/MS; JD/PhD. *Accreditation:* ABA. *Degree requirements:* For master's, thesis; for doctorate, thesis/dissertation (for some programs). *Entrance requirements:* For master's, language proficiency (LL M in Asian law); for doctorate, LSAT (for JD). Additional exam requirements/recommendations for international students: Required—TOEFL. *Expenses:* Contact institution. *Faculty research:* Asian, international and comparative law, intellectual property law, health law, environmental law, taxation.

University of Waterloo, Graduate Studies, Faculty of Arts, School of Accounting and Finance, Waterloo, ON N2L 3G1, Canada. Offers accounting (M Acc, PhD); finance (M Acc); taxation (M Tax). *Degree requirements:* For master's, thesis or alternative; for doctorate, thesis/dissertation. *Entrance requirements:* For master's, honors degree, minimum B average, resumé; for doctorate, GMAT, master's degree, minimum A-average, resume. Additional exam requirements/recommendations for international students: Required—TOEFL, TWE. Electronic applications accepted. *Expenses:* Contact institution. *Faculty research:* Auditing, management accounting.

University of Wisconsin–Madison, Graduate School, Wisconsin School of Business, Master of Accountancy Program, Madison, WI 53706-1380. Offers accountancy (M Acc); tax (M Acc). *Faculty:* 13 full-time (5 women). *Students:* 112 full-time (46 women); includes 9 minority (2 Black or African American, non-Hispanic/Latino; 5 Asian, non-Hispanic/Latino; 2 Hispanic/Latino), 13 international. Average age 22. 245 applicants, 43% accepted, 103 enrolled. In 2011, 87 degrees awarded. *Degree requirements:* For master's, minimum GPA of 3.0. *Entrance requirements:* For master's, GMAT, essays. Additional exam requirements/recommendations for international students: Required—TOEFL (minimum score 100 computer-based), Pearson Test of English. *Application deadline:* For fall admission, 9/15 for domestic and international students; for winter admission, 1/7 for domestic and international students. Application fee: $56. Electronic applications accepted. *Expenses:* Tuition, state resident: full-time $10,296; part-time $643.51 per credit. Tuition, nonresident: full-time $24,054; part-time $1503.40 per credit. *Required fees:* $70.06 per credit. Tuition and fees vary according to course load, campus/location, program and reciprocity agreements. *Financial support:* In 2011–12, 84 students received support, including 5 research assistantships with full tuition reimbursements available (averaging $4,695 per year), 32 teaching assistantships with full tuition reimbursements available (averaging $6,691 per year); career-related internships or fieldwork, scholarships/grants, and unspecified assistantships also available. Financial award application deadline: 5/1; financial award applicants required to submit FAFSA. *Faculty research:* Internal control deficiencies, impairment recognition, accounting misstatements, earnings restatements, voluntary disclosure. *Unit head:* Terry Warfield, Professor/Chair of Accounting and Information

Systems, 608-262-1028, E-mail: twarfield@bus.wisc.edu. *Application contact:* Kristen Ann Fuhremann, Director, 608-262-0316, Fax: 608-263-0477, E-mail: kfuhremann@bus.wisc.edu. Web site: http://bus.wisc.edu/degrees-programs/msmacc.

University of Wisconsin–Milwaukee, Graduate School, Sheldon B. Lubar School of Business, Milwaukee, WI 53201. Offers business administration (MBA); enterprise resource planning (Certificate); investment management (Certificate); management science (MS, PhD); nonprofit management and leadership (MS, Certificate); state and local taxation (Certificate); MS/MBA. *Accreditation:* AACSB. Part-time and evening/weekend programs available. *Faculty:* 50 full-time (11 women), 4 part-time/adjunct (2 women). *Students:* 293 full-time (100 women), 343 part-time (127 women); includes 73 minority (21 Black or African American, non-Hispanic/Latino; 2 American Indian or Alaska Native, non-Hispanic/Latino; 28 Asian, non-Hispanic/Latino; 3 Hispanic/Latino; 19 Two or more races, non-Hispanic/Latino), 66 international. Average age 32. 370 applicants, 46% accepted, 104 enrolled. In 2011, 255 master's, 9 doctorates awarded. *Degree requirements:* For master's, comprehensive exam (for some programs); for doctorate, comprehensive exam, thesis/dissertation. *Entrance requirements:* For master's and doctorate, GMAT or GRE General Test. Additional exam requirements/recommendations for international students: Required—TOEFL (minimum score 550 paper-based; 79 iBT), IELTS (minimum score 6.5). *Application deadline:* For fall admission, 1/1 priority date for domestic students; for spring admission, 9/1 for domestic students. Applications are processed on a rolling basis. Application fee: $56 ($96 for international students). Electronic applications accepted. *Expenses:* Contact institution. *Financial support:* In 2011–12, 5 fellowships with full tuition reimbursements, 2 research assistantships with full tuition reimbursements, 41 teaching assistantships with full tuition reimbursements were awarded; career-related internships or fieldwork, Federal Work-Study, health care benefits, unspecified assistantships, and project assistantships also available. Support available to part-time students. Financial award application deadline: 4/15; financial award applicants required to submit FAFSA. *Faculty research:* Applied management research in finance, MIS, marketing, operations research, organizational sciences. *Total annual research expenditures:* $620,657. *Unit head:* Timothy L. Smunt, Dean, 414-229-6256, Fax: 414-229-2372, E-mail: tsmunt@uwm.edu. *Application contact:* Matthew Jensen, 414-229-5403, E-mail: mba-ms@uwm.edu. Web site: http://www4.uwm.edu/business.

Villanova University, School of Law and Villanova School of Business, Tax Program, Villanova, PA 19085-1699. Offers LL M, JD/LL M. Part-time and evening/weekend programs available. *Entrance requirements:* For master's, LSAT, JD (LL M). Additional exam requirements/recommendations for international students: Required—TOEFL (minimum score 600 paper-based; 250 computer-based). *Expenses:* Contact institution. *Faculty research:* Taxation and estate planning, corporate tax planning, international taxation, state taxation.

Wake Forest University, Schools of Business, MS in Accountancy Program, Winston-Salem, NC 27106. Offers assurance services (MSA); tax consulting (MSA); transaction services (MSA). *Faculty:* 62 full-time (16 women), 41 part-time/adjunct (14 women). *Students:* 183 full-time (86 women); includes 33 minority (17 Black or African American, non-Hispanic/Latino; 1 American Indian or Alaska Native, non-Hispanic/Latino; 6 Asian, non-Hispanic/Latino; 9 Hispanic/Latino), 19 international. Average age 23. In 2011, 82 master's awarded. *Degree requirements:* For master's, 30 credit hours. *Entrance requirements:* For master's, GMAT, letters of recommendation, official transcripts, current resume or curriculum vitae. Additional exam requirements/recommendations for international students: Required—TOEFL (minimum score 600 paper-based; 250 computer-based; 100 iBT), Pearson Test of English. *Application deadline:* For fall admission, 6/1 for domestic and international students. Applications are processed on a rolling basis. Application fee: $100. Electronic applications accepted. *Financial support:* In 2011–12, 152 students received support. Career-related internships or fieldwork and scholarships/grants available. Financial award application deadline: 2/15; financial award applicants required to submit FAFSA. *Faculty research:* The influence of personal relationships on business decision-making and management of change; drivers of perceived value and consumer behavior; impact of accounting on auditing, financial, managerial, systems and taxation stakeholders; corporate governance and executive compensation; impact of operations strategies on competitiveness. *Unit head:* Jack Wilkerson, Senior Associate Dean of Accounting Programs, 336-758-5422, Fax: 336-758-5830, E-mail: busadmissions@wfu.edu. *Application contact:* Tamara Paquee, Administrative Assistant, 336-758-5422, Fax: 336-758-5830, E-mail: busadmissions@wfu.edu. Web site: http://www.business.wfu.edu/.

Walsh College of Accountancy and Business Administration, Graduate Programs, Program in Taxation, Troy, MI 48007-7006. Offers MST. Part-time and evening/weekend programs available. *Entrance requirements:* For master's, minimum GPA of 2.75, previous course work in individual income taxation and business. Additional exam requirements/recommendations for international students: Required—TOEFL. Electronic applications accepted.

Washington State University, Graduate School, College of Business, Department of Accounting, Pullman, WA 99164. Offers accounting and information systems (M Acc); accounting and taxation (M Acc). *Accreditation:* AACSB. *Faculty:* 9. *Students:* 53 full-time (31 women), 16 part-time (7 women); includes 57 minority (1 Black or African American, non-Hispanic/Latino; 54 Asian, non-Hispanic/Latino; 2 Hispanic/Latino), 21 international. Average age 24. 127 applicants, 39% accepted, 36 enrolled. In 2011, 25 master's awarded. *Degree requirements:* For master's, comprehensive exam (for some programs), thesis (for some programs), oral exam, research paper. *Entrance requirements:* For master's, GMAT (minimum score of 600), resume; statement of purpose identifying area of interest, experiences, and intended research focus; minimum GPA of 3.25. Additional exam requirements/recommendations for international students: Required—TOEFL (minimum score 580 paper-based; 237 computer-based), IELTS. *Application deadline:* For fall admission, 1/10 priority date for domestic students, 1/10 for international students. Applications are processed on a rolling basis. Application fee: $75. Electronic applications accepted. *Financial support:* In 2011–12, research assistantships (averaging $13,917 per year), 7 teaching assistantships with tuition reimbursements (averaging $18,204 per year) were awarded; Federal Work-Study, institutionally sponsored loans, tuition waivers (partial), and teaching associateships also available. Financial award application deadline: 3/1. *Faculty research:* Ethics, taxation, auditing. *Unit head:* Dr. John Sweeney, Chair, 509-335-8541, Fax: 509-335-4275, E-mail: jtsweeney@wsu.edu. *Application contact:* Graduate School Admissions, 800-GRADWSU, Fax: 509-335-1949, E-mail: gradsch@wsu.edu. Web site: http://www.business.wsu.edu/academics/Accounting/.

Wayne State University, Law School, Detroit, MI 48202. Offers corporate and finance law (LL M); labor and employment law (LL M); law (JD, PhD); taxation (LL M); United States law (LL M); JD/MA; JD/MADR; JD/MBA. *Accreditation:* ABA. Part-time and evening/weekend programs available. *Faculty:* 40 full-time (16 women), 21 part-time/adjunct (4 women). *Students:* 504 full-time (212 women), 96 part-time (45 women); includes 94 minority (36 Black or African American, non-Hispanic/Latino; 3 American Indian or Alaska Native, non-Hispanic/Latino; 38 Asian, non-Hispanic/Latino; 17 Hispanic/Latino), 14 international. Average age 27. 1,164 applicants, 45% accepted, 196 enrolled. In 2011, 17 master's, 198 doctorates awarded. *Degree requirements:* For master's, essay. *Entrance requirements:* For master's, JD; for doctorate, LSAT, LDAS report with LSAT scores, bachelor's degree from accredited institution, personal statement, transcripts from all U.S. undergraduate schools attended and an analysis and summary of the transcripts; letter of recommendation (up to two are accepted). Additional exam requirements/recommendations for international students: Required—TOEFL (minimum score 600 paper-based); Recommended—TWE. *Application deadline:* For fall admission, 3/15 priority date for domestic students, 3/15 for international students. Applications are processed on a rolling basis. Application fee: $50. Electronic applications accepted. *Expenses:* Contact institution. *Financial support:* Federal Work-Study and scholarships/grants available. Support available to part-time students. Financial award application deadline: 3/15; financial award applicants required to submit FAFSA. *Faculty research:* Constitutional law, intellectual property, commercial law, health law, tax law. *Total annual research expenditures:* $160,129. *Unit head:* Robert Ackerman, Dean, 313-577-9016, E-mail: ackerman@wayne.edu. *Application contact:* Erica M. Jackson, Assistant Dean of Admissions, 313-577-3937, E-mail: lawinquire@wayne.edu. Web site: http://www.law.wayne.edu/.

Wayne State University, School of Business Administration, Detroit, MI 48202. Offers accounting (MBA, MS); industrial relations (MBA); taxation (MST); JD/MBA. *Accreditation:* AACSB. Part-time and evening/weekend programs available. Postbaccalaureate distance learning degree programs offered. *Students:* 182 full-time (68 women), 731 part-time (305 women); includes 256 minority (144 Black or African American, non-Hispanic/Latino; 2 American Indian or Alaska Native, non-Hispanic/Latino; 85 Asian, non-Hispanic/Latino; 12 Hispanic/Latino; 13 Two or more races, non-Hispanic/Latino), 76 international. Average age 30. 675 applicants, 39% accepted, 181 enrolled. In 2011, 325 master's awarded. *Degree requirements:* For doctorate, thesis/dissertation. *Entrance requirements:* For master's, GMAT; for doctorate, GMAT (minimum score of 600), minimum undergraduate GPA 3.0, 3.5 upper-division or graduate; three letters of recommendation; brief essay. Additional exam requirements/recommendations for international students: Required—TOEFL (minimum score 550 paper-based; 213 computer-based); Recommended—TWE (minimum score 6). *Application deadline:* For fall admission, 6/1 priority date for domestic students, 5/1 for international students; for winter admission, 10/1 for domestic students, 9/1 for international students; for spring admission, 2/1 for domestic students, 1/1 for international students. Applications are processed on a rolling basis. Application fee: $50. Electronic applications accepted. *Expenses:* Tuition, state resident: part-time $512.85 per credit. Tuition, nonresident: part-time $1132.65 per credit. *Required fees:* $26.60 per credit. $199.65 per semester. Tuition and fees vary according to course load and program. *Financial support:* In 2011–12, 116 students received support, including 2 fellowships with tuition reimbursements available (averaging $18,000 per year), 2 teaching assistantships with tuition reimbursements available (averaging $1,800 per year); scholarships/grants, health care benefits, and unspecified assistantships also available. Support available to part-time students. Financial award applicants required to submit FAFSA. *Faculty research:* Corporate financial valuation, strategic advertising, information technology effectiveness, financial accounting and taxation, organizational performance and effectiveness. *Total annual research expenditures:* $257,637. *Unit head:* Dr. Margaret Williams, Interim Dean, 313-577-4501, Fax: 313-577-4557, E-mail: margaret.l.williams@wayne.edu. *Application contact:* Linda Zaddach, Assistant Dean, 313-577-4510, E-mail: l.s.zaddach@wayne.edu. Web site: http://business.wayne.edu/.

See Display on page 172 and Close-Up on page 261.

Weber State University, John B. Goddard School of Business and Economics, School of Accountancy, Ogden, UT 84408-1001. Offers accounting (M Acc); taxation (M Tax). *Accreditation:* AACSB. Part-time programs available. *Entrance requirements:* For master's, GMAT. *Faculty research:* Taxation, financial accounting, auditing, managerial accounting, accounting education.

Widener University, School of Business Administration, Program in Taxation, Chester, PA 19013-5792. Offers MS. Part-time and evening/weekend programs available. *Entrance requirements:* For master's, Certified Public Accountant Exam or GMAT. Electronic applications accepted. *Faculty research:* Financial planning, taxation fraud.

William Howard Taft University, Graduate Programs, W. Edwards Deming School of Business, Santa Ana, CA 92704. Offers taxation (MS).

Section 3
Advertising and Public Relations

This section contains a directory of institutions offering graduate work in electronic commerce. Additional information about programs listed in the directory but not augmented by an in-depth entry may be obtained by writing directly to the dean of a graduate school or chair of a department at the address given in the directory.

For programs offering related work, see also in this book *Business Administration and Management* and *Marketing.* In another guide in this series:

Graduate Programs in the Humanities, Arts & Social Sciences
See *Communication and Media*

CONTENTS

Program Directory

Advertising and Public Relations

Academy of Art University, Graduate Program, School of Advertising, San Francisco, CA 94105-3410. Offers MFA. Part-time programs available. Postbaccalaureate distance learning degree programs offered (no on-campus study). *Faculty:* 7 full-time (2 women), 28 part-time/adjunct (10 women). *Students:* 188 full-time (131 women), 99 part-time (59 women); includes 53 minority (22 Black or African American, non-Hispanic/Latino; 16 Asian, non-Hispanic/Latino; 13 Hispanic/Latino; 2 Two or more races, non-Hispanic/Latino), 118 international. Average age 28. 81 applicants. In 2011, 54 master's awarded. *Degree requirements:* For master's, final review. *Entrance requirements:* For master's, statement of intent; resume; portfolio/reel; official college transcripts. *Application deadline:* Applications are processed on a rolling basis. Application fee: $100. Electronic applications accepted. *Expenses: Tuition:* Full-time $20,160; part-time $840 per unit. *Required fees:* $90. *Financial support:* Career-related internships or fieldwork and Federal Work-Study available. Support available to part-time students. Financial award application deadline: 8/10; financial award applicants required to submit FAFSA. *Unit head:* 800-544-ARTS. *Application contact:* 800-544-ARTS, Fax: 415-263-4130, E-mail: info@academyart.edu. Web site: http://www.academyart.edu/advertising-school/index.html.

Ball State University, Graduate School, College of Communication, Information, and Media, Department of Journalism, Muncie, IN 47306-1099. Offers journalism (MA); public relations (MA). *Faculty:* 19 full-time (6 women), 1 part-time/adjunct (0 women). *Students:* 27 full-time (17 women), 44 part-time (27 women); includes 7 minority (5 Black or African American, non-Hispanic/Latino; 1 Asian, non-Hispanic/Latino; 1 Hispanic/Latino), 9 international. Average age 26. 65 applicants, 58% accepted, 15 enrolled. In 2011, 19 master's awarded. *Entrance requirements:* For master's, resume. Application fee: $50. Tuition and fees vary according to program and reciprocity agreements. *Financial support:* In 2011–12, 26 students received support, including 18 teaching assistantships with full tuition reimbursements available (averaging $7,703 per year); career-related internships or fieldwork also available. Financial award application deadline: 3/1. *Faculty research:* Image studies, readership surveys, audience perception studies. *Unit head:* William J. Willis, Chairperson, 765-285-8200, Fax: 765-285-7997. *Application contact:* Dan Waechter, Information Contact, 765-285-8200, Fax: 765-285-7997, E-mail: dwaechter@bsu.edu. Web site: http://www.bsu.edu/jounalism/.

Boston University, College of Communication, Department of Mass Communication, Advertising, and Public Relations, Boston, MA 02215. Offers advertising (MS); communication research (MS); communication studies (MS); public relations (MS); JD/MS. Part-time programs available. *Faculty:* 20 full-time, 28 part-time/adjunct. *Students:* 91 full-time (75 women), 44 part-time (29 women); includes 13 minority (3 Black or African American, non-Hispanic/Latino; 4 Asian, non-Hispanic/Latino; 6 Hispanic/Latino), 23 international. Average age 25. In 2011, 18 master's awarded. *Degree requirements:* For master's, comprehensive exam (for some programs), thesis (for some programs). *Entrance requirements:* For master's, GRE General Test, samples of written work. Additional exam requirements/recommendations for international students: Required—TOEFL (minimum score 600 paper-based; 250 computer-based; 100 iBT). *Application deadline:* For fall admission, 2/1 for domestic and international students. Application fee: $70. Electronic applications accepted. *Expenses: Tuition:* Full-time $40,848; part-time $1276 per credit hour. *Required fees:* $572; $286 per semester. *Financial support:* Research assistantships, teaching assistantships with partial tuition reimbursements, career-related internships or fieldwork, Federal Work-Study, institutionally sponsored loans, scholarships/grants, and unspecified assistantships available. Support available to part-time students. Financial award application deadline: 2/1; financial award applicants required to submit FAFSA. *Unit head:* T. Barton Carter, Chairman, 617-353-3482, E-mail: comlaw@bu.edu. *Application contact:* Manny Dotel, Administrator of Graduate Services, 617-353-3481, Fax: 617-358-0399, E-mail: comgrad@bu.edu. Web site: http://www.bu.edu/com/academics/masscomm-ad-pr/.

Boston University, Metropolitan College, Program in Advertising, Boston, MA 02215. Offers MS. Part-time and evening/weekend programs available. *Faculty:* 9 part-time/adjunct (3 women). *Students:* 32 part-time (21 women); includes 1 minority (Black or African American, non-Hispanic/Latino). Average age 28. In 2011, 39 master's awarded. *Entrance requirements:* For master's, undergraduate degree in appropriate field of study. *Application deadline:* Applications are processed on a rolling basis. Application fee: $70. Electronic applications accepted. *Expenses: Tuition:* Full-time $40,848; part-time $1276 per credit hour. *Required fees:* $572; $286 per semester. *Financial support:* Unspecified assistantships available. Support available to part-time students. Financial award applicants required to submit FAFSA. *Faculty research:* Communication and advertising. *Unit head:* Dr. Christopher Cakebread, Associate Professor, 617-353-3476, E-mail: ccakebr@bu.edu. *Application contact:* Sonia M. Parker, Assistant Dean, 617-353-2975, Fax: 617-353-2686, E-mail: soparker@bu.edu. Web site: http://www.bu.edu/met/advertising.

California State University, Fullerton, Graduate Studies, College of Communications, Department of Communications, Fullerton, CA 92834-9480. Offers advertising (MA); communications (MFA); entertainment and tourism (MA); journalism (MA); public relations (MA). Part-time programs available. *Students:* 31 full-time (21 women), 37 part-time (27 women); includes 23 minority (4 Black or African American, non-Hispanic/Latino; 8 Asian, non-Hispanic/Latino; 9 Hispanic/Latino; 2 Two or more races, non-Hispanic/Latino), 7 international. Average age 29. 96 applicants, 35% accepted, 22 enrolled. In 2011, 38 master's awarded. *Degree requirements:* For master's, project or thesis. *Entrance requirements:* For master's, GRE General Test. Application fee: $55. *Financial support:* Teaching assistantships, career-related internships or fieldwork, Federal Work-Study, institutionally sponsored loans, and scholarships/grants available. Support available to part-time students. Financial award application deadline: 3/1; financial award applicants required to submit FAFSA. *Unit head:* Dr. Tony Fellow, Chair, 657-278-3517. *Application contact:* Coordinator, 657-278-3832.

Central Connecticut State University, School of Graduate Studies, School of Arts and Sciences, Department of Communication, New Britain, CT 06050-4010. Offers organizational communication (MS); public relations/promotions (Certificate). Part-time and evening/weekend programs available. *Faculty:* 12 full-time (4 women), 5 part-time/adjunct (1 woman). *Students:* 6 full-time (1 woman), 29 part-time (21 women); includes 6 minority (3 Black or African American, non-Hispanic/Latino; 2 Hispanic/Latino; 1 Two or more races, non-Hispanic/Latino), 1 international. Average age 32. 28 applicants, 75% accepted, 17 enrolled. In 2011, 9 master's, 1 other advanced degree awarded. *Degree requirements:* For master's, comprehensive exam, thesis or alternative; for Certificate, qualifying exam. *Entrance requirements:* For master's, minimum undergraduate GPA of 3.0. Additional exam requirements/recommendations for international students: Required—TOEFL (minimum score 550 paper-based; 213 computer-based). *Application deadline:* For fall admission, 6/1 for domestic students, 5/1 for international students; for spring admission, 11/1 for domestic and international students. Applications are processed on a rolling basis. Application fee: $50. Electronic applications accepted. *Expenses: Tuition, area resident:* Full-time $5137; part-time $482 per credit. Tuition, state resident: full-time $7707; part-time $494 per credit. Tuition, nonresident: full-time $14,311; part-time $494 per credit. *Required fees:* $3865. One-time fee: $62 part-time. *Financial support:* In 2011–12, 5 students received support, including 2 research assistantships; career-related internships or fieldwork, Federal Work-Study, scholarships/grants, and unspecified assistantships also available. Support available to part-time students. Financial award application deadline: 4/15; financial award applicants required to submit FAFSA. *Faculty research:* Organizational communication, mass communication, intercultural communication, political communication, information management. *Unit head:* Dr. Glynis Fitzgerald, Chair, 860-832-2690, E-mail: fitzgeraldg@ccsu.edu. *Application contact:* Patricia Gardner, Associate Director of Graduate Studies, 860-832-2350, Fax: 860-832-2352, E-mail: graduateadmissions@ccsu.edu. Web site: http://www.ccsu.edu/page.cfm?p=8896.

Clarion University of Pennsylvania, Office of Graduate Programs, Department of Communication, Clarion, PA 16214. Offers mass media arts and journalism (MS); public relations (Certificate). Part-time programs available. *Students:* 18 full-time (13 women), 38 part-time (27 women); includes 16 minority (9 Black or African American, non-Hispanic/Latino; 1 American Indian or Alaska Native, non-Hispanic/Latino; 5 Hispanic/Latino; 1 Two or more races, non-Hispanic/Latino), 1 international. Average age 32. In 2011, 6 master's awarded. *Degree requirements:* For master's, comprehensive exam, thesis or alternative. *Entrance requirements:* For master's, minimum QPA of 3.0. Additional exam requirements/recommendations for international students: Required—TOEFL (minimum score 600 paper-based; 250 computer-based; 100 iBT). *Application deadline:* For fall admission, 8/1 priority date for domestic students, 4/15 for international students; for spring admission, 12/1 priority date for domestic students, 9/15 for international students. Applications are processed on a rolling basis. Application fee: $30. Electronic applications accepted. *Expenses:* Tuition, state resident: part-time $429 per credit. Tuition, nonresident: part-time $644 per credit. *Financial support:* Research assistantships with full tuition reimbursements available. Support available to part-time students. Financial award application deadline: 3/1. *Unit head:* Dr. Myrna Kuehn, Chair, 814-393-2245, Fax: 814-393-2186. *Application contact:* Dr. Brenda Sanders Dede, Assistant Vice President for Academic Affairs, 814-393-2337, Fax: 814-393-2030, E-mail: bdede@clarion.edu. Web site: http://www.clarion.edu/1063/.

Colorado State University, Graduate School, College of Liberal Arts, Department of Journalism and Technical Communication, Fort Collins, CO 80523-1785. Offers public communication and technology (MS, PhD); technical communication (MS). Part-time programs available. *Faculty:* 15 full-time (5 women). *Students:* 25 full-time (17 women), 37 part-time (26 women); includes 5 minority (3 Hispanic/Latino; 2 Two or more races, non-Hispanic/Latino), 6 international. Average age 33. 44 applicants, 36% accepted, 11 enrolled. In 2011, 10 master's awarded. *Degree requirements:* For master's, variable foreign language requirement, comprehensive exam (for some programs), thesis (for some programs); for doctorate, variable foreign language requirement, comprehensive exam (for some programs), thesis/dissertation (for some programs). *Entrance requirements:* For master's, GRE General Test, samples of written work, letters of recommendation, resume or curriculum vitae, 3 writing/communication projects; for doctorate, GRE General Test, master's degree, minimum GPA of 3.0, scholarly/professional work, letters of recommendation, statement of career plans, resume. Additional exam requirements/recommendations for international students: Required—TOEFL (minimum score 550 paper-based; 213 computer-based; 80 iBT). *Application deadline:* For fall admission, 2/15 priority date for domestic students, 12/15 for international students; for spring admission, 6/15 priority date for domestic students. Applications are processed on a rolling basis. Application fee: $50. Electronic applications accepted. *Expenses:* Tuition, state resident: full-time $7992. Tuition, nonresident: full-time $19,592. *Required fees:* $1735; $58 per credit. *Financial support:* In 2011–12, 35 students received support, including 1 fellowship with partial tuition reimbursement available (averaging $29,625 per year), 3 research assistantships with full and partial tuition reimbursements available (averaging $10,317 per year), 31 teaching assistantships with partial tuition reimbursements available (averaging $12,999 per year); career-related internships or fieldwork, Federal Work-Study, institutionally sponsored loans, scholarships/grants, traineeships, and unspecified assistantships also available. Support available to part-time students. Financial award application deadline: 3/1; financial award applicants required to submit FAFSA. *Faculty research:* Technical/science communication, public relations, health/risk communication, Web/new media technologies, environmental communication. *Total annual research expenditures:* $260,187. *Unit head:* Dr. Greg Luft, Chair, 970-491-1979, Fax: 970-491-2908, E-mail: greg.luft@colostate.edu. *Application contact:* Dr. Craig Trumbo, Graduate Program Coordinator, 970-491-2077, Fax: 970-491-2908, E-mail: craig.trumbo@colostate.edu. Web site: http://journalism.colostate.edu/.

DePaul University, College of Communication, Chicago, IL 60604-2287. Offers health communication (MA); journalism (MA); media and cinema studies (MA); organizational and multicultural communication (MA); public relations and advertising (MA); relational communication (MA). Part-time and evening/weekend programs available. *Faculty:* 51 full-time (28 women), 67 part-time/adjunct (41 women). *Students:* 193 full-time (152 women), 67 part-time (47 women); includes 80 minority (38 Black or African American, non-Hispanic/Latino; 15 Asian, non-Hispanic/Latino; 16 Hispanic/Latino; 1 Native Hawaiian or other Pacific Islander, non-Hispanic/Latino; 10 Two or more races, non-Hispanic/Latino), 14 international. Average age 27. *Degree requirements:* For master's, comprehensive exam or thesis/project. *Entrance requirements:* For master's, GRE General Test (for public relations and advertising), minimum GPA of 3.0, writing sample, letters of recommendation, resume, statement of purpose. Additional exam requirements/recommendations for international students: Required—TOEFL (minimum score 590 paper-based; 243 computer-based; 96 iBT). Application fee: $40. Electronic applications accepted. *Financial support:* Career-related internships or fieldwork, scholarships/grants, and tuition waivers (partial) available. Financial award applicants required to submit FAFSA. *Unit head:* Dr. Jacqueline Taylor, Dean, 773-325-7315. Web site: http://communication.depaul.edu/.

Emerson College, Graduate Studies, School of Communication, Department of Marketing Communication, Boston, MA 02116-4624. Offers global marketing communication and advertising (MA); integrated marketing communication (MA). *Entrance requirements:* For master's, GMAT or GRE General Test. Additional exam requirements/recommendations for international students: Required—TOEFL (minimum score 550 paper-based; 213 computer-based; 80 iBT), IELTS (minimum score 6.5). Electronic applications accepted.

George Mason University, College of Visual and Performing Arts, Program in Arts Management, Fairfax, VA 22030. Offers arts management (MA); entrepreneurship (Certificate); fund-raising and development in the arts (Certificate); marketing and public relations in the arts (Certificate); programming and project management (Certificate). *Accreditation:* NASAD. *Faculty:* 2 full-time (both women), 8 part-time/adjunct (3 women). *Students:* 48 full-time (40 women), 37 part-time (34 women); includes 17 minority (6

Black or African American, non-Hispanic/Latino; 4 Asian, non-Hispanic/Latino; 3 Hispanic/Latino; 4 Two or more races, non-Hispanic/Latino), 9 international. Average age 29. 105 applicants, 54% accepted, 22 enrolled. In 2011, 44 master's, 21 other advanced degrees awarded. *Degree requirements:* For master's, internship. *Entrance requirements:* For master's and Certificate, GRE (recommended), undergraduate degree with minimum GPA of 3.0, official transcripts, 2 letters of recommendation, statement of purpose, resume. Additional exam requirements/recommendations for international students: Required—TOEFL (minimum score 570 paper-based; 230 computer-based; 88 iBT), IELTS, Pearson Test of English. *Application deadline:* For fall admission, 3/1 for domestic students, 2/15 for international students; for spring admission, 10/15 for domestic students, 9/15 for international students. Application fee: $65 ($80 for international students). Electronic applications accepted. *Expenses:* Tuition, state resident: full-time $8750; part-time $364.58 per credit. Tuition, nonresident: full-time $24,092; part-time $1003.83 per credit. *Required fees:* $2514; $104.75 per credit. *Financial support:* In 2011–12, 2 students received support, including 2 teaching assistantships with full and partial tuition reimbursements available (averaging $8,649 per year); career-related internships or fieldwork, Federal Work-Study, scholarships/grants, unspecified assistantships, and health care benefits (full-time research and teaching assistantship recipient) also available. Financial award application deadline: 3/1; financial award applicants required to submit FAFSA. *Faculty research:* Information technology for arts managers, special topics in arts management, directions in gallery management, arts in society, public relations/marketing strategies for art organizations. *Unit head:* Richard Kamenitzer, Director, 703-993-9194, Fax: 703-993-9829, E-mail: rkamenit@gmu.edu. *Application contact:* Mathilde Speier, Information Contact, 703-993-8926, Fax: 703-993-9829, E-mail: mspeier@gmu.edu. Web site: http://artsmanagement.gmu.edu/arts-management-ma/.

Georgetown University, Graduate School of Arts and Sciences, School of Continuing Studies, Program in Public Relations and Corporate Communications, Washington, DC 20057. Offers MPS. *Degree requirements:* For master's, capstone course.

Golden Gate University, Ageno School of Business, San Francisco, CA 94105-2968. Offers accounting (MBA); business administration (EMBA, MBA, PMBA, DBA); finance (MBA, MS, Certificate); financial planning (MS, Certificate); healthcare information systems (Certificate); human resource management (MBA, MS); human resources management (Certificate); information systems (MS); information technology (MBA); information technology management (Certificate); integrated marketing and communications (MS, Certificate); international business (MBA); management (MBA); marketing (MBA, MS, Certificate); operations supply chain management (Certificate); psychology (MA, Certificate); public administration (EMPA); public relations (MS, Certificate); technical market analysis (Certificate); JD/MBA. Part-time and evening/weekend programs available. *Faculty:* 19 full-time (6 women), 241 part-time/adjunct (72 women). *Students:* 397 full-time (230 women), 779 part-time (432 women); includes 376 minority (105 Black or African American, non-Hispanic/Latino; 5 American Indian or Alaska Native, non-Hispanic/Latino; 161 Asian, non-Hispanic/Latino; 77 Hispanic/Latino; 12 Native Hawaiian or other Pacific Islander, non-Hispanic/Latino; 16 Two or more races, non-Hispanic/Latino), 265 international. Average age 34. 871 applicants, 64% accepted, 271 enrolled. In 2011, 550 master's, 13 doctorates awarded. *Degree requirements:* For doctorate, thesis/dissertation, qualifying examination. *Entrance requirements:* For master's, GMAT (MBA), minimum GPA of 2.5 (MS). Additional exam requirements/recommendations for international students: Required—TOEFL (minimum score 550 paper-based; 213 computer-based; 79 iBT). *Application deadline:* For fall admission, 5/15 for domestic and international students; for winter admission, 1/15 for domestic and international students; for spring admission, 9/15 for domestic and international students. Applications are processed on a rolling basis. Application fee: $70 ($110 for international students). Electronic applications accepted. *Expenses:* Contact institution. *Financial support:* Career-related internships or fieldwork, Federal Work-Study, institutionally sponsored loans, and scholarships/grants available. Support available to part-time students. Financial award applicants required to submit FAFSA. *Unit head:* Dr. Paul Fouts, Dean, 415-442-7026, Fax: 415-442-6579. *Application contact:* Angela Melero, Enrollment Services, 415-442-7800, Fax: 415-442-7807, E-mail: info@ggu.edu. Web site: http://www.ggu.edu/programs/business-and-management.

Immaculata University, College of Graduate Studies, Program in Applied Communication, Immaculata, PA 19345. Offers MA. Part-time and evening/weekend programs available. *Entrance requirements:* For master's, GRE, MAT. Additional exam requirements/recommendations for international students: Required—TOEFL, IELTS. Electronic applications accepted.

Iona College, School of Arts and Science, Department of Mass Communication, New Rochelle, NY 10801-1890. Offers non-profit public relations (Advanced Certificate); public relations (MA). *Accreditation:* ACEJMC (one or more programs are accredited). Part-time programs available. *Faculty:* 7 full-time (3 women), 2 part-time/adjunct (both women). *Students:* 11 full-time (9 women), 43 part-time (36 women); includes 15 minority (5 Black or African American, non-Hispanic/Latino; 1 Asian, non-Hispanic/Latino; 9 Hispanic/Latino), 3 international. Average age 27. 30 applicants, 60% accepted, 11 enrolled. In 2011, 18 master's, 2 other advanced degrees awarded. *Degree requirements:* For master's, comprehensive exam or thesis. *Entrance requirements:* For master's, GRE General Test, minimum GPA of 3.0. Additional exam requirements/recommendations for international students: Required—TOEFL (minimum score 550 paper-based; 213 computer-based). *Application deadline:* Applications are processed on a rolling basis. Application fee: $50. Electronic applications accepted. *Expenses:* Contact institution. *Financial support:* Career-related internships or fieldwork, scholarships/grants, tuition waivers (partial), and unspecified assistantships available. Support available to part-time students. Financial award application deadline: 4/15; financial award applicants required to submit FAFSA. *Faculty research:* Media ecology, new media, corporate communication, media images, organizational learning in public relations. *Unit head:* Br. Raymond Smith, Chair, 914-633-2354, E-mail: rrsmith@iona.edu. *Application contact:* Dr. Jeanne Zaino, Interim Dean, School of Arts and Science, 914-633-2112, Fax: 914-633-2023, E-mail: jzaino@iona.edu.

Kansas State University, Graduate School, College of Arts and Sciences, A. Q. Miller School of Journalism and Mass Communications, Manhattan, KS 66506. Offers advertising (MS); community journalism (MS); global communication (MS); health communication (MS); media management (MS); public relations (MS); risk communication (MS); strategic communications (MS). Part-time and evening/weekend programs available. *Faculty:* 15 full-time (7 women). *Students:* 13 full-time (9 women), 9 part-time (3 women); includes 3 minority (all Hispanic/Latino), 4 international. Average age 31. 22 applicants, 82% accepted, 7 enrolled. In 2011, 8 degrees awarded. *Degree requirements:* For master's, comprehensive exam, thesis. *Entrance requirements:* For master's, GRE General Test, minimum GPA of 3.0. Additional exam requirements/recommendations for international students: Required—TOEFL (minimum score 79 iBT). *Application deadline:* For fall admission, 2/1 priority date for domestic students, 2/1 for international students; for spring admission, 8/1 priority date for domestic students, 8/1 for international students. Applications are processed on a rolling basis. Application fee: $40 ($55 for international students). Electronic applications accepted. *Financial support:* In 2011–12, 10 students received support, including 3 research assistantships with full tuition reimbursements available (averaging $7,500 per year), 7 teaching assistantships with full tuition reimbursements available (averaging $7,500 per year); scholarships/grants, health care benefits, unspecified assistantships, and health insurance assistance also available. Financial award application deadline: 2/1; financial award applicants required to submit FAFSA. *Faculty research:* Health communication, risk communication, strategic communications, community journalism, global communication. *Total annual research expenditures:* $142,828. *Unit head:* Louise Benjamin, Director, 785-532-0959, Fax: 785-532-5484. *Application contact:* Dr. Nancy Muturi, Associate Director of Graduate Studies, 785-532-3890, Fax: 785-532-5484, E-mail: nmuturi@ksu.edu. Web site: http://jmc.ksu.edu/.

Lasell College, Graduate and Professional Studies in Communication, Newton, MA 02466-2709. Offers health communication (MSC); integrated marketing communication (MSC, Graduate Certificate); public relations (MSC, Graduate Certificate). Part-time and evening/weekend programs available. Postbaccalaureate distance learning degree programs offered (minimal on-campus study). *Faculty:* 3 full-time (all women), 4 part-time/adjunct (2 women). *Students:* 18 full-time (16 women), 29 part-time (26 women); includes 17 minority (7 Black or African American, non-Hispanic/Latino; 1 American Indian or Alaska Native, non-Hispanic/Latino; 2 Asian, non-Hispanic/Latino; 7 Hispanic/Latino), 7 international. Average age 30. 44 applicants, 68% accepted, 15 enrolled. In 2011, 10 master's awarded. *Entrance requirements:* For master's and Graduate Certificate, bachelor's degree from an accredited institution. Additional exam requirements/recommendations for international students: Required—TOEFL (minimum score 550 paper-based; 79 iBT), IELTS. *Application deadline:* For fall admission, 8/31 priority date for domestic students, 6/30 for international students; for spring admission, 12/31 priority date for domestic students, 10/31 for international students. Applications are processed on a rolling basis. Electronic applications accepted. *Expenses: Tuition:* Part-time $575 per credit. *Required fees:* $70 per semester. *Financial support:* Available to part-time students. Application deadline: 8/31; applicants required to submit FAFSA. *Unit head:* Dr. Joan Dolamore, Dean of Graduate and Professional Studies, 617-243-2485, Fax: 617-243-2450, E-mail: gradinfo@lasell.edu. *Application contact:* Adrienne Franciosi, Director of Graduate Admission, 617-243-2214, Fax: 617-243-2450, E-mail: gradinfo@lasell.edu. Web site: http://www.lasell.edu/Academics/Graduate-and-Professional-Studies/MS-in-Communication.html.

Lasell College, Graduate and Professional Studies in Management, Newton, MA 02466-2709. Offers elder care administration (MSM, Graduate Certificate); elder care marketing (MSM, Graduate Certificate); fundraising management (MSM, Graduate Certificate); human resource management (Graduate Certificate); human resources management (MSM); integrated marketing communication (Graduate Certificate); management (MSM, Graduate Certificate); marketing (MSM, Graduate Certificate); non-profit management (MSM, Graduate Certificate); project management (MSM, Graduate Certificate); public relations (Graduate Certificate). Part-time and evening/weekend programs available. Postbaccalaureate distance learning degree programs offered (no on-campus study). *Faculty:* 9 full-time (7 women), 20 part-time/adjunct (13 women). *Students:* 23 full-time (16 women), 92 part-time (65 women); includes 74 minority (8 Black or African American, non-Hispanic/Latino; 4 American Indian or Alaska Native, non-Hispanic/Latino; 53 Asian, non-Hispanic/Latino; 9 Hispanic/Latino), 14 international. Average age 30. 78 applicants, 67% accepted, 31 enrolled. In 2011, 49 master's, 7 other advanced degrees awarded. *Entrance requirements:* For master's and Graduate Certificate, bachelor's degree from an accredited institution. Additional exam requirements/recommendations for international students: Required—TOEFL (minimum score 550 paper-based; 213 computer-based; 79 iBT). *Application deadline:* For fall admission, 8/31 priority date for domestic students, 6/30 for international students; for spring admission, 12/31 priority date for domestic students, 10/31 for international students. Applications are processed on a rolling basis. Electronic applications accepted. *Expenses: Tuition:* Part-time $575 per credit. *Required fees:* $70 per semester. *Financial support:* Available to part-time students. Application deadline: 8/31; applicants required to submit FAFSA. *Unit head:* Dr. Joan Dolamore, Dean of Graduate and Professional Studies, 617-243-2485, Fax: 617-243-2450, E-mail: gradinfo@lasell.edu. *Application contact:* Adrienne Franciosi, Director of Graduate Admission, 617-243-2214, Fax: 617-243-2450, E-mail: gradinfo@lasell.edu. Web site: http://www.lasell.edu/Academics/Graduate-and-Professional-Studies/MS-in-Management.html.

La Sierra University, College of Arts and Sciences, Department of English and Communication, Riverside, CA 92515. Offers communication (MA), including public relations/advertising, theory emphasis; English (MA), including literary emphasis, writing emphasis. Part-time programs available. *Degree requirements:* For master's, one foreign language. *Entrance requirements:* For master's, GRE General Test.

Marquette University, Graduate School, College of Communication, Milwaukee, WI 53201-1881. Offers advertising and public relations (MA); broadcasting and electronic communications (MA); communications studies (MA); digital storytelling (Certificate); health, environment, science and sustainability (MA); journalism (MA); mass communications (MA). *Accreditation:* ACEJMC (one or more programs are accredited). Part-time and evening/weekend programs available. *Faculty:* 35 full-time (19 women), 37 part-time/adjunct (17 women). *Students:* 25 full-time (12 women), 30 part-time (22 women); includes 3 minority (2 Black or African American, non-Hispanic/Latino; 1 Two or more races, non-Hispanic/Latino), 6 international. Average age 29. 97 applicants, 45% accepted, 21 enrolled. In 2011, 21 master's, 6 other advanced degrees awarded. *Degree requirements:* For master's, comprehensive exam, thesis or alternative. *Entrance requirements:* For master's, GRE, official transcripts from all current and previous colleges/universities except Marquette, three letters of recommendation, statement of academic and professional goals. Additional exam requirements/recommendations for international students: Required—TOEFL (minimum score 530 paper-based; 78 computer-based). *Application deadline:* Applications are processed on a rolling basis. Application fee: $50. Electronic applications accepted. *Expenses: Tuition:* Full-time $17,010; part-time $945 per credit hour. Tuition and fees vary according to program. *Financial support:* In 2011–12, 41 students received support, including 2 fellowships with partial tuition reimbursements available (averaging $10,385 per year), 6 research assistantships with full tuition reimbursements available (averaging $13,285 per year), 12 teaching assistantships with full tuition reimbursements available (averaging $13,285 per year); career-related internships or fieldwork, scholarships/grants, health care benefits, tuition waivers (full and partial), and unspecified assistantships also available. Support available to part-time students. Financial award application deadline: 2/15. *Faculty research:* Urban journalism, gender and communication, intercultural communication, religious communication. *Total annual research expenditures:* $10,178. *Unit head:* Dr. Lori Bergen, Dean, 414-288-7133, Fax: 414-288-1578. *Application contact:* Craig Pierce, Assistant Dean of the Graduate School, 414-288-5740, Fax: 414-288-1902, E-mail: craig.pierce@marquette.edu. Web site: http://www.marquette.edu/comm/grad/index.shtml.

Michigan State University, The Graduate School, College of Communication Arts and Sciences, Department of Advertising, Public Relations and Retailing, East Lansing, MI 48824. Offers advertising (MA); public relations (MA); retailing (MS, PhD). *Entrance requirements:* Additional exam requirements/recommendations for international students: Required—TOEFL. Electronic applications accepted.

Advertising and Public Relations

Mississippi College, Graduate School, College of Arts and Sciences, School of Christian Studies and the Arts, Department of Communication, Clinton, MS 39058. Offers applied communication (MSC); public relations and corporate communication (MSC). Part-time programs available. *Degree requirements:* For master's, comprehensive exam, thesis optional. *Entrance requirements:* For master's, GRE or NTE, minimum GPA of 2.5. Additional exam requirements/recommendations for international students: Recommended—TOEFL, IELTS. Electronic applications accepted.

Monmouth University, The Graduate School, Department of Corporate and Public Communication, West Long Branch, NJ 07764-1898. Offers corporate and public communication (MA); human resources communication (Certificate); public relations (Certificate); public service communication specialist (Certificate). Part-time and evening/weekend programs available. *Faculty:* 9 full-time (6 women). *Students:* 6 full-time (4 women), 40 part-time (32 women); includes 4 minority (3 Black or African American, non-Hispanic/Latino; 1 Hispanic/Latino), 3 international. Average age 32. 22 applicants, 91% accepted, 12 enrolled. In 2011, 15 master's awarded. *Degree requirements:* For master's, comprehensive exam, project. *Entrance requirements:* For master's, GRE, minimum GPA of 3.0 in major, 2.75 overall. Additional exam requirements/recommendations for international students: Required—TOEFL (minimum score 550 paper-based; 213 computer-based; 79 iBT), IELTS (minimum score 5), Michigan English Language Assessment Battery (minimum score 77), Cambridge A, B, C. *Application deadline:* For fall admission, 7/15 priority date for domestic students, 6/1 for international students; for spring admission, 11/15 priority date for domestic students, 11/1 for international students. Applications are processed on a rolling basis. Application fee: $50. Electronic applications accepted. *Financial support:* In 2011–12, 20 students received support, including 22 fellowships (averaging $1,149 per year), 8 research assistantships (averaging $6,280 per year); scholarships/grants and unspecified assistantships also available. Support available to part-time students. Financial award applicants required to submit FAFSA. *Faculty research:* Service-learning, history of television, feminism and the media, executive communication, public relations pedagogy. *Unit head:* Dr. Shelia McAllister-Spooner, Program Director, 732-571-7553, Fax: 732-571-3609, E-mail: smcallis@monmouth.edu. *Application contact:* Kevin Roane, Director, Office of Graduate Admission, 732-571-3452, Fax: 732-263-5123, E-mail: gradadm@monmouth.edu. Web site: http://www.monmouth.edu/cpc.

Montana State University Billings, College of Arts and Sciences, Department of Communication and Theater, Billings, MT 59101-0298. Offers public relations (MS). Part-time programs available. Postbaccalaureate distance learning degree programs offered. *Degree requirements:* For master's, thesis optional. *Entrance requirements:* For master's, GRE General Test, minimum undergraduate GPA of 3.0, 3 letters of recommendation.

Montclair State University, The Graduate School, School of the Arts, Department of Communication Studies, Montclair, NJ 07043-1624. Offers MA. Part-time and evening/weekend programs available. *Students:* 14 full-time (10 women), 19 part-time (13 women); includes 10 minority (3 Black or African American, non-Hispanic/Latino; 1 Asian, non-Hispanic/Latino; 5 Hispanic/Latino; 1 Two or more races, non-Hispanic/Latino), 5 international. Average age 30. 37 applicants, 46% accepted, 14 enrolled. In 2011, 11 master's awarded. *Degree requirements:* For master's, comprehensive exam. *Entrance requirements:* For master's, GRE General Test, 2 letters of recommendation. Additional exam requirements/recommendations for international students: Required—TOEFL (minimum score 83 iBT) or IELTS (minimum score 6.5). *Application deadline:* For fall admission, 6/1 for international students; for spring admission, 10/1 for international students. Applications are processed on a rolling basis. Application fee: $60. Electronic applications accepted. *Financial support:* In 2011–12, 2 research assistantships with full tuition reimbursements (averaging $7,000 per year) were awarded; Federal Work-Study, scholarships/grants, and unspecified assistantships also available. Support available to part-time students. Financial award application deadline: 3/1; financial award applicants required to submit FAFSA. *Faculty research:* Organizational problem solving/innovation, social media, health communication, globalization, organizational change management. *Unit head:* Dr. Harry Haines, Chair, 973-655-4200. *Application contact:* Amy Aiello, Executive Director of The Graduate School, 973-655-5147, Fax: 973-655-7869, E-mail: graduate.school@montclair.edu.

New York University, School of Continuing and Professional Studies, Division of Programs in Business, Program in Public Relations and Corporate Communication, New York, NY 10012-1019. Offers corporate and organizational communication (MS); public relations management (MS). Part-time and evening/weekend programs available. *Faculty:* 1 (woman) full-time, 34 part-time/adjunct (10 women). *Students:* 82 full-time (68 women), 126 part-time (104 women); includes 32 minority (14 Black or African American, non-Hispanic/Latino; 10 Asian, non-Hispanic/Latino; 8 Hispanic/Latino), 40 international. Average age 29. 311 applicants, 55% accepted, 90 enrolled. In 2011, 51 master's awarded. *Degree requirements:* For master's, thesis. *Entrance requirements:* For master's, GRE/GMAT only upon request, relevant professional work, internship or volunteer experience. Additional exam requirements/recommendations for international students: Required—TOEFL (minimum score 600 paper-based; 250 computer-based; 100 iBT), IELTS (minimum score 7). *Application deadline:* For fall admission, 2/1 priority date for domestic students, 2/1 for international students; for spring admission, 10/15 priority date for domestic students, 8/15 for international students. Applications are processed on a rolling basis. Application fee: $150. Electronic applications accepted. *Financial support:* In 2011–12, 113 students received support, including 113 fellowships (averaging $2,437 per year). Financial award application deadline: 3/1; financial award applicants required to submit FAFSA. *Unit head:* John Doorley, Academic Chair and Clinical Assistant Professor, 212-998-7100. *Application contact:* Admissions Office, 212-998-7100, E-mail: scps.gradadmissions@nyu.edu. Web site: http://www.scps.nyu.edu/areas-of-study/public-relations.

Northern Kentucky University, Office of Graduate Programs, College of Informatics, Program in Communication, Highland Heights, KY 41099. Offers communication (MA); communication teaching (Certificate); documentary studies (Certificate); public relations (Certificate); relationships (Certificate). Part-time and evening/weekend programs available. *Faculty:* 5 full-time (2 women), 1 part-time/adjunct (0 women). *Students:* 11 full-time (9 women), 29 part-time (18 women); includes 5 minority (4 Black or African American, non-Hispanic/Latino; 1 Asian, non-Hispanic/Latino), 1 international. Average age 30. 28 applicants, 71% accepted, 10 enrolled. In 2011, 17 master's, 7 other advanced degrees awarded. *Degree requirements:* For master's, thesis (for some programs), capstone experience, internship. *Entrance requirements:* For master's, GRE, minimum GPA of 3.0, 3 letters of recommendation, letter of intent. Additional exam requirements/recommendations for international students: Required—TOEFL (minimum score 550 paper-based; 213 computer-based; 79 iBT); Recommended—IELTS (minimum score 6.5). *Application deadline:* For fall admission, 2/1 for domestic students, 6/1 for international students; for spring admission, 7/1 for domestic students, 10/1 for international students. Applications are processed on a rolling basis. Application fee: $40. Electronic applications accepted. *Expenses:* Tuition, state resident: full-time $7614; part-time $423 per credit hour. Tuition, nonresident: full-time $13,104; part-time $728 per credit hour. Tuition and fees vary according to degree level and reciprocity agreements. *Financial support:* Unspecified assistantships available. Financial award applicants required to submit FAFSA. *Faculty research:* Business/organizational communication, interpersonal/relational communication, public relations, communication teaching/pedagogy, media (production, criticism, popular culture). *Total annual research expenditures:* $29,000. *Unit head:* Dr. Jimmy Manning, Director, 859-572-1329, E-mail: manningj1@nku.edu. *Application contact:* Dr. Peg Griffin, Director of Graduate Programs, 859-572-6934, Fax: 859-572-6670, E-mail: griffinp@nku.edu. Web site: http://informatics.nku.edu/com/macom/index.php.

Northwestern University, Medill School of Journalism, Integrated Marketing Communications Program, Evanston, IL 60208. Offers advertising/sales promotion (MSIMC); direct database and e-commerce marketing (MSIMC); general studies (MSIMC); public relations (MSIMC). Part-time programs available. *Entrance requirements:* For master's, GRE General Test or GMAT, full-time work experience (preferred). Additional exam requirements/recommendations for international students: Required—TOEFL. Electronic applications accepted. *Faculty research:* Data mining, business to business marketing, values in advertising, political advertising.

Quinnipiac University, School of Communications, Program in Public Relations, Hamden, CT 06518-1940. Offers MS. Part-time and evening/weekend programs available. *Faculty:* 5 full-time (2 women), 5 part-time/adjunct (2 women). *Students:* 8 full-time (7 women), 2 part-time (both women); includes 2 minority (1 Black or African American, non-Hispanic/Latino; 1 Hispanic/Latino). 18 applicants, 72% accepted, 7 enrolled. *Entrance requirements:* For master's, GRE. Additional exam requirements/recommendations for international students: Required—TOEFL (minimum score 575 paper-based; 233 computer-based; 90 iBT), IELTS (minimum score 6.5). *Application deadline:* For fall admission, 7/31 priority date for domestic students; for spring admission, 12/15 priority date for domestic students. Applications are processed on a rolling basis. Application fee: $45. Electronic applications accepted. *Expenses: Tuition:* Part-time $855 per credit. *Required fees:* $35 per credit. *Financial support:* In 2011–12, 5 students received support. Federal Work-Study, scholarships/grants, tuition waivers (partial), and unspecified assistantships available. Support available to part-time students. Financial award application deadline: 4/30; financial award applicants required to submit FAFSA. *Faculty research:* Health care, international, investor relations, public diplomacy, non-profit, crisis management, ethics and professional responsibility. *Unit head:* Kathy Fitzpatrick, Professor, 203-582-3808, Fax: 203-582-3443, E-mail: graduate@quinnipiac.edu. *Application contact:* Katie Ludovico, Associate Director of Graduate Admissions, 203-582-8672, Fax: 203-582-3443, E-mail: katie.ludovico@quinnipiac.edu. Web site: http://www.quinnipiac.edu/gradpr.

Rowan University, Graduate School, College of Communication, Program in Public Relations, Glassboro, NJ 08028-1701. Offers MA. Part-time and evening/weekend programs available. *Degree requirements:* For master's, thesis. *Entrance requirements:* For master's, GRE General Test. Additional exam requirements/recommendations for international students: Required—TOEFL. Electronic applications accepted.

Royal Roads University, Graduate Studies, Applied Leadership and Management Program, Victoria, BC V9B 5Y2, Canada. Offers executive coaching (Graduate Certificate); health systems leadership (Graduate Certificate); project management (Graduate Certificate); public relations management (Graduate Certificate); strategic human resources management (Graduate Certificate).

Sacred Heart University, Graduate Programs, College of Arts and Sciences, Department of Communication and Media Studies, Fairfield, CT 06825-1000. Offers corporate communication and public relations (MA Comm); digital/multimedia journalism (MA Comm); digital/multimedia production (MA Comm).

San Diego State University, Graduate and Research Affairs, College of Professional Studies and Fine Arts, School of Communication, San Diego, CA 92182. Offers advertising and public relations (MA); critical-cultural studies (MA); interaction studies (MA); intercultural and international studies (MA); new media studies (MA); news and information studies (MA); telecommunications and media management (MA). *Degree requirements:* For master's, thesis. *Entrance requirements:* For master's, GRE General Test, 3 letters of recommendation. Additional exam requirements/recommendations for international students: Required—TOEFL. Electronic applications accepted.

Savannah College of Art and Design, Graduate School, Program in Advertising, Savannah, GA 31402-3146. Offers MA, MFA. Part-time programs available. *Faculty:* 12 full-time (4 women), 6 part-time/adjunct (1 woman). *Students:* 25 full-time (16 women), 5 part-time (2 women); includes 5 minority (4 Black or African American, non-Hispanic/Latino; 1 Hispanic/Latino), 10 international. Average age 27. 67 applicants, 22% accepted, 10 enrolled. In 2011, 24 master's awarded. *Degree requirements:* For master's, thesis, internships. *Entrance requirements:* For master's, portfolio. Additional exam requirements/recommendations for international students: Required—TOEFL (minimum score 400 paper-based; 50 computer-based). *Application deadline:* For fall admission, 4/1 priority date for domestic students, 4/1 for international students. Applications are processed on a rolling basis. Application fee: $35. Electronic applications accepted. *Expenses: Tuition:* Full-time $30,960; part-time $6880 per quarter. One-time fee: $500. *Financial support:* Fellowships, career-related internships or fieldwork, Federal Work-Study, and scholarships/grants available. Financial award application deadline: 4/1; financial award applicants required to submit FAFSA. *Unit head:* Luke Sullivan, Chair, 912-525-5974. *Application contact:* Elizabeth Mathis, Director of Graduate and International Enrollment, 912-525-5965, Fax: 912-525-5985, E-mail: emathis@scad.edu.

Southern Methodist University, Meadows School of the Arts, Temerlin Advertising Institute, Dallas, TX 75275. Offers MA. *Entrance requirements:* For master's, GRE, GMAT. Additional exam requirements/recommendations for international students: Required—TOEFL (minimum score 550 paper-based; 213 computer-based; 80 iBT). Electronic applications accepted.

Suffolk University, College of Arts and Sciences, Department of Communication and Journalism, Boston, MA 02108-2770. Offers communication studies (MAC); integrated marketing communication (MAC); public relations and advertising (MAC). Part-time and evening/weekend programs available. *Faculty:* 20 full-time (10 women), 1 part-time/adjunct (0 women). *Students:* 24 full-time (20 women), 16 part-time (14 women); includes 1 minority (Black or African American, non-Hispanic/Latino), 11 international. Average age 26. 100 applicants, 62% accepted, 20 enrolled. In 2011, 12 master's awarded. *Degree requirements:* For master's, thesis optional. *Entrance requirements:* For master's, GRE General Test, MAT, or GMAT, 2 letters of recommendation, resume. Additional exam requirements/recommendations for international students: Required—TOEFL (minimum score 550 paper-based; 213 computer-based; 80 iBT). *Application deadline:* For fall admission, 6/15 priority date for domestic students, 6/15 for international students; for spring admission, 11/1 priority date for domestic students, 11/1 for international students. Applications are processed on a rolling basis. Application fee: $50. Electronic applications accepted. *Expenses:* Contact institution. *Financial support:* In 2011–12, 27 students received support, including 23 fellowships with partial tuition reimbursements available (averaging $6,150 per year); career-related internships or fieldwork, Federal Work-Study, and institutionally sponsored loans also available. Support available to part-time students. Financial award application deadline: 4/1; financial award applicants required to submit FAFSA. *Faculty research:* New media and new markets for advertising, First Amendment issues with the Internet, gender and intercultural communication, organizational development. *Unit head:* Dr. Robert Rosenthal, Chair, 617-573-8502, Fax: 617-742-6982, E-mail: rrosenth@suffolk.edu. *Application contact:* Ellen Driscoll, Director of Graduate Admissions, 617-573-8302, Fax: 617-305-1733, E-mail: grad.admission@suffolk.edu.

Syracuse University, S. I. Newhouse School of Public Communications, Program in Advertising, Syracuse, NY 13244. Offers MA. *Students:* 20 full-time (17 women); includes 6 minority (2 Black or African American, non-Hispanic/Latino; 2 Asian, non-Hispanic/Latino; 2 Hispanic/Latino), 2 international. Average age 23. 85 applicants, 44% accepted, 20 enrolled. In 2011, 20 degrees awarded. *Degree requirements:* For master's, capstone course. *Entrance requirements:* For master's, GRE General Test. Additional exam requirements/recommendations for international students: Required—TOEFL (minimum score 600 paper-based; 250 computer-based; 100 iBT). *Application deadline:* For fall admission, 2/1 priority date for domestic students, 2/1 for international students. Application fee: $45. Electronic applications accepted. *Expenses: Tuition:* Part-time $1206 per credit. *Financial support:* Fellowships with full tuition reimbursements, research assistantships with partial tuition reimbursements, and teaching assistantships with full tuition reimbursements available. Financial award application deadline: 1/1. *Unit head:* James Tsao, Chair, 315-443-7401, Fax: 315-443-3946, E-mail: pcgrad@syr.edu. *Application contact:* Graduate Records Office, 315-443-5749, Fax: 315-443-1834, E-mail: pcgrad@syr.edu. Web site: http://newhouse.syr.edu/.

Syracuse University, S. I. Newhouse School of Public Communications, Program in Public Relations, Syracuse, NY 13244. Offers MS. *Students:* 39 full-time (29 women), 3 part-time (all women); includes 10 minority (4 Black or African American, non-Hispanic/Latino; 1 Asian, non-Hispanic/Latino; 5 Hispanic/Latino), 5 international. Average age 24. 203 applicants, 45% accepted, 33 enrolled. In 2011, 35 degrees awarded. *Degree requirements:* For master's, thesis (for some programs). *Entrance requirements:* For master's, GRE General Test. Additional exam requirements/recommendations for international students: Required—TOEFL (minimum score 600 paper-based; 250 computer-based; 100 iBT). *Application deadline:* For fall admission, 2/1 priority date for domestic students, 2/1 for international students. Application fee: $45. Electronic applications accepted. *Expenses: Tuition:* Part-time $1206 per credit. *Financial support:* Fellowships with full tuition reimbursements, research assistantships with partial tuition reimbursements, and teaching assistantships with partial tuition reimbursements available. Financial award application deadline: 2/1. *Unit head:* Brenda M. Wrigley, Chair, 315-443-1911, E-mail: newhouse@syr.edu. *Application contact:* Martha Coria, Graduate Records Office, 315-443-5749, Fax: 315-443-1834, E-mail: pcgrad@syr.edu. Web site: http://newhouse.syr.edu/.

Texas Christian University, College of Communication, Schieffer School of Journalism, Fort Worth, TX 76129-0002. Offers advertising/public relations (MS); news-editorial (MS). Part-time and evening/weekend programs available. *Faculty:* 14 full-time (9 women). *Students:* 8 full-time (6 women), 6 part-time (5 women); includes 3 minority (1 Black or African American, non-Hispanic/Latino; 2 Hispanic/Latino), 2 international. Average age 30. 27 applicants, 37% accepted, 7 enrolled. In 2011, 6 master's awarded. *Degree requirements:* For master's, thesis optional, written exam. *Entrance requirements:* For master's, GRE General Test. Additional exam requirements/recommendations for international students: Required—TOEFL. *Application deadline:* For fall admission, 3/1 for domestic and international students; for spring admission, 10/1 for domestic and international students. Applications are processed on a rolling basis. Application fee: $50. *Expenses: Tuition:* Full-time $20,250; part-time $1125 per credit hour. Part-time tuition and fees vary according to course load and program. *Financial support:* In 2011–12, 15 students received support, including 8 teaching assistantships (averaging $6,250 per year); tuition waivers (full and partial) and unspecified assistantships also available. Financial award application deadline: 3/1; financial award applicants required to submit FAFSA. *Unit head:* John Lumpkin, Director, 817-257-4908, E-mail: j.lumpkin@tcu.edu. *Application contact:* Dr. Julie O'Neil, Graduate Program Coordinator, 817-257-6966, E-mail: j.oneil@tcu.edu. Web site: http://www.schiefferschool.tcu.edu/.

Universidad Autonoma de Guadalajara, Graduate Programs, Guadalajara, Mexico. Offers administrative law and justice (LL M); advertising and corporate communications (MA); architecture (M Arch); business (MBA); computational science (MCC); education (Ed M, Ed D); English-Spanish translation (MA); entrepreneurship and management (MBA); integrated management of digital animation (MA); international business (MIB); international corporate law (LL M); internet technologies (MS); manufacturing systems (MMS); occupational health (MS); philosophy (MA, PhD); power electronics (MS); quality systems (MQS); renewable energy (MS); social evaluation of projects (MBA); strategic market research (MBA); tax law (MA); teaching mathematics (MA).

Université Laval, Faculty of Letters, Program in Public Relations, Québec, QC G1K 7P4, Canada. Offers Diploma. Part-time and evening/weekend programs available. *Entrance requirements:* For degree, knowledge of French, comprehension of written English. Electronic applications accepted.

The University of Alabama, Graduate School, College of Communication and Information Sciences, Department of Advertising and Public Relations, Tuscaloosa, AL 35487-0172. Offers MA. Part-time programs available. *Faculty:* 15 full-time (7 women). *Students:* 18 full-time (15 women), 9 part-time (7 women); includes 1 minority (Black or African American, non-Hispanic/Latino), 2 international. Average age 24. 83 applicants, 35% accepted, 16 enrolled. In 2011, 20 degrees awarded. *Degree requirements:* For master's, comprehensive exam, thesis or alternative. *Entrance requirements:* For master's, GRE (minimum score: 1000 verbal plus quantitative, 400 in each; 4.0 in writing), minimum undergraduate GPA of 3.0 for last 60 hours. Additional exam requirements/recommendations for international students: Required—TOEFL (minimum score 600 paper-based; 100 computer-based). *Application deadline:* For fall admission, 3/1 priority date for domestic students, 3/1 for international students. Applications are processed on a rolling basis. Application fee: $50 ($60 for international students). Electronic applications accepted. *Expenses:* Tuition, state resident: full-time $8600. Tuition, nonresident: full-time $21,900. *Financial support:* In 2011–12, 7 students received support, including 4 research assistantships with partial tuition reimbursements available, 3 teaching assistantships with full tuition reimbursements available; career-related internships or fieldwork, scholarships/grants, health care benefits, and unspecified assistantships also available. Financial award application deadline: 3/1. *Faculty research:* Advertising and public relations management, leadership, public opinion, political communication, advertising media, international communication, creativity, consumer privacy, crisis communication, sports communication, advertising and public relations history. *Total annual research expenditures:* $38,497. *Unit head:* Dr. Joseph Edward Phelps, Professor and Chairman, 205-348-8646, Fax: 205-348-2401, E-mail: phelps@apr.ua.edu. *Application contact:* Dr. Yorgo Pasadeos, Professor, 205-348-8641, Fax: 205-348-2401, E-mail: pasadeos@apr.ua.edu. Web site: http://www.apr.ua.edu.

University of Denver, Division of Arts, Humanities and Social Sciences, Department of Media, Film and Journalism Studies, Denver, CO 80208. Offers advertising management (MS); digital media studies (MA); international and intercultural communication (MA); media, film, and journalism studies (MA); strategic communication (MS). Part-time programs available. *Faculty:* 14 full-time (8 women), 3 part-time/adjunct (1 woman). *Students:* 31 full-time (29 women), 30 part-time (22 women); includes 11 minority (4 Asian, non-Hispanic/Latino; 7 Hispanic/Latino), 2 international. Average age 26. 109 applicants, 74% accepted, 33 enrolled. In 2011, 28 degrees awarded. *Degree requirements:* For master's, thesis (for some programs). *Entrance requirements:* For master's, GRE General Test, three letters of recommendation, personal statement. Additional exam requirements/recommendations for international students: Required—TOEFL (minimum score 620 paper-based; 105 iBT). *Application deadline:* Applications are processed on a rolling basis. Application fee: $60. Electronic applications accepted. *Financial support:* In 2011–12, 43 students received support, including 4 teaching assistantships with full and partial tuition reimbursements available (averaging $14,000 per year); career-related internships or fieldwork, Federal Work-Study, institutionally sponsored loans, scholarships/grants, and unspecified assistantships also available. Support available to part-time students. Financial award application deadline: 2/15; financial award applicants required to submit FAFSA. *Faculty research:* Youth and civic engagement. *Unit head:* Dr. Renee Botta, Chair, 303-871-7918, Fax: 303-871-4949, E-mail: rbotta@du.edu. *Application contact:* Information Contact, 303-871-2166, E-mail: mfjs@du.edu. Web site: http://www.du.edu/ahss/schools/mfjs/index.html.

University of Denver, University College, Denver, CO 80208. Offers arts and culture (MLS, Certificate), including art, literature, and culture, arts development and program management (Certificate), creative writing; environmental policy and management (MAS, Certificate), including energy and sustainability (Certificate), environmental assessment of nuclear power (Certificate), environmental health and safety (Certificate), environmental management, natural resource management (Certificate); geographic information systems (MAS, Certificate); global affairs (MLS, Certificate), including translation studies, world history and culture; healthcare leadership (MPH, Certificate), including healthcare policy, law, and ethics, medical and healthcare information technologies, strategic management of healthcare; information and communications technology (MCIS, Certificate), including database design and administration (Certificate), geographic information systems (MCIS), information security systems security (Certificate), information systems security (MCIS), project management (MCIS, MPS, Certificate), software design and administration (Certificate), software design and programming (MCIS), technology management, telecommunications technology (MCIS), Web design and development; leadership and organizations (MPS, Certificate), including human capital in organizations, philanthropic leadership, project management (MCIS, MPS, Certificate), strategic innovation and change; organizational and professional communication (MPS, Certificate), including alternative dispute resolution, organizational communication, organizational development and training, public relations and marketing; security management (MAS, Certificate), including emergency planning and response, information security (MAS), organizational security; strategic human resource management (MPS, Certificate), including global human resources (MPS), human resource management and development (MPS). Part-time and evening/weekend programs available. Postbaccalaureate distance learning degree programs offered (no on-campus study). *Faculty:* 204 part-time/adjunct (80 women). *Students:* 56 full-time (26 women), 1,096 part-time (647 women); includes 196 minority (81 Black or African American, non-Hispanic/Latino; 7 American Indian or Alaska Native, non-Hispanic/Latino; 30 Asian, non-Hispanic/Latino; 66 Hispanic/Latino; 3 Native Hawaiian or other Pacific Islander, non-Hispanic/Latino; 9 Two or more races, non-Hispanic/Latino), 76 international. Average age 36. 572 applicants, 95% accepted, 410 enrolled. In 2011, 404 master's, 123 other advanced degrees awarded. *Degree requirements:* For master's, capstone project. *Entrance requirements:* For master's, two letters of recommendation, personal statement, resume. Additional exam requirements/recommendations for international students: Required—TOEFL (minimum score 550 paper-based; 80 iBT). *Application deadline:* For fall admission, 7/20 priority date for domestic students, 6/8 for international students; for winter admission, 10/26 priority date for domestic students, 9/14 for international students; for spring admission, 2/1 priority date for domestic students, 12/14 for international students. Applications are processed on a rolling basis. Application fee: $75. Electronic applications accepted. *Expenses:* Contact institution. *Financial support:* Applicants required to submit FAFSA. *Unit head:* Dr. James Davis, Dean, 303-871-2291, Fax: 303-871-4047, E-mail: jdavis@du.edu. *Application contact:* Information Contact, 303-871-3155, Fax: 303-871-4047, E-mail: ucolinfo@du.edu. Web site: http://www.universitycollege.du.edu/.

University of Florida, Graduate School, College of Journalism and Communications, Department of Advertising, Gainesville, FL 32611. Offers M Adv. *Faculty:* 3 full-time (0 women). *Students:* 13 full-time (10 women), 2 part-time (both women); includes 2 minority (1 Asian, non-Hispanic/Latino; 1 Native Hawaiian or other Pacific Islander, non-Hispanic/Latino), 11 international. Average age 25. 87 applicants, 26% accepted, 6 enrolled. In 2011, 9 master's awarded. *Degree requirements:* For master's, thesis or terminal project. *Entrance requirements:* For master's, GRE General Test, minimum GPA of 3.0. Additional exam requirements/recommendations for international students: Required—TOEFL (minimum score 550 paper-based; 213 computer-based; 80 iBT), IELTS (minimum score 6). *Application deadline:* For fall admission, 4/1 for domestic students, 1/30 for international students. Applications are processed on a rolling basis. Application fee: $30. Electronic applications accepted. *Financial support:* Applicants required to submit FAFSA. *Faculty research:* Branding, information flow between clients and suppliers, message and media strategies, emotional response. *Unit head:* Dr. John C. Sutherland, Chair, 352-392-4046, Fax: 352-846-3015, E-mail: jsutherland@jou.ufl.edu. *Application contact:* Robyn Goodman, Graduate Coordinator, 352-392-2704, Fax: 352-392-1794, E-mail: rgoodman@jou.ufl.edu. Web site: http://www.jou.ufl.edu/academic/adv/.

University of Florida, Graduate School, College of Journalism and Communications, Department of Public Relations, Gainesville, FL 32611. Offers MAMC. *Faculty:* 7 full-time (4 women). *Entrance requirements:* For master's, GRE General Test, minimum GPA of 3.0. Additional exam requirements/recommendations for international students: Required—TOEFL (minimum score 550 paper-based; 213 computer-based; 80 iBT), IELTS (minimum score 6). *Application deadline:* For fall admission, 4/1 for domestic students, 1/30 for international students. Applications are processed on a rolling basis. Application fee: $30. *Financial support:* Applicants required to submit FAFSA. *Faculty research:* Social media/interactive media adoption and communication strategy; health and science communication, nonprofits, social marketing, public communications, and philanthropy; public relationships, partnerships and coalitions; strategic communication. *Total annual research expenditures:* $32,000. *Unit head:* Spiro K. Kiousis, Chair, 352-273-1222, E-mail: skiousis@jou.ufl.edu. *Application contact:* Juan C. Molleda, Graduate Coordinator, 352-273-1223, Fax: 352-392-3952, E-mail: jmolleda@jou.ufl.edu. Web site: http://www.jou.ufl.edu/academic/pr/.

University of Houston, College of Liberal Arts and Social Sciences, School of Communication, Houston, TX 77204. Offers health communication (MA); mass communication studies (MA); public relations studies (MA); speech communication (MA). Part-time programs available. *Degree requirements:* For master's, comprehensive exam (for some programs), thesis (for some programs), 30-33 hours. *Entrance requirements:* For master's, GRE. Additional exam requirements/recommendations for international students: Required—TOEFL. Electronic applications accepted.

University of Illinois at Urbana–Champaign, Graduate College, College of Media, Department of Advertising, Champaign, IL 61820. Offers MS. *Faculty:* 6 full-time (3 women), 1 (woman) part-time/adjunct. *Students:* 30 full-time (23 women); includes 2 minority (1 Black or African American, non-Hispanic/Latino; 1 Two or more races, non-Hispanic/Latino), 19 international. 102 applicants, 24% accepted, 19 enrolled. In 2011, 2 master's awarded. *Entrance requirements:* For master's, GMAT or GRE General Test, minimum GPA of 3.0. Additional exam requirements/recommendations for international students: Required—TOEFL (minimum score 610 paper-based; 253 computer-based; 102 iBT) or IELTS (minimum score 6.5). *Application deadline:* Applications are processed on a rolling basis. Application fee: $75 ($90 for international students). Electronic applications accepted. *Financial support:* In 2011–12, 4 fellowships, 1 research assistantship, 10 teaching assistantships were awarded; tuition waivers (full and partial) also available. *Faculty research:* Consumer behavior, persuasive communication. *Unit head:* Janet S. Slater, Interim Head, 217-333-1602, Fax: 217-244-3348, E-mail: slaterj@illinois.edu. *Application contact:* Janette Bradley-Wright, Office Administrator, 217-333-1602, Fax: 217-244-3348, E-mail: wjbradle@illinois.edu. Web site: http://www.media.illinois.edu/advertising/.

University of Maryland, College Park, Academic Affairs, College of Arts and Humanities, Department of Communication, College Park, MD 20742. Offers MA, PhD. *Faculty:* 24 full-time (12 women), 10 part-time/adjunct (8 women). *Students:* 56 full-time (43 women), 2 part-time (both women); includes 9 minority (2 Black or African American, non-Hispanic/Latino; 5 Asian, non-Hispanic/Latino; 2 Hispanic/Latino), 15 international. 215 applicants, 9% accepted, 11 enrolled. In 2011, 8 master's, 5 doctorates awarded. *Degree requirements:* For master's, thesis optional; for doctorate, comprehensive exam, thesis/dissertation. *Entrance requirements:* For master's, GRE General Test, minimum GPA of 3.0, sample of scholarly writing, 3 letters of recommendation; for doctorate, GRE General Test. Additional exam requirements/recommendations for international students: Required—TOEFL. *Application deadline:* For fall admission, 2/1 for domestic and international students. Applications are processed on a rolling basis. Application fee: $75. Electronic applications accepted. *Expenses: Tuition, area resident:* Part-time $525 per credit hour. Tuition, state resident: part-time $525 per credit hour. Tuition, nonresident: part-time $1131 per credit hour. *Required fees:* $386.31 per term. Tuition and fees vary according to program. *Financial support:* In 2011–12, 40 teaching assistantships with tuition reimbursements (averaging $16,913 per year) were awarded; fellowships with partial tuition reimbursements, Federal Work-Study, scholarships/grants, and unspecified assistantships also available. Support available to part-time students. Financial award applicants required to submit FAFSA. *Faculty research:* Health communication, interpersonal communication, persuasion, intercultural communication, contemporary rhetoric theory. *Unit head:* Dr. Elizabeth L. Toth, Chair, 301-405-0870, Fax: 301-314-9471, E-mail: eltoth@umd.edu. *Application contact:* Dr. Charles A. Caramello, Dean of Graduate School, 301-405-0358, Fax: 301-314-9305. Web site: http://www.comm.umd.edu/.

University of Miami, Graduate School, School of Communication, Coral Gables, FL 33124. Offers communication (PhD); communication studies (MA); film studies (MA, PhD); motion pictures (MFA), including production, producing, and screenwriting; print journalism (MA); public relations (MA); Spanish language journalism (MA); television broadcast journalism (MA). *Accreditation:* ACEJMC. Part-time programs available. *Degree requirements:* For master's, comprehensive exam (for some programs), thesis (for some programs); for doctorate, comprehensive exam, thesis/dissertation. *Entrance requirements:* For master's, GRE General Test; for doctorate, GRE General Test, master's thesis or scholarly research. Additional exam requirements/recommendations for international students: Required—TOEFL (minimum score 600 paper-based; 250 computer-based; 100 iBT). Electronic applications accepted. *Faculty research:* Communication studies, mass communication, international/interpersonal communication, film studies, journalism.

University of Nebraska–Lincoln, Graduate College, College of Arts and Sciences, Department of Communication Studies, Lincoln, NE 68588. Offers instructional communication (MA, PhD); interpersonal communication (MA, PhD); marketing, communication studies, and advertising (MA, PhD); organizational communication (MA, PhD); rhetoric and culture (MA, PhD). *Degree requirements:* For master's, thesis optional; for doctorate, comprehensive exam, thesis/dissertation. *Entrance requirements:* For master's and doctorate, GRE General Test, writing sample. Additional exam requirements/recommendations for international students: Required—TOEFL (minimum score 600 paper-based; 250 computer-based). Electronic applications accepted. *Faculty research:* Message strategies, gender communication, political communication, organizational communication, instructional communication.

University of Nebraska–Lincoln, Graduate College, College of Journalism and Mass Communications, Lincoln, NE 68588. Offers marketing, communication and advertising (MA); professional journalism (MA). Postbaccalaureate distance learning degree programs offered (no on-campus study). *Degree requirements:* For master's, thesis. *Entrance requirements:* For master's, samples of work. Additional exam requirements/recommendations for international students: Required—TOEFL (minimum score 600 paper-based; 250 computer-based). Electronic applications accepted. *Faculty research:* Interactive media and the Internet, community newspapers, children's radio, advertising involvement, telecommunications policy.

The University of North Carolina at Charlotte, Graduate School, College of Liberal Arts and Sciences, Department of Communication Studies, Charlotte, NC 28223-0001. Offers communication studies (Certificate); health communication (MA); media/rhetorical critical studies (MA); organizational communication (MA); public relations (MA). Part-time and evening/weekend programs available. *Faculty:* 13 full-time (6 women). *Students:* 12 full-time (10 women), 18 part-time (15 women); includes 6 minority (3 Black or African American, non-Hispanic/Latino; 2 Asian, non-Hispanic/Latino; 1 Two or more races, non-Hispanic/Latino), 1 international. Average age 27. 49 applicants, 49% accepted, 12 enrolled. In 2011, 12 master's, 1 other advanced degree awarded. Terminal master's awarded for partial completion of doctoral program. *Degree requirements:* For master's, project, thesis, or comprehensive exam. *Entrance requirements:* For master's, GRE General Test, minimum GPA of 2.75 overall. Additional exam requirements/recommendations for international students: Required—TOEFL (minimum score 557 paper-based; 220 computer-based; 83 iBT). *Application deadline:* For fall admission, 3/15 for domestic students, 5/1 for international students; for spring admission, 11/15 for domestic students, 10/1 for international students. Applications are processed on a rolling basis. Application fee: $55. Electronic applications accepted. *Expenses:* Tuition, state resident: full-time $3689. Tuition, nonresident: full-time $15,226. *Required fees:* $2198. Tuition and fees vary according to course load and program. *Financial support:* In 2011–12, 8 students received support, including 8 teaching assistantships (averaging $16,232 per year); career-related internships or fieldwork, institutionally sponsored loans, scholarships/grants, and unspecified assistantships also available. Support available to part-time students. Financial award application deadline: 4/1; financial award applicants required to submit FAFSA. *Faculty research:* Health literacy, systems of care and mental illness, the communication of emotions in gendered workplaces, international constructs of public relations managerial responsibilities, sports culture and the construction of social contracts, African-American oratory. *Total annual research expenditures:* $63,378. *Unit head:* Dr. Richard W. Leeman, Chair, 704-687-2086, Fax: 704-687-6900, E-mail: rwleeman@uncc.edu. *Application contact:* Kathy B. Giddings, Director of Graduate Admissions, 704-687-5503, Fax: 704-687-3279, E-mail: gradadm@uncc.edu. Web site: http://communications.uncc.edu/.

University of Oklahoma, Gaylord College of Journalism and Mass Communication, Program in Journalism and Mass Communication, Norman, OK 73019. Offers advertising and public relations (MA); broadcasting and electronic media (MA); journalism (MA); mass communication management (MA). Part-time programs available. *Students:* 32 full-time (19 women), 23 part-time (11 women); includes 4 minority (2 Black or African American, non-Hispanic/Latino; 1 American Indian or Alaska Native, non-Hispanic/Latino; 1 Hispanic/Latino), 9 international. Average age 29. 53 applicants, 47% accepted, 14 enrolled. In 2011, 18 degrees awarded. *Degree requirements:* For master's, thesis optional. *Entrance requirements:* For master's, GRE General Test, minimum GPA of 3.2, 9 hours of course work in journalism, course work in statistics. Additional exam requirements/recommendations for international students: Required—TOEFL (minimum score 600 paper-based; 100 iBT), TWE (minimum score 5). *Application deadline:* For fall admission, 2/1 for domestic students, 3/1 for international students; for spring admission, 11/1 for domestic students, 9/1 for international students. Application fee: $40 ($90 for international students). Electronic applications accepted. *Expenses:* Tuition, state resident: full-time $4087; part-time $170.30 per credit hour. Tuition, nonresident: full-time $14,875; part-time $619.80 per credit hour. *Required fees:* $2659; $100.25 per credit hour. Tuition and fees vary according to course load and degree level. *Financial support:* In 2011–12, 30 students received support. Career-related internships or fieldwork, institutionally sponsored loans, scholarships/grants, health care benefits, and unspecified assistantships available. Support available to part-time students. *Faculty research:* Organizational management, strategic communications, rhetorical theories and mass communication, interactive messaging and audience response, mass media history and law. *Unit head:* Dr. Joe Foote, Dean, 405-325-2721, Fax: 405-325-7565, E-mail: jfoote@ou.edu. *Application contact:* Kelly Storm, Graduate Advisor, 405-325-2722, Fax: 405-325-7565, E-mail: kstorm@ou.edu. Web site: http://www.ou.edu/content/gaylord/home/Audience/graduate_students.html.

University of Southern California, Graduate School, Annenberg School for Communication and Journalism, School of Journalism, Program in Strategic Public Relations, Los Angeles, CA 90089. Offers MA. Part-time programs available. *Students:* 120 full-time, 5 part-time; includes 40 minority (9 Black or African American, non-Hispanic/Latino; 15 Asian, non-Hispanic/Latino; 14 Hispanic/Latino; 1 Native Hawaiian or other Pacific Islander, non-Hispanic/Latino; 1 Two or more races, non-Hispanic/Latino), 36 international. Average age 24. 178 applicants, 68% accepted, 67 enrolled. In 2011, 43 master's awarded. *Degree requirements:* For master's, comprehensive exam, thesis optional. *Entrance requirements:* For master's, GRE General Test, resume, writing samples, letters of recommendation, statement of purpose. Additional exam requirements/recommendations for international students: Required—TOEFL (minimum score 280 computer-based; 114 iBT). *Application deadline:* For fall admission, 1/2 for domestic students, 12/2 for international students. Application fee: $85. Electronic applications accepted. *Financial support:* In 2011–12, 2 fellowships with full tuition reimbursements (averaging $52,000 per year) were awarded; career-related internships or fieldwork, Federal Work-Study, institutionally sponsored loans, scholarships/grants, health care benefits, and unspecified assistantships also available. Support available to part-time students. Financial award application deadline: 1/15; financial award applicants required to submit FAFSA. *Unit head:* Jerry Swerling, Director, 213-821-1275, E-mail: swerling@usc.edu. *Application contact:* Allyson Hill, Assistant Dean and Director of Admissions, 213-821-0770, Fax: 213-740-1933, E-mail: ascadm@usc.edu. Web site: http://www.annenberg.usc.edu/.

University of Southern Mississippi, Graduate School, College of Arts and Letters, School of Mass Communication and Journalism, Hattiesburg, MS 39406-0001. Offers mass communication (MA, MS, PhD); public relations (MS). Part-time programs available. *Faculty:* 10 full-time (3 women), 1 part-time/adjunct (0 women). *Students:* 38 full-time (27 women), 32 part-time (25 women); includes 23 minority (18 Black or African American, non-Hispanic/Latino; 3 Hispanic/Latino; 2 Two or more races, non-Hispanic/Latino), 9 international. Average age 34. 38 applicants, 68% accepted, 14 enrolled. In 2011, 22 master's, 8 doctorates awarded. *Degree requirements:* For master's, comprehensive exam, thesis optional; for doctorate, comprehensive exam, thesis/dissertation. *Entrance requirements:* For master's, GRE General Test, minimum GPA of 3.0 in field of study, 2.75 in last 2 years; for doctorate, GRE General Test, minimum GPA of 3.5. Additional exam requirements/recommendations for international students: Required—TOEFL, IELTS. *Application deadline:* For fall admission, 3/1 priority date for domestic students, 3/1 for international students; for spring admission, 1/10 priority date for domestic students, 1/10 for international students. Applications are processed on a rolling basis. Application fee: $50. *Financial support:* In 2011–12, 18 students received support, including 12 teaching assistantships with full tuition reimbursements available (averaging $8,000 per year); fellowships with full tuition reimbursements available, research assistantships with full tuition reimbursements available, career-related internships or fieldwork, Federal Work-Study, institutionally sponsored loans, scholarships/grants, health care benefits, and unspecified assistantships also available. Financial award application deadline: 3/15; financial award applicants required to submit FAFSA. *Unit head:* Dr. Christopher Campbell, Director, 601-266-5650, Fax: 601-266-4263. *Application contact:* Dr. Fei Xue, Graduate Coordinator, 601-266-5652, Fax: 601-266-6473, E-mail: fei.xue@usm.edu. Web site: http://www.usm.edu/mcj.

The University of Tennessee, Graduate School, College of Communication and Information, Knoxville, TN 37996. Offers advertising (MS, PhD); broadcasting (MS, PhD); communications (MS, PhD); information sciences (MS, PhD); journalism (MS, PhD); public relations (MS, PhD); speech communication (MS, PhD). *Accreditation:* ACEJMC (one or more programs are accredited at the [master's] level). Part-time and evening/weekend programs available. Postbaccalaureate distance learning degree programs offered (no on-campus study). *Degree requirements:* For master's, thesis or alternative; for doctorate, thesis/dissertation. *Entrance requirements:* For master's and doctorate, GRE General Test, minimum GPA of 2.7. Additional exam requirements/recommendations for international students: Required—TOEFL. Electronic applications accepted. *Expenses:* Tuition, state resident: full-time $8332; part-time $464 per credit hour. Tuition, nonresident: full-time $25,174; part-time $1400 per credit hour. *Required fees:* $1162; $56 per credit hour. Tuition and fees vary according to program.

The University of Texas at Austin, Graduate School, College of Communication, Department of Advertising, Austin, TX 78712-1111. Offers MA, PhD. *Entrance requirements:* For master's and doctorate, GRE General Test. *Application deadline:* For fall admission, 2/1 priority date for domestic students. Application fee: $50 ($75 for international students). Electronic applications accepted. *Financial support:* Fellowships with partial tuition reimbursements and teaching assistantships with partial tuition reimbursements available. Financial award application deadline: 2/1. *Faculty research:* Interactive advertising, advertising laws and ethics, advertising creativity, media planning and modeling, international advertising. *Unit head:* Dr. Isabella Cunningham, Chairman, 512-471-8126, E-mail: isabella.cunningham@austin.utexas.edu. *Application contact:* Dr. Gary B. Wilcox, Graduate Adviser, 512-471-0917. Web site: http://advertising.utexas.edu/.

The University of Texas–Pan American, College of Arts and Humanities, Department training and consulting (Graduate Certificate); strategic communication and media relations (Graduate Certificate); theatre (MA). *Accreditation:* NAST. Part-time and evening/weekend programs available. *Students:* 7 applicants, 100% accepted. *Degree requirements:* For master's, comprehensive exam, thesis or alternative. *Entrance requirements:* For master's, minimum GPA of 3.0. Additional exam requirements/ recommendations for international students: Required—TOEFL. Application fee: $0. Tuition and fees vary according to course load, program and student level. *Financial support:* Research assistantships, teaching assistantships, Federal Work-Study, and institutionally sponsored loans available. Support available to part-time students. Financial award application deadline: 6/1. *Faculty research:* Rhetorical theory, intercultural and mass communication, American theatre, multicultural theatre and drama, television and film. *Unit head:* Tom Grabowski, Chair, 956-665-3580, E-mail: tomgrab@utpa.edu. *Application contact:* Dr. Jeff McQuillen, Communication Graduate Coordinator, 956-665-2376, E-mail: mcquillen@utpa.edu. Web site: http://www.panam.edu/dept/comm/.

University of the Sacred Heart, Graduate Programs, Department of Communication, Program in Public Relations, San Juan, PR 00914-0383. Offers MA. Part-time and evening/weekend programs available. *Degree requirements:* For master's, thesis. *Entrance requirements:* For master's, EXADEP, minimum undergraduate GPA of 2.75, interview.

University of Wisconsin–Stevens Point, College of Fine Arts and Communication, Division of Communication, Stevens Point, WI 54481-3897. Offers interpersonal communication (MA); mass communication (MA); organizational communication (MA); public relations (MA). Part-time programs available. *Degree requirements:* For master's, thesis or alternative. *Entrance requirements:* For master's, GRE. Additional exam requirements/recommendations for international students: Required—TOEFL (minimum score 575 paper-based). *Faculty research:* Communication theory and research, film history.

Virginia Commonwealth University, Graduate School, College of Humanities and Sciences, School of Mass Communications, Brandcenter, Richmond, VA 23284-9005. Offers art direction (MS); communication strategy (MS); copywriting (MS); creative brand management (MS); creative media planning (MS). *Degree requirements:* For master's, comprehensive exam, thesis optional. *Entrance requirements:* For master's, GRE or GMAT, interview, portfolio. Additional exam requirements/recommendations for international students: Required—TOEFL (minimum score 600 paper-based; 250 computer-based; 100 iBT); Recommended—IELTS (minimum score 6.5). Electronic applications accepted. *Expenses:* Tuition, state resident: full-time $9133; part-time $507 per credit. Tuition, nonresident: full-time $18,777; part-time $1043 per credit. *Required fees:* $77 per credit. Tuition and fees vary according to degree level, campus/location, program and student level. *Faculty research:* Art direction, copywriting, communications strategy, creative brand management, creative technology.

Virginia Commonwealth University, Graduate School, College of Humanities and Sciences, School of Mass Communications, Program in Mass Communications, Richmond, VA 23284-9005. Offers multimedia journalism (MS); strategic public relations (MS). *Degree requirements:* For master's, comprehensive exam, thesis optional. *Entrance requirements:* For master's, GRE General Test. Additional exam requirements/ recommendations for international students: Required—TOEFL (minimum score 600 paper-based; 250 computer-based; 100 iBT); Recommended—IELTS (minimum score 6.5). Electronic applications accepted. *Expenses:* Tuition, state resident: full-time $9133; part-time $507 per credit. Tuition, nonresident: full-time $18,777; part-time $1043 per credit. *Required fees:* $77 per credit. Tuition and fees vary according to degree level, campus/location, program and student level. *Faculty research:* Multimedia journalism, strategic public relations.

Wayne State University, College of Fine, Performing and Communication Arts, Department of Communication, Detroit, MI 48202. Offers communication and new media (Certificate); communication education (MA); communication studies (MA, PhD); dispute resolution (MADR); journalism (MA); media arts (MA); media arts and studies (PhD); media studies (MA); public relations and organizational communication (MA); JD/ MADR. *Faculty:* 25 full-time (11 women), 4 part-time/adjunct (1 woman). *Students:* 64 full-time (43 women), 107 part-time (73 women); includes 44 minority (36 Black or African American, non-Hispanic/Latino; 2 American Indian or Alaska Native, non-Hispanic/Latino; 1 Asian, non-Hispanic/Latino; 5 Hispanic/Latino), 7 international. Average age 32. 65 applicants, 66% accepted, 31 enrolled. In 2011, 37 master's, 7 doctorates, 2 other advanced degrees awarded. *Degree requirements:* For master's, thesis, essay, or comprehensive exam; for doctorate, thesis/dissertation. *Entrance requirements:* For master's, minimum GPA of 3.0, sample of academic writing; for doctorate, GRE, minimum GPA of 3.3, MA; letters of recommendation; personal statement; sample of written scholarship. Additional exam requirements/ recommendations for international students: Required—TOEFL (minimum score 550 paper-based; 213 computer-based); Recommended—TWE (minimum score 6). *Application deadline:* For fall admission, 4/1 for domestic students, 6/1 for international students; for winter admission, 10/1 for international students; for spring admission, 2/1 for international students. Applications are processed on a rolling basis. Application fee: $30 ($50 for international students). Electronic applications accepted. *Expenses:* Tuition, state resident: part-time $512.85 per credit. Tuition, nonresident: part-time $1132.65 per credit. *Required fees:* $26.60 per credit. $199.65 per semester. Tuition and fees vary according to course load and program. *Financial support:* In 2011–12, 22 students received support, including 8 fellowships with tuition reimbursements available (averaging $14,956 per year), 1 research assistantship with tuition reimbursement available (averaging $23,000 per year), 19 teaching assistantships with tuition reimbursements available (averaging $14,620 per year); career-related internships or fieldwork also available. Financial award application deadline: 2/1. *Faculty research:* Rhetorical theory and criticism; mass media theory and research; argumentation; organizational communication; risk and crisis communication; interpersonal, family, and health communication. *Unit head:* Dr. Loraleigh Keashly, Chair, 313-577-2959, E-mail: ad8889@wayne.edu. *Application contact:* Dr. Pradeep Sopory, Graduate Studies Director, 313-577-3543, E-mail: psopory@wayne.edu. Web site: http://comm.wayne.edu/.

Webster University, School of Communications, Program in Advertising and Marketing Communications, St. Louis, MO 63119-3194. Offers MA. *Expenses: Tuition:* Full-time $10,890; part-time $605 per credit hour. Tuition and fees vary according to campus/ location and program.

Webster University, School of Communications, Program in Public Relations, St. Louis, MO 63119-3194. Offers MA. *Expenses: Tuition:* Full-time $10,890; part-time $605 per credit hour. Tuition and fees vary according to campus/location and program.

Section 4
Electronic Commerce

This section contains a directory of institutions offering graduate work in electronic commerce. Additional information about programs listed in the directory but not augmented by an in-depth entry may be obtained by writing directly to the dean of a graduate school or chair of a department at the address given in the directory.

CONTENTS

Program Directory

Displays and Close-Ups

See:

Electronic Commerce

Adelphi University, Robert B. Willumstad School of Business, MBA Program, Garden City, NY 11530-0701. Offers finance (MBA); management information systems (MBA); management/human resource management (MBA); marketing/e-commerce (MBA). *Accreditation:* AACSB. Part-time and evening/weekend programs available. *Students:* 258 full-time (121 women), 111 part-time (58 women); includes 67 minority (22 Black or African American, non-Hispanic/Latino; 18 Asian, non-Hispanic/Latino; 24 Hispanic/Latino; 3 Two or more races, non-Hispanic/Latino), 172 international. Average age 28. In 2011, 111 master's awarded. *Degree requirements:* For master's, capstone course. *Entrance requirements:* For master's, GMAT, 2 letters of recommendation. Additional exam requirements/recommendations for international students: Required—TOEFL (minimum score 550 paper-based; 213 computer-based; 80 iBT). *Application deadline:* For fall admission, 4/1 for international students; for spring admission, 11/1 for international students. Applications are processed on a rolling basis. Application fee: $50. Electronic applications accepted. *Expenses: Tuition:* Full-time $29,600; part-time $930 per credit. *Required fees:* $1100. *Financial support:* Research assistantships with full and partial tuition reimbursements, career-related internships or fieldwork, Federal Work-Study, institutionally sponsored loans, scholarships/grants, and unspecified assistantships available. Financial award application deadline: 3/1; financial award applicants required to submit FAFSA. *Faculty research:* Supply chain management, distribution channels, productivity benchmark analysis, data envelopment analysis, financial portfolio analysis. *Unit head:* Rakesh Gupta, 516-877-4670, Fax: 516-877-4607, E-mail: gradbusinquiries@adelphi.edu. *Application contact:* Christine Murphy, Director of Admissions, 516-877-3050, Fax: 516-877-3039, E-mail: graduateadmissions@adelphi.edu. Web site: http://business.adelphi.edu/degree-programs/graduate-degree-programs/m-b-a/.

See Display on page 68 and Close-Up on page 177.

Arkansas State University, Graduate School, College of Business, Department of Computer and Information Technology, Jonesboro, State University, AR 72467. Offers business education (SCCT); business technology education (MSE); information systems and e-commerce (MS). Part-time programs available. *Faculty:* 9 full-time (1 woman). *Students:* 4 full-time (2 women), 13 part-time (10 women); includes 5 minority (all Black or African American, non-Hispanic/Latino). Average age 36. 6 applicants, 100% accepted, 5 enrolled. In 2011, 13 master's awarded. *Degree requirements:* For master's, comprehensive exam, thesis or alternative. *Entrance requirements:* For master's, GRE General Test or MAT, appropriate bachelor's degree, official transcript, immunization records. Additional exam requirements/recommendations for international students: Required—TOEFL (minimum score 550 paper-based; 253 computer-based; 79 iBT), IELTS (minimum score 6), Pearson Test of English Academic (minimum score 56). *Application deadline:* For fall admission, 7/1 for domestic and international students; for spring admission, 11/15 for domestic students, 11/14 for international students. Applications are processed on a rolling basis. Application fee: $30 ($40 for international students). Electronic applications accepted. *Expenses:* Contact institution. *Financial support:* Career-related internships or fieldwork, scholarships/grants, and unspecified assistantships available. Financial award application deadline: 7/1; financial award applicants required to submit FAFSA. *Unit head:* Dr. John Robertson, Chair, 870-972-3416, Fax: 870-972-3868, E-mail: jfrobert@astate.edu. *Application contact:* Dr. Andrew Sustich, Dean of the Graduate School, 870-972-3029, Fax: 870-972-3857, E-mail: sustich@astate.edu. Web site: http://www.astate.edu/a/business/departments/computer-information-technology/.

Boston University, Metropolitan College, Department of Administrative Sciences, Boston, MA 02215. Offers banking and financial management (MSM); business continuity in emergency management (MSM); economics development and tourism management (MSAS); electronic commerce, systems, and technology (MSAS); financial economics (MSAS); innovation and technology (MSAS); insurance management (MSM); international market management (MSM); multinational commerce (MSAS); project management (MSM). *Accreditation:* AACSB. Part-time and evening/weekend programs available. Postbaccalaureate distance learning degree programs offered (no on-campus study). *Faculty:* 14 full-time (2 women), 21 part-time/adjunct (2 women). *Students:* 151 full-time (75 women), 106 part-time (51 women); includes 27 minority (6 Black or African American, non-Hispanic/Latino; 14 Asian, non-Hispanic/Latino; 7 Hispanic/Latino), 173 international. Average age 28. 500 applicants, 65% accepted, 194 enrolled. In 2011, 154 master's awarded. *Degree requirements:* For master's, thesis optional. *Entrance requirements:* For master's, 1 year of work experience, minimum GPA of 3.0. Additional exam requirements/recommendations for international students: Required—TOEFL (minimum score 560 paper-based; 220 computer-based; 84 iBT). *Application deadline:* Applications are processed on a rolling basis. Application fee: $70. Electronic applications accepted. *Expenses: Tuition:* Full-time $40,848; part-time $1276 per credit hour. *Required fees:* $572; $286 per semester. *Financial support:* In 2011–12, 15 students received support, including 7 research assistantships (averaging $10,000 per year); career-related internships or fieldwork, Federal Work-Study, and unspecified assistantships also available. *Faculty research:* International business, innovative process. *Unit head:* Dr. Kip Becker, Chairman, 617-353-3016, E-mail: adminsc@bu.edu. *Application contact:* Lucille Dicker, Administrative Sciences Department, 617-353-3016, E-mail: adminsc@bu.edu. Web site: http://www.bu.edu/met/programs/.

California State University, Fullerton, Graduate Studies, College of Business and Economics, Department of Information Systems and Decision Sciences, Fullerton, CA 92834-9480. Offers information systems (MS); information systems (decision sciences) (MS); information systems (e-commerce) (MS); information technology (MS); management science (MBA). Part-time programs available. *Students:* 15 full-time (2 women), 66 part-time (10 women); includes 35 minority (1 Black or African American, non-Hispanic/Latino; 23 Asian, non-Hispanic/Latino; 9 Hispanic/Latino; 2 Two or more races, non-Hispanic/Latino), 9 international. Average age 33. 82 applicants, 44% accepted, 30 enrolled. In 2011, 36 master's awarded. *Degree requirements:* For master's, project or thesis. *Entrance requirements:* For master's, GMAT, minimum AACSB index of 950. Application fee: $55. *Financial support:* Career-related internships or fieldwork, Federal Work-Study, institutionally sponsored loans, and scholarships/grants available. Support available to part-time students. Financial award application deadline: 3/1; financial award applicants required to submit FAFSA. *Unit head:* Dr. Bhushan Kapoor, Chair, 657-278-2221. *Application contact:* Admissions/Applications, 657-278-2371.

California State University, Fullerton, Graduate Studies, College of Business and Economics, Program in Business Administration, Fullerton, CA 92834-9480. Offers e-commerce (MBA); international business (MBA). *Accreditation:* AACSB. Part-time programs available. *Students:* 63 full-time (34 women), 89 part-time (35 women); includes 57 minority (2 Black or African American, non-Hispanic/Latino; 41 Asian, non-Hispanic/Latino; 10 Hispanic/Latino; 4 Two or more races, non-Hispanic/Latino), 36 international. Average age 28. 476 applicants, 40% accepted, 60 enrolled. In 2011, 31 master's awarded. *Degree requirements:* For master's, project or thesis. *Entrance requirements:* For master's, GMAT. *Financial support:* Career-related internships or fieldwork, Federal Work-Study, institutionally sponsored loans, and scholarships/grants available. Support available to part-time students. Financial award application deadline: 3/1; financial award applicants required to submit FAFSA. *Unit head:* Dr. Anil Puri, Dean, 657-773-2592. *Application contact:* Admissions/Applications, 657-278-2371.

Carnegie Mellon University, Tepper School of Business and School of Computer Science, Program in Electronic Commerce, Pittsburgh, PA 15213-3891. Offers MS. *Entrance requirements:* For master's, GRE General Test or GMAT. Additional exam requirements/recommendations for international students: Required—TOEFL.

Claremont Graduate University, Graduate Programs, School of Information Systems and Technology, Claremont, CA 91711-6160. Offers electronic commerce (MS, PhD); health information management (MS); information systems (Certificate); knowledge management (MS, PhD); systems development (MS, PhD); telecommunications and networking (MS, PhD); MBA/MS. Part-time programs available. *Faculty:* 7 full-time (1 woman), 1 part-time/adjunct (0 women). *Students:* 68 full-time (20 women), 26 part-time (10 women); includes 31 minority (5 Black or African American, non-Hispanic/Latino; 14 Asian, non-Hispanic/Latino; 9 Hispanic/Latino; 1 Native Hawaiian or other Pacific Islander, non-Hispanic/Latino; 2 Two or more races, non-Hispanic/Latino), 31 international. Average age 37. In 2011, 16 master's, 5 doctorates awarded. *Degree requirements:* For doctorate, comprehensive exam, thesis/dissertation, portfolio. *Entrance requirements:* For master's and doctorate, GMAT, GRE General Test. Additional exam requirements/recommendations for international students: Required—TOEFL (minimum score 550 paper-based; 213 computer-based; 80 iBT). *Application deadline:* For fall admission, 2/1 priority date for domestic students. Applications are processed on a rolling basis. Application fee: $60. Electronic applications accepted. *Expenses: Tuition:* Full-time $36,374; part-time $1581 per unit. *Required fees:* $165 per semester. *Financial support:* Fellowships, research assistantships, teaching assistantships, Federal Work-Study, institutionally sponsored loans, and scholarships/grants available. Support available to part-time students. Financial award application deadline: 2/15; financial award applicants required to submit FAFSA. *Faculty research:* GPSS, man-machine interaction, organizational aspects of computing, implementation of information systems, information systems practice. *Unit head:* Tom Horan, Dean, 909-607-9302, Fax: 909-621-8564, E-mail: tom.horan@cgu.edu. *Application contact:* Anondah Saide, Program Coordinator, 909-607-6006, E-mail: anonda.saide@cgu.edu. Web site: http://www.cgu.edu/pages/153.asp.

Columbia Southern University, MBA Program, Orange Beach, AL 36561. Offers electronic business and technology (MBA); finance (MBA); general (MBA); healthcare management (MBA); hospitality and tourism (MBA); human resources management (MBA); international management (MBA); marketing (MBA); project management (MBA); public administration (MBA); sport management (MBA). Part-time and evening/weekend programs available. Postbaccalaureate distance learning degree programs offered (no on-campus study). *Entrance requirements:* For master's, bachelor's degree from accredited/approved institution. Additional exam requirements/recommendations for international students: Required—TOEFL. Electronic applications accepted.

Dalhousie University, Faculty of Computer Science, Halifax , NS B3H 1W5, Canada. Offers computational biology and bioinformatics (M Sc); computer science (PhD); computer science (project-based) (MA Sc); computer science (thesis-based) (MC Sc); electronic commerce (MEC); health informatics (MHI). *Degree requirements:* For master's, thesis (for some programs); for doctorate, thesis/dissertation. *Entrance requirements:* Additional exam requirements/recommendations for international students: Required—1 of 5 approved tests: TOEFL, IELTS, CANTEST, CAEL, Michigan English Language Assessment Battery. Electronic applications accepted.

DePaul University, Charles H. Kellstadt Graduate School of Business, School of Accountancy and Management Information Systems, Chicago, IL 60604-2287. Offers accountancy (M Acc, MSA); business information technology (MS); e-business (MBA, MS); financial management and control (MBA); management accounting (MBA); management information systems (MBA); taxation (MST). Part-time and evening/weekend programs available. *Faculty:* 30 full-time (9 women), 54 part-time/adjunct (7 women). *Students:* 44 full-time (13 women), 22 part-time (4 women); includes 8 minority (2 Black or African American, non-Hispanic/Latino; 3 Asian, non-Hispanic/Latino; 2 Hispanic/Latino; 1 Two or more races, non-Hispanic/Latino), 4 international. Average age 29. In 2011, 141 master's awarded. *Entrance requirements:* For master's, GMAT, 2 letters of recommendation, resume. Additional exam requirements/recommendations for international students: Required—TOEFL (minimum score 550 paper-based; 213 computer-based). *Application deadline:* For fall admission, 7/1 for domestic students; for winter admission, 10/1 for domestic students; for spring admission, 2/1 for domestic students. Applications are processed on a rolling basis. Application fee: $60. *Financial support:* In 2011–12, 7 research assistantships with full tuition reimbursements (averaging $4,100 per year) were awarded; institutionally sponsored loans also available. Financial award application deadline: 4/2. *Faculty research:* Tax policy, property transactions, stock options as compensation, standards setting, activity-based costing in health care. *Unit head:* Kevin Stevens, Director, 312-362-6989, E-mail: kstevens@depaul.edu. *Application contact:* Christopher E. Kinsella, Director of Cohort MBA Programs, 312-362-8810, Fax: 312-362-6677, E-mail: kgsb@depaul.edu. Web site: http://accountancy.depaul.edu/.

DePaul University, College of Computing and Digital Media, Chicago, IL 60604. Offers animation (MA, MFA); applied technology (MS); business information technology (MS); cinema (MFA); cinema production (MS); computational finance (MS); computer and information sciences (PhD); computer game development (MS); computer graphics and motion technology (MS); computer information and network security (MS); computer science (MS); e-commerce technology (MS); human-computer interaction (MS); information systems (MS); information technology (MA); information technology project management (MS); network engineering and management (MS); predictive analytics (MS); screenwriting (MFA); software engineering (MS); JD/MA; JD/MS. Part-time and evening/weekend programs available. Postbaccalaureate distance learning degree programs offered (no on-campus study). *Faculty:* 64 full-time (16 women), 44 part-time/adjunct (5 women). *Students:* 969 full-time (250 women), 936 part-time (231 women); includes 566 minority (204 Black or African American, non-Hispanic/Latino; 3 American Indian or Alaska Native, non-Hispanic/Latino; 166 Asian, non-Hispanic/Latino; 135 Hispanic/Latino; 7 Native Hawaiian or other Pacific Islander, non-Hispanic/Latino; 51 Two or more races, non-Hispanic/Latino), 282 international. Average age 32. 1,040 applicants, 65% accepted, 324 enrolled. In 2011, 478 master's, 4 doctorates awarded. *Degree requirements:* For master's, thesis (for some programs); for doctorate, comprehensive exam, thesis/dissertation. *Entrance requirements:* For master's, GRE or GMAT (MS in computational finance only), bachelor's degree, resume (MS in predictive analytics only), IT experience (MS in information technology project management only), portfolio review (all MFA programs and MA in animation); for doctorate, GRE, master's degree in computer science. Additional exam requirements/recommendations for international students: Required—TOEFL (minimum score 550 paper-based; 213 computer-based; 80 iBT), IELTS (minimum score 6.5), Pearson Test of English (minimum score 53). *Application deadline:* For fall admission, 8/1 priority date for domestic students, 6/1 for international students; for winter admission, 12/1 priority date for domestic students, 10/1 for international students; for spring admission, 3/1 priority date for domestic students, 1/1 for international students. Applications are processed on a rolling basis. Application fee: $25. Electronic applications accepted. *Expenses:* Contact institution. *Financial support:* In 2011–12, 56 students received support, including 3 fellowships with full tuition reimbursements available (averaging $30,000 per year), 3 research assistantships with full and partial tuition reimbursements available (averaging $22,833 per year), 50 teaching assistantships (averaging $6,194 per year); Federal Work-Study, scholarships/grants, tuition waivers (full and partial), and unspecified assistantships also available. Support available to part-time students. Financial award application deadline: 4/30. *Faculty research:* Data mining, theoretical computer science, gaming, security, animation and film. *Total annual research expenditures:* $3.9 million. *Unit head:* Elly Kafritsas-Wessels, Senior Administrative Assistant, 312-362-5816, Fax: 312-362-5185, E-mail: ekafrits@cdm.depaul.edu. *Application contact:* James Parker, Director of Graduate Admission, 312-362-8714, Fax: 312-362-5179, E-mail: jparke29@cdm.depaul.edu. Web site: http://cdm.depaul.edu.

Eastern Michigan University, Graduate School, College of Business, Programs in Business Administration, Ypsilanti, MI 48197. Offers business administration (MBA, Graduate Certificate); computer information systems (Graduate Certificate); e-business (MBA, Graduate Certificate); enterprise business intelligence (MBA); entrepreneurship (MBA, Graduate Certificate); finance (MBA, Graduate Certificate); human resources (MBA); human resources management (Graduate Certificate); information systems (MBA); internal auditing (MBA); international business (MBA, Graduate Certificate); marketing management (Graduate Certificate); nonprofit management (MBA); organizational development (Graduate Certificate); supply chain management (MBA, Graduate Certificate). *Accreditation:* AACSB. Part-time programs available. Postbaccalaureate distance learning degree programs offered (no on-campus study). *Students:* 79 full-time (39 women), 287 part-time (143 women); includes 55 minority (22 Black or African American, non-Hispanic/Latino; 24 Asian, non-Hispanic/Latino; 6 Hispanic/Latino; 3 Two or more races, non-Hispanic/Latino), 238 international. Average age 32. 317 applicants, 62% accepted, 89 enrolled. In 2011, 102 master's, 58 other advanced degrees awarded. *Entrance requirements:* For master's, GMAT (minimum score 450), minimum cumulative undergraduate GPA of 2.75. Additional exam requirements/recommendations for international students: Required—TOEFL. *Application deadline:* For fall admission, 5/15 for domestic students, 5/1 for international students; for winter admission, 10/15 for domestic students, 10/1 for international students; for spring admission, 3/15 for domestic students, 3/1 for international students. Applications are processed on a rolling basis. Application fee: $35. *Expenses:* Tuition, state resident: full-time $10,367; part-time $432 per credit hour. Tuition, nonresident: full-time $20,435; part-time $851 per credit hour. *Required fees:* $39 per credit hour. $46 per semester. One-time fee: $100. Tuition and fees vary according to course level, degree level and reciprocity agreements. *Financial support:* Fellowships, research assistantships with full tuition reimbursements, teaching assistantships with full tuition reimbursements, career-related internships or fieldwork, Federal Work-Study, institutionally sponsored loans, scholarships/grants, tuition waivers (partial), and unspecified assistantships available. Support available to part-time students. Financial award applicants required to submit FAFSA. *Unit head:* K. Michelle Henry, Director, Academic Services, 734-487-4444, Fax: 734-483-1316, E-mail: mhenry1@emich.edu. *Application contact:* Beste Windes, Advisor, 734-487-4444, Fax: 734-483-1316, E-mail: bwindes@emich.edu. Web site: http://www.emich.edu/public/cob/gr/grad.html.

Ellis University, MBA Program, Chicago, IL 60606-7204. Offers e-commerce (MBA); finance (MBA); general business (MBA); global management (MBA); health care administration (MBA); leadership (MBA); management of information systems (MBA); marketing (MBA); professional accounting (MBA); project management (MBA); public accounting (MBA); risk management (MBA).

Fairleigh Dickinson University, Metropolitan Campus, University College: Arts, Sciences, and Professional Studies, School of Computer Sciences and Engineering, Program in E-Commerce, Teaneck, NJ 07666-1914. Offers MS.

Florida Institute of Technology, Graduate Programs, Extended Studies Division, Melbourne, FL 32901-6975. Offers acquisition and contract management (MS); aerospace engineering (MS); business administration (MBA); computer information systems (MS); computer science (MS); electrical engineering (MS); engineering management (MS); human resources management (MS); logistics management (MS), including humanitarian and disaster relief logistics; management (MS), including acquisition and contract management, e-business, human resources management, information systems, logistics management, management, transportation management; material acquisition management (MS); mechanical engineering (MS); operations research (MS); project management (MS), including information systems, operations research; public administration (MPA); quality management (MS); software engineering (MS); space systems (MS); space systems management (MS); supply chain management (MS); systems management (MS), including information systems, operations research. Part-time and evening/weekend programs available. Postbaccalaureate distance learning degree programs offered (no on-campus study). *Faculty:* 9 full-time (2 women), 105 part-time/adjunct (24 women). *Students:* 113 full-time (52 women), 1,150 part-time (484 women); includes 496 minority (332 Black or African American, non-Hispanic/Latino; 11 American Indian or Alaska Native, non-Hispanic/Latino; 42 Asian, non-Hispanic/Latino; 71 Hispanic/Latino; 2 Native Hawaiian or other Pacific Islander, non-Hispanic/Latino; 38 Two or more races, non-Hispanic/Latino), 11 international. Average age 35. 568 applicants, 56% accepted, 296 enrolled. In 2011, 471 master's awarded. *Degree requirements:* For master's, comprehensive exam (for some programs), capstone course. *Entrance requirements:* For master's, GMAT or resume showing 8 years of supervised experience, minimum GPA of 3.0, 2 letters of recommendation, resume. Additional exam requirements/recommendations for international students: Required—TOEFL (minimum score 550 paper-based; 213 computer-based; 79 iBT). *Application deadline:* For fall admission, 4/1 for international students; for spring admission, 9/30 for international students. Applications are processed on a rolling basis. Application fee: $0. Electronic applications accepted. *Expenses:* Contact institution. *Financial support:* Application deadline: 3/1; applicants required to submit FAFSA. *Unit head:* Dr. Theodore R. Richardson, III, Senior Associate Dean, 321-674-8123, Fax: 321-674-7597, E-mail: trichardson@fit.edu. *Application contact:* Carolyn Farrior, Director of Graduate Admissions, Online Learning and Off-Campus Programs, 321-674-7118, Fax: 321-674-8216, E-mail: cfarrior@fit.edu. Web site: http://es.fit.edu.

Florida Institute of Technology, Graduate Programs, Nathan M. Bisk College of Business, Online Programs, Melbourne, FL 32901-6975. Offers accounting (MBA); accounting and finance (MBA); business administration (MBA); finance (MBA); healthcare management (MBA); information technology (MS); information technology cybersecurity (MS); information technology management (MBA); international business (MBA); Internet marketing (MBA); management (MBA); marketing (MBA); project management (MBA). Part-time and evening/weekend programs available. Postbaccalaureate distance learning degree programs offered (no on-campus study). *Faculty:* 47 part-time/adjunct (15 women). *Students:* 8 full-time (4 women), 1,122 part-time (547 women); includes 418 minority (271 Black or African American, non-Hispanic/Latino; 5 American Indian or Alaska Native, non-Hispanic/Latino; 55 Asian, non-Hispanic/Latino; 81 Hispanic/Latino; 6 Native Hawaiian or other Pacific Islander, non-Hispanic/Latino), 23 international. Average age 36. In 2011, 329 master's awarded. *Entrance requirements:* For master's, GMAT or resume showing 8 years of supervised experience, 2 letters of recommendation, resume, competency in math past college algebra. Additional exam requirements/recommendations for international students: Required—TOEFL (minimum score 550 paper-based; 213 computer-based; 79 iBT). *Application deadline:* For fall admission, 4/1 for international students; for spring admission, 9/30 for international students. Applications are processed on a rolling basis. Electronic applications accepted. *Expenses:* Contact institution. *Financial support:* Available to part-time students. Application deadline: 3/1; applicants required to submit FAFSA. *Unit head:* Dr. Mary S. Bonhomme, Dean, Florida Tech Online/Associate Provost for Online Learning, 321-674-8202, Fax: 321-674-8216, E-mail: bonhomme@fit.edu. *Application contact:* Carolyn Farrior, Director of Graduate Admissions, Online Learning and Off-Campus Programs, 321-674-7118, Fax: 321-674-8216, E-mail: cfarrior@fit.edu. Web site: http://online.fit.edu.

George Mason University, Volgenau School of Engineering, Department of Computer Science, Fairfax, VA 22030. Offers computer games technology (Certificate); computer networking (Certificate); computer science (MS, PhD); database management (Certificate); electronic commerce (Certificate); foundations of information systems (Certificate); information engineering (Certificate); information security and assurance (MS, Certificate); information systems (MS); intelligent agents (Certificate); software architecture (Certificate); software engineering (MS, Certificate); software engineering for C41 (Certificate); Web-based software engineering (Certificate). MS program offered jointly with Old Dominion University, University of Virginia, Virginia Commonwealth University, and Virginia Polytechnic Institute and State University. *Faculty:* 40 full-time (9 women), 17 part-time/adjunct (0 women). *Students:* 208 full-time (52 women), 357 part-time (75 women); includes 98 minority (17 Black or African American, non-Hispanic/Latino; 63 Asian, non-Hispanic/Latino; 14 Hispanic/Latino; 4 Two or more races, non-Hispanic/Latino), 205 international. Average age 30. 882 applicants, 52% accepted, 137 enrolled. In 2011, 164 master's, 5 doctorates, 28 other advanced degrees awarded. *Degree requirements:* For master's, thesis optional; for doctorate, comprehensive exam, thesis/dissertation. *Entrance requirements:* For master's, GRE, proof of financial support; 2 official college transcripts; resume; self-evaluation form; official bank statement; photocopy of passport; 3 letters of recommendation; baccalaureate degree related to computer science; minimum GPA of 3.0 in last 2 years of undergraduate work; 1 year beyond 1st-year calculus; personal goals statement; for doctorate, GRE, personal goals statement; 2 official copies of transcripts; self-evaluation form; 3 letters of recommendation; photocopy of passport; proof of financial support; official bank statement; resume; 4-year baccalaureate degree with strong background in computer science. Additional exam requirements/recommendations for international students: Required—TOEFL (minimum score 575 paper-based; 230 computer-based; 88 iBT), IELTS, Pearson Test of English. *Application deadline:* For fall admission, 1/15 priority date for domestic students; for spring admission, 8/15 priority date for domestic students. Application fee: $65 ($80 for international students). Electronic applications accepted. *Expenses:* Tuition, state resident: full-time $8750; part-time $364.58 per credit. Tuition, nonresident: full-time $24,092; part-time $1003.83 per credit. *Required fees:* $2514; $104.75 per credit. *Financial support:* In 2011–12, 100 students received support, including 3 fellowships (averaging $18,000 per year), 50 research assistantships (averaging $15,232 per year), 47 teaching assistantships (averaging $11,675 per year); career-related internships or fieldwork, Federal Work-Study, scholarships/grants, unspecified assistantships, and health care benefits (full-time research or teaching assistantship recipients) also available. Support available to part-time students. Financial award application deadline: 3/1; financial award applicants required to submit FAFSA. *Faculty research:* Artificial intelligence, image processing/graphics, parallel/distributed systems, software engineering systems. *Total annual research expenditures:* $1.9 million. *Unit head:* Sanjeev Setia, Chair, 703-993-4098, Fax: 703-993-1710, E-mail: setia@gmu.edu. *Application contact:* Michele Pieper, Administrative Assistant, 703-993-9483, Fax: 703-993-1710, E-mail: mpieper@gmu.edu. Web site: http://cs.gmu.edu/.

Georgia Institute of Technology, Graduate Studies and Research, College of Management, Program in Business Administration, Atlanta, GA 30332-0001. Offers accounting (MBA); e-commerce (Certificate); engineering entrepreneurship (MBA); entrepreneurship (Certificate); finance (MBA); information technology management (MBA); international business (MBA, Certificate); management of technology (Certificate); marketing (MBA); operations management (MBA); organizational behavior (MBA); strategic management (MBA). *Accreditation:* AACSB.

Hawai`i Pacific University, College of Business Administration, Honolulu, HI 96813. Offers accounting/CPA (MBA); e-business (MBA); economics (MBA); finance (MBA); human resource management (MA, MBA); information systems (MBA, MSIS), including knowledge management (MSIS), software engineering (MSIS), telecommunications security (MSIS); international business (MBA); management (MBA); marketing (MBA); organizational change (MA, MBA); travel industry management (MBA). Part-time and evening/weekend programs available. *Faculty:* 15 full-time (5 women), 11 part-time/adjunct (4 women). *Students:* 297 full-time (133 women), 183 part-time (87 women); includes 282 minority (17 Black or African American, non-Hispanic/Latino; 131 Asian, non-Hispanic/Latino; 43 Hispanic/Latino; 10 Native Hawaiian or other Pacific Islander, non-Hispanic/Latino; 81 Two or more races, non-Hispanic/Latino). Average age 30. 302 applicants, 82% accepted, 160 enrolled. In 2011, 141 master's awarded. *Degree requirements:* For master's, thesis. *Entrance requirements:* For master's, GMAT. Additional exam requirements/recommendations for international students: Recommended—TOEFL (minimum score 550 paper-based; 213 computer-based; 80 iBT), TWE (minimum score 5). *Application deadline:* For fall admission, 2/15 priority date for domestic students; for spring admission, 10/15 priority date for domestic students. Applications are processed on a rolling basis. Application fee: $50. Electronic applications accepted. *Expenses: Tuition:* Full-time $13,230; part-time $735 per credit. Tuition and fees vary according to course load and program. *Financial support:* In 2011–12, 103 students received support. Research assistantships, career-related internships or fieldwork, Federal Work-Study, scholarships/grants, tuition waivers, and unspecified assistantships available. Financial award application deadline: 3/1; financial award applicants required to submit FAFSA. *Faculty research:* Statistical control process as used by management, studies in comparative cross-cultural management styles, not-for-profit management. *Unit head:* Dr. Deborah Crown, Dean, 808-544-0275, Fax: 808-544-0283, E-mail: dcrown@hpu.edu. *Application contact:* Chad Schempp, Director of Graduate Admissions, 808-543-8035, Fax: 808-544-0280, E-mail: graduate@hpu.edu. Web site: http://www.hpu.edu/mba.

See Display on page 98 and Close-Up on page 221.

HEC Montreal, School of Business Administration, Graduate Diplomas Programs in Administration, Program in E-Business, Montréal, QC H3T 2A7, Canada. Offers

Electronic Commerce

Graduate Diploma. All courses are given in French. Part-time programs available. *Students:* 14 full-time (6 women), 58 part-time (20 women). 69 applicants, 51% accepted, 28 enrolled. In 2011, 26 Graduate Diplomas awarded. *Degree requirements:* For Graduate Diploma, one foreign language. *Entrance requirements:* For degree, bachelor's degree in administration or equivalent. *Application deadline:* For fall admission, 4/15 for domestic and international students; for winter admission, 9/15 for domestic and international students. Application fee: $80 Canadian dollars. Electronic applications accepted. Application fee is waived when completed online. *Expenses:* Contact institution. *Financial support:* Scholarships/grants available. Financial award application deadline: 9/2. *Unit head:* Silvia Ponce, Director, 514-340-6393, E-mail: silvia.ponce@hec.ca. *Application contact:* Jo Anne Audet, Administrative Director, 514-340-1315, Fax: 514-340-6411, E-mail: joanne.audet@hec.ca. Web site: http://www.hec.ca/programmes_formations/des/dess/dess_affaires_electroniques/index.html.

HEC Montreal, School of Business Administration, Master of Science Programs in Administration, Program in Electronic Commerce, Montréal, QC H3T 2A7, Canada. Offers M Sc. Program offered jointly with University of Montreal. Part-time programs available. *Students:* 16 full-time (8 women), 23 part-time (10 women). 45 applicants, 42% accepted, 8 enrolled. In 2011, 24 master's awarded. *Degree requirements:* For master's, one foreign language. *Entrance requirements:* For master's, bachelor's degree in law, management, information systems or related field. *Application deadline:* For fall admission, 4/1 for domestic and international students. Application fee: $80 Canadian dollars. Electronic applications accepted. Application fee is waived when completed online. *Expenses:* Contact institution. *Financial support:* Research assistantships and teaching assistantships available. Financial award application deadline: 9/2. *Unit head:* Olivier Gerbe, Co-Director, 514-340-6855, Fax: 514-340-6132, E-mail: olivier.gerbe@hec.ca. *Application contact:* Jo Anne Audet, Administrative Director, 514-340-1315, Fax: 514-340-6411, E-mail: joanne.audet@hec.ca. Web site: http://www.hec.ca/programmes_formations/des/maitrises_professionnelles/maitrise_commerce_electronique/index.html.

Instituto Tecnológico y de Estudios Superiores de Monterrey, Campus Central de Veracruz, Graduate Programs, Córdoba, Mexico. Offers administration (MA); administration of information technologies (MTI); computer sciences (MCC); education (MEE); educational institution administration (MAD); educational technology (MTE); electronic commerce (MCE); finance (MAF); humanistic studies (MEH); international business for Latin America (MNL); marketing (MMT); science (MCP). Part-time and evening/weekend programs available. Postbaccalaureate distance learning degree programs offered (minimal on-campus study). *Degree requirements:* For master's, thesis (for some programs). *Entrance requirements:* For master's, PAEP College Board. Electronic applications accepted.

Instituto Tecnológico y de Estudios Superiores de Monterrey, Campus Ciudad Juárez, Program in Electronic Commerce, Ciudad Juárez, Mexico. Offers MEC.

Instituto Tecnológico y de Estudios Superiores de Monterrey, Campus Estado de México, Professional and Graduate Division, Estado de Mexico, Mexico. Offers administration of information technologies (MITA); architecture (M Arch); business administration (GMBA, MBA); computer sciences (MCS, PhD); education (M Ed); educational institution administration (MAD); educational technology and innovation (PhD); electronic commerce (MEC); environmental systems (MS); finance (MAF); humanistic studies (MHS); information sciences and knowledge management (MISKM); information systems (MS); manufacturing systems (MS); marketing (MEM); quality systems and productivity (MS); science and materials engineering (PhD); telecommunications management (MTM). Part-time programs available. Postbaccalaureate distance learning degree programs offered (minimal on-campus study). *Degree requirements:* For master's, one foreign language, thesis (for some programs); for doctorate, one foreign language, thesis/dissertation. *Entrance requirements:* For master's, E-PAEP 500, interview; for doctorate, E-PAEP 500, research proposal. Additional exam requirements/recommendations for international students: Required—TOEFL (minimum score 550 paper-based). *Faculty research:* Surface treatments by plasmas, mechanical properties, robotics, graphical computing, mechatronics security protocols.

Instituto Tecnológico y de Estudios Superiores de Monterrey, Campus Irapuato, Graduate Programs, Irapuato, Mexico. Offers administration (MBA); administration of information technology (MAIT); administration of telecommunications (MAT); architecture (M Arch); computer science (MCS); education (M Ed); educational administration (MEA); educational innovation and technology (DEIT); educational technology (MET); electronic commerce (MBA); environmental administration and planning (MEAP); environmental systems (MES); finances (MBA); humanistic studies (MHS); international management for Latin American executives (MIMLAE); library and information science (MLIS); manufacturing quality management (MMQM); marketing research (MBA).

Lewis University, College of Business, Graduate School of Management, Program in Business Administration, Romeoville, IL 60446. Offers accounting (MBA); custom elective option (MBA); e-business (MBA); finance (MBA); healthcare management (MBA); human resources management (MBA); information security (MBA); international business (MBA); management information systems (MBA); marketing (MBA); project management (MBA); technology and operations management (MBA). Part-time and evening/weekend programs available. *Students:* 112 full-time (60 women), 232 part-time (118 women); includes 104 minority (62 Black or African American, non-Hispanic/Latino; 1 American Indian or Alaska Native, non-Hispanic/Latino; 7 Asian, non-Hispanic/Latino; 33 Hispanic/Latino; 1 Native Hawaiian or other Pacific Islander, non-Hispanic/Latino), 9 international. Average age 28. In 2011, 99 master's awarded. *Entrance requirements:* For master's, interview, bachelor's degree, resume, 2 recommendations. Additional exam requirements/recommendations for international students: Required—TOEFL (minimum score 550 paper-based; 213 computer-based). *Application deadline:* For fall admission, 8/15 priority date for domestic students, 5/1 for international students; for spring admission, 11/15 for international students. Applications are processed on a rolling basis. Application fee: $40. Electronic applications accepted. *Financial support:* Career-related internships or fieldwork, Federal Work-Study, scholarships/grants, and unspecified assistantships available. Financial award application deadline: 5/1; financial award applicants required to submit FAFSA. *Unit head:* Dr. Maureen Culleeney, Academic Program Director, 815-838-0500 Ext. 5631, E-mail: culleema@lewisu.edu. *Application contact:* Michele Ryan, Director of Admission, 815-838-0500 Ext. 5384, E-mail: gsm@lewisu.edu.

Mercy College, School of Liberal Arts, Program in Internet Business Systems, Dobbs Ferry, NY 10522-1189. Offers Web strategy and design (MS, Certificate). Part-time and evening/weekend programs available. Postbaccalaureate distance learning degree programs offered (no on-campus study). *Entrance requirements:* For master's, interview, resume, 2 letters of recommendation, 2-page written personal statement. Additional exam requirements/recommendations for international students: Required—TOEFL (minimum score 600 paper-based; 250 computer-based; 100 iBT), IELTS (minimum score 8). Electronic applications accepted. *Expenses:* Contact institution. *Faculty research:* Internet business systems, Internet marketing, Web design, Internet technologies.

Northwestern University, Medill School of Journalism, Integrated Marketing Communications Program, Evanston, IL 60208. Offers advertising/sales promotion (MSIMC); direct database and e-commerce marketing (MSIMC); general studies (MSIMC); public relations (MSIMC). Part-time programs available. *Entrance requirements:* For master's, GRE General Test or GMAT, full-time work experience (preferred). Additional exam requirements/recommendations for international students: Required—TOEFL. Electronic applications accepted. *Faculty research:* Data mining, business to business marketing, values in advertising, political advertising.

Pace University, Seidenberg School of Computer Science and Information Systems, New York, NY 10038. Offers computer communications and networks (Certificate); computer science (MS); computing studies (DPS); information systems (MS); Internet technologies for e-commerce (Certificate); Internet technology (MS); object-oriented programming (Certificate); security and information assurance (Certificate); software development and engineering (MS); telecommunications (MS, Certificate). Part-time and evening/weekend programs available. *Students:* 82 full-time (19 women), 356 part-time (99 women); includes 175 minority (64 Black or African American, non-Hispanic/Latino; 1 American Indian or Alaska Native, non-Hispanic/Latino; 59 Asian, non-Hispanic/Latino; 47 Hispanic/Latino; 4 Two or more races, non-Hispanic/Latino), 72 international. Average age 37. 304 applicants, 67% accepted, 92 enrolled. In 2011, 136 master's, 9 doctorates, 32 other advanced degrees awarded. *Entrance requirements:* For master's, GRE General Test. Additional exam requirements/recommendations for international students: Required—TOEFL. *Application deadline:* For fall admission, 7/31 priority date for domestic students; for spring admission, 11/30 for domestic students. Applications are processed on a rolling basis. Application fee: $70. Electronic applications accepted. *Expenses:* Contact institution. *Financial support:* Research assistantships and career-related internships or fieldwork available. Support available to part-time students. Financial award applicants required to submit FAFSA. *Unit head:* Dr. Constance Knapp, Interim Dean, 914-773-3750, Fax: 914-773-3533, E-mail: cknapp@pace.edu. *Application contact:* Susan Ford-Goldschein, Director of Graduate Admissions, 914-422-4283, Fax: 914-422-4287, E-mail: gradwp@pace.edu. Web site: http://www.pace.edu/.

Polytechnic Institute of New York University, Department of Technology Management, Brooklyn, NY 11201-2990. Offers construction management (Advanced Certificate); electronic business management (Advanced Certificate); entrepreneurship (Advanced Certificate); human resources management (Advanced Certificate); information management (Advanced Certificate); management (MS); management of technology (MS); organizational behavior (MS, Advanced Certificate); project management (Advanced Certificate); technology management (MBA, PhD, Advanced Certificate); telecommunications and information management (MS); telecommunications management (Advanced Certificate). Part-time and evening/weekend programs available. *Faculty:* 6 full-time (1 woman), 32 part-time/adjunct (4 women). *Students:* 185 full-time (84 women), 94 part-time (41 women); includes 56 minority (15 Black or African American, non-Hispanic/Latino; 31 Asian, non-Hispanic/Latino; 10 Hispanic/Latino), 143 international. Average age 30. 467 applicants, 48% accepted, 123 enrolled. In 2011, 174 master's, 1 doctorate awarded. *Degree requirements:* For master's, comprehensive exam (for some programs), thesis (for some programs); for doctorate, comprehensive exam, thesis/dissertation. *Entrance requirements:* For master's, GMAT, minimum B average in undergraduate course work. Additional exam requirements/recommendations for international students: Required—TOEFL (minimum score 550 paper-based; 213 computer-based; 80 iBT); Recommended—IELTS (minimum score 6.5). *Application deadline:* For fall admission, 7/31 priority date for domestic students, 4/30 for international students; for spring admission, 12/31 priority date for domestic students, 11/30 for international students. Applications are processed on a rolling basis. Application fee: $75. Electronic applications accepted. *Expenses: Tuition:* Full-time $22,464; part-time $1248 per credit. *Required fees:* $501 per semester. *Financial support:* In 2011–12, 1 fellowship (averaging $26,400 per year) was awarded; research assistantships, teaching assistantships, institutionally sponsored loans, scholarships/grants, and unspecified assistantships also available. Support available to part-time students. *Unit head:* Prof. Bharadwaj Rao, Head, 718-260-3617, Fax: 718-260-3874, E-mail: brao@poly.edu. *Application contact:* JeanCarlo Bonilla, Director of Graduate Enrollment Management, 718-260-3182, Fax: 718-260-3624, E-mail: gradinfo@poly.edu. Web site: http://www.managementdept.poly.edu.

Regis University, College for Professional Studies, School of Computer and Information Sciences, Denver, CO 80221-1099. Offers database administration with Oracle (Certificate); database development (Certificate); database technologies (M Sc); enterprise Java software development (Certificate); enterprise resource planning (Certificate); executive information technologies (Certificate); information assurance (M Sc, Certificate); information technology management (M Sc); software engineering (M Sc, Certificate); software engineering and database technologies (M Sc); storage area networks (Certificate); systems engineering (M Sc, Certificate). Offered at Boulder Campus, Northwest Denver Campus, Southeast Denver Campus, Fort Collins Campus, Colorado Springs Campus, and Broomfield Campus. Part-time and evening/weekend programs available. Postbaccalaureate distance learning degree programs offered (no on-campus study). *Degree requirements:* For master's, thesis, final research project. *Entrance requirements:* For master's, 2 years of related experience, resume, interview; for Certificate, 2 years of related experience, resumé. Additional exam requirements/recommendations for international students: Required—TOEFL (minimum score 213 computer-based), TWE (minimum score 5) or university-based test. Electronic applications accepted. *Expenses:* Contact institution. *Faculty research:* Secure Virtual Laboratory Architecture, Joint IA project with W2C06 Institute, Information Policy, OLTP and OLAP Technologies, knowledge management, software architectures.

Stevens Institute of Technology, Graduate School, Wesley J. Howe School of Technology Management, Program in Information Systems, Hoboken, NJ 07030. Offers computer science (MS); e-commerce (MS); enterprise systems (MS); entrepreneurial information technology (MS); information architecture (MS); information management (MS, Certificate); information security (MS); information technology in financial services industry (MS); information technology in the pharmaceutical industry (MS); information technology outsourcing management (MS); project management (MS, Certificate); software engineering (MS); telecommunications (MS). *Degree requirements:* For master's, thesis optional. *Entrance requirements:* For master's, GMAT, GRE General Test. Additional exam requirements/recommendations for international students: Required—TOEFL. Electronic applications accepted.

Universidad del Este, Graduate School, Carolina, PR 00984. Offers accounting (MBA); adult education (M Ed); agribusiness (MBA); criminal justice and criminology (MA); curriculum and instruction - early education (M Ed); curriculum and instruction - elementary (M Ed); curriculum and instruction - English (M Ed); curriculum and instruction - Spanish (M Ed); human resources (MBA); information security management (MBA); information technology and Web business development (MBA); management (MBA); public policy (MPA); social work (MA), including clinical social work; special education (M Ed); strategic leadership (MBA).

Université de Montréal, Faculty of Arts and Sciences, Department of Computer Science and Operational Research, Montréal, QC H3C 3J7, Canada. Offers computer systems (M Sc, PhD); electronic commerce (M Sc). Part-time programs available. Terminal master's awarded for partial completion of doctoral program. *Degree requirements:* For master's, one foreign language, thesis; for doctorate, one foreign language, thesis/dissertation, general exam. *Entrance requirements:* For master's, B Sc in related field; for doctorate, MA or M Sc in related field. Electronic applications accepted. *Faculty research:* Optimization statistics, programming languages, telecommunications, theoretical computer science, artificial intelligence.

Université de Sherbrooke, Faculty of Administration, Program in E-Commerce, Sherbrooke, QC J1K 2R1, Canada. Offers M Sc. *Faculty:* 4 full-time (0 women), 7 part-time/adjunct (1 woman). *Students:* 18 full-time (7 women). Average age 25. 56 applicants, 39% accepted, 17 enrolled. In 2011, 14 master's awarded. *Degree requirements:* For master's, one foreign language, thesis. *Entrance requirements:* For master's, bachelor's degree in related field, minimum GPA of 3.0 (on 4.3 scale), letters of reference, fluency in French. *Application deadline:* For fall admission, 4/30 for domestic students, 1/15 for international students. Applications are processed on a rolling basis. Application fee: $70. Electronic applications accepted. *Faculty research:* RFID, B2B, Web social NW, Web value concept. *Unit head:* Prof. Julien Bilodeau, Director, Graduate Programs in Business, 819-821-8000 Ext. 62355, E-mail: julien.bilodeau@usherbrooke.ca. *Application contact:* Marie-Claude Drouin, Assistant to the Director, 819-821-7685, Fax: 819-821-7966.

Université Laval, Faculty of Administrative Sciences, Programs in Business Administration, Québec, QC G1K 7P4, Canada. Offers accounting (MBA); agri-food management (MBA); electronic business (MBA, Diploma); factory management and logistics (MBA); finance (MBA); firm management (MBA); geomatic management (MBA); information technology management (MBA); international management (MBA); management (MBA); management accounting (MBA, Diploma); marketing (MBA); modeling and organizational decision (MBA); occupational health and safety management (MBA); pharmacy management (MBA); social and environmental responsibility (MBA); technological entrepreneurship (Diploma). *Accreditation:* AACSB. Part-time and evening/weekend programs available. Postbaccalaureate distance learning degree programs offered (no on-campus study). *Entrance requirements:* For master's and Diploma, knowledge of French and English. Electronic applications accepted.

University at Buffalo, the State University of New York, Graduate School, College of Arts and Sciences, Department of Economics, Buffalo, NY 14260. Offers economics (MA, MS, PhD); financial economics (Certificate); health services (Certificate); information and Internet economics (Certificate); international economics (Certificate); law and regulation (Certificate); urban and regional economics (Certificate). Part-time programs available. *Faculty:* 19 full-time (3 women), 7 part-time/adjunct (2 women). *Students:* 218 full-time (82 women); includes 7 minority (2 Black or African American, non-Hispanic/Latino; 5 Asian, non-Hispanic/Latino), 184 international. Average age 24. 413 applicants, 65% accepted, 94 enrolled. In 2011, 108 master's, 8 doctorates, 4 other advanced degrees awarded. Terminal master's awarded for partial completion of doctoral program. *Degree requirements:* For master's, comprehensive exam; for doctorate, comprehensive exam, thesis/dissertation, field and theory exams. *Entrance requirements:* For master's, GRE General Test or GMAT; for doctorate, GRE General Test. Additional exam requirements/recommendations for international students: Required—TOEFL (minimum score 550 paper-based; 213 computer-based; 79 iBT), TWE. *Application deadline:* For fall admission, 1/15 priority date for domestic students, 1/15 for international students. Applications are processed on a rolling basis. Application fee: $75. Electronic applications accepted. *Financial support:* In 2011–12, 24 students received support, including 10 fellowships with full tuition reimbursements available (averaging $12,779 per year), 1 research assistantship with full tuition reimbursement available (averaging $13,500 per year), 12 teaching assistantships with full tuition reimbursements available (averaging $13,364 per year); Federal Work-Study, health care benefits, and unspecified assistantships also available. Financial award application deadline: 2/1; financial award applicants required to submit FAFSA. *Faculty research:* Human capital, international economics, econometrics, applied economics, urban economics, economic growth and development. *Unit head:* Dr. Isaac Ehrlich, Chair, 716-645-8670, Fax: 716-645-2127, E-mail: mgtehrl@buffalo.edu. *Application contact:* Dr. Nagesh Revankar, Director of Graduate Studies, 716-645-2121 Ext. 428, Fax: 716-645-2127, E-mail: ecorevan@buffalo.edu. Web site: http://www.economics.buffalo.edu/.

The University of Akron, Graduate School, College of Business Administration, Department of Management, Program in Electronic Business, Akron, OH 44325. Offers MBA. *Students:* 1 full-time (0 women), all international. Average age 28. 2 applicants, 0% accepted, 0 enrolled. In 2011, 1 master's awarded. *Entrance requirements:* For master's, GMAT, minimum GPA of 2.75, two letters of recommendation, statement of purpose, resume. Additional exam requirements/recommendations for international students: Required—TOEFL (minimum score 550 paper-based; 213 computer-based; 79 iBT). *Application deadline:* For fall admission, 7/15 for domestic and international students; for spring admission, 11/15 for domestic and international students. Applications are processed on a rolling basis. Application fee: $30 ($40 for international students). Electronic applications accepted. *Expenses:* Tuition, state resident: full-time $7038; part-time $391 per credit hour. Tuition, nonresident: full-time $12,051; part-time $670 per credit hour. *Required fees:* $1274; $34 per credit hour. *Unit head:* Dr. B. S. Vijayaraman, Head, 330-972-5442, E-mail: bsv@uakron.edu. *Application contact:* Dr. Susan Hanlon, Director of Graduate Business Programs, 330-972-7043, Fax: 330-972-6588, E-mail: shanlon@uakron.edu.

University of Colorado Denver, Business School, Program in Marketing, Denver, CO 80217. Offers brand management and marketing communication (MS); global marketing (MS); high-tech and entrepreneurial marketing (MS); Internet marketing (MS); marketing for sustainability (MS); marketing research (MS); sports and entertainment marketing (MS). Part-time and evening/weekend programs available. *Students:* 39 full-time (29 women), 11 part-time (6 women); includes 4 minority (3 Hispanic/Latino; 1 Two or more races, non-Hispanic/Latino), 8 international. Average age 28. 40 applicants, 65% accepted, 16 enrolled. In 2011, 8 master's awarded. *Degree requirements:* For master's, 30 semester hours (21 of marketing core courses, 9 of graduate marketing electives). *Entrance requirements:* For master's, GMAT, resume, essay, two letters of recommendation, financial statements (for international applicants). Additional exam requirements/recommendations for international students: Required—TOEFL (minimum score 525 paper-based; 197 computer-based; 71 iBT). *Application deadline:* For fall admission, 4/15 priority date for domestic students, 3/15 for international students; for spring admission, 10/15 priority date for domestic students, 10/1 for international students. Applications are processed on a rolling basis. Application fee: $50 ($75 for international students). Electronic applications accepted. *Expenses:* Contact institution. *Financial support:* Federal Work-Study and scholarships/grants available. Support available to part-time students. Financial award application deadline: 4/1; financial award applicants required to submit FAFSA. *Faculty research:* Marketing issues in the Chinese environment, impact of individual difference and contextual factors on the risk-taking behaviors of managers making new-business creation decisions, attribution theory perspective of conflict between marketers and engineers, organizational identity and identification, international market entry strategies. *Unit head:* Dr. David Forlani, Associate Professor/Director of Marketing Programs, 303-315-8420, E-mail: david.forlani@ucdenver.edu. *Application contact:* Shelly Townley, Admissions Director, Graduate Programs, 303-315-8202, E-mail: shelly.townley@ucdenver.edu. Web site: http://www.ucdenver.edu/academics/colleges/business/degrees/ms/marketing/Pages/Marketing.aspx.

University of Florida, Graduate School, Warrington College of Business Administration, Hough Graduate School of Business, Programs in Business Administration, Gainesville, FL 32611. Offers accounting (MBA); arts administration (MBA); business strategy and public policy (MBA); competitive strategy (MBA); decision and information sciences (MBA); electronic commerce (MBA); finance (MBA); general business (MBA); global management (MBA); Graham-Buffett security analysis (MBA); health administration (MBA); human resources management (MBA); international studies (MBA); Latin American business (MBA); management (MBA); marketing (MBA); sports administration (MBA); JD/MBA; MBA/MS; MBA/PhD; MBA/Pharm D; MD/MBA. *Accreditation:* AACSB. Part-time and evening/weekend programs available. *Faculty:* 71 full-time (10 women). *Students:* 412 full-time (111 women), 467 part-time (135 women); includes 235 minority (39 Black or African American, non-Hispanic/Latino; 7 American Indian or Alaska Native, non-Hispanic/Latino; 79 Asian, non-Hispanic/Latino; 109 Hispanic/Latino; 1 Native Hawaiian or other Pacific Islander, non-Hispanic/Latino), 44 international. Average age 32. 589 applicants, 52% accepted, 247 enrolled. In 2011, 505 master's awarded. *Degree requirements:* For master's, capstone course. *Entrance requirements:* For master's, GMAT, minimum GPA of 3.0, interview. Additional exam requirements/recommendations for international students: Required—TOEFL (minimum score 550 paper-based; 213 computer-based; 80 iBT), IELTS (minimum score 6). *Application deadline:* For fall admission, 7/1 for domestic students, 1/1 for international students; for spring admission, 12/1 for domestic and international students. Applications are processed on a rolling basis. Application fee: $30. Electronic applications accepted. *Financial support:* Teaching assistantships, career-related internships or fieldwork, scholarships/grants, and unspecified assistantships available. Support available to part-time students. Financial award applicants required to submit FAFSA. *Faculty research:* Accounting, finance, insurance, management, real estate, urban analysis marketing. *Unit head:* Prof. Alexander D. Sevilla, Assistant Dean/Director, 352-273-3252 Ext. 1206, E-mail: alex.sevilla@warrington.ufl.edu. *Application contact:* Prof. Kelli Gust, Associate Director, 352-273-3255, Fax: 352-392-8791, E-mail: kelly.gust@warrington.ufl.edu. Web site: http://www.floridamba.ufl.edu/.

University of New Brunswick Saint John, MBA Program, Saint John, NB E2L 4L5, Canada. Offers administration (MBA); electronic commerce (MBA); international business (MBA); natural resource management (MBA). Part-time programs available. *Faculty:* 19 full-time (4 women), 14 part-time/adjunct (8 women). *Students:* 58 full-time (24 women), 130 part-time (46 women). 93 applicants, 78% accepted, 25 enrolled. In 2011, 36 master's awarded. *Entrance requirements:* For master's, GMAT, minimum GPA of 3.0. Additional exam requirements/recommendations for international students: Required—TOEFL (minimum score 580 paper-based; 237 computer-based), IELTS (minimum score 7), TWE (minimum score 4.5). *Application deadline:* For fall admission, 5/15 for domestic and international students. Applications are processed on a rolling basis. Application fee: $100. Electronic applications accepted. *Expenses:* Contact institution. *Financial support:* In 2011–12, 4 students received support. Career-related internships or fieldwork and scholarships/grants available. *Faculty research:* Business use of weblogs and podcasts to communicate, corporate governance, high-involvement work systems, international competitiveness, supply chain management and logistics. *Unit head:* Henryk Sterniczuk, Director of Graduate Studies, 506-648-5573, Fax: 506-648-5574, E-mail: sterncz@unbsj.ca. *Application contact:* Tammy Morin, Secretary, 506-648-5746, Fax: 506-648-5574, E-mail: tmorin@unbsj.ca. Web site: http://www.mba.unbsj.ca.

University of North Florida, Coggin College of Business, MBA Program, Jacksonville, FL 32224. Offers accounting (MBA); construction management (MBA); e-commerce (MBA); economics (MBA); finance (MBA); human resource management (MBA); international business (MBA); logistics (MBA); management applications (MBA). *Accreditation:* AACSB. Part-time and evening/weekend programs available. *Faculty:* 19 full-time (6 women), 1 part-time/adjunct (0 women). *Students:* 145 full-time (57 women), 277 part-time (108 women); includes 67 minority (19 Black or African American, non-Hispanic/Latino; 21 Asian, non-Hispanic/Latino; 20 Hispanic/Latino; 7 Two or more races, non-Hispanic/Latino), 34 international. Average age 29. 200 applicants, 48% accepted, 70 enrolled. In 2011, 153 master's awarded. *Entrance requirements:* For master's, GMAT or GRE, U.S. bachelor's degree from regionally-accredited university or equivalent foreign degree. Additional exam requirements/recommendations for international students: Required—TOEFL (minimum score 550 paper-based; 213 computer-based; 79 iBT). *Application deadline:* For fall admission, 7/1 priority date for domestic students, 5/1 for international students; for spring admission, 11/1 priority date for domestic students, 10/1 for international students. Applications are processed on a rolling basis. Application fee: $30. *Expenses:* Tuition, state resident: full-time $8793; part-time $366.38 per credit hour. Tuition, nonresident: full-time $23,502; part-time $979.24 per credit hour. *Required fees:* $1384; $57.66 per credit hour. Tuition and fees vary according to course load and program. *Financial support:* In 2011–12, 55 students received support, including 1 teaching assistantship (averaging $5,333 per year); research assistantships, Federal Work-Study, and tuition waivers (partial) also available. Support available to part-time students. Financial award application deadline: 4/1; financial award applicants required to submit FAFSA. *Faculty research:* Performance measures, costing, and inventory issues in logistics and supply chain management; inter-organizational systems; international management and marketing practices; e-commerce; organizational learning and socialization processes. *Total annual research expenditures:* $7,686. *Unit head:* Dr. C. Bruce Kavan, Chair, 904-620-2780, Fax: 904-620-2832. *Application contact:* Cheryl Campbell, Graduate Advisor, 904-620-2575, Fax: 904-620-2832, E-mail: ccampbell@unf.edu. Web site: http://www.unf.edu/coggin/academics/graduate/mba.aspx.

University of Ottawa, Faculty of Graduate and Postdoctoral Studies, Interdisciplinary Programs, Ottawa, ON K1N 6N5, Canada. Offers e-business (Certificate); e-commerce (Certificate); finance (Certificate); health services and policies research (Diploma); population health (PhD); population health risk assessment and management (Certificate); public management and governance (Certificate); systems science (Certificate).

University of Ottawa, Faculty of Graduate and Postdoctoral Studies, Program in E-Business Technologies, Ottawa, ON K1N 6N5, Canada. Offers M Sc, MEBT. *Degree requirements:* For master's, thesis or alternative, project. *Entrance requirements:* For master's, honours degree or equivalent, minimum B average.

University of Phoenix–Austin Campus, School of Business, Austin, TX 78759. Offers accounting (MBA); business administration (MBA); business and management (MBA); e-business (MBA); global management (MBA); human resources management (MBA, MM); management (MM); marketing (MBA); public administration (MBA). Postbaccalaureate distance learning degree programs offered.

University of Phoenix–Chicago Campus, College of Information Systems and Technology, Schaumburg, IL 60173-4399. Offers e-business (MBA); information systems (MIS); management (MM); technology management (MBA). Evening/weekend programs available. *Degree requirements:* For master's, thesis (for some programs).

Electronic Commerce

Entrance requirements: For master's, 3 years of work experience, minimum undergraduate GPA of 3.0. Additional exam requirements/recommendations for international students: Required—TOEFL (minimum score 550 paper-based; 213 computer-based; 79 iBT). Electronic applications accepted.

University of Phoenix–Cincinnati Campus, College of Information Systems and Technology, West Chester, OH 45069-4875. Offers electronic business (MBA); information systems (MIS); technology management (MBA). Evening/weekend programs available. Postbaccalaureate distance learning degree programs offered. *Degree requirements:* For master's, thesis (for some programs). *Entrance requirements:* For master's, minimum undergraduate GPA of 2.5, 3 years of work experience. Additional exam requirements/recommendations for international students: Required—TOEFL (minimum score 550 paper-based; 213 computer-based; 79 iBT). Electronic applications accepted.

University of Phoenix–Columbus Georgia Campus, College of Information Systems and Technology, Columbus, GA 31904-6321. Offers e-business (MBA); information systems (MIS); technology management (MBA). Evening/weekend programs available. Postbaccalaureate distance learning degree programs offered. *Degree requirements:* For master's, thesis (for some programs). *Entrance requirements:* For master's, minimum undergraduate GPA of 3.0, 3 years of work experience. Additional exam requirements/recommendations for international students: Required—TOEFL (minimum score 550 paper-based; 213 computer-based; 79 iBT). Electronic applications accepted.

University of Phoenix–Dallas Campus, College of Information Systems and Technology, Dallas, TX 75251-2009. Offers e-business (MBA); information systems (MIS); technology management (MBA). Evening/weekend programs available. *Degree requirements:* For master's, thesis (for some programs). *Entrance requirements:* For master's, minimum undergraduate GPA of 3.0, 3 years of work experience. Additional exam requirements/recommendations for international students: Required—TOEFL (minimum score 550 paper-based; 213 computer-based; 79 iBT). Electronic applications accepted.

University of Phoenix–Denver Campus, College of Information Systems and Technology, Lone Tree, CO 80124-5453. Offers e-business (MBA); management (MIS); technology management (MBA). Evening/weekend programs available. Postbaccalaureate distance learning degree programs offered. *Degree requirements:* For master's, thesis (for some programs). *Entrance requirements:* For master's, minimum undergraduate GPA of 3.0, 3 years of work experience. Additional exam requirements/recommendations for international students: Required—TOEFL (minimum score 550 paper-based; 213 computer-based; 79 iBT). Electronic applications accepted.

University of Phoenix–Denver Campus, School of Business, Lone Tree, CO 80124-5453. Offers accountancy (MSA); accounting (MBA); business administration (MBA); e-business (MBA); global management (MBA); human resources management (MBA, MM); management (MM); marketing (MBA); public administration (MBA, MM). Evening/weekend programs available. Postbaccalaureate distance learning degree programs offered. *Degree requirements:* For master's, thesis (for some programs). *Entrance requirements:* For master's, minimum undergraduate GPA of 3.0, 3 years work experience. Additional exam requirements/recommendations for international students: Required—TOEFL (minimum score 550 paper-based; 213 computer-based; 79 iBT). Electronic applications accepted.

University of Phoenix–Houston Campus, College of Information Systems and Technology, Houston, TX 77079-2004. Offers e-business (MBA); information systems (MIS); technology management (MBA). Evening/weekend programs available. Postbaccalaureate distance learning degree programs offered. *Degree requirements:* For master's, comprehensive exam (for some programs), thesis. *Entrance requirements:* For master's, minimum undergraduate GPA of 3.0, 3 years of work experience. Additional exam requirements/recommendations for international students: Required—TOEFL (minimum score 550 paper-based; 213 computer-based; 79 iBT). Electronic applications accepted.

University of Phoenix–Madison Campus, School of Business, Madison, WI 53718-2416. Offers accounting (MBA); business and management (MBA); e-business (MBA); global management (MBA); human resources management (MBA, MM); management (MM); marketing (MBA); public administration (MBA).

University of Phoenix–Memphis Campus, School of Business, Cordova, TN 38018. Offers accounting (MBA); business and management (MBA); e-business (MBA); global management (MBA); human resources management (MBA, MM); management (MM); marketing (MBA); public administration (MBA, MM).

University of Phoenix–New Mexico Campus, College of Information Systems and Technology, Albuquerque, NM 87113-1570. Offers e-business (MBA); information systems (MS); technology management (MBA). Evening/weekend programs available. *Degree requirements:* For master's, thesis (for some programs). *Entrance requirements:* For master's, minimum undergraduate GPA of 3.0, 3 years of work experience. Additional exam requirements/recommendations for international students: Required—TOEFL (minimum score 550 paper-based; 213 computer-based; 79 iBT). Electronic applications accepted.

University of Phoenix–Oklahoma City Campus, College of Information Systems and Technology, Oklahoma City, OK 73116-8244. Offers e-business (MBA); technology management (MBA). Evening/weekend programs available. *Degree requirements:* For master's, thesis (for some programs). *Entrance requirements:* For master's, minimum undergraduate GPA of 3.0, 3 years of work experience. Additional exam requirements/recommendations for international students: Required—TOEFL (minimum score 550 paper-based; 213 computer-based; 79 iBT). Electronic applications accepted.

University of Phoenix–Pittsburgh Campus, College of Information Systems and Technology, Pittsburgh, PA 15276. Offers e-business (MBA); information systems (MIS); technology management (MBA). Evening/weekend programs available. *Degree requirements:* For master's, thesis (for some programs). *Entrance requirements:* For master's, minimum undergraduate GPA of 3.0, 3 years work experience. Additional exam requirements/recommendations for international students: Required—TOEFL (minimum score 550 paper-based; 213 computer-based; 79 iBT). Electronic applications accepted.

University of Phoenix–Raleigh Campus, School of Business, Raleigh, NC 27606. Offers accounting (MBA); business administration (MBA); e-business (MBA); global management (MBA); human resources management (MBA); marketing (MBA).

University of Phoenix–San Antonio Campus, School of Business, San Antonio, TX 78230. Offers accounting (MBA); business administration (MBA); e-business (MBA); global management (MBA); human resources management (MBA, MM); management (MM); marketing (MBA); public administration (MBA, MM).

University of San Francisco, School of Management, Masagung Graduate School of Management, Program in Business Administration, San Francisco, CA 94117-1080. Offers business economics (MBA); e-business (MBA); entrepreneurship (MBA); finance (MBA); international business (MBA); management (MBA); marketing (MBA); telecommunications management and policy (MBA); JD/MBA; MSN/MBA. *Accreditation:* AACSB. *Faculty:* 18 full-time (4 women), 18 part-time/adjunct (9 women). *Students:* 247 full-time (122 women), 9 part-time (3 women); includes 85 minority (5 Black or African American, non-Hispanic/Latino; 55 Asian, non-Hispanic/Latino; 16 Hispanic/Latino; 1 Native Hawaiian or other Pacific Islander, non-Hispanic/Latino; 8 Two or more races, non-Hispanic/Latino), 38 international. Average age 29. 552 applicants, 55% accepted, 99 enrolled. In 2011, 173 master's awarded. *Entrance requirements:* For master's, GMAT, minimum undergraduate GPA of 3.2. Additional exam requirements/recommendations for international students: Required—TOEFL. *Application deadline:* For fall admission, 7/1 priority date for domestic students; for spring admission, 11/30 for domestic students. Applications are processed on a rolling basis. Application fee: $55 ($65 for international students). *Expenses: Tuition:* Full-time $20,070; part-time $1115 per unit. Tuition and fees vary according to course load, campus/location and program. *Financial support:* In 2011–12, 33 students received support. Fellowships available. Financial award application deadline: 3/2; financial award applicants required to submit FAFSA. *Faculty research:* International financial markets, technology transfer licensing, international marketing, strategic planning. *Total annual research expenditures:* $50,000. *Unit head:* Kelly Brookes, Director, 415-422-2221, Fax: 415-422-6315. *Application contact:* Director, MBA Program, 415-422-2221, Fax: 415-422-6315, E-mail: mba@usfca.edu.

The University of Texas at Dallas, Naveen Jindal School of Management, Program in Management and Administrative Sciences, Richardson, TX 75080. Offers electronic commerce (MS); finance (MS); healthcare administration (MS); information systems (MS); innovation and entrepreneurship (MS); international management (MS); leadership in organizations (MS); marketing (MS); operations (MS); organizations (MS); real estate (MS); strategy (MS). *Accreditation:* AACSB. Part-time and evening/weekend programs available. *Faculty:* 26 full-time (6 women), 9 part-time/adjunct (2 women). *Students:* 128 full-time (69 women), 169 part-time (95 women); includes 76 minority (18 Black or African American, non-Hispanic/Latino; 1 American Indian or Alaska Native, non-Hispanic/Latino; 37 Asian, non-Hispanic/Latino; 15 Hispanic/Latino; 1 Native Hawaiian or other Pacific Islander, non-Hispanic/Latino; 4 Two or more races, non-Hispanic/Latino), 77 international. Average age 34. 220 applicants, 63% accepted, 68 enrolled. In 2011, 58 master's awarded. *Degree requirements:* For master's, thesis optional. *Entrance requirements:* For master's, GMAT. Additional exam requirements/recommendations for international students: Required—TOEFL (minimum score 550 paper-based; 215 computer-based). *Application deadline:* For fall admission, 7/15 for domestic students, 5/1 for international students; for spring admission, 11/15 for domestic students, 9/1 for international students. Applications are processed on a rolling basis. Application fee: $50 ($100 for international students). Electronic applications accepted. *Expenses:* Tuition, state resident: full-time $11,170; part-time $620.56 per credit hour. Tuition, nonresident: full-time $20,212; part-time $1122.89 per credit hour. *Financial support:* In 2011–12, 68 students received support, including 7 teaching assistantships with partial tuition reimbursements available (averaging $16,200 per year); research assistantships with partial tuition reimbursements available, career-related internships or fieldwork, Federal Work-Study, institutionally sponsored loans, scholarships/grants, and unspecified assistantships also available. Support available to part-time students. Financial award application deadline: 4/30; financial award applicants required to submit FAFSA. *Faculty research:* Integrated and detailed knowledge of functional areas of management, analytical tools for effective appraisal and decision-making. *Unit head:* Dr. Gregory Dess, Area Coordinator, 972-883-4439, E-mail: gdess@utdallas.edu. *Application contact:* James Parker, Assistant Director, 972-883-5842, E-mail: jparker@utdallas.edu. Web site: http://jindal.utdallas.edu/academic-areas/organizations-strategy-and-international-management/.

West Chester University of Pennsylvania, College of Business and Public Affairs, The School of Business, West Chester, PA 19383. Offers business (Certificate); business administration: technology/electronic (MBA); economics and finance (MBA); general business (MBA). *Accreditation:* AACSB. Part-time and evening/weekend programs available. Postbaccalaureate distance learning degree programs offered (minimal on-campus study). *Faculty:* 8 part-time/adjunct (4 women). *Students:* 2 full-time (both women), 78 part-time (23 women); includes 12 minority (5 Black or African American, non-Hispanic/Latino; 7 Asian, non-Hispanic/Latino), 3 international. Average age 34. 66 applicants, 47% accepted, 19 enrolled. In 2011, 9 master's, 1 other advanced degree awarded. *Degree requirements:* For master's, minimum GPA of 3.0. *Entrance requirements:* For master's, GMAT, statement of professional goals, resume, two letters of recommendation, transcripts. Additional exam requirements/recommendations for international students: Required—TOEFL (minimum score 550 paper-based; 213 computer-based; 80 iBT). *Application deadline:* For fall admission, 4/15 priority date for domestic students, 3/15 for international students; for spring admission, 10/15 priority date for domestic students, 9/1 for international students. Applications are processed on a rolling basis. Application fee: $45. Electronic applications accepted. *Expenses:* Tuition, state resident: full-time $7488; part-time $416 per credit. Tuition, nonresident: full-time $11,232; part-time $624 per credit. *Required fees:* $1784.64; $67.59 per credit. Tuition and fees vary according to program. *Financial support:* Unspecified assistantships available. Support available to part-time students. Financial award application deadline: 2/15; financial award applicants required to submit FAFSA. *Unit head:* Dr. Paul Christ, MBA Director and Graduate Coordinator, 610-425-5000, E-mail: mba@wcupa.edu. *Application contact:* Office of Graduate Studies, 610-436-2943, Fax: 610-436-2763, E-mail: gradstudy@wcupa.edu. Web site: http://www.wcumba.org/.

Section 5
Entrepreneurship

This section contains a directory of institutions offering graduate work in entrepreneurship. Additional information about programs listed in the directory but not augmented by an in-depth entry may be obtained by writing directly to the dean of a graduate school or chair of a department at the address given in the directory.

For programs offering related work, see also in this book *Business Administration and Management, International Business,* and *Education (Business Education)*

CONTENTS

Program Directory

Displays and Close-Ups

See:

Entrepreneurship

American College of Thessaloniki, Department of Business Administration, Pylea, Greece. Offers banking and finance (MBA); entrepreneurship (MBA, Certificate); finance (Certificate); management (MBA, Certificate); marketing (MBA, Certificate). Part-time and evening/weekend programs available. *Degree requirements:* For master's, thesis. *Entrance requirements:* For master's, bachelor's degree. Additional exam requirements/recommendations for international students: Recommended—TOEFL. Electronic applications accepted.

American Public University System, AMU/APU Graduate Programs, Charles Town, WV 25414. Offers accounting (MBA, MS); administration and supervision (M Ed); criminal justice (MA); emergency and disaster management (MA); entrepreneurship (MBA); environmental policy and management (MS), including environmental planning, environmental sustainability, fish and wildlife management, general (MA, MS), global environmental management; finance (MBA); general (MBA); global business management (MBA); guidance and counseling (M Ed); history (MA), including American history, ancient and classical history, European history, global history, military and diplomatic history, public history; homeland security (MA); homeland security resource allocation (MBA); humanities (MA); information technology (MS), including digital forensics, enterprise software development, information assurance and security, IT project management; information technology management (MBA); intelligence studies (MA), including criminal intelligence, general (MA, MS), homeland security, intelligence analysis, intelligence collection, intelligence operations, terrorism studies; international relations and conflict resolution (MA), including comparative and security issues, conflict resolution, international and transnational security issues, peacekeeping; legal studies (MA); management (MA), including defense management, general (MA, MS), human resource management, organizational leadership, public administration, reverse logistics, strategic consulting; marketing (MBA); military history (MA), including American military history, American revolution, civil war, war since 1946, World War II; military studies (MA), including air warfare, asymmetrical warfare, joint warfare, land warfare, naval warfare, strategic leadership; national security studies (MA), including general (MA, MS), homeland security, regional security studies, security and intelligence analysis, terrorism studies; nonprofit management (MBA); political science (MA), including American politics and government, comparative government and development, public policy; psychology (MA); public administration (MA, MPA), including disaster management (MPA), environmental policy (MA), health policy (MPA), human resources (MPA), national security (MPA), organizational management (MPA), security management (MPA); public health (MA, MPH), including emergency management (MPH), environmental health (MPH), public administration (MA); reverse logistics management (MA); security management (MA); space studies (MS), including aerospace science, planetary science; sports and health sciences (MS); sports management (MS), including coaching theory and strategy, sports administration; teaching (M Ed), including curriculum and instruction for elementary teachers, elementary, elementary reading, English language learners, instructional leadership, online learning, secondary social sciences, special education; transportation and logistics management (MA), including maritime engineering management. Programs offered via distance learning only. Part-time and evening/weekend programs available. Postbaccalaureate distance learning degree programs offered (no on-campus study). *Faculty:* 445 full-time (241 women), 1,360 part-time/adjunct (617 women). *Students:* 688 full-time (338 women), 10,168 part-time (3,706 women); includes 3,130 minority (1,007 Black or African American, non-Hispanic/Latino; 103 American Indian or Alaska Native, non-Hispanic/Latino; 825 Asian, non-Hispanic/Latino; 810 Hispanic/Latino; 51 Native Hawaiian or other Pacific Islander, non-Hispanic/Latino; 334 Two or more races, non-Hispanic/Latino), 134 international. Average age 35. In 2011, 2,386 master's awarded. *Degree requirements:* For master's, comprehensive exam or practicum. *Entrance requirements:* For master's, official transcript showing earned bachelor's degree from institution accredited by recognized accrediting body. Additional exam requirements/recommendations for international students: Required—TOEFL (minimum score 550 paper-based; 213 computer-based), IELTS (minimum score 6.5). *Application deadline:* Applications are processed on a rolling basis. Application fee: $0. Electronic applications accepted. *Expenses: Tuition:* Part-time $325 per credit hour. *Financial support:* Applicants required to submit FAFSA. *Faculty research:* Military history, criminal justice, management performance, national security. *Unit head:* Dr. Karan Powell, Executive Vice President and Provost, 877-468-6268, Fax: 304-724-3780. *Application contact:* Terry Grant, Vice President of Enrollment Management, 877-468-6268, Fax: 304-724-3780, E-mail: info@apus.edu. Web site: http://www.apus.edu.

American University, Kogod School of Business, Master of Business Administration Program, Washington, DC 20016-8044. Offers accounting (MBA); consulting (MBA), including business systems consulting, management consulting; entrepreneurship (MBA); entrepreneurship (Certificate); finance (MBA); global emerging markets (MBA); leadership and strategic human capital management (MBA); marketing (MBA); real estate (MBA); MBA/JD; MBA/LL M; MBA/MA. Part-time and evening/weekend programs available. *Faculty:* 13 full-time (6 women). *Students:* 96 full-time (43 women), 104 part-time (35 women); includes 49 minority (14 Black or African American, non-Hispanic/Latino; 16 Asian, non-Hispanic/Latino; 16 Hispanic/Latino; 1 Native Hawaiian or other Pacific Islander, non-Hispanic/Latino; 2 Two or more races, non-Hispanic/Latino), 22 international. Average age 29. 340 applicants, 52% accepted, 52 enrolled. In 2011, 124 master's awarded. *Entrance requirements:* For master's, GMAT, resume, personal statement, interview. Additional exam requirements/recommendations for international students: Required—TOEFL. *Application deadline:* For fall admission, 2/1 priority date for domestic students; for spring admission, 10/1 priority date for domestic students. Applications are processed on a rolling basis. Application fee: $100. *Expenses:* Contact institution. *Financial support:* In 2011–12, 19 students received support. Fellowships, research assistantships with partial tuition reimbursements available, career-related internships or fieldwork, Federal Work-Study, and institutionally sponsored loans available. Support available to part-time students. Financial award application deadline: 2/1. *Faculty research:* Information technology, decision-aiding methodology, negotiation. *Unit head:* Dr. Stevan R. Holmberg, Chair, 202-885-1921, Fax: 202-885-1916, E-mail: sholmbe@american.edu. *Application contact:* Shannon Demko, Director of Admissions, 202-885-1968, Fax: 202-885-1078, E-mail: demko@american.edu. Web site: http://www.american.edu/kogod/.

American University, School of International Service, Washington, DC 20016-8071. Offers comparative and international disability policy (MA); comparative and regional studies (Certificate); cross-cultural communication (Certificate); development management (MS); ethics, peace, and global affairs (MA); European studies (Certificate); global environmental policy (MA, Certificate); global information technology (Certificate); international affairs (MA), including comparative and international disability policy, comparative and regional studies, international economic relations, international politics, natural resources and sustainable development, U.S. foreign policy; international communication (MA, Certificate); international development (MA, Certificate); international economic policy (Certificate); international economic relations (Certificate); international media (MA); international peace and conflict resolution (MA, Certificate); international politics (Certificate); international relations (PhD); international service (MIS); peacebuilding (Certificate); social enterprise (MA); the Americas (Certificate); United States foreign policy (Certificate); JD/MA. Part-time and evening/weekend programs available. Postbaccalaureate distance learning degree programs offered (no on-campus study). *Faculty:* 108 full-time (45 women), 51 part-time/adjunct (23 women). *Students:* 595 full-time (375 women), 399 part-time (243 women); includes 201 minority (64 Black or African American, non-Hispanic/Latino; 6 American Indian or Alaska Native, non-Hispanic/Latino; 53 Asian, non-Hispanic/Latino; 66 Hispanic/Latino; 12 Two or more races, non-Hispanic/Latino), 153 international. Average age 27. 2,096 applicants, 63% accepted, 370 enrolled. In 2011, 331 master's, 2 doctorates, 2 other advanced degrees awarded. Terminal master's awarded for partial completion of doctoral program. *Degree requirements:* For master's, one foreign language, comprehensive exam, thesis or alternative; for doctorate, one foreign language, comprehensive exam, thesis/dissertation, research practicum; for Certificate, minimum 15 credit hours related course work. *Entrance requirements:* For master's, GRE, 24 credits of course work in related social sciences, minimum GPA of 3.5, 2 letters of recommendation, bachelor's degree, resume, statement of purpose; for doctorate, GRE, 3 letters of recommendation, 24 credits in related social sciences; for Certificate, bachelor's degree. Additional exam requirements/recommendations for international students: Required—TOEFL (minimum score 600 paper-based; 250 computer-based; 100 iBT). *Application deadline:* For fall admission, 1/15 priority date for domestic students; for spring admission, 10/1 priority date for domestic students. Applications are processed on a rolling basis. Application fee: $50. *Expenses: Tuition:* Full-time $24,264; part-time $1348 per credit hour. *Required fees:* $430. Tuition and fees vary according to course load and program. *Financial support:* Fellowships with partial tuition reimbursements, research assistantships with partial tuition reimbursements, teaching assistantships with partial tuition reimbursements, career-related internships or fieldwork, Federal Work-Study, institutionally sponsored loans, and scholarships/grants available. Financial award application deadline: 1/15. *Faculty research:* International intellectual property, international environmental issues, international law and legal order, international telecommunications/technology, international sustainable development. *Unit head:* Dr. James Goldgeier, Dean, 202-885-1603, Fax: 202-885-2494, E-mail: goldgeier@american.edu. *Application contact:* Amanda Taylor, Director of Graduate Admissions and Financial Aid, 202-885-2496, Fax: 202-885-1109, E-mail: ataylor@american.edu. Web site: http://www.american.edu/sis/.

Arizona State University, College of Technology and Innovation, Department of Technology Management, Mesa, AZ 85212. Offers technology (aviation management and human factors) (MS); technology (environmental technology management) (MS); technology (global technology and development) (MS); technology (graphic information technology) (MS); technology (management of technology) (MS). Part-time and evening/weekend programs available. Postbaccalaureate distance learning degree programs offered (minimal on-campus study). *Degree requirements:* For master's, thesis or applied project and oral defense; interactive Program of Study (iPOS) submitted before completing 50 percent of required credit hours. *Entrance requirements:* For master's, GRE, minimum GPA of 3.0 or equivalent in last 2 years of work leading to bachelor's degree. Additional exam requirements/recommendations for international students: Required—TOEFL (minimum score 83 iBT), TOEFL, IELTS, or Pearson Test of English. Electronic applications accepted. *Faculty research:* Digital imaging, digital publishing, Internet development/e-commerce, information aviation human factors, pilot selection, databases, multimedia, commercial digital photography, digital workflow, computer graphics modeling and animation, information design, sociotechnology, visual and technical literacy, environmental management, quality management, project management, industrial ethics, hazardous materials, environmental chemistry.

Azusa Pacific University, School of Business and Management, Azusa, CA 91702-7000. Offers business administration (MBA); diversity for strategic advantage (MA); entrepreneurship (MBA); finance (MBA); human and organizational development (MA); human resources and organizational development (MBA); human resources management (MA); international business (MBA); marketing (MBA); non-profit management (MA); organizational development and change (MA); performance improvement (MA); public administration (MA); strategic management (MBA). Part-time and evening/weekend programs available. *Degree requirements:* For master's, thesis (for some programs), final project. *Entrance requirements:* For master's, GMAT, minimum GPA of 3.0. Additional exam requirements/recommendations for international students: Required—TOEFL (minimum score 600 paper-based). *Expenses:* Contact institution. *Faculty research:* Gender issues, financial risk, leadership and ethics, marketing strategy.

Babson College, F. W. Olin Graduate School of Business, Wellesley, Babson Park, MA 02457-0310. Offers accounting (MSA); advanced management (Certificate); business administration (MBA); global entrepreneurship (MS); technological entrepreneurship (MS). *Accreditation:* AACSB. Part-time and evening/weekend programs available. Postbaccalaureate distance learning degree programs offered (minimal on-campus study). *Entrance requirements:* For master's, GMAT, 2 years of work experience, resume, letters of recommendation. Additional exam requirements/recommendations for international students: Required—TOEFL (minimum score 100 iBT), IELTS (minimum score 6.5). Electronic applications accepted. *Faculty research:* Entrepreneurship, sustainability, global markets, process of innovation, social media and advertising.

Bakke Graduate University, Programs in Pastoral Ministry and Business, Seattle, WA 98104. Offers business (MBA); global urban leadership (MA); social and civic entrepreneurship (MA); transformational leadership for the global city (D Min). Part-time programs available. Postbaccalaureate distance learning degree programs offered (minimal on-campus study). *Degree requirements:* For master's, thesis; for doctorate, thesis/dissertation. *Entrance requirements:* For master's, 2 years of ministry experience, BA in Biblical studies or theology; for doctorate, 3 years of ministry experience, M Div. Additional exam requirements/recommendations for international students: Required—TOEFL (minimum score 60 computer-based). Electronic applications accepted. *Faculty research:* Theological systems, church management, worship.

Baldwin Wallace University, Graduate Programs, Division of Business, Program in Entrepreneurship, Berea, OH 44017-2088. Offers MBA. Part-time and evening/weekend programs available. *Students:* 22 full-time (11 women), 10 part-time (3 women); includes 5 minority (all Black or African American, non-Hispanic/Latino), 3 international. Average age 32. 16 applicants, 81% accepted, 7 enrolled. In 2011, 10 master's awarded. *Degree requirements:* For master's, minimum overall GPA of 3.0, completion of all required courses. *Entrance requirements:* For master's, GMAT, bachelor's degree in any field, work experience, minimum GPA of 3.0. Additional exam requirements/recommendations for international students: Required—TOEFL (minimum score 523 paper-based; 193 computer-based; 70 iBT). *Application deadline:* For fall admission, 7/

25 priority date for domestic students, 4/30 for international students; for spring admission, 12/15 priority date for domestic students, 9/30 for international students. Applications are processed on a rolling basis. Application fee: $25. Electronic applications accepted. Application fee is waived when completed online. *Expenses:* Contact institution. *Financial support:* Career-related internships or fieldwork available. Support available to part-time students. Financial award application deadline: 5/1. *Unit head:* Ven Ochaya, Director, 440-826-2391, Fax: 440-826-3868, E-mail: vochaya@bw.edu. *Application contact:* Laura Spencer, Graduate Application Specialist, 440-826-2191, Fax: 440-826-3868, E-mail: lspencer@bw.edu. Web site: http://www.bw.edu/academics/bus/programs/entre/.

Bay Path College, Program in Entrepreneurial Thinking and Innovative Practices, Longmeadow, MA 01106-2292. Offers MBA. Part-time and evening/weekend programs available. Postbaccalaureate distance learning degree programs offered (no on-campus study). *Students:* 12 full-time (9 women), 61 part-time (53 women); includes 15 minority (8 Black or African American, non-Hispanic/Latino; 1 American Indian or Alaska Native, non-Hispanic/Latino; 1 Asian, non-Hispanic/Latino; 5 Hispanic/Latino). Average age 33. 64 applicants, 75% accepted, 35 enrolled. In 2011, 43 master's awarded. *Entrance requirements:* For master's, GMAT. *Application deadline:* Applications are processed on a rolling basis. Application fee: $45. Electronic applications accepted. Application fee is waived when completed online. *Expenses: Tuition:* Part-time $665 per credit. Tuition and fees vary according to program. *Financial support:* In 2011–12, 12 students received support. Scholarships/grants available. Financial award applicants required to submit FAFSA. *Application contact:* Lisa Adams, Director of Graduate Admissions, 413-565-1317, Fax: 413-565-1250, E-mail: ladams@baypath.edu.

Benedictine University, Graduate Programs, Program in Business Administration, Lisle, IL 60532-0900. Offers accounting (MBA); entrepreneurship and managing innovation (MBA); financial management (MBA); health administration (MBA); human resource management (MBA); information systems security (MBA); international business (MBA); management consulting (MBA); management information systems (MBA); marketing management (MBA); operations management and logistics (MBA); organizational leadership (MBA); MBA/MPH; MBA/MS. Part-time and evening/weekend programs available. Postbaccalaureate distance learning degree programs offered (minimal on-campus study). *Faculty:* 4 full-time (2 women), 24 part-time/adjunct (3 women). *Students:* 165 full-time (101 women), 766 part-time (381 women); includes 201 minority (118 Black or African American, non-Hispanic/Latino; 4 American Indian or Alaska Native, non-Hispanic/Latino; 37 Asian, non-Hispanic/Latino; 40 Hispanic/Latino; 2 Native Hawaiian or other Pacific Islander, non-Hispanic/Latino), 14 international. Average age 34. 313 applicants, 73% accepted, 166 enrolled. In 2011, 379 master's awarded. *Entrance requirements:* For master's, GMAT. Additional exam requirements/recommendations for international students: Required—TOEFL (minimum score 550 paper-based; 213 computer-based). *Application deadline:* For fall admission, 9/1 for domestic students; for winter admission, 12/1 for domestic students; for spring admission, 2/15 for domestic students. Applications are processed on a rolling basis. Application fee: $40. Electronic applications accepted. *Financial support:* Career-related internships or fieldwork and health care benefits available. Support available to part-time students. *Faculty research:* Strategic leadership in professional organizations, sociology of professions, organizational change, social identity theory, applications to change management. *Unit head:* Dr. Sharon Borowicz, Director, 630-829-6219, E-mail: sborowicz@ben.edu. *Application contact:* Kari Gibbons, Director, Admissions, 630-829-6200, Fax: 630-829-6584, E-mail: kgibbons@ben.edu.

Bernard M. Baruch College of the City University of New York, Zicklin School of Business, Department of Management, New York, NY 10010-5585. Offers entrepreneurship (MBA); management (PhD); operations management (MBA); organizational behavior/human resources management (MBA); sustainable business (MBA). PhD offered jointly with Graduate School and University Center of the City University of New York. Part-time and evening/weekend programs available. *Degree requirements:* For doctorate, comprehensive exam, thesis/dissertation. *Entrance requirements:* For master's, GMAT, 2 letters of recommendation, resume, 2 years of work experience; for doctorate, GMAT. Additional exam requirements/recommendations for international students: Required—TOEFL (minimum score 590 paper-based; 243 computer-based), TWE.

Bernard M. Baruch College of the City University of New York, Zicklin School of Business, International Executive MS Programs, New York, NY 10010-5585. Offers entrepreneurship (MS). Part-time and evening/weekend programs available. *Entrance requirements:* For master's, GMAT, 2 letters of recommendation, resume, 2 years of work experience. Additional exam requirements/recommendations for international students: Required—TOEFL (minimum score 590 paper-based; 243 computer-based), TWE (minimum score 5).

Brandeis University, Graduate School of Arts and Sciences, Program in Computer Science and IT Entrepreneurship, Waltham, MA 02454-9110. Offers MA. Part-time programs available. *Faculty:* 13 full-time (3 women), 4 part-time/adjunct (2 women). *Students:* 10 full-time (4 women), 2 part-time (0 women), 7 international. 35 applicants, 69% accepted, 9 enrolled. *Degree requirements:* For master's, practicum. *Entrance requirements:* For master's, GRE recommended, but not required, official transcript(s), 2 letters of recommendation, curriculum vitae or resume, statement of purpose. Additional exam requirements/recommendations for international students: Required—TOEFL (minimum score 600 paper-based; 250 computer-based; 100 iBT); Recommended—IELTS (minimum score 7). *Application deadline:* Applications are processed on a rolling basis. Application fee: $75. Electronic applications accepted. *Financial support:* In 2011–12, teaching assistantships with partial tuition reimbursements (averaging $3,200 per year) were awarded; institutionally sponsored loans, scholarships/grants, and tuition waivers (partial) also available. Support available to part-time students. Financial award application deadline: 4/15; financial award applicants required to submit FAFSA. *Faculty research:* Software development, IT entrepreneurship, business, computer science, information technology, entrepreneurship. *Unit head:* Prof. Fernando Colon Osorio, Director of Graduate Studies, 781-736-4586, E-mail: fcco@brandeis.edu. *Application contact:* David F. Cotter, Assistant Dean, Graduate School of Arts and Sciences, 781-736-3410, Fax: 781-736-3412, E-mail: gradschool@brandeis.edu. Web site: http://www.brandeis.edu/it-entrepreneurship/index.html.

California Intercontinental University, School of Business, Diamond Bar, CA 91765. Offers banking and finance (MBA); entrepreneurship and business management (DBA); global business leadership (DBA); international management and marketing (MBA); organizational management and human resource management (MBA).

California Lutheran University, Graduate Studies, School of Management, Thousand Oaks, CA 91360-2787. Offers business (IMBA); computer science (MS); econometrics (MBA); economics (MS); entrepreneurship (MBA, Certificate); finance (MBA, Certificate); financial planning (MBA, Certificate); information systems and technology (MS); information technology management (MBA, Certificate); international business (MBA, Certificate); management and organization behavior (MBA); management and organizational behavior (Certificate); marketing (MBA, Certificate); microeconomics (MBA); nonprofit and social enterprise (MBA). Part-time and evening/weekend programs available. Postbaccalaureate distance learning degree programs offered (no on-campus study). *Entrance requirements:* For master's, GMAT, interview, minimum GPA of 3.0. *Expenses:* Contact institution.

California State University, East Bay, Office of Academic Programs and Graduate Studies, College of Business and Economics, Business Administration, MBA Program, Hayward, CA 94542-3000. Offers entrepreneurship (MBA); finance (MBA); global innovators (MBA); human resources and organizational behavior (MBA); information technology management (MBA); marketing management (MBA); operations and supply chain management (MBA); strategy and international business (MBA). Part-time and evening/weekend programs available. *Faculty:* 11 full-time (3 women). *Students:* 80 full-time (42 women), 141 part-time (61 women); includes 70 minority (5 Black or African American, non-Hispanic/Latino; 46 Asian, non-Hispanic/Latino; 13 Hispanic/Latino; 1 Native Hawaiian or other Pacific Islander, non-Hispanic/Latino; 5 Two or more races, non-Hispanic/Latino), 69 international. Average age 31. 371 applicants, 36% accepted, 79 enrolled. In 2011, 254 master's awarded. *Degree requirements:* For master's, comprehensive exam or thesis. *Entrance requirements:* For master's, GMAT (minimum 20th percentile verbal and quantitative section), bachelor's degree, minimum GPA of 2.75. Additional exam requirements/recommendations for international students: Required—TOEFL (minimum score 550 paper-based; 213 computer-based; 79 iBT). *Application deadline:* For fall admission, 6/30 for domestic and international students. Applications are processed on a rolling basis. Application fee: $55. Electronic applications accepted. *Expenses:* Contact institution. *Financial support:* Career-related internships or fieldwork, Federal Work-Study, institutionally sponsored loans, and scholarships/grants available. Support available to part-time students. Financial award application deadline: 3/2; financial award applicants required to submit FAFSA. *Unit head:* Dr. Terri Swartz, Dean, 510-885-3291, Fax: 510-885-4884, E-mail: terri.swartz@csueastbay.edu. *Application contact:* Prof. Joanna Lee, Director, CBE Graduate Programs, 510-885-3517, Fax: 510-885-2176, E-mail: joanna.lee@csueastbay.edu. Web site: http://www20.csueastbay.edu/ecat/graduate-chapters/g-buad.html#mba.

California State University, East Bay, Office of Academic Programs and Graduate Studies, College of Business and Economics, Department of Marketing, Option in Entrepreneurship, Hayward, CA 94542-3000. Offers MBA. *Entrance requirements:* Additional exam requirements/recommendations for international students: Required—TOEFL (minimum score 550 paper-based; 213 computer-based). *Application deadline:* For fall admission, 6/30 for domestic and international students. *Expenses:* Tuition, state resident: full-time $6738; part-time $1302 per quarter. Tuition, nonresident: full-time $12,690; part-time $2294 per quarter. *Required fees:* $449 per quarter. Tuition and fees vary according to degree level, program and reciprocity agreements. *Financial support:* Career-related internships or fieldwork, Federal Work-Study, institutionally sponsored loans, and scholarships/grants available. Support available to part-time students. Financial award applicants required to submit FAFSA. *Unit head:* Dr. Nan Maxwell, Chair, 510-885-4336, Fax: 510-885-4796, E-mail: nan.maxwell@csueastbay.edu. *Application contact:* Donna Wiley, Interim Associate Director, 510-885-2928, Fax: 510-885-4777, E-mail: donna.wiley@csueastbay.edu.

California State University, Fullerton, Graduate Studies, College of Business and Economics, Department of Management, Fullerton, CA 92834-9480. Offers entrepreneurship (MBA); management (MBA). *Accreditation:* AACSB. Part-time programs available. *Students:* 12 full-time (3 women), 51 part-time (19 women); includes 32 minority (1 Black or African American, non-Hispanic/Latino; 22 Asian, non-Hispanic/Latino; 8 Hispanic/Latino; 1 Two or more races, non-Hispanic/Latino), 5 international. Average age 28. 2 applicants, 50% accepted, 1 enrolled. In 2011, 39 master's awarded. *Degree requirements:* For master's, project or thesis. *Entrance requirements:* For master's, GMAT, minimum AACSB index of 950. Application fee: $55. *Financial support:* Career-related internships or fieldwork, Federal Work-Study, institutionally sponsored loans, and scholarships/grants available. Support available to part-time students. Financial award application deadline: 3/1; financial award applicants required to submit FAFSA. *Unit head:* Dr. Ellen Dumond, Chair, 657-278-2251. *Application contact:* Admissions/Applications, 657-278-2371.

California State University, San Bernardino, Graduate Studies, College of Business and Public Administration, Master in Business Administration Program, San Bernardino, CA 92407. Offers accounting (MBA); entrepreneurship (MBA); executives (MBA); finance (MBA); global business (MBA); information assurance and security management (MBA); information management (MBA); management (MBA); marketing (MBA); professionals (MBA); supply chain management (MBA). *Accreditation:* AACSB. Part-time and evening/weekend programs available. Postbaccalaureate distance learning degree programs offered (no on-campus study). *Faculty:* 58 full-time (11 women), 26 part-time/adjunct (9 women). *Students:* 80 full-time (31 women), 137 part-time (56 women); includes 82 minority (19 Black or African American, non-Hispanic/Latino; 3 American Indian or Alaska Native, non-Hispanic/Latino; 20 Asian, non-Hispanic/Latino; 37 Hispanic/Latino; 3 Two or more races, non-Hispanic/Latino), 65 international. Average age 30. 217 applicants, 65% accepted, 79 enrolled. In 2011, 120 master's awarded. *Degree requirements:* For master's, comprehensive exam, thesis optional, portfolio, 48 units, minimum GPA of 3.0. *Entrance requirements:* For master's, GMAT, minimum GPA of 2.5. Additional exam requirements/recommendations for international students: Required—TOEFL (minimum score 550 paper-based; 213 computer-based; 79 iBT). *Application deadline:* For fall admission, 7/12 priority date for domestic students, 7/12 for international students; for winter admission, 10/26 priority date for domestic students, 10/26 for international students; for spring admission, 1/25 priority date for domestic students, 1/25 for international students. Applications are processed on a rolling basis. Application fee: $55. Electronic applications accepted. *Expenses:* Contact institution. *Financial support:* In 2011–12, 56 students received support, including 34 fellowships (averaging $3,732 per year), 18 research assistantships (averaging $2,193 per year), 4 teaching assistantships (averaging $2,606 per year); career-related internships or fieldwork, Federal Work-Study, institutionally sponsored loans, scholarships/grants, and unspecified assistantships also available. Support available to part-time students. Financial award application deadline: 3/1; financial award applicants required to submit FAFSA. *Faculty research:* Fraud, Stock Exchange, small business, logistics, job analysis. *Total annual research expenditures:* $4.8 million. *Unit head:* Dr. Lawrence C. Rose, Dean, 909-537-3703, Fax: 909-537-7026, E-mail: lrose@csusb.edu. *Application contact:* Dr. Sandra Kamusikiri, Associate Vice-President/Dean of Graduate Studies, 909-537-7058, Fax: 909-537-5078, E-mail: skamusik@csusb.edu. Web site: http://mba.csusb.edu/.

Cambridge College, School of Management, Cambridge, MA 02138-5304. Offers business negotiation and conflict resolution (M Mgt); general business (M Mgt); health care informatics (M Mgt); health care management (M Mgt); leadership in human and organizational dynamics (M Mgt); non-profit and public organization management (M Mgt); small business development (M Mgt); technology management (M Mgt). Part-time and evening/weekend programs available. *Degree requirements:* For master's, thesis, seminars. *Entrance requirements:* For master's, resume, 2 professional references. Additional exam requirements/recommendations for international students: Required—TOEFL (minimum score 550 paper-based; 213 computer-based; 79 iBT); Recommended—IELTS (minimum score 6). Electronic applications accepted. *Expenses:* Contact institution. *Faculty research:* Negotiation, mediation and conflict resolution; leadership; management of diverse organizations; case studies and simulation methodologies for management education, digital as a second language: social networking for digital immigrants, non-profit and public management.

Cameron University, Office of Graduate Studies, Program in Entrepreneurial Studies, Lawton, OK 73505-6377. Offers MS. Part-time and evening/weekend programs available. Postbaccalaureate distance learning degree programs offered (no on-campus study). *Degree requirements:* For master's, comprehensive exam. *Entrance requirements:* Additional exam requirements/recommendations for international students: Required—TOEFL (minimum score 550 paper-based; 213 computer-based). Electronic applications accepted. *Faculty research:* Entrepreneurial competition, new venture creation, legal issues, electronic commerce.

Capital University, School of Management, Columbus, OH 43209-2394. Offers entrepreneurship (MBA); finance (MBA); leadership (MBA); marketing (MBA); MBA/JD; MBA/LL M; MBA/MSN; MBA/MT. *Accreditation:* ACBSP. Part-time and evening/weekend programs available. *Faculty:* 17 full-time (7 women), 23 part-time/adjunct (1 woman). *Students:* 175 part-time (75 women). Average age 31. 59 applicants, 81% accepted, 43 enrolled. In 2011, 1 degree awarded. *Degree requirements:* For master's, research project. *Entrance requirements:* For master's, GMAT, 2 years of work experience. Additional exam requirements/recommendations for international students: Required—TOEFL (minimum score 550 paper-based; 80 computer-based); Recommended—IELTS (minimum score 6.5). *Application deadline:* For fall admission, 7/1 priority date for domestic students; for winter admission, 11/1 priority date for domestic students; for spring admission, 4/1 priority date for domestic students. Applications are processed on a rolling basis. Application fee: $25. Electronic applications accepted. *Financial support:* In 2011–12, 2 fellowships (averaging $1,000 per year) were awarded; scholarships/grants and tuition waivers (full) also available. Support available to part-time students. Financial award application deadline: 8/1; financial award applicants required to submit FAFSA. *Faculty research:* Taxation, public policy, health care, management of non-profits. *Unit head:* Dr. Keirsten Moore, Assistant Dean, School of Management and Leadership, 614-236-6670, Fax: 614-296-6540, E-mail: kmoore@capital.edu. *Application contact:* Jacob Wilk, Assistant Director of Adult and Graduate Education Recruitment, 614-236-6546, Fax: 614-236-6923, E-mail: jwilk@capital.edu. Web site: http://www.capital.edu/capital-mba/.

Carlos Albizu University, Miami Campus, Graduate Programs, Miami, FL 33172-2209. Offers clinical psychology (Psy D); entrepreneurship (MBA); exceptional student education (MS); industrial/organizational psychology (MS); marriage and family therapy (MS); mental health counseling (MS); nonprofit management (MBA); organizational management (MBA); psychology (MS); school counseling (MS); teaching English as a second language (MS). *Accreditation:* APA. Part-time and evening/weekend programs available. *Faculty:* 19 full-time (12 women), 53 part-time/adjunct (27 women). *Students:* 524 full-time (431 women), 216 part-time (169 women); includes 563 minority (50 Black or African American, non-Hispanic/Latino; 1 American Indian or Alaska Native, non-Hispanic/Latino; 4 Asian, non-Hispanic/Latino; 492 Hispanic/Latino; 16 Native Hawaiian or other Pacific Islander, non-Hispanic/Latino), 17 international. Average age 31. 174 applicants, 67% accepted, 116 enrolled. In 2011, 157 master's, 21 doctorates awarded. Terminal master's awarded for partial completion of doctoral program. *Degree requirements:* For master's, one foreign language, comprehensive exam, integrative project (MBA), research project (exceptional student education, teaching English as a second language); for doctorate, one foreign language, comprehensive exam, internship, project. *Entrance requirements:* For master's, 3 letters of recommendation, interview, minimum GPA of 3.0, resume, statement of purpose, official transcripts; for doctorate, 3 letters of recommendation, minimum GPA of 3.0, resume, interview, statement of purpose, official transcripts. Additional exam requirements/recommendations for international students: Required—Michigan Test of English Language Proficiency. *Application deadline:* For fall admission, 4/1 priority date for domestic students, 5/1 for international students; for spring admission, 11/1 priority date for domestic students, 9/1 for international students. Applications are processed on a rolling basis. Application fee: $50. Electronic applications accepted. *Expenses: Tuition:* Full-time $9360; part-time $520 per credit. *Required fees:* $298 per term. Tuition and fees vary according to course load, degree level and program. *Financial support:* In 2011–12, 106 students received support. Federal Work-Study, scholarships/grants, and tuition discounts available. Financial award application deadline: 6/1; financial award applicants required to submit FAFSA. *Faculty research:* Psychotherapy, forensic psychology, neuropsychology, marketing strategy, entrepreneurship, special education. *Unit head:* Dr. Carmen S. Roca, Chancellor, 305-593-1223 Ext. 120, Fax: 305-629-8052, E-mail: croca@albizu.edu. *Application contact:* Vanessa Almendarez, Administrative Assistant, 305-593-1223 Ext. 137, Fax: 305-593-1854, E-mail: valmendarez@albizu.edu.

Carlow University, School of Management, MBA Program, Pittsburgh, PA 15213-3165. Offers business administration (MBA); innovation management (MBA); technology management (MBA). Part-time and evening/weekend programs available. Postbaccalaureate distance learning degree programs offered (no on-campus study). *Students:* 84 full-time (70 women), 24 part-time (17 women); includes 25 minority (22 Black or African American, non-Hispanic/Latino; 3 Hispanic/Latino). Average age 32. 138 applicants, 44% accepted, 46 enrolled. In 2011, 38 master's awarded. *Entrance requirements:* For master's, minimum undergraduate GPA of 3.0; essay; resume; transcripts; two recommendations. Additional exam requirements/recommendations for international students: Required—TOEFL (minimum score 550 paper-based; 213 computer-based). *Application deadline:* Applications are processed on a rolling basis. Application fee: $20. Electronic applications accepted. Application fee is waived when completed online. *Expenses: Tuition:* Full-time $10,290; part-time $686 per credit. Tuition and fees vary according to course load, degree level and program. *Unit head:* Dr. Enrique Mu, Director, MBA Program, 412-578-8729, Fax: 412-587-6367, E-mail: muex@carlow.edu. *Application contact:* Jo Danhires, Administrative Assistant, Admissions, 412-578-6088, Fax: 412-578-6321, E-mail: gradstudies@carlow.edu. Web site: http://gradstudies.carlow.edu/management/mba.html.

Carnegie Mellon University, College of Humanities and Social Sciences, Department of Social and Decision Sciences, Pittsburgh, PA 15213-3891. Offers behavioral decision research (PhD); behavioral decision research and psychology (PhD); social and decision science (PhD); strategy, entrepeneurship, and technological change (PhD). Terminal master's awarded for partial completion of doctoral program. *Degree requirements:* For doctorate, comprehensive exam, thesis/dissertation, research paper. *Entrance requirements:* For doctorate, GRE General Test. Additional exam requirements/recommendations for international students: Required—TOEFL. Electronic applications accepted. *Faculty research:* Organization theory, political science, sociology, technology studies.

Clemson University, Graduate School, College of Business and Behavioral Science, Program in Business Administration, Clemson, SC 29634. Offers entrepreneurship and innovation (MBA). *Accreditation:* AACSB. Part-time and evening/weekend programs available. *Faculty:* 30 full-time (6 women). *Students:* 83 full-time (26 women), 171 part-time (60 women); includes 30 minority (14 Black or African American, non-Hispanic/Latino; 5 Asian, non-Hispanic/Latino; 10 Hispanic/Latino; 1 Two or more races, non-Hispanic/Latino), 25 international. Average age 33. 229 applicants, 61% accepted, 94 enrolled. In 2011, 109 degrees awarded. *Entrance requirements:* For master's, GMAT. Additional exam requirements/recommendations for international students: Required—TOEFL. *Application deadline:* For fall admission, 7/1 priority date for domestic students, 4/15 for international students; for spring admission, 11/1 for international students. Applications are processed on a rolling basis. Application fee: $70 ($80 for international students). Electronic applications accepted. *Financial support:* In 2011–12, 16 students received support, including 4 fellowships with full and partial tuition reimbursements available (averaging $2,307 per year), 9 research assistantships with partial tuition reimbursements available (averaging $9,333 per year), 1 teaching assistantship with partial tuition reimbursement available (averaging $6,000 per year); institutionally sponsored loans and scholarships/grants also available. Financial award application deadline: 5/1; financial award applicants required to submit FAFSA. *Unit head:* Dr. Gregory Pickett, Director, 864-656-3975, Fax: 864-656-0947. *Application contact:* Deanna Burns, Director of Admissions, 864-656-8173, E-mail: dchambe@clemson.edu. Web site: http://www.clemson.edu/cbbs/departments/mba/.

Cogswell Polytechnical College, Program in Entrepreneurship and Innovation, Sunnyvale, CA 94089-1299. Offers MA.

Columbia University, Graduate School of Business, MBA Program, New York, NY 10027. Offers accounting (MBA); decision, risk, and operations (MBA); entrepreneurship (MBA); finance and economics (MBA); healthcare and pharmaceutical management (MBA); human resource management (MBA); international business (MBA); leadership and ethics (MBA); management (MBA); marketing (MBA); media (MBA); private equity (MBA); real estate (MBA); social enterprise (MBA); value investing (MBA); DDS/MBA; JD/MBA; MBA/MIA; MBA/MPH; MBA/MS; MD/MBA. *Entrance requirements:* For master's, GMAT, 2 letters of recommendation. Additional exam requirements/recommendations for international students: Required—TOEFL. Electronic applications accepted. *Expenses:* Contact institution. *Faculty research:* Human decision making and behavioral research; real estate market and mortgage defaults; financial crisis and corporate governance; international business; security analysis and accounting.

Dallas Baptist University, College of Business, Business Administration Program, Dallas, TX 75211-9299. Offers accounting (MBA); business communication (MBA); conflict resolution management (MBA); entrepreneurship (MBA); finance (MBA); health care management (MBA); international business (MBA); leading the non-profit organization (MBA); management (MBA); management information systems (MBA); marketing (MBA); project management (MBA); technology and engineering management (MBA). *Accreditation:* ACBSP. Part-time and evening/weekend programs available. *Entrance requirements:* For master's, GMAT, minimum GPA of 3.0. Additional exam requirements/recommendations for international students: Required—TOEFL, IELTS. *Application deadline:* Applications are processed on a rolling basis. Application fee: $25. Electronic applications accepted. *Expenses: Tuition:* Full-time $12,060; part-time $670 per credit hour. *Required fees:* $100; $50 per semester. *Financial support:* Federal Work-Study, institutionally sponsored loans, scholarships/grants, and tuition waivers (full and partial) available. Support available to part-time students. Financial award applicants required to submit FAFSA. *Faculty research:* Sports management, services marketing, retailing, strategic management, financial planning/investments. *Unit head:* Dr. Sandra S. Reid, Director, 214-333-5280, Fax: 214-333-5293, E-mail: graduate@dbu.edu. *Application contact:* Kit P. Montgomery, Director of Graduate Programs, 214-333-5242, Fax: 214-333-5579, E-mail: graduate@dbu.edu. Web site: http://www3.dbu.edu/graduate/mba.asp.

DePaul University, Charles H. Kellstadt Graduate School of Business, Department of Management, Chicago, IL 60604-2287. Offers entrepreneurship (MBA); health sector management (MBA); human resource management (MBA, MSHR); leadership/change management (MBA); management planning and strategy (MBA); operations management (MBA). Part-time and evening/weekend programs available. *Faculty:* 36 full-time (7 women), 35 part-time/adjunct (16 women). *Students:* 280 full-time (116 women), 121 part-time (47 women); includes 78 minority (20 Black or African American, non-Hispanic/Latino; 37 Asian, non-Hispanic/Latino; 16 Hispanic/Latino; 1 Native Hawaiian or other Pacific Islander, non-Hispanic/Latino; 4 Two or more races, non-Hispanic/Latino), 33 international. Average age 30. In 2011, 112 master's awarded. *Entrance requirements:* For master's, GMAT, GRE (MSHR), 2 letters of recommendation, resume. Additional exam requirements/recommendations for international students: Required—TOEFL (minimum score 550 paper-based; 213 computer-based). *Application deadline:* For fall admission, 7/1 for domestic students; for winter admission, 10/1 for domestic students; for spring admission, 2/1 for domestic students. Applications are processed on a rolling basis. Application fee: $60. Electronic applications accepted. *Financial support:* Research assistantships available. Financial award application deadline: 4/1. *Faculty research:* Growth management, creativity and innovation, quality management and business process design, entrepreneurship. *Unit head:* Robert T. Ryan, Assistant Dean and Director, 312-362-8810, Fax: 312-362-6677, E-mail: rryan1@depaul.edu. *Application contact:* Christopher E. Kinsella, Director of Cohort MBA Programs, 312-362-8810, Fax: 312-362-6677, E-mail: kgsb@depaul.edu.

Eastern Michigan University, Graduate School, College of Business, Programs in Business Administration, Ypsilanti, MI 48197. Offers business administration (MBA, Graduate Certificate); computer information systems (Graduate Certificate); e-business (MBA, Graduate Certificate); enterprise business intelligence (MBA); entrepreneurship (MBA, Graduate Certificate); finance (MBA, Graduate Certificate); human resources (MBA); human resources management (Graduate Certificate); information systems (MBA); internal auditing (MBA); international business (MBA, Graduate Certificate); marketing management (Graduate Certificate); nonprofit management (MBA); organizational development (Graduate Certificate); supply chain management (MBA, Graduate Certificate). *Accreditation:* AACSB. Part-time programs available. Postbaccalaureate distance learning degree programs offered (no on-campus study). *Students:* 79 full-time (39 women), 287 part-time (143 women); includes 55 minority (22 Black or African American, non-Hispanic/Latino; 24 Asian, non-Hispanic/Latino; 6 Hispanic/Latino; 3 Two or more races, non-Hispanic/Latino), 238 international. Average age 32. 317 applicants, 62% accepted, 89 enrolled. In 2011, 102 master's, 58 other advanced degrees awarded. *Entrance requirements:* For master's, GMAT (minimum score 450), minimum cumulative undergraduate GPA of 2.75. Additional exam requirements/recommendations for international students: Required—TOEFL. *Application deadline:* For fall admission, 5/15 for domestic students, 5/1 for international students; for winter admission, 10/15 for domestic students, 10/1 for international students; for spring admission, 3/15 for domestic students, 3/1 for international students. Applications are processed on a rolling basis. Application fee: $35. *Expenses:* Tuition, state resident: full-time $10,367; part-time $432 per credit hour. Tuition, nonresident: full-time $20,435; part-time $851 per credit hour. *Required fees:* $39 per credit hour. $46 per semester. One-time fee: $100. Tuition and fees vary according to course level, degree level and reciprocity agreements. *Financial support:* Fellowships, research assistantships with full tuition reimbursements, teaching assistantships with full tuition reimbursements, career-related internships or fieldwork, Federal Work-Study, institutionally sponsored loans, scholarships/grants, tuition waivers (partial), and unspecified assistantships available. Support available to part-time students. Financial award applicants required to submit FAFSA. *Unit head:* K. Michelle Henry, Director, Academic Services, 734-487-4444, Fax: 734-483-1316, E-mail: mhenry1@emich.edu.

Application contact: Beste Windes, Advisor, 734-487-4444, Fax: 734-483-1316, E-mail: bwindes@emich.edu. Web site: http://www.emich.edu/public/cob/gr/grad.html.

East Tennessee State University, School of Graduate Studies, College of Business and Technology, Department of Engineering Technology, Surveying and Digital Media, Johnson City, TN 37614. Offers entrepreneurial leadership (Postbaccalaureate Certificate); technology (MS), including digital media, engineering technology, entrepreneurial leadership. Part-time programs available. *Faculty:* 16 full-time (1 woman), 2 part-time/adjunct (0 women). *Students:* 24 full-time (7 women), 17 part-time (2 women); includes 9 minority (4 Black or African American, non-Hispanic/Latino; 2 Asian, non-Hispanic/Latino; 2 Hispanic/Latino; 1 Two or more races, non-Hispanic/Latino), 2 international. Average age 32. 37 applicants, 68% accepted, 9 enrolled. In 2011, 24 master's awarded. *Degree requirements:* For master's, comprehensive exam, thesis optional, strategic experience, capstone; for Postbaccalaureate Certificate, strategic experience. *Entrance requirements:* For master's, bachelor's degree in technical or related area, minimum GPA of 3.0; for Postbaccalaureate Certificate, minimum GPA of 2.5, three letters of recommendation. Additional exam requirements/recommendations for international students: Required—TOEFL (minimum score 550 paper-based; 213 computer-based; 79 iBT). *Application deadline:* For fall admission, 6/1 for domestic students, 4/30 for international students; for spring admission, 11/1 for domestic students, 9/30 for international students. Application fee: $35 ($45 for international students). Electronic applications accepted. *Expenses:* Tuition, state resident: full-time $7312; part-time $350 per credit hour. Tuition, nonresident: full-time $18,490; part-time $621 per credit hour. *Required fees:* $63 per credit hour. Tuition and fees vary according to course load and program. *Financial support:* In 2011–12, 20 students received support, including 12 research assistantships with full tuition reimbursements available (averaging $6,000 per year); career-related internships or fieldwork, institutionally sponsored loans, scholarships/grants, and unspecified assistantships also available. Financial award application deadline: 7/1; financial award applicants required to submit FAFSA. *Faculty research:* Computer-integrated manufacturing, alternative energy, sustainability, CAD/CAM, organizational change. *Unit head:* Dr. Keith V. Johnson, Chair, 423-439-7822, Fax: 423-439-7750, E-mail: johnsonk@etsu.edu. *Application contact:* Bethany Glassbrenner, Graduate Specialist, 423-439-6165, Fax: 423-439-5624, E-mail: glassbrenner@etsu.edu.

Fairfield University, Charles F. Dolan School of Business, Fairfield, CT 06824-5195. Offers accounting (MBA, MS, CAS); accounting information systems (MBA, CAS); entrepreneurship (MBA, CAS); finance (MBA, MS, CAS); general management (MBA, CAS); human resource management (MBA, CAS); information systems and operations (MBA); information systems and operations management (CAS); international business (MBA, CAS); marketing (MBA, CAS); taxation (MBA, CAS). *Accreditation:* AACSB. Part-time and evening/weekend programs available. *Faculty:* 23 full-time (9 women), 3 part-time/adjunct (1 woman). *Students:* 87 full-time (37 women), 118 part-time (42 women); includes 13 minority (4 Black or African American, non-Hispanic/Latino; 4 Asian, non-Hispanic/Latino; 5 Hispanic/Latino), 9 international. Average age 29. 126 applicants, 47% accepted, 35 enrolled. In 2011, 90 master's awarded. *Degree requirements:* For master's, capstone course. *Entrance requirements:* For master's, GMAT (minimum score 500), 2 letters of reference, resume, minimum GPA of 3.0. Additional exam requirements/recommendations for international students: Required—TOEFL (minimum score 550 paper-based; 213 computer-bases; 80 iBT) or IELTS (minimum score 6.5). *Application deadline:* For fall admission, 5/15 for international students; for spring admission, 10/15 for international students. Applications are processed on a rolling basis. Application fee: $60. Electronic applications accepted. *Expenses:* Contact institution. *Financial support:* In 2011–12, 50 students received support, including 2 research assistantships (averaging $6,500 per year); scholarships/grants, unspecified assistantships, and merit-based one-time entrance scholarship also available. Financial award applicants required to submit FAFSA. *Faculty research:* Optimization strategies, international finance, consumer behavior, financial market volatility, Internet marketing, supply chain analysis, tax issues. *Unit head:* Dr. Donald Gibson, Dean, 203-254-4000 Ext. 4070, Fax: 203-254-4105, E-mail: dgibson@fairfield.edu. *Application contact:* Marianne Gumpper, Director of Graduate and Continuing Studies Admission, 203-254-4184, Fax: 203-254-4073, E-mail: gradadmis@fairfield.edu. Web site: http://www.fairfield.edu/dsb/dsb_grad_1.html.

Fairleigh Dickinson University, College at Florham, Silberman College of Business, Departments of Management, Marketing, and Entrepreneurial Studies, Program in Entrepreneurial Studies, Madison, NJ 07940-1099. Offers MBA, Certificate.

Fairleigh Dickinson University, Metropolitan Campus, Silberman College of Business, Departments of Management, Marketing, and Entrepreneurial Studies, Program in Entrepreneurial Studies, Teaneck, NJ 07666-1914. Offers MBA, Certificate.

Felician College, Program in Business, Lodi, NJ 07644-2117. Offers innovation and entrepreneurship (MBA). Part-time and evening/weekend programs available. *Students:* 3 full-time (2 women), 80 part-time (46 women); includes 16 minority (8 Black or African American, non-Hispanic/Latino; 3 Asian, non-Hispanic/Latino; 5 Hispanic/Latino), 5 international. 28 applicants, 89% accepted, 24 enrolled. *Entrance requirements:* For master's, GMAT. *Application deadline:* Applications are processed on a rolling basis. Application fee: $40. *Expenses: Tuition:* Part-time $925 per credit. *Required fees:* $262.50 per semester. Part-time tuition and fees vary according to class time and student level. *Unit head:* Dr. Beth Castiglia, Dean, Division of Business and Management Services, 201-559-6140, E-mail: mctaggartp@felician.edu. *Application contact:* Nicole Vitale, Assistant Director of Graduate Admissions, 201-559-6077, Fax: 201-559-6138, E-mail: graduate@felician.edu. Web site: http://www.felician.edu/divisions/business-management-sciences/graduate.

See Display on page 93 and Close-Up on page 219.

Florida Atlantic University, College of Business, Department of Management Programs, Boca Raton, FL 33431-0991. Offers global entrepreneurship (MBA); international business (MBA, MS); management (PhD). *Faculty:* 30 full-time (10 women), 24 part-time/adjunct (9 women). *Students:* 299 full-time (121 women), 459 part-time (199 women); includes 297 minority (99 Black or African American, non-Hispanic/Latino; 1 American Indian or Alaska Native, non-Hispanic/Latino; 45 Asian, non-Hispanic/Latino; 136 Hispanic/Latino; 1 Native Hawaiian or other Pacific Islander, non-Hispanic/Latino; 15 Two or more races, non-Hispanic/Latino), 40 international. Average age 33. 725 applicants, 51% accepted, 132 enrolled. In 2011, 259 master's, 4 doctorates awarded. *Entrance requirements:* For master's, GMAT or GRE General Test, minimum GPA of 3.0 in last 60 hours of course work. Additional exam requirements/recommendations for international students: Required—TOEFL (minimum score 600 paper-based; 250 computer-based). *Application deadline:* For fall admission, 7/25 for domestic students, 2/15 for international students; for spring admission, 12/10 for domestic students, 7/15 for international students. Applications are processed on a rolling basis. Application fee: $30. Electronic applications accepted. *Expenses: Tuition, area resident:* Part-time $343.02 per credit hour. Tuition, state resident: full-time $8232. Tuition, nonresident: full-time $23,931; part-time $997.14 per credit hour. *Financial support:* Research assistantships with full tuition reimbursements, career-related internships or fieldwork, tuition waivers (partial), and unspecified assistantships available. *Faculty research:* Sports administration, healthcare, policy, finance, real estate, senior living. *Unit head:* Dr. Peggy Golden, Chair, 561-297-2675, E-mail: golden@fau.edu. *Application contact:* Fredrick G. Taylor, Graduate Adviser, 561-297-3196, Fax: 561-297-1315, E-mail: ftaylor@fau.edu. Web site: http://business.fau.edu/departments/management/index.aspx.

George Mason University, College of Visual and Performing Arts, Program in Arts Management, Fairfax, VA 22030. Offers arts management (MA); entrepreneurship (Certificate); fund-raising and development in the arts (Certificate); marketing and public relations in the arts (Certificate); programming and project management (Certificate). *Accreditation:* NASAD. *Faculty:* 2 full-time (both women), 8 part-time/adjunct (3 women). *Students:* 48 full-time (40 women), 37 part-time (34 women); includes 17 minority (6 Black or African American, non-Hispanic/Latino; 4 Asian, non-Hispanic/Latino; 3 Hispanic/Latino; 4 Two or more races, non-Hispanic/Latino), 9 international. Average age 29. 105 applicants, 54% accepted, 22 enrolled. In 2011, 44 master's, 21 other advanced degrees awarded. *Degree requirements:* For master's, internship. *Entrance requirements:* For master's and Certificate, GRE (recommended), undergraduate degree with minimum GPA of 3.0, official transcripts, 2 letters of recommendation, statement of purpose, resume. Additional exam requirements/recommendations for international students: Required—TOEFL (minimum score 570 paper-based; 230 computer-based; 88 iBT), IELTS, Pearson Test of English. *Application deadline:* For fall admission, 3/1 for domestic students, 2/15 for international students; for spring admission, 10/15 for domestic students, 9/15 for international students. Application fee: $65 ($80 for international students). Electronic applications accepted. *Expenses:* Tuition, state resident: full-time $8750; part-time $364.58 per credit. Tuition, nonresident: full-time $24,092; part-time $1003.83 per credit. *Required fees:* $2514; $104.75 per credit. *Financial support:* In 2011–12, 2 students received support, including 2 teaching assistantships with full and partial tuition reimbursements available (averaging $8,649 per year); career-related internships or fieldwork, Federal Work-Study, scholarships/grants, unspecified assistantships, and health care benefits (full-time research and teaching assistantship recipient) also available. Financial award application deadline: 3/1; financial award applicants required to submit FAFSA. *Faculty research:* Information technology for arts managers, special topics in arts management, directions in gallery management, arts in society, public relations/marketing strategies for art organizations. *Unit head:* Richard Kamenitzer, Director, 703-993-9194, Fax: 703-993-9829, E-mail: rkamenit@gmu.edu. *Application contact:* Mathilde Speier, Information Contact, 703-993-8926, Fax: 703-993-9829, E-mail: mspeier@gmu.edu. Web site: http://artsmanagement.gmu.edu/arts-management-ma/.

Georgia Institute of Technology, Graduate Studies and Research, College of Management, Program in Business Administration, Atlanta, GA 30332-0001. Offers accounting (MBA); e-commerce (Certificate); engineering entrepreneurship (MBA); entrepreneurship (Certificate); finance (MBA); information technology management (MBA); international business (MBA, Certificate); management of technology (Certificate); marketing (MBA); operations management (MBA); organizational behavior (MBA); strategic management (MBA). *Accreditation:* AACSB.

Georgia State University, J. Mack Robinson College of Business, Department of Managerial Sciences, Atlanta, GA 30302-3083. Offers business analysis (MBA, MS); decision sciences (PhD); entrepreneurship (MBA); human resources management (MBA, MS); management (MBA, PhD); operations management (MBA, MS); organization change (MS); personnel employee relations (PhD); strategic management (PhD). *Accreditation:* AACSB. Part-time and evening/weekend programs available. *Degree requirements:* For doctorate, thesis/dissertation. *Entrance requirements:* For master's and doctorate, GMAT. Additional exam requirements/recommendations for international students: Required—TOEFL (minimum score 610 paper-based; 255 computer-based; 101 iBT). Electronic applications accepted. *Faculty research:* Abusive supervision, entrepreneurship, time series and neural networks, organizational controls, inventory control systems.

Georgia State University, J. Mack Robinson College of Business, Program in General Business Administration, Atlanta, GA 30302-3083. Offers accounting/information systems (MBA); economics (MBA, MS); enterprise risk management (MBA); general business (MBA); general business administration (EMBA, PMBA); information systems consulting (MBA); information systems risk management (MBA); international business and information technology (MBA); international entrepreneurship (MBA); MBA/JD. *Accreditation:* AACSB. Part-time and evening/weekend programs available. *Entrance requirements:* For master's, GMAT. Additional exam requirements/recommendations for international students: Required—TOEFL (minimum score 610 paper-based; 255 computer-based; 101 iBT). Electronic applications accepted.

Grand Canyon University, College of Business, Phoenix, AZ 85017-1097. Offers accounting (MBA); corporate business administration (MBA); disaster preparedness and crisis management (MBA); executive fire service leadership (MS); finance (MBA); general management (MBA); government and policy (MPA); health care management (MPA); health systems management (MBA); human resource management (MBA); innovation (MBA); leadership (MBA, MS); management of information system (MBA); marketing (MBA); project-based (MBA); six sigma (MBA); strategic human resource management (MBA). *Accreditation:* ACBSP. Part-time and evening/weekend programs available. Postbaccalaureate distance learning degree programs offered (no on-campus study). *Entrance requirements:* For master's, equivalent of two years full-time professional work experience. Additional exam requirements/recommendations for international students: Required—TOEFL (minimum score 575 paper-based; 233 computer-based; 90 iBT), IELTS (minimum score 7). Electronic applications accepted.

Harrisburg University of Science and Technology, Program in Information Systems Engineering and Management, Harrisburg, PA 17101. Offers digital government specialization (MS); digital health specialization (MS); entrepreneurship specialization (MS). Part-time programs available. *Degree requirements:* For master's, comprehensive exam, thesis optional. *Entrance requirements:* For master's, baccalaureate degree. Additional exam requirements/recommendations for international students: Required—TOEFL (minimum score 520 paper-based; 200 computer-based; 80 iBT). Electronic applications accepted.

Hult International Business School, Program in Business Administration - Hult London Campus, London, MA WC 1B 4JP, United Kingdom. Offers entrepreneurship (MBA); international business (MBA); international finance (MBA); marketing (MBA). Part-time programs available. *Degree requirements:* For master's, comprehensive exam, thesis, internship. *Entrance requirements:* Additional exam requirements/recommendations for international students: Required—TOEFL (minimum score 580 paper-based; 237 computer-based), TWE (minimum score 5). Electronic applications accepted.

The International University of Monaco, Graduate Programs, Monte Carlo, Monaco. Offers entrepreneurship (EMBA, MBA); financial engineering (M Sc); hedge fund and private equity (M Sc); international marketing (EMBA, MBA); international wealth management (M Sc); luxury goods and services (EMBA, M Sc, MBA); wealth and asset management (EMBA, MBA). Part-time programs available. *Degree requirements:* For master's, comprehensive exam (for some programs), applied research project. *Entrance requirements:* Additional exam requirements/recommendations for international students: Required—TOEFL (minimum score 550 paper-based; 213 computer-based),

Entrepreneurship

IELTS. Electronic applications accepted. *Faculty research:* Gaming, leadership, disintermediation.

Jones International University, School of Business, Centennial, CO 80112. Offers accounting (MBA); business communication (MABC); entrepreneurship (MABC, MBA); finance (MBA); global enterprise management (MBA); health care management (MBA); information security management (MBA); information technology management (MBA); leadership and influence (MABC); leading the customer-driven organization (MABC); negotiation and conflict management (MBA); project management (MABC, MBA). Program only offered online. Part-time and evening/weekend programs available. Postbaccalaureate distance learning degree programs offered (no on-campus study). *Degree requirements:* For master's, capstone project. *Entrance requirements:* For master's, minimum cumulative GPA of 2.5. Additional exam requirements/ recommendations for international students: Recommended—TOEFL (minimum score 550 paper-based; 213 computer-based). Electronic applications accepted.

Kaplan University, Davenport Campus, School of Business, Davenport, IA 52807-2095. Offers business administration (MBA); change leadership (MS); entrepreneurship (MBA); finance (MBA); health care management (MBA, MS); human resource (MBA); international business (MBA); management (MS); marketing (MBA); project management (MBA, MS); supply chain management and logistics (MBA, MS). Part-time and evening/weekend programs available. Postbaccalaureate distance learning degree programs offered (no on-campus study). *Entrance requirements:* Additional exam requirements/recommendations for international students: Required—TOEFL (minimum score 550 paper-based; 218 computer-based; 80 iBT). Electronic applications accepted.

Lamar University, College of Graduate Studies, College of Business, Beaumont, TX 77710. Offers accounting (MBA); experiential business and entrepreneurship (MBA); financial management (MBA); healthcare administration (MBA); information systems (MBA); management (MBA). *Accreditation:* AACSB. Part-time and evening/weekend programs available. *Faculty:* 18 full-time (5 women), 5 part-time/adjunct (0 women). *Students:* 74 full-time (33 women), 72 part-time (27 women); includes 24 minority (7 Black or African American, non-Hispanic/Latino; 9 Asian, non-Hispanic/Latino; 8 Hispanic/Latino), 34 international. Average age 29. 69 applicants, 84% accepted, 16 enrolled. In 2011, 62 master's awarded. *Degree requirements:* For master's, comprehensive exam (for some programs), thesis optional. *Entrance requirements:* For master's, GMAT. Additional exam requirements/recommendations for international students: Required—TOEFL (minimum score 525 paper-based; 197 computer-based). *Application deadline:* For fall admission, 3/15 priority date for domestic students; for spring admission, 10/1 priority date for domestic students. Applications are processed on a rolling basis. Application fee: $25 ($50 for international students). *Expenses:* Tuition, state resident: full-time $5430; part-time $272 per credit hour. Tuition, nonresident: full-time $11,540; part-time $577 per credit hour. *Required fees:* $1916. *Financial support:* In 2011–12, 12 students received support, including 4 research assistantships with partial tuition reimbursements available; fellowships with tuition reimbursements available, career-related internships or fieldwork, Federal Work-Study, institutionally sponsored loans, scholarships/grants, and tuition waivers (partial) also available. Support available to part-time students. Financial award application deadline: 4/1; financial award applicants required to submit FAFSA. *Faculty research:* Marketing, finance, quantitative methods, management information systems, legal, environmental. *Unit head:* Dr. Enrique R. Venta, Dean, 409-880-8604, Fax: 409-880-8088, E-mail: henry.venta@lamar.edu. *Application contact:* Dr. Brad Mayer, Professor and Associate Dean, 409-880-2383, Fax: 409-880-8605, E-mail: bradley.mayer@lamar.edu. Web site: http://mba.lamar.edu.

Lenoir-Rhyne University, Graduate Programs, Charles M. Snipes School of Business, Hickory, NC 28601. Offers accounting (MBA); entrepreneurship (MBA); global leadership (MBA); leadership development (MBA). *Accreditation:* ACBSP. Part-time and evening/weekend programs available. *Degree requirements:* For master's, capstone course. *Entrance requirements:* For master's, GMAT, minimum undergraduate GPA of 2.7, graduate 3.0. Additional exam requirements/recommendations for international students: Required—TOEFL (minimum score 600 paper-based). Electronic applications accepted. *Expenses:* Contact institution.

LIM College, MBA Program, New York, NY 10022-5268. Offers entrepreneurship (MBA); fashion management (MBA). *Entrance requirements:* For master's, interview. Additional exam requirements/recommendations for international students: Required—TOEFL (minimum score 550 paper-based; 213 computer-based; 80 iBT), IELTS (minimum score 6.5).

Lincoln University, School of Graduate Studies and Continuing Education, Jefferson City, MO 65102. Offers business administration (MBA), including accounting, entrepreneurship, management, public administration and policy; educational leadership (Ed S), including elementary leadership, secondary leadership, superintendency; guidance and counseling (M Ed), including community/agency counseling, elementary school, secondary school; history (MA); school administration and supervision (M Ed), including elementary school administration, secondary school administration, special education administration; school teaching (M Ed), including elementary school teaching, secondary school teaching; social science (MA), including history, political science, sociology; sociology (MA); sociology/criminal justice (MA). Part-time and evening/weekend programs available. *Degree requirements:* For master's and Ed S, comprehensive exam, thesis optional. *Entrance requirements:* For master's and Ed S, GRE, MAT or GMAT, minimum GPA of 2.75 in major, 2.5 overall; 3 letters of recommendation; minimum C average in English composition; personal statement of purpose. Additional exam requirements/recommendations for international students: Required—TOEFL (minimum score 500 paper-based; 173 computer-based; 61 iBT). *Faculty research:* Suicide prevention.

Lindenwood University, Graduate Programs, School of Business and Entrepreneurship, St. Charles, MO 63301-1695. Offers accounting (MBA, MS); business administration (MBA); entrepreneurial studies (MBA, MS); finance (MBA, MS); human resource management (MBA); human resources (MS); international business (MBA, MS); management (MBA, MS); management information systems (MBA, MS); marketing (MBA, MS); public management (MBA, MS); sport management (MA); supply chain management (MBA). *Accreditation:* ACBSP. Part-time and evening/weekend programs available. *Faculty:* 20 full-time (8 women), 17 part-time/adjunct (5 women). *Students:* 165 full-time (66 women), 223 part-time (100 women); includes 59 minority (48 Black or African American, non-Hispanic/Latino; 4 Asian, non-Hispanic/Latino; 2 Native Hawaiian or other Pacific Islander, non-Hispanic/Latino; 5 Two or more races, non-Hispanic/ Latino), 140 international. Average age 29. 156 applicants, 76% accepted, 103 enrolled. In 2011, 205 degrees awarded. *Degree requirements:* For master's, comprehensive exam (for some programs), thesis (for some programs). *Entrance requirements:* For master's, interview, minimum GPA of 3.0, letter of recommendation. Additional exam requirements/recommendations for international students: Required—TOEFL (minimum score 550 paper-based; 213 computer-based; 80 iBT). *Application deadline:* For fall admission, 8/15 priority date for domestic students, 8/15 for international students; for winter admission, 1/9 priority date for domestic students, 1/9 for international students; for spring admission, 3/12 priority date for domestic students, 3/12 for international students. Applications are processed on a rolling basis. Application fee: $30 ($100 for international students). Electronic applications accepted. *Expenses: Tuition:* Full-time $13,650; part-time $395 per credit hour. *Required fees:* $150 per semester. Tuition and fees vary according to course level and course load. *Financial support:* In 2011–12, 206 students received support. Career-related internships or fieldwork, Federal Work-Study, institutionally sponsored loans, and tuition waivers (partial) available. Financial award application deadline: 6/30; financial award applicants required to submit FAFSA. *Unit head:* Roger Ellis, Dean, 636-949-4839, E-mail: rellis@lindenwood.edu. *Application contact:* Brett Barger, Dean of Evening Admissions and Extension Campuses, 636-949-4934, Fax: 636-949-4109, E-mail: adultadmissions@lindenwood.edu. Web site: http://www.lindenwood.edu.

Long Island University–Hudson at Rockland, Graduate School, Master of Business Administration Program, Orangeburg, NY 10962. Offers business administration (Post Master's Certificate); entrepreneurship (MBA); finance (MBA); healthcare sector management (MBA); management (MBA). Part-time and evening/weekend programs available. *Entrance requirements:* For master's, GMAT, college transcripts, two letters of recommendation, personal statement, resume.

Marquette University, Graduate School of Management, Program in Business Administration, Milwaukee, WI 53201-1881. Offers business administration (MBA); economics (MBA); entrepreneurship (Certificate); finance (MBA); human resources (MBA); international business (MBA); management information systems (MBA); marketing (MBA); operations and supply chain management (MBA); sports business (MBA); JD/MBA; MBA/MA; MBA/MSN. *Accreditation:* AACSB. Part-time and evening/ weekend programs available. *Students:* 42 full-time (14 women), 335 part-time (94 women); includes 24 minority (5 Black or African American, non-Hispanic/Latino; 1 American Indian or Alaska Native, non-Hispanic/Latino; 15 Asian, non-Hispanic/Latino; 3 Hispanic/Latino), 29 international. Average age 31. 182 applicants, 59% accepted, 103 enrolled. In 2011, 128 master's awarded. *Degree requirements:* For Certificate, business plan. *Entrance requirements:* For master's, GMAT or GRE, letters of recommendation. Additional exam requirements/recommendations for international students: Required—TOEFL (minimum score 550 paper-based; 85 computer-based; 88 iBT), IELTS (minimum score 6.5), Pearson Test of English. *Application deadline:* For fall admission, 2/15 for domestic and international students. Applications are processed on a rolling basis. Application fee: $50. Electronic applications accepted. *Expenses: Tuition:* Full-time $17,010; part-time $945 per credit hour. Tuition and fees vary according to program. *Financial support:* In 2011–12, 4 fellowships, 11 teaching assistantships were awarded; research assistantships, Federal Work-Study, institutionally sponsored loans, scholarships/grants, and tuition waivers (full and partial) also available. Support available to part-time students. Financial award application deadline: 2/15. *Faculty research:* Ethics in the professions, services marketing, technology impact on decision-making, mentoring. *Unit head:* Dr. Jeanne Simmons, Graduate Director, 414-288-7145, Fax: 414-288-1660, E-mail: jeanne.simmons@marquette.edu. *Application contact:* Debra Leutermann, Admissions Coordinator, 414-288-8064, Fax: 414-288-1902, E-mail: debra.leutermann@marquette.edu. Web site: http://business.marquette.edu/ academics/mba.

Marquette University, Graduate School of Management, Program in Entrepreneurship, Milwaukee, WI 53201-1881. Offers Graduate Certificate. *Students:* 5 part-time (3 women). Average age 26. 6 applicants, 83% accepted, 5 enrolled. *Entrance requirements:* Additional exam requirements/recommendations for international students: Required—TOEFL (minimum score 530 paper-based; 78 computer-based). *Application deadline:* Applications are processed on a rolling basis. Application fee: $50. Electronic applications accepted. *Expenses: Tuition:* Full-time $17,010; part-time $945 per credit hour. Tuition and fees vary according to program. *Financial support:* Application deadline: 2/15. *Unit head:* Dr. Jeanne Simmons, Associate Dean, 414-288-7145, Fax: 414-288-8078. *Application contact:* Debra Leutermann, Admissions Coordinator, 414-288-8064, Fax: 414-288-8078, E-mail: debra.leutermann@marquette.edu.

McGill University, Faculty of Graduate and Postdoctoral Studies, Desautels Faculty of Management, Montréal, QC H3A 2T5, Canada. Offers administration (PhD); entrepreneurial studies (MBA); finance (MBA); general management (Post Master's Certificate); information systems (MBA); international business (MBA); international practicing management (MM); management (MBA); management for development (MBA); manufacturing management (MMM); marketing (MBA); operations management (MBA); public accountancy (Diploma); strategic management (MBA); MBA/LL B; MD/ MBA. MMM offered jointly with Faculty of Engineering; PhD with Concordia University, HEC Montreal, Université de Montréal, Université du Québec à Montréal.

Mercyhurst College, Graduate Studies, Program in Organizational Leadership, Erie, PA 16546. Offers accounting (MS); entrepreneurship (MS); higher education administration (MS); human resources (MS); nonprofit management (MS); organizational leadership (Certificate); sports leadership (MS). Part-time and evening/ weekend programs available. *Faculty:* 1 full-time (0 women), 11 part-time/adjunct (4 women). *Students:* 42 full-time (16 women), 22 part-time (15 women); includes 5 minority (3 Black or African American, non-Hispanic/Latino; 1 American Indian or Alaska Native, non-Hispanic/Latino; 1 Hispanic/Latino), 9 international. Average age 30. 60 applicants, 62% accepted, 25 enrolled. In 2011, 27 master's, 2 other advanced degrees awarded. *Degree requirements:* For master's, thesis. *Entrance requirements:* For master's, GRE General Test or MAT, interview, resume, essay, three professional references, transcripts. Additional exam requirements/recommendations for international students: Required—TOEFL. *Application deadline:* For fall admission, 8/1 priority date for domestic students, 7/1 for international students; for winter admission, 11/1 for domestic students, 10/1 for international students; for spring admission, 2/1 for domestic students, 1/1 for international students. Applications are processed on a rolling basis. Application fee: $35. Electronic applications accepted. *Expenses: Tuition:* Part-time $570 per credit. *Required fees:* $90 per term. Tuition and fees vary according to program. *Financial support:* In 2011–12, 16 students received support, including 112 research assistantships with full and partial tuition reimbursements available (averaging $6,000 per year); career-related internships or fieldwork and unspecified assistantships also available. Support available to part-time students. Financial award application deadline: 5/1; financial award applicants required to submit FAFSA. *Faculty research:* Leadership training, organizational communication, leadership pedagogy. *Unit head:* Dr. Gilbert Jacobs, Director, 814-824-2390, E-mail: gjacobs@mercyhurst.edu. *Application contact:* Sarah Murphy, Academic Coordinator, 814-824-2297, Fax: 814-824-2055, E-mail: smurphy@mercyhurst.edu.

Michigan Technological University, Graduate School, Institute for Leadership and Innovation, Houghton, MI 49931. Offers Graduate Certificate. *Students:* 2 applicants, 0% accepted, 0 enrolled. In 2011, 3 Graduate Certificates awarded. *Expenses:* Tuition, state resident: full-time $12,636; part-time $702 per credit. Tuition, nonresident: full-time $12,636; part-time $702 per credit. *Required fees:* $226; $226 per year. *Total annual research expenditures:* $91,931. *Unit head:* Dr. Robert O. Warrington, Dean, 906-487-4371, Fax: 906-487-2770, E-mail: row@mtu.edu. *Application contact:* Carol T. Wingerson, Senior Staff Assistant, 906-487-2327, Fax: 906-487-2463, E-mail: gradadms@mtu.edu. Web site: http://www.iis.mtu.edu/.

Mount St. Mary's College, Graduate Division, Program in Business Administration, Los Angeles, CA 90049-1599. Offers entrepreneurship (MBA); nonprofit management (MBA); organizational leadership (MBA); project management (MBA). Evening/weekend programs available. *Entrance requirements:* Additional exam requirements/recommendations for international students: Required—TOEFL. *Application deadline:* For fall admission, 6/30 for domestic students. Electronic applications accepted. *Expenses:* Contact institution. *Financial support:* Scholarships/grants available. Financial award application deadline: 3/15; financial award applicants required to submit FAFSA. *Unit head:* Dr. Janet Robinson, Director, 310-954-4153, E-mail: jrobinson@msmc.la.edu. Web site: http://www.msmc.la.edu/graduate-programs/mba.asp.

North Carolina State University, Graduate School, Poole College of Management, Program in Business Administration, Raleigh, NC 27695. Offers biosciences management (MBA); entrepreneurship and technology commercialization (MBA); financial management (MBA); innovation management (MBA); marketing management (MBA); services management (MBA); supply chain management (MBA). *Accreditation:* AACSB. Part-time programs available. *Degree requirements:* For master's, thesis optional. *Entrance requirements:* For master's, GMAT, interview, 3 letters of recommendation. Additional exam requirements/recommendations for international students: Required—TOEFL (minimum score 600 paper-based; 250 computer-based; 100 iBT). Electronic applications accepted. *Faculty research:* Manufacturing strategy, information systems, technology commercialization, managing research and development, historical stock returns.

See Display on page 116 and Close-Up on page 225.

Northeastern University, School of Technological Entrepreneurship, Boston, MA 02115. Offers MS. Part-time programs available. *Faculty:* 7 full-time, 3 part-time/adjunct. *Students:* 22 full-time, 1 part-time. 38 applicants, 87% accepted, 22 enrolled. In 2011, 13 master's awarded. *Entrance requirements:* For master's, GRE or GMAT, BS, minimum GPA of 3.0. Additional exam requirements/recommendations for international students: Required—TOEFL. *Application deadline:* For fall admission, 7/1 for international students. Applications are processed on a rolling basis. Application fee: $50. Electronic applications accepted. *Unit head:* Dr. Paul M. Zavracky, Dean, 617-373-2788, Fax: 617-373-7490, E-mail: ste@neu.edu. *Application contact:* Information Contact, 617-373-2788, Fax: 617-373-7490, E-mail: ste@neu.edu. Web site: http://www.ste.neu.edu.

Oakland University, Graduate Study and Lifelong Learning, School of Business Administration, Department of Management and Marketing, Rochester, MI 48309-4401. Offers business administration (MBA); entrepreneurship (Certificate); general management (Certificate); human resource management (Certificate); international business (Certificate); marketing (Certificate).

Oral Roberts University, School of Business, Tulsa, OK 74171. Offers accounting (MBA); entrepreneurship (MBA); finance (MBA); international business (MBA); management (MBA); marketing (MBA); non-profit management (MBA); not for profit management (MNM). *Accreditation:* ACBSP. Part-time programs available. Postbaccalaureate distance learning degree programs offered (minimal on-campus study). *Degree requirements:* For master's, thesis optional. *Entrance requirements:* For master's, minimum cumulative GPA of 3.0. Additional exam requirements/recommendations for international students: Required—TOEFL (minimum score 550 paper-based; 213 computer-based; 79 iBT). Electronic applications accepted. *Faculty research:* Social media, international business and marketing.

Pace University, Lubin School of Business, Program in Management, New York, NY 10038. Offers entrepreneurial studies (MBA); executive management (MBA); human resource management (MBA, MS); management (MBA); strategic management (MBA). Part-time and evening/weekend programs available. *Students:* 44 full-time (24 women), 89 part-time (53 women); includes 28 minority (9 Black or African American, non-Hispanic/Latino; 1 American Indian or Alaska Native, non-Hispanic/Latino; 12 Asian, non-Hispanic/Latino; 4 Hispanic/Latino; 2 Two or more races, non-Hispanic/Latino), 33 international. Average age 30. 244 applicants, 52% accepted, 36 enrolled. In 2011, 33 master's awarded. *Entrance requirements:* For master's, GMAT, GRE. Additional exam requirements/recommendations for international students: Required—TOEFL. *Application deadline:* For fall admission, 7/31 priority date for domestic students; for spring admission, 11/30 for domestic students. Applications are processed on a rolling basis. Application fee: $70. Electronic applications accepted. *Expenses: Tuition:* Part-time $990 per credit. *Required fees:* $168 per semester. Tuition and fees vary according to course load and degree level. *Financial support:* Research assistantships, career-related internships or fieldwork, and Federal Work-Study available. Support available to part-time students. Financial award applicants required to submit FAFSA. *Unit head:* Dr. John C. Byrne, Chairperson, 212-618-6581, E-mail: jbyrne@pace.edu. *Application contact:* Susan Ford-Goldschein, Director of Graduate Admissions, 212-346-1531, Fax: 212-346-1585, E-mail: gradnyc@pace.edu. Web site: http://www.pace.edu/.

Park University, College of Graduate and Professional Studies, Kansas City, MO 54105. Offers adult education (M Ed); at-risk students (M Ed); disaster and emergency management (MPA); educational administration (M Ed); entrepreneurship (MBA); general business (MBA); general education (M Ed); government/business relations (MPA); healthcare/services management (MBA, MPA); international business (MBA); K-12 certification (MAT); management information systems (MBA); management of information systems (MPA); middle school certification (MAT); multi-cultural education (M Ed); nonprofit management (MPA); public management (MPA); school law (M Ed); secondary school certification (MAT); special education (M Ed). Part-time and evening/weekend programs available. Postbaccalaureate distance learning degree programs offered (no on-campus study). *Degree requirements:* For master's, comprehensive exam, thesis (for some programs). *Entrance requirements:* For master's, GRE, GMAT, teacher certification (M Ed). Additional exam requirements/recommendations for international students: Required—TOEFL (minimum score 550 paper-based). Electronic applications accepted. *Faculty research:* Literacy, leadership, brain based research, multicultural education, diversity.

Peru State College, Graduate Programs, Program in Organizational Management, Peru, NE 68421. Offers MS. Program offered online only. Part-time programs available. *Degree requirements:* For master's, thesis (for some programs). *Expenses:* Contact institution. *Faculty research:* Emotional intelligence.

Polytechnic Institute of New York University, Department of Chemical and Biological Sciences, Major in Biotechnology and Entrepreneurship, Brooklyn, NY 11201-2990. Offers MS. *Students:* 17 full-time (11 women), 8 part-time (1 woman); includes 1 minority (Asian, non-Hispanic/Latino), 18 international. Average age 24. 62 applicants, 48% accepted, 22 enrolled. In 2011, 10 degrees awarded. *Entrance requirements:* Additional exam requirements/recommendations for international students: Required—TOEFL (minimum score 550 paper-based; 213 computer-based; 80 iBT); Recommended—IELTS (minimum score 6.5). *Application deadline:* For fall admission, 7/31 priority date for domestic students, 4/30 for international students; for spring admission, 12/31 priority date for domestic students, 10/30 for international students. Applications are processed on a rolling basis. Application fee: $75. Electronic applications accepted. *Expenses: Tuition:* Full-time $22,464; part-time $1248 per credit. *Required fees:* $501 per semester. *Financial support:* Institutionally sponsored loans, scholarships/grants, and unspecified assistantships available. Support available to part-time students. *Unit head:* Dr. Bruce Garetz, Department Head, 718-260-3287, E-mail: bgaretz@poly.edu. *Application contact:* JeanCarlo Bonilla, Director, Graduate Enrollment Management, 718-260-3182, Fax: 718-260-3624, E-mail: gradinfo@poly.edu.

Polytechnic Institute of New York University, Department of Technology Management, Brooklyn, NY 11201-2990. Offers construction management (Advanced Certificate); electronic business management (Advanced Certificate); entrepreneurship (Advanced Certificate); human resources management (Advanced Certificate); information management (Advanced Certificate); management (MS); management of technology (MS); organizational behavior (MS, Advanced Certificate); project management (Advanced Certificate); technology management (MBA, PhD, Advanced Certificate); telecommunications and information management (MS); telecommunications management (Advanced Certificate). Part-time and evening/weekend programs available. *Faculty:* 6 full-time (1 woman), 32 part-time/adjunct (4 women). *Students:* 185 full-time (84 women), 94 part-time (41 women); includes 56 minority (15 Black or African American, non-Hispanic/Latino; 31 Asian, non-Hispanic/Latino; 10 Hispanic/Latino), 143 international. Average age 30. 467 applicants, 48% accepted, 123 enrolled. In 2011, 174 master's, 1 doctorate awarded. *Degree requirements:* For master's, comprehensive exam (for some programs), thesis (for some programs); for doctorate, comprehensive exam, thesis/dissertation. *Entrance requirements:* For master's, GMAT, minimum B average in undergraduate course work. Additional exam requirements/recommendations for international students: Required—TOEFL (minimum score 550 paper-based; 213 computer-based; 80 iBT); Recommended—IELTS (minimum score 6.5). *Application deadline:* For fall admission, 7/31 priority date for domestic students, 4/30 for international students; for spring admission, 12/31 priority date for domestic students, 11/30 for international students. Applications are processed on a rolling basis. Application fee: $75. Electronic applications accepted. *Expenses: Tuition:* Full-time $22,464; part-time $1248 per credit. *Required fees:* $501 per semester. *Financial support:* In 2011–12, 1 fellowship (averaging $26,400 per year) was awarded; research assistantships, teaching assistantships, institutionally sponsored loans, scholarships/grants, and unspecified assistantships also available. Support available to part-time students. *Unit head:* Prof. Bharadwaj Rao, Head, 718-260-3617, Fax: 718-260-3874, E-mail: brao@poly.edu. *Application contact:* JeanCarlo Bonilla, Director of Graduate Enrollment Management, 718-260-3182, Fax: 718-260-3624, E-mail: gradinfo@poly.edu. Web site: http://www.managementdept.poly.edu.

Pontificia Universidad Catolica Madre y Maestra, Graduate School, Faculty of Social and Administrative Sciences, Santiago, Dominican Republic. Offers business administration (MBA), including business development, finance, international business, management skills (M Mgmt, MBA), marketing, operations, strategic cost management, strategy, tourist destination planning and management; law (LL M), including civil law, corporate business law, criminal law, international relations, real estate law; management (M Mgmt), including higher financial management, insurance program administration, management skills (M Mgmt, MBA); psychology (MA), including clinical child and adolescent psychology, forensic psychology; strategic human resources (EMBA).

Post University, Program in Business Administration, Waterbury, CT 06723-2540. Offers business administration (MBA); corporate innovation (MBA); entrepreneurship (MBA); finance (MBA); leadership (MBA); marketing (MBA). Postbaccalaureate distance learning degree programs offered.

Providence College, School of Business, Providence, RI 02918. Offers accounting (MBA); entrepreneurship (MBA); finance (MBA); international business (MBA); management (MBA); marketing (MBA); not-for-profit organizations (MBA). Part-time and evening/weekend programs available. *Faculty:* 11 full-time (4 women), 6 part-time/adjunct (1 woman). *Students:* 52 full-time (21 women), 49 part-time (17 women); includes 8 minority (3 Black or African American, non-Hispanic/Latino; 2 Asian, non-Hispanic/Latino; 3 Two or more races, non-Hispanic/Latino), 6 international. Average age 26. 49 applicants, 80% accepted, 25 enrolled. In 2011, 57 master's awarded. *Degree requirements:* For master's, thesis optional. *Entrance requirements:* For master's, GMAT. Additional exam requirements/recommendations for international students: Required—TOEFL (minimum score 550 paper-based; 213 computer-based; 80 iBT). *Application deadline:* For fall admission, 8/1 priority date for domestic students, 8/1 for international students; for spring admission, 12/1 priority date for domestic students, 12/1 for international students. Applications are processed on a rolling basis. Application fee: $55. *Expenses:* Contact institution. *Financial support:* In 2011–12, 34 research assistantships with full tuition reimbursements (averaging $8,400 per year) were awarded; Federal Work-Study, institutionally sponsored loans, and unspecified assistantships also available. Support available to part-time students. Financial award application deadline: 8/1; financial award applicants required to submit FAFSA. *Unit head:* Dr. Catherine L. Pastille, Director, MBA Program, 401-865-1654, Fax: 401-865-2978, E-mail: cpastill@providence.edu. *Application contact:* Katherine A. Follett, Administrative Coordinator, 401-865-2333, Fax: 401-865-2978, E-mail: kfollett@providence.edu. Web site: http://www.providence.edu/business/Pages/default.aspx.

Queen's University at Kingston, Queens School of Business, Program in Business Administration, Kingston, ON K7L 3N6, Canada. Offers consulting and project management (MBA); finance (MBA); innovation and entrepreneurship (MBA); marketing (MBA). *Accreditation:* AACSB. *Degree requirements:* For master's, thesis optional, research project. *Entrance requirements:* For master's, GMAT, minimum B+ average. Additional exam requirements/recommendations for international students: Required—TOEFL. Electronic applications accepted. *Faculty research:* Management fundamentals, strategic thinking, global business, innovation and change, leadership.

Regent University, Graduate School, School of Global Leadership and Entrepreneurship, Virginia Beach, VA 23464-9800. Offers business administration (MBA), including management general; leadership (Certificate); management (MA); organizational leadership (MA, PhD), including ecclesial leadership (PhD), entrepreneurial leadership (PhD), human resource development (PhD); strategic foresight (MA); strategic leadership (DSL), including global consulting, leadership coaching, strategic foresight. Part-time and evening/weekend programs available. Postbaccalaureate distance learning degree programs offered (minimal on-campus study). *Faculty:* 13 full-time (3 women), 4 part-time/adjunct (1 woman). *Students:* 27 full-time (11 women), 589 part-time (241 women); includes 183 minority (143 Black or African American, non-Hispanic/Latino; 3 American Indian or Alaska Native, non-Hispanic/Latino; 15 Asian, non-Hispanic/Latino; 22 Hispanic/Latino), 128 international. Average age 41. 225 applicants, 57% accepted, 85 enrolled. In 2011, 80 master's, 38 doctorates awarded. *Degree requirements:* For master's, thesis or alternative, 3 credit hour culminating experience; for doctorate, thesis/dissertation. *Entrance requirements:* For master's, GRE, GMAT, minimum undergraduate GPA of 2.75, computer literacy survey, 2 recommendations, resume, transcripts, essay; for doctorate, GRE, GMAT, sample of writing, minimum 3 years of relevant experience, computer literacy survey, 2 recommendations, resume, essay, transcripts; for Certificate, writing sample, resume, transcripts. Additional exam requirements/recommendations for international students: Required—TOEFL (minimum score 577 paper-based; 233 computer-based). *Application deadline:* For fall admission, 5/1 priority date for domestic students; for spring admission, 10/1 priority date for domestic students. Applications are processed on a rolling basis. Application fee: $50. Electronic applications accepted. *Expenses:* Contact institution. *Financial support:* Career-related internships or fieldwork, scholarships/grants, and tuition waivers (full and partial) available. Support available to part-time students. Financial award application deadline: 9/1. *Faculty research:* Servant leadership, ethics and values, telecommuting and family values, organizational communications, distance education. *Unit head:* Dr. Bruce Winston, Dean, 757-352-4306, Fax: 757-352-4634, E-mail: brucwin@regent.edu. *Application contact:* Matthew Chadwick, Director of Enrollment Support Services, 800-373-5504, Fax: 757-352-4381, E-mail: admissions@regent.edu.

Rensselaer Polytechnic Institute, Graduate School, Lally School of Management and Technology, Troy, NY 12180-3590. Offers business (MBA); financial engineering and risk analysis (MS); management (MS, PhD); technology, commercialization, and entrepreneurship (MS). *Accreditation:* AACSB. Part-time and evening/weekend programs available. *Degree requirements:* For doctorate, thesis/dissertation. *Entrance requirements:* For master's, GMAT, 2 letters of recommendation, resume; for doctorate, GMAT or GRE General Test, 2 letters of recommendation. Additional exam requirements/recommendations for international students: Required—TOEFL (minimum score 600 paper-based; 250 computer-based; 100 iBT); Recommended—IELTS (minimum score 7). Electronic applications accepted. *Faculty research:* Technological entrepreneurship, operations management, new product development and marketing, finance and financial engineering and risk analytics, information systems.

Rochester Institute of Technology, Graduate Enrollment Services, E. Philip Saunders College of Business, Program in Innovation Management, Rochester, NY 14623-5603. Offers MS. Part-time programs available. *Students:* 5 full-time (all women), 6 part-time (1 woman); includes 1 minority (Hispanic/Latino), 5 international. Average age 29. 14 applicants, 43% accepted, 5 enrolled. In 2011, 2 master's awarded. *Degree requirements:* For master's, project or research paper. *Entrance requirements:* For master's, GMAT or GRE. Additional exam requirements/recommendations for international students: Required—TOEFL (minimum score 580 paper-based; 237 computer-based; 92 iBT) or IELTS (minimum score 7). Application fee: $50. Electronic applications accepted. *Expenses: Tuition:* Full-time $34,659; part-time $963 per credit hour. *Required fees:* $228; $76 per quarter. *Unit head:* Melissa Ellison, Graduate Program Director, 585-475-2354, E-mail: maescb@rit.edu. *Application contact:* Diane Ellison, Assistant Vice President and Director, Graduate Enrollment Services, 585-475-2229, Fax: 585-475-7164, E-mail: gradinfo@rit.edu. Web site: http://saunders.rit.edu/programs/graduate/innovation_management/.

Rollins College, Crummer Graduate School of Business, Winter Park, FL 32789-4499. Offers entrepreneurship (MBA); finance (MBA); international business (MBA); management (MBA); marketing (MBA); operations and technology management (MBA). *Accreditation:* AACSB. Part-time and evening/weekend programs available. Postbaccalaureate distance learning degree programs offered (minimal on-campus study). *Faculty:* 23 full-time (3 women), 6 part-time/adjunct (4 women). *Students:* 257 full-time (95 women), 121 part-time (39 women); includes 75 minority (12 Black or African American, non-Hispanic/Latino; 1 American Indian or Alaska Native, non-Hispanic/Latino; 20 Asian, non-Hispanic/Latino; 39 Hispanic/Latino; 3 Two or more races, non-Hispanic/Latino), 27 international. Average age 28. 363 applicants, 44% accepted, 100 enrolled. In 2011, 213 master's awarded. *Degree requirements:* For master's, minimum GPA of 2.85. *Entrance requirements:* For master's, GMAT or GRE, official transcripts, two letters of recommendation, essay, current resume/curriculum vitae, interview. Additional exam requirements/recommendations for international students: Required—TOEFL (minimum score 100 iBT) or IELTS (minimum score 7). *Application deadline:* Applications are processed on a rolling basis. Application fee: $50. Electronic applications accepted. *Expenses:* Contact institution. *Financial support:* In 2011–12, 258 students received support. Federal Work-Study and scholarships/grants available. Support available to part-time students. Financial award applicants required to submit FAFSA. *Faculty research:* Sustainability, world financial markets, international business, market research, strategic marketing. *Unit head:* Dr. Craig M. McAllaster, Dean, 407-646-2249, Fax: 407-646-1550, E-mail: cmcallaster@rollins.edu. *Application contact:* Eva Gauthier Oleksiw, Admissions Coordinator, 407-646-2405, Fax: 407-646-1550, E-mail: mbaadmissions@rollins.edu. Web site: http://www.rollins.edu/mba/.

Rowan University, Graduate School, William G. Rohrer College of Business, Department of Management, Program in Entrepreneurship, Glassboro, NJ 08028-1701. Offers MBA. Part-time and evening/weekend programs available. *Degree requirements:* For master's, comprehensive exam, thesis. *Entrance requirements:* For master's, GRE General Test. Additional exam requirements/recommendations for international students: Required—TOEFL. Electronic applications accepted.

San Diego State University, Graduate and Research Affairs, College of Business Administration, Department of Management, San Diego, CA 92182. Offers entrepreneurship (MS); human resources management (MS); management science (MS). Part-time and evening/weekend programs available. *Degree requirements:* For master's, thesis or alternative. *Entrance requirements:* For master's, GMAT, resume, letters of reference. Additional exam requirements/recommendations for international students: Required—TOEFL. Electronic applications accepted.

Santa Clara University, Leavey School of Business, Program in Business Administration, Santa Clara, CA 95053. Offers accounting (MBA); entrepreneurship (MBA); executive business administration (EMBA); finance (MBA); food and agribusiness (MBA); international business (MBA); leading people and organizations (MBA); managing technology and innovation (MBA); marketing management (MBA); supply chain management (MBA). *Accreditation:* AACSB. Part-time and evening/weekend programs available. *Students:* 196 full-time (80 women), 669 part-time (224 women); includes 302 minority (12 Black or African American, non-Hispanic/Latino; 246 Asian, non-Hispanic/Latino; 35 Hispanic/Latino; 6 Native Hawaiian or other Pacific Islander, non-Hispanic/Latino; 3 Two or more races, non-Hispanic/Latino), 186 international. Average age 32. 365 applicants, 74% accepted, 199 enrolled. In 2011, 366 degrees awarded. *Degree requirements:* For master's, thesis or alternative. *Entrance requirements:* For master's, GMAT, GRE. Additional exam requirements/recommendations for international students: Required—TOEFL (minimum score 600 paper-based; 250 computer-based; 100 iBT). *Application deadline:* For fall admission, 6/1 for domestic and international students; for spring admission, 1/19 for domestic students, 1/17 for international students. Applications are processed on a rolling basis. Application fee: $75 ($100 for international students). Electronic applications accepted. *Expenses:* Contact institution. *Financial support:* In 2011–12, 350 students received support. Fellowships with partial tuition reimbursements available, research assistantships with partial tuition reimbursements available, career-related internships or fieldwork, Federal Work-Study, institutionally sponsored loans, scholarships/grants, health care benefits, and unspecified assistantships available. Support available to part-time students. Financial award application deadline: 6/1; financial award applicants required to submit FAFSA. *Unit head:* Elizabeth B. Ford, Senior Assistant Dean, 408-554-2752, Fax: 408-554-4571, E-mail: eford@scu.edu. *Application contact:* Tammy Fox, Assistant Director, Graduate Business Admissions, 408-554-7858, E-mail: tkfox@scu.edu.

Seton Hill University, Program in Business Administration, Greensburg, PA 15601. Offers entrepreneurship (MBA, Certificate); management (MBA). Part-time and evening/weekend programs available. *Faculty:* 5 full-time (3 women), 7 part-time/adjunct (1 woman). *Students:* 30 full-time (14 women), 55 part-time (26 women); includes 4 minority (2 Black or African American, non-Hispanic/Latino; 1 American Indian or Alaska Native, non-Hispanic/Latino; 1 Hispanic/Latino), 6 international. In 2011, 35 master's awarded. *Entrance requirements:* For master's, resume, 3 letters of recommendation, personal statement, transcripts. Additional exam requirements/recommendations for international students: Required—TOEFL (minimum score 600 paper-based; 250 computer-based; 100 iBT), IELTS (minimum score 6.5). *Application deadline:* Applications are processed on a rolling basis. Application fee: $0. Electronic applications accepted. *Expenses: Tuition:* Full-time $13,446; part-time $747 per credit. *Required fees:* $700; $25 per credit. $50 per term. *Financial support:* Federal Work-Study and tuition discounts available. *Faculty research:* Entrepreneurship, leadership and strategy, knowledge management. *Unit head:* Dr. Douglas Nelson, Director, 724-830-4738, E-mail: dnelson@setonhill.edu. *Application contact:* Laurel Komarny, Program Counselor, 724-838-4209, E-mail: komarny@setonhill.edu. Web site: http://www.setonhill.edu/academics/mba/index.cfm.

Simmons College, School of Management, Boston, MA 02115. Offers communications management (MS); entrepreneurship (Certificate); health administration (MHA); health care administration (CAGS); management (MBA); MS/MA. *Accreditation:* AACSB. *Unit head:* Cathy Minehan, Dean. *Application contact:* 617-521-3840, Fax: 617-521-3880, E-mail: somadm@simmons.edu. Web site: http://www.simmons.edu/som.

South Carolina State University, School of Graduate Studies, Department of Business Administration, Orangeburg, SC 29117-0001. Offers agribusiness (MBA); entrepreneurship (MBA). Part-time and evening/weekend programs available. *Faculty:* 4 full-time (1 woman). *Students:* 8 full-time (5 women), 3 part-time (1 woman); includes 10 minority (6 Black or African American, non-Hispanic/Latino; 3 Asian, non-Hispanic/Latino; 1 Hispanic/Latino), 1 international. Average age 28. 12 applicants, 100% accepted, 8 enrolled. In 2011, 3 master's awarded. *Degree requirements:* For master's, comprehensive exam, business plan. *Entrance requirements:* For master's, GMAT, minimum GPA of 2.8. Additional exam requirements/recommendations for international students: Required—TOEFL. *Application deadline:* For fall admission, 6/15 for domestic and international students; for spring admission, 11/1 for domestic and international students. Applications are processed on a rolling basis. Application fee: $25. Electronic applications accepted. *Expenses:* Tuition, state resident: full-time $8688; part-time $514 per credit hour. Tuition, nonresident: full-time $17,600; part-time $1009 per credit hour. *Required fees:* $570. *Financial support:* In 2011–12, 4 fellowships (averaging $5,542 per year) were awarded; research assistantships, career-related internships or fieldwork, Federal Work-Study, institutionally sponsored loans, and unspecified assistantships also available. Financial award application deadline: 6/1. *Faculty research:* Small farm income and profitability, agricultural credit, aquaculture, low-input sustainable agriculture, rural development. *Unit head:* Dr. Gerald Gonsalves, Chair, 803-536-7138, Fax: 803-536-8078, E-mail: ggonsalv@scsu.edu. *Application contact:* Dr. Stacey Settle, MBA Director, 803-536-8300, Fax: 803-516-4651, E-mail: ssettle@scsu.edu.

Southeast Missouri State University, School of Graduate Studies, Harrison College of Business, Cape Girardeau, MO 63701-4799. Offers accounting (MBA); entrepreneurship (MBA); financial management (MBA); general management (MBA); health administration (MBA); industrial management (MBA); international business (MBA); sport management (MBA). *Accreditation:* AACSB. Part-time and evening/weekend programs available. Postbaccalaureate distance learning degree programs offered (no on-campus study). *Faculty:* 31 full-time (10 women). *Students:* 49 full-time (23 women), 77 part-time (30 women); includes 5 minority (1 Black or African American, non-Hispanic/Latino; 1 American Indian or Alaska Native, non-Hispanic/Latino; 2 Hispanic/Latino; 1 Two or more races, non-Hispanic/Latino), 35 international. Average age 27. 78 applicants, 69% accepted, 43 enrolled. In 2011, 47 master's awarded. *Degree requirements:* For master's, variable foreign language requirement, comprehensive exam, applied research project related to field. *Entrance requirements:* For master's, GMAT (minimum score of 450), minimum undergraduate GPA of 2.5, C or better in prerequisite courses. Additional exam requirements/recommendations for international students: Required—TOEFL (minimum score 550 paper-based; 213 computer-based; 79 iBT); Recommended—IELTS (minimum score 6). *Application deadline:* For fall admission, 8/1 for domestic students, 7/1 for international students; for spring admission, 11/21 for domestic students, 11/1 for international students. Applications are processed on a rolling basis. Application fee: $30 ($40 for international students). Electronic applications accepted. *Expenses:* Tuition, state resident: full-time $4896; part-time $272 per credit hour. Tuition, nonresident: full-time $8649; part-time $480.50 per credit hour. *Financial support:* In 2011–12, 46 students received support, including 12 teaching assistantships with full tuition reimbursements available (averaging $7,600 per year); career-related internships or fieldwork, Federal Work-Study, scholarships/grants, tuition waivers (full), and unspecified assistantships also available. Financial award application deadline: 6/30; financial award applicants required to submit FAFSA. *Faculty research:* Human resources, laws impacting accounting, advertising. *Unit head:* Dr. Kenneth A. Heischmidt, Director, Graduate Programs in Business, 573-651-5116, Fax: 573-651-5032, E-mail: kheischmidt@semo.edu. *Application contact:* Gail Amick, Administrative Secretary, 573-651-2049, Fax: 573-651-2001, E-mail: gamick@semo.edu. Web site: http://www.semo.edu/mba.

Southern Methodist University, Cox School of Business, MBA Program, Dallas, TX 75275. Offers accounting (MBA); finance (MBA); financial consulting (MBA); general business (MBA); information technology and operations management (MBA); management (MBA); marketing (MBA); real estate (MBA); strategy and entrepreneurship (MBA). Part-time and evening/weekend programs available. *Entrance requirements:* For master's, GMAT. Additional exam requirements/recommendations for international students: Required—TOEFL. Electronic applications accepted. *Expenses:* Contact institution. *Faculty research:* Corporate finance, financial reporting, modeling consumer decision-making, competition between national brands and store brands, institutional determinants of firms' strategy.

Southern Methodist University, Cox School of Business, Program in Entrepreneurship, Dallas, TX 75275. Offers MS.

South University, Graduate Programs, College of Business, Savannah, GA 31406. Offers corrections (MBA); entrepreneurship and small business (MBA); healthcare administration (MBA); hospitality management (MBA); leadership (MS); sustainability (MBA).

See Close-Up on page 241.

South University, Program in Business Administration, Atlanta, GA. Offers Accelerated MBA. Program offered by South University, Savannah Campus at Atlanta Learning Site.

See Close-Up on page 229.

Stevens Institute of Technology, Graduate School, Wesley J. Howe School of Technology Management, Program in Information Systems, Hoboken, NJ 07030. Offers computer science (MS); e-commerce (MS); enterprise systems (MS); entrepreneurial information technology (MS); information architecture (MS); information management (MS, Certificate); information security (MS); information technology in financial services industry (MS); information technology in the pharmaceutical industry (MS); information technology outsourcing management (MS); project management (MS, Certificate); software engineering (MS); telecommunications (MS). *Degree requirements:* For master's, thesis optional. *Entrance requirements:* For master's, GMAT, GRE General Test. Additional exam requirements/recommendations for international students: Required—TOEFL. Electronic applications accepted.

Stratford University, School of Graduate Studies, Falls Church, VA 22043. Offers accounting (MS); business administration (IMBA, MBA); enterprise business management (MS); entrepreneurial management (MS); information assurance (MS); information systems (MS); software engineering (MS); telecommunications (MS). Part-time and evening/weekend programs available. Postbaccalaureate distance learning degree programs offered (no on-campus study). *Degree requirements:* For master's, comprehensive exam, capstone project. *Entrance requirements:* For master's, GRE or GMAT, baccalaureate degree. Additional exam requirements/recommendations for international students: Required—TOEFL (minimum score 213 computer-based, 79 iBT) or IELTS (6.5). Electronic applications accepted.

Suffolk University, Sawyer Business School, Master of Business Administration Program, Boston, MA 02108-2770. Offers accounting (MBA); business administration (APC); corporate financial executive track (MBA); entrepreneurship (MBA); executive business administration (EMBA); finance (MBA); global business administration (GMBA); health administration (MBA); international business (MBA); marketing (MBA); organizational behavior (MBA); strategic management (MBA); taxation (MBA); JD/MBA; MBA/GDPA; MBA/MHA; MBA/MSA; MBA/MSF; MBA/MST. *Accreditation:* AACSB. Part-time and evening/weekend programs available. Postbaccalaureate distance learning degree programs offered (no on-campus study). *Faculty:* 98 full-time (30 women), 14 part-time/adjunct (3 women). *Students:* 139 full-time (49 women), 321 part-time (138 women); includes 53 minority (17 Black or African American, non-Hispanic/Latino; 1 American Indian or Alaska Native, non-Hispanic/Latino; 21 Asian, non-Hispanic/Latino; 11 Hispanic/Latino; 1 Native Hawaiian or other Pacific Islander, non-Hispanic/Latino; 2 Two or more races, non-Hispanic/Latino), 64 international. Average age 30. 437 applicants, 61% accepted, 121 enrolled. In 2011, 283 master's awarded. *Entrance requirements:* For master's, GMAT, minimum undergraduate GPA of 2.75 (MBA), 5 years of managerial experience (EMBA). Additional exam requirements/recommendations for international students: Required—TOEFL (minimum score 550 paper-based; 213 computer-based). *Application deadline:* For fall admission, 6/15 priority date for domestic students, 6/15 for international students; for spring admission, 11/1 priority date for domestic students, 11/1 for international students. Applications are processed on a rolling basis. Application fee: $50. Electronic applications accepted. Tuition and fees vary according to program. *Financial support:* In 2011–12, 273 students received support, including 73 fellowships with full and partial tuition reimbursements available (averaging $12,415 per year); career-related internships or fieldwork, Federal Work-Study, and institutionally sponsored loans also available. Support available to part-time students. Financial award application deadline: 4/1; financial award applicants required to submit FAFSA. *Faculty research:* Foreign investments; career strategies and boundaryless careers; corporate ethics codes; interest rates, inflation, and growth options; innovation and product development performance. *Unit head:* Lillian Hallberg, Assistant Dean of Graduate Programs/Director of MBA Programs, 617-573-8306, E-mail: lhallber@suffolk.edu. *Application contact:* Ellen Driscoll, Director of Graduate Admissions, 617-573-8302, Fax: 617-305-1733, E-mail: grad.admission@suffolk.edu. Web site: http://www.suffolk.edu/mba.

Syracuse University, Martin J. Whitman School of Management, Program in Business Administration, Syracuse, NY 13244. Offers accounting (MBA); entrepreneurship (MBA); finance (MBA); marketing (MBA); supply chain management (MBA). Postbaccalaureate distance learning degree programs offered (minimal on-campus study). *Faculty:* 79 full-time (20 women), 25 part-time/adjunct (6 women). *Students:* 116 full-time (43 women), 188 part-time (58 women); includes 62 minority (33 Black or African American, non-Hispanic/Latino; 1 American Indian or Alaska Native, non-Hispanic/Latino; 13 Asian, non-Hispanic/Latino; 9 Hispanic/Latino; 1 Native Hawaiian or other Pacific Islander, non-Hispanic/Latino; 5 Two or more races, non-Hispanic/Latino), 44 international. Average age 33. 276 applicants, 49% accepted, 77 enrolled. In 2011, 132 master's awarded. *Entrance requirements:* For master's, GMAT, 2 letters of recommendation. Additional exam requirements/recommendations for international students: Required—TOEFL (minimum score 600 paper-based; 250 computer-based; 100 iBT). *Application deadline:* For fall admission, 1/15 priority date for domestic students, 1/15 for international students. Applications are processed on a rolling basis. Application fee: $75. Electronic applications accepted. *Expenses: Tuition:* Part-time $1206 per credit. *Financial support:* In 2011–12, 17 students received support. Fellowships with full and partial tuition reimbursements available, teaching assistantships with partial tuition reimbursements available, career-related internships or fieldwork, scholarships/grants, tuition waivers (partial), unspecified assistantships, and paid hourly positions available. Support available to part-time students. Financial award application deadline: 3/1. *Unit head:* Prof. Dennis Gillen, Chair and Associate Professor of Management, 315-443-3432, Fax: 315-443-9517, E-mail: dgillen@syr.edu. *Application contact:* Josh LaFave, Director, Graduate Enrollment, 315-443-3497, Fax: 315-443-9517, E-mail: mbainfo@syr.edu. Web site: http://whitman.syr.edu/ftmba/.

Syracuse University, Martin J. Whitman School of Management, Program in Entrepreneurship and Emerging Enterprises, Syracuse, NY 13244. Offers MS. *Students:* 7 full-time (3 women). Average age 22. 29 applicants, 34% accepted, 7 enrolled. In 2011, 1 master's awarded. *Entrance requirements:* For master's, GMAT. Additional exam requirements/recommendations for international students: Required—TOEFL. *Application deadline:* For fall admission, 1/1 priority date for domestic students, 1/1 for international students. Application fee: $75. Electronic applications accepted. *Expenses: Tuition:* Part-time $1206 per credit. *Financial support:* Fellowships with full tuition reimbursements and research assistantships with full and partial tuition reimbursements available. *Unit head:* Dr. George Burman, Chair and Professor of Entrepreneurship, 315-443-3602, E-mail: gburman@syr.edu. *Application contact:* Josh LaFave, Director of Graduate Enrollment, 315-443-3497, Fax: 315-443-9517, E-mail: mbainfo@syr.edu. Web site: http://whitman.syr.edu/Academics/EEE/.

Syracuse University, School of Information Studies, Program in Information Innovation, Syracuse, NY 13244. Offers CAS. Part-time and evening/weekend programs available. Postbaccalaureate distance learning degree programs offered. *Students:* 3 applicants, 100% accepted, 0 enrolled. *Entrance requirements:* Additional exam requirements/recommendations for international students: Required—TOEFL (minimum score 100 iBT). *Application deadline:* For fall admission, 2/1 priority date for domestic students, 1/1 for international students. Applications are processed on a rolling basis. Application fee: $75. Electronic applications accepted. *Expenses: Tuition:* Part-time $1206 per credit. *Unit head:* Elizabeth Liddy, Dean, 315-443-2736. *Application contact:* Susan Corieri, Director of Enrollment Management, 315-443-2575, E-mail: ischool@syr.edu. Web site: http://ischool.syr.edu/academics/graduate/infoinnovation/index.aspx.

See Display on page 1637 and Close-Up on page 1653.

Temple University, Fox School of Business, Doctoral Programs in Business, Philadelphia, PA 19122-6096. Offers accounting (PhD); entrepreneurship (PhD); finance (PhD); international business (PhD); management information systems (PhD); marketing (PhD); risk management and insurance (PhD); statistics (PhD); strategic management (PhD); tourism and sport (PhD). *Accreditation:* AACSB. *Degree requirements:* For doctorate, thesis/dissertation. *Entrance requirements:* For doctorate, GRE General Test, GMAT, minimum GPA of 3.0, master's degree. Additional exam requirements/recommendations for international students: Required—TOEFL (minimum score 600 paper-based; 250 computer-based; 100 iBT), IELTS (minimum score 7.5). Electronic applications accepted. *Expenses:* Tuition, state resident: full-time $12,366; part-time $687 per credit hour. Tuition, nonresident: full-time $17,298; part-time $961 per credit hour. *Required fees:* $590; $213 per year.

Texas Tech University, Graduate School, Rawls College of Business Administration, Programs in Business Administration, Lubbock, TX 79409. Offers agricultural business (MBA); business administration (IMBA); business statistics (MBA); entrepreneurship and innovation (MBA); general business (MBA); health organization management (MBA); international business (MBA); management and leadership skills (MBA); management information systems (MBA); marketing (MBA); real estate (MBA); JD/MBA; MBA/M Arch; MBA/MA; MBA/MD; MBA/MS; MBA/Pharm D. Part-time and evening/weekend programs available. *Faculty:* 49 full-time (8 women), 2 part-time/adjunct (0 women). *Students:* 195 full-time (55 women), 397 part-time (101 women); includes 123 minority (27 Black or African American, non-Hispanic/Latino; 4 American Indian or Alaska Native, non-Hispanic/Latino; 31 Asian, non-Hispanic/Latino; 61 Hispanic/Latino), 38 international. Average age 31. 374 applicants, 83% accepted, 255 enrolled. In 2011, 256 degrees awarded. *Degree requirements:* For master's, capstone course. *Entrance requirements:* For master's, GMAT, holistic review of academic credentials. Additional exam requirements/recommendations for international students: Required—TOEFL (minimum score 550 paper-based; 213 computer-based; 79 iBT). *Application deadline:* For fall admission, 4/1 priority date for domestic students, 1/15 for international students; for spring admission, 9/1 priority date for domestic students, 6/15 for international students. Applications are processed on a rolling basis. Application fee: $50 ($75 for international students). Electronic applications accepted. *Expenses:* Tuition, state resident: full-time $5899; part-time $245.80 per credit hour. Tuition, nonresident: full-time $13,411; part-time $558.80 per credit hour. *Required fees:* $2680.60; $86.50 per credit hour. $920.30 per semester. *Financial support:* In 2011–12, 22 research assistantships (averaging $8,800 per year) were awarded; teaching assistantships, career-related internships or fieldwork, Federal Work-Study, scholarships/grants, health care benefits, and unspecified assistantships also available. Support available to part-time students. Financial award applicants required to submit FAFSA. *Unit head:* Dr. W. Jay Conover, Director, 806-742-1546, Fax: 806-742-3958, E-mail: jay.conover@ttu.edu. *Application contact:* Elizabeth Stuart, Director, Graduate Services Center, 806-742-3184, Fax: 806-742-3958, E-mail: ba_grad@ttu.edu. Web site: http://mba.ba.ttu.edu/.

United States International University, School of Business Administration, Nairobi, Kenya. Offers business administration (GEMBA); entrepreneurship (MBA); finance (MBA); human resource management (MBA); information technology management (MBA); integrated studies (MBA); international business administration (MBA); management and organizational development (MS); marketing (MBA); organizational development (EMS); strategic management (MBA). Part-time and evening/weekend programs available. *Degree requirements:* For master's, thesis. *Entrance requirements:* For master's, GMAT, 2 letters of reference, resume. Additional exam requirements/recommendations for international students: Required—TOEFL (minimum score 550 paper-based; 213 computer-based). *Faculty research:* Marketing in small business enterprises, total quality management in Kenya.

Université Laval, Faculty of Administrative Sciences, Programs in Business Administration, Québec, QC G1K 7P4, Canada. Offers accounting (MBA); agri-food management (MBA); electronic business (MBA, Diploma); factory management and logistics (MBA); finance (MBA); firm management (MBA); geomatic management (MBA); information technology management (MBA); international management (MBA); management (MBA); management accounting (MBA, Diploma); marketing (MBA); modeling and organizational decision (MBA); occupational health and safety management (MBA); pharmacy management (MBA); social and environmental responsibility (MBA); technological entrepreneurship (Diploma). *Accreditation:* AACSB. Part-time and evening/weekend programs available. Postbaccalaureate distance learning degree programs offered (no on-campus study). *Entrance requirements:* For master's and Diploma, knowledge of French and English. Electronic applications accepted.

The University of Akron, Graduate School, College of Business Administration, Department of Management, Program in Entrepreneurship, Akron, OH 44325. Offers MBA. *Students:* 1 full-time (0 women), 1 part-time (0 women), 1 international. Average age 31. 3 applicants, 33% accepted, 1 enrolled. *Entrance requirements:* For master's, GMAT, minimum GPA of 2.75, two letters of recommendation, statement of purpose, resume. Additional exam requirements/recommendations for international students: Required—TOEFL (minimum score 550 paper-based; 213 computer-based; 79 iBT). *Application deadline:* For fall admission, 7/15 for domestic and international students; for spring admission, 11/15 for domestic and international students. Application fee: $30 ($40 for international students). Electronic applications accepted. *Expenses:* Tuition, state resident: full-time $7038; part-time $391 per credit hour. Tuition, nonresident: full-time $12,051; part-time $670 per credit hour. *Required fees:* $1274; $34 per credit hour. *Unit head:* Dr. Steven Ash, Head, 330-972-6429, E-mail: ash@uakron.edu. *Application contact:* Dr. Susan Hanlon, Director of Graduate Business Programs, 330-972-7043, Fax: 330-972-6588, E-mail: shanlon@uakron.edu. Web site: http://www.uakron.edu/cba/cba-home/dept-cent-inst/fitzgerald/advisory-board.dot.

The University of Alabama in Huntsville, School of Graduate Studies, College of Business Administration, Department of Management and Marketing, Huntsville, AL 35899. Offers federal contract procurement (Certificate); management (MBA), including acquisition management, entrepreneurship, federal contract accounting, finance, human resource management, logistics and supply chain management, marketing, project management; supply chain management (Certificate); technology and innovation management (Certificate). *Accreditation:* AACSB. Part-time and evening/weekend programs available. *Faculty:* 11 full-time (2 women), 3 part-time/adjunct (0 women). *Students:* 52 full-time (25 women), 145 part-time (68 women); includes 28 minority (14 Black or African American, non-Hispanic/Latino; 4 American Indian or Alaska Native, non-Hispanic/Latino; 7 Asian, non-Hispanic/Latino; 2 Hispanic/Latino; 1 Two or more races, non-Hispanic/Latino), 15 international. Average age 31. 103 applicants, 73% accepted, 65 enrolled. In 2011, 76 master's awarded. *Degree requirements:* For master's, comprehensive exam, thesis or alternative. *Entrance requirements:* For master's, GMAT (minimum score 500), minimum AACSB index of 1080. Additional exam requirements/recommendations for international students: Required—TOEFL (minimum score 550 paper-based; 213 computer-based; 62 iBT). *Application deadline:* For fall admission, 8/1 for domestic students, 4/1 for international students; for spring admission, 12/1 for domestic students, 9/1 for international students. Applications are processed on a rolling basis. Application fee: $40 ($50 for international students). Electronic applications accepted. *Expenses:* Tuition, state resident: full-time $7830; part-time $473.50 per credit. Tuition, nonresident: full-time $18,748; part-time $1128.33 per credit. Tuition and fees vary according to course load and program. *Financial support:* In 2011–12, 12 students received support, including 7 research assistantships with full tuition reimbursements available (averaging $9,829 per year), 4 teaching assistantships with full tuition reimbursements available (averaging $8,000 per year);

career-related internships or fieldwork, Federal Work-Study, institutionally sponsored loans, scholarships/grants, health care benefits, and unspecified assistantships also available. Support available to part-time students. Financial award application deadline: 4/1; financial award applicants required to submit FAFSA. *Faculty research:* Strategic human resources, corporate governance, cross-function integration and the management of research and development, determinants of team performance. *Total annual research expenditures:* $3.4 million. *Unit head:* Dr. Cynthia Gramm, Chair, 256-824-6913, Fax: 256-824-6328, E-mail: cynthia.gramm@uah.edu. *Application contact:* Jennifer Pettitt, Director of Graduate Programs, 256-824-6681, Fax: 256-824-7571, E-mail: jennifer.pettitt@uah.edu.

University of Bridgeport, School of Business, Bridgeport, CT 06604. Offers accounting (MBA); finance (MBA); general business (MBA); global financial services (MBA); human resource management (MBA); information systems and knowledge management (MBA); international business (MBA); management (MBA); marketing (MBA); operations management (MBA); small business and entrepreneurship (MBA); specialized business (MBA). Part-time and evening/weekend programs available. *Faculty:* 11 full-time (2 women), 39 part-time/adjunct (8 women). *Students:* 198 full-time (105 women), 94 part-time (47 women); includes 38 minority (16 Black or African American, non-Hispanic/Latino; 9 Asian, non-Hispanic/Latino; 10 Hispanic/Latino; 3 Two or more races, non-Hispanic/Latino), 227 international. Average age 28. 835 applicants, 56% accepted, 57 enrolled. In 2011, 155 master's awarded. *Degree requirements:* For master's, thesis optional. *Entrance requirements:* For master's, GMAT. Additional exam requirements/recommendations for international students: Recommended—TOEFL (minimum score 550 paper-based; 213 computer-based; 80 iBT), IELTS (minimum score 6.5). *Application deadline:* For fall admission, 8/1 priority date for domestic students, 8/1 for international students; for spring admission, 12/1 priority date for domestic students, 12/1 for international students. Applications are processed on a rolling basis. Application fee: $50. Electronic applications accepted. *Expenses:* Contact institution. *Financial support:* In 2011–12, 69 students received support. Fellowships, research assistantships, teaching assistantships, career-related internships or fieldwork, Federal Work-Study, institutionally sponsored loans, and tuition waivers (partial) available. Support available to part-time students. Financial award application deadline: 6/1; financial award applicants required to submit FAFSA. *Unit head:* Dr. Robert Gilmore, Dean, 203-576-4384, Fax: 203-576-4388, E-mail: rgilmore@bridgeport.edu. *Application contact:* Karissa Peckham, Dean of Admissions, 203-576-4552, Fax: 203-576-4941, E-mail: mba@bridgeport.edu. Web site: http://www.bridgeport.edu.

University of Central Florida, College of Business Administration, Department of Management, Orlando, FL 32816. Offers entrepreneurship (Graduate Certificate); management (MSM); technology ventures (Graduate Certificate). *Accreditation:* AACSB. *Faculty:* 27 full-time (8 women), 4 part-time/adjunct (2 women). *Students:* 6 part-time (3 women); includes 1 minority (Hispanic/Latino), 2 international. Average age 29. 20 applicants, 80% accepted, 6 enrolled. In 2011, 1 master's, 8 other advanced degrees awarded. *Entrance requirements:* For master's, GMAT, minimum GPA of 3.0 in last 60 hours. *Application deadline:* For fall admission, 2/1 priority date for domestic students; for spring admission, 11/1 priority date for domestic students. Application fee: $30. Electronic applications accepted. *Expenses:* Tuition, state resident: part-time $277.08 per credit hour. Tuition, nonresident: part-time $277.08 per credit hour. Part-time tuition and fees vary according to degree level and program. *Financial support:* Fellowships, research assistantships, and teaching assistantships available. *Unit head:* Dr. Stephen Goodman, Chair, 407-823-2675, Fax: 407-823-3725, E-mail: sgoodman@bus.ucf.edu. *Application contact:* Judy Ryder, Director, Graduate Admissions, 407-823-2364, Fax: 407-823-0219, E-mail: jryder@bus.ucf.edu. Web site: http://www.graduatecatalog.ucf.edu/programs/program.aspx?id=1080&program=Management MS.

University of Chicago, Booth School of Business, Full-Time MBA Program, Chicago, IL 60637. Offers accounting (MBA); analytic finance (MBA); analytic management (MBA); business administration (PhD); econometrics and statistics (MBA); economics (MBA); entrepreneurship (MBA); finance (MBA); general management (MBA); health administration and policy (Certificate); human resource management (MBA); international business (IMBA, MBA); managerial and organizational behavior (MBA); marketing management (MBA); operations management (MBA); strategic management (MBA); MBA/AM; MBA/JD; MBA/MA; MBA/MD; MBA/MPP. *Accreditation:* AACSB. Part-time and evening/weekend programs available. *Faculty:* 166 full-time, 32 part-time/adjunct. *Students:* 1,160 full-time (412 women); includes 316 minority (61 Black or African American, non-Hispanic/Latino; 173 Asian, non-Hispanic/Latino; 63 Hispanic/Latino; 19 Two or more races, non-Hispanic/Latino), 378 international. Average age 28. 4,169 applicants, 575 enrolled. In 2011, 1,423 master's, 19 doctorates awarded. Terminal master's awarded for partial completion of doctoral program. *Entrance requirements:* For master's, GMAT, 2 letters of recommendation, 3 essays, resume, interview. Additional exam requirements/recommendations for international students: Required—TOEFL (minimum score 600 paper-based; 250 computer-based; 104 iBT), IELTS. *Application deadline:* For fall admission, 10/12 priority date for domestic students, 10/12 for international students; for winter admission, 1/4 for domestic and international students; for spring admission, 4/4 for domestic and international students. Application fee: $200. Electronic applications accepted. *Expenses:* Contact institution. *Financial support:* Fellowships available. Financial award applicants required to submit FAFSA. *Faculty research:* Finance, marketing, economics, entrepreneurship, strategy, management. *Unit head:* Stacey Kole, Deputy Dean, 773-702-7121. *Application contact:* Kurt Ahlm, Associate Dean of Student Recruitment and Admissions, 773-702-7369, Fax: 773-702-9085, E-mail: admissions@chicagobooth.edu. Web site: http://chicagobooth.edu/.

University of Colorado Boulder, Leeds School of Business, Division of Business Administration, Boulder, CO 80309. Offers accounting (MS, PhD); finance (PhD); information systems (PhD); marketing (PhD); operations (PhD); strategic, organizational, and entrepreneurial studies (PhD). *Students:* 129 full-time (65 women), 6 part-time (0 women); includes 15 minority (1 Black or African American, non-Hispanic/Latino; 8 Asian, non-Hispanic/Latino; 5 Hispanic/Latino; 1 Two or more races, non-Hispanic/Latino), 21 international. Average age 27. 332 applicants, 9% accepted, 13 enrolled. In 2011, 53 master's, 6 doctorates awarded. *Entrance requirements:* For master's, GMAT, minimum undergraduate GPA of 3.0. *Application deadline:* For fall admission, 3/31 for domestic and international students; for spring admission, 10/31 for domestic and international students. Application fee: $50 ($60 for international students). Electronic applications accepted. *Financial support:* In 2011–12, 61 students received support, including 24 fellowships (averaging $3,398 per year), 19 research assistantships with full and partial tuition reimbursements available (averaging $27,830 per year), 15 teaching assistantships with full and partial tuition reimbursements available (averaging $25,615 per year); institutionally sponsored loans, scholarships/grants, health care benefits, and unspecified assistantships also available. Financial award applicants required to submit FAFSA. *Application contact:* E-mail: leedsphd@colorado.edu. Web site: http://leeds.colorado.edu/phdprog.

University of Colorado Denver, Business School, Master of Business Administration Program, Denver, CO 80217. Offers business intelligence (MBA); business strategy (MBA); business to business marketing (MBA); business to consumer marketing (MBA); change management (MBA); corporate financial management (MBA); enterprise technology management (MBA); entrepreneurship (MBA); health administration (MBA), including financial management, health administration, health information technologies, international health management and policy; human resources management (MBA); investment management (MBA); managing for sustainability (MBA); services management (MBA); sports and entertainment management (MBA). *Accreditation:* AACSB. Part-time and evening/weekend programs available. Postbaccalaureate distance learning degree programs offered (no on-campus study). *Students:* 784 full-time (306 women), 203 part-time (81 women); includes 135 minority (18 Black or African American, non-Hispanic/Latino; 5 American Indian or Alaska Native, non-Hispanic/Latino; 50 Asian, non-Hispanic/Latino; 58 Hispanic/Latino; 4 Two or more races, non-Hispanic/Latino), 38 international. Average age 31. 433 applicants, 76% accepted, 212 enrolled. In 2011, 326 master's awarded. *Degree requirements:* For master's, 48 semester hours, including 30 of core courses, 3 in international business, and 15 in electives from over 50 other graduate business courses. *Entrance requirements:* For master's, GMAT, resume, official transcripts, essay, two letters of recommendation, financial statements (for international applicants). Additional exam requirements/recommendations for international students: Required—TOEFL (minimum score 560 paper-based; 197 computer-based; 83 iBT). *Application deadline:* For fall admission, 4/15 priority date for domestic students, 3/15 for international students; for spring admission, 10/15 priority date for domestic students, 10/1 for international students. Applications are processed on a rolling basis. Application fee: $50 ($75 for international students). Electronic applications accepted. *Expenses:* Contact institution. *Financial support:* Scholarships/grants available. Support available to part-time students. Financial award application deadline: 4/1; financial award applicants required to submit FAFSA. *Faculty research:* Marketing, management, entrepreneurship, finance, health administration. *Unit head:* Elizabeth Cooperman, Professor of Finance and Managing for Sustainability/MBA Program Director, 303-315-8422, E-mail: elizabeth.cooperman@ucdenver.edu. *Application contact:* Shelly Townley, Admissions Director, Graduate Programs, 303-315-8202, E-mail: shelly.townley@ucdenver.edu. Web site: http://www.ucdenver.edu/academics/colleges/business/degrees/ms/accounting/Pages/Accounting.aspx.

University of Colorado Denver, Business School, Program in Management and Organization, Denver, CO 80217. Offers communications management (MS); entrepreneurship and innovation (MS); global management (MS); human resources management (MS); leadership and management (MS); sports and entertainment management (MS). *Accreditation:* AACSB. Part-time and evening/weekend programs available. Postbaccalaureate distance learning degree programs offered (no on-campus study). *Students:* 29 full-time (14 women), 14 part-time (10 women); includes 3 minority (2 Asian, non-Hispanic/Latino; 1 Hispanic/Latino), 5 international. Average age 31. 32 applicants, 63% accepted, 14 enrolled. In 2011, 22 master's awarded. *Degree requirements:* For master's, 30 semester hours (12 of required courses, 12 of management electives, and 6 of free electives). *Entrance requirements:* For master's, GMAT, resume, two letters of recommendation, essay, financial statements (for international applicants). Additional exam requirements/recommendations for international students: Required—TOEFL (minimum score 525 paper-based; 197 computer-based; 71 iBT). *Application deadline:* For fall admission, 4/15 priority date for domestic students, 3/15 for international students; for spring admission, 10/15 priority date for domestic students, 10/1 for international students. Applications are processed on a rolling basis. Application fee: $50 ($75 for international students). Electronic applications accepted. *Expenses:* Contact institution. *Financial support:* Federal Work-Study and scholarships/grants available. Support available to part-time students. Financial award application deadline: 4/1; financial award applicants required to submit FAFSA. *Faculty research:* Human resource management, management of catastrophe, turnaround strategies. *Unit head:* Dr. Kenneth Bettenhausen, Associate Professor/Director of MS in Management, 303-315-8425, E-mail: kenneth.bettenhausen@ucdenver.edu. *Application contact:* Shelly Townley, Admissions Director, Graduate Programs, 303-315-8202, E-mail: shelly.townley@ucdenver.edu. Web site: http://www.ucdenver.edu/academics/colleges/business/degrees/ms/management/Pages/Management.aspx.

University of Colorado Denver, College of Engineering and Applied Science, Department of Bioengineering, Aurora, CO 80045-2560. Offers bioengineering (PhD); clinical application (PhD); clinical imaging (MS); commercialization of medical technologies (MS, PhD); device design and entrepreneurship (MS); research (MS). Part-time programs available. *Faculty:* 3 full-time (1 woman). *Students:* 38 full-time (13 women), 1 part-time; includes 7 minority (3 Black or African American, non-Hispanic/Latino; 2 Asian, non-Hispanic/Latino; 1 Hispanic/Latino; 1 Two or more races, non-Hispanic/Latino), 2 international. Average age 27. 56 applicants, 48% accepted, 24 enrolled. Terminal master's awarded for partial completion of doctoral program. *Degree requirements:* For master's, thesis or alternative, 30 credit hours; for doctorate, comprehensive exam, thesis/dissertation, 36 credit hours of classwork (18 core, 18 elective), additional 30 hours of thesis work, three formal examinations, approval of dissertations. *Entrance requirements:* For master's and doctorate, GRE, transcripts, three letters of recommendation, resume, statement of purpose. Additional exam requirements/recommendations for international students: Required—TOEFL (minimum score 550 paper-based; 213 computer-based; 79 iBT), TOEFL (minimum score 600 paper-based; 250 computer-based; 100 iBT) for Ph D. *Application deadline:* For fall admission, 2/15 for domestic students. Application fee: $50. Electronic applications accepted. *Expenses:* Contact institution. *Financial support:* Fellowships, research assistantships, teaching assistantships, and Federal Work-Study available. Financial award application deadline: 4/1; financial award applicants required to submit FAFSA. *Faculty research:* Imaging and biophotonics, cardiovascular biomechanics and hemodynamics, orthopedic biomechanics, ophthalmology, neuroscience engineering, diabetes, surgery and urological sciences. *Unit head:* Dr. Robin Shandas, Chair, 303-724-4196, E-mail: robin.shandas@ucdenver.edu. *Application contact:* Graduate School Admissions, 303-556-2704, E-mail: admissions@ucdenver.edu. Web site: http://bioengineering.ucdenver.edu/.

University of Delaware, Alfred Lerner College of Business and Economics, Department of Economics, Newark, DE 19716. Offers economic education (PhD); economics (MA, MS, PhD); economics for entrepreneurship and educators (MA); MA/MBA. Part-time programs available. *Degree requirements:* For master's, comprehensive exam, thesis (for some programs), mathematics review exam, research project; for doctorate, comprehensive exam, thesis/dissertation, field exam. *Entrance requirements:* For master's, GMAT or GRE General Test, minimum GPA of 2.5; for doctorate, GRE General Test, minimum GPA of 3.5 in graduate economics course work. Additional exam requirements/recommendations for international students: Required—TOEFL (minimum score 550 paper-based; 225 computer-based). Electronic applications accepted. *Faculty research:* Applied quantitative economics, industrial organization, resource economics, monetary economics, labor economics.

University of Hawaii at Manoa, Graduate Division, Shidler College of Business, The Pacific Asian Center for Entrepreneurship and E-Business (PACE), Honolulu, HI 96822. Offers entrepreneurship (Graduate Certificate). Part-time programs available. *Entrance requirements:* Additional exam requirements/recommendations for international students: Required—TOEFL (minimum score 500 paper-based; 61 iBT).

University of Hawaii at Manoa, Graduate Division, Shidler College of Business, Program in Business Administration, Honolulu, HI 96822. Offers Asian business studies (MBA); Chinese business studies (MBA); decision sciences (MBA); entrepreneurship (MBA); finance (MBA); finance and banking (MBA); human resources management (MBA); information management (MBA); information technology (MBA); international business (MBA); Japanese business studies (MBA); marketing (MBA); organizational behavior (MBA); organizational management (MBA); real estate (MBA); student-designed track (MBA). *Accreditation:* AACSB. Part-time and evening/weekend programs available. *Degree requirements:* For master's, thesis optional. *Entrance requirements:* For master's, GMAT, minimum GPA of 3.0. Additional exam requirements/recommendations for international students: Required—TOEFL (minimum score 600 paper-based; 250 computer-based; 100 iBT), IELTS (minimum score 7). *Expenses:* Contact institution.

University of Houston–Victoria, School of Business Administration, Victoria, TX 77901-4450. Offers accounting (MBA); economic development and entrepreneurship (MS); finance (GMBA, MBA); general business (MBA); international business (MBA); management (GMBA, MBA); marketing (MBA). *Accreditation:* AACSB. Part-time and evening/weekend programs available. Postbaccalaureate distance learning degree programs offered (minimal on-campus study). *Entrance requirements:* For master's, GMAT. Additional exam requirements/recommendations for international students: Required—TOEFL (minimum score 550 paper-based; 213 computer-based). Electronic applications accepted. *Faculty research:* Economic development, marketing, finance.

University of Louisville, Graduate School, College of Business, MBA Programs, Louisville, KY 40292-0001. Offers entrepreneurship (MBA); global business (MBA); health sector management (weekend format) (MBA). *Accreditation:* AACSB. Part-time and evening/weekend programs available. *Faculty:* 28 full-time (8 women), 3 part-time/adjunct (1 woman). *Students:* 111 full-time (35 women), 112 part-time (33 women); includes 19 minority (4 Black or African American, non-Hispanic/Latino; 1 American Indian or Alaska Native, non-Hispanic/Latino; 7 Asian, non-Hispanic/Latino; 3 Hispanic/Latino; 4 Two or more races, non-Hispanic/Latino), 12 international. Average age 29. 223 applicants, 53% accepted, 94 enrolled. In 2011, 119 degrees awarded. *Degree requirements:* For master's, international learning experience. *Entrance requirements:* For master's, GMAT, 2 letters of reference, personal interview, resume, personal statement, college transcript(s). Additional exam requirements/recommendations for international students: Required—TOEFL (minimum score 83 iBT). *Application deadline:* For fall admission, 7/1 for domestic students; for spring admission, 12/1 for domestic students. Applications are processed on a rolling basis. Application fee: $50. *Expenses:* Tuition, state resident: full-time $9692; part-time $539 per credit hour. Tuition, nonresident: full-time $20,168; part-time $1121 per credit hour. Tuition and fees vary according to program and reciprocity agreements. *Financial support:* In 2011–12, 16 students received support, including 3 fellowships with full tuition reimbursements available (averaging $15,500 per year), 10 research assistantships with full tuition reimbursements available (averaging $12,000 per year); health care benefits and unspecified assistantships also available. Financial award application deadline: 3/31; financial award applicants required to submit FAFSA. *Faculty research:* Entrepreneurship, venture capital, retailing/franchising, corporate governance and leadership, supply chain management. *Unit head:* Dr. R. Charles Moyer, Dean, 502-852-6443, Fax: 502-852-7557, E-mail: charlie.moyer@louisville.edu. *Application contact:* L. Eddie Smith, Director of IT and Master's Programs Admissions/Recruiting Manager, 502-852-7257, Fax: 502-852-4901, E-mail: eddie.smith@louisville.edu. Web site: http://business.louisville.edu/mba.

University of Louisville, Graduate School, College of Business, PhD Program in Entrepreneurship, Louisville, KY 40292-0001. Offers PhD. *Faculty:* 17 full-time (5 women), 6 part-time/adjunct (0 women). *Students:* 12 full-time (2 women); includes 1 minority (Asian, non-Hispanic/Latino), 6 international. Average age 34. In 2011, 2 doctorates awarded. *Degree requirements:* For doctorate, comprehensive exam, thesis/dissertation, paper of sufficient quality for journal publication. *Entrance requirements:* For doctorate, GMAT, 3 letters of recommendation, curriculum vitae, personal interview. Additional exam requirements/recommendations for international students: Required—TOEFL (minimum score 83 iBT). *Application deadline:* For fall admission, 12/31 priority date for domestic students, 3/31 for international students. Applications are processed on a rolling basis. Application fee: $50. Electronic applications accepted. *Expenses:* Tuition, state resident: full-time $9692; part-time $539 per credit hour. Tuition, nonresident: full-time $20,168; part-time $1121 per credit hour. Tuition and fees vary according to program and reciprocity agreements. *Financial support:* In 2011–12, 11 students received support, including 1 fellowship with full tuition reimbursement available (averaging $21,000 per year), 8 research assistantships with full tuition reimbursements available (averaging $21,000 per year), 3 teaching assistantships with full tuition reimbursements available (averaging $10,000 per year); scholarships/grants, health care benefits, and unspecified assistantships also available. Financial award application deadline: 3/15; financial award applicants required to submit FAFSA. *Faculty research:* Entrepreneurship, supply chain management, venture capital, retailing/franchising, corporate governance. *Total annual research expenditures:* $146,460. *Unit head:* Dr. Charles Moyer, Dean, 502-852-6443, Fax: 502-852-7557, E-mail: charlie.moyer@louisville.edu. *Application contact:* Dr. David Dubofsky, Director, 502-852-3016, Fax: 502-852-6072, E-mail: d.dubofsky@louisville.edu. Web site: http://business.louisville.edu/entrepreneurshipphd.

University of Massachusetts Lowell, College of Management, Lowell, MA 01854-2881. Offers business administration (MBA); foundations of business (Graduate Certificate); new venture creation (Graduate Certificate). *Accreditation:* AACSB. Part-time and evening/weekend programs available. *Entrance requirements:* For master's, GMAT.

University of Missouri–Kansas City, Henry W. Bloch School of Management, Kansas City, MO 64110-2499. Offers accounting (MS); business administration (MBA); entrepreneurial real estate (MERE); entrepreneurship and innovation (PhD); finance (MS); public affairs (MPA, PhD); JD/MBA; LL M/MPA. PhD (interdisciplinary) offered through the School of Graduate Studies. *Accreditation:* AACSB; NASPAA. Part-time and evening/weekend programs available. *Faculty:* 51 full-time (14 women), 29 part-time/adjunct (9 women). *Students:* 272 full-time (126 women), 407 part-time (180 women); includes 91 minority (43 Black or African American, non-Hispanic/Latino; 20 Asian, non-Hispanic/Latino; 19 Hispanic/Latino; 9 Two or more races, non-Hispanic/Latino), 49 international. Average age 30. 397 applicants, 63% accepted, 202 enrolled. In 2011, 257 master's awarded. Terminal master's awarded for partial completion of doctoral program. *Entrance requirements:* For master's, GMAT, GRE, 2 writing essays, 2 references; support of employer; for doctorate, GRE, minimum GPA of 3.0. Additional exam requirements/recommendations for international students: Required—TOEFL (minimum score 550 paper-based; 213 computer-based; 80 iBT). *Application deadline:* For fall admission, 5/1 priority date for domestic students, 5/1 for international students; for spring admission, 10/1 priority date for domestic students, 10/1 for international students. Applications are processed on a rolling basis. Application fee: $45 ($50 for international students). Electronic applications accepted. *Expenses:* Tuition, state resident: full-time $5798; part-time $322.10 per credit hour. Tuition, nonresident: full-time $14,969; part-time $831.60 per credit hour. *Required fees:* $93.51 per credit hour. *Financial support:* In 2011–12, 29 research assistantships with partial tuition reimbursements (averaging $11,490 per year), 3 teaching assistantships with partial tuition reimbursements (averaging $11,600 per year) were awarded; career-related internships or fieldwork, Federal Work-Study, institutionally sponsored loans, scholarships/grants, tuition waivers (full and partial), and unspecified assistantships also available. Support available to part-time students. Financial award application deadline: 3/1; financial award applicants required to submit FAFSA. *Faculty research:* Entrepreneurship, finance, non-profit, risk management. *Unit head:* Dr. Teng-Kee Tan, Dean, 816-235-2215, Fax: 816-235-2206. *Application contact:* 816-235-1111, E-mail: admit@umkc.edu. Web site: http://www.bloch.umkc.edu.

University of Nevada, Las Vegas, Graduate College, College of Business, Department of Management, Las Vegas, NV 89154. Offers management (Certificate); new venture management (Certificate). *Students:* 2 part-time (1 woman); includes 1 minority (Two or more races, non-Hispanic/Latino). Average age 27. 1 applicant, 100% accepted, 1 enrolled. *Application deadline:* For fall admission, 6/15 for domestic students, 5/1 for international students; for spring admission, 11/15 for domestic students, 10/1 for international students. Electronic applications accepted. *Faculty research:* Supply chain management, business strategy, human resource management, entrepreneurship, business ethics. *Unit head:* Dr. Keong Leong, Chair/Professor, 702-895-1762, E-mail: keong.leong@unlv.edu. *Application contact:* Graduate College Admissions Evaluator, 702-895-3320, Fax: 702-895-4180, E-mail: gradcollege@unlv.edu. Web site: http://business.unlv.edu/management/.

University of New Brunswick Fredericton, School of Graduate Studies, Faculty of Business Administration, Fredericton, NB E3B 5A3, Canada. Offers business administration (MBA); engineering management (MBA); entrepreneurship (MBA); sports and recreation management (MBA); MBA/LL B. Part-time programs available. *Faculty:* 23 full-time (3 women), 5 part-time/adjunct (2 women). *Students:* 50 full-time (10 women), 27 part-time (12 women). In 2011, 46 master's awarded. *Degree requirements:* For master's, thesis optional. *Entrance requirements:* For master's, GMAT (minimum score 550), minimum GPA of 3.0; 3-5 years work experience. Additional exam requirements/recommendations for international students: Required—TOEFL (minimum score 580 paper-based; 92 iBT) or IELTS (minimum score 7). *Application deadline:* For fall admission, 3/1 priority date for domestic students. Applications are processed on a rolling basis. Application fee: $50 Canadian dollars. *Financial support:* In 2011–12, 7 fellowships, 1 research assistantship (averaging $4,500 per year), 17 teaching assistantships (averaging $2,250 per year) were awarded. *Faculty research:* Accounting and auditing practices, human resource management, the non-profit sector, marketing, strategic management, entrepreneurship, investment practices, supply chain management, operations management. *Unit head:* Judy Roy, Director of Graduate Studies, 506-458-7307, Fax: 506-453-3561, E-mail: jroy@unb.ca. *Application contact:* Marilyn Davis, Acting Graduate Secretary, 506-453-4766, Fax: 506-453-3561, E-mail: mbacontact@unb.ca. Web site: http://www.business.unbf.ca.

University of Phoenix–Puerto Rico Campus, School of Business, Guaynabo, PR 00968. Offers accounting (MBA); energy management (MBA); global management (MBA); human resource management (MBA); marketing (MBA); project management (MBA); small business administration (MBA). Evening/weekend programs available. *Degree requirements:* For master's, thesis (for some programs). *Entrance requirements:* For master's, minimum undergraduate GPA of 3.0, 3 years work experience. Additional exam requirements/recommendations for international students: Required—TOEFL (minimum score 550 paper-based; 213 computer-based; 79 iBT). Electronic applications accepted.

University of Portland, Dr. Robert B. Pamplin, Jr. School of Business, Portland, OR 97203-5798. Offers business administration (MBA); entrepreneurship (MBA); finance (MBA, MS); health care management (MBA); marketing (MBA); nonprofit management (EMBA); operations and technology management (MBA); sustainability (MBA). *Accreditation:* AACSB. Part-time and evening/weekend programs available. *Faculty:* 13 full-time (1 woman), 8 part-time/adjunct (1 woman). *Students:* 50 full-time (13 women), 90 part-time (41 women); includes 19 minority (1 Black or African American, non-Hispanic/Latino; 1 American Indian or Alaska Native, non-Hispanic/Latino; 8 Asian, non-Hispanic/Latino; 5 Hispanic/Latino; 2 Native Hawaiian or other Pacific Islander, non-Hispanic/Latino; 2 Two or more races, non-Hispanic/Latino), 18 international. Average age 31. In 2011, 54 master's awarded. *Entrance requirements:* For master's, GMAT, minimum GPA of 3.0, resume, 2 letters of recommendation. Additional exam requirements/recommendations for international students: Required—TOEFL (minimum score 570 paper-based; 89 iBT), IELTS (minimum score 7). *Application deadline:* For fall admission, 7/15 priority date for domestic students, 7/15 for international students; for spring admission, 12/15 priority date for domestic students, 12/15 for international students. Applications are processed on a rolling basis. Application fee: $50. *Expenses:* Contact institution. *Financial support:* Federal Work-Study, scholarships/grants, and tuition waivers (partial) available. Support available to part-time students. Financial award application deadline: 3/1; financial award applicants required to submit FAFSA. *Unit head:* Dr. Howard Feldman, Associate Dean, 503-943-7224, E-mail: feldman@up.edu. *Application contact:* Melissa McCarthy, Academic Specialist, 503-943-7225, E-mail: mccarthy@up.edu. Web site: http://business.up.edu/.

University of Rochester, Hajim School of Engineering and Applied Sciences, Center for Entrepreneurship, Rochester, NY 14627-0360. Offers technical entrepreneurship and management (TEAM) (MS), including biomedical engineering, chemical engineering, computer science, electrical and computer engineering, energy and the environment, materials science, mechanical engineering, optics. *Faculty:* 61 full-time (8 women), 5 part-time/adjunct (1 woman). *Students:* 18 full-time (5 women), 3 part-time (1 woman); includes 4 minority (1 Asian, non-Hispanic/Latino; 3 Hispanic/Latino), 12 international. Average age 23. 134 applicants, 48% accepted, 21 enrolled. *Degree requirements:* For master's, comprehensive exam. *Entrance requirements:* For master's, GRE or GMAT, technical concentration of interest, 3 letters of recommendation, personal statement, official transcript. Additional exam requirements/recommendations for international students: Required—TOEFL or IELTS. *Application deadline:* For fall admission, 2/1 for domestic and international students. Applications are processed on a rolling basis. Application fee: $60. Electronic applications accepted. *Expenses: Tuition:* Full-time $41,040. *Financial support:* Career-related internships or fieldwork and scholarships/grants available. Financial award application deadline: 2/1. *Faculty research:* High efficiency solar cells, macromolecular self-assembly, digital signal processing, memory hierarchy management, molecular and physical mechanisms in cell migration. *Unit head:* Duncan T. Moore, Vice Provost for Entrepreneurship, 585-275-5248, Fax: 585-473-6745, E-mail: moore@optics.rochester.edu. *Application contact:* Andrea M. Galati, Executive Director, 585-276-3407, Fax: 585-276-2357, E-mail: andrea.galati@rochester.edu. Web site: http://www.rochester.edu/team.

University of San Francisco, College of Arts and Sciences, Web Science Program, San Francisco, CA 94117-1080. Offers MS. *Faculty:* 5 full-time (3 women). *Students:* 16 full-time (1 woman), 5 part-time (0 women); includes 4 minority (2 Black or African American, non-Hispanic/Latino; 1 Asian, non-Hispanic/Latino; 1 Hispanic/Latino), 7 international. Average age 29. 30 applicants, 67% accepted, 8 enrolled. In 2011, 12 master's awarded. *Expenses: Tuition:* Full-time $20,070; part-time $1115 per unit. Tuition and fees vary according to course load, campus/location and program. *Financial* *support:* In 2011–12, 6 students received support. *Unit head:* Terence Parr, Graduate Director, 415-422-6530, Fax: 415-422-5800. *Application contact:* Mark Landerghini, Graduate Adviser, 415-422-5135, E-mail: asgraduate@usfca.edu. Web site: http://www1.cs.usfca.edu/grad/msws.

University of San Francisco, School of Management, Masagung Graduate School of Management, Joint Master of Global Entrepreneurship and Management Program, San Francisco, CA 94117-1080. Offers MGEM. Program offered jointly with IQS in Barcelona, Spain and Fu Jen Catholic University in Taipei, Taiwan. *Faculty:* 2 full-time (both women), 2 part-time/adjunct (0 women). *Students:* 35 full-time (17 women); includes 6 minority (1 Black or African American, non-Hispanic/Latino; 1 Asian, non-Hispanic/Latino; 3 Hispanic/Latino; 1 Two or more races, non-Hispanic/Latino), 18 international. Average age 24. 65 applicants, 69% accepted, 35 enrolled. In 2011, 27 master's awarded. *Expenses: Tuition:* Full-time $20,070; part-time $1115 per unit. Tuition and fees vary according to course load, campus/location and program. *Financial support:* In 2011–12, 9 students received support. *Unit head:* Dr. Sidaoui Mouwafac, 415-422-6771, Fax: 415-422-2502. *Application contact:* Director, MBA Program, 415-422-2221, Fax: 415-422-6315, E-mail: mba@usfca.edu. Web site: http://www.usfca.edu/jmgem/.

University of San Francisco, School of Management, Masagung Graduate School of Management, Program in Business Administration, San Francisco, CA 94117-1080. Offers business economics (MBA); e-business (MBA); entrepreneurship (MBA); finance (MBA); international business (MBA); management (MBA); marketing (MBA); telecommunications management and policy (MBA); JD/MBA; MSN/MBA. *Accreditation:* AACSB. *Faculty:* 18 full-time (4 women), 18 part-time/adjunct (9 women). *Students:* 247 full-time (122 women), 9 part-time (3 women); includes 85 minority (5 Black or African American, non-Hispanic/Latino; 55 Asian, non-Hispanic/Latino; 16 Hispanic/Latino; 1 Native Hawaiian or other Pacific Islander, non-Hispanic/Latino; 8 Two or more races, non-Hispanic/Latino), 38 international. Average age 29. 552 applicants, 55% accepted, 99 enrolled. In 2011, 173 master's awarded. *Entrance requirements:* For master's, GMAT, minimum undergraduate GPA of 3.2. Additional exam requirements/recommendations for international students: Required—TOEFL. *Application deadline:* For fall admission, 7/1 priority date for domestic students; for spring admission, 11/30 for domestic students. Applications are processed on a rolling basis. Application fee: $55 ($65 for international students). *Expenses: Tuition:* Full-time $20,070; part-time $1115 per unit. Tuition and fees vary according to course load, campus/location and program. *Financial support:* In 2011–12, 33 students received support. Fellowships available. Financial award application deadline: 3/2; financial award applicants required to submit FAFSA. *Faculty research:* International financial markets, technology transfer licensing, international marketing, strategic planning. *Total annual research expenditures:* $50,000. *Unit head:* Kelly Brookes, Director, 415-422-2221, Fax: 415-422-6315. *Application contact:* Director, MBA Program, 415-422-2221, Fax: 415-422-6315, E-mail: mba@usfca.edu.

University of Sioux Falls, Vucurevich School of Business, Sioux Falls, SD 57105-1699. Offers entrepreneurial leadership (MBA); general management (MBA); health care management (MBA); marketing (MBA). Part-time and evening/weekend programs available. *Faculty:* 8 full-time (3 women), 7 part-time/adjunct (2 women). *Students:* 119 part-time (60 women); includes 2 minority (1 Black or African American, non-Hispanic/Latino; 1 Asian, non-Hispanic/Latino). 50 applicants, 90% accepted, 45 enrolled. *Degree requirements:* For master's, project. *Entrance requirements:* For master's, minimum GPA of 3.0. Additional exam requirements/recommendations for international students: Required—TOEFL. Application fee: $25. *Expenses:* Contact institution. *Financial support:* Institutionally sponsored loans, scholarships/grants, and tuition waivers (full) available. Financial award applicants required to submit FAFSA. *Unit head:* Rebecca T. Murdock, MBA Director, 605-575-2068, E-mail: mba@usiouxfalls.edu. *Application contact:* Student Contact, 605-331-6680. Web site: http://www.usiouxfalls.edu/mba.

University of South Florida, Graduate School, College of Business, Center for Entrepreneurship, Tampa, FL 33620-9951. Offers MS, Graduate Certificate. Part-time and evening/weekend programs available. *Students:* 38 full-time (17 women), 53 part-time (22 women); includes 23 minority (8 Black or African American, non-Hispanic/Latino; 1 Asian, non-Hispanic/Latino; 12 Hispanic/Latino; 2 Two or more races, non-Hispanic/Latino), 13 international. Average age 32. 62 applicants, 73% accepted, 26 enrolled. In 2011, 37 master's awarded. *Degree requirements:* For master's, thesis optional. *Entrance requirements:* For master's, minimum undergraduate GPA of 3.0 in last 60 hours, two letters of recommendation, letter of interest, statement of purpose, interview. Additional exam requirements/recommendations for international students: Required—TOEFL (minimum score 550 paper-based; 213 computer-based; 79 iBT) or IELTS (minimum score 6.5). *Application deadline:* For fall admission, 2/15 for domestic students, 1/2 for international students; for spring admission, 10/15 for domestic students, 6/1 for international students. Applications are processed on a rolling basis. Application fee: $30. Electronic applications accepted. *Total annual research expenditures:* $58,300. *Unit head:* Dr. Michael W. Fountain, Director, 813-974-7900, Fax: 813-974-7663, E-mail: fountain@usf.edu. *Application contact:* Lu Thompson, Assistant Director, Graduate Studies, 813-974-7900, Fax: 813-974-4518, E-mail: entrepreneurship@usf.edu. Web site: http://www.ce.usf.edu/.

The University of Tampa, John H. Sykes College of Business, Tampa, FL 33606-1490. Offers accounting (MS); entrepreneurship (MBA); finance (MBA, MS); information systems management (MBA); innovation management (MBA); international business (MBA); marketing (MBA, MS); nonprofit management (MBA). *Accreditation:* AACSB. Part-time and evening/weekend programs available. *Faculty:* 38 full-time (14 women), 5 part-time/adjunct (1 woman). *Students:* 161 full-time (65 women), 193 part-time (82 women); includes 65 minority (11 Black or African American, non-Hispanic/Latino; 1 American Indian or Alaska Native, non-Hispanic/Latino; 8 Asian, non-Hispanic/Latino; 39 Hispanic/Latino; 2 Native Hawaiian or other Pacific Islander, non-Hispanic/Latino; 4 Two or more races, non-Hispanic/Latino), 58 international. Average age 29. 837 applicants, 41% accepted, 196 enrolled. In 2011, 259 degrees awarded. *Degree requirements:* For master's, capstone. *Entrance requirements:* For master's, GMAT or GRE, 4-year undergraduate degree, minimum GPA of 3.0, professional experience (for Executive MBA). Additional exam requirements/recommendations for international students: Required—TOEFL (minimum score 577 paper-based; 230 computer-based; 90 iBT); Recommended—IELTS (minimum score 7.5). *Application deadline:* Applications are processed on a rolling basis. Application fee: $40. Electronic applications accepted. *Expenses: Tuition:* Full-time $8320; part-time $520 per credit hour. *Required fees:* $40 per semester. Tuition and fees vary according to program. *Financial support:* In 2011–12, 124 students received support. Career-related internships or fieldwork, scholarships/grants, unspecified assistantships, and grants available. Financial award applicants required to submit FAFSA. *Faculty research:* Job market signaling, on-line shopping behaviors and social media, the Tampa Bay economy, digital literacy, entrepreneurship in small businesses. *Unit head:* Dennis Nostrand, Vice President, Enrollment/Admissions, 813-257-1808, E-mail: dnostrand@ut.edu. *Application contact:* Charlene Tobie, Associate Director of Admissions, 813-257-3566, E-mail: ctobie@ut.edu. Web site: http://ut.edu/graduate.

The University of Texas at Austin, Graduate School, McCombs School of Business, Program in Technology Commercialization, Austin, TX 78712-1111. Offers MS. Twelve-month program, beginning in May, with classes held every other Friday and Saturday. Evening/weekend programs available. Postbaccalaureate distance learning degree programs offered (no on-campus study). *Degree requirements:* For master's, year-long global teaming project. *Entrance requirements:* For master's, GRE General Test or GMAT. Additional exam requirements/recommendations for international students: Required—TOEFL (minimum score 550 paper-based; 213 computer-based; 79 iBT). *Application deadline:* For spring admission, 2/1 priority date for domestic students, 2/1 for international students. Applications are processed on a rolling basis. Application fee: $50 ($75 for international students). Electronic applications accepted. *Expenses:* Contact institution. *Financial support:* Institutionally sponsored loans and scholarships/grants available. Financial award application deadline: 2/15; financial award applicants required to submit FAFSA. *Faculty research:* Technology transfer; entrepreneurship; commercialization; research, development and innovation. *Unit head:* Dr. Gary M. Cadenhead, Director, 512-471-2227, Fax: 512-475-8903, E-mail: gary.cadenhead@mccombs.utexas.edu. *Application contact:* Marketing Coordinator, 512-475-8900, Fax: 512-475-8903, E-mail: mstc@ic2.utexas.edu. Web site: http://www.ic2.utexas.edu/mstc.

The University of Texas at Dallas, Naveen Jindal School of Management, Program in Innovation and Entrepreneurship, Richardson, TX 75080. Offers MS. Part-time and evening/weekend programs available. *Faculty:* 2 part-time/adjunct (0 women). *Students:* 3 full-time (1 woman), 10 part-time (2 women); includes 6 minority (1 Black or African American, non-Hispanic/Latino; 1 American Indian or Alaska Native, non-Hispanic/Latino; 2 Asian, non-Hispanic/Latino; 2 Hispanic/Latino), 1 international. Average age 33. 27 applicants, 56% accepted, 7 enrolled. In 2011, 1 master's awarded. *Degree requirements:* For master's, thesis optional. *Entrance requirements:* For master's, GMAT, minimum GPA of 3.0 in upper-level course work in field. Additional exam requirements/recommendations for international students: Required—TOEFL (minimum score 550 paper-based; 215 computer-based). *Application deadline:* For fall admission, 7/15 for domestic students, 5/1 for international students; for spring admission, 11/15 for domestic students, 9/1 for international students. Applications are processed on a rolling basis. Application fee: $50 ($100 for international students). Electronic applications accepted. *Expenses:* Tuition, state resident: full-time $11,170; part-time $620.56 per credit hour. Tuition, nonresident: full-time $20,212; part-time $1122.89 per credit hour. *Financial support:* In 2011–12, 2 students received support. Research assistantships with partial tuition reimbursements available, teaching assistantships with partial tuition reimbursements available, career-related internships or fieldwork, Federal Work-Study, institutionally sponsored loans, scholarships/grants, and unspecified assistantships available. Support available to part-time students. Financial award application deadline: 4/30; financial award applicants required to submit FAFSA. *Unit head:* Dr. Joseph C. Picken, Program Director, 972-883-4986, E-mail: jpicken@utdallas.edu. *Application contact:* James Parker, Assistant Director, Graduate Recruitment, 972-883-5842, E-mail: jparker@utdallas.edu. Web site: http://jindal.utdallas.edu/academic-programs/masters-programs/master-of-science-in-innovation-and-entrepreneurship/.

The University of Texas at Dallas, Naveen Jindal School of Management, Program in Management and Administrative Sciences, Richardson, TX 75080. Offers electronic commerce (MS); finance (MS); healthcare administration (MS); information systems (MS); innovation and entrepreneurship (MS); international management (MS); leadership in organizations (MS); marketing (MS); operations (MS); organizations (MS); real estate (MS); strategy (MS). *Accreditation:* AACSB. Part-time and evening/weekend programs available. *Faculty:* 26 full-time (6 women), 9 part-time/adjunct (2 women). *Students:* 128 full-time (69 women), 169 part-time (95 women); includes 76 minority (18 Black or African American, non-Hispanic/Latino; 1 American Indian or Alaska Native, non-Hispanic/Latino; 37 Asian, non-Hispanic/Latino; 15 Hispanic/Latino; 1 Native Hawaiian or other Pacific Islander, non-Hispanic/Latino; 4 Two or more races, non-Hispanic/Latino), 77 international. Average age 34. 220 applicants, 63% accepted, 68 enrolled. In 2011, 58 master's awarded. *Degree requirements:* For master's, thesis optional. *Entrance requirements:* For master's, GMAT. Additional exam requirements/recommendations for international students: Required—TOEFL (minimum score 550 paper-based; 215 computer-based). *Application deadline:* For fall admission, 7/15 for domestic students, 5/1 for international students; for spring admission, 11/15 for domestic students, 9/1 for international students. Applications are processed on a rolling basis. Application fee: $50 ($100 for international students). Electronic applications accepted. *Expenses:* Tuition, state resident: full-time $11,170; part-time $620.56 per credit hour. Tuition, nonresident: full-time $20,212; part-time $1122.89 per credit hour. *Financial support:* In 2011–12, 68 students received support, including 7 teaching assistantships with partial tuition reimbursements available (averaging $16,200 per year); research assistantships with partial tuition reimbursements available, career-related internships or fieldwork, Federal Work-Study, institutionally sponsored loans, scholarships/grants, and unspecified assistantships also available. Support available to part-time students. Financial award application deadline: 4/30; financial award applicants required to submit FAFSA. *Faculty research:* Integrated and detailed knowledge of functional areas of management, analytical tools for effective appraisal and decision-making. *Unit head:* Dr. Gregory Dess, Area Coordinator, 972-883-4439, E-mail: gdess@utdallas.edu. *Application contact:* James Parker, Assistant Director, 972-883-5842, E-mail: jparker@utdallas.edu. Web site: http://jindal.utdallas.edu/academic-areas/organizations-strategy-and-international-management/.

University of the Incarnate Word, School of Graduate Studies and Research, Dreeben School of Education, Programs in Education, San Antonio, TX 78209-6397. Offers adult education (M Ed, MA); cross-cultural education (M Ed, MA); early childhood literacy (M Ed, MA); general education (M Ed, MA); higher education (PhD); instructional technology (M Ed, MA); international education and entrepreneurship (PhD); kinesiology (M Ed, MA); literacy (M Ed, MA); organizational leadership (PhD); organizational learning and learning (M Ed, MA); reading (M Ed, MA); special education (M Ed, MA); teacher leadership (M Ed, MA). Part-time and evening/weekend programs available. *Faculty:* 14 full-time (8 women), 10 part-time/adjunct (9 women). *Students:* 13 full-time (7 women), 197 part-time (129 women); includes 111 minority (23 Black or African American, non-Hispanic/Latino; 2 American Indian or Alaska Native, non-Hispanic/Latino; 1 Asian, non-Hispanic/Latino; 85 Hispanic/Latino), 26 international. Average age 41. 78 applicants, 79% accepted, 34 enrolled. In 2011, 21 master's, 12 doctorates awarded. *Degree requirements:* For master's, capstone; for doctorate, thesis/dissertation, qualifying exam. *Entrance requirements:* For master's, baccalaureate degree; minimum foundation GPA of 2.5; interview; for doctorate, master's degree; interview; supervised writing sample. Additional exam requirements/recommendations for international students: Required—TOEFL (minimum score 560 paper-based; 220 computer-based; 83 iBT). *Application deadline:* Applications are processed on a rolling basis. Application fee: $20. Electronic applications accepted. *Expenses: Tuition:* Part-time $725 per credit hour. Tuition and fees vary according to degree level. *Financial support:* In 2011–12, 5 research assistantships were awarded; Federal Work-Study and scholarships/grants also available. Financial award applicants required to submit FAFSA. *Unit head:* Dr. Denise Staudt, Dean, Dreeben School of Education, 210-829-2762, E-mail: staudt@uiwtx.edu. *Application contact:* Andrea Cyterski-Acosta, Dean of Enrollment, 210-829-6005, Fax: 210-829-3921, E-mail: admis@uiwtx.edu. Web site: http://www.uiw.edu/education/index.htm.

The University of Toledo, College of Graduate Studies, College of Business and Innovation, Department of Management, Toledo, OH 43606-3390. Offers administration (MBA); entrepreneurship (MBA); executive management (MBA); general administration (MBA); human resource management (MBA); leadership (MBA). Part-time and evening/weekend programs available. *Faculty:* 8. *Students:* 61 full-time (20 women), 147 part-time (48 women); includes 20 minority (14 Black or African American, non-Hispanic/Latino; 1 American Indian or Alaska Native, non-Hispanic/Latino; 2 Asian, non-Hispanic/Latino; 3 Hispanic/Latino), 96 international. Average age 27. 82 applicants, 72% accepted, 53 enrolled. In 2011, 84 master's awarded. *Entrance requirements:* For master's, GMAT, minimum GPA of 2.7 for all prior academic work, three letters of recommendation, statement of purpose, transcripts from all prior institutions attended. Additional exam requirements/recommendations for international students: Required—TOEFL (minimum score 550 paper-based; 213 computer-based; 80 iBT), IELTS (minimum score 6.5). *Application deadline:* For fall admission, 1/15 priority date for domestic students, 1/15 for international students. Applications are processed on a rolling basis. Application fee: $45 ($75 for international students). Electronic applications accepted. *Financial support:* In 2011–12, 39 research assistantships with tuition reimbursements (averaging $5,241 per year) were awarded; career-related internships or fieldwork, Federal Work-Study, institutionally sponsored loans, scholarships/grants, tuition waivers (full and partial), unspecified assistantships, and administrative assistantships also available. Support available to part-time students. *Faculty research:* Stress, deviation, workplace, globalization, recruitment. *Unit head:* Dr. Sonny Ariss, Chair, 419-530-2366. *Application contact:* Graduate School Office, 419-530-4723, Fax: 419-530-4724, E-mail: grdsch@utnet.utoledo.edu. Web site: http://www.utoledo.edu/business/MGMT/MGMTCCD/MGMT.html.

University of Waterloo, Graduate Studies, Centre for Business, Entrepreneurship and Technology, Waterloo, ON N2L 3G1, Canada. Offers MBET. *Entrance requirements:* For master's, honors degree. Additional exam requirements/recommendations for international students: Required—TOEFL (minimum score 550 paper-based; 213 computer-based), TWE. Electronic applications accepted.

The University of Western Ontario, Richard Ivey School of Business, London, ON N6A 3K7, Canada. Offers business (EMBA, PhD); corporate strategy and leadership elective (MBA); entrepreneurship elective (MBA); finance elective (MBA); health sector stream (MBA); international management elective (MBA); marketing elective (MBA); JD/MBA. *Degree requirements:* For master's, thesis (for some programs); for doctorate, thesis/dissertation. *Entrance requirements:* For master's, GMAT, 2 years of full-time work experience, interview. Additional exam requirements/recommendations for international students: Required—TOEFL (minimum score 100 computer; 100 iBT) or IELTS (minimium score 6). Electronic applications accepted. *Faculty research:* Strategy, organizational behavior, international business, finance, operations management.

Wake Forest University, Schools of Business, Full-time MBA Program, Winston-Salem, NC 27106. Offers consulting/general management (MBA); entrepreneurship (MBA); finance (MBA); health (MBA); marketing (MBA); operations management (MBA); JD/MBA; MD/MBA; MSA/MBA. *Accreditation:* AACSB. *Faculty:* 62 full-time (16 women), 41 part-time/adjunct (14 women). *Students:* 120 full-time (28 women); includes 14 minority (8 Black or African American, non-Hispanic/Latino; 4 Asian, non-Hispanic/Latino; 1 Hispanic/Latino; 1 Two or more races, non-Hispanic/Latino), 28 international. Average age 28. In 2011, 62 master's awarded. *Degree requirements:* For master's, 65.5 credit hours. *Entrance requirements:* For master's, GMAT or GRE, letters of recommendation, official transcripts, current resume or curriculum vitae, 2 years of work experience. Additional exam requirements/recommendations for international students: Required—TOEFL (minimum score 600 paper-based; 250 computer-based; 100 iBT), Pearson Test of English. *Application deadline:* For fall admission, 4/15 for domestic and international students. Applications are processed on a rolling basis. Application fee: $100. Electronic applications accepted. *Expenses:* Contact institution. *Financial support:* In 2011–12, 84 students received support. Career-related internships or fieldwork, scholarships/grants, and unspecified assistantships available. Financial award application deadline: 2/15; financial award applicants required to submit FAFSA. *Faculty research:* The influence of personal relationships on business decision-making and management of change; drivers of perceived value and consumer behavior; impact of accounting on auditing, financial, managerial, systems and taxation stakeholders; corporate governance and executive compensation; impact of operations strategies on competitiveness. *Unit head:* Jon Duchac, Director, Full-time MBA Program, 336-758-5422, Fax: 336-758-5830, E-mail: busadmissions@wfu.edu. *Application contact:* Tamara Paquee, Administrative Assistant, 336-758-5422, Fax: 336-758-5830, E-mail: busadmissions@wfu.edu. Web site: http://www.business.wfu.edu/.

Walden University, Graduate Programs, School of Management, Minneapolis, MN 55401. Offers accounting (MS, DBA), including accounting for the professional (MS), CPA (MS), self-designed (MS); accounting and management (MS), including accounting for strategic managers, self-designed; accounting for managers (MBA); advanced project management (Post-Graduate Certificate); applied project management (Post-Graduate Certificate); corporate finance (MBA); entrepreneurship (MBA, DBA); finance (DBA); global management (MS); global supply chain management (DBA); healthcare management (MBA, DBA); healthcare system improvement (MBA); human resource management (MBA, MS, PhD), including functional human resource management (MS), integrating functional and strategic human resource management (MS), organizational strategy (MS); information systems management (DBA); international business (MBA, DBA); leadership (MBA, MS, DBA), including entrepreneurship (MS), general management (MS), human resources leadership (MS), innovation and technology (MS), leader development (MS), leading sustainability (MS), project management (MS), self-designed (MS); management (MS), including healthcare management; managers as leaders (MS); marketing (MBA, DBA); project management (MBA, MS, DBA); research strategies (MS); risk management (MBA); self-designed (MBA, DBA, PhD); social impact management (DBA); strategies for sustainability (MBA); strategy and operations (MS); sustainable management (MS); technology (MBA); technology entrepreneurship (DBA); technology management (MS). Part-time and evening/weekend programs available. Postbaccalaureate distance learning degree programs offered (minimal on-campus study). *Faculty:* 32 full-time (14 women), 275 part-time/adjunct (98 women). *Students:* 3,962 full-time (2,095 women), 1,557 part-time (959 women); includes 3,003 minority (2,510 Black or African American, non-Hispanic/Latino; 25 American Indian or Alaska Native, non-Hispanic/Latino; 140 Asian, non-Hispanic/Latino; 240 Hispanic/Latino; 9 Native Hawaiian or other Pacific Islander, non-Hispanic/Latino; 79 Two or more races, non-Hispanic/Latino), 395 international. Average age 41. In 2011, 586 master's, 87 doctorates, 4 other advanced degrees awarded. *Degree requirements:* For doctorate, thesis/dissertation (for some programs), residency. *Entrance requirements:* For master's, bachelor's degree or equivalent in related field; minimum GPA of 2.5; official transcripts; goal statement; access to computer and Internet; for doctorate, master's degree or equivalent in related field; minimum GPA of 3.0; 3 years of related professional/academic experience (preferred). Additional exam requirements/recommendations for international students: Required—TOEFL (minimum score 550 paper-based; 213 computer-based), IELTS (minimum score 6.5), Michigan English Language Assessment Battery (minimum score 82). *Application deadline:* Applications are processed on a rolling basis. Application fee: $50. Electronic applications accepted. *Financial support:* Federal Work-Study, scholarships/grants, unspecified assistantships, and family tuition reduction, active duty/veteran tuition reduction, group tuition reduction, interest-free payment plans, employee tuition reduction available. Support available to part-time students. Financial award applicants required to submit FAFSA. *Unit head:* Dr. William Schulz, III, Associate Dean, 800-925-3368. *Application contact:* Jennifer Hall, Vice President of Enrollment Management, 866-4-WALDEN, E-mail: info@waldenu.edu. Web site: http://www.waldenu.edu/Colleges-and-Schools/College-of-Management-and-Technology.htm.

West Chester University of Pennsylvania, College of Education, Department of Professional and Secondary Education, West Chester, PA 19383. Offers education for sustainability (Certificate); entrepreneurial education (Certificate); secondary education (M Ed, Teaching Certificate); teaching and learning with technology (Certificate). Part-time programs available. *Faculty:* 1 (woman) full-time, 9 part-time/adjunct (7 women). *Students:* 5 full-time (all women), 26 part-time (11 women); includes 4 minority (2 Black or African American, non-Hispanic/Latino; 1 Asian, non-Hispanic/Latino; 1 Two or more races, non-Hispanic/Latino). Average age 33. 34 applicants, 56% accepted, 10 enrolled. In 2011, 6 master's, 4 Certificates awarded. *Degree requirements:* For master's, comprehensive exam, thesis (for some programs). *Entrance requirements:* For master's, teaching certification (strongly recommended). Additional exam requirements/recommendations for international students: Required—TOEFL (minimum score 550 paper-based; 213 computer-based; 80 iBT). *Application deadline:* For fall admission, 4/15 priority date for domestic students, 3/15 for international students; for spring admission, 10/15 priority date for domestic students, 9/1 for international students. Applications are processed on a rolling basis. Application fee: $45. Electronic applications accepted. *Expenses:* Tuition, state resident: full-time $7488; part-time $416 per credit. Tuition, nonresident: full-time $11,232; part-time $624 per credit. *Required fees:* $1784.64; $67.59 per credit. Tuition and fees vary according to program. *Financial support:* Unspecified assistantships available. Support available to part-time students. Financial award application deadline: 2/15; financial award applicants required to submit FAFSA. *Faculty research:* Technology integration: preparing our teachers for the twenty-first century, critical pedagogy. *Unit head:* Dr. John Elmore, Chair, 610-436-6934, Fax: 610-436-3102, E-mail: jelmore@wcupa.edu. *Application contact:* Dr. David Bolton, Graduate Coordinator, 610-436-6914, Fax: 610-436-3102, E-mail: dbolton@wcupa.edu. Web site: http://www.wcupa.edu/_academics/sch_sed.prof&seced/.

Western Carolina University, Graduate School, College of Business, Program in Entrepreneurship, Cullowhee, NC 28723. Offers ME. Part-time and evening/weekend programs available. Postbaccalaureate distance learning degree programs offered (no on-campus study). *Students:* 3 full-time (1 woman), 45 part-time (18 women); includes 15 minority (8 Black or African American, non-Hispanic/Latino; 2 Asian, non-Hispanic/Latino; 3 Hispanic/Latino; 2 Two or more races, non-Hispanic/Latino), 2 international. Average age 37. 34 applicants, 88% accepted, 26 enrolled. In 2011, 20 master's awarded. *Entrance requirements:* For master's, GMAT or GRE General Test. Additional exam requirements/recommendations for international students: Required—TOEFL (minimum score 550 paper-based; 270 computer-based; 79 iBT). *Application deadline:* For fall admission, 5/1 priority date for domestic students; for spring admission, 9/1 priority date for domestic students. Applications are processed on a rolling basis. Application fee: $50. *Expenses:* Tuition, state resident: full-time $3348. Tuition, nonresident: full-time $12,933. *Required fees:* $3155. *Financial support:* Fellowships, research assistantships with full and partial tuition reimbursements, teaching assistantships with full and partial tuition reimbursements, institutionally sponsored loans, scholarships/grants, and unspecified assistantships available. Financial award application deadline: 3/31; financial award applicants required to submit FAFSA. *Unit head:* Dr. Robert Carton, Director, 828-227-3894, Fax: 828-227-7414, E-mail: rcarton@email.wcu.edu. *Application contact:* Admissions Specialist for Entrepreneurship, 828-227-7398, Fax: 828-227-7480, E-mail: gradsch@email.wcu.edu. Web site: http://online.wcu.edu/entrepreneurship/index.html.

Wilkes University, College of Graduate and Professional Studies, Jay S. Sidhu School of Business and Leadership, Wilkes-Barre, PA 18766-0002. Offers accounting (MBA); entrepreneurship (MBA); finance (MBA); health care administration (MBA); human resource management (MBA); international business (MBA); marketing (MBA); operations management (MBA); organizational leadership and development (MBA). *Accreditation:* ACBSP. Part-time and evening/weekend programs available. *Students:* 48 full-time (20 women), 134 part-time (62 women); includes 12 minority (2 Black or African American, non-Hispanic/Latino; 5 Asian, non-Hispanic/Latino; 2 Hispanic/Latino; 3 Two or more races, non-Hispanic/Latino), 9 international. Average age 30. In 2011, 69 master's awarded. *Entrance requirements:* For master's, GMAT. Additional exam requirements/recommendations for international students: Required—TOEFL (minimum score 550 paper-based; 213 computer-based; 79 iBT). *Application deadline:* Applications are processed on a rolling basis. Application fee: $45 ($65 for international students). Electronic applications accepted. *Expenses:* Contact institution. *Financial support:* Federal Work-Study and unspecified assistantships available. Financial award application deadline: 3/1; financial award applicants required to submit FAFSA. *Unit head:* Dr. Jeffrey Alves, Dean, 570-408-4702, Fax: 570-408-7846, E-mail: jeffrey.alves@wilkes.edu. *Application contact:* Erin Sutzko, Director of Extended Learning, 570-408-4253, Fax: 570-408-7846, E-mail: erin.sutzko@wilkes.edu. Web site: http://www.wilkes.edu/pages/457.asp.

Yorktown University, School of Business, Denver, CO 80246. Offers entrepreneurship (MBA); sport management (MBA).

Section 6
Facilities and Entertainment Management

This section contains a directory of institutions offering graduate work in facilities management. Additional information about programs listed in the directory but not augmented by an in-depth entry may be obtained by writing directly to the dean of a graduate school or chair of a department at the address given in the directory.

For programs offering related work, see also in this book *Business Administration and Management.*

CONTENTS

Program Directories

Entertainment Management

California Intercontinental University, Hollywood College of the Entertainment Industry, Diamond Bar, CA 91765. Offers Hollywood and entertainment management (MBA).

Carnegie Mellon University, Heinz College, School of Public Policy and Management, Master of Entertainment Industry Management Program, Pittsburgh, PA 15213-3891. Offers MEIM. *Accreditation:* AACSB. *Entrance requirements:* For master's, GRE or GMAT, college-level course in advanced algebra/pre-calculus; college-level courses in economics and statistics (recommended). Additional exam requirements/recommendations for international students: Required—TOEFL or IELTS.

Columbia College Chicago, Graduate School, Department of Arts, Entertainment and Media Management, Chicago, IL 60605-1996. Offers arts, entertainment and media management (MA), including media management, music business management, performing arts management, visual arts management. Evening/weekend programs available. *Degree requirements:* For master's, thesis, internship. *Entrance requirements:* For master's, self-assessment essay. Additional exam requirements/recommendations for international students: Required—TOEFL (minimum score 550 paper-based; 213 computer-based). Electronic applications accepted.

Dowling College, School of Business, Oakdale, NY 11769-1999. Offers aviation management (MBA, Certificate); banking and finance (MBA, Certificate); corporate finance (MBA); financial planning (Certificate); health care management (MBA, Certificate); human resource management (Certificate); information systems management (MBA); management and leadership (MBA); marketing (Certificate); project management (Certificate); public management (MBA, Certificate); sport, event and entertainment management (Certificate); JD/MBA. Part-time and evening/weekend programs available. Postbaccalaureate distance learning degree programs offered (minimal on-campus study). *Faculty:* 10 full-time (4 women), 54 part-time/adjunct (6 women). *Students:* 237 full-time (99 women), 403 part-time (199 women); includes 186 minority (95 Black or African American, non-Hispanic/Latino; 62 Asian, non-Hispanic/Latino; 28 Hispanic/Latino; 1 Native Hawaiian or other Pacific Islander, non-Hispanic/Latino), 1 international. Average age 35. 345 applicants, 83% accepted, 193 enrolled. In 2011, 350 master's, 7 other advanced degrees awarded. *Degree requirements:* For master's, comprehensive exam, thesis optional. *Entrance requirements:* For master's, minimum GPA of 2.8, 2 letters of recommendation, courses or seminar in accounting and finance, resume. Additional exam requirements/recommendations for international students: Required—TOEFL (minimum score 550 paper-based). *Application deadline:* For fall admission, 9/1 priority date for domestic students; for winter admission, 1/1 priority date for domestic students; for spring admission, 2/1 priority date for domestic students. Applications are processed on a rolling basis. Application fee: $50. Electronic applications accepted. *Expenses: Tuition:* Full-time $19,162; part-time $933 per credit. *Required fees:* $1330; $700 per year. Tuition and fees vary according to course load. *Financial support:* Career-related internships or fieldwork and Federal Work-Study available. Support available to part-time students. Financial award application deadline: 6/30; financial award applicants required to submit FAFSA. *Faculty research:* International finance, computer applications, labor relations, executive development. *Unit head:* Antonia Loschiavo, Assistant Dean, 631-244-3266, Fax: 631-244-1018, E-mail: loschiat@dowling.edu. *Application contact:* Ronnie S. Macdonald, Assistant Vice President for Enrollment Services/Dean of Admissions, 631-244-3357, Fax: 631-244-1059, E-mail: macdonar@dowling.edu.

Full Sail University, Entertainment Business Master of Science Program - Campus, Winter Park, FL 32792-7437. Offers MS.

Full Sail University, Entertainment Business Master of Science Program - Online, Winter Park, FL 32792-7437. Offers MS. Postbaccalaureate distance learning degree programs offered. *Entrance requirements:* Additional exam requirements/recommendations for international students: Required—TOEFL (minimum score 550 paper-based; 213 computer-based; 79 iBT).

Hofstra University, Frank G. Zarb School of Business, Department of Management, Entrepreneurship and General Management, Hempstead, NY 11549. Offers business administration (MBA), including health services management, management, sports and entertainment management; general management (Advanced Certificate); human resource management (MS, Advanced Certificate). Part-time and evening/weekend programs available. Postbaccalaureate distance learning degree programs offered (minimal on-campus study). *Faculty:* 7 full-time (2 women), 8 part-time/adjunct (1 woman). *Students:* 92 full-time (36 women), 151 part-time (62 women); includes 58 minority (25 Black or African American, non-Hispanic/Latino; 23 Asian, non-Hispanic/Latino; 10 Hispanic/Latino), 24 international. Average age 32. 227 applicants, 72% accepted, 93 enrolled. In 2011, 74 master's awarded. *Degree requirements:* For master's, thesis optional, capstone course (for MBA); thesis (for MS); minimum GPA of 3.0. *Entrance requirements:* For master's, GMAT/GRE, 2 letters of recommendation; resume; essay. Additional exam requirements/recommendations for international students: Required—TOEFL (minimum score 550 paper-based; 213 computer-based; 80 iBT); Recommended—IELTS (minimum score 6). *Application deadline:* Applications are processed on a rolling basis. Application fee: $70 ($75 for international students). Electronic applications accepted. *Expenses:* Contact institution. *Financial support:* In 2011–12, 23 students received support, including 18 fellowships with full and partial tuition reimbursements available (averaging $5,605 per year), 1 research assistantship with full and partial tuition reimbursement available (averaging $11,370 per year); career-related internships or fieldwork, Federal Work-Study, institutionally sponsored loans, scholarships/grants, tuition waivers (full and partial), and unspecified assistantships also available. Support available to part-time students. Financial award applicants required to submit FAFSA. *Faculty research:* Business/personal ethics, sustainability, innovation, decision-making, supply chain management, learning and pedagogical issues, family business, small business, entrepreneurship. *Unit head:* Dr. Li-Lian Gao, Chairperson, 516-463-5729, Fax: 516-463-4834, E-mail: mgblzg@hofstra.edu. *Application contact:* Carol Drummer, Dean of Graduate Admissions, 516-463-4876, Fax: 516-463-4664, E-mail: gradstudent@hofstra.edu. Web site: http://www.hofstra.edu/Academics/Colleges/Zarb/MGMT/.

Maryville University of Saint Louis, The John E. Simon School of Business, St. Louis, MO 63141-7299. Offers accounting (MBA, PGC); business studies (PGC); management (MBA, PGC); marketing (MBA, PGC); process and project management (MBA, PGC); sport and entertainment management (MBA, PGC). *Accreditation:* ACBSP. Part-time and evening/weekend programs available. *Faculty:* 8 full-time (3 women), 14 part-time/adjunct (5 women). *Students:* 19 full-time (10 women), 114 part-time (56 women); includes 13 minority (7 Black or African American, non-Hispanic/Latino; 3 Asian, non-Hispanic/Latino; 2 Hispanic/Latino; 1 Two or more races, non-Hispanic/Latino), 3 international. Average age 31. In 2011, 56 master's awarded. *Entrance requirements:* For master's, GMAT (unless applicant possesses undergraduate business degree with minimum cumulative GPA of 3.0, or has completed master's degree from accredited university or one early access course prior to undergraduate degree). Additional exam requirements/recommendations for international students: Required—TOEFL (minimum score 85 iBT). *Application deadline:* Applications are processed on a rolling basis. Application fee: $40 ($60 for international students). Electronic applications accepted. *Expenses: Tuition:* Full-time $21,922; part-time $675 per credit hour. *Required fees:* $233.75 per semester. *Financial support:* Career-related internships or fieldwork, Federal Work-Study, tuition waivers (partial), and campus employment available. Financial award application deadline: 3/1; financial award applicants required to submit FAFSA. *Faculty research:* International business, e-marketing, strategic planning, interpersonal management skills, financial analysis. *Unit head:* Dr. Pamela Horwitz, Dean, 314-529-9418, Fax: 314-529-9975, E-mail: horwitz@maryville.edu. *Application contact:* Kathy Dougherty, Director of MBA Programs, 314-529-9382, Fax: 314-529-9975, E-mail: business@maryville.edu. Web site: http://www.maryville.edu/academics-bu-mba.

Universidad Autonoma de Guadalajara, Graduate Programs, Guadalajara, Mexico. Offers administrative law and justice (LL M); advertising and corporate communications (MA); architecture (M Arch); business (MBA); computational science (MCC); education (Ed M, Ed D); English-Spanish translation (MA); entrepreneurship and management (MBA); integrated management of digital animation (MA); international business (MIB); international corporate law (LL M); internet technologies (MS); manufacturing systems (MMS); occupational health (MS); philosophy (MA, PhD); power electronics (MS); quality systems (MQS); renewable energy (MS); social evaluation of projects (MBA); strategic market research (MBA); tax law (MA); teaching mathematics (MA).

University of Colorado Denver, Business School, Master of Business Administration Program, Denver, CO 80217. Offers business intelligence (MBA); business strategy (MBA); business to business marketing (MBA); business to consumer marketing (MBA); change management (MBA); corporate financial management (MBA); enterprise technology management (MBA); entrepreneurship (MBA); health administration (MBA), including financial management, health administration, health information technologies, international health management and policy; human resources management (MBA); investment management (MBA); managing for sustainability (MBA); services management (MBA); sports and entertainment management (MBA). *Accreditation:* AACSB. Part-time and evening/weekend programs available. Postbaccalaureate distance learning degree programs offered (no on-campus study). *Students:* 784 full-time (306 women), 203 part-time (81 women); includes 135 minority (18 Black or African American, non-Hispanic/Latino; 5 American Indian or Alaska Native, non-Hispanic/Latino; 50 Asian, non-Hispanic/Latino; 58 Hispanic/Latino; 4 Two or more races, non-Hispanic/Latino), 38 international. Average age 31. 433 applicants, 76% accepted, 212 enrolled. In 2011, 326 master's awarded. *Degree requirements:* For master's, 48 semester hours, including 30 of core courses, 3 in international business, and 15 in electives from over 50 other graduate business courses. *Entrance requirements:* For master's, GMAT, resume, official transcripts, essay, two letters of recommendation, financial statements (for international applicants). Additional exam requirements/recommendations for international students: Required—TOEFL (minimum score 560 paper-based; 197 computer-based; 83 iBT). *Application deadline:* For fall admission, 4/15 priority date for domestic students, 3/15 for international students; for spring admission, 10/15 priority date for domestic students, 10/1 for international students. Applications are processed on a rolling basis. Application fee: $50 ($75 for international students). Electronic applications accepted. *Expenses:* Contact institution. *Financial support:* Scholarships/grants available. Support available to part-time students. Financial award application deadline: 4/1; financial award applicants required to submit FAFSA. *Faculty research:* Marketing, management, entrepreneurship, finance, health administration. *Unit head:* Elizabeth Cooperman, Professor of Finance and Managing for Sustainability/MBA Program Director, 303-315-8422, E-mail: elizabeth.cooperman@ucdenver.edu. *Application contact:* Shelly Townley, Admissions Director, Graduate Programs, 303-315-8202, E-mail: shelly.townley@ucdenver.edu. Web site: http://www.ucdenver.edu/academics/colleges/business/degrees/ms/accounting/Pages/Accounting.aspx.

University of Colorado Denver, Business School, Program in Management and Organization, Denver, CO 80217. Offers communications management (MS); entrepreneurship and innovation (MS); global management (MS); human resources management (MS); leadership and management (MS); sports and entertainment management (MS). *Accreditation:* AACSB. Part-time and evening/weekend programs available. Postbaccalaureate distance learning degree programs offered (no on-campus study). *Students:* 29 full-time (14 women), 14 part-time (10 women); includes 3 minority (2 Asian, non-Hispanic/Latino; 1 Hispanic/Latino), 5 international. Average age 31. 32 applicants, 63% accepted, 14 enrolled. In 2011, 22 master's awarded. *Degree requirements:* For master's, 30 semester hours (12 of required courses, 12 of management electives, and 6 of free electives). *Entrance requirements:* For master's, GMAT, resume, two letters of recommendation, essay, financial statements (for international applicants). Additional exam requirements/recommendations for international students: Required—TOEFL (minimum score 525 paper-based; 197 computer-based; 71 iBT). *Application deadline:* For fall admission, 4/15 priority date for domestic students, 3/15 for international students; for spring admission, 10/15 priority date for domestic students, 10/1 for international students. Applications are processed on a rolling basis. Application fee: $50 ($75 for international students). Electronic applications accepted. *Expenses:* Contact institution. *Financial support:* Federal Work-Study and scholarships/grants available. Support available to part-time students. Financial award application deadline: 4/1; financial award applicants required to submit FAFSA. *Faculty research:* Human resource management, management of catastrophe, turnaround strategies. *Unit head:* Dr. Kenneth Bettenhausen, Associate Professor/Director of MS in Management, 303-315-8425, E-mail: kenneth.bettenhausen@ucdenver.edu. *Application contact:* Shelly Townley, Admissions Director, Graduate Programs, 303-315-8202, E-mail: shelly.townley@ucdenver.edu. Web site: http://www.ucdenver.edu/academics/colleges/business/degrees/ms/management/Pages/Management.aspx.

University of Colorado Denver, Business School, Program in Marketing, Denver, CO 80217. Offers brand management and marketing communication (MS); global marketing (MS); high-tech and entrepreneurial marketing (MS); Internet marketing (MS); marketing for sustainability (MS); marketing research (MS); sports and entertainment marketing (MS). Part-time and evening/weekend programs available. *Students:* 39 full-time (29 women), 11 part-time (6 women); includes 4 minority (3 Hispanic/Latino; 1 Two or more races, non-Hispanic/Latino), 8 international. Average age 28. 40 applicants, 65% accepted, 16 enrolled. In 2011, 8 master's awarded. *Degree requirements:* For master's, 30 semester hours (21 of marketing core courses, 9 of graduate marketing electives). *Entrance requirements:* For master's, GMAT, resume, essay, two letters of recommendation, financial statements (for international applicants). Additional exam requirements/recommendations for international students: Required—TOEFL (minimum score 525 paper-based; 197 computer-based; 71 iBT). *Application deadline:* For fall admission, 4/15 priority date for domestic students, 3/15 for international students; for spring admission, 10/15 priority date for domestic students, 10/1 for international students. Applications are processed on a rolling basis. Application fee: $50 ($75 for international students). Electronic applications accepted. *Expenses:* Contact institution. *Financial support:* Federal Work-Study and scholarships/grants available. Support available to part-time students. Financial award application deadline: 4/1; financial award applicants required to submit FAFSA. *Faculty research:* Marketing issues in the Chinese environment, impact of individual difference and contextual factors on the risk-taking behaviors of managers making new-business creation decisions, attribution theory perspective of conflict between marketers and engineers, organizational identity and identification, international market entry strategies. *Unit head:* Dr. David Forlani, Associate Professor/Director of Marketing Programs, 303-315-8420, E-mail: david.forlani@ucdenver.edu. *Application contact:* Shelly Townley, Admissions Director, Graduate Programs, 303-315-8202, E-mail: shelly.townley@ucdenver.edu. Web site: http://www.ucdenver.edu/academics/colleges/business/degrees/ms/marketing/Pages/Marketing.aspx.

University of Dallas, Graduate School of Management, Irving, TX 75062-4736. Offers accounting (MBA, MM, MS); business management (MBA, MM); corporate finance (MBA, MM); financial services (MBA); global business (MBA, MM); health services management (MBA, MM); human resource management (MBA, MM); information assurance (MBA, MM, MS); information technology (MBA, MM, MS); information technology service management (MBA, MM, MS); marketing management (MBA, MM); organization development (MBA, MM); project management (MBA, MM); sports and entertainment management (MBA, MM); strategic leadership (MBA, MM); supply chain management (MBA); supply chain management and market logistics (MM). *Accreditation:* ACBSP. Part-time and evening/weekend programs available. Postbaccalaureate distance learning degree programs offered (no on-campus study). *Entrance requirements:* Additional exam requirements/recommendations for international students: Required—TOEFL. Electronic applications accepted. *Expenses:* Contact institution.

University of Massachusetts Amherst, Graduate School, Interdisciplinary Programs, Dual Degree Program in Business Administration and Civil Engineering, Amherst, MA 01003. Offers MSCE/MBA. Part-time programs available. *Entrance requirements:* Additional exam requirements/recommendations for international students: Required—TOEFL (minimum score 600 paper-based; 250 computer-based; 100 iBT), IELTS (minimum score 7). *Application deadline:* For fall admission, 2/1 for domestic and international students. Applications are processed on a rolling basis. Application fee: $50 ($65 for international students). Electronic applications accepted. Tuition and fees vary according to course load, campus/location and program. *Financial support:* Career-related internships or fieldwork, Federal Work-Study, scholarships/grants, traineeships, health care benefits, tuition waivers (full), and unspecified assistantships available. Support available to part-time students. Financial award application deadline: 2/1; financial award applicants required to submit FAFSA. *Unit head:* Dr. Sanjay Arwade, Graduate Program Director, 413-545-0686, Fax: 413-545-2840, E-mail: muriel@ecs.umass.edu. *Application contact:* Lindsay DeSantis, Interim Supervisor of Admissions, 413-545-0722, Fax: 413-577-0010, E-mail: gradadm@grad.umass.edu. Web site: http://www-new.ecs.umass.edu/degrees#MBA.

University of South Carolina, The Graduate School, College of Hospitality, Retail, and Sport Management, Department of Sport and Entertainment Management, Columbia, SC 29208. Offers live sport and entertainment events (MS); public assembly facilities management (MS). Part-time programs available. *Degree requirements:* For master's, comprehensive exam, thesis optional. *Entrance requirements:* For master's, GRE General Test or GMAT (preferred), minimum GPA of 3.0. Additional exam requirements/recommendations for international students: Required—TOEFL (minimum score 570 paper-based; 230 computer-based; 70 iBT). Electronic applications accepted. *Expenses:* Contact institution. *Faculty research:* Public assembly marketing, operations, box office, booking and scheduling, law/economic impacts.

Valparaiso University, Graduate School, Program in Arts and Entertainment Administration, Valparaiso, IN 46383. Offers MA. Part-time and evening/weekend programs available. *Students:* 2 full-time (1 woman), 2 part-time (both women); includes 1 minority (Hispanic/Latino), 1 international. Average age 28. In 2011, 1 master's awarded. *Degree requirements:* For master's, internship or research project. *Entrance requirements:* Additional exam requirements/recommendations for international students: Required—TOEFL (minimum score 550 paper-based; 213 computer-based; 80 iBT). *Application deadline:* Applications are processed on a rolling basis. Application fee: $30 ($50 for international students). Electronic applications accepted. *Expenses: Tuition:* Part-time $560 per credit hour. Tuition and fees vary according to course load and program. *Financial support:* Available to part-time students. Applicants required to submit FAFSA. *Unit head:* Dr. David L. Rowland, Dean, Graduate School and Continuing Education/Associate Provost, 219-464-5313, Fax: 219-464-5381, E-mail: david.rowland@valpo.edu. *Application contact:* Dustin Jesch, Coordinator, U.S. Student Engagement, 219-464-5313, Fax: 219-464-5381, E-mail: dustin.jesch@valpo.edu. Web site: http://www.valpo.edu/grad/aea/index.php.

Facilities Management

Cornell University, Graduate School, Graduate Fields of Human Ecology, Field of Design and Environmental Analysis, Ithaca, NY 14853. Offers applied research in human-environment relations (MS); facilities planning and management (MS); housing and design (MS); human factors and ergonomics (MS); human-environment relations (MS); interior design (MA, MPS). *Faculty:* 15 full-time (6 women). *Students:* 22 full-time (18 women); includes 6 minority (1 Black or African American, non-Hispanic/Latino; 4 Asian, non-Hispanic/Latino; 1 Hispanic/Latino), 7 international. Average age 26. 61 applicants, 33% accepted, 13 enrolled. In 2011, 12 master's awarded. *Degree requirements:* For master's, thesis. *Entrance requirements:* For master's, GRE General Test, portfolio or slides of recent work; bachelor's degree in interior design, architecture or related design discipline; 2 letters of recommendation. Additional exam requirements/recommendations for international students: Required—TOEFL (minimum score 600 paper-based; 250 computer-based; 105 iBT). *Application deadline:* For fall admission, 2/1 priority date for domestic students. Application fee: $95. Electronic applications accepted. *Financial support:* In 2011–12, 13 students received support, including 1 fellowship with full tuition reimbursement available, 2 research assistantships with full tuition reimbursements available, 9 teaching assistantships with full tuition reimbursements available; institutionally sponsored loans, scholarships/grants, health care benefits, tuition waivers (full and partial), and unspecified assistantships also available. Financial award applicants required to submit FAFSA. *Faculty research:* Facility planning and management, environmental psychology, housing, interior design, ergonomics and human factors. *Unit head:* Director of Graduate Studies, 607-255-2168, Fax: 607-255-0305. *Application contact:* Graduate Field Assistant, 607-255-2168, Fax: 607-255-0305, E-mail: deagrad@cornell.edu. Web site: http://www.gradschool.cornell.edu/fields.php?id-77&a-2.

Indiana University of Pennsylvania, School of Graduate Studies and Research, College of Health and Human Services, Department of Health and Physical Education, Indiana, PA 15705-1087. Offers aquatics administration and facilities management (MS); exercise science (MS); health and physical education (M Ed); sport science/exercise science (MS); sport science/sport management (MS); sports science/sport studies (MS). Part-time programs available. *Faculty:* 10 full-time (6 women). *Students:* 57 full-time (23 women), 17 part-time (8 women); includes 10 minority (5 Black or African American, non-Hispanic/Latino; 1 American Indian or Alaska Native, non-Hispanic/Latino; 1 Asian, non-Hispanic/Latino; 1 Hispanic/Latino; 2 Two or more races, non-Hispanic/Latino), 4 international. Average age 26. 106 applicants, 61% accepted, 44 enrolled. In 2011, 44 master's awarded. *Degree requirements:* For master's, thesis optional. *Entrance requirements:* For master's, 2 letters of recommendation. Additional exam requirements/recommendations for international students: Required—TOEFL (minimum score 540 paper-based; 207 computer-based). *Application deadline:* Applications are processed on a rolling basis. Application fee: $50. Electronic applications accepted. *Expenses:* Tuition, state resident: full-time $7488; part-time $416 per credit. Tuition, nonresident: full-time $11,232; part-time $624 per credit. *Required fees:* $2070; $192.20 per credit. $90 per semester. *Financial support:* In 2011–12, 15 research assistantships with full and partial tuition reimbursements (averaging $4,896 per year) were awarded; fellowships also available. Financial award application deadline: 4/15; financial award applicants required to submit FAFSA. *Unit head:* Dr. Elaine Blair, Chairperson, 724-357-2770, E-mail: eblair@iup.edu. *Application contact:* Dr. Dolores Brzycki, Associate Dean, 724-357-2088, E-mail: dolores.brzycki@iup.edu. Web site: http://www.iup.edu/upper.aspx?id=216.

Indiana University–Purdue University Fort Wayne, College of Engineering, Technology, and Computer Science, Program in Technology, Fort Wayne, IN 46805-1499. Offers facilities and construction management (MS); industrial technology/manufacturing (MS); information technology/advanced computer applications (MS). Part-time programs available. *Faculty:* 14 full-time (5 women). *Students:* 1 full-time (0 women), 18 part-time (1 woman); includes 3 minority (1 Black or African American, non-Hispanic/Latino; 1 Asian, non-Hispanic/Latino; 1 Hispanic/Latino), 3 international. Average age 32. 9 applicants, 100% accepted, 7 enrolled. In 2011, 5 master's awarded. *Entrance requirements:* For master's, minimum GPA of 3.0. Additional exam requirements/recommendations for international students: Required—TOEFL (minimum score 550 paper-based; 213 computer-based; 77 iBT), TWE. *Application deadline:* For fall admission, 7/15 for domestic students, 5/15 for international students; for spring admission, 12/1 for domestic students, 10/15 for international students. Applications are processed on a rolling basis. Application fee: $55 ($60 for international students). Electronic applications accepted. *Financial support:* Career-related internships or fieldwork, scholarships/grants, and unspecified assistantships available. Support available to part-time students. Financial award application deadline: 3/1; financial award applicants required to submit FAFSA. *Unit head:* Dr. Max Yen, Dean, 260-481-6839, Fax: 260-481-5734, E-mail: yens@ipfw.edu. *Application contact:* Dr. Gary Steffen, Chair, 260-481-6344, Fax: 260-481-5734, E-mail: steffen@ipfw.edu. Web site: http://www.ipfw.edu/etcs.

Maastricht School of Management, Graduate Programs, Maastricht, Netherlands. Offers business administration (MBA, DBA, PhD); facility management (Exec MBA); management (M Sc); sustainability (Exec MBA).

Massachusetts Maritime Academy, Program in Facilities Management, Buzzards Bay, MA 02532-1803. Offers MS. Part-time and evening/weekend programs available. *Entrance requirements:* For master's, GRE or GMAT, interview.

Pratt Institute, School of Architecture, Program in Facilities Management, New York, NY 10011. Offers MS. Part-time programs available. *Faculty:* 1 (woman) full-time, 5 part-time/adjunct (0 women). *Students:* 16 full-time (7 women), 3 part-time (0 women); includes 9 minority (2 Black or African American, non-Hispanic/Latino; 2 Asian, non-Hispanic/Latino; 5 Hispanic/Latino), 3 international. Average age 34. 10 applicants, 80% accepted, 4 enrolled. In 2011, 6 master's awarded. *Degree requirements:* For master's, thesis. *Entrance requirements:* For master's, writing sample, bachelor's degree, transcripts, letters of recommendation, portfolio. Additional exam requirements/recommendations for international students: Required—TOEFL (minimum score 550 paper-based; 213 computer-based; 79 iBT). *Application deadline:* For fall admission, 1/5 for domestic and international students; for spring admission, 10/1 for domestic and international students. Applications are processed on a rolling basis. Application fee: $50 ($90 for international students). Electronic applications accepted. *Expenses: Tuition:* Full-time $24,084; part-time $1338 per credit. *Financial support:* Career-related internships or fieldwork, Federal Work-Study, institutionally sponsored loans, scholarships/grants, health care benefits, and unspecified assistantships available. Support available to part-time students. Financial award application deadline: 2/1; financial award applicants required to submit FAFSA. *Faculty research:* Benchmarking, organizational studies, resource planning and management, computer-aided facilities management, value analysis. *Unit head:* Harriet Markis, Chairperson, 212-647-7524, Fax: 212-367-2497, E-mail: hmarkis@pratt.edu. *Application contact:* Young Hah, Director of Graduate Admissions, 718-636-3683, Fax: 718-399-4242, E-mail: yhah@pratt.edu. Web site: http://www.pratt.edu/academics/architecture/sustainable_planning/facilities_management.

Université Laval, Faculty of Administrative Sciences, Programs in Business Administration, Québec, QC G1K 7P4, Canada. Offers accounting (MBA); agri-food management (MBA); electronic business (MBA, Diploma); factory management and logistics (MBA); finance (MBA); firm management (MBA); geomatic management (MBA); information technology management (MBA); international management (MBA); management (MBA); management accounting (MBA, Diploma); marketing (MBA); modeling and organizational decision (MBA); occupational health and safety management (MBA); pharmacy management (MBA); social and environmental responsibility (MBA); technological entrepreneurship (Diploma). *Accreditation:* AACSB. Part-time and evening/weekend programs available. Postbaccalaureate distance learning degree programs offered (no on-campus study). *Entrance requirements:* For master's and Diploma, knowledge of French and English. Electronic applications accepted.

University of California, Berkeley, UC Berkeley Extension, Certificate Programs in Engineering, Construction and Facilities Management, Berkeley, CA 94720-1500. Offers construction management (Certificate); HVAC (Certificate); integrated circuit design and techniques (online) (Certificate). Postbaccalaureate distance learning degree programs offered.

The University of Kansas, Graduate Studies, School of Architecture, Design, and Planning, Department of Architecture, Lawrence, KS 66045. Offers academic track (MA); architecture (PhD); facility management (Certificate); management track (MA); professional track (M Arch); M Arch/MBA; M Arch/MUP. *Faculty:* 21 full-time (4 women). *Students:* 143 full-time (64 women), 25 part-time (14 women); includes 16 minority (4 Black or African American, non-Hispanic/Latino; 3 Asian, non-Hispanic/Latino; 7 Hispanic/Latino; 2 Two or more races, non-Hispanic/Latino), 18 international. Average age 27. 132 applicants, 54% accepted, 34 enrolled. In 2011, 131 degrees awarded. Terminal master's awarded for partial completion of doctoral program. *Degree requirements:* For master's, thesis or alternative, 1 summer abroad; for doctorate, comprehensive exam, thesis/dissertation. *Entrance requirements:* For master's, portfolio, minimum GPA of 3.0, letters of recommendation; for doctorate, GRE, portfolio, master's degree, letters of recommendation. Additional exam requirements/recommendations for international students: Required—TOEFL. *Application deadline:* For fall admission, 3/1 for domestic and international students; for spring admission, 11/1 for domestic and international students. Applications are processed on a rolling basis. Application fee: $55 ($65 for international students). Electronic applications accepted. Tuition and fees vary according to course load, campus/location, program and reciprocity agreements. *Financial support:* Fellowships, research assistantships with partial tuition reimbursements, teaching assistantships with full and partial tuition reimbursements, scholarships/grants, health care benefits, and unspecified assistantships available. Financial award application deadline: 2/1; financial award applicants required to submit FAFSA. *Faculty research:* Design build, sustainability, emergent technology, healthy places, urban design. *Unit head:* Prof. Nils Gore, Interim Chair, 785-864-2700, Fax: 785-864-5185, E-mail: archku@ku.edu. *Application contact:* Gera Elliott, Admissions Coordinator, 785-864-3167, Fax: 785-864-5185, E-mail: archku@ku.edu. Web site: http://www.saup.ku.edu/.

University of New Haven, Graduate School, School of Business, Program in Sports Management, West Haven, CT 06516-1916. Offers facility management (MS); management of sports industries (Certificate); sports management (MS). *Students:* 23 full-time (6 women), 9 part-time (2 women); includes 4 minority (2 Black or African American, non-Hispanic/Latino; 1 Hispanic/Latino; 1 Two or more races, non-Hispanic/Latino), 4 international. Average age 27. 16 applicants, 100% accepted, 13 enrolled. In 2011, 30 master's, 1 other advanced degree awarded. *Entrance requirements:* For master's, GMAT, minimum GPA of 2.7. Additional exam requirements/recommendations for international students: Required—TOEFL (minimum score 520 paper-based; 190 computer-based; 70 iBT); Recommended—IELTS (minimum score 5.5). *Application deadline:* For fall admission, 5/31 for international students; for winter admission, 10/15 for international students; for spring admission, 1/15 for international students. Applications are processed on a rolling basis. Application fee: $50. Electronic applications accepted. *Expenses: Tuition:* Part-time $750 per credit. *Financial support:* Research assistantships with partial tuition reimbursements, teaching assistantships with partial tuition reimbursements, career-related internships or fieldwork, Federal Work-Study, scholarships/grants, tuition waivers, and unspecified assistantships available. Support available to part-time students. Financial award applicants required to submit FAFSA. *Unit head:* Dr. Gil B. Fried, Head, 203-932-7081. *Application contact:* Eloise Gormley, Director of Graduate Admissions, 203-932-7449, Fax: 203-932-7137, E-mail: gradinfo@newhaven.edu. Web site: http://www.newhaven.edu/6851/.

Section 7
Hospitality Management

This section contains a directory of institutions offering graduate work in hospitality management. Additional information about programs listed in the directory but not augmented by an in-depth entry may be obtained by writing directly to the dean of a graduate school or chair of a department at the address given in the directory.

For programs offering related work, see also in this book *Business Administration and Management* and *Advertising and Public Relations.* In the other guides in this series:

Graduate Programs in the Biological/Biomedical Sciences & Health-Related Medical Professions

See *Health Services*

Graduate Programs in the Physical Sciences, Mathematics, Agricultural Sciences, the Environment & Natural Resources

See *Agricultural and Food Sciences (Food Science and Technology)*

CONTENTS

Program Directories

Displays and Close-Ups

See:

Hospitality Management

American International College, School of Business Administration, MBA Program, Springfield, MA 01109-3189. Offers accounting (MBA); corporate/public communication (MBA); finance (MBA); general business (MBA); hospitality, hotel and service management (MBA); international business (MBA); international business practice (MBA); management (MBA); management information systems (MBA); marketing (MBA). International business practice program developed in cooperation with the Mountbatten Institute.

Auburn University, Graduate School, College of Human Sciences, Department of Nutrition and Food Science, Auburn University, AL 36849. Offers global hospitality and retailing (Graduate Certificate); nutrition (MS, PhD). Part-time programs available. *Faculty:* 13 full-time (5 women). *Students:* 23 full-time (15 women), 25 part-time (16 women); includes 5 minority (4 Black or African American, non-Hispanic/Latino; 1 Asian, non-Hispanic/Latino), 19 international. Average age 29. 56 applicants, 38% accepted, 11 enrolled. In 2011, 4 master's, 2 doctorates awarded. *Degree requirements:* For master's, thesis (for some programs); for doctorate, thesis/dissertation. *Entrance requirements:* For master's and doctorate, GRE General Test. *Application deadline:* For fall admission, 7/7 for domestic students; for spring admission, 11/24 for domestic students. Applications are processed on a rolling basis. Application fee: $50 ($60 for international students). Electronic applications accepted. *Expenses:* Tuition, state resident: full-time $7290; part-time $405 per credit hour. Tuition, nonresident: full-time $21,870; part-time $1215 per credit hour. *International tuition:* $22,000 full-time. *Required fees:* $1402. *Financial support:* Research assistantships, teaching assistantships, career-related internships or fieldwork, and Federal Work-Study available. Support available to part-time students. Financial award application deadline: 3/15; financial award applicants required to submit FAFSA. *Faculty research:* Food quality and safety, diet, food supply, physical activity in maintenance of health, prevention of selected chronic disease states. *Unit head:* Dr. Martin O'Neill, Head, 334-844-3266. *Application contact:* Dr. George Flowers, Dean of the Graduate School, 334-844-2125. Web site: http://www.humsci.auburn.edu/nufs/.

California State University, Long Beach, Graduate Studies, College of Health and Human Services, Department of Family and Consumer Sciences, Master of Science in Nutritional Science Program, Long Beach, CA 90840. Offers food science (MS); hospitality foodservice and hotel management (MS); nutritional science (MS). Part-time programs available. *Students:* 32 full-time (29 women), 23 part-time (all women); includes 18 minority (2 Black or African American, non-Hispanic/Latino; 6 Asian, non-Hispanic/Latino; 5 Hispanic/Latino; 5 Two or more races, non-Hispanic/Latino). Average age 27. 108 applicants, 32% accepted, 21 enrolled. In 2011, 11 master's awarded. *Degree requirements:* For master's, thesis, oral presentation of thesis or directed project. *Entrance requirements:* For master's, GRE, minimum GPA of 2.5 in last 60 units. *Application deadline:* For fall admission, 5/1 for domestic students. Applications are processed on a rolling basis. Application fee: $55. Electronic applications accepted. *Financial support:* Federal Work-Study, institutionally sponsored loans, and scholarships/grants available. Financial award application deadline: 3/2. *Faculty research:* Protein and water-soluble vitamins, sensory evaluation of foods, mineral deficiencies in humans, child nutrition, minerals and blood pressure. *Unit head:* Dr. M. Sue Stanley, Chair, 562-985-4484, Fax: 562-985-4414, E-mail: stanleym@csulb.edu. *Application contact:* Dr. Mary Jacob, Graduate Coordinator, 562-985-4484, Fax: 562-985-4414, E-mail: marjacob@csulb.edu.

California State University, Northridge, Graduate Studies, College of Health and Human Development, Department of Recreation and Tourism Management, Northridge, CA 91330. Offers hospitality and tourism (MS); recreational sport management/campus recreation (MS). *Degree requirements:* For master's, thesis (for some programs). *Entrance requirements:* For master's, GRE (if cumulative undergraduate GPA less than 3.0). Additional exam requirements/recommendations for international students: Required—TOEFL.

Columbia Southern University, MBA Program, Orange Beach, AL 36561. Offers electronic business and technology (MBA); finance (MBA); general (MBA); healthcare management (MBA); hospitality and tourism (MBA); human resources management (MBA); international management (MBA); marketing (MBA); project management (MBA); public administration (MBA); sport management (MBA). Part-time and evening/weekend programs available. Postbaccalaureate distance learning degree programs offered (no on-campus study). *Entrance requirements:* For master's, bachelor's degree from accredited/approved institution. Additional exam requirements/recommendations for international students: Required—TOEFL. Electronic applications accepted.

Cornell University, Graduate School, Field of Hotel Administration, Ithaca, NY 14853. Offers hospitality management (MMH); hotel administration (MS, PhD). *Faculty:* 43 full-time (12 women). *Students:* 66 full-time (32 women); includes 18 minority (12 Asian, non-Hispanic/Latino; 4 Hispanic/Latino; 2 Two or more races, non-Hispanic/Latino), 31 international. Average age 29. 149 applicants, 49% accepted, 66 enrolled. In 2011, 68 master's, 4 doctorates awarded. Terminal master's awarded for partial completion of doctoral program. *Degree requirements:* For master's, thesis (MS); for doctorate, comprehensive exam, thesis/dissertation. *Entrance requirements:* For master's and doctorate, GMAT, 1 academic and 1 employer letter of recommendation, 2 interviews. Additional exam requirements/recommendations for international students: Required—TOEFL (minimum score 600 paper-based; 250 computer-based). *Application deadline:* For fall admission, 2/1 for domestic students. Application fee: $95. Electronic applications accepted. *Financial support:* In 2011–12, 12 students received support, including 2 fellowships with full tuition reimbursements available, 1 teaching assistantship with full tuition reimbursement available; research assistantships with full tuition reimbursements available, institutionally sponsored loans, scholarships/grants, health care benefits, tuition waivers (full and partial), and unspecified assistantships also available. Financial award applicants required to submit FAFSA. *Faculty research:* Hospitality finance; property-asset management; real estate; management, strategy, and human resources; organizational communication. *Unit head:* Director of Graduate Studies, 607-255-7245. *Application contact:* Graduate Field Assistant, 607-255-6376, E-mail: mmh@cornell.edu. Web site: http://www.gradschool.cornell.edu/fields.php?id-82&a-2.

Drexel University, Goodwin College of Professional Studies, School of Technology and Professional Studies, Philadelphia, PA 19104-2875. Offers construction management (MS); engineering technology (MS); food science (MS); hospitality management (MS); professional studies: creativity studies (MS); professional studies: e-learning leadership (MS); professional studies: homeland security management (MS); project management (MS); property management (MS); sport management (MS). Postbaccalaureate distance learning degree programs offered.

Eastern Michigan University, Graduate School, College of Technology, School of Technology Studies, Program in Hotel and Restaurant Management, Ypsilanti, MI 48197. Offers MS, Graduate Certificate. Part-time and evening/weekend programs available. Postbaccalaureate distance learning degree programs offered (minimal on-campus study). *Students:* 4 full-time (2 women), 6 part-time (4 women); includes 4 minority (3 Black or African American, non-Hispanic/Latino; 1 Two or more races, non-Hispanic/Latino), 2 international. Average age 31. 15 applicants, 73% accepted, 5 enrolled. In 2011, 4 degrees awarded. *Entrance requirements:* Additional exam requirements/recommendations for international students: Required—TOEFL. *Application deadline:* Applications are processed on a rolling basis. Application fee: $35. *Expenses:* Tuition, state resident: full-time $10,367; part-time $432 per credit hour. Tuition, nonresident: full-time $20,435; part-time $851 per credit hour. *Required fees:* $39 per credit hour. $46 per semester. One-time fee: $100. Tuition and fees vary according to course level, degree level and reciprocity agreements. *Financial support:* Fellowships, research assistantships with full tuition reimbursements, teaching assistantships with full tuition reimbursements, career-related internships or fieldwork, Federal Work-Study, institutionally sponsored loans, scholarships/grants, tuition waivers (partial), and unspecified assistantships available. Support available to part-time students. Financial award applicants required to submit FAFSA. *Unit head:* Dr. Susan Gregory, Program Coordinator, 734-487-0845, Fax: 734-487-7690, E-mail: susan.gregory@emich.edu. *Application contact:* Graduate Admissions, 734-487-2400, Fax: 734-487-6559, E-mail: graduate.admissions@emich.edu.

East Stroudsburg University of Pennsylvania, Graduate School, College of Business and Management, Department of Hotel, Restaurant and Tourism Management, East Stroudsburg, PA 18301-2999. Offers management and leadership (MS). Part-time and evening/weekend programs available. *Degree requirements:* For master's, comprehensive exam. *Entrance requirements:* For master's, GRE or GMAT, 3 letters of recommendation. Additional exam requirements/recommendations for international students: Required—TOEFL (minimum score 560 paper-based; 220 computer-based; 83 iBT).

Ecole Hôtelière de Lausanne, Program in Hospitality Administration, Lausanne, Switzerland. Offers MHA. *Degree requirements:* For master's, project.

Endicott College, Apicius International School of Hospitality, Florence, MA 50122, Italy. Offers organizational management (M Ed). Program held entirely in Florence, Italy. *Degree requirements:* For master's, thesis. *Entrance requirements:* For master's, MAT or GRE, 250-500 word essay explaining professional goals, official transcripts of all academic work, bachelor's degree, two letters of recommendation, personal interview. *Application deadline:* For fall admission, 6/30 for domestic and international students. Application fee: $50. Tuition and fees vary according to degree level and program. *Financial support:* Applicants required to submit FAFSA. *Application contact:* Dr. Mary Huegel, Dean of Graduate and Professional Studies, 978-232-2084, Fax: 978-232-3000, E-mail: mhuegel@endicott.edu. Web site: http://www.apicius.it.

ESSEC Business School, Graduate Programs, Paris, France. Offers business administration (PhD); executive business administration (MBA); global business administration (MBA); hospitality management (MBA); international luxury brand management (MBA); management (MSM).

Fairleigh Dickinson University, College at Florham, Anthony J. Petrocelli College of Continuing Studies, International School of Hospitality and Tourism Management, Madison, NJ 07940-1099. Offers hospitality management studies (MS).

Fairleigh Dickinson University, Metropolitan Campus, Anthony J. Petrocelli College of Continuing Studies, International School of Hospitality and Tourism Management, Teaneck, NJ 07666-1914. Offers hospitality management (MS).

Florida International University, School of Hospitality and Tourism Management, Hospitality Management Program, Miami, FL 33199. Offers MS. Part-time and evening/weekend programs available. Postbaccalaureate distance learning degree programs offered. *Entrance requirements:* For master's, minimum GPA of 3.0, letters of recommendation, 5 years of management experience (for executive track). Additional exam requirements/recommendations for international students: Required—TOEFL (minimum score 550 paper-based; 213 computer-based). Electronic applications accepted.

The George Washington University, School of Business, Department of Tourism and Hospitality Management, Washington, DC 20052. Offers event and meeting management (MTA); event management (Professional Certificate); hospitality management (MTA, Professional Certificate); sport management (MTA); sports business management (Professional Certificate); sustainable tourism destination management (MTA); tourism administration (MTA); tourism and hospitality management (MBA); tourism destination management (Professional Certificate). Part-time programs available. Postbaccalaureate distance learning degree programs offered. *Faculty:* 9 full-time (5 women), 11 part-time/adjunct (5 women). *Students:* 84 full-time (62 women), 107 part-time (77 women); includes 43 minority (27 Black or African American, non-Hispanic/Latino; 2 American Indian or Alaska Native, non-Hispanic/Latino; 5 Asian, non-Hispanic/Latino; 9 Hispanic/Latino), 38 international. Average age 30. 152 applicants, 74% accepted, 56 enrolled. In 2011, 69 master's awarded. *Degree requirements:* For master's, comprehensive exam, thesis. *Entrance requirements:* For master's, GRE General Test. Additional exam requirements/recommendations for international students: Required—TOEFL. *Application deadline:* For fall admission, 4/1 priority date for domestic students; for spring admission, 10/1 for domestic students. Applications are processed on a rolling basis. Application fee: $75. *Financial support:* In 2011–12, 32 students received support. Fellowships, teaching assistantships, career-related internships or fieldwork, Federal Work-Study, institutionally sponsored loans, and tuition waivers (partial) available. Financial award application deadline: 4/1. *Faculty research:* Tourism policy, tourism impact forecasting, geotourism. *Unit head:* Susan M. Phillips, Dean, 202-994-6380, E-mail: gwsbdean@gwu.edu. *Application contact:* Kristin Williams, Assistant Vice President for Graduate and Special Enrollment Management, 202-994-0467, Fax: 202-994-0371, E-mail: ksw@gwu.edu. Web site: http://business.gwu.edu/tourism/.

Glion Institute of Higher Education, Graduate Programs, Glion-sur-Montreux, Switzerland. Offers hospitality organizational training (M Ed); hotel management with leadership (MBA); hotel management with marketing (MBA); international hospitality management (MBA). Evening/weekend programs available.

Husson University, School of Graduate and Professional Studies, Master of Business Administration Program, Bangor, ME 04401-2999. Offers general (corporate) (MSB); health care management (MSB); hospitality management (MSB); nonprofit management (MSB). Part-time and evening/weekend programs available. *Faculty:* 9 full-time (3 women), 12 part-time/adjunct (2 women). *Students:* 111 full-time (66 women), 60 part-time (37 women); includes 8 minority (3 Black or African American, non-Hispanic/Latino; 1 American Indian or Alaska Native, non-Hispanic/Latino; 2 Asian, non-Hispanic/Latino; 2 Hispanic/Latino). 67 applicants, 35 enrolled. In 2011, 90 master's awarded. *Degree requirements:* For master's, comprehensive exam (for some programs), thesis optional.

Entrance requirements: For master's, GMAT or GRE, minimum GPA of 3.0. Additional exam requirements/recommendations for international students: Required—TOEFL (minimum score 550 paper-based). *Application deadline:* Applications are processed on a rolling basis. Application fee: $40. Electronic applications accepted. *Expenses:* Contact institution. *Financial support:* In 2011–12, 1 student received support. Career-related internships or fieldwork, Federal Work-Study, scholarships/grants, and unspecified assistantships available. Financial award application deadline: 4/15; financial award applicants required to submit FAFSA. *Unit head:* Dr. Ronald Nykiel, Dean, College of Business, 207-941-7111, E-mail: nykielr@husson.edu. *Application contact:* Kristen M. Card, Director of Graduate Admissions, 207-404-5660, Fax: 207-941-7935, E-mail: cardk@husson.edu. Web site: http://www.husson.edu/mba.

Iowa State University of Science and Technology, Department of Apparel, Education Studies, and Hospitality Management, Ames, IA 50011-1121. Offers family and consumer sciences education and studies (M Ed, MS, PhD); foodservice and lodging management (MFCS, MS, PhD); textiles and clothing (MFCS, MS, PhD). *Degree requirements:* For doctorate, thesis/dissertation. *Entrance requirements:* For master's and doctorate, GRE General Test. Additional exam requirements/recommendations for international students: Required—TOEFL (minimum score 550 paper-based; 79 iBT), IELTS (minimum score 6.5). *Application deadline:* For fall admission, 2/1 priority date for domestic students, 2/1 for international students. Application fee: $40 ($90 for international students). *Unit head:* Dr. Ann Marie Fiore, Director of Graduate Education, 515-294-9303, E-mail: amfiore@iastate.edu. *Application contact:* Ann Marie Fiore, Application Contact, 515-294-9303, E-mail: amfiore@iastate.edu. Web site: http://www.aeshm.hs.iastate.edu/graduate-programs/amd/.

Johnson & Wales University, The Alan Shawn Feinstein Graduate School, MAT Program in Teacher Education, Providence, RI 02903-3703. Offers business education and secondary special education (MAT); elementary education and elementary special education (MAT); elementary education and elementary/secondary special education (MAT); elementary education and secondary special education (MAT); food service education (MAT). Part-time and evening/weekend programs available. *Entrance requirements:* For master's, MAT, minimum GPA of 2.75. Additional exam requirements/recommendations for international students: Required—TOEFL (minimum score 550 paper-based; 210 computer-based) or IELTS (recommended). *Faculty research:* Secondary education, student teaching, educational reform, evaluation procedures.

Johnson & Wales University, The Alan Shawn Feinstein Graduate School, MBA Program in Global Business Leadership, Providence, RI 02903-3703. Offers accounting (MBA); enhanced accounting (MBA); hospitality (MBA). Part-time programs available. *Entrance requirements:* For master's, minimum GPA of 2.75. Additional exam requirements/recommendations for international students: Required—TOEFL (minimum score 550 paper-based; 210 computer-based) or IELTS (recommended); Recommended—TWE. *Faculty research:* International banking, global economy, international trade, cultural differences.

Kansas State University, Graduate School, College of Human Ecology, Department of Hospitality Management and Dietetics, Manhattan, KS 66506. Offers dietetics (MS); food service hospitality management and dietetics administration (MS). Part-time programs available. *Faculty:* 9 full-time (6 women). *Students:* 12 full-time (9 women), 15 part-time (12 women); includes 4 minority (1 American Indian or Alaska Native, non-Hispanic/Latino; 2 Asian, non-Hispanic/Latino; 1 Hispanic/Latino), 1 international. Average age 29. 22 applicants, 64% accepted, 6 enrolled. In 2011, 3 master's awarded. *Degree requirements:* For master's, thesis or alternative, residency. *Entrance requirements:* Additional exam requirements/recommendations for international students: Required—TOEFL. *Application deadline:* For fall admission, 2/1 priority date for domestic students, 2/1 for international students; for spring admission, 8/1 priority date for domestic students, 8/1 for international students. Applications are processed on a rolling basis. Application fee: $40 ($55 for international students). Electronic applications accepted. *Financial support:* In 2011–12, 2 fellowships (averaging $15,000 per year), 8 research assistantships (averaging $16,413 per year), 6 teaching assistantships with full and partial tuition reimbursements (averaging $12,167 per year) were awarded; Federal Work-Study, institutionally sponsored loans, scholarships/grants, and unspecified assistantships also available. Support available to part-time students. Financial award application deadline: 3/1; financial award applicants required to submit FAFSA. *Faculty research:* Customer satisfaction, brand loyalty, food safety and biosecurity issues in foodservice operations; gerontology and the hospitality industry; education, training, and career development in dietetics and hospitality. *Total annual research expenditures:* $224,290. *Unit head:* Jeannie Sneed, Head, 785-532-5507, Fax: 785-532-5522, E-mail: jsneed@ksu.edu. *Application contact:* Ashley Lignitz, Administrative Specialist, 785-532-5521, Fax: 785-532-5522, E-mail: lignitz@ksu.edu. Web site: http://www.he.k-state.edu/hmd/.

Kansas State University, Graduate School, College of Human Ecology, Program in Human Ecology, Manhattan, KS 66506. Offers apparel and textiles (PhD); family life education and consultation (PhD); food service and hospitality management (PhD); lifespan and human development (PhD); marriage and family therapy (PhD); personal financial planning (PhD). *Students:* 40 full-time (25 women), 49 part-time (26 women); includes 15 minority (11 Black or African American, non-Hispanic/Latino; 1 Asian, non-Hispanic/Latino; 2 Hispanic/Latino; 1 Two or more races, non-Hispanic/Latino), 15 international. Average age 39. 48 applicants, 44% accepted, 6 enrolled. In 2011, 8 doctorates awarded. *Degree requirements:* For doctorate, thesis/dissertation. *Application deadline:* For fall admission, 2/1 priority date for domestic students, 2/1 for international students; for spring admission, 8/1 priority date for domestic students, 8/1 for international students. Applications are processed on a rolling basis. Application fee: $40 ($55 for international students). Electronic applications accepted. *Financial support:* Application deadline: 3/1. *Unit head:* Virginia Moxley, Dean, 785-532-5500, Fax: 785-532-5504, E-mail: moxley@ksu.edu. *Application contact:* Connie Fechter, Application Contact, 785-532-1473, Fax: 785-532-3796, E-mail: fechter@ksu.edu.

Kent State University, Graduate School of Education, Health, and Human Services, School of Foundations, Leadership and Administration, Program in Hospitality and Tourism Management, Kent, OH 44242-0001. Offers MS. Part-time programs available. *Faculty:* 6 full-time (4 women), 4 part-time/adjunct (3 women). *Students:* 18 full-time (13 women), 7 part-time (4 women); includes 2 minority (1 Black or African American, non-Hispanic/Latino; 1 Asian, non-Hispanic/Latino). 36 applicants, 53% accepted. In 2011, 5 master's awarded. *Degree requirements:* For master's, thesis optional. *Entrance requirements:* For master's, minimum GPA of 3.0, 3 letters of recommendation, resume, goals statement. Additional exam requirements/recommendations for international students: Required—TOEFL (minimum score 550 paper-based; 213 computer-based; 80 iBT). *Application deadline:* Applications are processed on a rolling basis. Application fee: $30 ($60 for international students). Electronic applications accepted. *Expenses:* Tuition, state resident: full-time $8136; part-time $452 per credit hour. Tuition, nonresident: full-time $14,292; part-time $794 per credit hour. *Financial support:* In 2011–12, 4 students received support, including 2 fellowships (averaging $8,500 per year), 1 research assistantship with full tuition reimbursement available (averaging $8,500 per year); Federal Work-Study, scholarships/grants, and unspecified assistantships also available. Financial award application deadline: 2/1; financial award applicants required to submit FAFSA. *Faculty research:* Training human service workers, health care services for older adults, early adolescent development, care-giving arrangements with aging families, peace and war. *Unit head:* Barb Scheule, Coordinator, 330-672-3796, E-mail: bscheule@kent.edu. *Application contact:* Nancy Miller, Academic Program Coordinator, 330-672-2576, Fax: 330-672-9162, E-mail: ogs@kent.edu.

Lasell College, Graduate and Professional Studies in Sport Management, Newton, MA 02466-2709. Offers sport hospitality management (MS, Graduate Certificate); sport leadership (MS, Graduate Certificate); sport non-profit management (MS, Graduate Certificate). Part-time programs available. Postbaccalaureate distance learning degree programs offered (no on-campus study). *Faculty:* 1 (woman) full-time, 4 part-time/adjunct (3 women). *Students:* 13 full-time (5 women), 20 part-time (10 women); includes 10 minority (4 Black or African American, non-Hispanic/Latino; 2 American Indian or Alaska Native, non-Hispanic/Latino; 4 Hispanic/Latino). Average age 28. 30 applicants, 63% accepted, 9 enrolled. *Entrance requirements:* For master's and Graduate Certificate, bachelor's degree from an accredited institution. Additional exam requirements/recommendations for international students: Required—TOEFL (minimum score 550 paper-based; 213 computer-based; 79 iBT), IELTS. *Application deadline:* For fall admission, 8/31 priority date for domestic students, 6/30 for international students; for spring admission, 12/31 priority date for domestic students, 10/31 for international students. Applications are processed on a rolling basis. Electronic applications accepted. *Expenses: Tuition:* Part-time $575 per credit. *Required fees:* $70 per semester. *Financial support:* Available to part-time students. Application deadline: 8/31; applicants required to submit FAFSA. *Unit head:* Dr. Joan Dolamore, Dean of Graduate and Professional Studies, 617-243-2485, Fax: 617-243-2450, E-mail: gradinfo@lasell.edu. *Application contact:* Adrienne Franciosi, Director of Graduate Admission, 617-243-2214, Fax: 617-243-2450, E-mail: gradinfo@lasell.edu. Web site: http://www.lasell.edu/Academics/Graduate-and-Professional-Studies/MS-in-Sport-Management-.html.

Lynn University, College of Business and Management, Boca Raton, FL 33431-5598. Offers aviation management (MBA); financial valuation and investment management (MBA); hospitality management (MBA); international business (MBA); marketing (MBA); mass communication and media management (MBA); sports and athletics administration (MBA). Part-time and evening/weekend programs available. Postbaccalaureate distance learning degree programs offered. *Degree requirements:* For master's, project. *Entrance requirements:* For master's, GMAT or GRE, minimum undergraduate GPA of 3.0, resume, 2 letters of recommendation. Additional exam requirements/recommendations for international students: Required—TOEFL (minimum score 550 paper-based; 213 computer-based). Electronic applications accepted. *Faculty research:* Labor relations, dynamic balance in leisure-time skills, ethics in athletics, hotel development.

Michigan State University, The Graduate School, Eli Broad Graduate School of Management, The School of Hospitality Business, East Lansing, MI 48824. Offers foodservice business management (MS); hospitality business management (MS). *Degree requirements:* For master's, research project. *Entrance requirements:* For master's, GRE General Test, minimum GPA of 3.0 in last 2 years of undergraduate course work, working knowledge of computers, resume, 3 letters of recommendation, specified college-level coursework or work experience. Additional exam requirements/recommendations for international students: Required—TOEFL (minimum score 580 paper-based; 237 computer-based). Electronic applications accepted. *Faculty research:* Corporate food service management, entrepreneurial and food service management, hospitality business.

New York University, School of Continuing and Professional Studies, The Preston Robert Tisch Center for Hospitality, Tourism, and Sports Management, Program in Hospitality Industry Studies, New York, NY 10012-1019. Offers brand strategy (MS); hospitality industry studies (Advanced Certificate); hotel finance (MS). Part-time and evening/weekend programs available. *Faculty:* 13 full-time (5 women), 20 part-time/adjunct (4 women). *Students:* 22 full-time (14 women), 30 part-time (16 women); includes 11 minority (3 Black or African American, non-Hispanic/Latino; 4 Asian, non-Hispanic/Latino; 4 Hispanic/Latino), 14 international. Average age 29. 83 applicants, 58% accepted, 20 enrolled. In 2011, 17 master's, 4 other advanced degrees awarded. *Degree requirements:* For master's, thesis. *Entrance requirements:* For master's, GRE/GMAT only upon request, relevant professional work, internship or volunteer experience. Additional exam requirements/recommendations for international students: Required—TOEFL (minimum score 600 paper-based; 250 computer-based; 100 iBT), IELTS (minimum score 7). *Application deadline:* For fall admission, 2/1 priority date for domestic students, 2/1 for international students; for spring admission, 10/15 priority date for domestic students, 8/15 for international students. Applications are processed on a rolling basis. Application fee: $150. Electronic applications accepted. *Financial support:* In 2011–12, 51 students received support, including 35 fellowships (averaging $3,034 per year); scholarships/grants also available. Support available to part-time students. Financial award application deadline: 2/15; financial award applicants required to submit FAFSA. *Application contact:* Admissions Office, 212-998-7100, E-mail: scps.gradadmissions@nyu.edu. Web site: http://www.scps.nyu.edu/areas-of-study/tisch/graduate-programs/ms-hospitality-industry-studies/.

New York University, Steinhardt School of Culture, Education, and Human Development, Department of Nutrition, Food Studies, and Public Health, Program in Food Studies and Food Management, New York, NY 10012-1019. Offers food studies (MA), including food culture, food systems; food studies and food management (PhD). Part-time programs available. *Degree requirements:* For master's, thesis (for some programs); for doctorate, thesis/dissertation. *Entrance requirements:* For doctorate, GRE General Test, interview. Additional exam requirements/recommendations for international students: Required—TOEFL. Electronic applications accepted. *Faculty research:* Cultural and social history of food, food systems and agriculture, food and aesthetics, political economy of food.

The Ohio State University, Graduate School, College of Education and Human Ecology, Department of Consumer Sciences, Columbus, OH 43210. Offers family resource management (MS, PhD); fashion and retail studies (MS, PhD); hospitality management (MS, PhD). *Faculty:* 16. *Students:* 17 full-time (13 women), 14 part-time (12 women); includes 3 minority (all Asian, non-Hispanic/Latino), 19 international. Average age 33. In 2011, 3 master's, 1 doctorate awarded. *Entrance requirements:* Additional exam requirements/recommendations for international students: Required—TOEFL (minimum score 550 paper-based; 79 iBT), Michigan English Language Assessment Battery (minimum score 82). *Application deadline:* Applications are processed on a rolling basis. Application fee: $40 ($50 for international students). Electronic applications accepted. *Expenses:* Tuition, state resident: full-time $11,400. Tuition, nonresident: full-time $28,125. Tuition and fees vary according to course load, degree level, campus/location and program. *Unit head:* Jonathan Fox, Interim Chair, 614-292-4561, E-mail: jfox@ehe.osu.edu. *Application contact:* Graduate Admissions, 614-292-6031, Fax: 614-292-3656, E-mail: gradadmissions@osu.edu. Web site: http://ehe.osu.edu/cs/.

The Ohio State University, Graduate School, College of Education and Human Ecology, Department of Human Nutrition, Columbus, OH 43210. Offers food service management (MS, PhD); foods (MS, PhD); nutrition (MS, PhD). *Accreditation:* AND.

Faculty: 14. *Students:* 20 full-time (16 women), 13 part-time (8 women); includes 2 minority (both Black or African American, non-Hispanic/Latino), 16 international. Average age 29. In 2011, 5 master's, 8 doctorates awarded. *Degree requirements:* For master's, thesis optional; for doctorate, thesis/dissertation. *Entrance requirements:* For master's and doctorate, GRE General Test. Additional exam requirements/recommendations for international students: Required—TOEFL (minimum score 577 paper-based; 233 computer-based). *Application deadline:* For fall admission, 8/15 priority date for domestic students, 7/1 for international students; for winter admission, 12/1 priority date for domestic students, 11/1 for international students; for spring admission, 3/1 priority date for domestic students, 2/1 for international students. Applications are processed on a rolling basis. Application fee: $40 ($50 for international students). Electronic applications accepted. *Expenses:* Tuition, state resident: full-time $11,400. Tuition, nonresident: full-time $28,125. Tuition and fees vary according to course load, degree level, campus/location and program. *Financial support:* Fellowships, research assistantships, teaching assistantships, Federal Work-Study, and institutionally sponsored loans available. Support available to part-time students. *Unit head:* James E. Kinder, Chair, 614-292-4356, Fax: 614-292-8880, E-mail: kinder.15@osu.edu. *Application contact:* Graduate Admissions, 614-292-6031, Fax: 614-292-3656, E-mail: gradadmissions@osu.edu. Web site: http://ehe.osu.edu/hn/.

Oklahoma State University, College of Human Environmental Sciences, School of Hotel and Restaurant Administration, Stillwater, OK 74078. Offers MS, PhD. *Faculty:* 14 full-time (5 women), 4 part-time/adjunct (1 woman). *Students:* 11 full-time (10 women), 36 part-time (22 women); includes 6 minority (1 Black or African American, non-Hispanic/Latino; 1 Asian, non-Hispanic/Latino; 4 Hispanic/Latino), 30 international. Average age 36. 9 applicants, 22% accepted, 0 enrolled. In 2011, 6 master's, 6 doctorates awarded. *Degree requirements:* For master's, thesis (for some programs); for doctorate, comprehensive exam, thesis/dissertation. *Entrance requirements:* For master's and doctorate, GRE or GMAT. Additional exam requirements/recommendations for international students: Required—TOEFL (minimum score 550 paper-based; 79 iBT). *Application deadline:* For fall admission, 3/1 for international students; for spring admission, 8/1 for international students. Applications are processed on a rolling basis. Application fee: $40 ($75 for international students). Electronic applications accepted. *Expenses:* Tuition, state resident: full-time $4044; part-time $168.50 per credit hour. Tuition, nonresident: full-time $16,008; part-time $667 per credit hour. *Required fees:* $2122; $88.45 per credit hour. One-time fee: $50. Tuition and fees vary according to course load and campus/location. *Financial support:* In 2011–12, 9 research assistantships (averaging $8,181 per year), 9 teaching assistantships (averaging $9,769 per year) were awarded; career-related internships or fieldwork, Federal Work-Study, scholarships/grants, health care benefits, tuition waivers (partial), and unspecified assistantships also available. Support available to part-time students. Financial award application deadline: 3/1; financial award applicants required to submit FAFSA. *Faculty research:* Hotel operations and management, restaurant/food service management, hospitality education, hospitality human resources management, tourism. *Unit head:* Dr. Bill Ryan, Interim Head, 405-744-6713, Fax: 405-744-6299. *Application contact:* Dr. Sheryl Tucker, Dean, 405-744-7099, Fax: 405-744-0355, E-mail: grad-i@okstate.edu. Web site: http://humansciences.okstate.edu/hrad/.

Penn State University Park, Graduate School, College of Health and Human Development, School of Hospitality Management, State College, University Park, PA 16802-1503. Offers MS, PhD. *Unit head:* Dr. Ann C. Crouter, Dean, 814-865-1428, Fax: 814-865-3282, E-mail: ac1@psu.edu. *Application contact:* Cynthia E. Nicosia, Director, Graduate Enrollment Services, 814-865-1795, Fax: 814-865-4627, E-mail: cey1@psu.edu. Web site: http://www.hhdev.psu.edu/shm.

Pontificia Universidad Catolica Madre y Maestra, Graduate School, Faculty of Social and Administrative Sciences, Santiago, Dominican Republic. Offers business administration (MBA), including business development, finance, international business, management skills (M Mgmt, MBA), marketing, operations, strategic cost management, strategy, tourist destination planning and management; law (LL M), including civil law, corporate business law, criminal law, international relations, real estate law; management (M Mgmt), including higher financial management, insurance program administration, management skills (M Mgmt, MBA); psychology (MA), including clinical child and adolescent psychology, forensic psychology; strategic human resources (EMBA).

Purdue University, Graduate School, College of Health and Human Sciences, Department of Hospitality and Tourism Management, West Lafayette, IN 47907. Offers MS, PhD. *Faculty:* 16 full-time (5 women). *Students:* 75 full-time (56 women), 6 part-time (2 women); includes 3 minority (2 Asian, non-Hispanic/Latino; 1 Hispanic/Latino), 69 international. Average age 27. 179 applicants, 38% accepted, 33 enrolled. In 2011, 8 master's, 7 doctorates awarded. *Degree requirements:* For master's, thesis; for doctorate, thesis/dissertation. *Entrance requirements:* For master's, GMAT with minimum score of 550 total or GRE General Test Combined (new) verbal and quantitative score of 290 or higher (each: minimum of 145) or combined (previous) verbal and quantitative score of 1000 or higher (each minimum of 500), minimum GPA of 3.0; for doctorate, GMAT with minimum score of 550 total or GRE General Test Combined (new) verbal and quantitative score of 290 or higher (each: minimum of 145) or combined (previous) verbal and quantitative score of 1000 or higher (each minimum of 500), minimum undergraduate GPA of 3.0; master's degree with minimum GPA of 3.0 or equivalent. Additional exam requirements/recommendations for international students: Required—TOEFL (minimum score 550 computer-based; 77 iBT), TWE. *Application deadline:* For fall admission, 1/20 priority date for domestic students, 1/20 for international students; for spring admission, 9/20 for domestic and international students. Applications are processed on a rolling basis. Application fee: $60 ($75 for international students). Electronic applications accepted. *Financial support:* Research assistantships, teaching assistantships, and career-related internships or fieldwork available. Support available to part-time students. Financial award applicants required to submit FAFSA. *Faculty research:* Human resources, marketing, hotel and restaurant operations, food product and equipment development, tourism development. *Unit head:* Dr. Richard F. Ghiselli, Head, 765-494-2636, E-mail: ghiselli@purdue.edu. *Application contact:* Maria D. Campos, Graduate Contact, 765-494-9811, E-mail: camposm@purdue.edu. Web site: http://www.cfs.purdue.edu/HTM/.

Rochester Institute of Technology, Graduate Enrollment Services, College of Applied Science and Technology, School of International Hospitality and Service Innovation, Department of Hospitality and Service Management, Program in Hospitality and Tourism Management, Rochester, NY 14623-5603. Offers MS. *Degree requirements:* For master's, thesis or project. *Entrance requirements:* For master's, minimum GPA of 3.0. Additional exam requirements/recommendations for international students: Required—TOEFL (minimum score 550 paper-based; 213 computer-based; 79 iBT) or IELTS (minimum score 6.5). *Application deadline:* For fall admission, 2/15 priority date for domestic students, 2/15 for international students; for winter admission, 11/1 priority date for domestic students, 10/1 for international students; for spring admission, 2/1 priority date for domestic students, 1/1 for international students. Applications are processed on a rolling basis. *Expenses: Tuition:* Full-time $34,659; part-time $963 per credit hour. *Required fees:* $228; $76 per quarter. *Financial support:* Research assistantships with partial tuition reimbursements, teaching assistantships with partial tuition reimbursements, career-related internships or fieldwork, scholarships/grants, and unspecified assistantships available. Support available to part-time students. Financial award application deadline: 2/15; financial award applicants required to submit FAFSA. *Unit head:* Dr. Linda Underhill, Chair, 585-475-7359, Fax: 585-475-5099, E-mail: lmuism@rit.edu. *Application contact:* Diane Ellison, Assistant Vice President, Graduate Enrollment Services, 585-475-2229, Fax: 585-475-7164, E-mail: gradinfo@rit.edu.

Rochester Institute of Technology, Graduate Enrollment Services, College of Applied Science and Technology, School of International Hospitality and Service Innovation, Department of Service Systems, Program in Service Leadership and Innovation, Rochester, NY 14623-5603. Offers MS. Part-time and evening/weekend programs available. Postbaccalaureate distance learning degree programs offered (no on-campus study). *Students:* 19 full-time (14 women), 43 part-time (22 women); includes 1 minority (Black or African American, non-Hispanic/Latino), 25 international. Average age 30. 117 applicants, 50% accepted, 48 enrolled. In 2011, 64 master's awarded. *Degree requirements:* For master's, thesis or alternative. *Entrance requirements:* For master's, minimum GPA of 3.0. Additional exam requirements/recommendations for international students: Required—TOEFL (minimum score 550 paper-based; 213 computer-based; 79 iBT) or IELTS (minimum score 6.5). *Application deadline:* For fall admission, 2/15 priority date for domestic students, 2/15 for international students; for winter admission, 11/1 for domestic and international students; for spring admission, 2/1 for domestic and international students. Applications are processed on a rolling basis. Application fee: $50. Electronic applications accepted. *Expenses: Tuition:* Full-time $34,659; part-time $963 per credit hour. *Required fees:* $228; $76 per quarter. *Financial support:* Research assistantships with partial tuition reimbursements, teaching assistantships with partial tuition reimbursements, career-related internships or fieldwork, institutionally sponsored loans, scholarships/grants, and unspecified assistantships available. Support available to part-time students. Financial award application deadline: 2/15; financial award applicants required to submit FAFSA. *Faculty research:* Global resource development, service/product innovation and implementation. *Unit head:* Dr. Linda Underhill, Department Chair, 585-475-7359, E-mail: lmuism@rit.edu. *Application contact:* Diane Ellison, Assistant Vice President, Graduate Enrollment Services, 585-475-2229, Fax: 585-475-7164, E-mail: gradinfo@rit.edu. Web site: http://www.rit.edu/cast/servicesystems/service-leadership-and-innovation.php.

Roosevelt University, Graduate Division, College of Professional Studies, Program in Hospitality Management, Chicago, IL 60605. Offers MS. *Degree requirements:* For master's, thesis. *Entrance requirements:* For master's, minimum GPA of 2.75, work experience.

Royal Roads University, Graduate Studies, Tourism and Hotel Management Program, Victoria, BC V9B 5Y2, Canada. Offers destination development (Graduate Certificate); international hotel management (MA); sustainable tourism (Graduate Certificate); tourism leadership (Graduate Certificate); tourism management (MA).

Schiller International University, MBA Programs, Florida, Program in International Hotel and Tourism Management, Largo, FL 33770. Offers MBA. *Degree requirements:* For master's, thesis optional. *Entrance requirements:* Additional exam requirements/recommendations for international students: Required—TOEFL (minimum score 550 paper-based; 213 computer-based).

South Dakota State University, Graduate School, College of Education and Human Sciences, Department of Nutrition, Food Science and Hospitality, Brookings, SD 57007. Offers dietetics (MS); nutrition, food science and hospitality (MFCS); nutritional sciences (MS, PhD). Part-time programs available. *Degree requirements:* For master's, comprehensive exam (for some programs), thesis (for some programs), oral exam. *Entrance requirements:* Additional exam requirements/recommendations for international students: Required—TOEFL (minimum score 525 paper-based). *Faculty research:* Food chemistry, bone density, functional food, nutrition education, nutrition biochemistry.

Southern New Hampshire University, School of Business, Manchester, NH 03106-1045. Offers accounting (MS); business administration (MBA, Certificate), including accounting (Certificate), business administration (MBA), finance (Certificate), forensic accounting (Certificate), human resources management (Certificate), international business (Certificate), international sport management (Certificate), leadership of not for profit organizations (Certificate), marketing (Certificate), operations management (Certificate), sport management (Certificate), taxation (Certificate); finance (MS); hospitality and tourism leadership (Certificate); information technology (MS, Certificate); information technology/international business (Certificate); integrated marketing communications (Certificate); international business (MS, DBA); marketing (MS); operations and project management (MS); organizational leadership (MS); project management (Certificate); sport management (MS); MBA/Certificate. *Accreditation:* ACBSP. Part-time and evening/weekend programs available. Postbaccalaureate distance learning degree programs offered (no on-campus study). Terminal master's awarded for partial completion of doctoral program. *Degree requirements:* For master's, one foreign language, comprehensive exam (for some programs), thesis or alternative; for doctorate, one foreign language, comprehensive exam, thesis/dissertation. *Entrance requirements:* For master's, minimum GPA of 2.5; for doctorate, GMAT. Additional exam requirements/recommendations for international students: Required—TOEFL (minimum score 500 paper-based). Electronic applications accepted.

South University, Graduate Programs, College of Business, Savannah, GA 31406. Offers corrections (MBA); entrepreneurship and small business (MBA); healthcare administration (MBA); hospitality management (MBA); leadership (MS); sustainability (MBA).

See Close-Up on page 241.

South University, Program in Business Administration, Atlanta, GA. Offers Accelerated MBA. Program offered by South University, Savannah Campus at Atlanta Learning Site.

See Close-Up on page 229.

Stratford University, Program in International Hospitality Management, Baltimore, MD 21202-3230. Offers MS. Part-time and evening/weekend programs available. Postbaccalaureate distance learning degree programs offered.

Strayer University, Graduate Studies, Washington, DC 20005-2603. Offers accounting (MS); acquisition (MBA); business administration (MBA); communications technology (MS); educational management (M Ed); finance (MBA); health services administration (MHSA); hospitality and tourism management (MBA); human resource management (MBA); information systems (MS), including computer security management, decision support system management, enterprise resource management, network management, software engineering management, systems development management; management (MBA); management information systems (MS); marketing (MBA); professional accounting (MS), including accounting information systems, controllership, taxation; public administration (MPA); supply chain management (MBA); technology in education (M Ed). Programs also offered at campus locations in Birmingham, AL; Chamblee, GA; Cobb County, GA; Morrow, GA; White Marsh, MD; Charleston, SC; Columbia, SC; Greensboro, NC; Greenville, SC; Lexington, KY; Louisville, KY; Nashville, TN; North Raleigh, NC; Washington, DC. Part-time and evening/weekend programs available. Postbaccalaureate distance learning degree programs offered (minimal on-campus study). *Degree requirements:* For master's, thesis. *Entrance requirements:* For master's, GMAT, GRE General Test, bachelor's degree from an accredited college or university, minimum undergraduate GPA of 2.75. Electronic applications accepted.

Temple University, Fox School of Business, Doctoral Programs in Business, Philadelphia, PA 19122-6096. Offers accounting (PhD); entrepreneurship (PhD); finance (PhD); international business (PhD); management information systems (PhD); marketing (PhD); risk management and insurance (PhD); statistics (PhD); strategic management (PhD); tourism and sport (PhD). *Accreditation:* AACSB. *Degree requirements:* For doctorate, thesis/dissertation. *Entrance requirements:* For doctorate, GRE General Test, GMAT, minimum GPA of 3.0, master's degree. Additional exam requirements/recommendations for international students: Required—TOEFL (minimum score 600 paper-based; 250 computer-based; 100 iBT), IELTS (minimum score 7.5). Electronic applications accepted. *Expenses:* Tuition, state resident: full-time $12,366; part-time $687 per credit hour. Tuition, nonresident: full-time $17,298; part-time $961 per credit hour. *Required fees:* $590; $213 per year.

Temple University, School of Tourism and Hospitality Management, Program in Tourism and Hospitality Management, Philadelphia, PA 19122-6096. Offers MTHM. Part-time and evening/weekend programs available. *Faculty:* 8 full-time (2 women). *Students:* 15 full-time (14 women), 3 part-time (2 women); includes 3 minority (1 Black or African American, non-Hispanic/Latino; 1 American Indian or Alaska Native, non-Hispanic/Latino; 1 Asian, non-Hispanic/Latino), 6 international. Average age 25. 31 applicants, 77% accepted, 9 enrolled. In 2011, 9 master's awarded. *Entrance requirements:* For master's, GRE General Test or MAT, minimum of 2 years professional experience, minimum undergraduate GPA of 3.0. Additional exam requirements/recommendations for international students: Required—TOEFL (minimum score 550 paper-based; 213 computer-based; 79 iBT). *Application deadline:* For fall admission, 4/1 priority date for domestic students, 12/15 for international students; for spring admission, 9/30 priority date for domestic students, 8/1 for international students. Application fee: $50. Electronic applications accepted. *Expenses:* Tuition, state resident: full-time $12,366; part-time $687 per credit hour. Tuition, nonresident: full-time $17,298; part-time $961 per credit hour. *Required fees:* $590; $213 per year. *Financial support:* Teaching assistantships available. Financial award application deadline: 1/15; financial award applicants required to submit FAFSA. *Unit head:* Dr. Seoki Lee, Director, Master's Programs, 215-204-0543, E-mail: seokilee@temple.edu. *Application contact:* Tara Schumacher, Coordinator of Outreach, 215-204-6575, Fax: 215-204-8781, E-mail: tara.schumacher@temple.edu. Web site: http://www.temple.edu/STHM/pstudents/tourismhospprograms.htm.

Texas Tech University, Graduate School, College of Human Sciences, Department of Nutrition, Hospitality, and Retailing, Program in Hospitality Administration, Lubbock, TX 79409. Offers PhD. *Students:* 27 full-time (10 women), 12 part-time (6 women); includes 2 minority (both Hispanic/Latino), 28 international. Average age 35. 10 applicants, 70% accepted, 2 enrolled. In 2011, 7 doctorates awarded. *Degree requirements:* For doctorate, thesis/dissertation. *Entrance requirements:* For doctorate, GRE General Test. Additional exam requirements/recommendations for international students: Required—TOEFL (minimum score 550 paper-based; 213 computer-based; 79 iBT). *Application deadline:* For fall admission, 6/1 priority date for domestic students, 1/15 for international students; for spring admission, 9/1 priority date for domestic students, 6/15 for international students. Applications are processed on a rolling basis. Application fee: $50 ($75 for international students). Electronic applications accepted. *Expenses:* Tuition, state resident: full-time $5899; part-time $245.80 per credit hour. Tuition, nonresident: full-time $13,411; part-time $558.80 per credit hour. *Required fees:* $2680.60; $86.50 per credit hour. $920.30 per semester. *Financial support:* Application deadline: 4/15; applicants required to submit FAFSA. *Unit head:* Dr. Shane Blum, Chair, 806-742-3068 Ext. 253, Fax: 806-742-3042, E-mail: shane.blum@ttu.edu. *Application contact:* Dr. Betty Stout, Associate Professor, 806-742-3068 Ext. 233, E-mail: betty.stout@ttu.edu. Web site: http://www.depts.ttu.edu/hs/nhr/rhim/program_doctoral.php.

Texas Tech University, Graduate School, College of Human Sciences, Department of Nutrition, Hospitality, and Retailing, Program in Hospitality and Retail Management, Lubbock, TX 79409. Offers MS. Part-time programs available. *Students:* 18 full-time (13 women), 1 (woman) part-time; includes 3 minority (all Hispanic/Latino), 2 international. Average age 28. 8 applicants, 75% accepted, 6 enrolled. In 2011, 12 master's awarded. *Degree requirements:* For master's, thesis or alternative. *Entrance requirements:* For master's, GRE General Test. Additional exam requirements/recommendations for international students: Required—TOEFL (minimum score 550 paper-based; 213 computer-based; 79 iBT). *Application deadline:* For fall admission, 6/1 priority date for domestic students, 1/15 for international students; for spring admission, 9/1 priority date for domestic students, 6/15 for international students. Applications are processed on a rolling basis. Application fee: $50 ($75 for international students). Electronic applications accepted. *Expenses:* Tuition, state resident: full-time $5899; part-time $245.80 per credit hour. Tuition, nonresident: full-time $13,411; part-time $558.80 per credit hour. *Required fees:* $2680.60; $86.50 per credit hour. $920.30 per semester. *Financial support:* Application deadline: 4/15; applicants required to submit FAFSA. *Faculty research:* Community engagement and food supply development and security, tourism, lodging and human resource management, rural tourism. *Unit head:* Dr. Shane Blum, Chairperson, 806-742-3068 Ext. 253, Fax: 806-742-3042, E-mail: shane.blum@ttu.edu. *Application contact:* Dr. Deborah Fowler, Advisor, 806-742-3068 Ext. 253, Fax: 806-742-3042, E-mail: deborah.fowler@ttu.edu. Web site: http://www.depts.ttu.edu/hs/nhr/rhim.

Troy University, Graduate School, College of Business, Program in Management, Troy, AL 36082. Offers applied management (MSM); healthcare management (MSM); human resources management (MSM); information systems (MSM); international hospitality management (MSM); international management (MSM); leadership and organizational effectiveness (MSM); public management (MS, MSM). *Accreditation:* ACBSP. Evening/weekend programs available. *Faculty:* 21 full-time (6 women), 7 part-time/adjunct (2 women). *Students:* 52 full-time (33 women), 284 part-time (183 women); includes 222 minority (186 Black or African American, non-Hispanic/Latino; 5 American Indian or Alaska Native, non-Hispanic/Latino; 11 Asian, non-Hispanic/Latino; 13 Hispanic/Latino; 1 Native Hawaiian or other Pacific Islander, non-Hispanic/Latino; 6 Two or more races, non-Hispanic/Latino). Average age 35. 157 applicants, 76% accepted, 55 enrolled. In 2011, 234 master's awarded. *Degree requirements:* For master's, Graduate Educational Testing Service Major Field Test, capstone exam, minimum GPA of 3.0. *Entrance requirements:* For master's, GMAT (minimum score 500) or GRE General Test (minimum score 900), minimum GPA of 2.5, bachelor's degree, letter of recommendation. Additional exam requirements/recommendations for international students: Required—TOEFL (minimum score 523 paper-based; 193 computer-based; 70 iBT), IELTS (minimum score 6), or ACT COMPASS ESL (minimum listening, reading, and grammar score 270). *Application deadline:* Applications are processed on a rolling basis. Application fee: $50. Electronic applications accepted. *Expenses:* Contact institution. *Unit head:* Dr. Edward Merkel, Director, Graduate Business Programs, 334-670-3194, Fax: 334-670-3599, E-mail: emerkel@troy.edu. *Application contact:* Brenda K. Campbell, Director of Graduate Admissions, 334-670-3178, Fax: 334-670-3733, E-mail: bcamp@troy.edu.

The University of Alabama, Graduate School, College of Human Environmental Sciences, Department of Human Nutrition and Hospitality Management, Tuscaloosa, AL 35487. Offers MSHES. Part-time programs available. Postbaccalaureate distance learning degree programs offered (no on-campus study). *Faculty:* 7 full-time (5 women). *Students:* 11 full-time (9 women), 77 part-time (all women); includes 12 minority (7 Black or African American, non-Hispanic/Latino; 2 Asian, non-Hispanic/Latino; 3 Hispanic/Latino). Average age 30. 54 applicants, 59% accepted, 25 enrolled. In 2011, 34 degrees awarded. *Degree requirements:* For master's, comprehensive exam, thesis optional. *Entrance requirements:* For master's, minimum GPA of 3.0. Additional exam requirements/recommendations for international students: Required—TOEFL. *Application deadline:* For fall admission, 7/6 for domestic students. Applications are processed on a rolling basis. Application fee: $50 ($60 for international students). Electronic applications accepted. *Expenses:* Tuition, state resident: full-time $8600. Tuition, nonresident: full-time $21,900. *Financial support:* In 2011–12, 4 students received support, including 2 research assistantships (averaging $8,100 per year), 4 teaching assistantships (averaging $8,100 per year); career-related internships or fieldwork also available. Financial award application deadline: 3/15. *Faculty research:* Maternal and child nutrition, childhood obesity, community nutrition interventions, geriatric nutrition, family eating patterns, food chemistry, phytochemicals, dietary antioxidants. *Total annual research expenditures:* $60,305. *Unit head:* Dr. Mary K. Meyer, Chair/Professor, 205-348-6150, Fax: 205-348-3789, E-mail: mkmeyer@ches.ua.edu. *Application contact:* Patrick D. Fuller, Admissions Officer, 205-348-5923, Fax: 205-348-0400, E-mail: patrick.d.fuller@ua.edu. Web site: http://www.ches.ua.edu/.

The University of Alabama, Graduate School, College of Human Environmental Sciences, Program in Human Environmental Science, Tuscaloosa, AL 35487. Offers family financial planning and counseling (MS); interactive technology (MS); quality management (MS); restaurant and meeting management (MS); rural community health (MS); sport management (MS). *Faculty:* 1 full-time (0 women). *Students:* 80 full-time (53 women), 93 part-time (55 women); includes 51 minority (42 Black or African American, non-Hispanic/Latino; 3 American Indian or Alaska Native, non-Hispanic/Latino; 3 Hispanic/Latino; 3 Two or more races, non-Hispanic/Latino), 1 international. Average age 33. 118 applicants, 79% accepted, 75 enrolled. In 2011, 83 degrees awarded. *Degree requirements:* For master's, comprehensive exam. *Entrance requirements:* For master's, GRE (for some specializations), minimum GPA of 3.0. Additional exam requirements/recommendations for international students: Required—TOEFL. *Application deadline:* Applications are processed on a rolling basis. Application fee: $50 ($60 for international students). Electronic applications accepted. *Expenses:* Tuition, state resident: full-time $8600. Tuition, nonresident: full-time $21,900. *Faculty research:* Hospitality management, sports medicine education, technology and education. *Unit head:* Dr. Milla D. Boschung, Dean, 205-348-6250, Fax: 205-348-1786, E-mail: mboschun@ches.ua.edu. *Application contact:* Dr. Stuart Usdan, Associate Dean, 205-348-6150, Fax: 205-348-7899, E-mail: susdan@ches.ua.edu.

University of Central Florida, Rosen College of Hospitality Management, Orlando, FL 32816. Offers hospitality and tourism management (MS). *Faculty:* 47 full-time (17 women), 27 part-time/adjunct (11 women). *Students:* 61 full-time (45 women), 46 part-time (33 women); includes 16 minority (7 Black or African American, non-Hispanic/Latino; 4 Asian, non-Hispanic/Latino; 5 Hispanic/Latino), 35 international. Average age 27. 115 applicants, 57% accepted, 46 enrolled. In 2011, 29 master's awarded. *Degree requirements:* For master's, thesis or alternative. *Entrance requirements:* For master's, GMAT or GRE, minimum GPA of 3.0 in last 60 hours. Additional exam requirements/recommendations for international students: Required—TOEFL. *Application deadline:* For fall admission, 2/1 for domestic students. Application fee: $30. Electronic applications accepted. *Expenses:* Tuition, state resident: part-time $277.08 per credit hour. Tuition, nonresident: part-time $277.08 per credit hour. Part-time tuition and fees vary according to degree level and program. *Financial support:* In 2011–12, 9 students received support, including 8 fellowships with partial tuition reimbursements available (averaging $4,400 per year), 1 teaching assistantship (averaging $7,100 per year). *Unit head:* Dr. Abraham C. Pizam, Dean, 407-903-8010, E-mail: abraham.pizam@ucf.edu. *Application contact:* Barbara Rodriguez, Director, Admissions and Registration, 407-823-2766, Fax: 407-823-6442, E-mail: gradadmissions@ucf.edu. Web site: http://www.hospitality.ucf.edu/.

University of Delaware, Alfred Lerner College of Business and Economics, Program in Hospitality Information Management, Newark, DE 19716. Offers MS. *Entrance requirements:* Additional exam requirements/recommendations for international students: Required—TOEFL (minimum score 550 paper-based; 213 computer-based). Electronic applications accepted. *Faculty research:* Foodservice, lodging and tourism management.

The University of Findlay, Graduate and Professional Studies, College of Business, Findlay, OH 45840-3653. Offers health care management (MBA); hospitality management (MBA); organizational leadership (MBA); public management (MBA). Part-time and evening/weekend programs available. Postbaccalaureate distance learning degree programs offered (no on-campus study). *Faculty:* 18 full-time (5 women), 1 part-time/adjunct (0 women). *Students:* 25 full-time (15 women), 184 part-time (100 women); includes 13 minority (3 Black or African American, non-Hispanic/Latino; 7 Asian, non-Hispanic/Latino; 3 Hispanic/Latino), 78 international. Average age 25. 72 applicants, 82% accepted, 24 enrolled. In 2011, 168 master's awarded. *Degree requirements:* For master's, thesis, cumulative project. *Entrance requirements:* For master's, GMAT or GRE, bachelor's degree from accredited institution, minimum undergraduate GPA of 3.0. Additional exam requirements/recommendations for international students: Required—TOEFL (minimum score 550 paper-based; 213 computer-based; 80 iBT). *Application deadline:* Applications are processed on a rolling basis. Application fee: $25. Electronic applications accepted. *Expenses:* Contact institution. *Financial support:* In 2011–12, 5 research assistantships with full and partial tuition reimbursements (averaging $4,200 per year) were awarded; career-related internships or fieldwork, Federal Work-Study, health care benefits, and unspecified assistantships also available. Financial award application deadline: 4/1; financial award applicants required to submit FAFSA. *Faculty research:* Health care management, operations and logistics management. *Unit head:* Dr. Paul Sears, Dean, 419-434-4704, Fax: 419-434-4822. *Application contact:* Heather Riffle, Assistant Director, Graduate and Professional Studies, 419-434-4640, Fax: 419-434-5517, E-mail: riffle@findlay.edu. Web site: http://www.findlay.edu/.

University of Guelph, Graduate Studies, College of Management and Economics, MBA Program, Guelph, ON N1G 2W1, Canada. Offers food and agribusiness management (MBA); hospitality and tourism management (MBA). Part-time and evening/weekend programs available. Postbaccalaureate distance learning degree programs offered (minimal on-campus study). *Entrance requirements:* For master's, minimum B-average, minimum of 3 years of relevant work experience. Additional exam requirements/recommendations for international students: Required—TOEFL (minimum score 550 paper-based; 213 computer-based). Electronic applications accepted. *Faculty research:* Marketing, operations management, business policy, financial management, organizational behavior.

University of Houston, Conrad N. Hilton College of Hotel and Restaurant Management, Houston, TX 77204. Offers hospitality management (MS). Part-time programs available. *Degree requirements:* For master's, practicum or thesis. *Entrance requirements:* For master's, GMAT or GRE General Test. Additional exam requirements/recommendations for international students: Required—TOEFL (minimum score 100 iBT) or IELTS (minimum score 7). Electronic applications accepted. *Faculty research:* Catering, tourism, hospitality marketing, security and risk management, purchasing and financial information usage.

University of Kentucky, Graduate School, College of Agriculture, Program in Hospitality and Dietetic Administration, Lexington, KY 40506-0032. Offers MS. *Degree requirements:* For master's, comprehensive exam, thesis optional. *Entrance requirements:* For master's, GRE General Test, minimum undergraduate GPA of 2.75. Additional exam requirements/recommendations for international students: Required—TOEFL (minimum score 550 paper-based; 213 computer-based). Electronic applications accepted.

University of Massachusetts Amherst, Graduate School, Isenberg School of Management, Program in Management, Amherst, MA 01003. Offers accounting (PhD); business administration (MBA); business administration/sport management (MBA/MS); finance (PhD); hospitality and tourism management (PhD); management science (PhD); marketing (PhD); organization studies (PhD); sport management (PhD); strategic management (PhD); MBA/MS; MPH/MPPA. *Accreditation:* AACSB. Part-time programs available. *Faculty:* 61 full-time (14 women). *Students:* 92 full-time (34 women), 9 part-time (3 women); includes 8 minority (1 Black or African American, non-Hispanic/Latino; 4 Asian, non-Hispanic/Latino; 3 Hispanic/Latino), 47 international. Average age 33. 340 applicants, 15% accepted, 29 enrolled. In 2011, 31 master's, 13 doctorates awarded. Terminal master's awarded for partial completion of doctoral program. *Degree requirements:* For doctorate, comprehensive exam, thesis/dissertation. *Entrance requirements:* For master's and doctorate, GMAT. Additional exam requirements/recommendations for international students: Required—TOEFL (minimum score 550 paper-based; 213 computer-based; 80 iBT), IELTS (minimum score 6.5). *Application deadline:* For fall admission, 1/20 for domestic and international students. Applications are processed on a rolling basis. Application fee: $50 ($65 for international students). Electronic applications accepted. Tuition and fees vary according to course load, campus/location and program. *Financial support:* Fellowships with full and partial tuition reimbursements, research assistantships with full and partial tuition reimbursements, teaching assistantships with full and partial tuition reimbursements, career-related internships or fieldwork, Federal Work-Study, scholarships/grants, traineeships, health care benefits, tuition waivers (full and partial), and unspecified assistantships available. Support available to part-time students. Financial award application deadline: 1/20. *Unit head:* Dr. William Woodridge, Chair, 413-545-5675, Fax: 413-577-2234. *Application contact:* Lindsay DeSantis, Interim Supervisor of Admissions, 413-545-0722, Fax: 413-577-0010, E-mail: gradadm@grad.umass.edu. Web site: http://www.isenberg.umass.edu/.

University of Missouri, Graduate School, College of Agriculture, Food and Natural Resources, Department of Food Science, Columbia, MO 65211. Offers food science (MS, PhD); foods and food systems management (MS); human nutrition (MS). *Faculty:* 12 full-time (4 women), 2 part-time/adjunct (0 women). *Students:* 37 full-time (23 women), 11 part-time (3 women); includes 1 minority (Hispanic/Latino), 31 international. Average age 26. 67 applicants, 37% accepted, 16 enrolled. In 2011, 7 degrees awarded. Terminal master's awarded for partial completion of doctoral program. *Degree requirements:* For doctorate, comprehensive exam, thesis/dissertation. *Entrance requirements:* For master's, GRE General Test (minimum score: Verbal and Quantitative 1000 with neither section below 400, Analytical 3.5), minimum GPA of 3.0; BS in food science from accredited university; for doctorate, GRE General Test (minimum score: Verbal and Quantitative 1000 with neither section below 400, Analytical 3.5), minimum GPA of 3.0; BS and MS in food science from accredited university. Additional exam requirements/recommendations for international students: Required—TOEFL (minimum score 550 paper-based; 79 iBT). *Application deadline:* For fall admission, 4/1 priority date for domestic students; for winter admission, 10/1 priority date for domestic students. Applications are processed on a rolling basis. Application fee: $55 ($75 for international students). Electronic applications accepted. *Expenses:* Tuition, state resident: full-time $5881. Tuition, nonresident: full-time $15,183. *Required fees:* $952. Tuition and fees vary according to campus/location and program. *Financial support:* Fellowships, research assistantships with tuition reimbursements, teaching assistantships with tuition reimbursements, institutionally sponsored loans, scholarships/grants, health care benefits, and unspecified assistantships available. Support available to part-time students. *Faculty research:* Food chemistry, food analysis, food microbiology, food engineering and process control, functional foods, meat science and processing technology. *Unit head:* Dr. Jinglu Tan, Department Chair, 573-882-2369, E-mail: tanj@missouri.edu. *Application contact:* JoAnn Lewis, 573-882-4113, E-mail: lewisj@missouri.edu. Web site: http://foodscience.missouri.edu/graduate/.

University of Nevada, Las Vegas, Graduate College, William F. Harrah College of Hotel Administration, Program in Hotel Administration, Las Vegas, NV 89154-6013. Offers hospitality administration (MHA, PhD); hospitality administration-Singapore (MHA); hotel administration (MS). MHA program also offered in Singapore. Part-time programs available. Postbaccalaureate distance learning degree programs offered (no on-campus study). *Faculty:* 31 full-time (8 women), 14 part-time/adjunct (4 women). *Students:* 48 full-time (28 women), 95 part-time (43 women); includes 21 minority (6 Black or African American, non-Hispanic/Latino; 1 American Indian or Alaska Native, non-Hispanic/Latino; 5 Asian, non-Hispanic/Latino; 5 Hispanic/Latino; 4 Two or more races, non-Hispanic/Latino), 45 international. Average age 32. 161 applicants, 37% accepted, 35 enrolled. In 2011, 83 master's, 4 doctorates awarded. *Degree requirements:* For master's, comprehensive exam, thesis (for some programs), professional paper; for doctorate, comprehensive exam, thesis/dissertation, dissertation defense, seminar. *Entrance requirements:* Additional exam requirements/recommendations for international students: Required—TOEFL (minimum score 550 paper-based; 213 computer-based; 80 iBT), IELTS (minimum score 7). *Application deadline:* For fall admission, 2/1 priority date for domestic students, 5/1 for international students; for spring admission, 10/1 priority date for domestic students, 10/1 for international students. Applications are processed on a rolling basis. Application fee: $60 ($95 for international students). Electronic applications accepted. *Financial support:* In 2011–12, 29 students received support, including 16 research assistantships with partial tuition reimbursements available (averaging $9,852 per year), 13 teaching assistantships with partial tuition reimbursements available (averaging $11,933 per year); institutionally sponsored loans, scholarships/grants, health care benefits, and unspecified assistantships also available. Financial award application deadline: 3/1. *Faculty research:* Sustainable development and green strategies, self-service technology applications, branding and brand equity, employee engagement and leadership, pricing and loyalty in foodservice operations. *Total annual research expenditures:* $87,917. *Unit head:* Dr. Pearl Brewer, Chair/Professor, 702-895-3643, Fax: 702-895-4872, E-mail: pearl.brewer@unlv.edu. *Application contact:* Graduate College Admissions Evaluator, 702-895-3320, Fax: 702-895-4180, E-mail: gradcollege@unlv.edu. Web site: http://hotel.unlv.edu.

University of New Orleans, Graduate School, College of Business Administration, School of Hotel, Restaurant, and Tourism Administration, Program in Hospitality and Tourism Management, New Orleans, LA 70148. Offers MS. *Entrance requirements:* Additional exam requirements/recommendations for international students: Required—TOEFL (minimum score 550 paper-based; 213 computer-based; 79 iBT).

University of North Texas, Toulouse Graduate School, School of Merchandising and Hospitality Management, Denton, TX 76203. Offers hospitality management (MS); merchandising (MS). Part-time programs available. Postbaccalaureate distance learning degree programs offered (no on-campus study). *Degree requirements:* For master's, comprehensive exam, thesis or alternative. *Entrance requirements:* For master's, GRE General Test or GMAT, minimum GPA of 2.8, course work in major area, 3 references, resume. Additional exam requirements/recommendations for international students: Recommended—TOEFL (minimum score 550 paper-based; 213 computer-based; 79 iBT). Electronic applications accepted. *Expenses:* Tuition, state resident: part-time $100 per credit hour. Tuition, nonresident: part-time $413 per credit hour. *Faculty research:* Management, hospitality, merchandising, globalization, consumer behavior and experiences.

University of South Carolina, The Graduate School, College of Hospitality, Retail, and Sport Management, School of Hotel, Restaurant and Tourism Management, Columbia, SC 29208. Offers MIHTM. *Entrance requirements:* For master's, GMAT or GRE General Test, minimum GPA of 3.0, 2 letters of recommendation. Electronic applications accepted. *Faculty research:* Corporate strategy and management practices, sustainable tourism, club management, tourism technology, revenue management.

University of South Florida Sarasota-Manatee, School of Hotel and Restaurant Management, Sarasota, FL 34243. Offers hospitality management (MS). Part-time programs available. *Faculty:* 3 full-time (1 woman). *Students:* 4 full-time (2 women), 3 part-time (2 women); includes 1 minority (Hispanic/Latino), 2 international. Average age 32. 13 applicants, 69% accepted, 7 enrolled. *Entrance requirements:* For master's, GRE/GMAT. Additional exam requirements/recommendations for international students: Required—TOEFL or IELTS. *Application deadline:* For fall admission, 6/1 for domestic students, 3/15 for international students; for spring admission, 10/15 for domestic students, 8/15 for international students. Applications are processed on a rolling basis. Application fee: $30. Electronic applications accepted. *Expenses:* Tuition, state resident: full-time $9301; part-time $387.55 per credit hour. Tuition, nonresident: full-time $19,412; part-time $808.85 per credit hour. *Required fees:* $15; $5 per semester. One-time fee: $30. *Financial support:* In 2011–12, 2 students received support, including 2 research assistantships (averaging $9,180 per year); Federal Work-Study, scholarships/grants, health care benefits, and unspecified assistantships also available. Support available to part-time students. Financial award application deadline: 3/1; financial award applicants required to submit FAFSA. *Faculty research:* Technology's impact on hospitality industry, hospitality accounting and cost control, international tourism development, service quality. *Unit head:* Dr. Cihan Cobanoglu, Dean, 941-359-4244, E-mail: cihan@sar.usf.edu. *Application contact:* Jo Lynn Raudebaugh, Graduate Admissions Advisor, 941-359-4587. Web site: http://www.sarasota.usf.edu/Academics/SHRM/.

The University of Tennessee, Graduate School, College of Education, Health and Human Sciences, Department of Consumer and Industry Services Management, Program in Hotel, Restaurant, and Tourism Management, Knoxville, TN 37996. Offers hospitality management (MS); tourism (MS). Part-time programs available. *Degree requirements:* For master's, thesis or alternative. *Entrance requirements:* For master's, GRE General Test, minimum GPA of 2.7. Additional exam requirements/recommendations for international students: Required—TOEFL. Electronic applications accepted. *Expenses:* Tuition, state resident: full-time $8332; part-time $464 per credit hour. Tuition, nonresident: full-time $25,174; part-time $1400 per credit hour. *Required fees:* $1162; $56 per credit hour. Tuition and fees vary according to program.

Virginia Polytechnic Institute and State University, Graduate School, Pamplin College of Business, Department of Hospitality and Tourism Management, Blacksburg, VA 24061. Offers MS, PhD. *Degree requirements:* For master's, comprehensive exam (for some programs), thesis (for some programs); for doctorate, comprehensive exam (for some programs), thesis/dissertation (for some programs). *Entrance requirements:* For master's and doctorate, GRE. Additional exam requirements/recommendations for international students: Required—TOEFL (minimum score 550 paper-based; 213 computer-based). *Application deadline:* For fall admission, 7/1 for domestic and international students; for spring admission, 12/1 for domestic and international students. Applications are processed on a rolling basis. Application fee: $65. Electronic applications accepted. *Expenses:* Tuition, state resident: full-time $10,048; part-time $558.25 per credit hour. Tuition, nonresident: full-time $19,497; part-time $1083.25 per credit hour. *Required fees:* $405 per semester. Tuition and fees vary according to course load, campus/location and program. *Financial support:* In 2011–12, 1 research assistantship with full tuition reimbursement (averaging $12,053 per year), 3 teaching assistantships with full tuition reimbursements (averaging $12,861 per year) were awarded; career-related internships or fieldwork, Federal Work-Study, scholarships/grants, health care benefits, and unspecified assistantships also available. Financial award application deadline: 1/15. *Faculty research:* Human resource management, service management, marketing, strategy and finance tourist behavior. *Unit head:* Dr. Rick R. Perdue, Unit Head, 540-231-5515, Fax: 540-231-8313, E-mail: rick.perdue@vt.edu. *Application contact:* Nancy McGehee, Information Contact, 540-231-1201, Fax: 540-231-8313, E-mail: nmcgehee@vt.edu. Web site: http://www.htm.pamplin.vt.edu/.

Travel and Tourism

Arizona State University, College of Public Programs, School of Community Resources and Development, Phoenix, AZ 85004-0685. Offers community resources and development (PhD); nonprofit leadership and management (Graduate Certificate); nonprofit studies (MNpS); recreation and tourism studies (MS). Part-time and evening/weekend programs available. Terminal master's awarded for partial completion of doctoral program. *Degree requirements:* For master's, thesis or alternative, interactive

Program of Study (iPOS) submitted before completing 50 percent of required credit hours; for doctorate, comprehensive exam, thesis/dissertation, interactive Program of Study (iPOS) submitted before completing 50 percent of required credit hours. *Entrance requirements:* For master's and doctorate, GRE, minimum GPA of 3.0 or equivalent in last 2 years of work leading to bachelor's degree. Additional exam requirements/recommendations for international students: Required—TOEFL (minimum score 80 iBT), TOEFL, IELTS, or Pearson Test of English. Electronic applications accepted. *Expenses:* Contact institution.

Boston University, Metropolitan College, Department of Administrative Sciences, Boston, MA 02215. Offers banking and financial management (MSM); business continuity in emergency management (MSM); economics development and tourism management (MSAS); electronic commerce, systems, and technology (MSAS); financial economics (MSAS); innovation and technology (MSAS); insurance management (MSM); international market management (MSM); multinational commerce (MSAS); project management (MSM). *Accreditation:* AACSB. Part-time and evening/weekend programs available. Postbaccalaureate distance learning degree programs offered (no on-campus study). *Faculty:* 14 full-time (2 women), 21 part-time/adjunct (2 women). *Students:* 151 full-time (75 women), 106 part-time (51 women); includes 27 minority (6 Black or African American, non-Hispanic/Latino; 14 Asian, non-Hispanic/Latino; 7 Hispanic/Latino), 173 international. Average age 28. 500 applicants, 65% accepted, 194 enrolled. In 2011, 154 master's awarded. *Degree requirements:* For master's, thesis optional. *Entrance requirements:* For master's, 1 year of work experience, minimum GPA of 3.0. Additional exam requirements/recommendations for international students: Required—TOEFL (minimum score 560 paper-based; 220 computer-based; 84 iBT). *Application deadline:* Applications are processed on a rolling basis. Application fee: $70. Electronic applications accepted. *Expenses: Tuition:* Full-time $40,848; part-time $1276 per credit hour. *Required fees:* $572; $286 per semester. *Financial support:* In 2011–12, 15 students received support, including 7 research assistantships (averaging $10,000 per year); career-related internships or fieldwork, Federal Work-Study, and unspecified assistantships also available. *Faculty research:* International business, innovative process. *Unit head:* Dr. Kip Becker, Chairman, 617-353-3016, E-mail: adminsc@bu.edu. *Application contact:* Lucille Dicker, Administrative Sciences Department, 617-353-3016, E-mail: adminsc@bu.edu. Web site: http://www.bu.edu/met/programs/.

California State University, East Bay, Office of Academic Programs and Graduate Studies, College of Education and Allied Studies, Department of Hospitality, Recreation and Tourism, Hayward, CA 94542-3000. Offers recreation and tourism (MS). Part-time and evening/weekend programs available. Postbaccalaureate distance learning degree programs offered (no on-campus study). *Faculty:* 3 full-time (2 women), 1 (woman) part-time/adjunct. *Students:* 32 full-time (21 women), 22 part-time (13 women); includes 16 minority (5 Black or African American, non-Hispanic/Latino; 5 Asian, non-Hispanic/Latino; 4 Hispanic/Latino; 2 Two or more races, non-Hispanic/Latino). Average age 36. 38 applicants, 74% accepted, 24 enrolled. In 2011, 11 master's awarded. *Degree requirements:* For master's, thesis optional. *Entrance requirements:* For master's, minimum GPA of 2.75; 2 years' related work experience; 3 letters of recommendation; resume; baccalaureate degree. Additional exam requirements/recommendations for international students: Required—TOEFL (minimum score 550 paper-based; 237 computer-based). *Application deadline:* For fall admission, 6/30 for domestic and international students. Applications are processed on a rolling basis. Application fee: $55. Electronic applications accepted. *Expenses:* Tuition, state resident: full-time $6738; part-time $1302 per quarter. Tuition, nonresident: full-time $12,690; part-time $2294 per quarter. *Required fees:* $449 per quarter. Tuition and fees vary according to degree level, program and reciprocity agreements. *Financial support:* Federal Work-Study, institutionally sponsored loans, and scholarships/grants available. Support available to part-time students. Financial award application deadline: 3/2; financial award applicants required to submit FAFSA. *Faculty research:* Leisure, online vs. F2F learning, risk management, leadership, tourism consumer behavior. *Unit head:* Dr. Melany Spielman, Chair/Recreation Graduate Advisor, 510-885-3043, E-mail: melany.spielman@csueastbay.edu. Web site: http://www20.csueastbay.edu/ceas/departments/hrt/.

California State University, Fullerton, Graduate Studies, College of Communications, Department of Communications, Fullerton, CA 92834-9480. Offers advertising (MA); communications (MFA); entertainment and tourism (MA); journalism (MA); public relations (MA). Part-time programs available. *Students:* 31 full-time (21 women), 37 part-time (27 women); includes 23 minority (4 Black or African American, non-Hispanic/Latino; 8 Asian, non-Hispanic/Latino; 9 Hispanic/Latino; 2 Two or more races, non-Hispanic/Latino), 7 international. Average age 29. 96 applicants, 35% accepted, 22 enrolled. In 2011, 38 master's awarded. *Degree requirements:* For master's, project or thesis. *Entrance requirements:* For master's, GRE General Test. Application fee: $55. *Financial support:* Teaching assistantships, career-related internships or fieldwork, Federal Work-Study, institutionally sponsored loans, and scholarships/grants available. Support available to part-time students. Financial award application deadline: 3/1; financial award applicants required to submit FAFSA. *Unit head:* Dr. Tony Fellow, Chair, 657-278-3517. *Application contact:* Coordinator, 657-278-3832.

California State University, Northridge, Graduate Studies, College of Health and Human Development, Department of Recreation and Tourism Management, Northridge, CA 91330. Offers hospitality and tourism (MS); recreational sport management/campus recreation (MS). *Degree requirements:* For master's, thesis (for some programs). *Entrance requirements:* For master's, GRE (if cumulative undergraduate GPA less than 3.0). Additional exam requirements/recommendations for international students: Required—TOEFL.

Clemson University, Graduate School, College of Health, Education, and Human Development, Department of Parks, Recreation, and Tourism Management, Clemson, SC 29634. Offers MS, PhD. Part-time programs available. Postbaccalaureate distance learning degree programs offered (no on-campus study). *Faculty:* 17 full-time (7 women). *Students:* 61 full-time (29 women), 7 part-time (6 women); includes 1 minority (Hispanic/Latino), 21 international. Average age 32. 116 applicants, 80% accepted, 26 enrolled. In 2011, 6 master's, 5 doctorates awarded. *Degree requirements:* For master's, thesis (for some programs); for doctorate, thesis/dissertation. *Entrance requirements:* For master's, GRE General Test, minimum undergraduate GPA of 3.0; for doctorate, GRE General Test, minimum graduate GPA of 3.0. Additional exam requirements/recommendations for international students: Required—TOEFL. *Application deadline:* For fall admission, 5/1 priority date for domestic students; for spring admission, 10/1 for domestic students. Applications are processed on a rolling basis. Application fee: $70 ($80 for international students). Electronic applications accepted. *Financial support:* In 2011–12, 50 students received support, including 2 research assistantships with partial tuition reimbursements available (averaging $9,400 per year), 66 teaching assistantships with partial tuition reimbursements available (averaging $5,350 per year); fellowships with full and partial tuition reimbursements available, career-related internships or fieldwork, scholarships/grants, health care benefits, tuition waivers (partial), and unspecified assistantships also available. Support available to part-time students. Financial award application deadline: 1/15; financial award applicants required to submit FAFSA. *Faculty research:* Recreation resource management, leisure behavior, therapeutic recreation, community leisure . *Total annual research expenditures:* $380,421. *Unit head:* Dr. Brett A. Wright, Chair, 864-656-3036, Fax: 864-656-2226, E-mail: wright@clemson.edu. *Application contact:* Dr. Denise M. Anderson, Graduate Coordinator, 864-656-5679, Fax: 864-656-2226, E-mail: dander2@clemson.edu. Web site: http://www.hehd.clemson.edu/prtm/.

Eastern Michigan University, Graduate School, College of Arts and Sciences, Department of Geography and Geology, Program in Historic Preservation, Ypsilanti, MI 48197. Offers heritage interpretation and tourism (MS); historic preservation (MS, Graduate Certificate). Part-time and evening/weekend programs available. Postbaccalaureate distance learning degree programs offered (minimal on-campus study). *Students:* 11 full-time (9 women), 65 part-time (48 women); includes 1 minority (Black or African American, non-Hispanic/Latino). Average age 34. 39 applicants, 79% accepted, 18 enrolled. In 2011, 15 master's, 3 other advanced degrees awarded. *Entrance requirements:* Additional exam requirements/recommendations for international students: Required—TOEFL. *Application deadline:* Applications are processed on a rolling basis. Application fee: $35. *Expenses:* Tuition, state resident: full-time $10,367; part-time $432 per credit hour. Tuition, nonresident: full-time $20,435; part-time $851 per credit hour. *Required fees:* $39 per credit hour. $46 per semester. One-time fee: $100. Tuition and fees vary according to course level, degree level and reciprocity agreements. *Financial support:* Fellowships, research assistantships with full tuition reimbursements, teaching assistantships with full tuition reimbursements, career-related internships or fieldwork, Federal Work-Study, institutionally sponsored loans, scholarships/grants, tuition waivers (partial), and unspecified assistantships available. Support available to part-time students. Financial award applicants required to submit FAFSA. *Unit head:* Dr. Richard Sambrook, Department Head, 734-487-0218, Fax: 734-487-6979, E-mail: rsambroo@emich.edu. *Application contact:* Dr. Ted Ligibel, Program Advisor, 734-487-0232, Fax: 734-487-6979, E-mail: tligibel@emich.edu.

East Stroudsburg University of Pennsylvania, Graduate School, College of Business and Management, Department of Hotel, Restaurant and Tourism Management, East Stroudsburg, PA 18301-2999. Offers management and leadership (MS). Part-time and evening/weekend programs available. *Degree requirements:* For master's, comprehensive exam. *Entrance requirements:* For master's, GRE or GMAT, 3 letters of recommendation. Additional exam requirements/recommendations for international students: Required—TOEFL (minimum score 560 paper-based; 220 computer-based; 83 iBT).

Florida Atlantic University, College of Design and Social Inquiry, School of Urban and Regional Planning, Boca Raton, FL 33431-0991. Offers economic development and tourism (Certificate); environmental planning (Certificate); sustainable community planning (Certificate); urban and regional planning (MURP); visual planning technology (Certificate). *Accreditation:* ACSP. Part-time and evening/weekend programs available. *Faculty:* 7 full-time (5 women), 4 part-time/adjunct (3 women). *Students:* 22 full-time (12 women), 10 part-time (5 women); includes 17 minority (6 Black or African American, non-Hispanic/Latino; 1 Asian, non-Hispanic/Latino; 10 Hispanic/Latino), 1 international. Average age 30. 53 applicants, 57% accepted, 6 enrolled. In 2011, 19 master's awarded. *Entrance requirements:* For master's, GRE General Test, minimum GPA of 3.0. Additional exam requirements/recommendations for international students: Required—TOEFL. *Application deadline:* For fall admission, 5/1 priority date for domestic students, 2/15 for international students; for spring admission, 11/1 priority date for domestic students, 7/15 for international students. Applications are processed on a rolling basis. Application fee: $30. *Expenses: Tuition, area resident:* Part-time $343.02 per credit hour. Tuition, state resident: full-time $8232. Tuition, nonresident: full-time $23,931; part-time $997.14 per credit hour. *Financial support:* Fellowships with full tuition reimbursements, research assistantships, career-related internships or fieldwork, Federal Work-Study, institutionally sponsored loans, and tuition waivers (partial) available. Financial award application deadline: 4/1. *Faculty research:* Growth management, urban design, computer applications/geographical information systems, environmental planning. *Unit head:* Dr. Jaap Vos, Chair, 954-762-5653, Fax: 954-762-5673, E-mail: jvos@fau.edu. *Application contact:* Dr. Sofia Do Espirito Santo, 954-762-5158, E-mail: ssanto@fau.edu. Web site: http://www.fau.edu/durp/.

The George Washington University, School of Business, Department of Tourism and Hospitality Management, Washington, DC 20052. Offers event and meeting management (MTA); event management (Professional Certificate); hospitality management (MTA, Professional Certificate); sport management (MTA); sports business management (Professional Certificate); sustainable tourism destination management (MTA); tourism administration (MTA); tourism and hospitality management (MBA); tourism destination management (Professional Certificate). Part-time programs available. Postbaccalaureate distance learning degree programs offered. *Faculty:* 9 full-time (5 women), 11 part-time/adjunct (5 women). *Students:* 84 full-time (62 women), 107 part-time (77 women); includes 43 minority (27 Black or African American, non-Hispanic/Latino; 2 American Indian or Alaska Native, non-Hispanic/Latino; 5 Asian, non-Hispanic/Latino; 9 Hispanic/Latino), 38 international. Average age 30. 152 applicants, 74% accepted, 56 enrolled. In 2011, 69 master's awarded. *Degree requirements:* For master's, comprehensive exam, thesis. *Entrance requirements:* For master's, GRE General Test. Additional exam requirements/recommendations for international students: Required—TOEFL. *Application deadline:* For fall admission, 4/1 priority date for domestic students; for spring admission, 10/1 for domestic students. Applications are processed on a rolling basis. Application fee: $75. *Financial support:* In 2011–12, 32 students received support. Fellowships, teaching assistantships, career-related internships or fieldwork, Federal Work-Study, institutionally sponsored loans, and tuition waivers (partial) available. Financial award application deadline: 4/1. *Faculty research:* Tourism policy, tourism impact forecasting, geotourism. *Unit head:* Susan M. Phillips, Dean, 202-994-6380, E-mail: gwsbdean@gwu.edu. *Application contact:* Kristin Williams, Assistant Vice President for Graduate and Special Enrollment Management, 202-994-0467, Fax: 202-994-0371, E-mail: ksw@gwu.edu. Web site: http://business.gwu.edu/tourism/.

Hawai`i Pacific University, College of Business Administration, Honolulu, HI 96813. Offers accounting/CPA (MBA); e-business (MBA); economics (MBA); finance (MBA); human resource management (MA, MBA); information systems (MBA, MSIS), including knowledge management (MSIS), software engineering (MSIS), telecommunications security (MSIS); international business (MBA); management (MBA); marketing (MBA); organizational change (MA, MBA); travel industry management (MBA). Part-time and evening/weekend programs available. *Faculty:* 15 full-time (5 women), 11 part-time/adjunct (4 women). *Students:* 297 full-time (133 women), 183 part-time (87 women); includes 282 minority (17 Black or African American, non-Hispanic/Latino; 131 Asian, non-Hispanic/Latino; 43 Hispanic/Latino; 10 Native Hawaiian or other Pacific Islander, non-Hispanic/Latino; 81 Two or more races, non-Hispanic/Latino). Average age 30. 302 applicants, 82% accepted, 160 enrolled. In 2011, 141 master's awarded. *Degree requirements:* For master's, thesis. *Entrance requirements:* For master's, GMAT. Additional exam requirements/recommendations for international students: Recommended—TOEFL (minimum score 550 paper-based; 213 computer-based; 80 iBT), TWE (minimum score 5). *Application deadline:* For fall admission, 2/15 priority date for domestic students; for spring admission, 10/15 priority date for domestic students. Applications are processed on a rolling basis. Application fee: $50. Electronic applications accepted. *Expenses: Tuition:* Full-time $13,230; part-time $735 per credit.

Tuition and fees vary according to course load and program. *Financial support:* In 2011–12, 103 students received support. Research assistantships, career-related internships or fieldwork, Federal Work-Study, scholarships/grants, tuition waivers, and unspecified assistantships available. Financial award application deadline: 3/1; financial award applicants required to submit FAFSA. *Faculty research:* Statistical control process as used by management, studies in comparative cross-cultural management styles, not-for-profit management. *Unit head:* Dr. Deborah Crown, Dean, 808-544-0275, Fax: 808-544-0283, E-mail: dcrown@hpu.edu. *Application contact:* Chad Schempp, Director of Graduate Admissions, 808-543-8035, Fax: 808-544-0280, E-mail: graduate@hpu.edu. Web site: http://www.hpu.edu/mba.

See Display on page 98 and Close-Up on page 221.

Indiana University Bloomington, School of Health, Physical Education and Recreation, Department of Recreation, Park, and Tourism Studies, Bloomington, IN 47405-7000. Offers leisure behavior (PhD); outdoor recreation (MS); recreation administration (MS); recreational sports administration (MS); therapeutic recreation (MS); tourism management (MS). *Faculty:* 16 full-time (6 women), 2 part-time/adjunct (both women). *Students:* 61 full-time (32 women), 22 part-time (20 women); includes 9 minority (4 Black or African American, non-Hispanic/Latino; 1 Asian, non-Hispanic/Latino; 1 Hispanic/Latino; 3 Two or more races, non-Hispanic/Latino), 22 international. Average age 31. 48 applicants, 73% accepted, 18 enrolled. In 2011, 17 master's, 6 doctorates awarded. Terminal master's awarded for partial completion of doctoral program. *Degree requirements:* For master's, thesis optional; for doctorate, thesis/dissertation. *Entrance requirements:* For master's, GRE General Test, minimum GPA of 2.8; for doctorate, GRE General Test, minimum GPA of 3.0 (undergraduate), 3.5 (graduate). Additional exam requirements/recommendations for international students: Required—TOEFL. *Application deadline:* For fall admission, 1/1 for international students; for spring admission, 9/1 for international students. Applications are processed on a rolling basis. Application fee: $55 ($65 for international students). *Financial support:* Fellowships, research assistantships, teaching assistantships with partial tuition reimbursements, career-related internships or fieldwork, Federal Work-Study, institutionally sponsored loans, scholarships/grants, tuition waivers (partial), unspecified assistantships, and fee remissions available. Financial award application deadline: 3/1. *Faculty research:* Leisure counseling, gerontology, special populations, planning and development. *Unit head:* Bryan McCormick, Chair, 812-855-3482, E-mail: bmccormi@indiana.edu. *Application contact:* Program Office, 812-855-4711, Fax: 812-855-3998, E-mail: recpark@indiana.edu. Web site: http://www.indiana.edu/~recpark/.

Kent State University, Graduate School of Education, Health, and Human Services, School of Foundations, Leadership and Administration, Program in Hospitality and Tourism Management, Kent, OH 44242-0001. Offers MS. Part-time programs available. *Faculty:* 6 full-time (4 women), 4 part-time/adjunct (3 women). *Students:* 18 full-time (13 women), 7 part-time (4 women); includes 2 minority (1 Black or African American, non-Hispanic/Latino; 1 Asian, non-Hispanic/Latino). 36 applicants, 53% accepted. In 2011, 5 master's awarded. *Degree requirements:* For master's, thesis optional. *Entrance requirements:* For master's, minimum GPA of 3.0, 3 letters of recommendation, resume, goals statement. Additional exam requirements/recommendations for international students: Required—TOEFL (minimum score 550 paper-based; 213 computer-based; 80 iBT). *Application deadline:* Applications are processed on a rolling basis. Application fee: $30 ($60 for international students). Electronic applications accepted. *Expenses:* Tuition, state resident: full-time $8136; part-time $452 per credit hour. Tuition, nonresident: full-time $14,292; part-time $794 per credit hour. *Financial support:* In 2011–12, 4 students received support, including 2 fellowships (averaging $8,500 per year), 1 research assistantship with full tuition reimbursement available (averaging $8,500 per year); Federal Work-Study, scholarships/grants, and unspecified assistantships also available. Financial award application deadline: 2/1; financial award applicants required to submit FAFSA. *Faculty research:* Training human service workers, health care services for older adults, early adolescent development, caregiving arrangements with aging families, peace and war. *Unit head:* Barb Scheule, Coordinator, 330-672-3796, E-mail: bscheule@kent.edu. *Application contact:* Nancy Miller, Academic Program Coordinator, 330-672-2576, Fax: 330-672-9162, E-mail: ogs@kent.edu.

New York University, School of Continuing and Professional Studies, The Preston Robert Tisch Center for Hospitality, Tourism, and Sports Management, Program in Tourism Management, New York, NY 10012-1019. Offers MS, Advanced Certificate. Part-time and evening/weekend programs available. *Faculty:* 13 full-time (5 women), 13 part-time/adjunct (8 women). *Students:* 15 full-time (9 women), 15 part-time (10 women); includes 5 minority (1 Black or African American, non-Hispanic/Latino; 3 Asian, non-Hispanic/Latino; 1 Hispanic/Latino), 12 international. Average age 32. 43 applicants, 63% accepted, 21 enrolled. In 2011, 8 master's awarded. *Degree requirements:* For master's, thesis. *Entrance requirements:* For master's, GRE/GMAT only upon request, relevant professional work, internship or volunteer experience. Additional exam requirements/recommendations for international students: Required—TOEFL (minimum score 600 paper-based; 250 computer-based; 100 iBT), IELTS (minimum score 7). *Application deadline:* For fall admission, 2/1 priority date for domestic students, 2/1 for international students; for spring admission, 10/15 priority date for domestic students, 8/15 for international students. Applications are processed on a rolling basis. Application fee: $150. Electronic applications accepted. *Financial support:* In 2011–12, 27 students received support, including 23 fellowships (averaging $5,124 per year), 4 research assistantships (averaging $5,000 per year); career-related internships or fieldwork, Federal Work-Study, and scholarships/grants also available. Financial award application deadline: 2/15; financial award applicants required to submit FAFSA. *Faculty research:* Tourism planning for national parks and protected areas, leadership and organizational behavior issues. *Application contact:* Office of Admissions, 212-998-7100, E-mail: scps.gradadmissions@nyu.edu. Web site: http://www.scps.nyu.edu/areas-of-study/tisch/graduate-programs/ms-tourism-travel-management/.

North Carolina State University, Graduate School, College of Natural Resources, Department of Parks, Recreation and Tourism Management, Raleigh, NC 27695. Offers natural resource management (MPRTM, MS); park and recreation management (MPRTM, MS); parks, recreation and tourism management (PhD); recreational sport management (MPRTM, MS); spatial information science (MPRTM, MS); tourism policy and development (MPRTM, MS). *Degree requirements:* For master's, thesis (for some programs); for doctorate, thesis/dissertation. *Entrance requirements:* For master's and doctorate, GRE General Test. Additional exam requirements/recommendations for international students: Required—TOEFL. Electronic applications accepted. *Faculty research:* Tourism policy and development, spatial information systems, natural resource management, recreational sports management, park and recreation management.

Old Dominion University, Darden College of Education, Program in Physical Education, Recreation and Tourism Studies Emphasis, Norfolk, VA 23529. Offers MS Ed. Part-time and evening/weekend programs available. Postbaccalaureate distance learning degree programs offered (minimal on-campus study). *Faculty:* 1 full-time (0 women). *Students:* 3 part-time (2 women); includes 2 minority (both Black or African American, non-Hispanic/Latino). Average age 28. 10 applicants, 60% accepted, 3 enrolled. In 2011, 9 master's awarded. *Degree requirements:* For master's, comprehensive exam, thesis or alternative, internship, research project. *Entrance requirements:* For master's, GRE, minimum GPA of 2.8 overall, 3.0 in major. Additional exam requirements/recommendations for international students: Required—TOEFL (minimum score 500 paper-based; 200 computer-based). *Application deadline:* For fall admission, 6/1 for domestic students. Application fee: $50. Electronic applications accepted. *Expenses:* Tuition, state resident: full-time $9096; part-time $379 per credit. Tuition, nonresident: full-time $23,064; part-time $961 per credit. *Required fees:* $127 per semester. One-time fee: $50. *Financial support:* In 2011–12, 1 student received support, including 1 research assistantship with partial tuition reimbursement available (averaging $9,000 per year); career-related internships or fieldwork, scholarships/grants, and unspecified assistantships also available. Financial award application deadline: 3/1; financial award applicants required to submit FAFSA. *Faculty research:* Ethnicity and recreation, recreation programming, recreation and resiliency, tourism development, dog parks, sense of community and urban parks. *Total annual research expenditures:* $12,000. *Unit head:* Dr. Edwin Gomez, Graduate Program Director, 757-683-4995, Fax: 757-683-4270, E-mail: egomez@odu.edu. *Application contact:* Nechell Bonds, Director of Admissions, 757-683-3685, Fax: 757-683-3255, E-mail: gradadmit@odu.edu.

Penn State University Park, Graduate School, College of Health and Human Development, Department of Recreation, Park and Tourism Management, State College, University Park, PA 16802-1503. Offers M Ed, MS, PhD. *Unit head:* Dr. Ann C. Crouter, Dean, 814-865-1428, Fax: 814-865-3282, E-mail: ac1@psu.edu. *Application contact:* Cynthia E. Nicosia, Director, Graduate Enrollment Services, 814-865-1795, Fax: 814-865-4627, E-mail: cey1@psu.edu. Web site: http://www.hhdev.psu.edu/rptm/.

Pontificia Universidad Catolica Madre y Maestra, Graduate School, Faculty of Social and Administrative Sciences, Santiago, Dominican Republic. Offers business administration (MBA), including business development, finance, international business, management skills (M Mgmt, MBA), marketing, operations, strategic cost management, strategy, tourist destination planning and management; law (LL M), including civil law, corporate business law, criminal law, international relations, real estate law; management (M Mgmt), including higher financial management, insurance program administration, management skills (M Mgmt, MBA); psychology (MA), including clinical child and adolescent psychology, forensic psychology; strategic human resources (EMBA).

Purdue University, Graduate School, College of Health and Human Sciences, Department of Hospitality and Tourism Management, West Lafayette, IN 47907. Offers MS, PhD. *Faculty:* 16 full-time (5 women). *Students:* 75 full-time (56 women), 6 part-time (2 women); includes 3 minority (2 Asian, non-Hispanic/Latino; 1 Hispanic/Latino), 69 international. Average age 27. 179 applicants, 38% accepted, 33 enrolled. In 2011, 8 master's, 7 doctorates awarded. *Degree requirements:* For master's, thesis; for doctorate, thesis/dissertation. *Entrance requirements:* For master's, GMAT with minimum score of 550 total or GRE General Test Combined (new) verbal and quantitative score of 290 or higher (each: minimum of 145) or combined (previous) verbal and quantitative score of 1000 or higher (each minimum of 500), minimum GPA of 3.0; for doctorate, GMAT with minimum score of 550 total or GRE General Test Combined (new) verbal and quantitative score of 290 or higher (each: minimum of 145) or combined (previous) verbal and quantitative score of 1000 or higher (each minimum of 500), minimum undergraduate GPA of 3.0; master's degree with minimum GPA of 3.0 or equivalent. Additional exam requirements/recommendations for international students: Required—TOEFL (minimum score 550 computer-based; 77 iBT), TWE. *Application deadline:* For fall admission, 1/20 priority date for domestic students, 1/20 for international students; for spring admission, 9/20 for domestic and international students. Applications are processed on a rolling basis. Application fee: $60 ($75 for international students). Electronic applications accepted. *Financial support:* Research assistantships, teaching assistantships, and career-related internships or fieldwork available. Support available to part-time students. Financial award applicants required to submit FAFSA. *Faculty research:* Human resources, marketing, hotel and restaurant operations, food product and equipment development, tourism development. *Unit head:* Dr. Richard F. Ghiselli, Head, 765-494-2636, E-mail: ghiselli@purdue.edu. *Application contact:* Maria D. Campos, Graduate Contact, 765-494-9811, E-mail: camposm@purdue.edu. Web site: http://www.cfs.purdue.edu/HTM/.

Rochester Institute of Technology, Graduate Enrollment Services, College of Applied Science and Technology, School of International Hospitality and Service Innovation, Department of Hospitality and Service Management, Program in Hospitality and Tourism Management, Rochester, NY 14623-5603. Offers MS. *Degree requirements:* For master's, thesis or project. *Entrance requirements:* For master's, minimum GPA of 3.0. Additional exam requirements/recommendations for international students: Required—TOEFL (minimum score 550 paper-based; 213 computer-based; 79 iBT) or IELTS (minimum score 6.5). *Application deadline:* For fall admission, 2/15 priority date for domestic students, 2/15 for international students; for winter admission, 11/1 priority date for domestic students, 10/1 for international students; for spring admission, 2/1 priority date for domestic students, 1/1 for international students. Applications are processed on a rolling basis. *Expenses: Tuition:* Full-time $34,659; part-time $963 per credit hour. *Required fees:* $228; $76 per quarter. *Financial support:* Research assistantships with partial tuition reimbursements, teaching assistantships with partial tuition reimbursements, career-related internships or fieldwork, scholarships/grants, and unspecified assistantships available. Support available to part-time students. Financial award application deadline: 2/15; financial award applicants required to submit FAFSA. *Unit head:* Dr. Linda Underhill, Chair, 585-475-7359, Fax: 585-475-5099, E-mail: lmuism@rit.edu. *Application contact:* Diane Ellison, Assistant Vice President, Graduate Enrollment Services, 585-475-2229, Fax: 585-475-7164, E-mail: gradinfo@rit.edu.

Rochester Institute of Technology, Graduate Enrollment Services, College of Applied Science and Technology, School of International Hospitality and Service Innovation, Department of Service Systems, Program in Service Leadership and Innovation, Rochester, NY 14623-5603. Offers MS. Part-time and evening/weekend programs available. Postbaccalaureate distance learning degree programs offered (no on-campus study). *Students:* 19 full-time (14 women), 43 part-time (22 women); includes 1 minority (Black or African American, non-Hispanic/Latino), 25 international. Average age 30. 117 applicants, 50% accepted, 48 enrolled. In 2011, 64 master's awarded. *Degree requirements:* For master's, thesis or alternative. *Entrance requirements:* For master's, minimum GPA of 3.0. Additional exam requirements/recommendations for international students: Required—TOEFL (minimum score 550 paper-based; 213 computer-based; 79 iBT) or IELTS (minimum score 6.5). *Application deadline:* For fall admission, 2/15 priority date for domestic students, 2/15 for international students; for winter admission, 11/1 for domestic and international students; for spring admission, 2/1 for domestic and international students. Applications are processed on a rolling basis. Application fee: $50. Electronic applications accepted. *Expenses: Tuition:* Full-time $34,659; part-time $963 per credit hour. *Required fees:* $228; $76 per quarter. *Financial support:* Research assistantships with partial tuition reimbursements, teaching assistantships with partial tuition reimbursements, career-related internships or fieldwork, institutionally sponsored loans, scholarships/grants, and unspecified assistantships available. Support available to part-time students. Financial award application deadline: 2/15; financial award applicants required to submit FAFSA. *Faculty research:* Global resource development, service/product innovation and implementation. *Unit head:* Dr. Linda Underhill, Department Chair, 585-475-7359, E-mail: lmuism@rit.edu. *Application contact:* Diane Ellison, Assistant Vice President, Graduate Enrollment Services, 585-475-2229, Fax: 585-475-7164, E-mail: gradinfo@rit.edu. Web site: http://www.rit.edu/cast/servicesystems/service-leadership-and-innovation.php.

Royal Roads University, Graduate Studies, Tourism and Hotel Management Program, Victoria, BC V9B 5Y2, Canada. Offers destination development (Graduate Certificate); international hotel management (MA); sustainable tourism (Graduate Certificate); tourism leadership (Graduate Certificate); tourism management (MA).

Schiller International University, MBA Programs, Florida, Program in International Hotel and Tourism Management, Largo, FL 33770. Offers MBA. *Degree requirements:* For master's, thesis optional. *Entrance requirements:* Additional exam requirements/recommendations for international students: Required—TOEFL (minimum score 550 paper-based; 213 computer-based).

Strayer University, Graduate Studies, Washington, DC 20005-2603. Offers accounting (MS); acquisition (MBA); business administration (MBA); communications technology (MS); educational management (M Ed); finance (MBA); health services administration (MHSA); hospitality and tourism management (MBA); human resource management (MBA); information systems (MS), including computer security management, decision support system management, enterprise resource management, network management, software engineering management, systems development management; management (MBA); management information systems (MS); marketing (MBA); professional accounting (MS), including accounting information systems, controllership, taxation; public administration (MPA); supply chain management (MBA); technology in education (M Ed). Programs also offered at campus locations in Birmingham, AL; Chamblee, GA; Cobb County, GA; Morrow, GA; White Marsh, MD; Charleston, SC; Columbia, SC; Greensboro, NC; Greenville, SC; Lexington, KY; Louisville, KY; Nashville, TN; North Raleigh, NC; Washington, DC. Part-time and evening/weekend programs available. Postbaccalaureate distance learning degree programs offered (minimal on-campus study). *Degree requirements:* For master's, thesis. *Entrance requirements:* For master's, GMAT, GRE General Test, bachelor's degree from an accredited college or university, minimum undergraduate GPA of 2.75. Electronic applications accepted.

Syracuse University, Falk College of Sport and Human Dynamics, Program in Sport Venue and Event Management, Syracuse, NY 13244. Offers MS. *Entrance requirements:* For master's, GRE, undergraduate transcripts, three recommendations, resume, personal statement. Additional exam requirements/recommendations for international students: Required—TOEFL. *Expenses: Tuition:* Part-time $1206 per credit. *Unit head:* Dr. Diane Lyden Murphy, Dean, 315-443-5582, Fax: 315-443-2562, E-mail: falk@syr.edu. *Application contact:* Felecia Otero, Director of College Admissions, 315-443-5555, Fax: 315-443-2562, E-mail: falk@syr.edu. Web site: http://falk.syr.edu/SportManagement/Default.aspx.

Temple University, School of Tourism and Hospitality Management, Program in Tourism and Hospitality Management, Philadelphia, PA 19122-6096. Offers MTHM. Part-time and evening/weekend programs available. *Faculty:* 8 full-time (2 women). *Students:* 15 full-time (14 women), 3 part-time (2 women); includes 3 minority (1 Black or African American, non-Hispanic/Latino; 1 American Indian or Alaska Native, non-Hispanic/Latino; 1 Asian, non-Hispanic/Latino), 6 international. Average age 25. 31 applicants, 77% accepted, 9 enrolled. In 2011, 9 master's awarded. *Entrance requirements:* For master's, GRE General Test or MAT, minimum of 2 years professional experience, minimum undergraduate GPA of 3.0. Additional exam requirements/recommendations for international students: Required—TOEFL (minimum score 550 paper-based; 213 computer-based; 79 iBT). *Application deadline:* For fall admission, 4/1 priority date for domestic students, 12/15 for international students; for spring admission, 9/30 priority date for domestic students, 8/1 for international students. Application fee: $50. Electronic applications accepted. *Expenses:* Tuition, state resident: full-time $12,366; part-time $687 per credit hour. Tuition, nonresident: full-time $17,298; part-time $961 per credit hour. *Required fees:* $590; $213 per year. *Financial support:* Teaching assistantships available. Financial award application deadline: 1/15; financial award applicants required to submit FAFSA. *Unit head:* Dr. Seoki Lee, Director, Master's Programs, 215-204-0543, E-mail: seokilee@temple.edu. *Application contact:* Tara Schumacher, Coordinator of Outreach, 215-204-6575, Fax: 215-204-8781, E-mail: tara.schumacher@temple.edu. Web site: http://www.temple.edu/STHM/pstudents/tourismhospprograms.htm.

Tropical Agriculture Research and Higher Education Center, Graduate School, Turrialba, Costa Rica. Offers agribusiness management (MS); agroforestry systems (PhD); development practices (MS); ecological agriculture (MS); environmental socioeconomics (MS); forestry in tropical and subtropical zones (PhD); integrated watershed management (MS); international sustainable tourism (MS); management and conservation of tropical rainforests and biodiversity (MS); tropical agriculture (PhD); tropical agroforestry (MS). *Entrance requirements:* For master's, GRE, 2 years of related professional experience, letters of recommendation; for doctorate, GRE, 4 letters of recommendation, letter of support from employing organization, master's degree in agronomy, biological sciences, forestry, natural resources or related field. Additional exam requirements/recommendations for international students: Required—TOEFL (minimum score 550 paper-based; 213 computer-based). Electronic applications accepted. *Faculty research:* Biodiversity in fragmented landscapes, ecosystem management, integrated pest management, environmental livestock production, biotechnology carbon balances in diverse land uses.

Université du Québec à Trois-Rivières, Graduate Programs, Program in Leisure, Culture and Tourism Sciences, Trois-Rivières, QC G9A 5H7, Canada. Offers MA, DESS. Part-time programs available. *Degree requirements:* For master's, thesis optional. *Entrance requirements:* For master's, appropriate bachelor's degree, proficiency in French.

University of Central Florida, Rosen College of Hospitality Management, Orlando, FL 32816. Offers hospitality and tourism management (MS). *Faculty:* 47 full-time (17 women), 27 part-time/adjunct (11 women). *Students:* 61 full-time (45 women), 46 part-time (33 women); includes 16 minority (7 Black or African American, non-Hispanic/Latino; 4 Asian, non-Hispanic/Latino; 5 Hispanic/Latino), 35 international. Average age 27. 115 applicants, 57% accepted, 46 enrolled. In 2011, 29 master's awarded. *Degree requirements:* For master's, thesis or alternative. *Entrance requirements:* For master's, GMAT or GRE, minimum GPA of 3.0 in last 60 hours. Additional exam requirements/recommendations for international students: Required—TOEFL. *Application deadline:* For fall admission, 2/1 for domestic students. Application fee: $30. Electronic applications accepted. *Expenses:* Tuition, state resident: part-time $277.08 per credit hour. Tuition, nonresident: part-time $277.08 per credit hour. Part-time tuition and fees vary according to degree level and program. *Financial support:* In 2011–12, 9 students received support, including 8 fellowships with partial tuition reimbursements available (averaging $4,400 per year), 1 teaching assistantship (averaging $7,100 per year). *Unit head:* Dr. Abraham C. Pizam, Dean, 407-903-8010, E-mail: abraham.pizam@ucf.edu. *Application contact:* Barbara Rodriguez, Director, Admissions and Registration, 407-823-2766, Fax: 407-823-6442, E-mail: gradadmissions@ucf.edu. Web site: http://www.hospitality.ucf.edu/.

University of Hawaii at Manoa, Graduate Division, School of Travel Industry Management, Honolulu, HI 96822. Offers MS. Part-time programs available. *Degree requirements:* For master's, thesis optional. *Entrance requirements:* For master's, GRE General Test, minimum GPA of 3.0. Additional exam requirements/recommendations for international students: Required—TOEFL (minimum score 560 paper-based; 220 computer-based; 83 iBT), IELTS (minimum score 5). Electronic applications accepted. *Faculty research:* Travel information technology, tourism development and policy, transportation management and policy, hospitality management, sustainable tourism development.

University of Massachusetts Amherst, Graduate School, Isenberg School of Management, Program in Management, Amherst, MA 01003. Offers accounting (PhD); business administration (MBA); business administration/sport management (MBA/MS); finance (PhD); hospitality and tourism management (PhD); management science (PhD); marketing (PhD); organization studies (PhD); sport management (PhD); strategic management (PhD); MBA/MS; MPH/MPPA. *Accreditation:* AACSB. Part-time programs available. *Faculty:* 61 full-time (14 women). *Students:* 92 full-time (34 women), 9 part-time (3 women); includes 8 minority (1 Black or African American, non-Hispanic/Latino; 4 Asian, non-Hispanic/Latino; 3 Hispanic/Latino), 47 international. Average age 33. 340 applicants, 15% accepted, 29 enrolled. In 2011, 31 master's, 13 doctorates awarded. Terminal master's awarded for partial completion of doctoral program. *Degree requirements:* For doctorate, comprehensive exam, thesis/dissertation. *Entrance requirements:* For master's and doctorate, GMAT. Additional exam requirements/recommendations for international students: Required—TOEFL (minimum score 550 paper-based; 213 computer-based; 80 iBT), IELTS (minimum score 6.5). *Application deadline:* For fall admission, 1/20 for domestic and international students. Applications are processed on a rolling basis. Application fee: $50 ($65 for international students). Electronic applications accepted. Tuition and fees vary according to course load, campus/location and program. *Financial support:* Fellowships with full and partial tuition reimbursements, research assistantships with full and partial tuition reimbursements, teaching assistantships with full and partial tuition reimbursements, career-related internships or fieldwork, Federal Work-Study, scholarships/grants, traineeships, health care benefits, tuition waivers (full and partial), and unspecified assistantships available. Support available to part-time students. Financial award application deadline: 1/20. *Unit head:* Dr. William Woodridge, Chair, 413-545-5675, Fax: 413-577-2234. *Application contact:* Lindsay DeSantis, Interim Supervisor of Admissions, 413-545-0722, Fax: 413-577-0010, E-mail: gradadm@grad.umass.edu. Web site: http://www.isenberg.umass.edu/.

University of New Orleans, Graduate School, College of Business Administration, School of Hotel, Restaurant, and Tourism Administration, Program in Hospitality and Tourism Management, New Orleans, LA 70148. Offers MS. *Entrance requirements:* Additional exam requirements/recommendations for international students: Required—TOEFL (minimum score 550 paper-based; 213 computer-based; 79 iBT).

University of South Africa, College of Economic and Management Sciences, Pretoria, South Africa. Offers accounting (D Admin, D Com); accounting science (DA); auditing (D Admin, D Com); business administration (M Tech); business economics (D Admin); business leadership (DBL); business management (D Admin, D Com); economic management analysis (M Tech); economics (D Admin, D Com, PhD); human resource development (M Tech); industrial psychology (D Admin, D Com, PhD); logistics (D Com); marketing (M Tech); public administration (D Admin, D Com, DPA, PhD); public management (M Tech); quantitative management (D Admin, D Com); real estate (M Tech); statistics (D Admin, PhD); tourism management (D Admin, D Com); transport economics (D Admin, D Com).

University of South Carolina, The Graduate School, College of Hospitality, Retail, and Sport Management, School of Hotel, Restaurant and Tourism Management, Columbia, SC 29208. Offers MIHTM. *Entrance requirements:* For master's, GMAT or GRE General Test, minimum GPA of 3.0, 2 letters of recommendation. Electronic applications accepted. *Faculty research:* Corporate strategy and management practices, sustainable tourism, club management, tourism technology, revenue management.

The University of Tennessee, Graduate School, College of Education, Health and Human Sciences, Department of Consumer and Industry Services Management, Program in Hotel, Restaurant, and Tourism Management, Knoxville, TN 37996. Offers hospitality management (MS); tourism (MS). Part-time programs available. *Degree requirements:* For master's, thesis or alternative. *Entrance requirements:* For master's, GRE General Test, minimum GPA of 2.7. Additional exam requirements/recommendations for international students: Required—TOEFL. Electronic applications accepted. *Expenses:* Tuition, state resident: full-time $8332; part-time $464 per credit hour. Tuition, nonresident: full-time $25,174; part-time $1400 per credit hour. *Required fees:* $1162; $56 per credit hour. Tuition and fees vary according to program.

University of Waterloo, Graduate Studies, Faculty of Environment, Program in Tourism Policy and Planning, Waterloo, ON N2L 3G1, Canada. Offers MAES. Part-time programs available. *Degree requirements:* For master's, research paper. *Entrance requirements:* For master's, honors degree in related field, minimum B average. Additional exam requirements/recommendations for international students: Required—TOEFL, TWE. Electronic applications accepted. *Faculty research:* Urban and regional economics, regional economic development, strategic planning, environmental economics, economic geography.

Virginia Polytechnic Institute and State University, Graduate School, Pamplin College of Business, Department of Hospitality and Tourism Management, Blacksburg, VA 24061. Offers MS, PhD. *Degree requirements:* For master's, comprehensive exam (for some programs), thesis (for some programs); for doctorate, comprehensive exam (for some programs), thesis/dissertation (for some programs). *Entrance requirements:* For master's and doctorate, GRE. Additional exam requirements/recommendations for international students: Required—TOEFL (minimum score 550 paper-based; 213 computer-based). *Application deadline:* For fall admission, 7/1 for domestic and international students; for spring admission, 12/1 for domestic and international students. Applications are processed on a rolling basis. Application fee: $65. Electronic applications accepted. *Expenses:* Tuition, state resident: full-time $10,048; part-time $558.25 per credit hour. Tuition, nonresident: full-time $19,497; part-time $1083.25 per credit hour. *Required fees:* $405 per semester. Tuition and fees vary according to course load, campus/location and program. *Financial support:* In 2011–12, 1 research assistantship with full tuition reimbursement (averaging $12,053 per year), 3 teaching assistantships with full tuition reimbursements (averaging $12,861 per year) were awarded; career-related internships or fieldwork, Federal Work-Study, scholarships/grants, health care benefits, and unspecified assistantships also available. Financial award application deadline: 1/15. *Faculty research:* Human resource management, service management, marketing, strategy and finance tourist behavior. *Unit head:* Dr. Rick R. Perdue, Unit Head, 540-231-5515, Fax: 540-231-8313, E-mail: rick.perdue@vt.edu. *Application contact:* Nancy McGehee, Information Contact, 540-231-1201, Fax: 540-231-8313, E-mail: nmcgehee@vt.edu. Web site: http://www.htm.pamplin.vt.edu/.

Western Illinois University, School of Graduate Studies, College of Education and Human Services, Department of Recreation, Park, and Tourism Administration, Macomb, IL 61455-1390. Offers MS. Part-time programs available. *Students:* 28 full-time (16 women), 9 part-time (4 women); includes 3 minority (2 Black or African American, non-Hispanic/Latino; 1 Asian, non-Hispanic/Latino), 4 international. Average age 28. 25 applicants, 80% accepted. In 2011, 28 master's awarded. *Degree requirements:* For master's, thesis or alternative. *Entrance requirements:* Additional exam requirements/recommendations for international students: Required—TOEFL (minimum score 550 paper-based; 213 computer-based; 80 iBT). *Application deadline:* Applications are processed on a rolling basis. Application fee: $30. Electronic applications accepted. *Expenses:* Tuition, state resident: part-time $281.16 per credit hour. Tuition, nonresident: part-time $562.32 per credit hour. Part-time tuition and fees vary according to campus/location and reciprocity agreements. *Financial support:* In 2011–12, 23 students received support, including 23 research assistantships with full tuition reimbursements available (averaging $7,360 per year). Financial award applicants required to submit FAFSA. *Unit head:* Dr. K. Dale Adkins, Chairperson, 309-298-1967. *Application contact:* Dr. Nancy Parsons, Assistant Director of Graduate Studies, 309-298-1806, Fax: 309-298-2345, E-mail: grad-office@wiu.edu. Web site: http://www.wiu.edu/rpta.

Section 8
Human Resources

This section contains a directory of institutions offering graduate work in human resources, followed by in-depth entries submitted by institutions that chose to prepare detailed program descriptions. Additional information about programs listed in the directory but not augmented by an in-depth entry may be obtained by writing directly to the dean of a graduate school or chair of a department at the address given in the directory.

For programs offering related work, see also in this book *Business Administration and Management, Advertising and Public Relations, Hospitality Management, Industrial and Manufacturing Management,* and *Organizational Behavior.* In another guide in this series:

Graduate Programs in the Humanities, Arts & Social Sciences

See Public, Regional, and Industrial Affairs (Industrial and Labor Relations)

CONTENTS

Program Directories

Displays and Close-Ups

See also:

Human Resources Development

Abilene Christian University, Graduate School, College of Arts and Sciences, Department of Communication, Program in Organizational and Human Resource Development, Abilene, TX 79699-9100. Offers MS. Part-time and evening/weekend programs available. Postbaccalaureate distance learning degree programs offered (no on-campus study). *Students:* 12 full-time (10 women), 76 part-time (56 women); includes 31 minority (16 Black or African American, non-Hispanic/Latino; 1 Asian, non-Hispanic/Latino; 10 Hispanic/Latino; 4 Two or more races, non-Hispanic/Latino), 3 international. 64 applicants, 45% accepted, 18 enrolled. In 2011, 46 master's awarded. *Degree requirements:* For master's, thesis. *Entrance requirements:* Additional exam requirements/recommendations for international students: Required—TOEFL (minimum score 550 paper-based; 213 computer-based; 80 iBT), IELTS (minimum score 6). *Application deadline:* For fall admission, 8/15 priority date for domestic students; for winter admission, 10/1 priority date for domestic students; for spring admission, 12/15 priority date for domestic students. Applications are processed on a rolling basis. Application fee: $100. Electronic applications accepted. *Expenses: Tuition:* Full-time $14,168; part-time $787 per hour. *Required fees:* $82 per hour. $10 per term. *Financial support:* Available to part-time students. Application deadline: 4/1; applicants required to submit FAFSA. *Unit head:* Dr. Jonathan Camp, Graduate Director, 325-674-2136, E-mail: jwc03b@acu.edu. *Application contact:* David Pittman, Graduate Admissions Counselor, 325-674-2656, Fax: 325-674-6717, E-mail: gradinfo@acu.edu. Web site: http://acuonline.acu.edu/.

Adler Graduate School, Program in Adlerian Counseling and Psychotherapy, Richfield, MN 55423. Offers art therapy (MA); career development (MA); clinical mental health counseling (MA); marriage and family therapy (MA); non-clinical Adlerian studies (MA); online Adlerian studies (MA); parent coaching (Certificate); personal and professional life coaching (Certificate); school counseling (MA). Part-time and evening/weekend programs available. *Faculty:* 10 full-time (3 women), 44 part-time/adjunct (31 women). *Students:* 359 part-time (291 women). *Degree requirements:* For master's, thesis or alternative, 500-700 hour internship (depending on license choice). *Entrance requirements:* For master's, personal goal statement, three letters of reference, resume or work history, official transcripts. *Application deadline:* Applications are processed on a rolling basis. Application fee: $50. Electronic applications accepted. *Expenses: Tuition:* Full-time $8730; part-time $485 per credit. *Required fees:* $270. Tuition and fees vary according to course load. *Financial support:* Career-related internships or fieldwork and tuition waivers available. Support available to part-time students. Financial award applicants required to submit FAFSA. *Unit head:* Dr. Dan Haugen, President, 612-861-7554 Ext. 107, Fax: 612-861-7559, E-mail: haugen@alfredadler.edu. *Application contact:* Evelyn B. Haas, Director of Student Services and Admissions, 612-861-7554 Ext. 103, Fax: 612-861-7559, E-mail: ev@alfredadler.edu. Web site: http://www.alfredadler.edu/academics/index.htm.

Amberton University, Graduate School, Program in Human Relations and Business, Garland, TX 75041-5595. Offers MA, MS. Part-time and evening/weekend programs available. *Entrance requirements:* For master's, minimum GPA of 3.0.

American International College, School of Arts, Education and Sciences, Center for Human Resource Development, Springfield, MA 01109-3189. Offers MA. Evening/weekend programs available. *Degree requirements:* For master's, practicum, project. *Entrance requirements:* For master's, minimum B- average in undergraduate course work, writing sample. Additional exam requirements/recommendations for international students: Required—TOEFL. Electronic applications accepted. *Faculty research:* Faculty development, teaching/training effectiveness.

Antioch University Los Angeles, Graduate Programs, Program in Organizational Management, Culver City, CA 90230. Offers human resource development (MA); leadership (MA); organizational development (MA). Part-time and evening/weekend programs available. *Entrance requirements:* For master's, interview. Additional exam requirements/recommendations for international students: Required—TOEFL. *Faculty research:* Systems thinking and chaos theory, technology and organizational structure, nonprofit management, power and empowerment.

Azusa Pacific University, School of Business and Management, Program in Human and Organizational Development, Azusa, CA 91702-7000. Offers MA. Part-time and evening/weekend programs available. *Degree requirements:* For master's, comprehensive exam, final project. *Entrance requirements:* For master's, minimum GPA of 3.0.

Barry University, School of Education, Program in Human Resource Development and Administration, Miami Shores, FL 33161-6695. Offers MS. Part-time and evening/weekend programs available. *Degree requirements:* For master's, comprehensive exam, practicum. *Entrance requirements:* For master's, GRE General Test or MAT, minimum GPA of 3.0. Electronic applications accepted.

Barry University, School of Education, Program in Leadership and Education, Miami Shores, FL 33161-6695. Offers educational technology (PhD); exceptional student education (PhD); higher education administration (PhD); human resource development (PhD); leadership (PhD). Part-time and evening/weekend programs available. *Degree requirements:* For doctorate, thesis/dissertation. *Entrance requirements:* For doctorate, GRE General Test, minimum GPA of 3.25. Electronic applications accepted.

Bowie State University, Graduate Programs, Program in Human Resource Development, Bowie, MD 20715-9465. Offers MA. Part-time and evening/weekend programs available. *Faculty:* 4 full-time (3 women), 4 part-time/adjunct (2 women). *Students:* 56 full-time (43 women), 58 part-time (43 women); includes 107 minority (101 Black or African American, non-Hispanic/Latino; 2 Asian, non-Hispanic/Latino; 4 Hispanic/Latino), 4 international. Average age 31. 35 applicants, 100% accepted, 22 enrolled. In 2011, 30 master's awarded. *Degree requirements:* For master's, comprehensive exam, thesis optional, research paper. *Entrance requirements:* For master's, minimum GPA of 2.5. *Application deadline:* For fall admission, 4/1 priority date for domestic students, 4/1 for international students; for spring admission, 11/1 priority date for domestic students, 11/1 for international students. Applications are processed on a rolling basis. Application fee: $40. Electronic applications accepted. *Expenses:* Tuition, state resident: full-time $4140; part-time $3105 per semester. Tuition, nonresident: full-time $7836; part-time $5877 per semester. *Required fees:* $1715; $648 per semester. *Financial support:* Career-related internships or fieldwork and institutionally sponsored loans available. Support available to part-time students. Financial award application deadline: 4/1. *Unit head:* Dr. Marsha Jackson, Coordinator, 301-860-3108, E-mail: mjackson@bowiestate.edu. *Application contact:* Angela Issac, Information Contact, 301-860-4000.

California State University, Sacramento, Office of Graduate Studies, College of Business Administration, Sacramento, CA 95819-6088. Offers accountancy (MS); business administration (MBA); human resources (MBA); urban land development (MBA). *Accreditation:* AACSB. Part-time and evening/weekend programs available. *Faculty:* 61 full-time (19 women), 28 part-time/adjunct (7 women). *Students:* 39 full-time, 91 part-time; includes 40 minority (6 Black or African American, non-Hispanic/Latino; 2 American Indian or Alaska Native, non-Hispanic/Latino; 12 Asian, non-Hispanic/Latino; 11 Hispanic/Latino; 4 Native Hawaiian or other Pacific Islander, non-Hispanic/Latino; 5 Two or more races, non-Hispanic/Latino), 16 international. Average age 29. 330 applicants, 64% accepted, 54 enrolled. In 2011, 212 master's awarded. *Degree requirements:* For master's, thesis or alternative, writing proficiency exam. *Entrance requirements:* For master's, GMAT. Additional exam requirements/recommendations for international students: Required—TOEFL. *Application deadline:* For fall admission, 2/1 for domestic students, 3/1 for international students; for spring admission, 9/15 for domestic students, 9/30 for international students. Applications are processed on a rolling basis. Application fee: $55. Electronic applications accepted. *Financial support:* Research assistantships, teaching assistantships, career-related internships or fieldwork, and Federal Work-Study available. Support available to part-time students. Financial award applicants required to submit FAFSA. *Unit head:* Dr. Sanjay Varshney, Dean, 916-278-6942, Fax: 916-278-5793, E-mail: cba@csus.edu. *Application contact:* Jose Martinez, Outreach and Graduate Diversity Coordinator, 916-278-6470, Fax: 916-278-5669, E-mail: martinj@skymail.csus.edu. Web site: http://www.cba.csus.edu.

Claremont Graduate University, Graduate Programs, School of Behavioral and Organizational Sciences, Department of Psychology, Claremont, CA 91711-6160. Offers advanced study in evaluation (Certificate); cognitive psychology (MA, PhD); developmental psychology (MA, PhD); evaluation and applied research methods (MA, PhD); health behavior research and evaluation (MA, PhD); human resource development and evaluation (MA); industrial/organizational psychology (MA, PhD); organizational behavior (MA, PhD); organizational psychology (MA, PhD); social psychology (MA, PhD); MBA/PhD. Part-time programs available. *Faculty:* 15 full-time (7 women), 6 part-time/adjunct (2 women). *Students:* 226 full-time (145 women), 29 part-time (23 women); includes 66 minority (16 Black or African American, non-Hispanic/Latino; 1 American Indian or Alaska Native, non-Hispanic/Latino; 25 Asian, non-Hispanic/Latino; 17 Hispanic/Latino; 1 Native Hawaiian or other Pacific Islander, non-Hispanic/Latino; 6 Two or more races, non-Hispanic/Latino), 28 international. Average age 30. In 2011, 60 master's, 15 doctorates, 7 other advanced degrees awarded. Terminal master's awarded for partial completion of doctoral program. *Entrance requirements:* For master's and doctorate, GRE General Test. Additional exam requirements/recommendations for international students: Required—TOEFL (minimum score 550 paper-based; 213 computer-based; 80 iBT). *Application deadline:* For fall admission, 1/15 priority date for domestic students. Applications are processed on a rolling basis. Application fee: $60. Electronic applications accepted. *Expenses: Tuition:* Full-time $36,374; part-time $1581 per unit. *Required fees:* $165 per semester. *Financial support:* Fellowships, research assistantships, teaching assistantships, Federal Work-Study, institutionally sponsored loans, scholarships/grants, and tuition waivers (full and partial) available. Support available to part-time students. Financial award application deadline: 2/15; financial award applicants required to submit FAFSA. *Faculty research:* Social intervention, diversity in organizations, eyewitness memory, aging and cognition, drug policy. *Unit head:* Stewart Donaldson, Dean, 909-607-9001, Fax: 909-621-8905, E-mail: stewart.donaldson@cgu.edu. *Application contact:* John LaVelle, Director, External Affairs, 909-607-9016, Fax: 909-621-8905, E-mail: john.lavelle@cgu.edu. Web site: http://www.cgu.edu/pages/502.asp.

Clemson University, Graduate School, College of Health, Education, and Human Development, Eugene T. Moore School of Education, Program in Human Resource Development, Clemson, SC 29634. Offers MHRD. Part-time and evening/weekend programs available. Postbaccalaureate distance learning degree programs offered (no on-campus study). *Students:* 1 (woman) full-time, 76 part-time (52 women); includes 23 minority (17 Black or African American, non-Hispanic/Latino; 1 American Indian or Alaska Native, non-Hispanic/Latino; 4 Hispanic/Latino; 1 Two or more races, non-Hispanic/Latino). Average age 36. 64 applicants, 91% accepted, 41 enrolled. In 2011, 28 master's awarded. *Degree requirements:* For master's, comprehensive exam. *Entrance requirements:* For master's, GRE General Test. Additional exam requirements/recommendations for international students: Required—TOEFL; Recommended—IELTS. *Application deadline:* For fall admission, 7/1 for domestic students. Application fee: $70 ($80 for international students). Electronic applications accepted. *Expenses:* Contact institution. *Financial support:* In 2011–12, 2 students received support. Application deadline: 6/1; applicants required to submit FAFSA. *Faculty research:* Organizational development, human performance improvement, attachment theory, social constructivism, technology-mediated teaching and learning, corporate universities. *Unit head:* Dr. Michael J. Padilla, Director/Associate Dean, 864-656-4444, Fax: 864-656-0311, E-mail: pmcgee@clemson.edu. *Application contact:* Dr. David Fleming, Coordinator, 864-656-1881, Fax: 864-656-0311, E-mail: dflemin@clemson.edu. Web site: http://www.hehd.clemson.edu/MHRD/SoE_Webpage/MHRD.html.

The College of New Rochelle, Graduate School, Division of Human Services, Program in Career Development, New Rochelle, NY 10805-2308. Offers MS. Part-time programs available. *Degree requirements:* For master's, fieldwork, internship. *Entrance requirements:* For master's, interview, minimum GPA of 3.0, writing sample. *Faculty research:* Technology.

Drexel University, Goodwin College of Professional Studies, School of Education, Program in Human Resource Development, Philadelphia, PA 19104-2875. Offers MS.

Florida International University, College of Education, Department of Educational Leadership and Policy Studies, Miami, FL 33199. Offers adult education (MS); adult education in human resource development (Ed D); clinical mental health counseling (MS); conflict resolution and consensus building (Certificate); counselor education (MS); educational administration and supervision (Ed D); educational leadership (MS, Certificate, Ed S); higher education (Ed D); higher education administration (MS); human resource development (MS); instruction in urban settings (MS); international/intercultural education (MS); learning technologies (MS); multicultural-bilingual (MS); multicultural-TESOL (MS); recreation and sport management (MS); recreation therapy (MS); rehabilitation counseling (MS); school counseling (MS); school psychology (Ed S); urban education (MS). Part-time and evening/weekend programs available. *Degree requirements:* For doctorate, thesis/dissertation. *Entrance requirements:* For master's, minimum GPA of 3.0; for doctorate and other advanced degree, GRE General Test. Additional exam requirements/recommendations for international students: Required—TOEFL (minimum score 550 paper-based; 213 computer-based; 80 iBT), IELTS (minimum score 6.3). Electronic applications accepted.

Florida State University, The Graduate School, College of Education, Department of Educational Psychology and Learning Systems, Program in Instructional Systems, Tallahassee, FL 32306. Offers instructional systems (MS, PhD, Ed S); open and distance learning (MS); performance improvement and human resources (MS). *Faculty:* 6 full-time (4 women), 1 (woman) part-time/adjunct. *Students:* 68 full-time (47 women),

78 part-time (48 women); includes 19 minority (8 Black or African American, non-Hispanic/Latino; 1 American Indian or Alaska Native, non-Hispanic/Latino; 6 Asian, non-Hispanic/Latino; 4 Hispanic/Latino), 48 international. Average age 36. 60 applicants, 27% accepted, 7 enrolled. In 2011, 31 master's, 3 doctorates awarded. *Median time to degree:* Of those who began their doctoral program in fall 2003, 50% received their degree in 8 years or less. *Degree requirements:* For master's and Ed S, comprehensive exam, thesis optional; for doctorate, comprehensive exam, thesis/dissertation. *Entrance requirements:* For master's, doctorate, and Ed S, GRE General Test, minimum GPA of 3.0. Additional exam requirements/recommendations for international students: Required—TOEFL (minimum score 550 paper-based; 213 computer-based; 80 iBT). *Application deadline:* For fall admission, 7/1 for domestic and international students; for winter admission, 11/1 for domestic and international students; for spring admission, 3/1 for domestic and international students. Applications are processed on a rolling basis. Application fee: $30. Electronic applications accepted. *Expenses:* Tuition, state resident: full-time $9474; part-time $350.88 per credit hour. Tuition, nonresident: full-time $16,236; part-time $601.34 per credit hour. *Required fees:* $630 per semester. One-time fee: $20. Tuition and fees vary according to course load and campus/location. *Financial support:* Fellowships with full and partial tuition reimbursements, research assistantships with full and partial tuition reimbursements, teaching assistantships with full and partial tuition reimbursements, career-related internships or fieldwork, scholarships/grants, health care benefits, and unspecified assistantships available. Financial award applicants required to submit FAFSA. *Faculty research:* Human performance improvement, educational semiotics, development of software tools to measure online interaction among learners. *Unit head:* Dr. Vanessa Dennen, Program Leader, 850-644-8783, Fax: 850-644-8776, E-mail: vdennen@fsu.edu. *Application contact:* Mary Kate McKee, Program Coordinator, 850-644-8792, Fax: 850-644-8776, E-mail: mmckee@campus.fsu.edu.

Friends University, Graduate School, Wichita, KS 67213. Offers accounting (MBA); business administration (MBA); business law (MBL); Christian ministry (MACM); environment science (MSES); family therapy (MSFT); global leadership and management (MA); health care leadership (MHCL); management information systems (MMIS); operations management (MSOM); organization development (MSOD); teaching (MAT). Part-time and evening/weekend programs available. Postbaccalaureate distance learning degree programs offered (no on-campus study). *Faculty:* 14 full-time (5 women), 2 part-time/adjunct (1 woman). *Students:* 158 full-time (114 women), 616 part-time (367 women); includes 159 minority (83 Black or African American, non-Hispanic/Latino; 12 American Indian or Alaska Native, non-Hispanic/Latino; 26 Asian, non-Hispanic/Latino; 22 Hispanic/Latino; 2 Native Hawaiian or other Pacific Islander, non-Hispanic/Latino; 14 Two or more races, non-Hispanic/Latino). Average age 36. 497 applicants, 68% accepted, 256 enrolled. In 2011, 341 degrees awarded. *Degree requirements:* For master's, research project. *Entrance requirements:* For master's, bachelor's degree from accredited institution, official transcripts from institution granting bachelor's degree, interview with program director, letter(s) of recommendation. Additional exam requirements/recommendations for international students: Required—TOEFL (minimum score 560 paper-based; 220 computer-based). *Application deadline:* Applications are processed on a rolling basis. Application fee: $45 ($65 for international students). Electronic applications accepted. *Expenses: Tuition:* Part-time $601 per credit hour. One-time fee: $45 full-time. Tuition and fees vary according to campus/location and program. *Financial support:* Applicants required to submit FAFSA. *Unit head:* Dr. Evelyn Hume, Dean, 800-794-6945 Ext. 5859, Fax: 316-295-5040, E-mail: evelyn_hume@friends.edu. *Application contact:* Jeanette Hanson, Executive Director of Adult Recruitment, 800-794-6945, Fax: 316-295-5050, E-mail: jeanette@friends.edu. Web site: http://www.friends.edu.

The George Washington University, Graduate School of Education and Human Development, Department of Human and Organizational Learning, Program in Essentials of Human Resource Development, Washington, DC 20052. Offers Graduate Certificate. *Entrance requirements:* For degree, two letters of recommendation, resume, statement of purpose. Electronic applications accepted.

The George Washington University, Graduate School of Education and Human Development, Department of Human and Organizational Learning, Program in Human Resource Development, Washington, DC 20052. Offers MA. Part-time and evening/weekend programs available. *Entrance requirements:* For master's, GRE, MAT, or GMAT, two letters of recommendtion, statement of purpose, official transcripts, resume. Additional exam requirements/recommendations for international students: Required—TOEFL or IELTS. Electronic applications accepted.

The George Washington University, Graduate School of Education and Human Development, Department of Human and Organizational Learning, Program in Leadership Development, Washington, DC 20052. Offers Graduate Certificate. *Degree requirements:* For Graduate Certificate, practicum. *Entrance requirements:* For degree, two letters of recommendation, resume, statement of purpose. Electronic applications accepted.

Grantham University, Mark Skousen School of Business, Kansas City, MO 64153. Offers business administration (MBA); business intelligence (MS); information management (MBA); information management technology (MS); information technology (MS); performance improvement (MS); project management (MBA, MSIM). Part-time and evening/weekend programs available. Postbaccalaureate distance learning degree programs offered (no on-campus study). *Degree requirements:* For master's, capstone project. *Entrance requirements:* For master's, bachelor's degree from accredited degree-granting institution. Additional exam requirements/recommendations for international students: Required—TOEFL (minimum score 500 paper-based; 213 computer-based; 61 iBT). Electronic applications accepted.

Illinois Institute of Technology, Graduate College, College of Psychology, Chicago, IL 60616. Offers clinical psychology (PhD); industrial/organizational psychology (PhD); personnel/human resource development (MS); rehabilitation (PhD); rehabilitation counseling (MS). *Accreditation:* APA (one or more programs are accredited); CORE. Part-time and evening/weekend programs available. Terminal master's awarded for partial completion of doctoral program. *Degree requirements:* For master's, thesis (for some programs); for doctorate, comprehensive exam, thesis/dissertation, 96-108 credit hours, internship (for clinical and industrial/organizational specializations). *Entrance requirements:* For master's, GRE General Test (minimum score 900 Quantitative and Verbal, 2.5 Analytical Writing), minimum high school GPA of 3.0; at least 18 credit hours of undergraduate study in psychology with at least one course each in experimental psychology and statistics; official transcripts; 3 letters of recommendation; personal statement; for doctorate, GRE General Test (minimum score 1000 Quantitative and Verbal, 3.0 Analytical Writing), minimum high school GPA of 3.0; at least 18 credit hours of undergraduate study in psychology with at least one course each in experimental psychology and statistics; official transcripts; 3 letters of recommendation; personal statement. Additional exam requirements/recommendations for international students: Required—TOEFL (minimum score 550 paper-based; 213 computer-based; 80 iBT); Recommended—IELTS (minimum score 5.5). Electronic applications accepted. *Faculty research:* Health psychology, behavioral medicine, attachment, child social and emotional development, educational assessment.

Indiana State University, College of Graduate and Professional Studies, College of Technology, Department of Industrial Technology Education, Terre Haute, IN 47809. Offers career and technical education (MS); human resource development (MS); technology education (MS); MA/MS. *Accreditation:* NCATE (one or more programs are accredited). *Entrance requirements:* For master's, bachelor's degree in industrial technology or related field. Additional exam requirements/recommendations for international students: Required—TOEFL. Electronic applications accepted.

Indiana Tech, Program in Business Administration, Fort Wayne, IN 46803-1297. Offers accounting (MBA); health care administration (MBA); human resources (MBA); management (MBA); marketing (MBA). Part-time and evening/weekend programs available. Postbaccalaureate distance learning degree programs offered (no on-campus study). *Entrance requirements:* For master's, GMAT, minimum undergraduate GPA of 2.5, 3 letters of recommendation. Electronic applications accepted.

Indiana University of Pennsylvania, School of Graduate Studies and Research, Eberly College of Business and Information Technology, Department of Technology Support and Training, Program in Business/Workforce Development, Indiana, PA 15705-1087. Offers M Ed. *Faculty:* 3 full-time (2 women). *Students:* 1 (woman) full-time, 1 (woman) part-time. Average age 40. 25 applicants, 28% accepted, 2 enrolled. In 2011, 13 master's awarded. *Degree requirements:* For master's, thesis optional. *Entrance requirements:* For master's, 2 letters of recommendation. Additional exam requirements/recommendations for international students: Required—TOEFL (minimum score 540 paper-based; 207 computer-based). *Application deadline:* Applications are processed on a rolling basis. Application fee: $50. Electronic applications accepted. *Expenses:* Tuition, state resident: full-time $7488; part-time $416 per credit. Tuition, nonresident: full-time $11,232; part-time $624 per credit. *Required fees:* $2070; $192.20 per credit. $90 per semester. *Financial support:* In 2011–12, 1 research assistantship with full and partial tuition reimbursement (averaging $2,970 per year) was awarded; career-related internships or fieldwork and Federal Work-Study also available. Support available to part-time students. Financial award application deadline: 4/15; financial award applicants required to submit FAFSA. *Unit head:* Dr. Dawn Woodland, Graduate Coordinator, 724-357-5736, E-mail: woodland@iup.edu. *Application contact:* Dr. Dawn Woodland, Graduate Coordinator, 724-357-5736, E-mail: woodland@iup.edu. Web site: http://www.iup.edu/page.aspx?id=42103.

Inter American University of Puerto Rico, Metropolitan Campus, Graduate Programs, Program in Human Resources, San Juan, PR 00919-1293. Offers MBA. *Degree requirements:* For master's, comprehensive exam. *Entrance requirements:* For master's, GRE or EXADEP, interview. Electronic applications accepted.

Inter American University of Puerto Rico, San Germán Campus, Graduate Studies Center, Program in Business Administration, San Germán, PR 00683-5008. Offers accounting (MBA); finance (MBA); human resources (MBA, PhD); industrial relations (MBA); information sciences (MBA); management (MBA); marketing (MBA). Part-time and evening/weekend programs available. *Degree requirements:* For master's, comprehensive exam. *Entrance requirements:* For master's, GRE General Test or EXADEP, minimum GPA of 3.0. *Application deadline:* For fall admission, 4/30 priority date for domestic students; for spring admission, 11/15 for domestic students. Applications are processed on a rolling basis. Application fee: $31. *Expenses: Required fees:* $213 per semester. *Financial support:* Teaching assistantships, Federal Work-Study, and unspecified assistantships available. *Unit head:* Dr. Elba T. Irizarry, Director of Graduate Studies Center, 787-264-1912 Ext. 7357, Fax: 787-892-6350, E-mail: elbat@sg.inter.edu.

Iowa State University of Science and Technology, Department of Educational Leadership and Policy Studies, Ames, IA 50011. Offers counselor education (M Ed, MS); educational administration (M Ed, MS); educational leadership (PhD); higher education (M Ed, MS); organizational learning and human resource development (M Ed, MS); research and evaluation (MS); student affairs (MS). *Degree requirements:* For master's, thesis or alternative; for doctorate, thesis/dissertation. *Entrance requirements:* For master's and doctorate, GRE General Test. Additional exam requirements/recommendations for international students: Required—TOEFL (minimum score 560 paper-based; 83 iBT), IELTS (minimum score 6.5). *Application deadline:* For fall admission, 1/1 priority date for domestic students, 1/1 for international students. Application fee: $40 ($90 for international students). Electronic applications accepted. *Unit head:* Dr. Daniel Robinson, Director of Graduate Education, 515-294-1241, Fax: 515-294-4942, E-mail: edldrshp@iastate.edu. *Application contact:* Judy Weiland, Application Contact, 515-294-1241, Fax: 515-294-4942, E-mail: eldrshp@iastate.edu. Web site: http://www.elps.hs.iastate.edu/.

John F. Kennedy University, School of Management, Program in Career Development, Pleasant Hill, CA 94523-4817. Offers career coaching (Certificate); career development (MA, Certificate). Part-time and evening/weekend programs available. *Degree requirements:* For master's, thesis or alternative. *Entrance requirements:* For master's, interview. Additional exam requirements/recommendations for international students: Required—TOEFL.

The Johns Hopkins University, Carey Business School, Management Programs, Baltimore, MD 21218-2699. Offers leadership development (Certificate); organization development and human resources (MS); skilled facilitator (Certificate). Evening/weekend programs available. *Degree requirements:* For master's, 36 credits including final project. *Entrance requirements:* For master's and Certificate, minimum GPA of 3.0, resume, work experience, two letters of recommendation. Additional exam requirements/recommendations for international students: Required—TOEFL (minimum score 600 paper-based; 250 computer-based; 100 iBT). Electronic applications accepted. *Faculty research:* Agency theory and theory of the firm, technological entrepreneurship, technology policy and economic development, strategic human resources management, ethics and stakeholder theory.

Kentucky State University, College of Professional Studies, Frankfort, KY 40601. Offers public administration (MPA), including human resource management, international development, management information systems, nonprofit management; special education (MA). Part-time and evening/weekend programs available. Postbaccalaureate distance learning degree programs offered (minimal on-campus study). *Faculty:* 12 full-time (4 women), 2 part-time/adjunct (both women). *Students:* 88 full-time (57 women), 79 part-time (42 women); includes 104 minority (101 Black or African American, non-Hispanic/Latino; 1 Asian, non-Hispanic/Latino; 2 Hispanic/Latino), 2 international. Average age 34. 124 applicants, 62% accepted, 45 enrolled. In 2011, 38 master's awarded. *Degree requirements:* For master's, comprehensive exam, thesis optional. *Entrance requirements:* For master's, GMAT, GRE. Additional exam requirements/recommendations for international students: Required—TOEFL (minimum score 525 paper-based; 173 computer-based). *Application deadline:* Applications are processed on a rolling basis. Application fee: $30 ($100 for international students). Electronic applications accepted. *Expenses:* Tuition, state resident: full-time $6192; part-time $344 per credit hour. Tuition, nonresident: full-time $9522; part-time $529 per credit hour. *Required fees:* $450; $25 per credit hour. Tuition and fees vary according to course load. *Financial support:* In 2011–12, 46 students received support, including 4 research assistantships (averaging $10,975 per year); career-related internships or fieldwork, scholarships/grants, tuition waivers (partial), and unspecified assistantships also available. Financial award application deadline: 4/15; financial award applicants required to submit FAFSA. *Unit head:* Dr. Gashaw Lake, Dean, 502-597-6105, Fax: 502-597-6715, E-mail: gashaw.lake@kysu.edu. *Application contact:* Dr. Titilayo Ufomata, Acting Director of Graduate Studies, 502-597-6443, E-mail: titilayo.ufomata@kysu.edu. Web site: http://www.kysu.edu/academics/collegesAndSchools/collegeofprofessionalstudies/.

Lincoln Memorial University, Carter and Moyers School of Education, Harrogate, TN 37752-1901. Offers administration and supervision (M Ed, Ed S); counseling and guidance (M Ed); curriculum and instruction (M Ed, Ed D, Ed S); English (M Ed); executive leadership (Ed D); higher education administration (Ed D); human resource development (Ed D); leadership and administration (Ed D). Part-time and evening/weekend programs available. Postbaccalaureate distance learning degree programs offered. *Degree requirements:* For master's, comprehensive exam, thesis optional; for Ed S, comprehensive exam. *Entrance requirements:* For master's, PRAXIS, NTE, GRE, MAT, letters of recommendation; for Ed S, graduate transcripts. Additional exam requirements/recommendations for international students: Recommended—TOEFL. *Faculty research:* Brain compatible teaching and learning; poverty in Appalachia; leadership for change; ethics, moral responsibility and social justice; human and organizational learning.

Louisiana State University and Agricultural and Mechanical College, Graduate School, College of Agriculture, School of Human Resource Education and Workforce Development, Baton Rouge, LA 70803. Offers agriculture and extension education and youth development (MS, PhD); career and technical education (MS, PhD); comprehensive vocational education (MS, PhD); extension and international education (MS, PhD); human resource and leadership development (MS, PhD); industrial education (MS); vocational agriculture education (MS, PhD); vocational business education (MS); vocational home economics education (MS). *Accreditation:* NCATE. Part-time programs available. *Faculty:* 9 full-time (5 women), 3 part-time/adjunct (0 women). *Students:* 51 full-time (36 women), 85 part-time (59 women); includes 28 minority (23 Black or African American, non-Hispanic/Latino; 1 Asian, non-Hispanic/Latino; 4 Hispanic/Latino), 3 international. Average age 36. 29 applicants, 83% accepted, 20 enrolled. In 2011, 15 master's, 17 doctorates awarded. Terminal master's awarded for partial completion of doctoral program. *Degree requirements:* For master's, thesis (for some programs); for doctorate, thesis/dissertation. *Entrance requirements:* For master's and doctorate, GRE General Test, minimum GPA of 3.0. Additional exam requirements/recommendations for international students: Required—TOEFL (minimum score 550 paper-based; 213 computer-based; 79 iBT) or IELTS (minimum score 6.5). *Application deadline:* For fall admission, 1/25 priority date for domestic students, 5/15 for international students; for spring admission, 10/15 for international students. Applications are processed on a rolling basis. Application fee: $50 ($70 for international students). Electronic applications accepted. *Financial support:* In 2011–12, 84 students received support, including 3 fellowships with full and partial tuition reimbursements available (averaging $14,986 per year), 4 research assistantships with full and partial tuition reimbursements available (averaging $12,000 per year), 11 teaching assistantships with partial tuition reimbursements available (averaging $13,300 per year); career-related internships or fieldwork, Federal Work-Study, institutionally sponsored loans, health care benefits, tuition waivers (full and partial), and unspecified assistantships also available. Financial award application deadline: 3/1; financial award applicants required to submit FAFSA. *Faculty research:* Adult education, history and philosophy of vocational education, curriculum and instruction, career decision-making. *Unit head:* Dr. Michael F. Burnett, Director, 225-578-5748, Fax: 225-578-2526, E-mail: vocbur@lsu.edu. Web site: http://www.lsu.edu/hrleader/.

Manhattanville College, Graduate Studies, Humanities and Social Sciences Programs, Program in Organizational Management and Human Resource Development, Purchase, NY 10577-2132. Offers MS. Part-time and evening/weekend programs available. *Degree requirements:* For master's, thesis. *Entrance requirements:* For master's, interview, 2 letters of recommendation. Additional exam requirements/recommendations for international students: Required—TOEFL.

Marquette University, Graduate School of Management, Program in Human Resources, Milwaukee, WI 53201-1881. Offers MSHR. Part-time and evening/weekend programs available. *Students:* 17 full-time (14 women), 23 part-time (19 women); includes 2 minority (1 Black or African American, non-Hispanic/Latino; 1 Hispanic/Latino), 22 international. Average age 26. 110 applicants, 49% accepted, 15 enrolled. In 2011, 13 master's awarded. *Entrance requirements:* For master's, GMAT or GRE General Test, letters of recommendation. Additional exam requirements/recommendations for international students: Required—TOEFL (minimum score 550 paper-based; 85 computer-based; 88 iBT), IELTS (minimum score 6.5), Pearson Test of English. *Application deadline:* For fall admission, 2/15 for domestic and international students. Applications are processed on a rolling basis. Application fee: $50. Electronic applications accepted. *Expenses: Tuition:* Full-time $17,010; part-time $945 per credit hour. Tuition and fees vary according to program. *Financial support:* In 2011–12, 3 teaching assistantships were awarded; fellowships, research assistantships, Federal Work-Study, institutionally sponsored loans, and tuition waivers (full and partial) also available. Support available to part-time students. Financial award application deadline: 2/15. *Faculty research:* Diversity, mentoring, executive compensation. *Unit head:* Dr. Timothy Keaveny, Management Chair, 414-288-3643. *Application contact:* Dr. Jeanne Simmons, Associate Dean, 414-288-5126, Fax: 414-288-1902, E-mail: jeanne.simmons@marquette.edu. Web site: http://business.marquette.edu/academics/mshr.

McDaniel College, Graduate and Professional Studies, Program in Human Resources Development, Westminster, MD 21157-4390. Offers MS. Part-time and evening/weekend programs available. *Degree requirements:* For master's, portfolio, internship. *Entrance requirements:* For master's, letters of reference (3). Additional exam requirements/recommendations for international students: Required—TOEFL (minimum score 213 computer-based).

Midwestern State University, Graduate Studies, College of Education, Program in Counseling, Wichita Falls, TX 76308. Offers general counseling (MA); human resource development (MA); school counseling (M Ed); training and development (MA). Part-time and evening/weekend programs available. *Degree requirements:* For master's, comprehensive exam, thesis (for some programs). *Entrance requirements:* For master's, GRE General Test, MAT, or GMAT, valid teaching certificate (M Ed). Additional exam requirements/recommendations for international students: Required—TOEFL (minimum score 550 paper-based; 213 computer-based). Electronic applications accepted. *Faculty research:* Social development of students with disabilities, autism, criminal justice counseling, conflict resolution issues, leadership.

Mississippi State University, College of Education, Department of Instructional Systems and Workforce Development, Mississippi State, MS 39762. Offers MS, MSIT, Ed D, PhD, Ed S. *Faculty:* 9 full-time (6 women), 1 (woman) part-time/adjunct. *Students:* 24 full-time (15 women), 84 part-time (66 women); includes 61 minority (59 Black or African American, non-Hispanic/Latino; 2 Asian, non-Hispanic/Latino), 2 international. Average age 37. 36 applicants, 56% accepted, 17 enrolled. In 2011, 18 master's, 4 doctorates, 4 other advanced degrees awarded. *Degree requirements:* For master's, thesis optional, comprehensive oral or written exam; for doctorate, thesis/dissertation, comprehensive oral and written exam; for Ed S, thesis, comprehensive written exam. *Entrance requirements:* For master's, GRE, minimum GPA of 2.75 in junior and senior courses; for doctorate and Ed S, GRE. Additional exam requirements/recommendations for international students: Required—TOEFL (minimum score 550 paper-based; 213 computer-based; 79 iBT); Recommended—IELTS (minimum score 6.5). *Application deadline:* For fall admission, 7/1 for domestic students, 5/1 for international students; for spring admission, 11/1 for domestic students, 9/1 for international students. Applications are processed on a rolling basis. Application fee: $40. Electronic applications accepted. *Expenses:* Tuition, state resident: full-time $5805; part-time $322.50 per credit hour. Tuition, nonresident: full-time $14,670; part-time $815 per credit hour. *Financial support:* In 2011–12, 1 teaching assistantship with full tuition reimbursement (averaging $10,800 per year) was awarded; Federal Work-Study, institutionally sponsored loans, and unspecified assistantships also available. Financial award application deadline: 4/1; financial award applicants required to submit FAFSA. *Faculty research:* Computer technology, nontraditional students, interactive video, instructional technology, educational leadership. *Unit head:* Dr. Connie Forde, Professor and Department Head, 662-325-7258, Fax: 662-325-7599, E-mail: cforde@colled.msstate.edu. *Application contact:* Dr. James Adams, Associate Professor and Graduate Coordinator, 662-325-7563, Fax: 662-325-7258, E-mail: jadams@colled.msstate.edu. Web site: http://www.msstate.edu/dept/teched/.

Moravian College, Moravian College Comenius Center, Business and Management Programs, Bethlehem, PA 18018-6650. Offers accounting (MBA); general management (MBA); health care management (MBA); human resource management (MBA); leadership (MSHRM); learning and performance management (MSHRM); supply chain management (MBA). Part-time and evening/weekend programs available. *Entrance requirements:* For master's, GMAT. Additional exam requirements/recommendations for international students: Required—TOEFL (minimum score 550 paper-based; 260 computer-based; 90 iBT). *Expenses:* Contact institution. *Faculty research:* Leadership, change management, human resources.

National Louis University, College of Management and Business, Chicago, IL 60603. Offers business administration (MBA); human resource management and development (MS); management (MS). Part-time and evening/weekend programs available. *Students:* 71 full-time (48 women), 56 part-time (36 women); includes 80 minority (32 Black or African American, non-Hispanic/Latino; 1 American Indian or Alaska Native, non-Hispanic/Latino; 3 Asian, non-Hispanic/Latino; 42 Hispanic/Latino; 2 Two or more races, non-Hispanic/Latino). Average age 37. In 2011, 73 master's awarded. *Entrance requirements:* For master's, college-administered critical thinking and writing skills test, minimum GPA of 3.0, resume, 3 references. Additional exam requirements/recommendations for international students: Required—TOEFL (minimum score 550 paper-based; 213 computer-based; 79 iBT). *Application deadline:* Applications are processed on a rolling basis. Application fee: $40. *Financial support:* Federal Work-Study, institutionally sponsored loans, and scholarships/grants available. Support available to part-time students. Financial award applicants required to submit FAFSA. *Unit head:* Walter Roetlger, Executive Dean, 312-261-3073, Fax: 312-261-3073, E-mail: chris.multhauf@nl.edu. *Application contact:* Ken Kasprzak, Director of Admissions, 800-443-5522 Ext. 5718, Fax: 847-947-5575, E-mail: kkasprzak@nl.edu. Web site: http://www3.nl.edu/graduate/business_admin.cfm.

New York University, School of Continuing and Professional Studies, Division of Programs in Business, Program in Leadership and Human Capital Management, New York, NY 10012-1019. Offers benefits and compensation (Advanced Certificate); human resource development (MS); human resource management (MS, Advanced Certificate); organizational and executive coaching (Advanced Certificate); organizational effectiveness (MS). Part-time and evening/weekend programs available. Postbaccalaureate distance learning degree programs offered (no on-campus study). *Faculty:* 40 part-time/adjunct (15 women). *Students:* 32 full-time (19 women), 172 part-time (141 women); includes 29 minority (12 Black or African American, non-Hispanic/Latino; 8 Asian, non-Hispanic/Latino; 8 Hispanic/Latino; 1 Native Hawaiian or other Pacific Islander, non-Hispanic/Latino), 24 international. Average age 32. 196 applicants, 61% accepted, 62 enrolled. In 2011, 74 master's, 13 other advanced degrees awarded. *Degree requirements:* For master's, thesis. *Entrance requirements:* For master's, GRE/GMAT only upon request, relevant professional work, internship or volunteer experience. Additional exam requirements/recommendations for international students: Required—TOEFL (minimum score 600 paper-based; 250 computer-based; 100 iBT), IELTS (minimum score 7). *Application deadline:* For fall admission, 2/1 priority date for domestic students, 2/1 for international students; for spring admission, 10/15 priority date for domestic students, 8/15 for international students. Applications are processed on a rolling basis. Application fee: $150. Electronic applications accepted. *Financial support:* In 2011–12, 89 students received support, including 89 fellowships (averaging $1,838 per year). *Application contact:* Admissions Office, 212-998-7100, E-mail: scps.gradadmissions@nyu.edu. Web site: http://www.scps.nyu.edu/areas-of-study/leadership/.

North Carolina State University, Graduate School, College of Education, Department of Adult and Higher Education, Program in Human Resource Development, Raleigh, NC 27695. Offers MS. *Degree requirements:* For master's, thesis. *Entrance requirements:* For master's, GRE, 3 letters of recommendation, resume.

Northeastern Illinois University, Graduate College, College of Education, Department of Educational Leadership and Development, Program in Human Resource Development, Chicago, IL 60625-4699. Offers educational leadership (MA); human resource development (MA). Part-time and evening/weekend programs available. *Degree requirements:* For master's, comprehensive papers. *Entrance requirements:* For master's, minimum GPA of 2.75, BA in human resource development. Additional exam requirements/recommendations for international students: Required—TOEFL (minimum score 550 paper-based; 213 computer-based; 79 iBT). Electronic applications accepted. *Faculty research:* Analogics, development of expertise, case-based instruction, action science organizational development, theoretical model building.

Oakland University, Graduate Study and Lifelong Learning, School of Education and Human Services, Department of Human Resource Development, Rochester, MI 48309-4401. Offers MTD. *Entrance requirements:* For master's, minimum GPA of 3.0 for unconditional admission. Additional exam requirements/recommendations for international students: Required—TOEFL (minimum score 550 paper-based; 213 computer-based). Electronic applications accepted.

Ottawa University, Graduate Studies-Kansas City, Overland Park, KS 66211. Offers business administration (MBA); human resources (MA). Part-time and evening/weekend programs available. Postbaccalaureate distance learning degree programs offered (minimal on-campus study). *Degree requirements:* For master's, thesis or alternative. *Entrance requirements:* For master's, resume, 3 letters of recommendation. Additional exam requirements/recommendations for international students: Required—TOEFL (minimum score 550 paper-based; 213 computer-based). Electronic applications accepted. *Expenses:* Contact institution.

Penn State Great Valley, Graduate Studies, Management Division, Malvern, PA 19355-1488. Offers M Fin, MBA, MLD. *Accreditation:* AACSB. *Unit head:* Dr. Daniel Indro, Division Head, 610-725-5283, Fax: 610-725-5224, E-mail: dci1@psu.edu.

Application contact: 610-648-3242, Fax: 610-889-1334. Web site: http://www.sgps.psu.edu/current/academicprograms/management/default.ashx.

Penn State University Park, Graduate School, College of Education, Department of Learning and Performance Systems, State College, University Park, PA 16802-1503. Offers adult education (M Ed, D Ed, PhD, Certificate); instructional systems (M Ed, MS, D Ed, PhD); workforce education and development (M Ed, MS, PhD). *Unit head:* Dr. David H. Monk, Dean, 814-865-2526, Fax: 814-865-0555, E-mail: dhm6@psu.edu. *Application contact:* Cynthia E. Nicosia, Director, Graduate Enrollment Services, 814-865-1834, E-mail: cey1@psu.edu. Web site: http://www.ed.psu.edu/educ/lps/dept-lps.

Penn State University Park, Graduate School, College of the Liberal Arts, Department of Labor and Employment Relations, State College, University Park, PA 16802-1503. Offers MPS, MS. Postbaccalaureate distance learning degree programs offered. *Unit head:* Dr. Susan Welch, Dean, 814-865-7691, Fax: 814-863-2085, E-mail: swelch@psu.edu. *Application contact:* Cynthia E. Nicosia, Director, Graduate Enrollment Services, 814-865-1795, Fax: 814-865-4627, E-mail: cey1@psu.edu. Web site: http://lser.la.psu.edu.

Pittsburg State University, Graduate School, College of Technology, Department of Technology and Workforce Learning, Program in Human Resource Development, Pittsburg, KS 66762. Offers MS. *Degree requirements:* For master's, thesis or alternative.

Regent University, Graduate School, School of Global Leadership and Entrepreneurship, Virginia Beach, VA 23464-9800. Offers business administration (MBA), including management general; leadership (Certificate); management (MA); organizational leadership (MA, PhD), including ecclesial leadership (PhD), entrepreneurial leadership (PhD), human resource development (PhD); strategic foresight (MA); strategic leadership (DSL), including global consulting, leadership coaching, strategic foresight. Part-time and evening/weekend programs available. Postbaccalaureate distance learning degree programs offered (minimal on-campus study). *Faculty:* 13 full-time (3 women), 4 part-time/adjunct (1 woman). *Students:* 27 full-time (11 women), 589 part-time (241 women); includes 183 minority (143 Black or African American, non-Hispanic/Latino; 3 American Indian or Alaska Native, non-Hispanic/Latino; 15 Asian, non-Hispanic/Latino; 22 Hispanic/Latino), 128 international. Average age 41. 225 applicants, 57% accepted, 85 enrolled. In 2011, 80 master's, 38 doctorates awarded. *Degree requirements:* For master's, thesis or alternative, 3 credit hour culminating experience; for doctorate, thesis/dissertation. *Entrance requirements:* For master's, GRE, GMAT, minimum undergraduate GPA of 2.75, computer literacy survey, 2 recommendations, resume, transcripts, essay; for doctorate, GRE, GMAT, sample of writing, minimum 3 years of relevant experience, computer literacy survey, 2 recommendations, resume, essay, transcripts; for Certificate, writing sample, resume, transcripts. Additional exam requirements/recommendations for international students: Required—TOEFL (minimum score 577 paper-based; 233 computer-based). *Application deadline:* For fall admission, 5/1 priority date for domestic students; for spring admission, 10/1 priority date for domestic students. Applications are processed on a rolling basis. Application fee: $50. Electronic applications accepted. *Expenses:* Contact institution. *Financial support:* Career-related internships or fieldwork, scholarships/grants, and tuition waivers (full and partial) available. Support available to part-time students. Financial award application deadline: 9/1. *Faculty research:* Servant leadership, ethics and values, telecommuting and family values, organizational communications, distance education. *Unit head:* Dr. Bruce Winston, Dean, 757-352-4306, Fax: 757-352-4634, E-mail: brucwin@regent.edu. *Application contact:* Matthew Chadwick, Director of Enrollment Support Services, 800-373-5504, Fax: 757-352-4381, E-mail: admissions@regent.edu.

Rochester Institute of Technology, Graduate Enrollment Services, College of Applied Science and Technology, School of International Hospitality and Service Innovation, Department of Service Systems, Program in Human Resources Development, Rochester, NY 14623-5603. Offers MS. Part-time and evening/weekend programs available. *Students:* 25 full-time (16 women), 33 part-time (27 women); includes 8 minority (5 Black or African American, non-Hispanic/Latino; 2 Hispanic/Latino; 1 Two or more races, non-Hispanic/Latino), 27 international. Average age 33. 99 applicants, 40% accepted, 23 enrolled. In 2011, 21 master's awarded. *Degree requirements:* For master's, thesis or alternative. *Entrance requirements:* For master's, minimum GPA of 3.0. Additional exam requirements/recommendations for international students: Required—TOEFL (minimum score 570 paper-based; 230 computer-based; 88 iBT) or IELTS (minimum score 6.5). *Application deadline:* For fall admission, 2/15 priority date for domestic students, 2/15 for international students; for winter admission, 11/1 for domestic and international students; for spring admission, 2/1 for domestic and international students. Applications are processed on a rolling basis. Application fee: $50. Electronic applications accepted. *Expenses: Tuition:* Full-time $34,659; part-time $963 per credit hour. *Required fees:* $228; $76 per quarter. *Financial support:* Research assistantships with partial tuition reimbursements, teaching assistantships with partial tuition reimbursements, career-related internships or fieldwork, scholarships/grants, and unspecified assistantships available. Support available to part-time students. Financial award application deadline: 2/15; financial award applicants required to submit FAFSA. *Faculty research:* Global resource development, service/product innovation and implementation. *Unit head:* Dr. Linda Underhill, Director, 585-475-7359, Fax: 585-475-5099, E-mail: lmuism@rit.edu. *Application contact:* Diane Ellison, Assistant Vice President, Graduate Enrollment Services, 585-475-2229, Fax: 585-475-7164, E-mail: gradinfo@rit.edu. Web site: http://www.rit.edu/cast/servicesystems/human-resources-development.php.

Rollins College, Hamilton Holt School, Master of Human Resources Program, Winter Park, FL 32789. Offers MHR. Part-time and evening/weekend programs available. *Faculty:* 3 full-time (0 women), 3 part-time/adjunct (1 woman). *Students:* 4 full-time (all women), 51 part-time (45 women); includes 25 minority (13 Black or African American, non-Hispanic/Latino; 1 Asian, non-Hispanic/Latino; 10 Hispanic/Latino; 1 Two or more races, non-Hispanic/Latino), 1 international. Average age 32. 21 applicants, 95% accepted, 19 enrolled. In 2011, 23 master's awarded. *Degree requirements:* For master's, thesis optional. *Entrance requirements:* For master's, GMAT or GRE, official transcripts, two letters of recommendation, essay, current resume. Additional exam requirements/recommendations for international students: Required—TOEFL (minimum score 550 paper-based; 213 computer-based; 80 iBT). *Application deadline:* For fall admission, 4/1 for domestic students; for spring admission, 12/1 for domestic students. Application fee: $50. *Expenses:* Contact institution. *Financial support:* In 2011–12, 35 students received support. Federal Work-Study, scholarships/grants, and unspecified assistantships available. Support available to part-time students. Financial award applicants required to submit FAFSA. *Unit head:* Dr. Donald Rogers, Faculty Director, 407-646-2348, E-mail: drogers@rollins.edu. *Application contact:* Tonya Parker, Coordinator of Records and Registration, 407-646-2653, Fax: 407-646-1551, E-mail: tparker@rollins.edu. Web site: http://www.rollins.edu/holt/graduate/mhr.html.

Roosevelt University, Graduate Division, College of Professional Studies, Program in Training and Development, Chicago, IL 60605. Offers MA. *Degree requirements:* For master's, thesis. *Entrance requirements:* For master's, minimum GPA of 2.75, relevant work experience.

St. John Fisher College, Ronald L. Bittner School of Business, Organizational Learning and Human Resource Development Program, Rochester, NY 14618-3597. Offers MS. Part-time and evening/weekend programs available. *Faculty:* 1 full-time (0 women), 4 part-time/adjunct (1 woman). *Students:* 5 full-time (3 women), 18 part-time (13 women); includes 9 minority (4 Black or African American, non-Hispanic/Latino; 1 American Indian or Alaska Native, non-Hispanic/Latino; 1 Asian, non-Hispanic/Latino; 3 Hispanic/Latino). Average age 31. 27 applicants, 70% accepted, 14 enrolled. In 2011, 20 master's awarded. *Degree requirements:* For master's, capstone project, professional portfolio. *Entrance requirements:* For master's, 2 letters of recommendation, personal statement, current resume. Additional exam requirements/recommendations for international students: Required—TOEFL (minimum score 575 paper-based; 233 computer-based; 80 iBT). *Application deadline:* Applications are processed on a rolling basis. Application fee: $30. Electronic applications accepted. *Expenses: Tuition:* Part-time $735 per credit. One-time fee: $50 part-time. Tuition and fees vary according to course load, degree level and program. *Financial support:* In 2011–12, 3 students received support. Scholarships/grants available. Financial award applicants required to submit FAFSA. *Faculty research:* Empowerment, leadership, group dynamics, team learning, project management. *Unit head:* Edward Ciaschi, Program Director, 585-385-5266, E-mail: eciaschi@sjfc.edu. *Application contact:* Jose Perales, Director of Graduate Admissions, 585-385-8067, E-mail: jperales@sjfc.edu.

Salve Regina University, Program in Business Administration, Newport, RI 02840-4192. Offers business administration (MBA); business studies (Certificate); human resources management (Certificate); management (Certificate); organizational development (Certificate). Part-time and evening/weekend programs available. Postbaccalaureate distance learning degree programs offered (minimal on-campus study). *Faculty:* 2 full-time (1 woman), 15 part-time/adjunct (6 women). *Students:* 35 full-time (14 women), 86 part-time (41 women); includes 10 minority (5 Black or African American, non-Hispanic/Latino; 3 Asian, non-Hispanic/Latino; 2 Hispanic/Latino), 3 international. *Entrance requirements:* For master's, GMAT, GRE General Test, or MAT, 6 undergraduate credits each in accounting, economics, quantitative analysis and calculus or statistics. Additional exam requirements/recommendations for international students: Required—TOEFL (minimum score 600 paper-based; 250 computer-based; 100 iBT) or IELTS. *Application deadline:* For fall admission, 3/15 priority date for domestic students, 3/15 for international students; for spring admission, 9/15 priority date for domestic students, 9/15 for international students. Applications are processed on a rolling basis. Application fee: $60. Electronic applications accepted. *Expenses: Tuition:* Full-time $7740; part-time $430 per credit. *Required fees:* $40 per semester. Tuition and fees vary according to program. *Financial support:* Career-related internships or fieldwork and Federal Work-Study available. Support available to part-time students. Financial award application deadline: 3/1; financial award applicants required to submit FAFSA. *Unit head:* Dr. Arlene Nicholas, Director, 401-341-3280, E-mail: arlene.nicholas@salve.edu. *Application contact:* Kelly Alverson, Associate Director of Graduate Admissions, 401-341-2153, Fax: 401-341-2973, E-mail: kelly.alverson@salve.edu. Web site: http://www.salve.edu/graduatestudies/programs/gmt/.

Southern New Hampshire University, School of Education, Manchester, NH 03106-1045. Offers business education (MS); child development (M Ed); computer technology education (Certificate); curriculum and instruction (M Ed); education (M Ed, CAS); elementary education (M Ed); general special education (Certificate); school business administrator (Certificate); secondary education (M Ed); training and development (Certificate). Part-time and evening/weekend programs available. Postbaccalaureate distance learning degree programs offered (no on-campus study). *Degree requirements:* For master's, comprehensive exam (for some programs), thesis or alternative. *Entrance requirements:* For master's, PRAXIS I, minimum GPA of 2.75. Additional exam requirements/recommendations for international students: Required—TOEFL (minimum score 550 paper-based; 213 computer-based). Electronic applications accepted. *Expenses:* Contact institution.

Suffolk University, College of Arts and Sciences, Department of Education and Human Services, Boston, MA 02108-2770. Offers administration of higher education (M Ed, CAGS), including administration of higher education (M Ed), leadership (CAGS); human resource, learning and performance (MS, CAGS, Graduate Certificate), including global human resources (Graduate Certificate), human resources (MS, Graduate Certificate), organizational development (CAGS, Graduate Certificate), organizational learning and development (MS, Graduate Certificate); mental health counseling (MS, CAGS); school counseling (M Ed, CAGS); school teaching (M Ed, CAGS), including foundations of education (M Ed), middle school teaching (M Ed), secondary school teaching (M Ed); MPA/MSMHC; MS/Certificate. Part-time and evening/weekend programs available. *Faculty:* 10 full-time (6 women), 7 part-time/adjunct (3 women). *Students:* 53 full-time (39 women), 131 part-time (112 women); includes 21 minority (7 Black or African American, non-Hispanic/Latino; 2 American Indian or Alaska Native, non-Hispanic/Latino; 5 Asian, non-Hispanic/Latino; 5 Hispanic/Latino; 2 Two or more races, non-Hispanic/Latino), 9 international. Average age 28. 158 applicants, 73% accepted, 60 enrolled. In 2011, 72 master's, 8 other advanced degrees awarded. *Entrance requirements:* For master's, GRE General Test or MAT, 2 letters of recommendation, resume. Additional exam requirements/recommendations for international students: Required—TOEFL (minimum score 550 paper-based; 213 computer-based; 80 iBT). *Application deadline:* For fall admission, 6/15 priority date for domestic students, 6/15 for international students; for spring admission, 11/1 priority date for domestic students, 11/1 for international students. Applications are processed on a rolling basis. Application fee: $50. Electronic applications accepted. *Expenses:* Contact institution. *Financial support:* In 2011–12, 102 students received support, including 30 fellowships with full and partial tuition reimbursements available (averaging $10,664 per year); career-related internships or fieldwork, Federal Work-Study, and institutionally sponsored loans also available. Support available to part-time students. Financial award application deadline: 4/1; financial award applicants required to submit FAFSA. *Faculty research:* Predicting competent Head Start preschools, cultural differences. *Unit head:* Dr. Krisanne Bursik, Associate Dean and Acting Chair, 617-573-8261, Fax: 617-305-1743, E-mail: kbursik@suffolk.edu. *Application contact:* Ellen Driscoll, Director of Graduate Admissions, 617-573-8302, Fax: 617-305-1733, E-mail: grad.admission@suffolk.edu. Web site: http://www.suffolk.edu/college/9785.html.

Syracuse University, Martin J. Whitman School of Management, PhD Program in Business Administration, Syracuse, NY 13244. Offers accounting (PhD); finance (PhD); management information systems (PhD); managerial statistics (PhD); marketing (PhD); operations management (PhD); organizational behavior (PhD); strategy and human resources (PhD); supply chain management (PhD). *Faculty:* 79 full-time (20 women), 25 part-time/adjunct (6 women). *Students:* 32 full-time (10 women); includes 6 minority (3 Black or African American, non-Hispanic/Latino; 2 Asian, non-Hispanic/Latino; 1 Hispanic/Latino), 18 international. Average age 32. 260 applicants, 8% accepted, 12 enrolled. In 2011, 2 doctorates awarded. *Degree requirements:* For doctorate, comprehensive exam, thesis/dissertation, summer research paper. *Entrance requirements:* For doctorate, GMAT or GRE General Test, 3 recommendations. Additional exam requirements/recommendations for international students: Required—TOEFL (minimum score 600 paper-based; 250 computer-based; 100 iBT). *Application deadline:* For fall admission, 2/15 priority date for domestic students, 2/15 for international students. Applications are processed on a rolling basis. Application fee: $65. Electronic applications accepted. *Expenses: Tuition:* Part-time $1206 per credit. *Financial support:* In 2011–12, 1 fellowship with full tuition reimbursement (averaging $19,570 per year), 30 teaching assistantships with full tuition reimbursements (averaging $17,000 per year) were awarded; research assistantships with full tuition reimbursements, health care benefits, and unspecified assistantships also available. Financial award application deadline: 1/30. *Faculty research:* Marketing models, market microstructure, supply chain, auditing, corporate governance. *Unit head:* Dr. Eunkyu Lee, Director of the PhD Program, 315-443-3429, E-mail: elee06@syr.edu. *Application contact:* Carol Hilleges, Administrative Specialist, 315-443-9601, Fax: 315-443-3671, E-mail: clhilleg@syr.edu. Web site: http://whitman.syr.edu/phd/.

Texas A&M University, College of Education and Human Development, Department of Educational Administration and Human Resource Development, College Station, TX 77843. Offers adult education (PhD); higher education administration (MS, PhD); human resource development (MS, PhD); public school administration (M Ed, Ed D, PhD). Part-time programs available. *Faculty:* 31. *Students:* 126 full-time (88 women), 270 part-time (156 women); includes 162 minority (65 Black or African American, non-Hispanic/Latino; 2 American Indian or Alaska Native, non-Hispanic/Latino; 15 Asian, non-Hispanic/Latino; 77 Hispanic/Latino; 3 Two or more races, non-Hispanic/Latino), 23 international. Average age 37. In 2011, 91 master's, 30 doctorates awarded. *Degree requirements:* For master's, thesis optional; for doctorate, thesis/dissertation. *Entrance requirements:* For master's, GRE General Test, writing exam, interview, professional experience; for doctorate, GRE General Test, writing exam, interview/presentation, professional experience. Additional exam requirements/recommendations for international students: Required—TOEFL. *Application deadline:* For fall admission, 12/1 for domestic and international students; for spring admission, 8/15 for domestic and international students. Application fee: $50 ($75 for international students). Electronic applications accepted. *Expenses:* Tuition, state resident: full-time $5437; part-time $226.55 per credit hour. Tuition, nonresident: full-time $12,949; part-time $539.55 per credit hour. *Required fees:* $2741. *Financial support:* In 2011–12, fellowships (averaging $20,000 per year), research assistantships (averaging $12,000 per year) were awarded; career-related internships or fieldwork and institutionally sponsored loans also available. Support available to part-time students. Financial award application deadline: 3/1; financial award applicants required to submit FAFSA. *Faculty research:* Higher education administration, public school administration, student affairs. *Unit head:* Dr. Fred M. Nafukho, Head, 979-862-3395, Fax: 979-862-4347, E-mail: fnafukho@tamu.edu. *Application contact:* Joyce Nelson, Director of Academic Advising, 979-847-9098, Fax: 979-862-4347, E-mail: jnelson@tamu.edu. Web site: http://eahr.tamu.edu.

Towson University, Program in Human Resource Development, Towson, MD 21252-0001. Offers MS. Part-time and evening/weekend programs available. *Students:* 63 full-time (48 women), 194 part-time (152 women); includes 65 minority (46 Black or African American, non-Hispanic/Latino; 2 American Indian or Alaska Native, non-Hispanic/Latino; 7 Asian, non-Hispanic/Latino; 7 Hispanic/Latino; 3 Two or more races, non-Hispanic/Latino), 4 international. *Degree requirements:* For master's, comprehensive exam, internship (for educational leadership track). *Entrance requirements:* For master's, 2 letters of recommendation, minimum GPA of 3.0. Additional exam requirements/recommendations for international students: Required—TOEFL. *Application deadline:* Applications are processed on a rolling basis. Application fee: $50. Electronic applications accepted. *Expenses:* Tuition, state resident: part-time $337 per credit. Tuition, nonresident: part-time $709 per credit. *Required fees:* $99 per credit. *Financial support:* Application deadline: 4/1; applicants required to submit FAFSA. *Unit head:* Alan Clardy, Graduate Program Director, 410-704-3069, E-mail: aclardy@towson.edu.

Universidad Central del Este, Graduate School, San Pedro de Macoris, Dominican Republic. Offers environmental engineering (ME); financial management (M Ad); higher education (M Ed), including higher education management, higher education pedagogy; human resources (M Ad). *Entrance requirements:* For master's, letters of recommendation.

Universidad Iberoamericana, Graduate School, Santo Domingo D.N., Dominican Republic. Offers business administration (MBA, PMBA); constitutional law (LL M); dentistry (DMD); educational management (MA); integrated marketing communication (MA); psychopedagogical intervention (M Ed); real estate law (LL M); strategic management of human talent (MM).

University of Bridgeport, School of Arts and Sciences, Department of Counseling, Bridgeport, CT 06604. Offers clinical mental health counseling (MS); college student personnel (MS); community counseling (MS); human resource development (MS); human service (MS). Part-time and evening/weekend programs available. *Faculty:* 7 full-time (4 women), 13 part-time/adjunct (7 women). *Students:* 26 full-time (22 women), 98 part-time (73 women); includes 76 minority (52 Black or African American, non-Hispanic/Latino; 1 Asian, non-Hispanic/Latino; 18 Hispanic/Latino; 5 Two or more races, non-Hispanic/Latino), 2 international. Average age 36. 99 applicants, 47% accepted, 34 enrolled. In 2011, 23 master's awarded. *Degree requirements:* For master's, thesis, project. *Entrance requirements:* Additional exam requirements/recommendations for international students: Recommended—TOEFL (minimum score 550 paper-based; 213 computer-based; 80 iBT), IELTS (minimum score 6.5). *Application deadline:* For fall admission, 8/1 priority date for domestic students, 8/1 for international students; for spring admission, 12/1 priority date for domestic students, 12/1 for international students. Applications are processed on a rolling basis. Application fee: $50. Electronic applications accepted. *Expenses: Tuition:* Full-time $22,880; part-time $700 per credit. *Required fees:* $1870; $95 per semester. Tuition and fees vary according to course load and program. *Financial support:* In 2011–12, 27 students received support. Fellowships, research assistantships, teaching assistantships, career-related internships or fieldwork, Federal Work-Study, and institutionally sponsored loans available. Support available to part-time students. Financial award application deadline: 6/1; financial award applicants required to submit FAFSA. *Faculty research:* Corporate elder care programs. *Unit head:* Dr. Sara L. Connolly, Director, Division of Counseling and Human Resources, 203-576-4183, Fax: 203-576-4219, E-mail: sconnoll@bridgeport.edu. *Application contact:* Karissa Peckham, Dean of Admissions, 203-576-4552, Fax: 203-576-4941, E-mail: admit@bridgeport.edu.

University of California, Los Angeles, Graduate Division, UCLA Anderson School of Management, Los Angeles, CA 90095-1481. Offers accounting (PhD); Asia Pacific (EMBA); business administration (EMBA, MBA); decisions, operations and technology management (PhD); finance (PhD); financial engineering (MFE); global economics and management (PhD); Latin America (EMBA); management and organizations (PhD); marketing (PhD); strategy (PhD); DDS/MBA; MBA/JD; MBA/MD; MBA/MLAS; MBA/MLIS; MBA/MPH; MBA/MPP; MBA/MSCS; MBA/MSN; MBA/MUP. *Accreditation:* AACSB. Part-time programs available. *Faculty:* 90 full-time (14 women), 62 part-time/adjunct (14 women). *Students:* 1,103 full-time (312 women), 842 part-time (223 women); includes 663 minority (18 Black or African American, non-Hispanic/Latino; 510 Asian, non-Hispanic/Latino; 46 Hispanic/Latino; 2 Native Hawaiian or other Pacific Islander, non-Hispanic/Latino; 87 Two or more races, non-Hispanic/Latino), 469 international. 4,737 applicants, 32% accepted, 875 enrolled. In 2011, 759 master's, 6 doctorates awarded. *Degree requirements:* For master's, comprehensive exam, field study consulting project (for MBA); thesis/dissertation (for MFE); for doctorate, comprehensive exam, thesis/dissertation, oral and written qualifying exams. *Entrance requirements:* For master's, GMAT (for MBA); GMAT or GRE General Test (for MFE), 4-year bachelor's degree or equivalent; for doctorate, GMAT or GRE General Test, 4-year bachelor's degree from regionally-accredited institution; minimum GPA of 3.0. Additional exam requirements/recommendations for international students: Required—TOEFL (minimum score 560 paper-based; 220 computer-based; 87 iBT), IELTS (minimum score 7). *Application deadline:* For fall admission, 10/26 for domestic and international students; for winter admission, 1/11 for domestic and international students; for spring admission, 4/18 for domestic and international students. Application fee: $200. Electronic applications accepted. *Expenses:* Contact institution. *Financial support:* In 2011–12, 600 students received support. Fellowships, research assistantships, teaching assistantships, career-related internships or fieldwork, institutionally sponsored loans, scholarships/grants, health care benefits, and tuition waivers (partial) available. Financial award application deadline: 4/15; financial award applicants required to submit FAFSA. *Unit head:* Judy D. Olian, Dean, 310-825-7982, Fax: 310-206-2073, E-mail: judy.olian@anderson.ucla.edu. *Application contact:* Robert Weiler, Assistant Dean, Director of MBA Admissions and Financial Aid, 310-825-6944, Fax: 310-825-8582, E-mail: mba.admissions@anderson.ucla.edu. Web site: http://www.anderson.ucla.edu/.

See Display on page 141 and Close-Up on page 249.

University of Connecticut, Graduate School, Center for Continuing Studies, Program in Human Resource Management, Storrs, CT 06269. Offers labor relations (MPS); personnel (MPS).

University of Denver, University College, Denver, CO 80208. Offers arts and culture (MLS, Certificate), including art, literature, and culture, arts development and program management (Certificate), creative writing; environmental policy and management (MAS, Certificate), including energy and sustainability (Certificate), environmental assessment of nuclear power (Certificate), environmental health and safety (Certificate), environmental management, natural resource management (Certificate); geographic information systems (MAS, Certificate); global affairs (MLS, Certificate), including translation studies, world history and culture; healthcare leadership (MPH, Certificate), including healthcare policy, law, and ethics, medical and healthcare information technologies, strategic management of healthcare; information and communications technology (MCIS, Certificate), including database design and administration (Certificate), geographic information systems (MCIS), information security systems security (Certificate), information systems security (MCIS), project management (MCIS, MPS, Certificate), software design and administration (Certificate), software design and programming (MCIS), technology management, telecommunications technology (MCIS), Web design and development; leadership and organizations (MPS, Certificate), including human capital in organizations, philanthropic leadership, project management (MCIS, MPS, Certificate), strategic innovation and change; organizational and professional communication (MPS, Certificate), including alternative dispute resolution, organizational communication, organizational development and training, public relations and marketing; security management (MAS, Certificate), including emergency planning and response, information security (MAS), organizational security; strategic human resource management (MPS, Certificate), including global human resources (MPS), human resource management and development (MPS). Part-time and evening/weekend programs available. Postbaccalaureate distance learning degree programs offered (no on-campus study). *Faculty:* 204 part-time/adjunct (80 women). *Students:* 56 full-time (26 women), 1,096 part-time (647 women); includes 196 minority (81 Black or African American, non-Hispanic/Latino; 7 American Indian or Alaska Native, non-Hispanic/Latino; 30 Asian, non-Hispanic/Latino; 66 Hispanic/Latino; 3 Native Hawaiian or other Pacific Islander, non-Hispanic/Latino; 9 Two or more races, non-Hispanic/Latino), 76 international. Average age 36. 572 applicants, 95% accepted, 410 enrolled. In 2011, 404 master's, 123 other advanced degrees awarded. *Degree requirements:* For master's, capstone project. *Entrance requirements:* For master's, two letters of recommendation, personal statement, resume. Additional exam requirements/recommendations for international students: Required—TOEFL (minimum score 550 paper-based; 80 iBT). *Application deadline:* For fall admission, 7/20 priority date for domestic students, 6/8 for international students; for winter admission, 10/26 priority date for domestic students, 9/14 for international students; for spring admission, 2/1 priority date for domestic students, 12/14 for international students. Applications are processed on a rolling basis. Application fee: $75. Electronic applications accepted. *Expenses:* Contact institution. *Financial support:* Applicants required to submit FAFSA. *Unit head:* Dr. James Davis, Dean, 303-871-2291, Fax: 303-871-4047, E-mail: jdavis@du.edu. *Application contact:* Information Contact, 303-871-3155, Fax: 303-871-4047, E-mail: ucolinfo@du.edu. Web site: http://www.universitycollege.du.edu/.

University of Houston, College of Technology, Department of Human Development and Consumer Science, Houston, TX 77204. Offers future studies in commerce (MS); human resources development (MS). Part-time programs available. *Degree requirements:* For master's, project or thesis. *Entrance requirements:* For master's, GMAT, MAT. Additional exam requirements/recommendations for international students: Required—TOEFL (minimum score 550 paper-based; 79 iBT). Electronic applications accepted.

University of Illinois at Urbana–Champaign, Graduate College, College of Education, Department of Human Resource Education, Champaign, IL 61820. Offers Ed M, MS, Ed D, PhD, CAS, MBA/M Ed. Part-time and evening/weekend programs available. Postbaccalaureate distance learning degree programs offered (no on-campus study). *Faculty:* 6 full-time (1 woman). *Students:* 48 full-time (21 women), 118 part-time (81 women); includes 30 minority (19 Black or African American, non-Hispanic/Latino; 6 Asian, non-Hispanic/Latino; 5 Hispanic/Latino), 38 international. 104 applicants, 63% accepted, 29 enrolled. In 2011, 87 master's, 9 doctorates, 3 other advanced degrees awarded. *Entrance requirements:* For master's, minimum GPA of 3.0; for doctorate, GRE, minimum GPA of 3.0. Additional exam requirements/recommendations for international students: Required—TOEFL (minimum score 96 iBT). *Application deadline:* Applications are processed on a rolling basis. Application fee: $75 ($90 for international students). Electronic applications accepted. *Financial support:* In 2011–12, 3 fellowships, 8 research assistantships, 11 teaching assistantships were awarded; tuition waivers (full and partial) also available. *Unit head:* James D. Anderson, Head, 217-333-7404, Fax: 217-244-5632, E-mail: janders@illinois.edu. *Application contact:* Laura Ketchum, Secretary, 217-333-0807, Fax: 217-244-5632, E-mail: lirle@illinois.edu. Web site: http://education.illinois.edu/hre/index.html.

University of Louisville, Graduate School, College of Education and Human Development, Department of Leadership, Foundations and Human Resource Education, Louisville, KY 40292-0001. Offers educational leadership and organizational development (Ed D, PhD); higher education (MA); human resource education (MS); P-12 educational administration (M Ed, Ed S). *Accreditation:* NCATE. Part-time and evening/weekend programs available. Postbaccalaureate distance learning degree programs offered. *Degree requirements:* For doctorate, comprehensive exam, thesis/dissertation. *Entrance requirements:* For master's, doctorate, and Ed S, GRE General Test. Additional exam requirements/recommendations for international students: Required—TOEFL (minimum score 560 paper-based; 210 computer-based; 83 iBT). Electronic applications accepted. *Expenses:* Tuition, state resident: full-time $9692;

part-time $539 per credit hour. Tuition, nonresident: full-time $20,168; part-time $1121 per credit hour. Tuition and fees vary according to program and reciprocity agreements. *Faculty research:* Evaluation of methods and programs to improve elementary and secondary education; research on organizational and human resource development; student access, retention and success in post-secondary education; educational policy analysis; multivariate quantitative research methods.

University of Minnesota, Twin Cities Campus, Graduate School, College of Education and Human Development, Department of Organizational Leadership, Policy and Development, Program in Human Resource Development, Minneapolis, MN 55455-0213. Offers M Ed, MA, Ed D, PhD, Certificate. *Students:* 21 full-time (14 women), 30 part-time (24 women); includes 11 minority (5 Black or African American, non-Hispanic/Latino; 1 American Indian or Alaska Native, non-Hispanic/Latino; 4 Asian, non-Hispanic/Latino; 1 Hispanic/Latino), 8 international. Average age 33. 49 applicants, 73% accepted, 30 enrolled. In 2011, 28 master's, 84 other advanced degrees awarded. Application fee: $55. *Unit head:* Dr. Rebecca Ropers-Huilman, Chair, 612-624-1006, Fax: 612-624-3377, E-mail: ropers@umn.edu. *Application contact:* Dr. Jennifer Engler, Assistant Dean, 612-626-2887, Fax: 612-626-7496, E-mail: engle009@umn.edu. Web site: http://cehd.umn.edu/WHRE//HRD.

University of Missouri–St. Louis, Graduate School, Program in Public Policy Administration, St. Louis, MO 63121. Offers health policy (MPPA); local government management (MPPA, Certificate); managing human resources and organization (MPPA); nonprofit organization management (MPPA); nonprofit organization management and leadership (Certificate); policy research and analysis (MPPA). *Accreditation:* NASPAA. Part-time and evening/weekend programs available. *Faculty:* 10 full-time (5 women), 9 part-time/adjunct (4 women). *Students:* 33 full-time (17 women), 76 part-time (48 women); includes 30 minority (25 Black or African American, non-Hispanic/Latino; 2 American Indian or Alaska Native, non-Hispanic/Latino; 1 Asian, non-Hispanic/Latino; 2 Hispanic/Latino), 9 international. Average age 32. 68 applicants, 50% accepted, 27 enrolled. In 2011, 23 master's, 22 Certificates awarded. *Entrance requirements:* For master's, 3 letters of recommendation. Additional exam requirements/recommendations for international students: Required—TOEFL (minimum score 550 paper-based; 213 computer-based). *Application deadline:* For fall admission, 7/1 priority date for domestic students, 7/1 for international students; for spring admission, 12/1 priority date for domestic students, 12/1 for international students. Applications are processed on a rolling basis. Application fee: $35 ($40 for international students). Electronic applications accepted. *Expenses:* Tuition, state resident: full-time $6273; part-time $3866 per year. Tuition, nonresident: full-time $14,969; part-time $9980 per year. *Required fees:* $315 per year. *Financial support:* In 2011–12, 2 research assistantships with full and partial tuition reimbursements (averaging $12,000 per year) were awarded; career-related internships or fieldwork also available. Financial award application deadline: 4/1; financial award applicants required to submit FAFSA. *Faculty research:* Urban policy, public finance, evaluation. *Unit head:* Dr. Deborah Balser, Director, 314-516-5145, Fax: 314-516-5210, E-mail: balserd@msx.umsl.edu. *Application contact:* 314-516-5458, Fax: 314-516-6996, E-mail: gradadm@umsl.edu. Web site: http://www.umsl.edu/divisions/graduate/mppa/.

University of Nebraska at Omaha, Graduate Studies, College of Communication, Fine Arts and Media, School of Communication, Omaha, NE 68182. Offers communication (MA); human resources and training (Certificate). Part-time and evening/weekend programs available. *Faculty:* 23 full-time (11 women). *Students:* 3 full-time (all women), 47 part-time (36 women); includes 9 minority (5 Black or African American, non-Hispanic/Latino; 2 Asian, non-Hispanic/Latino; 1 Hispanic/Latino; 1 Two or more races, non-Hispanic/Latino), 2 international. Average age 31. 35 applicants, 57% accepted, 13 enrolled. In 2011, 9 master's, 3 other advanced degrees awarded. *Degree requirements:* For master's, comprehensive exam, thesis (for some programs). *Entrance requirements:* For master's, minimum GPA of 3.25, 15 undergraduate communication courses, resume, statement of purpose, 3 letters of recommendation. Additional exam requirements/recommendations for international students: Required—TOEFL (minimum score 550 paper-based; 213 computer-based; 80 iBT). *Application deadline:* For fall admission, 3/1 priority date for domestic students; for spring admission, 10/1 priority date for domestic students. Applications are processed on a rolling basis. Application fee: $45. Electronic applications accepted. *Financial support:* In 2011–12, 20 students received support, including 9 teaching assistantships with tuition reimbursements available; fellowships, research assistantships with tuition reimbursements available, Federal Work-Study, institutionally sponsored loans, scholarships/grants, tuition waivers (partial), and unspecified assistantships also available. Support available to part-time students. Financial award application deadline: 3/1; financial award applicants required to submit FAFSA. *Unit head:* Dr. Jeremy Lipschultz, Director, 402-554-2600. *Application contact:* Dr. Barbara Pickering, Student Contact, 402-554-2600.

University of Nevada, Las Vegas, Graduate College, Greenspun College of Urban Affairs, School of Environmental and Public Affairs, Las Vegas, NV 89154-4030. Offers crisis and emergency management (MS); environmental science (MS, PhD); non-profit management (Certificate); public administration (MPA); public affairs (PhD); public management (Certificate); solar and renewabale energy (Certificate); urban leadership (MA); workforce development and organizational leadership (PhD). Part-time programs available. *Faculty:* 28 full-time (10 women), 53 part-time/adjunct (11 women). *Students:* 49 full-time (19 women), 117 part-time (57 women); includes 62 minority (31 Black or African American, non-Hispanic/Latino; 1 American Indian or Alaska Native, non-Hispanic/Latino; 4 Asian, non-Hispanic/Latino; 21 Hispanic/Latino; 5 Two or more races, non-Hispanic/Latino), 5 international. Average age 36. 94 applicants, 66% accepted, 47 enrolled. In 2011, 46 master's, 4 doctorates, 4 other advanced degrees awarded. *Degree requirements:* For master's, comprehensive exam (for some programs), thesis; for doctorate, comprehensive exam (for some programs), thesis/dissertation. *Entrance requirements:* Additional exam requirements/recommendations for international students: Required—TOEFL (minimum score 550 paper-based; 213 computer-based; 80 iBT), IELTS (minimum score 7). *Application deadline:* For fall admission, 2/15 priority date for domestic students, 5/1 for international students; for spring admission, 11/15 priority date for domestic students, 10/1 for international students. Applications are processed on a rolling basis. Application fee: $60 ($95 for international students). Electronic applications accepted. *Financial support:* In 2011–12, 33 students received support, including 20 research assistantships with partial tuition reimbursements available (averaging $11,193 per year), 13 teaching assistantships with partial tuition reimbursements available (averaging $10,928 per year); institutionally sponsored loans, scholarships/grants, health care benefits, and unspecified assistantships also available. Financial award application deadline: 3/1. *Faculty research:* Community and organizational resilience; environmental decision-making and management; budgeting and human resource/workforce management; urban design, sustainability and governance; public and non-profit management. *Total annual research expenditures:* $1.3 million. *Unit head:* Dr. Christopher Stream, Chair/Associate Professor, 702-895-5120, Fax: 702-895-4436, E-mail: chris.stream@unlv.edu. *Application contact:* Graduate College Admissions Evaluator, 702-895-3320, Fax: 702-895-4180, E-mail: gradcollege@unlv.edu. Web site: http://sepa.unlv.edu/.

University of Oklahoma, College of Arts and Sciences, Department of Human Relations, Norman, OK 73019. Offers human relations (MHR), including affirmative action, chemical addictions counseling, family relations, general, human resources, juvenile justice; human relations licensure (Graduate Certificate). Part-time and evening/weekend programs available. Postbaccalaureate distance learning degree programs offered (minimal on-campus study). *Faculty:* 27 full-time (18 women), 2 part-time/adjunct (1 woman). *Students:* 327 full-time (207 women), 537 part-time (328 women); includes 343 minority (203 Black or African American, non-Hispanic/Latino; 42 American Indian or Alaska Native, non-Hispanic/Latino; 22 Asian, non-Hispanic/Latino; 45 Hispanic/Latino; 31 Two or more races, non-Hispanic/Latino), 15 international. Average age 34. 317 applicants, 90% accepted, 201 enrolled. In 2011, 310 degrees awarded. *Degree requirements:* For master's, thesis optional. *Entrance requirements:* For master's, minimum GPA of 3.0 in last 60 hours of undergraduate course work, resume, 3 letters of reference. Additional exam requirements/recommendations for international students: Required—TOEFL (minimum score 550 paper-based; 79 iBT). *Application deadline:* For fall admission, 4/1 priority date for domestic students, 3/1 for international students; for spring admission, 11/1 for domestic students, 9/1 for international students. Applications are processed on a rolling basis. Application fee: $40 ($90 for international students). Electronic applications accepted. *Expenses:* Tuition, state resident: full-time $4087; part-time $170.30 per credit hour. Tuition, nonresident: full-time $14,875; part-time $619.80 per credit hour. *Required fees:* $2659; $100.25 per credit hour. Tuition and fees vary according to course load and degree level. *Financial support:* In 2011–12, 358 students received support, including 12 research assistantships with partial tuition reimbursements available (averaging $11,021 per year), 5 teaching assistantships (averaging $11,124 per year); career-related internships or fieldwork, scholarships/grants, and unspecified assistantships also available. Financial award applicants required to submit FAFSA. *Faculty research:* Non-profit organizations, high risk youth, trauma, women's studies, impact of war on women and children. *Total annual research expenditures:* $62,927. *Unit head:* Dr. Susan Marcus-Mendoza, Chair, 405-325-1756, Fax: 405-325-4402, E-mail: smmendoza@ou.edu. *Application contact:* Lawana Miller, Admissions Coordinator, 405-325-1756, Fax: 405-325-4402, E-mail: lmiller@ou.edu. Web site: http://www.ou.edu/cas/hr.

University of Regina, Faculty of Graduate Studies and Research, Faculty of Education, Department of Human Resources Development, Regina, SK S4S 0A2, Canada. Offers MHRD. Part-time programs available. *Faculty:* 3 full-time (2 women). *Students:* 5 full-time (3 women), 10 part-time (9 women). 10 applicants, 70% accepted. In 2011, 6 master's awarded. *Degree requirements:* For master's, practicum, project, or thesis. *Entrance requirements:* For master's, 4-year B Ed, two years of teaching experience. Additional exam requirements/recommendations for international students: Required—TOEFL (minimum score 580 paper-based; 80 iBT), IELTS (minimum score 6.5). *Application deadline:* 2/15 for domestic and international students. Application fee: $100. Electronic applications accepted. *Financial support:* In 2011–12, 1 fellowship (averaging $6,000 per year), 3 teaching assistantships (averaging $2,298 per year) were awarded; research assistantships and scholarships/grants also available. Financial award application deadline: 6/15. *Faculty research:* Foundations of adult development, theory and practice of adult education and human resource development; design and assessment of curriculum and instruction; planning and curriculum development; learning and the workplace. *Unit head:* Dr. Rod Dolmage, Associate Dean, Research and Graduate Programs, 306-585-4816, Fax: 306-585-5387, E-mail: rod.dolmage@uregina.ca. *Application contact:* Tania Gates, Graduate Program Coordinator, 306-585-4506, Fax: 306-585-5387, E-mail: edgrad@uregina.ca.

The University of Scranton, College of Graduate and Continuing Education, Department of Health Administration and Human Resources, Program in Human Resources, Scranton, PA 18510. Offers MS. Part-time and evening/weekend programs available. *Students:* 92 full-time (75 women), 39 part-time (31 women); includes 23 minority (17 Black or African American, non-Hispanic/Latino; 4 Asian, non-Hispanic/Latino; 1 Hispanic/Latino; 1 Native Hawaiian or other Pacific Islander, non-Hispanic/Latino), 2 international. Average age 32. 46 applicants, 100% accepted. *Degree requirements:* For master's, capstone experience. *Entrance requirements:* Additional exam requirements/recommendations for international students: Required—TOEFL (minimum score 550 paper-based; 173 computer-based), IELTS (minimum score 5.5). Application fee: $0. *Financial support:* Fellowships, teaching assistantships, and career-related internships or fieldwork available. Financial award application deadline: 3/1. *Unit head:* Dr. Daniel J. West, Chair, 570-941-4126, Fax: 570-941-4201, E-mail: westd1@scranton.edu. *Application contact:* Joseph M. Roback, Director of Admissions, 570-941-4385, Fax: 570-941-5928, E-mail: robackj2@scranton.edu. Web site: http://academic.uofs.edu/department/hahr/.

The University of Scranton, College of Graduate and Continuing Education, Department of Health Administration and Human Resources, Program in Human Resources Administration, Scranton, PA 18510. Offers human resources (MS); human resources development (MS); organizational leadership (MS). Part-time and evening/weekend programs available. *Students:* 3 full-time (all women). Average age 36. 70 applicants, 80% accepted. In 2011, 5 master's awarded. *Degree requirements:* For master's, capstone experience. *Entrance requirements:* For master's, minimum GPA of 2.75. Additional exam requirements/recommendations for international students: Required—TOEFL (minimum score 500 paper-based; 173 computer-based), IELTS (minimum score 5.5). *Application deadline:* Applications are processed on a rolling basis. Application fee: $0. *Financial support:* Fellowships, teaching assistantships, career-related internships or fieldwork, Federal Work-Study, and unspecified assistantships available. Support available to part-time students. Financial award application deadline: 3/1. *Unit head:* Dr. Daniel West, Director, 570-941-6218, E-mail: westd1@scranton.edu. *Application contact:* Joseph M. Roback, Director of Admissions, 570-941-4385, Fax: 570-941-5928, E-mail: robackj2@scranton.edu.

University of South Africa, College of Economic and Management Sciences, Pretoria, South Africa. Offers accounting (D Admin, D Com); accounting science (DA); auditing (D Admin, D Com); business administration (M Tech); business economics (D Admin); business leadership (DBL); business management (D Admin, D Com); economic management analysis (M Tech); economics (D Admin, D Com, PhD); human resource development (M Tech); industrial psychology (D Admin, D Com, PhD); logistics (D Com); marketing (M Tech); public administration (D Admin, D Com, DPA, PhD); public management (M Tech); quantitative management (D Admin, D Com); real estate (M Tech); statistics (D Admin, PhD); tourism management (D Admin, D Com); transport economics (D Admin, D Com).

The University of Tennessee, Graduate School, College of Business Administration, Program in Human Resource Development, Knoxville, TN 37996. Offers teacher licensure (MS); training and development (MS). Part-time programs available. *Degree requirements:* For master's, thesis. *Entrance requirements:* For master's, GRE General Test, minimum GPA of 2.7. Electronic applications accepted. *Expenses:* Tuition, state resident: full-time $8332; part-time $464 per credit hour. Tuition, nonresident: full-time $25,174; part-time $1400 per credit hour. *Required fees:* $1162; $56 per credit hour. Tuition and fees vary according to program.

The University of Texas at Tyler, College of Business and Technology, School of Human Resource Development and Technology, Tyler, TX 75799-0001. Offers human resource development (MS, PhD); industrial management (MS). Part-time and evening/weekend programs available. Postbaccalaureate distance learning degree programs offered (no on-campus study). *Degree requirements:* For master's, comprehensive exam. *Entrance requirements:* For master's, GRE General Test or MAT. Additional exam requirements/recommendations for international students: Required—TOEFL (minimum score 79 computer-based). Electronic applications accepted. *Faculty research:* Human resource development.

University of Wisconsin–Milwaukee, Graduate School, College of Letters and Sciences, Interdepartmental Program in Human Resources and Labor Relations, Milwaukee, WI 53201-0413. Offers human resources and labor relations (MHRLR); international human resources and labor relations (Certificate); mediation and negotiation (Certificate). Part-time programs available. *Faculty:* 2 full-time (0 women). *Students:* 14 full-time (8 women), 24 part-time (21 women); includes 7 minority (6 Black or African American, non-Hispanic/Latino; 1 American Indian or Alaska Native, non-Hispanic/Latino), 3 international. Average age 30. 31 applicants, 61% accepted, 11 enrolled. In 2011, 21 degrees awarded. *Entrance requirements:* For master's, GMAT or GRE General Test. Additional exam requirements/recommendations for international students: Required—TOEFL (minimum score 550 paper-based; 79 iBT), IELTS (minimum score 6.5). *Application deadline:* For fall admission, 1/1 priority date for domestic students; for spring admission, 9/1 for domestic students. Applications are processed on a rolling basis. Application fee: $56 ($96 for international students). Electronic applications accepted. One-time fee: $506.10 full-time. Tuition and fees vary according to course load and reciprocity agreements. *Financial support:* Career-related internships or fieldwork available. Support available to part-time students. Financial award application deadline: 4/15; financial award applicants required to submit FAFSA. *Unit head:* Susan M. Donohue-Davies, Representative, 414-299-4009, Fax: 414-229-5915, E-mail: suedono@uwm.edu. *Application contact:* General Information Contact, 414-229-4982, Fax: 414-229-6967, E-mail: gradschool@uwm.edu. Web site: http://www.uwm.edu/dept/MHRLR/.

University of Wisconsin–Stout, Graduate School, College of Technology, Engineering, and Management, Program in Training and Development, Menomonie, WI 54751. Offers MS. Part-time programs available. *Degree requirements:* For master's, thesis. *Entrance requirements:* For master's, minimum GPA of 2.75. Additional exam requirements/recommendations for international students: Required—TOEFL (minimum score 500 paper-based; 173 computer-based; 61 iBT). Electronic applications accepted. *Faculty research:* Organizational behavior, performance, learning and performance, strategic planning.

Villanova University, Graduate School of Liberal Arts and Sciences, Department of Human Resource Development, Villanova, PA 19085-1699. Offers MS. Part-time and evening/weekend programs available. Postbaccalaureate distance learning degree programs offered (no on-campus study). *Faculty:* 5 full-time (3 women), 20 part-time/adjunct (10 women). *Students:* 211 full-time (155 women), 250 part-time (187 women); includes 126 minority (63 Black or African American, non-Hispanic/Latino; 2 American Indian or Alaska Native, non-Hispanic/Latino; 13 Asian, non-Hispanic/Latino; 36 Hispanic/Latino; 3 Native Hawaiian or other Pacific Islander, non-Hispanic/Latino; 9 Two or more races, non-Hispanic/Latino), 8 international. Average age 38. 196 applicants, 86% accepted, 141 enrolled. In 2011, 93 master's awarded. *Degree requirements:* For master's, comprehensive exam. *Entrance requirements:* For master's, GRE General Test, minimum GPA of 3.0. Additional exam requirements/recommendations for international students: Required—TOEFL. *Application deadline:* For fall admission, 5/1 for international students; for spring admission, 10/15 for international students. Applications are processed on a rolling basis. Application fee: $50. Electronic applications accepted. *Expenses: Tuition:* Part-time $675 per credit. Part-time tuition and fees vary according to degree level and program. *Financial support:* Research assistantships, career-related internships or fieldwork, Federal Work-Study, and unspecified assistantships available. Financial award applicants required to submit FAFSA. *Unit head:* Dr. David F. Bush, Director, 610-519-4746, E-mail: david.bush@villanova.edu. *Application contact:* Dr. Adele Lindenmeyr, Dean, Graduate School of Liberal Arts and Sciences, 610-519-7093, Fax: 610-519-7096. Web site: http://www.villanova.edu/artsci/hrd/.

Virginia Commonwealth University, Graduate School, School of Education, Program in Adult Learning, Richmond, VA 23284-9005. Offers adult literacy (M Ed); human resource development (M Ed); teaching and learning with technology (M Ed). *Accreditation:* NCATE. Part-time programs available. *Entrance requirements:* For master's, GRE General Test or MAT. Additional exam requirements/recommendations for international students: Required—TOEFL (minimum score 600 paper-based; 250 computer-based; 100 iBT). Electronic applications accepted. *Expenses:* Tuition, state resident: full-time $9133; part-time $507 per credit. Tuition, nonresident: full-time $18,777; part-time $1043 per credit. *Required fees:* $77 per credit. Tuition and fees vary according to degree level, campus/location, program and student level. *Faculty research:* Adult development and learning, program planning and evaluation.

Walden University, Graduate Programs, Richard W. Riley College of Education and Leadership, Minneapolis, MN 55401. Offers administrator leadership for teaching and learning (Ed D, Ed S); adult education (Ed D, Ed S); adult learning (MS, Postbaccalaureate Certificate), including developmental education (MS), online teaching (MS), teaching adults English as a second language (MS), training and performance management (MS); college teaching and learning (Ed D, Ed S, Postbaccalaureate Certificate); curriculum, instruction and assessment (Ed D, Postbaccalaureate Certificate); curriculum, instruction, and professional development (Ed S); developmental education (Postbaccalaureate Certificate); early childhood administration, management, and leadership (Postbaccalaureate Certificate); early childhood education (birth-grade 3) (MAT); early childhood public policy and advocacy (Postbaccalaureate Certificate); early childhood studies (MS), including administration, management and leadership, early childhood public policy and advocacy, teaching adults in the early childhood field, teaching and diversity; education (MS, PhD), including adolescent literacy and technology (grades 6-12) (MS), adult education leadership (PhD), assessment, evaluation, and accountability (PhD), community college leadership (PhD), curriculum, instruction, and assessment, early childhood education (PhD), educational technology (PhD), elementary reading and literacy (MS), elementary reading and mathematics (MS), general program, global and comparative education (PhD), higher education (PhD), integrating technology in the classroom (MS), K-12 educational leadership (PhD), leadership, policy and change (PhD), learning, instruction and innovation (PhD), literacy and learning in the content areas (MS), mathematics (grades 6-8) (MS), mathematics (grades K-5) (MS), middle level education (grades 5-8) (MS), professional development (MS), science (grades K-8) (MS), self-designed (PhD), special education (PhD), special education (non-licensure) (MS), teacher leadership (grades K-12) (MS), teaching English language learners (grades K-12) (MS); educational leadership and administration (principal preparation) (Ed S); educational technology (Ed S); elementary reading and literacy (Postbaccalaureate Certificate); engaging culturally diverse learners (Postbaccalaureate Certificate); enrollment management and institutional marketing (Postbaccalaureate Certificate); higher education (MS), including college teaching and learning, enrollment management and institutional planning, global higher education, leadership for student success, online and distance learning; higher education leadership (Ed D); instructional design (Postbaccalaureate Certificate); instructional design and technology (MS), including general program (MS, PhD), online learning, training and performance improvement; integrating technology in the classroom (Postbaccalaureate Certificate); online teaching for adult learners (Postbaccalaureate Certificate); professional development (Postbaccalaureate Certificate); reading and literacy leadership (Ed D); science K-8 (Postbaccalaureate Certificate); special education (Ed D, Ed S); special education: emotional/behavioral disorders (K-12) (MAT); special education: learning disabilities (K-12) (MAT); teacher leadership (Ed D, Ed S, Postbaccalaureate Certificate); training and performance management (Postbaccalaureate Certificate). Part-time and evening/weekend programs available. Postbaccalaureate distance learning degree programs offered (minimal on-campus study). *Faculty:* 71 full-time (48 women), 853 part-time/adjunct (585 women). *Students:* 11,326 full-time (9,212 women), 2,148 part-time (1,795 women); includes 5,346 minority (4,403 Black or African American, non-Hispanic/Latino; 76 American Indian or Alaska Native, non-Hispanic/Latino; 140 Asian, non-Hispanic/Latino; 561 Hispanic/Latino; 21 Native Hawaiian or other Pacific Islander, non-Hispanic/Latino; 145 Two or more races, non-Hispanic/Latino), 322 international. Average age 39. In 2011, 3,477 master's, 318 doctorates, 471 other advanced degrees awarded. *Degree requirements:* For doctorate, thesis/dissertation (for some programs), residency; for other advanced degree, residency (for some programs). *Entrance requirements:* For master's, bachelor's degree or equivalent in related field; minimum GPA of 2.5; official transcripts; goal statement; access to computer and Internet; for doctorate, master's degree or equivalent in related field; minimum GPA of 3.0; official transcripts; three years' related professional/academic experience (preferred); access to computer and Internet; for other advanced degree, master's degree or equivalent in related field; minimum GPA of 3.0; 3 years related professional/academic experience (preferred); access to computer and Internet (Ed S). Additional exam requirements/recommendations for international students: Required—TOEFL (minimum score 550 paper-based; 213 computer-based), IELTS (minimum score 6.5), or Michigan English Language Assessment Battery (minimum score 82). *Application deadline:* Applications are processed on a rolling basis. Application fee: $50. Electronic applications accepted. *Financial support:* Federal Work-Study, scholarships/grants, unspecified assistantships, and family tuition reduction, active duty/veteran tuition reduction, group tuition reduction, interest-free payment plans, employee tuition reduction available. Support available to part-time students. Financial award applicants required to submit FAFSA. *Unit head:* Dr. Kate Steffens, Dean, 800-925-3368. *Application contact:* Jennifer Hall, Vice President of Enrollment Management, 866-4-WALDEN, E-mail: info@waldenu.edu. Web site: http://www.waldenu.edu/Colleges-and-Schools/College-of-Education-and-Leadership.htm.

Webster University, George Herbert Walker School of Business and Technology, Department of Business, St. Louis, MO 63119-3194. Offers business (MA); business and organizational security management (MBA); computer resources and information management (MBA); environmental management (MBA); finance (MA, MBA); health services management (MBA); human resources development (MBA); human resources management (MBA); international business (MA, MBA); management and leadership (MBA); marketing (MBA); procurement and acquisitions management (MBA); telecommunications management (MBA). *Accreditation:* ACBSP. Part-time and evening/weekend programs available. Postbaccalaureate distance learning degree programs offered (no on-campus study). *Degree requirements:* For master's, comprehensive exam (for some programs), thesis (for some programs). *Entrance requirements:* Additional exam requirements/recommendations for international students: Required—TOEFL. *Expenses: Tuition:* Full-time $10,890; part-time $605 per credit hour. Tuition and fees vary according to campus/location and program.

Webster University, George Herbert Walker School of Business and Technology, Department of Management, St. Louis, MO 63119-3194. Offers business and organizational security management (MA); computer resources and information management (MA); environmental management (MS); government contracting (Certificate); health care management (MA); health services management (MA); human resources development (MA); human resources management (MA); management (DM); management and leadership (MA); marketing (MA); nonprofit management (Certificate); procurement and acquisitions management (MA); public administration (MA); quality management (MA); space systems operations management (MS); telecommunications management (MA). *Accreditation:* ACBSP. Part-time and evening/weekend programs available. Postbaccalaureate distance learning degree programs offered (no on-campus study). *Degree requirements:* For master's, thesis (for some programs); for doctorate, thesis/dissertation, written exam. *Entrance requirements:* For doctorate, GMAT, 3 years of work experience, MBA. Additional exam requirements/recommendations for international students: Required—TOEFL. *Expenses: Tuition:* Full-time $10,890; part-time $605 per credit hour. Tuition and fees vary according to campus/location and program.

Western Carolina University, Graduate School, College of Education and Allied Professions, Department of Human Services, Cullowhee, NC 28723. Offers counseling (M Ed, MA Ed, MS), including community counseling (M Ed, MS), school counseling (MA Ed); human resources (MS). *Accreditation:* ACA (one or more programs are accredited). Part-time and evening/weekend programs available. Postbaccalaureate distance learning degree programs offered. *Students:* 114 full-time (87 women), 280 part-time (206 women); includes 44 minority (27 Black or African American, non-Hispanic/Latino; 2 American Indian or Alaska Native, non-Hispanic/Latino; 4 Asian, non-Hispanic/Latino; 8 Hispanic/Latino; 3 Two or more races, non-Hispanic/Latino), 7 international. Average age 35. 224 applicants, 78% accepted, 124 enrolled. In 2011, 125 master's awarded. *Degree requirements:* For master's, comprehensive exam, thesis or alternative. *Entrance requirements:* For master's, GRE General Test, appropriate undergraduate degree with minimum GPA of 3.0, 3 recommendations, writing sample, resume. Additional exam requirements/recommendations for international students: Required—TOEFL (minimum score 550 paper-based; 270 computer-based; 79 iBT). *Application deadline:* For fall admission, 2/1 for domestic students. Applications are processed on a rolling basis. Application fee: $50. *Expenses:* Tuition, state resident: full-time $3348. Tuition, nonresident: full-time $12,933. *Required fees:* $3155. *Financial support:* Fellowships, research assistantships with full and partial tuition reimbursements, teaching assistantships with full and partial tuition reimbursements, career-related internships or fieldwork, institutionally sponsored loans, scholarships/grants, and unspecified assistantships available. Financial award application deadline: 3/31; financial award applicants required to submit FAFSA. *Faculty research:* Marital and family development, spirituality in counseling, home school law, sexuality education, employee recruitment/retention. *Unit head:* Dr. Dale Brotherton, Department Head, 828-227-3284, E-mail: brotherton@email.wcu.edu. *Application contact:* Admissions Specialist for Human Services, 828-227-7398, Fax: 828-227-7480, E-mail: gradsch@email.wcu.edu. Web site: http://www.wcu.edu/3065.asp.

Western Michigan University, Graduate College, College of Education and Human Development, Department of Counselor Education and Counseling Psychology, Kalamazoo, MI 49008. Offers counseling psychology (MA, PhD); counselor education (MA, PhD); human resources development (MA). *Accreditation:* ACA (one or more programs are accredited); APA (one or more programs are accredited); CORE; NCATE. *Degree requirements:* For doctorate, thesis/dissertation, oral exams. *Entrance requirements:* For doctorate, GRE General Test.

Western Seminary, Graduate Programs, Program in Ministry and Leadership, Portland, OR 97215-3367. Offers chaplaincy (MA); coaching (MA); Jewish ministry (MA); pastoral care to women (MA); youth ministry (MA). *Degree requirements:* For master's, practicum. *Entrance requirements:* Additional exam requirements/recommendations for international students: Required—TOEFL.

William Woods University, Graduate and Adult Studies, Fulton, MO 65251-1098. Offers administration (Ed S); agriculture (MBA); athletic/activities administration (M Ed); curriculum and instruction (M Ed); curriculum leadership (Ed S); elementary administration (M Ed); health management (MBA); human resources (MBA); principalship (Ed S); secondary administration (M Ed); special education director (M Ed). Evening/weekend programs available. *Degree requirements:* For master's, capstone course (MBA), action research (M Ed); for Ed S, field experience. *Entrance requirements:* For master's, 2 recommendations, resumé, BA/BS; teaching certification (M Ed); course work in economics and accounting (MBA); for Ed S, M Ed, 2 letters of recommendation, resume, teaching certification. Additional exam requirements/recommendations for international students: Required—TOEFL (minimum score 550 paper-based). Electronic applications accepted.

Xavier University, College of Social Sciences, Health and Education, School of Education, Department of Educational Leadership and Human Resource Development, Program in Human Resource Development, Cincinnati, OH 45207. Offers MS. Part-time and evening/weekend programs available. *Faculty:* 2 full-time (both women), 3 part-time/adjunct (0 women). *Students:* 67 part-time (53 women); includes 17 minority (13 Black or African American, non-Hispanic/Latino; 3 Asian, non-Hispanic/Latino; 1 Two or more races, non-Hispanic/Latino), 1 international. Average age 33. 38 applicants, 97% accepted, 31 enrolled. In 2011, 28 master's awarded. *Entrance requirements:* For master's, GRE or MAT, resume, goal statement, two references. Additional exam requirements/recommendations for international students: Required—TOEFL (minimum score 550 paper-based; 213 computer-based; 79 iBT). *Application deadline:* For fall admission, 8/1 priority date for domestic students, 8/1 for international students. Applications are processed on a rolling basis. Application fee: $35. Electronic applications accepted. *Expenses:* Contact institution. *Financial support:* Teaching assistantships and unspecified assistantships available. Financial award applicants required to submit FAFSA. *Faculty research:* Graduate education, group dynamics, organizational behavior, reflection-in-action. *Unit head:* Dr. Brenda Levya-Gardner, Associate Professor/Director, 513-745-4287, Fax: 513-745-1052, E-mail: gardner@xavier.edu. *Application contact:* Roger Bosse, Graduate Services Director, 513-745-3357, Fax: 513-745-1048, E-mail: bosse@xavier.edu. Web site: http://www.xavier.edu/hrd/.

Human Resources Management

Adelphi University, Robert B. Willumstad School of Business, Certificate Program in Human Resource Management, Garden City, NY 11530-0701. Offers Certificate. Part-time and evening/weekend programs available. *Students:* 1 (woman) full-time, 3 part-time (2 women); includes 2 minority (both Hispanic/Latino). Average age 25. In 2011, 3 Certificates awarded. *Entrance requirements:* For degree, GMAT or master's degree. Additional exam requirements/recommendations for international students: Required—TOEFL (minimum score 550 paper-based; 213 computer-based; 80 iBT). *Application deadline:* For fall admission, 4/1 for international students; for spring admission, 11/1 for international students. Applications are processed on a rolling basis. Application fee: $50. Electronic applications accepted. *Expenses: Tuition:* Full-time $29,600; part-time $930 per credit. *Required fees:* $1100. *Financial support:* Application deadline: 3/1; applicants required to submit FAFSA. *Unit head:* Brian Rothschild, Assistant Dean, 516-877-4670, Fax: 516-877-4607, E-mail: gradbusinquiries@adelphi.edu. *Application contact:* Christine Murphy, Director of Admissions, 516-877-3050, Fax: 516-877-3039, E-mail: graduateadmissions@adelphi.edu. Web site: http://academics.adelphi.edu/business-programs/advanced-certificate-hr-study.php.

Adelphi University, Robert B. Willumstad School of Business, MBA Program, Garden City, NY 11530-0701. Offers finance (MBA); management information systems (MBA); management/human resource management (MBA); marketing/e-commerce (MBA). *Accreditation:* AACSB. Part-time and evening/weekend programs available. *Students:* 258 full-time (121 women), 111 part-time (58 women); includes 67 minority (22 Black or African American, non-Hispanic/Latino; 18 Asian, non-Hispanic/Latino; 24 Hispanic/Latino; 3 Two or more races, non-Hispanic/Latino), 172 international. Average age 28. In 2011, 111 master's awarded. *Degree requirements:* For master's, capstone course. *Entrance requirements:* For master's, GMAT, 2 letters of recommendation. Additional exam requirements/recommendations for international students: Required—TOEFL (minimum score 550 paper-based; 213 computer-based; 80 iBT). *Application deadline:* For fall admission, 4/1 for international students; for spring admission, 11/1 for international students. Applications are processed on a rolling basis. Application fee: $50. Electronic applications accepted. *Expenses: Tuition:* Full-time $29,600; part-time $930 per credit. *Required fees:* $1100. *Financial support:* Research assistantships with full and partial tuition reimbursements, career-related internships or fieldwork, Federal Work-Study, institutionally sponsored loans, scholarships/grants, and unspecified assistantships available. Financial award application deadline: 3/1; financial award applicants required to submit FAFSA. *Faculty research:* Supply chain management, distribution channels, productivity benchmark analysis, data envelopment analysis, financial portfolio analysis. *Unit head:* Rakesh Gupta, 516-877-4670, Fax: 516-877-4607, E-mail: gradbusinquiries@adelphi.edu. *Application contact:* Christine Murphy, Director of Admissions, 516-877-3050, Fax: 516-877-3039, E-mail: graduateadmissions@adelphi.edu. Web site: http://business.adelphi.edu/degree-programs/graduate-degree-programs/m-b-a/.

See Display on page 68 and Close-Up on page 177.

Alabama Agricultural and Mechanical University, School of Graduate Studies, School of Education, Department of Counseling and Special Education, Huntsville, AL 35811. Offers communicative disorders (M Ed, MS); psychology and counseling (MS, Ed S), including clinical psychology (MS), counseling and guidance, counseling psychology (MS), personnel management (MS), psychometry (MS), school psychology (MS); special education (M Ed, MS). *Accreditation:* CORE; NCATE. Part-time and evening/weekend programs available. *Degree requirements:* For master's, comprehensive exam. *Entrance requirements:* For master's, GRE General Test. Additional exam requirements/recommendations for international students: Required—TOEFL (minimum score 500 paper-based; 173 computer-based; 61 iBT). *Faculty research:* Increasing numbers of minorities in special education and speech-language pathology.

Albany State University, College of Arts and Humanities, Albany, GA 31705-2717. Offers English education (M Ed); public administration (MPA), including community and economic development administration, criminal justice administration, general administration, health administration and policy, human resources management, public policy, water resources management; social work (MSW). Part-time programs available. *Faculty:* 13 full-time (6 women). *Students:* 47 full-time (38 women), 38 part-time (22 women); includes 77 minority (all Black or African American, non-Hispanic/Latino), 1 international. Average age 35. 43 applicants, 70% accepted, 23 enrolled. In 2011, 20 master's awarded. *Degree requirements:* For master's, comprehensive exam, professional portfolio (for MPA), internship, capstone report. *Entrance requirements:* For master's, GRE, MAT, minimum GPA of 3.0, official transcript, pre-medical record/certificate of immunization, letters of reference. *Application deadline:* For fall admission, 6/1 for domestic students, 5/1 for international students; for spring admission, 11/1 for domestic students, 10/1 for international students. Applications are processed on a rolling basis. Application fee: $20. Electronic applications accepted. *Expenses:* Tuition, state resident: full-time $3204; part-time $178 per credit hour. Tuition, nonresident: full-time $12,816; part-time $712 per credit hour. *Required fees:* $379 per semester. *Financial support:* Application deadline: 4/15; applicants required to submit FAFSA. *Faculty research:* HIV prevention for minority students . *Total annual research expenditures:* $2,000. *Unit head:* Dr. Leroy Bynum, Dean, 229-430-1877, Fax: 229-430-4296, E-mail: leroy.bynum@asurams.edu. *Application contact:* Jeffrey Pierce, II, Graduate Admissions Counselor, 229-430-4646, Fax: 229-430-4105, E-mail: jeffrey.pierce@asurams.edu. Web site: http://asu-sacs.asurams.edu/ASUCatalog/Graduate/index.html.

Amberton University, Graduate School, Program in Human Relations and Business, Garland, TX 75041-5595. Offers MA, MS. Part-time and evening/weekend programs available. *Entrance requirements:* For master's, minimum GPA of 3.0.

American InterContinental University Online, Program in Business Administration, Hoffman Estates, IL 60192. Offers accounting and finance (MBA); finance (MBA); healthcare management (MBA); human resource management (MBA); international business (MBA); management (MBA); marketing (MBA); operations management (MBA); organizational psychology and development (MBA); project management (MBA). Evening/weekend programs available. Postbaccalaureate distance learning degree programs offered (no on-campus study). *Entrance requirements:* Additional exam requirements/recommendations for international students: Required—TOEFL (minimum score 550 paper-based; 213 computer-based). Electronic applications accepted.

American InterContinental University South Florida, Program in International Business, Weston, FL 33326. Offers accounting and finance (MBA); human resource management (MBA); management (MBA); marketing (MBA). Part-time and evening/weekend programs available. Postbaccalaureate distance learning degree programs offered. Electronic applications accepted.

American Public University System, AMU/APU Graduate Programs, Charles Town, WV 25414. Offers accounting (MBA, MS); administration and supervision (M Ed); criminal justice (MA); emergency and disaster management (MA); entrepreneurship (MBA); environmental policy and management (MS), including environmental planning, environmental sustainability, fish and wildlife management, general (MA, MS), global environmental management; finance (MBA); general (MBA); global business management (MBA); guidance and counseling (M Ed); history (MA), including American history, ancient and classical history, European history, global history, military and diplomatic history, public history; homeland security (MA); homeland security resource allocation (MBA); humanities (MA); information technology (MS), including digital forensics, enterprise software development, information assurance and security, IT project management; information technology management (MBA); intelligence studies (MA), including criminal intelligence, general (MA, MS), homeland security, intelligence analysis, intelligence collection, intelligence operations, terrorism studies; international relations and conflict resolution (MA), including comparative and security issues, conflict resolution, international and transnational security issues, peacekeeping; legal studies (MA); management (MA), including defense management, general (MA, MS), human resource management, organizational leadership, public administration, reverse logistics, strategic consulting; marketing (MBA); military history (MA), including American military history, American revolution, civil war, war since 1946, World War II; military studies (MA), including air warfare, asymmetrical warfare, joint warfare, land warfare, naval warfare, strategic leadership; national security studies (MA), including general (MA, MS), homeland security, regional security studies, security and intelligence analysis, terrorism studies; nonprofit management (MBA); political science (MA), including American politics and government, comparative government and development, public policy; psychology (MA); public administration (MA, MPA), including disaster management (MPA), environmental policy (MA), health policy (MPA), human resources (MPA), national security (MPA), organizational management (MPA), security management (MPA); public health (MA, MPH), including emergency management (MPH), environmental health (MPH), public administration (MA); reverse logistics management (MA); security management (MA); space studies (MS), including aerospace science, planetary science; sports and health sciences (MS); sports management (MS), including coaching theory and strategy, sports administration; teaching (M Ed), including curriculum and instruction for elementary teachers, elementary, elementary reading, English language learners, instructional leadership, online learning, secondary social sciences, special education; transportation and logistics management (MA), including maritime engineering management. Programs offered via distance learning only. Part-time and evening/weekend programs available. Postbaccalaureate distance learning degree programs offered (no on-campus study). *Faculty:* 445 full-time (241 women), 1,360 part-time/adjunct (617 women). *Students:* 688 full-time (338 women), 10,168 part-time (3,706 women); includes 3,130 minority (1,007 Black or African American, non-Hispanic/Latino; 103 American Indian or Alaska Native, non-Hispanic/Latino; 825 Asian, non-Hispanic/Latino; 810 Hispanic/Latino; 51 Native Hawaiian or other Pacific Islander, non-Hispanic/Latino; 334 Two or more races, non-Hispanic/Latino), 134 international. Average age 35. In 2011, 2,386 master's awarded. *Degree requirements:* For master's, comprehensive exam or practicum. *Entrance requirements:* For master's, official transcript showing earned bachelor's degree from institution accredited by recognized accrediting body. Additional exam requirements/recommendations for international students: Required—TOEFL (minimum score 550 paper-based; 213 computer-based), IELTS (minimum score 6.5). *Application deadline:* Applications are processed on a rolling basis. Application fee: $0. Electronic applications accepted. *Expenses: Tuition:* Part-time $325 per credit hour. *Financial support:*

Human Resources Management

Applicants required to submit FAFSA. *Faculty research:* Military history, criminal justice, management performance, national security. *Unit head:* Dr. Karan Powell, Executive Vice President and Provost, 877-468-6268, Fax: 304-724-3780. *Application contact:* Terry Grant, Vice President of Enrollment Management, 877-468-6268, Fax: 304-724-3780, E-mail: info@apus.edu. Web site: http://www.apus.edu.

American University, Kogod School of Business, Master of Business Administration Program, Washington, DC 20016-8044. Offers accounting (MBA); consulting (MBA), including business systems consulting, management consulting; entrepreneurship (MBA); entrepreneurship (Certificate); finance (MBA); global emerging markets (MBA); leadership and strategic human capital management (MBA); marketing (MBA); real estate (MBA); MBA/JD; MBA/LL M; MBA/MA. Part-time and evening/weekend programs available. *Faculty:* 13 full-time (6 women). *Students:* 96 full-time (43 women), 104 part-time (35 women); includes 49 minority (14 Black or African American, non-Hispanic/Latino; 16 Asian, non-Hispanic/Latino; 16 Hispanic/Latino; 1 Native Hawaiian or other Pacific Islander, non-Hispanic/Latino; 2 Two or more races, non-Hispanic/Latino), 22 international. Average age 29. 340 applicants, 52% accepted, 52 enrolled. In 2011, 124 master's awarded. *Entrance requirements:* For master's, GMAT, resume, personal statement, interview. Additional exam requirements/recommendations for international students: Required—TOEFL. *Application deadline:* For fall admission, 2/1 priority date for domestic students; for spring admission, 10/1 priority date for domestic students. Applications are processed on a rolling basis. Application fee: $100. *Expenses:* Contact institution. *Financial support:* In 2011–12, 19 students received support. Fellowships, research assistantships with partial tuition reimbursements available, career-related internships or fieldwork, Federal Work-Study, and institutionally sponsored loans available. Support available to part-time students. Financial award application deadline: 2/1. *Faculty research:* Information technology, decision-aiding methodology, negotiation. *Unit head:* Dr. Stevan R. Holmberg, Chair, 202-885-1921, Fax: 202-885-1916, E-mail: sholmbe@american.edu. *Application contact:* Shannon Demko, Director of Admissions, 202-885-1968, Fax: 202-885-1078, E-mail: demko@american.edu. Web site: http://www.american.edu/kogod/.

Ashworth College, Graduate Programs, Norcross, GA 30092. Offers business administration (MBA); criminal justice (MS); health care administration (MBA, MS); human resource management (MBA, MS); international business (MBA); management (MS); marketing (MBA, MS).

Assumption College, Graduate Studies, Department of Business Studies, Worcester, MA 01609-1296. Offers accounting (MBA); business administration (CAGS); finance/economics (MBA); general business (MBA); human resources (MBA); international business (MBA); management (MBA); marketing (MBA); nonprofit leadership (MBA). Part-time and evening/weekend programs available. *Faculty:* 4 full-time (0 women), 16 part-time/adjunct (4 women). *Students:* 8 full-time (5 women), 133 part-time (65 women); includes 18 minority (8 Black or African American, non-Hispanic/Latino; 1 American Indian or Alaska Native, non-Hispanic/Latino; 2 Asian, non-Hispanic/Latino; 7 Hispanic/Latino), 3 international. Average age 30. 100 applicants, 75% accepted, 52 enrolled. In 2011, 53 master's, 1 other advanced degree awarded. *Degree requirements:* For master's, thesis, capstone. *Entrance requirements:* For master's and CAGS, 3 letters of recommendation, resume, essay. Additional exam requirements/recommendations for international students: Required—TOEFL (minimum score 540 paper-based; 200 computer-based; 76 iBT), IELTS (minimum score 6). *Application deadline:* For fall admission, 10/1 for domestic and international students; for winter admission, 2/1 for domestic and international students; for spring admission, 4/1 for domestic and international students. Applications are processed on a rolling basis. Application fee: $30. Electronic applications accepted. *Expenses: Tuition:* Full-time $9414; part-time $523 per credit. *Required fees:* $20 per term. Full-time tuition and fees vary according to course load and program. *Financial support:* In 2011–12, 14 students received support. Scholarships/grants, tuition waivers (partial), and unspecified assistantships available. Financial award application deadline: 5/1; financial award applicants required to submit FAFSA. *Faculty research:* Workplace diversity, dynamics of team interaction, utilization of leased employees, experiential learning project on due diligence market for prostheses. *Unit head:* Michael Lewis, Director, 508-767-7372, Fax: 508-767-7252, E-mail: milewis@assumption.edu. *Application contact:* Laura Lawrence, Graduate Programs Operations Manager, 508-767-7387, Fax: 508-767-7030, E-mail: graduate@assumption.edu. Web site: http://graduate.assumption.edu/mba/mba-assumption.

Auburn University, Graduate School, College of Business, Department of Management, Auburn University, AL 36849. Offers human resource management (PhD); management (MS, PhD); management information systems (MS, PhD). *Accreditation:* AACSB. Part-time programs available. *Faculty:* 26 full-time (5 women), 1 part-time/adjunct (0 women). *Students:* 15 full-time (5 women), 14 part-time (3 women); includes 4 minority (3 Black or African American, non-Hispanic/Latino; 1 Asian, non-Hispanic/Latino), 6 international. Average age 35. 66 applicants, 24% accepted, 8 enrolled. In 2011, 2 doctorates awarded. *Degree requirements:* For master's, thesis (for some programs); for doctorate, thesis/dissertation. *Entrance requirements:* For master's, GMAT, GRE General Test (MS); for doctorate, GMAT, GRE General Test. Additional exam requirements/recommendations for international students: Required—TOEFL. *Application deadline:* For fall admission, 7/7 for domestic students; for spring admission, 11/24 for domestic students. Applications are processed on a rolling basis. Application fee: $50 ($60 for international students). Electronic applications accepted. *Expenses:* Tuition, state resident: full-time $7290; part-time $405 per credit hour. Tuition, nonresident: full-time $21,870; part-time $1215 per credit hour. *International tuition:* $22,000 full-time. *Required fees:* $1402. *Financial support:* Teaching assistantships and Federal Work-Study available. Support available to part-time students. Financial award application deadline: 3/15; financial award applicants required to submit FAFSA. *Unit head:* Dr. Christopher Shook, Head, 334-844-9565. *Application contact:* Dr. George Flowers, Dean of the Graduate School, 334-844-2125. Web site: http://business.auburn.edu/academics/departments/department-of-management/.

Azusa Pacific University, School of Business and Management, Azusa, CA 91702-7000. Offers business administration (MBA); diversity for strategic advantage (MA); entrepreneurship (MBA); finance (MBA); human and organizational development (MA); human resources and organizational development (MBA); human resources management (MA); international business (MBA); marketing (MBA); non-profit management (MA); organizational development and change (MA); performance improvement (MA); public administration (MA); strategic management (MBA). Part-time and evening/weekend programs available. *Degree requirements:* For master's, thesis (for some programs), final project. *Entrance requirements:* For master's, GMAT, minimum GPA of 3.0. Additional exam requirements/recommendations for international students: Required—TOEFL (minimum score 600 paper-based). *Expenses:* Contact institution. *Faculty research:* Gender issues, financial risk, leadership and ethics, marketing strategy.

Baker College Center for Graduate Studies - Online, Graduate Programs, Flint, MI 48507-9843. Offers accounting (MBA); business administration (DBA); finance (MBA); general business (MBA); health care management (MBA); human resources management (MBA); information management (MBA); leadership studies (MBA); management information systems (MSIS); marketing (MBA). Part-time and evening/weekend programs available. Postbaccalaureate distance learning degree programs offered. *Degree requirements:* For master's, portfolio. *Entrance requirements:* For master's, 3 years of work experience, minimum undergraduate GPA of 2.5, writing sample, 3 letters of recommendation; for doctorate, MBA or acceptable related master's degree from accredited association, 5 years work experience, minimum graduate GPA of 3.25, writing sample, 3 professional references. Additional exam requirements/recommendations for international students: Required—TOEFL (minimum score 550 paper-based; 213 computer-based). Electronic applications accepted.

Baldwin Wallace University, Graduate Programs, Division of Business, Program in Human Resources, Berea, OH 44017-2088. Offers MBA. Part-time and evening/weekend programs available. *Students:* 15 full-time (12 women), 18 part-time (16 women); includes 10 minority (5 Black or African American, non-Hispanic/Latino; 1 Asian, non-Hispanic/Latino; 3 Hispanic/Latino; 1 Two or more races, non-Hispanic/Latino). Average age 37. 8 applicants, 63% accepted, 4 enrolled. In 2011, 19 master's awarded. *Degree requirements:* For master's, minimum overall GPA of 3.0, completion of all required courses. *Entrance requirements:* For master's, GMAT, bachelor's degree in any field, work experience, minimum GPA of 3.0. Additional exam requirements/recommendations for international students: Required—TOEFL (minimum score 523 paper-based; 193 computer-based; 70 iBT). *Application deadline:* For fall admission, 7/25 priority date for domestic students, 4/30 for international students; for spring admission, 12/15 priority date for domestic students, 9/30 for international students. Applications are processed on a rolling basis. Application fee: $25. Electronic applications accepted. Application fee is waived when completed online. *Expenses: Tuition:* Full-time $17,016; part-time $727 per credit hour. Tuition and fees vary according to program. *Financial support:* Career-related internships or fieldwork available. Support available to part-time students. Financial award application deadline: 5/1. *Unit head:* Dr. Dale Kramer, Director, 440-826-3331, Fax: 440-826-3868, E-mail: dkramer@bw.edu. *Application contact:* Laura Spencer, Graduate Application Specialist, 440-826-2191, Fax: 440-826-3868, E-mail: lspencer@bw.edu. Web site: http://www.bw.edu/academics/bus/programs/humres.

Barry University, School of Education, Graduate Certificate Programs, Miami Shores, FL 33161-6695. Offers advanced teaching and learning with technology (Certificate); distance education (Certificate); higher education technology integration (Certificate); human resources: not for profit and religious organizations (Certificate); K-12 technology integration (Certificate).

Bellevue University, Graduate School, College of Business, Bellevue, NE 68005-3098. Offers acquisition and contract management (MS); business administration (MBA); finance (MS); human capital management (PhD); management (MSM).

Benedictine University, Graduate Programs, Program in Business Administration, Lisle, IL 60532-0900. Offers accounting (MBA); entrepreneurship and managing innovation (MBA); financial management (MBA); health administration (MBA); human resource management (MBA); information systems security (MBA); international business (MBA); management consulting (MBA); management information systems (MBA); marketing management (MBA); operations management and logistics (MBA); organizational leadership (MBA); MBA/MPH; MBA/MS. Part-time and evening/weekend programs available. Postbaccalaureate distance learning degree programs offered (minimal on-campus study). *Faculty:* 4 full-time (2 women), 24 part-time/adjunct (3 women). *Students:* 165 full-time (101 women), 766 part-time (381 women); includes 201 minority (118 Black or African American, non-Hispanic/Latino; 4 American Indian or Alaska Native, non-Hispanic/Latino; 37 Asian, non-Hispanic/Latino; 40 Hispanic/Latino; 2 Native Hawaiian or other Pacific Islander, non-Hispanic/Latino), 14 international. Average age 34. 313 applicants, 73% accepted, 166 enrolled. In 2011, 379 master's awarded. *Entrance requirements:* For master's, GMAT. Additional exam requirements/recommendations for international students: Required—TOEFL (minimum score 550 paper-based; 213 computer-based). *Application deadline:* For fall admission, 9/1 for domestic students; for winter admission, 12/1 for domestic students; for spring admission, 2/15 for domestic students. Applications are processed on a rolling basis. Application fee: $40. Electronic applications accepted. *Financial support:* Career-related internships or fieldwork and health care benefits available. Support available to part-time students. *Faculty research:* Strategic leadership in professional organizations, sociology of professions, organizational change, social identity theory, applications to change management. *Unit head:* Dr. Sharon Borowicz, Director, 630-829-6219, E-mail: sborowicz@ben.edu. *Application contact:* Kari Gibbons, Director, Admissions, 630-829-6200, Fax: 630-829-6584, E-mail: kgibbons@ben.edu.

Bernard M. Baruch College of the City University of New York, Zicklin School of Business, Department of Management, New York, NY 10010-5585. Offers entrepreneurship (MBA); management (PhD); operations management (MBA); organizational behavior/human resources management (MBA); sustainable business (MBA). PhD offered jointly with Graduate School and University Center of the City University of New York. Part-time and evening/weekend programs available. *Degree requirements:* For doctorate, comprehensive exam, thesis/dissertation. *Entrance requirements:* For master's, GMAT, 2 letters of recommendation, resume, 2 years of work experience; for doctorate, GMAT. Additional exam requirements/recommendations for international students: Required—TOEFL (minimum score 590 paper-based; 243 computer-based), TWE.

Brandman University, School of Business and Professional Studies, Irvine, CA 92618. Offers business administration (MBA); human resources (MS); organizational leadership (MA); public administration (MPA).

Briar Cliff University, Program in Human Resource Management, Sioux City, IA 51104-0100. Offers MA. Part-time and evening/weekend programs available. *Degree requirements:* For master's, thesis optional. *Entrance requirements:* For master's, minimum undergraduate GPA of 2.77. Electronic applications accepted. *Faculty research:* Diversity in the workplace.

Brigham Young University, Graduate Studies, Marriott School of Management, Master of Public Administration Program, Provo, UT 84602. Offers finance (MPA); human resources (MPA); local government (MPA); nonprofit management (MPA); JD/MPA. *Faculty:* 17 full-time (2 women), 14 part-time/adjunct (4 women). *Students:* 119 full-time (61 women); includes 16 minority (1 American Indian or Alaska Native, non-Hispanic/Latino; 6 Asian, non-Hispanic/Latino; 5 Hispanic/Latino; 4 Native Hawaiian or other Pacific Islander, non-Hispanic/Latino), 13 international. Average age 27. 132 applicants, 57% accepted, 61 enrolled. In 2011, 57 master's awarded. *Entrance requirements:* For master's, GRE or GMAT, minimum GPA of 3.0. Additional exam requirements/recommendations for international students: Required—TOEFL (minimum score 580 paper-based; 85 iBT), IELTS (minimum score 7). *Application deadline:* For fall admission, 1/15 for domestic and international students. Application fee: $50. Electronic applications accepted. *Expenses: Tuition:* Full-time $5760; part-time $320 per credit. Tuition and fees vary according to student's religious affiliation. *Financial support:* In 2011–12, 93 students received support. Career-related internships or fieldwork and scholarships/grants available. Financial award application deadline: 3/1; financial award applicants required to submit FAFSA. *Faculty research:* Taxes, budgeting, nonprofit, ethics, decision modeling, work balance, organizational behavior. *Unit head:* Dr. David W. Hart, Director, 801-422-4221, Fax: 801-422-0311, E-mail: mpa@byu.edu.

Application contact: Catherine Cooper, Associate Director, 801-422-4221, E-mail: mpa@byu.edu. Web site: http://marriottschool.byu.edu/mpa.

Buffalo State College, State University of New York, The Graduate School, Faculty of Applied Science and Education, Department of Educational Foundations, Program in Adult Education, Buffalo, NY 14222-1095. Offers adult education (MS, Certificate); human resources development (Certificate). Part-time and evening/weekend programs available. Postbaccalaureate distance learning degree programs offered (no on-campus study). *Degree requirements:* For master's, comprehensive exam. *Entrance requirements:* Additional exam requirements/recommendations for international students: Required—TOEFL (minimum score 550 paper-based; 213 computer-based).

California Coast University, School of Administration and Management, Santa Ana, CA 92701. Offers business marketing (MBA); health care management (MBA); human resource management (MBA); management (MBA, MS). Postbaccalaureate distance learning degree programs offered (no on-campus study). Electronic applications accepted.

California Intercontinental University, School of Business, Diamond Bar, CA 91765. Offers banking and finance (MBA); entrepreneurship and business management (DBA); global business leadership (DBA); international management and marketing (MBA); organizational management and human resource management (MBA).

California State University, East Bay, Office of Academic Programs and Graduate Studies, College of Business and Economics, Business Administration, MBA Program, Hayward, CA 94542-3000. Offers entrepreneurship (MBA); finance (MBA); global innovators (MBA); human resources and organizational behavior (MBA); information technology management (MBA); marketing management (MBA); operations and supply chain management (MBA); strategy and international business (MBA). Part-time and evening/weekend programs available. *Faculty:* 11 full-time (3 women). *Students:* 80 full-time (42 women), 141 part-time (61 women); includes 70 minority (5 Black or African American, non-Hispanic/Latino; 46 Asian, non-Hispanic/Latino; 13 Hispanic/Latino; 1 Native Hawaiian or other Pacific Islander, non-Hispanic/Latino; 5 Two or more races, non-Hispanic/Latino), 69 international. Average age 31. 371 applicants, 36% accepted, 79 enrolled. In 2011, 254 master's awarded. *Degree requirements:* For master's, comprehensive exam or thesis. *Entrance requirements:* For master's, GMAT (minimum 20th percentile verbal and quantitative section), bachelor's degree, minimum GPA of 2.75. Additional exam requirements/recommendations for international students: Required—TOEFL (minimum score 550 paper-based; 213 computer-based; 79 iBT). *Application deadline:* For fall admission, 6/30 for domestic and international students. Applications are processed on a rolling basis. Application fee: $55. Electronic applications accepted. *Expenses:* Contact institution. *Financial support:* Career-related internships or fieldwork, Federal Work-Study, institutionally sponsored loans, and scholarships/grants available. Support available to part-time students. Financial award application deadline: 3/2; financial award applicants required to submit FAFSA. *Unit head:* Dr. Terri Swartz, Dean, 510-885-3291, Fax: 510-885-4884, E-mail: terri.swartz@csueastbay.edu. *Application contact:* Prof. Joanna Lee, Director, CBE Graduate Programs, 510-885-3517, Fax: 510-885-2176, E-mail: joanna.lee@csueastbay.edu. Web site: http://www20.csueastbay.edu/ecat/graduate-chapters/g-buad.html#mba.

California State University, East Bay, Office of Academic Programs and Graduate Studies, College of Business and Economics, Option in Human Resources and Organizational Behavior, Hayward, CA 94542-3000. Offers MBA. Part-time and evening/weekend programs available. *Degree requirements:* For master's, comprehensive exam or thesis. *Entrance requirements:* For master's, GMAT, minimum GPA of 2.75. Additional exam requirements/recommendations for international students: Required—TOEFL (minimum score 550 paper-based; 213 computer-based). *Application deadline:* For fall admission, 6/30 for domestic and international students. Application fee: $55. Electronic applications accepted. *Expenses:* Tuition, state resident: full-time $6738; part-time $1302 per quarter. Tuition, nonresident: full-time $12,690; part-time $2294 per quarter. *Required fees:* $449 per quarter. Tuition and fees vary according to degree level, program and reciprocity agreements. *Financial support:* Fellowships, career-related internships or fieldwork, Federal Work-Study, institutionally sponsored loans, and scholarships/grants available. Support available to part-time students. Financial award application deadline: 3/2; financial award applicants required to submit FAFSA. *Unit head:* Dr. Xinjian Lu, Chair, 510-885-3307, Fax: 510-885-2660, E-mail: xinjian.lu@csueastbay.edu. *Application contact:* Dr. Donna Wiley, Interim Associate Director, 510-885-2928, Fax: 510-885-4777, E-mail: donna.wiley@csueastbay.edu. Web site: http://www.cbe.csueastbay.edu/mgmt/.

California State University, East Bay, Office of Academic Programs and Graduate Studies, College of Letters, Arts, and Social Sciences, Department of Public Affairs and Administration, Program in Public Administration, Hayward, CA 94542-3000. Offers health care administration (MPA); management of human resources and change (MPA); public management and policy analysis (MPA). Part-time and evening/weekend programs available. *Faculty:* 5 full-time (1 woman). *Students:* 10 full-time (5 women), 135 part-time (92 women); includes 81 minority (25 Black or African American, non-Hispanic/Latino; 25 Asian, non-Hispanic/Latino; 23 Hispanic/Latino; 4 Native Hawaiian or other Pacific Islander, non-Hispanic/Latino; 4 Two or more races, non-Hispanic/Latino), 4 international. Average age 33. 132 applicants, 51% accepted, 45 enrolled. In 2011, 77 master's awarded. *Degree requirements:* For master's, comprehensive exam (for some programs), comprehensive exam or thesis. *Entrance requirements:* For master's, minimum GPA of 2.5; statement of purpose; 2 letters of recommendation; professional resume/curriculum vitae. Additional exam requirements/recommendations for international students: Required—TOEFL (minimum score 550 paper-based; 213 computer-based; 79 iBT). *Application deadline:* For fall admission, 6/18 for domestic and international students. Application fee: $55. Electronic applications accepted. *Expenses:* Tuition, state resident: full-time $6738; part-time $1302 per quarter. Tuition, nonresident: full-time $12,690; part-time $2294 per quarter. *Required fees:* $449 per quarter. Tuition and fees vary according to degree level, program and reciprocity agreements. *Financial support:* Fellowships, teaching assistantships, career-related internships or fieldwork, Federal Work-Study, institutionally sponsored loans, and scholarships/grants available. Support available to part-time students. Financial award application deadline: 3/2; financial award applicants required to submit FAFSA. *Unit head:* Dr. Toni Fogarty, Coordinator, 510-885-3282, Fax: 510-885-3726, E-mail: toni.fogarty@csueastbay.edu. *Application contact:* Prof. Michael Moon, Public Administration Graduate Advisor, 510-885-2545, Fax: 510-885-3726, E-mail: michael.moon@csueastbay.edu. Web site: http://class.csueastbay.edu/publicadmin/Public_Admin.php.

California State University, Sacramento, Office of Graduate Studies, College of Business Administration, Sacramento, CA 95819-6088. Offers accountancy (MS); business administration (MBA); human resources (MBA); urban land development (MBA). *Accreditation:* AACSB. Part-time and evening/weekend programs available. *Faculty:* 61 full-time (19 women), 28 part-time/adjunct (7 women). *Students:* 39 full-time, 91 part-time; includes 40 minority (6 Black or African American, non-Hispanic/Latino; 2 American Indian or Alaska Native, non-Hispanic/Latino; 12 Asian, non-Hispanic/Latino; 11 Hispanic/Latino; 4 Native Hawaiian or other Pacific Islander, non-Hispanic/Latino; 5 Two or more races, non-Hispanic/Latino), 16 international. Average age 29. 330 applicants, 64% accepted, 54 enrolled. In 2011, 212 master's awarded. *Degree requirements:* For master's, thesis or alternative, writing proficiency exam. *Entrance requirements:* For master's, GMAT. Additional exam requirements/recommendations for international students: Required—TOEFL. *Application deadline:* For fall admission, 2/1 for domestic students, 3/1 for international students; for spring admission, 9/15 for domestic students, 9/30 for international students. Applications are processed on a rolling basis. Application fee: $55. Electronic applications accepted. *Financial support:* Research assistantships, teaching assistantships, career-related internships or fieldwork, and Federal Work-Study available. Support available to part-time students. Financial award applicants required to submit FAFSA. *Unit head:* Dr. Sanjay Varshney, Dean, 916-278-6942, Fax: 916-278-5793, E-mail: cba@csus.edu. *Application contact:* Jose Martinez, Outreach and Graduate Diversity Coordinator, 916-278-6470, Fax: 916-278-5669, E-mail: martinj@skymail.csus.edu. Web site: http://www.cba.csus.edu.

Capella University, School of Business and Technology, Minneapolis, MN 55402. Offers accounting (MBA), including system design and programming; business (Certificate), including human resource management (MS, PhD, Certificate), information technology management (MS, PhD, Certificate), leadership (MBA, MS, PhD, Certificate); finance (MBA); general business (MBA); health care management (MBA); information technology (MS, Certificate), including general information technology (MS), information security, network architecture and design (MS), professional projects management (Certificate), project management and leadership (MS), system design and development (MS),); information technology management (MBA); marketing (MBA); organization and management (MBA, MS, PhD), including general business (PhD), general organization and management (MBA, MS), human resource management (MS, PhD, Certificate), information technology management (MS, PhD, Certificate), leadership (MBA, MS, PhD, Certificate); project management (MBA). Part-time and evening/weekend programs available. Postbaccalaureate distance learning degree programs offered (minimal on-campus study). Terminal master's awarded for partial completion of doctoral program. *Degree requirements:* For master's, thesis optional, integrative project; for doctorate, comprehensive exam, thesis/dissertation. *Entrance requirements:* Additional exam requirements/recommendations for international students: Required—TOEFL (minimum score 550 paper-based; 213 computer-based), TWE (minimum score 4). Electronic applications accepted. *Faculty research:* Business policies: strategic, corporate, and financial management; interplay of technological, organizational and social change.

Caribbean University, Graduate School, Bayamón, PR 00960-0493. Offers administration and supervision (MA Ed); criminal justice (MA); curriculum and instruction (MA Ed, PhD), including elementary education (MA Ed), English education (MA Ed), history education (MA Ed), mathematics education (MA Ed), primary education (MA Ed), science education (MA Ed), Spanish education (MA Ed); educational technology in instructional systems (MA Ed); gerontology (MSN); human resources (MBA); museology, archiving and art history (MA Ed); neonatal pediatrics (MSN); physical education (MA Ed); special education (MA Ed). *Entrance requirements:* For master's, interview, minimum GPA of 2.5.

Case Western Reserve University, Weatherhead School of Management, Department of Marketing and Policy Studies, Division of Labor and Human Resource Policy, Cleveland, OH 44106. Offers MBA. Part-time and evening/weekend programs available. *Entrance requirements:* For master's, GMAT. *Faculty research:* Strategic human resource management, negotiations and conflict management, human resources in high performance organizations, international human resources management, union management relations and collective bargaining.

The Catholic University of America, Metropolitan School of Professional Studies, Washington, DC 20064. Offers human resource management (MA); management (MSM). Part-time and evening/weekend programs available. *Faculty:* 45 part-time/adjunct (18 women). *Students:* 37 full-time (24 women), 129 part-time (83 women); includes 74 minority (50 Black or African American, non-Hispanic/Latino; 1 American Indian or Alaska Native, non-Hispanic/Latino; 8 Asian, non-Hispanic/Latino; 13 Hispanic/Latino; 1 Native Hawaiian or other Pacific Islander, non-Hispanic/Latino; 1 Two or more races, non-Hispanic/Latino), 15 international. Average age 36. 143 applicants, 48% accepted, 49 enrolled. In 2011, 43 degrees awarded. *Degree requirements:* For master's, minimum GPA of 3.0, capstone course. *Entrance requirements:* For master's, statement of purpose, official copies of academic transcripts, three letters of recommendation, resume. Additional exam requirements/recommendations for international students: Required—TOEFL (minimum score 237 computer-based; 93 iBT). *Application deadline:* For fall admission, 8/1 priority date for domestic students, 7/15 for international students; for spring admission, 12/1 priority date for domestic students, 10/15 for international students. Application fee: $55. *Expenses: Tuition:* Full-time $35,260; part-time $1380 per credit. *Required fees:* $80; $40 per semester hour. One-time fee: $425. *Total annual research expenditures:* $438,319. *Unit head:* Dr. Sara Thompson, Dean, 202-319-5256, Fax: 202-319-6032, E-mail: thompsons@cua.edu. *Application contact:* Andrew Woodall, Director of Graduate Admissions, 202-319-5057, Fax: 202-319-6533, E-mail: cua-admissions@cua.edu. Web site: http://metro.cua.edu/.

Central Michigan University, Central Michigan University Global Campus, Program in Administration, Mount Pleasant, MI 48859. Offers acquisitions administration (MSA, Certificate); general administration (MSA, Certificate); health services administration (MSA, Certificate); human resources administration (MSA, Certificate); information resource management (MSA, Certificate); international administration (MSA, Certificate); leadership (MSA, Certificate); public administration (MSA, Certificate); research administration (MSA, Certificate). Part-time and evening/weekend programs available. Postbaccalaureate distance learning degree programs offered (no on-campus study). *Students:* Average age 38. *Entrance requirements:* For master's, minimum GPA of 2.7 in major. *Application deadline:* Applications are processed on a rolling basis. Application fee: $50. Electronic applications accepted. *Financial support:* Scholarships/grants available. Support available to part-time students. Financial award applicants required to submit FAFSA. *Unit head:* Dr. Nana Korsah, Director, 989-774-6525, E-mail: korsa1na@cmich.edu. *Application contact:* 877-268-4636, E-mail: cmuglobal@cmich.edu.

Central Michigan University, College of Graduate Studies, College of Business Administration, Department of Management, Mount Pleasant, MI 48859. Offers human resource management (MBA); international business (MBA). *Degree requirements:* For master's, thesis or alternative. *Entrance requirements:* For master's, GMAT. Electronic applications accepted. *Faculty research:* Human resource accounting, valuation, and liability; international business and economic issues; entrepreneurial leadership; technology management and strategy; electronic commerce and neural networks.

Central Michigan University, College of Graduate Studies, Interdisciplinary Administration Programs, Mount Pleasant, MI 48859. Offers acquisitions administration (MSA, Graduate Certificate); general administration (MSA, Graduate Certificate); health services administration (MSA, Graduate Certificate); human resource administration (Graduate Certificate); human resources administration (MSA); information resource management (MSA, Graduate Certificate); international administration (MSA, Graduate Certificate); leadership (MSA, Graduate Certificate); organizational communication (MSA, Graduate Certificate); public administration (MSA, Graduate Certificate); recreation and park administration (MSA); sport administration (MSA). *Accreditation:* AACSB. Part-time and evening/weekend programs available. Postbaccalaureate distance learning degree programs offered (no on-campus study). *Degree requirements:* For master's, thesis or alternative. *Entrance requirements:* For master's, bachelor's degree with minimum GPA of 2.7. Electronic applications accepted. *Faculty research:* Interdisciplinary studies in acquisitions administration, health services administration, sport administration, recreation and park administration, and international administration.

City University of Seattle, Graduate Division, School of Management, Bellevue, WA 98005. Offers accounting (Certificate); change leadership (MBA, Certificate); computer systems (MS); finance (Certificate); financial management (MBA); general management (MBA); general management-Europe (MBA); global marketing (MBA); human resources management (Certificate); individualized study (MBA); information security (MS); information systems (MBA); leadership (MA); marketing (MBA, Certificate); project management (MBA, MS, Certificate); sustainable business (Certificate); technology management (MBA, Certificate). Part-time and evening/weekend programs available. Postbaccalaureate distance learning degree programs offered (no on-campus study). *Faculty:* 6 full-time (2 women), 95 part-time/adjunct (33 women). *Students:* 397 full-time (193 women), 283 part-time (137 women); includes 127 minority (67 Black or African American, non-Hispanic/Latino; 5 American Indian or Alaska Native, non-Hispanic/Latino; 33 Asian, non-Hispanic/Latino; 15 Hispanic/Latino; 1 Native Hawaiian or other Pacific Islander, non-Hispanic/Latino; 6 Two or more races, non-Hispanic/Latino), 117 international. Average age 36. 151 applicants, 100% accepted, 151 enrolled. In 2011, 369 master's, 32 other advanced degrees awarded. *Degree requirements:* For master's, comprehensive exam (for some programs), thesis (for some programs). *Entrance requirements:* Additional exam requirements/recommendations for international students: Required—TOEFL (minimum score 567 paper-based; 227 computer-based; 87 iBT); Recommended—IELTS. *Application deadline:* For fall admission, 9/1 for international students; for winter admission, 12/1 for international students; for spring admission, 3/1 for international students. Applications are processed on a rolling basis. Application fee: $50. Electronic applications accepted. *Financial support:* Federal Work-Study and scholarships/grants available. Support available to part-time students. Financial award applicants required to submit FAFSA. *Unit head:* Dr. Kurt Kirstein, Dean, 425-637-1010 Ext. 5456, Fax: 425-709-5363, E-mail: kdkirstein@cityu.edu. *Application contact:* Alysa Borelli, Director, Recruiting, 888-422-4898, Fax: 425-709-5363, E-mail: info@cityu.edu. Web site: http://www.cityu.edu/programs/som/index.aspx.

Claremont Graduate University, Graduate Programs, School of Behavioral and Organizational Sciences, Program in Human Resources Design, Claremont, CA 91711-6160. Offers MS. Part-time and evening/weekend programs available. *Students:* 26 full-time (13 women), 5 part-time (4 women); includes 8 minority (3 Black or African American, non-Hispanic/Latino; 4 Asian, non-Hispanic/Latino; 1 Two or more races, non-Hispanic/Latino), 18 international. Average age 28. In 2011, 19 master's awarded. *Entrance requirements:* For master's, GMAT or GRE General Test. Additional exam requirements/recommendations for international students: Required—TOEFL (minimum score 550 paper-based; 213 computer-based; 80 iBT). *Application deadline:* For fall admission, 1/15 priority date for domestic students. Applications are processed on a rolling basis. Application fee: $60. Electronic applications accepted. *Expenses: Tuition:* Full-time $36,374; part-time $1581 per unit. *Required fees:* $165 per semester. *Financial support:* Fellowships, Federal Work-Study, institutionally sponsored loans, and scholarships/grants available. Support available to part-time students. Financial award application deadline: 2/15; financial award applicants required to submit FAFSA. *Unit head:* Katie Ear, Administrative Director, 909-607-1916, Fax: 909-621-8905, E-mail: katie.ear@cgu.edu. *Application contact:* Freddie Zadi, Program Assistant, 909-607-3286, Fax: 909-621-8905, E-mail: hrd@cgu.edu. Web site: http://www.cgu.edu/pages/672.asp.

Clemson University, Graduate School, College of Health, Education, and Human Development, Eugene T. Moore School of Education, Program in Human Resource Development, Clemson, SC 29634. Offers MHRD. Part-time and evening/weekend programs available. Postbaccalaureate distance learning degree programs offered (no on-campus study). *Students:* 1 (woman) full-time, 76 part-time (52 women); includes 23 minority (17 Black or African American, non-Hispanic/Latino; 1 American Indian or Alaska Native, non-Hispanic/Latino; 4 Hispanic/Latino; 1 Two or more races, non-Hispanic/Latino). Average age 36. 64 applicants, 91% accepted, 41 enrolled. In 2011, 28 master's awarded. *Degree requirements:* For master's, comprehensive exam. *Entrance requirements:* For master's, GRE General Test. Additional exam requirements/recommendations for international students: Required—TOEFL; Recommended—IELTS. *Application deadline:* For fall admission, 7/1 for domestic students. Application fee: $70 ($80 for international students). Electronic applications accepted. *Expenses:* Contact institution. *Financial support:* In 2011–12, 2 students received support. Application deadline: 6/1; applicants required to submit FAFSA. *Faculty research:* Organizational development, human performance improvement, attachment theory, social constructivism, technology-mediated teaching and learning, corporate universities. *Unit head:* Dr. Michael J. Padilla, Director/Associate Dean, 864-656-4444, Fax: 864-656-0311, E-mail: pmcgee@clemson.edu. *Application contact:* Dr. David Fleming, Coordinator, 864-656-1881, Fax: 864-656-0311, E-mail: dflemin@clemson.edu. Web site: http://www.hehd.clemson.edu/MHRD/SoE_Webpage/MHRD.html.

Cleveland State University, College of Graduate Studies, Monte Ahuja College of Business, Department of Management and Labor Relations, Cleveland, OH 44115. Offers labor relations and human resources (MLRHR). Part-time and evening/weekend programs available. *Faculty:* 10 full-time (6 women), 8 part-time/adjunct (2 women). *Students:* 28 full-time (17 women), 42 part-time (31 women); includes 7 minority (4 Black or African American, non-Hispanic/Latino; 1 Hispanic/Latino; 2 Two or more races, non-Hispanic/Latino), 19 international. Average age 28. 91 applicants, 63% accepted, 28 enrolled. In 2011, 27 master's awarded. *Entrance requirements:* For master's, GMAT or GRE, minimum GPA of 3.0. Additional exam requirements/recommendations for international students: Required—TOEFL (minimum score 525 paper-based; 197 computer-based). *Application deadline:* For fall admission, 7/15 for domestic students; for spring admission, 12/15 for domestic students. Applications are processed on a rolling basis. Application fee: $30. Electronic applications accepted. *Expenses:* Tuition, state resident: full-time $6416; part-time $494 per credit hour. Tuition, nonresident: full-time $12,074; part-time $929 per credit hour. *Financial support:* In 2011–12, 3 students received support, including 3 research assistantships with full and partial tuition reimbursements available (averaging $6,960 per year); career-related internships or fieldwork, tuition waivers (full), and unspecified assistantships also available. Financial award application deadline: 5/1; financial award applicants required to submit FAFSA. *Faculty research:* Personality, individual differences, employment interviews, HR planning. *Unit head:* Dr. Timothy G. DeGroot, Chairperson, 216-687-4747, Fax: 216-687-4708, E-mail: t.degroot@csuohio.edu. Web site: http://www.csuohio.edu/cba/mlr/.

Colorado Technical University Colorado Springs, Graduate Studies, Program in Management, Colorado Springs, CO 80907-3896. Offers accounting (MBA, MSA); business administration (MBA); finance (MBA); human resources management (MBA); logistics/supply chain management (MBA); management (DM); marketing (MBA); mediation and dispute resolution (MBA); operations management (MBA); project management (MBA); technology management (MBA). Part-time and evening/weekend programs available. Postbaccalaureate distance learning degree programs offered. *Degree requirements:* For master's, thesis or alternative; for doctorate, thesis/dissertation. *Entrance requirements:* For doctorate, minimum graduate GPA of 3.0, 5 years of related work experience. *Faculty research:* Sexual harassment, performance evaluation, critical thinking.

Colorado Technical University Denver South, Programs in Business Administration and Management, Aurora, CO 80014. Offers accounting (MBA); business administration (MBA); business administration and management (EMBA); finance (MBA); human resource management (MBA); marketing (MBA); mediation and dispute resolution (MBA); operations management (MBA); project management (MBA); technology management (MBA). Part-time and evening/weekend programs available. *Degree requirements:* For master's, thesis or alternative. *Entrance requirements:* For master's, minimum undergraduate GPA of 3.0, resume.

Colorado Technical University Sioux Falls, Programs in Business Administration and Management, Sioux Falls, SD 57108. Offers business administration (MBA); business management (MSM); health science management (MSM); human resources management (MSM); information technology (MSM); organizational leadership (MSM); project management (MBA); technology management (MBA). Evening/weekend programs available. *Degree requirements:* For master's, thesis optional. *Entrance requirements:* For master's, minimum 2 years work experience, resume.

Columbia Southern University, MBA Program, Orange Beach, AL 36561. Offers electronic business and technology (MBA); finance (MBA); general (MBA); healthcare management (MBA); hospitality and tourism (MBA); human resources management (MBA); international management (MBA); marketing (MBA); project management (MBA); public administration (MBA); sport management (MBA). Part-time and evening/weekend programs available. Postbaccalaureate distance learning degree programs offered (no on-campus study). *Entrance requirements:* For master's, bachelor's degree from accredited/approved institution. Additional exam requirements/recommendations for international students: Required—TOEFL. Electronic applications accepted.

Columbia University, Graduate School of Business, MBA Program, New York, NY 10027. Offers accounting (MBA); decision, risk, and operations (MBA); entrepreneurship (MBA); finance and economics (MBA); healthcare and pharmaceutical management (MBA); human resource management (MBA); international business (MBA); leadership and ethics (MBA); management (MBA); marketing (MBA); media (MBA); private equity (MBA); real estate (MBA); social enterprise (MBA); value investing (MBA); DDS/MBA; JD/MBA; MBA/MIA; MBA/MPH; MBA/MS; MD/MBA. *Entrance requirements:* For master's, GMAT, 2 letters of recommendation. Additional exam requirements/recommendations for international students: Required—TOEFL. Electronic applications accepted. *Expenses:* Contact institution. *Faculty research:* Human decision making and behavioral research; real estate market and mortgage defaults; financial crisis and corporate governance; international business; security analysis and accounting.

Concordia University, St. Paul, College of Business and Organizational Leadership, St. Paul, MN 55104-5494. Offers business and organizational leadership (MBA); criminal justice leadership (MA); health care management (MBA); human resources management (MA); leadership and management (MA). *Accreditation:* ACBSP. Evening/weekend programs available. Postbaccalaureate distance learning degree programs offered (minimal on-campus study). *Faculty:* 16 full-time (6 women), 31 part-time/adjunct (12 women). *Students:* 417 full-time (230 women), 11 part-time (5 women); includes 83 minority (40 Black or African American, non-Hispanic/Latino; 2 American Indian or Alaska Native, non-Hispanic/Latino; 25 Asian, non-Hispanic/Latino; 5 Hispanic/Latino; 1 Native Hawaiian or other Pacific Islander, non-Hispanic/Latino; 10 Two or more races, non-Hispanic/Latino), 5 international. Average age 35. 316 applicants, 74% accepted, 198 enrolled. In 2011, 204 master's awarded. *Application deadline:* Applications are processed on a rolling basis. Application fee: $50. Electronic applications accepted. *Expenses: Tuition:* Full-time $8100; part-time $435 per credit. Tuition and fees vary according to program. *Financial support:* Applicants required to submit FAFSA. *Unit head:* Dr. Bruce Corrie, Dean, 651-641-8226, Fax: 651-641-8807, E-mail: corrie@csp.edu. *Application contact:* Kimberly Craig, Director of Graduate and Cohort Admission, 651-603-6223, Fax: 651-603-6320, E-mail: craig@csp.edu.

Concordia University Wisconsin, Graduate Programs, School of Business and Legal Studies, MBA Program, Mequon, WI 53097-2402. Offers finance (MBA); health care administration (MBA); human resource management (MBA); international business (MBA); international business-bilingual English/Chinese (MBA); management (MBA); management information systems (MBA); managerial communications (MBA); marketing (MBA); public administration (MBA); risk management (MBA). Postbaccalaureate distance learning degree programs offered (minimal on-campus study). *Students:* 308 full-time (146 women), 536 part-time (288 women); includes 126 minority (76 Black or African American, non-Hispanic/Latino; 9 American Indian or Alaska Native, non-Hispanic/Latino; 15 Asian, non-Hispanic/Latino; 12 Hispanic/Latino; 14 Two or more races, non-Hispanic/Latino), 276 international. Average age 35. In 2011, 110 master's awarded. *Degree requirements:* For master's, comprehensive exam, thesis or alternative. *Entrance requirements:* Additional exam requirements/recommendations for international students: Required—TOEFL. *Application deadline:* For fall admission, 8/1 priority date for domestic students; for spring admission, 1/15 for domestic students. Applications are processed on a rolling basis. Application fee: $50. *Expenses:* Contact institution. *Financial support:* Application deadline: 8/1. *Unit head:* Dr. David Borst, Director, 262-243-4298, Fax: 262-243-4428, E-mail: david.borst@cuw.edu. *Application contact:* Mary Eberhardt, Graduate Admissions, 262-243-4551, Fax: 262-243-4428, E-mail: mary.eberhardt@cuw.edu.

Cornell University, Graduate School, Graduate Fields of Industrial and Labor Relations, Ithaca, NY 14853. Offers collective bargaining, labor law and labor history (MILR, MPS, MS, PhD); economic and social statistics (MILR); human resource studies (MILR, MPS, MS, PhD); industrial and labor relations problems (MILR, MPS, MS, PhD); international and comparative labor (MILR, MPS, MS, PhD); labor economics (MILR, MPS, MS, PhD); organizational behavior (MILR, MPS, MS, PhD). *Faculty:* 55 full-time (14 women). *Students:* 164 full-time (97 women); includes 37 minority (13 Black or African American, non-Hispanic/Latino; 2 American Indian or Alaska Native, non-Hispanic/Latino; 15 Asian, non-Hispanic/Latino; 7 Hispanic/Latino), 60 international. Average age 31. 335 applicants, 27% accepted, 63 enrolled. In 2011, 67 master's, 4 doctorates awarded. *Degree requirements:* For master's, thesis (MS); for doctorate, comprehensive exam, thesis/dissertation, teaching experience. *Entrance requirements:* For master's and doctorate, GMAT or GRE General Test, 2 academic recommendations. Additional exam requirements/recommendations for international students: Required—TOEFL (minimum score 550 paper-based; 213 computer-based; 77 iBT). Application fee: $95. Electronic applications accepted. *Expenses:* Contact institution. *Financial support:* In 2011–12, 73 students received support, including 23 fellowships with full tuition reimbursements available, 30 research assistantships with full tuition reimbursements available, 24 teaching assistantships with full tuition reimbursements available; institutionally sponsored loans, scholarships/grants, health care benefits, tuition waivers (full and partial), and unspecified assistantships also available. Financial award applicants required to submit FAFSA. *Unit head:* Director of Graduate Studies, 607-255-1522. *Application contact:* Graduate Field Assistant, 607-

255-1522, E-mail: ilrgradapplicant@cornell.edu. Web site: http://www.gradschool.cornell.edu/fields.php?id-85&a-2.

Dallas Baptist University, College of Business, Management Program, Dallas, TX 75211-9299. Offers conflict resolution management (MA); general management (MA); health care management (MA); human resource management (MA). Part-time and evening/weekend programs available. *Entrance requirements:* For master's, GRE General Test, minimum GPA of 3.0. Additional exam requirements/recommendations for international students: Required—TOEFL, IELTS. *Application deadline:* Applications are processed on a rolling basis. Application fee: $25. Electronic applications accepted. *Expenses: Tuition:* Full-time $12,060; part-time $670 per credit hour. *Required fees:* $100; $50 per semester. *Financial support:* Federal Work-Study, institutionally sponsored loans, scholarships/grants, and tuition waivers (full and partial) available. Support available to part-time students. Financial award applicants required to submit FAFSA. *Faculty research:* Organizational behavior, conflict personalities. *Unit head:* Joanne Hix, Director, 214-333-5280, Fax: 214-333-5293, E-mail: graduate@dbu.edu. *Application contact:* Kit P. Montgomery, Director of Graduate Programs, 214-333-5242, Fax: 214-333-5579, E-mail: graduate@dbu.edu. Web site: http://www3.dbu.edu/graduate/maom.asp.

Davenport University, Sneden Graduate School, Grand Rapids, MI 49512. Offers accounting (MBA); business administration (EMBA); finance (MBA); health care management (MBA); human resources (MBA); information assurance (MS); public health (MPH); strategic management (MBA). Evening/weekend programs available. *Entrance requirements:* For master's, GMAT, minimum undergraduate GPA of 2.75. Additional exam requirements/recommendations for international students: Required—TOEFL. Electronic applications accepted. *Faculty research:* Leadership, management, marketing, organizational culture.

Davenport University, Sneden Graduate School, Warren, MI 48092-5209. Offers accounting (MBA); business administration (EMBA); finance (MBA); health care management (MBA); human resources management (MBA); information assurance (MS); public health (MPH); strategic management (MBA). *Entrance requirements:* For master's, minimum undergraduate GPA of 2.7.

Davenport University, Sneden Graduate School, Dearborn, MI 48126-3799. Offers accounting (MBA); business administration (EMBA); finance (MBA); health care management (MBA); human resources management (MBA); information assurance (MS); marketing (MBA); public health (MPH); strategic management (MBA). Part-time and evening/weekend programs available. Postbaccalaureate distance learning degree programs offered (no on-campus study). *Entrance requirements:* For master's, minimum GPA of 2.7, previous course work in accounting and statistics. *Faculty research:* Accounting, international accounting, social and environmental accounting, finance.

DePaul University, Charles H. Kellstadt Graduate School of Business, Department of Management, Chicago, IL 60604-2287. Offers entrepreneurship (MBA); health sector management (MBA); human resource management (MBA, MSHR); leadership/change management (MBA); management planning and strategy (MBA); operations management (MBA). Part-time and evening/weekend programs available. *Faculty:* 36 full-time (7 women), 35 part-time/adjunct (16 women). *Students:* 280 full-time (116 women), 121 part-time (47 women); includes 78 minority (20 Black or African American, non-Hispanic/Latino; 37 Asian, non-Hispanic/Latino; 16 Hispanic/Latino; 1 Native Hawaiian or other Pacific Islander, non-Hispanic/Latino; 4 Two or more races, non-Hispanic/Latino), 33 international. Average age 30. In 2011, 112 master's awarded. *Entrance requirements:* For master's, GMAT, GRE (MSHR), 2 letters of recommendation, resume. Additional exam requirements/recommendations for international students: Required—TOEFL (minimum score 550 paper-based; 213 computer-based). *Application deadline:* For fall admission, 7/1 for domestic students; for winter admission, 10/1 for domestic students; for spring admission, 2/1 for domestic students. Applications are processed on a rolling basis. Application fee: $60. Electronic applications accepted. *Financial support:* Research assistantships available. Financial award application deadline: 4/1. *Faculty research:* Growth management, creativity and innovation, quality management and business process design, entrepreneurship. *Unit head:* Robert T. Ryan, Assistant Dean and Director, 312-362-8810, Fax: 312-362-6677, E-mail: rryan1@depaul.edu. *Application contact:* Christopher E. Kinsella, Director of Cohort MBA Programs, 312-362-8810, Fax: 312-362-6677, E-mail: kgsb@depaul.edu.

DeSales University, Graduate Division, MBA Program, Center Valley, PA 18034-9568. Offers accounting (MBA); computer information systems (MBA); finance (MBA); health care systems management (MBA); human resources management (MBA); management (MBA); marketing (MBA); project management (MBA); self-design (MBA). *Accreditation:* ACBSP. Part-time programs available. Postbaccalaureate distance learning degree programs offered (no on-campus study). *Entrance requirements:* For master's, GMAT, minimum GPA of 3.0, 2 years of work experience. Additional exam requirements/recommendations for international students: Required—TOEFL. *Application deadline:* Applications are processed on a rolling basis. Electronic applications accepted. Tuition and fees vary according to degree level. *Faculty research:* Quality improvement, executive development, productivity, cross-cultural managerial differences, leadership. *Unit head:* Dr. David Gilfoil, Director, 610-282-1100 Ext. 1828, Fax: 610-282-2869, E-mail: david.gilfoil@desales.edu. *Application contact:* Caryn Stopper, Director of Graduate Admissions, 610-282-1100 Ext. 1768, Fax: 610-282-0525, E-mail: caryn.stopper@desales.edu.

DeVry University, Keller Graduate School of Management, Downers Grove, IL 60515. Offers accounting and financial management (MAFM); business administration (MBA); human resources management (MHRM); information systems management (MISM); network and communications management (MNCM); project management (MPM); public administration (MPA).

Dowling College, School of Business, Oakdale, NY 11769-1999. Offers aviation management (MBA, Certificate); banking and finance (MBA, Certificate); corporate finance (MBA); financial planning (Certificate); health care management (MBA, Certificate); human resource management (Certificate); information systems management (MBA); management and leadership (MBA); marketing (Certificate); project management (Certificate); public management (MBA, Certificate); sport, event and entertainment management (Certificate); JD/MBA. Part-time and evening/weekend programs available. Postbaccalaureate distance learning degree programs offered (minimal on-campus study). *Faculty:* 10 full-time (4 women), 54 part-time/adjunct (6 women). *Students:* 237 full-time (99 women), 403 part-time (199 women); includes 186 minority (95 Black or African American, non-Hispanic/Latino; 62 Asian, non-Hispanic/Latino; 28 Hispanic/Latino; 1 Native Hawaiian or other Pacific Islander, non-Hispanic/Latino), 1 international. Average age 35. 345 applicants, 83% accepted, 193 enrolled. In 2011, 350 master's, 7 other advanced degrees awarded. *Degree requirements:* For master's, comprehensive exam, thesis optional. *Entrance requirements:* For master's, minimum GPA of 2.8, 2 letters of recommendation, courses or seminar in accounting and finance, resume. Additional exam requirements/recommendations for international students: Required—TOEFL (minimum score 550 paper-based). *Application deadline:* For fall admission, 9/1 priority date for domestic students; for winter admission, 1/1 priority date for domestic students; for spring admission, 2/1 priority date for domestic students. Applications are processed on a rolling basis. Application fee: $50. Electronic applications accepted. *Expenses: Tuition:* Full-time $19,162; part-time $933 per credit. *Required fees:* $1330; $700 per year. Tuition and fees vary according to course load. *Financial support:* Career-related internships or fieldwork and Federal Work-Study available. Support available to part-time students. Financial award application deadline: 6/30; financial award applicants required to submit FAFSA. *Faculty research:* International finance, computer applications, labor relations, executive development. *Unit head:* Antonia Loschiavo, Assistant Dean, 631-244-3266, Fax: 631-244-1018, E-mail: loschiat@dowling.edu. *Application contact:* Ronnie S. Macdonald, Assistant Vice President for Enrollment Services/Dean of Admissions, 631-244-3357, Fax: 631-244-1059, E-mail: macdonar@dowling.edu.

East Central University, School of Graduate Studies, Department of Human Resources, Ada, OK 74820-6899. Offers administration (MSHR); counseling (MSHR); criminal justice (MSHR); rehabilitation counseling (MSHR). *Accreditation:* CORE. Part-time and evening/weekend programs available. *Degree requirements:* For master's, thesis optional. *Entrance requirements:* For master's, GRE General Test, MAT, minimum GPA of 2.5. Electronic applications accepted.

Eastern Michigan University, Graduate School, College of Arts and Sciences, Department of Political Science, Programs in Public Administration, Ypsilanti, MI 48197. Offers local government management (Graduate Certificate); management of public healthcare services (Graduate Certificate); public administration (MPA, Graduate Certificate); public budget management (Graduate Certificate); public land planning (Graduate Certificate); public management (Graduate Certificate); public personnel management (Graduate Certificate); public policy analysis (Graduate Certificate). *Accreditation:* NASPAA. *Students:* 21 full-time (12 women), 124 part-time (62 women); includes 48 minority (36 Black or African American, non-Hispanic/Latino; 1 American Indian or Alaska Native, non-Hispanic/Latino; 4 Asian, non-Hispanic/Latino; 5 Hispanic/Latino; 2 Two or more races, non-Hispanic/Latino), 2 international. Average age 33. 68 applicants, 68% accepted, 26 enrolled. In 2011, 20 master's, 15 other advanced degrees awarded. Application fee: $35. *Expenses:* Tuition, state resident: full-time $10,367; part-time $432 per credit hour. Tuition, nonresident: full-time $20,435; part-time $851 per credit hour. *Required fees:* $39 per credit hour. $46 per semester. One-time fee: $100. Tuition and fees vary according to course level, degree level and reciprocity agreements. *Unit head:* Dr. Joseph Ohren, Program Director, 734-487-2522, Fax: 734-487-3340, E-mail: joseph.ohren@emich.edu. *Application contact:* Graduate Admissions, 734-487-2400, Fax: 734-487-6559, E-mail: graduate.admissions@emich.edu.

Eastern Michigan University, Graduate School, College of Business, Department of Management, Program in Human Resources Management and Organizational Development, Ypsilanti, MI 48197. Offers MSHROD. Part-time and evening/weekend programs available. Postbaccalaureate distance learning degree programs offered (minimal on-campus study). *Students:* 30 full-time (22 women), 52 part-time (39 women); includes 18 minority (12 Black or African American, non-Hispanic/Latino; 4 Asian, non-Hispanic/Latino; 1 Hispanic/Latino; 1 Two or more races, non-Hispanic/Latino), 26 international. Average age 30. 50 applicants, 58% accepted, 10 enrolled. In 2011, 64 degrees awarded. *Degree requirements:* For master's, thesis optional. *Entrance requirements:* For master's, GMAT. Additional exam requirements/recommendations for international students: Required—TOEFL. *Application deadline:* Applications are processed on a rolling basis. Application fee: $35. *Expenses:* Tuition, state resident: full-time $10,367; part-time $432 per credit hour. Tuition, nonresident: full-time $20,435; part-time $851 per credit hour. *Required fees:* $39 per credit hour. $46 per semester. One-time fee: $100. Tuition and fees vary according to course level, degree level and reciprocity agreements. *Financial support:* Fellowships, research assistantships with full tuition reimbursements, teaching assistantships with full tuition reimbursements, career-related internships or fieldwork, Federal Work-Study, institutionally sponsored loans, scholarships/grants, tuition waivers (partial), and unspecified assistantships available. Support available to part-time students. Financial award applicants required to submit FAFSA. *Unit head:* Dr. Fraya Wagner-Marsh, Advisor, 734-787-3240, Fax: 734-487-4100, E-mail: fraya.wagner@emich.edu. *Application contact:* K. Michelle Henry, Director, Academic Services, 734-487-4444, Fax: 734-483-1316, E-mail: mhenry1@emich.edu. Web site: http://www.emich.edu/public/cob/management/mshrod.

Eastern Michigan University, Graduate School, College of Business, Programs in Business Administration, Ypsilanti, MI 48197. Offers business administration (MBA, Graduate Certificate); computer information systems (Graduate Certificate); e-business (MBA, Graduate Certificate); enterprise business intelligence (MBA); entrepreneurship (MBA, Graduate Certificate); finance (MBA, Graduate Certificate); human resources (MBA); human resources management (Graduate Certificate); information systems (MBA); internal auditing (MBA); international business (MBA, Graduate Certificate); marketing management (Graduate Certificate); nonprofit management (MBA); organizational development (Graduate Certificate); supply chain management (MBA, Graduate Certificate). *Accreditation:* AACSB. Part-time programs available. Postbaccalaureate distance learning degree programs offered (no on-campus study). *Students:* 79 full-time (39 women), 287 part-time (143 women); includes 55 minority (22 Black or African American, non-Hispanic/Latino; 24 Asian, non-Hispanic/Latino; 6 Hispanic/Latino; 3 Two or more races, non-Hispanic/Latino), 238 international. Average age 32. 317 applicants, 62% accepted, 89 enrolled. In 2011, 102 master's, 58 other advanced degrees awarded. *Entrance requirements:* For master's, GMAT (minimum score 450), minimum cumulative undergraduate GPA of 2.75. Additional exam requirements/recommendations for international students: Required—TOEFL. *Application deadline:* For fall admission, 5/15 for domestic students, 5/1 for international students; for winter admission, 10/15 for domestic students, 10/1 for international students; for spring admission, 3/15 for domestic students, 3/1 for international students. Applications are processed on a rolling basis. Application fee: $35. *Expenses:* Tuition, state resident: full-time $10,367; part-time $432 per credit hour. Tuition, nonresident: full-time $20,435; part-time $851 per credit hour. *Required fees:* $39 per credit hour. $46 per semester. One-time fee: $100. Tuition and fees vary according to course level, degree level and reciprocity agreements. *Financial support:* Fellowships, research assistantships with full tuition reimbursements, teaching assistantships with full tuition reimbursements, career-related internships or fieldwork, Federal Work-Study, institutionally sponsored loans, scholarships/grants, tuition waivers (partial), and unspecified assistantships available. Support available to part-time students. Financial award applicants required to submit FAFSA. *Unit head:* K. Michelle Henry, Director, Academic Services, 734-487-4444, Fax: 734-483-1316, E-mail: mhenry1@emich.edu. *Application contact:* Beste Windes, Advisor, 734-487-4444, Fax: 734-483-1316, E-mail: bwindes@emich.edu. Web site: http://www.emich.edu/public/cob/gr/grad.html.

Emmanuel College, Graduate and Professional Programs, Graduate Programs in Management, Boston, MA 02115. Offers biopharmaceutical leadership (MSM); human resource management (MSM, Graduate Certificate); management (MSM); management and leadership (Graduate Certificate); research administration (MSM, Graduate Certificate). Part-time and evening/weekend programs available. Postbaccalaureate distance learning degree programs offered (no on-campus study). *Faculty:* 60 part-time/adjunct (24 women). *Students:* 6 full-time (4 women); 216 part-time (155 women); includes 53 minority (28 Black or African American, non-Hispanic/Latino; 1 American

Indian or Alaska Native, non-Hispanic/Latino; 10 Asian, non-Hispanic/Latino; 14 Hispanic/Latino). Average age 34. 61 applicants, 75% accepted, 39 enrolled. In 2011, 76 master's, 29 other advanced degrees awarded. *Degree requirements:* For master's, thesis or alternative, 36 credits, including a 6-credit capstone project. *Entrance requirements:* For master's, interview, essay, resume, 2 letters of recommendation, bachelor's degree; for Graduate Certificate, transcripts from all regionally-accredited institutions attended (showing proof of bachelor's degree completion), 2 letters of recommendation, essay, resume, interview. Additional exam requirements/recommendations for international students: Required—TOEFL (minimum score 600 paper-based; 250 computer-based; 106 iBT) or IELTS (minimum score 6.5). *Application deadline:* For fall admission, 7/31 priority date for domestic students; for spring admission, 11/30 priority date for domestic students. Applications are processed on a rolling basis. Application fee: $0. Electronic applications accepted. *Expenses: Tuition:* Part-time $2139 per course. Tuition and fees vary according to program and reciprocity agreements. *Financial support:* Applicants required to submit FAFSA. *Unit head:* Dr. Joyce DeLeo, Vice President of Academic Affairs, 617-735-9700, Fax: 617-507-0434, E-mail: gpp@emmanuel.edu. *Application contact:* Enrollment Counselor, 617-735-9700, Fax: 617-507-0434, E-mail: gpp@emmanuel.edu. Web site: http://gpp.emmanuel.edu.

Emmanuel College, Graduate and Professional Programs, Program in Human Resource Management, Boston, MA 02115. Offers MS, Certificate. Part-time and evening/weekend programs available. *Faculty:* 1 (woman) full-time, 15 part-time/adjunct (4 women). *Students:* 4 full-time (all women), 75 part-time (58 women); includes 17 minority (11 Black or African American, non-Hispanic/Latino; 1 American Indian or Alaska Native, non-Hispanic/Latino; 1 Asian, non-Hispanic/Latino; 4 Hispanic/Latino). Average age 32. 28 applicants, 82% accepted, 23 enrolled. In 2011, 16 master's, 5 other advanced degrees awarded. *Entrance requirements:* For master's, interview, resume, 2 letters of recommendation, essay, bachelor's degree; for Certificate, interview, resume, letter of recommendation. Additional exam requirements/recommendations for international students: Required—TOEFL (minimum score 600 paper-based; 250 computer-based). *Application deadline:* For fall admission, 8/15 priority date for domestic students; for spring admission, 12/8 priority date for domestic students. Applications are processed on a rolling basis. Application fee: $50. Electronic applications accepted. *Expenses: Tuition:* Part-time $2139 per course. Tuition and fees vary according to program and reciprocity agreements. *Unit head:* Dr. Judith Marley, Dean, Graduate and Professional Programs, 617-735-9700, Fax: 617-507-0434, E-mail: gpp@emmanuel.edu. *Application contact:* Enrollment Counselor, 617-735-9700, Fax: 617-507-0434, E-mail: gpp@emmanuel.edu.

Everest University, Department of Business Administration, Tampa, FL 33614-5899. Offers accounting (MBA); human resources (MBA); international business (MBA). Part-time and evening/weekend programs available. *Degree requirements:* For master's, thesis optional. *Entrance requirements:* For master's, GMAT or GRE General Test, minimum GPA of 3.0.

Everest University, Program in Business Administration, Orlando, FL 32819. Offers accounting (MBA); general management (MBA); human resources (MBA); international management (MBA).

Fairfield University, Charles F. Dolan School of Business, Fairfield, CT 06824-5195. Offers accounting (MBA, MS, CAS); accounting information systems (MBA, CAS); entrepreneurship (MBA, CAS); finance (MBA, MS, CAS); general management (MBA, CAS); human resource management (MBA, CAS); information systems and operations (MBA); information systems and operations management (CAS); international business (MBA, CAS); marketing (MBA, CAS); taxation (MBA, CAS). *Accreditation:* AACSB. Part-time and evening/weekend programs available. *Faculty:* 23 full-time (9 women), 3 part-time/adjunct (1 woman). *Students:* 87 full-time (37 women), 118 part-time (42 women); includes 13 minority (4 Black or African American, non-Hispanic/Latino; 4 Asian, non-Hispanic/Latino; 5 Hispanic/Latino), 9 international. Average age 29. 126 applicants, 47% accepted, 35 enrolled. In 2011, 90 master's awarded. *Degree requirements:* For master's, capstone course. *Entrance requirements:* For master's, GMAT (minimum score 500), 2 letters of reference, resume, minimum GPA of 3.0. Additional exam requirements/recommendations for international students: Required—TOEFL (minimum score 550 paper-based; 213 computer-bases; 80 iBT) or IELTS (minimum score 6.5). *Application deadline:* For fall admission, 5/15 for international students; for spring admission, 10/15 for international students. Applications are processed on a rolling basis. Application fee: $60. Electronic applications accepted. *Expenses:* Contact institution. *Financial support:* In 2011–12, 50 students received support, including 2 research assistantships (averaging $6,500 per year); scholarships/grants, unspecified assistantships, and merit-based one-time entrance scholarship also available. Financial award applicants required to submit FAFSA. *Faculty research:* Optimization strategies, international finance, consumer behavior, financial market volatility, Internet marketing, supply chain analysis, tax issues. *Unit head:* Dr. Donald Gibson, Dean, 203-254-4000 Ext. 4070, Fax: 203-254-4105, E-mail: dgibson@fairfield.edu. *Application contact:* Marianne Gumpper, Director of Graduate and Continuing Studies Admission, 203-254-4184, Fax: 203-254-4073, E-mail: gradadmis@fairfield.edu. Web site: http://www.fairfield.edu/dsb/dsb_grad_1.html.

Fairleigh Dickinson University, College at Florham, Silberman College of Business, Center for Human Resource Management Studies, Program in Human Resource Management, Madison, NJ 07940-1099. Offers MBA, MA/MBA.

Fairleigh Dickinson University, Metropolitan Campus, Silberman College of Business, Center for Human Resources Management Studies, Program in Human Resource Management, Teaneck, NJ 07666-1914. Offers MBA, Certificate.

Fitchburg State University, Division of Graduate and Continuing Education, Program in Business Administration, Fitchburg, MA 01420-2697. Offers accounting (MBA); human resource management (MBA); management (MBA). Part-time and evening/weekend programs available. Postbaccalaureate distance learning degree programs offered (no on-campus study). *Students:* 24 full-time (9 women), 57 part-time (29 women); includes 10 minority (6 Black or African American, non-Hispanic/Latino; 2 Hispanic/Latino; 2 Two or more races, non-Hispanic/Latino), 10 international. Average age 32. 32 applicants, 97% accepted, 27 enrolled. In 2011, 61 master's awarded. *Entrance requirements:* Additional exam requirements/recommendations for international students: Required—TOEFL (minimum score 550 paper-based; 213 computer-based; 79 iBT). *Application deadline:* For fall admission, 7/15 for international students; for spring admission, 12/1 for international students. Applications are processed on a rolling basis. Application fee: $25 ($50 for international students). Electronic applications accepted. *Expenses:* Tuition, state resident: full-time $2700; part-time $150 per credit. Tuition, nonresident: full-time $2700; part-time $150 per credit. *Required fees:* $2286; $127 per credit. *Financial support:* In 2011–12, research assistantships with partial tuition reimbursements (averaging $5,500 per year) were awarded; Federal Work-Study, scholarships/grants, and unspecified assistantships also available. Support available to part-time students. Financial award application deadline: 3/1; financial award applicants required to submit FAFSA. *Unit head:* Joseph McAloon, Chair, 978-665-3745, Fax: 978-665-3658, E-mail: gce@fitchburgstate.edu. *Application contact:* Kay Reynolds, Director of Admissions, 978-665-3144, Fax: 978-665-4540, E-mail: admissions@fitchburgstate.edu. Web site: http://www.fitchburgstate.edu.

Florida Institute of Technology, Graduate Programs, Extended Studies Division, Melbourne, FL 32901-6975. Offers acquisition and contract management (MS); aerospace engineering (MS); business administration (MBA); computer information systems (MS); computer science (MS); electrical engineering (MS); engineering management (MS); human resources management (MS); logistics management (MS), including humanitarian and disaster relief logistics; management (MS), including acquisition and contract management, e-business, human resources management, information systems, logistics management, management, transportation management; material acquisition management (MS); mechanical engineering (MS); operations research (MS); project management (MS), including information systems, operations research; public administration (MPA); quality management (MS); software engineering (MS); space systems (MS); space systems management (MS); supply chain management (MS); systems management (MS), including information systems, operations research. Part-time and evening/weekend programs available. Postbaccalaureate distance learning degree programs offered (no on-campus study). *Faculty:* 9 full-time (2 women), 105 part-time/adjunct (24 women). *Students:* 113 full-time (52 women), 1,150 part-time (484 women); includes 496 minority (332 Black or African American, non-Hispanic/Latino; 11 American Indian or Alaska Native, non-Hispanic/Latino; 42 Asian, non-Hispanic/Latino; 71 Hispanic/Latino; 2 Native Hawaiian or other Pacific Islander, non-Hispanic/Latino; 38 Two or more races, non-Hispanic/Latino), 11 international. Average age 35. 568 applicants, 56% accepted, 296 enrolled. In 2011, 471 master's awarded. *Degree requirements:* For master's, comprehensive exam (for some programs), capstone course. *Entrance requirements:* For master's, GMAT or resume showing 8 years of supervised experience, minimum GPA of 3.0, 2 letters of recommendation, resume. Additional exam requirements/recommendations for international students: Required—TOEFL (minimum score 550 paper-based; 213 computer-based; 79 iBT). *Application deadline:* For fall admission, 4/1 for international students; for spring admission, 9/30 for international students. Applications are processed on a rolling basis. Application fee: $0. Electronic applications accepted. *Expenses:* Contact institution. *Financial support:* Application deadline: 3/1; applicants required to submit FAFSA. *Unit head:* Dr. Theodore R. Richardson, III, Senior Associate Dean, 321-674-8123, Fax: 321-674-7597, E-mail: trichardson@fit.edu. *Application contact:* Carolyn Farrior, Director of Graduate Admissions, Online Learning and Off-Campus Programs, 321-674-7118, Fax: 321-674-8216, E-mail: cfarrior@fit.edu. Web site: http://es.fit.edu.

Florida International University, Alvah H. Chapman, Jr. Graduate School of Business, Department of Management and International Business, Human Resources Management Program, Miami, FL 33199. Offers MSHRM. Part-time and evening/weekend programs available. *Entrance requirements:* For master's, GRE (minimum score of 1000) or GMAT (minimum score of 500), minimum GPA of 3.0 (upper-level coursework); two letters of recommendation; letter of intent; minimum of five years of professional (exempt) experience, of which at least two years are in HR field. Additional exam requirements/recommendations for international students: Required—TOEFL (minimum score 550 paper-based; 213 computer-based; 80 iBT) or IELTS (minimum score 6.5). Electronic applications accepted. *Expenses:* Contact institution. *Faculty research:* Compensation, labor issues, labor law, human resource strategy.

Fordham University, Graduate School of Education, Division of Educational Leadership, Administration and Policy, New York, NY 10023. Offers administration and supervision (MSE, Adv C); administration and supervision for church leaders (PhD); educational administration and supervision (Ed D, PhD); human resource program administration (MS). *Accreditation:* NCATE. *Degree requirements:* For doctorate, thesis/dissertation. *Entrance requirements:* For doctorate, MAT, GRE General Test. *Expenses: Tuition:* Full-time $30,480; part-time $1270 per credit. *Required fees:* $586; $293 per semester.

Framingham State University, Division of Graduate and Continuing Education, Program in Human Resource Management, Framingham, MA 01701-9101. Offers MA. Part-time and evening/weekend programs available.

Franklin Pierce University, Graduate Studies, Rindge, NH 03461-0060. Offers curriculum and instruction (M Ed); emerging network technologies (Graduate Certificate); energy and sustainability studies (MBA); health administration (MBA, Graduate Certificate); human resource management (MBA, Graduate Certificate); information technology (MBA); information technology management (MS); leadership (MBA, DA); nursing (MS); physical therapy (DPT); physician assistant studies (MPAS); special education (M Ed); sports management (MBA). *Accreditation:* APTA. Part-time programs available. Postbaccalaureate distance learning degree programs offered (no on-campus study). *Degree requirements:* For master's, concentrated original research projects; student teaching; fieldwork and/or internship; leadership project; PRAXIS I and II (for M Ed); for doctorate, concentrated original research projects, clinical fieldwork and/or internship, leadership project. *Entrance requirements:* For master's, minimum GPA of 2.5, 3 letters of recommendation; competencies in accounting, economics, statistics, and computer skills through life experience or undergraduate coursework (for MBA); certification/e-portfolio, minimum C grade in all education courses (for M Ed); license to practice as RN (for MS in nursing); for doctorate, GRE, BA/BS, 3 letters of recommendation, personal mission statement, interview, writing sample, minimum cumulative GPA of 2.8, master's degree (for DA); 80 hours of observation/work in PT settings, completion of anatomy, chemistry, physics, and statistics, minimum GPA of 3.0 (for DPT). Additional exam requirements/recommendations for international students: Required—TOEFL (minimum score 550 paper-based; 195 computer-based; 61 iBT). Electronic applications accepted. *Faculty research:* Evidence-based practice in sports physical therapy, human resource management in economic crisis, leadership in nursing, innovation in sports facility management, differentiated learning and understanding by design.

Gannon University, School of Graduate Studies, College of Engineering and Business, School of Business, Program in Human Resources Management, Erie, PA 16541-0001. Offers Certificate. Part-time and evening/weekend programs available. *Students:* 1 applicant, 0% accepted, 0 enrolled. *Entrance requirements:* For degree, GMAT. Additional exam requirements/recommendations for international students: Required—TOEFL (minimum score 79 iBT). *Application deadline:* Applications are processed on a rolling basis. Application fee: $25. Electronic applications accepted. *Financial support:* Application deadline: 7/1; applicants required to submit FAFSA. *Unit head:* Dr. Donna Mottilla, Director, 814-871-7780, E-mail: mottilla001@gannon.edu. *Application contact:* Kara Morgan, Director of Graduate Admissions, 814-871-5831, Fax: 814-871-5827, E-mail: graduate@gannon.edu.

George Fox University, School of Business, Newberg, OR 97132-2697. Offers finance (MBA); management (DBA); management/general (MBA); marketing (DBA); organizational strategy (MBA); strategic human resource management (MBA). MBA offered part-time and full-time in Newberg, OR, and in Portland, OR. Part-time and evening/weekend programs available. Postbaccalaureate distance learning degree programs offered (minimal on-campus study). *Faculty:* 9 full-time (2 women), 6 part-time/adjunct (0 women). *Students:* 24 full-time (11 women), 239 part-time (81 women); includes 33 minority (4 Black or African American, non-Hispanic/Latino; 1 American Indian or Alaska Native, non-Hispanic/Latino; 14 Asian, non-Hispanic/Latino; 10 Hispanic/Latino; 4 Two or more races, non-Hispanic/Latino), 13 international. Average

age 37. In 2011, 101 master's, 6 doctorates awarded. *Degree requirements:* For master's, capstone project; for doctorate, credit-applied research project. *Entrance requirements:* For master's, resume (5 years professional experience); 3 professional references; interview; financial e-learning course, official transcripts; for doctorate, GRE or GMAT, resume; personal mission statement; academic research writing sample; official transcript from each college/university attended; three professional references. Additional exam requirements/recommendations for international students: Required—TOEFL (minimum score 577 paper-based; 233 computer-based; 90 iBT) or IELTS (minimum score 7). *Application deadline:* For fall admission, 8/1 for domestic and international students; for spring admission, 12/1 for domestic and international students. Applications are processed on a rolling basis. Application fee: $40. Electronic applications accepted. *Expenses:* Contact institution. *Financial support:* Applicants required to submit FAFSA. *Unit head:* Dr. Dirk Barram, Professor/Dean, 800-631-0921. *Application contact:* Robin Halverson, Admissions Counselor, 800-493-4937, Fax: 503-554-6111, E-mail: mba@georgefox.edu. Web site: http://www.georgefox.edu/business/index.html.

George Mason University, School of Public Policy, Program in Organization Development and Knowledge Management, Arlington, VA 22201. Offers MS. *Faculty:* 54 full-time (18 women), 20 part-time/adjunct (8 women). *Students:* 59 full-time (38 women), 17 part-time (15 women); includes 21 minority (9 Black or African American, non-Hispanic/Latino; 1 American Indian or Alaska Native, non-Hispanic/Latino; 4 Asian, non-Hispanic/Latino; 6 Hispanic/Latino; 1 Two or more races, non-Hispanic/Latino), 3 international. Average age 37. 60 applicants, 58% accepted, 29 enrolled. In 2011, 39 master's awarded. *Degree requirements:* For master's, thesis or alternative. *Entrance requirements:* For master's, GRE (for students seeking merit-based scholarships), bachelor's degree with minimum GPA of 3.0, current resume, 2 letters of recommendation, expanded goals statement, 2 copies of official transcripts. Additional exam requirements/recommendations for international students: Required—TOEFL (minimum score 575 paper-based; 230 computer-based; 88 iBT), IELTS, Pearson Test of English. *Application deadline:* For fall admission, 6/1 priority date for domestic students, 5/1 for international students; for spring admission, 12/1 priority date for domestic students, 11/1 for international students. Applications are processed on a rolling basis. Application fee: $65 ($80 for international students). Electronic applications accepted. *Expenses:* Contact institution. *Financial support:* Career-related internships or fieldwork, Federal Work-Study, scholarships/grants, unspecified assistantships, and health care benefits (full-time research or teaching assistantship recipients) available. Financial award application deadline: 3/1; financial award applicants required to submit FAFSA. *Unit head:* Tojo Joseph Thatchenkery, Director, 703-993-3808, Fax: 703-993-8215, E-mail: thatchen@gmu.edu. *Application contact:* Tennille Haegele, Director, Graduate Admissions, 703-993-8099, Fax: 703-993-4876, E-mail: spp@gmu.edu. Web site: http://policy.gmu.edu/Home/AcademicProfessionalPrograms/MastersPrograms/OrganizationDevelopmentKnowledgeManagement/tabid/106/Default.aspx.

Georgetown University, Graduate School of Arts and Sciences, School of Continuing Studies, Washington, DC 20057. Offers American studies (MALS); Catholic studies (MALS); classical civilizations (MALS); disability studies (MPS); ethics and the professions (MALS); human resources management (MPS); humanities (MALS); individualized study (MALS); international affairs (MALS); Islam and Muslim-Christian relations (MALS); journalism (MPS); liberal studies (DLS); literature and society (MALS); medieval and early modern European studies (MALS); public relations and corporate communications (MPS); real estate (MPS); religious studies (MALS); social and public policy (MALS); sports industry management (MPS); the theory and practice of American democracy (MALS); visual culture (MALS). *Entrance requirements:* Additional exam requirements/recommendations for international students: Required—TOEFL.

The George Washington University, Columbian College of Arts and Sciences, Department of Organizational Sciences and Communication, Washington, DC 20052. Offers human resources management (MA); industrial/organizational psychology (PhD); organizational management (MA). Part-time and evening/weekend programs available. *Faculty:* 9 full-time (6 women), 25 part-time/adjunct (16 women). *Students:* 28 full-time (22 women), 39 part-time (32 women); includes 15 minority (5 Black or African American, non-Hispanic/Latino; 2 Asian, non-Hispanic/Latino; 7 Hispanic/Latino; 1 Native Hawaiian or other Pacific Islander, non-Hispanic/Latino), 4 international. Average age 28. 80 applicants, 95% accepted, 37 enrolled. In 2011, 29 master's awarded. *Degree requirements:* For master's, comprehensive exam. *Entrance requirements:* For master's, GRE General Test, minimum GPA of 3.0. Additional exam requirements/recommendations for international students: Required—TOEFL (minimum score 500 paper-based; 213 computer-based; 80 iBT). *Application deadline:* For fall admission, 1/15 priority date for domestic students, 1/15 for international students; for spring admission, 10/1 priority date for domestic students, 9/1 for international students. Applications are processed on a rolling basis. Application fee: $75. Electronic applications accepted. *Financial support:* Federal Work-Study and institutionally sponsored loans available. *Unit head:* Dr. David Costanza, Acting Director, 202-994-1875, Fax: 202-994-1881, E-mail: dconstanz@gwu.edu. *Application contact:* Information Contact, 202-994-1880, Fax: 202-994-1881. Web site: http://www.gwu.edu/~orgsci/.

Georgia State University, J. Mack Robinson College of Business, Department of Managerial Sciences, Atlanta, GA 30302-3083. Offers business analysis (MBA, MS); decision sciences (PhD); entrepreneurship (MBA); human resources management (MBA, MS); management (MBA, PhD); operations management (MBA, MS); organization change (MS); personnel employee relations (PhD); strategic management (PhD). *Accreditation:* AACSB. Part-time and evening/weekend programs available. *Degree requirements:* For doctorate, thesis/dissertation. *Entrance requirements:* For master's and doctorate, GMAT. Additional exam requirements/recommendations for international students: Required—TOEFL (minimum score 610 paper-based; 255 computer-based; 101 iBT). Electronic applications accepted. *Faculty research:* Abusive supervision, entrepreneurship, time series and neural networks, organizational controls, inventory control systems.

Golden Gate University, Ageno School of Business, San Francisco, CA 94105-2968. Offers accounting (MBA); business administration (EMBA, MBA, PMBA, DBA); finance (MBA, MS, Certificate); financial planning (MS, Certificate); healthcare information systems (Certificate); human resource management (MBA, MS); human resources management (Certificate); information systems (MS); information technology (MBA); information technology management (Certificate); integrated marketing and communications (MS, Certificate); international business (MBA); management (MBA); marketing (MBA, MS, Certificate); operations supply chain management (Certificate); psychology (MA, Certificate); public administration (EMPA); public relations (MS, Certificate); technical market analysis (Certificate); JD/MBA. Part-time and evening/weekend programs available. *Faculty:* 19 full-time (6 women), 241 part-time/adjunct (72 women). *Students:* 397 full-time (230 women), 779 part-time (432 women); includes 376 minority (105 Black or African American, non-Hispanic/Latino; 5 American Indian or Alaska Native, non-Hispanic/Latino; 161 Asian, non-Hispanic/Latino; 77 Hispanic/Latino; 12 Native Hawaiian or other Pacific Islander, non-Hispanic/Latino; 16 Two or more races, non-Hispanic/Latino), 265 international. Average age 34. 871 applicants, 64% accepted, 271 enrolled. In 2011, 550 master's, 13 doctorates awarded. *Degree requirements:* For doctorate, thesis/dissertation, qualifying examination. *Entrance requirements:* For master's, GMAT (MBA), minimum GPA of 2.5 (MS). Additional exam requirements/recommendations for international students: Required—TOEFL (minimum score 550 paper-based; 213 computer-based; 79 iBT). *Application deadline:* For fall admission, 5/15 for domestic and international students; for winter admission, 1/15 for domestic and international students; for spring admission, 9/15 for domestic and international students. Applications are processed on a rolling basis. Application fee: $70 ($110 for international students). Electronic applications accepted. *Expenses:* Contact institution. *Financial support:* Career-related internships or fieldwork, Federal Work-Study, institutionally sponsored loans, and scholarships/grants available. Support available to part-time students. Financial award applicants required to submit FAFSA. *Unit head:* Dr. Paul Fouts, Dean, 415-442-7026, Fax: 415-442-6579. *Application contact:* Angela Melero, Enrollment Services, 415-442-7800, Fax: 415-442-7807, E-mail: info@ggu.edu. Web site: http://www.ggu.edu/programs/business-and-management.

Goldey-Beacom College, Graduate Program, Wilmington, DE 19808-1999. Offers business administration (MBA); finance (MS); financial management (MBA); health care management (MBA); human resource management (MBA); information technology (MBA); international business management (MBA); major finance (MBA); major taxation (MBA); management (MM); marketing management (MBA); taxation (MBA, MS). *Accreditation:* ACBSP. Part-time and evening/weekend programs available. *Faculty:* 19 full-time (7 women), 35 part-time/adjunct (12 women). *Students:* 58 full-time (32 women), 388 part-time (164 women); includes 89 minority (34 Black or African American, non-Hispanic/Latino; 2 American Indian or Alaska Native, non-Hispanic/Latino; 44 Asian, non-Hispanic/Latino; 9 Hispanic/Latino), 229 international. Average age 30. In 2011, 243 master's awarded. *Entrance requirements:* For master's, GMAT, MAT, GRE, minimum GPA of 3.0. Additional exam requirements/recommendations for international students: Required—TOEFL (minimum score 65 computer-based); Recommended—IELTS (minimum score 5). *Application deadline:* Applications are processed on a rolling basis. Application fee: $0. Electronic applications accepted. *Expenses: Tuition:* Full-time $15,750; part-time $875 per credit. *Required fees:* $10 per credit. *Financial support:* Scholarships/grants available. Support available to part-time students. Financial award application deadline: 4/1; financial award applicants required to submit FAFSA. *Unit head:* Larry W. Eby, Director of Admissions, 302-225-6289, Fax: 302-996-5408, E-mail: ebylw@gbc.edu. *Application contact:* Ashley E. Mashington, Graduate Admissions Representative, 302-225-6259, Fax: 302-996-5408, E-mail: mashina@gbc.edu. Web site: http://www.gbc.edu/programs/graduate/.

Grambling State University, School of Graduate Studies and Research, College of Arts and Sciences, Program in Public Administration, Grambling, LA 71270. Offers health service administration (MPA); human resource management (MPA); public management (MPA); state and local government (MPA). *Accreditation:* NASPAA. Part-time programs available. *Degree requirements:* For master's, comprehensive exam (for some programs), thesis optional. *Entrance requirements:* For master's, GRE, minimum GPA of 2.75 on last degree. Additional exam requirements/recommendations for international students: Required—TOEFL (minimum score 500 paper-based; 173 computer-based; 61 iBT). Electronic applications accepted. *Expenses:* Tuition, state resident: full-time $3546; part-time $192 per credit hour. Tuition, nonresident: full-time $3456; part-time $192 per credit hour. *Required fees:* $1829; $1829 per semester hour.

Grand Canyon University, College of Business, Phoenix, AZ 85017-1097. Offers accounting (MBA); corporate business administration (MBA); disaster preparedness and crisis management (MBA); executive fire service leadership (MS); finance (MBA); general management (MBA); government and policy (MPA); health care management (MPA); health systems management (MBA); human resource management (MBA); innovation (MBA); leadership (MBA, MS); management of information system (MBA); marketing (MBA); project-based (MBA); six sigma (MBA); strategic human resource management (MBA). *Accreditation:* ACBSP. Part-time and evening/weekend programs available. Postbaccalaureate distance learning degree programs offered (no on-campus study). *Entrance requirements:* For master's, equivalent of two years full-time professional work experience. Additional exam requirements/recommendations for international students: Required—TOEFL (minimum score 575 paper-based; 233 computer-based; 90 iBT), IELTS (minimum score 7). Electronic applications accepted.

Hawai`i Pacific University, College of Business Administration, Program in Human Resource Management, Honolulu, HI 96813. Offers MA. Part-time and evening/weekend programs available. *Faculty:* 2 full-time (1 woman). *Students:* 32 full-time (19 women), 16 part-time (14 women); includes 25 minority (4 Black or African American, non-Hispanic/Latino; 10 Asian, non-Hispanic/Latino; 1 Hispanic/Latino; 1 Native Hawaiian or other Pacific Islander, non-Hispanic/Latino; 9 Two or more races, non-Hispanic/Latino). Average age 31. 34 applicants, 97% accepted, 19 enrolled. In 2011, 22 master's awarded. *Entrance requirements:* Additional exam requirements/recommendations for international students: Required—TOEFL (minimum score 550 paper-based; 213 computer-based; 80 iBT), IELTS (minimum score 6), TWE (minimum score 5). *Application deadline:* Applications are processed on a rolling basis. Application fee: $50. Electronic applications accepted. *Expenses: Tuition:* Full-time $13,230; part-time $735 per credit. Tuition and fees vary according to course load and program. *Financial support:* In 2011–12, 9 students received support. Career-related internships or fieldwork, Federal Work-Study, scholarships/grants, tuition waivers, and unspecified assistantships available. *Unit head:* Dr. Cheryl Crozier Garcia, Program Chair, 808-544-1178, Fax: 808-566-2403, E-mail: ccrozier@campus.hpu.edu. *Application contact:* Chad Schempp, Director of Graduate Admissions, 808-543-8035, Fax: 808-544-0280, E-mail: graduate@hpu.edu.

See Display on next page and Close-Up on page 439.

HEC Montreal, School of Business Administration, Master of Science Programs in Administration, Program in Human Resources Management, Montréal, QC H3T 2A7, Canada. Offers M Sc. All courses are given in French. Part-time programs available. *Students:* 32 full-time (27 women), 14 part-time (11 women). 54 applicants, 31% accepted, 11 enrolled. In 2011, 23 master's awarded. *Degree requirements:* For master's, one foreign language, thesis. *Entrance requirements:* For master's, Test de francais international (TFI) with minimum score of 850 (for those who have never studied in French), BBA, undergraduate degree in another field, degree deemed equivalent by program director and minimum GPA of 3.0 on 4.3 scale. *Application deadline:* For fall admission, 3/15 for domestic and international students; for winter admission, 9/15 for domestic and international students. Application fee: $80 Canadian dollars. Electronic applications accepted. Application fee is waived when completed online. *Expenses:* Contact institution. *Financial support:* Fellowships, research assistantships, teaching assistantships, and scholarships/grants available. Financial award application deadline: 9/2. *Unit head:* Dr. Claude Laurin, Director, 514-340-6485, Fax: 514-340-6880, E-mail: claude.laurin@hec.ca. *Application contact:* Virginie Lefebvre, Administrative Director, 514-340-6112, Fax: 514-340-6411, E-mail: virginie.lefebvre@hec.ca. Web site: http://www.hec.ca/en/programs_training/msc/options/hr_management/index.html.

Herzing University Online, Program in Business Administration, Milwaukee, WI 53203. Offers accounting (MBA); business administration (MBA); business management (MBA); healthcare management (MBA); human resources (MBA); marketing (MBA);

project management (MBA); technology management (MBA). Postbaccalaureate distance learning degree programs offered (no on-campus study).

Hofstra University, Frank G. Zarb School of Business, Department of Management, Entrepreneurship and General Management, Hempstead, NY 11549. Offers business administration (MBA), including health services management, management, sports and entertainment management; general management (Advanced Certificate); human resource management (MS, Advanced Certificate). Part-time and evening/weekend programs available. Postbaccalaureate distance learning degree programs offered (minimal on-campus study). *Faculty:* 7 full-time (2 women), 8 part-time/adjunct (1 woman). *Students:* 92 full-time (36 women), 151 part-time (62 women); includes 58 minority (25 Black or African American, non-Hispanic/Latino; 23 Asian, non-Hispanic/Latino; 10 Hispanic/Latino), 24 international. Average age 32. 227 applicants, 72% accepted, 93 enrolled. In 2011, 74 master's awarded. *Degree requirements:* For master's, thesis optional, capstone course (for MBA); thesis (for MS); minimum GPA of 3.0. *Entrance requirements:* For master's, GMAT/GRE, 2 letters of recommendation; resume; essay. Additional exam requirements/recommendations for international students: Required—TOEFL (minimum score 550 paper-based; 213 computer-based; 80 iBT); Recommended—IELTS (minimum score 6). *Application deadline:* Applications are processed on a rolling basis. Application fee: $70 ($75 for international students). Electronic applications accepted. *Expenses:* Contact institution. *Financial support:* In 2011–12, 23 students received support, including 18 fellowships with full and partial tuition reimbursements available (averaging $5,605 per year), 1 research assistantship with full and partial tuition reimbursement available (averaging $11,370 per year); career-related internships or fieldwork, Federal Work-Study, institutionally sponsored loans, scholarships/grants, tuition waivers (full and partial), and unspecified assistantships also available. Support available to part-time students. Financial award applicants required to submit FAFSA. *Faculty research:* Business/personal ethics, sustainability, innovation, decision-making, supply chain management, learning and pedagogical issues, family business, small business, entrepreneurship. *Unit head:* Dr. Li-Lian Gao, Chairperson, 516-463-5729, Fax: 516-463-4834, E-mail: mgblzg@hofstra.edu. *Application contact:* Carol Drummer, Dean of Graduate Admissions, 516-463-4876, Fax: 516-463-4664, E-mail: gradstudent@hofstra.edu. Web site: http://www.hofstra.edu/Academics/Colleges/Zarb/MGMT/.

Holy Family University, Graduate School, School of Business Administration, Program in Human Resources Management, Philadelphia, PA 19114. Offers MS. Part-time and evening/weekend programs available. *Entrance requirements:* For master's, GMAT, BS or BA, minimum GPA of 3.0. Electronic applications accepted.

See Display on next page and Close-Up on page 441.

Hood College, Graduate School, Department of Economics and Management, Frederick, MD 21701-8575. Offers accounting (MBA); administration and management (MBA); finance (MBA); human resource management (MBA); information systems (MBA); marketing (MBA); public management (MBA). *Accreditation:* ACBSP. Part-time and evening/weekend programs available. *Degree requirements:* For master's, capstone/final research project. *Entrance requirements:* For master's, minimum GPA of 2.75, resume, letters of recommendation. Additional exam requirements/recommendations for international students: Required—TOEFL (minimum score 575 paper-based; 231 computer-based; 89 iBT). Electronic applications accepted. *Faculty research:* Corporate strategy and sustainable competitive advantages, business ethics, entrepreneurship, investments management, economic development.

Houston Baptist University, College of Business and Economics, Program in Human Resources Management, Houston, TX 77074-3298. Offers MSHRM. Part-time and evening/weekend programs available. *Entrance requirements:* For master's, GMAT, minimum GPA of 2.5. Additional exam requirements/recommendations for international students: Required—TOEFL (minimum score 550 paper-based; 213 computer-based). *Expenses:* Contact institution.

Howard University, School of Business, Graduate Programs in Business, Washington, DC 20059-0002. Offers accounting (MBA); entrepreneurship (MBA); finance (MBA); general management (MBA); human resources management (MBA); information systems (MBA); international business (MBA); marketing (MBA); supply chain management (MBA); JD/MBA. *Accreditation:* AACSB. Part-time and evening/weekend programs available. Postbaccalaureate distance learning degree programs offered (no on-campus study). *Entrance requirements:* For master's, GMAT, minimum 1 year post undergraduate work experience, resume, 3 letters of recommendation, advanced college algebra. Additional exam requirements/recommendations for international students: Required—TOEFL. *Faculty research:* Marketing research in multi-ethnic populations, U.S. trade policies and international relations, risk management (finance).

Indiana Tech, Program in Business Administration, Fort Wayne, IN 46803-1297. Offers accounting (MBA); health care administration (MBA); human resources (MBA); management (MBA); marketing (MBA). Part-time and evening/weekend programs available. Postbaccalaureate distance learning degree programs offered (no on-campus study). *Entrance requirements:* For master's, GMAT, minimum undergraduate GPA of 2.5, 3 letters of recommendation. Electronic applications accepted.

Indiana Wesleyan University, College of Adult and Professional Studies, Graduate Studies in Business, Marion, IN 46953. Offers accounting (MBA); applied management (MBA); business administration (MBA); health care (MBA); human resources (MBA); management (MS). Part-time and evening/weekend programs available. Postbaccalaureate distance learning degree programs offered (no on-campus study). *Degree requirements:* For master's, applied business or management project. *Entrance requirements:* For master's, minimum GPA of 2.5, 2 years of related work experience. Additional exam requirements/recommendations for international students: Required—TOEFL (minimum score 550 paper-based; 213 computer-based). Electronic applications accepted.

Instituto Tecnologico de Santo Domingo, Graduate School, Area of Business, Santo Domingo, Dominican Republic. Offers banking and securities markets (M Mgmt); corporate finance (M Mgmt); human resources management (M Mgmt, Certificate); international trade management (M Mgmt); marketing (M Mgmt); organizational development (M Mgmt); quality and productivity management (Certificate); tax management and planning (M Mgmt); upper management (M Mgmt).

Instituto Tecnologico de Santo Domingo, Graduate School, Area of Engineering, Santo Domingo, Dominican Republic. Offers construction administration (MS, Certificate); data telecommunications (M Eng, MS, Certificate); industrial engineering (M Eng, Certificate); industrial management (M Mgmt); information technology (Certificate); maintenance engineering (M Eng); occupational hazard prevention (M Mgmt); production management (Certificate); quantitative methods (Certificate); sanitary and environmental engineering (M Eng); structural engineering (M Eng); systems engineering and electronic data processing (Certificate); transportation (Certificate).

Instituto Tecnológico y de Estudios Superiores de Monterrey, Campus Cuernavaca, Programs in Business Administration, Temixco, Mexico. Offers finance (MA); human resources management (MA); international business (MA); marketing (MA).

Inter American University of Puerto Rico, Aguadilla Campus, Graduate School, Aguadilla, PR 00605. Offers accounting (MBA); counseling psychology specializing in family (MS); criminal justice (MA); educative management and leadership (MA); elementary education (M Ed); finance (MBA); human resources (MBA); industrial management (MBA); management information systems (MBA); marketing (MBA). Part-time and evening/weekend programs available. *Degree requirements:* For master's, comprehensive exam. *Entrance requirements:* For master's, EXADEP, 2 letters of recommendation, minimum GPA of 2.5. Electronic applications accepted.

Inter American University of Puerto Rico, Arecibo Campus, Program in Business Administration, Arecibo, PR 00614-4050. Offers accounting (MBA); finance (MBA); human resources (MBA).

Inter American University of Puerto Rico, Bayamón Campus, Graduate School, Bayamón, PR 00957. Offers biology (MS), including environmental sciences and ecology, molecular biotechnology; human resources (MBA). Part-time and evening/weekend programs available. *Faculty:* 6 full-time (2 women), 2 part-time/adjunct (1 woman). *Students:* 7 full-time (6 women), 120 part-time (83 women); all minorities (1 Asian, non-Hispanic/Latino; 120 Hispanic/Latino; 6 Two or more races, non-Hispanic/Latino). Average age 29. *Degree requirements:* For master's, comprehensive exam, research project. *Entrance requirements:* For master's, EXADEP, GRE General Test, letters of recommendation. *Application deadline:* For fall admission, 7/1 for domestic students, 5/1 for international students; for winter admission, 11/15 priority date for domestic students, 11/15 for international students; for spring admission, 2/15 priority date for domestic students, 2/15 for international students. Application fee: $31. *Unit head:* Prof. Juan F. Martinez, Chancellor, 787-279-1200 Ext. 2295, Fax: 787-279-2205, E-mail: jmartinez@bayamon.inter.edu. *Application contact:* Carlos Alicea, Director of Admission, 787-279-1200 Ext. 2017, Fax: 787-279-2205, E-mail: calicea@bayamon.inter.edu.

Inter American University of Puerto Rico, Metropolitan Campus, Graduate Programs, Program in Human Resources, San Juan, PR 00919-1293. Offers MBA. *Degree requirements:* For master's, comprehensive exam. *Entrance requirements:* For master's, GRE or EXADEP, interview. Electronic applications accepted.

Inter American University of Puerto Rico, Ponce Campus, Graduate School, Mercedita, PR 00715-1602. Offers accounting (MBA); biology (M Ed); chemistry (M Ed); criminal justice (MA); elementary education (M Ed); English as a Second Language (M Ed); finance (MBA); history (M Ed); human resources (MBA); marketing (MBA); mathematics (M Ed); Spanish (M Ed). *Entrance requirements:* For master's, minimum GPA of 2.5.

Inter American University of Puerto Rico, San Germán Campus, Graduate Studies Center, Program in Business Administration, San Germán, PR 00683-5008. Offers accounting (MBA); finance (MBA); human resources (MBA, PhD); industrial relations (MBA); information sciences (MBA); management (MBA); marketing (MBA). Part-time and evening/weekend programs available. *Degree requirements:* For master's, comprehensive exam. *Entrance requirements:* For master's, GRE General Test or EXADEP, minimum GPA of 3.0. *Application deadline:* For fall admission, 4/30 priority date for domestic students; for spring admission, 11/15 for domestic students. Applications are processed on a rolling basis. Application fee: $31. *Expenses: Required fees:* $213 per semester. *Financial support:* Teaching assistantships, Federal Work-Study, and unspecified assistantships available. *Unit head:* Dr. Elba T. Irizarry, Director of Graduate Studies Center, 787-264-1912 Ext. 7357, Fax: 787-892-6350, E-mail: elbat@sg.inter.edu.

International College of the Cayman Islands, Graduate Program in Management, Newlands, Cayman Islands. Offers business administration (MBA); management (MS), including education, human resources. Part-time and evening/weekend programs available. *Degree requirements:* For master's, comprehensive exam. *Entrance requirements:* Additional exam requirements/recommendations for international students: Recommended—TOEFL. *Faculty research:* International human resources administration.

Iona College, Hagan School of Business, Department of Management, New Rochelle, NY 10801-1890. Offers business administration (MBA); health care management (MBA, AC); human resource management (MBA, PMC); long term care services management (AC); management (MBA, PMC). Part-time and evening/weekend programs available. *Faculty:* 7 full-time (1 woman), 4 part-time/adjunct (1 woman). *Students:* 29 full-time (13 women), 112 part-time (55 women); includes 27 minority (10 Black or African American, non-Hispanic/Latino; 8 Asian, non-Hispanic/Latino; 9 Hispanic/Latino). Average age 32. 60 applicants, 65% accepted, 30 enrolled. In 2011, 64 master's, 13 other advanced degrees awarded. *Entrance requirements:* For master's, GMAT, 2 letters of recommendation; for other advanced degree, GMAT. Additional exam requirements/recommendations for international students: Required—TOEFL (minimum score 550 paper-based; 213 computer-based; 80 iBT). *Application deadline:* For fall admission, 8/15 priority date for domestic students, 8/1 for international students; for winter admission, 11/15 priority date for domestic students, 11/1 for international students; for spring admission, 2/15 priority date for domestic students, 2/1 for international students. Applications are processed on a rolling basis. Application fee: $50. Electronic applications accepted. *Expenses:* Contact institution. *Financial support:* Scholarships/grants, tuition waivers (partial), and unspecified assistantships available. Support available to part-time students. Financial award application deadline: 4/15; financial award applicants required to submit FAFSA. *Faculty research:* Information systems, strategic management, corporate values and ethics. *Unit head:* Dr. Fredrica Rudell, Acting Chair, 914-637-2748, E-mail: frudell@iona.edu. *Application contact:* Ben Fan, Director of MBA Admissions, 914-633-2289, Fax: 914-637-2708, E-mail: sfan@iona.edu.

Kaplan University, Davenport Campus, School of Business, Davenport, IA 52807-2095. Offers business administration (MBA); change leadership (MS); entrepreneurship (MBA); finance (MBA); health care management (MBA, MS); human resource (MBA); international business (MBA); management (MS); marketing (MBA); project management (MBA, MS); supply chain management and logistics (MBA, MS). Part-time and evening/weekend programs available. Postbaccalaureate distance learning degree programs offered (no on-campus study). *Entrance requirements:* Additional exam requirements/recommendations for international students: Required—TOEFL (minimum score 550 paper-based; 218 computer-based; 80 iBT). Electronic applications accepted.

La Roche College, School of Graduate Studies and Adult Education, Program in Human Resources Management, Pittsburgh, PA 15237-5898. Offers MS, Certificate. *Accreditation:* ACBSP. Part-time and evening/weekend programs available. *Faculty:* 2 full-time (both women), 7 part-time/adjunct (3 women). *Students:* 5 full-time (2 women), 51 part-time (43 women); includes 3 minority (2 Black or African American, non-Hispanic/Latino; 1 Asian, non-Hispanic/Latino), 4 international. Average age 35. 15 applicants, 73% accepted, 8 enrolled. In 2011, 26 master's awarded. *Entrance requirements:* For master's, GMAT, GRE or MAT, minimum GPA of 3.0 during previous 2 years. Additional exam requirements/recommendations for international students: Recommended—TOEFL (minimum score 550 paper-based; 220 computer-based). *Application deadline:* For fall admission, 8/15 priority date for domestic students, 8/15 for international students; for spring admission, 12/15 priority date for domestic students, 12/15 for international students. Applications are processed on a rolling basis. Application fee: $50. Electronic applications accepted. *Expenses: Tuition:* Full-time $11,250; part-time $625 per credit hour. *Financial support:* Unspecified assistantships available. Financial award application deadline: 3/31; financial award applicants required to submit FAFSA. *Faculty research:* Personnel administration, human resources development. *Unit head:* Dr. Jean Forti, Coordinator, 412-536-1193, Fax: 412-536-1179, E-mail: fortij1@laroche.edu. *Application contact:* Hope Schiffgens, Director of Graduate Studies and Adult Education, 412-536-1266, Fax: 412-536-1283, E-mail: schombh1@laroche.edu.

Human Resources Management

Lasell College, Graduate and Professional Studies in Management, Newton, MA 02466-2709. Offers elder care administration (MSM, Graduate Certificate); elder care marketing (MSM, Graduate Certificate); fundraising management (MSM, Graduate Certificate); human resource management (Graduate Certificate); human resources management (MSM); integrated marketing communication (Graduate Certificate); management (MSM, Graduate Certificate); marketing (MSM, Graduate Certificate); non-profit management (MSM, Graduate Certificate); project management (MSM, Graduate Certificate); public relations (Graduate Certificate). Part-time and evening/weekend programs available. Postbaccalaureate distance learning degree programs offered (no on-campus study). *Faculty:* 9 full-time (7 women), 20 part-time/adjunct (13 women). *Students:* 23 full-time (16 women), 92 part-time (65 women); includes 74 minority (8 Black or African American, non-Hispanic/Latino; 4 American Indian or Alaska Native, non-Hispanic/Latino; 53 Asian, non-Hispanic/Latino; 9 Hispanic/Latino), 14 international. Average age 30. 78 applicants, 67% accepted, 31 enrolled. In 2011, 49 master's, 7 other advanced degrees awarded. *Entrance requirements:* For master's and Graduate Certificate, bachelor's degree from an accredited institution. Additional exam requirements/recommendations for international students: Required—TOEFL (minimum score 550 paper-based; 213 computer-based; 79 iBT). *Application deadline:* For fall admission, 8/31 priority date for domestic students, 6/30 for international students; for spring admission, 12/31 priority date for domestic students, 10/31 for international students. Applications are processed on a rolling basis. Electronic applications accepted. *Expenses: Tuition:* Part-time $575 per credit. *Required fees:* $70 per semester. *Financial support:* Available to part-time students. Application deadline: 8/31; applicants required to submit FAFSA. *Unit head:* Dr. Joan Dolamore, Dean of Graduate and Professional Studies, 617-243-2485, Fax: 617-243-2450, E-mail: gradinfo@lasell.edu. *Application contact:* Adrienne Franciosi, Director of Graduate Admission, 617-243-2214, Fax: 617-243-2450, E-mail: gradinfo@lasell.edu. Web site: http://www.lasell.edu/Academics/Graduate-and-Professional-Studies/MS-in-Management.html.

La Sierra University, School of Business and Management, Riverside, CA 92515. Offers accounting (MBA); finance (MBA); general management (MBA); human resources management (MBA); leadership, values, and ethics for business and management (Certificate); marketing (MBA). *Degree requirements:* For master's, research project. *Entrance requirements:* For master's, GMAT, minimum GPA of 3.0. Additional exam requirements/recommendations for international students: Required—TOEFL. *Faculty research:* Financial econometrics, institutional assessment and strategic planning, legal issues in management, behavioral finance, content of financial reports.

Lewis University, College of Business, Graduate School of Management, Program in Business Administration, Romeoville, IL 60446. Offers accounting (MBA); custom elective option (MBA); e-business (MBA); finance (MBA); healthcare management (MBA); human resources management (MBA); information security (MBA); international business (MBA); management information systems (MBA); marketing (MBA); project management (MBA); technology and operations management (MBA). Part-time and evening/weekend programs available. *Students:* 112 full-time (60 women), 232 part-time (118 women); includes 104 minority (62 Black or African American, non-Hispanic/Latino; 1 American Indian or Alaska Native, non-Hispanic/Latino; 7 Asian, non-Hispanic/Latino; 33 Hispanic/Latino; 1 Native Hawaiian or other Pacific Islander, non-Hispanic/Latino), 9 international. Average age 28. In 2011, 99 master's awarded. *Entrance requirements:* For master's, interview, bachelor's degree, resume, 2 recommendations. Additional exam requirements/recommendations for international students: Required—TOEFL (minimum score 550 paper-based; 213 computer-based). *Application deadline:* For fall admission, 8/15 priority date for domestic students, 5/1 for international students; for spring admission, 11/15 for international students. Applications are processed on a rolling basis. Application fee: $40. Electronic applications accepted. *Financial support:* Career-related internships or fieldwork, Federal Work-Study, scholarships/grants, and unspecified assistantships available. Financial award application deadline: 5/1; financial award applicants required to submit FAFSA. *Unit head:* Dr. Maureen Culleeney, Academic Program Director, 815-838-0500 Ext. 5631, E-mail: culleema@lewisu.edu. *Application contact:* Michele Ryan, Director of Admission, 815-838-0500 Ext. 5384, E-mail: gsm@lewisu.edu.

Lincoln University, Graduate Center, Lincoln University, PA 19352. Offers administration (MSA), including finance, human resources management; early childhood education (M Ed); elementary education (M Ed); human services (M Hum Svcs); reading (MSR). Evening/weekend programs available. *Degree requirements:* For master's, thesis. *Entrance requirements:* For master's, 5 years of work experience in human services. *Faculty research:* Gerontology/minority aging, computers in composition instruction.

Lincoln University, Graduate Studies, Oakland, CA 94612. Offers finance and investments (DBA); finance management and investment banking (MBA); general business (MBA); human resource management (MBA, DBA); international business (MBA); management information systems (MBA). Part-time and evening/weekend programs available. *Faculty:* 10 full-time (4 women), 15 part-time/adjunct (3 women). *Students:* 272 full-time (124 women), 1 part-time (0 women). *Degree requirements:* For master's, research project (thesis), internship report, or comprehensive exam; for doctorate, comprehensive exam, thesis/dissertation. *Entrance requirements:* For master's, minimum GPA of 2.7; for doctorate, GMAT (minimum score: 550), GRE (minimum score: 1000), or equivalent test results (waived for master's degree with minimum cumulative GPA of 3.3). Additional exam requirements/recommendations for international students: Required—TOEFL (minimum score 525 paper-based; 195 computer-based; 71 iBT) or IELTS (minimum score 5.5) for MBA; TOEFL (minimum score 550 paper-based; 213 computer-based; 79 iBT) or IELTS (minimum score 6) for DBA. *Application deadline:* For fall admission, 7/2 priority date for domestic students, 7/2 for international students; for spring admission, 11/25 priority date for domestic students, 11/25 for international students. Applications are processed on a rolling basis. Application fee: $75. Electronic applications accepted. *Financial support:* Teaching assistantships, career-related internships or fieldwork, and scholarships/grants available. *Unit head:* Dr. Marshall Burak, Director of Graduate Programs, 510-628-8016, Fax: 510-628-8012, E-mail: mburak@lincolnuca.edu. *Application contact:* Peggy Au, Director of Admissions and Records, 510-628-8010, Fax: 510-628-8012, E-mail: admissions@lincolnuca.edu. Web site: http://www.lincolnuca.edu/.

Lindenwood University, Graduate Programs, College of Individualized Education, St. Charles, MO 63301-1695. Offers administration (MSA); business administration (MBA); communications (MA); criminal justice and administration (MS); gerontology (MA); health management (MS); human resource management (MS); information technology (MBA, Certificate); managing information technology (MS); writing (MFA). Part-time and evening/weekend programs available. *Faculty:* 18 full-time (9 women), 128 part-time/adjunct (53 women). *Students:* 858 full-time (586 women), 69 part-time (43 women); includes 330 minority (296 Black or African American, non-Hispanic/Latino; 9 American Indian or Alaska Native, non-Hispanic/Latino; 4 Asian, non-Hispanic/Latino; 1 Hispanic/Latino; 20 Two or more races, non-Hispanic/Latino), 16 international. Average age 35. 229 applicants, 80% accepted, 172 enrolled. In 2011, 428 degrees awarded. *Degree requirements:* For master's, thesis (for some programs), 1 colloquium per term. *Entrance requirements:* For master's, interview, minimum GPA of 3.0. Additional exam requirements/recommendations for international students: Required—TOEFL (minimum score 550 paper-based; 213 computer-based; 80 iBT). *Application deadline:* For fall admission, 10/1 priority date for domestic students, 10/1 for international students; for winter admission, 1/7 priority date for domestic students, 1/7 for international students; for spring admission, 4/7 priority date for domestic students, 4/7 for international students. Applications are processed on a rolling basis. Application fee: $30 ($100 for international students). Electronic applications accepted. *Expenses: Tuition:* Full-time $13,650; part-time $395 per credit hour. *Required fees:* $150 per semester. Tuition and fees vary according to course level and course load. *Financial support:* In 2011–12, 386 students received support. Career-related internships or fieldwork, institutionally sponsored loans, tuition waivers (partial), and unspecified assistantships available. Financial award application deadline: 6/30; financial award applicants required to submit FAFSA. *Unit head:* Dan Kemper, Dean, 636-949-4501, Fax: 636-949-4505, E-mail: dkemper@lindenwood.edu. *Application contact:* Brett Barger, Dean of Evening Admissions and Extension Campuses, 636-949-4934, Fax: 636-949-4109, E-mail: adultadmissions@lindenwood.edu.

Lindenwood University, Graduate Programs, School of Business and Entrepreneurship, St. Charles, MO 63301-1695. Offers accounting (MBA, MS); business administration (MBA); entrepreneurial studies (MBA, MS); finance (MBA, MS); human resource management (MBA); human resources (MS); international business (MBA, MS); management (MBA, MS); management information systems (MBA, MS); marketing (MBA, MS); public management (MBA, MS); sport management (MA); supply chain management (MBA). *Accreditation:* ACBSP. Part-time and evening/weekend programs available. *Faculty:* 20 full-time (8 women), 17 part-time/adjunct (5 women). *Students:* 165 full-time (66 women), 223 part-time (100 women); includes 59 minority (48 Black or African American, non-Hispanic/Latino; 4 Asian, non-Hispanic/Latino; 2 Native Hawaiian or other Pacific Islander, non-Hispanic/Latino; 5 Two or more races, non-Hispanic/Latino), 140 international. Average age 29. 156 applicants, 76% accepted, 103 enrolled. In 2011, 205 degrees awarded. *Degree requirements:* For master's, comprehensive exam (for some programs), thesis (for some programs). *Entrance requirements:* For master's, interview, minimum GPA of 3.0, letter of recommendation. Additional exam requirements/recommendations for international students: Required—TOEFL (minimum score 550 paper-based; 213 computer-based; 80 iBT). *Application deadline:* For fall admission, 8/15 priority date for domestic students, 8/15 for international students; for winter admission, 1/9 priority date for domestic students, 1/9 for international students; for spring admission, 3/12 priority date for domestic students, 3/12 for international students. Applications are processed on a rolling basis. Application fee: $30 ($100 for international students). Electronic applications accepted. *Expenses: Tuition:* Full-time $13,650; part-time $395 per credit hour. *Required fees:* $150 per semester. Tuition and fees vary according to course level and course load. *Financial support:* In 2011–12, 206 students received support. Career-related internships or fieldwork, Federal Work-Study, institutionally sponsored loans, and tuition waivers (partial) available. Financial award application deadline: 6/30; financial award applicants required to submit FAFSA. *Unit head:* Roger Ellis, Dean, 636-949-4839, E-mail: rellis@lindenwood.edu. *Application contact:* Brett Barger, Dean of Evening Admissions and Extension Campuses, 636-949-4934, Fax: 636-949-4109, E-mail: adultadmissions@lindenwood.edu. Web site: http://www.lindenwood.edu.

Lipscomb University, College of Business, Nashville, TN 37204-3951. Offers accounting (MBA); business administration (general) (MBA); conflict management (MBA); financial services (MBA); healthcare management (MBA); human resources (MHR); leadership (MBA); nonprofit management (MBA); sports management (MBA); sustainability (MBA). *Accreditation:* ACBSP. Part-time and evening/weekend programs available. *Faculty:* 13 full-time (3 women), 7 part-time/adjunct (1 woman). *Students:* 51 full-time (21 women), 83 part-time (48 women); includes 20 minority (16 Black or African American, non-Hispanic/Latino; 3 Asian, non-Hispanic/Latino; 1 Hispanic/Latino), 1 international. Average age 33. 190 applicants, 43% accepted, 54 enrolled. In 2011, 85 master's awarded. *Entrance requirements:* For master's, GMAT, interview, 2 references, resume. Additional exam requirements/recommendations for international students: Required—TOEFL (minimum score 570 paper-based; 230 computer-based). *Application deadline:* For fall admission, 6/15 for domestic students, 2/1 for international students; for winter admission, 6/1 for international students; for spring admission, 11/15 for domestic students. Applications are processed on a rolling basis. Application fee: $50 ($75 for international students). Electronic applications accepted. *Expenses:* Contact institution. *Financial support:* Career-related internships or fieldwork, scholarships/grants, tuition waivers (partial), and unspecified assistantships available. Support available to part-time students. Financial award application deadline: 7/1; financial award applicants required to submit FAFSA. *Faculty research:* Impact of spirituality on organization commitment, leadership, psychological empowerment, training. *Unit head:* Dr. Mike Kendrick, Associate Dean of Graduate Business Programs, 615-966-1833, Fax: 615-966-1818, E-mail: mikekendrick@lipscomb.edu. *Application contact:* Lisa Shacklett, Executive Director of Enrollment and Marketing, 615-966-5968, E-mail: lisa.shacklett@lipscomb.edu. Web site: http://mba.lipscomb.edu.

Long Island University–Brooklyn Campus, School of Business, Public Administration and Information Sciences, Program in Human Resources Management, Brooklyn, NY 11201-8423. Offers MS. *Entrance requirements:* For master's, GMAT or GRE, 2 letters of recommendation. Additional exam requirements/recommendations for international students: Required—TOEFL (minimum score 500 paper-based; 173 computer-based).

Loyola University Chicago, Graduate School of Business, Institute of Human Resources and Employee Relations, Chicago, IL 60660. Offers MSHR. Part-time programs available. *Entrance requirements:* For master's, GMAT or GRE General Test, letters of recommendation. Additional exam requirements/recommendations for international students: Required—TOEFL (minimum score 550 paper-based; 213 computer-based; 80 iBT). *Expenses:* Contact institution. *Faculty research:* Human resource management, labor relations, global human resource management, organizational development, compensation.

Marquette University, Graduate School of Management, Executive MBA Program, Milwaukee, WI 53201-1881. Offers economics (MBA); finance (MBA); human resources (MBA); international business (MBA); management information systems (MBA); marketing (MBA); operations and supply chain management (MBA); sports business (MBA). *Accreditation:* AACSB. *Students:* 50 full-time (15 women); includes 4 minority (1 Black or African American, non-Hispanic/Latino; 3 Asian, non-Hispanic/Latino), 3 international. Average age 37. 37 applicants, 81% accepted, 29 enrolled. In 2011, 36 master's awarded. *Degree requirements:* For master's, international trip. *Entrance requirements:* For master's, GMAT or GRE, two letters of recommendation, official transcripts from current and previous colleges/universities. Additional exam requirements/recommendations for international students: Required—TOEFL (minimum score 550 paper-based; 85 computer-based; 88 iBT), IELTS (minimum score 6.5), Pearson Test of English. *Application deadline:* For fall admission, 2/15 for domestic and international students. Application fee: $50. Electronic applications accepted. *Expenses:* Contact institution. *Financial support:* Application deadline: 2/15. *Faculty research:* International trade and finance, customer relationship management, consumer satisfaction, customer service . *Unit head:* Dr. Jeanne Simmons, Graduate Director,

414-288-7145, Fax: 414-288-1660, E-mail: jeanne.simmons@marquette.edu. *Application contact:* Debra Leutermann, Admissions Coordinator, 414-288-7145, Fax: 414-288-8078, E-mail: debra.leutermann@marquette.edu. Web site: http://www.busadm.mu.edu/emba/.

Marquette University, Graduate School of Management, Program in Business Administration, Milwaukee, WI 53201-1881. Offers business administration (MBA); economics (MBA); entrepreneurship (Certificate); finance (MBA); human resources (MBA); international business (MBA); management information systems (MBA); marketing (MBA); operations and supply chain management (MBA); sports business (MBA); JD/MBA; MBA/MA; MBA/MSN. *Accreditation:* AACSB. Part-time and evening/weekend programs available. *Students:* 42 full-time (14 women), 335 part-time (94 women); includes 24 minority (5 Black or African American, non-Hispanic/Latino; 1 American Indian or Alaska Native, non-Hispanic/Latino; 15 Asian, non-Hispanic/Latino; 3 Hispanic/Latino), 29 international. Average age 31. 182 applicants, 59% accepted, 103 enrolled. In 2011, 128 master's awarded. *Degree requirements:* For Certificate, business plan. *Entrance requirements:* For master's, GMAT or GRE, letters of recommendation. Additional exam requirements/recommendations for international students: Required—TOEFL (minimum score 550 paper-based; 85 computer-based; 88 iBT), IELTS (minimum score 6.5), Pearson Test of English. *Application deadline:* For fall admission, 2/15 for domestic and international students. Applications are processed on a rolling basis. Application fee: $50. Electronic applications accepted. *Expenses: Tuition:* Full-time $17,010; part-time $945 per credit hour. Tuition and fees vary according to program. *Financial support:* In 2011–12, 4 fellowships, 11 teaching assistantships were awarded; research assistantships, Federal Work-Study, institutionally sponsored loans, scholarships/grants, and tuition waivers (full and partial) also available. Support available to part-time students. Financial award application deadline: 2/15. *Faculty research:* Ethics in the professions, services marketing, technology impact on decision-making, mentoring. *Unit head:* Dr. Jeanne Simmons, Graduate Director, 414-288-7145, Fax: 414-288-1660, E-mail: jeanne.simmons@marquette.edu. *Application contact:* Debra Leutermann, Admissions Coordinator, 414-288-8064, Fax: 414-288-1902, E-mail: debra.leutermann@marquette.edu. Web site: http://business.marquette.edu/academics/mba.

Marquette University, Graduate School of Management, Program in Human Resources, Milwaukee, WI 53201-1881. Offers MSHR. Part-time and evening/weekend programs available. *Students:* 17 full-time (14 women), 23 part-time (19 women); includes 2 minority (1 Black or African American, non-Hispanic/Latino; 1 Hispanic/Latino), 22 international. Average age 26. 110 applicants, 49% accepted, 15 enrolled. In 2011, 13 master's awarded. *Entrance requirements:* For master's, GMAT or GRE General Test, letters of recommendation. Additional exam requirements/recommendations for international students: Required—TOEFL (minimum score 550 paper-based; 85 computer-based; 88 iBT), IELTS (minimum score 6.5), Pearson Test of English. *Application deadline:* For fall admission, 2/15 for domestic and international students. Applications are processed on a rolling basis. Application fee: $50. Electronic applications accepted. *Expenses: Tuition:* Full-time $17,010; part-time $945 per credit hour. Tuition and fees vary according to program. *Financial support:* In 2011–12, 3 teaching assistantships were awarded; fellowships, research assistantships, Federal Work-Study, institutionally sponsored loans, and tuition waivers (full and partial) also available. Support available to part-time students. Financial award application deadline: 2/15. *Faculty research:* Diversity, mentoring, executive compensation. *Unit head:* Dr. Timothy Keaveny, Management Chair, 414-288-3643. *Application contact:* Dr. Jeanne Simmons, Associate Dean, 414-288-5126, Fax: 414-288-1902, E-mail: jeanne.simmons@marquette.edu. Web site: http://business.marquette.edu/academics/mshr.

Marshall University, Academic Affairs Division, College of Business, Program in Human Resource Management, Huntington, WV 25755. Offers MS. Part-time and evening/weekend programs available. *Students:* 33 full-time (22 women), 25 part-time (14 women); includes 6 minority (5 Black or African American, non-Hispanic/Latino; 1 Hispanic/Latino), 10 international. Average age 28. In 2011, 34 master's awarded. *Degree requirements:* For master's, comprehensive assessment. *Entrance requirements:* For master's, GMAT or GRE General Test. *Application deadline:* Applications are processed on a rolling basis. Application fee: $40. *Financial support:* Tuition waivers (full) available. Support available to part-time students. Financial award applicants required to submit FAFSA. *Unit head:* Dr. Andrew Sikula, Associate Dean, 304-746-1956, E-mail: sikula@marshall.edu. *Application contact:* Wesley Spradlin, Information Contact, 304-746-8964, Fax: 304-746-1902, E-mail: spradlin2@marshall.edu.

Marygrove College, Graduate Division, Program in Human Resource Management, Detroit, MI 48221-2599. Offers MA. *Entrance requirements:* For master's, interview, writing sample.

Marymount University, School of Business Administration, Program in Human Resource Management, Arlington, VA 22207-4299. Offers human resource management (MA, Certificate); instructional design (Certificate); organization development (Certificate). Part-time and evening/weekend programs available. *Faculty:* 3 full-time (1 woman), 1 part-time/adjunct (0 women). *Students:* 10 full-time (9 women), 68 part-time (56 women); includes 37 minority (16 Black or African American, non-Hispanic/Latino; 8 Asian, non-Hispanic/Latino; 11 Hispanic/Latino; 1 Native Hawaiian or other Pacific Islander, non-Hispanic/Latino; 1 Two or more races, non-Hispanic/Latino), 4 international. Average age 31. 34 applicants, 91% accepted, 27 enrolled. In 2011, 17 master's, 14 other advanced degrees awarded. *Degree requirements:* For master's, thesis or alternative. *Entrance requirements:* For master's, GMAT or GRE General Test, resume; for Certificate, resume. Additional exam requirements/recommendations for international students: Required—TOEFL (minimum score 600 paper-based; 250 computer-based; 96 iBT), IELTS (minimum score 6.5). *Application deadline:* For fall admission, 7/1 priority date for domestic students, 7/1 for international students; for spring admission, 11/15 for domestic students, 11/16 for international students. Applications are processed on a rolling basis. Application fee: $40. Electronic applications accepted. *Expenses: Tuition:* Part-time $770 per credit hour. *Required fees:* $8 per credit hour. One-time fee: $180 full-time. *Financial support:* In 2011–12, 3 students received support. Research assistantships with full tuition reimbursements available, career-related internships or fieldwork, Federal Work-Study, scholarships/grants, and unspecified assistantships available. Support available to part-time students. Financial award applicants required to submit FAFSA. *Unit head:* Dr. Virginia Bianco-Mathis, Chair/Director, 703-284-5957, Fax: 703-527-3830, E-mail: virginia.bianco-mathis@marymount.edu. *Application contact:* Francesca Reed, Director, Graduate Admissions, 703-284-5901, Fax: 703-527-3815, E-mail: grad.admissions@marymount.edu. Web site: http://www.marymount.edu/academics/programs/hrMgt.

McKendree University, Graduate Programs, Master of Business Administration Program, Lebanon, IL 62254-1299. Offers business administration (MBA); human resource management (MBA); international business (MBA). Part-time and evening/weekend programs available. Postbaccalaureate distance learning degree programs offered (no on-campus study). *Entrance requirements:* For master's, official transcripts from all institutions attended, essay, minimum GPA of 3.0, three references, resume. Additional exam requirements/recommendations for international students: Required—TOEFL. Electronic applications accepted.

McMaster University, School of Graduate Studies, Faculty of Business, Program in Human Resources and Management, Hamilton, ON L8S 4M2, Canada. Offers MBA, PhD. Part-time programs available. *Degree requirements:* For doctorate, comprehensive exam, thesis/dissertation. *Entrance requirements:* For master's, GMAT; for doctorate, GMAT or GRE, master's degree, minimum B+ average. Additional exam requirements/recommendations for international students: Required—TOEFL (minimum score 580 paper-based; 237 computer-based). *Faculty research:* Leadership, occupational mental health, work attitudes, human resources recruitment, change and stress management strategies.

Mercy College, School of Business, Program in Human Resource Management, Dobbs Ferry, NY 10522-1189. Offers MS, AC. Part-time and evening/weekend programs available. Postbaccalaureate distance learning degree programs offered (no on-campus study). *Entrance requirements:* For master's, undergraduate transcripts, interview, two letters of reference, resume. Additional exam requirements/recommendations for international students: Required—TOEFL (minimum score 600 paper-based; 250 computer-based; 100 iBT), IELTS (minimum score 8). Electronic applications accepted. *Expenses:* Contact institution. *Faculty research:* Team building, motivation, leadership, training, productivity.

Mercyhurst College, Graduate Studies, Program in Organizational Leadership, Erie, PA 16546. Offers accounting (MS); entrepreneurship (MS); higher education administration (MS); human resources (MS); nonprofit management (MS); organizational leadership (Certificate); sports leadership (MS). Part-time and evening/weekend programs available. *Faculty:* 1 full-time (0 women), 11 part-time/adjunct (4 women). *Students:* 42 full-time (16 women), 22 part-time (15 women); includes 5 minority (3 Black or African American, non-Hispanic/Latino; 1 American Indian or Alaska Native, non-Hispanic/Latino; 1 Hispanic/Latino), 9 international. Average age 30. 60 applicants, 62% accepted, 25 enrolled. In 2011, 27 master's, 2 other advanced degrees awarded. *Degree requirements:* For master's, thesis. *Entrance requirements:* For master's, GRE General Test or MAT, interview, resume, essay, three professional references, transcripts. Additional exam requirements/recommendations for international students: Required—TOEFL. *Application deadline:* For fall admission, 8/1 priority date for domestic students, 7/1 for international students; for winter admission, 11/1 for domestic students, 10/1 for international students; for spring admission, 2/1 for domestic students, 1/1 for international students. Applications are processed on a rolling basis. Application fee: $35. Electronic applications accepted. *Expenses: Tuition:* Part-time $570 per credit. *Required fees:* $90 per term. Tuition and fees vary according to program. *Financial support:* In 2011–12, 16 students received support, including 112 research assistantships with full and partial tuition reimbursements available (averaging $6,000 per year); career-related internships or fieldwork and unspecified assistantships also available. Support available to part-time students. Financial award application deadline: 5/1; financial award applicants required to submit FAFSA. *Faculty research:* Leadership training, organizational communication, leadership pedagogy. *Unit head:* Dr. Gilbert Jacobs, Director, 814-824-2390, E-mail: gjacobs@mercyhurst.edu. *Application contact:* Sarah Murphy, Academic Coordinator, 814-824-2297, Fax: 814-824-2055, E-mail: smurphy@mercyhurst.edu.

Michigan State University, The Graduate School, College of Social Science, School of Labor and Industrial Relations, East Lansing, MI 48824. Offers human resources and labor relations (MLRHR); industrial relations and human resources (PhD). *Entrance requirements:* Additional exam requirements/recommendations for international students: Required—TOEFL.

Moravian College, Moravian College Comenius Center, Business and Management Programs, Bethlehem, PA 18018-6650. Offers accounting (MBA); general management (MBA); health care management (MBA); human resource management (MBA); leadership (MSHRM); learning and performance management (MSHRM); supply chain management (MBA). Part-time and evening/weekend programs available. *Entrance requirements:* For master's, GMAT. Additional exam requirements/recommendations for international students: Required—TOEFL (minimum score 550 paper-based; 260 computer-based; 90 iBT). *Expenses:* Contact institution. *Faculty research:* Leadership, change management, human resources.

National Louis University, College of Management and Business, Chicago, IL 60603. Offers business administration (MBA); human resource management and development (MS); management (MS). Part-time and evening/weekend programs available. *Students:* 71 full-time (48 women), 56 part-time (36 women); includes 80 minority (32 Black or African American, non-Hispanic/Latino; 1 American Indian or Alaska Native, non-Hispanic/Latino; 3 Asian, non-Hispanic/Latino; 42 Hispanic/Latino; 2 Two or more races, non-Hispanic/Latino). Average age 37. In 2011, 73 master's awarded. *Entrance requirements:* For master's, college-administered critical thinking and writing skills test, minimum GPA of 3.0, resume, 3 references. Additional exam requirements/recommendations for international students: Required—TOEFL (minimum score 550 paper-based; 213 computer-based; 79 iBT). *Application deadline:* Applications are processed on a rolling basis. Application fee: $40. *Financial support:* Federal Work-Study, institutionally sponsored loans, and scholarships/grants available. Support available to part-time students. Financial award applicants required to submit FAFSA. *Unit head:* Walter Roetlger, Executive Dean, 312-261-3073, Fax: 312-261-3073, E-mail: chris.multhauf@nl.edu. *Application contact:* Ken Kasprzak, Director of Admissions, 800-443-5522 Ext. 5718, Fax: 847-947-5575, E-mail: kkasprzak@nl.edu. Web site: http://www3.nl.edu/graduate/business_admin.cfm.

National University, Academic Affairs, School of Business and Management, Department of Leadership and Human Resource Management, La Jolla, CA 92037-1011. Offers human resources management (MA); management information systems (MS); organizational leadership (MS). Part-time and evening/weekend programs available. Postbaccalaureate distance learning degree programs offered (no on-campus study). *Degree requirements:* For master's, thesis. *Entrance requirements:* For master's, interview, minimum GPA of 2.5. Additional exam requirements/recommendations for international students: Required—TOEFL (minimum score 550 paper-based; 213 computer-based; 79 iBT), IELTS (minimum score 6). *Application deadline:* Applications are processed on a rolling basis. Application fee: $60 ($65 for international students). Electronic applications accepted. *Financial support:* Career-related internships or fieldwork, institutionally sponsored loans, scholarships/grants, and tuition waivers (partial) available. Support available to part-time students. Financial award application deadline: 6/30; financial award applicants required to submit FAFSA. *Unit head:* Dr. Bruce Buchowicz, Chair, 858-642-8439, Fax: 858-642-8740, E-mail: bbuchowicz@nu.edu. *Application contact:* Dominick Giovanniello, Associate Regional Dean, 800-NAT-UNIV, Fax: 858-541-7792, E-mail: dgiovann@nu.edu. Web site: http://www.nu.edu/OurPrograms/SchoolOfBusinessAndManagement/LeadershipAndHumanResourceManagement.html.

Nazareth College of Rochester, Graduate Studies, Department of Business, Program in Human Resource Management, Rochester, NY 14618-3790. Offers MS. *Entrance requirements:* For master's, minimum GPA of 3.0.

Human Resources Management

New Mexico Highlands University, Graduate Studies, School of Business, Las Vegas, NM 87701. Offers business administration (MBA), including government nonprofit management, human resource management, international business, management, management information systems. *Accreditation:* ACBSP. *Faculty:* 20 full-time (5 women). *Students:* 63 full-time (40 women), 146 part-time (76 women); includes 131 minority (9 Black or African American, non-Hispanic/Latino; 8 American Indian or Alaska Native, non-Hispanic/Latino; 1 Asian, non-Hispanic/Latino; 110 Hispanic/Latino; 2 Native Hawaiian or other Pacific Islander, non-Hispanic/Latino; 1 Two or more races, non-Hispanic/Latino), 25 international. Average age 33. 99 applicants, 79% accepted, 49 enrolled. In 2011, 43 master's awarded. *Degree requirements:* For master's, comprehensive exam, thesis or alternative. *Entrance requirements:* For master's, minimum undergraduate GPA of 3.0. Additional exam requirements/recommendations for international students: Required—TOEFL (minimum score 540 paper-based; 207 computer-based). *Application deadline:* For fall admission, 8/1 priority date for domestic students. Applications are processed on a rolling basis. Application fee: $15. *Expenses:* Tuition, state resident: full-time $2767; part-time $146 per credit hour. Tuition, nonresident: full-time $4879; part-time $234 per credit hour. *International tuition:* $5436 full-time. *Required fees:* $737. *Financial support:* In 2011–12, 29 students received support. Career-related internships or fieldwork, Federal Work-Study, institutionally sponsored loans, scholarships/grants, tuition waivers (full and partial), and unspecified assistantships available. Support available to part-time students. Financial award application deadline: 3/1; financial award applicants required to submit FAFSA. *Faculty research:* Real estate valuation, studying expert judgments in complex accounting, decision environments, green marketing, environmentalism, marketing research methodology. *Unit head:* Dr. Margaret Young, Dean, 505-454-3522, Fax: 505-454-3354, E-mail: young_m@nmhu.edu. *Application contact:* Diane Trujillo, Administrative Assistant, Graduate Studies, 505-454-3266, Fax: 505-426-2117, E-mail: dtrujillo@nmhu.edu. Web site: http://www.nmhu.edu/business/.

New York Institute of Technology, Graduate Division, School of Management, Program in Human Resources Management and Labor Relations, Old Westbury, NY 11568-8000. Offers human resources administration (Advanced Certificate); human resources management and labor relations (MS); labor relations (Advanced Certificate). Part-time and evening/weekend programs available. *Students:* 33 full-time (21 women), 59 part-time (46 women); includes 32 minority (17 Black or African American, non-Hispanic/Latino; 1 American Indian or Alaska Native, non-Hispanic/Latino; 6 Asian, non-Hispanic/Latino; 8 Hispanic/Latino), 26 international. Average age 31. In 2011, 45 degrees awarded. *Degree requirements:* For master's, comprehensive exam, thesis optional. *Entrance requirements:* For master's, GRE, minimum QPA of 2.85, interview, 2 letters of recommendation. *Application deadline:* For fall admission, 7/1 priority date for domestic students; for spring admission, 12/1 priority date for domestic students. Applications are processed on a rolling basis. Application fee: $50. Electronic applications accepted. *Expenses: Tuition:* Part-time $930 per credit hour. *Financial support:* Fellowships, research assistantships, career-related internships or fieldwork, institutionally sponsored loans, and tuition waivers (full and partial) available. Support available to part-time students. Financial award applicants required to submit FAFSA. *Faculty research:* Ethics in industrial relations, employee relations, public sector labor relations, benefits. *Unit head:* William Ninehan, Director, 646-273-6071, Fax: 516-686-7425, E-mail: wninehan@nyit.edu. *Application contact:* Dr. Jacquelyn Nealon, Vice President for Enrollment Services, 516-686-7925, Fax: 516-686-7597, E-mail: jnealon@nyit.edu.

New York University, Robert F. Wagner Graduate School of Public Service, Program in Public Administration, New York, NY 10012. Offers public administration (PhD); public and nonprofit management and policy (MPA, Advanced Certificate), including developmental administration (Advanced Certificate), financial management and public finance, human resources management (Advanced Certificate), international administration (Advanced Certificate), management (MPA), management for public and nonprofit organizations (Advanced Certificate), public policy analysis, quantitative analysis and computer applications (Advanced Certificate), urban public policy (Advanced Certificate); JD/MPA; MBA/MPA; MPA/MA. *Accreditation:* NASPAA (one or more programs are accredited). Part-time programs available. *Faculty:* 32 full-time (13 women), 41 part-time/adjunct (22 women). *Students:* 431 full-time (323 women), 131 part-time (98 women); includes 148 minority (35 Black or African American, non-Hispanic/Latino; 53 Asian, non-Hispanic/Latino; 38 Hispanic/Latino; 1 Native Hawaiian or other Pacific Islander, non-Hispanic/Latino; 21 Two or more races, non-Hispanic/Latino), 62 international. Average age 28. 1,063 applicants, 58% accepted, 205 enrolled. In 2011, 213 master's, 8 doctorates awarded. *Degree requirements:* For master's, thesis or alternative, capstone end event; for doctorate, one foreign language, thesis/dissertation. *Entrance requirements:* Additional exam requirements/recommendations for international students: Required—TOEFL, IELTS, TWE. *Application deadline:* For fall admission, 1/15 for domestic students, 1/5 for international students; for spring admission, 10/15 for domestic students, 9/15 for international students. Application fee: $85. Electronic applications accepted. *Expenses:* Contact institution. *Financial support:* In 2011–12, 118 students received support, including 117 fellowships (averaging $13,500 per year); career-related internships or fieldwork, Federal Work-Study, scholarships/grants, health care benefits, and unspecified assistantships also available. Support available to part-time students. Financial award application deadline: 1/5; financial award applicants required to submit FAFSA. *Unit head:* Katty Jones, Director, Program Services, 212-998-7411, Fax: 212-995-4164, E-mail: katty.jones@nyu.edu. *Application contact:* Christopher Alexander, Communications Coordinator, 212-998-7414, Fax: 212-995-4611, E-mail: wagner.admissions@nyu.edu. Web site: http://www.nyu.edu.wagner/.

New York University, School of Continuing and Professional Studies, Division of Programs in Business, Program in Leadership and Human Capital Management, New York, NY 10012-1019. Offers benefits and compensation (Advanced Certificate); human resource development (MS); human resource management (MS, Advanced Certificate); organizational and executive coaching (Advanced Certificate); organizational effectiveness (MS). Part-time and evening/weekend programs available. Postbaccalaureate distance learning degree programs offered (no on-campus study). *Faculty:* 40 part-time/adjunct (15 women). *Students:* 32 full-time (19 women), 172 part-time (141 women); includes 29 minority (12 Black or African American, non-Hispanic/Latino; 8 Asian, non-Hispanic/Latino; 8 Hispanic/Latino; 1 Native Hawaiian or other Pacific Islander, non-Hispanic/Latino), 24 international. Average age 32. 196 applicants, 61% accepted, 62 enrolled. In 2011, 74 master's, 13 other advanced degrees awarded. *Degree requirements:* For master's, thesis. *Entrance requirements:* For master's, GRE/GMAT only upon request, relevant professional work, internship or volunteer experience. Additional exam requirements/recommendations for international students: Required—TOEFL (minimum score 600 paper-based; 250 computer-based; 100 iBT), IELTS (minimum score 7). *Application deadline:* For fall admission, 2/1 priority date for domestic students, 2/1 for international students; for spring admission, 10/15 priority date for domestic students, 8/15 for international students. Applications are processed on a rolling basis. Application fee: $150. Electronic applications accepted. *Financial support:* In 2011–12, 89 students received support, including 89 fellowships (averaging $1,838 per year). *Application contact:* Admissions Office, 212-998-7100, E-mail: scps.gradadmissions@nyu.edu. Web site: http://www.scps.nyu.edu/areas-of-study/leadership/.

North Central College, Graduate and Continuing Education Programs, Department of Business, Program in Business Administration, Naperville, IL 60566-7063. Offers change management (MBA); finance (MBA); human resource management (MBA); management (MBA); marketing (MBA). Part-time and evening/weekend programs available. *Faculty:* 14 full-time (4 women), 13 part-time/adjunct (3 women). *Students:* 41 full-time (15 women), 66 part-time (31 women); includes 19 minority (2 Black or African American, non-Hispanic/Latino; 1 American Indian or Alaska Native, non-Hispanic/Latino; 12 Asian, non-Hispanic/Latino; 4 Hispanic/Latino), 1 international. Average age 30. 116 applicants, 66% accepted, 50 enrolled. In 2011, 63 master's awarded. *Degree requirements:* For master's, thesis optional, project. *Entrance requirements:* For master's, interview. Additional exam requirements/recommendations for international students: Required—TOEFL (minimum score 577 paper-based; 233 computer-based; 90 iBT). *Application deadline:* For fall admission, 8/15 for domestic students; for winter admission, 12/1 for domestic students; for spring admission, 2/1 for domestic students. Application fee: $25. *Financial support:* In 2011–12, 8 students received support. Scholarships/grants available. Support available to part-time students. *Unit head:* Dr. Jean Clifton, MBA Program Coordinator, 630-637-5244, E-mail: jmclifton@noctrl.edu. *Application contact:* Wendy Kulpinski, Director of Graduate and Continuing Education Admission, 630-637-5808, Fax: 630-637-5844, E-mail: wekulpinski@noctrl.edu.

North Greenville University, T. Walter Brashier Graduate School, Greer, SC 29651. Offers Christian ministry (MCM, D Min); education (M Ed); financial planning (MBA); human resources (MBA). Part-time and evening/weekend programs available. Postbaccalaureate distance learning degree programs offered (no on-campus study). *Faculty:* 8 full-time (3 women), 15 part-time/adjunct (0 women). *Students:* 55 full-time (33 women), 148 part-time (53 women); includes 48 minority (37 Black or African American, non-Hispanic/Latino; 1 American Indian or Alaska Native, non-Hispanic/Latino; 3 Asian, non-Hispanic/Latino; 5 Hispanic/Latino; 2 Two or more races, non-Hispanic/Latino). Average age 32. 180 applicants, 98% accepted, 170 enrolled. In 2011, 58 master's awarded. *Degree requirements:* For master's, comprehensive exam (for some programs), thesis or alternative, capstone course. *Entrance requirements:* For master's, minimum GPA of 2.25 overall, 2.5 in major; for doctorate, MAT. Additional exam requirements/recommendations for international students: Required—TOEFL (minimum score 550 paper-based; 213 computer-based). *Application deadline:* For fall admission, 8/1 for domestic students, 6/1 for international students; for winter admission, 1/1 for domestic students, 10/1 for international students; for spring admission, 3/1 for domestic students, 1/1 for international students. Applications are processed on a rolling basis. Application fee: $30. Electronic applications accepted. *Financial support:* In 2011–12, 112 students received support, including 1 research assistantship (averaging $2,000 per year); Federal Work-Study, institutionally sponsored loans, scholarships/grants, tuition waivers (partial), and unspecified assistantships also available. Support available to part-time students. Financial award applicants required to submit FAFSA. *Faculty research:* Organizational behavior, church growth, homiletics, human resources, business strategy. *Unit head:* Dr. Joseph Samuel Isgett, Jr., Vice President for Graduate Studies, 864-877-3052, Fax: 864-877-1653, E-mail: sisgett@ngu.edu. *Application contact:* Tawana P. Scott, Dean of Graduate Enrollment, 864-877-1598, Fax: 864-877-1653, E-mail: tscott@ngu.edu. Web site: http://www.ngu.edu/gradschool.php.

Notre Dame de Namur University, Division of Academic Affairs, School of Business and Management, Department of Business Administration, Belmont, CA 94002-1908. Offers business administration (MBA); finance (MBA); human resource management (MBA); marketing (MBA). Part-time and evening/weekend programs available. *Faculty:* 7 full-time (1 woman), 6 part-time/adjunct (0 women). *Students:* 42 full-time (16 women), 104 part-time (67 women); includes 56 minority (6 Black or African American, non-Hispanic/Latino; 26 Asian, non-Hispanic/Latino; 20 Hispanic/Latino; 2 Native Hawaiian or other Pacific Islander, non-Hispanic/Latino; 2 Two or more races, non-Hispanic/Latino), 23 international. Average age 34. 167 applicants, 40% accepted, 39 enrolled. In 2011, 33 degrees awarded. *Entrance requirements:* For master's, minimum GPA of 2.5. Additional exam requirements/recommendations for international students: Required—TOEFL (minimum score 550 paper-based; 213 computer-based; 79 iBT). *Application deadline:* For fall admission, 8/1 priority date for domestic students; for spring admission, 12/1 priority date for domestic students. Applications are processed on a rolling basis. Application fee: $60. Electronic applications accepted. *Expenses: Tuition:* Full-time $14,220; part-time $790 per credit. *Required fees:* $35 per semester. Tuition and fees vary according to program. *Financial support:* Available to part-time students. Applicants required to submit FAFSA. *Unit head:* Jordan Holtzman, Director, 650-508-3637, E-mail: jholtzman@ndnu.edu. *Application contact:* Candace Hallmark, Associate Director of Admissions, 650-508-3600, Fax: 650-508-3426, E-mail: grad.admit@ndnu.edu. Web site: http://www.ndnu.edu/academics/schools-programs/school-business/.

Notre Dame de Namur University, Division of Academic Affairs, School of Business and Management, Department of Public Administration, Belmont, CA 94002-1908. Offers human resource management (MPA); public administration (MPA); public affairs administration (MPA). Part-time and evening/weekend programs available. Postbaccalaureate distance learning degree programs offered (no on-campus study). *Faculty:* 3 full-time (1 woman), 4 part-time/adjunct (2 women). *Students:* 24 full-time (12 women), 39 part-time (24 women); includes 24 minority (4 Black or African American, non-Hispanic/Latino; 7 Asian, non-Hispanic/Latino; 11 Hispanic/Latino; 1 Native Hawaiian or other Pacific Islander, non-Hispanic/Latino; 1 Two or more races, non-Hispanic/Latino), 15 international. Average age 32. 92 applicants, 46% accepted, 22 enrolled. In 2011, 19 master's awarded. *Entrance requirements:* For master's, interview, minimum GPA of 2.5. Additional exam requirements/recommendations for international students: Required—TOEFL (minimum score 550 paper-based; 213 computer-based; 79 iBT). *Application deadline:* For fall admission, 8/1 priority date for domestic students; for spring admission, 12/1 priority date for domestic students. Applications are processed on a rolling basis. Application fee: $60. Electronic applications accepted. *Expenses: Tuition:* Full-time $14,220; part-time $790 per credit. *Required fees:* $35 per semester. Tuition and fees vary according to program. *Financial support:* Available to part-time students. Applicants required to submit FAFSA. *Unit head:* Jordan Holtzman, Director, 650-508-3637, E-mail: jholtzman@ndnu.edu. *Application contact:* Candace Hallmark, Associate Director of Admissions, 650-508-3600, Fax: 650-508-3426, E-mail: grad.admit@ndnu.edu.

Nova Southeastern University, H. Wayne Huizenga School of Business and Entrepreneurship, Fort Lauderdale, FL 33314-7796. Offers accounting (M Acc); business administration (MBA, DBA); human resource management (MSHRM); international business administration (MIBA); leadership (MS); public administration (MPA, DPA); real estate development (MS); taxation (M Tax); JD/MBA; Pharm D/MBA. Part-time and evening/weekend programs available. Postbaccalaureate distance learning degree programs offered (minimal on-campus study). *Students:* 229 full-time (112 women), 3,506 part-time (2,109 women); includes 2,506 minority (1,256 Black or African American, non-Hispanic/Latino; 8 American Indian or Alaska Native, non-Hispanic/Latino; 146 Asian, non-Hispanic/Latino; 1,058 Hispanic/Latino; 4 Native Hawaiian or other Pacific Islander, non-Hispanic/Latino; 34 Two or more races, non-

Hispanic/Latino), 174 international. Average age 33. In 2011, 1,252 master's, 17 doctorates awarded. *Degree requirements:* For master's, thesis optional; for doctorate, comprehensive exam, thesis/dissertation. *Entrance requirements:* For doctorate, GMAT. Additional exam requirements/recommendations for international students: Required—TOEFL (minimum score 550 paper-based; 213 computer-based; 79 iBT), IELTS (minimum score 6). *Application deadline:* Applications are processed on a rolling basis. Application fee: $50. Electronic applications accepted. *Financial support:* In 2011–12, 2 students received support. Federal Work-Study and scholarships/grants available. Support available to part-time students. Financial award applicants required to submit FAFSA. *Faculty research:* Reputation management, call centers, international social capital, corporate earnings guidance, corporate governance. *Unit head:* Dr. D. Michael Fields, Dean, 954-262-5005, E-mail: fieldsm@nova.edu. *Application contact:* Karen Goldberg, Associate Director of Recruitment and Special Events, 954-262-5039, Fax: 954-262-3822, E-mail: karen@nova.edu. Web site: http://www.huizenga.nova.edu.

Oakland University, Graduate Study and Lifelong Learning, School of Business Administration, Department of Management and Marketing, Rochester, MI 48309-4401. Offers business administration (MBA); entrepreneurship (Certificate); general management (Certificate); human resource management (Certificate); international business (Certificate); marketing (Certificate).

The Ohio State University, Graduate School, Max M. Fisher College of Business, Program in Labor and Human Resources, Columbus, OH 43210. Offers MLHR, PhD. *Faculty:* 28. *Students:* 83 full-time (61 women), 38 part-time (27 women); includes 25 minority (8 Black or African American, non-Hispanic/Latino; 10 Asian, non-Hispanic/Latino; 4 Hispanic/Latino; 3 Two or more races, non-Hispanic/Latino), 18 international. Average age 28. In 2011, 22 master's, 1 doctorate awarded. *Degree requirements:* For master's, thesis optional; for doctorate, thesis/dissertation. *Entrance requirements:* For master's and doctorate, GRE General Test. Additional exam requirements/recommendations for international students: Required—Michigan English Language Assessment Battery (minimum score 82); Recommended—TOEFL (minimum score 600 paper-based; 250 computer-based). *Application deadline:* For fall admission, 8/15 priority date for domestic students, 7/1 for international students; for winter admission, 12/1 priority date for domestic students, 11/1 for international students; for spring admission, 3/1 priority date for domestic students, 2/1 for international students. Applications are processed on a rolling basis. Application fee: $40 ($50 for international students). Electronic applications accepted. *Expenses:* Tuition, state resident: full-time $11,400. Tuition, nonresident: full-time $28,125. Tuition and fees vary according to course load, degree level, campus/location and program. *Financial support:* Fellowships, research assistantships, teaching assistantships, Federal Work-Study, and institutionally sponsored loans available. Support available to part-time students. *Unit head:* David Greenberger, Chair, 614-292-5291, E-mail: greenberger.1@osu.edu. *Application contact:* Graduate Admissions, 614-292-6031, Fax: 614-292-3656, E-mail: gradadmissions@osu.edu. Web site: http://fisher.osu.edu/mlhr/.

Ottawa University, Graduate Studies-Arizona, Programs in Business, Ottawa, KS 66067-3399. Offers business administration (MBA); finance (MBA); human resources (MA, MBA); leadership (MBA); marketing (MBA). Programs offered in Mesa, Phoenix, Tempe and West Valley, AZ. Part-time and evening/weekend programs available. Postbaccalaureate distance learning degree programs offered. *Degree requirements:* For master's, thesis or alternative. *Entrance requirements:* For master's, minimum undergraduate GPA of 3.0. Additional exam requirements/recommendations for international students: Required—TOEFL (minimum score 550 paper-based; 213 computer-based). Electronic applications accepted.

Pace University, Lubin School of Business, Program in Management, New York, NY 10038. Offers entrepreneurial studies (MBA); executive management (MBA); human resource management (MBA, MS); management (MBA); strategic management (MBA). Part-time and evening/weekend programs available. *Students:* 44 full-time (24 women), 89 part-time (53 women); includes 28 minority (9 Black or African American, non-Hispanic/Latino; 1 American Indian or Alaska Native, non-Hispanic/Latino; 12 Asian, non-Hispanic/Latino; 4 Hispanic/Latino; 2 Two or more races, non-Hispanic/Latino), 33 international. Average age 30. 244 applicants, 52% accepted, 36 enrolled. In 2011, 33 master's awarded. *Entrance requirements:* For master's, GMAT, GRE. Additional exam requirements/recommendations for international students: Required—TOEFL. *Application deadline:* For fall admission, 7/31 priority date for domestic students; for spring admission, 11/30 for domestic students. Applications are processed on a rolling basis. Application fee: $70. Electronic applications accepted. *Expenses: Tuition:* Part-time $990 per credit. *Required fees:* $168 per semester. Tuition and fees vary according to course load and degree level. *Financial support:* Research assistantships, career-related internships or fieldwork, and Federal Work-Study available. Support available to part-time students. Financial award applicants required to submit FAFSA. *Unit head:* Dr. John C. Byrne, Chairperson, 212-618-6581, E-mail: jbyrne@pace.edu. *Application contact:* Susan Ford-Goldschein, Director of Graduate Admissions, 212-346-1531, Fax: 212-346-1585, E-mail: gradnyc@pace.edu. Web site: http://www.pace.edu/.

Penn State University Park, Graduate School, College of the Liberal Arts, Department of Labor and Employment Relations, State College, University Park, PA 16802-1503. Offers MPS, MS. Postbaccalaureate distance learning degree programs offered. *Unit head:* Dr. Susan Welch, Dean, 814-865-7691, Fax: 814-863-2085, E-mail: swelch@psu.edu. *Application contact:* Cynthia E. Nicosia, Director, Graduate Enrollment Services, 814-865-1795, Fax: 814-865-4627, E-mail: cey1@psu.edu. Web site: http://lser.la.psu.edu.

Polytechnic Institute of New York University, Department of Technology Management, Brooklyn, NY 11201-2990. Offers construction management (Advanced Certificate); electronic business management (Advanced Certificate); entrepreneurship (Advanced Certificate); human resources management (Advanced Certificate); information management (Advanced Certificate); management (MS); management of technology (MS); organizational behavior (MS, Advanced Certificate); project management (Advanced Certificate); technology management (MBA, PhD, Advanced Certificate); telecommunications and information management (MS); telecommunications management (Advanced Certificate). Part-time and evening/weekend programs available. *Faculty:* 6 full-time (1 woman), 32 part-time/adjunct (4 women). *Students:* 185 full-time (84 women), 94 part-time (41 women); includes 56 minority (15 Black or African American, non-Hispanic/Latino; 31 Asian, non-Hispanic/Latino; 10 Hispanic/Latino), 143 international. Average age 30. 467 applicants, 48% accepted, 123 enrolled. In 2011, 174 master's, 1 doctorate awarded. *Degree requirements:* For master's, comprehensive exam (for some programs), thesis (for some programs); for doctorate, comprehensive exam, thesis/dissertation. *Entrance requirements:* For master's, GMAT, minimum B average in undergraduate course work. Additional exam requirements/recommendations for international students: Required—TOEFL (minimum score 550 paper-based; 213 computer-based; 80 iBT); Recommended—IELTS (minimum score 6.5). *Application deadline:* For fall admission, 7/31 priority date for domestic students, 4/30 for international students; for spring admission, 12/31 priority date for domestic students, 11/30 for international students. Applications are processed on a rolling basis. Application fee: $75. Electronic applications accepted. *Expenses: Tuition:* Full-time $22,464; part-time $1248 per credit. *Required fees:* $501 per semester. *Financial support:* In 2011–12, 1 fellowship (averaging $26,400 per year) was awarded; research assistantships, teaching assistantships, institutionally sponsored loans, scholarships/grants, and unspecified assistantships also available. Support available to part-time students. *Unit head:* Prof. Bharadwaj Rao, Head, 718-260-3617, Fax: 718-260-3874, E-mail: brao@poly.edu. *Application contact:* JeanCarlo Bonilla, Director of Graduate Enrollment Management, 718-260-3182, Fax: 718-260-3624, E-mail: gradinfo@poly.edu. Web site: http://www.managementdept.poly.edu.

Polytechnic University of Puerto Rico, Miami Campus, Graduate School, Miami, FL 33166. Offers accounting (MBA); business administration (MBA); construction management (MEM); environmental management (MEM); finance (MBA); human resources management (MBA); logistics and supply chain management (MBA); management of international enterprises (MBA); manufacturing management (MEM); marketing management (MBA); project management (MBA). Part-time and evening/weekend programs available. Postbaccalaureate distance learning degree programs offered (no on-campus study). *Entrance requirements:* For master's, minimum GPA of 3.0. Electronic applications accepted.

Polytechnic University of Puerto Rico, Orlando Campus, Graduate School, Winter Park, FL 32792. Offers accounting (MBA); business administration (MBA); construction management (MEM); engineering management (MEM); environmental management (MEM); finance (MBA); human resources management (MBA); management of international enterprises (MBA); management of technology (MBA); manufacturing management (MEM). Part-time and evening/weekend programs available. Postbaccalaureate distance learning degree programs offered (no on-campus study). *Entrance requirements:* For master's, minimum GPA of 3.0. Additional exam requirements/recommendations for international students: Recommended—TOEFL. Electronic applications accepted.

Pontifical Catholic University of Puerto Rico, College of Business Administration, Program in Human Resources, Ponce, PR 00717-0777. Offers MBA, Professional Certificate. Part-time and evening/weekend programs available. *Degree requirements:* For master's, thesis. *Entrance requirements:* For master's, GRE, interview, minimum GPA of 2.75.

Pontificia Universidad Catolica Madre y Maestra, Graduate School, Faculty of Social and Administrative Sciences, Santiago, Dominican Republic. Offers business administration (MBA), including business development, finance, international business, management skills (M Mgmt, MBA), marketing, operations, strategic cost management, strategy, tourist destination planning and management; law (LL M), including civil law, corporate business law, criminal law, international relations, real estate law; management (M Mgmt), including higher financial management, insurance program administration, management skills (M Mgmt, MBA); psychology (MA), including clinical child and adolescent psychology, forensic psychology; strategic human resources (EMBA).

Purdue University, Graduate School, Krannert School of Management, Doctoral Program in Organizational Behavior and Human Resource Management, West Lafayette, IN 47907-2056. Offers PhD. *Students:* 6 full-time (3 women); includes 2 minority (1 Black or African American, non-Hispanic/Latino; 1 Asian, non-Hispanic/Latino). Average age 32. 80 applicants, 0% accepted, 0 enrolled. In 2011, 3 doctorates awarded. *Degree requirements:* For doctorate, comprehensive exam, thesis/dissertation, dissertation proposal, dissertation defense. *Entrance requirements:* For doctorate, GMAT or GRE, bachelor's degree, two semesters of calculus, one semester each of linear algebra and statistics. Additional exam requirements/recommendations for international students: Required—TOEFL (minimum score 575 paper-based; 233 computer-based); Recommended—TWE. *Application deadline:* For fall admission, 1/15 priority date for domestic students, 1/15 for international students. Application fee: $55. Electronic applications accepted. *Financial support:* In 2011–12, 1 fellowship with full tuition reimbursement (averaging $25,000 per year), research assistantships with partial tuition reimbursements (averaging $18,000 per year), teaching assistantships with partial tuition reimbursements (averaging $18,000 per year) were awarded; scholarships/grants, health care benefits, tuition waivers (full and partial), unspecified assistantships, and travel funds to present at a major conference also available. Support available to part-time students. Financial award application deadline: 1/15. *Faculty research:* Human resource management, organizational behavior. *Unit head:* Dr. P. Christopher Earley, Dean/Professor, 765-494-4366. *Application contact:* Krannert PhD Admissions, 765-494-4375, Fax: 765-494-0136, E-mail: krannertphd@purdue.edu. Web site: http://www.krannert.purdue.edu/programs/phd/.

Purdue University, Graduate School, Krannert School of Management, Master of Science in Human Resource Management Program, West Lafayette, IN 47907. Offers MSHRM. *Faculty:* 81 full-time (19 women), 2 part-time/adjunct (0 women). *Students:* 50 full-time (26 women); includes 10 minority (4 Black or African American, non-Hispanic/Latino; 2 Asian, non-Hispanic/Latino; 2 Hispanic/Latino; 2 Two or more races, non-Hispanic/Latino), 28 international. Average age 25. 215 applicants, 20% accepted, 22 enrolled. In 2011, 27 master's awarded. *Entrance requirements:* For master's, GMAT or GRE, essays, recommendation letters, work experience/internship, minimum GPA of 3.0, four-year baccalaureate degree. Additional exam requirements/recommendations for international students: Required—TOEFL (minimum score 550 paper, 213 computer, 77 iBT), IELTS (minimum score 6.5), or Pearson Test of English. *Application deadline:* For fall admission, 11/1 for domestic and international students; for winter admission, 1/10 for domestic students, 2/1 for international students; for spring admission, 3/1 for domestic students. Applications are processed on a rolling basis. Application fee: $60 ($75 for international students). Electronic applications accepted. *Financial support:* Research assistantships, teaching assistantships, scholarships/grants, and unspecified assistantships available. Financial award applicants required to submit FAFSA. *Faculty research:* Performance periods and the dynamics of the performance-risk relationship, reactions to unfair events in computer-mediated groups: a test of uncertainty management theory, influences on job search self-efficacy of spouses of military personnel, Cross-Cultural Social Intelligence: An Assessment for Employees Working in Cross-National Contexts, Will You Trust Your New Boss? The Role of Affective Reactions to Leadership Succession. *Unit head:* Dr. P. Christopher Earley, Dean/Professor of Management, 765-494-4366. *Application contact:* Brian Precious, Director of Admissions, Marketing, Recruiting and Entrepreneurial Outreach, 765-494-0773, Fax: 765-494-9841, E-mail: krannertmasters@purdue.edu. Web site: http://masters.krannert.purdue.edu/programs/mshrm/.

Quincy University, Program in Business Administration, Quincy, IL 62301-2699. Offers business administration (MBA); human resource management (MBA). Part-time and evening/weekend programs available. *Faculty:* 3 full-time (2 women). *Students:* 4 full-time (0 women), 22 part-time (12 women), 1 international. In 2011, 15 master's awarded. *Entrance requirements:* For master's, GMAT, previous course work in accounting, economics, finance, management or marketing, and statistics. Additional exam requirements/recommendations for international students: Required—TOEFL (minimum score 550 paper-based; 79 iBT). *Application deadline:* Applications are processed on a rolling basis. Application fee: $25. Electronic applications accepted. *Expenses:* Contact institution. *Financial support:* Applicants required to submit FAFSA. *Faculty research:* Macroeconomic forecasting, business ethics/social responsibility. *Unit head:* Dr. John Palmer, Director, 217-228-5432 Ext. 3070, E-mail: palmejo@quincy.edu. *Application* *contact:* Office of Admissions, 217-228-5210, Fax: 217-228-5479, E-mail: admissions@quincy.edu. Web site: http://www.quincy.edu/academics/graduate-programs/business-administation.

Regent's American College London, Webster Graduate School, London, United Kingdom. Offers business (MBA); finance (MS); human resources (MA); information technology management (MA); international business (MA); international non-governmental organizations (MA); international relations (MA); management and leadership (MA); marketing (MA). Part-time programs available.

Regis University, College for Professional Studies, School of Management, Denver, CO 80221-1099. Offers accounting (MS, Certificate); executive international management (Certificate); executive leadership (Certificate); executive project management (Certificate); finance and accounting (MBA); general business administration (MBA); health care management (MBA); human resource management and leadership (MSOL); information technology leadership and management (MSOL); international business (MBA); marketing (MBA); operations management (MBA); organizational leadership and management (MSOL); project leadership and management (MSOL); project management (Certificate); strategic business management (Certificate); strategic human resource management (Certificate); strategic management (MBA). Offered at Colorado Springs Campus, Northwest Denver Campus, Southeast Denver Campus, Fort Collins Campus, Broomfield Campus, Henderson (Nevada) Campus, and Summerlin (Nevada) Campus and online. Part-time and evening/weekend programs available. Postbaccalaureate distance learning degree programs offered (no on-campus study). *Degree requirements:* For master's, thesis optional, capstone project. *Entrance requirements:* For master's, GMAT or essays, interview, 2 years of full-time business work experience, resume; for Certificate, GMAT. Additional exam requirements/recommendations for international students: Required—TOEFL, TWE (minimum score 5) or university-based test. Electronic applications accepted. *Faculty research:* Impact of information technology on small business regulation of accounting, international project financing, mineral development, delivery of healthcare to rural indigenous communities.

Robert Morris University, Graduate Studies, School of Business, Moon Township, PA 15108-1189. Offers business administration (MBA); human resource management (MS); nonprofit management (MS); taxation (MS). *Accreditation:* AACSB. Part-time and evening/weekend programs available. Postbaccalaureate distance learning degree programs offered (no on-campus study). *Faculty:* 29 full-time (11 women), 3 part-time/adjunct (0 women). *Students:* 190 part-time (91 women); includes 11 minority (9 Black or African American, non-Hispanic/Latino; 1 Asian, non-Hispanic/Latino; 1 Hispanic/Latino), 4 international. *Entrance requirements:* For master's, GMAT, letters of recommendation. Additional exam requirements/recommendations for international students: Required—TOEFL (minimum score 550 paper-based; 213 computer-based; 79 iBT). *Application deadline:* For fall admission, 7/1 priority date for domestic students, 7/1 for international students; for spring admission, 11/1 priority date for domestic students, 11/1 for international students. Applications are processed on a rolling basis. Application fee: $35. Electronic applications accepted. *Expenses: Tuition:* Part-time $810 per credit. *Required fees:* $15 per course. Tuition and fees vary according to degree level. *Financial support:* Research assistantships with partial tuition reimbursements, Federal Work-Study, institutionally sponsored loans, and unspecified assistantships available. Support available to part-time students. Financial award application deadline: 5/1; financial award applicants required to submit FAFSA. *Unit head:* Dr. Patrick J. Litzinger, Interim Dean, 412-397-6383, Fax: 412-397-2217, E-mail: litzinger@rmu.edu. *Application contact:* Deborah Roach, Assistant Dean, Graduate Admissions, 412-397-5200, Fax: 412-397-2425, E-mail: graduateadmissions@rmu.edu. Web site: http://www.rmu.edu/web/cms/schools/sbus/.

Robert Morris University Illinois, Morris Graduate School of Management, Chicago, IL 60605. Offers accounting (MBA); accounting/finance (MBA); design and media (MM); health care administration (MM); higher education administration (MM); human resource management (MBA); information systems (MIS); law enforcement administration (MM); management (MBA); management/finance (MIS); management/human resource management (MBA); sports administration (MM). Part-time and evening/weekend programs available. *Faculty:* 7 full-time (1 woman), 21 part-time/adjunct (5 women). *Students:* 296 full-time (172 women), 216 part-time (136 women); includes 273 minority (160 Black or African American, non-Hispanic/Latino; 1 American Indian or Alaska Native, non-Hispanic/Latino; 32 Asian, non-Hispanic/Latino; 78 Hispanic/Latino; 2 Two or more races, non-Hispanic/Latino), 28 international. Average age 32. 247 applicants, 69% accepted, 152 enrolled. In 2011, 244 master's awarded. *Entrance requirements:* Additional exam requirements/recommendations for international students: Required—TOEFL (minimum score 550 paper-based; 173 computer-based). *Application deadline:* Applications are processed on a rolling basis. Application fee: $20 ($100 for international students). Electronic applications accepted. *Expenses: Tuition:* Full-time $13,800; part-time $2300 per course. *Financial support:* In 2011–12, 643 students received support. Federal Work-Study, scholarships/grants, tuition waivers, and leadership and athletic scholarships available. Support available to part-time students. Financial award applicants required to submit FAFSA. *Unit head:* Kayed Akkawi, Dean, 312-935-6025, Fax: 312-935-6020, E-mail: kakkawi@robertmorris.edu. *Application contact:* Fernando Villeda, Dean of Morris Graduate School of Management, 312-935-6050, Fax: 312-935-6020, E-mail: fvilleda@robertmorris.edu.

Rollins College, Hamilton Holt School, Master of Human Resources Program, Winter Park, FL 32789. Offers MHR. Part-time and evening/weekend programs available. *Faculty:* 3 full-time (0 women), 3 part-time/adjunct (1 woman). *Students:* 4 full-time (all women), 51 part-time (45 women); includes 25 minority (13 Black or African American, non-Hispanic/Latino; 1 Asian, non-Hispanic/Latino; 10 Hispanic/Latino; 1 Two or more races, non-Hispanic/Latino), 1 international. Average age 32. 21 applicants, 95% accepted, 19 enrolled. In 2011, 23 master's awarded. *Degree requirements:* For master's, thesis optional. *Entrance requirements:* For master's, GMAT or GRE, official transcripts, two letters of recommendation, essay, current resume. Additional exam requirements/recommendations for international students: Required—TOEFL (minimum score 550 paper-based; 213 computer-based; 80 iBT). *Application deadline:* For fall admission, 4/1 for domestic students; for spring admission, 12/1 for domestic students. Application fee: $50. *Expenses:* Contact institution. *Financial support:* In 2011–12, 35 students received support. Federal Work-Study, scholarships/grants, and unspecified assistantships available. Support available to part-time students. Financial award applicants required to submit FAFSA. *Unit head:* Dr. Donald Rogers, Faculty Director, 407-646-2348, E-mail: drogers@rollins.edu. *Application contact:* Tonya Parker, Coordinator of Records and Registration, 407-646-2653, Fax: 407-646-1551, E-mail: tparker@rollins.edu. Web site: http://www.rollins.edu/holt/graduate/mhr.html.

Roosevelt University, Graduate Division, Walter E. Heller College of Business Administration, Program in Human Resource Management, Chicago, IL 60605. Offers MSHRM.

Royal Roads University, Graduate Studies, Applied Leadership and Management Program, Victoria, BC V9B 5Y2, Canada. Offers executive coaching (Graduate Certificate); health systems leadership (Graduate Certificate); project management (Graduate Certificate); public relations management (Graduate Certificate); strategic human resources management (Graduate Certificate).

Royal Roads University, Graduate Studies, Faculty of Management, Victoria, BC V9B 5Y2, Canada. Offers digital technologies management (MBA); executive management (MBA), including global aviation management, knowledge management, leadership; human resources management (MBA). Postbaccalaureate distance learning degree programs offered (minimal on-campus study). *Degree requirements:* For master's, thesis. *Entrance requirements:* For master's, 5-7 years of related work experience. Additional exam requirements/recommendations for international students: Required—TOEFL (paper-based 570; computer-based 233) or IELTS (paper-based 7) (recommended). Electronic applications accepted. *Expenses:* Contact institution. *Faculty research:* Global venture analysis standards; computer assisted venture opportunity screening; teaching philosophies, instructions and methods.

Rutgers, The State University of New Jersey, Newark, Graduate School, Program in Public Administration, Newark, NJ 07102. Offers health care administration (MPA); human resources administration (MPA); public administration (PhD); public management (MPA); public policy analysis (MPA); urban systems and issues (MPA). *Accreditation:* NASPAA (one or more programs are accredited). Part-time and evening/weekend programs available. *Degree requirements:* For master's, comprehensive exam, thesis or alternative; for doctorate, thesis/dissertation. *Entrance requirements:* For master's, GRE, minimum undergraduate B average; for doctorate, GRE, MPA, minimum B average. Electronic applications accepted. *Faculty research:* Government finance, municipal and state government, public productivity.

Rutgers, The State University of New Jersey, New Brunswick, School of Management and Labor Relations, Program in Human Resource Management, Piscataway, NJ 08854-8097. Offers MHRM. Part-time and evening/weekend programs available. *Entrance requirements:* For master's, GMAT or GRE General Test, 3 letters of recommendation. Additional exam requirements/recommendations for international students: Required—TOEFL (minimum score 575 paper-based; 233 computer-based). Electronic applications accepted. *Expenses:* Contact institution. *Faculty research:* Human resource policy and planning, employee ownership and profit sharing, compensation and appraisal of performance, law and public policy, computers and decision making.

Rutgers, The State University of New Jersey, New Brunswick, School of Management and Labor Relations, Program in Industrial Relations and Human Resources, Piscataway, NJ 08854-8097. Offers PhD. Part-time programs available. *Degree requirements:* For doctorate, comprehensive exam, thesis/dissertation. *Entrance requirements:* For doctorate, GRE or GMAT, 3 letters of recommendation. Additional exam requirements/recommendations for international students: Required—TOEFL (minimum score 575 paper-based; 233 computer-based; 91 iBT). Electronic applications accepted. *Faculty research:* Strategic human resources, labor relations, organizational change, worker representation.

Sage Graduate School, School of Management, Program in Business Administration, Troy, NY 12180-4115. Offers business strategy (MBA); finance (MBA); human resources (MBA); marketing (MBA); JD/MBA. Part-time and evening/weekend programs available. *Faculty:* 2 full-time (both women), 8 part-time/adjunct (1 woman). *Students:* 20 full-time (10 women), 55 part-time (36 women); includes 10 minority (2 Black or African American, non-Hispanic/Latino; 4 Asian, non-Hispanic/Latino; 3 Hispanic/Latino; 1 Two or more races, non-Hispanic/Latino), 1 international. Average age 31. 51 applicants, 55% accepted, 19 enrolled. In 2011, 10 degrees awarded. *Entrance requirements:* For master's, minimum GPA of 2.75, resume, 2 letters of recommendation. Additional exam requirements/recommendations for international students: Required—TOEFL (minimum score 550 paper-based; 213 computer-based). *Application deadline:* Applications are processed on a rolling basis. Application fee: $40. *Expenses: Tuition:* Full-time $11,880; part-time $660 per credit hour. Tuition and fees vary according to program. *Financial support:* Fellowships, research assistantships, Federal Work-Study, scholarships/grants, and unspecified assistantships available. Support available to part-time students. Financial award application deadline: 3/1; financial award applicants required to submit FAFSA. *Unit head:* Dr. Daniel Robeson, Dean, School of Management, 518-292-8637, Fax: 518-292-1964, E-mail: robesd@sage.edu. *Application contact:* Wendy D. Diefendorf, Director of Graduate and Adult Admission, 518-244-2443, Fax: 518-244-6880, E-mail: diefew@sage.edu.

St. Ambrose University, College of Business, Program in Business Administration, Davenport, IA 52803-2898. Offers business administration (DBA); health care (MBA); human resources (MBA). *Accreditation:* ACBSP. Part-time and evening/weekend programs available. *Faculty:* 17 full-time (4 women), 4 part-time/adjunct (1 woman). *Students:* 44 full-time (21 women), 208 part-time (92 women); includes 23 minority (7 Black or African American, non-Hispanic/Latino; 2 American Indian or Alaska Native, non-Hispanic/Latino; 3 Asian, non-Hispanic/Latino; 11 Hispanic/Latino), 5 international. Average age 34. 133 applicants, 80% accepted, 74 enrolled. In 2011, 110 master's, 2 doctorates awarded. *Degree requirements:* For master's, comprehensive exam (for some programs), thesis or alternative, capstone seminar; for doctorate, comprehensive exam, thesis/dissertation, oral and written exams. *Entrance requirements:* For master's, GMAT; for doctorate, GMAT, master's degree. Additional exam requirements/recommendations for international students: Required—TOEFL. *Application deadline:* For fall admission, 8/15 priority date for domestic students; for winter admission, 12/15 for domestic students; for spring admission, 1/1 for domestic students. Applications are processed on a rolling basis. Application fee: $25. Electronic applications accepted. *Expenses:* Contact institution. *Financial support:* In 2011–12, 54 students received support, including 5 research assistantships with partial tuition reimbursements available (averaging $3,600 per year); career-related internships or fieldwork, scholarships/grants, tuition waivers (partial), and unspecified assistantships also available. Financial award application deadline: 3/15; financial award applicants required to submit FAFSA. *Unit head:* Dr. Linda K. Brown, MBA Director, 563-333-6343, Fax: 563-333-6243, E-mail: brownlindak@sau.edu. *Application contact:* Elizabeth Loveless, Director of Graduate Student Recruitment, 563-333-6271, Fax: 563-333-6268, E-mail: lovelesselizabethb@sau.edu. Web site: http://www.sau.edu/mba.

Saint Francis University, Graduate School of Business and Human Resource Management, Loretto, PA 15940. Offers business administration (MBA); human resource management (MHRM). Part-time and evening/weekend programs available. *Faculty:* 8 full-time (2 women), 25 part-time/adjunct (12 women). *Students:* 39 full-time (17 women), 141 part-time (66 women); includes 5 minority (3 Black or African American, non-Hispanic/Latino; 2 Asian, non-Hispanic/Latino). Average age 30. 35 applicants, 86% accepted, 20 enrolled. In 2011, 66 degrees awarded. *Degree requirements:* For master's, comprehensive exam (for some programs), thesis (for some programs). *Entrance requirements:* For master's, GMAT (waived if undergraduate QPA is 3.3 or above), 2 letters of recommendation, minimum GPA of 2.75, two essays. Additional exam requirements/recommendations for international students: Required—TOEFL (minimum score 550 paper-based; 213 computer-based; 57 iBT). *Application deadline:* For fall admission, 8/15 priority date for domestic students, 8/15 for international students; for spring admission, 12/1 priority date for domestic students, 12/1 for international students. Applications are processed on a rolling basis. Application fee: $30. *Expenses:* Contact institution. *Financial support:* Fellowships with partial tuition reimbursements, career-related internships or fieldwork, and unspecified assistantships available. Financial award application deadline: 8/15. *Unit head:* Dr.

Randy Frye, Director, Graduate Business Programs and Human Resource Management, 814-472-3041, Fax: 814-472-3174, E-mail: rfrye@francis.edu. *Application contact:* Nicole Marie Bauman, Coordinator, Graduate Business Programs and Human Resource Management, 814-472-3026, Fax: 814-472-3369, E-mail: nbauman@francis.edu. Web site: http://www.francis.edu.

St. Joseph's College, Long Island Campus, Program in Management, Patchogue, NY 11772-2399. Offers health care (AC); health care management (MS); human resource management (AC); human resources management (MS); organizational management (MS).

Saint Joseph's University, Erivan K. Haub School of Business, MS Program in Managing Human Capital, Philadelphia, PA 19131-1395. Offers MS. Part-time and evening/weekend programs available. *Students:* 2 full-time (both women), 25 part-time (18 women); includes 11 minority (8 Black or African American, non-Hispanic/Latino; 1 Asian, non-Hispanic/Latino; 2 Hispanic/Latino), 1 international. Average age 34. In 2011, 16 master's awarded. *Entrance requirements:* For master's, MAT, GRE, or GMAT, 2 letters of recommendation, resume, personal statement. Additional exam requirements/recommendations for international students: Required—TOEFL (minimum score 550 paper-based; 213 computer-based; 80 iBT) , IELTS (minimum score 6.5), or Pearson Test of English (minimum score 60). *Application deadline:* For fall admission, 7/15 priority date for domestic students, 5/15 for international students; for spring admission, 11/15 priority date for domestic students, 10/15 for international students. Applications are processed on a rolling basis. Application fee: $35. Electronic applications accepted. *Expenses: Tuition:* Part-time $735 per credit hour. Tuition and fees vary according to degree level and program. *Financial support:* Unspecified assistantships available. Financial award application deadline: 5/1; financial award applicants required to submit FAFSA. *Unit head:* Dr. Patricia Rafferty, Director, MS in Business Intelligence and MS in Human Resource Management Programs, 610-660-1318, Fax: 610-660-1229, E-mail: patricia.rafferty@sju.edu. *Application contact:* Dr. Patricia Rafferty, Director, MS in Business Intelligence and MS in Human Resource Management Programs, 610-660-1318, Fax: 610-660-1229, E-mail: patricia.rafferty@sju.edu. Web site: http://www.sju.edu/hsb/hr.

See Display below and Close-Up on page 443.

Saint Joseph's University, Erivan K. Haub School of Business, Professional MBA Program, Philadelphia, PA 19131-1395. Offers accounting (MBA); finance (MBA), including finance; general business (MBA); health and medical services administration (MBA); human resource management (MBA); international business (MBA); international marketing (MBA); management (MBA); marketing (MBA); DO/MBA. DO/MBA offered jointly with Philadelphia College of Osteopathic Medicine. Part-time and evening/weekend programs available. Postbaccalaureate distance learning degree programs offered (no on-campus study). *Students:* 98 full-time (42 women), 528 part-time (208 women); includes 102 minority (47 Black or African American, non-Hispanic/Latino; 1 American Indian or Alaska Native, non-Hispanic/Latino; 28 Asian, non-Hispanic/Latino; 20 Hispanic/Latino; 1 Native Hawaiian or other Pacific Islander, non-Hispanic/Latino; 5 Two or more races, non-Hispanic/Latino), 45 international. Average age 31. In 2011, 290 master's awarded. *Entrance requirements:* For master's, GMAT or GRE, 2 letters of recommendation, resume, personal statement. Additional exam requirements/recommendations for international students: Required—TOEFL (minimum score 550 paper-based; 213 computer-based; 80 iBT), IELTS (minimum score 6.5), or Pearson Test of English (minimum score 60). *Application deadline:* For fall admission, 7/15 priority date for domestic students, 4/15 for international students; for spring admission, 11/15 priority date for domestic students, 10/15 for international students. Applications are processed on a rolling basis. Application fee: $35. Electronic applications accepted. *Expenses: Tuition:* Part-time $735 per credit hour. Tuition and fees vary according to degree level and program. *Financial support:* Scholarships/grants and unspecified assistantships available. Financial award application deadline: 5/1; financial award applicants required to submit FAFSA. *Unit head:* Adele C. Foley, Associate Dean/Director, Graduate Business Programs, 610-660-1691, Fax: 610-660-1599, E-mail: afoley@sju.edu. *Application contact:* Dr. Janine N. Guerra, Associate Director, Professional MBA Program, 610-660-1695, Fax: 610-660-1599, E-mail: jguerra@sju.edu. Web site: http://www.sju.edu/mba.

Saint Leo University, Graduate Business Studies, Saint Leo, FL 33574-6665. Offers accounting (MBA); business (MBA); health services management (MBA); human resource management (MBA); information security management (MBA); marketing (MBA); sport business (MBA). Part-time and evening/weekend programs available. Postbaccalaureate distance learning degree programs offered (no on-campus study). *Faculty:* 39 full-time (7 women), 56 part-time/adjunct (17 women). *Students:* 1,506 full-time (901 women); includes 620 minority (480 Black or African American, non-Hispanic/Latino; 5 American Indian or Alaska Native, non-Hispanic/Latino; 21 Asian, non-Hispanic/Latino; 100 Hispanic/Latino; 1 Native Hawaiian or other Pacific Islander, non-Hispanic/Latino; 13 Two or more races, non-Hispanic/Latino), 20 international. Average age 38. In 2011, 574 master's awarded. *Entrance requirements:* For master's, GMAT (minimum score 500 if applicant does not have 5 years of professional work experience), bachelor's degree with minimum GPA of 3.0 in the last 60 hours of coursework from regionally-accredited college or university; 5 years of professional work experience; resume; 2 letters of recommendation. Additional exam requirements/recommendations for international students: Required—TOEFL (minimum score 550 paper-based; 213 computer-based; 80 iBT). *Application deadline:* For fall admission, 7/1 priority date for domestic students, 7/1 for international students; for spring admission, 11/12 priority date for domestic students, 11/1 for international students. Applications are processed on a rolling basis. Application fee: $80. Electronic applications accepted. *Expenses: Tuition:* Full-time $11,340; part-time $630 per semester hour. Tuition and fees vary according to campus/location and program. *Financial support:* In 2011–12, 72 students received support. Career-related internships or fieldwork, Federal Work-Study, scholarships/grants, and health care benefits available. Financial award application deadline: 3/1; financial award applicants required to submit FAFSA. *Unit head:* Dr. Lorrie McGovern, Director, 352-588-7390, Fax: 352-588-8585, E-mail: mbaslu@saintleo.edu. *Application contact:* Jared Welling, Director of Graduate Admission, 800-707-8846, Fax: 352-588-7873, E-mail: grad.admissions@saintleo.edu. Web site: http://www.saintleo.edu/Academics/School-of-Business/Graduate-Degree-Programs.

Saint Mary's University of Minnesota, Schools of Graduate and Professional Programs, Graduate School of Business and Technology, Human Resource Management Program, Winona, MN 55987-1399. Offers MA. *Unit head:* Janet Dunn, Director, 612-238-4546, E-mail: jdunn@smumn.edu. *Application contact:* Yasin Alsaidi, Director of Admissions for Graduate and Professional Programs, 612-728-5207, Fax: 612-728-5121, E-mail: yalsaidi@smumn.edu. Web site: http://www.smumn.edu/graduate-home/areas-of-study/graduate-school-of-business-technology/ma-in-human-resource-management.

Saint Peter's University, Graduate Business Programs, MBA Program, Jersey City, NJ 07306-5997. Offers finance (MBA); health care administration (MBA); human resource management (MBA); international business (MBA); management (MBA); management information systems (MBA); marketing (MBA); risk management (MBA); MBA/MS. Part-time and evening/weekend programs available. *Entrance requirements:* Additional exam requirements/recommendations for international students: Required—TOEFL (minimum score 79 computer-based). Electronic applications accepted. *Faculty research:* Finance, health care management, human resource management, international business, management, management information systems, marketing, risk management.

Human Resources Management

St. Thomas University, School of Business, Department of Management, Miami Gardens, FL 33054-6459. Offers accounting (MBA); general management (MSM, Certificate); health management (MBA, MSM, Certificate); human resource management (MBA, MSM, Certificate); international business (MBA, MIB, MSM, Certificate); justice administration (MSM, Certificate); management accounting (MSM, Certificate); public management (MSM, Certificate); sports administration (MS). Part-time and evening/weekend programs available. *Degree requirements:* For master's, comprehensive exam. *Entrance requirements:* For master's, interview, minimum GPA of 3.0 or GMAT. Additional exam requirements/recommendations for international students: Required—TOEFL (minimum score 550 paper-based; 213 computer-based; 79 iBT). Electronic applications accepted.

Salve Regina University, Program in Business Administration, Newport, RI 02840-4192. Offers business administration (MBA); business studies (Certificate); human resources management (Certificate); management (Certificate); organizational development (Certificate). Part-time and evening/weekend programs available. Postbaccalaureate distance learning degree programs offered (minimal on-campus study). *Faculty:* 2 full-time (1 woman), 15 part-time/adjunct (6 women). *Students:* 35 full-time (14 women), 86 part-time (41 women); includes 10 minority (5 Black or African American, non-Hispanic/Latino; 3 Asian, non-Hispanic/Latino; 2 Hispanic/Latino), 3 international. *Entrance requirements:* For master's, GMAT, GRE General Test, or MAT, 6 undergraduate credits each in accounting, economics, quantitative analysis and calculus or statistics. Additional exam requirements/recommendations for international students: Required—TOEFL (minimum score 600 paper-based; 250 computer-based; 100 iBT) or IELTS. *Application deadline:* For fall admission, 3/15 priority date for domestic students, 3/15 for international students; for spring admission, 9/15 priority date for domestic students, 9/15 for international students. Applications are processed on a rolling basis. Application fee: $60. Electronic applications accepted. *Expenses: Tuition:* Full-time $7740; part-time $430 per credit. *Required fees:* $40 per semester. Tuition and fees vary according to program. *Financial support:* Career-related internships or fieldwork and Federal Work-Study available. Support available to part-time students. Financial award application deadline: 3/1; financial award applicants required to submit FAFSA. *Unit head:* Dr. Arlene Nicholas, Director, 401-341-3280, E-mail: arlene.nicholas@salve.edu. *Application contact:* Kelly Alverson, Associate Director of Graduate Admissions, 401-341-2153, Fax: 401-341-2973, E-mail: kelly.alverson@salve.edu. Web site: http://www.salve.edu/graduatestudies/programs/gmt/.

Salve Regina University, Program in Management, Newport, RI 02840-4192. Offers business studies (Certificate); holistic leadership and management (Certificate); human resources management (Certificate); law enforcement leadership (MS); leadership and change management (Certificate); management (Certificate); organizational development (Certificate). Part-time and evening/weekend programs available. Postbaccalaureate distance learning degree programs offered (minimal on-campus study). *Faculty:* 2 full-time (1 woman), 15 part-time/adjunct (6 women). *Students:* 9 full-time (6 women), 40 part-time (20 women); includes 2 minority (both Black or African American, non-Hispanic/Latino). *Entrance requirements:* For master's, GMAT, GRE General Test, or MAT. Additional exam requirements/recommendations for international students: Required—TOEFL (minimum score 600 paper-based; 250 computer-based; 100 iBT). *Application deadline:* For fall admission, 3/15 priority date for domestic students, 3/5 for international students; for spring admission, 3/15 priority date for domestic students, 9/15 for international students. Applications are processed on a rolling basis. Application fee: $60. Electronic applications accepted. *Expenses: Tuition:* Full-time $7740; part-time $430 per credit. *Required fees:* $40 per semester. Tuition and fees vary according to program. *Financial support:* Career-related internships or fieldwork and Federal Work-Study available. Support available to part-time students. Financial award application deadline: 3/1; financial award applicants required to submit FAFSA. *Unit head:* Dr. Arlene Nicholas, Director, 401-341-3280, E-mail: arlene.nicholas@salve.edu. *Application contact:* Kelly Alverson, Associate Director of Graduate Admissions, 401-341-2153, Fax: 401-341-2973, E-mail: kelly.alverson@salve.edu. Web site: http://www.salve.edu/graduatestudies/programs/mgt/.

San Diego State University, Graduate and Research Affairs, College of Business Administration, Department of Management, San Diego, CA 92182. Offers entrepreneurship (MS); human resources management (MS); management science (MS). Part-time and evening/weekend programs available. *Degree requirements:* For master's, thesis or alternative. *Entrance requirements:* For master's, GMAT, resume, letters of reference. Additional exam requirements/recommendations for international students: Required—TOEFL. Electronic applications accepted.

Southern New Hampshire University, School of Business, Manchester, NH 03106-1045. Offers accounting (MS); business administration (MBA, Certificate), including accounting (Certificate), business administration (MBA), finance (Certificate), forensic accounting (Certificate), human resources management (Certificate), international business (Certificate), international sport management (Certificate), leadership of not for profit organizations (Certificate), marketing (Certificate), operations management (Certificate), sport management (Certificate), taxation (Certificate); finance (MS); hospitality and tourism leadership (Certificate); information technology (MS, Certificate); information technology/international business (Certificate); integrated marketing communications (Certificate); international business (MS, DBA); marketing (MS); operations and project management (MS); organizational leadership (MS); project management (Certificate); sport management (MS); MBA/Certificate. *Accreditation:* ACBSP. Part-time and evening/weekend programs available. Postbaccalaureate distance learning degree programs offered (no on-campus study). Terminal master's awarded for partial completion of doctoral program. *Degree requirements:* For master's, one foreign language, comprehensive exam (for some programs), thesis or alternative; for doctorate, one foreign language, comprehensive exam, thesis/dissertation. *Entrance requirements:* For master's, minimum GPA of 2.5; for doctorate, GMAT. Additional exam requirements/recommendations for international students: Required—TOEFL (minimum score 500 paper-based). Electronic applications accepted.

Stevens Institute of Technology, Graduate School, Wesley J. Howe School of Technology Management, Program in Management, Hoboken, NJ 07030. Offers general management (MS); global innovation management (MS); human resource management (MS); information management (MS); project management (MS); technology commercialization (MS); technology management (MS). Part-time programs available. *Degree requirements:* For master's, thesis optional. *Entrance requirements:* For master's, GMAT, GRE General Test. Additional exam requirements/recommendations for international students: Required—TOEFL. Electronic applications accepted. *Faculty research:* Industrial economics.

Stony Brook University, State University of New York, Graduate School, College of Business, Program in Business Administration, Stony Brook, NY 11794. Offers finance (MBA, Certificate); health care management (MBA, Certificate); human resource management (Certificate); human resources (MBA); information systems management (MBA, Certificate); management (MBA); marketing (MBA).

Stony Brook University, State University of New York, School of Professional Development, Stony Brook, NY 11794. Offers biology-grade 7-12 (MAT); chemistry-grade 7-12 (MAT); coaching (Graduate Certificate); coaching online (Graduate Certificate); computer integrated engineering (Graduate Certificate); earth science-grade 7-12 (MAT); educational computing (Graduate Certificate); educational leadership (Advanced Certificate); English-grade 7-12 (MAT); environmental management (Graduate Certificate); environmental/occupational health and safety (Graduate Certificate); French-grade 7-12 (MAT); German-grade 7-12 (MAT); human resource management (Graduate Certificate); human resource management online (Graduate Certificate); information systems management (Graduate Certificate); Italian-grade 7-12 (MAT); liberal studies (MA); liberal studies online (MAT); mathematics-grade 7-12 (MAT); operation research (Graduate Certificate); physics-grade 7-12 (MAT); professional studies online (MPS); school administration and supervision (Graduate Certificate); school building leadership (Graduate Certificate); school district administration (Graduate Certificate); school district business leadership (Advanced Certificate); school district leadership (Graduate Certificate); social science and the professions (MPS), including environmental waste management, human resource management; social studies-grade 7-12 (MAT); Spanish-grade 7-12 (MAT); waste management (Graduate Certificate). Part-time and evening/weekend programs available. Postbaccalaureate distance learning degree programs offered. *Degree requirements:* For master's, one foreign language, thesis or alternative.

Strayer University, Graduate Studies, Washington, DC 20005-2603. Offers accounting (MS); acquisition (MBA); business administration (MBA); communications technology (MS); educational management (M Ed); finance (MBA); health services administration (MHSA); hospitality and tourism management (MBA); human resource management (MBA); information systems (MS), including computer security management, decision support system management, enterprise resource management, network management, software engineering management, systems development management; management (MBA); management information systems (MS); marketing (MBA); professional accounting (MS), including accounting information systems, controllership, taxation; public administration (MPA); supply chain management (MBA); technology in education (M Ed). Programs also offered at campus locations in Birmingham, AL; Chamblee, GA; Cobb County, GA; Morrow, GA; White Marsh, MD; Charleston, SC; Columbia, SC; Greensboro, NC; Greenville, SC; Lexington, KY; Louisville, KY; Nashville, TN; North Raleigh, NC; Washington, DC. Part-time and evening/weekend programs available. Postbaccalaureate distance learning degree programs offered (minimal on-campus study). *Degree requirements:* For master's, thesis. *Entrance requirements:* For master's, GMAT, GRE General Test, bachelor's degree from an accredited college or university, minimum undergraduate GPA of 2.75. Electronic applications accepted.

Tarleton State University, College of Graduate Studies, College of Business Administration, Department of Management, Marketing, and Administrative Systems, Stephenville, TX 76402. Offers human resource management (MS); management and leadership (MS). Part-time and evening/weekend programs available. Postbaccalaureate distance learning degree programs offered. *Faculty:* 10 full-time (1 woman), 6 part-time/adjunct (3 women). *Students:* 21 full-time (12 women), 136 part-time (91 women); includes 44 minority (26 Black or African American, non-Hispanic/Latino; 1 American Indian or Alaska Native, non-Hispanic/Latino; 2 Asian, non-Hispanic/Latino; 14 Hispanic/Latino; 1 Two or more races, non-Hispanic/Latino). Average age 33. 51 applicants, 86% accepted, 35 enrolled. In 2011, 18 master's awarded. *Degree requirements:* For master's, comprehensive exam. *Entrance requirements:* For master's, GRE, minimum GPA of 3.0. Additional exam requirements/recommendations for international students: Required—TOEFL (minimum score 550 paper-based; 213 computer-based; 80 iBT). *Application deadline:* For fall admission, 8/5 priority date for domestic students; for spring admission, 12/1 for domestic students. Applications are processed on a rolling basis. Application fee: $30 ($130 for international students). Electronic applications accepted. *Expenses:* Tuition, state resident: full-time $3131.46; part-time $174 per credit hour. Tuition, nonresident: full-time $8225; part-time $457 per credit hour. *Required fees:* $1446. Tuition and fees vary according to course load and campus/location. *Financial support:* Research assistantships, teaching assistantships, Federal Work-Study, scholarships/grants, and unspecified assistantships available. Financial award application deadline: 5/1; financial award applicants required to submit FAFSA. *Unit head:* Dr. Rusty Freed, Head, 254-968-9277, Fax: 254-968-9737, E-mail: freed@tarleton.edu. *Application contact:* Information Contact, 254-968-9104, Fax: 254-968-9670, E-mail: gradoffice@tarleton.edu. Web site: http://www.tarleton.edu/~mmas.

Temple University, Fox School of Business, MBA Programs, Philadelphia, PA 19122-6096. Offers accounting (MBA); business management (MBA); financial management (MBA); healthcare and life sciences innovation (MBA); human resource management (MBA); international business (IMBA); IT management (MBA); marketing management (MBA); pharmaceutical management (MBA); strategic management (EMBA, MBA). EMBA offered in Philadelphia, PA and Tokyo, Japan. *Accreditation:* AACSB. Part-time and evening/weekend programs available. Postbaccalaureate distance learning degree programs offered (minimal on-campus study). *Entrance requirements:* For master's, GMAT, minimum undergraduate GPA of 3.0. Additional exam requirements/recommendations for international students: Required—TOEFL (minimum score 600 paper-based; 250 computer-based; 100 iBT), IELTS (minimum score 7.5). *Expenses:* Tuition, state resident: full-time $12,366; part-time $687 per credit hour. Tuition, nonresident: full-time $17,298; part-time $961 per credit hour. *Required fees:* $590; $213 per year.

Temple University, Fox School of Business, Specialized Master's Programs, Philadelphia, PA 19122-6096. Offers accountancy (MS); actuarial science (MS); finance (MS); financial engineering (MS); human resource management (MS); marketing (MS); statistics (MS). *Accreditation:* AACSB. Part-time programs available. *Entrance requirements:* For master's, GRE General Test or GMAT, minimum undergraduate GPA of 3.0. Additional exam requirements/recommendations for international students: Required—TOEFL (minimum score 600 paper-based; 250 computer-based; 100 iBT), IELTS (minimum score 7.5). *Expenses:* Tuition, state resident: full-time $12,366; part-time $687 per credit hour. Tuition, nonresident: full-time $17,298; part-time $961 per credit hour. *Required fees:* $590; $213 per year.

Tennessee Technological University, Graduate School, College of Business, Cookeville, TN 38505. Offers accounting (MBA); finance (MBA); human resource management (MBA); international business (MBA); management information systems (MBA); risk management & insurance (MBA). *Accreditation:* AACSB. Part-time and evening/weekend programs available. Postbaccalaureate distance learning degree programs offered (no on-campus study). *Faculty:* 28 full-time (5 women). *Students:* 45 full-time (19 women), 135 part-time (51 women); includes 13 minority (4 Black or African American, non-Hispanic/Latino; 5 Asian, non-Hispanic/Latino; 3 Hispanic/Latino; 1 Native Hawaiian or other Pacific Islander, non-Hispanic/Latino), 2 international. Average age 25. 193 applicants, 59% accepted, 70 enrolled. In 2011, 89 master's awarded. *Entrance requirements:* For master's, GMAT. Additional exam requirements/recommendations for international students: Required—TOEFL (minimum score 550 paper-based; 79 iBT), IELTS (minimum score 5.5), Pearson Test of English Academic. *Application deadline:* For fall admission, 8/1 for domestic students, 5/1 for international students; for spring admission, 12/1 for domestic students, 10/1 for international students. Application fee: $25 ($30 for international students). Electronic applications accepted. *Expenses:* Tuition, state resident: full-time $8094; part-time $422 per credit hour. Tuition, nonresident: full-time $20,574; part-time $1046 per credit hour. *Financial* *support:* In 2011–12, 5 fellowships (averaging $10,000 per year), 18 research assistantships (averaging $4,000 per year), teaching assistantships (averaging $4,000 per year) were awarded. Support available to part-time students. Financial award application deadline: 4/1. *Unit head:* Dr. Tom Timmerman, Director, 931-372-3600, Fax: 931-372-6249. *Application contact:* Shelia K. Kendrick, Coordinator of Graduate Admissions, 931-372-3808, Fax: 931-372-3497, E-mail: skendrick@tntech.edu. Web site: http://www.tntech.edu/mba.

Tennessee Technological University, Graduate School, Program of Professional Studies, Cookeville, TN 38505. Offers human resources leadership (MPS); strategic leadership (MPS); training and development (MPS). Part-time and evening/weekend programs available. Postbaccalaureate distance learning degree programs offered (no on-campus study). *Students:* 2 full-time (both women), 31 part-time (19 women); includes 5 minority (3 Black or African American, non-Hispanic/Latino; 1 American Indian or Alaska Native, non-Hispanic/Latino; 1 Hispanic/Latino). 17 applicants, 71% accepted, 7 enrolled. In 2011, 10 master's awarded. *Degree requirements:* For master's, comprehensive exam, thesis or alternative. *Entrance requirements:* For master's, GRE. Additional exam requirements/recommendations for international students: Required—TOEFL (minimum score 550 paper-based; 79 iBT), IELTS (minimum score 5.5), Pearson Test of English Academic. *Application deadline:* For fall admission, 8/1 for domestic students, 5/1 for international students; for spring admission, 12/1 for domestic students, 10/1 for international students. Application fee: $25 ($30 for international students). Electronic applications accepted. *Expenses:* Tuition, state resident: full-time $8094; part-time $422 per credit hour. Tuition, nonresident: full-time $20,574; part-time $1046 per credit hour. *Financial support:* Application deadline: 4/1. *Unit head:* Dr. Susan A. Elkins, Dean, School of Interdisciplinary Studies, 931-372-3394, Fax: 372-372-3499, E-mail: selkins@tntech.edu. *Application contact:* Shelia K. Kendrick, Coordinator of Graduate Admissions, 931-372-3808, Fax: 931-372-3497, E-mail: skendrick@tntech.edu.

Texas A&M University, Mays Business School, Department of Management, College Station, TX 77843. Offers human resource management (MS); management (PhD). *Faculty:* 27. *Students:* 71 full-time (46 women), 1 (woman) part-time; includes 12 minority (4 Black or African American, non-Hispanic/Latino; 5 Asian, non-Hispanic/Latino; 3 Hispanic/Latino), 6 international. Average age 31. 76 applicants, 28% accepted. In 2011, 32 master's, 2 doctorates awarded. Terminal master's awarded for partial completion of doctoral program. *Degree requirements:* For master's, comprehensive exam; for doctorate, thesis/dissertation. *Entrance requirements:* For master's, GMAT or GRE; for doctorate, GMAT or GRE General Test. Additional exam requirements/recommendations for international students: Required—TOEFL. *Application deadline:* For fall admission, 3/1 priority date for domestic students; for spring admission, 8/1 for domestic students. Applications are processed on a rolling basis. Application fee: $50 ($75 for international students). *Expenses:* Tuition, state resident: full-time $5437; part-time $226.55 per credit hour. Tuition, nonresident: full-time $12,949; part-time $539.55 per credit hour. *Required fees:* $2741. *Financial support:* In 2011–12, 25 students received support. Fellowships, research assistantships, teaching assistantships, career-related internships or fieldwork, and institutionally sponsored loans available. Financial award application deadline: 2/1. *Faculty research:* Strategic and human resource management, business and public policy, organizational behavior, organizational theory. *Unit head:* Dr. Ricky W. Griffin, Head, 979-862-3962, Fax: 979-845-9641, E-mail: rgriffin@mays.tamu.edu. *Application contact:* Kristi Mora, Senior Academic Advisor II, 979-845-6127, E-mail: kmora@mays.tamu.edu. Web site: http://mays.tamu.edu/mgmt/.

Texas A&M University–San Antonio, School of Business, San Antonio, TX 78224. Offers business administration (MBA); enterprise resource planning systems (MBA); finance (MBA); healthcare management (MBA); human resources management (MBA); information assurance and security (MBA); international business (MBA); professional accounting (MPA); project management (MBA); supply chain management (MBA). Part-time and evening/weekend programs available. *Faculty:* 18 full-time (6 women), 1 part-time/adjunct (0 women). *Students:* 91 full-time (45 women), 278 part-time (150 women). Average age 33. In 2011, 20 master's awarded. *Entrance requirements:* For master's, GMAT. Additional exam requirements/recommendations for international students: Required—TOEFL (minimum score 550 paper-based; 213 computer-based; 80 iBT), IELTS (minimum score 6). *Application deadline:* For fall admission, 7/1 priority date for domestic students, 6/1 for international students; for spring admission, 11/15 priority date for domestic students, 10/1 for international students. Applications are processed on a rolling basis. Application fee: $35 ($50 for international students). Electronic applications accepted. *Expenses:* Tuition, state resident: part-time $691.11 per course. Tuition, nonresident: part-time $1621.11 per course. *Financial support:* Application deadline: 3/31; applicants required to submit FAFSA. *Unit head:* Dr. Tracy Hurley, MBA Coordinator, 210-932-6200, E-mail: tracy.hurley@tamusa.tamus.edu. *Application contact:* Melissa A. Villanueva, Graduate Admissions Specialist, 210-932-6200, Fax: 210-932-6209, E-mail: melissa.villanueva@tamusa.tamus.edu. Web site: http://www.tamusa.tamus.edu.

Thomas College, Graduate School, Programs in Business, Waterville, ME 04901-5097. Offers business (MBA); computer technology education (MS); education (MS); human resource management (MBA). Part-time and evening/weekend programs available. *Entrance requirements:* For master's, GMAT, GRE, MAT or minimum GPA of 3.3 in first 3 graduate-level courses. Additional exam requirements/recommendations for international students: Recommended—TOEFL.

Thomas Edison State College, School of Business and Management, Program in Human Resources Management, Trenton, NJ 08608-1176. Offers MSHRM, Graduate Certificate. Part-time programs available. Postbaccalaureate distance learning degree programs offered (no on-campus study). *Students:* 106 part-time (76 women); includes 45 minority (29 Black or African American, non-Hispanic/Latino; 3 Asian, non-Hispanic/Latino; 13 Hispanic/Latino), 3 international. Average age 41. In 2011, 18 master's, 2 other advanced degrees awarded. *Degree requirements:* For master's, final/capstone project. *Entrance requirements:* For master's, bachelor's degree from a regionally-accredited college or university; minimum 2 letters of recommendation; 3-5 years of related working experience; current resume. Additional exam requirements/recommendations for international students: Required—TOEFL (minimum score 550 paper-based; 213 computer-based; 79 iBT). *Application deadline:* For fall admission, 8/15 priority date for domestic students, 8/15 for international students; for winter admission, 11/15 priority date for domestic students, 11/15 for international students; for spring admission, 2/15 priority date for domestic students, 2/15 for international students. Applications are processed on a rolling basis. Application fee: $75. Electronic applications accepted. *Financial support:* Applicants required to submit FAFSA. *Unit head:* Dr. Susan Gilbert, Dean, School of Business and Management, 609-984-1130, Fax: 609-984-3898, E-mail: info@tesc.edu. *Application contact:* David Hoftiezer, Director of Admissions, 888-442-8372, Fax: 609-984-8447, E-mail: admissions@tesc.edu. Web site: http://www.tesc.edu/business/mshrm/.

Tiffin University, Program in Business Administration, Tiffin, OH 44883-2161. Offers finance (MBA); general management (MBA); healthcare administration (MBA); human resources (MBA); international business (MBA); leadership (MBA); marketing (MBA); sports management (MBA). *Accreditation:* ACBSP. Part-time and evening/weekend programs available. Postbaccalaureate distance learning degree programs offered (no on-campus study). *Faculty:* 30 full-time (15 women), 22 part-time/adjunct (6 women). *Students:* 209 full-time (107 women), 340 part-time (172 women); includes 112 minority (91 Black or African American, non-Hispanic/Latino; 4 Asian, non-Hispanic/Latino; 17 Hispanic/Latino), 71 international. Average age 31. 237 applicants, 76% accepted. In 2011, 170 master's awarded. *Entrance requirements:* For master's, minimum undergraduate GPA of 2.5, work experience. Additional exam requirements/recommendations for international students: Required—TOEFL (minimum score 550 paper-based; 213 computer-based; 79 iBT). *Application deadline:* For fall admission, 8/15 for domestic students, 8/1 for international students; for spring admission, 1/9 for domestic students, 12/1 for international students. Applications are processed on a rolling basis. Electronic applications accepted. *Expenses: Tuition:* Full-time $11,200; part-time $700 per credit. Tuition and fees vary according to program. *Financial support:* Available to part-time students. Application deadline: 7/31; applicants required to submit FAFSA. *Faculty research:* Small business, executive development operations, research and statistical analysis, market research, management information systems. *Unit head:* Dr. Lillian Schumacher, Dean of the School of Business, 419-448-3053, Fax: 419-443-5002, E-mail: schumacherlb@tiffin.edu. *Application contact:* Nikki Hintze, Director of Graduate Admissions and Student Services, 800-968-6446 Ext. 3445, Fax: 419-443-5002, E-mail: hintzenm@tiffin.edu. Web site: http://www.tiffin.edu/graduateprograms/.

Trident University International, College of Business Administration, Program in Business Administration, Cypress, CA 90630. Offers business administration (PhD); conflict and negotiation management (MBA); criminal justice administration (MBA); entrepreneurship (MBA); finance (MBA); general management (MBA); government accounting (MBA); human resource management (MBA); information security and digital assurance management (MBA); information technology management (MBA); international business (MBA); logistics management (MBA); marketing (MBA); project management (MBA); public management (MBA); quality management (MBA); strategic leadership (MBA). Part-time and evening/weekend programs available. Postbaccalaureate distance learning degree programs offered (no on-campus study). *Degree requirements:* For doctorate, comprehensive exam, thesis/dissertation, defense of dissertation. *Entrance requirements:* For master's, minimum GPA of 2.5 (students with GPA 3.0 or greater may transfer up to 30% of graduate level credits); for doctorate, minimum GPA of 3.4, curriculum vitae, course work in research methods or statistics. Additional exam requirements/recommendations for international students: Required—TOEFL. Electronic applications accepted.

Trinity Washington University, School of Professional Studies, Washington, DC 20017-1094. Offers business administration (MBA); communication (MA); international security studies (MA); organizational management (MSA), including federal program management, human resource management, nonprofit management, organizational development, public and community health. Part-time and evening/weekend programs available. *Degree requirements:* For master's, thesis (for some programs), capstone project (MSA). *Entrance requirements:* For master's, minimum GPA of 2.5. Additional exam requirements/recommendations for international students: Required—TOEFL (minimum score 550 paper-based; 213 computer-based).

Troy University, Graduate School, College of Arts and Sciences, Program in Public Administration, Troy, AL 36082. Offers education (MPA); environmental management (MPA); government contracting (MPA); health care administration (MPA); justice administration (MPA); national security affairs (MPA); nonprofit management (MPA); public human resources management (MPA); public management (MPA). *Accreditation:* NASPAA. Part-time and evening/weekend programs available. Postbaccalaureate distance learning degree programs offered (no on-campus study). *Faculty:* 17 full-time (10 women), 10 part-time/adjunct (3 women). *Students:* 97 full-time (71 women), 400 part-time (259 women); includes 298 minority (264 Black or African American, non-Hispanic/Latino; 5 American Indian or Alaska Native, non-Hispanic/Latino; 15 Asian, non-Hispanic/Latino; 11 Hispanic/Latino; 3 Two or more races, non-Hispanic/Latino). Average age 33. 323 applicants, 63% accepted, 97 enrolled. In 2011, 249 master's awarded. *Degree requirements:* For master's, capstone course, minimum GPA of 3.0, admission to candidacy. *Entrance requirements:* For master's, GRE (minimum score of 920), MAT (minimum score of 400) or GMAT (minimum score of 490), minimum undergraduate GPA of 2.5, letter of recommendation, essay. Additional exam requirements/recommendations for international students: Required—TOEFL (minimum score 523 paper-based; 193 computer-based; 70 iBT), IELTS (minimum score 6). *Application deadline:* Applications are processed on a rolling basis. Application fee: $50. Electronic applications accepted. *Expenses:* Tuition, state resident: full-time $6960; part-time $290 per credit hour. Tuition, nonresident: full-time $13,920; part-time $580 per credit hour. *Required fees:* $386 per term. *Financial support:* Available to part-time students. Applicants required to submit FAFSA. *Unit head:* Dr. Charles Kruprick, Chairman, 334-670-5968, Fax: 334-670-5647, E-mail: ckrupnickl@troy.edu. *Application contact:* Brenda K. Campbell, Director of Graduate Admissions, 334-670-3178, Fax: 334-670-3733, E-mail: bcamp@troy.edu.

Troy University, Graduate School, College of Business, Program in Human Resources Management, Troy, AL 36082. Offers MS. Part-time and evening/weekend programs available. *Faculty:* 14 full-time (5 women), 6 part-time/adjunct (5 women). *Students:* 50 full-time (34 women), 299 part-time (235 women); includes 286 minority (270 Black or African American, non-Hispanic/Latino; 4 Asian, non-Hispanic/Latino; 9 Hispanic/Latino; 3 Two or more races, non-Hispanic/Latino). Average age 34. 153 applicants, 76% accepted, 60 enrolled. In 2011, 196 master's awarded. *Degree requirements:* For master's, minimum GPA of 3.0; admission to candidacy. *Entrance requirements:* For master's, GMAT (minimum score 500) or GRE General Test (minimum score 900), minimum GPA of 2.5; letter of recommendation; bachelor's degree. Additional exam requirements/recommendations for international students: Required—TOEFL (minimum score 523 paper-based; 193 computer-based; 70 iBT), IELTS (minimum score 6), or ACT COMPASS ESL (minimum listening, reading, and grammar score 270). *Application deadline:* Applications are processed on a rolling basis. Application fee: $50. *Expenses:* Tuition, state resident: full-time $6960; part-time $290 per credit hour. Tuition, nonresident: full-time $13,920; part-time $580 per credit hour. *Required fees:* $386 per term. *Unit head:* Dr. Edward Merkel, Director, Graduate Business Programs, 334-241-3194, E-mail: emerkel@troy.edu. *Application contact:* Brenda K. Campbell, Director of Graduate Admissions, 334-670-3178, Fax: 334-670-3733, E-mail: bcamp@troy.edu.

Troy University, Graduate School, College of Business, Program in Management, Troy, AL 36082. Offers applied management (MSM); healthcare management (MSM); human resources management (MSM); information systems (MSM); international hospitality management (MSM); international management (MSM); leadership and organizational effectiveness (MSM); public management (MS, MSM). *Accreditation:* ACBSP. Evening/weekend programs available. *Faculty:* 21 full-time (6 women), 7 part-time/adjunct (2 women). *Students:* 52 full-time (33 women), 284 part-time (183 women); includes 222 minority (186 Black or African American, non-Hispanic/Latino; 5 American Indian or Alaska Native, non-Hispanic/Latino; 11 Asian, non-Hispanic/Latino; 13 Hispanic/Latino; 1 Native Hawaiian or other Pacific Islander, non-Hispanic/Latino; 6 Two or more races, non-Hispanic/Latino). Average age 35. 157 applicants, 76% accepted, 55 enrolled. In 2011, 234 master's awarded. *Degree requirements:* For master's, Graduate

Educational Testing Service Major Field Test, capstone exam, minimum GPA of 3.0. *Entrance requirements:* For master's, GMAT (minimum score 500) or GRE General Test (minimum score 900), minimum GPA of 2.5, bachelor's degree, letter of recommendation. Additional exam requirements/recommendations for international students: Required—TOEFL (minimum score 523 paper-based; 193 computer-based; 70 iBT), IELTS (minimum score 6), or ACT COMPASS ESL (minimum listening, reading, and grammar score 270). *Application deadline:* Applications are processed on a rolling basis. Application fee: $50. Electronic applications accepted. *Expenses:* Contact institution. *Unit head:* Dr. Edward Merkel, Director, Graduate Business Programs, 334-670-3194, Fax: 334-670-3599, E-mail: emerkel@troy.edu. *Application contact:* Brenda K. Campbell, Director of Graduate Admissions, 334-670-3178, Fax: 334-670-3733, E-mail: bcamp@troy.edu.

Union Graduate College, School of Management, Schenectady, NY 12308-3107. Offers business administration (MBA); financial management (Certificate); general management (Certificate); health systems administration (MBA, Certificate); human resources (Certificate). *Accreditation:* AACSB. Part-time and evening/weekend programs available. *Faculty:* 18 full-time (4 women), 25 part-time/adjunct (4 women). *Students:* 122 full-time (53 women), 102 part-time (59 women); includes 47 minority (6 Black or African American, non-Hispanic/Latino; 35 Asian, non-Hispanic/Latino; 4 Hispanic/Latino; 2 Two or more races, non-Hispanic/Latino), 5 international. Average age 27. 101 applicants, 75% accepted, 68 enrolled. In 2011, 73 master's, 9 other advanced degrees awarded. *Degree requirements:* For master's, internship, capstone course. *Entrance requirements:* For master's, GMAT, GRE, minimum GPA of 3.0, 3 letters of recommendation. Additional exam requirements/recommendations for international students: Required—TOEFL (minimum score 550 paper-based; 213 computer-based). *Application deadline:* Applications are processed on a rolling basis. Application fee: $60. *Expenses: Tuition:* Full-time $22,000; part-time $775 per credit. One-time fee: $410 full-time. Tuition and fees vary according to course load and program. *Financial support:* In 2011–12, 79 students received support. Research assistantships, career-related internships or fieldwork, Federal Work-Study, scholarships/grants, health care benefits, and tuition waivers (partial) available. Support available to part-time students. Financial award applicants required to submit FAFSA. *Unit head:* Bela Musits, Dean, 518-631-9890, Fax: 518-631-9902, E-mail: musitsb@uniongraduatecollege.edu. *Application contact:* Diane Trzaskos, Admissions Coordinator, 518-631-9837, Fax: 518-631-9901, E-mail: trzaskod@uniongraduatecollege.edu. Web site: http://www.uniongraduatecollege.edu.

United States International University, School of Business Administration, Nairobi, Kenya. Offers business administration (GEMBA); entrepreneurship (MBA); finance (MBA); human resource management (MBA); information technology management (MBA); integrated studies (MBA); international business administration (MBA); management and organizational development (MS); marketing (MBA); organizational development (EMS); strategic management (MBA). Part-time and evening/weekend programs available. *Degree requirements:* For master's, thesis. *Entrance requirements:* For master's, GMAT, 2 letters of reference, resume. Additional exam requirements/recommendations for international students: Required—TOEFL (minimum score 550 paper-based; 213 computer-based). *Faculty research:* Marketing in small business enterprises, total quality management in Kenya.

Universidad del Este, Graduate School, Carolina, PR 00984. Offers accounting (MBA); adult education (M Ed); agribusiness (MBA); criminal justice and criminology (MA); curriculum and instruction - early education (M Ed); curriculum and instruction - elementary (M Ed); curriculum and instruction - English (M Ed); curriculum and instruction - Spanish (M Ed); human resources (MBA); information security management (MBA); information technology and Web business development (MBA); management (MBA); public policy (MPA); social work (MA), including clinical social work; special education (M Ed); strategic leadership (MBA).

Universidad del Turabo, Graduate Programs, School in Business Administration, Program in Human Resources, Gurabo, PR 00778-3030. Offers MBA. *Students:* 39 full-time (30 women), 68 part-time (58 women); includes 95 minority (all Hispanic/Latino). Average age 32. 70 applicants, 80% accepted, 42 enrolled. In 2011, 58 master's awarded. *Unit head:* Marcelino Rivera, Dean, 787-743-7979 Ext. 4117. *Application contact:* Virginia Gonzalez, Admissions Officer, 787-746-3009.

Universidad Metropolitana, School of Business Administration, Program in Human Resources Management, San Juan, PR 00928-1150. Offers MBA. Part-time programs available.

University at Albany, State University of New York, School of Business, Department of Management, Albany, NY 12222-0001. Offers human resource systems (MBA). *Degree requirements:* For master's, field study project. *Entrance requirements:* For master's, GMAT. Additional exam requirements/recommendations for international students: Required—TOEFL (minimum score 550 paper-based; 213 computer-based). Electronic applications accepted. *Faculty research:* Leadership, strategic management, performance appraisal, franchising, job satisfaction.

University at Buffalo, the State University of New York, Graduate School, Graduate School of Education, Department of Educational Leadership and Policy, Buffalo, NY 14260. Offers educational administration (Ed M, PhD); educational culture, policy and society (PhD); general education (Ed M); higher education administration (Ed M, PhD); school building leadership (LIFTS) (Certificate); school business and human resource administration (Certificate); school district business leadership (LIFTS) (Certificate); school district leadership (LIFTS) (Certificate). Part-time and evening/weekend programs available. *Faculty:* 12 full-time (7 women), 9 part-time/adjunct (7 women). *Students:* 79 full-time (55 women), 136 part-time (76 women); includes 47 minority (24 Black or African American, non-Hispanic/Latino; 1 American Indian or Alaska Native, non-Hispanic/Latino; 9 Asian, non-Hispanic/Latino; 13 Hispanic/Latino), 17 international. Average age 35. 194 applicants, 40% accepted, 73 enrolled. In 2011, 44 master's, 18 doctorates, 25 other advanced degrees awarded. *Degree requirements:* For master's, comprehensive exam (for some programs), thesis optional; for doctorate, comprehensive exam, thesis/dissertation. *Entrance requirements:* For doctorate, GRE General Test or MAT, writing sample. Additional exam requirements/recommendations for international students: Required—TOEFL (minimum score 550 paper-based; 213 computer-based; 79 iBT). *Application deadline:* For fall admission, 3/1 priority date for domestic students, 3/1 for international students; for spring admission, 11/15 priority date for domestic students, 10/1 for international students. Applications are processed on a rolling basis. Application fee: $50. Electronic applications accepted. *Financial support:* In 2011–12, 21 fellowships (averaging $10,298 per year), 9 research assistantships (averaging $11,955 per year) were awarded; career-related internships or fieldwork, Federal Work-Study, institutionally sponsored loans, health care benefits, and unspecified assistantships also available. Financial award application deadline: 3/15; financial award applicants required to submit FAFSA. *Faculty research:* College access and choice, school leadership preparation and practice, public policy, curriculum and pedagogy, comparative and international education. *Unit head:* Dr. William C. Barba, Chairman, 716-645-2471, Fax: 716-645-2481, E-mail: barba@buffalo.edu. *Application contact:* Bonnie Reed, Admissions Assistant, 716-645-2110, Fax: 716-645-7937, E-mail: brfisher@buffalo.edu. Web site: http://gse.buffalo.edu/elp.

The University of Akron, Graduate School, College of Business Administration, Department of Management, Program in Human Resources, Akron, OH 44325. Offers MSM. *Students:* 5 full-time (all women), 3 part-time (all women); includes 1 minority (Asian, non-Hispanic/Latino), 1 international. Average age 30. 8 applicants, 13% accepted, 1 enrolled. In 2011, 5 master's awarded. *Entrance requirements:* For master's, GMAT, minimum GPA of 2.75, two letters of recommendation, statement of purpose, resume. Additional exam requirements/recommendations for international students: Required—TOEFL (minimum score 550 paper-based; 213 computer-based; 79 iBT). *Application deadline:* For fall admission, 7/15 for domestic and international students; for spring admission, 11/15 for domestic and international students. Application fee: $30 ($40 for international students). Electronic applications accepted. *Expenses:* Tuition, state resident: full-time $7038; part-time $391 per credit hour. Tuition, nonresident: full-time $12,051; part-time $670 per credit hour. *Required fees:* $1274; $34 per credit hour. *Unit head:* Dr. Steve Ash, Interim Chair, 330-972-6086, Fax: 330-972-6588, E-mail: ash@uakron.edu. *Application contact:* Dr. Susan Hanlon, Director of Graduate Business Programs, 330-972-7043, Fax: 330-972-6588, E-mail: shanlon@uakron.edu.

The University of Alabama in Huntsville, School of Graduate Studies, College of Business Administration, Department of Management and Marketing, Huntsville, AL 35899. Offers federal contract procurement (Certificate); management (MBA), including acquisition management, entrepreneurship, federal contract accounting, finance, human resource management, logistics and supply chain management, marketing, project management; supply chain management (Certificate); technology and innovation management (Certificate). *Accreditation:* AACSB. Part-time and evening/weekend programs available. *Faculty:* 11 full-time (2 women), 3 part-time/adjunct (0 women). *Students:* 52 full-time (25 women), 145 part-time (68 women); includes 28 minority (14 Black or African American, non-Hispanic/Latino; 4 American Indian or Alaska Native, non-Hispanic/Latino; 7 Asian, non-Hispanic/Latino; 2 Hispanic/Latino; 1 Two or more races, non-Hispanic/Latino), 15 international. Average age 31. 103 applicants, 73% accepted, 65 enrolled. In 2011, 76 master's awarded. *Degree requirements:* For master's, comprehensive exam, thesis or alternative. *Entrance requirements:* For master's, GMAT (minimum score 500), minimum AACSB index of 1080. Additional exam requirements/recommendations for international students: Required—TOEFL (minimum score 550 paper-based; 213 computer-based; 62 iBT). *Application deadline:* For fall admission, 8/1 for domestic students, 4/1 for international students; for spring admission, 12/1 for domestic students, 9/1 for international students. Applications are processed on a rolling basis. Application fee: $40 ($50 for international students). Electronic applications accepted. *Expenses:* Tuition, state resident: full-time $7830; part-time $473.50 per credit. Tuition, nonresident: full-time $18,748; part-time $1128.33 per credit. Tuition and fees vary according to course load and program. *Financial support:* In 2011–12, 12 students received support, including 7 research assistantships with full tuition reimbursements available (averaging $9,829 per year), 4 teaching assistantships with full tuition reimbursements available (averaging $8,000 per year); career-related internships or fieldwork, Federal Work-Study, institutionally sponsored loans, scholarships/grants, health care benefits, and unspecified assistantships also available. Support available to part-time students. Financial award application deadline: 4/1; financial award applicants required to submit FAFSA. *Faculty research:* Strategic human resources, corporate governance, cross-function integration and the management of research and development, determinants of team performance. *Total annual research expenditures:* $3.4 million. *Unit head:* Dr. Cynthia Gramm, Chair, 256-824-6913, Fax: 256-824-6328, E-mail: cynthia.gramm@uah.edu. *Application contact:* Jennifer Pettitt, Director of Graduate Programs, 256-824-6681, Fax: 256-824-7571, E-mail: jennifer.pettitt@uah.edu.

University of Bridgeport, School of Business, Bridgeport, CT 06604. Offers accounting (MBA); finance (MBA); general business (MBA); global financial services (MBA); human resource management (MBA); information systems and knowledge management (MBA); international business (MBA); management (MBA); marketing (MBA); operations management (MBA); small business and entrepreneurship (MBA); specialized business (MBA). Part-time and evening/weekend programs available. *Faculty:* 11 full-time (2 women), 39 part-time/adjunct (8 women). *Students:* 198 full-time (105 women), 94 part-time (47 women); includes 38 minority (16 Black or African American, non-Hispanic/Latino; 9 Asian, non-Hispanic/Latino; 10 Hispanic/Latino; 3 Two or more races, non-Hispanic/Latino), 227 international. Average age 28. 835 applicants, 56% accepted, 57 enrolled. In 2011, 155 master's awarded. *Degree requirements:* For master's, thesis optional. *Entrance requirements:* For master's, GMAT. Additional exam requirements/recommendations for international students: Recommended—TOEFL (minimum score 550 paper-based; 213 computer-based; 80 iBT), IELTS (minimum score 6.5). *Application deadline:* For fall admission, 8/1 priority date for domestic students, 8/1 for international students; for spring admission, 12/1 priority date for domestic students, 12/1 for international students. Applications are processed on a rolling basis. Application fee: $50. Electronic applications accepted. *Expenses:* Contact institution. *Financial support:* In 2011–12, 69 students received support. Fellowships, research assistantships, teaching assistantships, career-related internships or fieldwork, Federal Work-Study, institutionally sponsored loans, and tuition waivers (partial) available. Support available to part-time students. Financial award application deadline: 6/1; financial award applicants required to submit FAFSA. *Unit head:* Dr. Robert Gilmore, Dean, 203-576-4384, Fax: 203-576-4388, E-mail: rgilmore@bridgeport.edu. *Application contact:* Karissa Peckham, Dean of Admissions, 203-576-4552, Fax: 203-576-4941, E-mail: mba@bridgeport.edu. Web site: http://www.bridgeport.edu.

University of California, Berkeley, UC Berkeley Extension, Certificate Programs in Business, Berkeley, CA 94720-1500. Offers accounting (Certificate); business administration (Certificate); finance (Certificate); human resource management (Certificate); management (Certificate); marketing (Certificate); project management (Certificate). *Accreditation:* AACSB. Postbaccalaureate distance learning degree programs offered.

University of Chicago, Booth School of Business, Full-Time MBA Program, Chicago, IL 60637. Offers accounting (MBA); analytic finance (MBA); analytic management (MBA); business administration (PhD); econometrics and statistics (MBA); economics (MBA); entrepreneurship (MBA); finance (MBA); general management (MBA); health administration and policy (Certificate); human resource management (MBA); international business (IMBA, MBA); managerial and organizational behavior (MBA); marketing management (MBA); operations management (MBA); strategic management (MBA); MBA/AM; MBA/JD; MBA/MA; MBA/MD; MBA/MPP. *Accreditation:* AACSB. Part-time and evening/weekend programs available. *Faculty:* 166 full-time, 32 part-time/adjunct. *Students:* 1,160 full-time (412 women); includes 316 minority (61 Black or African American, non-Hispanic/Latino; 173 Asian, non-Hispanic/Latino; 63 Hispanic/Latino; 19 Two or more races, non-Hispanic/Latino), 378 international. Average age 28. 4,169 applicants, 575 enrolled. In 2011, 1,423 master's, 19 doctorates awarded. Terminal master's awarded for partial completion of doctoral program. *Entrance requirements:* For master's, GMAT, 2 letters of recommendation, 3 essays, resume, interview. Additional exam requirements/recommendations for international students: Required—TOEFL (minimum score 600 paper-based; 250 computer-based; 104 iBT), IELTS. *Application deadline:* For fall admission, 10/12 priority date for domestic students, 10/12 for international students; for winter admission, 1/4 for domestic and international students; for spring admission, 4/4 for domestic and international students. Application fee: $200. Electronic applications accepted. *Expenses:* Contact institution. *Financial support:* Fellowships available. Financial award applicants required to submit FAFSA. *Faculty research:* Finance, marketing, economics, entrepreneurship, strategy, management. *Unit head:* Stacey Kole, Deputy Dean, 773-702-7121. *Application contact:* Kurt Ahlm, Associate Dean of Student Recruitment and Admissions, 773-702-7369, Fax: 773-702-9085, E-mail: admissions@chicagobooth.edu. Web site: http://chicagobooth.edu/.

University of Colorado Denver, Business School, Master of Business Administration Program, Denver, CO 80217. Offers business intelligence (MBA); business strategy (MBA); business to business marketing (MBA); business to consumer marketing (MBA); change management (MBA); corporate financial management (MBA); enterprise technology management (MBA); entrepreneurship (MBA); health administration (MBA), including financial management, health administration, health information technologies, international health management and policy; human resources management (MBA); investment management (MBA); managing for sustainability (MBA); services management (MBA); sports and entertainment management (MBA). *Accreditation:* AACSB. Part-time and evening/weekend programs available. Postbaccalaureate distance learning degree programs offered (no on-campus study). *Students:* 784 full-time (306 women), 203 part-time (81 women); includes 135 minority (18 Black or African American, non-Hispanic/Latino; 5 American Indian or Alaska Native, non-Hispanic/Latino; 50 Asian, non-Hispanic/Latino; 58 Hispanic/Latino; 4 Two or more races, non-Hispanic/Latino), 38 international. Average age 31. 433 applicants, 76% accepted, 212 enrolled. In 2011, 326 master's awarded. *Degree requirements:* For master's, 48 semester hours, including 30 of core courses, 3 in international business, and 15 in electives from over 50 other graduate business courses. *Entrance requirements:* For master's, GMAT, resume, official transcripts, essay, two letters of recommendation, financial statements (for international applicants). Additional exam requirements/recommendations for international students: Required—TOEFL (minimum score 560 paper-based; 197 computer-based; 83 iBT). *Application deadline:* For fall admission, 4/15 priority date for domestic students, 3/15 for international students; for spring admission, 10/15 priority date for domestic students, 10/1 for international students. Applications are processed on a rolling basis. Application fee: $50 ($75 for international students). Electronic applications accepted. *Expenses:* Contact institution. *Financial support:* Scholarships/grants available. Support available to part-time students. Financial award application deadline: 4/1; financial award applicants required to submit FAFSA. *Faculty research:* Marketing, management, entrepreneurship, finance, health administration. *Unit head:* Elizabeth Cooperman, Professor of Finance and Managing for Sustainability/MBA Program Director, 303-315-8422, E-mail: elizabeth.cooperman@ucdenver.edu. *Application contact:* Shelly Townley, Admissions Director, Graduate Programs, 303-315-8202, E-mail: shelly.townley@ucdenver.edu. Web site: http://www.ucdenver.edu/academics/colleges/business/degrees/ms/accounting/Pages/Accounting.aspx.

University of Colorado Denver, Business School, Program in Management and Organization, Denver, CO 80217. Offers communications management (MS); entrepreneurship and innovation (MS); global management (MS); human resources management (MS); leadership and management (MS); sports and entertainment management (MS). *Accreditation:* AACSB. Part-time and evening/weekend programs available. Postbaccalaureate distance learning degree programs offered (no on-campus study). *Students:* 29 full-time (14 women), 14 part-time (10 women); includes 3 minority (2 Asian, non-Hispanic/Latino; 1 Hispanic/Latino), 5 international. Average age 31. 32 applicants, 63% accepted, 14 enrolled. In 2011, 22 master's awarded. *Degree requirements:* For master's, 30 semester hours (12 of required courses, 12 of management electives, and 6 of free electives). *Entrance requirements:* For master's, GMAT, resume, two letters of recommendation, essay, financial statements (for international applicants). Additional exam requirements/recommendations for international students: Required—TOEFL (minimum score 525 paper-based; 197 computer-based; 71 iBT). *Application deadline:* For fall admission, 4/15 priority date for domestic students, 3/15 for international students; for spring admission, 10/15 priority date for domestic students, 10/1 for international students. Applications are processed on a rolling basis. Application fee: $50 ($75 for international students). Electronic applications accepted. *Expenses:* Contact institution. *Financial support:* Federal Work-Study and scholarships/grants available. Support available to part-time students. Financial award application deadline: 4/1; financial award applicants required to submit FAFSA. *Faculty research:* Human resource management, management of catastrophe, turnaround strategies. *Unit head:* Dr. Kenneth Bettenhausen, Associate Professor/Director of MS in Management, 303-315-8425, E-mail: kenneth.bettenhausen@ucdenver.edu. *Application contact:* Shelly Townley, Admissions Director, Graduate Programs, 303-315-8202, E-mail: shelly.townley@ucdenver.edu. Web site: http://www.ucdenver.edu/academics/colleges/business/degrees/ms/management/Pages/Management.aspx.

University of Connecticut, Graduate School, Center for Continuing Studies, Program in Human Resource Management, Storrs, CT 06269. Offers labor relations (MPS); personnel (MPS).

University of Dallas, Graduate School of Management, Irving, TX 75062-4736. Offers accounting (MBA, MM, MS); business management (MBA, MM); corporate finance (MBA, MM); financial services (MBA); global business (MBA, MM); health services management (MBA, MM); human resource management (MBA, MM); information assurance (MBA, MM, MS); information technology (MBA, MM, MS); information technology service management (MBA, MM, MS); marketing management (MBA, MM); organization development (MBA, MM); project management (MBA, MM); sports and entertainment management (MBA, MM); strategic leadership (MBA, MM); supply chain management (MBA); supply chain management and market logistics (MM). *Accreditation:* ACBSP. Part-time and evening/weekend programs available. Postbaccalaureate distance learning degree programs offered (no on-campus study). *Entrance requirements:* Additional exam requirements/recommendations for international students: Required—TOEFL. Electronic applications accepted. *Expenses:* Contact institution.

University of Denver, University College, Denver, CO 80208. Offers arts and culture (MLS, Certificate), including art, literature, and culture, arts development and program management (Certificate), creative writing; environmental policy and management (MAS, Certificate), including energy and sustainability (Certificate), environmental assessment of nuclear power (Certificate), environmental health and safety (Certificate), environmental management, natural resource management (Certificate); geographic information systems (MAS, Certificate); global affairs (MLS, Certificate), including translation studies, world history and culture; healthcare leadership (MPH, Certificate), including healthcare policy, law, and ethics, medical and healthcare information technologies, strategic management of healthcare; information and communications technology (MCIS, Certificate), including database design and administration (Certificate), geographic information systems (MCIS), information security systems security (Certificate), information systems security (MCIS), project management (MCIS, MPS, Certificate), software design and administration (Certificate), software design and programming (MCIS), technology management, telecommunications technology (MCIS), Web design and development; leadership and organizations (MPS, Certificate), including human capital in organizations, philanthropic leadership, project management (MCIS, MPS, Certificate), strategic innovation and change; organizational and professional communication (MPS, Certificate), including alternative dispute resolution, organizational communication, organizational development and training, public relations and marketing; security management (MAS, Certificate), including emergency planning and response, information security (MAS), organizational security; strategic human resource management (MPS, Certificate), including global human resources (MPS), human resource management and development (MPS). Part-time and evening/weekend programs available. Postbaccalaureate distance learning degree programs offered (no on-campus study). *Faculty:* 204 part-time/adjunct (80 women). *Students:* 56 full-time (26 women), 1,096 part-time (647 women); includes 196 minority (81 Black or African American, non-Hispanic/Latino; 7 American Indian or Alaska Native, non-Hispanic/Latino; 30 Asian, non-Hispanic/Latino; 66 Hispanic/Latino; 3 Native Hawaiian or other Pacific Islander, non-Hispanic/Latino; 9 Two or more races, non-Hispanic/Latino), 76 international. Average age 36. 572 applicants, 95% accepted, 410 enrolled. In 2011, 404 master's, 123 other advanced degrees awarded. *Degree requirements:* For master's, capstone project. *Entrance requirements:* For master's, two letters of recommendation, personal statement, resume. Additional exam requirements/recommendations for international students: Required—TOEFL (minimum score 550 paper-based; 80 iBT). *Application deadline:* For fall admission, 7/20 priority date for domestic students, 6/8 for international students; for winter admission, 10/26 priority date for domestic students, 9/14 for international students; for spring admission, 2/1 priority date for domestic students, 12/14 for international students. Applications are processed on a rolling basis. Application fee: $75. Electronic applications accepted. *Expenses:* Contact institution. *Financial support:* Applicants required to submit FAFSA. *Unit head:* Dr. James Davis, Dean, 303-871-2291, Fax: 303-871-4047, E-mail: jdavis@du.edu. *Application contact:* Information Contact, 303-871-3155, Fax: 303-871-4047, E-mail: ucolinfo@du.edu. Web site: http://www.universitycollege.du.edu/.

University of Florida, Graduate School, Warrington College of Business Administration, Hough Graduate School of Business, Programs in Business Administration, Gainesville, FL 32611. Offers accounting (MBA); arts administration (MBA); business strategy and public policy (MBA); competitive strategy (MBA); decision and information sciences (MBA); electronic commerce (MBA); finance (MBA); general business (MBA); global management (MBA); Graham-Buffett security analysis (MBA); health administration (MBA); human resources management (MBA); international studies (MBA); Latin American business (MBA); management (MBA); marketing (MBA); sports administration (MBA); JD/MBA; MBA/MS; MBA/PhD; MBA/Pharm D; MD/MBA. *Accreditation:* AACSB. Part-time and evening/weekend programs available. *Faculty:* 71 full-time (10 women). *Students:* 412 full-time (111 women), 467 part-time (135 women); includes 235 minority (39 Black or African American, non-Hispanic/Latino; 7 American Indian or Alaska Native, non-Hispanic/Latino; 79 Asian, non-Hispanic/Latino; 109 Hispanic/Latino; 1 Native Hawaiian or other Pacific Islander, non-Hispanic/Latino), 44 international. Average age 32. 589 applicants, 52% accepted, 247 enrolled. In 2011, 505 master's awarded. *Degree requirements:* For master's, capstone course. *Entrance requirements:* For master's, GMAT, minimum GPA of 3.0, interview. Additional exam requirements/recommendations for international students: Required—TOEFL (minimum score 550 paper-based; 213 computer-based; 80 iBT), IELTS (minimum score 6). *Application deadline:* For fall admission, 7/1 for domestic students, 1/1 for international students; for spring admission, 12/1 for domestic and international students. Applications are processed on a rolling basis. Application fee: $30. Electronic applications accepted. *Financial support:* Teaching assistantships, career-related internships or fieldwork, scholarships/grants, and unspecified assistantships available. Support available to part-time students. Financial award applicants required to submit FAFSA. *Faculty research:* Accounting, finance, insurance, management, real estate, urban analysis marketing. *Unit head:* Prof. Alexander D. Sevilla, Assistant Dean/Director, 352-273-3252 Ext. 1206, E-mail: alex.sevilla@warrington.ufl.edu. *Application contact:* Prof. Kelli Gust, Associate Director, 352-273-3255, Fax: 352-392-8791, E-mail: kelly.gust@warrington.ufl.edu. Web site: http://www.floridamba.ufl.edu/.

University of Georgia, College of Education, Department of Lifelong Education, Administration and Policy, Athens, GA 30602. Offers adult education (M Ed, Ed D, PhD, Ed S); educational administration and policy (M Ed, PhD, Ed S); educational leadership (Ed D); human resource and organizational design (M Ed). *Accreditation:* NCATE. *Faculty:* 25 full-time (18 women), 1 part-time/adjunct (0 women). *Students:* 74 full-time (56 women), 216 part-time (136 women); includes 73 minority (62 Black or African American, non-Hispanic/Latino; 4 Asian, non-Hispanic/Latino; 3 Hispanic/Latino; 4 Two or more races, non-Hispanic/Latino), 23 international. Average age 37. 123 applicants, 64% accepted, 45 enrolled. In 2011, 54 master's, 19 doctorates, 14 other advanced degrees awarded. *Entrance requirements:* For master's and Ed S, GRE General Test or MAT; for doctorate, GRE General Test. *Application deadline:* For fall admission, 7/1 priority date for domestic students; for spring admission, 11/15 for domestic students. Application fee: $50. Electronic applications accepted. *Unit head:* Dr. Janette Hill, Head, 706-542-4035, Fax: 706-542-5873, E-mail: janette@.uga.edu. *Application contact:* Dr. Robert B. Hill, Graduate Coordinator, 706-542-4016, Fax: 706-542-5873, E-mail: bobhill@uga.edu. Web site: http://www.coe.uga.edu/leap/.

University of Georgia, College of Education, Department of Workforce Education, Leadership and Social Foundations, Athens, GA 30602. Offers educational leadership (Ed D); human resources and organization design (M Ed); occupational studies (MAT, Ed D, PhD, Ed S); social foundations of education (PhD). *Accreditation:* NCATE. *Faculty:* 14 full-time (7 women). *Students:* 27 full-time (15 women), 70 part-time (46 women); includes 24 minority (23 Black or African American, non-Hispanic/Latino; 1 Native Hawaiian or other Pacific Islander, non-Hispanic/Latino), 5 international. Average age 37. 40 applicants, 63% accepted, 8 enrolled. In 2011, 16 master's, 23 doctorates, 5 other advanced degrees awarded. *Entrance requirements:* For master's, GRE General Test, MAT; for doctorate, GRE General Test; for Ed S, GRE General Test or MAT. *Application deadline:* For fall admission, 7/1 priority date for domestic students; for spring admission, 11/15 for domestic students. Application fee: $50. Electronic applications accepted. *Financial support:* Fellowships, research assistantships, teaching assistantships, and unspecified assistantships available. *Unit head:* Dr. Roger B. Hill, Interim Head, 706-542-4100, Fax: 706-542-4054, E-mail: rbhill@uga.edu. *Application contact:* Dr. Robert C. Wicklein, Graduate Coordinator, 706-542-4503, Fax: 706-542-4054, E-mail: wickone@uga.edu. Web site: http://www.coe.uga.edu/welsf/.

University of Hawaii at Manoa, Graduate Division, Shidler College of Business, Program in Business Administration, Honolulu, HI 96822. Offers Asian business studies (MBA); Chinese business studies (MBA); decision sciences (MBA); entrepreneurship (MBA); finance (MBA); finance and banking (MBA); human resources management (MBA); information management (MBA); information technology (MBA); international business (MBA); Japanese business studies (MBA); marketing (MBA); organizational behavior (MBA); organizational management (MBA); real estate (MBA); student-designed track (MBA). *Accreditation:* AACSB. Part-time and evening/weekend programs available. *Degree requirements:* For master's, thesis optional. *Entrance requirements:* For master's, GMAT, minimum GPA of 3.0. Additional exam requirements/recommendations for international students: Required—TOEFL (minimum score 600 paper-based; 250 computer-based; 100 iBT), IELTS (minimum score 7). *Expenses:* Contact institution.

University of Hawaii at Manoa, Graduate Division, Shidler College of Business, Program in Human Resources Management, Honolulu, HI 96822. Offers MHRM. Part-time programs available. *Entrance requirements:* Additional exam requirements/recommendations for international students: Required—TOEFL (minimum score 600 paper-based; 250 computer-based; 100 iBT), IELTS (minimum score 7). *Expenses:* Contact institution.

University of Houston–Clear Lake, School of Business, Program in Administrative Science, Houston, TX 77058-1098. Offers environmental management (MS); human resource management (MA). *Accreditation:* CAHME (one or more programs are accredited). Part-time and evening/weekend programs available. *Degree requirements:* For master's, thesis optional. *Entrance requirements:* For master's, GMAT. Additional exam requirements/recommendations for international students: Required—TOEFL (minimum score 550 paper-based; 213 computer-based). Electronic applications accepted.

University of Illinois at Urbana–Champaign, Graduate College, College of Education, Department of Education Policy, Organization, and Leadership, Champaign, IL 61820. Offers educational organization and leadership (Ed M, MS, Ed D, PhD, CAS); educational policy studies (Ed M, MA, PhD); human resource education (Ed M, MS, Ed D, PhD, CAS). Part-time programs available. Postbaccalaureate distance learning degree programs offered (minimal on-campus study). *Faculty:* 30 full-time (13 women), 3 part-time/adjunct (2 women). *Students:* 185 full-time (117 women), 391 part-time (249 women); includes 199 minority (107 Black or African American, non-Hispanic/Latino; 3 American Indian or Alaska Native, non-Hispanic/Latino; 28 Asian, non-Hispanic/Latino; 49 Hispanic/Latino; 12 Two or more races, non-Hispanic/Latino), 52 international. 327 applicants, 60% accepted, 100 enrolled. In 2011, 201 master's, 34 doctorates, 3 other advanced degrees awarded. *Entrance requirements:* For master's, minimum GPA of 3.0; for doctorate, GRE General Test, minimum GPA of 3.0, writing samples, interview. Additional exam requirements/recommendations for international students: Required—TOEFL (minimum score 620 paper-based; 260 computer-based; 105 iBT). *Application deadline:* Applications are processed on a rolling basis. Application fee: $75 ($90 for international students). Electronic applications accepted. *Financial support:* In 2011–12, 29 fellowships, 60 research assistantships, 60 teaching assistantships were awarded; tuition waivers (full and partial) also available. *Unit head:* James Anderson, Head, 217-333-2446, Fax: 217-244-5632, E-mail: janders@illinois.edu. *Application contact:* Rebecca Grady, 217-265-5404, Fax: 217-244-5632, E-mail: rgrady@illinois.edu. Web site: http://education.illinois.edu/epol.

University of Illinois at Urbana–Champaign, Graduate College, School of Labor and Employment Relations, Champaign, IL 61820. Offers human resources and industrial relations (MHRIR, PhD); MHRIR/JD; MHRIR/MBA. Part-time programs available. *Faculty:* 14 full-time (5 women), 2 part-time/adjunct (0 women). *Students:* 182 full-time (128 women), 9 part-time (7 women); includes 45 minority (18 Black or African American, non-Hispanic/Latino; 17 Asian, non-Hispanic/Latino; 7 Hispanic/Latino; 3 Two or more races, non-Hispanic/Latino), 63 international. 347 applicants, 37% accepted, 82 enrolled. In 2011, 108 master's, 1 doctorate awarded. Terminal master's awarded for partial completion of doctoral program. *Entrance requirements:* For master's and doctorate, GRE or GMAT, minimum GPA of 3.0. Additional exam requirements/recommendations for international students: Required—TOEFL (minimum score 590 paper-based; 243 computer-based; 96 iBT) or IELTS (minimum score 6.5). Application fee: $75 ($90 for international students). Electronic applications accepted. *Financial support:* In 2011–12, 10 fellowships, 10 research assistantships, 3 teaching assistantships were awarded; tuition waivers (full and partial) also available. *Unit head:* Dr. Joel E. Cutcher-Gershenfeld, Dean, 217-333-1482, Fax: 217-244-9290, E-mail: joelcg@illinois.edu. *Application contact:* Elizabeth Barker, Director of Student Services, 217-333-2381, Fax: 217-244-9290, E-mail: ebarker@illinois.edu. Web site: http://www.ler.illinois.edu.

University of Lethbridge, School of Graduate Studies, Lethbridge, AB T1K 3M4, Canada. Offers accounting (MScM); addictions counseling (M Sc); agricultural biotechnology (M Sc); agricultural studies (M Sc, MA); anthropology (MA); archaeology (MA); art (MA, MFA); biochemistry (M Sc); biological sciences (M Sc); biomolecular science (PhD); biosystems and biodiversity (PhD); Canadian studies (MA); chemistry (M Sc); computer science (M Sc); computer science and geographical information science (M Sc); counseling psychology (M Ed); dramatic arts (MA); earth, space, and physical science (PhD); economics (MA); educational leadership (M Ed); English (MA); environmental science (M Sc); evolution and behavior (PhD); exercise science (M Sc); finance (MScM); French (MA); French/German (MA); French/Spanish (MA); general education (M Ed); general management (MScM); geography (M Sc, MA); German (MA); health science (M Sc); history (MA); human resource management and labour relations (MScM); individualized multidisciplinary (M Sc, MA); information systems (MScM); international management (MScM); kinesiology (M Sc, MA); management (M Sc, MA); marketing (MScM); mathematics (M Sc); music (M Mus, MA); Native American studies (MA); neuroscience (M Sc, PhD); new media (MA); nursing (M Sc); philosophy (MA); physics (M Sc); policy and strategy (MScM); political science (MA); psychology (M Sc, MA); religious studies (MA); social sciences (MA); sociology (MA); theatre and dramatic arts (MFA); theoretical and computational science (PhD); urban and regional studies (MA); women's studies (MA). Part-time and evening/weekend programs available. *Degree requirements:* For doctorate, comprehensive exam, thesis/dissertation. *Entrance requirements:* For master's, GMAT (M Sc in management), bachelor's degree in related field, minimum GPA of 3.0 during previous 20 graded semester courses, 2 years teaching or related experience (M Ed); for doctorate, master's degree, minimum graduate GPA of 3.5. Additional exam requirements/recommendations for international students: Required—TOEFL. *Faculty research:* Movement and brain plasticity, gibberellin physiology, photosynthesis, carbon cycling, molecular properties of main-group ring components.

University of Louisville, Graduate School, College of Arts and Sciences, Department of Urban and Public Affairs, Louisville, KY 40208. Offers public administration (MPA), including human resources management, non-profit management, public policy and administration; urban and public affairs (PhD), including urban planning and development, urban policy and administration; urban planning (MUP), including administration of planning organizations, housing and community development, land use and environmental planning, spatial analysis. Part-time and evening/weekend programs available. Terminal master's awarded for partial completion of doctoral program. *Degree requirements:* For master's, internship; for doctorate, comprehensive exam, thesis/dissertation. *Entrance requirements:* For master's, GRE General Test, minimum GPA of 3.0; for doctorate, GRE General Test, master's degree in appropriate field. Additional exam requirements/recommendations for international students: Required—TOEFL (minimum score 550 paper-based; 213 computer-based; 79 iBT). Electronic applications accepted. *Expenses:* Tuition, state resident: full-time $9692; part-time $539 per credit hour. Tuition, nonresident: full-time $20,168; part-time $1121 per credit hour. Tuition and fees vary according to program and reciprocity agreements. *Faculty research:* Housing and community development, performance-based budgeting, environmental policy and natural hazards, sustainability, real estate development, comparative urban development.

University of Mary, Gary Tharaldson School of Business, Bismarck, ND 58504-9652. Offers accountancy (MBA); business administration (MBA); health care (MBA); human resource management (MBA); management (MBA); project management (MPM); strategic leadership (MSSL). Part-time and evening/weekend programs available. *Faculty:* 8 full-time (5 women), 66 part-time/adjunct (22 women). *Students:* 340 full-time (190 women), 189 part-time (91 women); includes 69 minority (28 Black or African American, non-Hispanic/Latino; 25 American Indian or Alaska Native, non-Hispanic/Latino; 7 Asian, non-Hispanic/Latino; 7 Hispanic/Latino; 1 Native Hawaiian or other Pacific Islander, non-Hispanic/Latino; 1 Two or more races, non-Hispanic/Latino), 14 international. Average age 35. 207 applicants, 95% accepted, 148 enrolled. In 2011, 265 master's awarded. *Degree requirements:* For master's, strategic planning seminar. *Entrance requirements:* For master's, minimum GPA of 2.5. Additional exam requirements/recommendations for international students: Required—TOEFL (minimum score 500 paper-based; 197 computer-based; 71 iBT). *Application deadline:* Applications are processed on a rolling basis. Application fee: $40. *Financial support:* Application deadline: 8/1; applicants required to submit FAFSA. *Unit head:* Dr. Shanda Traiser, Director of the School of Accelerated and Distance Education, 701-355-8160, Fax: 701-255-7687, E-mail: straiser@umary.edu. *Application contact:* Wayne G. Maruska, Graduate Program Advisor, 701-355-8134, Fax: 701-255-7687, E-mail: wmaruska@umary.edu.

University of Minnesota, Twin Cities Campus, Carlson School of Management, Program in Human Resources and Industrial Relations, Minneapolis, MN 55455-0213. Offers MA, PhD. *Accreditation:* AACSB. Part-time and evening/weekend programs available. *Faculty:* 16 full-time (9 women), 8 part-time/adjunct (4 women). *Students:* 145 full-time (90 women), 59 part-time (50 women); includes 29 minority (8 Black or African American, non-Hispanic/Latino; 1 American Indian or Alaska Native, non-Hispanic/Latino; 15 Asian, non-Hispanic/Latino; 5 Hispanic/Latino), 46 international. Average age 26. 410 applicants, 32% accepted, 76 enrolled. In 2011, 90 degrees awarded. Terminal master's awarded for partial completion of doctoral program. *Degree requirements:* For master's, thesis or alternative, 48 course credits; for doctorate, comprehensive exam, thesis/dissertation. *Entrance requirements:* For master's, GMAT or GRE General Test, undergraduate degree from accredited institution, course in microeconomics; for doctorate, GRE General Test or GMAT, undergraduate degree from accredited institution, course in microeconomics. Additional exam requirements/recommendations for international students: Required—TOEFL (minimum score 550 paper-based; 79 iBT: 21 writing, 19 reading). *Application deadline:* For fall admission, 6/15 for domestic and international students; for spring admission, 10/15 for domestic and international students. Applications are processed on a rolling basis. Application fee: $75 ($95 for international students). *Expenses:* Contact institution. *Financial support:* In 2011–12, 60 students received support, including 2 fellowships with full tuition reimbursements available (averaging $6,500 per year), 12 research assistantships with full tuition reimbursements available (averaging $14,000 per year), 25 teaching assistantships with full and partial tuition reimbursements available (averaging $12,000 per year); career-related internships or fieldwork, Federal Work-Study, institutionally sponsored loans, and tuition waivers (full and partial) also available. Support available to part-time students. Financial award application deadline: 2/1; financial award applicants required to submit FAFSA. *Faculty research:* Staffing, training, and development; compensation and benefits; organization theory; collective bargaining. *Total annual research expenditures:* $13,660. *Unit head:* Stacy Doepner-Hove, Director of Master's Program in HRIR, 612-625-8732, Fax: 612-624-8360, E-mail: doepn002@umn.edu. *Application contact:* Patti Blair, Admissions Coordinator, 612-624-5704, Fax: 612-624-8360, E-mail: hrirgrad@umn.edu. Web site: http://www.csom.umn.edu/chrls/.

University of Missouri–St. Louis, College of Business Administration, Program in Business Administration, St. Louis, MO 63121. Offers accounting (MBA); business administration (Certificate); finance (MBA); human resource management (Certificate); information systems (MBA); logistics and supply chain management (MBA, Certificate); marketing (MBA); marketing management (Certificate); operations management (MBA). *Accreditation:* AACSB. Part-time and evening/weekend programs available. *Faculty:* 32 full-time (7 women), 10 part-time/adjunct (2 women). *Students:* 126 full-time (48 women), 305 part-time (141 women); includes 61 minority (25 Black or African American, non-Hispanic/Latino; 23 Asian, non-Hispanic/Latino; 9 Hispanic/Latino; 1 Native Hawaiian or other Pacific Islander, non-Hispanic/Latino; 3 Two or more races, non-Hispanic/Latino), 47 international. Average age 30. 241 applicants, 70% accepted, 134 enrolled. In 2011, 150 master's, 1 doctorate, 19 other advanced degrees awarded. *Entrance requirements:* For master's, GMAT, 2 letters of recommendation. Additional exam requirements/recommendations for international students: Required—TOEFL (minimum score 550 paper-based; 213 computer-based). *Application deadline:* For fall admission, 7/1 for domestic and international students; for spring admission, 12/1 for domestic and international students. Applications are processed on a rolling basis. Application fee: $35 ($40 for international students). Electronic applications accepted. *Expenses:* Tuition, state resident: full-time $6273; part-time $3866 per year. Tuition, nonresident: full-time $14,969; part-time $9980 per year. *Required fees:* $315 per year. *Financial support:* In 2011–12, 32 research assistantships with full and partial tuition reimbursements (averaging $6,000 per year), 6 teaching assistantships with full and partial tuition reimbursements (averaging $12,276 per year) were awarded; career-related internships or fieldwork, Federal Work-Study, and institutionally sponsored loans also available. Support available to part-time students. Financial award application deadline: 4/1; financial award applicants required to submit FAFSA. *Faculty research:* Human resources, strategic management, marketing strategy, consumer behavior product development, advertising. *Unit head:* Karl Kottemann, Assistant Director, 314-516-5885, Fax: 314-516-6420, E-mail: mba@umsl.edu. *Application contact:* 314-516-5458, Fax: 314-516-6996, E-mail: gradadm@umsl.edu. Web site: http://www.umsl.edu/divisions/business/mbaonline/mbaprog.htm.

University of New Haven, Graduate School, College of Arts and Sciences, Program in Industrial and Organizational Psychology, West Haven, CT 06516-1916. Offers conflict management (MA); human resource management (MA); industrial organizational psychology (MA); organizational development (MA); psychology of conflict management (Certificate). Part-time and evening/weekend programs available. *Students:* 93 full-time (66 women), 25 part-time (19 women); includes 20 minority (12 Black or African American, non-Hispanic/Latino; 1 Asian, non-Hispanic/Latino; 5 Hispanic/Latino; 2 Two or more races, non-Hispanic/Latino), 13 international. 67 applicants, 97% accepted, 50 enrolled. In 2011, 56 master's awarded. *Degree requirements:* For master's, thesis or alternative. *Entrance requirements:* Additional exam requirements/recommendations for international students: Required—TOEFL (minimum score 520 paper-based; 190 computer-based; 70 iBT); Recommended—IELTS (minimum score 5.5). *Application deadline:* For fall admission, 5/31 for international students; for winter admission, 10/15 for international students; for spring admission, 1/15 for international students. Applications are processed on a rolling basis. Application fee: $50. Electronic applications accepted. *Expenses:* Contact institution. *Financial support:* Research assistantships with partial tuition reimbursements, teaching assistantships with partial tuition reimbursements, career-related internships or fieldwork, Federal Work-Study, scholarships/grants, tuition waivers, and unspecified assistantships available. Support available to part-time students. Financial award applicants required to submit FAFSA. *Unit head:* Dr. Stuart D. Sidle, Coordinator, 203-932-7341. *Application contact:* Eloise Gormley, Information Contact, 203-932-7449. Web site: http://www.newhaven.edu/4730/.

University of New Haven, Graduate School, School of Business, Program in Business Administration, West Haven, CT 06516-1916. Offers accounting (MBA, Certificate), including CPA (MBA); business management (Certificate); business policy and strategy (MBA); finance (MBA), including CFA; global marketing (MBA); human resource management (Certificate); human resources management (MBA); international business (Certificate); marketing (Certificate); sports management (MBA); telecommunications management (Certificate); MBA/MPA. Part-time and evening/weekend programs available. *Students:* 215 full-time (106 women), 182 part-time (87 women); includes 73 minority (38 Black or African American, non-Hispanic/Latino; 2 American Indian or Alaska Native, non-Hispanic/Latino; 22 Asian, non-Hispanic/Latino; 11 Hispanic/Latino), 129 international. 179 applicants, 97% accepted, 93 enrolled. In 2011, 197 master's, 28 other advanced degrees awarded. *Degree requirements:* For master's, thesis or alternative. *Entrance requirements:* For master's, GMAT. Additional exam requirements/recommendations for international students: Required—TOEFL (minimum score 520 paper-based; 190 computer-based; 70 iBT), IELTS (minimum score 5.5). *Application deadline:* For fall admission, 5/31 for international students; for winter admission, 10/15 for international students; for spring admission, 1/15 for international students. Applications are processed on a rolling basis. Application fee: $50. Electronic applications accepted. *Expenses:* Contact institution. *Financial support:* Research assistantships with partial tuition reimbursements, teaching assistantships with partial tuition reimbursements, Federal Work-Study, scholarships/grants, health care benefits, tuition waivers, and unspecified assistantships available. Support available to part-time students. Financial award applicants required to submit FAFSA. *Unit head:* Charles Coleman, Chairman, 203-932-7375. *Application contact:* Eloise Gormley, Director of Graduate Admissions, 203-932-7449, Fax: 203-932-7137, E-mail: gradinfo@newhaven.edu. Web site: http://www.newhaven.edu/7433/.

University of New Haven, Graduate School, School of Business, Program in Public Administration, West Haven, CT 06516-1916. Offers personnel and labor relations (MPA); public administration (MPA, Certificate), including city management (MPA), community-clinical services (MPA), health care management (MPA), long-term health care (MPA), personnel and labor relations (MPA), public administration (Certificate), public management (Certificate), public personnel management (Certificate); MBA/MPA. Part-time and evening/weekend programs available. *Students:* 50 full-time (21 women), 19 part-time (9 women); includes 17 minority (14 Black or African American, non-Hispanic/Latino; 2 Asian, non-Hispanic/Latino; 1 Hispanic/Latino), 13 international. 23 applicants, 100% accepted, 13 enrolled. In 2011, 23 master's, 14 other advanced degrees awarded. *Degree requirements:* For master's, thesis or alternative. *Entrance requirements:* Additional exam requirements/recommendations for international students: Required—TOEFL (minimum score 520 paper-based; 190 computer-based; 70 iBT); Recommended—IELTS (minimum score 5.5). *Application deadline:* For fall admission, 5/31 for international students; for winter admission, 10/15 for international students; for spring admission, 1/15 for international students. Applications are processed on a rolling basis. Application fee: $50. Electronic applications accepted. *Expenses:* Contact institution. *Financial support:* Research assistantships with partial tuition reimbursements, teaching assistantships with partial tuition reimbursements, career-related internships or fieldwork, Federal Work-Study, scholarships/grants, tuition waivers, and unspecified assistantships available. Support available to part-time students. Financial award application deadline: 5/1; financial award applicants required to submit FAFSA. *Unit head:* Cynthia Conrad, Chair, 203-932-7486. *Application contact:* Eloise Gormley, Director of Graduate Admissions, 203-932-7449, Fax: 203-932-7137, E-mail: gradinfo@newhaven.edu. Web site: http://www.newhaven.edu/6854/.

University of New Mexico, Graduate School, College of Arts and Sciences, Department of Economics, Albuquerque, NM 87131-2039. Offers environmental/natural resources (MA, PhD); international/development (MA, PhD); labor/human resources (MA, PhD); public finance (MA, PhD). Part-time programs available. *Faculty:* 14 full-time (7 women), 8 part-time/adjunct (1 woman). *Students:* 37 full-time (9 women), 25 part-time (6 women); includes 10 minority (3 Asian, non-Hispanic/Latino; 6 Hispanic/Latino; 1 Two or more races, non-Hispanic/Latino), 17 international. Average age 35. 61 applicants, 49% accepted, 14 enrolled. In 2011, 10 master's, 3 doctorates awarded. Terminal master's awarded for partial completion of doctoral program. *Degree requirements:* For master's, comprehensive exam, thesis (for some programs); for doctorate, comprehensive exam, thesis/dissertation. *Entrance requirements:* For master's and doctorate, GRE General Test, 3 letters of recommendation, letter of intent, curriculum vitae. Additional exam requirements/recommendations for international students: Required—TOEFL (minimum score 520 paper-based; 190 computer-based; 68 iBT). *Application deadline:* For fall admission, 3/1 priority date for domestic students, 3/1 for international students. Applications are processed on a rolling basis. Application fee: $50. Electronic applications accepted. *Financial support:* In 2011–12, 47 students received support, including 3 fellowships with tuition reimbursements available (averaging $3,611 per year), 14 research assistantships with tuition reimbursements available (averaging $7,791 per year), 15 teaching assistantships with tuition reimbursements available (averaging $7,467 per year); career-related internships or fieldwork, Federal Work-Study, scholarships/grants, health care benefits, and unspecified assistantships also available. Support available to part-time students. Financial award application deadline: 3/1; financial award applicants required to submit FAFSA. *Faculty research:* Core theory, econometrics, public finance, international/development economics, labor/human resource economics, environmental/natural resource economics. *Total annual research expenditures:* $1.8 million. *Unit head:* Dr. Robert Berrens, Chair, 505-277-5304, Fax: 505-277-9445, E-mail: rberrens@unm.edu. *Application contact:* Rikk Murphy, Academic Advisor, 505-277-3056, Fax: 505-277-9445, E-mail: rikk@unm.edu. Web site: http://econ.unm.edu.

University of New Mexico, Robert O. Anderson Graduate School of Management, Department of Organizational Studies, Albuquerque, NM 87131. Offers human resources management (MBA); policy and planning (MBA). Part-time and evening/weekend programs available. *Faculty:* 12 full-time (6 women), 16 part-time/adjunct (10 women). In 2011, 74 master's awarded. *Degree requirements:* For master's, minimum GPA of 3.0. *Entrance requirements:* For master's, GMAT or GRE. Additional exam requirements/recommendations for international students: Required—TOEFL (minimum score 550 paper-based; 213 computer-based; 79 iBT). *Application deadline:* For fall admission, 4/1 priority date for domestic students, 4/1 for international students; for spring admission, 10/1 priority date for domestic students, 10/1 for international students. Applications are processed on a rolling basis. Application fee: $50. Electronic applications accepted. *Financial support:* Fellowships, research assistantships, career-related internships or fieldwork, Federal Work-Study, scholarships/grants, and unspecified assistantships available. Support available to part-time students. Financial award application deadline: 6/1. *Faculty research:* Business ethics and social corporate responsibility, diversity, human resources, organizational strategy, organizational behavior. *Unit head:* Dr. Jacqueline Hood, Chair, 505-277-6471, Fax: 505-277-7108. *Application contact:* Megan Conner, Director, Student Services, 505-277-3290, Fax: 505-277-8436, E-mail: mconner@mgt.unm.edu.

University of North Florida, Coggin College of Business, MBA Program, Jacksonville, FL 32224. Offers accounting (MBA); construction management (MBA); e-commerce (MBA); economics (MBA); finance (MBA); human resource management (MBA); international business (MBA); logistics (MBA); management applications (MBA). *Accreditation:* AACSB. Part-time and evening/weekend programs available. *Faculty:* 19 full-time (6 women), 1 part-time/adjunct (0 women). *Students:* 145 full-time (57 women), 277 part-time (108 women); includes 67 minority (19 Black or African American, non-Hispanic/Latino; 21 Asian, non-Hispanic/Latino; 20 Hispanic/Latino; 7 Two or more races, non-Hispanic/Latino), 34 international. Average age 29. 200 applicants, 48% accepted, 70 enrolled. In 2011, 153 master's awarded. *Entrance requirements:* For master's, GMAT or GRE, U.S. bachelor's degree from regionally-accredited university or equivalent foreign degree. Additional exam requirements/recommendations for international students: Required—TOEFL (minimum score 550 paper-based; 213 computer-based; 79 iBT). *Application deadline:* For fall admission, 7/1 priority date for domestic students, 5/1 for international students; for spring admission, 11/1 priority date for domestic students, 10/1 for international students. Applications are processed on a rolling basis. Application fee: $30. *Expenses:* Tuition, state resident: full-time $8793; part-time $366.38 per credit hour. Tuition, nonresident: full-time $23,502; part-time $979.24 per credit hour. *Required fees:* $1384; $57.66 per credit hour. Tuition and fees vary according to course load and program. *Financial support:* In 2011–12, 55 students received support, including 1 teaching assistantship (averaging $5,333 per year); research assistantships, Federal Work-Study, and tuition waivers (partial) also available. Support available to part-time students. Financial award application deadline: 4/1; financial award applicants required to submit FAFSA. *Faculty research:* Performance measures, costing, and inventory issues in logistics and supply chain management; inter-organizational systems; international management and marketing practices; e-commerce; organizational learning and socialization processes. *Total annual research expenditures:* $7,686. *Unit head:* Dr. C. Bruce Kavan, Chair, 904-620-2780, Fax: 904-620-2832. *Application contact:* Cheryl Campbell, Graduate Advisor, 904-620-2575, Fax: 904-620-2832, E-mail: ccampbell@unf.edu. Web site: http://www.unf.edu/coggin/academics/graduate/mba.aspx.

University of Oklahoma, College of Arts and Sciences, Department of Psychology, Program in Organizational Dynamics, Tulsa, OK 74135. Offers organizational dynamics (MA), including human resource management, organizational dynamics, technical project management. Part-time and evening/weekend programs available. *Students:* 13 full-time (8 women), 21 part-time (10 women); includes 11 minority (2 Black or African American, non-Hispanic/Latino; 1 American Indian or Alaska Native, non-Hispanic/Latino; 2 Asian, non-Hispanic/Latino; 4 Hispanic/Latino; 1 Native Hawaiian or other Pacific Islander, non-Hispanic/Latino; 1 Two or more races, non-Hispanic/Latino), 1 international. Average age 36. 8 applicants, 75% accepted, 4 enrolled. In 2011, 14 degrees awarded. *Entrance requirements:* For master's, minimum GPA of 3.0 in last 60 hours of undergraduate course work. Additional exam requirements/recommendations for international students: Required—TOEFL (minimum score 550 paper-based; 79 iBT). *Application deadline:* For fall admission, 4/15 priority date for domestic students, 3/1 for international students; for spring admission, 11/1 for domestic students, 9/1 for international students. Applications are processed on a rolling basis. Application fee: $40 ($90 for international students). Electronic applications accepted. *Expenses:* Tuition, state resident: full-time $4087; part-time $170.30 per credit hour. Tuition, nonresident: full-time $14,875; part-time $619.80 per credit hour. *Required fees:* $2659; $100.25 per credit hour. Tuition and fees vary according to course load and degree level. *Financial support:* In 2011–12, 7 students received support. Scholarships/grants, health care benefits, and unspecified assistantships available. Financial award application deadline: 3/1; financial award applicants required to submit FAFSA. *Faculty research:* Academic integrity, organizational behavior, interdisciplinary teams, shared leadership. *Unit head:* Dr. Jorge Mendoza, Chair, 405-325-4511, Fax: 405-325-4737, E-mail: jmendoza@ou.edu. *Application contact:* Jennifer Kisamore, Graduate Liaison, 918-660-3603, Fax: 918-660-3383, E-mail: jkisamore@ou.edu. Web site: http://tulsagrad.ou.edu/odyn/.

University of Phoenix–Atlanta Campus, School of Business, Sandy Springs, GA 30350-4153. Offers accounting (MBA); business administration (MBA); global management (MBA); human resources management (MBA, MM); management (MM); marketing (MBA); public administration (MM). Evening/weekend programs available. Postbaccalaureate distance learning degree programs offered. *Degree requirements:* For master's, thesis (for some programs). *Entrance requirements:* For master's, minimum undergraduate GPA of 3.0, 3 years of work experience. Additional exam requirements/recommendations for international students: Required—TOEFL (minimum score 550 paper-based; 213 computer-based; 79 iBT).

University of Phoenix–Augusta Campus, School of Business, Augusta, GA 30909-4583. Offers accounting (MBA); business administration (MBA); business and management (MBA, MM); global management (MBA); human resources management (MBA, MM); management (MM); marketing (MBA); public administration (MBA, MM). Postbaccalaureate distance learning degree programs offered.

University of Phoenix–Austin Campus, School of Business, Austin, TX 78759. Offers accounting (MBA); business administration (MBA); business and management (MBA); e-business (MBA); global management (MBA); human resources management (MBA, MM); management (MM); marketing (MBA); public administration (MBA). Postbaccalaureate distance learning degree programs offered.

University of Phoenix–Bay Area Campus, School of Business, San Jose, CA 95134-1805. Offers accountancy (MS); accounting (MBA); business administration (MBA, DBA); energy management (MBA); global management (MBA); health care management (MBA); human resource management (MBA); human resources management (MM); management (MM); marketing (MBA); organizational leadership (DM); project management (MBA); public administration (MPA); technology management (MBA). Evening/weekend programs available. Postbaccalaureate distance learning degree programs offered (no on-campus study). *Degree requirements:* For master's, thesis (for some programs). *Entrance requirements:* For master's, minimum undergraduate GPA of 3.0, 3 years of work experience. Additional exam requirements/recommendations for international students: Required—TOEFL (minimum score 550 paper-based; 213 computer-based; 79 iBT). Electronic applications accepted.

University of Phoenix–Birmingham Campus, College of Graduate Business and Management, Birmingham, AL 35244. Offers accounting (MBA); business administration (MBA); global management (MBA); human resources management (MBA, MM); management (MM); marketing (MBA); public administration (MM).

University of Phoenix–Central Florida Campus, School of Business, Maitland, FL 32751-7057. Offers accounting (MBA); business administration (MBA); business and management (MM); global management (MBA); human resources management (MBA, MM); management (MM); marketing (MBA); public administration (MBA, MM). Evening/weekend programs available. *Degree requirements:* For master's, thesis (for some programs). *Entrance requirements:* For master's, minimum undergraduate GPA of 3.0, 3 years work experience. Additional exam requirements/recommendations for international students: Required—TOEFL (minimum score 550 paper-based; 213 computer-based; 79 iBT). Electronic applications accepted.

Human Resources Management

University of Phoenix–Central Valley Campus, School of Business, Fresno, CA 93720-1562. Offers accounting (MBA); business administration (MBA); global management (MBA); human resources management (MBA, MM); management (MM); marketing (MBA); public administration (MBA, MM).

University of Phoenix–Chattanooga Campus, School of Business, Chattanooga, TN 37421-3707. Offers accounting (MBA); business administration (MBA); business and management (MBA); global management (MBA); human resources management (MBA, MM); management (MM); marketing (MBA); public administration (MBA, MM). Postbaccalaureate distance learning degree programs offered.

University of Phoenix–Cheyenne Campus, School of Business, Cheyenne, WY 82009. Offers global management (MBA); human resources management (MBA, MM); management (MM); marketing (MBA); public administration (MBA, MM). Postbaccalaureate distance learning degree programs offered.

University of Phoenix–Chicago Campus, School of Business, Schaumburg, IL 60173-4399. Offers business administration (MBA); global management (MBA); human resources management (MBA); information systems (MIS); management (MM). Evening/weekend programs available. *Degree requirements:* For master's, thesis (for some programs). *Entrance requirements:* For master's, minimum undergraduate GPA of 3.0, 3 years of work experience. Additional exam requirements/recommendations for international students: Required—TOEFL (minimum score 550 paper-based; 213 computer-based; 79 iBT). Electronic applications accepted.

University of Phoenix–Cincinnati Campus, School of Business, West Chester, OH 45069-4875. Offers accounting (MBA); business administration (MBA); global management (MBA); human resources management (MBA, MM); management (MM); marketing (MBA); public administration (MM). Evening/weekend programs available. *Degree requirements:* For master's, thesis (for some programs). *Entrance requirements:* For master's, minimum undergraduate GPA of 3.0, 3 years of work experience. Additional exam requirements/recommendations for international students: Required—TOEFL (minimum score 550 paper-based; 213 computer-based; 79 iBT). Electronic applications accepted.

University of Phoenix–Cleveland Campus, School of Business, Independence, OH 44131-2194. Offers accounting (MBA); business administration (MBA); global management (MBA); human resources management (MBA, MM); management (MM); marketing (MBA); public administration (MBA, MM). Evening/weekend programs available. Postbaccalaureate distance learning degree programs offered (no on-campus study). *Degree requirements:* For master's, thesis (for some programs). *Entrance requirements:* For master's, minimum undergraduate GPA of 3.0, 3 years of work experience. Additional exam requirements/recommendations for international students: Required—TOEFL (minimum score 550 paper-based; 213 computer-based; 79 iBT). Electronic applications accepted.

University of Phoenix–Columbus Georgia Campus, School of Business, Columbus, GA 31904-6321. Offers accounting (MBA); business administration (MBA); global management (MBA); human resources management (MBA, MM); management (MM); marketing (MBA); public administration (MBA). Evening/weekend programs available. *Degree requirements:* For master's, thesis (for some programs). *Entrance requirements:* For master's, minimum undergraduate GPA of 3.0, 3 years of work experience. Additional exam requirements/recommendations for international students: Required—TOEFL (minimum score 550 paper-based; 213 computer-based; 79 iBT). Electronic applications accepted.

University of Phoenix–Columbus Ohio Campus, School of Business, Columbus, OH 43240-4032. Offers accounting (MBA); business administration (MBA); global management (MBA); human resources management (MBA, MM); management (MM); marketing (MBA); public administration (MM). Evening/weekend programs available. Postbaccalaureate distance learning degree programs offered. *Degree requirements:* For master's, thesis (for some programs). *Entrance requirements:* For master's, minimum undergraduate GPA of 3.0, 3 years of work experience. Additional exam requirements/recommendations for international students: Required—TOEFL (minimum score 550 paper-based; 213 computer-based; 79 iBT). Electronic applications accepted.

University of Phoenix–Dallas Campus, School of Business, Dallas, TX 75251-2009. Offers accounting (MBA); business administration (MBA); global management (MBA); human resources management (MBA, MM); management (MM); marketing (MBA); public administration (MBA, MM). Evening/weekend programs available. Postbaccalaureate distance learning degree programs offered. *Degree requirements:* For master's, thesis (for some programs). *Entrance requirements:* For master's, 3 years of work experience, minimum undergraduate GPA of 3.0. Additional exam requirements/recommendations for international students: Required—TOEFL (minimum score 550 paper-based; 213 computer-based; 79 iBT). Electronic applications accepted.

University of Phoenix–Denver Campus, School of Business, Lone Tree, CO 80124-5453. Offers accountancy (MSA); accounting (MBA); business administration (MBA); e-business (MBA); global management (MBA); human resources management (MBA, MM); management (MM); marketing (MBA); public administration (MBA, MM). Evening/weekend programs available. Postbaccalaureate distance learning degree programs offered. *Degree requirements:* For master's, thesis (for some programs). *Entrance requirements:* For master's, minimum undergraduate GPA of 3.0, 3 years work experience. Additional exam requirements/recommendations for international students: Required—TOEFL (minimum score 550 paper-based; 213 computer-based; 79 iBT). Electronic applications accepted.

University of Phoenix–Des Moines Campus, School of Business, Des Moines, IA 50266. Offers accounting (MBA); business administration (MBA); global management (MBA); human resources management (MBA, MM); management (MM); marketing (MBA); public administration (MBA, MM). Postbaccalaureate distance learning degree programs offered.

University of Phoenix–Eastern Washington Campus, School of Business, Spokane Valley, WA 99212-2531. Offers accounting (MBA); business administration (MBA); human resources management (MBA); marketing (MBA); public administration (MBA). Evening/weekend programs available. *Degree requirements:* For master's, thesis (for some programs). *Entrance requirements:* For master's, minimum undergraduate GPA of 3.0, 3 years of work experience. Additional exam requirements/recommendations for international students: Required—TOEFL (minimum score 550 paper-based; 213 computer-based; 79 iBT). Electronic applications accepted.

University of Phoenix–Harrisburg Campus, School of Business, Harrisburg, PA 17112. Offers accounting (MBA); business administration (MBA); business and management (MBA); global management (MBA); human resources management (MBA, MM); management (MM); marketing (MBA); public administration (MBA, MM). Postbaccalaureate distance learning degree programs offered.

University of Phoenix–Hawaii Campus, School of Business, Honolulu, HI 96813-4317. Offers accounting (MBA); business administration (MBA); global management (MBA); human resources management (MBA, MM); management (MM); marketing (MBA); public administration (MBA, MM). Evening/weekend programs available. *Degree requirements:* For master's, thesis (for some programs). *Entrance requirements:* For master's, minimum undergraduate GPA of 3.0, 3 years of work experience. Additional exam requirements/recommendations for international students: Required—TOEFL (minimum score 550 paper-based; 213 computer-based; 79 iBT). Electronic applications accepted.

University of Phoenix–Houston Campus, School of Business, Houston, TX 77079-2004. Offers accounting (MBA); business administration (MBA); global management (MBA); human resources management (MBA, MM); management (MM); marketing (MBA); public administration (MBA, MM). Evening/weekend programs available. Postbaccalaureate distance learning degree programs offered. *Degree requirements:* For master's, thesis (for some programs). *Entrance requirements:* For master's, 3 years of work experience, minimum undergraduate GPA of 3.0. Additional exam requirements/recommendations for international students: Required—TOEFL (minimum score 550 paper-based; 213 computer-based; 79 iBT). Electronic applications accepted.

University of Phoenix–Idaho Campus, School of Business, Meridian, ID 83642-5114. Offers accounting (MBA); administration (MBA); global management (MBA); human resources management (MBA, MM); management (MM); marketing (MBA); public administration (MM). Evening/weekend programs available. Postbaccalaureate distance learning degree programs offered. *Degree requirements:* For master's, thesis (for some programs). *Entrance requirements:* For master's, 3 years of work experience, minimum undergraduate GPA of 3.0. Additional exam requirements/recommendations for international students: Required—TOEFL (minimum score 550 paper-based; 213 computer-based). Electronic applications accepted.

University of Phoenix–Indianapolis Campus, School of Business, Indianapolis, IN 46250-932. Offers accounting (MBA); business administration (MBA); global management (MBA); human resources management (MBA, MM); management (MM); marketing (MBA); public administration (MM). Evening/weekend programs available. *Degree requirements:* For master's, thesis (for some programs). *Entrance requirements:* For master's, minimum undergraduate GPA of 3.0, 3 years of work experience. Additional exam requirements/recommendations for international students: Required—TOEFL (minimum score 550 paper-based; 213 computer-based). Electronic applications accepted.

University of Phoenix–Jersey City Campus, School of Business, Jersey City, NJ 07310. Offers accounting (MBA); business administration (MBA); global management (MBA); human resources management (MBA, MM); management (MM); marketing (MBA); public administration (MBA, MM).

University of Phoenix–Kansas City Campus, School of Business, Kansas City, MO 64131-4517. Offers accounting (MBA); business administration (MBA); global management (MBA); human resources management (MBA, MM); management (MM); marketing (MBA); public administration (MBA). Evening/weekend programs available. *Degree requirements:* For master's, thesis (for some programs). *Entrance requirements:* For master's, minimum undergraduate GPA of 3.0, 3 years of work experience. Additional exam requirements/recommendations for international students: Required—TOEFL (minimum score 550 paper-based; 213 computer-based). Electronic applications accepted.

University of Phoenix–Las Vegas Campus, School of Business, Las Vegas, NV 89128. Offers accounting (MBA); business administration (MBA); global management (MBA); human resources management (MBA, MM); management (MM); marketing (MBA); public administration (MM). Evening/weekend programs available. Postbaccalaureate distance learning degree programs offered (no on-campus study). *Degree requirements:* For master's, thesis (for some programs). *Entrance requirements:* For master's, minimum undergraduate GPA of 3.0, 3 years of work experience. Additional exam requirements/recommendations for international students: Required—TOEFL (minimum score 550 paper-based; 213 computer-based; 79 iBT). Electronic applications accepted.

University of Phoenix–Louisiana Campus, School of Business, Metairie, LA 70001-2082. Offers accounting (MBA); business administration (MBA); global management (MBA); human resources management (MBA, MM); management (MM); marketing (MBA); public administration (MBA). Evening/weekend programs available. *Degree requirements:* For master's, thesis (for some programs). *Entrance requirements:* For master's, minimum undergraduate GPA of 3.0, 3 years work experience. Additional exam requirements/recommendations for international students: Required—TOEFL (minimum score 550 paper-based; 213 computer-based; 79 iBT). Electronic applications accepted.

University of Phoenix–Madison Campus, School of Business, Madison, WI 53718-2416. Offers accounting (MBA); business and management (MBA); e-business (MBA); global management (MBA); human resources management (MBA, MM); management (MM); marketing (MBA); public administration (MBA).

University of Phoenix–Memphis Campus, School of Business, Cordova, TN 38018. Offers accounting (MBA); business and management (MBA); e-business (MBA); global management (MBA); human resources management (MBA, MM); management (MM); marketing (MBA); public administration (MBA, MM).

University of Phoenix–Milwaukee Campus, School of Business, Milwaukee, WI 53045. Offers accounting (MS); business administration (MBA, DBA); human resources management (MM); management (MM); organizational leadership (DM); public administration (MPA).

University of Phoenix–Minneapolis/St. Louis Park Campus, School of Business, St. Louis Park, MN 55426. Offers accounting (MBA); business administration (MBA); global management (MBA); human resources management (MBA); management (MM); marketing (MBA); public administration (MBA).

University of Phoenix–Nashville Campus, School of Business, Nashville, TN 37214-5048. Offers business administration (MBA); human resources management (MBA); management (MM). Evening/weekend programs available. *Degree requirements:* For master's, thesis (for some programs). *Entrance requirements:* For master's, minimum undergraduate GPA of 3.0, 3 years of work experience. Additional exam requirements/recommendations for international students: Required—TOEFL (minimum score 550 paper-based; 213 computer-based; 79 iBT). Electronic applications accepted.

University of Phoenix–New Mexico Campus, School of Business, Albuquerque, NM 87113-1570. Offers accounting (MBA); business administration (MBA); global management (MBA); human resources management (MBA, MM); management (MM); marketing (MBA). Evening/weekend programs available. *Degree requirements:* For master's, thesis (for some programs). *Entrance requirements:* For master's, 3 years of work experience, minimum undergraduate GPA of 3.0. Additional exam requirements/recommendations for international students: Required—TOEFL (minimum score 550 paper-based; 213 computer-based; 79 iBT). Electronic applications accepted.

University of Phoenix–Northern Nevada Campus, School of Business, Reno, NV 89521-5862. Offers accounting (MBA); business administration (MBA); global management (MBA); human resources management (MBA, MM); management (MM); marketing (MBA); public administration (MBA, MM).

University of Phoenix–North Florida Campus, School of Business, Jacksonville, FL 32216-0959. Offers accounting (MBA); business administration (MBA); global management (MBA); human resources management (MBA, MM); management (MM);

marketing (MBA); public administration (MBA, MM). Evening/weekend programs available. *Degree requirements:* For master's, thesis (for some programs). *Entrance requirements:* For master's, minimum undergraduate GPA of 3.0, 3 years work experience. Additional exam requirements/recommendations for international students: Required—TOEFL (minimum score 550 paper-based; 213 computer-based; 79 iBT). Electronic applications accepted.

University of Phoenix–Northwest Arkansas Campus, School of Business, Rogers, AR 72756-9615. Offers accounting (MBA); business and management (MBA); global management (MBA); human resources management (MBA, MM); management (MM); marketing (MBA); public administration (MBA, MM).

University of Phoenix–Oklahoma City Campus, School of Business, Oklahoma City, OK 73116-8244. Offers accounting (MBA); business administration (MBA); global management (MBA); human resource management (MBA); management (MM); marketing (MBA). Evening/weekend programs available. *Degree requirements:* For master's, thesis (for some programs). *Entrance requirements:* For master's, minimum undergraduate GPA of 3.0, 3 years of work experience. Additional exam requirements/recommendations for international students: Required—TOEFL (minimum score 550 paper-based; 213 computer-based; 79 iBT). Electronic applications accepted.

University of Phoenix–Omaha Campus, School of Business, Omaha, NE 68154-5240. Offers accounting (MBA); business and management (MBA); global management (MBA); human resources management (MBA, MM); management (MM); marketing (MBA); public administration (MBA, MM).

University of Phoenix–Online Campus, School of Business, Phoenix, AZ 85034-7209. Offers accountancy (MS); accounting (MBA); business administration (MBA); energy management (MBA); global management (MBA); health care management (MBA); human resource management (MBA); human resources management (MM); international (MM); management (MM); marketing (MBA, Graduate Certificate); organizational management (MA); project management (MBA, Graduate Certificate); public administration (MBA, MM, MPA); technology management (MBA). Evening/weekend programs available. Postbaccalaureate distance learning degree programs offered. *Students:* 18,883 full-time (11,868 women); includes 6,302 minority (4,182 Black or African American, non-Hispanic/Latino; 121 American Indian or Alaska Native, non-Hispanic/Latino; 478 Asian, non-Hispanic/Latino; 1,252 Hispanic/Latino; 121 Native Hawaiian or other Pacific Islander, non-Hispanic/Latino; 148 Two or more races, non-Hispanic/Latino), 1,000 international. Average age 37. *Entrance requirements:* Additional exam requirements/recommendations for international students: Required—TOEFL, TOEIC (Test of English as an International Communication), Berlitz Online English Proficiency Exam, Pearson Test of English, or IELTS. *Application deadline:* Applications are processed on a rolling basis. Application fee: $45. Electronic applications accepted. *Expenses: Tuition:* Full-time $17,160. *Required fees:* $920. One-time fee: $45 full-time. Full-time tuition and fees vary according to course load, degree level, campus/location and program. *Financial support:* Scholarships/grants available. Financial award applicants required to submit FAFSA. *Application contact:* 866-766-0766. Web site: http://www.phoenix.edu/colleges_divisions/business.html.

University of Phoenix–Oregon Campus, School of Business, Tigard, OR 97223. Offers accounting (MBA); business administration (MBA); global management (MBA); human resource management (MM); human resources management (MBA); management (MM); marketing (MBA); public administration (MM). Evening/weekend programs available. *Degree requirements:* For master's, thesis (for some programs). *Entrance requirements:* For master's, minimum undergraduate GPA of 3.0, 3 years of work experience. Additional exam requirements/recommendations for international students: Required—TOEFL (minimum score 550 paper-based; 213 computer-based; 79 iBT). Electronic applications accepted.

University of Phoenix–Philadelphia Campus, School of Business, Wayne, PA 19087-2121. Offers accounting (MBA); business administration (MBA); global management (MBA); human resources management (MBA, MM); management (MM); marketing (MBA); public administration (MM). Evening/weekend programs available. *Degree requirements:* For master's, thesis (for some programs). *Entrance requirements:* For master's, minimum undergraduate GPA of 3.0, 3 years work experience. Additional exam requirements/recommendations for international students: Required—TOEFL (minimum score 550 paper-based; 213 computer-based; 79 iBT). Electronic applications accepted.

University of Phoenix–Phoenix Main Campus, School of Business, Tempe, AZ 85282-2371. Offers accounting (MBA, MS); business administration (MBA); energy management (MBA); global management (MBA); health care management (MBA); human resource management (MBA); management (MM); marketing (MBA); project management (MBA); public administration (MPA); technology management (MBA). Evening/weekend programs available. Postbaccalaureate distance learning degree programs offered. *Students:* 1,151 full-time (531 women); includes 310 minority (99 Black or African American, non-Hispanic/Latino; 10 American Indian or Alaska Native, non-Hispanic/Latino; 39 Asian, non-Hispanic/Latino; 130 Hispanic/Latino; 15 Native Hawaiian or other Pacific Islander, non-Hispanic/Latino; 17 Two or more races, non-Hispanic/Latino), 63 international. Average age 34. *Entrance requirements:* Additional exam requirements/recommendations for international students: Required—TOEFL, TOEIC (Test of English as an International Communication), Berlitz Online English Proficiency Exam, Pearson Test of English, or IELTS. *Application deadline:* Applications are processed on a rolling basis. Application fee: $45. Electronic applications accepted. *Expenses:* Contact institution. *Financial support:* Scholarships/grants available. Financial award applicants required to submit FAFSA. *Application contact:* 866-766-0766. Web site: http://www.phoenix.edu/colleges_divisions/business.html.

University of Phoenix–Pittsburgh Campus, School of Business, Pittsburgh, PA 15276. Offers accounting (MBA); business administration (MBA); global management (MBA); human resources management (MBA, MM); management (MM); marketing (MBA); public administration (MBA, MM). Evening/weekend programs available. *Degree requirements:* For master's, thesis (for some programs). *Entrance requirements:* For master's, minimum undergraduate GPA of 3.0, 3 years work experience. Additional exam requirements/recommendations for international students: Required—TOEFL (minimum score 550 paper-based; 213 computer-based; 79 iBT). Electronic applications accepted.

University of Phoenix–Puerto Rico Campus, School of Business, Guaynabo, PR 00968. Offers accounting (MBA); energy management (MBA); global management (MBA); human resource management (MBA); marketing (MBA); project management (MBA); small business administration (MBA). Evening/weekend programs available. *Degree requirements:* For master's, thesis (for some programs). *Entrance requirements:* For master's, minimum undergraduate GPA of 3.0, 3 years work experience. Additional exam requirements/recommendations for international students: Required—TOEFL (minimum score 550 paper-based; 213 computer-based; 79 iBT). Electronic applications accepted.

University of Phoenix–Raleigh Campus, School of Business, Raleigh, NC 27606. Offers accounting (MBA); business administration (MBA); e-business (MBA); global management (MBA); human resources management (MBA); marketing (MBA).

University of Phoenix–Richmond Campus, School of Business, Richmond, VA 23230. Offers accounting (MBA); business administration (MBA); global management (MBA); human resources management (MBA, MM); management (MM); marketing (MBA); public administration (MBA, MM). Evening/weekend programs available. *Degree requirements:* For master's, thesis (for some programs). *Entrance requirements:* For master's, minimum undergraduate GPA of 3.0, 3 years work experience. Additional exam requirements/recommendations for international students: Required—TOEFL (minimum score 550 paper-based; 213 computer-based; 79 iBT). Electronic applications accepted.

University of Phoenix–Sacramento Valley Campus, School of Business, Sacramento, CA 95833-3632. Offers accounting (MBA); business administration (MBA); global management (MBA); human resources management (MBA, MM); management (MM); marketing (MBA); public administration (MBA, MM). Evening/weekend programs available. *Degree requirements:* For master's, thesis (for some programs). *Entrance requirements:* For master's, minimum undergraduate GPA of 3.0, 3 years work experience. Additional exam requirements/recommendations for international students: Required—TOEFL (minimum score 550 paper-based; 213 computer-based; 79 iBT). Electronic applications accepted.

University of Phoenix–St. Louis Campus, School of Business, St. Louis, MO 63043-4828. Offers accounting (MBA); business administration (MBA); global management (MBA); human resources management (MBA, MM); management (MM); marketing (MBA); public administration (MM). Evening/weekend programs available. *Degree requirements:* For master's, thesis (for some programs). *Entrance requirements:* For master's, 3 years of work experience, minimum undergraduate GPA of 3.0. Additional exam requirements/recommendations for international students: Required—TOEFL (minimum score 550 paper-based; 213 computer-based; 79 iBT). Electronic applications accepted.

University of Phoenix–San Antonio Campus, School of Business, San Antonio, TX 78230. Offers accounting (MBA); business administration (MBA); e-business (MBA); global management (MBA); human resources management (MBA, MM); management (MM); marketing (MBA); public administration (MBA, MM).

University of Phoenix–San Diego Campus, School of Business, San Diego, CA 92123. Offers accounting (MBA); business administration (MBA); global management (MBA); human resources management (MBA, MM); management (MM); marketing (MBA); public administration (MBA). Evening/weekend programs available. *Degree requirements:* For master's, thesis (for some programs). *Entrance requirements:* For master's, 3 years of work experience, minimum undergraduate GPA of 3.0. Additional exam requirements/recommendations for international students: Required—TOEFL (minimum score 550 paper-based; 213 computer-based; 79 iBT). Electronic applications accepted.

University of Phoenix–Savannah Campus, School of Business, Savannah, GA 31405-7400. Offers accounting (MBA); business administration (MBA); global management (MBA); human resources management (MBA, MM); management (MM); marketing (MBA); public administration (MBA, MM).

University of Phoenix–Southern Arizona Campus, School of Business, Tucson, AZ 85711. Offers accountancy (MS); accounting (MBA); business administration (MBA); global management (MBA); human resources management (MBA); management (MM); marketing (MBA). Evening/weekend programs available. *Degree requirements:* For master's, thesis (for some programs). *Entrance requirements:* For master's, minimum undergraduate GPA of 3.0, 3 years of work experience. Additional exam requirements/recommendations for international students: Required—TOEFL (minimum score 550 paper-based; 213 computer-based; 79 iBT). Electronic applications accepted.

University of Phoenix–Southern California Campus, School of Business, Costa Mesa, CA 92626. Offers accounting (MIS); business administration (MBA); energy management (MBA); global management (MBA); health care management (MBA); human resource management (MBA); management (MM); marketing (MBA); project management (MBA); public administration (MPA); technology management (MBA). Evening/weekend programs available. Postbaccalaureate distance learning degree programs offered. *Students:* 699 full-time (341 women); includes 318 minority (124 Black or African American, non-Hispanic/Latino; 4 American Indian or Alaska Native, non-Hispanic/Latino; 44 Asian, non-Hispanic/Latino; 124 Hispanic/Latino; 15 Native Hawaiian or other Pacific Islander, non-Hispanic/Latino; 7 Two or more races, non-Hispanic/Latino), 29 international. Average age 38. *Entrance requirements:* Additional exam requirements/recommendations for international students: Required—TOEFL, TOEIC (Test of English as an International Communication), Berlitz Online English Proficiency Exam, Pearson Test of English, or IELTS. *Application deadline:* Applications are processed on a rolling basis. Application fee: $45. Electronic applications accepted. *Expenses:* Contact institution. *Financial support:* Scholarships/grants available. Financial award applicants required to submit FAFSA. *Application contact:* 866-766-0766. Web site: http://www.phoenix.edu/colleges_divisions/business.html.

University of Phoenix–Southern Colorado Campus, School of Business, Colorado Springs, CO 80919-2335. Offers accounting (MBA); business administration (MBA); global management (MBA); human resources management (MBA, MM); management (MM); marketing (MBA); public administration (MM). Evening/weekend programs available. *Degree requirements:* For master's, thesis (for some programs). *Entrance requirements:* For master's, minimum undergraduate GPA of 3.0, 3 years of work experience. Additional exam requirements/recommendations for international students: Required—TOEFL (minimum score 550 paper-based; 213 computer-based; 79 iBT). Electronic applications accepted.

University of Phoenix–South Florida Campus, School of Business, Fort Lauderdale, FL 33309. Offers accounting (MBA); business administration (MBA); global management (MBA); human resource management (MBA); human resources management (MM); management (MM); marketing (MBA); public administration (MBA, MM). Evening/weekend programs available. *Degree requirements:* For master's, thesis (for some programs). *Entrance requirements:* For master's, minimum undergraduate GPA of 3.0, 3 years work experience. Additional exam requirements/recommendations for international students: Required—TOEFL (minimum score 550 paper-based; 213 computer-based; 79 iBT). Electronic applications accepted.

University of Phoenix–Springfield Campus, School of Business, Springfield, MO 65804-7211. Offers accounting (MBA); business administration (MBA); global management (MBA); human resources management (MBA, MM); management (MM); marketing (MBA); public administration (MBA, MM).

University of Phoenix–Tulsa Campus, School of Business, Tulsa, OK 74134-1412. Offers accounting (MBA); business (MM); business administration (MBA); global management (MBA); human resources management (MBA); marketing (MBA). Evening/weekend programs available. *Degree requirements:* For master's, thesis (for some programs). *Entrance requirements:* For master's, minimum undergraduate GPA of 3.0, 3 years work experience. Additional exam requirements/recommendations for international students: Required—TOEFL (minimum score 550 paper-based; 213 computer-based; 79 iBT).

Human Resources Management

University of Phoenix–Utah Campus, School of Business, Salt Lake City, UT 84123-4617. Offers accounting (MBA); business administration (MBA); global management (MBA); human resource management (MBA, MM); management (MM); marketing (MBA); technology management (MBA). Evening/weekend programs available. *Degree requirements:* For master's, thesis (for some programs). *Entrance requirements:* For master's, minimum undergraduate GPA of 3.0, 3 years of work experience. Additional exam requirements/recommendations for international students: Required—TOEFL (minimum score 550 paper-based; 213 computer-based; 79 iBT). Electronic applications accepted.

University of Phoenix–Vancouver Campus, John Sperling School of Business, College of Graduate Business and Management, Burnaby, BC V5C 6G9, Canada. Offers accounting (MBA); business administration (MBA); global management (MBA); human resources management (MBA, MM); marketing (MBA). Evening/weekend programs available. *Degree requirements:* For master's, thesis (for some programs). *Entrance requirements:* For master's, minimum undergraduate GPA of 3.0, 3 years of work experience. Additional exam requirements/recommendations for international students: Required—TOEFL (minimum score 550 paper-based; 213 computer-based; 79 iBT). Electronic applications accepted.

University of Phoenix–Washington D.C. Campus, School of Business, Washington, DC 20001. Offers accountancy (MS); business administration (MBA, DBA); human resources management (MM); management (MM); organizational leadership (DM); public administration (MPA).

University of Phoenix–West Florida Campus, School of Business, Temple Terrace, FL 33637. Offers accounting (MBA); business administration (MBA); global management (MBA); human resources management (MBA, MM); management (MM); marketing (MBA); public administration (MBA, MM). Evening/weekend programs available. *Degree requirements:* For master's, thesis (for some programs). *Entrance requirements:* For master's, 3 years of work experience, minimum undergraduate GPA of 3.0. Additional exam requirements/recommendations for international students: Required—TOEFL (minimum score 550 paper-based; 213 computer-based; 79 iBT). Electronic applications accepted.

University of Pittsburgh, Katz Graduate School of Business, Doctoral Program in Business Administration, Pittsburgh, PA 15260. Offers accounting (PhD); finance (PhD); information systems (PhD); marketing (PhD); operations/decision sciences/artificial intelligence (PhD); organizational behavior and human resource management (PhD); strategic planning (PhD). *Accreditation:* AACSB. *Faculty:* 54 full-time (16 women). *Students:* 51 full-time (21 women); includes 9 minority (4 Black or African American, non-Hispanic/Latino; 4 Asian, non-Hispanic/Latino; 1 Hispanic/Latino), 23 international. 373 applicants, 7% accepted, 10 enrolled. In 2011, 6 doctorates awarded. *Degree requirements:* For doctorate, comprehensive exam, thesis/dissertation. *Entrance requirements:* For doctorate, GMAT or GRE. Additional exam requirements/recommendations for international students: Required—TOEFL. *Application deadline:* For fall admission, 2/1 priority date for domestic students, 2/1 for international students. Applications are processed on a rolling basis. Application fee: $50. Electronic applications accepted. *Expenses:* Tuition, state resident: full-time $18,774; part-time $760 per credit. Tuition, nonresident: full-time $30,736; part-time $1258 per credit. *Required fees:* $740; $200 per term. Tuition and fees vary according to program. *Financial support:* In 2011–12, 38 students received support, including 29 research assistantships with full tuition reimbursements available (averaging $19,400 per year), 10 teaching assistantships with full tuition reimbursements available (averaging $24,700 per year); fellowships, Federal Work-Study, scholarships/grants, health care benefits, and unspecified assistantships also available. Financial award application deadline: 2/1. *Faculty research:* Accounting statements and reporting, corporate finance, information systems processes, structures and decision-making, consumer behavior and marketing models. *Total annual research expenditures:* $254,031. *Unit head:* Dr. Dennis Galletta, Director, 412-648-1699, Fax: 412-624-3633, E-mail: galletta@katz.pitt.edu. *Application contact:* Carrie Woods, Assistant Director, 412-648-1525, Fax: 412-624-3633, E-mail: cawoods@katz.pitt.edu. Web site: http://www.business.pitt.edu/katz/phd/.

University of Pittsburgh, Katz Graduate School of Business, Master of Business Administration Programs, Pittsburgh , PA 15260. Offers finance (MBA); information systems (MBA); marketing (MBA); operations management (MBA); organizational behavior and human resource management (MBA); organizational leadership (Certificate); strategy, environment and organizations (MBA); technology, innovation and entrepreneurship (Certificate); MBA/JD; MBA/MIB; MBA/MPIA; MBA/MSE; MBA/MSIS; MID/MBA. *Accreditation:* AACSB. Part-time and evening/weekend programs available. *Faculty:* 62 full-time (17 women), 21 part-time/adjunct (4 women). *Students:* 179 full-time (63 women), 572 part-time (373 women); includes 69 minority (29 Black or African American, non-Hispanic/Latino; 24 Asian, non-Hispanic/Latino; 16 Hispanic/Latino), 83 international. Average age 29. 391 applicants, 42% accepted, 78 enrolled. *Degree requirements:* For master's, minimum GPA of 3.0. *Entrance requirements:* For master's, GMAT, recommendations, undergraduate transcripts, essay, resume, interview, bachelor's degree. Additional exam requirements/recommendations for international students: Required—TOEFL (minimum score 600 paper, 250 computer, 100 iBT) or IELTS. *Application deadline:* For fall admission, 4/1 priority date for domestic students, 2/1 for international students. Application fee: $50. Electronic applications accepted. *Expenses:* Tuition, state resident: full-time $18,774; part-time $760 per credit. Tuition, nonresident: full-time $30,736; part-time $1258 per credit. *Required fees:* $740; $200 per term. Tuition and fees vary according to program. *Financial support:* In 2011–12, 58 students received support. Career-related internships or fieldwork and scholarships/grants available. Financial award application deadline: 3/1; financial award applicants required to submit FAFSA. *Faculty research:* Accounting statements and reporting, corporate finance, information systems processes, structures and decision-making, consumer behavior and marketing models. *Unit head:* William T. Valenta, Assistant Dean/Director, 412-648-1610, Fax: 412-648-1659, E-mail: wtvalenta@katz.pitt.edu. *Application contact:* Thomas Keller, Director of MBA Admissions, 412-648-1700, Fax: 412-648-1659, E-mail: mba@katz.pitt.edu. Web site: http://www.business.pitt.edu/katz/mba/.

University of Puerto Rico, Mayagüez Campus, Graduate Studies, College of Business Administration, Mayagüez, PR 00681-9000. Offers business administration (MBA); finance (MBA); human resources (MBA); industrial management (MBA). Part-time and evening/weekend programs available. *Students:* 46 full-time (30 women), 16 part-time (9 women); includes 59 minority (all Hispanic/Latino), 3 international. 18 applicants, 44% accepted, 5 enrolled. In 2011, 14 master's awarded. *Degree requirements:* For master's, comprehensive exam. *Entrance requirements:* For master's, GMAT or EXADEP, bachelor's degree with courses in calculus, microeconomics, accounting and statistics. Additional exam requirements/recommendations for international students: Required—TOEFL (minimum score 500 paper-based; 173 computer-based). *Application deadline:* For fall admission, 2/15 for domestic and international students; for spring admission, 9/15 for domestic and international students. Applications are processed on a rolling basis. Application fee: $25. Tuition and fees vary according to course level and course load. *Financial support:* In 2011–12, 4 students received support, including 4 teaching assistantships (averaging $8,500 per year); Federal Work-Study and institutionally sponsored loans also available. *Faculty research:* Organizational studies, management, accounting. *Total annual research expenditures:* $20,000. *Unit head:* Dr. Rosario Ortiz, Graduate Student Coordinator, 787-265-3800, Fax: 787-832-5320, E-mail: rosario.ortiz@upr.edu. *Application contact:* Milagros Soto, Student Administrator, 787-265-3887, Fax: 787-832-5320, E-mail: milagros.soto1@upr.edu. Web site: http://enterprise.uprm.edu/.

University of Puerto Rico, Río Piedras, College of Business Administration, San Juan, PR 00931-3300. Offers accounting (MBA); finance (MBA, PhD); general business (MBA); human resources management (MBA); international trade and business (MBA, PhD); marketing (MBA); operations management (MBA); quantitative methods (MBA). *Accreditation:* ACBSP. Part-time programs available. *Degree requirements:* For master's, comprehensive exam, thesis or alternative, research project. *Entrance requirements:* For master's, GMAT or PAEG, minimum GPA of 3.0, letter of recommendation; for doctorate, GMAT, PAEG, minimum GPA of 3.0, master degree. *Faculty research:* Management.

University of Regina, Faculty of Graduate Studies and Research, Kenneth Levene Graduate School of Business, Program in Human Resources Management, Regina, SK S4S 0A2, Canada. Offers MHRM, Master's Certificate. Part-time programs available. *Faculty:* 32 full-time (12 women), 10 part-time/adjunct (0 women). *Students:* 12 full-time (5 women), 15 part-time (11 women). 44 applicants, 45% accepted. In 2011, 24 master's awarded. *Degree requirements:* For master's, project. *Entrance requirements:* For master's, GMAT, two years relevant work experience. Additional exam requirements/recommendations for international students: Required—TOEFL (minimum score 580 paper-based; 80 iBT), IELTS (minimum score 6.5). *Application deadline:* Applications are processed on a rolling basis. Application fee: $100. Electronic applications accepted. *Expenses:* Contact institution. *Financial support:* In 2011–12, 4 teaching assistantships (averaging $2,298 per year) were awarded; fellowships, research assistantships, and scholarships/grants also available. Financial award application deadline: 6/15. *Faculty research:* Human behavior in organizations, labor relations and collective bargaining, organization theory, staffing organizations, human resources systems analysis. *Unit head:* Dr. Morina Rennie, Dean, 306-585-4162, Fax: 306-585-4805, E-mail: morina.rennie@uregina.ca. *Application contact:* Steve Wield, Manager, Graduate Programs, 306-337-8463, Fax: 306-585-5361, E-mail: steve.wield@uregina.ca.

University of Rhode Island, Graduate School, Labor Research Center, Kingston, RI 02881. Offers labor relations and human resources (MS); MS/JD. Part-time and evening/weekend programs available. *Faculty:* 1 full-time (0 women). *Students:* 7 full-time (4 women), 32 part-time (24 women); includes 6 minority (2 Black or African American, non-Hispanic/Latino; 2 Asian, non-Hispanic/Latino; 2 Hispanic/Latino), 1 international. In 2011, 7 master's awarded. *Entrance requirements:* For master's, GRE, MAT, GMAT, or LSAT, 2 letters of recommendation. Additional exam requirements/recommendations for international students: Required—TOEFL (minimum score 550 paper-based; 213 computer-based). *Application deadline:* For fall admission, 7/15 for domestic students, 2/1 for international students; for spring admission, 11/15 for domestic students, 7/15 for international students. Application fee: $65. Electronic applications accepted. *Expenses:* Tuition, state resident: full-time $10,432; part-time $580 per credit hour. Tuition, nonresident: full-time $23,130; part-time $1285 per credit hour. *Required fees:* $1362; $36 per credit hour. $35 per semester. One-time fee: $130. *Financial support:* In 2011–12, 2 teaching assistantships with full tuition reimbursements (averaging $13,894 per year) were awarded; institutionally sponsored loans also available. Financial award application deadline: 2/1; financial award applicants required to submit FAFSA. *Unit head:* Dr. Richard W. Scholl, Director, 401-874-4347, Fax: 401-874-2954, E-mail: rscholl@uri.edu. *Application contact:* Nasser H. Zawia, Dean of the Graduate School, 401-874-5909, Fax: 401-874-5787, E-mail: nzawia@uri.edu. Web site: http://www.uri.edu/research/lrc/.

University of St. Thomas, Graduate Studies, School of Education, Program in Organization Learning and Development, St. Paul, MN 55105-1096. Offers e-learning (Certificate); human resource management (Certificate); learning technology (MA); organization development (Ed D, Certificate); strategic resources and change leadership (MA). Part-time and evening/weekend programs available. Postbaccalaureate distance learning degree programs offered (minimal on-campus study). *Faculty:* 6 full-time (4 women), 15 part-time/adjunct (8 women). *Students:* 6 full-time (all women), 125 part-time (96 women); includes 26 minority (13 Black or African American, non-Hispanic/Latino; 5 Asian, non-Hispanic/Latino; 4 Hispanic/Latino; 1 Native Hawaiian or other Pacific Islander, non-Hispanic/Latino; 3 Two or more races, non-Hispanic/Latino), 9 international. Average age 38. 40 applicants, 85% accepted, 28 enrolled. In 2011, 31 master's, 9 doctorates awarded. *Degree requirements:* For master's, practicum; for doctorate, comprehensive exam, thesis/dissertation. *Entrance requirements:* For master's, minimum GPA of 3.0, 2 letters of reference, personal statement, 2-5 years of organization experience; for doctorate, minimum GPA of 3.5, interview, 5-7 years of OD or leadership experience; for Certificate, minimum graduate GPA of 3.25. Additional exam requirements/recommendations for international students: Required—TOEFL (minimum score 550 paper-based; 213 computer-based). *Application deadline:* For fall admission, 8/1 priority date for domestic students, 8/1 for international students; for winter admission, 12/1 priority date for domestic students, 12/1 for international students; for spring admission, 12/1 priority date for domestic students, 12/1 for international students. Applications are processed on a rolling basis. Application fee: $50. Electronic applications accepted. *Expenses:* Contact institution. *Financial support:* In 2011–12, 1 student received support. Fellowships, research assistantships, institutionally sponsored loans, and scholarships/grants available. Support available to part-time students. Financial award applicants required to submit FAFSA. *Faculty research:* Workplace conflict, physician leaders, virtual teams, technology use in schools/workplace, developing masterful practitioners. *Unit head:* Dr. David W. Jamieson, Department Chair, 651-962-4387, Fax: 651-962-4169, E-mail: djamieson@stthomas.edu. *Application contact:* Liz G. Knight, Program Manager, 651-962-4459, Fax: 651-962-4169, E-mail: egknight@stthomas.edu. Web site: http://www.stthomas.edu/education.

The University of Scranton, College of Graduate and Continuing Education, Department of Health Administration and Human Resources, Program in Human Resources Administration, Scranton, PA 18510. Offers human resources (MS); human resources development (MS); organizational leadership (MS). Part-time and evening/weekend programs available. *Students:* 3 full-time (all women). Average age 36. 70 applicants, 80% accepted. In 2011, 5 master's awarded. *Degree requirements:* For master's, capstone experience. *Entrance requirements:* For master's, minimum GPA of 2.75. Additional exam requirements/recommendations for international students: Required—TOEFL (minimum score 500 paper-based; 173 computer-based), IELTS (minimum score 5.5). *Application deadline:* Applications are processed on a rolling basis. Application fee: $0. *Financial support:* Fellowships, teaching assistantships, career-related internships or fieldwork, Federal Work-Study, and unspecified assistantships available. Support available to part-time students. Financial award application deadline: 3/1. *Unit head:* Dr. Daniel West, Director, 570-941-6218, E-mail: westd1@scranton.edu. *Application contact:* Joseph M. Roback, Director of Admissions, 570-941-4385, Fax: 570-941-5928, E-mail: robackj2@scranton.edu.

University of South Carolina, The Graduate School, Darla Moore School of Business, Human Resources Program, Columbia, SC 29208. Offers MHR, JD/MHR. Part-time programs available. *Degree requirements:* For master's, internship. *Entrance requirements:* For master's, GMAT or GRE, minimum GPA of 3.0. Additional exam requirements/recommendations for international students: Required—TOEFL (minimum score 250 computer-based; 100 iBT); Recommended—IELTS. Electronic applications accepted. *Expenses:* Contact institution. *Faculty research:* Management and compensation, performance appraisal, work values, grievance systems, union formation, group behavior.

The University of Texas at Arlington, Graduate School, College of Business, Department of Management, Arlington, TX 76019. Offers human resources (MSHRM). Part-time and evening/weekend programs available. *Faculty:* 14 full-time (5 women). *Students:* 35 full-time (17 women), 35 part-time (22 women); includes 16 minority (7 Black or African American, non-Hispanic/Latino; 1 Asian, non-Hispanic/Latino; 6 Hispanic/Latino; 1 Native Hawaiian or other Pacific Islander, non-Hispanic/Latino; 1 Two or more races, non-Hispanic/Latino), 20 international. 94 applicants, 67% accepted, 54 enrolled. In 2011, 14 degrees awarded. *Degree requirements:* For master's, thesis optional. *Entrance requirements:* For master's, GMAT/GRE. Additional exam requirements/recommendations for international students: Required—TOEFL (minimum score 550 paper-based; 213 computer-based; 79 iBT). *Application deadline:* For fall admission, 6/5 priority date for domestic students, 4/1 for international students; for spring admission, 10/15 for domestic students, 9/15 for international students. Applications are processed on a rolling basis. Application fee: $40 ($70 for international students). *Financial support:* In 2011–12, 16 teaching assistantships (averaging $15,594 per year) were awarded; career-related internships or fieldwork, scholarships/grants, and unspecified assistantships also available. Support available to part-time students. Financial award application deadline: 6/1; financial award applicants required to submit FAFSA. *Faculty research:* Compensations, training, diversity, strategic human resources. *Unit head:* Dr. Abdul Rasheed, Chair, 817-272-3166, Fax: 817-272-3122, E-mail: abdul@uta.edu. *Application contact:* Dennis Veit, Graduate Advisor, 817-272-3865, Fax: 817-272-3122, E-mail: dveit@uta.edu. Web site: http://www.management.uta.edu/.

University of the Sacred Heart, Graduate Programs, Department of Business Administration, Program in Human Resource Management, San Juan, PR 00914-0383. Offers MBA. Part-time and evening/weekend programs available. *Degree requirements:* For master's, thesis. *Entrance requirements:* For master's, EXADEP, minimum undergraduate GPA of 2.75, interview.

The University of Toledo, College of Graduate Studies, College of Business and Innovation, Department of Management, Toledo, OH 43606-3390. Offers administration (MBA); entrepreneurship (MBA); executive management (MBA); general administration (MBA); human resource management (MBA); leadership (MBA). Part-time and evening/weekend programs available. *Faculty:* 8. *Students:* 61 full-time (20 women), 147 part-time (48 women); includes 20 minority (14 Black or African American, non-Hispanic/Latino; 1 American Indian or Alaska Native, non-Hispanic/Latino; 2 Asian, non-Hispanic/Latino; 3 Hispanic/Latino), 96 international. Average age 27. 82 applicants, 72% accepted, 53 enrolled. In 2011, 84 master's awarded. *Entrance requirements:* For master's, GMAT, minimum GPA of 2.7 for all prior academic work, three letters of recommendation, statement of purpose, transcripts from all prior institutions attended. Additional exam requirements/recommendations for international students: Required—TOEFL (minimum score 550 paper-based; 213 computer-based; 80 iBT), IELTS (minimum score 6.5). *Application deadline:* For fall admission, 1/15 priority date for domestic students, 1/15 for international students. Applications are processed on a rolling basis. Application fee: $45 ($75 for international students). Electronic applications accepted. *Financial support:* In 2011–12, 39 research assistantships with tuition reimbursements (averaging $5,241 per year) were awarded; career-related internships or fieldwork, Federal Work-Study, institutionally sponsored loans, scholarships/grants, tuition waivers (full and partial), unspecified assistantships, and administrative assistantships also available. Support available to part-time students. *Faculty research:* Stress, deviation, workplace, globalization, recruitment. *Unit head:* Dr. Sonny Ariss, Chair, 419-530-2366. *Application contact:* Graduate School Office, 419-530-4723, Fax: 419-530-4724, E-mail: grdsch@utnet.utoledo.edu. Web site: http://www.utoledo.edu/business/MGMT/MGMTCCD/MGMT.html.

University of Toronto, School of Graduate Studies, Faculty of Arts and Science, Centre for Industrial Relations and Human Resources, Toronto, ON M5S 1A1, Canada. Offers MIRHR, PhD. Part-time programs available. *Degree requirements:* For doctorate, thesis/dissertation. *Entrance requirements:* For master's, GRE or GMAT (for applicants who completed degree outside of Canada), minimum B+ in final 2 years of bachelor's degree completion, 2 letters of reference, resume; for doctorate, GRE or GMAT, MIR or equivalent, minimum B+ average, 3 letters of reference, resume. Additional exam requirements/recommendations for international students: Required—TOEFL (minimum score 600 paper-based; 100 iBT), IELTS, TWE (minimum score 5), Michigan English Language Assessment Battery, or COPE. Electronic applications accepted. *Expenses:* Contact institution.

University of Wisconsin–Madison, Graduate School, Wisconsin School of Business, Doctoral Program in Management and Human Resources, Madison, WI 53706-1380. Offers PhD. *Faculty:* 12 full-time (2 women), 7 part-time/adjunct (3 women). *Students:* 9 full-time (3 women), 4 international. Average age 30. 58 applicants, 5% accepted, 1 enrolled. In 2011, 2 degrees awarded. *Median time to degree:* Of those who began their doctoral program in fall 2003, 75% received their degree in 8 years or less. *Degree requirements:* For doctorate, comprehensive exam, thesis/dissertation. *Entrance requirements:* For doctorate, GMAT or GRE. Additional exam requirements/recommendations for international students: Required—Pearson Test of English (minimum score 73; written 80); Recommended—TOEFL (minimum score 623 paper-based; 263 computer-based; 106 iBT), IELTS (minimum score 7.5). *Application deadline:* For fall admission, 12/15 priority date for domestic students, 12/15 for international students. Application fee: $56. Electronic applications accepted. *Expenses:* Contact institution. *Financial support:* In 2011–12, 10 students received support, including fellowships with tuition reimbursements available (averaging $18,756 per year), research assistantships with full tuition reimbursements available (averaging $16,506 per year), 10 teaching assistantships with full tuition reimbursements available (averaging $14,088 per year); Federal Work-Study, institutionally sponsored loans, scholarships/grants, health care benefits, and unspecified assistantships also available. Financial award application deadline: 2/1; financial award applicants required to submit FAFSA. *Faculty research:* Employee compensation, performance for work groups, small business management, venture financing, arts industry. *Unit head:* Prof. Barry Gerhart, Chair, 608-262-3895, E-mail: bgerhart@bus.wisc.edu. *Application contact:* Belle Heberling, Assistant Director for Research Programs, 608-262-3749, Fax: 608-890-0180, E-mail: phd@bus.wisc.edu. Web site: http://www.bus.wisc.edu/phd/.

University of Wisconsin–Madison, Graduate School, Wisconsin School of Business, Wisconsin Full-Time MBA Program, Madison, WI 53706-1380. Offers applied security analysis (MBA); arts administration (MBA); brand and product management (MBA); corporate finance and investment banking (MBA); marketing research (MBA); operations and technology management (MBA); real estate (MBA); risk management and insurance (MBA); strategic human resource management (MBA); supply chain management (MBA). *Faculty:* 32 full-time (6 women), 27 part-time/adjunct (7 women). *Students:* 228 full-time (75 women); includes 53 minority (16 Black or African American, non-Hispanic/Latino; 25 Asian, non-Hispanic/Latino; 10 Hispanic/Latino; 2 Native Hawaiian or other Pacific Islander, non-Hispanic/Latino), 28 international. Average age 28. 509 applicants, 30% accepted, 111 enrolled. In 2011, 120 master's awarded. *Degree requirements:* For master's, thesis (for arts administration). *Entrance requirements:* For master's, GMAT, bachelor's or equivalent degree, 2 years of work experience, letters of recommendation. Additional exam requirements/recommendations for international students: Required—TOEFL (minimum score 600 paper-based; 250 computer-based; 100 iBT), IELTS. *Application deadline:* For fall admission, 11/4 for domestic and international students; for winter admission, 2/3 for domestic and international students; for spring admission, 4/27 for domestic and international students. Applications are processed on a rolling basis. Application fee: $56. Electronic applications accepted. *Expenses:* Tuition, state resident: full-time $10,296; part-time $643.51 per credit. Tuition, nonresident: full-time $24,054; part-time $1503.40 per credit. *Required fees:* $70.06 per credit. Tuition and fees vary according to course load, campus/location, program and reciprocity agreements. *Financial support:* In 2011–12, 176 students received support, including 20 fellowships with full and partial tuition reimbursements available (averaging $18,756 per year), 128 research assistantships with full tuition reimbursements available (averaging $25,185 per year), 28 teaching assistantships with full tuition reimbursements available (averaging $25,097 per year); scholarships/grants, health care benefits, and unspecified assistantships also available. Financial award application deadline: 4/27; financial award applicants required to submit FAFSA. *Faculty research:* Market consequences of International Financial Reporting Standards (IFRS), inter-firm relationships and strategic partnerships, application of Bayesian statistical methods and applied probability models to understanding individuals' behaviors in the context of customer relationship management (CRM) applications, liquidity provision and the structure of financial markets, strategic management of global startups. *Unit head:* Dr. Larry "Chip" W. Hunter, Associate Dean of Master's Programs, 608-265-3494, Fax: 608-265-4192, E-mail: lhunter@bus.wisc.edu. *Application contact:* Maria Reis, Assistant Director of MBA Marketing and Recruiting, 608-262-4000, Fax: 608-265-4192, E-mail: mreis@bus.wisc.edu. Web site: http://www.bus.wisc.edu/mba.

University of Wisconsin–Whitewater, School of Graduate Studies, College of Business and Economics, Program in Business Administration, Whitewater, WI 53190-1790. Offers finance (MBA); human resource management (MBA); information technology management (MBA); international business (MBA); management (MBA); marketing (MBA); operations and supply chain management (MBA). *Accreditation:* AACSB. Part-time and evening/weekend programs available. Postbaccalaureate distance learning degree programs offered (no on-campus study). *Students:* 170 full-time (53 women), 538 part-time (213 women); includes 130 minority (28 Black or African American, non-Hispanic/Latino; 87 Asian, non-Hispanic/Latino; 15 Hispanic/Latino). Average age 31. 448 applicants, 33% accepted, 120 enrolled. In 2011, 304 master's awarded. *Entrance requirements:* For master's, GMAT or GRE, minimum AACSB index of 1000, minimum GPA of 2.75. Additional exam requirements/recommendations for international students: Required—TOEFL (minimum score 550 paper-based; 213 computer-based; 80 iBT), IELTS (minimum score 6). *Application deadline:* For fall admission, 7/15 for domestic and international students; for spring admission, 12/1 for domestic and international students. Applications are processed on a rolling basis. Application fee: $56. Electronic applications accepted. *Expenses:* Tuition, state resident: full-time $4088. Tuition, nonresident: full-time $8817. Tuition and fees vary according to program. *Financial support:* In 2011–12, research assistantships (averaging $7,245 per year) were awarded; Federal Work-Study, unspecified assistantships, and out-of-state fee waivers also available. Support available to part-time students. Financial award application deadline: 3/15; financial award applicants required to submit FAFSA. *Faculty research:* Interface between social institutions and individual behavior, technology and innovation management, occupational mental health, workplace deviance and workplace romance. *Unit head:* Dr. John Chenoweth, Associate Dean, 262-472-1945, Fax: 262-472-4863, E-mail: chenowej@uww.edu.

Upper Iowa University, Online Master's Programs, Fayette, IA 52142-1857. Offers accounting (MBA); corporate financial management (MBA); global business (MBA); health and human services (MPA); higher education administration (MHEA); homeland security (MPA); human resources management (MBA); justice administration (MPA); organizational development (MBA); public personnel management (MPA); quality management (MBA). MBA also available at Madison, WI campus. Part-time programs available. Postbaccalaureate distance learning degree programs offered (no on-campus study). *Degree requirements:* For master's, research project. *Entrance requirements:* For master's, GMAT, GRE, or minimum GPA of 2.7 during last 60 hours. Additional exam requirements/recommendations for international students: Required—TOEFL (minimum score 570 paper-based; 230 computer-based). Electronic applications accepted. *Faculty research:* Total quality management, CQI, teams, organization culture and climate, management.

Utah State University, School of Graduate Studies, College of Business, Program in Human Resource Management, Logan, UT 84322. Offers MS. Part-time and evening/weekend programs available. Postbaccalaureate distance learning degree programs offered. *Entrance requirements:* For master's, GMAT or GRE, minimum GPA of 3.0. Additional exam requirements/recommendations for international students: Required—TOEFL. Electronic applications accepted. *Expenses:* Contact institution. *Faculty research:* International human resources, aging workforce.

Virginia International University, School of Business, Fairfax, VA 22030. Offers accounting (MBA); executive management (Graduate Certificate); global logistics (MBA); health care management (MBA); human resources management (MBA); international business management (MBA); international finance (MBA); marketing management (MBA). Part-time programs available. *Entrance requirements:* For master's and Graduate Certificate, bachelor's degree. Additional exam requirements/recommendations for international students: Required—TOEFL (minimum score 550 paper-based; 213 computer-based; 80 iBT), IELTS (minimum score 6). Electronic applications accepted.

Walden University, Graduate Programs, School of Management, Minneapolis, MN 55401. Offers accounting (MS, DBA), including accounting for the professional (MS), CPA (MS), self-designed (MS); accounting and management (MS), including accounting for strategic managers, self-designed; accounting for managers (MBA); advanced project management (Post-Graduate Certificate); applied project management (Post-Graduate Certificate); corporate finance (MBA); entrepreneurship (MBA, DBA); finance (DBA); global management (MS); global supply chain management (DBA); healthcare management (MBA, DBA); healthcare system improvement (MBA); human resource management (MBA, MS, PhD), including functional human resource management (MS), integrating functional and strategic human resource management (MS), organizational strategy (MS); information systems management (DBA); international business (MBA, DBA); leadership (MBA, MS, DBA), including entrepreneurship (MS), general management (MS), human resources leadership (MS), innovation and technology (MS), leader development (MS), leading sustainability (MS), project management (MS), self-designed (MS); management (MS), including healthcare management; managers as leaders (MS); marketing (MBA, DBA); project management (MBA, MS, DBA); research strategies (MS); risk management (MBA); self-designed (MBA, DBA, PhD); social impact management (DBA); strategies for sustainability (MBA); strategy and operations (MS); sustainable management (MS); technology (MBA); technology entrepreneurship (DBA); technology management (MS). Part-time and evening/weekend programs available. Postbaccalaureate distance learning degree programs offered (minimal on-campus study). *Faculty:* 32 full-time (14 women), 275 part-time/adjunct (98 women). *Students:* 3,962 full-time (2,095 women), 1,557 part-time (959 women); includes 3,003 minority (2,510 Black or African American, non-Hispanic/Latino; 25 American Indian or Alaska Native, non-Hispanic/Latino; 140 Asian, non-Hispanic/Latino; 240 Hispanic/Latino; 9 Native Hawaiian or other Pacific Islander, non-Hispanic/Latino; 79 Two or more races, non-Hispanic/Latino), 395 international. Average age 41. In 2011, 586 master's, 87 doctorates, 4 other advanced degrees awarded. *Degree requirements:* For doctorate, thesis/dissertation (for some programs), residency. *Entrance requirements:* For master's, bachelor's degree or equivalent in related field; minimum GPA of 2.5; official transcripts; goal statement; access to computer and Internet; for doctorate, master's degree or equivalent in related field; minimum GPA of 3.0; 3 years of related professional/academic experience (preferred). Additional exam requirements/recommendations for international students: Required—TOEFL (minimum score 550 paper-based; 213 computer-based), IELTS (minimum score 6.5), Michigan English Language Assessment Battery (minimum score 82). *Application deadline:* Applications are processed on a rolling basis. Application fee: $50. Electronic applications accepted. *Financial support:* Federal Work-Study, scholarships/grants, unspecified assistantships, and family tuition reduction, active duty/veteran tuition reduction, group tuition reduction, interest-free payment plans, employee tuition reduction available. Support available to part-time students. Financial award applicants required to submit FAFSA. *Unit head:* Dr. William Schulz, III, Associate Dean, 800-925-3368. *Application contact:* Jennifer Hall, Vice President of Enrollment Management, 866-4-WALDEN, E-mail: info@waldenu.edu. Web site: http://www.waldenu.edu/Colleges-and-Schools/College-of-Management-and-Technology.htm.

Wayland Baptist University, Graduate Programs, Programs in Business Administration/Management, Plainview, TX 79072-6998. Offers general business (MBA); health care administration (MBA); human resource management (MBA); international management (MBA); management (MA, MBA), including health care administration (MA), human resource management (MA), organization management (MA); management information systems (MBA). Part-time and evening/weekend programs available. Postbaccalaureate distance learning degree programs offered (no on-campus study). *Degree requirements:* For master's, capstone course. *Entrance requirements:* For master's, GMAT, GRE or MAT. Additional exam requirements/recommendations for international students: Required—TOEFL (minimum score 500 paper-based; 173 computer-based; 61 iBT). Electronic applications accepted.

Waynesburg University, Graduate and Professional Studies, Waynesburg, PA 15370-1222. Offers business (MBA), including finance, health systems, human resources, leadership, market development; counseling (MA), including addictions counseling, clinical mental health; education (MAT); nursing (MSN), including administration, education, informatics, palliative care; nursing practice (DNP); special education (M Ed); technology (M Ed); MSN/MBA. *Accreditation:* AACN. Part-time and evening/weekend programs available. *Degree requirements:* For doctorate, thesis/dissertation. *Entrance requirements:* Additional exam requirements/recommendations for international students: Required—TOEFL. Electronic applications accepted.

Wayne State University, College of Liberal Arts and Sciences, Department of Economics, Detroit, MI 48202. Offers health economics (MA, PhD); industrial organization (MA, PhD); international economics (MA, PhD); labor and human resources (MA, PhD); JD/MA. *Students:* 54 full-time (19 women), 16 part-time (8 women); includes 13 minority (9 Black or African American, non-Hispanic/Latino; 4 Asian, non-Hispanic/Latino), 26 international. Average age 31. 94 applicants, 54% accepted, 16 enrolled. In 2011, 6 master's, 6 doctorates awarded. *Degree requirements:* For master's, comprehensive exam, thesis optional; for doctorate, thesis/dissertation. *Entrance requirements:* For master's, minimum GPA of 3.0, prior coursework in intermediate microeconomic and macroeconomic theory, statistics, and elementary calculus; for doctorate, GRE, minimum GPA of 3.0, prior coursework in intermediate microeconomic and macroeconomic theory, statistics, and elementary calculus. Additional exam requirements/recommendations for international students: Required—TOEFL (minimum score 550 paper-based; 213 computer-based); Recommended—TWE (minimum score 5.5). *Application deadline:* For fall admission, 6/1 priority date for domestic students, 5/1 for international students; for winter admission, 10/1 priority date for domestic students, 9/1 for international students; for spring admission, 2/1 priority date for domestic students, 1/1 for international students. Applications are processed on a rolling basis. Application fee: $50. Electronic applications accepted. *Expenses:* Tuition, state resident: part-time $512.85 per credit. Tuition, nonresident: part-time $1132.65 per credit. *Required fees:* $26.60 per credit. $199.65 per semester. Tuition and fees vary according to course load and program. *Financial support:* In 2011–12, 23 students received support, including 3 fellowships with tuition reimbursements available (averaging $15,805 per year), 1 research assistantship with tuition reimbursement available (averaging $17,453 per year), 19 teaching assistantships with tuition reimbursements available (averaging $15,713 per year); scholarships/grants, health care benefits, and unspecified assistantships also available. Support available to part-time students. Financial award application deadline: 3/1. *Faculty research:* Health economics, international economics, macro economics, urban and labor economics, econometrics. *Total annual research expenditures:* $56,699. *Unit head:* Dr. Li Way Lee, Chair, 313-577-3345, Fax: 313-577-0149, E-mail: aa1313@wayne.edu. *Application contact:* Dr. Allen Goodman, Director, 313-577-3235, E-mail: allen.goodman@wayne.edu. Web site: http://www.clas.wayne.edu/economics/.

Wayne State University, College of Liberal Arts and Sciences, Department of Political Science, Program in Public Administration, Detroit, MI 48202. Offers aging policy and management (MPA); criminal justice policy and management (MPA); economic development policy and management (MPA); health services policy and management (MPA); human resources management (MPA); information technology management (MPA); non-profit management (MPA); organizational behavior and management (MPA); public budgeting and financial management (MPA); public policy analysis and program evaluation (MPA); social welfare policy and management (MPA); urban policy and management (MPA). *Accreditation:* NASPAA. Evening/weekend programs available. *Students:* 22 full-time (17 women), 45 part-time (33 women); includes 19 minority (16 Black or African American, non-Hispanic/Latino; 1 American Indian or Alaska Native, non-Hispanic/Latino; 2 Hispanic/Latino), 1 international. Average age 31. 75 applicants, 28% accepted, 11 enrolled. In 2011, 20 master's awarded. *Degree requirements:* For master's, comprehensive exam. *Entrance requirements:* For master's, GRE General Test. Additional exam requirements/recommendations for international students: Required—TOEFL (minimum score 550 paper-based; 213 computer-based); Recommended—TWE (minimum score 5.5). *Application deadline:* For fall admission, 6/1 priority date for domestic students, 5/1 for international students; for winter admission, 10/1 priority date for domestic students, 9/1 for international students; for spring admission, 2/1 priority date for domestic students, 1/1 for international students. Applications are processed on a rolling basis. Application fee: $50. Electronic applications accepted. *Expenses:* Tuition, state resident: part-time $512.85 per credit. Tuition, nonresident: part-time $1132.65 per credit. *Required fees:* $26.60 per credit. $199.65 per semester. Tuition and fees vary according to course load and program. *Financial support:* In 2011–12, 7 students received support. Scholarships/grants available. *Faculty research:* Urban politics, urban education, state administration. *Unit head:* Dr. Brady Baybeck, Director, 313-577-2630, E-mail: mpa@wayne.edu. Web site: http://clasweb.clas.wayne.edu/mapa.

Wayne State University, College of Liberal Arts and Sciences, Program in Employment and Labor Relations, Detroit, MI 48202. Offers MA. *Expenses:* Tuition, state resident: part-time $512.85 per credit. Tuition, nonresident: part-time $1132.65 per credit. *Required fees:* $26.60 per credit. $199.65 per semester. Tuition and fees vary according to course load and program.

Webster University, George Herbert Walker School of Business and Technology, Department of Business, St. Louis, MO 63119-3194. Offers business (MA); business and organizational security management (MBA); computer resources and information management (MBA); environmental management (MBA); finance (MA, MBA); health services management (MBA); human resources development (MBA); human resources management (MBA); international business (MA, MBA); management and leadership (MBA); marketing (MBA); procurement and acquisitions management (MBA); telecommunications management (MBA). *Accreditation:* ACBSP. Part-time and evening/weekend programs available. Postbaccalaureate distance learning degree programs offered (no on-campus study). *Degree requirements:* For master's, comprehensive exam (for some programs), thesis (for some programs). *Entrance requirements:* Additional exam requirements/recommendations for international students: Required—TOEFL. *Expenses: Tuition:* Full-time $10,890; part-time $605 per credit hour. Tuition and fees vary according to campus/location and program.

Webster University, George Herbert Walker School of Business and Technology, Department of Management, St. Louis, MO 63119-3194. Offers business and organizational security management (MA); computer resources and information management (MA); environmental management (MS); government contracting (Certificate); health care management (MA); health services management (MA); human resources development (MA); human resources management (MA); management (DM); management and leadership (MA); marketing (MA); nonprofit management (Certificate); procurement and acquisitions management (MA); public administration (MA); quality management (MA); space systems operations management (MS); telecommunications management (MA). *Accreditation:* ACBSP. Part-time and evening/weekend programs available. Postbaccalaureate distance learning degree programs offered (no on-campus study). *Degree requirements:* For master's, thesis (for some programs); for doctorate, thesis/dissertation, written exam. *Entrance requirements:* For doctorate, GMAT, 3 years of work experience, MBA. Additional exam requirements/recommendations for international students: Required—TOEFL. *Expenses: Tuition:* Full-time $10,890; part-time $605 per credit hour. Tuition and fees vary according to campus/location and program.

West Chester University of Pennsylvania, College of Business and Public Affairs, Department of Political Science, West Chester, PA 19383. Offers general public administration (MPA); human resource management (MPA, Certificate); non profit administration (Certificate); nonprofit administration (MPA); public administration (Certificate); training and development (MPA). Part-time and evening/weekend programs available. *Faculty:* 1 (woman) full-time, 6 part-time/adjunct (3 women). *Students:* 49 full-time (27 women), 57 part-time (37 women); includes 42 minority (38 Black or African American, non-Hispanic/Latino; 4 Hispanic/Latino), 2 international. Average age 29. 72 applicants, 65% accepted, 39 enrolled. In 2011, 100 degrees awarded. *Degree requirements:* For master's, capstone project. *Entrance requirements:* For master's and Certificate, statement of professional goals, resume, two letters of reference. Additional exam requirements/recommendations for international students: Required—TOEFL (minimum score 550 paper-based; 213 computer-based; 80 iBT). *Application deadline:* For fall admission, 4/15 priority date for domestic students, 3/15 for international students; for spring admission, 10/15 priority date for domestic students, 9/1 for international students. Applications are processed on a rolling basis. Application fee: $45. Electronic applications accepted. *Expenses:* Tuition, state resident: full-time $7488; part-time $416 per credit. Tuition, nonresident: full-time $11,232; part-time $624 per credit. *Required fees:* $1784.64; $67.59 per credit. Tuition and fees vary according to program. *Financial support:* Unspecified assistantships available. Support available to part-time students. Financial award application deadline: 2/15; financial award applicants required to submit FAFSA. *Faculty research:* Public policy, economic development, public opinion, urban politics, public administration . *Unit head:* Dr. Christopher Fiorentino, Dean, College of Business and Public Affairs, 610-436-2930, Fax: 610-436-3170, E-mail: cfiorentino@wcupa.edu. *Application contact:* Dr. Lorraine Bernotsky, Graduate Coordinator, 610-436-2438, Fax: 610-436-3047, E-mail: lbernotsky@wcupa.edu.

Widener University, School of Business Administration, Program in Human Resource Management, Chester, PA 19013-5792. Offers MHR, MS, Psy D/MHR. Part-time and evening/weekend programs available. *Entrance requirements:* For master's, GMAT, GRE, or MAT, minimum GPA of 2.5. Electronic applications accepted. *Faculty research:* Training and development, collective bargaining and arbitration, business communication.

Wilfrid Laurier University, Faculty of Graduate and Postdoctoral Studies, School of Business and Economics, Department of Business, Waterloo, ON N2L 3C5, Canada. Offers accounting (PhD); finance (M Fin); financial economics (PhD); marketing (PhD); operations and supply chain management (PhD); organizational behavior and human resource management (M Sc); organizational behaviour and human resource management (PhD); supply chain management (M Sc); technology management (EMTM). Part-time and evening/weekend programs available. *Degree requirements:* For master's, thesis optional; for doctorate, comprehensive exam, thesis/dissertation. *Entrance requirements:* For master's, GMAT, 4-year honors degree with minimum B+ average; for doctorate, GMAT, master's degree, minimum B+ average. Additional exam requirements/recommendations for international students: Required—TOEFL (minimum score 89 iBT). Electronic applications accepted. *Faculty research:* Financial economics, management and organizational behavior, operations and supply chain management.

Wilkes University, College of Graduate and Professional Studies, Jay S. Sidhu School of Business and Leadership, Wilkes-Barre, PA 18766-0002. Offers accounting (MBA); entrepreneurship (MBA); finance (MBA); health care administration (MBA); human resource management (MBA); international business (MBA); marketing (MBA); operations management (MBA); organizational leadership and development (MBA). *Accreditation:* ACBSP. Part-time and evening/weekend programs available. *Students:* 48 full-time (20 women), 134 part-time (62 women); includes 12 minority (2 Black or African American, non-Hispanic/Latino; 5 Asian, non-Hispanic/Latino; 2 Hispanic/Latino; 3 Two or more races, non-Hispanic/Latino), 9 international. Average age 30. In 2011, 69 master's awarded. *Entrance requirements:* For master's, GMAT. Additional exam requirements/recommendations for international students: Required—TOEFL (minimum score 550 paper-based; 213 computer-based; 79 iBT). *Application deadline:* Applications are processed on a rolling basis. Application fee: $45 ($65 for international students). Electronic applications accepted. *Expenses:* Contact institution. *Financial support:* Federal Work-Study and unspecified assistantships available. Financial award application deadline: 3/1; financial award applicants required to submit FAFSA. *Unit head:* Dr. Jeffrey Alves, Dean, 570-408-4702, Fax: 570-408-7846, E-mail: jeffrey.alves@wilkes.edu. *Application contact:* Erin Sutzko, Director of Extended Learning, 570-408-4253, Fax: 570-408-7846, E-mail: erin.sutzko@wilkes.edu. Web site: http://www.wilkes.edu/pages/457.asp.

Wilmington University, College of Business, New Castle, DE 19720-6491. Offers accounting (MBA, MS); business administration (MBA, DBA); environmental stewardship (MBA); finance (MBA); health care administration (MBA, MSM); homeland security (MBA, MSM); human resource management (MSM); management information systems (MBA, MSN); marketing (MSM); marketing management (MBA); military leadership (MSM); organizational leadership (MBA, MSM); public administration (MSM). Part-time and evening/weekend programs available. *Faculty:* 4 full-time (0 women). *Students:* 266 full-time (121 women), 700 part-time (505 women). Average age 34. *Entrance requirements:* Additional exam requirements/recommendations for international students: Required—TOEFL (minimum score 500 paper-based; 173 computer-based). *Application deadline:* Applications are processed on a rolling basis. Application fee: $35. Electronic applications accepted. *Expenses: Tuition:* Part-time $534 per credit hour. *Required fees:* $25 per term. *Financial support:* Applicants required to submit FAFSA. *Unit head:* Dr. Donald W. Durandetta, Dean, 302-356-6780, E-mail: donald.w.durandetta@wilmu.edu. *Application contact:* Chris Ferguson, Director of Admissions, 302-356-4636 Ext. 256, Fax: 302-328-5164, E-mail: inquire@wilmcoll.edu. Web site: http://www.wilmu.edu/business/.

York University, Faculty of Graduate Studies, Atkinson Faculty of Liberal and Professional Studies, Program in Human Resources Management, Toronto, ON M3J 1P3, Canada. Offers MHRM, PhD. Part-time programs available. *Degree requirements:* For master's, thesis or alternative. *Entrance requirements:* Additional exam requirements/recommendations for international students: Required—TOEFL (minimum score 600 paper-based; 250 computer-based). Electronic applications accepted.

HAWAI'I PACIFIC UNIVERSITY

Program in Human Resource Management

Programs of Study

Successful management of an organization's human capital requires a logical, consistent strategy for moving people into, around, and out of the organization. Human resource (HR) professionals collaborate with other senior managers to ensure that all employees work efficiently and effectively to accomplish the organization's mission and goals. Generally, HR professionals are expected to be strong subject-matter experts in six distinct bodies of HR knowledge: strategic management; workforce planning and employment; employee and labor relations; compensation and benefits management; human resource development; and occupational health, safety, and security. Hawai'i Pacific University's Master of Arts in human resource management program (MAHRM) is built around these bodies of knowledge, to ensure that students successfully completing the classes are prepared to face and conquer the challenges posed by the growing complexity and competitiveness of the business and economic environments.

It is the mission of the MAHRM program to prepare students to enter human resource management as a career field, to position themselves to exploit promotion opportunities in the discipline, or to segue into the HR field as managers after successful careers in other management disciplines. Hawai'i Pacific University (HPU) is committed to preparing its students to become HR generalists, specialists, managers, and executives, as their career phase, maturity level, and personal motivation dictates.

The MAHRM requires a minimum of 36 semester hours of graduate work: 33 semester hours of core courses, and 3 semester hours of capstone courses.

Research Facilities

To support graduate studies, HPU's Meader and Atherton libraries offer over 110,000 bound volumes, 350,000 microfiche items, and periodical subscriptions to 1,500 print titles and 30,000 electronic journals. Databases of public and state university libraries, legislative information, and business-oriented statistical data are also available in the library or online. Students can access HPU's library databases, course information, their academic information, and an e-mail account through Pipeline, the University's internal Web site for students. The University's accessible on-campus computer center houses more than 420 computers with specialized software to support graduate academic programs. HPU also provides free Wi-Fi, so students have wireless access to Pipeline resources anywhere on campus. A significant number of online courses are available as well.

Financial Aid

The University participates in all federal financial aid programs designated for graduate students. These programs provide aid in the form of subsidized (need-based) and unsubsidized (non-need-based) Federal Stafford Student Loans. Through these loans, funds may be available to cover a student's entire cost of education. To apply for aid, students must submit the Free Application for Federal Student Aid (FAFSA) beginning January 1.

The University also offers several types of institutional graduate scholarships to new full-time, degree-seeking students. U.S. citizens, permanent residents, and international students who have a demonstrated financial need may apply. HPU's graduate scholarships include the Graduate Trustee Scholarship of $6000 ($3000/semester), the Graduate Dean Scholarship of $4000 ($2000/semester), and the Graduate Kokua Scholarship of $2000 ($1000/semester). Factors that may be considered when evaluating requests are previous academic record, community involvement and service, and professional work experience and achievement.

In order to be eligible for the best award package, students should apply by HPU's priority deadline of March 1. Applications received after the priority deadline will be awarded on a funds-available basis. Mailing of student award letters usually begins by the end of March. Applicants will be notified by mail as decisions are made.

Cost of Study

Tuition for graduate students enrolled in fall and spring semesters is determined on a per-credit basis; full-time status for a graduate student is 9 credits. Tuition for the optional winter and summer sessions is also determined on a per-credit basis. For the 2012–13 academic year, full-time tuition is $13,590 for most graduate degree programs, including the MAHRM program. Other expenses, including books, personal expenses, fees, and a student bus pass, are estimated at $3285.

Living and Housing Costs

The University has off-campus housing for graduate students and an apartment referral service. The cost of living in off-campus apartments is approximately $12,482 for a double-occupancy room. Additional graduate housing information is available online at www.hpu.edu/housing.

Student Group

University enrollment currently stands at approximately 8,200, including more than 1,200 graduate students. All fifty states and more than 100 countries are represented at HPU, one of the most culturally diverse universities in America.

Location

Hawai'i Pacific University combines the excitement of an urban, downtown campus with the serenity of a residential campus. The urban campus is ideally located in downtown Honolulu, the business and financial center of the Pacific. The downtown campus comprises seven buildings in the center of Honolulu's business district and is home to the College of Business Administration and the College of Humanities and Social Sciences.

Eight miles away, situated on 135 acres in Kaneohe, the windward Hawai'i Loa campus is the site of the College of Nursing and Health Sciences and the College of Natural and Computational Sciences. The Hawai'i Loa campus has residence halls, dining commons, the Educational Technology Center, a student center, and outdoor recreational facilities, including a soccer field, tennis courts, a softball field, and an exercise room.

HPU is affiliated with the Oceanic Institute, an aquaculture research facility located on a 56-acre site at Makapu'u Point on the windward coast of Oahu, Hawaii. All three sites are linked by HPU shuttle, and easily accessed by public transportation as well.

Notably, the downtown campus location is within walking distance of shopping and dining. Iolani Palace, the only royal palace in the United States, is a few blocks away, as are the State Capitol, City Hall, and the Blaisdell Concert Hall. The Honolulu Academy of Arts,

Hawai'i Pacific University

Museum of Contemporary Art, Waikiki Aquarium, Honolulu Zoo, and many other cultural attractions are located nearby.

The University

Hawai'i Pacific University is a private, nonprofit university with approximately 8,200 students. Founded in 1965, HPU prides itself on maintaining strong academic programs, small class sizes, individual attention to students, and a diverse faculty and student population. HPU is recognized as a Best in the West college by the Princeton Review and *U.S. News & World Report* and a Best Buy by *Barron's* business magazine. HPU offers more than fifty acclaimed undergraduate programs and fourteen distinguished graduate programs. The University has a faculty of more than 500, a student-faculty ratio of 15:1, and an average class size of fewer than 25 students. A wide range of counseling and other student support services are available. There are more than fifty student organizations on campus, including the Graduate Student Organization.

Applying

Students must have a baccalaureate degree from an accredited college or university in the United States or an equivalent degree from another country. Applicants should complete and forward a graduate admissions application, send in the $50 nonrefundable application fee, have official transcripts sent from all colleges or universities previously attended, and forward two letters of recommendation. A personal statement about the applicant's academic and career goals is required; submitting a resume is optional. Applicants who have taken the Graduate Record Examination (GRE) should have their scores sent directly to the Graduate Admissions Office. International students should submit scores of a recognized English proficiency test such as TOEFL. Admissions decisions are made on a rolling basis, and applicants are notified between one and two weeks after all documents have been submitted. Applicants are encouraged to submit their applications online.

Correspondence and Information

Graduate Admissions
Hawai'i Pacific University
1164 Bishop Street, #911
Honolulu, Hawaii 96813
Phone: 808-543-8034
866-GRAD-HPU (toll-free)
Fax: 808-544-0280
E-mail: graduate@hpu.edu

THE FACULTY AND THEIR RESEARCH

Cheryl Crozier Garcia, MAHRM Program Chair; Ph.D., Walden; SPHR, GPHR.

Gerald W. Glover, Affiliate Professor of Management and Organizational Change; Ph.D., Florida.

Edgar Palafox, Instructor of Human Resource Management; M.B.A., Hawai'i Pacific; PHR.

Larry Rowland, Department of Financial Economics and Information Systems Chair; Ed.D., USC.

William A. Sodeman, Department of Management and Marketing Chair; Ph.D., Georgia

Richard T. Ward, Associate Professor of Management; Ed.D., USC.

HOLY FAMILY UNIVERSITY

School of Business Administration
Master of Science in Human Resources Management Program

Programs of Study

Since its founding in 2000, Holy Family University's Master of Science (M.S.) in Human Resources Management program has trained more than 100 professionals in this dynamic, growing field. This program meets the core competencies for the human resource (HR) profession set forth by the Society of Human Resource Management Professionals (SHRM).

The program, which is accredited by the Accreditation Council for Business Schools and Programs, provides an excellent theoretical and practical foundation. With a graduate degree in human resources from Holy Family University, students are prepared for careers in both human resources management and general management. In addition, Holy Family's student SHRM chapter provides ongoing professional development and networking opportunities.

The M.S. in Human Resources Management program requires 33 credits, which can be completed in six semesters or less than two years. Classes are offered at the University's easily accessible main campus in Northeast Philadelphia.

Research Facilities

The University library currently houses more than 124,000 items, including more than 4,000 DVDs and videos selected to support the learning, teaching, and informational needs of the University community. The library offers print and online access to the full text of over 13,000 journals and periodicals. Over two dozen full-text databases are available on and off campus, including Academic Search Premier, WilsonWeb OmniFile, CINAHL, and PsycARTICLES. In addition, the Library has over 8,500 electronic books available from home or campus via NetLibrary and other interfaces.

Financial Aid

Holy Family is committed to helping adults further their education by consistently maintaining competitive tuition rates. Most graduate students are eligible for Federal Stafford Loans when attending with a half-time enrollment status (6 graduate credits) or greater.

For more information, potential students may contact the Financial Aid Office via e-mail at finaid@holyfamily.edu or by phone at 267-341-3233.

Cost of Study

Tuition for Holy Family's traditional graduate programs is $655 per credit hour.

Living and Housing Costs

Holy Family University does not provide graduate student housing; however, there are numerous housing options available in the nearby area.

Student Group

Approximately 45 students, nearly all studying part-time, are enrolled in the graduate-level Human Resources Management program.

Student Outcomes

Nearly all of Holy Family's M.S. degree holders have secured management-level jobs in human resources departments. Many have been promoted to managerial positions, and others have ascended to vice presidencies.

Location

The School of Business Administration, in which the master's program in human resource management is based, is on Holy Family's Northeast Philadelphia campus. Located less than a mile from Bucks County, Holy Family offers the benefits of a big city in a quiet, parklike suburban setting. With easy access to regional rail lines, city bus routes, and nearby expressways, the University is conveniently located for students throughout Greater Philadelphia.

The University

Holy Family University prides itself on programs that offer students real-world experience. This focus on preparedness and student outcomes is designed to help graduates stand out, with distinction.

Respect for the individual, the dignity of the human person—these values are taught, lived, and form the foundation of Holy Family University. Concern for moral values and social justice guides the University's programs and enriches the student's education and experience.

Applying

Holy Family University has a rolling admissions policy. Applicants must submit a statement of goals, official transcripts, two letters of reference, and the application fee.

Correspondence and Information

Graduate Admissions Office
Holy Family University
9801 Frankford Avenue
Philadelphia, Pennsylvania 19114
United States
Phone: 267-341-3327
Fax: 215-637-1478
E-mail: gradstudy@holyfamily.edu
Web site: http://www.holyfamily.edu

Holy Family University

THE FACULTY

Anthony DiPrimio, Professor; Ph.D., Temple, 1978. Economics, management.

Thomas Martin, Professor; Ph.D., Pennsylvania, 1970. Digital forensics, hybrid education, intelligent classrooms, use of technology in education, cloud computing, educating the Third World, e-discovery, enterprise security including an emphasis on data exfiltration, IPv6 tunneling inside IPv4 Networks, deep packet inspection, biometrics, GPS, encryption, information security, data communications, computer networks, entrepreneurship, starting a new company in high technology.

SAINT JOSEPH'S UNIVERSITY

Master of Science in Managing Human Capital

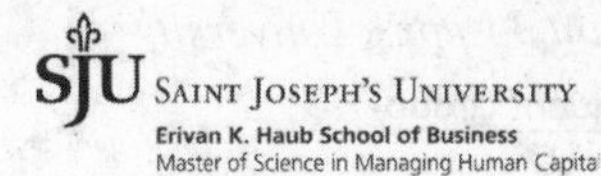

Program of Study

The Master of Science in Managing Human Capital program is offered within the Erivan K. Haub School of Business, making it one of the few institutions in the region to offer advanced business credentials in the field of human capital management within an AACSB International–accredited institution. This specialized professional program is designed to equip students with an advanced level of expertise and enables twenty-first century professionals to become strategic partners within their organizations. This program is appropriate for the early careerist, as well as for experienced professionals seeking to develop advanced credentials and skills for a highly complex, competitive, and global environment.

Graduate students in the Managing Human Capital program are exposed to the latest applications and theories to add value to their organizations through their greatest asset, their people. The program combines the concepts of strategic management, ethics, finance, and law with traditional human resource/human capital functional content (e.g., technology, compensation, staffing, negotiation, and organizational development) and culminates with the capstone human capital management course. The goal of the M.S. in Managing Human Capital program is to enhance students' abilities to perform as strategic partners with their colleagues by developing a sound foundation in finance, marketing, and accounting. A broad array of electives allows students to develop expertise in specific areas of human resources and human capital management. Students may also take elective courses in the University's other graduate programs.

The Master of Science in Managing Human Capital program at Saint Joseph's University is endorsed by the Society of Human Resource Management (SHRM) as having its curriculum aligned with the guidelines offered by SHRM. Saint Joseph's University is also ranked by U.S. News & World Report, The Princeton Review, and Business Week as one of the nation's outstanding schools. The program offers the opportunity to study on a part- or full-time basis, allowing all students to be employed during their course of study.

Research Facilities

Saint Joseph's University opened its newest building, Mandeville Hall, in 1998. This technologically advanced, $25-million building is a three-story, 89,000-square-foot facility that houses the Erivan K. Haub School of Business, the Center for Food Marketing Research, and the Academy of Food Marketing. Included in the building are classrooms, a lecture hall, seminar rooms, research facilities, computer labs, a 180-seat Teletorium equipped for teleconferencing (with a translation booth for international presentations), faculty and administrative offices, and informational gathering spaces. Many of the teaching areas are equipped with interactive communication multimedia technology, which greatly enhances pedagogical possibilities.

One of the most innovative concepts is a suite of classrooms that includes two moot board rooms, a preparation seminar room, a video room, and meeting breakout rooms. These rooms are modeled after the moot court concept in law schools. They accommodate the teachings of real-world situations through dramatizations and analysis of interactive business negotiations. They are equipped with stepped, semicircular seating that surrounds a boardroom table. Video cameras are available to record sessions for later replay or for simultaneous projection to the Teletorium or off-site locations around the globe.

The Francis A. Drexel Library and Post Learning Commons contains a business collection of approximately 350,000 bound volumes, 1,400 periodical subscriptions, 840,500 microforms, more than 2,750 videos, and Fortune 500 annual reports. The business print collection also contains nearly half of the Harvard Core, a list of more than 3,500 books recommended by the Harvard Business School, and it serves as a selective depository for U.S. government documents. The library has an online public-access catalog for searching its holdings and the holdings of other university libraries. The catalog is accessible from remote locations via the University's academic computer. There are 100 computer terminals available to Saint Joseph's students, and many online services are available to M.B.A. students. The Instructional Media Center (IMC) at Saint Joseph's University offers students assistance with presentation materials. The IMC has nearly 1,200 videotapes, which can be viewed in the IMC or signed out if needed as part of a presentation.

Services at the Career Development Center include individual career counseling, job search advising, access to alumni contact lists, and the career resource library, which contains occupational information, employer literature/directories, and current employment listings. Workshops are offered on resume writing, interviewing, and job-search techniques. Graduating students can also participate in on-campus recruiting. In addition, job search assistance is available in the form of a resume referral program.

Financial Aid

Through guaranteed loan agreements with lending institutions and state agencies such as the Pennsylvania Higher Education Assistance Agency (PHEAA) and the New Jersey Department of Higher Education, students can secure long-term loans at a low interest rate. The University initiates an electronic loan application and forwards it to its guarantor, the PHEAA. Stafford loans can be subsidized or unsubsidized. All full- or half-time students (at least 6 credits per semester) are eligible to apply for federal aid. Students may elect to finance part of their tuition through a deferred-payment program offered by the University.

Cost of Study

Tuition for the 2012–13 academic year is $892 per credit hour.

Living and Housing Costs

Off-campus apartments are available within walking distance of both the campus and the local train station.

Saint Joseph's University

Student Group

Students in this program include professionals with all levels of experience, who work full time and complete their graduate degrees on a part-time basis. The program also includes early careerists who have decided to study on a full-time basis after completing their undergraduate studies. The Master of Science in Managing Human Capital program houses the SJU-SHRM student chapter, which allows students throughout the University to network with each other, as well as those in the professional community.

Location

Saint Joseph's University is located in eastern Pennsylvania in the suburbs of Philadelphia, only 15 minutes from downtown Center City.

The University

Founded by the Society of Jesus in 1851, Saint Joseph's University advances the professional and personal ambitions of men and women by providing a demanding, yet supportive, educational experience. One of only 142 schools with a Phi Beta Kappa chapter and AACSB International–business school accreditation, Saint Joseph's is home to 3,900 full-time undergraduates and 3,400 graduate, part-time, and doctoral students. Steeped in the 450-year Jesuit tradition of scholarship and service, the University strives to be recognized as the preeminent comprehensive Catholic university in the Northeast.

Saint Joseph's Erivan K. Haub School of Business is AACSB International–accredited and consistently ranked as among the best academic institutions in the United States.

Applying

Applications are accepted on a rolling admission basis. Students applying to the Master of Science in Managing Human Capital program must have a baccalaureate degree from an accredited college or university. Applicants must submit an online application, the application fee, official transcripts, an official test score (GMAT, GRE, or MAT), two letters of recommendation, a resume, and a personal statement. International students must also submit TOEFL scores (for those whose native language is not English) and an affidavit of support. International applicants are required to submit an official course-by-course credentials evaluation of their undergraduate work. Students are strongly advised to register with World Education Services (WES). Application deadlines for international students are July 15 for the fall, November 15 for the spring, April 1 for summer session I, and May 15 for summer session II.

Correspondence and Information

Patricia D. Rafferty, Ed.D.
Director
Erivan K. Haub School of Business
Saint Joseph's University
5600 City Avenue
Philadelphia, Pennsylvania 19131-1395
Phone: 610-660-1318
E-mail: patricia.rafferty@sju.edu
Web site: http://www.sju.edu/hsb/hr

THE FACULTY

Lucy Ford, Assistant Professor; Ph.D.
John J. McCall, Professor of Philosophy and Management; Ph.D.
William McDevitt, Associate Professor; J.D.
Eric Patton, Assistant Professor; Ph.D.
Claire Simmers, Chair of Department of Management, Professor; M.B.A., Ph.D.
David Steingard, Professor; Ph.D.
C. Ken Weidner, Assistant Professor; M.B.A., Ph.D.

Section 9
Industrial and Manufacturing Management

This section contains a directory of institutions offering graduate work in industrial and manufacturing management. Additional information about programs listed in the directory but not augmented by an in-depth entry may be obtained by writing directly to the dean of a graduate school or chair of a department at the address given in the directory.

For programs offering related work, see also in this book *Business Administration and Management* and *Human Resources.* In another guide in this series:

Graduate Programs in the Humanities, Arts & Social Sciences

See *Public, Regional, and Industrial Affairs (Industrial and Labor Relations)*

CONTENTS

Program Directory

Display and Close-Up

See:

Industrial and Manufacturing Management

American InterContinental University Online, Program in Business Administration, Hoffman Estates, IL 60192. Offers accounting and finance (MBA); finance (MBA); healthcare management (MBA); human resource management (MBA); international business (MBA); management (MBA); marketing (MBA); operations management (MBA); organizational psychology and development (MBA); project management (MBA). Evening/weekend programs available. Postbaccalaureate distance learning degree programs offered (no on-campus study). *Entrance requirements:* Additional exam requirements/recommendations for international students: Required—TOEFL (minimum score 550 paper-based; 213 computer-based). Electronic applications accepted.

The American University in Cairo, School of Sciences and Engineering, Department of Mechanical Engineering, Cairo, Egypt. Offers mechanical engineering (MS); product development and systems management (M Eng). *Expenses: Tuition:* Part-time $932 per credit hour. Tuition and fees vary according to course load, degree level and program. *Unit head:* Dr. Salah El-Haggar, Chair, 20-2-2615-3065, E-mail: elhaggar@aucegypt.edu. *Application contact:* Wesley Clark, Director of North American Admissions and Financial Aid, 212-646-810-9433 Ext. 4547, E-mail: wclark@aucnyo.edu. Web site: http://www.aucegypt.edu/sse/meng/.

Bernard M. Baruch College of the City University of New York, Zicklin School of Business, Department of Management, New York, NY 10010-5585. Offers entrepreneurship (MBA); management (PhD); operations management (MBA); organizational behavior/human resources management (MBA); sustainable business (MBA). PhD offered jointly with Graduate School and University Center of the City University of New York. Part-time and evening/weekend programs available. *Degree requirements:* For doctorate, comprehensive exam, thesis/dissertation. *Entrance requirements:* For master's, GMAT, 2 letters of recommendation, resume, 2 years of work experience; for doctorate, GMAT. Additional exam requirements/recommendations for international students: Required—TOEFL (minimum score 590 paper-based; 243 computer-based), TWE.

California Polytechnic State University, San Luis Obispo, Orfalea College of Business, Department of Business and Technology, San Luis Obispo, CA 93407. Offers MS. Part-time programs available. *Faculty:* 1 full-time (0 women). *Students:* 2 part-time (0 women). Average age 23. 1 applicant, 100% accepted, 1 enrolled. *Degree requirements:* For master's, thesis or alternative. *Entrance requirements:* For master's, GRE General Test or GMAT, minimum GPA of 2.8 in last 90 quarter units of course work, 2 letters of recommendation. Additional exam requirements/recommendations for international students: Required—TOEFL (minimum score 550 paper-based; 213 computer-based) or IELTS (minimum score 6). *Application deadline:* For fall admission, 7/1 for domestic students, 11/30 for international students. Applications are processed on a rolling basis. Application fee: $55. Electronic applications accepted. *Expenses:* Tuition, state resident: full-time $6738. Tuition, nonresident: full-time $17,898. *Required fees:* $2449. *Financial support:* Career-related internships or fieldwork, Federal Work-Study, institutionally sponsored loans, and scholarships/grants available. Support available to part-time students. Financial award application deadline: 3/2; financial award applicants required to submit FAFSA. *Faculty research:* Valve chain management, packing science and technology, technology entrepreneurship and innovation, industrial processes and systems. *Unit head:* Dr. Bradford Anderson, Graduate Coordinator, 805-756-5210, Fax: 805-756-6111, E-mail: bpanders@calpoly.edu.

California State University, East Bay, Office of Academic Programs and Graduate Studies, College of Business and Economics, Program in Information Technology Management, Option in Operations and Supply Chain Management, Hayward, CA 94542-3000. Offers MBA. *Degree requirements:* For master's, comprehensive exam or thesis. *Entrance requirements:* For master's, GMAT, minimum GPA of 2.75. Additional exam requirements/recommendations for international students: Required—TOEFL (minimum score 550 paper-based; 213 computer-based). *Application deadline:* For fall admission, 6/30 for domestic and international students. Application fee: $55. Electronic applications accepted. *Expenses:* Tuition, state resident: full-time $6738; part-time $1302 per quarter. Tuition, nonresident: full-time $12,690; part-time $2294 per quarter. *Required fees:* $449 per quarter. Tuition and fees vary according to degree level, program and reciprocity agreements. *Financial support:* Fellowships, career-related internships or fieldwork, Federal Work-Study, institutionally sponsored loans, and scholarships/grants available. Support available to part-time students. Financial award application deadline: 3/1; financial award applicants required to submit FAFSA. *Unit head:* Prof. Xinjian Lu, Chair, 510-885-3307, E-mail: xinjian.lu@csueastbay.edu. *Application contact:* Donna Wiley, Interim Associate Director, 510-885-2928, Fax: 510-885-4777, E-mail: donna.wiley@csueastbay.edu.

Carnegie Mellon University, Carnegie Institute of Technology and School of Design, Program in Product Development, Pittsburgh, PA 15213-3891. Offers MPD. *Entrance requirements:* For master's, GRE General Test, undergraduate degree in engineering, industrial design, or related fields, 3 letters of reference, 2 years of professional experience. Additional exam requirements/recommendations for international students: Required—TOEFL or TSE.

Carnegie Mellon University, College of Fine Arts, School of Design, Pittsburgh, PA 15213-3891. Offers communication planning and information design (M Des); design (PhD); design theory (PhD); interaction design (M Des, PhD); new product development (PhD); product development (MPD); typography and information design (PhD). *Accreditation:* NASAD.

Carnegie Mellon University, Tepper School of Business, Program in Management of Manufacturing and Automation, Pittsburgh, PA 15213-3891. Offers PhD. *Degree requirements:* For doctorate, thesis/dissertation.

Case Western Reserve University, Weatherhead School of Management, Department of Operations, Cleveland, OH 44106. Offers management (MS, MSM), including finance (MS), information systems (MS), marketing (MS), operations research, quality management (MS), supply chain (MSM); management for liberal arts graduates (MSM); operations research (PhD); MBA/MSM. Part-time programs available. *Degree requirements:* For doctorate, thesis/dissertation. *Entrance requirements:* For master's, GRE General Test; for doctorate, GMAT, GRE General Test. *Faculty research:* Mathematical finance, mathematical programming, scheduling, stochastic optimization, environmental/energy models.

Central Connecticut State University, School of Graduate Studies, School of Technology, Department of Manufacturing and Construction Management, New Britain, CT 06050-4010. Offers construction management (MS, Certificate); lean manufacturing and Six Sigma (Certificate); supply chain and logistics (Certificate); technology management (MS). Part-time and evening/weekend programs available. *Faculty:* 18 full-time (4 women), 26 part-time/adjunct (2 women). *Students:* 23 full-time (5 women), 89 part-time (22 women); includes 18 minority (10 Black or African American, non-Hispanic/Latino; 7 Asian, non-Hispanic/Latino; 1 Hispanic/Latino), 7 international. Average age 36. 68 applicants, 78% accepted, 39 enrolled. In 2011, 25 master's, 1 other advanced degree awarded. *Degree requirements:* For master's, comprehensive exam, thesis or alternative; for Certificate, qualifying exam. *Entrance requirements:* For master's, minimum undergraduate GPA of 2.7. Additional exam requirements/recommendations for international students: Required—TOEFL (minimum score 550 paper-based; 213 computer-based). *Application deadline:* For fall admission, 6/1 for domestic students, 5/1 for international students; for spring admission, 11/1 for domestic and international students. Applications are processed on a rolling basis. Application fee: $50. Electronic applications accepted. *Expenses: Tuition, area resident:* Full-time $5137; part-time $482 per credit. Tuition, state resident: full-time $7707; part-time $494 per credit. Tuition, nonresident: full-time $14,311; part-time $494 per credit. *Required fees:* $3865. One-time fee: $62 part-time. *Financial support:* In 2011–12, 9 students received support, including 7 research assistantships; career-related internships or fieldwork, Federal Work-Study, scholarships/grants, and unspecified assistantships also available. Support available to part-time students. Financial award application deadline: 4/15; financial award applicants required to submit FAFSA. *Faculty research:* All aspects of middle management, technical supervision in the workplace. *Unit head:* Dr. Jacob Kovel, Chair, 860-832-1830, E-mail: kovelj@ccsu.edu. *Application contact:* Patricia Gardner, Associate Director of Graduate Studies, 860-832-2350, Fax: 860-832-2352, E-mail: graduateadmissions@ccsu.edu. Web site: http://www.ccsu.edu/page.cfm?p=6497.

Central Michigan University, College of Graduate Studies, College of Science and Technology, Department of Engineering Technology, Mount Pleasant, MI 48859. Offers industrial management and technology (MA). Part-time programs available. *Degree requirements:* For master's, thesis or alternative. Electronic applications accepted. *Faculty research:* Computer applications, manufacturing process control, mechanical engineering automation, industrial technology.

Cleveland State University, College of Graduate Studies, Monte Ahuja College of Business, Doctor of Business Administration Program, Cleveland, OH 44115. Offers finance (DBA); global business (DBA); information systems (DBA); marketing (DBA); operations management (DBA). *Accreditation:* AACSB. Part-time and evening/weekend programs available. *Faculty:* 50 full-time (11 women). *Students:* 4 full-time (1 woman), 34 part-time (12 women); includes 3 minority (1 Black or African American, non-Hispanic/Latino; 2 Asian, non-Hispanic/Latino), 11 international. Average age 40. In 2011, 5 doctorates awarded. *Degree requirements:* For doctorate, comprehensive exam, thesis/dissertation, oral dissertation defense. *Entrance requirements:* For doctorate, GMAT, MBA or equivalent. Additional exam requirements/recommendations for international students: Required—TOEFL (minimum score 550 paper-based; 213 computer-based; 79 iBT). *Application deadline:* For spring admission, 2/28 priority date for domestic students, 2/28 for international students. Application fee: $30. Electronic applications accepted. *Expenses:* Tuition, state resident: full-time $6416; part-time $494 per credit hour. Tuition, nonresident: full-time $12,074; part-time $929 per credit hour. *Financial support:* In 2011–12, 5 research assistantships with full tuition reimbursements (averaging $12,700 per year), 4 teaching assistantships with full tuition reimbursements (averaging $12,700 per year) were awarded; tuition waivers (full) and unspecified assistantships also available. *Faculty research:* Supply chain management, international business, strategic management, risk analysis, consumer behavior. *Unit head:* Dr. Raj Shekhar G. Javalgi, Director, 216-687-3786, Fax: 216-687-9354, E-mail: r.javalgi@csuohio.edu. *Application contact:* Melinda J. Arnold, Administrative Secretary, 216-687-6952, Fax: 216-687-9257, E-mail: m.arnold@csuohio.edu. Web site: http://www.csuohio.edu/business/academics/doctoral.html.

Colorado Technical University Colorado Springs, Graduate Studies, Program in Management, Colorado Springs, CO 80907-3896. Offers accounting (MBA, MSA); business administration (MBA); finance (MBA); human resources management (MBA); logistics/supply chain management (MBA); management (DM); marketing (MBA); mediation and dispute resolution (MBA); operations management (MBA); project management (MBA); technology management (MBA). Part-time and evening/weekend programs available. Postbaccalaureate distance learning degree programs offered. *Degree requirements:* For master's, thesis or alternative; for doctorate, thesis/dissertation. *Entrance requirements:* For doctorate, minimum graduate GPA of 3.0, 5 years of related work experience. *Faculty research:* Sexual harassment, performance evaluation, critical thinking.

Colorado Technical University Denver South, Programs in Business Administration and Management, Aurora, CO 80014. Offers accounting (MBA); business administration (MBA); business administration and management (EMBA); finance (MBA); human resource management (MBA); marketing (MBA); mediation and dispute resolution (MBA); operations management (MBA); project management (MBA); technology management (MBA). Part-time and evening/weekend programs available. *Degree requirements:* For master's, thesis or alternative. *Entrance requirements:* For master's, minimum undergraduate GPA of 3.0, resume.

DePaul University, Charles H. Kellstadt Graduate School of Business, Department of Management, Chicago, IL 60604-2287. Offers entrepreneurship (MBA); health sector management (MBA); human resource management (MBA, MSHR); leadership/change management (MBA); management planning and strategy (MBA); operations management (MBA). Part-time and evening/weekend programs available. *Faculty:* 36 full-time (7 women), 35 part-time/adjunct (16 women). *Students:* 280 full-time (116 women), 121 part-time (47 women); includes 78 minority (20 Black or African American, non-Hispanic/Latino; 37 Asian, non-Hispanic/Latino; 16 Hispanic/Latino; 1 Native Hawaiian or other Pacific Islander, non-Hispanic/Latino; 4 Two or more races, non-Hispanic/Latino), 33 international. Average age 30. In 2011, 112 master's awarded. *Entrance requirements:* For master's, GMAT, GRE (MSHR), 2 letters of recommendation, resume. Additional exam requirements/recommendations for international students: Required—TOEFL (minimum score 550 paper-based; 213 computer-based). *Application deadline:* For fall admission, 7/1 for domestic students; for winter admission, 10/1 for domestic students; for spring admission, 2/1 for domestic students. Applications are processed on a rolling basis. Application fee: $60. Electronic applications accepted. *Financial support:* Research assistantships available. Financial award application deadline: 4/1. *Faculty research:* Growth management, creativity and innovation, quality management and business process design, entrepreneurship. *Unit head:* Robert T. Ryan, Assistant Dean and Director, 312-362-8810, Fax: 312-362-6677, E-mail: rryan1@depaul.edu. *Application contact:* Christopher E. Kinsella, Director of Cohort MBA Programs, 312-362-8810, Fax: 312-362-6677, E-mail: kgsb@depaul.edu.

East Carolina University, Graduate School, College of Technology and Computer Science, Department of Technology Systems, Greenville, NC 27858-4353. Offers computer network professional (Certificate); industrial technology (MS), including computer networking management, digital communications, industrial distribution and logistics, information security, manufacturing, performance improvement, quality systems; information assurance (Certificate); Lean Six Sigma Black Belt (Certificate);

occupational safety (MS); technology management (PhD); Website developer (Certificate). *Entrance requirements:* For master's and Certificate, GRE General Test or MAT, minimum GPA of 2.5; for doctorate, GRE General Test, related work experience. *Application deadline:* For fall admission, 6/1 priority date for domestic students. Applications are processed on a rolling basis. Application fee: $50. *Expenses:* Tuition, state resident: full-time $3557; part-time $444.63 per semester hour. Tuition, nonresident: full-time $14,351; part-time $1793.88 per semester hour. *Required fees:* $2016; $252 per semester hour. Part-time tuition and fees vary according to course load, campus/location and program. *Financial support:* Application deadline: 6/1. *Unit head:* Dr. Tijjani Mohammed, Interim Chair, 252-328-9668, E-mail: mohammedt@ecu.edu. Web site: http://www.ecu.edu/cs-tecs/techsystems/.

Embry-Riddle Aeronautical University–Worldwide, Worldwide Headquarters - Graduate Degrees and Programs, Program in Aeronautics, Daytona Beach, FL 32114-3900. Offers aeronautical science (MAS); air transportation management (Graduate Certificate); airport planning design and development (Graduate Certificate); aviation/aerospace industrial management (Graduate Certificate); aviation/aerospace safety (Graduate Certificate); instructional system design (Graduate Certificate). Part-time and evening/weekend programs available. Postbaccalaureate distance learning degree programs offered (minimal on-campus study). *Faculty:* 24 full-time (2 women), 177 part-time/adjunct (20 women). *Students:* 1,684 full-time (248 women), 1,771 part-time (239 women); includes 497 minority (154 Black or African American, non-Hispanic/Latino; 20 American Indian or Alaska Native, non-Hispanic/Latino; 58 Asian, non-Hispanic/Latino; 251 Hispanic/Latino; 3 Native Hawaiian or other Pacific Islander, non-Hispanic/Latino; 11 Two or more races, non-Hispanic/Latino), 32 international. Average age 36. 913 applicants, 77% accepted, 330 enrolled. In 2011, 1032 degrees awarded. *Degree requirements:* For master's, comprehensive exam (for some programs), thesis optional. *Entrance requirements:* Additional exam requirements/recommendations for international students: Recommended—TOEFL (minimum score 550 paper-based; 213 computer-based; 79 iBT). *Application deadline:* Applications are processed on a rolling basis. Application fee: $50. Electronic applications accepted. *Expenses: Tuition:* Part-time $395 per credit hour. Tuition and fees vary according to degree level and program. *Financial support:* In 2011–12, 570 students received support. Available to part-time students. Applicants required to submit FAFSA. *Faculty research:* Unmanned aircraft system (UAS) operations, human factors, crash investigation, reliability and hazard analysis, aviation security. *Unit head:* Dr. Katherine A. Moran, Department Chair, 360-597-4560, E-mail: morank@erau.edu. *Application contact:* Linda Dammer, Director of Admissions, 386-226-6396 Ext. 1, Fax: 386-226-6984, E-mail: worldwide@erau.edu.

Friends University, Graduate School, Wichita, KS 67213. Offers accounting (MBA); business administration (MBA); business law (MBL); Christian ministry (MACM); environment science (MSES); family therapy (MSFT); global leadership and management (MA); health care leadership (MHCL); management information systems (MMIS); operations management (MSOM); organization development (MSOD); teaching (MAT). Part-time and evening/weekend programs available. Postbaccalaureate distance learning degree programs offered (no on-campus study). *Faculty:* 14 full-time (5 women), 2 part-time/adjunct (1 woman). *Students:* 158 full-time (114 women), 616 part-time (367 women); includes 159 minority (83 Black or African American, non-Hispanic/Latino; 12 American Indian or Alaska Native, non-Hispanic/Latino; 26 Asian, non-Hispanic/Latino; 22 Hispanic/Latino; 2 Native Hawaiian or other Pacific Islander, non-Hispanic/Latino; 14 Two or more races, non-Hispanic/Latino). Average age 36. 497 applicants, 68% accepted, 256 enrolled. In 2011, 341 degrees awarded. *Degree requirements:* For master's, research project. *Entrance requirements:* For master's, bachelor's degree from accredited institution, official transcripts from institution granting bachelor's degree, interview with program director, letter(s) of recommendation. Additional exam requirements/recommendations for international students: Required—TOEFL (minimum score 560 paper-based; 220 computer-based). *Application deadline:* Applications are processed on a rolling basis. Application fee: $45 ($65 for international students). Electronic applications accepted. *Expenses: Tuition:* Part-time $601 per credit hour. One-time fee: $45 full-time. Tuition and fees vary according to campus/location and program. *Financial support:* Applicants required to submit FAFSA. *Unit head:* Dr. Evelyn Hume, Dean, 800-794-6945 Ext. 5859, Fax: 316-295-5040, E-mail: evelyn_hume@friends.edu. *Application contact:* Jeanette Hanson, Executive Director of Adult Recruitment, 800-794-6945, Fax: 316-295-5050, E-mail: jeanette@friends.edu. Web site: http://www.friends.edu.

Georgetown University, Graduate School of Arts and Sciences, Department of Economics, Washington, DC 20057. Offers econometrics (PhD); economic development (PhD); economic theory (PhD); industrial organization (PhD); international macro and finance (PhD); international trade (PhD); labor economics (PhD); macroeconomics (PhD); public economics and political economics (PhD); MA/PhD; MS/MA. *Degree requirements:* For doctorate, comprehensive exam, thesis/dissertation. *Entrance requirements:* For doctorate, GRE General Test. Additional exam requirements/recommendations for international students: Required—TOEFL. *Faculty research:* International economics, economic development.

Harvard University, Harvard Business School, Doctoral Programs in Management, Boston, MA 02163. Offers accounting and management (DBA); business economics (PhD); health policy management (PhD); management (DBA); marketing (DBA); organizational behavior (PhD); science, technology and management (PhD); strategy (DBA); technology and operations management (DBA). *Degree requirements:* For doctorate, comprehensive exam (for some programs), thesis/dissertation. *Entrance requirements:* For doctorate, GRE General Test or GMAT. Additional exam requirements/recommendations for international students: Required—TOEFL. *Expenses: Tuition:* Full-time $36,304. *Required fees:* $1186. Full-time tuition and fees vary according to program.

HEC Montreal, School of Business Administration, Master of Science Programs in Administration, Program in Production and Operations Management, Montréal, QC H3T 2A7, Canada. Offers M Sc. Part-time programs available. *Students:* 24 full-time (12 women), 7 part-time (5 women). 25 applicants, 52% accepted, 7 enrolled. In 2011, 10 master's awarded. *Degree requirements:* For master's, one foreign language, thesis. *Entrance requirements:* For master's, Test de francais international (TFI) with minimum score of 850 (for those who have never studied in French), BBA, undergraduate degree in another field, degree deemed equivalent by program director and minimum GPA of 3.0 on 4.3 scale. *Application deadline:* For fall admission, 3/15 for domestic and international students; for winter admission, 9/15 for domestic and international students. Application fee: $80 Canadian dollars. Electronic applications accepted. Application fee is waived when completed online. *Expenses:* Contact institution. *Financial support:* Fellowships, research assistantships, teaching assistantships, and scholarships/grants available. Financial award application deadline: 9/2. *Unit head:* Dr. Claude Laurin, Director, 514-340-6485, Fax: 514-340-6880, E-mail: claude.laurin@hec.ca. *Application contact:* Virginie Lefebvre, Administrative Director, 514-340-6112, Fax: 514-340-6411, E-mail: virginie.lefebvre@hec.ca. Web site: http://www.hec.ca/en/programs_training/msc/options/operation_prod_management/index.html.

Illinois Institute of Technology, Graduate College, School of Applied Technology, Program in Industrial Technology and Management, Chicago, IL 60616-3793. Offers MITO. Part-time and evening/weekend programs available. Postbaccalaureate distance learning degree programs offered (no on-campus study). *Entrance requirements:* For master's, GRE (minimum score 900 Quantitative and Verbal, 2.5 Analytical Writing), bachelor's degree with minimum cumulative undergraduate GPA of 3.0 (or its equivalent) from accredited institution. Additional exam requirements/recommendations for international students: Required—TOEFL (minimum score 523 paper-based; 70 iBT); Recommended—IELTS (minimum score 5.5). Electronic applications accepted. *Faculty research:* Industrial logistics, industrial facilities, manufacturing technology, entrepreneurship, energy options.

Instituto Tecnologico de Santo Domingo, Graduate School, Area of Engineering, Santo Domingo, Dominican Republic. Offers construction administration (MS, Certificate); data telecommunications (M Eng, MS, Certificate); industrial engineering (M Eng, Certificate); industrial management (M Mgmt); information technology (Certificate); maintenance engineering (M Eng); occupational hazard prevention (M Mgmt); production management (Certificate); quantitative methods (Certificate); sanitary and environmental engineering (M Eng); structural engineering (M Eng); systems engineering and electronic data processing (Certificate); transportation (Certificate).

Instituto Tecnológico y de Estudios Superiores de Monterrey, Campus Estado de México, Professional and Graduate Division, Estado de Mexico, Mexico. Offers administration of information technologies (MITA); architecture (M Arch); business administration (GMBA, MBA); computer sciences (MCS, PhD); education (M Ed); educational institution administration (MAD); educational technology and innovation (PhD); electronic commerce (MEC); environmental systems (MS); finance (MAF); humanistic studies (MHS); information sciences and knowledge management (MISKM); information systems (MS); manufacturing systems (MS); marketing (MEM); quality systems and productivity (MS); science and materials engineering (PhD); telecommunications management (MTM). Part-time programs available. Postbaccalaureate distance learning degree programs offered (minimal on-campus study). *Degree requirements:* For master's, one foreign language, thesis (for some programs); for doctorate, one foreign language, thesis/dissertation. *Entrance requirements:* For master's, E-PAEP 500, interview; for doctorate, E-PAEP 500, research proposal. Additional exam requirements/recommendations for international students: Required—TOEFL (minimum score 550 paper-based). *Faculty research:* Surface treatments by plasmas, mechanical properties, robotics, graphical computing, mechatronics security protocols.

Instituto Tecnológico y de Estudios Superiores de Monterrey, Campus Irapuato, Graduate Programs, Irapuato, Mexico. Offers administration (MBA); administration of information technology (MAIT); administration of telecommunications (MAT); architecture (M Arch); computer science (MCS); education (M Ed); educational administration (MEA); educational innovation and technology (DEIT); educational technology (MET); electronic commerce (MBA); environmental administration and planning (MEAP); environmental systems (MES); finances (MBA); humanistic studies (MHS); international management for Latin American executives (MIMLAE); library and information science (MLIS); manufacturing quality management (MMQM); marketing research (MBA).

Inter American University of Puerto Rico, Metropolitan Campus, Graduate Programs, Program in Industrial Management, San Juan, PR 00919-1293. Offers MBA. *Degree requirements:* For master's, comprehensive exam. *Entrance requirements:* For master's, GRE or EXADEP, interview. Electronic applications accepted.

Inter American University of Puerto Rico, San Germán Campus, Graduate Studies Center, Program in Business Administration, San Germán, PR 00683-5008. Offers accounting (MBA); finance (MBA); human resources (MBA, PhD); industrial relations (MBA); information sciences (MBA); management (MBA); marketing (MBA). Part-time and evening/weekend programs available. *Degree requirements:* For master's, comprehensive exam. *Entrance requirements:* For master's, GRE General Test or EXADEP, minimum GPA of 3.0. *Application deadline:* For fall admission, 4/30 priority date for domestic students; for spring admission, 11/15 for domestic students. Applications are processed on a rolling basis. Application fee: $31. *Expenses: Required fees:* $213 per semester. *Financial support:* Teaching assistantships, Federal Work-Study, and unspecified assistantships available. *Unit head:* Dr. Elba T. Irizarry, Director of Graduate Studies Center, 787-264-1912 Ext. 7357, Fax: 787-892-6350, E-mail: elbat@sg.inter.edu.

International Technological University, Program in Industrial Management, Santa Clara, CA 95050. Offers MIM.

Kansas State University, Graduate School, College of Human Ecology, Department of Apparel, Textiles, and Interior Design, Manhattan, KS 66506. Offers design (MS); general apparel and textiles (MS); marketing (MS); merchandising (MS); product development (MS). Postbaccalaureate distance learning degree programs offered (no on-campus study). *Faculty:* 9 full-time (7 women), 1 (woman) part-time/adjunct. *Students:* 8 full-time (all women), 26 part-time (24 women); includes 10 minority (3 Black or African American, non-Hispanic/Latino; 3 Asian, non-Hispanic/Latino; 2 Hispanic/Latino; 2 Two or more races, non-Hispanic/Latino), 2 international. Average age 28. 24 applicants, 17% accepted, 4 enrolled. In 2011, 11 master's awarded. *Degree requirements:* For master's, comprehensive exam (for some programs), thesis (for some programs). *Entrance requirements:* For master's, GRE General Test (except for merchandising applicants), minimum undergraduate GPA of 3.0. Additional exam requirements/recommendations for international students: Required—TOEFL (minimum score 550 paper-based; 213 computer-based; 79 iBT). *Application deadline:* For fall admission, 2/1 priority date for domestic students, 2/1 for international students; for spring admission, 8/1 priority date for domestic students, 8/1 for international students. Applications are processed on a rolling basis. Application fee: $40 ($55 for international students). Electronic applications accepted. *Financial support:* In 2011–12, 4 teaching assistantships with full tuition reimbursements (averaging $10,208 per year) were awarded; research assistantships, career-related internships or fieldwork, Federal Work-Study, institutionally sponsored loans, and scholarships/grants also available. Support available to part-time students. Financial award application deadline: 3/1; financial award applicants required to submit FAFSA. *Faculty research:* Apparel marketing and consumer behavior, protective and functional clothing and textiles, social and environmental responsibility, apparel design, new product development. *Total annual research expenditures:* $43,034. *Unit head:* Barbara G. Anderson, Head, 785-532-6993, Fax: 785-532-3796, E-mail: barbara@ksu.edu. *Application contact:* Gina Jackson, Application Contact, 785-532-6693, Fax: 785-532-3796, E-mail: gjackson@ksu.edu. Web site: http://www.he.k-state.edu/atid/.

Lawrence Technological University, College of Management, Southfield, MI 48075-1058. Offers business administration (MBA, DBA); business administration international (MBA); global leadership and management (MS); global operations and project management (MS); information systems (MS); information technology (DM); operations management (MS). *Accreditation:* ACBSP. Part-time and evening/weekend programs available. *Faculty:* 12 full-time (6 women), 39 part-time/adjunct (11 women). *Students:* 10 full-time (4 women), 518 part-time (228 women); includes 183 minority (123 Black or African American, non-Hispanic/Latino; 2 American Indian or Alaska Native, non-Hispanic/Latino; 44 Asian, non-Hispanic/Latino; 11 Hispanic/Latino; 3 Two or more races, non-Hispanic/Latino), 50 international. Average age 36. 420 applicants, 45% accepted, 97 enrolled. In 2011, 177 master's, 14 doctorates awarded. *Degree requirements:* For master's, thesis (for some programs). *Entrance requirements:* For master's, GMAT. Additional exam requirements/recommendations for international students: Required—TOEFL (minimum score 550 paper-based; 213 computer-based; 79 iBT). *Application deadline:* For fall admission, 7/27 priority date for domestic students, 5/23 for international students; for spring admission, 11/15 priority date for domestic students, 11/15 for international students. Applications are processed on a rolling basis. Application fee: $50. Electronic applications accepted. *Financial support:* In 2011–12, 122 students received support. Federal Work-Study and institutionally sponsored loans available. Support available to part-time students. Financial award application deadline: 4/1; financial award applicants required to submit FAFSA. *Unit head:* Dr. Alan McCord, Interim Dean, 248-204-3050, E-mail: mgtdean@ltu.edu. *Application contact:* Jane Rohrback, Director of Admissions, 248-204-3160, Fax: 248-204-2228, E-mail: admissions@ltu.edu. Web site: http://www.ltu.edu/management/index.asp.

Marist College, Graduate Programs, School of Management, Poughkeepsie, NY 12601-1387. Offers business administration (MBA, Adv C), including business administration (MBA), executive leadership (Adv C), production management (Adv C); public administration (MPA); technology management (MS). Part-time and evening/weekend programs available. Postbaccalaureate distance learning degree programs offered (no on-campus study). *Entrance requirements:* For master's, GMAT (MBA), GRE General Test(MPA), resume, letters of recommendation. Additional exam requirements/recommendations for international students: Required—TOEFL (minimum score 550 paper-based; 213 computer-based; 80 iBT); Recommended—IELTS (minimum score 6.5). Electronic applications accepted.

Marquette University, Graduate School of Management, Executive MBA Program, Milwaukee, WI 53201-1881. Offers economics (MBA); finance (MBA); human resources (MBA); international business (MBA); management information systems (MBA); marketing (MBA); operations and supply chain management (MBA); sports business (MBA). *Accreditation:* AACSB. *Students:* 50 full-time (15 women); includes 4 minority (1 Black or African American, non-Hispanic/Latino; 3 Asian, non-Hispanic/Latino), 3 international. Average age 37. 37 applicants, 81% accepted, 29 enrolled. In 2011, 36 master's awarded. *Degree requirements:* For master's, international trip. *Entrance requirements:* For master's, GMAT or GRE, two letters of recommendation, official transcripts from current and previous colleges/universities. Additional exam requirements/recommendations for international students: Required—TOEFL (minimum score 550 paper-based; 85 computer-based; 88 iBT), IELTS (minimum score 6.5), Pearson Test of English. *Application deadline:* For fall admission, 2/15 for domestic and international students. Application fee: $50. Electronic applications accepted. *Expenses:* Contact institution. *Financial support:* Application deadline: 2/15. *Faculty research:* International trade and finance, customer relationship management, consumer satisfaction, customer service . *Unit head:* Dr. Jeanne Simmons, Graduate Director, 414-288-7145, Fax: 414-288-1660, E-mail: jeanne.simmons@marquette.edu. *Application contact:* Debra Leutermann, Admissions Coordinator, 414-288-7145, Fax: 414-288-8078, E-mail: debra.leutermann@marquette.edu. Web site: http://www.busadm.mu.edu/emba/.

Marquette University, Graduate School of Management, Program in Business Administration, Milwaukee, WI 53201-1881. Offers business administration (MBA); economics (MBA); entrepreneurship (Certificate); finance (MBA); human resources (MBA); international business (MBA); management information systems (MBA); marketing (MBA); operations and supply chain management (MBA); sports business (MBA); JD/MBA; MBA/MA; MBA/MSN. *Accreditation:* AACSB. Part-time and evening/weekend programs available. *Students:* 42 full-time (14 women), 335 part-time (94 women); includes 24 minority (5 Black or African American, non-Hispanic/Latino; 1 American Indian or Alaska Native, non-Hispanic/Latino; 15 Asian, non-Hispanic/Latino; 3 Hispanic/Latino), 29 international. Average age 31. 182 applicants, 59% accepted, 103 enrolled. In 2011, 128 master's awarded. *Degree requirements:* For Certificate, business plan. *Entrance requirements:* For master's, GMAT or GRE, letters of recommendation. Additional exam requirements/recommendations for international students: Required—TOEFL (minimum score 550 paper-based; 85 computer-based; 88 iBT), IELTS (minimum score 6.5), Pearson Test of English. *Application deadline:* For fall admission, 2/15 for domestic and international students. Applications are processed on a rolling basis. Application fee: $50. Electronic applications accepted. *Expenses: Tuition:* Full-time $17,010; part-time $945 per credit hour. Tuition and fees vary according to program. *Financial support:* In 2011–12, 4 fellowships, 11 teaching assistantships were awarded; research assistantships, Federal Work-Study, institutionally sponsored loans, scholarships/grants, and tuition waivers (full and partial) also available. Support available to part-time students. Financial award application deadline: 2/15. *Faculty research:* Ethics in the professions, services marketing, technology impact on decision-making, mentoring. *Unit head:* Dr. Jeanne Simmons, Graduate Director, 414-288-7145, Fax: 414-288-1660, E-mail: jeanne.simmons@marquette.edu. *Application contact:* Debra Leutermann, Admissions Coordinator, 414-288-8064, Fax: 414-288-1902, E-mail: debra.leutermann@marquette.edu. Web site: http://business.marquette.edu/academics/mba.

McGill University, Faculty of Graduate and Postdoctoral Studies, Desautels Faculty of Management, Montréal, QC H3A 2T5, Canada. Offers administration (PhD); entrepreneurial studies (MBA); finance (MBA); general management (Post Master's Certificate); information systems (MBA); international business (MBA); international practicing management (MM); management (MBA); management for development (MBA); manufacturing management (MMM); marketing (MBA); operations management (MBA); public accountancy (Diploma); strategic management (MBA); MBA/LL B; MD/MBA. MMM offered jointly with Faculty of Engineering; PhD with Concordia University, HEC Montreal, Université de Montréal, Université du Québec à Montréal.

McGill University, Faculty of Graduate and Postdoctoral Studies, Faculty of Engineering, Department of Mechanical Engineering and Desautels Faculty of Management, Master in Manufacturing Management, Montréal, QC H3A 2T5, Canada. Offers MMM.

Milwaukee School of Engineering, Rader School of Business, Program in New Product Management, Milwaukee, WI 53202-3109. Offers MS. Part-time and evening/weekend programs available. *Faculty:* 1 full-time (0 women), 2 part-time/adjunct (1 woman). *Students:* 2 full-time (1 woman), 10 part-time (3 women); includes 2 minority (1 Asian, non-Hispanic/Latino; 1 Hispanic/Latino). Average age 30. 5 applicants, 60% accepted, 3 enrolled. In 2011, 6 master's awarded. *Degree requirements:* For master's, thesis, thesis defense or capstone project. *Entrance requirements:* For master's, GRE General Test or GMAT, 2 letters of recommendation. Additional exam requirements/recommendations for international students: Required—TOEFL (minimum score 550 paper-based; 213 computer-based; 79 iBT) or IELTS; Recommended—IELTS (minimum score 6.5). *Application deadline:* Applications are processed on a rolling basis. Electronic applications accepted. Application fee is waived when completed online. *Expenses: Tuition:* Full-time $17,550; part-time $650 per credit hour. *Financial support:* In 2011–12, 3 students received support. Career-related internships or fieldwork available. Support available to part-time students. Financial award applicants required to submit FAFSA. *Faculty research:* New product development, product research and design, product development. *Unit head:* Dr. Kathy Faggiani, Director, 414-277-2711, E-mail: faggiani@msoe.com. *Application contact:* Katie Gassenhuber, Graduate Program Associate, 800-321-6763, Fax: 414-277-7208, E-mail: gassenhuber@msoe.edu.

Northeastern State University, Graduate College, College of Business and Technology, Program in Industrial Management, Tahlequah, OK 74464-2399. Offers MS. Part-time and evening/weekend programs available. *Faculty:* 3 full-time (0 women). *Students:* 4 full-time (0 women), 15 part-time (5 women); includes 8 minority (2 Black or African American, non-Hispanic/Latino; 5 American Indian or Alaska Native, non-Hispanic/Latino; 1 Asian, non-Hispanic/Latino), 1 international. In 2011, 4 master's awarded. *Degree requirements:* For master's, synergistic experience. *Entrance requirements:* For master's, GRE, MAT, minimum GPA of 2.5. Additional exam requirements/recommendations for international students: Required—TOEFL (minimum score 213 computer-based). *Application deadline:* For fall admission, 6/1 priority date for domestic students. Applications are processed on a rolling basis. Application fee: $25. Electronic applications accepted. *Financial support:* Teaching assistantships and Federal Work-Study available. Financial award application deadline: 3/1. *Unit head:* Dr. Michael Turner, Chair, 918-456-5511 Ext. 2970, Fax: 918-458-2337, E-mail: turne003@nsuok.edu. *Application contact:* Margie Railey, Administrative Assistant, 918-456-5511 Ext. 2093, Fax: 918-458-2061, E-mail: railey@nsouk.edu.

Northern Illinois University, Graduate School, College of Engineering and Engineering Technology, Department of Technology, De Kalb, IL 60115-2854. Offers industrial management (MS). Part-time and evening/weekend programs available. *Faculty:* 14 full-time (1 woman), 1 part-time/adjunct (0 women). *Students:* 20 full-time (5 women), 28 part-time (6 women); includes 13 minority (7 Black or African American, non-Hispanic/Latino; 3 Asian, non-Hispanic/Latino; 1 Hispanic/Latino; 2 Two or more races, non-Hispanic/Latino), 6 international. Average age 33. 33 applicants, 58% accepted, 11 enrolled. In 2011, 28 master's awarded. *Degree requirements:* For master's, thesis optional. *Entrance requirements:* For master's, GRE General Test, minimum GPA of 2.75. Additional exam requirements/recommendations for international students: Required—TOEFL (minimum score 550 paper-based; 213 computer-based). *Application deadline:* For fall admission, 6/1 for domestic students, 5/1 for international students; for spring admission, 11/1 for domestic students, 10/1 for international students. Applications are processed on a rolling basis. Application fee: $40. Electronic applications accepted. *Financial support:* In 2011–12, 2 research assistantships with full tuition reimbursements, 12 teaching assistantships with full tuition reimbursements were awarded; fellowships with full tuition reimbursements, career-related internships or fieldwork, Federal Work-Study, scholarships/grants, tuition waivers (full), and unspecified assistantships also available. Support available to part-time students. Financial award applicants required to submit FAFSA. *Faculty research:* Digital control, intelligent systems, engineering graphic design, occupational safety, ergonomics. *Unit head:* Dr. Clifford Mirman, Chair, 815-753-1349, Fax: 815-753-3702, E-mail: mirman@ceet.niu.edu. *Application contact:* Graduate School Office, 815-753-0395, E-mail: gradsch@niu.edu. Web site: http://www.niu.edu/tech/graduate/index.shtml.

Oakland University, Graduate Study and Lifelong Learning, School of Business Administration, Department of Decision and Information Sciences, Rochester, MI 48309-4401. Offers information technology management (MS); management information systems (Certificate); production and operations management (Certificate).

Penn State University Park, Graduate School, Intercollege Graduate Programs, Intercollege Program in Quality and Manufacturing Management, State College, University Park, PA 16802-1503. Offers MMM. *Unit head:* Dr. Jose A. Ventura, Co-Director, 814-865-5802, Fax: 814-863-4745, E-mail: jav1@psu.edu. *Application contact:* Cynthia E. Nicosia, Director, Graduate Enrollment Services, 814-865-1795, Fax: 814-865-4627, E-mail: cey1@psu.edu.

Polytechnic University of Puerto Rico, Graduate School, Hato Rey, PR 00919. Offers business administration (MBA), including computer information systems, general management, management of information systems, management of international enterprises; civil engineering (ME, MS); computer engineering (ME, MS); computer science (MCS, MS); electrical engineering (ME, MS); engineering management (MEM); environmental management (MEM); landscape architecture (M Land Arch); manufacturing competitiveness (MMC, MS); manufacturing engineering (ME, MS); mechanical engineering (M Mech E). Part-time and evening/weekend programs available. *Entrance requirements:* For master's, 3 letters of recommendation.

Polytechnic University of Puerto Rico, Miami Campus, Graduate School, Miami, FL 33166. Offers accounting (MBA); business administration (MBA); construction management (MEM); environmental management (MEM); finance (MBA); human resources management (MBA); logistics and supply chain management (MBA); management of international enterprises (MBA); manufacturing management (MEM); marketing management (MBA); project management (MBA). Part-time and evening/weekend programs available. Postbaccalaureate distance learning degree programs offered (no on-campus study). *Entrance requirements:* For master's, minimum GPA of 3.0. Electronic applications accepted.

Polytechnic University of Puerto Rico, Orlando Campus, Graduate School, Winter Park, FL 32792. Offers accounting (MBA); business administration (MBA); construction management (MEM); engineering management (MEM); environmental management (MEM); finance (MBA); human resources management (MBA); management of international enterprises (MBA); management of technology (MBA); manufacturing management (MEM). Part-time and evening/weekend programs available. Postbaccalaureate distance learning degree programs offered (no on-campus study). *Entrance requirements:* For master's, minimum GPA of 3.0. Additional exam requirements/recommendations for international students: Recommended—TOEFL. Electronic applications accepted.

Portland State University, Graduate Studies, Maseeh College of Engineering and Computer Science, Department of Engineering and Technology Management, Portland, OR 97207-0751. Offers engineering and technology management (M Eng); engineering management (MS); manufacturing engineering (ME); manufacturing management (M Eng); systems science/engineering management (PhD); MS/MBA; MS/MS. Part-time and evening/weekend programs available. *Degree requirements:* For master's, thesis optional; for doctorate, one foreign language, thesis/dissertation, oral and written exams. *Entrance requirements:* For master's, minimum GPA of 3.0 in upper-division course work, BS in civil engineering; for doctorate, GRE General Test, GRE Subject Test, minimum GPA of 3.0 in upper-division course work. Additional exam requirements/recommendations for international students: Required—TOEFL (minimum score 550 paper-based; 213 computer-based). *Faculty research:* Scheduling, hierarchical decision modeling, operations research, knowledge-based information systems.

Purdue University, Graduate School, Krannert School of Management, Master of Science in Industrial Administration Program, West Lafayette, IN 47907. Offers MSIA. *Faculty:* 81 full-time (19 women), 2 part-time/adjunct (0 women). *Students:* 16 full-time (4 women); includes 3 minority (1 Black or African American, non-Hispanic/Latino; 2 Asian, non-Hispanic/Latino), 27 international. Average age 27. 53 applicants, 55% accepted, 16 enrolled. In 2011, 20 master's awarded. *Entrance requirements:* For master's, GMAT or GRE, work experience, essays, minimum GPA of 3.0, four-year baccalaureate degree, letters of recommendation. Additional exam requirements/recommendations for international students: Required—TOEFL (minimum score 550 paper, 213 computer, 77 iBT), IELTS (minimum score 6.5), or Pearson Test of English. *Application deadline:* For fall admission, 11/1 for domestic and international students; for winter admission, 1/10 for domestic students, 2/1 for international students; for spring admission, 3/1 for domestic students. Applications are processed on a rolling basis. Application fee: $60 ($75 for international students). Electronic applications accepted. *Financial support:* Applicants required to submit FAFSA. *Unit head:* Dr. P. Christopher Earley, Dean/Professor of Management, 765-494-4366. *Application contact:* Brian Precious, Director of Admissions, Marketing, Recruiting and Entrepreneurial Outreach, 765-494-0773, Fax: 765-494-9841, E-mail: krannertmasters@purdue.edu. Web site: http://masters.krannert.purdue.edu/programs/msia/.

Regis University, College for Professional Studies, School of Management, Denver, CO 80221-1099. Offers accounting (MS, Certificate); executive international management (Certificate); executive leadership (Certificate); executive project management (Certificate); finance and accounting (MBA); general business administration (MBA); health care management (MBA); human resource management and leadership (MSOL); information technology leadership and management (MSOL); international business (MBA); marketing (MBA); operations management (MBA); organizational leadership and management (MSOL); project leadership and management (MSOL); project management (Certificate); strategic business management (Certificate); strategic human resource management (Certificate); strategic management (MBA). Offered at Colorado Springs Campus, Northwest Denver Campus, Southeast Denver Campus, Fort Collins Campus, Broomfield Campus, Henderson (Nevada) Campus, and Summerlin (Nevada) Campus and online. Part-time and evening/weekend programs available. Postbaccalaureate distance learning degree programs offered (no on-campus study). *Degree requirements:* For master's, thesis optional, capstone project. *Entrance requirements:* For master's, GMAT or essays, interview, 2 years of full-time business work experience, resume; for Certificate, GMAT. Additional exam requirements/recommendations for international students: Required—TOEFL, TWE (minimum score 5) or university-based test. Electronic applications accepted. *Faculty research:* Impact of information technology on small business regulation of accounting, international project financing, mineral development, delivery of healthcare to rural indigenous communities.

Rochester Institute of Technology, Graduate Enrollment Services, College of Applied Science and Technology, School of Engineering Technology, Department of Civil Engineering Technology, Environmental Management and Safety, Program in Facility Management, Rochester, NY 14623-5603. Offers MS. Part-time programs available. Postbaccalaureate distance learning degree programs offered (no on-campus study). *Students:* 2 full-time (0 women), 19 part-time (7 women); includes 5 minority (2 Black or African American, non-Hispanic/Latino; 1 Asian, non-Hispanic/Latino; 2 Hispanic/Latino). Average age 39. 22 applicants, 50% accepted, 9 enrolled. In 2011, 5 master's awarded. *Degree requirements:* For master's, thesis or alternative, project. *Entrance requirements:* For master's, minimum GPA of 3.0. Additional exam requirements/recommendations for international students: Required—TOEFL (minimum score 550 paper-based; 213 computer-based; 79 iBT) or IELTS (minimum score 6.5). *Application deadline:* For fall admission, 2/15 priority date for domestic students, 2/15 for international students; for winter admission, 11/1 priority date for domestic students, 10/1 for international students; for spring admission, 2/1 priority date for domestic students, 1/1 for international students. Applications are processed on a rolling basis. Application fee: $50. Electronic applications accepted. *Expenses: Tuition:* Full-time $34,659; part-time $963 per credit hour. *Required fees:* $228; $76 per quarter. *Financial support:* Career-related internships or fieldwork and scholarships/grants available. Support available to part-time students. Financial award applicants required to submit FAFSA. *Faculty research:* Sustainability. *Unit head:* Dr. Jeff Rogers, Graduate Program Director, 585-475-4185, E-mail: jwrite@rit.edu. *Application contact:* Diane Ellison, Assistant Vice President, Graduate Enrollment Services, 585-475-2229, Fax: 585-475-7164, E-mail: gradinfo@rit.edu. Web site: http://www.rit.edu/cast/cetems/ms-in-facility-management.php.

Rochester Institute of Technology, Graduate Enrollment Services, College of Applied Science and Technology, School of Engineering Technology, Department of Electrical, Computer and Telecommunications Engineering Technology, Rochester, NY 14623-5603. Offers facility management (MS); manufacturing and mechanical systems integration (MS); telecommunications engineering technology (MS). Part-time and evening/weekend programs available. Postbaccalaureate distance learning degree programs offered (no on-campus study). *Students:* 54 full-time (13 women), 34 part-time (6 women); includes 7 minority (4 Black or African American, non-Hispanic/Latino; 1 Asian, non-Hispanic/Latino; 1 Hispanic/Latino; 1 Two or more races, non-Hispanic/Latino), 70 international. Average age 26. 154 applicants, 55% accepted, 32 enrolled. In 2011, 24 master's awarded. *Degree requirements:* For master's, thesis. *Entrance requirements:* For master's, GRE, minimum GPA of 3.0. Additional exam requirements/recommendations for international students: Required—TOEFL (minimum score 550 paper-based; 213 computer-based; 79 iBT) or IELTS (minimum score 6.5). *Application deadline:* For fall admission, 2/15 priority date for domestic students, 2/15 for international students; for winter admission, 11/1 for domestic and international students; for spring admission, 2/1 for domestic and international students. Applications are processed on a rolling basis. Application fee: $50. Electronic applications accepted. *Expenses: Tuition:* Full-time $34,659; part-time $963 per credit hour. *Required fees:* $228; $76 per quarter. *Financial support:* Research assistantships with partial tuition reimbursements, teaching assistantships with partial tuition reimbursements, career-related internships or fieldwork, and unspecified assistantships available. Support available to part-time students. Financial award application deadline: 2/15; financial award applicants required to submit FAFSA. *Faculty research:* Fiber optic networks, next generation networks, project management. *Unit head:* Michael Eastman, Department Chair, 585-475-7787, Fax: 585-475-2178, E-mail: mgeiee@rit.edu. *Application contact:* Diane Ellison, Assistant Vice President, Graduate Enrollment Services, 585-475-2229, Fax: 585-475-7164, E-mail: gradinfo@rit.edu. Web site: http://www.rit.edu/cast/ectet/.

Rochester Institute of Technology, Graduate Enrollment Services, Kate Gleason College of Engineering, Program in Manufacturing Leadership, Rochester, NY 14623-5603. Offers MS. Part-time and evening/weekend programs available. Postbaccalaureate distance learning degree programs offered (minimal on-campus study). *Students:* 11 full-time (7 women), 34 part-time (13 women); includes 5 minority (3 Black or African American, non-Hispanic/Latino; 2 Hispanic/Latino), 11 international. Average age 30. 23 applicants, 87% accepted, 20 enrolled. In 2011, 9 degrees awarded. *Degree requirements:* For master's, capstone. *Entrance requirements:* For master's, GMAT, minimum GPA of 2.5. Additional exam requirements/recommendations for international students: Required—TOEFL (minimum score 570 paper-based; 230 computer-based; 88 iBT) or IELTS (minimum score 6.5). *Application deadline:* For fall admission, 2/15 priority date for domestic students, 2/15 for international students. Applications are processed on a rolling basis. Application fee: $50. *Expenses: Tuition:* Full-time $34,659; part-time $963 per credit hour. *Required fees:* $228; $76 per quarter. *Financial support:* Institutionally sponsored loans and scholarships/grants available. Support available to part-time students. Financial award applicants required to submit FAFSA. *Faculty research:* Supply chain management, global manufacturing and operations, lean thinking, leadership. *Unit head:* Mark Smith, Graduate Program Director, 585-475-7971, Fax: 585-475-7955, E-mail: mmlmail@rit.edu. *Application contact:* Diane Ellison, Assistant Vice President, Graduate Enrollment Services, 585-475-2229, Fax: 585-475-7164, E-mail: gradinfo@rit.edu. Web site: http://www.rit.edu/kgcoe/mml/.

San Jose State University, Graduate Studies and Research, Lucas Graduate School of Business, Programs in Business Administration, San Jose, CA 95192-0001. Offers MBA. *Accreditation:* AACSB. *Degree requirements:* For master's, comprehensive exam, thesis or alternative. *Entrance requirements:* For master's, GMAT, minimum GPA of 3.0. Electronic applications accepted.

Southeast Missouri State University, School of Graduate Studies, Harrison College of Business, Cape Girardeau, MO 63701-4799. Offers accounting (MBA); entrepreneurship (MBA); financial management (MBA); general management (MBA); health administration (MBA); industrial management (MBA); international business (MBA); sport management (MBA). *Accreditation:* AACSB. Part-time and evening/weekend programs available. Postbaccalaureate distance learning degree programs offered (no on-campus study). *Faculty:* 31 full-time (10 women). *Students:* 49 full-time (23 women), 77 part-time (30 women); includes 5 minority (1 Black or African American, non-Hispanic/Latino; 1 American Indian or Alaska Native, non-Hispanic/Latino; 2 Hispanic/Latino; 1 Two or more races, non-Hispanic/Latino), 35 international. Average age 27. 78 applicants, 69% accepted, 43 enrolled. In 2011, 47 master's awarded. *Degree requirements:* For master's, variable foreign language requirement, comprehensive exam, applied research project related to field. *Entrance requirements:* For master's, GMAT (minimum score of 450), minimum undergraduate GPA of 2.5, C or better in prerequisite courses. Additional exam requirements/recommendations for international students: Required—TOEFL (minimum score 550 paper-based; 213 computer-based; 79 iBT); Recommended—IELTS (minimum score 6). *Application deadline:* For fall admission, 8/1 for domestic students, 7/1 for international students; for spring admission, 11/21 for domestic students, 11/1 for international students. Applications are processed on a rolling basis. Application fee: $30 ($40 for international students). Electronic applications accepted. *Expenses:* Tuition, state resident: full-time $4896; part-time $272 per credit hour. Tuition, nonresident: full-time $8649; part-time $480.50 per credit hour. *Financial support:* In 2011–12, 46 students received support, including 12 teaching assistantships with full tuition reimbursements available (averaging $7,600 per year); career-related internships or fieldwork, Federal Work-Study, scholarships/grants, tuition waivers (full), and unspecified assistantships also available. Financial award application deadline: 6/30; financial award applicants required to submit FAFSA. *Faculty research:* Human resources, laws impacting accounting, advertising. *Unit head:* Dr. Kenneth A. Heischmidt, Director, Graduate Programs in Business, 573-651-5116, Fax: 573-651-5032, E-mail: kheischmidt@semo.edu. *Application contact:* Gail Amick, Administrative Secretary, 573-651-2049, Fax: 573-651-2001, E-mail: gamick@semo.edu. Web site: http://www.semo.edu/mba.

Stevens Institute of Technology, Graduate School, Charles V. Schaefer Jr. School of Engineering, Department of Mechanical Engineering, Program in Integrated Product Development, Hoboken, NJ 07030. Offers armament engineering (M Eng); computer and electrical engineering (M Eng); manufacturing technologies (M Eng); systems reliability and design (M Eng).

Syracuse University, Martin J. Whitman School of Management, PhD Program in Business Administration, Syracuse, NY 13244. Offers accounting (PhD); finance (PhD); management information systems (PhD); managerial statistics (PhD); marketing (PhD); operations management (PhD); organizational behavior (PhD); strategy and human resources (PhD); supply chain management (PhD). *Faculty:* 79 full-time (20 women), 25 part-time/adjunct (6 women). *Students:* 32 full-time (10 women); includes 6 minority (3 Black or African American, non-Hispanic/Latino; 2 Asian, non-Hispanic/Latino; 1 Hispanic/Latino), 18 international. Average age 32. 260 applicants, 8% accepted, 12 enrolled. In 2011, 2 doctorates awarded. *Degree requirements:* For doctorate, comprehensive exam, thesis/dissertation, summer research paper. *Entrance requirements:* For doctorate, GMAT or GRE General Test, 3 recommendations. Additional exam requirements/recommendations for international students: Required—TOEFL (minimum score 600 paper-based; 250 computer-based; 100 iBT). *Application deadline:* For fall admission, 2/15 priority date for domestic students, 2/15 for international students. Applications are processed on a rolling basis. Application fee: $65. Electronic applications accepted. *Expenses: Tuition:* Part-time $1206 per credit. *Financial support:* In 2011–12, 1 fellowship with full tuition reimbursement (averaging $19,570 per year), 30 teaching assistantships with full tuition reimbursements (averaging $17,000 per year) were awarded; research assistantships with full tuition reimbursements, health care benefits, and unspecified assistantships also available. Financial award application deadline: 1/30. *Faculty research:* Marketing models, market microstructure, supply chain, auditing, corporate governance. *Unit head:* Dr. Eunkyu Lee, Director of the PhD Program, 315-443-3429, E-mail: elee06@syr.edu. *Application contact:* Carol Hilleges, Administrative Specialist, 315-443-9601, Fax: 315-443-3671, E-mail: clhilleg@syr.edu. Web site: http://whitman.syr.edu/phd/.

Texas A&M University, Mays Business School, Department of Information and Operations Management, College Station, TX 77843. Offers management information systems (MS, PhD); management science (PhD); production and operations management (PhD). *Faculty:* 16. *Students:* 172 full-time (61 women), 5 part-time (1 woman); includes 9 minority (5 Asian, non-Hispanic/Latino; 4 Hispanic/Latino), 121 international. Average age 31. In 2011, 96 master's awarded. Terminal master's awarded for partial completion of doctoral program. *Degree requirements:* For master's, comprehensive exam; for doctorate, thesis/dissertation. *Entrance requirements:* For master's, GMAT; for doctorate, GMAT or GRE General Test. Additional exam requirements/recommendations for international students: Required—TOEFL. *Application deadline:* For fall admission, 3/1 priority date for domestic students; for spring admission, 8/1 for domestic students. Applications are processed on a rolling basis. Application fee: $50 ($75 for international students). *Expenses:* Tuition, state resident: full-time $5437; part-time $226.55 per credit hour. Tuition, nonresident: full-time $12,949; part-time $539.55 per credit hour. *Required fees:* $2741. *Financial support:* In 2011–12, 51 students received support. Fellowships, research assistantships, teaching assistantships, career-related internships or fieldwork, Federal Work-Study, and institutionally sponsored loans available. Financial award application deadline: 2/1. *Unit head:* Dr. Rich Metters, Head, 979-845-1148, E-mail: rmetters@mays.tamu.edu. *Application contact:* Ted Boone, Graduate Advisor, 979-845-0809, E-mail: tboone@mays.tamu.edu. Web site: http://mays.tamu.edu/info/.

Texas Tech University, Graduate School, Rawls College of Business Administration, Area of Information Systems and Quantitative Sciences, Lubbock, TX 79409. Offers business statistics (MS, PhD); healthcare management (MS); management information systems (MS, PhD); production and operations management (MS, PhD); risk management (MS). Part-time programs available. *Faculty:* 15 full-time (0 women). *Students:* 46 full-time (13 women), 8 part-time (0 women); includes 4 minority (1 American Indian or Alaska Native, non-Hispanic/Latino; 1 Asian, non-Hispanic/Latino; 2 Hispanic/Latino), 38 international. Average age 27. 101 applicants, 65% accepted, 18 enrolled. In 2011, 35 master's, 2 doctorates awarded. Terminal master's awarded for partial completion of doctoral program. *Degree requirements:* For master's, comprehensive exam or capstone course; for doctorate, thesis/dissertation, qualifying exams. *Entrance requirements:* For master's and doctorate, GMAT, holistic profile of academic credentials. Additional exam requirements/recommendations for international students: Required—TOEFL (minimum score 550 paper-based; 213 computer-based; 79 iBT). *Application deadline:* For fall admission, 4/1 priority date for domestic students, 1/15 for international students; for spring admission, 9/1 priority date for domestic students, 6/15 for international students. Applications are processed on a rolling basis. Application fee: $50 ($75 for international students). Electronic applications accepted. *Expenses:* Tuition, state resident: full-time $5899; part-time $245.80 per credit hour. Tuition, nonresident: full-time $13,411; part-time $558.80 per credit hour. *Required fees:* $2680.60; $86.50 per credit hour. $920.30 per semester. *Financial support:* In 2011–12, 5 research assistantships (averaging $16,160 per year), 5 teaching assistantships (averaging $18,000 per year) were awarded; Federal Work-Study, scholarships/grants, and unspecified assistantships also available. *Faculty research:* Database management systems, systems management and engineering, expert systems and adaptive knowledge-based sciences, statistical analysis and design. *Unit head:* Dr. Glenn Browne, Area Coordinator, 806-834-0969, Fax: 806-742-3193, E-mail: glenn.browne@ttu.edu. *Application contact:* Elizabeth Stuart, Director, Graduate Services Center, 806-742-3184, Fax: 806-742-3958, E-mail: ba_grad@ttu.edu. Web site: http://is.ba.ttu.edu.

Universidad de las Américas–Puebla, Division of Graduate Studies, School of Engineering, Program in Industrial Engineering, Puebla, Mexico. Offers industrial engineering (MS); production management (M Adm). Part-time and evening/weekend programs available. *Degree requirements:* For master's, one foreign language, thesis. *Faculty research:* Textile industry, quality control.

Universidad de las Américas–Puebla, Division of Graduate Studies, School of Engineering, Program in Manufacturing Administration, Puebla, Mexico. Offers MS. *Faculty research:* Operations research, construction.

The University of Alabama, Graduate School, Manderson Graduate School of Business, Department of Information Systems, Statistics, and Management Science, Program in Operations Management, Tuscaloosa, AL 35487. Offers MS, PhD. *Accreditation:* AACSB. Part-time programs available. Postbaccalaureate distance learning degree programs offered (no on-campus study). *Faculty:* 9 full-time (1 woman). *Students:* 32 full-time (6 women), 26 part-time (8 women); includes 7 minority (3 Black or African American, non-Hispanic/Latino; 2 Asian, non-Hispanic/Latino; 1 Hispanic/Latino; 1 Two or more races, non-Hispanic/Latino), 11 international. Average age 31. 62 applicants, 42% accepted, 14 enrolled. In 2011, 34 master's, 1 doctorate awarded. Terminal master's awarded for partial completion of doctoral program. *Median time to degree:* Of those who began their doctoral program in fall 2003, 75% received their degree in 8 years or less. *Degree requirements:* For master's, comprehensive exam, business calculus; for doctorate, comprehensive exam, thesis/dissertation. *Entrance requirements:* For master's, GMAT or GRE; for doctorate, GRE or GMAT. Additional exam requirements/recommendations for international students: Required—TOEFL (minimum score 550 paper-based; 213 computer-based), IELTS (minimum score 6.5). *Application deadline:* For spring admission, 3/1 priority date for domestic students, 3/1 for international students. Applications are processed on a rolling basis. Application fee: $50 ($60 for international students). Electronic applications accepted. *Expenses:* Tuition, state resident: full-time $8600. Tuition, nonresident: full-time $21,900. *Financial support:* In 2011–12, 11 students received support, including 7 teaching assistantships with full tuition reimbursements available (averaging $13,500 per year); scholarships/grants and health care benefits also available. Financial award application deadline: 3/1. *Faculty research:* Supply chain management, inventory, simulation, logistics. *Unit head:* Dr. Charles R. Sox, Head, 205-348-8992, Fax: 205-348-0560, E-mail: csox@cba.ua.edu. *Application contact:* Dana Merchant, Administrative Secretary, 205-348-8904, E-mail: dmerchan@cba.ua.edu.

University of Arkansas, Graduate School, College of Engineering, Department of Industrial Engineering, Operations Management Program, Fayetteville, AR 72701-1201. Offers MS. Part-time and evening/weekend programs available. Postbaccalaureate distance learning degree programs offered. *Students:* 34 full-time (14 women), 459 part-time (110 women); includes 107 minority (64 Black or African American, non-Hispanic/Latino; 6 American Indian or Alaska Native, non-Hispanic/Latino; 12 Asian, non-Hispanic/Latino; 15 Hispanic/Latino; 1 Native Hawaiian or other Pacific Islander, non-Hispanic/Latino; 9 Two or more races, non-Hispanic/Latino), 22 international. 137 applicants, 94% accepted. In 2011, 183 master's awarded. *Degree requirements:* For master's, thesis optional. *Application deadline:* For fall admission, 4/1 for international students; for spring admission, 10/1 for international students. Applications are processed on a rolling basis. Application fee: $0. Electronic applications accepted. *Financial support:* In 2011–12, 2 research assistantships were awarded; fellowships, teaching assistantships, and institutionally sponsored loans also available. *Unit head:* Dr. Kim Needy, Departmental Chair, 479-575-7426, E-mail: kneedy@uark.edu. *Application contact:* Dr. Edward A. Pohl, Director and Chairman of Studies, 479-575-3156, Fax: 479-575-8431, E-mail: epohl@uark.edu. Web site: http://www.opnsmgmt.uark.edu/.

University of Bridgeport, School of Business, Bridgeport, CT 06604. Offers accounting (MBA); finance (MBA); general business (MBA); global financial services (MBA); human resource management (MBA); information systems and knowledge management (MBA); international business (MBA); management (MBA); marketing (MBA); operations management (MBA); small business and entrepreneurship (MBA); specialized business (MBA). Part-time and evening/weekend programs available. *Faculty:* 11 full-time (2 women), 39 part-time/adjunct (8 women). *Students:* 198 full-time (105 women), 94 part-time (47 women); includes 38 minority (16 Black or African American, non-Hispanic/Latino; 9 Asian, non-Hispanic/Latino; 10 Hispanic/Latino; 3 Two or more races, non-Hispanic/Latino), 227 international. Average age 28. 835 applicants, 56% accepted, 57 enrolled. In 2011, 155 master's awarded. *Degree requirements:* For master's, thesis optional. *Entrance requirements:* For master's, GMAT. Additional exam requirements/recommendations for international students: Recommended—TOEFL (minimum score 550 paper-based; 213 computer-based; 80 iBT), IELTS (minimum score 6.5). *Application deadline:* For fall admission, 8/1 priority date for domestic students, 8/1 for international students; for spring admission, 12/1 priority date for domestic students, 12/1 for international students. Applications are processed on a rolling basis. Application fee: $50. Electronic applications accepted. *Expenses:* Contact institution. *Financial support:* In 2011–12, 69 students received support. Fellowships, research assistantships, teaching assistantships, career-related internships or fieldwork, Federal Work-Study, institutionally sponsored loans, and tuition waivers (partial) available. Support available to part-time students. Financial award application deadline: 6/1; financial award applicants required to submit FAFSA. *Unit head:* Dr. Robert Gilmore, Dean, 203-576-4384, Fax: 203-576-4388, E-mail: rgilmore@bridgeport.edu. *Application contact:* Karissa Peckham, Dean of Admissions, 203-576-4552, Fax: 203-576-4941, E-mail: mba@bridgeport.edu. Web site: http://www.bridgeport.edu.

University of California, Berkeley, Graduate Division, Haas School of Business, PhD in Business Administration Program, Berkeley, CA 94720-1500. Offers accounting (PhD); business and public policy (PhD); finance (PhD); management of organizations (PhD); marketing (PhD); operations management (PhD); real estate (PhD). *Accreditation:* AACSB. *Faculty:* 77 full-time (18 women), 152 part-time/adjunct (24 women). *Students:* 79 full-time (25 women); includes 13 minority (12 Asian, non-Hispanic/Latino; 1 Hispanic/Latino), 34 international. Average age 30. 547 applicants, 5% accepted, 15 enrolled. In 2011, 14 doctorates awarded. *Degree requirements:* For doctorate, comprehensive exam, thesis/dissertation, written preliminary exams, oral qualifying exam. *Entrance requirements:* For doctorate, GMAT or GRE, minimum GPA of 3.0 in undergraduate and graduate coursework. Additional exam requirements/recommendations for international students: Required—TOEFL (minimum score 570 paper-based; 230 computer-based; 70 iBT), IELTS (minimum score 7). *Application deadline:* For fall admission, 12/10 for domestic and international students. Application fee: $80 ($100 for international students). Electronic applications accepted. *Financial support:* In 2011–12, 66 students received support, including 58 fellowships with full and partial tuition reimbursements available (averaging $29,000 per year), 77 teaching assistantships with full and partial tuition reimbursements available; research assistantships with full and partial tuition reimbursements available, scholarships/grants, health care benefits, tuition waivers (full), unspecified assistantships, and transit pass, travel grants also available. Financial award application deadline: 12/10; financial award applicants required to submit FAFSA. *Faculty research:* Accounting, business and public policy, finance, management of organizations, marketing, operations and information technology management, real estate. *Unit head:* Dr. Sunil Dutta, Director, 510-642-1229, Fax: 510-643-4255, E-mail: kimg@haas.berkeley.edu. *Application contact:* Kim Guilfoyle, Director, Student Affairs, 510-642-3944, Fax: 510-643-4255, E-mail: kimg@haas.berkeley.edu. Web site: http://www.haas.berkeley.edu/Phd/.

University of California, Los Angeles, Graduate Division, UCLA Anderson School of Management, Los Angeles, CA 90095-1481. Offers accounting (PhD); Asia Pacific (EMBA); business administration (EMBA, MBA); decisions, operations and technology management (PhD); finance (PhD); financial engineering (MFE); global economics and management (PhD); Latin America (EMBA); management and organizations (PhD); marketing (PhD); strategy (PhD); DDS/MBA; MBA/JD; MBA/MD; MBA/MLAS; MBA/MLIS; MBA/MPH; MBA/MPP; MBA/MSCS; MBA/MSN; MBA/MUP. *Accreditation:* AACSB. Part-time programs available. *Faculty:* 90 full-time (14 women), 62 part-time/adjunct (14 women). *Students:* 1,103 full-time (312 women), 842 part-time (223 women); includes 663 minority (18 Black or African American, non-Hispanic/Latino; 510 Asian, non-Hispanic/Latino; 46 Hispanic/Latino; 2 Native Hawaiian or other Pacific Islander, non-Hispanic/Latino; 87 Two or more races, non-Hispanic/Latino), 469 international. 4,737 applicants, 32% accepted, 875 enrolled. In 2011, 759 master's, 6 doctorates awarded. *Degree requirements:* For master's, comprehensive exam, field study consulting project (for MBA); thesis/dissertation (for MFE); for doctorate, comprehensive exam, thesis/dissertation, oral and written qualifying exams. *Entrance requirements:* For master's, GMAT (for MBA); GMAT or GRE General Test (for MFE), 4-year bachelor's degree or equivalent; for doctorate, GMAT or GRE General Test, 4-year bachelor's degree from regionally-accredited institution; minimum GPA of 3.0. Additional exam requirements/recommendations for international students: Required—TOEFL (minimum score 560 paper-based; 220 computer-based; 87 iBT), IELTS (minimum score 7). *Application deadline:* For fall admission, 10/26 for domestic and international students; for winter admission, 1/11 for domestic and international students; for spring admission, 4/18 for domestic and international students. Application fee: $200. Electronic applications accepted. *Expenses:* Contact institution. *Financial support:* In 2011–12, 600 students received support. Fellowships, research assistantships, teaching assistantships, career-related internships or fieldwork, institutionally sponsored loans, scholarships/grants, health care benefits, and tuition waivers (partial) available. Financial award application deadline: 4/15; financial award applicants required to submit FAFSA. *Unit head:* Judy D. Olian, Dean, 310-825-7982, Fax: 310-206-2073, E-mail: judy.olian@anderson.ucla.edu. *Application contact:* Robert Weiler, Assistant Dean, Director of MBA Admissions and Financial Aid, 310-825-6944, Fax: 310-825-8582, E-mail: mba.admissions@anderson.ucla.edu. Web site: http://www.anderson.ucla.edu/.

See Display on page 141 and Close-Up on page 249.

University of Central Missouri, The Graduate School, College of Science and Technology, Warrensburg, MO 64093. Offers applied mathematics (MS); aviation safety (MS); biology (MS); computer science (MS); environmental studies (MA); industrial management (MS); mathematics (MS); technology (MS); technology management (PhD). PhD is offered jointly with Indiana State University. Part-time programs available. Postbaccalaureate distance learning degree programs offered. *Entrance requirements:* Additional exam requirements/recommendations for international students: Required—TOEFL (minimum score 550 paper-based; 79 computer-based). Electronic applications accepted.

University of Cincinnati, Graduate School, Carl H. Lindner College of Business, PhD Programs, Cincinnati, OH 45221. Offers accounting (PhD); finance (PhD); information systems (PhD); management (PhD); marketing (PhD); quantitative analysis and operations management (PhD). *Faculty:* 56 full-time (13 women). *Students:* 34 full-time (12 women), 12 part-time (4 women); includes 2 minority (1 Asian, non-Hispanic/Latino; 1 Hispanic/Latino), 25 international. Average age 29. 120 applicants, 13% accepted, 10 enrolled. In 2011, 8 degrees awarded. *Median time to degree:* Of those who began their doctoral program in fall 2003, 65% received their degree in 8 years or less. *Degree requirements:* For doctorate, comprehensive exam, thesis/dissertation. *Entrance requirements:* For doctorate, GMAT, GRE, transcripts, essays, resume, letters of recommendation. Additional exam requirements/recommendations for international students: Required—TOEFL (minimum score 600 paper-based; 250 computer-based; 100 iBT). *Application deadline:* For fall admission, 2/1 for domestic and international students. Application fee: $65 ($70 for international students). Electronic applications accepted. *Expenses:* Contact institution. *Financial support:* In 2011–12, 39 students received support, including 30 research assistantships with full and partial tuition reimbursements available (averaging $14,640 per year); scholarships/grants, tuition waivers (full and partial), and unspecified assistantships also available. Financial award application deadline: 2/1; financial award applicants required to submit FAFSA. *Unit head:* Dr. Suzanne Masterson, Director, 513-556-7125, Fax: 513-556-5499, E-mail: suzanne.masterson@uc.edu. *Application contact:* Deborah Schildknecht, Assistant Director, 513-556-7190, Fax: 513-558-7006, E-mail: deborah.schildknecht@uc.edu. Web site: http://www.business.uc.edu/phd.

The University of Manchester, School of Mechanical, Aerospace and Civil Engineering, Manchester, United Kingdom. Offers advanced manufacturing technology (M Ent); aerospace engineering (M Phil, M Sc, PhD); civil engineering (M Phil, M Sc, PhD); environmental engineering (M Phil, PhD); management of projects (M Phil, M Sc, PhD); mechanical engineering (M Phil, M Sc, PhD); mechanical engineering design (M Ent); nuclear engineering (M Phil, D Eng, PhD).

University of Minnesota, Twin Cities Campus, Carlson School of Management, Doctoral Program in Business Administration, Minneapolis, MN 55455-0213. Offers accounting (PhD); finance (PhD); information and decision sciences (PhD); marketing (PhD); operations and management science (PhD); strategic management and organization (PhD). *Faculty:* 104 full-time (30 women). *Students:* 74 full-time (30 women); includes 8 minority (5 Asian, non-Hispanic/Latino; 3 Hispanic/Latino), 50 international. Average age 30. 320 applicants, 8% accepted, 15 enrolled. In 2011, 13 doctorates awarded. *Degree requirements:* For doctorate, comprehensive exam, thesis/dissertation, written and oral preliminary exams, proposal defense, final defense. *Entrance requirements:* For doctorate, GMAT, GRE General Test. Additional exam requirements/recommendations for international students: Required—TOEFL (minimum score 600 paper-based; 250 computer-based; 100 iBT); Recommended—IELTS (minimum score 7.5). *Application deadline:* For fall admission, 12/31 for domestic and international students. Applications are processed on a rolling basis. Application fee: $75 ($95 for international students). Electronic applications accepted. *Expenses:* Contact institution. *Financial support:* In 2011–12, 66 students received support, including 112 fellowships with full tuition reimbursements available (averaging $6,700 per year), 55 research assistantships with full tuition reimbursements available (averaging $6,750 per year), 54 teaching assistantships with full tuition reimbursements available (averaging $6,750 per year); institutionally sponsored loans, scholarships/grants, health care benefits, and unspecified assistantships also available. Financial award application deadline: 12/31. *Faculty research:* Corporate strategy, finance, entrepreneurship, marketing, information and decision science, operations, accounting, quality management. *Unit head:* Dr. Shawn P. Curley, Director, 612-624-6546, Fax: 612-624-8221, E-mail: curley@umn.edu. *Application contact:* Earlene K. Bronson, Assistant Director, 612-624-0875, Fax: 612-624-8221, E-mail: brons003@umn.edu. Web site: http://www.csom.umn.edu/phd-BA/.

University of Missouri–St. Louis, College of Business Administration, Program in Business Administration, St. Louis, MO 63121. Offers accounting (MBA); business administration (Certificate); finance (MBA); human resource management (Certificate); information systems (MBA); logistics and supply chain management (MBA, Certificate); marketing (MBA); marketing management (Certificate); operations management (MBA). *Accreditation:* AACSB. Part-time and evening/weekend programs available. *Faculty:* 32 full-time (7 women), 10 part-time/adjunct (2 women). *Students:* 126 full-time (48 women), 305 part-time (141 women); includes 61 minority (25 Black or African American, non-Hispanic/Latino; 23 Asian, non-Hispanic/Latino; 9 Hispanic/Latino; 1 Native Hawaiian or other Pacific Islander, non-Hispanic/Latino; 3 Two or more races, non-Hispanic/Latino), 47 international. Average age 30. 241 applicants, 70% accepted, 134 enrolled. In 2011, 150 master's, 1 doctorate, 19 other advanced degrees awarded. *Entrance requirements:* For master's, GMAT, 2 letters of recommendation. Additional exam requirements/recommendations for international students: Required—TOEFL (minimum score 550 paper-based; 213 computer-based). *Application deadline:* For fall admission, 7/1 for domestic and international students; for spring admission, 12/1 for domestic and international students. Applications are processed on a rolling basis. Application fee: $35 ($40 for international students). Electronic applications accepted. *Expenses:* Tuition, state resident: full-time $6273; part-time $3866 per year. Tuition, nonresident: full-time $14,969; part-time $9980 per year. *Required fees:* $315 per year. *Financial support:* In 2011–12, 32 research assistantships with full and partial tuition reimbursements (averaging $6,000 per year), 6 teaching assistantships with full and partial tuition reimbursements (averaging $12,276 per year) were awarded; career-related internships or fieldwork, Federal Work-Study, and institutionally sponsored loans also available. Support available to part-time students. Financial award application deadline: 4/1; financial award applicants required to submit FAFSA. *Faculty research:* Human resources, strategic management, marketing strategy, consumer behavior product development, advertising. *Unit head:* Karl Kottemann, Assistant Director, 314-516-5885, Fax: 314-516-6420, E-mail: mba@umsl.edu. *Application contact:* 314-516-5458, Fax: 314-516-6996, E-mail: gradadm@umsl.edu. Web site: http://www.umsl.edu/divisions/business/mbaonline/mbaprog.htm.

University of New Haven, Graduate School, Tagliatela College of Engineering, Program in Engineering and Operations Management, West Haven, CT 06516-1916. Offers MS. *Students:* 3 full-time (1 woman), 38 part-time (4 women); includes 6 minority (3 Black or African American, non-Hispanic/Latino; 3 Asian, non-Hispanic/Latino), 3 international. 30 applicants, 97% accepted, 14 enrolled. *Entrance requirements:* For master's, five or more years' experience in a supervisory role in engineering, technical staff support, engineering or systems management, project management, systems engineering, manufacturing, logistics, industrial engineering, military operations, or quality assurance. Additional exam requirements/recommendations for international students: Required—TOEFL (minimum score 520 paper-based; 190 computer-based; 70 iBT); Recommended—IELTS (minimum score 5.5). *Application deadline:* For fall admission, 5/31 for international students; for winter admission, 10/15 for international students; for spring admission, 1/15 for international students. Application fee: $50. *Expenses: Tuition:* Part-time $750 per credit. *Unit head:* Dr. John Sarris, Chair, 203-932-7146. *Application contact:* Eloise Gormley, Director of Graduate Admissions, 203-932-7449, Fax: 203-932-7137, E-mail: gradinfo@newhaven.edu. Web site: http://www.newhaven.edu/88389/.

University of Pittsburgh, Katz Graduate School of Business, Master of Business Administration Programs, Pittsburgh , PA 15260. Offers finance (MBA); information systems (MBA); marketing (MBA); operations management (MBA); organizational behavior and human resource management (MBA); organizational leadership (Certificate); strategy, environment and organizations (MBA); technology, innovation and entrepreneurship (Certificate); MBA/JD; MBA/MIB; MBA/MPIA; MBA/MSE; MBA/MSIS; MID/MBA. *Accreditation:* AACSB. Part-time and evening/weekend programs available. *Faculty:* 62 full-time (17 women), 21 part-time/adjunct (4 women). *Students:* 179 full-time (63 women), 572 part-time (373 women); includes 69 minority (29 Black or African American, non-Hispanic/Latino; 24 Asian, non-Hispanic/Latino; 16 Hispanic/Latino), 83 international. Average age 29. 391 applicants, 42% accepted, 78 enrolled. *Degree requirements:* For master's, minimum GPA of 3.0. *Entrance requirements:* For master's, GMAT, recommendations, undergraduate transcripts, essay, resume, interview, bachelor's degree. Additional exam requirements/recommendations for international students: Required—TOEFL (minimum score 600 paper, 250 computer, 100 iBT) or IELTS. *Application deadline:* For fall admission, 4/1 priority date for domestic students, 2/1 for international students. Application fee: $50. Electronic applications accepted. *Expenses:* Tuition, state resident: full-time $18,774; part-time $760 per credit. Tuition, nonresident: full-time $30,736; part-time $1258 per credit. *Required fees:* $740; $200 per term. Tuition and fees vary according to program. *Financial support:* In 2011–12, 58 students received support. Career-related internships or fieldwork and scholarships/grants available. Financial award application deadline: 3/1; financial award applicants required to submit FAFSA. *Faculty research:* Accounting statements and reporting, corporate finance, information systems processes, structures and decision-making, consumer behavior and marketing models. *Unit head:* William T. Valenta, Assistant Dean/Director, 412-648-1610, Fax: 412-648-1659, E-mail: wtvalenta@katz.pitt.edu. *Application contact:* Thomas Keller, Director of MBA Admissions, 412-648-1700, Fax: 412-648-1659, E-mail: mba@katz.pitt.edu. Web site: http://www.business.pitt.edu/katz/mba/.

University of Puerto Rico, Mayagüez Campus, Graduate Studies, College of Business Administration, Mayagüez, PR 00681-9000. Offers business administration (MBA); finance (MBA); human resources (MBA); industrial management (MBA). Part-time and evening/weekend programs available. *Students:* 46 full-time (30 women), 16 part-time (9 women); includes 59 minority (all Hispanic/Latino), 3 international. 18 applicants, 44% accepted, 5 enrolled. In 2011, 14 master's awarded. *Degree requirements:* For master's, comprehensive exam. *Entrance requirements:* For master's, GMAT or EXADEP, bachelor's degree with courses in calculus, microeconomics, accounting and statistics. Additional exam requirements/recommendations for international students: Required—TOEFL (minimum score 500 paper-based; 173 computer-based). *Application deadline:* For fall admission, 2/15 for domestic and international students; for spring admission, 9/15 for domestic and international students. Applications are processed on a rolling basis. Application fee: $25. Tuition and fees vary according to course level and course load. *Financial support:* In 2011–12, 4 students received support, including 4 teaching assistantships (averaging $8,500 per year); Federal Work-Study and institutionally sponsored loans also available. *Faculty research:* Organizational studies, management, accounting. *Total annual research expenditures:* $20,000. *Unit head:* Dr. Rosario Ortiz, Graduate Student Coordinator, 787-265-3800, Fax: 787-832-5320, E-mail: rosario.ortiz@upr.edu. *Application contact:* Milagros Soto, Student Administrator, 787-265-3887, Fax: 787-832-5320, E-mail: milagros.soto1@upr.edu. Web site: http://enterprise.uprm.edu/.

University of Puerto Rico, Río Piedras, College of Business Administration, San Juan, PR 00931-3300. Offers accounting (MBA); finance (MBA, PhD); general business (MBA); human resources management (MBA); international trade and business (MBA, PhD); marketing (MBA, PhD); operations management (MBA); quantitative methods (MBA). *Accreditation:* ACBSP. Part-time programs available. *Degree requirements:* For master's, comprehensive exam, thesis or alternative, research project. *Entrance requirements:* For master's, GMAT or PAEG, minimum GPA of 3.0, letter of recommendation; for doctorate, GMAT, PAEG, minimum GPA of 3.0, master degree. *Faculty research:* Management.

University of Rhode Island, Graduate School, College of Business Administration, Kingston, RI 02881. Offers accounting (MS); business administration (MBA, PhD), including finance and insurance (PhD), management (PhD), marketing (PhD), operations and supply chain management (MBA); finance (MBA); general business (MBA); management (MBA); marketing (MBA); supply chain management (MBA). *Accreditation:* AACSB. Part-time and evening/weekend programs available. *Faculty:* 56 full-time (15 women), 8 part-time/adjunct (4 women). *Students:* 93 full-time (40 women), 226 part-time (90 women); includes 35 minority (7 Black or African American, non-Hispanic/Latino; 1 American Indian or Alaska Native, non-Hispanic/Latino; 15 Asian, non-Hispanic/Latino; 11 Hispanic/Latino; 1 Two or more races, non-Hispanic/Latino), 24 international. In 2011, 78 master's, 3 doctorates awarded. *Degree requirements:* For master's, comprehensive exam (for some programs), thesis optional; for doctorate, comprehensive exam, thesis/dissertation. *Entrance requirements:* For master's, GMAT or GRE, 2 letters of recommendation, resume; for doctorate, GMAT or GRE, 3 letters of recommendation, resume. Additional exam requirements/recommendations for international students: Required—TOEFL (minimum score 575 paper-based; 233 computer-based; 91 iBT). Application fee: $65. Electronic applications accepted. *Expenses:* Tuition, state resident: full-time $10,432; part-time $580 per credit hour. Tuition, nonresident: full-time $23,130; part-time $1285 per credit hour. *Required fees:* $1362; $36 per credit hour. $35 per semester. One-time fee: $130. *Financial support:* In 2011–12, 13 teaching assistantships with full and partial tuition reimbursements (averaging $13,020 per year) were awarded. Financial award applicants required to submit FAFSA. *Unit head:* Dr. Mark Higgins, Dean, 401-874-4244, Fax: 401-874-4312, E-mail: markhiggins@uri.edu. *Application contact:* Lisa Lancellotta, Coordinator, MBA Programs, 401-874-4241, Fax: 401-874-4312, E-mail: mba@uri.edu. Web site: http://www.cba.uri.edu/.

University of Southern Indiana, Graduate Studies, College of Science, Engineering, and Education, Program in Industrial Management, Evansville, IN 47712-3590. Offers MS. Part-time and evening/weekend programs available. *Faculty:* 2 full-time (1 woman). *Students:* 9 part-time (2 women). Average age 33. 2 applicants, 100% accepted, 2 enrolled. *Degree requirements:* For master's, project. *Entrance requirements:* For master's, minimum GPA of 2.5, BS in engineering or engineering technology. Additional exam requirements/recommendations for international students: Required—TOEFL (minimum score 550 paper-based; 213 computer-based; 79 iBT), IELTS (minimum score 6). *Application deadline:* For fall admission, 8/15 priority date for domestic students, 3/1 for international students. Applications are processed on a rolling basis. Application fee: $35. Electronic applications accepted. *Expenses:* Tuition, state resident: full-time $5044; part-time $280.21 per credit hour. Tuition, nonresident: full-time $9949; part-time $552.71 per credit hour. *Required fees:* $240; $22.75 per term. Tuition and fees vary according to course load and reciprocity agreements. *Financial support:* Federal Work-Study, scholarships/grants, tuition waivers (full and partial), and unspecified assistantships available. Financial award application deadline: 3/1; financial award applicants required to submit FAFSA. *Unit head:* Dr. David E. Schultz, Director, 812-464-1881, E-mail: dschultz@usi.edu. *Application contact:* Dr. Wes Durham, Director, Graduate Studies, 812-465-7015, Fax: 812-464-1956, E-mail: wdurham@usi.edu. Web site: http://www.usi.edu/science/engineering/msim-program-objectives.asp.

The University of Tennessee, Graduate School, College of Business Administration, Program in Business Administration, Knoxville, TN 37996. Offers accounting (PhD); finance (MBA, PhD); logistics and transportation (MBA, PhD); management (PhD); marketing (MBA, PhD); operations management (MBA); professional business administration (MBA); statistics (PhD); JD/MBA; MS/MBA; Pharm D/MBA. Pharm D/MBA offered jointly with The University of Tennessee Health Science Center. *Accreditation:* AACSB. Postbaccalaureate distance learning degree programs offered. *Degree requirements:* For master's, thesis or alternative; for doctorate, thesis/dissertation. *Entrance requirements:* For master's and doctorate, GMAT, minimum GPA of 2.7. Additional exam requirements/recommendations for international students: Required—TOEFL. Electronic applications accepted. *Expenses:* Tuition, state resident: full-time $8332; part-time $464 per credit hour. Tuition, nonresident: full-time $25,174; part-time $1400 per credit hour. *Required fees:* $1162; $56 per credit hour. Tuition and fees vary according to program.

The University of Texas at Arlington, Graduate School, College of Business, Program in Business Administration, Arlington, TX 76019. Offers accounting (PhD); business statistics (PhD); finance (MBA, PhD); information systems (MBA, PhD); management (MBA, PhD); marketing (MBA, PhD); operations management (MBA, PhD); real estate (MBA). *Accreditation:* AACSB. Part-time and evening/weekend programs available. *Students:* 505 full-time (189 women), 369 part-time (140 women); includes 199 minority (58 Black or African American, non-Hispanic/Latino; 2 American Indian or Alaska Native, non-Hispanic/Latino; 70 Asian, non-Hispanic/Latino; 56 Hispanic/Latino; 1 Native Hawaiian or other Pacific Islander, non-Hispanic/Latino; 12 Two or more races, non-Hispanic/Latino), 306 international. 416 applicants, 81% accepted, 234 enrolled. In 2011, 495 master's, 3 doctorates awarded. *Degree requirements:* For master's, thesis optional; for doctorate, comprehensive exam, thesis/dissertation. *Entrance requirements:* For master's, GMAT or GRE; for doctorate, GMAT, minimum GPA of 3.0 (undergraduate), 3.4 (graduate); 30 hours of graduate course work. Additional exam requirements/recommendations for international students: Required—TOEFL (minimum score 550 paper-based; 213 computer-based; 79 iBT). *Application deadline:* For fall admission, 6/1 for domestic students, 4/1 for international students; for spring admission, 10/15 for domestic students, 9/15 for international students. Applications are processed on a rolling basis. Application fee: $40 ($70 for international students).

Industrial and Manufacturing Management

Electronic applications accepted. *Financial support:* Career-related internships or fieldwork, scholarships/grants, and unspecified assistantships available. Support available to part-time students. Financial award application deadline: 6/1; financial award applicants required to submit FAFSA. *Unit head:* Dr. Edmund Prater, Director of PhD Programs, 817-272-2131, Fax: 817-272-5799. *Application contact:* Melanie McGee, Director of MBA Program, 817-272-3005, Fax: 817-272-5799, E-mail: mwmcgee@uta.edu.

The University of Texas at Austin, Graduate School, McCombs School of Business, Department of Information, Risk, and Operations Management, Austin, TX 78712-1111. Offers information management (MBA); information systems (PhD); risk analysis and decision making (PhD); risk management (MBA); supply chain and operations management (MBA, PhD). *Degree requirements:* For doctorate, thesis/dissertation. *Entrance requirements:* For doctorate, GMAT or GRE. *Application deadline:* For fall admission, 1/2 for domestic students. Applications are processed on a rolling basis. Application fee: $50 ($75 for international students). Electronic applications accepted. *Financial support:* Fellowships with full and partial tuition reimbursements, research assistantships, and teaching assistantships with partial tuition reimbursements available. Financial award application deadline: 1/2. *Faculty research:* Stochastic processing and queuing, discrete nonlinear and large-scale optimization simulation, quality assurance logistics, distributed artificial intelligence, organizational modeling. *Unit head:* Dr. Prabhudev Konana, Chair, 512-471-5219, E-mail: prabhudev.konana@mccombs.utexas.edu. Web site: http://www.mccombs.utexas.edu/dept/irom/.

The University of Texas at Tyler, College of Business and Technology, School of Human Resource Development and Technology, Tyler, TX 75799-0001. Offers human resource development (MS, PhD); industrial management (MS). Part-time and evening/weekend programs available. Postbaccalaureate distance learning degree programs offered (no on-campus study). *Degree requirements:* For master's, comprehensive exam. *Entrance requirements:* For master's, GRE General Test or MAT. Additional exam requirements/recommendations for international students: Required—TOEFL (minimum score 79 computer-based). Electronic applications accepted. *Faculty research:* Human resource development.

The University of Toledo, College of Graduate Studies, College of Business and Innovation, Department of Information Operations and Technology Management, Toledo, OH 43606-3390. Offers information systems (MBA); manufacturing management (PhD); operations management (MBA); supply chain management (Certificate). Part-time and evening/weekend programs available. *Faculty:* 11. *Students:* 16 full-time (5 women), 36 part-time (9 women); includes 7 minority (5 Black or African American, non-Hispanic/Latino; 1 Asian, non-Hispanic/Latino; 1 Hispanic/Latino), 20 international. Average age 33. 41 applicants, 51% accepted, 10 enrolled. In 2011, 15 master's, 5 doctorates awarded. *Degree requirements:* For doctorate, thesis/dissertation. *Entrance requirements:* For master's, doctorate, and Certificate, GMAT, minimum GPA of 2.7 for all prior academic work, three letters of recommendation, statement of purpose, transcripts from all prior institutions attended. Additional exam requirements/recommendations for international students: Required—TOEFL (minimum score 550 paper-based; 213 computer-based; 80 iBT), IELTS (minimum score 6.5). *Application deadline:* For fall admission, 1/15 priority date for domestic students, 1/15 for international students. Applications are processed on a rolling basis. Application fee: $45 ($75 for international students). Electronic applications accepted. *Financial support:* In 2011–12, 23 research assistantships with full and partial tuition reimbursements (averaging $9,500 per year) were awarded; career-related internships or fieldwork, Federal Work-Study, institutionally sponsored loans, scholarships/grants, tuition waivers (full and partial), unspecified assistantships, and administrative assistantships also available. Support available to part-time students. *Unit head:* Dr. T. S. Ragu-Nathan, Chair, 419-530-2420. *Application contact:* Graduate School Office, 419-530-4723, Fax: 419-530-4724, E-mail: grdsch@utnet.utoledo.edu. Web site: http://www.utoledo.edu/business/index.html.

Virginia Commonwealth University, Graduate School, da Vinci Center for Innovation, Richmond, VA 23284-9005. Offers product innovation (MPI). Part-time programs available. *Entrance requirements:* For master's, bachelor's degree or equivalent from accredited college or university; minimum undergraduate GPA of 3.0 for at least the last two years of undergraduate work; letter of recommendation; statement of intent; interview. Additional exam requirements/recommendations for international students: Required—TOEFL. *Application deadline:* For fall admission, 5/31 for domestic students; for spring admission, 10/15 for domestic students. *Expenses:* Tuition, state resident: full-time $9133; part-time $507 per credit. Tuition, nonresident: full-time $18,777; part-time $1043 per credit. *Required fees:* $77 per credit. Tuition and fees vary according to degree level, campus/location, program and student level. *Unit head:* Dr. Kenneth Kahn, Director, 804-828-7188. *Application contact:* Seth Caskey, Program Coordinator, 804-828-7188, E-mail: swcaskey@vcu.edu. Web site: http://www.davincicenter.vcu.edu/.

Wake Forest University, Schools of Business, Full-time MBA Program, Winston-Salem, NC 27106. Offers consulting/general management (MBA); entrepreneurship (MBA); finance (MBA); health (MBA); marketing (MBA); operations management (MBA); JD/MBA; MD/MBA; MSA/MBA. *Accreditation:* AACSB. *Faculty:* 62 full-time (16 women), 41 part-time/adjunct (14 women). *Students:* 120 full-time (28 women); includes 14 minority (8 Black or African American, non-Hispanic/Latino; 4 Asian, non-Hispanic/Latino; 1 Hispanic/Latino; 1 Two or more races, non-Hispanic/Latino), 28 international. Average age 28. In 2011, 62 master's awarded. *Degree requirements:* For master's, 65.5 credit hours. *Entrance requirements:* For master's, GMAT or GRE, letters of recommendation, official transcripts, current resume or curriculum vitae, 2 years of work experience. Additional exam requirements/recommendations for international students: Required—TOEFL (minimum score 600 paper-based; 250 computer-based; 100 iBT), Pearson Test of English. *Application deadline:* For fall admission, 4/15 for domestic and international students. Applications are processed on a rolling basis. Application fee: $100. Electronic applications accepted. *Expenses:* Contact institution. *Financial support:* In 2011–12, 84 students received support. Career-related internships or fieldwork, scholarships/grants, and unspecified assistantships available. Financial award application deadline: 2/15; financial award applicants required to submit FAFSA. *Faculty research:* The influence of personal relationships on business decision-making and management of change; drivers of perceived value and consumer behavior; impact of accounting on auditing, financial, managerial, systems and taxation stakeholders; corporate governance and executive compensation; impact of operations strategies on competitiveness. *Unit head:* Jon Duchac, Director, Full-time MBA Program, 336-758-5422, Fax: 336-758-5830, E-mail: busadmissions@wfu.edu. *Application contact:* Tamara Paquee, Administrative Assistant, 336-758-5422, Fax: 336-758-5830, E-mail: busadmissions@wfu.edu. Web site: http://www.business.wfu.edu/.

Washington State University, Graduate School, College of Business, Business Administration Programs, Pullman, WA 99164. Offers business administration (MBA, PhD), including accounting (PhD), finance (PhD), management and operations (PhD), management information systems (PhD), marketing (PhD). *Accreditation:* AACSB. *Faculty:* 47. *Students:* 93 full-time (35 women), 94 part-time (32 women); includes 25 minority (4 Black or African American, non-Hispanic/Latino; 2 American Indian or Alaska Native, non-Hispanic/Latino; 11 Asian, non-Hispanic/Latino; 7 Hispanic/Latino; 1 Two or more races, non-Hispanic/Latino), 33 international. Average age 31. 310 applicants, 31% accepted, 67 enrolled. In 2011, 15 doctorates awarded. *Degree requirements:* For master's, comprehensive exam (for some programs), thesis (for some programs), final presentation; for doctorate, comprehensive exam, thesis/dissertation, oral and written exams. *Entrance requirements:* For master's and doctorate, GMAT, minimum GPA of 3.0, 3 letters of recommendation. Additional exam requirements/recommendations for international students: Required—TOEFL. *Application deadline:* For fall admission, 3/1 priority date for domestic students, 3/1 for international students; for spring admission, 6/1 priority date for domestic students, 6/1 for international students. Applications are processed on a rolling basis. Application fee: $75. Electronic applications accepted. *Financial support:* In 2011–12, 102 students received support, including 36 teaching assistantships with full and partial tuition reimbursements available (averaging $18,204 per year); career-related internships or fieldwork, Federal Work-Study, institutionally sponsored loans, health care benefits, tuition waivers (partial), unspecified assistantships, and teaching associateships also available. Financial award application deadline: 4/1. *Total annual research expenditures:* $344,000. *Unit head:* Dr. Eric Spangenberg, Dean, 509-335-8150, E-mail: ers@wsu.edu. *Application contact:* Graduate School Admissions, 800-GRADWSU, Fax: 509-335-1949, E-mail: gradsch@wsu.edu.

Wayne State University, College of Liberal Arts and Sciences, Department of Economics, Detroit, MI 48202. Offers health economics (MA, PhD); industrial organization (MA, PhD); international economics (MA, PhD); labor and human resources (MA, PhD); JD/MA. *Students:* 54 full-time (19 women), 16 part-time (8 women); includes 13 minority (9 Black or African American, non-Hispanic/Latino; 4 Asian, non-Hispanic/Latino), 26 international. Average age 31. 94 applicants, 54% accepted, 16 enrolled. In 2011, 6 master's, 6 doctorates awarded. *Degree requirements:* For master's, comprehensive exam, thesis optional; for doctorate, thesis/dissertation. *Entrance requirements:* For master's, minimum GPA of 3.0, prior coursework in intermediate microeconomic and macroeconomic theory, statistics, and elementary calculus; for doctorate, GRE, minimum GPA of 3.0, prior coursework in intermediate microeconomic and macroeconomic theory, statistics, and elementary calculus. Additional exam requirements/recommendations for international students: Required—TOEFL (minimum score 550 paper-based; 213 computer-based); Recommended—TWE (minimum score 5.5). *Application deadline:* For fall admission, 6/1 priority date for domestic students, 5/1 for international students; for winter admission, 10/1 priority date for domestic students, 9/1 for international students; for spring admission, 2/1 priority date for domestic students, 1/1 for international students. Applications are processed on a rolling basis. Application fee: $50. Electronic applications accepted. *Expenses:* Tuition, state resident: part-time $512.85 per credit. Tuition, nonresident: part-time $1132.65 per credit. *Required fees:* $26.60 per credit. $199.65 per semester. Tuition and fees vary according to course load and program. *Financial support:* In 2011–12, 23 students received support, including 3 fellowships with tuition reimbursements available (averaging $15,805 per year), 1 research assistantship with tuition reimbursement available (averaging $17,453 per year), 19 teaching assistantships with tuition reimbursements available (averaging $15,713 per year); scholarships/grants, health care benefits, and unspecified assistantships also available. Support available to part-time students. Financial award application deadline: 3/1. *Faculty research:* Health economics, international economics, macro economics, urban and labor economics, econometrics. *Total annual research expenditures:* $56,699. *Unit head:* Dr. Li Way Lee, Chair, 313-577-3345, Fax: 313-577-0149, E-mail: aa1313@wayne.edu. *Application contact:* Dr. Allen Goodman, Director, 313-577-3235, E-mail: allen.goodman@wayne.edu. Web site: http://www.clas.wayne.edu/economics/.

Wilkes University, College of Graduate and Professional Studies, Jay S. Sidhu School of Business and Leadership, Wilkes-Barre, PA 18766-0002. Offers accounting (MBA); entrepreneurship (MBA); finance (MBA); health care administration (MBA); human resource management (MBA); international business (MBA); marketing (MBA); operations management (MBA); organizational leadership and development (MBA). *Accreditation:* ACBSP. Part-time and evening/weekend programs available. *Students:* 48 full-time (20 women), 134 part-time (62 women); includes 12 minority (2 Black or African American, non-Hispanic/Latino; 5 Asian, non-Hispanic/Latino; 2 Hispanic/Latino; 3 Two or more races, non-Hispanic/Latino), 9 international. Average age 30. In 2011, 69 master's awarded. *Entrance requirements:* For master's, GMAT. Additional exam requirements/recommendations for international students: Required—TOEFL (minimum score 550 paper-based; 213 computer-based; 79 iBT). *Application deadline:* Applications are processed on a rolling basis. Application fee: $45 ($65 for international students). Electronic applications accepted. *Expenses:* Contact institution. *Financial support:* Federal Work-Study and unspecified assistantships available. Financial award application deadline: 3/1; financial award applicants required to submit FAFSA. *Unit head:* Dr. Jeffrey Alves, Dean, 570-408-4702, Fax: 570-408-7846, E-mail: jeffrey.alves@wilkes.edu. *Application contact:* Erin Sutzko, Director of Extended Learning, 570-408-4253, Fax: 570-408-7846, E-mail: erin.sutzko@wilkes.edu. Web site: http://www.wilkes.edu/pages/457.asp.

Section 10
Insurance and Actuarial Science

This section contains a directory of institutions offering graduate work in insurance and actuarial science. Additional information about programs listed in the directory but not augmented by an in-depth entry may be obtained by writing directly to the dean of a graduate school or chair of a department at the address given in the directory.

For programs offering related work, see also in this book *Business Administration and Management.*

CONTENTS

Program Directories

Actuarial Science

Ball State University, Graduate School, College of Sciences and Humanities, Department of Mathematical Sciences, Program in Actuarial Science, Muncie, IN 47306-1099. Offers MA. *Faculty:* 20. *Students:* 23 full-time (9 women), 7 part-time (4 women), 11 international. Average age 27. 45 applicants, 78% accepted, 16 enrolled. In 2011, 16 master's awarded. *Entrance requirements:* For master's, GMAT. Application fee: $50. Tuition and fees vary according to program and reciprocity agreements. *Financial support:* In 2011–12, 20 students received support, including 20 teaching assistantships with full tuition reimbursements available (averaging $13,765 per year). Financial award application deadline: 3/1. *Unit head:* Dr. Sheryl Smith, Director, 765-285-8681, Fax: 765-285-1721. *Application contact:* Dr. Hanspeter Fischer, Director of Graduate Programs, 765-285-8640, Fax: 765-285-1721. Web site: http://cms.bsu.edu/Academics/CollegesandDepartments/Math/AcademicsAdmissions/Programs/Masters/ActuarialScience.aspx.

Boston University, Metropolitan College, Department of Actuarial Science, Boston, MA 02215. Offers MS. Part-time and evening/weekend programs available. *Faculty:* 3 full-time (1 woman), 6 part-time/adjunct (1 woman). *Students:* 43 full-time (17 women), 57 part-time (26 women); includes 18 minority (1 Black or African American, non-Hispanic/Latino; 15 Asian, non-Hispanic/Latino; 2 Hispanic/Latino), 54 international. Average age 25. 168 applicants, 55% accepted, 47 enrolled. In 2011, 31 master's awarded. *Entrance requirements:* For master's, prerequisite coursework in calculus. Additional exam requirements/recommendations for international students: Required—TOEFL (minimum score 550 paper-based; 213 computer-based; 84 iBT). *Application deadline:* For fall admission, 5/31 priority date for domestic students, 5/15 for international students; for spring admission, 10/31 priority date for domestic students, 10/15 for international students. Applications are processed on a rolling basis. Application fee: $70. Electronic applications accepted. *Expenses: Tuition:* Full-time $40,848; part-time $1276 per credit hour. *Required fees:* $572; $286 per semester. *Financial support:* In 2011–12, 1 research assistantship with full tuition reimbursement (averaging $19,300 per year), 6 teaching assistantships with full tuition reimbursements (averaging $19,300 per year) were awarded; career-related internships or fieldwork, scholarships/grants, and unspecified assistantships also available. *Faculty research:* Survival models, life contingencies, numerical analysis, operations research, compound interest. *Unit head:* Lois K. Horwitz, Chairman, 617-353-8758, Fax: 617-353-8757, E-mail: lhorwitz@bu.edu. *Application contact:* Andrea Cozzi, Administrative Coordinator, 617-353-8758, Fax: 617-353-8757, E-mail: actuary@bu.edu. Web site: http://www.bu.edu/actuary/.

California State University, East Bay, Office of Academic Programs and Graduate Studies, College of Science, Department of Statistics and Biostatistics, Statistics Program, Hayward, CA 94542-3000. Offers actuarial science (MS); applied statistics (MS); computational statistics (MS); mathematical statistics (MS). Part-time and evening/weekend programs available. *Faculty:* 4 full-time (1 woman), 1 part-time/adjunct. *Students:* 19 full-time (6 women), 74 part-time (31 women); includes 32 minority (1 Black or African American, non-Hispanic/Latino; 24 Asian, non-Hispanic/Latino; 6 Hispanic/Latino; 1 Two or more races, non-Hispanic/Latino), 30 international. Average age 30. 82 applicants, 72% accepted, 30 enrolled. In 2011, 49 master's awarded. *Degree requirements:* For master's, comprehensive exam. *Entrance requirements:* For master's, letters of recommendation, minimum GPA of 3.0, math through lower-division calculus. Additional exam requirements/recommendations for international students: Required—TOEFL (minimum score 550 paper-based; 213 computer-based). *Application deadline:* For fall admission, 6/30 for domestic and international students. Application fee: $55. Electronic applications accepted. *Expenses:* Tuition, state resident: full-time $6738; part-time $1302 per quarter. Tuition, nonresident: full-time $12,690; part-time $2294 per quarter. *Required fees:* $449 per quarter. Tuition and fees vary according to degree level, program and reciprocity agreements. *Financial support:* Fellowships, career-related internships or fieldwork, Federal Work-Study, institutionally sponsored loans, scholarships/grants, and unspecified assistantships available. Support available to part-time students. Financial award application deadline: 3/2; financial award applicants required to submit FAFSA. *Unit head:* Dr. Eric Suess, Chair, 510-885-3435, Fax: 510-885-4714, E-mail: eric.suess@csueastbay.edu. *Application contact:* Prof. Mitchell Watnik, Statistics Graduate Coordinator, 510-885-4130, Fax: 510-885-4714, E-mail: mitchell.watnik@csueastbay.edu. Web site: http://www.sci.csueastbay.edu/statistics/.

Central Connecticut State University, School of Graduate Studies, School of Arts and Sciences, Department of Mathematical Sciences, New Britain, CT 06050-4010. Offers data mining (MS, Certificate); mathematics (MA, MS, Certificate, Sixth Year Certificate), including actuarial science (MA), computer science (MA), statistics (MA). Part-time and evening/weekend programs available. *Faculty:* 33 full-time (10 women), 66 part-time/adjunct (26 women). *Students:* 19 full-time (9 women), 119 part-time (68 women); includes 23 minority (5 Black or African American, non-Hispanic/Latino; 8 Asian, non-Hispanic/Latino; 8 Hispanic/Latino; 2 Two or more races, non-Hispanic/Latino), 4 international. Average age 37. 65 applicants, 57% accepted, 24 enrolled. In 2011, 24 master's awarded. *Degree requirements:* For master's, comprehensive exam, thesis or alternative; for other advanced degree, qualifying exam. *Entrance requirements:* For master's, minimum undergraduate GPA of 2.7. Additional exam requirements/recommendations for international students: Required—TOEFL (minimum score 550 paper-based; 213 computer-based). *Application deadline:* For fall admission, 5/1 for domestic and international students; for spring admission, 11/1 for domestic and international students. Applications are processed on a rolling basis. Application fee: $50. Electronic applications accepted. *Expenses: Tuition, area resident:* Full-time $5137; part-time $482 per credit. Tuition, state resident: full-time $7707; part-time $494 per credit. Tuition, nonresident: full-time $14,311; part-time $494 per credit. *Required fees:* $3865. One-time fee: $62 part-time. *Financial support:* In 2011–12, 5 students received support. Career-related internships or fieldwork, Federal Work-Study, scholarships/grants, and unspecified assistantships available. Support available to part-time students. Financial award application deadline: 4/15; financial award applicants required to submit FAFSA. *Faculty research:* Statistics, actuarial mathematics, computer systems and engineering, computer programming techniques, operations research. *Unit head:* Dr. Jeffrey McGowan, Chair, 860-832-2835, E-mail: mcgowan@ccsu.edu. *Application contact:* Patricia Gardner, Associate Director of Graduate Studies, 860-832-2350, Fax: 860-832-2352, E-mail: graduateadmissions@ccsu.edu. Web site: http://www.math.ccsu.edu/.

Columbia University, School of Continuing Education, Program in Actuarial Science, New York, NY 10027. Offers MS. Part-time programs available. *Degree requirements:* For master's, comprehensive exam. *Entrance requirements:* For master's, minimum GPA of 3.0, knowledge of economics, linear algebra, calculus. Additional exam requirements/recommendations for international students: Required—American Language Program placement test. Electronic applications accepted.

DePaul University, College of Science and Health, Department of Mathematical Sciences, Chicago, IL 60614. Offers applied mathematics (MS), including actuarial science or statistics; applied statistics (MS, Certificate); mathematics education (MA). Part-time and evening/weekend programs available. *Faculty:* 23 full-time (6 women), 18 part-time/adjunct (5 women). *Students:* 122 full-time (57 women), 63 part-time (23 women); includes 52 minority (19 Black or African American, non-Hispanic/Latino; 18 Asian, non-Hispanic/Latino; 10 Hispanic/Latino; 1 Native Hawaiian or other Pacific Islander, non-Hispanic/Latino; 4 Two or more races, non-Hispanic/Latino), 15 international. Average age 30. 40 applicants, 100% accepted. In 2011, 30 master's awarded. *Degree requirements:* For master's, comprehensive exam. *Entrance requirements:* Additional exam requirements/recommendations for international students: Required—TOEFL. *Application deadline:* For fall admission, 7/30 for domestic students, 6/30 for international students; for winter admission, 11/30 for domestic students, 10/31 for international students; for spring admission, 2/15 for domestic students. Applications are processed on a rolling basis. Application fee: $25. *Financial support:* In 2011–12, 12 students received support, including research assistantships with partial tuition reimbursements available (averaging $6,000 per year); teaching assistantships and tuition waivers (full) also available. Financial award application deadline: 4/30. *Faculty research:* Verbally prime algebras, enveloping algebras of Lie, superalgebras and related rings, harmonic analysis, estimation theory. *Unit head:* Dr. Ahmed I. Zayed, Chairperson, 773-325-7806, Fax: 773-325-7807, E-mail: azayed@depaul.edu. *Application contact:* Ann Spittle, Director of Graduate Admissions, 312-362-8300, Fax: 312-362-5749, E-mail: admitdpu@depaul.edu. Web site: http://depaul.edu/~math.

George Mason University, College of Science, Department of Mathematical Sciences, Fairfax, VA 22030. Offers actuarial sciences (Certificate); mathematics (MS, PhD). *Faculty:* 32 full-time (8 women), 11 part-time/adjunct (4 women). *Students:* 19 full-time (6 women), 38 part-time (14 women); includes 9 minority (2 Black or African American, non-Hispanic/Latino; 4 Asian, non-Hispanic/Latino; 3 Hispanic/Latino), 5 international. Average age 32. 82 applicants, 49% accepted, 20 enrolled. In 2011, 3 master's, 1 doctorate, 3 other advanced degrees awarded. *Degree requirements:* For master's, comprehensive exam, thesis optional. *Entrance requirements:* For master's, GRE, 3 letters of recommendation; official college transcripts; expanded goals statement; resume; for doctorate, GRE (recommended), master's degree in math or undergraduate coursework with math preparation with minimum GPA of 3.0 in last 60 credits; 2 copies of official transcripts; 3 letters of recommendation; expanded goals statement; for Certificate, 3 letters of recommendation; official transcripts. Additional exam requirements/recommendations for international students: Required—TOEFL (minimum score 570 paper-based; 230 computer-based; 88 iBT), IELTS, Pearson Test of English. *Application deadline:* For fall admission, 4/15 priority date for domestic students; for spring admission, 11/1 priority date for domestic students. Application fee: $65 ($80 for international students). Electronic applications accepted. *Expenses:* Tuition, state resident: full-time $8750; part-time $364.58 per credit. Tuition, nonresident: full-time $24,092; part-time $1003.83 per credit. *Required fees:* $2514; $104.75 per credit. *Financial support:* In 2011–12, 20 students received support, including 3 fellowships with full tuition reimbursements available (averaging $18,000 per year), 6 research assistantships with full and partial tuition reimbursements available (averaging $15,794 per year), 11 teaching assistantships with full and partial tuition reimbursements available (averaging $20,249 per year); career-related internships or fieldwork, Federal Work-Study, scholarships/grants, unspecified assistantships, and health care benefits (full-time research or teaching assistantship recipients) also available. Support available to part-time students. Financial award application deadline: 3/1; financial award applicants required to submit FAFSA. *Faculty research:* Nonlinear dynamics and topology, with an emphasis on global bifurcations and chaos; numerical and theoretical methods of dynamical systems. *Total annual research expenditures:* $922,388. *Unit head:* Stephen H. Sapperstone, Acting Chair, 703-993-1462, Fax: 703-993-1491, E-mail: sap@gmu.edu. *Application contact:* Walter D. Morris, Jr., Graduate Coordinator, 703-993-1481, Fax: 703-993-1491, E-mail: wmorris@gmu.edu. Web site: http://math.gmu.edu/.

Georgia State University, J. Mack Robinson College of Business, Department of Risk Management and Insurance, Program in Actuarial Science, Atlanta, GA 30302-3083. Offers MAS, MBA. Part-time and evening/weekend programs available. *Entrance requirements:* For master's, GMAT, GRE. Additional exam requirements/recommendations for international students: Required—TOEFL (minimum score 610 paper-based; 255 computer-based; 101 iBT). Electronic applications accepted.

Maryville University of Saint Louis, College of Arts and Sciences, St. Louis, MO 63141-7299. Offers actuarial science (MS); organizational leadership (MA); strategic communication and leadership (MA). Part-time and evening/weekend programs available. *Faculty:* 8 full-time (7 women). *Students:* 16 full-time (9 women), 24 part-time (19 women); includes 6 minority (3 Black or African American, non-Hispanic/Latino; 1 American Indian or Alaska Native, non-Hispanic/Latino; 1 Asian, non-Hispanic/Latino; 1 Two or more races, non-Hispanic/Latino), 5 international. Average age 31. In 2011, 8 master's awarded. *Entrance requirements:* For master's, GRE with minimum score of 600 (MS), strong mathematics background, 2 letters of recommendation, and personal statement (MS). Additional exam requirements/recommendations for international students: Required—TOEFL (minimum score 550 paper-based; 213 computer-based; 80 iBT). *Application deadline:* Applications are processed on a rolling basis. Application fee: $40 ($60 for international students). Electronic applications accepted. *Expenses: Tuition:* Full-time $21,922; part-time $675 per credit hour. *Required fees:* $233.75 per semester. *Financial support:* Application deadline: 3/1; applicants required to submit FAFSA. *Unit head:* Dr. Dan Sparling, Dean, 314-529-9436, Fax: 314-529-9965, E-mail: dsparling@maryville.edu. *Application contact:* Dr. Donna Payne, Vice President, Adult and Online Education, 314-529-9676, Fax: 314-529-9927, E-mail: dpayne@maryville.edu. Web site: http://www.maryville.edu/academics-as-actuarialscience-master.

Roosevelt University, Graduate Division, College of Arts and Sciences, Department of Mathematics and Actuarial Science, Program in Mathematics, Chicago, IL 60605. Offers mathematical sciences (MS), including actuarial science. Part-time and evening/weekend programs available. *Faculty research:* Statistics, mathematics education, finite groups, computers in mathematics.

St. John's University, The Peter J. Tobin College of Business, School of Risk Management and Actuarial Science, Queens, NY 11439. Offers enterprise risk management (MS); management of risk (MS); risk management (MBA). Postbaccalaureate distance learning degree programs offered (no on-campus study). *Students:* 56 full-time (24 women), 28 part-time (10 women); includes 14 minority (3 Black or African American, non-Hispanic/Latino; 4 Asian, non-Hispanic/Latino; 5 Hispanic/Latino; 2 Two or more races, non-Hispanic/Latino), 50 international. Average age 26. 84 applicants, 71% accepted, 28 enrolled. In 2011, 28 master's awarded. *Degree requirements:* For master's, comprehensive exam (for some programs), thesis optional. *Entrance requirements:* For master's, GMAT or GRE (for MS), 2 letters of recommendation, resume, transcripts, essay. Additional exam requirements/recommendations for international students: Required—TOEFL (minimum score 600 paper-based; 250 computer-based; 100 iBT), IELTS (minimum score 7). *Application deadline:* For fall admission, 5/1 priority date for domestic students, 5/1 for international students; for spring admission, 11/1 priority date for domestic students, 11/1 for international students. Applications are processed on a rolling basis. Application fee: $50. Electronic applications accepted. *Expenses:* Contact institution. *Financial support:* Research assistantships, scholarships/grants, and unspecified assistantships available. *Faculty research:* Insurance company operations and financial analysis, enterprise risk management, risk theory and modeling, credibility theory and actuarial price modeling, international insurance. *Unit head:* Dr. W. Jean Kwon, Chair. *Application contact:* Carol J. Swanberg, Assistant Dean/Director of Graduate Admissions, 718-990-1345, Fax: 718-990-5242, E-mail: tobingradnyc@stjohns.edu.

Simon Fraser University, Graduate Studies, Faculty of Science, Department of Statistics and Actuarial Science, Burnaby, BC V5A 1S6, Canada. Offers M Sc, PhD. Part-time programs available. *Degree requirements:* For master's, participation in consulting, project; for doctorate, comprehensive exam, thesis/dissertation. *Entrance requirements:* For master's, minimum GPA of 3.0; for doctorate, minimum GPA of 3.5. Additional exam requirements/recommendations for international students: Required—TOEFL. Electronic applications accepted. *Faculty research:* Biostatistics, experimental design, envirometrics, statistical computing, statistical theory.

Temple University, Fox School of Business, Specialized Master's Programs, Philadelphia, PA 19122-6096. Offers accountancy (MS); actuarial science (MS); finance (MS); financial engineering (MS); human resource management (MS); marketing (MS); statistics (MS). *Accreditation:* AACSB. Part-time programs available. *Entrance requirements:* For master's, GRE General Test or GMAT, minimum undergraduate GPA of 3.0. Additional exam requirements/recommendations for international students: Required—TOEFL (minimum score 600 paper-based; 250 computer-based; 100 iBT), IELTS (minimum score 7.5). *Expenses:* Tuition, state resident: full-time $12,366; part-time $687 per credit hour. Tuition, nonresident: full-time $17,298; part-time $961 per credit hour. *Required fees:* $590; $213 per year.

Université du Québec à Montréal, Graduate Programs, Program in Actuarial Sciences, Montréal, QC H3C 3P8, Canada. Offers Diploma. Part-time programs available. *Entrance requirements:* For degree, appropriate bachelor's degree or equivalent and proficiency in French.

University of Central Florida, College of Sciences, Department of Statistics and Actuarial Science, Orlando, FL 32816. Offers SAS data mining (Certificate); statistical computing (MS). Part-time and evening/weekend programs available. *Faculty:* 11 full-time (2 women), 2 part-time/adjunct (0 women). *Students:* 38 full-time (17 women), 25 part-time (9 women); includes 17 minority (7 Black or African American, non-Hispanic/Latino; 6 Asian, non-Hispanic/Latino; 4 Hispanic/Latino), 18 international. Average age 30. 60 applicants, 82% accepted, 32 enrolled. In 2011, 16 master's, 10 other advanced degrees awarded. *Degree requirements:* For master's, comprehensive exam. *Entrance requirements:* For master's, GRE General Test, minimum GPA of 3.0 in last 60 hours. Additional exam requirements/recommendations for international students: Required—TOEFL. *Application deadline:* For fall admission, 7/15 for domestic students; for spring admission, 12/1 for domestic students. Application fee: $30. Electronic applications accepted. *Expenses:* Tuition, state resident: part-time $277.08 per credit hour. Tuition, nonresident: part-time $277.08 per credit hour. Part-time tuition and fees vary according to degree level and program. *Financial support:* In 2011–12, 19 students received support, including 2 fellowships with partial tuition reimbursements available (averaging $7,000 per year), 1 research assistantship with partial tuition reimbursement available (averaging $5,300 per year), 16 teaching assistantships with partial tuition reimbursements available (averaging $11,600 per year); career-related internships or fieldwork, Federal Work-Study, institutionally sponsored loans, tuition waivers (partial), and unspecified assistantships also available. Financial award application deadline: 3/1; financial award applicants required to submit FAFSA. *Faculty research:* Multivariate analysis, quality control, shrinkage estimation. *Unit head:* Dr. David Nickerson, Chair, 407-823-2289, Fax: 407-823-5419, E-mail: david.nickerson@ucf.edu. *Application contact:* Barbara Rodriguez, Director, Admissions and Registration, 407-823-2766, Fax: 407-823-6442, E-mail: gradadmissions@ucf.edu. Web site: http://statistics.cos.ucf.edu/.

University of Connecticut, Graduate School, College of Liberal Arts and Sciences, Department of Mathematics, Storrs, CT 06269. Offers applied financial mathematics (MS); mathematics (MS, PhD), including actuarial science, mathematics. *Degree requirements:* For doctorate, thesis/dissertation. *Entrance requirements:* For master's and doctorate, GRE General Test, GRE Subject Test. Additional exam requirements/recommendations for international students: Required—TOEFL (minimum score 550 paper-based; 213 computer-based). Electronic applications accepted.

University of Connecticut, Graduate School, College of Liberal Arts and Sciences, Department of Mathematics, Field of Mathematics, Program in Actuarial Science, Storrs, CT 06269. Offers MS, PhD. *Degree requirements:* For master's, comprehensive exam. *Entrance requirements:* Additional exam requirements/recommendations for international students: Required—TOEFL (minimum score 550 paper-based; 213 computer-based). Electronic applications accepted.

University of Illinois at Urbana–Champaign, Graduate College, College of Liberal Arts and Sciences, Department of Mathematics, Champaign, IL 61820. Offers applied mathematics (MS); applied mathematics: actuarial science (MS); mathematics (MS, PhD); teaching of mathematics (MS). *Faculty:* 64 full-time (6 women), 9 part-time/adjunct (0 women). *Students:* 166 full-time (52 women), 36 part-time (13 women); includes 16 minority (7 Asian, non-Hispanic/Latino; 5 Hispanic/Latino; 4 Two or more races, non-Hispanic/Latino), 111 international. 455 applicants, 23% accepted, 48 enrolled. In 2011, 32 master's, 26 doctorates awarded. *Entrance requirements:* For master's and doctorate, GRE General Test, GRE Subject Test (math), minimum GPA of 3.0. Additional exam requirements/recommendations for international students: Required—TOEFL (minimum score 550 paper-based; 213 computer-based). *Application deadline:* Applications are processed on a rolling basis. Application fee: $75 ($90 for international students). Electronic applications accepted. *Financial support:* In 2011–12, 26 fellowships, 44 research assistantships, 152 teaching assistantships were awarded; tuition waivers (full and partial) also available. *Unit head:* Matthew Ando, Chair, 217-244-2846, Fax: 217-333-9576, E-mail: mando@illinois.edu. *Application contact:* Marci Blocher, Office Support Specialist, 217-333-5749, Fax: 217-333-9576, E-mail: mblocher@illinois.edu. Web site: http://math.illinois.edu/.

The University of Iowa, Graduate College, College of Liberal Arts and Sciences, Department of Statistics and Actuarial Science, Iowa City, IA 52242-1316. Offers MS, PhD. *Degree requirements:* For master's, thesis optional, exam; for doctorate, comprehensive exam, thesis/dissertation. *Entrance requirements:* For master's and doctorate, GRE General Test, minimum GPA of 3.0. Additional exam requirements/recommendations for international students: Required—TOEFL (minimum score 550 paper-based; 213 computer-based; 81 iBT). Electronic applications accepted.

The University of Manchester, School of Mathematics, Manchester, United Kingdom. Offers actuarial science (PhD); applied mathematics (M Phil, PhD); applied numerical computing (M Phil, PhD); financial mathematics (M Phil, PhD); mathematical logic (M Phil); probability (M Phil, PhD); pure mathematics (M Phil, PhD); statistics (M Phil, PhD).

University of Nebraska–Lincoln, Graduate College, College of Business Administration, Interdepartmental Area of Actuarial Science, Lincoln, NE 68588. Offers MS. *Entrance requirements:* For master's, GRE. Additional exam requirements/recommendations for international students: Required—TOEFL (minimum score 550 paper-based; 213 computer-based). Electronic applications accepted. *Faculty research:* Risk theory, pensions, actuarial finance, decision theory, stochastic calculus.

University of Northern Iowa, Graduate College, College of Humanities, Arts and Sciences, Department of Mathematics, Cedar Falls, IA 50614. Offers industrial mathematics (PSM), including actuarial science, continuous quality improvement, mathematical computing and modeling; mathematics (MA), including mathematics, secondary; mathematics for middle grades 4-8 (MA). Part-time programs available. *Students:* 13 full-time (6 women), 23 part-time (17 women); includes 2 minority (1 Black or African American, non-Hispanic/Latino; 1 Asian, non-Hispanic/Latino), 6 international. 35 applicants, 74% accepted, 11 enrolled. In 2011, 19 master's awarded. *Degree requirements:* For master's, comprehensive exam (for some programs), thesis or alternative. *Entrance requirements:* For master's, minimum GPA of 3.0. Additional exam requirements/recommendations for international students: Required—TOEFL (minimum score 600 paper-based; 250 computer-based; 100 iBT). *Application deadline:* For fall admission, 8/1 priority date for domestic students. Applications are processed on a rolling basis. Application fee: $50 ($70 for international students). Electronic applications accepted. *Expenses:* Tuition, state resident: full-time $7476. Tuition, nonresident: full-time $16,410. *Required fees:* $942. *Financial support:* Career-related internships or fieldwork, Federal Work-Study, scholarships/grants, and tuition waivers (full and partial) available. Support available to part-time students. Financial award application deadline: 2/1. *Unit head:* Dr. Douglas Mupasiri, Interim Head, 319-273-2012, Fax: 319-273-2546, E-mail: douglas.mupasiri@uni.edu. *Application contact:* Laurie S. Russell, Record Analyst, 319-273-2623, Fax: 319-273-2885, E-mail: laurie.russell@uni.edu. Web site: http://www.math.uni.edu/.

The University of Texas at Austin, Graduate School, College of Natural Sciences, Department of Mathematics, Austin, TX 78712-1111. Offers MA, PhD. *Entrance requirements:* For master's and doctorate, GRE General Test. *Application deadline:* For fall admission, 2/1 priority date for domestic students. Application fee: $50 ($75 for international students). Electronic applications accepted. *Financial support:* Fellowships and teaching assistantships with partial tuition reimbursements available. Financial award application deadline: 2/1. *Unit head:* Dr. Alan Reid, Chair, 512-471-3153, E-mail: areid@math.utexas.edu. *Application contact:* Dr. Dan Knopf, Graduate Adviser, 512-471-8131, E-mail: danknopf@math.utexas.edu. Web site: http://www.ma.utexas.edu/academics/graduate/.

University of Waterloo, Graduate Studies, Faculty of Mathematics, Department of Statistics and Actuarial Science, Waterloo, ON N2L 3G1, Canada. Offers actuarial science (M Math, PhD); biostatistics (PhD); statistics (M Math, PhD); statistics-biostatistics (M Math); statistics-computing (M Math); statistics-finance (M Math). *Degree requirements:* For master's, research paper or thesis; for doctorate, comprehensive exam, thesis/dissertation. *Entrance requirements:* For master's, honors degree in field, minimum B+ average; for doctorate, master's degree, minimum B+ average. Additional exam requirements/recommendations for international students: Required—TOEFL (minimum score 600 paper-based; 250 computer-based; 90 iBT), TWE (minimum score 4.5). Electronic applications accepted. *Faculty research:* Data analysis, risk theory, inference, stochastic processes, quantitative finance.

University of Wisconsin–Madison, Graduate School, Wisconsin School of Business, MS Program in Actuarial Science, Madison, WI 53706-1380. Offers MS. *Faculty:* 5 full-time (2 women), 1 part-time/adjunct (0 women). *Students:* 8 full-time (1 woman); includes 1 minority (Black or African American, non-Hispanic/Latino), 2 international. Average age 24. 67 applicants, 10% accepted, 3 enrolled. In 2011, 8 master's awarded. *Entrance requirements:* For master's, GMAT or GRE. Additional exam requirements/recommendations for international students: Required—Pearson Test of English (minimum score 73; written 80); Recommended—TOEFL (minimum score 623 paper-based; 263 computer-based; 106 iBT), IELTS (minimum score 7.5). *Application deadline:* For fall admission, 3/15 for domestic and international students. Application fee: $56. Electronic applications accepted. *Expenses:* Contact institution. *Financial support:* In 2011–12, 2 students received support, including 2 teaching assistantships with full tuition reimbursements available (averaging $9,392 per year); Federal Work-Study, institutionally sponsored loans, scholarships/grants, health care benefits, and unspecified assistantships also available. Financial award application deadline: 3/15; financial award applicants required to submit FAFSA. *Faculty research:* Fuzzy logic, business forecasting, health insurance, international insurance. *Unit head:* Prof. Marjorie Rosenberg, Chair, 608-262-1683, E-mail: mrosenberg@bus.wisc.edu. *Application contact:* Belle Heberling, Assistant Director for Research Programs, 608-262-3749, Fax: 608-890-0180, E-mail: ms@bus.wisc.edu. Web site: http://www.bus.wisc.edu/MS.

Insurance

Florida State University, The Graduate School, College of Business, Tallahassee, FL 32306-1110. Offers accounting (M Acc), including accounting information services, assurance services, corporate accounting, taxation; business administration (MBA, PhD), including accounting (PhD), finance (PhD), management information systems (PhD), marketing (PhD), organizational behavior (PhD), risk management and insurance (PhD), strategic management (PhD); finance (MS); insurance (MSM); management information systems (MS); marketing (MS); JD/MBA; MSW/MBA. *Accreditation:* AACSB. Part-time programs available. Postbaccalaureate distance learning degree programs offered (no on-campus study). *Faculty:* 107 full-time (31 women). *Students:* 196 full-time (76 women), 310 part-time (109 women); includes 89 minority (27 Black or African

American, non-Hispanic/Latino; 1 American Indian or Alaska Native, non-Hispanic/Latino; 31 Asian, non-Hispanic/Latino; 30 Hispanic/Latino). Average age 30. 702 applicants, 33% accepted, 205 enrolled. In 2011, 268 master's, 17 doctorates awarded. Terminal master's awarded for partial completion of doctoral program. *Degree requirements:* For doctorate, comprehensive exam, thesis/dissertation. *Entrance requirements:* For master's, GMAT, work experience (MBA, MS), minimum GPA of 3.0, letters of recommendation; for doctorate, GMAT, minimum graduate GPA of 3.5, letters of recommendation. Additional exam requirements/recommendations for international students: Required—TOEFL (minimum score 600 paper-based; 80 computer-based); Recommended—IELTS (minimum score 6.5). *Application deadline:* For fall admission, 6/1 for domestic students, 5/1 for international students; for spring admission, 10/1 for domestic students, 9/1 for international students. Applications are processed on a rolling basis. Application fee: $30. Electronic applications accepted. *Expenses:* Tuition, state resident: full-time $9474; part-time $350.88 per credit hour. Tuition, nonresident: full-time $16,236; part-time $601.34 per credit hour. *Required fees:* $630 per semester. One-time fee: $20. Tuition and fees vary according to course load and campus/location. *Financial support:* In 2011–12, 86 students received support, including 12 fellowships with full tuition reimbursements available (averaging $7,161 per year), 30 research assistantships with full tuition reimbursements available (averaging $6,000 per year), 43 teaching assistantships with full tuition reimbursements available (averaging $15,000 per year); career-related internships or fieldwork, scholarships/grants, health care benefits, tuition waivers (full and partial), and unspecified assistantships also available. Support available to part-time students. Financial award application deadline: 1/1. *Unit head:* Dr. Caryn Beck-Dudley, Dean, 850-644-3090, Fax: 850-644-0915. *Application contact:* Lisa Beverly, Director, Graduate Programs Admissions, 850-644-6458, Fax: 850-644-0588, E-mail: lbeverly@cob.fsu.edu. Web site: http://www.cob.fsu.edu/grad/.

Georgia State University, J. Mack Robinson College of Business, Department of Risk Management and Insurance, Program in Risk Management and Insurance, Atlanta, GA 30302-3083. Offers MBA, MS, PhD, Certificate. Part-time and evening/weekend programs available. *Degree requirements:* For doctorate, comprehensive exam, thesis/dissertation. *Entrance requirements:* For master's and doctorate, GMAT, GRE. Additional exam requirements/recommendations for international students: Required—TOEFL (minimum score 610 paper-based; 255 computer-based; 101 iBT). Electronic applications accepted.

Pontificia Universidad Catolica Madre y Maestra, Graduate School, Faculty of Social and Administrative Sciences, Santiago, Dominican Republic. Offers business administration (MBA), including business development, finance, international business, management skills (M Mgmt, MBA), marketing, operations, strategic cost management, strategy, tourist destination planning and management; law (LL M), including civil law, corporate business law, criminal law, international relations, real estate law; management (M Mgmt), including higher financial management, insurance program administration, management skills (M Mgmt, MBA); psychology (MA), including clinical child and adolescent psychology, forensic psychology; strategic human resources (EMBA).

St. John's University, The Peter J. Tobin College of Business, School of Risk Management and Actuarial Science, Queens, NY 11439. Offers enterprise risk management (MS); management of risk (MS); risk management (MBA). Postbaccalaureate distance learning degree programs offered (no on-campus study). *Students:* 56 full-time (24 women), 28 part-time (10 women); includes 14 minority (3 Black or African American, non-Hispanic/Latino; 4 Asian, non-Hispanic/Latino; 5 Hispanic/Latino; 2 Two or more races, non-Hispanic/Latino), 50 international. Average age 26. 84 applicants, 71% accepted, 28 enrolled. In 2011, 28 master's awarded. *Degree requirements:* For master's, comprehensive exam (for some programs), thesis optional. *Entrance requirements:* For master's, GMAT or GRE (for MS), 2 letters of recommendation, resume, transcripts, essay. Additional exam requirements/recommendations for international students: Required—TOEFL (minimum score 600 paper-based; 250 computer-based; 100 iBT), IELTS (minimum score 7). *Application deadline:* For fall admission, 5/1 priority date for domestic students, 5/1 for international students; for spring admission, 11/1 priority date for domestic students, 11/1 for international students. Applications are processed on a rolling basis. Application fee: $50. Electronic applications accepted. *Expenses:* Contact institution. *Financial support:* Research assistantships, scholarships/grants, and unspecified assistantships available. *Faculty research:* Insurance company operations and financial analysis, enterprise risk management, risk theory and modeling, credibility theory and actuarial price modeling, international insurance. *Unit head:* Dr. W. Jean Kwon, Chair. *Application contact:* Carol J. Swanberg, Assistant Dean/Director of Graduate Admissions, 718-990-1345, Fax: 718-990-5242, E-mail: tobingradnyc@stjohns.edu.

Temple University, Fox School of Business, Doctoral Programs in Business, Philadelphia, PA 19122-6096. Offers accounting (PhD); entrepreneurship (PhD); finance (PhD); international business (PhD); management information systems (PhD); marketing (PhD); risk management and insurance (PhD); statistics (PhD); strategic management (PhD); tourism and sport (PhD). *Accreditation:* AACSB. *Degree requirements:* For doctorate, thesis/dissertation. *Entrance requirements:* For doctorate, GRE General Test, GMAT, minimum GPA of 3.0, master's degree. Additional exam requirements/recommendations for international students: Required—TOEFL (minimum score 600 paper-based; 250 computer-based; 100 iBT), IELTS (minimum score 7.5). Electronic applications accepted. *Expenses:* Tuition, state resident: full-time $12,366; part-time $687 per credit hour. Tuition, nonresident: full-time $17,298; part-time $961 per credit hour. *Required fees:* $590; $213 per year.

Tennessee Technological University, Graduate School, College of Business, Cookeville, TN 38505. Offers accounting (MBA); finance (MBA); human resource management (MBA); international business (MBA); management information systems (MBA); risk management & insurance (MBA). *Accreditation:* AACSB. Part-time and evening/weekend programs available. Postbaccalaureate distance learning degree programs offered (no on-campus study). *Faculty:* 28 full-time (5 women). *Students:* 45 full-time (19 women), 135 part-time (51 women); includes 13 minority (4 Black or African American, non-Hispanic/Latino; 5 Asian, non-Hispanic/Latino; 3 Hispanic/Latino; 1 Native Hawaiian or other Pacific Islander, non-Hispanic/Latino), 2 international. Average age 25. 193 applicants, 59% accepted, 70 enrolled. In 2011, 89 master's awarded. *Entrance requirements:* For master's, GMAT. Additional exam requirements/recommendations for international students: Required—TOEFL (minimum score 550 paper-based; 79 iBT), IELTS (minimum score 5.5), Pearson Test of English Academic. *Application deadline:* For fall admission, 8/1 for domestic students, 5/1 for international students; for spring admission, 12/1 for domestic students, 10/1 for international students. Application fee: $25 ($30 for international students). Electronic applications accepted. *Expenses:* Tuition, state resident: full-time $8094; part-time $422 per credit hour. Tuition, nonresident: full-time $20,574; part-time $1046 per credit hour. *Financial support:* In 2011–12, 5 fellowships (averaging $10,000 per year), 18 research assistantships (averaging $4,000 per year), teaching assistantships (averaging $4,000 per year) were awarded. Support available to part-time students. Financial award application deadline: 4/1. *Unit head:* Dr. Tom Timmerman, Director, 931-372-3600, Fax: 931-372-6249. *Application contact:* Shelia K. Kendrick, Coordinator of Graduate Admissions, 931-372-3808, Fax: 931-372-3497, E-mail: skendrick@tntech.edu. Web site: http://www.tntech.edu/mba.

Thomas M. Cooley Law School, JD and LL M Programs, Lansing, MI 48901-3038. Offers administrative law (public law) (JD); business transactions (JD); Canadian law (JD); Constitutional law and civil rights (public law) (JD); corporate law and finance (LL M); environmental law (public law) (JD); general practice (JD); insurance (LL M); intellectual property (LL M, JD); international law (JD); litigation (JD); self-directed (LL M, JD); taxation (LL M, JD); U.S. law for foreign attorneys (LL M); JD/MBA; JD/MPA; JD/MSW. *Accreditation:* ABA. Part-time and evening/weekend programs available. Postbaccalaureate distance learning degree programs offered (no on-campus study). *Faculty:* 131 full-time (55 women), 286 part-time/adjunct (93 women). *Students:* 781 full-time (368 women), 2,964 part-time (1,450 women); includes 1,055 minority (543 Black or African American, non-Hispanic/Latino; 19 American Indian or Alaska Native, non-Hispanic/Latino; 179 Asian, non-Hispanic/Latino; 205 Hispanic/Latino; 9 Native Hawaiian or other Pacific Islander, non-Hispanic/Latino; 100 Two or more races, non-Hispanic/Latino), 220 international. Average age 30. 4,032 applicants, 80% accepted, 1161 enrolled. In 2011, 40 master's, 999 doctorates awarded. *Degree requirements:* For master's, thesis optional; for doctorate, minimum of 3 credits of clinical experience. *Entrance requirements:* For master's, JD or LL B; for doctorate, LSAT. Additional exam requirements/recommendations for international students: Required—TOEFL. *Application deadline:* For fall admission, 9/1 for domestic and international students; for winter admission, 1/1 for domestic and international students; for spring admission, 5/1 for domestic and international students. Applications are processed on a rolling basis. Electronic applications accepted. *Expenses: Tuition:* Full-time $34,300; part-time $1225 per credit hour. *Required fees:* $40; $40 per year. Tuition and fees vary according to degree level and student level. *Financial support:* In 2011–12, 2,324 students received support. Career-related internships or fieldwork, Federal Work-Study, scholarships/grants, traineeships, and unspecified assistantships available. Support available to part-time students. Financial award applicants required to submit FAFSA. *Faculty research:* Wrongful convictions, civil rights, environmental law, litigation techniques, data mining, intellectual property, practical and skills-based legal education. *Unit head:* Don LeDuc, President and Dean, 517-371-5140 Ext. 2009, Fax: 517-334-5152. *Application contact:* Dr. Paul Zelenski, Associate Dean of Enrollment and Student Services, 517-371-5140 Ext. 2244, Fax: 517-334-5718, E-mail: admissions@cooley.edu. Web site: http://www.cooley.edu/.

University of Colorado Denver, Business School, Program in Finance, Denver, CO 80217. Offers economics (MS); finance (MS); financial analysis and management (MS); financial and commodities risk management (MS); risk management and insurance (MS); MS/MBA. Part-time and evening/weekend programs available. *Students:* 60 full-time (19 women), 33 part-time (11 women); includes 9 minority (5 Asian, non-Hispanic/Latino; 3 Hispanic/Latino; 1 Two or more races, non-Hispanic/Latino), 27 international. Average age 30. 83 applicants, 59% accepted, 24 enrolled. In 2011, 45 master's awarded. *Degree requirements:* For master's, 30 semester hours (18 of required core courses, 9 of finance electives, and 3 of free elective). *Entrance requirements:* For master's, GMAT, essay, resume, two letters of recommendation, financial statements (for international students). Additional exam requirements/recommendations for international students: Required—TOEFL (minimum score 525 paper-based; 197 computer-based; 70 iBT), IELTS (minimum score 6). *Application deadline:* For fall admission, 4/15 priority date for domestic students, 3/15 for international students; for spring admission, 10/15 priority date for domestic students, 10/1 for international students. Applications are processed on a rolling basis. Application fee: $50 ($75 for international students). Electronic applications accepted. *Expenses:* Contact institution. *Financial support:* Federal Work-Study and scholarships/grants available. Support available to part-time students. Financial award application deadline: 4/1; financial award applicants required to submit FAFSA. *Faculty research:* Corporate governance, debt maturity policies, regulation and financial markets, option management strategies. *Unit head:* Dr. Ajeyo Banerjee, Associate Professor/Director of MS in Finance Program, 303-315-8456, E-mail: ajeyo.banerjee@ucdenver.edu. *Application contact:* Shelly Townley, Admissions Director, Graduate Programs, 303-315-8202, E-mail: shelly.townley@ucdenver.edu. Web site: http://www.ucdenver.edu/academics/colleges/business/degrees/ms/finance/Pages/Finance.aspx.

University of Florida, Graduate School, Warrington College of Business Administration, Hough Graduate School of Business, Department of Finance, Insurance and Real Estate, Gainesville, FL 32611. Offers finance (MS, PhD); financial services (Certificate); insurance (PhD); real estate and urban analysis (MS, PhD); JD/MBA. *Faculty:* 13 full-time (0 women). *Students:* 107 full-time (28 women), 10 part-time (2 women); includes 20 minority (6 Black or African American, non-Hispanic/Latino; 8 Asian, non-Hispanic/Latino; 6 Hispanic/Latino), 31 international. Average age 26. 245 applicants, 2% accepted, 3 enrolled. In 2011, 103 master's, 2 doctorates awarded. Terminal master's awarded for partial completion of doctoral program. *Degree requirements:* For master's, comprehensive exam, thesis; for doctorate, comprehensive exam, thesis/dissertation. *Entrance requirements:* For master's, GMAT or GRE General Test, minimum GPA of 3.0 for last 60 hours of undergraduate degree, work experience (preferred); for doctorate, GMAT or GRE General Test, minimum GPA of 3.0. Additional exam requirements/recommendations for international students: Required—TOEFL (minimum score 550 paper-based; 213 computer-based; 80 iBT), IELTS (minimum score 6). *Application deadline:* For fall admission, 1/15 priority date for domestic students, 1/15 for international students. Applications are processed on a rolling basis. Application fee: $30. Electronic applications accepted. *Financial support:* Fellowships, research assistantships, teaching assistantships, career-related internships or fieldwork, scholarships/grants, and unspecified assistantships available. Financial award application deadline: 1/15; financial award applicants required to submit FAFSA. *Faculty research:* Banking, empirical corporate finance, hedge funds. *Unit head:* Dr. Mahendrarajah Nimalendran, Chair, 352-392-9526, Fax: 352-392-0301, E-mail: nimal@ufl.edu. *Application contact:* Mark J. Flannery, Graduate Coordinator, 352-392-3184, Fax: 352-392-0301, E-mail: flannery@ufl.edu. Web site: http://www.cba.ufl.edu/fire/.

University of Pennsylvania, Wharton School, Insurance and Risk Management Department, Philadelphia, PA 19104. Offers MBA, PhD. *Degree requirements:* For doctorate, thesis/dissertation. *Entrance requirements:* For master's, GMAT; for doctorate, GMAT or GRE. *Expenses: Tuition:* Full-time $26,660; part-time $4944 per course. *Required fees:* $2318; $291 per course. Tuition and fees vary according to course load, degree level and program. *Faculty research:* Fair rate of return in insurance economics of pension plans, insurance regulation, malpractice insurance, actuarial science, genetic testing and life insurance.

University of Wisconsin–Madison, Graduate School, Wisconsin School of Business, Doctoral Program in Actuarial Science, Risk Management and Insurance, Madison, WI 53706-1380. Offers PhD. *Faculty:* 6 full-time (2 women), 2 part-time/adjunct (0 women). *Students:* 8 full-time (5 women), 6 international. Average age 29. 20 applicants, 10% accepted, 1 enrolled. In 2011, 1 doctorate awarded. *Degree requirements:* For doctorate, comprehensive exam, thesis/dissertation. *Entrance requirements:* For doctorate, GMAT or GRE General Test. Additional exam requirements/recommendations for international students: Required—Pearson Test of English (minimum score 73; written 80); Recommended—TOEFL (minimum score 623 paper-based; 263 computer-based; 106 iBT), IELTS (minimum score 7.5). *Application deadline:* For fall admission, 12/15 priority date for domestic students, 12/15 for international students. Application fee: $56. Electronic applications accepted. *Expenses:* Contact institution. *Financial support:* In 2011–12, 7 students received support, including fellowships with full tuition reimbursements available (averaging $18,756 per year), research assistantships with full tuition reimbursements available (averaging $16,506 per year), 7 teaching assistantships with full tuition reimbursements available (averaging $14,088 per year); Federal Work-Study, institutionally sponsored loans, scholarships/grants, health care benefits, and unspecified assistantships also available. Financial award application deadline: 2/1; financial award applicants required to submit FAFSA. *Faculty research:* Superfund, health insurance, workers compensation, employee benefits, fuzzy logic. *Unit head:* Prof. Mark Browne, Chair, 608-262-3030, E-mail: mbrowne@bus.wisc.edu. *Application contact:* Belle Heberling, Assistant Director for Research Programs, 608-262-3749, Fax: 608-890-0180, E-mail: phd@bus.wisc.edu. Web site: http://www.bus.wisc.edu/phd.

University of Wisconsin–Madison, Graduate School, Wisconsin School of Business, Wisconsin Full-Time MBA Program, Madison, WI 53706-1380. Offers applied security analysis (MBA); arts administration (MBA); brand and product management (MBA); corporate finance and investment banking (MBA); marketing research (MBA); operations and technology management (MBA); real estate (MBA); risk management and insurance (MBA); strategic human resource management (MBA); supply chain management (MBA). *Faculty:* 32 full-time (6 women), 27 part-time/adjunct (7 women). *Students:* 228 full-time (75 women); includes 53 minority (16 Black or African American, non-Hispanic/Latino; 25 Asian, non-Hispanic/Latino; 10 Hispanic/Latino; 2 Native Hawaiian or other Pacific Islander, non-Hispanic/Latino), 28 international. Average age 28. 509 applicants, 30% accepted, 111 enrolled. In 2011, 120 master's awarded. *Degree requirements:* For master's, thesis (for arts administration). *Entrance requirements:* For master's, GMAT, bachelor's or equivalent degree, 2 years of work experience, letters of recommendation. Additional exam requirements/ recommendations for international students: Required—TOEFL (minimum score 600 paper-based; 250 computer-based; 100 iBT), IELTS. *Application deadline:* For fall admission, 11/4 for domestic and international students; for winter admission, 2/3 for domestic and international students; for spring admission, 4/27 for domestic and international students. Applications are processed on a rolling basis. Application fee: $56. Electronic applications accepted. *Expenses:* Tuition, state resident: full-time $10,296; part-time $643.51 per credit. Tuition, nonresident: full-time $24,054; part-time $1503.40 per credit. *Required fees:* $70.06 per credit. Tuition and fees vary according to course load, campus/location, program and reciprocity agreements. *Financial support:* In 2011–12, 176 students received support, including 20 fellowships with full and partial tuition reimbursements available (averaging $18,756 per year), 128 research assistantships with full tuition reimbursements available (averaging $25,185 per year), 28 teaching assistantships with full tuition reimbursements available (averaging $25,097 per year); scholarships/grants, health care benefits, and unspecified assistantships also available. Financial award application deadline: 4/27; financial award applicants required to submit FAFSA. *Faculty research:* Market consequences of International Financial Reporting Standards (IFRS), inter-firm relationships and strategic partnerships, application of Bayesian statistical methods and applied probability models to understanding individuals' behaviors in the context of customer relationship management (CRM) applications, liquidity provision and the structure of financial markets, strategic management of global startups. *Unit head:* Dr. Larry "Chip" W. Hunter, Associate Dean of Master's Programs, 608-265-3494, Fax: 608-265-4192, E-mail: lhunter@bus.wisc.edu. *Application contact:* Maria Reis, Assistant Director of MBA Marketing and Recruiting, 608-262-4000, Fax: 608-265-4192, E-mail: mreis@bus.wisc.edu. Web site: http://www.bus.wisc.edu/mba.

Virginia Commonwealth University, Graduate School, School of Business, Program in Finance, Insurance, and Real Estate, Richmond, VA 23284-9005. Offers MS. *Faculty:* 11 full-time (0 women). *Entrance requirements:* For master's, GMAT. Additional exam requirements/recommendations for international students: Required—TOEFL (minimum score 600 paper-based; 250 computer-based; 100 iBT); Recommended—IELTS (minimum score 6.5). *Application deadline:* For fall admission, 6/1 for domestic students; for spring admission, 11/1 for domestic students. Applications are processed on a rolling basis. Application fee: $50. Electronic applications accepted. *Expenses:* Tuition, state resident: full-time $9133; part-time $507 per credit. Tuition, nonresident: full-time $18,777; part-time $1043 per credit. *Required fees:* $77 per credit. Tuition and fees vary according to degree level, campus/location, program and student level. *Financial support:* Fellowships, research assistantships, teaching assistantships, Federal Work-Study, institutionally sponsored loans, and tuition waivers (full and partial) available. Financial award application deadline: 3/15; financial award applicants required to submit FAFSA. *Unit head:* Dr. Nanda Rangan, Chair, 804-828-6002, Fax: 804-828-7174, E-mail: nkrangan@vcu.edu. *Application contact:* Jana P. McQuaid, Assistant Dean, Master's Programs, 804-828-4622, Fax: 804-828-7174, E-mail: jpmcquaid@vcu.edu. Web site: http://www.business.vcu.edu/graduate.html.

Section 11
International Business

This section contains a directory of institutions offering graduate work in international business. Additional information about programs listed in the directory but not augmented by an in-depth entry may be obtained by writing directly to the dean of a graduate school or chair of a department at the address given in the directory.

For programs offering related work, see also in this book *Business Administration and Management, Entrepreneurship, Industrial and Manufacturing Management,* and *Organizational Behavior.* In another guide in this series:

Graduate Programs in the Humanities, Arts & Social Sciences

See *Political Science and International Affairs* and *Public, Regional, and Industrial Affairs*

CONTENTS

International Business

Alliant International University–México City, School of Management, Mexico City, Mexico. Offers business administration (MBA); international business administration (MIBA); international studies (MA), including international relations. Part-time and evening/weekend programs available. *Faculty:* 7 part-time/adjunct (3 women). *Students:* 9. Average age 33. In 2011, 9 master's awarded. *Degree requirements:* For master's, thesis (for some programs). *Entrance requirements:* For master's, GMAT or GRE (depending on program), minimum GPA of 3.0, letters of recommendation. Additional exam requirements/recommendations for international students: Required—TOEFL (minimum score 550 paper-based; 213 computer-based), TWE (minimum score 5). *Application deadline:* For fall admission, 8/1 priority date for domestic students, 8/1 for international students; for spring admission, 12/1 priority date for domestic students, 12/1 for international students. Applications are processed on a rolling basis. Application fee: $45. Electronic applications accepted. *Financial support:* Research assistantships, teaching assistantships, career-related internships or fieldwork, Federal Work-Study, institutionally sponsored loans, and scholarships/grants available. Support available to part-time students. Financial award application deadline: 2/15; financial award applicants required to submit FAFSA. *Faculty research:* Global economy, international relations. *Unit head:* Dr. Chet Haskell, Dean, 858-635-4696, E-mail: contacto@alliantmexico.com. *Application contact:* Lesly Gutierrez Garcia, Coordinator of Admissions and Student Services, (+5255) 5525-7651, E-mail: contacto@alliantmexico.com. Web site: http://www.alliantmexico.com.

American InterContinental University Atlanta, Program in Global Technology Management, Atlanta, GA 30328. Offers MBA. Part-time and evening/weekend programs available. Postbaccalaureate distance learning degree programs offered. *Entrance requirements:* For master's, interview. Electronic applications accepted. *Faculty research:* E-commerce, service quality leadership, human resources management.

American InterContinental University London, Program in Business Administration, London, United Kingdom. Offers international business (MBA). *Degree requirements:* For master's, thesis optional. *Entrance requirements:* For master's, interview, professional experience. Additional exam requirements/recommendations for international students: Required—TOEFL or IELTS recommended. Electronic applications accepted.

American InterContinental University Online, Program in Business Administration, Hoffman Estates, IL 60192. Offers accounting and finance (MBA); finance (MBA); healthcare management (MBA); human resource management (MBA); international business (MBA); management (MBA); marketing (MBA); operations management (MBA); organizational psychology and development (MBA); project management (MBA). Evening/weekend programs available. Postbaccalaureate distance learning degree programs offered (no on-campus study). *Entrance requirements:* Additional exam requirements/recommendations for international students: Required—TOEFL (minimum score 550 paper-based; 213 computer-based). Electronic applications accepted.

American InterContinental University South Florida, Program in International Business, Weston, FL 33326. Offers accounting and finance (MBA); human resource management (MBA); management (MBA); marketing (MBA). Part-time and evening/weekend programs available. Postbaccalaureate distance learning degree programs offered. Electronic applications accepted.

American International College, School of Business Administration, MBA Program, Springfield, MA 01109-3189. Offers accounting (MBA); corporate/public communication (MBA); finance (MBA); general business (MBA); hospitality, hotel and service management (MBA); international business (MBA); international business practice (MBA); management (MBA); management information systems (MBA); marketing (MBA). International business practice program developed in cooperation with the Mountbatten Institute.

American Public University System, AMU/APU Graduate Programs, Charles Town, WV 25414. Offers accounting (MBA, MS); administration and supervision (M Ed); criminal justice (MA); emergency and disaster management (MA); entrepreneurship (MBA); environmental policy and management (MS), including environmental planning, environmental sustainability, fish and wildlife management, general (MA, MS), global environmental management; finance (MBA); general (MBA); global business management (MBA); guidance and counseling (M Ed); history (MA), including American history, ancient and classical history, European history, global history, military and diplomatic history, public history; homeland security (MA); homeland security resource allocation (MBA); humanities (MA); information technology (MS), including digital forensics, enterprise software development, information assurance and security, IT project management; information technology management (MBA); intelligence studies (MA), including criminal intelligence, general (MA, MS), homeland security, intelligence analysis, intelligence collection, intelligence operations, terrorism studies; international relations and conflict resolution (MA), including comparative and security issues, conflict resolution, international and transnational security issues, peacekeeping; legal studies (MA); management (MA), including defense management, general (MA, MS), human resource management, organizational leadership, public administration, reverse logistics, strategic consulting; marketing (MBA); military history (MA), including American military history, American revolution, civil war, war since 1946, World War II; military studies (MA), including air warfare, asymmetrical warfare, joint warfare, land warfare, naval warfare, strategic leadership; national security studies (MA), including general (MA, MS), homeland security, regional security studies, security and intelligence analysis, terrorism studies; nonprofit management (MBA); political science (MA), including American politics and government, comparative government and development, public policy; psychology (MA); public administration (MA, MPA), including disaster management (MPA), environmental policy (MA), health policy (MPA), human resources (MPA), national security (MPA), organizational management (MPA), security management (MPA); public health (MA, MPH), including emergency management (MPH), environmental health (MPH), public administration (MA); reverse logistics management (MA); security management (MA); space studies (MS), including aerospace science, planetary science; sports and health sciences (MS); sports management (MS), including coaching theory and strategy, sports administration; teaching (M Ed), including curriculum and instruction for elementary teachers, elementary, elementary reading, English language learners, instructional leadership, online learning, secondary social sciences, special education; transportation and logistics management (MA), including maritime engineering management. Programs offered via distance learning only. Part-time and evening/weekend programs available. Postbaccalaureate distance learning degree programs offered (no on-campus study). *Faculty:* 445 full-time (241 women), 1,360 part-time/adjunct (617 women). *Students:* 688 full-time (338 women), 10,168 part-time (3,706 women); includes 3,130 minority (1,007 Black or African American, non-Hispanic/Latino; 103 American Indian or Alaska Native, non-Hispanic/Latino; 825 Asian, non-Hispanic/Latino; 810 Hispanic/Latino; 51 Native Hawaiian or other Pacific Islander, non-Hispanic/Latino; 334 Two or more races, non-Hispanic/Latino), 134 international. Average age 35. In 2011, 2,386 master's awarded. *Degree requirements:* For master's, comprehensive exam or practicum. *Entrance requirements:* For master's, official transcript showing earned bachelor's degree from institution accredited by recognized accrediting body. Additional exam requirements/recommendations for international students: Required—TOEFL (minimum score 550 paper-based; 213 computer-based), IELTS (minimum score 6.5). *Application deadline:* Applications are processed on a rolling basis. Application fee: $0. Electronic applications accepted. *Expenses: Tuition:* Part-time $325 per credit hour. *Financial support:* Applicants required to submit FAFSA. *Faculty research:* Military history, criminal justice, management performance, national security. *Unit head:* Dr. Karan Powell, Executive Vice President and Provost, 877-468-6268, Fax: 304-724-3780. *Application contact:* Terry Grant, Vice President of Enrollment Management, 877-468-6268, Fax: 304-724-3780, E-mail: info@apus.edu. Web site: http://www.apus.edu.

American University, Kogod School of Business, Department of International Business, Washington, DC 20016-8044. Offers Certificate. Part-time and evening/weekend programs available. *Faculty:* 12 full-time (4 women), 2 part-time/adjunct (1 woman). *Students:* 1 part-time (0 women). Average age 29. In 2011, 1 degree awarded. *Entrance requirements:* For degree, bachelor's degree. Additional exam requirements/recommendations for international students: Required—TOEFL. *Application deadline:* For fall admission, 2/1 priority date for domestic students; for spring admission, 10/1 priority date for domestic students. Applications are processed on a rolling basis. Application fee: $100. *Expenses:* Contact institution. *Financial support:* Fellowships, research assistantships with partial tuition reimbursements, career-related internships or fieldwork, Federal Work-Study, and institutionally sponsored loans available. Support available to part-time students. Financial award application deadline: 2/1; financial award applicants required to submit FAFSA. *Faculty research:* Financial risk in the multinational corporation, emerging security markets, import/export issues, joint ventures in China, Japanese management. *Unit head:* Dr. Heather Elms, Chair, 202-885-1967, Fax: 202-885-1992, E-mail: elms@american.edu. *Application contact:* Shannon Demko, Associate Director of Graduate Admissions, 202-885-1968, Fax: 202-885-1078, E-mail: demko@american.edu. Web site: http://www.american.edu/kogod/.

The American University in Dubai, Master in Business Administration Program, Dubai, United Arab Emirates. Offers general (MBA); healthcare management (MBA); international finance (MBA); international marketing (MBA); management of construction enterprises (MBA). Part-time and evening/weekend programs available. *Degree requirements:* For master's, thesis optional. *Entrance requirements:* For master's, GMAT, Interview. Additional exam requirements/recommendations for international students: Required—TOEFL (minimum score 550 paper-based; 213 computer-based; 79 iBT). Electronic applications accepted.

The American University of Paris, Graduate Programs, Paris, France. Offers cross-cultural and sustainable business management (MA); cultural translation (MA); global communications (MA); global communications and civil society (MA); international affairs, conflict resolution and civil society development (MA); Middle East and Islamic studies (MA); Middle East and Islamic studies and international affairs (MA); public policy and international affairs (MA); public policy and international law (MA). *Faculty:* 14 full-time (3 women). *Students:* 142 full-time (98 women), 59 part-time (41 women). *Degree requirements:* For master's, thesis. *Entrance requirements:* For master's, minimum undergraduate GPA of 3.0. Additional exam requirements/recommendations for international students: Recommended—TOEFL, IELTS. *Application deadline:* For fall admission, 4/15 for international students; for spring admission, 11/15 for international students. Applications are processed on a rolling basis. Application fee: $75. Electronic applications accepted. Tuition and fees charges are reported in euros. *Expenses: Tuition:* Full-time 25,060 euros; part-time 784 euros per credit. *Required fees:* 784 euros per credit. *Financial support:* Scholarships/grants available. Financial award applicants required to submit FAFSA. *Unit head:* Dr. Celeste Schenck, President, 33 1 40 62 06 59, E-mail: president@aup.fr. *Application contact:* International Admissions Counselor, 33-1 40 62 07 20, Fax: 33-1 47 05 34 32, E-mail: admissions@aup.edu. Web site: http://aup.edu/main/academics/graduate.htm.

Argosy University, Atlanta, College of Business, Atlanta, GA 30328. Offers accounting (DBA); corporate compliance (MBA); customized professional concentration (MBA, DBA); finance (MBA); healthcare administration (MBA); information systems (DBA); information systems management (MBA); international business (MBA, DBA); management (MBA, MSM, DBA); marketing (MBA, DBA).

See Close-Up on page 179.

Argosy University, Chicago, College of Business, Chicago, IL 60601. Offers accounting (DBA); customized professional concentration (MBA, DBA); finance (MBA); fraud examination (MBA); global business sustainability (DBA); healthcare administration (MBA); information systems (DBA); information systems management (MBA); international business (MBA, DBA); management (MBA, MSM, DBA); marketing (MBA, DBA); organizational leadership (Ed D); public administration (MBA); sustainable management (MBA). Postbaccalaureate distance learning degree programs offered (minimal on-campus study).

See Close-Up on page 181.

Argosy University, Dallas, College of Business, Farmers Branch, TX 75244. Offers accounting (DBA, AGC); corporate compliance (MBA, Graduate Certificate); customized professional concentration (MBA); finance (MBA, Graduate Certificate); fraud examination (MBA, Graduate Certificate); global business sustainability (DBA, AGC); healthcare administration (Graduate Certificate); healthcare management (MBA); information systems (MBA, DBA, AGC); information systems management (Graduate Certificate); international business (MBA, DBA, AGC, Graduate Certificate); management (MBA, DBA, AGC, Graduate Certificate); marketing (MBA, DBA, AGC, Graduate Certificate); public administration (MBA, Graduate Certificate); sustainable management (MBA, Graduate Certificate).

See Close-Up on page 183.

Argosy University, Denver, College of Business, Denver, CO 80231. Offers accounting (DBA); corporate compliance (MBA); customized professional concentration (MBA, DBA); finance (MBA); fraud examination (MBA); global business sustainability (DBA); healthcare administration (MBA); information systems (DBA); information systems management (MBA); international business (MBA, DBA); management (MBA, MSM, DBA); marketing (MBA, DBA); organizational leadership (Ed D); public administration (MBA); sustainable management (MBA).

See Close-Up on page 185.

Argosy University, Hawai`i, College of Business, Honolulu, HI 96813. Offers accounting (DBA); corporate compliance (MBA); customized professional concentration

(MBA, DBA); finance (MBA, Certificate); fraud examination (MBA); global business sustainability (DBA); healthcare administration (MBA, Certificate); information systems (DBA); information systems management (MBA, Certificate); international business (MBA, DBA, Certificate); management (MBA, MSM, DBA); marketing (MBA, DBA, Certificate); organizational leadership (Ed D); public administration (MBA); sustainable management (MBA).

See Close-Up on page 187.

Argosy University, Inland Empire, College of Business, San Bernardino, CA 92408. Offers accounting (DBA); corporate compliance (MBA); customized professional concentration (MBA, DBA); finance (MBA); fraud examination (MBA); global business sustainability (DBA); healthcare administration (MBA); information systems (DBA); information systems management (MBA); international business (MBA, DBA); management (MBA, MSM, DBA); marketing (MBA, DBA); organizational leadership (Ed D); public administration (MBA); sustainable management (MBA).

See Close-Up on page 189.

Argosy University, Los Angeles, College of Business, Santa Monica, CA 90045. Offers accounting (DBA); corporate compliance (MBA); customized professional concentration (MBA, DBA); finance (MBA); fraud examination (MBA); global business sustainability (DBA); healthcare administration (MBA); information systems (DBA); information systems management (MBA); international business (MBA, DBA); management (MBA, MSM, DBA); marketing (MBA, DBA); organizational leadership (Ed D); public administration (MBA); sustainable management (MBA).

See Close-Up on page 191.

Argosy University, Nashville, College of Business, Nashville, TN 37214. Offers accounting (DBA); customized professional concentration (MBA, DBA); finance (MBA); healthcare administration (MBA); information systems (MBA, DBA); international business (MBA, DBA); management (MBA, MSM, DBA); marketing (MBA, DBA).

See Close-Up on page 193.

Argosy University, Orange County, College of Business, Orange, CA 92868. Offers accounting (DBA, Adv C); corporate compliance (MBA); customized professional concentration (MBA, DBA); finance (MBA, Certificate); fraud examination (MBA); global business sustainability (DBA); healthcare administration (MBA, Certificate); information systems (DBA, Adv C, Certificate); information systems management (MBA); international business (MBA, DBA, Adv C, Certificate); management (MBA, MSM, DBA, Adv C); marketing (MBA, DBA, Adv C, Certificate); organizational leadership (Ed D); public administration (MBA, Certificate); sustainable management (MBA).

See Close-Up on page 195.

Argosy University, Phoenix, College of Business, Phoenix, AZ 85021. Offers accounting (DBA); corporate compliance (MBA); customized professional concentration (MBA, DBA); finance (MBA); fraud examination (MBA); global business sustainability (DBA); healthcare administration (MBA); information systems (DBA); information systems management (MBA); international business (MBA, DBA); management (MBA, DBA); marketing (MBA, DBA); public administration (MBA); sustainable management (MBA).

See Close-Up on page 197.

Argosy University, Salt Lake City, College of Business, Draper, UT 84020. Offers accounting (DBA); corporate compliance (MBA); customized professional concentration (MBA, DBA); finance (MBA); fraud examination (MBA); global business sustainability (DBA); healthcare administration (MBA); information systems (DBA); information systems management (MBA); international business (MBA, DBA); management (MBA, DBA); marketing (MBA, DBA); public administration (MBA); sustainable management (MBA).

See Close-Up on page 199.

Argosy University, San Diego, College of Business, San Diego, CA 92108. Offers accounting (DBA); corporate compliance (MBA); customized professional concentration (MBA, DBA); finance (MBA); fraud examination (MBA); global business sustainability (DBA); information systems (DBA); information systems management (MBA); international business (MBA, DBA); management (MBA, MSM, DBA); marketing (MBA, DBA); organizational leadership (Ed D); public administration (MBA).

See Close-Up on page 201.

Argosy University, San Francisco Bay Area, College of Business, Alameda, CA 94501. Offers accounting (DBA); corporate compliance (MBA); customized professional concentration (MBA, DBA); finance (MBA); fraud examination (MBA); global business sustainability (DBA); healthcare administration (MBA); information systems (DBA); information systems management (MBA); international business (MBA, DBA); management (MBA, MSM, DBA); marketing (MBA, DBA); organizational leadership (Ed D); public administration (MBA); sustainable management (MBA).

See Close-Up on page 203.

Argosy University, Sarasota, College of Business, Sarasota, FL 34235. Offers accounting (DBA, Adv C); corporate compliance (MBA, DBA, Certificate); customized professional concentration (MBA, DBA); finance (MBA, Certificate); fraud examination (MBA, Certificate); global business sustainability (DBA, Adv C); healthcare administration (MBA, Certificate); information systems (DBA, Adv C, Certificate); information systems management (MBA); international business (MBA, DBA, Adv C, Certificate); management (MBA, MSM, DBA, Adv C, Certificate); marketing (MBA, DBA, Adv C, Certificate); organizational leadership (Ed D); public administration (MBA, Certificate); sustainable management (MBA, Certificate).

See Close-Up on page 205.

Argosy University, Schaumburg, College of Business, Schaumburg, IL 60173-5403. Offers accounting (DBA, Adv C); customized professional concentration (MBA, DBA); finance (MBA, Certificate); fraud examination (MBA); global business sustainability (DBA); healthcare administration (MBA, Certificate); information systems (DBA, Adv C, Certificate); information systems management (MBA); international business (MBA, DBA, Adv C, Certificate); management (MBA, MSM, DBA, Adv C, Certificate); marketing (MBA, DBA, Adv C, Certificate); organizational leadership (Ed D); public administration (MBA); sustainable management (MBA).

See Close-Up on page 9999.

Argosy University, Seattle, College of Business, Seattle, WA 98121. Offers accounting (DBA); corporate compliance (MBA); customized professional concentration (MBA, DBA); finance (MBA); fraud examination (MBA); global business sustainability (DBA); healthcare administration (MBA); information systems (DBA); information systems management (MBA); international business (MBA, DBA); management (MBA, MSM, DBA); marketing (MBA, DBA); organizational leadership (Ed D); public administration (MBA); sustainable management (MBA).

See Close-Up on page 209.

Argosy University, Tampa, College of Business, Tampa, FL 33607. Offers accounting (DBA); corporate compliance (MBA); customized professional concentration (MBA, DBA); finance (MBA); fraud examination (MBA); global business sustainability (DBA); healthcare administration (MBA); information systems (DBA); information systems management (MBA); international business (MBA, DBA); management (MBA, MSM, DBA); marketing (MBA, DBA); organizational leadership (Ed D); public administration (MBA); sustainable management (MBA).

See Close-Up on page 211.

Argosy University, Twin Cities, College of Business, Eagan, MN 55121. Offers accounting (DBA); customized professional concentration (MBA, DBA); finance (MBA); fraud examination (MBA); global business sustainability (DBA); healthcare administration (MBA); information systems (DBA); information systems management (MBA); international business (MBA, DBA); management (MBA, MSM, DBA); marketing (MBA, DBA); organizational leadership (Ed D); public administration (MBA); sustainable management (MBA).

See Close-Up on page 213.

Argosy University, Washington DC, College of Business, Arlington, VA 22209. Offers accounting (DBA); customized professional concentration (MBA, DBA); finance (MBA); fraud examination (MBA); global business sustainability (DBA); healthcare administration (MBA); information systems (DBA); information systems management (MBA); international business (MBA, DBA, Certificate); management (MBA, MSM, DBA); marketing (MBA, DBA, Certificate); organizational leadership (Ed D); public administration (MBA); sustainable management (MBA).

See Close-Up on page 215.

Ashworth College, Graduate Programs, Norcross, GA 30092. Offers business administration (MBA); criminal justice (MS); health care administration (MBA, MS); human resource management (MBA, MS); international business (MBA); management (MS); marketing (MBA, MS).

Assumption College, Graduate Studies, Department of Business Studies, Worcester, MA 01609-1296. Offers accounting (MBA); business administration (CAGS); finance/economics (MBA); general business (MBA); human resources (MBA); international business (MBA); management (MBA); marketing (MBA); nonprofit leadership (MBA). Part-time and evening/weekend programs available. *Faculty:* 4 full-time (0 women), 16 part-time/adjunct (4 women). *Students:* 8 full-time (5 women), 133 part-time (65 women); includes 18 minority (8 Black or African American, non-Hispanic/Latino; 1 American Indian or Alaska Native, non-Hispanic/Latino; 2 Asian, non-Hispanic/Latino; 7 Hispanic/Latino), 3 international. Average age 30. 100 applicants, 75% accepted, 52 enrolled. In 2011, 53 master's, 1 other advanced degree awarded. *Degree requirements:* For master's, thesis, capstone. *Entrance requirements:* For master's and CAGS, 3 letters of recommendation, resume, essay. Additional exam requirements/recommendations for international students: Required—TOEFL (minimum score 540 paper-based; 200 computer-based; 76 iBT), IELTS (minimum score 6). *Application deadline:* For fall admission, 10/1 for domestic and international students; for winter admission, 2/1 for domestic and international students; for spring admission, 4/1 for domestic and international students. Applications are processed on a rolling basis. Application fee: $30. Electronic applications accepted. *Expenses: Tuition:* Full-time $9414; part-time $523 per credit. *Required fees:* $20 per term. Full-time tuition and fees vary according to course load and program. *Financial support:* In 2011–12, 14 students received support. Scholarships/grants, tuition waivers (partial), and unspecified assistantships available. Financial award application deadline: 5/1; financial award applicants required to submit FAFSA. *Faculty research:* Workplace diversity, dynamics of team interaction, utilization of leased employees, experiential learning project on due diligence market for prostheses. *Unit head:* Michael Lewis, Director, 508-767-7372, Fax: 508-767-7252, E-mail: milewis@assumption.edu. *Application contact:* Laura Lawrence, Graduate Programs Operations Manager, 508-767-7387, Fax: 508-767-7030, E-mail: graduate@assumption.edu. Web site: http://graduate.assumption.edu/mba/mba-assumption.

Avila University, School of Business, Kansas City, MO 64145-1698. Offers accounting (MBA); finance (MBA); general management (MBA); health care administration (MBA); international business (MBA); management information systems (MBA); marketing (MBA). Part-time and evening/weekend programs available. *Faculty:* 9 full-time (3 women), 14 part-time/adjunct (5 women). *Students:* 102 full-time (49 women), 53 part-time (31 women); includes 36 minority (29 Black or African American, non-Hispanic/Latino; 1 American Indian or Alaska Native, non-Hispanic/Latino; 3 Asian, non-Hispanic/Latino; 2 Hispanic/Latino; 1 Native Hawaiian or other Pacific Islander, non-Hispanic/Latino), 33 international. Average age 32. 25 applicants, 76% accepted, 19 enrolled. In 2011, 59 master's awarded. *Degree requirements:* For master's, comprehensive exam, capstone course. *Entrance requirements:* For master's, GMAT (minimum score 420), minimum GPA of 3.0, interview. Additional exam requirements/recommendations for international students: Required—TOEFL (minimum score 550 paper-based). *Application deadline:* For fall admission, 7/30 priority date for domestic students, 7/30 for international students; for winter admission, 11/30 priority date for domestic students, 11/30 for international students; for spring admission, 2/28 priority date for domestic students, 2/28 for international students. Applications are processed on a rolling basis. Application fee: $0. Electronic applications accepted. *Expenses:* Contact institution. *Financial support:* In 2011–12, 102 students received support. Career-related internships or fieldwork and competitive merit scholarships available. Support available to part-time students. Financial award applicants required to submit FAFSA. *Faculty research:* Leadership characteristics, financial hedging, group dynamics. *Unit head:* Dr. Richard Woodall, Dean, 816-501-3720, Fax: 816-501-2463, E-mail: richard.woodall@avila.edu. *Application contact:* JoAnna Giffin, MBA Admissions Director, 816-501-3601, Fax: 816-501-2463, E-mail: joanna.giffin@avila.edu. Web site: http://www.avila.edu/mba.

Azusa Pacific University, School of Behavioral and Applied Sciences, Department of Higher Education and Organizational Leadership, Program in Global Leadership, Azusa, CA 91702-7000. Offers MA.

Azusa Pacific University, School of Business and Management, Azusa, CA 91702-7000. Offers business administration (MBA); diversity for strategic advantage (MA); entrepreneurship (MBA); finance (MBA); human and organizational development (MA); human resources and organizational development (MBA); human resources management (MA); international business (MBA); marketing (MBA); non-profit management (MA); organizational development and change (MA); performance improvement (MA); public administration (MA); strategic management (MBA). Part-time and evening/weekend programs available. *Degree requirements:* For master's, thesis (for some programs), final project. *Entrance requirements:* For master's, GMAT, minimum GPA of 3.0. Additional exam requirements/recommendations for international students: Required—TOEFL (minimum score 600 paper-based). *Expenses:* Contact institution. *Faculty research:* Gender issues, financial risk, leadership and ethics, marketing strategy.

Baldwin Wallace University, Graduate Programs, Division of Business, Program in International Management, Berea, OH 44017-2088. Offers MBA. Part-time and evening/weekend programs available. *Students:* 24 full-time (8 women), 21 part-time (13 women); includes 13 minority (2 Black or African American, non-Hispanic/Latino; 8 Asian, non-Hispanic/Latino; 3 Hispanic/Latino), 6 international. Average age 32. 13 applicants, 77% accepted, 4 enrolled. In 2011, 12 master's awarded. *Degree requirements:* For master's, one foreign language, minimum overall GPA of 3.0, completion of all required courses. *Entrance requirements:* For master's, GMAT, interview, work experience, bachelor's degree in any field. Additional exam requirements/recommendations for international students: Required—TOEFL (minimum score 523 paper-based; 193 computer-based; 70 iBT). *Application deadline:* For fall admission, 7/25 priority date for domestic students, 4/30 for international students; for spring admission, 12/15 priority date for domestic students, 9/30 for international students. Applications are processed on a rolling basis. Application fee: $25. Electronic applications accepted. Application fee is waived when completed online. *Expenses:* Contact institution. *Financial support:* Career-related internships or fieldwork available. Support available to part-time students. Financial award application deadline: 5/1; financial award applicants required to submit FAFSA. *Faculty research:* International finance, systems approach, international marketing. *Unit head:* Harvey Hopson, Director, 440-826-2137, Fax: 440-826-3868, E-mail: hhopson@bw.edu. *Application contact:* Laura Spencer, Graduate Application Specialist, 440-826-2191, Fax: 440-826-3868, E-mail: lspencer@bw.edu. Web site: http://www.bw.edu/academics/bus/programs/imba/.

Barry University, Andreas School of Business, Graduate Certificate Programs, Miami Shores, FL 33161-6695. Offers finance (Certificate); health services administration (Certificate); international business (Certificate); management (Certificate); management information systems (Certificate); marketing (Certificate).

Benedictine University, Graduate Programs, Program in Business Administration, Lisle, IL 60532-0900. Offers accounting (MBA); entrepreneurship and managing innovation (MBA); financial management (MBA); health administration (MBA); human resource management (MBA); information systems security (MBA); international business (MBA); management consulting (MBA); management information systems (MBA); marketing management (MBA); operations management and logistics (MBA); organizational leadership (MBA); MBA/MPH; MBA/MS. Part-time and evening/weekend programs available. Postbaccalaureate distance learning degree programs offered (minimal on-campus study). *Faculty:* 4 full-time (2 women), 24 part-time/adjunct (3 women). *Students:* 165 full-time (101 women), 766 part-time (381 women); includes 201 minority (118 Black or African American, non-Hispanic/Latino; 4 American Indian or Alaska Native, non-Hispanic/Latino; 37 Asian, non-Hispanic/Latino; 40 Hispanic/Latino; 2 Native Hawaiian or other Pacific Islander, non-Hispanic/Latino), 14 international. Average age 34. 313 applicants, 73% accepted, 166 enrolled. In 2011, 379 master's awarded. *Entrance requirements:* For master's, GMAT. Additional exam requirements/recommendations for international students: Required—TOEFL (minimum score 550 paper-based; 213 computer-based). *Application deadline:* For fall admission, 9/1 for domestic students; for winter admission, 12/1 for domestic students; for spring admission, 2/15 for domestic students. Applications are processed on a rolling basis. Application fee: $40. Electronic applications accepted. *Financial support:* Career-related internships or fieldwork and health care benefits available. Support available to part-time students. *Faculty research:* Strategic leadership in professional organizations, sociology of professions, organizational change, social identity theory, applications to change management. *Unit head:* Dr. Sharon Borowicz, Director, 630-829-6219, E-mail: sborowicz@ben.edu. *Application contact:* Kari Gibbons, Director, Admissions, 630-829-6200, Fax: 630-829-6584, E-mail: kgibbons@ben.edu.

Bernard M. Baruch College of the City University of New York, Zicklin School of Business, Department of Marketing and International Business, New York, NY 10010-5585. Offers international business (MBA); marketing (MBA, MS, PhD). PhD offered jointly with Graduate School and University Center of the City University of New York. Part-time and evening/weekend programs available. *Degree requirements:* For doctorate, comprehensive exam, thesis/dissertation. *Entrance requirements:* For master's, GMAT, 2 letters of recommendation, resume, 2 years of work experience; for doctorate, GMAT. Additional exam requirements/recommendations for international students: Required—TOEFL (minimum score 590 paper-based; 243 computer-based), TWE (minimum score 5).

Bernard M. Baruch College of the City University of New York, Zicklin School of Business, International Executive MS Programs, New York, NY 10010-5585. Offers entrepreneurship (MS). Part-time and evening/weekend programs available. *Entrance requirements:* For master's, GMAT, 2 letters of recommendation, resume, 2 years of work experience. Additional exam requirements/recommendations for international students: Required—TOEFL (minimum score 590 paper-based; 243 computer-based), TWE (minimum score 5).

Boston University, Metropolitan College, Department of Administrative Sciences, Boston, MA 02215. Offers banking and financial management (MSM); business continuity in emergency management (MSM); economics development and tourism management (MSAS); electronic commerce, systems, and technology (MSAS); financial economics (MSAS); innovation and technology (MSAS); insurance management (MSM); international market management (MSM); multinational commerce (MSAS); project management (MSM). *Accreditation:* AACSB. Part-time and evening/weekend programs available. Postbaccalaureate distance learning degree programs offered (no on-campus study). *Faculty:* 14 full-time (2 women), 21 part-time/adjunct (2 women). *Students:* 151 full-time (75 women), 106 part-time (51 women); includes 27 minority (6 Black or African American, non-Hispanic/Latino; 14 Asian, non-Hispanic/Latino; 7 Hispanic/Latino), 173 international. Average age 28. 500 applicants, 65% accepted, 194 enrolled. In 2011, 154 master's awarded. *Degree requirements:* For master's, thesis optional. *Entrance requirements:* For master's, 1 year of work experience, minimum GPA of 3.0. Additional exam requirements/recommendations for international students: Required—TOEFL (minimum score 560 paper-based; 220 computer-based; 84 iBT). *Application deadline:* Applications are processed on a rolling basis. Application fee: $70. Electronic applications accepted. *Expenses: Tuition:* Full-time $40,848; part-time $1276 per credit hour. *Required fees:* $572; $286 per semester. *Financial support:* In 2011–12, 15 students received support, including 7 research assistantships (averaging $10,000 per year); career-related internships or fieldwork, Federal Work-Study, and unspecified assistantships also available. *Faculty research:* International business, innovative process. *Unit head:* Dr. Kip Becker, Chairman, 617-353-3016, E-mail: adminsc@bu.edu. *Application contact:* Lucille Dicker, Administrative Sciences Department, 617-353-3016, E-mail: adminsc@bu.edu. Web site: http://www.bu.edu/met/programs/.

Brandeis University, International Business School, Waltham, MA 02454-9110. Offers finance (MSF); international business (MBA); international economic policy (MBA); international economics and finance (MA, PhD); international finance (MBA); socially responsible business (MBA). Part-time and evening/weekend programs available. Terminal master's awarded for partial completion of doctoral program. *Degree requirements:* For master's, one foreign language, semester abroad; for doctorate, thesis/dissertation. *Entrance requirements:* For master's, GMAT or GRE General Test (MA), GMAT (MBAi, MSF); for doctorate, GRE General Test. Additional exam requirements/recommendations for international students: Required—TOEFL (minimum score 600 paper-based; 250 computer-based), IELTS (minimum score 7). Electronic applications accepted. *Faculty research:* International finance and business, trade policy, macroeconomics, Asian economic issues, developmental economics.

Brooklyn College of the City University of New York, Division of Graduate Studies, Department of Economics, Brooklyn, NY 11210-2889. Offers accounting (MS); business economics (MS), including economic analysis, global business and finance; economics (MA). Part-time and evening/weekend programs available. *Degree requirements:* For master's, comprehensive exam, thesis or alternative. *Entrance requirements:* For master's, GMAT (for MS), 2 letters of recommendation. Additional exam requirements/recommendations for international students: Required—TOEFL (minimum score 550 paper-based; 213 computer-based; 79 iBT). Electronic applications accepted. *Faculty research:* Econometrics, environmental economics, microeconomics, macroeconomics, taxation.

California Intercontinental University, School of Business, Diamond Bar, CA 91765. Offers banking and finance (MBA); entrepreneurship and business management (DBA); global business leadership (DBA); international management and marketing (MBA); organizational management and human resource management (MBA).

California Lutheran University, Graduate Studies, School of Management, Thousand Oaks, CA 91360-2787. Offers business (IMBA); computer science (MS); econometrics (MBA); economics (MS); entrepreneurship (MBA, Certificate); finance (MBA, Certificate); financial planning (MBA, Certificate); information systems and technology (MS); information technology management (MBA, Certificate); international business (MBA, Certificate); management and organization behavior (MBA); management and organizational behavior (Certificate); marketing (MBA, Certificate); microeconomics (MBA); nonprofit and social enterprise (MBA). Part-time and evening/weekend programs available. Postbaccalaureate distance learning degree programs offered (no on-campus study). *Entrance requirements:* For master's, GMAT, interview, minimum GPA of 3.0. *Expenses:* Contact institution.

California State University, East Bay, Office of Academic Programs and Graduate Studies, College of Business and Economics, Business Administration, MBA Program, Hayward, CA 94542-3000. Offers entrepreneurship (MBA); finance (MBA); global innovators (MBA); human resources and organizational behavior (MBA); information technology management (MBA); marketing management (MBA); operations and supply chain management (MBA); strategy and international business (MBA). Part-time and evening/weekend programs available. *Faculty:* 11 full-time (3 women). *Students:* 80 full-time (42 women), 141 part-time (61 women); includes 70 minority (5 Black or African American, non-Hispanic/Latino; 46 Asian, non-Hispanic/Latino; 13 Hispanic/Latino; 1 Native Hawaiian or other Pacific Islander, non-Hispanic/Latino; 5 Two or more races, non-Hispanic/Latino), 69 international. Average age 31. 371 applicants, 36% accepted, 79 enrolled. In 2011, 254 master's awarded. *Degree requirements:* For master's, comprehensive exam or thesis. *Entrance requirements:* For master's, GMAT (minimum 20th percentile verbal and quantitative section), bachelor's degree, minimum GPA of 2.75. Additional exam requirements/recommendations for international students: Required—TOEFL (minimum score 550 paper-based; 213 computer-based; 79 iBT). *Application deadline:* For fall admission, 6/30 for domestic and international students. Applications are processed on a rolling basis. Application fee: $55. Electronic applications accepted. *Expenses:* Contact institution. *Financial support:* Career-related internships or fieldwork, Federal Work-Study, institutionally sponsored loans, and scholarships/grants available. Support available to part-time students. Financial award application deadline: 3/2; financial award applicants required to submit FAFSA. *Unit head:* Dr. Terri Swartz, Dean, 510-885-3291, Fax: 510-885-4884, E-mail: terri.swartz@csueastbay.edu. *Application contact:* Prof. Joanna Lee, Director, CBE Graduate Programs, 510-885-3517, Fax: 510-885-2176, E-mail: joanna.lee@csueastbay.edu. Web site: http://www20.csueastbay.edu/ecat/graduate-chapters/g-buad.html#mba.

California State University, East Bay, Office of Academic Programs and Graduate Studies, College of Business and Economics, Program in Information Technology Management, Option in Strategy and International Business, Hayward, CA 94542-3000. Offers MBA. Part-time and evening/weekend programs available. *Degree requirements:* For master's, comprehensive exam or thesis. *Entrance requirements:* For master's, GMAT, minimum GPA of 2.75. Additional exam requirements/recommendations for international students: Required—TOEFL (minimum score 550 paper-based; 213 computer-based). *Application deadline:* For fall admission, 6/30 for domestic and international students. Application fee: $55. *Expenses:* Tuition, state resident: full-time $6738; part-time $1302 per quarter. Tuition, nonresident: full-time $12,690; part-time $2294 per quarter. *Required fees:* $449 per quarter. Tuition and fees vary according to degree level, program and reciprocity agreements. *Financial support:* Career-related internships or fieldwork, Federal Work-Study, institutionally sponsored loans, and scholarships/grants available. Support available to part-time students. Financial award application deadline: 3/1. *Unit head:* Dr. Xinjian Lu, Chair, 510-885-3307, E-mail: xinjian.lu@csueastbay.edu. *Application contact:* Donna Wiley, Interim Associate Director, 510-885-2928, Fax: 510-885-4777, E-mail: donna.wiley@csueastbay.edu. Web site: http://www.cbe.csueastbay.edu/mgmt/.

California State University, Fullerton, Graduate Studies, College of Business and Economics, Program in Business Administration, Fullerton, CA 92834-9480. Offers e-commerce (MBA); international business (MBA). *Accreditation:* AACSB. Part-time programs available. *Students:* 63 full-time (34 women), 89 part-time (35 women); includes 57 minority (2 Black or African American, non-Hispanic/Latino; 41 Asian, non-Hispanic/Latino; 10 Hispanic/Latino; 4 Two or more races, non-Hispanic/Latino), 36 international. Average age 28. 476 applicants, 40% accepted, 60 enrolled. In 2011, 31 master's awarded. *Degree requirements:* For master's, project or thesis. *Entrance requirements:* For master's, GMAT. *Financial support:* Career-related internships or fieldwork, Federal Work-Study, institutionally sponsored loans, and scholarships/grants available. Support available to part-time students. Financial award application deadline: 3/1; financial award applicants required to submit FAFSA. *Unit head:* Dr. Anil Puri, Dean, 657-773-2592. *Application contact:* Admissions/Applications, 657-278-2371.

California State University, Los Angeles, Graduate Studies, College of Business and Economics, Department of Marketing, Los Angeles, CA 90032-8530. Offers international business (MBA, MS); marketing management (MBA, MS). Part-time and evening/weekend programs available. *Faculty:* 1 full-time (0 women), 1 part-time/adjunct (0 women). *Students:* 9 full-time (5 women), 11 part-time (7 women); includes 4 minority (2 Asian, non-Hispanic/Latino; 2 Hispanic/Latino), 12 international. Average age 27. 93 applicants, 38% accepted, 11 enrolled. In 2011, 13 master's awarded. *Degree requirements:* For master's, comprehensive exam (MBA), thesis (MS). *Entrance requirements:* For master's, GMAT, minimum GPA of 2.5 during previous 2 years of course work. Additional exam requirements/recommendations for international students: Required—TOEFL (minimum score 550 paper-based; 213 computer-based). *Application deadline:* For fall admission, 5/1 for domestic and international students. Applications are processed on a rolling basis. Application fee: $55. Electronic applications accepted. *Expenses:* Tuition, state resident: full-time $8225. *Financial support:* Career-related internships or fieldwork and Federal Work-Study available. Support available to part-time students. Financial award application deadline: 3/1. *Unit head:* Dr. Tyrone Jackson, Chair, 323-343-2960, Fax: 323-343-5462, E-mail: tjackso4@calstatela.edu. *Application contact:* Dr. Karin Brown, Acting Associate Dean of Graduate Studies, 323-343-3820,

Fax: 323-343-5653, E-mail: kbrown5@calstatela.edu. Web site: http://cbe.calstatela.edu/mkt/.

California State University, San Bernardino, Graduate Studies, College of Business and Public Administration, Master in Business Administration Program, San Bernardino, CA 92407. Offers accounting (MBA); entrepreneurship (MBA); executives (MBA); finance (MBA); global business (MBA); information assurance and security management (MBA); information management (MBA); management (MBA); marketing (MBA); professionals (MBA); supply chain management (MBA). *Accreditation:* AACSB. Part-time and evening/weekend programs available. Postbaccalaureate distance learning degree programs offered (no on-campus study). *Faculty:* 58 full-time (11 women), 26 part-time/adjunct (9 women). *Students:* 80 full-time (31 women), 137 part-time (56 women); includes 82 minority (19 Black or African American, non-Hispanic/Latino; 3 American Indian or Alaska Native, non-Hispanic/Latino; 20 Asian, non-Hispanic/Latino; 37 Hispanic/Latino; 3 Two or more races, non-Hispanic/Latino), 65 international. Average age 30. 217 applicants, 65% accepted, 79 enrolled. In 2011, 120 master's awarded. *Degree requirements:* For master's, comprehensive exam, thesis optional, portfolio, 48 units, minimum GPA of 3.0. *Entrance requirements:* For master's, GMAT, minimum GPA of 2.5. Additional exam requirements/recommendations for international students: Required—TOEFL (minimum score 550 paper-based; 213 computer-based; 79 iBT). *Application deadline:* For fall admission, 7/12 priority date for domestic students, 7/12 for international students; for winter admission, 10/26 priority date for domestic students, 10/26 for international students; for spring admission, 1/25 priority date for domestic students, 1/25 for international students. Applications are processed on a rolling basis. Application fee: $55. Electronic applications accepted. *Expenses:* Contact institution. *Financial support:* In 2011–12, 56 students received support, including 34 fellowships (averaging $3,732 per year), 18 research assistantships (averaging $2,193 per year), 4 teaching assistantships (averaging $2,606 per year); career-related internships or fieldwork, Federal Work-Study, institutionally sponsored loans, scholarships/grants, and unspecified assistantships also available. Support available to part-time students. Financial award application deadline: 3/1; financial award applicants required to submit FAFSA. *Faculty research:* Fraud, Stock Exchange, small business, logistics, job analysis. *Total annual research expenditures:* $4.8 million. *Unit head:* Dr. Lawrence C. Rose, Dean, 909-537-3703, Fax: 909-537-7026, E-mail: lrose@csusb.edu. *Application contact:* Dr. Sandra Kamusikiri, Associate Vice-President/Dean of Graduate Studies, 909-537-7058, Fax: 909-537-5078, E-mail: skamusik@csusb.edu. Web site: http://mba.csusb.edu/.

Canisius College, Graduate Division, Richard J. Wehle School of Business, Department of Management and Marketing, Buffalo, NY 14208-1098. Offers accelerated business administration (1 year) (MBA); business administration (MBA); international business (MS). *Accreditation:* AACSB. Part-time and evening/weekend programs available. *Faculty:* 35 full-time (7 women), 11 part-time/adjunct (5 women). *Students:* 102 full-time (42 women), 150 part-time (67 women); includes 29 minority (20 Black or African American, non-Hispanic/Latino; 1 American Indian or Alaska Native, non-Hispanic/Latino; 5 Asian, non-Hispanic/Latino; 1 Hispanic/Latino; 2 Two or more races, non-Hispanic/Latino), 10 international. Average age 28. 173 applicants, 66% accepted, 84 enrolled. In 2011, 97 master's awarded. *Entrance requirements:* For master's, GMAT, transcripts. Additional exam requirements/recommendations for international students: Required—TOEFL. *Application deadline:* For fall admission, 7/1 priority date for domestic students; for spring admission, 11/1 priority date for domestic students. Applications are processed on a rolling basis. Application fee: $25. Electronic applications accepted. *Financial support:* Research assistantships, career-related internships or fieldwork, Federal Work-Study, scholarships/grants, and unspecified assistantships available. Support available to part-time students. Financial award application deadline: 4/30; financial award applicants required to submit FAFSA. *Faculty research:* Global leadership effectiveness, global supply chain management, quality management. *Unit head:* Dr. Gordon W. Meyers, Chair, Management, Entrepreneurship and International Business, 716-888-2634, E-mail: meyerg@canisius.edu. *Application contact:* Jim Bagwell, Director, Graduate Programs, 716-888-2545, Fax: 716-888-3290, E-mail: bagwellj@canisius.edu. Web site: http://www.canisius.edu/academics/gradhome.asp.

Central European University, Graduate Studies, Department of Legal Studies, Budapest, Hungary. Offers comparative Constitutional law (LL M); human rights (LL M, MA); international business law (LL M); law and economics (LL M, MA); legal studies (SJD). *Faculty:* 7 full-time (2 women), 31 part-time/adjunct (8 women). *Students:* 104 full-time (58 women). Average age 27. 474 applicants, 22% accepted, 80 enrolled. In 2011, 36 master's, 7 doctorates awarded. Terminal master's awarded for partial completion of doctoral program. *Degree requirements:* For master's, one foreign language, thesis; for doctorate, one foreign language, comprehensive exam, thesis/dissertation. *Entrance requirements:* For master's and doctorate, LSAT, CEU admissions exams. Additional exam requirements/recommendations for international students: Required—TOEFL (minimum score 570 paper-based; 230 computer-based); Recommended—IELTS (minimum score 6.5). *Application deadline:* For fall admission, 1/24 for domestic and international students. Application fee: $0. Electronic applications accepted. *Expenses:* Contact institution. *Financial support:* In 2011–12, 85 students received support, including 88 fellowships with full and partial tuition reimbursements available (averaging $6,100 per year); career-related internships or fieldwork, institutionally sponsored loans, scholarships/grants, and tuition waivers (full and partial) also available. Financial award application deadline: 1/5. *Faculty research:* Institutional, constitutional and human rights in European Union law; biomedical law and reproductive rights; data protection law; Islamic banking and finance. *Unit head:* Dr. Stefan Messmann, Head, 361-327-3274, Fax: 361-327-3198, E-mail: legalst@ceu.hu. *Application contact:* Maria Balla, Coordinator, 361-327-3204, Fax: 361-327-3198, E-mail: ballam@ceu.hu. Web site: http://www.ceu.hu/legal/.

Central Michigan University, College of Graduate Studies, College of Business Administration, Department of Management, Mount Pleasant, MI 48859. Offers human resource management (MBA); international business (MBA). *Degree requirements:* For master's, thesis or alternative. *Entrance requirements:* For master's, GMAT. Electronic applications accepted. *Faculty research:* Human resource accounting, valuation, and liability; international business and economic issues; entrepreneurial leadership; technology management and strategy; electronic commerce and neural networks.

Central Michigan University, College of Graduate Studies, Interdisciplinary Administration Programs, Mount Pleasant, MI 48859. Offers acquisitions administration (MSA, Graduate Certificate); general administration (MSA, Graduate Certificate); health services administration (MSA, Graduate Certificate); human resource administration (Graduate Certificate); human resources administration (MSA); information resource management (MSA, Graduate Certificate); international administration (MSA, Graduate Certificate); leadership (MSA, Graduate Certificate); organizational communication (MSA, Graduate Certificate); public administration (MSA, Graduate Certificate); recreation and park administration (MSA); sport administration (MSA). *Accreditation:* AACSB. Part-time and evening/weekend programs available. Postbaccalaureate distance learning degree programs offered (no on-campus study). *Degree requirements:* For master's, thesis or alternative. *Entrance requirements:* For master's, bachelor's degree with minimum GPA of 2.7. Electronic applications accepted. *Faculty research:* Interdisciplinary studies in acquisitions administration, health services administration, sport administration, recreation and park administration, and international administration.

City University of Seattle, Graduate Division, School of Management, Bellevue, WA 98005. Offers accounting (Certificate); change leadership (MBA, Certificate); computer systems (MS); finance (Certificate); financial management (MBA); general management (MBA); general management-Europe (MBA); global marketing (MBA); human resources management (Certificate); individualized study (MBA); information security (MS); information systems (MBA); leadership (MA); marketing (MBA, Certificate); project management (MBA, MS, Certificate); sustainable business (Certificate); technology management (MBA, Certificate). Part-time and evening/weekend programs available. Postbaccalaureate distance learning degree programs offered (no on-campus study). *Faculty:* 6 full-time (2 women), 95 part-time/adjunct (33 women). *Students:* 397 full-time (193 women), 283 part-time (137 women); includes 127 minority (67 Black or African American, non-Hispanic/Latino; 5 American Indian or Alaska Native, non-Hispanic/Latino; 33 Asian, non-Hispanic/Latino; 15 Hispanic/Latino; 1 Native Hawaiian or other Pacific Islander, non-Hispanic/Latino; 6 Two or more races, non-Hispanic/Latino), 117 international. Average age 36. 151 applicants, 100% accepted, 151 enrolled. In 2011, 369 master's, 32 other advanced degrees awarded. *Degree requirements:* For master's, comprehensive exam (for some programs), thesis (for some programs). *Entrance requirements:* Additional exam requirements/recommendations for international students: Required—TOEFL (minimum score 567 paper-based; 227 computer-based; 87 iBT); Recommended—IELTS. *Application deadline:* For fall admission, 9/1 for international students; for winter admission, 12/1 for international students; for spring admission, 3/1 for international students. Applications are processed on a rolling basis. Application fee: $50. Electronic applications accepted. *Financial support:* Federal Work-Study and scholarships/grants available. Support available to part-time students. Financial award applicants required to submit FAFSA. *Unit head:* Dr. Kurt Kirstein, Dean, 425-637-1010 Ext. 5456, Fax: 425-709-5363, E-mail: kdkirstein@cityu.edu. *Application contact:* Alysa Borelli, Director, Recruiting, 888-422-4898, Fax: 425-709-5363, E-mail: info@cityu.edu. Web site: http://www.cityu.edu/programs/som/index.aspx.

Clark University, Graduate School, Graduate School of Management, Business Administration Program, Worcester, MA 01610-1477. Offers accounting (MBA); finance (MBA); global business (MBA); health care management (MBA); management (MBA); management of information technology (MBA); marketing (MBA). *Accreditation:* AACSB. Part-time and evening/weekend programs available. *Students:* 103 full-time (47 women), 108 part-time (41 women); includes 16 minority (7 Black or African American, non-Hispanic/Latino; 5 Asian, non-Hispanic/Latino; 4 Hispanic/Latino), 69 international. Average age 30. 371 applicants, 48% accepted, 77 enrolled. In 2011, 112 master's awarded. *Degree requirements:* For master's, thesis optional. *Application deadline:* For fall admission, 6/1 priority date for domestic students; for spring admission, 12/1 priority date for domestic students. Applications are processed on a rolling basis. Application fee: $50. Electronic applications accepted. *Expenses: Tuition:* Full-time $37,000; part-time $1156 per credit hour. *Financial support:* In 2011–12, research assistantships with partial tuition reimbursements (averaging $4,800 per year), teaching assistantships with partial tuition reimbursements (averaging $4,800 per year) were awarded; fellowships, career-related internships or fieldwork, Federal Work-Study, institutionally sponsored loans, and tuition waivers (partial) also available. Support available to part-time students. Financial award application deadline: 5/31. *Faculty research:* Marketing, accounting, human resource management, management information systems, business finance. *Unit head:* Dr. Catherine Usoff, Dean, 508-793-8822, Fax: 508-793-8822, E-mail: clarkmba@clarku.edu. *Application contact:* Patrick Oroszko, Enrollment and Marketing Director, 508-793-8822, Fax: 508-793-8822, E-mail: clarkmba@clarku.edu. Web site: http://www.clarku.edu/gsom/prospective/mba/.

Clayton State University, School of Graduate Studies, Program in Business Administration, Morrow, GA 30260-0285. Offers accounting (MBA); international business (MBA); supply chain management (MBA). *Accreditation:* AACSB. Part-time and evening/weekend programs available. *Faculty:* 12 full-time (3 women). *Students:* 35 full-time (13 women), 85 part-time (25 women); includes 85 minority (78 Black or African American, non-Hispanic/Latino; 1 American Indian or Alaska Native, non-Hispanic/Latino; 3 Asian, non-Hispanic/Latino; 2 Hispanic/Latino; 1 Two or more races, non-Hispanic/Latino), 3 international. Average age 36. 62 applicants, 87% accepted, 47 enrolled. In 2011, 38 master's awarded. *Degree requirements:* For master's, thesis. *Entrance requirements:* For master's, GMAT, 3 letters of recommendation; statement of purpose; 2 official transcripts. Additional exam requirements/recommendations for international students: Required—TOEFL (minimum score 550 paper-based; 213 computer-based; 80 iBT). *Application deadline:* For fall admission, 6/15 priority date for domestic students, 5/1 for international students; for spring admission, 11/15 priority date for domestic students, 9/1 for international students. Applications are processed on a rolling basis. Application fee: $75. Electronic applications accepted. *Expenses:* Contact institution. *Financial support:* Application deadline: 7/1; applicants required to submit FAFSA. *Unit head:* Dr. Judith Ogden, Graduate Program Director, Master of Business Administration, 678-466-4509, E-mail: judithogden@clayton.edu. *Application contact:* Michelle Terrell, Program Manager, 678-466-4500, Fax: 648-466-4599, E-mail: michelleterrell@clayton.edu. Web site: http://business.clayton.edu/MBA/.

Cleveland State University, College of Graduate Studies, Monte Ahuja College of Business, Department of Marketing, Cleveland, OH 44115. Offers global business (Graduate Certificate); marketing (MBA, DBA); marketing analytics (Graduate Certificate). *Faculty:* 12 full-time (4 women), 6 part-time/adjunct (3 women). *Students:* 1 full-time (0 women), 10 part-time (3 women); includes 1 minority (Black or African American, non-Hispanic/Latino), 1 international. Average age 43. 3 applicants, 33% accepted, 1 enrolled. In 2011, 3 other advanced degrees awarded. *Expenses:* Tuition, state resident: full-time $6416; part-time $494 per credit hour. Tuition, nonresident: full-time $12,074; part-time $929 per credit hour. *Financial support:* In 2011–12, 4 students received support, including 4 research assistantships (averaging $9,744 per year); tuition waivers (partial) also available. Financial award application deadline: 6/30; financial award applicants required to submit FAFSA. *Unit head:* Dr. Thomas W. Whipple, Chair, 216-687-4771, Fax: 216-687-5135, E-mail: t.whipple@csuohio.edu. *Application contact:* Dr. Thomas W. Whipple, Chair, 216-687-4771, Fax: 216-687-9354, E-mail: t.whipple@csuohio.edu. Web site: http://www.csuohio.edu/cba/mkt/.

Cleveland State University, College of Graduate Studies, Monte Ahuja College of Business, Doctor of Business Administration Program, Cleveland, OH 44115. Offers finance (DBA); global business (DBA); information systems (DBA); marketing (DBA); operations management (DBA). *Accreditation:* AACSB. Part-time and evening/weekend programs available. *Faculty:* 50 full-time (11 women). *Students:* 4 full-time (1 woman), 34 part-time (12 women); includes 3 minority (1 Black or African American, non-Hispanic/Latino; 2 Asian, non-Hispanic/Latino), 11 international. Average age 40. In 2011, 5 doctorates awarded. *Degree requirements:* For doctorate, comprehensive exam, thesis/dissertation, oral dissertation defense. *Entrance requirements:* For doctorate, GMAT, MBA or equivalent. Additional exam requirements/recommendations for international students: Required—TOEFL (minimum score 550 paper-based; 213 computer-based; 79 iBT). *Application deadline:* For spring admission, 2/28 priority date for domestic students, 2/28 for international students. Application fee: $30. Electronic applications accepted. *Expenses:* Tuition, state resident: full-time $6416; part-time $494 per credit hour. Tuition, nonresident: full-time $12,074; part-time $929 per credit hour. *Financial support:* In 2011–12, 5 research assistantships with full tuition reimbursements (averaging $12,700 per year), 4 teaching assistantships with full tuition reimbursements (averaging $12,700 per year) were awarded; tuition waivers (full) and unspecified assistantships also available. *Faculty research:* Supply chain management, international business, strategic management, risk analysis, consumer behavior. *Unit head:* Dr. Raj Shekhar G. Javalgi, Director, 216-687-3786, Fax: 216-687-9354, E-mail: r.javalgi@csuohio.edu. *Application contact:* Melinda J. Arnold, Administrative Secretary, 216-687-6952, Fax: 216-687-9257, E-mail: m.arnold@csuohio.edu. Web site: http://www.csuohio.edu/business/academics/doctoral.html.

Columbia Southern University, MBA Program, Orange Beach, AL 36561. Offers electronic business and technology (MBA); finance (MBA); general (MBA); healthcare management (MBA); hospitality and tourism (MBA); human resources management (MBA); international management (MBA); marketing (MBA); project management (MBA); public administration (MBA); sport management (MBA). Part-time and evening/weekend programs available. Postbaccalaureate distance learning degree programs offered (no on-campus study). *Entrance requirements:* For master's, bachelor's degree from accredited/approved institution. Additional exam requirements/recommendations for international students: Required—TOEFL. Electronic applications accepted.

Columbia University, Graduate School of Business, Executive MBA Global Program, New York, NY 10027. Offers EMBA. Program offered jointly with London Business School. *Entrance requirements:* For master's, GMAT, 2 letters of reference, interview, minimum 5 years of work experience, curriculum vitae or resume, employer support. Additional exam requirements/recommendations for international students: Recommended—TOEFL, IELTS. Electronic applications accepted. *Expenses:* Contact institution.

Columbia University, Graduate School of Business, MBA Program, New York, NY 10027. Offers accounting (MBA); decision, risk, and operations (MBA); entrepreneurship (MBA); finance and economics (MBA); healthcare and pharmaceutical management (MBA); human resource management (MBA); international business (MBA); leadership and ethics (MBA); management (MBA); marketing (MBA); media (MBA); private equity (MBA); real estate (MBA); social enterprise (MBA); value investing (MBA); DDS/MBA; JD/MBA; MBA/MIA; MBA/MPH; MBA/MS; MD/MBA. *Entrance requirements:* For master's, GMAT, 2 letters of recommendation. Additional exam requirements/recommendations for international students: Required—TOEFL. Electronic applications accepted. *Expenses:* Contact institution. *Faculty research:* Human decision making and behavioral research; real estate market and mortgage defaults; financial crisis and corporate governance; international business; security analysis and accounting.

Concordia University Wisconsin, Graduate Programs, School of Business and Legal Studies, MBA Program, Mequon, WI 53097-2402. Offers finance (MBA); health care administration (MBA); human resource management (MBA); international business (MBA); international business-bilingual English/Chinese (MBA); management (MBA); management information systems (MBA); managerial communications (MBA); marketing (MBA); public administration (MBA); risk management (MBA). Postbaccalaureate distance learning degree programs offered (minimal on-campus study). *Students:* 308 full-time (146 women), 536 part-time (288 women); includes 126 minority (76 Black or African American, non-Hispanic/Latino; 9 American Indian or Alaska Native, non-Hispanic/Latino; 15 Asian, non-Hispanic/Latino; 12 Hispanic/Latino; 14 Two or more races, non-Hispanic/Latino), 276 international. Average age 35. In 2011, 110 master's awarded. *Degree requirements:* For master's, comprehensive exam, thesis or alternative. *Entrance requirements:* Additional exam requirements/recommendations for international students: Required—TOEFL. *Application deadline:* For fall admission, 8/1 priority date for domestic students; for spring admission, 1/15 for domestic students. Applications are processed on a rolling basis. Application fee: $50. *Expenses:* Contact institution. *Financial support:* Application deadline: 8/1. *Unit head:* Dr. David Borst, Director, 262-243-4298, Fax: 262-243-4428, E-mail: david.borst@cuw.edu. *Application contact:* Mary Eberhardt, Graduate Admissions, 262-243-4551, Fax: 262-243-4428, E-mail: mary.eberhardt@cuw.edu.

Copenhagen Business School, Graduate Programs, Copenhagen, Denmark. Offers business administration (Exec MBA, MBA, PhD); business administration and information systems (M Sc); business, language and culture (M Sc); economics and business administration (M Sc); health management (MHM); international business and politics (M Sc); public administration (MPA); shipping and logistics (Exec MBA); technology, market and organization (MBA).

Daemen College, Department of Accounting/Information Systems, Amherst, NY 14226-3592. Offers global business (MS), including accounting, global business, management information systems, marketing. Part-time and evening/weekend programs available. *Degree requirements:* For master's, minimum GPA of 3.0. *Entrance requirements:* For master's, GMAT if undergraduate GPA is less than 3.0, 2 letters of recommendation; goal statement; transcripts; demonstration of satisfactory oral and written English. Additional exam requirements/recommendations for international students: Required—TOEFL (minimum score 500 paper-based; 173 computer-based; 63 iBT), IELTS (minimum score 5.5). Electronic applications accepted. *Faculty research:* Internationalization of small business, cultural influences on business practices, international human resource practices.

Dallas Baptist University, College of Business, Business Administration Program, Dallas, TX 75211-9299. Offers accounting (MBA); business communication (MBA); conflict resolution management (MBA); entrepreneurship (MBA); finance (MBA); health care management (MBA); international business (MBA); leading the non-profit organization (MBA); management (MBA); management information systems (MBA); marketing (MBA); project management (MBA); technology and engineering management (MBA). *Accreditation:* ACBSP. Part-time and evening/weekend programs available. *Entrance requirements:* For master's, GMAT, minimum GPA of 3.0. Additional exam requirements/recommendations for international students: Required—TOEFL, IELTS. *Application deadline:* Applications are processed on a rolling basis. Application fee: $25. Electronic applications accepted. *Expenses: Tuition:* Full-time $12,060; part-time $670 per credit hour. *Required fees:* $100; $50 per semester. *Financial support:* Federal Work-Study, institutionally sponsored loans, scholarships/grants, and tuition waivers (full and partial) available. Support available to part-time students. Financial award applicants required to submit FAFSA. *Faculty research:* Sports management, services marketing, retailing, strategic management, financial planning/investments. *Unit head:* Dr. Sandra S. Reid, Director, 214-333-5280, Fax: 214-333-5293, E-mail: graduate@dbu.edu. *Application contact:* Kit P. Montgomery, Director of Graduate Programs, 214-333-5242, Fax: 214-333-5579, E-mail: graduate@dbu.edu. Web site: http://www3.dbu.edu/graduate/mba.asp.

Dallas Baptist University, Gary Cook School of Leadership, Program in Global Leadership, Dallas, TX 75211-9299. Offers business communication (MA); East Asian studies (MA); ESL (MA); general studies (MA); global leadership (MA); global studies (MA); international business (MA); leading the nonprofit organization (MA); missions (MA); small group ministry (MA); MA/MA. Part-time and evening/weekend programs available. *Entrance requirements:* For master's, minimum GPA of 3.0. Additional exam requirements/recommendations for international students: Required—TOEFL, IELTS. Application fee: $25. *Expenses: Tuition:* Full-time $12,060; part-time $670 per credit hour. *Required fees:* $100; $50 per semester. *Financial support:* Federal Work-Study, institutionally sponsored loans, scholarships/grants, and tuition waivers (full and partial) available. Support available to part-time students. Financial award applicants required to submit FAFSA. *Unit head:* Dr. Bob Garrett, Director, 214-333-5508, Fax: 214-333-5689, E-mail: graduate@dbu.edu. *Application contact:* Kit P. Montgomery, Director of Graduate Programs, 214-333-5242, Fax: 214-333-5579, E-mail: graduate@dbu.edu. Web site: http://www3.dbu.edu/leadership/globalleadership.asp.

Delaware Valley College, MBA Program, Doylestown, PA 18901-2697. Offers accounting (MBA); food and agribusiness (MBA); general business (MBA); online global executive leadership (MBA). Part-time and evening/weekend programs available. Postbaccalaureate distance learning degree programs offered (no on-campus study). *Entrance requirements:* For master's, minimum undergraduate GPA of 3.0. *Expenses:* Contact institution.

DePaul University, Charles H. Kellstadt Graduate School of Business and College of Liberal Arts and Sciences, Department of Economics, Chicago, IL 60604-2287. Offers applied economics (MBA); business strategy (MBA); economics and policy analysis (MA); international business (MBA). Part-time and evening/weekend programs available. *Faculty:* 26 full-time (5 women), 21 part-time/adjunct (5 women). *Students:* 72 full-time (20 women), 27 part-time (13 women); includes 18 minority (7 Black or African American, non-Hispanic/Latino; 7 Asian, non-Hispanic/Latino; 4 Hispanic/Latino), 8 international. Average age 28. In 2011, 7 master's awarded. *Degree requirements:* For master's, thesis optional. *Entrance requirements:* For master's, GMAT (MBA), GRE (MS). Additional exam requirements/recommendations for international students: Required—TOEFL. *Application deadline:* For fall admission, 7/1 for domestic students; for winter admission, 10/1 for domestic students; for spring admission, 2/1 for domestic students. Applications are processed on a rolling basis. Application fee: $40. Electronic applications accepted. *Financial support:* In 2011–12, 3 students received support, including 2 research assistantships with partial tuition reimbursements available (averaging $9,999 per year). Support available to part-time students. *Faculty research:* Forensic economics, game theory sports, economics of education, banking in Poland and Thailand. *Unit head:* Dr. Thomas D. Donley, Chairperson, 312-362-8887, Fax: 312-362-5452, E-mail: tdonley@depaul.edu. *Application contact:* Gabriella Bucci, Director of Graduate Program, 773-362-6787, Fax: 312-362-5452, E-mail: gbucci@depaul.edu. Web site: http://economics.depaul.edu/.

Dominican University of California, Graduate Programs, School of Business and Leadership, Program in Global Management, San Rafael, CA 94901-2298. Offers MBA. Part-time programs available. *Students:* 24 full-time (12 women), 19 part-time (9 women); includes 12 minority (3 Black or African American, non-Hispanic/Latino; 1 Asian, non-Hispanic/Latino; 8 Hispanic/Latino), 16 international. Average age 30. 59 applicants, 53% accepted, 18 enrolled. In 2011, 20 master's awarded. *Degree requirements:* For master's, thesis or alternative, capstone. *Entrance requirements:* For master's, minimum GPA of 3.0. Additional exam requirements/recommendations for international students: Required—TOEFL (minimum score 550 paper-based; 213 computer-based; 80 iBT), IELTS (minimum score 7). *Application deadline:* For fall admission, 6/15 priority date for domestic students, 6/15 for international students; for spring admission, 11/15 priority date for domestic students, 11/15 for international students. Applications are processed on a rolling basis. Application fee: $40. Electronic applications accepted. *Expenses: Tuition:* Full-time $15,660. *Required fees:* $300. Tuition and fees vary according to program. *Financial support:* In 2011–12, 13 students received support. Scholarships/grants available. Support available to part-time students. Financial award application deadline: 3/2; financial award applicants required to submit FAFSA. *Unit head:* Sue Stavn, Assistant Dean, 415-482-2418, Fax: 415-459-3206, E-mail: sue.stavn@dominican.edu.

Duquesne University, School of Leadership and Professional Advancement, Pittsburgh, PA 15282-0001. Offers leadership (MS), including business ethics, community leadership, global leadership, information technology, leadership, liberal studies, professional administration, sports leadership. Part-time and evening/weekend programs available. Postbaccalaureate distance learning degree programs offered (no on-campus study). *Faculty:* 1 full-time (0 women), 88 part-time/adjunct (39 women). *Students:* 311 full-time (134 women), 151 part-time (68 women); includes 109 minority (69 Black or African American, non-Hispanic/Latino; 3 American Indian or Alaska Native, non-Hispanic/Latino; 11 Asian, non-Hispanic/Latino; 19 Hispanic/Latino; 1 Native Hawaiian or other Pacific Islander, non-Hispanic/Latino; 6 Two or more races, non-Hispanic/Latino), 9 international. Average age 35. 172 applicants, 73% accepted, 107 enrolled. In 2011, 67 degrees awarded. *Degree requirements:* For master's, capstone course. *Entrance requirements:* For master's, professional work experience, 500-word essay, resume, interview. Additional exam requirements/recommendations for international students: Required—TOEFL (minimum score 80 iBT). *Application deadline:* Applications are processed on a rolling basis. Application fee: $0. Electronic applications accepted. Application fee is waived when completed online. *Expenses: Tuition:* Full-time $16,596; part-time $922 per credit. *Required fees:* $1584; $88 per credit. Tuition and fees vary according to program. *Financial support:* Applicants required to submit FAFSA. *Unit head:* Dr. Dorothy Bassett, Dean, 412-396-2141, Fax: 412-396-4711, E-mail: bassettd@duq.edu. *Application contact:* Marianne Leister, Director of Student Services, 412-396-4933, Fax: 412-396-5072, E-mail: leister@duq.edu. Web site: http://www.duq.edu/leadership.

D'Youville College, Department of Business, Buffalo, NY 14201-1084. Offers business administration (MBA); international business (MS). Part-time and evening/weekend programs available. *Faculty:* 4 full-time (1 woman), 7 part-time/adjunct (2 women). *Students:* 54 full-time (25 women), 16 part-time (9 women); includes 16 minority (6 Black or African American, non-Hispanic/Latino; 2 Asian, non-Hispanic/Latino; 7 Hispanic/Latino; 1 Two or more races, non-Hispanic/Latino), 15 international. Average age 28. 87 applicants, 47% accepted, 26 enrolled. In 2011, 28 master's awarded. *Degree requirements:* For master's, one foreign language, project or thesis. *Entrance requirements:* For master's, minimum GPA of 3.0. Additional exam requirements/recommendations for international students: Required—TOEFL (minimum score 500 paper-based; 173 computer-based). *Application deadline:* For fall admission, 5/1 for international students; for spring admission, 9/1 for international students. Applications are processed on a rolling basis. Application fee: $25. Electronic applications accepted. *Expenses: Tuition:* Full-time $18,960; part-time $790 per credit hour. *Required fees:* $310. Tuition and fees vary according to degree level and program. *Financial support:* In 2011–12, 1 research assistantship with partial tuition reimbursement (averaging $3,000 per year) was awarded; career-related internships or fieldwork, Federal Work-Study, and scholarships/grants also available. Support available to part-time students. Financial award application deadline: 3/1; financial award applicants required to submit FAFSA. *Faculty research:* Assessment, accreditation, supply chain, online learning, adult learning. *Unit head:* Dr. Dion Daly, Chair, 716-829-8176, Fax: 716-829-7760. *Application contact:* Linda Fisher, Graduate Admissions Director, 716-829-8400, Fax: 716-829-7900, E-mail: graduateadmissions@dyc.edu. Web site: http://www.dyc.edu/academics/business/index.asp.

Eastern Michigan University, Graduate School, College of Arts and Sciences, Department of World Languages, Program in Language and International Trade, Ypsilanti, MI 48197. Offers MA. Evening/weekend programs available. *Students:* 1 (woman) full-time, 5 part-time (2 women); includes 1 minority (Black or African American, non-Hispanic/Latino), 2 international. Average age 27. 3 applicants, 100% accepted, 1 enrolled. In 2011, 2 degrees awarded. *Degree requirements:* For master's, one foreign language. *Entrance requirements:* Additional exam requirements/recommendations for international students: Required—TOEFL. *Application deadline:* Applications are processed on a rolling basis. Application fee: $35. *Expenses:* Tuition, state resident: full-time $10,367; part-time $432 per credit hour. Tuition, nonresident: full-time $20,435; part-time $851 per credit hour. *Required fees:* $39 per credit hour. $46 per semester. One-time fee: $100. Tuition and fees vary according to course level, degree level and reciprocity agreements. *Financial support:* Fellowships, research assistantships with full tuition reimbursements, teaching assistantships with full tuition reimbursements, career-related internships or fieldwork, Federal Work-Study, institutionally sponsored loans, scholarships/grants, tuition waivers (partial), and unspecified assistantships available. Support available to part-time students. Financial award applicants required to submit FAFSA. *Unit head:* Dr. Rosemary Weston-Gil, Department Head, 734-487-0130, Fax: 734-487-3411, E-mail: rweston3@emich.edu. *Application contact:* Dr. Genevieve Peden, Program Advisor, 734-487-1498, Fax: 734-487-3411, E-mail: gpeden@emich.edu.

Eastern Michigan University, Graduate School, College of Arts and Sciences, Department of World Languages, Programs in Foreign Languages, Ypsilanti, MI 48197. Offers French (MA); German (MA); German for business (Graduate Certificate); Hispanic language and cultures (Graduate Certificate); Japanese business practices (Graduate Certificate); Spanish (MA). Part-time and evening/weekend programs available. Postbaccalaureate distance learning degree programs offered (minimal on-campus study). *Students:* 12 part-time (9 women); includes 6 minority (1 Black or African American, non-Hispanic/Latino; 1 Asian, non-Hispanic/Latino; 4 Hispanic/Latino). Average age 44. 9 applicants, 67% accepted, 5 enrolled. In 2011, 3 degrees awarded. *Degree requirements:* For master's, one foreign language, thesis optional. *Entrance requirements:* Additional exam requirements/recommendations for international students: Required—TOEFL. *Application deadline:* Applications are processed on a rolling basis. Application fee: $35. *Expenses:* Tuition, state resident: full-time $10,367; part-time $432 per credit hour. Tuition, nonresident: full-time $20,435; part-time $851 per credit hour. *Required fees:* $39 per credit hour. $46 per semester. One-time fee: $100. Tuition and fees vary according to course level, degree level and reciprocity agreements. *Financial support:* Fellowships, research assistantships with full tuition reimbursements, teaching assistantships with full tuition reimbursements, career-related internships or fieldwork, Federal Work-Study, institutionally sponsored loans, scholarships/grants, tuition waivers (partial), and unspecified assistantships available. Support available to part-time students. Financial award applicants required to submit FAFSA. *Unit head:* Dr. Rosemary Weston-Gil, Department Head, 734-487-0130, Fax: 734-487-3411, E-mail: rweston3@emich.edu. *Application contact:* Dr. Genevieve Peden, Program Advisor, 734-487-1498, Fax: 734-487-3411, E-mail: gpeden@emich.edu.

Eastern Michigan University, Graduate School, College of Business, Programs in Business Administration, Ypsilanti, MI 48197. Offers business administration (MBA, Graduate Certificate); computer information systems (Graduate Certificate); e-business (MBA, Graduate Certificate); enterprise business intelligence (MBA); entrepreneurship (MBA, Graduate Certificate); finance (MBA, Graduate Certificate); human resources (MBA); human resources management (Graduate Certificate); information systems (MBA); internal auditing (MBA); international business (MBA, Graduate Certificate); marketing management (Graduate Certificate); nonprofit management (MBA); organizational development (Graduate Certificate); supply chain management (MBA, Graduate Certificate). *Accreditation:* AACSB. Part-time programs available. Postbaccalaureate distance learning degree programs offered (no on-campus study). *Students:* 79 full-time (39 women), 287 part-time (143 women); includes 55 minority (22 Black or African American, non-Hispanic/Latino; 24 Asian, non-Hispanic/Latino; 6 Hispanic/Latino; 3 Two or more races, non-Hispanic/Latino), 238 international. Average age 32. 317 applicants, 62% accepted, 89 enrolled. In 2011, 102 master's, 58 other advanced degrees awarded. *Entrance requirements:* For master's, GMAT (minimum score 450), minimum cumulative undergraduate GPA of 2.75. Additional exam requirements/recommendations for international students: Required—TOEFL. *Application deadline:* For fall admission, 5/15 for domestic students, 5/1 for international students; for winter admission, 10/15 for domestic students, 10/1 for international students; for spring admission, 3/15 for domestic students, 3/1 for international students. Applications are processed on a rolling basis. Application fee: $35. *Expenses:* Tuition, state resident: full-time $10,367; part-time $432 per credit hour. Tuition, nonresident: full-time $20,435; part-time $851 per credit hour. *Required fees:* $39 per credit hour. $46 per semester. One-time fee: $100. Tuition and fees vary according to course level, degree level and reciprocity agreements. *Financial support:* Fellowships, research assistantships with full tuition reimbursements, teaching assistantships with full tuition reimbursements, career-related internships or fieldwork, Federal Work-Study, institutionally sponsored loans, scholarships/grants, tuition waivers (partial), and unspecified assistantships available. Support available to part-time students. Financial award applicants required to submit FAFSA. *Unit head:* K. Michelle Henry, Director, Academic Services, 734-487-4444, Fax: 734-483-1316, E-mail: mhenry1@emich.edu. *Application contact:* Beste Windes, Advisor, 734-487-4444, Fax: 734-483-1316, E-mail: bwindes@emich.edu. Web site: http://www.emich.edu/public/cob/gr/grad.html.

Ellis University, MBA Program, Chicago, IL 60606-7204. Offers e-commerce (MBA); finance (MBA); general business (MBA); global management (MBA); health care administration (MBA); leadership (MBA); management of information systems (MBA); marketing (MBA); professional accounting (MBA); project management (MBA); public accounting (MBA); risk management (MBA).

Emerson College, Graduate Studies, School of Communication, Department of Marketing Communication, Program in Global Marketing Communication and Advertising, Boston, MA 02116-4624. Offers MA. *Entrance requirements:* For master's, GMAT or GRE General Test. Additional exam requirements/recommendations for international students: Required—TOEFL (minimum score 550 paper-based; 213 computer-based; 80 iBT), IELTS (minimum score 6.5). Electronic applications accepted. *Faculty research:* International business, marketing.

ESSEC Business School, Graduate Programs, Paris, France. Offers business administration (PhD); executive business administration (MBA); global business administration (MBA); hospitality management (MBA); international luxury brand management (MBA); management (MSM).

Everest University, Department of Business Administration, Tampa, FL 33614-5899. Offers accounting (MBA); human resources (MBA); international business (MBA). Part-time and evening/weekend programs available. *Degree requirements:* For master's, thesis optional. *Entrance requirements:* For master's, GMAT or GRE General Test, minimum GPA of 3.0.

Everest University, Program in Business Administration, Orlando, FL 32819. Offers accounting (MBA); general management (MBA); human resources (MBA); international management (MBA).

Fairfield University, Charles F. Dolan School of Business, Fairfield, CT 06824-5195. Offers accounting (MBA, MS, CAS); accounting information systems (MBA, CAS); entrepreneurship (MBA, CAS); finance (MBA, MS, CAS); general management (MBA, CAS); human resource management (MBA, CAS); information systems and operations (MBA); information systems and operations management (CAS); international business (MBA, CAS); marketing (MBA, CAS); taxation (MBA, CAS). *Accreditation:* AACSB. Part-time and evening/weekend programs available. *Faculty:* 23 full-time (9 women), 3 part-time/adjunct (1 woman). *Students:* 87 full-time (37 women), 118 part-time (42 women); includes 13 minority (4 Black or African American, non-Hispanic/Latino; 4 Asian, non-Hispanic/Latino; 5 Hispanic/Latino), 9 international. Average age 29. 126 applicants, 47% accepted, 35 enrolled. In 2011, 90 master's awarded. *Degree requirements:* For master's, capstone course. *Entrance requirements:* For master's, GMAT (minimum score 500), 2 letters of reference, resume, minimum GPA of 3.0. Additional exam requirements/recommendations for international students: Required—TOEFL (minimum score 550 paper-based; 213 computer-bases; 80 iBT) or IELTS (minimum score 6.5). *Application deadline:* For fall admission, 5/15 for international students; for spring admission, 10/15 for international students. Applications are processed on a rolling basis. Application fee: $60. Electronic applications accepted. *Expenses:* Contact institution. *Financial support:* In 2011–12, 50 students received support, including 2 research assistantships (averaging $6,500 per year); scholarships/grants, unspecified assistantships, and merit-based one-time entrance scholarship also available. Financial award applicants required to submit FAFSA. *Faculty research:* Optimization strategies, international finance, consumer behavior, financial market volatility, Internet marketing, supply chain analysis, tax issues. *Unit head:* Dr. Donald Gibson, Dean, 203-254-4000 Ext. 4070, Fax: 203-254-4105, E-mail: dgibson@fairfield.edu. *Application contact:* Marianne Gumpper, Director of Graduate and Continuing Studies Admission, 203-254-4184, Fax: 203-254-4073, E-mail: gradadmis@fairfield.edu. Web site: http://www.fairfield.edu/dsb/dsb_grad_1.html.

Fairleigh Dickinson University, College at Florham, Silberman College of Business, Department of Economics, Finance, and International Business, Program in International Business, Madison, NJ 07940-1099. Offers MBA, Certificate.

Fairleigh Dickinson University, Metropolitan Campus, Silberman College of Business, Department of Economics, Finance and International Business, Program in International Business, Teaneck, NJ 07666-1914. Offers MBA.

Florida Atlantic University, College of Business, Department of Management Programs, Boca Raton, FL 33431-0991. Offers global entrepreneurship (MBA); international business (MBA, MS); management (PhD). *Faculty:* 30 full-time (10 women), 24 part-time/adjunct (9 women). *Students:* 299 full-time (121 women), 459 part-time (199 women); includes 297 minority (99 Black or African American, non-Hispanic/Latino; 1 American Indian or Alaska Native, non-Hispanic/Latino; 45 Asian, non-Hispanic/Latino; 136 Hispanic/Latino; 1 Native Hawaiian or other Pacific Islander, non-Hispanic/Latino; 15 Two or more races, non-Hispanic/Latino), 40 international. Average age 33. 725 applicants, 51% accepted, 132 enrolled. In 2011, 259 master's, 4 doctorates awarded. *Entrance requirements:* For master's, GMAT or GRE General Test, minimum GPA of 3.0 in last 60 hours of course work. Additional exam requirements/recommendations for international students: Required—TOEFL (minimum score 600 paper-based; 250 computer-based). *Application deadline:* For fall admission, 7/25 for domestic students, 2/15 for international students; for spring admission, 12/10 for domestic students, 7/15 for international students. Applications are processed on a rolling basis. Application fee: $30. Electronic applications accepted. *Expenses: Tuition, area resident:* Part-time $343.02 per credit hour. Tuition, state resident: full-time $8232. Tuition, nonresident: full-time $23,931; part-time $997.14 per credit hour. *Financial support:* Research assistantships with full tuition reimbursements, career-related internships or fieldwork, tuition waivers (partial), and unspecified assistantships available. *Faculty research:* Sports administration, healthcare, policy, finance, real estate, senior living. *Unit head:* Dr. Peggy Golden, Chair, 561-297-2675, E-mail: golden@fau.edu. *Application contact:* Fredrick G. Taylor, Graduate Adviser, 561-297-3196, Fax: 561-297-1315, E-mail: ftaylor@fau.edu. Web site: http://business.fau.edu/departments/management/index.aspx.

Florida Institute of Technology, Graduate Programs, Nathan M. Bisk College of Business, Online Programs, Melbourne, FL 32901-6975. Offers accounting (MBA); accounting and finance (MBA); business administration (MBA); finance (MBA); healthcare management (MBA); information technology (MS); information technology cybersecurity (MS); information technology management (MBA); international business (MBA); Internet marketing (MBA); management (MBA); marketing (MBA); project management (MBA). Part-time and evening/weekend programs available. Postbaccalaureate distance learning degree programs offered (no on-campus study). *Faculty:* 47 part-time/adjunct (15 women). *Students:* 8 full-time (4 women), 1,122 part-time (547 women); includes 418 minority (271 Black or African American, non-Hispanic/Latino; 5 American Indian or Alaska Native, non-Hispanic/Latino; 55 Asian, non-Hispanic/Latino; 81 Hispanic/Latino; 6 Native Hawaiian or other Pacific Islander, non-Hispanic/Latino), 23 international. Average age 36. In 2011, 329 master's awarded. *Entrance requirements:* For master's, GMAT or resume showing 8 years of supervised experience, 2 letters of recommendation, resume, competency in math past college algebra. Additional exam requirements/recommendations for international students: Required—TOEFL (minimum score 550 paper-based; 213 computer-based; 79 iBT). *Application deadline:* For fall admission, 4/1 for international students; for spring admission, 9/30 for international students. Applications are processed on a rolling basis. Electronic applications accepted. *Expenses:* Contact institution. *Financial support:* Available to part-time students. Application deadline: 3/1; applicants required to submit FAFSA. *Unit head:* Dr. Mary S. Bonhomme, Dean, Florida Tech Online/Associate Provost for Online Learning, 321-674-8202, Fax: 321-674-8216, E-mail: bonhomme@fit.edu. *Application contact:* Carolyn Farrior, Director of Graduate Admissions, Online Learning and Off-Campus Programs, 321-674-7118, Fax: 321-674-8216, E-mail: cfarrior@fit.edu. Web site: http://online.fit.edu.

Florida International University, Alvah H. Chapman, Jr. Graduate School of Business, Department of Management and International Business, International Business Program, Miami, FL 33199. Offers MIB. Part-time and evening/weekend programs available. *Entrance requirements:* For master's, GRE or GMAT, minimum GPA of 3.0 (upper-level coursework), letter of intent, bachelor's degree in business administration or related area, resume, at least two years of work experience. Additional exam requirements/recommendations for international students: Required—TOEFL (minimum score 550 paper-based; 213 computer-based; 80 iBT) or IELTS (minimum score 6.5). Electronic applications accepted. *Expenses:* Contact institution. *Faculty research:* Strategy, international business, multinational corporations.

Friends University, Graduate School, Wichita, KS 67213. Offers accounting (MBA); business administration (MBA); business law (MBL); Christian ministry (MACM); environment science (MSES); family therapy (MSFT); global leadership and management (MA); health care leadership (MHCL); management information systems (MMIS); operations management (MSOM); organization development (MSOD); teaching

(MAT). Part-time and evening/weekend programs available. Postbaccalaureate distance learning degree programs offered (no on-campus study). *Faculty:* 14 full-time (5 women), 2 part-time/adjunct (1 woman). *Students:* 158 full-time (114 women), 616 part-time (367 women); includes 159 minority (83 Black or African American, non-Hispanic/Latino; 12 American Indian or Alaska Native, non-Hispanic/Latino; 26 Asian, non-Hispanic/Latino; 22 Hispanic/Latino; 2 Native Hawaiian or other Pacific Islander, non-Hispanic/Latino; 14 Two or more races, non-Hispanic/Latino). Average age 36. 497 applicants, 68% accepted, 256 enrolled. In 2011, 341 degrees awarded. *Degree requirements:* For master's, research project. *Entrance requirements:* For master's, bachelor's degree from accredited institution, official transcripts from institution granting bachelor's degree, interview with program director, letter(s) of recommendation. Additional exam requirements/recommendations for international students: Required—TOEFL (minimum score 560 paper-based; 220 computer-based). *Application deadline:* Applications are processed on a rolling basis. Application fee: $45 ($65 for international students). Electronic applications accepted. *Expenses: Tuition:* Part-time $601 per credit hour. One-time fee: $45 full-time. Tuition and fees vary according to campus/location and program. *Financial support:* Applicants required to submit FAFSA. *Unit head:* Dr. Evelyn Hume, Dean, 800-794-6945 Ext. 5859, Fax: 316-295-5040, E-mail: evelyn_hume@friends.edu. *Application contact:* Jeanette Hanson, Executive Director of Adult Recruitment, 800-794-6945, Fax: 316-295-5050, E-mail: jeanette@friends.edu. Web site: http://www.friends.edu.

George Mason University, College of Humanities and Social Sciences, Program in Global Affairs, Fairfax, VA 22030. Offers MA. *Expenses:* Tuition, state resident: full-time $8750; part-time $364.58 per credit. Tuition, nonresident: full-time $24,092; part-time $1003.83 per credit. *Required fees:* $2514; $104.75 per credit. *Application contact:* Laura Layland, Graduate Admissions Assistant, 703-993-2409, E-mail: llayland@gmu.edu.

Georgetown University, Graduate School of Arts and Sciences, Department of Economics, Washington, DC 20057. Offers econometrics (PhD); economic development (PhD); economic theory (PhD); industrial organization (PhD); international macro and finance (PhD); international trade (PhD); labor economics (PhD); macroeconomics (PhD); public economics and political economics (PhD); MA/PhD; MS/MA. *Degree requirements:* For doctorate, comprehensive exam, thesis/dissertation. *Entrance requirements:* For doctorate, GRE General Test. Additional exam requirements/recommendations for international students: Required—TOEFL. *Faculty research:* International economics, economic development.

Georgetown University, Graduate School of Arts and Sciences, McDonough School of Business, Washington, DC 20057. Offers business administration (IEMBA, MBA). *Accreditation:* AACSB. *Entrance requirements:* For master's, GMAT. Additional exam requirements/recommendations for international students: Required—TOEFL. *Expenses:* Contact institution.

Georgetown University, Law Center, Washington, DC 20001. Offers global health law (LL M); individualized study (LL M); international business and economic law (LL M); law (JD, SJD); national security law (LL M); securities and financial regulation (LL M); taxation (LL M); JD/LL M; JD/MA; JD/MBA; JD/MPH; JD/PhD. *Accreditation:* ABA. Part-time and evening/weekend programs available. *Degree requirements:* For master's, thesis; for doctorate, thesis/dissertation (for some programs). *Entrance requirements:* For master's, JD, LL B, or first law degree earned in country of origin; for doctorate, LSAT (for JD). Additional exam requirements/recommendations for international students: Required—TOEFL. *Expenses:* Contact institution. *Faculty research:* Constitutional law, legal history, jurisprudence.

The George Washington University, Elliott School of International Affairs, Program in International Trade and Investment Policy, Washington, DC 20052. Offers MA, JD/MA, MBA/MA. Part-time and evening/weekend programs available. *Students:* 37 full-time (19 women), 13 part-time (8 women); includes 5 minority (1 Black or African American, non-Hispanic/Latino; 1 American Indian or Alaska Native, non-Hispanic/Latino; 1 Asian, non-Hispanic/Latino; 2 Two or more races, non-Hispanic/Latino), 15 international. Average age 26. 102 applicants, 65% accepted, 22 enrolled. In 2011, 27 master's awarded. *Degree requirements:* For master's, one foreign language, capstone project. *Entrance requirements:* For master's, GRE General Test, 2 years of a modern foreign language, 2 semesters of introductory economics. Additional exam requirements/recommendations for international students: Required—TOEFL. *Application deadline:* For fall admission, 2/1 for domestic students; for spring admission, 10/1 for domestic students. Application fee: $75. Electronic applications accepted. *Financial support:* In 2011–12, 11 students received support. Fellowships with tuition reimbursements available, research assistantships with tuition reimbursements available, career-related internships or fieldwork, Federal Work-Study, institutionally sponsored loans, and tuition waivers available. Financial award application deadline: 1/15. *Unit head:* Steven Suranovic, Director, 202-994-7579, Fax: 202-994-5477, E-mail: smsuran@gwu.edu. *Application contact:* Jeff V. Miles, Director of Graduate Admissions, 202-994-7050, Fax: 202-994-9537, E-mail: esiagrad@gwu.edu. Web site: http://www.gwu.edu/~elliott/academics/grad/itip/.

The George Washington University, School of Business, Department of International Business, Washington, DC 20052. Offers MBA, PhD, MBA/MA. Part-time and evening/weekend programs available. *Faculty:* 18 full-time (8 women), 3 part-time/adjunct (1 woman). *Degree requirements:* For doctorate, thesis/dissertation. *Entrance requirements:* For master's, GMAT; for doctorate, GMAT or GRE. Additional exam requirements/recommendations for international students: Required—TOEFL. *Application deadline:* For fall admission, 4/1 priority date for domestic students; for spring admission, 10/1 for domestic students. Applications are processed on a rolling basis. Application fee: $75. *Financial support:* Fellowships, teaching assistantships, career-related internships or fieldwork, Federal Work-Study, and institutionally sponsored loans available. Financial award application deadline: 4/1. *Faculty research:* International trade, competitiveness, business management. *Unit head:* Reid Click, Chair, 202-994-7130, E-mail: rclick@gwu.edu. *Application contact:* Kristin Williams, Assistant Vice President for Graduate and Special Enrollment Management, 202-994-0467, Fax: 202-994-0371, E-mail: ksw@gwu.edu. Web site: http://www.ibusdept.com/.

Georgia Institute of Technology, Graduate Studies and Research, College of Management, Program in Business Administration, Atlanta, GA 30332-0001. Offers accounting (MBA); e-commerce (Certificate); engineering entrepreneurship (MBA); entrepreneurship (Certificate); finance (MBA); information technology management (MBA); international business (MBA, Certificate); management of technology (Certificate); marketing (MBA); operations management (MBA); organizational behavior (MBA); strategic management (MBA). *Accreditation:* AACSB.

Georgia State University, J. Mack Robinson College of Business, Institute of International Business, Atlanta, GA 30303. Offers MBA, MIB, MIB/MAPOLS. Part-time and evening/weekend programs available. *Entrance requirements:* For master's, GMAT. Additional exam requirements/recommendations for international students: Required—TOEFL (minimum score 610 paper-based; 255 computer-based; 101 iBT). Electronic applications accepted. *Faculty research:* Emerging markets, international business strategy, international business transactions, multi-international enterprise, international buyer seller relations.

Georgia State University, J. Mack Robinson College of Business, Program in General Business Administration, Atlanta, GA 30302-3083. Offers accounting/information systems (MBA); economics (MBA, MS); enterprise risk management (MBA); general business (MBA); general business administration (EMBA, PMBA); information systems consulting (MBA); information systems risk management (MBA); international business and information technology (MBA); international entrepreneurship (MBA); MBA/JD. *Accreditation:* AACSB. Part-time and evening/weekend programs available. *Entrance requirements:* For master's, GMAT. Additional exam requirements/recommendations for international students: Required—TOEFL (minimum score 610 paper-based; 255 computer-based; 101 iBT). Electronic applications accepted.

Golden Gate University, Ageno School of Business, San Francisco, CA 94105-2968. Offers accounting (MBA); business administration (EMBA, MBA, PMBA, DBA); finance (MBA, MS, Certificate); financial planning (MS, Certificate); healthcare information systems (Certificate); human resource management (MBA, MS); human resources management (Certificate); information systems (MS); information technology (MBA); information technology management (Certificate); integrated marketing and communications (MS, Certificate); international business (MBA); management (MBA); marketing (MBA, MS, Certificate); operations supply chain management (Certificate); psychology (MA, Certificate); public administration (EMPA); public relations (MS, Certificate); technical market analysis (Certificate); JD/MBA. Part-time and evening/weekend programs available. *Faculty:* 19 full-time (6 women), 241 part-time/adjunct (72 women). *Students:* 397 full-time (230 women), 779 part-time (432 women); includes 376 minority (105 Black or African American, non-Hispanic/Latino; 5 American Indian or Alaska Native, non-Hispanic/Latino; 161 Asian, non-Hispanic/Latino; 77 Hispanic/Latino; 12 Native Hawaiian or other Pacific Islander, non-Hispanic/Latino; 16 Two or more races, non-Hispanic/Latino), 265 international. Average age 34. 871 applicants, 64% accepted, 271 enrolled. In 2011, 550 master's, 13 doctorates awarded. *Degree requirements:* For doctorate, thesis/dissertation, qualifying examination. *Entrance requirements:* For master's, GMAT (MBA), minimum GPA of 2.5 (MS). Additional exam requirements/recommendations for international students: Required—TOEFL (minimum score 550 paper-based; 213 computer-based; 79 iBT). *Application deadline:* For fall admission, 5/15 for domestic and international students; for winter admission, 1/15 for domestic and international students; for spring admission, 9/15 for domestic and international students. Applications are processed on a rolling basis. Application fee: $70 ($110 for international students). Electronic applications accepted. *Expenses:* Contact institution. *Financial support:* Career-related internships or fieldwork, Federal Work-Study, institutionally sponsored loans, and scholarships/grants available. Support available to part-time students. Financial award applicants required to submit FAFSA. *Unit head:* Dr. Paul Fouts, Dean, 415-442-7026, Fax: 415-442-6579. *Application contact:* Angela Melero, Enrollment Services, 415-442-7800, Fax: 415-442-7807, E-mail: info@ggu.edu. Web site: http://www.ggu.edu/programs/business-and-management.

Goldey-Beacom College, Graduate Program, Wilmington, DE 19808-1999. Offers business administration (MBA); finance (MS); financial management (MBA); health care management (MBA); human resource management (MBA); information technology (MBA); international business management (MBA); major finance (MBA); major taxation (MBA); management (MM); marketing management (MBA); taxation (MBA, MS). *Accreditation:* ACBSP. Part-time and evening/weekend programs available. *Faculty:* 19 full-time (7 women), 35 part-time/adjunct (12 women). *Students:* 58 full-time (32 women), 388 part-time (164 women); includes 89 minority (34 Black or African American, non-Hispanic/Latino; 2 American Indian or Alaska Native, non-Hispanic/Latino; 44 Asian, non-Hispanic/Latino; 9 Hispanic/Latino), 229 international. Average age 30. In 2011, 243 master's awarded. *Entrance requirements:* For master's, GMAT, MAT, GRE, minimum GPA of 3.0. Additional exam requirements/recommendations for international students: Required—TOEFL (minimum score 65 computer-based); Recommended—IELTS (minimum score 5). *Application deadline:* Applications are processed on a rolling basis. Application fee: $0. Electronic applications accepted. *Expenses: Tuition:* Full-time $15,750; part-time $875 per credit. *Required fees:* $10 per credit. *Financial support:* Scholarships/grants available. Support available to part-time students. Financial award application deadline: 4/1; financial award applicants required to submit FAFSA. *Unit head:* Larry W. Eby, Director of Admissions, 302-225-6289, Fax: 302-996-5408, E-mail: ebylw@gbc.edu. *Application contact:* Ashley E. Mashington, Graduate Admissions Representative, 302-225-6259, Fax: 302-996-5408, E-mail: mashina@gbc.edu. Web site: http://www.gbc.edu/programs/graduate/.

Harding University, Paul R. Carter College of Business Administration, Searcy, AR 72149-0001. Offers health care management (MBA); information technology management (MBA); international business (MBA); leadership and organizational management (MBA). *Accreditation:* ACBSP. Part-time and evening/weekend programs available. Postbaccalaureate distance learning degree programs offered (no on-campus study). *Faculty:* 30 part-time/adjunct (6 women). *Students:* 60 full-time (25 women), 140 part-time (63 women); includes 33 minority (26 Black or African American, non-Hispanic/Latino; 1 American Indian or Alaska Native, non-Hispanic/Latino; 3 Asian, non-Hispanic/Latino; 1 Hispanic/Latino; 2 Two or more races, non-Hispanic/Latino), 24 international. Average age 30. 65 applicants, 98% accepted, 64 enrolled. In 2011, 120 master's awarded. *Degree requirements:* For master's, portfolio. *Entrance requirements:* For master's, GMAT (minimum score of 500) or GRE (minimum score of 300), minimum GPA of 3.0, 2 letters of recommendation, resume, 3 essays, all official transcripts. Additional exam requirements/recommendations for international students: Required—TOEFL (minimum score 550 paper-based; 213 computer-based; 79 iBT). *Application deadline:* For fall admission, 8/1 priority date for domestic students, 8/1 for international students; for spring admission, 12/1 priority date for domestic students, 12/1 for international students. Applications are processed on a rolling basis. Application fee: $40. *Expenses: Tuition:* Full-time $10,512; part-time $584 per credit hour. *Required fees:* $500; $25 per credit hour. Tuition and fees vary according to course load, degree level and program. *Financial support:* In 2011–12, 19 students received support. Unspecified assistantships available. Financial award application deadline: 7/30; financial award applicants required to submit FAFSA. *Unit head:* Glen Metheny, Director of Graduate Studies, 501-279-5851, Fax: 501-279-4805, E-mail: gmetheny@harding.edu. *Application contact:* Melanie Kiihnl, Recruiting Manager/Director of Marketing, 501-279-4523, Fax: 501-279-4805, E-mail: mba@harding.edu. Web site: http://www.harding.edu/mba.

Hawai`i Pacific University, College of Business Administration, Honolulu, HI 96813. Offers accounting/CPA (MBA); e-business (MBA); economics (MBA); finance (MBA); human resource management (MA, MBA); information systems (MBA, MSIS), including knowledge management (MSIS), software engineering (MSIS), telecommunications security (MSIS); international business (MBA); management (MBA); marketing (MBA); organizational change (MA, MBA); travel industry management (MBA). Part-time and evening/weekend programs available. *Faculty:* 15 full-time (5 women), 11 part-time/adjunct (4 women). *Students:* 297 full-time (133 women), 183 part-time (87 women); includes 282 minority (17 Black or African American, non-Hispanic/Latino; 131 Asian, non-Hispanic/Latino; 43 Hispanic/Latino; 10 Native Hawaiian or other Pacific Islander, non-Hispanic/Latino; 81 Two or more races, non-Hispanic/Latino). Average age 30. 302 applicants, 82% accepted, 160 enrolled. In 2011, 141 master's awarded. *Degree requirements:* For master's, thesis. *Entrance requirements:* For master's, GMAT.

Additional exam requirements/recommendations for international students: Recommended—TOEFL (minimum score 550 paper-based; 213 computer-based; 80 iBT), TWE (minimum score 5). *Application deadline:* For fall admission, 2/15 priority date for domestic students; for spring admission, 10/15 priority date for domestic students. Applications are processed on a rolling basis. Application fee: $50. Electronic applications accepted. *Expenses: Tuition:* Full-time $13,230; part-time $735 per credit. Tuition and fees vary according to course load and program. *Financial support:* In 2011–12, 103 students received support. Research assistantships, career-related internships or fieldwork, Federal Work-Study, scholarships/grants, tuition waivers, and unspecified assistantships available. Financial award application deadline: 3/1; financial award applicants required to submit FAFSA. *Faculty research:* Statistical control process as used by management, studies in comparative cross-cultural management styles, not-for-profit management. *Unit head:* Dr. Deborah Crown, Dean, 808-544-0275, Fax: 808-544-0283, E-mail: dcrown@hpu.edu. *Application contact:* Chad Schempp, Director of Graduate Admissions, 808-543-8035, Fax: 808-544-0280, E-mail: graduate@hpu.edu. Web site: http://www.hpu.edu/mba.

See Display on page 98 and Close-Up on page 221.

HEC Montreal, School of Business Administration, Master of Science Programs in Administration, Program in International Business, Montréal, QC H3T 2A7, Canada. Offers M Sc. Part-time programs available. *Students:* 54 full-time (24 women), 16 part-time (10 women). 62 applicants, 50% accepted, 16 enrolled. In 2011, 25 master's awarded. *Degree requirements:* For master's, one foreign language, thesis. *Entrance requirements:* For master's, Test de francais international (TFI) with minimum score of 850 (for those who have never studied in French), BBA, undergraduate degree in another field, degree deemed equivalent by program director and minimum GPA of 3.0 on 4.3 scale. *Application deadline:* For fall admission, 3/15 for domestic and international students; for winter admission, 9/15 for domestic and international students. Application fee: $80. Electronic applications accepted. Application fee is waived when completed online. *Expenses:* Tuition, state resident: full-time $2601.36. Tuition, nonresident: full-time $7030. *International tuition:* $17,474.04 full-time. *Required fees:* $1381.77. Tuition and fees vary according to degree level and program. *Financial support:* Research assistantships and teaching assistantships available. Financial award application deadline: 9/2. *Unit head:* Dr. Claude Laurin, Director, 514-340-6485, Fax: 514-340-6880, E-mail: claude.laurin@hec.ca. *Application contact:* Virginie Lefebvre, Administrative Director, 514-340-6112, Fax: 514-340-6411, E-mail: virginie.lefebvre@hec.ca. Web site: http://www.hec.ca/en/programs_training/msc/options/international_business/index.html.

Hofstra University, Frank G. Zarb School of Business, Department of Marketing and International Business, Hempstead, NY 11549. Offers business administration (MBA), including international business, marketing; international business (Advanced Certificate); marketing (MS, Advanced Certificate); marketing research (MS). Part-time and evening/weekend programs available. *Faculty:* 9 full-time (0 women), 3 part-time/adjunct (0 women). *Students:* 91 full-time (54 women), 39 part-time (20 women); includes 11 minority (2 Black or African American, non-Hispanic/Latino; 3 Asian, non-Hispanic/Latino; 6 Hispanic/Latino), 73 international. Average age 27. 260 applicants, 71% accepted, 46 enrolled. In 2011, 43 master's awarded. *Degree requirements:* For master's, capstone course (MBA), thesis (MS), minimum GPA of 3.0. *Entrance requirements:* For master's, GMAT or GRE, 2 letters of recommendation, resume, essay. Additional exam requirements/recommendations for international students: Required—TOEFL (minimum score 550 paper-based; 213 computer-based; 80 iBT); Recommended—IELTS (minimum score 6). *Application deadline:* Applications are processed on a rolling basis. Application fee: $70 ($75 for international students). Electronic applications accepted. *Expenses:* Contact institution. *Financial support:* In 2011–12, 19 students received support, including 18 fellowships with full and partial tuition reimbursements available (averaging $7,371 per year); research assistantships with full and partial tuition reimbursements available, career-related internships or fieldwork, Federal Work-Study, institutionally sponsored loans, scholarships/grants, tuition waivers (full and partial), and unspecified assistantships also available. Support available to part-time students. Financial award applicants required to submit FAFSA. *Faculty research:* Outsourcing, global alliances, retailing, Web marketing, cross-cultural age research. *Unit head:* Dr. Benny Barak, Chairperson, 516-463-5707, Fax: 516-463-4834, E-mail: mktbzb@hofstra.edu. *Application contact:* Carol Drummer, Dean of Graduate Admissions, 516-463-4876, Fax: 516-463-4664, E-mail: gradstudent@hofstra.edu. Web site: http://www.hofstra.edu/business/.

Hope International University, School of Graduate and Professional Studies, Program in Business Administration, Fullerton, CA 92831-3138. Offers general management (MBA, MSM); international development (MBA, MSM); marketing management (MBA, MSM); non-profit management (MBA, MSM). Part-time programs available. Postbaccalaureate distance learning degree programs offered (no on-campus study). *Degree requirements:* For master's, comprehensive exam (for some programs), thesis (for some programs), project. *Entrance requirements:* For master's, minimum GPA of 3.0; 2 references. Additional exam requirements/recommendations for international students: Required—TOEFL (minimum score 550 paper-based; 213 computer-based; 86 iBT); Recommended—IELTS (minimum score 6.5). Electronic applications accepted. *Expenses:* Contact institution.

Howard University, School of Business, Graduate Programs in Business, Washington, DC 20059-0002. Offers accounting (MBA); entrepreneurship (MBA); finance (MBA); general management (MBA); human resources management (MBA); information systems (MBA); international business (MBA); marketing (MBA); supply chain management (MBA); JD/MBA. *Accreditation:* AACSB. Part-time and evening/weekend programs available. Postbaccalaureate distance learning degree programs offered (no on-campus study). *Entrance requirements:* For master's, GMAT, minimum 1 year post undergraduate work experience, resume, 3 letters of recommendation, advanced college algebra. Additional exam requirements/recommendations for international students: Required—TOEFL. *Faculty research:* Marketing research in multi-ethnic populations, U.S. trade policies and international relations, risk management (finance).

Hult International Business School, Program in Business Administration - Hult London Campus, London, MA WC 1B 4JP, United Kingdom. Offers entrepreneurship (MBA); international business (MBA); international finance (MBA); marketing (MBA). Part-time programs available. *Degree requirements:* For master's, comprehensive exam, thesis, internship. *Entrance requirements:* Additional exam requirements/recommendations for international students: Required—TOEFL (minimum score 580 paper-based; 237 computer-based), TWE (minimum score 5). Electronic applications accepted.

Hult International Business School, Program in International Business, Cambridge, MA 02141. Offers MIB.

Hult International Business School, Program in International Business - Hult Dubai Campus, Dubai, MA 02141, United Arab Emirates. Offers MIB.

Hult International Business School, Program in International Business - Hult London Campus, London, MA WC 1B 4JP, United Kingdom. Offers MIB.

Hult International Business School, Program in International Business - Hult San Francisco Campus, San Francisco, CA 94133. Offers MIB.

Indiana Tech, Program in Global Leadership, Fort Wayne, IN 46803-1297. Offers PhD. Part-time and evening/weekend programs available. Postbaccalaureate distance learning degree programs offered (minimal on-campus study). *Entrance requirements:* For doctorate, GMAT, LSAT, GRE, or MAT, transcripts from accredited institutions, essay, resume, interview. Electronic applications accepted.

Instituto Tecnologico de Santo Domingo, Graduate School, Area of Business, Santo Domingo, Dominican Republic. Offers banking and securities markets (M Mgmt); corporate finance (M Mgmt); human resources management (M Mgmt, Certificate); international trade management (M Mgmt); marketing (M Mgmt); organizational development (M Mgmt); quality and productivity management (Certificate); tax management and planning (M Mgmt); upper management (M Mgmt).

Instituto Tecnologico de Santo Domingo, Graduate School, Area of Humanities and Social Sciences, Santo Domingo, Dominican Republic. Offers accounting (Certificate); adult education (Certificate); applied linguistics (MA); economics (MA); education (M Ed); educational psychology (MA, Certificate); gender and development (MA, Certificate); humanistic studies (MA); international marketing management (Certificate); international relations in the Caribbean basin (Certificate); intervention systems in family therapy (MA); linguistic and literary communication (Certificate); pedagogical support (MA); social science education (M Ed); sustainable human development (MA); terminal illness and death psychology (Certificate); youth and adult education (M Ed).

Instituto Tecnológico y de Estudios Superiores de Monterrey, Campus Central de Veracruz, Graduate Programs, Córdoba, Mexico. Offers administration (MA); administration of information technologies (MTI); computer sciences (MCC); education (MEE); educational institution administration (MAD); educational technology (MTE); electronic commerce (MCE); finance (MAF); humanistic studies (MEH); international business for Latin America (MNL); marketing (MMT); science (MCP). Part-time and evening/weekend programs available. Postbaccalaureate distance learning degree programs offered (minimal on-campus study). *Degree requirements:* For master's, thesis (for some programs). *Entrance requirements:* For master's, PAEP College Board. Electronic applications accepted.

Instituto Tecnológico y de Estudios Superiores de Monterrey, Campus Chihuahua, Graduate Programs, Chihuahua, Mexico. Offers computer systems engineering (Ingeniero); electrical engineering (Ingeniero); electromechanical engineering (Ingeniero); electronic engineering (Ingeniero); engineering administration (MEA); industrial engineering (MIE, Ingeniero); international trade (MIT); mechanical engineering (Ingeniero).

Instituto Tecnológico y de Estudios Superiores de Monterrey, Campus Ciudad de México, Virtual University Division, Ciudad de Mexico, Mexico. Offers administration of information technologies (MA); computer sciences (MA); education (MA, PhD); educational technology (MA); environmental engineering (MA); environmental systems (MA); humanistic studies (MA); industrial engineering (MA); international business for Latin America (MA); quality systems (MA); quality systems and productivity (MA). Part-time and evening/weekend programs available. Postbaccalaureate distance learning degree programs offered (minimal on-campus study). *Entrance requirements:* For master's and doctorate, Instituto entrance exam. Additional exam requirements/recommendations for international students: Required—TOEFL.

Instituto Tecnológico y de Estudios Superiores de Monterrey, Campus Cuernavaca, Programs in Business Administration, Temixco, Mexico. Offers finance (MA); human resources management (MA); international business (MA); marketing (MA).

Instituto Tecnológico y de Estudios Superiores de Monterrey, Campus Irapuato, Graduate Programs, Irapuato, Mexico. Offers administration (MBA); administration of information technology (MAIT); administration of telecommunications (MAT); architecture (M Arch); computer science (MCS); education (M Ed); educational administration (MEA); educational innovation and technology (DEIT); educational technology (MET); electronic commerce (MBA); environmental administration and planning (MEAP); environmental systems (MES); finances (MBA); humanistic studies (MHS); international management for Latin American executives (MIMLAE); library and information science (MLIS); manufacturing quality management (MMQM); marketing research (MBA).

Instituto Tecnológico y de Estudios Superiores de Monterrey, Campus Monterrey, Graduate School of Business Administration and Leadership, Program in Business Administration, Monterrey, Mexico. Offers business administration (MA, MBA); finance (M Sc); international business (M Sc); marketing (M Sc). *Accreditation:* AACSB. Part-time programs available. *Degree requirements:* For master's, one foreign language, thesis. *Entrance requirements:* For master's, GMAT. Additional exam requirements/recommendations for international students: Required—TOEFL. *Faculty research:* Technology management, quality management, organizational theory and behavior.

Inter American University of Puerto Rico, Metropolitan Campus, Graduate Programs, Program in International Business, San Juan, PR 00919-1293. Offers international business (MIB); interregional and international business (PhD).

The International University of Monaco, Graduate Programs, Monte Carlo, Monaco. Offers entrepreneurship (EMBA, MBA); financial engineering (M Sc); hedge fund and private equity (M Sc); international marketing (EMBA, MBA); international wealth management (M Sc); luxury goods and services (EMBA, M Sc, MBA); wealth and asset management (EMBA, MBA). Part-time programs available. *Degree requirements:* For master's, comprehensive exam (for some programs), applied research project. *Entrance requirements:* Additional exam requirements/recommendations for international students: Required—TOEFL (minimum score 550 paper-based; 213 computer-based), IELTS. Electronic applications accepted. *Faculty research:* Gaming, leadership, disintermediation.

Iona College, Hagan School of Business, Department of Marketing and International Business, New Rochelle, NY 10801-1890. Offers international business (AC, PMC); marketing (MBA). Part-time and evening/weekend programs available. *Faculty:* 3 full-time (all women), 3 part-time/adjunct (0 women). *Students:* 10 full-time (4 women), 27 part-time (14 women); includes 6 minority (2 Black or African American, non-Hispanic/Latino; 4 Hispanic/Latino). Average age 26. 20 applicants, 70% accepted, 12 enrolled. In 2011, 26 master's, 64 other advanced degrees awarded. *Entrance requirements:* For master's, GMAT, 2 letters of recommendation; for other advanced degree, GMAT. Additional exam requirements/recommendations for international students: Required—TOEFL (minimum score 550 paper-based; 213 computer-based; 80 iBT). *Application deadline:* For fall admission, 8/15 priority date for domestic students, 8/1 for international students; for winter admission, 11/15 priority date for domestic students, 11/1 for international students; for spring admission, 2/15 priority date for domestic students, 2/1 for international students. Applications are processed on a rolling basis. Application fee: $50. Electronic applications accepted. *Expenses:* Contact institution. *Financial support:* Scholarships/grants, tuition waivers (partial), and unspecified assistantships available. Support available to part-time students. Financial award application deadline: 4/15; financial award applicants required to submit FAFSA. *Faculty research:* Business ethics, international retailing, mega-marketing, consumer behavior and consumer confidence. *Unit head:* Dr. Frederica E. Rudell, Chair, 914-637-2748, E-mail: frudell@iona.edu. *Application contact:* Ben Fan, Director of MBA Admissions, 914-633-2289, Fax: 914-637-2708, E-mail: sfan@iona.edu. Web site: http://www.iona.edu/hagan/.

John Marshall Law School, Graduate and Professional Programs, Chicago, IL 60604-3968. Offers employee benefits (LL M, MS); global legal studies (LL M); information technology (MS); information technology and privacy law (LL M); intellectual property (LL M, MS); international business and trade (LL M); law (JD); real estate (LL M, MS); taxation (LL M, MS); trial advocacy (LL M); JD/LL M; JD/MA; JD/MBA; JD/MPA. JD/MBA offered jointly with Dominican University; JD/MA and JD/MPA with Roosevelt University. *Accreditation:* ABA. Part-time and evening/weekend programs available. *Faculty:* 69 full-time (22 women), 133 part-time/adjunct (40 women). *Students:* 1,305 full-time (598 women), 368 part-time (180 women); includes 385 minority (148 Black or African American, non-Hispanic/Latino; 15 American Indian or Alaska Native, non-Hispanic/Latino; 108 Asian, non-Hispanic/Latino; 110 Hispanic/Latino; 2 Native Hawaiian or other Pacific Islander, non-Hispanic/Latino; 2 Two or more races, non-Hispanic/Latino), 40 international. Average age 27. 3,513 applicants, 48% accepted, 365 enrolled. In 2011, 86 master's, 403 doctorates awarded. *Degree requirements:* For master's, 24 credits; for doctorate, 90 credits. *Entrance requirements:* For master's, JD; for doctorate, LSAT. Additional exam requirements/recommendations for international students: Required—TOEFL. *Application deadline:* For fall admission, 3/1 priority date for domestic students, 3/1 for international students; for spring admission, 10/15 priority date for domestic students, 10/15 for international students. Applications are processed on a rolling basis. Application fee: $0. Electronic applications accepted. *Expenses:* Contact institution. *Financial support:* In 2011–12, 1,350 students received support. Scholarships/grants and tuition waivers (full and partial) available. Support available to part-time students. Financial award application deadline: 6/1; financial award applicants required to submit FAFSA. *Unit head:* John Corkery, Dean, 312-427-2737. *Application contact:* William B. Powers, Associate Dean of Admission and Student Affairs, 800-537-4280, Fax: 312-427-5136, E-mail: admission@jmls.edu.

Johnson & Wales University, The Alan Shawn Feinstein Graduate School, MBA Program in Global Business Leadership, Providence, RI 02903-3703. Offers accounting (MBA); enhanced accounting (MBA); hospitality (MBA). Part-time programs available. *Entrance requirements:* For master's, minimum GPA of 2.75. Additional exam requirements/recommendations for international students: Required—TOEFL (minimum score 550 paper-based; 210 computer-based) or IELTS (recommended); Recommended—TWE. *Faculty research:* International banking, global economy, international trade, cultural differences.

Kaplan University, Davenport Campus, School of Business, Davenport, IA 52807-2095. Offers business administration (MBA); change leadership (MS); entrepreneurship (MBA); finance (MBA); health care management (MBA, MS); human resource (MBA); international business (MBA); management (MS); marketing (MBA); project management (MBA, MS); supply chain management and logistics (MBA, MS). Part-time and evening/weekend programs available. Postbaccalaureate distance learning degree programs offered (no on-campus study). *Entrance requirements:* Additional exam requirements/recommendations for international students: Required—TOEFL (minimum score 550 paper-based; 218 computer-based; 80 iBT). Electronic applications accepted.

Kean University, Nathan Weiss Graduate College, Program in Global Management, Union, NJ 07083. Offers executive management (MBA); global management (MBA). *Faculty:* 5 full-time (3 women). *Students:* 37 full-time (22 women), 32 part-time (17 women); includes 40 minority (18 Black or African American, non-Hispanic/Latino; 7 Asian, non-Hispanic/Latino; 15 Hispanic/Latino), 13 international. Average age 32. 26 applicants, 65% accepted, 9 enrolled. In 2011, 31 master's awarded. *Degree requirements:* For master's, one foreign language, internship or study abroad. *Entrance requirements:* For master's, GMAT, minimum GPA of 3.0, 3 letters of recommendation, prerequisite business courses, transcripts, personal essay, interview; 5 years of experience, resume, and personal statement (for executive management option). Additional exam requirements/recommendations for international students: Required—TOEFL (minimum score 79 iBT). *Application deadline:* For fall admission, 6/1 for domestic and international students; for spring admission, 12/1 for domestic and international students. Applications are processed on a rolling basis. Application fee: $75 ($150 for international students). Electronic applications accepted. *Expenses:* Tuition, state resident: full-time $11,302; part-time $550 per credit. Tuition, nonresident: full-time $15,318; part-time $674 per credit. *Required fees:* $2849; $130 per credit. Tuition and fees vary according to degree level. *Financial support:* In 2011–12, 10 research assistantships with full tuition reimbursements (averaging $3,263 per year) were awarded; unspecified assistantships also available. Financial award applicants required to submit FAFSA. *Unit head:* Dr. Veysel Yucetepe, Program Coordinator, 908-737-5980, E-mail: vyucetep@kean.edu. *Application contact:* Reenat Hasan, Admissions Counselor, 908-737-5923, Fax: 908-737-5925, E-mail: rhasan@exchange.kean.edu. Web site: http://www.kean.edu/KU/MBA-Global-Management.

Keiser University, Doctor of Business Administration Program, Fort Lauderdale, FL 33309. Offers global business (DBA); global organizational leadership (DBA); marketing (DBA).

Keiser University, Master of Business Administration Program, Fort Lauderdale, FL 33309. Offers accounting (MBA); health services management (MBA); international business (MBA); leadership for managers (MBA); marketing (MBA). Leadership for Managers and International Business concentrations also offered in Spanish. Part-time programs available. Postbaccalaureate distance learning degree programs offered (minimal on-campus study). *Entrance requirements:* For master's, minimum GPA of 2.7 from an accredited institution. Additional exam requirements/recommendations for international students: Required—TOEFL. Electronic applications accepted.

Lake Forest Graduate School of Management, The Immersion MBA Program (iMBA), Lake Forest, IL 60045. Offers global business (MBA). Postbaccalaureate distance learning degree programs offered (no on-campus study). *Expenses: Tuition:* Part-time $2932 per unit. *Required fees:* $50 per unit.

Lake Forest Graduate School of Management, The Leadership MBA Program (LMBA), Lake Forest, IL 60045. Offers finance (MBA); global business (MBA); healthcare management (MBA); management (MBA); marketing (MBA); organizational behavior (MBA). Part-time and evening/weekend programs available. *Faculty:* 136 part-time/adjunct (41 women). *Students:* 734 part-time (306 women); includes 161 minority (34 Black or African American, non-Hispanic/Latino; 4 American Indian or Alaska Native, non-Hispanic/Latino; 87 Asian, non-Hispanic/Latino; 14 Hispanic/Latino; 4 Native Hawaiian or other Pacific Islander, non-Hispanic/Latino; 18 Two or more races, non-Hispanic/Latino). Average age 38. In 2011, 213 master's awarded. *Entrance requirements:* For master's, 4 years of work experience in field, interview, 2 letters of recommendation. *Application deadline:* For fall admission, 7/1 for domestic students; for winter admission, 1/5 for domestic students; for spring admission, 3/1 for domestic students. Applications are processed on a rolling basis. Application fee: $75. Electronic applications accepted. *Expenses: Tuition:* Part-time $2932 per unit. *Required fees:* $50 per unit. *Financial support:* Scholarships/grants available. Support available to part-time students. Financial award applicants required to submit FAFSA. *Unit head:* Chris Multhauf, Executive Vice President of Educational Programs and Solutions, 847-574-5270, Fax: 847-295-3656, E-mail: cmulthauf@lfgsm.edu. *Application contact:* Carolyn Brune, Director of Admissions, 800-737-4MBA, Fax: 847-295-3656, E-mail: admiss@lfgsm.edu. Web site: http://www.lakeforestmba.edu/lake_forest_mba_program/LFGSM-Leadership-MBA.aspx.

Lawrence Technological University, College of Management, Southfield, MI 48075-1058. Offers business administration (MBA, DBA); business administration international (MBA); global leadership and management (MS); global operations and project management (MS); information systems (MS); information technology (DM); operations management (MS). *Accreditation:* ACBSP. Part-time and evening/weekend programs available. *Faculty:* 12 full-time (6 women), 39 part-time/adjunct (11 women). *Students:* 10 full-time (4 women), 518 part-time (228 women); includes 183 minority (123 Black or African American, non-Hispanic/Latino; 2 American Indian or Alaska Native, non-Hispanic/Latino; 44 Asian, non-Hispanic/Latino; 11 Hispanic/Latino; 3 Two or more races, non-Hispanic/Latino), 50 international. Average age 36. 420 applicants, 45% accepted, 97 enrolled. In 2011, 177 master's, 14 doctorates awarded. *Degree requirements:* For master's, thesis (for some programs). *Entrance requirements:* For master's, GMAT. Additional exam requirements/recommendations for international students: Required—TOEFL (minimum score 550 paper-based; 213 computer-based; 79 iBT). *Application deadline:* For fall admission, 7/27 priority date for domestic students, 5/23 for international students; for spring admission, 11/15 priority date for domestic students, 11/15 for international students. Applications are processed on a rolling basis. Application fee: $50. Electronic applications accepted. *Financial support:* In 2011–12, 122 students received support. Federal Work-Study and institutionally sponsored loans available. Support available to part-time students. Financial award application deadline: 4/1; financial award applicants required to submit FAFSA. *Unit head:* Dr. Alan McCord, Interim Dean, 248-204-3050, E-mail: mgtdean@ltu.edu. *Application contact:* Jane Rohrback, Director of Admissions, 248-204-3160, Fax: 248-204-2228, E-mail: admissions@ltu.edu. Web site: http://www.ltu.edu/management/index.asp.

Lewis University, College of Business, Graduate School of Management, Program in Business Administration, Romeoville, IL 60446. Offers accounting (MBA); custom elective option (MBA); e-business (MBA); finance (MBA); healthcare management (MBA); human resources management (MBA); information security (MBA); international business (MBA); management information systems (MBA); marketing (MBA); project management (MBA); technology and operations management (MBA). Part-time and evening/weekend programs available. *Students:* 112 full-time (60 women), 232 part-time (118 women); includes 104 minority (62 Black or African American, non-Hispanic/Latino; 1 American Indian or Alaska Native, non-Hispanic/Latino; 7 Asian, non-Hispanic/Latino; 33 Hispanic/Latino; 1 Native Hawaiian or other Pacific Islander, non-Hispanic/Latino), 9 international. Average age 28. In 2011, 99 master's awarded. *Entrance requirements:* For master's, interview, bachelor's degree, resume, 2 recommendations. Additional exam requirements/recommendations for international students: Required—TOEFL (minimum score 550 paper-based; 213 computer-based). *Application deadline:* For fall admission, 8/15 priority date for domestic students, 5/1 for international students; for spring admission, 11/15 for international students. Applications are processed on a rolling basis. Application fee: $40. Electronic applications accepted. *Financial support:* Career-related internships or fieldwork, Federal Work-Study, scholarships/grants, and unspecified assistantships available. Financial award application deadline: 5/1; financial award applicants required to submit FAFSA. *Unit head:* Dr. Maureen Culleeney, Academic Program Director, 815-838-0500 Ext. 5631, E-mail: culleema@lewisu.edu. *Application contact:* Michele Ryan, Director of Admission, 815-838-0500 Ext. 5384, E-mail: gsm@lewisu.edu.

Lincoln University, Graduate Studies, Oakland, CA 94612. Offers finance and investments (DBA); finance management and investment banking (MBA); general business (MBA); human resource management (MBA, DBA); international business (MBA); management information systems (MBA). Part-time and evening/weekend programs available. *Faculty:* 10 full-time (4 women), 15 part-time/adjunct (3 women). *Students:* 272 full-time (124 women), 1 part-time (0 women). *Degree requirements:* For master's, research project (thesis), internship report, or comprehensive exam; for doctorate, comprehensive exam, thesis/dissertation. *Entrance requirements:* For master's, minimum GPA of 2.7; for doctorate, GMAT (minimum score: 550), GRE (minimum score: 1000), or equivalent test results (waived for master's degree with minimum cumulative GPA of 3.3). Additional exam requirements/recommendations for international students: Required—TOEFL (minimum score 525 paper-based; 195 computer-based; 71 iBT) or IELTS (minimum score 5.5) for MBA; TOEFL (minimum score 550 paper-based; 213 computer-based; 79 iBT) or IELTS (minimum score 6) for DBA. *Application deadline:* For fall admission, 7/2 priority date for domestic students, 7/2 for international students; for spring admission, 11/25 priority date for domestic students, 11/25 for international students. Applications are processed on a rolling basis. Application fee: $75. Electronic applications accepted. *Financial support:* Teaching assistantships, career-related internships or fieldwork, and scholarships/grants available. *Unit head:* Dr. Marshall Burak, Director of Graduate Programs, 510-628-8016, Fax: 510-628-8012, E-mail: mburak@lincolnuca.edu. *Application contact:* Peggy Au, Director of Admissions and Records, 510-628-8010, Fax: 510-628-8012, E-mail: admissions@lincolnuca.edu. Web site: http://www.lincolnuca.edu/.

Lindenwood University, Graduate Programs, School of Business and Entrepreneurship, St. Charles, MO 63301-1695. Offers accounting (MBA, MS); business administration (MBA); entrepreneurial studies (MBA, MS); finance (MBA, MS); human resource management (MBA); human resources (MS); international business (MBA, MS); management (MBA, MS); management information systems (MBA, MS); marketing (MBA, MS); public management (MBA, MS); sport management (MA); supply chain management (MBA). *Accreditation:* ACBSP. Part-time and evening/weekend programs available. *Faculty:* 20 full-time (8 women), 17 part-time/adjunct (5 women). *Students:* 165 full-time (66 women), 223 part-time (100 women); includes 59 minority (48 Black or African American, non-Hispanic/Latino; 4 Asian, non-Hispanic/Latino; 2 Native Hawaiian or other Pacific Islander, non-Hispanic/Latino; 5 Two or more races, non-Hispanic/Latino), 140 international. Average age 29. 156 applicants, 76% accepted, 103 enrolled. In 2011, 205 degrees awarded. *Degree requirements:* For master's, comprehensive exam (for some programs), thesis (for some programs). *Entrance requirements:* For master's, interview, minimum GPA of 3.0, letter of recommendation. Additional exam requirements/recommendations for international students: Required—TOEFL (minimum score 550 paper-based; 213 computer-based; 80 iBT). *Application deadline:* For fall admission, 8/15 priority date for domestic students, 8/15 for international students; for winter admission, 1/9 priority date for domestic students, 1/9 for international students; for spring admission, 3/12 priority date for domestic students, 3/12 for international students. Applications are processed on a rolling basis. Application fee: $30 ($100 for international students). Electronic applications accepted. *Expenses: Tuition:* Full-time $13,650; part-time $395 per credit hour. *Required fees:* $150 per semester. Tuition and fees vary according to course level and course load. *Financial support:* In 2011–12, 206 students received support. Career-related internships or fieldwork, Federal Work-Study, institutionally sponsored loans, and tuition waivers (partial) available. Financial award application deadline: 6/30; financial award applicants required to submit FAFSA. *Unit head:* Roger Ellis, Dean, 636-949-4839, E-mail: rellis@lindenwood.edu. *Application* *contact:* Brett Barger, Dean of Evening Admissions and Extension Campuses, 636-949-4934, Fax: 636-949-4109, E-mail: adultadmissions@lindenwood.edu. Web site: http://www.lindenwood.edu.

Long Island University–C. W. Post Campus, College of Management, School of Business, Brookville, NY 11548-1300. Offers accounting and taxation (Certificate); business administration (Certificate); finance (MBA, Certificate); general business administration (MBA); international business (MBA, Certificate); management (MBA, Certificate); management information systems (MBA, Certificate); marketing (MBA, Certificate). *Accreditation:* AACSB. Part-time and evening/weekend programs available. *Entrance requirements:* For master's, GMAT, resume, minimum GPA of 3.0, 2 letters of recommendation. Additional exam requirements/recommendations for international students: Required—TOEFL (minimum score 527 paper-based; 197 computer-based). Electronic applications accepted. *Faculty research:* Financial markets, consumer behavior.

Loyola University Maryland, Graduate Programs, Sellinger School of Business and Management, Program in Business Administration, Baltimore, MD 21210-2699. Offers accounting (MBA); finance (MBA); general business (MBA); information systems operations management (MBA); international business (MBA); management (MBA); marketing (MBA). *Accreditation:* AACSB. Part-time and evening/weekend programs available. *Faculty:* 61 full-time (12 women), 29 part-time/adjunct (4 women). *Students:* 50 full-time (15 women), 547 part-time (210 women); includes 98 minority (39 Black or African American, non-Hispanic/Latino; 1 American Indian or Alaska Native, non-Hispanic/Latino; 28 Asian, non-Hispanic/Latino; 18 Hispanic/Latino; 2 Native Hawaiian or other Pacific Islander, non-Hispanic/Latino; 10 Two or more races, non-Hispanic/Latino), 15 international. Average age 30. In 2011, 232 master's awarded. *Entrance requirements:* For master's, GMAT (for some programs). Additional exam requirements/recommendations for international students: Required—TOEFL (minimum score 550 paper-based; 213 computer-based). *Application deadline:* For fall admission, 8/1 priority date for domestic students; for spring admission, 12/1 priority date for domestic students. Application fee: $50. Electronic applications accepted. *Financial support:* Research assistantships and unspecified assistantships available. Financial award application deadline: 4/15; financial award applicants required to submit FAFSA. *Unit head:* Dr. Karyl Leggio, Dean, 410-617-2301, E-mail: kbleggio@loyola.edu. *Application contact:* Maureen Faux, Executive Director, Graduate Admissions, 410-617-5020, Fax: 410-617-2002, E-mail: graduate@loyola.edu.

Lynn University, College of Business and Management, Boca Raton, FL 33431-5598. Offers aviation management (MBA); financial valuation and investment management (MBA); hospitality management (MBA); international business (MBA); marketing (MBA); mass communication and media management (MBA); sports and athletics administration (MBA). Part-time and evening/weekend programs available. Postbaccalaureate distance learning degree programs offered. *Degree requirements:* For master's, project. *Entrance requirements:* For master's, GMAT or GRE, minimum undergraduate GPA of 3.0, resume, 2 letters of recommendation. Additional exam requirements/recommendations for international students: Required—TOEFL (minimum score 550 paper-based; 213 computer-based). Electronic applications accepted. *Faculty research:* Labor relations, dynamic balance in leisure-time skills, ethics in athletics, hotel development.

Madonna University, School of Business, Livonia, MI 48150-1173. Offers business administration (MBA); international business (MSBA); leadership studies (MSBA); leadership studies in criminal justice (MSBA); quality and operations management (MSBA). Part-time and evening/weekend programs available. Postbaccalaureate distance learning degree programs offered (minimal on-campus study). *Degree requirements:* For master's, thesis (for some programs), foreign language proficiency (international business). *Entrance requirements:* For master's, GMAT, GRE General Test, minimum GPA of 3.0. Electronic applications accepted. *Faculty research:* Management, women in management, future studies.

Maine Maritime Academy, Department of Graduate Studies, Program in Global Supply Chain Management, Castine, ME 04420. Offers MS, Certificate, Diploma. Part-time programs available. *Degree requirements:* For master's, capstone course. *Entrance requirements:* For master's, GMAT or GRE, letters of recommendation. Additional exam requirements/recommendations for international students: Required—TOEFL.

Maine Maritime Academy, Department of Graduate Studies, Program in International Business, Castine, ME 04420. Offers MS, Certificate, Diploma. Part-time programs available. *Degree requirements:* For master's, thesis optional, capstone course. *Entrance requirements:* Additional exam requirements/recommendations for international students: Required—TOEFL.

Manhattanville College, Graduate Studies, Humanities and Social Sciences Programs, Program in International Management, Purchase, NY 10577-2132. Offers MS. Part-time and evening/weekend programs available. *Entrance requirements:* Additional exam requirements/recommendations for international students: Required—TOEFL.

Marquette University, Graduate School of Management, Executive MBA Program, Milwaukee, WI 53201-1881. Offers economics (MBA); finance (MBA); human resources (MBA); international business (MBA); management information systems (MBA); marketing (MBA); operations and supply chain management (MBA); sports business (MBA). *Accreditation:* AACSB. *Students:* 50 full-time (15 women); includes 4 minority (1 Black or African American, non-Hispanic/Latino; 3 Asian, non-Hispanic/Latino), 3 international. Average age 37. 37 applicants, 81% accepted, 29 enrolled. In 2011, 36 master's awarded. *Degree requirements:* For master's, international trip. *Entrance requirements:* For master's, GMAT or GRE, two letters of recommendation, official transcripts from current and previous colleges/universities. Additional exam requirements/recommendations for international students: Required—TOEFL (minimum score 550 paper-based; 85 computer-based; 88 iBT), IELTS (minimum score 6.5), Pearson Test of English. *Application deadline:* For fall admission, 2/15 for domestic and international students. Application fee: $50. Electronic applications accepted. *Expenses:* Contact institution. *Financial support:* Application deadline: 2/15. *Faculty research:* International trade and finance, customer relationship management, consumer satisfaction, customer service . *Unit head:* Dr. Jeanne Simmons, Graduate Director, 414-288-7145, Fax: 414-288-1660, E-mail: jeanne.simmons@marquette.edu. *Application contact:* Debra Leutermann, Admissions Coordinator, 414-288-7145, Fax: 414-288-8078, E-mail: debra.leutermann@marquette.edu. Web site: http://www.busadm.mu.edu/emba/.

Marquette University, Graduate School of Management, Program in Business Administration, Milwaukee, WI 53201-1881. Offers business administration (MBA); economics (MBA); entrepreneurship (Certificate); finance (MBA); human resources (MBA); international business (MBA); management information systems (MBA); marketing (MBA); operations and supply chain management (MBA); sports business (MBA); JD/MBA; MBA/MA; MBA/MSN. *Accreditation:* AACSB. Part-time and evening/weekend programs available. *Students:* 42 full-time (14 women), 335 part-time (94 women); includes 24 minority (5 Black or African American, non-Hispanic/Latino; 1 American Indian or Alaska Native, non-Hispanic/Latino; 15 Asian, non-Hispanic/Latino; 3 Hispanic/Latino), 29 international. Average age 31. 182 applicants, 59% accepted, 103 enrolled. In 2011, 128 master's awarded. *Degree requirements:* For Certificate, business plan. *Entrance requirements:* For master's, GMAT or GRE, letters of recommendation. Additional exam requirements/recommendations for international students: Required—TOEFL (minimum score 550 paper-based; 85 computer-based; 88 iBT), IELTS (minimum score 6.5), Pearson Test of English. *Application deadline:* For fall admission, 2/15 for domestic and international students. Applications are processed on a rolling basis. Application fee: $50. Electronic applications accepted. *Expenses: Tuition:* Full-time $17,010; part-time $945 per credit hour. Tuition and fees vary according to program. *Financial support:* In 2011–12, 4 fellowships, 11 teaching assistantships were awarded; research assistantships, Federal Work-Study, institutionally sponsored loans, scholarships/grants, and tuition waivers (full and partial) also available. Support available to part-time students. Financial award application deadline: 2/15. *Faculty research:* Ethics in the professions, services marketing, technology impact on decision-making, mentoring. *Unit head:* Dr. Jeanne Simmons, Graduate Director, 414-288-7145, Fax: 414-288-1660, E-mail: jeanne.simmons@marquette.edu. *Application contact:* Debra Leutermann, Admissions Coordinator, 414-288-8064, Fax: 414-288-1902, E-mail: debra.leutermann@marquette.edu. Web site: http://business.marquette.edu/academics/mba.

McGill University, Faculty of Graduate and Postdoctoral Studies, Desautels Faculty of Management, Montréal, QC H3A 2T5, Canada. Offers administration (PhD); entrepreneurial studies (MBA); finance (MBA); general management (Post Master's Certificate); information systems (MBA); international business (MBA); international practicing management (MM); management (MBA); management for development (MBA); manufacturing management (MMM); marketing (MBA); operations management (MBA); public accountancy (Diploma); strategic management (MBA); MBA/LL B; MD/MBA. MMM offered jointly with Faculty of Engineering; PhD with Concordia University, HEC Montreal, Université de Montréal, Université du Québec à Montréal.

McKendree University, Graduate Programs, Master of Business Administration Program, Lebanon, IL 62254-1299. Offers business administration (MBA); human resource management (MBA); international business (MBA). Part-time and evening/weekend programs available. Postbaccalaureate distance learning degree programs offered (no on-campus study). *Entrance requirements:* For master's, official transcripts from all institutions attended, essay, minimum GPA of 3.0, three references, resume. Additional exam requirements/recommendations for international students: Required—TOEFL. Electronic applications accepted.

MidAmerica Nazarene University, Graduate Studies in Management, Olathe, KS 66062-1899. Offers management (MBA); organizational administration (MA), including finance, international business, leadership, non-profit. Evening/weekend programs available. *Entrance requirements:* For master's, mathematical assessment, minimum undergraduate GPA of 3.0, letters of recommendation. Additional exam requirements/recommendations for international students: Required—TOEFL. Electronic applications accepted. *Faculty research:* Economic development, international finance, business development, employee evaluation.

Milwaukee School of Engineering, Rader School of Business, Program in Marketing and Export Management, Milwaukee, WI 53202-3109. Offers MS. Part-time and evening/weekend programs available. *Faculty:* 1 full-time (0 women), 1 part-time/adjunct (0 women). *Students:* 5 part-time (4 women). Average age 27. 2 applicants, 50% accepted, 0 enrolled. In 2011, 1 master's awarded. *Degree requirements:* For master's, thesis, thesis defense or capstone project. *Entrance requirements:* For master's, GRE General Test or GMAT, 2 letters of recommendation. Additional exam requirements/recommendations for international students: Recommended—TOEFL (minimum score 550 paper-based; 213 computer-based; 79 iBT), IELTS. *Application deadline:* Applications are processed on a rolling basis. Application fee: $0. Electronic applications accepted. Application fee is waived when completed online. *Expenses: Tuition:* Full-time $17,550; part-time $650 per credit hour. *Financial support:* In 2011–12, 4 students received support. Career-related internships or fieldwork available. Support available to part-time students. Financial award applicants required to submit FAFSA. *Unit head:* Dr. Kathy Faggiani, Director, 414-277-2711, Fax: 414-277-2711, E-mail: faggiani@msoe.edu. *Application contact:* Katie Gassenhuber, Graduate Admissions Director, 800-321-6763, Fax: 414-277-7208, E-mail: gassenhuber@msoe.edu.

Montclair State University, The Graduate School, School of Business, Post Master's Certificate Program in International Business, Montclair, NJ 07043-1624. Offers Post Master's Certificate. *Students:* Average age 29. *Entrance requirements:* For degree, essay. Additional exam requirements/recommendations for international students: Required—TOEFL (minimum score 83 iBT) or IELTS. *Application deadline:* For fall admission, 6/1 for international students; for spring admission, 10/1 for international students. Applications are processed on a rolling basis. Application fee: $60. Electronic applications accepted. *Financial support:* Federal Work-Study, scholarships/grants, and unspecified assistantships available. Support available to part-time students. Financial award application deadline: 3/1; financial award applicants required to submit FAFSA. *Unit head:* Dr. Chandana Chakraborty, Head, 973-655-4280. *Application contact:* Amy Aiello, Executive Director of The Graduate School, 973-655-5147, Fax: 973-655-7869, E-mail: graduate.school@montclair.edu. Web site: http://business.montclair.edu/.

Monterey Institute of International Studies, Graduate School of International Policy and Management, Fisher International MBA Program, Monterey, CA 93940-2691. Offers MBA. *Accreditation:* AACSB. *Degree requirements:* For master's, one foreign language, thesis. *Entrance requirements:* For master's, GMAT, minimum GPA of 3.0, proficiency in a foreign language. Additional exam requirements/recommendations for international students: Required—TOEFL (minimum score 550 paper-based; 213 computer-based; 80 iBT). Electronic applications accepted. *Expenses: Tuition:* Full-time $32,800; part-time $1560 per credit. *Required fees:* $28 per semester. *Faculty research:* Cross-cultural consumer behavior, foreign direct investment, marketing and entrepreneurial orientation, political risk analysis and area studies, managing international human resources.

National University, Academic Affairs, School of Business and Management, Department of Management and Marketing, La Jolla, CA 92037-1011. Offers business administration (GMBA); global management (MGM). GMBA offered in Spanish. Part-time and evening/weekend programs available. Postbaccalaureate distance learning degree programs offered (no on-campus study). *Students:* 157 applicants, 100% accepted, 134 enrolled. *Degree requirements:* For master's, thesis. *Entrance requirements:* For master's, interview, minimum GPA of 2.5. Additional exam requirements/recommendations for international students: Required—TOEFL (minimum score 550 paper-based; 213 computer-based; 79 iBT), IELTS (minimum score 6). *Application deadline:* Applications are processed on a rolling basis. Application fee: $60 ($65 for international students). Electronic applications accepted. *Financial support:* Career-related internships or fieldwork, institutionally sponsored loans, scholarships/grants, and tuition waivers (partial) available. Support available to part-time students. Financial award application deadline: 6/30; financial award applicants required to submit FAFSA. *Unit head:* Dr. Ramon Corona, Chair, 858-642-8427, Fax: 858-642-8406, E-mail: rcorona@nu.edu. *Application contact:* Dominick Giovanniello, Associate Regional Dean, 800-NAT-UNIV, Fax: 858-541-7792, E-mail: dgiovann@nu.edu. Web site: http://www.nu.edu/OurPrograms/SchoolOfBusinessAndManagement/ManagementAndMarketing.html.

International Business

New Jersey Institute of Technology, Office of Graduate Studies, School of Management, Program in International Business, Newark, NJ 07102. Offers MS. Part-time and evening/weekend programs available. *Students:* 11 full-time (8 women), 1 part-time (0 women); includes 1 minority (Hispanic/Latino), 10 international. Average age 26. 58 applicants, 52% accepted, 7 enrolled. In 2011, 5 master's awarded. *Entrance requirements:* Additional exam requirements/recommendations for international students: Required—TOEFL (minimum score 550 paper-based; 213 computer-based; 79 iBT). *Application deadline:* For fall admission, 6/1 priority date for domestic students, 5/1 for international students; for spring admission, 11/15 priority date for domestic students, 11/15 for international students. Applications are processed on a rolling basis. Application fee: $65. Electronic applications accepted. *Expenses:* Tuition, state resident: full-time $7980; part-time $867 per credit. Tuition, nonresident: full-time $11,336; part-time $1196 per credit. *Required fees:* $230 per credit. *Financial support:* Fellowships available. Financial award application deadline: 1/15. *Unit head:* Dr. Robert English, Interim Dean, 973-596-3224, Fax: 973-596-3074, E-mail: robert.english@njit.edu. *Application contact:* Kathryn Kelly, Director of Admissions, 973-596-3300, Fax: 973-596-3461, E-mail: admissions@njit.edu. Web site: http://som.njit.edu/academics/graduate/ms-intlbusiness.php.

Newman University, MBA Program, Wichita, KS 67213-2097. Offers finance (MBA); international business (MBA); leadership (MBA); management (MBA); technology (MBA). Part-time programs available. *Faculty:* 4 full-time (1 woman), 7 part-time/adjunct (2 women). *Students:* 28 full-time (7 women), 83 part-time (28 women); includes 31 minority (8 Black or African American, non-Hispanic/Latino; 1 American Indian or Alaska Native, non-Hispanic/Latino; 9 Asian, non-Hispanic/Latino; 9 Hispanic/Latino; 1 Native Hawaiian or other Pacific Islander, non-Hispanic/Latino; 3 Two or more races, non-Hispanic/Latino), 23 international. Average age 31. 63 applicants, 70% accepted, 38 enrolled. In 2011, 49 master's awarded. *Degree requirements:* For master's, thesis optional. *Entrance requirements:* For master's, interview; minimum GPA of 3.0; 3 letters of recommendation; course work in algebra, statistics, macroeconomics, and financial accounting. Additional exam requirements/recommendations for international students: Required—TOEFL (minimum score 600 paper-based; 250 computer-based; 100 iBT). *Application deadline:* For fall admission, 8/1 priority date for domestic students, 7/15 for international students; for winter admission, 1/1 priority date for domestic students; for spring admission, 1/1 priority date for domestic students, 11/15 for international students. Applications are processed on a rolling basis. Application fee: $25 ($40 for international students). Electronic applications accepted. *Expenses:* Contact institution. *Financial support:* In 2011–12, 18 students received support. Federal Work-Study available. Financial award application deadline: 8/15; financial award applicants required to submit FAFSA. *Unit head:* Dr. Wendy Munday, Director of MBA Program, 316-942-4291 Ext. 2296, Fax: 316-942-4483, E-mail: mundayw@newmanu.edu. *Application contact:* Linda Kay Sabala, Director of Graduate Admissions, 316-942-4291 Ext. 2230, Fax: 316-942-4483, E-mail: sabalal@newmanu.edu. Web site: http://www.newmanu.edu.

New Mexico Highlands University, Graduate Studies, School of Business, Las Vegas, NM 87701. Offers business administration (MBA), including government nonprofit management, human resource management, international business, management, management information systems. *Accreditation:* ACBSP. *Faculty:* 20 full-time (5 women). *Students:* 63 full-time (40 women), 146 part-time (76 women); includes 131 minority (9 Black or African American, non-Hispanic/Latino; 8 American Indian or Alaska Native, non-Hispanic/Latino; 1 Asian, non-Hispanic/Latino; 110 Hispanic/Latino; 2 Native Hawaiian or other Pacific Islander, non-Hispanic/Latino; 1 Two or more races, non-Hispanic/Latino), 25 international. Average age 33. 99 applicants, 79% accepted, 49 enrolled. In 2011, 43 master's awarded. *Degree requirements:* For master's, comprehensive exam, thesis or alternative. *Entrance requirements:* For master's, minimum undergraduate GPA of 3.0. Additional exam requirements/recommendations for international students: Required—TOEFL (minimum score 540 paper-based; 207 computer-based). *Application deadline:* For fall admission, 8/1 priority date for domestic students. Applications are processed on a rolling basis. Application fee: $15. *Expenses:* Tuition, state resident: full-time $2767; part-time $146 per credit hour. Tuition, nonresident: full-time $4879; part-time $234 per credit hour. *International tuition:* $5436 full-time. *Required fees:* $737. *Financial support:* In 2011–12, 29 students received support. Career-related internships or fieldwork, Federal Work-Study, institutionally sponsored loans, scholarships/grants, tuition waivers (full and partial), and unspecified assistantships available. Support available to part-time students. Financial award application deadline: 3/1; financial award applicants required to submit FAFSA. *Faculty research:* Real estate valuation, studying expert judgments in complex accounting, decision environments, green marketing, environmentalism, marketing research methodology. *Unit head:* Dr. Margaret Young, Dean, 505-454-3522, Fax: 505-454-3354, E-mail: young_m@nmhu.edu. *Application contact:* Diane Trujillo, Administrative Assistant, Graduate Studies, 505-454-3266, Fax: 505-426-2117, E-mail: dtrujillo@nmhu.edu. Web site: http://www.nmhu.edu/business/.

New York Institute of Technology, Graduate Division, School of Management, Program in Business Administration, Old Westbury, NY 11568-8000. Offers accounting (Advanced Certificate); business administration (MBA); finance (Advanced Certificate); international business (Advanced Certificate); management of information systems (Advanced Certificate); marketing (Advanced Certificate). Part-time and evening/weekend programs available. *Students:* 331 full-time (131 women), 508 part-time (211 women); includes 74 minority (26 Black or African American, non-Hispanic/Latino; 27 Asian, non-Hispanic/Latino; 15 Hispanic/Latino; 6 Two or more races, non-Hispanic/Latino), 214 international. Average age 28. In 2011, 449 degrees awarded. *Degree requirements:* For master's, thesis (for some programs). *Entrance requirements:* For master's, minimum QPA of 2.85. Additional exam requirements/recommendations for international students: Required—TOEFL (minimum score 550 paper-based; 213 computer-based). *Application deadline:* For fall admission, 7/1 priority date for domestic students; for spring admission, 12/1 priority date for domestic students. Applications are processed on a rolling basis. Application fee: $50. Electronic applications accepted. *Expenses: Tuition:* Part-time $930 per credit hour. *Financial support:* Fellowships, research assistantships with partial tuition reimbursements, institutionally sponsored loans, tuition waivers (full and partial), and unspecified assistantships available. Support available to part-time students. Financial award applicants required to submit FAFSA. *Faculty research:* Instructor performance appraisal; relationship between TOEFL, GMAT, GRE, and performance in foreign students. *Unit head:* Dr. Stephen Hartman, Director, 516-686-7691, E-mail: shartman@nyit.edu. *Application contact:* Dr. Jacquelyn Nealon, Vice President for Enrollment Services, 516-686-7925, Fax: 516-686-7597, E-mail: jnealon@nyit.edu.

New York University, Graduate School of Arts and Science, Department of Politics, New York, NY 10012-1019. Offers political campaign management (MA); politics (MA, PhD); JD/MA; MBA/MA. Part-time programs available. *Faculty:* 30 full-time (4 women). *Students:* 187 full-time (94 women), 52 part-time (24 women); includes 28 minority (4 Black or African American, non-Hispanic/Latino; 16 Asian, non-Hispanic/Latino; 6 Hispanic/Latino; 2 Two or more races, non-Hispanic/Latino), 111 international. Average age 28. 811 applicants, 46% accepted, 104 enrolled. In 2011, 63 master's, 12 doctorates awarded. Terminal master's awarded for partial completion of doctoral program. *Degree requirements:* For master's, one foreign language, thesis or alternative; for doctorate, 2 foreign languages, comprehensive exam, thesis/dissertation. *Entrance requirements:* For master's, GRE General Test; for doctorate, GRE General Test, master's degree in political science, minimum GPA of 2.5. Additional exam requirements/recommendations for international students: Required—TOEFL. *Application deadline:* For fall admission, 12/18 priority date for domestic students, 12/18 for international students. Application fee: $90. *Financial support:* Fellowships with tuition reimbursements, teaching assistantships with tuition reimbursements, career-related internships or fieldwork, Federal Work-Study, and institutionally sponsored loans available. Financial award application deadline: 12/18; financial award applicants required to submit FAFSA. *Faculty research:* Comparative politics, democratic theory and practice, rational choice, political economy, international relations. *Unit head:* Michael Gilligan, Director of PhD Program, 212-998-8500, Fax: 212-995-4184, E-mail: politics.phd@nyu.edu. *Application contact:* Shinasi Rama, Director of Master's Program, 212-998-8500, Fax: 212-995-4184, E-mail: politics.masters@nyu.edu. Web site: http://www.nyu.edu/gsas/dept/politics/.

New York University, School of Continuing and Professional Studies, Schack Institute of Real Estate, Program in Real Estate, New York, NY 10012-1019. Offers real estate (MS, Advanced Certificate), including finance and investment (MS), strategic real estate management (MS); real estate development (MS, Advanced Certificate), including business of development (MS), community development (MS), global real estate (MS), sustainable development (MS). Part-time and evening/weekend programs available. *Faculty:* 10 full-time (3 women), 94 part-time/adjunct (17 women). *Students:* 111 full-time (36 women), 352 part-time (75 women); includes 37 minority (9 Black or African American, non-Hispanic/Latino; 1 American Indian or Alaska Native, non-Hispanic/Latino; 21 Asian, non-Hispanic/Latino; 6 Hispanic/Latino), 50 international. Average age 31. 279 applicants, 63% accepted, 99 enrolled. In 2011, 186 master's, 28 other advanced degrees awarded. *Degree requirements:* For master's, thesis, capstone. *Entrance requirements:* For master's, GRE/GMAT only upon request, relevant professional work, internship or volunteer experience. Additional exam requirements/recommendations for international students: Required—TOEFL (minimum score 600 paper-based; 250 computer-based; 100 iBT), IELTS (minimum score 7). *Application deadline:* For fall admission, 2/1 priority date for domestic students, 2/1 for international students; for spring admission, 10/15 priority date for domestic students, 8/15 for international students. Applications are processed on a rolling basis. Application fee: $150. Electronic applications accepted. *Financial support:* In 2011–12, 225 students received support, including 201 fellowships (averaging $2,349 per year); scholarships/grants also available. Support available to part-time students. Financial award application deadline: 3/2. *Faculty research:* Economics and market cycles, international property rights, comparative metropolitan economies, current market trends. *Unit head:* Rosemary Scanlon, Divisional Dean. *Application contact:* Office of Admissions, 212-998-7100, E-mail: scps.gradadmissions@nyu.edu. Web site: http://www.scps.nyu.edu/areas-of-study/real-estate/graduate-programs/.

Norwich University, College of Graduate and Continuing Studies, Master of Arts in Diplomacy Program, Northfield, VT 05663. Offers international commerce (MA); international conflict management (MA); international terrorism (MA). Evening/weekend programs available. *Faculty:* 1 full-time (0 women), 23 part-time/adjunct (5 women). *Students:* 132 full-time (44 women); includes 27 minority (12 Black or African American, non-Hispanic/Latino; 5 Asian, non-Hispanic/Latino; 9 Hispanic/Latino; 1 Native Hawaiian or other Pacific Islander, non-Hispanic/Latino). Average age 34. 155 applicants, 38% accepted, 57 enrolled. In 2011, 209 master's awarded. *Degree requirements:* For master's, comprehensive exam, thesis optional. *Entrance requirements:* For master's, minimum undergraduate GPA of 2.75. Additional exam requirements/recommendations for international students: Required—TOEFL. *Application deadline:* For fall admission, 8/10 for domestic and international students; for winter admission, 11/7 for domestic and international students; for spring admission, 2/6 for domestic and international students. Applications are processed on a rolling basis. Application fee: $50. Electronic applications accepted. *Expenses: Tuition:* Full-time $16,174. *Required fees:* $2130. Full-time tuition and fees vary according to program. *Financial support:* In 2011–12, 24 students received support. Scholarships/grants available. Financial award applicants required to submit FAFSA. *Unit head:* Dr. Lasha Tchantouridze, Program Director, 802-485-2095, Fax: 802-485-2533, E-mail: ltchanto@norwich.edu. *Application contact:* Fianna Verret, Assistant Program Director, 802-485-2783, Fax: 802-485-2533, E-mail: fverret@norwich.edu. Web site: http://diplomacy.norwich.edu/.

Nova Southeastern University, H. Wayne Huizenga School of Business and Entrepreneurship, Fort Lauderdale, FL 33314-7796. Offers accounting (M Acc); business administration (MBA, DBA); human resource management (MSHRM); international business administration (MIBA); leadership (MS); public administration (MPA, DPA); real estate development (MS); taxation (M Tax); JD/MBA; Pharm D/MBA. Part-time and evening/weekend programs available. Postbaccalaureate distance learning degree programs offered (minimal on-campus study). *Students:* 229 full-time (112 women), 3,506 part-time (2,109 women); includes 2,506 minority (1,256 Black or African American, non-Hispanic/Latino; 8 American Indian or Alaska Native, non-Hispanic/Latino; 146 Asian, non-Hispanic/Latino; 1,058 Hispanic/Latino; 4 Native Hawaiian or other Pacific Islander, non-Hispanic/Latino; 34 Two or more races, non-Hispanic/Latino), 174 international. Average age 33. In 2011, 1,252 master's, 17 doctorates awarded. *Degree requirements:* For master's, thesis optional; for doctorate, comprehensive exam, thesis/dissertation. *Entrance requirements:* For doctorate, GMAT. Additional exam requirements/recommendations for international students: Required—TOEFL (minimum score 550 paper-based; 213 computer-based; 79 iBT), IELTS (minimum score 6). *Application deadline:* Applications are processed on a rolling basis. Application fee: $50. Electronic applications accepted. *Financial support:* In 2011–12, 2 students received support. Federal Work-Study and scholarships/grants available. Support available to part-time students. Financial award applicants required to submit FAFSA. *Faculty research:* Reputation management, call centers, international social capital, corporate earnings guidance, corporate governance. *Unit head:* Dr. D. Michael Fields, Dean, 954-262-5005, E-mail: fieldsm@nova.edu. *Application contact:* Karen Goldberg, Associate Director of Recruitment and Special Events, 954-262-5039, Fax: 954-262-3822, E-mail: karen@nova.edu. Web site: http://www.huizenga.nova.edu.

Oakland University, Graduate Study and Lifelong Learning, School of Business Administration, Department of Management and Marketing, Rochester, MI 48309-4401. Offers business administration (MBA); entrepreneurship (Certificate); general management (Certificate); human resource management (Certificate); international business (Certificate); marketing (Certificate).

Oklahoma City University, Meinders School of Business, Program in Business Administration, Oklahoma City, OK 73106-1402. Offers finance (MBA); health administration (MBA); information technology (MBA); integrated marketing communications (MBA); international business (MBA); marketing (MBA); JD/MBA. *Accreditation:* ACBSP. Part-time and evening/weekend programs available. *Faculty:* 15 full-time (6 women), 14 part-time/adjunct (6 women). *Students:* 136 full-time (59 women), 112 part-time (34 women); includes 38 minority (14 Black or African American, non-Hispanic/Latino; 4 American Indian or Alaska Native, non-Hispanic/Latino; 11 Asian, non-Hispanic/Latino; 3 Hispanic/Latino; 6 Two or more races, non-Hispanic/Latino), 100 international. Average age 30. 252 applicants, 83% accepted, 30 enrolled.

In 2011, 148 master's awarded. *Degree requirements:* For master's, comprehensive exam. *Entrance requirements:* For master's, GRE or GMAT. Additional exam requirements/recommendations for international students: Required—TOEFL (minimum score 560 paper-based; 220 computer-based; 83 iBT). *Application deadline:* Applications are processed on a rolling basis. Application fee: $50 ($70 for international students). Electronic applications accepted. *Expenses: Tuition:* Full-time $16,848; part-time $936 per credit hour. *Required fees:* $2070; $115 per credit hour. One-time fee: $300. *Financial support:* Career-related internships or fieldwork, Federal Work-Study, institutionally sponsored loans, and tuition waivers (partial) available. Support available to part-time students. Financial award application deadline: 6/1; financial award applicants required to submit FAFSA. *Faculty research:* Management information systems, international business strategies. *Unit head:* Dr. Steven Agee, Dean, 405-208-5130, Fax: 405-208-5098, E-mail: sagee@okcu.edu. *Application contact:* Michelle Cook, Director, Graduate Admissions, 800-633-7242, Fax: 405-208-5916, E-mail: gadmissions@okcu.edu. Web site: http://msb.okcu.edu/graduate/.

Old Dominion University, College of Business and Public Administration, MBA Program, Norfolk, VA 23529. Offers business and economic forecasting (MBA); financial analysis and valuation (MBA); information technology and enterprise integration (MBA); international business (MBA); maritime and port management (MBA); public administration (MBA). *Accreditation:* AACSB. Part-time and evening/weekend programs available. *Faculty:* 66 full-time (15 women), 6 part-time/adjunct (1 woman). *Students:* 69 full-time (21 women), 230 part-time (85 women); includes 49 minority (22 Black or African American, non-Hispanic/Latino; 1 American Indian or Alaska Native, non-Hispanic/Latino; 10 Asian, non-Hispanic/Latino; 3 Hispanic/Latino; 1 Native Hawaiian or other Pacific Islander, non-Hispanic/Latino; 12 Two or more races, non-Hispanic/Latino), 19 international. Average age 31. 177 applicants, 43% accepted, 53 enrolled. In 2011, 115 master's awarded. *Entrance requirements:* For master's, GMAT, GRE, letter of reference, resume, coursework in calculus, essay. Additional exam requirements/recommendations for international students: Required—TOEFL (minimum score 550 paper-based; 213 computer-based; 80 iBT). *Application deadline:* For fall admission, 6/1 priority date for domestic students, 4/15 for international students; for spring admission, 11/1 priority date for domestic students, 10/1 for international students. Applications are processed on a rolling basis. Application fee: $75. Electronic applications accepted. *Expenses:* Tuition, state resident: full-time $9096; part-time $379 per credit. Tuition, nonresident: full-time $23,064; part-time $961 per credit. *Required fees:* $127 per semester. One-time fee: $50. *Financial support:* In 2011–12, 44 students received support, including 90 research assistantships with partial tuition reimbursements available (averaging $8,900 per year); career-related internships or fieldwork, scholarships/grants, and unspecified assistantships also available. Support available to part-time students. Financial award application deadline: 2/15; financial award applicants required to submit FAFSA. *Faculty research:* International business, buyer behavior, financial markets, strategy, operations research, maritime and transportation economics. *Unit head:* Dr. Larry Filer, Graduate Program Director, 757-683-3585, Fax: 757-683-5750, E-mail: mbainfo@odu.edu. *Application contact:* Shanna Wood, MBA Program Manager, 757-683-3585, Fax: 757-683-5750, E-mail: mbainfo@odu.edu. Web site: http://bpa.odu.edu/mba/.

Oral Roberts University, School of Business, Tulsa, OK 74171. Offers accounting (MBA); entrepreneurship (MBA); finance (MBA); international business (MBA); management (MBA); marketing (MBA); non-profit management (MBA); not for profit management (MNM). *Accreditation:* ACBSP. Part-time programs available. Postbaccalaureate distance learning degree programs offered (minimal on-campus study). *Degree requirements:* For master's, thesis optional. *Entrance requirements:* For master's, minimum cumulative GPA of 3.0. Additional exam requirements/recommendations for international students: Required—TOEFL (minimum score 550 paper-based; 213 computer-based; 79 iBT). Electronic applications accepted. *Faculty research:* Social media, international business and marketing.

Pace University, Lubin School of Business, International Business Program, New York, NY 10038. Offers MBA. Part-time and evening/weekend programs available. *Students:* 7 full-time (3 women), 35 part-time (19 women); includes 15 minority (3 Black or African American, non-Hispanic/Latino; 9 Asian, non-Hispanic/Latino; 3 Hispanic/Latino), 13 international. Average age 27. 77 applicants, 48% accepted, 14 enrolled. In 2011, 19 master's awarded. *Entrance requirements:* For master's, GMAT, GRE. Additional exam requirements/recommendations for international students: Required—TOEFL. *Application deadline:* For fall admission, 7/31 priority date for domestic students; for spring admission, 11/30 for domestic students. Applications are processed on a rolling basis. Application fee: $70. Electronic applications accepted. *Expenses: Tuition:* Part-time $990 per credit. *Required fees:* $168 per semester. Tuition and fees vary according to course load and degree level. *Financial support:* Research assistantships, career-related internships or fieldwork, and Federal Work-Study available. Support available to part-time students. Financial award applicants required to submit FAFSA. *Unit head:* Dr. Lawrence Bridwell, Chairperson, 914-422-4156, E-mail: lbridwell@pace.edu. *Application contact:* Susan Ford-Goldschein, Director of Graduate Admissions, 212-346-1531, Fax: 212-346-1585, E-mail: gradnyc@pace.edu. Web site: http://www.pace.edu/.

Pacific States University, College of Business, Los Angeles, CA 90006. Offers accounting (MBA); finance (MBA); international business (MBA, DBA); management of information technology (MBA); real estate management (MBA). Part-time and evening/weekend programs available. Postbaccalaureate distance learning degree programs offered (no on-campus study). *Faculty:* 6 full-time (2 women), 14 part-time/adjunct (0 women). *Students:* 157 full-time (70 women); includes 13 minority (2 Black or African American, non-Hispanic/Latino; 8 Asian, non-Hispanic/Latino; 3 Native Hawaiian or other Pacific Islander, non-Hispanic/Latino), 140 international. Average age 31. 42 applicants, 83% accepted, 33 enrolled. *Degree requirements:* For doctorate, comprehensive exam, thesis/dissertation. *Entrance requirements:* For master's, minimum undergraduate GPA of 2.5 during last 90 hours of course work. Additional exam requirements/recommendations for international students: Required—TOEFL (minimum score 133 computer-based; 45 iBT), IELTS (minimum score 4.5). *Application deadline:* For fall admission, 8/15 priority date for domestic students; for winter admission, 10/15 priority date for domestic students; for spring admission, 1/15 priority date for domestic students. Applications are processed on a rolling basis. Application fee: $100. *Expenses: Tuition:* Full-time $11,040; part-time $345 per credit hour. *Required fees:* $150 per quarter. *Financial support:* Scholarships/grants available. Financial award applicants required to submit FAFSA. *Application contact:* Zolzaya Enkhbayar, Interim Registrar, 323-731-2383, Fax: 323-731-7276, E-mail: registrar@psuca.edu.

Park University, College of Graduate and Professional Studies, Kansas City, MO 54105. Offers adult education (M Ed); at-risk students (M Ed); disaster and emergency management (MPA); educational administration (M Ed); entrepreneurship (MBA); general business (MBA); general education (M Ed); government/business relations (MPA); healthcare/services management (MBA, MPA); international business (MBA); K-12 certification (MAT); management information systems (MBA); management of information systems (MPA); middle school certification (MAT); multi-cultural education (M Ed); nonprofit management (MPA); public management (MPA); school law (M Ed); secondary school certification (MAT); special education (M Ed). Part-time and evening/weekend programs available. Postbaccalaureate distance learning degree programs offered (no on-campus study). *Degree requirements:* For master's, comprehensive exam, thesis (for some programs). *Entrance requirements:* For master's, GRE, GMAT, teacher certification (M Ed). Additional exam requirements/recommendations for international students: Required—TOEFL (minimum score 550 paper-based). Electronic applications accepted. *Faculty research:* Literacy, leadership, brain based research, multicultural education, diversity.

Pepperdine University, Graziadio School of Business and Management, International MBA Program, Malibu, CA 90263. Offers IMBA. *Students:* 17 full-time (8 women); includes 2 minority (1 Asian, non-Hispanic/Latino; 1 Hispanic/Latino), 1 international. 25 applicants, 52% accepted, 13 enrolled. In 2011, 7 master's awarded. *Entrance requirements:* For master's, GMAT or GRE, two letters of recommendation. Additional exam requirements/recommendations for international students: Required—TOEFL. *Application deadline:* For fall admission, 5/1 for domestic students, 4/1 for international students. Application fee: $75. Electronic applications accepted. *Unit head:* Dr. Linda A. Livingstone, Dean, Graziadio School of Business and Management, 310-568-5689, Fax: 310-568-5766, E-mail: linda.livingstone@pepperdine.edu. *Application contact:* Darrell Eriksen, Director of Admission and Student Accounts, Graziadio School of Business and Management, 310-568-5525, E-mail: darrell.eriksen@pepperdine.edu. Web site: http://bschool.pepperdine.edu/programs/international-mba/.

Pepperdine University, Graziadio School of Business and Management, MS in Global Business Program, Malibu, CA 90263. Offers MS. *Entrance requirements:* For master's, GMAT or GRE, two letters of recommendation. Additional exam requirements/recommendations for international students: Required—TOEFL.

Philadelphia University, School of Business Administration, Program in Business Administration, Philadelphia, PA 19144. Offers business administration (MBA); finance (MBA); health care management (MBA); international business (MBA); marketing (MBA); MBA/MS. Part-time and evening/weekend programs available. Postbaccalaureate distance learning degree programs offered (no on-campus study). *Entrance requirements:* For master's, GMAT. Additional exam requirements/recommendations for international students: Required—TOEFL (minimum score 550 paper-based; 213 computer-based; 79 iBT).

Polytechnic University of Puerto Rico, Graduate School, Hato Rey, PR 00919. Offers business administration (MBA), including computer information systems, general management, management of information systems, management of international enterprises; civil engineering (ME, MS); computer engineering (ME, MS); computer science (MCS, MS); electrical engineering (ME, MS); engineering management (MEM); environmental management (MEM); landscape architecture (M Land Arch); manufacturing competitiveness (MMC, MS); manufacturing engineering (ME, MS); mechanical engineering (M Mech E). Part-time and evening/weekend programs available. *Entrance requirements:* For master's, 3 letters of recommendation.

Polytechnic University of Puerto Rico, Miami Campus, Graduate School, Miami, FL 33166. Offers accounting (MBA); business administration (MBA); construction management (MEM); environmental management (MEM); finance (MBA); human resources management (MBA); logistics and supply chain management (MBA); management of international enterprises (MBA); manufacturing management (MEM); marketing management (MBA); project management (MBA). Part-time and evening/weekend programs available. Postbaccalaureate distance learning degree programs offered (no on-campus study). *Entrance requirements:* For master's, minimum GPA of 3.0. Electronic applications accepted.

Polytechnic University of Puerto Rico, Orlando Campus, Graduate School, Winter Park, FL 32792. Offers accounting (MBA); business administration (MBA); construction management (MEM); engineering management (MEM); environmental management (MEM); finance (MBA); human resources management (MBA); management of international enterprises (MBA); management of technology (MBA); manufacturing management (MEM). Part-time and evening/weekend programs available. Postbaccalaureate distance learning degree programs offered (no on-campus study). *Entrance requirements:* For master's, minimum GPA of 3.0. Additional exam requirements/recommendations for international students: Recommended—TOEFL. Electronic applications accepted.

Pontifical Catholic University of Puerto Rico, College of Business Administration, Program in International Business, Ponce, PR 00717-0777. Offers MBA. Part-time and evening/weekend programs available. *Entrance requirements:* For master's, GRE, interview, minimum GPA of 2.75.

Pontificia Universidad Catolica Madre y Maestra, Graduate School, Faculty of Social and Administrative Sciences, Santiago, Dominican Republic. Offers business administration (MBA), including business development, finance, international business, management skills (M Mgmt, MBA), marketing, operations, strategic cost management, strategy, tourist destination planning and management; law (LL M), including civil law, corporate business law, criminal law, international relations, real estate law; management (M Mgmt), including higher financial management, insurance program administration, management skills (M Mgmt, MBA); psychology (MA), including clinical child and adolescent psychology, forensic psychology; strategic human resources (EMBA).

Portland State University, Graduate Studies, School of Business Administration, Program in International Management, Portland, OR 97207-0751. Offers MIM. Part-time and evening/weekend programs available. *Degree requirements:* For master's, field study trip to China and Japan. *Entrance requirements:* For master's, GMAT, GRE General Test, minimum GPA of 2.75, resume, 2 letters of recommendation. Additional exam requirements/recommendations for international students: Required—TOEFL (minimum score 550 paper-based; 213 computer-based).

Providence College, School of Business, Providence, RI 02918. Offers accounting (MBA); entrepreneurship (MBA); finance (MBA); international business (MBA); management (MBA); marketing (MBA); not-for-profit organizations (MBA). Part-time and evening/weekend programs available. *Faculty:* 11 full-time (4 women), 6 part-time/adjunct (1 woman). *Students:* 52 full-time (21 women), 49 part-time (17 women); includes 8 minority (3 Black or African American, non-Hispanic/Latino; 2 Asian, non-Hispanic/Latino; 3 Two or more races, non-Hispanic/Latino), 6 international. Average age 26. 49 applicants, 80% accepted, 25 enrolled. In 2011, 57 master's awarded. *Degree requirements:* For master's, thesis optional. *Entrance requirements:* For master's, GMAT. Additional exam requirements/recommendations for international students: Required—TOEFL (minimum score 550 paper-based; 213 computer-based; 80 iBT). *Application deadline:* For fall admission, 8/1 priority date for domestic students, 8/1 for international students; for spring admission, 12/1 priority date for domestic students, 12/1 for international students. Applications are processed on a rolling basis. Application fee: $55. *Expenses:* Contact institution. *Financial support:* In 2011–12, 34 research assistantships with full tuition reimbursements (averaging $8,400 per year) were awarded; Federal Work-Study, institutionally sponsored loans, and unspecified assistantships also available. Support available to part-time students. Financial award application deadline: 8/1; financial award applicants required to submit FAFSA. *Unit head:* Dr. Catherine L. Pastille, Director, MBA Program, 401-865-1654, Fax: 401-865-2978, E-mail: cpastill@providence.edu. *Application contact:* Katherine A. Follett,

Administrative Coordinator, 401-865-2333, Fax: 401-865-2978, E-mail: kfollett@providence.edu. Web site: http://www.providence.edu/business/Pages/default.aspx.

Purdue University, Graduate School, Krannert School of Management, International Master's in Management Program, West Lafayette, IN 47907. Offers MBA. *Faculty:* 8 full-time (3 women), 15 part-time/adjunct (1 woman). *Students:* 61 full-time (10 women); includes 11 minority (2 Black or African American, non-Hispanic/Latino; 7 Asian, non-Hispanic/Latino; 2 Hispanic/Latino), 42 international. Average age 35. 53 applicants, 81% accepted, 32 enrolled. In 2011, 31 master's awarded. *Entrance requirements:* For master's, letters of recommendation, essays, transcripts, resume. *Application deadline:* For fall admission, 2/28 for domestic students, 2/15 for international students. Applications are processed on a rolling basis. Application fee: $60 ($75 for international students). Electronic applications accepted. *Financial support:* Scholarships/grants and tuition waivers (partial) available. Financial award application deadline: 2/1; financial award applicants required to submit FAFSA. *Faculty research:* Dimensions of trust, communities of practice and networks, business in Latin America. *Unit head:* Dr. Aldas P. Kriauciunas, Executive Director, 765-496-1860, Fax: 765-494-0862, E-mail: akriauci@purdue.edu. *Application contact:* JoAnn Whitford, Assistant Director of Admissions, 765-494-4580, Fax: 765-494-0862, E-mail: jwhitfor@purdue.edu. Web site: http://www.krannert.purdue.edu/programs/executive/imm/home.asp.

Regent's American College London, Webster Graduate School, London, United Kingdom. Offers business (MBA); finance (MS); human resources (MA); information technology management (MA); international business (MA); international non-governmental organizations (MA); international relations (MA); management and leadership (MA); marketing (MA). Part-time programs available.

Regis University, College for Professional Studies, School of Management, Denver, CO 80221-1099. Offers accounting (MS, Certificate); executive international management (Certificate); executive leadership (Certificate); executive project management (Certificate); finance and accounting (MBA); general business administration (MBA); health care management (MBA); human resource management and leadership (MSOL); information technology leadership and management (MSOL); international business (MBA); marketing (MBA); operations management (MBA); organizational leadership and management (MSOL); project leadership and management (MSOL); project management (Certificate); strategic business management (Certificate); strategic human resource management (Certificate); strategic management (MBA). Offered at Colorado Springs Campus, Northwest Denver Campus, Southeast Denver Campus, Fort Collins Campus, Broomfield Campus, Henderson (Nevada) Campus, and Summerlin (Nevada) Campus and online. Part-time and evening/weekend programs available. Postbaccalaureate distance learning degree programs offered (no on-campus study). *Degree requirements:* For master's, thesis optional, capstone project. *Entrance requirements:* For master's, GMAT or essays, interview, 2 years of full-time business work experience, resume; for Certificate, GMAT. Additional exam requirements/recommendations for international students: Required—TOEFL, TWE (minimum score 5) or university-based test. Electronic applications accepted. *Faculty research:* Impact of information technology on small business regulation of accounting, international project financing, mineral development, delivery of healthcare to rural indigenous communities.

Rochester Institute of Technology, Graduate Enrollment Services, E. Philip Saunders College of Business, Program in Management, Rochester, NY 14623-5603. Offers MS. Part-time and evening/weekend programs available. *Students:* 1 part-time (0 women). 26 applicants, 23% accepted, 0 enrolled. In 2011, 1 master's awarded. *Degree requirements:* For master's, comprehensive exam (for some programs), thesis (for some programs). *Entrance requirements:* For master's, GMAT, minimum GPA of 2.5. Additional exam requirements/recommendations for international students: Required—TOEFL (minimum score 580 paper-based; 237 computer-based; 92 iBT) or IELTS (minimum score 7). *Application deadline:* For fall admission, 2/15 priority date for domestic students, 2/15 for international students; for winter admission, 11/1 priority date for domestic students, 10/1 for international students; for spring admission, 2/1 priority date for domestic students, 1/1 for international students. Applications are processed on a rolling basis. Application fee: $50. *Expenses: Tuition:* Full-time $34,659; part-time $963 per credit hour. *Required fees:* $228; $76 per quarter. *Financial support:* Research assistantships with partial tuition reimbursements, teaching assistantships with partial tuition reimbursements, career-related internships or fieldwork, scholarships/grants, and unspecified assistantships available. Support available to part-time students. Financial award applicants required to submit FAFSA. *Faculty research:* Strategic and managerial issues associated with manufacturing and production systems, total quality management (TQM), technology-based entrepreneurship. *Unit head:* Melissa Ellison, Graduate Program Director, 585-475-2354, E-mail: maescb@rit.edu. *Application contact:* Diane Ellison, Assistant Vice President, Graduate Enrollment Services, 585-475-2229, Fax: 585-475-7164, E-mail: gradinfo@rit.edu. Web site: http://saunders.rit.edu/graduate/index.php.

Rollins College, Crummer Graduate School of Business, Winter Park, FL 32789-4499. Offers entrepreneurship (MBA); finance (MBA); international business (MBA); management (MBA); marketing (MBA); operations and technology management (MBA). *Accreditation:* AACSB. Part-time and evening/weekend programs available. Postbaccalaureate distance learning degree programs offered (minimal on-campus study). *Faculty:* 23 full-time (3 women), 6 part-time/adjunct (4 women). *Students:* 257 full-time (95 women), 121 part-time (39 women); includes 75 minority (12 Black or African American, non-Hispanic/Latino; 1 American Indian or Alaska Native, non-Hispanic/Latino; 20 Asian, non-Hispanic/Latino; 39 Hispanic/Latino; 3 Two or more races, non-Hispanic/Latino), 27 international. Average age 28. 363 applicants, 44% accepted, 100 enrolled. In 2011, 213 master's awarded. *Degree requirements:* For master's, minimum GPA of 2.85. *Entrance requirements:* For master's, GMAT or GRE, official transcripts, two letters of recommendation, essay, current resume/curriculum vitae, interview. Additional exam requirements/recommendations for international students: Required—TOEFL (minimum score 100 iBT) or IELTS (minimum score 7). *Application deadline:* Applications are processed on a rolling basis. Application fee: $50. Electronic applications accepted. *Expenses:* Contact institution. *Financial support:* In 2011–12, 258 students received support. Federal Work-Study and scholarships/grants available. Support available to part-time students. Financial award applicants required to submit FAFSA. *Faculty research:* Sustainability, world financial markets, international business, market research, strategic marketing. *Unit head:* Dr. Craig M. McAllaster, Dean, 407-646-2249, Fax: 407-646-1550, E-mail: cmcallaster@rollins.edu. *Application contact:* Eva Gauthier Oleksiw, Admissions Coordinator, 407-646-2405, Fax: 407-646-1550, E-mail: mbaadmissions@rollins.edu. Web site: http://www.rollins.edu/mba/.

Roosevelt University, Graduate Division, Walter E. Heller College of Business Administration, Program in International Business, Chicago, IL 60605. Offers MSIB. Part-time and evening/weekend programs available. *Degree requirements:* For master's, one foreign language. *Entrance requirements:* For master's, GMAT.

Rutgers, The State University of New Jersey, Newark, Graduate School, Program in Management, Newark, NJ 07102. Offers accounting (PhD); accounting information systems (PhD); computer information systems (PhD); finance (PhD); information technology (PhD); international business (PhD); management science (PhD); marketing (PhD); organization management (PhD). Program offered jointly with New Jersey Institute of Technology. *Accreditation:* AACSB. *Degree requirements:* For doctorate, thesis/dissertation, cumulative exams. *Entrance requirements:* For doctorate, GMAT or GRE General Test, minimum undergraduate B average. Additional exam requirements/recommendations for international students: Required—TOEFL. Electronic applications accepted. *Faculty research:* Technology management, leadership and teams, consumer behavior, financial and markets, logistics.

Rutgers, The State University of New Jersey, Newark, Rutgers Business School–Newark and New Brunswick, Doctoral Programs in Management, Newark, NJ 07102. Offers accounting (PhD); accounting information systems (PhD); economics (PhD); finance (PhD); individualized study (PhD); information technology (PhD); international business (PhD); management science (PhD); marketing science (PhD); organizational management (PhD); science, technology and management (PhD); supply chain management (PhD). *Degree requirements:* For doctorate, comprehensive exam, thesis/dissertation. *Entrance requirements:* For doctorate, GRE or GMAT. Additional exam requirements/recommendations for international students: Required—TOEFL (minimum score 550 paper-based; 213 computer-based; 79 iBT). Electronic applications accepted.

St. Edward's University, School of Management and Business, Area of Business Administration, Austin, TX 78704. Offers accounting (MBA); business management (MBA); finance (Certificate); global entrepreneurship (MBA); marketing (MBA, Certificate). Part-time and evening/weekend programs available. *Students:* 35 full-time (14 women), 218 part-time (114 women); includes 102 minority (22 Black or African American, non-Hispanic/Latino; 1 American Indian or Alaska Native, non-Hispanic/Latino; 11 Asian, non-Hispanic/Latino; 62 Hispanic/Latino; 1 Native Hawaiian or other Pacific Islander, non-Hispanic/Latino; 5 Two or more races, non-Hispanic/Latino), 14 international. Average age 32. 94 applicants, 71% accepted, 48 enrolled. In 2011, 104 master's awarded. *Degree requirements:* For master's, minimum of 24 resident hours. *Entrance requirements:* For master's, GMAT or GRE General Test, minimum GPA of 2.75 in last 60 hours of course work. Additional exam requirements/recommendations for international students: Required—TOEFL (minimum score 550 paper-based; 213 computer-based; 79 iBT) or IELTS (minimum score 6). *Application deadline:* For fall admission, 7/1 for domestic and international students; for spring admission, 11/1 for domestic and international students. Applications are processed on a rolling basis. Application fee: $45 ($50 for international students). Electronic applications accepted. *Expenses: Tuition:* Full-time $17,550; part-time $975 per credit hour. *Required fees:* $50 per trimester. Full-time tuition and fees vary according to course load and program. *Unit head:* Dr. Stan Horner, Director, 512-428-1279, Fax: 512-448-8492, E-mail: stanleyh@stedwards.edu. *Application contact:* Sarah Hennes, Graduate Admissions Coordinator, 512-448-8600, Fax: 512-428-1032, E-mail: sarahhe@stedwards.edu. Web site: http://www.stedwards.edu.

St. John's University, The Peter J. Tobin College of Business, Program in International Business, Queens, NY 11439. Offers MBA, Adv C. Part-time and evening/weekend programs available. *Students:* 32 full-time (19 women), 12 part-time (7 women); includes 8 minority (4 Black or African American, non-Hispanic/Latino; 2 Asian, non-Hispanic/Latino; 2 Hispanic/Latino), 16 international. Average age 25. 25 applicants, 72% accepted, 8 enrolled. In 2011, 22 master's awarded. *Degree requirements:* For master's, comprehensive exam (for some programs), thesis optional. *Entrance requirements:* For master's, GMAT, 2 letters of recommendation, resume, transcripts, essay; for Adv C, 2 letters of recommendation, resume, undergraduate and graduate transcripts, essay, MBA. Additional exam requirements/recommendations for international students: Required—TOEFL (minimum score 600 paper-based; 250 computer-based; 100 iBT), IELTS (minimum score 7). *Application deadline:* For fall admission, 5/1 priority date for domestic students, 5/1 for international students; for spring admission, 11/1 priority date for domestic students, 11/1 for international students. Applications are processed on a rolling basis. Application fee: $50. Electronic applications accepted. *Expenses:* Contact institution. *Financial support:* Research assistantships, scholarships/grants, and unspecified assistantships available. Support available to part-time students. Financial award application deadline: 3/1; financial award applicants required to submit FAFSA. *Unit head:* Dr. Victoria L. Shoaf, Dean. *Application contact:* Carol J. Swanberg, Assistant Dean/Director of Graduate Admissions, 718-990-1345, Fax: 718-990-5242, E-mail: tobingradnyc@stjohns.edu.

Saint Joseph's University, Erivan K. Haub School of Business, MS Program in International Marketing, Philadelphia, PA 19131-1395. Offers MS. Part-time and evening/weekend programs available. *Students:* 45 full-time (28 women), 12 part-time (8 women); includes 5 minority (3 Black or African American, non-Hispanic/Latino; 1 American Indian or Alaska Native, non-Hispanic/Latino; 1 Hispanic/Latino), 40 international. Average age 26. In 2011, 18 master's awarded. *Entrance requirements:* For master's, GMAT or GRE, 2 letters of recommendation, resume, personal statement. Additional exam requirements/recommendations for international students: Required—TOEFL (minimum score 550 paper-based; 213 computer-based; 80 iBT), IELTS (minimum score 6.5), or Pearson Test of English (minimum score 60). *Application deadline:* For fall admission, 7/15 priority date for domestic students; for spring admission, 11/15 priority date for domestic students. Applications are processed on a rolling basis. Application fee: $35. Electronic applications accepted. *Expenses: Tuition:* Part-time $735 per credit hour. Tuition and fees vary according to degree level and program. *Financial support:* In 2011–12, 2 research assistantships with partial tuition reimbursements (averaging $8,000 per year) were awarded; unspecified assistantships also available. Financial award application deadline: 5/1; financial award applicants required to submit FAFSA. *Faculty research:* Export marketing, global marketing, international marketing research, new product development, emerging markets, international consumer behavior. *Unit head:* Christine Kaczmar-Russo, Director, 610-660-1238, Fax: 610-660-3239, E-mail: ckaczmar@sju.edu. *Application contact:* Karena Whitmore, Administrative Assistant, MS Programs, 610-660-3211, Fax: 610-660-1599, E-mail: kwhitmor@sju.edu. Web site: http://www.sju.edu/academics/hsb/grad/mim/.

Saint Joseph's University, Erivan K. Haub School of Business, Professional MBA Program, Philadelphia, PA 19131-1395. Offers accounting (MBA); finance (MBA), including finance; general business (MBA); health and medical services administration (MBA); human resource management (MBA); international business (MBA); international marketing (MBA); management (MBA); marketing (MBA); DO/MBA. DO/MBA offered jointly with Philadelphia College of Osteopathic Medicine. Part-time and evening/weekend programs available. Postbaccalaureate distance learning degree programs offered (no on-campus study). *Students:* 98 full-time (42 women), 528 part-time (208 women); includes 102 minority (47 Black or African American, non-Hispanic/Latino; 1 American Indian or Alaska Native, non-Hispanic/Latino; 28 Asian, non-Hispanic/Latino; 20 Hispanic/Latino; 1 Native Hawaiian or other Pacific Islander, non-Hispanic/Latino; 5 Two or more races, non-Hispanic/Latino), 45 international. Average age 31. In 2011, 290 master's awarded. *Entrance requirements:* For master's, GMAT or GRE, 2 letters of recommendation, resume, personal statement. Additional exam requirements/recommendations for international students: Required—TOEFL (minimum score 550 paper-based; 213 computer-based; 80 iBT), IELTS (minimum score 6.5), or Pearson Test of English (minimum score 60). *Application deadline:* For fall admission, 7/15 priority date for domestic students, 4/15 for international students; for spring admission, 11/15 priority date for domestic students, 10/15 for international students. Applications are processed on a rolling basis. Application fee: $35. Electronic applications accepted. *Expenses: Tuition:* Part-time $735 per credit hour. Tuition and fees vary according to degree level and program. *Financial support:* Scholarships/grants and unspecified assistantships available. Financial award application deadline: 5/1; financial award applicants required to submit FAFSA. *Unit head:* Adele C. Foley, Associate Dean/Director, Graduate Business Programs, 610-660-1691, Fax: 610-660-1599, E-mail: afoley@sju.edu. *Application contact:* Dr. Janine N. Guerra, Associate Director, Professional MBA Program, 610-660-1695, Fax: 610-660-1599, E-mail: jguerra@sju.edu. Web site: http://www.sju.edu/mba.

Saint Louis University, Graduate Education, John Cook School of Business, Boeing Institute of International Business, St. Louis, MO 63103-2097. Offers business administration (PhD), including international business and marketing; executive international business (EMIB); international business (MBA). Part-time and evening/weekend programs available. *Degree requirements:* For master's, thesis, study abroad; for doctorate, comprehensive exam, thesis/dissertation. *Entrance requirements:* For master's, GMAT, work experience. Additional exam requirements/recommendations for international students: Required—TOEFL (minimum score 525 paper-based; 194 computer-based). *Expenses:* Contact institution. *Faculty research:* Foreign direct investment, technology transfer, emerging markets, Asian business, Latin American business.

St. Mary's University, Graduate School, Bill Greehey School of Business, MBA Program, San Antonio, TX 78228-8507. Offers finance (MBA); international business (MBA); management (MBA). Part-time and evening/weekend programs available. Postbaccalaureate distance learning degree programs offered (minimal on-campus study). *Degree requirements:* For master's, comprehensive exam. *Entrance requirements:* For master's, GMAT. Additional exam requirements/recommendations for international students: Required—TOEFL (minimum score 570 paper-based; 230 computer-based; 80 iBT).

Saint Mary's University of Minnesota, Schools of Graduate and Professional Programs, Graduate School of Business and Technology, International Business Program, Winona, MN 55987-1399. Offers MA. *Unit head:* Dushan Knezevich, Director, 612-728-5156, E-mail: dknezevi@smumn.edu. *Application contact:* Yasin Alsaidi, Director of Admissions for Graduate and Professional Programs, 612-728-5207, E-mail: yalsaidi@smumn.edu. Web site: http://www.smumn.edu/graduate-home/areas-of-study/graduate-school-of-business-technology/ma-in-international-business-twin-cities.

Saint Peter's University, Graduate Business Programs, MBA Program, Jersey City, NJ 07306-5997. Offers finance (MBA); health care administration (MBA); human resource management (MBA); international business (MBA); management (MBA); management information systems (MBA); marketing (MBA); risk management (MBA); MBA/MS. Part-time and evening/weekend programs available. *Entrance requirements:* Additional exam requirements/recommendations for international students: Required—TOEFL (minimum score 79 computer-based). Electronic applications accepted. *Faculty research:* Finance, health care management, human resource management, international business, management, management information systems, marketing, risk management.

St. Thomas University, School of Business, Department of Management, Miami Gardens, FL 33054-6459. Offers accounting (MBA); general management (MSM, Certificate); health management (MBA, MSM, Certificate); human resource management (MBA, MSM, Certificate); international business (MBA, MIB, MSM, Certificate); justice administration (MSM, Certificate); management accounting (MSM, Certificate); public management (MSM, Certificate); sports administration (MS). Part-time and evening/weekend programs available. *Degree requirements:* For master's, comprehensive exam. *Entrance requirements:* For master's, interview, minimum GPA of 3.0 or GMAT. Additional exam requirements/recommendations for international students: Required—TOEFL (minimum score 550 paper-based; 213 computer-based; 79 iBT). Electronic applications accepted.

Salem International University, School of Business, Salem, WV 26426-0500. Offers information security (MBA); international business (MBA). Part-time programs available. Postbaccalaureate distance learning degree programs offered (no on-campus study). *Entrance requirements:* For master's, minimum undergraduate GPA of 2.5, course work in business, resume. Additional exam requirements/recommendations for international students: Recommended—TOEFL (minimum score 550 paper-based; 213 computer-based), IELTS (minimum score 6.5). Electronic applications accepted. *Expenses:* Contact institution. *Faculty research:* Organizational behavior strategy, marketing services.

Santa Clara University, Leavey School of Business, Program in Business Administration, Santa Clara, CA 95053. Offers accounting (MBA); entrepreneurship (MBA); executive business administration (EMBA); finance (MBA); food and agribusiness (MBA); international business (MBA); leading people and organizations (MBA); managing technology and innovation (MBA); marketing management (MBA); supply chain management (MBA). *Accreditation:* AACSB. Part-time and evening/weekend programs available. *Students:* 196 full-time (80 women), 669 part-time (224 women); includes 302 minority (12 Black or African American, non-Hispanic/Latino; 246 Asian, non-Hispanic/Latino; 35 Hispanic/Latino; 6 Native Hawaiian or other Pacific Islander, non-Hispanic/Latino; 3 Two or more races, non-Hispanic/Latino), 186 international. Average age 32. 365 applicants, 74% accepted, 199 enrolled. In 2011, 366 degrees awarded. *Degree requirements:* For master's, thesis or alternative. *Entrance requirements:* For master's, GMAT, GRE. Additional exam requirements/recommendations for international students: Required—TOEFL (minimum score 600 paper-based; 250 computer-based; 100 iBT). *Application deadline:* For fall admission, 6/1 for domestic and international students; for spring admission, 1/19 for domestic students, 1/17 for international students. Applications are processed on a rolling basis. Application fee: $75 ($100 for international students). Electronic applications accepted. *Expenses:* Contact institution. *Financial support:* In 2011–12, 350 students received support. Fellowships with partial tuition reimbursements available, research assistantships with partial tuition reimbursements available, career-related internships or fieldwork, Federal Work-Study, institutionally sponsored loans, scholarships/grants, health care benefits, and unspecified assistantships available. Support available to part-time students. Financial award application deadline: 6/1; financial award applicants required to submit FAFSA. *Unit head:* Elizabeth B. Ford, Senior Assistant Dean, 408-554-2752, Fax: 408-554-4571, E-mail: eford@scu.edu. *Application contact:* Tammy Fox, Assistant Director, Graduate Business Admissions, 408-554-7858, E-mail: tkfox@scu.edu.

Schiller International University, MBA Program, Madrid, Spain, Madrid, Spain. Offers international business (MBA). Part-time programs available. *Degree requirements:* For master's, comprehensive exam, thesis optional. *Entrance requirements:* Additional exam requirements/recommendations for international students: Required—TOEFL (minimum score 550 paper-based; 213 computer-based).

Schiller International University, MBA Program Paris, France, Paris, France. Offers international business (MBA). Bilingual French/English MBA available for native French speakers. Part-time and evening/weekend programs available. Postbaccalaureate distance learning degree programs offered (no on-campus study). *Degree requirements:* For master's, comprehensive exam, thesis or alternative. *Entrance requirements:* Additional exam requirements/recommendations for international students: Required—TOEFL (minimum score 550 paper-based; 213 computer-based).

Schiller International University, MBA Programs, Florida, Program in International Business, Largo, FL 33770. Offers MBA. Part-time and evening/weekend programs available. Postbaccalaureate distance learning degree programs offered (no on-campus study). *Degree requirements:* For master's, thesis optional. *Entrance requirements:* Additional exam requirements/recommendations for international students: Required—TOEFL (minimum score 550 paper-based; 213 computer-based).

Schiller International University, MBA Programs, Heidelberg, Germany, Heidelberg, Germany. Offers international business (MBA, MIM); management of information technology (MBA). Part-time and evening/weekend programs available. *Degree requirements:* For master's, thesis optional. *Entrance requirements:* Additional exam requirements/recommendations for international students: Required—TOEFL (minimum score 550 paper-based; 213 computer-based). *Faculty research:* Leadership, international economy, foreign direct investment.

Schiller International University, MBA Program, Strasbourg, France Campus, Strasbourg, France. Offers international business (MBA). Part-time and evening/weekend programs available. Postbaccalaureate distance learning degree programs offered (no on-campus study). *Degree requirements:* For master's, oral comprehensive exam or thesis. *Entrance requirements:* Additional exam requirements/recommendations for international students: Recommended—TOEFL (minimum score 550 paper-based; 213 computer-based).

Seton Hall University, Stillman School of Business, Department of International Business, South Orange, NJ 07079-2697. Offers MBA, Certificate. Part-time and evening/weekend programs available. *Faculty:* 5 full-time (1 woman), 2 part-time/adjunct (0 women). *Students:* 11 full-time (5 women), 11 part-time (4 women); includes 7 minority (2 Black or African American, non-Hispanic/Latino; 2 Asian, non-Hispanic/Latino; 3 Hispanic/Latino). Average age 28. 20 applicants, 55% accepted, 9 enrolled. In 2011, 1 master's awarded. *Entrance requirements:* For master's, GMAT, GRE or CPA, advanced degree from AACSB institution, MS in a business discipline, professional degree (MD, JD, PhD, DVM, DDS, etc.), minimum undergraduate GPA of 3.0; for Certificate, master's degree. Additional exam requirements/recommendations for international students: Required—TOEFL (minimum score 102 iBT), IELTS or Pearson Test of English. *Application deadline:* For fall admission, 5/31 priority date for domestic students, 3/31 for international students; for spring admission, 10/31 priority date for domestic students. Applications are processed on a rolling basis. Application fee: $75. Electronic applications accepted. *Expenses:* Contact institution. *Financial support:* In 2011–12, 1 student received support, including research assistantships with full tuition reimbursements available (averaging $35,610 per year); career-related internships or fieldwork, scholarships/grants, and unspecified assistantships also available. Support available to part-time students. Financial award application deadline: 6/30; financial award applicants required to submit FAFSA. *Faculty research:* International marketing, Asian financial markets, economics in eastern Europe and accounting in the Middle East. *Unit head:* Dr. Laurence McCarthy, 973-275-2957, Fax: 973-275-2465, E-mail: laurence.mccarthy@shu.edu. *Application contact:* Catherine Bianchi, Director of Graduate Admissions, 973-761-9262, Fax: 973-761-9208, E-mail: catherine.bianchi@shu.edu. Web site: http://www.shu.edu/academics/business/international-business.

Seton Hall University, Stillman School of Business, Programs in Business Administration, South Orange, NJ 07079-2697. Offers accounting (MBA); finance (MBA); information technology management (MBA); international business (MBA); management (MBA); marketing (MBA); sport management (MBA); supply chain management (MBA). Part-time and evening/weekend programs available. *Faculty:* 37 full-time (9 women), 19 part-time/adjunct (1 woman). *Students:* 166 full-time (65 women), 284 part-time (131 women); includes 113 minority (21 Black or African American, non-Hispanic/Latino; 81 Asian, non-Hispanic/Latino; 9 Hispanic/Latino; 2 Native Hawaiian or other Pacific Islander, non-Hispanic/Latino). Average age 29. 459 applicants, 59% accepted, 208 enrolled. In 2011, 210 master's awarded. *Degree requirements:* For master's, 20 hours of community service (Social Responsibility Project). *Entrance requirements:* For master's, GMAT, GRE or CPA, advanced degree from AACSB institution, MS in a business discipline, professional degree (MD, JD, PhD, DVM, DDS, etc.), minimum undergraduate GPA of 3.0. Additional exam requirements/recommendations for international students: Required—TOEFL (minimum score 102 iBT), IELTS or Pearson Test of English. *Application deadline:* For fall admission, 5/31 priority date for domestic students, 3/31 for international students; for spring admission, 10/31 priority date for domestic students, 9/30 for international students. Applications are processed on a rolling basis. Application fee: $75. Electronic applications accepted. *Expenses: Tuition:* Part-time $1033 per credit hour. *Required fees:* $85 per semester. *Financial support:* In 2011–12, research assistantships with full tuition reimbursements (averaging $35,610 per year) were awarded; career-related internships or fieldwork, Federal Work-Study, scholarships/grants, and unspecified assistantships also available. Support available to part-time students. Financial award application deadline: 6/30; financial award applicants required to submit FAFSA. *Faculty research:* Financial, hedge funds, international business, legal issues, disclosure and branding. *Unit head:* Dr. Joyce A. Strawser, Dean, 973-761-9013, Fax: 973-761-9217, E-mail: joyce.strawser@shu.edu. *Application contact:* Catherine Bianchi, Director of Graduate Admissions, 973-761-9262, Fax: 973-761-9208, E-mail: catherine.bianchi@shu.edu. Web site: http://www.shu.edu/academics/business.

Simon Fraser University, Graduate Studies, Faculty of Business Administration, Burnaby, BC V5A 1S6, Canada. Offers business administration (EMBA, PhD); financial management (MA); general business (MBA); global asset and wealth management (MBA); management of technology/biotechnology (MBA); MBA/MRM. *Accreditation:* AACSB. Postbaccalaureate distance learning degree programs offered. *Degree requirements:* For master's, thesis or written project. *Entrance requirements:* For master's, minimum GPA of 3.0. Additional exam requirements/recommendations for international students: Required—TOEFL. *Expenses:* Contact institution. *Faculty research:* Leadership, marketing and technology, wealth management.

SIT Graduate Institute, Graduate Programs, Master's Programs in Intercultural Service, Leadership, and Management, Brattleboro, VT 05302-0676. Offers conflict transformation (MA); intercultural service, leadership, and management (MA); international education (MA); sustainable development (MA). Postbaccalaureate distance learning degree programs offered (minimal on-campus study). *Degree requirements:* For master's, one foreign language, thesis. *Entrance requirements:* For master's, 3 letters of reference. Additional exam requirements/recommendations for international students: Required—TOEFL. *Faculty research:* Intercultural communication, conflict resolution, advising and training, world issues, international business.

Southeast Missouri State University, School of Graduate Studies, Harrison College of Business, Cape Girardeau, MO 63701-4799. Offers accounting (MBA); entrepreneurship (MBA); financial management (MBA); general management (MBA); health administration (MBA); industrial management (MBA); international business (MBA); sport management (MBA). *Accreditation:* AACSB. Part-time and evening/weekend programs available. Postbaccalaureate distance learning degree programs offered (no on-campus study). *Faculty:* 31 full-time (10 women). *Students:* 49 full-time (23 women), 77 part-time (30 women); includes 5 minority (1 Black or African American, non-Hispanic/Latino; 1 American Indian or Alaska Native, non-Hispanic/Latino; 2 Hispanic/Latino; 1 Two or more races, non-Hispanic/Latino), 35 international. Average age 27. 78 applicants, 69% accepted, 43 enrolled. In 2011, 47 master's awarded. *Degree requirements:* For master's, variable foreign language requirement, comprehensive exam, applied research project related to field. *Entrance requirements:* For master's, GMAT (minimum score of 450), minimum undergraduate GPA of 2.5, C or better in prerequisite courses. Additional exam requirements/recommendations for international students: Required—TOEFL (minimum score 550 paper-based; 213 computer-based; 79 iBT); Recommended—IELTS (minimum score 6). *Application deadline:* For fall admission, 8/1 for domestic students, 7/1 for international students; for spring admission, 11/21 for domestic students, 11/1 for international students. Applications are processed on a rolling basis. Application fee: $30 ($40 for international students). Electronic applications accepted. *Expenses:* Tuition, state resident: full-time $4896; part-time $272 per credit hour. Tuition, nonresident: full-time $8649; part-time $480.50 per credit hour. *Financial support:* In 2011–12, 46 students received support, including 12 teaching assistantships with full tuition reimbursements available (averaging $7,600 per year); career-related internships or fieldwork, Federal Work-Study, scholarships/grants, tuition waivers (full), and unspecified assistantships also available. Financial award application deadline: 6/30; financial award applicants required to submit FAFSA. *Faculty research:* Human resources, laws impacting accounting, advertising. *Unit head:* Dr. Kenneth A. Heischmidt, Director, Graduate Programs in Business, 573-651-5116, Fax: 573-651-5032, E-mail: kheischmidt@semo.edu. *Application contact:* Gail Amick, Administrative Secretary, 573-651-2049, Fax: 573-651-2001, E-mail: gamick@semo.edu. Web site: http://www.semo.edu/mba.

Southern New Hampshire University, School of Business, Manchester, NH 03106-1045. Offers accounting (MS); business administration (MBA, Certificate), including accounting (Certificate), business administration (MBA), finance (Certificate), forensic accounting (Certificate), human resources management (Certificate), international business (Certificate), international sport management (Certificate), leadership of not for profit organizations (Certificate), marketing (Certificate), operations management (Certificate), sport management (Certificate), taxation (Certificate); finance (MS); hospitality and tourism leadership (Certificate); information technology (MS, Certificate); information technology/international business (Certificate); integrated marketing communications (Certificate); international business (MS, DBA); marketing (MS); operations and project management (MS); organizational leadership (MS); project management (Certificate); sport management (MS); MBA/Certificate. *Accreditation:* ACBSP. Part-time and evening/weekend programs available. Postbaccalaureate distance learning degree programs offered (no on-campus study). Terminal master's awarded for partial completion of doctoral program. *Degree requirements:* For master's, one foreign language, comprehensive exam (for some programs), thesis or alternative; for doctorate, one foreign language, comprehensive exam, thesis/dissertation. *Entrance requirements:* For master's, minimum GPA of 2.5; for doctorate, GMAT. Additional exam requirements/recommendations for international students: Required—TOEFL (minimum score 500 paper-based). Electronic applications accepted.

Stevens Institute of Technology, Graduate School, Wesley J. Howe School of Technology Management, Program in Management, Hoboken, NJ 07030. Offers general management (MS); global innovation management (MS); human resource management (MS); information management (MS); project management (MS); technology commercialization (MS); technology management (MS). Part-time programs available. *Degree requirements:* For master's, thesis optional. *Entrance requirements:* For master's, GMAT, GRE General Test. Additional exam requirements/recommendations for international students: Required—TOEFL. Electronic applications accepted. *Faculty research:* Industrial economics.

Suffolk University, College of Arts and Sciences, Department of Economics, Boston, MA 02108-2770. Offers economic policy (MSEP); economics (MSE, PhD); international economics (MSIE); JD/MSIE. Part-time and evening/weekend programs available. *Faculty:* 13 full-time (3 women). *Students:* 18 full-time (6 women), 17 part-time (4 women); includes 6 minority (1 Black or African American, non-Hispanic/Latino; 3 Asian, non-Hispanic/Latino; 2 Hispanic/Latino), 14 international. Average age 27. 120 applicants, 53% accepted, 15 enrolled. In 2011, 8 master's, 5 doctorates awarded. *Degree requirements:* For doctorate, comprehensive exam, thesis/dissertation. *Entrance requirements:* For master's, GRE General Test or GMAT, 2 letters of recommendation, resume; for doctorate, GRE General Test, 3 letters of recommendation. Additional exam requirements/recommendations for international students: Required—TOEFL (minimum score 550 paper-based; 213 computer-based; 80 iBT). *Application deadline:* For fall admission, 6/15 priority date for domestic students, 6/15 for international students; for spring admission, 11/1 priority date for domestic students, 11/1 for international students. Applications are processed on a rolling basis. Application fee: $50. Electronic applications accepted. *Expenses:* Contact institution. *Financial support:* In 2011–12, 29 students received support, including 28 fellowships with full and partial tuition reimbursements available (averaging $13,237 per year); career-related internships or fieldwork, Federal Work-Study, and institutionally sponsored loans also available. Support available to part-time students. Financial award application deadline: 4/1; financial award applicants required to submit FAFSA. *Faculty research:* Trade demands, fair tax, smoking, multinational firms, charitable giving, fair tax. *Unit head:* Dr. David Tuerck, Chairperson, 617-573-8259, Fax: 617-994-4216, E-mail: dtuerck@suffolk.edu. *Application contact:* Ellen Driscoll, Director of Graduate Admissions, 617-573-8302, Fax: 617-305-1733, E-mail: grad.admission@suffolk.edu. Web site: http://www.suffolk.edu/economics.

Suffolk University, Sawyer Business School, Master of Business Administration Program, Boston, MA 02108-2770. Offers accounting (MBA); business administration (APC); corporate financial executive track (MBA); entrepreneurship (MBA); executive business administration (EMBA); finance (MBA); global business administration (GMBA); health administration (MBA); international business (MBA); marketing (MBA); organizational behavior (MBA); strategic management (MBA); taxation (MBA); JD/MBA; MBA/GDPA; MBA/MHA; MBA/MSA; MBA/MSF; MBA/MST. *Accreditation:* AACSB. Part-time and evening/weekend programs available. Postbaccalaureate distance learning degree programs offered (no on-campus study). *Faculty:* 98 full-time (30 women), 14 part-time/adjunct (3 women). *Students:* 139 full-time (49 women), 321 part-time (138 women); includes 53 minority (17 Black or African American, non-Hispanic/Latino; 1 American Indian or Alaska Native, non-Hispanic/Latino; 21 Asian, non-Hispanic/Latino; 11 Hispanic/Latino; 1 Native Hawaiian or other Pacific Islander, non-Hispanic/Latino; 2 Two or more races, non-Hispanic/Latino), 64 international. Average age 30. 437 applicants, 61% accepted, 121 enrolled. In 2011, 283 master's awarded. *Entrance requirements:* For master's, GMAT, minimum undergraduate GPA of 2.75 (MBA), 5 years of managerial experience (EMBA). Additional exam requirements/recommendations for international students: Required—TOEFL (minimum score 550 paper-based; 213 computer-based). *Application deadline:* For fall admission, 6/15 priority date for domestic students, 6/15 for international students; for spring admission, 11/1 priority date for domestic students, 11/1 for international students. Applications are processed on a rolling basis. Application fee: $50. Electronic applications accepted. Tuition and fees vary according to program. *Financial support:* In 2011–12, 273 students received support, including 73 fellowships with full and partial tuition reimbursements available (averaging $12,415 per year); career-related internships or fieldwork, Federal Work-Study, and institutionally sponsored loans also available. Support available to part-time students. Financial award application deadline: 4/1; financial award applicants required to submit FAFSA. *Faculty research:* Foreign investments; career strategies and boundaryless careers; corporate ethics codes; interest rates, inflation, and growth options; innovation and product development performance. *Unit head:* Lillian Hallberg, Assistant Dean of Graduate Programs/Director of MBA Programs, 617-573-8306, E-mail: lhallber@suffolk.edu. *Application contact:* Ellen Driscoll, Director of Graduate Admissions, 617-573-8302, Fax: 617-305-1733, E-mail: grad.admission@suffolk.edu. Web site: http://www.suffolk.edu/mba.

Taylor University, Master of Business Administration Program, Upland, IN 46989-1001. Offers emerging business strategies (MBA); global leadership (MBA). Part-time programs available. *Faculty:* 1 full-time (0 women), 5 part-time/adjunct (0 women). *Students:* 42 full-time (13 women), 6 part-time (1 woman); includes 3 minority (1 Black or African American, non-Hispanic/Latino; 2 Hispanic/Latino). Average age 35. 27 applicants, 85% accepted, 22 enrolled. In 2011, 26 master's awarded. *Application deadline:* Applications are processed on a rolling basis. Application fee: $100. *Expenses: Tuition:* Full-time $9800; part-time $570 per credit hour. *Required fees:* $72 per semester. One-time fee: $100. Tuition and fees vary according to program. *Financial support:* Applicants required to submit FAFSA. *Unit head:* Dr. Evan Wood, Interim Chair, 260-627-9663, E-mail: evwood@taylor.edu. *Application contact:* Wendy Speakman, Program Director, 866-471-6062, Fax: 260-492-0452, E-mail: wnspeakman@taylor.edu. Web site: http://www.taylor.edu/mba/.

Temple University, Fox School of Business, Doctoral Programs in Business, Philadelphia, PA 19122-6096. Offers accounting (PhD); entrepreneurship (PhD); finance (PhD); international business (PhD); management information systems (PhD); marketing (PhD); risk management and insurance (PhD); statistics (PhD); strategic management (PhD); tourism and sport (PhD). *Accreditation:* AACSB. *Degree requirements:* For doctorate, thesis/dissertation. *Entrance requirements:* For doctorate, GRE General Test, GMAT, minimum GPA of 3.0, master's degree. Additional exam requirements/recommendations for international students: Required—TOEFL (minimum score 600 paper-based; 250 computer-based; 100 iBT), IELTS (minimum score 7.5). Electronic applications accepted. *Expenses:* Tuition, state resident: full-time $12,366; part-time $687 per credit hour. Tuition, nonresident: full-time $17,298; part-time $961 per credit hour. *Required fees:* $590; $213 per year.

Temple University, Fox School of Business, MBA Programs, Philadelphia, PA 19122-6096. Offers accounting (MBA); business management (MBA); financial management (MBA); healthcare and life sciences innovation (MBA); human resource management (MBA); international business (IMBA); IT management (MBA); marketing management (MBA); pharmaceutical management (MBA); strategic management (EMBA, MBA). EMBA offered in Philadelphia, PA and Tokyo, Japan. *Accreditation:* AACSB. Part-time and evening/weekend programs available. Postbaccalaureate distance learning degree programs offered (minimal on-campus study). *Entrance requirements:* For master's, GMAT, minimum undergraduate GPA of 3.0. Additional exam requirements/recommendations for international students: Required—TOEFL (minimum score 600 paper-based; 250 computer-based; 100 iBT), IELTS (minimum score 7.5). *Expenses:* Tuition, state resident: full-time $12,366; part-time $687 per credit hour. Tuition, nonresident: full-time $17,298; part-time $961 per credit hour. *Required fees:* $590; $213 per year.

Tennessee Technological University, Graduate School, College of Business, Cookeville, TN 38505. Offers accounting (MBA); finance (MBA); human resource management (MBA); international business (MBA); management information systems (MBA); risk management & insurance (MBA). *Accreditation:* AACSB. Part-time and evening/weekend programs available. Postbaccalaureate distance learning degree programs offered (no on-campus study). *Faculty:* 28 full-time (5 women). *Students:* 45 full-time (19 women), 135 part-time (51 women); includes 13 minority (4 Black or African American, non-Hispanic/Latino; 5 Asian, non-Hispanic/Latino; 3 Hispanic/Latino; 1 Native Hawaiian or other Pacific Islander, non-Hispanic/Latino), 2 international. Average age 25. 193 applicants, 59% accepted, 70 enrolled. In 2011, 89 master's awarded. *Entrance requirements:* For master's, GMAT. Additional exam requirements/recommendations for international students: Required—TOEFL (minimum score 550 paper-based; 79 iBT), IELTS (minimum score 5.5), Pearson Test of English Academic. *Application deadline:* For fall admission, 8/1 for domestic students, 5/1 for international students; for spring admission, 12/1 for domestic students, 10/1 for international students. Application fee: $25 ($30 for international students). Electronic applications accepted. *Expenses:* Tuition, state resident: full-time $8094; part-time $422 per credit hour. Tuition, nonresident: full-time $20,574; part-time $1046 per credit hour. *Financial support:* In 2011–12, 5 fellowships (averaging $10,000 per year), 18 research assistantships (averaging $4,000 per year), teaching assistantships (averaging $4,000 per year) were awarded. Support available to part-time students. Financial award application deadline: 4/1. *Unit head:* Dr. Tom Timmerman, Director, 931-372-3600, Fax: 931-372-6249. *Application contact:* Shelia K. Kendrick, Coordinator of Graduate Admissions, 931-372-3808, Fax: 931-372-3497, E-mail: skendrick@tntech.edu. Web site: http://www.tntech.edu/mba.

Texas A&M International University, Office of Graduate Studies and Research, College of Business Administration, Division of International Business and Technology Studies, Laredo, TX 78041-1900. Offers information systems (MSIS); international trade (MBA). *Faculty:* 12 full-time (1 woman), 1 part-time/adjunct (0 women). *Students:* 29 full-time (8 women), 20 part-time (5 women); includes 12 minority (3 Black or African American, non-Hispanic/Latino; 2 Asian, non-Hispanic/Latino; 7 Hispanic/Latino), 32 international. Average age 28. 111 applicants, 22% accepted, 11 enrolled. In 2011, 19 master's awarded. *Degree requirements:* For master's, thesis (for some programs). *Entrance requirements:* For master's, GMAT or GRE General Test. Additional exam requirements/recommendations for international students: Required—TOEFL (minimum score 550 paper-based; 213 computer-based; 79 iBT). *Application deadline:* For fall admission, 4/30 priority date for domestic students, 4/30 for international students; for spring admission, 11/30 for domestic students, 10/1 for international students. Applications are processed on a rolling basis. Application fee: $35 ($50 for international students). *Expenses:* Tuition, state resident: full-time $5063. *Financial support:* In 2011–12, 8 students received support, including 2 fellowships, 5 research assistantships, 1 teaching assistantship; Federal Work-Study, institutionally sponsored loans, and scholarships/grants also available. Support available to part-time students. *Unit head:* Dr. S. Srinivasan, Chair, 956-326-2520, Fax: 956-326-2494, E-mail: srini@tamiu.edu. *Application contact:* Imelda Lopez, Graduate Admissions Counselor, 956-326-2485, Fax: 956-326-2459, E-mail: lopez@tamiu.edu. Web site: http://www.tamiu.edu/ssb/divisions.php?optN-220.

Texas A&M University–Corpus Christi, Graduate Studies and Research, College of Business, Corpus Christi, TX 78412-5503. Offers accounting (M Acc); health care administration (MBA); international business (MBA). *Accreditation:* AACSB. Part-time and evening/weekend programs available. *Degree requirements:* For master's, comprehensive exam, thesis (for some programs). *Entrance requirements:* For master's,

GMAT. Additional exam requirements/recommendations for international students: Required—TOEFL. Electronic applications accepted.

Texas A&M University–San Antonio, School of Business, San Antonio, TX 78224. Offers business administration (MBA); enterprise resource planning systems (MBA); finance (MBA); healthcare management (MBA); human resources management (MBA); information assurance and security (MBA); international business (MBA); professional accounting (MPA); project management (MBA); supply chain management (MBA). Part-time and evening/weekend programs available. *Faculty:* 18 full-time (6 women), 1 part-time/adjunct (0 women). *Students:* 91 full-time (45 women), 278 part-time (150 women). Average age 33. In 2011, 20 master's awarded. *Entrance requirements:* For master's, GMAT. Additional exam requirements/recommendations for international students: Required—TOEFL (minimum score 550 paper-based; 213 computer-based; 80 iBT), IELTS (minimum score 6). *Application deadline:* For fall admission, 7/1 priority date for domestic students, 6/1 for international students; for spring admission, 11/15 priority date for domestic students, 10/1 for international students. Applications are processed on a rolling basis. Application fee: $35 ($50 for international students). Electronic applications accepted. *Expenses:* Tuition, state resident: part-time $691.11 per course. Tuition, nonresident: part-time $1621.11 per course. *Financial support:* Application deadline: 3/31; applicants required to submit FAFSA. *Unit head:* Dr. Tracy Hurley, MBA Coordinator, 210-932-6200, E-mail: tracy.hurley@tamusa.tamus.edu. *Application contact:* Melissa A. Villanueva, Graduate Admissions Specialist, 210-932-6200, Fax: 210-932-6209, E-mail: melissa.villanueva@tamusa.tamus.edu. Web site: http://www.tamusa.tamus.edu.

Texas Tech University, Graduate School, Rawls College of Business Administration, Programs in Business Administration, Lubbock, TX 79409. Offers agricultural business (MBA); business administration (IMBA); business statistics (MBA); entrepreneurship and innovation (MBA); general business (MBA); health organization management (MBA); international business (MBA); management and leadership skills (MBA); management information systems (MBA); marketing (MBA); real estate (MBA); JD/MBA; MBA/M Arch; MBA/MA; MBA/MD; MBA/MS; MBA/Pharm D. Part-time and evening/weekend programs available. *Faculty:* 49 full-time (8 women), 2 part-time/adjunct (0 women). *Students:* 195 full-time (55 women), 397 part-time (101 women); includes 123 minority (27 Black or African American, non-Hispanic/Latino; 4 American Indian or Alaska Native, non-Hispanic/Latino; 31 Asian, non-Hispanic/Latino; 61 Hispanic/Latino), 38 international. Average age 31. 374 applicants, 83% accepted, 255 enrolled. In 2011, 256 degrees awarded. *Degree requirements:* For master's, capstone course. *Entrance requirements:* For master's, GMAT, holistic review of academic credentials. Additional exam requirements/recommendations for international students: Required—TOEFL (minimum score 550 paper-based; 213 computer-based; 79 iBT). *Application deadline:* For fall admission, 4/1 priority date for domestic students, 1/15 for international students; for spring admission, 9/1 priority date for domestic students, 6/15 for international students. Applications are processed on a rolling basis. Application fee: $50 ($75 for international students). Electronic applications accepted. *Expenses:* Tuition, state resident: full-time $5899; part-time $245.80 per credit hour. Tuition, nonresident: full-time $13,411; part-time $558.80 per credit hour. *Required fees:* $2680.60; $86.50 per credit hour. $920.30 per semester. *Financial support:* In 2011–12, 22 research assistantships (averaging $8,800 per year) were awarded; teaching assistantships, career-related internships or fieldwork, Federal Work-Study, scholarships/grants, health care benefits, and unspecified assistantships also available. Support available to part-time students. Financial award applicants required to submit FAFSA. *Unit head:* Dr. W. Jay Conover, Director, 806-742-1546, Fax: 806-742-3958, E-mail: jay.conover@ttu.edu. *Application contact:* Elizabeth Stuart, Director, Graduate Services Center, 806-742-3184, Fax: 806-742-3958, E-mail: ba_grad@ttu.edu. Web site: http://mba.ba.ttu.edu/.

Thunderbird School of Global Management, Executive MBA Program–Glendale, Glendale, AZ 85306. Offers global management (MBA). Part-time and evening/weekend programs available. *Faculty:* 18 full-time (5 women). *Students:* 95 part-time (19 women); includes 26 minority (3 Black or African American, non-Hispanic/Latino; 2 American Indian or Alaska Native, non-Hispanic/Latino; 12 Asian, non-Hispanic/Latino; 7 Hispanic/Latino; 2 Two or more races, non-Hispanic/Latino), 23 international. Average age 39. 61 applicants, 98% accepted, 47 enrolled. In 2011, 52 master's awarded. *Degree requirements:* For master's, one foreign language. *Entrance requirements:* For master's, 8 years of full-time work experience, 3 years of management experience, company sponsorship, mid-management position. Additional exam requirements/recommendations for international students: Recommended—TOEFL. *Application deadline:* For fall admission, 6/10 priority date for domestic students, 4/30 for international students. Applications are processed on a rolling basis. Application fee: $125. Electronic applications accepted. *Expenses:* Contact institution. *Financial support:* In 2011–12, 25 students received support. Application deadline: 6/7; applicants required to submit FAFSA. *Faculty research:* Management, social enterprise, cross-cultural communication, finance, marketing. *Unit head:* Barbara Carpenter, Associate Vice President, EMBA Programs, 602-978-7921, Fax: 602-978-7463, E-mail: barbara.carpenter@thunderbird.edu. *Application contact:* Jay Bryant, Director of Admissions, 602-978-7294, Fax: 602-439-5432, E-mail: jay.bryant@thunderbird.edu. Web site: http://www.thunderbird.edu.

Thunderbird School of Global Management, Global MBA Program for Latin American Managers, Glendale, AZ 85306. Offers GMBA. Offered jointly with Instituto Tecnológico y de Estudios Superiores de Monterrey. Part-time and evening/weekend programs available. Postbaccalaureate distance learning degree programs offered. *Students:* 266 part-time (78 women); includes 6 minority (1 American Indian or Alaska Native, non-Hispanic/Latino; 1 Asian, non-Hispanic/Latino; 4 Hispanic/Latino), 256 international. Average age 31. 194 applicants, 89% accepted, 115 enrolled. In 2011, 121 master's awarded. *Entrance requirements:* For master's, GMAT or PAEP (Pruebade Admisiona Estudios Posgrado), minimum GPA of 3.0, 2 years of work experience. Additional exam requirements/recommendations for international students: Required—TOEFL (minimum score 550 paper-based; 213 computer-based; 79 iBT). *Application deadline:* For spring admission, 4/25 priority date for domestic students, 4/25 for international students. Application fee: $125. *Expenses:* Contact institution. *Financial support:* Scholarships/grants available. Financial award application deadline: 4/30. *Faculty research:* Globalization impact on Latin American business, doing business in Latin America, international marketing in Latin America. *Unit head:* Dr. Bert Valencia, Vice President, 602-978-7534, Fax: 602-978-7729, E-mail: globalmba@thunderbird.edu. *Application contact:* Jay Bryant, Director of Admissions, 602-978-7294, Fax: 602-439-5432, E-mail: jay.bryant@thunderbird.edu. Web site: http://www.thunderbird.edu.

Thunderbird School of Global Management, GMBA - On Demand Program, Glendale, AZ 85306-6000. Offers GMBA. Part-time programs available. Postbaccalaureate distance learning degree programs offered (minimal on-campus study). *Students:* 134 part-time (48 women); includes 15 minority (3 Black or African American, non-Hispanic/Latino; 4 Asian, non-Hispanic/Latino; 5 Hispanic/Latino; 3 Two or more races, non-Hispanic/Latino), 30 international. Average age 32. 54 applicants, 80% accepted, 31 enrolled. In 2011, 55 master's awarded. *Entrance requirements:* For master's, GMAT. Additional exam requirements/recommendations for international students: Required—TOEFL. *Application deadline:* For fall admission, 6/10 for domestic students, 4/30 for international students. Application fee: $125. *Expenses:* *Tuition:* Full-time $43,080; part-time $1436 per credit. *Financial support:* Scholarships/grants available. Financial award application deadline: 2/15. *Unit head:* Dr. Bert Valencia, Vice President, 602-978-7534, Fax: 602-978-7729, E-mail: globalmba@thunderbird.edu. *Application contact:* Jay Bryant, Director of Admissions, 602-978-7294, Fax: 602-439-5432, E-mail: jay.bryant@thunderbird.edu. Web site: http://www.thunderbird.edu.

Thunderbird School of Global Management, Master's Programs in Global Management, Glendale, AZ 85306. Offers global affairs and management (MA); global management (MS). *Accreditation:* AACSB. *Students:* 141 full-time (78 women); includes 12 minority (1 Black or African American, non-Hispanic/Latino; 2 Asian, non-Hispanic/Latino; 4 Hispanic/Latino; 5 Two or more races, non-Hispanic/Latino), 90 international. 132 applicants, 84% accepted, 70 enrolled. In 2011, 79 master's awarded. *Degree requirements:* For master's, one foreign language. *Entrance requirements:* For master's, GMAT/GRE. Additional exam requirements/recommendations for international students: Required—TOEFL. *Application deadline:* For fall admission, 6/10 for domestic students, 4/30 for international students. Application fee: $125. *Expenses:* *Tuition:* Full-time $43,080; part-time $1436 per credit. *Financial support:* Career-related internships or fieldwork, Federal Work-Study, scholarships/grants, and unspecified assistantships available. *Unit head:* Dr. Glenn Fong, Unit Head, 602-978-7156. *Application contact:* Jay Bryant, Director of Admissions, 602-978-7294, Fax: 602-439-5432, E-mail: jay.bryant@thunderbird.edu.

Tiffin University, Program in Business Administration, Tiffin, OH 44883-2161. Offers finance (MBA); general management (MBA); healthcare administration (MBA); human resources (MBA); international business (MBA); leadership (MBA); marketing (MBA); sports management (MBA). *Accreditation:* ACBSP. Part-time and evening/weekend programs available. Postbaccalaureate distance learning degree programs offered (no on-campus study). *Faculty:* 30 full-time (15 women), 22 part-time/adjunct (6 women). *Students:* 209 full-time (107 women), 340 part-time (172 women); includes 112 minority (91 Black or African American, non-Hispanic/Latino; 4 Asian, non-Hispanic/Latino; 17 Hispanic/Latino), 71 international. Average age 31. 237 applicants, 76% accepted. In 2011, 170 master's awarded. *Entrance requirements:* For master's, minimum undergraduate GPA of 2.5, work experience. Additional exam requirements/recommendations for international students: Required—TOEFL (minimum score 550 paper-based; 213 computer-based; 79 iBT). *Application deadline:* For fall admission, 8/15 for domestic students, 8/1 for international students; for spring admission, 1/9 for domestic students, 12/1 for international students. Applications are processed on a rolling basis. Electronic applications accepted. *Expenses:* *Tuition:* Full-time $11,200; part-time $700 per credit. Tuition and fees vary according to program. *Financial support:* Available to part-time students. Application deadline: 7/31; applicants required to submit FAFSA. *Faculty research:* Small business, executive development operations, research and statistical analysis, market research, management information systems. *Unit head:* Dr. Lillian Schumacher, Dean of the School of Business, 419-448-3053, Fax: 419-443-5002, E-mail: schumacherlb@tiffin.edu. *Application contact:* Nikki Hintze, Director of Graduate Admissions and Student Services, 800-968-6446 Ext. 3445, Fax: 419-443-5002, E-mail: hintzenm@tiffin.edu. Web site: http://www.tiffin.edu/graduateprograms/.

Trident University International, College of Business Administration, Program in Business Administration, Cypress, CA 90630. Offers business administration (PhD); conflict and negotiation management (MBA); criminal justice administration (MBA); entrepreneurship (MBA); finance (MBA); general management (MBA); government accounting (MBA); human resource management (MBA); information security and digital assurance management (MBA); information technology management (MBA); international business (MBA); logistics management (MBA); marketing (MBA); project management (MBA); public management (MBA); quality management (MBA); strategic leadership (MBA). Part-time and evening/weekend programs available. Postbaccalaureate distance learning degree programs offered (no on-campus study). *Degree requirements:* For doctorate, comprehensive exam, thesis/dissertation, defense of dissertation. *Entrance requirements:* For master's, minimum GPA of 2.5 (students with GPA 3.0 or greater may transfer up to 30% of graduate level credits); for doctorate, minimum GPA of 3.4, curriculum vitae, course work in research methods or statistics. Additional exam requirements/recommendations for international students: Required—TOEFL. Electronic applications accepted.

Trinity Western University, School of Graduate Studies, Program in Business Administration, Langley, BC V2Y 1Y1, Canada. Offers international business (MBA); management of the growing enterprise (MBA); non-profit and charitable organization management (MBA). Part-time programs available. Postbaccalaureate distance learning degree programs offered (minimal on-campus study). *Degree requirements:* For master's, thesis or alternative, applied project. *Entrance requirements:* For master's, GMAT (minimum score of 550 recommended). Additional exam requirements/recommendations for international students: Required—TOEFL (minimum score 600 paper-based; 250 computer-based; 100 iBT), IELTS. Electronic applications accepted.

Troy University, Graduate School, College of Business, Program in Management, Troy, AL 36082. Offers applied management (MSM); healthcare management (MSM); human resources management (MSM); information systems (MSM); international hospitality management (MSM); international management (MSM); leadership and organizational effectiveness (MSM); public management (MS, MSM). *Accreditation:* ACBSP. Evening/weekend programs available. *Faculty:* 21 full-time (2 women), 7 part-time/adjunct (2 women). *Students:* 52 full-time (33 women), 284 part-time (183 women); includes 222 minority (186 Black or African American, non-Hispanic/Latino; 5 American Indian or Alaska Native, non-Hispanic/Latino; 11 Asian, non-Hispanic/Latino; 13 Hispanic/Latino; 1 Native Hawaiian or other Pacific Islander, non-Hispanic/Latino; 6 Two or more races, non-Hispanic/Latino). Average age 35. 157 applicants, 76% accepted, 55 enrolled. In 2011, 234 master's awarded. *Degree requirements:* For master's, Graduate Educational Testing Service Major Field Test, capstone exam, minimum GPA of 3.0. *Entrance requirements:* For master's, GMAT (minimum score 500) or GRE General Test (minimum score 900), minimum GPA of 2.5, bachelor's degree, letter of recommendation. Additional exam requirements/recommendations for international students: Required—TOEFL (minimum score 523 paper-based; 193 computer-based; 70 iBT), IELTS (minimum score 6), or ACT COMPASS ESL (minimum listening, reading, and grammar score 270). *Application deadline:* Applications are processed on a rolling basis. Application fee: $50. Electronic applications accepted. *Expenses:* Contact institution. *Unit head:* Dr. Edward Merkel, Director, Graduate Business Programs, 334-670-3194, Fax: 334-670-3599, E-mail: emerkel@troy.edu. *Application contact:* Brenda K. Campbell, Director of Graduate Admissions, 334-670-3178, Fax: 334-670-3733, E-mail: bcamp@troy.edu.

Tufts University, Fletcher School of Law and Diplomacy, Medford, MA 02155. Offers LL M, MA, MALD, MIB, PhD, DVM/MA, JD/MALD, MALD/MA, MALD/MBA, MALD/MS, MD/MA. Postbaccalaureate distance learning degree programs offered (minimal on-campus study). *Degree requirements:* For master's, one foreign language, thesis; for doctorate, one foreign language, comprehensive exam, thesis/dissertation, dissertation defense. *Entrance requirements:* For master's and doctorate, GMAT or GRE General Test. Additional exam requirements/recommendations for international students: Required—TOEFL (minimum score 600 paper-based; 250 computer-based; 100 iBT), IELTS (minimum score 7). Electronic applications accepted. *Expenses:* Contact institution. *Faculty research:* Negotiation and conflict resolution, international organizations, international business and economic law, security studies, development economics.

United States International University, School of Business Administration, Nairobi, Kenya. Offers business administration (GEMBA); entrepreneurship (MBA); finance (MBA); human resource management (MBA); information technology management (MBA); integrated studies (MBA); international business administration (MBA); management and organizational development (MS); marketing (MBA); organizational development (EMS); strategic management (MBA). Part-time and evening/weekend programs available. *Degree requirements:* For master's, thesis. *Entrance requirements:* For master's, GMAT, 2 letters of reference, resume. Additional exam requirements/recommendations for international students: Required—TOEFL (minimum score 550 paper-based; 213 computer-based). *Faculty research:* Marketing in small business enterprises, total quality management in Kenya.

Universidad Autonoma de Guadalajara, Graduate Programs, Guadalajara, Mexico. Offers administrative law and justice (LL M); advertising and corporate communications (MA); architecture (M Arch); business (MBA); computational science (MCC); education (Ed M, Ed D); English-Spanish translation (MA); entrepreneurship and management (MBA); integrated management of digital animation (MA); international business (MIB); international corporate law (LL M); internet technologies (MS); manufacturing systems (MMS); occupational health (MS); philosophy (MA, PhD); power electronics (MS); quality systems (MQS); renewable energy (MS); social evaluation of projects (MBA); strategic market research (MBA); tax law (MA); teaching mathematics (MA).

Universidad Metropolitana, School of Business Administration, Program in International Business, San Juan, PR 00928-1150. Offers MBA.

Université de Sherbrooke, Faculty of Administration, Program in International Business, Sherbrooke, QC J1K 2R1, Canada. Offers M Sc. *Faculty:* 3 full-time (0 women), 3 part-time/adjunct (1 woman). *Students:* 56 full-time (31 women), 2 part-time (1 woman). Average age 24. 116 applicants, 59% accepted, 29 enrolled. In 2011, 32 master's awarded. *Degree requirements:* For master's, one foreign language, thesis. *Entrance requirements:* For master's, bachelor's degree in related field, minimum GPA of 3.0 (on 4.3 scale). *Application deadline:* For fall admission, 4/30 for domestic students, 1/15 for international students. Applications are processed on a rolling basis. Application fee: $70. Electronic applications accepted. *Unit head:* Prof. Julien Bilodeau, Director, Graduate Programs in Business, 819-821-8000 Ext. 62355. *Application contact:* Marie-Claude Drouin, Programs Director's Assistant, 819-821-8000 Ext. 63301.

Université du Québec, École nationale d'administration publique, Graduate Program in Public Administration, Program in International Administration, Quebec, QC G1K 9E5, Canada. Offers MAP, Diploma. Part-time programs available. *Entrance requirements:* For degree, appropriate bachelor's degree, proficiency in French.

Université Laval, Faculty of Administrative Sciences, Programs in Business Administration, Québec, QC G1K 7P4, Canada. Offers accounting (MBA); agri-food management (MBA); electronic business (MBA, Diploma); factory management and logistics (MBA); finance (MBA); firm management (MBA); geomatic management (MBA); information technology management (MBA); international management (MBA); management (MBA); management accounting (MBA, Diploma); marketing (MBA); modeling and organizational decision (MBA); occupational health and safety management (MBA); pharmacy management (MBA); social and environmental responsibility (MBA); technological entrepreneurship (Diploma). *Accreditation:* AACSB. Part-time and evening/weekend programs available. Postbaccalaureate distance learning degree programs offered (no on-campus study). *Entrance requirements:* For master's and Diploma, knowledge of French and English. Electronic applications accepted.

University at Buffalo, the State University of New York, Graduate School, College of Arts and Sciences, Department of Geography, Buffalo, NY 14260. Offers earth systems science (MA); economic geography and international business and world trade (MA); environmental modeling and analysis (MA); geographic information science (MA, Certificate); geography (MA, PhD); transportation and business geographics (MA, Certificate); urban and regional geography (MA); MA/MBA. *Faculty:* 15 full-time (7 women), 1 part-time/adjunct (0 women). *Students:* 102 full-time (38 women), 20 part-time (10 women); includes 61 minority (1 Black or African American, non-Hispanic/Latino; 55 Asian, non-Hispanic/Latino; 5 Hispanic/Latino), 1 international. 167 applicants, 33% accepted, 29 enrolled. In 2011, 21 master's, 5 doctorates awarded. Terminal master's awarded for partial completion of doctoral program. *Degree requirements:* For master's, thesis (for some programs), project or portfolio; for doctorate, thesis/dissertation. *Entrance requirements:* For master's, GRE General Test, minimum GPA of 2.9; for doctorate, GRE General Test, minimum GPA of 3.0. Additional exam requirements/recommendations for international students: Required—TOEFL (minimum score 550 paper-based; 213 computer-based; 79 iBT). *Application deadline:* For fall admission, 7/1 priority date for domestic students, 1/10 for international students; for spring admission, 12/1 priority date for domestic students, 10/1 for international students. Applications are processed on a rolling basis. Application fee: $75. Electronic applications accepted. *Financial support:* In 2011–12, 13 students received support, including 8 fellowships with full tuition reimbursements available (averaging $4,750 per year), 13 teaching assistantships with full tuition reimbursements available (averaging $13,520 per year); research assistantships with full tuition reimbursements available, career-related internships or fieldwork, Federal Work-Study, institutionally sponsored loans, traineeships, health care benefits, and unspecified assistantships also available. Financial award application deadline: 1/10. *Faculty research:* International business and world trade, geographic information systems and cartography, transportation, urban and regional analysis, physical and environmental geography. *Total annual research expenditures:* $630,314. *Unit head:* Dr. Sharmistha Bagchi-Sen, Chairman, 716-645-0473, Fax: 716-645-2329, E-mail: geosbs@buffalo.edu. *Application contact:* Betsy Abraham, Graduate Secretary, 716-645-0471, Fax: 716-645-2329, E-mail: babraham@buffalo.edu. Web site: http://www.geog.buffalo.edu/.

The University of Akron, Graduate School, College of Business Administration, Department of Marketing, Akron, OH 44325. Offers international business (MBA); international business for international executive (MBA); strategic marketing (MBA); JD/MBA. Part-time and evening/weekend programs available. *Faculty:* 12 full-time (2 women), 3 part-time/adjunct (1 woman). *Students:* 24 full-time (9 women), 20 part-time (16 women); includes 4 minority (1 Black or African American, non-Hispanic/Latino; 2 Hispanic/Latino; 1 Two or more races, non-Hispanic/Latino), 10 international. Average age 27. 42 applicants, 45% accepted, 13 enrolled. In 2011, 18 master's awarded. *Entrance requirements:* For master's, GMAT, minimum GPA of 2.75, two letters of recommendation, statement of purpose, resume. Additional exam requirements/recommendations for international students: Required—TOEFL (minimum score 550 paper-based; 213 computer-based; 79 iBT). *Application deadline:* For fall admission, 7/15 for domestic and international students; for spring admission, 11/15 for domestic and international students. Application fee: $30 ($40 for international students). Electronic applications accepted. *Expenses:* Tuition, state resident: full-time $7038; part-time $391 per credit hour. Tuition, nonresident: full-time $12,051; part-time $670 per credit hour. *Required fees:* $1274; $34 per credit hour. *Financial support:* In 2011–12, 10 teaching assistantships with full tuition reimbursements were awarded. *Faculty research:* Multi-channel marketing, direct interactive marketing, strategic retailing, marketing strategy and telemarketing. *Total annual research expenditures:* $19,735. *Unit head:* Dr. William Baker, Chair, 330-972-8466, E-mail: wbaker@uakron.edu. *Application contact:* Dr. Susan Hanlon, Director of Graduate Business Programs, 330-972-7043, Fax: 330-972-6588, E-mail: shanlon@uakron.edu. Web site: http://www.uakron.edu/cba/cba-home/dept-cent-inst/marketing/index.dot.

The University of Akron, Graduate School, College of Business Administration, Program in International Business, Akron, OH 44325. Offers MBA, JD/MBA. Part-time and evening/weekend programs available. *Students:* 7 full-time (4 women), 6 part-time (5 women); includes 2 minority (1 Black or African American, non-Hispanic/Latino; 1 Asian, non-Hispanic/Latino), 4 international. Average age 26. 18 applicants, 50% accepted, 4 enrolled. In 2011, 5 master's awarded. *Entrance requirements:* For master's, GMAT, minimum GPA of 2.75, two letters of recommendation, resume, statement of purpose. Additional exam requirements/recommendations for international students: Required—TOEFL (minimum score 550 paper-based; 213 computer-based; 79 iBT). *Application deadline:* For fall admission, 7/15 for domestic and international students; for spring admission, 11/15 for domestic and international students. Application fee: $30 ($40 for international students). Electronic applications accepted. *Expenses:* Tuition, state resident: full-time $7038; part-time $391 per credit hour. Tuition, nonresident: full-time $12,051; part-time $670 per credit hour. *Required fees:* $1274; $34 per credit hour. *Financial support:* In 2011–12, 1 research assistantship with full tuition reimbursement, 2 teaching assistantships with full tuition reimbursements were awarded. *Unit head:* Dr. Ravi Krovi, Interim Dean, 330-972-7442, E-mail: cbadean@uakron.edu. *Application contact:* Dr. Susan Hanlon, Director of Graduate Business Programs, 330-972-7043, Fax: 330-972-6588, E-mail: shanlon@uakron.edu.

University of Alberta, Faculty of Graduate Studies and Research, Program in Business Administration, Edmonton, AB T6G 2E1, Canada. Offers international business (MBA); leisure and sport management (MBA); natural resources and energy (MBA); technology commercialization (MBA); MBA/LL B; MBA/M Ag; MBA/M Eng; MBA/MF; MBA/PhD. *Accreditation:* AACSB. Part-time and evening/weekend programs available. *Degree requirements:* For master's, thesis or alternative. *Entrance requirements:* For master's, GMAT. Additional exam requirements/recommendations for international students: Required—TOEFL (minimum score 600 paper-based; 250 computer-based). Electronic applications accepted. *Faculty research:* Natural resources and energy/management and policy/family enterprise/international business/healthcare research management.

University of Bridgeport, School of Business, Bridgeport, CT 06604. Offers accounting (MBA); finance (MBA); general business (MBA); global financial services (MBA); human resource management (MBA); information systems and knowledge management (MBA); international business (MBA); management (MBA); marketing (MBA); operations management (MBA); small business and entrepreneurship (MBA); specialized business (MBA). Part-time and evening/weekend programs available. *Faculty:* 11 full-time (2 women), 39 part-time/adjunct (8 women). *Students:* 198 full-time (105 women), 94 part-time (47 women); includes 38 minority (16 Black or African American, non-Hispanic/Latino; 9 Asian, non-Hispanic/Latino; 10 Hispanic/Latino; 3 Two or more races, non-Hispanic/Latino), 227 international. Average age 28. 835 applicants, 56% accepted, 57 enrolled. In 2011, 155 master's awarded. *Degree requirements:* For master's, thesis optional. *Entrance requirements:* For master's, GMAT. Additional exam requirements/recommendations for international students: Recommended—TOEFL (minimum score 550 paper-based; 213 computer-based; 80 iBT), IELTS (minimum score 6.5). *Application deadline:* For fall admission, 8/1 priority date for domestic students, 8/1 for international students; for spring admission, 12/1 priority date for domestic students, 12/1 for international students. Applications are processed on a rolling basis. Application fee: $50. Electronic applications accepted. *Expenses:* Contact institution. *Financial support:* In 2011–12, 69 students received support. Fellowships, research assistantships, teaching assistantships, career-related internships or fieldwork, Federal Work-Study, institutionally sponsored loans, and tuition waivers (partial) available. Support available to part-time students. Financial award application deadline: 6/1; financial award applicants required to submit FAFSA. *Unit head:* Dr. Robert Gilmore, Dean, 203-576-4384, Fax: 203-576-4388, E-mail: rgilmore@bridgeport.edu. *Application contact:* Karissa Peckham, Dean of Admissions, 203-576-4552, Fax: 203-576-4941, E-mail: mba@bridgeport.edu. Web site: http://www.bridgeport.edu.

The University of British Columbia, Sauder School of Business, Doctoral Program in Commerce and Business Administration, Vancouver, BC V6T 1Z1, Canada. Offers accounting (PhD); finance (PhD); international business (PhD); management information systems (PhD); management science (PhD); marketing (PhD); organizational behavior (PhD); strategy and business economics (PhD); transportation and logistics (PhD); urban land economics (PhD). *Degree requirements:* For doctorate, comprehensive exam, thesis/dissertation. *Entrance requirements:* For doctorate, GMAT or GRE. Additional exam requirements/recommendations for international students: Required—TOEFL (minimum score 600 paper-based; 250 computer-based; 100 iBT). Electronic applications accepted.

University of California, Berkeley, UC Berkeley Extension, International Diploma Programs, Berkeley, CA 94720-1500. Offers business administration (Certificate); finance (Certificate); global business management (Certificate); marketing (Certificate); project management (Certificate). *Accreditation:* AACSB.

University of California, Los Angeles, Graduate Division, UCLA Anderson School of Management, Los Angeles, CA 90095-1481. Offers accounting (PhD); Asia Pacific (EMBA); business administration (EMBA, MBA); decisions, operations and technology management (PhD); finance (PhD); financial engineering (MFE); global economics and management (PhD); Latin America (EMBA); management and organizations (PhD); marketing (PhD); strategy (PhD); DDS/MBA; MBA/JD; MBA/MD; MBA/MLAS; MBA/MLIS; MBA/MPH; MBA/MPP; MBA/MSCS; MBA/MSN; MBA/MUP. *Accreditation:* AACSB. Part-time programs available. *Faculty:* 90 full-time (14 women), 62 part-time/adjunct (14 women). *Students:* 1,103 full-time (312 women), 842 part-time (223 women); includes 663 minority (18 Black or African American, non-Hispanic/Latino; 510 Asian, non-Hispanic/Latino; 46 Hispanic/Latino; 2 Native Hawaiian or other Pacific Islander, non-Hispanic/Latino; 87 Two or more races, non-Hispanic/Latino), 469 international. 4,737 applicants, 32% accepted, 875 enrolled. In 2011, 759 master's, 6 doctorates awarded. *Degree requirements:* For master's, comprehensive exam, field study consulting project (for MBA); thesis/dissertation (for MFE); for doctorate, comprehensive exam, thesis/dissertation, oral and written qualifying exams. *Entrance requirements:* For master's, GMAT (for MBA); GMAT or GRE General Test (for MFE), 4-year bachelor's degree or equivalent; for doctorate, GMAT or GRE General Test, 4-year bachelor's degree from regionally-accredited institution; minimum GPA of 3.0. Additional exam requirements/recommendations for international students: Required—TOEFL (minimum score 560 paper-based; 220 computer-based; 87 iBT), IELTS (minimum score 7). *Application deadline:* For fall admission, 10/26 for domestic and international students; for winter admission, 1/11 for domestic and international students; for spring admission, 4/18 for domestic and international students. Application fee: $200. Electronic applications accepted. *Expenses:* Contact institution. *Financial support:* In 2011–12, 600 students received support. Fellowships, research assistantships, teaching assistantships, career-related internships or fieldwork, institutionally sponsored loans, scholarships/grants, health care benefits, and tuition waivers (partial) available. Financial award application deadline: 4/15; financial award applicants required to submit FAFSA. *Unit head:* Judy D. Olian, Dean, 310-825-7982, Fax: 310-206-2073, E-mail: judy.olian@anderson.ucla.edu. *Application contact:* Robert Weiler, Assistant Dean, Director of MBA Admissions and Financial Aid, 310-825-6944, Fax: 310-825-8582, E-mail: mba.admissions@anderson.ucla.edu. Web site: http://www.anderson.ucla.edu/.

See Display on page 141 and Close-Up on page 249.

University of Chicago, Booth School of Business, Executive MBA Program Asia, Singapore, IL 238466, Singapore. Offers MBA. Part-time programs available. *Entrance requirements:* For master's, interview, letter of company support, 3 letters of recommendation, resume. Additional exam requirements/recommendations for international students: Recommended—TOEFL (minimum score 600 paper-based; 250 computer-based). Electronic applications accepted. *Expenses:* Contact institution. *Faculty research:* Finance, marketing, international business, general management, strategy.

University of Chicago, Booth School of Business, Executive MBA Program Europe, London, IL EC2V 5HA, United Kingdom. Offers MBA. Part-time programs available. *Entrance requirements:* For master's, interview, 3 letters of recommendation, letter of company support, resume. Additional exam requirements/recommendations for international students: Recommended—TOEFL (minimum score 600 paper-based; 250 computer-based). Electronic applications accepted. *Expenses:* Contact institution. *Faculty research:* Finance, marketing, international business, general management, strategy.

University of Chicago, Booth School of Business, Executive MBA Program North America, Chicago, IL 60611. Offers MBA. Part-time programs available. *Entrance requirements:* For master's, interview, company-sponsored letter, 3 letters of recommendation, resume. Additional exam requirements/recommendations for international students: Required—TOEFL (minimum score 600 paper-based; 250 computer-based), IELTS. Electronic applications accepted. *Expenses:* Contact institution. *Faculty research:* Finance, marketing, international business, general management, strategy.

University of Chicago, Booth School of Business, Full-Time MBA Program, Chicago, IL 60637. Offers accounting (MBA); analytic finance (MBA); analytic management (MBA); business administration (PhD); econometrics and statistics (MBA); economics (MBA); entrepreneurship (MBA); finance (MBA); general management (MBA); health administration and policy (Certificate); human resource management (MBA); international business (IMBA, MBA); managerial and organizational behavior (MBA); marketing management (MBA); operations management (MBA); strategic management (MBA); MBA/AM; MBA/JD; MBA/MA; MBA/MD; MBA/MPP. *Accreditation:* AACSB. Part-time and evening/weekend programs available. *Faculty:* 166 full-time, 32 part-time/adjunct. *Students:* 1,160 full-time (412 women); includes 316 minority (61 Black or African American, non-Hispanic/Latino; 173 Asian, non-Hispanic/Latino; 63 Hispanic/Latino; 19 Two or more races, non-Hispanic/Latino), 378 international. Average age 28. 4,169 applicants, 575 enrolled. In 2011, 1,423 master's, 19 doctorates awarded. Terminal master's awarded for partial completion of doctoral program. *Entrance requirements:* For master's, GMAT, 2 letters of recommendation, 3 essays, resume, interview. Additional exam requirements/recommendations for international students: Required—TOEFL (minimum score 600 paper-based; 250 computer-based; 104 iBT), IELTS. *Application deadline:* For fall admission, 10/12 priority date for domestic students, 10/12 for international students; for winter admission, 1/4 for domestic and international students; for spring admission, 4/4 for domestic and international students. Application fee: $200. Electronic applications accepted. *Expenses:* Contact institution. *Financial support:* Fellowships available. Financial award applicants required to submit FAFSA. *Faculty research:* Finance, marketing, economics, entrepreneurship, strategy, management. *Unit head:* Stacey Kole, Deputy Dean, 773-702-7121. *Application contact:* Kurt Ahlm, Associate Dean of Student Recruitment and Admissions, 773-702-7369, Fax: 773-702-9085, E-mail: admissions@chicagobooth.edu. Web site: http://chicagobooth.edu/.

University of Chicago, Booth School of Business, International MBA Program, Chicago, IL 60637-1513. Offers IMBA. *Accreditation:* AACSB. *Degree requirements:* For master's, one foreign language, study abroad. *Entrance requirements:* For master's, GMAT, 2 letters of recommendation. Additional exam requirements/recommendations for international students: Required—TOEFL (minimum score 600 paper-based; 250 computer-based), IELTS. Electronic applications accepted.

University of Colorado Denver, Business School, Program in Global Energy Management, Denver, CO 80217. Offers MS. Postbaccalaureate distance learning degree programs offered (minimal on-campus study). *Students:* 59 full-time (15 women); includes 6 minority (1 Black or African American, non-Hispanic/Latino; 1 Asian, non-Hispanic/Latino; 4 Hispanic/Latino), 2 international. Average age 34. 27 applicants, 93% accepted, 17 enrolled. In 2011, 53 master's awarded. *Degree requirements:* For master's, 36 semester credit hours. *Entrance requirements:* For master's, GMAT if less than three years of experience in the energy industry and no undergraduate degree in energy sciences or engineering, minimum of 5 years' experience in energy industry. Additional exam requirements/recommendations for international students: Required—TOEFL (minimum score 525 paper-based; 71 iBT). *Application deadline:* For fall admission, 6/1 for domestic and international students; for winter admission, 12/1 for domestic and international students. Application fee: $50 ($75 for international students). Electronic applications accepted. *Expenses:* Contact institution. *Financial support:* Application deadline: 4/1; applicants required to submit FAFSA. *Unit head:* Wayne Cascio, Chair in Global Leadership Management, 303-315-8434, E-mail: wayne.cascio@ucdenver.edu. *Application contact:* Shelly Townley, Admissions Coordinator, 303-315-8202, Fax: 303-556-5904, E-mail: shelly.townley@ucdenver.edu. Web site: http://www.ucdenver.edu/academics/colleges/business/degrees/ms/gem/Pages/Overview.aspx.

University of Colorado Denver, Business School, Program in International Business, Denver, CO 80217. Offers MSIB. Part-time and evening/weekend programs available. *Students:* 23 full-time (12 women), 3 part-time (1 woman); includes 4 minority (3 Asian, non-Hispanic/Latino; 1 Hispanic/Latino), 6 international. Average age 28. 18 applicants, 61% accepted, 4 enrolled. In 2011, 19 master's awarded. *Degree requirements:* For master's, one foreign language, thesis optional, 42 credit hours. *Entrance requirements:* For master's, GMAT, resume, essay, two letters of recommendation, financial statements (for international applicants). Additional exam requirements/recommendations for international students: Required—TOEFL (minimum score 525 paper-based; 197 computer-based; 71 iBT). *Application deadline:* For fall admission, 4/15 priority date for domestic students, 3/15 for international students; for spring admission, 10/15 priority date for domestic students, 10/1 for international students. Applications are processed on a rolling basis. Application fee: $50 ($75 for international students). Electronic applications accepted. *Expenses:* Contact institution. *Financial support:* Federal Work-Study and scholarships/grants available. Support available to part-time students. Financial award application deadline: 4/1; financial award applicants required to submit FAFSA. *Faculty research:* Foreign direct investment, international business strategies, cross-cultural management, internationalization of research and development, global leadership development. *Unit head:* Dr. Manuel Serapio, Associate Professor/Director of MS in International Business, 303-315-8436, E-mail: manuel.serapio@ucdenver.edu. *Application contact:* Shelly Townley, Admissions Director, Graduate Programs, 303-315-8202, E-mail: shelly.townley@ucdenver.edu. Web site: http://www.ucdenver.edu/academics/colleges/business/degrees/ms/ib/Pages/International-Business.aspx.

University of Colorado Denver, Business School, Program in Management and Organization, Denver, CO 80217. Offers communications management (MS); entrepreneurship and innovation (MS); global management (MS); human resources management (MS); leadership and management (MS); sports and entertainment management (MS). *Accreditation:* AACSB. Part-time and evening/weekend programs available. Postbaccalaureate distance learning degree programs offered (no on-campus study). *Students:* 29 full-time (14 women), 14 part-time (10 women); includes 3 minority (2 Asian, non-Hispanic/Latino; 1 Hispanic/Latino), 5 international. Average age 31. 32 applicants, 63% accepted, 14 enrolled. In 2011, 22 master's awarded. *Degree requirements:* For master's, 30 semester hours (12 of required courses, 12 of management electives, and 6 of free electives). *Entrance requirements:* For master's, GMAT, resume, two letters of recommendation, essay, financial statements (for international applicants). Additional exam requirements/recommendations for international students: Required—TOEFL (minimum score 525 paper-based; 197 computer-based; 71 iBT). *Application deadline:* For fall admission, 4/15 priority date for domestic students, 3/15 for international students; for spring admission, 10/15 priority date for domestic students, 10/1 for international students. Applications are processed on a rolling basis. Application fee: $50 ($75 for international students). Electronic applications accepted. *Expenses:* Contact institution. *Financial support:* Federal Work-Study and scholarships/grants available. Support available to part-time students. Financial award application deadline: 4/1; financial award applicants required to submit FAFSA. *Faculty research:* Human resource management, management of catastrophe, turnaround strategies. *Unit head:* Dr. Kenneth Bettenhausen, Associate Professor/Director of MS in Management, 303-315-8425, E-mail: kenneth.bettenhausen@ucdenver.edu. *Application contact:* Shelly Townley, Admissions Director, Graduate Programs, 303-315-8202, E-mail: shelly.townley@ucdenver.edu. Web site: http://www.ucdenver.edu/academics/colleges/business/degrees/ms/management/Pages/Management.aspx.

University of Colorado Denver, Business School, Program in Marketing, Denver, CO 80217. Offers brand management and marketing communication (MS); global marketing (MS); high-tech and entrepreneurial marketing (MS); Internet marketing (MS); marketing for sustainability (MS); marketing research (MS); sports and entertainment marketing (MS). Part-time and evening/weekend programs available. *Students:* 39 full-time (29 women), 11 part-time (6 women); includes 4 minority (3 Hispanic/Latino; 1 Two or more races, non-Hispanic/Latino), 8 international. Average age 28. 40 applicants, 65% accepted, 16 enrolled. In 2011, 8 master's awarded. *Degree requirements:* For master's, 30 semester hours (21 of marketing core courses, 9 of graduate marketing electives). *Entrance requirements:* For master's, GMAT, resume, essay, two letters of recommendation, financial statements (for international applicants). Additional exam requirements/recommendations for international students: Required—TOEFL (minimum score 525 paper-based; 197 computer-based; 71 iBT). *Application deadline:* For fall admission, 4/15 priority date for domestic students, 3/15 for international students; for spring admission, 10/15 priority date for domestic students, 10/1 for international students. Applications are processed on a rolling basis. Application fee: $50 ($75 for international students). Electronic applications accepted. *Expenses:* Contact institution. *Financial support:* Federal Work-Study and scholarships/grants available. Support available to part-time students. Financial award application deadline: 4/1; financial award applicants required to submit FAFSA. *Faculty research:* Marketing issues in the Chinese environment, impact of individual difference and contextual factors on the risk-taking behaviors of managers making new-business creation decisions, attribution theory perspective of conflict between marketers and engineers, organizational identity and identification, international market entry strategies. *Unit head:* Dr. David Forlani, Associate Professor/Director of Marketing Programs, 303-315-8420, E-mail: david.forlani@ucdenver.edu. *Application contact:* Shelly Townley, Admissions Director, Graduate Programs, 303-315-8202, E-mail: shelly.townley@ucdenver.edu. Web site: http://www.ucdenver.edu/academics/colleges/business/degrees/ms/marketing/Pages/Marketing.aspx.

University of Dallas, Graduate School of Management, Irving, TX 75062-4736. Offers accounting (MBA, MM, MS); business management (MBA, MM); corporate finance (MBA, MM); financial services (MBA); global business (MBA, MM); health services management (MBA, MM); human resource management (MBA, MM); information assurance (MBA, MM, MS); information technology (MBA, MM, MS); information technology service management (MBA, MM, MS); marketing management (MBA, MM); organization development (MBA, MM); project management (MBA, MM); sports and entertainment management (MBA, MM); strategic leadership (MBA, MM); supply chain management (MBA); supply chain management and market logistics (MM). *Accreditation:* ACBSP. Part-time and evening/weekend programs available. Postbaccalaureate distance learning degree programs offered (no on-campus study). *Entrance requirements:* Additional exam requirements/recommendations for international students: Required—TOEFL. Electronic applications accepted. *Expenses:* Contact institution.

University of Denver, Daniels College of Business, Programs in International Business/Management, Denver, CO 80208. Offers IMBA, MBA. *Accreditation:* AACSB. *Students:* 65 full-time (22 women), 13 part-time (10 women); includes 12 minority (2 Black or African American, non-Hispanic/Latino; 1 American Indian or Alaska Native, non-Hispanic/Latino; 3 Asian, non-Hispanic/Latino; 5 Hispanic/Latino; 1 Two or more races, non-Hispanic/Latino), 5 international. Average age 28. 87 applicants, 85% accepted, 34 enrolled. In 2011, 39 degrees awarded. *Degree requirements:* For master's, one foreign language. *Entrance requirements:* For master's, GRE General Test or GMAT, two letters of recommendation, essay. Additional exam requirements/recommendations for international students: Required—TOEFL (minimum score 570 paper-based; 88 iBT). *Application deadline:* For fall admission, 5/15 priority date for domestic students. Applications are processed on a rolling basis. Application fee: $100. Electronic applications accepted. *Financial support:* In 2011–12, 47 students received support. Career-related internships or fieldwork, Federal Work-Study, institutionally sponsored loans, and scholarships/grants available. Support available to part-time students. Financial award application deadline: 2/15; financial award applicants required to submit FAFSA. *Unit head:* Leslie Carter, Associate Director, 303-871-2037, E-mail: leslie.carter@du.edu. *Application contact:* Tara Stenbakken, Graduate Admissions Manager, 303-871-4211, E-mail: tara.stenbakken@du.edu.

University of Denver, Josef Korbel School of International Studies, Denver, CO 80210. Offers conflict resolution (MA); global finance, trade and economic integration (MA); global health affairs (Certificate); homeland security (Certificate); humanitarian assistance (Certificate); international administration (MA); international development (MA); international human rights (MA); international security (MA); international studies (MA, PhD). Part-time programs available. *Faculty:* 41 full-time (14 women), 33 part-time/adjunct (8 women). *Students:* 440 full-time (270 women), 38 part-time (22 women);

includes 54 minority (6 Black or African American, non-Hispanic/Latino; 2 American Indian or Alaska Native, non-Hispanic/Latino; 16 Asian, non-Hispanic/Latino; 20 Hispanic/Latino; 1 Native Hawaiian or other Pacific Islander, non-Hispanic/Latino; 9 Two or more races, non-Hispanic/Latino), 35 international. Average age 27. 940 applicants, 75% accepted, 256 enrolled. In 2011, 257 master's, 7 doctorates, 43 other advanced degrees awarded. *Degree requirements:* For master's, one foreign language, thesis (for some programs); for doctorate, one foreign language, comprehensive exam, thesis/dissertation, two extended research papers. *Entrance requirements:* For master's, GRE General Test, Official transcript from each undergraduate institution, two letters of recommendation, statement of purpose, resume/curriculum vitae; for doctorate, GRE General Test, official transcript from each undergraduate institution, three letters of recommendation, statement of purpose, resume/curriculum vitae; for Certificate, official transcript from each undergraduate institution, two letters of recommendation, statement of purpose, resume/curriculum vitae. Additional exam requirements/recommendations for international students: Required—TOEFL (minimum score 587 paper-based; 95 iBT). *Application deadline:* For fall admission, 1/15 priority date for domestic students, 12/15 for international students. Application fee: $60. Electronic applications accepted. *Financial support:* In 2011–12, 261 students received support, including 3 teaching assistantships with partial tuition reimbursements available (averaging $5,222 per year); career-related internships or fieldwork, Federal Work-Study, institutionally sponsored loans, scholarships/grants, and unspecified assistantships also available. Support available to part-time students. Financial award application deadline: 2/15; financial award applicants required to submit FAFSA. *Faculty research:* Human rights and international security, international politics and economics, economic-social and political development, international technology analysis and management. *Unit head:* Christopher R. Hill, Dean, 303-871-2359, Fax: 303-871-2456, E-mail: christopher.r.hill@du.edu. *Application contact:* Brad Miller, Director of Graduate Admissions, 303-871-2989, Fax: 303-871-2124, E-mail: brad.miller@du.edu. Web site: http://www.du.edu/korbel/.

University of Florida, Graduate School, Warrington College of Business Administration, Hough Graduate School of Business, Department of Management, Gainesville, FL 32611. Offers geriatric care management (MSM); health care risk management (MSM); international business (MAIB); management (MSM, PhD). *Accreditation:* AACSB. Postbaccalaureate distance learning degree programs offered. *Faculty:* 11 full-time (2 women). *Students:* 235 full-time (122 women), 75 part-time (44 women); includes 85 minority (18 Black or African American, non-Hispanic/Latino; 19 Asian, non-Hispanic/Latino; 48 Hispanic/Latino), 60 international. Average age 25. 58 applicants, 78% accepted, 40 enrolled. In 2011, 239 master's, 2 doctorates awarded. *Degree requirements:* For master's, comprehensive exam, thesis; for doctorate, comprehensive exam, thesis/dissertation. *Entrance requirements:* For master's and doctorate, GMAT or GRE General Test, minimum GPA of 3.0. Additional exam requirements/recommendations for international students: Required—TOEFL (minimum score 550 paper-based; 213 computer-based; 80 iBT), IELTS (minimum score 6). *Application deadline:* For fall admission, 1/1 for domestic and international students. Applications are processed on a rolling basis. Application fee: $30. Electronic applications accepted. *Financial support:* Fellowships, research assistantships, teaching assistantships, and unspecified assistantships available. Financial award applicants required to submit FAFSA. *Faculty research:* Job attitudes, personality and individual differences, organizational entry and exit, knowledge management, competitive dynamics. *Unit head:* Dr. Robert E. Thomas, Chair, 352-392-0136, Fax: 352-392-6020, E-mail: rethomas@ufl.edu. *Application contact:* Dr. Jason A. Colquitt, Graduate Coordinator, 352-846-0507, Fax: 352-392-6020, E-mail: colquitt@ufl.edu. Web site: http://www.cba.ufl.edu/mang/.

University of Florida, Graduate School, Warrington College of Business Administration, Hough Graduate School of Business, Programs in Business Administration, Gainesville, FL 32611. Offers accounting (MBA); arts administration (MBA); business strategy and public policy (MBA); competitive strategy (MBA); decision and information sciences (MBA); electronic commerce (MBA); finance (MBA); general business (MBA); global management (MBA); Graham-Buffett security analysis (MBA); health administration (MBA); human resources management (MBA); international studies (MBA); Latin American business (MBA); management (MBA); marketing (MBA); sports administration (MBA); JD/MBA; MBA/MS; MBA/PhD; MBA/Pharm D; MD/MBA. *Accreditation:* AACSB. Part-time and evening/weekend programs available. *Faculty:* 71 full-time (10 women). *Students:* 412 full-time (111 women), 467 part-time (135 women); includes 235 minority (39 Black or African American, non-Hispanic/Latino; 7 American Indian or Alaska Native, non-Hispanic/Latino; 79 Asian, non-Hispanic/Latino; 109 Hispanic/Latino; 1 Native Hawaiian or other Pacific Islander, non-Hispanic/Latino), 44 international. Average age 32. 589 applicants, 52% accepted, 247 enrolled. In 2011, 505 master's awarded. *Degree requirements:* For master's, capstone course. *Entrance requirements:* For master's, GMAT, minimum GPA of 3.0, interview. Additional exam requirements/recommendations for international students: Required—TOEFL (minimum score 550 paper-based; 213 computer-based; 80 iBT), IELTS (minimum score 6). *Application deadline:* For fall admission, 7/1 for domestic students, 1/1 for international students; for spring admission, 12/1 for domestic and international students. Applications are processed on a rolling basis. Application fee: $30. Electronic applications accepted. *Financial support:* Teaching assistantships, career-related internships or fieldwork, scholarships/grants, and unspecified assistantships available. Support available to part-time students. Financial award applicants required to submit FAFSA. *Faculty research:* Accounting, finance, insurance, management, real estate, urban analysis marketing. *Unit head:* Prof. Alexander D. Sevilla, Assistant Dean/Director, 352-273-3252 Ext. 1206, E-mail: alex.sevilla@warrington.ufl.edu. *Application contact:* Prof. Kelli Gust, Associate Director, 352-273-3255, Fax: 352-392-8791, E-mail: kelly.gust@warrington.ufl.edu. Web site: http://www.floridamba.ufl.edu/.

University of Florida, Levin College of Law, Gainesville, FL 32611. Offers comparative law (LL M); environmental law (LL M); international taxation (LL M); law (JD); taxation (LL M, SJD). *Accreditation:* ABA. *Faculty:* 77 full-time (37 women), 36 part-time/adjunct (10 women). *Students:* 1,111 full-time (476 women); includes 257 minority (68 Black or African American, non-Hispanic/Latino; 14 American Indian or Alaska Native, non-Hispanic/Latino; 57 Asian, non-Hispanic/Latino; 118 Hispanic/Latino), 45 international. Average age 24. 3,024 applicants, 29% accepted, 295 enrolled. In 2011, 406 doctorates awarded. *Entrance requirements:* For doctorate, LSAT (for JD). Additional exam requirements/recommendations for international students: Required—TOEFL (minimum score 250 computer-based; 100 iBT). *Application deadline:* For fall admission, 3/15 for domestic and international students. Applications are processed on a rolling basis. Application fee: $30. Electronic applications accepted. *Financial support:* In 2011–12, 291 students received support, including 34 research assistantships (averaging $9,867 per year); Federal Work-Study, institutionally sponsored loans, scholarships/grants, health care benefits, and unspecified assistantships also available. Financial award application deadline: 4/15; financial award applicants required to submit FAFSA. *Faculty research:* Environmental and land use law, taxation, dispute resolution, family law, Constitutional law. *Unit head:* Robert Jerry, Dean, 352-273-0600, Fax: 352-392-8727, E-mail: jerryr@law.ufl.edu. *Application contact:* Michelle Adorno, Assistant Dean for Admissions, 352-273-0890, Fax: 352-392-4087, E-mail: madorno@law.ufl.edu. Web site: http://www.law.ufl.edu/.

University of Hawaii at Manoa, Graduate Division, Shidler College of Business, Program in Business Administration, Honolulu, HI 96822. Offers Asian business studies (MBA); Chinese business studies (MBA); decision sciences (MBA); entrepreneurship (MBA); finance (MBA); finance and banking (MBA); human resources management (MBA); information management (MBA); information technology (MBA); international business (MBA); Japanese business studies (MBA); marketing (MBA); organizational behavior (MBA); organizational management (MBA); real estate (MBA); student-designed track (MBA). *Accreditation:* AACSB. Part-time and evening/weekend programs available. *Degree requirements:* For master's, thesis optional. *Entrance requirements:* For master's, GMAT, minimum GPA of 3.0. Additional exam requirements/recommendations for international students: Required—TOEFL (minimum score 600 paper-based; 250 computer-based; 100 iBT), IELTS (minimum score 7). *Expenses:* Contact institution.

University of Hawaii at Manoa, Graduate Division, Shidler College of Business, Program in International Management, Honolulu, HI 96822. Offers Asian finance (PhD); global information technology management (PhD); international accounting (PhD); international marketing (PhD); international organization and strategy (PhD). Part-time programs available. *Degree requirements:* For doctorate, comprehensive exam, thesis/dissertation. *Entrance requirements:* For doctorate, GMAT or GRE General Test, minimum GPA of 3.0. Additional exam requirements/recommendations for international students: Required—TOEFL (minimum score 600 paper-based; 250 computer-based; 100 iBT), IELTS (minimum score 7). *Expenses:* Contact institution.

University of Houston–Victoria, School of Business Administration, Victoria, TX 77901-4450. Offers accounting (MBA); economic development and entrepreneurship (MS); finance (GMBA, MBA); general business (MBA); international business (MBA); management (GMBA, MBA); marketing (MBA). *Accreditation:* AACSB. Part-time and evening/weekend programs available. Postbaccalaureate distance learning degree programs offered (minimal on-campus study). *Entrance requirements:* For master's, GMAT. Additional exam requirements/recommendations for international students: Required—TOEFL (minimum score 550 paper-based; 213 computer-based). Electronic applications accepted. *Faculty research:* Economic development, marketing, finance.

University of Kentucky, Graduate School, Patterson School of Diplomacy and International Commerce, Lexington, KY 40506-0027. Offers MA. *Degree requirements:* For master's, one foreign language, comprehensive exam, statistics. *Entrance requirements:* For master's, GRE General Test, minimum undergraduate GPA of 3.0. Additional exam requirements/recommendations for international students: Required—TOEFL (minimum score 550 paper-based; 213 computer-based; 79 iBT). Electronic applications accepted. *Faculty research:* International relations, foreign and defense policy, cross-cultural negotiation, international science and technology, diplomacy, international economics and development, geopolitical modeling.

University of La Verne, College of Business and Public Management, Graduate Programs in Business Administration, La Verne, CA 91750-4443. Offers accounting (MBA); executive management (MBA-EP); finance (MBA, MBA-EP); health services management (MBA); information technology (MBA, MBA-EP); international business (MBA, MBA-EP); leadership (MBA-EP); managed care (MBA); management (MBA, MBA-EP); marketing (MBA, MBA-EP). Part-time and evening/weekend programs available. *Faculty:* 34 full-time (15 women), 38 part-time/adjunct (13 women). *Students:* 525 full-time (243 women), 231 part-time (114 women); includes 199 minority (27 Black or African American, non-Hispanic/Latino; 1 American Indian or Alaska Native, non-Hispanic/Latino; 55 Asian, non-Hispanic/Latino; 113 Hispanic/Latino; 3 Two or more races, non-Hispanic/Latino), 436 international. Average age 28. In 2011, 403 master's awarded. *Entrance requirements:* For master's, minimum undergraduate GPA of 3.0, 2 letters of recommendation, resume. Additional exam requirements/recommendations for international students: Required—TOEFL (minimum score 550 paper-based; 213 computer-based). *Application deadline:* Applications are processed on a rolling basis. Application fee: $50. *Expenses:* Contact institution. *Financial support:* Career-related internships or fieldwork, institutionally sponsored loans, and scholarships/grants available. Financial award application deadline: 3/2; financial award applicants required to submit FAFSA. *Unit head:* Dr. Abe Helou, Chairperson, 909-593-3511 Ext. 4211, Fax: 909-392-2704, E-mail: ihelou@laverne.edu. *Application contact:* Rina Lazarian, Program and Admission Specialist, 909-593-3511 Ext. 4819, Fax: 909-392-2704, E-mail: cbpm@ulv.edu.

University of Lethbridge, School of Graduate Studies, Lethbridge, AB T1K 3M4, Canada. Offers accounting (MScM); addictions counseling (M Sc); agricultural biotechnology (M Sc); agricultural studies (M Sc, MA); anthropology (MA); archaeology (MA); art (MA, MFA); biochemistry (M Sc); biological sciences (M Sc); biomolecular science (PhD); biosystems and biodiversity (PhD); Canadian studies (MA); chemistry (M Sc); computer science (M Sc); computer science and geographical information science (M Sc); counseling psychology (M Ed); dramatic arts (MA); earth, space, and physical science (PhD); economics (MA); educational leadership (M Ed); English (MA); environmental science (M Sc); evolution and behavior (PhD); exercise science (M Sc); finance (MScM); French (MA); French/German (MA); French/Spanish (MA); general education (M Ed); general management (MScM); geography (M Sc, MA); German (MA); health science (M Sc); history (MA); human resource management and labour relations (MScM); individualized multidisciplinary (M Sc, MA); information systems (MScM); international management (MScM); kinesiology (M Sc, MA); management (M Sc, MA); marketing (MScM); mathematics (M Sc); music (M Mus, MA); Native American studies (MA); neuroscience (M Sc, PhD); new media (MA); nursing (M Sc); philosophy (MA); physics (M Sc); policy and strategy (MScM); political science (MA); psychology (M Sc, MA); religious studies (MA); social sciences (MA); sociology (MA); theatre and dramatic arts (MFA); theoretical and computational science (PhD); urban and regional studies (MA); women's studies (MA). Part-time and evening/weekend programs available. *Degree requirements:* For doctorate, comprehensive exam, thesis/dissertation. *Entrance requirements:* For master's, GMAT (M Sc in management), bachelor's degree in related field, minimum GPA of 3.0 during previous 20 graded semester courses, 2 years teaching or related experience (M Ed); for doctorate, master's degree, minimum graduate GPA of 3.5. Additional exam requirements/recommendations for international students: Required—TOEFL. *Faculty research:* Movement and brain plasticity, gibberellin physiology, photosynthesis, carbon cycling, molecular properties of main-group ring components.

University of Louisville, Graduate School, College of Business, MBA Programs, Louisville, KY 40292-0001. Offers entrepreneurship (MBA); global business (MBA); health sector management (weekend format) (MBA). *Accreditation:* AACSB. Part-time and evening/weekend programs available. *Faculty:* 28 full-time (8 women), 3 part-time/adjunct (1 woman). *Students:* 111 full-time (35 women), 112 part-time (33 women); includes 19 minority (4 Black or African American, non-Hispanic/Latino; 1 American Indian or Alaska Native, non-Hispanic/Latino; 7 Asian, non-Hispanic/Latino; 3 Hispanic/Latino; 4 Two or more races, non-Hispanic/Latino), 12 international. Average age 29. 223 applicants, 53% accepted, 94 enrolled. In 2011, 119 degrees awarded. *Degree requirements:* For master's, international learning experience. *Entrance requirements:* For master's, GMAT, 2 letters of reference, personal interview, resume, personal statement, college transcript(s). Additional exam requirements/recommendations for international students: Required—TOEFL (minimum score 83 iBT). *Application deadline:*

For fall admission, 7/1 for domestic students; for spring admission, 12/1 for domestic students. Applications are processed on a rolling basis. Application fee: $50. *Expenses:* Tuition, state resident: full-time $9692; part-time $539 per credit hour. Tuition, nonresident: full-time $20,168; part-time $1121 per credit hour. Tuition and fees vary according to program and reciprocity agreements. *Financial support:* In 2011–12, 16 students received support, including 3 fellowships with full tuition reimbursements available (averaging $15,500 per year), 10 research assistantships with full tuition reimbursements available (averaging $12,000 per year); health care benefits and unspecified assistantships also available. Financial award application deadline: 3/31; financial award applicants required to submit FAFSA. *Faculty research:* Entrepreneurship, venture capital, retailing/franchising, corporate governance and leadership, supply chain management. *Unit head:* Dr. R. Charles Moyer, Dean, 502-852-6443, Fax: 502-852-7557, E-mail: charlie.moyer@louisville.edu. *Application contact:* L. Eddie Smith, Director of IT and Master's Programs Admissions/Recruiting Manager, 502-852-7257, Fax: 502-852-4901, E-mail: eddie.smith@louisville.edu. Web site: http://business.louisville.edu/mba.

University of Maryland University College, Graduate School of Management and Technology, Program in International Management, Adelphi, MD 20783. Offers MIM, Certificate. Offered evenings and weekends only. Part-time and evening/weekend programs available. Postbaccalaureate distance learning degree programs offered (no on-campus study). *Students:* 7 full-time (3 women), 234 part-time (131 women); includes 117 minority (85 Black or African American, non-Hispanic/Latino; 1 American Indian or Alaska Native, non-Hispanic/Latino; 11 Asian, non-Hispanic/Latino; 16 Hispanic/Latino; 4 Two or more races, non-Hispanic/Latino), 9 international. Average age 34. 94 applicants, 100% accepted, 57 enrolled. In 2011, 58 master's, 13 Certificates awarded. *Degree requirements:* For master's, thesis or alternative. *Application deadline:* Applications are processed on a rolling basis. Application fee: $50. Electronic applications accepted. *Financial support:* Federal Work-Study and scholarships/grants available. Support available to part-time students. Financial award application deadline: 6/1; financial award applicants required to submit FAFSA. *Unit head:* Dr. Robert Jerome, Director, 240-684-2400, Fax: 240-684-2401, E-mail: rjerome@umuc.edu. *Application contact:* Coordinator, Graduate Admissions, 800-888-8682, Fax: 240-684-2151, E-mail: newgrad@umuc.edu. Web site: http://www.umuc.edu/grad/iman.shtml.

University of Massachusetts Dartmouth, Graduate School, Charlton College of Business, Program in Business Administration, North Dartmouth, MA 02747-2300. Offers accounting (Postbaccalaureate Certificate); business administration (MBA); business foundation (online) (Graduate Certificate); finance (PMC); international business (online) (Graduate Certificate); leadership (online) (Graduate Certificate); management (Postbaccalaureate Certificate); marketing (Postbaccalaureate Certificate); supply chain management (PMC). *Accreditation:* AACSB. Part-time programs available. *Faculty:* 35 full-time (11 women), 26 part-time/adjunct (7 women). *Students:* 81 full-time (29 women), 119 part-time (56 women); includes 17 minority (6 Black or African American, non-Hispanic/Latino; 1 American Indian or Alaska Native, non-Hispanic/Latino; 3 Asian, non-Hispanic/Latino; 5 Hispanic/Latino; 2 Two or more races, non-Hispanic/Latino), 42 international. Average age 31. 132 applicants, 92% accepted, 68 enrolled. In 2011, 91 master's, 18 other advanced degrees awarded. *Entrance requirements:* For master's, GMAT, statement of intent, resume, 3 letters of recommendation; for other advanced degree, statement of intent, resume, 3 letters of recommendation. Additional exam requirements/recommendations for international students: Required—TOEFL (minimum score 500 paper-based; 200 computer-based; 72 iBT). *Application deadline:* For fall admission, 3/1 for domestic students, 2/1 for international students; for spring admission, 11/1 for domestic students, 10/15 for international students. Application fee: $40 ($60 for international students). Electronic applications accepted. *Expenses:* Tuition, state resident: full-time $2071; part-time $86.29 per credit. Tuition, nonresident: full-time $8099; part-time $337.46 per credit. *Required fees:* $438.58 per credit. Part-time tuition and fees vary according to class time, course load, degree level and reciprocity agreements. *Financial support:* Research assistantships, teaching assistantships, Federal Work-Study, and unspecified assistantships available. Support available to part-time students. Financial award application deadline: 3/1; financial award applicants required to submit FAFSA. *Faculty research:* Global business environment, e-commerce, managing diversity, agile manufacturing, green business. *Total annual research expenditures:* $8,653. *Unit head:* Stephanie Jacobsen, Program Coordinator, 508-999-8543, Fax: 508-999-8646, E-mail: s.jacobsen@umassd.edu. *Application contact:* Elan Turcotte-Shamski, Graduate Admissions Officer, 508-999-8604, Fax: 508-999-8183, E-mail: graduate@umassd.edu. Web site: http://www.umassd.edu/charlton/.

University of Memphis, Graduate School, Fogelman College of Business and Economics, Program in Business Administration, Memphis, TN 38152. Offers accounting (MBA, PhD); economics (MBA, PhD); executive business administration (MBA); finance (PhD); finance, insurance, and real estate (MBA, MS); international business administration (IMBA); management (MBA, MS, PhD); management information systems (MBA, MS, PhD); management science (MBA); marketing (MBA, MS); marketing and supply chain management (PhD); real estate development (MS); JD/MBA. *Accreditation:* AACSB. *Degree requirements:* For master's, comprehensive exam; for doctorate, comprehensive exam, thesis/dissertation. *Entrance requirements:* For master's, GMAT, resume; for doctorate, GMAT, interview, minimum GPA of 3.4, resume, letter of recommendation. Additional exam requirements/recommendations for international students: Required—TOEFL (minimum score 550 paper-based; 220 computer-based). *Faculty research:* Competitive business strategy, finance microstructures, supply chain management innovations, health care economics, litigation risks and corporate audits.

University of Miami, Graduate School, School of Business Administration, Program in Business Administration, Coral Gables, FL 33124. Offers accounting (MBA); computer information systems (MBA); executive and professional (MBA), including international business, management; finance (MBA); international business (MBA); management (MBA); management science (MBA); marketing (MBA); professional management (MSPM); JD/MBA; MBA/MSIE. *Accreditation:* AACSB. Evening/weekend programs available. *Degree requirements:* For master's, comprehensive exam. *Entrance requirements:* For master's, GMAT. Additional exam requirements/recommendations for international students: Required—TOEFL (minimum score 550 paper-based; 213 computer-based; 59 iBT). Electronic applications accepted. *Faculty research:* Leadership, e-commerce, supply chain management.

University of Michigan–Dearborn, College of Business, Dearborn, MI 48128-1491. Offers accounting (MBA, MS); business analytics (MS); finance (MBA, MS); information systems (MS); international business (MBA); management (MBA); management information systems (MBA); marketing (MBA); supply chain management (MBA, MS); MBA/MHSA; MBA/MSE; MBA/MSF; MBA/MSIS; MSF/MSA. *Accreditation:* AACSB. Part-time and evening/weekend programs available. Postbaccalaureate distance learning degree programs offered (no on-campus study). *Faculty:* 50 full-time (6 women), 32 part-time/adjunct (18 women). *Students:* 65 full-time (29 women), 356 part-time (121 women); includes 79 minority (19 Black or African American, non-Hispanic/Latino; 36 American Indian or Alaska Native, non-Hispanic/Latino; 15 Hispanic/Latino; 1 Native Hawaiian or other Pacific Islander, non-Hispanic/Latino; 8 Two or more races, non-Hispanic/Latino), 80 international. Average age 28. 175 applicants, 53% accepted, 68 enrolled. In 2011, 173 master's awarded. *Entrance requirements:* For master's, GMAT or GRE, 2 years of work experience (MBA); course work in computer applications, statistics, and pre-calculus or finite mathematics; 18 credits of accounting course work beyond introductory courses (MS in accounting). Additional exam requirements/recommendations for international students: Required—TOEFL (minimum score 560 paper-based; 220 computer-based; 84 iBT), IELTS. *Application deadline:* For fall admission, 8/1 priority date for domestic students, 6/1 for international students; for winter admission, 12/1 priority date for domestic students, 10/1 for international students; for spring admission, 4/1 priority date for domestic students, 2/1 for international students. Applications are processed on a rolling basis. Application fee: $60. Electronic applications accepted. *Expenses:* Contact institution. *Financial support:* Career-related internships or fieldwork, Federal Work-Study, and scholarships/grants available. Support available to part-time students. Financial award application deadline: 9/1; financial award applicants required to submit FAFSA. *Faculty research:* Cultural diversity, buyer-supplier relations, error detection in data, economic evolution. *Unit head:* Dr. Lee Redding, Interim Dean, 313-593-5248, Fax: 313-271-9835, E-mail: lredding@umd.umich.edu. *Application contact:* Joan Doherty, Academic Advisor/Counselor, 313-593-5460, Fax: 313-271-9838, E-mail: gradbusiness@umd.umich.edu. Web site: http://www.cob.umd.umich.edu.

University of New Brunswick Saint John, MBA Program, Saint John, NB E2L 4L5, Canada. Offers administration (MBA); electronic commerce (MBA); international business (MBA); natural resource management (MBA). Part-time programs available. *Faculty:* 19 full-time (4 women), 14 part-time/adjunct (8 women). *Students:* 58 full-time (24 women), 130 part-time (46 women). 93 applicants, 78% accepted, 25 enrolled. In 2011, 36 master's awarded. *Entrance requirements:* For master's, GMAT, minimum GPA of 3.0. Additional exam requirements/recommendations for international students: Required—TOEFL (minimum score 580 paper-based; 237 computer-based), IELTS (minimum score 7), TWE (minimum score 4.5). *Application deadline:* For fall admission, 5/15 for domestic and international students. Applications are processed on a rolling basis. Application fee: $100. Electronic applications accepted. *Expenses:* Contact institution. *Financial support:* In 2011–12, 4 students received support. Career-related internships or fieldwork and scholarships/grants available. *Faculty research:* Business use of weblogs and podcasts to communicate, corporate governance, high-involvement work systems, international competitiveness, supply chain management and logistics. *Unit head:* Henryk Sterniczuk, Director of Graduate Studies, 506-648-5573, Fax: 506-648-5574, E-mail: sternicz@unbsj.ca. *Application contact:* Tammy Morin, Secretary, 506-648-5746, Fax: 506-648-5574, E-mail: tmorin@unbsj.ca. Web site: http://www.mba.unbsj.ca.

University of New Haven, Graduate School, School of Business, Program in Business Administration, West Haven, CT 06516-1916. Offers accounting (MBA, Certificate), including CPA (MBA); business management (Certificate); business policy and strategy (MBA); finance (MBA), including CFA; global marketing (MBA); human resource management (Certificate); human resources management (MBA); international business (Certificate); marketing (Certificate); sports management (MBA); telecommunications management (Certificate); MBA/MPA. Part-time and evening/weekend programs available. *Students:* 215 full-time (106 women), 182 part-time (87 women); includes 73 minority (38 Black or African American, non-Hispanic/Latino; 2 American Indian or Alaska Native, non-Hispanic/Latino; 22 Asian, non-Hispanic/Latino; 11 Hispanic/Latino), 129 international. 179 applicants, 97% accepted, 93 enrolled. In 2011, 197 master's, 28 other advanced degrees awarded. *Degree requirements:* For master's, thesis or alternative. *Entrance requirements:* For master's, GMAT. Additional exam requirements/recommendations for international students: Required—TOEFL (minimum score 520 paper-based; 190 computer-based; 70 iBT), IELTS (minimum score 5.5). *Application deadline:* For fall admission, 5/31 for international students; for winter admission, 10/15 for international students; for spring admission, 1/15 for international students. Applications are processed on a rolling basis. Application fee: $50. Electronic applications accepted. *Expenses:* Contact institution. *Financial support:* Research assistantships with partial tuition reimbursements, teaching assistantships with partial tuition reimbursements, Federal Work-Study, scholarships/grants, health care benefits, tuition waivers, and unspecified assistantships available. Support available to part-time students. Financial award applicants required to submit FAFSA. *Unit head:* Charles Coleman, Chairman, 203-932-7375. *Application contact:* Eloise Gormley, Director of Graduate Admissions, 203-932-7449, Fax: 203-932-7137, E-mail: gradinfo@newhaven.edu. Web site: http://www.newhaven.edu/7433/.

University of New Mexico, Robert O. Anderson Graduate School of Management, Department of Finance, International, Technology and Entrepreneurship, Albuquerque, NM 87131-1221. Offers finance (MBA); international management (MBA); international management in Latin America (MBA); management of technology (MBA). Part-time and evening/weekend programs available. *Faculty:* 14 full-time (2 women), 17 part-time/adjunct (4 women). In 2011, 53 master's awarded. *Degree requirements:* For master's, minimum GPA of 3.0. *Entrance requirements:* For master's, GMAT or GRE. Additional exam requirements/recommendations for international students: Required—TOEFL (minimum score 550 paper-based; 213 computer-based; 79 iBT). *Application deadline:* For fall admission, 4/1 priority date for domestic students, 4/1 for international students; for spring admission, 10/1 priority date for domestic students, 10/1 for international students. Applications are processed on a rolling basis. Application fee: $50. Electronic applications accepted. *Financial support:* Fellowships, research assistantships, career-related internships or fieldwork, Federal Work-Study, scholarships/grants, and unspecified assistantships available. Support available to part-time students. Financial award application deadline: 6/1. *Faculty research:* Corporate finance, investments, management in Latin America, management of technology, entrepreneurship. *Unit head:* Dr. Leslie Boni, Chair, 505-277-6471, Fax: 505-277-7108. *Application contact:* Megan Conner, Director, Student Services, 505-277-3290, Fax: 505-277-8436, E-mail: mconner@mgt.unm.edu.

University of North Florida, Coggin College of Business, MBA Program, Jacksonville, FL 32224. Offers accounting (MBA); construction management (MBA); e-commerce (MBA); economics (MBA); finance (MBA); human resource management (MBA); international business (MBA); logistics (MBA); management applications (MBA). *Accreditation:* AACSB. Part-time and evening/weekend programs available. *Faculty:* 19 full-time (6 women), 1 part-time/adjunct (0 women). *Students:* 145 full-time (57 women), 277 part-time (108 women); includes 67 minority (19 Black or African American, non-Hispanic/Latino; 21 Asian, non-Hispanic/Latino; 20 Hispanic/Latino; 7 Two or more races, non-Hispanic/Latino), 34 international. Average age 29. 200 applicants, 48% accepted, 70 enrolled. In 2011, 153 master's awarded. *Entrance requirements:* For master's, GMAT or GRE, U.S. bachelor's degree from regionally-accredited university or equivalent foreign degree. Additional exam requirements/recommendations for international students: Required—TOEFL (minimum score 550 paper-based; 213 computer-based; 79 iBT). *Application deadline:* For fall admission, 7/1 priority date for domestic students, 5/1 for international students; for spring admission, 11/1 priority date for domestic students, 10/1 for international students. Applications are processed on a rolling basis. Application fee: $30. *Expenses:* Tuition, state resident: full-time $8793; part-time $366.38 per credit hour. Tuition, nonresident: full-time $23,502; part-time $979.24 per credit hour. *Required fees:* $1384; $57.66 per credit hour. Tuition and fees vary according to course load and program. *Financial support:* In 2011–12, 55 students received support, including 1 teaching assistantship (averaging $5,333 per year); research assistantships, Federal Work-Study, and tuition waivers (partial) also available. Support available to part-time students. Financial award application deadline: 4/1; financial award applicants required to submit FAFSA. *Faculty research:* Performance measures, costing, and inventory issues in logistics and supply chain management; inter-organizational systems; international management and marketing practices; e-commerce; organizational learning and socialization processes. *Total annual research expenditures:* $7,686. *Unit head:* Dr. C. Bruce Kavan, Chair, 904-620-2780, Fax: 904-620-2832. *Application contact:* Cheryl Campbell, Graduate Advisor, 904-620-2575, Fax: 904-620-2832, E-mail: ccampbell@unf.edu. Web site: http://www.unf.edu/coggin/academics/graduate/mba.aspx.

University of Pennsylvania, School of Arts and Sciences and Wharton School, Joseph H. Lauder Institute of Management and International Studies, Philadelphia, PA 19104. Offers international studies (MA); management and international studies (MBA); MBA/MA. Applications must be made concurrently and separately to the Wharton MBA program. *Degree requirements:* For master's, one foreign language, thesis. *Entrance requirements:* For master's, GMAT or GRE, advanced proficiency in a non-native language (Arabic, Chinese, French, German, Hindi, Japanese, Portuguese, Russian, or Spanish). Additional exam requirements/recommendations for international students: Required—TOEFL. Electronic applications accepted. *Expenses:* Contact institution. *Faculty research:* Finance, marketing, strategy, operations management, multinational management.

University of Phoenix–Atlanta Campus, School of Business, Sandy Springs, GA 30350-4153. Offers accounting (MBA); business administration (MBA); global management (MBA); human resources management (MBA, MM); management (MM); marketing (MBA); public administration (MM). Evening/weekend programs available. Postbaccalaureate distance learning degree programs offered. *Degree requirements:* For master's, thesis (for some programs). *Entrance requirements:* For master's, minimum undergraduate GPA of 3.0, 3 years of work experience. Additional exam requirements/recommendations for international students: Required—TOEFL (minimum score 550 paper-based; 213 computer-based; 79 iBT).

University of Phoenix–Augusta Campus, School of Business, Augusta, GA 30909-4583. Offers accounting (MBA); business administration (MBA); business and management (MBA, MM); global management (MBA); human resources management (MBA, MM); management (MM); marketing (MBA); public administration (MBA, MM). Postbaccalaureate distance learning degree programs offered.

University of Phoenix–Austin Campus, School of Business, Austin, TX 78759. Offers accounting (MBA); business administration (MBA); business and management (MBA); e-business (MBA); global management (MBA); human resources management (MBA, MM); management (MM); marketing (MBA); public administration (MBA). Postbaccalaureate distance learning degree programs offered.

University of Phoenix–Bay Area Campus, School of Business, San Jose, CA 95134-1805. Offers accountancy (MS); accounting (MBA); business administration (MBA, DBA); energy management (MBA); global management (MBA); health care management (MBA); human resource management (MBA); human resources management (MM); management (MM); marketing (MBA); organizational leadership (DM); project management (MBA); public administration (MPA); technology management (MBA). Evening/weekend programs available. Postbaccalaureate distance learning degree programs offered (no on-campus study). *Degree requirements:* For master's, thesis (for some programs). *Entrance requirements:* For master's, minimum undergraduate GPA of 3.0, 3 years of work experience. Additional exam requirements/recommendations for international students: Required—TOEFL (minimum score 550 paper-based; 213 computer-based; 79 iBT). Electronic applications accepted.

University of Phoenix–Birmingham Campus, College of Graduate Business and Management, Birmingham, AL 35244. Offers accounting (MBA); business administration (MBA); global management (MBA); human resources management (MBA, MM); management (MM); marketing (MBA); public administration (MM).

University of Phoenix–Boston Campus, School of Business, Braintree, MA 02184-4949. Offers administration (MBA); global management (MBA). Evening/weekend programs available. *Degree requirements:* For master's, thesis (for some programs). *Entrance requirements:* For master's, 3 years of work experience, minimum undergraduate GPA of 3.0. Additional exam requirements/recommendations for international students: Required—TOEFL (minimum score 550 paper-based; 213 computer-based; 79 iBT).

University of Phoenix–Central Florida Campus, School of Business, Maitland, FL 32751-7057. Offers accounting (MBA); business administration (MBA); business and management (MM); global management (MBA); human resources management (MBA, MM); management (MM); marketing (MBA); public administration (MBA, MM). Evening/weekend programs available. *Degree requirements:* For master's, thesis (for some programs). *Entrance requirements:* For master's, minimum undergraduate GPA of 3.0, 3 years work experience. Additional exam requirements/recommendations for international students: Required—TOEFL (minimum score 550 paper-based; 213 computer-based; 79 iBT). Electronic applications accepted.

University of Phoenix–Central Valley Campus, School of Business, Fresno, CA 93720-1562. Offers accounting (MBA); business administration (MBA); global management (MBA); human resources management (MBA, MM); management (MM); marketing (MBA); public administration (MBA, MM).

University of Phoenix–Charlotte Campus, School of Business, Charlotte, NC 28273-3409. Offers accounting (MBA); business administration (MBA); global management (MBA). Evening/weekend programs available. *Degree requirements:* For master's, thesis (for some programs). *Entrance requirements:* For master's, minimum undergraduate GPA of 3.0, 3 years work experience. Additional exam requirements/recommendations for international students: Required—TOEFL (minimum score 550 paper-based; 213 computer-based; 79 iBT). Electronic applications accepted.

University of Phoenix–Chattanooga Campus, School of Business, Chattanooga, TN 37421-3707. Offers accounting (MBA); business administration (MBA); business and management (MBA); global management (MBA); human resources management (MBA, MM); management (MM); marketing (MBA); public administration (MBA, MM). Postbaccalaureate distance learning degree programs offered.

University of Phoenix–Cheyenne Campus, School of Business, Cheyenne, WY 82009. Offers global management (MBA); human resources management (MBA, MM); management (MM); marketing (MBA); public administration (MBA, MM). Postbaccalaureate distance learning degree programs offered.

University of Phoenix–Chicago Campus, School of Business, Schaumburg, IL 60173-4399. Offers business administration (MBA); global management (MBA); human resources management (MBA); information systems (MIS); management (MM). Evening/weekend programs available. *Degree requirements:* For master's, thesis (for some programs). *Entrance requirements:* For master's, minimum undergraduate GPA of 3.0, 3 years of work experience. Additional exam requirements/recommendations for international students: Required—TOEFL (minimum score 550 paper-based; 213 computer-based; 79 iBT). Electronic applications accepted.

University of Phoenix–Cincinnati Campus, School of Business, West Chester, OH 45069-4875. Offers accounting (MBA); business administration (MBA); global management (MBA); human resources management (MBA, MM); management (MM); marketing (MBA); public administration (MM). Evening/weekend programs available. *Degree requirements:* For master's, thesis (for some programs). *Entrance requirements:* For master's, minimum undergraduate GPA of 3.0, 3 years of work experience. Additional exam requirements/recommendations for international students: Required—TOEFL (minimum score 550 paper-based; 213 computer-based; 79 iBT). Electronic applications accepted.

University of Phoenix–Cleveland Campus, School of Business, Independence, OH 44131-2194. Offers accounting (MBA); business administration (MBA); global management (MBA); human resources management (MBA, MM); management (MM); marketing (MBA); public administration (MBA, MM). Evening/weekend programs available. Postbaccalaureate distance learning degree programs offered (no on-campus study). *Degree requirements:* For master's, thesis (for some programs). *Entrance requirements:* For master's, minimum undergraduate GPA of 3.0, 3 years of work experience. Additional exam requirements/recommendations for international students: Required—TOEFL (minimum score 550 paper-based; 213 computer-based; 79 iBT). Electronic applications accepted.

University of Phoenix–Columbus Georgia Campus, School of Business, Columbus, GA 31904-6321. Offers accounting (MBA); business administration (MBA); global management (MBA); human resources management (MBA, MM); management (MM); marketing (MBA); public administration (MBA). Evening/weekend programs available. *Degree requirements:* For master's, thesis (for some programs). *Entrance requirements:* For master's, minimum undergraduate GPA of 3.0, 3 years of work experience. Additional exam requirements/recommendations for international students: Required—TOEFL (minimum score 550 paper-based; 213 computer-based; 79 iBT). Electronic applications accepted.

University of Phoenix–Columbus Ohio Campus, School of Business, Columbus, OH 43240-4032. Offers accounting (MBA); business administration (MBA); global management (MBA); human resources management (MBA, MM); management (MM); marketing (MBA); public administration (MM). Evening/weekend programs available. Postbaccalaureate distance learning degree programs offered. *Degree requirements:* For master's, thesis (for some programs). *Entrance requirements:* For master's, minimum undergraduate GPA of 3.0, 3 years of work experience. Additional exam requirements/recommendations for international students: Required—TOEFL (minimum score 550 paper-based; 213 computer-based; 79 iBT). Electronic applications accepted.

University of Phoenix–Dallas Campus, School of Business, Dallas, TX 75251-2009. Offers accounting (MBA); business administration (MBA); global management (MBA); human resources management (MBA, MM); management (MM); marketing (MBA); public administration (MBA, MM). Evening/weekend programs available. Postbaccalaureate distance learning degree programs offered. *Degree requirements:* For master's, thesis (for some programs). *Entrance requirements:* For master's, 3 years of work experience, minimum undergraduate GPA of 3.0. Additional exam requirements/recommendations for international students: Required—TOEFL (minimum score 550 paper-based; 213 computer-based; 79 iBT). Electronic applications accepted.

University of Phoenix–Denver Campus, School of Business, Lone Tree, CO 80124-5453. Offers accountancy (MSA); accounting (MBA); business administration (MBA); e-business (MBA); global management (MBA); human resources management (MBA, MM); management (MM); marketing (MBA); public administration (MBA, MM). Evening/weekend programs available. Postbaccalaureate distance learning degree programs offered. *Degree requirements:* For master's, thesis (for some programs). *Entrance requirements:* For master's, minimum undergraduate GPA of 3.0, 3 years work experience. Additional exam requirements/recommendations for international students: Required—TOEFL (minimum score 550 paper-based; 213 computer-based; 79 iBT). Electronic applications accepted.

University of Phoenix–Des Moines Campus, School of Business, Des Moines, IA 50266. Offers accounting (MBA); business administration (MBA); global management (MBA); human resources management (MBA, MM); management (MM); marketing (MBA); public administration (MBA, MM). Postbaccalaureate distance learning degree programs offered.

University of Phoenix–Harrisburg Campus, School of Business, Harrisburg, PA 17112. Offers accounting (MBA); business administration (MBA); business and management (MBA); global management (MBA); human resources management (MBA, MM); management (MM); marketing (MBA); public administration (MBA, MM). Postbaccalaureate distance learning degree programs offered.

University of Phoenix–Hawaii Campus, School of Business, Honolulu, HI 96813-4317. Offers accounting (MBA); business administration (MBA); global management (MBA); human resources management (MBA, MM); management (MM); marketing (MBA); public administration (MBA, MM). Evening/weekend programs available. *Degree requirements:* For master's, thesis (for some programs). *Entrance requirements:* For master's, minimum undergraduate GPA of 3.0, 3 years of work experience. Additional exam requirements/recommendations for international students: Required—TOEFL (minimum score 550 paper-based; 213 computer-based; 79 iBT). Electronic applications accepted.

University of Phoenix–Houston Campus, School of Business, Houston, TX 77079-2004. Offers accounting (MBA); business administration (MBA); global management (MBA); human resources management (MBA, MM); management (MM); marketing (MBA); public administration (MBA, MM). Evening/weekend programs available. Postbaccalaureate distance learning degree programs offered. *Degree requirements:* For master's, thesis (for some programs). *Entrance requirements:* For master's, 3 years of work experience, minimum undergraduate GPA of 3.0. Additional exam requirements/recommendations for international students: Required—TOEFL (minimum score 550 paper-based; 213 computer-based; 79 iBT). Electronic applications accepted.

University of Phoenix–Idaho Campus, School of Business, Meridian, ID 83642-5114. Offers accounting (MBA); administration (MBA); global management (MBA); human resources management (MBA, MM); management (MM); marketing (MBA); public administration (MM). Evening/weekend programs available. Postbaccalaureate distance learning degree programs offered. *Degree requirements:* For master's, thesis (for some programs). *Entrance requirements:* For master's, 3 years of work experience, minimum undergraduate GPA of 3.0. Additional exam requirements/recommendations for international students: Required—TOEFL (minimum score 550 paper-based; 213 computer-based). Electronic applications accepted.

University of Phoenix–Indianapolis Campus, School of Business, Indianapolis, IN 46250-932. Offers accounting (MBA); business administration (MBA); global management (MBA); human resources management (MBA, MM); management (MM); marketing (MBA); public administration (MM). Evening/weekend programs available. *Degree requirements:* For master's, thesis (for some programs). *Entrance requirements:* For master's, minimum undergraduate GPA of 3.0, 3 years of work experience.

Additional exam requirements/recommendations for international students: Required—TOEFL (minimum score 550 paper-based; 213 computer-based). Electronic applications accepted.

University of Phoenix–Jersey City Campus, School of Business, Jersey City, NJ 07310. Offers accounting (MBA); business administration (MBA); global management (MBA); human resources management (MBA, MM); management (MM); marketing (MBA); public administration (MBA, MM).

University of Phoenix–Kansas City Campus, School of Business, Kansas City, MO 64131-4517. Offers accounting (MBA); business administration (MBA); global management (MBA); human resources management (MBA, MM); management (MM); marketing (MBA); public administration (MBA). Evening/weekend programs available. *Degree requirements:* For master's, thesis (for some programs). *Entrance requirements:* For master's, minimum undergraduate GPA of 3.0, 3 years of work experience. Additional exam requirements/recommendations for international students: Required—TOEFL (minimum score 550 paper-based; 213 computer-based). Electronic applications accepted.

University of Phoenix–Las Vegas Campus, School of Business, Las Vegas, NV 89128. Offers accounting (MBA); business administration (MBA); global management (MBA); human resources management (MBA, MM); management (MM); marketing (MBA); public administration (MM). Evening/weekend programs available. Postbaccalaureate distance learning degree programs offered (no on-campus study). *Degree requirements:* For master's, thesis (for some programs). *Entrance requirements:* For master's, minimum undergraduate GPA of 3.0, 3 years of work experience. Additional exam requirements/recommendations for international students: Required—TOEFL (minimum score 550 paper-based; 213 computer-based; 79 iBT). Electronic applications accepted.

University of Phoenix–Louisiana Campus, School of Business, Metairie, LA 70001-2082. Offers accounting (MBA); business administration (MBA); global management (MBA); human resources management (MBA, MM); management (MM); marketing (MBA); public administration (MBA). Evening/weekend programs available. *Degree requirements:* For master's, thesis (for some programs). *Entrance requirements:* For master's, minimum undergraduate GPA of 3.0, 3 years work experience. Additional exam requirements/recommendations for international students: Required—TOEFL (minimum score 550 paper-based; 213 computer-based; 79 iBT). Electronic applications accepted.

University of Phoenix–Madison Campus, School of Business, Madison, WI 53718-2416. Offers accounting (MBA); business and management (MBA); e-business (MBA); global management (MBA); human resources management (MBA, MM); management (MM); marketing (MBA); public administration (MBA).

University of Phoenix–Maryland Campus, School of Business, Columbia, MD 21045-5424. Offers global management (MBA); technology management (MBA). Evening/weekend programs available. Postbaccalaureate distance learning degree programs offered. *Students:* 121 full-time (58 women); includes 65 minority (59 Black or African American, non-Hispanic/Latino; 3 Asian, non-Hispanic/Latino; 1 Hispanic/Latino; 2 Two or more races, non-Hispanic/Latino), 3 international. Average age 41. *Entrance requirements:* Additional exam requirements/recommendations for international students: Required—TOEFL, TOEIC (Test of English as an International Communication), Berlitz Online English Proficiency Exam, PTE (Pearson Test of English), or IELTS. *Application deadline:* Applications are processed on a rolling basis. Application fee: $45. Electronic applications accepted. *Expenses: Tuition:* Full-time $17,098. *Required fees:* $915. One-time fee: $45 full-time. Full-time tuition and fees vary according to course load, campus/location and program. *Financial support:* Scholarships/grants available. Financial award applicants required to submit FAFSA. *Application contact:* 866-766-0766. Web site: http://www.phoenix.edu/colleges_divisions/business.html.

University of Phoenix–Memphis Campus, School of Business, Cordova, TN 38018. Offers accounting (MBA); business and management (MBA); e-business (MBA); global management (MBA); human resources management (MBA, MM); management (MM); marketing (MBA); public administration (MBA, MM).

University of Phoenix–Minneapolis/St. Louis Park Campus, School of Business, St. Louis Park, MN 55426. Offers accounting (MBA); business administration (MBA); global management (MBA); human resources management (MBA); management (MM); marketing (MBA); public administration (MBA).

University of Phoenix–New Mexico Campus, School of Business, Albuquerque, NM 87113-1570. Offers accounting (MBA); business administration (MBA); global management (MBA); human resources management (MBA, MM); management (MM); marketing (MBA). Evening/weekend programs available. *Degree requirements:* For master's, thesis (for some programs). *Entrance requirements:* For master's, 3 years of work experience, minimum undergraduate GPA of 3.0. Additional exam requirements/recommendations for international students: Required—TOEFL (minimum score 550 paper-based; 213 computer-based; 79 iBT). Electronic applications accepted.

University of Phoenix–Northern Nevada Campus, School of Business, Reno, NV 89521-5862. Offers accounting (MBA); business administration (MBA); global management (MBA); human resources management (MBA, MM); management (MM); marketing (MBA); public administration (MBA, MM).

University of Phoenix–North Florida Campus, School of Business, Jacksonville, FL 32216-0959. Offers accounting (MBA); business administration (MBA); global management (MBA); human resources management (MBA, MM); management (MM); marketing (MBA); public administration (MBA, MM). Evening/weekend programs available. *Degree requirements:* For master's, thesis (for some programs). *Entrance requirements:* For master's, minimum undergraduate GPA of 3.0, 3 years work experience. Additional exam requirements/recommendations for international students: Required—TOEFL (minimum score 550 paper-based; 213 computer-based; 79 iBT). Electronic applications accepted.

University of Phoenix–Northwest Arkansas Campus, School of Business, Rogers, AR 72756-9615. Offers accounting (MBA); business and management (MBA); global management (MBA); human resources management (MBA, MM); management (MM); marketing (MBA); public administration (MBA, MM).

University of Phoenix–Oklahoma City Campus, School of Business, Oklahoma City, OK 73116-8244. Offers accounting (MBA); business administration (MBA); global management (MBA); human resource management (MBA); management (MM); marketing (MBA). Evening/weekend programs available. *Degree requirements:* For master's, thesis (for some programs). *Entrance requirements:* For master's, minimum undergraduate GPA of 3.0, 3 years of work experience. Additional exam requirements/recommendations for international students: Required—TOEFL (minimum score 550 paper-based; 213 computer-based; 79 iBT). Electronic applications accepted.

University of Phoenix–Omaha Campus, School of Business, Omaha, NE 68154-5240. Offers accounting (MBA); business and management (MBA); global management (MBA); human resources management (MBA, MM); management (MM); marketing (MBA); public administration (MBA, MM).

University of Phoenix–Online Campus, School of Business, Phoenix, AZ 85034-7209. Offers accountancy (MS); accounting (MBA); business administration (MBA); energy management (MBA); global management (MBA); health care management (MBA); human resource management (MBA); human resources management (MM); international (MM); management (MM); marketing (MBA, Graduate Certificate); organizational management (MA); project management (MBA, Graduate Certificate); public administration (MBA, MM, MPA); technology management (MBA). Evening/weekend programs available. Postbaccalaureate distance learning degree programs offered. *Students:* 18,883 full-time (11,868 women); includes 6,302 minority (4,182 Black or African American, non-Hispanic/Latino; 121 American Indian or Alaska Native, non-Hispanic/Latino; 478 Asian, non-Hispanic/Latino; 1,252 Hispanic/Latino; 121 Native Hawaiian or other Pacific Islander, non-Hispanic/Latino; 148 Two or more races, non-Hispanic/Latino), 1,000 international. Average age 37. *Entrance requirements:* Additional exam requirements/recommendations for international students: Required—TOEFL, TOEIC (Test of English as an International Communication), Berlitz Online English Proficiency Exam, Pearson Test of English, or IELTS. *Application deadline:* Applications are processed on a rolling basis. Application fee: $45. Electronic applications accepted. *Expenses: Tuition:* Full-time $17,160. *Required fees:* $920. One-time fee: $45 full-time. Full-time tuition and fees vary according to course load, degree level, campus/location and program. *Financial support:* Scholarships/grants available. Financial award applicants required to submit FAFSA. *Application contact:* 866-766-0766. Web site: http://www.phoenix.edu/colleges_divisions/business.html.

University of Phoenix–Oregon Campus, School of Business, Tigard, OR 97223. Offers accounting (MBA); business administration (MBA); global management (MBA); human resource management (MM); human resources management (MBA); management (MM); marketing (MBA); public administration (MM). Evening/weekend programs available. *Degree requirements:* For master's, thesis (for some programs). *Entrance requirements:* For master's, minimum undergraduate GPA of 3.0, 3 years of work experience. Additional exam requirements/recommendations for international students: Required—TOEFL (minimum score 550 paper-based; 213 computer-based; 79 iBT). Electronic applications accepted.

University of Phoenix–Philadelphia Campus, School of Business, Wayne, PA 19087-2121. Offers accounting (MBA); business administration (MBA); global management (MBA); human resources management (MBA, MM); management (MM); marketing (MBA); public administration (MM). Evening/weekend programs available. *Degree requirements:* For master's, thesis (for some programs). *Entrance requirements:* For master's, minimum undergraduate GPA of 3.0, 3 years work experience. Additional exam requirements/recommendations for international students: Required—TOEFL (minimum score 550 paper-based; 213 computer-based; 79 iBT). Electronic applications accepted.

University of Phoenix–Phoenix Main Campus, School of Business, Tempe, AZ 85282-2371. Offers accounting (MBA, MS); business administration (MBA); energy management (MBA); global management (MBA); health care management (MBA); human resource management (MBA); management (MM); marketing (MBA); project management (MBA); public administration (MPA); technology management (MBA). Evening/weekend programs available. Postbaccalaureate distance learning degree programs offered. *Students:* 1,151 full-time (531 women); includes 310 minority (99 Black or African American, non-Hispanic/Latino; 10 American Indian or Alaska Native, non-Hispanic/Latino; 39 Asian, non-Hispanic/Latino; 130 Hispanic/Latino; 15 Native Hawaiian or other Pacific Islander, non-Hispanic/Latino; 17 Two or more races, non-Hispanic/Latino), 63 international. Average age 34. *Entrance requirements:* Additional exam requirements/recommendations for international students: Required—TOEFL, TOEIC (Test of English as an International Communication), Berlitz Online English Proficiency Exam, Pearson Test of English, or IELTS. *Application deadline:* Applications are processed on a rolling basis. Application fee: $45. Electronic applications accepted. *Expenses:* Contact institution. *Financial support:* Scholarships/grants available. Financial award applicants required to submit FAFSA. *Application contact:* 866-766-0766. Web site: http://www.phoenix.edu/colleges_divisions/business.html.

University of Phoenix–Pittsburgh Campus, School of Business, Pittsburgh, PA 15276. Offers accounting (MBA); business administration (MBA); global management (MBA); human resources management (MBA, MM); management (MM); marketing (MBA); public administration (MBA, MM). Evening/weekend programs available. *Degree requirements:* For master's, thesis (for some programs). *Entrance requirements:* For master's, minimum undergraduate GPA of 3.0, 3 years work experience. Additional exam requirements/recommendations for international students: Required—TOEFL (minimum score 550 paper-based; 213 computer-based; 79 iBT). Electronic applications accepted.

University of Phoenix–Puerto Rico Campus, School of Business, Guaynabo, PR 00968. Offers accounting (MBA); energy management (MBA); global management (MBA); human resource management (MBA); marketing (MBA); project management (MBA); small business administration (MBA). Evening/weekend programs available. *Degree requirements:* For master's, thesis (for some programs). *Entrance requirements:* For master's, minimum undergraduate GPA of 3.0, 3 years work experience. Additional exam requirements/recommendations for international students: Required—TOEFL (minimum score 550 paper-based; 213 computer-based; 79 iBT). Electronic applications accepted.

University of Phoenix–Raleigh Campus, School of Business, Raleigh, NC 27606. Offers accounting (MBA); business administration (MBA); e-business (MBA); global management (MBA); human resources management (MBA); marketing (MBA).

University of Phoenix–Richmond Campus, School of Business, Richmond, VA 23230. Offers accounting (MBA); business administration (MBA); global management (MBA); human resources management (MBA, MM); management (MM); marketing (MBA); public administration (MBA, MM). Evening/weekend programs available. *Degree requirements:* For master's, thesis (for some programs). *Entrance requirements:* For master's, minimum undergraduate GPA of 3.0, 3 years work experience. Additional exam requirements/recommendations for international students: Required—TOEFL (minimum score 550 paper-based; 213 computer-based; 79 iBT). Electronic applications accepted.

University of Phoenix–Sacramento Valley Campus, School of Business, Sacramento, CA 95833-3632. Offers accounting (MBA); business administration (MBA); global management (MBA); human resources management (MBA, MM); management (MM); marketing (MBA); public administration (MBA, MM). Evening/weekend programs available. *Degree requirements:* For master's, thesis (for some programs). *Entrance requirements:* For master's, minimum undergraduate GPA of 3.0, 3 years work experience. Additional exam requirements/recommendations for international students: Required—TOEFL (minimum score 550 paper-based; 213 computer-based; 79 iBT). Electronic applications accepted.

University of Phoenix–St. Louis Campus, School of Business, St. Louis, MO 63043-4828. Offers accounting (MBA); business administration (MBA); global management (MBA); human resources management (MBA, MM); management (MM); marketing (MBA); public administration (MM). Evening/weekend programs available. *Degree requirements:* For master's, thesis (for some programs). *Entrance requirements:* For master's, 3 years of work experience, minimum undergraduate GPA of 3.0. Additional exam requirements/recommendations for international students: Required—TOEFL (minimum score 550 paper-based; 213 computer-based; 79 iBT). Electronic applications accepted.

University of Phoenix–San Antonio Campus, School of Business, San Antonio, TX 78230. Offers accounting (MBA); business administration (MBA); e-business (MBA); global management (MBA); human resources management (MBA, MM); management (MM); marketing (MBA); public administration (MBA, MM).

University of Phoenix–San Diego Campus, School of Business, San Diego, CA 92123. Offers accounting (MBA); business administration (MBA); global management (MBA); human resources management (MBA, MM); management (MM); marketing (MBA); public administration (MBA). Evening/weekend programs available. *Degree requirements:* For master's, thesis (for some programs). *Entrance requirements:* For master's, 3 years of work experience, minimum undergraduate GPA of 3.0. Additional exam requirements/recommendations for international students: Required—TOEFL (minimum score 550 paper-based; 213 computer-based; 79 iBT). Electronic applications accepted.

University of Phoenix–Savannah Campus, School of Business, Savannah, GA 31405-7400. Offers accounting (MBA); business administration (MBA); global management (MBA); human resources management (MBA, MM); management (MM); marketing (MBA); public administration (MBA, MM).

University of Phoenix–Southern Arizona Campus, School of Business, Tucson, AZ 85711. Offers accountancy (MS); accounting (MBA); business administration (MBA); global management (MBA); human resources management (MBA); management (MM); marketing (MBA). Evening/weekend programs available. *Degree requirements:* For master's, thesis (for some programs). *Entrance requirements:* For master's, minimum undergraduate GPA of 3.0, 3 years of work experience. Additional exam requirements/recommendations for international students: Required—TOEFL (minimum score 550 paper-based; 213 computer-based; 79 iBT). Electronic applications accepted.

University of Phoenix–Southern California Campus, School of Business, Costa Mesa, CA 92626. Offers accounting (MIS); business administration (MBA); energy management (MBA); global management (MBA); health care management (MBA); human resource management (MBA); management (MM); marketing (MBA); project management (MBA); public administration (MPA); technology management (MBA). Evening/weekend programs available. Postbaccalaureate distance learning degree programs offered. *Students:* 699 full-time (341 women); includes 318 minority (124 Black or African American, non-Hispanic/Latino; 4 American Indian or Alaska Native, non-Hispanic/Latino; 44 Asian, non-Hispanic/Latino; 124 Hispanic/Latino; 15 Native Hawaiian or other Pacific Islander, non-Hispanic/Latino; 7 Two or more races, non-Hispanic/Latino), 29 international. Average age 38. *Entrance requirements:* Additional exam requirements/recommendations for international students: Required—TOEFL, TOEIC (Test of English as an International Communication), Berlitz Online English Proficiency Exam, Pearson Test of English, or IELTS. *Application deadline:* Applications are processed on a rolling basis. Application fee: $45. Electronic applications accepted. *Expenses:* Contact institution. *Financial support:* Scholarships/grants available. Financial award applicants required to submit FAFSA. *Application contact:* 866-766-0766. Web site: http://www.phoenix.edu/colleges_divisions/business.html.

University of Phoenix–Southern Colorado Campus, School of Business, Colorado Springs, CO 80919-2335. Offers accounting (MBA); business administration (MBA); global management (MBA); human resources management (MBA, MM); management (MM); marketing (MBA); public administration (MM). Evening/weekend programs available. *Degree requirements:* For master's, thesis (for some programs). *Entrance requirements:* For master's, minimum undergraduate GPA of 3.0, 3 years of work experience. Additional exam requirements/recommendations for international students: Required—TOEFL (minimum score 550 paper-based; 213 computer-based; 79 iBT). Electronic applications accepted.

University of Phoenix–South Florida Campus, School of Business, Fort Lauderdale, FL 33309. Offers accounting (MBA); business administration (MBA); global management (MBA); human resource management (MBA); human resources management (MM); management (MM); marketing (MBA); public administration (MBA, MM). Evening/weekend programs available. *Degree requirements:* For master's, thesis (for some programs). *Entrance requirements:* For master's, minimum undergraduate GPA of 3.0, 3 years work experience. Additional exam requirements/recommendations for international students: Required—TOEFL (minimum score 550 paper-based; 213 computer-based; 79 iBT). Electronic applications accepted.

University of Phoenix–Springfield Campus, School of Business, Springfield, MO 65804-7211. Offers accounting (MBA); business administration (MBA); global management (MBA); human resources management (MBA, MM); management (MM); marketing (MBA); public administration (MBA, MM).

University of Phoenix–Tulsa Campus, School of Business, Tulsa, OK 74134-1412. Offers accounting (MBA); business (MM); business administration (MBA); global management (MBA); human resources management (MBA); marketing (MBA). Evening/weekend programs available. *Degree requirements:* For master's, thesis (for some programs). *Entrance requirements:* For master's, minimum undergraduate GPA of 3.0, 3 years work experience. Additional exam requirements/recommendations for international students: Required—TOEFL (minimum score 550 paper-based; 213 computer-based; 79 iBT).

University of Phoenix–Utah Campus, School of Business, Salt Lake City, UT 84123-4617. Offers accounting (MBA); business administration (MBA); global management (MBA); human resource management (MBA, MM); management (MM); marketing (MBA); technology management (MBA). Evening/weekend programs available. *Degree requirements:* For master's, thesis (for some programs). *Entrance requirements:* For master's, minimum undergraduate GPA of 3.0, 3 years of work experience. Additional exam requirements/recommendations for international students: Required—TOEFL (minimum score 550 paper-based; 213 computer-based; 79 iBT). Electronic applications accepted.

University of Phoenix–Vancouver Campus, John Sperling School of Business, College of Graduate Business and Management, Burnaby, BC V5C 6G9, Canada. Offers accounting (MBA); business administration (MBA); global management (MBA); human resources management (MBA, MM); marketing (MBA). Evening/weekend programs available. *Degree requirements:* For master's, thesis (for some programs). *Entrance requirements:* For master's, minimum undergraduate GPA of 3.0, 3 years of work experience. Additional exam requirements/recommendations for international students: Required—TOEFL (minimum score 550 paper-based; 213 computer-based; 79 iBT). Electronic applications accepted.

University of Phoenix–West Florida Campus, School of Business, Temple Terrace, FL 33637. Offers accounting (MBA); business administration (MBA); global management (MBA); human resources management (MBA, MM); management (MM); marketing (MBA); public administration (MBA, MM). Evening/weekend programs available. *Degree requirements:* For master's, thesis (for some programs). *Entrance requirements:* For master's, 3 years of work experience, minimum undergraduate GPA of 3.0. Additional exam requirements/recommendations for international students: Required—TOEFL (minimum score 550 paper-based; 213 computer-based; 79 iBT). Electronic applications accepted.

University of Pittsburgh, Katz Graduate School of Business, Augsburg Executive Fellows Program, Pittsburgh, PA 15260. Offers MBA. *Faculty:* 62 full-time (17 women), 21 part-time/adjunct (4 women). *Students:* 16 full-time (3 women), all international. Average age 34. *Degree requirements:* For master's, one foreign language, 7-week stay at Katz Graduate School as full-time student. *Entrance requirements:* For master's, admission to the MBA program at the University of Augsburg, Germany. Additional exam requirements/recommendations for international students: Required—TOEFL (minimum score 600 paper-based; 250 computer-based; 100 iBT) or IELTS. *Application deadline:* For spring admission, 7/1 for international students. *Expenses:* Contact institution. *Faculty research:* Accounting statements and reporting, corporate finance, information systems processes, structures and decision-making, consumer behavior and marketing models. *Unit head:* William T. Valenta, Assistant Dean, MBA Programs, 412-648-1610, Fax: 412-648-1659, E-mail: wtvalenta@katz.pitt.edu. *Application contact:* Patricia Hermenault, Director, Special International and Dual Degree Programs, 412-383-8835, Fax: 412-648-1659, E-mail: hermenault@katz.pitt.edu. Web site: http://www.business.pitt.edu/katz/mba/academics/courses/international/international-students.php.

University of Pittsburgh, Katz Graduate School of Business, MBA/Master of International Business Dual Degree Program, Pittsburgh, PA 15260. Offers MBA/MIB. Part-time and evening/weekend programs available. *Faculty:* 62 full-time (17 women), 21 part-time/adjunct (4 women). *Students:* 1 full-time (0 women), 6 part-time (5 women); includes 1 minority (Hispanic/Latino). Average age 29. 25 applicants, 28% accepted, 5 enrolled. *Entrance requirements:* Additional exam requirements/recommendations for international students: Required—TOEFL (minimum score 600 paper-based; 250 computer-based; 100 iBT) or IELTS. *Application deadline:* For fall admission, 4/1 priority date for domestic students, 2/1 for international students. Application fee: $50. Electronic applications accepted. *Expenses:* Tuition, state resident: full-time $18,774; part-time $760 per credit. Tuition, nonresident: full-time $30,736; part-time $1258 per credit. *Required fees:* $740; $200 per term. Tuition and fees vary according to program. *Financial support:* In 2011–12, 5 students received support. Career-related internships or fieldwork and scholarships/grants available. Financial award application deadline: 3/1; financial award applicants required to submit FAFSA. *Faculty research:* Transitional economies, incentives and governance; corporate finance, mergers and acquisitions; global information systems and structures; consumer behavior and marketing models; entrepreneurship and globalization. *Unit head:* William T. Valenta, Assistant Dean/Director, 412-648-1610, Fax: 412-648-1659, E-mail: wtvalenta@katz.pitt.edu. *Application contact:* Thomas Keller, Director of MBA Admissions, 412-648-1700, Fax: 412-648-1659, E-mail: mba@katz.pitt.edu. Web site: http://www.business.pitt.edu/katz/mba/academics/programs/mba-mib.php.

University of Puerto Rico, Río Piedras, College of Business Administration, San Juan, PR 00931-3300. Offers accounting (MBA); finance (MBA, PhD); general business (MBA); human resources management (MBA); international trade and business (MBA, PhD); marketing (MBA); operations management (MBA); quantitative methods (MBA). *Accreditation:* ACBSP. Part-time programs available. *Degree requirements:* For master's, comprehensive exam, thesis or alternative, research project. *Entrance requirements:* For master's, GMAT or PAEG, minimum GPA of 3.0, letter of recommendation; for doctorate, GMAT, PAEG, minimum GPA of 3.0, master degree. *Faculty research:* Management.

University of Regina, Faculty of Graduate Studies and Research, Kenneth Levene Graduate School of Business, Program in Business Administration, Regina, SK S4S 0A2, Canada. Offers business (Master's Certificate); business administration (MBA); executive business administration (MBA); international business (MBA); leadership (M Admin); organizational leadership (Master's Certificate); project management (Master's Certificate). Part-time and evening/weekend programs available. *Faculty:* 32 full-time (12 women), 10 part-time/adjunct (0 women). *Students:* 83 full-time (32 women), 51 part-time (26 women). 117 applicants, 75% accepted. In 2011, 35 master's awarded. *Degree requirements:* For master's, project. *Entrance requirements:* For master's, GMAT, two years relevant work experience. Additional exam requirements/recommendations for international students: Required—TOEFL (minimum score 580 paper-based; 80 iBT), IELTS (minimum score 6.5). *Application deadline:* Applications are processed on a rolling basis. Application fee: $100. Electronic applications accepted. *Expenses:* Contact institution. *Financial support:* In 2011–12, 6 fellowships (averaging $6,000 per year), 9 teaching assistantships (averaging $2,298 per year) were awarded; research assistantships and scholarships/grants also available. Financial award application deadline: 6/15. *Faculty research:* Business policy and strategy, production and operations management, human behavior in organizations, financial management, social issues in business. *Unit head:* Dr. Morina Rennie, Dean, 306-585-4162, Fax: 306-585-4805, E-mail: morina.rennie@uregina.ca. *Application contact:* Steve Wield, Manager, Graduate Programs, 306-337-8463, Fax: 306-585-5361, E-mail: steve.wield@uregina.ca.

University of San Diego, School of Business Administration, Masters in International Business Administration (IMBA) Program, San Diego, CA 92110-2492. Offers IMBA, JD/IMBA. *Students:* 28 full-time (14 women), 12 part-time (6 women); includes 6 minority (2 Asian, non-Hispanic/Latino; 3 Hispanic/Latino; 1 Two or more races, non-Hispanic/Latino), 11 international. Average age 29. In 2011, 28 master's awarded. *Degree requirements:* For master's, one foreign language, community service, capstone project. *Entrance requirements:* For master's, GMAT, minimum GPA of 3.0, minimum 2 years of full-time work experience. Additional exam requirements/recommendations for international students: Required—TOEFL (minimum score 580 paper-based; 237 computer-based; 92 iBT), TWE. *Application deadline:* For fall admission, 4/1 for domestic students. Applications are processed on a rolling basis. Application fee: $80. Electronic applications accepted. *Expenses: Tuition:* Full-time $22,482; part-time $1249 per unit. *Required fees:* $224. Full-time tuition and fees vary according to course load and degree level. *Financial support:* In 2011–12, 32 students received support. Career-related internships or fieldwork, Federal Work-Study, institutionally sponsored loans, scholarships/grants, and unspecified assistantships available. Support available to part-time students. Financial award application deadline: 4/1; financial award applicants required to submit FAFSA. *Faculty research:* Exchange rate forecasting, corporate governance, performance of private equity funds, economic geography, food banking. *Unit head:* Dr. Manzur Rahman, Academic Director, MBA Programs, 619-260-4886, E-mail: mba@sandiego.edu. *Application contact:* Monica Mahon, Associate Director of Graduate Admissions, 619-260-4524, Fax: 619-260-4158, E-mail: grads@sandiego.edu. Web site: http://www.sandiego.edu/business/programs/graduate/MBA/MBA_Programs/International_MBA/.

University of San Diego, School of Business Administration, Program in Global Leadership, San Diego, CA 92110-2492. Offers MS. Postbaccalaureate distance learning degree programs offered (minimal on-campus study). *Students:* 24 full-time (9 women), 65 part-time (19 women); includes 30 minority (6 Black or African American, non-Hispanic/Latino; 1 American Indian or Alaska Native, non-Hispanic/Latino; 8 Asian, non-Hispanic/Latino; 12 Hispanic/Latino; 1 Native Hawaiian or other Pacific Islander, non-Hispanic/Latino; 2 Two or more races, non-Hispanic/Latino), 2 international. Average age 34. In 2011, 54 master's awarded. *Entrance requirements:* For master's, minimum GPA of 3.0, minimum 2 years of work experience. Additional exam requirements/recommendations for international students: Required—TOEFL (minimum score 580 paper-based; 237 computer-based; 92 iBT), TWE. *Application deadline:* Applications are processed on a rolling basis. Application fee: $80. Electronic applications accepted. *Expenses: Tuition:* Full-time $22,482; part-time $1249 per unit. *Required fees:* $224. Full-time tuition and fees vary according to course load and degree level. *Financial support:* In 2011–12, 42 students received support. Scholarships/grants available. Financial award application deadline: 4/1; financial award applicants required to submit FAFSA. *Unit head:* Stephanie Kiesel, Director, 619-260-8850, E-mail: skiesel@sandiego.edu. *Application contact:* Monica Mahon, Associate Director of Graduate Admissions, 619-260-4524, Fax: 619-260-4158, E-mail: grads@sandiego.edu. Web site: http://www.sandiego.edu/business/programs/graduate/leadership/global_leadership/.

University of San Francisco, School of Law, Master of Law Program, San Francisco, CA 94117-1080. Offers intellectual property and technology law (LL M); international transactions and comparative law (LL M). *Faculty:* 15 full-time (7 women), 49 part-time/adjunct (18 women). *Students:* 15 full-time (7 women), 3 part-time (2 women), 14 international. Average age 30. 125 applicants, 62% accepted, 17 enrolled. In 2011, 23 master's awarded. *Entrance requirements:* For master's, law degree from U.S. or foreign school (intellectual property and technology law), law degree from foreign school (international transactions and comparative law). Application fee: $60. *Expenses: Tuition:* Full-time $20,070; part-time $1115 per unit. Tuition and fees vary according to course load, campus/location and program. *Financial support:* In 2011–12, 13 students received support. *Unit head:* Eldon Reiley, Director, Fax: 415-422-5440. *Application contact:* Program Assistant, 415-422-5100, E-mail: masterlaws@usfca.edu.

University of San Francisco, School of Management, Masagung Graduate School of Management, Joint Master of Global Entrepreneurship and Management Program, San Francisco, CA 94117-1080. Offers MGEM. Program offered jointly with IQS in Barcelona, Spain and Fu Jen Catholic University in Taipei, Taiwan. *Faculty:* 2 full-time (both women), 2 part-time/adjunct (0 women). *Students:* 35 full-time (17 women); includes 6 minority (1 Black or African American, non-Hispanic/Latino; 1 Asian, non-Hispanic/Latino; 3 Hispanic/Latino; 1 Two or more races, non-Hispanic/Latino), 18 international. Average age 24. 65 applicants, 69% accepted, 35 enrolled. In 2011, 27 master's awarded. *Expenses: Tuition:* Full-time $20,070; part-time $1115 per unit. Tuition and fees vary according to course load, campus/location and program. *Financial support:* In 2011–12, 9 students received support. *Unit head:* Dr. Sidaoui Mouwafac, 415-422-6771, Fax: 415-422-2502. *Application contact:* Director, MBA Program, 415-422-2221, Fax: 415-422-6315, E-mail: mba@usfca.edu. Web site: http://www.usfca.edu/jmgem/.

University of San Francisco, School of Management, Masagung Graduate School of Management, Program in Business Administration, San Francisco, CA 94117-1080. Offers business economics (MBA); e-business (MBA); entrepreneurship (MBA); finance (MBA); international business (MBA); management (MBA); marketing (MBA); telecommunications management and policy (MBA); JD/MBA; MSN/MBA. *Accreditation:* AACSB. *Faculty:* 18 full-time (4 women), 18 part-time/adjunct (9 women). *Students:* 247 full-time (122 women), 9 part-time (3 women); includes 85 minority (5 Black or African American, non-Hispanic/Latino; 55 Asian, non-Hispanic/Latino; 16 Hispanic/Latino; 1 Native Hawaiian or other Pacific Islander, non-Hispanic/Latino; 8 Two or more races, non-Hispanic/Latino), 38 international. Average age 29. 552 applicants, 55% accepted, 99 enrolled. In 2011, 173 master's awarded. *Entrance requirements:* For master's, GMAT, minimum undergraduate GPA of 3.2. Additional exam requirements/recommendations for international students: Required—TOEFL. *Application deadline:* For fall admission, 7/1 priority date for domestic students; for spring admission, 11/30 for domestic students. Applications are processed on a rolling basis. Application fee: $55 ($65 for international students). *Expenses: Tuition:* Full-time $20,070; part-time $1115 per unit. Tuition and fees vary according to course load, campus/location and program. *Financial support:* In 2011–12, 33 students received support. Fellowships available. Financial award application deadline: 3/2; financial award applicants required to submit FAFSA. *Faculty research:* International financial markets, technology transfer licensing, international marketing, strategic planning. *Total annual research expenditures:* $50,000. *Unit head:* Kelly Brookes, Director, 415-422-2221, Fax: 415-422-6315. *Application contact:* Director, MBA Program, 415-422-2221, Fax: 415-422-6315, E-mail: mba@usfca.edu.

University of Saskatchewan, College of Graduate Studies and Research, Edwards School of Business, Program in Business Administration, Saskatoon, SK S7N 5A2, Canada. Offers agribusiness management (MBA); biotechnology management (MBA); health services management (MBA); indigenous management (MBA); international business management (MBA).

University of Saskatchewan, College of Graduate Studies and Research, School of Public Policy, Saskatoon, SK S7N 5A2, Canada. Offers MIT, MPA, MPP, PhD.

The University of Scranton, College of Graduate and Continuing Education, Program in Business Administration, Scranton, PA 18510. Offers accounting (MBA); finance (MBA); general business administration (MBA); health care management (MBA); international business (MBA); management information systems (MBA); marketing (MBA); operations management (MBA). *Accreditation:* AACSB. Part-time and evening/weekend programs available. Postbaccalaureate distance learning degree programs offered (no on-campus study). *Faculty:* 34 full-time (8 women). *Students:* 276 full-time (94 women), 243 part-time (88 women); includes 14 minority (10 Black or African American, non-Hispanic/Latino; 3 Asian, non-Hispanic/Latino; 1 Hispanic/Latino), 49 international. Average age 33. 358 applicants, 80% accepted. In 2011, 101 master's awarded. *Degree requirements:* For master's, capstone experience. *Entrance requirements:* For master's, GMAT, minimum GPA of 2.75. Additional exam requirements/recommendations for international students: Required—TOEFL (minimum score 500 paper-based; 173 computer-based), IELTS (minimum score 5.5). *Application deadline:* Applications are processed on a rolling basis. Application fee: $0. *Financial support:* In 2011–12, 12 students received support, including 12 teaching assistantships with full and partial tuition reimbursements available (averaging $8,433 per year); fellowships, career-related internships or fieldwork, Federal Work-Study, and unspecified assistantships also available. Support available to part-time students. Financial award application deadline: 3/1. *Faculty research:* Financial markets, strategic impact of total quality management, internal accounting controls, consumer preference, information systems and the Internet. *Unit head:* Dr. Murli Rajan, Director, 570-941-4043, Fax: 570-941-4342. *Application contact:* Joseph M. Roback, Director of Admissions, 570-941-4385, Fax: 570-941-5928, E-mail: robackj2@scranton.edu. Web site: http://www.academic.scranton.edu/department/mba/.

University of South Carolina, The Graduate School, Darla Moore School of Business, International Business Administration Program, Columbia, SC 29208. Offers IMBA. *Degree requirements:* For master's, one foreign language, field consulting project/internship. *Entrance requirements:* For master's, GMAT or GRE, minimum two years of work experience. Additional exam requirements/recommendations for international students: Required—TOEFL (minimum score 250 computer-based; 100 iBT); Recommended—IELTS. Electronic applications accepted. *Expenses:* Contact institution.

The University of Tampa, John H. Sykes College of Business, Tampa, FL 33606-1490. Offers accounting (MS); entrepreneurship (MBA); finance (MBA, MS); information systems management (MBA); innovation management (MBA); international business (MBA); marketing (MBA, MS); nonprofit management (MBA). *Accreditation:* AACSB. Part-time and evening/weekend programs available. *Faculty:* 38 full-time (14 women), 5 part-time/adjunct (1 woman). *Students:* 161 full-time (65 women), 193 part-time (82 women); includes 65 minority (11 Black or African American, non-Hispanic/Latino; 1 American Indian or Alaska Native, non-Hispanic/Latino; 8 Asian, non-Hispanic/Latino; 39 Hispanic/Latino; 2 Native Hawaiian or other Pacific Islander, non-Hispanic/Latino; 4 Two or more races, non-Hispanic/Latino), 58 international. Average age 29. 837 applicants, 41% accepted, 196 enrolled. In 2011, 259 degrees awarded. *Degree requirements:* For master's, capstone. *Entrance requirements:* For master's, GMAT or GRE, 4-year undergraduate degree, minimum GPA of 3.0, professional experience (for Executive MBA). Additional exam requirements/recommendations for international students: Required—TOEFL (minimum score 577 paper-based; 230 computer-based; 90 iBT); Recommended—IELTS (minimum score 7.5). *Application deadline:* Applications are processed on a rolling basis. Application fee: $40. Electronic applications accepted. *Expenses: Tuition:* Full-time $8320; part-time $520 per credit hour. *Required fees:* $40 per semester. Tuition and fees vary according to program. *Financial support:* In 2011–12, 124 students received support. Career-related internships or fieldwork, scholarships/grants, unspecified assistantships, and grants available. Financial award applicants required to submit FAFSA. *Faculty research:* Job market signaling, on-line shopping behaviors and social media, the Tampa Bay economy, digital literacy, entrepreneurship in small businesses. *Unit head:* Dennis Nostrand, Vice President, Enrollment/Admissions, 813-257-1808, E-mail: dnostrand@ut.edu. *Application contact:* Charlene Tobie, Associate Director of Admissions, 813-257-3566, E-mail: ctobie@ut.edu. Web site: http://ut.edu/graduate.

The University of Texas at Dallas, Naveen Jindal School of Management, Program in Accounting, Richardson, TX 75080. Offers assurance services (MS); corporate accounting (MS); internal audit (MS); taxation (MS). *Accreditation:* AACSB. *Faculty:* 16 full-time (4 women), 11 part-time/adjunct (5 women). *Students:* 398 full-time (258 women), 402 part-time (238 women); includes 136 minority (18 Black or African American, non-Hispanic/Latino; 1 American Indian or Alaska Native, non-Hispanic/Latino; 79 Asian, non-Hispanic/Latino; 28 Hispanic/Latino; 10 Two or more races, non-Hispanic/Latino), 411 international. Average age 28. 825 applicants, 59% accepted, 308 enrolled. In 2011, 314 master's awarded. *Entrance requirements:* For master's, GMAT, minimum GPA of 3.0 in upper-level course work in field. Additional exam requirements/recommendations for international students: Required—TOEFL (minimum score 550 paper-based; 215 computer-based). *Application deadline:* For fall admission, 7/15 for domestic students, 5/1 for international students; for spring admission, 11/15 for domestic students, 9/1 for international students. Applications are processed on a rolling basis. Application fee: $50 ($100 for international students). Electronic applications accepted. *Expenses:* Tuition, state resident: full-time $11,170; part-time $620.56 per credit hour. Tuition, nonresident: full-time $20,212; part-time $1122.89 per credit hour. *Financial support:* In 2011–12, 257 students received support, including 5 teaching assistantships with partial tuition reimbursements available (averaging $10,050 per year); research assistantships with partial tuition reimbursements available, career-related internships or fieldwork, Federal Work-Study, institutionally sponsored loans, scholarships/grants, and unspecified assistantships also available. Support available to part-time students. Financial award application deadline: 4/30; financial award applicants required to submit FAFSA. *Faculty research:* Privatization and accounting/auditing, corporate performance and executive compensation, risk management, information technology in accounting. *Unit head:* Amy Troutman, Associate Area Coordinator, 972-883-6719, Fax: 972-883-6823, E-mail: amybass@utdallas.edu. *Application contact:* Jennifer Johnson, Director, Graduate Accounting Programs, 972-883-5912, E-mail: jennifer.johnson@utdallas.edu. Web site: http://jindal.utdallas.edu/academic-areas/accounting/.

The University of Texas at Dallas, Naveen Jindal School of Management, Program in Business Administration, Richardson, TX 75080. Offers cohort (MBA); executive business administration (EMBA); global leadership (EMBA); global online (MBA); healthcare management (EMBA); product lifecycle and supply chain management (EMBA); professional business administration (MBA); project management (EMBA). *Accreditation:* AACSB. Part-time and evening/weekend programs available. Postbaccalaureate distance learning degree programs offered (no on-campus study). *Faculty:* 88 full-time (16 women), 52 part-time/adjunct (13 women). *Students:* 390 full-time (129 women), 658 part-time (207 women); includes 291 minority (42 Black or African American, non-Hispanic/Latino; 4 American Indian or Alaska Native, non-Hispanic/Latino; 168 Asian, non-Hispanic/Latino; 66 Hispanic/Latino; 11 Two or more races, non-Hispanic/Latino), 161 international. Average age 32. 872 applicants, 51% accepted, 323 enrolled. In 2011, 471 master's awarded. *Degree requirements:* For master's, thesis optional. *Entrance requirements:* For master's, GMAT, 10 years of business experience (EMBA), minimum GPA of 3.0. Additional exam requirements/recommendations for international students: Required—TOEFL (minimum score 550 paper-based; 215 computer-based). *Application deadline:* For fall admission, 7/15 for domestic students, 5/1 for international students; for spring admission, 11/15 for domestic students, 9/1 for international students. Applications are processed on a rolling basis. Application fee: $50 ($100 for international students). Electronic applications accepted. *Expenses:* Contact institution. *Financial support:* In 2011–12, 223 students received support, including 1 research assistantship with partial tuition reimbursement available (averaging $13,400 per year), 24 teaching assistantships with partial tuition reimbursements available (averaging $10,050 per year); career-related internships or fieldwork, Federal Work-Study, institutionally sponsored loans, scholarships/grants, and unspecified assistantships also available. Support available to part-time students. Financial award application deadline: 4/30; financial award applicants required to submit FAFSA. *Faculty research:* Production scheduling, trade and finance, organizational decision-making, life/work planning. *Unit head:* Lisa Shatz, Director, Full-time MBA Program, 972-883-6191, E-mail: lisa.shatz@utdallas.edu. *Application contact:* James Parker, Assistant Director, 972-883-5842, E-mail: jparker@utdallas.edu. Web site: http://jindal.utdallas.edu/academic-programs/mba-programs/.

The University of Texas at Dallas, Naveen Jindal School of Management, Program in International Management, Richardson, TX 75080. Offers MS, PhD. Part-time and evening/weekend programs available. *Faculty:* 12 full-time (3 women), 9 part-time/adjunct (2 women). *Students:* 30 full-time (17 women), 15 part-time (9 women); includes 9 minority (3 Black or African American, non-Hispanic/Latino; 5 Asian, non-Hispanic/Latino; 1 Hispanic/Latino), 19 international. Average age 29. 138 applicants, 22% accepted, 14 enrolled. In 2011, 9 master's, 1 doctorate awarded. *Degree requirements:* For doctorate, thesis/dissertation. *Entrance requirements:* For master's and doctorate, GMAT. Additional exam requirements/recommendations for international students: Required—TOEFL (minimum score 550 paper-based; 215 computer-based). *Application deadline:* For fall admission, 7/15 for domestic students, 5/1 for international students; for spring admission, 11/15 for domestic students, 9/1 for international students. Applications are processed on a rolling basis. Application fee: $50 ($100 for international students). Electronic applications accepted. *Expenses:* Tuition, state resident: full-time $11,170; part-time $620.56 per credit hour. Tuition, nonresident: full-time $20,212; part-time $1122.89 per credit hour. *Financial support:* In 2011–12, 26 students received support, including 1 research assistantship with partial tuition reimbursement available (averaging $21,600 per year), 11 teaching assistantships with partial tuition reimbursements available (averaging $16,364 per year); Federal Work-Study, institutionally sponsored loans, scholarships/grants, and unspecified assistantships also available. Support available to part-time students. Financial award application deadline: 4/30; financial award applicants required to submit FAFSA. *Faculty research:* International accounting, international trade and finance, economic development, international economics. *Unit head:* Dr. Mike W. Peng, PhD Program Director, 972-883-2714, Fax: 972-883-5977, E-mail: mikepeng@utdallas.edu. *Application contact:* Dr. Habte Woldu, Master's Program Director, 972-883-6357, Fax: 972-883-5977, E-mail: wolduh@utdallas.edu. Web site: http://jindal.utdallas.edu/academic-programs/phd-programs/.

The University of Texas at Dallas, Naveen Jindal School of Management, Program in Management and Administrative Sciences, Richardson, TX 75080. Offers electronic commerce (MS); finance (MS); healthcare administration (MS); information systems (MS); innovation and entrepreneurship (MS); international management (MS); leadership in organizations (MS); marketing (MS); operations (MS); organizations (MS); real estate (MS); strategy (MS). *Accreditation:* AACSB. Part-time and evening/weekend programs available. *Faculty:* 26 full-time (6 women), 9 part-time/adjunct (2 women). *Students:* 128 full-time (69 women), 169 part-time (95 women); includes 76 minority (18 Black or African American, non-Hispanic/Latino; 1 American Indian or Alaska Native, non-Hispanic/Latino; 37 Asian, non-Hispanic/Latino; 15 Hispanic/Latino; 1 Native Hawaiian or other Pacific Islander, non-Hispanic/Latino; 4 Two or more races, non-Hispanic/Latino), 77 international. Average age 34. 220 applicants, 63% accepted, 68 enrolled. In 2011, 58 master's awarded. *Degree requirements:* For master's, thesis optional. *Entrance requirements:* For master's, GMAT. Additional exam requirements/recommendations for international students: Required—TOEFL (minimum score 550 paper-based; 215 computer-based). *Application deadline:* For fall admission, 7/15 for domestic students, 5/1 for international students; for spring admission, 11/15 for domestic students, 9/1 for international students. Applications are processed on a rolling basis. Application fee: $50 ($100 for international students). Electronic applications accepted. *Expenses:* Tuition, state resident: full-time $11,170; part-time $620.56 per credit hour. Tuition, nonresident: full-time $20,212; part-time $1122.89 per credit hour. *Financial support:* In 2011–12, 68 students received support, including 7 teaching assistantships with partial tuition reimbursements available (averaging $16,200 per year); research assistantships with partial tuition reimbursements available, career-related internships or fieldwork, Federal Work-Study, institutionally sponsored loans, scholarships/grants, and unspecified assistantships also available. Support available to part-time students. Financial award application deadline: 4/30; financial award applicants required to submit FAFSA. *Faculty research:* Integrated and detailed knowledge of functional areas of management, analytical tools for effective appraisal and decision-making. *Unit head:* Dr. Gregory Dess, Area Coordinator, 972-883-4439, E-mail: gdess@utdallas.edu. *Application contact:* James Parker, Assistant Director, 972-883-5842, E-mail: jparker@utdallas.edu. Web site: http://jindal.utdallas.edu/academic-areas/organizations-strategy-and-international-management/.

The University of Texas at El Paso, Graduate School, College of Business Administration, Programs in Business Administration, El Paso, TX 79968-0001. Offers business administration (MBA, Certificate); international business (PhD). *Accreditation:* AACSB. Part-time and evening/weekend programs available. Postbaccalaureate distance learning degree programs offered (no on-campus study). *Students:* 345 (147 women); includes 200 minority (5 Black or African American, non-Hispanic/Latino; 7 Asian, non-Hispanic/Latino; 188 Hispanic/Latino), 95 international. Average age 34. 135 applicants, 67% accepted, 73 enrolled. In 2011, 42 master's awarded. *Entrance requirements:* For master's, GMAT, minimum GPA of 2.7. Additional exam requirements/recommendations for international students: Required—TOEFL. *Application deadline:* For fall admission, 7/1 priority date for domestic students, 3/1 for international students; for spring admission, 11/1 priority date for domestic students, 9/1 for international students. Applications are processed on a rolling basis. Application fee: $15 ($65 for international students). Electronic applications accepted. *Financial support:* In 2011–12, research assistantships with partial tuition reimbursements (averaging $18,750 per year), teaching assistantships with partial tuition reimbursements (averaging $15,000 per year) were awarded; Federal Work-Study, institutionally sponsored loans, and tuition waivers (partial) also available. Financial award application deadline: 3/15; financial award applicants required to submit FAFSA. *Unit head:* Laura M. Uribarri, Director, 915-747-5379, Fax: 915-747-5147, E-mail: mba@utep.edu. *Application contact:* Dr. Benjamin Flores, Interim Dean of the Graduate School, 915-747-5491, Fax: 915-747-5788, E-mail: bflores@utep.edu.

See Display on page 163 and Close-Up on page 259.

The University of Texas at San Antonio, College of Business, General Business Program, San Antonio, TX 78249-0617. Offers business (MBA); business administration (PhD), including accounting, business administration, finance, information technology, management and organization studies, marketing; information systems (MBA); international business (MBA); management accounting (MBA); management of technology (MBA); marketing management (MBA); taxation (MBA). *Students:* 170 full-time (52 women), 120 part-time (49 women); includes 90 minority (14 Black or African American, non-Hispanic/Latino; 2 American Indian or Alaska Native, non-Hispanic/Latino; 15 Asian, non-Hispanic/Latino; 55 Hispanic/Latino; 1 Native Hawaiian or other Pacific Islander, non-Hispanic/Latino; 3 Two or more races, non-Hispanic/Latino), 37 international. Average age 32. 395 applicants, 45% accepted, 133 enrolled. In 2011, 95 master's, 8 doctorates awarded. *Entrance requirements:* Additional exam requirements/recommendations for international students: Required—TOEFL (minimum score 500 paper-based; 61 iBT), IELTS (minimum score 5). *Application deadline:* For fall admission, 7/1 for domestic students, 4/1 for international students; for spring admission, 11/1 for domestic students, 9/1 for international students. Application fee: $45 ($85 for international students). *Expenses:* Tuition, state resident: full-time $3148; part-time $2176 per semester. Tuition, nonresident: full-time $8782; part-time $5932 per semester. *Required fees:* $719 per semester. *Financial support:* In 2011–12, fellowships (averaging $22,000 per year), research assistantships (averaging $10,000 per year), teaching assistantships (averaging $10,000 per year) were awarded. *Unit head:* Dr. Lynda Y. de la Vinna, Dean, 210-458-4317, Fax: 210-458-4308, E-mail: lynda.delavina@utsa.edu. *Application contact:* Katherine Pope, Director of Graduate Student Services, 210-458-7316, Fax: 210-458-4398, E-mail: katherine.pope@utsa.edu. Web site: http://business.utsa.edu.

University of the Incarnate Word, School of Graduate Studies and Research, H-E-B School of Business and Administration, Programs in Administration, San Antonio, TX 78209-6397. Offers adult education (MAA); applied administration (MAA); communication arts (MAA); healthcare administration (MAA); instructional technology (MAA); international business (Certificate); nutrition (MAA); organizational development (MAA, Certificate); project management (Certificate); sports management (MAA). Part-time and evening/weekend programs available. Postbaccalaureate distance learning degree programs offered (no on-campus study). *Faculty:* 23 full-time (10 women), 26 part-time/adjunct (12 women). *Students:* 25 full-time (18 women), 54 part-time (33 women); includes 50 minority (10 Black or African American, non-Hispanic/Latino; 40 Hispanic/Latino), 5 international. Average age 34. 35 applicants, 94% accepted, 19 enrolled. In 2011, 38 master's awarded. *Degree requirements:* For master's, capstone. *Entrance requirements:* For master's, GRE, GMAT, undergraduate degree, minimum GPA of 2.5. Additional exam requirements/recommendations for international students: Required—TOEFL (minimum score 560 paper-based; 220 computer-based; 83 iBT). *Application deadline:* Applications are processed on a rolling basis. Application fee: $20. Electronic applications accepted. *Expenses: Tuition:* Part-time $725 per credit hour. Tuition and fees vary according to degree level. *Financial support:* Federal Work-Study and scholarships/grants available. Financial award applicants required to submit FAFSA. *Unit head:* Dr. Mark Teachout, MAA Programs Director, 210-829-3177, Fax: 210-805-3564, E-mail: teachout@uiwtx.edu. *Application contact:* Andrea Cyterski-Acosta, Dean of Enrollment, 210-829-6005, Fax: 210-829-3921, E-mail: admis@uiwtx.edu. Web site: http://www.uiw.edu/maa/index.htm and http://www.uiw.edu/maa/admissions.html.

University of the Incarnate Word, School of Graduate Studies and Research, H-E-B School of Business and Administration, Programs in Business Administration, San Antonio, TX 78209-6397. Offers general business (MBA); international business (MBA); international business strategy (MBA); sports management (MBA). *Accreditation:* ACBSP. Part-time and evening/weekend programs available. Postbaccalaureate distance learning degree programs offered. *Faculty:* 23 full-time (10 women), 26 part-time/adjunct (12 women). *Students:* 78 full-time (38 women), 93 part-time (46 women); includes 85 minority (11 Black or African American, non-Hispanic/Latino; 5 Asian, non-Hispanic/Latino; 68 Hispanic/Latino; 1 Native Hawaiian or other Pacific Islander, non-Hispanic/Latino), 42 international. Average age 28. 114 applicants, 96% accepted, 40 enrolled. In 2011, 83 master's awarded. *Degree requirements:* For master's, capstone. *Entrance requirements:* For master's, GMAT (minimum score 450), undergraduate degree with minimum overall GPA of 2.5. Additional exam requirements/recommendations for international students: Required—TOEFL (minimum score 560 paper-based; 220 computer-based; 83 iBT). *Application deadline:* Applications are processed on a rolling basis. Application fee: $20. Electronic applications accepted. *Expenses: Tuition:* Part-time $725 per credit hour. Tuition and fees vary according to degree level. *Financial support:* Federal Work-Study and scholarships/grants available. Financial award applicants required to submit FAFSA. *Unit head:* Dr. Jeannie Scott, Acting Dean, 210-283-5002, Fax: 210-805-3564, E-mail: scott@uiwtx.edu. *Application contact:* Andrea Cyterski-Acosta, Dean of Enrollment, 210-829-6005, Fax: 210-829-3921, E-mail: admis@uiwtx.edu. Web site: http://www.uiw.edu/mba/index.htm and http://www.uiw.edu/mba/admission.html.

University of the West, Department of Business Administration, Rosemead, CA 91770. Offers business administration (EMBA); finance (MBA); information technology and management (MBA); international business (MBA); nonprofit organization management (MBA). Part-time and evening/weekend programs available. *Entrance requirements:* Additional exam requirements/recommendations for international students: Required—TOEFL.

University of Tulsa, Graduate School, Collins College of Business, Master of Business Administration Program, Tulsa, OK 74104-3189. Offers accounting (MBA); business administration (MBA); energy management (MBA); finance (MBA); international business (MBA); management information systems (MBA); taxation (MBA); JD/MBA; MBA/MSCS; MBA/MSF. *Accreditation:* AACSB. Part-time and evening/weekend programs available. *Faculty:* 32 full-time (6 women). *Students:* 56 full-time (29 women), 28 part-time (7 women); includes 7 minority (1 Black or African American, non-Hispanic/Latino; 2 American Indian or Alaska Native, non-Hispanic/Latino; 2 Asian, non-Hispanic/Latino; 2 Hispanic/Latino), 16 international. Average age 26. 70 applicants, 67% accepted, 29 enrolled. In 2011, 35 master's awarded. *Entrance requirements:* For master's, GMAT. Additional exam requirements/recommendations for international students: Required—TOEFL (minimum score 577 paper-based; 233 computer-based; 91 iBT), IELTS (minimum score 6.5). *Application deadline:* Applications are processed on a rolling basis. Application fee: $40. Electronic applications accepted. *Expenses: Tuition:* Full-time $17,748; part-time $986 per hour. *Required fees:* $5 per contact hour. $75 per semester. Tuition and fees vary according to program. *Financial support:* In 2011–12, 30 students received support, including 30 teaching assistantships (averaging $11,044 per year); fellowships, research assistantships, career-related internships or fieldwork, institutionally sponsored loans, scholarships/grants, health care benefits, tuition waivers (full and partial), and unspecified assistantships also available. Support available to part-time students. Financial award application deadline: 2/1; financial award applicants required to submit FAFSA. *Faculty research:* Accounting, energy management, finance, international business, management information systems, taxation. *Unit head:* Dr. Linda Nichols, Associate Dean of the Collins College of Business, 918-631-2242, Fax: 918-631-2142, E-mail: linda-nichols@utulsa.edu. *Application contact:* Information Contact, 918-631-2242, E-mail: graduate-business@utulsa.edu. Web site: http://www.cba.utulsa.edu/.

University of Washington, Graduate School, Interdisciplinary Program in Global Trade, Transportation and Logistics Studies, Seattle, WA 98195. Offers Certificate.

University of Washington, Graduate School, Michael G. Foster School of Business, Seattle, WA 98195-3233. Offers auditing and assurance (MP Acc); business (PhD); business administration (evening) (MBA); business administration (full-time) (MBA); executive business administration (MBA); global business administration (MBA); global executive business administration (MBA); taxation (MP Acc); technology management (MBA); JD/MBA; MBA/MAIS; MBA/MHA. *Accreditation:* AACSB. Part-time programs available. *Faculty:* 100 full-time (28 women), 55 part-time/adjunct (22 women). *Students:* 385 full-time (116 women), 483 part-time (118 women); includes 183 minority (16 Black or African American, non-Hispanic/Latino; 2 American Indian or Alaska Native, non-Hispanic/Latino; 133 Asian, non-Hispanic/Latino; 25 Hispanic/Latino; 2 Native Hawaiian or other Pacific Islander, non-Hispanic/Latino; 5 Two or more races, non-Hispanic/Latino), 178 international. Average age 32. 1,367 applicants, 76% accepted, 868 enrolled. In 2011, 458 master's, 12 doctorates awarded. Terminal master's awarded for partial completion of doctoral program. *Degree requirements:* For doctorate, comprehensive exam, thesis/dissertation. *Entrance requirements:* For master's, GMAT; for doctorate, GMAT, GRE. Additional exam requirements/recommendations for international students: Required—TOEFL (minimum score 600 paper-based; 250 computer-based; 100 iBT). *Application deadline:* For fall admission, 3/15 for domestic students, 1/20 for international students. Application fee: $75. Electronic applications accepted. *Expenses:* Contact institution. *Financial support:* Fellowships with partial tuition reimbursements, research assistantships with partial tuition reimbursements, teaching assistantships with partial tuition reimbursements, Federal Work-Study, institutionally sponsored loans, and scholarships/grants available. Financial award application deadline: 2/28; financial award applicants required to submit FAFSA. *Faculty research:* Finance, marketing, organizational behavior, information technology, strategy. *Unit head:* Dr. James Jiambalvo, Dean, 206-543-4750. *Application contact:* Erin Ernst, Assistant Director of Admissions, 206-543-4661, Fax: 206-616-7351, E-mail: mba@u.washington.edu. Web site: http://www.foster.washington.edu/mba.

The University of Western Ontario, Richard Ivey School of Business, London, ON N6A 3K7, Canada. Offers business (EMBA, PhD); corporate strategy and leadership elective (MBA); entrepreneurship elective (MBA); finance elective (MBA); health sector stream (MBA); international management elective (MBA); marketing elective (MBA); JD/MBA. *Degree requirements:* For master's, thesis (for some programs); for doctorate, thesis/dissertation. *Entrance requirements:* For master's, GMAT, 2 years of full-time work experience, interview. Additional exam requirements/recommendations for international students: Required—TOEFL (minimum score 100 computer; 100 iBT) or IELTS (minimium score 6). Electronic applications accepted. *Faculty research:* Strategy, organizational behavior, international business, finance, operations management.

University of Wisconsin–Milwaukee, Graduate School, College of Letters and Sciences, Interdepartmental Program in Human Resources and Labor Relations, Milwaukee, WI 53201-0413. Offers human resources and labor relations (MHRLR); international human resources and labor relations (Certificate); mediation and negotiation (Certificate). Part-time programs available. *Faculty:* 2 full-time (0 women). *Students:* 14 full-time (8 women), 24 part-time (21 women); includes 7 minority (6 Black or African American, non-Hispanic/Latino; 1 American Indian or Alaska Native, non-Hispanic/Latino), 3 international. Average age 30. 31 applicants, 61% accepted, 11 enrolled. In 2011, 21 degrees awarded. *Entrance requirements:* For master's, GMAT or GRE General Test. Additional exam requirements/recommendations for international students: Required—TOEFL (minimum score 550 paper-based; 79 iBT), IELTS (minimum score 6.5). *Application deadline:* For fall admission, 1/1 priority date for domestic students; for spring admission, 9/1 for domestic students. Applications are processed on a rolling basis. Application fee: $56 ($96 for international students). Electronic applications accepted. One-time fee: $506.10 full-time. Tuition and fees vary according to course load and reciprocity agreements. *Financial support:* Career-related internships or fieldwork available. Support available to part-time students. Financial award application deadline: 4/15; financial award applicants required to submit FAFSA. *Unit head:* Susan M. Donohue-Davies, Representative, 414-299-4009, Fax: 414-229-5915, E-mail: suedono@uwm.edu. *Application contact:* General Information Contact, 414-229-4982, Fax: 414-229-6967, E-mail: gradschool@uwm.edu. Web site: http://www.uwm.edu/dept/MHRLR/.

University of Wisconsin–Oshkosh, Graduate Studies, College of Business, Program in Global Business Administration, Oshkosh, WI 54901. Offers GMBA. *Degree requirements:* For master's, integrative seminar, study abroad. *Entrance requirements:* For master's, GMAT, GRE, letters of recommendation. Additional exam requirements/recommendations for international students: Required—TOEFL (minimum score 79 iBT).

University of Wisconsin–Whitewater, School of Graduate Studies, College of Business and Economics, Program in Business Administration, Whitewater, WI 53190-1790. Offers finance (MBA); human resource management (MBA); information technology management (MBA); international business (MBA); management (MBA); marketing (MBA); operations and supply chain management (MBA). *Accreditation:* AACSB. Part-time and evening/weekend programs available. Postbaccalaureate distance learning degree programs offered (no on-campus study). *Students:* 170 full-time (53 women), 538 part-time (213 women); includes 130 minority (28 Black or African American, non-Hispanic/Latino; 87 Asian, non-Hispanic/Latino; 15 Hispanic/Latino). Average age 31. 448 applicants, 33% accepted, 120 enrolled. In 2011, 304 master's awarded. *Entrance requirements:* For master's, GMAT or GRE, minimum AACSB index of 1000, minimum GPA of 2.75. Additional exam requirements/recommendations for international students: Required—TOEFL (minimum score 550 paper-based; 213 computer-based; 80 iBT), IELTS (minimum score 6). *Application deadline:* For fall admission, 7/15 for domestic and international students; for spring admission, 12/1 for domestic and international students. Applications are processed on a rolling basis. Application fee: $56. Electronic applications accepted. *Expenses:* Tuition, state resident: full-time $4088. Tuition, nonresident: full-time $8817. Tuition and fees vary according to program. *Financial support:* In 2011–12, research assistantships (averaging $7,245 per year) were awarded; Federal Work-Study, unspecified assistantships, and out-of-state fee waivers also available. Support available to part-time students. Financial award application deadline: 3/15; financial award applicants required to submit FAFSA. *Faculty research:* Interface between social institutions and individual behavior, technology and innovation management, occupational mental health, workplace deviance and workplace romance. *Unit head:* Dr. John Chenoweth, Associate Dean, 262-472-1945, Fax: 262-472-4863, E-mail: chenowej@uww.edu.

Upper Iowa University, Online Master's Programs, Fayette, IA 52142-1857. Offers accounting (MBA); corporate financial management (MBA); global business (MBA); health and human services (MPA); higher education administration (MHEA); homeland security (MPA); human resources management (MBA); justice administration (MPA); organizational development (MBA); public personnel management (MPA); quality management (MBA). MBA also available at Madison, WI campus. Part-time programs available. Postbaccalaureate distance learning degree programs offered (no on-campus study). *Degree requirements:* For master's, research project. *Entrance requirements:* For master's, GMAT, GRE, or minimum GPA of 2.7 during last 60 hours. Additional exam requirements/recommendations for international students: Required—TOEFL (minimum score 570 paper-based; 230 computer-based). Electronic applications accepted. *Faculty research:* Total quality management, CQI, teams, organization culture and climate, management.

Valparaiso University, Graduate School, Program in International Commerce and Policy, Valparaiso, IN 46383. Offers MS, JD/MS. Part-time and evening/weekend programs available. *Students:* 31 full-time (10 women), 14 part-time (9 women); includes 4 minority (2 Black or African American, non-Hispanic/Latino; 1 Asian, non-Hispanic/Latino; 1 Hispanic/Latino), 35 international. Average age 25. In 2011, 34 master's awarded. *Entrance requirements:* For master's, minimum GPA of 3.0. Additional exam requirements/recommendations for international students: Required—TOEFL (minimum score 550 paper-based; 213 computer-based; 80 iBT). *Application deadline:* Applications are processed on a rolling basis. Application fee: $30 ($50 for international students). Electronic applications accepted. *Expenses: Tuition:* Part-time $560 per credit hour. Tuition and fees vary according to course load and program. *Financial support:* Available to part-time students. Applicants required to submit FAFSA. *Unit head:* Dr. David L. Rowland, Dean, Graduate School and Continuing Education/Associate Provost, 219-464-5313, Fax: 219-464-5381, E-mail: david.rowland@valpo.edu. *Application contact:* Dustin Jesch, Coordinator, U.S. Student Engagement, 219-464-5313, Fax: 219-464-5381, E-mail: dustin.jesch@valpo.edu. Web site: http://valpo.edu/grad/icp/.

Vancouver Island University, Master of Business Administration Program, Nanaimo, BC V9R 5S5, Canada. Offers international business (MBA), including finance, marketing. Program offered jointly with University of Hertfordshire. *Accreditation:* ACBSP. Part-time programs available. *Faculty:* 23 full-time (3 women), 3 part-time/adjunct (2 women). *Students:* 135 full-time (59 women), 2 part-time (0 women); includes 9 minority (1 Black or African American, non-Hispanic/Latino; 2 American Indian or Alaska Native, non-Hispanic/Latino; 5 Asian, non-Hispanic/Latino; 1 Hispanic/Latino), 102 international. Average age 27. 632 applicants, 46% accepted, 135 enrolled. In 2011, 145 master's awarded. *Degree requirements:* For master's, thesis. *Entrance requirements:* Additional exam requirements/recommendations for international students: Required—TOEFL (minimum score 550 paper-based; 213 computer-based). *Application deadline:* For fall admission, 2/28 priority date for domestic students, 2/28 for international students; for winter admission, 4/30 for domestic and international students. Applications are processed on a rolling basis. Application fee: $150. Electronic applications accepted. *Financial support:* In 2011–12, 8 students received support. Scholarships/grants available. *Faculty research:* Tourism development, entrepreneurship, organizational development, strategic planning, international business strategy, intercultural team work. *Unit head:* Brock Dykeman, Director, 250-740-6178, Fax: 250-740-6551, E-mail: brock.dykeman@viu.ca. *Application contact:* Jane Kelly, International Admissions Manager, 250-740-6384, Fax: 250-740-6471, E-mail: kellyj@mala.bc.ca. Web site: http://www.viu.ca/mba/index.asp.

Villanova University, Villanova School of Business, MBA - The Fast Track Program, Villanova, PA 19085. Offers finance (MBA); health care management (MBA); international business (MBA); management information systems (MBA); marketing (MBA); real estate (MBA); strategic management (MBA). *Accreditation:* AACSB. Part-time and evening/weekend programs available. *Faculty:* 101 full-time (32 women), 38 part-time/adjunct (8 women). *Students:* 123 part-time (46 women); includes 14 minority (1 Black or African American, non-Hispanic/Latino; 3 American Indian or Alaska Native, non-Hispanic/Latino; 5 Asian, non-Hispanic/Latino; 1 Hispanic/Latino; 4 Two or more races, non-Hispanic/Latino). Average age 29. In 2011, 53 master's awarded. *Degree requirements:* For master's, minimum GPA of 3.0. *Entrance requirements:* For master's, GMAT, work experience. Additional exam requirements/recommendations for international students: Required—TOEFL (minimum score 550 paper-based; 213 computer-based; 80 iBT). *Application deadline:* For fall admission, 6/30 for domestic and international students. Application fee: $50. Electronic applications accepted. *Expenses: Tuition:* Part-time $675 per credit. Part-time tuition and fees vary according to degree level and program. *Financial support:* Scholarships/grants available. Financial award application deadline: 6/30; financial award applicants required to submit FAFSA. *Faculty research:* Business analytics; creativity, innovation and entrepreneurship; global leadership; marketing and public policy; real estate; church management. *Unit head:* Kristy Irwin, Director of Recruitment and Marketing, 610-519-6288, Fax: 610-519-6273, E-mail: kristy.irwin@villanova.edu. *Application contact:* Meredith L. Lockyer, Assistant Director, 610-519-7016, Fax: 610-519-6273, E-mail: meredith.lockyer@villanova.edu. Web site: http://www.mba.villanova.edu.

Villanova University, Villanova School of Business, MBA - The Flex Track Program, Villanova, PA 19085. Offers finance (MBA); health care management (MBA); international business (MBA); management information systems (MBA); marketing (MBA); real estate (MBA); strategic management (MBA); JD/MBA. *Accreditation:* AACSB. Part-time and evening/weekend programs available. Postbaccalaureate distance learning degree programs offered (minimal on-campus study). *Faculty:* 101 full-time (32 women), 38 part-time/adjunct (8 women). *Students:* 18 full-time (9 women), 412 part-time (127 women); includes 45 minority (7 Black or African American, non-Hispanic/Latino; 1 American Indian or Alaska Native, non-Hispanic/Latino; 25 Asian, non-Hispanic/Latino; 4 Hispanic/Latino; 1 Native Hawaiian or other Pacific Islander, non-Hispanic/Latino; 7 Two or more races, non-Hispanic/Latino). Average age 30. In 2011, 150 master's awarded. *Degree requirements:* For master's, minimum GPA of 3.0. *Entrance requirements:* For master's, GMAT, work experience. Additional exam requirements/recommendations for international students: Required—TOEFL (minimum score 550 paper-based; 213 computer-based; 80 iBT). *Application deadline:* For fall admission, 6/30 for domestic and international students; for winter admission, 11/15 for domestic and international students; for spring admission, 3/30 for domestic students, 3/31 for international students. Applications are processed on a rolling basis. Application fee: $50. Electronic applications accepted. *Expenses: Tuition:* Part-time $675 per credit. Part-time tuition and fees vary according to degree level and program. *Financial support:* In 2011–12, 18 research assistantships with full tuition reimbursements (averaging $13,100 per year) were awarded; scholarships/grants and unspecified assistantships also available. Financial award application deadline: 6/30; financial award applicants required to submit FAFSA. *Faculty research:* Business analytics; creativity, innovation and entrepreneurship; global leadership; marketing and public policy; real estate; church management. *Unit head:* Kristy Irwin, Director of Recruitment and Marketing, 610-610-6288, Fax: 610-519-6273, E-mail: kristy.irwin@villanova.edu. *Application contact:* Meredity L. Lockyer, Assistant Director, 610-519-7016, Fax: 610-519-6273, E-mail: meredith.lockyer@villanova.edu. Web site: http://www.mba.villanova.edu.

Virginia International University, School of Business, Fairfax, VA 22030. Offers accounting (MBA); executive management (Graduate Certificate); global logistics (MBA); health care management (MBA); human resources management (MBA); international business management (MBA); international finance (MBA); marketing management (MBA). Part-time programs available. *Entrance requirements:* For master's and Graduate Certificate, bachelor's degree. Additional exam requirements/recommendations for international students: Required—TOEFL (minimum score 550 paper-based; 213 computer-based; 80 iBT), IELTS (minimum score 6). Electronic applications accepted.

Wagner College, Division of Graduate Studies, Department of Business Administration, Program in International Business, Staten Island, NY 10301-4495. Offers MBA. Part-time and evening/weekend programs available. *Faculty:* 1 full-time (0 women), 1 part-time/adjunct (0 women). *Students:* 5 full-time (3 women); includes 4 minority (1 Asian, non-Hispanic/Latino; 3 Hispanic/Latino). Average age 30. 2 applicants, 100% accepted, 1 enrolled. In 2011, 4 master's awarded. *Degree requirements:* For master's, thesis optional. *Entrance requirements:* For master's, GMAT, minimum GPA of 2.6. Additional exam requirements/recommendations for international students: Required—TOEFL (minimum score 550 paper-based; 217 computer-based; 79 iBT). *Application deadline:* For fall admission, 5/1 priority date for domestic students, 3/1 for international students; for spring admission, 11/1 priority date for domestic students, 10/1 for international students. Applications are processed on a rolling basis. Application fee: $50 ($80 for international students). *Expenses: Tuition:* Full-time $16,200; part-time $890 per credit. *Financial support:* Career-related internships or fieldwork, unspecified assistantships, and alumni fellowship grant available. Financial award applicants required to submit FAFSA. *Unit head:* Dr. Cathyann Tully, Director, 718-390-3439, Fax: 718-420-4274, E-mail: cathyann.tully@wagner.edu. *Application contact:* Patricia Clancy, Assistant Coordinator of Graduate Studies, 718-420-4464, Fax: 718-390-3105, E-mail: patricia.clancy@wagner.edu.

Walden University, Graduate Programs, School of Management, Minneapolis, MN 55401. Offers accounting (MS, DBA), including accounting for the professional (MS), CPA (MS), self-designed (MS); accounting and management (MS), including accounting for strategic managers, self-designed; accounting for managers (MBA); advanced project management (Post-Graduate Certificate); applied project management (Post-Graduate Certificate); corporate finance (MBA); entrepreneurship (MBA, DBA); finance (DBA); global management (MS); global supply chain management (DBA); healthcare management (MBA, DBA); healthcare system improvement (MBA); human resource management (MBA, MS, PhD), including functional human resource management (MS), integrating functional and strategic human resource management (MS), organizational strategy (MS); information systems management (DBA); international business (MBA,

DBA); leadership (MBA, MS, DBA), including entrepreneurship (MS), general management (MS), human resources leadership (MS), innovation and technology (MS), leader development (MS), leading sustainability (MS), project management (MS), self-designed (MS); management (MS), including healthcare management; managers as leaders (MS); marketing (MBA, DBA); project management (MBA, MS, DBA); research strategies (MS); risk management (MBA); self-designed (MBA, DBA, PhD); social impact management (DBA); strategies for sustainability (MBA); strategy and operations (MS); sustainable management (MS); technology (MBA); technology entrepreneurship (DBA); technology management (MS). Part-time and evening/weekend programs available. Postbaccalaureate distance learning degree programs offered (minimal on-campus study). *Faculty:* 32 full-time (14 women), 275 part-time/adjunct (98 women). *Students:* 3,962 full-time (2,095 women), 1,557 part-time (959 women); includes 3,003 minority (2,510 Black or African American, non-Hispanic/Latino; 25 American Indian or Alaska Native, non-Hispanic/Latino; 140 Asian, non-Hispanic/Latino; 240 Hispanic/Latino; 9 Native Hawaiian or other Pacific Islander, non-Hispanic/Latino; 79 Two or more races, non-Hispanic/Latino), 395 international. Average age 41. In 2011, 586 master's, 87 doctorates, 4 other advanced degrees awarded. *Degree requirements:* For doctorate, thesis/dissertation (for some programs), residency. *Entrance requirements:* For master's, bachelor's degree or equivalent in related field; minimum GPA of 2.5; official transcripts; goal statement; access to computer and Internet; for doctorate, master's degree or equivalent in related field; minimum GPA of 3.0; 3 years of related professional/academic experience (preferred). Additional exam requirements/recommendations for international students: Required—TOEFL (minimum score 550 paper-based; 213 computer-based), IELTS (minimum score 6.5), Michigan English Language Assessment Battery (minimum score 82). *Application deadline:* Applications are processed on a rolling basis. Application fee: $50. Electronic applications accepted. *Financial support:* Federal Work-Study, scholarships/grants, unspecified assistantships, and family tuition reduction, active duty/veteran tuition reduction, group tuition reduction, interest-free payment plans, employee tuition reduction available. Support available to part-time students. Financial award applicants required to submit FAFSA. *Unit head:* Dr. William Schulz, III, Associate Dean, 800-925-3368. *Application contact:* Jennifer Hall, Vice President of Enrollment Management, 866-4-WALDEN, E-mail: info@waldenu.edu. Web site: http://www.waldenu.edu/Colleges-and-Schools/College-of-Management-and-Technology.htm.

Washington State University, Graduate School, College of Agricultural, Human, and Natural Resource Sciences, School of Economic Sciences, Program in Economics, Pullman, WA 99164. Offers applied economics (MA); economics (MA, PhD); international business economics (Certificate). *Faculty:* 26. *Students:* 66 full-time (25 women), 3 part-time (1 woman); includes 5 minority (2 Black or African American, non-Hispanic/Latino; 1 American Indian or Alaska Native, non-Hispanic/Latino; 1 Asian, non-Hispanic/Latino; 1 Hispanic/Latino), 41 international. Average age 28. 124 applicants, 19% accepted, 18 enrolled. In 2011, 10 doctorates awarded. *Degree requirements:* For master's, comprehensive exam (for some programs), thesis (for some programs), oral exam; for doctorate, comprehensive exam, thesis/dissertation, oral exam, written exam, field exams. *Entrance requirements:* For master's, GRE General Test, statement of purpose, three letters of reference, copies of all transcripts; for doctorate, GRE General Test or GMAT, statement of purpose, three letters of reference, copies of all transcripts. Additional exam requirements/recommendations for international students: Required—TOEFL, IELTS. *Application deadline:* For fall admission, 1/10 priority date for domestic students, 1/10 for international students. Applications are processed on a rolling basis. Application fee: $75. *Financial support:* In 2011–12, 16 research assistantships (averaging $18,204 per year), 7 teaching assistantships (averaging $18,204 per year) were awarded; career-related internships or fieldwork, Federal Work-Study, institutionally sponsored loans, tuition waivers (partial), and teaching associateships also available. Financial award application deadline: 4/1; financial award applicants required to submit FAFSA. *Faculty research:* Economic theory and quantitative methods, applied microeconomics. *Total annual research expenditures:* $1 million. *Unit head:* Dr. Ron C. Mittelhammer, Director, 509-335-1706, Fax: 509-335-1173, E-mail: mittelha@wsu.edu. *Application contact:* Graduate School Admissions, 800-GRADWSU, Fax: 509-335-1949, E-mail: gradsch@wsu.edu. Web site: http://cahnrs-cms.wsu.edu/ses/graduatestudies/.

Wayland Baptist University, Graduate Programs, Programs in Business Administration/Management, Plainview, TX 79072-6998. Offers general business (MBA); health care administration (MBA); human resource management (MBA); international management (MBA); management (MA, MBA), including health care administration (MA), human resource management (MA), organization management (MA); management information systems (MBA). Part-time and evening/weekend programs available. Postbaccalaureate distance learning degree programs offered (no on-campus study). *Degree requirements:* For master's, capstone course. *Entrance requirements:* For master's, GMAT, GRE or MAT. Additional exam requirements/recommendations for international students: Required—TOEFL (minimum score 500 paper-based; 173 computer-based; 61 iBT). Electronic applications accepted.

Webster University, George Herbert Walker School of Business and Technology, Department of Business, St. Louis, MO 63119-3194. Offers business (MA); business and organizational security management (MBA); computer resources and information management (MBA); environmental management (MBA); finance (MA, MBA); health services management (MBA); human resources development (MBA); human resources management (MBA); international business (MA, MBA); management and leadership (MBA); marketing (MBA); procurement and acquisitions management (MBA); telecommunications management (MBA). *Accreditation:* ACBSP. Part-time and evening/weekend programs available. Postbaccalaureate distance learning degree programs offered (no on-campus study). *Degree requirements:* For master's, comprehensive exam (for some programs), thesis (for some programs). *Entrance requirements:* Additional exam requirements/recommendations for international students: Required—TOEFL. *Expenses: Tuition:* Full-time $10,890; part-time $605 per credit hour. Tuition and fees vary according to campus/location and program.

Western International University, Graduate Programs in Business, Master of Business Administration Program in International Business, Phoenix, AZ 85021-2718. Offers MBA. Part-time and evening/weekend programs available. Postbaccalaureate distance learning degree programs offered (no on-campus study). *Entrance requirements:* For master's, minimum GPA of 2.75. Additional exam requirements/recommendations for international students: Required—TOEFL (minimum score 550 paper-based; 213 computer-based; 79 iBT), TWE (minimum score 5), or IELTS (minimum score 6.5). Electronic applications accepted.

Whitworth University, School of Global Commerce and Management, Spokane, WA 99251-0001. Offers international management (MBA, MIM). Part-time and evening/weekend programs available. *Faculty:* 5 full-time (1 woman), 9 part-time/adjunct (2 women). *Students:* 12 full-time (8 women), 11 part-time (7 women); includes 6 minority (2 Black or African American, non-Hispanic/Latino; 2 Asian, non-Hispanic/Latino; 1 Native Hawaiian or other Pacific Islander, non-Hispanic/Latino; 1 Two or more races, non-Hispanic/Latino), 4 international. Average age 31. 24 applicants, 46% accepted, 8 enrolled. In 2011, 16 degrees awarded. *Degree requirements:* For master's, foreign language (MBA in international management, MIM). *Entrance requirements:* For master's, GMAT or GRE, minimum GPA of 3.0; two letters of recommendation; resume; completion of prerequisite courses in micro-economics, macro-economics, financial accounting, finance, and marketing. Additional exam requirements/recommendations for international students: Required—TOEFL (minimum score 213 computer-based; 88 iBT), TWE. *Application deadline:* For fall admission, 8/1 priority date for domestic students, 8/1 for international students; for spring admission, 1/8 priority date for domestic students. Applications are processed on a rolling basis. Application fee: $35. Electronic applications accepted. Tuition and fees vary according to program. *Financial support:* In 2011–12, 9 students received support. Scholarships/grants available. Financial award applicants required to submit FAFSA. *Faculty research:* International business (European, Central America and Asian topics), entrepreneurship and business plan development. *Unit head:* John Hengesh, Director, Graduate Studies in Business, 509-777-4455, Fax: 509-777-3723, E-mail: jhengesh@whitworth.edu. *Application contact:* Susan Cook, Admissions Manager, Graduate Studies, 509-777-4298, Fax: 509-777-3723, E-mail: scook@whitworth.edu. Web site: http://www.whitworth.edu/sgcm.

Wilkes University, College of Graduate and Professional Studies, Jay S. Sidhu School of Business and Leadership, Wilkes-Barre, PA 18766-0002. Offers accounting (MBA); entrepreneurship (MBA); finance (MBA); health care administration (MBA); human resource management (MBA); international business (MBA); marketing (MBA); operations management (MBA); organizational leadership and development (MBA). *Accreditation:* ACBSP. Part-time and evening/weekend programs available. *Students:* 48 full-time (20 women), 134 part-time (62 women); includes 12 minority (2 Black or African American, non-Hispanic/Latino; 5 Asian, non-Hispanic/Latino; 2 Hispanic/Latino; 3 Two or more races, non-Hispanic/Latino), 9 international. Average age 30. In 2011, 69 master's awarded. *Entrance requirements:* For master's, GMAT. Additional exam requirements/recommendations for international students: Required—TOEFL (minimum score 550 paper-based; 213 computer-based; 79 iBT). *Application deadline:* Applications are processed on a rolling basis. Application fee: $45 ($65 for international students). Electronic applications accepted. *Expenses:* Contact institution. *Financial support:* Federal Work-Study and unspecified assistantships available. Financial award application deadline: 3/1; financial award applicants required to submit FAFSA. *Unit head:* Dr. Jeffrey Alves, Dean, 570-408-4702, Fax: 570-408-7846, E-mail: jeffrey.alves@wilkes.edu. *Application contact:* Erin Sutzko, Director of Extended Learning, 570-408-4253, Fax: 570-408-7846, E-mail: erin.sutzko@wilkes.edu. Web site: http://www.wilkes.edu/pages/457.asp.

Wright State University, School of Graduate Studies, Raj Soin College of Business, Department of Management, Dayton, OH 45435. Offers flexible business (MBA); health care management (MBA); international business (MBA); management, innovation and change (MBA); project management (MBA); supply chain management (MBA); MBA/MS. *Entrance requirements:* For master's, GMAT, minimum AACSB index of 1000. Additional exam requirements/recommendations for international students: Required—TOEFL.

Xavier University, Williams College of Business, Master of Business Administration Program, Cincinnati, OH 45207. Offers business administration (Exec MBA, MBA); business intelligence (MBA); finance (MBA); health industry (MBA); international business (MBA); management information systems (MBA); marketing (MBA); MBA/MHSA; MSN/MBA. *Accreditation:* AACSB. Part-time and evening/weekend programs available. *Faculty:* 45 full-time (17 women), 13 part-time/adjunct (4 women). *Students:* 188 full-time (63 women), 630 part-time (206 women); includes 112 minority (36 Black or African American, non-Hispanic/Latino; 3 American Indian or Alaska Native, non-Hispanic/Latino; 52 Asian, non-Hispanic/Latino; 17 Hispanic/Latino; 1 Native Hawaiian or other Pacific Islander, non-Hispanic/Latino; 3 Two or more races, non-Hispanic/Latino), 45 international. Average age 30. 319 applicants, 63% accepted, 149 enrolled. In 2011, 403 master's awarded. *Degree requirements:* For master's, capstone course. *Entrance requirements:* For master's, GMAT or GRE. Additional exam requirements/recommendations for international students: Required—TOEFL (minimum score 550 paper-based; 213 computer-based; 80 iBT). *Application deadline:* For fall admission, 8/1 priority date for domestic students, 5/1 for international students; for spring admission, 12/1 priority date for domestic students, 9/1 for international students. Applications are processed on a rolling basis. Application fee: $0. Electronic applications accepted. *Expenses:* Contact institution. *Financial support:* In 2011–12, 176 students received support. Scholarships/grants, tuition waivers (partial), and unspecified assistantships available. Financial award application deadline: 3/1; financial award applicants required to submit FAFSA. *Unit head:* Dr. Hema Krishnan, Associate Dean, 513-745-3420, Fax: 513-745-3455, E-mail: krishnan@xavier.edu. *Application contact:* Anna Marie Whelan, Assistant Director, MBA Programs, 513-745-3525, Fax: 513-745-2929, E-mail: whelana@xavier.edu. Web site: http://www.xavier.edu/williams/mba/.

York University, Faculty of Graduate Studies, Schulich School of Business, Toronto, ON M3J 1P3, Canada. Offers administration (PhD); business (MBA); finance (MF); international business (IMBA); public administration (MPA); MBA/JD; MBA/MA; MBA/MFA. Part-time and evening/weekend programs available. *Faculty:* 112 full-time (35 women), 191 part-time/adjunct (61 women). *Students:* 706 full-time (240 women), 401 part-time (136 women). Average age 28. 1,621 applicants, 46% accepted, 439 enrolled. In 2011, 528 master's, 10 doctorates awarded. *Degree requirements:* For master's, advanced proficiency in a second language, work term (IMBA); for doctorate, comprehensive exam, thesis/dissertation. *Entrance requirements:* For master's, GMAT (GRE acceptable for MF), minimum GPA of 3.0 (3.3 for MF); for doctorate, GMAT or GRE, minimum GPA of 3.3. Additional exam requirements/recommendations for international students: Required—TOEFL (minimum score 600 paper-based; 100 iBT), IELTS (minimum score 7), York English Language Test (minimum score 1). *Application deadline:* For fall admission, 5/1 for domestic students, 2/1 for international students; for winter admission, 10/1 for domestic students, 9/1 for international students. Applications are processed on a rolling basis. Application fee: $150. Electronic applications accepted. *Financial support:* In 2011–12, 800 students received support, including fellowships (averaging $5,000 per year), research assistantships (averaging $3,000 per year), teaching assistantships (averaging $7,000 per year); career-related internships or fieldwork, scholarships/grants, and bursaries for part-time students also available. Financial award application deadline: 2/1. *Faculty research:* Accounting, finance, marketing, operations management and information systems, organizational studies, strategic management. *Unit head:* Dezso Horvath, Dean, 416-736-5070, E-mail: dhorvath@schulich.yorku.ca. *Application contact:* Graduate Admissions, 416-736-5060, Fax: 416-650-8174, E-mail: admissions@schulich.yorku.ca. Web site: http://www.schulich.yorku.ca.

See Display on page 175 and Close-Up on page 263.

Section 12
Management Information Systems

This section contains a directory of institutions offering graduate work in management information systems, followed by in-depth entries submitted by institutions that chose to prepare detailed program descriptions. Additional information about programs listed in the directory but not augmented by an in-depth entry may be obtained by writing directly to the dean of a graduate school or chair of a department at the address given in the directory.

For programs offering related work, see also in this book *Business Administration and Management.* In another guide in this series:

Graduate Programs in Engineering & Applied Sciences

See *Computer Science and Information Technology* and *Management of Engineering and Technology*

CONTENTS

Program Directory

Displays and Close-Ups

See also:

Management Information Systems

Adelphi University, Robert B. Willumstad School of Business, MBA Program, Garden City, NY 11530-0701. Offers finance (MBA); management information systems (MBA); management/human resource management (MBA); marketing/e-commerce (MBA). *Accreditation:* AACSB. Part-time and evening/weekend programs available. *Students:* 258 full-time (121 women), 111 part-time (58 women); includes 67 minority (22 Black or African American, non-Hispanic/Latino; 18 Asian, non-Hispanic/Latino; 24 Hispanic/Latino; 3 Two or more races, non-Hispanic/Latino), 172 international. Average age 28. In 2011, 111 master's awarded. *Degree requirements:* For master's, capstone course. *Entrance requirements:* For master's, GMAT, 2 letters of recommendation. Additional exam requirements/recommendations for international students: Required—TOEFL (minimum score 550 paper-based; 213 computer-based; 80 iBT). *Application deadline:* For fall admission, 4/1 for international students; for spring admission, 11/1 for international students. Applications are processed on a rolling basis. Application fee: $50. Electronic applications accepted. *Expenses: Tuition:* Full-time $29,600; part-time $930 per credit. *Required fees:* $1100. *Financial support:* Research assistantships with full and partial tuition reimbursements, career-related internships or fieldwork, Federal Work-Study, institutionally sponsored loans, scholarships/grants, and unspecified assistantships available. Financial award application deadline: 3/1; financial award applicants required to submit FAFSA. *Faculty research:* Supply chain management, distribution channels, productivity benchmark analysis, data envelopment analysis, financial portfolio analysis. *Unit head:* Rakesh Gupta, 516-877-4670, Fax: 516-877-4607, E-mail: gradbusinquiries@adelphi.edu. *Application contact:* Christine Murphy, Director of Admissions, 516-877-3050, Fax: 516-877-3039, E-mail: graduateadmissions@adelphi.edu. Web site: http://business.adelphi.edu/degree-programs/graduate-degree-programs/m-b-a/.

See Display on page 68 and Close-Up on page 177.

Air Force Institute of Technology, Graduate School of Engineering and Management, Department of Systems and Engineering Management, Dayton, OH 45433-7765. Offers cost analysis (MS); environmental and engineering management (MS); environmental engineering science (MS); information resource/systems management (MS). *Accreditation:* ABET. Part-time programs available. *Degree requirements:* For master's, thesis. *Entrance requirements:* For master's, GRE, GMAT, minimum GPA of 3.0.

American InterContinental University Atlanta, Program in Information Technology, Atlanta, GA 30328. Offers MIT. Part-time and evening/weekend programs available. *Degree requirements:* For master's, technical proficiency demonstration. *Entrance requirements:* For master's, Computer Programmer Aptitude Battery Exam, interview. Electronic applications accepted. *Faculty research:* Operating systems, security issues, networks and routing, computer hardware.

American InterContinental University London, Program in Information Technology, London, United Kingdom. Offers MIT. *Degree requirements:* For master's, thesis optional. *Entrance requirements:* For master's, interview, professional experience. Electronic applications accepted.

American International College, School of Business Administration, MBA Program, Springfield, MA 01109-3189. Offers accounting (MBA); corporate/public communication (MBA); finance (MBA); general business (MBA); hospitality, hotel and service management (MBA); international business (MBA); international business practice (MBA); management (MBA); management information systems (MBA); marketing (MBA). International business practice program developed in cooperation with the Mountbatten Institute.

American Public University System, AMU/APU Graduate Programs, Charles Town, WV 25414. Offers accounting (MBA, MS); administration and supervision (M Ed); criminal justice (MA); emergency and disaster management (MA); entrepreneurship (MBA); environmental policy and management (MS), including environmental planning, environmental sustainability, fish and wildlife management, general (MA, MS), global environmental management; finance (MBA); general (MBA); global business management (MBA); guidance and counseling (M Ed); history (MA), including American history, ancient and classical history, European history, global history, military and diplomatic history, public history; homeland security (MA); homeland security resource allocation (MBA); humanities (MA); information technology (MS), including digital forensics, enterprise software development, information assurance and security, IT project management; information technology management (MBA); intelligence studies (MA), including criminal intelligence, general (MA, MS), homeland security, intelligence analysis, intelligence collection, intelligence operations, terrorism studies; international relations and conflict resolution (MA), including comparative and security issues, conflict resolution, international and transnational security issues, peacekeeping; legal studies (MA); management (MA), including defense management, general (MA, MS), human resource management, organizational leadership, public administration, reverse logistics, strategic consulting; marketing (MBA); military history (MA), including American military history, American revolution, civil war, war since 1946, World War II; military studies (MA), including air warfare, asymmetrical warfare, joint warfare, land warfare, naval warfare, strategic leadership; national security studies (MA), including general (MA, MS), homeland security, regional security studies, security and intelligence analysis, terrorism studies; nonprofit management (MBA); political science (MA), including American politics and government, comparative government and development, public policy; psychology (MA); public administration (MA, MPA), including disaster management (MPA), environmental policy (MA), health policy (MPA), human resources (MPA), national security (MPA), organizational management (MPA), security management (MPA); public health (MA, MPH), including emergency management (MPH), environmental health (MPH), public administration (MA); reverse logistics management (MA); security management (MA); space studies (MS), including aerospace science, planetary science; sports and health sciences (MS); sports management (MS), including coaching theory and strategy, sports administration; teaching (M Ed), including curriculum and instruction for elementary teachers, elementary, elementary reading, English language learners, instructional leadership, online learning, secondary social sciences, special education; transportation and logistics management (MA), including maritime engineering management. Programs offered via distance learning only. Part-time and evening/weekend programs available. Postbaccalaureate distance learning degree programs offered (no on-campus study). *Faculty:* 445 full-time (241 women), 1,360 part-time/adjunct (617 women). *Students:* 688 full-time (338 women), 10,168 part-time (3,706 women); includes 3,130 minority (1,007 Black or African American, non-Hispanic/Latino; 103 American Indian or Alaska Native, non-Hispanic/Latino; 825 Asian, non-Hispanic/Latino; 810 Hispanic/Latino; 51 Native Hawaiian or other Pacific Islander, non-Hispanic/Latino; 334 Two or more races, non-Hispanic/Latino), 134 international. Average age 35. In 2011, 2,386 master's awarded. *Degree requirements:* For master's, comprehensive exam or practicum. *Entrance requirements:* For master's, official transcript showing earned bachelor's degree from institution accredited by recognized accrediting body. Additional exam requirements/recommendations for international students: Required—TOEFL (minimum score 550 paper-based; 213 computer-based), IELTS (minimum score 6.5). *Application deadline:* Applications are processed on a rolling basis. Application fee: $0. Electronic applications accepted. *Expenses: Tuition:* Part-time $325 per credit hour. *Financial support:* Applicants required to submit FAFSA. *Faculty research:* Military history, criminal justice, management performance, national security. *Unit head:* Dr. Karan Powell, Executive Vice President and Provost, 877-468-6268, Fax: 304-724-3780. *Application contact:* Terry Grant, Vice President of Enrollment Management, 877-468-6268, Fax: 304-724-3780, E-mail: info@apus.edu. Web site: http://www.apus.edu.

American Sentinel University, Graduate Programs, Aurora, CO 80014. Offers business administration (MBA); business intelligence (MS); computer science (MSCS); health information management (MS); healthcare (MBA); information systems (MSIS); nursing (MSN). Part-time and evening/weekend programs available. Postbaccalaureate distance learning degree programs offered (no on-campus study). *Entrance requirements:* Additional exam requirements/recommendations for international students: Required—TOEFL (minimum score 600 paper-based; 215 computer-based). Electronic applications accepted.

American University, Kogod School of Business, Master of Business Administration Program, Washington, DC 20016-8044. Offers accounting (MBA); consulting (MBA), including business systems consulting, management consulting; entrepreneurship (MBA); entrepreneurship (Certificate); finance (MBA); global emerging markets (MBA); leadership and strategic human capital management (MBA); marketing (MBA); real estate (MBA); MBA/JD; MBA/LL M; MBA/MA. Part-time and evening/weekend programs available. *Faculty:* 13 full-time (6 women). *Students:* 96 full-time (43 women), 104 part-time (35 women); includes 49 minority (14 Black or African American, non-Hispanic/Latino; 16 Asian, non-Hispanic/Latino; 16 Hispanic/Latino; 1 Native Hawaiian or other Pacific Islander, non-Hispanic/Latino; 2 Two or more races, non-Hispanic/Latino), 22 international. Average age 29. 340 applicants, 52% accepted, 52 enrolled. In 2011, 124 master's awarded. *Entrance requirements:* For master's, GMAT, resume, personal statement, interview. Additional exam requirements/recommendations for international students: Required—TOEFL. *Application deadline:* For fall admission, 2/1 priority date for domestic students; for spring admission, 10/1 priority date for domestic students. Applications are processed on a rolling basis. Application fee: $100. *Expenses:* Contact institution. *Financial support:* In 2011–12, 19 students received support. Fellowships, research assistantships with partial tuition reimbursements available, career-related internships or fieldwork, Federal Work-Study, and institutionally sponsored loans available. Support available to part-time students. Financial award application deadline: 2/1. *Faculty research:* Information technology, decision-aiding methodology, negotiation. *Unit head:* Dr. Stevan R. Holmberg, Chair, 202-885-1921, Fax: 202-885-1916, E-mail: sholmbe@american.edu. *Application contact:* Shannon Demko, Director of Admissions, 202-885-1968, Fax: 202-885-1078, E-mail: demko@american.edu. Web site: http://www.american.edu/kogod/.

American University, School of International Service, Washington, DC 20016-8071. Offers comparative and international disability policy (MA); comparative and regional studies (Certificate); cross-cultural communication (Certificate); development management (MS); ethics, peace, and global affairs (MA); European studies (Certificate); global environmental policy (MA, Certificate); global information technology (Certificate); international affairs (MA), including comparative and international disability policy, comparative and regional studies, international economic relations, international politics, natural resources and sustainable development, U.S. foreign policy; international communication (MA, Certificate); international development (MA, Certificate); international economic policy (Certificate); international economic relations (Certificate); international media (MA); international peace and conflict resolution (MA, Certificate); international politics (Certificate); international relations (PhD); international service (MIS); peacebuilding (Certificate); social enterprise (MA); the Americas (Certificate); United States foreign policy (Certificate); JD/MA. Part-time and evening/weekend programs available. Postbaccalaureate distance learning degree programs offered (no on-campus study). *Faculty:* 108 full-time (45 women), 51 part-time/adjunct (23 women). *Students:* 595 full-time (375 women), 399 part-time (243 women); includes 201 minority (64 Black or African American, non-Hispanic/Latino; 6 American Indian or Alaska Native, non-Hispanic/Latino; 53 Asian, non-Hispanic/Latino; 66 Hispanic/Latino; 12 Two or more races, non-Hispanic/Latino), 153 international. Average age 27. 2,096 applicants, 63% accepted, 370 enrolled. In 2011, 331 master's, 2 doctorates, 2 other advanced degrees awarded. Terminal master's awarded for partial completion of doctoral program. *Degree requirements:* For master's, one foreign language, comprehensive exam, thesis or alternative; for doctorate, one foreign language, comprehensive exam, thesis/dissertation, research practicum; for Certificate, minimum 15 credit hours related course work. *Entrance requirements:* For master's, GRE, 24 credits of course work in related social sciences, minimum GPA of 3.5, 2 letters of recommendation, bachelor's degree, resume, statement of purpose; for doctorate, GRE, 3 letters of recommendation, 24 credits in related social sciences; for Certificate, bachelor's degree. Additional exam requirements/recommendations for international students: Required—TOEFL (minimum score 600 paper-based; 250 computer-based; 100 iBT). *Application deadline:* For fall admission, 1/15 priority date for domestic students; for spring admission, 10/1 priority date for domestic students. Applications are processed on a rolling basis. Application fee: $50. *Expenses: Tuition:* Full-time $24,264; part-time $1348 per credit hour. *Required fees:* $430. Tuition and fees vary according to course load and program. *Financial support:* Fellowships with partial tuition reimbursements, research assistantships with partial tuition reimbursements, teaching assistantships with partial tuition reimbursements, career-related internships or fieldwork, Federal Work-Study, institutionally sponsored loans, and scholarships/grants available. Financial award application deadline: 1/15. *Faculty research:* International intellectual property, international environmental issues, international law and legal order, international telecommunications/technology, international sustainable development. *Unit head:* Dr. James Goldgeier, Dean, 202-885-1603, Fax: 202-885-2494, E-mail: goldgeier@american.edu. *Application contact:* Amanda Taylor, Director of Graduate Admissions and Financial Aid, 202-885-2496, Fax: 202-885-1109, E-mail: ataylor@american.edu. Web site: http://www.american.edu/sis/.

The American University in Cairo, School of Sciences and Engineering, Department of Mechanical Engineering, Cairo, Egypt. Offers mechanical engineering (MS); product development and systems management (M Eng). *Expenses: Tuition:* Part-time $932 per credit hour. Tuition and fees vary according to course load, degree level and program. *Unit head:* Dr. Salah El-Haggar, Chair, 20-2-2615-3065, E-mail: elhaggar@aucegypt.edu. *Application contact:* Wesley Clark, Director of North American Admissions and Financial Aid, 212-646-810-9433 Ext. 4547, E-mail: wclark@aucnyo.edu. Web site: http://www.aucegypt.edu/sse/meng/.

Argosy University, Atlanta, College of Business, Atlanta, GA 30328. Offers accounting (DBA); corporate compliance (MBA); customized professional concentration (MBA,

DBA); finance (MBA); healthcare administration (MBA); information systems (DBA); information systems management (MBA); international business (MBA, DBA); management (MBA, MSM, DBA); marketing (MBA, DBA).

See Close-Up on page 179.

Argosy University, Chicago, College of Business, Chicago, IL 60601. Offers accounting (DBA); customized professional concentration (MBA, DBA); finance (MBA); fraud examination (MBA); global business sustainability (DBA); healthcare administration (MBA); information systems (DBA); information systems management (MBA); international business (MBA, DBA); management (MBA, MSM, DBA); marketing (MBA, DBA); organizational leadership (Ed D); public administration (MBA); sustainable management (MBA). Postbaccalaureate distance learning degree programs offered (minimal on-campus study).

See Close-Up on page 181.

Argosy University, Dallas, College of Business, Farmers Branch, TX 75244. Offers accounting (DBA, AGC); corporate compliance (MBA, Graduate Certificate); customized professional concentration (MBA); finance (MBA, Graduate Certificate); fraud examination (MBA, Graduate Certificate); global business sustainability (DBA, AGC); healthcare administration (Graduate Certificate); healthcare management (MBA); information systems (MBA, DBA, AGC); information systems management (Graduate Certificate); international business (MBA, DBA, AGC, Graduate Certificate); management (MBA, DBA, AGC, Graduate Certificate); marketing (MBA, DBA, AGC, Graduate Certificate); public administration (MBA, Graduate Certificate); sustainable management (MBA, Graduate Certificate).

See Close-Up on page 183.

Argosy University, Denver, College of Business, Denver, CO 80231. Offers accounting (DBA); corporate compliance (MBA); customized professional concentration (MBA, DBA); finance (MBA); fraud examination (MBA); global business sustainability (DBA); healthcare administration (MBA); information systems (DBA); information systems management (MBA); international business (MBA, DBA); management (MBA, MSM, DBA); marketing (MBA, DBA); organizational leadership (Ed D); public administration (MBA); sustainable management (MBA).

See Close-Up on page 185.

Argosy University, Hawai`i, College of Business, Honolulu, HI 96813. Offers accounting (DBA); corporate compliance (MBA); customized professional concentration (MBA, DBA); finance (MBA, Certificate); fraud examination (MBA); global business sustainability (DBA); healthcare administration (MBA, Certificate); information systems (DBA); information systems management (MBA, Certificate); international business (MBA, DBA, Certificate); management (MBA, MSM, DBA); marketing (MBA, DBA, Certificate); organizational leadership (Ed D); public administration (MBA); sustainable management (MBA).

See Close-Up on page 187.

Argosy University, Inland Empire, College of Business, San Bernardino, CA 92408. Offers accounting (DBA); corporate compliance (MBA); customized professional concentration (MBA, DBA); finance (MBA); fraud examination (MBA); global business sustainability (DBA); healthcare administration (MBA); information systems (DBA); information systems management (MBA); international business (MBA, DBA); management (MBA, MSM, DBA); marketing (MBA, DBA); organizational leadership (Ed D); public administration (MBA); sustainable management (MBA).

See Close-Up on page 189.

Argosy University, Los Angeles, College of Business, Santa Monica, CA 90045. Offers accounting (DBA); corporate compliance (MBA); customized professional concentration (MBA, DBA); finance (MBA); fraud examination (MBA); global business sustainability (DBA); healthcare administration (MBA); information systems (DBA); information systems management (MBA); international business (MBA, DBA); management (MBA, MSM, DBA); marketing (MBA, DBA); organizational leadership (Ed D); public administration (MBA); sustainable management (MBA).

See Close-Up on page 191.

Argosy University, Nashville, College of Business, Nashville, TN 37214. Offers accounting (DBA); customized professional concentration (MBA, DBA); finance (MBA); healthcare administration (MBA); information systems (MBA, DBA); international business (MBA, DBA); management (MBA, MSM, DBA); marketing (MBA, DBA).

See Close-Up on page 9999.

Argosy University, Orange County, College of Business, Orange, CA 92868. Offers accounting (DBA, Adv C); corporate compliance (MBA); customized professional concentration (MBA, DBA); finance (MBA, Certificate); fraud examination (MBA); global business sustainability (DBA); healthcare administration (MBA, Certificate); information systems (DBA, Adv C, Certificate); information systems management (MBA); international business (MBA, DBA, Adv C, Certificate); management (MBA, MSM, DBA, Adv C); marketing (MBA, DBA, Adv C, Certificate); organizational leadership (Ed D); public administration (MBA, Certificate); sustainable management (MBA).

See Close-Up on page 195.

Argosy University, Phoenix, College of Business, Phoenix, AZ 85021. Offers accounting (DBA); corporate compliance (MBA); customized professional concentration (MBA, DBA); finance (MBA); fraud examination (MBA); global business sustainability (DBA); healthcare administration (MBA); information systems (DBA); information systems management (MBA); international business (MBA, DBA); management (MBA, DBA); marketing (MBA, DBA); public administration (MBA); sustainable management (MBA).

See Close-Up on page 197.

Argosy University, Salt Lake City, College of Business, Draper, UT 84020. Offers accounting (DBA); corporate compliance (MBA); customized professional concentration (MBA, DBA); finance (MBA); fraud examination (MBA); global business sustainability (DBA); healthcare administration (MBA); information systems (DBA); information systems management (MBA); international business (MBA, DBA); management (MBA, DBA); marketing (MBA, DBA); public administration (MBA); sustainable management (MBA).

See Close-Up on page 199.

Argosy University, San Diego, College of Business, San Diego, CA 92108. Offers accounting (DBA); corporate compliance (MBA); customized professional concentration (MBA, DBA); finance (MBA); fraud examination (MBA); global business sustainability (DBA); information systems (DBA); information systems management (MBA); international business (MBA, DBA); management (MBA, MSM, DBA); marketing (MBA, DBA); organizational leadership (Ed D); public administration (MBA).

See Close-Up on page 201.

Argosy University, San Francisco Bay Area, College of Business, Alameda, CA 94501. Offers accounting (DBA); corporate compliance (MBA); customized professional concentration (MBA, DBA); finance (MBA); fraud examination (MBA); global business sustainability (DBA); healthcare administration (MBA); information systems (DBA); information systems management (MBA); international business (MBA, DBA); management (MBA, MSM, DBA); marketing (MBA, DBA); organizational leadership (Ed D); public administration (MBA); sustainable management (MBA).

See Close-Up on page 203.

Argosy University, Sarasota, College of Business, Sarasota, FL 34235. Offers accounting (DBA, Adv C); corporate compliance (MBA, DBA, Certificate); customized professional concentration (MBA, DBA); finance (MBA, Certificate); fraud examination (MBA, Certificate); global business sustainability (DBA, Adv C); healthcare administration (MBA, Certificate); information systems (DBA, Adv C, Certificate); information systems management (MBA); international business (MBA, DBA, Adv C, Certificate); management (MBA, MSM, DBA, Adv C, Certificate); marketing (MBA, DBA, Adv C, Certificate); organizational leadership (Ed D); public administration (MBA, Certificate); sustainable management (MBA, Certificate).

See Close-Up on page 205.

Argosy University, Schaumburg, College of Business, Schaumburg, IL 60173-5403. Offers accounting (DBA, Adv C); customized professional concentration (MBA, DBA); finance (MBA, Certificate); fraud examination (MBA); global business sustainability (DBA); healthcare administration (MBA, Certificate); information systems (DBA, Adv C, Certificate); information systems management (MBA); international business (MBA, DBA, Adv C, Certificate); management (MBA, MSM, DBA, Adv C, Certificate); marketing (MBA, DBA, Adv C, Certificate); organizational leadership (Ed D); public administration (MBA); sustainable management (MBA).

See Close-Up on page 207.

Argosy University, Seattle, College of Business, Seattle, WA 98121. Offers accounting (DBA); corporate compliance (MBA); customized professional concentration (MBA, DBA); finance (MBA); fraud examination (MBA); global business sustainability (DBA); healthcare administration (MBA); information systems (DBA); information systems management (MBA); international business (MBA, DBA); management (MBA, MSM, DBA); marketing (MBA, DBA); organizational leadership (Ed D); public administration (MBA); sustainable management (MBA).

See Close-Up on page 209.

Argosy University, Tampa, College of Business, Tampa, FL 33607. Offers accounting (DBA); corporate compliance (MBA); customized professional concentration (MBA, DBA); finance (MBA); fraud examination (MBA); global business sustainability (DBA); healthcare administration (MBA); information systems (DBA); information systems management (MBA); international business (MBA, DBA); management (MBA, MSM, DBA); marketing (MBA, DBA); organizational leadership (Ed D); public administration (MBA); sustainable management (MBA).

See Close-Up on page 211.

Argosy University, Twin Cities, College of Business, Eagan, MN 55121. Offers accounting (DBA); customized professional concentration (MBA, DBA); finance (MBA); fraud examination (MBA); global business sustainability (DBA); healthcare administration (MBA); information systems (DBA); information systems management (MBA); international business (MBA, DBA); management (MBA, MSM, DBA); marketing (MBA, DBA); organizational leadership (Ed D); public administration (MBA); sustainable management (MBA).

See Close-Up on page 213.

Argosy University, Washington DC, College of Business, Arlington, VA 22209. Offers accounting (DBA); customized professional concentration (MBA, DBA); finance (MBA); fraud examination (MBA); global business sustainability (DBA); healthcare administration (MBA); information systems (DBA); information systems management (MBA); international business (MBA, DBA, Certificate); management (MBA, MSM, DBA); marketing (MBA, DBA, Certificate); organizational leadership (Ed D); public administration (MBA); sustainable management (MBA).

See Close-Up on page 215.

Arizona State University, College of Technology and Innovation, Department of Technology Management, Mesa, AZ 85212. Offers technology (aviation management and human factors) (MS); technology (environmental technology management) (MS); technology (global technology and development) (MS); technology (graphic information technology) (MS); technology (management of technology) (MS). Part-time and evening/weekend programs available. Postbaccalaureate distance learning degree programs offered (minimal on-campus study). *Degree requirements:* For master's, thesis or applied project and oral defense; interactive Program of Study (iPOS) submitted before completing 50 percent of required credit hours. *Entrance requirements:* For master's, GRE, minimum GPA of 3.0 or equivalent in last 2 years of work leading to bachelor's degree. Additional exam requirements/recommendations for international students: Required—TOEFL (minimum score 83 iBT), TOEFL, IELTS, or Pearson Test of English. Electronic applications accepted. *Faculty research:* Digital imaging, digital publishing, Internet development/e-commerce, information aviation human factors, pilot selection, databases, multimedia, commercial digital photography, digital workflow, computer graphics modeling and animation, information design, sociotechnology, visual and technical literacy, environmental management, quality management, project management, industrial ethics, hazardous materials, environmental chemistry.

Arizona State University, W. P. Carey School of Business, Department of Information Systems, Tempe, AZ 85287-4606. Offers business administration (computer information systems) (PhD); information management (MS); MBA/MS. Evening/weekend programs available. Postbaccalaureate distance learning degree programs offered (no on-campus study). Terminal master's awarded for partial completion of doctoral program. *Degree requirements:* For master's, thesis or alternative, applied project, interactive Program of Study (iPOS) submitted before completing 50 percent of required credit hours; for doctorate, comprehensive exam, thesis/dissertation, interactive Program of Study (iPOS) submitted before completing 50 percent of required credit hours. *Entrance requirements:* For master's, 2 years of full-time related work experience, bachelor's degree in related field from accredited university, resume, essay, 2 letters of recommendation, official transcripts; for doctorate, GMAT, MBA, 2 years of full-time related work experience (recommended), bachelor's degree in related field from accredited university, 3 letters of recommendation, resume, personal statement. Additional exam requirements/recommendations for international students: Required—TOEFL (minimum score 550 paper-based; 213 computer-based; 80 iBT), IELTS (minimum score 6.5). Electronic applications accepted. *Expenses:* Contact institution. *Faculty research:* Strategy and technology, technology investments and firm valuation, Internet e-commerce, IT enablement for emergency preparedness and response, information supply chain, collaborative computing and security/privacy issues for e-health, enterprise information systems and their application to management control systems.

Management Information Systems

Arizona State University, W. P. Carey School of Business, Program in Business Administration, Tempe, AZ 85287-4906. Offers accountancy (PhD); agribusiness (PhD); business administration (MBA); finance (PhD); financial management and markets (MBA); information management (MBA); information systems (PhD); management (PhD); marketing (PhD); strategic marketing and services leadership (MBA); supply chain financial management (MBA); supply chain management (MBA, PhD); JD/MBA; MBA/M Acc; MBA/M Arch. *Accreditation:* AACSB. Part-time and evening/weekend programs available. Postbaccalaureate distance learning degree programs offered (minimal on-campus study). Terminal master's awarded for partial completion of doctoral program. *Degree requirements:* For master's, thesis or alternative, internship, interactive Program of Study (iPOS) submitted before completing 50 percent of required credit hours; for doctorate, comprehensive exam, thesis/dissertation, interactive Program of Study (iPOS) submitted before completing 50 percent of required credit hours. *Entrance requirements:* For master's, GMAT, minimum GPA of 3.0 in last 2 years of work leading to bachelor's degree, 2 letters of recommendation, professional resume, official transcripts, 3 essays; for doctorate, GMAT or GRE, minimum GPA of 3.0 in last 2 years of work leading to bachelor's degree, 3 letters of recommendation, resume, personal statement/essay. Additional exam requirements/recommendations for international students: Required—TOEFL (minimum score 550 paper-based; 213 computer-based; 80 iBT), IELTS (minimum score 6.5). Electronic applications accepted. *Expenses:* Contact institution.

Arkansas State University, Graduate School, College of Business, Department of Computer and Information Technology, Jonesboro, State University, AR 72467. Offers business education (SCCT); business technology education (MSE); information systems and e-commerce (MS). Part-time programs available. *Faculty:* 9 full-time (1 woman). *Students:* 4 full-time (2 women), 13 part-time (10 women); includes 5 minority (all Black or African American, non-Hispanic/Latino). Average age 36. 6 applicants, 100% accepted, 5 enrolled. In 2011, 13 master's awarded. *Degree requirements:* For master's, comprehensive exam, thesis or alternative. *Entrance requirements:* For master's, GRE General Test or MAT, appropriate bachelor's degree, official transcript, immunization records. Additional exam requirements/recommendations for international students: Required—TOEFL (minimum score 550 paper-based; 253 computer-based; 79 iBT), IELTS (minimum score 6), Pearson Test of English Academic (minimum score 56). *Application deadline:* For fall admission, 7/1 for domestic and international students; for spring admission, 11/15 for domestic students, 11/14 for international students. Applications are processed on a rolling basis. Application fee: $30 ($40 for international students). Electronic applications accepted. *Expenses:* Contact institution. *Financial support:* Career-related internships or fieldwork, scholarships/grants, and unspecified assistantships available. Financial award application deadline: 7/1; financial award applicants required to submit FAFSA. *Unit head:* Dr. John Robertson, Chair, 870-972-3416, Fax: 870-972-3868, E-mail: jfrobert@astate.edu. *Application contact:* Dr. Andrew Sustich, Dean of the Graduate School, 870-972-3029, Fax: 870-972-3857, E-mail: sustich@astate.edu. Web site: http://www.astate.edu/a/business/departments/computer-information-technology/.

Aspen University, Programs in Information Management, Denver, CO 80246. Offers information management (MS); information systems (Certificate). Part-time and evening/weekend programs available. Postbaccalaureate distance learning degree programs offered (no on-campus study). Electronic applications accepted.

Auburn University, Graduate School, College of Business, Department of Management, Auburn University, AL 36849. Offers human resource management (PhD); management (MS, PhD); management information systems (MS, PhD). *Accreditation:* AACSB. Part-time programs available. *Faculty:* 26 full-time (5 women), 1 part-time/adjunct (0 women). *Students:* 15 full-time (5 women), 14 part-time (3 women); includes 4 minority (3 Black or African American, non-Hispanic/Latino; 1 Asian, non-Hispanic/Latino), 6 international. Average age 35. 66 applicants, 24% accepted, 8 enrolled. In 2011, 2 doctorates awarded. *Degree requirements:* For master's, thesis (for some programs); for doctorate, thesis/dissertation. *Entrance requirements:* For master's, GMAT, GRE General Test (MS); for doctorate, GMAT, GRE General Test. Additional exam requirements/recommendations for international students: Required—TOEFL. *Application deadline:* For fall admission, 7/7 for domestic students; for spring admission, 11/24 for domestic students. Applications are processed on a rolling basis. Application fee: $50 ($60 for international students). Electronic applications accepted. *Expenses:* Tuition, state resident: full-time $7290; part-time $405 per credit hour. Tuition, nonresident: full-time $21,870; part-time $1215 per credit hour. *International tuition:* $22,000 full-time. *Required fees:* $1402. *Financial support:* Teaching assistantships and Federal Work-Study available. Support available to part-time students. Financial award application deadline: 3/15; financial award applicants required to submit FAFSA. *Unit head:* Dr. Christopher Shook, Head, 334-844-9565. *Application contact:* Dr. George Flowers, Dean of the Graduate School, 334-844-2125. Web site: http://business.auburn.edu/academics/departments/department-of-management/.

Avila University, School of Business, Kansas City, MO 64145-1698. Offers accounting (MBA); finance (MBA); general management (MBA); health care administration (MBA); international business (MBA); management information systems (MBA); marketing (MBA). Part-time and evening/weekend programs available. *Faculty:* 9 full-time (3 women), 14 part-time/adjunct (5 women). *Students:* 102 full-time (49 women), 53 part-time (31 women); includes 36 minority (29 Black or African American, non-Hispanic/Latino; 1 American Indian or Alaska Native, non-Hispanic/Latino; 3 Asian, non-Hispanic/Latino; 2 Hispanic/Latino; 1 Native Hawaiian or other Pacific Islander, non-Hispanic/Latino), 33 international. Average age 32. 25 applicants, 76% accepted, 19 enrolled. In 2011, 59 master's awarded. *Degree requirements:* For master's, comprehensive exam, capstone course. *Entrance requirements:* For master's, GMAT (minimum score 420), minimum GPA of 3.0, interview. Additional exam requirements/recommendations for international students: Required—TOEFL (minimum score 550 paper-based). *Application deadline:* For fall admission, 7/30 priority date for domestic students, 7/30 for international students; for winter admission, 11/30 priority date for domestic students, 11/30 for international students; for spring admission, 2/28 priority date for domestic students, 2/28 for international students. Applications are processed on a rolling basis. Application fee: $0. Electronic applications accepted. *Expenses:* Contact institution. *Financial support:* In 2011–12, 102 students received support. Career-related internships or fieldwork and competitive merit scholarships available. Support available to part-time students. Financial award applicants required to submit FAFSA. *Faculty research:* Leadership characteristics, financial hedging, group dynamics. *Unit head:* Dr. Richard Woodall, Dean, 816-501-3720, Fax: 816-501-2463, E-mail: richard.woodall@avila.edu. *Application contact:* JoAnna Giffin, MBA Admissions Director, 816-501-3601, Fax: 816-501-2463, E-mail: joanna.giffin@avila.edu. Web site: http://www.avila.edu/mba.

Baker College Center for Graduate Studies - Online, Graduate Programs, Flint, MI 48507-9843. Offers accounting (MBA); business administration (DBA); finance (MBA); general business (MBA); health care management (MBA); human resources management (MBA); information management (MBA); leadership studies (MBA); management information systems (MSIS); marketing (MBA). Part-time and evening/weekend programs available. Postbaccalaureate distance learning degree programs offered. *Degree requirements:* For master's, portfolio. *Entrance requirements:* For master's, 3 years of work experience, minimum undergraduate GPA of 2.5, writing sample, 3 letters of recommendation; for doctorate, MBA or acceptable related master's degree from accredited association, 5 years work experience, minimum graduate GPA of 3.25, writing sample, 3 professional references. Additional exam requirements/recommendations for international students: Required—TOEFL (minimum score 550 paper-based; 213 computer-based). Electronic applications accepted.

Barry University, Andreas School of Business, Graduate Certificate Programs, Miami Shores, FL 33161-6695. Offers finance (Certificate); health services administration (Certificate); international business (Certificate); management (Certificate); management information systems (Certificate); marketing (Certificate).

Baylor University, Graduate School, Hankamer School of Business, Department of Information Systems, Waco, TX 76798-8005. Offers information systems (MSIS, PhD); information systems management (MBA); MBA/MSIS. *Faculty:* 12 full-time (4 women). *Students:* 22 full-time (5 women), 5 part-time (0 women); includes 3 minority (2 Black or African American, non-Hispanic/Latino; 1 Hispanic/Latino), 10 international. In 2011, 5 master's awarded. *Entrance requirements:* For master's, GMAT; for doctorate, GMAT, GRE. Additional exam requirements/recommendations for international students: Required—TOEFL. *Application deadline:* For fall admission, 8/1 for domestic students; for spring admission, 12/1 for domestic students. Applications are processed on a rolling basis. Application fee: $25. *Financial support:* Research assistantships, career-related internships or fieldwork, and Federal Work-Study available. *Faculty research:* Computer personnel, group systems, information technology standards and infrastructure, international information systems, technology and the learning environment. *Unit head:* Dr. Gary Carini, Associate Dean, 254-710-4091, Fax: 254-710-1091, E-mail: gary_carini@baylor.edu. *Application contact:* Laurie Wilson, Director, Graduate Business Programs, 254-710-4163, Fax: 254-710-1066, E-mail: laurie_wilson@baylor.edu. Web site: http://hsb.baylor.edu/isy/.

Bay Path College, Program in Communications and Information Management, Longmeadow, MA 01106-2292. Offers MS. Part-time and evening/weekend programs available. Postbaccalaureate distance learning degree programs offered (no on-campus study). *Students:* 17 full-time (16 women), 40 part-time (36 women); includes 9 minority (7 Black or African American, non-Hispanic/Latino; 1 Asian, non-Hispanic/Latino; 1 Hispanic/Latino), 1 international. Average age 35. 67 applicants, 66% accepted, 34 enrolled. In 2011, 24 master's awarded. *Application deadline:* Applications are processed on a rolling basis. Application fee: $45. Electronic applications accepted. Application fee is waived when completed online. *Expenses: Tuition:* Part-time $665 per credit. Tuition and fees vary according to program. *Financial support:* In 2011–12, 13 students received support. Scholarships/grants available. Financial award applicants required to submit FAFSA. *Application contact:* Lisa Adams, Director of Graduate Admissions, 413-565-1317, Fax: 413-565-1250, E-mail: ladams@baypath.edu. Web site: http://www.baypath.edu/.

Bellarmine University, School of Continuing and Professional Studies, Louisville, KY 40205-0671. Offers MAIT. Part-time and evening/weekend programs available. *Faculty:* 1 full-time (0 women), 4 part-time/adjunct (0 women). *Students:* 25 part-time (2 women); includes 2 minority (1 Black or African American, non-Hispanic/Latino; 1 Asian, non-Hispanic/Latino). Average age 31. In 2011, 11 master's awarded. *Entrance requirements:* For master's, GRE or GMAT, minimum GPA of 2.75, two letters of recommendation. Additional exam requirements/recommendations for international students: Required—TOEFL (minimum score 550 paper-based; 213 computer-based; 80 iBT). Application fee: $25. *Expenses:* Contact institution. *Unit head:* Dr. Michael D. Mattei, Dean, 502-272-8441, E-mail: mmattei@bellarmine.edu. *Application contact:* Dr. Sara Pettingill, Dean of Graduate Admission, 502-272-8401, E-mail: spettingill@bellarmine.edu. Web site: http://www.bellarmine.edu/ce/MAIT.asp.

Bellevue University, Graduate School, College of Information Technology, Bellevue, NE 68005-3098. Offers computer information systems (MS); cybersecurity (MS); management of information systems (MS); project management (MPM).

Benedictine University, Graduate Programs, Program in Business Administration, Lisle, IL 60532-0900. Offers accounting (MBA); entrepreneurship and managing innovation (MBA); financial management (MBA); health administration (MBA); human resource management (MBA); information systems security (MBA); international business (MBA); management consulting (MBA); management information systems (MBA); marketing management (MBA); operations management and logistics (MBA); organizational leadership (MBA); MBA/MPH; MBA/MS. Part-time and evening/weekend programs available. Postbaccalaureate distance learning degree programs offered (minimal on-campus study). *Faculty:* 4 full-time (2 women), 24 part-time/adjunct (3 women). *Students:* 165 full-time (101 women), 766 part-time (381 women); includes 201 minority (118 Black or African American, non-Hispanic/Latino; 4 American Indian or Alaska Native, non-Hispanic/Latino; 37 Asian, non-Hispanic/Latino; 40 Hispanic/Latino; 2 Native Hawaiian or other Pacific Islander, non-Hispanic/Latino), 14 international. Average age 34. 313 applicants, 73% accepted, 166 enrolled. In 2011, 379 master's awarded. *Entrance requirements:* For master's, GMAT. Additional exam requirements/recommendations for international students: Required—TOEFL (minimum score 550 paper-based; 213 computer-based). *Application deadline:* For fall admission, 9/1 for domestic students; for winter admission, 12/1 for domestic students; for spring admission, 2/15 for domestic students. Applications are processed on a rolling basis. Application fee: $40. Electronic applications accepted. *Financial support:* Career-related internships or fieldwork and health care benefits available. Support available to part-time students. *Faculty research:* Strategic leadership in professional organizations, sociology of professions, organizational change, social identity theory, applications to change management. *Unit head:* Dr. Sharon Borowicz, Director, 630-829-6219, E-mail: sborowicz@ben.edu. *Application contact:* Kari Gibbons, Director, Admissions, 630-829-6200, Fax: 630-829-6584, E-mail: kgibbons@ben.edu.

Benedictine University, Graduate Programs, Program in Management Information Systems, Lisle, IL 60532-0900. Offers MS, MBA/MS, MPH/MS. Part-time programs available. *Faculty:* 2 full-time (1 woman), 6 part-time/adjunct (1 woman). *Students:* 61 full-time (17 women), 21 part-time (6 women); includes 2 minority (1 Black or African American, non-Hispanic/Latino; 1 Hispanic/Latino), 3 international. Average age 36. 106 applicants, 95% accepted, 82 enrolled. In 2011, 76 master's awarded. *Entrance requirements:* For master's, GMAT. Additional exam requirements/recommendations for international students: Required—TOEFL (minimum score 550 paper-based; 213 computer-based). *Application deadline:* For fall admission, 9/1 for domestic students; for winter admission, 12/1 for domestic students; for spring admission, 2/15 for domestic students. Applications are processed on a rolling basis. Application fee: $40. Electronic applications accepted. *Financial support:* Career-related internships or fieldwork and health care benefits available. Support available to part-time students. *Faculty research:* Technology management, knowledge management, electronic commerce, information security. *Unit head:* Dr. Barbara Ozog, Director, 630-829-6218, E-mail: bozog@ben.edu. *Application contact:* Kari Gibbons, Associate Vice President, Enrollment Center, 630-829-6200, Fax: 630-829-6584, E-mail: kgibbons@ben.edu.

Bernard M. Baruch College of the City University of New York, Zicklin School of Business, Department of Statistics and Computer Information Systems, Program in Information Systems, New York, NY 10010-5585. Offers MBA, MS, PhD. Part-time and evening/weekend programs available. Terminal master's awarded for partial completion of doctoral program. *Degree requirements:* For master's, thesis or alternative; for doctorate, comprehensive exam, thesis/dissertation. *Entrance requirements:* For master's, GMAT, 2 letters of recommendation, resume, 2 years of work experience; for doctorate, GMAT. Additional exam requirements/recommendations for international students: Required—TOEFL (minimum score 590 paper-based; 243 computer-based), TWE (minimum score 5).

Boise State University, Graduate College, College of Business and Economics, Program in Information Technology Management, Boise, ID 83725-0399. Offers MBA. Part-time programs available. *Entrance requirements:* For master's, GMAT, minimum GPA of 3.0. Additional exam requirements/recommendations for international students: Required—TOEFL. Electronic applications accepted.

Boston University, Metropolitan College, Department of Computer Science, Boston, MA 02215. Offers computer information systems (MS), including computer networks, database management and business intelligence, health informatics, IT project management, security, Web application development; computer science (MS), including computer networks, security; telecommunications (MS), including security. Evening/weekend programs available. Postbaccalaureate distance learning degree programs offered. *Faculty:* 12 full-time (2 women), 28 part-time/adjunct (2 women). *Students:* 25 full-time (6 women), 732 part-time (167 women); includes 208 minority (51 Black or African American, non-Hispanic/Latino; 1 American Indian or Alaska Native, non-Hispanic/Latino; 104 Asian, non-Hispanic/Latino; 43 Hispanic/Latino; 1 Native Hawaiian or other Pacific Islander, non-Hispanic/Latino; 8 Two or more races, non-Hispanic/Latino), 86 international. Average age 35. 260 applicants, 67% accepted, 143 enrolled. In 2011, 143 master's awarded. *Degree requirements:* For master's, thesis optional. *Entrance requirements:* For master's, 3 letters of recommendation, professional resume. Additional exam requirements/recommendations for international students: Required—TOEFL (minimum score 550 paper-based; 213 computer-based; 80 iBT). *Application deadline:* For fall admission, 6/1 for international students; for spring admission, 10/1 for international students. Applications are processed on a rolling basis. Application fee: $70. Electronic applications accepted. *Expenses: Tuition:* Full-time $40,848; part-time $1276 per credit hour. *Required fees:* $572; $286 per semester. *Financial support:* In 2011–12, 9 research assistantships (averaging $5,000 per year) were awarded; career-related internships or fieldwork and unspecified assistantships also available. Support available to part-time students. Financial award applicants required to submit FAFSA. *Faculty research:* Medical informatics, Web technologies, telecom and networks, security and forensics, software engineering, programming languages, multimedia and AI, information systems and IT project management. *Unit head:* Dr. Lubomir Chitkushev, Chairman, 617-353-2566, Fax: 617-353-2367, E-mail: csinfo@bu.edu. *Application contact:* Kim Richards, Program Coordinator, 617-353-2566, Fax: 617-353-2367, E-mail: kimrich@bu.edu. Web site: http://www.bu.edu/csmet/.

Bowie State University, Graduate Programs, Program in Management Information Systems, Bowie, MD 20715-9465. Offers information systems analyst (Certificate); management information systems (MS). Part-time and evening/weekend programs available. *Faculty:* 4 full-time (0 women). *Students:* 28 full-time (7 women), 47 part-time (18 women); includes 61 minority (60 Black or African American, non-Hispanic/Latino; 1 Asian, non-Hispanic/Latino), 4 international. Average age 33. 14 applicants, 86% accepted, 12 enrolled. In 2011, 42 master's awarded. *Degree requirements:* For master's, comprehensive exam, thesis optional, research paper. *Entrance requirements:* For master's, minimum GPA of 2.5. *Application deadline:* For fall admission, 9/1 priority date for domestic students, 4/1 for international students; for spring admission, 11/1 priority date for domestic students, 11/1 for international students. Applications are processed on a rolling basis. Application fee: $40. Electronic applications accepted. *Expenses:* Tuition, state resident: full-time $4140; part-time $3105 per semester. Tuition, nonresident: full-time $7836; part-time $5877 per semester. *Required fees:* $1715; $648 per semester. *Financial support:* Career-related internships or fieldwork and institutionally sponsored loans available. Financial award application deadline: 4/1. *Unit head:* Dr. David Anyiwo, Coordinator, 301-860-3626, Fax: 301-860-3644, E-mail: danyiwo@bowiestate.edu. *Application contact:* Angela Issac, Information Contact, 301-860-4000.

Brandeis University, Rabb School of Continuing Studies, Division of Graduate Professional Studies, Information Technology Management Program, Waltham, MA 02454-9110. Offers MS. Part-time programs available. Postbaccalaureate distance learning degree programs offered (no on-campus study). *Faculty:* 2 full-time (both women), 34 part-time/adjunct (8 women). *Students:* 67 part-time (13 women); includes 17 minority (4 Black or African American, non-Hispanic/Latino; 12 Asian, non-Hispanic/Latino; 1 Hispanic/Latino). Average age 35. 5 applicants, 100% accepted, 4 enrolled. In 2011, 26 master's awarded. *Entrance requirements:* For master's, resume, official transcripts, recommendations, goal statements. Additional exam requirements/recommendations for international students: Recommended—TOEFL (minimum score 600 paper-based; 250 computer-based; 100 iBT). *Application deadline:* For fall admission, 6/15 priority date for domestic students; for winter admission, 10/15 priority date for domestic students; for spring admission, 2/15 priority date for domestic students. Applications are processed on a rolling basis. Application fee: $50. Electronic applications accepted. *Unit head:* Dr. Cynthia Phillips, Program Chair, 781-736-8787, Fax: 781-736-3420, E-mail: cynthiap@brandeis.edu. *Application contact:* Frances Stearns, Associate Director of Admissions and Student Services, 781-736-8785, Fax: 781-736-3420, E-mail: fstearns@brandeis.edu. Web site: http://www.brandeis.edu/gps.

Brigham Young University, Graduate Studies, Marriott School of Management, Master of Information Systems Program, Provo, UT 84602. Offers MISM. *Faculty:* 12 full-time (1 woman), 5 part-time/adjunct (1 woman). *Students:* 42 full-time (2 women); includes 1 minority (Asian, non-Hispanic/Latino), 4 international. Average age 25. 71 applicants, 66% accepted, 42 enrolled. In 2011, 48 master's awarded. *Entrance requirements:* For master's, GMAT, minimum GPA of 3.0 in last 60 hours of course work. Additional exam requirements/recommendations for international students: Required—TOEFL (minimum score 580 paper-based; 237 computer-based). *Application deadline:* For fall admission, 3/1 for domestic and international students. Application fee: $50. Electronic applications accepted. *Expenses: Tuition:* Full-time $5760; part-time $320 per credit. Tuition and fees vary according to student's religious affiliation. *Financial support:* In 2011–12, 29 students received support. Research assistantships, teaching assistantships, career-related internships or fieldwork, and scholarships/grants available. Financial award application deadline: 3/1. *Faculty research:* Research standards - faculty career development in information systems, electronic commerce technology and standards, collaborative tools and methods, technology for fraud detection and prevention, ethical issues in the information systems field. *Unit head:* Dr. Marshall B. Romney, Director, 801-422-3247, Fax: 801-422-0573, E-mail: marshall_romney@byu.edu. *Application contact:* Ann E. Sumsion, Program Assistant, 801-422-3247, Fax: 801-422-0573, E-mail: mism@byu.edu. Web site: http://marriottschool.byu.edu/mism.

Broadview University–West Jordan, Graduate Programs, West Jordan, UT 84088. Offers business administration (MBA); health care management (MSM); information technology (MSM); managerial leadership (MSM).

California Intercontinental University, School of Information Technology, Diamond Bar, CA 91765. Offers information systems and enterprise resource management (DBA); information systems and knowledge management (MBA); project and quality management (MBA).

California Lutheran University, Graduate Studies, School of Management, Thousand Oaks, CA 91360-2787. Offers business (IMBA); computer science (MS); econometrics (MBA); economics (MS); entrepreneurship (MBA, Certificate); finance (MBA, Certificate); financial planning (MBA, Certificate); information systems and technology (MS); information technology management (MBA, Certificate); international business (MBA, Certificate); management and organization behavior (MBA); management and organizational behavior (Certificate); marketing (MBA, Certificate); microeconomics (MBA); nonprofit and social enterprise (MBA). Part-time and evening/weekend programs available. Postbaccalaureate distance learning degree programs offered (no on-campus study). *Entrance requirements:* For master's, GMAT, interview, minimum GPA of 3.0. *Expenses:* Contact institution.

California State Polytechnic University, Pomona, Academic Affairs, College of Business Administration, Master of Science in Business Administration Program, Pomona, CA 91768-2557. Offers information systems auditing (MS). *Students:* 1 (woman) full-time, 15 part-time (6 women); includes 9 minority (5 Asian, non-Hispanic/Latino; 2 Hispanic/Latino; 2 Two or more races, non-Hispanic/Latino), 1 international. Average age 32. 25 applicants, 24% accepted, 5 enrolled. In 2011, 6 master's awarded. *Application deadline:* Applications are processed on a rolling basis. Application fee: $55. Electronic applications accepted. *Expenses:* Tuition, state resident: full-time $6738. Tuition, nonresident: full-time $12,300. *Required fees:* $657. Tuition and fees vary according to course load and program. *Unit head:* Dr. Richard S. Lapidus, Dean, 909-869-2400, Fax: 909-869-6799, E-mail: rslapidus@csupomona.edu. *Application contact:* Dr. Gregory Carlton, Graduate Coordinator, 909-869-5190, E-mail: ghcarlton@csupomona.edu. Web site: http://cba.csupomona.edu/graduateprograms/.

California State University, East Bay, Office of Academic Programs and Graduate Studies, College of Business and Economics, Business Administration, MBA Program, Hayward, CA 94542-3000. Offers entrepreneurship (MBA); finance (MBA); global innovators (MBA); human resources and organizational behavior (MBA); information technology management (MBA); marketing management (MBA); operations and supply chain management (MBA); strategy and international business (MBA). Part-time and evening/weekend programs available. *Faculty:* 11 full-time (3 women). *Students:* 80 full-time (42 women), 141 part-time (61 women); includes 70 minority (5 Black or African American, non-Hispanic/Latino; 46 Asian, non-Hispanic/Latino; 13 Hispanic/Latino; 1 Native Hawaiian or other Pacific Islander, non-Hispanic/Latino; 5 Two or more races, non-Hispanic/Latino), 69 international. Average age 31. 371 applicants, 36% accepted, 79 enrolled. In 2011, 254 master's awarded. *Degree requirements:* For master's, comprehensive exam or thesis. *Entrance requirements:* For master's, GMAT (minimum 20th percentile verbal and quantitative section), bachelor's degree, minimum GPA of 2.75. Additional exam requirements/recommendations for international students: Required—TOEFL (minimum score 550 paper-based; 213 computer-based; 79 iBT). *Application deadline:* For fall admission, 6/30 for domestic and international students. Applications are processed on a rolling basis. Application fee: $55. Electronic applications accepted. *Expenses:* Contact institution. *Financial support:* Career-related internships or fieldwork, Federal Work-Study, institutionally sponsored loans, and scholarships/grants available. Support available to part-time students. Financial award application deadline: 3/2; financial award applicants required to submit FAFSA. *Unit head:* Dr. Terri Swartz, Dean, 510-885-3291, Fax: 510-885-4884, E-mail: terri.swartz@csueastbay.edu. *Application contact:* Prof. Joanna Lee, Director, CBE Graduate Programs, 510-885-3517, Fax: 510-885-2176, E-mail: joanna.lee@csueastbay.edu. Web site: http://www20.csueastbay.edu/ecat/graduate-chapters/g-buad.html#mba.

California State University, East Bay, Office of Academic Programs and Graduate Studies, College of Business and Economics, Program in Information Technology Management, Hayward, CA 94542-3000. Offers MBA. Part-time and evening/weekend programs available. *Faculty:* 37 full-time (7 women), 8 part-time/adjunct (3 women). *Students:* Average age 32. *Degree requirements:* For master's, comprehensive exam or thesis. *Entrance requirements:* For master's, GMAT, minimum GPA of 2.75. Additional exam requirements/recommendations for international students: Required—TOEFL (minimum score 550 paper-based; 213 computer-based). *Application deadline:* For fall admission, 6/30 for domestic and international students. Application fee: $55. Electronic applications accepted. *Expenses:* Tuition, state resident: full-time $6738; part-time $1302 per quarter. Tuition, nonresident: full-time $12,690; part-time $2294 per quarter. *Required fees:* $449 per quarter. Tuition and fees vary according to degree level, program and reciprocity agreements. *Financial support:* Career-related internships or fieldwork, Federal Work-Study, and institutionally sponsored loans available. Support available to part-time students. Financial award application deadline: 3/2; financial award applicants required to submit FAFSA. *Unit head:* Dr. Xinjian Lu, Chair, 510-885-3307, Fax: 510-885-2165, E-mail: xinjian.lu@csueastbay.edu. *Application contact:* Donna Wiley, Interim Associate Director, 510-885-2928, Fax: 510-885-4777.

California State University, Fullerton, Graduate Studies, College of Business and Economics, Department of Information Systems and Decision Sciences, Fullerton, CA 92834-9480. Offers information systems (MS); information systems (decision sciences) (MS); information systems (e-commerce) (MS); information technology (MS); management science (MBA). Part-time programs available. *Students:* 15 full-time (2 women), 66 part-time (10 women); includes 35 minority (1 Black or African American, non-Hispanic/Latino; 23 Asian, non-Hispanic/Latino; 9 Hispanic/Latino; 2 Two or more races, non-Hispanic/Latino), 9 international. Average age 33. 82 applicants, 44% accepted, 30 enrolled. In 2011, 36 master's awarded. *Degree requirements:* For master's, project or thesis. *Entrance requirements:* For master's, GMAT, minimum AACSB index of 950. Application fee: $55. *Financial support:* Career-related internships or fieldwork, Federal Work-Study, institutionally sponsored loans, and scholarships/grants available. Support available to part-time students. Financial award application deadline: 3/1; financial award applicants required to submit FAFSA. *Unit head:* Dr. Bhushan Kapoor, Chair, 657-278-2221. *Application contact:* Admissions/Applications, 657-278-2371.

California State University, Los Angeles, Graduate Studies, College of Business and Economics, Department of Information Systems, Los Angeles, CA 90032-8530. Offers business information systems (MBA); management (MS); management information systems (MS); office management (MBA). Part-time and evening/weekend programs available. *Faculty:* 2 full-time (1 woman), 1 part-time/adjunct (0 women). *Students:* 3 full-time (1 woman), 8 part-time (3 women); includes 4 minority (3 Asian, non-Hispanic/Latino; 1 Hispanic/Latino), 3 international. Average age 32. 20 applicants, 20% accepted, 2 enrolled. In 2011, 26 master's awarded. *Degree requirements:* For master's, comprehensive exam (MBA), thesis (MS). *Entrance requirements:* For master's, GMAT, minimum GPA of 2.5 during previous 2 years of course work. Additional exam requirements/recommendations for international students: Required—TOEFL (minimum score 550 paper-based; 213 computer-based). *Application deadline:* For fall admission, 5/1 for domestic and international students. Applications are processed on a rolling basis. Application fee: $55. Electronic applications accepted. *Expenses:* Tuition, state resident: full-time $8225. *Financial support:* Career-related internships or fieldwork and Federal Work-Study available. Support available to part-time students. Financial award application deadline: 3/1. *Unit head:* Dr. Nanda Ganesen, Chair, 323-343-2983, E-mail:

nganesa@calstatela.edu. *Application contact:* Dr. Karin Brown, Acting Associate Dean of Graduate Studies, 323-343-3820, Fax: 323-343-5653, E-mail: kbrown5@calstatela.edu.

California State University, Monterey Bay, College of Science, Media Arts and Technology, School of Information Technology and Communication Design, Seaside, CA 93955-8001. Offers interdisciplinary studies (MA), including instructional science and technology; management and information technology (MA). *Degree requirements:* For master's, capstone or thesis. *Entrance requirements:* For master's, GRE, 2 letters of recommendation, minimum GPA of 3.0, technology screening assessment. Additional exam requirements/recommendations for international students: Required—TOEFL (minimum score 550 paper-based; 213 computer-based; 71 iBT). Electronic applications accepted. *Faculty research:* Electronic commerce, e-learning, knowledge management, international business, business and public policy.

California State University, San Bernardino, Graduate Studies, College of Business and Public Administration, Master in Business Administration Program, San Bernardino, CA 92407. Offers accounting (MBA); entrepreneurship (MBA); executives (MBA); finance (MBA); global business (MBA); information assurance and security management (MBA); information management (MBA); management (MBA); marketing (MBA); professionals (MBA); supply chain management (MBA). *Accreditation:* AACSB. Part-time and evening/weekend programs available. Postbaccalaureate distance learning degree programs offered (no on-campus study). *Faculty:* 58 full-time (11 women), 26 part-time/adjunct (9 women). *Students:* 80 full-time (31 women), 137 part-time (56 women); includes 82 minority (19 Black or African American, non-Hispanic/Latino; 3 American Indian or Alaska Native, non-Hispanic/Latino; 20 Asian, non-Hispanic/Latino; 37 Hispanic/Latino; 3 Two or more races, non-Hispanic/Latino), 65 international. Average age 30. 217 applicants, 65% accepted, 79 enrolled. In 2011, 120 master's awarded. *Degree requirements:* For master's, comprehensive exam, thesis optional, portfolio, 48 units, minimum GPA of 3.0. *Entrance requirements:* For master's, GMAT, minimum GPA of 2.5. Additional exam requirements/recommendations for international students: Required—TOEFL (minimum score 550 paper-based; 213 computer-based; 79 iBT). *Application deadline:* For fall admission, 7/12 priority date for domestic students, 7/12 for international students; for winter admission, 10/26 priority date for domestic students, 10/26 for international students; for spring admission, 1/25 priority date for domestic students, 1/25 for international students. Applications are processed on a rolling basis. Application fee: $55. Electronic applications accepted. *Expenses:* Contact institution. *Financial support:* In 2011–12, 56 students received support, including 34 fellowships (averaging $3,732 per year), 18 research assistantships (averaging $2,193 per year), 4 teaching assistantships (averaging $2,606 per year); career-related internships or fieldwork, Federal Work-Study, institutionally sponsored loans, scholarships/grants, and unspecified assistantships also available. Support available to part-time students. Financial award application deadline: 3/1; financial award applicants required to submit FAFSA. *Faculty research:* Fraud, Stock Exchange, small business, logistics, job analysis. *Total annual research expenditures:* $4.8 million. *Unit head:* Dr. Lawrence C. Rose, Dean, 909-537-3703, Fax: 909-537-7026, E-mail: lrose@csusb.edu. *Application contact:* Dr. Sandra Kamusikiri, Associate Vice-President/Dean of Graduate Studies, 909-537-7058, Fax: 909-537-5078, E-mail: skamusik@csusb.edu. Web site: http://mba.csusb.edu/.

Capella University, School of Business and Technology, Minneapolis, MN 55402. Offers accounting (MBA), including system design and programming; business (Certificate), including human resource management (MS, PhD, Certificate), information technology management (MS, PhD, Certificate), leadership (MBA, MS, PhD, Certificate); finance (MBA); general business (MBA); health care management (MBA); information technology (MS, Certificate), including general information technology (MS), information security, network architecture and design (MS), professional projects management (Certificate), project management and leadership (MS), system design and development (MS),); information technology management (MBA); marketing (MBA); organization and management (MBA, MS, PhD), including general business (PhD), general organization and management (MBA, MS), human resource management (MS, PhD, Certificate), information technology management (MS, PhD, Certificate), leadership (MBA, MS, PhD, Certificate); project management (MBA). Part-time and evening/weekend programs available. Postbaccalaureate distance learning degree programs offered (minimal on-campus study). Terminal master's awarded for partial completion of doctoral program. *Degree requirements:* For master's, thesis optional, integrative project; for doctorate, comprehensive exam, thesis/dissertation. *Entrance requirements:* Additional exam requirements/recommendations for international students: Required—TOEFL (minimum score 550 paper-based; 213 computer-based), TWE (minimum score 4). Electronic applications accepted. *Faculty research:* Business policies: strategic, corporate, and financial management; interplay of technological, organizational and social change.

Capitol College, Graduate Programs, Laurel, MD 20708-9759. Offers business administration (MBA); computer science (MS); electrical engineering (MS); information and telecommunications systems management (MS); information architecture (MS); network security (MS). Part-time and evening/weekend programs available. Postbaccalaureate distance learning degree programs offered (no on-campus study). *Entrance requirements:* For master's, minimum GPA of 3.0. Electronic applications accepted.

Carnegie Mellon University, Heinz College Australia, Master of Science in Information Technology Program (Adelaide, South Australia), Adelaide, PA 5000, Australia. Offers MSIT. *Entrance requirements:* For master's, GRE or GMAT, college-level course in advanced algebra/pre-calculus; college-level courses in economics and statistics (recommended). Additional exam requirements/recommendations for international students: Required—TOEFL or IELTS.

Carnegie Mellon University, Heinz College, School of Information Systems and Management, Master of Information Systems Management Program, Pittsburgh, PA 15213-3891. Offers MISM. *Entrance requirements:* For master's, GRE or GMAT, college-level course in advanced algebra/pre-calculus; college-level courses in economics and statistics (recommended). Additional exam requirements/recommendations for international students: Required—TOEFL or IELTS.

Carnegie Mellon University, Heinz College, School of Information Systems and Management, Master of Science in Information Security Policy and Management Program, Pittsburgh, PA 15213-3891. Offers MSISPM. *Entrance requirements:* For master's, GRE or GMAT, college-level course in advanced algebra/pre-calculus; college-level courses in economics and statistics (recommended). Additional exam requirements/recommendations for international students: Required—TOEFL or IELTS.

Carnegie Mellon University, Heinz College, School of Information Systems and Management, Program in Information Technology, Pittsburgh, PA 15213-3891. Offers MSIT.

Carnegie Mellon University, Tepper School of Business, Program in Information Systems, Pittsburgh, PA 15213-3891. Offers PhD. *Degree requirements:* For doctorate, thesis/dissertation. *Entrance requirements:* For doctorate, GRE General Test.

Case Western Reserve University, Weatherhead School of Management, Department of Information Systems, Cleveland, OH 44106. Offers MBA. Part-time and evening/weekend programs available. *Entrance requirements:* For master's, GMAT. *Faculty research:* Decision support, business forecasting systems, design and use of information systems, artificial intelligence, executive information systems.

Case Western Reserve University, Weatherhead School of Management, Department of Operations, Cleveland, OH 44106. Offers management (MS, MSM), including finance (MS), information systems (MS), marketing (MS), operations research, quality management (MS), supply chain (MSM); management for liberal arts graduates (MSM); operations research (PhD); MBA/MSM. Part-time programs available. *Degree requirements:* For doctorate, thesis/dissertation. *Entrance requirements:* For master's, GRE General Test; for doctorate, GMAT, GRE General Test. *Faculty research:* Mathematical finance, mathematical programming, scheduling, stochastic optimization, environmental/energy models.

Central European University, CEU Business School, Budapest, Hungary. Offers executive business administration (EMBA); finance (MBA); general management (MBA); information technology management (MBA); marketing (MBA); real estate management (MBA). Part-time and evening/weekend programs available. *Faculty:* 17 full-time (4 women), 12 part-time/adjunct (1 woman). *Students:* 31 full-time (12 women), 84 part-time (16 women). Average age 34. 162 applicants, 35% accepted, 31 enrolled. In 2011, 83 degrees awarded. *Degree requirements:* For master's, one foreign language. *Entrance requirements:* For master's, GMAT. Additional exam requirements/recommendations for international students: Required—TOEFL (minimum score 570 paper-based; 230 computer-based); Recommended—IELTS (minimum score 6.5). *Application deadline:* For fall admission, 5/15 priority date for domestic students, 5/22 for international students; for winter admission, 11/15 priority date for domestic students, 11/10 for international students. Applications are processed on a rolling basis. Application fee: $0. Electronic applications accepted. Tuition charges are reported in euros. *Expenses: Tuition:* Full-time 11,000 euros. *Financial support:* Tuition waivers (partial) available. *Faculty research:* Social and ethical business, marketing, international business. *Unit head:* Dr. Mel Horwitch, Dean and Managing Director, 361-887-5050, E-mail: mhorwitch@ceubusiness.com. *Application contact:* Agnes Schram, Admissions Manager, 361-887-5111, Fax: 361-887-5133, E-mail: mba@ceubusiness.com. Web site: http://www.ceubusiness.com.

Central Michigan University, Central Michigan University Global Campus, Program in Administration, Mount Pleasant, MI 48859. Offers acquisitions administration (MSA, Certificate); general administration (MSA, Certificate); health services administration (MSA, Certificate); human resources administration (MSA, Certificate); information resource management (MSA, Certificate); international administration (MSA, Certificate); leadership (MSA, Certificate); public administration (MSA, Certificate); research administration (MSA, Certificate). Part-time and evening/weekend programs available. Postbaccalaureate distance learning degree programs offered (no on-campus study). *Students:* Average age 38. *Entrance requirements:* For master's, minimum GPA of 2.7 in major. *Application deadline:* Applications are processed on a rolling basis. Application fee: $50. Electronic applications accepted. *Financial support:* Scholarships/grants available. Support available to part-time students. Financial award applicants required to submit FAFSA. *Unit head:* Dr. Nana Korsah, Director, 989-774-6525, E-mail: korsa1na@cmich.edu. *Application contact:* 877-268-4636, E-mail: cmuglobal@cmich.edu.

Central Michigan University, College of Graduate Studies, College of Business Administration, Department of Business Information Systems, Mount Pleasant, MI 48859. Offers business computing (Graduate Certificate); information systems (MS), including enterprise software, general business, systems applications. Part-time and evening/weekend programs available. *Degree requirements:* For master's, thesis or alternative. Electronic applications accepted. *Faculty research:* Enterprise software, electronic commerce, decision support systems, ethical issues in information systems, information technology management and teaching issues.

Central Michigan University, College of Graduate Studies, Interdisciplinary Administration Programs, Mount Pleasant, MI 48859. Offers acquisitions administration (MSA, Graduate Certificate); general administration (MSA, Graduate Certificate); health services administration (MSA, Graduate Certificate); human resource administration (Graduate Certificate); human resources administration (MSA); information resource management (MSA, Graduate Certificate); international administration (MSA, Graduate Certificate); leadership (MSA, Graduate Certificate); organizational communication (MSA, Graduate Certificate); public administration (MSA, Graduate Certificate); recreation and park administration (MSA); sport administration (MSA). *Accreditation:* AACSB. Part-time and evening/weekend programs available. Postbaccalaureate distance learning degree programs offered (no on-campus study). *Degree requirements:* For master's, thesis or alternative. *Entrance requirements:* For master's, bachelor's degree with minimum GPA of 2.7. Electronic applications accepted. *Faculty research:* Interdisciplinary studies in acquisitions administration, health services administration, sport administration, recreation and park administration, and international administration.

Charleston Southern University, Program in Business, Charleston, SC 29423-8087. Offers accounting (MBA); finance (MBA); health care administration (MBA); information systems (MBA); organizational development (MBA). Part-time and evening/weekend programs available. *Degree requirements:* For master's, thesis optional. *Entrance requirements:* For master's, GMAT. Additional exam requirements/recommendations for international students: Required—TOEFL (minimum score 550 paper-based; 213 computer-based; 79 iBT).

City University of Seattle, Graduate Division, School of Management, Bellevue, WA 98005. Offers accounting (Certificate); change leadership (MBA, Certificate); computer systems (MS); finance (Certificate); financial management (MBA); general management (MBA); general management-Europe (MBA); global marketing (MBA); human resources management (Certificate); individualized study (MBA); information security (MS); information systems (MBA); leadership (MA); marketing (MBA, Certificate); project management (MBA, MS, Certificate); sustainable business (Certificate); technology management (MBA, Certificate). Part-time and evening/weekend programs available. Postbaccalaureate distance learning degree programs offered (no on-campus study). *Faculty:* 6 full-time (2 women), 95 part-time/adjunct (33 women). *Students:* 397 full-time (193 women), 283 part-time (137 women); includes 127 minority (67 Black or African American, non-Hispanic/Latino; 5 American Indian or Alaska Native, non-Hispanic/Latino; 33 Asian, non-Hispanic/Latino; 15 Hispanic/Latino; 1 Native Hawaiian or other Pacific Islander, non-Hispanic/Latino; 6 Two or more races, non-Hispanic/Latino), 117 international. Average age 36. 151 applicants, 100% accepted, 151 enrolled. In 2011, 369 master's, 32 other advanced degrees awarded. *Degree requirements:* For master's, comprehensive exam (for some programs), thesis (for some programs). *Entrance requirements:* Additional exam requirements/recommendations for international students: Required—TOEFL (minimum score 567 paper-based; 227 computer-based; 87 iBT); Recommended—IELTS. *Application deadline:* For fall admission, 9/1 for international students; for winter admission, 12/1 for international students; for spring admission, 3/1 for international students. Applications are processed on a rolling basis. Application fee: $50. Electronic applications accepted. *Financial support:* Federal Work-Study and scholarships/grants available. Support available to part-time students. Financial award applicants required to submit FAFSA. *Unit head:* Dr. Kurt Kirstein,

Dean, 425-637-1010 Ext. 5456, Fax: 425-709-5363, E-mail: kdkirstein@cityu.edu. *Application contact:* Alysa Borelli, Director, Recruiting, 888-422-4898, Fax: 425-709-5363, E-mail: info@cityu.edu. Web site: http://www.cityu.edu/programs/som/index.aspx.

Claremont Graduate University, Graduate Programs, School of Information Systems and Technology, Claremont, CA 91711-6160. Offers electronic commerce (MS, PhD); health information management (MS); information systems (Certificate); knowledge management (MS, PhD); systems development (MS, PhD); telecommunications and networking (MS, PhD); MBA/MS. Part-time programs available. *Faculty:* 7 full-time (1 woman), 1 part-time/adjunct (0 women). *Students:* 68 full-time (20 women), 26 part-time (10 women); includes 31 minority (5 Black or African American, non-Hispanic/Latino; 14 Asian, non-Hispanic/Latino; 9 Hispanic/Latino; 1 Native Hawaiian or other Pacific Islander, non-Hispanic/Latino; 2 Two or more races, non-Hispanic/Latino), 31 international. Average age 37. In 2011, 16 master's, 5 doctorates awarded. *Degree requirements:* For doctorate, comprehensive exam, thesis/dissertation, portfolio. *Entrance requirements:* For master's and doctorate, GMAT, GRE General Test. Additional exam requirements/recommendations for international students: Required—TOEFL (minimum score 550 paper-based; 213 computer-based; 80 iBT). *Application deadline:* For fall admission, 2/1 priority date for domestic students. Applications are processed on a rolling basis. Application fee: $60. Electronic applications accepted. *Expenses: Tuition:* Full-time $36,374; part-time $1581 per unit. *Required fees:* $165 per semester. *Financial support:* Fellowships, research assistantships, teaching assistantships, Federal Work-Study, institutionally sponsored loans, and scholarships/grants available. Support available to part-time students. Financial award application deadline: 2/15; financial award applicants required to submit FAFSA. *Faculty research:* GPSS, man-machine interaction, organizational aspects of computing, implementation of information systems, information systems practice. *Unit head:* Tom Horan, Dean, 909-607-9302, Fax: 909-621-8564, E-mail: tom.horan@cgu.edu. *Application contact:* Anondah Saide, Program Coordinator, 909-607-6006, E-mail: anonda.saide@cgu.edu. Web site: http://www.cgu.edu/pages/153.asp.

Clark University, Graduate School, Graduate School of Management, Business Administration Program, Worcester, MA 01610-1477. Offers accounting (MBA); finance (MBA); global business (MBA); health care management (MBA); management (MBA); management of information technology (MBA); marketing (MBA). *Accreditation:* AACSB. Part-time and evening/weekend programs available. *Students:* 103 full-time (47 women), 108 part-time (41 women); includes 16 minority (7 Black or African American, non-Hispanic/Latino; 5 Asian, non-Hispanic/Latino; 4 Hispanic/Latino), 69 international. Average age 30. 371 applicants, 48% accepted, 77 enrolled. In 2011, 112 master's awarded. *Degree requirements:* For master's, thesis optional. *Application deadline:* For fall admission, 6/1 priority date for domestic students; for spring admission, 12/1 priority date for domestic students. Applications are processed on a rolling basis. Application fee: $50. Electronic applications accepted. *Expenses: Tuition:* Full-time $37,000; part-time $1156 per credit hour. *Financial support:* In 2011–12, research assistantships with partial tuition reimbursements (averaging $4,800 per year), teaching assistantships with partial tuition reimbursements (averaging $4,800 per year) were awarded; fellowships, career-related internships or fieldwork, Federal Work-Study, institutionally sponsored loans, and tuition waivers (partial) also available. Support available to part-time students. Financial award application deadline: 5/31. *Faculty research:* Marketing, accounting, human resource management, management information systems, business finance. *Unit head:* Dr. Catherine Usoff, Dean, 508-793-8822, Fax: 508-793-8822, E-mail: clarkmba@clarku.edu. *Application contact:* Patrick Oroszko, Enrollment and Marketing Director, 508-793-8822, Fax: 508-793-8822, E-mail: clarkmba@clarku.edu. Web site: http://www.clarku.edu/gsom/prospective/mba/.

Cleveland State University, College of Graduate Studies, Monte Ahuja College of Business, Department of Computer and Information Science, Cleveland, OH 44115. Offers computer and information science (MCIS); information systems (DBA). Part-time and evening/weekend programs available. *Faculty:* 12 full-time (2 women), 3 part-time/adjunct (2 women). *Students:* 18 full-time (8 women), 70 part-time (15 women); includes 6 minority (3 Black or African American, non-Hispanic/Latino; 3 Asian, non-Hispanic/Latino), 51 international. Average age 27. 344 applicants, 71% accepted, 34 enrolled. In 2011, 34 master's awarded. Terminal master's awarded for partial completion of doctoral program. *Degree requirements:* For master's, thesis optional; for doctorate, comprehensive exam, thesis/dissertation. *Entrance requirements:* For master's, GRE or GMAT, minimum GPA of 2.75; for doctorate, GRE or GMAT, MBA, MCIS or equivalent. Additional exam requirements/recommendations for international students: Required—TOEFL (minimum score 525 paper-based; 197 computer-based; 78 iBT). *Application deadline:* For fall admission, 7/15 priority date for domestic students, 5/15 for international students; for spring admission, 12/15 priority date for domestic students. Applications are processed on a rolling basis. Application fee: $30. Electronic applications accepted. *Expenses:* Tuition, state resident: full-time $6416; part-time $494 per credit hour. Tuition, nonresident: full-time $12,074; part-time $929 per credit hour. *Financial support:* In 2011–12, 21 students received support, including 7 research assistantships with full and partial tuition reimbursements available (averaging $7,800 per year), 2 teaching assistantships with full and partial tuition reimbursements available (averaging $16,000 per year); career-related internships or fieldwork, tuition waivers (full), and unspecified assistantships also available. *Faculty research:* Artificial intelligence, object-oriented analysis, database design, software efficiency, distributed system, geographical information systems. *Total annual research expenditures:* $7,500. *Unit head:* Dr. Santosh K. Misra, Chairman, 216-687-4760, Fax: 216-687-5448, E-mail: s.misra@csuohio.edu. *Application contact:* 216-687-4760, Fax: 216-687-9354, E-mail: s.misra@csuohio.edu. Web site: http://cis.csuohio.edu/.

Cleveland State University, College of Graduate Studies, Monte Ahuja College of Business, Doctor of Business Administration Program, Cleveland, OH 44115. Offers finance (DBA); global business (DBA); information systems (DBA); marketing (DBA); operations management (DBA). *Accreditation:* AACSB. Part-time and evening/weekend programs available. *Faculty:* 50 full-time (11 women). *Students:* 4 full-time (1 woman), 34 part-time (12 women); includes 3 minority (1 Black or African American, non-Hispanic/Latino; 2 Asian, non-Hispanic/Latino), 11 international. Average age 40. In 2011, 5 doctorates awarded. *Degree requirements:* For doctorate, comprehensive exam, thesis/dissertation, oral dissertation defense. *Entrance requirements:* For doctorate, GMAT, MBA or equivalent. Additional exam requirements/recommendations for international students: Required—TOEFL (minimum score 550 paper-based; 213 computer-based; 79 iBT). *Application deadline:* For spring admission, 2/28 priority date for domestic students, 2/28 for international students. Application fee: $30. Electronic applications accepted. *Expenses:* Tuition, state resident: full-time $6416; part-time $494 per credit hour. Tuition, nonresident: full-time $12,074; part-time $929 per credit hour. *Financial support:* In 2011–12, 5 research assistantships with full tuition reimbursements (averaging $12,700 per year), 4 teaching assistantships with full tuition reimbursements (averaging $12,700 per year) were awarded; tuition waivers (full) and unspecified assistantships also available. *Faculty research:* Supply chain management, international business, strategic management, risk analysis, consumer behavior. *Unit head:* Dr. Raj Shekhar G. Javalgi, Director, 216-687-3786, Fax: 216-687-9354, E-mail: r.javalgi@csuohio.edu. *Application contact:* Melinda J. Arnold, Administrative Secretary, 216-687-6952, Fax: 216-687-9257, E-mail: m.arnold@csuohio.edu. Web site: http://www.csuohio.edu/business/academics/doctoral.html.

College of Charleston, Graduate School, School of Sciences and Mathematics, Program in Computer and Information Sciences, Charleston, SC 29424-0001. Offers MS. Program offered jointly with The Citadel, The Military College of South Carolina. Part-time and evening/weekend programs available. *Faculty:* 11 full-time (3 women). *Students:* 6 full-time (1 woman), 18 part-time (2 women); includes 2 minority (1 American Indian or Alaska Native, non-Hispanic/Latino; 1 Asian, non-Hispanic/Latino), 2 international. Average age 32. 13 applicants, 62% accepted, 8 enrolled. In 2011, 6 degrees awarded. *Degree requirements:* For master's, thesis optional. *Entrance requirements:* For master's, GRE. Additional exam requirements/recommendations for international students: Required—TOEFL (minimum score 81 iBT). *Application deadline:* For fall admission, 6/1 for domestic students; for spring admission, 11/1 for domestic students. Application fee: $45. Electronic applications accepted. *Expenses:* Tuition, state resident: full-time $5455; part-time $455 per credit. Tuition, nonresident: full-time $13,917; part-time $1160 per credit. *Financial support:* In 2011–12, research assistantships (averaging $12,400 per year) were awarded; Federal Work-Study, scholarships/grants, and unspecified assistantships also available. Support available to part-time students. Financial award application deadline: 4/1; financial award applicants required to submit FAFSA. *Unit head:* Dr. Renee McCauley, Director, 843-953-3187, E-mail: mccauleyr@cofc.edu. *Application contact:* Susan Hallatt, Director of Graduate Admissions, 843-953-5614, Fax: 843-953-1434, E-mail: hallatts@cofc.edu.

The College of St. Scholastica, Graduate Studies, Department of Computer Information Systems, Duluth, MN 55811-4199. Offers MA, Certificate. Part-time programs available. Postbaccalaureate distance learning degree programs offered (minimal on-campus study). *Faculty:* 1 full-time (0 women), 4 part-time/adjunct (0 women). *Students:* 12 full-time (3 women), 9 part-time (4 women); includes 3 minority (1 American Indian or Alaska Native, non-Hispanic/Latino; 2 Asian, non-Hispanic/Latino). Average age 35. 21 applicants, 81% accepted, 7 enrolled. In 2011, 10 master's awarded. *Degree requirements:* For master's, thesis. *Entrance requirements:* For master's, minimum GPA of 2.8. Additional exam requirements/recommendations for international students: Required—TOEFL (minimum score 550 paper-based; 213 computer-based; 79 iBT). *Application deadline:* For fall admission, 8/1 priority date for domestic students, 8/1 for international students; for spring admission, 11/15 priority date for domestic students, 11/15 for international students. Application fee: $50. *Expenses:* Contact institution. *Financial support:* In 2011–12, 1 teaching assistantship (averaging $2,235 per year) was awarded. Support available to part-time students. Financial award applicants required to submit FAFSA. *Faculty research:* Organization acceptance of software development methodologies. *Unit head:* Brandon Olson, Program Coordinator, 218-723-6199, E-mail: bolson@css.edu. *Application contact:* Lindsay Lahti, Director of Graduate and Extended Studies Recruitment, 218-733-2240, Fax: 218-733-2275, E-mail: gradstudies@css.edu. Web site: http://grad.css.edu/cis/.

Colorado State University, Graduate School, College of Business, Department of Computer Information Systems, Fort Collins, CO 80523-1277. Offers MSBA. Part-time programs available. *Faculty:* 11 full-time (2 women). *Students:* Average age 31. *Degree requirements:* For master's, thesis or alternative, project. *Entrance requirements:* For master's, GMAT, minimum GPA of 3.0. Additional exam requirements/recommendations for international students: Required—TOEFL (minimum score 565 paper-based; 227 computer-based; 86 iBT). *Application deadline:* For fall admission, 7/15 for domestic students, 4/1 for international students. Applications are processed on a rolling basis. Application fee: $50. Electronic applications accepted. *Expenses:* Tuition, state resident: full-time $7992. Tuition, nonresident: full-time $19,592. *Required fees:* $1735; $58 per credit. *Financial support:* In 2011–12, 1 student received support, including 1 research assistantship (averaging $10,275 per year); fellowships, teaching assistantships with full and partial tuition reimbursements available, career-related internships or fieldwork, Federal Work-Study, scholarships/grants, traineeships, and unspecified assistantships also available. Support available to part-time students. Financial award application deadline: 3/1; financial award applicants required to submit FAFSA. *Faculty research:* Decision-making, object-oriented design, database research, electronic marketing, e-commerce. *Total annual research expenditures:* $20,898. *Unit head:* Dr. Jon D. Clark, Chair, 970-491-1618, Fax: 970-491-5205, E-mail: jon.clark@business.colostate.edu. *Application contact:* Janet Estes, Associate Dean of Graduate Programs, 970-491-4612, Fax: 970-491-5205, E-mail: janet.estes@colostate.edu. Web site: http://www.biz.colostate.edu/cis/Pages/default.aspx.

Colorado Technical University Sioux Falls, Programs in Business Administration and Management, Sioux Falls, SD 57108. Offers business administration (MBA); business management (MSM); health science management (MSM); human resources management (MSM); information technology (MSM); organizational leadership (MSM); project management (MBA); technology management (MBA). Evening/weekend programs available. *Degree requirements:* For master's, thesis optional. *Entrance requirements:* For master's, minimum 2 years work experience, resume.

Concordia University Wisconsin, Graduate Programs, School of Business and Legal Studies, MBA Program, Mequon, WI 53097-2402. Offers finance (MBA); health care administration (MBA); human resource management (MBA); international business (MBA); international business-bilingual English/Chinese (MBA); management (MBA); management information systems (MBA); managerial communications (MBA); marketing (MBA); public administration (MBA); risk management (MBA). Postbaccalaureate distance learning degree programs offered (minimal on-campus study). *Students:* 308 full-time (146 women), 536 part-time (288 women); includes 126 minority (76 Black or African American, non-Hispanic/Latino; 9 American Indian or Alaska Native, non-Hispanic/Latino; 15 Asian, non-Hispanic/Latino; 12 Hispanic/Latino; 14 Two or more races, non-Hispanic/Latino), 276 international. Average age 35. In 2011, 110 master's awarded. *Degree requirements:* For master's, comprehensive exam, thesis or alternative. *Entrance requirements:* Additional exam requirements/recommendations for international students: Required—TOEFL. *Application deadline:* For fall admission, 8/1 priority date for domestic students; for spring admission, 1/15 for domestic students. Applications are processed on a rolling basis. Application fee: $50. *Expenses:* Contact institution. *Financial support:* Application deadline: 8/1. *Unit head:* Dr. David Borst, Director, 262-243-4298, Fax: 262-243-4428, E-mail: david.borst@cuw.edu. *Application contact:* Mary Eberhardt, Graduate Admissions, 262-243-4551, Fax: 262-243-4428, E-mail: mary.eberhardt@cuw.edu.

Copenhagen Business School, Graduate Programs, Copenhagen, Denmark. Offers business administration (Exec MBA, MBA, PhD); business administration and information systems (M Sc); business, language and culture (M Sc); economics and business administration (M Sc); health management (MHM); international business and politics (M Sc); public administration (MPA); shipping and logistics (Exec MBA); technology, market and organization (MBA).

Creighton University, Graduate School, Eugene C. Eppley College of Business Administration, Omaha, NE 68178-0001. Offers business administration (MBA); information technology management (MS); securities and portfolio management (MSAPM); JD/MBA; MBA/MS-ITM; MBA/MSAPM; MD/MBA; MS ITM/JD; Pharm D/MBA. *Accreditation:* AACSB. Part-time and evening/weekend programs available. Postbaccalaureate distance learning degree programs offered (minimal on-campus

(52 women); includes 39 minority (23 Black or African American, non-Hispanic/Latino; 2 American Indian or Alaska Native, non-Hispanic/Latino; 4 Asian, non-Hispanic/Latino; 7 Hispanic/Latino; 3 Native Hawaiian or other Pacific Islander, non-Hispanic/Latino), 16 international. Average age 32. 130 applicants, 98% accepted, 120 enrolled. In 2011, 130 master's awarded. *Degree requirements:* For master's, thesis optional. *Entrance requirements:* For master's, GMAT, resume, 2 letters of recommendation. Additional exam requirements/recommendations for international students: Required—TOEFL (minimum score 550 paper-based; 213 computer-based; 80 iBT). *Application deadline:* For fall admission, 7/1 priority date for domestic students, 3/1 for international students; for winter admission, 10/1 priority date for domestic students, 7/1 for international students; for spring admission, 4/1 priority date for domestic students, 10/1 for international students. Applications are processed on a rolling basis. Application fee: $50. Electronic applications accepted. *Expenses: Tuition:* Full-time $12,672; part-time $704 per credit hour. *Required fees:* $1410; $136 per semester. Tuition and fees vary according to campus/location and reciprocity agreements. *Financial support:* In 2011–12, 10 fellowships with partial tuition reimbursements (averaging $8,448 per year) were awarded; career-related internships or fieldwork, tuition waivers (partial), and unspecified assistantships also available. Financial award application deadline: 3/1. *Faculty research:* Small business issues, economics. *Unit head:* Dr. Deborah Wells, Associate Dean for Graduate Programs, 402-280-2841, E-mail: deborahwells@creighton.edu. *Application contact:* Gail Hafer, Assistant Dean, 402-280-2829, Fax: 402-280-2172, E-mail: ghafer@creighton.edu. Web site: http://business.creighton.edu.

Daemen College, Department of Accounting/Information Systems, Amherst, NY 14226-3592. Offers global business (MS), including accounting, global business, management information systems, marketing. Part-time and evening/weekend programs available. *Degree requirements:* For master's, minimum GPA of 3.0. *Entrance requirements:* For master's, GMAT if undergraduate GPA is less than 3.0, 2 letters of recommendation; goal statement; transcripts; demonstration of satisfactory oral and written English. Additional exam requirements/recommendations for international students: Required—TOEFL (minimum score 500 paper-based; 173 computer-based; 63 iBT), IELTS (minimum score 5.5). Electronic applications accepted. *Faculty research:* Internationalization of small business, cultural influences on business practices, international human resource practices.

Dalhousie University, Faculty of Management, Centre for Advanced Management Education, Halifax, NS B3H 3J5, Canada. Offers financial services (MBA); information management (MIM); management (MPA); natural resources (MBA). Part-time programs available. Postbaccalaureate distance learning degree programs offered. *Entrance requirements:* For master's, GMAT, minimum GPA of 3.0, resume. Additional exam requirements/recommendations for international students: Required—TOEFL, IELTS, CANTEST, CAEL, or Michigan English Language Assessment Battery. Electronic applications accepted.

Dallas Baptist University, College of Business, Business Administration Program, Dallas, TX 75211-9299. Offers accounting (MBA); business communication (MBA); conflict resolution management (MBA); entrepreneurship (MBA); finance (MBA); health care management (MBA); international business (MBA); leading the non-profit organization (MBA); management (MBA); management information systems (MBA); marketing (MBA); project management (MBA); technology and engineering management (MBA). *Accreditation:* ACBSP. Part-time and evening/weekend programs available. *Entrance requirements:* For master's, GMAT, minimum GPA of 3.0. Additional exam requirements/recommendations for international students: Required—TOEFL, IELTS. *Application deadline:* Applications are processed on a rolling basis. Application fee: $25. Electronic applications accepted. *Expenses: Tuition:* Full-time $12,060; part-time $670 per credit hour. *Required fees:* $100; $50 per semester. *Financial support:* Federal Work-Study, institutionally sponsored loans, scholarships/grants, and tuition waivers (full and partial) available. Support available to part-time students. Financial award applicants required to submit FAFSA. *Faculty research:* Sports management, services marketing, retailing, strategic management, financial planning/investments. *Unit head:* Dr. Sandra S. Reid, Director, 214-333-5280, Fax: 214-333-5293, E-mail: graduate@dbu.edu. *Application contact:* Kit P. Montgomery, Director of Graduate Programs, 214-333-5242, Fax: 214-333-5579, E-mail: graduate@dbu.edu. Web site: http://www3.dbu.edu/graduate/mba.asp.

Dallas Baptist University, Professional Development Program, Dallas, TX 75211-9299. Offers accounting (MA); church leadership (MA); counseling (MA); criminal justice (MA); English as a second language (MA); finance (MA); higher education (MA); leadership studies (MA); management (MA); management information systems (MA); marketing (MA); missions (MA); professional life coaching (MA). Part-time and evening/weekend programs available. *Entrance requirements:* For master's, minimum GPA of 3.0. Additional exam requirements/recommendations for international students: Required—TOEFL, IELTS. Application fee: $25. *Expenses: Tuition:* Full-time $12,060; part-time $670 per credit hour. *Required fees:* $100; $50 per semester. *Financial support:* Federal Work-Study, institutionally sponsored loans, scholarships/grants, and tuition waivers (full and partial) available. Support available to part-time students. Financial award applicants required to submit FAFSA. *Unit head:* Angela Fogle, Acting Director, 214-333-6830, Fax: 214-333-5558, E-mail: graduate@dbu.edu. *Application contact:* Kit P. Montgomery, Director of Graduate Programs, 214-333-5242, Fax: 214-333-5579, E-mail: graduate@dbu.edu. Web site: http://www3.dbu.edu/graduate/mapd.asp.

DePaul University, Charles H. Kellstadt Graduate School of Business, School of Accountancy and Management Information Systems, Chicago, IL 60604-2287. Offers accountancy (M Acc, MSA); business information technology (MS); e-business (MBA, MS); financial management and control (MBA); management accounting (MBA); management information systems (MBA); taxation (MST). Part-time and evening/weekend programs available. *Faculty:* 30 full-time (9 women), 54 part-time/adjunct (7 women). *Students:* 44 full-time (13 women), 22 part-time (4 women); includes 8 minority (2 Black or African American, non-Hispanic/Latino; 3 Asian, non-Hispanic/Latino; 2 Hispanic/Latino; 1 Two or more races, non-Hispanic/Latino), 4 international. Average age 29. In 2011, 141 master's awarded. *Entrance requirements:* For master's, GMAT, 2 letters of recommendation, resume. Additional exam requirements/recommendations for international students: Required—TOEFL (minimum score 550 paper-based; 213 computer-based). *Application deadline:* For fall admission, 7/1 for domestic students; for winter admission, 10/1 for domestic students; for spring admission, 2/1 for domestic students. Applications are processed on a rolling basis. Application fee: $60. *Financial support:* In 2011–12, 7 research assistantships with full tuition reimbursements (averaging $4,100 per year) were awarded; institutionally sponsored loans also available. Financial award application deadline: 4/2. *Faculty research:* Tax policy, property transactions, stock options as compensation, standards setting, activity-based costing in health care. *Unit head:* Kevin Stevens, Director, 312-362-6989, E-mail: kstevens@depaul.edu. *Application contact:* Christopher E. Kinsella, Director of Cohort MBA Programs, 312-362-8810, Fax: 312-362-6677, E-mail: kgsb@depaul.edu. Web site: http://accountancy.depaul.edu/.

DePaul University, College of Computing and Digital Media, Chicago, IL 60604. Offers animation (MA, MFA); applied technology (MS); business information technology (MS); cinema (MFA); cinema production (MS); computational finance (MS); computer and information sciences (PhD); computer game development (MS); computer graphics and motion technology (MS); computer information and network security (MS); computer science (MS); e-commerce technology (MS); human-computer interaction (MS); information systems (MS); information technology (MA); information technology project management (MS); network engineering and management (MS); predictive analytics (MS); screenwriting (MFA); software engineering (MS); JD/MA; JD/MS. Part-time and evening/weekend programs available. Postbaccalaureate distance learning degree programs offered (no on-campus study). *Faculty:* 64 full-time (16 women), 44 part-time/adjunct (5 women). *Students:* 969 full-time (250 women), 936 part-time (231 women); includes 566 minority (204 Black or African American, non-Hispanic/Latino; 3 American Indian or Alaska Native, non-Hispanic/Latino; 166 Asian, non-Hispanic/Latino; 135 Hispanic/Latino; 7 Native Hawaiian or other Pacific Islander, non-Hispanic/Latino; 51 Two or more races, non-Hispanic/Latino), 282 international. Average age 32. 1,040 applicants, 65% accepted, 324 enrolled. In 2011, 478 master's, 4 doctorates awarded. *Degree requirements:* For master's, thesis (for some programs); for doctorate, comprehensive exam, thesis/dissertation. *Entrance requirements:* For master's, GRE or GMAT (MS in computational finance only), bachelor's degree, resume (MS in predictive analytics only), IT experience (MS in information technology project management only), portfolio review (all MFA programs and MA in animation); for doctorate, GRE, master's degree in computer science. Additional exam requirements/recommendations for international students: Required—TOEFL (minimum score 550 paper-based; 213 computer-based; 80 iBT), IELTS (minimum score 6.5), Pearson Test of English (minimum score 53). *Application deadline:* For fall admission, 8/1 priority date for domestic students, 6/1 for international students; for winter admission, 12/1 priority date for domestic students, 10/1 for international students; for spring admission, 3/1 priority date for domestic students, 1/1 for international students. Applications are processed on a rolling basis. Application fee: $25. Electronic applications accepted. *Expenses:* Contact institution. *Financial support:* In 2011–12, 56 students received support, including 3 fellowships with full tuition reimbursements available (averaging $30,000 per year), 3 research assistantships with full and partial tuition reimbursements available (averaging $22,833 per year), 50 teaching assistantships (averaging $6,194 per year); Federal Work-Study, scholarships/grants, tuition waivers (full and partial), and unspecified assistantships also available. Support available to part-time students. Financial award application deadline: 4/30. *Faculty research:* Data mining, theoretical computer science, gaming, security, animation and film. *Total annual research expenditures:* $3.9 million. *Unit head:* Elly Kafritsas-Wessels, Senior Administrative Assistant, 312-362-5816, Fax: 312-362-5185, E-mail: ekafrits@cdm.depaul.edu. *Application contact:* James Parker, Director of Graduate Admission, 312-362-8714, Fax: 312-362-5179, E-mail: jparke29@cdm.depaul.edu. Web site: http://cdm.depaul.edu.

DeSales University, Graduate Division, MBA Program, Center Valley, PA 18034-9568. Offers accounting (MBA); computer information systems (MBA); finance (MBA); health care systems management (MBA); human resources management (MBA); management (MBA); marketing (MBA); project management (MBA); self-design (MBA). *Accreditation:* ACBSP. Part-time programs available. Postbaccalaureate distance learning degree programs offered (no on-campus study). *Entrance requirements:* For master's, GMAT, minimum GPA of 3.0, 2 years of work experience. Additional exam requirements/recommendations for international students: Required—TOEFL. *Application deadline:* Applications are processed on a rolling basis. Electronic applications accepted. Tuition and fees vary according to degree level. *Faculty research:* Quality improvement, executive development, productivity, cross-cultural managerial differences, leadership. *Unit head:* Dr. David Gilfoil, Director, 610-282-1100 Ext. 1828, Fax: 610-282-2869, E-mail: david.gilfoil@desales.edu. *Application contact:* Caryn Stopper, Director of Graduate Admissions, 610-282-1100 Ext. 1768, Fax: 610-282-0525, E-mail: caryn.stopper@desales.edu.

DeVry University, Keller Graduate School of Management, Downers Grove, IL 60515. Offers accounting and financial management (MAFM); business administration (MBA); human resources management (MHRM); information systems management (MISM); network and communications management (MNCM); project management (MPM); public administration (MPA).

Dowling College, School of Business, Oakdale, NY 11769-1999. Offers aviation management (MBA, Certificate); banking and finance (MBA, Certificate); corporate finance (MBA); financial planning (Certificate); health care management (MBA, Certificate); human resource management (Certificate); information systems management (MBA); management and leadership (MBA); marketing (Certificate); project management (Certificate); public management (MBA, Certificate); sport, event and entertainment management (Certificate); JD/MBA. Part-time and evening/weekend programs available. Postbaccalaureate distance learning degree programs offered (minimal on-campus study). *Faculty:* 10 full-time (4 women), 54 part-time/adjunct (6 women). *Students:* 237 full-time (99 women), 403 part-time (199 women); includes 186 minority (95 Black or African American, non-Hispanic/Latino; 62 Asian, non-Hispanic/Latino; 28 Hispanic/Latino; 1 Native Hawaiian or other Pacific Islander, non-Hispanic/Latino), 1 international. Average age 35. 345 applicants, 83% accepted, 193 enrolled. In 2011, 350 master's, 7 other advanced degrees awarded. *Degree requirements:* For master's, comprehensive exam, thesis optional. *Entrance requirements:* For master's, minimum GPA of 2.8, 2 letters of recommendation, courses or seminar in accounting and finance, resume. Additional exam requirements/recommendations for international students: Required—TOEFL (minimum score 550 paper-based). *Application deadline:* For fall admission, 9/1 priority date for domestic students; for winter admission, 1/1 priority date for domestic students; for spring admission, 2/1 priority date for domestic students. Applications are processed on a rolling basis. Application fee: $50. Electronic applications accepted. *Expenses: Tuition:* Full-time $19,162; part-time $933 per credit. *Required fees:* $1330; $700 per year. Tuition and fees vary according to course load. *Financial support:* Career-related internships or fieldwork and Federal Work-Study available. Support available to part-time students. Financial award application deadline: 6/30; financial award applicants required to submit FAFSA. *Faculty research:* International finance, computer applications, labor relations, executive development. *Unit head:* Antonia Loschiavo, Assistant Dean, 631-244-3266, Fax: 631-244-1018, E-mail: loschiat@dowling.edu. *Application contact:* Ronnie S. Macdonald, Assistant Vice President for Enrollment Services/Dean of Admissions, 631-244-3357, Fax: 631-244-1059, E-mail: macdonar@dowling.edu.

Duquesne University, School of Leadership and Professional Advancement, Pittsburgh, PA 15282-0001. Offers leadership (MS), including business ethics, community leadership, global leadership, information technology, leadership, liberal studies, professional administration, sports leadership. Part-time and evening/weekend programs available. Postbaccalaureate distance learning degree programs offered (no on-campus study). *Faculty:* 1 full-time (0 women), 88 part-time/adjunct (39 women). *Students:* 311 full-time (134 women), 151 part-time (68 women); includes 109 minority (69 Black or African American, non-Hispanic/Latino; 3 American Indian or Alaska Native, non-Hispanic/Latino; 11 Asian, non-Hispanic/Latino; 19 Hispanic/Latino; 1 Native Hawaiian or other Pacific Islander, non-Hispanic/Latino; 6 Two or more races, non-Hispanic/Latino), 9 international. Average age 35. 172 applicants, 73% accepted, 107 enrolled. In 2011, 67 degrees awarded. *Degree requirements:* For master's, capstone course. *Entrance requirements:* For master's, professional work experience, 500-word essay, resume, interview. Additional exam requirements/recommendations for international students: Required—TOEFL (minimum score 80 iBT). *Application deadline:* Applications are processed on a rolling basis. Application fee: $0. Electronic applications accepted. Application fee is waived when completed online. *Expenses: Tuition:* Full-time $16,596; part-time $922 per credit. *Required fees:* $1584; $88 per credit. Tuition and fees vary according to program. *Financial support:* Applicants required to submit FAFSA. *Unit head:* Dr. Dorothy Bassett, Dean, 412-396-2141, Fax: 412-396-4711, E-mail: bassettd@duq.edu. *Application contact:* Marianne Leister, Director of Student Services, 412-396-4933, Fax: 412-396-5072, E-mail: leister@duq.edu. Web site: http://www.duq.edu/leadership.

East Carolina University, Graduate School, College of Technology and Computer Science, Department of Technology Systems, Greenville, NC 27858-4353. Offers computer network professional (Certificate); industrial technology (MS), including computer networking management, digital communications, industrial distribution and logistics, information security, manufacturing, performance improvement, quality systems; information assurance (Certificate); Lean Six Sigma Black Belt (Certificate); occupational safety (MS); technology management (PhD); Website developer (Certificate). *Entrance requirements:* For master's and Certificate, GRE General Test or MAT, minimum GPA of 2.5; for doctorate, GRE General Test, related work experience. *Application deadline:* For fall admission, 6/1 priority date for domestic students. Applications are processed on a rolling basis. Application fee: $50. *Expenses:* Tuition, state resident: full-time $3557; part-time $444.63 per semester hour. Tuition, nonresident: full-time $14,351; part-time $1793.88 per semester hour. *Required fees:* $2016; $252 per semester hour. Part-time tuition and fees vary according to course load, campus/location and program. *Financial support:* Application deadline: 6/1. *Unit head:* Dr. Tijjani Mohammed, Interim Chair, 252-328-9668, E-mail: mohammedt@ecu.edu. Web site: http://www.ecu.edu/cs-tecs/techsystems/.

Eastern Michigan University, Graduate School, College of Business, Department of Computer Information Systems, Ypsilanti, MI 48197. Offers information systems (MSIS). Part-time and evening/weekend programs available. *Faculty:* 12 full-time (1 woman). *Students:* 38 full-time (13 women), 27 part-time (11 women); includes 6 minority (5 Black or African American, non-Hispanic/Latino; 1 Asian, non-Hispanic/Latino), 44 international. Average age 27. 70 applicants, 56% accepted, 15 enrolled. In 2011, 20 degrees awarded. *Entrance requirements:* Additional exam requirements/recommendations for international students: Required—TOEFL. *Application deadline:* For fall admission, 5/15 priority date for domestic students, 5/1 for international students; for winter admission, 10/15 priority date for domestic students, 10/1 for international students; for spring admission, 3/15 priority date for domestic students, 3/1 for international students. Applications are processed on a rolling basis. Application fee: $35. *Expenses:* Tuition, state resident: full-time $10,367; part-time $432 per credit hour. Tuition, nonresident: full-time $20,435; part-time $851 per credit hour. *Required fees:* $39 per credit hour. $46 per semester. One-time fee: $100. Tuition and fees vary according to course level, degree level and reciprocity agreements. *Financial support:* Fellowships, research assistantships with full tuition reimbursements, teaching assistantships with full tuition reimbursements, career-related internships or fieldwork, Federal Work-Study, institutionally sponsored loans, scholarships/grants, tuition waivers (partial), and unspecified assistantships available. Support available to part-time students. Financial award applicants required to submit FAFSA. *Unit head:* Dr. David Mielke, Interim Department Head, 734-487-2454, Fax: 734-487-1941, E-mail: d.mielke@emich.edu. *Application contact:* K. Michelle Henry, Interim Director, Graduate Programs, 734-487-4444, Fax: 734-483-1316, E-mail: mhenry1@emich.edu. Web site: http://www.cis.emich.edu.

Eastern Michigan University, Graduate School, College of Business, Programs in Business Administration, Ypsilanti, MI 48197. Offers business administration (MBA, Graduate Certificate); computer information systems (Graduate Certificate); e-business (MBA, Graduate Certificate); enterprise business intelligence (MBA); entrepreneurship (MBA, Graduate Certificate); finance (MBA, Graduate Certificate); human resources (MBA); human resources management (Graduate Certificate); information systems (MBA); internal auditing (MBA); international business (MBA, Graduate Certificate); marketing management (Graduate Certificate); nonprofit management (MBA); organizational development (Graduate Certificate); supply chain management (MBA, Graduate Certificate). *Accreditation:* AACSB. Part-time programs available. Postbaccalaureate distance learning degree programs offered (no on-campus study). *Students:* 79 full-time (39 women), 287 part-time (143 women); includes 55 minority (22 Black or African American, non-Hispanic/Latino; 24 Asian, non-Hispanic/Latino; 6 Hispanic/Latino; 3 Two or more races, non-Hispanic/Latino), 238 international. Average age 32. 317 applicants, 62% accepted, 89 enrolled. In 2011, 102 master's, 58 other advanced degrees awarded. *Entrance requirements:* For master's, GMAT (minimum score 450), minimum cumulative undergraduate GPA of 2.75. Additional exam requirements/recommendations for international students: Required—TOEFL. *Application deadline:* For fall admission, 5/15 for domestic students, 5/1 for international students; for winter admission, 10/15 for domestic students, 10/1 for international students; for spring admission, 3/15 for domestic students, 3/1 for international students. Applications are processed on a rolling basis. Application fee: $35. *Expenses:* Tuition, state resident: full-time $10,367; part-time $432 per credit hour. Tuition, nonresident: full-time $20,435; part-time $851 per credit hour. *Required fees:* $39 per credit hour. $46 per semester. One-time fee: $100. Tuition and fees vary according to course level, degree level and reciprocity agreements. *Financial support:* Fellowships, research assistantships with full tuition reimbursements, teaching assistantships with full tuition reimbursements, career-related internships or fieldwork, Federal Work-Study, institutionally sponsored loans, scholarships/grants, tuition waivers (partial), and unspecified assistantships available. Support available to part-time students. Financial award applicants required to submit FAFSA. *Unit head:* K. Michelle Henry, Director, Academic Services, 734-487-4444, Fax: 734-483-1316, E-mail: mhenry1@emich.edu. *Application contact:* Beste Windes, Advisor, 734-487-4444, Fax: 734-483-1316, E-mail: bwindes@emich.edu. Web site: http://www.emich.edu/public/cob/gr/grad.html.

East Tennessee State University, School of Graduate Studies, College of Business and Technology, Department of Computer and Information Sciences, Johnson City, TN 37614. Offers applied computer science (MS); information technology (MS). Part-time and evening/weekend programs available. *Faculty:* 16 full-time (3 women), 1 part-time/adjunct (0 women). *Students:* 33 full-time (2 women), 19 part-time (4 women); includes 2 minority (1 Hispanic/Latino; 1 Two or more races, non-Hispanic/Latino), 10 international. Average age 30. 42 applicants, 55% accepted, 15 enrolled. In 2011, 21 master's awarded. *Degree requirements:* For master's, comprehensive exam, thesis optional, capstone. *Entrance requirements:* For master's, GRE General Test, minimum GPA of 2.5, three letters of recommendation. Additional exam requirements/recommendations for international students: Required—TOEFL (minimum score 550 paper-based; 213 computer-based; 79 iBT). *Application deadline:* For fall admission, 6/1 for domestic students, 4/30 for international students; for spring admission, 11/1 for domestic students, 9/30 for international students. Application fee: $35 ($45 for international students). Electronic applications accepted. *Expenses:* Tuition, state resident: full-time $7312; part-time $350 per credit hour. Tuition, nonresident: full-time $18,490; part-time $621 per credit hour. *Required fees:* $63 per credit hour. Tuition and fees vary according to course load and program. *Financial support:* In 2011–12, 29 students received support, including 9 research assistantships with full tuition reimbursements available (averaging $9,000 per year), 15 teaching assistantships with full tuition reimbursements available (averaging $10,000 per year); career-related internships or fieldwork, institutionally sponsored loans, scholarships/grants, and unspecified assistantships also available. Financial award application deadline: 7/1; financial award applicants required to submit FAFSA. *Faculty research:* Security, enterprise resource planning, high performance computing, optimization, software engineering. *Unit head:* Dr. Terry Countermine, Chair, 423-439-5328, Fax: 423-439-7119, E-mail: counter@etsu.edu. *Application contact:* Bethany Glassbrenner, Graduate Specialist, 423-439-6165, Fax: 423-439-5624, E-mail: glassbrenner@etsu.edu.

Ellis University, MBA Program, Chicago, IL 60606-7204. Offers e-commerce (MBA); finance (MBA); general business (MBA); global management (MBA); health care administration (MBA); leadership (MBA); management of information systems (MBA); marketing (MBA); professional accounting (MBA); project management (MBA); public accounting (MBA); risk management (MBA).

Elmhurst College, Graduate Programs, Program in Computer Information Systems, Elmhurst, IL 60126-3296. Offers MS. Part-time and evening/weekend programs available. Postbaccalaureate distance learning degree programs offered (minimal on-campus study). *Faculty:* 2 full-time (1 woman). *Students:* 15 part-time (5 women); includes 3 minority (2 Asian, non-Hispanic/Latino; 1 Hispanic/Latino). Average age 32. 15 applicants, 60% accepted, 8 enrolled. In 2011, 6 master's awarded. *Entrance requirements:* For master's, 3 recommendations, resume, statement of purpose. Additional exam requirements/recommendations for international students: Required—TOEFL (minimum score 550 paper-based; 213 computer-based). *Application deadline:* Applications are processed on a rolling basis. Application fee: $0. Electronic applications accepted. *Expenses: Tuition:* Part-time $700 per semester hour. *Financial support:* In 2011–12, 2 students received support. Federal Work-Study and scholarships/grants available. Support available to part-time students. Financial award application deadline: 6/1; financial award applicants required to submit FAFSA. *Unit head:* Elizabeth D. Kuebler, Director of Adult and Graduate Admission, 630-617-3300, Fax: 630-617-5501, E-mail: oaga@elmhurst.edu. *Application contact:* Elizabeth D. Kuebler, Director of Adult and Graduate Admission, 630-617-3300, Fax: 630-617-5501, E-mail: oaga@elmhurst.edu.

Emory University, Goizueta Business School, Doctoral Program in Business, Atlanta, GA 30322-1100. Offers accounting (PhD); finance (PhD); information systems (PhD); marketing (PhD); organization and management (PhD). *Faculty:* 56 full-time (13 women). *Students:* 37 full-time (17 women); includes 21 minority (20 Asian, non-Hispanic/Latino; 1 Hispanic/Latino). Average age 29. 240 applicants, 6% accepted, 11 enrolled. In 2011, 5 doctorates awarded. *Degree requirements:* For doctorate, comprehensive exam, thesis/dissertation. *Entrance requirements:* For doctorate, GMAT (strongly preferred) or GRE. Additional exam requirements/recommendations for international students: Required—TOEFL (minimum score 250 computer-based). *Application deadline:* For fall admission, 1/3 priority date for domestic students, 1/1 for international students. Application fee: $50. Electronic applications accepted. *Expenses: Tuition:* Full-time $34,800. *Required fees:* $1300. *Financial support:* In 2011–12, 37 students received support. *Unit head:* Dr. Lawrence Benveniste, Dean, 404-727-6377, Fax: 404-727-0868, E-mail: larry_benveniste@bus.emory.edu. *Application contact:* Allison Gilmore, Director of Admissions and Student Services, 404-727-6353, Fax: 404-727-5337, E-mail: phd@bus.emory.edu.

Endicott College, Van Loan School of Graduate and Professional Studies, Program in Information Technology, Beverly, MA 01915-2096. Offers MSIT. *Faculty:* 1 full-time (0 women), 2 part-time/adjunct (0 women). *Students:* 6 part-time (2 women). Average age 31. 3 applicants, 33% accepted, 1 enrolled. In 2011, 3 master's awarded. *Degree requirements:* For master's, thesis. *Entrance requirements:* For master's, GRE or MAT, two letters of recommendation. Additional exam requirements/recommendations for international students: Required—TOEFL. *Application deadline:* Applications are processed on a rolling basis. Application fee: $50. Electronic applications accepted. *Expenses:* Contact institution. *Financial support:* Applicants required to submit FAFSA. *Unit head:* Dr. Richard Benedetto, Associate Dean of Graduate School, 978-232-2744, Fax: 978-232-3000, E-mail: rbenedet@endicott.edu. *Application contact:* Richard Benedetto, Associate Dean of Graduate School, 978-232-2744, Fax: 978-232-3000, E-mail: rbenedet@endicott.edu.

Fairfield University, Charles F. Dolan School of Business, Fairfield, CT 06824-5195. Offers accounting (MBA, MS, CAS); accounting information systems (MBA, CAS); entrepreneurship (MBA, CAS); finance (MBA, MS, CAS); general management (MBA, CAS); human resource management (MBA, CAS); information systems and operations (MBA); information systems and operations management (CAS); international business (MBA, CAS); marketing (MBA, CAS); taxation (MBA, CAS). *Accreditation:* AACSB. Part-time and evening/weekend programs available. *Faculty:* 23 full-time (9 women), 3 part-time/adjunct (1 woman). *Students:* 87 full-time (37 women), 118 part-time (42 women); includes 13 minority (4 Black or African American, non-Hispanic/Latino; 4 Asian, non-Hispanic/Latino; 5 Hispanic/Latino), 9 international. Average age 29. 126 applicants, 47% accepted, 35 enrolled. In 2011, 90 master's awarded. *Degree requirements:* For master's, capstone course. *Entrance requirements:* For master's, GMAT (minimum score 500), 2 letters of reference, resume, minimum GPA of 3.0. Additional exam requirements/recommendations for international students: Required—TOEFL (minimum score 550 paper-based; 213 computer-bases; 80 iBT) or IELTS (minimum score 6.5). *Application deadline:* For fall admission, 5/15 for international students; for spring admission, 10/15 for international students. Applications are processed on a rolling basis. Application fee: $60. Electronic applications accepted. *Expenses:* Contact institution. *Financial support:* In 2011–12, 50 students received support, including 2 research assistantships (averaging $6,500 per year); scholarships/grants, unspecified assistantships, and merit-based one-time entrance scholarship also available. Financial award applicants required to submit FAFSA. *Faculty research:* Optimization strategies, international finance, consumer behavior, financial market volatility, Internet marketing, supply chain analysis, tax issues. *Unit head:* Dr. Donald Gibson, Dean, 203-254-4000 Ext. 4070, Fax: 203-254-4105, E-mail: dgibson@fairfield.edu. *Application contact:* Marianne Gumpper, Director of Graduate and Continuing Studies Admission, 203-254-4184, Fax: 203-254-4073, E-mail: gradadmis@fairfield.edu. Web site: http://www.fairfield.edu/dsb/dsb_grad_1.html.

Fairleigh Dickinson University, Metropolitan Campus, Silberman College of Business, Departments of Management, Marketing, and Entrepreneurial Studies, Program in Management, Teaneck, NJ 07666-1914. Offers management (MBA); management information systems (Certificate). *Accreditation:* AACSB.

Fairleigh Dickinson University, Metropolitan Campus, University College: Arts, Sciences, and Professional Studies, School of Computer Sciences and Engineering, Program in Management Information Systems, Teaneck, NJ 07666-1914. Offers MS.

Ferris State University, College of Business, Big Rapids, MI 49307. Offers business intelligence (MBA); design and innovation management (MBA); incident response (MBA); information security and intelligence (MS, MSISM), including business intelligence (MS), incident response (MSISM), project management (MSISM); management tools and concepts (MBA); project management (MBA). *Accreditation:* ACBSP. Part-time and evening/weekend programs available. Postbaccalaureate distance learning degree programs offered (minimal on-campus study). *Faculty:* 9 full-time (3 women), 2 part-time/adjunct (both women). *Students:* 22 full-time (7 women), 98 part-time (50 women); includes 14 minority (3 Black or African American, non-Hispanic/Latino; 4 American Indian or Alaska Native, non-Hispanic/Latino; 2 Asian, non-Hispanic/Latino; 2 Hispanic/Latino; 3 Two or more races, non-Hispanic/Latino), 3 international. Average age 34. 58 applicants, 79% accepted, 10 enrolled. In 2011, 56 master's awarded. *Degree requirements:* For master's, comprehensive exam, thesis (for MSISM). *Entrance requirements:* For master's, GRE or GMAT (waived if GPA is 3.5 or better), minimum GPA of 3.0 in junior/senior level classes, 2.75 overall; writing sample; 3 letters of reference; resume. Additional exam requirements/recommendations for international students: Required—TOEFL (minimum score 500 paper-based; 173 computer-based; 67 iBT). *Application deadline:* For fall admission, 7/1 priority date for domestic students, 6/15 for international students; for winter admission, 11/1 priority date for domestic students, 10/15 for international students; for spring admission, 3/1 priority date for domestic students, 2/15 for international students. Applications are processed on a rolling basis. Application fee: $30. Electronic applications accepted. Application fee is waived when completed online. *Financial support:* Career-related internships or fieldwork, Federal Work-Study, scholarships/grants, and unspecified assistantships available. Support available to part-time students. Financial award application deadline: 3/15; financial award applicants required to submit FAFSA. *Faculty research:* Quality improvement, client/server end-user computing, information management and policy, security, digital forensics. *Unit head:* Dr. David Steenstra, Department Chair, 231-591-2168, Fax: 231-591-3548, E-mail: yosts@ferris.edu. *Application contact:* Shannon Yost, Department Secretary, 231-591-2168, Fax: 231-591-3548, E-mail: yosts@ferris.edu. Web site: http://cbgp.ferris.edu/.

Florida Agricultural and Mechanical University, Division of Graduate Studies, Research, and Continuing Education, School of Business and Industry, Tallahassee, FL 32307-3200. Offers accounting (MBA); finance (MBA); management information systems (MBA); marketing (MBA). *Degree requirements:* For master's, residency. *Entrance requirements:* For master's, GMAT, minimum GPA of 3.0.

Florida Atlantic University, College of Business, Department of Information Technology and Operations Management, Boca Raton, FL 33431-0991. Offers management information systems (MS). *Faculty:* 16 full-time (6 women), 4 part-time/adjunct (0 women). *Students:* 31 full-time (23 women), 45 part-time (23 women); includes 35 minority (17 Black or African American, non-Hispanic/Latino; 7 Asian, non-Hispanic/Latino; 7 Hispanic/Latino; 4 Two or more races, non-Hispanic/Latino), 6 international. Average age 30. 91 applicants, 37% accepted, 14 enrolled. In 2011, 28 master's awarded. *Degree requirements:* For master's, thesis optional. *Entrance requirements:* For master's, GMAT, minimum GPA of 3.0. Additional exam requirements/recommendations for international students: Required—TOEFL (minimum score 600 paper-based; 250 computer-based). *Application deadline:* For fall admission, 7/1 priority date for domestic students, 2/15 for international students; for spring admission, 4/1 priority date for domestic students, 1/15 for international students. Applications are processed on a rolling basis. Application fee: $30. Electronic applications accepted. *Expenses: Tuition, area resident:* Part-time $343.02 per credit hour. Tuition, state resident: full-time $8232. Tuition, nonresident: full-time $23,931; part-time $997.14 per credit hour. *Financial support:* Research assistantships, teaching assistantships, career-related internships or fieldwork, Federal Work-Study, institutionally sponsored loans, tuition waivers (partial), and unspecified assistantships available. Support available to part-time students. Financial award application deadline: 3/1; financial award applicants required to submit FAFSA. *Unit head:* Dr. Tamara Dinev, Chair, 561-297-3675. *Application contact:* Fredrick G. Taylor, Graduate Adviser, 561-297-3196, Fax: 561-297-1315, E-mail: ftaylor@fau.edu. Web site: http://business.fau.edu/departments/information-technology-operations-management/index.aspx.

Florida Institute of Technology, Graduate Programs, College of Engineering, Computer Science Department, Melbourne, FL 32901-6975. Offers computer information systems (MS); computer science (MS, PhD); software engineering (MS). Part-time and evening/weekend programs available. *Faculty:* 14 full-time (1 woman), 11 part-time/adjunct (1 woman). *Students:* 73 full-time (14 women), 63 part-time (14 women); includes 9 minority (4 Black or African American, non-Hispanic/Latino; 2 Asian, non-Hispanic/Latino; 2 Hispanic/Latino; 1 Two or more races, non-Hispanic/Latino), 81 international. Average age 29. 342 applicants, 64% accepted, 40 enrolled. In 2011, 37 master's, 4 doctorates awarded. *Degree requirements:* For master's, comprehensive exam (for some programs), thesis optional, final exam, seminar, or internship (for non-thesis option); for doctorate, comprehensive exam, thesis/dissertation, publication in journal, teaching experience (strongly encouraged), specialized research program. *Entrance requirements:* For master's, GRE General Test, minimum GPA of 3.0, 3 letters of recommendation; for doctorate, GRE General Test, GRE Subject Test in computer science (recommended), 3 letters of recommendation, minimum GPA of 3.5, resume, statement of objectives. Additional exam requirements/recommendations for international students: Required—TOEFL (minimum score 550 paper-based; 213 computer-based; 79 iBT). *Application deadline:* For fall admission, 4/1 for international students; for spring admission, 9/30 for international students. Applications are processed on a rolling basis. Application fee: $0. Electronic applications accepted. *Expenses: Tuition:* Full-time $19,620; part-time $1090 per credit hour. Tuition and fees vary according to campus/location. *Financial support:* In 2011–12, 1 research assistantship with full and partial tuition reimbursement (averaging $4,500 per year), 12 teaching assistantships with full and partial tuition reimbursements (averaging $12,103 per year) were awarded; career-related internships or fieldwork, institutionally sponsored loans, tuition waivers (partial), unspecified assistantships, and tuition remissions also available. Support available to part-time students. Financial award application deadline: 3/1; financial award applicants required to submit FAFSA. *Faculty research:* Artificial intelligence, software engineering, management and processes, programming languages, database systems. *Total annual research expenditures:* $741,031. *Unit head:* Dr. William D. Shoaff, Department Head, 321-674-8066, Fax: 321-674-7046, E-mail: wds@cs.fit.edu. *Application contact:* Cheryl A. Brown, Associate Director of Graduate Admissions, 321-674-7581, Fax: 321-723-9468, E-mail: cbrown@fit.edu. Web site: http://coe.fit.edu/cs.

Florida Institute of Technology, Graduate Programs, Extended Studies Division, Melbourne, FL 32901-6975. Offers acquisition and contract management (MS); aerospace engineering (MS); business administration (MBA); computer information systems (MS); computer science (MS); electrical engineering (MS); engineering management (MS); human resources management (MS); logistics management (MS), including humanitarian and disaster relief logistics; management (MS), including acquisition and contract management, e-business, human resources management, information systems, logistics management, management, transportation management; material acquisition management (MS); mechanical engineering (MS); operations research (MS); project management (MS), including information systems, operations research; public administration (MPA); quality management (MS); software engineering (MS); space systems (MS); space systems management (MS); supply chain management (MS); systems management (MS), including information systems, operations research. Part-time and evening/weekend programs available. Postbaccalaureate distance learning degree programs offered (no on-campus study). *Faculty:* 9 full-time (2 women), 105 part-time/adjunct (24 women). *Students:* 113 full-time (52 women), 1,150 part-time (484 women); includes 496 minority (332 Black or African American, non-Hispanic/Latino; 11 American Indian or Alaska Native, non-Hispanic/Latino; 42 Asian, non-Hispanic/Latino; 71 Hispanic/Latino; 2 Native Hawaiian or other Pacific Islander, non-Hispanic/Latino; 38 Two or more races, non-Hispanic/Latino), 11 international. Average age 35. 568 applicants, 56% accepted, 296 enrolled. In 2011, 471 master's awarded. *Degree requirements:* For master's, comprehensive exam (for some programs), capstone course. *Entrance requirements:* For master's, GMAT or resume showing 8 years of supervised experience, minimum GPA of 3.0, 2 letters of recommendation, resume. Additional exam requirements/recommendations for international students: Required—TOEFL (minimum score 550 paper-based; 213 computer-based; 79 iBT). *Application deadline:* For fall admission, 4/1 for international students; for spring admission, 9/30 for international students. Applications are processed on a rolling basis. Application fee: $0. Electronic applications accepted. *Expenses:* Contact institution. *Financial support:* Application deadline: 3/1; applicants required to submit FAFSA. *Unit head:* Dr. Theodore R. Richardson, III, Senior Associate Dean, 321-674-8123, Fax: 321-674-7597, E-mail: trichardson@fit.edu. *Application contact:* Carolyn Farrior, Director of Graduate Admissions, Online Learning and Off-Campus Programs, 321-674-7118, Fax: 321-674-8216, E-mail: cfarrior@fit.edu. Web site: http://es.fit.edu.

Florida Institute of Technology, Graduate Programs, Nathan M. Bisk College of Business, Online Programs, Melbourne, FL 32901-6975. Offers accounting (MBA); accounting and finance (MBA); business administration (MBA); finance (MBA); healthcare management (MBA); information technology (MS); information technology cybersecurity (MS); information technology management (MBA); international business (MBA); Internet marketing (MBA); management (MBA); marketing (MBA); project management (MBA). Part-time and evening/weekend programs available. Postbaccalaureate distance learning degree programs offered (no on-campus study). *Faculty:* 47 part-time/adjunct (15 women). *Students:* 8 full-time (4 women), 1,122 part-time (547 women); includes 418 minority (271 Black or African American, non-Hispanic/Latino; 5 American Indian or Alaska Native, non-Hispanic/Latino; 55 Asian, non-Hispanic/Latino; 81 Hispanic/Latino; 6 Native Hawaiian or other Pacific Islander, non-Hispanic/Latino), 23 international. Average age 36. In 2011, 329 master's awarded. *Entrance requirements:* For master's, GMAT or resume showing 8 years of supervised experience, 2 letters of recommendation, resume, competency in math past college algebra. Additional exam requirements/recommendations for international students: Required—TOEFL (minimum score 550 paper-based; 213 computer-based; 79 iBT). *Application deadline:* For fall admission, 4/1 for international students; for spring admission, 9/30 for international students. Applications are processed on a rolling basis. Electronic applications accepted. *Expenses:* Contact institution. *Financial support:* Available to part-time students. Application deadline: 3/1; applicants required to submit FAFSA. *Unit head:* Dr. Mary S. Bonhomme, Dean, Florida Tech Online/Associate Provost for Online Learning, 321-674-8202, Fax: 321-674-8216, E-mail: bonhomme@fit.edu. *Application contact:* Carolyn Farrior, Director of Graduate Admissions, Online Learning and Off-Campus Programs, 321-674-7118, Fax: 321-674-8216, E-mail: cfarrior@fit.edu. Web site: http://online.fit.edu.

Florida International University, Alvah H. Chapman, Jr. Graduate School of Business, Department of Decision Sciences and Information Systems, Miami, FL 33199. Offers MSMIS. Part-time and evening/weekend programs available. *Entrance requirements:* For master's, GMAT or GRE, minimum GPA of 3.0 (upper-level coursework); letter of intent; resume. Additional exam requirements/recommendations for international students: Required—TOEFL (minimum score 550 paper-based; 213 computer-based; 80 iBT) or IELTS. Electronic applications accepted. *Expenses:* Contact institution. *Faculty research:* Artificial intelligence, data warehouses, operations management.

Florida State University, The Graduate School, College of Business, Tallahassee, FL 32306-1110. Offers accounting (M Acc), including accounting information services, assurance services, corporate accounting, taxation; business administration (MBA, PhD), including accounting (PhD), finance (PhD), management information systems (PhD), marketing (PhD), organizational behavior (PhD), risk management and insurance (PhD), strategic management (PhD); finance (MS); insurance (MSM); management information systems (MS); marketing (MS); JD/MBA; MSW/MBA. *Accreditation:* AACSB. Part-time programs available. Postbaccalaureate distance learning degree programs offered (no on-campus study). *Faculty:* 107 full-time (31 women). *Students:* 196 full-time (76 women), 310 part-time (109 women); includes 89 minority (27 Black or African American, non-Hispanic/Latino; 1 American Indian or Alaska Native, non-Hispanic/Latino; 31 Asian, non-Hispanic/Latino; 30 Hispanic/Latino). Average age 30. 702 applicants, 33% accepted, 205 enrolled. In 2011, 268 master's, 17 doctorates awarded. Terminal master's awarded for partial completion of doctoral program. *Degree requirements:* For doctorate, comprehensive exam, thesis/dissertation. *Entrance requirements:* For master's, GMAT, work experience (MBA, MS), minimum GPA of 3.0, letters of recommendation; for doctorate, GMAT, minimum graduate GPA of 3.5, letters of recommendation. Additional exam requirements/recommendations for international students: Required—TOEFL (minimum score 600 paper-based; 80 computer-based); Recommended—IELTS (minimum score 6.5). *Application deadline:* For fall admission, 6/1 for domestic students, 5/1 for international students; for spring admission, 10/1 for domestic students, 9/1 for international students. Applications are processed on a rolling basis. Application fee: $30. Electronic applications accepted. *Expenses:* Tuition, state resident: full-time $9474; part-time $350.88 per credit hour. Tuition, nonresident: full-time $16,236; part-time $601.34 per credit hour. *Required fees:* $630 per semester. One-time fee: $20. Tuition and fees vary according to course load and campus/location. *Financial support:* In 2011–12, 86 students received support, including 12 fellowships with full tuition reimbursements available (averaging $7,161 per year), 30 research assistantships with full tuition reimbursements available (averaging $6,000 per year), 43 teaching assistantships with full tuition reimbursements available (averaging $15,000 per year); career-related internships or fieldwork, scholarships/grants, health care benefits, tuition waivers (full and partial), and unspecified assistantships also available. Support available to part-time students. Financial award application deadline: 1/1. *Unit head:* Dr. Caryn Beck-Dudley, Dean, 850-644-3090, Fax: 850-644-0915. *Application contact:* Lisa Beverly, Director, Graduate Programs Admissions, 850-644-6458, Fax: 850-644-0588, E-mail: lbeverly@cob.fsu.edu. Web site: http://www.cob.fsu.edu/grad/.

Fordham University, Graduate School of Business, New York, NY 10023. Offers accounting (MBA); communications and media management (MBA); executive business administration (EMBA); finance (MBA, MS); information systems (MBA, MS); management systems (MBA); marketing (MBA); media management (MS); taxation (MS); taxation and accounting (MTA);); JD/MBA; MBA/MIM; MS/MBA. MBA/MIM offered jointly with Thunderbird School of Global Management. *Accreditation:* AACSB. Part-time and evening/weekend programs available. *Entrance requirements:* For master's, GMAT, 2 letters of recommendation, resume. Additional exam requirements/recommendations for international students: Required—TOEFL (minimum score 600 paper-based; 250 computer-based; 100 iBT). Electronic applications accepted. *Expenses:* Contact institution.

Franklin Pierce University, Graduate Studies, Rindge, NH 03461-0060. Offers curriculum and instruction (M Ed); emerging network technologies (Graduate

Certificate); energy and sustainability studies (MBA); health administration (MBA, Graduate Certificate); human resource management (MBA, Graduate Certificate); information technology (MBA); information technology management (MS); leadership (MBA, DA); nursing (MS); physical therapy (DPT); physician assistant studies (MPAS); special education (M Ed); sports management (MBA). *Accreditation:* APTA. Part-time programs available. Postbaccalaureate distance learning degree programs offered (no on-campus study). *Degree requirements:* For master's, concentrated original research projects; student teaching; fieldwork and/or internship; leadership project; PRAXIS I and II (for M Ed); for doctorate, concentrated original research projects, clinical fieldwork and/or internship, leadership project. *Entrance requirements:* For master's, minimum GPA of 2.5, 3 letters of recommendation; competencies in accounting, economics, statistics, and computer skills through life experience or undergraduate coursework (for MBA); certification/e-portfolio, minimum C grade in all education courses (for M Ed); license to practice as RN (for MS in nursing); for doctorate, GRE, BA/BS, 3 letters of recommendation, personal mission statement, interview, writing sample, minimum cumulative GPA of 2.8, master's degree (for DA); 80 hours of observation/work in PT settings, completion of anatomy, chemistry, physics, and statistics, minimum GPA of 3.0 (for DPT). Additional exam requirements/recommendations for international students: Required—TOEFL (minimum score 550 paper-based; 195 computer-based; 61 iBT). Electronic applications accepted. *Faculty research:* Evidence-based practice in sports physical therapy, human resource management in economic crisis, leadership in nursing, innovation in sports facility management, differentiated learning and understanding by design.

Friends University, Graduate School, Wichita, KS 67213. Offers accounting (MBA); business administration (MBA); business law (MBL); Christian ministry (MACM); environment science (MSES); family therapy (MSFT); global leadership and management (MA); health care leadership (MHCL); management information systems (MMIS); operations management (MSOM); organization development (MSOD); teaching (MAT). Part-time and evening/weekend programs available. Postbaccalaureate distance learning degree programs offered (no on-campus study). *Faculty:* 14 full-time (5 women), 2 part-time/adjunct (1 woman). *Students:* 158 full-time (114 women), 616 part-time (367 women); includes 159 minority (83 Black or African American, non-Hispanic/Latino; 12 American Indian or Alaska Native, non-Hispanic/Latino; 26 Asian, non-Hispanic/Latino; 22 Hispanic/Latino; 2 Native Hawaiian or other Pacific Islander, non-Hispanic/Latino; 14 Two or more races, non-Hispanic/Latino). Average age 36. 497 applicants, 68% accepted, 256 enrolled. In 2011, 341 degrees awarded. *Degree requirements:* For master's, research project. *Entrance requirements:* For master's, bachelor's degree from accredited institution, official transcripts from institution granting bachelor's degree, interview with program director, letter(s) of recommendation. Additional exam requirements/recommendations for international students: Required—TOEFL (minimum score 560 paper-based; 220 computer-based). *Application deadline:* Applications are processed on a rolling basis. Application fee: $45 ($65 for international students). Electronic applications accepted. *Expenses: Tuition:* Part-time $601 per credit hour. One-time fee: $45 full-time. Tuition and fees vary according to campus/location and program. *Financial support:* Applicants required to submit FAFSA. *Unit head:* Dr. Evelyn Hume, Dean, 800-794-6945 Ext. 5859, Fax: 316-295-5040, E-mail: evelyn_hume@friends.edu. *Application contact:* Jeanette Hanson, Executive Director of Adult Recruitment, 800-794-6945, Fax: 316-295-5050, E-mail: jeanette@friends.edu. Web site: http://www.friends.edu.

George Mason University, School of Management, Fairfax, VA 22030. Offers accounting (MS); business administration (EMBA, MBA); management of secure information systems (MS); real estate development (MS); technology management (MS). Part-time and evening/weekend programs available. Postbaccalaureate distance learning degree programs offered. *Faculty:* 79 full-time (25 women), 49 part-time/adjunct (14 women). *Students:* 170 full-time (65 women), 349 part-time (113 women); includes 116 minority (30 Black or African American, non-Hispanic/Latino; 1 American Indian or Alaska Native, non-Hispanic/Latino; 64 Asian, non-Hispanic/Latino; 15 Hispanic/Latino; 1 Native Hawaiian or other Pacific Islander, non-Hispanic/Latino; 5 Two or more races, non-Hispanic/Latino), 49 international. Average age 30. 408 applicants, 58% accepted, 152 enrolled. In 2011, 273 master's awarded. *Entrance requirements:* For master's, GMAT. Additional exam requirements/recommendations for international students: Required—TOEFL (minimum score 570 paper-based; 230 computer-based; 88 iBT), IELTS, Pearson Test of English. *Application deadline:* Applications are processed on a rolling basis. Application fee: $65 ($80 for international students). Electronic applications accepted. *Expenses:* Tuition, state resident: full-time $8750; part-time $364.58 per credit. Tuition, nonresident: full-time $24,092; part-time $1003.83 per credit. *Required fees:* $2514; $104.75 per credit. *Financial support:* In 2011–12, 50 students received support, including 35 research assistantships with full and partial tuition reimbursements available (averaging $9,267 per year), 19 teaching assistantships with full and partial tuition reimbursements available (averaging $8,253 per year); career-related internships or fieldwork, Federal Work-Study, scholarships/grants, unspecified assistantships, and health care benefits (full-time research or teaching assistantship recipients) also available. Financial award application deadline: 3/1; financial award applicants required to submit FAFSA. *Faculty research:* Current leading global issues: offshore outsourcing, international financial risk, comparative systems of innovation. *Total annual research expenditures:* $382,706. *Unit head:* Jorge Haddock, Dean, 703-993-1875, E-mail: jhaddock@gmu.edu. *Application contact:* Melanie Pflugshaupt, Administrative Coordinator to Dean's Office, 703-993-3638, E-mail: mpflugsh@gmu.edu. Web site: http://som.gmu.edu/.

George Mason University, Volgenau School of Engineering, Department of Computer Science, Fairfax, VA 22030. Offers computer games technology (Certificate); computer networking (Certificate); computer science (MS, PhD); database management (Certificate); electronic commerce (Certificate); foundations of information systems (Certificate); information engineering (Certificate); information security and assurance (MS, Certificate); information systems (MS); intelligent agents (Certificate); software architecture (Certificate); software engineering (MS, Certificate); software engineering for C41 (Certificate); Web-based software engineering (Certificate). MS program offered jointly with Old Dominion University, University of Virginia, Virginia Commonwealth University, and Virginia Polytechnic Institute and State University. *Faculty:* 40 full-time (9 women), 17 part-time/adjunct (0 women). *Students:* 208 full-time (52 women), 357 part-time (75 women); includes 98 minority (17 Black or African American, non-Hispanic/Latino; 63 Asian, non-Hispanic/Latino; 14 Hispanic/Latino; 4 Two or more races, non-Hispanic/Latino), 205 international. Average age 30. 882 applicants, 52% accepted, 137 enrolled. In 2011, 164 master's, 5 doctorates, 28 other advanced degrees awarded. *Degree requirements:* For master's, thesis optional; for doctorate, comprehensive exam, thesis/dissertation. *Entrance requirements:* For master's, GRE, proof of financial support; 2 official college transcripts; resume; self-evaluation form; official bank statement; photocopy of passport; 3 letters of recommendation; baccalaureate degree related to computer science; minimum GPA of 3.0 in last 2 years of undergraduate work; 1 year beyond 1st-year calculus; personal goals statement; for doctorate, GRE, personal goals statement; 2 official copies of transcripts; self-evaluation form; 3 letters of recommendation; photocopy of passport; proof of financial support; official bank statement; resume; 4-year baccalaureate degree with strong background in computer science. Additional exam requirements/recommendations for international students: Required—TOEFL (minimum score 575 paper-based; 230 computer-based; 88 iBT), IELTS, Pearson Test of English. *Application deadline:* For fall admission, 1/15 priority date for domestic students; for spring admission, 8/15 priority date for domestic students. Application fee: $65 ($80 for international students). Electronic applications accepted. *Expenses:* Tuition, state resident: full-time $8750; part-time $364.58 per credit. Tuition, nonresident: full-time $24,092; part-time $1003.83 per credit. *Required fees:* $2514; $104.75 per credit. *Financial support:* In 2011–12, 100 students received support, including 3 fellowships (averaging $18,000 per year), 50 research assistantships (averaging $15,232 per year), 47 teaching assistantships (averaging $11,675 per year); career-related internships or fieldwork, Federal Work-Study, scholarships/grants, unspecified assistantships, and health care benefits (full-time research or teaching assistantship recipients) also available. Support available to part-time students. Financial award application deadline: 3/1; financial award applicants required to submit FAFSA. *Faculty research:* Artificial intelligence, image processing/graphics, parallel/distributed systems, software engineering systems. *Total annual research expenditures:* $1.9 million. *Unit head:* Sanjeev Setia, Chair, 703-993-4098, Fax: 703-993-1710, E-mail: setia@gmu.edu. *Application contact:* Michele Pieper, Administrative Assistant, 703-993-9483, Fax: 703-993-1710, E-mail: mpieper@gmu.edu. Web site: http://cs.gmu.edu/.

The George Washington University, School of Business, Department of Information Systems and Technology Management, Washington, DC 20052. Offers information and decision systems (PhD); information systems (MSIST); information systems development (MSIST); information systems management (MBA); information systems project management (MSIST); management information systems (MSIST); management of science, technology, and innovation (MBA, PhD). Programs also offered in Ashburn and Arlington, VA. Part-time and evening/weekend programs available. *Faculty:* 12 full-time (4 women), 5 part-time/adjunct (2 women). *Students:* 111 full-time (37 women), 144 part-time (47 women); includes 87 minority (36 Black or African American, non-Hispanic/Latino; 1 American Indian or Alaska Native, non-Hispanic/Latino; 30 Asian, non-Hispanic/Latino; 19 Hispanic/Latino; 1 Two or more races, non-Hispanic/Latino), 45 international. Average age 33. 231 applicants, 72% accepted, 93 enrolled. In 2011, 86 master's, 3 doctorates awarded. *Entrance requirements:* For master's, GMAT. Additional exam requirements/recommendations for international students: Required—TOEFL. *Application deadline:* For fall admission, 4/1 priority date for domestic students; for spring admission, 10/1 for domestic students. Applications are processed on a rolling basis. Application fee: $75. *Financial support:* In 2011–12, 35 students received support. Fellowships, teaching assistantships, career-related internships or fieldwork, Federal Work-Study, institutionally sponsored loans, and tuition waivers available. Financial award application deadline: 4/1. *Faculty research:* Expert systems, decision support systems. *Unit head:* Richard G. Donnelly, Chair, 202-994-4364, E-mail: rgd@gwu.edu. *Application contact:* Kristin Williams, Assistant Vice President for Graduate and Special Enrollment Management, 202-994-0467, Fax: 202-994-0371, E-mail: ksw@gwu.edu.

Georgia College & State University, Graduate School, The J. Whitney Bunting School of Business, Milledgeville, GA 31061. Offers accountancy (MACCT); accounting (MBA); business (MBA); health services administration (MBA); information systems (MIS); management information services (MBA). *Accreditation:* AACSB. Part-time and evening/weekend programs available. Postbaccalaureate distance learning degree programs offered (no on-campus study). *Students:* 61 full-time (26 women), 134 part-time (55 women); includes 34 minority (18 Black or African American, non-Hispanic/Latino; 9 Asian, non-Hispanic/Latino; 5 Hispanic/Latino; 2 Two or more races, non-Hispanic/Latino), 17 international. Average age 30. 162 applicants, 41% accepted, 45 enrolled. In 2011, 99 master's awarded. *Entrance requirements:* For master's, GMAT or GRE. Additional exam requirements/recommendations for international students: Recommended—TOEFL (minimum score 550 paper-based; 213 computer-based; 79 iBT). *Application deadline:* For fall admission, 7/1 priority date for domestic students, 4/1 for international students; for spring admission, 11/15 priority date for domestic students, 8/1 for international students. Applications are processed on a rolling basis. Application fee: $40. Electronic applications accepted. *Expenses:* Tuition, state resident: full-time $4806; part-time $267 per credit hour. Tuition, nonresident: full-time $17,802; part-time $989 per credit hour. *Required fees:* $936 per semester. Tuition and fees vary according to course load and campus/location. *Financial support:* In 2011–12, 34 research assistantships with full tuition reimbursements were awarded; career-related internships or fieldwork and unspecified assistantships also available. Support available to part-time students. Financial award application deadline: 3/1; financial award applicants required to submit FAFSA. *Unit head:* Dr. Matthew Liao-Troth, Dean, School of Business, 478-445-5497, E-mail: matthew.liao-troth@gcsu.edu. *Application contact:* Lynn Hanson, Director of Graduate Programs, 478-445-5115, E-mail: lynn.hanson@gcsu.edu. Web site: http://www.gcsu.edu/business/graduateprograms/index.htm.

Georgia Institute of Technology, Graduate Studies and Research, College of Management, Program in Business Administration, Atlanta, GA 30332-0001. Offers accounting (MBA); e-commerce (Certificate); engineering entrepreneurship (MBA); entrepreneurship (Certificate); finance (MBA); information technology management (MBA); international business (MBA, Certificate); management of technology (Certificate); marketing (MBA); operations management (MBA); organizational behavior (MBA); strategic management (MBA). *Accreditation:* AACSB.

Georgia Institute of Technology, Graduate Studies and Research, College of Management, Program in Management, Atlanta, GA 30332-0001. Offers accounting (PhD); finance (PhD); information technology management (PhD); marketing (PhD); operations management (PhD); organizational behavior (PhD); quantitative and computational finance (MS); strategic management (PhD). *Accreditation:* AACSB. *Degree requirements:* For doctorate, comprehensive exam, thesis/dissertation, oral exams. *Entrance requirements:* For master's and doctorate, GMAT. Additional exam requirements/recommendations for international students: Required—TOEFL. *Faculty research:* MIS, management of technology, international business, entrepreneurship, operations management.

Georgia Southern University, Jack N. Averitt College of Graduate Studies, College of Business Administration, Enterprise Resources Planning Certificate Program, Statesboro, GA 30460. Offers Graduate Certificate. Postbaccalaureate distance learning degree programs offered. *Students:* 13 part-time (6 women); includes 8 minority (7 Black or African American, non-Hispanic/Latino; 1 Asian, non-Hispanic/Latino), 1 international. Average age 46. 17 applicants, 100% accepted, 12 enrolled. *Entrance requirements:* For degree, bachelor's degree or equivalent with minimum cumulative GPA of 2.7; official copies of all transcripts; resume with three references; personal statement. Application fee: $50. *Expenses:* Tuition, state resident: full-time $6300; part-time $263 per semester hour. Tuition, nonresident: full-time $25,174; part-time $1049 per semester hour. *Required fees:* $1872. *Faculty research:* ERP and business intelligence (BI) synergies, cloud-based and on-demand ERP solutions, IT artifact in ERP-centered supply chain information systems, impact of bring your own device (BYOD) policies on deployment of enterprise systems mobile applications, career readiness of SAP University Alliances students for positions in ERP user and consulting firms. *Unit head:* Dr. Camille Rogers, Coordinator, 912-478-0194, E-mail: cfrogers@georgiasouthern.edu. *Application contact:* Amanda Gilliland, Coordinator for Graduate

Student Recruitment, 912-478-5384, Fax: 912-478-0740, E-mail: gradadmissions@georgiasouthern.edu. Web site: http://cit.georgiasouthern.edu/is/erp-certificate.html.

Georgia State University, J. Mack Robinson College of Business, Department of Computer Information Systems, Atlanta, GA 30302-3083. Offers MBA, MSIS, PhD. Part-time and evening/weekend programs available. Terminal master's awarded for partial completion of doctoral program. *Degree requirements:* For doctorate, thesis/dissertation. *Entrance requirements:* For master's and doctorate, GMAT. Additional exam requirements/recommendations for international students: Required—TOEFL (minimum score 610 paper-based; 255 computer-based; 101 iBT).

Georgia State University, J. Mack Robinson College of Business, Program in General Business Administration, Atlanta, GA 30302-3083. Offers accounting/information systems (MBA); economics (MBA, MS); enterprise risk management (MBA); general business (MBA); general business administration (EMBA, PMBA); information systems consulting (MBA); information systems risk management (MBA); international business and information technology (MBA); international entrepreneurship (MBA); MBA/JD. *Accreditation:* AACSB. Part-time and evening/weekend programs available. *Entrance requirements:* For master's, GMAT. Additional exam requirements/recommendations for international students: Required—TOEFL (minimum score 610 paper-based; 255 computer-based; 101 iBT). Electronic applications accepted.

Globe University–Woodbury, Minnesota School of Business, Woodbury, MN 55125. Offers business administration (MBA); health care management (MSM); information technology (MSM); managerial leadership (MSM).

Golden Gate University, Ageno School of Business, San Francisco, CA 94105-2968. Offers accounting (MBA); business administration (EMBA, MBA, PMBA, DBA); finance (MBA, MS, Certificate); financial planning (MS, Certificate); healthcare information systems (Certificate); human resource management (MBA, MS); human resources management (Certificate); information systems (MS); information technology (MBA); information technology management (Certificate); integrated marketing and communications (MS, Certificate); international business (MBA); management (MBA); marketing (MBA, MS, Certificate); operations supply chain management (Certificate); psychology (MA, Certificate); public administration (EMPA); public relations (MS, Certificate); technical market analysis (Certificate); JD/MBA. Part-time and evening/weekend programs available. *Faculty:* 19 full-time (6 women), 241 part-time/adjunct (72 women). *Students:* 397 full-time (230 women), 779 part-time (432 women); includes 376 minority (105 Black or African American, non-Hispanic/Latino; 5 American Indian or Alaska Native, non-Hispanic/Latino; 161 Asian, non-Hispanic/Latino; 77 Hispanic/Latino; 12 Native Hawaiian or other Pacific Islander, non-Hispanic/Latino; 16 Two or more races, non-Hispanic/Latino), 265 international. Average age 34. 871 applicants, 64% accepted, 271 enrolled. In 2011, 550 master's, 13 doctorates awarded. *Degree requirements:* For doctorate, thesis/dissertation, qualifying examination. *Entrance requirements:* For master's, GMAT (MBA), minimum GPA of 2.5 (MS). Additional exam requirements/recommendations for international students: Required—TOEFL (minimum score 550 paper-based; 213 computer-based; 79 iBT). *Application deadline:* For fall admission, 5/15 for domestic and international students; for winter admission, 1/15 for domestic and international students; for spring admission, 9/15 for domestic and international students. Applications are processed on a rolling basis. Application fee: $70 ($110 for international students). Electronic applications accepted. *Expenses:* Contact institution. *Financial support:* Career-related internships or fieldwork, Federal Work-Study, institutionally sponsored loans, and scholarships/grants available. Support available to part-time students. Financial award applicants required to submit FAFSA. *Unit head:* Dr. Paul Fouts, Dean, 415-442-7026, Fax: 415-442-6579. *Application contact:* Angela Melero, Enrollment Services, 415-442-7800, Fax: 415-442-7807, E-mail: info@ggu.edu. Web site: http://www.ggu.edu/programs/business-and-management.

Goldey-Beacom College, Graduate Program, Wilmington, DE 19808-1999. Offers business administration (MBA); finance (MS); financial management (MBA); health care management (MBA); human resource management (MBA); information technology (MBA); international business management (MBA); major finance (MBA); major taxation (MBA); management (MM); marketing management (MBA); taxation (MBA, MS). *Accreditation:* ACBSP. Part-time and evening/weekend programs available. *Faculty:* 19 full-time (7 women), 35 part-time/adjunct (12 women). *Students:* 58 full-time (32 women), 388 part-time (164 women); includes 89 minority (34 Black or African American, non-Hispanic/Latino; 2 American Indian or Alaska Native, non-Hispanic/Latino; 44 Asian, non-Hispanic/Latino; 9 Hispanic/Latino), 229 international. Average age 30. In 2011, 243 master's awarded. *Entrance requirements:* For master's, GMAT, MAT, GRE, minimum GPA of 3.0. Additional exam requirements/recommendations for international students: Required—TOEFL (minimum score 65 computer-based); Recommended—IELTS (minimum score 5). *Application deadline:* Applications are processed on a rolling basis. Application fee: $0. Electronic applications accepted. *Expenses: Tuition:* Full-time $15,750; part-time $875 per credit. *Required fees:* $10 per credit. *Financial support:* Scholarships/grants available. Support available to part-time students. Financial award application deadline: 4/1; financial award applicants required to submit FAFSA. *Unit head:* Larry W. Eby, Director of Admissions, 302-225-6289, Fax: 302-996-5408, E-mail: ebylw@gbc.edu. *Application contact:* Ashley E. Mashington, Graduate Admissions Representative, 302-225-6259, Fax: 302-996-5408, E-mail: mashina@gbc.edu. Web site: http://www.gbc.edu/programs/graduate/.

Governors State University, College of Business and Public Administration, Program in Management Information Systems, University Park, IL 60484. Offers MS. *Students:* 7 full-time (4 women), 12 part-time (4 women); includes 10 minority (7 Black or African American, non-Hispanic/Latino; 3 Hispanic/Latino), 3 international. Average age 35. Application fee: $25. *Unit head:* Dr. Ellen Foster-Curtis, Dean, College of Business and Public Administration, 708-534-4930, Fax: 708-534-8457, E-mail: efostercurtis@govst.edu.

Graduate School and University Center of the City University of New York, Graduate Studies, Program in Business, New York, NY 10016-4039. Offers accounting (PhD); behavioral science (PhD); finance (PhD); management planning systems (PhD). *Degree requirements:* For doctorate, thesis/dissertation. *Entrance requirements:* For doctorate, GMAT, writing sample (15 pages). Additional exam requirements/recommendations for international students: Required—TOEFL. Electronic applications accepted.

Grand Canyon University, College of Business, Phoenix, AZ 85017-1097. Offers accounting (MBA); corporate business administration (MBA); disaster preparedness and crisis management (MBA); executive fire service leadership (MS); finance (MBA); general management (MBA); government and policy (MPA); health care management (MPA); health systems management (MBA); human resource management (MBA); innovation (MBA); leadership (MBA, MS); management of information system (MBA); marketing (MBA); project-based (MBA); six sigma (MBA); strategic human resource management (MBA). *Accreditation:* ACBSP. Part-time and evening/weekend programs available. Postbaccalaureate distance learning degree programs offered (no on-campus study). *Entrance requirements:* For master's, equivalent of two years full-time professional work experience. Additional exam requirements/recommendations for international students: Required—TOEFL (minimum score 575 paper-based; 233 computer-based; 90 iBT), IELTS (minimum score 7). Electronic applications accepted.

Grand Valley State University, Padnos College of Engineering and Computing, School of Computing and Information Systems, Allendale, MI 49401-9403. Offers computer information systems (MS), including databases, distributed systems, management of information systems, object-oriented systems, software engineering. Part-time and evening/weekend programs available. *Degree requirements:* For master's, thesis or alternative. *Entrance requirements:* For master's, GMAT or GRE General Test. Additional exam requirements/recommendations for international students: Required—TOEFL. Electronic applications accepted. *Faculty research:* Object technology, distributed computing, information systems management database, software engineering.

Grantham University, Mark Skousen School of Business, Kansas City, MO 64153. Offers business administration (MBA); business intelligence (MS); information management (MBA); information management technology (MS); information technology (MS); performance improvement (MS); project management (MBA, MSIM). Part-time and evening/weekend programs available. Postbaccalaureate distance learning degree programs offered (no on-campus study). *Degree requirements:* For master's, capstone project. *Entrance requirements:* For master's, bachelor's degree from accredited degree-granting institution. Additional exam requirements/recommendations for international students: Required—TOEFL (minimum score 500 paper-based; 213 computer-based; 61 iBT). Electronic applications accepted.

Harrisburg University of Science and Technology, Program in Information Systems Engineering and Management, Harrisburg, PA 17101. Offers digital government specialization (MS); digital health specialization (MS); entrepreneurship specialization (MS). Part-time programs available. *Degree requirements:* For master's, comprehensive exam, thesis optional. *Entrance requirements:* For master's, baccalaureate degree. Additional exam requirements/recommendations for international students: Required—TOEFL (minimum score 520 paper-based; 200 computer-based; 80 iBT). Electronic applications accepted.

Hawai`i Pacific University, College of Business Administration, Program in Information Systems, Honolulu, HI 96813. Offers knowledge management (MSIS); software engineering (MSIS); telecommunications security (MSIS). Part-time and evening/weekend programs available. *Faculty:* 9 full-time (2 women), 3 part-time/adjunct (1 woman). *Students:* 46 full-time (7 women), 51 part-time (9 women); includes 64 minority (6 Black or African American, non-Hispanic/Latino; 29 Asian, non-Hispanic/Latino; 10 Hispanic/Latino; 2 Native Hawaiian or other Pacific Islander, non-Hispanic/Latino; 17 Two or more races, non-Hispanic/Latino). Average age 32. 52 applicants, 83% accepted, 23 enrolled. In 2011, 52 master's awarded. *Expenses: Tuition:* Full-time $13,230; part-time $735 per credit. Tuition and fees vary according to course load and program. *Financial support:* In 2011–12, 12 students received support. Career-related internships or fieldwork, Federal Work-Study, scholarships/grants, tuition waivers, and unspecified assistantships available. *Unit head:* Dr. Gordon Jones, Dean, 808-544-1181, Fax: 808-544-0247, E-mail: gjones@hpu.edu. *Application contact:* Chad Schempp, Director of Graduate Admissions, 808-543-8035, Fax: 808-544-0280, E-mail: graduate@hpu.edu.

See Display on next page and Close-Up on page 527.

HEC Montreal, School of Business Administration, Master of Science Programs in Administration, Program in Information Technologies, Montréal, QC H3T 2A7, Canada. Offers M Sc. All courses are given in French. Part-time programs available. *Students:* 26 full-time (4 women), 5 part-time (3 women). 29 applicants, 55% accepted, 13 enrolled. In 2011, 15 master's awarded. *Degree requirements:* For master's, one foreign language, thesis. *Entrance requirements:* For master's, Test de francais international (TFI) with minimum score of 850 (for those who have never studied in French), BBA, undergraduate degree in another field, degree deemed equivalent by program director and minimum GPA of 3.0 on 4.3 scale. *Application deadline:* For fall admission, 3/15 for domestic and international students; for winter admission, 9/15 for domestic and international students. Application fee: $80 Canadian dollars. Electronic applications accepted. Application fee is waived when completed online. *Expenses:* Contact institution. *Financial support:* Fellowships, research assistantships, teaching assistantships, and scholarships/grants available. Financial award application deadline: 9/2. *Unit head:* Dr. Claude Laurin, Director, 514-340-6485, Fax: 514-340-6880, E-mail: claude.laurin@hec.ca. *Application contact:* Virginie Lefebvre, Administrative Director, 514-340-6112, Fax: 514-340-6411, E-mail: virginie.lefebvre@hec.ca. Web site: http://www.hec.ca/en/programs_training/msc/options/information_technologies/index.html.

Hodges University, Graduate Programs, Naples, FL 34119. Offers business administration (MBA); criminal justice (MS); education (MPS); information systems management (MIS); legal studies (MS); management (MSM); mental health counseling (MS); public administration (MPA). Part-time and evening/weekend programs available. Postbaccalaureate distance learning degree programs offered (no on-campus study). *Faculty:* 22 full-time (9 women), 3 part-time/adjunct (2 women). *Students:* 28 full-time (21 women), 237 part-time (156 women); includes 76 minority (35 Black or African American, non-Hispanic/Latino; 5 Asian, non-Hispanic/Latino; 36 Hispanic/Latino). Average age 36. 92 applicants, 91% accepted, 81 enrolled. *Degree requirements:* For master's, comprehensive exam (for some programs), thesis (for some programs). *Entrance requirements:* For master's, in-house entrance exam. Additional exam requirements/recommendations for international students: Recommended—TOEFL. *Application deadline:* Applications are processed on a rolling basis. Application fee: $50. Electronic applications accepted. *Expenses: Tuition:* Full-time $11,340; part-time $630 per credit hour. *Required fees:* $250 per term. *Financial support:* In 2011–12, 200 students received support. Federal Work-Study and scholarships/grants available. Financial award application deadline: 7/9; financial award applicants required to submit FAFSA. *Unit head:* Terry McMahan, President, 239-513-1122, Fax: 239-598-6253, E-mail: tmcmahan@hodges.edu. *Application contact:* Rita Lampus, Vice President of Student Enrollment Management, 239-513-1122, Fax: 239-598-6253, E-mail: rlampus@hodges.edu.

Hofstra University, Frank G. Zarb School of Business, Department of Information Technology and Quantitative Methods, Hempstead, NY 11549. Offers business administration (MBA), including information technology, quality management; information technology (MS, Advanced Certificate). Part-time and evening/weekend programs available. *Faculty:* 9 full-time (2 women), 2 part-time/adjunct (0 women). *Students:* 16 full-time (3 women), 14 part-time (3 women); includes 6 minority (2 Black or African American, non-Hispanic/Latino; 3 Asian, non-Hispanic/Latino; 1 Hispanic/Latino), 8 international. Average age 29. 42 applicants, 76% accepted, 9 enrolled. In 2011, 4 master's awarded. *Degree requirements:* For master's, capstone course (for MBA); thesis (for MS); minimum GPA of 3.0. *Entrance requirements:* For master's, GMAT/GRE, 2 letters of recommendation; resume; essay; for Advanced Certificate, GMAT/GRE, 2 letters of recommendation; resume. Additional exam requirements/recommendations for international students: Required—TOEFL (minimum score 550 paper-based; 213 computer-based; 80 iBT); Recommended—IELTS (minimum score 6). *Application deadline:* Applications are processed on a rolling basis. Application fee: $70 ($75 for international students). Electronic applications accepted. *Expenses:*

Contact institution. *Financial support:* In 2011–12, 5 students received support, including 5 fellowships with full and partial tuition reimbursements available (averaging $6,680 per year); research assistantships with full and partial tuition reimbursements available, career-related internships or fieldwork, Federal Work-Study, institutionally sponsored loans, scholarships/grants, tuition waivers (full and partial), and unspecified assistantships also available. Support available to part-time students. Financial award applicants required to submit FAFSA. *Faculty research:* IT Outsourcing, IT Strategy, SAP and enterprise systems, data mining/electronic medical records, IT and crisis management, inventory theory and modeling, forecasting. *Unit head:* Dr. Mohammed H. Tafti, Chairperson, 516-463-5720, E-mail: acsmht@hofstra.edu. *Application contact:* Carol Drummer, Dean of Graduate Admissions, 516-463-4876, Fax: 516-463-4664, E-mail: gradstudent@hofstra.edu. Web site: http://www.hofstra.edu/business/.

Holy Family University, Graduate School, School of Business Administration, Program in Information Systems Management, Philadelphia, PA 19114. Offers MS. Part-time and evening/weekend programs available. *Entrance requirements:* For master's, BA or BS, minimum GPA of 3.0, 2 letters of recommenation. Electronic applications accepted.

See Display on next page and Close-Up on page 529.

Hood College, Graduate School, Department of Economics and Management, Frederick, MD 21701-8575. Offers accounting (MBA); administration and management (MBA); finance (MBA); human resource management (MBA); information systems (MBA); marketing (MBA); public management (MBA). *Accreditation:* ACBSP. Part-time and evening/weekend programs available. *Degree requirements:* For master's, capstone/final research project. *Entrance requirements:* For master's, minimum GPA of 2.75, resume, letters of recommendation. Additional exam requirements/ recommendations for international students: Required—TOEFL (minimum score 575 paper-based; 231 computer-based; 89 iBT). Electronic applications accepted. *Faculty research:* Corporate strategy and sustainable competitive advantages, business ethics, entrepreneurship, investments management, economic development.

Howard University, School of Business, Graduate Programs in Business, Washington, DC 20059-0002. Offers accounting (MBA); entrepreneurship (MBA); finance (MBA); general management (MBA); human resources management (MBA); information systems (MBA); international business (MBA); marketing (MBA); supply chain management (MBA); JD/MBA. *Accreditation:* AACSB. Part-time and evening/weekend programs available. Postbaccalaureate distance learning degree programs offered (no on-campus study). *Entrance requirements:* For master's, GMAT, minimum 1 year post undergraduate work experience, resume, 3 letters of recommendation, advanced college algebra. Additional exam requirements/recommendations for international students: Required—TOEFL. *Faculty research:* Marketing research in multi-ethnic populations, U.S. trade policies and international relations, risk management (finance).

Idaho State University, Office of Graduate Studies, College of Business, Pocatello, ID 83209-8020. Offers business administration (MBA, Postbaccalaureate Certificate); computer information systems (MS, Postbaccalaureate Certificate). *Accreditation:* AACSB. Part-time programs available. *Degree requirements:* For master's, comprehensive exam, thesis (for some programs), oral exam; for Postbaccalaureate Certificate, comprehensive exam, thesis (for some programs), 6 hours of clerkship. *Entrance requirements:* For master's, GMAT, GRE General Test, minimum GPA of 3.0, resume outlining work experience, 2 letters of reference; for Postbaccalaureate Certificate, GMAT, GRE General Test, minimum upper-level GPA of 3.0, resume of work experience. Additional exam requirements/recommendations for international students: Required—TOEFL (minimum score 550 paper-based; 213 computer-based; 80 iBT). Electronic applications accepted. *Faculty research:* Information assurance, computer information technology, finance management, marketing.

Illinois Institute of Technology, Graduate College, College of Science and Letters, Department of Computer Science, Chicago, IL 60616-3793. Offers business (MCS); computer networking and telecommunications (MCS); computer science (MCS, MS, PhD); information systems (MCS); software engineering (MCS); teaching (MST). Part-time and evening/weekend programs available. Postbaccalaureate distance learning degree programs offered (no on-campus study). Terminal master's awarded for partial completion of doctoral program. *Degree requirements:* For master's, thesis optional; for doctorate, comprehensive exam, thesis/dissertation. *Entrance requirements:* For master's, GRE General Test (minimum scores: 1000 Quantitative and Verbal, 3.0 Analytical Writing), minimum undergraduate GPA of 3.0; for doctorate, GRE General Test (minimum scores: 1100 Quantitative and Verbal, 3.5 Analytical Writing), minimum undergraduate GPA of 3.0. Additional exam requirements/recommendations for international students: Required—TOEFL (minimum score 523 paper-based; 70 iBT). Electronic applications accepted. *Faculty research:* Algorithms, data structures, artificial intelligences, computer architecture, computer graphics, computer networking and telecommunications.

Illinois Institute of Technology, Graduate College, College of Science and Letters, Lewis Department of Humanities, Chicago, IL 60616-3793. Offers information architecture (MS); technical communication (PhD); technical communication and information design (MS). Part-time programs available. *Degree requirements:* For master's, comprehensive exam, thesis or alternative; for doctorate, comprehensive exam, thesis/dissertation. *Entrance requirements:* For master's and doctorate, GRE General Test (minimum score 500 Quantitative, 500 Verbal, and 3.0 Analytical Writing), minimum undergraduate GPA of 3.0. Additional exam requirements/recommendations for international students: Required—TOEFL (minimum score 523 paper-based; 70 iBT). Electronic applications accepted. *Faculty research:* Aesthetics, document and online design, ethics in the professions, history of art and architecture, humanizing technology.

Illinois Institute of Technology, Graduate College, School of Applied Technology, Program in Information Technology and Management, Chicago, IL 60616-3793. Offers MITM. Part-time and evening/weekend programs available. Postbaccalaureate distance learning degree programs offered (no on-campus study). *Entrance requirements:* For master's, GRE (minimum score 900 Quantitative and Verbal, 2.5 Analytical Writing), bachelor's degree with minimum cumulative undergraduate GPA of 3.0 (or its equivalent) from accredited institution. Additional exam requirements/recommendations for international students: Required—TOEFL (minimum score 523 paper-based; 70 iBT); Recommended—IELTS (minimum score 5.5). Electronic applications accepted. *Faculty research:* Database design, voice over IP, process engineering, object-oriented programming, computer networking, online design, system administration.

Illinois State University, Graduate School, College of Applied Science and Technology, School of Information Technology, Normal, IL 61790-2200. Offers MS. *Entrance requirements:* For master's, GRE General Test, minimum GPA of 3.0 in last 60 hours; proficiency in COBOL, FORTRAN, Pascal, or P12. *Faculty research:* Graduate practicum training in network support.

Indiana University Bloomington, School of Public and Environmental Affairs, Public Affairs Programs, Bloomington, IN 47405. Offers comparative and international affairs (MPA); economic development (MPA); energy (MPA); environmental policy (PhD); environmental policy and natural resource management (MPA); hazardous materials management (Certificate); information systems (MPA); international development (MPA); local government management (MPA); nonprofit management (MPA, Certificate); policy analysis (MPA); public budgeting and financial management (Certificate); public finance (PhD); public financial administration (MPA); public management (MPA, PhD, Certificate); public policy analysis (PhD); social entrepreneurship (Certificate); specialized public affairs (MPA); sustainability and sustainable development (MPA); JD/MPA; MPA/MA; MPA/MIS; MPA/MLS; MSES/MPA. *Accreditation:* NASPAA (one or more programs are accredited). Part-time programs available. *Faculty:* 80 full-time (30 women), 102 part-time/adjunct (43 women). *Students:* 338 full-time, 30 part-time; includes 27 minority (7 Black or African American, non-Hispanic/Latino; 2 American Indian or Alaska Native, non-Hispanic/Latino; 10 Asian, non-Hispanic/Latino; 8 Hispanic/Latino), 56 international. Average age 24. 501 applicants, 148 enrolled. In 2011, 172 master's, 7 doctorates awarded. *Degree requirements:* For master's, core classes, capstone, internship; for doctorate, comprehensive exam, thesis/dissertation. *Entrance requirements:* For master's, GRE General Test or GMAT, official transcripts, 3 letters of recommendation, resume, personal statement; for doctorate, GRE General Test or LSAT, official transcripts, 3 letters of recommendation, resume or curriculum vitae, statement of purpose. Additional exam requirements/recommendations for international students: Required—TOEFL (minimum score 600 paper-based; 96 iBT); Recommended—IELTS (minimum score 7). *Application deadline:* For fall admission, 2/1 priority date for domestic students, 12/1 for international students. Applications are processed on a rolling basis. Application fee: $55 ($65 for international students). Electronic applications accepted. *Financial support:* Fellowships with partial tuition reimbursements, research assistantships with partial tuition reimbursements, teaching assistantships with partial tuition reimbursements, career-related internships or fieldwork, Federal Work-Study, scholarships/grants, health care benefits, unspecified assistantships, and Service Corps programs available. Financial award application deadline: 2/1; financial award applicants required to submit FAFSA. *Faculty research:* Comparative and international affairs, environmental policy and resource management, policy analysis, public finance, public management, urban management, nonprofit management, energy policy, social policy, public finance. *Unit head:* Jennifer Forney, Director of Graduate Student Services, 812-855-9485, Fax: 812-856-3665, E-mail: speampo@indiana.edu. *Application contact:* Admissions Assistant, 812-855-2840, E-mail: speaapps@indiana.edu. Web site: http://www.indiana.edu/~spea/prospective_students/masters/.

Indiana University South Bend, School of Business and Economics, South Bend, IN 46634-7111. Offers accounting (MSA); business administration (MBA); management of information technologies (MS). Part-time and evening/weekend programs available. *Faculty:* 17 full-time (2 women), 3 part-time/adjunct (1 woman). *Students:* 78 full-time (31 women), 112 part-time (50 women); includes 17 minority (6 Black or African American, non-Hispanic/Latino; 1 American Indian or Alaska Native, non-Hispanic/Latino; 4 Asian, non-Hispanic/Latino; 5 Hispanic/Latino; 1 Two or more races, non-Hispanic/Latino), 70 international. Average age 32. 65 applicants, 74% accepted, 23 enrolled. In 2011, 37 master's awarded. *Entrance requirements:* For master's, GMAT. Additional exam requirements/recommendations for international students: Required—TOEFL (minimum score 550 paper-based; 213 computer-based). *Application deadline:* For fall admission, 7/1 priority date for domestic students, 7/1 for international students; for spring admission, 11/1 priority date for domestic students, 11/1 for international students. Applications are processed on a rolling basis. Application fee: $50 ($60 for international students). *Expenses:* Contact institution. *Financial support:* In 2011–12, 1 fellowship (averaging $3,846 per year) was awarded; Federal Work-Study and institutionally sponsored loans also available. Support available to part-time students. Financial award applicants required to submit FAFSA. *Faculty research:* Financial accounting, consumer research, capital budgeting research, business strategy research. *Unit head:* Robert H. Ducoffe, Dean, 574-520-4228, Fax: 574-520-4866. *Application contact:* Sharon Peterson, Secretary, 574-520-4138, Fax: 574-520-4866, E-mail: speterso@iusb.edu. Web site: http://www.iusb.edu/~buse/grad.

Instituto Tecnológico y de Estudios Superiores de Monterrey, Campus Central de Veracruz, Graduate Programs, Córdoba, Mexico. Offers administration (MA); administration of information technologies (MTI); computer sciences (MCC); education (MEE); educational institution administration (MAD); educational technology (MTE); electronic commerce (MCE); finance (MAF); humanistic studies (MEH); international business for Latin America (MNL); marketing (MMT); science (MCP). Part-time and evening/weekend programs available. Postbaccalaureate distance learning degree programs offered (minimal on-campus study). *Degree requirements:* For master's, thesis (for some programs). *Entrance requirements:* For master's, PAEP College Board. Electronic applications accepted.

Instituto Tecnológico y de Estudios Superiores de Monterrey, Campus Ciudad de México, Virtual University Division, Ciudad de Mexico, Mexico. Offers administration of information technologies (MA); computer sciences (MA); education (MA, PhD); educational technology (MA); environmental engineering (MA); environmental systems (MA); humanistic studies (MA); industrial engineering (MA); international business for Latin America (MA); quality systems (MA); quality systems and productivity (MA). Part-time and evening/weekend programs available. Postbaccalaureate distance learning degree programs offered (minimal on-campus study). *Entrance requirements:* For master's and doctorate, Instituto entrance exam. Additional exam requirements/recommendations for international students: Required—TOEFL.

Instituto Tecnológico y de Estudios Superiores de Monterrey, Campus Ciudad Juárez, Program in Administration of Information Technology, Ciudad Juárez, Mexico. Offers MAIT.

Instituto Tecnológico y de Estudios Superiores de Monterrey, Campus Ciudad Obregón, Program in Administration of Information Technology, Ciudad Obregón, Mexico. Offers MATI.

Instituto Tecnológico y de Estudios Superiores de Monterrey, Campus Estado de México, Professional and Graduate Division, Estado de Mexico, Mexico. Offers administration of information technologies (MITA); architecture (M Arch); business administration (GMBA, MBA); computer sciences (MCS, PhD); education (M Ed); educational institution administration (MAD); educational technology and innovation (PhD); electronic commerce (MEC); environmental systems (MS); finance (MAF); humanistic studies (MHS); information sciences and knowledge management (MISKM); information systems (MS); manufacturing systems (MS); marketing (MEM); quality systems and productivity (MS); science and materials engineering (PhD); telecommunications management (MTM). Part-time programs available. Postbaccalaureate distance learning degree programs offered (minimal on-campus study). *Degree requirements:* For master's, one foreign language, thesis (for some programs); for doctorate, one foreign language, thesis/dissertation. *Entrance requirements:* For master's, E-PAEP 500, interview; for doctorate, E-PAEP 500, research proposal. Additional exam requirements/recommendations for international students: Required—TOEFL (minimum score 550 paper-based). *Faculty research:* Surface treatments by plasmas, mechanical properties, robotics, graphical computing, mechatronics security protocols.

Instituto Tecnológico y de Estudios Superiores de Monterrey, Campus Irapuato, Graduate Programs, Irapuato, Mexico. Offers administration (MBA); administration of information technology (MAIT); administration of telecommunications (MAT); architecture (M Arch); computer science (MCS); education (M Ed); educational administration (MEA); educational innovation and technology (DEIT); educational technology (MET); electronic commerce (MBA); environmental administration and planning (MEAP); environmental systems (MES); finances (MBA); humanistic studies (MHS); international management for Latin American executives (MIMLAE); library and information science (MLIS); manufacturing quality management (MMQM); marketing research (MBA).

Instituto Tecnológico y de Estudios Superiores de Monterrey, Campus Laguna, Graduate School, Torreón, Mexico. Offers business administration (MBA); industrial engineering (MIE); management information systems (MS). Part-time programs available. *Entrance requirements:* For master's, GMAT. *Faculty research:* Computer communications from home to the university.

Inter American University of Puerto Rico, Aguadilla Campus, Graduate School, Aguadilla, PR 00605. Offers accounting (MBA); counseling psychology specializing in family (MS); criminal justice (MA); educative management and leadership (MA); elementary education (M Ed); finance (MBA); human resources (MBA); industrial management (MBA); management information systems (MBA); marketing (MBA). Part-time and evening/weekend programs available. *Degree requirements:* For master's, comprehensive exam. *Entrance requirements:* For master's, EXADEP, 2 letters of recommendation, minimum GPA of 2.5. Electronic applications accepted.

Inter American University of Puerto Rico, Metropolitan Campus, Graduate Programs, Program in Management Information Systems, San Juan, PR 00919-1293. Offers MBA.

Iowa State University of Science and Technology, Program in Business and Technology, Ames, IA 50011-1350. Offers PhD. *Entrance requirements:* Additional exam requirements/recommendations for international students: Required—TOEFL (minimum score 600 paper-based; 100 iBT), IELTS (minimum score 7). *Application deadline:* For fall admission, 1/16 for domestic students. Electronic applications accepted. *Unit head:* Dr. Sridhar Ramaswami, Director of Graduate Education, 515-294-5341, Fax: 515-294-6060, E-mail: dmm@iastate.edu. *Application contact:* Deborah Martinez, Information Contact, 515-294-2474, Fax: 515-294-6060, E-mail: dmm@iastate.edu. Web site: http://www.business.iastate.edu/phd/.

Iowa State University of Science and Technology, Program in Logistics, Operations, and Management Information Systems, Ames, IA 50011-1350. Offers information systems (MS). *Degree requirements:* For master's, thesis or alternative. *Entrance requirements:* For master's, GMAT. Additional exam requirements/recommendations for international students: Recommended—TOEFL (minimum score 570 paper-based; 88 iBT), IELTS (minimum score 7). *Application deadline:* For fall admission, 6/1 priority date for domestic students, 3/1 for international students; for spring admission, 11/1 priority date for domestic students, 3/1 for international students. Application fee: $40 ($90 for international students). Electronic applications accepted. *Unit head:* Dr. Qing Hu, Director of Graduate Education, 515-294-8118, Fax: 515-294-2446, E-mail: busgrad@iastate.edu. *Application contact:* Debbie Johnson, 515-294-8118, Fax: 515-294-2446, E-mail: busgrad@iastate.edu. Web site: http://www.business.iastate.edu/masters/msis.

John Marshall Law School, Graduate and Professional Programs, Chicago, IL 60604-3968. Offers employee benefits (LL M, MS); global legal studies (LL M); information technology (MS); information technology and privacy law (LL M); intellectual property (LL M, MS); international business and trade (LL M); law (JD); real estate (LL M, MS); taxation (LL M, MS); trial advocacy (LL M); JD/LL M; JD/MA; JD/MBA; JD/MPA. JD/MBA offered jointly with Dominican University; JD/MA and JD/MPA with Roosevelt University. *Accreditation:* ABA. Part-time and evening/weekend programs available. *Faculty:* 69 full-time (22 women), 133 part-time/adjunct (40 women). *Students:* 1,305 full-time (598 women), 368 part-time (180 women); includes 385 minority (148 Black or African American, non-Hispanic/Latino; 15 American Indian or Alaska Native, non-Hispanic/Latino; 108 Asian, non-Hispanic/Latino; 110 Hispanic/Latino; 2 Native Hawaiian or other Pacific Islander, non-Hispanic/Latino; 2 Two or more races, non-Hispanic/Latino), 40 international. Average age 27. 3,513 applicants, 48% accepted, 365 enrolled. In 2011, 86 master's, 403 doctorates awarded. *Degree requirements:* For master's, 24 credits; for doctorate, 90 credits. *Entrance requirements:* For master's, JD; for doctorate, LSAT. Additional exam requirements/recommendations for international students: Required—TOEFL. *Application deadline:* For fall admission, 3/1 priority date for domestic students, 3/1 for international students; for spring admission, 10/15 priority date for domestic students, 10/15 for international students. Applications are processed on a rolling basis. Application fee: $0. Electronic applications accepted. *Expenses:* Contact institution. *Financial support:* In 2011–12, 1,350 students received support. Scholarships/grants and tuition waivers (full and partial) available. Support available to part-time students. Financial award application deadline: 6/1; financial award applicants required to submit FAFSA. *Unit head:* John Corkery, Dean, 312-427-2737. *Application contact:* William B. Powers, Associate Dean of Admission and Student Affairs, 800-537-4280, Fax: 312-427-5136, E-mail: admission@jmls.edu.

The Johns Hopkins University, Carey Business School, Information Technology Programs, Baltimore, MD 21218-2699. Offers competitive intelligence (Certificate); information security management (Certificate); information systems (MS); MBA/MSIS. Part-time and evening/weekend programs available. *Degree requirements:* For master's, 36 credits including final project. *Entrance requirements:* For master's and Certificate, minimum GPA of 3.0, resume, work experience, two letters of recommendation. Additional exam requirements/recommendations for international students: Required—TOEFL (minimum score 600 paper-based; 250 computer-based; 100 iBT). Electronic applications accepted. *Faculty research:* Information security, healthcare information systems.

The Johns Hopkins University, Engineering Program for Professionals, Part-time Program in Information Systems and Technology, Baltimore, MD 21218-2699. Offers MS, Post-Master's Certificate. Part-time and evening/weekend programs available. Electronic applications accepted.

Kaplan University, Davenport Campus, School of Information Technology, Davenport, IA 52807-2095. Offers decision support systems (MS); information security and assurance (MS). Part-time and evening/weekend programs available. Postbaccalaureate distance learning degree programs offered (no on-campus study). *Entrance requirements:* Additional exam requirements/recommendations for international students: Required—TOEFL (minimum score 550 paper-based; 218 computer-based; 80 iBT).

Kean University, College of Natural, Applied and Health Sciences, Program in Computer Information Systems, Union, NJ 07083. Offers MS. *Faculty:* 7 full-time (2 women). *Students:* 2 full-time (1 woman); includes 1 minority (Hispanic/Latino), 1 international. Average age 23. 3 applicants, 100% accepted, 2 enrolled. *Entrance requirements:* For master's, undergraduate degree in computer science or closely-related field, minimum GPA of 3.0, official transcripts, 2 letters of recommendation, professional resume/curriculum vitae, personal statement. Additional exam requirements/recommendations for international students: Required—TOEFL (minimum score 79 iBT). *Application deadline:* For fall admission, 6/1 for domestic and international students; for spring admission, 12/1 for domestic and international students. Applications are processed on a rolling basis. Application fee: $75 ($150 for international students). Electronic applications accepted. *Expenses:* Tuition, state resident: full-time $11,302; part-time $550 per credit. Tuition, nonresident: full-time $15,318; part-time $674 per credit. *Required fees:* $2849; $130 per credit. Tuition and fees vary according to degree level. *Financial support:* In 2011–12, 1 research assistantship (averaging $3,263 per year) was awarded; tuition waivers (full) and unspecified assistantships also available. Financial award applicants required to submit FAFSA. *Unit head:* Dr. Jing-Chiou Liou, Program Coordinator, 908-737-3803, E-mail: jliou@kean.edu. *Application contact:* Reenat Hasan, Admissions Counselor, 908-737-5923, Fax: 908-737-5925, E-mail: hasanr@kean.edu.

Kent State University, College of Business Administration, Doctoral Program in Management Systems, Kent, OH 44242-0001. Offers PhD. *Faculty:* 19 full-time (6 women). *Students:* 11 full-time (3 women), 7 international. Average age 36. 13 applicants, 15% accepted, 0 enrolled. In 2011, 4 doctorates awarded. *Degree requirements:* For doctorate, comprehensive exam, thesis/dissertation, oral defense. *Entrance requirements:* For doctorate, GMAT or GRE. Additional exam requirements/recommendations for international students: Required—TOEFL (minimum score 600 paper-based; 250 computer-based; 100 iBT). *Application deadline:* For fall admission, 2/1 for domestic students, 1/1 for international students. Application fee: $30 ($60 for international students). Electronic applications accepted. *Expenses:* Tuition, state resident: full-time $8136; part-time $452 per credit hour. Tuition, nonresident: full-time $14,292; part-time $794 per credit hour. *Financial support:* In 2011–12, 14 students received support, including 8 teaching assistantships with full tuition reimbursements available (averaging $16,000 per year); Federal Work-Study also available. Financial award application deadline: 2/1; financial award applicants required to submit FAFSA. *Unit head:* Dr. O. Felix Offodile, Chair and Professor, 330-672-2750, Fax: 330-672-2953, E-mail: foffodil@kent.edu. *Application contact:* Felecia A. Urbanek, Coordinator, Graduate Programs, 330-672-2282, Fax: 330-672-7303, E-mail: gradbus@kent.edu. Web site: http://www.kent.edu/business/Grad/phd/index.cfm.

Kentucky State University, College of Professional Studies, Frankfort, KY 40601. Offers public administration (MPA), including human resource management, international development, management information systems, nonprofit management; special education (MA). Part-time and evening/weekend programs available. Postbaccalaureate distance learning degree programs offered (minimal on-campus study). *Faculty:* 12 full-time (4 women), 2 part-time/adjunct (both women). *Students:* 88 full-time (57 women), 79 part-time (42 women); includes 104 minority (101 Black or African American, non-Hispanic/Latino; 1 Asian, non-Hispanic/Latino; 2 Hispanic/Latino), 2 international. Average age 34. 124 applicants, 62% accepted, 45 enrolled. In 2011, 38 master's awarded. *Degree requirements:* For master's, comprehensive exam, thesis optional. *Entrance requirements:* For master's, GMAT, GRE. Additional exam requirements/recommendations for international students: Required—TOEFL (minimum score 525 paper-based; 173 computer-based). *Application deadline:* Applications are processed on a rolling basis. Application fee: $30 ($100 for international students). Electronic applications accepted. *Expenses:* Tuition, state resident: full-time $6192; part-time $344 per credit hour. Tuition, nonresident: full-time $9522; part-time $529 per credit hour. *Required fees:* $450; $25 per credit hour. Tuition and fees vary according to course load. *Financial support:* In 2011–12, 46 students received support, including 4 research assistantships (averaging $10,975 per year); career-related internships or fieldwork, scholarships/grants, tuition waivers (partial), and unspecified assistantships also available. Financial award application deadline: 4/15; financial award applicants required to submit FAFSA. *Unit head:* Dr. Gashaw Lake, Dean, 502-597-6105, Fax: 502-597-6715, E-mail: gashaw.lake@kysu.edu. *Application contact:* Dr. Titilayo Ufomata, Acting Director of Graduate Studies, 502-597-6443, E-mail: titilayo.ufomata@kysu.edu. Web site: http://www.kysu.edu/academics/collegesAndSchools/collegeofprofessionalstudies/.

Lawrence Technological University, College of Management, Southfield, MI 48075-1058. Offers business administration (MBA, DBA); business administration international (MBA); global leadership and management (MS); global operations and project management (MS); information systems (MS); information technology (DM); operations management (MS). *Accreditation:* ACBSP. Part-time and evening/weekend programs available. *Faculty:* 12 full-time (6 women), 39 part-time/adjunct (11 women). *Students:* 10 full-time (4 women), 518 part-time (228 women); includes 183 minority (123 Black or African American, non-Hispanic/Latino; 2 American Indian or Alaska Native, non-Hispanic/Latino; 44 Asian, non-Hispanic/Latino; 11 Hispanic/Latino; 3 Two or more races, non-Hispanic/Latino), 50 international. Average age 36. 420 applicants, 45% accepted, 97 enrolled. In 2011, 177 master's, 14 doctorates awarded. *Degree requirements:* For master's, thesis (for some programs). *Entrance requirements:* For master's, GMAT. Additional exam requirements/recommendations for international students: Required—TOEFL (minimum score 550 paper-based; 213 computer-based; 79 iBT). *Application deadline:* For fall admission, 7/27 priority date for domestic students, 5/23 for international students; for spring admission, 11/15 priority date for domestic students, 11/15 for international students. Applications are processed on a rolling basis. Application fee: $50. Electronic applications accepted. *Financial support:* In 2011–12, 122 students received support. Federal Work-Study and institutionally sponsored loans available. Support available to part-time students. Financial award application deadline: 4/1; financial award applicants required to submit FAFSA. *Unit head:* Dr. Alan McCord, Interim Dean, 248-204-3050, E-mail: mgtdean@ltu.edu. *Application contact:* Jane Rohrback, Director of Admissions, 248-204-3160, Fax: 248-204-2228, E-mail: admissions@ltu.edu. Web site: http://www.ltu.edu/management/index.asp.

Lewis University, College of Business, Graduate School of Management, Program in Business Administration, Romeoville, IL 60446. Offers accounting (MBA); custom elective option (MBA); e-business (MBA); finance (MBA); healthcare management (MBA); human resources management (MBA); information security (MBA); international business (MBA); management information systems (MBA); marketing (MBA); project management (MBA); technology and operations management (MBA). Part-time and evening/weekend programs available. *Students:* 112 full-time (60 women), 232 part-time (118 women); includes 104 minority (62 Black or African American, non-Hispanic/Latino; 1 American Indian or Alaska Native, non-Hispanic/Latino; 7 Asian, non-Hispanic/Latino; 33 Hispanic/Latino; 1 Native Hawaiian or other Pacific Islander, non-Hispanic/Latino), 9 international. Average age 28. In 2011, 99 master's awarded. *Entrance requirements:* For master's, interview, bachelor's degree, resume, 2 recommendations. Additional exam requirements/recommendations for international students: Required—TOEFL (minimum score 550 paper-based; 213 computer-based). *Application deadline:* For fall admission, 8/15 priority date for domestic students, 5/1 for international students; for spring admission, 11/15 for international students. Applications are processed on a rolling basis. Application fee: $40. Electronic applications accepted. *Financial support:* Career-related internships or fieldwork, Federal Work-Study, scholarships/grants, and unspecified assistantships available. Financial award application deadline: 5/1; financial award applicants required to submit FAFSA. *Unit head:* Dr. Maureen Culleeney, Academic Program Director, 815-838-0500 Ext. 5631, E-mail: culleema@lewisu.edu. *Application contact:* Michele Ryan, Director of Admission, 815-838-0500 Ext. 5384, E-mail: gsm@lewisu.edu.

Lincoln University, Graduate Studies, Oakland, CA 94612. Offers finance and investments (DBA); finance management and investment banking (MBA); general business (MBA); human resource management (MBA, DBA); international business (MBA); management information systems (MBA). Part-time and evening/weekend programs available. *Faculty:* 10 full-time (4 women), 15 part-time/adjunct (3 women). *Students:* 272 full-time (124 women), 1 part-time (0 women). *Degree requirements:* For master's, research project (thesis), internship report, or comprehensive exam; for doctorate, comprehensive exam, thesis/dissertation. *Entrance requirements:* For master's, minimum GPA of 2.7; for doctorate, GMAT (minimum score: 550), GRE (minimum score: 1000), or equivalent test results (waived for master's degree with minimum cumulative GPA of 3.3). Additional exam requirements/recommendations for international students: Required—TOEFL (minimum score 525 paper-based; 195 computer-based; 71 iBT) or IELTS (minimum score 5.5) for MBA; TOEFL (minimum score 550 paper-based; 213 computer-based; 79 iBT) or IELTS (minimum score 6) for DBA. *Application deadline:* For fall admission, 7/2 priority date for domestic students, 7/2 for international students; for spring admission, 11/25 priority date for domestic students, 11/25 for international students. Applications are processed on a rolling basis. Application fee: $75. Electronic applications accepted. *Financial support:* Teaching assistantships, career-related internships or fieldwork, and scholarships/grants available. *Unit head:* Dr. Marshall Burak, Director of Graduate Programs, 510-628-8016, Fax: 510-628-8012, E-mail: mburak@lincolnuca.edu. *Application contact:* Peggy Au, Director of Admissions and Records, 510-628-8010, Fax: 510-628-8012, E-mail: admissions@lincolnuca.edu. Web site: http://www.lincolnuca.edu/.

Lindenwood University, Graduate Programs, College of Individualized Education, St. Charles, MO 63301-1695. Offers administration (MSA); business administration (MBA); communications (MA); criminal justice and administration (MS); gerontology (MA); health management (MS); human resource management (MS); information technology (MBA, Certificate); managing information technology (MS); writing (MFA). Part-time and evening/weekend programs available. *Faculty:* 18 full-time (9 women), 128 part-time/adjunct (53 women). *Students:* 858 full-time (586 women), 69 part-time (43 women); includes 330 minority (296 Black or African American, non-Hispanic/Latino; 9 American Indian or Alaska Native, non-Hispanic/Latino; 4 Asian, non-Hispanic/Latino; 1 Hispanic/Latino; 20 Two or more races, non-Hispanic/Latino), 16 international. Average age 35. 229 applicants, 80% accepted, 172 enrolled. In 2011, 428 degrees awarded. *Degree requirements:* For master's, thesis (for some programs), 1 colloquium per term. *Entrance requirements:* For master's, interview, minimum GPA of 3.0. Additional exam requirements/recommendations for international students: Required—TOEFL (minimum score 550 paper-based; 213 computer-based; 80 iBT). *Application deadline:* For fall admission, 10/1 priority date for domestic students, 10/1 for international students; for winter admission, 1/7 priority date for domestic students, 1/7 for international students; for spring admission, 4/7 priority date for domestic students, 4/7 for international students. Applications are processed on a rolling basis. Application fee: $30 ($100 for international students). Electronic applications accepted. *Expenses: Tuition:* Full-time $13,650; part-time $395 per credit hour. *Required fees:* $150 per semester. Tuition and fees vary according to course level and course load. *Financial support:* In 2011–12, 386 students received support. Career-related internships or fieldwork, institutionally sponsored loans, tuition waivers (partial), and unspecified assistantships available. Financial award application deadline: 6/30; financial award applicants required to submit FAFSA. *Unit head:* Dan Kemper, Dean, 636-949-4501, Fax: 636-949-4505, E-mail: dkemper@lindenwood.edu. *Application contact:* Brett Barger, Dean of Evening Admissions and Extension Campuses, 636-949-4934, Fax: 636-949-4109, E-mail: adultadmissions@lindenwood.edu.

Lindenwood University, Graduate Programs, School of Business and Entrepreneurship, St. Charles, MO 63301-1695. Offers accounting (MBA, MS); business administration (MBA); entrepreneurial studies (MBA, MS); finance (MBA, MS); human resource management (MBA); human resources (MS); international business (MBA, MS); management (MBA, MS); management information systems (MBA, MS); marketing (MBA, MS); public management (MBA, MS); sport management (MA); supply chain management (MBA). *Accreditation:* ACBSP. Part-time and evening/weekend programs available. *Faculty:* 20 full-time (8 women), 17 part-time/adjunct (5 women). *Students:* 165 full-time (66 women), 223 part-time (100 women); includes 59 minority (48 Black or African American, non-Hispanic/Latino; 4 Asian, non-Hispanic/Latino; 2 Native Hawaiian or other Pacific Islander, non-Hispanic/Latino; 5 Two or more races, non-Hispanic/Latino), 140 international. Average age 29. 156 applicants, 76% accepted, 103 enrolled. In 2011, 205 degrees awarded. *Degree requirements:* For master's, comprehensive exam (for some programs), thesis (for some programs). *Entrance requirements:* For master's, interview, minimum GPA of 3.0, letter of recommendation. Additional exam requirements/recommendations for international students: Required—TOEFL (minimum score 550 paper-based; 213 computer-based; 80 iBT). *Application deadline:* For fall admission, 8/15 priority date for domestic students, 8/15 for international students; for winter admission, 1/9 priority date for domestic students, 1/9 for international students; for spring admission, 3/12 priority date for domestic students, 3/12 for international students. Applications are processed on a rolling basis. Application fee: $30 ($100 for international students). Electronic applications accepted. *Expenses: Tuition:* Full-time $13,650; part-time $395 per credit hour. *Required fees:* $150 per semester. Tuition and fees vary according to course level and course load. *Financial support:* In 2011–12, 206 students received support. Career-related internships or fieldwork, Federal Work-Study, institutionally sponsored loans, and tuition waivers (partial) available. Financial award application deadline: 6/30; financial award applicants required to submit FAFSA. *Unit head:* Roger Ellis, Dean, 636-949-4839, E-mail: rellis@lindenwood.edu. *Application contact:* Brett Barger, Dean of Evening Admissions and Extension Campuses, 636-949-4934, Fax: 636-949-4109, E-mail: adultadmissions@lindenwood.edu. Web site: http://www.lindenwood.edu.

Long Island University–C. W. Post Campus, College of Management, School of Business, Brookville, NY 11548-1300. Offers accounting and taxation (Certificate); business administration (Certificate); finance (MBA, Certificate); general business administration (MBA); international business (MBA, Certificate); management (MBA, Certificate); management information systems (MBA, Certificate); marketing (MBA, Certificate). *Accreditation:* AACSB. Part-time and evening/weekend programs available. *Entrance requirements:* For master's, GMAT, resume, minimum GPA of 3.0, 2 letters of recommendation. Additional exam requirements/recommendations for international students: Required—TOEFL (minimum score 527 paper-based; 197 computer-based). Electronic applications accepted. *Faculty research:* Financial markets, consumer behavior.

Louisiana State University and Agricultural and Mechanical College, Graduate School, E. J. Ourso College of Business, Department of Information Systems and Decision Sciences, Baton Rouge, LA 70803. Offers MS, PhD. *Faculty:* 14 full-time (5 women). *Students:* 19 full-time (5 women), 4 part-time (2 women); includes 5 minority (2 Black or African American, non-Hispanic/Latino; 2 Asian, non-Hispanic/Latino; 1 Hispanic/Latino), 2 international. Average age 30. 27 applicants, 37% accepted, 2 enrolled. In 2011, 6 master's, 2 doctorates awarded. Terminal master's awarded for partial completion of doctoral program. *Degree requirements:* For master's, comprehensive exam, thesis optional; for doctorate, comprehensive exam, thesis/dissertation. *Entrance requirements:* For master's, GMAT or GRE General Test; for doctorate, GMAT or GRE. Additional exam requirements/recommendations for international students: Required—TOEFL (minimum score 550 paper-based; 213 computer-based; 79 iBT). *Application deadline:* For fall admission, 1/25 priority date for domestic students, 5/15 for international students; for spring admission, 10/15 for international students. Applications are processed on a rolling basis. Application fee: $50 ($70 for international students). Electronic applications accepted. *Financial support:* In 2011–12, 16 students received support, including 9 research assistantships with full and partial tuition reimbursements available (averaging $18,084 per year), 3 teaching assistantships with full and partial tuition reimbursements available (averaging $8,933 per year); fellowships, Federal Work-Study, institutionally sponsored loans, scholarships/grants, health care benefits, tuition waivers (full and partial), and unspecified assistantships also available. Support available to part-time students. Financial award applicants required to submit FAFSA. *Faculty research:* Healthcare informatics, outsourcing, information systems management, operations management. *Total annual research expenditures:* $258,367. *Unit head:* Dr. Helmut Schneider, Department Head, 225-578-2516, Fax: 225-578-2511, E-mail: hschnei@lsu.edu. *Application contact:* Dr. Rudy Hirschheim, Graduate Adviser, 225-578-2514, Fax: 225-578-2511, E-mail: rudy@lsu.edu. Web site: http://business.lsu.edu/isds.

Loyola University Chicago, Graduate School of Business, Information Systems and Operations Management Department, Chicago, IL 60660. Offers information systems management (MS). Part-time and evening/weekend programs available. *Entrance requirements:* For master's, GMAT, letters of recommendation. Additional exam requirements/recommendations for international students: Required—TOEFL (minimum score 550 paper-based; 213 computer-based; 80 iBT). Electronic applications accepted. *Expenses:* Contact institution. *Faculty research:* Strategic use of IT, database design data warehousing, e-business, applications of data mining.

Loyola University Maryland, Graduate Programs, Sellinger School of Business and Management, Program in Business Administration, Baltimore, MD 21210-2699. Offers accounting (MBA); finance (MBA); general business (MBA); information systems operations management (MBA); international business (MBA); management (MBA); marketing (MBA). *Accreditation:* AACSB. Part-time and evening/weekend programs available. *Faculty:* 61 full-time (12 women), 29 part-time/adjunct (4 women). *Students:* 50 full-time (15 women), 547 part-time (210 women); includes 98 minority (39 Black or African American, non-Hispanic/Latino; 1 American Indian or Alaska Native, non-Hispanic/Latino; 28 Asian, non-Hispanic/Latino; 18 Hispanic/Latino; 2 Native Hawaiian or other Pacific Islander, non-Hispanic/Latino; 10 Two or more races, non-Hispanic/Latino), 15 international. Average age 30. In 2011, 232 master's awarded. *Entrance requirements:* For master's, GMAT (for some programs). Additional exam requirements/recommendations for international students: Required—TOEFL (minimum score 550 paper-based; 213 computer-based). *Application deadline:* For fall admission, 8/1 priority date for domestic students; for spring admission, 12/1 priority date for domestic students. Application fee: $50. Electronic applications accepted. *Financial support:* Research assistantships and unspecified assistantships available. Financial award application deadline: 4/15; financial award applicants required to submit FAFSA. *Unit head:* Dr. Karyl Leggio, Dean, 410-617-2301, E-mail: kbleggio@loyola.edu. *Application contact:* Maureen Faux, Executive Director, Graduate Admissions, 410-617-5020, Fax: 410-617-2002, E-mail: graduate@loyola.edu.

Marist College, Graduate Programs, School of Computer Science and Mathematics, Poughkeepsie, NY 12601-1387. Offers computer science/software development (MS); information systems (MS, Adv C); technology management (MS). Part-time and evening/weekend programs available. Postbaccalaureate distance learning degree programs offered (minimal on-campus study). *Entrance requirements:* For master's, resume. Additional exam requirements/recommendations for international students: Required—TOEFL (minimum score 550 paper-based; 213 computer-based; 80 iBT); Recommended—IELTS (minimum score 6.5). Electronic applications accepted. *Faculty research:* Data quality, artificial intelligence, imaging, analysis of algorithms, distributed systems and applications.

Marquette University, Graduate School of Management, Executive MBA Program, Milwaukee, WI 53201-1881. Offers economics (MBA); finance (MBA); human resources (MBA); international business (MBA); management information systems (MBA); marketing (MBA); operations and supply chain management (MBA); sports business (MBA). *Accreditation:* AACSB. *Students:* 50 full-time (15 women); includes 4 minority (1 Black or African American, non-Hispanic/Latino; 3 Asian, non-Hispanic/Latino), 3 international. Average age 37. 37 applicants, 81% accepted, 29 enrolled. In 2011, 36 master's awarded. *Degree requirements:* For master's, international trip. *Entrance requirements:* For master's, GMAT or GRE, two letters of recommendation, official transcripts from current and previous colleges/universities. Additional exam requirements/recommendations for international students: Required—TOEFL (minimum score 550 paper-based; 85 computer-based; 88 iBT), IELTS (minimum score 6.5), Pearson Test of English. *Application deadline:* For fall admission, 2/15 for domestic and international students. Application fee: $50. Electronic applications accepted. *Expenses:* Contact institution. *Financial support:* Application deadline: 2/15. *Faculty research:* International trade and finance, customer relationship management, consumer satisfaction, customer service . *Unit head:* Dr. Jeanne Simmons, Graduate Director, 414-288-7145, Fax: 414-288-1660, E-mail: jeanne.simmons@marquette.edu. *Application contact:* Debra Leutermann, Admissions Coordinator, 414-288-7145, Fax: 414-288-8078, E-mail: debra.leutermann@marquette.edu. Web site: http://www.busadm.mu.edu/emba/.

Marquette University, Graduate School of Management, Program in Business Administration, Milwaukee, WI 53201-1881. Offers business administration (MBA); economics (MBA); entrepreneurship (Certificate); finance (MBA); human resources (MBA); international business (MBA); management information systems (MBA); marketing (MBA); operations and supply chain management (MBA); sports business (MBA); JD/MBA; MBA/MA; MBA/MSN. *Accreditation:* AACSB. Part-time and evening/weekend programs available. *Students:* 42 full-time (14 women), 335 part-time (94 women); includes 24 minority (5 Black or African American, non-Hispanic/Latino; 1 American Indian or Alaska Native, non-Hispanic/Latino; 15 Asian, non-Hispanic/Latino; 3 Hispanic/Latino), 29 international. Average age 31. 182 applicants, 59% accepted, 103 enrolled. In 2011, 128 master's awarded. *Degree requirements:* For Certificate, business plan. *Entrance requirements:* For master's, GMAT or GRE, letters of recommendation. Additional exam requirements/recommendations for international students: Required—TOEFL (minimum score 550 paper-based; 85 computer-based; 88 iBT), IELTS (minimum score 6.5), Pearson Test of English. *Application deadline:* For fall admission, 2/15 for domestic and international students. Applications are processed on a rolling basis. Application fee: $50. Electronic applications accepted. *Expenses: Tuition:* Full-time $17,010; part-time $945 per credit hour. Tuition and fees vary according to program. *Financial support:* In 2011–12, 4 fellowships, 11 teaching assistantships were awarded; research assistantships, Federal Work-Study, institutionally sponsored loans, scholarships/grants, and tuition waivers (full and partial) also available. Support available to part-time students. Financial award application deadline: 2/15. *Faculty research:* Ethics in the professions, services marketing, technology impact on decision-making, mentoring. *Unit head:* Dr. Jeanne Simmons, Graduate Director, 414-288-7145, Fax: 414-288-1660, E-mail: jeanne.simmons@marquette.edu. *Application contact:* Debra Leutermann, Admissions Coordinator, 414-288-8064, Fax: 414-288-1902, E-mail: debra.leutermann@marquette.edu. Web site: http://business.marquette.edu/academics/mba.

Marymount University, School of Business Administration, Program in Information Technology, Arlington, VA 22207-4299. Offers computer security and information assurance (Certificate); health care informatics (Certificate); information technology (MS, Certificate); information technology project management: technology leadership (Certificate). Part-time and evening/weekend programs available. *Faculty:* 6 full-time (2 women), 9 part-time/adjunct (0 women). *Students:* 37 full-time (14 women), 32 part-time (13 women); includes 19 minority (9 Black or African American, non-Hispanic/Latino; 6 Asian, non-Hispanic/Latino; 3 Hispanic/Latino; 1 Two or more races, non-Hispanic/

Latino), 30 international. Average age 30. 47 applicants, 98% accepted, 36 enrolled. In 2011, 28 master's, 10 other advanced degrees awarded. *Degree requirements:* For master's, thesis or alternative. *Entrance requirements:* For master's, GMAT or GRE General Test, interview, resume, bachelor's degree in computer-related field or degree in another subject with a post-baccalaureate certificate in a computer-related field; for Certificate, resume. Additional exam requirements/recommendations for international students: Required—TOEFL (minimum score 600 paper-based; 250 computer-based; 96 iBT), IELTS (minimum score 6.5). *Application deadline:* For fall admission, 7/1 priority date for domestic students, 7/1 for international students; for spring admission, 11/15 for domestic students, 11/16 for international students. Applications are processed on a rolling basis. Application fee: $40. Electronic applications accepted. *Expenses: Tuition:* Part-time $770 per credit hour. *Required fees:* $8 per credit hour. One-time fee: $180 full-time. *Financial support:* In 2011–12, 7 students received support. Research assistantships with full tuition reimbursements available, career-related internships or fieldwork, Federal Work-Study, scholarships/grants, and unspecified assistantships available. Support available to part-time students. Financial award applicants required to submit FAFSA. *Unit head:* Dr. Diane Murphy, Chair, 703-284-5958, Fax: 703-527-3830, E-mail: diane.murphy@marymount.edu. *Application contact:* Francesca Reed, Director, Graduate Admissions, 703-284-5901, Fax: 703-527-3815, E-mail: grad.admissions@marymount.edu. Web site: http://www.marymount.edu/academics/programs/infoTechMS.

Marywood University, Academic Affairs, College of Liberal Arts and Sciences, Department of Business and Managerial Science, Emphasis in Management Information Systems, Scranton, PA 18509-1598. Offers MBA, MS. *Entrance requirements:* Additional exam requirements/recommendations for international students: Required—TOEFL (minimum score 550 paper-based; 213 computer-based; 79 iBT). *Application deadline:* For fall admission, 4/1 priority date for domestic students, 3/31 for international students; for spring admission, 11/1 priority date for domestic students, 8/31 for international students. Applications are processed on a rolling basis. Application fee: $35. Electronic applications accepted. *Financial support:* Career-related internships or fieldwork, scholarships/grants, and unspecified assistantships available. Support available to part-time students. Financial award application deadline: 6/30; financial award applicants required to submit FAFSA. *Faculty research:* Systems design. *Unit head:* Dr. Arthur Comstock, Chair, 570-348-6274, E-mail: comstock@marywood.edu. *Application contact:* Tammy Manka, Assistant Director of Graduate Admissions, 570-348-6211 Ext. 2322, E-mail: tmanka@marywood.edu. Web site: http://www.marywood.edu/business/graduate/mis.html.

McGill University, Faculty of Graduate and Postdoctoral Studies, Desautels Faculty of Management, Montréal, QC H3A 2T5, Canada. Offers administration (PhD); entrepreneurial studies (MBA); finance (MBA); general management (Post Master's Certificate); information systems (MBA); international business (MBA); international practicing management (MM); management (MBA); management for development (MBA); manufacturing management (MMM); marketing (MBA); operations management (MBA); public accountancy (Diploma); strategic management (MBA); MBA/LL B; MD/MBA. MMM offered jointly with Faculty of Engineering; PhD with Concordia University, HEC Montreal, Université de Montréal, Université du Québec à Montréal.

McMaster University, School of Graduate Studies, Faculty of Business, Program in Information Systems, Hamilton, ON L8S 4M2, Canada. Offers PhD. Part-time programs available. *Degree requirements:* For doctorate, comprehensive exam, thesis/dissertation. *Entrance requirements:* For doctorate, GMAT or GRE General Test, master's degree, minimum B+ average. Additional exam requirements/recommendations for international students: Required—TOEFL (minimum score 580 paper-based; 237 computer-based). *Faculty research:* Information systems, operations management, web-based decision support systems, web-based agents, financial engineering.

Metropolitan State University, College of Management, St. Paul, MN 55106-5000. Offers business administration (MBA, DBA); database administration (Graduate Certificate); healthcare information technology management (Graduate Certificate); information assurance security (Graduate Certificate); management information systems (MMIS); MIS generalist (Graduate Certificate); MIS systems analysis and design (Graduate Certificate); project management (Graduate Certificate); public and nonprofit administration (MPNA). Part-time and evening/weekend programs available. *Students:* 63 full-time (41 women), 409 part-time (192 women); includes 94 minority (38 Black or African American, non-Hispanic/Latino; 33 Asian, non-Hispanic/Latino; 14 Hispanic/Latino; 9 Two or more races, non-Hispanic/Latino), 61 international. Average age 35. *Degree requirements:* For master's, thesis optional, computer language (MMIS). *Entrance requirements:* For master's, GMAT (MBA), resume. Additional exam requirements/recommendations for international students: Required—TOEFL (minimum score 550 paper-based; 213 computer-based). *Application deadline:* For fall admission, 7/15 for international students; for winter admission, 11/15 for international students; for spring admission, 3/15 for international students. Applications are processed on a rolling basis. Application fee: $20. Electronic applications accepted. *Expenses:* Tuition, state resident: full-time $5799.06; part-time $322.17 per credit. Tuition, nonresident: full-time $11,411; part-time $633.92 per credit. Tuition and fees vary according to degree level, program and reciprocity agreements. *Financial support:* Research assistantships with partial tuition reimbursements, career-related internships or fieldwork, and Federal Work-Study available. Support available to part-time students. Financial award applicants required to submit FAFSA. *Faculty research:* Yugoslav economic system, workers' cooperatives, participative management and job enrichment, global business systems. *Unit head:* Dr. Paul Huo, Dean, 612-659-7271, Fax: 612-659-7268, E-mail: paul.huo@metrostate.edu. Web site: http://choose.metrostate.edu/comgradprograms.

Michigan State University, The Graduate School, College of Communication Arts and Sciences, Department of Telecommunication, Information Studies, and Media, East Lansing, MI 48824. Offers digital media arts and technology (MA); information and telecommunication management (MA); information, policy and society (MA); serious game design (MA). *Entrance requirements:* Additional exam requirements/recommendations for international students: Required—TOEFL. Electronic applications accepted.

Michigan State University, The Graduate School, Eli Broad Graduate School of Management, Department of Accounting and Information Systems, East Lansing, MI 48824. Offers accounting (MS); business administration (PhD). *Accreditation:* AACSB. *Entrance requirements:* Additional exam requirements/recommendations for international students: Required—TOEFL. Electronic applications accepted.

Middle Tennessee State University, College of Graduate Studies, Jennings A. Jones College of Business, Department of Computer Information Systems, Murfreesboro, TN 37132. Offers MS. Part-time and evening/weekend programs available. Postbaccalaureate distance learning degree programs offered. *Faculty:* 15 full-time (6 women). *Students:* 11 full-time (4 women), 44 part-time (10 women); includes 19 minority (11 Black or African American, non-Hispanic/Latino; 4 Asian, non-Hispanic/Latino; 3 Hispanic/Latino; 1 Two or more races, non-Hispanic/Latino). Average age 33. 33 applicants, 73% accepted. In 2011, 25 master's awarded. *Entrance requirements:* Additional exam requirements/recommendations for international students: Required—TOEFL (minimum score 525 paper-based; 195 computer-based; 71 iBT) or IELTS (minimum score 6). *Application deadline:* For fall admission, 6/1 for domestic and international students. Applications are processed on a rolling basis. Application fee: $25 ($30 for international students). Electronic applications accepted. *Expenses:* Tuition, state resident: full-time $10,008. Tuition, nonresident: full-time $25,056. *Financial support:* In 2011–12, 8 students received support. Tuition waivers available. Support available to part-time students. Financial award application deadline: 5/1; financial award applicants required to submit FAFSA. *Faculty research:* Safety and security, project management. *Unit head:* Dr. Stanley E. Gambill, Chair, 615-898-2362, Fax: 615-898-5187, E-mail: stan.gambill@mtsu.edu. *Application contact:* Dr. Michael D. Allen, Dean and Vice Provost for Research, 615-898-2840, Fax: 615-904-8020, E-mail: michael.allen@mtsu.edu.

Minnesota State University Mankato, College of Graduate Studies, College of Science, Engineering and Technology, Department of Information Systems and Technology, Mankato, MN 56001. Offers database technologies (Certificate); information technology (MS). *Students:* 9 full-time (1 woman), 22 part-time (4 women). *Degree requirements:* For master's, comprehensive exam, thesis or alternative. *Entrance requirements:* For master's, GRE General Test, minimum GPA of 3.0 during previous 2 years. Additional exam requirements/recommendations for international students: Required—TOEFL (minimum score 550 paper-based; 213 computer-based; 80 iBT). *Application deadline:* For fall admission, 7/1 priority date for domestic students; for spring admission, 11/1 for domestic students. Applications are processed on a rolling basis. Electronic applications accepted. *Financial support:* Research assistantships with full tuition reimbursements, teaching assistantships with full tuition reimbursements, and unspecified assistantships available. Financial award application deadline: 3/15; financial award applicants required to submit FAFSA. *Unit head:* Dr. Mahbubur Syed, Graduate Coordinator, 507-389-3226. *Application contact:* 507-389-2321, E-mail: grad@mnsu.edu. Web site: http://cset.mnsu.edu/ist/.

Minot State University, Graduate School, Information Systems Program, Minot, ND 58707-0002. Offers MSIS. Part-time programs available. Postbaccalaureate distance learning degree programs offered (minimal on-campus study).

Mississippi State University, College of Business, Department of Management and Information Systems, Mississippi State, MS 39762. Offers business administration (PhD), including management; information systems (MSIS). Part-time programs available. *Faculty:* 13 full-time (4 women), 1 (woman) part-time/adjunct. *Students:* 22 full-time (8 women), 9 part-time (2 women); includes 8 minority (1 Black or African American, non-Hispanic/Latino; 5 Asian, non-Hispanic/Latino; 1 Hispanic/Latino; 1 Two or more races, non-Hispanic/Latino), 5 international. Average age 31. 72 applicants, 28% accepted, 16 enrolled. In 2011, 7 master's, 1 doctorate awarded. *Degree requirements:* For master's, comprehensive exam; for doctorate, comprehensive exam, thesis/dissertation. *Entrance requirements:* For master's, GMAT, minimum GPA of 3.0 in last 60 hours of course work; for doctorate, GMAT, minimum graduate GPA of 3.25 in last 60 hours. Additional exam requirements/recommendations for international students: Required—TOEFL (minimum score 575 paper-based; 233 computer-based; 90 iBT); Recommended—IELTS (minimum score 7). *Application deadline:* For fall admission, 7/1 for domestic students, 5/1 for international students; for spring admission, 11/1 for domestic students, 9/1 for international students. Applications are processed on a rolling basis. Application fee: $40. Electronic applications accepted. *Expenses:* Tuition, state resident: full-time $5805; part-time $322.50 per credit hour. Tuition, nonresident: full-time $14,670; part-time $815 per credit hour. *Financial support:* In 2011–12, 6 teaching assistantships (averaging $12,270 per year) were awarded; Federal Work-Study and institutionally sponsored loans also available. Financial award applicants required to submit FAFSA. *Faculty research:* Electronic commerce, management of information technology. *Unit head:* Dr. Rodney Pearson, Department Head and Professor of Information Systems, 662-325-3928, Fax: 662-325-8651, E-mail: rodney.pearson@msstate.edu. *Application contact:* Dr. Barbara Spencer, Associate Dean for Research and Outreach, 662-325-1891, Fax: 662-325-8161, E-mail: bspencer@cobian.msstate.edu. Web site: http://misweb.cbi.msstate.edu/~COBI/faculty/departments/mainpage.shtml?MIS.

Missouri State University, Graduate College, College of Business Administration, Department of Computer Information Systems, Springfield, MO 65897. Offers computer information systems (MS); secondary education (MS Ed), including business. Part-time and evening/weekend programs available. Postbaccalaureate distance learning degree programs offered (no on-campus study). *Faculty:* 13 full-time (2 women), 5 part-time/adjunct (0 women). *Students:* 28 full-time (5 women), 2 part-time (1 woman); includes 2 minority (1 Asian, non-Hispanic/Latino; 1 Two or more races, non-Hispanic/Latino), 2 international. Average age 38. 20 applicants, 90% accepted, 11 enrolled. In 2011, 13 master's awarded. *Degree requirements:* For master's, thesis optional. *Entrance requirements:* For master's, GMAT, 3 years of work experience in computer information systems, minimum GPA of 2.75 (MS), 9-12 teaching certification (MS Ed). Additional exam requirements/recommendations for international students: Required—TOEFL (minimum score 550 paper-based; 213 computer-based; 79 iBT). *Application deadline:* For fall admission, 7/20 priority date for domestic students, 5/1 for international students; for spring admission, 12/20 priority date for domestic students, 9/1 for international students. Applications are processed on a rolling basis. Application fee: $35 ($50 for international students). Electronic applications accepted. *Expenses:* Contact institution. *Financial support:* Federal Work-Study, institutionally sponsored loans, scholarships/grants, and unspecified assistantships available. Support available to part-time students. Financial award application deadline: 3/31; financial award applicants required to submit FAFSA. *Faculty research:* Decision support systems, algorithms in Visual Basic, end-user satisfaction, information security. *Unit head:* Dr. Jerry Chin, Head, 417-836-4131, Fax: 417-836-6907, E-mail: jerrychin@missouristate.edu. *Application contact:* Misty Stewart, Coordinator of Graduate Admissions and Recruitment, 417-836-6079, Fax: 417-836-6200, E-mail: mistystewart@missouristate.edu. Web site: http://mscis.missouristate.edu.

Missouri Western State University, Program in Applied Science, St. Joseph, MO 64507-2294. Offers chemistry (MAS); engineering technology management (MAS); human factors and usability testing (MAS); information technology management (MAS). Part-time programs available. *Application deadline:* For fall admission, 7/15 for domestic and international students; for spring admission, 10/1 for domestic and international students. Electronic applications accepted. *Expenses:* Tuition, state resident: full-time $4697; part-time $261 per credit hour. Tuition, nonresident: full-time $9355; part-time $520 per credit hour. *Required fees:* $343; $19.10 per credit hour. $30 per semester. Tuition and fees vary according to course load. *Application contact:* Dr. Brian C. Cronk, Dean of the Graduate School, 816-271-4394, E-mail: graduate@missouriwestern.edu.

Montclair State University, The Graduate School, School of Business, Post Master's Certificate Program in Management Information Systems, Montclair, NJ 07043-1624. Offers MBA, Certificate, Post Master's Certificate. Part-time and evening/weekend programs available. *Students:* Average age 30. *Entrance requirements:* For degree, essay. Additional exam requirements/recommendations for international students: Required—TOEFL (minimum score 83 iBT) or IELTS (minimum score 6.5). *Application deadline:* For fall admission, 6/1 for international students; for spring admission, 10/1 for international students. Applications are processed on a rolling basis. Application fee: $60. Electronic applications accepted. *Financial support:* Federal Work-Study, scholarships/grants, and unspecified assistantships available. Support available to part-time students. Financial award application deadline: 3/1; financial award applicants required to submit FAFSA. *Faculty research:* Search engine optimization; trust and privacy online; data mining; teaching in hybrid and online environments; counterproductive work behavior and its effect on organizations, employees and customers; social identity and identification in organizations. *Unit head:* Dr. Richard Peterson, Head, 973-655-4269. *Application contact:* Amy Aiello, Director of Graduate Admissions and Operations, 973-655-5147, Fax: 973-655-7869, E-mail: graduate.school@montclair.edu. Web site: http://business.montclair.edu/.

Morehead State University, Graduate Programs, College of Business and Public Affairs, Department of Information Systems, Morehead, KY 40351. Offers MSIS. *Entrance requirements:* For master's, GRE, GMAT. Additional exam requirements/recommendations for international students: Required—TOEFL (minimum score 525 paper-based). Electronic applications accepted.

Morehead State University, Graduate Programs, College of Business and Public Affairs, School of Business Administration, Morehead, KY 40351. Offers business administration (MBA); information systems (MSIS); sport management (MA). Part-time and evening/weekend programs available. *Entrance requirements:* For master's, GRE or GMAT. Additional exam requirements/recommendations for international students: Required—TOEFL (minimum score 500 paper-based; 173 computer-based). Electronic applications accepted.

National University, Academic Affairs, School of Business and Management, Department of Leadership and Human Resource Management, La Jolla, CA 92037-1011. Offers human resources management (MA); management information systems (MS); organizational leadership (MS). Part-time and evening/weekend programs available. Postbaccalaureate distance learning degree programs offered (no on-campus study). *Degree requirements:* For master's, thesis. *Entrance requirements:* For master's, interview, minimum GPA of 2.5. Additional exam requirements/recommendations for international students: Required—TOEFL (minimum score 550 paper-based; 213 computer-based; 79 iBT), IELTS (minimum score 6). *Application deadline:* Applications are processed on a rolling basis. Application fee: $60 ($65 for international students). Electronic applications accepted. *Financial support:* Career-related internships or fieldwork, institutionally sponsored loans, scholarships/grants, and tuition waivers (partial) available. Support available to part-time students. Financial award application deadline: 6/30; financial award applicants required to submit FAFSA. *Unit head:* Dr. Bruce Buchowicz, Chair, 858-642-8439, Fax: 858-642-8740, E-mail: bbuchowicz@nu.edu. *Application contact:* Dominick Giovanniello, Associate Regional Dean, 800-NAT-UNIV, Fax: 858-541-7792, E-mail: dgiovann@nu.edu. Web site: http://www.nu.edu/OurPrograms/SchoolOfBusinessAndManagement/LeadershipAndHumanResourceManagement.html.

National University, Academic Affairs, School of Engineering, Technology and Media, Department of Computer Science, Information and Media Systems, La Jolla, CA 92037-1011. Offers computer science (MS); cyber security and information assurance (MS); management information systems (MS). Part-time and evening/weekend programs available. Postbaccalaureate distance learning degree programs offered (no on-campus study). *Degree requirements:* For master's, thesis. *Entrance requirements:* For master's, interview, minimum GPA of 2.5. Additional exam requirements/recommendations for international students: Required—TOEFL (minimum score 550 paper-based; 213 computer-based; 79 iBT), IELTS (minimum score 6). *Application deadline:* Applications are processed on a rolling basis. Application fee: $60 ($65 for international students). Electronic applications accepted. *Financial support:* Career-related internships or fieldwork, institutionally sponsored loans, scholarships/grants, and tuition waivers (partial) available. Support available to part-time students. Financial award application deadline: 6/30; financial award applicants required to submit FAFSA. *Unit head:* Dr. Alireza M. Farahani, 858-309-3438, Fax: 858-309-3420, E-mail: afarahan@nu.edu. *Application contact:* Dominick Giovanniello, Associate Regional Dean, 800-NAT-UNIV, Fax: 858-541-7792, E-mail: dgiovann@nu.edu. Web site: http://www.nu.edu/OurPrograms/SchoolOfEngineeringAndTechnology/ComputerScienceAndInformationSystems.html.

Naval Postgraduate School, Departments and Academic Groups, Department of Information Sciences, Monterey, CA 93943. Offers electronic warfare systems engineering (MS); information sciences (PhD); information systems and operations (MS); information technology management (MS); information warfare systems engineering (MS); knowledge superiority (Certificate); remote sensing intelligence (MS); system technology (command, control and communications) (MS). Program open only to commissioned officers of the United States and friendly nations and selected United States federal civilian employees. Part-time programs available. *Faculty:* 54 full-time (5 women), 5 part-time/adjunct (1 woman). *Students:* 169 full-time (2 women), 38 part-time (4 women); includes 51 minority (19 Black or African American, non-Hispanic/Latino; 1 American Indian or Alaska Native, non-Hispanic/Latino; 16 Asian, non-Hispanic/Latino; 15 Hispanic/Latino), 36 international. Average age 41. In 2011, 65 master's, 1 doctorate awarded. *Degree requirements:* For master's, thesis (for some programs); for doctorate, thesis/dissertation. *Faculty research:* Designing inter-organisational collectivities for dynamic fit: stability, manoeuvrability and application in disaster relief endeavours; system self-awareness and related methods for Improving the use and understanding of data within DoD; evaluating a macrocognition model of team collaboration using real-world data from the Haiti relief effort; cyber distortion in command and control; performance and QoS in service-based systems. *Total annual research expenditures:* $12.4 million. *Unit head:* Prof. Dan Boger, Department Chair, 831-656-3671, E-mail: dboger@nps.edu. Web site: http://nps.edu/Academics/Schools/GSOIS/Departments/IS/index.html.

Naval Postgraduate School, Departments and Academic Groups, School of Business and Public Policy, Monterey, CA 93943. Offers acquisitions and contract management (MBA); business administration (EMBA, MBA); contract management (MS); defense business management (MBA); defense systems analysis (MS), including management; defense systems management (international) (MBA); executive management (MBA); financial management (MBA); information systems management (MBA); manpower systems analysis (MS); material logistics support management (MBA); program management (MS); resource planning/management for international defense (MBA); supply chain management (MBA); systems acquisition management (MBA); transportation management (MBA). Program only open to commissioned officers of the United States and friendly nations and selected United States federal civilian employees. *Accreditation:* AACSB; NASPAA. Part-time programs available. Postbaccalaureate distance learning degree programs offered (minimal on-campus study). *Faculty:* 67 full-time (15 women), 32 part-time/adjunct (12 women). *Students:* 307 full-time (29 women), 327 part-time (71 women); includes 149 minority (55 Black or African American, non-Hispanic/Latino; 5 American Indian or Alaska Native, non-Hispanic/Latino; 46 Asian, non-Hispanic/Latino; 43 Hispanic/Latino), 44 international. Average age 42. In 2011, 295 master's awarded. *Degree requirements:* For master's, thesis (for some programs), terminal project/capstone (for some programs). *Faculty research:* U. S. and European public procurement policies for small and medium-sized enterprises, examining external validity criticisms in the choice of students as subjects in accounting experiment studies, assurance of learning in contract management education, contracting for cloud computing: opportunities and risks, NPS, Apple App Store as a business model supporting U. S. Navy requirements. *Total annual research expenditures:* $9 million. *Unit head:* Raymond Franck, Department Chair, 831-656-3614, E-mail: refranck@nps.edu. *Application contact:* Acting Director of Admissions. Web site: http://www.nps.edu/Academics/Schools/GSBPP/index.html.

New England Institute of Technology, Program in Information Technology, Warwick, RI 02886-2244. Offers MS. *Degree requirements:* For master's, project. Web site: http://www.neit.edu/Programs/Masters-Degree/Information-Technology.

New Jersey Institute of Technology, Office of Graduate Studies, College of Computing Science, Program in Information Systems, Program in Business and Information Systems, Newark, NJ 07102. Offers MS. *Students:* 19 full-time (5 women), 41 part-time (14 women); includes 31 minority (9 Black or African American, non-Hispanic/Latino; 13 Asian, non-Hispanic/Latino; 9 Hispanic/Latino), 12 international. Average age 32. 102 applicants, 62% accepted, 22 enrolled. In 2011, 28 master's awarded. *Entrance requirements:* Additional exam requirements/recommendations for international students: Required—TOEFL (minimum score 550 paper-based; 213 computer-based; 79 iBT). *Application deadline:* For fall admission, 6/1 for domestic students, 5/1 for international students; for spring admission, 11/15 for domestic and international students. Applications are processed on a rolling basis. Application fee: $65. Electronic applications accepted. *Expenses:* Tuition, state resident: full-time $7980; part-time $867 per credit. Tuition, nonresident: full-time $11,336; part-time $1196 per credit. *Required fees:* $230 per credit. *Financial support:* Application deadline: 1/15. *Unit head:* Dr. Michael P. Bieber, Associate Chair, 973-596-2681, Fax: 973-596-2986, E-mail: michael.p.bieber@njit.edu. *Application contact:* Kathryn Kelly, Director of Admissions, 973-596-3300, Fax: 973-596-3461, E-mail: admissions@njit.edu. Web site: http://is.njit.edu/academics/graduate/msbis/index.php.

New Jersey Institute of Technology, Office of Graduate Studies, College of Computing Science, Program in Information Systems, Program in Information Systems, Newark, NJ 07102. Offers MS, PhD. *Students:* 71 full-time (23 women), 109 part-time (28 women); includes 68 minority (19 Black or African American, non-Hispanic/Latino; 30 Asian, non-Hispanic/Latino; 18 Hispanic/Latino; 1 Native Hawaiian or other Pacific Islander, non-Hispanic/Latino), 50 international. Average age 33. 271 applicants, 65% accepted, 50 enrolled. In 2011, 71 master's, 1 doctorate awarded. *Entrance requirements:* For doctorate, GRE. Additional exam requirements/recommendations for international students: Required—TOEFL (minimum score 550 paper-based; 213 computer-based; 79 iBT). *Application deadline:* For fall admission, 6/1 priority date for domestic students, 5/1 for international students; for spring admission, 11/15 priority date for domestic students, 11/15 for international students. Applications are processed on a rolling basis. Application fee: $65. Electronic applications accepted. Application fee is waived when completed online. *Expenses:* Tuition, state resident: full-time $7980; part-time $867 per credit. Tuition, nonresident: full-time $11,336; part-time $1196 per credit. *Required fees:* $230 per credit. *Financial support:* Application deadline: 1/15. *Unit head:* Dr. Michael P. Bieber, Associate Chair, 973-596-2681, Fax: 973-596-2986, E-mail: michael.p.bieber@njit.edu. *Application contact:* Kathryn Kelly, Director of Admissions, 973-596-3300, Fax: 973-596-3461, E-mail: admissions@njit.edu.

Newman University, MBA Program, Wichita, KS 67213-2097. Offers finance (MBA); international business (MBA); leadership (MBA); management (MBA); technology (MBA). Part-time programs available. *Faculty:* 4 full-time (1 woman), 7 part-time/adjunct (2 women). *Students:* 28 full-time (7 women), 83 part-time (28 women); includes 31 minority (8 Black or African American, non-Hispanic/Latino; 1 American Indian or Alaska Native, non-Hispanic/Latino; 9 Asian, non-Hispanic/Latino; 9 Hispanic/Latino; 1 Native Hawaiian or other Pacific Islander, non-Hispanic/Latino; 3 Two or more races, non-Hispanic/Latino), 23 international. Average age 31. 63 applicants, 70% accepted, 38 enrolled. In 2011, 49 master's awarded. *Degree requirements:* For master's, thesis optional. *Entrance requirements:* For master's, interview; minimum GPA of 3.0; 3 letters of recommendation; course work in algebra, statistics, macroeconomics, and financial accounting. Additional exam requirements/recommendations for international students: Required—TOEFL (minimum score 600 paper-based; 250 computer-based; 100 iBT). *Application deadline:* For fall admission, 8/1 priority date for domestic students, 7/15 for international students; for winter admission, 1/1 priority date for domestic students; for spring admission, 1/1 priority date for domestic students, 11/15 for international students. Applications are processed on a rolling basis. Application fee: $25 ($40 for international students). Electronic applications accepted. *Expenses:* Contact institution. *Financial support:* In 2011–12, 18 students received support. Federal Work-Study available. Financial award application deadline: 8/15; financial award applicants required to submit FAFSA. *Unit head:* Dr. Wendy Munday, Director of MBA Program, 316-942-4291 Ext. 2296, Fax: 316-942-4483, E-mail: mundayw@newmanu.edu. *Application contact:* Linda Kay Sabala, Director of Graduate Admissions, 316-942-4291 Ext. 2230, Fax: 316-942-4483, E-mail: sabalal@newmanu.edu. Web site: http://www.newmanu.edu.

New Mexico Highlands University, Graduate Studies, School of Business, Las Vegas, NM 87701. Offers business administration (MBA), including government nonprofit management, human resource management, international business, management, management information systems. *Accreditation:* ACBSP. *Faculty:* 20 full-time (5 women). *Students:* 63 full-time (40 women), 146 part-time (76 women); includes 131 minority (9 Black or African American, non-Hispanic/Latino; 8 American Indian or Alaska Native, non-Hispanic/Latino; 1 Asian, non-Hispanic/Latino; 110 Hispanic/Latino; 2 Native Hawaiian or other Pacific Islander, non-Hispanic/Latino; 1 Two or more races, non-Hispanic/Latino), 25 international. Average age 33. 99 applicants, 79% accepted, 49 enrolled. In 2011, 43 master's awarded. *Degree requirements:* For master's, comprehensive exam, thesis or alternative. *Entrance requirements:* For master's, minimum undergraduate GPA of 3.0. Additional exam requirements/recommendations for international students: Required—TOEFL (minimum score 540 paper-based; 207 computer-based). *Application deadline:* For fall admission, 8/1 priority date for domestic students. Applications are processed on a rolling basis. Application fee: $15. *Expenses:* Tuition, state resident: full-time $2767; part-time $146 per credit hour. Tuition, nonresident: full-time $4879; part-time $234 per credit hour. *International tuition:* $5436 full-time. *Required fees:* $737. *Financial support:* In 2011–12, 29 students received support. Career-related internships or fieldwork, Federal Work-Study, institutionally sponsored loans, scholarships/grants, tuition waivers (full and partial), and unspecified assistantships available. Support available to part-time students. Financial award application deadline: 3/1; financial award applicants required to submit FAFSA. *Faculty research:* Real estate valuation, studying expert judgments in complex accounting, decision environments, green marketing, environmentalism, marketing research methodology. *Unit head:* Dr. Margaret Young, Dean, 505-454-3522, Fax: 505-454-3354, E-mail: young_m@nmhu.edu. *Application contact:* Diane Trujillo, Administrative Assistant, Graduate Studies, 505-454-3266, Fax: 505-426-2117, E-mail: dtrujillo@nmhu.edu. Web site: http://www.nmhu.edu/business/.

New York Institute of Technology, Graduate Division, School of Management, Program in Business Administration, Old Westbury, NY 11568-8000. Offers accounting (Advanced Certificate); business administration (MBA); finance (Advanced Certificate); international business (Advanced Certificate); management of information systems (Advanced Certificate); marketing (Advanced Certificate). Part-time and evening/

weekend programs available. *Students:* 331 full-time (131 women), 508 part-time (211 women); includes 74 minority (26 Black or African American, non-Hispanic/Latino; 27 Asian, non-Hispanic/Latino; 15 Hispanic/Latino; 6 Two or more races, non-Hispanic/ Latino), 214 international. Average age 28. In 2011, 449 degrees awarded. *Degree requirements:* For master's, thesis (for some programs). *Entrance requirements:* For master's, minimum QPA of 2.85. Additional exam requirements/recommendations for international students: Required—TOEFL (minimum score 550 paper-based; 213 computer-based). *Application deadline:* For fall admission, 7/1 priority date for domestic students; for spring admission, 12/1 priority date for domestic students. Applications are processed on a rolling basis. Application fee: $50. Electronic applications accepted. *Expenses: Tuition:* Part-time $930 per credit hour. *Financial support:* Fellowships, research assistantships with partial tuition reimbursements, institutionally sponsored loans, tuition waivers (full and partial), and unspecified assistantships available. Support available to part-time students. Financial award applicants required to submit FAFSA. *Faculty research:* Instructor performance appraisal; relationship between TOEFL, GMAT, GRE, and performance in foreign students. *Unit head:* Dr. Stephen Hartman, Director, 516-686-7691, E-mail: shartman@nyit.edu. *Application contact:* Dr. Jacquelyn Nealon, Vice President for Enrollment Services, 516-686-7925, Fax: 516-686-7597, E-mail: jnealon@nyit.edu.

New York University, Leonard N. Stern School of Business, Department of Information, Operations and Management Sciences, New York, NY 10012-1019. Offers information systems (MBA, PhD); operations management (MBA, PhD); statistics (MBA, PhD). *Faculty research:* Knowledge management, economics of information, computer-supported groups and communities financial information systems, data mining and business intelligence.

New York University, School of Continuing and Professional Studies, Division of Programs in Business, Graduate Programs in Management and Systems, New York, NY 10012-1019. Offers core business competencies (Advanced Certificate); database technologies (MS); enterprise and risk management (Advanced Certificate); enterprise risk management (MS); information technologies (Advanced Certificate); strategy and leadership (MS, Advanced Certificate); systems management (MS). Part-time and evening/weekend programs available. Postbaccalaureate distance learning degree programs offered (no on-campus study). *Faculty:* 2 full-time (0 women), 43 part-time/ adjunct (7 women). *Students:* 30 full-time (15 women), 222 part-time (89 women); includes 49 minority (14 Black or African American, non-Hispanic/Latino; 20 Asian, non-Hispanic/Latino; 14 Hispanic/Latino; 1 Two or more races, non-Hispanic/Latino), 39 international. Average age 35. 178 applicants, 54% accepted, 50 enrolled. In 2011, 69 master's, 15 other advanced degrees awarded. *Degree requirements:* For master's, thesis, capstone project. *Entrance requirements:* For master's, GRE/GMAT only upon request, relevant professional work, internship or volunteer experience. Additional exam requirements/recommendations for international students: Required—TOEFL (minimum score 600 paper-based; 250 computer-based; 100 iBT), IELTS (minimum score 7). *Application deadline:* For fall admission, 2/1 priority date for domestic students, 2/1 for international students; for spring admission, 10/15 priority date for domestic students, 8/ 15 for international students. Applications are processed on a rolling basis. Application fee: $150. Electronic applications accepted. *Financial support:* In 2011–12, 94 students received support, including 94 fellowships (averaging $1,704 per year). *Unit head:* Anthony Pennings, Visiting Clinical Assistant Professor. *Application contact:* Admissions Office, 212-998-7100, E-mail: scps.gradadmissions@nyu.edu. Web site: http:// www.scps.nyu.edu/areas-of-study/information-technology/.

North Carolina Agricultural and Technical State University, School of Graduate Studies, School of Technology, Department of Electronics, Computer, and Information Technology, Greensboro, NC 27411. Offers electronics and computer technology (MSIT, MSTM); information technology (MSIT, MSTM).

North Central College, Graduate and Continuing Education Programs, Department of Business, Program in Management Information Systems, Naperville, IL 60566-7063. Offers MS. Part-time and evening/weekend programs available. *Faculty:* 11 full-time (2 women), 5 part-time/adjunct (1 woman). *Students:* 4 full-time (1 woman), 4 part-time (0 women); includes 3 minority (1 Black or African American, non-Hispanic/Latino; 2 Asian, non-Hispanic/Latino), 1 international. Average age 37. 4 applicants, 50% accepted, 2 enrolled. In 2011, 1 master's awarded. *Degree requirements:* For master's, thesis optional, project. *Entrance requirements:* For master's, interview. Additional exam requirements/recommendations for international students: Required—TOEFL (minimum score 577 paper-based; 233 computer-based; 90 iBT). *Application deadline:* For fall admission, 8/15 for domestic students; for winter admission, 12/1 for domestic students; for spring admission, 2/1 for domestic students. Applications are processed on a rolling basis. Application fee: $25. *Expenses:* Contact institution. *Financial support:* Scholarships/grants available. Support available to part-time students. *Unit head:* Dr. Caroline St Clair, Program Coordinator, Management Information Systems, 630-637-5171, Fax: 630-637-5172, E-mail: cstclair@noctrl.edu. *Application contact:* Wendy Kulpinski, Director of Graduate and Continuing Education Admission, 630-637-5808, Fax: 630-637-5844, E-mail: wekulpinski@noctrl.edu.

Northeastern University, College of Computer and Information Science, Boston, MA 02115-5096. Offers computer and information science (PhD); computer science (MS); health informatics (MS); information assurance (MS). Part-time and evening/weekend programs available. *Faculty:* 28 full-time, 3 part-time/adjunct. *Students:* 337 full-time (91 women), 90 part-time (52 women). 1,045 applicants, 56% accepted, 150 enrolled. In 2011, 88 master's, 7 doctorates awarded. Terminal master's awarded for partial completion of doctoral program. *Degree requirements:* For master's, thesis optional; for doctorate, comprehensive exam, thesis/dissertation. *Entrance requirements:* For master's and doctorate, GRE General Test. Additional exam requirements/ recommendations for international students: Required—TOEFL or IELTS. *Application deadline:* For fall admission, 7/15 for domestic students, 5/1 for international students; for spring admission, 10/15 for domestic students, 9/1 for international students. Applications are processed on a rolling basis. Application fee: $50. Electronic applications accepted. *Expenses:* Contact institution. *Financial support:* In 2011–12, 59 students received support, including 1 fellowship, 40 research assistantships with full tuition reimbursements available (averaging $18,260 per year), 33 teaching assistantships with full tuition reimbursements available (averaging $18,260 per year); career-related internships or fieldwork, Federal Work-Study, institutionally sponsored loans, scholarships/grants, and unspecified assistantships also available. Financial award application deadline: 1/15. *Faculty research:* Programming languages, artificial intelligence, human-computer interaction, database management, network security. *Unit head:* Dr. Larry A. Finkelstein, Dean, 617-373-2462, Fax: 617-373-5121. *Application contact:* Dr. Agnes Chan, Associate Dean and Director of Graduate Program, 617-373-2462, Fax: 617-373-5121, E-mail: gradschool@ccs.neu.edu. Web site: http:// www.ccs.neu.edu/.

Northern Illinois University, Graduate School, College of Business, Department of Operations Management and Information Systems, De Kalb, IL 60115-2854. Offers management information systems (MS). Part-time programs available. *Faculty:* 11 full-time (3 women), 3 part-time/adjunct (0 women). *Students:* 32 full-time (6 women), 32 part-time (7 women); includes 10 minority (6 Asian, non-Hispanic/Latino; 3 Hispanic/ Latino; 1 Two or more races, non-Hispanic/Latino), 22 international. Average age 27. 58 applicants, 64% accepted, 22 enrolled. In 2011, 33 master's awarded. *Degree requirements:* For master's, computer language. *Entrance requirements:* For master's, GMAT, minimum GPA of 2.75. Additional exam requirements/recommendations for international students: Required—TOEFL (minimum score 550 paper-based; 213 computer-based). *Application deadline:* For fall admission, 6/1 for domestic students, 5/ 1 for international students; for spring admission, 11/1 for domestic students, 10/1 for international students. Applications are processed on a rolling basis. Application fee: $40. Electronic applications accepted. *Financial support:* In 2011–12, 1 research assistantship with full tuition reimbursement, 17 teaching assistantships with full tuition reimbursements were awarded; fellowships with full tuition reimbursements, career-related internships or fieldwork, Federal Work-Study, scholarships/grants, tuition waivers (full), and unspecified assistantships also available. Support available to part-time students. Financial award applicants required to submit FAFSA. *Faculty research:* Affordability of home ownership, Web portal competition intranet, electronic commerce, corporate-academic alliances. *Unit head:* Dr. Chang Liu, Chair, 815-753-3021, Fax: 815-753-7460. *Application contact:* Steve Kispert, Office of Graduate Studies in Business, 815-753-6372, E-mail: skispert@niu.edu. Web site: http://www.cob.niu.edu/omis/.

Northwestern University, The Graduate School, School of Communication, Department of Communication Studies, Communication Systems Strategy and Management Program, Evanston, IL 60208. Offers MSC. Part-time programs available. Electronic applications accepted.

Northwestern University, School of Continuing Studies, Program in Information Systems, Evanston, IL 60208. Offers database and Internet technologies (MS); information systems management (MS); information systems security (MS); software project management and development (MS).

Northwest Missouri State University, Graduate School, Melvin and Valorie Booth College of Business and Professional Studies, Program in Information Technology Management, Maryville, MO 64468-6001. Offers MBA. Part-time programs available. *Faculty:* 15 full-time (4 women). *Students:* 3 full-time (1 woman), 2 part-time (0 women), 3 international. 3 applicants, 100% accepted, 1 enrolled. In 2011, 7 master's awarded. *Degree requirements:* For master's, comprehensive exam. *Entrance requirements:* For master's, GMAT/GRE, minimum GPA of 2.5. Additional exam requirements/ recommendations for international students: Required—TOEFL (minimum score 550 paper-based; 213 computer-based). *Application deadline:* For fall admission, 7/1 for domestic and international students; for spring admission, 12/1 for domestic students, 11/15 for international students. Application fee: $0 ($50 for international students). *Financial support:* In 2011–12, research assistantships with full tuition reimbursements (averaging $6,000 per year), teaching assistantships with full tuition reimbursements (averaging $6,000 per year) were awarded. Financial award application deadline: 4/1; financial award applicants required to submit FAFSA. *Unit head:* Dr. Joni Adkins, Head, 660-562-1185. *Application contact:* Dr. Gregory Haddock, Dean of Graduate School, 660-562-1145, Fax: 660-562-1096, E-mail: gradsch@nwmissouri.edu.

Norwich University, College of Graduate and Continuing Studies, Master of Science in Information Assurance Program, Northfield, VT 05663. Offers business continuity management (MS); continuity of governmental operations (MS); managing cyber crime and digital incidents (MS). Evening/weekend programs available. *Faculty:* 21 part-time/ adjunct (4 women). *Students:* 39 full-time (3 women); includes 8 minority (3 Black or African American, non-Hispanic/Latino; 3 Asian, non-Hispanic/Latino; 1 Hispanic/Latino; 1 Native Hawaiian or other Pacific Islander, non-Hispanic/Latino). Average age 39. 13 applicants, 100% accepted, 13 enrolled. In 2011, 67 degrees awarded. *Entrance requirements:* For master's, minimum undergraduate GPA of 2.75. Additional exam requirements/recommendations for international students: Required—TOEFL (minimum score 550 paper-based; 212 computer-based; 83 iBT). *Application deadline:* For fall admission, 8/10 for domestic and international students; for winter admission, 11/7 for domestic and international students; for spring admission, 2/6 for domestic and international students. Applications are processed on a rolling basis. Application fee: $50. Electronic applications accepted. *Expenses: Tuition:* Full-time $16,174. *Required fees:* $2130. Full-time tuition and fees vary according to program. *Financial support:* In 2011–12, 36 students received support. Scholarships/grants available. Financial award applicants required to submit FAFSA. *Unit head:* Dr. Gary Kessler, Director, 802-485-2729, Fax: 802-485-2533, E-mail: kesslerg@norwich.edu. *Application contact:* Elizabeth Templeton, Assistant Director, 802-485-2757, Fax: 802-485-2533, E-mail: etemplet@ norwich.edu. Web site: http://infoassurance.norwich.edu/.

Nova Southeastern University, Graduate School of Computer and Information Sciences, Fort Lauderdale, FL 33314-7796. Offers computer information systems (MS, PhD); computer science (MS, PhD); computing technology in education (PhD); information security (MS); information systems (PhD); information technology (MS); information technology in education (MS); management information systems (MS). Part-time and evening/weekend programs available. Postbaccalaureate distance learning degree programs offered (no on-campus study). *Faculty:* 20 full-time (5 women), 21 part-time/adjunct (3 women). *Students:* 130 full-time (37 women), 960 part-time (291 women); includes 496 minority (221 Black or African American, non-Hispanic/Latino; 4 American Indian or Alaska Native, non-Hispanic/Latino; 78 Asian, non-Hispanic/Latino; 178 Hispanic/Latino; 15 Two or more races, non-Hispanic/Latino), 49 international. Average age 41. 486 applicants, 45% accepted. In 2011, 131 master's, 39 doctorates awarded. Terminal master's awarded for partial completion of doctoral program. *Degree requirements:* For master's, thesis optional; for doctorate, thesis/dissertation. *Entrance requirements:* For master's, minimum undergraduate GPA of 2.5; 3.0 in major; for doctorate, master's degree, minimum graduate GPA of 3.25. Additional exam requirements/recommendations for international students: Required—TOEFL (minimum score 213 computer-based; 79 iBT), IELTS (minimum score 6). *Application deadline:* Applications are processed on a rolling basis. Application fee: $50. Electronic applications accepted. *Expenses:* Contact institution. *Financial support:* Federal Work-Study, scholarships/grants, and unspecified assistantships available. Support available to part-time students. Financial award application deadline: 5/1. *Faculty research:* Artificial intelligence, database management, human-computer interaction, distance education, information security. *Unit head:* Dr. Eric S. Ackerman, Interim Dean, 954-262-7300. *Application contact:* 954-262-2000, Fax: 954-262-2752, E-mail: scisinfo@ nova.edu. Web site: http://www.scis.nova.edu/.

Oakland University, Graduate Study and Lifelong Learning, School of Business Administration, Department of Decision and Information Sciences, Rochester, MI 48309-4401. Offers information technology management (MS); management information systems (Certificate); production and operations management (Certificate).

The Ohio State University, Graduate School, Max M. Fisher College of Business, Department of Accounting and Management Information Systems, Columbus, OH 43210. Offers M Acc, MA, MS, PhD. *Accreditation:* AACSB. *Faculty:* 18. *Students:* 81 full-time (51 women), 8 part-time (2 women); includes 7 minority (2 Black or African American, non-Hispanic/Latino; 2 Asian, non-Hispanic/Latino; 2 Hispanic/Latino; 1 Two or more races, non-Hispanic/Latino), 35 international. Average age 25. In 2011, 89 master's awarded. Terminal master's awarded for partial completion of doctoral program. *Degree requirements:* For doctorate, thesis/dissertation. *Entrance requirements:* For master's and doctorate, GMAT (preferred) or GRE. Additional exam requirements/recommendations for international students: Required—TOEFL (minimum score 600 paper-based; 250 computer-based), Michigan English Language Assessment Battery (minimum score 82). *Application deadline:* For fall admission, 8/15 priority date for domestic students, 7/1 for international students; for winter admission, 12/1 priority date for domestic students, 11/1 for international students; for spring admission, 3/1 priority date for domestic students, 2/1 for international students. Applications are processed on a rolling basis. Application fee: $40 ($50 for international students). Electronic applications accepted. *Expenses:* Tuition, state resident: full-time $11,400. Tuition, nonresident: full-time $28,125. Tuition and fees vary according to course load, degree level, campus/location and program. *Financial support:* Fellowships, research assistantships, teaching assistantships, career-related internships or fieldwork, Federal Work-Study, and institutionally sponsored loans available. Support available to part-time students. *Faculty research:* Artificial intelligence, protocol analysis, database design in decision-supporting systems. *Unit head:* J. Richard Dietrich, Chair, 614-247-6299, Fax: 614-292-2118, E-mail: dietrich.59@osu.edu. *Application contact:* Graduate Admissions, 614-292-6031, Fax: 614-292-3656, E-mail: gradadmissions@osu.edu. Web site: http://fisher.osu.edu/departments/accounting-and-mis/.

Oklahoma City University, Meinders School of Business, Program in Business Administration, Oklahoma City, OK 73106-1402. Offers finance (MBA); health administration (MBA); information technology (MBA); integrated marketing communications (MBA); international business (MBA); marketing (MBA); JD/MBA. *Accreditation:* ACBSP. Part-time and evening/weekend programs available. *Faculty:* 15 full-time (6 women), 14 part-time/adjunct (6 women). *Students:* 136 full-time (59 women), 112 part-time (34 women); includes 38 minority (14 Black or African American, non-Hispanic/Latino; 4 American Indian or Alaska Native, non-Hispanic/Latino; 11 Asian, non-Hispanic/Latino; 3 Hispanic/Latino; 6 Two or more races, non-Hispanic/Latino), 100 international. Average age 30. 252 applicants, 83% accepted, 30 enrolled. In 2011, 148 master's awarded. *Degree requirements:* For master's, comprehensive exam. *Entrance requirements:* For master's, GRE or GMAT. Additional exam requirements/recommendations for international students: Required—TOEFL (minimum score 560 paper-based; 220 computer-based; 83 iBT). *Application deadline:* Applications are processed on a rolling basis. Application fee: $50 ($70 for international students). Electronic applications accepted. *Expenses: Tuition:* Full-time $16,848; part-time $936 per credit hour. *Required fees:* $2070; $115 per credit hour. One-time fee: $300. *Financial support:* Career-related internships or fieldwork, Federal Work-Study, institutionally sponsored loans, and tuition waivers (partial) available. Support available to part-time students. Financial award application deadline: 6/1; financial award applicants required to submit FAFSA. *Faculty research:* Management information systems, international business strategies. *Unit head:* Dr. Steven Agee, Dean, 405-208-5130, Fax: 405-208-5098, E-mail: sagee@okcu.edu. *Application contact:* Michelle Cook, Director, Graduate Admissions, 800-633-7242, Fax: 405-208-5916, E-mail: gadmissions@okcu.edu. Web site: http://msb.okcu.edu/graduate/.

Oklahoma State University, Spears School of Business, Department of Management Science and Information Systems, Stillwater, OK 74078. Offers management information systems (MS); management science and information systems (PhD); telecommunications management (MS). Part-time programs available. Postbaccalaureate distance learning degree programs offered. *Faculty:* 17 full-time (3 women), 2 part-time/adjunct (0 women). *Students:* 57 full-time (12 women), 75 part-time (9 women); includes 10 minority (3 Black or African American, non-Hispanic/Latino; 3 American Indian or Alaska Native, non-Hispanic/Latino; 1 Asian, non-Hispanic/Latino; 2 Hispanic/Latino; 1 Two or more races, non-Hispanic/Latino), 54 international. Average age 30. 280 applicants, 37% accepted, 50 enrolled. In 2011, 60 degrees awarded. *Degree requirements:* For master's, thesis or alternative; for doctorate, comprehensive exam, thesis/dissertation. *Entrance requirements:* For master's and doctorate, GRE or GMAT. Additional exam requirements/recommendations for international students: Required—TOEFL (minimum score 550 paper-based; 79 iBT). *Application deadline:* For fall admission, 3/1 for international students; for spring admission, 8/1 for international students. Applications are processed on a rolling basis. Application fee: $40 ($75 for international students). Electronic applications accepted. *Expenses:* Tuition, state resident: full-time $4044; part-time $168.50 per credit hour. Tuition, nonresident: full-time $16,008; part-time $667 per credit hour. *Required fees:* $2122; $88.45 per credit hour. One-time fee: $50. Tuition and fees vary according to course load and campus/location. *Financial support:* In 2011–12, 1 research assistantship (averaging $4,200 per year), 12 teaching assistantships (averaging $13,083 per year) were awarded; career-related internships or fieldwork, Federal Work-Study, scholarships/grants, health care benefits, tuition waivers (partial), and unspecified assistantships also available. Support available to part-time students. Financial award application deadline: 3/1; financial award applicants required to submit FAFSA. *Unit head:* Dr. Rick Wilson, Head, 405-744-3551, Fax: 405-744-5180. *Application contact:* Dr. Sheryl Tucker, Dean, 405-744-7099, Fax: 405-744-0355, E-mail: grad-i@okstate.edu. Web site: http://spears.okstate.edu/msis.

Old Dominion University, College of Business and Public Administration, MBA Program, Norfolk, VA 23529. Offers business and economic forecasting (MBA); financial analysis and valuation (MBA); information technology and enterprise integration (MBA); international business (MBA); maritime and port management (MBA); public administration (MBA). *Accreditation:* AACSB. Part-time and evening/weekend programs available. *Faculty:* 66 full-time (15 women), 6 part-time/adjunct (1 woman). *Students:* 69 full-time (21 women), 230 part-time (85 women); includes 49 minority (22 Black or African American, non-Hispanic/Latino; 1 American Indian or Alaska Native, non-Hispanic/Latino; 10 Asian, non-Hispanic/Latino; 3 Hispanic/Latino; 1 Native Hawaiian or other Pacific Islander, non-Hispanic/Latino; 12 Two or more races, non-Hispanic/Latino), 19 international. Average age 31. 177 applicants, 43% accepted, 53 enrolled. In 2011, 115 master's awarded. *Entrance requirements:* For master's, GMAT, GRE, letter of reference, resume, coursework in calculus, essay. Additional exam requirements/recommendations for international students: Required—TOEFL (minimum score 550 paper-based; 213 computer-based; 80 iBT). *Application deadline:* For fall admission, 6/1 priority date for domestic students, 4/15 for international students; for spring admission, 11/1 priority date for domestic students, 10/1 for international students. Applications are processed on a rolling basis. Application fee: $75. Electronic applications accepted. *Expenses:* Tuition, state resident: full-time $9096; part-time $379 per credit. Tuition, nonresident: full-time $23,064; part-time $961 per credit. *Required fees:* $127 per semester. One-time fee: $50. *Financial support:* In 2011–12, 44 students received support, including 90 research assistantships with partial tuition reimbursements available (averaging $8,900 per year); career-related internships or fieldwork, scholarships/grants, and unspecified assistantships also available. Support available to part-time students. Financial award application deadline: 2/15; financial award applicants required to submit FAFSA. *Faculty research:* International business, buyer behavior, financial markets, strategy, operations research, maritime and transportation economics. *Unit head:* Dr. Larry Filer, Graduate Program Director, 757-683-3585, Fax: 757-683-5750, E-mail: mbainfo@odu.edu. *Application contact:* Shanna Wood, MBA Program Manager, 757-683-3585, Fax: 757-683-5750, E-mail: mbainfo@odu.edu. Web site: http://bpa.odu.edu/mba/.

Our Lady of the Lake University of San Antonio, School of Business and Leadership, Program in Information Systems and Security, San Antonio, TX 78207-4689. Offers MS. Postbaccalaureate distance learning degree programs offered.

Pace University, Lubin School of Business, Information Systems Program, New York, NY 10038. Offers MBA. Part-time and evening/weekend programs available. *Students:* 3 full-time (1 woman), 18 part-time (3 women); includes 5 minority (all Asian, non-Hispanic/Latino), 10 international. Average age 29. 28 applicants, 50% accepted, 4 enrolled. In 2011, 6 master's awarded. *Entrance requirements:* For master's, GMAT, GRE. Additional exam requirements/recommendations for international students: Required—TOEFL. *Application deadline:* For fall admission, 7/31 priority date for domestic students; for spring admission, 11/30 for domestic students. Applications are processed on a rolling basis. Application fee: $70. Electronic applications accepted. *Expenses: Tuition:* Part-time $990 per credit. *Required fees:* $168 per semester. Tuition and fees vary according to course load and degree level. *Financial support:* Research assistantships, career-related internships or fieldwork, and Federal Work-Study available. Support available to part-time students. Financial award applicants required to submit FAFSA. *Unit head:* Dr. John Molluzzo, Chair, 212-346-1780, E-mail: jmulluzzo@pace.edu. *Application contact:* Susan Ford-Goldschein, Director of Graduate Admissions, 212-346-1531, Fax: 212-346-1585, E-mail: gradnyc@pace.edu. Web site: http://www.pace.edu/.

Pacific States University, College of Business, Los Angeles, CA 90006. Offers accounting (MBA); finance (MBA); international business (MBA, DBA); management of information technology (MBA); real estate management (MBA). Part-time and evening/weekend programs available. Postbaccalaureate distance learning degree programs offered (no on-campus study). *Faculty:* 6 full-time (2 women), 14 part-time/adjunct (0 women). *Students:* 157 full-time (70 women); includes 13 minority (2 Black or African American, non-Hispanic/Latino; 8 Asian, non-Hispanic/Latino; 3 Native Hawaiian or other Pacific Islander, non-Hispanic/Latino), 140 international. Average age 31. 42 applicants, 83% accepted, 33 enrolled. *Degree requirements:* For doctorate, comprehensive exam, thesis/dissertation. *Entrance requirements:* For master's, minimum undergraduate GPA of 2.5 during last 90 hours of course work. Additional exam requirements/recommendations for international students: Required—TOEFL (minimum score 133 computer-based; 45 iBT), IELTS (minimum score 4.5). *Application deadline:* For fall admission, 8/15 priority date for domestic students; for winter admission, 10/15 priority date for domestic students; for spring admission, 1/15 priority date for domestic students. Applications are processed on a rolling basis. Application fee: $100. *Expenses: Tuition:* Full-time $11,040; part-time $345 per credit hour. *Required fees:* $150 per quarter. *Financial support:* Scholarships/grants available. Financial award applicants required to submit FAFSA. *Application contact:* Zolzaya Enkhbayar, Interim Registrar, 323-731-2383, Fax: 323-731-7276, E-mail: registrar@psuca.edu.

Pacific States University, College of Computer Science and Information Systems, Los Angeles, CA 90006. Offers computer science (MS); information systems (MS). Part-time and evening/weekend programs available. *Faculty:* 4 part-time/adjunct (0 women). *Students:* 19 full-time (3 women); includes 1 minority (Asian, non-Hispanic/Latino), 17 international. Average age 27. 9 applicants, 78% accepted, 6 enrolled. *Entrance requirements:* For master's, bachelor's degree in physics, engineering, computer science, or applied mathematics; minimum undergraduate GPA of 2.5 during last 90 hours of course work. Additional exam requirements/recommendations for international students: Required—TOEFL (minimum score 450 paper-based; 133 computer-based; 45 iBT), IELTS (minimum score 4.5). *Application deadline:* For fall admission, 8/15 priority date for domestic students; for winter admission, 10/15 priority date for domestic students; for spring admission, 1/15 priority date for domestic students. Applications are processed on a rolling basis. Application fee: $100. *Expenses: Tuition:* Full-time $11,040; part-time $345 per credit hour. *Required fees:* $150 per quarter. *Financial support:* Scholarships/grants available. Financial award applicants required to submit FAFSA. *Application contact:* Zolzaya Enkhbayar, Interim Registrar, 323-731-2383, Fax: 323-731-7276, E-mail: registrar@psuca.edu.

Park University, College of Graduate and Professional Studies, Kansas City, MO 54105. Offers adult education (M Ed); at-risk students (M Ed); disaster and emergency management (MPA); educational administration (M Ed); entrepreneurship (MBA); general business (MBA); general education (M Ed); government/business relations (MPA); healthcare/services management (MBA, MPA); international business (MBA); K-12 certification (MAT); management information systems (MBA); management of information systems (MPA); middle school certification (MAT); multi-cultural education (M Ed); nonprofit management (MPA); public management (MPA); school law (M Ed); secondary school certification (MAT); special education (M Ed). Part-time and evening/weekend programs available. Postbaccalaureate distance learning degree programs offered (no on-campus study). *Degree requirements:* For master's, comprehensive exam, thesis (for some programs). *Entrance requirements:* For master's, GRE, GMAT, teacher certification (M Ed). Additional exam requirements/recommendations for international students: Required—TOEFL (minimum score 550 paper-based). Electronic applications accepted. *Faculty research:* Literacy, leadership, brain based research, multicultural education, diversity.

Penn State Harrisburg, Graduate School, School of Business Administration, Middletown, PA 17057-4898. Offers business administration (MBA); information systems (MS). Part-time and evening/weekend programs available. *Unit head:* Dr. Stephen P. Schappe, Director, 717-948-6141, E-mail: sxs28@psu.edu. *Application contact:* Robert Coffman, Director of Admissions, 717-948-6250, Fax: 717-948-6325, E-mail: ric1@psu.edu. Web site: http://harrisburg.psu.edu/business-administration/.

Polytechnic Institute of New York University, Department of Technology Management, Brooklyn, NY 11201-2990. Offers construction management (Advanced Certificate); electronic business management (Advanced Certificate); entrepreneurship (Advanced Certificate); human resources management (Advanced Certificate); information management (Advanced Certificate); management (MS); management of technology (MS); organizational behavior (MS, Advanced Certificate); project management (Advanced Certificate); technology management (MBA, PhD, Advanced Certificate); telecommunications and information management (MS); telecommunications management (Advanced Certificate). Part-time and evening/weekend programs available. *Faculty:* 6 full-time (1 woman), 32 part-time/adjunct (4 women). *Students:* 185 full-time (84 women), 94 part-time (41 women); includes 56 minority (15 Black or African American, non-Hispanic/Latino; 31 Asian, non-Hispanic/Latino; 10 Hispanic/Latino), 143 international. Average age 30. 467 applicants, 48% accepted, 123 enrolled. In 2011, 174 master's, 1 doctorate awarded. *Degree requirements:* For master's, comprehensive exam (for some programs), thesis (for some programs); for doctorate, comprehensive exam, thesis/dissertation. *Entrance requirements:* For master's, GMAT, minimum B average in undergraduate course work. Additional exam requirements/recommendations for international students: Required—TOEFL (minimum score 550 paper-based; 213 computer-based; 80 iBT); Recommended—IELTS (minimum score 6.5). *Application deadline:* For fall admission, 7/31 priority date for domestic students, 4/30 for international students; for spring admission, 12/31 priority date for domestic students, 11/30 for international students. Applications are processed on a rolling basis. Application fee: $75. Electronic applications accepted. *Expenses: Tuition:* Full-time $22,464; part-time $1248 per credit. *Required fees:* $501 per semester. *Financial support:* In 2011–12, 1 fellowship (averaging $26,400 per year) was awarded; research assistantships, teaching assistantships, institutionally sponsored loans, scholarships/grants, and unspecified assistantships also available. Support available to part-time students. *Unit head:* Prof. Bharadwaj Rao, Head, 718-260-3617, Fax: 718-260-3874, E-mail: brao@poly.edu. *Application contact:* JeanCarlo Bonilla, Director of Graduate Enrollment Management, 718-260-3182, Fax: 718-260-3624, E-mail: gradinfo@poly.edu. Web site: http://www.managementdept.poly.edu.

Polytechnic University of Puerto Rico, Graduate School, Hato Rey, PR 00919. Offers business administration (MBA), including computer information systems, general management, management of information systems, management of international enterprises; civil engineering (ME, MS); computer engineering (ME, MS); computer science (MCS, MS); electrical engineering (ME, MS); engineering management (MEM); environmental management (MEM); landscape architecture (M Land Arch); manufacturing competitiveness (MMC, MS); manufacturing engineering (ME, MS); mechanical engineering (M Mech E). Part-time and evening/weekend programs available. *Entrance requirements:* For master's, 3 letters of recommendation.

Pontifical Catholic University of Puerto Rico, College of Business Administration, Program in Management Information Systems, Ponce, PR 00717-0777. Offers MBA, Professional Certificate. Part-time and evening/weekend programs available. *Degree requirements:* For master's, thesis. *Entrance requirements:* For master's, GRE, interview, minimum GPA of 2.75.

Prairie View A&M University, College of Engineering, Prairie View, TX 77446-0519. Offers computer information systems (MSCIS); computer science (MSCS); electrical engineering (MSEE, PhDEE); engineering (MS Engr). Part-time and evening/weekend programs available. *Degree requirements:* For master's, thesis (for some programs); for doctorate, comprehensive exam, thesis/dissertation. *Entrance requirements:* For master's, GRE General Test, bachelor's degree in engineering from an ABET accredited institution; for doctorate, GRE. Additional exam requirements/recommendations for international students: Required—TOEFL (minimum score 550 paper-based). Electronic applications accepted. *Faculty research:* Applied radiation research, thermal science, computational fluid dynamics, analog mixed signal, aerial space battlefield.

Quinnipiac University, School of Business, Program in Business Administration, Hamden, CT 06518-1940. Offers chartered financial analyst (MBA); finance (MBA); healthcare management (MBA); information systems management (MBA); marketing (MBA); supply chain management (MBA); JD/MBA. *Accreditation:* AACSB. Part-time and evening/weekend programs available. Postbaccalaureate distance learning degree programs offered (no on-campus study). *Faculty:* 19 full-time (4 women), 2 part-time/adjunct (1 woman). *Students:* 89 full-time (36 women), 129 part-time (50 women); includes 16 minority (5 Black or African American, non-Hispanic/Latino; 5 Asian, non-Hispanic/Latino; 6 Hispanic/Latino), 19 international. Average age 29. 206 applicants, 81% accepted, 139 enrolled. In 2011, 95 master's awarded. *Entrance requirements:* For master's, GMAT or GRE, minimum GPA of 3.0. Additional exam requirements/recommendations for international students: Required—TOEFL (minimum score 575 paper-based; 233 computer-based; 90 iBT), IELTS (minimum score 6.5). *Application deadline:* For fall admission, 7/30 priority date for domestic students, 4/30 for international students; for spring admission, 12/15 priority date for domestic students, 9/15 for international students. Applications are processed on a rolling basis. Application fee: $45. Electronic applications accepted. *Expenses: Tuition:* Part-time $855 per credit. *Required fees:* $35 per credit. *Financial support:* In 2011–12, 23 students received support. Career-related internships or fieldwork, Federal Work-Study, scholarships/grants, tuition waivers (partial), and unspecified assistantships available. Support available to part-time students. Financial award application deadline: 4/15; financial award applicants required to submit FAFSA. *Faculty research:* Financial markets and investments, international business, supply chain management, health care management, corporate governance. *Unit head:* Lisa Braiewa, MBA Program Director, 203-582-3710, Fax: 203-582-8664, E-mail: lisa.braiewa@quinnipiac.edu. *Application contact:* Katie Ludovico, 800-462-1944, Fax: 203-582-3443, E-mail: katie.ludovico@quinnipiac.edu. Web site: http://www.quinnipiac.edu/mba.

Quinnipiac University, School of Business, Program in Information Technology, Hamden, CT 06518-1940. Offers MS. Part-time and evening/weekend programs available. *Faculty:* 2 full-time (0 women), 1 part-time/adjunct (0 women). *Students:* 4 full-time (2 women), 40 part-time (7 women); includes 6 minority (2 Black or African American, non-Hispanic/Latino; 1 American Indian or Alaska Native, non-Hispanic/Latino; 2 Asian, non-Hispanic/Latino; 1 Hispanic/Latino), 1 international. Average age 24. 35 applicants, 83% accepted, 28 enrolled. In 2011, 3 master's awarded. *Entrance requirements:* For master's, minimum GPA of 2.75; course work in computer language programming, management, accounting foundation. Additional exam requirements/recommendations for international students: Required—TOEFL (minimum score 575 paper-based; 233 computer-based; 90 iBT), IELTS (minimum score 6.5). *Application deadline:* For fall admission, 7/30 priority date for domestic students, 4/30 for international students; for spring admission, 12/15 priority date for domestic students, 9/15 for international students. Applications are processed on a rolling basis. Application fee: $45. Electronic applications accepted. *Expenses: Tuition:* Part-time $855 per credit. *Required fees:* $35 per credit. *Financial support:* In 2011–12, 2 students received support. Federal Work-Study, tuition waivers (partial), and unspecified assistantships available. Support available to part-time students. Financial award application deadline: 4/15. *Faculty research:* Data management and warehousing, peer-to-peer counseling, decision support systems. *Unit head:* Lisa Braiewa, Program Director, 203-582-3710, Fax: 203-582-8664, E-mail: lisa.braiewa@quinnipiac.edu. *Application contact:* Katharina Wagner, Online Admissions Coordinator, 877-403-4277, Fax: 203-582-3352, E-mail: quonlineadmissions@quinnipiac.edu. Web site: http://www.quinnipiac.edu/qu-online/academics/degree-programs/ms-in-information-technology.

Regent's American College London, Webster Graduate School, London, United Kingdom. Offers business (MBA); finance (MS); human resources (MA); information technology management (MA); international business (MA); international non-governmental organizations (MA); international relations (MA); management and leadership (MA); marketing (MA). Part-time programs available.

Regis University, College for Professional Studies, School of Computer and Information Sciences, Denver, CO 80221-1099. Offers database administration with Oracle (Certificate); database development (Certificate); database technologies (M Sc); enterprise Java software development (Certificate); enterprise resource planning (Certificate); executive information technologies (Certificate); information assurance (M Sc, Certificate); information technology management (M Sc); software engineering (M Sc, Certificate); software engineering and database technologies (M Sc); storage area networks (Certificate); systems engineering (M Sc, Certificate). Offered at Boulder Campus, Northwest Denver Campus, Southeast Denver Campus, Fort Collins Campus, Colorado Springs Campus, and Broomfield Campus. Part-time and evening/weekend programs available. Postbaccalaureate distance learning degree programs offered (no on-campus study). *Degree requirements:* For master's, thesis, final research project. *Entrance requirements:* For master's, 2 years of related experience, resume, interview; for Certificate, 2 years of related experience, resumé. Additional exam requirements/recommendations for international students: Required—TOEFL (minimum score 213 computer-based), TWE (minimum score 5) or university-based test. Electronic applications accepted. *Expenses:* Contact institution. *Faculty research:* Secure Virtual Laboratory Architecture, Joint IA project with W2C06 Institute, Information Policy, OLTP and OLAP Technologies, knowledge management, software architectures.

Rivier University, School of Graduate Studies, Department of Computer Information Systems, Nashua, NH 03060. Offers MS. Part-time programs available.

Robert Morris University, Graduate Studies, School of Communications and Information Systems, Moon Township, PA 15108-1189. Offers communication and information systems (MS); competitive intelligence systems (MS); information security and assurance (MS); information systems and communications (D Sc); information systems management (MS); information technology project management (MS); Internet information systems (MS); organizational leadership (MS). Part-time and evening/weekend programs available. Postbaccalaureate distance learning degree programs offered (no on-campus study). *Faculty:* 28 full-time (9 women), 9 part-time/adjunct (3 women). *Students:* 231 part-time (68 women); includes 41 minority (31 Black or African American, non-Hispanic/Latino; 8 Asian, non-Hispanic/Latino; 2 Hispanic/Latino), 16 international. *Degree requirements:* For doctorate, thesis/dissertation. *Entrance requirements:* For doctorate, employer letter of endorsement, interview. Additional exam requirements/recommendations for international students: Required—TOEFL (minimum score 550 paper-based; 213 computer-based; 79 iBT). *Application deadline:* For fall admission, 7/1 priority date for domestic students, 7/1 for international students; for spring admission, 11/1 priority date for domestic students, 11/1 for international students. Applications are processed on a rolling basis. Application fee: $35. Electronic applications accepted. *Expenses:* Contact institution. *Financial support:* Research assistantships with partial tuition reimbursements, institutionally sponsored loans, and unspecified assistantships available. Support available to part-time students. Financial award application deadline: 5/1. *Unit head:* Dr. Barbara J. Levine, Dean, 412-397-2591, Fax: 412-397-2481, E-mail: levine@rmu.edu. *Application contact:* Deborah Roach, Assistant Dean, Graduate Admissions, 412-397-5200, Fax: 412-397-2425, E-mail: graduateadmissions@rmu.edu. Web site: http://www.rmu.edu/web/cms/schools/scis/.

Robert Morris University Illinois, Morris Graduate School of Management, Chicago, IL 60605. Offers accounting (MBA); accounting/finance (MBA); design and media (MM); health care administration (MM); higher education administration (MM); human resource management (MBA); information systems (MIS); law enforcement administration (MM); management (MBA); management/finance (MIS); management/human resource management (MBA); sports administration (MM). Part-time and evening/weekend programs available. *Faculty:* 7 full-time (1 woman), 21 part-time/adjunct (5 women). *Students:* 296 full-time (172 women), 216 part-time (136 women); includes 273 minority (160 Black or African American, non-Hispanic/Latino; 1 American Indian or Alaska Native, non-Hispanic/Latino; 32 Asian, non-Hispanic/Latino; 78 Hispanic/Latino; 2 Two or more races, non-Hispanic/Latino), 28 international. Average age 32. 247 applicants, 69% accepted, 152 enrolled. In 2011, 244 master's awarded. *Entrance requirements:* Additional exam requirements/recommendations for international students: Required—TOEFL (minimum score 550 paper-based; 173 computer-based). *Application deadline:* Applications are processed on a rolling basis. Application fee: $20 ($100 for international students). Electronic applications accepted. *Expenses: Tuition:* Full-time $13,800; part-time $2300 per course. *Financial support:* In 2011–12, 643 students received support. Federal Work-Study, scholarships/grants, tuition waivers, and leadership and athletic scholarships available. Support available to part-time students. Financial award applicants required to submit FAFSA. *Unit head:* Kayed Akkawi, Dean, 312-935-6025, Fax: 312-935-6020, E-mail: kakkawi@robertmorris.edu. *Application contact:* Fernando Villeda, Dean of Morris Graduate School of Management, 312-935-6050, Fax: 312-935-6020, E-mail: fvilleda@robertmorris.edu.

Rochester Institute of Technology, Graduate Enrollment Services, B. Thomas Golisano College of Computing and Information Sciences, Department of Networking, Security and Systems Administration, Program in Computing Security and Information Assurance, Rochester, NY 14623-5603. Offers MS. Part-time programs available. *Students:* 14 full-time (1 woman), 12 part-time (2 women), 12 international. Average age 33. 46 applicants, 57% accepted, 12 enrolled. In 2011, 2 master's awarded. *Degree requirements:* For master's, thesis. *Entrance requirements:* For master's, GRE, minimum GPA of 3.0. Additional exam requirements/recommendations for international students: Required—TOEFL (minimum score 600 paper-based; 250 computer-based; 100 iBT) or IELTS (minimum score 7.0). *Application deadline:* Applications are processed on a rolling basis. Application fee: $50. Electronic applications accepted. *Expenses: Tuition:* Full-time $34,659; part-time $963 per credit hour. *Required fees:* $228; $76 per quarter. *Financial support:* Research assistantships with partial tuition reimbursements, teaching assistantships with partial tuition reimbursements, career-related internships or fieldwork, scholarships/grants, and unspecified assistantships available. Support available to part-time students. Financial award applicants required to submit FAFSA. *Unit head:* Prof. Dianne Bills, Graduate Program Director, 585-475-2700, Fax: 585-475-6584, E-mail: informaticsgrad@rit.edu. *Application contact:* Diane Ellison, Assistant Vice President, Graduate Enrollment Services, 585-475-2229, Fax: 585-475-7164, E-mail: gradinfo@rit.edu.

Roosevelt University, Graduate Division, Walter E. Heller College of Business Administration, Program in Information Systems, Chicago, IL 60605. Offers MSIS. Part-time and evening/weekend programs available. *Entrance requirements:* For master's, GMAT.

Rowan University, Graduate School, William G. Rohrer College of Business, Department of Marketing and Business Information Systems, Glassboro, NJ 08028-1701. Offers MBA. Part-time and evening/weekend programs available. *Degree requirements:* For master's, comprehensive exam, thesis. *Entrance requirements:* For master's, GRE General Test. Additional exam requirements/recommendations for international students: Required—TOEFL. Electronic applications accepted.

Rutgers, The State University of New Jersey, Newark, Graduate School, Program in Management, Newark, NJ 07102. Offers accounting (PhD); accounting information systems (PhD); computer information systems (PhD); finance (PhD); information technology (PhD); international business (PhD); management science (PhD); marketing (PhD); organization management (PhD). Program offered jointly with New Jersey Institute of Technology. *Accreditation:* AACSB. *Degree requirements:* For doctorate, thesis/dissertation, cumulative exams. *Entrance requirements:* For doctorate, GMAT or GRE General Test, minimum undergraduate B average. Additional exam requirements/recommendations for international students: Required—TOEFL. Electronic applications accepted. *Faculty research:* Technology management, leadership and teams, consumer behavior, financial and markets, logistics.

Rutgers, The State University of New Jersey, Newark, Rutgers Business School–Newark and New Brunswick, Doctoral Programs in Management, Newark, NJ 07102. Offers accounting (PhD); accounting information systems (PhD); economics (PhD); finance (PhD); individualized study (PhD); information technology (PhD); international business (PhD); management science (PhD); marketing science (PhD); organizational management (PhD); science, technology and management (PhD); supply chain management (PhD). *Degree requirements:* For doctorate, comprehensive exam, thesis/dissertation. *Entrance requirements:* For doctorate, GRE or GMAT. Additional exam requirements/recommendations for international students: Required—TOEFL (minimum score 550 paper-based; 213 computer-based; 79 iBT). Electronic applications accepted.

Management Information Systems

Sacred Heart University, Graduate Programs, College of Arts and Sciences, Department of Computer Science and Information Technology, Fairfield, CT 06825-1000. Offers computer science (MS); database (CPS); information technology (MS, CPS); information technology and network security (CPS); interactive multimedia (CPS); Web development (CPS). Part-time and evening/weekend programs available. *Degree requirements:* For master's, thesis optional. *Entrance requirements:* Additional exam requirements/recommendations for international students: Required—TOEFL (minimum score 550 paper-based; 213 computer-based). Electronic applications accepted. *Faculty research:* Contemporary market software.

St. Edward's University, School of Management and Business, Program in Computer Information Systems, Austin, TX 78704. Offers MS. Part-time and evening/weekend programs available. *Students:* 8 full-time (0 women), 13 part-time (1 woman); includes 7 minority (1 Black or African American, non-Hispanic/Latino; 1 Asian, non-Hispanic/Latino; 4 Hispanic/Latino; 1 Two or more races, non-Hispanic/Latino), 1 international. Average age 39. In 2011, 16 master's awarded. *Degree requirements:* For master's, minimum of 24 resident hours. *Entrance requirements:* For master's, GMAT or GRE General Test, minimum GPA of 2.75 in last 60 hours of course work. Additional exam requirements/recommendations for international students: Required—TOEFL (minimum score 550 paper-based; 213 computer-based; 79 iBT) or IELTS (minimum score 6). *Application deadline:* For fall admission, 7/1 for domestic and international students; for spring admission, 11/1 for domestic and international students. Applications are processed on a rolling basis. Application fee: $45 ($50 for international students). Electronic applications accepted. *Expenses: Tuition:* Full-time $17,550; part-time $975 per credit hour. *Required fees:* $50 per trimester. Full-time tuition and fees vary according to course load and program. *Faculty research:* System design. *Unit head:* Dwight D. Daniel, Director, 512-448-8460, Fax: 512-428-8492, E-mail: dwightd@stedwards.edu. *Application contact:* Gloria Candelaria, Graduate Admissions Coordinator, 512-448-8600, Fax: 512-428-1032, E-mail: gloriaca@stedwards.edu. Web site: http://www.stedwards.edu.

St. John's University, The Peter J. Tobin College of Business, Department of Computer Information Systems and Decision Sciences, Queens, NY 11439. Offers business analytics (MBA); computer information systems for managers (Adv C). Part-time and evening/weekend programs available. *Students:* 6 full-time (3 women), 8 part-time (0 women); includes 4 minority (1 Black or African American, non-Hispanic/Latino; 2 Asian, non-Hispanic/Latino; 1 Hispanic/Latino), 1 international. Average age 26. 8 applicants, 75% accepted, 4 enrolled. In 2011, 5 master's awarded. *Degree requirements:* For master's, comprehensive exam (for some programs), thesis optional. *Entrance requirements:* For master's, GMAT, 2 letters of recommendation, resume, transcripts, essay. Additional exam requirements/recommendations for international students: Required—TOEFL (minimum score 600 paper-based; 250 computer-based; 100 iBT), IELTS (minimum score 7). *Application deadline:* For fall admission, 5/1 priority date for domestic students, 5/1 for international students; for spring admission, 11/1 priority date for domestic students, 11/1 for international students. Applications are processed on a rolling basis. Application fee: $50. Electronic applications accepted. *Expenses:* Contact institution. *Financial support:* Research assistantships, scholarships/grants, and unspecified assistantships available. Support available to part-time students. Financial award application deadline: 3/1; financial award applicants required to submit FAFSA. *Unit head:* Dr. Victor Lu, Chair. *Application contact:* Carol J. Swanberg, Assistant Dean/Director of Graduate Admissions, 718-990-1345, Fax: 718-990-5242, E-mail: tobingradnyc@stjohns.edu.

Saint Joseph's University, Erivan K. Haub School of Business, MS Program in Business Intelligence, Philadelphia, PA 19131-1395. Offers business intelligence (MS). Part-time and evening/weekend programs available. Postbaccalaureate distance learning degree programs offered (no on-campus study). *Students:* 21 full-time (8 women), 97 part-time (29 women); includes 22 minority (8 Black or African American, non-Hispanic/Latino; 6 Asian, non-Hispanic/Latino; 6 Hispanic/Latino; 2 Two or more races, non-Hispanic/Latino), 17 international. Average age 35. In 2011, 40 master's awarded. *Entrance requirements:* For master's, GMAT or GRE, 2 letters of recommendation, resume, personal statement. Additional exam requirements/recommendations for international students: Required—TOEFL (minimum score 550 paper-based; 213 computer-based; 80 iBT), IELTS (minimum score 6.5), or Pearson Test of English (minimum score 60). *Application deadline:* For fall admission, 7/15 priority date for domestic students, 4/15 for international students; for spring admission, 11/15 priority date for domestic students, 10/15 for international students. Applications are processed on a rolling basis. Application fee: $35. Electronic applications accepted. *Expenses: Tuition:* Part-time $735 per credit hour. Tuition and fees vary according to degree level and program. *Financial support:* In 2011–12, teaching assistantships with partial tuition reimbursements (averaging $2,500 per year) were awarded; unspecified assistantships also available. Financial award application deadline: 5/1; financial award applicants required to submit FAFSA. *Unit head:* Dr. Patricia Rafferty, Director, MS in Business Intelligence and MS in Human Resource Management Programs, 610-660-1318, Fax: 610-660-1229, E-mail: patricia.rafferty@sju.edu. *Application contact:* Dr. Patricia Rafferty, Director, MS in Business Intelligence and MS in Human Resource Management Programs, 610-660-1318, Fax: 610-660-1229, E-mail: patricia.rafferty@sju.edu. Web site: http://www.sju.edu/hsb/bi/.

See Display below and Close-Up on page 531.

Saint Peter's University, Graduate Business Programs, MBA Program, Jersey City, NJ 07306-5997. Offers finance (MBA); health care administration (MBA); human resource management (MBA); international business (MBA); management (MBA); management information systems (MBA); marketing (MBA); risk management (MBA); MBA/MS. Part-time and evening/weekend programs available. *Entrance requirements:* Additional exam requirements/recommendations for international students: Required—TOEFL (minimum score 79 computer-based). Electronic applications accepted. *Faculty research:* Finance, health care management, human resource management, international business, management, management information systems, marketing, risk management.

San Diego State University, Graduate and Research Affairs, College of Business Administration, Department of Management Information Systems, San Diego, CA 92182. Offers information systems (MS). Evening/weekend programs available. *Degree requirements:* For master's, thesis or alternative. *Entrance requirements:* For master's, GMAT, resume, letters of reference. Additional exam requirements/recommendations for international students: Required—TOEFL. Electronic applications accepted.

San Jose State University, Graduate Studies and Research, Lucas Graduate School of Business, Programs in Business Administration, San Jose, CA 95192-0001. Offers MBA. *Accreditation:* AACSB. *Degree requirements:* For master's, comprehensive exam, thesis or alternative. *Entrance requirements:* For master's, GMAT, minimum GPA of 3.0. Electronic applications accepted.

Santa Clara University, Leavey School of Business, Program in Information Systems, Santa Clara, CA 95053. Offers MSIS. Part-time programs available. *Students:* 27 full-time (12 women), 46 part-time (22 women); includes 11 minority (8 Asian, non-Hispanic/Latino; 2 Hispanic/Latino; 1 Native Hawaiian or other Pacific Islander, non-Hispanic/Latino), 42 international. Average age 28. 66 applicants, 91% accepted, 30 enrolled. In 2011, 37 degrees awarded. *Degree requirements:* For master's, capstone project. *Entrance requirements:* For master's, GMAT, GRE. Additional exam requirements/recommendations for international students: Required—TOEFL (minimum score 600 paper-based; 250 computer-based; 100 iBT). *Application deadline:* For fall admission, 6/1 for domestic and international students; for spring admission, 1/19 for domestic and international students. Applications are processed on a rolling basis. Application fee: $75 ($100 for international students). Electronic applications accepted. *Expenses:* Contact institution. *Financial support:* In 2011–12, 25 students received support. Fellowships with partial tuition reimbursements available, research assistantships with partial tuition reimbursements available, career-related internships or fieldwork, Federal Work-Study, institutionally sponsored loans, scholarships/grants, health care benefits, and unspecified assistantships available. Support available to part-time students. Financial award application deadline: 6/1; financial award applicants required to submit FAFSA. *Unit head:* Manoochehr Ghiassi, Faculty Director, MSIS Program, 408-554-4687, E-mail: mghiassi@scu.edu. *Application contact:* Tiffiny Gillingham, Assistant Director, MSIS Admissions, 408-551-7047, Fax: 408-554-2331, E-mail: tgillingham@scu.edu.

Schiller International University, MBA Programs, Florida, Program in Information Technology, Largo, FL 33770. Offers MBA. *Entrance requirements:* Additional exam requirements/recommendations for international students: Required—TOEFL.

Schiller International University, MBA Programs, Heidelberg, Germany, Heidelberg, Germany. Offers international business (MBA, MIM); management of information technology (MBA). Part-time and evening/weekend programs available. *Degree requirements:* For master's, thesis optional. *Entrance requirements:* Additional exam requirements/recommendations for international students: Required—TOEFL (minimum score 550 paper-based; 213 computer-based). *Faculty research:* Leadership, international economy, foreign direct investment.

Seattle Pacific University, Master's Degree in Information Systems Management (MS-ISM) Program, Seattle, WA 98119-1997. Offers MS. Part-time programs available. *Entrance requirements:* For master's, GMAT, minimum GPA of 3.0. Additional exam requirements/recommendations for international students: Required—TOEFL (minimum score 225 computer-based). Electronic applications accepted.

Shippensburg University of Pennsylvania, School of Graduate Studies, College of Arts and Sciences, Department of Sociology and Anthropology, Shippensburg, PA 17257-2299. Offers organizational development and leadership (MS), including business, communications, environmental management, higher education structure and policy, historical administration, individual and organizational development, management information systems, public organizations, social structures and organizations. Part-time and evening/weekend programs available. *Faculty:* 3 full-time (all women). *Students:* 12 full-time (6 women), 40 part-time (34 women); includes 6 minority (3 Black or African American, non-Hispanic/Latino; 2 Asian, non-Hispanic/Latino; 1 Two or more races, non-Hispanic/Latino), 2 international. Average age 33. 52 applicants, 46% accepted, 16 enrolled. In 2011, 34 master's awarded. *Degree requirements:* For master's, capstone experience including internship. *Entrance requirements:* For master's, interview (if GPA less than 2.75), resume, personal goals statement. Additional exam requirements/recommendations for international students: Required—TOEFL (minimum score 580 paper-based; 237 computer-based); Recommended—IELTS (minimum score 6). *Application deadline:* For fall admission, 4/30 for international students; for spring admission, 9/30 for international students. Applications are processed on a rolling basis. Application fee: $30. Electronic applications accepted. *Expenses: Tuition, area resident:* Part-time $416 per credit. Tuition, state resident: part-time $416 per credit. Tuition, nonresident: part-time $624 per credit. *Required fees:* $119 per credit. *Financial support:* In 2011–12, 9 research assistantships with full tuition reimbursements (averaging $5,000 per year) were awarded; career-related internships or fieldwork, scholarships/grants, unspecified assistantships, and resident hall director and student payroll positions also available. Support available to part-time students. Financial award applicants required to submit FAFSA. *Unit head:* Dr. Barbara Denison, Program Coordinator, 717-477-1735, Fax: 717-477-4011, E-mail: bjdeni@ship.edu. *Application contact:* Jeremy R. Goshorn, Assistant Dean of Graduate Admissions, 717-477-1231, Fax: 717-477-4016, E-mail: jrgoshorn@ship.edu. Web site: http://www.ship.edu/odl/.

Southeastern Oklahoma State University, School of Arts and Sciences, Durant, OK 74701-0609. Offers biology (MT); computer information systems (MT); occupational safety and health (MT). Part-time and evening/weekend programs available. *Faculty:* 12 full-time (4 women), 1 part-time/adjunct (0 women). *Students:* 17 full-time (6 women), 45 part-time (8 women); includes 18 minority (1 Black or African American, non-Hispanic/Latino; 15 American Indian or Alaska Native, non-Hispanic/Latino; 2 Hispanic/Latino), 2 international. Average age 28. 19 applicants, 95% accepted, 18 enrolled. *Degree requirements:* For master's, thesis optional. *Entrance requirements:* For master's, minimum GPA of 3.0 in last 60 hours or 2.75 overall. Additional exam requirements/recommendations for international students: Required—TOEFL (minimum score 550 paper-based; 213 computer-based; 79 iBT). *Application deadline:* For fall admission, 8/1 for domestic students, 6/1 for international students; for spring admission, 1/5 for domestic students, 11/1 for international students. Application fee: $20 ($55 for international students). Electronic applications accepted. *Expenses:* Tuition, state resident: full-time $3537; part-time $173.95 per credit hour. Tuition, nonresident: full-time $8673; part-time $459.30 per credit hour. *Required fees:* $22.55 per credit hour. *Financial support:* In 2011–12, 8 students received support. Fellowships, research assistantships, teaching assistantships, Federal Work-Study, and institutionally sponsored loans available. Support available to part-time students. Financial award application deadline: 6/15; financial award applicants required to submit FAFSA. *Unit head:* Dr. Teresa Golden, Graduate Coordinator, 580-745-2286, E-mail: tgolden@se.edu. *Application contact:* Carrie Williamson, Graduate Secretary, 580-745-2220, Fax: 580-745-7474, E-mail: cwilliamson@se.edu. Web site: http://www.se.edu/arts-and-sciences/.

Southern Illinois University Edwardsville, Graduate School, School of Business, Department of Computer Management and Information Systems, Edwardsville, IL 62026. Offers MS. Part-time and evening/weekend programs available. *Faculty:* 9 full-time (5 women). *Students:* 9 full-time (1 woman), 16 part-time (5 women); includes 4 minority (3 Black or African American, non-Hispanic/Latino; 1 Asian, non-Hispanic/Latino), 5 international. 38 applicants, 21% accepted. In 2011, 15 master's awarded. *Degree requirements:* For master's, thesis or alternative, final exam. *Entrance requirements:* For master's, GMAT. Additional exam requirements/recommendations for international students: Required—TOEFL (minimum score 550 paper-based; 213 computer-based; 79 iBT), IELTS (minimum score 6.5). *Application deadline:* For fall admission, 7/22 for domestic students, 6/1 for international students; for spring admission, 12/10 for domestic students, 10/1 for international students. Applications are processed on a rolling basis. Application fee: $30. Electronic applications accepted. Tuition and fees vary according to course load and program. *Financial support:* Fellowships, research assistantships, teaching assistantships with tuition reimbursements, institutionally sponsored loans, scholarships/grants, and unspecified assistantships available. Financial award application deadline: 3/1; financial award applicants required to submit FAFSA. *Unit head:* Dr. Douglas Bock, Chair, 618-650-2504, E-mail: dbock@siue.edu. *Application contact:* Dr. Jo Ellen Moore, Director, 618-650-5816, E-mail: joemoor@siue.edu. Web site: http://www.siue.edu/business/cmis/.

Southern Illinois University Edwardsville, Graduate School, School of Business, Program in Business Administration, Specialization in Management Information Systems, Edwardsville, IL 62026. Offers MBA. Part-time programs available. In 2011, 5 master's awarded. *Degree requirements:* For master's, thesis or alternative, final exam. *Entrance requirements:* For master's, GMAT. Additional exam requirements/recommendations for international students: Required—TOEFL (minimum score 550 paper-based; 213 computer-based; 79 iBT), IELTS (minimum score 6.5). *Application deadline:* For fall admission, 7/23 for domestic students, 6/1 for international students; for spring admission, 12/10 for domestic students, 10/1 for international students. Applications are processed on a rolling basis. Application fee: $30. Electronic applications accepted. Tuition and fees vary according to course load and program. *Financial support:* Fellowships with full tuition reimbursements, research assistantships with full tuition reimbursements, teaching assistantships with full tuition reimbursements, career-related internships or fieldwork, Federal Work-Study, institutionally sponsored loans, scholarships/grants, traineeships, and unspecified assistantships available. Support available to part-time students. Financial award application deadline: 3/1; financial award applicants required to submit FAFSA. *Unit head:* Dr. Janice Joplin, Director, 618-650-3412, E-mail: jjoplin@siue.edu. *Application contact:* Michelle Robinson, Coordinator of Graduate Recruitment, 618-650-2811, Fax: 618-650-3523, E-mail: michero@siue.edu. Web site: http://www.siue.edu/business/mba/mis-specialization.shtml.

Southern Methodist University, Cox School of Business, MBA Program, Dallas, TX 75275. Offers accounting (MBA); finance (MBA); financial consulting (MBA); general business (MBA); information technology and operations management (MBA); management (MBA); marketing (MBA); real estate (MBA); strategy and entrepreneurship (MBA). Part-time and evening/weekend programs available. *Entrance requirements:* For master's, GMAT. Additional exam requirements/recommendations for international students: Required—TOEFL. Electronic applications accepted. *Expenses:* Contact institution. *Faculty research:* Corporate finance, financial reporting, modeling consumer decision-making, competition between national brands and store brands, institutional determinants of firms' strategy.

Southern New Hampshire University, School of Business, Manchester, NH 03106-1045. Offers accounting (MS); business administration (MBA, Certificate), including accounting (Certificate), business administration (MBA), finance (Certificate), forensic accounting (Certificate), human resources management (Certificate), international business (Certificate), international sport management (Certificate), leadership of not for profit organizations (Certificate), marketing (Certificate), operations management (Certificate), sport management (Certificate), taxation (Certificate); finance (MS); hospitality and tourism leadership (Certificate); information technology (MS, Certificate); information technology/international business (Certificate); integrated marketing communications (Certificate); international business (MS, DBA); marketing (MS); operations and project management (MS); organizational leadership (MS); project management (Certificate); sport management (MS); MBA/Certificate. *Accreditation:* ACBSP. Part-time and evening/weekend programs available. Postbaccalaureate distance learning degree programs offered (no on-campus study). Terminal master's awarded for partial completion of doctoral program. *Degree requirements:* For master's, one foreign language, comprehensive exam (for some programs), thesis or alternative; for doctorate, one foreign language, comprehensive exam, thesis/dissertation. *Entrance requirements:* For master's, minimum GPA of 2.5; for doctorate, GMAT. Additional exam requirements/recommendations for international students: Required—TOEFL (minimum score 500 paper-based). Electronic applications accepted.

Southern University at New Orleans, School of Graduate Studies, New Orleans, LA 70126-1009. Offers criminal justice (MA); management information systems (MS); museum studies (MA); social work (MSW). *Accreditation:* CSWE. Part-time and evening/weekend programs available. *Faculty:* 28 full-time (12 women), 3 part-time/adjunct (2 women). *Students:* 230 full-time (180 women), 210 part-time (174 women); includes 393 minority (385 Black or African American, non-Hispanic/Latino; 2 American Indian or Alaska Native, non-Hispanic/Latino; 4 Asian, non-Hispanic/Latino; 2 Hispanic/Latino). Average age 35. In 2011, 157 master's awarded. *Degree requirements:* For master's, thesis. *Entrance requirements:* For master's, GRE/GMAT. Additional exam requirements/recommendations for international students: Required—TOEFL. *Application deadline:* Applications are processed on a rolling basis. Application fee: $25 ($35 for international students). *Expenses:* Tuition, state resident: part-time $747 per credit hour. Tuition, nonresident: part-time $747 per credit hour. *Financial support:* Fellowships, career-related internships or fieldwork, and institutionally sponsored loans available. *Application contact:* Deidrea Hazure, Administrative Specialist/Graduate Studies Admissions Coordinator, 504-284-5486, Fax: 504-284-5506, E-mail: dhazure@suno.edu. Web site: http://www.suno.edu/Colleges/Graduate_Studies/.

Stevens Institute of Technology, Graduate School, Wesley J. Howe School of Technology Management, Doctoral Program in Technology Management, Hoboken, NJ 07030. Offers information management (PhD); technology management (PhD); telecommunications management (PhD). Part-time and evening/weekend programs available. Postbaccalaureate distance learning degree programs offered (minimal on-campus study). *Entrance requirements:* Additional exam requirements/recommendations for international students: Required—TOEFL. Electronic applications accepted.

Stevens Institute of Technology, Graduate School, Wesley J. Howe School of Technology Management, Program in Business Administration, Hoboken, NJ 07030. Offers engineering management (MBA); financial engineering (MBA); information management (MBA); information technology in financial services (MBA); information technology in the pharmaceutical industry (MBA); information technology outsourcing (MBA); pharmaceutical management (MBA); project management (MBA); technology management (MBA); telecommunications management (MBA).

Stevens Institute of Technology, Graduate School, Wesley J. Howe School of Technology Management, Program in Information Systems, Hoboken, NJ 07030. Offers computer science (MS); e-commerce (MS); enterprise systems (MS); entrepreneurial information technology (MS); information architecture (MS); information management (MS, Certificate); information security (MS); information technology in financial services industry (MS); information technology in the pharmaceutical industry (MS); information technology outsourcing management (MS); project management (MS, Certificate); software engineering (MS); telecommunications (MS). *Degree requirements:* For master's, thesis optional. *Entrance requirements:* For master's, GMAT, GRE General Test. Additional exam requirements/recommendations for international students: Required—TOEFL. Electronic applications accepted.

Stevens Institute of Technology, Graduate School, Wesley J. Howe School of Technology Management, Program in Management, Hoboken, NJ 07030. Offers general management (MS); global innovation management (MS); human resource management (MS); information management (MS); project management (MS); technology commercialization (MS); technology management (MS). Part-time programs available. *Degree requirements:* For master's, thesis optional. *Entrance requirements:* For master's, GMAT, GRE General Test. Additional exam requirements/recommendations for international students: Required—TOEFL. Electronic applications accepted. *Faculty research:* Industrial economics.

Stony Brook University, State University of New York, Graduate School, College of Business, Program in Business Administration, Stony Brook, NY 11794. Offers finance

(MBA, Certificate); health care management (MBA, Certificate); human resource management (Certificate); human resources (MBA); information systems management (MBA, Certificate); management (MBA); marketing (MBA).

Stony Brook University, State University of New York, Graduate School, College of Engineering and Applied Sciences, Department of Computer Science, Stony Brook, NY 11794. Offers computer science (MS, PhD); information systems (Certificate); information systems engineering (MS); software engineering (Certificate). *Degree requirements:* For master's, thesis or alternative; for doctorate, comprehensive exam, thesis/dissertation. *Entrance requirements:* For master's and doctorate, GRE General Test. Additional exam requirements/recommendations for international students: Required—TOEFL. *Faculty research:* Artificial intelligence, computer architecture, database management systems, VLSI, operating systems.

Stony Brook University, State University of New York, School of Professional Development, Stony Brook, NY 11794. Offers biology-grade 7-12 (MAT); chemistry-grade 7-12 (MAT); coaching (Graduate Certificate); coaching online (Graduate Certificate); computer integrated engineering (Graduate Certificate); earth science-grade 7-12 (MAT); educational computing (Graduate Certificate); educational leadership (Advanced Certificate); English-grade 7-12 (MAT); environmental management (Graduate Certificate); environmental/occupational health and safety (Graduate Certificate); French-grade 7-12 (MAT); German-grade 7-12 (MAT); human resource management (Graduate Certificate); human resource management online (Graduate Certificate); information systems management (Graduate Certificate); Italian-grade 7-12 (MAT); liberal studies (MA); liberal studies online (MAT); mathematics-grade 7-12 (MAT); operation research (Graduate Certificate); physics-grade 7-12 (MAT); professional studies online (MPS); school administration and supervision (Graduate Certificate); school building leadership (Graduate Certificate); school district administration (Graduate Certificate); school district business leadership (Advanced Certificate); school district leadership (Graduate Certificate); social science and the professions (MPS), including environmental waste management, human resource management; social studies-grade 7-12 (MAT); Spanish-grade 7-12 (MAT); waste management (Graduate Certificate). Part-time and evening/weekend programs available. Postbaccalaureate distance learning degree programs offered. *Degree requirements:* For master's, one foreign language, thesis or alternative.

Stratford University, School of Graduate Studies, Falls Church, VA 22043. Offers accounting (MS); business administration (IMBA, MBA); enterprise business management (MS); entrepreneurial management (MS); information assurance (MS); information systems (MS); software engineering (MS); telecommunications (MS). Part-time and evening/weekend programs available. Postbaccalaureate distance learning degree programs offered (no on-campus study). *Degree requirements:* For master's, comprehensive exam, capstone project. *Entrance requirements:* For master's, GRE or GMAT, baccalaureate degree. Additional exam requirements/recommendations for international students: Required—TOEFL (minimum score 213 computer-based, 79 iBT) or IELTS (6.5). Electronic applications accepted.

Strayer University, Graduate Studies, Washington, DC 20005-2603. Offers accounting (MS); acquisition (MBA); business administration (MBA); communications technology (MS); educational management (M Ed); finance (MBA); health services administration (MHSA); hospitality and tourism management (MBA); human resource management (MBA); information systems (MS), including computer security management, decision support system management, enterprise resource management, network management, software engineering management, systems development management; management (MBA); management information systems (MS); marketing (MBA); professional accounting (MS), including accounting information systems, controllership, taxation; public administration (MPA); supply chain management (MBA); technology in education (M Ed). Programs also offered at campus locations in Birmingham, AL; Chamblee, GA; Cobb County, GA; Morrow, GA; White Marsh, MD; Charleston, SC; Columbia, SC; Greensboro, NC; Greenville, SC; Lexington, KY; Louisville, KY; Nashville, TN; North Raleigh, NC; Washington, DC. Part-time and evening/weekend programs available. Postbaccalaureate distance learning degree programs offered (minimal on-campus study). *Degree requirements:* For master's, thesis. *Entrance requirements:* For master's, GMAT, GRE General Test, bachelor's degree from an accredited college or university, minimum undergraduate GPA of 2.75. Electronic applications accepted.

Syracuse University, Martin J. Whitman School of Management, PhD Program in Business Administration, Syracuse, NY 13244. Offers accounting (PhD); finance (PhD); management information systems (PhD); managerial statistics (PhD); marketing (PhD); operations management (PhD); organizational behavior (PhD); strategy and human resources (PhD); supply chain management (PhD). *Faculty:* 79 full-time (20 women), 25 part-time/adjunct (6 women). *Students:* 32 full-time (10 women); includes 6 minority (3 Black or African American, non-Hispanic/Latino; 2 Asian, non-Hispanic/Latino; 1 Hispanic/Latino), 18 international. Average age 32. 260 applicants, 8% accepted, 12 enrolled. In 2011, 2 doctorates awarded. *Degree requirements:* For doctorate, comprehensive exam, thesis/dissertation, summer research paper. *Entrance requirements:* For doctorate, GMAT or GRE General Test, 3 recommendations. Additional exam requirements/recommendations for international students: Required—TOEFL (minimum score 600 paper-based; 250 computer-based; 100 iBT). *Application deadline:* For fall admission, 2/15 priority date for domestic students, 2/15 for international students. Applications are processed on a rolling basis. Application fee: $65. Electronic applications accepted. *Expenses: Tuition:* Part-time $1206 per credit. *Financial support:* In 2011–12, 1 fellowship with full tuition reimbursement (averaging $19,570 per year), 30 teaching assistantships with full tuition reimbursements (averaging $17,000 per year) were awarded; research assistantships with full tuition reimbursements, health care benefits, and unspecified assistantships also available. Financial award application deadline: 1/30. *Faculty research:* Marketing models, market microstructure, supply chain, auditing, corporate governance. *Unit head:* Dr. Eunkyu Lee, Director of the PhD Program, 315-443-3429, E-mail: elee06@syr.edu. *Application contact:* Carol Hilleges, Administrative Specialist, 315-443-9601, Fax: 315-443-3671, E-mail: clhilleg@syr.edu. Web site: http://whitman.syr.edu/phd/.

Syracuse University, School of Information Studies, Program in Data Science, Syracuse, NY 13244. Offers CAS. Part-time and evening/weekend programs available. Postbaccalaureate distance learning degree programs offered. *Students:* 5 applicants, 100% accepted, 0 enrolled. *Entrance requirements:* Additional exam requirements/recommendations for international students: Required—TOEFL (minimum score 100 iBT). *Application deadline:* For fall admission, 2/1 for domestic and international students. Applications are processed on a rolling basis. Application fee: $75. Electronic applications accepted. *Expenses: Tuition:* Part-time $1206 per credit. *Unit head:* Elizabeth Liddy, Dean, 315-443-2736. *Application contact:* Susan Corieri, Director of Enrollment Management, 315-443-2575, E-mail: ischool@syr.edu. Web site: http://ischool.syr.edu/.

See Display on page 1637 and Close-Up on page 1653.

Syracuse University, School of Information Studies, Program in Information Management, Syracuse, NY 13244. Offers MS, DPS. Part-time and evening/weekend programs available. Postbaccalaureate distance learning degree programs offered (minimal on-campus study). *Students:* 199 full-time (69 women), 146 part-time (40 women); includes 85 minority (29 Black or African American, non-Hispanic/Latino; 2 American Indian or Alaska Native, non-Hispanic/Latino; 16 Asian, non-Hispanic/Latino; 31 Hispanic/Latino; 7 Two or more races, non-Hispanic/Latino), 144 international. Average age 29. 606 applicants, 54% accepted, 130 enrolled. In 2011, 123 master's, 2 doctorates awarded. *Entrance requirements:* For master's, GRE General Test. Additional exam requirements/recommendations for international students: Required—TOEFL (minimum score 100 iBT). *Application deadline:* For fall admission, 2/15 priority date for domestic students, 2/15 for international students; for spring admission, 10/15 priority date for domestic students, 10/15 for international students. Applications are processed on a rolling basis. Application fee: $75. Electronic applications accepted. *Expenses: Tuition:* Part-time $1206 per credit. *Financial support:* Fellowships with tuition reimbursements, research assistantships with partial tuition reimbursements, teaching assistantships with partial tuition reimbursements, and scholarships/grants available. Financial award application deadline: 1/1; financial award applicants required to submit FAFSA. *Unit head:* David Dischiave, Director, 315-443-4681, Fax: 315-443-6886, E-mail: ddischia@syr.edu. *Application contact:* Susan Corieri, Director of Enrollment Management, 315-443-2575, E-mail: ischool@syr.edu. Web site: http://ischool.syr.edu/.

See Display on page 1637 and Close-Up on page 1653.

Syracuse University, School of Information Studies, Program in Information Security Management, Syracuse, NY 13244. Offers CAS. Part-time and evening/weekend programs available. Postbaccalaureate distance learning degree programs offered. *Students:* 7 part-time (2 women), 3 international. Average age 36. 48 applicants, 73% accepted, 1 enrolled. In 2011, 38 degrees awarded. *Entrance requirements:* Additional exam requirements/recommendations for international students: Required—TOEFL (minimum score 100 iBT). *Application deadline:* For fall admission, 2/1 priority date for domestic students, 2/1 for international students; for spring admission, 10/15 priority date for domestic students, 10/15 for international students. Applications are processed on a rolling basis. Application fee: $75. Electronic applications accepted. *Expenses: Tuition:* Part-time $1206 per credit. *Financial support:* Application deadline: 1/1; applicants required to submit FAFSA. *Unit head:* Joon S. Park, Head, 315-443-2911, E-mail: ischool@syr.edu. *Application contact:* Susan Corieri, Director of Enrollment Management, 315-443-2575, E-mail: ischool@syr.edu. Web site: http://ischool.syr.edu/.

See Display on page 1637 and Close-Up on page 1653.

Syracuse University, School of Information Studies, Program in Information Systems and Telecommunications Management, Syracuse, NY 13244. Offers CAS. Part-time and evening/weekend programs available. Postbaccalaureate distance learning degree programs offered. *Students:* 2 full-time (0 women), 15 part-time (5 women); includes 2 minority (1 Black or African American, non-Hispanic/Latino; 1 Hispanic/Latino), 3 international. Average age 33. 16 applicants, 75% accepted, 8 enrolled. In 2011, 11 degrees awarded. *Entrance requirements:* Additional exam requirements/recommendations for international students: Required—TOEFL (minimum score 100 iBT). *Application deadline:* For fall admission, 2/1 priority date for domestic students, 2/1 for international students; for spring admission, 10/15 priority date for domestic students, 10/15 for international students. Applications are processed on a rolling basis. Application fee: $75. Electronic applications accepted. *Expenses: Tuition:* Part-time $1206 per credit. *Financial support:* Fellowships with full tuition reimbursements, research assistantships with partial tuition reimbursements, and teaching assistantships with partial tuition reimbursements available. Financial award application deadline: 1/1; financial award applicants required to submit FAFSA. *Unit head:* David Dischiave, Director, 315-443-4681, Fax: 315-443-6886, E-mail: ddischia@syr.edu. *Application contact:* Susan Corieri, Director of Enrollment Management, 315-443-2575, E-mail: ischool@syr.edu. Web site: http://ischool.syr.edu/.

See Display on page 1637 and Close-Up on page 1653.

Tarleton State University, College of Graduate Studies, College of Business Administration, Department of Computer Information Systems, Stephenville, TX 76402. Offers information systems (MS). Part-time and evening/weekend programs available. *Faculty:* 4 full-time (1 woman), 1 part-time/adjunct (0 women). *Students:* 20 full-time (6 women), 52 part-time (14 women); includes 16 minority (6 Black or African American, non-Hispanic/Latino; 3 Asian, non-Hispanic/Latino; 5 Hispanic/Latino; 2 Two or more races, non-Hispanic/Latino), 6 international. Average age 34. 18 applicants, 94% accepted, 15 enrolled. In 2011, 31 master's awarded. *Degree requirements:* For master's, comprehensive exam. *Entrance requirements:* For master's, GRE, minimum GPA of 3.0. Additional exam requirements/recommendations for international students: Required—TOEFL (minimum score 550 paper-based; 213 computer-based; 80 iBT). *Application deadline:* For fall admission, 8/5 priority date for domestic students; for spring admission, 12/1 for domestic students. Applications are processed on a rolling basis. Application fee: $30 ($130 for international students). Electronic applications accepted. *Expenses:* Tuition, state resident: full-time $3131.46; part-time $174 per credit hour. Tuition, nonresident: full-time $8225; part-time $457 per credit hour. *Required fees:* $1446. Tuition and fees vary according to course load and campus/location. *Financial support:* Research assistantships and teaching assistantships available. Financial award application deadline: 5/1; financial award applicants required to submit FAFSA. *Unit head:* Dr. Leah Shultz, Interim Department Head, 254-968-9169, Fax: 254-968-9345, E-mail: lschult@tarleton.edu. *Application contact:* Information Contact, 254-968-9104, Fax: 254-968-9670, E-mail: gradoffice@tarleton.edu. Web site: http://www.tarleton.edu/~cis.

Temple University, Fox School of Business, Doctoral Programs in Business, Philadelphia, PA 19122-6096. Offers accounting (PhD); entrepreneurship (PhD); finance (PhD); international business (PhD); management information systems (PhD); marketing (PhD); risk management and insurance (PhD); statistics (PhD); strategic management (PhD); tourism and sport (PhD). *Accreditation:* AACSB. *Degree requirements:* For doctorate, thesis/dissertation. *Entrance requirements:* For doctorate, GRE General Test, GMAT, minimum GPA of 3.0, master's degree. Additional exam requirements/recommendations for international students: Required—TOEFL (minimum score 600 paper-based; 250 computer-based; 100 iBT), IELTS (minimum score 7.5). Electronic applications accepted. *Expenses:* Tuition, state resident: full-time $12,366; part-time $687 per credit hour. Tuition, nonresident: full-time $17,298; part-time $961 per credit hour. *Required fees:* $590; $213 per year.

Tennessee Technological University, Graduate School, College of Business, Cookeville, TN 38505. Offers accounting (MBA); finance (MBA); human resource management (MBA); international business (MBA); management information systems (MBA); risk management & insurance (MBA). *Accreditation:* AACSB. Part-time and evening/weekend programs available. Postbaccalaureate distance learning degree programs offered (no on-campus study). *Faculty:* 28 full-time (5 women). *Students:* 45 full-time (19 women), 135 part-time (51 women); includes 13 minority (4 Black or African American, non-Hispanic/Latino; 5 Asian, non-Hispanic/Latino; 3 Hispanic/Latino; 1 Native Hawaiian or other Pacific Islander, non-Hispanic/Latino), 2 international. Average age 25. 193 applicants, 59% accepted, 70 enrolled. In 2011, 89 master's awarded. *Entrance requirements:* For master's, GMAT. Additional exam requirements/recommendations for international students: Required—TOEFL (minimum score 550 paper-based; 79 iBT), IELTS (minimum score 5.5), Pearson Test of English Academic.

Application deadline: For fall admission, 8/1 for domestic students, 5/1 for international students; for spring admission, 12/1 for domestic students, 10/1 for international students. Application fee: $25 ($30 for international students). Electronic applications accepted. *Expenses:* Tuition, state resident: full-time $8094; part-time $422 per credit hour. Tuition, nonresident: full-time $20,574; part-time $1046 per credit hour. *Financial support:* In 2011–12, 5 fellowships (averaging $10,000 per year), 18 research assistantships (averaging $4,000 per year), teaching assistantships (averaging $4,000 per year) were awarded. Support available to part-time students. Financial award application deadline: 4/1. *Unit head:* Dr. Tom Timmerman, Director, 931-372-3600, Fax: 931-372-6249. *Application contact:* Shelia K. Kendrick, Coordinator of Graduate Admissions, 931-372-3808, Fax: 931-372-3497, E-mail: skendrick@tntech.edu. Web site: http://www.tntech.edu/mba.

Texas A&M International University, Office of Graduate Studies and Research, College of Business Administration, Division of International Business and Technology Studies, Laredo, TX 78041-1900. Offers information systems (MSIS); international trade (MBA). *Faculty:* 12 full-time (1 woman), 1 part-time/adjunct (0 women). *Students:* 29 full-time (8 women), 20 part-time (5 women); includes 12 minority (3 Black or African American, non-Hispanic/Latino; 2 Asian, non-Hispanic/Latino; 7 Hispanic/Latino), 32 international. Average age 28. 111 applicants, 22% accepted, 11 enrolled. In 2011, 19 master's awarded. *Degree requirements:* For master's, thesis (for some programs). *Entrance requirements:* For master's, GMAT or GRE General Test. Additional exam requirements/recommendations for international students: Required—TOEFL (minimum score 550 paper-based; 213 computer-based; 79 iBT). *Application deadline:* For fall admission, 4/30 priority date for domestic students, 4/30 for international students; for spring admission, 11/30 for domestic students, 10/1 for international students. Applications are processed on a rolling basis. Application fee: $35 ($50 for international students). *Expenses:* Tuition, state resident: full-time $5063. *Financial support:* In 2011–12, 8 students received support, including 2 fellowships, 5 research assistantships, 1 teaching assistantship; Federal Work-Study, institutionally sponsored loans, and scholarships/grants also available. Support available to part-time students. *Unit head:* Dr. S. Srinivasan, Chair, 956-326-2520, Fax: 956-326-2494, E-mail: srini@tamiu.edu. *Application contact:* Imelda Lopez, Graduate Admissions Counselor, 956-326-2485, Fax: 956-326-2459, E-mail: lopez@tamiu.edu. Web site: http://www.tamiu.edu/ssb/divisions.php?optN-220.

Texas A&M University, Mays Business School, Department of Information and Operations Management, College Station, TX 77843. Offers management information systems (MS, PhD); management science (PhD); production and operations management (PhD). *Faculty:* 16. *Students:* 172 full-time (61 women), 5 part-time (1 woman); includes 9 minority (5 Asian, non-Hispanic/Latino; 4 Hispanic/Latino), 121 international. Average age 31. In 2011, 96 master's awarded. Terminal master's awarded for partial completion of doctoral program. *Degree requirements:* For master's, comprehensive exam; for doctorate, thesis/dissertation. *Entrance requirements:* For master's, GMAT; for doctorate, GMAT or GRE General Test. Additional exam requirements/recommendations for international students: Required—TOEFL. *Application deadline:* For fall admission, 3/1 priority date for domestic students; for spring admission, 8/1 for domestic students. Applications are processed on a rolling basis. Application fee: $50 ($75 for international students). *Expenses:* Tuition, state resident: full-time $5437; part-time $226.55 per credit hour. Tuition, nonresident: full-time $12,949; part-time $539.55 per credit hour. *Required fees:* $2741. *Financial support:* In 2011–12, 51 students received support. Fellowships, research assistantships, teaching assistantships, career-related internships or fieldwork, Federal Work-Study, and institutionally sponsored loans available. Financial award application deadline: 2/1. *Unit head:* Dr. Rich Metters, Head, 979-845-1148, E-mail: rmetters@mays.tamu.edu. *Application contact:* Ted Boone, Graduate Advisor, 979-845-0809, E-mail: tboone@mays.tamu.edu. Web site: http://mays.tamu.edu/info/.

Texas A&M University–San Antonio, School of Business, San Antonio, TX 78224. Offers business administration (MBA); enterprise resource planning systems (MBA); finance (MBA); healthcare management (MBA); human resources management (MBA); information assurance and security (MBA); international business (MBA); professional accounting (MPA); project management (MBA); supply chain management (MBA). Part-time and evening/weekend programs available. *Faculty:* 18 full-time (6 women), 1 part-time/adjunct (0 women). *Students:* 91 full-time (45 women), 278 part-time (150 women). Average age 33. In 2011, 20 master's awarded. *Entrance requirements:* For master's, GMAT. Additional exam requirements/recommendations for international students: Required—TOEFL (minimum score 550 paper-based; 213 computer-based; 80 iBT), IELTS (minimum score 6). *Application deadline:* For fall admission, 7/1 priority date for domestic students, 6/1 for international students; for spring admission, 11/15 priority date for domestic students, 10/1 for international students. Applications are processed on a rolling basis. Application fee: $35 ($50 for international students). Electronic applications accepted. *Expenses:* Tuition, state resident: part-time $691.11 per course. Tuition, nonresident: part-time $1621.11 per course. *Financial support:* Application deadline: 3/31; applicants required to submit FAFSA. *Unit head:* Dr. Tracy Hurley, MBA Coordinator, 210-932-6200, E-mail: tracy.hurley@tamusa.tamus.edu. *Application contact:* Melissa A. Villanueva, Graduate Admissions Specialist, 210-932-6200, Fax: 210-932-6209, E-mail: melissa.villanueva@tamusa.tamus.edu. Web site: http://www.tamusa.tamus.edu.

Texas Southern University, Jesse H. Jones School of Business, Program in Management Information Systems, Houston, TX 77004-4584. Offers MS. Electronic applications accepted.

Texas State University–San Marcos, Graduate School, Emmett and Miriam McCoy College of Business Administration, Program in Accounting and Information Technology, San Marcos, TX 78666. Offers MS. *Faculty:* 7 full-time (2 women). *Students:* 6 full-time (2 women), 11 part-time (4 women); includes 2 minority (both Asian, non-Hispanic/Latino), 3 international. Average age 33. 11 applicants, 82% accepted, 3 enrolled. In 2011, 7 master's awarded. *Degree requirements:* For master's, comprehensive exam. *Entrance requirements:* For master's, GMAT, official transcript from each college or university attended, 2 letters of recommendation, resume. Additional exam requirements/recommendations for international students: Required—TOEFL (minimum score 550 paper-based; 213 computer-based; 78 iBT). *Application deadline:* For fall admission, 6/1 for domestic and international students; for spring admission, 10/1 for domestic and international students. Application fee: $40 ($90 for international students). *Expenses:* Tuition, state resident: full-time $6408; part-time $3204 per semester. Tuition, nonresident: full-time $14,832; part-time $7416 per semester. *Required fees:* $1824; $912 per semester. Tuition and fees vary according to course load. *Financial support:* In 2011–12, 8 students received support, including 2 teaching assistantships (averaging $10,283 per year); research assistantships, Federal Work-Study, institutionally sponsored loans, scholarships/grants, health care benefits, and unspecified assistantships also available. Support available to part-time students. *Unit head:* Dr. Robert Davis, Associate Dean, 512-245-3591, Fax: 512-245-7973, E-mail: rd23@txstate.edu. *Application contact:* Dr. J. Michael Willoughby, Dean of Graduate School, 512-245-2581, Fax: 512-245-8365, E-mail: gradcollege@txstate.edu.

Texas Tech University, Graduate School, Rawls College of Business Administration, Area of Information Systems and Quantitative Sciences, Lubbock, TX 79409. Offers business statistics (MS, PhD); healthcare management (MS); management information systems (MS, PhD); production and operations management (MS, PhD); risk management (MS). Part-time programs available. *Faculty:* 15 full-time (0 women). *Students:* 46 full-time (13 women), 8 part-time (0 women); includes 4 minority (1 American Indian or Alaska Native, non-Hispanic/Latino; 1 Asian, non-Hispanic/Latino; 2 Hispanic/Latino), 38 international. Average age 27. 101 applicants, 65% accepted, 18 enrolled. In 2011, 35 master's, 2 doctorates awarded. Terminal master's awarded for partial completion of doctoral program. *Degree requirements:* For master's, comprehensive exam or capstone course; for doctorate, thesis/dissertation, qualifying exams. *Entrance requirements:* For master's and doctorate, GMAT, holistic profile of academic credentials. Additional exam requirements/recommendations for international students: Required—TOEFL (minimum score 550 paper-based; 213 computer-based; 79 iBT). *Application deadline:* For fall admission, 4/1 priority date for domestic students, 1/15 for international students; for spring admission, 9/1 priority date for domestic students, 6/15 for international students. Applications are processed on a rolling basis. Application fee: $50 ($75 for international students). Electronic applications accepted. *Expenses:* Tuition, state resident: full-time $5899; part-time $245.80 per credit hour. Tuition, nonresident: full-time $13,411; part-time $558.80 per credit hour. *Required fees:* $2680.60; $86.50 per credit hour. $920.30 per semester. *Financial support:* In 2011–12, 5 research assistantships (averaging $16,160 per year), 5 teaching assistantships (averaging $18,000 per year) were awarded; Federal Work-Study, scholarships/grants, and unspecified assistantships also available. *Faculty research:* Database management systems, systems management and engineering, expert systems and adaptive knowledge-based sciences, statistical analysis and design. *Unit head:* Dr. Glenn Browne, Area Coordinator, 806-834-0969, Fax: 806-742-3193, E-mail: glenn.browne@ttu.edu. *Application contact:* Elizabeth Stuart, Director, Graduate Services Center, 806-742-3184, Fax: 806-742-3958, E-mail: ba_grad@ttu.edu. Web site: http://is.ba.ttu.edu.

Texas Tech University, Graduate School, Rawls College of Business Administration, Programs in Business Administration, Lubbock, TX 79409. Offers agricultural business (MBA); business administration (IMBA); business statistics (MBA); entrepreneurship and innovation (MBA); general business (MBA); health organization management (MBA); international business (MBA); management and leadership skills (MBA); management information systems (MBA); marketing (MBA); real estate (MBA); JD/MBA; MBA/M Arch; MBA/MA; MBA/MD; MBA/MS; MBA/Pharm D. Part-time and evening/weekend programs available. *Faculty:* 49 full-time (8 women), 2 part-time/adjunct (0 women). *Students:* 195 full-time (55 women), 397 part-time (101 women); includes 123 minority (27 Black or African American, non-Hispanic/Latino; 4 American Indian or Alaska Native, non-Hispanic/Latino; 31 Asian, non-Hispanic/Latino; 61 Hispanic/Latino), 38 international. Average age 31. 374 applicants, 83% accepted, 255 enrolled. In 2011, 256 degrees awarded. *Degree requirements:* For master's, capstone course. *Entrance requirements:* For master's, GMAT, holistic review of academic credentials. Additional exam requirements/recommendations for international students: Required—TOEFL (minimum score 550 paper-based; 213 computer-based; 79 iBT). *Application deadline:* For fall admission, 4/1 priority date for domestic students, 1/15 for international students; for spring admission, 9/1 priority date for domestic students, 6/15 for international students. Applications are processed on a rolling basis. Application fee: $50 ($75 for international students). Electronic applications accepted. *Expenses:* Tuition, state resident: full-time $5899; part-time $245.80 per credit hour. Tuition, nonresident: full-time $13,411; part-time $558.80 per credit hour. *Required fees:* $2680.60; $86.50 per credit hour. $920.30 per semester. *Financial support:* In 2011–12, 22 research assistantships (averaging $8,800 per year) were awarded; teaching assistantships, career-related internships or fieldwork, Federal Work-Study, scholarships/grants, health care benefits, and unspecified assistantships also available. Support available to part-time students. Financial award applicants required to submit FAFSA. *Unit head:* Dr. W. Jay Conover, Director, 806-742-1546, Fax: 806-742-3958, E-mail: jay.conover@ttu.edu. *Application contact:* Elizabeth Stuart, Director, Graduate Services Center, 806-742-3184, Fax: 806-742-3958, E-mail: ba_grad@ttu.edu. Web site: http://mba.ba.ttu.edu/.

Touro College, Graduate School of Technology, New York, NY 10010. Offers information systems (MS); instructional technology (MS); Web and multimedia design (MA). *Students:* 87 full-time (17 women), 19 part-time (17 women); includes 46 minority (15 Black or African American, non-Hispanic/Latino; 15 Asian, non-Hispanic/Latino; 9 Hispanic/Latino; 7 Native Hawaiian or other Pacific Islander, non-Hispanic/Latino), 2 international. *Unit head:* Dr. Isaac Herskowitz, Dean of the Graduate School of Technology, 202-463-0400 Ext. 5231, E-mail: ssac.herskowitz@touro.edu. Web site: http://www.touro.edu/gst/.

Towson University, Program in Applied Information Technology, Towson, MD 21252-0001. Offers applied information technology (MS, PhD); database management systems (Postbaccalaureate Certificate); information security and assurance (Postbaccalaureate Certificate); information systems management (Postbaccalaureate Certificate); Internet applications development (Postbaccalaureate Certificate); networking technologies (Postbaccalaureate Certificate); software engineering (Postbaccalaureate Certificate). *Students:* 145 full-time (32 women), 270 part-time (78 women); includes 151 minority (96 Black or African American, non-Hispanic/Latino; 35 Asian, non-Hispanic/Latino; 17 Hispanic/Latino; 1 Native Hawaiian or other Pacific Islander, non-Hispanic/Latino; 2 Two or more races, non-Hispanic/Latino), 93 international. *Expenses:* Tuition, state resident: part-time $337 per credit. Tuition, nonresident: part-time $709 per credit. *Required fees:* $99 per credit. *Unit head:* Mike O'Leary, Graduate Program Director, 410-704-4757, E-mail: moleary@towson.edu.

Trident University International, College of Business Administration, Program in Business Administration, Cypress, CA 90630. Offers business administration (PhD); conflict and negotiation management (MBA); criminal justice administration (MBA); entrepreneurship (MBA); finance (MBA); general management (MBA); government accounting (MBA); human resource management (MBA); information security and digital assurance management (MBA); information technology management (MBA); international business (MBA); logistics management (MBA); marketing (MBA); project management (MBA); public management (MBA); quality management (MBA); strategic leadership (MBA). Part-time and evening/weekend programs available. Postbaccalaureate distance learning degree programs offered (no on-campus study). *Degree requirements:* For doctorate, comprehensive exam, thesis/dissertation, defense of dissertation. *Entrance requirements:* For master's, minimum GPA of 2.5 (students with GPA 3.0 or greater may transfer up to 30% of graduate level credits); for doctorate, minimum GPA of 3.4, curriculum vitae, course work in research methods or statistics. Additional exam requirements/recommendations for international students: Required—TOEFL. Electronic applications accepted.

Trident University International, College of Information Systems, Cypress, CA 90630. Offers business intelligence (Certificate); information technology management (MS). Part-time and evening/weekend programs available. Postbaccalaureate distance learning degree programs offered (no on-campus study). *Entrance requirements:* For master's, minimum GPA of 2.5 (students with GPA 3.0 or greater may transfer up to 30% of graduate level credits); undergraduate degree completed within the past 5 years. Additional exam requirements/recommendations for international students: Required—TOEFL (minimum score 525 paper-based). Electronic applications accepted.

Management Information Systems

Troy University, Graduate School, College of Business, Program in Business Administration, Troy, AL 36082. Offers accounting (EMBA, MBA); criminal justice (EMBA); finance (MBA); general management (EMBA, MBA); healthcare management (EMBA); information systems (EMBA, MBA); international economic development (MBA). *Accreditation:* ACBSP. Part-time and evening/weekend programs available. *Faculty:* 50 full-time (14 women), 12 part-time/adjunct (0 women). *Students:* 326 full-time (168 women), 596 part-time (358 women); includes 524 minority (402 Black or African American, non-Hispanic/Latino; 12 American Indian or Alaska Native, non-Hispanic/Latino; 85 Asian, non-Hispanic/Latino; 21 Hispanic/Latino; 4 Two or more races, non-Hispanic/Latino). Average age 29. 644 applicants, 67% accepted, 204 enrolled. In 2011, 388 master's awarded. *Degree requirements:* For master's, minimum GPA of 3.0, capstone course, research course. *Entrance requirements:* For master's, GMAT (minimum score 500) or GRE General Test (minimum score 900), minimum GPA of 2.5; letter of recommendation, bachelor's degree. Additional exam requirements/recommendations for international students: Required—TOEFL (minimum score 523 paper-based; 193 computer-based; 70 iBT), IELTS (minimum score 6), or ACT COMPASS ESL (minimum listening, reading, and grammar score 270). *Application deadline:* Applications are processed on a rolling basis. Application fee: $50. *Expenses:* Tuition, state resident: full-time $6960; part-time $290 per credit hour. Tuition, nonresident: full-time $13,920; part-time $580 per credit hour. *Required fees:* $386 per term. *Unit head:* Dr. Edward Merkel, Director, Graduate Business Programs, 334-670-3194, Fax: 334-670-3599, E-mail: emerkel@troy.edu. *Application contact:* Brenda K. Campbell, Director of Graduate Admissions, 334-670-3178, Fax: 334-670-3733, E-mail: bcamp@troy.edu.

Troy University, Graduate School, College of Business, Program in Management, Troy, AL 36082. Offers applied management (MSM); healthcare management (MSM); human resources management (MSM); information systems (MSM); international hospitality management (MSM); international management (MSM); leadership and organizational effectiveness (MSM); public management (MS, MSM). *Accreditation:* ACBSP. Evening/weekend programs available. *Faculty:* 21 full-time (6 women), 7 part-time/adjunct (2 women). *Students:* 52 full-time (33 women), 284 part-time (183 women); includes 222 minority (186 Black or African American, non-Hispanic/Latino; 5 American Indian or Alaska Native, non-Hispanic/Latino; 11 Asian, non-Hispanic/Latino; 13 Hispanic/Latino; 1 Native Hawaiian or other Pacific Islander, non-Hispanic/Latino; 6 Two or more races, non-Hispanic/Latino). Average age 35. 157 applicants, 76% accepted, 55 enrolled. In 2011, 234 master's awarded. *Degree requirements:* For master's, Graduate Educational Testing Service Major Field Test, capstone exam, minimum GPA of 3.0. *Entrance requirements:* For master's, GMAT (minimum score 500) or GRE General Test (minimum score 900), minimum GPA of 2.5, bachelor's degree, letter of recommendation. Additional exam requirements/recommendations for international students: Required—TOEFL (minimum score 523 paper-based; 193 computer-based; 70 iBT), IELTS (minimum score 6), or ACT COMPASS ESL (minimum listening, reading, and grammar score 270). *Application deadline:* Applications are processed on a rolling basis. Application fee: $50. Electronic applications accepted. *Expenses:* Contact institution. *Unit head:* Dr. Edward Merkel, Director, Graduate Business Programs, 334-670-3194, Fax: 334-670-3599, E-mail: emerkel@troy.edu. *Application contact:* Brenda K. Campbell, Director of Graduate Admissions, 334-670-3178, Fax: 334-670-3733, E-mail: bcamp@troy.edu.

United States International University, School of Business Administration, Nairobi, Kenya. Offers business administration (GEMBA); entrepreneurship (MBA); finance (MBA); human resource management (MBA); information technology management (MBA); integrated studies (MBA); international business administration (MBA); management and organizational development (MS); marketing (MBA); organizational development (EMS); strategic management (MBA). Part-time and evening/weekend programs available. *Degree requirements:* For master's, thesis. *Entrance requirements:* For master's, GMAT, 2 letters of reference, resume. Additional exam requirements/recommendations for international students: Required—TOEFL (minimum score 550 paper-based; 213 computer-based). *Faculty research:* Marketing in small business enterprises, total quality management in Kenya.

Universidad del Este, Graduate School, Carolina, PR 00984. Offers accounting (MBA); adult education (M Ed); agribusiness (MBA); criminal justice and criminology (MA); curriculum and instruction - early education (M Ed); curriculum and instruction - elementary (M Ed); curriculum and instruction - English (M Ed); curriculum and instruction - Spanish (M Ed); human resources (MBA); information security management (MBA); information technology and Web business development (MBA); management (MBA); public policy (MPA); social work (MA), including clinical social work; special education (M Ed); strategic leadership (MBA).

Universidad del Turabo, Graduate Programs, School in Business Administration, Program in Management of Information Systems, Gurabo, PR 00778-3030. Offers DBA. *Students:* 4 full-time (2 women), 21 part-time (7 women); includes 20 minority (all Hispanic/Latino). Average age 41. 5 applicants, 80% accepted, 3 enrolled. In 2011, 4 degrees awarded. *Unit head:* Marcelino Rivera, Dean, 787-743-7979 Ext. 4117. *Application contact:* Virginia Gonzalez, Admissions Officer, 787-746-3009.

Universidad Metropolitana, School of Business Administration, Program in Management Information Systems, San Juan, PR 00928-1150. Offers MBA.

Université de Sherbrooke, Faculty of Administration, Program in Governance, Audit and Security of Information Technology, Longueuil, QC J4K0A8, Canada. Offers M Adm. Part-time and evening/weekend programs available. Postbaccalaureate distance learning degree programs offered. *Faculty:* 1 full-time (0 women), 12 part-time/adjunct (2 women). *Students:* 25 part-time (4 women). Average age 40. 35 applicants, 31% accepted, 8 enrolled. In 2011, 3 master's awarded. *Degree requirements:* For master's, thesis. *Entrance requirements:* For master's, bachelor's degree, related work experience. *Application deadline:* For fall admission, 4/30 priority date for domestic students. Applications are processed on a rolling basis. Application fee: $70. Electronic applications accepted. *Unit head:* Prof. Julien Bilodeau, Director, Graduate Programs in Business, 819-821-8000 Ext. 62355, E-mail: julien.bilodeau@usherbrooke.ca. *Application contact:* Lyne Cantin, Assistant to the Director, 450-463-1835 Ext. 61768, Fax: 450-670-1848, E-mail: lyne.cantin@usherbrooke.ca. Web site: http://gouvauditsecurti.adm@USherbrooke.ca.

Université de Sherbrooke, Faculty of Administration, Program in Management Information Systems, Sherbrooke, QC J1K 2R1, Canada. Offers M Sc. *Faculty:* 8 full-time (2 women), 1 part-time/adjunct (0 women). *Students:* 28 full-time (6 women). Average age 29. 70 applicants, 79% accepted, 21 enrolled. In 2011, 12 master's awarded. *Degree requirements:* For master's, one foreign language, thesis. *Entrance requirements:* For master's, bachelor's degree in related field, minimum GPA of 3.0 (on 4.3 scale). *Application deadline:* For fall admission, 4/30 for domestic students, 1/15 for international students. Applications are processed on a rolling basis. Application fee: $70. Electronic applications accepted. *Faculty research:* Project management in IT, IT governance, business intelligence, IT performance. *Unit head:* Prof. Julien Bilodeau, Director, Graduate Programs in Business, 819-821-8000 Ext. 62355. *Application contact:* Marie-Claude Drouin, Assistant to the Director, 819-821-8000 Ext. 63301.

Université de Sherbrooke, Faculty of Sciences, Centre de Formation en Technologies de L'information, Sherbrooke, QC J1K 2R1, Canada. Offers M Sc, Diploma. Electronic applications accepted.

Université du Québec à Montréal, Graduate Programs, Program in Management Information Systems, Montréal, QC H3C 3P8, Canada. Offers M Sc, M Sc A. Part-time programs available. *Entrance requirements:* For master's, appropriate bachelor's degree or equivalent and proficiency in French.

Université Laval, Faculty of Administrative Sciences, Programs in Business Administration, Québec, QC G1K 7P4, Canada. Offers accounting (MBA); agri-food management (MBA); electronic business (MBA, Diploma); factory management and logistics (MBA); finance (MBA); firm management (MBA); geomatic management (MBA); information technology management (MBA); international management (MBA); management (MBA); management accounting (MBA, Diploma); marketing (MBA); modeling and organizational decision (MBA); occupational health and safety management (MBA); pharmacy management (MBA); social and environmental responsibility (MBA); technological entrepreneurship (Diploma). *Accreditation:* AACSB. Part-time and evening/weekend programs available. Postbaccalaureate distance learning degree programs offered (no on-campus study). *Entrance requirements:* For master's and Diploma, knowledge of French and English. Electronic applications accepted.

University at Buffalo, the State University of New York, Graduate School, School of Engineering and Applied Sciences, Department of Computer Science and Engineering, Buffalo, NY 14260. Offers computer science and engineering (MS, PhD); information assurance (Certificate). Part-time programs available. *Faculty:* 36 full-time (4 women). *Students:* 367 full-time (73 women), 13 part-time (1 woman); includes 4 minority (2 Black or African American, non-Hispanic/Latino; 1 Asian, non-Hispanic/Latino; 1 Hispanic/Latino), 341 international. Average age 25. 1,632 applicants, 40% accepted, 134 enrolled. In 2011, 120 master's, 12 doctorates awarded. Terminal master's awarded for partial completion of doctoral program. *Degree requirements:* For master's, thesis or alternative; for doctorate, thesis/dissertation, comprehensive qualifying exam. *Entrance requirements:* For master's and doctorate, GRE General Test. Additional exam requirements/recommendations for international students: Required—TOEFL (minimum score 550 paper-based; 213 computer-based; 79 iBT). *Application deadline:* For fall admission, 8/15 for domestic and international students. Application fee: $75. Electronic applications accepted. *Financial support:* In 2011–12, 103 students received support, including 5 fellowships with full tuition reimbursements available (averaging $28,900 per year), 53 research assistantships with full tuition reimbursements available (averaging $27,600 per year), 43 teaching assistantships with full tuition reimbursements available (averaging $24,000 per year); career-related internships or fieldwork, Federal Work-Study, institutionally sponsored loans, health care benefits, tuition waivers (partial), and unspecified assistantships also available. Financial award application deadline: 12/15; financial award applicants required to submit FAFSA. *Faculty research:* Bioinformatics, pattern recognition, computer networks and security, theory and algorithms, databases and data mining. *Total annual research expenditures:* $7.1 million. *Unit head:* Dr. Aidong Zhang, Chairman, 716-645-3180, Fax: 716-645-3464, E-mail: azhang@buffalo.edu. *Application contact:* Dr. Jan Chomicki, Director of Graduate Studies, 716-645-4735, Fax: 716-645-3464, E-mail: chomicki@buffalo.edu. Web site: http://www.cse.buffalo.edu/.

University at Buffalo, the State University of New York, Graduate School, School of Management, Buffalo, NY 14260. Offers accounting (MS); business administration (EMBA, MBA, PMBA); finance (MS), including financial engineering, financial management; management (PhD); management information systems (MS); supply chains and operations management (MS); Au D/MBA; JD/MBA; M Arch/MBA; MA/MBA; MD/MBA; MPH/MBA; MSW/MBA; Pharm D/MBA. *Accreditation:* AACSB. Part-time and evening/weekend programs available. *Degree requirements:* For master's, thesis (for some programs); for doctorate, comprehensive exam, thesis/dissertation. *Entrance requirements:* For master's, GMAT (MBA, MS in accounting), GRE or GMAT (for all other MS concentrations); for doctorate, GMAT or GRE. Additional exam requirements/recommendations for international students: Required—TOEFL (minimum score 230 computer-based; 95 iBT). Electronic applications accepted. *Expenses:* Contact institution. *Faculty research:* Earnings management and electronic information assurance, supply chains and operations management, corporate financing and asset pricing, consumer behavior and quantitative modeling of marketing behavior, leadership and politics in organizations.

The University of Akron, Graduate School, College of Business Administration, Department of Management, Program in Information Systems Management, Akron, OH 44325. Offers MSM. *Students:* 5 full-time (3 women), 7 part-time (2 women), 8 international. Average age 29. 20 applicants, 35% accepted, 3 enrolled. In 2011, 10 master's awarded. *Entrance requirements:* For master's, GMAT or GRE if applicant has two years of work experience, minimum GPA of 2.75, two letters of recommendation, statement of purpose, resume. Additional exam requirements/recommendations for international students: Required—TOEFL (minimum score 550 paper-based; 213 computer-based; 79 iBT). *Application deadline:* For fall admission, 7/15 for domestic students, 7/1 for international students; for spring admission, 11/15 for domestic and international students. Application fee: $30 ($40 for international students). Electronic applications accepted. *Expenses:* Tuition, state resident: full-time $7038; part-time $391 per credit hour. Tuition, nonresident: full-time $12,051; part-time $670 per credit hour. *Required fees:* $1274; $34 per credit hour. *Unit head:* Dr. B. S. Vijayaraman, Head, 330-972-5442, E-mail: bsv@uakron.edu. *Application contact:* Dr. Susan Hanlon, Director of Graduate Business Programs, 330-972-7043, Fax: 330-972-6588, E-mail: shanlon@uakron.edu.

The University of Alabama in Huntsville, School of Graduate Studies, College of Business Administration, Department of Accounting and Finance, Huntsville, AL 35899. Offers accounting (M Acc), including CPA preparatory with an emphasis in taxation, CPA preparatory with emphasis in assurance and financial reporting, general accounting, information systems audit and control (ISAC). *Accreditation:* AACSB. Part-time and evening/weekend programs available. *Faculty:* 7 full-time (2 women), 4 part-time/adjunct (1 woman). *Students:* 21 full-time (14 women), 28 part-time (13 women); includes 8 minority (6 Black or African American, non-Hispanic/Latino; 1 American Indian or Alaska Native, non-Hispanic/Latino; 1 Asian, non-Hispanic/Latino), 4 international. Average age 33. 30 applicants, 70% accepted, 19 enrolled. In 2011, 24 master's awarded. *Degree requirements:* For master's, comprehensive exam, thesis or alternative. *Entrance requirements:* For master's, GMAT (minimum score 500), minimum AACSB index of 1080. Additional exam requirements/recommendations for international students: Required—TOEFL (minimum score 550 paper-based; 213 computer-based; 62 iBT). *Application deadline:* For fall admission, 8/1 for domestic students, 4/1 for international students; for spring admission, 12/1 for domestic students, 9/1 for international students. Applications are processed on a rolling basis. Application fee: $40 ($50 for international students). Electronic applications accepted. *Expenses:* Tuition, state resident: full-time $7830; part-time $473.50 per credit. Tuition, nonresident: full-time $18,748; part-time $1128.33 per credit. Tuition and fees vary according to course load and program. *Financial support:* In 2011–12, 5 students received support, including 1 research assistantship with full tuition reimbursement available (averaging $14,400 per year), 2 teaching assistantships with full tuition reimbursements available (averaging $5,000 per year); career-related internships or fieldwork, Federal Work-Study, institutionally sponsored loans, scholarships/grants, health care benefits, and unspecified assistantships also available. Support available to part-time students. Financial award application deadline: 4/1; financial award applicants required to submit FAFSA. *Faculty research:* Accounting information systems, emerging technologies in accounting, behavioral accounting, state and local taxation, financial accounting. *Total annual research expenditures:* $66,318. *Unit head:* Dr. John Burnett, Interim Chair, 256-824-2923, Fax: 256-824-2929, E-mail: burnettj@uah.edu. *Application contact:* Jennifer Pettitt, Director of Graduate Programs, 256-824-6681, Fax: 256-824-7571, E-mail: jennifer.pettitt@uah.edu.

The University of Alabama in Huntsville, School of Graduate Studies, College of Business Administration, Department of Economics and Information Systems, Huntsville, AL 35899. Offers enterprise resource planning (Certificate); information assurance (Certificate); information systems (MSIS). Part-time and evening/weekend programs available. *Faculty:* 11 full-time (2 women), 3 part-time/adjunct (1 woman). *Students:* 11 full-time (4 women), 24 part-time (6 women); includes 6 minority (1 Black or African American, non-Hispanic/Latino; 2 American Indian or Alaska Native, non-Hispanic/Latino; 3 Asian, non-Hispanic/Latino). Average age 34. 31 applicants, 55% accepted, 14 enrolled. In 2011, 12 master's, 10 other advanced degrees awarded. *Degree requirements:* For master's, comprehensive exam, thesis or alternative. *Entrance requirements:* For master's, GMAT (minimum score 500), minimum AACSB index of 1080. Additional exam requirements/recommendations for international students: Required—TOEFL (minimum score 550 paper-based; 213 computer-based; 62 iBT). *Application deadline:* For fall admission, 8/1 for domestic students, 4/1 for international students; for spring admission, 12/1 for domestic students, 9/1 for international students. Applications are processed on a rolling basis. Application fee: $40 ($50 for international students). Electronic applications accepted. *Expenses:* Tuition, state resident: full-time $7830; part-time $473.50 per credit. Tuition, nonresident: full-time $18,748; part-time $1128.33 per credit. Tuition and fees vary according to course load and program. *Financial support:* In 2011–12, 2 students received support, including 1 research assistantship with full tuition reimbursement available (averaging $14,400 per year), 1 teaching assistantship with full tuition reimbursement available (averaging $8,000 per year); career-related internships or fieldwork, Federal Work-Study, institutionally sponsored loans, scholarships/grants, health care benefits, and unspecified assistantships also available. Support available to part-time students. Financial award application deadline: 4/1; financial award applicants required to submit FAFSA. *Faculty research:* Supply chain management, incomplete contract and dynamic bargaining in technology investment, personalization at e-commerce sites, workflow management, real options modeling of technology competition. *Total annual research expenditures:* $306,953. *Unit head:* Dr. Allen W. Wilhite, Chair, 256-824-6591, Fax: 256-824-6328, E-mail: wilhitea@uah.edu. *Application contact:* Jennifer Pettitt, Director of Graduate Programs, 256-824-6681, Fax: 256-824-7571, E-mail: jennifer.pettitt@uah.edu.

The University of Alabama in Huntsville, School of Graduate Studies, Interdisciplinary Studies, Interdisciplinary Program in Information Assurance and Cybersecurity, Huntsville, AL 35899. Offers computer engineering (MS), including computer science; information systems (Certificate). Part-time and evening/weekend programs available. *Faculty:* 6 full-time (0 women), 3 part-time/adjunct (0 women). *Students:* 5 full-time (4 women), 17 part-time (5 women); includes 7 minority (4 Black or African American, non-Hispanic/Latino; 2 Asian, non-Hispanic/Latino; 1 Hispanic/Latino). Average age 37. 15 applicants, 67% accepted, 8 enrolled. In 2011, 2 master's awarded. *Degree requirements:* For master's, comprehensive exam, thesis or alternative, thesis: 24 hours course work plus 6-hour thesis. *Entrance requirements:* For master's, GRE General Test, minimum GPA of 3.0; for Certificate, GMAT, minimum GPA of 3.0. Additional exam requirements/recommendations for international students: Required—TOEFL (minimum score 550 paper-based; 213 computer-based; 62 iBT). *Application deadline:* For fall admission, 7/15 for domestic students, 4/1 for international students; for spring admission, 11/30 for domestic students, 9/1 for international students. Applications are processed on a rolling basis. Application fee: $40 ($50 for international students). Electronic applications accepted. *Expenses:* Tuition, state resident: full-time $7830; part-time $473.50 per credit. Tuition, nonresident: full-time $18,748; part-time $1128.33 per credit. Tuition and fees vary according to course load and program. *Financial support:* Career-related internships or fieldwork, Federal Work-Study, institutionally sponsored loans, scholarships/grants, health care benefits, and unspecified assistantships available. Support available to part-time students. Financial award application deadline: 4/1; financial award applicants required to submit FAFSA. *Faculty research:* Service discovery, enterprise security, security metrics, cryptography, network security. *Unit head:* Dr. Rhonda Kay Gaede, Dean of Graduate Studies, 256-824-6002, Fax: 256-824-6405, E-mail: deangrad@uah.edu. *Application contact:* Jennifer Pettitt, College of Business Administration Director of Graduate Programs, 256-824-6681, Fax: 256-824-7572, E-mail: jennifer.pettitt@uah.edu. Web site: http://www.cs.uah.edu/admissions/msias.html.

The University of Arizona, Eller College of Management, Department of Management Information Systems, Tucson, AZ 85721. Offers MS. *Faculty:* 13 full-time (5 women), 1 part-time/adjunct (0 women). *Students:* 155 full-time (47 women), 11 part-time (5 women); includes 12 minority (4 Asian, non-Hispanic/Latino; 4 Hispanic/Latino; 4 Two or more races, non-Hispanic/Latino), 135 international. Average age 26. 393 applicants, 66% accepted, 58 enrolled. In 2011, 78 master's awarded. *Degree requirements:* For master's, thesis or alternative. *Entrance requirements:* For master's, GMAT or GRE General Test, 2 letters of recommendation, resume. Additional exam requirements/recommendations for international students: Required—TOEFL (minimum score 550 paper-based; 213 computer-based; 80 iBT). *Application deadline:* For fall admission, 1/15 for domestic and international students. Applications are processed on a rolling basis. Application fee: $75. Electronic applications accepted. *Expenses:* Tuition, state resident: full-time $10,840. Tuition, nonresident: full-time $25,802. *Financial support:* In 2011–12, 14 research assistantships with full tuition reimbursements (averaging $20,412 per year), 26 teaching assistantships with full tuition reimbursements (averaging $20,412 per year) were awarded; career-related internships or fieldwork, Federal Work-Study, scholarships/grants, health care benefits, tuition waivers (partial), and unspecified assistantships also available. Financial award application deadline: 3/15. *Faculty research:* Group decision support systems, domestic and international computing issues, expert systems, data management and structures. *Total annual research expenditures:* $887,026. *Unit head:* Dr. Paulo Goes, Department Head, 520-621-2429, Fax: 520-621-2775, E-mail: pgoes@eller.arizona.edu. *Application contact:* Cinda Van Winkle, 520-621-2387, E-mail: admissions_mis@eller.arizona.edu. Web site: http://mis.eller.arizona.edu/.

University of Arkansas, Graduate School, Sam M. Walton College of Business Administration, Department of Information Systems, Fayetteville, AR 72701-1201. Offers MIS. Part-time and evening/weekend programs available. *Students:* 16 full-time (7 women), 28 part-time (8 women); includes 5 minority (2 Asian, non-Hispanic/Latino; 3 Hispanic/Latino), 18 international. In 2011, 21 master's awarded. *Entrance requirements:* For master's, GMAT. Application fee: $40 ($50 for international students). *Financial support:* In 2011–12, 18 research assistantships, 7 teaching assistantships were awarded; fellowships with tuition reimbursements also available. Financial award application deadline: 4/1. *Unit head:* Dr. Rajir Sabherwal, Department Head, 479-575-4500, E-mail: rsaberwal@walton.uark.edu. *Application contact:* Dr. Paul Cronan, Graduate Coordinator, 479-575-6130, E-mail: cronan@uark.edu. Web site: http://gsb.uark.edu/.

University of Arkansas at Little Rock, Graduate School, College of Business Administration, Little Rock, AR 72204-1099. Offers accountancy (M Acc, Graduate Certificate); business administration (MBA); construction management (Graduate Certificate); management (Graduate Certificate); management information system (MIS); management information systems (Graduate Certificate); management information systems leadership (Graduate Certificate); taxation (MS, Graduate Certificate). *Accreditation:* AACSB. Part-time and evening/weekend programs available. *Entrance requirements:* For master's, GMAT, minimum undergraduate GPA of 2.7. Additional exam requirements/recommendations for international students: Required—TOEFL (minimum score 525 paper-based; 195 computer-based).

University of Atlanta, Graduate Programs, Atlanta, GA 30360. Offers business (MS); business administration (Exec MBA, MBA); computer science (MS); educational leadership (MS, Ed D); healthcare administration (MS, D Sc, Graduate Certificate); information technology for management (Graduate Certificate); international project management (Graduate Certificate); law (JD); managerial science (DBA); project management (Graduate Certificate); social science (MS). Postbaccalaureate distance learning degree programs offered. *Entrance requirements:* For master's, minimum cumulative GPA of 2.5.

University of Baltimore, Graduate School, Merrick School of Business, Department of Accounting and Management Information Systems, Baltimore, MD 21201-5779. Offers accounting and business advisory services (MS); accounting fundamentals (Graduate Certificate); forensic accounting (Graduate Certificate). Part-time and evening/weekend programs available. *Entrance requirements:* For master's, GMAT. Additional exam requirements/recommendations for international students: Required—TOEFL (minimum score 550 paper-based; 213 computer-based). Electronic applications accepted. *Faculty research:* Health care, accounting and administration, managerial accounting, financial accounting theory, accounting information.

University of Bridgeport, School of Business, Bridgeport, CT 06604. Offers accounting (MBA); finance (MBA); general business (MBA); global financial services (MBA); human resource management (MBA); information systems and knowledge management (MBA); international business (MBA); management (MBA); marketing (MBA); operations management (MBA); small business and entrepreneurship (MBA); specialized business (MBA). Part-time and evening/weekend programs available. *Faculty:* 11 full-time (2 women), 39 part-time/adjunct (8 women). *Students:* 198 full-time (105 women), 94 part-time (47 women); includes 38 minority (16 Black or African American, non-Hispanic/Latino; 9 Asian, non-Hispanic/Latino; 10 Hispanic/Latino; 3 Two or more races, non-Hispanic/Latino), 227 international. Average age 28. 835 applicants, 56% accepted, 57 enrolled. In 2011, 155 master's awarded. *Degree requirements:* For master's, thesis optional. *Entrance requirements:* For master's, GMAT. Additional exam requirements/recommendations for international students: Recommended—TOEFL (minimum score 550 paper-based; 213 computer-based; 80 iBT), IELTS (minimum score 6.5). *Application deadline:* For fall admission, 8/1 priority date for domestic students, 8/1 for international students; for spring admission, 12/1 priority date for domestic students, 12/1 for international students. Applications are processed on a rolling basis. Application fee: $50. Electronic applications accepted. *Expenses:* Contact institution. *Financial support:* In 2011–12, 69 students received support. Fellowships, research assistantships, teaching assistantships, career-related internships or fieldwork, Federal Work-Study, institutionally sponsored loans, and tuition waivers (partial) available. Support available to part-time students. Financial award application deadline: 6/1; financial award applicants required to submit FAFSA. *Unit head:* Dr. Robert Gilmore, Dean, 203-576-4384, Fax: 203-576-4388, E-mail: rgilmore@bridgeport.edu. *Application contact:* Karissa Peckham, Dean of Admissions, 203-576-4552, Fax: 203-576-4941, E-mail: mba@bridgeport.edu. Web site: http://www.bridgeport.edu.

The University of British Columbia, Sauder School of Business, Doctoral Program in Commerce and Business Administration, Vancouver, BC V6T 1Z1, Canada. Offers accounting (PhD); finance (PhD); international business (PhD); management information systems (PhD); management science (PhD); marketing (PhD); organizational behavior (PhD); strategy and business economics (PhD); transportation and logistics (PhD); urban land economics (PhD). *Degree requirements:* For doctorate, comprehensive exam, thesis/dissertation. *Entrance requirements:* For doctorate, GMAT or GRE. Additional exam requirements/recommendations for international students: Required—TOEFL (minimum score 600 paper-based; 250 computer-based; 100 iBT). Electronic applications accepted.

University of California, Berkeley, UC Berkeley Extension, Certificate Programs in Computer Technology and Information Management, Berkeley, CA 94720-1500. Offers information systems and management (Postbaccalaureate Certificate); UNIX/LINUX system administration (Certificate). Postbaccalaureate distance learning degree programs offered.

University of California, Los Angeles, Graduate Division, UCLA Anderson School of Management, Los Angeles, CA 90095-1481. Offers accounting (PhD); Asia Pacific (EMBA); business administration (EMBA, MBA); decisions, operations and technology management (PhD); finance (PhD); financial engineering (MFE); global economics and management (PhD); Latin America (EMBA); management and organizations (PhD); marketing (PhD); strategy (PhD); DDS/MBA; MBA/JD; MBA/MD; MBA/MLAS; MBA/MLIS; MBA/MPH; MBA/MPP; MBA/MSCS; MBA/MSN; MBA/MUP. *Accreditation:* AACSB. Part-time programs available. *Faculty:* 90 full-time (14 women), 62 part-time/adjunct (14 women). *Students:* 1,103 full-time (312 women), 842 part-time (223 women); includes 663 minority (18 Black or African American, non-Hispanic/Latino; 510 Asian, non-Hispanic/Latino; 46 Hispanic/Latino; 2 Native Hawaiian or other Pacific Islander, non-Hispanic/Latino; 87 Two or more races, non-Hispanic/Latino), 469 international. 4,737 applicants, 32% accepted, 875 enrolled. In 2011, 759 master's, 6 doctorates awarded. *Degree requirements:* For master's, comprehensive exam, field study consulting project (for MBA); thesis/dissertation (for MFE); for doctorate, comprehensive exam, thesis/dissertation, oral and written qualifying exams. *Entrance requirements:* For master's, GMAT (for MBA); GMAT or GRE General Test (for MFE), 4-year bachelor's degree or equivalent; for doctorate, GMAT or GRE General Test, 4-year bachelor's degree from regionally-accredited institution; minimum GPA of 3.0. Additional exam requirements/recommendations for international students: Required—TOEFL (minimum score 560 paper-based; 220 computer-based; 87 iBT), IELTS (minimum score 7). *Application deadline:* For fall admission, 10/26 for domestic and international students; for winter admission, 1/11 for domestic and international students; for spring admission, 4/18 for domestic and international students. Application fee: $200. Electronic applications accepted. *Expenses:* Contact institution. *Financial support:* In 2011–12, 600 students received support. Fellowships, research assistantships, teaching assistantships, career-related internships or fieldwork, institutionally sponsored loans, scholarships/grants, health care benefits, and tuition waivers (partial) available. Financial award application deadline: 4/15; financial award applicants required to submit FAFSA. *Unit head:* Judy D. Olian, Dean, 310-825-7982, Fax: 310-206-2073, E-mail: judy.olian@anderson.ucla.edu. *Application contact:* Robert Weiler, Assistant Dean,

Management Information Systems

Director of MBA Admissions and Financial Aid, 310-825-6944, Fax: 310-825-8582, E-mail: mba.admissions@anderson.ucla.edu. Web site: http://www.anderson.ucla.edu/.

See Display on page 141 and Close-Up on page 249.

University of California, Santa Cruz, Division of Graduate Studies, Jack Baskin School of Engineering, Department of Technology and Information Management, Santa Cruz, CA 95064. Offers MS, PhD. Terminal master's awarded for partial completion of doctoral program. *Degree requirements:* For master's, thesis, 2 seminars; for doctorate, thesis/dissertation, 2 seminars. *Entrance requirements:* For master's and doctorate, GRE General Test; GRE Subject Test preferably in computer science, engineering, physics, or mathematics (highly recommended), minimum GPA of 3.5. Additional exam requirements/recommendations for international students: Required—TOEFL (minimum score 570 paper-based; 230 computer-based; 89 iBT); Recommended—IELTS (minimum score 8). Electronic applications accepted. *Faculty research:* Integration of information systems, technology, and business management.

University of Central Missouri, The Graduate School, Harmon College of Business Administration, Warrensburg, MO 64093. Offers accountancy (MA); accounting (MBA); ethical strategic leadership (MBA); finance (MBA); general business (MBA); information systems (MBA); information technology (MS); marketing (MBA). Part-time programs available. Postbaccalaureate distance learning degree programs offered. *Entrance requirements:* Additional exam requirements/recommendations for international students: Required—TOEFL (minimum score 550 paper-based; 79 computer-based). Electronic applications accepted.

University of Cincinnati, Graduate School, Carl H. Lindner College of Business, MS Program, Cincinnati, OH 45221. Offers accounting (MS); information systems (MS); marketing (MS); quantitative analysis (MS). Part-time and evening/weekend programs available. *Faculty:* 79 full-time (22 women), 71 part-time/adjunct (24 women). *Students:* 171 full-time (75 women), 106 part-time (46 women); includes 19 minority (6 Black or African American, non-Hispanic/Latino; 1 American Indian or Alaska Native, non-Hispanic/Latino; 7 Asian, non-Hispanic/Latino; 2 Hispanic/Latino; 3 Two or more races, non-Hispanic/Latino), 114 international. 404 applicants, 77% accepted, 125 enrolled. *Degree requirements:* For master's, thesis (for some programs). *Entrance requirements:* For master's, GMAT, GRE, resume, transcripts, essays, letters of recommendation. Additional exam requirements/recommendations for international students: Required—TOEFL (minimum score 600 paper-based; 250 computer-based; 100 iBT). *Application deadline:* For fall admission, 1/15 priority date for domestic students, 4/1 for international students. Applications are processed on a rolling basis. Application fee: $65 ($70 for international students). Electronic applications accepted. *Expenses:* Contact institution. *Financial support:* In 2011–12, 10 teaching assistantships with full and partial tuition reimbursements (averaging $5,400 per year) were awarded; scholarships/grants, tuition waivers (full and partial), and unspecified assistantships also available. Financial award application deadline: 2/1; financial award applicants required to submit FAFSA. *Unit head:* Dr. David Szymanski, Dean, 513-556-7001, Fax: 513-556-4891, E-mail: will.mcintosh@uc.edu. *Application contact:* Dona Clary, Director, Graduate Programs Office, 513-556-3546, Fax: 513-558-7006, E-mail: dona.clary@uc.edu.

University of Cincinnati, Graduate School, Carl H. Lindner College of Business, PhD Programs, Cincinnati, OH 45221. Offers accounting (PhD); finance (PhD); information systems (PhD); management (PhD); marketing (PhD); quantitative analysis and operations management (PhD). *Faculty:* 56 full-time (13 women). *Students:* 34 full-time (12 women), 12 part-time (4 women); includes 2 minority (1 Asian, non-Hispanic/Latino; 1 Hispanic/Latino), 25 international. Average age 29. 120 applicants, 13% accepted, 10 enrolled. In 2011, 8 degrees awarded. *Median time to degree:* Of those who began their doctoral program in fall 2003, 65% received their degree in 8 years or less. *Degree requirements:* For doctorate, comprehensive exam, thesis/dissertation. *Entrance requirements:* For doctorate, GMAT, GRE, transcripts, essays, resume, letters of recommendation. Additional exam requirements/recommendations for international students: Required—TOEFL (minimum score 600 paper-based; 250 computer-based; 100 iBT). *Application deadline:* For fall admission, 2/1 for domestic and international students. Application fee: $65 ($70 for international students). Electronic applications accepted. *Expenses:* Contact institution. *Financial support:* In 2011–12, 39 students received support, including 30 research assistantships with full and partial tuition reimbursements available (averaging $14,640 per year); scholarships/grants, tuition waivers (full and partial), and unspecified assistantships also available. Financial award application deadline: 2/1; financial award applicants required to submit FAFSA. *Unit head:* Dr. Suzanne Masterson, Director, 513-556-7125, Fax: 513-556-5499, E-mail: suzanne.masterson@uc.edu. *Application contact:* Deborah Schildknecht, Assistant Director, 513-556-7190, Fax: 513-558-7006, E-mail: deborah.schildknecht@uc.edu. Web site: http://www.business.uc.edu/phd.

University of Colorado Boulder, Leeds School of Business, Division of Business Administration, Boulder, CO 80309. Offers accounting (MS, PhD); finance (PhD); information systems (PhD); marketing (PhD); operations (PhD); strategic, organizational, and entrepreneurial studies (PhD). *Students:* 129 full-time (65 women), 6 part-time (0 women); includes 15 minority (1 Black or African American, non-Hispanic/Latino; 8 Asian, non-Hispanic/Latino; 5 Hispanic/Latino; 1 Two or more races, non-Hispanic/Latino), 21 international. Average age 27. 332 applicants, 9% accepted, 13 enrolled. In 2011, 53 master's, 6 doctorates awarded. *Entrance requirements:* For master's, GMAT, minimum undergraduate GPA of 3.0. *Application deadline:* For fall admission, 3/31 for domestic and international students; for spring admission, 10/31 for domestic and international students. Application fee: $50 ($60 for international students). Electronic applications accepted. *Financial support:* In 2011–12, 61 students received support, including 24 fellowships (averaging $3,398 per year), 19 research assistantships with full and partial tuition reimbursements available (averaging $27,830 per year), 15 teaching assistantships with full and partial tuition reimbursements available (averaging $25,615 per year); institutionally sponsored loans, scholarships/grants, health care benefits, and unspecified assistantships also available. Financial award applicants required to submit FAFSA. *Application contact:* E-mail: leedsphd@colorado.edu. Web site: http://leeds.colorado.edu/phdprog.

University of Colorado Denver, Business School, Program in Computer Science and Information Systems, Denver, CO 80217. Offers PhD. *Students:* 12 full-time (2 women), 6 part-time (2 women); includes 2 minority (both Asian, non-Hispanic/Latino), 7 international. Average age 37. 16 applicants, 56% accepted, 6 enrolled. In 2011, 1 doctorate awarded. *Degree requirements:* For doctorate, comprehensive exam, thesis/dissertation. *Entrance requirements:* For doctorate, GMAT or GRE General Test, letters of recommendation, portfolio essay describing applicant's motivation and initial plan for doctoral study. Additional exam requirements/recommendations for international students: Required—TOEFL (minimum score 525 paper-based; 197 computer-based; 71 iBT). *Application deadline:* For fall admission, 4/15 priority date for domestic students, 3/15 for international students; for spring admission, 10/15 priority date for domestic students, 10/1 for international students. Applications are processed on a rolling basis. Application fee: $50 ($75 for international students). Electronic applications accepted. *Expenses:* Contact institution. *Financial support:* Research assistantships, teaching assistantships, Federal Work-Study, institutionally sponsored loans, and scholarships/grants available. Support available to part-time students. Financial award application deadline: 4/1; financial award applicants required to submit FAFSA. *Faculty research:* Design science of information systems, information system economics, organizational impacts of information technology, high performance parallel and distributed systems, performance measurement and prediction. *Unit head:* Dr. Michael Mannino, Associate Professor/Co-Director, 303-315-8427, E-mail: michael.mannino@ucdenver.edu. *Application contact:* Shelly Townley, Admissions Coordinator, 303-315-8202, Fax: 303-556-5904, E-mail: shelly.townley@ucdenver.edu. Web site: http://business.cudenver.edu/Disciplines/InfoSystems/PhD/index.htm.

University of Colorado Denver, Business School, Program in Information Systems, Denver, CO 80217. Offers accounting and information systems audit and control (PhD); business intelligence (MS); enterprise technology management (MS); geographic information systems (MS); health information technology management (MS); web and mobile computing (MS). Part-time and evening/weekend programs available. Postbaccalaureate distance learning degree programs offered (no on-campus study). *Students:* 53 full-time (17 women), 34 part-time (5 women); includes 13 minority (1 Black or African American, non-Hispanic/Latino; 9 Asian, non-Hispanic/Latino; 3 Hispanic/Latino), 11 international. Average age 34. 36 applicants, 61% accepted, 12 enrolled. In 2011, 16 master's awarded. *Degree requirements:* For master's, 30 credit hours. *Entrance requirements:* For master's, GMAT, resume, essay, two letters of recommendation, financial statements (for international applicants). Additional exam requirements/recommendations for international students: Required—TOEFL (minimum score 525 paper-based; 197 computer-based; 71 iBT). *Application deadline:* For fall admission, 4/15 priority date for domestic students, 3/15 for international students; for spring admission, 10/15 priority date for domestic students, 10/1 for international students. Applications are processed on a rolling basis. Application fee: $50 ($75 for international students). Electronic applications accepted. *Expenses:* Contact institution. *Financial support:* Federal Work-Study and scholarships/grants available. Support available to part-time students. Financial award application deadline: 4/1; financial award applicants required to submit FAFSA. *Faculty research:* Human-computer interaction, expert systems, database management, electronic commerce, object-oriented software development. *Unit head:* Dr. Jahangir Karimi, Director of Information Systems Programs, 303-315-8430, E-mail: jahangir.karimi@ucdenver.edu. *Application contact:* Shelly Townley, Admissions Director, Graduate Programs, 303-315-8202, E-mail: shelly.townley@ucdenver.edu. Web site: http://ucdenver.edu/academics/colleges/business/degrees/ms/IS/Pages/Information-Systems.aspx.

University of Dallas, Graduate School of Management, Irving, TX 75062-4736. Offers accounting (MBA, MM, MS); business management (MBA, MM); corporate finance (MBA, MM); financial services (MBA); global business (MBA, MM); health services management (MBA, MM); human resource management (MBA, MM); information assurance (MBA, MM, MS); information technology (MBA, MM, MS); information technology service management (MBA, MM, MS); marketing management (MBA, MM); organization development (MBA, MM); project management (MBA, MM); sports and entertainment management (MBA, MM); strategic leadership (MBA, MM); supply chain management (MBA); supply chain management and market logistics (MM). *Accreditation:* ACBSP. Part-time and evening/weekend programs available. Postbaccalaureate distance learning degree programs offered (no on-campus study). *Entrance requirements:* Additional exam requirements/recommendations for international students: Required—TOEFL. Electronic applications accepted. *Expenses:* Contact institution.

University of Delaware, Alfred Lerner College of Business and Economics, Department of Accounting and Management Information Systems and Department of Electrical and Computer Engineering, Program in Information Systems and Technology Management, Newark, DE 19716. Offers MS. Part-time and evening/weekend programs available. *Entrance requirements:* For master's, GRE or GMAT, 2 letters of recommendation, resume, minimum GPA of 2.75. Additional exam requirements/recommendations for international students: Required—TOEFL (minimum score 600 paper-based; 250 computer-based). *Faculty research:* Security, developer trust, XML.

University of Denver, University College, Denver, CO 80208. Offers arts and culture (MLS, Certificate), including art, literature, and culture, arts development and program management (Certificate), creative writing; environmental policy and management (MAS, Certificate), including energy and sustainability (Certificate), environmental assessment of nuclear power (Certificate), environmental health and safety (Certificate), environmental management, natural resource management (Certificate); geographic information systems (MAS, Certificate); global affairs (MLS, Certificate), including translation studies, world history and culture; healthcare leadership (MPH, Certificate), including healthcare policy, law, and ethics, medical and healthcare information technologies, strategic management of healthcare; information and communications technology (MCIS, Certificate), including database design and administration (Certificate), geographic information systems (MCIS), information security systems security (Certificate), information systems security (MCIS), project management (MCIS, MPS, Certificate), software design and administration (Certificate), software design and programming (MCIS), technology management, telecommunications technology (MCIS), Web design and development; leadership and organizations (MPS, Certificate), including human capital in organizations, philanthropic leadership, project management (MCIS, MPS, Certificate), strategic innovation and change; organizational and professional communication (MPS, Certificate), including alternative dispute resolution, organizational communication, organizational development and training, public relations and marketing; security management (MAS, Certificate), including emergency planning and response, information security (MAS), organizational security; strategic human resource management (MPS, Certificate), including global human resources (MPS), human resource management and development (MPS). Part-time and evening/weekend programs available. Postbaccalaureate distance learning degree programs offered (no on-campus study). *Faculty:* 204 part-time/adjunct (80 women). *Students:* 56 full-time (26 women), 1,096 part-time (647 women); includes 196 minority (81 Black or African American, non-Hispanic/Latino; 7 American Indian or Alaska Native, non-Hispanic/Latino; 30 Asian, non-Hispanic/Latino; 66 Hispanic/Latino; 3 Native Hawaiian or other Pacific Islander, non-Hispanic/Latino; 9 Two or more races, non-Hispanic/Latino), 76 international. Average age 36. 572 applicants, 95% accepted, 410 enrolled. In 2011, 404 master's, 123 other advanced degrees awarded. *Degree requirements:* For master's, capstone project. *Entrance requirements:* For master's, two letters of recommendation, personal statement, resume. Additional exam requirements/recommendations for international students: Required—TOEFL (minimum score 550 paper-based; 80 iBT). *Application deadline:* For fall admission, 7/20 priority date for domestic students, 6/8 for international students; for winter admission, 10/26 priority date for domestic students, 9/14 for international students; for spring admission, 2/1 priority date for domestic students, 12/14 for international students. Applications are processed on a rolling basis. Application fee: $75. Electronic applications accepted. *Expenses:* Contact institution. *Financial support:* Applicants required to submit FAFSA. *Unit head:* Dr. James Davis, Dean, 303-871-2291, Fax: 303-871-4047, E-mail: jdavis@du.edu. *Application contact:* Information Contact, 303-871-3155, Fax: 303-871-4047, E-mail: ucolinfo@du.edu. Web site: http://www.universitycollege.du.edu/.

University of Detroit Mercy, College of Business Administration, Program in Computer Information Systems, Detroit, MI 48221. Offers MSCIS. Part-time and evening/weekend programs available. *Degree requirements:* For master's, thesis or alternative. *Entrance requirements:* For master's, minimum GPA of 3.75.

University of Florida, Graduate School, Warrington College of Business Administration, Hough Graduate School of Business, Department of Information Systems and Operations Management, Gainesville, FL 32611. Offers information systems and operations management (MS, PhD); supply chain management (MS). *Faculty:* 13 full-time (2 women). *Students:* 203 full-time (77 women), 27 part-time (5 women); includes 31 minority (6 Black or African American, non-Hispanic/Latino; 13 Asian, non-Hispanic/Latino; 12 Hispanic/Latino), 148 international. Average age 25. 383 applicants, 79% accepted, 77 enrolled. In 2011, 89 master's, 2 doctorates awarded. Terminal master's awarded for partial completion of doctoral program. *Degree requirements:* For doctorate, thesis/dissertation. *Entrance requirements:* For master's, GMAT or GRE General Test, minimum GPA of 3.0; for doctorate, GMAT (minimum score 650) or GRE General Test (minimum score 1350 verbal and quantitative combined), minimum GPA of 3.0. Additional exam requirements/recommendations for international students: Required—TOEFL (minimum score 550 paper-based; 213 computer-based; 80 iBT), IELTS (minimum score 6), IELTS (minimum score 6) or Michigan English Language Assessment Battery (minimum score 77) also required for some. *Application deadline:* For fall admission, 4/1 priority date for domestic students, 3/1 for international students; for spring admission, 10/15 for domestic students, 10/1 for international students. Applications are processed on a rolling basis. Application fee: $30. *Financial support:* Fellowships, research assistantships, teaching assistantships, and unspecified assistantships available. Financial award application deadline: 2/1; financial award applicants required to submit FAFSA. *Faculty research:* Expert systems, nonconvex optimization, manufacturing management, production and operation management, telecommunication. *Unit head:* Dr. Gary J. Koehler, Chair, 352-846-2090, Fax: 352-392-5438, E-mail: koehler@ufl.edu. *Application contact:* Dr. Anand A. Paul, Graduate Coordinator for PhD Program, 352-392-9600, Fax: 352-392-5438, E-mail: paulaa@ufl.edu. Web site: http://www.cba.ufl.edu/isom/.

University of Georgia, Terry College of Business, Department of Management Information Systems, Athens, GA 30602. Offers PhD. *Faculty:* 8 full-time (2 women). *Students:* 1 full-time (0 women), 27 part-time (10 women); includes 10 minority (5 Black or African American, non-Hispanic/Latino; 2 Asian, non-Hispanic/Latino; 1 Hispanic/Latino; 2 Two or more races, non-Hispanic/Latino). Average age 34. 55 applicants, 62% accepted, 23 enrolled. *Unit head:* Dr. Richard Watson, Head, 706-542-3706, E-mail: rwatson@terry.uga.edu. *Application contact:* Dr. Marie-Claude Bourdreau, Graduate Coordinator, 706-583-0887, E-mail: mcboudre@terry.uga.edu. Web site: http://www.terry.uga.edu/mis/.

University of Hawaii at Manoa, Graduate Division, College of Social Sciences, School of Communications, Program in Telecommunication and Information Resource Management, Honolulu, HI 96822. Offers Graduate Certificate. Part-time programs available. *Entrance requirements:* Additional exam requirements/recommendations for international students: Required—TOEFL (minimum score 500 paper-based; 173 computer-based; 61 iBT), IELTS (minimum score 5).

University of Hawaii at Manoa, Graduate Division, Shidler College of Business, Program in Accounting, Honolulu, HI 96822. Offers accounting (M Acc); accounting law (M Acc); information systems (M Acc); taxation (M Acc). Part-time programs available. *Entrance requirements:* For master's, GMAT, bachelor's degree in accounting, minimum GPA of 3.0. Additional exam requirements/recommendations for international students: Required—TOEFL (minimum score 550 paper-based; 213 computer-based; 79 iBT), IELTS (minimum score 5). *Faculty research:* International accounting, current tax topics, insurance industry financial reporting, behavioral accounting, auditing.

University of Hawaii at Manoa, Graduate Division, Shidler College of Business, Program in Business Administration, Honolulu, HI 96822. Offers Asian business studies (MBA); Chinese business studies (MBA); decision sciences (MBA); entrepreneurship (MBA); finance (MBA); finance and banking (MBA); human resources management (MBA); information management (MBA); information technology (MBA); international business (MBA); Japanese business studies (MBA); marketing (MBA); organizational behavior (MBA); organizational management (MBA); real estate (MBA); student-designed track (MBA). *Accreditation:* AACSB. Part-time and evening/weekend programs available. *Degree requirements:* For master's, thesis optional. *Entrance requirements:* For master's, GMAT, minimum GPA of 3.0. Additional exam requirements/recommendations for international students: Required—TOEFL (minimum score 600 paper-based; 250 computer-based; 100 iBT), IELTS (minimum score 7). *Expenses:* Contact institution.

University of Hawaii at Manoa, Graduate Division, Shidler College of Business, Program in International Management, Honolulu, HI 96822. Offers Asian finance (PhD); global information technology management (PhD); international accounting (PhD); international marketing (PhD); international organization and strategy (PhD). Part-time programs available. *Degree requirements:* For doctorate, comprehensive exam, thesis/dissertation. *Entrance requirements:* For doctorate, GMAT or GRE General Test, minimum GPA of 3.0. Additional exam requirements/recommendations for international students: Required—TOEFL (minimum score 600 paper-based; 250 computer-based; 100 iBT), IELTS (minimum score 7). *Expenses:* Contact institution.

University of Houston–Clear Lake, School of Business, Program in Management Information Systems, Houston, TX 77058-1098. Offers MS. Part-time programs available. *Entrance requirements:* For master's, GMAT. Additional exam requirements/recommendations for international students: Required—TOEFL (minimum score 550 paper-based; 213 computer-based).

University of Illinois at Chicago, Graduate College, Liautaud Graduate School of Business, Department of Information and Decision Sciences, Chicago, IL 60607-7128. Offers business statistics (PhD); management information systems (MS, PhD). Part-time and evening/weekend programs available. *Degree requirements:* For doctorate, thesis/dissertation. *Entrance requirements:* For doctorate, GMAT, minimum GPA of 2.75. Additional exam requirements/recommendations for international students: Required—TOEFL. Electronic applications accepted.

University of Illinois at Springfield, Graduate Programs, College of Business and Management, Program in Management Information Systems, Springfield, IL 62703-5407. Offers MS. Part-time and evening/weekend programs available. Postbaccalaureate distance learning degree programs offered (no on-campus study). *Faculty:* 7 full-time (1 woman). *Students:* 47 full-time (14 women), 143 part-time (48 women); includes 54 minority (21 Black or African American, non-Hispanic/Latino; 1 American Indian or Alaska Native, non-Hispanic/Latino; 18 Asian, non-Hispanic/Latino; 10 Hispanic/Latino; 1 Native Hawaiian or other Pacific Islander, non-Hispanic/Latino; 3 Two or more races, non-Hispanic/Latino), 44 international. Average age 35. 184 applicants, 65% accepted, 38 enrolled. In 2011, 46 master's awarded. *Degree requirements:* For master's, project, closure seminar. *Entrance requirements:* For master's, GMAT or GRE General Test, competency in a structured, high-level programming language; minimum undergraduate GPA of 3.0. Additional exam requirements/recommendations for international students: Required—TOEFL (minimum score 500 paper-based; 176 computer-based; 61 iBT). *Application deadline:* Applications are processed on a rolling basis. Application fee: $50 ($60 for international students). Electronic applications accepted. *Expenses:* Tuition, state resident: full-time $6978; part-time $290.75 per credit hour. Tuition, nonresident: full-time $15,282; part-time $636.75 per credit hour. *Required fees:* $2106; $87.75 per credit hour. *Financial support:* In 2011–12, fellowships with full tuition reimbursements (averaging $8,550 per year), research assistantships with full tuition reimbursements (averaging $8,550 per year), teaching assistantships with full tuition reimbursements (averaging $8,550 per year) were awarded; career-related internships or fieldwork, Federal Work-Study, scholarships/grants, health care benefits, and unspecified assistantships also available. Support available to part-time students. Financial award application deadline: 11/15; financial award applicants required to submit FAFSA. *Unit head:* Dr. Rassule Hadidi, Program Administrator, 217-206-6067, Fax: 217-206-7543, E-mail: hadidi.rassule@uis.edu. *Application contact:* Dr. Lynn Pardie, Office of Graduate Studies, 800-252-8533, Fax: 217-206-7623, E-mail: lpard1@uis.edu.

The University of Kansas, Graduate Studies, School of Engineering, Program in Information Technology, Lawrence, KS 66045. Offers MS. Part-time and evening/weekend programs available. *Faculty:* 36. *Students:* 2 full-time (1 woman), 16 part-time (2 women); includes 3 minority (all Asian, non-Hispanic/Latino), 3 international. Average age 35. 14 applicants, 36% accepted, 4 enrolled. In 2011, 7 degrees awarded. *Degree requirements:* For master's, thesis optional, exam. *Entrance requirements:* For master's, GRE. Additional exam requirements/recommendations for international students: Required—TOEFL (minimum score 600 paper-based; 250 computer-based; 100 iBT). *Application deadline:* For fall admission, 3/1 priority date for domestic students, 3/1 for international students; for spring admission, 10/1 priority date for domestic students, 10/1 for international students. Applications are processed on a rolling basis. Application fee: $55 ($65 for international students). Electronic applications accepted. Tuition and fees vary according to course load, campus/location, program and reciprocity agreements. *Faculty research:* Information security and privacy, game theory, graph theory, software process improvement, resilient and survivable networks, object orientation technology. *Unit head:* Dr. Glenn Prescott, Chairperson, 785-864-4620, Fax: 785-864-3226. *Application contact:* Pam Shadoin, Assistant to Graduate Director, 785-864-4487, Fax: 785-864-3226, E-mail: eecs_graduate@ku.edu. Web site: http://eecs.ku.edu/prospective_students/graduate/masters#information_technology.

University of La Verne, College of Business and Public Management, Graduate Programs in Business Administration, La Verne, CA 91750-4443. Offers accounting (MBA); executive management (MBA-EP); finance (MBA, MBA-EP); health services management (MBA); information technology (MBA, MBA-EP); international business (MBA, MBA-EP); leadership (MBA-EP); managed care (MBA); management (MBA, MBA-EP); marketing (MBA, MBA-EP). Part-time and evening/weekend programs available. *Faculty:* 34 full-time (15 women), 38 part-time/adjunct (13 women). *Students:* 525 full-time (243 women), 231 part-time (114 women); includes 199 minority (27 Black or African American, non-Hispanic/Latino; 1 American Indian or Alaska Native, non-Hispanic/Latino; 55 Asian, non-Hispanic/Latino; 113 Hispanic/Latino; 3 Two or more races, non-Hispanic/Latino), 436 international. Average age 28. In 2011, 403 master's awarded. *Entrance requirements:* For master's, minimum undergraduate GPA of 3.0, 2 letters of recommendation, resume. Additional exam requirements/recommendations for international students: Required—TOEFL (minimum score 550 paper-based; 213 computer-based). *Application deadline:* Applications are processed on a rolling basis. Application fee: $50. *Expenses:* Contact institution. *Financial support:* Career-related internships or fieldwork, institutionally sponsored loans, and scholarships/grants available. Financial award application deadline: 3/2; financial award applicants required to submit FAFSA. *Unit head:* Dr. Abe Helou, Chairperson, 909-593-3511 Ext. 4211, Fax: 909-392-2704, E-mail: ihelou@laverne.edu. *Application contact:* Rina Lazarian, Program and Admission Specialist, 909-593-3511 Ext. 4819, Fax: 909-392-2704, E-mail: cbpm@ulv.edu.

University of La Verne, Regional Campus Administration, Graduate Programs, Central Coast/Vandenberg Air Force Base Campuses, La Verne, CA 91750-4443. Offers business (MBA-EP), including health services management, information technology; health administration (MHA); leadership and management (MS). *Entrance requirements:* For master's, 2 letters of recommendation, resume. *Expenses:* Contact institution.

University of La Verne, Regional Campus Administration, Graduate Programs, Inland Empire Campus, Rancho Cucamonga, CA 91730. Offers business (MBA-EP), including health services management, information technology, management, marketing; leadership and management (MS). *Entrance requirements:* For master's, 2 letters of recommendation, resume. *Expenses:* Contact institution.

University of Lethbridge, School of Graduate Studies, Lethbridge, AB T1K 3M4, Canada. Offers accounting (MScM); addictions counseling (M Sc); agricultural biotechnology (M Sc); agricultural studies (M Sc, MA); anthropology (MA); archaeology (MA); art (MA, MFA); biochemistry (M Sc); biological sciences (M Sc); biomolecular science (PhD); biosystems and biodiversity (PhD); Canadian studies (MA); chemistry (M Sc); computer science (M Sc); computer science and geographical information science (M Sc); counseling psychology (M Ed); dramatic arts (MA); earth, space, and physical science (PhD); economics (MA); educational leadership (M Ed); English (MA); environmental science (M Sc); evolution and behavior (PhD); exercise science (M Sc); finance (MScM); French (MA); French/German (MA); French/Spanish (MA); general education (M Ed); general management (MScM); geography (M Sc, MA); German (MA); health science (M Sc); history (MA); human resource management and labour relations (MScM); individualized multidisciplinary (M Sc, MA); information systems (MScM); international management (MScM); kinesiology (M Sc, MA); management (M Sc, MA); marketing (MScM); mathematics (M Sc); music (M Mus, MA); Native American studies (MA); neuroscience (M Sc, PhD); new media (MA); nursing (M Sc); philosophy (MA); physics (M Sc); policy and strategy (MScM); political science (MA); psychology (M Sc, MA); religious studies (MA); social sciences (MA); sociology (MA); theatre and dramatic arts (MFA); theoretical and computational science (PhD); urban and regional studies (MA); women's studies (MA). Part-time and evening/weekend programs available. *Degree requirements:* For doctorate, comprehensive exam, thesis/dissertation. *Entrance requirements:* For master's, GMAT (M Sc in management), bachelor's degree in related field, minimum GPA of 3.0 during previous 20 graded semester courses, 2 years teaching or related experience (M Ed); for doctorate, master's degree, minimum graduate GPA of 3.5. Additional exam requirements/recommendations for international students: Required—TOEFL. *Faculty research:* Movement and brain plasticity, gibberellin physiology, photosynthesis, carbon cycling, molecular properties of main-group ring components.

University of Maine, Graduate School, Interdisciplinary Program in Information Systems, Orono, ME 04469. Offers MS. Part-time programs available. *Students:* 3 full-time (1 woman), 2 part-time (0 women); includes 1 minority (Hispanic/Latino), 1 international. Average age 32. 6 applicants, 50% accepted, 3 enrolled. In 2011, 2 degrees awarded. *Entrance requirements:* For master's, GRE General Test or GMAT. Additional exam requirements/recommendations for international students: Required—TOEFL. *Application deadline:* For fall admission, 2/1 priority date for domestic students. Applications are processed on a rolling basis. Application fee: $65. Electronic applications accepted. *Expenses:* Tuition, state resident: full-time $5016. Tuition, nonresident: full-time $14,424. *Financial support:* In 2011–12, 5 research assistantships (averaging $30,000 per year), 1 teaching assistantship with full tuition reimbursement (averaging $13,600 per year) were awarded; Federal Work-Study also available. *Total annual research expenditures:* $327,609. *Unit head:* Dr. Harland Onsrud, Coordinator, 207-581-2175, Fax: 207-581-2206, E-mail: graduate@maine.edu. *Application contact:* Scott G. Delcourt, Associate Dean of the Graduate School, 207-581-3291, Fax: 207-581-3232, E-mail: graduate@maine.edu. Web site: http://www2.umaine.edu/graduate/.

University of Management and Technology, Program in Computer Science and Information Technology, Arlington, VA 22209. Offers computer science (MS); information technology (AC); information technology project management (MS); management information systems (MS); project management (AC); software engineering (MS). Part-time and evening/weekend programs available. Postbaccalaureate distance learning degree programs offered (no on-campus study). *Entrance requirements:* For master's, 3 recommendations, resume. Additional exam requirements/recommendations for international students: Required—TOEFL (minimum score 550 paper-based; 213 computer-based). Electronic applications accepted.

University of Mary Hardin-Baylor, Graduate Studies in Business Administration, Belton, TX 76513. Offers accounting (MBA); information systems management (MBA); management (MBA). Part-time and evening/weekend programs available. *Faculty:* 11 full-time (4 women), 5 part-time/adjunct (3 women). *Students:* 48 full-time (26 women), 23 part-time (12 women); includes 19 minority (7 Black or African American, non-Hispanic/Latino; 1 Asian, non-Hispanic/Latino; 11 Hispanic/Latino), 29 international. Average age 29. 102 applicants, 69% accepted, 25 enrolled. In 2011, 11 master's awarded. *Degree requirements:* For master's, comprehensive exam. *Entrance requirements:* For master's, GMAT, minimum GPA of 3.0, work experience, interview. *Application deadline:* For fall admission, 6/1 priority date for domestic students; for spring admission, 11/1 for domestic students. Applications are processed on a rolling basis. Application fee: $35 ($135 for international students). Electronic applications accepted. *Expenses: Tuition:* Full-time $12,780. *Required fees:* $2350. *Financial support:* Federal Work-Study and scholarships (for some active duty military personnel only) available. Financial award applicants required to submit FAFSA. *Unit head:* Dr. Terry Fox, Program Director, 254-295-5406, E-mail: terry.fox@umhb.edu. *Application contact:* Melissa Ford, Director of Graduate Admissions, 254-295-4020, Fax: 254-295-5301, E-mail: mford@umhb.edu.

University of Mary Hardin-Baylor, Graduate Studies in Information Systems, Belton, TX 76513. Offers MS. Part-time and evening/weekend programs available. *Faculty:* 3 full-time (1 woman). *Students:* 40 full-time (12 women), 11 part-time (6 women); includes 1 minority (Asian, non-Hispanic/Latino), 45 international. Average age 25. 123 applicants, 93% accepted, 10 enrolled. In 2011, 12 master's awarded. *Degree requirements:* For master's, comprehensive exam. *Entrance requirements:* For master's, minimum GPA of 3.0, work experience, interview. *Application deadline:* For fall admission, 6/1 priority date for domestic students; for spring admission, 11/1 for domestic students. Applications are processed on a rolling basis. Application fee: $35 ($135 for international students). Electronic applications accepted. *Expenses: Tuition:* Full-time $12,780. *Required fees:* $2350. *Financial support:* Federal Work-Study and scholarships (for some active duty military personnel only) available. Support available to part-time students. Financial award applicants required to submit FAFSA. *Unit head:* Dr. Nancy Bonner, Director of MSIS Program, 254-295-5405, E-mail: nbonner@umhb.edu. *Application contact:* Melissa Ford, Director of Graduate Admissions, 254-295-4020, Fax: 254-295-5301, E-mail: mford@umhb.edu.

University of Maryland University College, Graduate School of Management and Technology, Program in Financial Management and Information Systems, Adelphi, MD 20783. Offers MS, Certificate. Part-time and evening/weekend programs available. Postbaccalaureate distance learning degree programs offered (no on-campus study). *Students:* 4 full-time (2 women), 169 part-time (80 women); includes 107 minority (80 Black or African American, non-Hispanic/Latino; 15 Asian, non-Hispanic/Latino; 9 Hispanic/Latino; 3 Two or more races, non-Hispanic/Latino), 4 international. Average age 34. 63 applicants, 100% accepted, 25 enrolled. In 2011, 39 degrees awarded. *Degree requirements:* For master's, thesis or alternative. *Application deadline:* Applications are processed on a rolling basis. Application fee: $50. Electronic applications accepted. *Financial support:* Federal Work-Study and scholarships/grants available. Support available to part-time students. Financial award application deadline: 6/1; financial award applicants required to submit FAFSA. *Unit head:* Dr. Jayanta Sen, Director, 240-684-2400, Fax: 240-684-2401, E-mail: jsen@umuc.edu. *Application contact:* Coordinator, Graduate Admissions, 800-888-8682, Fax: 240-684-2151, E-mail: newgrad@umuc.edu. Web site: http://www.umuc.edu/programs/grad/fmis/.

University of Mary Washington, College of Business, Fredericksburg, VA 22401-5358. Offers business administration (MBA); management information systems (MSMIS). Part-time and evening/weekend programs available. *Faculty:* 11 full-time (4 women), 9 part-time/adjunct (1 woman). *Students:* 107 full-time (57 women), 253 part-time (123 women); includes 100 minority (78 Black or African American, non-Hispanic/Latino; 1 American Indian or Alaska Native, non-Hispanic/Latino; 8 Asian, non-Hispanic/Latino; 13 Hispanic/Latino), 5 international. Average age 36. 82 applicants, 61% accepted, 34 enrolled. In 2011, 85 master's awarded. *Entrance requirements:* For master's, GMAT or GRE, minimum GPA of 3.0. Additional exam requirements/recommendations for international students: Required—TOEFL (minimum score 570 paper-based; 230 computer-based; 88 iBT), IELTS (minimum score 6.5). *Application deadline:* For fall admission, 6/1 priority date for domestic students, 6/1 for international students; for spring admission, 10/1 for domestic and international students. Application fee: $50. Electronic applications accepted. *Financial support:* Available to part-time students. Application deadline: 3/15; applicants required to submit FAFSA. *Faculty research:* Management of IT offshoring, boundary theory and co-creation matrix: hermeneutics perspectives, text and image mining, queuing theory and supply chain, organizational learning. *Unit head:* Dr. Lynne D. Richardson, Dean, 540-654-2470, Fax: 540-654-2430, E-mail: lynne.richardson@umw.edu. *Application contact:* Matthew E. Mejia, Associate Dean of Admissions, 540-286-8088, Fax: 540-286-8085, E-mail: mmejia@umw.edu. Web site: http://business.umw.edu/.

University of Memphis, Graduate School, Fogelman College of Business and Economics, Program in Business Administration, Memphis, TN 38152. Offers accounting (MBA, PhD); economics (MBA, PhD); executive business administration (MBA); finance (PhD); finance, insurance, and real estate (MBA, MS); international business administration (IMBA); management (MBA, MS, PhD); management information systems (MBA, MS, PhD); management science (MBA); marketing (MBA, MS); marketing and supply chain management (PhD); real estate development (MS); JD/MBA. *Accreditation:* AACSB. *Degree requirements:* For master's, comprehensive exam; for doctorate, comprehensive exam, thesis/dissertation. *Entrance requirements:* For master's, GMAT, resume; for doctorate, GMAT, interview, minimum GPA of 3.4, resume, letter of recommendation. Additional exam requirements/recommendations for international students: Required—TOEFL (minimum score 550 paper-based; 220 computer-based). *Faculty research:* Competitive business strategy, finance microstructures, supply chain management innovations, health care economics, litigation risks and corporate audits.

University of Miami, Graduate School, School of Business Administration, Program in Business Administration, Coral Gables, FL 33124. Offers accounting (MBA); computer information systems (MBA); executive and professional (MBA), including international business, management; finance (MBA); international business (MBA); management (MBA); management science (MBA); marketing (MBA); professional management (MSPM); JD/MBA; MBA/MSIE. *Accreditation:* AACSB. Evening/weekend programs available. *Degree requirements:* For master's, comprehensive exam. *Entrance requirements:* For master's, GMAT. Additional exam requirements/recommendations for international students: Required—TOEFL (minimum score 550 paper-based; 213 computer-based; 59 iBT). Electronic applications accepted. *Faculty research:* Leadership, e-commerce, supply chain management.

University of Michigan–Dearborn, College of Business, Dearborn, MI 48128-1491. Offers accounting (MBA, MS); business analytics (MS); finance (MBA, MS); information systems (MS); international business (MBA); management (MBA); management information systems (MBA); marketing (MBA); supply chain management (MBA, MS); MBA/MHSA; MBA/MSE; MBA/MSF; MBA/MSIS; MSF/MSA. *Accreditation:* AACSB. Part-time and evening/weekend programs available. Postbaccalaureate distance learning degree programs offered (no on-campus study). *Faculty:* 50 full-time (6 women), 32 part-time/adjunct (18 women). *Students:* 65 full-time (29 women), 356 part-time (121 women); includes 79 minority (19 Black or African American, non-Hispanic/Latino; 36 American Indian or Alaska Native, non-Hispanic/Latino; 15 Hispanic/Latino; 1 Native Hawaiian or other Pacific Islander, non-Hispanic/Latino; 8 Two or more races, non-Hispanic/Latino), 80 international. Average age 28. 175 applicants, 53% accepted, 68 enrolled. In 2011, 173 master's awarded. *Entrance requirements:* For master's, GMAT or GRE, 2 years of work experience (MBA); course work in computer applications, statistics, and pre-calculus or finite mathematics; 18 credits of accounting course work beyond introductory courses (MS in accounting). Additional exam requirements/recommendations for international students: Required—TOEFL (minimum score 560 paper-based; 220 computer-based; 84 iBT), IELTS. *Application deadline:* For fall admission, 8/1 priority date for domestic students, 6/1 for international students; for winter admission, 12/1 priority date for domestic students, 10/1 for international students; for spring admission, 4/1 priority date for domestic students, 2/1 for international students. Applications are processed on a rolling basis. Application fee: $60. Electronic applications accepted. *Expenses:* Contact institution. *Financial support:* Career-related internships or fieldwork, Federal Work-Study, and scholarships/grants available. Support available to part-time students. Financial award application deadline: 9/1; financial award applicants required to submit FAFSA. *Faculty research:* Cultural diversity, buyer-supplier relations, error detection in data, economic evolution. *Unit head:* Dr. Lee Redding, Interim Dean, 313-593-5248, Fax: 313-271-9835, E-mail: lredding@umd.umich.edu. *Application contact:* Joan Doherty, Academic Advisor/Counselor, 313-593-5460, Fax: 313-271-9838, E-mail: gradbusiness@umd.umich.edu. Web site: http://www.cob.umd.umich.edu.

University of Minnesota, Twin Cities Campus, Carlson School of Management, Carlson Full-Time MBA Program, Minneapolis, MN 55455. Offers finance (MBA); information technology (MBA); management (MBA); marketing (MBA); medical industry orientation (MBA); supply chain and operations (MBA); JD/MBA; MBA/MPP; MD/MBA; MHA/MBA; Pharm D/MBA. *Accreditation:* AACSB. *Faculty:* 58 full-time (17 women), 23 part-time/adjunct (5 women). *Students:* 172 full-time (54 women); includes 16 minority (4 Black or African American, non-Hispanic/Latino; 10 Asian, non-Hispanic/Latino; 2 Two or more races, non-Hispanic/Latino), 41 international. Average age 28. 538 applicants, 41% accepted, 99 enrolled. In 2011, 97 master's awarded. *Entrance requirements:* For master's, GMAT or GRE. Additional exam requirements/recommendations for international students: Required—TOEFL (minimum score 580 paper-based; 240 computer-based; 84 iBT), IELTS (minimum score 7), or Pearson Test of English. *Application deadline:* For fall admission, 4/1 for domestic students, 2/1 for international students. Application fee: $60 ($90 for international students). Electronic applications accepted. *Expenses:* Contact institution. *Financial support:* In 2011–12, 116 students received support, including 116 fellowships with full and partial tuition reimbursements available (averaging $18,702 per year); research assistantships with partial tuition reimbursements available, teaching assistantships with partial tuition reimbursements available, career-related internships or fieldwork, Federal Work-Study, institutionally sponsored loans, scholarships/grants, health care benefits, and unspecified assistantships also available. Financial award application deadline: 4/1; financial award applicants required to submit FAFSA. *Faculty research:* Finance and accounting: financial reporting, asset pricing models and corporate finance; information and decision sciences: on-line auctions, information transparency and recommender systems; marketing: psychological influences on consumer behavior, brand equity, pricing and marketing channels; operations: lean manufacturing, quality management and global supply chains; strategic management and organization: global strategy, networks, entrepreneurship and innovation, sustainability. *Unit head:* Philip J. Miller, Assistant Dean, MBA Programs and Graduate Business Career Center, 612-625-5555, Fax: 612-625-1012, E-mail: mba@umn.edu. *Application contact:* Linh Gilles, Director of Admissions and Recruiting, 612-625-5555, Fax: 612-625-1012, E-mail: ftmba@umn.edu. Web site: http://www.csom.umn.edu/MBA/full-time/.

University of Minnesota, Twin Cities Campus, Carlson School of Management, Carlson Part-Time MBA Program, Minneapolis, MN 55455. Offers finance (MBA); information technology (MBA); management (MBA); marketing (MBA); supply chain and operations (MBA). Part-time and evening/weekend programs available. *Faculty:* 63 full-time (16 women), 27 part-time/adjunct (4 women). *Students:* 1,459 part-time (463 women); includes 94 minority (11 Black or African American, non-Hispanic/Latino; 3 American Indian or Alaska Native, non-Hispanic/Latino; 68 Asian, non-Hispanic/Latino; 10 Hispanic/Latino; 2 Two or more races, non-Hispanic/Latino), 72 international. Average age 28. 336 applicants, 86% accepted, 256 enrolled. In 2011, 479 master's awarded. *Entrance requirements:* For master's, GMAT or GRE. Additional exam requirements/recommendations for international students: Required—TOEFL (minimum score 580 paper-based; 240 computer-based; 84 iBT), IELTS (minimum score 7), or Pearson Test of English. *Application deadline:* For fall admission, 5/1 priority date for domestic students, 5/1 for international students; for spring admission, 10/1 priority date for domestic students, 10/1 for international students. Applications are processed on a rolling basis. Application fee: $60 ($90 for international students). Electronic applications accepted. *Expenses:* Contact institution. *Financial support:* Applicants required to submit FAFSA. *Faculty research:* Finance and accounting: financial reporting, asset pricing models and corporate finance; information and decision sciences: on-line auctions, information transparency and recommender systems; marketing: psychological influences on consumer behavior, brand equity, pricing and marketing channels; operations: lean manufacturing, quality management and global supply chains; strategic management and organization: global strategy, networks, entrepreneurship and innovation, sustainability. *Unit head:* Philip J. Miller, Assistant Dean, MBA Programs and Graduate Business Career Center, 612-624-2039, Fax: 612-625-1012, E-mail: mba@umn.edu. *Application contact:* Linh Gilles, Director of Admissions and Recruiting, 612-625-5555, Fax: 612-625-1012, E-mail: ptmba@umn.edu. Web site: http://www.carlsonschool.umn.edu/ptmba.

University of Minnesota, Twin Cities Campus, Carlson School of Management, Doctoral Program in Business Administration, Minneapolis, MN 55455-0213. Offers accounting (PhD); finance (PhD); information and decision sciences (PhD); marketing (PhD); operations and management science (PhD); strategic management and organization (PhD). *Faculty:* 104 full-time (30 women). *Students:* 74 full-time (30 women); includes 8 minority (5 Asian, non-Hispanic/Latino; 3 Hispanic/Latino), 50 international. Average age 30. 320 applicants, 8% accepted, 15 enrolled. In 2011, 13 doctorates awarded. *Degree requirements:* For doctorate, comprehensive exam, thesis/dissertation, written and oral preliminary exams, proposal defense, final defense. *Entrance requirements:* For doctorate, GMAT, GRE General Test. Additional exam requirements/recommendations for international students: Required—TOEFL (minimum score 600 paper-based; 250 computer-based; 100 iBT); Recommended—IELTS (minimum score 7.5). *Application deadline:* For fall admission, 12/31 for domestic and international students. Applications are processed on a rolling basis. Application fee: $75 ($95 for international students). Electronic applications accepted. *Expenses:* Contact institution. *Financial support:* In 2011–12, 66 students received support, including 112 fellowships with full tuition reimbursements available (averaging $6,700 per year), 55 research assistantships with full tuition reimbursements available (averaging $6,750 per year), 54 teaching assistantships with full tuition reimbursements available (averaging $6,750 per year); institutionally sponsored loans, scholarships/grants, health care benefits, and unspecified assistantships also available. Financial award application deadline: 12/31. *Faculty research:* Corporate strategy, finance, entrepreneurship, marketing, information and decision science, operations, accounting, quality management. *Unit head:* Dr. Shawn P. Curley, Director, 612-624-6546, Fax: 612-624-8221, E-mail: curley@umn.edu. *Application contact:* Earlene K. Bronson, Assistant Director, 612-624-0875, Fax: 612-624-8221, E-mail: brons003@umn.edu. Web site: http://www.csom.umn.edu/phd-BA/.

University of Mississippi, Graduate School, School of Business Administration, Oxford, University, MS 38677. Offers business administration (MBA, PhD); systems management (MS); JD/MBA. *Accreditation:* AACSB. *Students:* 75 full-time (20 women), 58 part-time (19 women); includes 11 minority (8 Black or African American, non-Hispanic/Latino; 1 Hispanic/Latino; 2 Two or more races, non-Hispanic/Latino), 10 international. *Degree requirements:* For doctorate, thesis/dissertation. *Entrance requirements:* For master's, GMAT, minimum GPA of 3.0; for doctorate, GMAT. Additional exam requirements/recommendations for international students: Required—TOEFL. *Application deadline:* For fall admission, 2/1 for domestic students; for spring admission, 10/1 for domestic students. Applications are processed on a rolling basis. Application fee: $25. Electronic applications accepted. *Financial support:* Fellowships, career-related internships or fieldwork, scholarships/grants, tuition waivers (full), and unspecified assistantships available. Financial award application deadline: 3/1; financial award applicants required to submit FAFSA. *Unit head:* Dr. Ken Cyree, Dean, 662-915-5820, Fax: 662-915-5821, E-mail: info@bus.olemiss.edu. *Application contact:* Dr. Christy M. Wyandt, Associate Dean, 662-915-7474, Fax: 662-915-7577, E-mail: cwyandt@olemiss.edu. Web site: http://www.olemissbusiness.com/.

University of Missouri–St. Louis, College of Business Administration, Program in Business Administration, St. Louis, MO 63121. Offers accounting (MBA); business administration (Certificate); finance (MBA); human resource management (Certificate); information systems (MBA); logistics and supply chain management (MBA, Certificate); marketing (MBA); marketing management (Certificate); operations management (MBA). *Accreditation:* AACSB. Part-time and evening/weekend programs available. *Faculty:* 32 full-time (7 women), 10 part-time/adjunct (2 women). *Students:* 126 full-time (48 women), 305 part-time (141 women); includes 61 minority (25 Black or African American, non-Hispanic/Latino; 23 Asian, non-Hispanic/Latino; 9 Hispanic/Latino; 1 Native Hawaiian or other Pacific Islander, non-Hispanic/Latino; 3 Two or more races, non-Hispanic/Latino), 47 international. Average age 30. 241 applicants, 70% accepted, 134 enrolled. In 2011, 150 master's, 1 doctorate, 19 other advanced degrees awarded. *Entrance requirements:* For master's, GMAT, 2 letters of recommendation. Additional exam requirements/recommendations for international students: Required—TOEFL (minimum score 550 paper-based; 213 computer-based). *Application deadline:* For fall admission, 7/1 for domestic and international students; for spring admission, 12/1 for domestic and international students. Applications are processed on a rolling basis. Application fee: $35 ($40 for international students). Electronic applications accepted. *Expenses:* Tuition, state resident: full-time $6273; part-time $3866 per year. Tuition, nonresident: full-time $14,969; part-time $9980 per year. *Required fees:* $315 per year. *Financial support:* In 2011–12, 32 research assistantships with full and partial tuition reimbursements (averaging $6,000 per year), 6 teaching assistantships with full and partial tuition reimbursements (averaging $12,276 per year) were awarded; career-related internships or fieldwork, Federal Work-Study, and institutionally sponsored loans also available. Support available to part-time students. Financial award application deadline: 4/1; financial award applicants required to submit FAFSA. *Faculty research:* Human resources, strategic management, marketing strategy, consumer behavior product development, advertising. *Unit head:* Karl Kottemann, Assistant Director, 314-516-5885, Fax: 314-516-6420, E-mail: mba@umsl.edu. *Application contact:* 314-516-5458, Fax: 314-516-6996, E-mail: gradadm@umsl.edu. Web site: http://www.umsl.edu/divisions/business/mbaonline/mbaprog.htm.

University of Missouri–St. Louis, College of Business Administration, Program in Information Systems, St. Louis, MO 63121. Offers information systems (MS); logistics and supply chain management (PhD). Part-time and evening/weekend programs available. *Faculty:* 6 full-time (2 women), 4 part-time/adjunct (0 women). *Students:* 2 full-time (0 women), 18 part-time (2 women); includes 2 minority (both Asian, non-Hispanic/Latino), 3 international. Average age 33. 14 applicants, 57% accepted, 2 enrolled. In 2011, 11 degrees awarded. *Entrance requirements:* For master's, GMAT, 2 letters of recommendation. Additional exam requirements/recommendations for international students: Required—TOEFL (minimum score 550 paper-based; 213 computer-based). *Application deadline:* For fall admission, 7/1 priority date for domestic students, 7/1 for international students; for spring admission, 12/1 priority date for domestic students, 12/1 for international students. Applications are processed on a rolling basis. Application fee: $35 ($40 for international students). Electronic applications accepted. *Expenses:* Tuition, state resident: full-time $6273; part-time $3866 per year. Tuition, nonresident: full-time $14,969; part-time $9980 per year. *Required fees:* $315 per year. *Financial support:* Career-related internships or fieldwork, Federal Work-Study, and institutionally sponsored loans available. Support available to part-time students. Financial award application deadline: 4/1; financial award applicants required to submit FAFSA. *Faculty research:* International information systems, telecommunications, systems development, information systems sourcing. *Unit head:* Karl Kottemann, Assistant Director, 314-516-5885, Fax: 314-516-6420, E-mail: mba@umsl.edu. *Application contact:* 314-516-5458, Fax: 314-516-6996, E-mail: gradadm@umsl.edu. Web site: http://www.umsl.edu/divisions/business/mis/ms_req_mis.html.

University of Nebraska at Omaha, Graduate Studies, College of Information Science and Technology, Department of Information Systems and Quantitative Analysis, Omaha, NE 68182. Offers information assurance (Certificate); information technology (PhD); management information systems (MS); project management (Certificate); systems analysis and design (Certificate). Part-time and evening/weekend programs available. *Faculty:* 14 full-time (7 women). *Students:* 69 full-time (23 women), 87 part-time (26 women); includes 17 minority (4 Black or African American, non-Hispanic/Latino; 7 Asian, non-Hispanic/Latino; 4 Hispanic/Latino; 2 Two or more races, non-Hispanic/Latino), 75 international. Average age 32. 142 applicants, 43% accepted, 49 enrolled. In 2011, 38 master's, 3 doctorates, 29 other advanced degrees awarded. *Degree requirements:* For master's, comprehensive exam, thesis (for some programs); for doctorate, comprehensive exam, thesis/dissertation. *Entrance requirements:* For master's, GMAT or GRE General Test; for doctorate, GMAT or GRE General Test, letters of recommendation, writing sample, resume. Additional exam requirements/recommendations for international students: Required—TOEFL (minimum score 575 paper-based; 230 computer-based; 89 iBT). *Application deadline:* For fall admission, 2/15 for domestic students; for spring admission, 9/15 for domestic students. Applications are processed on a rolling basis. Application fee: $45. Electronic applications accepted. *Financial support:* In 2011–12, 31 students received support, including 25 research assistantships with tuition reimbursements available, 3 teaching assistantships with tuition reimbursements available; fellowships, career-related internships or fieldwork, Federal Work-Study, scholarships/grants, tuition waivers (partial), and unspecified assistantships also available. Financial award application deadline: 3/1; financial award applicants required to submit FAFSA. *Unit head:* Dr. Ilze Zigurs, Chairperson, 402-554-3770. *Application contact:* Carla Frakes, Information Contact, 402-554-2423.

University of Nebraska–Lincoln, Graduate College, College of Agricultural Sciences and Natural Resources, Program in Mechanized Systems Management, Lincoln, NE 68588. Offers MS. *Degree requirements:* For master's, thesis optional. *Entrance requirements:* For master's, GRE General Test. Additional exam requirements/recommendations for international students: Required—TOEFL (minimum score 550 paper-based; 213 computer-based). Electronic applications accepted. *Faculty research:* Irrigation management, agricultural power and machinery systems, sensors and controls, food/industrial materials handling and processing systems.

University of Nevada, Las Vegas, Graduate College, College of Business, Department of Management Information Systems, Las Vegas, NV 89154-6034. Offers MS, Certificate. *Faculty:* 9 full-time (1 woman), 2 part-time/adjunct (0 women). *Students:* 22 full-time (7 women), 22 part-time (8 women); includes 22 minority (4 Black or African American, non-Hispanic/Latino; 8 Asian, non-Hispanic/Latino; 3 Hispanic/Latino; 1 Native Hawaiian or other Pacific Islander, non-Hispanic/Latino; 6 Two or more races, non-Hispanic/Latino), 12 international. Average age 31. 41 applicants, 80% accepted, 12 enrolled. In 2011, 22 master's, 3 other advanced degrees awarded. *Entrance requirements:* For master's and Certificate, GMAT or GRE. Additional exam requirements/recommendations for international students: Required—TOEFL (minimum score 550 paper-based; 213 computer-based; 80 iBT), IELTS (minimum score 7). *Application deadline:* For fall admission, 6/15 priority date for domestic students, 5/1 for international students; for spring admission, 11/15 priority date for domestic students, 10/1 for international students. Applications are processed on a rolling basis. Application fee: $60 ($95 for international students). Electronic applications accepted. *Financial support:* In 2011–12, 8 students received support, including 8 teaching assistantships with partial tuition reimbursements available (averaging $9,298 per year); institutionally sponsored loans, scholarships/grants, health care benefits, and unspecified assistantships also available. Financial award application deadline: 3/1. *Faculty research:* Engineering, design science, system development, technology adoption, IT sourcing. *Unit head:* Dr. Marcus Rothenberger, Chair/Associate Professor, 702-895-3676, Fax: 702-895-0802, E-mail: marcus.rothenberger@unlv.edu. *Application contact:* Graduate College Admissions Evaluator, 702-895-3320, Fax: 702-895-4180, E-mail: gradcollege@unlv.edu. Web site: http://business.unlv.edu/mis/content.asp?content-75.

University of Nevada, Reno, Graduate School, College of Business Administration, Department of Information Systems, Reno, NV 89557. Offers MS. *Degree requirements:* For master's, thesis optional. *Entrance requirements:* For master's, GRE or GMAT, minimum GPA of 2.75. Additional exam requirements/recommendations for international students: Required—TOEFL (minimum score 500 paper-based; 173 computer-based; 61 iBT), IELTS (minimum score 6). Electronic applications accepted.

University of New Hampshire, Graduate School Manchester Campus, Manchester, NH 03101. Offers business administration (MBA); counseling (M Ed); education (M Ed, MAT); educational administration and supervision (M Ed, Ed S); information technology (MS); management of technology (MS); public administration (MPA); public health (MPH, Certificate); social work (MSW); software systems engineering (Certificate). Part-time and evening/weekend programs available. *Students:* 78 full-time (50 women), 130 part-time (65 women); includes 62 minority (2 Black or African American, non-Hispanic/Latino; 56 Asian, non-Hispanic/Latino; 4 Hispanic/Latino), 4 international. Average age 34. 132 applicants, 55% accepted, 57 enrolled. In 2011, 66 master's, 9 other advanced degrees awarded. *Degree requirements:* For master's, thesis or alternative. *Entrance requirements:* Additional exam requirements/recommendations for international students: Required—TOEFL (minimum score 550 paper-based; 213 computer-based; 80 iBT). *Application deadline:* For fall admission, 6/1 for domestic students, 4/1 for international students; for spring admission, 12/1 for domestic students. Applications are processed on a rolling basis. Application fee: $65. Electronic applications accepted. *Expenses:* Tuition, state resident: full-time $12,360; part-time $687 per credit hour. Tuition, nonresident: full-time $25,680; part-time $1058 per credit hour. *International tuition:* $29,550 full-time. *Required fees:* $1666; $833 per course. $416.50 per semester. Tuition and fees vary according to course load and degree level. *Financial support:* In 2011–12, 11 students received support, including 2 teaching assistantships; fellowships, research assistantships, Federal Work-Study, scholarships/grants, health care benefits, and unspecified assistantships also available. Support available to part-time students. Financial award application deadline: 3/1; financial award applicants required to submit FAFSA. *Unit head:* Candice Brown, Director, 603-641-4313, E-mail: unhm.gradcenter@unh.edu. *Application contact:* Graduate Admissions Office, 603-862-3000, Fax: 603-862-0275, E-mail: grad.school@unh.edu. Web site: http://www.gradschool.unh.edu/manchester/.

University of New Mexico, Robert O. Anderson Graduate School of Management, Department of Marketing, Information and Decision Sciences, Albuquerque, NM 87131. Offers information assurance (MBA); management information systems (MBA); marketing management (MBA); operations management (MBA). Part-time and evening/weekend programs available. *Faculty:* 14 full-time (4 women), 11 part-time/adjunct (5 women). In 2011, 74 master's awarded. *Degree requirements:* For master's, minimum GPA of 3.0. *Entrance requirements:* For master's, GMAT or GRE. Additional exam requirements/recommendations for international students: Required—TOEFL (minimum score 550 paper-based; 213 computer-based; 79 iBT). *Application deadline:* For fall admission, 4/1 priority date for domestic students, 4/1 for international students; for spring admission, 10/1 priority date for domestic students, 10/1 for international students. Applications are processed on a rolling basis. Application fee: $50. Electronic applications accepted. *Financial support:* Fellowships, research assistantships, career-related internships or fieldwork, Federal Work-Study, scholarships/grants, and unspecified assistantships available. Support available to part-time students. Financial award application deadline: 6/1. *Faculty research:* Marketing, operations, information science. *Unit head:* Dr. Steve Yourstone, Chair, 505-277-6471, Fax: 505-277-7108. *Application contact:* Megan Conner, Director, Student Services, 505-277-3290, Fax: 505-277-8436, E-mail: mconner@mgt.unm.edu.

The University of North Carolina at Chapel Hill, Kenan-Flagler Business School, Doctoral Program in Business Administration, Chapel Hill, NC 27599. Offers accounting (PhD); finance (PhD); marketing (PhD); operations management (PhD); organizational behavior (PhD); strategy (PhD). *Accreditation:* AACSB. *Degree requirements:* For doctorate, thesis/dissertation. *Entrance requirements:* For doctorate, GMAT or GRE General Test. Electronic applications accepted. *Expenses:* Contact institution.

The University of North Carolina at Charlotte, Graduate School, Belk College of Business, Department of Business Information Systems and Operation Management, Charlotte, NC 28223-0001. Offers information and technology management (MBA); supply chain management (MBA). *Faculty:* 14 full-time (5 women). *Expenses:* Tuition, state resident: full-time $3689. Tuition, nonresident: full-time $15,226. *Required fees:* $2198. Tuition and fees vary according to course load and program. *Unit head:* Dr. Joe Mazzola, Interim Dean, 704-687-7577, Fax: 704-687-4014, E-mail: jmazzola@uncc.edu. *Application contact:* Kathy B. Giddings, Director of Graduate Admissions, 704-687-5503, Fax: 704-687-3279, E-mail: gradadm@uncc.edu. Web site: http://belkcollege.uncc.edu/about-college/departments/bisom.

The University of North Carolina at Greensboro, Graduate School, Bryan School of Business and Economics, Department of Information Systems and Operations Management, Greensboro, NC 27412-5001. Offers information systems (PhD); information technology (Certificate); information technology and management (MS); supply chain management (Certificate). *Entrance requirements:* For master's, GMAT, GRE General Test. Additional exam requirements/recommendations for international students: Required—TOEFL. Electronic applications accepted.

University of North Florida, College of Computing, Engineering, and Construction, School of Computing, Jacksonville, FL 32224. Offers computer science (MS); information systems (MS); software engineering (MS). Part-time programs available. *Faculty:* 14 full-time (3 women). *Students:* 7 full-time (3 women), 39 part-time (10 women); includes 15 minority (7 Black or African American, non-Hispanic/Latino; 4 Asian, non-Hispanic/Latino; 2 Hispanic/Latino; 2 Two or more races, non-Hispanic/Latino), 14 international. Average age 30. 30 applicants, 63% accepted, 5 enrolled. In 2011, 4 master's awarded. *Degree requirements:* For master's, thesis. *Entrance requirements:* For master's, GRE General Test, minimum GPA of 3.0 in last 60 hours of course work. Additional exam requirements/recommendations for international students: Required—TOEFL (minimum score 500 paper-based; 173 computer-based; 61 iBT). *Application deadline:* For fall admission, 7/1 for domestic students, 5/1 for international students; for spring admission, 11/1 for domestic students, 10/1 for international students. Applications are processed on a rolling basis. Application fee: $30. Electronic applications accepted. *Expenses:* Tuition, state resident: full-time $8793; part-time $366.38 per credit hour. Tuition, nonresident: full-time $23,502; part-time $979.24 per credit hour. *Required fees:* $1384; $57.66 per credit hour. Tuition and fees vary according to course load and program. *Financial support:* In 2011–12, 12 students received support, including 1 research assistantship (averaging $1,000 per year); teaching assistantships, Federal Work-Study, scholarships/grants, and unspecified assistantships also available. Financial award application deadline: 4/1; financial award applicants required to submit FAFSA. *Total annual research expenditures:* $91,012. *Unit head:* Dr. Neal Coulter, Dean, 904-620-1350, E-mail: ncoulter@unf.edu. *Application contact:* Lillith Richardson, Assistant Director, The Graduate School, 904-620-1360, Fax: 904-620-1362, E-mail: graduateschool@unf.edu. Web site: http://www.unf.edu/ccec/computing/.

University of North Texas, Toulouse Graduate School, College of Business, Department of Information Technology and Decision Sciences, Denton, TX 76203. Offers business computer information systems (PhD); decision technologies (MS); information technology (MS); management science (PhD). Part-time and evening/weekend programs available. *Degree requirements:* For doctorate, comprehensive exam, thesis/dissertation. *Entrance requirements:* For master's, GMAT; for doctorate, GMAT or GRE General Test. Additional exam requirements/recommendations for international students: Recommended—TOEFL (minimum score 550 paper-based; 213 computer-based; 79 iBT). Electronic applications accepted. *Expenses:* Tuition, state resident: part-time $100 per credit hour. Tuition, nonresident: part-time $413 per credit hour. *Faculty research:* Large scale IS, business intelligence, security, applied statistics, quality and reliability management.

University of Oklahoma, Michael F. Price College of Business, Division of Management Information Systems, Norman, OK 73019. Offers MS, Graduate Certificate. Part-time and evening/weekend programs available. *Faculty:* 9 full-time (3 women). *Students:* 18 full-time (5 women), 11 part-time (0 women); includes 1 minority (Asian, non-Hispanic/Latino), 4 international. Average age 28. 13 applicants, 38% accepted, 3 enrolled. In 2011, 13 degrees awarded. *Entrance requirements:* Additional exam requirements/recommendations for international students: Required—TOEFL (minimum score 550 paper-based; 79 iBT). *Application deadline:* For fall admission, 3/15 for domestic students, 3/1 for international students; for spring admission, 11/1 for domestic students, 9/1 for international students. Applications are processed on a rolling basis. Application fee: $40 ($90 for international students). Electronic applications accepted. *Expenses:* Tuition, state resident: full-time $4087; part-time $170.30 per credit hour. Tuition, nonresident: full-time $14,875; part-time $619.80 per credit hour. *Required fees:* $2659; $100.25 per credit hour. Tuition and fees vary according to course load and degree level. *Financial support:* In 2011–12, 11 students received support, including 8 research assistantships with full tuition reimbursements available (averaging $10,513 per year), 12 teaching assistantships with full tuition reimbursements available (averaging $13,705 per year); scholarships/grants and unspecified assistantships also available. Financial award applicants required to submit FAFSA. *Faculty research:* IT enabled teams, business value of IT, knowledge management, technology adoption. *Total annual research expenditures:* $89,212. *Unit head:* Laku Chidambaram, Director, 405-325-5721, Fax: 405-325-2096, E-mail: laku@ou.edu. *Application contact:* Amber Hasbrook, Academic Counselor, 405-325-4107, Fax: 405-325-7753, E-mail: amber.hasbrook@ou.edu. Web site: http://price.ou.edu/mis/mis_in_mis.aspx.

See Display on page 153 and Close-Up on page 253.

University of Oregon, Graduate School, Interdisciplinary Program in Applied Information Management, Eugene, OR 97403. Offers MS. Part-time programs available. Postbaccalaureate distance learning degree programs offered (no on-campus study). *Degree requirements:* For master's, project. *Entrance requirements:* Additional exam requirements/recommendations for international students: Required—TOEFL. Electronic applications accepted. *Expenses:* Contact institution. *Faculty research:* Business management, information design.

University of Pennsylvania, Wharton School, Operations and Information Management Department, Philadelphia, PA 19104. Offers MBA, PhD. Terminal master's awarded for partial completion of doctoral program. *Degree requirements:* For master's, thesis, preliminary exams; for doctorate, thesis/dissertation, preliminary exams. *Entrance requirements:* For master's, GMAT, GRE; for doctorate, GRE. Electronic applications accepted. *Expenses: Tuition:* Full-time $26,660; part-time $4944 per course. *Required fees:* $2318; $291 per course. Tuition and fees vary according to course load, degree level and program. *Faculty research:* Supply chain management, operations research, economics of information systems, risk analysis, electronic commerce.

University of Phoenix–Atlanta Campus, College of Information Systems and Technology, Sandy Springs, GA 30350-4153. Offers information systems (MIS); technology management (MBA). Evening/weekend programs available. *Degree requirements:* For master's, thesis (for some programs). *Entrance requirements:* For master's, 3 years of work experience, minimum undergraduate GPA of 3.0. Additional exam requirements/recommendations for international students: Required—TOEFL (minimum score 550 paper-based; 213 computer-based; 79 iBT). Electronic applications accepted.

University of Phoenix–Augusta Campus, College of Information Systems and Technology, Augusta, GA 30909-4583. Offers information systems (MIS); technology management (MBA).

University of Phoenix–Austin Campus, College of Information Systems and Technology, Austin, TX 78759. Offers information systems (MIS); technology management (MBA).

University of Phoenix–Bay Area Campus, College of Information Systems and Technology, San Jose, CA 95134-1805. Offers information systems (MIS); organizational leadership/information systems and technology (DM). Evening/weekend programs available. *Degree requirements:* For master's, thesis (for some programs). *Entrance requirements:* For master's, minimum undergraduate GPA of 3.0, 3 years of work experience. Additional exam requirements/recommendations for international students: Required—TOEFL (minimum score 550 paper-based; 213 computer-based; 79 iBT). Electronic applications accepted.

University of Phoenix–Birmingham Campus, College of Information Systems and Technology, Birmingham, AL 35244. Offers information systems (MIS); technology management (MBA).

University of Phoenix–Boston Campus, College of Information Systems and Technology, Braintree, MA 02184-4949. Offers technology management (MBA). Evening/weekend programs available. *Degree requirements:* For master's, thesis (for some programs). *Entrance requirements:* For master's, minimum GPA of 3.0, 3 years of work experience. Additional exam requirements/recommendations for international students: Required—TOEFL (minimum score 550 paper-based; 213 computer-based; 79 iBT). Electronic applications accepted.

University of Phoenix–Central Florida Campus, College of Information Systems and Technology, Maitland, FL 32751-7057. Offers management (MIS); technology management (MBA). Evening/weekend programs available. *Degree requirements:* For master's, thesis (for some programs). *Entrance requirements:* For master's, minimum undergraduate GPA of 3.0, 3 years work experience. Additional exam requirements/recommendations for international students: Required—TOEFL (minimum score 550 paper-based; 213 computer-based; 79 iBT). Electronic applications accepted.

University of Phoenix–Central Valley Campus, College of Information Systems and Technology, Fresno, CA 93720-1562. Offers information systems (MIS); technology management (MBA).

University of Phoenix–Charlotte Campus, College of Information Systems and Technology, Charlotte, NC 28273-3409. Offers information systems (MIS); information systems management (MISM); technology management (MBA). Evening/weekend programs available. *Degree requirements:* For master's, thesis (for some programs). *Entrance requirements:* For master's, minimum undergraduate GPA of 3.0, 3 years work experience. Additional exam requirements/recommendations for international students: Required—TOEFL (minimum score 550 paper-based; 213 computer-based; 79 iBT). Electronic applications accepted.

University of Phoenix–Chattanooga Campus, College of Information Systems and Technology, Chattanooga, TN 37421-3707. Offers information systems (MIS); technology management (MBA). Postbaccalaureate distance learning degree programs offered.

University of Phoenix–Cheyenne Campus, College of Information Systems and Technology, Cheyenne, WY 82009. Offers information systems (MIS); technology management (MBA).

University of Phoenix–Chicago Campus, College of Information Systems and Technology, Schaumburg, IL 60173-4399. Offers e-business (MBA); information systems (MIS); management (MM); technology management (MBA). Evening/weekend programs available. *Degree requirements:* For master's, thesis (for some programs). *Entrance requirements:* For master's, 3 years of work experience, minimum undergraduate GPA of 3.0. Additional exam requirements/recommendations for international students: Required—TOEFL (minimum score 550 paper-based; 213 computer-based; 79 iBT). Electronic applications accepted.

University of Phoenix–Cincinnati Campus, College of Information Systems and Technology, West Chester, OH 45069-4875. Offers electronic business (MBA); information systems (MIS); technology management (MBA). Evening/weekend programs available. Postbaccalaureate distance learning degree programs offered. *Degree requirements:* For master's, thesis (for some programs). *Entrance requirements:* For master's, minimum undergraduate GPA of 2.5, 3 years of work experience. Additional exam requirements/recommendations for international students: Required—TOEFL (minimum score 550 paper-based; 213 computer-based; 79 iBT). Electronic applications accepted.

University of Phoenix–Cleveland Campus, College of Information Systems and Technology, Independence, OH 44131-2194. Offers information management (MIS); technology management (MBA). Evening/weekend programs available. Postbaccalaureate distance learning degree programs offered (no on-campus study). *Degree requirements:* For master's, thesis (for some programs). *Entrance requirements:* For master's, minimum undergraduate GPA of 3.0, 3 years of work experience. Additional exam requirements/recommendations for international students: Required—TOEFL (minimum score 550 paper-based; 213 computer-based; 79 iBT). Electronic applications accepted.

University of Phoenix–Columbus Georgia Campus, College of Information Systems and Technology, Columbus, GA 31904-6321. Offers e-business (MBA); information systems (MIS); technology management (MBA). Evening/weekend programs available. Postbaccalaureate distance learning degree programs offered. *Degree requirements:* For master's, thesis (for some programs). *Entrance requirements:* For master's, minimum undergraduate GPA of 3.0, 3 years of work experience. Additional exam requirements/recommendations for international students: Required—TOEFL (minimum score 550 paper-based; 213 computer-based; 79 iBT). Electronic applications accepted.

University of Phoenix–Columbus Ohio Campus, College of Information Systems and Technology, Columbus, OH 43240-4032. Offers information systems (MIS); technology management (MBA). Postbaccalaureate distance learning degree programs offered.

University of Phoenix–Dallas Campus, College of Information Systems and Technology, Dallas, TX 75251-2009. Offers e-business (MBA); information systems (MIS); technology management (MBA). Evening/weekend programs available. *Degree requirements:* For master's, thesis (for some programs). *Entrance requirements:* For master's, minimum undergraduate GPA of 3.0, 3 years of work experience. Additional exam requirements/recommendations for international students: Required—TOEFL (minimum score 550 paper-based; 213 computer-based; 79 iBT). Electronic applications accepted.

University of Phoenix–Denver Campus, College of Information Systems and Technology, Lone Tree, CO 80124-5453. Offers e-business (MBA); management (MIS); technology management (MBA). Evening/weekend programs available. Postbaccalaureate distance learning degree programs offered. *Degree requirements:* For master's, thesis (for some programs). *Entrance requirements:* For master's, minimum undergraduate GPA of 3.0, 3 years of work experience. Additional exam requirements/recommendations for international students: Required—TOEFL (minimum score 550 paper-based; 213 computer-based; 79 iBT). Electronic applications accepted.

University of Phoenix–Des Moines Campus, College of Information Systems and Technology, Des Moines, IA 50266. Offers information systems (MIS); technology management (MBA). Postbaccalaureate distance learning degree programs offered.

University of Phoenix–Eastern Washington Campus, College of Information Systems and Technology, Spokane Valley, WA 99212-2531. Offers technology management (MBA).

University of Phoenix–Harrisburg Campus, College of Information Systems and Technology, Harrisburg, PA 17112. Offers information systems (MIS); technology management (MBA). Postbaccalaureate distance learning degree programs offered.

University of Phoenix–Hawaii Campus, College of Information Systems and Technology, Honolulu, HI 96813-4317. Offers information systems (MIS); technology management (MBA). Evening/weekend programs available. *Degree requirements:* For master's, thesis (for some programs). *Entrance requirements:* For master's, minimum undergraduate GPA of 3.0, 3 years of work experience. Additional exam requirements/recommendations for international students: Required—TOEFL (minimum score 550 paper-based; 213 computer-based; 79 iBT). Electronic applications accepted.

University of Phoenix–Houston Campus, College of Information Systems and Technology, Houston, TX 77079-2004. Offers e-business (MBA); information systems (MIS); technology management (MBA). Evening/weekend programs available. Postbaccalaureate distance learning degree programs offered. *Degree requirements:* For master's, comprehensive exam (for some programs), thesis. *Entrance requirements:* For master's, minimum undergraduate GPA of 3.0, 3 years of work experience. Additional exam requirements/recommendations for international students: Required—TOEFL (minimum score 550 paper-based; 213 computer-based; 79 iBT). Electronic applications accepted.

University of Phoenix–Idaho Campus, College of Information Systems and Technology, Meridian, ID 83642-5114. Offers information systems (MIS); technology management (MBA). Evening/weekend programs available. *Degree requirements:* For master's, thesis (for some programs). *Entrance requirements:* For master's, minimum undergraduate GPA of 3.0, 3 years of work experience. Additional exam requirements/recommendations for international students: Required—TOEFL (minimum score 550 paper-based; 213 computer-based). Electronic applications accepted.

University of Phoenix–Indianapolis Campus, College of Information Systems and Technology, Indianapolis, IN 46250-932. Offers information systems (MIS); technology management (MBA). Evening/weekend programs available. *Degree requirements:* For master's, thesis (for some programs). *Entrance requirements:* For master's, minimum undergraduate GPA of 3.0, 3 years of work experience. Additional exam requirements/recommendations for international students: Required—TOEFL (minimum score 550 paper-based; 213 computer-based). Electronic applications accepted.

University of Phoenix–Jersey City Campus, College of Information Systems and Technology, Jersey City, NJ 07310. Offers information systems (MIS); technology management (MBA). Postbaccalaureate distance learning degree programs offered.

University of Phoenix–Las Vegas Campus, College of Information Systems and Technology, Las Vegas, NV 89128. Offers information systems (MIS); technology management (MBA). Evening/weekend programs available. *Degree requirements:* For master's, thesis (for some programs). *Entrance requirements:* For master's, minimum undergraduate GPA of 3.0, 3 years of work experience. Additional exam requirements/recommendations for international students: Required—TOEFL (minimum score 550 paper-based; 213 computer-based; 79 iBT). Electronic applications accepted.

University of Phoenix–Louisiana Campus, College of Information Systems and Technology, Metairie, LA 70001-2082. Offers information systems/management (MIS); technology management (MBA). Evening/weekend programs available. *Degree requirements:* For master's, thesis (for some programs). *Entrance requirements:* For master's, minimum undergraduate GPA of 3.0, 3 years work experience. Additional exam requirements/recommendations for international students: Required—TOEFL (minimum score 550 paper-based; 213 computer-based). Electronic applications accepted.

University of Phoenix–Madison Campus, College of Information Systems and Technology, Madison, WI 53718-2416. Offers information systems (MIS); management (MIS); technology management (MBA).

University of Phoenix–Memphis Campus, College of Information Systems and Technology, Cordova, TN 38018. Offers information systems (MIS); technology management (MBA).

University of Phoenix–Metro Detroit Campus, College of Information Systems and Technology, Troy, MI 48098-2623. Offers MIS. Evening/weekend programs available. *Degree requirements:* For master's, thesis (for some programs). *Entrance requirements:* For master's, minimum undergraduate GPA of 3.0, 3 years work experience. Additional exam requirements/recommendations for international students: Required—TOEFL (minimum score 550 paper-based; 213 computer-based; 79 iBT). Electronic applications accepted.

University of Phoenix–Milwaukee Campus, College of Information Systems and Technology, Milwaukee, WI 53045. Offers information systems (MIS); organziational leadership/information systems and technology (DM).

University of Phoenix–Nashville Campus, College of Information Systems and Technology, Nashville, TN 37214-5048. Offers technology management (MBA). Evening/weekend programs available. *Degree requirements:* For master's, thesis (for some programs). *Entrance requirements:* For master's, 3 years of work experience, minimum undergraduate GPA of 3.0. Additional exam requirements/recommendations for international students: Required—TOEFL (minimum score 550 paper-based; 213 computer-based; 79 iBT). Electronic applications accepted.

University of Phoenix–New Mexico Campus, College of Information Systems and Technology, Albuquerque, NM 87113-1570. Offers e-business (MBA); information systems (MS); technology management (MBA). Evening/weekend programs available. *Degree requirements:* For master's, thesis (for some programs). *Entrance requirements:* For master's, minimum undergraduate GPA of 3.0, 3 years of work experience. Additional exam requirements/recommendations for international students: Required—TOEFL (minimum score 550 paper-based; 213 computer-based; 79 iBT). Electronic applications accepted.

University of Phoenix–Northern Nevada Campus, College of Information Systems and Technology, Reno, NV 89521-5862. Offers information systems (MIS); technology management (MBA).

University of Phoenix–Northern Virginia Campus, College of Information Systems and Technology, Reston, VA 20190. Offers MIS. Evening/weekend programs available. Postbaccalaureate distance learning degree programs offered. *Entrance requirements:* For master's, 3 years working experience, minimum GPA of 2.5 from accredited university, citizen of the United States or valid visa. Additional exam requirements/recommendations for international students: Required—TOEFL (minimum score 79 iBT), TOEFL (minimum score 213 paper, 79 iBT), TOEIC, IELTS or Berlitz. Electronic applications accepted.

University of Phoenix–North Florida Campus, College of Information Systems and Technology, Jacksonville, FL 32216-0959. Offers information systems (MIS); management (MIS). Evening/weekend programs available. *Degree requirements:* For master's, thesis (for some programs). *Entrance requirements:* For master's, minimum undergraduate GPA of 3.0, 3 years work experience. Additional exam requirements/recommendations for international students: Required—TOEFL (minimum score 550 paper-based; 213 computer-based; 79 iBT). Electronic applications accepted.

University of Phoenix–Northwest Arkansas Campus, College of Information Systems and Technology, Rogers, AR 72756-9615. Offers information systems (MIS); technology management (MBA).

University of Phoenix–Oklahoma City Campus, College of Information Systems and Technology, Oklahoma City, OK 73116-8244. Offers e-business (MBA); technology management (MBA). Evening/weekend programs available. *Degree requirements:* For master's, thesis (for some programs). *Entrance requirements:* For master's, minimum undergraduate GPA of 3.0, 3 years of work experience. Additional exam requirements/recommendations for international students: Required—TOEFL (minimum score 550 paper-based; 213 computer-based; 79 iBT). Electronic applications accepted.

University of Phoenix–Omaha Campus, College of Information Systems and Technology, Omaha, NE 68154-5240. Offers information systems (MIS); technology management (MBA).

University of Phoenix–Online Campus, College of Information Systems and Technology, Phoenix, AZ 85034-7209. Offers information systems (MIS). Evening/weekend programs available. Postbaccalaureate distance learning degree programs offered. *Students:* 1,742 full-time (594 women); includes 604 minority (386 Black or African American, non-Hispanic/Latino; 13 American Indian or Alaska Native, non-Hispanic/Latino; 54 Asian, non-Hispanic/Latino; 113 Hispanic/Latino; 19 Native Hawaiian or other Pacific Islander, non-Hispanic/Latino; 19 Two or more races, non-Hispanic/Latino), 112 international. Average age 38. *Entrance requirements:* Additional exam requirements/recommendations for international students: Required—TOEFL, TOEIC (Test of English as an International Communication), Berlitz Online English Proficiency Exam, Pearson Test of English, or IELTS. *Application deadline:* Applications are processed on a rolling basis. Application fee: $45. Electronic applications accepted. *Expenses: Tuition:* Full-time $17,160. *Required fees:* $920. One-time fee: $45 full-time. Full-time tuition and fees vary according to course load, degree level, campus/location and program. *Financial support:* Scholarships/grants available. Financial award applicants required to submit FAFSA. *Unit head:* Dr. Blair Smith, Dean/Executive Director. *Application contact:* 866-766-0766. Web site: http://www.phoenix.edu/colleges_divisions/technology.html.

University of Phoenix–Oregon Campus, College of Information Systems and Technology, Tigard, OR 97223. Offers information systems (MIS); technology management (MBA). Evening/weekend programs available. *Degree requirements:* For master's, thesis (for some programs). *Entrance requirements:* For master's, minimum undergraduate GPA of 2.5, 3 years work experience. Additional exam requirements/recommendations for international students: Required—TOEFL (minimum score 550 paper-based; 213 computer-based; 79 iBT). Electronic applications accepted.

University of Phoenix–Philadelphia Campus, College of Information Systems and Technology, Wayne, PA 19087-2121. Offers information systems (MIS); technology management (MBA). Evening/weekend programs available. *Degree requirements:* For master's, thesis (for some programs). *Entrance requirements:* For master's, 3 years of work experience, minimum undergraduate GPA of 3.0. Additional exam requirements/recommendations for international students: Required—TOEFL (minimum score 550 paper-based; 213 computer-based; 79 iBT). Electronic applications accepted.

University of Phoenix–Pittsburgh Campus, College of Information Systems and Technology, Pittsburgh, PA 15276. Offers e-business (MBA); information systems (MIS); technology management (MBA). Evening/weekend programs available. *Degree requirements:* For master's, thesis (for some programs). *Entrance requirements:* For master's, minimum undergraduate GPA of 3.0, 3 years work experience. Additional exam requirements/recommendations for international students: Required—TOEFL (minimum score 550 paper-based; 213 computer-based; 79 iBT). Electronic applications accepted.

University of Phoenix–Raleigh Campus, College of Information Systems and Technology, Raleigh, NC 27606. Offers information systems and technology (MIS); management (MIS); technology management (MBA).

University of Phoenix–Richmond Campus, College of Information Systems and Technology, Richmond, VA 23230. Offers information systems (MIS); technology management (MBA). Evening/weekend programs available. *Degree requirements:* For master's, thesis (for some programs). *Entrance requirements:* For master's, minimum undergraduate GPA of 3.0, 3 years work experience. Additional exam requirements/recommendations for international students: Required—TOEFL (minimum score 500 paper-based; 213 computer-based; 79 iBT). Electronic applications accepted.

University of Phoenix–Sacramento Valley Campus, College of Information Systems and Technology, Sacramento, CA 95833-3632. Offers management (MIS); technology management (MBA). Evening/weekend programs available. *Degree requirements:* For master's, thesis (for some programs). *Entrance requirements:* For master's, minimum undergraduate GPA of 3.0, 3 years work experience. Additional exam requirements/recommendations for international students: Required—TOEFL (minimum score 550 paper-based; 213 computer-based; 79 iBT). Electronic applications accepted.

University of Phoenix–St. Louis Campus, College of Information Systems and Technology, St. Louis, MO 63043-4828. Offers information systems (MIS); technology management (MBA). Evening/weekend programs available. *Degree requirements:* For master's, thesis (for some programs). *Entrance requirements:* For master's, minimum undergraduate GPA of 3.0, 3 years of work experience. Additional exam requirements/recommendations for international students: Required—TOEFL (minimum score 550 paper-based; 213 computer-based). Electronic applications accepted.

University of Phoenix–San Antonio Campus, College of Information Systems and Technology, San Antonio, TX 78230. Offers information systems (MIS); technology management (MBA).

University of Phoenix–San Diego Campus, College of Information Systems and Technology, San Diego, CA 92123. Offers management (MIS); technology management (MBA). Evening/weekend programs available. *Degree requirements:* For master's, thesis (for some programs). *Entrance requirements:* For master's, minimum undergraduate GPA of 3.0, 3 years work experience. Additional exam requirements/

recommendations for international students: Required—TOEFL (minimum score 550 paper-based; 213 computer-based; 79 iBT). Electronic applications accepted.

University of Phoenix–Savannah Campus, College of Information Systems and Technology, Savannah, GA 31405-7400. Offers information systems and technology (MIS); technology management (MBA).

University of Phoenix–Southern Arizona Campus, College of Information Systems and Technology, Tucson, AZ 85711. Offers information systems (MIS); technology management (MBA). Evening/weekend programs available. *Degree requirements:* For master's, thesis (for some programs). *Entrance requirements:* For master's, minimum undergraduate GPA of 3.0, 3 years of work experience. Additional exam requirements/recommendations for international students: Required—TOEFL (minimum score 550 paper-based; 213 computer-based; 79 iBT). Electronic applications accepted.

University of Phoenix–Southern California Campus, College of Information Systems and Technology, Costa Mesa, CA 92626. Offers MIS. Evening/weekend programs available. Postbaccalaureate distance learning degree programs offered. *Entrance requirements:* Additional exam requirements/recommendations for international students: Required—TOEFL, TOEIC (Test of English as an International Communication), Berlitz Online English Proficiency Exam, Pearson Test of English, or IELTS. *Application deadline:* Applications are processed on a rolling basis. Application fee: $45. Electronic applications accepted. *Expenses:* Contact institution. *Financial support:* Scholarships/grants available. Financial award applicants required to submit FAFSA. *Unit head:* Blair Smith, Dean/Executive Director. *Application contact:* 866-766-0766. Web site: http://www.phoenix.edu/colleges_divisions/technology.html.

University of Phoenix–Southern Colorado Campus, College of Information Systems and Technology, Colorado Springs, CO 80919-2335. Offers technology management (MBA). Evening/weekend programs available. *Degree requirements:* For master's, thesis (for some programs). *Entrance requirements:* For master's, minimum undergraduate GPA of 3.0, 3 years of work experience. Additional exam requirements/recommendations for international students: Required—TOEFL (minimum score 550 paper-based; 213 computer-based; 79 iBT). Electronic applications accepted.

University of Phoenix–South Florida Campus, College of Information Systems and Technology, Fort Lauderdale, FL 33309. Offers management (MIS); technology management (MBA). Evening/weekend programs available. *Degree requirements:* For master's, thesis (for some programs). *Entrance requirements:* For master's, minimum undergraduate GPA of 3.0, 3 years of work experience. Additional exam requirements/recommendations for international students: Required—TOEFL (minimum score 550 paper-based; 213 computer-based; 79 iBT). Electronic applications accepted.

University of Phoenix–Springfield Campus, College of Information Systems and Technology, Springfield, MO 65804-7211. Offers information systems (MIS); technology management (MBA).

University of Phoenix–Tulsa Campus, College of Information Systems and Technology, Tulsa, OK 74134-1412. Offers information systems and technology (MIS); technology management (MBA).

University of Phoenix–Utah Campus, College of Information Systems and Technology, Salt Lake City, UT 84123-4617. Offers MIS. Evening/weekend programs available. *Degree requirements:* For master's, thesis (for some programs). *Entrance requirements:* For master's, minimum undergraduate GPA of 2.5, 3 years work experience. Additional exam requirements/recommendations for international students: Required—TOEFL (minimum score 550 paper-based; 213 computer-based; 79 iBT). Electronic applications accepted.

University of Phoenix–Vancouver Campus, John Sperling School of Business, College of Information Systems and Technology, Burnaby, BC V5C 6G9, Canada. Offers technology management (MBA). Evening/weekend programs available. *Degree requirements:* For master's, thesis (for some programs). *Entrance requirements:* For master's, minimum undergraduate GPA of 3.0, 3 years of work experience. Additional exam requirements/recommendations for international students: Required—TOEFL (minimum score 550 paper-based; 213 computer-based; 79 iBT). Electronic applications accepted.

University of Phoenix–Washington D.C. Campus, College of Information Systems and Technology, Washington, DC 20001. Offers information systems (MIS); organizational leadership/information systems and technology (DM).

University of Phoenix–West Florida Campus, College of Information Systems and Technology, Temple Terrace, FL 33637. Offers information systems (MIS); technology management (MBA). Evening/weekend programs available. *Degree requirements:* For master's, thesis (for some programs). *Entrance requirements:* For master's, minimum undergraduate GPA of 3.0, 3 years work experience. Additional exam requirements/recommendations for international students: Required—TOEFL (minimum score 550 paper-based; 213 computer-based; 79 iBT). Electronic applications accepted.

University of Pittsburgh, Katz Graduate School of Business, Doctoral Program in Business Administration, Pittsburgh, PA 15260. Offers accounting (PhD); finance (PhD); information systems (PhD); marketing (PhD); operations/decision sciences/artificial intelligence (PhD); organizational behavior and human resource management (PhD); strategic planning (PhD). *Accreditation:* AACSB. *Faculty:* 54 full-time (16 women). *Students:* 51 full-time (21 women); includes 9 minority (4 Black or African American, non-Hispanic/Latino; 4 Asian, non-Hispanic/Latino; 1 Hispanic/Latino), 23 international. 373 applicants, 7% accepted, 10 enrolled. In 2011, 6 doctorates awarded. *Degree requirements:* For doctorate, comprehensive exam, thesis/dissertation. *Entrance requirements:* For doctorate, GMAT or GRE. Additional exam requirements/recommendations for international students: Required—TOEFL. *Application deadline:* For fall admission, 2/1 priority date for domestic students, 2/1 for international students. Applications are processed on a rolling basis. Application fee: $50. Electronic applications accepted. *Expenses:* Tuition, state resident: full-time $18,774; part-time $760 per credit. Tuition, nonresident: full-time $30,736; part-time $1258 per credit. *Required fees:* $740; $200 per term. Tuition and fees vary according to program. *Financial support:* In 2011–12, 38 students received support, including 29 research assistantships with full tuition reimbursements available (averaging $19,400 per year), 10 teaching assistantships with full tuition reimbursements available (averaging $24,700 per year); fellowships, Federal Work-Study, scholarships/grants, health care benefits, and unspecified assistantships also available. Financial award application deadline: 2/1. *Faculty research:* Accounting statements and reporting, corporate finance, information systems processes, structures and decision-making, consumer behavior and marketing models. *Total annual research expenditures:* $254,031. *Unit head:* Dr. Dennis Galletta, Director, 412-648-1699, Fax: 412-624-3633, E-mail: galletta@katz.pitt.edu. *Application contact:* Carrie Woods, Assistant Director, 412-648-1525, Fax: 412-624-3633, E-mail: cawoods@katz.pitt.edu. Web site: http://www.business.pitt.edu/katz/phd/.

University of Pittsburgh, Katz Graduate School of Business, Master of Business Administration Programs, Pittsburgh , PA 15260. Offers finance (MBA); information systems (MBA); marketing (MBA); operations management (MBA); organizational behavior and human resource management (MBA); organizational leadership (Certificate); strategy, environment and organizations (MBA); technology, innovation and entrepreneurship (Certificate); MBA/JD; MBA/MIB; MBA/MPIA; MBA/MSE; MBA/MSIS; MID/MBA. *Accreditation:* AACSB. Part-time and evening/weekend programs available. *Faculty:* 62 full-time (17 women), 21 part-time/adjunct (4 women). *Students:* 179 full-time (63 women), 572 part-time (373 women); includes 69 minority (29 Black or African American, non-Hispanic/Latino; 24 Asian, non-Hispanic/Latino; 16 Hispanic/Latino), 83 international. Average age 29. 391 applicants, 42% accepted, 78 enrolled. *Degree requirements:* For master's, minimum GPA of 3.0. *Entrance requirements:* For master's, GMAT, recommendations, undergraduate transcripts, essay, resume, interview, bachelor's degree. Additional exam requirements/recommendations for international students: Required—TOEFL (minimum score 600 paper, 250 computer, 100 iBT) or IELTS. *Application deadline:* For fall admission, 4/1 priority date for domestic students, 2/1 for international students. Application fee: $50. Electronic applications accepted. *Expenses:* Tuition, state resident: full-time $18,774; part-time $760 per credit. Tuition, nonresident: full-time $30,736; part-time $1258 per credit. *Required fees:* $740; $200 per term. Tuition and fees vary according to program. *Financial support:* In 2011–12, 58 students received support. Career-related internships or fieldwork and scholarships/grants available. Financial award application deadline: 3/1; financial award applicants required to submit FAFSA. *Faculty research:* Accounting statements and reporting, corporate finance, information systems processes, structures and decision-making, consumer behavior and marketing models. *Unit head:* William T. Valenta, Assistant Dean/Director, 412-648-1610, Fax: 412-648-1659, E-mail: wtvalenta@katz.pitt.edu. *Application contact:* Thomas Keller, Director of MBA Admissions, 412-648-1700, Fax: 412-648-1659, E-mail: mba@katz.pitt.edu. Web site: http://www.business.pitt.edu/katz/mba/.

University of Pittsburgh, Katz Graduate School of Business, MBA/MS in Management of Information Systems Program, Pittsburgh, PA 15206. Offers MBA/MS. Part-time and evening/weekend programs available. *Faculty:* 62 full-time (17 women), 21 part-time/adjunct (4 women). *Students:* 6 full-time (0 women), 17 part-time (4 women); includes 4 minority (2 Black or African American, non-Hispanic/Latino; 2 Hispanic/Latino), 2 international. Average age 23. 16 applicants, 56% accepted, 5 enrolled. *Entrance requirements:* Additional exam requirements/recommendations for international students: Required—TOEFL (minimum score 600 paper-based; 250 computer-based; 100 iBT) or IELTS. *Application deadline:* For fall admission, 4/1 priority date for domestic students, 2/1 for international students. Application fee: $50. Electronic applications accepted. *Expenses:* Tuition, state resident: full-time $18,774; part-time $760 per credit. Tuition, nonresident: full-time $30,736; part-time $1258 per credit. *Required fees:* $740; $200 per term. Tuition and fees vary according to program. *Financial support:* In 2011–12, 3 students received support. Career-related internships or fieldwork and scholarships/grants available. Financial award application deadline: 3/1; financial award applicants required to submit FAFSA. *Faculty research:* Social media and their impacts on organizations, information technology adoption and diffusion, economics of information systems, software acquisition and implementation, human-computer interaction. *Unit head:* William T. Valenta, Assistant Dean/Director of MBA Programs, 412-648-1610, Fax: 412-648-1659, E-mail: wtvalenta@katz.pitt.edu. *Application contact:* Thomas Keller, Director, MBA Admissions, 412-648-1700, Fax: 412-648-1659, E-mail: mba@katz.pitt.edu. Web site: http://www.business.pitt.edu/katz/mba/academics/programs/mba-mis.php.

University of Redlands, School of Business, Redlands, CA 92373-0999. Offers business (MBA); information technology (MS); management (MA). Evening/weekend programs available. *Entrance requirements:* For master's, minimum GPA of 3.0, 2 letters of recommendation. *Faculty research:* Human resources management, educational leadership, humanities, teacher education.

University of St. Thomas, Graduate Studies, Graduate Programs in Software, Saint Paul, MN 55105. Offers advanced studies in software engineering (Certificate); business analysis (Certificate); computer security (Certificate); information systems (Certificate); software design and development (Certificate); software engineering (MS); software management (MS); software systems (MSS); MS/MBA. Part-time and evening/weekend programs available. *Faculty:* 5 full-time (0 women), 15 part-time/adjunct (1 woman). *Students:* 34 full-time (7 women), 314 part-time (79 women); includes 99 minority (48 Black or African American, non-Hispanic/Latino; 1 American Indian or Alaska Native, non-Hispanic/Latino; 45 Asian, non-Hispanic/Latino; 4 Hispanic/Latino; 1 Two or more races, non-Hispanic/Latino), 70 international. Average age 35. 155 applicants, 85% accepted, 79 enrolled. In 2011, 84 master's, 9 other advanced degrees awarded. *Degree requirements:* For master's, thesis optional. *Entrance requirements:* For master's, bachelor's degree earned in U.S. or equivalent international degree. Additional exam requirements/recommendations for international students: Required—TOEFL (minimum score 80 iBT). *Application deadline:* For fall admission, 8/1 priority date for domestic students, 5/1 for international students; for spring admission, 1/1 priority date for domestic students, 10/1 for international students. Applications are processed on a rolling basis. Application fee: $50. Electronic applications accepted. *Expenses:* Contact institution. *Financial support:* Federal Work-Study, institutionally sponsored loans, and scholarships/grants available. Financial award application deadline: 4/1. *Faculty research:* Data mining, distributed databases, computer security, big data. *Unit head:* Dr. Bhabani Misra, Director, 651-962-5508, Fax: 651-962-5543, E-mail: bsmisra@stthomas.edu. *Application contact:* Douglas J. Stubeda, Assistant Director, 651-962-5503, Fax: 651-962-5543, E-mail: djstubeda@stthomas.edu. Web site: http://www.stthomas.edu/gradsoftware/.

University of San Francisco, School of Management, Program in Information Systems, San Francisco, CA 94117-1080. Offers MS. Part-time and evening/weekend programs available. *Faculty:* 2 full-time (0 women), 5 part-time/adjunct (2 women). *Students:* 54 full-time (16 women); includes 28 minority (3 Black or African American, non-Hispanic/Latino; 15 Asian, non-Hispanic/Latino; 8 Hispanic/Latino; 1 Native Hawaiian or other Pacific Islander, non-Hispanic/Latino; 1 Two or more races, non-Hispanic/Latino), 6 international. Average age 38. 49 applicants, 57% accepted, 18 enrolled. In 2011, 17 master's awarded. *Degree requirements:* For master's, thesis. *Entrance requirements:* For master's, minimum GPA of 3.0. Application fee: $55 ($65 for international students). *Expenses: Tuition:* Full-time $20,070; part-time $1115 per unit. Tuition and fees vary according to course load, campus/location and program. *Financial support:* In 2011–12, 2 students received support. Application deadline: 3/2; applicants required to submit FAFSA. *Unit head:* Dr. Moira Gunn, Director, 415-422-2592. *Application contact:* Advising Office, 415-422-6000, E-mail: graduate@usfca.edu.

The University of Scranton, College of Graduate and Continuing Education, Program in Business Administration, Scranton, PA 18510. Offers accounting (MBA); finance (MBA); general business administration (MBA); health care management (MBA); international business (MBA); management information systems (MBA); marketing (MBA); operations management (MBA). *Accreditation:* AACSB. Part-time and evening/weekend programs available. Postbaccalaureate distance learning degree programs offered (no on-campus study). *Faculty:* 34 full-time (8 women). *Students:* 276 full-time (94 women), 243 part-time (88 women); includes 14 minority (10 Black or African American, non-Hispanic/Latino; 3 Asian, non-Hispanic/Latino; 1 Hispanic/Latino), 49 international. Average age 33. 358 applicants, 80% accepted. In 2011, 101 master's awarded. *Degree requirements:* For master's, capstone experience. *Entrance requirements:* For master's, GMAT, minimum GPA of 2.75. Additional exam requirements/recommendations for international students: Required—TOEFL (minimum score 500 paper-based; 173 computer-based), IELTS (minimum score 5.5). *Application deadline:* Applications are processed on a rolling basis. Application fee: $0. *Financial support:* In 2011–12, 12 students received support, including 12 teaching assistantships with full and partial tuition reimbursements available (averaging $8,433 per year); fellowships, career-related internships or fieldwork, Federal Work-Study, and unspecified assistantships also available. Support available to part-time students. Financial award application deadline: 3/1. *Faculty research:* Financial markets, strategic impact of total quality management, internal accounting controls, consumer preference, information systems and the Internet. *Unit head:* Dr. Murli Rajan, Director, 570-941-4043, Fax: 570-941-4342. *Application contact:* Joseph M. Roback, Director of Admissions, 570-941-4385, Fax: 570-941-5928, E-mail: robackj2@scranton.edu. Web site: http://www.academic.scranton.edu/department/mba/.

University of South Africa, College of Science, Engineering and Technology, Pretoria, South Africa. Offers chemical engineering (M Tech); information technology (M Tech).

University of South Alabama, Graduate School, School of Computer and Information Sciences, Mobile, AL 36688-0002. Offers computer science (MS); information systems (MS). Part-time and evening/weekend programs available. *Faculty:* 8 full-time (0 women). *Students:* 70 full-time (18 women), 16 part-time (4 women); includes 6 minority (4 Black or African American, non-Hispanic/Latino; 1 Asian, non-Hispanic/Latino; 1 Native Hawaiian or other Pacific Islander, non-Hispanic/Latino), 51 international. 103 applicants, 74% accepted, 20 enrolled. In 2011, 44 master's awarded. *Degree requirements:* For master's, thesis optional, project. *Entrance requirements:* For master's, GRE General Test. *Application deadline:* For fall admission, 7/15 priority date for domestic students, 6/15 for international students; for spring admission, 12/1 for domestic students, 11/1 for international students. Applications are processed on a rolling basis. Application fee: $35. *Expenses:* Tuition, state resident: full-time $7968; part-time $332 per credit hour. Tuition, nonresident: full-time $15,936; part-time $664 per credit hour. *Financial support:* Research assistantships, career-related internships or fieldwork, and institutionally sponsored loans available. Support available to part-time students. Financial award application deadline: 4/1. *Faculty research:* Numerical analysis, artificial intelligence, simulation, medical applications, software engineering. *Unit head:* Dr. Roy Daigle, Director of Graduate Studies, 251-460-6390. *Application contact:* Dr. B. Keith Harrison, Dean of the Graduate School, 251-460-6310, Fax: 251-461-1513, E-mail: kharriso@usouthal.edu. Web site: http://www.cis.usouthal.edu.

University of Southern Mississippi, Graduate School, College of Business, School of Accountancy and Information Systems, Hattiesburg, MS 39406-0001. Offers accountancy (MPA). *Accreditation:* AACSB. Part-time and evening/weekend programs available. *Faculty:* 7 full-time (4 women), 2 part-time/adjunct (both women). *Students:* 26 full-time (18 women), 6 part-time (5 women); includes 2 minority (1 Black or African American, non-Hispanic/Latino; 1 Hispanic/Latino). Average age 26. 23 applicants, 78% accepted, 16 enrolled. In 2011, 14 degrees awarded. *Degree requirements:* For master's, comprehensive exam. *Entrance requirements:* For master's, GMAT, minimum GPA of 2.75 on last 60 hours. Additional exam requirements/recommendations for international students: Required—TOEFL, IELTS. *Application deadline:* For fall admission, 7/15 priority date for domestic students, 7/15 for international students; for spring admission, 11/15 priority date for domestic students, 11/15 for international students. Applications are processed on a rolling basis. Application fee: $50. Electronic applications accepted. *Financial support:* In 2011–12, 7 research assistantships with full tuition reimbursements (averaging $7,200 per year) were awarded; Federal Work-Study, institutionally sponsored loans, scholarships/grants, health care benefits, and unspecified assistantships also available. Support available to part-time students. Financial award application deadline: 3/15; financial award applicants required to submit FAFSA. *Faculty research:* Bank liquidity, subchapter S corporations, internal auditing, governmental accounting, inflation accounting. *Unit head:* Dr. Skip Hughes, Director, 601-266-4322, Fax: 601-266-4639. *Application contact:* Dr. Michael Dugan, Director of Graduate Studies, 601-266-4641, Fax: 601-266-5814. Web site: http://www.usm.edu/graduateschool/table.php.

University of South Florida, Graduate School, College of Business, Department of Business Administration, Tampa, FL 33620-9951. Offers entrepreneurship (MBA); information systems (PhD); leadership and organizational effectiveness (MSM); management and organization (MBA); management information systems (MS); marketing (PhD). *Accreditation:* AACSB. Part-time and evening/weekend programs available. *Faculty:* 4 full-time (2 women), 1 part-time/adjunct (0 women). *Students:* 139 full-time (47 women), 156 part-time (55 women); includes 60 minority (11 Black or African American, non-Hispanic/Latino; 1 American Indian or Alaska Native, non-Hispanic/Latino; 22 Asian, non-Hispanic/Latino; 25 Hispanic/Latino; 1 Two or more races, non-Hispanic/Latino), 68 international. Average age 30. 300 applicants, 44% accepted, 92 enrolled. In 2011, 120 master's awarded. *Degree requirements:* For master's, comprehensive exam, thesis (for some programs); for doctorate, comprehensive exam, thesis/dissertation, 90 credit hours, minimum GPA of 3.0. *Entrance requirements:* For master's, GMAT (preferred) or GRE, minimum GPA of 3.0 in last 60 hours of course work, at least two letters of recommendation, statement of purpose, two years of significant professional work experience, resume; for doctorate, GMAT (preferred) or GRE, minimum GPA of 3.0 in last 60 hours of course work, at least two letters of recommendation, personal statement, interview. Additional exam requirements/recommendations for international students: Required—TOEFL (minimum score 550 paper-based; 213 computer-based; 79 iBT) or IELTS (minimum score 6.5). *Application deadline:* For fall admission, 6/1 for domestic students, 1/2 for international students; for spring admission, 10/15 for domestic students, 6/1 for international students. Application fee: $30. *Financial support:* Scholarships/grants, health care benefits, and unspecified assistantships available. Financial award applicants required to submit FAFSA. *Unit head:* Dr. Jacqueline Reck, Associate Dean, 813-974-6721, Fax: 813-974-4518, E-mail: jreck@usf.edu. *Application contact:* Irene Hurst, Assistant Director, Graduate Studies, 813-974-3335, Fax: 813-974-4518, E-mail: hurst@usf.edu. Web site: http://www.coba.usf.edu.

University of South Florida, Graduate School, College of Business, Information Systems and Decision Sciences Department, Tampa, FL 33620-9951. Offers business administration (PhD), including management information systems; management information systems (MS). Part-time programs available. *Faculty:* 14 full-time (2 women), 11 part-time/adjunct (2 women). *Students:* 55 full-time (18 women), 33 part-time (5 women); includes 16 minority (4 Black or African American, non-Hispanic/Latino; 1 American Indian or Alaska Native, non-Hispanic/Latino; 4 Asian, non-Hispanic/Latino; 7 Hispanic/Latino), 33 international. Average age 29. 130 applicants, 61% accepted, 29 enrolled. In 2011, 28 master's awarded. Terminal master's awarded for partial completion of doctoral program. *Degree requirements:* For master's, thesis or alternative, 33 credit hours, minimum GPA of 3.0; for doctorate, comprehensive exam, thesis/dissertation. *Entrance requirements:* For master's, GMAT or GRE, minimum GPA of 3.0 in last 60 hours, at least two letters of recommendation, statement of purpose, relevant work experience; for doctorate, GMAT or GRE, minimum GPA of 3.0 in last 60 hours, at least two letters of recommendation, statement of purpose, interview. Additional exam requirements/recommendations for international students: Required—TOEFL (minimum score 550 paper-based; 213 computer-based; 79 iBT) or IELTS (minimum score 6.5). *Application deadline:* For fall admission, 6/1 for domestic students, 1/2 for international students; for spring admission, 10/30 for domestic students, 6/1 for international students. Applications are processed on a rolling basis. Application fee: $30. Electronic applications accepted. *Financial support:* In 2011–12, 30 students received support, including 8 research assistantships with tuition reimbursements available (averaging $11,972 per year), 22 teaching assistantships with tuition reimbursements available (averaging $9,002 per year); scholarships/grants, health care benefits, and unspecified assistantships also available. Financial award applicants required to submit FAFSA. *Faculty research:* Business intelligence, software engineering, health informatics, information technology adoption, organizational impacts of IT. *Total annual research expenditures:* $108,606. *Unit head:* Dr. Kaushal Chari, Chair/Program Director, 813-974-5524, Fax: 813-974-6749, E-mail: kchari@usf.edu. *Application contact:* Judy Oates, Program Coordinator, 813-974-5524, Fax: 813-974-6749, E-mail: joates@usf.edu. Web site: http://business.usf.edu/faculty/isds/.

University of South Florida–Polytechnic, College of Technology and Innovation, Lakeland, FL 33803. Offers business administration (MBA); information technology (MSIT).

The University of Tampa, John H. Sykes College of Business, Tampa, FL 33606-1490. Offers accounting (MS); entrepreneurship (MBA); finance (MBA, MS); information systems management (MBA); innovation management (MBA); international business (MBA); marketing (MBA, MS); nonprofit management (MBA). *Accreditation:* AACSB. Part-time and evening/weekend programs available. *Faculty:* 38 full-time (14 women), 5 part-time/adjunct (1 woman). *Students:* 161 full-time (65 women), 193 part-time (82 women); includes 65 minority (11 Black or African American, non-Hispanic/Latino; 1 American Indian or Alaska Native, non-Hispanic/Latino; 8 Asian, non-Hispanic/Latino; 39 Hispanic/Latino; 2 Native Hawaiian or other Pacific Islander, non-Hispanic/Latino; 4 Two or more races, non-Hispanic/Latino), 58 international. Average age 29. 837 applicants, 41% accepted, 196 enrolled. In 2011, 259 degrees awarded. *Degree requirements:* For master's, capstone. *Entrance requirements:* For master's, GMAT or GRE, 4-year undergraduate degree, minimum GPA of 3.0, professional experience (for Executive MBA). Additional exam requirements/recommendations for international students: Required—TOEFL (minimum score 577 paper-based; 230 computer-based; 90 iBT); Recommended—IELTS (minimum score 7.5). *Application deadline:* Applications are processed on a rolling basis. Application fee: $40. Electronic applications accepted. *Expenses: Tuition:* Full-time $8320; part-time $520 per credit hour. *Required fees:* $40 per semester. Tuition and fees vary according to program. *Financial support:* In 2011–12, 124 students received support. Career-related internships or fieldwork, scholarships/grants, unspecified assistantships, and grants available. Financial award applicants required to submit FAFSA. *Faculty research:* Job market signaling, on-line shopping behaviors and social media, the Tampa Bay economy, digital literacy, entrepreneurship in small businesses. *Unit head:* Dennis Nostrand, Vice President, Enrollment/Admissions, 813-257-1808, E-mail: dnostrand@ut.edu. *Application contact:* Charlene Tobie, Associate Director of Admissions, 813-257-3566, E-mail: ctobie@ut.edu. Web site: http://ut.edu/graduate.

The University of Texas at Arlington, Graduate School, College of Business, Department of Information Systems and Operations Management, Arlington, TX 76019. Offers information systems (MS, PhD). Part-time and evening/weekend programs available. *Faculty:* 14 full-time (2 women). *Students:* 38 full-time (13 women), 26 part-time (5 women); includes 17 minority (6 Black or African American, non-Hispanic/Latino; 6 Asian, non-Hispanic/Latino; 4 Hispanic/Latino; 1 Two or more races, non-Hispanic/Latino), 17 international. 129 applicants, 57% accepted, 39 enrolled. In 2011, 15 master's, 1 doctorate awarded. *Degree requirements:* For master's, thesis optional; for doctorate, comprehensive exam, thesis/dissertation. *Entrance requirements:* For master's, GMAT, minimum GPA of 3.0; for doctorate, GMAT/GRE. Additional exam requirements/recommendations for international students: Required—TOEFL (minimum score 550 paper-based; 213 computer-based; 79 iBT). *Application deadline:* For fall admission, 6/1 for domestic students, 4/1 for international students; for spring admission, 10/15 for domestic students, 9/15 for international students. Applications are processed on a rolling basis. Application fee: $40 ($70 for international students). *Financial support:* In 2011–12, 7 students received support, including 15 teaching assistantships (averaging $15,693 per year); career-related internships or fieldwork, scholarships/grants, and unspecified assistantships also available. Support available to part-time students. Financial award application deadline: 6/1; financial award applicants required to submit FAFSA. *Faculty research:* Database modeling, strategic issues in information systems, simulations, production operations management. *Unit head:* Dr. R. C. Baker, Chair, 817-272-3502, Fax: 817-272-5801, E-mail: rcbaker@uta.edu. *Application contact:* Dr. Carolyn Davis, Graduate Advisor, 817-272-7399, Fax: 817-272-5801, E-mail: carolynd@exchange.uta.edu. Web site: http://wweb.uta.edu/insyopma.

The University of Texas at Arlington, Graduate School, College of Business, Program in Business Administration, Arlington, TX 76019. Offers accounting (PhD); business statistics (PhD); finance (MBA, PhD); information systems (MBA, PhD); management (MBA, PhD); marketing (MBA, PhD); operations management (MBA, PhD); real estate (MBA). *Accreditation:* AACSB. Part-time and evening/weekend programs available. *Students:* 505 full-time (189 women), 369 part-time (140 women); includes 199 minority (58 Black or African American, non-Hispanic/Latino; 2 American Indian or Alaska Native, non-Hispanic/Latino; 70 Asian, non-Hispanic/Latino; 56 Hispanic/Latino; 1 Native Hawaiian or other Pacific Islander, non-Hispanic/Latino; 12 Two or more races, non-Hispanic/Latino), 306 international. 416 applicants, 81% accepted, 234 enrolled. In 2011, 495 master's, 3 doctorates awarded. *Degree requirements:* For master's, thesis optional; for doctorate, comprehensive exam, thesis/dissertation. *Entrance requirements:* For master's, GMAT or GRE; for doctorate, GMAT, minimum GPA of 3.0 (undergraduate), 3.4 (graduate); 30 hours of graduate course work. Additional exam requirements/recommendations for international students: Required—TOEFL (minimum score 550 paper-based; 213 computer-based; 79 iBT). *Application deadline:* For fall admission, 6/1 for domestic students, 4/1 for international students; for spring admission, 10/15 for domestic students, 9/15 for international students. Applications are processed on a rolling basis. Application fee: $40 ($70 for international students). Electronic applications accepted. *Financial support:* Career-related internships or fieldwork, scholarships/grants, and unspecified assistantships available. Support available to part-time students. Financial award application deadline: 6/1; financial award applicants required to submit FAFSA. *Unit head:* Dr. Edmund Prater, Director of PhD Programs, 817-272-2131, Fax: 817-272-5799. *Application contact:* Melanie McGee, Director of MBA Program, 817-272-3005, Fax: 817-272-5799, E-mail: mwmcgee@uta.edu.

The University of Texas at Austin, Graduate School, McCombs School of Business, Department of Information, Risk, and Operations Management, Austin, TX 78712-1111. Offers information management (MBA); information systems (PhD); risk analysis and decision making (PhD); risk management (MBA); supply chain and operations management (MBA, PhD). *Degree requirements:* For doctorate, thesis/dissertation. *Entrance requirements:* For doctorate, GMAT or GRE. *Application deadline:* For fall admission, 1/2 for domestic students. Applications are processed on a rolling basis. Application fee: $50 ($75 for international students). Electronic applications accepted. *Financial support:* Fellowships with full and partial tuition reimbursements, research assistantships, and teaching assistantships with partial tuition reimbursements available. Financial award application deadline: 1/2. *Faculty research:* Stochastic processing and queuing, discrete nonlinear and large-scale optimization simulation, quality assurance logistics, distributed artificial intelligence, organizational modeling. *Unit head:* Dr. Prabhudev Konana, Chair, 512-471-5219, E-mail: prabhudev.konana@mccombs.utexas.edu. Web site: http://www.mccombs.utexas.edu/dept/irom/.

The University of Texas at Dallas, Naveen Jindal School of Management, Program in Information Systems and Operations Management, Richardson, TX 75080. Offers health care systems (MS); information technology consulting (MS). Part-time and evening/weekend programs available. *Faculty:* 14 full-time (0 women), 5 part-time/adjunct (1 woman). *Students:* 172 full-time (66 women), 117 part-time (38 women); includes 33 minority (6 Black or African American, non-Hispanic/Latino; 18 Asian, non-Hispanic/Latino; 7 Hispanic/Latino; 2 Two or more races, non-Hispanic/Latino), 220 international. Average age 27. 510 applicants, 63% accepted, 99 enrolled. In 2011, 128 master's awarded. *Degree requirements:* For master's, thesis optional. *Entrance requirements:* For master's, GMAT. Additional exam requirements/recommendations for international students: Required—TOEFL (minimum score 550 paper-based; 215 computer-based). *Application deadline:* For fall admission, 7/15 for domestic students, 5/1 for international students; for spring admission, 11/15 for domestic students, 9/1 for international students. Applications are processed on a rolling basis. Application fee: $50 ($100 for international students). Electronic applications accepted. *Expenses:* Tuition, state resident: full-time $11,170; part-time $620.56 per credit hour. Tuition, nonresident: full-time $20,212; part-time $1122.89 per credit hour. *Financial support:* In 2011–12, 97 students received support, including 1 research assistantship with partial tuition reimbursement available (averaging $14,832 per year), 7 teaching assistantships with partial tuition reimbursements available (averaging $10,050 per year); career-related internships or fieldwork, Federal Work-Study, institutionally sponsored loans, scholarships/grants, and unspecified assistantships also available. Support available to part-time students. Financial award application deadline: 4/30; financial award applicants required to submit FAFSA. *Faculty research:* Technology marketing, measuring information work productivity, electronic commerce, decision support systems, data quality. *Unit head:* Dr. Mark Thouin, Director, 972-883-4011, E-mail: mark.thouin@utdallas.edu. *Application contact:* James Parker, Assistant Director, 972-883-5842, E-mail: jparker@utdallas.edu. Web site: http://jindal.utdallas.edu/academic-areas/information-systems-and-operations-management/.

The University of Texas at Dallas, Naveen Jindal School of Management, Program in Management and Administrative Sciences, Richardson, TX 75080. Offers electronic commerce (MS); finance (MS); healthcare administration (MS); information systems (MS); innovation and entrepreneurship (MS); international management (MS); leadership in organizations (MS); marketing (MS); operations (MS); organizations (MS); real estate (MS); strategy (MS). *Accreditation:* AACSB. Part-time and evening/weekend programs available. *Faculty:* 26 full-time (6 women), 9 part-time/adjunct (2 women). *Students:* 128 full-time (69 women), 169 part-time (95 women); includes 76 minority (18 Black or African American, non-Hispanic/Latino; 1 American Indian or Alaska Native, non-Hispanic/Latino; 37 Asian, non-Hispanic/Latino; 15 Hispanic/Latino; 1 Native Hawaiian or other Pacific Islander, non-Hispanic/Latino; 4 Two or more races, non-Hispanic/Latino), 77 international. Average age 34. 220 applicants, 63% accepted, 68 enrolled. In 2011, 58 master's awarded. *Degree requirements:* For master's, thesis optional. *Entrance requirements:* For master's, GMAT. Additional exam requirements/recommendations for international students: Required—TOEFL (minimum score 550 paper-based; 215 computer-based). *Application deadline:* For fall admission, 7/15 for domestic students, 5/1 for international students; for spring admission, 11/15 for domestic students, 9/1 for international students. Applications are processed on a rolling basis. Application fee: $50 ($100 for international students). Electronic applications accepted. *Expenses:* Tuition, state resident: full-time $11,170; part-time $620.56 per credit hour. Tuition, nonresident: full-time $20,212; part-time $1122.89 per credit hour. *Financial support:* In 2011–12, 68 students received support, including 7 teaching assistantships with partial tuition reimbursements available (averaging $16,200 per year); research assistantships with partial tuition reimbursements available, career-related internships or fieldwork, Federal Work-Study, institutionally sponsored loans, scholarships/grants, and unspecified assistantships also available. Support available to part-time students. Financial award application deadline: 4/30; financial award applicants required to submit FAFSA. *Faculty research:* Integrated and detailed knowledge of functional areas of management, analytical tools for effective appraisal and decision-making. *Unit head:* Dr. Gregory Dess, Area Coordinator, 972-883-4439, E-mail: gdess@utdallas.edu. *Application contact:* James Parker, Assistant Director, 972-883-5842, E-mail: jparker@utdallas.edu. Web site: http://jindal.utdallas.edu/academic-areas/organizations-strategy-and-international-management/.

The University of Texas at Dallas, Naveen Jindal School of Management, Programs in Management Science, Richardson, TX 75080. Offers accounting (PhD); finance (PhD); information systems (PhD); marketing (PhD); operations management (PhD). *Accreditation:* AACSB. Part-time and evening/weekend programs available. *Faculty:* 14 full-time (4 women). *Students:* 75 full-time (30 women), 8 part-time (4 women); includes 5 minority (4 Asian, non-Hispanic/Latino; 1 Two or more races, non-Hispanic/Latino), 71 international. Average age 31. 224 applicants, 11% accepted, 20 enrolled. In 2011, 10 doctorates awarded. *Degree requirements:* For doctorate, thesis/dissertation. *Entrance requirements:* For doctorate, GMAT, minimum GPA of 3.0. Additional exam requirements/recommendations for international students: Required—TOEFL (minimum score 550 paper-based; 215 computer-based). *Application deadline:* For fall admission, 7/15 for domestic students, 5/1 for international students; for spring admission, 11/15 for domestic students, 9/1 for international students. Applications are processed on a rolling basis. Application fee: $50 ($100 for international students). Electronic applications accepted. *Expenses:* Tuition, state resident: full-time $11,170; part-time $620.56 per credit hour. Tuition, nonresident: full-time $20,212; part-time $1122.89 per credit hour. *Financial support:* In 2011–12, 76 students received support, including 3 research assistantships with partial tuition reimbursements available (averaging $21,600 per year), 68 teaching assistantships with partial tuition reimbursements available (averaging $16,162 per year); career-related internships or fieldwork, Federal Work-Study, institutionally sponsored loans, scholarships/grants, and unspecified assistantships also available. Support available to part-time students. Financial award application deadline: 4/30; financial award applicants required to submit FAFSA. *Faculty research:* Empirical generalizations in marketing, diffusion of generations of technology, stochastic brand-choice theory, acceptance of trade deals by supermarkets, nonparametric estimations of market share response. *Unit head:* Dr. Sumit Sarkar, Program Director, 972-883-2745, Fax: 972-883-5977, E-mail: som_phd.@utdallas.edu. *Application contact:* LeeAnne Sloane, Coordinator, 972-883-2745, Fax: 972-883-5977, E-mail: som_phd@utdallas.edu. Web site: http://jindal.utdallas.edu/academic-programs/phd-programs/management-science/.

The University of Texas at San Antonio, College of Business, General Business Program, San Antonio, TX 78249-0617. Offers business (MBA); business administration (PhD), including accounting, business administration, finance, information technology, management and organization studies, marketing; information systems (MBA); international business (MBA); management accounting (MBA); management of technology (MBA); marketing management (MBA); taxation (MBA). *Students:* 170 full-time (52 women), 120 part-time (49 women); includes 90 minority (14 Black or African American, non-Hispanic/Latino; 2 American Indian or Alaska Native, non-Hispanic/Latino; 15 Asian, non-Hispanic/Latino; 55 Hispanic/Latino; 1 Native Hawaiian or other Pacific Islander, non-Hispanic/Latino; 3 Two or more races, non-Hispanic/Latino), 37 international. Average age 32. 395 applicants, 45% accepted, 133 enrolled. In 2011, 95 master's, 8 doctorates awarded. *Entrance requirements:* Additional exam requirements/recommendations for international students: Required—TOEFL (minimum score 500 paper-based; 61 iBT), IELTS (minimum score 5). *Application deadline:* For fall admission, 7/1 for domestic students, 4/1 for international students; for spring admission, 11/1 for domestic students, 9/1 for international students. Application fee: $45 ($85 for international students). *Expenses:* Tuition, state resident: full-time $3148; part-time $2176 per semester. Tuition, nonresident: full-time $8782; part-time $5932 per semester. *Required fees:* $719 per semester. *Financial support:* In 2011–12, fellowships (averaging $22,000 per year), research assistantships (averaging $10,000 per year), teaching assistantships (averaging $10,000 per year) were awarded. *Unit head:* Dr. Lynda Y. de la Vinna, Dean, 210-458-4317, Fax: 210-458-4308, E-mail: lynda.delavina@utsa.edu. *Application contact:* Katherine Pope, Director of Graduate Student Services, 210-458-7316, Fax: 210-458-4398, E-mail: katherine.pope@utsa.edu. Web site: http://business.utsa.edu.

The University of Texas–Pan American, College of Engineering and Computer Science, Department of Computer Science, Edinburg, TX 78539. Offers computer science (MS); information technology (MS). Part-time and evening/weekend programs available. Postbaccalaureate distance learning degree programs offered (minimal on-campus study). *Degree requirements:* For master's, final written exam, project. *Entrance requirements:* For master's, GRE General Test, minimum GPA of 3.0 in last 60 hours. Additional exam requirements/recommendations for international students: Required—TOEFL. *Application deadline:* For fall admission, 7/1 priority date for domestic students; for spring admission, 11/1 priority date for domestic students. Applications are processed on a rolling basis. Application fee: $0. Tuition and fees vary according to course load, program and student level. *Financial support:* Research assistantships, teaching assistantships, career-related internships or fieldwork, Federal Work-Study, and scholarships/grants available. Support available to part-time students. Financial award applicants required to submit FAFSA. *Faculty research:* Artificial intelligence, distributed systems, Internet computing, theoretical computer sciences, information visualization. *Unit head:* Dr. Zhixiang Chen, Chair, 956-665-3520, E-mail: zchen@utpa.edu. *Application contact:* Dr. Richard Fowler, Graduate Coordinator, 956-665-3453, E-mail: fowler@utpa.edu. Web site: http://www.cs.panam.edu/.

University of the Sacred Heart, Graduate Programs, Department of Business Administration, Program in Information Systems Management, San Juan, PR 00914-0383. Offers MBA. Part-time and evening/weekend programs available. *Degree requirements:* For master's, thesis. *Entrance requirements:* For master's, EXADEP, minimum undergraduate GPA of 2.75, interview.

University of the West, Department of Business Administration, Rosemead, CA 91770. Offers business administration (EMBA); finance (MBA); information technology and management (MBA); international business (MBA); nonprofit organization management (MBA). Part-time and evening/weekend programs available. *Entrance requirements:* Additional exam requirements/recommendations for international students: Required—TOEFL.

The University of Toledo, College of Graduate Studies, College of Business and Innovation, Department of Information Operations and Technology Management, Toledo, OH 43606-3390. Offers information systems (MBA); manufacturing management (PhD); operations management (MBA); supply chain management (Certificate). Part-time and evening/weekend programs available. *Faculty:* 11. *Students:* 16 full-time (5 women), 36 part-time (9 women); includes 7 minority (5 Black or African American, non-Hispanic/Latino; 1 Asian, non-Hispanic/Latino; 1 Hispanic/Latino), 20 international. Average age 33. 41 applicants, 51% accepted, 10 enrolled. In 2011, 15 master's, 5 doctorates awarded. *Degree requirements:* For doctorate, thesis/dissertation. *Entrance requirements:* For master's, doctorate, and Certificate, GMAT, minimum GPA of 2.7 for all prior academic work, three letters of recommendation, statement of purpose, transcripts from all prior institutions attended. Additional exam requirements/recommendations for international students: Required—TOEFL (minimum score 550 paper-based; 213 computer-based; 80 iBT), IELTS (minimum score 6.5). *Application deadline:* For fall admission, 1/15 priority date for domestic students, 1/15 for international students. Applications are processed on a rolling basis. Application fee: $45 ($75 for international students). Electronic applications accepted. *Financial support:* In 2011–12, 23 research assistantships with full and partial tuition reimbursements (averaging $9,500 per year) were awarded; career-related internships or fieldwork, Federal Work-Study, institutionally sponsored loans, scholarships/grants, tuition waivers (full and partial), unspecified assistantships, and administrative assistantships also available. Support available to part-time students. *Unit head:* Dr. T. S. Ragu-Nathan, Chair, 419-530-2420. *Application contact:* Graduate School Office, 419-530-4723, Fax: 419-530-4724, E-mail: grdsch@utnet.utoledo.edu. Web site: http://www.utoledo.edu/business/index.html.

University of Tulsa, Graduate School, Collins College of Business, Master of Business Administration Program, Tulsa, OK 74104-3189. Offers accounting (MBA); business administration (MBA); energy management (MBA); finance (MBA); international business (MBA); management information systems (MBA); taxation (MBA); JD/MBA; MBA/MSCS; MBA/MSF. *Accreditation:* AACSB. Part-time and evening/weekend programs available. *Faculty:* 32 full-time (6 women). *Students:* 56 full-time (29 women), 28 part-time (7 women); includes 7 minority (1 Black or African American, non-Hispanic/Latino; 2 American Indian or Alaska Native, non-Hispanic/Latino; 2 Asian, non-Hispanic/Latino; 2 Hispanic/Latino), 16 international. Average age 26. 70 applicants, 67% accepted, 29 enrolled. In 2011, 35 master's awarded. *Entrance requirements:* For master's, GMAT. Additional exam requirements/recommendations for international students: Required—TOEFL (minimum score 577 paper-based; 233 computer-based; 91 iBT), IELTS (minimum score 6.5). *Application deadline:* Applications are processed on a rolling basis. Application fee: $40. Electronic applications accepted. *Expenses: Tuition:* Full-time $17,748; part-time $986 per hour. *Required fees:* $5 per contact hour. $75 per semester. Tuition and fees vary according to program. *Financial support:* In 2011–12, 30 students received support, including 30 teaching assistantships (averaging $11,044 per year); fellowships, research assistantships, career-related internships or fieldwork, institutionally sponsored loans, scholarships/grants, health care benefits, tuition waivers (full and partial), and unspecified assistantships also available. Support available to part-time students. Financial award application deadline: 2/1; financial award applicants required to submit FAFSA. *Faculty research:* Accounting, energy management, finance, international business, management information systems, taxation. *Unit head:* Dr. Linda Nichols, Associate Dean of the Collins College of Business, 918-631-2242, Fax: 918-631-2142, E-mail: linda-nichols@utulsa.edu. *Application contact:* Information Contact, 918-631-2242, E-mail: graduate-business@utulsa.edu. Web site: http://www.cba.utulsa.edu/.

University of Utah, Graduate School, David Eccles School of Business, Department of Operations and Information Systems, Salt Lake City, UT 84112-1107. Offers information systems (MS). *Faculty:* 14 full-time (2 women). *Students:* 37 full-time (8 women), 25 part-time (3 women); includes 8 minority (4 Asian, non-Hispanic/Latino; 2 Hispanic/

Latino; 2 Two or more races, non-Hispanic/Latino), 5 international. Average age 29. 67 applicants, 52% accepted, 32 enrolled. In 2011, 37 degrees awarded. *Entrance requirements:* For master's, GMAT/GRE, minimum undergraduate GPA of 3.0. Additional exam requirements/recommendations for international students: Required—TOEFL (minimum score 600 paper-based; 250 computer-based; 100 iBT), IELTS (minimum score 7). *Application deadline:* For fall admission, 3/1 priority date for domestic students, 3/1 for international students. Applications are processed on a rolling basis. Application fee: $55 ($65 for international students). Electronic applications accepted. *Financial support:* In 2011–12, 4 students received support. Graduate assistantships available. Financial award application deadline: 3/1; financial award applicants required to submit FAFSA. *Faculty research:* Data management, IT security, economics of information systems, Web and data mining, applications and management of IT in healthcare. *Total annual research expenditures:* $115,012. *Unit head:* Dr. Olivia Sheng, Head, 801-585-9071, E-mail: actos@business.utah.edu. *Application contact:* Andrea Chmelik, Academic Coordinator, 801-585-1719, Fax: 801-581-3666, E-mail: andrea.chmelik@business.utah.edu. Web site: http://www.business.utah.edu/infosystems/.

University of Virginia, McIntire School of Commerce, Program in Management of Information Technology, Charlottesville, VA 22903. Offers MS. *Students:* 1 (woman) full-time, 70 part-time (17 women); includes 20 minority (2 Black or African American, non-Hispanic/Latino; 15 Asian, non-Hispanic/Latino; 2 Hispanic/Latino; 1 Two or more races, non-Hispanic/Latino), 3 international. Average age 38. In 2011, 68 master's awarded. *Entrance requirements:* For master's, GMAT, 2 recommendations. Additional exam requirements/recommendations for international students: Required—TOEFL (minimum score 620 paper-based; 270 computer-based). *Application deadline:* For fall admission, 9/15 priority date for domestic students, 1/15 for international students. Applications are processed on a rolling basis. Application fee: $75. Electronic applications accepted. *Expenses:* Contact institution. *Financial support:* Fellowships and Federal Work-Study available. Financial award application deadline: 2/15; financial award applicants required to submit FAFSA. *Unit head:* Stefano Grazioli, Director, 434-982-2973, E-mail: grazioli@virginia.edu. *Application contact:* Emma Candalier, Associate Director of Graduate Recruiting, 434-243-4992, Fax: 434-924-4511, E-mail: ecandalier@virginia.edu.

University of Wisconsin–Madison, Graduate School, Wisconsin School of Business, Doctoral Program in Accounting and Information Systems, Madison, WI 53706-1380. Offers PhD. *Accreditation:* AACSB. *Faculty:* 10 full-time (3 women), 5 part-time/adjunct (2 women). *Students:* 12 full-time (8 women); includes 1 minority (American Indian or Alaska Native, non-Hispanic/Latino), 2 international. Average age 29. 64 applicants, 8% accepted, 3 enrolled. In 2011, 2 doctorates awarded. *Degree requirements:* For doctorate, comprehensive exam, thesis/dissertation. *Entrance requirements:* For doctorate, GMAT or GRE. Additional exam requirements/recommendations for international students: Required—Pearson Test of English (minimum score 73; written 80); Recommended—TOEFL (minimum score 623 paper-based; 263 computer-based; 106 iBT), IELTS (minimum score 7.5). *Application deadline:* For fall admission, 12/15 priority date for domestic students, 12/15 for international students. Application fee: $56. Electronic applications accepted. *Expenses:* Contact institution. *Financial support:* In 2011–12, 12 students received support, including 1 fellowship with full tuition reimbursement available (averaging $18,756 per year), research assistantships with full tuition reimbursements available (averaging $16,506 per year), 11 teaching assistantships with full tuition reimbursements available (averaging $14,088 per year); Federal Work-Study, institutionally sponsored loans, scholarships/grants, health care benefits, and unspecified assistantships also available. Financial award application deadline: 2/1. *Faculty research:* Auditing, financial reporting, economic theory, strategy, computer models. *Unit head:* Prof. Jon Davis, Chair, 608-263-4264. *Application contact:* Belle Heberling, Assistant Director for Research Programs, 608-262-3749, Fax: 608-890-0180, E-mail: phd@bus.wisc.edu. Web site: http://www.bus.wisc.edu/phd.

University of Wisconsin–Madison, Graduate School, Wisconsin School of Business, Doctoral Program in Operations and Information Management, Madison, WI 53706-1380. Offers information systems (PhD); operations management (PhD). *Faculty:* 8 full-time (0 women), 4 part-time/adjunct (0 women). *Students:* 3 full-time (0 women), 2 international. Average age 38. 33 applicants, 3% accepted, 1 enrolled. *Degree requirements:* For doctorate, comprehensive exam, thesis/dissertation. *Entrance requirements:* For doctorate, GMAT or GRE General Test. Additional exam requirements/recommendations for international students: Required—Pearson Test of English (minimum score 73; written 80); Recommended—TOEFL (minimum score 623 paper-based; 263 computer-based; 106 iBT), IELTS (minimum score 7.5). *Application deadline:* For fall admission, 12/15 priority date for domestic students, 12/15 for international students. Application fee: $56. Electronic applications accepted. *Expenses:* Tuition, state resident: full-time $10,296; part-time $643.51 per credit. Tuition, nonresident: full-time $24,054; part-time $1503.40 per credit. *Required fees:* $70.06 per credit. Tuition and fees vary according to course load, campus/location, program and reciprocity agreements. *Financial support:* In 2011–12, 3 students received support, including 3 fellowships with full tuition reimbursements available (averaging $18,756 per year), research assistantships with full tuition reimbursements available (averaging $16,506 per year), teaching assistantships with full tuition reimbursements available (averaging $14,088 per year); Federal Work-Study, institutionally sponsored loans, scholarships/grants, health care benefits, and unspecified assistantships also available. Financial award application deadline: 2/1; financial award applicants required to submit FAFSA. *Faculty research:* Supply-chain management, reorganization of the factory, creating continuous innovation, transportation economics, organizational economics. *Unit head:* Prof. James G. Morris, Chair, 608-262-1284, E-mail: jmorris@bus.wisc.edu. *Application contact:* Belle Heberling, Assistant Director for Research Programs, 608-262-3749, Fax: 608-890-0180, E-mail: phd@bus.wisc.edu. Web site: http://bus.wisc.edu/phd.

Utah State University, School of Graduate Studies, College of Business, Department of Business Information Systems, Logan, UT 84322. Offers business education (MS); business information systems (MS); business information systems and education (Ed D); education (PhD). Part-time programs available. Terminal master's awarded for partial completion of doctoral program. *Degree requirements:* For master's, thesis optional; for doctorate, thesis/dissertation. *Entrance requirements:* For master's, GMAT, minimum GPA of 3.2; for doctorate, GRE General Test, minimum GPA of 3.0. Additional exam requirements/recommendations for international students: Required—TOEFL. *Faculty research:* Oral and written communication, methods of teaching, CASE tools, object-oriented programming, decision support systems.

Valparaiso University, Graduate School, Program in Information Technology and Management, Valparaiso, IN 46383. Offers MS. Part-time and evening/weekend programs available. *Students:* 18 full-time (4 women), 17 part-time (5 women), 26 international. Average age 28. In 2011, 21 master's awarded. *Entrance requirements:* For master's, minimum GPA of 3.0; minor or equivalent in computer science, information technology, or a related field. Additional exam requirements/recommendations for international students: Required—TOEFL (minimum score 550 paper-based; 213 computer-based; 80 iBT). *Application deadline:* Applications are processed on a rolling basis. Application fee: $30 ($50 for international students). Electronic applications accepted. *Expenses: Tuition:* Part-time $560 per credit hour. Tuition and fees vary according to course load and program. *Financial support:* Available to part-time students. Applicants required to submit FAFSA. *Unit head:* Dr. David L. Rowland, Dean, Graduate School and Continuing Education/Associate Provost, 219-464-5313, Fax: 219-464-5381, E-mail: david.rowland@valpo.edu. *Application contact:* Dustin Jesch, Coordinator, U.S. Student Engagement, 219-464-5313, Fax: 219-464-5381, E-mail: dustin.jesch@valpo.edu. Web site: http://valpo.edu/grad/it/.

Villanova University, Villanova School of Business, MBA - The Fast Track Program, Villanova, PA 19085. Offers finance (MBA); health care management (MBA); international business (MBA); management information systems (MBA); marketing (MBA); real estate (MBA); strategic management (MBA). *Accreditation:* AACSB. Part-time and evening/weekend programs available. *Faculty:* 101 full-time (32 women), 38 part-time/adjunct (8 women). *Students:* 123 part-time (46 women); includes 14 minority (1 Black or African American, non-Hispanic/Latino; 3 American Indian or Alaska Native, non-Hispanic/Latino; 5 Asian, non-Hispanic/Latino; 1 Hispanic/Latino; 4 Two or more races, non-Hispanic/Latino). Average age 29. In 2011, 53 master's awarded. *Degree requirements:* For master's, minimum GPA of 3.0. *Entrance requirements:* For master's, GMAT, work experience. Additional exam requirements/recommendations for international students: Required—TOEFL (minimum score 550 paper-based; 213 computer-based; 80 iBT). *Application deadline:* For fall admission, 6/30 for domestic and international students. Application fee: $50. Electronic applications accepted. *Expenses: Tuition:* Part-time $675 per credit. Part-time tuition and fees vary according to degree level and program. *Financial support:* Scholarships/grants available. Financial award application deadline: 6/30; financial award applicants required to submit FAFSA. *Faculty research:* Business analytics; creativity, innovation and entrepreneurship; global leadership; marketing and public policy; real estate; church management. *Unit head:* Kristy Irwin, Director of Recruitment and Marketing, 610-519-6288, Fax: 610-519-6273, E-mail: kristy.irwin@villanova.edu. *Application contact:* Meredith L. Lockyer, Assistant Director, 610-519-7016, Fax: 610-519-6273, E-mail: meredith.lockyer@villanova.edu. Web site: http://www.mba.villanova.edu.

Villanova University, Villanova School of Business, MBA - The Flex Track Program, Villanova, PA 19085. Offers finance (MBA); health care management (MBA); international business (MBA); management information systems (MBA); marketing (MBA); real estate (MBA); strategic management (MBA); JD/MBA. *Accreditation:* AACSB. Part-time and evening/weekend programs available. Postbaccalaureate distance learning degree programs offered (minimal on-campus study). *Faculty:* 101 full-time (32 women), 38 part-time/adjunct (8 women). *Students:* 18 full-time (9 women), 412 part-time (127 women); includes 45 minority (7 Black or African American, non-Hispanic/Latino; 1 American Indian or Alaska Native, non-Hispanic/Latino; 25 Asian, non-Hispanic/Latino; 4 Hispanic/Latino; 1 Native Hawaiian or other Pacific Islander, non-Hispanic/Latino; 7 Two or more races, non-Hispanic/Latino). Average age 30. In 2011, 150 master's awarded. *Degree requirements:* For master's, minimum GPA of 3.0. *Entrance requirements:* For master's, GMAT, work experience. Additional exam requirements/recommendations for international students: Required—TOEFL (minimum score 550 paper-based; 213 computer-based; 80 iBT). *Application deadline:* For fall admission, 6/30 for domestic and international students; for winter admission, 11/15 for domestic and international students; for spring admission, 3/30 for domestic students, 3/31 for international students. Applications are processed on a rolling basis. Application fee: $50. Electronic applications accepted. *Expenses: Tuition:* Part-time $675 per credit. Part-time tuition and fees vary according to degree level and program. *Financial support:* In 2011–12, 18 research assistantships with full tuition reimbursements (averaging $13,100 per year) were awarded; scholarships/grants and unspecified assistantships also available. Financial award application deadline: 6/30; financial award applicants required to submit FAFSA. *Faculty research:* Business analytics; creativity, innovation and entrepreneurship; global leadership; marketing and public policy; real estate; church management. *Unit head:* Kristy Irwin, Director of Recruitment and Marketing, 610-610-6288, Fax: 610-519-6273, E-mail: kristy.irwin@villanova.edu. *Application contact:* Meredity L. Lockyer, Assistant Director, 610-519-7016, Fax: 610-519-6273, E-mail: meredith.lockyer@villanova.edu. Web site: http://www.mba.villanova.edu.

Virginia Commonwealth University, Graduate School, School of Business, Program in Information Systems, Richmond, VA 23284-9005. Offers MS, PhD. *Faculty:* 13 full-time (3 women). *Students:* 27 full-time (5 women), 18 part-time (4 women); includes 16 minority (11 Black or African American, non-Hispanic/Latino; 5 Asian, non-Hispanic/Latino), 3 international. 27 applicants, 44% accepted, 7 enrolled. In 2011, 31 master's awarded. *Degree requirements:* For doctorate, thesis/dissertation. *Entrance requirements:* For master's, GMAT. Additional exam requirements/recommendations for international students: Required—TOEFL (minimum score 600 paper-based; 250 computer-based; 100 iBT); Recommended—IELTS (minimum score 6.5). *Application deadline:* For fall admission, 7/1 for domestic students; for spring admission, 11/1 for domestic students. Applications are processed on a rolling basis. Application fee: $50. Electronic applications accepted. *Expenses:* Tuition, state resident: full-time $9133; part-time $507 per credit. Tuition, nonresident: full-time $18,777; part-time $1043 per credit. *Required fees:* $77 per credit. Tuition and fees vary according to degree level, campus/location, program and student level. *Financial support:* Fellowships, research assistantships, teaching assistantships, Federal Work-Study, institutionally sponsored loans, and tuition waivers (full and partial) available. Financial award application deadline: 3/15; financial award applicants required to submit FAFSA. *Unit head:* Dr. Richard Redmond, Chair, 804-828-1737, Fax: 804-828-3199, E-mail: rtredmon@vcu.edu. *Application contact:* Jana P. McQuaid, Assistant Dean, Master's Programs, 804-828-4622, Fax: 804-828-7174, E-mail: jpmcquaid@vcu.edu. Web site: http://www.business.vcu.edu/graduate.html.

Virginia International University, School of Computer Information Systems, Fairfax, VA 22030. Offers computer science (MS); information systems (MS). Part-time programs available. *Entrance requirements:* For master's, bachelor's degree. Additional exam requirements/recommendations for international students: Required—TOEFL (minimum score 550 paper-based; 213 computer-based; 80 iBT), IELTS. Electronic applications accepted.

Virginia Polytechnic Institute and State University, Graduate School, Intercollege, Program in Information Technology, Blacksburg, VA 24061. Offers MIT. *Degree requirements:* For master's, comprehensive exam (for some programs), thesis (for some programs). *Entrance requirements:* For master's, GRE. Additional exam requirements/recommendations for international students: Required—TOEFL (minimum score 550 paper-based; 213 computer-based). *Application deadline:* For fall admission, 7/1 for domestic and international students; for spring admission, 12/1 for domestic and international students. Applications are processed on a rolling basis. Application fee: $65. Electronic applications accepted. *Expenses:* Tuition, state resident: full-time $10,048; part-time $558.25 per credit hour. Tuition, nonresident: full-time $19,497; part-time $1083.25 per credit hour. *Required fees:* $405 per semester. Tuition and fees vary according to course load, campus/location and program. *Financial support:* Career-related internships or fieldwork, Federal Work-Study, scholarships/grants, health care benefits, and unspecified assistantships available. Financial award application deadline: 1/15. *Unit head:* Dr. Thomas T. Sheehan, Unit Head, 703-538-8361, Fax: 703-538-8415, E-mail: thsheeha@vt.edu. *Application contact:* Cindy Rubens, Information Contact, 703-

818-8464, Fax: 703-538-8415, E-mail: crubens@vt.edu. Web site: http://www.vtmit.vt.edu/index.php.

Virginia Polytechnic Institute and State University, Graduate School, Pamplin College of Business, Department of Business Information Technology, Blacksburg, VA 24061. Offers PhD. *Degree requirements:* For doctorate, comprehensive exam (for some programs), thesis/dissertation (for some programs). *Entrance requirements:* For doctorate, GRE. Additional exam requirements/recommendations for international students: Required—TOEFL (minimum score 550 paper-based; 213 computer-based). *Application deadline:* For fall admission, 7/1 for domestic and international students; for spring admission, 12/1 for domestic students, 11/1 for international students. Applications are processed on a rolling basis. Application fee: $65. Electronic applications accepted. *Expenses:* Tuition, state resident: full-time $10,048; part-time $558.25 per credit hour. Tuition, nonresident: full-time $19,497; part-time $1083.25 per credit hour. *Required fees:* $405 per semester. Tuition and fees vary according to course load, campus/location and program. *Financial support:* Research assistantships with full tuition reimbursements, teaching assistantships with full tuition reimbursements, career-related internships or fieldwork, Federal Work-Study, scholarships/grants, health care benefits, and unspecified assistantships available. Financial award application deadline: 1/15. *Faculty research:* Mathematical programming, computer simulation, decision support systems, production/operations research, information technology. *Unit head:* Dr. Bernard W. Taylor, III, Unit Head, 540-231-6596, Fax: 540-231-7916, E-mail: betaylo3@vt.edu. *Application contact:* Cliff Ragsdale, Information Contact, 540-231-4697, Fax: 540-231-7916, E-mail: cliff.ragsdale@vt.edu. Web site: http://www.bit.vt.edu/.

Virginia Polytechnic Institute and State University, VT Online, Blacksburg, VA 24061. Offers advanced transportation systems (Certificate); aerospace engineering (MS); agricultural and life sciences (MSLFS); business information systems (Graduate Certificate); career and technical education (MS); civil engineering (MS); computer engineering (M Eng, MS); decision support systems (Graduate Certificate); eLearning leadership (MA); electrical engineering (M Eng, MS); engineering administration (MEA); environmental engineering (Certificate); environmental politics and policy (Graduate Certificate); environmental sciences and engineering (MS); foundations of political analysis (Graduate Certificate); health product risk management (Graduate Certificate); industrial and systems engineering (MS); information policy and society (Graduate Certificate); information security (Graduate Certificate); information technology (MIT); instructional technology (MA); integrative STEM education (MA Ed); liberal arts (Graduate Certificate); life sciences: health product risk management (MS); natural resources (MNR, Graduate Certificate); networking (Graduate Certificate); nonprofit and nongovernmental organization management (Graduate Certificate); ocean engineering (MS); political science (MA); security studies (Graduate Certificate); software development (Graduate Certificate). *Expenses:* Tuition, state resident: full-time $10,048; part-time $558.25 per credit hour. Tuition, nonresident: full-time $19,497; part-time $1083.25 per credit hour. *Required fees:* $405 per semester. Tuition and fees vary according to course load, campus/location and program. *Application contact:* Graduate School Applications General Assistance, 540-231-8636, Fax: 540-231-2039, E-mail: gradappl@vt.edu. Web site: http://www.vto.vt.edu/.

Walden University, Graduate Programs, School of Information Systems and Technology, Minneapolis, MN 55401. Offers information systems (MS, Certificate); information systems management (MISM); information technology (MS). Part-time and evening/weekend programs available. Postbaccalaureate distance learning degree programs offered (minimal on-campus study). *Faculty:* 3 full-time (1 woman), 30 part-time/adjunct (10 women). *Students:* 175 full-time (71 women), 176 part-time (73 women); includes 163 minority (122 Black or African American, non-Hispanic/Latino; 5 American Indian or Alaska Native, non-Hispanic/Latino; 13 Asian, non-Hispanic/Latino; 14 Hispanic/Latino; 1 Native Hawaiian or other Pacific Islander, non-Hispanic/Latino; 8 Two or more races, non-Hispanic/Latino), 37 international. Average age 37. In 2011, 83 master's awarded. *Entrance requirements:* For master's, bachelor's degree or equivalent in related field; minimum GPA of 2.5; official transcripts; goal statement; access to computer and Internet. Additional exam requirements/recommendations for international students: Required—TOEFL (minimum score 550 paper-based; 213 computer-based), IELTS (minimum score 6.5). *Financial support:* Federal Work-Study, scholarships/grants, unspecified assistantships, and family tuition reduction, active duty/veteran tuition reduction, group tuition reduction, interest-free payment plans, employee tuition reduction available. Support available to part-time students. Financial award applicants required to submit FAFSA. *Unit head:* Colin Wightman, Interim Associate Dean, 866-492-5336. *Application contact:* Jennifer Hall, Vice President of Enrollment Management, 866-4-WALDEN, E-mail: info@walden.edu.

Walden University, Graduate Programs, School of Management, Minneapolis, MN 55401. Offers accounting (MS, DBA), including accounting for the professional (MS), CPA (MS), self-designed (MS); accounting and management (MS), including accounting for strategic managers, self-designed; accounting for managers (MBA); advanced project management (Post-Graduate Certificate); applied project management (Post-Graduate Certificate); corporate finance (MBA); entrepreneurship (MBA, DBA); finance (DBA); global management (MS); global supply chain management (DBA); healthcare management (MBA, DBA); healthcare system improvement (MBA); human resource management (MBA, MS, PhD), including functional human resource management (MS), integrating functional and strategic human resource management (MS), organizational strategy (MS); information systems management (DBA); international business (MBA, DBA); leadership (MBA, MS, DBA), including entrepreneurship (MS), general management (MS), human resources leadership (MS), innovation and technology (MS), leader development (MS), leading sustainability (MS), project management (MS), self-designed (MS); management (MS), including healthcare management; managers as leaders (MS); marketing (MBA, DBA); project management (MBA, MS, DBA); research strategies (MS); risk management (MBA); self-designed (MBA, DBA, PhD); social impact management (DBA); strategies for sustainability (MBA); strategy and operations (MS); sustainable management (MS); technology (MBA); technology entrepreneurship (DBA); technology management (MS). Part-time and evening/weekend programs available. Postbaccalaureate distance learning degree programs offered (minimal on-campus study). *Faculty:* 32 full-time (14 women), 275 part-time/adjunct (98 women). *Students:* 3,962 full-time (2,095 women), 1,557 part-time (959 women); includes 3,003 minority (2,510 Black or African American, non-Hispanic/Latino; 25 American Indian or Alaska Native, non-Hispanic/Latino; 140 Asian, non-Hispanic/Latino; 240 Hispanic/Latino; 9 Native Hawaiian or other Pacific Islander, non-Hispanic/Latino; 79 Two or more races, non-Hispanic/Latino), 395 international. Average age 41. In 2011, 586 master's, 87 doctorates, 4 other advanced degrees awarded. *Degree requirements:* For doctorate, thesis/dissertation (for some programs), residency. *Entrance requirements:* For master's, bachelor's degree or equivalent in related field; minimum GPA of 2.5; official transcripts; goal statement; access to computer and Internet; for doctorate, master's degree or equivalent in related field; minimum GPA of 3.0; 3 years of related professional/academic experience (preferred). Additional exam requirements/recommendations for international students: Required—TOEFL (minimum score 550 paper-based; 213 computer-based), IELTS (minimum score 6.5), Michigan English Language Assessment Battery (minimum score 82). *Application deadline:* Applications are processed on a rolling basis. Application fee: $50. Electronic applications accepted. *Financial support:* Federal Work-Study, scholarships/grants, unspecified assistantships, and family tuition reduction, active duty/veteran tuition reduction, group tuition reduction, interest-free payment plans, employee tuition reduction available. Support available to part-time students. Financial award applicants required to submit FAFSA. *Unit head:* Dr. William Schulz, III, Associate Dean, 800-925-3368. *Application contact:* Jennifer Hall, Vice President of Enrollment Management, 866-4-WALDEN, E-mail: info@waldenu.edu. Web site: http://www.waldenu.edu/Colleges-and-Schools/College-of-Management-and-Technology.htm.

Walsh College of Accountancy and Business Administration, Graduate Programs, Program in Business Information Technology, Troy, MI 48007-7006. Offers MSBIT.

Washington State University, Graduate School, College of Business, Business Administration Programs, Pullman, WA 99164. Offers business administration (MBA, PhD), including accounting (PhD), finance (PhD), management and operations (PhD), management information systems (PhD), marketing (PhD). *Accreditation:* AACSB. *Faculty:* 47. *Students:* 93 full-time (35 women), 94 part-time (32 women); includes 25 minority (4 Black or African American, non-Hispanic/Latino; 2 American Indian or Alaska Native, non-Hispanic/Latino; 11 Asian, non-Hispanic/Latino; 7 Hispanic/Latino; 1 Two or more races, non-Hispanic/Latino), 33 international. Average age 31. 310 applicants, 31% accepted, 67 enrolled. In 2011, 15 doctorates awarded. *Degree requirements:* For master's, comprehensive exam (for some programs), thesis (for some programs), final presentation; for doctorate, comprehensive exam, thesis/dissertation, oral and written exams. *Entrance requirements:* For master's and doctorate, GMAT, minimum GPA of 3.0, 3 letters of recommendation. Additional exam requirements/recommendations for international students: Required—TOEFL. *Application deadline:* For fall admission, 3/1 priority date for domestic students, 3/1 for international students; for spring admission, 6/1 priority date for domestic students, 6/1 for international students. Applications are processed on a rolling basis. Application fee: $75. Electronic applications accepted. *Financial support:* In 2011–12, 102 students received support, including 36 teaching assistantships with full and partial tuition reimbursements available (averaging $18,204 per year); career-related internships or fieldwork, Federal Work-Study, institutionally sponsored loans, health care benefits, tuition waivers (partial), unspecified assistantships, and teaching associateships also available. Financial award application deadline: 4/1. *Total annual research expenditures:* $344,000. *Unit head:* Dr. Eric Spangenberg, Dean, 509-335-8150, E-mail: ers@wsu.edu. *Application contact:* Graduate School Admissions, 800-GRADWSU, Fax: 509-335-1949, E-mail: gradsch@wsu.edu.

Washington State University, Graduate School, College of Business, Department of Accounting, Pullman, WA 99164. Offers accounting and information systems (M Acc); accounting and taxation (M Acc). *Accreditation:* AACSB. *Faculty:* 9. *Students:* 53 full-time (31 women), 16 part-time (7 women); includes 57 minority (1 Black or African American, non-Hispanic/Latino; 54 Asian, non-Hispanic/Latino; 2 Hispanic/Latino), 21 international. Average age 24. 127 applicants, 39% accepted, 36 enrolled. In 2011, 25 master's awarded. *Degree requirements:* For master's, comprehensive exam (for some programs), thesis (for some programs), oral exam, research paper. *Entrance requirements:* For master's, GMAT (minimum score of 600), resume; statement of purpose identifying area of interest, experiences, and intended research focus; minimum GPA of 3.25. Additional exam requirements/recommendations for international students: Required—TOEFL (minimum score 580 paper-based; 237 computer-based), IELTS. *Application deadline:* For fall admission, 1/10 priority date for domestic students, 1/10 for international students. Applications are processed on a rolling basis. Application fee: $75. Electronic applications accepted. *Financial support:* In 2011–12, research assistantships (averaging $13,917 per year), 7 teaching assistantships with tuition reimbursements (averaging $18,204 per year) were awarded; Federal Work-Study, institutionally sponsored loans, tuition waivers (partial), and teaching associateships also available. Financial award application deadline: 3/1. *Faculty research:* Ethics, taxation, auditing. *Unit head:* Dr. John Sweeney, Chair, 509-335-8541, Fax: 509-335-4275, E-mail: jtsweeney@wsu.edu. *Application contact:* Graduate School Admissions, 800-GRADWSU, Fax: 509-335-1949, E-mail: gradsch@wsu.edu. Web site: http://www.business.wsu.edu/academics/Accounting/.

Wayland Baptist University, Graduate Programs, Programs in Business Administration/Management, Plainview, TX 79072-6998. Offers general business (MBA); health care administration (MBA); human resource management (MBA); international management (MBA); management (MA, MBA), including health care administration (MA), human resource management (MA), organization management (MA); management information systems (MBA). Part-time and evening/weekend programs available. Postbaccalaureate distance learning degree programs offered (no on-campus study). *Degree requirements:* For master's, capstone course. *Entrance requirements:* For master's, GMAT, GRE or MAT. Additional exam requirements/recommendations for international students: Required—TOEFL (minimum score 500 paper-based; 173 computer-based; 61 iBT). Electronic applications accepted.

Wayne State University, College of Liberal Arts and Sciences, Department of Political Science, Program in Public Administration, Detroit, MI 48202. Offers aging policy and management (MPA); criminal justice policy and management (MPA); economic development policy and management (MPA); health services policy and management (MPA); human resources management (MPA); information technology management (MPA); non-profit management (MPA); organizational behavior and management (MPA); public budgeting and financial management (MPA); public policy analysis and program evaluation (MPA); social welfare policy and management (MPA); urban policy and management (MPA). *Accreditation:* NASPAA. Evening/weekend programs available. *Students:* 22 full-time (17 women), 45 part-time (33 women); includes 19 minority (16 Black or African American, non-Hispanic/Latino; 1 American Indian or Alaska Native, non-Hispanic/Latino; 2 Hispanic/Latino), 1 international. Average age 31. 75 applicants, 28% accepted, 11 enrolled. In 2011, 20 master's awarded. *Degree requirements:* For master's, comprehensive exam. *Entrance requirements:* For master's, GRE General Test. Additional exam requirements/recommendations for international students: Required—TOEFL (minimum score 550 paper-based; 213 computer-based); Recommended—TWE (minimum score 5.5). *Application deadline:* For fall admission, 6/1 priority date for domestic students, 5/1 for international students; for winter admission, 10/1 priority date for domestic students, 9/1 for international students; for spring admission, 2/1 priority date for domestic students, 1/1 for international students. Applications are processed on a rolling basis. Application fee: $50. Electronic applications accepted. *Expenses:* Tuition, state resident: part-time $512.85 per credit. Tuition, nonresident: part-time $1132.65 per credit. *Required fees:* $26.60 per credit. $199.65 per semester. Tuition and fees vary according to course load and program. *Financial support:* In 2011–12, 7 students received support. Scholarships/grants available. *Faculty research:* Urban politics, urban education, state administration. *Unit head:* Dr. Brady Baybeck, Director, 313-577-2630, E-mail: mpa@wayne.edu. Web site: http://clasweb.clas.wayne.edu/mapa.

Wayne State University, School of Library and Information Science, Detroit, MI 48202. Offers archival administration (MLIS, Certificate); arts and museum librarianship (Certificate); general librarianship (MLIS); health sciences librarianship (MLIS); information management for librarians (Certificate); information science (MLIS); law librarianship (MLIS); library and information science (MLIS, Spec), including academic libraries (MLIS); organization of information (MLIS); public libraries (MLIS); public library services to children and young adults (MLIS, Certificate); records and information management (Certificate); records management (MLIS); references services (MLIS); school library media (Spec); school library media specialist endorsement (MLIS); special libraries (MLIS); urban librarianship (Certificate); urban libraries (MLIS); MLIS/MA. *Accreditation:* ALA (one or more programs are accredited). Part-time and evening/weekend programs available. Postbaccalaureate distance learning degree programs offered (no on-campus study). *Faculty:* 13 full-time (8 women), 25 part-time/adjunct (19 women). *Students:* 121 full-time (93 women), 447 part-time (346 women); includes 57 minority (37 Black or African American, non-Hispanic/Latino; 1 American Indian or Alaska Native, non-Hispanic/Latino; 4 Asian, non-Hispanic/Latino; 7 Hispanic/Latino; 8 Two or more races, non-Hispanic/Latino), 4 international. Average age 33. 336 applicants, 62% accepted, 135 enrolled. In 2011, 212 master's, 38 other advanced degrees awarded. *Entrance requirements:* For master's and other advanced degree, GRE or MAT (if undergraduate GPA is between 2.5 and 2.99), minimum undergraduate GPA of 3.0 or graduate degree, personal statement, new student orientation. Additional exam requirements/recommendations for international students: Required—TOEFL (minimum score 550 paper-based; 213 computer-based); Recommended—TWE (minimum score 5.5). *Application deadline:* For fall admission, 7/1 for domestic students, 5/1 for international students; for winter admission, 10/1 for domestic students, 9/1 for international students; for spring admission, 3/15 for domestic students, 1/1 for international students. Applications are processed on a rolling basis. Application fee: $50. Electronic applications accepted. *Expenses:* Tuition, state resident: part-time $512.85 per credit. Tuition, nonresident: part-time $1132.65 per credit. *Required fees:* $26.60 per credit. $199.65 per semester. Tuition and fees vary according to course load and program. *Financial support:* In 2011–12, 1 research assistantship with tuition reimbursement (averaging $12,250 per year) was awarded; fellowships with tuition reimbursements, career-related internships or fieldwork, Federal Work-Study, institutionally sponsored loans, scholarships/grants, and unspecified assistantships also available. Support available to part-time students. Financial award application deadline: 5/15. *Faculty research:* Convergence of academic libraries and other academic services, competitive intelligence and data mining, impact of digitization on libraries, international librarianship, consumer health information, urban library issues, human-computer interaction, universal access to libraries and instructional support services. *Unit head:* Dr. Sandra Yee, Dean, 313-577-4059, Fax: 313-577-7563, E-mail: aj0533@wayne.edu. *Application contact:* Dr. Stephen Fredericks, Associate Dean and Director, 313-577-7563, E-mail: bajjaly@wayne.edu. Web site: http://www.lisp.wayne.edu/.

Webster University, George Herbert Walker School of Business and Technology, Department of Business, St. Louis, MO 63119-3194. Offers business (MA); business and organizational security management (MBA); computer resources and information management (MBA); environmental management (MBA); finance (MA, MBA); health services management (MBA); human resources development (MBA); human resources management (MBA); international business (MA, MBA); management and leadership (MBA); marketing (MBA); procurement and acquisitions management (MBA); telecommunications management (MBA). *Accreditation:* ACBSP. Part-time and evening/weekend programs available. Postbaccalaureate distance learning degree programs offered (no on-campus study). *Degree requirements:* For master's, comprehensive exam (for some programs), thesis (for some programs). *Entrance requirements:* Additional exam requirements/recommendations for international students: Required—TOEFL. *Expenses: Tuition:* Full-time $10,890; part-time $605 per credit hour. Tuition and fees vary according to campus/location and program.

Webster University, George Herbert Walker School of Business and Technology, Department of Management, St. Louis, MO 63119-3194. Offers business and organizational security management (MA); computer resources and information management (MA); environmental management (MS); government contracting (Certificate); health care management (MA); health services management (MA); human resources development (MA); human resources management (MA); management (DM); management and leadership (MA); marketing (MA); nonprofit management (Certificate); procurement and acquisitions management (MA); public administration (MA); quality management (MA); space systems operations management (MS); telecommunications management (MA). *Accreditation:* ACBSP. Part-time and evening/weekend programs available. Postbaccalaureate distance learning degree programs offered (no on-campus study). *Degree requirements:* For master's, thesis (for some programs); for doctorate, thesis/dissertation, written exam. *Entrance requirements:* For doctorate, GMAT, 3 years of work experience, MBA. Additional exam requirements/recommendations for international students: Required—TOEFL. *Expenses: Tuition:* Full-time $10,890; part-time $605 per credit hour. Tuition and fees vary according to campus/location and program.

Webster University, George Herbert Walker School of Business and Technology, Department of Mathematics and Computer Science, St. Louis, MO 63119-3194. Offers computer science/distributed systems (MS, Certificate); decision support systems (Certificate); web services (Certificate). Part-time and evening/weekend programs available. Postbaccalaureate distance learning degree programs offered (no on-campus study). *Entrance requirements:* For master's, 36 hours of graduate course work. Additional exam requirements/recommendations for international students: Required—TOEFL. *Expenses: Tuition:* Full-time $10,890; part-time $605 per credit hour. Tuition and fees vary according to campus/location and program. *Faculty research:* Databases, computer information systems networks, operating systems, computer architecture.

West Chester University of Pennsylvania, College of Arts and Sciences, Department of Computer Science, West Chester, PA 19383. Offers computer science (MS); computer security (Certificate); information systems (Certificate); Web technology (Certificate). Part-time and evening/weekend programs available. *Faculty:* 7 part-time/adjunct (1 woman). *Students:* 5 full-time (0 women), 18 part-time (1 woman); includes 1 minority (Black or African American, non-Hispanic/Latino), 6 international. Average age 27. 37 applicants, 49% accepted, 13 enrolled. In 2011, 3 master's, 1 other advanced degree awarded. *Degree requirements:* For master's, thesis optional. *Entrance requirements:* For master's, GRE, two letters of recommendation; for Certificate, BS. Additional exam requirements/recommendations for international students: Required—TOEFL (minimum score 550 paper-based; 213 computer-based; 80 iBT). *Application deadline:* For fall admission, 4/15 priority date for domestic students, 3/15 for international students; for spring admission, 10/15 priority date for domestic students, 9/1 for international students. Applications are processed on a rolling basis. Application fee: $45. Electronic applications accepted. *Expenses:* Tuition, state resident: full-time $7488; part-time $416 per credit. Tuition, nonresident: full-time $11,232; part-time $624 per credit. *Required fees:* $1784.64; $67.59 per credit. Tuition and fees vary according to program. *Financial support:* Unspecified assistantships available. Support available to part-time students. Financial award application deadline: 2/15; financial award applicants required to submit FAFSA. *Faculty research:* Automata theory, compilers, non well-founded sets, security in sensor and mobile ad-hoc networks, intrusion detection, security and trust in pervasive computing, economic modeling of security protocols. *Unit head:* Dr. James Fabrey, Chair, 610-436-2204, E-mail: jfabrey@wcupa.edu. *Application contact:* Dr. Afrand Agah, Graduate Coordinator, 610-430-4419, E-mail: aagah@wcupa.edu. Web site: http://www.cs.wcupa.edu/.

Western Governors University, College of Business, Salt Lake City, UT 84107. Offers information technology management (MBA); management and strategy (MBA); strategic leadership (MBA). Evening/weekend programs available. *Students:* 1,665 full-time (684 women); includes 430 minority (202 Black or African American, non-Hispanic/Latino; 18 American Indian or Alaska Native, non-Hispanic/Latino; 72 Asian, non-Hispanic/Latino; 97 Hispanic/Latino; 2 Native Hawaiian or other Pacific Islander, non-Hispanic/Latino; 39 Two or more races, non-Hispanic/Latino), 31 international. Average age 38. In 2011, 388 master's awarded. *Degree requirements:* For master's, capstone project. *Entrance requirements:* For master's, Readiness Assessment, commitment counseling discussion, transcript submissions, completion of orientation. Additional exam requirements/recommendations for international students: Required—TOEFL (minimum score 450 paper-based; 80 iBT). *Application deadline:* Applications are processed on a rolling basis. Application fee: $65. Electronic applications accepted. *Expenses: Tuition:* Full-time $6500. Full-time tuition and fees vary according to program. *Financial support:* Scholarships/grants and tuition waivers (partial) available. Financial award applicants required to submit FAFSA. *Application contact:* Enrollment Department, 866-225-5948, Fax: 801-274-3306, E-mail: info@wgu.edu.

Western International University, Graduate Programs in Business, MBA Program in Information Technology, Phoenix, AZ 85021-2718. Offers MBA. Evening/weekend programs available. Postbaccalaureate distance learning degree programs offered (no on-campus study). *Degree requirements:* For master's, thesis. *Entrance requirements:* For master's, minimum GPA of 2.75.

Wilmington University, College of Business, New Castle, DE 19720-6491. Offers accounting (MBA, MS); business administration (MBA, DBA); environmental stewardship (MBA); finance (MBA); health care administration (MBA, MSM); homeland security (MBA, MSM); human resource management (MSM); management information systems (MBA, MSN); marketing (MSM); marketing management (MBA); military leadership (MSM); organizational leadership (MBA, MSM); public administration (MSM). Part-time and evening/weekend programs available. *Faculty:* 4 full-time (0 women). *Students:* 266 full-time (121 women), 700 part-time (505 women). Average age 34. *Entrance requirements:* Additional exam requirements/recommendations for international students: Required—TOEFL (minimum score 500 paper-based; 173 computer-based). *Application deadline:* Applications are processed on a rolling basis. Application fee: $35. Electronic applications accepted. *Expenses: Tuition:* Part-time $534 per credit hour. *Required fees:* $25 per term. *Financial support:* Applicants required to submit FAFSA. *Unit head:* Dr. Donald W. Durandetta, Dean, 302-356-6780, E-mail: donald.w.durandetta@wilmu.edu. *Application contact:* Chris Ferguson, Director of Admissions, 302-356-4636 Ext. 256, Fax: 302-328-5164, E-mail: inquire@wilmcoll.edu. Web site: http://www.wilmu.edu/business/.

Wilmington University, College of Technology, New Castle, DE 19720-6491. Offers corporate training skills (MS); information assurance (MS); information systems technologies (MS); Internet/web design (MS); management and management information systems (MS). Part-time and evening/weekend programs available. *Faculty:* 1 full-time (0 women). *Students:* 21 full-time (8 women), 63 part-time (24 women). Average age 36. *Entrance requirements:* Additional exam requirements/recommendations for international students: Required—TOEFL (minimum score 500 paper-based; 173 computer-based). *Application deadline:* Applications are processed on a rolling basis. Application fee: $35. Electronic applications accepted. *Expenses: Tuition:* Part-time $534 per credit hour. *Required fees:* $25 per term. *Unit head:* Dr. Edward L. Guthrie, Dean, 302-356-6870. *Application contact:* Laura Morris, Director of Admissions, 302-295-1179, Fax: 302-328-5164, E-mail: inquire@wilmcoll.edu. Web site: http://www.wilmu.edu/technology/.

Winston-Salem State University, Program in Computer Science and Information Technology, Winston-Salem, NC 27110-0003. Offers MS. Part-time programs available. *Degree requirements:* For master's, thesis optional. *Entrance requirements:* For master's, GRE, resume. Electronic applications accepted. *Faculty research:* Artificial intelligence, network protocols, software engineering.

Worcester Polytechnic Institute, Graduate Studies and Research, School of Business, Worcester, MA 01609-2280. Offers information technology (MS), including information security management; management (Graduate Certificate); marketing and technological innovation (MS); operations design and leadership (MS); technology (MBA, MS). *Accreditation:* AACSB. Part-time and evening/weekend programs available. Postbaccalaureate distance learning degree programs offered (minimal on-campus study). *Faculty:* 12 full-time (7 women), 12 part-time/adjunct (2 women). *Students:* 108 full-time (64 women), 206 part-time (55 women); includes 27 minority (4 Black or African American, non-Hispanic/Latino; 12 Asian, non-Hispanic/Latino; 4 Hispanic/Latino; 7 Two or more races, non-Hispanic/Latino), 131 international. 596 applicants, 48% accepted, 131 enrolled. In 2011, 75 master's awarded. *Degree requirements:* For master's, thesis optional. *Entrance requirements:* For master's, GMAT (MBA), GMAT or GRE General Test (MS), resume; for Graduate Certificate, GMAT or GRE General Test, statement of purpose, 3 letters of recommendation. Additional exam requirements/recommendations for international students: Required—TOEFL (minimum score 563 paper-based; 223 computer-based; 84 iBT), IELTS (minimum score 7). *Application deadline:* For fall admission, 6/1 priority date for domestic students, 6/1 for international students; for spring admission, 11/1 priority date for domestic students, 10/1 for international students. Applications are processed on a rolling basis. Application fee: $70. Electronic applications accepted. *Financial support:* Career-related internships or fieldwork, institutionally sponsored loans, scholarships/grants, and unspecified assistantships available. Financial award application deadline: 6/1; financial award applicants required to submit FAFSA. *Faculty research:* Organizational aesthetics, resistance in organizations, dynamics of product innovation, economic approaches to productivity, corporate earnings forecasts and value relevance, ERP implementation, improving Web accessibility, information quality assessment, measuring strategic and transactional IT, website quality, service operations modeling, healthcare operations and performance analysis, entrepreneurship, leadership and change. *Unit head:* Dr. Mark Rice, Dean, 508-831-4665, Fax: 508-831-5218, E-mail: rice@wpi.edu. *Application contact:* Peggy Caisse, Recruiting Operations Coordinator, 508-831-4665, Fax: 508-831-5720, E-mail: mcaisse@wpi.edu. Web site: http://www.biz.wpi.edu/Graduate/.

Wright State University, School of Graduate Studies, Raj Soin College of Business, Department of Information Systems and Operations Management, Information Systems Program, Dayton, OH 45435. Offers MIS.

Xavier University, Williams College of Business, Master of Business Administration Program, Cincinnati, OH 45207. Offers business administration (Exec MBA, MBA); business intelligence (MBA); finance (MBA); health industry (MBA); international business (MBA); management information systems (MBA); marketing (MBA); MBA/MHSA; MSN/MBA. *Accreditation:* AACSB. Part-time and evening/weekend programs available. *Faculty:* 45 full-time (17 women), 13 part-time/adjunct (4 women). *Students:* 188 full-time (63 women), 630 part-time (206 women); includes 112 minority (36 Black or African American, non-Hispanic/Latino; 3 American Indian or Alaska Native, non-Hispanic/Latino; 52 Asian, non-Hispanic/Latino; 17 Hispanic/Latino; 1 Native Hawaiian or other Pacific Islander, non-Hispanic/Latino; 3 Two or more races, non-Hispanic/Latino), 45 international. Average age 30. 319 applicants, 63% accepted, 149 enrolled. In 2011, 403 master's awarded. *Degree requirements:* For master's, capstone course.

Management Information Systems

Entrance requirements: For master's, GMAT or GRE. Additional exam requirements/recommendations for international students: Required—TOEFL (minimum score 550 paper-based; 213 computer-based; 80 iBT). *Application deadline:* For fall admission, 8/1 priority date for domestic students, 5/1 for international students; for spring admission, 12/1 priority date for domestic students, 9/1 for international students. Applications are processed on a rolling basis. Application fee: $0. Electronic applications accepted. *Expenses:* Contact institution. *Financial support:* In 2011–12, 176 students received support. Scholarships/grants, tuition waivers (partial), and unspecified assistantships available. Financial award application deadline: 3/1; financial award applicants required to submit FAFSA. *Unit head:* Dr. Hema Krishnan, Associate Dean, 513-745-3420, Fax: 513-745-3455, E-mail: krishnan@xavier.edu. *Application contact:* Anna Marie Whelan, Assistant Director, MBA Programs, 513-745-3525, Fax: 513-745-2929, E-mail: whelana@xavier.edu. Web site: http://www.xavier.edu/williams/mba/.

HAWAI'I PACIFIC UNIVERSITY

Master of Science in Information Systems

Program of Study

The Master of Science in Information Systems (M.S.I.S.) program at Hawai'i Pacific University (HPU) is designed to create a generation of decision makers and experts in information technology, systems design, and problem solving with automated resources. The program uses an integrated approach of experimentation, testing, and analysis that leads to an understanding of the importance of well-crafted information and knowledge systems. The full-time M.S.I.S. program is designed to be completed in eighteen to twenty-four months through a combination of rigorous course work and experiential learning, enhanced by state-of-the-art technology. High-tech classroom facilities, online information databases, the Frear Technology Center, expert faculty members, and a dynamic campus environment provide students with an enriching and unique learning experience.

Students have the opportunity to work with professional faculty members on a one-on-one basis due to an average class size of less than 25 students. As a result, students frequently develop strong mentoring relationships with faculty members. Since the program attracts the world's leading professionals, participants can build a lifelong network of business contacts, thus gaining an enormous career advantage in today's competitive marketplace.

Students taking the 36-credit program have the option to take three elective courses that match individual interests or they may pursue concentrations in the following areas: knowledge management, software engineering, telecommunication, or decision sciences. Students may also choose to complement their degree with a professional certificate in areas such as electronic commerce or organizational change, among others.

Research Facilities

To support graduate studies, HPU's Meader and Atherton Libraries hold more than 110,000 bound volumes, 350,000 microfiche items, and periodical subscriptions to 1,500 print titles and 30,000 electronic journals. Databases of public and state university libraries, legislative information, and business-oriented statistical data are also available in the library or online. Students can access HPU's library databases, course information, their academic information, and an e-mail account through Pipeline, the University's internal Web site for students. The University's accessible on-campus computer center houses more than 420 computers with specialized software to support graduate academic programs. HPU also provides free Wi-Fi service so that students can wirelessly access Pipeline resources anywhere on campus using laptops. A significant number of online courses are available as well.

Financial Aid

The University participates in all federal financial aid programs designated for graduate students. These programs provide aid in the form of subsidized (need-based) and unsubsidized (non-need-based) Federal Stafford Student Loans. Through these loans, funds may be available to cover a student's entire cost of education. To apply for aid, students must submit the Free Application for Federal Student Aid (FAFSA) beginning January 1.

The University also offers several types of institutional graduate scholarships to new, full-time, degree-seeking students. U.S. citizens, permanent residents, and international students who have a demonstrated financial need may apply. HPU's graduate scholarships include the Graduate Trustee Scholarship of $6000 ($3000 for two semesters), the Graduate Dean Scholarship of $4000 ($2000 for two semesters), and the Graduate Kokua Scholarship of $2000 ($1000 for two semesters). Factors that may be considered when evaluating requests are previous academic record, community involvement and service, and professional work experience and achievement.

In order to be eligible for the best award package, students should apply by HPU's priority deadline of March 1. Applications received after the priority deadline will be awarded on a funds-available basis. Mailing of student award letters usually begins by the end of March. Applicants will be notified by mail as decisions are made.

Cost of Study

Tuition for graduate students enrolled in fall and spring semesters is determined on a per-credit basis; full-time status for a graduate student is 9 credits. Tuition for the optional winter and summer sessions is also determined on a per-credit basis. For the 2012–13 academic year (excluding winter and summer sessions), full-time tuition is $13,590 for most graduate degree programs, including the M.S.I.S. program. Other expenses, including books, personal expenses, fees, and a student bus pass are estimated at $3285.

Living and Housing Costs

The University has off-campus housing for graduate students and an apartment referral service. The cost of living in off-campus apartments is approximately $12,482 for a double occupancy room. Additional housing information is available online at www.hpu.edu/housing.

Student Group

University enrollment currently stands at more than 8,200. HPU is one of the most culturally diverse universities in America with students from all fifty U.S. states and more than 100 countries.

Location

Hawai'i Pacific combines the excitement of an urban, downtown campus with the serenity of a residential campus. The urban campus is ideally located in downtown Honolulu, the business and financial center of the Pacific. The downtown campus is composed of seven buildings in the center of Honolulu's business district and is home to the College of Business Administration and the College of Humanities and Social Sciences.

Eight miles away, situated on 135 acres in Kaneohe, the windward Hawai'i Loa campus is the site of the College of Nursing and Health Sciences and the College of Natural and Computational Sciences. The Hawai'i Loa campus has residence halls; dining commons; the Educational Technology Center; a student center; and outdoor recreational facilities including a soccer field, tennis courts, a softball field, and an exercise room.

Hawai'i Pacific University

HPU is affiliated with the Oceanic Institute, an aquaculture research facility located on a 56-acre site at Makapu'u Point on the windward coast of Oahu, Hawaii. All three sites are linked by HPU shuttle and easily accessible by public transportation.

The downtown campus location is within walking distance of shopping and dining. Iolani Palace, the only royal palace in the United States, is a few blocks away, as are the State Capitol, City Hall, and the Blaisdell Concert Hall. The Honolulu Academy of Arts, Museum of Contemporary Art, Waikiki Aquarium, Honolulu Zoo, and many other cultural attractions are also located nearby.

The University

HPU is a private, nonprofit university with approximately 8,200 students. Founded in 1965, HPU prides itself on maintaining strong academic programs, small class sizes, individual attention to students, and a diverse faculty and student population. Students may choose from more than fifty acclaimed undergraduate programs and fourteen distinguished graduate programs.

HPU is recognized as a Best in the West college by The Princeton Review and *U.S. News & World Report* and a Best Buy by *Barron's* business magazine.

HPU boasts more than 500 full- and part-time faculty members from around the world with outstanding academic and professional credentials. HPU's student-centered approach and low student to faculty ratio of 15:1 naturally results in personal attention and one-on-one guidance. The average class size is under 25.

A wide range of counseling and other student support services are available. There are more than fifty student organizations on campus, including the Graduate Student Organization.

Applying

Students must have a baccalaureate degree from an accredited college or university in the United States or an equivalent degree from another country. Applicants should complete and forward a Graduate Admissions Application, send in the $50 nonrefundable application fee, have official transcripts sent from all colleges or universities previously attended, and forward two letters of recommendation. A personal statement about the applicant's academic and career goals is required; submitting a resume is optional. Applicants who have taken the Graduate Management Admission Test (GMAT) or the Graduate Record Examination (GRE) should have their scores sent directly to the Graduate Admissions Office. International students should submit scores from a recognized English proficiency test, such as the TOEFL. Admissions decisions are made on a rolling basis. Applicants are notified between one and two weeks after all documents have been submitted. Applicants are encouraged to submit their applications online.

Correspondence and Information

Graduate Admissions
Hawai'i Pacific University
1164 Bishop Street, Suite 911
Honolulu, Hawaii 96813
Phone: 808-544-1135
866-GRAD-HPU (toll-free)
Fax: 808-544-0280
E-mail: graduate@hpu.edu
Web site: http://www.hpu.edu/hpumsis

THE FACULTY AND THEIR RESEARCH

Richard Chepkevich, Instructor in Computer Science/Information Systems; M.S.S.M., USC.

Cathrine Linnes, Assistant Professor of Information Systems; Ph.D., Nova Southeastern.

Kenneth Rossi, Assistant Professor of Information Systems; Ed.D., USC.

Lawrence Rowland, Department Chair and Assistant Professor of Information Systems; Ed.D., USC.

William A. Sodeman, Associate Professor of Information Systems and Department Chair of Management and Marketing; Ph.D., Georgia.

Edward Souza, Affiliate Instructor of Information Systems; M.S. Hawai'i Pacific.

HOLY FAMILY UNIVERSITY

School of Business Administration
Master of Science in Information Systems Management

Programs of Study

Holy Family University's master's degree program in Information Systems Management offers students the leading-edge knowledge and skills necessary to succeed in a global, technology-driven business environment.

The Master of Science in Information Systems Management, which is accredited by the Accreditation Council for Business Schools and Programs, blends business and technological education and is ideal for a wide range of working professionals who are seeking a leadership role in the field of information systems. Those with an information systems background will acquire critical management and operational skills allowing them to assume leadership positions within their organizations. Those with no technology background will be given a comprehensive understanding of information systems and the pivotal role it plays in virtually every business discipline.

The program prepares students to manage a broad array of computer resources and technology issues for organizations of all sizes. Course work includes in-depth study of networks, information security, computer forensics, project management, business finance and marketing, human resources management, communications applications, current topics in information systems, e-commerce, and other advanced topics, with an emphasis on management techniques.

The M.S. in Information Systems Management requires 33 credits, which can be completed in six semesters, or less than two years. Classes are offered primarily at Holy Family's easily accessible main campus in Northeast Philadelphia and occasionally at the University's Newtown, Bucks County, Pennsylvania site.

Research Facilities

The University library currently houses more than 124,000 items, including more than 4,000 DVDs and videos selected to support the learning, teaching, and informational needs of the University community. The library offers print and online access to the full text of over 13,000 journals and periodicals. Over two dozen full-text databases are available on and off campus, including Academic Search Premier, WilsonWeb OmniFile, CINAHL, and PsycARTICLES. In addition, the library has over 8,500 electronic books available from home or campus via NetLibrary and other interfaces.

Financial Aid

Holy Family is committed to helping adults further their education by consistently maintaining competitive tuition rates. Most graduate students are eligible for Federal Stafford Loans when attending with a half-time enrollment status (6 graduate credits) or greater.

For more information, potential students may contact the Financial Aid Office via e-mail at finaid@holyfamily.edu or by phone at 267-341-3233.

Cost of Study

Tuition for Holy Family's traditional graduate programs is $655 per credit hour.

Living and Housing Costs

Holy Family University does not provide graduate student housing; however, there are numerous housing options available in the nearby area.

Student Group

Approximately 20 students, nearly all studying part-time, are enrolled in the graduate Information Systems Management program.

Student Outcomes

Because of its emphasis on both information technology and leadership, the program produces graduates with the flexibility to assume leadership roles in information systems management and in managerial positions.

Location

The School of Business Administration, in which the master's program in Information Systems Management is based, is on Holy Family's Northeast Philadelphia campus. Located less than a mile from Bucks County, Holy Family offers the benefits of a big city in a quiet, parklike suburban setting. With easy access to regional rail lines, city bus routes, and nearby expressways, the University is conveniently located for students throughout Greater Philadelphia.

The University

Holy Family University prides itself on programs that offer students real-world experience. This focus on preparedness and student outcomes is designed to help graduates stand out, with distinction.

Respect for the individual, the dignity of the human person—these values are taught, lived, and form the foundation of Holy Family University. Concern for moral values and social justice guides the University's programs and enriches the student's education and experience.

Applying

Holy Family University has a rolling admissions policy. Applicants must submit a statement of goals, official transcripts, two letters of reference, and the application fee.

Correspondence and Information

Graduate Admissions Office
Holy Family University
9801 Frankford Avenue
Philadelphia, Pennsylvania 19114
United States
Phone: 267-341-3327
Fax: 215-637-1478
E-mail: gradstudy@holyfamily.edu
Web site: http://www.holyfamily.edu

Holy Family University

THE FACULTY

Anthony DiPrimio, Professor; Ph.D., Temple, 1978. Economics, management.

Thomas Martin, Professor; Ph.D., Pennsylvania, 1970. Digital forensics, hybrid education, intelligent classrooms, use of technology in education, cloud computing, educating the Third World, e-discovery, enterprise security including an emphasis on data exfiltration, IPv6 tunneling inside IPv4 Networks, deep packet inspection, biometrics, GPS, encryption, information security, data communications, computer networks, entrepreneurship, starting a new company in high technology.

SAINT JOSEPH'S UNIVERSITY

Master of Science in Business Intelligence

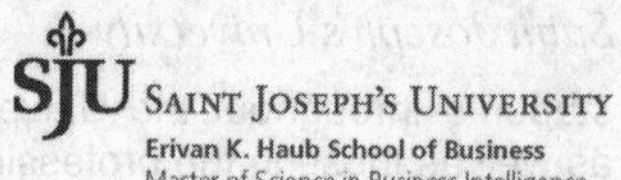

Program of Study

The Master of Science in Business Intelligence program is offered within the Erivan K. Haub School of Business. It is one of the few institutions in the region to offer an advanced business intelligence (BI) education within a business context. This specialized professional program is designed to equip students with an advanced level of expertise in the area of data-driven decision-making. Gaining these crucial analytical skills enable twenty-first century professionals to become strategic partners within their organizations. This program is appropriate for the early careerist, as well as for experienced professionals seeking to develop advanced credentials and skills in a highly complex, competitive, and global environment.

Graduate students in the M.S. in Business Intelligence program are exposed to the latest applications and theories in order to use data to advance an organization's strategic priorities. Through this program, students will develop analytic skills across diverse industries. As organizations seek to create value from the exponentially growing amount of data, they need leaders with strong analytical capabilities to understand this data in order to make smarter decisions and improve performance. Saint Joseph's graduate BI program prepares students to meet this demand.

The Master of Science in Business Intelligence program at Saint Joseph's University is endorsed by SAS, one of the leaders in data analysis tools. Saint Joseph's University is also ranked by *U.S. News & World Report*, The Princeton Review, and *Business Week* as one of the nation's outstanding schools. The program offers the opportunity to study on a part- or full-time basis, allowing all students to be employed during their course of study.

Research Facilities

Saint Joseph's University opened its newest building, Mandeville Hall, in 1998. This technologically advanced, $25-million building is a three-story, 89,000-square-foot facility that houses the Erivan K. Haub School of Business, the Center for Food Marketing Research, and the Academy of Food Marketing. Included in the building are classrooms, a lecture hall, seminar rooms, research facilities, computer labs, a 180-seat Teletorium equipped for teleconferencing (with a translation booth for international presentations), faculty and administrative offices, and informational gathering spaces. Many of the teaching areas are equipped with interactive multimedia communication technology, which greatly enhances pedagogical possibilities.

One of the most innovative concepts is a suite of classrooms that includes two moot board rooms, a preparation seminar room, a video room, and meeting breakout rooms. These rooms are modeled after the moot court concept in law schools. They accommodate teaching real-world situations through dramatizations and analysis of interactive business negotiations. They are equipped with stepped, semicircular seating that surrounds a boardroom table. Video cameras are available to record sessions for later replay or for simultaneous projection to the Teletorium or off-site locations around the globe.

The Francis A. Drexel Library and Post Learning Commons contain a business collection of approximately 350,000 bound volumes, 1,400 periodical subscriptions, 840,500 microforms, more than 2,750 videos, and Fortune 500 annual reports. The business print collection also contains nearly half of the Harvard Core, a list of more than 3,500 books recommended by the Harvard Business School, and it serves as a selective depository for U.S. government documents. The library has an online public-access catalog for searching its holdings and the holdings of other university libraries. The catalog is accessible from remote locations via the University's academic computer. There are 100 computer terminals available to Saint Joseph's students, and many online services are available to M.B.A. students. The Instructional Media Center (IMC) at Saint Joseph's University offers students assistance with presentation materials. The IMC has nearly 1,200 videotapes, which can be viewed in the IMC or signed out if needed as part of a presentation.

Services at the Career Development Center include individual career counseling, job search advising, access to alumni contact lists, and the career resource library, which contains occupational information, employer literature/directories, and current employment listings. Workshops are offered on resume writing, interviewing, and job-search techniques. Graduating students can also participate in on-campus recruiting. In addition, job search assistance is available in the form of a resume referral program.

Financial Aid

Through guaranteed loan agreements with lending institutions and state agencies such as the Pennsylvania Higher Education Assistance Agency (PHEAA) and the New Jersey Department of Higher Education, students can secure long-term loans at a low interest rate. The University initiates an electronic loan application and forwards it to its guarantor, the PHEAA. Stafford loans can be subsidized or unsubsidized. All full- or half-time students (at least 6 credits per semester) are eligible to apply for federal aid. Students may elect to finance part of their tuition through a deferred-payment program offered by the University.

Cost of Study

Tuition for the 2012–13 academic year is $892 per credit hour.

Living and Housing Costs

Off-campus apartments are available within walking distance of both the campus and the local train station.

Student Group

Students in this program include professionals with all levels of experience, who work full time and complete their graduate degrees on a part-time basis. The program also includes early careerists who have decided to study on a full-time basis after completing their undergraduate studies. The Master of Science in Business Intelligence program offers multiple opportunities for students throughout the University to network with each other, as well as those in the professional community.

Location

Saint Joseph's University is located in eastern Pennsylvania in the suburbs of Philadelphia, only 15 minutes from downtown Center City.

The University

Founded by the Society of Jesus in 1851, Saint Joseph's University advances the professional and personal ambitions of men and women by providing a demanding, yet supportive, educational experience. One of only 142 schools with a Phi Beta Kappa chapter and AACSB International business school accreditation, Saint Joseph's is home to 3,900 full-time undergraduates and 3,400 graduate, part-time, and doctoral students. Steeped in the 450-year Jesuit tradition of scholarship and service, the University strives to be recognized as the preeminent comprehensive Catholic university in the Northeast.

Saint Joseph's Erivan K. Haub School of Business is AACSB International–accredited and consistently ranked among the best academic institutions in the United States.

Applying

Applications are accepted on a rolling admission basis. Students applying to the Master of Science in Business Intelligence program must have a baccalaureate degree from an accredited college or university. Applicants must submit an online application, the application fee, official transcripts, an official test score (GMAT, GRE), two letters of recommendation, a resume, and a personal statement. International students must also submit TOEFL scores (for those whose native language is not English) and an affidavit of support. International applicants are required to submit an official course-by-course credentials evaluation of their undergraduate work. Students are strongly advised to register with World Education Services (WES). Application deadlines for international students are July 15 for the fall, November 15 for the spring, April 1 for summer session I, and May 15 for summer session II.

Correspondence and Information

Patricia D. Rafferty, Ed.D.
Director
Erivan K. Haub School of Business
Saint Joseph's University 5600 City Avenue
Philadelphia, Pennsylvania 19131-1395
Phone: 610-660-1318
E-mail: patricia.rafferty@sju.edu
Web site: http://www.sju.edu/hsb/bi

THE FACULTY

Richard Herschel, Chair of Department of Decision and System Sciences, Professor; Ph.D.
Ronald Klimberg, Professor; Ph.D.
Rashmi, Malhotra, Associate Professor; Ph.D.
Virginia Miori, MSBI Academic Coordinator, Professor; Ph.D.
John Yi, Assistant Professor; Ph.D.

Section 13
Management Strategy and Policy

This section contains a directory of institutions offering graduate work in management strategy and policy. Additional information about programs listed in the directory but not augmented by an in-depth entry may be obtained by writing directly to the dean of a graduate school or chair of a department at the address given in the directory.

For programs offering related work, see also in this book *Business Administration and Management.* In another guide in this series:

Graduate Programs in the Humanities, Arts & Social Sciences

See *Public, Regional, and Industrial Affairs (Industrial and Labor Relations)*

CONTENTS

Program Directories

Displays and Close-Ups

See:

Management Strategy and Policy

American Public University System, AMU/APU Graduate Programs, Charles Town, WV 25414. Offers accounting (MBA, MS); administration and supervision (M Ed); criminal justice (MA); emergency and disaster management (MA); entrepreneurship (MBA); environmental policy and management (MS), including environmental planning, environmental sustainability, fish and wildlife management, general (MA, MS), global environmental management; finance (MBA); general (MBA); global business management (MBA); guidance and counseling (M Ed); history (MA), including American history, ancient and classical history, European history, global history, military and diplomatic history, public history; homeland security (MA); homeland security resource allocation (MBA); humanities (MA); information technology (MS), including digital forensics, enterprise software development, information assurance and security, IT project management; information technology management (MBA); intelligence studies (MA), including criminal intelligence, general (MA, MS), homeland security, intelligence analysis, intelligence collection, intelligence operations, terrorism studies; international relations and conflict resolution (MA), including comparative and security issues, conflict resolution, international and transnational security issues, peacekeeping; legal studies (MA); management (MA), including defense management, general (MA, MS), human resource management, organizational leadership, public administration, reverse logistics, strategic consulting; marketing (MBA); military history (MA), including American military history, American revolution, civil war, war since 1946, World War II; military studies (MA), including air warfare, asymmetrical warfare, joint warfare, land warfare, naval warfare, strategic leadership; national security studies (MA), including general (MA, MS), homeland security, regional security studies, security and intelligence analysis, terrorism studies; nonprofit management (MBA); political science (MA), including American politics and government, comparative government and development, public policy; psychology (MA); public administration (MA, MPA), including disaster management (MPA), environmental policy (MA), health policy (MPA), human resources (MPA), national security (MPA), organizational management (MPA), security management (MPA); public health (MA, MPH), including emergency management (MPH), environmental health (MPH), public administration (MA); reverse logistics management (MA); security management (MA); space studies (MS), including aerospace science, planetary science; sports and health sciences (MS); sports management (MS), including coaching theory and strategy, sports administration; teaching (M Ed), including curriculum and instruction for elementary teachers, elementary, elementary reading, English language learners, instructional leadership, online learning, secondary social sciences, special education; transportation and logistics management (MA), including maritime engineering management. Programs offered via distance learning only. Part-time and evening/weekend programs available. Postbaccalaureate distance learning degree programs offered (no on-campus study). *Faculty:* 445 full-time (241 women), 1,360 part-time/adjunct (617 women). *Students:* 688 full-time (338 women), 10,168 part-time (3,706 women); includes 3,130 minority (1,007 Black or African American, non-Hispanic/Latino; 103 American Indian or Alaska Native, non-Hispanic/Latino; 825 Asian, non-Hispanic/Latino; 810 Hispanic/Latino; 51 Native Hawaiian or other Pacific Islander, non-Hispanic/Latino; 334 Two or more races, non-Hispanic/Latino), 134 international. Average age 35. In 2011, 2,386 master's awarded. *Degree requirements:* For master's, comprehensive exam or practicum. *Entrance requirements:* For master's, official transcript showing earned bachelor's degree from institution accredited by recognized accrediting body. Additional exam requirements/recommendations for international students: Required—TOEFL (minimum score 550 paper-based; 213 computer-based), IELTS (minimum score 6.5). *Application deadline:* Applications are processed on a rolling basis. Application fee: $0. Electronic applications accepted. *Expenses: Tuition:* Part-time $325 per credit hour. *Financial support:* Applicants required to submit FAFSA. *Faculty research:* Military history, criminal justice, management performance, national security. *Unit head:* Dr. Karan Powell, Executive Vice President and Provost, 877-468-6268, Fax: 304-724-3780. *Application contact:* Terry Grant, Vice President of Enrollment Management, 877-468-6268, Fax: 304-724-3780, E-mail: info@apus.edu. Web site: http://www.apus.edu.

Antioch University Midwest, Graduate Programs, Program in Management and Leading Change, Yellow Springs, OH 45387-1609. Offers MA. Part-time and evening/weekend programs available. Postbaccalaureate distance learning degree programs offered (minimal on-campus study). *Faculty:* 3 part-time/adjunct (2 women). *Students:* 24 full-time (15 women), 2 part-time (both women); includes 12 minority (11 Black or African American, non-Hispanic/Latino; 1 Hispanic/Latino). Average age 38. 44 applicants, 66% accepted, 21 enrolled. In 2011, 21 master's awarded. *Entrance requirements:* For master's, resume, goal statement, interview. *Application deadline:* For fall admission, 9/1 for domestic students; for winter admission, 12/1 for domestic students; for spring admission, 3/10 for domestic students. Applications are processed on a rolling basis. Application fee: $50. Electronic applications accepted. *Expenses:* Contact institution. *Financial support:* Federal Work-Study available. Financial award applicants required to submit FAFSA. *Unit head:* Dr. Stephen Brzezinski, Chair, 937-769-1860, Fax: 937-769-1807, E-mail: sbrzezinski@antioch.edu. *Application contact:* Deena Kent-Hummel, Director of Admissions, 937-769-1816, Fax: 937-769-1804, E-mail: dkent@antioch.edu. Web site: http://midwest.antioch.edu.

Azusa Pacific University, School of Business and Management, Azusa, CA 91702-7000. Offers business administration (MBA); diversity for strategic advantage (MA); entrepreneurship (MBA); finance (MBA); human and organizational development (MA); human resources and organizational development (MBA); human resources management (MA); international business (MBA); marketing (MBA); non-profit management (MA); organizational development and change (MA); performance improvement (MA); public administration (MA); strategic management (MBA). Part-time and evening/weekend programs available. *Degree requirements:* For master's, thesis (for some programs), final project. *Entrance requirements:* For master's, GMAT, minimum GPA of 3.0. Additional exam requirements/recommendations for international students: Required—TOEFL (minimum score 600 paper-based). *Expenses:* Contact institution. *Faculty research:* Gender issues, financial risk, leadership and ethics, marketing strategy.

Black Hills State University, Graduate Studies, Program in Strategic Leadership, Spearfish, SD 57799. Offers MS. *Entrance requirements:* Additional exam requirements/recommendations for international students: Required—TOEFL (minimum score 500 paper-based; 171 computer-based; 60 iBT).

Boston University, Metropolitan College, Department of Computer Science, Boston, MA 02215. Offers computer information systems (MS), including computer networks, database management and business intelligence, health informatics, IT project management, security, Web application development; computer science (MS), including computer networks, security; telecommunications (MS), including security. Evening/weekend programs available. Postbaccalaureate distance learning degree programs offered. *Faculty:* 12 full-time (2 women), 28 part-time/adjunct (2 women). *Students:* 25 full-time (6 women), 732 part-time (167 women); includes 208 minority (51 Black or African American, non-Hispanic/Latino; 1 American Indian or Alaska Native, non-Hispanic/Latino; 104 Asian, non-Hispanic/Latino; 43 Hispanic/Latino; 1 Native Hawaiian or other Pacific Islander, non-Hispanic/Latino; 8 Two or more races, non-Hispanic/Latino), 86 international. Average age 35. 260 applicants, 67% accepted, 143 enrolled. In 2011, 143 master's awarded. *Degree requirements:* For master's, thesis optional. *Entrance requirements:* For master's, 3 letters of recommendation, professional resume. Additional exam requirements/recommendations for international students: Required—TOEFL (minimum score 550 paper-based; 213 computer-based; 80 iBT). *Application deadline:* For fall admission, 6/1 for international students; for spring admission, 10/1 for international students. Applications are processed on a rolling basis. Application fee: $70. Electronic applications accepted. *Expenses: Tuition:* Full-time $40,848; part-time $1276 per credit hour. *Required fees:* $572; $286 per semester. *Financial support:* In 2011–12, 9 research assistantships (averaging $5,000 per year) were awarded; career-related internships or fieldwork and unspecified assistantships also available. Support available to part-time students. Financial award applicants required to submit FAFSA. *Faculty research:* Medical informatics, Web technologies, telecom and networks, security and forensics, software engineering, programming languages, multimedia and AI, information systems and IT project management. *Unit head:* Dr. Lubomir Chitkushev, Chairman, 617-353-2566, Fax: 617-353-2367, E-mail: csinfo@bu.edu. *Application contact:* Kim Richards, Program Coordinator, 617-353-2566, Fax: 617-353-2367, E-mail: kimrich@bu.edu. Web site: http://www.bu.edu/csmet/.

California Miramar University, Program in Strategic Leadership, San Diego, CA 92126. Offers MS. *Degree requirements:* For master's, capstone project.

California State University, East Bay, Office of Academic Programs and Graduate Studies, College of Business and Economics, Business Administration, MBA Program, Hayward, CA 94542-3000. Offers entrepreneurship (MBA); finance (MBA); global innovators (MBA); human resources and organizational behavior (MBA); information technology management (MBA); marketing management (MBA); operations and supply chain management (MBA); strategy and international business (MBA). Part-time and evening/weekend programs available. *Faculty:* 11 full-time (3 women). *Students:* 80 full-time (42 women), 141 part-time (61 women); includes 70 minority (5 Black or African American, non-Hispanic/Latino; 46 Asian, non-Hispanic/Latino; 13 Hispanic/Latino; 1 Native Hawaiian or other Pacific Islander, non-Hispanic/Latino; 5 Two or more races, non-Hispanic/Latino), 69 international. Average age 31. 371 applicants, 36% accepted, 79 enrolled. In 2011, 254 master's awarded. *Degree requirements:* For master's, comprehensive exam or thesis. *Entrance requirements:* For master's, GMAT (minimum 20th percentile verbal and quantitative section), bachelor's degree, minimum GPA of 2.75. Additional exam requirements/recommendations for international students: Required—TOEFL (minimum score 550 paper-based; 213 computer-based; 79 iBT). *Application deadline:* For fall admission, 6/30 for domestic and international students. Applications are processed on a rolling basis. Application fee: $55. Electronic applications accepted. *Expenses:* Contact institution. *Financial support:* Career-related internships or fieldwork, Federal Work-Study, institutionally sponsored loans, and scholarships/grants available. Support available to part-time students. Financial award application deadline: 3/2; financial award applicants required to submit FAFSA. *Unit head:* Dr. Terri Swartz, Dean, 510-885-3291, Fax: 510-885-4884, E-mail: terri.swartz@csueastbay.edu. *Application contact:* Prof. Joanna Lee, Director, CBE Graduate Programs, 510-885-3517, Fax: 510-885-2176, E-mail: joanna.lee@csueastbay.edu. Web site: http://www20.csueastbay.edu/ecat/graduate-chapters/g-buad.html#mba.

California State University, East Bay, Office of Academic Programs and Graduate Studies, College of Business and Economics, Program in Information Technology Management, Option in Strategy and International Business, Hayward, CA 94542-3000. Offers MBA. Part-time and evening/weekend programs available. *Degree requirements:* For master's, comprehensive exam or thesis. *Entrance requirements:* For master's, GMAT, minimum GPA of 2.75. Additional exam requirements/recommendations for international students: Required—TOEFL (minimum score 550 paper-based; 213 computer-based). *Application deadline:* For fall admission, 6/30 for domestic and international students. Application fee: $55. *Expenses:* Tuition, state resident: full-time $6738; part-time $1302 per quarter. Tuition, nonresident: full-time $12,690; part-time $2294 per quarter. *Required fees:* $449 per quarter. Tuition and fees vary according to degree level, program and reciprocity agreements. *Financial support:* Career-related internships or fieldwork, Federal Work-Study, institutionally sponsored loans, and scholarships/grants available. Support available to part-time students. Financial award application deadline: 3/1. *Unit head:* Dr. Xinjian Lu, Chair, 510-885-3307, E-mail: xinjian.lu@csueastbay.edu. *Application contact:* Donna Wiley, Interim Associate Director, 510-885-2928, Fax: 510-885-4777, E-mail: donna.wiley@csueastbay.edu. Web site: http://www.cbe.csueastbay.edu/mgmt/.

Case Western Reserve University, Weatherhead School of Management, Department of Marketing and Policy Studies, Cleveland, OH 44106. Offers labor and human resource policy (MBA); management policy (MBA); marketing (MBA). Part-time and evening/weekend programs available. *Entrance requirements:* For master's, GMAT.

Claremont Graduate University, Graduate Programs, Peter F. Drucker and Masatoshi Ito Graduate School of Management, Program in Executive Management, Claremont, CA 91711-6160. Offers advanced management (MS); executive management (EMBA); leadership (Certificate); management (MA, PhD, Certificate); strategy (Certificate). *Accreditation:* AACSB. Part-time programs available. *Faculty:* 1 full-time (0 women). *Students:* 25 full-time (6 women), 64 part-time (28 women); includes 47 minority (8 Black or African American, non-Hispanic/Latino; 19 Asian, non-Hispanic/Latino; 16 Hispanic/Latino; 4 Two or more races, non-Hispanic/Latino), 4 international. Average age 43. In 2011, 41 master's, 1 doctorate, 95 other advanced degrees awarded. *Entrance requirements:* Additional exam requirements/recommendations for international students: Required—TOEFL (minimum score 550 paper-based; 213 computer-based; 80 iBT). *Application deadline:* For fall admission, 2/15 priority date for domestic students. Applications are processed on a rolling basis. Application fee: $60. Electronic applications accepted. *Expenses:* Contact institution. *Financial support:* Federal Work-Study, institutionally sponsored loans, and scholarships/grants available. Support available to part-time students. Financial award application deadline: 2/15; financial award applicants required to submit FAFSA. *Faculty research:* Strategy and leadership, brand management, cost management and control, organizational transformation, general management. *Unit head:* Christina Wassenaar, Director, 909-607-7812, Fax: 909-607-9104, E-mail: christina.wassenaar@cgu.edu. *Application contact:* Albert Ramos, Admissions Coordinator, 909-621-8067, Fax: 909-621-8551, E-mail: albert.ramos@cgu.edu. Web site: http://www.cgu.edu/pages/1247.asp.

Davenport University, Sneden Graduate School, Grand Rapids, MI 49512. Offers accounting (MBA); business administration (EMBA); finance (MBA); health care management (MBA); human resources (MBA); information assurance (MS); public health (MPH); strategic management (MBA). Evening/weekend programs available.

Entrance requirements: For master's, GMAT, minimum undergraduate GPA of 2.75. Additional exam requirements/recommendations for international students: Required—TOEFL. Electronic applications accepted. *Faculty research:* Leadership, management, marketing, organizational culture.

Davenport University, Sneden Graduate School, Dearborn, MI 48126-3799. Offers accounting (MBA); business administration (EMBA); finance (MBA); health care management (MBA); human resources management (MBA); information assurance (MS); marketing (MBA); public health (MPH); strategic management (MBA). Part-time and evening/weekend programs available. Postbaccalaureate distance learning degree programs offered (no on-campus study). *Entrance requirements:* For master's, minimum GPA of 2.7, previous course work in accounting and statistics. *Faculty research:* Accounting, international accounting, social and environmental accounting, finance.

Defiance College, Program in Business Administration, Defiance, OH 43512-1610. Offers criminal justice (MBA); health care (MBA); leadership (MBA); sport management (MBA). Part-time and evening/weekend programs available. *Faculty:* 3 full-time (0 women), 2 part-time/adjunct (1 woman). *Students:* 49 part-time (21 women); includes 2 minority (both Hispanic/Latino). *Degree requirements:* For master's, thesis. *Entrance requirements:* For master's, minimum GPA of 2.5. Additional exam requirements/recommendations for international students: Recommended—TOEFL. *Application deadline:* For fall admission, 8/1 for domestic and international students. Applications are processed on a rolling basis. Application fee: $25. *Expenses: Tuition:* Full-time $10,800; part-time $450 per credit hour. *Required fees:* $95; $35 per semester. *Unit head:* Dr. Susan Wajert, Coordinator, 419-783-2372, Fax: 419-784-0426, E-mail: swajert@defiance.edu. *Application contact:* Sally Bissell, Director of Continuing Education, 419-783-2350, Fax: 419-784-0426, E-mail: sbissell@defiance.edu. Web site: http://www.defiance.edu.

DePaul University, Charles H. Kellstadt Graduate School of Business and College of Liberal Arts and Sciences, Department of Economics, Chicago, IL 60604-2287. Offers applied economics (MBA); business strategy (MBA); economics and policy analysis (MA); international business (MBA). Part-time and evening/weekend programs available. *Faculty:* 26 full-time (5 women), 21 part-time/adjunct (5 women). *Students:* 72 full-time (20 women), 27 part-time (13 women); includes 18 minority (7 Black or African American, non-Hispanic/Latino; 7 Asian, non-Hispanic/Latino; 4 Hispanic/Latino), 8 international. Average age 28. In 2011, 7 master's awarded. *Degree requirements:* For master's, thesis optional. *Entrance requirements:* For master's, GMAT (MBA), GRE (MS). Additional exam requirements/recommendations for international students: Required—TOEFL. *Application deadline:* For fall admission, 7/1 for domestic students; for winter admission, 10/1 for domestic students; for spring admission, 2/1 for domestic students. Applications are processed on a rolling basis. Application fee: $40. Electronic applications accepted. *Financial support:* In 2011–12, 3 students received support, including 2 research assistantships with partial tuition reimbursements available (averaging $9,999 per year). Support available to part-time students. *Faculty research:* Forensic economics, game theory sports, economics of education, banking in Poland and Thailand. *Unit head:* Dr. Thomas D. Donley, Chairperson, 312-362-8887, Fax: 312-362-5452, E-mail: tdonley@depaul.edu. *Application contact:* Gabriella Bucci, Director of Graduate Program, 773-362-6787, Fax: 312-362-5452, E-mail: gbucci@depaul.edu. Web site: http://economics.depaul.edu/.

DePaul University, Charles H. Kellstadt Graduate School of Business, Department of Management, Chicago, IL 60604-2287. Offers entrepreneurship (MBA); health sector management (MBA); human resource management (MBA, MSHR); leadership/change management (MBA); management planning and strategy (MBA); operations management (MBA). Part-time and evening/weekend programs available. *Faculty:* 36 full-time (7 women), 35 part-time/adjunct (16 women). *Students:* 280 full-time (116 women), 121 part-time (47 women); includes 78 minority (20 Black or African American, non-Hispanic/Latino; 37 Asian, non-Hispanic/Latino; 16 Hispanic/Latino; 1 Native Hawaiian or other Pacific Islander, non-Hispanic/Latino; 4 Two or more races, non-Hispanic/Latino), 33 international. Average age 30. In 2011, 112 master's awarded. *Entrance requirements:* For master's, GMAT, GRE (MSHR), 2 letters of recommendation, resume. Additional exam requirements/recommendations for international students: Required—TOEFL (minimum score 550 paper-based; 213 computer-based). *Application deadline:* For fall admission, 7/1 for domestic students; for winter admission, 10/1 for domestic students; for spring admission, 2/1 for domestic students. Applications are processed on a rolling basis. Application fee: $60. Electronic applications accepted. *Financial support:* Research assistantships available. Financial award application deadline: 4/1. *Faculty research:* Growth management, creativity and innovation, quality management and business process design, entrepreneurship. *Unit head:* Robert T. Ryan, Assistant Dean and Director, 312-362-8810, Fax: 312-362-6677, E-mail: rryan1@depaul.edu. *Application contact:* Christopher E. Kinsella, Director of Cohort MBA Programs, 312-362-8810, Fax: 312-362-6677, E-mail: kgsb@depaul.edu.

DePaul University, Charles H. Kellstadt Graduate School of Business, Department of Marketing, Chicago, IL 60604-2287. Offers brand management (MBA); customer relationship management (MBA); integrated marketing communication (MBA); marketing analysis (MSMA); marketing and management (MBA); marketing strategy and analysis (MBA); marketing strategy and planning (MBA); new product management (MBA); sales leadership (MBA). Part-time and evening/weekend programs available. *Faculty:* 23 full-time (4 women), 15 part-time/adjunct (6 women). *Students:* 163 full-time (84 women), 71 part-time (36 women); includes 29 minority (6 Black or African American, non-Hispanic/Latino; 18 Asian, non-Hispanic/Latino; 5 Hispanic/Latino), 38 international. Average age 28. In 2011, 88 master's awarded. *Entrance requirements:* For master's, GMAT, 2 letters of recommendation, resume. Additional exam requirements/recommendations for international students: Required—TOEFL (minimum score 550 paper-based; 213 computer-based). *Application deadline:* For fall admission, 7/1 for domestic students; for winter admission, 10/1 for domestic students; for spring admission, 2/1 for domestic students. Applications are processed on a rolling basis. Application fee: $60. Electronic applications accepted. *Financial support:* In 2011–12, 6 research assistantships with partial tuition reimbursements (averaging $2,500 per year) were awarded. Financial award application deadline: 4/30. *Faculty research:* International and marketing role in developing economics, Internet marketing, direct marketing, consumer behavior, new product development processes. *Total annual research expenditures:* $100,000. *Unit head:* Dr. Suzanne Louise Fogel, Chairperson/Associate Professor, 312-362-5150, Fax: 312-362-5647, E-mail: sfogel@depaul.edu. *Application contact:* Director of MBA Programs, 312-362-8810, Fax: 312-362-6677, E-mail: kgsb@depaul.edu.

Dominican University of California, Graduate Programs, School of Business and Leadership, MBA in Strategic Leadership Program, San Rafael, CA 94901-2298. Offers MBA. Part-time and evening/weekend programs available. *Students:* 6 full-time (2 women), 7 part-time (6 women); includes 5 minority (all Hispanic/Latino), 1 international. Average age 38. 45 applicants, 40% accepted, 11 enrolled. In 2011, 8 master's awarded. *Degree requirements:* For master's, thesis or alternative, capstone. *Entrance requirements:* For master's, minimum GPA of 3.0. Additional exam requirements/recommendations for international students: Required—TOEFL (minimum score 550 paper-based; 213 computer-based; 80 iBT), IELTS (minimum score 7). *Application deadline:* For fall admission, 6/15 priority date for domestic students, 6/15 for international students. Applications are processed on a rolling basis. Application fee: $40. Electronic applications accepted. *Expenses:* Contact institution. *Financial support:* In 2011–12, 2 students received support. Scholarships/grants available. Support available to part-time students. Financial award application deadline: 3/2; financial award applicants required to submit FAFSA. *Unit head:* Sue Stavn, Assistant Dean, 415-482-2418, Fax: 415-459-3206, E-mail: sue.stavn@dominican.edu. Web site: http://www.dominican.edu/academics/businesslead/mba/mbasl.

Drexel University, LeBow College of Business, Program in Business Administration, Philadelphia, PA 19104-2875. Offers business administration (MBA, PhD, APC), including accounting (MBA, PhD), decision sciences (PhD), economics (MBA, PhD), finance (MBA, PhD), legal studies (MBA), management (MBA), marketing (MBA, PhD), organizational sciences (PhD), quantitative methods (MBA), strategic management (PhD). *Accreditation:* AACSB. Part-time and evening/weekend programs available. Postbaccalaureate distance learning degree programs offered (minimal on-campus study). Terminal master's awarded for partial completion of doctoral program. *Entrance requirements:* For master's, GMAT, minimum GPA of 2.75; for doctorate, GMAT. Additional exam requirements/recommendations for international students: Required—TOEFL. Electronic applications accepted. *Faculty research:* Decision support systems, individual and group behavior, operations research, techniques and strategy.

Duquesne University, School of Leadership and Professional Advancement, Pittsburgh, PA 15282-0001. Offers leadership (MS), including business ethics, community leadership, global leadership, information technology, leadership, liberal studies, professional administration, sports leadership. Part-time and evening/weekend programs available. Postbaccalaureate distance learning degree programs offered (no on-campus study). *Faculty:* 1 full-time (0 women), 88 part-time/adjunct (39 women). *Students:* 311 full-time (134 women), 151 part-time (68 women); includes 109 minority (69 Black or African American, non-Hispanic/Latino; 3 American Indian or Alaska Native, non-Hispanic/Latino; 11 Asian, non-Hispanic/Latino; 19 Hispanic/Latino; 1 Native Hawaiian or other Pacific Islander, non-Hispanic/Latino; 6 Two or more races, non-Hispanic/Latino), 9 international. Average age 35. 172 applicants, 73% accepted, 107 enrolled. In 2011, 67 degrees awarded. *Degree requirements:* For master's, capstone course. *Entrance requirements:* For master's, professional work experience, 500-word essay, resume, interview. Additional exam requirements/recommendations for international students: Required—TOEFL (minimum score 80 iBT). *Application deadline:* Applications are processed on a rolling basis. Application fee: $0. Electronic applications accepted. Application fee is waived when completed online. *Expenses: Tuition:* Full-time $16,596; part-time $922 per credit. *Required fees:* $1584; $88 per credit. Tuition and fees vary according to program. *Financial support:* Applicants required to submit FAFSA. *Unit head:* Dr. Dorothy Bassett, Dean, 412-396-2141, Fax: 412-396-4711, E-mail: bassettd@duq.edu. *Application contact:* Marianne Leister, Director of Student Services, 412-396-4933, Fax: 412-396-5072, E-mail: leister@duq.edu. Web site: http://www.duq.edu/leadership.

East Tennessee State University, School of Graduate Studies, School of Continuing Studies and Academic Outreach, Johnson City, TN 37614. Offers archival studies (MALS, Postbaccalaureate Certificate); gender and diversity (MALS); strategic leadership (MPS); training and development (MPS). Part-time programs available. Postbaccalaureate distance learning degree programs offered (no on-campus study). *Faculty:* 7 full-time (3 women), 1 (woman) part-time/adjunct. *Students:* 28 full-time (21 women), 50 part-time (40 women); includes 13 minority (6 Black or African American, non-Hispanic/Latino; 1 American Indian or Alaska Native, non-Hispanic/Latino; 2 Hispanic/Latino; 4 Two or more races, non-Hispanic/Latino). Average age 41. 49 applicants, 55% accepted, 24 enrolled. In 2011, 14 master's, 2 other advanced degrees awarded. *Degree requirements:* For master's, comprehensive exam, thesis optional, professional project. *Entrance requirements:* For master's, GRE General Test, minimum GPA of 2.75, professional portfolio, three letters of recommendation, interview, writing sample; for Postbaccalaureate Certificate, minimum GPA of 2.5, three letters of recommendation, interview. Additional exam requirements/recommendations for international students: Required—TOEFL (minimum score 550 paper-based; 213 computer-based; 79 iBT). *Application deadline:* For fall admission, 6/1 for domestic students, 4/30 for international students; for spring admission, 11/1 for domestic students, 9/30 for international students. Application fee: $35 ($45 for international students). Electronic applications accepted. *Expenses:* Tuition, state resident: full-time $7312; part-time $350 per credit hour. Tuition, nonresident: full-time $18,490; part-time $621 per credit hour. *Required fees:* $63 per credit hour. Tuition and fees vary according to course load and program. *Financial support:* In 2011–12, 20 students received support, including 6 research assistantships with full tuition reimbursements available (averaging $6,000 per year); institutionally sponsored loans, scholarships/grants, and unspecified assistantships also available. Financial award application deadline: 7/1; financial award applicants required to submit FAFSA. *Faculty research:* Appalachian studies, women's and gender studies, interdisciplinary theory, regional and Southern cultures. *Unit head:* Dr. Rick E. Osborn, Dean, 423-439-4223, Fax: 423-439-7091, E-mail: osbornr@etsu.edu. *Application contact:* Mary Duncan, Graduate Specialist, 423-439-4302, Fax: 423-439-5624, E-mail: duncanm@etsu.edu.

Florida State University, The Graduate School, College of Business, Tallahassee, FL 32306-1110. Offers accounting (M Acc), including accounting information services, assurance services, corporate accounting, taxation; business administration (MBA, PhD), including accounting (PhD), finance (PhD), management information systems (PhD), marketing (PhD), organizational behavior (PhD), risk management and insurance (PhD), strategic management (PhD); finance (MS); insurance (MSM); management information systems (MS); marketing (MS); JD/MBA; MSW/MBA. *Accreditation:* AACSB. Part-time programs available. Postbaccalaureate distance learning degree programs offered (no on-campus study). *Faculty:* 107 full-time (31 women). *Students:* 196 full-time (76 women), 310 part-time (109 women); includes 89 minority (27 Black or African American, non-Hispanic/Latino; 1 American Indian or Alaska Native, non-Hispanic/Latino; 31 Asian, non-Hispanic/Latino; 30 Hispanic/Latino). Average age 30. 702 applicants, 33% accepted, 205 enrolled. In 2011, 268 master's, 17 doctorates awarded. Terminal master's awarded for partial completion of doctoral program. *Degree requirements:* For doctorate, comprehensive exam, thesis/dissertation. *Entrance requirements:* For master's, GMAT, work experience (MBA, MS), minimum GPA of 3.0, letters of recommendation; for doctorate, GMAT, minimum graduate GPA of 3.5, letters of recommendation. Additional exam requirements/recommendations for international students: Required—TOEFL (minimum score 600 paper-based; 80 computer-based); Recommended—IELTS (minimum score 6.5). *Application deadline:* For fall admission, 6/1 for domestic students, 5/1 for international students; for spring admission, 10/1 for domestic students, 9/1 for international students. Applications are processed on a rolling basis. Application fee: $30. Electronic applications accepted. *Expenses:* Tuition, state resident: full-time $9474; part-time $350.88 per credit hour. Tuition, nonresident: full-time $16,236; part-time $601.34 per credit hour. *Required fees:* $630 per semester. One-time fee: $20. Tuition and fees vary according to course load and campus/location. *Financial support:* In 2011–12, 86 students received support, including 12 fellowships with full tuition reimbursements available (averaging $7,161 per year), 30 research assistantships with full tuition reimbursements available (averaging $6,000 per year), 43 teaching assistantships with full tuition reimbursements available (averaging $15,000 per year); career-related internships or fieldwork, scholarships/grants, health care benefits, tuition waivers (full and partial), and unspecified assistantships also available. Support available to part-time students. Financial award application deadline: 1/1. *Unit head:* Dr. Caryn Beck-Dudley, Dean, 850-644-3090, Fax: 850-644-0915. *Application contact:* Lisa Beverly, Director, Graduate Programs Admissions, 850-644-6458, Fax: 850-644-0588, E-mail: lbeverly@cob.fsu.edu. Web site: http://www.cob.fsu.edu/grad/.

Franklin Pierce University, Graduate Studies, Rindge, NH 03461-0060. Offers curriculum and instruction (M Ed); emerging network technologies (Graduate Certificate); energy and sustainability studies (MBA); health administration (MBA, Graduate Certificate); human resource management (MBA, Graduate Certificate); information technology (MBA); information technology management (MS); leadership (MBA, DA); nursing (MS); physical therapy (DPT); physician assistant studies (MPAS); special education (M Ed); sports management (MBA). *Accreditation:* APTA. Part-time programs available. Postbaccalaureate distance learning degree programs offered (no on-campus study). *Degree requirements:* For master's, concentrated original research projects; student teaching; fieldwork and/or internship; leadership project; PRAXIS I and II (for M Ed); for doctorate, concentrated original research projects, clinical fieldwork and/or internship, leadership project. *Entrance requirements:* For master's, minimum GPA of 2.5, 3 letters of recommendation; competencies in accounting, economics, statistics, and computer skills through life experience or undergraduate coursework (for MBA); certification/e-portfolio, minimum C grade in all education courses (for M Ed); license to practice as RN (for MS in nursing); for doctorate, GRE, BA/BS, 3 letters of recommendation, personal mission statement, interview, writing sample, minimum cumulative GPA of 2.8, master's degree (for DA); 80 hours of observation/work in PT settings, completion of anatomy, chemistry, physics, and statistics, minimum GPA of 3.0 (for DPT). Additional exam requirements/recommendations for international students: Required—TOEFL (minimum score 550 paper-based; 195 computer-based; 61 iBT). Electronic applications accepted. *Faculty research:* Evidence-based practice in sports physical therapy, human resource management in economic crisis, leadership in nursing, innovation in sports facility management, differentiated learning and understanding by design.

Freed-Hardeman University, Program in Business Administration, Henderson, TN 38340-2399. Offers accounting (MBA); corporate responsibility (MBA); leadership (MBA). *Accreditation:* ACBSP. Part-time and evening/weekend programs available. Postbaccalaureate distance learning degree programs offered (no on-campus study). *Entrance requirements:* For master's, GMAT. Additional exam requirements/ recommendations for international students: Required—TOEFL (minimum score 500 paper-based; 173 computer-based).

The George Washington University, School of Business, Department of Strategic Management and Public Policy, Washington, DC 20052. Offers MBA, PhD. Part-time and evening/weekend programs available. *Faculty:* 15 full-time (4 women), 8 part-time/ adjunct (0 women). *Students:* 239 full-time (86 women), 7 part-time (4 women); includes 54 minority (14 Black or African American, non-Hispanic/Latino; 25 Asian, non-Hispanic/ Latino; 11 Hispanic/Latino; 1 Native Hawaiian or other Pacific Islander, non-Hispanic/ Latino; 3 Two or more races, non-Hispanic/Latino), 71 international. Average age 29. 440 applicants, 73% accepted. In 2011, 112 master's awarded. *Degree requirements:* For doctorate, thesis/dissertation. *Entrance requirements:* For master's, GMAT; for doctorate, GMAT or GRE. Additional exam requirements/recommendations for international students: Required—TOEFL. *Application deadline:* For fall admission, 4/1 priority date for domestic students; for spring admission, 10/1 for domestic students. Applications are processed on a rolling basis. Application fee: $75. *Financial support:* In 2011–12, 1 student received support. Fellowships, teaching assistantships, career-related internships or fieldwork, Federal Work-Study, and institutionally sponsored loans available. Financial award application deadline: 4/1. *Unit head:* Dr. Mark Starik, Chair, 202-994-6677, E-mail: starik@gwu.edu. *Application contact:* Kristin Williams, Assistant Vice President for Graduate and Special Enrollment Management, 202-994-0467, Fax: 202-994-0371, E-mail: ksw@gwu.edu. Web site: http://business.gwu.edu/smpp/.

Georgia Institute of Technology, Graduate Studies and Research, College of Management, Program in Business Administration, Atlanta, GA 30332-0001. Offers accounting (MBA); e-commerce (Certificate); engineering entrepreneurship (MBA); entrepreneurship (Certificate); finance (MBA); information technology management (MBA); international business (MBA, Certificate); management of technology (Certificate); marketing (MBA); operations management (MBA); organizational behavior (MBA); strategic management (MBA). *Accreditation:* AACSB.

Georgia Institute of Technology, Graduate Studies and Research, College of Management, Program in Management, Atlanta, GA 30332-0001. Offers accounting (PhD); finance (PhD); information technology management (PhD); marketing (PhD); operations management (PhD); organizational behavior (PhD); quantitative and computational finance (MS); strategic management (PhD). *Accreditation:* AACSB. *Degree requirements:* For doctorate, comprehensive exam, thesis/dissertation, oral exams. *Entrance requirements:* For master's and doctorate, GMAT. Additional exam requirements/recommendations for international students: Required—TOEFL. *Faculty research:* MIS, management of technology, international business, entrepreneurship, operations management.

Georgia State University, J. Mack Robinson College of Business, Department of Managerial Sciences, Atlanta, GA 30302-3083. Offers business analysis (MBA, MS); decision sciences (PhD); entrepreneurship (MBA); human resources management (MBA, MS); management (MBA, PhD); operations management (MBA, MS); organization change (MS); personnel employee relations (PhD); strategic management (PhD). *Accreditation:* AACSB. Part-time and evening/weekend programs available. *Degree requirements:* For doctorate, thesis/dissertation. *Entrance requirements:* For master's and doctorate, GMAT. Additional exam requirements/recommendations for international students: Required—TOEFL (minimum score 610 paper-based; 255 computer-based; 101 iBT). Electronic applications accepted. *Faculty research:* Abusive supervision, entrepreneurship, time series and neural networks, organizational controls, inventory control systems.

Grantham University, Mark Skousen School of Business, Kansas City, MO 64153. Offers business administration (MBA); business intelligence (MS); information management (MBA); information management technology (MS); information technology (MS); performance improvement (MS); project management (MBA, MSIM). Part-time and evening/weekend programs available. Postbaccalaureate distance learning degree programs offered (no on-campus study). *Degree requirements:* For master's, capstone project. *Entrance requirements:* For master's, bachelor's degree from accredited degree-granting institution. Additional exam requirements/recommendations for international students: Required—TOEFL (minimum score 500 paper-based; 213 computer-based; 61 iBT). Electronic applications accepted.

Harvard University, Harvard Business School, Doctoral Programs in Management, Boston, MA 02163. Offers accounting and management (DBA); business economics (PhD); health policy management (PhD); management (DBA); marketing (DBA); organizational behavior (PhD); science, technology and management (PhD); strategy (DBA); technology and operations management (DBA). *Degree requirements:* For doctorate, comprehensive exam (for some programs), thesis/dissertation. *Entrance requirements:* For doctorate, GRE General Test or GMAT. Additional exam requirements/recommendations for international students: Required—TOEFL. *Expenses: Tuition:* Full-time $36,304. *Required fees:* $1186. Full-time tuition and fees vary according to program.

HEC Montreal, School of Business Administration, Master of Science Programs in Administration, Program in Business Intelligence, Montréal, QC H3T 2A7, Canada. Offers M Sc. All courses are given in French. Part-time programs available. *Students:* 23 full-time (9 women), 6 part-time (1 woman). 18 applicants, 61% accepted, 7 enrolled. In 2011, 10 master's awarded. *Degree requirements:* For master's, one foreign language, thesis. *Entrance requirements:* For master's, Test de francais international (TFI) with minimum score of 850 (for those who have never studied in French), BBA, undergraduate degree in another field, degree deemed equivalent by program director and minimum GPA of 3.0 on 4.3 scale. *Application deadline:* For fall admission, 3/15 for domestic and international students; for winter admission, 9/15 for domestic and international students. Application fee: $80 Canadian dollars. Electronic applications accepted. Application fee is waived when completed online. *Expenses:* Contact institution. *Financial support:* Fellowships, research assistantships, teaching assistantships, and scholarships/grants available. Financial award application deadline: 9/2. *Unit head:* Dr. Claude Laurin, Director, 514-340-6485, Fax: 514-340-6880, E-mail: claude.laurin@hec.ca. *Application contact:* Virginie Lefebvre, Administrative Director, 514-340-6112, Fax: 514-340-6411, E-mail: virginie.lefebvre@hec.ca. Web site: http://www.hec.ca/en/programs_training/msc/options/business_intelligence/index.html.

HEC Montreal, School of Business Administration, Master of Science Programs in Administration, Program in Strategy, Montréal, QC H3T 2A7, Canada. Offers M Sc. All courses are given in French. Part-time programs available. *Students:* 39 full-time (15 women), 10 part-time (8 women). 32 applicants, 59% accepted, 12 enrolled. In 2011, 2 master's awarded. *Degree requirements:* For master's, one foreign language, thesis. *Entrance requirements:* For master's, Test de francais international (TFI) with minimum score of 850 (for those who have never studied in French), BBA, undergraduate degree in another field, degree deemed equivalent by program director and minimum GPA of 3.0 on 4.3 scale. *Application deadline:* For fall admission, 3/15 for domestic and international students; for winter admission, 9/15 for domestic and international students. Application fee: $80. Electronic applications accepted. Application fee is waived when completed online. *Expenses:* Contact institution. *Financial support:* Scholarships/grants available. Financial award application deadline: 9/2. *Unit head:* Claude Laurin, Director, 514-340-6485, Fax: 514-340-6880, E-mail: claude.laurin@hec.ca. *Application contact:* Virginie Lefebvre, Administrative Director, 514-340-6112, Fax: 514-340-6411, E-mail: virginie.lefebvre@hec.ca.

Lamar University, College of Graduate Studies, College of Business, Beaumont, TX 77710. Offers accounting (MBA); experiential business and entrepreneurship (MBA); financial management (MBA); healthcare administration (MBA); information systems (MBA); management (MBA). *Accreditation:* AACSB. Part-time and evening/weekend programs available. *Faculty:* 18 full-time (5 women), 5 part-time/adjunct (0 women). *Students:* 74 full-time (33 women), 72 part-time (27 women); includes 24 minority (7 Black or African American, non-Hispanic/Latino; 9 Asian, non-Hispanic/Latino; 8 Hispanic/Latino), 34 international. Average age 29. 69 applicants, 84% accepted, 16 enrolled. In 2011, 62 master's awarded. *Degree requirements:* For master's, comprehensive exam (for some programs), thesis optional. *Entrance requirements:* For master's, GMAT. Additional exam requirements/recommendations for international students: Required—TOEFL (minimum score 525 paper-based; 197 computer-based). *Application deadline:* For fall admission, 3/15 priority date for domestic students; for spring admission, 10/1 priority date for domestic students. Applications are processed on a rolling basis. Application fee: $25 ($50 for international students). *Expenses:* Tuition, state resident: full-time $5430; part-time $272 per credit hour. Tuition, nonresident: full-time $11,540; part-time $577 per credit hour. *Required fees:* $1916. *Financial support:* In 2011–12, 12 students received support, including 4 research assistantships with partial tuition reimbursements available; fellowships with tuition reimbursements available, career-related internships or fieldwork, Federal Work-Study, institutionally sponsored loans, scholarships/grants, and tuition waivers (partial) also available. Support available to part-time students. Financial award application deadline: 4/1; financial award applicants required to submit FAFSA. *Faculty research:* Marketing, finance, quantitative methods, management information systems, legal, environmental. *Unit head:* Dr. Enrique R. Venta, Dean, 409-880-8604, Fax: 409-880-8088, E-mail: henry.venta@lamar.edu. *Application contact:* Dr. Brad Mayer, Professor and Associate Dean, 409-880-2383, Fax: 409-880-8605, E-mail: bradley.mayer@lamar.edu. Web site: http://mba.lamar.edu.

LeTourneau University, School of Graduate and Professional Studies, Longview, TX 75607-7001. Offers business administration (MBA); counseling (MA); education (M Ed); engineering (M Sc); health care administration (MS); psychology (MA); strategic leadership (MSL). Part-time and evening/weekend programs available. Postbaccalaureate distance learning degree programs offered (no on-campus study). *Faculty:* 19 full-time (5 women), 62 part-time/adjunct (25 women). *Students:* 12 full-time (6 women), 347 part-time (273 women); includes 191 minority (162 Black or African American, non-Hispanic/Latino; 2 American Indian or Alaska Native, non-Hispanic/ Latino; 3 Asian, non-Hispanic/Latino; 20 Hispanic/Latino; 1 Native Hawaiian or other Pacific Islander, non-Hispanic/Latino; 3 Two or more races, non-Hispanic/Latino), 1 international. Average age 37. 138 applicants, 90% accepted, 120 enrolled. In 2011, 129 master's awarded. *Degree requirements:* For master's, thesis (for some programs). *Entrance requirements:* For master's, GRE (for counseling and engineering programs), minimum GPA of 2.8 (3.0 for counseling and engineering programs). Additional exam requirements/recommendations for international students: Required—TOEFL. *Application deadline:* Applications are processed on a rolling basis. Electronic applications accepted. *Expenses: Tuition:* Full-time $13,020; part-time $620 per credit hour. *Financial support:* In 2011–12, 15 students received support, including 5 research assistantships (averaging $9,600 per year); institutionally sponsored loans and unspecified assistantships also available. *Unit head:* Dr. Carol Green, Vice President, 903-233-4010, Fax: 903-233-3227, E-mail: carolgreen@letu.edu. *Application contact:* Chris Fontaine, Assistant Vice President for Enrollment Management and Marketing, 903-233-4071, Fax: 903-233-3227, E-mail: chrisfontaine@letu.edu. Web site: http://www.adults.letu.edu/.

Manhattanville College, Graduate Studies, Humanities and Social Sciences Programs, Program in Leadership and Strategic Management, Purchase, NY 10577-2132. Offers MS. Part-time and evening/weekend programs available. *Degree requirements:* For master's, thesis. *Entrance requirements:* For master's, 2 letters of recommendation, interview. Additional exam requirements/recommendations for international students: Required—TOEFL.

McGill University, Faculty of Graduate and Postdoctoral Studies, Desautels Faculty of Management, Montréal, QC H3A 2T5, Canada. Offers administration (PhD); entrepreneurial studies (MBA); finance (MBA); general management (Post Master's Certificate); information systems (MBA); international business (MBA); international practicing management (MM); management (MBA); management for development (MBA); manufacturing management (MMM); marketing (MBA); operations management (MBA); public accountancy (Diploma); strategic management (MBA); MBA/LL B; MD/

MBA. MMM offered jointly with Faculty of Engineering; PhD with Concordia University, HEC Montreal, Université de Montréal, Université du Québec à Montréal.

Middle Tennessee State University, College of Graduate Studies, University College, Murfreesboro, TN 37132. Offers M Ed, MPS, MSN, Graduate Certificate. Part-time and evening/weekend programs available. Postbaccalaureate distance learning degree programs offered. *Students:* 6 full-time (5 women), 226 part-time (190 women); includes 50 minority (30 Black or African American, non-Hispanic/Latino; 2 American Indian or Alaska Native, non-Hispanic/Latino; 5 Asian, non-Hispanic/Latino; 4 Hispanic/Latino; 9 Two or more races, non-Hispanic/Latino). Average age 37. 192 applicants, 96% accepted, 32 enrolled. In 2011, 41 master's, 1 other advanced degree awarded. *Entrance requirements:* Additional exam requirements/recommendations for international students: Required—TOEFL (minimum score 525 paper-based; 195 computer-based; 71 iBT) or IELTS (minimum score 6). *Application deadline:* For fall admission, 6/1 for domestic and international students. Applications are processed on a rolling basis. Application fee: $25 ($30 for international students). *Expenses:* Tuition, state resident: full-time $10,008. Tuition, nonresident: full-time $25,056. *Financial support:* In 2011–12, 2 students received support. Tuition waivers available. Support available to part-time students. Financial award application deadline: 5/1. *Unit head:* Dr. Mike Boyle, Dean, 615-494-7714, Fax: 615-896-7925, E-mail: mike.boyle@mtsu.edu. *Application contact:* Dr. Michael D. Allen, Dean and Vice Provost for Research, 615-898-2840, Fax: 615-904-8020, E-mail: michael.allen@mtsu.edu.

Mountain State University, School of Graduate Studies, Program in Strategic Leadership, Beckley, WV 25802-9003. Offers MSSL. Part-time and evening/weekend programs available. Postbaccalaureate distance learning degree programs offered (no on-campus study). *Faculty:* 3 full-time (0 women), 14 part-time/adjunct (7 women). *Students:* 184 full-time (91 women), 6 part-time (3 women); includes 57 minority (40 Black or African American, non-Hispanic/Latino; 6 Asian, non-Hispanic/Latino; 10 Hispanic/Latino; 1 Two or more races, non-Hispanic/Latino), 2 international. Average age 39. 130 applicants, 44% accepted, 43 enrolled. In 2011, 196 master's awarded. *Degree requirements:* For master's, thesis or alternative. *Entrance requirements:* Additional exam requirements/recommendations for international students: Required—TOEFL (minimum score 550 paper-based; 213 computer-based); Recommended—IELTS (minimum score 6.5). *Application deadline:* For fall admission, 5/31 priority date for domestic students, 5/31 for international students. Applications are processed on a rolling basis. Application fee: $25 ($50 for international students). Electronic applications accepted. *Financial support:* Federal Work-Study, scholarships/grants, and unspecified assistantships available. Support available to part-time students. Financial award applicants required to submit FAFSA. *Unit head:* Dr. William White, Dean, School of Leadership and Professional Development/Interim Dean, School of Graduate Studies, 304-929-1658, Fax: 304-929-1637, E-mail: wwhite@mountainstate.edu.

Neumann University, Program in Strategic Leadership, Aston, PA 19014-1298. Offers MS. Electronic applications accepted.

New England College, Program in Management, Henniker, NH 03242-3293. Offers accounting (MSA); healthcare administration (MS); international relations (MA); marketing management (MS); nonprofit leadership (MS); project management (MS); strategic leadership (MS). Part-time and evening/weekend programs available. *Degree requirements:* For master's, independent research project. Electronic applications accepted.

New York University, Leonard N. Stern School of Business, Department of Management and Organizations, New York, NY 10012-1019. Offers management organizations (MBA); organization theory (PhD); organizational behavior (PhD); strategy (PhD). *Faculty research:* Strategic management, managerial cognition, interpersonal processes, conflict and negotiation.

New York University, School of Continuing and Professional Studies, Division of Programs in Business, Graduate Programs in Management and Systems, New York, NY 10012-1019. Offers core business competencies (Advanced Certificate); database technologies (MS); enterprise and risk management (Advanced Certificate); enterprise risk management (MS); information technologies (Advanced Certificate); strategy and leadership (MS, Advanced Certificate); systems management (MS). Part-time and evening/weekend programs available. Postbaccalaureate distance learning degree programs offered (no on-campus study). *Faculty:* 2 full-time (0 women), 43 part-time/adjunct (7 women). *Students:* 30 full-time (15 women), 222 part-time (89 women); includes 49 minority (14 Black or African American, non-Hispanic/Latino; 20 Asian, non-Hispanic/Latino; 14 Hispanic/Latino; 1 Two or more races, non-Hispanic/Latino), 39 international. Average age 35. 178 applicants, 54% accepted, 50 enrolled. In 2011, 69 master's, 15 other advanced degrees awarded. *Degree requirements:* For master's, thesis, capstone project. *Entrance requirements:* For master's, GRE/GMAT only upon request, relevant professional work, internship or volunteer experience. Additional exam requirements/recommendations for international students: Required—TOEFL (minimum score 600 paper-based; 250 computer-based; 100 iBT), IELTS (minimum score 7). *Application deadline:* For fall admission, 2/1 priority date for domestic students, 2/1 for international students; for spring admission, 10/15 priority date for domestic students, 8/15 for international students. Applications are processed on a rolling basis. Application fee: $150. Electronic applications accepted. *Financial support:* In 2011–12, 94 students received support, including 94 fellowships (averaging $1,704 per year). *Unit head:* Anthony Pennings, Visiting Clinical Assistant Professor. *Application contact:* Admissions Office, 212-998-7100, E-mail: scps.gradadmissions@nyu.edu. Web site: http://www.scps.nyu.edu/areas-of-study/information-technology/.

New York University, School of Continuing and Professional Studies, Schack Institute of Real Estate, Program in Real Estate, New York, NY 10012-1019. Offers real estate (MS, Advanced Certificate), including finance and investment (MS), strategic real estate management (MS); real estate development (MS, Advanced Certificate), including business of development (MS), community development (MS), global real estate (MS), sustainable development (MS). Part-time and evening/weekend programs available. *Faculty:* 10 full-time (3 women), 94 part-time/adjunct (17 women). *Students:* 111 full-time (36 women), 352 part-time (75 women); includes 37 minority (9 Black or African American, non-Hispanic/Latino; 1 American Indian or Alaska Native, non-Hispanic/Latino; 21 Asian, non-Hispanic/Latino; 6 Hispanic/Latino), 50 international. Average age 31. 279 applicants, 63% accepted, 99 enrolled. In 2011, 186 master's, 28 other advanced degrees awarded. *Degree requirements:* For master's, thesis, capstone. *Entrance requirements:* For master's, GRE/GMAT only upon request, relevant professional work, internship or volunteer experience. Additional exam requirements/recommendations for international students: Required—TOEFL (minimum score 600 paper-based; 250 computer-based; 100 iBT), IELTS (minimum score 7). *Application deadline:* For fall admission, 2/1 priority date for domestic students, 2/1 for international students; for spring admission, 10/15 priority date for domestic students, 8/15 for international students. Applications are processed on a rolling basis. Application fee: $150. Electronic applications accepted. *Financial support:* In 2011–12, 225 students received support, including 201 fellowships (averaging $2,349 per year); scholarships/grants also available. Support available to part-time students. Financial award application deadline: 3/2. *Faculty research:* Economics and market cycles, international property rights, comparative metropolitan economies, current market trends. *Unit head:* Rosemary Scanlon, Divisional Dean. *Application contact:* Office of Admissions, 212-998-7100, E-mail: scps.gradadmissions@nyu.edu. Web site: http://www.scps.nyu.edu/areas-of-study/real-estate/graduate-programs/.

North Central College, Graduate and Continuing Education Programs, Department of Business, Program in Business Administration, Naperville, IL 60566-7063. Offers change management (MBA); finance (MBA); human resource management (MBA); management (MBA); marketing (MBA). Part-time and evening/weekend programs available. *Faculty:* 14 full-time (4 women), 13 part-time/adjunct (3 women). *Students:* 41 full-time (15 women), 66 part-time (31 women); includes 19 minority (2 Black or African American, non-Hispanic/Latino; 1 American Indian or Alaska Native, non-Hispanic/Latino; 12 Asian, non-Hispanic/Latino; 4 Hispanic/Latino), 1 international. Average age 30. 116 applicants, 66% accepted, 50 enrolled. In 2011, 63 master's awarded. *Degree requirements:* For master's, thesis optional, project. *Entrance requirements:* For master's, interview. Additional exam requirements/recommendations for international students: Required—TOEFL (minimum score 577 paper-based; 233 computer-based; 90 iBT). *Application deadline:* For fall admission, 8/15 for domestic students; for winter admission, 12/1 for domestic students; for spring admission, 2/1 for domestic students. Application fee: $25. *Financial support:* In 2011–12, 8 students received support. Scholarships/grants available. Support available to part-time students. *Unit head:* Dr. Jean Clifton, MBA Program Coordinator, 630-637-5244, E-mail: jmclifton@noctrl.edu. *Application contact:* Wendy Kulpinski, Director of Graduate and Continuing Education Admission, 630-637-5808, Fax: 630-637-5844, E-mail: wekulpinski@noctrl.edu.

Northwestern University, The Graduate School, Kellogg School of Management, Program in Managerial Economics and Strategy, Evanston, IL 60208. Offers PhD. Admissions and degree offered through The Graduate School. *Degree requirements:* For doctorate, comprehensive exam, thesis/dissertation. *Entrance requirements:* For doctorate, GMAT or GRE General Test. Additional exam requirements/recommendations for international students: Required—TOEFL. Electronic applications accepted. *Faculty research:* Competitive strategy and organization, managerial economics, decision sciences, game theory, operations management.

Northwestern University, School of Continuing Studies, Program in Predictive Analytics, Evanston, IL 60208. Offers MS. Postbaccalaureate distance learning degree programs offered. *Entrance requirements:* For master's, official transcripts, two letters of recommendation, statement of purpose, current resume or curriculum vitae. Additional exam requirements/recommendations for international students: Required—TOEFL (minimum score 600 paper-based, 250 computer-based, or 100 iBT) or IELTS (minimum score 7).

Pace University, Lubin School of Business, Program in Management, New York, NY 10038. Offers entrepreneurial studies (MBA); executive management (MBA); human resource management (MBA, MS); management (MBA); strategic management (MBA). Part-time and evening/weekend programs available. *Students:* 44 full-time (24 women), 89 part-time (53 women); includes 28 minority (9 Black or African American, non-Hispanic/Latino; 1 American Indian or Alaska Native, non-Hispanic/Latino; 12 Asian, non-Hispanic/Latino; 4 Hispanic/Latino; 2 Two or more races, non-Hispanic/Latino), 33 international. Average age 30. 244 applicants, 52% accepted, 36 enrolled. In 2011, 33 master's awarded. *Entrance requirements:* For master's, GMAT, GRE. Additional exam requirements/recommendations for international students: Required—TOEFL. *Application deadline:* For fall admission, 7/31 priority date for domestic students; for spring admission, 11/30 for domestic students. Applications are processed on a rolling basis. Application fee: $70. Electronic applications accepted. *Expenses: Tuition:* Part-time $990 per credit. *Required fees:* $168 per semester. Tuition and fees vary according to course load and degree level. *Financial support:* Research assistantships, career-related internships or fieldwork, and Federal Work-Study available. Support available to part-time students. Financial award applicants required to submit FAFSA. *Unit head:* Dr. John C. Byrne, Chairperson, 212-618-6581, E-mail: jbyrne@pace.edu. *Application contact:* Susan Ford-Goldschein, Director of Graduate Admissions, 212-346-1531, Fax: 212-346-1585, E-mail: gradnyc@pace.edu. Web site: http://www.pace.edu/.

Pontificia Universidad Catolica Madre y Maestra, Graduate School, Faculty of Social and Administrative Sciences, Santiago, Dominican Republic. Offers business administration (MBA), including business development, finance, international business, management skills (M Mgmt, MBA), marketing, operations, strategic cost management, strategy, tourist destination planning and management; law (LL M), including civil law, corporate business law, criminal law, international relations, real estate law; management (M Mgmt), including higher financial management, insurance program administration, management skills (M Mgmt, MBA); psychology (MA), including clinical child and adolescent psychology, forensic psychology; strategic human resources (EMBA).

Regent University, Graduate School, School of Global Leadership and Entrepreneurship, Virginia Beach, VA 23464-9800. Offers business administration (MBA), including management general; leadership (Certificate); management (MA); organizational leadership (MA, PhD), including ecclesial leadership (PhD), entrepreneurial leadership (PhD), human resource development (PhD); strategic foresight (MA); strategic leadership (DSL), including global consulting, leadership coaching, strategic foresight. Part-time and evening/weekend programs available. Postbaccalaureate distance learning degree programs offered (minimal on-campus study). *Faculty:* 13 full-time (3 women), 4 part-time/adjunct (1 woman). *Students:* 27 full-time (11 women), 589 part-time (241 women); includes 183 minority (143 Black or African American, non-Hispanic/Latino; 3 American Indian or Alaska Native, non-Hispanic/Latino; 15 Asian, non-Hispanic/Latino; 22 Hispanic/Latino), 128 international. Average age 41. 225 applicants, 57% accepted, 85 enrolled. In 2011, 80 master's, 38 doctorates awarded. *Degree requirements:* For master's, thesis or alternative, 3 credit hour culminating experience; for doctorate, thesis/dissertation. *Entrance requirements:* For master's, GRE, GMAT, minimum undergraduate GPA of 2.75, computer literacy survey, 2 recommendations, resume, transcripts, essay; for doctorate, GRE, GMAT, sample of writing, minimum 3 years of relevant experience, computer literacy survey, 2 recommendations, resume, essay, transcripts; for Certificate, writing sample, resume, transcripts. Additional exam requirements/recommendations for international students: Required—TOEFL (minimum score 577 paper-based; 233 computer-based). *Application deadline:* For fall admission, 5/1 priority date for domestic students; for spring admission, 10/1 priority date for domestic students. Applications are processed on a rolling basis. Application fee: $50. Electronic applications accepted. *Expenses:* Contact institution. *Financial support:* Career-related internships or fieldwork, scholarships/grants, and tuition waivers (full and partial) available. Support available to part-time students. Financial award application deadline: 9/1. *Faculty research:* Servant leadership, ethics and values, telecommuting and family values, organizational communications, distance education. *Unit head:* Dr. Bruce Winston, Dean, 757-352-4306, Fax: 757-352-4634, E-mail: brucwin@regent.edu. *Application contact:* Matthew Chadwick, Director of Enrollment Support Services, 800-373-5504, Fax: 757-352-4381, E-mail: admissions@regent.edu.

Regis University, College for Professional Studies, School of Management, Denver, CO 80221-1099. Offers accounting (MS, Certificate); executive international management (Certificate); executive leadership (Certificate); executive project management (Certificate); finance and accounting (MBA); general business administration (MBA); health care management (MBA); human resource management and leadership (MSOL); information technology leadership and management (MSOL); international business (MBA); marketing (MBA); operations management (MBA); organizational leadership and management (MSOL); project leadership and management (MSOL); project management (Certificate); strategic business management (Certificate); strategic human resource management (Certificate); strategic management (MBA). Offered at Colorado Springs Campus, Northwest Denver Campus, Southeast Denver Campus, Fort Collins Campus, Broomfield Campus, Henderson (Nevada) Campus, and Summerlin (Nevada) Campus and online. Part-time and evening/weekend programs available. Postbaccalaureate distance learning degree programs offered (no on-campus study). *Degree requirements:* For master's, thesis optional, capstone project. *Entrance requirements:* For master's, GMAT or essays, interview, 2 years of full-time business work experience, resume; for Certificate, GMAT. Additional exam requirements/recommendations for international students: Required—TOEFL, TWE (minimum score 5) or university-based test. Electronic applications accepted. *Faculty research:* Impact of information technology on small business regulation of accounting, international project financing, mineral development, delivery of healthcare to rural indigenous communities.

Roberts Wesleyan College, Division of Business, Rochester, NY 14624-1997. Offers nonprofit leadership (Certificate); strategic leadership (MS); strategic marketing (MS). Evening/weekend programs available. *Degree requirements:* For master's, thesis or alternative. *Entrance requirements:* For master's, GMAT, minimum GPA of 2.75, verifiable work experience. *Expenses:* Contact institution.

Sage Graduate School, School of Management, Program in Business Administration, Troy, NY 12180-4115. Offers business strategy (MBA); finance (MBA); human resources (MBA); marketing (MBA); JD/MBA. Part-time and evening/weekend programs available. *Faculty:* 2 full-time (both women), 8 part-time/adjunct (1 woman). *Students:* 20 full-time (10 women), 55 part-time (36 women); includes 10 minority (2 Black or African American, non-Hispanic/Latino; 4 Asian, non-Hispanic/Latino; 3 Hispanic/Latino; 1 Two or more races, non-Hispanic/Latino), 1 international. Average age 31. 51 applicants, 55% accepted, 19 enrolled. In 2011, 10 degrees awarded. *Entrance requirements:* For master's, minimum GPA of 2.75, resume, 2 letters of recommendation. Additional exam requirements/recommendations for international students: Required—TOEFL (minimum score 550 paper-based; 213 computer-based). *Application deadline:* Applications are processed on a rolling basis. Application fee: $40. *Expenses: Tuition:* Full-time $11,880; part-time $660 per credit hour. Tuition and fees vary according to program. *Financial support:* Fellowships, research assistantships, Federal Work-Study, scholarships/grants, and unspecified assistantships available. Support available to part-time students. Financial award application deadline: 3/1; financial award applicants required to submit FAFSA. *Unit head:* Dr. Daniel Robeson, Dean, School of Management, 518-292-8637, Fax: 518-292-1964, E-mail: robesd@sage.edu. *Application contact:* Wendy D. Diefendorf, Director of Graduate and Adult Admission, 518-244-2443, Fax: 518-244-6880, E-mail: diefew@sage.edu.

St. John's University, The Peter J. Tobin College of Business, Department of Computer Information Systems and Decision Sciences, Queens, NY 11439. Offers business analytics (MBA); computer information systems for managers (Adv C). Part-time and evening/weekend programs available. *Students:* 6 full-time (3 women), 8 part-time (0 women); includes 4 minority (1 Black or African American, non-Hispanic/Latino; 2 Asian, non-Hispanic/Latino; 1 Hispanic/Latino), 1 international. Average age 26. 8 applicants, 75% accepted, 4 enrolled. In 2011, 5 master's awarded. *Degree requirements:* For master's, comprehensive exam (for some programs), thesis optional. *Entrance requirements:* For master's, GMAT, 2 letters of recommendation, resume, transcripts, essay. Additional exam requirements/recommendations for international students: Required—TOEFL (minimum score 600 paper-based; 250 computer-based; 100 iBT), IELTS (minimum score 7). *Application deadline:* For fall admission, 5/1 priority date for domestic students, 5/1 for international students; for spring admission, 11/1 priority date for domestic students, 11/1 for international students. Applications are processed on a rolling basis. Application fee: $50. Electronic applications accepted. *Expenses:* Contact institution. *Financial support:* Research assistantships, scholarships/grants, and unspecified assistantships available. Support available to part-time students. Financial award application deadline: 3/1; financial award applicants required to submit FAFSA. *Unit head:* Dr. Victor Lu, Chair. *Application contact:* Carol J. Swanberg, Assistant Dean/Director of Graduate Admissions, 718-990-1345, Fax: 718-990-5242, E-mail: tobingradnyc@stjohns.edu.

Saint Joseph's University, Erivan K. Haub School of Business, MS Program in Business Intelligence, Philadelphia, PA 19131-1395. Offers business intelligence (MS). Part-time and evening/weekend programs available. Postbaccalaureate distance learning degree programs offered (no on-campus study). *Students:* 21 full-time (8 women), 97 part-time (29 women); includes 22 minority (8 Black or African American, non-Hispanic/Latino; 6 Asian, non-Hispanic/Latino; 6 Hispanic/Latino; 2 Two or more races, non-Hispanic/Latino), 17 international. Average age 35. In 2011, 40 master's awarded. *Entrance requirements:* For master's, GMAT or GRE, 2 letters of recommendation, resume, personal statement. Additional exam requirements/recommendations for international students: Required—TOEFL (minimum score 550 paper-based; 213 computer-based; 80 iBT), IELTS (minimum score 6.5), or Pearson Test of English (minimum score 60). *Application deadline:* For fall admission, 7/15 priority date for domestic students, 4/15 for international students; for spring admission, 11/15 priority date for domestic students, 10/15 for international students. Applications are processed on a rolling basis. Application fee: $35. Electronic applications accepted. *Expenses: Tuition:* Part-time $735 per credit hour. Tuition and fees vary according to degree level and program. *Financial support:* In 2011–12, teaching assistantships with partial tuition reimbursements (averaging $2,500 per year) were awarded; unspecified assistantships also available. Financial award application deadline: 5/1; financial award applicants required to submit FAFSA. *Unit head:* Dr. Patricia Rafferty, Director, MS in Business Intelligence and MS in Human Resource Management Programs, 610-660-1318, Fax: 610-660-1229, E-mail: patricia.rafferty@sju.edu. *Application contact:* Dr. Patricia Rafferty, Director, MS in Business Intelligence and MS in Human Resource Management Programs, 610-660-1318, Fax: 610-660-1229, E-mail: patricia.rafferty@sju.edu. Web site: http://www.sju.edu/hsb/bi/.

See Display on page 508 and Close-Up on page 531.

Saint Mary-of-the-Woods College, Program in Leadership Development, Saint Mary-of-the-Woods, IN 47876. Offers MLD.

Salve Regina University, Holistic Graduate Programs, Newport, RI 02840-4192. Offers holistic counseling (MA); holistic leadership (MA, CAGS); holistic leadership and change management (CAGS); holistic leadership and management (CAGS); holistic studies (CAGS); mental health counseling (CAGS); professional applications of the expressive and creative arts (CAGS). Part-time and evening/weekend programs available. *Faculty:* 2 full-time (1 woman), 13 part-time/adjunct (10 women). *Students:* 14 full-time (12 women), 75 part-time (67 women). *Degree requirements:* For master's, internship, project. *Entrance requirements:* For master's, GMAT, GRE General Test, or MAT. Additional exam requirements/recommendations for international students: Required—TOEFL (minimum score 600 paper-based; 250 computer-based; 100 iBT) or IELTS. *Application deadline:* For fall admission, 3/15 priority date for domestic students, 3/15 for international students; for spring admission, 9/15 priority date for domestic students, 9/15 for international students. Applications are processed on a rolling basis. Application fee: $60. Electronic applications accepted. *Expenses: Tuition:* Full-time $7740; part-time $430 per credit. *Required fees:* $40 per semester. Tuition and fees vary according to program. *Financial support:* Career-related internships or fieldwork and Federal Work-Study available. Support available to part-time students. Financial award application deadline: 3/1; financial award applicants required to submit FAFSA. *Unit head:* Dr. Nancy Gordon, Director, 401-341-3290, Fax: 401-341-2977, E-mail: nancy.gordon@salve.edu. *Application contact:* Kelly Alverson, Associate Director of Graduate Admissions, 401-341-2153, Fax: 401-341-2973, E-mail: kelly.alverson@salve.edu. Web site: http://www.salve.edu/academics/graduateStudies/programs/hs/.

Salve Regina University, Program in Management, Newport, RI 02840-4192. Offers business studies (Certificate); holistic leadership and management (Certificate); human resources management (Certificate); law enforcement leadership (MS); leadership and change management (Certificate); management (Certificate); organizational development (Certificate). Part-time and evening/weekend programs available. Postbaccalaureate distance learning degree programs offered (minimal on-campus study). *Faculty:* 2 full-time (1 woman), 15 part-time/adjunct (6 women). *Students:* 9 full-time (6 women), 40 part-time (20 women); includes 2 minority (both Black or African American, non-Hispanic/Latino). *Entrance requirements:* For master's, GMAT, GRE General Test, or MAT. Additional exam requirements/recommendations for international students: Required—TOEFL (minimum score 600 paper-based; 250 computer-based; 100 iBT). *Application deadline:* For fall admission, 3/15 priority date for domestic students, 3/5 for international students; for spring admission, 3/15 priority date for domestic students, 9/15 for international students. Applications are processed on a rolling basis. Application fee: $60. Electronic applications accepted. *Expenses: Tuition:* Full-time $7740; part-time $430 per credit. *Required fees:* $40 per semester. Tuition and fees vary according to program. *Financial support:* Career-related internships or fieldwork and Federal Work-Study available. Support available to part-time students. Financial award application deadline: 3/1; financial award applicants required to submit FAFSA. *Unit head:* Dr. Arlene Nicholas, Director, 401-341-3280, E-mail: arlene.nicholas@salve.edu. *Application contact:* Kelly Alverson, Associate Director of Graduate Admissions, 401-341-2153, Fax: 401-341-2973, E-mail: kelly.alverson@salve.edu. Web site: http://www.salve.edu/graduatestudies/programs/mgt/.

Southern Methodist University, Cox School of Business, MBA Program, Dallas, TX 75275. Offers accounting (MBA); finance (MBA); financial consulting (MBA); general business (MBA); information technology and operations management (MBA); management (MBA); marketing (MBA); real estate (MBA); strategy and entrepreneurship (MBA). Part-time and evening/weekend programs available. *Entrance requirements:* For master's, GMAT. Additional exam requirements/recommendations for international students: Required—TOEFL. Electronic applications accepted. *Expenses:* Contact institution. *Faculty research:* Corporate finance, financial reporting, modeling consumer decision-making, competition between national brands and store brands, institutional determinants of firms' strategy.

Stevens Institute of Technology, Graduate School, Wesley J. Howe School of Technology Management, Program in Management, Hoboken, NJ 07030. Offers general management (MS); global innovation management (MS); human resource management (MS); information management (MS); project management (MS); technology commercialization (MS); technology management (MS). Part-time programs available. *Degree requirements:* For master's, thesis optional. *Entrance requirements:* For master's, GMAT, GRE General Test. Additional exam requirements/recommendations for international students: Required—TOEFL. Electronic applications accepted. *Faculty research:* Industrial economics.

Suffolk University, Sawyer Business School, Master of Business Administration Program, Boston, MA 02108-2770. Offers accounting (MBA); business administration (APC); corporate financial executive track (MBA); entrepreneurship (MBA); executive business administration (EMBA); finance (MBA); global business administration (GMBA); health administration (MBA); international business (MBA); marketing (MBA); organizational behavior (MBA); strategic management (MBA); taxation (MBA); JD/MBA; MBA/GDPA; MBA/MHA; MBA/MSA; MBA/MSF; MBA/MST. *Accreditation:* AACSB. Part-time and evening/weekend programs available. Postbaccalaureate distance learning degree programs offered (no on-campus study). *Faculty:* 98 full-time (30 women), 14 part-time/adjunct (3 women). *Students:* 139 full-time (49 women), 321 part-time (138 women); includes 53 minority (17 Black or African American, non-Hispanic/Latino; 1 American Indian or Alaska Native, non-Hispanic/Latino; 21 Asian, non-Hispanic/Latino; 11 Hispanic/Latino; 1 Native Hawaiian or other Pacific Islander, non-Hispanic/Latino; 2 Two or more races, non-Hispanic/Latino), 64 international. Average age 30. 437 applicants, 61% accepted, 121 enrolled. In 2011, 283 master's awarded. *Entrance requirements:* For master's, GMAT, minimum undergraduate GPA of 2.75 (MBA), 5 years of managerial experience (EMBA). Additional exam requirements/recommendations for international students: Required—TOEFL (minimum score 550 paper-based; 213 computer-based). *Application deadline:* For fall admission, 6/15 priority date for domestic students, 6/15 for international students; for spring admission, 11/1 priority date for domestic students, 11/1 for international students. Applications are processed on a rolling basis. Application fee: $50. Electronic applications accepted. Tuition and fees vary according to program. *Financial support:* In 2011–12, 273 students received support, including 73 fellowships with full and partial tuition reimbursements available (averaging $12,415 per year); career-related internships or fieldwork, Federal Work-Study, and institutionally sponsored loans also available. Support available to part-time students. Financial award application deadline: 4/1; financial award applicants required to submit FAFSA. *Faculty research:* Foreign investments; career strategies and boundaryless careers; corporate ethics codes; interest rates, inflation, and growth options; innovation and product development performance. *Unit head:* Lillian Hallberg, Assistant Dean of Graduate Programs/Director of MBA Programs, 617-573-8306, E-mail: lhallber@suffolk.edu. *Application contact:* Ellen Driscoll, Director of Graduate Admissions, 617-573-8302, Fax: 617-305-1733, E-mail: grad.admission@suffolk.edu. Web site: http://www.suffolk.edu/mba.

Syracuse University, Martin J. Whitman School of Management, PhD Program in Business Administration, Syracuse, NY 13244. Offers accounting (PhD); finance (PhD); management information systems (PhD); managerial statistics (PhD); marketing (PhD); operations management (PhD); organizational behavior (PhD); strategy and human resources (PhD); supply chain management (PhD). *Faculty:* 79 full-time (20 women), 25 part-time/adjunct (6 women). *Students:* 32 full-time (10 women); includes 6 minority (3 Black or African American, non-Hispanic/Latino; 2 Asian, non-Hispanic/Latino; 1 Hispanic/Latino), 18 international. Average age 32. 260 applicants, 8% accepted, 12 enrolled. In 2011, 2 doctorates awarded. *Degree requirements:* For doctorate, comprehensive exam, thesis/dissertation, summer research paper. *Entrance requirements:* For doctorate, GMAT or GRE General Test, 3 recommendations. Additional exam requirements/recommendations for international students: Required—TOEFL (minimum score 600 paper-based; 250 computer-based; 100 iBT). *Application deadline:* For fall admission, 2/15 priority date for domestic students, 2/15 for international students. Applications are processed on a rolling basis. Application fee: $65. Electronic applications accepted. *Expenses: Tuition:* Part-time $1206 per credit.

Financial support: In 2011–12, 1 fellowship with full tuition reimbursement (averaging $19,570 per year), 30 teaching assistantships with full tuition reimbursements (averaging $17,000 per year) were awarded; research assistantships with full tuition reimbursements, health care benefits, and unspecified assistantships also available. Financial award application deadline: 1/30. *Faculty research:* Marketing models, market microstructure, supply chain, auditing, corporate governance. *Unit head:* Dr. Eunkyu Lee, Director of the PhD Program, 315-443-3429, E-mail: elee06@syr.edu. *Application contact:* Carol Hilleges, Administrative Specialist, 315-443-9601, Fax: 315-443-3671, E-mail: clhilleg@syr.edu. Web site: http://whitman.syr.edu/phd/.

Taylor University, Master of Business Administration Program, Upland, IN 46989-1001. Offers emerging business strategies (MBA); global leadership (MBA). Part-time programs available. *Faculty:* 1 full-time (0 women), 5 part-time/adjunct (0 women). *Students:* 42 full-time (13 women), 6 part-time (1 woman); includes 3 minority (1 Black or African American, non-Hispanic/Latino; 2 Hispanic/Latino). Average age 35. 27 applicants, 85% accepted, 22 enrolled. In 2011, 26 master's awarded. *Application deadline:* Applications are processed on a rolling basis. Application fee: $100. *Expenses: Tuition:* Full-time $9800; part-time $570 per credit hour. *Required fees:* $72 per semester. One-time fee: $100. Tuition and fees vary according to program. *Financial support:* Applicants required to submit FAFSA. *Unit head:* Dr. Evan Wood, Interim Chair, 260-627-9663, E-mail: evwood@taylor.edu. *Application contact:* Wendy Speakman, Program Director, 866-471-6062, Fax: 260-492-0452, E-mail: wnspeakman@taylor.edu. Web site: http://www.taylor.edu/mba/.

Temple University, Fox School of Business, Doctoral Programs in Business, Philadelphia, PA 19122-6096. Offers accounting (PhD); entrepreneurship (PhD); finance (PhD); international business (PhD); management information systems (PhD); marketing (PhD); risk management and insurance (PhD); statistics (PhD); strategic management (PhD); tourism and sport (PhD). *Accreditation:* AACSB. *Degree requirements:* For doctorate, thesis/dissertation. *Entrance requirements:* For doctorate, GRE General Test, GMAT, minimum GPA of 3.0, master's degree. Additional exam requirements/recommendations for international students: Required—TOEFL (minimum score 600 paper-based; 250 computer-based; 100 iBT), IELTS (minimum score 7.5). Electronic applications accepted. *Expenses:* Tuition, state resident: full-time $12,366; part-time $687 per credit hour. Tuition, nonresident: full-time $17,298; part-time $961 per credit hour. *Required fees:* $590; $213 per year.

Tennessee Technological University, Graduate School, Program of Professional Studies, Cookeville, TN 38505. Offers human resources leadership (MPS); strategic leadership (MPS); training and development (MPS). Part-time and evening/weekend programs available. Postbaccalaureate distance learning degree programs offered (no on-campus study). *Students:* 2 full-time (both women), 31 part-time (19 women); includes 5 minority (3 Black or African American, non-Hispanic/Latino; 1 American Indian or Alaska Native, non-Hispanic/Latino; 1 Hispanic/Latino). 17 applicants, 71% accepted, 7 enrolled. In 2011, 10 master's awarded. *Degree requirements:* For master's, comprehensive exam, thesis or alternative. *Entrance requirements:* For master's, GRE. Additional exam requirements/recommendations for international students: Required—TOEFL (minimum score 550 paper-based; 79 iBT), IELTS (minimum score 5.5), Pearson Test of English Academic. *Application deadline:* For fall admission, 8/1 for domestic students, 5/1 for international students; for spring admission, 12/1 for domestic students, 10/1 for international students. Application fee: $25 ($30 for international students). Electronic applications accepted. *Expenses:* Tuition, state resident: full-time $8094; part-time $422 per credit hour. Tuition, nonresident: full-time $20,574; part-time $1046 per credit hour. *Financial support:* Application deadline: 4/1. *Unit head:* Dr. Susan A. Elkins, Dean, School of Interdisciplinary Studies, 931-372-3394, Fax: 372-372-3499, E-mail: selkins@tntech.edu. *Application contact:* Shelia K. Kendrick, Coordinator of Graduate Admissions, 931-372-3808, Fax: 931-372-3497, E-mail: skendrick@tntech.edu.

Towson University, Program in Management and Leadership Development, Towson, MD 21252-0001. Offers Postbaccalaureate Certificate. Part-time and evening/weekend programs available. *Students:* 10 full-time (9 women), 22 part-time (16 women); includes 14 minority (8 Black or African American, non-Hispanic/Latino; 2 Asian, non-Hispanic/Latino; 4 Hispanic/Latino), 1 international. *Entrance requirements:* For degree, minimum GPA of 3.0, letter of intent. Application fee: $50. *Expenses:* Tuition, state resident: part-time $337 per credit. Tuition, nonresident: part-time $709 per credit. *Required fees:* $99 per credit. *Unit head:* Alan Clardy, Graduate Program Director, 410-704-3069, E-mail: aclardy@towson.edu.

Tufts University, Graduate School of Arts and Sciences, Graduate Certificate Programs, Program Evaluation Program, Medford, MA 02155. Offers Certificate. Part-time and evening/weekend programs available. Electronic applications accepted. *Expenses:* Contact institution.

United States International University, School of Business Administration, Nairobi, Kenya. Offers business administration (GEMBA); entrepreneurship (MBA); finance (MBA); human resource management (MBA); information technology management (MBA); integrated studies (MBA); international business administration (MBA); management and organizational development (MS); marketing (MBA); organizational development (EMS); strategic management (MBA). Part-time and evening/weekend programs available. *Degree requirements:* For master's, thesis. *Entrance requirements:* For master's, GMAT, 2 letters of reference, resume. Additional exam requirements/recommendations for international students: Required—TOEFL (minimum score 550 paper-based; 213 computer-based). *Faculty research:* Marketing in small business enterprises, total quality management in Kenya.

Universidad del Este, Graduate School, Carolina, PR 00984. Offers accounting (MBA); adult education (M Ed); agribusiness (MBA); criminal justice and criminology (MA); curriculum and instruction - early education (M Ed); curriculum and instruction - elementary (M Ed); curriculum and instruction - English (M Ed); curriculum and instruction - Spanish (M Ed); human resources (MBA); information security management (MBA); information technology and Web business development (MBA); management (MBA); public policy (MPA); social work (MA), including clinical social work; special education (M Ed); strategic leadership (MBA).

The University of Arizona, Eller College of Management, Department of Management, Tucson, AZ 85721. Offers PhD. Evening/weekend programs available. *Faculty:* 13 full-time (2 women). *Students:* 108 full-time (37 women), 15 part-time (7 women); includes 12 minority (2 Black or African American, non-Hispanic/Latino; 3 Asian, non-Hispanic/Latino; 3 Hispanic/Latino; 4 Two or more races, non-Hispanic/Latino), 65 international. Average age 30. 373 applicants, 29% accepted, 47 enrolled. In 2011, 15 doctorates awarded. *Entrance requirements:* Additional exam requirements/recommendations for international students: Required—TOEFL (minimum score 550 paper-based; 213 computer-based; 79 iBT). *Application deadline:* For fall admission, 1/15 for domestic and international students. Applications are processed on a rolling basis. Application fee: $75. Electronic applications accepted. *Expenses:* Tuition, state resident: full-time $10,840. Tuition, nonresident: full-time $25,802. *Financial support:* In 2011–12, 8 research assistantships with full tuition reimbursements (averaging $26,100 per year) were awarded; teaching assistantships with full tuition reimbursements, career-related internships or fieldwork, Federal Work-Study, institutionally sponsored loans, scholarships/grants, health care benefits, tuition waivers (partial), and unspecified assistantships also available. Financial award application deadline: 3/15. *Faculty research:* Organizational behavior, human resources, decision-making, health economics and finance, immigration. *Total annual research expenditures:* $267,161. *Unit head:* Dr. Stephen Gilliland, Department Head, 520-621-9324, Fax: 520-621-4171, E-mail: sgill@eller.arizona.edu. *Application contact:* Information Contact, 520-621-1053, Fax: 520-621-4171. Web site: http://www.management.eller.arizona.edu/.

The University of British Columbia, Sauder School of Business, Doctoral Program in Commerce and Business Administration, Vancouver, BC V6T 1Z1, Canada. Offers accounting (PhD); finance (PhD); international business (PhD); management information systems (PhD); management science (PhD); marketing (PhD); organizational behavior (PhD); strategy and business economics (PhD); transportation and logistics (PhD); urban land economics (PhD). *Degree requirements:* For doctorate, comprehensive exam, thesis/dissertation. *Entrance requirements:* For doctorate, GMAT or GRE. Additional exam requirements/recommendations for international students: Required—TOEFL (minimum score 600 paper-based; 250 computer-based; 100 iBT). Electronic applications accepted.

University of Calgary, Faculty of Graduate Studies, Centre for Military and Strategic Studies, Calgary, AB T2N 1N4, Canada. Offers MSS, PhD. PhD offered in special cases only. Part-time programs available. *Degree requirements:* For master's, thesis; for doctorate, comprehensive exam, thesis/dissertation. *Entrance requirements:* For master's, minimum GPA of 3.4. Additional exam requirements/recommendations for international students: Recommended—TOEFL (minimum score 550 paper-based). *Faculty research:* Military history, Israeli studies, strategic studies, int'l relations, Arctic security.

University of California, Los Angeles, Graduate Division, UCLA Anderson School of Management, Los Angeles, CA 90095-1481. Offers accounting (PhD); Asia Pacific (EMBA); business administration (EMBA, MBA); decisions, operations and technology management (PhD); finance (PhD); financial engineering (MFE); global economics and management (PhD); Latin America (EMBA); management and organizations (PhD); marketing (PhD); strategy (PhD); DDS/MBA; MBA/JD; MBA/MD; MBA/MLAS; MBA/MLIS; MBA/MPH; MBA/MPP; MBA/MSCS; MBA/MSN; MBA/MUP. *Accreditation:* AACSB. Part-time programs available. *Faculty:* 90 full-time (14 women), 62 part-time/adjunct (14 women). *Students:* 1,103 full-time (312 women), 842 part-time (223 women); includes 663 minority (18 Black or African American, non-Hispanic/Latino; 510 Asian, non-Hispanic/Latino; 46 Hispanic/Latino; 2 Native Hawaiian or other Pacific Islander, non-Hispanic/Latino; 87 Two or more races, non-Hispanic/Latino), 469 international. 4,737 applicants, 32% accepted, 875 enrolled. In 2011, 759 master's, 6 doctorates awarded. *Degree requirements:* For master's, comprehensive exam, field study consulting project (for MBA); thesis/dissertation (for MFE); for doctorate, comprehensive exam, thesis/dissertation, oral and written qualifying exams. *Entrance requirements:* For master's, GMAT (for MBA); GMAT or GRE General Test (for MFE), 4-year bachelor's degree or equivalent; for doctorate, GMAT or GRE General Test, 4-year bachelor's degree from regionally-accredited institution; minimum GPA of 3.0. Additional exam requirements/recommendations for international students: Required—TOEFL (minimum score 560 paper-based; 220 computer-based; 87 iBT), IELTS (minimum score 7). *Application deadline:* For fall admission, 10/26 for domestic and international students; for winter admission, 1/11 for domestic and international students; for spring admission, 4/18 for domestic and international students. Application fee: $200. Electronic applications accepted. *Expenses:* Contact institution. *Financial support:* In 2011–12, 600 students received support. Fellowships, research assistantships, teaching assistantships, career-related internships or fieldwork, institutionally sponsored loans, scholarships/grants, health care benefits, and tuition waivers (partial) available. Financial award application deadline: 4/15; financial award applicants required to submit FAFSA. *Unit head:* Judy D. Olian, Dean, 310-825-7982, Fax: 310-206-2073, E-mail: judy.olian@anderson.ucla.edu. *Application contact:* Robert Weiler, Assistant Dean, Director of MBA Admissions and Financial Aid, 310-825-6944, Fax: 310-825-8582, E-mail: mba.admissions@anderson.ucla.edu. Web site: http://www.anderson.ucla.edu/.

See Display on page 141 and Close-Up on page 249.

University of Central Missouri, The Graduate School, Harmon College of Business Administration, Warrensburg, MO 64093. Offers accountancy (MA); accounting (MBA); ethical strategic leadership (MBA); finance (MBA); general business (MBA); information systems (MBA); information technology (MS); marketing (MBA). Part-time programs available. Postbaccalaureate distance learning degree programs offered. *Entrance requirements:* Additional exam requirements/recommendations for international students: Required—TOEFL (minimum score 550 paper-based; 79 computer-based). Electronic applications accepted.

University of Chicago, Booth School of Business, Full-Time MBA Program, Chicago, IL 60637. Offers accounting (MBA); analytic finance (MBA); analytic management (MBA); business administration (PhD); econometrics and statistics (MBA); economics (MBA); entrepreneurship (MBA); finance (MBA); general management (MBA); health administration and policy (Certificate); human resource management (MBA); international business (IMBA, MBA); managerial and organizational behavior (MBA); marketing management (MBA); operations management (MBA); strategic management (MBA); MBA/AM; MBA/JD; MBA/MA; MBA/MD; MBA/MPP. *Accreditation:* AACSB. Part-time and evening/weekend programs available. *Faculty:* 166 full-time, 32 part-time/adjunct. *Students:* 1,160 full-time (412 women); includes 316 minority (61 Black or African American, non-Hispanic/Latino; 173 Asian, non-Hispanic/Latino; 63 Hispanic/Latino; 19 Two or more races, non-Hispanic/Latino), 378 international. Average age 28. 4,169 applicants, 575 enrolled. In 2011, 1,423 master's, 19 doctorates awarded. Terminal master's awarded for partial completion of doctoral program. *Entrance requirements:* For master's, GMAT, 2 letters of recommendation, 3 essays, resume, interview. Additional exam requirements/recommendations for international students: Required—TOEFL (minimum score 600 paper-based; 250 computer-based; 104 iBT), IELTS. *Application deadline:* For fall admission, 10/12 priority date for domestic students, 10/12 for international students; for winter admission, 1/4 for domestic and international students; for spring admission, 4/4 for domestic and international students. Application fee: $200. Electronic applications accepted. *Expenses:* Contact institution. *Financial support:* Fellowships available. Financial award applicants required to submit FAFSA. *Faculty research:* Finance, marketing, economics, entrepreneurship, strategy, management. *Unit head:* Stacey Kole, Deputy Dean, 773-702-7121. *Application contact:* Kurt Ahlm, Associate Dean of Student Recruitment and Admissions, 773-702-7369, Fax: 773-702-9085, E-mail: admissions@chicagobooth.edu. Web site: http://chicagobooth.edu/.

University of Colorado Denver, Business School, Master of Business Administration Program, Denver, CO 80217. Offers business intelligence (MBA); business strategy (MBA); business to business marketing (MBA); business to consumer marketing (MBA); change management (MBA); corporate financial management (MBA); enterprise technology management (MBA); entrepreneurship (MBA); health administration (MBA), including financial management, health administration, health information technologies, international health management and policy; human resources management (MBA); investment management (MBA); managing for sustainability (MBA); services management (MBA); sports and entertainment management (MBA). *Accreditation:* AACSB. Part-time and evening/weekend programs available. Postbaccalaureate distance learning degree programs offered (no on-campus study). *Students:* 784 full-time (306 women), 203 part-time (81 women); includes 135 minority (18 Black or African American, non-Hispanic/Latino; 5 American Indian or Alaska Native, non-Hispanic/Latino; 50 Asian, non-Hispanic/Latino; 58 Hispanic/Latino; 4 Two or more races, non-Hispanic/Latino), 38 international. Average age 31. 433 applicants, 76% accepted, 212 enrolled. In 2011, 326 master's awarded. *Degree requirements:* For master's, 48 semester hours, including 30 of core courses, 3 in international business, and 15 in electives from over 50 other graduate business courses. *Entrance requirements:* For master's, GMAT, resume, official transcripts, essay, two letters of recommendation, financial statements (for international applicants). Additional exam requirements/recommendations for international students: Required—TOEFL (minimum score 560 paper-based; 197 computer-based; 83 iBT). *Application deadline:* For fall admission, 4/15 priority date for domestic students, 3/15 for international students; for spring admission, 10/15 priority date for domestic students, 10/1 for international students. Applications are processed on a rolling basis. Application fee: $50 ($75 for international students). Electronic applications accepted. *Expenses:* Contact institution. *Financial support:* Scholarships/grants available. Support available to part-time students. Financial award application deadline: 4/1; financial award applicants required to submit FAFSA. *Faculty research:* Marketing, management, entrepreneurship, finance, health administration. *Unit head:* Elizabeth Cooperman, Professor of Finance and Managing for Sustainability/MBA Program Director, 303-315-8422, E-mail: elizabeth.cooperman@ucdenver.edu. *Application contact:* Shelly Townley, Admissions Director, Graduate Programs, 303-315-8202, E-mail: shelly.townley@ucdenver.edu. Web site: http://www.ucdenver.edu/academics/colleges/business/degrees/ms/accounting/Pages/Accounting.aspx.

University of Dallas, Graduate School of Management, Irving, TX 75062-4736. Offers accounting (MBA, MM, MS); business management (MBA, MM); corporate finance (MBA, MM); financial services (MBA); global business (MBA, MM); health services management (MBA, MM); human resource management (MBA, MM); information assurance (MBA, MM, MS); information technology (MBA, MM, MS); information technology service management (MBA, MM, MS); marketing management (MBA, MM); organization development (MBA, MM); project management (MBA, MM); sports and entertainment management (MBA, MM); strategic leadership (MBA, MM); supply chain management (MBA); supply chain management and market logistics (MM). *Accreditation:* ACBSP. Part-time and evening/weekend programs available. Postbaccalaureate distance learning degree programs offered (no on-campus study). *Entrance requirements:* Additional exam requirements/recommendations for international students: Required—TOEFL. Electronic applications accepted. *Expenses:* Contact institution.

University of Denver, Daniels College of Business, Department of Business Information and Analytics, Denver, CO 80208. Offers business intelligence (MS); data mining (MS). *Faculty:* 12 full-time (2 women), 2 part-time/adjunct (0 women). *Entrance requirements:* Additional exam requirements/recommendations for international students: Required—TOEFL (minimum score 570 paper-based; 88 iBT). *Application deadline:* For fall admission, 1/15 priority date for domestic students. Applications are processed on a rolling basis. Application fee: $60. Electronic applications accepted. *Financial support:* Career-related internships or fieldwork, Federal Work-Study, institutionally sponsored loans, and scholarships/grants available. Support available to part-time students. Financial award application deadline: 2/15; financial award applicants required to submit FAFSA. *Unit head:* Dr. Anthony Hayter, Professor, 303-871-4341, E-mail: anthony.hayter@du.edu. *Application contact:* Information Contact, 303-871-3416. Web site: http://daniels.du.edu/schoolsdepartments/dbia/index.html.

University of Florida, Graduate School, Warrington College of Business Administration, Hough Graduate School of Business, Programs in Business Administration, Gainesville, FL 32611. Offers accounting (MBA); arts administration (MBA); business strategy and public policy (MBA); competitive strategy (MBA); decision and information sciences (MBA); electronic commerce (MBA); finance (MBA); general business (MBA); global management (MBA); Graham-Buffett security analysis (MBA); health administration (MBA); human resources management (MBA); international studies (MBA); Latin American business (MBA); management (MBA); marketing (MBA); sports administration (MBA); JD/MBA; MBA/MS; MBA/PhD; MBA/Pharm D; MD/MBA. *Accreditation:* AACSB. Part-time and evening/weekend programs available. *Faculty:* 71 full-time (10 women). *Students:* 412 full-time (111 women), 467 part-time (135 women); includes 235 minority (39 Black or African American, non-Hispanic/Latino; 7 American Indian or Alaska Native, non-Hispanic/Latino; 79 Asian, non-Hispanic/Latino; 109 Hispanic/Latino; 1 Native Hawaiian or other Pacific Islander, non-Hispanic/Latino), 44 international. Average age 32. 589 applicants, 52% accepted, 247 enrolled. In 2011, 505 master's awarded. *Degree requirements:* For master's, capstone course. *Entrance requirements:* For master's, GMAT, minimum GPA of 3.0, interview. Additional exam requirements/recommendations for international students: Required—TOEFL (minimum score 550 paper-based; 213 computer-based; 80 iBT), IELTS (minimum score 6). *Application deadline:* For fall admission, 7/1 for domestic students, 1/1 for international students; for spring admission, 12/1 for domestic and international students. Applications are processed on a rolling basis. Application fee: $30. Electronic applications accepted. *Financial support:* Teaching assistantships, career-related internships or fieldwork, scholarships/grants, and unspecified assistantships available. Support available to part-time students. Financial award applicants required to submit FAFSA. *Faculty research:* Accounting, finance, insurance, management, real estate, urban analysis marketing. *Unit head:* Prof. Alexander D. Sevilla, Assistant Dean/Director, 352-273-3252 Ext. 1206, E-mail: alex.sevilla@warrington.ufl.edu. *Application contact:* Prof. Kelli Gust, Associate Director, 352-273-3255, Fax: 352-392-8791, E-mail: kelly.gust@warrington.ufl.edu. Web site: http://www.floridamba.ufl.edu/.

University of Illinois at Urbana–Champaign, Graduate College, College of Education, Department of Education Policy, Organization, and Leadership, Champaign, IL 61820. Offers educational organization and leadership (Ed M, MS, Ed D, PhD, CAS); educational policy studies (Ed M, MA, PhD); human resource education (Ed M, MS, Ed D, PhD, CAS). Part-time programs available. Postbaccalaureate distance learning degree programs offered (minimal on-campus study). *Faculty:* 30 full-time (13 women), 3 part-time/adjunct (2 women). *Students:* 185 full-time (117 women), 391 part-time (249 women); includes 199 minority (107 Black or African American, non-Hispanic/Latino; 3 American Indian or Alaska Native, non-Hispanic/Latino; 28 Asian, non-Hispanic/Latino; 49 Hispanic/Latino; 12 Two or more races, non-Hispanic/Latino), 52 international. 327 applicants, 60% accepted, 100 enrolled. In 2011, 201 master's, 34 doctorates, 3 other advanced degrees awarded. *Entrance requirements:* For master's, minimum GPA of 3.0; for doctorate, GRE General Test, minimum GPA of 3.0, writing samples, interview. Additional exam requirements/recommendations for international students: Required—TOEFL (minimum score 620 paper-based; 260 computer-based; 105 iBT). *Application deadline:* Applications are processed on a rolling basis. Application fee: $75 ($90 for international students). Electronic applications accepted. *Financial support:* In 2011–12, 29 fellowships, 60 research assistantships, 60 teaching assistantships were awarded; tuition waivers (full and partial) also available. *Unit head:* James Anderson, Head, 217-333-2446, Fax: 217-244-5632, E-mail: janders@illinois.edu. *Application contact:* Rebecca Grady, 217-265-5404, Fax: 217-244-5632, E-mail: rgrady@illinois.edu. Web site: http://education.illinois.edu/epol.

The University of Iowa, Henry B. Tippie College of Business, Henry B. Tippie School of Management, Iowa City, IA 52242-1316. Offers finance (MBA); investment management (MBA); marketing (MBA); process and operations excellence (MBA); strategic innovation (MBA); JD/MBA; MBA/MA; MBA/MD; MBA/MHA; MBA/MSN. *Accreditation:* AACSB. Part-time and evening/weekend programs available. *Faculty:* 62 full-time (19 women), 26 part-time/adjunct (6 women). *Students:* 153 full-time (34 women), 876 part-time (288 women); includes 87 minority (16 Black or African American, non-Hispanic/Latino; 4 American Indian or Alaska Native, non-Hispanic/Latino; 43 Asian, non-Hispanic/Latino; 24 Hispanic/Latino), 130 international. Average age 32. 697 applicants, 66% accepted, 362 enrolled. In 2011, 361 master's awarded. *Degree requirements:* For master's, minimum GPA of 2.75. *Entrance requirements:* For master's, GMAT, quality work experience and leadership as shown through resume, references, and essays. Additional exam requirements/recommendations for international students: Required—TOEFL (minimum score 600 paper-based; 250 computer-based; 100 iBT), IELTS (minimum score 7). *Application deadline:* For fall admission, 7/30 for domestic students, 4/15 for international students; for spring admission, 12/15 for domestic and international students. Applications are processed on a rolling basis. Application fee: $60 ($100 for international students). Electronic applications accepted. *Expenses:* Contact institution. *Financial support:* In 2011–12, 110 students received support, including 110 fellowships (averaging $9,059 per year), 82 research assistantships with partial tuition reimbursements available (averaging $8,609 per year), 16 teaching assistantships with partial tuition reimbursements available (averaging $14,530 per year); career-related internships or fieldwork, scholarships/grants, health care benefits, and unspecified assistantships also available. Financial award application deadline: 4/15; financial award applicants required to submit FAFSA. *Faculty research:* Capital markets, econometrics, optimization, investments and empirical corporate finance, Iowa electronic markets. *Unit head:* Prof. Jarjisu Sa-Aadu, Associate Dean, MBA Programs, 800-622-4692, Fax: 319-335-3604, E-mail: jsa-aadu@uiowa.edu. *Application contact:* Jodi Schafer, Director of Admissions and Financial Aid, 319-335-0864, Fax: 319-335-3604, E-mail: jodi-schafer@uiowa.edu. Web site: http://tippie.uiowa.edu/mba.

University of Lethbridge, School of Graduate Studies, Lethbridge, AB T1K 3M4, Canada. Offers accounting (MScM); addictions counseling (M Sc); agricultural biotechnology (M Sc); agricultural studies (M Sc, MA); anthropology (MA); archaeology (MA); art (MA, MFA); biochemistry (M Sc); biological sciences (M Sc); biomolecular science (PhD); biosystems and biodiversity (PhD); Canadian studies (MA); chemistry (M Sc); computer science (M Sc); computer science and geographical information science (M Sc); counseling psychology (M Ed); dramatic arts (MA); earth, space, and physical science (PhD); economics (MA); educational leadership (M Ed); English (MA); environmental science (M Sc); evolution and behavior (PhD); exercise science (M Sc); finance (MScM); French (MA); French/German (MA); French/Spanish (MA); general education (M Ed); general management (MScM); geography (M Sc, MA); German (MA); health science (M Sc); history (MA); human resource management and labour relations (MScM); individualized multidisciplinary (M Sc, MA); information systems (MScM); international management (MScM); kinesiology (M Sc, MA); management (M Sc, MA); marketing (MScM); mathematics (M Sc); music (M Mus, MA); Native American studies (MA); neuroscience (M Sc, PhD); new media (MA); nursing (M Sc); philosophy (MA); physics (M Sc); policy and strategy (MScM); political science (MA); psychology (M Sc, MA); religious studies (MA); social sciences (MA); sociology (MA); theatre and dramatic arts (MFA); theoretical and computational science (PhD); urban and regional studies (MA); women's studies (MA). Part-time and evening/weekend programs available. *Degree requirements:* For doctorate, comprehensive exam, thesis/dissertation. *Entrance requirements:* For master's, GMAT (M Sc in management), bachelor's degree in related field, minimum GPA of 3.0 during previous 20 graded semester courses, 2 years teaching or related experience (M Ed); for doctorate, master's degree, minimum graduate GPA of 3.5. Additional exam requirements/recommendations for international students: Required—TOEFL. *Faculty research:* Movement and brain plasticity, gibberellin physiology, photosynthesis, carbon cycling, molecular properties of main-group ring components.

University of Mary, Gary Tharaldson School of Business, Bismarck, ND 58504-9652. Offers accountancy (MBA); business administration (MBA); health care (MBA); human resource management (MBA); management (MBA); project management (MPM); strategic leadership (MSSL). Part-time and evening/weekend programs available. *Faculty:* 8 full-time (5 women), 66 part-time/adjunct (22 women). *Students:* 340 full-time (190 women), 189 part-time (91 women); includes 69 minority (28 Black or African American, non-Hispanic/Latino; 25 American Indian or Alaska Native, non-Hispanic/Latino; 7 Asian, non-Hispanic/Latino; 7 Hispanic/Latino; 1 Native Hawaiian or other Pacific Islander, non-Hispanic/Latino; 1 Two or more races, non-Hispanic/Latino), 14 international. Average age 35. 207 applicants, 95% accepted, 148 enrolled. In 2011, 265 master's awarded. *Degree requirements:* For master's, strategic planning seminar. *Entrance requirements:* For master's, minimum GPA of 2.5. Additional exam requirements/recommendations for international students: Required—TOEFL (minimum score 500 paper-based; 197 computer-based; 71 iBT). *Application deadline:* Applications are processed on a rolling basis. Application fee: $40. *Financial support:* Application deadline: 8/1; applicants required to submit FAFSA. *Unit head:* Dr. Shanda Traiser, Director of the School of Accelerated and Distance Education, 701-355-8160, Fax: 701-255-7687, E-mail: straiser@umary.edu. *Application contact:* Wayne G. Maruska, Graduate Program Advisor, 701-355-8134, Fax: 701-255-7687, E-mail: wmaruska@umary.edu.

University of Massachusetts Amherst, Graduate School, Isenberg School of Management, Program in Management, Amherst, MA 01003. Offers accounting (PhD); business administration (MBA); business administration/sport management (MBA/MS); finance (PhD); hospitality and tourism management (PhD); management science (PhD); marketing (PhD); organization studies (PhD); sport management (PhD); strategic management (PhD); MBA/MS; MPH/MPPA. *Accreditation:* AACSB. Part-time programs available. *Faculty:* 61 full-time (14 women). *Students:* 92 full-time (34 women), 9 part-time (3 women); includes 8 minority (1 Black or African American, non-Hispanic/Latino; 4 Asian, non-Hispanic/Latino; 3 Hispanic/Latino), 47 international. Average age 33. 340 applicants, 15% accepted, 29 enrolled. In 2011, 31 master's, 13 doctorates awarded. Terminal master's awarded for partial completion of doctoral program. *Degree requirements:* For doctorate, comprehensive exam, thesis/dissertation. *Entrance requirements:* For master's and doctorate, GMAT. Additional exam requirements/recommendations for international students: Required—TOEFL (minimum score 550 paper-based; 213 computer-based; 80 iBT), IELTS (minimum score 6.5). *Application deadline:* For fall admission, 1/20 for domestic and international students. Applications are processed on a rolling basis. Application fee: $50 ($65 for international students). Electronic applications accepted. Tuition and fees vary according to course load, campus/location and program. *Financial support:* Fellowships with full and partial tuition reimbursements, research assistantships with full and partial tuition reimbursements, teaching assistantships with full and partial tuition reimbursements, career-related internships or fieldwork, Federal Work-Study, scholarships/grants, traineeships, health care benefits, tuition waivers (full and partial), and unspecified assistantships available. Support available to part-time students. Financial award application deadline: 1/20. *Unit* *head:* Dr. William Woodridge, Chair, 413-545-5675, Fax: 413-577-2234. *Application contact:* Lindsay DeSantis, Interim Supervisor of Admissions, 413-545-0722, Fax: 413-577-0010, E-mail: gradadm@grad.umass.edu. Web site: http://www.isenberg.umass.edu/.

University of Michigan–Dearborn, College of Business, Dearborn, MI 48128-1491. Offers accounting (MBA, MS); business analytics (MS); finance (MBA, MS); information systems (MS); international business (MBA); management (MBA); management information systems (MBA); marketing (MBA); supply chain management (MBA, MS); MBA/MHSA; MBA/MSE; MBA/MSF; MBA/MSIS; MSF/MSA. *Accreditation:* AACSB. Part-time and evening/weekend programs available. Postbaccalaureate distance learning degree programs offered (no on-campus study). *Faculty:* 50 full-time (6 women), 32 part-time/adjunct (18 women). *Students:* 65 full-time (29 women), 356 part-time (121 women); includes 79 minority (19 Black or African American, non-Hispanic/Latino; 36 American Indian or Alaska Native, non-Hispanic/Latino; 15 Hispanic/Latino; 1 Native Hawaiian or other Pacific Islander, non-Hispanic/Latino; 8 Two or more races, non-Hispanic/Latino), 80 international. Average age 28. 175 applicants, 53% accepted, 68 enrolled. In 2011, 173 master's awarded. *Entrance requirements:* For master's, GMAT or GRE, 2 years of work experience (MBA); course work in computer applications, statistics, and pre-calculus or finite mathematics; 18 credits of accounting course work beyond introductory courses (MS in accounting). Additional exam requirements/recommendations for international students: Required—TOEFL (minimum score 560 paper-based; 220 computer-based; 84 iBT), IELTS. *Application deadline:* For fall admission, 8/1 priority date for domestic students, 6/1 for international students; for winter admission, 12/1 priority date for domestic students, 10/1 for international students; for spring admission, 4/1 priority date for domestic students, 2/1 for international students. Applications are processed on a rolling basis. Application fee: $60. Electronic applications accepted. *Expenses:* Contact institution. *Financial support:* Career-related internships or fieldwork, Federal Work-Study, and scholarships/grants available. Support available to part-time students. Financial award application deadline: 9/1; financial award applicants required to submit FAFSA. *Faculty research:* Cultural diversity, buyer-supplier relations, error detection in data, economic evolution. *Unit head:* Dr. Lee Redding, Interim Dean, 313-593-5248, Fax: 313-271-9835, E-mail: lredding@umd.umich.edu. *Application contact:* Joan Doherty, Academic Advisor/Counselor, 313-593-5460, Fax: 313-271-9838, E-mail: gradbusiness@umd.umich.edu. Web site: http://www.cob.umd.umich.edu.

University of Minnesota, Twin Cities Campus, Carlson School of Management, Doctoral Program in Business Administration, Minneapolis, MN 55455-0213. Offers accounting (PhD); finance (PhD); information and decision sciences (PhD); marketing (PhD); operations and management science (PhD); strategic management and organization (PhD). *Faculty:* 104 full-time (30 women). *Students:* 74 full-time (30 women); includes 8 minority (5 Asian, non-Hispanic/Latino; 3 Hispanic/Latino), 50 international. Average age 30. 320 applicants, 8% accepted, 15 enrolled. In 2011, 13 doctorates awarded. *Degree requirements:* For doctorate, comprehensive exam, thesis/dissertation, written and oral preliminary exams, proposal defense, final defense. *Entrance requirements:* For doctorate, GMAT, GRE General Test. Additional exam requirements/recommendations for international students: Required—TOEFL (minimum score 600 paper-based; 250 computer-based; 100 iBT); Recommended—IELTS (minimum score 7.5). *Application deadline:* For fall admission, 12/31 for domestic and international students. Applications are processed on a rolling basis. Application fee: $75 ($95 for international students). Electronic applications accepted. *Expenses:* Contact institution. *Financial support:* In 2011–12, 66 students received support, including 112 fellowships with full tuition reimbursements available (averaging $6,700 per year), 55 research assistantships with full tuition reimbursements available (averaging $6,750 per year), 54 teaching assistantships with full tuition reimbursements available (averaging $6,750 per year); institutionally sponsored loans, scholarships/grants, health care benefits, and unspecified assistantships also available. Financial award application deadline: 12/31. *Faculty research:* Corporate strategy, finance, entrepreneurship, marketing, information and decision science, operations, accounting, quality management. *Unit head:* Dr. Shawn P. Curley, Director, 612-624-6546, Fax: 612-624-8221, E-mail: curley@umn.edu. *Application contact:* Earlene K. Bronson, Assistant Director, 612-624-0875, Fax: 612-624-8221, E-mail: brons003@umn.edu. Web site: http://www.csom.umn.edu/phd-BA/.

University of New Haven, Graduate School, School of Business, Program in Business Administration, West Haven, CT 06516-1916. Offers accounting (MBA, Certificate), including CPA (MBA); business management (Certificate); business policy and strategy (MBA); finance (MBA), including CFA; global marketing (MBA); human resource management (Certificate); human resources management (MBA); international business (Certificate); marketing (Certificate); sports management (MBA); telecommunications management (Certificate); MBA/MPA. Part-time and evening/weekend programs available. *Students:* 215 full-time (106 women), 182 part-time (87 women); includes 73 minority (38 Black or African American, non-Hispanic/Latino; 2 American Indian or Alaska Native, non-Hispanic/Latino; 22 Asian, non-Hispanic/Latino; 11 Hispanic/Latino), 129 international. 179 applicants, 97% accepted, 93 enrolled. In 2011, 197 master's, 28 other advanced degrees awarded. *Degree requirements:* For master's, thesis or alternative. *Entrance requirements:* For master's, GMAT. Additional exam requirements/recommendations for international students: Required—TOEFL (minimum score 520 paper-based; 190 computer-based; 70 iBT), IELTS (minimum score 5.5). *Application deadline:* For fall admission, 5/31 for international students; for winter admission, 10/15 for international students; for spring admission, 1/15 for international students. Applications are processed on a rolling basis. Application fee: $50. Electronic applications accepted. *Expenses:* Contact institution. *Financial support:* Research assistantships with partial tuition reimbursements, teaching assistantships with partial tuition reimbursements, Federal Work-Study, scholarships/grants, health care benefits, tuition waivers, and unspecified assistantships available. Support available to part-time students. Financial award applicants required to submit FAFSA. *Unit head:* Charles Coleman, Chairman, 203-932-7375. *Application contact:* Eloise Gormley, Director of Graduate Admissions, 203-932-7449, Fax: 203-932-7137, E-mail: gradinfo@newhaven.edu. Web site: http://www.newhaven.edu/7433/.

University of New Mexico, Robert O. Anderson Graduate School of Management, Department of Marketing, Information and Decision Sciences, Albuquerque, NM 87131. Offers information assurance (MBA); management information systems (MBA); marketing management (MBA); operations management (MBA). Part-time and evening/weekend programs available. *Faculty:* 14 full-time (4 women), 11 part-time/adjunct (5 women). In 2011, 74 master's awarded. *Degree requirements:* For master's, minimum GPA of 3.0. *Entrance requirements:* For master's, GMAT or GRE. Additional exam requirements/recommendations for international students: Required—TOEFL (minimum score 550 paper-based; 213 computer-based; 79 iBT). *Application deadline:* For fall admission, 4/1 priority date for domestic students, 4/1 for international students; for spring admission, 10/1 priority date for domestic students, 10/1 for international students. Applications are processed on a rolling basis. Application fee: $50. Electronic applications accepted. *Financial support:* Fellowships, research assistantships, career-related internships or fieldwork, Federal Work-Study, scholarships/grants, and unspecified assistantships available. Support available to part-time students. Financial award application deadline: 6/1. *Faculty research:* Marketing, operations, information science. *Unit head:* Dr. Steve Yourstone, Chair, 505-277-6471, Fax: 505-277-7108. *Application contact:* Megan Conner, Director, Student Services, 505-277-3290, Fax: 505-277-8436, E-mail: mconner@mgt.unm.edu.

University of New Mexico, Robert O. Anderson Graduate School of Management, Department of Organizational Studies, Albuquerque, NM 87131. Offers human resources management (MBA); policy and planning (MBA). Part-time and evening/weekend programs available. *Faculty:* 12 full-time (6 women), 16 part-time/adjunct (10 women). In 2011, 74 master's awarded. *Degree requirements:* For master's, minimum GPA of 3.0. *Entrance requirements:* For master's, GMAT or GRE. Additional exam requirements/recommendations for international students: Required—TOEFL (minimum score 550 paper-based; 213 computer-based; 79 iBT). *Application deadline:* For fall admission, 4/1 priority date for domestic students, 4/1 for international students; for spring admission, 10/1 priority date for domestic students, 10/1 for international students. Applications are processed on a rolling basis. Application fee: $50. Electronic applications accepted. *Financial support:* Fellowships, research assistantships, career-related internships or fieldwork, Federal Work-Study, scholarships/grants, and unspecified assistantships available. Support available to part-time students. Financial award application deadline: 6/1. *Faculty research:* Business ethics and social corporate responsibility, diversity, human resources, organizational strategy, organizational behavior. *Unit head:* Dr. Jacqueline Hood, Chair, 505-277-6471, Fax: 505-277-7108. *Application contact:* Megan Conner, Director, Student Services, 505-277-3290, Fax: 505-277-8436, E-mail: mconner@mgt.unm.edu.

The University of North Carolina at Chapel Hill, Kenan-Flagler Business School, Doctoral Program in Business Administration, Chapel Hill, NC 27599. Offers accounting (PhD); finance (PhD); marketing (PhD); operations management (PhD); organizational behavior (PhD); strategy (PhD). *Accreditation:* AACSB. *Degree requirements:* For doctorate, thesis/dissertation. *Entrance requirements:* For doctorate, GMAT or GRE General Test. Electronic applications accepted. *Expenses:* Contact institution.

University of Pittsburgh, Katz Graduate School of Business, Master of Business Administration Programs, Pittsburgh , PA 15260. Offers finance (MBA); information systems (MBA); marketing (MBA); operations management (MBA); organizational behavior and human resource management (MBA); organizational leadership (Certificate); strategy, environment and organizations (MBA); technology, innovation and entrepreneurship (Certificate); MBA/JD; MBA/MIB; MBA/MPIA; MBA/MSE; MBA/MSIS; MID/MBA. *Accreditation:* AACSB. Part-time and evening/weekend programs available. *Faculty:* 62 full-time (17 women), 21 part-time/adjunct (4 women). *Students:* 179 full-time (63 women), 572 part-time (373 women); includes 69 minority (29 Black or African American, non-Hispanic/Latino; 24 Asian, non-Hispanic/Latino; 16 Hispanic/Latino), 83 international. Average age 29. 391 applicants, 42% accepted, 78 enrolled. *Degree requirements:* For master's, minimum GPA of 3.0. *Entrance requirements:* For master's, GMAT, recommendations, undergraduate transcripts, essay, resumé, interview, bachelor's degree. Additional exam requirements/recommendations for international students: Required—TOEFL (minimum score 600 paper, 250 computer, 100 iBT) or IELTS. *Application deadline:* For fall admission, 4/1 priority date for domestic students, 2/1 for international students. Application fee: $50. Electronic applications accepted. *Expenses:* Tuition, state resident: full-time $18,774; part-time $760 per credit. Tuition, nonresident: full-time $30,736; part-time $1258 per credit. *Required fees:* $740; $200 per term. Tuition and fees vary according to program. *Financial support:* In 2011–12, 58 students received support. Career-related internships or fieldwork and scholarships/grants available. Financial award application deadline: 3/1; financial award applicants required to submit FAFSA. *Faculty research:* Accounting statements and reporting, corporate finance, information systems processes, structures and decision-making, consumer behavior and marketing models. *Unit head:* William T. Valenta, Assistant Dean/Director, 412-648-1610, Fax: 412-648-1659, E-mail: wtvalenta@katz.pitt.edu. *Application contact:* Thomas Keller, Director of MBA Admissions, 412-648-1700, Fax: 412-648-1659, E-mail: mba@katz.pitt.edu. Web site: http://www.business.pitt.edu/katz/mba/.

The University of Texas at Dallas, Naveen Jindal School of Management, Program in Management and Administrative Sciences, Richardson, TX 75080. Offers electronic commerce (MS); finance (MS); healthcare administration (MS); information systems (MS); innovation and entrepreneurship (MS); international management (MS); leadership in organizations (MS); marketing (MS); operations (MS); organizations (MS); real estate (MS); strategy (MS). *Accreditation:* AACSB. Part-time and evening/weekend programs available. *Faculty:* 26 full-time (6 women), 9 part-time/adjunct (2 women). *Students:* 128 full-time (69 women), 169 part-time (95 women); includes 76 minority (18 Black or African American, non-Hispanic/Latino; 1 American Indian or Alaska Native, non-Hispanic/Latino; 37 Asian, non-Hispanic/Latino; 15 Hispanic/Latino; 1 Native Hawaiian or other Pacific Islander, non-Hispanic/Latino; 4 Two or more races, non-Hispanic/Latino), 77 international. Average age 34. 220 applicants, 63% accepted, 68 enrolled. In 2011, 58 master's awarded. *Degree requirements:* For master's, thesis optional. *Entrance requirements:* For master's, GMAT. Additional exam requirements/recommendations for international students: Required—TOEFL (minimum score 550 paper-based; 215 computer-based). *Application deadline:* For fall admission, 7/15 for domestic students, 5/1 for international students; for spring admission, 11/15 for domestic students, 9/1 for international students. Applications are processed on a rolling basis. Application fee: $50 ($100 for international students). Electronic applications accepted. *Expenses:* Tuition, state resident: full-time $11,170; part-time $620.56 per credit hour. Tuition, nonresident: full-time $20,212; part-time $1122.89 per credit hour. *Financial support:* In 2011–12, 68 students received support, including 7 teaching assistantships with partial tuition reimbursements available (averaging $16,200 per year); research assistantships with partial tuition reimbursements available, career-related internships or fieldwork, Federal Work-Study, institutionally sponsored loans, scholarships/grants, and unspecified assistantships also available. Support available to part-time students. Financial award application deadline: 4/30; financial award applicants required to submit FAFSA. *Faculty research:* Integrated and detailed knowledge of functional areas of management, analytical tools for effective appraisal and decision-making. *Unit head:* Dr. Gregory Dess, Area Coordinator, 972-883-4439, E-mail: gdess@utdallas.edu. *Application contact:* James Parker, Assistant Director, 972-883-5842, E-mail: jparker@utdallas.edu. Web site: http://jindal.utdallas.edu/academic-areas/organizations-strategy-and-international-management/.

The University of Texas at Dallas, Naveen Jindal School of Management, Programs in Management Science, Richardson, TX 75080. Offers accounting (PhD); finance (PhD); information systems (PhD); marketing (PhD); operations management (PhD). *Accreditation:* AACSB. Part-time and evening/weekend programs available. *Faculty:* 14 full-time (4 women). *Students:* 75 full-time (30 women), 8 part-time (4 women); includes 5 minority (4 Asian, non-Hispanic/Latino; 1 Two or more races, non-Hispanic/Latino), 71 international. Average age 31. 224 applicants, 11% accepted, 20 enrolled. In 2011, 10 doctorates awarded. *Degree requirements:* For doctorate, thesis/dissertation. *Entrance requirements:* For doctorate, GMAT, minimum GPA of 3.0. Additional exam requirements/recommendations for international students: Required—TOEFL (minimum score 550 paper-based; 215 computer-based). *Application deadline:* For fall admission, 7/15 for domestic students, 5/1 for international students; for spring admission, 11/15 for domestic students, 9/1 for international students. Applications are processed on a rolling basis. Application fee: $50 ($100 for international students). Electronic applications accepted. *Expenses:* Tuition, state resident: full-time $11,170; part-time $620.56 per credit hour. Tuition, nonresident: full-time $20,212; part-time $1122.89 per credit hour. *Financial support:* In 2011–12, 76 students received support, including 3 research assistantships with partial tuition reimbursements available (averaging $21,600 per year), 68 teaching assistantships with partial tuition reimbursements available (averaging $16,162 per year); career-related internships or fieldwork, Federal Work-Study, institutionally sponsored loans, scholarships/grants, and unspecified assistantships also available. Support available to part-time students. Financial award application deadline: 4/30; financial award applicants required to submit FAFSA. *Faculty research:* Empirical generalizations in marketing, diffusion of generations of technology, stochastic brand-choice theory, acceptance of trade deals by supermarkets, nonparametric estimations of market share response. *Unit head:* Dr. Sumit Sarkar, Program Director, 972-883-2745, Fax: 972-883-5977, E-mail: som_phd.@utdallas.edu. *Application contact:* LeeAnne Sloane, Coordinator, 972-883-2745, Fax: 972-883-5977, E-mail: som_phd@utdallas.edu. Web site: http://jindal.utdallas.edu/academic-programs/phd-programs/management-science/.

The University of Western Ontario, Richard Ivey School of Business, London, ON N6A 3K7, Canada. Offers business (EMBA, PhD); corporate strategy and leadership elective (MBA); entrepreneurship elective (MBA); finance elective (MBA); health sector stream (MBA); international management elective (MBA); marketing elective (MBA); JD/MBA. *Degree requirements:* For master's, thesis (for some programs); for doctorate, thesis/dissertation. *Entrance requirements:* For master's, GMAT, 2 years of full-time work experience, interview. Additional exam requirements/recommendations for international students: Required—TOEFL (minimum score 100 computer; 100 iBT) or IELTS (minimium score 6). Electronic applications accepted. *Faculty research:* Strategy, organizational behavior, international business, finance, operations management.

University of West Florida, College of Professional Studies, Department of Applied Science, Technology and Administration, Program in Administration, Pensacola, FL 32514-5750. Offers acquisition and contract administration (MSA); biomedical/pharmaceutical (MSA); criminal justice administration (MSA); database administration (MSA); education leadership (MSA); healthcare administration (MSA); human performance technology (MSA); leadership (MSA); nursing administration (MSA); public administration (MSA); software engineering administration (MSA). Part-time and evening/weekend programs available. Postbaccalaureate distance learning degree programs offered (no on-campus study). *Students:* 36 full-time (28 women), 158 part-time (95 women); includes 61 minority (31 Black or African American, non-Hispanic/Latino; 4 American Indian or Alaska Native, non-Hispanic/Latino; 4 Asian, non-Hispanic/Latino; 17 Hispanic/Latino; 2 Native Hawaiian or other Pacific Islander, non-Hispanic/Latino; 3 Two or more races, non-Hispanic/Latino), 1 international. Average age 34. 102 applicants, 59% accepted, 40 enrolled. In 2011, 62 master's awarded. *Entrance requirements:* For master's, GRE General Test, letter of intent, names of references. Additional exam requirements/recommendations for international students: Required—TOEFL (minimum score 550 paper-based; 213 computer-based). *Application deadline:* For fall admission, 6/1 for domestic and international students; for spring admission, 10/1 for domestic and international students. Applications are processed on a rolling basis. Application fee: $30. *Expenses:* Tuition, state resident: full-time $5729; part-time $302 per credit hour. Tuition, nonresident: full-time $20,059; part-time $961 per credit hour. *Required fees:* $1509; $63 per credit hour. *Financial support:* Unspecified assistantships available. Financial award application deadline: 4/15; financial award applicants required to submit FAFSA. *Unit head:* Dr. Karen Rasmussen, Chairperson, 850-474-2301, Fax: 850-474-2804, E-mail: krasmuss@uwf.edu. *Application contact:* Terry McCray, Assistant Director of Graduate Admissions, 850-473-7718, Fax: 850-473-7714, E-mail: gradadmissions@uwf.edu. Web site: http://uwf.edu/msaprogram/.

University of West Florida, College of Professional Studies, Department of Research and Applied Studies, Pensacola, FL 32514-5750. Offers administration (MSA), including acquisition and contract administration, biomedical/pharmaceutical, criminal justice administration, database administration, education leadership, healthcare administration, human performance technology, leadership, nursing administration, public administration, software engineering and administration; college student personnel administration (M Ed), including college personnel administration, guidance and counseling; curriculum and instruction (M Ed, Ed S); educational leadership (M Ed); middle and secondary level education and ESOL (M Ed). Part-time and evening/weekend programs available. *Faculty:* 2 full-time (both women), 3 part-time/adjunct (2 women). *Students:* 26 full-time (15 women), 13 part-time (9 women); includes 8 minority (4 Black or African American, non-Hispanic/Latino; 2 American Indian or Alaska Native, non-Hispanic/Latino; 1 Hispanic/Latino; 1 Two or more races, non-Hispanic/Latino), 1 international. Average age 26. 51 applicants, 51% accepted, 16 enrolled. In 2011, 17 master's, 49 Ed Ss awarded. *Entrance requirements:* For master's, GRE or MAT, official transcripts; minimum undergraduate GPA of 3.0; letter of intent; three letters of recommendation; resume. Additional exam requirements/recommendations for international students: Required—TOEFL (minimum score 550 paper-based; 213 computer-based). *Application deadline:* For fall admission, 6/1 for domestic and international students; for spring admission, 10/1 for domestic and international students. Applications are processed on a rolling basis. Application fee: $30. *Expenses:* Tuition, state resident: full-time $5729; part-time $302 per credit hour. Tuition, nonresident: full-time $20,059; part-time $961 per credit hour. *Required fees:* $1509; $63 per credit hour. *Financial support:* In 2011–12, 33 fellowships (averaging $860 per year), 10 research assistantships (averaging $3,280 per year), 2 teaching assistantships (averaging $3,760 per year) were awarded; unspecified assistantships also available. Financial award application deadline: 4/15; financial award applicants required to submit FAFSA. *Unit head:* Dr. Joyce Nichols, Chairperson, 850-857-6042, E-mail: jcoleman0@uwf.edu. *Application contact:* Terry McCray, Assistant Director of Graduate Admissions, 850-473-7718, Fax: 850-473-7714, E-mail: gradadmissions@uwf.edu. Web site: http://uwf.edu/pcl/.

Villanova University, Villanova School of Business, MBA - The Fast Track Program, Villanova, PA 19085. Offers finance (MBA); health care management (MBA); international business (MBA); management information systems (MBA); marketing (MBA); real estate (MBA); strategic management (MBA). *Accreditation:* AACSB. Part-time and evening/weekend programs available. *Faculty:* 101 full-time (32 women), 38 part-time/adjunct (8 women). *Students:* 123 part-time (46 women); includes 14 minority (1 Black or African American, non-Hispanic/Latino; 3 American Indian or Alaska Native, non-Hispanic/Latino; 5 Asian, non-Hispanic/Latino; 1 Hispanic/Latino; 4 Two or more races, non-Hispanic/Latino). Average age 29. In 2011, 53 master's awarded. *Degree requirements:* For master's, minimum GPA of 3.0. *Entrance requirements:* For master's, GMAT, work experience. Additional exam requirements/recommendations for international students: Required—TOEFL (minimum score 550 paper-based; 213 computer-based; 80 iBT). *Application deadline:* For fall admission, 6/30 for domestic and international students. Application fee: $50. Electronic applications accepted. *Expenses: Tuition:* Part-time $675 per credit. Part-time tuition and fees vary according to degree level and program. *Financial support:* Scholarships/grants available. Financial award application deadline: 6/30; financial award applicants required to submit FAFSA. *Faculty research:* Business analytics; creativity, innovation and entrepreneurship; global leadership; marketing and public policy; real estate; church management. *Unit head:* Kristy Irwin, Director of Recruitment and Marketing, 610-519-6288, Fax: 610-519-6273, E-mail: kristy.irwin@villanova.edu. *Application contact:* Meredith L. Lockyer, Assistant Director, 610-519-7016, Fax: 610-519-6273, E-mail: meredith.lockyer@villanova.edu. Web site: http://www.mba.villanova.edu.

Villanova University, Villanova School of Business, MBA - The Flex Track Program, Villanova, PA 19085. Offers finance (MBA); health care management (MBA); international business (MBA); management information systems (MBA); marketing (MBA); real estate (MBA); strategic management (MBA); JD/MBA. *Accreditation:* AACSB. Part-time and evening/weekend programs available. Postbaccalaureate distance learning degree programs offered (minimal on-campus study). *Faculty:* 101 full-time (32 women), 38 part-time/adjunct (8 women). *Students:* 18 full-time (9 women), 412 part-time (127 women); includes 45 minority (7 Black or African American, non-Hispanic/Latino; 1 American Indian or Alaska Native, non-Hispanic/Latino; 25 Asian, non-Hispanic/Latino; 4 Hispanic/Latino; 1 Native Hawaiian or other Pacific Islander, non-Hispanic/Latino; 7 Two or more races, non-Hispanic/Latino). Average age 30. In 2011, 150 master's awarded. *Degree requirements:* For master's, minimum GPA of 3.0. *Entrance requirements:* For master's, GMAT, work experience. Additional exam requirements/recommendations for international students: Required—TOEFL (minimum score 550 paper-based; 213 computer-based; 80 iBT). *Application deadline:* For fall admission, 6/30 for domestic and international students; for winter admission, 11/15 for domestic and international students; for spring admission, 3/30 for domestic students, 3/31 for international students. Applications are processed on a rolling basis. Application fee: $50. Electronic applications accepted. *Expenses: Tuition:* Part-time $675 per credit. Part-time tuition and fees vary according to degree level and program. *Financial support:* In 2011–12, 18 research assistantships with full tuition reimbursements (averaging $13,100 per year) were awarded; scholarships/grants and unspecified assistantships also available. Financial award application deadline: 6/30; financial award applicants required to submit FAFSA. *Faculty research:* Business analytics; creativity, innovation and entrepreneurship; global leadership; marketing and public policy; real estate; church management. *Unit head:* Kristy Irwin, Director of Recruitment and Marketing, 610-610-6288, Fax: 610-519-6273, E-mail: kristy.irwin@villanova.edu. *Application contact:* Meredity L. Lockyer, Assistant Director, 610-519-7016, Fax: 610-519-6273, E-mail: meredith.lockyer@villanova.edu. Web site: http://www.mba.villanova.edu.

Virginia Commonwealth University, Graduate School, School of Business, Program in Decision Sciences and Business Analytics, Richmond, VA 23284-9005. Offers MBA, MS. *Entrance requirements:* For master's, GMAT. Additional exam requirements/recommendations for international students: Required—TOEFL (minimum score 600 paper-based; 250 computer-based; 100 iBT). *Application deadline:* For fall admission, 7/1 for domestic students; for spring admission, 11/1 for domestic students. Applications are processed on a rolling basis. Application fee: $50. Electronic applications accepted. *Expenses:* Tuition, state resident: full-time $9133; part-time $507 per credit. Tuition, nonresident: full-time $18,777; part-time $1043 per credit. *Required fees:* $77 per credit. Tuition and fees vary according to degree level, campus/location, program and student level. *Financial support:* Fellowships, research assistantships, teaching assistantships, Federal Work-Study, institutionally sponsored loans, and tuition waivers (full and partial) available. Financial award application deadline: 3/15; financial award applicants required to submit FAFSA. *Unit head:* Dr. E. G. Miller, Interim Chair, Department of Management, 804-827-7404, Fax: 804-828-8884, E-mail: egmiller@vcu.edu. *Application contact:* Jana P. McQuaid, Assistant Dean, Master's Programs, 804-828-4622, Fax: 804-828-7174, E-mail: jpmcquaid@vcu.edu. Web site: http://www.business.vcu.edu/graduate/dsba.html.

Walden University, Graduate Programs, School of Management, Minneapolis, MN 55401. Offers accounting (MS, DBA), including accounting for the professional (MS), CPA (MS), self-designed (MS); accounting and management (MS), including accounting for strategic managers, self-designed; accounting for managers (MBA); advanced project management (Post-Graduate Certificate); applied project management (Post-Graduate Certificate); corporate finance (MBA); entrepreneurship (MBA, DBA); finance (DBA); global management (MS); global supply chain management (DBA); healthcare management (MBA, DBA); healthcare system improvement (MBA); human resource management (MBA, MS, PhD), including functional human resource management (MS), integrating functional and strategic human resource management (MS), organizational strategy (MS); information systems management (DBA); international business (MBA, DBA); leadership (MBA, MS, DBA), including entrepreneurship (MS), general management (MS), human resources leadership (MS), innovation and technology (MS), leader development (MS), leading sustainability (MS), project management (MS), self-designed (MS); management (MS), including healthcare management; managers as leaders (MS); marketing (MBA, DBA); project management (MBA, MS, DBA); research strategies (MS); risk management (MBA); self-designed (MBA, DBA, PhD); social impact management (DBA); strategies for sustainability (MBA); strategy and operations (MS); sustainable management (MS); technology (MBA); technology entrepreneurship (DBA); technology management (MS). Part-time and evening/weekend programs available. Postbaccalaureate distance learning degree programs offered (minimal on-campus study). *Faculty:* 32 full-time (14 women), 275 part-time/adjunct (98 women). *Students:* 3,962 full-time (2,095 women), 1,557 part-time (959 women); includes 3,003 minority (2,510 Black or African American, non-Hispanic/Latino; 25 American Indian or Alaska Native, non-Hispanic/Latino; 140 Asian, non-Hispanic/Latino; 240 Hispanic/Latino; 9 Native Hawaiian or other Pacific Islander, non-Hispanic/Latino; 79 Two or more races, non-Hispanic/Latino), 395 international. Average age 41. In 2011, 586 master's, 87 doctorates, 4 other advanced degrees awarded. *Degree requirements:* For doctorate, thesis/dissertation (for some programs), residency. *Entrance requirements:* For master's, bachelor's degree or equivalent in related field; minimum GPA of 2.5; official transcripts; goal statement; access to computer and Internet; for doctorate, master's degree or equivalent in related field; minimum GPA of 3.0; 3 years of related professional/academic experience (preferred). Additional exam requirements/recommendations for international students: Required—TOEFL (minimum score 550 paper-based; 213 computer-based), IELTS (minimum score 6.5), Michigan English Language Assessment Battery (minimum score 82). *Application deadline:* Applications are processed on a rolling basis. Application fee: $50. Electronic applications accepted. *Financial support:* Federal Work-Study, scholarships/grants, unspecified assistantships, and family tuition reduction, active duty/veteran tuition reduction, group tuition reduction, interest-free payment plans, employee tuition reduction available. Support available to part-time students. Financial award applicants required to submit FAFSA. *Unit head:* Dr. William Schulz, III, Associate Dean, 800-925-3368. *Application contact:* Jennifer Hall, Vice President of Enrollment Management, 866-4-WALDEN, E-mail: info@waldenu.edu. Web site: http://www.waldenu.edu/Colleges-and-Schools/College-of-Management-and-Technology.htm.

Western Governors University, College of Business, Salt Lake City, UT 84107. Offers information technology management (MBA); management and strategy (MBA); strategic leadership (MBA). Evening/weekend programs available. *Students:* 1,665 full-time (684 women); includes 430 minority (202 Black or African American, non-Hispanic/Latino; 18 American Indian or Alaska Native, non-Hispanic/Latino; 72 Asian, non-Hispanic/Latino; 97 Hispanic/Latino; 2 Native Hawaiian or other Pacific Islander, non-Hispanic/Latino; 39 Two or more races, non-Hispanic/Latino), 31 international. Average age 38. In 2011, 388 master's awarded. *Degree requirements:* For master's, capstone project. *Entrance* *requirements:* For master's, Readiness Assessment, commitment counseling discussion, transcript submissions, completion of orientation. Additional exam requirements/recommendations for international students: Required—TOEFL (minimum score 450 paper-based; 80 iBT). *Application deadline:* Applications are processed on a rolling basis. Application fee: $65. Electronic applications accepted. *Expenses: Tuition:* Full-time $6500. Full-time tuition and fees vary according to program. *Financial support:* Scholarships/grants and tuition waivers (partial) available. Financial award applicants required to submit FAFSA. *Application contact:* Enrollment Department, 866-225-5948, Fax: 801-274-3306, E-mail: info@wgu.edu.

Western International University, Graduate Programs in Business, Master of Arts Program in Innovative Leadership, Phoenix, AZ 85021-2718. Offers MA. Part-time and evening/weekend programs available. Postbaccalaureate distance learning degree programs offered (no on-campus study). *Entrance requirements:* For master's, minimum GPA of 2.75. Additional exam requirements/recommendations for international students: Required—TOEFL (minimum score 550 paper-based; 213 computer-based; 79 iBT), TWE (minimum score 5), or IELTS (minimum score 6.5). Electronic applications accepted.

Xavier University, Williams College of Business, Master of Business Administration Program, Cincinnati, OH 45207. Offers business administration (Exec MBA, MBA); business intelligence (MBA); finance (MBA); health industry (MBA); international business (MBA); management information systems (MBA); marketing (MBA); MBA/MHSA; MSN/MBA. *Accreditation:* AACSB. Part-time and evening/weekend programs available. *Faculty:* 45 full-time (17 women), 13 part-time/adjunct (4 women). *Students:* 188 full-time (63 women), 630 part-time (206 women); includes 112 minority (36 Black or African American, non-Hispanic/Latino; 3 American Indian or Alaska Native, non-Hispanic/Latino; 52 Asian, non-Hispanic/Latino; 17 Hispanic/Latino; 1 Native Hawaiian or other Pacific Islander, non-Hispanic/Latino; 3 Two or more races, non-Hispanic/Latino), 45 international. Average age 30. 319 applicants, 63% accepted, 149 enrolled. In 2011, 403 master's awarded. *Degree requirements:* For master's, capstone course. *Entrance requirements:* For master's, GMAT or GRE. Additional exam requirements/recommendations for international students: Required—TOEFL (minimum score 550 paper-based; 213 computer-based; 80 iBT). *Application deadline:* For fall admission, 8/1 priority date for domestic students, 5/1 for international students; for spring admission, 12/1 priority date for domestic students, 9/1 for international students. Applications are processed on a rolling basis. Application fee: $0. Electronic applications accepted. *Expenses:* Contact institution. *Financial support:* In 2011–12, 176 students received support. Scholarships/grants, tuition waivers (partial), and unspecified assistantships available. Financial award application deadline: 3/1; financial award applicants required to submit FAFSA. *Unit head:* Dr. Hema Krishnan, Associate Dean, 513-745-3420, Fax: 513-745-3455, E-mail: krishnan@xavier.edu. *Application contact:* Anna Marie Whelan, Assistant Director, MBA Programs, 513-745-3525, Fax: 513-745-2929, E-mail: whelana@xavier.edu. Web site: http://www.xavier.edu/williams/mba/.

Sustainability Management

Alliant International University–San Francisco, School of Management, Presidio School of Management, San Francisco, CA 94133-1221. Offers sustainable management (MBA, MPA). Part-time programs available. *Faculty:* 6 full-time (3 women), 15 part-time/adjunct (8 women). *Students:* 175 full-time (88 women), 61 part-time (26 women); includes 15 minority (10 Asian, non-Hispanic/Latino; 5 Two or more races, non-Hispanic/Latino). Average age 35. *Entrance requirements:* For master's, letters of reference, essay. Additional exam requirements/recommendations for international students: Required—TOEFL (minimum score 100 iBT). *Application deadline:* For fall admission, 3/9 priority date for domestic students. Applications are processed on a rolling basis. Electronic applications accepted. *Financial support:* Application deadline: 3/9; applicants required to submit FAFSA. *Faculty research:* Sustainable management, renewable energy and clean technology, ecological economics, social entrepreneurship, urban sustainability. *Unit head:* Dr. Edward Quevedo, Interim Dean, 415-561-6555, E-mail: info@presidioedu.org. *Application contact:* Bethany Baugh, Director of Admissions, 415-561-6555, E-mail: admissions@presidioedu.org.

American University, Kogod School of Business, Program in Sustainability Management, Washington, DC 20016-8001. Offers MS. *Expenses: Tuition:* Full-time $24,264; part-time $1348 per credit hour. *Required fees:* $430. Tuition and fees vary according to course load and program. *Unit head:* Dr. Michael Ginzberg, Dean, 202-885-1900, Fax: 202-885-1955, E-mail: ginzberg@american.edu. *Application contact:* Shannon Demko, Director of Admissions, 202-885-1968, Fax: 202-885-1078, E-mail: demko@american.edu.

Anaheim University, Programs in Business Administration, Anaheim, CA 92806-5150. Offers online global (MBA); online green (MBA); professional (MBA); sustainable management (Certificate, Diploma). Postbaccalaureate distance learning degree programs offered.

Antioch University New England, Graduate School, Department of Organization and Management, Program in Organizational and Environmental Sustainability (Green MBA), Keene, NH 03431-3552. Offers MBA. Part-time programs available. *Entrance requirements:* For master's, GRE, resume, 3 letters of recommendation. Additional exam requirements/recommendations for international students: Required—TOEFL (minimum score 600 paper-based; 250 computer-based).

Aquinas College, School of Management, Grand Rapids, MI 49506-1799. Offers health care administration (M Mgt); marketing management (M Mgt); organizational leadership (M Min); sustainable business (M Mgt, MSB). Part-time and evening/weekend programs available. *Faculty:* 11 full-time (3 women), 7 part-time/adjunct (0 women). *Students:* 12 full-time (6 women), 56 part-time (32 women); includes 7 minority (3 Black or African American, non-Hispanic/Latino; 1 Asian, non-Hispanic/Latino; 3 Hispanic/Latino). *Entrance requirements:* For master's, GMAT, minimum undergraduate GPA of 2.75, 2 years of work experience. Additional exam requirements/recommendations for international students: Required—TOEFL (minimum score 550 paper-based; 213 computer-based). *Application deadline:* Applications are processed on a rolling basis. *Expenses:* Contact institution. *Financial support:* Scholarships/grants available. Support available to part-time students. Financial award application deadline: 3/15; financial award applicants required to submit FAFSA. *Unit head:* Brian DiVita, Director, 616-632-2922, Fax: 616-732-4489. *Application contact:* Lynn Atkins-Rykert, Administrative Assistant, 616-632-2924, Fax: 616-732-4489, E-mail: atkinlyn@aquinas.edu.

Argosy University, Chicago, College of Business, Chicago, IL 60601. Offers accounting (DBA); customized professional concentration (MBA, DBA); finance (MBA); fraud examination (MBA); global business sustainability (DBA); healthcare administration (MBA); information systems (DBA); information systems management (MBA); international business (MBA, DBA); management (MBA, MSM, DBA); marketing (MBA, DBA); organizational leadership (Ed D); public administration (MBA); sustainable management (MBA). Postbaccalaureate distance learning degree programs offered (minimal on-campus study).

See Close-Up on page 181.

Argosy University, Dallas, College of Business, Farmers Branch, TX 75244. Offers accounting (DBA, AGC); corporate compliance (MBA, Graduate Certificate); customized professional concentration (MBA); finance (MBA, Graduate Certificate); fraud examination (MBA, Graduate Certificate); global business sustainability (DBA, AGC); healthcare administration (Graduate Certificate); healthcare management (MBA); information systems (MBA, DBA, AGC); information systems management (Graduate Certificate); international business (MBA, DBA, AGC, Graduate Certificate); management (MBA, DBA, AGC, Graduate Certificate); marketing (MBA, DBA, AGC, Graduate Certificate); public administration (MBA, Graduate Certificate); sustainable management (MBA, Graduate Certificate).

See Close-Up on page 183.

Argosy University, Denver, College of Business, Denver, CO 80231. Offers accounting (DBA); corporate compliance (MBA); customized professional concentration (MBA, DBA); finance (MBA); fraud examination (MBA); global business sustainability (DBA); healthcare administration (MBA); information systems (DBA); information systems management (MBA); international business (MBA, DBA); management (MBA, MSM, DBA); marketing (MBA, DBA); organizational leadership (Ed D); public administration (MBA); sustainable management (MBA).

See Close-Up on page 185.

Argosy University, Hawai`i, College of Business, Honolulu, HI 96813. Offers accounting (DBA); corporate compliance (MBA); customized professional concentration (MBA, DBA); finance (MBA, Certificate); fraud examination (MBA); global business sustainability (DBA); healthcare administration (MBA, Certificate); information systems (DBA); information systems management (MBA, Certificate); international business (MBA, DBA, Certificate); management (MBA, MSM, DBA); marketing (MBA, DBA, Certificate); organizational leadership (Ed D); public administration (MBA); sustainable management (MBA).

See Close-Up on page 187.

Argosy University, Inland Empire, College of Business, San Bernardino, CA 92408. Offers accounting (DBA); corporate compliance (MBA); customized professional concentration (MBA, DBA); finance (MBA); fraud examination (MBA); global business sustainability (DBA); healthcare administration (MBA); information systems (DBA); information systems management (MBA); international business (MBA, DBA); management (MBA, MSM, DBA); marketing (MBA, DBA); organizational leadership (Ed D); public administration (MBA); sustainable management (MBA).

See Close-Up on page 189.

Argosy University, Los Angeles, College of Business, Santa Monica, CA 90045. Offers accounting (DBA); corporate compliance (MBA); customized professional concentration (MBA, DBA); finance (MBA); fraud examination (MBA); global business sustainability (DBA); healthcare administration (MBA); information systems (DBA); information systems management (MBA); international business (MBA, DBA); management (MBA, MSM, DBA); marketing (MBA, DBA); organizational leadership (Ed D); public administration (MBA); sustainable management (MBA).

See Close-Up on page 191.

Argosy University, Orange County, College of Business, Orange, CA 92868. Offers accounting (DBA, Adv C); corporate compliance (MBA); customized professional concentration (MBA, DBA); finance (MBA, Certificate); fraud examination (MBA); global business sustainability (DBA); healthcare administration (MBA, Certificate); information systems (DBA, Adv C, Certificate); information systems management (MBA); international business (MBA, DBA, Adv C, Certificate); management (MBA, MSM, DBA, Adv C); marketing (MBA, DBA, Adv C, Certificate); organizational leadership (Ed D); public administration (MBA, Certificate); sustainable management (MBA).

See Close-Up on page 195.

Argosy University, Phoenix, College of Business, Phoenix, AZ 85021. Offers accounting (DBA); corporate compliance (MBA); customized professional concentration (MBA, DBA); finance (MBA); fraud examination (MBA); global business sustainability (DBA); healthcare administration (MBA); information systems (DBA); information systems management (MBA); international business (MBA, DBA); management (MBA, DBA); marketing (MBA, DBA); public administration (MBA); sustainable management (MBA).

See Close-Up on page 197.

Argosy University, Salt Lake City, College of Business, Draper, UT 84020. Offers accounting (DBA); corporate compliance (MBA); customized professional concentration (MBA, DBA); finance (MBA); fraud examination (MBA); global business sustainability (DBA); healthcare administration (MBA); information systems (DBA); information systems management (MBA); international business (MBA, DBA); management (MBA, DBA); marketing (MBA, DBA); public administration (MBA); sustainable management (MBA).

See Close-Up on page 199.

Argosy University, San Francisco Bay Area, College of Business, Alameda, CA 94501. Offers accounting (DBA); corporate compliance (MBA); customized professional concentration (MBA, DBA); finance (MBA); fraud examination (MBA); global business sustainability (DBA); healthcare administration (MBA); information systems (DBA); information systems management (MBA); international business (MBA, DBA); management (MBA, MSM, DBA); marketing (MBA, DBA); organizational leadership (Ed D); public administration (MBA); sustainable management (MBA).

See Close-Up on page 203.

Argosy University, Sarasota, College of Business, Sarasota, FL 34235. Offers accounting (DBA, Adv C); corporate compliance (MBA, DBA, Certificate); customized professional concentration (MBA, DBA); finance (MBA, Certificate); fraud examination

(MBA, Certificate); global business sustainability (DBA, Adv C); healthcare administration (MBA, Certificate); information systems (DBA, Adv C, Certificate); information systems management (MBA); international business (MBA, DBA, Adv C, Certificate); management (MBA, MSM, DBA, Adv C, Certificate); marketing (MBA, DBA, Adv C, Certificate); organizational leadership (Ed D); public administration (MBA, Certificate); sustainable management (MBA, Certificate).

See Close-Up on page 205.

Argosy University, Schaumburg, College of Business, Schaumburg, IL 60173-5403. Offers accounting (DBA, Adv C); customized professional concentration (MBA, DBA); finance (MBA, Certificate); fraud examination (MBA); global business sustainability (DBA); healthcare administration (MBA, Certificate); information systems (DBA, Adv C, Certificate); information systems management (MBA); international business (MBA, DBA, Adv C, Certificate); management (MBA, MSM, DBA, Adv C, Certificate); marketing (MBA, DBA, Adv C, Certificate); organizational leadership (Ed D); public administration (MBA); sustainable management (MBA).

See Close-Up on page 207.

Argosy University, Seattle, College of Business, Seattle, WA 98121. Offers accounting (DBA); corporate compliance (MBA); customized professional concentration (MBA, DBA); finance (MBA); fraud examination (MBA); global business sustainability (DBA); healthcare administration (MBA); information systems (DBA); information systems management (MBA); international business (MBA, DBA); management (MBA, MSM, DBA); marketing (MBA, DBA); organizational leadership (Ed D); public administration (MBA); sustainable management (MBA).

See Close-Up on page 209.

Argosy University, Tampa, College of Business, Tampa, FL 33607. Offers accounting (DBA); corporate compliance (MBA); customized professional concentration (MBA, DBA); finance (MBA); fraud examination (MBA); global business sustainability (DBA); healthcare administration (MBA); information systems (DBA); information systems management (MBA); international business (MBA, DBA); management (MBA, MSM, DBA); marketing (MBA, DBA); organizational leadership (Ed D); public administration (MBA); sustainable management (MBA).

See Close-Up on page 211.

Argosy University, Twin Cities, College of Business, Eagan, MN 55121. Offers accounting (DBA); customized professional concentration (MBA, DBA); finance (MBA); fraud examination (MBA); global business sustainability (DBA); healthcare administration (MBA); information systems (DBA); information systems management (MBA); international business (MBA, DBA); management (MBA, MSM, DBA); marketing (MBA, DBA); organizational leadership (Ed D); public administration (MBA); sustainable management (MBA).

See Close-Up on page 213.

Argosy University, Washington DC, College of Business, Arlington, VA 22209. Offers accounting (DBA); customized professional concentration (MBA, DBA); finance (MBA); fraud examination (MBA); global business sustainability (DBA); healthcare administration (MBA); information systems (DBA); information systems management (MBA); international business (MBA, DBA, Certificate); management (MBA, MSM, DBA); marketing (MBA, DBA, Certificate); organizational leadership (Ed D); public administration (MBA); sustainable management (MBA).

See Close-Up on page 215.

Baldwin Wallace University, Graduate Programs, Division of Business, Program in Sustainability, Berea, OH 44017-2088. Offers MBA. Part-time and evening/weekend programs available. *Students:* 11 full-time (7 women), 3 part-time (all women); includes 3 minority (1 Hispanic/Latino; 2 Two or more races, non-Hispanic/Latino). Average age 34. 5 applicants, 100% accepted, 5 enrolled. *Degree requirements:* For master's, minimum overall GPA of 3.0, completion of all required courses. *Entrance requirements:* For master's, GMAT, bachelor's degree, minimum GPA of 3.0. Additional exam requirements/recommendations for international students: Required—TOEFL (minimum score 523 paper-based; 193 computer-based; 70 iBT). *Application deadline:* For fall admission, 7/25 for domestic students, 4/30 for international students; for spring admission, 12/15 for domestic students, 9/30 for international students. Application fee: $25. Application fee is waived when completed online. *Expenses: Tuition:* Full-time $17,016; part-time $727 per credit hour. Tuition and fees vary according to program. *Financial support:* Application deadline: 5/1; applicants required to submit FAFSA. *Unit head:* Ven Ochaya, Director, 440-826-2391, Fax: 440-826-3868, E-mail: vochaya@bw.edu. *Application contact:* Laura Spencer, Graduate Application Specialist, 440-826-2191, Fax: 440-826-3868, E-mail: lspencer@bw.edu. Web site: http://www.bw.edu/academics/bus/programs/smba/.

Bard College, Bard Center for Environmental Policy, Annandale-on-Hudson, NY 12504. Offers climate science and policy (MS, Professional Certificate), including agriculture (MS), ecosystems (MS); environmental policy (MS, Professional Certificate); sustainability (MBA); MS/JD; MS/MAT. Part-time programs available. *Degree requirements:* For master's, thesis, 4-month, full-time internship. *Entrance requirements:* For master's, GRE, coursework in statistics, chemistry and one other semester of college science; personal statement; curriculum vitae; 3 letters of recommendation; sample of written work. Additional exam requirements/recommendations for international students: Required—TOEFL (minimum score 600 paper-based; 250 computer-based; 100 iBT). Electronic applications accepted. *Expenses:* Contact institution. *Faculty research:* Climate and agriculture, alternative energy, environmental economics, environmental toxicology, EPA law, sustainable development, international relations, literature and composition, human rights, agronomy, advocacy, leadership.

Bernard M. Baruch College of the City University of New York, Zicklin School of Business, Department of Management, New York, NY 10010-5585. Offers entrepreneurship (MBA); management (PhD); operations management (MBA); organizational behavior/human resources management (MBA); sustainable business (MBA). PhD offered jointly with Graduate School and University Center of the City University of New York. Part-time and evening/weekend programs available. *Degree requirements:* For doctorate, comprehensive exam, thesis/dissertation. *Entrance requirements:* For master's, GMAT, 2 letters of recommendation, resume, 2 years of work experience; for doctorate, GMAT. Additional exam requirements/recommendations for international students: Required—TOEFL (minimum score 590 paper-based; 243 computer-based), TWE.

Brandeis University, International Business School, Waltham, MA 02454-9110. Offers finance (MSF); international business (MBA); international economic policy (MBA); international economics and finance (MA, PhD); international finance (MBA); socially responsible business (MBA). Part-time and evening/weekend programs available. Terminal master's awarded for partial completion of doctoral program. *Degree requirements:* For master's, one foreign language, semester abroad; for doctorate, thesis/dissertation. *Entrance requirements:* For master's, GMAT or GRE General Test (MA), GMAT (MBAi, MSF); for doctorate, GRE General Test. Additional exam requirements/recommendations for international students: Required—TOEFL (minimum score 600 paper-based; 250 computer-based), IELTS (minimum score 7). Electronic applications accepted. *Faculty research:* International finance and business, trade policy, macroeconomics, Asian economic issues, developmental economics.

Chatham University, Program in Business Administration, Pittsburgh, PA 15232-2826. Offers business administration (MBA); healthcare professionals (MBA); sustainability (MBA); women's leadership (MBA). Part-time and evening/weekend programs available. *Students:* 25 full-time (21 women), 53 part-time (45 women); includes 13 minority (7 Black or African American, non-Hispanic/Latino; 2 American Indian or Alaska Native, non-Hispanic/Latino; 2 Asian, non-Hispanic/Latino; 2 Hispanic/Latino), 5 international. Average age 32. 59 applicants, 64% accepted, 25 enrolled. In 2011, 21 master's awarded. *Entrance requirements:* For master's, minimum GPA of 3.0, letters of recommendation. Additional exam requirements/recommendations for international students: Required—TOEFL (minimum score 600 paper-based; 250 computer-based; 100 iBT), IELTS (minimum score 7), TWE. *Application deadline:* For fall admission, 4/1 for domestic and international students; for spring admission, 11/1 for domestic students, 10/1 for international students. Applications are processed on a rolling basis. Application fee: $45. Electronic applications accepted. Application fee is waived when completed online. *Expenses: Tuition:* Full-time $13,896. Tuition and fees vary according to program. *Financial support:* Applicants required to submit FAFSA. *Unit head:* Prof. Bruce Rosenthal, Director of Business and Entrepreneurship Program, 412-365-2433. *Application contact:* Michael May, Director of Graduate Admission, 412-365-1141, Fax: 412-365-1609, E-mail: gradadmissions@chatham.edu. Web site: http://www.chatham.edu/mba.

City University of Seattle, Graduate Division, School of Management, Bellevue, WA 98005. Offers accounting (Certificate); change leadership (MBA, Certificate); computer systems (MS); finance (Certificate); financial management (MBA); general management (MBA); general management-Europe (MBA); global marketing (MBA); human resources management (Certificate); individualized study (MBA); information security (MS); information systems (MBA); leadership (MA); marketing (MBA, Certificate); project management (MBA, MS, Certificate); sustainable business (Certificate); technology management (MBA, Certificate). Part-time and evening/weekend programs available. Postbaccalaureate distance learning degree programs offered (no on-campus study). *Faculty:* 6 full-time (2 women), 95 part-time/adjunct (33 women). *Students:* 397 full-time (193 women), 283 part-time (137 women); includes 127 minority (67 Black or African American, non-Hispanic/Latino; 5 American Indian or Alaska Native, non-Hispanic/Latino; 33 Asian, non-Hispanic/Latino; 15 Hispanic/Latino; 1 Native Hawaiian or other Pacific Islander, non-Hispanic/Latino; 6 Two or more races, non-Hispanic/Latino), 117 international. Average age 36. 151 applicants, 100% accepted, 151 enrolled. In 2011, 369 master's, 32 other advanced degrees awarded. *Degree requirements:* For master's, comprehensive exam (for some programs), thesis (for some programs). *Entrance requirements:* Additional exam requirements/recommendations for international students: Required—TOEFL (minimum score 567 paper-based; 227 computer-based; 87 iBT); Recommended—IELTS. *Application deadline:* For fall admission, 9/1 for international students; for winter admission, 12/1 for international students; for spring admission, 3/1 for international students. Applications are processed on a rolling basis. Application fee: $50. Electronic applications accepted. *Financial support:* Federal Work-Study and scholarships/grants available. Support available to part-time students. Financial award applicants required to submit FAFSA. *Unit head:* Dr. Kurt Kirstein, Dean, 425-637-1010 Ext. 5456, Fax: 425-709-5363, E-mail: kdkirstein@cityu.edu. *Application contact:* Alysa Borelli, Director, Recruiting, 888-422-4898, Fax: 425-709-5363, E-mail: info@cityu.edu. Web site: http://www.cityu.edu/programs/som/index.aspx.

Cleary University, Online Program in Business Administration, Ann Arbor, MI 48105-2659. Offers financial planning (MBA); financial planning (Graduate Certificate); green business strategy (MBA, Graduate Certificate); management (MBA); nonprofit management (MBA, Graduate Certificate); organizational leadership (MBA); public accounting (MBA). Part-time and evening/weekend programs available. Postbaccalaureate distance learning degree programs offered (no on-campus study). *Degree requirements:* For master's, thesis. *Entrance requirements:* For master's, bachelor's degree; minimum GPA of 2.5; professional resume indicating minimum 2 years management or related experience; undergraduate degree from an accredited college or university with at least 18 quarter hours (or 12 semester hours) of accounting study (for MBA in accounting). Additional exam requirements/recommendations for international students: Required—TOEFL (minimum score 550 paper-based; 213 computer-based; 79 iBT), Michigan English Language Assessment Battery (minimum score: 75). Electronic applications accepted.

Colorado State University, Graduate School, College of Business, Program in Global Social and Sustainable Enterprise, Fort Collins, CO 80523-1201. Offers MSBA. *Students:* 41 full-time (25 women), 2 part-time (1 woman); includes 7 minority (1 Black or African American, non-Hispanic/Latino; 1 American Indian or Alaska Native, non-Hispanic/Latino; 3 Asian, non-Hispanic/Latino; 2 Hispanic/Latino), 16 international. Average age 32. *Degree requirements:* For master's, variable foreign language requirement, comprehensive exam (for some programs), thesis, practicum. *Entrance requirements:* For master's, GMAT or GRE, 3 recommendations, current resume, minimum cumulative GPA of 3.0. Additional exam requirements/recommendations for international students: Required—TOEFL (minimum score 567 paper-based; 227 computer-based; 80 iBT); Recommended—IELTS (minimum score 6). *Application deadline:* For fall admission, 3/31 priority date for domestic students, 3/30 for international students. Application fee: $50. *Expenses:* Tuition, state resident: full-time $7992. Tuition, nonresident: full-time $19,592. *Required fees:* $1735; $58 per credit. *Financial support:* Fellowships with tuition reimbursements, research assistantships with tuition reimbursements, teaching assistantships, scholarships/grants, and unspecified assistantships available. Financial award application deadline: 3/31; financial award applicants required to submit FAFSA. *Faculty research:* Entrepreneurial and collective decision-making, entrepreneurship and sustainability, cooperative business analysis, organizational behavior, risk management. *Unit head:* Carl Hammerdorfer, Director, 970-491-8734, E-mail: carl.hammerdorfer@business.colostate.edu. *Application contact:* Sandy Dahlberg, Program Advisor, 970-491-6937, E-mail: sandy.dahlberg@colostate.edu. Web site: http://www.biz.colostate.edu/gsse/pages/default.aspx.

Columbia University, School of Continuing Education, Program in Sustainability Management, New York, NY 10027. Offers MS. Program offered in collaboration with Columbia University's Earth Institute. Part-time programs available. Electronic applications accepted.

Dominican University of California, Graduate Programs, School of Business and Leadership, MBA in Sustainable Enterprise Program, San Rafael, CA 94901-2298. Offers MBA. Part-time and evening/weekend programs available. *Students:* 36 full-time (18 women), 56 part-time (41 women); includes 21 minority (2 Black or African American, non-Hispanic/Latino; 6 Asian, non-Hispanic/Latino; 10 Hispanic/Latino; 3 Two or more races, non-Hispanic/Latino), 5 international. Average age 35. 56 applicants, 68% accepted, 26 enrolled. In 2011, 33 master's awarded. *Degree requirements:* For master's, thesis or alternative, capstone. *Entrance requirements:* For master's, minimum GPA of 3.0. Additional exam requirements/recommendations for international students:

Required—TOEFL (minimum score 550 paper-based; 213 computer-based; 80 iBT), IELTS (minimum score 7). *Application deadline:* For fall admission, 6/15 priority date for domestic students, 6/15 for international students; for spring admission, 11/15 priority date for domestic students, 11/15 for international students. Applications are processed on a rolling basis. Application fee: $40. Electronic applications accepted. *Expenses: Tuition:* Full-time $15,660. *Required fees:* $300. Tuition and fees vary according to program. *Financial support:* In 2011–12, 32 students received support. Scholarships/grants available. Support available to part-time students. Financial award application deadline: 3/2; financial award applicants required to submit FAFSA. *Unit head:* Elaine McCarty, Director, 415-458-3712, Fax: 415-459-3206, E-mail: elaine.mccarty@dominican.edu.

Edgewood College, Program in Business, Madison, WI 53711-1997. Offers accountancy (MS); accounting (MBA); business administration (MBA); finance (MBA); management (MBA); marketing (MBA); sustainability leadership (MBA). *Accreditation:* ACBSP. Part-time and evening/weekend programs available. *Students:* 24 full-time (15 women), 95 part-time (41 women); includes 9 minority (2 Black or African American, non-Hispanic/Latino; 4 Asian, non-Hispanic/Latino; 3 Hispanic/Latino), 7 international. Average age 33. In 2011, 43 master's awarded. *Entrance requirements:* For master's, GMAT (minimum score 430), minimum GPA of 2.75, 2 letters of recommendation. Additional exam requirements/recommendations for international students: Required—TOEFL (minimum score 213 computer-based). *Application deadline:* For fall admission, 8/15 for domestic students, 5/1 for international students; for spring admission, 1/8 for domestic students, 11/1 for international students. Applications are processed on a rolling basis. Application fee: $25. Electronic applications accepted. *Expenses: Tuition:* Part-time $747 per credit. Part-time tuition and fees vary according to program. *Financial support:* Career-related internships or fieldwork and scholarships/grants available. *Unit head:* Martin Preizler, Dean, 608-663-2898, Fax: 608-663-3291, E-mail: martinpreizler@edgewood.edu. *Application contact:* Joann Eastman, Admissions Counselor, 608-663-3250, Fax: 608-663-2214, E-mail: gps@edgewood.edu. Web site: http://www.edgewood.edu/Academics/Graduate.aspx.

Edgewood College, Program in Education, Madison, WI 53711-1997. Offers adult learning (MA Ed); bilingual teaching and learning (MA Ed); director of instruction (Certificate); director of special education and pupil services (Certificate); education (MA Ed); educational administration (MA Ed); educational leadership (Ed D); professional studies (MA Ed); program coordinator (Certificate); reading administration (MA Ed); school business administration (Certificate); school principalship K-12 (Certificate); special education (MA Ed); sustainability leadership (MA Ed); teaching and learning (MA Ed); teaching English to speakers of other languages (TESOL) (MA Ed). *Accreditation:* NCATE (one or more programs are accredited). Part-time and evening/weekend programs available. *Students:* 155 full-time (93 women), 152 part-time (116 women); includes 39 minority (13 Black or African American, non-Hispanic/Latino; 5 Asian, non-Hispanic/Latino; 17 Hispanic/Latino; 4 Two or more races, non-Hispanic/Latino), 9 international. Average age 36. In 2011, 39 master's, 32 doctorates awarded. *Degree requirements:* For master's, practicum, research project; for doctorate, comprehensive exam, thesis/dissertation. *Entrance requirements:* For master's, minimum GPA of 2.75, 2 letters of recommendation, personal statement; for doctorate, resume, letter of intent, 2 letters of recommendation, interview, writing sample. Additional exam requirements/recommendations for international students: Required—TOEFL (minimum score 525 paper-based; 197 computer-based; 72 iBT). *Application deadline:* For fall admission, 8/15 for domestic students, 5/1 for international students; for spring admission, 1/8 for domestic students, 11/1 for international students. Applications are processed on a rolling basis. Application fee: $25. Electronic applications accepted. *Expenses: Tuition:* Part-time $747 per credit. Part-time tuition and fees vary according to program. *Unit head:* Dr. Jane Belmore, Dean, 608-663-8336, Fax: 608-663-3291, E-mail: jbelmore@edgewood.edu. *Application contact:* Joann Eastman, Admissions Counselor, 608-663-3250, Fax: 608-663-2214, E-mail: gps@edgewood.edu. Web site: http://education.edgewood.edu/graduate.html.

Fairleigh Dickinson University, College at Florham, Silberman College of Business, Certificate Program in Managing Sustainability, Madison, NJ 07940-1099. Offers Certificate.

Franklin Pierce University, Graduate Studies, Rindge, NH 03461-0060. Offers curriculum and instruction (M Ed); emerging network technologies (Graduate Certificate); energy and sustainability studies (MBA); health administration (MBA, Graduate Certificate); human resource management (MBA, Graduate Certificate); information technology (MBA); information technology management (MS); leadership (MBA, DA); nursing (MS); physical therapy (DPT); physician assistant studies (MPAS); special education (M Ed); sports management (MBA). *Accreditation:* APTA. Part-time programs available. Postbaccalaureate distance learning degree programs offered (no on-campus study). *Degree requirements:* For master's, concentrated original research projects; student teaching; fieldwork and/or internship; leadership project; PRAXIS I and II (for M Ed); for doctorate, concentrated original research projects, clinical fieldwork and/or internship, leadership project. *Entrance requirements:* For master's, minimum GPA of 2.5, 3 letters of recommendation; competencies in accounting, economics, statistics, and computer skills through life experience or undergraduate coursework (for MBA); certification/e-portfolio, minimum C grade in all education courses (for M Ed); license to practice as RN (for MS in nursing); for doctorate, GRE, BA/BS, 3 letters of recommendation, personal mission statement, interview, writing sample, minimum cumulative GPA of 2.8, master's degree (for DA); 80 hours of observation/work in PT settings, completion of anatomy, chemistry, physics, and statistics, minimum GPA of 3.0 (for DPT). Additional exam requirements/recommendations for international students: Required—TOEFL (minimum score 550 paper-based; 195 computer-based; 61 iBT). Electronic applications accepted. *Faculty research:* Evidence-based practice in sports physical therapy, human resource management in economic crisis, leadership in nursing, innovation in sports facility management, differentiated learning and understanding by design.

Goddard College, Graduate Division, Master of Arts in Sustainable Business and Communities Program, Plainfield, VT 05667-9432. Offers MA. Postbaccalaureate distance learning degree programs offered (minimal on-campus study). *Degree requirements:* For master's, thesis. *Entrance requirements:* For master's, 3 letters of recommendation, study plan and resource list, interview.

Illinois Institute of Technology, Stuart School of Business, Program in Business Administration, Chicago, IL 60616-3793. Offers financial management (MBA); innovation and emerging enterprises (MBA); management science (MBA); marketing (MBA); sustainability (MBA); JD/MBA; M Des/MBA; MBA/MS. *Accreditation:* AACSB. Part-time and evening/weekend programs available. *Entrance requirements:* For master's, GRE (minimum score 1000) or GMAT (500). Additional exam requirements/recommendations for international students: Required—TOEFL (minimum score 600 paper-based; 85 iBT); Recommended—IELTS (minimum score 7). Electronic applications accepted. *Expenses:* Contact institution. *Faculty research:* Global management and marketing strategy, technological innovation, management science, financial management, knowledge management.

Indiana University Bloomington, School of Public and Environmental Affairs, Public Affairs Programs, Bloomington, IN 47405. Offers comparative and international affairs (MPA); economic development (MPA); energy (MPA); environmental policy (PhD); environmental policy and natural resource management (MPA); hazardous materials management (Certificate); information systems (MPA); international development (MPA); local government management (MPA); nonprofit management (MPA, Certificate); policy analysis (MPA); public budgeting and financial management (Certificate); public finance (PhD); public financial administration (MPA); public management (MPA, PhD, Certificate); public policy analysis (PhD); social entrepreneurship (Certificate); specialized public affairs (MPA); sustainability and sustainable development (MPA); JD/MPA; MPA/MA; MPA/MIS; MPA/MLS; MSES/MPA. *Accreditation:* NASPAA (one or more programs are accredited). Part-time programs available. *Faculty:* 80 full-time (30 women), 102 part-time/adjunct (43 women). *Students:* 338 full-time, 30 part-time; includes 27 minority (7 Black or African American, non-Hispanic/Latino; 2 American Indian or Alaska Native, non-Hispanic/Latino; 10 Asian, non-Hispanic/Latino; 8 Hispanic/Latino), 56 international. Average age 24. 501 applicants, 148 enrolled. In 2011, 172 master's, 7 doctorates awarded. *Degree requirements:* For master's, core classes, capstone, internship; for doctorate, comprehensive exam, thesis/dissertation. *Entrance requirements:* For master's, GRE General Test or GMAT, official transcripts, 3 letters of recommendation, resume, personal statement; for doctorate, GRE General Test or LSAT, official transcripts, 3 letters of recommendation, resume or curriculum vitae, statement of purpose. Additional exam requirements/recommendations for international students: Required—TOEFL (minimum score 600 paper-based; 96 iBT); Recommended—IELTS (minimum score 7). *Application deadline:* For fall admission, 2/1 priority date for domestic students, 12/1 for international students. Applications are processed on a rolling basis. Application fee: $55 ($65 for international students). Electronic applications accepted. *Financial support:* Fellowships with partial tuition reimbursements, research assistantships with partial tuition reimbursements, teaching assistantships with partial tuition reimbursements, career-related internships or fieldwork, Federal Work-Study, scholarships/grants, health care benefits, unspecified assistantships, and Service Corps programs available. Financial award application deadline: 2/1; financial award applicants required to submit FAFSA. *Faculty research:* Comparative and international affairs, environmental policy and resource management, policy analysis, public finance, public management, urban management, nonprofit management, energy policy, social policy, public finance. *Unit head:* Jennifer Forney, Director of Graduate Student Services, 812-855-9485, Fax: 812-856-3665, E-mail: speampo@indiana.edu. *Application contact:* Admissions Assistant, 812-855-2840, E-mail: speaapps@indiana.edu. Web site: http://www.indiana.edu/~spea/prospective_students/masters/.

Lipscomb University, College of Business, Nashville, TN 37204-3951. Offers accounting (MBA); business administration (general) (MBA); conflict management (MBA); financial services (MBA); healthcare management (MBA); human resources (MHR); leadership (MBA); nonprofit management (MBA); sports management (MBA); sustainability (MBA). *Accreditation:* ACBSP. Part-time and evening/weekend programs available. *Faculty:* 13 full-time (3 women), 7 part-time/adjunct (1 woman). *Students:* 51 full-time (21 women), 83 part-time (48 women); includes 20 minority (16 Black or African American, non-Hispanic/Latino; 3 Asian, non-Hispanic/Latino; 1 Hispanic/Latino), 1 international. Average age 33. 190 applicants, 43% accepted, 54 enrolled. In 2011, 85 master's awarded. *Entrance requirements:* For master's, GMAT, interview, 2 references, resume. Additional exam requirements/recommendations for international students: Required—TOEFL (minimum score 570 paper-based; 230 computer-based). *Application deadline:* For fall admission, 6/15 for domestic students, 2/1 for international students; for winter admission, 6/1 for international students; for spring admission, 11/15 for domestic students. Applications are processed on a rolling basis. Application fee: $50 ($75 for international students). Electronic applications accepted. *Expenses:* Contact institution. *Financial support:* Career-related internships or fieldwork, scholarships/grants, tuition waivers (partial), and unspecified assistantships available. Support available to part-time students. Financial award application deadline: 7/1; financial award applicants required to submit FAFSA. *Faculty research:* Impact of spirituality on organization commitment, leadership, psychological empowerment, training. *Unit head:* Dr. Mike Kendrick, Associate Dean of Graduate Business Programs, 615-966-1833, Fax: 615-966-1818, E-mail: mikekendrick@lipscomb.edu. *Application contact:* Lisa Shacklett, Executive Director of Enrollment and Marketing, 615-966-5968, E-mail: lisa.shacklett@lipscomb.edu. Web site: http://mba.lipscomb.edu.

Maastricht School of Management, Graduate Programs, Maastricht, Netherlands. Offers business administration (MBA, DBA, PhD); facility management (Exec MBA); management (M Sc); sustainability (Exec MBA).

Maharishi University of Management, Graduate Studies, Program in Business Administration, Fairfield, IA 52557. Offers accounting (MBA); business administration (PhD); sustainability (MBA). Evening/weekend programs available. Postbaccalaureate distance learning degree programs offered (minimal on-campus study). *Degree requirements:* For doctorate, thesis/dissertation. *Entrance requirements:* For master's, GMAT, minimum GPA of 3.0; for doctorate, minimum GPA of 3.0. Additional exam requirements/recommendations for international students: Required—TOEFL. *Faculty research:* Leadership, effects of the group dynamics of consciousness on the economy, innovation, employee development, cooperative strategy.

Marlboro College, Graduate School, Program in Business Administration, Marlboro, VT 05344. Offers managing for sustainability (MBA). Part-time and evening/weekend programs available. Postbaccalaureate distance learning degree programs offered (minimal on-campus study). *Degree requirements:* For master's, 60 credits including capstone project. *Entrance requirements:* For master's, letter of intent, essay, transcripts, 2 letters of recommendation. Electronic applications accepted.

Michigan Technological University, Graduate School, Sustainable Futures Institute, Houghton, MI 49931. Offers sustainability (Graduate Certificate). Part-time programs available. In 2011, 6 Graduate Certificates awarded. *Entrance requirements:* For degree, official transcripts, statement of purpose, 2 letters of recommendation. Additional exam requirements/recommendations for international students: Required—TOEFL (minimum score 79 iBT) or IELTS. *Expenses:* Tuition, state resident: full-time $12,636; part-time $702 per credit. Tuition, nonresident: full-time $12,636; part-time $702 per credit. *Required fees:* $226; $226 per year. *Financial support:* Career-related internships or fieldwork, Federal Work-Study, scholarships/grants, unspecified assistantships, and cooperative program available. Financial award applicants required to submit FAFSA. *Unit head:* Dr. David R. Shonnard, Director, 906-487-3132, Fax: 906-487-3213, E-mail: drshonna@mtu.edu. *Application contact:* Carol T. Wingerson, Senior Staff Assistant, 906-487-2327, Fax: 906-487-2463, E-mail: gradadms@mtu.edu. Web site: http://www.sfi.mtu.edu.

National University, Academic Affairs, School of Business and Management, Department of Accounting and Finance, La Jolla, CA 92037-1011. Offers accountancy (M Acc); business administration (MBA); sustainability management (MS). Part-time and evening/weekend programs available. Postbaccalaureate distance learning degree programs offered (no on-campus study). *Degree requirements:* For master's, thesis. *Entrance requirements:* For master's, interview, minimum GPA of 2.5. Additional exam requirements/recommendations for international students: Required—TOEFL (minimum score 550 paper-based; 213 computer-based; 79 iBT), IELTS (minimum score 6). *Application deadline:* Applications are processed on a rolling basis. Application fee: $60

Sustainability Management

($65 for international students). Electronic applications accepted. *Financial support:* Career-related internships or fieldwork, institutionally sponsored loans, scholarships/grants, and tuition waivers (partial) available. Support available to part-time students. Financial award application deadline: 6/30; financial award applicants required to submit FAFSA. *Unit head:* Dr. Farhang Mossavar-Rahmani, Chair, 858-642-8409, Fax: 858-642-8726, E-mail: fmossava@nu.edu. *Application contact:* Dominick Giovanniello, Associate Regional Dean, 800-NAT-UNIV, Fax: 858-541-7792, E-mail: dgiovann@nu.edu. Web site: http://www.nu.edu/OurPrograms/SchoolOfBusinessAndManagement/AccountingAndFinance.html.

National University, Academic Affairs, School of Engineering, Technology and Media, Department of Applied Engineering, La Jolla, CA 92037-1011. Offers engineering management (MS); environmental engineering (MS); homeland security and safety engineering (MS); project management (Certificate); security and safety engineering (Certificate); sustainability management (MS); wireless communications (MS). Part-time and evening/weekend programs available. Postbaccalaureate distance learning degree programs offered (no on-campus study). *Degree requirements:* For master's, thesis. *Entrance requirements:* For master's, interview, minimum GPA of 2.5. Additional exam requirements/recommendations for international students: Required—TOEFL (minimum score 550 paper-based; 213 computer-based; 79 iBT), IELTS (minimum score 6). *Application deadline:* Applications are processed on a rolling basis. Application fee: $60 ($65 for international students). Electronic applications accepted. *Financial support:* Career-related internships or fieldwork, institutionally sponsored loans, scholarships/grants, and tuition waivers (partial) available. Support available to part-time students. Financial award application deadline: 6/30; financial award applicants required to submit FAFSA. *Unit head:* Dr. Shekar Viswanathan, Chair and Associate Professor, 858-309-3416, Fax: 858-309-3420, E-mail: sviswana@nu.edu. *Application contact:* Dominick Giovanniello, Associate Regional Dean, 800-NAT-UNIV, Fax: 858-541-7792, E-mail: dgiovann@nu.edu. Web site: http://www.nu.edu/OurPrograms/SchoolOfEngineeringAndTechnology/AppliedEngineering.html.

The New School, Milano The New School for Management and Urban Policy, Program in Environmental Policy and Sustainability Management, New York, NY 10011. Offers MS.

Rochester Institute of Technology, Graduate Enrollment Services, Golisano Institute for Sustainability, Rochester, NY 14623-5603. Offers M Arch, MS, PhD. *Students:* 27 full-time (16 women), 2 part-time (1 woman); includes 4 minority (1 Black or African American, non-Hispanic/Latino; 3 Hispanic/Latino), 7 international. Average age 29. 72 applicants, 44% accepted, 23 enrolled. In 2011, 1 degree awarded. *Degree requirements:* For master's, comprehensive exam, thesis. *Entrance requirements:* For master's, GRE. Additional exam requirements/recommendations for international students: Required—TOEFL (minimum score 600 paper-based; 250 computer-based; 100 iBT) or IELTS (minimum score 6.5). *Application deadline:* For fall admission, 1/15 priority date for domestic students, 1/15 for international students. Applications are processed on a rolling basis. Application fee: $50. Electronic applications accepted. *Expenses: Tuition:* Full-time $34,659; part-time $963 per credit hour. *Required fees:* $228; $76 per quarter. *Faculty research:* Remanufacturing and resource recovery, sustainable production, sustainable mobility, systems modernization and sustainment, pollution prevention. *Unit head:* Dr. Nabil Nasr, Assistant Provost and Director, 585-475-2602, E-mail: info@sustainability.rit.edu. *Application contact:* Diane Ellison, Assistant Vice President, Graduate Enrollment Services, 585-475-2229, Fax: 585-475-7164, E-mail: gradinfo@rit.edu. Web site: http://www.sustainability.rit.edu/.

South University, Graduate Programs, College of Business, Savannah, GA 31406. Offers corrections (MBA); entrepreneurship and small business (MBA); healthcare administration (MBA); hospitality management (MBA); leadership (MS); sustainability (MBA).

See Close-Up on page 241.

South University, Program in Business Administration, Atlanta, GA. Offers Accelerated MBA. Program offered by South University, Savannah Campus at Atlanta Learning Site.

See Close-Up on page 229.

State University of New York College of Environmental Science and Forestry, Department of Paper and Bioprocess Engineering, Syracuse, NY 13210-2779. Offers biomaterials engineering (MS, PhD); bioprocess engineering (MPS, MS, PhD); paper science and engineering (MPS, MS, PhD); sustainable engineering management (MPS). *Degree requirements:* For master's, thesis; for doctorate, comprehensive exam, thesis/dissertation. *Entrance requirements:* For master's and doctorate, GRE General Test, minimum GPA of 3.0. Additional exam requirements/recommendations for international students: Required—TOEFL (minimum score 550 paper-based; 213 computer-based; 80 iBT), IELTS (minimum score 6). *Application deadline:* For fall admission, 2/1 priority date for domestic students, 2/1 for international students; for spring admission, 11/1 priority date for domestic students, 11/1 for international students. Applications are processed on a rolling basis. Application fee: $60. *Expenses:* Tuition, state resident: full-time $8870; part-time $370 per credit hour. Tuition, nonresident: full-time $15,160; part-time $632 per credit hour. *Required fees:* $60; $370 per credit hour. $350 per semester. One-time fee: $85. *Financial support:* Fellowships with full tuition reimbursements, research assistantships with full tuition reimbursements, teaching assistantships with full tuition reimbursements, career-related internships or fieldwork, Federal Work-Study, institutionally sponsored loans, scholarships/grants, health care benefits, and unspecified assistantships available. Support available to part-time students. Financial award application deadline: 6/30; financial award applicants required to submit FAFSA. *Total annual research expenditures:* $604,516. *Unit head:* Dr. Gary M. Scott, Chair, 315-470-6501, Fax: 315-470-6945, E-mail: gscott@esf.edu. *Application contact:* Dr. Dudley J. Raynal, Dean, Instruction and Graduate Studies, 315-470-6599, Fax: 315-470-6978, E-mail: esfgrad@esf.edu. Web site: http://www.esf.edu/pbe/.

University of California, Berkeley, UC Berkeley Extension, Certificate Programs in Sustainability Studies, Berkeley, CA 94720-1500. Offers leadership in sustainability and environmental management (Professional Certificate); solar energy and green building (Professional Certificate); sustainable design (Professional Certificate).

University of Colorado Denver, Business School, Master of Business Administration Program, Denver, CO 80217. Offers business intelligence (MBA); business strategy (MBA); business to business marketing (MBA); business to consumer marketing (MBA); change management (MBA); corporate financial management (MBA); enterprise technology management (MBA); entrepreneurship (MBA); health administration (MBA), including financial management, health administration, health information technologies, international health management and policy; human resources management (MBA); investment management (MBA); managing for sustainability (MBA); services management (MBA); sports and entertainment management (MBA). *Accreditation:* AACSB. Part-time and evening/weekend programs available. Postbaccalaureate distance learning degree programs offered (no on-campus study). *Students:* 784 full-time (306 women), 203 part-time (81 women); includes 135 minority (18 Black or African American, non-Hispanic/Latino; 5 American Indian or Alaska Native, non-Hispanic/Latino; 50 Asian, non-Hispanic/Latino; 58 Hispanic/Latino; 4 Two or more races, non-Hispanic/Latino), 38 international. Average age 31. 433 applicants, 76% accepted, 212 enrolled. In 2011, 326 master's awarded. *Degree requirements:* For master's, 48 semester hours, including 30 of core courses, 3 in international business, and 15 in electives from over 50 other graduate business courses. *Entrance requirements:* For master's, GMAT, resume, official transcripts, essay, two letters of recommendation, financial statements (for international applicants). Additional exam requirements/recommendations for international students: Required—TOEFL (minimum score 560 paper-based; 197 computer-based; 83 iBT). *Application deadline:* For fall admission, 4/15 priority date for domestic students, 3/15 for international students; for spring admission, 10/15 priority date for domestic students, 10/1 for international students. Applications are processed on a rolling basis. Application fee: $50 ($75 for international students). Electronic applications accepted. *Expenses:* Contact institution. *Financial support:* Scholarships/grants available. Support available to part-time students. Financial award application deadline: 4/1; financial award applicants required to submit FAFSA. *Faculty research:* Marketing, management, entrepreneurship, finance, health administration. *Unit head:* Elizabeth Cooperman, Professor of Finance and Managing for Sustainability/MBA Program Director, 303-315-8422, E-mail: elizabeth.cooperman@ucdenver.edu. *Application contact:* Shelly Townley, Admissions Director, Graduate Programs, 303-315-8202, E-mail: shelly.townley@ucdenver.edu. Web site: http://www.ucdenver.edu/academics/colleges/business/degrees/ms/accounting/Pages/Accounting.aspx.

University of Maine, Graduate School, College of Business, Public Policy and Health, The Maine Business School, Orono, ME 04469. Offers accounting (MBA); business and sustainability (MBA); finance (MBA); management (MBA). *Accreditation:* AACSB. Part-time and evening/weekend programs available. *Faculty:* 20 full-time (8 women), 6 part-time/adjunct (2 women). *Students:* 47 full-time (19 women), 15 part-time (2 women); includes 5 minority (1 American Indian or Alaska Native, non-Hispanic/Latino; 2 Asian, non-Hispanic/Latino; 2 Hispanic/Latino), 5 international. Average age 29. 41 applicants, 71% accepted, 24 enrolled. In 2011, 28 master's awarded. *Entrance requirements:* For master's, GMAT. Additional exam requirements/recommendations for international students: Required—TOEFL (minimum score 550 paper-based; 213 computer-based). *Application deadline:* For fall admission, 6/1 priority date for domestic students, 6/1 for international students; for spring admission, 11/1 priority date for domestic students, 11/1 for international students. Applications are processed on a rolling basis. Application fee: $65. Electronic applications accepted. *Expenses:* Contact institution. *Financial support:* In 2011–12, 16 students received support, including 3 teaching assistantships with full tuition reimbursements available (averaging $13,600 per year); career-related internships or fieldwork, Federal Work-Study, institutionally sponsored loans, scholarships/grants, tuition waivers (full and partial), and unspecified assistantships also available. Financial award application deadline: 3/1. *Faculty research:* Entrepreneurship, investment management, international markets, decision support systems, strategic planning. *Unit head:* Dr. Nory Jones, Director of Graduate Programs, 207-581-1971, Fax: 207-581-1930, E-mail: mba@maine.edu. *Application contact:* Scott G. Delcourt, Associate Dean of the Graduate School, 207-581-3291, Fax: 207-581-3232, E-mail: graduate@maine.edu. Web site: http://www.umaine.edu/business/.

University of Portland, Dr. Robert B. Pamplin, Jr. School of Business, Portland, OR 97203-5798. Offers business administration (MBA); entrepreneurship (MBA); finance (MBA, MS); health care management (MBA); marketing (MBA); nonprofit management (EMBA); operations and technology management (MBA); sustainability (MBA). *Accreditation:* AACSB. Part-time and evening/weekend programs available. *Faculty:* 13 full-time (1 woman), 8 part-time/adjunct (1 woman). *Students:* 50 full-time (13 women), 90 part-time (41 women); includes 19 minority (1 Black or African American, non-Hispanic/Latino; 1 American Indian or Alaska Native, non-Hispanic/Latino; 8 Asian, non-Hispanic/Latino; 5 Hispanic/Latino; 2 Native Hawaiian or other Pacific Islander, non-Hispanic/Latino; 2 Two or more races, non-Hispanic/Latino), 18 international. Average age 31. In 2011, 54 master's awarded. *Entrance requirements:* For master's, GMAT, minimum GPA of 3.0, resume, 2 letters of recommendation. Additional exam requirements/recommendations for international students: Required—TOEFL (minimum score 570 paper-based; 89 iBT), IELTS (minimum score 7). *Application deadline:* For fall admission, 7/15 priority date for domestic students, 7/15 for international students; for spring admission, 12/15 priority date for domestic students, 12/15 for international students. Applications are processed on a rolling basis. Application fee: $50. *Expenses:* Contact institution. *Financial support:* Federal Work-Study, scholarships/grants, and tuition waivers (partial) available. Support available to part-time students. Financial award application deadline: 3/1; financial award applicants required to submit FAFSA. *Unit head:* Dr. Howard Feldman, Associate Dean, 503-943-7224, E-mail: feldman@up.edu. *Application contact:* Melissa McCarthy, Academic Specialist, 503-943-7225, E-mail: mccarthy@up.edu. Web site: http://business.up.edu/.

University of Saskatchewan, College of Graduate Studies and Research, School of Environment and Sustainability, Saskatoon, SK S7N 5A2, Canada. Offers MES.

University of Southern Maine, School of Business, Portland, ME 04104-9300. Offers accounting (MBA); business administration (MBA); finance (MBA); health management and policy (MBA); sustainability (MBA); JD/MBA; MBA/MSA; MBA/MSN; MS/MBA. *Accreditation:* AACSB. Part-time and evening/weekend programs available. *Faculty:* 20 full-time (5 women), 2 part-time/adjunct (1 woman). *Students:* 28 full-time (9 women), 91 part-time (39 women), 1 international. Average age 33. 64 applicants, 72% accepted, 33 enrolled. *Entrance requirements:* For master's, GMAT, minimum AACSB index of 1100. Additional exam requirements/recommendations for international students: Required—TOEFL (minimum score 550 paper-based; 213 computer-based; 79 iBT). *Application deadline:* For fall admission, 8/1 priority date for domestic students, 5/1 for international students; for spring admission, 12/1 priority date for domestic students, 9/1 for international students. Applications are processed on a rolling basis. Application fee: $65. Electronic applications accepted. *Financial support:* In 2011–12, 3 research assistantships with partial tuition reimbursements (averaging $9,000 per year), 3 teaching assistantships with partial tuition reimbursements (averaging $9,000 per year) were awarded; career-related internships or fieldwork, Federal Work-Study, scholarships/grants, tuition waivers (full and partial), and unspecified assistantships also available. Support available to part-time students. Financial award application deadline: 2/15; financial award applicants required to submit FAFSA. *Faculty research:* Economic development, management information systems, real options, system dynamics, simulation. *Unit head:* John Voyer, Director, 207-780-4020, Fax: 207-780-4665, E-mail: voyer@usm.maine.edu. *Application contact:* Alice B. Cash, Assistant Director for Student Affairs, 207-780-4184, Fax: 207-780-4662, E-mail: acash@usm.maine.edu. Web site: http://www.usm.maine.edu/sb.

Walden University, Graduate Programs, School of Management, Minneapolis, MN 55401. Offers accounting (MS, DBA), including accounting for the professional (MS), CPA (MS), self-designed (MS); accounting and management (MS), including accounting for strategic managers, self-designed; accounting for managers (MBA); advanced project management (Post-Graduate Certificate); applied project management (Post-Graduate Certificate); corporate finance (MBA); entrepreneurship (MBA, DBA); finance (DBA); global management (MS); global supply chain management (DBA); healthcare management (MBA, DBA); healthcare system improvement (MBA); human resource management (MBA, MS, PhD), including functional human resource management (MS), integrating functional and strategic human resource management (MS), organizational strategy (MS); information systems management (DBA); international business (MBA, DBA); leadership (MBA, MS, DBA), including entrepreneurship (MS), general management (MS), human resources leadership (MS), innovation and technology (MS), leader development (MS), leading sustainability (MS), project management (MS), self-designed (MS); management (MS), including healthcare management; managers as leaders (MS); marketing (MBA, DBA); project management (MBA, MS, DBA); research strategies (MS); risk management (MBA); self-designed (MBA, DBA, PhD); social impact management (DBA); strategies for sustainability (MBA); strategy and operations (MS); sustainable management (MS); technology (MBA); technology entrepreneurship (DBA); technology management (MS). Part-time and evening/weekend programs available. Postbaccalaureate distance learning degree programs offered (minimal on-campus study). *Faculty:* 32 full-time (14 women), 275 part-time/adjunct (98 women). *Students:* 3,962 full-time (2,095 women), 1,557 part-time (959 women); includes 3,003 minority (2,510 Black or African American, non-Hispanic/Latino; 25 American Indian or Alaska Native, non-Hispanic/Latino; 140 Asian, non-Hispanic/Latino; 240 Hispanic/Latino; 9 Native Hawaiian or other Pacific Islander, non-Hispanic/Latino; 79 Two or more races, non-Hispanic/Latino), 395 international. Average age 41. In 2011, 586 master's, 87 doctorates, 4 other advanced degrees awarded. *Degree requirements:* For doctorate, thesis/dissertation (for some programs), residency. *Entrance requirements:* For master's, bachelor's degree or equivalent in related field; minimum GPA of 2.5; official transcripts; goal statement; access to computer and Internet; for doctorate, master's degree or equivalent in related field; minimum GPA of 3.0; 3 years of related professional/academic experience (preferred). Additional exam requirements/recommendations for international students: Required—TOEFL (minimum score 550 paper-based; 213 computer-based), IELTS (minimum score 6.5), Michigan English Language Assessment Battery (minimum score 82). *Application deadline:* Applications are processed on a rolling basis. Application fee: $50. Electronic applications accepted. *Financial support:* Federal Work-Study, scholarships/grants, unspecified assistantships, and family tuition reduction, active duty/veteran tuition reduction, group tuition reduction, interest-free payment plans, employee tuition reduction available. Support available to part-time students. Financial award applicants required to submit FAFSA. *Unit head:* Dr. William Schulz, III, Associate Dean, 800-925-3368. *Application contact:* Jennifer Hall, Vice President of Enrollment Management, 866-4-WALDEN, E-mail: info@waldenu.edu. Web site: http://www.waldenu.edu/Colleges-and-Schools/College-of-Management-and-Technology.htm.

Section 14
Marketing

This section contains a directory of institutions offering graduate work in marketing, followed by an in-depth entry submitted by an institution that chose to prepare a detailed program description. Additional information about programs listed in the directory but not augmented by an in-depth entry may be obtained by writing directly to the dean of a graduate school or chair of a department at the address given in the directory.

For programs offering related work, see also in this book *Advertising and Public Relations, Business Administration and Management,* and *Hospitality Management.* In another guide in this series:

Graduate Programs in the Humanities, Arts & Social Sciences
See *Communication and Media* and *Public, Regional, and Industrial Affairs*

CONTENTS

Program Directories

Displays and Close-Ups

See also:

Marketing

Adelphi University, Robert B. Willumstad School of Business, MBA Program, Garden City, NY 11530-0701. Offers finance (MBA); management information systems (MBA); management/human resource management (MBA); marketing/e-commerce (MBA). *Accreditation:* AACSB. Part-time and evening/weekend programs available. *Students:* 258 full-time (121 women), 111 part-time (58 women); includes 67 minority (22 Black or African American, non-Hispanic/Latino; 18 Asian, non-Hispanic/Latino; 24 Hispanic/Latino; 3 Two or more races, non-Hispanic/Latino), 172 international. Average age 28. In 2011, 111 master's awarded. *Degree requirements:* For master's, capstone course. *Entrance requirements:* For master's, GMAT, 2 letters of recommendation. Additional exam requirements/recommendations for international students: Required—TOEFL (minimum score 550 paper-based; 213 computer-based; 80 iBT). *Application deadline:* For fall admission, 4/1 for international students; for spring admission, 11/1 for international students. Applications are processed on a rolling basis. Application fee: $50. Electronic applications accepted. *Expenses: Tuition:* Full-time $29,600; part-time $930 per credit. *Required fees:* $1100. *Financial support:* Research assistantships with full and partial tuition reimbursements, career-related internships or fieldwork, Federal Work-Study, institutionally sponsored loans, scholarships/grants, and unspecified assistantships available. Financial award application deadline: 3/1; financial award applicants required to submit FAFSA. *Faculty research:* Supply chain management, distribution channels, productivity benchmark analysis, data envelopment analysis, financial portfolio analysis. *Unit head:* Rakesh Gupta, 516-877-4670, Fax: 516-877-4607, E-mail: gradbusinquiries@adelphi.edu. *Application contact:* Christine Murphy, Director of Admissions, 516-877-3050, Fax: 516-877-3039, E-mail: graduateadmissions@adelphi.edu. Web site: http://business.adelphi.edu/degree-programs/graduate-degree-programs/m-b-a/.

See Display on page 68 and Close-Up on page 177.

Alabama Agricultural and Mechanical University, School of Graduate Studies, School of Business, Department of Management and Marketing, Huntsville, AL 35811. Offers MBA. Part-time and evening/weekend programs available. *Degree requirements:* For master's, comprehensive exam, thesis optional. *Entrance requirements:* For master's, GMAT, minimum undergraduate GPA of 2.5. Additional exam requirements/recommendations for international students: Required—TOEFL (minimum score 500 paper-based; 173 computer-based; 61 iBT). Electronic applications accepted. *Faculty research:* Consumer behavior of blacks, small business marketing, economics of education, China in transition, international economics.

American College of Thessaloniki, Department of Business Administration, Pylea, Greece. Offers banking and finance (MBA); entrepreneurship (MBA, Certificate); finance (Certificate); management (MBA, Certificate); marketing (MBA, Certificate). Part-time and evening/weekend programs available. *Degree requirements:* For master's, thesis. *Entrance requirements:* For master's, bachelor's degree. Additional exam requirements/recommendations for international students: Recommended—TOEFL. Electronic applications accepted.

American InterContinental University Buckhead Campus, Program in Business Administration, Atlanta, GA 30326-1016. Offers accounting and finance (MBA); management (MBA); marketing (MBA). Evening/weekend programs available. Postbaccalaureate distance learning degree programs offered. *Entrance requirements:* For master's, minimum cumulative undergraduate GPA of 2.0. Additional exam requirements/recommendations for international students: Required—TOEFL (minimum score 530 paper-based; 230 computer-based). Electronic applications accepted. *Faculty research:* Leadership management, international advertising.

American InterContinental University Online, Program in Business Administration, Hoffman Estates, IL 60192. Offers accounting and finance (MBA); finance (MBA); healthcare management (MBA); human resource management (MBA); international business (MBA); management (MBA); marketing (MBA); operations management (MBA); organizational psychology and development (MBA); project management (MBA). Evening/weekend programs available. Postbaccalaureate distance learning degree programs offered (no on-campus study). *Entrance requirements:* Additional exam requirements/recommendations for international students: Required—TOEFL (minimum score 550 paper-based; 213 computer-based). Electronic applications accepted.

American InterContinental University South Florida, Program in International Business, Weston, FL 33326. Offers accounting and finance (MBA); human resource management (MBA); management (MBA); marketing (MBA). Part-time and evening/weekend programs available. Postbaccalaureate distance learning degree programs offered. Electronic applications accepted.

American International College, School of Business Administration, MBA Program, Springfield, MA 01109-3189. Offers accounting (MBA); corporate/public communication (MBA); finance (MBA); general business (MBA); hospitality, hotel and service management (MBA); international business (MBA); international business practice (MBA); management (MBA); management information systems (MBA); marketing (MBA). International business practice program developed in cooperation with the Mountbatten Institute.

American Public University System, AMU/APU Graduate Programs, Charles Town, WV 25414. Offers accounting (MBA, MS); administration and supervision (M Ed); criminal justice (MA); emergency and disaster management (MA); entrepreneurship (MBA); environmental policy and management (MS), including environmental planning, environmental sustainability, fish and wildlife management, general (MA, MS), global environmental management; finance (MBA); general (MBA); global business management (MBA); guidance and counseling (M Ed); history (MA), including American history, ancient and classical history, European history, global history, military and diplomatic history, public history; homeland security (MA); homeland security resource allocation (MBA); humanities (MA); information technology (MS), including digital forensics, enterprise software development, information assurance and security, IT project management; information technology management (MBA); intelligence studies (MA), including criminal intelligence, general (MA, MS), homeland security, intelligence analysis, intelligence collection, intelligence operations, terrorism studies; international relations and conflict resolution (MA), including comparative and security issues, conflict resolution, international and transnational security issues, peacekeeping; legal studies (MA); management (MA), including defense management, general (MA, MS), human resource management, organizational leadership, public administration, reverse logistics, strategic consulting; marketing (MBA); military history (MA), including American military history, American revolution, civil war, war since 1946, World War II; military studies (MA), including air warfare, asymmetrical warfare, joint warfare, land warfare, naval warfare, strategic leadership; national security studies (MA), including general (MA, MS), homeland security, regional security studies, security and intelligence analysis, terrorism studies; nonprofit management (MBA); political science (MA), including American politics and government, comparative government and development, public policy; psychology (MA); public administration (MA, MPA), including disaster management (MPA), environmental policy (MA), health policy (MPA), human resources (MPA), national security (MPA), organizational management (MPA), security management (MPA); public health (MA, MPH), including emergency management (MPH), environmental health (MPH), public administration (MA); reverse logistics management (MA); security management (MA); space studies (MS), including aerospace science, planetary science; sports and health sciences (MS); sports management (MS), including coaching theory and strategy, sports administration; teaching (M Ed), including curriculum and instruction for elementary teachers, elementary, elementary reading, English language learners, instructional leadership, online learning, secondary social sciences, special education; transportation and logistics management (MA), including maritime engineering management. Programs offered via distance learning only. Part-time and evening/weekend programs available. Postbaccalaureate distance learning degree programs offered (no on-campus study). *Faculty:* 445 full-time (241 women), 1,360 part-time/adjunct (617 women). *Students:* 688 full-time (338 women), 10,168 part-time (3,706 women); includes 3,130 minority (1,007 Black or African American, non-Hispanic/Latino; 103 American Indian or Alaska Native, non-Hispanic/Latino; 825 Asian, non-Hispanic/Latino; 810 Hispanic/Latino; 51 Native Hawaiian or other Pacific Islander, non-Hispanic/Latino; 334 Two or more races, non-Hispanic/Latino), 134 international. Average age 35. In 2011, 2,386 master's awarded. *Degree requirements:* For master's, comprehensive exam or practicum. *Entrance requirements:* For master's, official transcript showing earned bachelor's degree from institution accredited by recognized accrediting body. Additional exam requirements/recommendations for international students: Required—TOEFL (minimum score 550 paper-based; 213 computer-based), IELTS (minimum score 6.5). *Application deadline:* Applications are processed on a rolling basis. Application fee: $0. Electronic applications accepted. *Expenses: Tuition:* Part-time $325 per credit hour. *Financial support:* Applicants required to submit FAFSA. *Faculty research:* Military history, criminal justice, management performance, national security. *Unit head:* Dr. Karan Powell, Executive Vice President and Provost, 877-468-6268, Fax: 304-724-3780. *Application contact:* Terry Grant, Vice President of Enrollment Management, 877-468-6268, Fax: 304-724-3780, E-mail: info@apus.edu. Web site: http://www.apus.edu.

American University, Kogod School of Business, Master of Business Administration Program, Washington, DC 20016-8044. Offers accounting (MBA); consulting (MBA), including business systems consulting, management consulting; entrepreneurship (MBA); entrepreneurship (Certificate); finance (MBA); global emerging markets (MBA); leadership and strategic human capital management (MBA); marketing (MBA); real estate (MBA); MBA/JD; MBA/LL M; MBA/MA. Part-time and evening/weekend programs available. *Faculty:* 13 full-time (6 women). *Students:* 96 full-time (43 women), 104 part-time (35 women); includes 49 minority (14 Black or African American, non-Hispanic/Latino; 16 Asian, non-Hispanic/Latino; 16 Hispanic/Latino; 1 Native Hawaiian or other Pacific Islander, non-Hispanic/Latino; 2 Two or more races, non-Hispanic/Latino), 22 international. Average age 29. 340 applicants, 52% accepted, 52 enrolled. In 2011, 124 master's awarded. *Entrance requirements:* For master's, GMAT, resume, personal statement, interview. Additional exam requirements/recommendations for international students: Required—TOEFL. *Application deadline:* For fall admission, 2/1 priority date for domestic students; for spring admission, 10/1 priority date for domestic students. Applications are processed on a rolling basis. Application fee: $100. *Expenses:* Contact institution. *Financial support:* In 2011–12, 19 students received support. Fellowships, research assistantships with partial tuition reimbursements available, career-related internships or fieldwork, Federal Work-Study, and institutionally sponsored loans available. Support available to part-time students. Financial award application deadline: 2/1. *Faculty research:* Information technology, decision-aiding methodology, negotiation. *Unit head:* Dr. Stevan R. Holmberg, Chair, 202-885-1921, Fax: 202-885-1916, E-mail: sholmbe@american.edu. *Application contact:* Shannon Demko, Director of Admissions, 202-885-1968, Fax: 202-885-1078, E-mail: demko@american.edu. Web site: http://www.american.edu/kogod/.

The American University in Dubai, Master in Business Administration Program, Dubai, United Arab Emirates. Offers general (MBA); healthcare management (MBA); international finance (MBA); international marketing (MBA); management of construction enterprises (MBA). Part-time and evening/weekend programs available. *Degree requirements:* For master's, thesis optional. *Entrance requirements:* For master's, GMAT, Interview. Additional exam requirements/recommendations for international students: Required—TOEFL (minimum score 550 paper-based; 213 computer-based; 79 iBT). Electronic applications accepted.

Aquinas College, School of Management, Grand Rapids, MI 49506-1799. Offers health care administration (M Mgt); marketing management (M Mgt); organizational leadership (M Min); sustainable business (M Mgt, MSB). Part-time and evening/weekend programs available. *Faculty:* 11 full-time (3 women), 7 part-time/adjunct (0 women). *Students:* 12 full-time (6 women), 56 part-time (32 women); includes 7 minority (3 Black or African American, non-Hispanic/Latino; 1 Asian, non-Hispanic/Latino; 3 Hispanic/Latino). *Entrance requirements:* For master's, GMAT, minimum undergraduate GPA of 2.75, 2 years of work experience. Additional exam requirements/recommendations for international students: Required—TOEFL (minimum score 550 paper-based; 213 computer-based). *Application deadline:* Applications are processed on a rolling basis. *Expenses:* Contact institution. *Financial support:* Scholarships/grants available. Support available to part-time students. Financial award application deadline: 3/15; financial award applicants required to submit FAFSA. *Unit head:* Brian DiVita, Director, 616-632-2922, Fax: 616-732-4489. *Application contact:* Lynn Atkins-Rykert, Administrative Assistant, 616-632-2924, Fax: 616-732-4489, E-mail: atkinlyn@aquinas.edu.

Argosy University, Atlanta, College of Business, Atlanta, GA 30328. Offers accounting (DBA); corporate compliance (MBA); customized professional concentration (MBA, DBA); finance (MBA); healthcare administration (MBA); information systems (DBA); information systems management (MBA); international business (MBA, DBA); management (MBA, MSM, DBA); marketing (MBA, DBA).

See Close-Up on page 179.

Argosy University, Chicago, College of Business, Chicago, IL 60601. Offers accounting (DBA); customized professional concentration (MBA, DBA); finance (MBA); fraud examination (MBA); global business sustainability (DBA); healthcare administration (MBA); information systems (DBA); information systems management (MBA); international business (MBA, DBA); management (MBA, MSM, DBA); marketing (MBA, DBA); organizational leadership (Ed D); public administration (MBA); sustainable management (MBA). Postbaccalaureate distance learning degree programs offered (minimal on-campus study).

See Close-Up on page 181.

Argosy University, Dallas, College of Business, Farmers Branch, TX 75244. Offers accounting (DBA, AGC); corporate compliance (MBA, Graduate Certificate); customized professional concentration (MBA); finance (MBA, Graduate Certificate); fraud examination (MBA, Graduate Certificate); global business sustainability (DBA, AGC); healthcare administration (Graduate Certificate); healthcare management (MBA); information systems (MBA, DBA, AGC); information systems management (Graduate Certificate); international business (MBA, DBA, AGC, Graduate Certificate); management (MBA, DBA, AGC, Graduate Certificate); marketing (MBA, DBA, AGC, Graduate Certificate); public administration (MBA, Graduate Certificate); sustainable management (MBA, Graduate Certificate).

See Close-Up on page 183.

Argosy University, Denver, College of Business, Denver, CO 80231. Offers accounting (DBA); corporate compliance (MBA); customized professional concentration (MBA, DBA); finance (MBA); fraud examination (MBA); global business sustainability (DBA); healthcare administration (MBA); information systems (DBA); information systems management (MBA); international business (MBA, DBA); management (MBA, MSM, DBA); marketing (MBA, DBA); organizational leadership (Ed D); public administration (MBA); sustainable management (MBA).

See Close-Up on page 185.

Argosy University, Hawai`i, College of Business, Honolulu, HI 96813. Offers accounting (DBA); corporate compliance (MBA); customized professional concentration (MBA, DBA); finance (MBA, Certificate); fraud examination (MBA); global business sustainability (DBA); healthcare administration (MBA, Certificate); information systems (DBA); information systems management (MBA, Certificate); international business (MBA, DBA, Certificate); management (MBA, MSM, DBA); marketing (MBA, DBA, Certificate); organizational leadership (Ed D); public administration (MBA); sustainable management (MBA).

See Close-Up on page 187.

Argosy University, Inland Empire, College of Business, San Bernardino, CA 92408. Offers accounting (DBA); corporate compliance (MBA); customized professional concentration (MBA, DBA); finance (MBA); fraud examination (MBA); global business sustainability (DBA); healthcare administration (MBA); information systems (DBA); information systems management (MBA); international business (MBA, DBA); management (MBA, MSM, DBA); marketing (MBA, DBA); organizational leadership (Ed D); public administration (MBA); sustainable management (MBA).

See Close-Up on page 189.

Argosy University, Los Angeles, College of Business, Santa Monica, CA 90045. Offers accounting (DBA); corporate compliance (MBA); customized professional concentration (MBA, DBA); finance (MBA); fraud examination (MBA); global business sustainability (DBA); healthcare administration (MBA); information systems (DBA); information systems management (MBA); international business (MBA, DBA); management (MBA, MSM, DBA); marketing (MBA, DBA); organizational leadership (Ed D); public administration (MBA); sustainable management (MBA).

See Close-Up on page 191.

Argosy University, Nashville, College of Business, Nashville, TN 37214. Offers accounting (DBA); customized professional concentration (MBA, DBA); finance (MBA); healthcare administration (MBA); information systems (MBA, DBA); international business (MBA, DBA); management (MBA, MSM, DBA); marketing (MBA, DBA).

See Close-Up on page 193.

Argosy University, Orange County, College of Business, Orange, CA 92868. Offers accounting (DBA, Adv C); corporate compliance (MBA); customized professional concentration (MBA, DBA); finance (MBA, Certificate); fraud examination (MBA); global business sustainability (DBA); healthcare administration (MBA, Certificate); information systems (DBA, Adv C, Certificate); information systems management (MBA); international business (MBA, DBA, Adv C, Certificate); management (MBA, MSM, DBA, Adv C); marketing (MBA, DBA, Adv C, Certificate); organizational leadership (Ed D); public administration (MBA, Certificate); sustainable management (MBA).

See Close-Up on page 195.

Argosy University, Phoenix, College of Business, Phoenix, AZ 85021. Offers accounting (DBA); corporate compliance (MBA); customized professional concentration (MBA, DBA); finance (MBA); fraud examination (MBA); global business sustainability (DBA); healthcare administration (MBA); information systems (DBA); information systems management (MBA); international business (MBA, DBA); management (MBA, DBA); marketing (MBA, DBA); public administration (MBA); sustainable management (MBA).

See Close-Up on page 197.

Argosy University, Salt Lake City, College of Business, Draper, UT 84020. Offers accounting (DBA); corporate compliance (MBA); customized professional concentration (MBA, DBA); finance (MBA); fraud examination (MBA); global business sustainability (DBA); healthcare administration (MBA); information systems (DBA); information systems management (MBA); international business (MBA, DBA); management (MBA, DBA); marketing (MBA, DBA); public administration (MBA); sustainable management (MBA).

See Close-Up on page 199.

Argosy University, San Diego, College of Business, San Diego, CA 92108. Offers accounting (DBA); corporate compliance (MBA); customized professional concentration (MBA, DBA); finance (MBA); fraud examination (MBA); global business sustainability (DBA); information systems (DBA); information systems management (MBA); international business (MBA, DBA); management (MBA, MSM, DBA); marketing (MBA, DBA); organizational leadership (Ed D); public administration (MBA).

See Close-Up on page 201.

Argosy University, San Francisco Bay Area, College of Business, Alameda, CA 94501. Offers accounting (DBA); corporate compliance (MBA); customized professional concentration (MBA, DBA); finance (MBA); fraud examination (MBA); global business sustainability (DBA); healthcare administration (MBA); information systems (DBA); information systems management (MBA); international business (MBA, DBA); management (MBA, MSM, DBA); marketing (MBA, DBA); organizational leadership (Ed D); public administration (MBA); sustainable management (MBA).

See Close-Up on page 203.

Argosy University, Sarasota, College of Business, Sarasota, FL 34235. Offers accounting (DBA, Adv C); corporate compliance (MBA, DBA, Certificate); customized professional concentration (MBA, DBA); finance (MBA, Certificate); fraud examination (MBA, Certificate); global business sustainability (DBA, Adv C); healthcare administration (MBA, Certificate); information systems (DBA, Adv C, Certificate); information systems management (MBA); international business (MBA, DBA, Adv C, Certificate); management (MBA, MSM, DBA, Adv C, Certificate); marketing (MBA, DBA, Adv C, Certificate); organizational leadership (Ed D); public administration (MBA, Certificate); sustainable management (MBA, Certificate).

See Close-Up on page 205.

Argosy University, Schaumburg, College of Business, Schaumburg, IL 60173-5403. Offers accounting (DBA, Adv C); customized professional concentration (MBA, DBA); finance (MBA, Certificate); fraud examination (MBA); global business sustainability (DBA); healthcare administration (MBA, Certificate); information systems (DBA, Adv C, Certificate); information systems management (MBA); international business (MBA, DBA, Adv C, Certificate); management (MBA, MSM, DBA, Adv C, Certificate); marketing (MBA, DBA, Adv C, Certificate); organizational leadership (Ed D); public administration (MBA); sustainable management (MBA).

See Close-Up on page 207.

Argosy University, Seattle, College of Business, Seattle, WA 98121. Offers accounting (DBA); corporate compliance (MBA); customized professional concentration (MBA, DBA); finance (MBA); fraud examination (MBA); global business sustainability (DBA); healthcare administration (MBA); information systems (DBA); information systems management (MBA); international business (MBA, DBA); management (MBA, MSM, DBA); marketing (MBA, DBA); organizational leadership (Ed D); public administration (MBA); sustainable management (MBA).

See Close-Up on page 209.

Argosy University, Tampa, College of Business, Tampa, FL 33607. Offers accounting (DBA); corporate compliance (MBA); customized professional concentration (MBA, DBA); finance (MBA); fraud examination (MBA); global business sustainability (DBA); healthcare administration (MBA); information systems (DBA); information systems management (MBA); international business (MBA, DBA); management (MBA, MSM, DBA); marketing (MBA, DBA); organizational leadership (Ed D); public administration (MBA); sustainable management (MBA).

See Close-Up on page 211.

Argosy University, Twin Cities, College of Business, Eagan, MN 55121. Offers accounting (DBA); customized professional concentration (MBA, DBA); finance (MBA); fraud examination (MBA); global business sustainability (DBA); healthcare administration (MBA); information systems (DBA); information systems management (MBA); international business (MBA, DBA); management (MBA, MSM, DBA); marketing (MBA, DBA); organizational leadership (Ed D); public administration (MBA); sustainable management (MBA).

See Close-Up on page 213.

Argosy University, Washington DC, College of Business, Arlington, VA 22209. Offers accounting (DBA); customized professional concentration (MBA, DBA); finance (MBA); fraud examination (MBA); global business sustainability (DBA); healthcare administration (MBA); information systems (DBA); information systems management (MBA); international business (MBA, DBA, Certificate); management (MBA, MSM, DBA); marketing (MBA, DBA, Certificate); organizational leadership (Ed D); public administration (MBA); sustainable management (MBA).

See Close-Up on page 215.

Arizona State University, W. P. Carey School of Business, Department of Marketing, Tempe, AZ 85287-4106. Offers business administration (marketing) (PhD); real estate development (MRED). Part-time and evening/weekend programs available. Postbaccalaureate distance learning degree programs offered. *Degree requirements:* For master's, thesis or alternative, capstone project, interactive Program of Study (iPOS) submitted before completing 50 percent of required credit hours; for doctorate, comprehensive exam, thesis/dissertation, interactive Program of Study (iPOS) submitted before completing 50 percent of required credit hours. *Entrance requirements:* For master's, GMAT, GRE, or LSAT, minimum GPA of 3.0 in last 2 years of work leading to bachelor's degree, 3 personal references, resume, official transcripts, personal statement; for doctorate, GMAT, minimum GPA of 3.0 in last 2 years of work leading to bachelor's degree, 3 letters of recommendation, personal statement/essay. Additional exam requirements/recommendations for international students: Required—TOEFL (minimum score 550 paper-based; 213 computer-based; 80 iBT), IELTS (minimum score 6.5). Electronic applications accepted. *Expenses:* Contact institution. *Faculty research:* Service marketing and management, strategic marketing, customer portfolio management, characteristics and skills of high-performing managers, market orientation, market segmentation, consumer behavior, marketing strategy, new product development, management of innovation, social influences on consumption, e-commerce, market research methodology.

Arizona State University, W. P. Carey School of Business, Program in Business Administration, Tempe, AZ 85287-4906. Offers accountancy (PhD); agribusiness (PhD); business administration (MBA); finance (PhD); financial management and markets (MBA); information management (MBA); information systems (PhD); management (PhD); marketing (PhD); strategic marketing and services leadership (MBA); supply chain financial management (MBA); supply chain management (MBA, PhD); JD/MBA; MBA/M Acc; MBA/M Arch. *Accreditation:* AACSB. Part-time and evening/weekend programs available. Postbaccalaureate distance learning degree programs offered (minimal on-campus study). Terminal master's awarded for partial completion of doctoral program. *Degree requirements:* For master's, thesis or alternative, internship, interactive Program of Study (iPOS) submitted before completing 50 percent of required credit hours; for doctorate, comprehensive exam, thesis/dissertation, interactive Program of Study (iPOS) submitted before completing 50 percent of required credit hours. *Entrance requirements:* For master's, GMAT, minimum GPA of 3.0 in last 2 years of work leading to bachelor's degree, 2 letters of recommendation, professional resume, official transcripts, 3 essays; for doctorate, GMAT or GRE, minimum GPA of 3.0 in last 2 years of work leading to bachelor's degree, 3 letters of recommendation, resume, personal statement/essay. Additional exam requirements/recommendations for international students: Required—TOEFL (minimum score 550 paper-based; 213 computer-based; 80 iBT), IELTS (minimum score 6.5). Electronic applications accepted. *Expenses:* Contact institution.

Ashworth College, Graduate Programs, Norcross, GA 30092. Offers business administration (MBA); criminal justice (MS); health care administration (MBA, MS); human resource management (MBA, MS); international business (MBA); management (MS); marketing (MBA, MS).

Assumption College, Graduate Studies, Department of Business Studies, Worcester, MA 01609-1296. Offers accounting (MBA); business administration (CAGS); finance/economics (MBA); general business (MBA); human resources (MBA); international business (MBA); management (MBA); marketing (MBA); nonprofit leadership (MBA). Part-time and evening/weekend programs available. *Faculty:* 4 full-time (0 women), 16 part-time/adjunct (4 women). *Students:* 8 full-time (5 women), 133 part-time (65 women); includes 18 minority (8 Black or African American, non-Hispanic/Latino; 1 American Indian or Alaska Native, non-Hispanic/Latino; 2 Asian, non-Hispanic/Latino; 7 Hispanic/Latino), 3 international. Average age 30. 100 applicants, 75% accepted, 52 enrolled. In 2011, 53 master's, 1 other advanced degree awarded. *Degree requirements:* For master's, thesis, capstone. *Entrance requirements:* For master's and CAGS, 3 letters of recommendation, resume, essay. Additional exam requirements/recommendations for international students: Required—TOEFL (minimum score 540 paper-based; 200 computer-based; 76 iBT), IELTS (minimum score 6). *Application deadline:* For fall admission, 10/1 for domestic and international students; for winter admission, 2/1 for domestic and international students; for spring admission, 4/1 for domestic and international students. Applications are processed on a rolling basis. Application fee: $30. Electronic applications accepted. *Expenses: Tuition:* Full-time $9414; part-time $523 per credit. *Required fees:* $20 per term. Full-time tuition and fees vary according to course load and program. *Financial support:* In 2011–12, 14 students received support. Scholarships/grants, tuition waivers (partial), and unspecified assistantships available. Financial award application deadline: 5/1; financial award applicants required to submit FAFSA. *Faculty research:* Workplace diversity, dynamics of team interaction, utilization of leased employees, experiential learning project on due diligence market for prostheses. *Unit head:* Michael Lewis, Director, 508-767-7372, Fax: 508-767-7252, E-mail: milewis@assumption.edu. *Application contact:* Laura Lawrence, Graduate Programs Operations Manager, 508-767-7387, Fax: 508-767-7030, E-mail: graduate@assumption.edu. Web site: http://graduate.assumption.edu/mba/mba-assumption.

Avila University, School of Business, Kansas City, MO 64145-1698. Offers accounting (MBA); finance (MBA); general management (MBA); health care administration (MBA); international business (MBA); management information systems (MBA); marketing (MBA). Part-time and evening/weekend programs available. *Faculty:* 9 full-time (3 women), 14 part-time/adjunct (5 women). *Students:* 102 full-time (49 women), 53 part-time (31 women); includes 36 minority (29 Black or African American, non-Hispanic/Latino; 1 American Indian or Alaska Native, non-Hispanic/Latino; 3 Asian, non-Hispanic/Latino; 2 Hispanic/Latino; 1 Native Hawaiian or other Pacific Islander, non-Hispanic/Latino), 33 international. Average age 32. 25 applicants, 76% accepted, 19 enrolled. In 2011, 59 master's awarded. *Degree requirements:* For master's, comprehensive exam, capstone course. *Entrance requirements:* For master's, GMAT (minimum score 420), minimum GPA of 3.0, interview. Additional exam requirements/recommendations for international students: Required—TOEFL (minimum score 550 paper-based). *Application deadline:* For fall admission, 7/30 priority date for domestic students, 7/30 for international students; for winter admission, 11/30 priority date for domestic students, 11/30 for international students; for spring admission, 2/28 priority date for domestic students, 2/28 for international students. Applications are processed on a rolling basis. Application fee: $0. Electronic applications accepted. *Expenses:* Contact institution. *Financial support:* In 2011–12, 102 students received support. Career-related internships or fieldwork and competitive merit scholarships available. Support available to part-time students. Financial award applicants required to submit FAFSA. *Faculty research:* Leadership characteristics, financial hedging, group dynamics. *Unit head:* Dr. Richard Woodall, Dean, 816-501-3720, Fax: 816-501-2463, E-mail: richard.woodall@avila.edu. *Application contact:* JoAnna Giffin, MBA Admissions Director, 816-501-3601, Fax: 816-501-2463, E-mail: joanna.giffin@avila.edu. Web site: http://www.avila.edu/mba.

Azusa Pacific University, School of Business and Management, Azusa, CA 91702-7000. Offers business administration (MBA); diversity for strategic advantage (MA); entrepreneurship (MBA); finance (MBA); human and organizational development (MA); human resources and organizational development (MBA); human resources management (MA); international business (MBA); marketing (MBA); non-profit management (MA); organizational development and change (MA); performance improvement (MA); public administration (MA); strategic management (MBA). Part-time and evening/weekend programs available. *Degree requirements:* For master's, thesis (for some programs), final project. *Entrance requirements:* For master's, GMAT, minimum GPA of 3.0. Additional exam requirements/recommendations for international students: Required—TOEFL (minimum score 600 paper-based). *Expenses:* Contact institution. *Faculty research:* Gender issues, financial risk, leadership and ethics, marketing strategy.

Baker College Center for Graduate Studies - Online, Graduate Programs, Flint, MI 48507-9843. Offers accounting (MBA); business administration (DBA); finance (MBA); general business (MBA); health care management (MBA); human resources management (MBA); information management (MBA); leadership studies (MBA); management information systems (MSIS); marketing (MBA). Part-time and evening/weekend programs available. Postbaccalaureate distance learning degree programs offered. *Degree requirements:* For master's, portfolio. *Entrance requirements:* For master's, 3 years of work experience, minimum undergraduate GPA of 2.5, writing sample, 3 letters of recommendation; for doctorate, MBA or acceptable related master's degree from accredited association, 5 years work experience, minimum graduate GPA of 3.25, writing sample, 3 professional references. Additional exam requirements/recommendations for international students: Required—TOEFL (minimum score 550 paper-based; 213 computer-based). Electronic applications accepted.

Barry University, Andreas School of Business, Graduate Certificate Programs, Miami Shores, FL 33161-6695. Offers finance (Certificate); health services administration (Certificate); international business (Certificate); management (Certificate); management information systems (Certificate); marketing (Certificate).

Bayamón Central University, Graduate Programs, Program in Business Administration, Bayamón, PR 00960-1725. Offers accounting (MBA); finance (MBA); general business (MBA); management (MBA); marketing (MBA). Part-time and evening/weekend programs available. *Degree requirements:* For master's, comprehensive exam (for some programs). *Entrance requirements:* For master's, EXADEP, bachelor's degree in business or related field.

Benedictine University, Graduate Programs, Program in Business Administration, Lisle, IL 60532-0900. Offers accounting (MBA); entrepreneurship and managing innovation (MBA); financial management (MBA); health administration (MBA); human resource management (MBA); information systems security (MBA); international business (MBA); management consulting (MBA); management information systems (MBA); marketing management (MBA); operations management and logistics (MBA); organizational leadership (MBA); MBA/MPH; MBA/MS. Part-time and evening/weekend programs available. Postbaccalaureate distance learning degree programs offered (minimal on-campus study). *Faculty:* 4 full-time (2 women), 24 part-time/adjunct (3 women). *Students:* 165 full-time (101 women), 766 part-time (381 women); includes 201 minority (118 Black or African American, non-Hispanic/Latino; 4 American Indian or Alaska Native, non-Hispanic/Latino; 37 Asian, non-Hispanic/Latino; 40 Hispanic/Latino; 2 Native Hawaiian or other Pacific Islander, non-Hispanic/Latino), 14 international. Average age 34. 313 applicants, 73% accepted, 166 enrolled. In 2011, 379 master's awarded. *Entrance requirements:* For master's, GMAT. Additional exam requirements/recommendations for international students: Required—TOEFL (minimum score 550 paper-based; 213 computer-based). *Application deadline:* For fall admission, 9/1 for domestic students; for winter admission, 12/1 for domestic students; for spring admission, 2/15 for domestic students. Applications are processed on a rolling basis. Application fee: $40. Electronic applications accepted. *Financial support:* Career-related internships or fieldwork and health care benefits available. Support available to part-time students. *Faculty research:* Strategic leadership in professional organizations, sociology of professions, organizational change, social identity theory, applications to change management. *Unit head:* Dr. Sharon Borowicz, Director, 630-829-6219, E-mail: sborowicz@ben.edu. *Application contact:* Kari Gibbons, Director, Admissions, 630-829-6200, Fax: 630-829-6584, E-mail: kgibbons@ben.edu.

Bentley University, McCallum Graduate School of Business, Program in Marketing Analytics, Waltham, MA 02452-4705. Offers MSMA. Part-time and evening/weekend programs available. *Entrance requirements:* For master's, GMAT or GRE General Test. Additional exam requirements/recommendations for international students: Required—TOEFL (minimum score 600 paper-based; 250 computer-based; 100 IBT) or IELTS (minimum score 7). Electronic applications accepted. *Faculty research:* Marketing information processing, blogging and social media, customer lifetime value and customer relationship management, measuring and improving productivity, online consumer behavior.

Bernard M. Baruch College of the City University of New York, Zicklin School of Business, Department of Marketing and International Business, New York, NY 10010-5585. Offers international business (MBA); marketing (MBA, MS, PhD). PhD offered jointly with Graduate School and University Center of the City University of New York. Part-time and evening/weekend programs available. *Degree requirements:* For doctorate, comprehensive exam, thesis/dissertation. *Entrance requirements:* For master's, GMAT, 2 letters of recommendation, resume, 2 years of work experience; for doctorate, GMAT. Additional exam requirements/recommendations for international students: Required—TOEFL (minimum score 590 paper-based; 243 computer-based), TWE (minimum score 5).

California Coast University, School of Administration and Management, Santa Ana, CA 92701. Offers business marketing (MBA); health care management (MBA); human resource management (MBA); management (MBA, MS). Postbaccalaureate distance learning degree programs offered (no on-campus study). Electronic applications accepted.

California Intercontinental University, School of Business, Diamond Bar, CA 91765. Offers banking and finance (MBA); entrepreneurship and business management (DBA); global business leadership (DBA); international management and marketing (MBA); organizational management and human resource management (MBA).

California Lutheran University, Graduate Studies, School of Management, Thousand Oaks, CA 91360-2787. Offers business (IMBA); computer science (MS); econometrics (MBA); economics (MS); entrepreneurship (MBA, Certificate); finance (MBA, Certificate); financial planning (MBA, Certificate); information systems and technology (MS); information technology management (MBA, Certificate); international business (MBA, Certificate); management and organization behavior (MBA); management and organizational behavior (Certificate); marketing (MBA, Certificate); microeconomics (MBA); nonprofit and social enterprise (MBA). Part-time and evening/weekend programs available. Postbaccalaureate distance learning degree programs offered (no on-campus study). *Entrance requirements:* For master's, GMAT, interview, minimum GPA of 3.0. *Expenses:* Contact institution.

California State University, East Bay, Office of Academic Programs and Graduate Studies, College of Business and Economics, Business Administration, MBA Program, Hayward, CA 94542-3000. Offers entrepreneurship (MBA); finance (MBA); global innovators (MBA); human resources and organizational behavior (MBA); information technology management (MBA); marketing management (MBA); operations and supply chain management (MBA); strategy and international business (MBA). Part-time and evening/weekend programs available. *Faculty:* 11 full-time (3 women). *Students:* 80 full-time (42 women), 141 part-time (61 women); includes 70 minority (5 Black or African American, non-Hispanic/Latino; 46 Asian, non-Hispanic/Latino; 13 Hispanic/Latino; 1 Native Hawaiian or other Pacific Islander, non-Hispanic/Latino; 5 Two or more races, non-Hispanic/Latino), 69 international. Average age 31. 371 applicants, 36% accepted, 79 enrolled. In 2011, 254 master's awarded. *Degree requirements:* For master's, comprehensive exam or thesis. *Entrance requirements:* For master's, GMAT (minimum 20th percentile verbal and quantitative section), bachelor's degree, minimum GPA of 2.75. Additional exam requirements/recommendations for international students: Required—TOEFL (minimum score 550 paper-based; 213 computer-based; 79 iBT). *Application deadline:* For fall admission, 6/30 for domestic and international students. Applications are processed on a rolling basis. Application fee: $55. Electronic applications accepted. *Expenses:* Contact institution. *Financial support:* Career-related internships or fieldwork, Federal Work-Study, institutionally sponsored loans, and scholarships/grants available. Support available to part-time students. Financial award application deadline: 3/2; financial award applicants required to submit FAFSA. *Unit head:* Dr. Terri Swartz, Dean, 510-885-3291, Fax: 510-885-4884, E-mail: terri.swartz@csueastbay.edu. *Application contact:* Prof. Joanna Lee, Director, CBE Graduate Programs, 510-885-3517, Fax: 510-885-2176, E-mail: joanna.lee@csueastbay.edu. Web site: http://www20.csueastbay.edu/ecat/graduate-chapters/g-buad.html#mba.

California State University, East Bay, Office of Academic Programs and Graduate Studies, College of Business and Economics, Department of Marketing, Option in Marketing Management, Hayward, CA 94542-3000. Offers MBA. Part-time and evening/weekend programs available. *Degree requirements:* For master's, comprehensive exam or thesis. *Entrance requirements:* For master's, GMAT, minimum GPA of 2.75. Additional exam requirements/recommendations for international students: Required—TOEFL (minimum score 550 paper-based; 213 computer-based). *Application deadline:* For fall admission, 6/30 for domestic and international students. Application fee: $55. Electronic applications accepted. *Expenses:* Tuition, state resident: full-time $6738; part-time $1302 per quarter. Tuition, nonresident: full-time $12,690; part-time $2294 per quarter. *Required fees:* $449 per quarter. Tuition and fees vary according to degree level, program and reciprocity agreements. *Financial support:* Fellowships, teaching assistantships, career-related internships or fieldwork, Federal Work-Study, institutionally sponsored loans, and scholarships/grants available. Support available to part-time students. Financial award application deadline: 3/1; financial award applicants required to submit FAFSA. *Unit head:* Dr. Nan Maxwell, Chair, 510-885-4336, E-mail: nan.maxwell@csueastbay.edu. *Application contact:* Donna Wiley, Interim Associate Director, 510-885-2928, Fax: 510-885-4777, E-mail: donna.wiley@csueastbay.edu. Web site: http://www.cbe.csueastbay.edu.

California State University, Fullerton, Graduate Studies, College of Business and Economics, Department of Marketing, Fullerton, CA 92834-9480. Offers marketing (MBA). Part-time programs available. *Students:* 13 full-time (6 women), 26 part-time (15 women); includes 15 minority (9 Asian, non-Hispanic/Latino; 5 Hispanic/Latino; 1 Two or more races, non-Hispanic/Latino), 11 international. Average age 27. 3 applicants, 100% accepted, 3 enrolled. In 2011, 15 master's awarded. *Degree requirements:* For master's, project or thesis. *Entrance requirements:* For master's, GMAT, minimum AACSB index of 950. Application fee: $55. *Financial support:* Career-related internships or fieldwork, Federal Work-Study, institutionally sponsored loans, and scholarships/grants available. Support available to part-time students. Financial award application deadline: 3/1; financial award applicants required to submit FAFSA. *Unit head:* Dr. Irene Lange, Chair, 657-278-2223. *Application contact:* Admissions/Applications, 657-278-2371.

California State University, Los Angeles, Graduate Studies, College of Business and Economics, Department of Marketing, Los Angeles, CA 90032-8530. Offers international business (MBA, MS); marketing management (MBA, MS). Part-time and evening/

weekend programs available. *Faculty:* 1 full-time (0 women), 1 part-time/adjunct (0 women). *Students:* 9 full-time (5 women), 11 part-time (7 women); includes 4 minority (2 Asian, non-Hispanic/Latino; 2 Hispanic/Latino), 12 international. Average age 27. 93 applicants, 38% accepted, 11 enrolled. In 2011, 13 master's awarded. *Degree requirements:* For master's, comprehensive exam (MBA), thesis (MS). *Entrance requirements:* For master's, GMAT, minimum GPA of 2.5 during previous 2 years of course work. Additional exam requirements/recommendations for international students: Required—TOEFL (minimum score 550 paper-based; 213 computer-based). *Application deadline:* For fall admission, 5/1 for domestic and international students. Applications are processed on a rolling basis. Application fee: $55. Electronic applications accepted. *Expenses:* Tuition, state resident: full-time $8225. *Financial support:* Career-related internships or fieldwork and Federal Work-Study available. Support available to part-time students. Financial award application deadline: 3/1. *Unit head:* Dr. Tyrone Jackson, Chair, 323-343-2960, Fax: 323-343-5462, E-mail: tjackso4@calstatela.edu. *Application contact:* Dr. Karin Brown, Acting Associate Dean of Graduate Studies, 323-343-3820, Fax: 323-343-5653, E-mail: kbrown5@calstatela.edu. Web site: http://cbe.calstatela.edu/mkt/.

California State University, San Bernardino, Graduate Studies, College of Arts and Letters, Department of Communication Studies, San Bernardino, CA 92407-2397. Offers communication studies (MA); integrated marketing communication (MA). *Students:* 15 full-time (11 women), 13 part-time (8 women); includes 13 minority (1 Black or African American, non-Hispanic/Latino; 3 Asian, non-Hispanic/Latino; 8 Hispanic/Latino; 1 Two or more races, non-Hispanic/Latino), 2 international. Average age 26. 67 applicants, 36% accepted, 11 enrolled. In 2011, 13 master's awarded. *Degree requirements:* For master's, comprehensive exam, advancement to candidacy. *Entrance requirements:* Additional exam requirements/recommendations for international students: Required—TOEFL. *Application deadline:* For fall admission, 8/31 priority date for domestic students. Application fee: $55. *Expenses:* Tuition, state resident: full-time $7356. Tuition, nonresident: full-time $7356. *Required fees:* $1077. Tuition and fees vary according to program. *Unit head:* Dr. Treadwell Ruml, Chair, 909-537-5820, Fax: 909-537-7009, E-mail: truml@csusb.edu. *Application contact:* Sandra Kamusikiri, Director of Admissions, 909-5375058, Fax: 909-537-7034, E-mail: skamusik@csusb.edu.

California State University, San Bernardino, Graduate Studies, College of Business and Public Administration, Master in Business Administration Program, San Bernardino, CA 92407. Offers accounting (MBA); entrepreneurship (MBA); executives (MBA); finance (MBA); global business (MBA); information assurance and security management (MBA); information management (MBA); management (MBA); marketing (MBA); professionals (MBA); supply chain management (MBA). *Accreditation:* AACSB. Part-time and evening/weekend programs available. Postbaccalaureate distance learning degree programs offered (no on-campus study). *Faculty:* 58 full-time (11 women), 26 part-time/adjunct (9 women). *Students:* 80 full-time (31 women), 137 part-time (56 women); includes 82 minority (19 Black or African American, non-Hispanic/Latino; 3 American Indian or Alaska Native, non-Hispanic/Latino; 20 Asian, non-Hispanic/Latino; 37 Hispanic/Latino; 3 Two or more races, non-Hispanic/Latino), 65 international. Average age 30. 217 applicants, 65% accepted, 79 enrolled. In 2011, 120 master's awarded. *Degree requirements:* For master's, comprehensive exam, thesis optional, portfolio, 48 units, minimum GPA of 3.0. *Entrance requirements:* For master's, GMAT, minimum GPA of 2.5. Additional exam requirements/recommendations for international students: Required—TOEFL (minimum score 550 paper-based; 213 computer-based; 79 iBT). *Application deadline:* For fall admission, 7/12 priority date for domestic students, 7/12 for international students; for winter admission, 10/26 priority date for domestic students, 10/26 for international students; for spring admission, 1/25 priority date for domestic students, 1/25 for international students. Applications are processed on a rolling basis. Application fee: $55. Electronic applications accepted. *Expenses:* Contact institution. *Financial support:* In 2011–12, 56 students received support, including 34 fellowships (averaging $3,732 per year), 18 research assistantships (averaging $2,193 per year), 4 teaching assistantships (averaging $2,606 per year); career-related internships or fieldwork, Federal Work-Study, institutionally sponsored loans, scholarships/grants, and unspecified assistantships also available. Support available to part-time students. Financial award application deadline: 3/1; financial award applicants required to submit FAFSA. *Faculty research:* Fraud, Stock Exchange, small business, logistics, job analysis. *Total annual research expenditures:* $4.8 million. *Unit head:* Dr. Lawrence C. Rose, Dean, 909-537-3703, Fax: 909-537-7026, E-mail: lrose@csusb.edu. *Application contact:* Dr. Sandra Kamusikiri, Associate Vice-President/Dean of Graduate Studies, 909-537-7058, Fax: 909-537-5078, E-mail: skamusik@csusb.edu. Web site: http://mba.csusb.edu/.

Canisius College, Graduate Division, Richard J. Wehle School of Business, Department of Management and Marketing, Buffalo, NY 14208-1098. Offers accelerated business administration (1 year) (MBA); business administration (MBA); international business (MS). *Accreditation:* AACSB. Part-time and evening/weekend programs available. *Faculty:* 35 full-time (7 women), 11 part-time/adjunct (5 women). *Students:* 102 full-time (42 women), 150 part-time (67 women); includes 29 minority (20 Black or African American, non-Hispanic/Latino; 1 American Indian or Alaska Native, non-Hispanic/Latino; 5 Asian, non-Hispanic/Latino; 1 Hispanic/Latino; 2 Two or more races, non-Hispanic/Latino), 10 international. Average age 28. 173 applicants, 66% accepted, 84 enrolled. In 2011, 97 master's awarded. *Entrance requirements:* For master's, GMAT, transcripts. Additional exam requirements/recommendations for international students: Required—TOEFL. *Application deadline:* For fall admission, 7/1 priority date for domestic students; for spring admission, 11/1 priority date for domestic students. Applications are processed on a rolling basis. Application fee: $25. Electronic applications accepted. *Financial support:* Research assistantships, career-related internships or fieldwork, Federal Work-Study, scholarships/grants, and unspecified assistantships available. Support available to part-time students. Financial award application deadline: 4/30; financial award applicants required to submit FAFSA. *Faculty research:* Global leadership effectiveness, global supply chain management, quality management. *Unit head:* Dr. Gordon W. Meyers, Chair, Management, Entrepreneurship and International Business, 716-888-2634, E-mail: meyerg@canisius.edu. *Application contact:* Jim Bagwell, Director, Graduate Programs, 716-888-2545, Fax: 716-888-3290, E-mail: bagwellj@canisius.edu. Web site: http://www.canisius.edu/academics/gradhome.asp.

Capella University, School of Business and Technology, Minneapolis, MN 55402. Offers accounting (MBA), including system design and programming; business (Certificate), including human resource management (MS, PhD, Certificate), information technology management (MS, PhD, Certificate), leadership (MBA, MS, PhD, Certificate); finance (MBA); general business (MBA); health care management (MBA); information technology (MS, Certificate), including general information technology (MS), information security, network architecture and design (MS), professional projects management (Certificate), project management and leadership (MS), system design and development (MS),); information technology management (MBA); marketing (MBA); organization and management (MBA, MS, PhD), including general business (PhD), general organization and management (MBA, MS), human resource management (MS, PhD, Certificate), information technology management (MS, PhD, Certificate), leadership (MBA, MS, PhD, Certificate); project management (MBA). Part-time and evening/weekend programs available. Postbaccalaureate distance learning degree programs offered (minimal on-campus study). Terminal master's awarded for partial completion of doctoral program. *Degree requirements:* For master's, thesis optional, integrative project; for doctorate, comprehensive exam, thesis/dissertation. *Entrance requirements:* Additional exam requirements/recommendations for international students: Required—TOEFL (minimum score 550 paper-based; 213 computer-based), TWE (minimum score 4). Electronic applications accepted. *Faculty research:* Business policies: strategic, corporate, and financial management; interplay of technological, organizational and social change.

Capital University, School of Management, Columbus, OH 43209-2394. Offers entrepreneurship (MBA); finance (MBA); leadership (MBA); marketing (MBA); MBA/JD; MBA/LL M; MBA/MSN; MBA/MT. *Accreditation:* ACBSP. Part-time and evening/weekend programs available. *Faculty:* 17 full-time (7 women), 23 part-time/adjunct (1 woman). *Students:* 175 part-time (75 women). Average age 31. 59 applicants, 81% accepted, 43 enrolled. In 2011, 1 degree awarded. *Degree requirements:* For master's, research project. *Entrance requirements:* For master's, GMAT, 2 years of work experience. Additional exam requirements/recommendations for international students: Required—TOEFL (minimum score 550 paper-based; 80 computer-based); Recommended—IELTS (minimum score 6.5). *Application deadline:* For fall admission, 7/1 priority date for domestic students; for winter admission, 11/1 priority date for domestic students; for spring admission, 4/1 priority date for domestic students. Applications are processed on a rolling basis. Application fee: $25. Electronic applications accepted. *Financial support:* In 2011–12, 2 fellowships (averaging $1,000 per year) were awarded; scholarships/grants and tuition waivers (full) also available. Support available to part-time students. Financial award application deadline: 8/1; financial award applicants required to submit FAFSA. *Faculty research:* Taxation, public policy, health care, management of non-profits. *Unit head:* Dr. Keirsten Moore, Assistant Dean, School of Management and Leadership, 614-236-6670, Fax: 614-296-6540, E-mail: kmoore@capital.edu. *Application contact:* Jacob Wilk, Assistant Director of Adult and Graduate Education Recruitment, 614-236-6546, Fax: 614-236-6923, E-mail: jwilk@capital.edu. Web site: http://www.capital.edu/capital-mba/.

Carnegie Mellon University, Tepper School of Business, Program in Marketing, Pittsburgh, PA 15213-3891. Offers PhD. *Degree requirements:* For doctorate, thesis/dissertation.

Case Western Reserve University, Weatherhead School of Management, Department of Marketing and Policy Studies, Division of Marketing, Cleveland, OH 44106. Offers MBA. *Entrance requirements:* For master's, GMAT. *Faculty research:* Consumer decision making, global marketing, brand equity management, supply chain management, industrial and new technology marketing.

Case Western Reserve University, Weatherhead School of Management, Department of Operations, Cleveland, OH 44106. Offers management (MS, MSM), including finance (MS), information systems (MS), marketing (MS), operations research, quality management (MS), supply chain (MSM); management for liberal arts graduates (MSM); operations research (PhD); MBA/MSM. Part-time programs available. *Degree requirements:* For doctorate, thesis/dissertation. *Entrance requirements:* For master's, GRE General Test; for doctorate, GMAT, GRE General Test. *Faculty research:* Mathematical finance, mathematical programming, scheduling, stochastic optimization, environmental/energy models.

Central European University, CEU Business School, Budapest, Hungary. Offers executive business administration (EMBA); finance (MBA); general management (MBA); information technology management (MBA); marketing (MBA); real estate management (MBA). Part-time and evening/weekend programs available. *Faculty:* 17 full-time (4 women), 12 part-time/adjunct (1 woman). *Students:* 31 full-time (12 women), 84 part-time (16 women). Average age 34. 162 applicants, 35% accepted, 31 enrolled. In 2011, 83 degrees awarded. *Degree requirements:* For master's, one foreign language. *Entrance requirements:* For master's, GMAT. Additional exam requirements/recommendations for international students: Required—TOEFL (minimum score 570 paper-based; 230 computer-based); Recommended—IELTS (minimum score 6.5). *Application deadline:* For fall admission, 5/15 priority date for domestic students, 5/22 for international students; for winter admission, 11/15 priority date for domestic students, 11/10 for international students. Applications are processed on a rolling basis. Application fee: $0. Electronic applications accepted. Tuition charges are reported in euros. *Expenses: Tuition:* Full-time 11,000 euros. *Financial support:* Tuition waivers (partial) available. *Faculty research:* Social and ethical business, marketing, international business. *Unit head:* Dr. Mel Horwitch, Dean and Managing Director, 361-887-5050, E-mail: mhorwitch@ceubusiness.com. *Application contact:* Agnes Schram, Admissions Manager, 361-887-5111, Fax: 361-887-5133, E-mail: mba@ceubusiness.com. Web site: http://www.ceubusiness.com.

Central Michigan University, College of Graduate Studies, College of Business Administration, Department of Marketing and Hospitality Services Administration, Mount Pleasant, MI 48859. Offers marketing (MBA). Part-time and evening/weekend programs available. *Degree requirements:* For master's, thesis or alternative. *Entrance requirements:* For master's, GMAT. Electronic applications accepted. *Faculty research:* Consumer preferences and market assessment, marketing research and new product development, business economics and forecasting, SAP/marketing and logistics, services marketing and hospitality organizations.

City University of Seattle, Graduate Division, School of Management, Bellevue, WA 98005. Offers accounting (Certificate); change leadership (MBA, Certificate); computer systems (MS); finance (Certificate); financial management (MBA); general management (MBA); general management-Europe (MBA); global marketing (MBA); human resources management (Certificate); individualized study (MBA); information security (MS); information systems (MBA); leadership (MA); marketing (MBA, Certificate); project management (MBA, MS, Certificate); sustainable business (Certificate); technology management (MBA, Certificate). Part-time and evening/weekend programs available. Postbaccalaureate distance learning degree programs offered (no on-campus study). *Faculty:* 6 full-time (2 women), 95 part-time/adjunct (33 women). *Students:* 397 full-time (193 women), 283 part-time (137 women); includes 127 minority (67 Black or African American, non-Hispanic/Latino; 5 American Indian or Alaska Native, non-Hispanic/Latino; 33 Asian, non-Hispanic/Latino; 15 Hispanic/Latino; 1 Native Hawaiian or other Pacific Islander, non-Hispanic/Latino; 6 Two or more races, non-Hispanic/Latino), 117 international. Average age 36. 151 applicants, 100% accepted, 151 enrolled. In 2011, 369 master's, 32 other advanced degrees awarded. *Degree requirements:* For master's, comprehensive exam (for some programs), thesis (for some programs). *Entrance requirements:* Additional exam requirements/recommendations for international students: Required—TOEFL (minimum score 567 paper-based; 227 computer-based; 87 iBT); Recommended—IELTS. *Application deadline:* For fall admission, 9/1 for international students; for winter admission, 12/1 for international students; for spring admission, 3/1 for international students. Applications are processed on a rolling basis. Application fee: $50. Electronic applications accepted. *Financial support:* Federal Work-Study and scholarships/grants available. Support available to part-time students. Financial award applicants required to submit FAFSA. *Unit head:* Dr. Kurt Kirstein, Dean, 425-637-1010 Ext. 5456, Fax: 425-709-5363, E-mail: kdkirstein@cityu.edu. *Application contact:* Alysa Borelli, Director, Recruiting, 888-422-4898, Fax: 425-709-

5363, E-mail: info@cityu.edu. Web site: http://www.cityu.edu/programs/som/index.aspx.

Clark University, Graduate School, Graduate School of Management, Business Administration Program, Worcester, MA 01610-1477. Offers accounting (MBA); finance (MBA); global business (MBA); health care management (MBA); management (MBA); management of information technology (MBA); marketing (MBA). *Accreditation:* AACSB. Part-time and evening/weekend programs available. *Students:* 103 full-time (47 women), 108 part-time (41 women); includes 16 minority (7 Black or African American, non-Hispanic/Latino; 5 Asian, non-Hispanic/Latino; 4 Hispanic/Latino), 69 international. Average age 30. 371 applicants, 48% accepted, 77 enrolled. In 2011, 112 master's awarded. *Degree requirements:* For master's, thesis optional. *Application deadline:* For fall admission, 6/1 priority date for domestic students; for spring admission, 12/1 priority date for domestic students. Applications are processed on a rolling basis. Application fee: $50. Electronic applications accepted. *Expenses: Tuition:* Full-time $37,000; part-time $1156 per credit hour. *Financial support:* In 2011–12, research assistantships with partial tuition reimbursements (averaging $4,800 per year), teaching assistantships with partial tuition reimbursements (averaging $4,800 per year) were awarded; fellowships, career-related internships or fieldwork, Federal Work-Study, institutionally sponsored loans, and tuition waivers (partial) also available. Support available to part-time students. Financial award application deadline: 5/31. *Faculty research:* Marketing, accounting, human resource management, management information systems, business finance. *Unit head:* Dr. Catherine Usoff, Dean, 508-793-8822, Fax: 508-793-8822, E-mail: clarkmba@clarku.edu. *Application contact:* Patrick Oroszko, Enrollment and Marketing Director, 508-793-8822, Fax: 508-793-8822, E-mail: clarkmba@clarku.edu. Web site: http://www.clarku.edu/gsom/prospective/mba/.

Clemson University, Graduate School, College of Business and Behavioral Science, Department of Marketing, Clemson, SC 29634. Offers marketing (MS). Part-time programs available. *Faculty:* 11 full-time (2 women). *Students:* 10 full-time (7 women), 3 part-time (2 women), 5 international. Average age 26. 142 applicants, 20% accepted, 10 enrolled. In 2011, 5 master's awarded. *Entrance requirements:* For master's, GMAT or GRE, minimum GPA of 3.0, letters of recommendation. Additional exam requirements/recommendations for international students: Required—TOEFL. *Application deadline:* Applications are processed on a rolling basis. Application fee: $70 ($80 for international students). Electronic applications accepted. *Financial support:* In 2011–12, 6 students received support. Teaching assistantships with partial tuition reimbursements available, career-related internships or fieldwork, institutionally sponsored loans, scholarships/grants, health care benefits, and unspecified assistantships available. Support available to part-time students. Financial award applicants required to submit FAFSA. *Faculty research:* Marketing decision-making, marketing analysis, marketing strategy. *Unit head:* Dr. Greg Pickett, Head, 864-656-5294, E-mail: pgregor@clemson.edu. *Application contact:* Dr. Thomas Baker, Program Contact, 864-656-2397, Fax: 864-656-0138, E-mail: tbaker2@clemson.edu. Web site: http://business.clemson.edu/departments/marketing/mkt_about.htm.

Cleveland State University, College of Graduate Studies, Monte Ahuja College of Business, Department of Marketing, Cleveland, OH 44115. Offers global business (Graduate Certificate); marketing (MBA, DBA); marketing analytics (Graduate Certificate). *Faculty:* 12 full-time (4 women), 6 part-time/adjunct (3 women). *Students:* 1 full-time (0 women), 10 part-time (3 women); includes 1 minority (Black or African American, non-Hispanic/Latino), 1 international. Average age 43. 3 applicants, 33% accepted, 1 enrolled. In 2011, 3 other advanced degrees awarded. *Expenses:* Tuition, state resident: full-time $6416; part-time $494 per credit hour. Tuition, nonresident: full-time $12,074; part-time $929 per credit hour. *Financial support:* In 2011–12, 4 students received support, including 4 research assistantships (averaging $9,744 per year); tuition waivers (partial) also available. Financial award application deadline: 6/30; financial award applicants required to submit FAFSA. *Unit head:* Dr. Thomas W. Whipple, Chair, 216-687-4771, Fax: 216-687-5135, E-mail: t.whipple@csuohio.edu. *Application contact:* Dr. Thomas W. Whipple, Chair, 216-687-4771, Fax: 216-687-9354, E-mail: t.whipple@csuohio.edu. Web site: http://www.csuohio.edu/cba/mkt/.

Cleveland State University, College of Graduate Studies, Monte Ahuja College of Business, Doctor of Business Administration Program, Cleveland, OH 44115. Offers finance (DBA); global business (DBA); information systems (DBA); marketing (DBA); operations management (DBA). *Accreditation:* AACSB. Part-time and evening/weekend programs available. *Faculty:* 50 full-time (11 women). *Students:* 4 full-time (1 woman), 34 part-time (12 women); includes 3 minority (1 Black or African American, non-Hispanic/Latino; 2 Asian, non-Hispanic/Latino), 11 international. Average age 40. In 2011, 5 doctorates awarded. *Degree requirements:* For doctorate, comprehensive exam, thesis/dissertation, oral dissertation defense. *Entrance requirements:* For doctorate, GMAT, MBA or equivalent. Additional exam requirements/recommendations for international students: Required—TOEFL (minimum score 550 paper-based; 213 computer-based; 79 iBT). *Application deadline:* For spring admission, 2/28 priority date for domestic students, 2/28 for international students. Application fee: $30. Electronic applications accepted. *Expenses:* Tuition, state resident: full-time $6416; part-time $494 per credit hour. Tuition, nonresident: full-time $12,074; part-time $929 per credit hour. *Financial support:* In 2011–12, 5 research assistantships with full tuition reimbursements (averaging $12,700 per year), 4 teaching assistantships with full tuition reimbursements (averaging $12,700 per year) were awarded; tuition waivers (full) and unspecified assistantships also available. *Faculty research:* Supply chain management, international business, strategic management, risk analysis, consumer behavior. *Unit head:* Dr. Raj Shekhar G. Javalgi, Director, 216-687-3786, Fax: 216-687-9354, E-mail: r.javalgi@csuohio.edu. *Application contact:* Melinda J. Arnold, Administrative Secretary, 216-687-6952, Fax: 216-687-9257, E-mail: m.arnold@csuohio.edu. Web site: http://www.csuohio.edu/business/academics/doctoral.html.

Colorado Technical University Colorado Springs, Graduate Studies, Program in Management, Colorado Springs, CO 80907-3896. Offers accounting (MBA, MSA); business administration (MBA); finance (MBA); human resources management (MBA); logistics/supply chain management (MBA); management (DM); marketing (MBA); mediation and dispute resolution (MBA); operations management (MBA); project management (MBA); technology management (MBA). Part-time and evening/weekend programs available. Postbaccalaureate distance learning degree programs offered. *Degree requirements:* For master's, thesis or alternative; for doctorate, thesis/dissertation. *Entrance requirements:* For doctorate, minimum graduate GPA of 3.0, 5 years of related work experience. *Faculty research:* Sexual harassment, performance evaluation, critical thinking.

Colorado Technical University Denver South, Programs in Business Administration and Management, Aurora, CO 80014. Offers accounting (MBA); business administration (MBA); business administration and management (EMBA); finance (MBA); human resource management (MBA); marketing (MBA); mediation and dispute resolution (MBA); operations management (MBA); project management (MBA); technology management (MBA). Part-time and evening/weekend programs available. *Degree requirements:* For master's, thesis or alternative. *Entrance requirements:* For master's, minimum undergraduate GPA of 3.0, resume.

Columbia Southern University, MBA Program, Orange Beach, AL 36561. Offers electronic business and technology (MBA); finance (MBA); general (MBA); healthcare management (MBA); hospitality and tourism (MBA); human resources management (MBA); international management (MBA); marketing (MBA); project management (MBA); public administration (MBA); sport management (MBA). Part-time and evening/weekend programs available. Postbaccalaureate distance learning degree programs offered (no on-campus study). *Entrance requirements:* For master's, bachelor's degree from accredited/approved institution. Additional exam requirements/recommendations for international students: Required—TOEFL. Electronic applications accepted.

Columbia University, Graduate School of Business, Doctoral Program in Business, New York, NY 10027. Offers business (PhD), including accounting, decision, risk, and operations, finance and economics, management, marketing. *Accreditation:* AACSB. *Degree requirements:* For doctorate, comprehensive exam, thesis/dissertation, major field exam, research paper, thesis proposal. *Entrance requirements:* For doctorate, GMAT or GRE (finance), 2 letters of reference, resume. Additional exam requirements/recommendations for international students: Required—TOEFL. Electronic applications accepted. *Expenses:* Contact institution. *Faculty research:* Human decision making and behavioral research; real estate market and mortgage defaults; financial crisis and corporate governance; international business; security analysis and accounting.

Columbia University, Graduate School of Business, MBA Program, New York, NY 10027. Offers accounting (MBA); decision, risk, and operations (MBA); entrepreneurship (MBA); finance and economics (MBA); healthcare and pharmaceutical management (MBA); human resource management (MBA); international business (MBA); leadership and ethics (MBA); management (MBA); marketing (MBA); media (MBA); private equity (MBA); real estate (MBA); social enterprise (MBA); value investing (MBA); DDS/MBA; JD/MBA; MBA/MIA; MBA/MPH; MBA/MS; MD/MBA. *Entrance requirements:* For master's, GMAT, 2 letters of recommendation. Additional exam requirements/recommendations for international students: Required—TOEFL. Electronic applications accepted. *Expenses:* Contact institution. *Faculty research:* Human decision making and behavioral research; real estate market and mortgage defaults; financial crisis and corporate governance; international business; security analysis and accounting.

Concordia University Wisconsin, Graduate Programs, School of Business and Legal Studies, MBA Program, Mequon, WI 53097-2402. Offers finance (MBA); health care administration (MBA); human resource management (MBA); international business (MBA); international business-bilingual English/Chinese (MBA); management (MBA); management information systems (MBA); managerial communications (MBA); marketing (MBA); public administration (MBA); risk management (MBA). Postbaccalaureate distance learning degree programs offered (minimal on-campus study). *Students:* 308 full-time (146 women), 536 part-time (288 women); includes 126 minority (76 Black or African American, non-Hispanic/Latino; 9 American Indian or Alaska Native, non-Hispanic/Latino; 15 Asian, non-Hispanic/Latino; 12 Hispanic/Latino; 14 Two or more races, non-Hispanic/Latino), 276 international. Average age 35. In 2011, 110 master's awarded. *Degree requirements:* For master's, comprehensive exam, thesis or alternative. *Entrance requirements:* Additional exam requirements/recommendations for international students: Required—TOEFL. *Application deadline:* For fall admission, 8/1 priority date for domestic students; for spring admission, 1/15 for domestic students. Applications are processed on a rolling basis. Application fee: $50. *Expenses:* Contact institution. *Financial support:* Application deadline: 8/1. *Unit head:* Dr. David Borst, Director, 262-243-4298, Fax: 262-243-4428, E-mail: david.borst@cuw.edu. *Application contact:* Mary Eberhardt, Graduate Admissions, 262-243-4551, Fax: 262-243-4428, E-mail: mary.eberhardt@cuw.edu.

Cornell University, Graduate School, Graduate Field of Management, Ithaca, NY 14853-0001. Offers accounting (PhD); behavioral decision theory (PhD); finance (PhD); marketing (PhD); organizational behavior (PhD); production and operations management (PhD). *Accreditation:* AACSB. *Faculty:* 53 full-time (8 women). *Students:* 39 full-time (11 women); includes 2 minority (both Asian, non-Hispanic/Latino), 23 international. Average age 29. 424 applicants, 3% accepted, 8 enrolled. In 2011, 6 doctorates awarded. *Degree requirements:* For doctorate, comprehensive exam, thesis/dissertation. *Entrance requirements:* For doctorate, GMAT or GRE General Test. Additional exam requirements/recommendations for international students: Required—TOEFL (minimum score 600 paper-based; 250 computer-based; 77 iBT). *Application deadline:* For fall admission, 1/3 for domestic students. Application fee: $95. Electronic applications accepted. *Expenses:* Contact institution. *Financial support:* In 2011–12, 38 students received support, including 4 fellowships with full tuition reimbursements available, 33 research assistantships with full tuition reimbursements available, 2 teaching assistantships with full tuition reimbursements available; institutionally sponsored loans, scholarships/grants, health care benefits, tuition waivers (full and partial), and unspecified assistantships also available. Financial award applicants required to submit FAFSA. *Faculty research:* Operations and manufacturing. *Unit head:* Director of Graduate Studies, 607-255-3669. *Application contact:* Graduate Field Assistant, 607-255-9431, E-mail: js_phd@cornell.edu. Web site: http://www.gradschool.cornell.edu/fields.php?id-91&a-2.

Daemen College, Department of Accounting/Information Systems, Amherst, NY 14226-3592. Offers global business (MS), including accounting, global business, management information systems, marketing. Part-time and evening/weekend programs available. *Degree requirements:* For master's, minimum GPA of 3.0. *Entrance requirements:* For master's, GMAT if undergraduate GPA is less than 3.0, 2 letters of recommendation; goal statement; transcripts; demonstration of satisfactory oral and written English. Additional exam requirements/recommendations for international students: Required—TOEFL (minimum score 500 paper-based; 173 computer-based; 63 iBT), IELTS (minimum score 5.5). Electronic applications accepted. *Faculty research:* Internationalization of small business, cultural influences on business practices, international human resource practices.

Dallas Baptist University, College of Business, Business Administration Program, Dallas, TX 75211-9299. Offers accounting (MBA); business communication (MBA); conflict resolution management (MBA); entrepreneurship (MBA); finance (MBA); health care management (MBA); international business (MBA); leading the non-profit organization (MBA); management (MBA); management information systems (MBA); marketing (MBA); project management (MBA); technology and engineering management (MBA). *Accreditation:* ACBSP. Part-time and evening/weekend programs available. *Entrance requirements:* For master's, GMAT, minimum GPA of 3.0. Additional exam requirements/recommendations for international students: Required—TOEFL, IELTS. *Application deadline:* Applications are processed on a rolling basis. Application fee: $25. Electronic applications accepted. *Expenses: Tuition:* Full-time $12,060; part-time $670 per credit hour. *Required fees:* $100; $50 per semester. *Financial support:* Federal Work-Study, institutionally sponsored loans, scholarships/grants, and tuition waivers (full and partial) available. Support available to part-time students. Financial award applicants required to submit FAFSA. *Faculty research:* Sports management, services marketing, retailing, strategic management, financial planning/investments. *Unit head:* Dr. Sandra S. Reid, Director, 214-333-5280, Fax: 214-333-5293, E-mail: graduate@dbu.edu. *Application contact:* Kit P. Montgomery, Director of Graduate Programs, 214-333-5242, Fax: 214-333-5579, E-mail: graduate@dbu.edu. Web site: http://www3.dbu.edu/graduate/mba.asp.

Dallas Baptist University, Professional Development Program, Dallas, TX 75211-9299. Offers accounting (MA); church leadership (MA); counseling (MA); criminal justice

(MA); English as a second language (MA); finance (MA); higher education (MA); leadership studies (MA); management (MA); management information systems (MA); marketing (MA); missions (MA); professional life coaching (MA). Part-time and evening/weekend programs available. *Entrance requirements:* For master's, minimum GPA of 3.0. Additional exam requirements/recommendations for international students: Required—TOEFL, IELTS. Application fee: $25. *Expenses: Tuition:* Full-time $12,060; part-time $670 per credit hour. *Required fees:* $100; $50 per semester. *Financial support:* Federal Work-Study, institutionally sponsored loans, scholarships/grants, and tuition waivers (full and partial) available. Support available to part-time students. Financial award applicants required to submit FAFSA. *Unit head:* Angela Fogle, Acting Director, 214-333-6830, Fax: 214-333-5558, E-mail: graduate@dbu.edu. *Application contact:* Kit P. Montgomery, Director of Graduate Programs, 214-333-5242, Fax: 214-333-5579, E-mail: graduate@dbu.edu. Web site: http://www3.dbu.edu/graduate/mapd.asp.

Davenport University, Sneden Graduate School, Dearborn, MI 48126-3799. Offers accounting (MBA); business administration (EMBA); finance (MBA); health care management (MBA); human resources management (MBA); information assurance (MS); marketing (MBA); public health (MPH); strategic management (MBA). Part-time and evening/weekend programs available. Postbaccalaureate distance learning degree programs offered (no on-campus study). *Entrance requirements:* For master's, minimum GPA of 2.7, previous course work in accounting and statistics. *Faculty research:* Accounting, international accounting, social and environmental accounting, finance.

DePaul University, Charles H. Kellstadt Graduate School of Business, Department of Marketing, Chicago, IL 60604-2287. Offers brand management (MBA); customer relationship management (MBA); integrated marketing communication (MBA); marketing analysis (MSMA); marketing and management (MBA); marketing strategy and analysis (MBA); marketing strategy and planning (MBA); new product management (MBA); sales leadership (MBA). Part-time and evening/weekend programs available. *Faculty:* 23 full-time (4 women), 15 part-time/adjunct (6 women). *Students:* 163 full-time (84 women), 71 part-time (36 women); includes 29 minority (6 Black or African American, non-Hispanic/Latino; 18 Asian, non-Hispanic/Latino; 5 Hispanic/Latino), 38 international. Average age 28. In 2011, 88 master's awarded. *Entrance requirements:* For master's, GMAT, 2 letters of recommendation, resume. Additional exam requirements/recommendations for international students: Required—TOEFL (minimum score 550 paper-based; 213 computer-based). *Application deadline:* For fall admission, 7/1 for domestic students; for winter admission, 10/1 for domestic students; for spring admission, 2/1 for domestic students. Applications are processed on a rolling basis. Application fee: $60. Electronic applications accepted. *Financial support:* In 2011–12, 6 research assistantships with partial tuition reimbursements (averaging $2,500 per year) were awarded. Financial award application deadline: 4/30. *Faculty research:* International and marketing role in developing economics, Internet marketing, direct marketing, consumer behavior, new product development processes. *Total annual research expenditures:* $100,000. *Unit head:* Dr. Suzanne Louise Fogel, Chairperson/Associate Professor, 312-362-5150, Fax: 312-362-5647, E-mail: sfogel@depaul.edu. *Application contact:* Director of MBA Programs, 312-362-8810, Fax: 312-362-6677, E-mail: kgsb@depaul.edu.

DEREE - The American College of Greece, Graduate Programs, Athens, Greece. Offers applied psychology (MS); communication (MA); leadership (MS); marketing (MS).

DeSales University, Graduate Division, MBA Program, Center Valley, PA 18034-9568. Offers accounting (MBA); computer information systems (MBA); finance (MBA); health care systems management (MBA); human resources management (MBA); management (MBA); marketing (MBA); project management (MBA); self-design (MBA). *Accreditation:* ACBSP. Part-time programs available. Postbaccalaureate distance learning degree programs offered (no on-campus study). *Entrance requirements:* For master's, GMAT, minimum GPA of 3.0, 2 years of work experience. Additional exam requirements/recommendations for international students: Required—TOEFL. *Application deadline:* Applications are processed on a rolling basis. Electronic applications accepted. Tuition and fees vary according to degree level. *Faculty research:* Quality improvement, executive development, productivity, cross-cultural managerial differences, leadership. *Unit head:* Dr. David Gilfoil, Director, 610-282-1100 Ext. 1828, Fax: 610-282-2869, E-mail: david.gilfoil@desales.edu. *Application contact:* Caryn Stopper, Director of Graduate Admissions, 610-282-1100 Ext. 1768, Fax: 610-282-0525, E-mail: caryn.stopper@desales.edu.

Dowling College, School of Business, Oakdale, NY 11769-1999. Offers aviation management (MBA, Certificate); banking and finance (MBA, Certificate); corporate finance (MBA); financial planning (Certificate); health care management (MBA, Certificate); human resource management (Certificate); information systems management (MBA); management and leadership (MBA); marketing (Certificate); project management (Certificate); public management (MBA, Certificate); sport, event and entertainment management (Certificate); JD/MBA. Part-time and evening/weekend programs available. Postbaccalaureate distance learning degree programs offered (minimal on-campus study). *Faculty:* 10 full-time (4 women), 54 part-time/adjunct (6 women). *Students:* 237 full-time (99 women), 403 part-time (199 women); includes 186 minority (95 Black or African American, non-Hispanic/Latino; 62 Asian, non-Hispanic/Latino; 28 Hispanic/Latino; 1 Native Hawaiian or other Pacific Islander, non-Hispanic/Latino), 1 international. Average age 35. 345 applicants, 83% accepted, 193 enrolled. In 2011, 350 master's, 7 other advanced degrees awarded. *Degree requirements:* For master's, comprehensive exam, thesis optional. *Entrance requirements:* For master's, minimum GPA of 2.8, 2 letters of recommendation, courses or seminar in accounting and finance, resume. Additional exam requirements/recommendations for international students: Required—TOEFL (minimum score 550 paper-based). *Application deadline:* For fall admission, 9/1 priority date for domestic students; for winter admission, 1/1 priority date for domestic students; for spring admission, 2/1 priority date for domestic students. Applications are processed on a rolling basis. Application fee: $50. Electronic applications accepted. *Expenses: Tuition:* Full-time $19,162; part-time $933 per credit. *Required fees:* $1330; $700 per year. Tuition and fees vary according to course load. *Financial support:* Career-related internships or fieldwork and Federal Work-Study available. Support available to part-time students. Financial award application deadline: 6/30; financial award applicants required to submit FAFSA. *Faculty research:* International finance, computer applications, labor relations, executive development. *Unit head:* Antonia Loschiavo, Assistant Dean, 631-244-3266, Fax: 631-244-1018, E-mail: loschiat@dowling.edu. *Application contact:* Ronnie S. Macdonald, Assistant Vice President for Enrollment Services/Dean of Admissions, 631-244-3357, Fax: 631-244-1059, E-mail: macdonar@dowling.edu.

Drexel University, LeBow College of Business, Program in Business Administration, Philadelphia, PA 19104-2875. Offers business administration (MBA, PhD, APC), including accounting (MBA, PhD), decision sciences (PhD), economics (MBA, PhD), finance (MBA, PhD), legal studies (MBA), management (MBA), marketing (MBA, PhD), organizational sciences (PhD), quantitative methods (MBA), strategic management (PhD). *Accreditation:* AACSB. Part-time and evening/weekend programs available. Postbaccalaureate distance learning degree programs offered (minimal on-campus study). Terminal master's awarded for partial completion of doctoral program. *Entrance requirements:* For master's, GMAT, minimum GPA of 2.75; for doctorate, GMAT. Additional exam requirements/recommendations for international students: Required—TOEFL. Electronic applications accepted. *Faculty research:* Decision support systems, individual and group behavior, operations research, techniques and strategy.

Eastern Michigan University, Graduate School, Academic Affairs Division, Ypsilanti, MI 48197. Offers individualized studies (MA, MS); integrated marketing communications (MS). *Students:* 9 full-time (5 women), 85 part-time (64 women); includes 55 minority (47 Black or African American, non-Hispanic/Latino; 1 American Indian or Alaska Native, non-Hispanic/Latino; 1 Asian, non-Hispanic/Latino; 5 Hispanic/Latino; 1 Two or more races, non-Hispanic/Latino). Average age 33. 411 applicants, 89% accepted, 94 enrolled. In 2011, 2 degrees awarded. *Entrance requirements:* Additional exam requirements/recommendations for international students: Required—TOEFL. *Expenses:* Tuition, state resident: full-time $10,367; part-time $432 per credit hour. Tuition, nonresident: full-time $20,435; part-time $851 per credit hour. *Required fees:* $39 per credit hour. $46 per semester. One-time fee: $100. Tuition and fees vary according to course level, degree level and reciprocity agreements. *Unit head:* Dr. Deborah de Laski-Smith, Interim Dean, 734-487-0042, Fax: 734-487-0050, E-mail: deb.delaski-smith@emich.edu. *Application contact:* Graduate Admissions, 734-487-2400, Fax: 734-487-6559, E-mail: graduate.admissions@emich.edu.

Eastern Michigan University, Graduate School, College of Business, Department of Marketing, Program in Integrated Marketing Communications, Ypsilanti, MI 48197. Offers MS. *Students:* 22 full-time (18 women), 45 part-time (31 women); includes 22 minority (16 Black or African American, non-Hispanic/Latino; 2 American Indian or Alaska Native, non-Hispanic/Latino; 2 Asian, non-Hispanic/Latino; 2 Two or more races, non-Hispanic/Latino). Average age 33. 65 applicants, 54% accepted, 21 enrolled. In 2011, 35 degrees awarded. *Expenses:* Tuition, state resident: full-time $10,367; part-time $432 per credit hour. Tuition, nonresident: full-time $20,435; part-time $851 per credit hour. *Required fees:* $39 per credit hour. $46 per semester. One-time fee: $100. Tuition and fees vary according to course level, degree level and reciprocity agreements. *Unit head:* K. Michelle Henry, Director, Academic Services, 734-487-4444, Fax: 734-487-1316, E-mail: mhenry1@emich.edu. *Application contact:* Graduate Advisor.

Eastern Michigan University, Graduate School, College of Business, Programs in Business Administration, Ypsilanti, MI 48197. Offers business administration (MBA, Graduate Certificate); computer information systems (Graduate Certificate); e-business (MBA, Graduate Certificate); enterprise business intelligence (MBA); entrepreneurship (MBA, Graduate Certificate); finance (MBA, Graduate Certificate); human resources (MBA); human resources management (Graduate Certificate); information systems (MBA); internal auditing (MBA); international business (MBA, Graduate Certificate); marketing management (Graduate Certificate); nonprofit management (MBA); organizational development (Graduate Certificate); supply chain management (MBA, Graduate Certificate). *Accreditation:* AACSB. Part-time programs available. Postbaccalaureate distance learning degree programs offered (no on-campus study). *Students:* 79 full-time (39 women), 287 part-time (143 women); includes 55 minority (22 Black or African American, non-Hispanic/Latino; 24 Asian, non-Hispanic/Latino; 6 Hispanic/Latino; 3 Two or more races, non-Hispanic/Latino), 238 international. Average age 32. 317 applicants, 62% accepted, 89 enrolled. In 2011, 102 master's, 58 other advanced degrees awarded. *Entrance requirements:* For master's, GMAT (minimum score 450), minimum cumulative undergraduate GPA of 2.75. Additional exam requirements/recommendations for international students: Required—TOEFL. *Application deadline:* For fall admission, 5/15 for domestic students, 5/1 for international students; for winter admission, 10/15 for domestic students, 10/1 for international students; for spring admission, 3/15 for domestic students, 3/1 for international students. Applications are processed on a rolling basis. Application fee: $35. *Expenses:* Tuition, state resident: full-time $10,367; part-time $432 per credit hour. Tuition, nonresident: full-time $20,435; part-time $851 per credit hour. *Required fees:* $39 per credit hour. $46 per semester. One-time fee: $100. Tuition and fees vary according to course level, degree level and reciprocity agreements. *Financial support:* Fellowships, research assistantships with full tuition reimbursements, teaching assistantships with full tuition reimbursements, career-related internships or fieldwork, Federal Work-Study, institutionally sponsored loans, scholarships/grants, tuition waivers (partial), and unspecified assistantships available. Support available to part-time students. Financial award applicants required to submit FAFSA. *Unit head:* K. Michelle Henry, Director, Academic Services, 734-487-4444, Fax: 734-483-1316, E-mail: mhenry1@emich.edu. *Application contact:* Beste Windes, Advisor, 734-487-4444, Fax: 734-483-1316, E-mail: bwindes@emich.edu. Web site: http://www.emich.edu/public/cob/gr/grad.html.

Edgewood College, Program in Business, Madison, WI 53711-1997. Offers accountancy (MS); accounting (MBA); business administration (MBA); finance (MBA); management (MBA); marketing (MBA); sustainability leadership (MBA). *Accreditation:* ACBSP. Part-time and evening/weekend programs available. *Students:* 24 full-time (15 women), 95 part-time (41 women); includes 9 minority (2 Black or African American, non-Hispanic/Latino; 4 Asian, non-Hispanic/Latino; 3 Hispanic/Latino), 7 international. Average age 33. In 2011, 43 master's awarded. *Entrance requirements:* For master's, GMAT (minimum score 430), minimum GPA of 2.75, 2 letters of recommendation. Additional exam requirements/recommendations for international students: Required—TOEFL (minimum score 213 computer-based). *Application deadline:* For fall admission, 8/15 for domestic students, 5/1 for international students; for spring admission, 1/8 for domestic students, 11/1 for international students. Applications are processed on a rolling basis. Application fee: $25. Electronic applications accepted. *Expenses: Tuition:* Part-time $747 per credit. Part-time tuition and fees vary according to program. *Financial support:* Career-related internships or fieldwork and scholarships/grants available. *Unit head:* Martin Preizler, Dean, 608-663-2898, Fax: 608-663-3291, E-mail: martinpreizler@edgewood.edu. *Application contact:* Joann Eastman, Admissions Counselor, 608-663-3250, Fax: 608-663-2214, E-mail: gps@edgewood.edu. Web site: http://www.edgewood.edu/Academics/Graduate.aspx.

Ellis University, MBA Program, Chicago, IL 60606-7204. Offers e-commerce (MBA); finance (MBA); general business (MBA); global management (MBA); health care administration (MBA); leadership (MBA); management of information systems (MBA); marketing (MBA); professional accounting (MBA); project management (MBA); public accounting (MBA); risk management (MBA).

Emerson College, Graduate Studies, School of Communication, Department of Marketing Communication, Program in Integrated Marketing Communication, Boston, MA 02116-4624. Offers MA. Part-time and evening/weekend programs available. *Entrance requirements:* For master's, GMAT or GRE General Test. Additional exam requirements/recommendations for international students: Required—TOEFL (minimum score 550 paper-based; 213 computer-based; 80 iBT), IELTS (minimum score 6.5). Electronic applications accepted. *Faculty research:* Marketing, international business.

Emory University, Goizueta Business School, Doctoral Program in Business, Atlanta, GA 30322-1100. Offers accounting (PhD); finance (PhD); information systems (PhD); marketing (PhD); organization and management (PhD). *Faculty:* 56 full-time (13 women). *Students:* 37 full-time (17 women); includes 21 minority (20 Asian, non-Hispanic/Latino; 1 Hispanic/Latino). Average age 29. 240 applicants, 6% accepted, 11 enrolled. In 2011, 5 doctorates awarded. *Degree requirements:* For doctorate, comprehensive exam, thesis/dissertation. *Entrance requirements:* For doctorate, GMAT (strongly preferred) or GRE. Additional exam requirements/recommendations for international students: Required—TOEFL (minimum score 250 computer-based). *Application deadline:* For fall admission, 1/3 priority date for domestic students, 1/1 for international students. Application fee: $50. Electronic applications accepted. *Expenses: Tuition:* Full-time $34,800. *Required fees:* $1300. *Financial support:* In 2011–12, 37 students received support. *Unit head:* Dr. Lawrence Benveniste, Dean, 404-727-6377, Fax: 404-727-0868, E-mail: larry_benveniste@bus.emory.edu. *Application contact:* Allison Gilmore, Director of Admissions and Student Services, 404-727-6353, Fax: 404-727-5337, E-mail: phd@bus.emory.edu.

Fairfield University, Charles F. Dolan School of Business, Fairfield, CT 06824-5195. Offers accounting (MBA, MS, CAS); accounting information systems (MBA, CAS); entrepreneurship (MBA, CAS); finance (MBA, MS, CAS); general management (MBA, CAS); human resource management (MBA, CAS); information systems and operations (MBA); information systems and operations management (CAS); international business (MBA, CAS); marketing (MBA, CAS); taxation (MBA, CAS). *Accreditation:* AACSB. Part-time and evening/weekend programs available. *Faculty:* 23 full-time (9 women), 3 part-time/adjunct (1 woman). *Students:* 87 full-time (37 women), 118 part-time (42 women); includes 13 minority (4 Black or African American, non-Hispanic/Latino; 4 Asian, non-Hispanic/Latino; 5 Hispanic/Latino), 9 international. Average age 29. 126 applicants, 47% accepted, 35 enrolled. In 2011, 90 master's awarded. *Degree requirements:* For master's, capstone course. *Entrance requirements:* For master's, GMAT (minimum score 500), 2 letters of reference, resume, minimum GPA of 3.0. Additional exam requirements/recommendations for international students: Required—TOEFL (minimum score 550 paper-based; 213 computer-bases; 80 iBT) or IELTS (minimum score 6.5). *Application deadline:* For fall admission, 5/15 for international students; for spring admission, 10/15 for international students. Applications are processed on a rolling basis. Application fee: $60. Electronic applications accepted. *Expenses:* Contact institution. *Financial support:* In 2011–12, 50 students received support, including 2 research assistantships (averaging $6,500 per year); scholarships/grants, unspecified assistantships, and merit-based one-time entrance scholarship also available. Financial award applicants required to submit FAFSA. *Faculty research:* Optimization strategies, international finance, consumer behavior, financial market volatility, Internet marketing, supply chain analysis, tax issues. *Unit head:* Dr. Donald Gibson, Dean, 203-254-4000 Ext. 4070, Fax: 203-254-4105, E-mail: dgibson@fairfield.edu. *Application contact:* Marianne Gumpper, Director of Graduate and Continuing Studies Admission, 203-254-4184, Fax: 203-254-4073, E-mail: gradadmis@fairfield.edu. Web site: http://www.fairfield.edu/dsb/dsb_grad_1.html.

Fairleigh Dickinson University, College at Florham, Silberman College of Business, Departments of Management, Marketing, and Entrepreneurial Studies, Program in Marketing, Madison, NJ 07940-1099. Offers MBA, Certificate. *Entrance requirements:* For master's, GMAT.

Fairleigh Dickinson University, Metropolitan Campus, Silberman College of Business, Departments of Management, Marketing, and Entrepreneurial Studies, Program in Marketing, Teaneck, NJ 07666-1914. Offers MBA, Certificate.

Fashion Institute of Technology, School of Graduate Studies, Program in Cosmetics and Fragrance Marketing and Management, New York, NY 10001-5992. Offers MPS. *Degree requirements:* For master's, capstone seminar. *Entrance requirements:* Additional exam requirements/recommendations for international students: Required—TOEFL (minimum score 550 paper-based; 213 computer-based). Electronic applications accepted.

See Display below and Close-Up on page 581.

Florida Agricultural and Mechanical University, Division of Graduate Studies, Research, and Continuing Education, School of Business and Industry, Tallahassee, FL 32307-3200. Offers accounting (MBA); finance (MBA); management information systems (MBA); marketing (MBA). *Degree requirements:* For master's, residency. *Entrance requirements:* For master's, GMAT, minimum GPA of 3.0.

Florida Institute of Technology, Graduate Programs, Nathan M. Bisk College of Business, Online Programs, Melbourne, FL 32901-6975. Offers accounting (MBA); accounting and finance (MBA); business administration (MBA); finance (MBA); healthcare management (MBA); information technology (MS); information technology cybersecurity (MS); information technology management (MBA); international business (MBA); Internet marketing (MBA); management (MBA); marketing (MBA); project management (MBA). Part-time and evening/weekend programs available. Postbaccalaureate distance learning degree programs offered (no on-campus study). *Faculty:* 47 part-time/adjunct (15 women). *Students:* 8 full-time (4 women), 1,122 part-time (547 women); includes 418 minority (271 Black or African American, non-Hispanic/Latino; 5 American Indian or Alaska Native, non-Hispanic/Latino; 55 Asian, non-Hispanic/Latino; 81 Hispanic/Latino; 6 Native Hawaiian or other Pacific Islander, non-Hispanic/Latino), 23 international. Average age 36. In 2011, 329 master's awarded. *Entrance requirements:* For master's, GMAT or resume showing 8 years of supervised experience, 2 letters of recommendation, resume, competency in math past college algebra. Additional exam requirements/recommendations for international students: Required—TOEFL (minimum score 550 paper-based; 213 computer-based; 79 iBT). *Application deadline:* For fall admission, 4/1 for international students; for spring admission, 9/30 for international students. Applications are processed on a rolling basis. Electronic applications accepted. *Expenses:* Contact institution. *Financial support:* Available to part-time students. Application deadline: 3/1; applicants required to submit FAFSA. *Unit head:* Dr. Mary S. Bonhomme, Dean, Florida Tech Online/Associate Provost for Online Learning, 321-674-8202, Fax: 321-674-8216, E-mail: bonhomme@fit.edu. *Application contact:* Carolyn Farrior, Director of Graduate Admissions, Online Learning and Off-Campus Programs, 321-674-7118, Fax: 321-674-8216, E-mail: cfarrior@fit.edu. Web site: http://online.fit.edu.

Florida State University, The Graduate School, College of Business, Tallahassee, FL 32306-1110. Offers accounting (M Acc), including accounting information services, assurance services, corporate accounting, taxation; business administration (MBA, PhD), including accounting (PhD), finance (PhD), management information systems (PhD), marketing (PhD), organizational behavior (PhD), risk management and insurance (PhD), strategic management (PhD); finance (MS); insurance (MSM); management information systems (MS); marketing (MS); JD/MBA; MSW/MBA. *Accreditation:* AACSB. Part-time programs available. Postbaccalaureate distance learning degree programs offered (no on-campus study). *Faculty:* 107 full-time (31 women). *Students:* 196 full-time (76 women), 310 part-time (109 women); includes 89 minority (27 Black or African American, non-Hispanic/Latino; 1 American Indian or Alaska Native, non-Hispanic/Latino; 31 Asian, non-Hispanic/Latino; 30 Hispanic/Latino). Average age 30. 702 applicants, 33% accepted, 205 enrolled. In 2011, 268 master's, 17 doctorates awarded. Terminal master's awarded for partial completion of doctoral program. *Degree requirements:* For doctorate, comprehensive exam, thesis/dissertation. *Entrance requirements:* For master's, GMAT, work experience (MBA, MS), minimum GPA of 3.0, letters of recommendation; for doctorate, GMAT, minimum graduate GPA of 3.5, letters of recommendation. Additional exam requirements/recommendations for international students: Required—TOEFL (minimum score 600 paper-based; 80 computer-based); Recommended—IELTS (minimum score 6.5). *Application deadline:* For fall admission, 6/1 for domestic students, 5/1 for international students; for spring admission, 10/1 for domestic students, 9/1 for international students. Applications are processed on a rolling basis. Application fee: $30. Electronic applications accepted. *Expenses:* Tuition, state resident: full-time $9474; part-time $350.88 per credit hour. Tuition, nonresident: full-time $16,236; part-time $601.34 per credit hour. *Required fees:* $630 per semester.

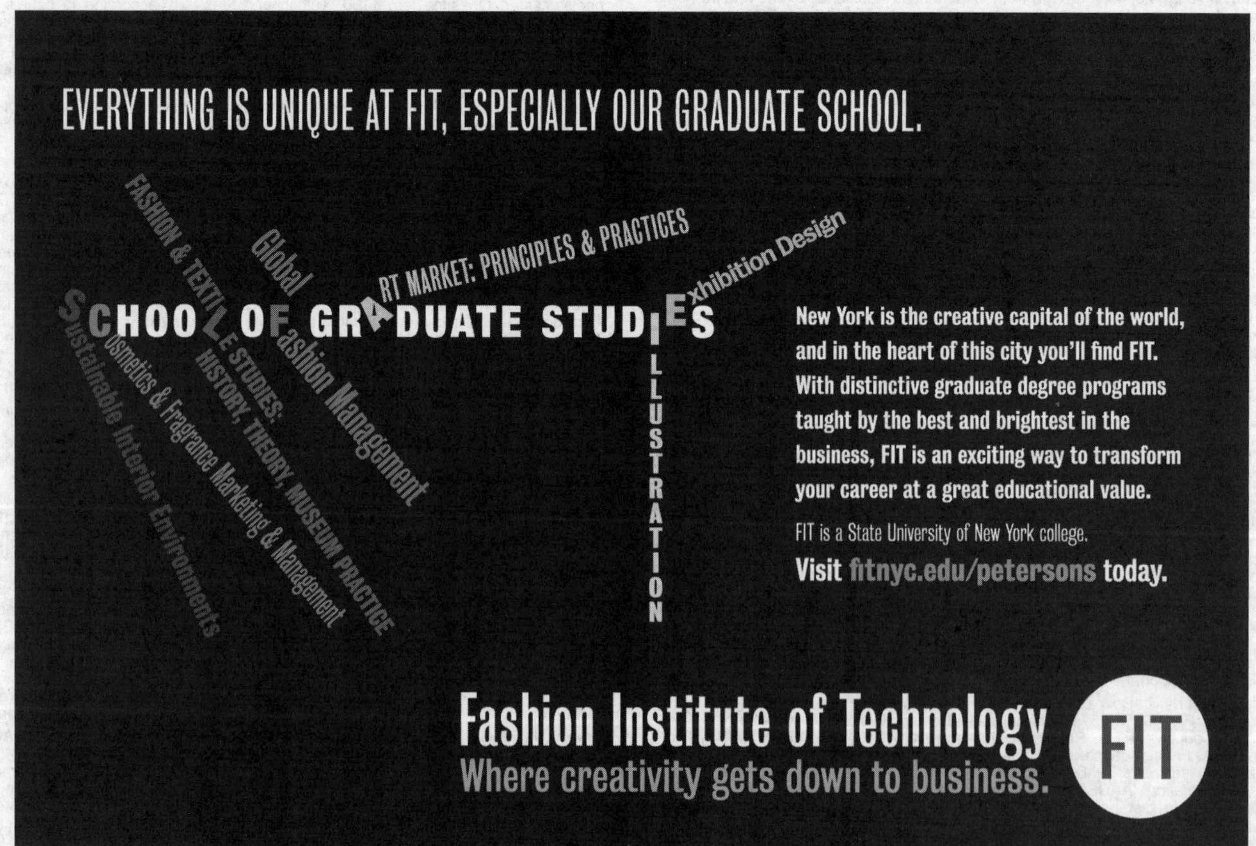

One-time fee: $20. Tuition and fees vary according to course load and campus/location. *Financial support:* In 2011–12, 86 students received support, including 12 fellowships with full tuition reimbursements available (averaging $7,161 per year), 30 research assistantships with full tuition reimbursements available (averaging $6,000 per year), 43 teaching assistantships with full tuition reimbursements available (averaging $15,000 per year); career-related internships or fieldwork, scholarships/grants, health care benefits, tuition waivers (full and partial), and unspecified assistantships also available. Support available to part-time students. Financial award application deadline: 1/1. *Unit head:* Dr. Caryn Beck-Dudley, Dean, 850-644-3090, Fax: 850-644-0915. *Application contact:* Lisa Beverly, Director, Graduate Programs Admissions, 850-644-6458, Fax: 850-644-0588, E-mail: lbeverly@cob.fsu.edu. Web site: http://www.cob.fsu.edu/grad/.

Florida State University, The Graduate School, College of Communication and Information, School of Communication, Tallahassee, FL 32306. Offers corporate and public communication (MS); integrated marketing communication (MA, MS); mass communication (PhD); media and communication studies (MA, MS); speech communication (PhD). Part-time programs available. *Faculty:* 24 full-time (9 women), 6 part-time/adjunct (1 woman). *Students:* 78 full-time (58 women), 131 part-time (82 women); includes 100 minority (26 Black or African American, non-Hispanic/Latino; 58 Asian, non-Hispanic/Latino; 16 Hispanic/Latino). Average age 24. 212 applicants, 60% accepted, 45 enrolled. In 2011, 132 master's, 7 doctorates awarded. *Degree requirements:* For master's, thesis (for some programs); for doctorate, comprehensive exam, thesis/dissertation. *Entrance requirements:* For master's, GRE General Test, minimum GPA of 3.0; for doctorate, GRE General Test, minimum GPA of 3.3 in graduate course work. Additional exam requirements/recommendations for international students: Required—TOEFL (minimum score 600 paper-based; 250 computer-based; 100 iBT). *Application deadline:* For fall admission, 7/1 priority date for domestic students, 5/1 for international students; for spring admission, 11/1 priority date for domestic students, 11/1 for international students. Applications are processed on a rolling basis. Application fee: $30. Electronic applications accepted. *Expenses:* Tuition, state resident: full-time $9474; part-time $350.88 per credit hour. Tuition, nonresident: full-time $16,236; part-time $601.34 per credit hour. *Required fees:* $630 per semester. One-time fee: $20. Tuition and fees vary according to course load and campus/location. *Financial support:* In 2011–12, 52 students received support, including 59 teaching assistantships with full tuition reimbursements available (averaging $14,000 per year); fellowships, research assistantships, career-related internships or fieldwork, Federal Work-Study, institutionally sponsored loans, scholarships/grants, tuition waivers (partial), and unspecified assistantships also available. Support available to part-time students. Financial award application deadline: 2/1; financial award applicants required to submit FAFSA. *Faculty research:* Communication technology and policy, marketing communication, communication content and effect, new communication/information technologies. *Total annual research expenditures:* $400,000. *Unit head:* Dr. Stephen D. McDowell, Director, 850-644-2276, Fax: 850-644-8642, E-mail: steve.mcdowell@cci.fsu.edu. *Application contact:* Natashia Hinson-Turner, Graduate Coordinator, 850-644-8746, Fax: 850-644-8642, E-mail: natashia.turner@cci.fsu.edu. Web site: http://www.cci.fsu.edu.

Fordham University, Graduate School of Business, New York, NY 10023. Offers accounting (MBA); communications and media management (MBA); executive business administration (EMBA); finance (MBA, MS); information systems (MBA, MS); management systems (MBA); marketing (MBA); media management (MS); taxation (MS); taxation and accounting (MTA);); JD/MBA; MBA/MIM; MS/MBA. MBA/MIM offered jointly with Thunderbird School of Global Management. *Accreditation:* AACSB. Part-time and evening/weekend programs available. *Entrance requirements:* For master's, GMAT, 2 letters of recommendation, resume. Additional exam requirements/recommendations for international students: Required—TOEFL (minimum score 600 paper-based; 250 computer-based; 100 iBT). Electronic applications accepted. *Expenses:* Contact institution.

Franklin University, Marketing and Communication Program, Columbus, OH 43215-5399. Offers MS. Part-time and evening/weekend programs available. *Entrance requirements:* For master's, minimum undergraduate GPA of 2.75. Additional exam requirements/recommendations for international students: Required—TOEFL (minimum score 550 paper-based; 213 computer-based). Electronic applications accepted.

Full Sail University, Internet Marketing Master of Science Program - Online, Winter Park, FL 32792-7437. Offers MS. Postbaccalaureate distance learning degree programs offered.

Gannon University, School of Graduate Studies, College of Engineering and Business, School of Business, Program in Marketing, Erie, PA 16541-0001. Offers Certificate. Part-time and evening/weekend programs available. *Entrance requirements:* For degree, GMAT. Additional exam requirements/recommendations for international students: Required—TOEFL (minimum score 79 iBT). *Application deadline:* Applications are processed on a rolling basis. Application fee: $25. Electronic applications accepted. *Financial support:* Application deadline: 7/1; applicants required to submit FAFSA. *Unit head:* Dr. Donna Mottilla, Director, 814-871-7780, E-mail: mottilla001@gannon.edu. *Application contact:* Kara Morgan, Director of Graduate Admissions, 814-871-5831, Fax: 814-871-5827, E-mail: graduate@gannon.edu.

George Fox University, School of Business, Newberg, OR 97132-2697. Offers finance (MBA); management (DBA); management/general (MBA); marketing (DBA); organizational strategy (MBA); strategic human resource management (MBA). MBA offered part-time and full-time in Newberg, OR, and in Portland, OR. Part-time and evening/weekend programs available. Postbaccalaureate distance learning degree programs offered (minimal on-campus study). *Faculty:* 9 full-time (2 women), 6 part-time/adjunct (0 women). *Students:* 24 full-time (11 women), 239 part-time (81 women); includes 33 minority (4 Black or African American, non-Hispanic/Latino; 1 American Indian or Alaska Native, non-Hispanic/Latino; 14 Asian, non-Hispanic/Latino; 10 Hispanic/Latino; 4 Two or more races, non-Hispanic/Latino), 13 international. Average age 37. In 2011, 101 master's, 6 doctorates awarded. *Degree requirements:* For master's, capstone project; for doctorate, credit-applied research project. *Entrance requirements:* For master's, resume (5 years professional experience); 3 professional references; interview; financial e-learning course, official transcripts; for doctorate, GRE or GMAT, resume; personal mission statement; academic research writing sample; official transcript from each college/university attended; three professional references. Additional exam requirements/recommendations for international students: Required—TOEFL (minimum score 577 paper-based; 233 computer-based; 90 iBT) or IELTS (minimum score 7). *Application deadline:* For fall admission, 8/1 for domestic and international students; for spring admission, 12/1 for domestic and international students. Applications are processed on a rolling basis. Application fee: $40. Electronic applications accepted. *Expenses:* Contact institution. *Financial support:* Applicants required to submit FAFSA. *Unit head:* Dr. Dirk Barram, Professor/Dean, 800-631-0921. *Application contact:* Robin Halverson, Admissions Counselor, 800-493-4937, Fax: 503-554-6111, E-mail: mba@georgefox.edu. Web site: http://www.georgefox.edu/business/index.html.

The George Washington University, School of Business, Department of Marketing, Washington, DC 20052. Offers MBA, PhD. Part-time and evening/weekend programs available. *Faculty:* 9 full-time (3 women), 6 part-time/adjunct (3 women). *Students:* 99 applicants, 27% accepted, 12 enrolled. In 2011, 5 master's awarded. *Degree requirements:* For doctorate, thesis/dissertation. *Entrance requirements:* For master's, GMAT; for doctorate, GMAT or GRE. Additional exam requirements/recommendations for international students: Required—TOEFL. *Application deadline:* For fall admission, 4/1 priority date for domestic students; for spring admission, 10/1 for domestic students. Applications are processed on a rolling basis. Application fee: $60. *Financial support:* Fellowships, teaching assistantships, career-related internships or fieldwork, Federal Work-Study, and institutionally sponsored loans available. Financial award application deadline: 4/1. *Faculty research:* Strategic marketing, marketing and public policy, marketing management. *Unit head:* Dr. Salah S. Hassan, Chair, 202-994-8200, E-mail: hassan@gwu.edu. *Application contact:* Kristin Williams, Assistant Vice President for Graduate and Special Enrollment Management, 202-994-0467, Fax: 202-994-0371, E-mail: ksw@gwu.edu. Web site: http://business.gwu.edu/marketing/.

Georgia Institute of Technology, Graduate Studies and Research, College of Management, Program in Business Administration, Atlanta, GA 30332-0001. Offers accounting (MBA); e-commerce (Certificate); engineering entrepreneurship (MBA); entrepreneurship (Certificate); finance (MBA); information technology management (MBA); international business (MBA, Certificate); management of technology (Certificate); marketing (MBA); operations management (MBA); organizational behavior (MBA); strategic management (MBA). *Accreditation:* AACSB.

Georgia Institute of Technology, Graduate Studies and Research, College of Management, Program in Management, Atlanta, GA 30332-0001. Offers accounting (PhD); finance (PhD); information technology management (PhD); marketing (PhD); operations management (PhD); organizational behavior (PhD); quantitative and computational finance (MS); strategic management (PhD). *Accreditation:* AACSB. *Degree requirements:* For doctorate, comprehensive exam, thesis/dissertation, oral exams. *Entrance requirements:* For master's and doctorate, GMAT. Additional exam requirements/recommendations for international students: Required—TOEFL. *Faculty research:* MIS, management of technology, international business, entrepreneurship, operations management.

Georgia State University, J. Mack Robinson College of Business, Department of Marketing, Atlanta, GA 30302-3083. Offers MBA, MS, PhD. Part-time and evening/weekend programs available. Terminal master's awarded for partial completion of doctoral program. *Degree requirements:* For doctorate, thesis/dissertation. *Entrance requirements:* For master's and doctorate, GMAT. Additional exam requirements/recommendations for international students: Required—TOEFL (minimum score 610 paper-based; 255 computer-based; 101 iBT). Electronic applications accepted. *Faculty research:* Business marketing; sales and sales management; international.

Golden Gate University, Ageno School of Business, San Francisco, CA 94105-2968. Offers accounting (MBA); business administration (EMBA, MBA, PMBA, DBA); finance (MBA, MS, Certificate); financial planning (MS, Certificate); healthcare information systems (Certificate); human resource management (MBA, MS); human resources management (Certificate); information systems (MS); information technology (MBA); information technology management (Certificate); integrated marketing and communications (MS, Certificate); international business (MBA); management (MBA); marketing (MBA, MS, Certificate); operations supply chain management (Certificate); psychology (MA, Certificate); public administration (EMPA); public relations (MS, Certificate); technical market analysis (Certificate); JD/MBA. Part-time and evening/weekend programs available. *Faculty:* 19 full-time (6 women), 241 part-time/adjunct (72 women). *Students:* 397 full-time (230 women), 779 part-time (432 women); includes 376 minority (105 Black or African American, non-Hispanic/Latino; 5 American Indian or Alaska Native, non-Hispanic/Latino; 161 Asian, non-Hispanic/Latino; 77 Hispanic/Latino; 12 Native Hawaiian or other Pacific Islander, non-Hispanic/Latino; 16 Two or more races, non-Hispanic/Latino), 265 international. Average age 34. 871 applicants, 64% accepted, 271 enrolled. In 2011, 550 master's, 13 doctorates awarded. *Degree requirements:* For doctorate, thesis/dissertation, qualifying examination. *Entrance requirements:* For master's, GMAT (MBA), minimum GPA of 2.5 (MS). Additional exam requirements/recommendations for international students: Required—TOEFL (minimum score 550 paper-based; 213 computer-based; 79 iBT). *Application deadline:* For fall admission, 5/15 for domestic and international students; for winter admission, 1/15 for domestic and international students; for spring admission, 9/15 for domestic and international students. Applications are processed on a rolling basis. Application fee: $70 ($110 for international students). Electronic applications accepted. *Expenses:* Contact institution. *Financial support:* Career-related internships or fieldwork, Federal Work-Study, institutionally sponsored loans, and scholarships/grants available. Support available to part-time students. Financial award applicants required to submit FAFSA. *Unit head:* Dr. Paul Fouts, Dean, 415-442-7026, Fax: 415-442-6579. *Application contact:* Angela Melero, Enrollment Services, 415-442-7800, Fax: 415-442-7807, E-mail: info@ggu.edu. Web site: http://www.ggu.edu/programs/business-and-management.

Goldey-Beacom College, Graduate Program, Wilmington, DE 19808-1999. Offers business administration (MBA); finance (MS); financial management (MBA); health care management (MBA); human resource management (MBA); information technology (MBA); international business management (MBA); major finance (MBA); major taxation (MBA); management (MM); marketing management (MBA); taxation (MBA, MS). *Accreditation:* ACBSP. Part-time and evening/weekend programs available. *Faculty:* 19 full-time (7 women), 35 part-time/adjunct (12 women). *Students:* 58 full-time (32 women), 388 part-time (164 women); includes 89 minority (34 Black or African American, non-Hispanic/Latino; 2 American Indian or Alaska Native, non-Hispanic/Latino; 44 Asian, non-Hispanic/Latino; 9 Hispanic/Latino), 229 international. Average age 30. In 2011, 243 master's awarded. *Entrance requirements:* For master's, GMAT, MAT, GRE, minimum GPA of 3.0. Additional exam requirements/recommendations for international students: Required—TOEFL (minimum score 65 computer-based); Recommended—IELTS (minimum score 5). *Application deadline:* Applications are processed on a rolling basis. Application fee: $0. Electronic applications accepted. *Expenses: Tuition:* Full-time $15,750; part-time $875 per credit. *Required fees:* $10 per credit. *Financial support:* Scholarships/grants available. Support available to part-time students. Financial award application deadline: 4/1; financial award applicants required to submit FAFSA. *Unit head:* Larry W. Eby, Director of Admissions, 302-225-6289, Fax: 302-996-5408, E-mail: ebylw@gbc.edu. *Application contact:* Ashley E. Mashington, Graduate Admissions Representative, 302-225-6259, Fax: 302-996-5408, E-mail: mashina@gbc.edu. Web site: http://www.gbc.edu/programs/graduate/.

Grand Canyon University, College of Business, Phoenix, AZ 85017-1097. Offers accounting (MBA); corporate business administration (MBA); disaster preparedness and crisis management (MBA); executive fire service leadership (MS); finance (MBA); general management (MBA); government and policy (MPA); health care management (MPA); health systems management (MBA); human resource management (MBA); innovation (MBA); leadership (MBA, MS); management of information system (MBA); marketing (MBA); project-based (MBA); six sigma (MBA); strategic human resource management (MBA). *Accreditation:* ACBSP. Part-time and evening/weekend programs available. Postbaccalaureate distance learning degree programs offered (no on-campus study). *Entrance requirements:* For master's, equivalent of two years full-time professional work experience. Additional exam requirements/recommendations for international students: Required—TOEFL (minimum score 575 paper-based; 233 computer-based; 90 iBT), IELTS (minimum score 7). Electronic applications accepted.

Harvard University, Harvard Business School, Doctoral Programs in Management, Boston, MA 02163. Offers accounting and management (DBA); business economics (PhD); health policy management (PhD); management (DBA); marketing (DBA); organizational behavior (PhD); science, technology and management (PhD); strategy (DBA); technology and operations management (DBA). *Degree requirements:* For doctorate, comprehensive exam (for some programs), thesis/dissertation. *Entrance requirements:* For doctorate, GRE General Test or GMAT. Additional exam requirements/recommendations for international students: Required—TOEFL. *Expenses: Tuition:* Full-time $36,304. *Required fees:* $1186. Full-time tuition and fees vary according to program.

Hawai`i Pacific University, College of Business Administration, Honolulu, HI 96813. Offers accounting/CPA (MBA); e-business (MBA); economics (MBA); finance (MBA); human resource management (MA, MBA); information systems (MBA, MSIS), including knowledge management (MSIS), software engineering (MSIS), telecommunications security (MSIS); international business (MBA); management (MBA); marketing (MBA); organizational change (MA, MBA); travel industry management (MBA). Part-time and evening/weekend programs available. *Faculty:* 15 full-time (5 women), 11 part-time/adjunct (4 women). *Students:* 297 full-time (133 women), 183 part-time (87 women); includes 282 minority (17 Black or African American, non-Hispanic/Latino; 131 Asian, non-Hispanic/Latino; 43 Hispanic/Latino; 10 Native Hawaiian or other Pacific Islander, non-Hispanic/Latino; 81 Two or more races, non-Hispanic/Latino). Average age 30. 302 applicants, 82% accepted, 160 enrolled. In 2011, 141 master's awarded. *Degree requirements:* For master's, thesis. *Entrance requirements:* For master's, GMAT. Additional exam requirements/recommendations for international students: Recommended—TOEFL (minimum score 550 paper-based; 213 computer-based; 80 iBT), TWE (minimum score 5). *Application deadline:* For fall admission, 2/15 priority date for domestic students; for spring admission, 10/15 priority date for domestic students. Applications are processed on a rolling basis. Application fee: $50. Electronic applications accepted. *Expenses: Tuition:* Full-time $13,230; part-time $735 per credit. Tuition and fees vary according to course load and program. *Financial support:* In 2011–12, 103 students received support. Research assistantships, career-related internships or fieldwork, Federal Work-Study, scholarships/grants, tuition waivers, and unspecified assistantships available. Financial award application deadline: 3/1; financial award applicants required to submit FAFSA. *Faculty research:* Statistical control process as used by management, studies in comparative cross-cultural management styles, not-for-profit management. *Unit head:* Dr. Deborah Crown, Dean, 808-544-0275, Fax: 808-544-0283, E-mail: dcrown@hpu.edu. *Application contact:* Chad Schempp, Director of Graduate Admissions, 808-543-8035, Fax: 808-544-0280, E-mail: graduate@hpu.edu. Web site: http://www.hpu.edu/mba.

See Display on page 98 and Close-Up on page 221.

HEC Montreal, School of Business Administration, Master of Science Programs in Administration, Program in Marketing, Montréal, QC H3T 2A7, Canada. Offers M Sc. Part-time programs available. *Students:* 111 full-time (65 women), 29 part-time (17 women). 115 applicants, 66% accepted, 42 enrolled. In 2011, 31 master's awarded. *Degree requirements:* For master's, one foreign language, thesis. *Entrance requirements:* For master's, Test de francais international (TFI) with minimum score of 850 (for those who have never studied in French), BBA, undergraduate degree in another field, degree deemed equivalent by program director and minimum GPA of 3.0 on 4.3 scale. *Application deadline:* For fall admission, 3/15 for domestic and international students; for winter admission, 9/15 for domestic and international students. Application fee: $80 Canadian dollars. Electronic applications accepted. Application fee is waived when completed online. *Expenses:* Contact institution. *Financial support:* Fellowships, research assistantships, teaching assistantships, and scholarships/grants available. Financial award application deadline: 9/2. *Unit head:* Dr. Claude Laurin, Director, 514-340-6485, Fax: 514-340-6880, E-mail: claude.laurin@hec.ca. *Application contact:* Virginie Lefebvre, Administrative Director, 514-340-6112, Fax: 514-340-6411, E-mail: virginie.lefebvre@hec.ca. Web site: http://www.hec.ca/en/programs_training/msc/options/marketing/index.html.

Herzing University Online, Program in Business Administration, Milwaukee, WI 53203. Offers accounting (MBA); business administration (MBA); business management (MBA); healthcare management (MBA); human resources (MBA); marketing (MBA); project management (MBA); technology management (MBA). Postbaccalaureate distance learning degree programs offered (no on-campus study).

Hofstra University, Frank G. Zarb School of Business, Department of Marketing and International Business, Hempstead, NY 11549. Offers business administration (MBA), including international business, marketing; international business (Advanced Certificate); marketing (MS, Advanced Certificate); marketing research (MS). Part-time and evening/weekend programs available. *Faculty:* 9 full-time (0 women), 3 part-time/adjunct (0 women). *Students:* 91 full-time (54 women), 39 part-time (20 women); includes 11 minority (2 Black or African American, non-Hispanic/Latino; 3 Asian, non-Hispanic/Latino; 6 Hispanic/Latino), 73 international. Average age 27. 260 applicants, 71% accepted, 46 enrolled. In 2011, 43 master's awarded. *Degree requirements:* For master's, capstone course (MBA), thesis (MS), minimum GPA of 3.0. *Entrance requirements:* For master's, GMAT or GRE, 2 letters of recommendation, resume, essay. Additional exam requirements/recommendations for international students: Required—TOEFL (minimum score 550 paper-based; 213 computer-based; 80 iBT); Recommended—IELTS (minimum score 6). *Application deadline:* Applications are processed on a rolling basis. Application fee: $70 ($75 for international students). Electronic applications accepted. *Expenses:* Contact institution. *Financial support:* In 2011–12, 19 students received support, including 18 fellowships with full and partial tuition reimbursements available (averaging $7,371 per year); research assistantships with full and partial tuition reimbursements available, career-related internships or fieldwork, Federal Work-Study, institutionally sponsored loans, scholarships/grants, tuition waivers (full and partial), and unspecified assistantships also available. Support available to part-time students. Financial award applicants required to submit FAFSA. *Faculty research:* Outsourcing, global alliances, retailing, Web marketing, cross-cultural age research. *Unit head:* Dr. Benny Barak, Chairperson, 516-463-5707, Fax: 516-463-4834, E-mail: mktbzb@hofstra.edu. *Application contact:* Carol Drummer, Dean of Graduate Admissions, 516-463-4876, Fax: 516-463-4664, E-mail: gradstudent@hofstra.edu. Web site: http://www.hofstra.edu/business/.

Holy Names University, Graduate Division, Department of Business, Oakland, CA 94619-1699. Offers energy and environment management (MBA); finance (MBA); management and leadership (MBA); marketing (MBA); sports management (MBA). Part-time and evening/weekend programs available. *Entrance requirements:* For master's, minimum undergraduate GPA of 2.6 overall, 3.0 in major. Additional exam requirements/recommendations for international students: Required—TOEFL (minimum score 550 paper-based; 213 computer-based; 80 iBT). *Faculty research:* Business ethics, sustainable economics, accounting models, cross-cultural management, diversity in organizations.

Hood College, Graduate School, Department of Economics and Management, Frederick, MD 21701-8575. Offers accounting (MBA); administration and management (MBA); finance (MBA); human resource management (MBA); information systems (MBA); marketing (MBA); public management (MBA). *Accreditation:* ACBSP. Part-time and evening/weekend programs available. *Degree requirements:* For master's, capstone/final research project. *Entrance requirements:* For master's, minimum GPA of 2.75, resume, letters of recommendation. Additional exam requirements/recommendations for international students: Required—TOEFL (minimum score 575 paper-based; 231 computer-based; 89 iBT). Electronic applications accepted. *Faculty research:* Corporate strategy and sustainable competitive advantages, business ethics, entrepreneurship, investments management, economic development.

Hope International University, School of Graduate and Professional Studies, Program in Business Administration, Fullerton, CA 92831-3138. Offers general management (MBA, MSM); international development (MBA, MSM); marketing management (MBA, MSM); non-profit management (MBA, MSM). Part-time programs available. Postbaccalaureate distance learning degree programs offered (no on-campus study). *Degree requirements:* For master's, comprehensive exam (for some programs), thesis (for some programs), project. *Entrance requirements:* For master's, minimum GPA of 3.0; 2 references. Additional exam requirements/recommendations for international students: Required—TOEFL (minimum score 550 paper-based; 213 computer-based; 86 iBT); Recommended—IELTS (minimum score 6.5). Electronic applications accepted. *Expenses:* Contact institution.

Howard University, School of Business, Graduate Programs in Business, Washington, DC 20059-0002. Offers accounting (MBA); entrepreneurship (MBA); finance (MBA); general management (MBA); human resources management (MBA); information systems (MBA); international business (MBA); marketing (MBA); supply chain management (MBA); JD/MBA. *Accreditation:* AACSB. Part-time and evening/weekend programs available. Postbaccalaureate distance learning degree programs offered (no on-campus study). *Entrance requirements:* For master's, GMAT, minimum 1 year post undergraduate work experience, resume, 3 letters of recommendation, advanced college algebra. Additional exam requirements/recommendations for international students: Required—TOEFL. *Faculty research:* Marketing research in multi-ethnic populations, U.S. trade policies and international relations, risk management (finance).

Hult International Business School, Program in Business Administration - Hult London Campus, London, MA WC 1B 4JP, United Kingdom. Offers entrepreneurship (MBA); international business (MBA); international finance (MBA); marketing (MBA). Part-time programs available. *Degree requirements:* For master's, comprehensive exam, thesis, internship. *Entrance requirements:* Additional exam requirements/recommendations for international students: Required—TOEFL (minimum score 580 paper-based; 237 computer-based), TWE (minimum score 5). Electronic applications accepted.

Illinois Institute of Technology, Stuart School of Business, Program in Business Administration, Chicago, IL 60616-3793. Offers financial management (MBA); innovation and emerging enterprises (MBA); management science (MBA); marketing (MBA); sustainability (MBA); JD/MBA; M Des/MBA; MBA/MS. *Accreditation:* AACSB. Part-time and evening/weekend programs available. *Entrance requirements:* For master's, GRE (minimum score 1000) or GMAT (500). Additional exam requirements/recommendations for international students: Required—TOEFL (minimum score 600 paper-based; 85 iBT); Recommended—IELTS (minimum score 7). Electronic applications accepted. *Expenses:* Contact institution. *Faculty research:* Global management and marketing strategy, technological innovation, management science, financial management, knowledge management.

Illinois Institute of Technology, Stuart School of Business, Program in Marketing Communication, Chicago, IL 60661. Offers MS, MBA/MS. Part-time and evening/weekend programs available. *Entrance requirements:* For master's, GRE (minimum score 1000) or GMAT (500). Additional exam requirements/recommendations for international students: Required—TOEFL (minimum score 600 paper-based; 85 iBT); Recommended—IELTS (minimum score 7). Electronic applications accepted. *Expenses:* Contact institution.

Indiana Tech, Program in Business Administration, Fort Wayne, IN 46803-1297. Offers accounting (MBA); health care administration (MBA); human resources (MBA); management (MBA); marketing (MBA). Part-time and evening/weekend programs available. Postbaccalaureate distance learning degree programs offered (no on-campus study). *Entrance requirements:* For master's, GMAT, minimum undergraduate GPA of 2.5, 3 letters of recommendation. Electronic applications accepted.

Instituto Tecnologico de Santo Domingo, Graduate School, Area of Business, Santo Domingo, Dominican Republic. Offers banking and securities markets (M Mgmt); corporate finance (M Mgmt); human resources management (M Mgmt, Certificate); international trade management (M Mgmt); marketing (M Mgmt); organizational development (M Mgmt); quality and productivity management (Certificate); tax management and planning (M Mgmt); upper management (M Mgmt).

Instituto Tecnologico de Santo Domingo, Graduate School, Area of Humanities and Social Sciences, Santo Domingo, Dominican Republic. Offers accounting (Certificate); adult education (Certificate); applied linguistics (MA); economics (MA); education (M Ed); educational psychology (MA, Certificate); gender and development (MA, Certificate); humanistic studies (MA); international marketing management (Certificate); international relations in the Caribbean basin (Certificate); intervention systems in family therapy (MA); linguistic and literary communication (Certificate); pedagogical support (MA); social science education (M Ed); sustainable human development (MA); terminal illness and death psychology (Certificate); youth and adult education (M Ed).

Instituto Tecnológico y de Estudios Superiores de Monterrey, Campus Central de Veracruz, Graduate Programs, Córdoba, Mexico. Offers administration (MA); administration of information technologies (MTI); computer sciences (MCC); education (MEE); educational institution administration (MAD); educational technology (MTE); electronic commerce (MCE); finance (MAF); humanistic studies (MEH); international business for Latin America (MNL); marketing (MMT); science (MCP). Part-time and evening/weekend programs available. Postbaccalaureate distance learning degree programs offered (minimal on-campus study). *Degree requirements:* For master's, thesis (for some programs). *Entrance requirements:* For master's, PAEP College Board. Electronic applications accepted.

Instituto Tecnológico y de Estudios Superiores de Monterrey, Campus Ciudad Obregón, Program in Marketing Technology, Ciudad Obregón, Mexico. Offers MMT.

Instituto Tecnológico y de Estudios Superiores de Monterrey, Campus Cuernavaca, Programs in Business Administration, Temixco, Mexico. Offers finance (MA); human resources management (MA); international business (MA); marketing (MA).

Instituto Tecnológico y de Estudios Superiores de Monterrey, Campus Estado de México, Professional and Graduate Division, Estado de Mexico, Mexico. Offers administration of information technologies (MITA); architecture (M Arch); business administration (GMBA, MBA); computer sciences (MCS, PhD); education (M Ed); educational institution administration (MAD); educational technology and innovation

(PhD); electronic commerce (MEC); environmental systems (MS); finance (MAF); humanistic studies (MHS); information sciences and knowledge management (MISKM); information systems (MS); manufacturing systems (MS); marketing (MEM); quality systems and productivity (MS); science and materials engineering (PhD); telecommunications management (MTM). Part-time programs available. Postbaccalaureate distance learning degree programs offered (minimal on-campus study). *Degree requirements:* For master's, one foreign language, thesis (for some programs); for doctorate, one foreign language, thesis/dissertation. *Entrance requirements:* For master's, E-PAEP 500, interview; for doctorate, E-PAEP 500, research proposal. Additional exam requirements/recommendations for international students: Required—TOEFL (minimum score 550 paper-based). *Faculty research:* Surface treatments by plasmas, mechanical properties, robotics, graphical computing, mechatronics security protocols.

Instituto Tecnológico y de Estudios Superiores de Monterrey, Campus Monterrey, Graduate School of Business Administration and Leadership, Program in Business Administration, Monterrey, Mexico. Offers business administration (MA, MBA); finance (M Sc); international business (M Sc); marketing (M Sc). *Accreditation:* AACSB. Part-time programs available. *Degree requirements:* For master's, one foreign language, thesis. *Entrance requirements:* For master's, GMAT. Additional exam requirements/recommendations for international students: Required—TOEFL. *Faculty research:* Technology management, quality management, organizational theory and behavior.

Inter American University of Puerto Rico, Aguadilla Campus, Graduate School, Aguadilla, PR 00605. Offers accounting (MBA); counseling psychology specializing in family (MS); criminal justice (MA); educative management and leadership (MA); elementary education (M Ed); finance (MBA); human resources (MBA); industrial management (MBA); management information systems (MBA); marketing (MBA). Part-time and evening/weekend programs available. *Degree requirements:* For master's, comprehensive exam. *Entrance requirements:* For master's, EXADEP, 2 letters of recommendation, minimum GPA of 2.5. Electronic applications accepted.

Inter American University of Puerto Rico, Guayama Campus, Department of Business Administration, Guayama, PR 00785. Offers marketing (MBA).

Inter American University of Puerto Rico, Metropolitan Campus, Graduate Programs, Program in Marketing, San Juan, PR 00919-1293. Offers MBA. *Degree requirements:* For master's, comprehensive exam. *Entrance requirements:* For master's, GRE or EXADEP, interview. Electronic applications accepted.

Inter American University of Puerto Rico, Ponce Campus, Graduate School, Mercedita, PR 00715-1602. Offers accounting (MBA); biology (M Ed); chemistry (M Ed); criminal justice (MA); elementary education (M Ed); English as a Second Language (M Ed); finance (MBA); history (M Ed); human resources (MBA); marketing (MBA); mathematics (M Ed); Spanish (M Ed). *Entrance requirements:* For master's, minimum GPA of 2.5.

Inter American University of Puerto Rico, San Germán Campus, Graduate Studies Center, Program in Business Administration, San Germán, PR 00683-5008. Offers accounting (MBA); finance (MBA); human resources (MBA, PhD); industrial relations (MBA); information sciences (MBA); management (MBA); marketing (MBA). Part-time and evening/weekend programs available. *Degree requirements:* For master's, comprehensive exam. *Entrance requirements:* For master's, GRE General Test or EXADEP, minimum GPA of 3.0. *Application deadline:* For fall admission, 4/30 priority date for domestic students; for spring admission, 11/15 for domestic students. Applications are processed on a rolling basis. Application fee: $31. *Expenses: Required fees:* $213 per semester. *Financial support:* Teaching assistantships, Federal Work-Study, and unspecified assistantships available. *Unit head:* Dr. Elba T. Irizarry, Director of Graduate Studies Center, 787-264-1912 Ext. 7357, Fax: 787-892-6350, E-mail: elbat@sg.inter.edu.

The International University of Monaco, Graduate Programs, Monte Carlo, Monaco. Offers entrepreneurship (EMBA, MBA); financial engineering (M Sc); hedge fund and private equity (M Sc); international marketing (EMBA, MBA); international wealth management (M Sc); luxury goods and services (EMBA, M Sc, MBA); wealth and asset management (EMBA, MBA). Part-time programs available. *Degree requirements:* For master's, comprehensive exam (for some programs), applied research project. *Entrance requirements:* Additional exam requirements/recommendations for international students: Required—TOEFL (minimum score 550 paper-based; 213 computer-based), IELTS. Electronic applications accepted. *Faculty research:* Gaming, leadership, disintermediation.

Iona College, Hagan School of Business, Department of Marketing and International Business, New Rochelle, NY 10801-1890. Offers international business (AC, PMC); marketing (MBA). Part-time and evening/weekend programs available. *Faculty:* 3 full-time (all women), 3 part-time/adjunct (0 women). *Students:* 10 full-time (4 women), 27 part-time (14 women); includes 6 minority (2 Black or African American, non-Hispanic/Latino; 4 Hispanic/Latino). Average age 26. 20 applicants, 70% accepted, 12 enrolled. In 2011, 26 master's, 64 other advanced degrees awarded. *Entrance requirements:* For master's, GMAT, 2 letters of recommendation; for other advanced degree, GMAT. Additional exam requirements/recommendations for international students: Required—TOEFL (minimum score 550 paper-based; 213 computer-based; 80 iBT). *Application deadline:* For fall admission, 8/15 priority date for domestic students, 8/1 for international students; for winter admission, 11/15 priority date for domestic students, 11/1 for international students; for spring admission, 2/15 priority date for domestic students, 2/1 for international students. Applications are processed on a rolling basis. Application fee: $50. Electronic applications accepted. *Expenses:* Contact institution. *Financial support:* Scholarships/grants, tuition waivers (partial), and unspecified assistantships available. Support available to part-time students. Financial award application deadline: 4/15; financial award applicants required to submit FAFSA. *Faculty research:* Business ethics, international retailing, mega-marketing, consumer behavior and consumer confidence. *Unit head:* Dr. Frederica E. Rudell, Chair, 914-637-2748, E-mail: frudell@iona.edu. *Application contact:* Ben Fan, Director of MBA Admissions, 914-633-2289, Fax: 914-637-2708, E-mail: sfan@iona.edu. Web site: http://www.iona.edu/hagan/.

The Johns Hopkins University, Carey Business School, Marketing Programs, Baltimore, MD 21218-2699. Offers MS. Part-time and evening/weekend programs available. *Degree requirements:* For master's, research project (MS). *Entrance requirements:* For master's, minimum GPA of 3.0, resume, work experience, two letters of recommendation. Additional exam requirements/recommendations for international students: Required—TOEFL (minimum score 600 paper-based; 250 computer-based; 100 iBT). Electronic applications accepted. *Faculty research:* Consumer behavior and advertising.

Kansas State University, Graduate School, College of Human Ecology, Department of Apparel, Textiles, and Interior Design, Manhattan, KS 66506. Offers design (MS); general apparel and textiles (MS); marketing (MS); merchandising (MS); product development (MS). Postbaccalaureate distance learning degree programs offered (no on-campus study). *Faculty:* 9 full-time (7 women), 1 (woman) part-time/adjunct. *Students:* 8 full-time (all women), 26 part-time (24 women); includes 10 minority (3 Black or African American, non-Hispanic/Latino; 3 Asian, non-Hispanic/Latino; 2 Hispanic/Latino; 2 Two or more races, non-Hispanic/Latino), 2 international. Average age 28. 24 applicants, 17% accepted, 4 enrolled. In 2011, 11 master's awarded. *Degree requirements:* For master's, comprehensive exam (for some programs), thesis (for some programs). *Entrance requirements:* For master's, GRE General Test (except for merchandising applicants), minimum undergraduate GPA of 3.0. Additional exam requirements/recommendations for international students: Required—TOEFL (minimum score 550 paper-based; 213 computer-based; 79 iBT). *Application deadline:* For fall admission, 2/1 priority date for domestic students, 2/1 for international students; for spring admission, 8/1 priority date for domestic students, 8/1 for international students. Applications are processed on a rolling basis. Application fee: $40 ($55 for international students). Electronic applications accepted. *Financial support:* In 2011–12, 4 teaching assistantships with full tuition reimbursements (averaging $10,208 per year) were awarded; research assistantships, career-related internships or fieldwork, Federal Work-Study, institutionally sponsored loans, and scholarships/grants also available. Support available to part-time students. Financial award application deadline: 3/1; financial award applicants required to submit FAFSA. *Faculty research:* Apparel marketing and consumer behavior, protective and functional clothing and textiles, social and environmental responsibility, apparel design, new product development. *Total annual research expenditures:* $43,034. *Unit head:* Barbara G. Anderson, Head, 785-532-6993, Fax: 785-532-3796, E-mail: barbara@ksu.edu. *Application contact:* Gina Jackson, Application Contact, 785-532-6693, Fax: 785-532-3796, E-mail: gjackson@ksu.edu. Web site: http://www.he.k-state.edu/atid/.

Kaplan University, Davenport Campus, School of Business, Davenport, IA 52807-2095. Offers business administration (MBA); change leadership (MS); entrepreneurship (MBA); finance (MBA); health care management (MBA, MS); human resource (MBA); international business (MBA); management (MS); marketing (MBA); project management (MBA, MS); supply chain management and logistics (MBA, MS). Part-time and evening/weekend programs available. Postbaccalaureate distance learning degree programs offered (no on-campus study). *Entrance requirements:* Additional exam requirements/recommendations for international students: Required—TOEFL (minimum score 550 paper-based; 218 computer-based; 80 iBT). Electronic applications accepted.

Keiser University, Doctor of Business Administration Program, Fort Lauderdale, FL 33309. Offers global business (DBA); global organizational leadership (DBA); marketing (DBA).

Keiser University, Master of Business Administration Program, Fort Lauderdale, FL 33309. Offers accounting (MBA); health services management (MBA); international business (MBA); leadership for managers (MBA); marketing (MBA). Leadership for Managers and International Business concentrations also offered in Spanish. Part-time programs available. Postbaccalaureate distance learning degree programs offered (minimal on-campus study). *Entrance requirements:* For master's, minimum GPA of 2.7 from an accredited institution. Additional exam requirements/recommendations for international students: Required—TOEFL. Electronic applications accepted.

Kent State University, College of Business Administration, Doctoral Program in Marketing, Kent, OH 44242-0001. Offers PhD. *Faculty:* 12 full-time (3 women). *Students:* 11 full-time (7 women); includes 1 minority (Asian, non-Hispanic/Latino), 4 international. Average age 31. 20 applicants, 40% accepted, 3 enrolled. In 2011, 3 doctorates awarded. *Degree requirements:* For doctorate, comprehensive exam, thesis/dissertation, oral defense. *Entrance requirements:* For doctorate, GMAT or GRE. Additional exam requirements/recommendations for international students: Required—TOEFL (minimum score 600 paper-based; 250 computer-based; 100 iBT). *Application deadline:* For fall admission, 2/1 for domestic students, 1/1 for international students. Application fee: $30 ($60 for international students). Electronic applications accepted. *Expenses:* Tuition, state resident: full-time $8136; part-time $452 per credit hour. Tuition, nonresident: full-time $14,292; part-time $794 per credit hour. *Financial support:* In 2011–12, 11 students received support, including 9 teaching assistantships with full tuition reimbursements available (averaging $17,000 per year); Federal Work-Study also available. Financial award application deadline: 2/1; financial award applicants required to submit FAFSA. *Faculty research:* Advertising effects, satisfaction, international marketing, high-tech marketing, personality and consumer behavior. *Unit head:* Dr. Pamela Grimm, Chair and Associate Professor, 330-672-2170, Fax: 330-672-5006, E-mail: pgrimm@kent.edu. *Application contact:* Felecia A. Urbanek, Coordinator, Graduate Programs, 330-672-2282, Fax: 330-672-7303, E-mail: gradbus@kent.edu. Web site: http://www.kent.edu/business/Grad/phd/index.cfm.

Lake Forest Graduate School of Management, The Leadership MBA Program (LMBA), Lake Forest, IL 60045. Offers finance (MBA); global business (MBA); healthcare management (MBA); management (MBA); marketing (MBA); organizational behavior (MBA). Part-time and evening/weekend programs available. *Faculty:* 136 part-time/adjunct (41 women). *Students:* 734 part-time (306 women); includes 161 minority (34 Black or African American, non-Hispanic/Latino; 4 American Indian or Alaska Native, non-Hispanic/Latino; 87 Asian, non-Hispanic/Latino; 14 Hispanic/Latino; 4 Native Hawaiian or other Pacific Islander, non-Hispanic/Latino; 18 Two or more races, non-Hispanic/Latino). Average age 38. In 2011, 213 master's awarded. *Entrance requirements:* For master's, 4 years of work experience in field, interview, 2 letters of recommendation. *Application deadline:* For fall admission, 7/1 for domestic students; for winter admission, 1/5 for domestic students; for spring admission, 3/1 for domestic students. Applications are processed on a rolling basis. Application fee: $75. Electronic applications accepted. *Expenses: Tuition:* Part-time $2932 per unit. *Required fees:* $50 per unit. *Financial support:* Scholarships/grants available. Support available to part-time students. Financial award applicants required to submit FAFSA. *Unit head:* Chris Multhauf, Executive Vice President of Educational Programs and Solutions, 847-574-5270, Fax: 847-295-3656, E-mail: cmulthauf@lfgsm.edu. *Application contact:* Carolyn Brune, Director of Admissions, 800-737-4MBA, Fax: 847-295-3656, E-mail: admiss@lfgsm.edu. Web site: http://www.lakeforestmba.edu/lake_forest_mba_program/LFGSM-Leadership-MBA.aspx.

Lasell College, Graduate and Professional Studies in Communication, Newton, MA 02466-2709. Offers health communication (MSC); integrated marketing communication (MSC, Graduate Certificate); public relations (MSC, Graduate Certificate). Part-time and evening/weekend programs available. Postbaccalaureate distance learning degree programs offered (minimal on-campus study). *Faculty:* 3 full-time (all women), 4 part-time/adjunct (2 women). *Students:* 18 full-time (16 women), 29 part-time (26 women); includes 17 minority (7 Black or African American, non-Hispanic/Latino; 1 American Indian or Alaska Native, non-Hispanic/Latino; 2 Asian, non-Hispanic/Latino; 7 Hispanic/Latino), 7 international. Average age 30. 44 applicants, 68% accepted, 15 enrolled. In 2011, 10 master's awarded. *Entrance requirements:* For master's and Graduate Certificate, bachelor's degree from an accredited institution. Additional exam requirements/recommendations for international students: Required—TOEFL (minimum score 550 paper-based; 79 iBT), IELTS. *Application deadline:* For fall admission, 8/31 priority date for domestic students, 6/30 for international students; for spring admission, 12/31 priority date for domestic students, 10/31 for international students. Applications are processed on a rolling basis. Electronic applications accepted. *Expenses: Tuition:* Part-time $575 per credit. *Required fees:* $70 per semester. *Financial support:* Available to part-time students. Application deadline: 8/31; applicants required to submit FAFSA. *Unit head:* Dr. Joan Dolamore, Dean of Graduate and Professional Studies, 617-243-2485, Fax: 617-243-2450, E-mail: gradinfo@lasell.edu. *Application contact:*

Marketing

Adrienne Franciosi, Director of Graduate Admission, 617-243-2214, Fax: 617-243-2450, E-mail: gradinfo@lasell.edu. Web site: http://www.lasell.edu/Academics/Graduate-and-Professional-Studies/MS-in-Communication.html.

Lasell College, Graduate and Professional Studies in Management, Newton, MA 02466-2709. Offers elder care administration (MSM, Graduate Certificate); elder care marketing (MSM, Graduate Certificate); fundraising management (MSM, Graduate Certificate); human resource management (Graduate Certificate); human resources management (MSM); integrated marketing communication (Graduate Certificate); management (MSM, Graduate Certificate); marketing (MSM, Graduate Certificate); non-profit management (MSM, Graduate Certificate); project management (MSM, Graduate Certificate); public relations (Graduate Certificate). Part-time and evening/weekend programs available. Postbaccalaureate distance learning degree programs offered (no on-campus study). *Faculty:* 9 full-time (7 women), 20 part-time/adjunct (13 women). *Students:* 23 full-time (16 women), 92 part-time (65 women); includes 74 minority (8 Black or African American, non-Hispanic/Latino; 4 American Indian or Alaska Native, non-Hispanic/Latino; 53 Asian, non-Hispanic/Latino; 9 Hispanic/Latino), 14 international. Average age 30. 78 applicants, 67% accepted, 31 enrolled. In 2011, 49 master's, 7 other advanced degrees awarded. *Entrance requirements:* For master's and Graduate Certificate, bachelor's degree from an accredited institution. Additional exam requirements/recommendations for international students: Required—TOEFL (minimum score 550 paper-based; 213 computer-based; 79 iBT). *Application deadline:* For fall admission, 8/31 priority date for domestic students, 6/30 for international students; for spring admission, 12/31 priority date for domestic students, 10/31 for international students. Applications are processed on a rolling basis. Electronic applications accepted. *Expenses: Tuition:* Part-time $575 per credit. *Required fees:* $70 per semester. *Financial support:* Available to part-time students. Application deadline: 8/31; applicants required to submit FAFSA. *Unit head:* Dr. Joan Dolamore, Dean of Graduate and Professional Studies, 617-243-2485, Fax: 617-243-2450, E-mail: gradinfo@lasell.edu. *Application contact:* Adrienne Franciosi, Director of Graduate Admission, 617-243-2214, Fax: 617-243-2450, E-mail: gradinfo@lasell.edu. Web site: http://www.lasell.edu/Academics/Graduate-and-Professional-Studies/MS-in-Management.html.

La Sierra University, School of Business and Management, Riverside, CA 92515. Offers accounting (MBA); finance (MBA); general management (MBA); human resources management (MBA); leadership, values, and ethics for business and management (Certificate); marketing (MBA). *Degree requirements:* For master's, research project. *Entrance requirements:* For master's, GMAT, minimum GPA of 3.0. Additional exam requirements/recommendations for international students: Required—TOEFL. *Faculty research:* Financial econometrics, institutional assessment and strategic planning, legal issues in management, behavioral finance, content of financial reports.

Lewis University, College of Business, Graduate School of Management, Program in Business Administration, Romeoville, IL 60446. Offers accounting (MBA); custom elective option (MBA); e-business (MBA); finance (MBA); healthcare management (MBA); human resources management (MBA); information security (MBA); international business (MBA); management information systems (MBA); marketing (MBA); project management (MBA); technology and operations management (MBA). Part-time and evening/weekend programs available. *Students:* 112 full-time (60 women), 232 part-time (118 women); includes 104 minority (62 Black or African American, non-Hispanic/Latino; 1 American Indian or Alaska Native, non-Hispanic/Latino; 7 Asian, non-Hispanic/Latino; 33 Hispanic/Latino; 1 Native Hawaiian or other Pacific Islander, non-Hispanic/Latino), 9 international. Average age 28. In 2011, 99 master's awarded. *Entrance requirements:* For master's, interview, bachelor's degree, resume, 2 recommendations. Additional exam requirements/recommendations for international students: Required—TOEFL (minimum score 550 paper-based; 213 computer-based). *Application deadline:* For fall admission, 8/15 priority date for domestic students, 5/1 for international students; for spring admission, 11/15 for international students. Applications are processed on a rolling basis. Application fee: $40. Electronic applications accepted. *Financial support:* Career-related internships or fieldwork, Federal Work-Study, scholarships/grants, and unspecified assistantships available. Financial award application deadline: 5/1; financial award applicants required to submit FAFSA. *Unit head:* Dr. Maureen Culleeney, Academic Program Director, 815-838-0500 Ext. 5631, E-mail: culleema@lewisu.edu. *Application contact:* Michele Ryan, Director of Admission, 815-838-0500 Ext. 5384, E-mail: gsm@lewisu.edu.

Lindenwood University, Graduate Programs, School of Business and Entrepreneurship, St. Charles, MO 63301-1695. Offers accounting (MBA, MS); business administration (MBA); entrepreneurial studies (MBA, MS); finance (MBA, MS); human resource management (MBA); human resources (MS); international business (MBA, MS); management (MBA, MS); management information systems (MBA, MS); marketing (MBA, MS); public management (MBA, MS); sport management (MA); supply chain management (MBA). *Accreditation:* ACBSP. Part-time and evening/weekend programs available. *Faculty:* 20 full-time (8 women), 17 part-time/adjunct (5 women). *Students:* 165 full-time (66 women), 223 part-time (100 women); includes 59 minority (48 Black or African American, non-Hispanic/Latino; 4 Asian, non-Hispanic/Latino; 2 Native Hawaiian or other Pacific Islander, non-Hispanic/Latino; 5 Two or more races, non-Hispanic/Latino), 140 international. Average age 29. 156 applicants, 76% accepted, 103 enrolled. In 2011, 205 degrees awarded. *Degree requirements:* For master's, comprehensive exam (for some programs), thesis (for some programs). *Entrance requirements:* For master's, interview, minimum GPA of 3.0, letter of recommendation. Additional exam requirements/recommendations for international students: Required—TOEFL (minimum score 550 paper-based; 213 computer-based; 80 iBT). *Application deadline:* For fall admission, 8/15 priority date for domestic students, 8/15 for international students; for winter admission, 1/9 priority date for domestic students, 1/9 for international students; for spring admission, 3/12 priority date for domestic students, 3/12 for international students. Applications are processed on a rolling basis. Application fee: $30 ($100 for international students). Electronic applications accepted. *Expenses: Tuition:* Full-time $13,650; part-time $395 per credit hour. *Required fees:* $150 per semester. Tuition and fees vary according to course level and course load. *Financial support:* In 2011–12, 206 students received support. Career-related internships or fieldwork, Federal Work-Study, institutionally sponsored loans, and tuition waivers (partial) available. Financial award application deadline: 6/30; financial award applicants required to submit FAFSA. *Unit head:* Roger Ellis, Dean, 636-949-4839, E-mail: rellis@lindenwood.edu. *Application contact:* Brett Barger, Dean of Evening Admissions and Extension Campuses, 636-949-4934, Fax: 636-949-4109, E-mail: adultadmissions@lindenwood.edu. Web site: http://www.lindenwood.edu.

Long Island University–C. W. Post Campus, College of Management, School of Business, Brookville, NY 11548-1300. Offers accounting and taxation (Certificate); business administration (Certificate); finance (MBA, Certificate); general business administration (MBA); international business (MBA, Certificate); management (MBA, Certificate); management information systems (MBA, Certificate); marketing (MBA, Certificate). *Accreditation:* AACSB. Part-time and evening/weekend programs available. *Entrance requirements:* For master's, GMAT, resume, minimum GPA of 3.0, 2 letters of recommendation. Additional exam requirements/recommendations for international students: Required—TOEFL (minimum score 527 paper-based; 197 computer-based). Electronic applications accepted. *Faculty research:* Financial markets, consumer behavior.

Louisiana State University and Agricultural and Mechanical College, Graduate School, E. J. Ourso College of Business, Department of Marketing, Baton Rouge, LA 70803. Offers business administration (PhD), including marketing. Part-time programs available. *Faculty:* 8 full-time (1 woman). *Students:* 4 full-time (3 women), 1 (woman) part-time, 2 international. Average age 32. In 2011, 1 doctorate awarded. *Degree requirements:* For doctorate, thesis/dissertation. *Entrance requirements:* Additional exam requirements/recommendations for international students: Required—TOEFL (minimum score 550 paper-based; 213 computer-based; 79 iBT) or IELTS (minimum score 6.5). *Application deadline:* For fall admission, 1/25 priority date for domestic students, 5/15 for international students; for spring admission, 10/15 for international students. Applications are processed on a rolling basis. Application fee: $50 ($70 for international students). Electronic applications accepted. *Financial support:* In 2011–12, 4 students received support, including 4 teaching assistantships with full and partial tuition reimbursements available (averaging $18,000 per year); fellowships, research assistantships with partial tuition reimbursements available, career-related internships or fieldwork, Federal Work-Study, institutionally sponsored loans, scholarships/grants, health care benefits, and unspecified assistantships also available. Support available to part-time students. Financial award applicants required to submit FAFSA. *Faculty research:* Consumer behavior, marketing strategy, global marketing, e-commerce, branding/brand equity. *Unit head:* Dr. Alvin C. Burns, Chair, 225-578-8786, Fax: 225-578-8616, E-mail: alburns@lsu.edu. *Application contact:* Dr. Judith Garretson Folse, Graduate Adviser, 225-578-6531, Fax: 225-578-8616, E-mail: folse@lsu.edu. Web site: http://www.business.lsu.edu/marketing.

Louisiana Tech University, Graduate School, College of Business, Department of Marketing, Ruston, LA 71272. Offers MBA, DBA. Part-time programs available. *Degree requirements:* For doctorate, thesis/dissertation. *Entrance requirements:* For master's and doctorate, GMAT.

Loyola University Chicago, Graduate School of Business, Marketing Department, Chicago, IL 60660. Offers integrated marketing communications (MS); marketing (MSIMC). Part-time and evening/weekend programs available. *Entrance requirements:* For master's, GMAT, v. Additional exam requirements/recommendations for international students: Required—TOEFL (minimum score 550 paper-based; 213 computer-based; 80 iBT). Electronic applications accepted. *Expenses:* Contact institution. *Faculty research:* Web performance metrics, new venture marketing strategies over consumption, benefit segmentation strategies.

Loyola University Maryland, Graduate Programs, Sellinger School of Business and Management, Program in Business Administration, Baltimore, MD 21210-2699. Offers accounting (MBA); finance (MBA); general business (MBA); information systems operations management (MBA); international business (MBA); management (MBA); marketing (MBA). *Accreditation:* AACSB. Part-time and evening/weekend programs available. *Faculty:* 61 full-time (12 women), 29 part-time/adjunct (4 women). *Students:* 50 full-time (15 women), 547 part-time (210 women); includes 98 minority (39 Black or African American, non-Hispanic/Latino; 1 American Indian or Alaska Native, non-Hispanic/Latino; 28 Asian, non-Hispanic/Latino; 18 Hispanic/Latino; 2 Native Hawaiian or other Pacific Islander, non-Hispanic/Latino; 10 Two or more races, non-Hispanic/Latino), 15 international. Average age 30. In 2011, 232 master's awarded. *Entrance requirements:* For master's, GMAT (for some programs). Additional exam requirements/recommendations for international students: Required—TOEFL (minimum score 550 paper-based; 213 computer-based). *Application deadline:* For fall admission, 8/1 priority date for domestic students; for spring admission, 12/1 priority date for domestic students. Application fee: $50. Electronic applications accepted. *Financial support:* Research assistantships and unspecified assistantships available. Financial award application deadline: 4/15; financial award applicants required to submit FAFSA. *Unit head:* Dr. Karyl Leggio, Dean, 410-617-2301, E-mail: kbleggio@loyola.edu. *Application contact:* Maureen Faux, Executive Director, Graduate Admissions, 410-617-5020, Fax: 410-617-2002, E-mail: graduate@loyola.edu.

Lynn University, College of Business and Management, Boca Raton, FL 33431-5598. Offers aviation management (MBA); financial valuation and investment management (MBA); hospitality management (MBA); international business (MBA); marketing (MBA); mass communication and media management (MBA); sports and athletics administration (MBA). Part-time and evening/weekend programs available. Postbaccalaureate distance learning degree programs offered. *Degree requirements:* For master's, project. *Entrance requirements:* For master's, GMAT or GRE, minimum undergraduate GPA of 3.0, resume, 2 letters of recommendation. Additional exam requirements/recommendations for international students: Required—TOEFL (minimum score 550 paper-based; 213 computer-based). Electronic applications accepted. *Faculty research:* Labor relations, dynamic balance in leisure-time skills, ethics in athletics, hotel development.

Manhattanville College, Graduate Studies, Humanities and Social Sciences Programs, Program in Integrated Marketing Communications, Purchase, NY 10577-2132. Offers MS. Part-time and evening/weekend programs available. *Entrance requirements:* Additional exam requirements/recommendations for international students: Required—TOEFL.

Marquette University, Graduate School of Management, Executive MBA Program, Milwaukee, WI 53201-1881. Offers economics (MBA); finance (MBA); human resources (MBA); international business (MBA); management information systems (MBA); marketing (MBA); operations and supply chain management (MBA); sports business (MBA). *Accreditation:* AACSB. *Students:* 50 full-time (15 women); includes 4 minority (1 Black or African American, non-Hispanic/Latino; 3 Asian, non-Hispanic/Latino), 3 international. Average age 37. 37 applicants, 81% accepted, 29 enrolled. In 2011, 36 master's awarded. *Degree requirements:* For master's, international trip. *Entrance requirements:* For master's, GMAT or GRE, two letters of recommendation, official transcripts from current and previous colleges/universities. Additional exam requirements/recommendations for international students: Required—TOEFL (minimum score 550 paper-based; 85 computer-based; 88 iBT), IELTS (minimum score 6.5), Pearson Test of English. *Application deadline:* For fall admission, 2/15 for domestic and international students. Application fee: $50. Electronic applications accepted. *Expenses:* Contact institution. *Financial support:* Application deadline: 2/15. *Faculty research:* International trade and finance, customer relationship management, consumer satisfaction, customer service . *Unit head:* Dr. Jeanne Simmons, Graduate Director, 414-288-7145, Fax: 414-288-1660, E-mail: jeanne.simmons@marquette.edu. *Application contact:* Debra Leutermann, Admissions Coordinator, 414-288-7145, Fax: 414-288-8078, E-mail: debra.leutermann@marquette.edu. Web site: http://www.busadm.mu.edu/emba/.

Marquette University, Graduate School of Management, Program in Business Administration, Milwaukee, WI 53201-1881. Offers business administration (MBA); economics (MBA); entrepreneurship (Certificate); finance (MBA); human resources (MBA); international business (MBA); management information systems (MBA); marketing (MBA); operations and supply chain management (MBA); sports business

(MBA); JD/MBA; MBA/MA; MBA/MSN. *Accreditation:* AACSB. Part-time and evening/weekend programs available. *Students:* 42 full-time (14 women), 335 part-time (94 women); includes 24 minority (5 Black or African American, non-Hispanic/Latino; 1 American Indian or Alaska Native, non-Hispanic/Latino; 15 Asian, non-Hispanic/Latino; 3 Hispanic/Latino), 29 international. Average age 31. 182 applicants, 59% accepted, 103 enrolled. In 2011, 128 master's awarded. *Degree requirements:* For Certificate, business plan. *Entrance requirements:* For master's, GMAT or GRE, letters of recommendation. Additional exam requirements/recommendations for international students: Required—TOEFL (minimum score 550 paper-based; 85 computer-based; 88 iBT), IELTS (minimum score 6.5), Pearson Test of English. *Application deadline:* For fall admission, 2/15 for domestic and international students. Applications are processed on a rolling basis. Application fee: $50. Electronic applications accepted. *Expenses: Tuition:* Full-time $17,010; part-time $945 per credit hour. Tuition and fees vary according to program. *Financial support:* In 2011–12, 4 fellowships, 11 teaching assistantships were awarded; research assistantships, Federal Work-Study, institutionally sponsored loans, scholarships/grants, and tuition waivers (full and partial) also available. Support available to part-time students. Financial award application deadline: 2/15. *Faculty research:* Ethics in the professions, services marketing, technology impact on decision-making, mentoring. *Unit head:* Dr. Jeanne Simmons, Graduate Director, 414-288-7145, Fax: 414-288-1660, E-mail: jeanne.simmons@marquette.edu. *Application contact:* Debra Leutermann, Admissions Coordinator, 414-288-8064, Fax: 414-288-1902, E-mail: debra.leutermann@marquette.edu. Web site: http://business.marquette.edu/academics/mba.

Marylhurst University, Department of Business Administration, Marylhurst, OR 97036-0261. Offers finance (MBA); general management (MBA); government policy and administration (MBA); green development (MBA); health care management (MBA); marketing (MBA); natural and organic resources (MBA); nonprofit management (MBA); organizational behavior (MBA); real estate (MBA); renewable energy (MBA); sustainable business (MBA). Part-time and evening/weekend programs available. Postbaccalaureate distance learning degree programs offered (no on-campus study). *Faculty:* 3 full-time (0 women), 36 part-time/adjunct (6 women). *Students:* 29 full-time (15 women), 675 part-time (373 women); includes 178 minority (59 Black or African American, non-Hispanic/Latino; 6 American Indian or Alaska Native, non-Hispanic/Latino; 34 Asian, non-Hispanic/Latino; 46 Hispanic/Latino; 4 Native Hawaiian or other Pacific Islander, non-Hispanic/Latino; 29 Two or more races, non-Hispanic/Latino), 14 international. Average age 37. 262 applicants, 91% accepted, 194 enrolled. In 2011, 352 master's awarded. *Degree requirements:* For master's, comprehensive exam, capstone course. *Entrance requirements:* For master's, GMAT (if GPA less than 3.0 and fewer than 5 years of work experience), interview, resume, 2 letters of recommendation. Additional exam requirements/recommendations for international students: Recommended—TOEFL (minimum score 550 paper-based; 213 computer-based; 80 iBT). *Application deadline:* For fall admission, 9/11 priority date for domestic students, 9/11 for international students; for winter admission, 12/15 priority date for domestic students, 12/15 for international students; for spring admission, 3/15 priority date for domestic students, 3/17 for international students. Applications are processed on a rolling basis. Application fee: $50. Electronic applications accepted. *Expenses: Tuition:* Full-time $14,796; part-time $548 per quarter hour. Tuition and fees vary according to program. *Financial support:* Scholarships/grants available. Support available to part-time students. Financial award applicants required to submit FAFSA. *Unit head:* David McNamee, Interim Chair, 503-636-8141, Fax: 503-697-5597, E-mail: mba@marylhurst.edu. *Application contact:* Maruska Lynch, Graduate Admissions Specialist, 800-634-9982 Ext. 6322, Fax: 503-699-6320, E-mail: admissions@marylhurst.edu. Web site: http://www.marylhurst.edu/.

Maryville University of Saint Louis, The John E. Simon School of Business, St. Louis, MO 63141-7299. Offers accounting (MBA, PGC); business studies (PGC); management (MBA, PGC); marketing (MBA, PGC); process and project management (MBA, PGC); sport and entertainment management (MBA, PGC). *Accreditation:* ACBSP. Part-time and evening/weekend programs available. *Faculty:* 8 full-time (3 women), 14 part-time/adjunct (5 women). *Students:* 19 full-time (10 women), 114 part-time (56 women); includes 13 minority (7 Black or African American, non-Hispanic/Latino; 3 Asian, non-Hispanic/Latino; 2 Hispanic/Latino; 1 Two or more races, non-Hispanic/Latino), 3 international. Average age 31. In 2011, 56 master's awarded. *Entrance requirements:* For master's, GMAT (unless applicant possesses undergraduate business degree with minimum cumulative GPA of 3.0, or has completed master's degree from accredited university or one early access course prior to undergraduate degree). Additional exam requirements/recommendations for international students: Required—TOEFL (minimum score 85 iBT). *Application deadline:* Applications are processed on a rolling basis. Application fee: $40 ($60 for international students). Electronic applications accepted. *Expenses: Tuition:* Full-time $21,922; part-time $675 per credit hour. *Required fees:* $233.75 per semester. *Financial support:* Career-related internships or fieldwork, Federal Work-Study, tuition waivers (partial), and campus employment available. Financial award application deadline: 3/1; financial award applicants required to submit FAFSA. *Faculty research:* International business, e-marketing, strategic planning, interpersonal management skills, financial analysis. *Unit head:* Dr. Pamela Horwitz, Dean, 314-529-9418, Fax: 314-529-9975, E-mail: horwitz@maryville.edu. *Application contact:* Kathy Dougherty, Director of MBA Programs, 314-529-9382, Fax: 314-529-9975, E-mail: business@maryville.edu. Web site: http://www.maryville.edu/academics-bu-mba.

McGill University, Faculty of Graduate and Postdoctoral Studies, Desautels Faculty of Management, Montréal, QC H3A 2T5, Canada. Offers administration (PhD); entrepreneurial studies (MBA); finance (MBA); general management (Post Master's Certificate); information systems (MBA); international business (MBA); international practicing management (MM); management (MBA); management for development (MBA); manufacturing management (MMM); marketing (MBA); operations management (MBA); public accountancy (Diploma); strategic management (MBA); MBA/LL B; MD/MBA. MMM offered jointly with Faculty of Engineering; PhD with Concordia University, HEC Montreal, Université de Montréal, Université du Québec à Montréal.

Melbourne Business School, Graduate Programs, Carlton, Australia. Offers business administration (Exec MBA, MBA); management (PhD); management science (PhD); marketing (PhD); social impact (Graduate Certificate); JD/MBA.

Michigan State University, The Graduate School, Eli Broad Graduate School of Management, Department of Marketing, East Lansing, MI 48824. Offers MBA, PhD.

Middle Tennessee State University, College of Graduate Studies, Jennings A. Jones College of Business, Department of Management and Marketing, Murfreesboro, TN 37132. Offers MBA. *Accreditation:* AACSB. Part-time and evening/weekend programs available. Postbaccalaureate distance learning degree programs offered. *Faculty:* 31 full-time (11 women), 2 part-time/adjunct (both women). *Students:* 51 full-time (20 women), 342 part-time (122 women); includes 118 minority (51 Black or African American, non-Hispanic/Latino; 2 American Indian or Alaska Native, non-Hispanic/Latino; 49 Asian, non-Hispanic/Latino; 7 Hispanic/Latino; 1 Native Hawaiian or other Pacific Islander, non-Hispanic/Latino; 8 Two or more races, non-Hispanic/Latino). Average age 30. 447 applicants, 49% accepted. In 2011, 132 master's awarded. *Degree requirements:* For master's, comprehensive exam. *Entrance requirements:* Additional exam requirements/recommendations for international students: Required—TOEFL (minimum score 525 paper-based; 195 computer-based; 71 iBT) or IELTS (minimum score 6). *Application deadline:* For fall admission, 6/1 for domestic and international students. Applications are processed on a rolling basis. Application fee: $25 ($30 for international students). Electronic applications accepted. *Expenses:* Tuition, state resident: full-time $10,008. Tuition, nonresident: full-time $25,056. *Financial support:* In 2011–12, 8 students received support. Tuition waivers available. Support available to part-time students. Financial award application deadline: 5/1; financial award applicants required to submit FAFSA. *Unit head:* Dr. Jill Austin, Chair, 615-898-2736, Fax: 615-898-5308, E-mail: jill.austin@mtsu.edu. *Application contact:* Dr. Michael D. Allen, Dean and Vice Provost for Research, 615-898-2840, Fax: 615-904-8020, E-mail: michael.allen@mtsu.edu.

Milwaukee School of Engineering, Rader School of Business, Program in Marketing and Export Management, Milwaukee, WI 53202-3109. Offers MS. Part-time and evening/weekend programs available. *Faculty:* 1 full-time (0 women), 1 part-time/adjunct (0 women). *Students:* 5 part-time (4 women). Average age 27. 2 applicants, 50% accepted, 0 enrolled. In 2011, 1 master's awarded. *Degree requirements:* For master's, thesis, thesis defense or capstone project. *Entrance requirements:* For master's, GRE General Test or GMAT, 2 letters of recommendation. Additional exam requirements/recommendations for international students: Recommended—TOEFL (minimum score 550 paper-based; 213 computer-based; 79 iBT), IELTS. *Application deadline:* Applications are processed on a rolling basis. Application fee: $0. Electronic applications accepted. Application fee is waived when completed online. *Expenses: Tuition:* Full-time $17,550; part-time $650 per credit hour. *Financial support:* In 2011–12, 4 students received support. Career-related internships or fieldwork available. Support available to part-time students. Financial award applicants required to submit FAFSA. *Unit head:* Dr. Kathy Faggiani, Director, 414-277-2711, Fax: 414-277-2711, E-mail: faggiani@msoe.edu. *Application contact:* Katie Gassenhuber, Graduate Admissions Director, 800-321-6763, Fax: 414-277-7208, E-mail: gassenhuber@msoe.edu.

Mississippi State University, College of Business, Department of Marketing, Quantitative Analysis and Business Law, Mississippi State, MS 39762. Offers business administration (MBA), including marketing. Part-time and evening/weekend programs available. *Faculty:* 10 full-time (3 women). *Students:* 7 full-time (3 women); includes 1 minority (Black or African American, non-Hispanic/Latino). Average age 33. 12 applicants, 33% accepted, 4 enrolled. In 2011, 1 degree awarded. *Degree requirements:* For doctorate, comprehensive exam, thesis/dissertation. *Entrance requirements:* For doctorate, GMAT, minimum GPA of 2.75 in last 60 undergraduate hours. Additional exam requirements/recommendations for international students: Required—TOEFL (minimum score 575 paper-based; 233 computer-based; 90 iBT); Recommended—IELTS (minimum score 6.5). *Application deadline:* For fall admission, 7/1 for domestic students, 5/1 for international students; for spring admission, 11/1 for domestic students, 9/1 for international students. Applications are processed on a rolling basis. Application fee: $40. Electronic applications accepted. *Expenses:* Tuition, state resident: full-time $5805; part-time $322.50 per credit hour. Tuition, nonresident: full-time $14,670; part-time $815 per credit hour. *Financial support:* In 2011–12, 3 teaching assistantships (averaging $12,270 per year) were awarded; Federal Work-Study, institutionally sponsored loans, and scholarships/grants also available. Financial award application deadline: 4/1; financial award applicants required to submit FAFSA. *Unit head:* Dr. Jason Lueg, Associate Professor and Department Head, 662-325-3163, Fax: 662-325-7012, E-mail: jlueg@cobilan.msstate.edu. *Application contact:* Dr. Barbara Spencer, Associate Dean for Research and Outreach, 662-325-1891, Fax: 662-325-8161, E-mail: gsbi@cobilan.msstate.edu. Web site: http://business.msstate.edu/marketing/.

Montclair State University, The Graduate School, School of Business, Post Master's Certificate Program in Marketing, Montclair, NJ 07043-1624. Offers MBA, Certificate, Post Master's Certificate. Part-time and evening/weekend programs available. *Students:* Average age 29. *Entrance requirements:* For degree, essay. Additional exam requirements/recommendations for international students: Required—TOEFL (minimum score 83 iBT) or IELTS (minimum score 6.5). *Application deadline:* For fall admission, 6/1 for international students; for spring admission, 10/1 for international students. Applications are processed on a rolling basis. Application fee: $60. Electronic applications accepted. *Financial support:* Federal Work-Study, scholarships/grants, and unspecified assistantships available. Support available to part-time students. Financial award application deadline: 3/1; financial award applicants required to submit FAFSA. *Faculty research:* Converting service marketing to tangibility, mathematical approaches to solving marketing problems, system dynamic modeling of brand management, attitudes toward safety in leisure facilities, marketing/retailing strategy and instruction. *Unit head:* Dr. Avinandan Mukherjee, Chair, 973-655-5126. *Application contact:* Amy Aiello, Executive Director of The Graduate School, 973-655-5147, Fax: 973-655-7869, E-mail: graduate.school@montclair.edu.

New England College, Program in Management, Henniker, NH 03242-3293. Offers accounting (MSA); healthcare administration (MS); international relations (MA); marketing management (MS); nonprofit leadership (MS); project management (MS); strategic leadership (MS). Part-time and evening/weekend programs available. *Degree requirements:* For master's, independent research project. Electronic applications accepted.

New Mexico State University, Graduate School, College of Business, Department of Marketing, Las Cruces, NM 88003-8001. Offers PhD. *Expenses:* Tuition, state resident: full-time $5004; part-time $208.50 per credit. Tuition, nonresident: full-time $17,446; part-time $726.90 per credit. *Financial support:* Research assistantships, teaching assistantships, scholarships/grants, and health care benefits available.

New York Institute of Technology, Graduate Division, School of Management, Program in Business Administration, Old Westbury, NY 11568-8000. Offers accounting (Advanced Certificate); business administration (MBA); finance (Advanced Certificate); international business (Advanced Certificate); management of information systems (Advanced Certificate); marketing (Advanced Certificate). Part-time and evening/weekend programs available. *Students:* 331 full-time (131 women), 508 part-time (211 women); includes 74 minority (26 Black or African American, non-Hispanic/Latino; 27 Asian, non-Hispanic/Latino; 15 Hispanic/Latino; 6 Two or more races, non-Hispanic/Latino), 214 international. Average age 28. In 2011, 449 degrees awarded. *Degree requirements:* For master's, thesis (for some programs). *Entrance requirements:* For master's, minimum QPA of 2.85. Additional exam requirements/recommendations for international students: Required—TOEFL (minimum score 550 paper-based; 213 computer-based). *Application deadline:* For fall admission, 7/1 priority date for domestic students; for spring admission, 12/1 priority date for domestic students. Applications are processed on a rolling basis. Application fee: $50. Electronic applications accepted. *Expenses: Tuition:* Part-time $930 per credit hour. *Financial support:* Fellowships, research assistantships with partial tuition reimbursements, institutionally sponsored loans, tuition waivers (full and partial), and unspecified assistantships available. Support available to part-time students. Financial award applicants required to submit FAFSA. *Faculty research:* Instructor performance appraisal; relationship between TOEFL, GMAT, GRE, and performance in foreign students. *Unit head:* Dr. Stephen Hartman, Director, 516-686-7691, E-mail: shartman@nyit.edu. *Application contact:* Dr. Jacquelyn

Nealon, Vice President for Enrollment Services, 516-686-7925, Fax: 516-686-7597, E-mail: jnealon@nyit.edu.

New York University, Leonard N. Stern School of Business, Department of Marketing, New York, NY 10012-1019. Offers entertainment, media and technology (MBA); general marketing (MBA); marketing (PhD); product management (MBA).

New York University, School of Continuing and Professional Studies, Division of Programs in Business, Program in Integrated Marketing, New York, NY 10012-1019. Offers brand management (MS); digital marketing (MS); marketing analytics (MS). Part-time and evening/weekend programs available. *Faculty:* 1 full-time (0 women), 26 part-time/adjunct (5 women). *Students:* 69 full-time (56 women), 102 part-time (79 women); includes 21 minority (3 Black or African American, non-Hispanic/Latino; 12 Asian, non-Hispanic/Latino; 6 Hispanic/Latino), 59 international. Average age 29. 337 applicants, 55% accepted, 96 enrolled. In 2011, 57 master's awarded. *Degree requirements:* For master's, comprehensive exam, thesis, capstone; writing of complete business plan. *Entrance requirements:* For master's, GRE/GMAT only upon request, relevant professional work, internship or volunteer experience. Additional exam requirements/recommendations for international students: Required—TOEFL (minimum score 600 paper-based; 250 computer-based; 100 iBT), IELTS (minimum score 7). *Application deadline:* For fall admission, 2/1 priority date for domestic students, 2/1 for international students; for spring admission, 10/15 priority date for domestic students, 8/15 for international students. Applications are processed on a rolling basis. Application fee: $150. Electronic applications accepted. *Financial support:* In 2011–12, 71 students received support, including 71 fellowships (averaging $1,868 per year); institutionally sponsored loans and scholarships/grants also available. Financial award application deadline: 3/1; financial award applicants required to submit FAFSA. *Faculty research:* Branding, digital marketing, Web analytics, consumer behavior, customer loyalty, campaign planning and management. *Application contact:* Admissions Office, 212-998-7100, E-mail: scps.gradadmissions@nyu.edu. Web site: http://www.scps.nyu.edu/areas-of-study/marketing/graduate-programs/ms-integrated-marketing/.

New York University, School of Continuing and Professional Studies, The Preston Robert Tisch Center for Hospitality, Tourism, and Sports Management, Program in Sports Business, New York, NY 10012-1019. Offers collegiate and professional sports operations (MS); marketing and media (MS); sports business (Advanced Certificate). Part-time and evening/weekend programs available. *Faculty:* 13 full-time (5 women), 26 part-time/adjunct (8 women). *Students:* 27 full-time (8 women), 41 part-time (18 women); includes 5 minority (3 Black or African American, non-Hispanic/Latino; 1 American Indian or Alaska Native, non-Hispanic/Latino; 1 Hispanic/Latino), 11 international. Average age 29. 140 applicants, 49% accepted, 22 enrolled. In 2011, 38 master's, 5 other advanced degrees awarded. *Degree requirements:* For master's, thesis. *Entrance requirements:* For master's, GRE/GMAT only upon request, relevant professional work, internship or volunteer experience. Additional exam requirements/recommendations for international students: Required—TOEFL (minimum score 600 paper-based; 250 computer-based; 100 iBT), IELTS (minimum score 7). *Application deadline:* For fall admission, 2/1 priority date for domestic students, 2/1 for international students; for spring admission, 10/15 priority date for domestic students, 8/15 for international students. Applications are processed on a rolling basis. Application fee: $150. Electronic applications accepted. *Financial support:* In 2011–12, 47 students received support, including 43 fellowships (averaging $3,033 per year); scholarships/grants also available. Support available to part-time students. Financial award application deadline: 2/15. *Faculty research:* Implications of college football's bowl coalition series from a legal, economic, and academic perspective; social history of sports. *Application contact:* Admissions Office, 212-998-7100, E-mail: scps.gradadmissions@nyu.edu. Web site: http://www.scps.nyu.edu/areas-of-study/tisch/graduate-programs/ms-sports-business/.

North Central College, Graduate and Continuing Education Programs, Department of Business, Program in Business Administration, Naperville, IL 60566-7063. Offers change management (MBA); finance (MBA); human resource management (MBA); management (MBA); marketing (MBA). Part-time and evening/weekend programs available. *Faculty:* 14 full-time (4 women), 13 part-time/adjunct (3 women). *Students:* 41 full-time (15 women), 66 part-time (31 women); includes 19 minority (2 Black or African American, non-Hispanic/Latino; 1 American Indian or Alaska Native, non-Hispanic/Latino; 12 Asian, non-Hispanic/Latino; 4 Hispanic/Latino), 1 international. Average age 30. 116 applicants, 66% accepted, 50 enrolled. In 2011, 63 master's awarded. *Degree requirements:* For master's, thesis optional, project. *Entrance requirements:* For master's, interview. Additional exam requirements/recommendations for international students: Required—TOEFL (minimum score 577 paper-based; 233 computer-based; 90 iBT). *Application deadline:* For fall admission, 8/15 for domestic students; for winter admission, 12/1 for domestic students; for spring admission, 2/1 for domestic students. Application fee: $25. *Financial support:* In 2011–12, 8 students received support. Scholarships/grants available. Support available to part-time students. *Unit head:* Dr. Jean Clifton, MBA Program Coordinator, 630-637-5244, E-mail: jmclifton@noctrl.edu. *Application contact:* Wendy Kulpinski, Director of Graduate and Continuing Education Admission, 630-637-5808, Fax: 630-637-5844, E-mail: wekulpinski@noctrl.edu.

Northeastern Illinois University, Graduate College, College of Business and Management, Chicago, IL 60625-4699. Offers accounting (MSA); finance (MBA); management (MBA); marketing (MBA). Part-time and evening/weekend programs available. *Degree requirements:* For master's, thesis optional. *Entrance requirements:* For master's, GMAT, minimum GPA of 2.75. Additional exam requirements/recommendations for international students: Required—TOEFL (minimum score 550 paper-based; 213 computer-based; 79 iBT). Electronic applications accepted. *Faculty research:* Perception of accountants and non-accountants toward future of the accounting industry, asynchronous learning outcomes, cost and efficiency of financial markets, impact of deregulation on airline industry, analysis of derivational instruments.

Northwestern University, The Graduate School, Kellogg School of Management, Department of Marketing, Evanston, IL 60208. Offers PhD. Admissions and degree offered through The Graduate School. *Degree requirements:* For doctorate, comprehensive exam, thesis/dissertation. *Entrance requirements:* For doctorate, GMAT or GRE General Test. Additional exam requirements/recommendations for international students: Required—TOEFL. Electronic applications accepted. *Faculty research:* Choice models, database and high-tech marketing, consumer information processing, ethnographic analysis of consumption, psychometric analysis of consumer behavior.

Northwestern University, Medill School of Journalism, Integrated Marketing Communications Program, Evanston, IL 60208. Offers advertising/sales promotion (MSIMC); direct database and e-commerce marketing (MSIMC); general studies (MSIMC); public relations (MSIMC). Part-time programs available. *Entrance requirements:* For master's, GRE General Test or GMAT, full-time work experience (preferred). Additional exam requirements/recommendations for international students: Required—TOEFL. Electronic applications accepted. *Faculty research:* Data mining, business to business marketing, values in advertising, political advertising.

Notre Dame de Namur University, Division of Academic Affairs, School of Business and Management, Department of Business Administration, Belmont, CA 94002-1908. Offers business administration (MBA); finance (MBA); human resource management (MBA); marketing (MBA). Part-time and evening/weekend programs available. *Faculty:* 7 full-time (1 woman), 6 part-time/adjunct (0 women). *Students:* 42 full-time (16 women), 104 part-time (67 women); includes 56 minority (6 Black or African American, non-Hispanic/Latino; 26 Asian, non-Hispanic/Latino; 20 Hispanic/Latino; 2 Native Hawaiian or other Pacific Islander, non-Hispanic/Latino; 2 Two or more races, non-Hispanic/Latino), 23 international. Average age 34. 167 applicants, 40% accepted, 39 enrolled. In 2011, 33 degrees awarded. *Entrance requirements:* For master's, minimum GPA of 2.5. Additional exam requirements/recommendations for international students: Required—TOEFL (minimum score 550 paper-based; 213 computer-based; 79 iBT). *Application deadline:* For fall admission, 8/1 priority date for domestic students; for spring admission, 12/1 priority date for domestic students. Applications are processed on a rolling basis. Application fee: $60. Electronic applications accepted. *Expenses: Tuition:* Full-time $14,220; part-time $790 per credit. *Required fees:* $35 per semester. Tuition and fees vary according to program. *Financial support:* Available to part-time students. Applicants required to submit FAFSA. *Unit head:* Jordan Holtzman, Director, 650-508-3637, E-mail: jholtzman@ndnu.edu. *Application contact:* Candace Hallmark, Associate Director of Admissions, 650-508-3600, Fax: 650-508-3426, E-mail: grad.admit@ndnu.edu. Web site: http://www.ndnu.edu/academics/schools-programs/school-business/.

Oakland University, Graduate Study and Lifelong Learning, School of Business Administration, Department of Management and Marketing, Rochester, MI 48309-4401. Offers business administration (MBA); entrepreneurship (Certificate); general management (Certificate); human resource management (Certificate); international business (Certificate); marketing (Certificate).

The Ohio State University, Graduate School, Max M. Fisher College of Business, Program in Marketing, Columbus, OH 43210. Offers MBA, MS, PhD. *Faculty:* 23. *Students:* 19 part-time (11 women); includes 2 minority (both Asian, non-Hispanic/Latino), 1 international. Average age 36. In 2011, 2 degrees awarded. *Entrance requirements:* Additional exam requirements/recommendations for international students: Required—TOEFL. *Expenses:* Tuition, state resident: full-time $11,400. Tuition, nonresident: full-time $28,125. Tuition and fees vary according to course load, degree level, campus/location and program. *Unit head:* Walter Zinn, Chair, 614-292-0797, E-mail: zinn.13@osu.edu. *Application contact:* Graduate Admissions, 614-292-6031, Fax: 614-292-3656, E-mail: gradadmissions@osu.edu. Web site: http://fisher.osu.edu/departments/marketing-and-logistics/master-programs.

Oklahoma City University, Meinders School of Business, Program in Business Administration, Oklahoma City, OK 73106-1402. Offers finance (MBA); health administration (MBA); information technology (MBA); integrated marketing communications (MBA); international business (MBA); marketing (MBA); JD/MBA. *Accreditation:* ACBSP. Part-time and evening/weekend programs available. *Faculty:* 15 full-time (6 women), 14 part-time/adjunct (6 women). *Students:* 136 full-time (59 women), 112 part-time (34 women); includes 38 minority (14 Black or African American, non-Hispanic/Latino; 4 American Indian or Alaska Native, non-Hispanic/Latino; 11 Asian, non-Hispanic/Latino; 3 Hispanic/Latino; 6 Two or more races, non-Hispanic/Latino), 100 international. Average age 30. 252 applicants, 83% accepted, 30 enrolled. In 2011, 148 master's awarded. *Degree requirements:* For master's, comprehensive exam. *Entrance requirements:* For master's, GRE or GMAT. Additional exam requirements/recommendations for international students: Required—TOEFL (minimum score 560 paper-based; 220 computer-based; 83 iBT). *Application deadline:* Applications are processed on a rolling basis. Application fee: $50 ($70 for international students). Electronic applications accepted. *Expenses: Tuition:* Full-time $16,848; part-time $936 per credit hour. *Required fees:* $2070; $115 per credit hour. One-time fee: $300. *Financial support:* Career-related internships or fieldwork, Federal Work-Study, institutionally sponsored loans, and tuition waivers (partial) available. Support available to part-time students. Financial award application deadline: 6/1; financial award applicants required to submit FAFSA. *Faculty research:* Management information systems, international business strategies. *Unit head:* Dr. Steven Agee, Dean, 405-208-5130, Fax: 405-208-5098, E-mail: sagee@okcu.edu. *Application contact:* Michelle Cook, Director, Graduate Admissions, 800-633-7242, Fax: 405-208-5916, E-mail: gadmissions@okcu.edu. Web site: http://msb.okcu.edu/graduate/.

Oklahoma State University, Spears School of Business, Department of Marketing, Stillwater, OK 74078. Offers business administration (PhD), including marketing; marketing (MBA). Part-time programs available. *Faculty:* 17 full-time (5 women), 15 part-time/adjunct (5 women). *Students:* 4 full-time (1 woman), 7 part-time (0 women); includes 2 minority (1 Asian, non-Hispanic/Latino; 1 Two or more races, non-Hispanic/Latino), 5 international. Average age 32. In 2011, 3 degrees awarded. *Degree requirements:* For master's, thesis or alternative; for doctorate, comprehensive exam, thesis/dissertation. *Entrance requirements:* For master's and doctorate, GRE or GMAT. Additional exam requirements/recommendations for international students: Required—TOEFL (minimum score 550 paper-based; 79 iBT). *Application deadline:* For fall admission, 3/1 for international students; for spring admission, 8/1 for international students. Applications are processed on a rolling basis. Application fee: $40 ($75 for international students). Electronic applications accepted. *Expenses:* Tuition, state resident: full-time $4044; part-time $168.50 per credit hour. Tuition, nonresident: full-time $16,008; part-time $667 per credit hour. *Required fees:* $2122; $88.45 per credit hour. One-time fee: $50. Tuition and fees vary according to course load and campus/location. *Financial support:* In 2011–12, 7 research assistantships (averaging $15,516 per year), 4 teaching assistantships (averaging $14,238 per year) were awarded; career-related internships or fieldwork, Federal Work-Study, scholarships/grants, health care benefits, tuition waivers (partial), and unspecified assistantships also available. Support available to part-time students. Financial award application deadline: 3/1; financial award applicants required to submit FAFSA. *Faculty research:* Decision-making (consumer, managerial, cross-functional), communication effects, services marketing, public policy and marketing, corporate image. *Unit head:* Dr. Joshua L. Wiener, Head, 405-744-5192, Fax: 405-744-5180. *Application contact:* Dr. Gordon Emslie, Dean, 405-744-6368, Fax: 405-744-0355, E-mail: grad-i@okstate.edu. Web site: http://spears.okstate.edu/marketing.

Old Dominion University, College of Business and Public Administration, Doctoral Program in Business Administration, Norfolk, VA 23529. Offers finance (PhD); information technology (PhD); marketing (PhD); strategic management (PhD). *Accreditation:* AACSB. *Faculty:* 21 full-time (2 women). *Students:* 51 full-time (17 women); includes 5 minority (3 Black or African American, non-Hispanic/Latino; 1 Asian, non-Hispanic/Latino; 1 Native Hawaiian or other Pacific Islander, non-Hispanic/Latino), 29 international. Average age 35. 47 applicants, 60% accepted, 12 enrolled. In 2011, 7 doctorates awarded. *Degree requirements:* For doctorate, comprehensive exam, thesis/dissertation. *Entrance requirements:* For doctorate, GMAT. Additional exam requirements/recommendations for international students: Required—TOEFL (minimum score 550 paper-based; 213 computer-based; 79 iBT). *Application deadline:* For fall admission, 4/1 priority date for domestic students, 4/1 for international students. Application fee: $50. Electronic applications accepted. *Expenses:* Tuition, state resident: full-time $9096; part-time $379 per credit. Tuition, nonresident: full-time $23,064; part-time $961 per credit. *Required fees:* $127 per semester. One-time fee: $50. *Financial support:* In 2011–12, 27 students received support, including 2 fellowships with full tuition reimbursements available (averaging $7,500 per year), 32 research assistantships with full tuition reimbursements available (averaging $7,500 per year), 12 teaching assistantships with full tuition reimbursements available (averaging $7,500 per year); scholarships/grants and unspecified assistantships also available. Financial award application deadline: 4/1; financial award applicants required to submit FAFSA. *Faculty research:* International business, buyer behavior, financial markets, strategy, operations research. *Unit head:* Dr. John B. Ford, Graduate Program Director, 757-683-3587, Fax: 757-683-4076, E-mail: jford@odu.edu. *Application contact:* Katrina Davenport, Program Coordinator, 757-683-5138, Fax: 757-683-4076, E-mail: kdavenpo@odu.edu. Web site: http://bpa.odu.edu/bpa/academics/baphd.shtml.

Oral Roberts University, School of Business, Tulsa, OK 74171. Offers accounting (MBA); entrepreneurship (MBA); finance (MBA); international business (MBA); management (MBA); marketing (MBA); non-profit management (MBA); not for profit management (MNM). *Accreditation:* ACBSP. Part-time programs available. Postbaccalaureate distance learning degree programs offered (minimal on-campus study). *Degree requirements:* For master's, thesis optional. *Entrance requirements:* For master's, minimum cumulative GPA of 3.0. Additional exam requirements/ recommendations for international students: Required—TOEFL (minimum score 550 paper-based; 213 computer-based; 79 iBT). Electronic applications accepted. *Faculty research:* Social media, international business and marketing.

Ottawa University, Graduate Studies-Arizona, Programs in Business, Ottawa, KS 66067-3399. Offers business administration (MBA); finance (MBA); human resources (MA, MBA); leadership (MBA); marketing (MBA). Programs offered in Mesa, Phoenix, Tempe and West Valley, AZ. Part-time and evening/weekend programs available. Postbaccalaureate distance learning degree programs offered. *Degree requirements:* For master's, thesis or alternative. *Entrance requirements:* For master's, minimum undergraduate GPA of 3.0. Additional exam requirements/recommendations for international students: Required—TOEFL (minimum score 550 paper-based; 213 computer-based). Electronic applications accepted.

Pace University, Lubin School of Business, Marketing Program, New York, NY 10038. Offers marketing management (MBA); marketing research (MBA). Part-time and evening/weekend programs available. *Students:* 19 full-time (7 women), 52 part-time (33 women); includes 12 minority (2 Black or African American, non-Hispanic/Latino; 5 Asian, non-Hispanic/Latino; 4 Hispanic/Latino; 1 Two or more races, non-Hispanic/ Latino), 35 international. Average age 27. 178 applicants, 40% accepted, 19 enrolled. In 2011, 24 master's awarded. *Entrance requirements:* For master's, GMAT, GRE. Additional exam requirements/recommendations for international students: Required—TOEFL. *Application deadline:* For fall admission, 7/31 priority date for domestic students; for spring admission, 11/30 for domestic students. Applications are processed on a rolling basis. Application fee: $70. Electronic applications accepted. *Expenses: Tuition:* Part-time $990 per credit. *Required fees:* $168 per semester. Tuition and fees vary according to course load and degree level. *Financial support:* Research assistantships, career-related internships or fieldwork, and Federal Work-Study available. Support available to part-time students. Financial award applicants required to submit FAFSA. *Unit head:* Dr. Mary M. Long, Chairperson, 212-618-6453, E-mail: mlong@pace.edu. *Application contact:* Susan Ford-Goldschein, Director of Graduate Admissions, 212-346-1531, Fax: 212-346-1585, E-mail: gradnyc@pace.edu. Web site: http://www.pace.edu/.

Philadelphia University, School of Business Administration, Program in Business Administration, Philadelphia, PA 19144. Offers business administration (MBA); finance (MBA); health care management (MBA); international business (MBA); marketing (MBA); MBA/MS. Part-time and evening/weekend programs available. Postbaccalaureate distance learning degree programs offered (no on-campus study). *Entrance requirements:* For master's, GMAT. Additional exam requirements/ recommendations for international students: Required—TOEFL (minimum score 550 paper-based; 213 computer-based; 79 iBT).

Polytechnic University of Puerto Rico, Miami Campus, Graduate School, Miami, FL 33166. Offers accounting (MBA); business administration (MBA); construction management (MEM); environmental management (MEM); finance (MBA); human resources management (MBA); logistics and supply chain management (MBA); management of international enterprises (MBA); manufacturing management (MEM); marketing management (MBA); project management (MBA). Part-time and evening/ weekend programs available. Postbaccalaureate distance learning degree programs offered (no on-campus study). *Entrance requirements:* For master's, minimum GPA of 3.0. Electronic applications accepted.

Pontifical Catholic University of Puerto Rico, College of Business Administration, Program in Marketing, Ponce, PR 00717-0777. Offers MBA. Part-time and evening/ weekend programs available. *Degree requirements:* For master's, thesis. *Entrance requirements:* For master's, GRE, interview, minimum GPA of 2.75.

Pontificia Universidad Catolica Madre y Maestra, Graduate School, Faculty of Social and Administrative Sciences, Santiago, Dominican Republic. Offers business administration (MBA), including business development, finance, international business, management skills (M Mgmt, MBA), marketing, operations, strategic cost management, strategy, tourist destination planning and management; law (LL M), including civil law, corporate business law, criminal law, international relations, real estate law; management (M Mgmt), including higher financial management, insurance program administration, management skills (M Mgmt, MBA); psychology (MA), including clinical child and adolescent psychology, forensic psychology; strategic human resources (EMBA).

Post University, Program in Business Administration, Waterbury, CT 06723-2540. Offers business administration (MBA); corporate innovation (MBA); entrepreneurship (MBA); finance (MBA); leadership (MBA); marketing (MBA). Postbaccalaureate distance learning degree programs offered.

Providence College, School of Business, Providence, RI 02918. Offers accounting (MBA); entrepreneurship (MBA); finance (MBA); international business (MBA); management (MBA); marketing (MBA); not-for-profit organizations (MBA). Part-time and evening/weekend programs available. *Faculty:* 11 full-time (4 women), 6 part-time/ adjunct (1 woman). *Students:* 52 full-time (21 women), 49 part-time (17 women); includes 8 minority (3 Black or African American, non-Hispanic/Latino; 2 Asian, non-Hispanic/Latino; 3 Two or more races, non-Hispanic/Latino), 6 international. Average age 26. 49 applicants, 80% accepted, 25 enrolled. In 2011, 57 master's awarded. *Degree requirements:* For master's, thesis optional. *Entrance requirements:* For master's, GMAT. Additional exam requirements/recommendations for international students: Required—TOEFL (minimum score 550 paper-based; 213 computer-based; 80 iBT). *Application deadline:* For fall admission, 8/1 priority date for domestic students, 8/1 for international students; for spring admission, 12/1 priority date for domestic students, 12/1 for international students. Applications are processed on a rolling basis. Application fee: $55. *Expenses:* Contact institution. *Financial support:* In 2011–12, 34 research assistantships with full tuition reimbursements (averaging $8,400 per year) were awarded; Federal Work-Study, institutionally sponsored loans, and unspecified assistantships also available. Support available to part-time students. Financial award application deadline: 8/1; financial award applicants required to submit FAFSA. *Unit head:* Dr. Catherine L. Pastille, Director, MBA Program, 401-865-1654, Fax: 401-865-2978, E-mail: cpastill@providence.edu. *Application contact:* Katherine A. Follett, Administrative Coordinator, 401-865-2333, Fax: 401-865-2978, E-mail: kfollett@providence.edu. Web site: http://www.providence.edu/business/Pages/default.aspx.

Queen's University at Kingston, Queens School of Business, Program in Business Administration, Kingston, ON K7L 3N6, Canada. Offers consulting and project management (MBA); finance (MBA); innovation and entrepreneurship (MBA); marketing (MBA). *Accreditation:* AACSB. *Degree requirements:* For master's, thesis optional, research project. *Entrance requirements:* For master's, GMAT, minimum B+ average. Additional exam requirements/recommendations for international students: Required—TOEFL. Electronic applications accepted. *Faculty research:* Management fundamentals, strategic thinking, global business, innovation and change, leadership.

Quinnipiac University, School of Business, Program in Business Administration, Hamden, CT 06518-1940. Offers chartered financial analyst (MBA); finance (MBA); healthcare management (MBA); information systems management (MBA); marketing (MBA); supply chain management (MBA); JD/MBA. *Accreditation:* AACSB. Part-time and evening/weekend programs available. Postbaccalaureate distance learning degree programs offered (no on-campus study). *Faculty:* 19 full-time (4 women), 2 part-time/ adjunct (1 woman). *Students:* 89 full-time (36 women), 129 part-time (50 women); includes 16 minority (5 Black or African American, non-Hispanic/Latino; 5 Asian, non-Hispanic/Latino; 6 Hispanic/Latino), 19 international. Average age 29. 206 applicants, 81% accepted, 139 enrolled. In 2011, 95 master's awarded. *Entrance requirements:* For master's, GMAT or GRE, minimum GPA of 3.0. Additional exam requirements/ recommendations for international students: Required—TOEFL (minimum score 575 paper-based; 233 computer-based; 90 iBT), IELTS (minimum score 6.5). *Application deadline:* For fall admission, 7/30 priority date for domestic students, 4/30 for international students; for spring admission, 12/15 priority date for domestic students, 9/15 for international students. Applications are processed on a rolling basis. Application fee: $45. Electronic applications accepted. *Expenses: Tuition:* Part-time $855 per credit. *Required fees:* $35 per credit. *Financial support:* In 2011–12, 23 students received support. Career-related internships or fieldwork, Federal Work-Study, scholarships/ grants, tuition waivers (partial), and unspecified assistantships available. Support available to part-time students. Financial award application deadline: 4/15; financial award applicants required to submit FAFSA. *Faculty research:* Financial markets and investments, international business, supply chain management, health care management, corporate governance. *Unit head:* Lisa Braiewa, MBA Program Director, 203-582-3710, Fax: 203-582-8664, E-mail: lisa.braiewa@quinnipiac.edu. *Application contact:* Katie Ludovico, 800-462-1944, Fax: 203-582-3443, E-mail: katie.ludovico@quinnipiac.edu. Web site: http://www.quinnipiac.edu/mba.

Regent's American College London, Webster Graduate School, London, United Kingdom. Offers business (MBA); finance (MS); human resources (MA); information technology management (MA); international business (MA); international non-governmental organizations (MA); international relations (MA); management and leadership (MA); marketing (MA). Part-time programs available.

Regis University, College for Professional Studies, School of Management, Denver, CO 80221-1099. Offers accounting (MS, Certificate); executive international management (Certificate); executive leadership (Certificate); executive project management (Certificate); finance and accounting (MBA); general business administration (MBA); health care management (MBA); human resource management and leadership (MSOL); information technology leadership and management (MSOL); international business (MBA); marketing (MBA); operations management (MBA); organizational leadership and management (MSOL); project leadership and management (MSOL); project management (Certificate); strategic business management (Certificate); strategic human resource management (Certificate); strategic management (MBA). Offered at Colorado Springs Campus, Northwest Denver Campus, Southeast Denver Campus, Fort Collins Campus, Broomfield Campus, Henderson (Nevada) Campus, and Summerlin (Nevada) Campus and online. Part-time and evening/weekend programs available. Postbaccalaureate distance learning degree programs offered (no on-campus study). *Degree requirements:* For master's, thesis optional, capstone project. *Entrance requirements:* For master's, GMAT or essays, interview, 2 years of full-time business work experience, resume; for Certificate, GMAT. Additional exam requirements/recommendations for international students: Required—TOEFL, TWE (minimum score 5) or university-based test. Electronic applications accepted. *Faculty research:* Impact of information technology on small business regulation of accounting, international project financing, mineral development, delivery of healthcare to rural indigenous communities.

Roberts Wesleyan College, Division of Business, Rochester, NY 14624-1997. Offers nonprofit leadership (Certificate); strategic leadership (MS); strategic marketing (MS). Evening/weekend programs available. *Degree requirements:* For master's, thesis or alternative. *Entrance requirements:* For master's, GMAT, minimum GPA of 2.75, verifiable work experience. *Expenses:* Contact institution.

Rollins College, Crummer Graduate School of Business, Winter Park, FL 32789-4499. Offers entrepreneurship (MBA); finance (MBA); international business (MBA); management (MBA); marketing (MBA); operations and technology management (MBA). *Accreditation:* AACSB. Part-time and evening/weekend programs available. Postbaccalaureate distance learning degree programs offered (minimal on-campus study). *Faculty:* 23 full-time (3 women), 6 part-time/adjunct (4 women). *Students:* 257 full-time (95 women), 121 part-time (39 women); includes 75 minority (12 Black or African American, non-Hispanic/Latino; 1 American Indian or Alaska Native, non-Hispanic/Latino; 20 Asian, non-Hispanic/Latino; 39 Hispanic/Latino; 3 Two or more races, non-Hispanic/Latino), 27 international. Average age 28. 363 applicants, 44% accepted, 100 enrolled. In 2011, 213 master's awarded. *Degree requirements:* For master's, minimum GPA of 2.85. *Entrance requirements:* For master's, GMAT or GRE, official transcripts, two letters of recommendation, essay, current resume/curriculum vitae, interview. Additional exam requirements/recommendations for international students: Required—TOEFL (minimum score 100 iBT) or IELTS (minimum score 7). *Application deadline:* Applications are processed on a rolling basis. Application fee: $50. Electronic applications accepted. *Expenses:* Contact institution. *Financial support:* In 2011–12, 258 students received support. Federal Work-Study and scholarships/grants available. Support available to part-time students. Financial award applicants required to submit FAFSA. *Faculty research:* Sustainability, world financial markets, international business, market research, strategic marketing. *Unit head:* Dr. Craig M. McAllaster, Dean, 407-646-2249, Fax: 407-646-1550, E-mail: cmcallaster@rollins.edu. *Application contact:* Eva Gauthier Oleksiw, Admissions Coordinator, 407-646-2405, Fax: 407-646-1550, E-mail: mbaadmissions@rollins.edu. Web site: http://www.rollins.edu/mba/.

Roosevelt University, Graduate Division, College of Arts and Sciences, Department of Communication, Program in Integrated Marketing Communications, Chicago, IL 60605. Offers MSIMC. Part-time and evening/weekend programs available. *Faculty research:* Print journalism, urban high school journalism.

Rowan University, Graduate School, William G. Rohrer College of Business, Department of Marketing and Business Information Systems, Glassboro, NJ 08028-1701. Offers MBA. Part-time and evening/weekend programs available. *Degree requirements:* For master's, comprehensive exam, thesis. *Entrance requirements:* For master's, GRE General Test. Additional exam requirements/recommendations for international students: Required—TOEFL. Electronic applications accepted.

Rutgers, The State University of New Jersey, Newark, Graduate School, Program in Management, Newark, NJ 07102. Offers accounting (PhD); accounting information systems (PhD); computer information systems (PhD); finance (PhD); information technology (PhD); international business (PhD); management science (PhD); marketing (PhD); organization management (PhD). Program offered jointly with New Jersey Institute of Technology. *Accreditation:* AACSB. *Degree requirements:* For doctorate, thesis/dissertation, cumulative exams. *Entrance requirements:* For doctorate, GMAT or GRE General Test, minimum undergraduate B average. Additional exam requirements/recommendations for international students: Required—TOEFL. Electronic applications accepted. *Faculty research:* Technology management, leadership and teams, consumer behavior, financial and markets, logistics.

Rutgers, The State University of New Jersey, Newark, Rutgers Business School–Newark and New Brunswick, Doctoral Programs in Management, Newark, NJ 07102. Offers accounting (PhD); accounting information systems (PhD); economics (PhD); finance (PhD); individualized study (PhD); information technology (PhD); international business (PhD); management science (PhD); marketing science (PhD); organizational management (PhD); science, technology and management (PhD); supply chain management (PhD). *Degree requirements:* For doctorate, comprehensive exam, thesis/dissertation. *Entrance requirements:* For doctorate, GRE or GMAT. Additional exam requirements/recommendations for international students: Required—TOEFL (minimum score 550 paper-based; 213 computer-based; 79 iBT). Electronic applications accepted.

Sacred Heart University, Graduate Programs, John F. Welch College of Business, Fairfield, CT 06825-1000. Offers accounting (MBA); finance (MBA); management (MBA); marketing (MBA). *Accreditation:* AACSB. Part-time and evening/weekend programs available. Postbaccalaureate distance learning degree programs offered. *Degree requirements:* For master's, thesis or alternative. *Entrance requirements:* For master's, GMAT (preferred) or GRE General Test. Additional exam requirements/recommendations for international students: Required—TOEFL (minimum score 550 paper-based; 213 computer-based; 75 iBT). Electronic applications accepted. *Expenses:* Contact institution. *Faculty research:* Management of organizations, international business management of technology.

Sage Graduate School, School of Management, Program in Business Administration, Troy, NY 12180-4115. Offers business strategy (MBA); finance (MBA); human resources (MBA); marketing (MBA); JD/MBA. Part-time and evening/weekend programs available. *Faculty:* 2 full-time (both women), 8 part-time/adjunct (1 woman). *Students:* 20 full-time (10 women), 55 part-time (36 women); includes 10 minority (2 Black or African American, non-Hispanic/Latino; 4 Asian, non-Hispanic/Latino; 3 Hispanic/Latino; 1 Two or more races, non-Hispanic/Latino), 1 international. Average age 31. 51 applicants, 55% accepted, 19 enrolled. In 2011, 10 degrees awarded. *Entrance requirements:* For master's, minimum GPA of 2.75, resume, 2 letters of recommendation. Additional exam requirements/recommendations for international students: Required—TOEFL (minimum score 550 paper-based; 213 computer-based). *Application deadline:* Applications are processed on a rolling basis. Application fee: $40. *Expenses: Tuition:* Full-time $11,880; part-time $660 per credit hour. Tuition and fees vary according to program. *Financial support:* Fellowships, research assistantships, Federal Work-Study, scholarships/grants, and unspecified assistantships available. Support available to part-time students. Financial award application deadline: 3/1; financial award applicants required to submit FAFSA. *Unit head:* Dr. Daniel Robeson, Dean, School of Management, 518-292-8637, Fax: 518-292-1964, E-mail: robesd@sage.edu. *Application contact:* Wendy D. Diefendorf, Director of Graduate and Adult Admission, 518-244-2443, Fax: 518-244-6880, E-mail: diefew@sage.edu.

St. Bonaventure University, School of Graduate Studies, Russell J. Jandoli School of Journalism and Mass Communication, St. Bonaventure, NY 14778-2284. Offers integrated marketing communications (MA). Evening/weekend programs available. *Faculty:* 2 full-time (1 woman), 4 part-time/adjunct (3 women). *Students:* 34 full-time (21 women), 8 part-time (5 women); includes 2 minority (both Black or African American, non-Hispanic/Latino), 1 international. Average age 28. 39 applicants, 85% accepted, 24 enrolled. In 2011, 34 master's awarded. *Entrance requirements:* For master's, GRE, writing sample, undergraduate transcript, letters of recommendation. Additional exam requirements/recommendations for international students: Required—TOEFL (minimum score 550 paper-based; 213 computer-based; 80 iBT). *Application deadline:* For fall admission, 6/15 priority date for domestic students, 2/1 for international students; for spring admission, 10/15 priority date for domestic students, 7/1 for international students. Applications are processed on a rolling basis. Application fee: $30. Electronic applications accepted. *Expenses: Tuition:* Part-time $670 per credit. *Financial support:* In 2011–12, 1 research assistantship with full and partial tuition reimbursement was awarded; Federal Work-Study, scholarships/grants, health care benefits, tuition waivers (partial), and unspecified assistantships also available. Support available to part-time students. Financial award application deadline: 4/15; financial award applicants required to submit FAFSA. *Unit head:* Br. Basil Valente, Program Director, 716-375-2585, E-mail: hoffmann@sbu.edu. *Application contact:* Dr. Bruce Campbell, Program Director, 716-375-2021, Fax: 716-375-4015, E-mail: gradsch@sbu.edu.

St. Edward's University, School of Management and Business, Area of Business Administration, Austin, TX 78704. Offers accounting (MBA); business management (MBA); finance (Certificate); global entrepreneurship (MBA); marketing (MBA, Certificate). Part-time and evening/weekend programs available. *Students:* 35 full-time (14 women), 218 part-time (114 women); includes 102 minority (22 Black or African American, non-Hispanic/Latino; 1 American Indian or Alaska Native, non-Hispanic/Latino; 11 Asian, non-Hispanic/Latino; 62 Hispanic/Latino; 1 Native Hawaiian or other Pacific Islander, non-Hispanic/Latino; 5 Two or more races, non-Hispanic/Latino), 14 international. Average age 32. 94 applicants, 71% accepted, 48 enrolled. In 2011, 104 master's awarded. *Degree requirements:* For master's, minimum of 24 resident hours. *Entrance requirements:* For master's, GMAT or GRE General Test, minimum GPA of 2.75 in last 60 hours of course work. Additional exam requirements/recommendations for international students: Required—TOEFL (minimum score 550 paper-based; 213 computer-based; 79 iBT) or IELTS (minimum score 6). *Application deadline:* For fall admission, 7/1 for domestic and international students; for spring admission, 11/1 for domestic and international students. Applications are processed on a rolling basis. Application fee: $45 ($50 for international students). Electronic applications accepted. *Expenses: Tuition:* Full-time $17,550; part-time $975 per credit hour. *Required fees:* $50 per trimester. Full-time tuition and fees vary according to course load and program. *Unit head:* Dr. Stan Horner, Director, 512-428-1279, Fax: 512-448-8492, E-mail: stanleyh@stedwards.edu. *Application contact:* Sarah Hennes, Graduate Admissions Coordinator, 512-448-8600, Fax: 512-428-1032, E-mail: sarahhe@stedwards.edu. Web site: http://www.stedwards.edu.

St. John's University, The Peter J. Tobin College of Business, Department of Marketing, Queens, NY 11439. Offers MBA, Adv C. Part-time and evening/weekend programs available. *Students:* 55 full-time (26 women), 18 part-time (12 women); includes 8 minority (4 Black or African American, non-Hispanic/Latino; 4 Asian, non-Hispanic/Latino), 35 international. Average age 26. 59 applicants, 71% accepted, 19 enrolled. In 2011, 37 master's awarded. *Degree requirements:* For master's, comprehensive exam (for some programs), thesis optional. *Entrance requirements:* For master's, GMAT, 2 letters of recommendation, resume, transcripts, essay; for Adv C, GMAT, 2 letters of recommendation, resume, undergraduate and graduate transcripts, essay, MBA. Additional exam requirements/recommendations for international students: Required—TOEFL (minimum score 600 paper-based; 250 computer-based; 100 iBT), IELTS (minimum score 7). *Application deadline:* For fall admission, 5/1 priority date for domestic students, 5/1 for international students; for spring admission, 11/1 priority date for domestic students, 11/1 for international students. Applications are processed on a rolling basis. Application fee: $50. Electronic applications accepted. *Expenses:* Contact institution. *Financial support:* Research assistantships, scholarships/grants, and unspecified assistantships available. Support available to part-time students. Financial award application deadline: 3/1; financial award applicants required to submit FAFSA. *Faculty research:* Global brand management, China's stimulus plan, measuring attitude, marketing in India, consumer decision-making. *Application contact:* Carol J. Swanberg, Assistant Dean/Director of Graduate Admissions, 718-990-1345, Fax: 718-990-5242, E-mail: tobingradnyc@stjohns.edu.

Saint Joseph's University, Erivan K. Haub School of Business, Executive Master's in Food Marketing Program, Philadelphia, PA 19131-1395. Offers MBA, MS. Part-time programs available. *Students:* 3 full-time (1 woman), 65 part-time (33 women); includes 7 minority (2 Black or African American, non-Hispanic/Latino; 1 Asian, non-Hispanic/Latino; 4 Hispanic/Latino), 2 international. Average age 36. In 2011, 12 master's awarded. *Entrance requirements:* For master's, 4 years of industry experience, interview or GMAT/GRE, 2 letters of recommendation, resume. Additional exam requirements/recommendations for international students: Required—TOEFL (minimum score 550 paper-based; 213 computer-based; 80 iBT), IELTS (minimum score 6.5), or Pearson Test of English (minimum score 60). *Application deadline:* For fall admission, 7/15 priority date for domestic students, 4/15 for international students; for spring admission, 11/15 priority date for domestic students, 10/15 for international students. Applications are processed on a rolling basis. Application fee: $0. Electronic applications accepted. *Expenses:* Contact institution. *Financial support:* In 2011–12, research assistantships with partial tuition reimbursements (averaging $4,000 per year), teaching assistantships (averaging $4,000 per year) were awarded; fellowships, institutionally sponsored loans, tuition waivers (partial), and unspecified assistantships also available. Financial award application deadline: 5/1; financial award applicants required to submit FAFSA. *Faculty research:* Marketing strategy, obesity, business ethics, bio-defense, international food marketing. *Unit head:* Christine Hartmann, Director, 610-660-1659, Fax: 610-660-3153, E-mail: chartman@sju.edu. *Application contact:* Amanda Basile, Program Administrator, 610-660-3151, Fax: 610-660-3153, E-mail: abasile@sju.edu. Web site: http://www.sju.edu/academics/hsb/grad/efm/.

Saint Joseph's University, Erivan K. Haub School of Business, MS Program in International Marketing, Philadelphia, PA 19131-1395. Offers MS. Part-time and evening/weekend programs available. *Students:* 45 full-time (28 women), 12 part-time (8 women); includes 5 minority (3 Black or African American, non-Hispanic/Latino; 1 American Indian or Alaska Native, non-Hispanic/Latino; 1 Hispanic/Latino), 40 international. Average age 26. In 2011, 18 master's awarded. *Entrance requirements:* For master's, GMAT or GRE, 2 letters of recommendation, resume, personal statement. Additional exam requirements/recommendations for international students: Required—TOEFL (minimum score 550 paper-based; 213 computer-based; 80 iBT), IELTS (minimum score 6.5), or Pearson Test of English (minimum score 60). *Application deadline:* For fall admission, 7/15 priority date for domestic students; for spring admission, 11/15 priority date for domestic students. Applications are processed on a rolling basis. Application fee: $35. Electronic applications accepted. *Expenses: Tuition:* Part-time $735 per credit hour. Tuition and fees vary according to degree level and program. *Financial support:* In 2011–12, 2 research assistantships with partial tuition reimbursements (averaging $8,000 per year) were awarded; unspecified assistantships also available. Financial award application deadline: 5/1; financial award applicants required to submit FAFSA. *Faculty research:* Export marketing, global marketing, international marketing research, new product development, emerging markets, international consumer behavior. *Unit head:* Christine Kaczmar-Russo, Director, 610-660-1238, Fax: 610-660-3239, E-mail: ckaczmar@sju.edu. *Application contact:* Karena Whitmore, Administrative Assistant, MS Programs, 610-660-3211, Fax: 610-660-1599, E-mail: kwhitmor@sju.edu. Web site: http://www.sju.edu/academics/hsb/grad/mim/.

Saint Joseph's University, Erivan K. Haub School of Business, Pharmaceutical and Healthcare Marketing MBA for Executives Program, Philadelphia, PA 19131-1395. Offers executive pharmaceutical marketing (Post Master's Certificate); pharmaceutical marketing (MBA). Part-time and evening/weekend programs available. Postbaccalaureate distance learning degree programs offered (minimal on-campus study). *Students:* 12 full-time (6 women), 107 part-time (58 women); includes 26 minority (11 Black or African American, non-Hispanic/Latino; 10 Asian, non-Hispanic/Latino; 4 Hispanic/Latino; 1 Two or more races, non-Hispanic/Latino), 3 international. Average age 38. In 2011, 20 master's awarded. *Entrance requirements:* For master's, 4 years of industry experience, letter of recommendation, resume, interview; for Post Master's Certificate, MBA, 4 years of industry experience, resume. Additional exam requirements/recommendations for international students: Required—TOEFL (minimum score 550 paper-based; 213 computer-based; 80 iBT), IELTS (minimum score 6.5), or Pearson Test of English (minimum score 60). *Application deadline:* For fall admission, 7/15 priority date for domestic students, 4/15 for international students; for spring admission, 11/15 priority date for domestic students, 10/15 for international students. Applications are processed on a rolling basis. Electronic applications accepted. *Expenses: Tuition:* Part-time $735 per credit hour. Tuition and fees vary according to degree level and program. *Financial support:* Scholarships/grants available. Financial award applicants required to submit FAFSA. *Faculty research:* Pharmaceutical strategy, Internet and pharmaceuticals, pharmaceutical promotion. *Unit head:* Terese W. Waldron, Director, 610-660-3150, Fax: 610-660-5160, E-mail: twaldron@sju.edu. *Application contact:* Christine Anderson, Senior Manager, Executive Relations and Industry Outreach, 610-660-3157, Fax: 610-660-3160, E-mail: christine.anderson@sju.edu. Web site: http://www.sju.edu/hsb/pharmaceutical_marketing/.

Saint Joseph's University, Erivan K. Haub School of Business, Professional MBA Program, Philadelphia, PA 19131-1395. Offers accounting (MBA); finance (MBA), including finance; general business (MBA); health and medical services administration (MBA); human resource management (MBA); international business (MBA); international marketing (MBA); management (MBA); marketing (MBA); DO/MBA. DO/MBA offered jointly with Philadelphia College of Osteopathic Medicine. Part-time and evening/weekend programs available. Postbaccalaureate distance learning degree programs offered (no on-campus study). *Students:* 98 full-time (42 women), 528 part-time (208 women); includes 102 minority (47 Black or African American, non-Hispanic/Latino; 1 American Indian or Alaska Native, non-Hispanic/Latino; 28 Asian, non-Hispanic/Latino; 20 Hispanic/Latino; 1 Native Hawaiian or other Pacific Islander, non-Hispanic/Latino; 5 Two or more races, non-Hispanic/Latino), 45 international. Average age 31. In 2011, 290 master's awarded. *Entrance requirements:* For master's, GMAT or GRE, 2 letters of recommendation, resume, personal statement. Additional exam requirements/recommendations for international students: Required—TOEFL (minimum score 550 paper-based; 213 computer-based; 80 iBT), IELTS (minimum score 6.5), or Pearson Test of English (minimum score 60). *Application deadline:* For fall admission, 7/

15 priority date for domestic students, 4/15 for international students; for spring admission, 11/15 priority date for domestic students, 10/15 for international students. Applications are processed on a rolling basis. Application fee: $35. Electronic applications accepted. *Expenses: Tuition:* Part-time $735 per credit hour. Tuition and fees vary according to degree level and program. *Financial support:* Scholarships/grants and unspecified assistantships available. Financial award application deadline: 5/1; financial award applicants required to submit FAFSA. *Unit head:* Adele C. Foley, Associate Dean/Director, Graduate Business Programs, 610-660-1691, Fax: 610-660-1599, E-mail: afoley@sju.edu. *Application contact:* Dr. Janine N. Guerra, Associate Director, Professional MBA Program, 610-660-1695, Fax: 610-660-1599, E-mail: jguerra@sju.edu. Web site: http://www.sju.edu/mba.

Saint Leo University, Graduate Business Studies, Saint Leo, FL 33574-6665. Offers accounting (MBA); business (MBA); health services management (MBA); human resource management (MBA); information security management (MBA); marketing (MBA); sport business (MBA). Part-time and evening/weekend programs available. Postbaccalaureate distance learning degree programs offered (no on-campus study). *Faculty:* 39 full-time (7 women), 56 part-time/adjunct (17 women). *Students:* 1,506 full-time (901 women); includes 620 minority (480 Black or African American, non-Hispanic/Latino; 5 American Indian or Alaska Native, non-Hispanic/Latino; 21 Asian, non-Hispanic/Latino; 100 Hispanic/Latino; 1 Native Hawaiian or other Pacific Islander, non-Hispanic/Latino; 13 Two or more races, non-Hispanic/Latino), 20 international. Average age 38. In 2011, 574 master's awarded. *Entrance requirements:* For master's, GMAT (minimum score 500 if applicant does not have 5 years of professional work experience), bachelor's degree with minimum GPA of 3.0 in the last 60 hours of coursework from regionally-accredited college or university; 5 years of professional work experience; resume; 2 letters of recommendation. Additional exam requirements/recommendations for international students: Required—TOEFL (minimum score 550 paper-based; 213 computer-based; 80 iBT). *Application deadline:* For fall admission, 7/1 priority date for domestic students, 7/1 for international students; for spring admission, 11/12 priority date for domestic students, 11/1 for international students. Applications are processed on a rolling basis. Application fee: $80. Electronic applications accepted. *Expenses: Tuition:* Full-time $11,340; part-time $630 per semester hour. Tuition and fees vary according to campus/location and program. *Financial support:* In 2011–12, 72 students received support. Career-related internships or fieldwork, Federal Work-Study, scholarships/grants, and health care benefits available. Financial award application deadline: 3/1; financial award applicants required to submit FAFSA. *Unit head:* Dr. Lorrie McGovern, Director, 352-588-7390, Fax: 352-588-8585, E-mail: mbaslu@saintleo.edu. *Application contact:* Jared Welling, Director of Graduate Admission, 800-707-8846, Fax: 352-588-7873, E-mail: grad.admissions@saintleo.edu. Web site: http://www.saintleo.edu/Academics/School-of-Business/Graduate-Degree-Programs.

Saint Peter's University, Graduate Business Programs, MBA Program, Jersey City, NJ 07306-5997. Offers finance (MBA); health care administration (MBA); human resource management (MBA); international business (MBA); management (MBA); management information systems (MBA); marketing (MBA); risk management (MBA); MBA/MS. Part-time and evening/weekend programs available. *Entrance requirements:* Additional exam requirements/recommendations for international students: Required—TOEFL (minimum score 79 computer-based). Electronic applications accepted. *Faculty research:* Finance, health care management, human resource management, international business, management, management information systems, marketing, risk management.

St. Thomas Aquinas College, Division of Business Administration, Sparkill, NY 10976. Offers business administration (MBA); finance (MBA); management (MBA); marketing (MBA). Part-time and evening/weekend programs available. *Entrance requirements:* For master's, GMAT. Additional exam requirements/recommendations for international students: Required—TOEFL. Electronic applications accepted.

Saint Xavier University, Graduate Studies, Graham School of Management, Chicago, IL 60655-3105. Offers employee health benefits (Certificate); finance (MBA); financial fraud examination and management (MBA, Certificate); financial planning (MBA, Certificate); generalist/individualized (MBA); health administration (MBA); managed care (Certificate); management (MBA); marketing (MBA); project management (MBA, Certificate); MBA/MS. *Accreditation:* ACBSP. Part-time and evening/weekend programs available. *Entrance requirements:* For master's, GMAT, minimum GPA of 3.0, 2 years of work experience. *Application deadline:* For fall admission, 8/15 for domestic students. Applications are processed on a rolling basis. Application fee: $35. Electronic applications accepted. *Expenses:* Contact institution. *Financial support:* Career-related internships or fieldwork available. Support available to part-time students. Financial award applicants required to submit FAFSA. *Unit head:* Dr. John E. Eber, Dean, 773-298-3601, Fax: 773-298-3601, E-mail: eber@sxu.edu. *Application contact:* Beth Gierach, Managing Director of Admission, 773-298-3053, Fax: 773-298-3076, E-mail: gierach@sxu.edu. Web site: http://www.sxu.edu/academics/colleges_schools/gsm/.

San Diego State University, Graduate and Research Affairs, College of Business Administration, Department of Marketing, San Diego, CA 92182. Offers MS. Part-time and evening/weekend programs available. *Degree requirements:* For master's, thesis or alternative. *Entrance requirements:* For master's, GMAT, resume, letters of reference. Additional exam requirements/recommendations for international students: Required—TOEFL. Electronic applications accepted.

Santa Clara University, Leavey School of Business, Program in Business Administration, Santa Clara, CA 95053. Offers accounting (MBA); entrepreneurship (MBA); executive business administration (EMBA); finance (MBA); food and agribusiness (MBA); international business (MBA); leading people and organizations (MBA); managing technology and innovation (MBA); marketing management (MBA); supply chain management (MBA). *Accreditation:* AACSB. Part-time and evening/weekend programs available. *Students:* 196 full-time (80 women), 669 part-time (224 women); includes 302 minority (12 Black or African American, non-Hispanic/Latino; 246 Asian, non-Hispanic/Latino; 35 Hispanic/Latino; 6 Native Hawaiian or other Pacific Islander, non-Hispanic/Latino; 3 Two or more races, non-Hispanic/Latino), 186 international. Average age 32. 365 applicants, 74% accepted, 199 enrolled. In 2011, 366 degrees awarded. *Degree requirements:* For master's, thesis or alternative. *Entrance requirements:* For master's, GMAT, GRE. Additional exam requirements/recommendations for international students: Required—TOEFL (minimum score 600 paper-based; 250 computer-based; 100 iBT). *Application deadline:* For fall admission, 6/1 for domestic and international students; for spring admission, 1/19 for domestic students, 1/17 for international students. Applications are processed on a rolling basis. Application fee: $75 ($100 for international students). Electronic applications accepted. *Expenses:* Contact institution. *Financial support:* In 2011–12, 350 students received support. Fellowships with partial tuition reimbursements available, research assistantships with partial tuition reimbursements available, career-related internships or fieldwork, Federal Work-Study, institutionally sponsored loans, scholarships/grants, health care benefits, and unspecified assistantships available. Support available to part-time students. Financial award application deadline: 6/1; financial award applicants required to submit FAFSA. *Unit head:* Elizabeth B. Ford, Senior Assistant Dean, 408-554-2752, Fax: 408-554-4571, E-mail: eford@scu.edu. *Application contact:* Tammy Fox, Assistant Director, Graduate Business Admissions, 408-554-7858, E-mail: tkfox@scu.edu.

Seton Hall University, Stillman School of Business, Programs in Business Administration, South Orange, NJ 07079-2697. Offers accounting (MBA); finance (MBA); information technology management (MBA); international business (MBA); management (MBA); marketing (MBA); sport management (MBA); supply chain management (MBA). Part-time and evening/weekend programs available. *Faculty:* 37 full-time (9 women), 19 part-time/adjunct (1 woman). *Students:* 166 full-time (65 women), 284 part-time (131 women); includes 113 minority (21 Black or African American, non-Hispanic/Latino; 81 Asian, non-Hispanic/Latino; 9 Hispanic/Latino; 2 Native Hawaiian or other Pacific Islander, non-Hispanic/Latino). Average age 29. 459 applicants, 59% accepted, 208 enrolled. In 2011, 210 master's awarded. *Degree requirements:* For master's, 20 hours of community service (Social Responsibility Project). *Entrance requirements:* For master's, GMAT, GRE or CPA, advanced degree from AACSB institution, MS in a business discipline, professional degree (MD, JD, PhD, DVM, DDS, etc.), minimum undergraduate GPA of 3.0. Additional exam requirements/recommendations for international students: Required—TOEFL (minimum score 102 iBT), IELTS or Pearson Test of English. *Application deadline:* For fall admission, 5/31 priority date for domestic students, 3/31 for international students; for spring admission, 10/31 priority date for domestic students, 9/30 for international students. Applications are processed on a rolling basis. Application fee: $75. Electronic applications accepted. *Expenses: Tuition:* Part-time $1033 per credit hour. *Required fees:* $85 per semester. *Financial support:* In 2011–12, research assistantships with full tuition reimbursements (averaging $35,610 per year) were awarded; career-related internships or fieldwork, Federal Work-Study, scholarships/grants, and unspecified assistantships also available. Support available to part-time students. Financial award application deadline: 6/30; financial award applicants required to submit FAFSA. *Faculty research:* Financial, hedge funds, international business, legal issues, disclosure and branding. *Unit head:* Dr. Joyce A. Strawser, Dean, 973-761-9013, Fax: 973-761-9217, E-mail: joyce.strawser@shu.edu. *Application contact:* Catherine Bianchi, Director of Graduate Admissions, 973-761-9262, Fax: 973-761-9208, E-mail: catherine.bianchi@shu.edu. Web site: http://www.shu.edu/academics/business.

Southern Adventist University, School of Business and Management, Collegedale, TN 37315-0370. Offers accounting (MBA); church administration (MSA); church and nonprofit leadership (MBA); financial management (MFM); healthcare administration (MBA); management (MBA); marketing management (MBA); outdoor education (MSA). Part-time and evening/weekend programs available. Postbaccalaureate distance learning degree programs offered (no on-campus study). *Entrance requirements:* For master's, GMAT. Additional exam requirements/recommendations for international students: Required—TOEFL (minimum score 600 paper-based; 250 computer-based; 100 iBT). Electronic applications accepted.

Southern Methodist University, Cox School of Business, MBA Program, Dallas, TX 75275. Offers accounting (MBA); finance (MBA); financial consulting (MBA); general business (MBA); information technology and operations management (MBA); management (MBA); marketing (MBA); real estate (MBA); strategy and entrepreneurship (MBA). Part-time and evening/weekend programs available. *Entrance requirements:* For master's, GMAT. Additional exam requirements/recommendations for international students: Required—TOEFL. Electronic applications accepted. *Expenses:* Contact institution. *Faculty research:* Corporate finance, financial reporting, modeling consumer decision-making, competition between national brands and store brands, institutional determinants of firms' strategy.

Southern New Hampshire University, School of Business, Manchester, NH 03106-1045. Offers accounting (MS); business administration (MBA, Certificate), including accounting (Certificate), business administration (MBA), finance (Certificate), forensic accounting (Certificate), human resources management (Certificate), international business (Certificate), international sport management (Certificate), leadership of not for profit organizations (Certificate), marketing (Certificate), operations management (Certificate), sport management (Certificate), taxation (Certificate); finance (MS); hospitality and tourism leadership (Certificate); information technology (MS, Certificate); information technology/international business (Certificate); integrated marketing communications (Certificate); international business (MS, DBA); marketing (MS); operations and project management (MS); organizational leadership (MS); project management (Certificate); sport management (MS); MBA/Certificate. *Accreditation:* ACBSP. Part-time and evening/weekend programs available. Postbaccalaureate distance learning degree programs offered (no on-campus study). Terminal master's awarded for partial completion of doctoral program. *Degree requirements:* For master's, one foreign language, comprehensive exam (for some programs), thesis or alternative; for doctorate, one foreign language, comprehensive exam, thesis/dissertation. *Entrance requirements:* For master's, minimum GPA of 2.5; for doctorate, GMAT. Additional exam requirements/recommendations for international students: Required—TOEFL (minimum score 500 paper-based). Electronic applications accepted.

Southwest Minnesota State University, Department of Business and Public Affairs, Marshall, MN 56258. Offers leadership (MBA); management (MBA); marketing (MBA). Part-time and evening/weekend programs available. Postbaccalaureate distance learning degree programs offered (no on-campus study). *Degree requirements:* For master's, thesis. *Entrance requirements:* For master's, GMAT (minimum score: 450). Additional exam requirements/recommendations for international students: Recommended—TOEFL (minimum score 550 paper-based; 213 computer-based; 79 iBT), IELTS. Electronic applications accepted.

Stephen F. Austin State University, Graduate School, College of Business, Program in Business Administration, Nacogdoches, TX 75962. Offers business (MBA); management and marketing (MBA). *Accreditation:* AACSB. Part-time and evening/weekend programs available. *Degree requirements:* For master's, comprehensive exam. *Entrance requirements:* For master's, GMAT, minimum AACSB index of 1000. Additional exam requirements/recommendations for international students: Required—TOEFL (minimum score 550 paper-based; 213 computer-based). *Faculty research:* Strategic implications, information search, multinational firms, philosophical guidance.

Stony Brook University, State University of New York, Graduate School, College of Business, Program in Business Administration, Stony Brook, NY 11794. Offers finance (MBA, Certificate); health care management (MBA, Certificate); human resource management (Certificate); human resources (MBA); information systems management (MBA, Certificate); management (MBA); marketing (MBA).

Strayer University, Graduate Studies, Washington, DC 20005-2603. Offers accounting (MS); acquisition (MBA); business administration (MBA); communications technology (MS); educational management (M Ed); finance (MBA); health services administration (MHSA); hospitality and tourism management (MBA); human resource management (MBA); information systems (MS), including computer security management, decision support system management, enterprise resource management, network management, software engineering management, systems development management; management (MBA); management information systems (MS); marketing (MBA); professional accounting (MS), including accounting information systems, controllership, taxation; public administration (MPA); supply chain management (MBA); technology in education

(M Ed). Programs also offered at campus locations in Birmingham, AL; Chamblee, GA; Cobb County, GA; Morrow, GA; White Marsh, MD; Charleston, SC; Columbia, SC; Greensboro, NC; Greenville, SC; Lexington, KY; Louisville, KY; Nashville, TN; North Raleigh, NC; Washington, DC. Part-time and evening/weekend programs available. Postbaccalaureate distance learning degree programs offered (minimal on-campus study). *Degree requirements:* For master's, thesis. *Entrance requirements:* For master's, GMAT, GRE General Test, bachelor's degree from an accredited college or university, minimum undergraduate GPA of 2.75. Electronic applications accepted.

Suffolk University, College of Arts and Sciences, Department of Communication and Journalism, Boston, MA 02108-2770. Offers communication studies (MAC); integrated marketing communication (MAC); public relations and advertising (MAC). Part-time and evening/weekend programs available. *Faculty:* 20 full-time (10 women), 1 part-time/adjunct (0 women). *Students:* 24 full-time (20 women), 16 part-time (14 women); includes 1 minority (Black or African American, non-Hispanic/Latino), 11 international. Average age 26. 100 applicants, 62% accepted, 20 enrolled. In 2011, 12 master's awarded. *Degree requirements:* For master's, thesis optional. *Entrance requirements:* For master's, GRE General Test, MAT, or GMAT, 2 letters of recommendation, resume. Additional exam requirements/recommendations for international students: Required—TOEFL (minimum score 550 paper-based; 213 computer-based; 80 iBT). *Application deadline:* For fall admission, 6/15 priority date for domestic students, 6/15 for international students; for spring admission, 11/1 priority date for domestic students, 11/1 for international students. Applications are processed on a rolling basis. Application fee: $50. Electronic applications accepted. *Expenses:* Contact institution. *Financial support:* In 2011–12, 27 students received support, including 23 fellowships with partial tuition reimbursements available (averaging $6,150 per year); career-related internships or fieldwork, Federal Work-Study, and institutionally sponsored loans also available. Support available to part-time students. Financial award application deadline: 4/1; financial award applicants required to submit FAFSA. *Faculty research:* New media and new markets for advertising, First Amendment issues with the Internet, gender and intercultural communication, organizational development. *Unit head:* Dr. Robert Rosenthal, Chair, 617-573-8502, Fax: 617-742-6982, E-mail: rrosenth@suffolk.edu. *Application contact:* Ellen Driscoll, Director of Graduate Admissions, 617-573-8302, Fax: 617-305-1733, E-mail: grad.admission@suffolk.edu.

Suffolk University, Sawyer Business School, Master of Business Administration Program, Boston, MA 02108-2770. Offers accounting (MBA); business administration (APC); corporate financial executive track (MBA); entrepreneurship (MBA); executive business administration (EMBA); finance (MBA); global business administration (GMBA); health administration (MBA); international business (MBA); marketing (MBA); organizational behavior (MBA); strategic management (MBA); taxation (MBA); JD/MBA; MBA/GDPA; MBA/MHA; MBA/MSA; MBA/MSF; MBA/MST. *Accreditation:* AACSB. Part-time and evening/weekend programs available. Postbaccalaureate distance learning degree programs offered (no on-campus study). *Faculty:* 98 full-time (30 women), 14 part-time/adjunct (3 women). *Students:* 139 full-time (49 women), 321 part-time (138 women); includes 53 minority (17 Black or African American, non-Hispanic/Latino; 1 American Indian or Alaska Native, non-Hispanic/Latino; 21 Asian, non-Hispanic/Latino; 11 Hispanic/Latino; 1 Native Hawaiian or other Pacific Islander, non-Hispanic/Latino; 2 Two or more races, non-Hispanic/Latino), 64 international. Average age 30. 437 applicants, 61% accepted, 121 enrolled. In 2011, 283 master's awarded. *Entrance requirements:* For master's, GMAT, minimum undergraduate GPA of 2.75 (MBA), 5 years of managerial experience (EMBA). Additional exam requirements/recommendations for international students: Required—TOEFL (minimum score 550 paper-based; 213 computer-based). *Application deadline:* For fall admission, 6/15 priority date for domestic students, 6/15 for international students; for spring admission, 11/1 priority date for domestic students, 11/1 for international students. Applications are processed on a rolling basis. Application fee: $50. Electronic applications accepted. Tuition and fees vary according to program. *Financial support:* In 2011–12, 273 students received support, including 73 fellowships with full and partial tuition reimbursements available (averaging $12,415 per year); career-related internships or fieldwork, Federal Work-Study, and institutionally sponsored loans also available. Support available to part-time students. Financial award application deadline: 4/1; financial award applicants required to submit FAFSA. *Faculty research:* Foreign investments; career strategies and boundaryless careers; corporate ethics codes; interest rates, inflation, and growth options; innovation and product development performance. *Unit head:* Lillian Hallberg, Assistant Dean of Graduate Programs/Director of MBA Programs, 617-573-8306, E-mail: lhallber@suffolk.edu. *Application contact:* Ellen Driscoll, Director of Graduate Admissions, 617-573-8302, Fax: 617-305-1733, E-mail: grad.admission@suffolk.edu. Web site: http://www.suffolk.edu/mba.

Syracuse University, Martin J. Whitman School of Management, PhD Program in Business Administration, Syracuse, NY 13244. Offers accounting (PhD); finance (PhD); management information systems (PhD); managerial statistics (PhD); marketing (PhD); operations management (PhD); organizational behavior (PhD); strategy and human resources (PhD); supply chain management (PhD). *Faculty:* 79 full-time (20 women), 25 part-time/adjunct (6 women). *Students:* 32 full-time (10 women); includes 6 minority (3 Black or African American, non-Hispanic/Latino; 2 Asian, non-Hispanic/Latino; 1 Hispanic/Latino), 18 international. Average age 32. 260 applicants, 8% accepted, 12 enrolled. In 2011, 2 doctorates awarded. *Degree requirements:* For doctorate, comprehensive exam, thesis/dissertation, summer research paper. *Entrance requirements:* For doctorate, GMAT or GRE General Test, 3 recommendations. Additional exam requirements/recommendations for international students: Required—TOEFL (minimum score 600 paper-based; 250 computer-based; 100 iBT). *Application deadline:* For fall admission, 2/15 priority date for domestic students, 2/15 for international students. Applications are processed on a rolling basis. Application fee: $65. Electronic applications accepted. *Expenses: Tuition:* Part-time $1206 per credit. *Financial support:* In 2011–12, 1 fellowship with full tuition reimbursement (averaging $19,570 per year), 30 teaching assistantships with full tuition reimbursements (averaging $17,000 per year) were awarded; research assistantships with full tuition reimbursements, health care benefits, and unspecified assistantships also available. Financial award application deadline: 1/30. *Faculty research:* Marketing models, market microstructure, supply chain, auditing, corporate governance. *Unit head:* Dr. Eunkyu Lee, Director of the PhD Program, 315-443-3429, E-mail: elee06@syr.edu. *Application contact:* Carol Hilleges, Administrative Specialist, 315-443-9601, Fax: 315-443-3671, E-mail: clhilleg@syr.edu. Web site: http://whitman.syr.edu/phd/.

Syracuse University, Martin J. Whitman School of Management, Program in Business Administration, Syracuse, NY 13244. Offers accounting (MBA); entrepreneurship (MBA); finance (MBA); marketing (MBA); supply chain management (MBA). Postbaccalaureate distance learning degree programs offered (minimal on-campus study). *Faculty:* 79 full-time (20 women), 25 part-time/adjunct (6 women). *Students:* 116 full-time (43 women), 188 part-time (58 women); includes 62 minority (33 Black or African American, non-Hispanic/Latino; 1 American Indian or Alaska Native, non-Hispanic/Latino; 13 Asian, non-Hispanic/Latino; 9 Hispanic/Latino; 1 Native Hawaiian or other Pacific Islander, non-Hispanic/Latino; 5 Two or more races, non-Hispanic/Latino), 44 international. Average age 33. 276 applicants, 49% accepted, 77 enrolled. In 2011, 132 master's awarded. *Entrance requirements:* For master's, GMAT, 2 letters of recommendation. Additional exam requirements/recommendations for international students: Required—TOEFL (minimum score 600 paper-based; 250 computer-based; 100 iBT). *Application deadline:* For fall admission, 1/15 priority date for domestic students, 1/15 for international students. Applications are processed on a rolling basis. Application fee: $75. Electronic applications accepted. *Expenses: Tuition:* Part-time $1206 per credit. *Financial support:* In 2011–12, 17 students received support. Fellowships with full and partial tuition reimbursements available, teaching assistantships with partial tuition reimbursements available, career-related internships or fieldwork, scholarships/grants, tuition waivers (partial), unspecified assistantships, and paid hourly positions available. Support available to part-time students. Financial award application deadline: 3/1. *Unit head:* Prof. Dennis Gillen, Chair and Associate Professor of Management, 315-443-3432, Fax: 315-443-9517, E-mail: dgillen@syr.edu. *Application contact:* Josh LaFave, Director, Graduate Enrollment, 315-443-3497, Fax: 315-443-9517, E-mail: mbainfo@syr.edu. Web site: http://whitman.syr.edu/ftmba/.

Temple University, Fox School of Business, Doctoral Programs in Business, Philadelphia, PA 19122-6096. Offers accounting (PhD); entrepreneurship (PhD); finance (PhD); international business (PhD); management information systems (PhD); marketing (PhD); risk management and insurance (PhD); statistics (PhD); strategic management (PhD); tourism and sport (PhD). *Accreditation:* AACSB. *Degree requirements:* For doctorate, thesis/dissertation. *Entrance requirements:* For doctorate, GRE General Test, GMAT, minimum GPA of 3.0, master's degree. Additional exam requirements/recommendations for international students: Required—TOEFL (minimum score 600 paper-based; 250 computer-based; 100 iBT), IELTS (minimum score 7.5). Electronic applications accepted. *Expenses:* Tuition, state resident: full-time $12,366; part-time $687 per credit hour. Tuition, nonresident: full-time $17,298; part-time $961 per credit hour. *Required fees:* $590; $213 per year.

Temple University, Fox School of Business, MBA Programs, Philadelphia, PA 19122-6096. Offers accounting (MBA); business management (MBA); financial management (MBA); healthcare and life sciences innovation (MBA); human resource management (MBA); international business (IMBA); IT management (MBA); marketing management (MBA); pharmaceutical management (MBA); strategic management (EMBA, MBA). EMBA offered in Philadelphia, PA and Tokyo, Japan. *Accreditation:* AACSB. Part-time and evening/weekend programs available. Postbaccalaureate distance learning degree programs offered (minimal on-campus study). *Entrance requirements:* For master's, GMAT, minimum undergraduate GPA of 3.0. Additional exam requirements/recommendations for international students: Required—TOEFL (minimum score 600 paper-based; 250 computer-based; 100 iBT), IELTS (minimum score 7.5). *Expenses:* Tuition, state resident: full-time $12,366; part-time $687 per credit hour. Tuition, nonresident: full-time $17,298; part-time $961 per credit hour. *Required fees:* $590; $213 per year.

Temple University, Fox School of Business, Specialized Master's Programs, Philadelphia, PA 19122-6096. Offers accountancy (MS); actuarial science (MS); finance (MS); financial engineering (MS); human resource management (MS); marketing (MS); statistics (MS). *Accreditation:* AACSB. Part-time programs available. *Entrance requirements:* For master's, GRE General Test or GMAT, minimum undergraduate GPA of 3.0. Additional exam requirements/recommendations for international students: Required—TOEFL (minimum score 600 paper-based; 250 computer-based; 100 iBT), IELTS (minimum score 7.5). *Expenses:* Tuition, state resident: full-time $12,366; part-time $687 per credit hour. Tuition, nonresident: full-time $17,298; part-time $961 per credit hour. *Required fees:* $590; $213 per year.

Texas A&M University, Mays Business School, Department of Marketing, College Station, TX 77843. Offers MS, PhD. *Faculty:* 9. *Students:* 60 full-time (41 women), 4 part-time (3 women); includes 8 minority (1 Black or African American, non-Hispanic/Latino; 2 Asian, non-Hispanic/Latino; 5 Hispanic/Latino), 14 international. Average age 30. 53 applicants, 25% accepted. In 2011, 31 master's, 1 doctorate awarded. Terminal master's awarded for partial completion of doctoral program. *Degree requirements:* For master's, comprehensive exam; for doctorate, thesis/dissertation. *Entrance requirements:* For master's, GMAT; for doctorate, GMAT or GRE General Test. Additional exam requirements/recommendations for international students: Required—TOEFL. *Application deadline:* For fall admission, 3/1 priority date for domestic students. Applications are processed on a rolling basis. Application fee: $50 ($75 for international students). *Expenses:* Tuition, state resident: full-time $5437; part-time $226.55 per credit hour. Tuition, nonresident: full-time $12,949; part-time $539.55 per credit hour. *Required fees:* $2741. *Financial support:* In 2011–12, 16 students received support. Fellowships, research assistantships, teaching assistantships, career-related internships or fieldwork, and institutionally sponsored loans available. Financial award application deadline: 2/1. *Faculty research:* Consumer behavior, innovation and product management, international marketing, marketing management and strategy, services marketing. *Unit head:* Rajan Varadarajan, Head, 979-845-5809, E-mail: rvaradarajan@mays.tamu.edu. *Application contact:* Stephen W. McDaniel, Advisor, 979-845-5801, E-mail: smcdaniel@mays.tamu.edu. Web site: http://mays.tamu.edu/mktg/.

Texas A&M University–Commerce, Graduate School, College of Business, MS Programs, Commerce, TX 75429-3011. Offers accounting (MS); economics (MA); finance (MS); management (MS); marketing (MS). Part-time programs available. *Degree requirements:* For master's, comprehensive exam, thesis (for some programs). *Entrance requirements:* For master's, GMAT or GRE General Test. Electronic applications accepted. *Faculty research:* Economic activity, forensic economics, volatility and finance, international economics.

Texas Tech University, Graduate School, Rawls College of Business Administration, Area of Marketing, Lubbock, TX 79409. Offers PhD. Part-time programs available. *Faculty:* 12 full-time (4 women). *Students:* 11 full-time (4 women), 8 international. Average age 36. 14 applicants, 36% accepted, 4 enrolled. *Degree requirements:* For doctorate, thesis/dissertation, qualifying exams. *Entrance requirements:* For doctorate, GMAT, holistic profile of academic credentials. Additional exam requirements/recommendations for international students: Required—TOEFL (minimum score 550 paper-based; 213 computer-based; 79 iBT). *Application deadline:* For fall admission, 2/1 priority date for domestic students, 1/15 for international students. Applications are processed on a rolling basis. Application fee: $50 ($75 for international students). Electronic applications accepted. *Expenses:* Tuition, state resident: full-time $5899; part-time $245.80 per credit hour. Tuition, nonresident: full-time $13,411; part-time $558.80 per credit hour. *Required fees:* $2680.60; $86.50 per credit hour. $920.30 per semester. *Financial support:* In 2011–12, 11 research assistantships (averaging $14,655 per year), 3 teaching assistantships (averaging $18,000 per year) were awarded; Federal Work-Study and scholarships/grants also available. *Faculty research:* Consumer behavior, macromarketing, marketing strategy and strategic planning. *Unit head:* Dr. Robert McDonald, Area Coordinator, 806-742-1175, Fax: 806-742-2199, E-mail: bob.mcdonald@ttu.edu. *Application contact:* Elizabeth Stuart, Director, Graduate Services Center, 806-742-3184, Fax: 806-742-3958, E-mail: ba_grad@ttu.edu. Web site: http://marketing.ba.ttu.edu.

Texas Tech University, Graduate School, Rawls College of Business Administration, Programs in Business Administration, Lubbock, TX 79409. Offers agricultural business (MBA); business administration (IMBA); business statistics (MBA); entrepreneurship and innovation (MBA); general business (MBA); health organization management (MBA); international business (MBA); management and leadership skills (MBA); management information systems (MBA); marketing (MBA); real estate (MBA); JD/MBA; MBA/M Arch; MBA/MA; MBA/MD; MBA/MS; MBA/Pharm D. Part-time and evening/weekend programs available. *Faculty:* 49 full-time (8 women), 2 part-time/adjunct (0 women). *Students:* 195 full-time (55 women), 397 part-time (101 women); includes 123 minority (27 Black or African American, non-Hispanic/Latino; 4 American Indian or Alaska Native, non-Hispanic/Latino; 31 Asian, non-Hispanic/Latino; 61 Hispanic/Latino), 38 international. Average age 31. 374 applicants, 83% accepted, 255 enrolled. In 2011, 256 degrees awarded. *Degree requirements:* For master's, capstone course. *Entrance requirements:* For master's, GMAT, holistic review of academic credentials. Additional exam requirements/recommendations for international students: Required—TOEFL (minimum score 550 paper-based; 213 computer-based; 79 iBT). *Application deadline:* For fall admission, 4/1 priority date for domestic students, 1/15 for international students; for spring admission, 9/1 priority date for domestic students, 6/15 for international students. Applications are processed on a rolling basis. Application fee: $50 ($75 for international students). Electronic applications accepted. *Expenses:* Tuition, state resident: full-time $5899; part-time $245.80 per credit hour. Tuition, nonresident: full-time $13,411; part-time $558.80 per credit hour. *Required fees:* $2680.60; $86.50 per credit hour. $920.30 per semester. *Financial support:* In 2011–12, 22 research assistantships (averaging $8,800 per year) were awarded; teaching assistantships, career-related internships or fieldwork, Federal Work-Study, scholarships/grants, health care benefits, and unspecified assistantships also available. Support available to part-time students. Financial award applicants required to submit FAFSA. *Unit head:* Dr. W. Jay Conover, Director, 806-742-1546, Fax: 806-742-3958, E-mail: jay.conover@ttu.edu. *Application contact:* Elizabeth Stuart, Director, Graduate Services Center, 806-742-3184, Fax: 806-742-3958, E-mail: ba_grad@ttu.edu. Web site: http://mba.ba.ttu.edu/.

Tiffin University, Program in Business Administration, Tiffin, OH 44883-2161. Offers finance (MBA); general management (MBA); healthcare administration (MBA); human resources (MBA); international business (MBA); leadership (MBA); marketing (MBA); sports management (MBA). *Accreditation:* ACBSP. Part-time and evening/weekend programs available. Postbaccalaureate distance learning degree programs offered (no on-campus study). *Faculty:* 30 full-time (15 women), 22 part-time/adjunct (6 women). *Students:* 209 full-time (107 women), 340 part-time (172 women); includes 112 minority (91 Black or African American, non-Hispanic/Latino; 4 Asian, non-Hispanic/Latino; 17 Hispanic/Latino), 71 international. Average age 31. 237 applicants, 76% accepted. In 2011, 170 master's awarded. *Entrance requirements:* For master's, minimum undergraduate GPA of 2.5, work experience. Additional exam requirements/recommendations for international students: Required—TOEFL (minimum score 550 paper-based; 213 computer-based; 79 iBT). *Application deadline:* For fall admission, 8/15 for domestic students, 8/1 for international students; for spring admission, 1/9 for domestic students, 12/1 for international students. Applications are processed on a rolling basis. Electronic applications accepted. *Expenses: Tuition:* Full-time $11,200; part-time $700 per credit. Tuition and fees vary according to program. *Financial support:* Available to part-time students. Application deadline: 7/31; applicants required to submit FAFSA. *Faculty research:* Small business, executive development operations, research and statistical analysis, market research, management information systems. *Unit head:* Dr. Lillian Schumacher, Dean of the School of Business, 419-448-3053, Fax: 419-443-5002, E-mail: schumacherlb@tiffin.edu. *Application contact:* Nikki Hintze, Director of Graduate Admissions and Student Services, 800-968-6446 Ext. 3445, Fax: 419-443-5002, E-mail: hintzenm@tiffin.edu. Web site: http://www.tiffin.edu/graduateprograms/.

Trident University International, College of Business Administration, Program in Business Administration, Cypress, CA 90630. Offers business administration (PhD); conflict and negotiation management (MBA); criminal justice administration (MBA); entrepreneurship (MBA); finance (MBA); general management (MBA); government accounting (MBA); human resource management (MBA); information security and digital assurance management (MBA); information technology management (MBA); international business (MBA); logistics management (MBA); marketing (MBA); project management (MBA); public management (MBA); quality management (MBA); strategic leadership (MBA). Part-time and evening/weekend programs available. Postbaccalaureate distance learning degree programs offered (no on-campus study). *Degree requirements:* For doctorate, comprehensive exam, thesis/dissertation, defense of dissertation. *Entrance requirements:* For master's, minimum GPA of 2.5 (students with GPA 3.0 or greater may transfer up to 30% of graduate level credits); for doctorate, minimum GPA of 3.4, curriculum vitae, course work in research methods or statistics. Additional exam requirements/recommendations for international students: Required—TOEFL. Electronic applications accepted.

United States International University, School of Business Administration, Nairobi, Kenya. Offers business administration (GEMBA); entrepreneurship (MBA); finance (MBA); human resource management (MBA); information technology management (MBA); integrated studies (MBA); international business administration (MBA); management and organizational development (MS); marketing (MBA); organizational development (EMS); strategic management (MBA). Part-time and evening/weekend programs available. *Degree requirements:* For master's, thesis. *Entrance requirements:* For master's, GMAT, 2 letters of reference, resume. Additional exam requirements/recommendations for international students: Required—TOEFL (minimum score 550 paper-based; 213 computer-based). *Faculty research:* Marketing in small business enterprises, total quality management in Kenya.

Universidad del Turabo, Graduate Programs, School in Business Administration, Program in Marketing, Gurabo, PR 00778-3030. Offers MBA. Part-time and evening/weekend programs available. *Students:* 22 full-time (12 women), 17 part-time (10 women); includes 35 minority (all Hispanic/Latino). Average age 30. 23 applicants, 96% accepted, 15 enrolled. In 2011, 17 master's awarded. *Entrance requirements:* For master's, GRE, EXADEP, interview. *Application deadline:* For fall admission, 8/5 for domestic students. Application fee: $25. *Unit head:* Marcelino Rivera, Dean, 787-743-7979 Ext. 4117. *Application contact:* Virginia Gonzalez, Admissions Officer, 787-746-3009.

Universidad Iberoamericana, Graduate School, Santo Domingo D.N., Dominican Republic. Offers business administration (MBA, PMBA); constitutional law (LL M); dentistry (DMD); educational management (MA); integrated marketing communication (MA); psychopedagogical intervention (M Ed); real estate law (LL M); strategic management of human talent (MM).

Universidad Metropolitana, School of Business Administration, Program in Marketing, San Juan, PR 00928-1150. Offers MBA. Part-time programs available. *Degree requirements:* For master's, thesis or alternative. *Entrance requirements:* For master's, GMAT, PAEG, interview. Electronic applications accepted.

Université de Sherbrooke, Faculty of Administration, Program in Marketing, Sherbrooke, QC J1K 2R1, Canada. Offers M Sc. *Faculty:* 8 full-time (5 women), 1 part-time/adjunct (0 women). *Students:* 17 full-time (11 women). Average age 24. 111 applicants, 43% accepted, 17 enrolled. In 2011, 21 master's awarded. *Degree requirements:* For master's, one foreign language, thesis. *Entrance requirements:* For master's, bachelor's degree in related field, minimum GPA of 3.0 (on 4.3 scale). *Application deadline:* For fall admission, 4/30 for domestic students, 1/15 for international students. Applications are processed on a rolling basis. Application fee: $70. Electronic applications accepted. *Faculty research:* Consumer behavior, sales force, branding, prices management. *Unit head:* Prof. Julien Bilodeau, Director, Graduate Programs in Business, 819-821-8000 Ext. 62355. *Application contact:* Marie-Claude Drouin, Programs Assistant Director, 819-821-8000 Ext. 63301.

Université Laval, Faculty of Administrative Sciences, Programs in Business Administration, Québec, QC G1K 7P4, Canada. Offers accounting (MBA); agri-food management (MBA); electronic business (MBA, Diploma); factory management and logistics (MBA); finance (MBA); firm management (MBA); geomatic management (MBA); information technology management (MBA); international management (MBA); management (MBA); management accounting (MBA, Diploma); marketing (MBA); modeling and organizational decision (MBA); occupational health and safety management (MBA); pharmacy management (MBA); social and environmental responsibility (MBA); technological entrepreneurship (Diploma). *Accreditation:* AACSB. Part-time and evening/weekend programs available. Postbaccalaureate distance learning degree programs offered (no on-campus study). *Entrance requirements:* For master's and Diploma, knowledge of French and English. Electronic applications accepted.

University at Albany, State University of New York, School of Business, Department of Marketing, Albany, NY 12222-0001. Offers MBA. *Degree requirements:* For master's, field study project. *Entrance requirements:* For master's, GMAT. Additional exam requirements/recommendations for international students: Required—TOEFL (minimum score 550 paper-based; 213 computer-based). Electronic applications accepted. *Faculty research:* Sales management, buyer-seller interaction, family decision making, sociological influence on consumption, health promotion.

The University of Akron, Graduate School, College of Business Administration, Department of Marketing, Akron, OH 44325. Offers international business (MBA); international business for international executive (MBA); strategic marketing (MBA); JD/MBA. Part-time and evening/weekend programs available. *Faculty:* 12 full-time (2 women), 3 part-time/adjunct (1 woman). *Students:* 24 full-time (9 women), 20 part-time (16 women); includes 4 minority (1 Black or African American, non-Hispanic/Latino; 2 Hispanic/Latino; 1 Two or more races, non-Hispanic/Latino), 10 international. Average age 27. 42 applicants, 45% accepted, 13 enrolled. In 2011, 18 master's awarded. *Entrance requirements:* For master's, GMAT, minimum GPA of 2.75, two letters of recommendation, statement of purpose, resume. Additional exam requirements/recommendations for international students: Required—TOEFL (minimum score 550 paper-based; 213 computer-based; 79 iBT). *Application deadline:* For fall admission, 7/15 for domestic and international students; for spring admission, 11/15 for domestic and international students. Application fee: $30 ($40 for international students). Electronic applications accepted. *Expenses:* Tuition, state resident: full-time $7038; part-time $391 per credit hour. Tuition, nonresident: full-time $12,051; part-time $670 per credit hour. *Required fees:* $1274; $34 per credit hour. *Financial support:* In 2011–12, 10 teaching assistantships with full tuition reimbursements were awarded. *Faculty research:* Multi-channel marketing, direct interactive marketing, strategic retailing, marketing strategy and telemarketing. *Total annual research expenditures:* $19,735. *Unit head:* Dr. William Baker, Chair, 330-972-8466, E-mail: wbaker@uakron.edu. *Application contact:* Dr. Susan Hanlon, Director of Graduate Business Programs, 330-972-7043, Fax: 330-972-6588, E-mail: shanlon@uakron.edu. Web site: http://www.uakron.edu/cba/cba-home/dept-cent-inst/marketing/index.dot.

The University of Alabama, Graduate School, Manderson Graduate School of Business, Department of Management and Marketing, Program in Marketing, Tuscaloosa, AL 35487. Offers MS, PhD. *Accreditation:* AACSB. *Faculty:* 11 full-time (3 women). *Students:* 68 full-time (28 women), 5 part-time (3 women); includes 4 minority (2 Black or African American, non-Hispanic/Latino; 1 Asian, non-Hispanic/Latino; 1 Hispanic/Latino), 15 international. Average age 26. 134 applicants, 46% accepted, 42 enrolled. In 2011, 41 master's, 3 doctorates awarded. Terminal master's awarded for partial completion of doctoral program. *Median time to degree:* Of those who began their doctoral program in fall 2003, 100% received their degree in 8 years or less. *Degree requirements:* For master's, internship; for doctorate, comprehensive exam, thesis/dissertation. *Entrance requirements:* For master's, GRE or GMAT; for doctorate, GRE or GMAT, minimum GPA of 3.0. Additional exam requirements/recommendations for international students: Required—TOEFL (minimum score 600 paper-based) or IELTS (minimum score 6.5). *Application deadline:* For fall admission, 4/1 priority date for domestic students, 4/1 for international students; for spring admission, 2/1 priority date for domestic students, 2/1 for international students. Applications are processed on a rolling basis. Application fee: $50 ($60 for international students). Electronic applications accepted. *Expenses:* Tuition, state resident: full-time $8600. Tuition, nonresident: full-time $21,900. *Financial support:* In 2011–12, 1 fellowship with full tuition reimbursement (averaging $15,000 per year), 5 research assistantships with full tuition reimbursements (averaging $25,000 per year), 5 teaching assistantships with full tuition reimbursements (averaging $25,000 per year) were awarded; scholarships/grants, health care benefits, and unspecified assistantships also available. *Faculty research:* Relationship marketing, consumer behavior, services marketing, professional selling, supply chain management. *Unit head:* Dr. Robert M. Morgan, Department Head, 205-348-6183, Fax: 205-348-6695, E-mail: rmorgan@cba.ua.edu. *Application contact:* Courtney Cox, Office Associate II, 205-348-6183, Fax: 205-348-6695, E-mail: crhodes@cba.ua.edu. Web site: http://cba.ua.edu/mkt.

The University of Alabama in Huntsville, School of Graduate Studies, College of Business Administration, Department of Management and Marketing, Huntsville, AL 35899. Offers federal contract procurement (Certificate); management (MBA), including acquisition management, entrepreneurship, federal contract accounting, finance, human resource management, logistics and supply chain management, marketing, project management; supply chain management (Certificate); technology and innovation management (Certificate). *Accreditation:* AACSB. Part-time and evening/weekend programs available. *Faculty:* 11 full-time (2 women), 3 part-time/adjunct (0 women). *Students:* 52 full-time (25 women), 145 part-time (68 women); includes 28 minority (14 Black or African American, non-Hispanic/Latino; 4 American Indian or Alaska Native, non-Hispanic/Latino; 7 Asian, non-Hispanic/Latino; 2 Hispanic/Latino; 1 Two or more races, non-Hispanic/Latino), 15 international. Average age 31. 103 applicants, 73% accepted, 65 enrolled. In 2011, 76 master's awarded. *Degree requirements:* For master's, comprehensive exam, thesis or alternative. *Entrance requirements:* For master's, GMAT (minimum score 500), minimum AACSB index of 1080. Additional exam requirements/recommendations for international students: Required—TOEFL (minimum score 550 paper-based; 213 computer-based; 62 iBT). *Application deadline:* For fall admission, 8/1 for domestic students, 4/1 for international students; for spring admission, 12/1 for domestic students, 9/1 for international students. Applications are processed on a rolling basis. Application fee: $40 ($50 for international students). Electronic applications accepted. *Expenses:* Tuition, state resident: full-time $7830; part-time $473.50 per credit. Tuition, nonresident: full-time $18,748; part-time $1128.33 per credit. Tuition and fees vary according to course load and program. *Financial support:* In 2011–12, 12 students received support, including 7 research assistantships with full tuition reimbursements available (averaging $9,829 per year), 4 teaching assistantships with full tuition reimbursements available (averaging $8,000 per year); career-related internships or fieldwork, Federal Work-Study, institutionally sponsored loans, scholarships/grants, health care benefits, and unspecified assistantships also available. Support available to part-time students. Financial award application deadline: 4/1; financial award applicants required to submit FAFSA. *Faculty research:* Strategic human resources, corporate governance, cross-function integration and the management of research and development, determinants of team performance. *Total annual research expenditures:* $3.4 million. *Unit head:* Dr. Cynthia Gramm, Chair, 256-824-6913, Fax: 256-824-6328, E-mail: cynthia.gramm@uah.edu. *Application contact:* Jennifer Pettitt, Director of Graduate Programs, 256-824-6681, Fax: 256-824-7571, E-mail: jennifer.pettitt@uah.edu.

University of Alberta, Faculty of Graduate Studies and Research, Doctoral Program in Business, Edmonton, AB T6G 2E1, Canada. Offers accounting (PhD); finance (PhD); human resources/industrial relations (PhD); management science (PhD); marketing (PhD); organizational analysis (PhD); MBA/PhD. *Accreditation:* AACSB. Part-time programs available. *Degree requirements:* For doctorate, comprehensive exam, thesis/dissertation. *Entrance requirements:* For doctorate, GMAT. Additional exam requirements/recommendations for international students: Required—TOEFL (minimum score 550 paper-based; 213 computer-based). Electronic applications accepted. *Faculty research:* Accounting, capital markets and corporate finance, organizational change and human resource management, marketing, strategic management.

The University of Arizona, Eller College of Management, Department of Marketing, Tucson, AZ 85721. Offers MS, PhD. *Faculty:* 11 full-time (4 women), 1 part-time/adjunct (0 women). *Degree requirements:* For doctorate, comprehensive exam, thesis/dissertation. *Entrance requirements:* For doctorate, GMAT (minimum score 600). Additional exam requirements/recommendations for international students: Required—TOEFL (minimum score 600 paper-based). *Application deadline:* For fall admission, 3/1 for domestic students, 12/1 for international students. Applications are processed on a rolling basis. Application fee: $75. Electronic applications accepted. *Expenses:* Tuition, state resident: full-time $10,840. Tuition, nonresident: full-time $25,802. *Financial support:* In 2011–12, 8 teaching assistantships with full tuition reimbursements (averaging $26,100 per year) were awarded; research assistantships with full tuition reimbursements, career-related internships or fieldwork, Federal Work-Study, scholarships/grants, health care benefits, tuition waivers (partial), and unspecified assistantships also available. Financial award application deadline: 2/1. *Faculty research:* Consumer behavior, customer relationship management, research methods, brand strategy, public policy. *Unit head:* Dr. Robert F. Lusch, Head, 520-621-7480, Fax: 520-621-7483, E-mail: rlusch@eller.arizona.edu. *Application contact:* Audrey L. Hambleton, Graduate Secretary, 520-621-1321, Fax: 520-621-7483, E-mail: audrey@eller.arizona.edu. Web site: http://marketing.eller.arizona.edu/.

University of Baltimore, Graduate School, Merrick School of Business, Department of Marketing, Baltimore, MD 21201-5779. Offers business/marketing and venturing (MS). Part-time and evening/weekend programs available. *Entrance requirements:* For master's, GMAT. Additional exam requirements/recommendations for international students: Required—TOEFL (minimum score 550 paper-based; 213 computer-based). Electronic applications accepted.

University of Bridgeport, School of Business, Bridgeport, CT 06604. Offers accounting (MBA); finance (MBA); general business (MBA); global financial services (MBA); human resource management (MBA); information systems and knowledge management (MBA); international business (MBA); management (MBA); marketing (MBA); operations management (MBA); small business and entrepreneurship (MBA); specialized business (MBA). Part-time and evening/weekend programs available. *Faculty:* 11 full-time (2 women), 39 part-time/adjunct (8 women). *Students:* 198 full-time (105 women), 94 part-time (47 women); includes 38 minority (16 Black or African American, non-Hispanic/Latino; 9 Asian, non-Hispanic/Latino; 10 Hispanic/Latino; 3 Two or more races, non-Hispanic/Latino), 227 international. Average age 28. 835 applicants, 56% accepted, 57 enrolled. In 2011, 155 master's awarded. *Degree requirements:* For master's, thesis optional. *Entrance requirements:* For master's, GMAT. Additional exam requirements/recommendations for international students: Recommended—TOEFL (minimum score 550 paper-based; 213 computer-based; 80 iBT), IELTS (minimum score 6.5). *Application deadline:* For fall admission, 8/1 priority date for domestic students, 8/1 for international students; for spring admission, 12/1 priority date for domestic students, 12/1 for international students. Applications are processed on a rolling basis. Application fee: $50. Electronic applications accepted. *Expenses:* Contact institution. *Financial support:* In 2011–12, 69 students received support. Fellowships, research assistantships, teaching assistantships, career-related internships or fieldwork, Federal Work-Study, institutionally sponsored loans, and tuition waivers (partial) available. Support available to part-time students. Financial award application deadline: 6/1; financial award applicants required to submit FAFSA. *Unit head:* Dr. Robert Gilmore, Dean, 203-576-4384, Fax: 203-576-4388, E-mail: rgilmore@bridgeport.edu. *Application contact:* Karissa Peckham, Dean of Admissions, 203-576-4552, Fax: 203-576-4941, E-mail: mba@bridgeport.edu. Web site: http://www.bridgeport.edu.

The University of British Columbia, Sauder School of Business, Doctoral Program in Commerce and Business Administration, Vancouver, BC V6T 1Z1, Canada. Offers accounting (PhD); finance (PhD); international business (PhD); management information systems (PhD); management science (PhD); marketing (PhD); organizational behavior (PhD); strategy and business economics (PhD); transportation and logistics (PhD); urban land economics (PhD). *Degree requirements:* For doctorate, comprehensive exam, thesis/dissertation. *Entrance requirements:* For doctorate, GMAT or GRE. Additional exam requirements/recommendations for international students: Required—TOEFL (minimum score 600 paper-based; 250 computer-based; 100 iBT). Electronic applications accepted.

University of California, Berkeley, Graduate Division, Haas School of Business, PhD in Business Administration Program, Berkeley, CA 94720-1500. Offers accounting (PhD); business and public policy (PhD); finance (PhD); management of organizations (PhD); marketing (PhD); operations management (PhD); real estate (PhD). *Accreditation:* AACSB. *Faculty:* 77 full-time (18 women), 152 part-time/adjunct (24 women). *Students:* 79 full-time (25 women); includes 13 minority (12 Asian, non-Hispanic/Latino; 1 Hispanic/Latino), 34 international. Average age 30. 547 applicants, 5% accepted, 15 enrolled. In 2011, 14 doctorates awarded. *Degree requirements:* For doctorate, comprehensive exam, thesis/dissertation, written preliminary exams, oral qualifying exam. *Entrance requirements:* For doctorate, GMAT or GRE, minimum GPA of 3.0 in undergraduate and graduate coursework. Additional exam requirements/recommendations for international students: Required—TOEFL (minimum score 570 paper-based; 230 computer-based; 70 iBT), IELTS (minimum score 7). *Application deadline:* For fall admission, 12/10 for domestic and international students. Application fee: $80 ($100 for international students). Electronic applications accepted. *Financial support:* In 2011–12, 66 students received support, including 58 fellowships with full and partial tuition reimbursements available (averaging $29,000 per year), 77 teaching assistantships with full and partial tuition reimbursements available; research assistantships with full and partial tuition reimbursements available, scholarships/grants, health care benefits, tuition waivers (full), unspecified assistantships, and transit pass, travel grants also available. Financial award application deadline: 12/10; financial award applicants required to submit FAFSA. *Faculty research:* Accounting, business and public policy, finance, management of organizations, marketing, operations and information technology management, real estate. *Unit head:* Dr. Sunil Dutta, Director, 510-642-1229, Fax: 510-643-4255, E-mail: kimg@haas.berkeley.edu. *Application contact:* Kim Guilfoyle, Director, Student Affairs, 510-642-3944, Fax: 510-643-4255, E-mail: kimg@haas.berkeley.edu. Web site: http://www.haas.berkeley.edu/Phd/.

University of California, Berkeley, UC Berkeley Extension, Certificate Programs in Business, Berkeley, CA 94720-1500. Offers accounting (Certificate); business administration (Certificate); finance (Certificate); human resource management (Certificate); management (Certificate); marketing (Certificate); project management (Certificate). *Accreditation:* AACSB. Postbaccalaureate distance learning degree programs offered.

University of California, Berkeley, UC Berkeley Extension, International Diploma Programs, Berkeley, CA 94720-1500. Offers business administration (Certificate); finance (Certificate); global business management (Certificate); marketing (Certificate); project management (Certificate). *Accreditation:* AACSB.

University of California, Los Angeles, Graduate Division, UCLA Anderson School of Management, Los Angeles, CA 90095-1481. Offers accounting (PhD); Asia Pacific (EMBA); business administration (EMBA, MBA); decisions, operations and technology management (PhD); finance (PhD); financial engineering (MFE); global economics and management (PhD); Latin America (EMBA); management and organizations (PhD); marketing (PhD); strategy (PhD); DDS/MBA; MBA/JD; MBA/MD; MBA/MLAS; MBA/MLIS; MBA/MPH; MBA/MPP; MBA/MSCS; MBA/MSN; MBA/MUP. *Accreditation:* AACSB. Part-time programs available. *Faculty:* 90 full-time (14 women), 62 part-time/adjunct (14 women). *Students:* 1,103 full-time (312 women), 842 part-time (223 women); includes 663 minority (18 Black or African American, non-Hispanic/Latino; 510 Asian, non-Hispanic/Latino; 46 Hispanic/Latino; 2 Native Hawaiian or other Pacific Islander, non-Hispanic/Latino; 87 Two or more races, non-Hispanic/Latino), 469 international. 4,737 applicants, 32% accepted, 875 enrolled. In 2011, 759 master's, 6 doctorates awarded. *Degree requirements:* For master's, comprehensive exam, field study consulting project (for MBA); thesis/dissertation (for MFE); for doctorate, comprehensive exam, thesis/dissertation, oral and written qualifying exams. *Entrance requirements:* For master's, GMAT (for MBA); GMAT or GRE General Test (for MFE), 4-year bachelor's degree or equivalent; for doctorate, GMAT or GRE General Test, 4-year bachelor's degree from regionally-accredited institution; minimum GPA of 3.0. Additional exam requirements/recommendations for international students: Required—TOEFL (minimum score 560 paper-based; 220 computer-based; 87 iBT), IELTS (minimum score 7). *Application deadline:* For fall admission, 10/26 for domestic and international students; for winter admission, 1/11 for domestic and international students; for spring admission, 4/18 for domestic and international students. Application fee: $200. Electronic applications accepted. *Expenses:* Contact institution. *Financial support:* In 2011–12, 600 students received support. Fellowships, research assistantships, teaching assistantships, career-related internships or fieldwork, institutionally sponsored loans, scholarships/grants, health care benefits, and tuition waivers (partial) available. Financial award application deadline: 4/15; financial award applicants required to submit FAFSA. *Unit head:* Judy D. Olian, Dean, 310-825-7982, Fax: 310-206-2073, E-mail: judy.olian@anderson.ucla.edu. *Application contact:* Robert Weiler, Assistant Dean, Director of MBA Admissions and Financial Aid, 310-825-6944, Fax: 310-825-8582, E-mail: mba.admissions@anderson.ucla.edu. Web site: http://www.anderson.ucla.edu/.

See Display on page 141 and Close-Up on page 249.

University of Central Missouri, The Graduate School, Harmon College of Business Administration, Warrensburg, MO 64093. Offers accountancy (MA); accounting (MBA); ethical strategic leadership (MBA); finance (MBA); general business (MBA); information systems (MBA); information technology (MS); marketing (MBA). Part-time programs available. Postbaccalaureate distance learning degree programs offered. *Entrance requirements:* Additional exam requirements/recommendations for international students: Required—TOEFL (minimum score 550 paper-based; 79 computer-based). Electronic applications accepted.

University of Chicago, Booth School of Business, Full-Time MBA Program, Chicago, IL 60637. Offers accounting (MBA); analytic finance (MBA); analytic management (MBA); business administration (PhD); econometrics and statistics (MBA); economics (MBA); entrepreneurship (MBA); finance (MBA); general management (MBA); health administration and policy (Certificate); human resource management (MBA); international business (IMBA, MBA); managerial and organizational behavior (MBA); marketing management (MBA); operations management (MBA); strategic management (MBA); MBA/AM; MBA/JD; MBA/MA; MBA/MD; MBA/MPP. *Accreditation:* AACSB. Part-time and evening/weekend programs available. *Faculty:* 166 full-time, 32 part-time/adjunct. *Students:* 1,160 full-time (412 women); includes 316 minority (61 Black or African American, non-Hispanic/Latino; 173 Asian, non-Hispanic/Latino; 63 Hispanic/Latino; 19 Two or more races, non-Hispanic/Latino), 378 international. Average age 28. 4,169 applicants, 575 enrolled. In 2011, 1,423 master's, 19 doctorates awarded. Terminal master's awarded for partial completion of doctoral program. *Entrance requirements:* For master's, GMAT, 2 letters of recommendation, 3 essays, resume, interview. Additional exam requirements/recommendations for international students: Required—TOEFL (minimum score 600 paper-based; 250 computer-based; 104 iBT), IELTS. *Application deadline:* For fall admission, 10/12 priority date for domestic students, 10/12 for international students; for winter admission, 1/4 for domestic and international students; for spring admission, 4/4 for domestic and international students. Application fee: $200. Electronic applications accepted. *Expenses:* Contact institution. *Financial support:* Fellowships available. Financial award applicants required to submit FAFSA. *Faculty research:* Finance, marketing, economics, entrepreneurship, strategy, management. *Unit head:* Stacey Kole, Deputy Dean, 773-702-7121. *Application contact:* Kurt Ahlm, Associate Dean of Student Recruitment and Admissions, 773-702-7369, Fax: 773-702-9085, E-mail: admissions@chicagobooth.edu. Web site: http://chicagobooth.edu/.

University of Cincinnati, Graduate School, Carl H. Lindner College of Business, MS Program, Cincinnati, OH 45221. Offers accounting (MS); information systems (MS); marketing (MS); quantitative analysis (MS). Part-time and evening/weekend programs available. *Faculty:* 79 full-time (22 women), 71 part-time/adjunct (24 women). *Students:* 171 full-time (75 women), 106 part-time (46 women); includes 19 minority (6 Black or African American, non-Hispanic/Latino; 1 American Indian or Alaska Native, non-Hispanic/Latino; 7 Asian, non-Hispanic/Latino; 2 Hispanic/Latino; 3 Two or more races, non-Hispanic/Latino), 114 international. 404 applicants, 77% accepted, 125 enrolled. *Degree requirements:* For master's, thesis (for some programs). *Entrance requirements:* For master's, GMAT, GRE, resume, transcripts, essays, letters of recommendation. Additional exam requirements/recommendations for international students: Required—TOEFL (minimum score 600 paper-based; 250 computer-based; 100 iBT). *Application deadline:* For fall admission, 1/15 priority date for domestic students, 4/1 for international students. Applications are processed on a rolling basis. Application fee: $65 ($70 for international students). Electronic applications accepted. *Expenses:* Contact institution. *Financial support:* In 2011–12, 10 teaching assistantships with full and partial tuition reimbursements (averaging $5,400 per year) were awarded; scholarships/grants, tuition waivers (full and partial), and unspecified assistantships also available. Financial award application deadline: 2/1; financial award applicants required to submit FAFSA. *Unit head:* Dr. David Szymanski, Dean, 513-556-7001, Fax: 513-556-4891, E-mail:

will.mcintosh@uc.edu. *Application contact:* Dona Clary, Director, Graduate Programs Office, 513-556-3546, Fax: 513-558-7006, E-mail: dona.clary@uc.edu.

University of Cincinnati, Graduate School, Carl H. Lindner College of Business, PhD Programs, Cincinnati, OH 45221. Offers accounting (PhD); finance (PhD); information systems (PhD); management (PhD); marketing (PhD); quantitative analysis and operations management (PhD). *Faculty:* 56 full-time (13 women). *Students:* 34 full-time (12 women), 12 part-time (4 women); includes 2 minority (1 Asian, non-Hispanic/Latino; 1 Hispanic/Latino), 25 international. Average age 29. 120 applicants, 13% accepted, 10 enrolled. In 2011, 8 degrees awarded. *Median time to degree:* Of those who began their doctoral program in fall 2003, 65% received their degree in 8 years or less. *Degree requirements:* For doctorate, comprehensive exam, thesis/dissertation. *Entrance requirements:* For doctorate, GMAT, GRE, transcripts, essays, resume, letters of recommendation. Additional exam requirements/recommendations for international students: Required—TOEFL (minimum score 600 paper-based; 250 computer-based; 100 iBT). *Application deadline:* For fall admission, 2/1 for domestic and international students. Application fee: $65 ($70 for international students). Electronic applications accepted. *Expenses:* Contact institution. *Financial support:* In 2011–12, 39 students received support, including 30 research assistantships with full and partial tuition reimbursements available (averaging $14,640 per year); scholarships/grants, tuition waivers (full and partial), and unspecified assistantships also available. Financial award application deadline: 2/1; financial award applicants required to submit FAFSA. *Unit head:* Dr. Suzanne Masterson, Director, 513-556-7125, Fax: 513-556-5499, E-mail: suzanne.masterson@uc.edu. *Application contact:* Deborah Schildknecht, Assistant Director, 513-556-7190, Fax: 513-558-7006, E-mail: deborah.schildknecht@uc.edu. Web site: http://www.business.uc.edu/phd.

University of Colorado Boulder, Leeds School of Business, Division of Business Administration, Boulder, CO 80309. Offers accounting (MS, PhD); finance (PhD); information systems (PhD); marketing (PhD); operations (PhD); strategic, organizational, and entrepreneurial studies (PhD). *Students:* 129 full-time (65 women), 6 part-time (0 women); includes 15 minority (1 Black or African American, non-Hispanic/Latino; 8 Asian, non-Hispanic/Latino; 5 Hispanic/Latino; 1 Two or more races, non-Hispanic/Latino), 21 international. Average age 27. 332 applicants, 9% accepted, 13 enrolled. In 2011, 53 master's, 6 doctorates awarded. *Entrance requirements:* For master's, GMAT, minimum undergraduate GPA of 3.0. *Application deadline:* For fall admission, 3/31 for domestic and international students; for spring admission, 10/31 for domestic and international students. Application fee: $50 ($60 for international students). Electronic applications accepted. *Financial support:* In 2011–12, 61 students received support, including 24 fellowships (averaging $3,398 per year), 19 research assistantships with full and partial tuition reimbursements available (averaging $27,830 per year), 15 teaching assistantships with full and partial tuition reimbursements available (averaging $25,615 per year); institutionally sponsored loans, scholarships/grants, health care benefits, and unspecified assistantships also available. Financial award applicants required to submit FAFSA. *Application contact:* E-mail: leedsphd@colorado.edu. Web site: http://leeds.colorado.edu/phdprog.

University of Colorado Denver, Business School, Master of Business Administration Program, Denver, CO 80217. Offers business intelligence (MBA); business strategy (MBA); business to business marketing (MBA); business to consumer marketing (MBA); change management (MBA); corporate financial management (MBA); enterprise technology management (MBA); entrepreneurship (MBA); health administration (MBA), including financial management, health administration, health information technologies, international health management and policy; human resources management (MBA); investment management (MBA); managing for sustainability (MBA); services management (MBA); sports and entertainment management (MBA). *Accreditation:* AACSB. Part-time and evening/weekend programs available. Postbaccalaureate distance learning degree programs offered (no on-campus study). *Students:* 784 full-time (306 women), 203 part-time (81 women); includes 135 minority (18 Black or African American, non-Hispanic/Latino; 5 American Indian or Alaska Native, non-Hispanic/Latino; 50 Asian, non-Hispanic/Latino; 58 Hispanic/Latino; 4 Two or more races, non-Hispanic/Latino), 38 international. Average age 31. 433 applicants, 76% accepted, 212 enrolled. In 2011, 326 master's awarded. *Degree requirements:* For master's, 48 semester hours, including 30 of core courses, 3 in international business, and 15 in electives from over 50 other graduate business courses. *Entrance requirements:* For master's, GMAT, resume, official transcripts, essay, two letters of recommendation, financial statements (for international applicants). Additional exam requirements/recommendations for international students: Required—TOEFL (minimum score 560 paper-based; 197 computer-based; 83 iBT). *Application deadline:* For fall admission, 4/15 priority date for domestic students, 3/15 for international students; for spring admission, 10/15 priority date for domestic students, 10/1 for international students. Applications are processed on a rolling basis. Application fee: $50 ($75 for international students). Electronic applications accepted. *Expenses:* Contact institution. *Financial support:* Scholarships/grants available. Support available to part-time students. Financial award application deadline: 4/1; financial award applicants required to submit FAFSA. *Faculty research:* Marketing, management, entrepreneurship, finance, health administration. *Unit head:* Elizabeth Cooperman, Professor of Finance and Managing for Sustainability/MBA Program Director, 303-315-8422, E-mail: elizabeth.cooperman@ucdenver.edu. *Application contact:* Shelly Townley, Admissions Director, Graduate Programs, 303-315-8202, E-mail: shelly.townley@ucdenver.edu. Web site: http://www.ucdenver.edu/academics/colleges/business/degrees/ms/accounting/Pages/Accounting.aspx.

University of Colorado Denver, Business School, Program in Marketing, Denver, CO 80217. Offers brand management and marketing communication (MS); global marketing (MS); high-tech and entrepreneurial marketing (MS); Internet marketing (MS); marketing for sustainability (MS); marketing research (MS); sports and entertainment marketing (MS). Part-time and evening/weekend programs available. *Students:* 39 full-time (29 women), 11 part-time (6 women); includes 4 minority (3 Hispanic/Latino; 1 Two or more races, non-Hispanic/Latino), 8 international. Average age 28. 40 applicants, 65% accepted, 16 enrolled. In 2011, 8 master's awarded. *Degree requirements:* For master's, 30 semester hours (21 of marketing core courses, 9 of graduate marketing electives). *Entrance requirements:* For master's, GMAT, resume, essay, two letters of recommendation, financial statements (for international applicants). Additional exam requirements/recommendations for international students: Required—TOEFL (minimum score 525 paper-based; 197 computer-based; 71 iBT). *Application deadline:* For fall admission, 4/15 priority date for domestic students, 3/15 for international students; for spring admission, 10/15 priority date for domestic students, 10/1 for international students. Applications are processed on a rolling basis. Application fee: $50 ($75 for international students). Electronic applications accepted. *Expenses:* Contact institution. *Financial support:* Federal Work-Study and scholarships/grants available. Support available to part-time students. Financial award application deadline: 4/1; financial award applicants required to submit FAFSA. *Faculty research:* Marketing issues in the Chinese environment, impact of individual difference and contextual factors on the risk-taking behaviors of managers making new-business creation decisions, attribution theory perspective of conflict between marketers and engineers, organizational identity and identification, international market entry strategies. *Unit head:* Dr. David Forlani, Associate Professor/Director of Marketing Programs, 303-315-8420, E-mail: david.forlani@ucdenver.edu. *Application contact:* Shelly Townley, Admissions Director, Graduate Programs, 303-315-8202, E-mail: shelly.townley@ucdenver.edu. Web site: http://www.ucdenver.edu/academics/colleges/business/degrees/ms/marketing/Pages/Marketing.aspx.

University of Connecticut, Graduate School, School of Business, Storrs, CT 06269. Offers accounting (MS, PhD); business administration (Exec MBA, MBA, PhD); finance (PhD); health care management and insurance studies (MBA); management (PhD); management consulting (MBA); marketing (PhD); marketing intelligence (MBA); MA/MBA; MBA/MSW. *Accreditation:* AACSB. *Degree requirements:* For master's, comprehensive exam; for doctorate, thesis/dissertation. *Entrance requirements:* For master's and doctorate, GMAT. Additional exam requirements/recommendations for international students: Required—TOEFL (minimum score 550 paper-based; 213 computer-based). Electronic applications accepted.

See Display on page 144 and Close-Up on page 251.

University of Dallas, Graduate School of Management, Irving, TX 75062-4736. Offers accounting (MBA, MM, MS); business management (MBA, MM); corporate finance (MBA, MM); financial services (MBA); global business (MBA, MM); health services management (MBA, MM); human resource management (MBA, MM); information assurance (MBA, MM, MS); information technology (MBA, MM, MS); information technology service management (MBA, MM, MS); marketing management (MBA, MM); organization development (MBA, MM); project management (MBA, MM); sports and entertainment management (MBA, MM); strategic leadership (MBA, MM); supply chain management (MBA); supply chain management and market logistics (MM). *Accreditation:* ACBSP. Part-time and evening/weekend programs available. Postbaccalaureate distance learning degree programs offered (no on-campus study). *Entrance requirements:* Additional exam requirements/recommendations for international students: Required—TOEFL. Electronic applications accepted. *Expenses:* Contact institution.

University of Dayton, School of Business Administration, Dayton, OH 45469-1300. Offers accounting (MBA); cyber security (MBA); finance (MBA); marketing (MBA); JD/MBA. *Accreditation:* AACSB. Part-time and evening/weekend programs available. *Faculty:* 23 full-time (6 women), 13 part-time/adjunct (2 women). *Students:* 170 full-time (72 women), 117 part-time (43 women); includes 26 minority (16 Black or African American, non-Hispanic/Latino; 6 Asian, non-Hispanic/Latino; 3 Hispanic/Latino; 1 Two or more races, non-Hispanic/Latino), 49 international. Average age 28. 366 applicants, 72% accepted, 126 enrolled. In 2011, 147 master's awarded. *Entrance requirements:* For master's, GMAT or GRE. Additional exam requirements/recommendations for international students: Required—TOEFL (minimum score 550 paper-based; 213 computer-based; 80 iBT); Recommended—IELTS (minimum score 6.5). *Application deadline:* For fall admission, 3/1 for international students; for winter admission, 7/1 for international students; for spring admission, 1/1 for international students. Applications are processed on a rolling basis. Application fee: $0 ($50 for international students). Electronic applications accepted. *Expenses:* Contact institution. *Financial support:* In 2011–12, 12 research assistantships with full and partial tuition reimbursements (averaging $7,020 per year) were awarded; career-related internships or fieldwork, institutionally sponsored loans, scholarships/grants, health care benefits, and unspecified assistantships also available. Support available to part-time students. Financial award application deadline: 3/15; financial award applicants required to submit FAFSA. *Faculty research:* Management information systems, economics, finance, entrepreneurship, marketing, accounting and cyber security. *Unit head:* Janice M. Glynn, Director, MBA Program, 937-229-3733, Fax: 937-229-3882, E-mail: glynn@udayton.edu. *Application contact:* Jeffrey Carter, Assistant Director, MBA Program, 937-229-3733, Fax: 937-229-3882, E-mail: jeff.carter@notes.udayton.edu. Web site: http://business.udayton.edu/mba/.

University of Denver, Daniels College of Business, Department of Marketing, Denver, CO 80208. Offers IMBA, MBA, MS. Part-time and evening/weekend programs available. *Faculty:* 11 full-time (4 women), 5 part-time/adjunct (3 women). *Students:* 22 full-time (12 women), 36 part-time (23 women); includes 2 minority (1 Black or African American, non-Hispanic/Latino; 1 Asian, non-Hispanic/Latino), 38 international. Average age 25. 236 applicants, 32% accepted, 24 enrolled. In 2011, 17 degrees awarded. *Entrance requirements:* For master's, GRE General Test or GMAT, essay, two letters of recommendation. Additional exam requirements/recommendations for international students: Required—TOEFL (minimum score 570 paper-based; 88 iBT). *Application deadline:* For fall admission, 11/15 priority date for domestic students; for spring admission, 10/1 priority date for domestic students. Applications are processed on a rolling basis. Application fee: $100. Electronic applications accepted. *Financial support:* In 2011–12, 14 students received support, including 4 teaching assistantships with full and partial tuition reimbursements available (averaging $1,656 per year); career-related internships or fieldwork, Federal Work-Study, institutionally sponsored loans, scholarships/grants, and unspecified assistantships also available. Support available to part-time students. Financial award application deadline: 2/15; financial award applicants required to submit FAFSA. *Faculty research:* Social policy issues in marketing, price bundling, marketing to the disabled, marketing to the elderly, international marketing and logistics. *Unit head:* Dr. Carol Johnson, Chair, 303-871-2276, Fax: 303-871-2323, E-mail: carol.johnson@du.edu. *Application contact:* Soumontha A. Colwell-Chanthaphonh, Assistant Director of Graduate Student Recruitment and Admissions, 303-871-2338, Fax: 303-871-2323, E-mail: soumontha.chanthaphonh@du.edu. Web site: http://www.daniels.du.edu/schoolsdepartments/marketing/.

University of Florida, Graduate School, Warrington College of Business Administration, Hough Graduate School of Business, Department of Marketing, Gainesville, FL 32611. Offers MA, MS, PhD. *Faculty:* 10 full-time (2 women). *Students:* 9 full-time (5 women), 2 part-time (1 woman); includes 1 minority (Asian, non-Hispanic/Latino), 6 international. Average age 31. 45 applicants, 0% accepted, 0 enrolled. In 2011, 2 doctorates awarded. Terminal master's awarded for partial completion of doctoral program. *Degree requirements:* For master's, comprehensive exam, thesis optional; for doctorate, comprehensive exam, thesis/dissertation. *Entrance requirements:* For master's and doctorate, GMAT or GRE General Test, minimum GPA of 3.0. Additional exam requirements/recommendations for international students: Required—TOEFL (minimum score 550 paper-based; 213 computer-based; 80 iBT), IELTS (minimum score 6). *Application deadline:* For fall admission, 2/1 for domestic and international students. Applications are processed on a rolling basis. Application fee: $30. Electronic applications accepted. *Financial support:* Career-related internships or fieldwork, institutionally sponsored loans, and unspecified assistantships available. Financial award application deadline: 2/1; financial award applicants required to submit FAFSA. *Faculty research:* Consumer behavior, decision-making, behavioral decision theory, marketing models, marketing strategy. *Unit head:* Dr. Joseph W. Alba, Chair, 352-273-3280, Fax: 352-846-0457, E-mail: joe.alba@warrington.ufl.edu. *Application contact:* Dr. Lyle A. Brenner, Graduate Coordinator, 352-273-3272, Fax: 352-846-0457, E-mail: lbrenner@ufl.edu. Web site: http://www.cba.ufl.edu/mkt/.

University of Florida, Graduate School, Warrington College of Business Administration, Hough Graduate School of Business, Programs in Business

Administration, Gainesville, FL 32611. Offers accounting (MBA); arts administration (MBA); business strategy and public policy (MBA); competitive strategy (MBA); decision and information sciences (MBA); electronic commerce (MBA); finance (MBA); general business (MBA); global management (MBA); Graham-Buffett security analysis (MBA); health administration (MBA); human resources management (MBA); international studies (MBA); Latin American business (MBA); management (MBA); marketing (MBA); sports administration (MBA); JD/MBA; MBA/MS; MBA/PhD; MBA/Pharm D; MD/MBA. *Accreditation:* AACSB. Part-time and evening/weekend programs available. *Faculty:* 71 full-time (10 women). *Students:* 412 full-time (111 women), 467 part-time (135 women); includes 235 minority (39 Black or African American, non-Hispanic/Latino; 7 American Indian or Alaska Native, non-Hispanic/Latino; 79 Asian, non-Hispanic/Latino; 109 Hispanic/Latino; 1 Native Hawaiian or other Pacific Islander, non-Hispanic/Latino), 44 international. Average age 32. 589 applicants, 52% accepted, 247 enrolled. In 2011, 505 master's awarded. *Degree requirements:* For master's, capstone course. *Entrance requirements:* For master's, GMAT, minimum GPA of 3.0, interview. Additional exam requirements/recommendations for international students: Required—TOEFL (minimum score 550 paper-based; 213 computer-based; 80 iBT), IELTS (minimum score 6). *Application deadline:* For fall admission, 7/1 for domestic students, 1/1 for international students; for spring admission, 12/1 for domestic and international students. Applications are processed on a rolling basis. Application fee: $30. Electronic applications accepted. *Financial support:* Teaching assistantships, career-related internships or fieldwork, scholarships/grants, and unspecified assistantships available. Support available to part-time students. Financial award applicants required to submit FAFSA. *Faculty research:* Accounting, finance, insurance, management, real estate, urban analysis marketing. *Unit head:* Prof. Alexander D. Sevilla, Assistant Dean/ Director, 352-273-3252 Ext. 1206, E-mail: alex.sevilla@warrington.ufl.edu. *Application contact:* Prof. Kelli Gust, Associate Director, 352-273-3255, Fax: 352-392-8791, E-mail: kelly.gust@warrington.ufl.edu. Web site: http://www.floridamba.ufl.edu/.

University of Hawaii at Manoa, Graduate Division, Shidler College of Business, Program in Business Administration, Honolulu, HI 96822. Offers Asian business studies (MBA); Chinese business studies (MBA); decision sciences (MBA); entrepreneurship (MBA); finance (MBA); finance and banking (MBA); human resources management (MBA); information management (MBA); information technology (MBA); international business (MBA); Japanese business studies (MBA); marketing (MBA); organizational behavior (MBA); organizational management (MBA); real estate (MBA); student-designed track (MBA). *Accreditation:* AACSB. Part-time and evening/weekend programs available. *Degree requirements:* For master's, thesis optional. *Entrance requirements:* For master's, GMAT, minimum GPA of 3.0. Additional exam requirements/ recommendations for international students: Required—TOEFL (minimum score 600 paper-based; 250 computer-based; 100 iBT), IELTS (minimum score 7). *Expenses:* Contact institution.

University of Hawaii at Manoa, Graduate Division, Shidler College of Business, Program in International Management, Honolulu, HI 96822. Offers Asian finance (PhD); global information technology management (PhD); international accounting (PhD); international marketing (PhD); international organization and strategy (PhD). Part-time programs available. *Degree requirements:* For doctorate, comprehensive exam, thesis/ dissertation. *Entrance requirements:* For doctorate, GMAT or GRE General Test, minimum GPA of 3.0. Additional exam requirements/recommendations for international students: Required—TOEFL (minimum score 600 paper-based; 250 computer-based; 100 iBT), IELTS (minimum score 7). *Expenses:* Contact institution.

University of Houston, Bauer College of Business, Marketing Program, Houston, TX 77204. Offers PhD. Part-time and evening/weekend programs available. *Degree requirements:* For doctorate, comprehensive exam, thesis/dissertation. *Entrance requirements:* For doctorate, GMAT or GRE. *Faculty research:* Accountancy and taxation, finance, international business, management.

University of Houston–Victoria, School of Business Administration, Victoria, TX 77901-4450. Offers accounting (MBA); economic development and entrepreneurship (MS); finance (GMBA, MBA); general business (MBA); international business (MBA); management (GMBA, MBA); marketing (MBA). *Accreditation:* AACSB. Part-time and evening/weekend programs available. Postbaccalaureate distance learning degree programs offered (minimal on-campus study). *Entrance requirements:* For master's, GMAT. Additional exam requirements/recommendations for international students: Required—TOEFL (minimum score 550 paper-based; 213 computer-based). Electronic applications accepted. *Faculty research:* Economic development, marketing, finance.

The University of Iowa, Henry B. Tippie College of Business, Department of Marketing, Iowa City, IA 52242-1316. Offers PhD. *Faculty:* 15 full-time (4 women), 15 part-time/ adjunct (3 women). *Students:* 11 full-time (4 women); includes 1 minority (Asian, non-Hispanic/Latino), 9 international. Average age 38. 30 applicants, 10% accepted, 2 enrolled. In 2011, 2 doctorates awarded. *Degree requirements:* For doctorate, comprehensive exam, thesis/dissertation, thesis defense. *Entrance requirements:* For doctorate, GMAT or GRE. Additional exam requirements/recommendations for international students: Required—TOEFL (minimum score 600 paper-based; 250 computer-based; 100 iBT). *Application deadline:* For fall admission, 1/15 for domestic and international students. Applications are processed on a rolling basis. Application fee: $60 ($100 for international students). Electronic applications accepted. *Financial support:* In 2011–12, 11 students received support, including 10 fellowships with full tuition reimbursements available, 11 teaching assistantships with full tuition reimbursements available (averaging $16,908 per year); institutionally sponsored loans, scholarships/grants, health care benefits, and unspecified assistantships also available. Financial award application deadline: 1/15. *Faculty research:* Judgments and decision-making under certainty; consumer behavior: cognitive neuroscience, attitudes and evaluation; hierarchical Bayesian estimation; marketing-finance interface; advertising effects. *Unit head:* Prof. Gary J. Russell, Department Executive Officer, 319-335-1013, Fax: 319-335-1956, E-mail: gary-j-russell@uiowa.edu. *Application contact:* Renea L. Jay, PhD Program Coordinator, 319-335-0830, Fax: 319-335-1956, E-mail: renea-jay@uiowa.edu. Web site: http://tippie.uiowa.edu/marketing/.

The University of Iowa, Henry B. Tippie College of Business, Henry B. Tippie School of Management, Iowa City, IA 52242-1316. Offers finance (MBA); investment management (MBA); marketing (MBA); process and operations excellence (MBA); strategic innovation (MBA); JD/MBA; MBA/MA; MBA/MD; MBA/MHA; MBA/MSN. *Accreditation:* AACSB. Part-time and evening/weekend programs available. *Faculty:* 62 full-time (19 women), 26 part-time/adjunct (6 women). *Students:* 153 full-time (34 women), 876 part-time (288 women); includes 87 minority (16 Black or African American, non-Hispanic/ Latino; 4 American Indian or Alaska Native, non-Hispanic/Latino; 43 Asian, non-Hispanic/Latino; 24 Hispanic/Latino), 130 international. Average age 32. 697 applicants, 66% accepted, 362 enrolled. In 2011, 361 master's awarded. *Degree requirements:* For master's, minimum GPA of 2.75. *Entrance requirements:* For master's, GMAT, quality work experience and leadership as shown through resume, references, and essays. Additional exam requirements/recommendations for international students: Required—TOEFL (minimum score 600 paper-based; 250 computer-based; 100 iBT), IELTS (minimum score 7). *Application deadline:* For fall admission, 7/30 for domestic students, 4/15 for international students; for spring admission, 12/15 for domestic and international students. Applications are processed on a rolling basis. Application fee: $60 ($100 for international students). Electronic applications accepted. *Expenses:* Contact institution. *Financial support:* In 2011–12, 110 students received support, including 110 fellowships (averaging $9,059 per year), 82 research assistantships with partial tuition reimbursements available (averaging $8,609 per year), 16 teaching assistantships with partial tuition reimbursements available (averaging $14,530 per year); career-related internships or fieldwork, scholarships/grants, health care benefits, and unspecified assistantships also available. Financial award application deadline: 4/15; financial award applicants required to submit FAFSA. *Faculty research:* Capital markets, econometrics, optimization, investments and empirical corporate finance, Iowa electronic markets. *Unit head:* Prof. Jarjisu Sa-Aadu, Associate Dean, MBA Programs, 800-622-4692, Fax: 319-335-3604, E-mail: jsa-aadu@uiowa.edu. *Application contact:* Jodi Schafer, Director of Admissions and Financial Aid, 319-335-0864, Fax: 319-335-3604, E-mail: jodi-schafer@uiowa.edu. Web site: http://tippie.uiowa.edu/mba.

University of La Verne, College of Business and Public Management, Graduate Programs in Business Administration, La Verne, CA 91750-4443. Offers accounting (MBA); executive management (MBA-EP); finance (MBA, MBA-EP); health services management (MBA); information technology (MBA, MBA-EP); international business (MBA, MBA-EP); leadership (MBA-EP); managed care (MBA); management (MBA, MBA-EP); marketing (MBA, MBA-EP). Part-time and evening/weekend programs available. *Faculty:* 34 full-time (15 women), 38 part-time/adjunct (13 women). *Students:* 525 full-time (243 women), 231 part-time (114 women); includes 199 minority (27 Black or African American, non-Hispanic/Latino; 1 American Indian or Alaska Native, non-Hispanic/Latino; 55 Asian, non-Hispanic/Latino; 113 Hispanic/Latino; 3 Two or more races, non-Hispanic/Latino), 436 international. Average age 28. In 2011, 403 master's awarded. *Entrance requirements:* For master's, minimum undergraduate GPA of 3.0, 2 letters of recommendation, resume. Additional exam requirements/recommendations for international students: Required—TOEFL (minimum score 550 paper-based; 213 computer-based). *Application deadline:* Applications are processed on a rolling basis. Application fee: $50. *Expenses:* Contact institution. *Financial support:* Career-related internships or fieldwork, institutionally sponsored loans, and scholarships/grants available. Financial award application deadline: 3/2; financial award applicants required to submit FAFSA. *Unit head:* Dr. Abe Helou, Chairperson, 909-593-3511 Ext. 4211, Fax: 909-392-2704, E-mail: ihelou@laverne.edu. *Application contact:* Rina Lazarian, Program and Admission Specialist, 909-593-3511 Ext. 4819, Fax: 909-392-2704, E-mail: cbpm@ulv.edu.

University of La Verne, Regional Campus Administration, Graduate Programs, Inland Empire Campus, Rancho Cucamonga, CA 91730. Offers business (MBA-EP), including health services management, information technology, management, marketing; leadership and management (MS). *Entrance requirements:* For master's, 2 letters of recommendation, resume. *Expenses:* Contact institution.

University of Massachusetts Amherst, Graduate School, Isenberg School of Management, Program in Management, Amherst, MA 01003. Offers accounting (PhD); business administration (MBA); business administration/sport management (MBA/MS); finance (PhD); hospitality and tourism management (PhD); management science (PhD); marketing (PhD); organization studies (PhD); sport management (PhD); strategic management (PhD); MBA/MS; MPH/MPPA. *Accreditation:* AACSB. Part-time programs available. *Faculty:* 61 full-time (14 women). *Students:* 92 full-time (34 women), 9 part-time (3 women); includes 8 minority (1 Black or African American, non-Hispanic/Latino; 4 Asian, non-Hispanic/Latino; 3 Hispanic/Latino), 47 international. Average age 33. 340 applicants, 15% accepted, 29 enrolled. In 2011, 31 master's, 13 doctorates awarded. Terminal master's awarded for partial completion of doctoral program. *Degree requirements:* For doctorate, comprehensive exam, thesis/dissertation. *Entrance requirements:* For master's and doctorate, GMAT. Additional exam requirements/ recommendations for international students: Required—TOEFL (minimum score 550 paper-based; 213 computer-based; 80 iBT), IELTS (minimum score 6.5). *Application deadline:* For fall admission, 1/20 for domestic and international students. Applications are processed on a rolling basis. Application fee: $50 ($65 for international students). Electronic applications accepted. Tuition and fees vary according to course load, campus/location and program. *Financial support:* Fellowships with full and partial tuition reimbursements, research assistantships with full and partial tuition reimbursements, teaching assistantships with full and partial tuition reimbursements, career-related internships or fieldwork, Federal Work-Study, scholarships/grants, traineeships, health care benefits, tuition waivers (full and partial), and unspecified assistantships available. Support available to part-time students. Financial award application deadline: 1/20. *Unit head:* Dr. William Woodridge, Chair, 413-545-5675, Fax: 413-577-2234. *Application contact:* Lindsay DeSantis, Interim Supervisor of Admissions, 413-545-0722, Fax: 413-577-0010, E-mail: gradadm@grad.umass.edu. Web site: http://www.isenberg.umass.edu/.

University of Massachusetts Dartmouth, Graduate School, Charlton College of Business, Program in Business Administration, North Dartmouth, MA 02747-2300. Offers accounting (Postbaccalaureate Certificate); business administration (MBA); business foundation (online) (Graduate Certificate); finance (PMC); international business (online) (Graduate Certificate); leadership (online) (Graduate Certificate); management (Postbaccalaureate Certificate); marketing (Postbaccalaureate Certificate); supply chain management (PMC). *Accreditation:* AACSB. Part-time programs available. *Faculty:* 35 full-time (11 women), 26 part-time/adjunct (7 women). *Students:* 81 full-time (29 women), 119 part-time (56 women); includes 17 minority (6 Black or African American, non-Hispanic/Latino; 1 American Indian or Alaska Native, non-Hispanic/Latino; 3 Asian, non-Hispanic/Latino; 5 Hispanic/Latino; 2 Two or more races, non-Hispanic/Latino), 42 international. Average age 31. 132 applicants, 92% accepted, 68 enrolled. In 2011, 91 master's, 18 other advanced degrees awarded. *Entrance requirements:* For master's, GMAT, statement of intent, resume, 3 letters of recommendation; for other advanced degree, statement of intent, resume, 3 letters of recommendation. Additional exam requirements/recommendations for international students: Required—TOEFL (minimum score 500 paper-based; 200 computer-based; 72 iBT). *Application deadline:* For fall admission, 3/1 for domestic students, 2/1 for international students; for spring admission, 11/1 for domestic students, 10/15 for international students. Application fee: $40 ($60 for international students). Electronic applications accepted. *Expenses:* Tuition, state resident: full-time $2071; part-time $86.29 per credit. Tuition, nonresident: full-time $8099; part-time $337.46 per credit. *Required fees:* $438.58 per credit. Part-time tuition and fees vary according to class time, course load, degree level and reciprocity agreements. *Financial support:* Research assistantships, teaching assistantships, Federal Work-Study, and unspecified assistantships available. Support available to part-time students. Financial award application deadline: 3/1; financial award applicants required to submit FAFSA. *Faculty research:* Global business environment, e-commerce, managing diversity, agile manufacturing, green business. *Total annual research expenditures:* $8,653. *Unit head:* Stephanie Jacobsen, Program Coordinator, 508-999-8543, Fax: 508-999-8646, E-mail: s.jacobsen@umassd.edu. *Application contact:* Elan Turcotte-Shamski, Graduate Admissions Officer, 508-999-8604, Fax: 508-999-8183, E-mail: graduate@umassd.edu. Web site: http://www.umassd.edu/charlton/.

University of Memphis, Graduate School, Fogelman College of Business and Economics, Program in Business Administration, Memphis, TN 38152. Offers accounting (MBA, PhD); economics (MBA, PhD); executive business administration (MBA); finance (PhD); finance, insurance, and real estate (MBA, MS); international business administration (IMBA); management (MBA, MS, PhD); management information systems (MBA, MS, PhD); management science (MBA); marketing (MBA, MS); marketing and supply chain management (PhD); real estate development (MS); JD/MBA. *Accreditation:* AACSB. *Degree requirements:* For master's, comprehensive exam; for doctorate, comprehensive exam, thesis/dissertation. *Entrance requirements:* For master's, GMAT, resume; for doctorate, GMAT, interview, minimum GPA of 3.4, resume, letter of recommendation. Additional exam requirements/recommendations for international students: Required—TOEFL (minimum score 550 paper-based; 220 computer-based). *Faculty research:* Competitive business strategy, finance microstructures, supply chain management innovations, health care economics, litigation risks and corporate audits.

University of Miami, Graduate School, School of Business Administration, Program in Business Administration, Coral Gables, FL 33124. Offers accounting (MBA); computer information systems (MBA); executive and professional (MBA), including international business, management; finance (MBA); international business (MBA); management (MBA); management science (MBA); marketing (MBA); professional management (MSPM); JD/MBA; MBA/MSIE. *Accreditation:* AACSB. Evening/weekend programs available. *Degree requirements:* For master's, comprehensive exam. *Entrance requirements:* For master's, GMAT. Additional exam requirements/recommendations for international students: Required—TOEFL (minimum score 550 paper-based; 213 computer-based; 59 iBT). Electronic applications accepted. *Faculty research:* Leadership, e-commerce, supply chain management.

University of Michigan–Dearborn, College of Business, Dearborn, MI 48128-1491. Offers accounting (MBA, MS); business analytics (MS); finance (MBA, MS); information systems (MS); international business (MBA); management (MBA); management information systems (MBA); marketing (MBA); supply chain management (MBA, MS); MBA/MHSA; MBA/MSE; MBA/MSF; MBA/MSIS; MSF/MSA. *Accreditation:* AACSB. Part-time and evening/weekend programs available. Postbaccalaureate distance learning degree programs offered (no on-campus study). *Faculty:* 50 full-time (6 women), 32 part-time/adjunct (18 women). *Students:* 65 full-time (29 women), 356 part-time (121 women); includes 79 minority (19 Black or African American, non-Hispanic/Latino; 36 American Indian or Alaska Native, non-Hispanic/Latino; 15 Hispanic/Latino; 1 Native Hawaiian or other Pacific Islander, non-Hispanic/Latino; 8 Two or more races, non-Hispanic/Latino), 80 international. Average age 28. 175 applicants, 53% accepted, 68 enrolled. In 2011, 173 master's awarded. *Entrance requirements:* For master's, GMAT or GRE, 2 years of work experience (MBA); course work in computer applications, statistics, and pre-calculus or finite mathematics; 18 credits of accounting course work beyond introductory courses (MS in accounting). Additional exam requirements/recommendations for international students: Required—TOEFL (minimum score 560 paper-based; 220 computer-based; 84 iBT), IELTS. *Application deadline:* For fall admission, 8/1 priority date for domestic students, 6/1 for international students; for winter admission, 12/1 priority date for domestic students, 10/1 for international students; for spring admission, 4/1 priority date for domestic students, 2/1 for international students. Applications are processed on a rolling basis. Application fee: $60. Electronic applications accepted. *Expenses:* Contact institution. *Financial support:* Career-related internships or fieldwork, Federal Work-Study, and scholarships/grants available. Support available to part-time students. Financial award application deadline: 9/1; financial award applicants required to submit FAFSA. *Faculty research:* Cultural diversity, buyer-supplier relations, error detection in data, economic evolution. *Unit head:* Dr. Lee Redding, Interim Dean, 313-593-5248, Fax: 313-271-9835, E-mail: lredding@umd.umich.edu. *Application contact:* Joan Doherty, Academic Advisor/Counselor, 313-593-5460, Fax: 313-271-9838, E-mail: gradbusiness@umd.umich.edu. Web site: http://www.cob.umd.umich.edu.

University of Minnesota, Twin Cities Campus, Carlson School of Management, Carlson Full-Time MBA Program, Minneapolis, MN 55455. Offers finance (MBA); information technology (MBA); management (MBA); marketing (MBA); medical industry orientation (MBA); supply chain and operations (MBA); JD/MBA; MBA/MPP; MD/MBA; MHA/MBA; Pharm D/MBA. *Accreditation:* AACSB. *Faculty:* 58 full-time (17 women), 23 part-time/adjunct (5 women). *Students:* 172 full-time (54 women); includes 16 minority (4 Black or African American, non-Hispanic/Latino; 10 Asian, non-Hispanic/Latino; 2 Two or more races, non-Hispanic/Latino), 41 international. Average age 28. 538 applicants, 41% accepted, 99 enrolled. In 2011, 97 master's awarded. *Entrance requirements:* For master's, GMAT or GRE. Additional exam requirements/recommendations for international students: Required—TOEFL (minimum score 580 paper-based; 240 computer-based; 84 iBT), IELTS (minimum score 7), or Pearson Test of English. *Application deadline:* For fall admission, 4/1 for domestic students, 2/1 for international students. Application fee: $60 ($90 for international students). Electronic applications accepted. *Expenses:* Contact institution. *Financial support:* In 2011–12, 116 students received support, including 116 fellowships with full and partial tuition reimbursements available (averaging $18,702 per year); research assistantships with partial tuition reimbursements available, teaching assistantships with partial tuition reimbursements available, career-related internships or fieldwork, Federal Work-Study, institutionally sponsored loans, scholarships/grants, health care benefits, and unspecified assistantships also available. Financial award application deadline: 4/1; financial award applicants required to submit FAFSA. *Faculty research:* Finance and accounting: financial reporting, asset pricing models and corporate finance; information and decision sciences: on-line auctions, information transparency and recommender systems; marketing: psychological influences on consumer behavior, brand equity, pricing and marketing channels; operations: lean manufacturing, quality management and global supply chains; strategic management and organization: global strategy, networks, entrepreneurship and innovation, sustainability. *Unit head:* Philip J. Miller, Assistant Dean, MBA Programs and Graduate Business Career Center, 612-625-5555, Fax: 612-625-1012, E-mail: mba@umn.edu. *Application contact:* Linh Gilles, Director of Admissions and Recruiting, 612-625-5555, Fax: 612-625-1012, E-mail: ftmba@umn.edu. Web site: http://www.csom.umn.edu/MBA/full-time/.

University of Minnesota, Twin Cities Campus, Carlson School of Management, Carlson Part-Time MBA Program, Minneapolis, MN 55455. Offers finance (MBA); information technology (MBA); management (MBA); marketing (MBA); supply chain and operations (MBA). Part-time and evening/weekend programs available. *Faculty:* 63 full-time (16 women), 27 part-time/adjunct (4 women). *Students:* 1,459 part-time (463 women); includes 94 minority (11 Black or African American, non-Hispanic/Latino; 3 American Indian or Alaska Native, non-Hispanic/Latino; 68 Asian, non-Hispanic/Latino; 10 Hispanic/Latino; 2 Two or more races, non-Hispanic/Latino), 72 international. Average age 28. 336 applicants, 86% accepted, 256 enrolled. In 2011, 479 master's awarded. *Entrance requirements:* For master's, GMAT or GRE. Additional exam requirements/recommendations for international students: Required—TOEFL (minimum score 580 paper-based; 240 computer-based; 84 iBT), IELTS (minimum score 7), or Pearson Test of English. *Application deadline:* For fall admission, 5/1 priority date for domestic students, 5/1 for international students; for spring admission, 10/1 priority date for domestic students, 10/1 for international students. Applications are processed on a rolling basis. Application fee: $60 ($90 for international students). Electronic applications accepted. *Expenses:* Contact institution. *Financial support:* Applicants required to submit FAFSA. *Faculty research:* Finance and accounting: financial reporting, asset pricing models and corporate finance; information and decision sciences: on-line auctions, information transparency and recommender systems; marketing: psychological influences on consumer behavior, brand equity, pricing and marketing channels; operations: lean manufacturing, quality management and global supply chains; strategic management and organization: global strategy, networks, entrepreneurship and innovation, sustainability. *Unit head:* Philip J. Miller, Assistant Dean, MBA Programs and Graduate Business Career Center, 612-624-2039, Fax: 612-625-1012, E-mail: mba@umn.edu. *Application contact:* Linh Gilles, Director of Admissions and Recruiting, 612-625-5555, Fax: 612-625-1012, E-mail: ptmba@umn.edu. Web site: http://www.carlsonschool.umn.edu/ptmba.

University of Minnesota, Twin Cities Campus, Carlson School of Management, Doctoral Program in Business Administration, Minneapolis, MN 55455-0213. Offers accounting (PhD); finance (PhD); information and decision sciences (PhD); marketing (PhD); operations and management science (PhD); strategic management and organization (PhD). *Faculty:* 104 full-time (30 women). *Students:* 74 full-time (30 women); includes 8 minority (5 Asian, non-Hispanic/Latino; 3 Hispanic/Latino), 50 international. Average age 30. 320 applicants, 8% accepted, 15 enrolled. In 2011, 13 doctorates awarded. *Degree requirements:* For doctorate, comprehensive exam, thesis/dissertation, written and oral preliminary exams, proposal defense, final defense. *Entrance requirements:* For doctorate, GMAT, GRE General Test. Additional exam requirements/recommendations for international students: Required—TOEFL (minimum score 600 paper-based; 250 computer-based; 100 iBT); Recommended—IELTS (minimum score 7.5). *Application deadline:* For fall admission, 12/31 for domestic and international students. Applications are processed on a rolling basis. Application fee: $75 ($95 for international students). Electronic applications accepted. *Expenses:* Contact institution. *Financial support:* In 2011–12, 66 students received support, including 112 fellowships with full tuition reimbursements available (averaging $6,700 per year), 55 research assistantships with full tuition reimbursements available (averaging $6,750 per year), 54 teaching assistantships with full tuition reimbursements available (averaging $6,750 per year); institutionally sponsored loans, scholarships/grants, health care benefits, and unspecified assistantships also available. Financial award application deadline: 12/31. *Faculty research:* Corporate strategy, finance, entrepreneurship, marketing, information and decision science, operations, accounting, quality management. *Unit head:* Dr. Shawn P. Curley, Director, 612-624-6546, Fax: 612-624-8221, E-mail: curley@umn.edu. *Application contact:* Earlene K. Bronson, Assistant Director, 612-624-0875, Fax: 612-624-8221, E-mail: brons003@umn.edu. Web site: http://www.csom.umn.edu/phd-BA/.

University of Missouri–St. Louis, College of Business Administration, Program in Business Administration, St. Louis, MO 63121. Offers accounting (MBA); business administration (Certificate); finance (MBA); human resource management (Certificate); information systems (MBA); logistics and supply chain management (MBA, Certificate); marketing (MBA); marketing management (Certificate); operations management (MBA). *Accreditation:* AACSB. Part-time and evening/weekend programs available. *Faculty:* 32 full-time (7 women), 10 part-time/adjunct (2 women). *Students:* 126 full-time (48 women), 305 part-time (141 women); includes 61 minority (25 Black or African American, non-Hispanic/Latino; 23 Asian, non-Hispanic/Latino; 9 Hispanic/Latino; 1 Native Hawaiian or other Pacific Islander, non-Hispanic/Latino; 3 Two or more races, non-Hispanic/Latino), 47 international. Average age 30. 241 applicants, 70% accepted, 134 enrolled. In 2011, 150 master's, 1 doctorate, 19 other advanced degrees awarded. *Entrance requirements:* For master's, GMAT, 2 letters of recommendation. Additional exam requirements/recommendations for international students: Required—TOEFL (minimum score 550 paper-based; 213 computer-based). *Application deadline:* For fall admission, 7/1 for domestic and international students; for spring admission, 12/1 for domestic and international students. Applications are processed on a rolling basis. Application fee: $35 ($40 for international students). Electronic applications accepted. *Expenses:* Tuition, state resident: full-time $6273; part-time $3866 per year. Tuition, nonresident: full-time $14,969; part-time $9980 per year. *Required fees:* $315 per year. *Financial support:* In 2011–12, 32 research assistantships with full and partial tuition reimbursements (averaging $6,000 per year), 6 teaching assistantships with full and partial tuition reimbursements (averaging $12,276 per year) were awarded; career-related internships or fieldwork, Federal Work-Study, and institutionally sponsored loans also available. Support available to part-time students. Financial award application deadline: 4/1; financial award applicants required to submit FAFSA. *Faculty research:* Human resources, strategic management, marketing strategy, consumer behavior product development, advertising. *Unit head:* Karl Kottemann, Assistant Director, 314-516-5885, Fax: 314-516-6420, E-mail: mba@umsl.edu. *Application contact:* 314-516-5458, Fax: 314-516-6996, E-mail: gradadm@umsl.edu. Web site: http://www.umsl.edu/divisions/business/mbaonline/mbaprog.htm.

University of Nebraska–Lincoln, Graduate College, College of Arts and Sciences, Department of Communication Studies, Lincoln, NE 68588. Offers instructional communication (MA, PhD); interpersonal communication (MA, PhD); marketing, communication studies, and advertising (MA, PhD); organizational communication (MA, PhD); rhetoric and culture (MA, PhD). *Degree requirements:* For master's, thesis optional; for doctorate, comprehensive exam, thesis/dissertation. *Entrance requirements:* For master's and doctorate, GRE General Test, writing sample. Additional exam requirements/recommendations for international students: Required—TOEFL (minimum score 600 paper-based; 250 computer-based). Electronic applications accepted. *Faculty research:* Message strategies, gender communication, political communication, organizational communication, instructional communication.

University of Nebraska–Lincoln, Graduate College, College of Business Administration, Interdepartmental Area of Business, Department of Marketing, Lincoln, NE 68588. Offers business (MA, PhD). *Degree requirements:* For doctorate, comprehensive exam, thesis/dissertation. *Entrance requirements:* For master's and doctorate, GMAT. Additional exam requirements/recommendations for international students: Required—TOEFL. Electronic applications accepted. *Faculty research:* Channel information, marketing research methodology, sales management, cross-cultural marketing, impact of new technology.

University of Nebraska–Lincoln, Graduate College, College of Journalism and Mass Communications, Lincoln, NE 68588. Offers marketing, communication and advertising (MA); professional journalism (MA). Postbaccalaureate distance learning degree programs offered (no on-campus study). *Degree requirements:* For master's, thesis. *Entrance requirements:* For master's, samples of work. Additional exam requirements/recommendations for international students: Required—TOEFL (minimum score 600 paper-based; 250 computer-based). Electronic applications accepted. *Faculty research:* Interactive media and the Internet, community newspapers, children's radio, advertising involvement, telecommunications policy.

University of New Brunswick Fredericton, School of Graduate Studies, Faculty of Forestry and Environmental Management, Fredericton, NB E3B 5A3, Canada. Offers ecological foundations of forest management (PhD); environmental management (MEM); forest engineering (M Sc FE, MFE); forest products marketing (MBA); forest resources (M Sc F, MF, PhD). Part-time programs available. *Faculty:* 22 full-time (3 women), 1 part-time/adjunct (0 women). *Students:* 72 full-time (27 women), 15 part-time

(12 women). In 2011, 13 master's, 4 doctorates awarded. *Degree requirements:* For master's, thesis; for doctorate, thesis/dissertation. *Entrance requirements:* For master's and doctorate, minimum GPA of 3.0. Additional exam requirements/recommendations for international students: Required—TWE (minimum score 4), TOEFL (minimum score 580 paper-based) or IELTS. *Application deadline:* For fall admission, 3/1 priority date for domestic students. Application fee: $50 Canadian dollars. Electronic applications accepted. *Financial support:* In 2011–12, 55 fellowships, 34 teaching assistantships were awarded. *Faculty research:* Forest machines, soils, and ecosystems; integrated forest management; forest meteorology; wood engineering; stream ecosystems dynamics; forest and natural resources policy; forest operations planning; wood technology and mechanics; forest road construction and engineering; forest, wildlife, insect, bird, and fire ecology; remote sensing; insect impacts; Silviculture; LiDAR analytics; integrated pest management; forest tree genetics; genetic resource conservation and sustainable management. *Unit head:* Dr. John Kershaw, Director of Graduate Studies, 506-453-4933, Fax: 506-453-3538, E-mail: kershaw@unb.ca. *Application contact:* Faith Sharpe, Graduate Secretary, 506-458-7520, Fax: 506-453-3538, E-mail: fsharpe@unb.ca. Web site: http://www.unb.ca/fredericton/forestry/.

University of New Haven, Graduate School, School of Business, Program in Business Administration, West Haven, CT 06516-1916. Offers accounting (MBA, Certificate), including CPA (MBA); business management (Certificate); business policy and strategy (MBA); finance (MBA), including CFA; global marketing (MBA); human resource management (Certificate); human resources management (MBA); international business (Certificate); marketing (Certificate); sports management (MBA); telecommunications management (Certificate); MBA/MPA. Part-time and evening/weekend programs available. *Students:* 215 full-time (106 women), 182 part-time (87 women); includes 73 minority (38 Black or African American, non-Hispanic/Latino; 2 American Indian or Alaska Native, non-Hispanic/Latino; 22 Asian, non-Hispanic/Latino; 11 Hispanic/Latino), 129 international. 179 applicants, 97% accepted, 93 enrolled. In 2011, 197 master's, 28 other advanced degrees awarded. *Degree requirements:* For master's, thesis or alternative. *Entrance requirements:* For master's, GMAT. Additional exam requirements/recommendations for international students: Required—TOEFL (minimum score 520 paper-based; 190 computer-based; 70 iBT), IELTS (minimum score 5.5). *Application deadline:* For fall admission, 5/31 for international students; for winter admission, 10/15 for international students; for spring admission, 1/15 for international students. Applications are processed on a rolling basis. Application fee: $50. Electronic applications accepted. *Expenses:* Contact institution. *Financial support:* Research assistantships with partial tuition reimbursements, teaching assistantships with partial tuition reimbursements, Federal Work-Study, scholarships/grants, health care benefits, tuition waivers, and unspecified assistantships available. Support available to part-time students. Financial award applicants required to submit FAFSA. *Unit head:* Charles Coleman, Chairman, 203-932-7375. *Application contact:* Eloise Gormley, Director of Graduate Admissions, 203-932-7449, Fax: 203-932-7137, E-mail: gradinfo@newhaven.edu. Web site: http://www.newhaven.edu/7433/.

University of New Mexico, Robert O. Anderson Graduate School of Management, Department of Marketing, Information and Decision Sciences, Albuquerque, NM 87131. Offers information assurance (MBA); management information systems (MBA); marketing management (MBA); operations management (MBA). Part-time and evening/weekend programs available. *Faculty:* 14 full-time (4 women), 11 part-time/adjunct (5 women). In 2011, 74 master's awarded. *Degree requirements:* For master's, minimum GPA of 3.0. *Entrance requirements:* For master's, GMAT or GRE. Additional exam requirements/recommendations for international students: Required—TOEFL (minimum score 550 paper-based; 213 computer-based; 79 iBT). *Application deadline:* For fall admission, 4/1 priority date for domestic students, 4/1 for international students; for spring admission, 10/1 priority date for domestic students, 10/1 for international students. Applications are processed on a rolling basis. Application fee: $50. Electronic applications accepted. *Financial support:* Fellowships, research assistantships, career-related internships or fieldwork, Federal Work-Study, scholarships/grants, and unspecified assistantships available. Support available to part-time students. Financial award application deadline: 6/1. *Faculty research:* Marketing, operations, information science. *Unit head:* Dr. Steve Yourstone, Chair, 505-277-6471, Fax: 505-277-7108. *Application contact:* Megan Conner, Director, Student Services, 505-277-3290, Fax: 505-277-8436, E-mail: mconner@mgt.unm.edu.

The University of North Carolina at Chapel Hill, Kenan-Flagler Business School, Doctoral Program in Business Administration, Chapel Hill, NC 27599. Offers accounting (PhD); finance (PhD); marketing (PhD); operations management (PhD); organizational behavior (PhD); strategy (PhD). *Accreditation:* AACSB. *Degree requirements:* For doctorate, thesis/dissertation. *Entrance requirements:* For doctorate, GMAT or GRE General Test. Electronic applications accepted. *Expenses:* Contact institution.

The University of North Carolina at Charlotte, Graduate School, Belk College of Business, Department of Marketing, Charlotte, NC 28223-0001. Offers MBA. *Faculty:* 7. *Expenses:* Tuition, state resident: full-time $3689. Tuition, nonresident: full-time $15,226. *Required fees:* $2198. Tuition and fees vary according to course load and program. *Unit head:* Dr. Sunil Erevelles, Chair, 704-687-7684, Fax: 704-687-6463, E-mail: sunil.erevelles@uncc.edu. *Application contact:* Kathy B. Giddings, Director of Graduate Admissions, 704-687-5503, Fax: 704-687-3279, E-mail: gradadm@uncc.edu. Web site: http://belkcollege.uncc.edu/about-college/departments/marketing.

The University of North Carolina at Greensboro, Graduate School, School of Human Environmental Sciences, Department of Consumer, Apparel, and Retail Studies, Greensboro, NC 27412-5001. Offers MS, PhD. *Degree requirements:* For master's, one foreign language; for doctorate, one foreign language, thesis/dissertation. *Entrance requirements:* For master's and doctorate, GRE General Test. Additional exam requirements/recommendations for international students: Required—TOEFL. Electronic applications accepted. *Faculty research:* Impact of phosphate removal, protective clothing for pesticide workers, fabric hand: subjective and objective measurements.

University of North Texas, Toulouse Graduate School, College of Business, Department of Marketing and Logistics, Denton, TX 76203-5017. Offers PhD. Part-time programs available. *Degree requirements:* For doctorate, comprehensive exam, thesis/dissertation, referred publication. *Entrance requirements:* For doctorate, GMAT (minimum score: 550). Additional exam requirements/recommendations for international students: Recommended—TOEFL (minimum score 550 paper-based; 213 computer-based; 79 iBT). *Expenses:* Tuition, state resident: part-time $100 per credit hour. Tuition, nonresident: part-time $413 per credit hour. *Faculty research:* Promotion, distribution channels, international distribution, sales management, consumer behavior, services marketing, NPD.

University of Oregon, Graduate School, Charles H. Lundquist College of Business, Department of Marketing, Eugene, OR 97403. Offers PhD. Part-time programs available. *Degree requirements:* For doctorate, thesis/dissertation, 2 comprehensive exams. *Entrance requirements:* For doctorate, GMAT. Additional exam requirements/recommendations for international students: Required—TOEFL. *Faculty research:* Consumer behavior, marketing research, international marketing, marketing management, price quality.

University of Pennsylvania, Wharton School, Marketing Department, Philadelphia, PA 19104. Offers MBA, PhD. Terminal master's awarded for partial completion of doctoral program. *Degree requirements:* For master's, thesis optional; for doctorate, thesis/dissertation. *Entrance requirements:* For doctorate, GMAT or GRE. *Expenses: Tuition:* Full-time $26,660; part-time $4944 per course. *Required fees:* $2318; $291 per course. Tuition and fees vary according to course load, degree level and program. *Faculty research:* Scanner data, consumer preferences, decision-making theory, modeling for marketing and e-business.

University of Phoenix–Atlanta Campus, School of Business, Sandy Springs, GA 30350-4153. Offers accounting (MBA); business administration (MBA); global management (MBA); human resources management (MBA, MM); management (MM); marketing (MBA); public administration (MM). Evening/weekend programs available. Postbaccalaureate distance learning degree programs offered. *Degree requirements:* For master's, thesis (for some programs). *Entrance requirements:* For master's, minimum undergraduate GPA of 3.0, 3 years of work experience. Additional exam requirements/recommendations for international students: Required—TOEFL (minimum score 550 paper-based; 213 computer-based; 79 iBT).

University of Phoenix–Augusta Campus, School of Business, Augusta, GA 30909-4583. Offers accounting (MBA); business administration (MBA); business and management (MBA, MM); global management (MBA); human resources management (MBA, MM); management (MM); marketing (MBA); public administration (MBA, MM). Postbaccalaureate distance learning degree programs offered.

University of Phoenix–Austin Campus, School of Business, Austin, TX 78759. Offers accounting (MBA); business administration (MBA); business and management (MBA); e-business (MBA); global management (MBA); human resources management (MBA, MM); management (MM); marketing (MBA); public administration (MBA). Postbaccalaureate distance learning degree programs offered.

University of Phoenix–Bay Area Campus, School of Business, San Jose, CA 95134-1805. Offers accountancy (MS); accounting (MBA); business administration (MBA, DBA); energy management (MBA); global management (MBA); health care management (MBA); human resource management (MBA); human resources management (MM); management (MM); marketing (MBA); organizational leadership (DM); project management (MBA); public administration (MPA); technology management (MBA). Evening/weekend programs available. Postbaccalaureate distance learning degree programs offered (no on-campus study). *Degree requirements:* For master's, thesis (for some programs). *Entrance requirements:* For master's, minimum undergraduate GPA of 3.0, 3 years of work experience. Additional exam requirements/recommendations for international students: Required—TOEFL (minimum score 550 paper-based; 213 computer-based; 79 iBT). Electronic applications accepted.

University of Phoenix–Birmingham Campus, College of Graduate Business and Management, Birmingham, AL 35244. Offers accounting (MBA); business administration (MBA); global management (MBA); human resources management (MBA, MM); management (MM); marketing (MBA); public administration (MM).

University of Phoenix–Central Florida Campus, School of Business, Maitland, FL 32751-7057. Offers accounting (MBA); business administration (MBA); business and management (MM); global management (MBA); human resources management (MBA, MM); management (MM); marketing (MBA); public administration (MBA, MM). Evening/weekend programs available. *Degree requirements:* For master's, thesis (for some programs). *Entrance requirements:* For master's, minimum undergraduate GPA of 3.0, 3 years work experience. Additional exam requirements/recommendations for international students: Required—TOEFL (minimum score 550 paper-based; 213 computer-based; 79 iBT). Electronic applications accepted.

University of Phoenix–Central Valley Campus, School of Business, Fresno, CA 93720-1562. Offers accounting (MBA); business administration (MBA); global management (MBA); human resources management (MBA, MM); management (MM); marketing (MBA); public administration (MBA, MM).

University of Phoenix–Chattanooga Campus, School of Business, Chattanooga, TN 37421-3707. Offers accounting (MBA); business administration (MBA); business and management (MBA); global management (MBA); human resources management (MBA, MM); management (MM); marketing (MBA); public administration (MBA, MM). Postbaccalaureate distance learning degree programs offered.

University of Phoenix–Cheyenne Campus, School of Business, Cheyenne, WY 82009. Offers global management (MBA); human resources management (MBA, MM); management (MM); marketing (MBA); public administration (MBA, MM). Postbaccalaureate distance learning degree programs offered.

University of Phoenix–Cincinnati Campus, School of Business, West Chester, OH 45069-4875. Offers accounting (MBA); business administration (MBA); global management (MBA); human resources management (MBA, MM); management (MM); marketing (MBA); public administration (MM). Evening/weekend programs available. *Degree requirements:* For master's, thesis (for some programs). *Entrance requirements:* For master's, minimum undergraduate GPA of 3.0, 3 years of work experience. Additional exam requirements/recommendations for international students: Required—TOEFL (minimum score 550 paper-based; 213 computer-based; 79 iBT). Electronic applications accepted.

University of Phoenix–Cleveland Campus, School of Business, Independence, OH 44131-2194. Offers accounting (MBA); business administration (MBA); global management (MBA); human resources management (MBA, MM); management (MM); marketing (MBA); public administration (MBA, MM). Evening/weekend programs available. Postbaccalaureate distance learning degree programs offered (no on-campus study). *Degree requirements:* For master's, thesis (for some programs). *Entrance requirements:* For master's, minimum undergraduate GPA of 3.0, 3 years of work experience. Additional exam requirements/recommendations for international students: Required—TOEFL (minimum score 550 paper-based; 213 computer-based; 79 iBT). Electronic applications accepted.

University of Phoenix–Columbus Georgia Campus, School of Business, Columbus, GA 31904-6321. Offers accounting (MBA); business administration (MBA); global management (MBA); human resources management (MBA, MM); management (MM); marketing (MBA); public administration (MBA). Evening/weekend programs available. *Degree requirements:* For master's, thesis (for some programs). *Entrance requirements:* For master's, minimum undergraduate GPA of 3.0, 3 years of work experience. Additional exam requirements/recommendations for international students: Required—TOEFL (minimum score 550 paper-based; 213 computer-based; 79 iBT). Electronic applications accepted.

University of Phoenix–Columbus Ohio Campus, School of Business, Columbus, OH 43240-4032. Offers accounting (MBA); business administration (MBA); global management (MBA); human resources management (MBA, MM); management (MM); marketing (MBA); public administration (MM). Evening/weekend programs available. Postbaccalaureate distance learning degree programs offered. *Degree requirements:* For master's, thesis (for some programs). *Entrance requirements:* For master's, minimum undergraduate GPA of 3.0, 3 years of work experience. Additional exam requirements/recommendations for international students: Required—TOEFL (minimum score 550 paper-based; 213 computer-based; 79 iBT). Electronic applications accepted.

University of Phoenix–Dallas Campus, School of Business, Dallas, TX 75251-2009. Offers accounting (MBA); business administration (MBA); global management (MBA); human resources management (MBA, MM); management (MM); marketing (MBA); public administration (MBA, MM). Evening/weekend programs available. Postbaccalaureate distance learning degree programs offered. *Degree requirements:* For master's, thesis (for some programs). *Entrance requirements:* For master's, 3 years of work experience, minimum undergraduate GPA of 3.0. Additional exam requirements/recommendations for international students: Required—TOEFL (minimum score 550 paper-based; 213 computer-based; 79 iBT). Electronic applications accepted.

University of Phoenix–Denver Campus, School of Business, Lone Tree, CO 80124-5453. Offers accountancy (MSA); accounting (MBA); business administration (MBA); e-business (MBA); global management (MBA); human resources management (MBA, MM); management (MM); marketing (MBA); public administration (MBA, MM). Evening/weekend programs available. Postbaccalaureate distance learning degree programs offered. *Degree requirements:* For master's, thesis (for some programs). *Entrance requirements:* For master's, minimum undergraduate GPA of 3.0, 3 years work experience. Additional exam requirements/recommendations for international students: Required—TOEFL (minimum score 550 paper-based; 213 computer-based; 79 iBT). Electronic applications accepted.

University of Phoenix–Des Moines Campus, School of Business, Des Moines, IA 50266. Offers accounting (MBA); business administration (MBA); global management (MBA); human resources management (MBA, MM); management (MM); marketing (MBA); public administration (MBA, MM). Postbaccalaureate distance learning degree programs offered.

University of Phoenix–Eastern Washington Campus, School of Business, Spokane Valley, WA 99212-2531. Offers accounting (MBA); business administration (MBA); human resources management (MBA); marketing (MBA); public administration (MBA). Evening/weekend programs available. *Degree requirements:* For master's, thesis (for some programs). *Entrance requirements:* For master's, minimum undergraduate GPA of 3.0, 3 years of work experience. Additional exam requirements/recommendations for international students: Required—TOEFL (minimum score 550 paper-based; 213 computer-based; 79 iBT). Electronic applications accepted.

University of Phoenix–Harrisburg Campus, School of Business, Harrisburg, PA 17112. Offers accounting (MBA); business administration (MBA); business and management (MBA); global management (MBA); human resources management (MBA, MM); management (MM); marketing (MBA); public administration (MBA, MM). Postbaccalaureate distance learning degree programs offered.

University of Phoenix–Hawaii Campus, School of Business, Honolulu, HI 96813-4317. Offers accounting (MBA); business administration (MBA); global management (MBA); human resources management (MBA, MM); management (MM); marketing (MBA); public administration (MBA, MM). Evening/weekend programs available. *Degree requirements:* For master's, thesis (for some programs). *Entrance requirements:* For master's, minimum undergraduate GPA of 3.0, 3 years of work experience. Additional exam requirements/recommendations for international students: Required—TOEFL (minimum score 550 paper-based; 213 computer-based; 79 iBT). Electronic applications accepted.

University of Phoenix–Houston Campus, School of Business, Houston, TX 77079-2004. Offers accounting (MBA); business administration (MBA); global management (MBA); human resources management (MBA, MM); management (MM); marketing (MBA); public administration (MBA, MM). Evening/weekend programs available. Postbaccalaureate distance learning degree programs offered. *Degree requirements:* For master's, thesis (for some programs). *Entrance requirements:* For master's, 3 years of work experience, minimum undergraduate GPA of 3.0. Additional exam requirements/recommendations for international students: Required—TOEFL (minimum score 550 paper-based; 213 computer-based; 79 iBT). Electronic applications accepted.

University of Phoenix–Idaho Campus, School of Business, Meridian, ID 83642-5114. Offers accounting (MBA); administration (MBA); global management (MBA); human resources management (MBA, MM); management (MM); marketing (MBA); public administration (MM). Evening/weekend programs available. Postbaccalaureate distance learning degree programs offered. *Degree requirements:* For master's, thesis (for some programs). *Entrance requirements:* For master's, 3 years of work experience, minimum undergraduate GPA of 3.0. Additional exam requirements/recommendations for international students: Required—TOEFL (minimum score 550 paper-based; 213 computer-based). Electronic applications accepted.

University of Phoenix–Indianapolis Campus, School of Business, Indianapolis, IN 46250-932. Offers accounting (MBA); business administration (MBA); global management (MBA); human resources management (MBA, MM); management (MM); marketing (MBA); public administration (MM). Evening/weekend programs available. *Degree requirements:* For master's, thesis (for some programs). *Entrance requirements:* For master's, minimum undergraduate GPA of 3.0, 3 years of work experience. Additional exam requirements/recommendations for international students: Required—TOEFL (minimum score 550 paper-based; 213 computer-based). Electronic applications accepted.

University of Phoenix–Jersey City Campus, School of Business, Jersey City, NJ 07310. Offers accounting (MBA); business administration (MBA); global management (MBA); human resources management (MBA, MM); management (MM); marketing (MBA); public administration (MBA, MM).

University of Phoenix–Kansas City Campus, School of Business, Kansas City, MO 64131-4517. Offers accounting (MBA); business administration (MBA); global management (MBA); human resources management (MBA, MM); management (MM); marketing (MBA); public administration (MBA). Evening/weekend programs available. *Degree requirements:* For master's, thesis (for some programs). *Entrance requirements:* For master's, minimum undergraduate GPA of 3.0, 3 years of work experience. Additional exam requirements/recommendations for international students: Required—TOEFL (minimum score 550 paper-based; 213 computer-based). Electronic applications accepted.

University of Phoenix–Las Vegas Campus, School of Business, Las Vegas, NV 89128. Offers accounting (MBA); business administration (MBA); global management (MBA); human resources management (MBA, MM); management (MM); marketing (MBA); public administration (MM). Evening/weekend programs available. Postbaccalaureate distance learning degree programs offered (no on-campus study). *Degree requirements:* For master's, thesis (for some programs). *Entrance requirements:* For master's, minimum undergraduate GPA of 3.0, 3 years of work experience. Additional exam requirements/recommendations for international students: Required—TOEFL (minimum score 550 paper-based; 213 computer-based; 79 iBT). Electronic applications accepted.

University of Phoenix–Louisiana Campus, School of Business, Metairie, LA 70001-2082. Offers accounting (MBA); business administration (MBA); global management (MBA); human resources management (MBA, MM); management (MM); marketing (MBA); public administration (MBA). Evening/weekend programs available. *Degree requirements:* For master's, thesis (for some programs). *Entrance requirements:* For master's, minimum undergraduate GPA of 3.0, 3 years work experience. Additional exam requirements/recommendations for international students: Required—TOEFL (minimum score 550 paper-based; 213 computer-based; 79 iBT). Electronic applications accepted.

University of Phoenix–Madison Campus, School of Business, Madison, WI 53718-2416. Offers accounting (MBA); business and management (MBA); e-business (MBA); global management (MBA); human resources management (MBA, MM); management (MM); marketing (MBA); public administration (MBA).

University of Phoenix–Memphis Campus, School of Business, Cordova, TN 38018. Offers accounting (MBA); business and management (MBA); e-business (MBA); global management (MBA); human resources management (MBA, MM); management (MM); marketing (MBA); public administration (MBA, MM).

University of Phoenix–Minneapolis/St. Louis Park Campus, School of Business, St. Louis Park, MN 55426. Offers accounting (MBA); business administration (MBA); global management (MBA); human resources management (MBA); management (MM); marketing (MBA); public administration (MBA).

University of Phoenix–New Mexico Campus, School of Business, Albuquerque, NM 87113-1570. Offers accounting (MBA); business administration (MBA); global management (MBA); human resources management (MBA, MM); management (MM); marketing (MBA). Evening/weekend programs available. *Degree requirements:* For master's, thesis (for some programs). *Entrance requirements:* For master's, 3 years of work experience, minimum undergraduate GPA of 3.0. Additional exam requirements/recommendations for international students: Required—TOEFL (minimum score 550 paper-based; 213 computer-based; 79 iBT). Electronic applications accepted.

University of Phoenix–Northern Nevada Campus, School of Business, Reno, NV 89521-5862. Offers accounting (MBA); business administration (MBA); global management (MBA); human resources management (MBA, MM); management (MM); marketing (MBA); public administration (MBA, MM).

University of Phoenix–North Florida Campus, School of Business, Jacksonville, FL 32216-0959. Offers accounting (MBA); business administration (MBA); global management (MBA); human resources management (MBA, MM); management (MM); marketing (MBA); public administration (MBA, MM). Evening/weekend programs available. *Degree requirements:* For master's, thesis (for some programs). *Entrance requirements:* For master's, minimum undergraduate GPA of 3.0, 3 years work experience. Additional exam requirements/recommendations for international students: Required—TOEFL (minimum score 550 paper-based; 213 computer-based; 79 iBT). Electronic applications accepted.

University of Phoenix–Northwest Arkansas Campus, School of Business, Rogers, AR 72756-9615. Offers accounting (MBA); business and management (MBA); global management (MBA); human resources management (MBA, MM); management (MM); marketing (MBA); public administration (MBA, MM).

University of Phoenix–Oklahoma City Campus, School of Business, Oklahoma City, OK 73116-8244. Offers accounting (MBA); business administration (MBA); global management (MBA); human resource management (MBA); management (MM); marketing (MBA). Evening/weekend programs available. *Degree requirements:* For master's, thesis (for some programs). *Entrance requirements:* For master's, minimum undergraduate GPA of 3.0, 3 years of work experience. Additional exam requirements/recommendations for international students: Required—TOEFL (minimum score 550 paper-based; 213 computer-based; 79 iBT). Electronic applications accepted.

University of Phoenix–Omaha Campus, School of Business, Omaha, NE 68154-5240. Offers accounting (MBA); business and management (MBA); global management (MBA); human resources management (MBA, MM); management (MM); marketing (MBA); public administration (MBA, MM).

University of Phoenix–Online Campus, School of Business, Phoenix, AZ 85034-7209. Offers accountancy (MS); accounting (MBA); business administration (MBA); energy management (MBA); global management (MBA); health care management (MBA); human resource management (MBA); human resources management (MM); international (MM); management (MM); marketing (MBA, Graduate Certificate); organizational management (MA); project management (MBA, Graduate Certificate); public administration (MBA, MM, MPA); technology management (MBA). Evening/weekend programs available. Postbaccalaureate distance learning degree programs offered. *Students:* 18,883 full-time (11,868 women); includes 6,302 minority (4,182 Black or African American, non-Hispanic/Latino; 121 American Indian or Alaska Native, non-Hispanic/Latino; 478 Asian, non-Hispanic/Latino; 1,252 Hispanic/Latino; 121 Native Hawaiian or other Pacific Islander, non-Hispanic/Latino; 148 Two or more races, non-Hispanic/Latino), 1,000 international. Average age 37. *Entrance requirements:* Additional exam requirements/recommendations for international students: Required—TOEFL, TOEIC (Test of English as an International Communication), Berlitz Online English Proficiency Exam, Pearson Test of English, or IELTS. *Application deadline:* Applications are processed on a rolling basis. Application fee: $45. Electronic applications accepted. *Expenses: Tuition:* Full-time $17,160. *Required fees:* $920. One-time fee: $45 full-time. Full-time tuition and fees vary according to course load, degree level, campus/location and program. *Financial support:* Scholarships/grants available. Financial award applicants required to submit FAFSA. *Application contact:* 866-766-0766. Web site: http://www.phoenix.edu/colleges_divisions/business.html.

University of Phoenix–Oregon Campus, School of Business, Tigard, OR 97223. Offers accounting (MBA); business administration (MBA); global management (MBA); human resource management (MM); human resources management (MBA); management (MM); marketing (MBA); public administration (MM). Evening/weekend programs available. *Degree requirements:* For master's, thesis (for some programs). *Entrance requirements:* For master's, minimum undergraduate GPA of 3.0, 3 years of work experience. Additional exam requirements/recommendations for international students: Required—TOEFL (minimum score 550 paper-based; 213 computer-based; 79 iBT). Electronic applications accepted.

University of Phoenix–Philadelphia Campus, School of Business, Wayne, PA 19087-2121. Offers accounting (MBA); business administration (MBA); global management (MBA); human resources management (MBA, MM); management (MM); marketing (MBA); public administration (MM). Evening/weekend programs available. *Degree requirements:* For master's, thesis (for some programs). *Entrance requirements:* For master's, minimum undergraduate GPA of 3.0, 3 years work experience. Additional exam requirements/recommendations for international students: Required—TOEFL (minimum score 550 paper-based; 213 computer-based; 79 iBT). Electronic applications accepted.

University of Phoenix–Phoenix Main Campus, School of Business, Tempe, AZ 85282-2371. Offers accounting (MBA, MS); business administration (MBA); energy management (MBA); global management (MBA); health care management (MBA); human resource management (MBA); management (MM); marketing (MBA); project management (MBA); public administration (MPA); technology management (MBA). Evening/weekend programs available. Postbaccalaureate distance learning degree programs offered. *Students:* 1,151 full-time (531 women); includes 310 minority (99 Black or African American, non-Hispanic/Latino; 10 American Indian or Alaska Native, non-Hispanic/Latino; 39 Asian, non-Hispanic/Latino; 130 Hispanic/Latino; 15 Native Hawaiian or other Pacific Islander, non-Hispanic/Latino; 17 Two or more races, non-Hispanic/Latino), 63 international. Average age 34. *Entrance requirements:* Additional exam requirements/recommendations for international students: Required—TOEFL, TOEIC (Test of English as an International Communication), Berlitz Online English Proficiency Exam, Pearson Test of English, or IELTS. *Application deadline:* Applications are processed on a rolling basis. Application fee: $45. Electronic applications accepted. *Expenses:* Contact institution. *Financial support:* Scholarships/grants available. Financial award applicants required to submit FAFSA. *Application contact:* 866-766-0766. Web site: http://www.phoenix.edu/colleges_divisions/business.html.

University of Phoenix–Pittsburgh Campus, School of Business, Pittsburgh, PA 15276. Offers accounting (MBA); business administration (MBA); global management (MBA); human resources management (MBA, MM); management (MM); marketing (MBA); public administration (MBA, MM). Evening/weekend programs available. *Degree requirements:* For master's, thesis (for some programs). *Entrance requirements:* For master's, minimum undergraduate GPA of 3.0, 3 years work experience. Additional exam requirements/recommendations for international students: Required—TOEFL (minimum score 550 paper-based; 213 computer-based; 79 iBT). Electronic applications accepted.

University of Phoenix–Puerto Rico Campus, School of Business, Guaynabo, PR 00968. Offers accounting (MBA); energy management (MBA); global management (MBA); human resource management (MBA); marketing (MBA); project management (MBA); small business administration (MBA). Evening/weekend programs available. *Degree requirements:* For master's, thesis (for some programs). *Entrance requirements:* For master's, minimum undergraduate GPA of 3.0, 3 years work experience. Additional exam requirements/recommendations for international students: Required—TOEFL (minimum score 550 paper-based; 213 computer-based; 79 iBT). Electronic applications accepted.

University of Phoenix–Raleigh Campus, School of Business, Raleigh, NC 27606. Offers accounting (MBA); business administration (MBA); e-business (MBA); global management (MBA); human resources management (MBA); marketing (MBA).

University of Phoenix–Richmond Campus, School of Business, Richmond, VA 23230. Offers accounting (MBA); business administration (MBA); global management (MBA); human resources management (MBA, MM); management (MM); marketing (MBA); public administration (MBA, MM). Evening/weekend programs available. *Degree requirements:* For master's, thesis (for some programs). *Entrance requirements:* For master's, minimum undergraduate GPA of 3.0, 3 years work experience. Additional exam requirements/recommendations for international students: Required—TOEFL (minimum score 550 paper-based; 213 computer-based; 79 iBT). Electronic applications accepted.

University of Phoenix–Sacramento Valley Campus, School of Business, Sacramento, CA 95833-3632. Offers accounting (MBA); business administration (MBA); global management (MBA); human resources management (MBA, MM); management (MM); marketing (MBA); public administration (MBA, MM). Evening/weekend programs available. *Degree requirements:* For master's, thesis (for some programs). *Entrance requirements:* For master's, minimum undergraduate GPA of 3.0, 3 years work experience. Additional exam requirements/recommendations for international students: Required—TOEFL (minimum score 550 paper-based; 213 computer-based; 79 iBT). Electronic applications accepted.

University of Phoenix–St. Louis Campus, School of Business, St. Louis, MO 63043-4828. Offers accounting (MBA); business administration (MBA); global management (MBA); human resources management (MBA, MM); management (MM); marketing (MBA); public administration (MM). Evening/weekend programs available. *Degree requirements:* For master's, thesis (for some programs). *Entrance requirements:* For master's, 3 years of work experience, minimum undergraduate GPA of 3.0. Additional exam requirements/recommendations for international students: Required—TOEFL (minimum score 550 paper-based; 213 computer-based; 79 iBT). Electronic applications accepted.

University of Phoenix–San Antonio Campus, School of Business, San Antonio, TX 78230. Offers accounting (MBA); business administration (MBA); e-business (MBA); global management (MBA); human resources management (MBA, MM); management (MM); marketing (MBA); public administration (MBA, MM).

University of Phoenix–San Diego Campus, School of Business, San Diego, CA 92123. Offers accounting (MBA); business administration (MBA); global management (MBA); human resources management (MBA, MM); management (MM); marketing (MBA); public administration (MBA). Evening/weekend programs available. *Degree requirements:* For master's, thesis (for some programs). *Entrance requirements:* For master's, 3 years of work experience, minimum undergraduate GPA of 3.0. Additional exam requirements/recommendations for international students: Required—TOEFL (minimum score 550 paper-based; 213 computer-based; 79 iBT). Electronic applications accepted.

University of Phoenix–Savannah Campus, School of Business, Savannah, GA 31405-7400. Offers accounting (MBA); business administration (MBA); global management (MBA); human resources management (MBA, MM); management (MM); marketing (MBA); public administration (MBA, MM).

University of Phoenix–Southern Arizona Campus, School of Business, Tucson, AZ 85711. Offers accountancy (MS); accounting (MBA); business administration (MBA); global management (MBA); human resources management (MBA); management (MM); marketing (MBA). Evening/weekend programs available. *Degree requirements:* For master's, thesis (for some programs). *Entrance requirements:* For master's, minimum undergraduate GPA of 3.0, 3 years of work experience. Additional exam requirements/recommendations for international students: Required—TOEFL (minimum score 550 paper-based; 213 computer-based; 79 iBT). Electronic applications accepted.

University of Phoenix–Southern California Campus, School of Business, Costa Mesa, CA 92626. Offers accounting (MIS); business administration (MBA); energy management (MBA); global management (MBA); health care management (MBA); human resource management (MBA); management (MM); marketing (MBA); project management (MBA); public administration (MPA); technology management (MBA). Evening/weekend programs available. Postbaccalaureate distance learning degree programs offered. *Students:* 699 full-time (341 women); includes 318 minority (124 Black or African American, non-Hispanic/Latino; 4 American Indian or Alaska Native, non-Hispanic/Latino; 44 Asian, non-Hispanic/Latino; 124 Hispanic/Latino; 15 Native Hawaiian or other Pacific Islander, non-Hispanic/Latino; 7 Two or more races, non-Hispanic/Latino), 29 international. Average age 38. *Entrance requirements:* Additional exam requirements/recommendations for international students: Required—TOEFL, TOEIC (Test of English as an International Communication), Berlitz Online English Proficiency Exam, Pearson Test of English, or IELTS. *Application deadline:* Applications are processed on a rolling basis. Application fee: $45. Electronic applications accepted. *Expenses:* Contact institution. *Financial support:* Scholarships/grants available. Financial award applicants required to submit FAFSA. *Application contact:* 866-766-0766. Web site: http://www.phoenix.edu/colleges_divisions/business.html.

University of Phoenix–Southern Colorado Campus, School of Business, Colorado Springs, CO 80919-2335. Offers accounting (MBA); business administration (MBA); global management (MBA); human resources management (MBA, MM); management (MM); marketing (MBA); public administration (MM). Evening/weekend programs available. *Degree requirements:* For master's, thesis (for some programs). *Entrance requirements:* For master's, minimum undergraduate GPA of 3.0, 3 years of work experience. Additional exam requirements/recommendations for international students: Required—TOEFL (minimum score 550 paper-based; 213 computer-based; 79 iBT). Electronic applications accepted.

University of Phoenix–South Florida Campus, School of Business, Fort Lauderdale, FL 33309. Offers accounting (MBA); business administration (MBA); global management (MBA); human resource management (MBA); human resources management (MM); management (MM); marketing (MBA); public administration (MBA, MM). Evening/weekend programs available. *Degree requirements:* For master's, thesis (for some programs). *Entrance requirements:* For master's, minimum undergraduate GPA of 3.0, 3 years work experience. Additional exam requirements/recommendations for international students: Required—TOEFL (minimum score 550 paper-based; 213 computer-based; 79 iBT). Electronic applications accepted.

University of Phoenix–Springfield Campus, School of Business, Springfield, MO 65804-7211. Offers accounting (MBA); business administration (MBA); global management (MBA); human resources management (MBA, MM); management (MM); marketing (MBA); public administration (MBA, MM).

University of Phoenix–Tulsa Campus, School of Business, Tulsa, OK 74134-1412. Offers accounting (MBA); business (MM); business administration (MBA); global management (MBA); human resources management (MBA); marketing (MBA). Evening/weekend programs available. *Degree requirements:* For master's, thesis (for some programs). *Entrance requirements:* For master's, minimum undergraduate GPA of 3.0, 3 years work experience. Additional exam requirements/recommendations for international students: Required—TOEFL (minimum score 550 paper-based; 213 computer-based; 79 iBT).

University of Phoenix–Utah Campus, School of Business, Salt Lake City, UT 84123-4617. Offers accounting (MBA); business administration (MBA); global management (MBA); human resource management (MBA, MM); management (MM); marketing (MBA); technology management (MBA). Evening/weekend programs available. *Degree requirements:* For master's, thesis (for some programs). *Entrance requirements:* For master's, minimum undergraduate GPA of 3.0, 3 years of work experience. Additional exam requirements/recommendations for international students: Required—TOEFL (minimum score 550 paper-based; 213 computer-based; 79 iBT). Electronic applications accepted.

University of Phoenix–Vancouver Campus, John Sperling School of Business, College of Graduate Business and Management, Burnaby, BC V5C 6G9, Canada. Offers accounting (MBA); business administration (MBA); global management (MBA); human resources management (MBA, MM); marketing (MBA). Evening/weekend programs available. *Degree requirements:* For master's, thesis (for some programs). *Entrance requirements:* For master's, minimum undergraduate GPA of 3.0, 3 years of work experience. Additional exam requirements/recommendations for international students: Required—TOEFL (minimum score 550 paper-based; 213 computer-based; 79 iBT). Electronic applications accepted.

University of Phoenix–West Florida Campus, School of Business, Temple Terrace, FL 33637. Offers accounting (MBA); business administration (MBA); global management (MBA); human resources management (MBA, MM); management (MM); marketing (MBA); public administration (MBA, MM). Evening/weekend programs available. *Degree requirements:* For master's, thesis (for some programs). *Entrance requirements:* For master's, 3 years of work experience, minimum undergraduate GPA of 3.0. Additional exam requirements/recommendations for international students: Required—TOEFL (minimum score 550 paper-based; 213 computer-based; 79 iBT). Electronic applications accepted.

University of Pittsburgh, Katz Graduate School of Business, Doctoral Program in Business Administration, Pittsburgh, PA 15260. Offers accounting (PhD); finance (PhD); information systems (PhD); marketing (PhD); operations/decision sciences/artificial intelligence (PhD); organizational behavior and human resource management (PhD); strategic planning (PhD). *Accreditation:* AACSB. *Faculty:* 54 full-time (16 women). *Students:* 51 full-time (21 women); includes 9 minority (4 Black or African American, non-Hispanic/Latino; 4 Asian, non-Hispanic/Latino; 1 Hispanic/Latino), 23 international. 373 applicants, 7% accepted, 10 enrolled. In 2011, 6 doctorates awarded. *Degree requirements:* For doctorate, comprehensive exam, thesis/dissertation. *Entrance requirements:* For doctorate, GMAT or GRE. Additional exam requirements/recommendations for international students: Required—TOEFL. *Application deadline:* For fall admission, 2/1 priority date for domestic students, 2/1 for international students. Applications are processed on a rolling basis. Application fee: $50. Electronic applications accepted. *Expenses:* Tuition, state resident: full-time $18,774; part-time $760 per credit. Tuition, nonresident: full-time $30,736; part-time $1258 per credit. *Required fees:* $740; $200 per term. Tuition and fees vary according to program. *Financial support:* In 2011–12, 38 students received support, including 29 research assistantships with full tuition reimbursements available (averaging $19,400 per year), 10 teaching assistantships with full tuition reimbursements available (averaging $24,700 per year); fellowships, Federal Work-Study, scholarships/grants, health care benefits, and unspecified assistantships also available. Financial award application deadline: 2/1. *Faculty research:* Accounting statements and reporting, corporate finance, information systems processes, structures and decision-making, consumer behavior and marketing models. *Total annual research expenditures:* $254,031. *Unit head:* Dr. Dennis Galletta, Director, 412-648-1699, Fax: 412-624-3633, E-mail: galletta@katz.pitt.edu. *Application contact:* Carrie Woods, Assistant Director, 412-648-1525, Fax: 412-624-3633, E-mail: cawoods@katz.pitt.edu. Web site: http://www.business.pitt.edu/katz/phd/.

University of Pittsburgh, Katz Graduate School of Business, Master of Business Administration Programs, Pittsburgh , PA 15260. Offers finance (MBA); information systems (MBA); marketing (MBA); operations management (MBA); organizational behavior and human resource management (MBA); organizational leadership (Certificate); strategy, environment and organizations (MBA); technology, innovation and entrepreneurship (Certificate); MBA/JD; MBA/MIB; MBA/MPIA; MBA/MSE; MBA/MSIS; MID/MBA. *Accreditation:* AACSB. Part-time and evening/weekend programs available. *Faculty:* 62 full-time (17 women), 21 part-time/adjunct (4 women). *Students:* 179 full-time (63 women), 572 part-time (373 women); includes 69 minority (29 Black or African American, non-Hispanic/Latino; 24 Asian, non-Hispanic/Latino; 16 Hispanic/Latino), 83 international. Average age 29. 391 applicants, 42% accepted, 78 enrolled. *Degree requirements:* For master's, minimum GPA of 3.0. *Entrance requirements:* For master's, GMAT, recommendations, undergraduate transcripts, essay, resume, interview, bachelor's degree. Additional exam requirements/recommendations for international students: Required—TOEFL (minimum score 600 paper, 250 computer, 100 iBT) or IELTS. *Application deadline:* For fall admission, 4/1 priority date for domestic students, 2/1 for international students. Application fee: $50. Electronic applications accepted. *Expenses:* Tuition, state resident: full-time $18,774; part-time $760 per credit. Tuition, nonresident: full-time $30,736; part-time $1258 per credit. *Required fees:* $740; $200 per term. Tuition and fees vary according to program. *Financial support:* In 2011–12, 58 students received support. Career-related internships or fieldwork and scholarships/grants available. Financial award application deadline: 3/1; financial award applicants required to submit FAFSA. *Faculty research:* Accounting statements and reporting, corporate finance, information systems processes, structures and decision-making, consumer behavior and marketing models. *Unit head:* William T. Valenta, Assistant Dean/Director, 412-648-1610, Fax: 412-648-1659, E-mail: wtvalenta@katz.pitt.edu. *Application contact:* Thomas Keller, Director of MBA Admissions, 412-648-1700, Fax: 412-648-1659, E-mail: mba@katz.pitt.edu. Web site: http://www.business.pitt.edu/katz/mba/.

University of Portland, Dr. Robert B. Pamplin, Jr. School of Business, Portland, OR 97203-5798. Offers business administration (MBA); entrepreneurship (MBA); finance (MBA, MS); health care management (MBA); marketing (MBA); nonprofit management (EMBA); operations and technology management (MBA); sustainability (MBA). *Accreditation:* AACSB. Part-time and evening/weekend programs available. *Faculty:* 13 full-time (1 woman), 8 part-time/adjunct (1 woman). *Students:* 50 full-time (13 women), 90 part-time (41 women); includes 19 minority (1 Black or African American, non-Hispanic/Latino; 1 American Indian or Alaska Native, non-Hispanic/Latino; 8 Asian, non-Hispanic/Latino; 5 Hispanic/Latino; 2 Native Hawaiian or other Pacific Islander, non-Hispanic/Latino; 2 Two or more races, non-Hispanic/Latino), 18 international. Average age 31. In 2011, 54 master's awarded. *Entrance requirements:* For master's, GMAT, minimum GPA of 3.0, resume, 2 letters of recommendation. Additional exam requirements/recommendations for international students: Required—TOEFL (minimum score 570 paper-based; 89 iBT), IELTS (minimum score 7). *Application deadline:* For fall admission, 7/15 priority date for domestic students, 7/15 for international students; for spring admission, 12/15 priority date for domestic students, 12/15 for international students. Applications are processed on a rolling basis. Application fee: $50. *Expenses:* Contact institution. *Financial support:* Federal Work-Study, scholarships/grants, and tuition waivers (partial) available. Support available to part-time students. Financial award application deadline: 3/1; financial award applicants required to submit FAFSA. *Unit head:* Dr. Howard Feldman, Associate Dean, 503-943-7224, E-mail: feldman@up.edu. *Application contact:* Melissa McCarthy, Academic Specialist, 503-943-7225, E-mail: mccarthy@up.edu. Web site: http://business.up.edu/.

University of Puerto Rico, Río Piedras, College of Business Administration, San Juan, PR 00931-3300. Offers accounting (MBA); finance (MBA, PhD); general business (MBA); human resources management (MBA); international trade and business (MBA, PhD); marketing (MBA); operations management (MBA); quantitative methods (MBA). *Accreditation:* ACBSP. Part-time programs available. *Degree requirements:* For master's, comprehensive exam, thesis or alternative, research project. *Entrance requirements:* For master's, GMAT or PAEG, minimum GPA of 3.0, letter of recommendation; for doctorate, GMAT, PAEG, minimum GPA of 3.0, master degree. *Faculty research:* Management.

University of Rhode Island, Graduate School, College of Business Administration, Kingston, RI 02881. Offers accounting (MS); business administration (MBA, PhD), including finance and insurance (PhD), management (PhD), marketing (PhD), operations and supply chain management (MBA); finance (MBA); general business (MBA); management (MBA); marketing (MBA); supply chain management (MBA). *Accreditation:* AACSB. Part-time and evening/weekend programs available. *Faculty:* 56 full-time (15 women), 8 part-time/adjunct (4 women). *Students:* 93 full-time (40 women), 226 part-time (90 women); includes 35 minority (7 Black or African American, non-Hispanic/Latino; 1 American Indian or Alaska Native, non-Hispanic/Latino; 15 Asian, non-Hispanic/Latino; 11 Hispanic/Latino; 1 Two or more races, non-Hispanic/Latino), 24 international. In 2011, 78 master's, 3 doctorates awarded. *Degree requirements:* For master's, comprehensive exam (for some programs), thesis optional; for doctorate, comprehensive exam, thesis/dissertation. *Entrance requirements:* For master's, GMAT or GRE, 2 letters of recommendation, resume; for doctorate, GMAT or GRE, 3 letters of recommendation, resume. Additional exam requirements/recommendations for international students: Required—TOEFL (minimum score 575 paper-based; 233 computer-based; 91 iBT). Application fee: $65. Electronic applications accepted. *Expenses:* Tuition, state resident: full-time $10,432; part-time $580 per credit hour. Tuition, nonresident: full-time $23,130; part-time $1285 per credit hour. *Required fees:* $1362; $36 per credit hour. $35 per semester. One-time fee: $130. *Financial support:* In 2011–12, 13 teaching assistantships with full and partial tuition reimbursements (averaging $13,020 per year) were awarded. Financial award applicants required to submit FAFSA. *Unit head:* Dr. Mark Higgins, Dean, 401-874-4244, Fax: 401-874-4312, E-mail: markhiggins@uri.edu. *Application contact:* Lisa Lancellotta, Coordinator, MBA Programs, 401-874-4241, Fax: 401-874-4312, E-mail: mba@uri.edu. Web site: http://www.cba.uri.edu/.

University of San Francisco, School of Management, Masagung Graduate School of Management, Program in Business Administration, San Francisco, CA 94117-1080. Offers business economics (MBA); e-business (MBA); entrepreneurship (MBA); finance (MBA); international business (MBA); management (MBA); marketing (MBA); telecommunications management and policy (MBA); JD/MBA; MSN/MBA. *Accreditation:* AACSB. *Faculty:* 18 full-time (4 women), 18 part-time/adjunct (9 women). *Students:* 247 full-time (122 women), 9 part-time (3 women); includes 85 minority (5 Black or African American, non-Hispanic/Latino; 55 Asian, non-Hispanic/Latino; 16 Hispanic/Latino; 1 Native Hawaiian or other Pacific Islander, non-Hispanic/Latino; 8 Two or more races, non-Hispanic/Latino), 38 international. Average age 29. 552 applicants, 55% accepted, 99 enrolled. In 2011, 173 master's awarded. *Entrance requirements:* For master's, GMAT, minimum undergraduate GPA of 3.2. Additional exam requirements/recommendations for international students: Required—TOEFL. *Application deadline:* For fall admission, 7/1 priority date for domestic students; for spring admission, 11/30 for domestic students. Applications are processed on a rolling basis. Application fee: $55 ($65 for international students). *Expenses: Tuition:* Full-time $20,070; part-time $1115 per unit. Tuition and fees vary according to course load, campus/location and program. *Financial support:* In 2011–12, 33 students received support. Fellowships available. Financial award application deadline: 3/2; financial award applicants required to submit FAFSA. *Faculty research:* International financial markets, technology transfer licensing, international marketing, strategic planning. *Total annual research expenditures:* $50,000. *Unit head:* Kelly Brookes, Director, 415-422-2221, Fax: 415-422-6315. *Application contact:* Director, MBA Program, 415-422-2221, Fax: 415-422-6315, E-mail: mba@usfca.edu.

University of Saskatchewan, College of Graduate Studies and Research, Edwards School of Business, Department of Management and Marketing, Saskatoon, SK S7N 5A2, Canada. Offers marketing (M Sc). Part-time programs available. *Degree requirements:* For master's, thesis. *Entrance requirements:* For master's, GMAT. Additional exam requirements/recommendations for international students: Required—TOEFL.

The University of Scranton, College of Graduate and Continuing Education, Program in Business Administration, Scranton, PA 18510. Offers accounting (MBA); finance (MBA); general business administration (MBA); health care management (MBA); international business (MBA); management information systems (MBA); marketing (MBA); operations management (MBA). *Accreditation:* AACSB. Part-time and evening/weekend programs available. Postbaccalaureate distance learning degree programs offered (no on-campus study). *Faculty:* 34 full-time (8 women). *Students:* 276 full-time (94 women), 243 part-time (88 women); includes 14 minority (10 Black or African American, non-Hispanic/Latino; 3 Asian, non-Hispanic/Latino; 1 Hispanic/Latino), 49 international. Average age 33. 358 applicants, 80% accepted. In 2011, 101 master's awarded. *Degree requirements:* For master's, capstone experience. *Entrance requirements:* For master's, GMAT, minimum GPA of 2.75. Additional exam requirements/recommendations for international students: Required—TOEFL (minimum score 500 paper-based; 173 computer-based), IELTS (minimum score 5.5). *Application deadline:* Applications are processed on a rolling basis. Application fee: $0. *Financial support:* In 2011–12, 12 students received support, including 12 teaching assistantships with full and partial tuition reimbursements available (averaging $8,433 per year); fellowships, career-related internships or fieldwork, Federal Work-Study, and unspecified assistantships also available. Support available to part-time students. Financial award application deadline: 3/1. *Faculty research:* Financial markets, strategic impact of total quality management, internal accounting controls, consumer preference, information systems and the Internet. *Unit head:* Dr. Murli Rajan, Director, 570-941-4043, Fax: 570-941-4342. *Application contact:* Joseph M. Roback, Director of Admissions, 570-941-4385, Fax: 570-941-5928, E-mail: robackj2@scranton.edu. Web site: http://www.academic.scranton.edu/department/mba/.

University of Sioux Falls, Vucurevich School of Business, Sioux Falls, SD 57105-1699. Offers entrepreneurial leadership (MBA); general management (MBA); health care management (MBA); marketing (MBA). Part-time and evening/weekend programs available. *Faculty:* 8 full-time (3 women), 7 part-time/adjunct (2 women). *Students:* 119 part-time (60 women); includes 2 minority (1 Black or African American, non-Hispanic/Latino; 1 Asian, non-Hispanic/Latino). 50 applicants, 90% accepted, 45 enrolled. *Degree requirements:* For master's, project. *Entrance requirements:* For master's, minimum GPA of 3.0. Additional exam requirements/recommendations for international students: Required—TOEFL. Application fee: $25. *Expenses:* Contact institution. *Financial support:* Institutionally sponsored loans, scholarships/grants, and tuition waivers (full) available. Financial award applicants required to submit FAFSA. *Unit head:* Rebecca T. Murdock, MBA Director, 605-575-2068, E-mail: mba@usiouxfalls.edu. *Application contact:* Student Contact, 605-331-6680. Web site: http://www.usiouxfalls.edu/mba.

University of South Africa, College of Economic and Management Sciences, Pretoria, South Africa. Offers accounting (D Admin, D Com); accounting science (DA); auditing (D Admin, D Com); business administration (M Tech); business economics (D Admin); business leadership (DBL); business management (D Admin, D Com); economic management analysis (M Tech); economics (D Admin, D Com, PhD); human resource development (M Tech); industrial psychology (D Admin, D Com, PhD); logistics (D Com); marketing (M Tech); public administration (D Admin, D Com, DPA, PhD); public management (M Tech); quantitative management (D Admin, D Com); real estate (M Tech); statistics (D Admin, PhD); tourism management (D Admin, D Com); transport economics (D Admin, D Com).

University of South Florida, Graduate School, College of Business, Department of Business Administration, Tampa, FL 33620-9951. Offers entrepreneurship (MBA); information systems (PhD); leadership and organizational effectiveness (MSM); management and organization (MBA); management information systems (MS); marketing (PhD). *Accreditation:* AACSB. Part-time and evening/weekend programs available. *Faculty:* 4 full-time (2 women), 1 part-time/adjunct (0 women). *Students:* 139 full-time (47 women), 156 part-time (55 women); includes 60 minority (11 Black or African American, non-Hispanic/Latino; 1 American Indian or Alaska Native, non-Hispanic/Latino; 22 Asian, non-Hispanic/Latino; 25 Hispanic/Latino; 1 Two or more races, non-Hispanic/Latino), 68 international. Average age 30. 300 applicants, 44% accepted, 92 enrolled. In 2011, 120 master's awarded. *Degree requirements:* For master's, comprehensive exam, thesis (for some programs); for doctorate, comprehensive exam, thesis/dissertation, 90 credit hours, minimum GPA of 3.0. *Entrance requirements:* For master's, GMAT (preferred) or GRE, minimum GPA of 3.0 in last 60 hours of course work, at least two letters of recommendation, statement of purpose, two years of significant professional work experience, resume; for doctorate, GMAT (preferred) or GRE, minimum GPA of 3.0 in last 60 hours of course work, at least two letters of recommendation, personal statement, interview. Additional exam requirements/recommendations for international students: Required—TOEFL (minimum score 550 paper-based; 213 computer-based; 79 iBT) or IELTS (minimum score 6.5). *Application deadline:* For fall admission, 6/1 for domestic students, 1/2 for international students; for spring admission, 10/15 for domestic students, 6/1 for international students. Application fee: $30. *Financial support:* Scholarships/grants, health care benefits, and unspecified assistantships available. Financial award applicants required to submit FAFSA. *Unit head:* Dr. Jacqueline Reck, Associate Dean, 813-974-6721, Fax: 813-974-4518, E-mail: jreck@usf.edu. *Application contact:* Irene Hurst, Assistant Director, Graduate Studies, 813-974-3335, Fax: 813-974-4518, E-mail: hurst@usf.edu. Web site: http://www.coba.usf.edu.

University of South Florida, Graduate School, College of Business, Department of Marketing, Tampa, FL 33620-9951. Offers business administration (PhD), including marketing; marketing (MSM). Part-time and evening/weekend programs available. *Faculty:* 10 full-time (4 women), 5 part-time/adjunct (1 woman). *Students:* 30 full-time (16 women), 14 part-time (13 women); includes 7 minority (1 Black or African American, non-Hispanic/Latino; 1 American Indian or Alaska Native, non-Hispanic/Latino; 1 Asian, non-Hispanic/Latino; 3 Hispanic/Latino; 1 Two or more races, non-Hispanic/Latino), 16 international. Average age 28. 59 applicants, 44% accepted, 18 enrolled. In 2011, 17 master's, 1 doctorate awarded. Terminal master's awarded for partial completion of doctoral program. *Degree requirements:* For master's, thesis or alternative; for doctorate, comprehensive exam, thesis/dissertation, 90 credit hours, minimum GPA of 3.0. *Entrance requirements:* For master's, GMAT (minimum score of 500), minimum GPA of 3.0 in last 60 hours, two letters of recommendation; for doctorate, GMAT (minimum score of 500), minimum GPA of 3.0 in last 60 hours, two letters of recommendation, personal statement, interview. Additional exam requirements/recommendations for international students: Required—TOEFL (minimum score 550 paper-based; 213 computer-based; 79 iBT) or IELTS (minimum score 6.5). *Application deadline:* For fall admission, 6/1 for domestic students, 1/2 for international students; for spring admission, 10/15 for domestic students, 6/1 for international students. Applications are processed on a rolling basis. Application fee: $30. Electronic applications accepted. *Financial support:* In 2011–12, 11 students received support, including 5 research assistantships (averaging $14,943 per year), 6 teaching assistantships (averaging $11,972 per year); health care benefits and unspecified assistantships also available. *Faculty research:* Consumer behavior, supply chain management, reverse logistics (product returns), pricing, branding. *Total annual research expenditures:* $84,694. *Unit head:* Dr. Miriam Stamps, Chair, 813-974-6205, Fax: 813-974-6175, E-mail: mstamps@usf.edu. *Application contact:* Dr. Paul Solomon, Program Director, 813-974-5995, Fax: 813-974-6175, E-mail: psolomon@usf.edu. Web site: http://business.usf.edu/faculty/marketing/index.asp.

Marketing

The University of Tampa, John H. Sykes College of Business, Tampa, FL 33606-1490. Offers accounting (MS); entrepreneurship (MBA); finance (MBA, MS); information systems management (MBA); innovation management (MBA); international business (MBA); marketing (MBA, MS); nonprofit management (MBA). *Accreditation:* AACSB. Part-time and evening/weekend programs available. *Faculty:* 38 full-time (14 women), 5 part-time/adjunct (1 woman). *Students:* 161 full-time (65 women), 193 part-time (82 women); includes 65 minority (11 Black or African American, non-Hispanic/Latino; 1 American Indian or Alaska Native, non-Hispanic/Latino; 8 Asian, non-Hispanic/Latino; 39 Hispanic/Latino; 2 Native Hawaiian or other Pacific Islander, non-Hispanic/Latino; 4 Two or more races, non-Hispanic/Latino), 58 international. Average age 29. 837 applicants, 41% accepted, 196 enrolled. In 2011, 259 degrees awarded. *Degree requirements:* For master's, capstone. *Entrance requirements:* For master's, GMAT or GRE, 4-year undergraduate degree, minimum GPA of 3.0, professional experience (for Executive MBA). Additional exam requirements/recommendations for international students: Required—TOEFL (minimum score 577 paper-based; 230 computer-based; 90 iBT); Recommended—IELTS (minimum score 7.5). *Application deadline:* Applications are processed on a rolling basis. Application fee: $40. Electronic applications accepted. *Expenses: Tuition:* Full-time $8320; part-time $520 per credit hour. *Required fees:* $40 per semester. Tuition and fees vary according to program. *Financial support:* In 2011–12, 124 students received support. Career-related internships or fieldwork, scholarships/grants, unspecified assistantships, and grants available. Financial award applicants required to submit FAFSA. *Faculty research:* Job market signaling, on-line shopping behaviors and social media, the Tampa Bay economy, digital literacy, entrepreneurship in small businesses. *Unit head:* Dennis Nostrand, Vice President, Enrollment/Admissions, 813-257-1808, E-mail: dnostrand@ut.edu. *Application contact:* Charlene Tobie, Associate Director of Admissions, 813-257-3566, E-mail: ctobie@ut.edu. Web site: http://ut.edu/graduate.

The University of Tennessee, Graduate School, College of Business Administration, Program in Business Administration, Knoxville, TN 37996. Offers accounting (PhD); finance (MBA, PhD); logistics and transportation (MBA, PhD); management (PhD); marketing (MBA, PhD); operations management (MBA); professional business administration (MBA); statistics (PhD); JD/MBA; MS/MBA; Pharm D/MBA. Pharm D/MBA offered jointly with The University of Tennessee Health Science Center. *Accreditation:* AACSB. Postbaccalaureate distance learning degree programs offered. *Degree requirements:* For master's, thesis or alternative; for doctorate, thesis/dissertation. *Entrance requirements:* For master's and doctorate, GMAT, minimum GPA of 2.7. Additional exam requirements/recommendations for international students: Required—TOEFL. Electronic applications accepted. *Expenses:* Tuition, state resident: full-time $8332; part-time $464 per credit hour. Tuition, nonresident: full-time $25,174; part-time $1400 per credit hour. *Required fees:* $1162; $56 per credit hour. Tuition and fees vary according to program.

The University of Texas at Arlington, Graduate School, College of Business, Department of Marketing, Arlington, TX 76019. Offers marketing (PhD); marketing research (MS). Part-time and evening/weekend programs available. *Faculty:* 10 full-time (2 women). *Students:* 30 full-time (19 women), 18 part-time (7 women); includes 6 minority (1 Black or African American, non-Hispanic/Latino; 3 Asian, non-Hispanic/Latino; 2 Hispanic/Latino), 20 international. 66 applicants, 50% accepted, 23 enrolled. In 2011, 13 master's, 2 doctorates awarded. *Degree requirements:* For master's, thesis optional; for doctorate, comprehensive exam, thesis/dissertation. *Entrance requirements:* For master's and doctorate, GMAT, GRE. Additional exam requirements/recommendations for international students: Required—TOEFL (minimum score 550 paper-based; 213 computer-based; 79 iBT). *Application deadline:* For fall admission, 6/1 for domestic students, 4/1 for international students; for spring admission, 10/15 for domestic students, 9/15 for international students. Applications are processed on a rolling basis. Application fee: $40 ($70 for international students). Electronic applications accepted. *Financial support:* In 2011–12, 8 teaching assistantships (averaging $17,425 per year) were awarded; career-related internships or fieldwork, scholarships/grants, and unspecified assistantships also available. Support available to part-time students. Financial award application deadline: 6/1; financial award applicants required to submit FAFSA. *Faculty research:* Marketing strategy, marketing research, international marketing. *Total annual research expenditures:* $30,000. *Unit head:* Dr. Greg Frazier, Interim Chair, 817-272-0264, Fax: 817-272-2854, E-mail: frazier@uta.edu. *Application contact:* Dr. Robert Rogers, MS Program Director, 817-272-2340, Fax: 817-272-2854, E-mail: msmr@uta.edu. Web site: http://wweb.uta.edu/marketing/.

The University of Texas at Arlington, Graduate School, College of Business, Program in Business Administration, Arlington, TX 76019. Offers accounting (PhD); business statistics (PhD); finance (MBA, PhD); information systems (MBA, PhD); management (MBA, PhD); marketing (MBA, PhD); operations management (MBA, PhD); real estate (MBA). *Accreditation:* AACSB. Part-time and evening/weekend programs available. *Students:* 505 full-time (189 women), 369 part-time (140 women); includes 199 minority (58 Black or African American, non-Hispanic/Latino; 2 American Indian or Alaska Native, non-Hispanic/Latino; 70 Asian, non-Hispanic/Latino; 56 Hispanic/Latino; 1 Native Hawaiian or other Pacific Islander, non-Hispanic/Latino; 12 Two or more races, non-Hispanic/Latino), 306 international. 416 applicants, 81% accepted, 234 enrolled. In 2011, 495 master's, 3 doctorates awarded. *Degree requirements:* For master's, thesis optional; for doctorate, comprehensive exam, thesis/dissertation. *Entrance requirements:* For master's, GMAT or GRE; for doctorate, GMAT, minimum GPA of 3.0 (undergraduate), 3.4 (graduate); 30 hours of graduate course work. Additional exam requirements/recommendations for international students: Required—TOEFL (minimum score 550 paper-based; 213 computer-based; 79 iBT). *Application deadline:* For fall admission, 6/1 for domestic students, 4/1 for international students; for spring admission, 10/15 for domestic students, 9/15 for international students. Applications are processed on a rolling basis. Application fee: $40 ($70 for international students). Electronic applications accepted. *Financial support:* Career-related internships or fieldwork, scholarships/grants, and unspecified assistantships available. Support available to part-time students. Financial award application deadline: 6/1; financial award applicants required to submit FAFSA. *Unit head:* Dr. Edmund Prater, Director of PhD Programs, 817-272-2131, Fax: 817-272-5799. *Application contact:* Melanie McGee, Director of MBA Program, 817-272-3005, Fax: 817-272-5799, E-mail: mwmcgee@uta.edu.

The University of Texas at Austin, Graduate School, McCombs School of Business, Department of Marketing, Austin, TX 78712-1111. Offers MBA, PhD. *Degree requirements:* For doctorate, comprehensive exam, thesis/dissertation. *Entrance requirements:* For doctorate, GMAT or GRE. *Application deadline:* For fall admission, 2/1 for domestic students. Application fee: $50 ($75 for international students). Electronic applications accepted. *Financial support:* Fellowships with full tuition reimbursements, teaching assistantships with partial tuition reimbursements, and tuition waivers (partial) available. Financial award application deadline: 2/1. *Faculty research:* Internet marketing, strategic marketing, buy behavior. *Unit head:* Wayne Hoyer, Chair, 512-471-1128, E-mail: wayne.hoyer@mccombs.utexas.edu. *Application contact:* Raj Raghunathan, Graduate Adviser, 512-471-2987, E-mail: raj.raghunathan@mccombs.utexas.edu. Web site: http://www.mccombs.utexas.edu/departments/marketing/.

The University of Texas at Dallas, Naveen Jindal School of Management, Program in Management and Administrative Sciences, Richardson, TX 75080. Offers electronic commerce (MS); finance (MS); healthcare administration (MS); information systems (MS); innovation and entrepreneurship (MS); international management (MS); leadership in organizations (MS); marketing (MS); operations (MS); organizations (MS); real estate (MS); strategy (MS). *Accreditation:* AACSB. Part-time and evening/weekend programs available. *Faculty:* 26 full-time (6 women), 9 part-time/adjunct (2 women). *Students:* 128 full-time (69 women), 169 part-time (95 women); includes 76 minority (18 Black or African American, non-Hispanic/Latino; 1 American Indian or Alaska Native, non-Hispanic/Latino; 37 Asian, non-Hispanic/Latino; 15 Hispanic/Latino; 1 Native Hawaiian or other Pacific Islander, non-Hispanic/Latino; 4 Two or more races, non-Hispanic/Latino), 77 international. Average age 34. 220 applicants, 63% accepted, 68 enrolled. In 2011, 58 master's awarded. *Degree requirements:* For master's, thesis optional. *Entrance requirements:* For master's, GMAT. Additional exam requirements/recommendations for international students: Required—TOEFL (minimum score 550 paper-based; 215 computer-based). *Application deadline:* For fall admission, 7/15 for domestic students, 5/1 for international students; for spring admission, 11/15 for domestic students, 9/1 for international students. Applications are processed on a rolling basis. Application fee: $50 ($100 for international students). Electronic applications accepted. *Expenses:* Tuition, state resident: full-time $11,170; part-time $620.56 per credit hour. Tuition, nonresident: full-time $20,212; part-time $1122.89 per credit hour. *Financial support:* In 2011–12, 68 students received support, including 7 teaching assistantships with partial tuition reimbursements available (averaging $16,200 per year); research assistantships with partial tuition reimbursements available, career-related internships or fieldwork, Federal Work-Study, institutionally sponsored loans, scholarships/grants, and unspecified assistantships also available. Support available to part-time students. Financial award application deadline: 4/30; financial award applicants required to submit FAFSA. *Faculty research:* Integrated and detailed knowledge of functional areas of management, analytical tools for effective appraisal and decision-making. *Unit head:* Dr. Gregory Dess, Area Coordinator, 972-883-4439, E-mail: gdess@utdallas.edu. *Application contact:* James Parker, Assistant Director, 972-883-5842, E-mail: jparker@utdallas.edu. Web site: http://jindal.utdallas.edu/academic-areas/organizations-strategy-and-international-management/.

The University of Texas at Dallas, Naveen Jindal School of Management, Programs in Management Science, Richardson, TX 75080. Offers accounting (PhD); finance (PhD); information systems (PhD); marketing (PhD); operations management (PhD). *Accreditation:* AACSB. Part-time and evening/weekend programs available. *Faculty:* 14 full-time (4 women). *Students:* 75 full-time (30 women), 8 part-time (4 women); includes 5 minority (4 Asian, non-Hispanic/Latino; 1 Two or more races, non-Hispanic/Latino), 71 international. Average age 31. 224 applicants, 11% accepted, 20 enrolled. In 2011, 10 doctorates awarded. *Degree requirements:* For doctorate, thesis/dissertation. *Entrance requirements:* For doctorate, GMAT, minimum GPA of 3.0. Additional exam requirements/recommendations for international students: Required—TOEFL (minimum score 550 paper-based; 215 computer-based). *Application deadline:* For fall admission, 7/15 for domestic students, 5/1 for international students; for spring admission, 11/15 for domestic students, 9/1 for international students. Applications are processed on a rolling basis. Application fee: $50 ($100 for international students). Electronic applications accepted. *Expenses:* Tuition, state resident: full-time $11,170; part-time $620.56 per credit hour. Tuition, nonresident: full-time $20,212; part-time $1122.89 per credit hour. *Financial support:* In 2011–12, 76 students received support, including 3 research assistantships with partial tuition reimbursements available (averaging $21,600 per year), 68 teaching assistantships with partial tuition reimbursements available (averaging $16,162 per year); career-related internships or fieldwork, Federal Work-Study, institutionally sponsored loans, scholarships/grants, and unspecified assistantships also available. Support available to part-time students. Financial award application deadline: 4/30; financial award applicants required to submit FAFSA. *Faculty research:* Empirical generalizations in marketing, diffusion of generations of technology, stochastic brand-choice theory, acceptance of trade deals by supermarkets, nonparametric estimations of market share response. *Unit head:* Dr. Sumit Sarkar, Program Director, 972-883-2745, Fax: 972-883-5977, E-mail: som_phd.@utdallas.edu. *Application contact:* LeeAnne Sloane, Coordinator, 972-883-2745, Fax: 972-883-5977, E-mail: som_phd@utdallas.edu. Web site: http://jindal.utdallas.edu/academic-programs/phd-programs/management-science/.

The University of Texas at San Antonio, College of Business, General Business Program, San Antonio, TX 78249-0617. Offers business (MBA); business administration (PhD), including accounting, business administration, finance, information technology, management and organization studies, marketing; information systems (MBA); international business (MBA); management accounting (MBA); management of technology (MBA); marketing management (MBA); taxation (MBA). *Students:* 170 full-time (52 women), 120 part-time (49 women); includes 90 minority (14 Black or African American, non-Hispanic/Latino; 2 American Indian or Alaska Native, non-Hispanic/Latino; 15 Asian, non-Hispanic/Latino; 55 Hispanic/Latino; 1 Native Hawaiian or other Pacific Islander, non-Hispanic/Latino; 3 Two or more races, non-Hispanic/Latino), 37 international. Average age 32. 395 applicants, 45% accepted, 133 enrolled. In 2011, 95 master's, 8 doctorates awarded. *Entrance requirements:* Additional exam requirements/recommendations for international students: Required—TOEFL (minimum score 500 paper-based; 61 iBT), IELTS (minimum score 5). *Application deadline:* For fall admission, 7/1 for domestic students, 4/1 for international students; for spring admission, 11/1 for domestic students, 9/1 for international students. Application fee: $45 ($85 for international students). *Expenses:* Tuition, state resident: full-time $3148; part-time $2176 per semester. Tuition, nonresident: full-time $8782; part-time $5932 per semester. *Required fees:* $719 per semester. *Financial support:* In 2011–12, fellowships (averaging $22,000 per year), research assistantships (averaging $10,000 per year), teaching assistantships (averaging $10,000 per year) were awarded. *Unit head:* Dr. Lynda Y. de la Vinna, Dean, 210-458-4317, Fax: 210-458-4308, E-mail: lynda.delavina@utsa.edu. *Application contact:* Katherine Pope, Director of Graduate Student Services, 210-458-7316, Fax: 210-458-4398, E-mail: katherine.pope@utsa.edu. Web site: http://business.utsa.edu.

The University of Texas–Pan American, College of Business Administration, Program in Business Administration, Edinburg, TX 78539. Offers business administration (MBA); finance (PhD); management (PhD); marketing (PhD). Part-time and evening/weekend programs available. Postbaccalaureate distance learning degree programs offered (no on-campus study). *Degree requirements:* For master's, thesis optional. *Entrance requirements:* For master's, GMAT, minimum GPA of 3.0. Additional exam requirements/recommendations for international students: Required—TOEFL (minimum score 500 paper-based). *Application deadline:* For fall admission, 7/25 priority date for domestic students, 7/1 for international students; for spring admission, 12/15 priority date for domestic students, 11/1 for international students. Applications are processed on a rolling basis. Application fee: $35. Electronic applications accepted. Tuition and fees vary according to course load, program and student level. *Financial support:* Research assistantships with partial tuition reimbursements, scholarships/grants, and unspecified assistantships available. *Faculty research:* Human resources, border region, entrepreneurship, marketing. *Unit head:* Business Administration Building, 956-

665-3313, E-mail: mbaprog@utpa.edu. Web site: http://portal.utpa.edu/utpa_main/daa_home/coba_new_home/coba_degrees/coba_graduate.

University of the Cumberlands, Graduate Programs in Education, Williamsburg, KY 40769-1372. Offers all grades (P-12) (M Ed); business and marketing (MA Ed, MAT); director of pupil personnel (Certificate); director of special education (Certificate); educational administration and supervision (Ed S); educational leadership (Ed D); elementary education (MA Ed, MAT); instructional leadership - principalship (MA Ed); instructional leadership - school principal (Certificate); middle school education (MA Ed, MAT); reading and writing (MA Ed); school counseling (MA Ed); school superintendent (Certificate); secondary education (MA Ed, MAT); special education (MAT); supervisor of instruction (Certificate); teacher leader (MA Ed). Part-time and evening/weekend programs available. Postbaccalaureate distance learning degree programs offered. *Degree requirements:* For master's, comprehensive exam. Electronic applications accepted.

University of the Sacred Heart, Graduate Programs, Department of Business Administration, Program in International Marketing, San Juan, PR 00914-0383. Offers MBA. Part-time and evening/weekend programs available. *Degree requirements:* For master's, thesis. *Entrance requirements:* For master's, EXADEP, minimum undergraduate GPA of 2.75, interview.

University of Virginia, McIntire School of Commerce, Program in Commerce, Charlottesville, VA 22903. Offers financial services (MSC); marketing and management (MSC). *Students:* 93 full-time (40 women); includes 14 minority (8 Asian, non-Hispanic/Latino; 5 Hispanic/Latino; 1 Two or more races, non-Hispanic/Latino), 16 international. Average age 22. 241 applicants, 59% accepted, 93 enrolled. In 2011, 72 master's awarded. *Entrance requirements:* For master's, GMAT, 2 letters of recommendation; prerequisite course work in financial accounting, microeconomics, and introduction to business. Additional exam requirements/recommendations for international students: Required—TOEFL (minimum score 600 paper-based; 250 computer-based; 100 iBT), IELTS (minimum score 7). *Application deadline:* For fall admission, 9/15 priority date for domestic students, 1/15 for international students. Applications are processed on a rolling basis. Application fee: $75. Electronic applications accepted. *Expenses:* Contact institution. *Financial support:* Scholarships/grants available. Financial award application deadline: 3/1; financial award applicants required to submit CSS PROFILE or FAFSA. *Unit head:* Ira C. Harris, Head, 434-924-8816, Fax: 434-924-7074, E-mail: ich3x@comm.virginia.edu. *Application contact:* Emma Candalier, Associate Director of Graduate Recruiting, 434-243-4992, Fax: 434-924-4511, E-mail: ecandalier@virginia.edu. Web site: http://www.commerce.virginia.edu/academic_programs/MSCommerce/Pages/index.aspx.

The University of Western Ontario, Richard Ivey School of Business, London, ON N6A 3K7, Canada. Offers business (EMBA, PhD); corporate strategy and leadership elective (MBA); entrepreneurship elective (MBA); finance elective (MBA); health sector stream (MBA); international management elective (MBA); marketing elective (MBA); JD/MBA. *Degree requirements:* For master's, thesis (for some programs); for doctorate, thesis/dissertation. *Entrance requirements:* For master's, GMAT, 2 years of full-time work experience, interview. Additional exam requirements/recommendations for international students: Required—TOEFL (minimum score 100 computer; 100 iBT) or IELTS (minimium score 6). Electronic applications accepted. *Faculty research:* Strategy, organizational behavior, international business, finance, operations management.

University of Wisconsin–Madison, Graduate School, Wisconsin School of Business, Doctoral Program in Marketing, Madison, WI 53706-1380. Offers PhD. *Faculty:* 12 full-time (3 women), 8 part-time/adjunct (4 women). *Students:* 7 full-time (all women); includes 1 minority (Asian, non-Hispanic/Latino), 4 international. Average age 29. 40 applicants, 8% accepted, 2 enrolled. In 2011, 1 doctorate awarded. *Degree requirements:* For doctorate, comprehensive exam, thesis/dissertation. *Entrance requirements:* For doctorate, GMAT or GRE. Additional exam requirements/recommendations for international students: Required—Pearson Test of English (minimum score 73; written 80); Recommended—TOEFL (minimum score 623 paper-based; 263 computer-based; 106 iBT), IELTS (minimum score 7.5). *Application deadline:* For fall admission, 12/15 priority date for domestic students, 12/15 for international students. Application fee: $56. Electronic applications accepted. *Expenses:* Contact institution. *Financial support:* In 2011–12, 7 students received support, including fellowships with full tuition reimbursements available (averaging $18,756 per year), research assistantships with full tuition reimbursements available (averaging $16,506 per year), 7 teaching assistantships with full tuition reimbursements available (averaging $14,088 per year); Federal Work-Study, institutionally sponsored loans, scholarships/grants, health care benefits, and unspecified assistantships also available. Financial award application deadline: 2/1; financial award applicants required to submit FAFSA. *Faculty research:* Marketing strategy, consumer behavior, channels of distribution, advertising, price promotions. *Unit head:* Prof. Aric Rindfleisch, Chair, 608-262-1942, Fax: 608-262-0394, E-mail: jnevin@bus.wisc.edu. *Application contact:* Belle Heberling, Assistant Director for Research Programs, 608-262-3749, Fax: 608-890-0180, E-mail: phd@bus.wisc.edu. Web site: http://www.bus.wisc.edu/phd.

University of Wisconsin–Whitewater, School of Graduate Studies, College of Business and Economics, Department of Business Education, Whitewater, WI 53190-1790. Offers business and marketing education (MS), including general, post secondary, secondary. *Accreditation:* NCATE. Part-time and evening/weekend programs available. Postbaccalaureate distance learning degree programs offered (no on-campus study). *Students:* 2 full-time (1 woman), 19 part-time (8 women); includes 1 minority (Hispanic/Latino). Average age 35. 5 applicants, 80% accepted, 2 enrolled. In 2011, 7 master's awarded. *Degree requirements:* For master's, thesis or alternative. *Entrance requirements:* For master's, interview, teaching license. Additional exam requirements/recommendations for international students: Required—TOEFL (minimum score 550 paper-based; 213 computer-based; 80 iBT), IELTS (minimum score 6). *Application deadline:* For fall admission, 7/15 priority date for domestic students, 7/15 for international students; for spring admission, 12/1 priority date for domestic students, 12/1 for international students. Applications are processed on a rolling basis. Application fee: $56. Electronic applications accepted. *Expenses:* Tuition, state resident: full-time $4088. Tuition, nonresident: full-time $8817. Tuition and fees vary according to program. *Financial support:* In 2011–12, 2 research assistantships (averaging $7,245 per year) were awarded; Federal Work-Study, unspecified assistantships, and out of state fee waiver also available. Support available to part-time students. Financial award application deadline: 3/15; financial award applicants required to submit FAFSA. *Faculty research:* Active learning and performance strategies, technology-enhanced formative assessment, computer-supported cooperative work, privacy surveillance. *Unit head:* Dr. Lila Waldman, Coordinator, 262-472-5475. *Application contact:* Sally A. Lange, School of Graduate Studies, 262-472-1006, Fax: 262-472-5027, E-mail: gradschl@uww.edu.

University of Wisconsin–Whitewater, School of Graduate Studies, College of Business and Economics, Program in Business Administration, Whitewater, WI 53190-1790. Offers finance (MBA); human resource management (MBA); information technology management (MBA); international business (MBA); management (MBA); marketing (MBA); operations and supply chain management (MBA). *Accreditation:* AACSB. Part-time and evening/weekend programs available. Postbaccalaureate distance learning degree programs offered (no on-campus study). *Students:* 170 full-time (53 women), 538 part-time (213 women); includes 130 minority (28 Black or African American, non-Hispanic/Latino; 87 Asian, non-Hispanic/Latino; 15 Hispanic/Latino). Average age 31. 448 applicants, 33% accepted, 120 enrolled. In 2011, 304 master's awarded. *Entrance requirements:* For master's, GMAT or GRE, minimum AACSB index of 1000, minimum GPA of 2.75. Additional exam requirements/recommendations for international students: Required—TOEFL (minimum score 550 paper-based; 213 computer-based; 80 iBT), IELTS (minimum score 6). *Application deadline:* For fall admission, 7/15 for domestic and international students; for spring admission, 12/1 for domestic and international students. Applications are processed on a rolling basis. Application fee: $56. Electronic applications accepted. *Expenses:* Tuition, state resident: full-time $4088. Tuition, nonresident: full-time $8817. Tuition and fees vary according to program. *Financial support:* In 2011–12, research assistantships (averaging $7,245 per year) were awarded; Federal Work-Study, unspecified assistantships, and out-of-state fee waivers also available. Support available to part-time students. Financial award application deadline: 3/15; financial award applicants required to submit FAFSA. *Faculty research:* Interface between social institutions and individual behavior, technology and innovation management, occupational mental health, workplace deviance and workplace romance. *Unit head:* Dr. John Chenoweth, Associate Dean, 262-472-1945, Fax: 262-472-4863, E-mail: chenowej@uww.edu.

Vancouver Island University, Master of Business Administration Program, Nanaimo, BC V9R 5S5, Canada. Offers international business (MBA), including finance, marketing. Program offered jointly with University of Hertfordshire. *Accreditation:* ACBSP. Part-time programs available. *Faculty:* 23 full-time (3 women), 3 part-time/adjunct (2 women). *Students:* 135 full-time (59 women), 2 part-time (0 women); includes 9 minority (1 Black or African American, non-Hispanic/Latino; 2 American Indian or Alaska Native, non-Hispanic/Latino; 5 Asian, non-Hispanic/Latino; 1 Hispanic/Latino), 102 international. Average age 27. 632 applicants, 46% accepted, 135 enrolled. In 2011, 145 master's awarded. *Degree requirements:* For master's, thesis. *Entrance requirements:* Additional exam requirements/recommendations for international students: Required—TOEFL (minimum score 550 paper-based; 213 computer-based). *Application deadline:* For fall admission, 2/28 priority date for domestic students, 2/28 for international students; for winter admission, 4/30 for domestic and international students. Applications are processed on a rolling basis. Application fee: $150. Electronic applications accepted. *Financial support:* In 2011–12, 8 students received support. Scholarships/grants available. *Faculty research:* Tourism development, entrepreneurship, organizational development, strategic planning, international business strategy, intercultural team work. *Unit head:* Brock Dykeman, Director, 250-740-6178, Fax: 250-740-6551, E-mail: brock.dykeman@viu.ca. *Application contact:* Jane Kelly, International Admissions Manager, 250-740-6384, Fax: 250-740-6471, E-mail: kellyj@mala.bc.ca. Web site: http://www.viu.ca/mba/index.asp.

Villanova University, Villanova School of Business, MBA - The Fast Track Program, Villanova, PA 19085. Offers finance (MBA); health care management (MBA); international business (MBA); management information systems (MBA); marketing (MBA); real estate (MBA); strategic management (MBA). *Accreditation:* AACSB. Part-time and evening/weekend programs available. *Faculty:* 101 full-time (32 women), 38 part-time/adjunct (8 women). *Students:* 123 part-time (46 women); includes 14 minority (1 Black or African American, non-Hispanic/Latino; 3 American Indian or Alaska Native, non-Hispanic/Latino; 5 Asian, non-Hispanic/Latino; 1 Hispanic/Latino; 4 Two or more races, non-Hispanic/Latino). Average age 29. In 2011, 53 master's awarded. *Degree requirements:* For master's, minimum GPA of 3.0. *Entrance requirements:* For master's, GMAT, work experience. Additional exam requirements/recommendations for international students: Required—TOEFL (minimum score 550 paper-based; 213 computer-based; 80 iBT). *Application deadline:* For fall admission, 6/30 for domestic and international students. Application fee: $50. Electronic applications accepted. *Expenses: Tuition:* Part-time $675 per credit. Part-time tuition and fees vary according to degree level and program. *Financial support:* Scholarships/grants available. Financial award application deadline: 6/30; financial award applicants required to submit FAFSA. *Faculty research:* Business analytics; creativity, innovation and entrepreneurship; global leadership; marketing and public policy; real estate; church management. *Unit head:* Kristy Irwin, Director of Recruitment and Marketing, 610-519-6288, Fax: 610-519-6273, E-mail: kristy.irwin@villanova.edu. *Application contact:* Meredith L. Lockyer, Assistant Director, 610-519-7016, Fax: 610-519-6273, E-mail: meredith.lockyer@villanova.edu. Web site: http://www.mba.villanova.edu.

Villanova University, Villanova School of Business, MBA - The Flex Track Program, Villanova, PA 19085. Offers finance (MBA); health care management (MBA); international business (MBA); management information systems (MBA); marketing (MBA); real estate (MBA); strategic management (MBA); JD/MBA. *Accreditation:* AACSB. Part-time and evening/weekend programs available. Postbaccalaureate distance learning degree programs offered (minimal on-campus study). *Faculty:* 101 full-time (32 women), 38 part-time/adjunct (8 women). *Students:* 18 full-time (9 women), 412 part-time (127 women); includes 45 minority (7 Black or African American, non-Hispanic/Latino; 1 American Indian or Alaska Native, non-Hispanic/Latino; 25 Asian, non-Hispanic/Latino; 4 Hispanic/Latino; 1 Native Hawaiian or other Pacific Islander, non-Hispanic/Latino; 7 Two or more races, non-Hispanic/Latino). Average age 30. In 2011, 150 master's awarded. *Degree requirements:* For master's, minimum GPA of 3.0. *Entrance requirements:* For master's, GMAT, work experience. Additional exam requirements/recommendations for international students: Required—TOEFL (minimum score 550 paper-based; 213 computer-based; 80 iBT). *Application deadline:* For fall admission, 6/30 for domestic and international students; for winter admission, 11/15 for domestic and international students; for spring admission, 3/30 for domestic students, 3/31 for international students. Applications are processed on a rolling basis. Application fee: $50. Electronic applications accepted. *Expenses: Tuition:* Part-time $675 per credit. Part-time tuition and fees vary according to degree level and program. *Financial support:* In 2011–12, 18 research assistantships with full tuition reimbursements (averaging $13,100 per year) were awarded; scholarships/grants and unspecified assistantships also available. Financial award application deadline: 6/30; financial award applicants required to submit FAFSA. *Faculty research:* Business analytics; creativity, innovation and entrepreneurship; global leadership; marketing and public policy; real estate; church management. *Unit head:* Kristy Irwin, Director of Recruitment and Marketing, 610-610-6288, Fax: 610-519-6273, E-mail: kristy.irwin@villanova.edu. *Application contact:* Meredity L. Lockyer, Assistant Director, 610-519-7016, Fax: 610-519-6273, E-mail: meredith.lockyer@villanova.edu. Web site: http://www.mba.villanova.edu.

Virginia Commonwealth University, Graduate School, School of Business, Program in Marketing and Business Law, Richmond, VA 23284-9005. Offers MS. *Entrance requirements:* For master's, GMAT. Additional exam requirements/recommendations for international students: Required—TOEFL (minimum score 600 paper-based; 250 computer-based; 100 iBT); Recommended—IELTS (minimum score 6.5). Electronic applications accepted. *Expenses:* Tuition, state resident: full-time $9133; part-time $507 per credit. Tuition, nonresident: full-time $18,777; part-time $1043 per credit. *Required fees:* $77 per credit. Tuition and fees vary according to degree level, campus/location, program and student level.

Virginia International University, School of Business, Fairfax, VA 22030. Offers accounting (MBA); executive management (Graduate Certificate); global logistics

(MBA); health care management (MBA); human resources management (MBA); international business management (MBA); international finance (MBA); marketing management (MBA). Part-time programs available. *Entrance requirements:* For master's and Graduate Certificate, bachelor's degree. Additional exam requirements/recommendations for international students: Required—TOEFL (minimum score 550 paper-based; 213 computer-based; 80 iBT), IELTS (minimum score 6). Electronic applications accepted.

Virginia Polytechnic Institute and State University, Graduate School, Pamplin College of Business, Department of Marketing, Blacksburg, VA 24061. Offers MS, PhD. *Degree requirements:* For master's, comprehensive exam (for some programs), thesis (for some programs); for doctorate, comprehensive exam (for some programs), thesis/dissertation (for some programs). *Entrance requirements:* For master's and doctorate, GRE. Additional exam requirements/recommendations for international students: Required—TOEFL (minimum score 550 paper-based; 213 computer-based). *Application deadline:* For fall admission, 7/1 for domestic and international students; for spring admission, 12/1 for domestic and international students. Applications are processed on a rolling basis. Application fee: $65. Electronic applications accepted. *Expenses:* Tuition, state resident: full-time $10,048; part-time $558.25 per credit hour. Tuition, nonresident: full-time $19,497; part-time $1083.25 per credit hour. *Required fees:* $405 per semester. Tuition and fees vary according to course load, campus/location and program. *Financial support:* In 2011–12, 6 teaching assistantships with full tuition reimbursements (averaging $13,692 per year) were awarded; career-related internships or fieldwork, Federal Work-Study, scholarships/grants, health care benefits, and unspecified assistantships also available. Financial award application deadline: 1/15; financial award applicants required to submit CSS PROFILE. *Faculty research:* Consumer behavior, marketing research, channels of distribution, advertising, marketing strategy. *Unit head:* Dr. Kent Nakamoto, Unit Head, 540-231-6949, Fax: 540-231-4487, E-mail: nakamoto@vt.edu. *Application contact:* David Brinberg, Information Contact, 540-231-7639, Fax: 540-231-4487, E-mail: dbrinber@vt.edu.

Wagner College, Division of Graduate Studies, Department of Business Administration, Program in Marketing, Staten Island, NY 10301-4495. Offers MBA. Part-time and evening/weekend programs available. *Faculty:* 1 (woman) part-time/adjunct. *Students:* 8 full-time (5 women), 6 part-time (2 women); includes 2 minority (both Hispanic/Latino), 1 international. Average age 30. 9 applicants, 100% accepted, 5 enrolled. In 2011, 7 master's awarded. *Degree requirements:* For master's, thesis optional. *Entrance requirements:* For master's, GMAT, minimum GPA of 2.6. Additional exam requirements/recommendations for international students: Required—TOEFL (minimum score 550 paper-based; 217 computer-based; 79 iBT). *Application deadline:* For fall admission, 4/1 priority date for domestic students, 3/1 for international students; for spring admission, 11/1 priority date for domestic students, 10/1 for international students. Applications are processed on a rolling basis. Application fee: $50 ($80 for international students). *Expenses: Tuition:* Full-time $16,200; part-time $890 per credit. *Financial support:* Career-related internships or fieldwork, unspecified assistantships, and alumni fellowship grant available. Financial award applicants required to submit FAFSA. *Unit head:* Prof. Cathyann Tully, Director, 718-390-3439, Fax: 718-420-4274, E-mail: cathyann.tully@wagner.edu. *Application contact:* Patricia Clancy, Assistant Coordinator of Graduate Studies, 718-420-4464, Fax: 718-390-3105, E-mail: patricia.clancy@wagner.edu.

Wake Forest University, Schools of Business, Full-time MBA Program, Winston-Salem, NC 27106. Offers consulting/general management (MBA); entrepreneurship (MBA); finance (MBA); health (MBA); marketing (MBA); operations management (MBA); JD/MBA; MD/MBA; MSA/MBA. *Accreditation:* AACSB. *Faculty:* 62 full-time (16 women), 41 part-time/adjunct (14 women). *Students:* 120 full-time (28 women); includes 14 minority (8 Black or African American, non-Hispanic/Latino; 4 Asian, non-Hispanic/Latino; 1 Hispanic/Latino; 1 Two or more races, non-Hispanic/Latino), 28 international. Average age 28. In 2011, 62 master's awarded. *Degree requirements:* For master's, 65.5 credit hours. *Entrance requirements:* For master's, GMAT or GRE, letters of recommendation, official transcripts, current resume or curriculum vitae, 2 years of work experience. Additional exam requirements/recommendations for international students: Required—TOEFL (minimum score 600 paper-based; 250 computer-based; 100 iBT), Pearson Test of English. *Application deadline:* For fall admission, 4/15 for domestic and international students. Applications are processed on a rolling basis. Application fee: $100. Electronic applications accepted. *Expenses:* Contact institution. *Financial support:* In 2011–12, 84 students received support. Career-related internships or fieldwork, scholarships/grants, and unspecified assistantships available. Financial award application deadline: 2/15; financial award applicants required to submit FAFSA. *Faculty research:* The influence of personal relationships on business decision-making and management of change; drivers of perceived value and consumer behavior; impact of accounting on auditing, financial, managerial, systems and taxation stakeholders; corporate governance and executive compensation; impact of operations strategies on competitiveness. *Unit head:* Jon Duchac, Director, Full-time MBA Program, 336-758-5422, Fax: 336-758-5830, E-mail: busadmissions@wfu.edu. *Application contact:* Tamara Paquee, Administrative Assistant, 336-758-5422, Fax: 336-758-5830, E-mail: busadmissions@wfu.edu. Web site: http://www.business.wfu.edu/.

Walden University, Graduate Programs, School of Management, Minneapolis, MN 55401. Offers accounting (MS, DBA), including accounting for the professional (MS), CPA (MS), self-designed (MS); accounting and management (MS), including accounting for strategic managers, self-designed; accounting for managers (MBA); advanced project management (Post-Graduate Certificate); applied project management (Post-Graduate Certificate); corporate finance (MBA); entrepreneurship (MBA, DBA); finance (DBA); global management (MS); global supply chain management (DBA); healthcare management (MBA, DBA); healthcare system improvement (MBA); human resource management (MBA, MS, PhD), including functional human resource management (MS), integrating functional and strategic human resource management (MS), organizational strategy (MS); information systems management (DBA); international business (MBA, DBA); leadership (MBA, MS, DBA), including entrepreneurship (MS), general management (MS), human resources leadership (MS), innovation and technology (MS), leader development (MS), leading sustainability (MS), project management (MS), self-designed (MS); management (MS), including healthcare management; managers as leaders (MS); marketing (MBA, DBA); project management (MBA, MS, DBA); research strategies (MS); risk management (MBA); self-designed (MBA, DBA, PhD); social impact management (DBA); strategies for sustainability (MBA); strategy and operations (MS); sustainable management (MS); technology (MBA); technology entrepreneurship (DBA); technology management (MS). Part-time and evening/weekend programs available. Postbaccalaureate distance learning degree programs offered (minimal on-campus study). *Faculty:* 32 full-time (14 women), 275 part-time/adjunct (98 women). *Students:* 3,962 full-time (2,095 women), 1,557 part-time (959 women); includes 3,003 minority (2,510 Black or African American, non-Hispanic/Latino; 25 American Indian or Alaska Native, non-Hispanic/Latino; 140 Asian, non-Hispanic/Latino; 240 Hispanic/Latino; 9 Native Hawaiian or other Pacific Islander, non-Hispanic/Latino; 79 Two or more races, non-Hispanic/Latino), 395 international. Average age 41. In 2011, 586 master's, 87 doctorates, 4 other advanced degrees awarded. *Degree requirements:* For doctorate, thesis/dissertation (for some programs), residency. *Entrance requirements:* For master's, bachelor's degree or equivalent in related field; minimum GPA of 2.5; official transcripts; goal statement; access to computer and Internet; for doctorate, master's degree or equivalent in related field; minimum GPA of 3.0; 3 years of related professional/academic experience (preferred). Additional exam requirements/recommendations for international students: Required—TOEFL (minimum score 550 paper-based; 213 computer-based), IELTS (minimum score 6.5), Michigan English Language Assessment Battery (minimum score 82). *Application deadline:* Applications are processed on a rolling basis. Application fee: $50. Electronic applications accepted. *Financial support:* Federal Work-Study, scholarships/grants, unspecified assistantships, and family tuition reduction, active duty/veteran tuition reduction, group tuition reduction, interest-free payment plans, employee tuition reduction available. Support available to part-time students. Financial award applicants required to submit FAFSA. *Unit head:* Dr. William Schulz, III, Associate Dean, 800-925-3368. *Application contact:* Jennifer Hall, Vice President of Enrollment Management, 866-4-WALDEN, E-mail: info@waldenu.edu. Web site: http://www.waldenu.edu/Colleges-and-Schools/College-of-Management-and-Technology.htm.

Walsh University, Graduate Studies, MBA Program, North Canton, OH 44720-3396. Offers health care management (MBA); integrated marketing communications (MBA); management (MBA). Part-time and evening/weekend programs available. *Faculty:* 7 full-time (2 women), 24 part-time/adjunct (7 women). *Students:* 21 full-time (11 women), 151 part-time (74 women); includes 13 minority (8 Black or African American, non-Hispanic/Latino; 2 American Indian or Alaska Native, non-Hispanic/Latino; 3 Hispanic/Latino). Average age 34. 62 applicants, 81% accepted, 45 enrolled. In 2011, 57 master's awarded. *Entrance requirements:* For master's, GMAT, minimum GPA of 3.0. Additional exam requirements/recommendations for international students: Required—TOEFL (minimum score 500 paper-based; 173 computer-based; 61 iBT). *Application deadline:* For fall admission, 7/15 priority date for domestic students. Applications are processed on a rolling basis. Application fee: $25. Electronic applications accepted. *Expenses: Tuition:* Full-time $10,170; part-time $565 per credit hour. *Financial support:* In 2011–12, 106 students received support, including 10 research assistantships with partial tuition reimbursements available (averaging $5,674 per year), 4 teaching assistantships (averaging $5,763 per year); tuition waivers (partial), unspecified assistantships, and tuition discounts also available. Support available to part-time students. Financial award application deadline: 12/31; financial award applicants required to submit FAFSA. *Faculty research:* Patient and physician satisfaction, advancing and improving learning with information technology, consumer-driven healthcare, branding and the service industry, service provider training and customer satisfaction. *Unit head:* Dr. Michael A. Petrochuk, Director of the MBA Program and Assistant Professor, 330-244-4764, Fax: 330-490-7359, E-mail: mpetrochuk@walsh.edu. *Application contact:* Audra Dice, Graduate and Transfer Admissions Counselor, 330-490-7181, Fax: 330-244-4925, E-mail: adice@walsh.edu. Web site: http://www.walsh.edu/mba-program.

Washington State University, Graduate School, College of Business, Business Administration Programs, Pullman, WA 99164. Offers business administration (MBA, PhD), including accounting (PhD), finance (PhD), management and operations (PhD), management information systems (PhD), marketing (PhD). *Accreditation:* AACSB. *Faculty:* 47. *Students:* 93 full-time (35 women), 94 part-time (32 women); includes 25 minority (4 Black or African American, non-Hispanic/Latino; 2 American Indian or Alaska Native, non-Hispanic/Latino; 11 Asian, non-Hispanic/Latino; 7 Hispanic/Latino; 1 Two or more races, non-Hispanic/Latino), 33 international. Average age 31. 310 applicants, 31% accepted, 67 enrolled. In 2011, 15 doctorates awarded. *Degree requirements:* For master's, comprehensive exam (for some programs), thesis (for some programs), final presentation; for doctorate, comprehensive exam, thesis/dissertation, oral and written exams. *Entrance requirements:* For master's and doctorate, GMAT, minimum GPA of 3.0, 3 letters of recommendation. Additional exam requirements/recommendations for international students: Required—TOEFL. *Application deadline:* For fall admission, 3/1 priority date for domestic students, 3/1 for international students; for spring admission, 6/1 priority date for domestic students, 6/1 for international students. Applications are processed on a rolling basis. Application fee: $75. Electronic applications accepted. *Financial support:* In 2011–12, 102 students received support, including 36 teaching assistantships with full and partial tuition reimbursements available (averaging $18,204 per year); career-related internships or fieldwork, Federal Work-Study, institutionally sponsored loans, health care benefits, tuition waivers (partial), unspecified assistantships, and teaching associateships also available. Financial award application deadline: 4/1. *Total annual research expenditures:* $344,000. *Unit head:* Dr. Eric Spangenberg, Dean, 509-335-8150, E-mail: ers@wsu.edu. *Application contact:* Graduate School Admissions, 800-GRADWSU, Fax: 509-335-1949, E-mail: gradsch@wsu.edu.

Webster University, George Herbert Walker School of Business and Technology, Department of Business, St. Louis, MO 63119-3194. Offers business (MA); business and organizational security management (MBA); computer resources and information management (MBA); environmental management (MBA); finance (MA, MBA); health services management (MBA); human resources development (MBA); human resources management (MBA); international business (MA, MBA); management and leadership (MBA); marketing (MBA); procurement and acquisitions management (MBA); telecommunications management (MBA). *Accreditation:* ACBSP. Part-time and evening/weekend programs available. Postbaccalaureate distance learning degree programs offered (no on-campus study). *Degree requirements:* For master's, comprehensive exam (for some programs), thesis (for some programs). *Entrance requirements:* Additional exam requirements/recommendations for international students: Required—TOEFL. *Expenses: Tuition:* Full-time $10,890; part-time $605 per credit hour. Tuition and fees vary according to campus/location and program.

Webster University, George Herbert Walker School of Business and Technology, Department of Management, St. Louis, MO 63119-3194. Offers business and organizational security management (MA); computer resources and information management (MA); environmental management (MS); government contracting (Certificate); health care management (MA); health services management (MA); human resources development (MA); human resources management (MA); management (DM); management and leadership (MA); marketing (MA); nonprofit management (Certificate); procurement and acquisitions management (MA); public administration (MA); quality management (MA); space systems operations management (MS); telecommunications management (MA). *Accreditation:* ACBSP. Part-time and evening/weekend programs available. Postbaccalaureate distance learning degree programs offered (no on-campus study). *Degree requirements:* For master's, thesis (for some programs); for doctorate, thesis/dissertation, written exam. *Entrance requirements:* For doctorate, GMAT, 3 years of work experience, MBA. Additional exam requirements/recommendations for international students: Required—TOEFL. *Expenses: Tuition:* Full-time $10,890; part-time $605 per credit hour. Tuition and fees vary according to campus/location and program.

Western International University, Graduate Programs in Business, Master of Business Administration Program in Marketing, Phoenix, AZ 85021-2718. Offers MBA. Part-time and evening/weekend programs available. Postbaccalaureate distance learning degree programs offered (no on-campus study). *Entrance requirements:* For master's, minimum GPA of 2.75. Additional exam requirements/recommendations for international students: Required—TOEFL (minimum score 550 paper-based; 213

computer-based; 79 iBT), TWE (minimum score 5), or IELTS (minimum score 6.5). Electronic applications accepted.

West Virginia University, Perley Isaac Reed School of Journalism, Program in Integrated Marketing Communications, Morgantown, WV 26506. Offers MS, Graduate Certificate. Part-time programs available. Postbaccalaureate distance learning degree programs offered (no on-campus study). *Entrance requirements:* For master's, GRE or GMAT (waived with minimum undergraduate GPA of 3.3 or at least 6 years of related professional experience), undergraduate transcript, resume; letters of recommendation (strongly recommended). Additional exam requirements/recommendations for international students: Required—TOEFL.

Wilfrid Laurier University, Faculty of Graduate and Postdoctoral Studies, School of Business and Economics, Department of Business, Waterloo, ON N2L 3C5, Canada. Offers accounting (PhD); finance (M Fin); financial economics (PhD); marketing (PhD); operations and supply chain management (PhD); organizational behavior and human resource management (M Sc); organizational behaviour and human resource management (PhD); supply chain management (M Sc); technology management (EMTM). Part-time and evening/weekend programs available. *Degree requirements:* For master's, thesis optional; for doctorate, comprehensive exam, thesis/dissertation. *Entrance requirements:* For master's, GMAT, 4-year honors degree with minimum B+ average; for doctorate, GMAT, master's degree, minimum B+ average. Additional exam requirements/recommendations for international students: Required—TOEFL (minimum score 89 iBT). Electronic applications accepted. *Faculty research:* Financial economics, management and organizational behavior, operations and supply chain management.

Wilkes University, College of Graduate and Professional Studies, Jay S. Sidhu School of Business and Leadership, Wilkes-Barre, PA 18766-0002. Offers accounting (MBA); entrepreneurship (MBA); finance (MBA); health care administration (MBA); human resource management (MBA); international business (MBA); marketing (MBA); operations management (MBA); organizational leadership and development (MBA). *Accreditation:* ACBSP. Part-time and evening/weekend programs available. *Students:* 48 full-time (20 women), 134 part-time (62 women); includes 12 minority (2 Black or African American, non-Hispanic/Latino; 5 Asian, non-Hispanic/Latino; 2 Hispanic/Latino; 3 Two or more races, non-Hispanic/Latino), 9 international. Average age 30. In 2011, 69 master's awarded. *Entrance requirements:* For master's, GMAT. Additional exam requirements/recommendations for international students: Required—TOEFL (minimum score 550 paper-based; 213 computer-based; 79 iBT). *Application deadline:* Applications are processed on a rolling basis. Application fee: $45 ($65 for international students). Electronic applications accepted. *Expenses:* Contact institution. *Financial support:* Federal Work-Study and unspecified assistantships available. Financial award application deadline: 3/1; financial award applicants required to submit FAFSA. *Unit head:* Dr. Jeffrey Alves, Dean, 570-408-4702, Fax: 570-408-7846, E-mail: jeffrey.alves@wilkes.edu. *Application contact:* Erin Sutzko, Director of Extended Learning, 570-408-4253, Fax: 570-408-7846, E-mail: erin.sutzko@wilkes.edu. Web site: http://www.wilkes.edu/pages/457.asp.

Wilmington University, College of Business, New Castle, DE 19720-6491. Offers accounting (MBA, MS); business administration (MBA, DBA); environmental stewardship (MBA); finance (MBA); health care administration (MBA, MSM); homeland security (MBA, MSM); human resource management (MSM); management information systems (MBA, MSN); marketing (MSM); marketing management (MBA); military leadership (MSM); organizational leadership (MBA, MSM); public administration (MSM). Part-time and evening/weekend programs available. *Faculty:* 4 full-time (0 women). *Students:* 266 full-time (121 women), 700 part-time (505 women). Average age 34. *Entrance requirements:* Additional exam requirements/recommendations for international students: Required—TOEFL (minimum score 500 paper-based; 173 computer-based). *Application deadline:* Applications are processed on a rolling basis. Application fee: $35. Electronic applications accepted. *Expenses: Tuition:* Part-time $534 per credit hour. *Required fees:* $25 per term. *Financial support:* Applicants required to submit FAFSA. *Unit head:* Dr. Donald W. Durandetta, Dean, 302-356-6780, E-mail: donald.w.durandetta@wilmu.edu. *Application contact:* Chris Ferguson, Director of Admissions, 302-356-4636 Ext. 256, Fax: 302-328-5164, E-mail: inquire@wilmcoll.edu. Web site: http://www.wilmu.edu/business/.

Worcester Polytechnic Institute, Graduate Studies and Research, School of Business, Worcester, MA 01609-2280. Offers information technology (MS), including information security management; management (Graduate Certificate); marketing and technological innovation (MS); operations design and leadership (MS); technology (MBA, MS). *Accreditation:* AACSB. Part-time and evening/weekend programs available. Postbaccalaureate distance learning degree programs offered (minimal on-campus study). *Faculty:* 12 full-time (7 women), 12 part-time/adjunct (2 women). *Students:* 108 full-time (64 women), 206 part-time (55 women); includes 27 minority (4 Black or African American, non-Hispanic/Latino; 12 Asian, non-Hispanic/Latino; 4 Hispanic/Latino; 7 Two or more races, non-Hispanic/Latino), 131 international. 596 applicants, 48% accepted, 131 enrolled. In 2011, 75 master's awarded. *Degree requirements:* For master's, thesis optional. *Entrance requirements:* For master's, GMAT (MBA), GMAT or GRE General Test (MS), resume; for Graduate Certificate, GMAT or GRE General Test, statement of purpose, 3 letters of recommendation. Additional exam requirements/recommendations for international students: Required—TOEFL (minimum score 563 paper-based; 223 computer-based; 84 iBT), IELTS (minimum score 7). *Application deadline:* For fall admission, 6/1 priority date for domestic students, 6/1 for international students; for spring admission, 11/1 priority date for domestic students, 10/1 for international students. Applications are processed on a rolling basis. Application fee: $70. Electronic applications accepted. *Financial support:* Career-related internships or fieldwork, institutionally sponsored loans, scholarships/grants, and unspecified assistantships available. Financial award application deadline: 6/1; financial award applicants required to submit FAFSA. *Faculty research:* Organizational aesthetics, resistance in organizations, dynamics of product innovation, economic approaches to productivity, corporate earnings forecasts and value relevance, ERP implementation, improving Web accessibility, information quality assessment, measuring strategic and transactional IT, website quality, service operations modeling, healthcare operations and performance analysis, entrepreneurship, leadership and change. *Unit head:* Dr. Mark Rice, Dean, 508-831-4665, Fax: 508-831-5218, E-mail: rice@wpi.edu. *Application contact:* Peggy Caisse, Recruiting Operations Coordinator, 508-831-4665, Fax: 508-831-5720, E-mail: mcaisse@wpi.edu. Web site: http://www.biz.wpi.edu/Graduate/.

Wright State University, School of Graduate Studies, Raj Soin College of Business, Department of Marketing, Dayton, OH 45435. Offers MBA, MBA/MS. *Entrance requirements:* For master's, GMAT, minimum AACSB index of 1000. Additional exam requirements/recommendations for international students: Required—TOEFL.

Xavier University, Williams College of Business, Master of Business Administration Program, Cincinnati, OH 45207. Offers business administration (Exec MBA, MBA); business intelligence (MBA); finance (MBA); health industry (MBA); international business (MBA); management information systems (MBA); marketing (MBA); MBA/MHSA; MSN/MBA. *Accreditation:* AACSB. Part-time and evening/weekend programs available. *Faculty:* 45 full-time (17 women), 13 part-time/adjunct (4 women). *Students:* 188 full-time (63 women), 630 part-time (206 women); includes 112 minority (36 Black or African American, non-Hispanic/Latino; 3 American Indian or Alaska Native, non-Hispanic/Latino; 52 Asian, non-Hispanic/Latino; 17 Hispanic/Latino; 1 Native Hawaiian or other Pacific Islander, non-Hispanic/Latino; 3 Two or more races, non-Hispanic/Latino), 45 international. Average age 30. 319 applicants, 63% accepted, 149 enrolled. In 2011, 403 master's awarded. *Degree requirements:* For master's, capstone course. *Entrance requirements:* For master's, GMAT or GRE. Additional exam requirements/recommendations for international students: Required—TOEFL (minimum score 550 paper-based; 213 computer-based; 80 iBT). *Application deadline:* For fall admission, 8/1 priority date for domestic students, 5/1 for international students; for spring admission, 12/1 priority date for domestic students, 9/1 for international students. Applications are processed on a rolling basis. Application fee: $0. Electronic applications accepted. *Expenses:* Contact institution. *Financial support:* In 2011–12, 176 students received support. Scholarships/grants, tuition waivers (partial), and unspecified assistantships available. Financial award application deadline: 3/1; financial award applicants required to submit FAFSA. *Unit head:* Dr. Hema Krishnan, Associate Dean, 513-745-3420, Fax: 513-745-3455, E-mail: krishnan@xavier.edu. *Application contact:* Anna Marie Whelan, Assistant Director, MBA Programs, 513-745-3525, Fax: 513-745-2929, E-mail: whelana@xavier.edu. Web site: http://www.xavier.edu/williams/mba/.

Yale University, Yale School of Management and Graduate School of Arts and Sciences, Doctoral Program in Management, New Haven, CT 06520. Offers accounting (PhD); financial economics (PhD); marketing (PhD); organizations and management (PhD). *Accreditation:* AACSB. *Faculty:* 42 full-time (8 women). *Students:* 33 full-time (9 women); includes 4 minority (all Asian, non-Hispanic/Latino), 16 international. 439 applicants, 3% accepted, 4 enrolled. In 2011, 2 doctorates awarded. *Degree requirements:* For doctorate, comprehensive exam, thesis/dissertation. *Entrance requirements:* For doctorate, GMAT or GRE General Test. Additional exam requirements/recommendations for international students: Required—TOEFL or IELTS. *Application deadline:* For fall admission, 1/2 for domestic and international students. Application fee: $100. Electronic applications accepted. *Expenses:* Contact institution. *Financial support:* In 2011–12, 31 students received support, including 31 fellowships with full tuition reimbursements available, 31 research assistantships with full tuition reimbursements available, 31 teaching assistantships with full tuition reimbursements available; institutionally sponsored loans, scholarships/grants, and health care benefits also available. Financial award application deadline: 1/2. *Faculty research:* Pricing of options and futures, term structure of interest rates, use of accounting numbers in debt contracts, product differentiation, e-commerce and marketing, behavioral finance. *Unit head:* Carla Mills, Registrar, 203-432-3955, Fax: 203-432-0342.

York College of Pennsylvania, Donald Graham School of Business, York, PA 17405-7199. Offers accounting (MBA); continuous improvement (MBA); finance (MBA); management (MBA); marketing (MBA); self-designed (MBA). *Accreditation:* ACBSP. Part-time and evening/weekend programs available. *Faculty:* 14 full-time (3 women), 1 part-time/adjunct (0 women). *Students:* 11 full-time (5 women), 99 part-time (40 women); includes 10 minority (5 Black or African American, non-Hispanic/Latino; 1 Asian, non-Hispanic/Latino; 3 Hispanic/Latino; 1 Two or more races, non-Hispanic/Latino), 1 international. Average age 29. 49 applicants, 80% accepted, 26 enrolled. In 2011, 33 master's awarded. *Entrance requirements:* For master's, GMAT. Additional exam requirements/recommendations for international students: Required—TOEFL (minimum score 530 paper-based; 200 computer-based; 72 iBT). *Application deadline:* For fall admission, 7/15 priority date for domestic students; for spring admission, 12/15 priority date for domestic students. Applications are processed on a rolling basis. Application fee: $50. Electronic applications accepted. *Expenses: Tuition:* Full-time $12,060; part-time $670 per credit hour. *Required fees:* $340 per semester. Tuition and fees vary according to degree level. *Financial support:* In 2011–12, 3 students received support. Scholarships/grants available. Financial award application deadline: 4/15; financial award applicants required to submit FAFSA. *Unit head:* Dr. David Greisler, MBA Director, 717-815-6410, Fax: 717-600-3999, E-mail: dgreisle@ycp.edu. *Application contact:* Brenda Adams, Assistant Director, MBA Program, 717-815-1749, Fax: 717-600-3999, E-mail: badams@ycp.edu. Web site: http://www.ycp.edu/mba.

Youngstown State University, Graduate School, Williamson College of Business Administration, Department of Marketing, Youngstown, OH 44555-0001. Offers MBA. Part-time and evening/weekend programs available. *Degree requirements:* For master's, thesis optional. *Entrance requirements:* For master's, GMAT, minimum GPA of 2.7. Additional exam requirements/recommendations for international students: Required—TOEFL. *Faculty research:* Media, international marketing, advanced marketing simulations, ethics in business.

Marketing Research

Hofstra University, Frank G. Zarb School of Business, Department of Marketing and International Business, Hempstead, NY 11549. Offers business administration (MBA), including international business, marketing; international business (Advanced Certificate); marketing (MS, Advanced Certificate); marketing research (MS). Part-time and evening/weekend programs available. *Faculty:* 9 full-time (0 women), 3 part-time/adjunct (0 women). *Students:* 91 full-time (54 women), 39 part-time (20 women); includes 11 minority (2 Black or African American, non-Hispanic/Latino; 3 Asian, non-Hispanic/Latino; 6 Hispanic/Latino), 73 international. Average age 27. 260 applicants, 71% accepted, 46 enrolled. In 2011, 43 master's awarded. *Degree requirements:* For master's, capstone course (MBA), thesis (MS), minimum GPA of 3.0. *Entrance requirements:* For master's, GMAT or GRE, 2 letters of recommendation, resume, essay. Additional exam requirements/recommendations for international students: Required—TOEFL (minimum score 550 paper-based; 213 computer-based; 80 iBT); Recommended—IELTS (minimum score 6). *Application deadline:* Applications are processed on a rolling basis. Application fee: $70 ($75 for international students). Electronic applications accepted. *Expenses:* Contact institution. *Financial support:* In 2011–12, 19 students received support, including 18 fellowships with full and partial tuition reimbursements available (averaging $7,371 per year); research assistantships with full and partial tuition reimbursements available, career-related internships or fieldwork, Federal Work-Study, institutionally sponsored loans, scholarships/grants, tuition waivers (full and partial), and unspecified assistantships also available. Support available to part-time students. Financial award applicants required to submit FAFSA. *Faculty research:* Outsourcing, global alliances, retailing, Web marketing, cross-cultural age research. *Unit head:* Dr. Benny Barak, Chairperson, 516-463-5707, Fax: 516-463-4834, E-mail: mktbzb@hofstra.edu. *Application contact:* Carol Drummer, Dean of Graduate Admissions, 516-463-4876, Fax: 516-463-4664, E-mail: gradstudent@hofstra.edu. Web site: http://www.hofstra.edu/business/.

Instituto Tecnológico y de Estudios Superiores de Monterrey, Campus Irapuato, Graduate Programs, Irapuato, Mexico. Offers administration (MBA); administration of information technology (MAIT); administration of telecommunications (MAT); architecture (M Arch); computer science (MCS); education (M Ed); educational administration (MEA); educational innovation and technology (DEIT); educational technology (MET); electronic commerce (MBA); environmental administration and planning (MEAP); environmental systems (MES); finances (MBA); humanistic studies (MHS); international management for Latin American executives (MIMLAE); library and information science (MLIS); manufacturing quality management (MMQM); marketing research (MBA).

Marquette University, Graduate School of Management, Department of Economics, Milwaukee, WI 53201-1881. Offers business economics (MSAE); financial economics (MSAE); international economics (MSAE); marketing research (MSAE); real estate economics (MSAE). Part-time and evening/weekend programs available. *Faculty:* 14 full-time (5 women), 3 part-time/adjunct (0 women). *Students:* 36 full-time (8 women), 37 part-time (13 women); includes 5 minority (2 Black or African American, non-Hispanic/Latino; 2 Hispanic/Latino; 1 Two or more races, non-Hispanic/Latino), 18 international. Average age 26. 120 applicants, 62% accepted, 27 enrolled. In 2011, 22 master's awarded. *Degree requirements:* For master's, comprehensive exam, professional project. *Entrance requirements:* For master's, GMAT or GRE General Test. Additional exam requirements/recommendations for international students: Required—TOEFL (minimum score 550 paper-based; 85 computer-based; 88 iBT), IELTS (minimum score 6.5), Pearson Test of English. *Application deadline:* For fall admission, 2/15 for domestic and international students. Applications are processed on a rolling basis. Application fee: $50. Electronic applications accepted. *Expenses: Tuition:* Full-time $17,010; part-time $945 per credit hour. Tuition and fees vary according to program. *Financial support:* In 2011–12, 2 fellowships, 7 teaching assistantships were awarded; research assistantships, Federal Work-Study, institutionally sponsored loans, scholarships/grants, and tuition waivers (full and partial) also available. Support available to part-time students. Financial award application deadline: 2/15. *Faculty research:* Monetary and fiscal policy in open economy, housing and regional migration, political economy of taxation and state/local government. *Total annual research expenditures:* $16,889. *Unit head:* Dr. Abdur Chowdhury, Chair, 414-288-6915, Fax: 414-288-5757. *Application contact:* Farrokh Nourzad, Information Contact, 414-288-3570. Web site: http://business.marquette.edu/academics/msae.

Pace University, Lubin School of Business, Marketing Program, New York, NY 10038. Offers marketing management (MBA); marketing research (MBA). Part-time and evening/weekend programs available. *Students:* 19 full-time (7 women), 52 part-time (33 women); includes 12 minority (2 Black or African American, non-Hispanic/Latino; 5 Asian, non-Hispanic/Latino; 4 Hispanic/Latino; 1 Two or more races, non-Hispanic/Latino), 35 international. Average age 27. 178 applicants, 40% accepted, 19 enrolled. In 2011, 24 master's awarded. *Entrance requirements:* For master's, GMAT, GRE. Additional exam requirements/recommendations for international students: Required—TOEFL. *Application deadline:* For fall admission, 7/31 priority date for domestic students; for spring admission, 11/30 for domestic students. Applications are processed on a rolling basis. Application fee: $70. Electronic applications accepted. *Expenses: Tuition:* Part-time $990 per credit. *Required fees:* $168 per semester. Tuition and fees vary according to course load and degree level. *Financial support:* Research assistantships, career-related internships or fieldwork, and Federal Work-Study available. Support available to part-time students. Financial award applicants required to submit FAFSA. *Unit head:* Dr. Mary M. Long, Chairperson, 212-618-6453, E-mail: mlong@pace.edu. *Application contact:* Susan Ford-Goldschein, Director of Graduate Admissions, 212-346-1531, Fax: 212-346-1585, E-mail: gradnyc@pace.edu. Web site: http://www.pace.edu/.

Southern Illinois University Edwardsville, Graduate School, School of Business, Department of Management and Marketing, Edwardsville, IL 62026. Offers marketing research (MMR). Part-time and evening/weekend programs available. *Faculty:* 18 full-time (5 women). *Students:* 10 full-time (4 women), 11 part-time (4 women); includes 5 minority (2 Asian, non-Hispanic/Latino; 3 Hispanic/Latino), 8 international. 24 applicants, 50% accepted. In 2011, 16 master's awarded. *Degree requirements:* For master's, comprehensive exam, final exam. *Entrance requirements:* For master's, GMAT. Additional exam requirements/recommendations for international students: Required—TOEFL (minimum score 550 paper-based; 213 computer-based; 79 iBT), IELTS (minimum score 6.5). *Application deadline:* For fall admission, 7/22 for domestic students, 6/1 for international students; for spring admission, 12/10 for domestic students, 10/1 for international students. Applications are processed on a rolling basis. Application fee: $30. Electronic applications accepted. Tuition and fees vary according to course load and program. *Financial support:* In 2011–12, 19 research assistantships with full tuition reimbursements (averaging $9,927 per year) were awarded; fellowships with full tuition reimbursements, teaching assistantships with full tuition reimbursements, institutionally sponsored loans, scholarships/grants, and unspecified assistantships also available. Financial award application deadline: 3/1; financial award applicants required to submit FAFSA. *Unit head:* Dr. Ralph Giacobbe, Chair, 618-650-2750, E-mail: rgiacob@siue.edu. *Application contact:* Dr. Ramana Madupalli, Program Director, 618-650-2701, E-mail: rmadupa@siue.edu. Web site: http://www.siue.edu/business/mgtmkt/.

Universidad Autonoma de Guadalajara, Graduate Programs, Guadalajara, Mexico. Offers administrative law and justice (LL M); advertising and corporate communications (MA); architecture (M Arch); business (MBA); computational science (MCC); education (Ed M, Ed D); English-Spanish translation (MA); entrepreneurship and management (MBA); integrated management of digital animation (MA); international business (MIB); international corporate law (LL M); internet technologies (MS); manufacturing systems (MMS); occupational health (MS); philosophy (MA, PhD); power electronics (MS); quality systems (MQS); renewable energy (MS); social evaluation of projects (MBA); strategic market research (MBA); tax law (MA); teaching mathematics (MA).

Universidad de las Americas, A.C., Program in Business Administration, Mexico City, Mexico. Offers finance (MBA); marketing research (MBA); production and quality (MBA).

University of Colorado Denver, Business School, Program in Marketing, Denver, CO 80217. Offers brand management and marketing communication (MS); global marketing (MS); high-tech and entrepreneurial marketing (MS); Internet marketing (MS); marketing for sustainability (MS); marketing research (MS); sports and entertainment marketing (MS). Part-time and evening/weekend programs available. *Students:* 39 full-time (29 women), 11 part-time (6 women); includes 4 minority (3 Hispanic/Latino; 1 Two or more races, non-Hispanic/Latino), 8 international. Average age 28. 40 applicants, 65% accepted, 16 enrolled. In 2011, 8 master's awarded. *Degree requirements:* For master's, 30 semester hours (21 of marketing core courses, 9 of graduate marketing electives). *Entrance requirements:* For master's, GMAT, resume, essay, two letters of recommendation, financial statements (for international applicants). Additional exam requirements/recommendations for international students: Required—TOEFL (minimum score 525 paper-based; 197 computer-based; 71 iBT). *Application deadline:* For fall admission, 4/15 priority date for domestic students, 3/15 for international students; for spring admission, 10/15 priority date for domestic students, 10/1 for international students. Applications are processed on a rolling basis. Application fee: $50 ($75 for international students). Electronic applications accepted. *Expenses:* Contact institution. *Financial support:* Federal Work-Study and scholarships/grants available. Support available to part-time students. Financial award application deadline: 4/1; financial award applicants required to submit FAFSA. *Faculty research:* Marketing issues in the Chinese environment, impact of individual difference and contextual factors on the risk-taking behaviors of managers making new-business creation decisions, attribution theory perspective of conflict between marketers and engineers, organizational identity and identification, international market entry strategies. *Unit head:* Dr. David Forlani, Associate Professor/Director of Marketing Programs, 303-315-8420, E-mail: david.forlani@ucdenver.edu. *Application contact:* Shelly Townley, Admissions Director, Graduate Programs, 303-315-8202, E-mail: shelly.townley@ucdenver.edu. Web site: http://www.ucdenver.edu/academics/colleges/business/degrees/ms/marketing/Pages/Marketing.aspx.

The University of Texas at Arlington, Graduate School, College of Business, Department of Marketing, Arlington, TX 76019. Offers marketing (PhD); marketing research (MS). Part-time and evening/weekend programs available. *Faculty:* 10 full-time (2 women). *Students:* 30 full-time (19 women), 18 part-time (7 women); includes 6 minority (1 Black or African American, non-Hispanic/Latino; 3 Asian, non-Hispanic/Latino; 2 Hispanic/Latino), 20 international. 66 applicants, 50% accepted, 23 enrolled. In 2011, 13 master's, 2 doctorates awarded. *Degree requirements:* For master's, thesis optional; for doctorate, comprehensive exam, thesis/dissertation. *Entrance requirements:* For master's and doctorate, GMAT, GRE. Additional exam requirements/recommendations for international students: Required—TOEFL (minimum score 550 paper-based; 213 computer-based; 79 iBT). *Application deadline:* For fall admission, 6/1 for domestic students, 4/1 for international students; for spring admission, 10/15 for domestic students, 9/15 for international students. Applications are processed on a rolling basis. Application fee: $40 ($70 for international students). Electronic applications accepted. *Financial support:* In 2011–12, 8 teaching assistantships (averaging $17,425 per year) were awarded; career-related internships or fieldwork, scholarships/grants, and unspecified assistantships also available. Support available to part-time students. Financial award application deadline: 6/1; financial award applicants required to submit FAFSA. *Faculty research:* Marketing strategy, marketing research, international marketing. *Total annual research expenditures:* $30,000. *Unit head:* Dr. Greg Frazier, Interim Chair, 817-272-0264, Fax: 817-272-2854, E-mail: frazier@uta.edu. *Application contact:* Dr. Robert Rogers, MS Program Director, 817-272-2340, Fax: 817-272-2854, E-mail: msmr@uta.edu. Web site: http://wweb.uta.edu/marketing/.

University of Wisconsin–Madison, Graduate School, Wisconsin School of Business, Wisconsin Full-Time MBA Program, Madison, WI 53706-1380. Offers applied security analysis (MBA); arts administration (MBA); brand and product management (MBA); corporate finance and investment banking (MBA); marketing research (MBA); operations and technology management (MBA); real estate (MBA); risk management and insurance (MBA); strategic human resource management (MBA); supply chain management (MBA). *Faculty:* 32 full-time (6 women), 27 part-time/adjunct (7 women). *Students:* 228 full-time (75 women); includes 53 minority (16 Black or African American, non-Hispanic/Latino; 25 Asian, non-Hispanic/Latino; 10 Hispanic/Latino; 2 Native Hawaiian or other Pacific Islander, non-Hispanic/Latino), 28 international. Average age 28. 509 applicants, 30% accepted, 111 enrolled. In 2011, 120 master's awarded. *Degree requirements:* For master's, thesis (for arts administration). *Entrance requirements:* For master's, GMAT, bachelor's or equivalent degree, 2 years of work experience, letters of recommendation. Additional exam requirements/recommendations for international students: Required—TOEFL (minimum score 600 paper-based; 250 computer-based; 100 iBT), IELTS. *Application deadline:* For fall admission, 11/4 for domestic and international students; for winter admission, 2/3 for domestic and international students; for spring admission, 4/27 for domestic and international students. Applications are processed on a rolling basis. Application fee: $56. Electronic applications accepted. *Expenses:* Tuition, state resident: full-time $10,296; part-time $643.51 per credit. Tuition, nonresident: full-time $24,054; part-time $1503.40 per credit. *Required fees:* $70.06 per credit. Tuition and fees vary according to course load, campus/location, program and reciprocity agreements. *Financial support:* In 2011–12, 176 students received support, including 20 fellowships with full and partial tuition reimbursements available (averaging $18,756 per year), 128 research assistantships with full tuition reimbursements available (averaging $25,185 per year), 28 teaching assistantships with full tuition reimbursements available (averaging $25,097 per year); scholarships/grants, health care benefits, and unspecified assistantships also available. Financial award application deadline: 4/27; financial award applicants required to submit FAFSA. *Faculty research:* Market consequences of International Financial Reporting Standards (IFRS), inter-firm relationships and strategic partnerships, application of Bayesian statistical methods and applied probability models to understanding individuals' behaviors in the context of customer relationship management (CRM) applications, liquidity provision and the structure of financial markets, strategic management of global startups. *Unit head:* Dr. Larry "Chip" W. Hunter, Associate Dean of Master's Programs, 608-265-3494, Fax: 608-265-4192, E-mail: lhunter@bus.wisc.edu. *Application contact:* Maria Reis, Assistant Director of MBA Marketing and Recruiting, 608-262-4000, Fax: 608-265-4192, E-mail: mreis@bus.wisc.edu. Web site: http://www.bus.wisc.edu/mba.

FASHION INSTITUTE OF TECHNOLOGY

State University of New York

M.P.S. in Cosmetics and Fragrance Marketing and Management

Program of Study

The Fashion Institute of Technology (FIT), a State University of New York (SUNY) college of art and design, business, and technology, is home to a mix of innovative achievers, creative thinkers, and industry pioneers. FIT fosters interdisciplinary initiatives, advances research, and provides access to an international network of professionals. With a reputation for excellence, FIT offers its diverse student body access to world-class faculty, dynamic and relevant curricula, and a superior education at an affordable cost. It offers seven programs of graduate study. The programs in Art Market: Principles and Practices; Exhibition Design; Fashion and Textile Studies: History, Theory, Museum Practice; and Sustainable Interior Environments lead to the Master of Arts (M.A.) degree. The Illustration program leads to the Master of Fine Arts (M.F.A.) degree. The Master of Professional Studies (M.P.S.) degree programs are Cosmetics and Fragrance Marketing and Management, and Global Fashion Management.

Cosmetics and Fragrance Marketing and Management is a 36-credit, part-time M.P.S. program designed to provide industry professionals with intensive training in high-level management skills while helping them build interdisciplinary, global perspectives. The curriculum focuses on building three skill sets that leaders in the cosmetics and fragrance industries have identified as crucial to managerial success: core business skills, such as management, corporate finance, international business, and management communication; marketing skills, such as advanced marketing theory, marketing communications, and market research and strategy; and technical and creative competencies, such as cosmetics and fragrance product knowledge, retail and creative management, and an intellectual foundation in beauty and fashion culture. An international component sends students to Europe and Asia to meet with industry leaders, talk with market research analysts, and visit diverse retail environments to develop a global business and cultural perspective. The program culminates in a capstone seminar.

Research Facilities

The School of Graduate Studies is primarily located in the campus's Shirley Goodman Resource Center, which also houses the Gladys Marcus Library and The Museum at FIT. School of Graduate Studies facilities include conference rooms; a fully equipped conservation laboratory; a multipurpose laboratory for conservation projects and the dressing of mannequins; storage facilities for costume and textile materials; a graduate student lounge with computer and printer access; a graduate student library reading room with computers, reference materials, and copies of past classes' qualifying and thesis papers; specialized wireless classrooms; traditional and digital illustration studios; and classrooms equipped with model stands, easels, and drafting tables.

The Gladys Marcus Library houses more than 300,000 volumes of print, nonprint, and digital resources. Specialized holdings include industry reference materials, manufacturers' catalogues, original fashion sketches and scrapbooks, photographs, portfolios of plates, and sample books. The FIT Digital Library provides access to over 90 searchable online databases.

The Museum at FIT houses one of the world's most important collections of clothing and textiles and is the only museum in New York City dedicated to the art of fashion. The permanent collection encompasses more than 50,000 garments and accessories dating from the eighteenth century to the present, with particular strength in twentieth-century fashion, as well as 30,000 textiles and 100,000 textile swatches. Each year, nearly 100,000 visitors are drawn to the museum's award-winning exhibitions and public programs.

Financial Aid

FIT directly administers its institutional grants, scholarships, and loans. Federal funding administered by the college may include Federal Perkins Loans, federally subsidized and unsubsidized Direct Loans for students, Grad PLUS loans, and the Federal Work-Study Program. Priority for institutionally administered funds is given to students enrolled and designated as full-time.

Cost of Study

Tuition for New York State residents is $4599 per semester, or $383 per credit. Out-of-state residents' tuition is $8352 per semester, or $696 per credit. Tuition and fees are subject to change at the discretion of FIT's Board of Trustees. Additional expenses—for class materials, textbooks, and travel—may apply and vary per program.

Living and Housing Costs

On-campus housing is available to graduate students. Traditional residence hall accommodations (including meal plan) cost from $6119 to $6299 per semester. Apartment-style housing options (not including meal plan) cost from $5241 to $9521 per semester.

Student Group

Enrollment in the School of Graduate Studies is approximately 200 students per academic year, allowing considerable individualized advisement. Students come to FIT from throughout the country and around the world.

Student Outcomes

Students in the Cosmetics and Fragrance Marketing and Management program maintain full-time employment in the industry while working toward their degree, which provides the basis for advancement to positions of upper-level managerial responsibility.

Location

FIT is located in Manhattan's Chelsea neighborhood, at the heart of the advertising, visual arts, marketing, fashion, business, design, and communications industries. Students are connected to New York City and gain unparalleled exposure to their field through guest lectures, field trips, internships, and sponsored competitions. The location provides access to major museums, galleries, and auction houses as well as dining, entertainment, and shopping options. The campus is near subway, bus, and commuter rail lines.

Applying

Applicants to all School of Graduate Studies programs must hold a baccalaureate degree in an appropriate major from a college or university, with a cumulative GPA of 3.0 or higher. International students from non-English-speaking countries are required to submit minimum TOEFL scores of 550 on the written test, 213 on the computer test, or 80 on the Internet test. Each major has additional, specialized prerequisites for admission; for detailed information, students should visit the School of Graduate Studies on FIT's Web site.

Domestic and international students use the same application when seeking admission. The deadline for Cosmetics and Fragrance Marketing and Management is March 15. After the deadline date, applicants are considered on a rolling admissions basis. Candidates may apply online at fitnyc.edu/gradstudies.

Correspondence and Information

School of Graduate Studies
Shirley Goodman Resource Center, Room E315
Fashion Institute of Technology
227 West 27 Street
New York, New York 10001-5992
Phone: 212-217-4300
Fax: 212-217-4301
E-mail: gradinfo@fitnyc.edu
Web sites: http://www.fitnyc.edu/gradstudies
http://www.fitnyc.edu/CFMM

THE FACULTY

A partial listing of faculty members is below. Guest lecturers are not included.

Stephan Kanlian, Chairperson; M.P.A., Pennsylvania.
Brooke Carlson, Sc.D., New Haven.
Dorothy C. Foster, J.D., Fordham.
Judy Galloway, A.B., Mary Baldwin.
Leslie Harris, M.P.S., Fashion Institute of Technology.
Mark Polson, M.P.S., Fashion Institute of Technology.
Cynthia Strite, Ph.D. candidate, Columbia Teachers College.
Mary Tumolo, former Vice President, Promotional Marketing, Lancôme, L'Oreal USA.
Rochelle Udell, M.S., Pratt.
Pamela Vaile, M.B.A., Pace.
Karen Young, B.A., Denver.
Jean Zimmerman, B.A., Florida.

Section 15
Nonprofit Management

This section contains a directory of institutions offering graduate work in nonprofit management. Additional information about programs listed in the directory but not augmented by an in-depth entry may be obtained by writing directly to the dean of a graduate school or chair of a department at the address given in the directory.

For programs offering related work, see also in this book *Accounting and Finance* and *Business Administration and Management*. In another guide in this series:

Graduate Programs in the Humanities, Arts & Social Sciences
See *Public, Regional, and Industrial Affairs*

CONTENTS

Program Directory

Nonprofit Management

American International College, School of Business Administration, Program in Nonprofit Management, Springfield, MA 01109-3189. Offers MS. Part-time programs available. *Entrance requirements:* Additional exam requirements/recommendations for international students: Required—TOEFL. Electronic applications accepted.

American Jewish University, Graduate School of Nonprofit Management, Program in Business Administration, Bel Air, CA 90077-1599. Offers general nonprofit administration (MBA); Jewish nonprofit administration (MBA). Part-time and evening/weekend programs available. *Degree requirements:* For master's, thesis, internship. *Entrance requirements:* For master's, GMAT or GRE General Test, interview, minimum undergraduate GPA of 3.0. Additional exam requirements/recommendations for international students: Required—TOEFL (minimum score 550 paper-based; 247 computer-based).

American Public University System, AMU/APU Graduate Programs, Charles Town, WV 25414. Offers accounting (MBA, MS); administration and supervision (M Ed); criminal justice (MA); emergency and disaster management (MA); entrepreneurship (MBA); environmental policy and management (MS), including environmental planning, environmental sustainability, fish and wildlife management, general (MA, MS), global environmental management; finance (MBA); general (MBA); global business management (MBA); guidance and counseling (M Ed); history (MA), including American history, ancient and classical history, European history, global history, military and diplomatic history, public history; homeland security (MA); homeland security resource allocation (MBA); humanities (MA); information technology (MS), including digital forensics, enterprise software development, information assurance and security, IT project management; information technology management (MBA); intelligence studies (MA), including criminal intelligence, general (MA, MS), homeland security, intelligence analysis, intelligence collection, intelligence operations, terrorism studies; international relations and conflict resolution (MA), including comparative and security issues, conflict resolution, international and transnational security issues, peacekeeping; legal studies (MA); management (MA), including defense management, general (MA, MS), human resource management, organizational leadership, public administration, reverse logistics, strategic consulting; marketing (MBA); military history (MA), including American military history, American revolution, civil war, war since 1946, World War II; military studies (MA), including air warfare, asymmetrical warfare, joint warfare, land warfare, naval warfare, strategic leadership; national security studies (MA), including general (MA, MS), homeland security, regional security studies, security and intelligence analysis, terrorism studies; nonprofit management (MBA); political science (MA), including American politics and government, comparative government and development, public policy; psychology (MA); public administration (MA, MPA), including disaster management (MPA), environmental policy (MA), health policy (MPA), human resources (MPA), national security (MPA), organizational management (MPA), security management (MPA); public health (MA, MPH), including emergency management (MPH), environmental health (MPH), public administration (MA); reverse logistics management (MA); security management (MA); space studies (MS), including aerospace science, planetary science; sports and health sciences (MS); sports management (MS), including coaching theory and strategy, sports administration; teaching (M Ed), including curriculum and instruction for elementary teachers, elementary, elementary reading, English language learners, instructional leadership, online learning, secondary social sciences, special education; transportation and logistics management (MA), including maritime engineering management. Programs offered via distance learning only. Part-time and evening/weekend programs available. Postbaccalaureate distance learning degree programs offered (no on-campus study). *Faculty:* 445 full-time (241 women), 1,360 part-time/adjunct (617 women). *Students:* 688 full-time (338 women), 10,168 part-time (3,706 women); includes 3,130 minority (1,007 Black or African American, non-Hispanic/Latino; 103 American Indian or Alaska Native, non-Hispanic/Latino; 825 Asian, non-Hispanic/Latino; 810 Hispanic/Latino; 51 Native Hawaiian or other Pacific Islander, non-Hispanic/Latino; 334 Two or more races, non-Hispanic/Latino), 134 international. Average age 35. In 2011, 2,386 master's awarded. *Degree requirements:* For master's, comprehensive exam or practicum. *Entrance requirements:* For master's, official transcript showing earned bachelor's degree from institution accredited by recognized accrediting body. Additional exam requirements/recommendations for international students: Required—TOEFL (minimum score 550 paper-based; 213 computer-based), IELTS (minimum score 6.5). *Application deadline:* Applications are processed on a rolling basis. Application fee: $0. Electronic applications accepted. *Expenses: Tuition:* Part-time $325 per credit hour. *Financial support:* Applicants required to submit FAFSA. *Faculty research:* Military history, criminal justice, management performance, national security. *Unit head:* Dr. Karan Powell, Executive Vice President and Provost, 877-468-6268, Fax: 304-724-3780. *Application contact:* Terry Grant, Vice President of Enrollment Management, 877-468-6268, Fax: 304-724-3780, E-mail: info@apus.edu. Web site: http://www.apus.edu.

American University, School of Public Affairs, Department of Public Administration, Washington, DC 20016-8070. Offers key executive leadership (MPA); leadership for organizational change (Certificate); non-profit management (Certificate); organization development (MSOD); public administration (MPA, PhD); public financial management (Certificate); public management (Certificate); public policy (MPP, Certificate), including public policy (MPP), public policy analysis (Certificate); public policy analysis (Certificate); LL M/MPA; MPA/JD; MPP/JD; MPP/LL M. Part-time and evening/weekend programs available. *Faculty:* 28 full-time (13 women), 14 part-time/adjunct (4 women). *Students:* 232 full-time (145 women), 240 part-time (145 women); includes 111 minority (62 Black or African American, non-Hispanic/Latino; 6 American Indian or Alaska Native, non-Hispanic/Latino; 21 Asian, non-Hispanic/Latino; 15 Hispanic/Latino; 7 Two or more races, non-Hispanic/Latino), 42 international. Average age 30. 809 applicants, 69% accepted, 172 enrolled. In 2011, 171 master's, 4 doctorates, 14 other advanced degrees awarded. *Degree requirements:* For master's, comprehensive exam; for doctorate, comprehensive exam, thesis/dissertation. *Entrance requirements:* For master's, GRE, statement of purpose; 2 recommendations, resume; for doctorate, GRE, 3 recommendations, statement of purpose, resume, writing sample; for Certificate, bachelor's degree. Additional exam requirements/recommendations for international students: Required—TOEFL. *Application deadline:* For fall admission, 2/1 for domestic students; for spring admission, 11/1 for domestic students. Application fee: $55. *Expenses: Tuition:* Full-time $24,264; part-time $1348 per credit hour. *Required fees:* $430. Tuition and fees vary according to course load and program. *Financial support:* Fellowships, research assistantships, teaching assistantships, career-related internships or fieldwork, Federal Work-Study, and institutionally sponsored loans available. Financial award application deadline: 2/1. *Faculty research:* Urban management, conservation politics, state and local budgeting, tax policy. *Unit head:* Dr. Jocelyn Johnston, Chair, 202-885-2608, Fax: 202-885-2347, E-mail: johnston@american.edu. *Application contact:* Brenda Manley, Admissions and Financial Aid Manager, 202-885-6202, Fax: 202-885-2355, E-mail: bmanley@american.edu. Web site: http://www.american.edu/spa/dpap/.

Arizona State University, College of Public Programs, School of Community Resources and Development, Phoenix, AZ 85004-0685. Offers community resources and development (PhD); nonprofit leadership and management (Graduate Certificate); nonprofit studies (MNpS); recreation and tourism studies (MS). Part-time and evening/weekend programs available. Terminal master's awarded for partial completion of doctoral program. *Degree requirements:* For master's, thesis or alternative, interactive Program of Study (iPOS) submitted before completing 50 percent of required credit hours; for doctorate, comprehensive exam, thesis/dissertation, interactive Program of Study (iPOS) submitted before completing 50 percent of required credit hours. *Entrance requirements:* For master's and doctorate, GRE, minimum GPA of 3.0 or equivalent in last 2 years of work leading to bachelor's degree. Additional exam requirements/recommendations for international students: Required—TOEFL (minimum score 80 iBT), TOEFL, IELTS, or Pearson Test of English. Electronic applications accepted. *Expenses:* Contact institution.

Arizona State University, College of Public Programs, School of Public Affairs, Phoenix, AZ 85004-0687. Offers public administration (nonprofit administration) (MPA); public administration (urban management) (MPA); public affairs (PhD); public policy (MPP); MPA/MSW. *Accreditation:* NASPAA (one or more programs are accredited). Part-time and evening/weekend programs available. Terminal master's awarded for partial completion of doctoral program. *Degree requirements:* For master's, thesis or alternative, policy analysis or capstone project; interactive Program of Study (iPOS) submitted before completing 50 percent of required credit hours; for doctorate, comprehensive exam, thesis/dissertation, interactive Program of Study (iPOS) submitted before completing 50 percent of required credit hours. *Entrance requirements:* For master's, GRE, minimum GPA of 3.0 or equivalent in last 2 years of work leading to bachelor's degree; for doctorate, GRE, minimum GPA of 3.0 or equivalent in last 2 years of work leading to bachelor's degree, 3 letters of recommendation, resume, statement of goals, samples of research reports. Additional exam requirements/recommendations for international students: Required—TOEFL (minimum score 600 paper-based; 213 computer-based; 100 iBT), IELTS (minimum score 6.5). Electronic applications accepted. *Expenses:* Contact institution.

Assumption College, Graduate Studies, Department of Business Studies, Worcester, MA 01609-1296. Offers accounting (MBA); business administration (CAGS); finance/economics (MBA); general business (MBA); human resources (MBA); international business (MBA); management (MBA); marketing (MBA); nonprofit leadership (MBA). Part-time and evening/weekend programs available. *Faculty:* 4 full-time (0 women), 16 part-time/adjunct (4 women). *Students:* 8 full-time (5 women), 133 part-time (65 women); includes 18 minority (8 Black or African American, non-Hispanic/Latino; 1 American Indian or Alaska Native, non-Hispanic/Latino; 2 Asian, non-Hispanic/Latino; 7 Hispanic/Latino), 3 international. Average age 30. 100 applicants, 75% accepted, 52 enrolled. In 2011, 53 master's, 1 other advanced degree awarded. *Degree requirements:* For master's, thesis, capstone. *Entrance requirements:* For master's and CAGS, 3 letters of recommendation, resume, essay. Additional exam requirements/recommendations for international students: Required—TOEFL (minimum score 540 paper-based; 200 computer-based; 76 iBT), IELTS (minimum score 6). *Application deadline:* For fall admission, 10/1 for domestic and international students; for winter admission, 2/1 for domestic and international students; for spring admission, 4/1 for domestic and international students. Applications are processed on a rolling basis. Application fee: $30. Electronic applications accepted. *Expenses: Tuition:* Full-time $9414; part-time $523 per credit. *Required fees:* $20 per term. Full-time tuition and fees vary according to course load and program. *Financial support:* In 2011–12, 14 students received support. Scholarships/grants, tuition waivers (partial), and unspecified assistantships available. Financial award application deadline: 5/1; financial award applicants required to submit FAFSA. *Faculty research:* Workplace diversity, dynamics of team interaction, utilization of leased employees, experiential learning project on due diligence market for prostheses. *Unit head:* Michael Lewis, Director, 508-767-7372, Fax: 508-767-7252, E-mail: milewis@assumption.edu. *Application contact:* Laura Lawrence, Graduate Programs Operations Manager, 508-767-7387, Fax: 508-767-7030, E-mail: graduate@assumption.edu. Web site: http://graduate.assumption.edu/mba/mba-assumption.

Azusa Pacific University, School of Business and Management, Azusa, CA 91702-7000. Offers business administration (MBA); diversity for strategic advantage (MA); entrepreneurship (MBA); finance (MBA); human and organizational development (MA); human resources and organizational development (MBA); human resources management (MA); international business (MBA); marketing (MBA); non-profit management (MA); organizational development and change (MA); performance improvement (MA); public administration (MA); strategic management (MBA). Part-time and evening/weekend programs available. *Degree requirements:* For master's, thesis (for some programs), final project. *Entrance requirements:* For master's, GMAT, minimum GPA of 3.0. Additional exam requirements/recommendations for international students: Required—TOEFL (minimum score 600 paper-based). *Expenses:* Contact institution. *Faculty research:* Gender issues, financial risk, leadership and ethics, marketing strategy.

Bay Path College, Program in Nonprofit Management and Philanthropy, Longmeadow, MA 01106-2292. Offers MS. Part-time and evening/weekend programs available. Postbaccalaureate distance learning degree programs offered (no on-campus study). *Students:* 14 full-time (12 women), 57 part-time (48 women); includes 12 minority (8 Black or African American, non-Hispanic/Latino; 1 American Indian or Alaska Native, non-Hispanic/Latino; 3 Hispanic/Latino). Average age 38. 59 applicants, 64% accepted, 29 enrolled. In 2011, 29 master's awarded. *Application deadline:* Applications are processed on a rolling basis. Application fee: $45. Electronic applications accepted. Application fee is waived when completed online. *Expenses: Tuition:* Part-time $665 per credit. Tuition and fees vary according to program. *Financial support:* In 2011–12, 27 students received support. Scholarships/grants available. Financial award applicants required to submit FAFSA. *Unit head:* Dr. Melissa Morriss-Olson, 413-565-1010, Fax: 413-565-1116, E-mail: mmolson@baypath.edu. *Application contact:* Lisa Adams, Director of Graduate Admissions, 413-565-1317, Fax: 413-565-1250, E-mail: ladams@baypath.edu.

Bay Path College, Program in Strategic Fundraising and Philanthropy, Longmeadow, MA 01106-2292. Offers higher education (MS); non-profit fundraising administration (MS). Part-time and evening/weekend programs available. Postbaccalaureate distance learning degree programs offered (no on-campus study). *Students:* 3 full-time (all women), 9 part-time (7 women), 1 international. Average age 30. 22 applicants, 73% accepted, 12 enrolled. In 2011, 4 master's awarded. *Application deadline:* Applications are processed on a rolling basis. Application fee: $45. Electronic applications accepted. Application fee is waived when completed online. *Expenses: Tuition:* Part-time $665 per credit. Tuition and fees vary according to program. *Financial support:* In 2011–12, 2 students received support. Scholarships/grants available. Financial award applicants required to submit FAFSA. *Application contact:* Lisa Adams, Director of Graduate Admissions, 413-565-1317, Fax: 413-565-1250, E-mail: ladams@baypath.edu.

Bernard M. Baruch College of the City University of New York, School of Public Affairs, Program in Public Administration, New York, NY 10010-5585. Offers general public administration (MPA); health care policy (MPA); nonprofit administration (MPA); policy analysis and evaluation (MPA); public management (MPA); MS/MPA. *Accreditation:* NASPAA. Part-time and evening/weekend programs available. *Faculty:* 45 full-time (17 women), 34 part-time/adjunct (12 women). *Students:* 177 full-time (121 women), 493 part-time (327 women); includes 347 minority (152 Black or African American, non-Hispanic/Latino; 2 American Indian or Alaska Native, non-Hispanic/Latino; 68 Asian, non-Hispanic/Latino; 107 Hispanic/Latino; 18 Two or more races, non-Hispanic/Latino). *Degree requirements:* For master's, thesis, capstone. *Entrance requirements:* For master's, GRE General Test. Additional exam requirements/recommendations for international students: Required—TOEFL. *Application deadline:* For fall admission, 4/1 priority date for domestic students, 4/1 for international students; for spring admission, 11/15 priority date for domestic students, 11/15 for international students. Applications are processed on a rolling basis. Application fee: $125. Electronic applications accepted. *Expenses:* Contact institution. *Financial support:* In 2011–12, fellowships (averaging $1,500 per year), research assistantships (averaging $12,000 per year) were awarded; career-related internships or fieldwork, Federal Work-Study, scholarships/grants, tuition waivers (partial), and unspecified assistantships also available. Support available to part-time students. Financial award application deadline: 5/15; financial award applicants required to submit FAFSA. *Faculty research:* Urbanization, population and poverty in the developing world, housing and community development, labor unions and housing, government-nongovernment relations, immigration policy, social network analysis, cross-sectoral governance, comparative healthcare systems, program evaluation, social welfare policy, health outcomes, educational policy and leadership, transnationalism, infant health, welfare reform, racial/ethnic disparities in health, urban politics, homelessness, race and ethnic relations. *Total annual research expenditures:* $2.6 million. *Unit head:* David S. Birdsell, Dean, 646-660-6700, Fax: 646-660-6721, E-mail: david.birdsell@baruch.cuny.edu. *Application contact:* Michael J. Lovaglio, Director of Student Affairs and Graduate Admissions, 646-660-6760, Fax: 646-660-6751, E-mail: michael.lovaglio@baruch.cuny.edu. Web site: http://www.baruch.cuny.edu/spa/.

Brandeis University, The Heller School for Social Policy and Management, Program in Nonprofit Management, Waltham, MA 02454-9110. Offers child, youth, and family management (MBA); health care management (MBA); social impact management (MBA); social policy and management (MBA); sustainable development (MBA); MBA/MA; MBA/MD. MBA/MD program offered in conjunction with Tufts University School of Medicine. *Accreditation:* AACSB. Part-time programs available. *Students:* 82 full-time (50 women), 7 part-time (5 women); includes 8 minority (2 Black or African American, non-Hispanic/Latino; 4 Asian, non-Hispanic/Latino; 2 Hispanic/Latino), 5 international. Average age 27. 130 applicants, 73% accepted, 56 enrolled. In 2011, 47 master's awarded. *Degree requirements:* For master's, team consulting project. *Entrance requirements:* For master's, GMAT (preferred) or GRE, 2 letters of recommendation, problem statement analysis, 3-5 years of professional experience. Additional exam requirements/recommendations for international students: Required—TOEFL (minimum score 600 paper-based; 250 computer-based; 100 iBT). *Application deadline:* For fall admission, 3/15 for domestic and international students. Applications are processed on a rolling basis. Application fee: $55. Electronic applications accepted. *Expenses:* Contact institution. *Financial support:* In 2011–12, 89 students received support. Career-related internships or fieldwork, scholarships/grants, and tuition waivers (partial) available. Support available to part-time students. Financial award application deadline: 3/15; financial award applicants required to submit FAFSA. *Faculty research:* Health care; children and families; elder and disabled services; social impact management; organizations in the non-profit, for-profit, or public sector. *Unit head:* Dr. Brenda Anderson, Program Director, 781-736-8423, E-mail: banderson@brandeis.edu. *Application contact:* Shana Sconyers, Assistant Director for Admissions and Financial Aid, 781-736-4229, E-mail: sconyers@brandeis.edu. Web site: http://heller.brandeis.edu/academic/mba.html.

Brigham Young University, Graduate Studies, Marriott School of Management, Master of Public Administration Program, Provo, UT 84602. Offers finance (MPA); human resources (MPA); local government (MPA); nonprofit management (MPA); JD/MPA. *Faculty:* 17 full-time (2 women), 14 part-time/adjunct (4 women). *Students:* 119 full-time (61 women); includes 16 minority (1 American Indian or Alaska Native, non-Hispanic/Latino; 6 Asian, non-Hispanic/Latino; 5 Hispanic/Latino; 4 Native Hawaiian or other Pacific Islander, non-Hispanic/Latino), 13 international. Average age 27. 132 applicants, 57% accepted, 61 enrolled. In 2011, 57 master's awarded. *Entrance requirements:* For master's, GRE or GMAT, minimum GPA of 3.0. Additional exam requirements/recommendations for international students: Required—TOEFL (minimum score 580 paper-based; 85 iBT), IELTS (minimum score 7). *Application deadline:* For fall admission, 1/15 for domestic and international students. Application fee: $50. Electronic applications accepted. *Expenses: Tuition:* Full-time $5760; part-time $320 per credit. Tuition and fees vary according to student's religious affiliation. *Financial support:* In 2011–12, 93 students received support. Career-related internships or fieldwork and scholarships/grants available. Financial award application deadline: 3/1; financial award applicants required to submit FAFSA. *Faculty research:* Taxes, budgeting, nonprofit, ethics, decision modeling, work balance, organizational behavior. *Unit head:* Dr. David W. Hart, Director, 801-422-4221, Fax: 801-422-0311, E-mail: mpa@byu.edu. *Application contact:* Catherine Cooper, Associate Director, 801-422-4221, E-mail: mpa@byu.edu. Web site: http://marriottschool.byu.edu/mpa.

California Lutheran University, Graduate Studies, School of Management, Thousand Oaks, CA 91360-2787. Offers business (IMBA); computer science (MS); econometrics (MBA); economics (MS); entrepreneurship (MBA, Certificate); finance (MBA, Certificate); financial planning (MBA, Certificate); information systems and technology (MS); information technology management (MBA, Certificate); international business (MBA, Certificate); management and organization behavior (MBA); management and organizational behavior (Certificate); marketing (MBA, Certificate); microeconomics (MBA); nonprofit and social enterprise (MBA). Part-time and evening/weekend programs available. Postbaccalaureate distance learning degree programs offered (no on-campus study). *Entrance requirements:* For master's, GMAT, interview, minimum GPA of 3.0. *Expenses:* Contact institution.

Cambridge College, School of Management, Cambridge, MA 02138-5304. Offers business negotiation and conflict resolution (M Mgt); general business (M Mgt); health care informatics (M Mgt); health care management (M Mgt); leadership in human and organizational dynamics (M Mgt); non-profit and public organization management (M Mgt); small business development (M Mgt); technology management (M Mgt). Part-time and evening/weekend programs available. *Degree requirements:* For master's, thesis, seminars. *Entrance requirements:* For master's, resume, 2 professional references. Additional exam requirements/recommendations for international students: Required—TOEFL (minimum score 550 paper-based; 213 computer-based; 79 iBT); Recommended—IELTS (minimum score 6). Electronic applications accepted. *Expenses:* Contact institution. *Faculty research:* Negotiation, mediation and conflict resolution; leadership; management of diverse organizations; case studies and simulation methodologies for management education, digital as a second language: social networking for digital immigrants, non-profit and public management.

Capella University, School of Human Services, Minneapolis, MN 55402. Offers addictions counseling (Certificate); counseling studies (MS, PhD); criminal justice (MS, PhD, Certificate); diversity studies (Certificate); general human services (MS, PhD); health care administration (MS, PhD, Certificate); management of nonprofit agencies (MS, PhD, Certificate); marital, couple and family counseling/therapy (MS); marriage and family services (Certificate); mental health counseling (MS); professional counseling (Certificate); social and community services (MS, PhD, Certificate). Part-time and evening/weekend programs available. Postbaccalaureate distance learning degree programs offered (minimal on-campus study). Terminal master's awarded for partial completion of doctoral program. *Degree requirements:* For master's, thesis optional, integrative project; for doctorate, comprehensive exam, thesis/dissertation. *Entrance requirements:* Additional exam requirements/recommendations for international students: Required—TOEFL (minimum score 550 paper-based; 213 computer-based), TWE (minimum score 4). Electronic applications accepted. *Faculty research:* Compulsive and addictive behaviors, substance abuse, assessment of psychopathology and neuropsychology.

Capella University, School of Public Service Leadership, Minneapolis, MN 55402. Offers criminal justice (MS, PhD); emergency management (MS, PhD); general human services (MS, PhD); general public administration (MPA, DPA); gerontology (MS); health care administration (MS, PhD); health management and policy (MSPH); management of nonprofit agencies (MS, PhD); nurse educator (MS); public safety leadership (MS, PhD); social and community services (MS, PhD); social behavioral sciences (MSPH).

Carlos Albizu University, Miami Campus, Graduate Programs, Miami, FL 33172-2209. Offers clinical psychology (Psy D); entrepreneurship (MBA); exceptional student education (MS); industrial/organizational psychology (MS); marriage and family therapy (MS); mental health counseling (MS); nonprofit management (MBA); organizational management (MBA); psychology (MS); school counseling (MS); teaching English as a second language (MS). *Accreditation:* APA. Part-time and evening/weekend programs available. *Faculty:* 19 full-time (12 women), 53 part-time/adjunct (27 women). *Students:* 524 full-time (431 women), 216 part-time (169 women); includes 563 minority (50 Black or African American, non-Hispanic/Latino; 1 American Indian or Alaska Native, non-Hispanic/Latino; 4 Asian, non-Hispanic/Latino; 492 Hispanic/Latino; 16 Native Hawaiian or other Pacific Islander, non-Hispanic/Latino), 17 international. Average age 31. 174 applicants, 67% accepted, 116 enrolled. In 2011, 157 master's, 21 doctorates awarded. Terminal master's awarded for partial completion of doctoral program. *Degree requirements:* For master's, one foreign language, comprehensive exam, integrative project (MBA), research project (exceptional student education, teaching English as a second language); for doctorate, one foreign language, comprehensive exam, internship, project. *Entrance requirements:* For master's, 3 letters of recommendation, interview, minimum GPA of 3.0, resume, statement of purpose, official transcripts; for doctorate, 3 letters of recommendation, minimum GPA of 3.0, resume, interview, statement of purpose, official transcripts. Additional exam requirements/recommendations for international students: Required—Michigan Test of English Language Proficiency. *Application deadline:* For fall admission, 4/1 priority date for domestic students, 5/1 for international students; for spring admission, 11/1 priority date for domestic students, 9/1 for international students. Applications are processed on a rolling basis. Application fee: $50. Electronic applications accepted. *Expenses: Tuition:* Full-time $9360; part-time $520 per credit. *Required fees:* $298 per term. Tuition and fees vary according to course load, degree level and program. *Financial support:* In 2011–12, 106 students received support. Federal Work-Study, scholarships/grants, and tuition discounts available. Financial award application deadline: 6/1; financial award applicants required to submit FAFSA. *Faculty research:* Psychotherapy, forensic psychology, neuropsychology, marketing strategy, entrepreneurship, special education. *Unit head:* Dr. Carmen S. Roca, Chancellor, 305-593-1223 Ext. 120, Fax: 305-629-8052, E-mail: croca@albizu.edu. *Application contact:* Vanessa Almendarez, Administrative Assistant, 305-593-1223 Ext. 137, Fax: 305-593-1854, E-mail: valmendarez@albizu.edu.

Case Western Reserve University, Weatherhead School of Management, Mandel Center for Nonprofit Organizations, Cleveland, OH 44106-7167. Offers MNO, CNM, JD/MNO, MNO/MSSA, MSSA/MNO. *Entrance requirements:* For master's, GMAT or GRE. Additional exam requirements/recommendations for international students: Required—TOEFL. *Expenses:* Contact institution. *Faculty research:* Leadership management of non-profit organizations, strategic alliances, economic analysis of non-profit organizations.

Chaminade University of Honolulu, Graduate Services, Program in Business Administration, Honolulu, HI 96816-1578. Offers accounting (MBA); business (MBA); not-for-profit (MBA); public sector (MBA). Part-time and evening/weekend programs available. *Faculty:* 5 full-time (1 woman), 17 part-time/adjunct (6 women). *Students:* 65 full-time (37 women), 50 part-time (23 women); includes 73 minority (6 Black or African American, non-Hispanic/Latino; 37 Asian, non-Hispanic/Latino; 6 Hispanic/Latino; 17 Native Hawaiian or other Pacific Islander, non-Hispanic/Latino; 7 Two or more races, non-Hispanic/Latino), 2 international. Average age 31. 52 applicants, 79% accepted, 29 enrolled. In 2011, 45 master's awarded. *Entrance requirements:* For master's, minimum GPA of 3.0, resume. Additional exam requirements/recommendations for international students: Required—TOEFL (minimum score 650 paper-based). *Application deadline:* For fall admission, 9/1 priority date for domestic students, 9/1 for international students; for winter admission, 12/1 priority date for domestic students, 12/1 for international students; for spring admission, 3/1 priority date for domestic students, 3/1 for international students. Applications are processed on a rolling basis. Application fee: $50. Electronic applications accepted. *Expenses: Required fees:* $600 per credit hour. One-time fee: $93 part-time. *Financial support:* In 2011–12, 35 students received support. Career-related internships or fieldwork, Federal Work-Study, and institutionally sponsored loans available. Support available to part-time students. Financial award application deadline: 3/1; financial award applicants required to submit FAFSA. *Faculty research:* Total quality management, international finance, not-for-profit accounting, service-learning in business contexts. *Unit head:* Dr. Scott J. Schroeder, Dean, 808-739-4611, Fax: 808-735-4734, E-mail: sschroed@chaminade.edu. *Application contact:* 808-739-4633, Fax: 808-739-8329, E-mail: gradserv@chaminade.edu. Web site: http://www.chaminade.edu/business_communication/mba/index.php.

Cleary University, Online Program in Business Administration, Ann Arbor, MI 48105-2659. Offers financial planning (MBA); financial planning (Graduate Certificate); green business strategy (MBA, Graduate Certificate); management (MBA); nonprofit management (MBA, Graduate Certificate); organizational leadership (MBA); public accounting (MBA). Part-time and evening/weekend programs available. Postbaccalaureate distance learning degree programs offered (no on-campus study). *Degree requirements:* For master's, thesis. *Entrance requirements:* For master's, bachelor's degree; minimum GPA of 2.5; professional resume indicating minimum 2 years management or related experience; undergraduate degree from an accredited college or university with at least 18 quarter hours (or 12 semester hours) of accounting study (for MBA in accounting). Additional exam requirements/recommendations for international students: Required—TOEFL (minimum score 550 paper-based; 213 computer-based; 79 iBT), Michigan English Language Assessment Battery (minimum score: 75). Electronic applications accepted.

Cleveland State University, College of Graduate Studies, Maxine Goodman Levin College of Urban Affairs, Program in Environmental Studies, Cleveland, OH 44115. Offers environmental nonprofit management (MAES); environmental planning (MAES); geographic information systems (Certificate); policy and administration (MAES); sustainable economic development (MAES); urban economic development (Certificate); urban real estate development and finance (Certificate); JD/MAES. Part-time and evening/weekend programs available. *Faculty:* 26 full-time (10 women), 3 part-time/adjunct (0 women). *Students:* 12 full-time (5 women), 23 part-time (12 women); includes 1 minority (Asian, non-Hispanic/Latino), 4 international. 18 applicants, 61% accepted, 6 enrolled. In 2011, 9 master's awarded. *Degree requirements:* For master's, thesis or alternative, exit project. *Entrance requirements:* For master's, GRE General Test (minimum score: verbal and quantitative in 40th percentile, analytical writing 4.0), minimum GPA of 3.0. Additional exam requirements/recommendations for international students: Required—TOEFL (minimum score 525 paper-based; 197 computer-based; 65 iBT). *Application deadline:* For fall admission, 7/15 priority date for domestic students, 5/15 for international students; for spring admission, 11/1 for international students. Applications are processed on a rolling basis. Application fee: $30. Electronic applications accepted. *Expenses:* Tuition, state resident: full-time $6416; part-time $494 per credit hour. Tuition, nonresident: full-time $12,074; part-time $929 per credit hour. *Financial support:* In 2011–12, 6 students received support, including 2 research assistantships with full and partial tuition reimbursements available (averaging $7,200 per year), 4 teaching assistantships with full and partial tuition reimbursements available (averaging $2,400 per year); career-related internships or fieldwork, scholarships/grants, traineeships, and unspecified assistantships also available. Support available to part-time students. Financial award application deadline: 3/1; financial award applicants required to submit FAFSA. *Faculty research:* Environmental policy and administration, environmental planning, geographic information systems (GIS), urban sustainability planning and management, energy policy, land re-use. *Unit head:* Dr. Sanda Kaufman, Director, 216-687-2367, Fax: 216-687-9342, E-mail: s.kaufman@csuohio.edu. *Application contact:* Joan Demko, Graduate Academic Program Specialist, 216-523-7522, Fax: 216-687-5398, E-mail: urbanprograms@csuohio.edu. Web site: http://urban.csuohio.edu/academics/graduate/maes/.

Cleveland State University, College of Graduate Studies, Maxine Goodman Levin College of Urban Affairs, Program in Nonprofit Administration and Leadership, Cleveland, OH 44115. Offers advanced fundraising (Certificate); local and urban management (Certificate); nonprofit administration and leadership (MNAL); nonprofit management (Certificate). Part-time and evening/weekend programs available. *Faculty:* 10 full-time (9 women), 8 part-time/adjunct (4 women). *Students:* 11 full-time (10 women), 20 part-time (17 women); includes 9 minority (7 Black or African American, non-Hispanic/Latino; 2 Asian, non-Hispanic/Latino). Average age 35. 45 applicants, 51% accepted, 12 enrolled. In 2011, 8 master's awarded. *Degree requirements:* For master's, thesis or alternative, capstone course. *Entrance requirements:* For master's, GRE (minimum score in 40th percentile verbal and quantitative, 4.0 analytical writing), minimum GPA of 3.0. Additional exam requirements/recommendations for international students: Required—TOEFL (minimum score 525 paper-based; 197 computer-based; 65 iBT). *Application deadline:* For fall admission, 7/15 priority date for domestic students, 5/15 for international students; for spring admission, 11/1 for international students. Applications are processed on a rolling basis. Application fee: $30. Electronic applications accepted. *Expenses:* Tuition, state resident: full-time $6416; part-time $494 per credit hour. Tuition, nonresident: full-time $12,074; part-time $929 per credit hour. *Financial support:* In 2011–12, 4 students received support, including 4 research assistantships with full and partial tuition reimbursements available (averaging $7,200 per year); career-related internships or fieldwork, scholarships/grants, traineeships, and unspecified assistantships also available. Support available to part-time students. Financial award application deadline: 3/1; financial award applicants required to submit FAFSA. *Faculty research:* Human resource management, volunteerism, performance measurement in nonprofits, government-nonprofit partnerships. *Unit head:* Dr. Mittie Davis Jones, Department Chair, 216-687-3861, Fax: 216-687-9342, E-mail: m.d.jones@csuohio.edu. *Application contact:* Joan Demko, Graduate Academic Program Specialist, 216-523-7522, Fax: 216-687-5398, E-mail: urbanprograms@csuohio.edu. Web site: http://urban.csuohio.edu/academics/graduate/mnal/.

Cleveland State University, College of Graduate Studies, Maxine Goodman Levin College of Urban Affairs, Program in Public Administration, Cleveland, OH 44115. Offers city management (MPA); economic development (MPA); healthcare administration (MPA); local and urban management (Certificate); non-profit management (Certificate); public financial management (MPA); public management (MPA); urban economic development (Certificate); JD/MPA. *Accreditation:* NASPAA. Part-time and evening/weekend programs available. *Faculty:* 26 full-time (10 women), 14 part-time/adjunct (8 women). *Students:* 36 full-time (22 women), 70 part-time (41 women); includes 31 minority (26 Black or African American, non-Hispanic/Latino; 1 American Indian or Alaska Native, non-Hispanic/Latino; 1 Asian, non-Hispanic/Latino; 2 Hispanic/Latino; 1 Two or more races, non-Hispanic/Latino), 4 international. Average age 36. 122 applicants, 52% accepted, 41 enrolled. In 2011, 45 master's awarded. *Degree requirements:* For master's, thesis or alternative, capstone course. *Entrance requirements:* For master's, GRE General Test (minimum scores in 40th percentile verbal and quantitative, 4.0 writing), minimum GPA of 3.0. Additional exam requirements/recommendations for international students: Required—TOEFL (minimum score 525 paper-based; 197 computer-based; 65 iBT). *Application deadline:* For fall admission, 7/15 priority date for domestic students, 5/15 for international students; for spring admission, 11/1 for international students. Applications are processed on a rolling basis. Application fee: $30. Electronic applications accepted. *Expenses:* Tuition, state resident: full-time $6416; part-time $494 per credit hour. Tuition, nonresident: full-time $12,074; part-time $929 per credit hour. *Financial support:* In 2011–12, 9 students received support, including 6 research assistantships with full and partial tuition reimbursements available (averaging $7,200 per year), 3 teaching assistantships with full and partial tuition reimbursements available (averaging $4,800 per year); career-related internships or fieldwork, scholarships/grants, traineeships, and unspecified assistantships also available. Support available to part-time students. Financial award application deadline: 3/1; financial award applicants required to submit FAFSA. *Faculty research:* Health care administration, public management, economic development, city management, nonprofit management. *Unit head:* Dr. Nancy Meyer-Emerick, Director, 216-687-2261, Fax: 216-687-9342, E-mail: n.meyeremerick@csuohio.edu. *Application contact:* Joan Demko, Graduate Academic Programs Specialist, 216-523-7522, Fax: 216-687-5398, E-mail: urbanprograms@csuohio.edu. Web site: http://urban.csuohio.edu/academics/graduate/mpa/.

The College at Brockport, State University of New York, School of Education and Human Services, Department of Public Administration, Brockport, NY 14420-2997. Offers arts administration (AGC); nonprofit management (AGC); public administration (MPA), including general public administration, health care management, nonprofit management. *Accreditation:* NASPAA. Part-time and evening/weekend programs available. *Students:* 24 full-time (20 women), 68 part-time (56 women); includes 19 minority (13 Black or African American, non-Hispanic/Latino; 4 Asian, non-Hispanic/Latino; 2 Hispanic/Latino). 49 applicants, 65% accepted, 21 enrolled. In 2011, 31 degrees awarded. *Degree requirements:* For master's, thesis or alternative. *Entrance requirements:* For master's, GRE or minimum GPA of 3.0, letters of recommendation, statement of objectives; current resume. Additional exam requirements/recommendations for international students: Required—TOEFL (minimum score 550 paper-based; 213 computer-based; 79 iBT). *Application deadline:* For fall admission, 3/1 priority date for domestic students, 3/1 for international students; for spring admission, 10/1 priority date for domestic students, 10/1 for international students. Application fee: $50. Electronic applications accepted. *Financial support:* In 2011–12, teaching assistantships with full tuition reimbursements (averaging $6,000 per year) were awarded; Federal Work-Study, scholarships/grants, and unspecified assistantships also available. Support available to part-time students. Financial award application deadline: 3/15; financial award applicants required to submit FAFSA. *Faculty research:* E-government, performance management, nonprofits and policy implementation, Medicaid and disabilities. *Unit head:* Dr. Ed Downey, Chairperson, 585-395-5568, Fax: 585-395-2172, E-mail: edowney@brockport.edu. *Application contact:* Dr. Ed Downey, Chairperson, 585-395-5568, Fax: 585-395-2172, E-mail: edowney@brockport.edu. Web site: http://www.brockport.edu/graduate/.

The College of Saint Rose, Graduate Studies, School of Business, Department of Not-for-Profit Management, Albany, NY 12203-1419. Offers Certificate. Part-time and evening/weekend programs available. *Entrance requirements:* For degree, minimum undergraduate GPA of 3.0 or GMAT. Additional exam requirements/recommendations for international students: Required—TOEFL (minimum score 550 paper-based; 213 computer-based). Electronic applications accepted.

Columbia University, School of Continuing Education, Program in Fundraising Management, New York, NY 10027. Offers MS. Part-time and evening/weekend programs available. *Degree requirements:* For master's, internship. *Entrance requirements:* For master's, BA with minimum GPA of 3.0. Additional exam requirements/recommendations for international students: Required—American Language Program placement test; Recommended—TOEFL. Electronic applications accepted. *Faculty research:* Fundraising for annual campaigns, capital campaigns, nonprofit financial management, research for fundraising and planned giving.

Corban University, Graduate School, The Corban MBA, Salem, OR 97301-9392. Offers management (MBA); non-profit management (MBA). Postbaccalaureate distance learning degree programs offered (no on-campus study).

Daemen College, Program in Executive Leadership and Change, Amherst, NY 14226-3592. Offers business (MS); health professions (MS); not-for-profit organizations (MS). Part-time and evening/weekend programs available. *Degree requirements:* For master's, thesis, cohort learning sequence (2 years for weekend cohort; 3 years for weeknight cohort). *Entrance requirements:* For master's, 2 letters of recommendation, interview, goal statement, official transcripts, resume. Additional exam requirements/recommendations for international students: Required—TOEFL (minimum score 500 paper-based; 173 computer-based; 63 iBT), IELTS (minimum score 5.5). Electronic applications accepted.

Dallas Baptist University, College of Business, Business Administration Program, Dallas, TX 75211-9299. Offers accounting (MBA); business communication (MBA); conflict resolution management (MBA); entrepreneurship (MBA); finance (MBA); health care management (MBA); international business (MBA); leading the non-profit organization (MBA); management (MBA); management information systems (MBA); marketing (MBA); project management (MBA); technology and engineering management (MBA). *Accreditation:* ACBSP. Part-time and evening/weekend programs available. *Entrance requirements:* For master's, GMAT, minimum GPA of 3.0. Additional exam requirements/recommendations for international students: Required—TOEFL, IELTS. *Application deadline:* Applications are processed on a rolling basis. Application fee: $25. Electronic applications accepted. *Expenses: Tuition:* Full-time $12,060; part-time $670 per credit hour. *Required fees:* $100; $50 per semester. *Financial support:* Federal Work-Study, institutionally sponsored loans, scholarships/grants, and tuition waivers (full and partial) available. Support available to part-time students. Financial award applicants required to submit FAFSA. *Faculty research:* Sports management, services marketing, retailing, strategic management, financial planning/investments. *Unit head:* Dr. Sandra S. Reid, Director, 214-333-5280, Fax: 214-333-5293, E-mail: graduate@dbu.edu. *Application contact:* Kit P. Montgomery, Director of Graduate Programs, 214-333-5242, Fax: 214-333-5579, E-mail: graduate@dbu.edu. Web site: http://www3.dbu.edu/graduate/mba.asp.

Dallas Baptist University, Gary Cook School of Leadership, Program in Christian Education, Dallas, TX 75211-9299. Offers adult ministry (MA); business ministry (MA); Christian studies (MA); collegiate ministry (MA); communication ministry (MA); counseling ministry (MA); family ministry (MA); general ministry (MA); leading the nonprofit organization (MA); missions ministry (MA); small group ministry (MA); student ministry (MA); worship ministry (MA); MA/MA. Part-time and evening/weekend programs available. *Entrance requirements:* For master's, minimum GPA of 3.0. Additional exam requirements/recommendations for international students: Required—TOEFL. *Application deadline:* Applications are processed on a rolling basis. Application fee: $25. Electronic applications accepted. *Expenses: Tuition:* Full-time $12,060; part-time $670 per credit hour. *Required fees:* $100; $50 per semester. *Financial support:* Federal Work-Study, institutionally sponsored loans, scholarships/grants, and tuition waivers (full and partial) available. Support available to part-time students. Financial award applicants required to submit FAFSA. *Unit head:* Dr. Judy Morris, Director, 214-333-5246, Fax: 214-333-5115, E-mail: graduate@dbu.edu. *Application contact:* Kit P. Montgomery, Director of Graduate Programs, 214-333-5242, Fax: 214-333-5579, E-mail: graduate@dbu.edu. Web site: http://www3.dbu.edu/leadership/mace/.

Dallas Baptist University, Gary Cook School of Leadership, Program in Global Leadership, Dallas, TX 75211-9299. Offers business communication (MA); East Asian studies (MA); ESL (MA); general studies (MA); global leadership (MA); global studies (MA); international business (MA); leading the nonprofit organization (MA); missions (MA); small group ministry (MA); MA/MA. Part-time and evening/weekend programs available. *Entrance requirements:* For master's, minimum GPA of 3.0. Additional exam requirements/recommendations for international students: Required—TOEFL, IELTS. Application fee: $25. *Expenses: Tuition:* Full-time $12,060; part-time $670 per credit hour. *Required fees:* $100; $50 per semester. *Financial support:* Federal Work-Study, institutionally sponsored loans, scholarships/grants, and tuition waivers (full and partial) available. Support available to part-time students. Financial award applicants required to submit FAFSA. *Unit head:* Dr. Bob Garrett, Director, 214-333-5508, Fax: 214-333-5689, E-mail: graduate@dbu.edu. *Application contact:* Kit P. Montgomery, Director of Graduate Programs, 214-333-5242, Fax: 214-333-5579, E-mail: graduate@dbu.edu. Web site: http://www3.dbu.edu/leadership/globalleadership.asp.

DePaul University, School of Public Service, Chicago, IL 60604. Offers administrative foundations (Certificate); community development (Certificate); financial administration management (Certificate); health administration (Certificate); health law and policy (MS); international public services (MS); leadership and policy studies (MS); metropolitan planning (Certificate); nonprofit leadership (Certificate); nonprofit management (MNM); public administration (MPA); public service management (MS), including association management, fundraising and philanthropy, healthcare administration, higher education administration, metropolitan planning; public services (Certificate); JD/MS. Part-time and evening/weekend programs available. Postbaccalaureate distance learning degree programs offered (minimal on-campus study). *Faculty:* 14 full-time (3 women), 43 part-time/adjunct (24 women). *Students:* 366 full-time (266 women), 316 part-time (216 women); includes 283 minority (143 Black or African American, non-Hispanic/Latino; 1 American Indian or Alaska Native, non-Hispanic/Latino; 35 Asian, non-Hispanic/Latino; 88 Hispanic/Latino; 16 Two or more races, non-Hispanic/Latino), 13 international. Average age 29. 162 applicants, 100% accepted, 94 enrolled. In 2011, 108 master's awarded. *Degree requirements:* For master's, thesis or integrative seminar. *Entrance requirements:* For master's, minimum GPA of 2.7. Additional exam requirements/recommendations for international students: Required—TOEFL (minimum score 550 paper-based; 213 computer-based; 80 iBT), IELTS (minimum score 6.5). *Application deadline:* Applications are processed on a rolling basis. Application fee: $40. Electronic applications accepted. *Financial support:* In 2011–12, 60 students received support, including 3 research assistantships with full tuition reimbursements available (averaging $7,000 per year); career-related internships or fieldwork, Federal Work-Study, institutionally sponsored loans, scholarships/grants, tuition waivers (partial), and unspecified assistantships also available. Support available to part-time students. Financial award application deadline: 7/1; financial award applicants required to submit FAFSA. *Faculty research:* Government financing, transportation, leadership, health care, volunteerism and organizational behavior, non-profit organizations. *Total annual research expenditures:* $20,000. *Unit head:* Dr. J. Patrick Murphy, Director, 312-362-5608, Fax: 312-362-5506, E-mail: jpmurphy@depaul.edu. *Application contact:* Megan B. Balderston, Director of Admissions and Marketing, 312-362-5565, Fax: 312-362-5506, E-mail: pubserv@depaul.edu. Web site: http://las.depaul.edu/sps/.

Eastern Michigan University, Graduate School, College of Business, Programs in Business Administration, Ypsilanti, MI 48197. Offers business administration (MBA, Graduate Certificate); computer information systems (Graduate Certificate); e-business (MBA, Graduate Certificate); enterprise business intelligence (MBA); entrepreneurship (MBA, Graduate Certificate); finance (MBA, Graduate Certificate); human resources (MBA); human resources management (Graduate Certificate); information systems (MBA); internal auditing (MBA); international business (MBA, Graduate Certificate); marketing management (Graduate Certificate); nonprofit management (MBA); organizational development (Graduate Certificate); supply chain management (MBA, Graduate Certificate). *Accreditation:* AACSB. Part-time programs available. Postbaccalaureate distance learning degree programs offered (no on-campus study). *Students:* 79 full-time (39 women), 287 part-time (143 women); includes 55 minority (22 Black or African American, non-Hispanic/Latino; 24 Asian, non-Hispanic/Latino; 6 Hispanic/Latino; 3 Two or more races, non-Hispanic/Latino), 238 international. Average age 32. 317 applicants, 62% accepted, 89 enrolled. In 2011, 102 master's, 58 other advanced degrees awarded. *Entrance requirements:* For master's, GMAT (minimum score 450), minimum cumulative undergraduate GPA of 2.75. Additional exam requirements/recommendations for international students: Required—TOEFL. *Application deadline:* For fall admission, 5/15 for domestic students, 5/1 for international students; for winter admission, 10/15 for domestic students, 10/1 for international students; for spring admission, 3/15 for domestic students, 3/1 for international students. Applications are processed on a rolling basis. Application fee: $35. *Expenses:* Tuition, state resident: full-time $10,367; part-time $432 per credit hour. Tuition, nonresident: full-time $20,435; part-time $851 per credit hour. *Required fees:* $39 per credit hour. $46 per semester. One-time fee: $100. Tuition and fees vary according to course level, degree level and reciprocity agreements. *Financial support:* Fellowships, research assistantships with full tuition reimbursements, teaching assistantships with full tuition reimbursements, career-related internships or fieldwork, Federal Work-Study, institutionally sponsored loans, scholarships/grants, tuition waivers (partial), and unspecified assistantships available. Support available to part-time students. Financial award applicants required to submit FAFSA. *Unit head:* K. Michelle Henry, Director, Academic Services, 734-487-4444, Fax: 734-483-1316, E-mail: mhenry1@emich.edu. *Application contact:* Beste Windes, Advisor, 734-487-4444, Fax: 734-483-1316, E-mail: bwindes@emich.edu. Web site: http://www.emich.edu/public/cob/gr/grad.html.

Eastern Michigan University, Graduate School, College of Health and Human Services, Interdisciplinary Program in Non-Profit Management, Ypsilanti, MI 48197. Offers Graduate Certificate. *Students:* 3 part-time (all women); includes 1 minority (Hispanic/Latino). Average age 42. 2 applicants, 50% accepted, 1 enrolled. In 2011, 3 degrees awarded. *Expenses:* Tuition, state resident: full-time $10,367; part-time $432 per credit hour. Tuition, nonresident: full-time $20,435; part-time $851 per credit hour. *Required fees:* $39 per credit hour. $46 per semester. One-time fee: $100. Tuition and fees vary according to course level, degree level and reciprocity agreements. *Unit head:* Dr. Marcia Bombyk, Program Coordinator, 734-487-4173, Fax: 734-487-8536, E-mail: marcia.bombyk@emich.edu. *Application contact:* Graduate Admissions, 734-487-2400, Fax: 734-487-6559, E-mail: graduate.admissions@emich.edu.

Eastern University, School of Leadership and Development, Program in Nonprofit Management, St. Davids, PA 19087-3696. Offers MS. *Entrance requirements:* For master's, minimum GPA of 2.5.

East Tennessee State University, School of Graduate Studies, College of Arts and Sciences, Department of Political Science, International Affairs and Public Administration, Johnson City, TN 37614. Offers city management (MCM); economic development (Postbaccalaureate Certificate); not-for-profit administration (MPA); planning and development (MPA); public financial management (MPA); urban planning (Postbaccalaureate Certificate). Part-time programs available. *Faculty:* 7 full-time (2 women), 1 part-time/adjunct (0 women). *Students:* 27 full-time (12 women), 12 part-time (4 women); includes 9 minority (5 Black or African American, non-Hispanic/Latino; 1 American Indian or Alaska Native, non-Hispanic/Latino; 3 Hispanic/Latino), 4 international. Average age 29. 32 applicants, 63% accepted, 15 enrolled. In 2011, 12 degrees awarded. *Degree requirements:* For master's, internship. *Entrance requirements:* For master's, GRE General Test, three letters of recommendation; for Postbaccalaureate Certificate, GRE General Test. Additional exam requirements/recommendations for international students: Required—TOEFL (minimum score 550 paper-based; 213 computer-based; 79 iBT). *Application deadline:* For fall admission, 6/1 for domestic students, 4/29 for international students; for spring admission, 11/1 for domestic students, 9/30 for international students. Application fee: $35 ($45 for international students). Electronic applications accepted. *Expenses:* Tuition, state resident: full-time $7312; part-time $350 per credit hour. Tuition, nonresident: full-time $18,490; part-time $621 per credit hour. *Required fees:* $63 per credit hour. Tuition and fees vary according to course load and program. *Financial support:* In 2011–12, 18 students received support, including 7 research assistantships with full tuition reimbursements available (averaging $6,000 per year); career-related internships or fieldwork, institutionally sponsored loans, scholarships/grants, and unspecified assistantships also available. Financial award application deadline: 7/1; financial award applicants required to submit FAFSA. *Faculty research:* American politics, comparative politics, international relations, public administration, public law. *Unit head:* Dr. Weixing Chen, Chair, 423-439-4217, Fax: 423-439-4348, E-mail: chen@etsu.edu. *Application contact:* Gail Powers, Graduate Specialist, 423-439-4703, Fax: 423-439-5624, E-mail: pwersg@etsu.edu.

Fairleigh Dickinson University, Metropolitan Campus, Anthony J. Petrocelli College of Continuing Studies, Public Administration Institute, Teaneck, NJ 07666-1914. Offers public administration (MPA, Certificate); public non-profit management (Certificate).

Florida Atlantic University, College of Design and Social Inquiry, School of Public Administration, Program in Nonprofit Management, Boca Raton, FL 33431-0991. Offers MNM. *Students:* 18 full-time (14 women), 36 part-time (31 women); includes 26 minority (16 Black or African American, non-Hispanic/Latino; 1 Asian, non-Hispanic/Latino; 7 Hispanic/Latino; 2 Two or more races, non-Hispanic/Latino), 1 international. Average age 33. 51 applicants, 88% accepted, 15 enrolled. In 2011, 13 master's awarded. *Degree requirements:* For master's, thesis optional. *Entrance requirements:* For master's, GRE, minimum GPA of 3.0. Additional exam requirements/recommendations for international students: Required—TOEFL. *Application deadline:* For fall admission, 5/1 priority date for domestic students, 2/15 for international students; for spring admission, 11/1 priority date for domestic students, 7/15 for international students. Application fee: $30. *Expenses: Tuition, area resident:* Part-time $343.02 per credit hour. Tuition, state resident: full-time $8232. Tuition, nonresident: full-time $23,931; part-time $997.14 per credit hour. *Financial support:* Career-related internships or fieldwork and institutionally sponsored loans available. *Faculty research:* Governance, nonprofit management, resource development, public and private nonprofit enterprise, accounting for government. *Unit head:* Dr. Ron Nyhan, Coordinator, 954-762-5664, E-mail: rcnyhan@fau.edu. *Application contact:* Dr. Sofia Do Espirito Santo, 954-762-5158, E-mail: ssanto@fau.edu. Web site: http://www.fau.edu/caupa/spa/mnm/index.html.

George Mason University, College of Humanities and Social Sciences, Department of Public and International Affairs, Fairfax, VA 22030. Offers association management (Certificate); biodefense (MS, PhD); emergency management and homeland security (Certificate); nonprofit management (Certificate); political science (MA, PhD); public administration (MPA); public management (Certificate). *Accreditation:* NASPAA (one or more programs are accredited). *Faculty:* 37 full-time (12 women), 38 part-time/adjunct (9 women). *Students:* 139 full-time (74 women), 316 part-time (178 women); includes 92 minority (31 Black or African American, non-Hispanic/Latino; 21 Asian, non-Hispanic/Latino; 27 Hispanic/Latino; 3 Native Hawaiian or other Pacific Islander, non-Hispanic/Latino; 10 Two or more races, non-Hispanic/Latino), 14 international. Average age 31. 505 applicants, 54% accepted, 134 enrolled. In 2011, 135 master's, 3 doctorates, 8 other advanced degrees awarded. *Entrance requirements:* For master's, GRE, GMAT or LSAT (for MPA); GRE (for MS in biodefense and MA in political science), expanded goals statement; 3 letters of recommendation; official transcripts; resume (for MPA); writing sample (for MS, MA); for doctorate, GRE (taken within the last 5 years), 3 letters of recommendation; expanded goals statement; resume; official transcript; writing sample; for Certificate, GRE, GMAT or LSAT, expanded goals statement; 3 letters of recommendation; official transcripts; resume. Additional exam requirements/recommendations for international students: Required—TOEFL (minimum score 570 paper-based; 230 computer-based; 88 iBT), IELTS, Pearson Test of English. Application fee: $65 ($80 for international students). Electronic applications accepted. *Expenses:* Tuition, state resident: full-time $8750; part-time $364.58 per credit. Tuition, nonresident: full-time $24,092; part-time $1003.83 per credit. *Required fees:* $2514; $104.75 per credit. *Financial support:* In 2011–12, 30 students received support, including 3 fellowships with full tuition reimbursements available (averaging $18,000 per year), 12 research assistantships with full and partial tuition reimbursements available (averaging $11,769 per year), 15 teaching assistantships with full and partial tuition reimbursements available (averaging $11,600 per year); career-related internships or fieldwork, Federal Work-Study, scholarships/grants, unspecified assistantships, and health care benefits (full-time research or teaching assistantship recipients) also available. Support available to part-time students. Financial award application deadline: 3/1; financial award applicants required to submit FAFSA. *Faculty research:* The Rehnquist Court and economic liberties; intersection of economic development with high-tech industry, telecommunications, and entrepreneurism; political economy of development; violence, terrorism and U. S. foreign policy; international security issues. *Total annual research expenditures:* $666,214. *Unit head:* Dr. Priscilla Regan, Chair, 703-993-1419, Fax: 703-993-1399, E-mail: pregan@gmu.edu. *Application contact:* Peg Koback, Education Support Specialist, 703-993-9466, E-mail: mkoback@gmu.edu. Web site: http://pia.gmu.edu/.

Georgia State University, Andrew Young School of Policy Studies, Department of Public Management and Policy, Atlanta, GA 30303. Offers disaster management (Certificate); non-profit management (Certificate); planning and economic development (Certificate); public administration (MPA), including criminal justice, management and finance, nonprofit management, planning and economic development, policy analysis and evaluation, public health; public policy (MPP, PhD), including disaster policy (MPP), nonprofit policy (MPP), planning and economic development policy (MPP), public finance policy (MPP), social policy (MPP); JD/MPA. *Accreditation:* NASPAA (one or more programs are accredited). Part-time and evening/weekend programs available. Terminal master's awarded for partial completion of doctoral program. *Degree requirements:* For master's, thesis optional; for doctorate, comprehensive exam, thesis/dissertation. *Entrance requirements:* For master's and doctorate, GRE General Test. Additional exam requirements/recommendations for international students: Required—TOEFL. Electronic applications accepted. *Faculty research:* Public management, policy analysis, public finance, planning and economic development, nonprofit leadership and policy.

Gratz College, Graduate Programs, Program in Jewish Non-Profit Management, Melrose Park, PA 19027. Offers Graduate Certificate. *Application contact:* Joanna Boeing Bratton, Director of Admissions, 215-635-7300 Ext. 140, Fax: 215-635-7399, E-mail: admissions@gratz.edu.

Hamline University, School of Business, St. Paul, MN 55104-1284. Offers business (MBA); nonprofit management (MA); public administration (MA, DPA); JD/MA; JD/MBA; LL M/MA; LL M/MBA; MA/MA; MBA/MA. Part-time and evening/weekend programs available. *Faculty:* 21 full-time (9 women), 44 part-time/adjunct (12 women). *Students:* 435 full-time (221 women), 117 part-time (63 women); includes 71 minority (44 Black or African American, non-Hispanic/Latino; 2 American Indian or Alaska Native, non-Hispanic/Latino; 17 Asian, non-Hispanic/Latino; 5 Hispanic/Latino; 3 Two or more races, non-Hispanic/Latino), 66 international. Average age 33. 316 applicants, 70% accepted, 149 enrolled. In 2011, 295 master's awarded. *Degree requirements:* For master's, thesis (for some programs); for doctorate, comprehensive exam, thesis/dissertation. *Entrance requirements:* For master's, personal statement, official transcripts, curriculum vitae, letters of recommendation, writing sample; for doctorate, personal statement, curriculum vitae, official transcripts, letters of recommendation, writing sample. Additional exam requirements/recommendations for international students: Required—TOEFL (minimum score 80 iBT). *Application deadline:* Applications are processed on a rolling basis. Application fee: $0 ($100 for international students). Electronic applications accepted. *Expenses: Tuition:* Full-time $3720; part-time $465 per credit. *Required fees:* $28 per year. Tuition and fees vary according to degree level, campus/location and program. *Financial support:* Federal Work-Study and scholarships/grants available. Support available to part-time students. Financial award applicants required to submit FAFSA. *Faculty research:* Liberal arts-based business programs, experiential learning, organizational process/politics, gender differences, social equity. *Unit head:* Dr. Anne McCarthy, Dean, 651-523-2284, Fax: 651-523-3098, E-mail: amccarthy02@gw.hamline.edu. *Application contact:* Michael Hand, Assistant Director, Graduate Admission, 651-523-2900, Fax: 651-523-3058, E-mail: mhand01@gw.hamline.edu. Web site: http://www.hamline.edu/business.

Hebrew Union College–Jewish Institute of Religion, School of Jewish Nonprofit Management, Los Angeles, CA 90007. Offers MA.

High Point University, Norcross Graduate School, High Point, NC 27262-3598. Offers business administration (MBA); educational leadership (M Ed); elementary education (M Ed); history (MA); nonprofit management (MA); secondary math (M Ed); special education (M Ed); strategic communication (MA); teaching elementary education k-6 (MAT); teaching secondary mathematics 9-12 (MAT). *Accreditation:* ACBSP; NCATE. Part-time and evening/weekend programs available. *Degree requirements:* For master's, comprehensive exam (for some programs), thesis (for some programs). *Entrance requirements:* For master's, GMAT (MBA), GRE, MAT, minimum GPA of 3.0. Additional exam requirements/recommendations for international students: Required—TOEFL (minimum score 550 paper-based). Electronic applications accepted.

Hope International University, School of Graduate and Professional Studies, Program in Business Administration, Fullerton, CA 92831-3138. Offers general management (MBA, MSM); international development (MBA, MSM); marketing management (MBA, MSM); non-profit management (MBA, MSM). Part-time programs available. Postbaccalaureate distance learning degree programs offered (no on-campus study). *Degree requirements:* For master's, comprehensive exam (for some programs), thesis (for some programs), project. *Entrance requirements:* For master's, minimum GPA of 3.0; 2 references. Additional exam requirements/recommendations for international students: Required—TOEFL (minimum score 550 paper-based; 213 computer-based; 86 iBT); Recommended—IELTS (minimum score 6.5). Electronic applications accepted. *Expenses:* Contact institution.

Husson University, School of Graduate and Professional Studies, Master of Business Administration Program, Bangor, ME 04401-2999. Offers general (corporate) (MSB); health care management (MSB); hospitality management (MSB); nonprofit management (MSB). Part-time and evening/weekend programs available. *Faculty:* 9 full-time (3 women), 12 part-time/adjunct (2 women). *Students:* 111 full-time (66 women), 60 part-time (37 women); includes 8 minority (3 Black or African American, non-Hispanic/Latino; 1 American Indian or Alaska Native, non-Hispanic/Latino; 2 Asian, non-Hispanic/Latino; 2 Hispanic/Latino). 67 applicants, 35 enrolled. In 2011, 90 master's awarded. *Degree requirements:* For master's, comprehensive exam (for some programs), thesis optional. *Entrance requirements:* For master's, GMAT or GRE, minimum GPA of 3.0. Additional exam requirements/recommendations for international students: Required—TOEFL (minimum score 550 paper-based). *Application deadline:* Applications are processed on a rolling basis. Application fee: $40. Electronic applications accepted. *Expenses:* Contact institution. *Financial support:* In 2011–12, 1 student received support. Career-related internships or fieldwork, Federal Work-Study, scholarships/grants, and unspecified assistantships available. Financial award application deadline: 4/15; financial award applicants required to submit FAFSA. *Unit head:* Dr. Ronald Nykiel, Dean, College of Business, 207-941-7111, E-mail: nykielr@husson.edu. *Application contact:* Kristen M. Card, Director of Graduate Admissions, 207-404-5660, Fax: 207-941-7935, E-mail: cardk@husson.edu. Web site: http://www.husson.edu/mba.

Indiana University Bloomington, School of Public and Environmental Affairs, Public Affairs Programs, Bloomington, IN 47405. Offers comparative and international affairs (MPA); economic development (MPA); energy (MPA); environmental policy (PhD); environmental policy and natural resource management (MPA); hazardous materials management (Certificate); information systems (MPA); international development (MPA); local government management (MPA); nonprofit management (MPA, Certificate); policy analysis (MPA); public budgeting and financial management (Certificate); public finance (PhD); public financial administration (MPA); public management (MPA, PhD, Certificate); public policy analysis (PhD); social entrepreneurship (Certificate); specialized public affairs (MPA); sustainability and sustainable development (MPA); JD/MPA; MPA/MA; MPA/MIS; MPA/MLS; MSES/MPA. *Accreditation:* NASPAA (one or more programs are accredited). Part-time programs available. *Faculty:* 80 full-time (30 women), 102 part-time/adjunct (43 women). *Students:* 338 full-time, 30 part-time; includes 27 minority (7 Black or African American, non-Hispanic/Latino; 2 American Indian or Alaska Native, non-Hispanic/Latino; 10 Asian, non-Hispanic/Latino; 8 Hispanic/Latino), 56 international. Average age 24. 501 applicants, 148 enrolled. In 2011, 172 master's, 7 doctorates awarded. *Degree requirements:* For master's, core classes, capstone, internship; for doctorate, comprehensive exam, thesis/dissertation. *Entrance requirements:* For master's, GRE General Test or GMAT, official transcripts, 3 letters of recommendation, resume, personal statement; for doctorate, GRE General Test or LSAT, official transcripts, 3 letters of recommendation, resume or curriculum vitae, statement of purpose. Additional exam requirements/recommendations for international students: Required—TOEFL (minimum score 600 paper-based; 96 iBT); Recommended—IELTS (minimum score 7). *Application deadline:* For fall admission, 2/1 priority date for domestic students, 12/1 for international students. Applications are processed on a rolling basis. Application fee: $55 ($65 for international students). Electronic applications accepted. *Financial support:* Fellowships with partial tuition reimbursements, research assistantships with partial tuition reimbursements, teaching assistantships with partial tuition reimbursements, career-related internships or fieldwork, Federal Work-Study, scholarships/grants, health care benefits, unspecified assistantships, and Service Corps programs available. Financial award application deadline: 2/1; financial award applicants required to submit FAFSA. *Faculty research:* Comparative and international affairs, environmental policy and resource management, policy analysis, public finance, public management, urban management, nonprofit management, energy policy, social policy, public finance. *Unit head:* Jennifer Forney, Director of Graduate Student Services, 812-855-9485, Fax: 812-856-3665, E-mail: speampo@indiana.edu. *Application contact:* Admissions Assistant, 812-855-2840, E-mail: speaapps@indiana.edu. Web site: http://www.indiana.edu/~spea/prospective_students/masters/.

Indiana University–Purdue University Indianapolis, School of Public and Environmental Affairs, Indianapolis, IN 46202. Offers criminal justice and public safety (MS); homeland security and emergency management (Graduate Certificate); library management (Graduate Certificate); nonprofit management (Graduate Certificate); public affairs (MPA); public management (Graduate Certificate); social entrepreneurship: nonprofit and public benefit organizations (Graduate Certificate); JD/MPA; MLS/NMC; MLS/PMC; MPA/MA. *Accreditation:* CAHME (one or more programs are accredited); NASPAA. Part-time and evening/weekend programs available. Postbaccalaureate distance learning degree programs offered (no on-campus study). *Faculty:* 24 full-time (8 women), 10 part-time/adjunct (2 women). *Students:* 204 full-time (124 women), 109 part-time (74 women); includes 61 minority (45 Black or African American, non-Hispanic/Latino; 1 American Indian or Alaska Native, non-Hispanic/Latino; 7 Asian, non-Hispanic/Latino; 8 Hispanic/Latino), 11 international. Average age 31. 214 applicants, 83% accepted, 147 enrolled. In 2011, 55 master's, 43 other advanced degrees awarded. *Entrance requirements:* For master's, GRE General Test, GMAT or LSAT, minimum GPA of 3.0 (preferred). *Application deadline:* For fall admission, 5/15 priority date for domestic students, 2/1 for international students; for spring admission, 2/15 priority date for domestic students, 9/15 for international students. Applications are processed on a rolling basis. Application fee: $60. Electronic applications accepted. *Financial support:* In 2011–12, 12 research assistantships with full tuition reimbursements (averaging $12,000 per year) were awarded; fellowships, teaching assistantships, career-related internships or fieldwork, Federal Work-Study, institutionally sponsored loans, and scholarships/grants also available. Support available to part-time students. Financial award application deadline: 3/1; financial award applicants required to submit FAFSA. *Faculty research:* Nonprofit and public management, public policy, urban policy, sustainability policy, disaster preparedness and recovery, vehicular safety, homicide, offender rehabilitation and re-entry. *Total annual research expenditures:* $1.6 million. *Unit head:* Dr. Terry L. Baumer, Executive Associate Dean, 317-274-2016, Fax: 317-274-5153, E-mail: tebaumer@iupui.edu. *Application contact:* Luke Bickel, Director of Graduate Programs, 317-274-4656, Fax: 317-278-9668, E-mail: lbickel@iupui.edu. Web site: http://www.spea.iupui.edu/.

Indiana University South Bend, School of Public and Environmental Affairs, South Bend, IN 46634-7111. Offers health systems administration and policy (MPA); health systems management (Certificate); nonprofit management (Certificate); public and community services administration and policy (MPA); public management (Certificate); urban affairs (Certificate). *Accreditation:* NASPAA. Part-time and evening/weekend programs available. *Faculty:* 4 full-time (1 woman). *Students:* 7 part-time (5 women); includes 3 minority (2 Black or African American, non-Hispanic/Latino; 1 Hispanic/Latino). Average age 43. In 2011, 6 master's awarded. *Entrance requirements:* For master's, GRE General Test, minimum undergraduate GPA of 2.5. *Application deadline:* For fall admission, 7/1 priority date for domestic students; for spring admission, 11/1 for domestic students. Applications are processed on a rolling basis. Application fee: $50 ($60 for international students). *Financial support:* Fellowships, research assistantships, career-related internships or fieldwork, Federal Work-Study; and institutionally sponsored loans available. Support available to part-time students. Financial award application deadline: 3/1; financial award applicants required to submit FAFSA. *Unit head:* Leda M. Hall, Dean, 574-520-4803. *Application contact:* Admissions Counselor, 574-520-4839, Fax: 574-520-4834, E-mail: graduate@iusb.edu.

Iona College, School of Arts and Science, Department of Mass Communication, New Rochelle, NY 10801-1890. Offers non-profit public relations (Advanced Certificate); public relations (MA). *Accreditation:* ACEJMC (one or more programs are accredited). Part-time programs available. *Faculty:* 7 full-time (3 women), 2 part-time/adjunct (both women). *Students:* 11 full-time (9 women), 43 part-time (36 women); includes 15 minority (5 Black or African American, non-Hispanic/Latino; 1 Asian, non-Hispanic/Latino; 9 Hispanic/Latino), 3 international. Average age 27. 30 applicants, 60% accepted, 11 enrolled. In 2011, 18 master's, 2 other advanced degrees awarded. *Degree requirements:* For master's, comprehensive exam or thesis. *Entrance requirements:* For master's, GRE General Test, minimum GPA of 3.0. Additional exam requirements/recommendations for international students: Required—TOEFL (minimum score 550 paper-based; 213 computer-based). *Application deadline:* Applications are processed on a rolling basis. Application fee: $50. Electronic applications accepted. *Expenses:* Contact institution. *Financial support:* Career-related internships or fieldwork, scholarships/grants, tuition waivers (partial), and unspecified assistantships available. Support available to part-time students. Financial award application deadline: 4/15; financial award applicants required to submit FAFSA. *Faculty research:* Media ecology, new media, corporate communication, media images, organizational learning in public relations. *Unit head:* Br. Raymond Smith, Chair, 914-633-2354, E-mail: rrsmith@iona.edu. *Application contact:* Dr. Jeanne Zaino, Interim Dean, School of Arts and Science, 914-633-2112, Fax: 914-633-2023, E-mail: jzaino@iona.edu.

John Carroll University, Graduate School, Program in Nonprofit Administration, University Heights, OH 44118-4581. Offers MA. Part-time and evening/weekend programs available. *Degree requirements:* For master's, thesis optional. *Entrance requirements:* For master's, minimum GPA of 3.0, interview. Additional exam requirements/recommendations for international students: Required—TOEFL. Electronic applications accepted.

Kean University, College of Business and Public Management, Program in Public Administration, Union, NJ 07083. Offers environmental management (MPA); health services administration (MPA); non-profit management (MPA); public administration (MPA). *Accreditation:* NASPAA. *Faculty:* 14 full-time (7 women). *Students:* 65 full-time (34 women), 77 part-time (41 women); includes 92 minority (68 Black or African American, non-Hispanic/Latino; 7 Asian, non-Hispanic/Latino; 17 Hispanic/Latino), 4 international. Average age 32. 69 applicants, 70% accepted, 32 enrolled. In 2011, 48 master's awarded. *Degree requirements:* For master's, thesis, internship, research seminar. *Entrance requirements:* For master's, minimum GPA of 3.0, 2 letters of recommendation, interview, writing sample, transcripts, resume. Additional exam requirements/recommendations for international students: Required—TOEFL (minimum score 79 iBT). *Application deadline:* For fall admission, 6/1 for domestic and international students; for spring admission, 12/1 for domestic and international students. Applications are processed on a rolling basis. Application fee: $75 ($150 for international students). Electronic applications accepted. *Expenses:* Tuition, state resident: full-time $11,302; part-time $550 per credit. Tuition, nonresident: full-time $15,318; part-time $674 per credit. *Required fees:* $2849; $130 per credit. Tuition and fees vary according to degree level. *Financial support:* In 2011–12, 14 research assistantships with full tuition reimbursements (averaging $3,263 per year) were awarded; unspecified assistantships also available. Financial award applicants required to submit FAFSA. *Unit head:* Dr. Patricia Moore, Program Coordinator, 908-737-4314, E-mail: pmoore@kean.edu. *Application contact:* Reenat Hasan, Admissions Counselor, 908-737-5923, Fax: 908-737-5925, E-mail: hasanr@kean.edu. Web site: http://www.kean.edu/KU/Public-Administration.

Kentucky State University, College of Professional Studies, Frankfort, KY 40601. Offers public administration (MPA), including human resource management, international development, management information systems, nonprofit management; special education (MA). Part-time and evening/weekend programs available. Postbaccalaureate distance learning degree programs offered (minimal on-campus study). *Faculty:* 12 full-time (4 women), 2 part-time/adjunct (both women). *Students:* 88 full-time (57 women), 79 part-time (42 women); includes 104 minority (101 Black or African American, non-Hispanic/Latino; 1 Asian, non-Hispanic/Latino; 2 Hispanic/Latino), 2 international. Average age 34. 124 applicants, 62% accepted, 45 enrolled. In 2011, 38 master's awarded. *Degree requirements:* For master's, comprehensive exam, thesis optional. *Entrance requirements:* For master's, GMAT, GRE. Additional exam requirements/recommendations for international students: Required—TOEFL (minimum score 525 paper-based; 173 computer-based). *Application deadline:* Applications are processed on a rolling basis. Application fee: $30 ($100 for international students). Electronic applications accepted. *Expenses:* Tuition, state resident: full-time $6192; part-time $344 per credit hour. Tuition, nonresident: full-time $9522; part-time $529 per credit hour. *Required fees:* $450; $25 per credit hour. Tuition and fees vary according to course load. *Financial support:* In 2011–12, 46 students received support, including 4 research assistantships (averaging $10,975 per year); career-related internships or fieldwork, scholarships/grants, tuition waivers (partial), and unspecified assistantships also available. Financial award application deadline: 4/15; financial award applicants required to submit FAFSA. *Unit head:* Dr. Gashaw Lake, Dean, 502-597-6105, Fax: 502-597-6715, E-mail: gashaw.lake@kysu.edu. *Application contact:* Dr. Titilayo Ufomata, Acting Director of Graduate Studies, 502-597-6443, E-mail: titilayo.ufomata@kysu.edu. Web site: http://www.kysu.edu/academics/collegesAndSchools/collegeofprofessionalstudies/.

Lasell College, Graduate and Professional Studies in Management, Newton, MA 02466-2709. Offers elder care administration (MSM, Graduate Certificate); elder care marketing (MSM, Graduate Certificate); fundraising management (MSM, Graduate Certificate); human resource management (Graduate Certificate); human resources management (MSM); integrated marketing communication (Graduate Certificate); management (MSM, Graduate Certificate); marketing (MSM, Graduate Certificate); non-profit management (MSM, Graduate Certificate); project management (MSM, Graduate Certificate); public relations (Graduate Certificate). Part-time and evening/weekend programs available. Postbaccalaureate distance learning degree programs offered (no on-campus study). *Faculty:* 9 full-time (7 women), 20 part-time/adjunct (13 women). *Students:* 23 full-time (16 women), 92 part-time (65 women); includes 74 minority (8 Black or African American, non-Hispanic/Latino; 4 American Indian or Alaska Native, non-Hispanic/Latino; 53 Asian, non-Hispanic/Latino; 9 Hispanic/Latino), 14 international. Average age 30. 78 applicants, 67% accepted, 31 enrolled. In 2011, 49 master's, 7 other advanced degrees awarded. *Entrance requirements:* For master's and Graduate Certificate, bachelor's degree from an accredited institution. Additional exam requirements/recommendations for international students: Required—TOEFL (minimum score 550 paper-based; 213 computer-based; 79 iBT). *Application deadline:* For fall admission, 8/31 priority date for domestic students, 6/30 for international students; for spring admission, 12/31 priority date for domestic students, 10/31 for international students. Applications are processed on a rolling basis. Electronic applications accepted. *Expenses: Tuition:* Part-time $575 per credit. *Required fees:* $70 per semester. *Financial support:* Available to part-time students. Application deadline: 8/31; applicants required to submit FAFSA. *Unit head:* Dr. Joan Dolamore, Dean of Graduate and Professional Studies, 617-243-2485, Fax: 617-243-2450, E-mail: gradinfo@lasell.edu. *Application contact:* Adrienne Franciosi, Director of Graduate Admission, 617-243-2214, Fax: 617-243-2450, E-mail: gradinfo@lasell.edu. Web site: http://www.lasell.edu/Academics/Graduate-and-Professional-Studies/MS-in-Management.html.

Lasell College, Graduate and Professional Studies in Sport Management, Newton, MA 02466-2709. Offers sport hospitality management (MS, Graduate Certificate); sport leadership (MS, Graduate Certificate); sport non-profit management (MS, Graduate Certificate). Part-time programs available. Postbaccalaureate distance learning degree programs offered (no on-campus study). *Faculty:* 1 (woman) full-time, 4 part-time/adjunct (3 women). *Students:* 13 full-time (5 women), 20 part-time (10 women); includes 10 minority (4 Black or African American, non-Hispanic/Latino; 2 American Indian or Alaska Native, non-Hispanic/Latino; 4 Hispanic/Latino). Average age 28. 30 applicants, 63% accepted, 9 enrolled. *Entrance requirements:* For master's and Graduate Certificate, bachelor's degree from an accredited institution. Additional exam requirements/recommendations for international students: Required—TOEFL (minimum score 550 paper-based; 213 computer-based; 79 iBT), IELTS. *Application deadline:* For fall admission, 8/31 priority date for domestic students, 6/30 for international students; for spring admission, 12/31 priority date for domestic students, 10/31 for international students. Applications are processed on a rolling basis. Electronic applications accepted. *Expenses: Tuition:* Part-time $575 per credit. *Required fees:* $70 per semester. *Financial support:* Available to part-time students. Application deadline: 8/31; applicants required to submit FAFSA. *Unit head:* Dr. Joan Dolamore, Dean of Graduate and Professional Studies, 617-243-2485, Fax: 617-243-2450, E-mail: gradinfo@lasell.edu. *Application contact:* Adrienne Franciosi, Director of Graduate Admission, 617-243-2214, Fax: 617-243-2450, E-mail: gradinfo@lasell.edu. Web site: http://www.lasell.edu/Academics/Graduate-and-Professional-Studies/MS-in-Sport-Management-.html.

Lewis University, College of Arts and Sciences, Program in Organizational Leadership, Romeoville, IL 60446. Offers higher education/student services (MA); non-for-profit management (MA); organizational management (MA); public administration (MA); training and development (MA). Part-time and evening/weekend programs available. Postbaccalaureate distance learning degree programs offered (no on-campus study). *Faculty:* 2 full-time (0 women), 9 part-time/adjunct (2 women). *Students:* 15 full-time (14 women), 193 part-time (143 women); includes 61 minority (50 Black or African American, non-Hispanic/Latino; 2 Asian, non-Hispanic/Latino; 9 Hispanic/Latino). Average age 36. In 2011, 46 master's awarded. *Entrance requirements:* For master's, bachelor's degree, at least 25 years of age, minimum of 3 years of work experience, minimum GPA of 3.0, letter of recommendation, interview. Additional exam requirements/recommendations for international students: Required—TOEFL (minimum score 550 paper-based; 213 computer-based). *Application deadline:* For fall admission, 5/1 for international students; for spring admission, 11/15 for international students. Applications are processed on a rolling basis. Application fee: $40. Electronic applications accepted. *Financial support:* Federal Work-Study, scholarships/grants, tuition waivers, and unspecified assistantships available. Financial award application deadline: 5/1; financial award applicants required to submit FAFSA. *Unit head:* Dr. Rich Walsh, Director, 815-838-0500, E-mail: walshri@lewisu.edu. *Application contact:* Julie Branchaw, Assistant Director, Graduate and Adult Admission, 815-836-5574, Fax: 815-836-5578, E-mail: branchju@lewisu.edu.

Lindenwood University, Graduate Programs, School of Human Services, St. Charles, MO 63301-1695. Offers nonprofit administration (MA); public administration (MPA). Part-time programs available. *Faculty:* 2 full-time (1 woman), 9 part-time/adjunct (4 women). *Students:* 2 full-time (1 woman), 36 part-time (29 women); includes 20 minority (18 Black or African American, non-Hispanic/Latino; 1 American Indian or Alaska Native, non-Hispanic/Latino; 1 Two or more races, non-Hispanic/Latino). Average age 34. 19 applicants, 74% accepted, 13 enrolled. In 2011, 11 degrees awarded. *Degree requirements:* For master's, minimum cumulative GPA of 3.0, directed internship, capstone project. *Entrance requirements:* Additional exam requirements/recommendations for international students: Required—TOEFL (minimum score 550 paper-based; 213 computer-based; 80 iBT). *Application deadline:* For fall admission, 8/26 priority date for domestic students, 8/26 for international students; for spring admission, 1/27 priority date for domestic students, 1/27 for international students. Applications are processed on a rolling basis. Application fee: $30 ($100 for international students). Electronic applications accepted. *Expenses: Tuition:* Full-time $13,650; part-time $395 per credit hour. *Required fees:* $150 per semester. Tuition and fees vary according to course level and course load. *Financial support:* In 2011–12, 12 students received support. Career-related internships or fieldwork, institutionally sponsored loans, tuition waivers, and unspecified assistantships available. Financial award application deadline: 6/30; financial award applicants required to submit FAFSA. *Unit head:* Carla Mueller, Dean, 636-949-4731, E-mail: cmueller@lindenwood.edu. *Application contact:* Brett Barger, Dean of Evening Admissions and Extension Campuses, 636-949-4934, Fax: 636-949-4109, E-mail: adultadmissions@lindenwood.edu. Web site: http://www.lindenwood.edu/humanServices/.

Lipscomb University, College of Business, Nashville, TN 37204-3951. Offers accounting (MBA); business administration (general) (MBA); conflict management (MBA); financial services (MBA); healthcare management (MBA); human resources (MHR); leadership (MBA); nonprofit management (MBA); sports management (MBA); sustainability (MBA). *Accreditation:* ACBSP. Part-time and evening/weekend programs available. *Faculty:* 13 full-time (3 women), 7 part-time/adjunct (1 woman). *Students:* 51 full-time (21 women), 83 part-time (48 women); includes 20 minority (16 Black or African American, non-Hispanic/Latino; 3 Asian, non-Hispanic/Latino; 1 Hispanic/Latino), 1 international. Average age 33. 190 applicants, 43% accepted, 54 enrolled. In 2011, 85 master's awarded. *Entrance requirements:* For master's, GMAT, interview, 2 references, resume. Additional exam requirements/recommendations for international students: Required—TOEFL (minimum score 570 paper-based; 230 computer-based). *Application deadline:* For fall admission, 6/15 for domestic students, 2/1 for international students; for winter admission, 6/1 for international students; for spring admission, 11/15 for domestic students. Applications are processed on a rolling basis. Application fee: $50 ($75 for international students). Electronic applications accepted. *Expenses:* Contact institution. *Financial support:* Career-related internships or fieldwork, scholarships/grants, tuition waivers (partial), and unspecified assistantships available. Support available to part-time students. Financial award application deadline: 7/1; financial award applicants required to submit FAFSA. *Faculty research:* Impact of spirituality on organization commitment, leadership, psychological empowerment, training. *Unit head:* Dr. Mike Kendrick, Associate Dean of Graduate Business Programs, 615-966-1833, Fax: 615-966-1818, E-mail: mikekendrick@lipscomb.edu. *Application contact:* Lisa Shacklett, Executive Director of Enrollment and Marketing, 615-966-5968, E-mail: lisa.shacklett@lipscomb.edu. Web site: http://mba.lipscomb.edu.

Long Island University–C. W. Post Campus, College of Management, Department of Health Care and Public Administration, Brookville, NY 11548-1300. Offers gerontology (Certificate); health care administration (MPA); health care administration/gerontology (MPA); nonprofit management (MPA, Certificate); public administration (MPA). *Accreditation:* NASPAA (one or more programs are accredited). Part-time and evening/weekend programs available. *Degree requirements:* For master's, thesis. *Entrance requirements:* For master's, GMAT, minimum GPA of 2.5; for Certificate, minimum GPA of 2.5. Electronic applications accepted. *Faculty research:* Critical issues in sexuality, social work in religious communities, gerontological social work.

Long Island University–C. W. Post Campus, School of Health Professions and Nursing, Master of Social Work Program, Brookville, NY 11548-1300. Offers alcohol and substance abuse (MSW); child and family welfare (MSW); forensic social work (MSW); gerontology (MSW); nonprofit management (MSW). *Accreditation:* CSWE.

Marquette University, Graduate School, College of Professional Studies, Milwaukee, WI 53201-1881. Offers criminal justice administration (MLS); dispute resolution (MDR, MLS); engineering (MLS); health care administration (MLS); law enforcement leadership and management (Certificate); leadership studies (Certificate); non-profit sector (MLS); public service (MAPS, MLS); sports leadership (MLS). Part-time and evening/weekend programs available. Postbaccalaureate distance learning degree programs offered (no on-campus study). *Faculty:* 9 full-time (8 women), 10 part-time/adjunct (5 women). *Students:* 26 full-time (13 women), 142 part-time (90 women); includes 29 minority (19 Black or African American, non-Hispanic/Latino; 1 American Indian or Alaska Native, non-Hispanic/Latino; 3 Asian, non-Hispanic/Latino; 5 Hispanic/Latino; 1 Two or more races, non-Hispanic/Latino), 3 international. Average age 37. 88 applicants, 78% accepted, 36 enrolled. In 2011, 36 master's, 29 Certificates awarded. *Degree requirements:* For master's, comprehensive exam (for some programs). *Entrance requirements:* For master's, GRE General Test (preferred), GMAT, or LSAT, official transcripts from all current and previous colleges/universities except Marquette, three letters of recommendation, statement of purpose. Additional exam requirements/recommendations for international students: Required—TOEFL. *Application deadline:* Applications are processed on a rolling basis. Application fee: $50. Electronic applications accepted. *Expenses: Tuition:* Full-time $17,010; part-time $945 per credit hour. Tuition and fees vary according to program. *Financial support:* In 2011–12, 9 students received support, including 8 fellowships with full tuition reimbursements available (averaging $16,247 per year). Financial award application deadline: 2/15. *Unit head:* Dr. Johnette Caulfield, Adjunct Assistant Professor/Director, 414-288-5556, E-mail: jay.caulfield@marquette.edu. *Application contact:* Craig Pierce, Assistant Director for Recruitment, 414-288-5740, Fax: 414-288-1902, E-mail: craig.pierce@marquette.edu.

Marylhurst University, Department of Business Administration, Marylhurst, OR 97036-0261. Offers finance (MBA); general management (MBA); government policy and administration (MBA); green development (MBA); health care management (MBA); marketing (MBA); natural and organic resources (MBA); nonprofit management (MBA); organizational behavior (MBA); real estate (MBA); renewable energy (MBA); sustainable business (MBA). Part-time and evening/weekend programs available. Postbaccalaureate distance learning degree programs offered (no on-campus study). *Faculty:* 3 full-time (0 women), 36 part-time/adjunct (6 women). *Students:* 29 full-time (15 women), 675 part-time (373 women); includes 178 minority (59 Black or African American, non-Hispanic/Latino; 6 American Indian or Alaska Native, non-Hispanic/Latino; 34 Asian, non-Hispanic/Latino; 46 Hispanic/Latino; 4 Native Hawaiian or other Pacific Islander, non-Hispanic/Latino; 29 Two or more races, non-Hispanic/Latino), 14 international. Average age 37. 262 applicants, 91% accepted, 194 enrolled. In 2011, 352 master's awarded. *Degree requirements:* For master's, comprehensive exam, capstone course. *Entrance requirements:* For master's, GMAT (if GPA less than 3.0 and fewer than 5 years of work experience), interview, resume, 2 letters of recommendation. Additional exam requirements/recommendations for international students: Recommended—TOEFL (minimum score 550 paper-based; 213 computer-based; 80 iBT). *Application deadline:* For fall admission, 9/11 priority date for domestic students, 9/11 for international students; for winter admission, 12/15 priority date for domestic students, 12/15 for international students; for spring admission, 3/15 priority date for domestic students, 3/17 for international students. Applications are processed on a rolling basis. Application fee: $50. Electronic applications accepted. *Expenses: Tuition:* Full-time $14,796; part-time $548 per quarter hour. Tuition and fees vary according to program. *Financial support:* Scholarships/grants available. Support available to part-time students. Financial award applicants required to submit FAFSA. *Unit head:* David McNamee, Interim Chair, 503-636-8141, Fax: 503-697-5597, E-mail: mba@marylhurst.edu. *Application contact:* Maruska Lynch, Graduate Admissions Specialist, 800-634-9982 Ext. 6322, Fax: 503-699-6320, E-mail: admissions@marylhurst.edu. Web site: http://www.marylhurst.edu/.

Marywood University, Academic Affairs, College of Health and Human Services, School of Social Work and Administrative Services, Program in Public Administration, Scranton, PA 18509-1598. Offers nonprofit management (MPA). *Students:* 3 full-time (0 women), 13 part-time (9 women). Average age 30. In 2011, 9 degrees awarded. *Entrance requirements:* Additional exam requirements/recommendations for international students: Required—TOEFL (minimum score 550 paper-based; 213

computer-based; 79 iBT). *Application deadline:* For fall admission, 4/1 priority date for domestic students, 3/31 for international students; for spring admission, 11/1 priority date for domestic students, 8/31 for international students. Applications are processed on a rolling basis. Application fee: $35. Electronic applications accepted. *Financial support:* Career-related internships or fieldwork, scholarships/grants, and unspecified assistantships available. Support available to part-time students. Financial award application deadline: 6/30; financial award applicants required to submit FAFSA. *Unit head:* Dr. Katrina Maurer, Co-Chairperson, 570-348-6275, E-mail: maurer@marywood.edu. *Application contact:* Tammy Manka, Assistant Director of Graduate Admissions, 866-279-9663, E-mail: tmanka@marywood.edu. Web site: http://www.marywood.edu/academics/gradcatalog/.

Mercyhurst College, Graduate Studies, Program in Organizational Leadership, Erie, PA 16546. Offers accounting (MS); entrepreneurship (MS); higher education administration (MS); human resources (MS); nonprofit management (MS); organizational leadership (Certificate); sports leadership (MS). Part-time and evening/weekend programs available. *Faculty:* 1 full-time (0 women), 11 part-time/adjunct (4 women). *Students:* 42 full-time (16 women), 22 part-time (15 women); includes 5 minority (3 Black or African American, non-Hispanic/Latino; 1 American Indian or Alaska Native, non-Hispanic/Latino; 1 Hispanic/Latino), 9 international. Average age 30. 60 applicants, 62% accepted, 25 enrolled. In 2011, 27 master's, 2 other advanced degrees awarded. *Degree requirements:* For master's, thesis. *Entrance requirements:* For master's, GRE General Test or MAT, interview, resume, essay, three professional references, transcripts. Additional exam requirements/recommendations for international students: Required—TOEFL. *Application deadline:* For fall admission, 8/1 priority date for domestic students, 7/1 for international students; for winter admission, 11/1 for domestic students, 10/1 for international students; for spring admission, 2/1 for domestic students, 1/1 for international students. Applications are processed on a rolling basis. Application fee: $35. Electronic applications accepted. *Expenses: Tuition:* Part-time $570 per credit. *Required fees:* $90 per term. Tuition and fees vary according to program. *Financial support:* In 2011–12, 16 students received support, including 112 research assistantships with full and partial tuition reimbursements available (averaging $6,000 per year); career-related internships or fieldwork and unspecified assistantships also available. Support available to part-time students. Financial award application deadline: 5/1; financial award applicants required to submit FAFSA. *Faculty research:* Leadership training, organizational communication, leadership pedagogy. *Unit head:* Dr. Gilbert Jacobs, Director, 814-824-2390, E-mail: gjacobs@mercyhurst.edu. *Application contact:* Sarah Murphy, Academic Coordinator, 814-824-2297, Fax: 814-824-2055, E-mail: smurphy@mercyhurst.edu.

Metropolitan State University, College of Management, St. Paul, MN 55106-5000. Offers business administration (MBA, DBA); database administration (Graduate Certificate); healthcare information technology management (Graduate Certificate); information assurance security (Graduate Certificate); management information systems (MMIS); MIS generalist (Graduate Certificate); MIS systems analysis and design (Graduate Certificate); project management (Graduate Certificate); public and nonprofit administration (MPNA). Part-time and evening/weekend programs available. *Students:* 63 full-time (41 women), 409 part-time (192 women); includes 94 minority (38 Black or African American, non-Hispanic/Latino; 33 Asian, non-Hispanic/Latino; 14 Hispanic/Latino; 9 Two or more races, non-Hispanic/Latino), 61 international. Average age 35. *Degree requirements:* For master's, thesis optional, computer language (MMIS). *Entrance requirements:* For master's, GMAT (MBA), resume. Additional exam requirements/recommendations for international students: Required—TOEFL (minimum score 550 paper-based; 213 computer-based). *Application deadline:* For fall admission, 7/15 for international students; for winter admission, 11/15 for international students; for spring admission, 3/15 for international students. Applications are processed on a rolling basis. Application fee: $20. Electronic applications accepted. *Expenses:* Tuition, state resident: full-time $5799.06; part-time $322.17 per credit. Tuition, nonresident: full-time $11,411; part-time $633.92 per credit. Tuition and fees vary according to degree level, program and reciprocity agreements. *Financial support:* Research assistantships with partial tuition reimbursements, career-related internships or fieldwork, and Federal Work-Study available. Support available to part-time students. Financial award applicants required to submit FAFSA. *Faculty research:* Yugoslav economic system, workers' cooperatives, participative management and job enrichment, global business systems. *Unit head:* Dr. Paul Huo, Dean, 612-659-7271, Fax: 612-659-7268, E-mail: paul.huo@metrostate.edu. Web site: http://choose.metrostate.edu/comgradprograms.

MidAmerica Nazarene University, Graduate Studies in Management, Olathe, KS 66062-1899. Offers management (MBA); organizational administration (MA), including finance, international business, leadership, non-profit. Evening/weekend programs available. *Entrance requirements:* For master's, mathematical assessment, minimum undergraduate GPA of 3.0, letters of recommendation. Additional exam requirements/recommendations for international students: Required—TOEFL. Electronic applications accepted. *Faculty research:* Economic development, international finance, business development, employee evaluation.

Mount St. Mary's College, Graduate Division, Program in Business Administration, Los Angeles, CA 90049-1599. Offers entrepreneurship (MBA); nonprofit management (MBA); organizational leadership (MBA); project management (MBA). Evening/weekend programs available. *Entrance requirements:* Additional exam requirements/recommendations for international students: Required—TOEFL. *Application deadline:* For fall admission, 6/30 for domestic students. Electronic applications accepted. *Expenses:* Contact institution. *Financial support:* Scholarships/grants available. Financial award application deadline: 3/15; financial award applicants required to submit FAFSA. *Unit head:* Dr. Janet Robinson, Director, 310-954-4153, E-mail: jrobinson@msmc.la.edu. Web site: http://www.msmc.la.edu/graduate-programs/mba.asp.

New England College, Program in Management, Henniker, NH 03242-3293. Offers accounting (MSA); healthcare administration (MS); international relations (MA); marketing management (MS); nonprofit leadership (MS); project management (MS); strategic leadership (MS). Part-time and evening/weekend programs available. *Degree requirements:* For master's, independent research project. Electronic applications accepted.

New Mexico Highlands University, Graduate Studies, School of Business, Las Vegas, NM 87701. Offers business administration (MBA), including government nonprofit management, human resource management, international business, management, management information systems. *Accreditation:* ACBSP. *Faculty:* 20 full-time (5 women). *Students:* 63 full-time (40 women), 146 part-time (76 women); includes 131 minority (9 Black or African American, non-Hispanic/Latino; 8 American Indian or Alaska Native, non-Hispanic/Latino; 1 Asian, non-Hispanic/Latino; 110 Hispanic/Latino; 2 Native Hawaiian or other Pacific Islander, non-Hispanic/Latino; 1 Two or more races, non-Hispanic/Latino), 25 international. Average age 33. 99 applicants, 79% accepted, 49 enrolled. In 2011, 43 master's awarded. *Degree requirements:* For master's, comprehensive exam, thesis or alternative. *Entrance requirements:* For master's, minimum undergraduate GPA of 3.0. Additional exam requirements/recommendations for international students: Required—TOEFL (minimum score 540 paper-based; 207 computer-based). *Application deadline:* For fall admission, 8/1 priority date for domestic students. Applications are processed on a rolling basis. Application fee: $15. *Expenses:* Tuition, state resident: full-time $2767; part-time $146 per credit hour. Tuition, nonresident: full-time $4879; part-time $234 per credit hour. *International tuition:* $5436 full-time. *Required fees:* $737. *Financial support:* In 2011–12, 29 students received support. Career-related internships or fieldwork, Federal Work-Study, institutionally sponsored loans, scholarships/grants, tuition waivers (full and partial), and unspecified assistantships available. Support available to part-time students. Financial award application deadline: 3/1; financial award applicants required to submit FAFSA. *Faculty research:* Real estate valuation, studying expert judgments in complex accounting, decision environments, green marketing, environmentalism, marketing research methodology. *Unit head:* Dr. Margaret Young, Dean, 505-454-3522, Fax: 505-454-3354, E-mail: young_m@nmhu.edu. *Application contact:* Diane Trujillo, Administrative Assistant, Graduate Studies, 505-454-3266, Fax: 505-426-2117, E-mail: dtrujillo@nmhu.edu. Web site: http://www.nmhu.edu/business/.

New Mexico Highlands University, Graduate Studies, School of Social Work, Las Vegas, NM 87701. Offers bilingual/bicultural social work practice (MSW); clinical practice (MSW); government non-profit management (MSW). *Accreditation:* CSWE. Part-time programs available. *Faculty:* 19 full-time (8 women). *Students:* 266 full-time (231 women), 82 part-time (68 women); includes 188 minority (15 Black or African American, non-Hispanic/Latino; 24 American Indian or Alaska Native, non-Hispanic/Latino; 2 Asian, non-Hispanic/Latino; 143 Hispanic/Latino; 1 Native Hawaiian or other Pacific Islander, non-Hispanic/Latino; 3 Two or more races, non-Hispanic/Latino), 7 international. Average age 36. 233 applicants, 88% accepted, 136 enrolled. In 2011, 151 master's awarded. *Degree requirements:* For master's, comprehensive exam, thesis or alternative. *Entrance requirements:* For master's, minimum undergraduate GPA of 3.0. Additional exam requirements/recommendations for international students: Required—TOEFL (minimum score 540 paper-based; 207 computer-based). *Application deadline:* For fall admission, 8/1 priority date for domestic students. Applications are processed on a rolling basis. Application fee: $15. *Expenses:* Tuition, state resident: full-time $2767; part-time $146 per credit hour. Tuition, nonresident: full-time $4879; part-time $234 per credit hour. *International tuition:* $5436 full-time. *Required fees:* $737. *Financial support:* In 2011–12, 17 students received support. Career-related internships or fieldwork, Federal Work-Study, institutionally sponsored loans, scholarships/grants, tuition waivers (partial), and unspecified assistantships available. Support available to part-time students. Financial award application deadline: 3/1; financial award applicants required to submit FAFSA. *Faculty research:* Treatment attrition among domestic violence batterers, children's health and mental health, Dejando Huellas: meeting the bilingual/bicultural needs of the Latino mental health patient, impact of culture on the therapeutic process, effects of generational gang involvement on adolescents' future. *Unit head:* Dr. Alfredo Garcia, Dean, 505-891-9053, Fax: 505-454-3290, E-mail: a_garcia@nmhu.edu. *Application contact:* LouAnn Romero, Administrative Assistant, Graduate Studies, 505-454-3087, E-mail: laromero@nmhu.edu.

The New School, Milano The New School for Management and Urban Policy, Program in Nonprofit Management, New York, NY 10011. Offers MS. Part-time and evening/weekend programs available. *Degree requirements:* For master's, thesis. *Entrance requirements:* For master's, interview. Additional exam requirements/recommendations for international students: Required—TOEFL (minimum score 600 paper-based; 250 computer-based; 100 iBT). Electronic applications accepted. *Faculty research:* Management of nonprofit organizations, fundraising in minority nonprofit organizations.

New York University, Robert F. Wagner Graduate School of Public Service, Program in Public Administration, New York, NY 10012. Offers public administration (PhD); public and nonprofit management and policy (MPA, Advanced Certificate), including developmental administration (Advanced Certificate), financial management and public finance, human resources management (Advanced Certificate), international administration (Advanced Certificate), management (MPA), management for public and nonprofit organizations (Advanced Certificate), public policy analysis, quantitative analysis and computer applications (Advanced Certificate), urban public policy (Advanced Certificate); JD/MPA; MBA/MPA; MPA/MA. *Accreditation:* NASPAA (one or more programs are accredited). Part-time programs available. *Faculty:* 32 full-time (13 women), 41 part-time/adjunct (22 women). *Students:* 431 full-time (323 women), 131 part-time (98 women); includes 148 minority (35 Black or African American, non-Hispanic/Latino; 53 Asian, non-Hispanic/Latino; 38 Hispanic/Latino; 1 Native Hawaiian or other Pacific Islander, non-Hispanic/Latino; 21 Two or more races, non-Hispanic/Latino), 62 international. Average age 28. 1,063 applicants, 58% accepted, 205 enrolled. In 2011, 213 master's, 8 doctorates awarded. *Degree requirements:* For master's, thesis or alternative, capstone end event; for doctorate, one foreign language, thesis/dissertation. *Entrance requirements:* Additional exam requirements/recommendations for international students: Required—TOEFL, IELTS, TWE. *Application deadline:* For fall admission, 1/15 for domestic students, 1/5 for international students; for spring admission, 10/15 for domestic students, 9/15 for international students. Application fee: $85. Electronic applications accepted. *Expenses:* Contact institution. *Financial support:* In 2011–12, 118 students received support, including 117 fellowships (averaging $13,500 per year); career-related internships or fieldwork, Federal Work-Study, scholarships/grants, health care benefits, and unspecified assistantships also available. Support available to part-time students. Financial award application deadline: 1/5; financial award applicants required to submit FAFSA. *Unit head:* Katty Jones, Director, Program Services, 212-998-7411, Fax: 212-995-4164, E-mail: katty.jones@nyu.edu. *Application contact:* Christopher Alexander, Communications Coordinator, 212-998-7414, Fax: 212-995-4611, E-mail: wagner.admissions@nyu.edu. Web site: http://www.nyu.edu.wagner/.

New York University, School of Continuing and Professional Studies, The George Heyman Jr. Center for Philanthropy and Fundraising, New York, NY 10012-1019. Offers fundraising and grantmaking (MS), including fundraising, grantmaking. Part-time and evening/weekend programs available. *Faculty:* 1 full-time (0 women), 19 part-time/adjunct (9 women). *Students:* 8 full-time (6 women), 44 part-time (37 women); includes 7 minority (5 Black or African American, non-Hispanic/Latino; 1 Asian, non-Hispanic/Latino; 1 Native Hawaiian or other Pacific Islander, non-Hispanic/Latino), 5 international. Average age 35. 31 applicants, 90% accepted, 23 enrolled. In 2011, 17 master's awarded. *Degree requirements:* For master's, thesis, capstone project. *Entrance requirements:* For master's, GRE/GMAT only upon request, relevant professional work, internship or volunteer experience. Additional exam requirements/recommendations for international students: Required—TOEFL (minimum score 600 paper-based; 250 computer-based; 100 iBT), IELTS (minimum score 7). *Application deadline:* For fall admission, 2/1 priority date for domestic students, 2/1 for international students; for spring admission, 10/15 priority date for domestic students, 8/15 for international students. Applications are processed on a rolling basis. Application fee: $150. Electronic applications accepted. *Financial support:* In 2011–12, 35 students received support, including 1 fellowship (averaging $1,600 per year); scholarships/grants also available. Support available to part-time students. Financial award application deadline: 8/15; financial award applicants required to submit FAFSA. *Unit head:* Levine Naomi, Chair and Executive Director. *Application contact:* Admissions Office, 212-998-7100, E-mail: scps.gradadmissions@nyu.edu. Web site: http://www.scps.nyu.edu/philanthropy.

North Carolina State University, Graduate School, College of Humanities and Social Sciences, School of Public and International Affairs, Raleigh, NC 27695. Offers international studies (MIS); nonprofit management (Certificate); public administration (MPA, PhD). *Accreditation:* NASPAA (one or more programs are accredited). Part-time and evening/weekend programs available. *Entrance requirements:* For master's, GRE General Test, minimum GPA of 3.0 during previous 2 years. Electronic applications accepted. *Faculty research:* Public sector leadership and ethics, financial management, management systems evaluation, computer applications, service delivery.

North Central College, Graduate and Continuing Education Programs, Program in Leadership Studies, Naperville, IL 60566-7063. Offers higher education leadership (MLS); professional leadership (MLS); social entrepreneurship (MLS); sports leadership (MLS). Part-time and evening/weekend programs available. *Faculty:* 9 full-time (1 woman), 11 part-time/adjunct (5 women). *Students:* 44 full-time (28 women), 32 part-time (20 women); includes 16 minority (9 Black or African American, non-Hispanic/Latino; 6 Hispanic/Latino; 1 Two or more races, non-Hispanic/Latino), 1 international. Average age 29. 69 applicants, 74% accepted, 32 enrolled. In 2011, 20 master's awarded. *Degree requirements:* For master's, thesis optional, project. *Entrance requirements:* For master's, interview. Additional exam requirements/recommendations for international students: Required—TOEFL (minimum score 570 paper-based; 233 computer-based; 90 iBT). *Application deadline:* For fall admission, 8/15 for domestic students; for winter admission, 12/1 for domestic students; for spring admission, 2/1 for domestic students. Applications are processed on a rolling basis. Application fee: $25. *Expenses:* Contact institution. *Financial support:* In 2011–12, 1 student received support. Scholarships/grants available. Support available to part-time students. *Unit head:* Dr. Thomas Cavenagh, Program Coordinator, Leadership Studies, 630-637-5285. *Application contact:* Wendy Kulpinski, Director of Graduate and Continuing Education Admission, 630-637-5808, Fax: 630-637-5844, E-mail: wekulpinski@noctrl.edu.

Northern Kentucky University, Office of Graduate Programs, College of Arts and Sciences, Program in Public Administration, Highland Heights, KY 41099. Offers non-profit management (Certificate); public administration (MPA). *Accreditation:* NASPAA. Part-time and evening/weekend programs available. *Students:* 15 full-time (10 women), 90 part-time (51 women); includes 14 minority (10 Black or African American, non-Hispanic/Latino; 2 Asian, non-Hispanic/Latino; 1 Hispanic/Latino; 1 Two or more races, non-Hispanic/Latino), 2 international. Average age 34. 49 applicants, 55% accepted, 19 enrolled. In 2011, 23 master's, 10 other advanced degrees awarded. *Degree requirements:* For master's, capstone. *Entrance requirements:* For master's, GRE, GMAT or MAT, 2 letters of recommendation, writing sample, minimum GPA of 2.75, essay, resume (for those in-career). Additional exam requirements/recommendations for international students: Required—TOEFL (minimum score 550 paper-based; 213 computer-based; 79 iBT); Recommended—IELTS (minimum score 6.5). *Application deadline:* For fall admission, 7/1 priority date for domestic students, 6/1 for international students; for spring admission, 12/1 priority date for domestic students, 10/1 for international students. Applications are processed on a rolling basis. Application fee: $40. Electronic applications accepted. *Expenses:* Tuition, state resident: full-time $7614; part-time $423 per credit hour. Tuition, nonresident: full-time $13,104; part-time $728 per credit hour. Tuition and fees vary according to degree level and reciprocity agreements. *Financial support:* Unspecified assistantships available. Financial award applicants required to submit FAFSA. *Faculty research:* Non-profit management, human resource management, local government, budgeting and finance, urban planning. *Unit head:* Dr. Shamima Ahmed, Director, 859-572-6402, Fax: 859-572-6184, E-mail: ahmed@nku.edu. *Application contact:* Beth Devantier, MPA Coordinator, 859-572-5326, Fax: 859-572-6184, E-mail: devantier@nku.edu. Web site: http://psc-cj.nku.edu/programs/public/masters/index.php.

North Park University, School of Business and Nonprofit Management, Chicago, IL 60625-4895. Offers MBA, MHEA, MHRM, MM, MNA. Part-time and evening/weekend programs available. Postbaccalaureate distance learning degree programs offered (no on-campus study). *Entrance requirements:* For master's, GMAT, GRE. Additional exam requirements/recommendations for international students: Required—TOEFL. *Expenses:* Contact institution.

Notre Dame of Maryland University, Graduate Studies, Program in Nonprofit Management, Baltimore, MD 21210-2476. Offers MA. Part-time and evening/weekend programs available. *Degree requirements:* For master's, thesis optional. *Entrance requirements:* For master's, minimum GPA of 3.0. Additional exam requirements/recommendations for international students: Required—TOEFL (minimum score 500 paper-based; 173 computer-based; 61 iBT). Electronic applications accepted.

Oklahoma City University, Petree College of Arts and Sciences, Division of Sociology and Justice Studies, Oklahoma City, OK 73106-1402. Offers applied sociology (MA), including nonprofit leadership; criminology (MCJ). Part-time and evening/weekend programs available. *Faculty:* 4 full-time (1 woman), 3 part-time/adjunct (2 women). *Students:* 17 full-time (9 women), 3 part-time (2 women); includes 15 minority (8 Black or African American, non-Hispanic/Latino; 2 American Indian or Alaska Native, non-Hispanic/Latino; 2 Hispanic/Latino; 3 Two or more races, non-Hispanic/Latino). Average age 29. 22 applicants, 86% accepted, 16 enrolled. In 2011, 11 master's awarded. *Degree requirements:* For master's, thesis or alternative. *Entrance requirements:* For master's, minimum GPA of 3.0, two letters of recommendation. Additional exam requirements/recommendations for international students: Required—TOEFL (minimum score 550 paper-based). *Application deadline:* Applications are processed on a rolling basis. Application fee: $30 ($70 for international students). Electronic applications accepted. *Expenses: Tuition:* Full-time $16,848; part-time $936 per credit hour. *Required fees:* $2070; $115 per credit hour. One-time fee: $300. *Financial support:* Career-related internships or fieldwork available. Financial award application deadline: 6/1; financial award applicants required to submit FAFSA. *Faculty research:* Victims, police, corrections, security, women and crime. *Unit head:* Robert Spinks, Director, 405-208-5368, Fax: 405-208-5447, E-mail: bspinks@okcu.edu. *Application contact:* Michelle Cook, Director, Admissions, 800-633-7242, Fax: 405-208-5916, E-mail: gadmissions@okcu.edu. Web site: http://www.okcu.edu/petree/soc/.

Oral Roberts University, School of Business, Tulsa, OK 74171. Offers accounting (MBA); entrepreneurship (MBA); finance (MBA); international business (MBA); management (MBA); marketing (MBA); non-profit management (MBA); not for profit management (MNM). *Accreditation:* ACBSP. Part-time programs available. Postbaccalaureate distance learning degree programs offered (minimal on-campus study). *Degree requirements:* For master's, thesis optional. *Entrance requirements:* For master's, minimum cumulative GPA of 3.0. Additional exam requirements/recommendations for international students: Required—TOEFL (minimum score 550 paper-based; 213 computer-based; 79 iBT). Electronic applications accepted. *Faculty research:* Social media, international business and marketing.

Our Lady of the Lake University of San Antonio, School of Business and Leadership, Program in Nonprofit Management, San Antonio, TX 78207-4689. Offers MS. Part-time and evening/weekend programs available. Postbaccalaureate distance learning degree programs offered.

Pace University, Dyson College of Arts and Sciences, Department of Public Administration, New York, NY 10038. Offers environmental management (MPA); government management (MPA); health care administration (MPA); management for public safety and homeland security (MA); nonprofit management (MPA); JD/MPA. Offered at White Plains, NY location only. Part-time and evening/weekend programs available. *Faculty:* 4 full-time (2 women), 6 part-time/adjunct (1 woman). *Students:* 66 full-time (41 women), 76 part-time (47 women); includes 73 minority (40 Black or African American, non-Hispanic/Latino; 1 American Indian or Alaska Native, non-Hispanic/Latino; 7 Asian, non-Hispanic/Latino; 21 Hispanic/Latino; 4 Two or more races, non-Hispanic/Latino), 10 international. Average age 31. 73 applicants, 89% accepted, 33 enrolled. In 2011, 49 master's awarded. *Degree requirements:* For master's, capstone project. *Entrance requirements:* For master's, GRE General Test. Additional exam requirements/recommendations for international students: Required—TOEFL. *Application deadline:* For fall admission, 8/1 priority date for domestic students; for spring admission, 12/1 priority date for domestic students. Applications are processed on a rolling basis. Application fee: $70. Electronic applications accepted. *Expenses: Tuition:* Part-time $990 per credit. *Required fees:* $168 per semester. Tuition and fees vary according to course load and degree level. *Financial support:* Research assistantships, career-related internships or fieldwork, Federal Work-Study, and tuition waivers (partial) available. Support available to part-time students. Financial award applicants required to submit FAFSA. *Unit head:* Dr. Farrokh Hormozi, Chairperson, 914-422-4285, E-mail: fhormozi@pace.edu. *Application contact:* Susan Ford-Goldschein, Director of Admissions, 914-422-4283, Fax: 914-422-4287, E-mail: gradwp@pace.edu.

Park University, College of Graduate and Professional Studies, Kansas City, MO 54105. Offers adult education (M Ed); at-risk students (M Ed); disaster and emergency management (MPA); educational administration (M Ed); entrepreneurship (MBA); general business (MBA); general education (M Ed); government/business relations (MPA); healthcare/services management (MBA, MPA); international business (MBA); K-12 certification (MAT); management information systems (MBA); management of information systems (MPA); middle school certification (MAT); multi-cultural education (M Ed); nonprofit management (MPA); public management (MPA); school law (M Ed); secondary school certification (MAT); special education (M Ed). Part-time and evening/weekend programs available. Postbaccalaureate distance learning degree programs offered (no on-campus study). *Degree requirements:* For master's, comprehensive exam, thesis (for some programs). *Entrance requirements:* For master's, GRE, GMAT, teacher certification (M Ed). Additional exam requirements/recommendations for international students: Required—TOEFL (minimum score 550 paper-based). Electronic applications accepted. *Faculty research:* Literacy, leadership, brain based research, multicultural education, diversity.

Providence College, School of Business, Providence, RI 02918. Offers accounting (MBA); entrepreneurship (MBA); finance (MBA); international business (MBA); management (MBA); marketing (MBA); not-for-profit organizations (MBA). Part-time and evening/weekend programs available. *Faculty:* 11 full-time (4 women), 6 part-time/adjunct (1 woman). *Students:* 52 full-time (21 women), 49 part-time (17 women); includes 8 minority (3 Black or African American, non-Hispanic/Latino; 2 Asian, non-Hispanic/Latino; 3 Two or more races, non-Hispanic/Latino), 6 international. Average age 26. 49 applicants, 80% accepted, 25 enrolled. In 2011, 57 master's awarded. *Degree requirements:* For master's, thesis optional. *Entrance requirements:* For master's, GMAT. Additional exam requirements/recommendations for international students: Required—TOEFL (minimum score 550 paper-based; 213 computer-based; 80 iBT). *Application deadline:* For fall admission, 8/1 priority date for domestic students, 8/1 for international students; for spring admission, 12/1 priority date for domestic students, 12/1 for international students. Applications are processed on a rolling basis. Application fee: $55. *Expenses:* Contact institution. *Financial support:* In 2011–12, 34 research assistantships with full tuition reimbursements (averaging $8,400 per year) were awarded; Federal Work-Study, institutionally sponsored loans, and unspecified assistantships also available. Support available to part-time students. Financial award application deadline: 8/1; financial award applicants required to submit FAFSA. *Unit head:* Dr. Catherine L. Pastille, Director, MBA Program, 401-865-1654, Fax: 401-865-2978, E-mail: cpastill@providence.edu. *Application contact:* Katherine A. Follett, Administrative Coordinator, 401-865-2333, Fax: 401-865-2978, E-mail: kfollett@providence.edu. Web site: http://www.providence.edu/business/Pages/default.aspx.

Regent University, Graduate School, Robertson School of Government, Virginia Beach, VA 23464-9800. Offers government (MA), including American government, international politics, political theory, public administration; public administration (MPA), including emergency management and homeland security, nonprofit administration and civil society organizations, public leadership and management. Part-time and evening/weekend programs available. Postbaccalaureate distance learning degree programs offered (minimal on-campus study). *Faculty:* 7 full-time (1 woman), 9 part-time/adjunct (1 woman). *Students:* 72 full-time (43 women), 79 part-time (38 women); includes 51 minority (45 Black or African American, non-Hispanic/Latino; 2 Asian, non-Hispanic/Latino; 4 Hispanic/Latino), 3 international. Average age 31. 146 applicants, 65% accepted, 60 enrolled. In 2011, 57 master's awarded. *Degree requirements:* For master's, thesis optional, internship. *Entrance requirements:* For master's, GRE General Test or LSAT, minimum undergraduate GPA of 3.0, writing sample, resume, interview, references. Additional exam requirements/recommendations for international students: Required—TOEFL (minimum score 577 paper-based; 233 computer-based). *Application deadline:* For fall admission, 5/1 priority date for domestic students; for spring admission, 11/1 priority date for domestic students. Applications are processed on a rolling basis. Application fee: $50. Electronic applications accepted. *Expenses:* Contact institution. *Financial support:* Career-related internships or fieldwork, scholarships/grants, tuition waivers (full and partial), and unspecified assistantships available. Support available to part-time students. Financial award application deadline: 9/1; financial award applicants required to submit FAFSA. *Faculty research:* Education reform, political character issues, social capital concerns, administrative ethics, Biblical law and public policy. *Unit head:* Dr. Gary Roberts, Interim Dean, 757-352-4962, Fax: 757-352-4735, E-mail: garyrob@regent.edu. *Application contact:* Matthew Chadwick, Director of Enrollment Support Services, 800-373-5504, Fax: 757-352-4381, E-mail: admissions@regent.edu. Web site: http://www.regent.edu/government/.

Regis University, College for Professional Studies, School of Humanities and Social Sciences, Program in Nonprofit Management, Denver, CO 80221-1099. Offers leadership (Certificate); nonprofit management (MNM). Offered at Northwest Denver Campus and Southeast Denver Campus. Part-time and evening/weekend programs available. Postbaccalaureate distance learning degree programs offered (no on-campus study). *Degree requirements:* For master's and Certificate, thesis optional, final research project. *Entrance requirements:* For master's, 2 years of significant paid or volunteer experience in a nonprofit organization or 400-hour practicum in nonprofit sector, resume, interview; for Certificate, 2 years of significant paid or volunteer experience in a nonprofit organization or 400-hour practicum in nonprofit sector; resumé. Additional exam requirements/recommendations for international students: Required—TOEFL (minimum score 213 computer-based) , TWE (minimum score 5), or university-based test. *Expenses:* Contact institution. *Faculty research:* International nonprofits, enterprise, grass roots nonprofits, leadership in non profit organizations.

Robert Morris University, Graduate Studies, School of Business, Moon Township, PA 15108-1189. Offers business administration (MBA); human resource management (MS); nonprofit management (MS); taxation (MS). *Accreditation:* AACSB. Part-time and evening/weekend programs available. Postbaccalaureate distance learning degree programs offered (no on-campus study). *Faculty:* 29 full-time (11 women), 3 part-time/adjunct (0 women). *Students:* 190 part-time (91 women); includes 11 minority (9 Black or African American, non-Hispanic/Latino; 1 Asian, non-Hispanic/Latino; 1 Hispanic/Latino), 4 international. *Entrance requirements:* For master's, GMAT, letters of recommendation. Additional exam requirements/recommendations for international students: Required—TOEFL (minimum score 550 paper-based; 213 computer-based; 79 iBT). *Application deadline:* For fall admission, 7/1 priority date for domestic students, 7/1 for international students; for spring admission, 11/1 priority date for domestic students, 11/1 for international students. Applications are processed on a rolling basis. Application fee: $35. Electronic applications accepted. *Expenses: Tuition:* Part-time $810 per credit. *Required fees:* $15 per course. Tuition and fees vary according to degree level. *Financial support:* Research assistantships with partial tuition reimbursements, Federal Work-Study, institutionally sponsored loans, and unspecified assistantships available. Support available to part-time students. Financial award application deadline: 5/1; financial award applicants required to submit FAFSA. *Unit head:* Dr. Patrick J. Litzinger, Interim Dean, 412-397-6383, Fax: 412-397-2217, E-mail: litzinger@rmu.edu. *Application contact:* Deborah Roach, Assistant Dean, Graduate Admissions, 412-397-5200, Fax: 412-397-2425, E-mail: graduateadmissions@rmu.edu. Web site: http://www.rmu.edu/web/cms/schools/sbus/.

Roberts Wesleyan College, Division of Business, Rochester, NY 14624-1997. Offers nonprofit leadership (Certificate); strategic leadership (MS); strategic marketing (MS). Evening/weekend programs available. *Degree requirements:* For master's, thesis or alternative. *Entrance requirements:* For master's, GMAT, minimum GPA of 2.75, verifiable work experience. *Expenses:* Contact institution.

St. Cloud State University, School of Graduate Studies, College of Public Affairs, Department of Economics, Program in Public and Nonprofit Institutions, St. Cloud, MN 56301-4498. Offers MS. Part-time programs available. *Degree requirements:* For master's, thesis or alternative. *Entrance requirements:* For master's, GRE General Test, minimum GPA of 2.75. Additional exam requirements/recommendations for international students: Required—Michigan English Language Assessment Battery; Recommended—TOEFL (minimum score 550 paper-based; 213 computer-based), IELTS (minimum score 6.5). Electronic applications accepted.

San Francisco State University, Division of Graduate Studies, College of Health and Human Services, Public Administration Program, San Francisco, CA 94132-1722. Offers nonprofit administration (MPA); policy making and analysis (MPA); public management (MPA); urban administration (MPA). *Accreditation:* NASPAA. *Unit head:* Dr. Genie Stowers, Chair, 415-817-4457, Fax: 415-338-1980, E-mail: gstowers@sfsu.edu. *Application contact:* Bridget McCracken, Director of Academic Services, 415-817-4455, E-mail: mpa@sfsu.edu. Web site: http://www.bss.sfsu.edu/~mpa.

Seton Hall University, College of Arts and Sciences, Department of Political Science and Public Affairs, South Orange, NJ 07079-2697. Offers healthcare administration (MHA, Graduate Certificate); nonprofit organization management (Graduate Certificate); public administration (MPA), including health policy and management, nonprofit organization management, public service: leadership, governance, and policy. *Accreditation:* NASPAA. Part-time and evening/weekend programs available. Postbaccalaureate distance learning degree programs offered (minimal on-campus study). *Degree requirements:* For master's, thesis or alternative, internship or practicum. *Entrance requirements:* Additional exam requirements/recommendations for international students: Required—TOEFL. Electronic applications accepted. *Expenses: Tuition:* Part-time $1033 per credit hour. *Required fees:* $85 per semester.

Southern Adventist University, School of Business and Management, Collegedale, TN 37315-0370. Offers accounting (MBA); church administration (MSA); church and nonprofit leadership (MBA); financial management (MFM); healthcare administration (MBA); management (MBA); marketing management (MBA); outdoor education (MSA). Part-time and evening/weekend programs available. Postbaccalaureate distance learning degree programs offered (no on-campus study). *Entrance requirements:* For master's, GMAT. Additional exam requirements/recommendations for international students: Required—TOEFL (minimum score 600 paper-based; 250 computer-based; 100 iBT). Electronic applications accepted.

Southern New Hampshire University, School of Business, Manchester, NH 03106-1045. Offers accounting (MS); business administration (MBA, Certificate), including accounting (Certificate), business administration (MBA), finance (Certificate), forensic accounting (Certificate), human resources management (Certificate), international business (Certificate), international sport management (Certificate), leadership of not for profit organizations (Certificate), marketing (Certificate), operations management (Certificate), sport management (Certificate), taxation (Certificate); finance (MS); hospitality and tourism leadership (Certificate); information technology (MS, Certificate); information technology/international business (Certificate); integrated marketing communications (Certificate); international business (MS, DBA); marketing (MS); operations and project management (MS); organizational leadership (MS); project management (Certificate); sport management (MS); MBA/Certificate. *Accreditation:* ACBSP. Part-time and evening/weekend programs available. Postbaccalaureate distance learning degree programs offered (no on-campus study). Terminal master's awarded for partial completion of doctoral program. *Degree requirements:* For master's, one foreign language, comprehensive exam (for some programs), thesis or alternative; for doctorate, one foreign language, comprehensive exam, thesis/dissertation. *Entrance requirements:* For master's, minimum GPA of 2.5; for doctorate, GMAT. Additional exam requirements/recommendations for international students: Required—TOEFL (minimum score 500 paper-based). Electronic applications accepted.

Spertus Institute of Jewish Studies, Graduate Programs, Program in Nonprofit Management, Chicago, IL 60605-1901. Offers MSNM. Part-time and evening/weekend programs available. *Faculty:* 35 part-time/adjunct (19 women). *Students:* 142 part-time (120 women); includes 112 minority (109 Black or African American, non-Hispanic/Latino; 1 Asian, non-Hispanic/Latino; 2 Hispanic/Latino). Average age 32. In 2011, 38 master's awarded. *Degree requirements:* For master's, one foreign language, thesis optional. *Entrance requirements:* For master's, interview, minimum GPA of 2.75, graduation from accredited undergraduate program. *Application deadline:* Applications are processed on a rolling basis. Application fee: $50. Electronic applications accepted. *Expenses: Tuition:* Full-time $18,750; part-time $350 per credit. *Financial support:* In 2011–12, 112 students received support. Applicants required to submit FAFSA. *Unit head:* Dr. Lynda Crawford, Associate Dean, 312-322-1720, Fax: 312-994-5360, E-mail: lcrawford@spertus.edu.

Suffolk University, Sawyer Business School, Department of Public Administration, Boston, MA 02108-2770. Offers nonprofit management (MPA); public administration (CASPA); state and local government (MPA); JD/MPA; MPA/MS. *Accreditation:* NASPAA (one or more programs are accredited). Part-time and evening/weekend programs available. *Faculty:* 9 full-time (4 women), 5 part-time/adjunct (2 women). *Students:* 42 full-time (26 women), 102 part-time (66 women); includes 33 minority (17 Black or African American, non-Hispanic/Latino; 5 Asian, non-Hispanic/Latino; 7 Hispanic/Latino; 4 Two or more races, non-Hispanic/Latino), 7 international. Average age 31. 119 applicants, 79% accepted, 43 enrolled. In 2011, 53 master's awarded. *Entrance requirements:* Additional exam requirements/recommendations for international students: Required—TOEFL (minimum score 550 paper-based; 213 computer-based; 80 iBT). *Application deadline:* For fall admission, 6/15 priority date for domestic students, 6/15 for international students; for spring admission, 11/1 priority date for domestic students, 11/1 for international students. Applications are processed on a rolling basis. Application fee: $50. Electronic applications accepted. *Expenses:* Contact institution. *Financial support:* In 2011–12, 109 students received support, including 64 fellowships with full and partial tuition reimbursements available (averaging $11,704 per year); career-related internships or fieldwork and Federal Work-Study also available. Support available to part-time students. Financial award application deadline: 4/1; financial award applicants required to submit FAFSA. *Faculty research:* Local government, health care, federal policy, mental health, HIV/AIDS. *Unit head:* Dr. Richard Beinecke, Chair, 617-573-8062, Fax: 617-227-4618, E-mail: rbeineck@suffolk.edu. *Application contact:* Ellen Driscoll, Director of Graduate Admissions, 617-573-8302, Fax: 617-305-1733, E-mail: grad.admission@suffolk.edu. Web site: http://www.suffolk.edu/mpa.

Texas A&M University, Bush School of Government and Public Service, College Station, TX 77843. Offers advanced international affairs (Certificate); China studies (Certificate); homeland security (Certificate); international affairs (MPIA); national security affairs (Certificate); nonprofit management (Certificate); public service and administration (MPSA). *Accreditation:* NASPAA. *Faculty:* 47. *Students:* 243 full-time (111 women), 91 part-time (44 women); includes 80 minority (16 Black or African American, non-Hispanic/Latino; 4 American Indian or Alaska Native, non-Hispanic/Latino; 11 Asian, non-Hispanic/Latino; 42 Hispanic/Latino; 1 Native Hawaiian or other Pacific Islander, non-Hispanic/Latino; 6 Two or more races, non-Hispanic/Latino), 26 international. Average age 24. In 2011, 107 master's awarded. *Degree requirements:* For master's, summer internship. *Entrance requirements:* For master's, GRE (preferred) or GMAT. Additional exam requirements/recommendations for international students: Recommended—TOEFL. *Application deadline:* For fall admission, 1/24 for domestic and international students. Application fee: $50 ($75 for international students). Electronic applications accepted. *Expenses:* Tuition, state resident: full-time $5437; part-time $226.55 per credit hour. Tuition, nonresident: full-time $12,949; part-time $539.55 per credit hour. *Required fees:* $2741. *Financial support:* In 2011–12, fellowships (averaging $11,000 per year), research assistantships (averaging $11,250 per year) were awarded; career-related internships or fieldwork, Federal Work-Study, and institutionally sponsored loans also available. Financial award application deadline: 2/1; financial award applicants required to submit FAFSA. *Faculty research:* Public policy, presidential studies, public leadership, economic policy, social policy. *Unit head:* Andrew H. Dean, Jr., Acting Dean, 979-862-8007, E-mail: admissions@bushschool.tamu.edu. *Application contact:* Director of Recruiting, 979-458-4767, Fax: 979-845-4155, E-mail: admissions@bushschool.tamu.edu. Web site: http://bush.tamu.edu/.

Trinity Washington University, School of Professional Studies, Washington, DC 20017-1094. Offers business administration (MBA); communication (MA); international security studies (MA); organizational management (MSA), including federal program management, human resource management, nonprofit management, organizational development, public and community health. Part-time and evening/weekend programs available. *Degree requirements:* For master's, thesis (for some programs), capstone project (MSA). *Entrance requirements:* For master's, minimum GPA of 2.5. Additional exam requirements/recommendations for international students: Required—TOEFL (minimum score 550 paper-based; 213 computer-based).

Trinity Western University, School of Graduate Studies, Program in Business Administration, Langley, BC V2Y 1Y1, Canada. Offers international business (MBA); management of the growing enterprise (MBA); non-profit and charitable organization management (MBA). Part-time programs available. Postbaccalaureate distance learning degree programs offered (minimal on-campus study). *Degree requirements:* For master's, thesis or alternative, applied project. *Entrance requirements:* For master's, GMAT (minimum score of 550 recommended). Additional exam requirements/recommendations for international students: Required—TOEFL (minimum score 600 paper-based; 250 computer-based; 100 iBT), IELTS. Electronic applications accepted.

Trinity Western University, School of Graduate Studies, Program in Leadership, Langley, BC V2Y 1Y1, Canada. Offers business (MA, Certificate); Christian ministry (MA); education (MA, Certificate); healthcare (MA, Certificate); non-profit (MA, Certificate). Postbaccalaureate distance learning degree programs offered (minimal on-campus study). *Degree requirements:* For master's, major project. *Entrance requirements:* For master's, minimum GPA of 2.7. Additional exam requirements/recommendations for international students: Required—TOEFL (minimum score 620 paper-based; 260 computer-based; 105 iBT). Electronic applications accepted. *Expenses:* Contact institution. *Faculty research:* Servant leadership.

Troy University, Graduate School, College of Arts and Sciences, Program in Public Administration, Troy, AL 36082. Offers education (MPA); environmental management (MPA); government contracting (MPA); health care administration (MPA); justice administration (MPA); national security affairs (MPA); nonprofit management (MPA); public human resources management (MPA); public management (MPA). *Accreditation:* NASPAA. Part-time and evening/weekend programs available. Postbaccalaureate distance learning degree programs offered (no on-campus study). *Faculty:* 17 full-time (10 women), 10 part-time/adjunct (3 women). *Students:* 97 full-time (71 women), 400 part-time (259 women); includes 298 minority (264 Black or African American, non-Hispanic/Latino; 5 American Indian or Alaska Native, non-Hispanic/Latino; 15 Asian, non-Hispanic/Latino; 11 Hispanic/Latino; 3 Two or more races, non-Hispanic/Latino). Average age 33. 323 applicants, 63% accepted, 97 enrolled. In 2011, 249 master's awarded. *Degree requirements:* For master's, capstone course, minimum GPA of 3.0, admission to candidacy. *Entrance requirements:* For master's, GRE (minimum score of 920), MAT (minimum score of 400) or GMAT (minimum score of 490), minimum undergraduate GPA of 2.5, letter of recommendation, essay. Additional exam requirements/recommendations for international students: Required—TOEFL (minimum score 523 paper-based; 193 computer-based; 70 iBT), IELTS (minimum score 6). *Application deadline:* Applications are processed on a rolling basis. Application fee: $50. Electronic applications accepted. *Expenses:* Tuition, state resident: full-time $6960; part-time $290 per credit hour. Tuition, nonresident: full-time $13,920; part-time $580 per credit hour. *Required fees:* $386 per term. *Financial support:* Available to part-time students. Applicants required to submit FAFSA. *Unit head:* Dr. Charles Kruprick, Chairman, 334-670-5968, Fax: 334-670-5647, E-mail: ckrupnickl@troy.edu. *Application contact:* Brenda K. Campbell, Director of Graduate Admissions, 334-670-3178, Fax: 334-670-3733, E-mail: bcamp@troy.edu.

Tufts University, Graduate School of Arts and Sciences, Graduate Certificate Programs, Management of Community Organizations Program, Medford, MA 02155. Offers Certificate. Part-time and evening/weekend programs available. Electronic applications accepted. *Expenses:* Contact institution.

University of Arkansas at Little Rock, Graduate School, College of Professional Studies, Program in Nonprofit Management, Little Rock, AR 72204-1099. Offers Graduate Certificate.

University of Central Florida, College of Health and Public Affairs, Department of Public Administration, Orlando, FL 32816. Offers emergency management and homeland security (Certificate); non-profit management (MNM, Certificate); public administration (MPA, Certificate); urban and regional planning (MS, Certificate). *Accreditation:* NASPAA. Part-time and evening/weekend programs available. *Faculty:* 16 full-time (9 women), 13 part-time/adjunct (4 women). *Students:* 102 full-time (79 women), 289 part-time (206 women); includes 142 minority (86 Black or African American, non-Hispanic/Latino; 12 Asian, non-Hispanic/Latino; 37 Hispanic/Latino; 3 Native Hawaiian or other Pacific Islander, non-Hispanic/Latino; 4 Two or more races, non-Hispanic/Latino), 8 international. Average age 31. 293 applicants, 73% accepted, 149 enrolled. In 2011, 80 master's, 31 other advanced degrees awarded. *Degree requirements:* For master's, comprehensive exam, thesis or alternative, research report. *Entrance requirements:* For master's, GRE General Test. *Application deadline:* For fall admission, 7/1 for domestic students; for spring admission, 12/1 for domestic students. Application fee: $30. Electronic applications accepted. *Expenses:* Tuition, state resident: part-time $277.08 per credit hour. Tuition, nonresident: part-time $277.08 per credit hour. Part-time tuition and fees vary according to degree level and program. *Financial support:* In 2011–12, 16 students received support, including 2 fellowships with partial tuition reimbursements available (averaging $7,500 per year), 16 research assistantships with partial tuition reimbursements available (averaging $5,400 per year); teaching assistantships with partial tuition reimbursements available, career-related internships or fieldwork, Federal Work-Study, institutionally sponsored loans, tuition waivers (partial), and unspecified assistantships also available. Financial award application deadline: 3/1; financial award applicants required to submit FAFSA. *Unit head:* Dr. Mary Ann Feldheim, Director, 407-823-3693, Fax: 407-823-5651, E-mail: mary.feldheim@ucf.edu. *Application contact:* Barbara Rodriguez, Director, Admissions and Registration, 407-823-2766, Fax: 407-823-6442, E-mail: gradadmissions@ucf.edu. Web site: http://www.cohpa.ucf.edu/pubadm/.

University of Colorado Denver, School of Public Affairs, Program in Public Affairs and Administration, Denver, CO 80127. Offers public administration (MPA), including domestic violence, emergency management and homeland security, environmental policy, management and law, homeland security and defense, local government, nonprofit management, public administration; public affairs (PhD). *Accreditation:* NASPAA. Part-time and evening/weekend programs available. Postbaccalaureate distance learning degree programs offered (no on-campus study). *Faculty:* 19 full-time (9 women), 14 part-time/adjunct (5 women). *Students:* 264 full-time (158 women), 177 part-time (100 women); includes 54 minority (17 Black or African American, non-Hispanic/Latino; 2 American Indian or Alaska Native, non-Hispanic/Latino; 11 Asian, non-Hispanic/Latino; 22 Hispanic/Latino; 2 Two or more races, non-Hispanic/Latino), 31 international. Average age 34. 215 applicants, 67% accepted, 96 enrolled. In 2011, 155 master's, 4 doctorates awarded. *Degree requirements:* For master's, thesis or alternative, 36-39 credit hours; for doctorate, comprehensive exam, thesis/dissertation, minimum of 66 semester hours, including at least 30 hours of doctoral dissertation. *Entrance requirements:* For master's and doctorate, GRE, resume, essay, transcripts, recommendations. Additional exam requirements/recommendations for international students: Required—TOEFL (minimum score 550 paper-based; 223 computer-based). *Application deadline:* For fall admission, 2/1 for domestic students; for spring admission, 10/15 priority date for domestic students. Application fee: $50 ($75 for international students). Electronic applications accepted. *Expenses:* Contact institution. *Financial support:* Fellowships with partial tuition reimbursements, research assistantships with partial tuition reimbursements, teaching assistantships with partial tuition reimbursements, Federal Work-Study, and scholarships/grants available. Support available to part-time students. Financial award application deadline: 4/1; financial award applicants required to submit FAFSA. *Faculty research:* Housing, education and the social and economic issues of vulnerable populations; nonprofit governance and management; education finance, effectiveness and reform; P-20 education initiatives; municipal government accountability. *Unit head:* Dr. Kathleen Beatty, Director of Executive MPA Program, 303-315-2485, Fax: 303-315-2229, E-mail: kathleen.beatty@ucdenver.edu. *Application contact:* Annie Davies, Director of Marketing, Community Outreach and Alumni Affairs, 303-315-2896, Fax: 303-315-2229, E-mail: annie.davies@ucdenver.edu. Web site: http://www.ucdenver.edu/academics/colleges/SPA/Academics/programs/PublicAffairsAdmin/Pages/index.aspx.

University of Connecticut, Graduate School, College of Liberal Arts and Sciences, Department of Public Policy, Field of Public Administration, Storrs, CT 06269. Offers nonprofit management (Graduate Certificate); public administration (MPA); public financial management (Graduate Certificate); JD/MPA; MPA/MSW. *Accreditation:* NASPAA. *Degree requirements:* For master's, comprehensive exam, internship. *Entrance requirements:* For master's, GRE General Test. Additional exam requirements/recommendations for international students: Required—TOEFL (minimum score 550 paper-based; 213 computer-based). Electronic applications accepted.

University of Georgia, School of Social Work, Athens, GA 30602. Offers MA, MSW, PhD, Certificate. *Accreditation:* CSWE (one or more programs are accredited). Part-time and evening/weekend programs available. *Faculty:* 20 full-time (13 women), 1 part-time/adjunct (0 women). *Students:* 300 full-time (256 women), 39 part-time (32 women); includes 83 minority (66 Black or African American, non-Hispanic/Latino; 5 Asian, non-Hispanic/Latino; 7 Hispanic/Latino; 5 Two or more races, non-Hispanic/Latino), 10 international. Average age 30. 397 applicants, 58% accepted, 160 enrolled. In 2011, 160 master's, 4 doctorates awarded. *Degree requirements:* For master's, thesis or alternative; for doctorate, one foreign language, thesis/dissertation. *Entrance requirements:* For master's and doctorate, GRE General Test. *Application deadline:* For fall admission, 7/1 priority date for domestic students, 7/1 for international students; for spring admission, 11/15 for domestic and international students. Applications are processed on a rolling basis. Application fee: $50. Electronic applications accepted. *Financial support:* In 2011–12, 39 students received support, including 4 fellowships (averaging $25,000 per year), 35 research assistantships with tuition reimbursements available (averaging $7,500 per year); teaching assistantships with tuition reimbursements available, career-related internships or fieldwork, Federal Work-Study, scholarships/grants, tuition waivers (full and partial), and unspecified assistantships also available. Support available to part-time students. Financial award application deadline: 2/10; financial award applicants required to submit FAFSA. *Faculty research:* Juvenile justice, substance abuse, civil rights and social justice, gerontology, social policy. *Total annual research expenditures:* $2.6 million. *Unit head:* Dr. Maurice C. Daniels, Dean, 706-542-5424, Fax: 706-542-3282, E-mail: daniels@uga.edu. *Application contact:* Dr. Jerome Schiele, Graduate Coordinator, 706-542-5429, Fax: 706-542-3282, E-mail: fschiele@uga.edu. Web site: http://www.ssw.uga.edu/.

University of La Verne, College of Business and Public Management, Program in Organizational Management and Leadership, La Verne, CA 91750-4443. Offers nonprofit management (Certificate); organizational leadership (Certificate); organizational management and leadership (MS). Part-time programs available. *Faculty:* 34 full-time (15 women), 38 part-time/adjunct (13 women). *Students:* 87 full-time (44 women), 78 part-time (56 women); includes 70 minority (13 Black or African American, non-Hispanic/Latino; 12 Asian, non-Hispanic/Latino; 43 Hispanic/Latino; 2 Two or more races, non-Hispanic/Latino), 48 international. Average age 33. In 2011, 138 master's awarded. *Degree requirements:* For master's, thesis or research project. *Entrance requirements:* For master's, minimum undergraduate GPA of 2.75, 2 letters of recommendation, interview, resume. Additional exam requirements/recommendations for international students: Required—TOEFL (minimum score 550 paper-based; 213 computer-based). *Application deadline:* Applications are processed on a rolling basis. Application fee: $50. *Expenses:* Contact institution. *Financial support:* Institutionally sponsored loans available. Financial award application deadline: 3/2; financial award applicants required to submit FAFSA. *Unit head:* Dr. Kathy Duncan, Program Director, 909-593-3511 Ext. 4415, E-mail: kduncan2@laverne.edu. *Application contact:* Program and Admissions Specialist, 909-593-3511 Ext. 4819, Fax: 909-392-2761, E-mail: cbpm@laverne.edu. Web site: http://laverne.edu/catalog/program/ms-leadership-and-management/.

University of Louisville, Graduate School, College of Arts and Sciences, Department of Urban and Public Affairs, Louisville, KY 40208. Offers public administration (MPA), including human resources management, non-profit management, public policy and administration; urban and public affairs (PhD), including urban planning and development, urban policy and administration; urban planning (MUP), including administration of planning organizations, housing and community development, land use and environmental planning, spatial analysis. Part-time and evening/weekend programs available. Terminal master's awarded for partial completion of doctoral program. *Degree requirements:* For master's, internship; for doctorate, comprehensive exam, thesis/dissertation. *Entrance requirements:* For master's, GRE General Test, minimum GPA of 3.0; for doctorate, GRE General Test, master's degree in appropriate field. Additional exam requirements/recommendations for international students: Required—TOEFL (minimum score 550 paper-based; 213 computer-based; 79 iBT). Electronic applications accepted. *Expenses:* Tuition, state resident: full-time $9692; part-time $539 per credit hour. Tuition, nonresident: full-time $20,168; part-time $1121 per credit hour. Tuition and fees vary according to program and reciprocity agreements. *Faculty research:* Housing and community development, performance-based budgeting, environmental policy and natural hazards, sustainability, real estate development, comparative urban development.

University of Memphis, Graduate School, College of Arts and Sciences, Division of Public and Nonprofit Administration, Memphis, TN 38152. Offers nonprofit administration (MPA); public management and policy (MPA); urban management and planning (MPA). *Accreditation:* NASPAA. Part-time and evening/weekend programs available. Postbaccalaureate distance learning degree programs offered (minimal on-campus study). *Degree requirements:* For master's, comprehensive exam, thesis or alternative, internship. *Entrance requirements:* For master's, GRE General Test, GMAT, or MAT, minimum GPA of 3.0. Additional exam requirements/recommendations for international students: Required—TOEFL. *Faculty research:* Nonprofit organization governance, local government management, community collaboration, urban problems, accountability.

University of Missouri, Graduate School, Harry S Truman School of Public Affairs, Columbia, MO 65211. Offers grantsmanship (Graduate Certificate); nonprofit management (Graduate Certificate); organizational change (Graduate Certificate); public affairs (MPA, PhD); public management (Graduate Certificate); science and public policy (Graduate Certificate). *Accreditation:* NASPAA. *Faculty:* 12 full-time (5 women). *Students:* 83 full-time (46 women), 70 part-time (36 women); includes 10 minority (3 Black or African American, non-Hispanic/Latino; 3 Asian, non-Hispanic/Latino; 2 Hispanic/Latino; 2 Two or more races, non-Hispanic/Latino), 40 international. Average age 31. 122 applicants, 61% accepted, 51 enrolled. In 2011, 54 master's, 22 other advanced degrees awarded. *Entrance requirements:* For master's, GRE General Test, minimum GPA of 3.0. Additional exam requirements/recommendations for international students: Required—TOEFL (minimum score 550 paper-based; 213 computer-based; 79 iBT). *Application deadline:* For fall admission, 2/15 priority date for domestic students. Applications are processed on a rolling basis. Application fee: $55 ($75 for international students). *Expenses:* Tuition, state resident: full-time $5881. Tuition, nonresident: full-time $15,183. *Required fees:* $952. Tuition and fees vary according to campus/location and program. *Financial support:* Fellowships, research assistantships, teaching assistantships, and institutionally sponsored loans available. *Faculty research:* Public service ethics, history and theory, organizational symbolism and culture; program evaluation and social policy, with special emphasis on child development, education and health policies; organization theory and applied psychoanalytic theory; foreign policy and international political economy; health care delivery for persons with disabilities and health policy; survival strategies employed by low-income households; rural economic development, fiscal and economic impact analysis. *Unit head:* Dr. Bart Wechsler, Director, E-mail: wechslerb@missouri.edu. *Application contact:* Jessica Hosey, 573-882-3471, E-mail: hoseyj@missouri.edu. Web site: http://truman.missouri.edu/.

University of Missouri–St. Louis, Graduate School, Program in Public Policy Administration, St. Louis, MO 63121. Offers health policy (MPPA); local government management (MPPA, Certificate); managing human resources and organization (MPPA); nonprofit organization management (MPPA); nonprofit organization management and leadership (Certificate); policy research and analysis (MPPA). *Accreditation:* NASPAA. Part-time and evening/weekend programs available. *Faculty:* 10 full-time (5 women), 9 part-time/adjunct (4 women). *Students:* 33 full-time (17 women), 76 part-time (48 women); includes 30 minority (25 Black or African American, non-Hispanic/Latino; 2 American Indian or Alaska Native, non-Hispanic/Latino; 1 Asian, non-Hispanic/Latino; 2 Hispanic/Latino), 9 international. Average age 32. 68 applicants, 50% accepted, 27 enrolled. In 2011, 23 master's, 22 Certificates awarded. *Entrance requirements:* For master's, 3 letters of recommendation. Additional exam requirements/recommendations for international students: Required—TOEFL (minimum score 550 paper-based; 213 computer-based). *Application deadline:* For fall admission, 7/1 priority date for domestic students, 7/1 for international students; for spring admission, 12/1 priority date for domestic students, 12/1 for international students. Applications are processed on a rolling basis. Application fee: $35 ($40 for international students). Electronic applications accepted. *Expenses:* Tuition, state resident: full-time $6273; part-time $3866 per year. Tuition, nonresident: full-time $14,969; part-time $9980 per year. *Required fees:* $315 per year. *Financial support:* In 2011–12, 2 research assistantships with full and partial tuition reimbursements (averaging $12,000 per year) were awarded; career-related internships or fieldwork also available. Financial award application deadline: 4/1; financial award applicants required to submit FAFSA. *Faculty research:* Urban policy, public finance, evaluation. *Unit head:* Dr. Deborah Balser, Director, 314-516-5145, Fax: 314-516-5210, E-mail: balserd@msx.umsl.edu. *Application contact:* 314-516-5458, Fax: 314-516-6996, E-mail: gradadm@umsl.edu. Web site: http://www.umsl.edu/divisions/graduate/mppa/.

University of Nevada, Las Vegas, Graduate College, Greenspun College of Urban Affairs, School of Environmental and Public Affairs, Las Vegas, NV 89154-4030. Offers crisis and emergency management (MS); environmental science (MS, PhD); non-profit management (Certificate); public administration (MPA); public affairs (PhD); public management (Certificate); solar and renewabale energy (Certificate); urban leadership (MA); workforce development and organizational leadership (PhD). Part-time programs available. *Faculty:* 28 full-time (10 women), 53 part-time/adjunct (11 women). *Students:* 49 full-time (19 women), 117 part-time (57 women); includes 62 minority (31 Black or

Nonprofit Management

African American, non-Hispanic/Latino; 1 American Indian or Alaska Native, non-Hispanic/Latino; 4 Asian, non-Hispanic/Latino; 21 Hispanic/Latino; 5 Two or more races, non-Hispanic/Latino), 5 international. Average age 36. 94 applicants, 66% accepted, 47 enrolled. In 2011, 46 master's, 4 doctorates, 4 other advanced degrees awarded. *Degree requirements:* For master's, comprehensive exam (for some programs), thesis; for doctorate, comprehensive exam (for some programs), thesis/dissertation. *Entrance requirements:* Additional exam requirements/recommendations for international students: Required—TOEFL (minimum score 550 paper-based; 213 computer-based; 80 iBT), IELTS (minimum score 7). *Application deadline:* For fall admission, 2/15 priority date for domestic students, 5/1 for international students; for spring admission, 11/15 priority date for domestic students, 10/1 for international students. Applications are processed on a rolling basis. Application fee: $60 ($95 for international students). Electronic applications accepted. *Financial support:* In 2011–12, 33 students received support, including 20 research assistantships with partial tuition reimbursements available (averaging $11,193 per year), 13 teaching assistantships with partial tuition reimbursements available (averaging $10,928 per year); institutionally sponsored loans, scholarships/grants, health care benefits, and unspecified assistantships also available. Financial award application deadline: 3/1. *Faculty research:* Community and organizational resilience; environmental decision-making and management; budgeting and human resource/workforce management; urban design, sustainability and governance; public and non-profit management. *Total annual research expenditures:* $1.3 million. *Unit head:* Dr. Christopher Stream, Chair/Associate Professor, 702-895-5120, Fax: 702-895-4436, E-mail: chris.stream@unlv.edu. *Application contact:* Graduate College Admissions Evaluator, 702-895-3320, Fax: 702-895-4180, E-mail: gradcollege@unlv.edu. Web site: http://sepa.unlv.edu/.

The University of North Carolina at Charlotte, Graduate School, College of Liberal Arts and Sciences, Department of Political Science, Charlotte, NC 28223-0001. Offers emergency management (Certificate); non-profit management (Certificate); public administration (MPA), including arts administration, emergency management, non-profit management, public finance; public finance (Certificate); urban management and policy (Certificate). *Accreditation:* NASPAA. Part-time and evening/weekend programs available. *Faculty:* 19 full-time (8 women), 2 part-time/adjunct (1 woman). *Students:* 25 full-time (12 women), 71 part-time (50 women); includes 29 minority (26 Black or African American, non-Hispanic/Latino; 1 Asian, non-Hispanic/Latino; 1 Hispanic/Latino; 1 Two or more races, non-Hispanic/Latino), 2 international. Average age 29. 53 applicants, 77% accepted, 22 enrolled. In 2011, 20 master's, 6 other advanced degrees awarded. Terminal master's awarded for partial completion of doctoral program. *Degree requirements:* For master's, thesis or alternative. *Entrance requirements:* For master's, GRE General Test or MAT, minimum GPA of 3.0 in undergraduate major, 2.75 overall. Additional exam requirements/recommendations for international students: Required—TOEFL (minimum score 557 paper-based; 220 computer-based; 83 iBT). *Application deadline:* For fall admission, 7/1 for domestic students, 5/1 for international students; for spring admission, 11/1 for domestic students, 10/1 for international students. Applications are processed on a rolling basis. Application fee: $65 ($75 for international students). Electronic applications accepted. *Expenses:* Tuition, state resident: full-time $3689. Tuition, nonresident: full-time $15,226. *Required fees:* $2198. Tuition and fees vary according to course load and program. *Financial support:* In 2011–12, 6 students received support, including 6 research assistantships (averaging $9,167 per year); career-related internships or fieldwork, Federal Work-Study, institutionally sponsored loans, scholarships/grants, and unspecified assistantships also available. Support available to part-time students. Financial award application deadline: 4/1; financial award applicants required to submit FAFSA. *Faculty research:* Terrorism, public administration, nonprofit and arts administration, educational policy, social policy. *Total annual research expenditures:* $168,058. *Unit head:* Dr. Theodore S. Arrington, Chair, 704-687-2571, Fax: 704-687-3497, E-mail: tarrngtn@uncc.edu. *Application contact:* Kathy B. Giddings, Director of Graduate Admissions, 704-687-5503, Fax: 704-687-3279, E-mail: gradadm@uncc.edu. Web site: http://www.popliticalscience.uncc.edu/mpa_handbook.html.

The University of North Carolina at Greensboro, Graduate School, College of Arts and Sciences, Department of Political Science, Greensboro, NC 27412-5001. Offers nonprofit management (Certificate); public affairs (MPA); urban and economic development (Certificate). *Accreditation:* NASPAA. *Degree requirements:* For master's, comprehensive exam. *Entrance requirements:* For master's, GRE General Test. Additional exam requirements/recommendations for international students: Required—TOEFL. Electronic applications accepted. *Faculty research:* U.S. Constitution, Canadian parliament, public management, ethical challenge of public service.

University of Northern Iowa, Graduate College, Program in Philanthropy and Nonprofit Development, Cedar Falls, IA 50614. Offers MA. *Students:* 15 part-time (12 women); includes 2 minority (1 Asian, non-Hispanic/Latino; 1 Hispanic/Latino). 22 applicants, 77% accepted, 14 enrolled. *Entrance requirements:* For master's, minimum GPA of 3.0; 3 letters of recommendation; experience in the philanthropy and/or nonprofit areas. Additional exam requirements/recommendations for international students: Required—TOEFL (minimum score 500 paper-based; 180 computer-based; 61 iBT). *Application deadline:* Applications are processed on a rolling basis. Application fee: $50 ($70 for international students). Electronic applications accepted. *Expenses:* Tuition, state resident: full-time $7476. Tuition, nonresident: full-time $16,410. *Required fees:* $942. *Financial support:* Application deadline: 2/1. *Unit head:* Dr. Rodney Dieser, Coordinator, 319-273-7775, Fax: 319-273-5958, E-mail: rodney.dieser@uni.edu. *Application contact:* Laurie S. Russell, Record Analyst, 319-273-2623, Fax: 319-273-2885, E-mail: laurie.russell@uni.edu.

University of North Florida, College of Arts and Sciences, Department of Political Science and Public Administration, Jacksonville, FL 32224. Offers nonprofit management (Graduate Certificate); public administration (MPA). *Accreditation:* NASPAA. Part-time programs available. *Faculty:* 11 full-time (4 women), 1 part-time/adjunct (0 women). *Students:* 19 full-time (9 women), 43 part-time (26 women); includes 45 minority (40 Black or African American, non-Hispanic/Latino; 1 American Indian or Alaska Native, non-Hispanic/Latino; 1 Asian, non-Hispanic/Latino; 2 Hispanic/Latino; 1 Two or more races, non-Hispanic/Latino), 2 international. Average age 31. 41 applicants, 51% accepted, 16 enrolled. In 2011, 25 master's awarded. *Degree requirements:* For master's, thesis or alternative, internship. *Entrance requirements:* For master's, GRE General Test, minimum GPA of 3.0 in last 60 hours, 2 letters of recommendation, interview. Additional exam requirements/recommendations for international students: Required—TOEFL (minimum score 500 paper-based; 173 computer-based; 61 iBT). *Application deadline:* For fall admission, 7/1 priority date for domestic students, 5/1 for international students; for spring admission, 11/1 priority date for domestic students, 10/1 for international students. Applications are processed on a rolling basis. Application fee: $30. Electronic applications accepted. *Expenses:* Tuition, state resident: full-time $8793; part-time $366.38 per credit hour. Tuition, nonresident: full-time $23,502; part-time $979.24 per credit hour. *Required fees:* $1384; $57.66 per credit hour. Tuition and fees vary according to course load and program. *Financial support:* In 2011–12, 15 students received support, including 1 research assistantship (averaging $1,666 per year), 1 teaching assistantship (averaging $3,222 per year); career-related internships or fieldwork, Federal Work-Study, scholarships/grants, tuition waivers (partial), and unspecified assistantships also available. Financial award application deadline: 4/1; financial award applicants required to submit FAFSA. *Faculty research:* America's usage of the Internet, use of information communication technologies by educators and children. *Total annual research expenditures:* $6,508. *Unit head:* Dr. Matthew T. Corrigan, Chair, 904-620-2977, Fax: 904-620-2979, E-mail: mcorriga@unf.edu. *Application contact:* Lillith Richardson, Assistant Director, The Graduate School, 904-620-1360, Fax: 907-620-1362, E-mail: graduateschool@unf.edu. Web site: http://www.unf.edu/coas/pspa/.

University of Notre Dame, Mendoza College of Business, Program in Nonprofit Administration, Notre Dame, IN 46556. Offers MNA. *Accreditation:* AACSB. Part-time programs available. Postbaccalaureate distance learning degree programs offered (minimal on-campus study). *Faculty:* 8 full-time (0 women), 10 part-time/adjunct (5 women). *Students:* 7 full-time (3 women), 62 part-time (40 women); includes 5 minority (1 Black or African American, non-Hispanic/Latino; 1 Asian, non-Hispanic/Latino; 3 Hispanic/Latino), 4 international. Average age 30. 80 applicants, 41% accepted, 29 enrolled. In 2011, 15 master's awarded. *Degree requirements:* For master's, thesis. *Entrance requirements:* For master's, GRE General Test; GMAT, work experience. Additional exam requirements/recommendations for international students: Required—TOEFL (minimum score 600 paper-based; 250 computer-based). *Application deadline:* For winter admission, 1/15 for domestic students; for spring admission, 3/31 for domestic students. Application fee: $60. Electronic applications accepted. *Expenses:* Contact institution. *Financial support:* In 2011–12, 42 students received support, including 42 fellowships (averaging $2,500 per year); institutionally sponsored loans and scholarships/grants also available. Support available to part-time students. *Unit head:* Thomas J. Harvey, Director, 574-631-7593, Fax: 574-631-6532, E-mail: harvey.18@nd.edu. *Application contact:* Kimberly M. Brennan, Program Manager, 574-631-3639, Fax: 574-631-6532, E-mail: brennan.53@nd.edu. Web site: http://business.nd.edu/mna/.

University of Pittsburgh, Graduate School of Public and International Affairs, Public Policy and Management Program for Mid-Career Professionals, Pittsburgh, PA 15260. Offers development planning (MPPM); international development (MPPM); international political economy (MPPM); international security studies (MPPM); management of non profit organizations (MPPM); metropolitan management and regional development (MPPM); policy analysis and evaluation (MPPM). Part-time programs available. *Faculty:* 26 full-time (12 women), 47 part-time/adjunct (19 women). *Students:* 18 full-time (5 women), 29 part-time (12 women); includes 7 minority (3 Black or African American, non-Hispanic/Latino; 1 Hispanic/Latino; 3 Two or more races, non-Hispanic/Latino), 12 international. Average age 38. 43 applicants, 51% accepted, 19 enrolled. In 2011, 26 master's awarded. *Degree requirements:* For master's, thesis optional, capstone seminar. *Entrance requirements:* For master's, 2 letters of recommendation, resume, 5 years of supervisory or budgetary experience. Additional exam requirements/recommendations for international students: Required—TOEFL (minimum score 600 paper-based; 250 computer-based; 100 iBT), TWE (minimum score 4); Recommended—IELTS (minimum score 7). *Application deadline:* For fall admission, 6/1 priority date for domestic students, 2/15 for international students; for spring admission, 1/1 priority date for domestic students, 8/1 for international students. Applications are processed on a rolling basis. Application fee: $50. Electronic applications accepted. *Expenses:* Tuition, state resident: full-time $18,774; part-time $760 per credit. Tuition, nonresident: full-time $30,736; part-time $1258 per credit. *Required fees:* $740; $200 per term. Tuition and fees vary according to program. *Financial support:* In 2011–12, 14 students received support. Scholarships/grants and tuition waivers (partial) available. Support available to part-time students. Financial award application deadline: 2/1. *Faculty research:* Nonprofit management, urban and regional affairs, policy analysis and evaluation, security and intelligence studies, global political economy, nongovernmental organizations, civil society, development planning and environmental sustainability, human security. *Total annual research expenditures:* $892,349. *Unit head:* Dr. George Dougherty, Jr., Director, Executive Education, 412-648-7603, Fax: 412-648-2605, E-mail: gwdjr@pitt.edu. *Application contact:* Michael T. Rizzi, Associate Director of Student Services, 412-648-7640, Fax: 412-648-7641, E-mail: rizzim@pitt.edu. Web site: http://www.gspia.pitt.edu/.

University of Portland, Dr. Robert B. Pamplin, Jr. School of Business, Portland, OR 97203-5798. Offers business administration (MBA); entrepreneurship (MBA); finance (MBA, MS); health care management (MBA); marketing (MBA); nonprofit management (EMBA); operations and technology management (MBA); sustainability (MBA). *Accreditation:* AACSB. Part-time and evening/weekend programs available. *Faculty:* 13 full-time (1 woman), 8 part-time/adjunct (1 woman). *Students:* 50 full-time (13 women), 90 part-time (41 women); includes 19 minority (1 Black or African American, non-Hispanic/Latino; 1 American Indian or Alaska Native, non-Hispanic/Latino; 8 Asian, non-Hispanic/Latino; 5 Hispanic/Latino; 2 Native Hawaiian or other Pacific Islander, non-Hispanic/Latino; 2 Two or more races, non-Hispanic/Latino), 18 international. Average age 31. In 2011, 54 master's awarded. *Entrance requirements:* For master's, GMAT, minimum GPA of 3.0, resume, 2 letters of recommendation. Additional exam requirements/recommendations for international students: Required—TOEFL (minimum score 570 paper-based; 89 iBT), IELTS (minimum score 7). *Application deadline:* For fall admission, 7/15 priority date for domestic students, 7/15 for international students; for spring admission, 12/15 priority date for domestic students, 12/15 for international students. Applications are processed on a rolling basis. Application fee: $50. *Expenses:* Contact institution. *Financial support:* Federal Work-Study, scholarships/grants, and tuition waivers (partial) available. Support available to part-time students. Financial award application deadline: 3/1; financial award applicants required to submit FAFSA. *Unit head:* Dr. Howard Feldman, Associate Dean, 503-943-7224, E-mail: feldman@up.edu. *Application contact:* Melissa McCarthy, Academic Specialist, 503-943-7225, E-mail: mccarthy@up.edu. Web site: http://business.up.edu/.

University of San Diego, School of Leadership and Education Sciences, Department of Leadership Studies, San Diego, CA 92110-2492. Offers higher education leadership (MA); leadership studies (MA, PhD); nonprofit leadership and management (MA, Certificate). Part-time and evening/weekend programs available. *Faculty:* 11 full-time (6 women), 16 part-time/adjunct (8 women). *Students:* 14 full-time (9 women), 202 part-time (139 women); includes 65 minority (16 Black or African American, non-Hispanic/Latino; 11 Asian, non-Hispanic/Latino; 30 Hispanic/Latino; 3 Native Hawaiian or other Pacific Islander, non-Hispanic/Latino; 5 Two or more races, non-Hispanic/Latino), 8 international. Average age 35. 236 applicants, 51% accepted, 75 enrolled. In 2011, 53 master's, 11 doctorates awarded. *Degree requirements:* For master's, thesis (for some programs), portfolio; for doctorate, comprehensive exam, thesis/dissertation. *Entrance requirements:* For master's, minimum GPA of 3.0, interview; for doctorate, GRE, master's degree, minimum GPA of 3.5 (recommended), interview, writing sample, resume. Additional exam requirements/recommendations for international students: Required—TOEFL (minimum score 580 paper-based; 237 computer-based; 83 iBT), TWE. *Application deadline:* For fall admission, 1/15 for domestic and international students. Application fee: $45. Electronic applications accepted. *Expenses: Tuition:* Full-time $22,482; part-time $1249 per unit. *Required fees:* $224. Full-time tuition and fees vary according to course load and degree level. *Financial support:* In 2011–12, 161 students received support. Career-related internships or fieldwork, Federal Work-Study, institutionally sponsored loans, unspecified assistantships, and stipends available. Support available to part-time students. Financial award application deadline: 4/1;

financial award applicants required to submit FAFSA. *Faculty research:* Higher education administration policy and relations, organizational leadership, nonprofits and philanthropy, student affairs leadership. *Unit head:* Dr. Cheryl Getz, Graduate Program Director, 619-260-4289, Fax: 619-260-6835, E-mail: cgetz@sandiego.edu. *Application contact:* Monica Mahon, Associate Director of Graduate Admissions, 619-260-4524, Fax: 619-260-4158, E-mail: grads@sandiego.edu. Web site: http://www.sandiego.edu/soles/programs/leadership_studies/.

University of San Francisco, School of Management, Program in Nonprofit Administration, San Francisco, CA 94117-1080. Offers MNA. *Faculty:* 2 full-time (0 women), 5 part-time/adjunct (4 women). *Students:* 70 full-time (50 women); includes 28 minority (7 Black or African American, non-Hispanic/Latino; 5 Asian, non-Hispanic/Latino; 11 Hispanic/Latino; 5 Two or more races, non-Hispanic/Latino), 4 international. Average age 33. 41 applicants, 88% accepted, 23 enrolled. In 2011, 29 master's awarded. *Degree requirements:* For master's, thesis optional. *Entrance requirements:* For master's, minimum GPA of 3.0. Application fee: $55 ($65 for international students). *Expenses: Tuition:* Full-time $20,070; part-time $1115 per unit. Tuition and fees vary according to course load, campus/location and program. *Financial support:* In 2011–12, 6 students received support. Application deadline: 3/2; applicants required to submit FAFSA. *Faculty research:* Philanthropy in ethnic communities. *Unit head:* Dr. Kathleen Fletcher, Director, 415-422-5121. *Application contact:* 415-422-6000, E-mail: graduate@usfca.edu.

University of Southern California, Graduate School, School of Policy, Planning, and Development, Master of Public Administration Program, Los Angeles, CA 90089. Offers nonprofit management and policy (Graduate Certificate); political management (Graduate Certificate); public administration (MPA); public management (Graduate Certificate); MPA/JD; MPA/M Pl; MPA/MA; MPA/MAJCS; MPA/MS; MPA/MSW. *Accreditation:* NASPAA (one or more programs are accredited). Part-time and evening/weekend programs available. Postbaccalaureate distance learning degree programs offered (minimal on-campus study). Terminal master's awarded for partial completion of doctoral program. *Degree requirements:* For master's, capstone, internship. *Entrance requirements:* For master's, GRE, GMAT. Additional exam requirements/recommendations for international students: Required—TOEFL (minimum score 600 paper-based; 250 computer-based; 100 iBT). Electronic applications accepted. *Faculty research:* Collaborative governance and decision-making, nonprofit management, environmental management, institutional analysis, local government, civic engagement.

University of Southern Maine, Edmund S. Muskie School of Public Service, Program in Public Policy and Management, Portland, ME 04104-9300. Offers child and family policy (Certificate); non-profit management (Certificate); public policy and management (MPPM); JD/MPPM. Part-time and evening/weekend programs available. Postbaccalaureate distance learning degree programs offered (minimal on-campus study). *Degree requirements:* For master's, thesis, capstone project, field experience. *Entrance requirements:* For master's, GRE General Test or LSAT. Additional exam requirements/recommendations for international students: Required—TOEFL. Electronic applications accepted. *Faculty research:* Sustainable communities, juvenile justice, program management, nonprofit management.

The University of Tampa, John H. Sykes College of Business, Tampa, FL 33606-1490. Offers accounting (MS); entrepreneurship (MBA); finance (MBA, MS); information systems management (MBA); innovation management (MBA); international business (MBA); marketing (MBA, MS); nonprofit management (MBA). *Accreditation:* AACSB. Part-time and evening/weekend programs available. *Faculty:* 38 full-time (14 women), 5 part-time/adjunct (1 woman). *Students:* 161 full-time (65 women), 193 part-time (82 women); includes 65 minority (11 Black or African American, non-Hispanic/Latino; 1 American Indian or Alaska Native, non-Hispanic/Latino; 8 Asian, non-Hispanic/Latino; 39 Hispanic/Latino; 2 Native Hawaiian or other Pacific Islander, non-Hispanic/Latino; 4 Two or more races, non-Hispanic/Latino), 58 international. Average age 29. 837 applicants, 41% accepted, 196 enrolled. In 2011, 259 degrees awarded. *Degree requirements:* For master's, capstone. *Entrance requirements:* For master's, GMAT or GRE, 4-year undergraduate degree, minimum GPA of 3.0, professional experience (for Executive MBA). Additional exam requirements/recommendations for international students: Required—TOEFL (minimum score 577 paper-based; 230 computer-based; 90 iBT); Recommended—IELTS (minimum score 7.5). *Application deadline:* Applications are processed on a rolling basis. Application fee: $40. Electronic applications accepted. *Expenses: Tuition:* Full-time $8320; part-time $520 per credit hour. *Required fees:* $40 per semester. Tuition and fees vary according to program. *Financial support:* In 2011–12, 124 students received support. Career-related internships or fieldwork, scholarships/grants, unspecified assistantships, and grants available. Financial award applicants required to submit FAFSA. *Faculty research:* Job market signaling, on-line shopping behaviors and social media, the Tampa Bay economy, digital literacy, entrepreneurship in small businesses. *Unit head:* Dennis Nostrand, Vice President, Enrollment/Admissions, 813-257-1808, E-mail: dnostrand@ut.edu. *Application contact:* Charlene Tobie, Associate Director of Admissions, 813-257-3566, E-mail: ctobie@ut.edu. Web site: http://ut.edu/graduate.

The University of Tennessee at Chattanooga, Graduate School, College of Arts and Sciences, Department of Political Science, Chattanooga, TN 37403. Offers local government management (MPA); non profit management (MPA); public administration (MPA); public administration and non-profit management (Postbaccalaureate Certificate). Part-time and evening/weekend programs available. *Faculty:* 6 full-time (2 women), 1 (woman) part-time/adjunct. *Students:* 19 full-time (13 women), 16 part-time (10 women); includes 7 minority (5 Black or African American, non-Hispanic/Latino; 1 Hispanic/Latino; 1 Two or more races, non-Hispanic/Latino). Average age 28. 20 applicants, 85% accepted, 13 enrolled. In 2011, 16 degrees awarded. *Degree requirements:* For master's, comprehensive exam, thesis or alternative, internship. *Entrance requirements:* For master's, GRE General Test. Additional exam requirements/recommendations for international students: Required—TOEFL (minimum score 550 paper-based; 213 computer-based; 79 iBT), IELTS (minimum score 6). *Application deadline:* For fall admission, 8/1 priority date for domestic students, 6/1 for international students; for spring admission, 12/1 priority date for domestic students, 10/1 for international students. Applications are processed on a rolling basis. Application fee: $35. Electronic applications accepted. *Expenses:* Tuition, state resident: full-time $6472; part-time $359 per credit hour. Tuition, nonresident: full-time $20,006; part-time $1111 per credit hour. *Required fees:* $1320; $160 per credit hour. *Financial support:* Career-related internships or fieldwork, scholarships/grants, and unspecified assistantships available. Support available to part-time students. *Faculty research:* Organizational cultures and renewal, management theory, public policy, policy analysis, nonprofit organization. *Total annual research expenditures:* $3,000. *Unit head:* Dr. Fouad M. Moughrabi, Head, 423-425-4281, Fax: 423-425-2373, E-mail: fouad-moughrabi@utc.edu. *Application contact:* Dr. Jerald Ainsworth, Dean of Graduate Studies, 423-425-4478, Fax: 423-425-5223, E-mail: jerald-ainsworth@utc.edu. Web site: http://www.utc.edu/Academic/PoliticalScience/.

University of the Sacred Heart, Graduate Programs, Program in Nonprofit Organization Administration, San Juan, PR 00914-0383. Offers MBA.

University of the West, Department of Business Administration, Rosemead, CA 91770. Offers business administration (EMBA); finance (MBA); information technology and management (MBA); international business (MBA); nonprofit organization management (MBA). Part-time and evening/weekend programs available. *Entrance requirements:* Additional exam requirements/recommendations for international students: Required—TOEFL.

The University of Toledo, College of Graduate Studies, College of Language, Literature and Social Sciences, Department of Political Science and Public Administration, Toledo, OH 43606-3390. Offers health care policy and administration (Certificate); management of non-profit organizations (Certificate); municipal administration (Certificate); political science (MA); JD/MPA. Part-time programs available. *Faculty:* 8. *Students:* 16 full-time (8 women), 23 part-time (11 women); includes 9 minority (5 Black or African American, non-Hispanic/Latino; 4 Hispanic/Latino), 1 international. Average age 31. 34 applicants, 59% accepted, 16 enrolled. In 2011, 13 master's, 7 other advanced degrees awarded. *Degree requirements:* For master's, comprehensive exam (for some programs), thesis. *Entrance requirements:* For master's, GRE General Test, minimum cumulative point-hour ratio of 2.7 (3.0 for MPA) for all previous academic work, three letters of recommendation, statement of purpose, transcripts from all prior institutions attended; for Certificate, minimum cumulative point-hour ratio of 2.7 for all previous academic work, three letters of recommendation, statement of purpose, transcripts from all prior institutions attended. Additional exam requirements/recommendations for international students: Required—TOEFL (minimum score 550 paper-based; 213 computer-based; 80 iBT), IELTS (minimum score 6.5). *Application deadline:* For fall admission, 1/15 priority date for domestic students, 1/15 for international students. Applications are processed on a rolling basis. Application fee: $45 ($75 for international students). Electronic applications accepted. *Financial support:* In 2011–12, 1 research assistantship with full and partial tuition reimbursement (averaging $9,000 per year), 10 teaching assistantships with full and partial tuition reimbursements (averaging $6,300 per year) were awarded; career-related internships or fieldwork, Federal Work-Study, institutionally sponsored loans, scholarships/grants, tuition waivers (full), and unspecified assistantships also available. Support available to part-time students. *Faculty research:* Economic development, health care, Third World, criminal justice, Eastern Europe. *Unit head:* Dr. Mark E. Denham, Chair, 419-530-4062, E-mail: mark.denham@utoledo.edu. *Application contact:* Graduate School Office, 419-530-4723, Fax: 419-530-4724, E-mail: grdsch@utnet.utoledo.edu. Web site: http://www.utoledo.edu/llss/.

University of Wisconsin–Milwaukee, Graduate School, School of Social Welfare, Department of Social Work, Milwaukee, WI 53201-0413. Offers applied gerontology (Certificate); marriage and family therapy (Certificate); non-profit management (Certificate); social work (MSW, PhD). *Accreditation:* CSWE. Part-time programs available. *Faculty:* 14 full-time (8 women). *Students:* 199 full-time (185 women), 89 part-time (76 women); includes 53 minority (25 Black or African American, non-Hispanic/Latino; 1 American Indian or Alaska Native, non-Hispanic/Latino; 6 Asian, non-Hispanic/Latino; 5 Hispanic/Latino; 16 Two or more races, non-Hispanic/Latino). Average age 30. 316 applicants, 59% accepted, 99 enrolled. In 2011, 105 degrees awarded. *Degree requirements:* For master's, thesis or alternative. *Entrance requirements:* For doctorate, GRE, bachelor's degree. Additional exam requirements/recommendations for international students: Required—TOEFL (minimum score 550 paper-based; 79 iBT), IELTS (minimum score 6.5). *Application deadline:* For fall admission, 1/1 priority date for domestic students; for spring admission, 9/1 for domestic students. Applications are processed on a rolling basis. Application fee: $56 ($96 for international students). Electronic applications accepted. One-time fee: $506.10 full-time. Tuition and fees vary according to course load and reciprocity agreements. *Financial support:* In 2011–12, 5 fellowships, 4 research assistantships, 3 teaching assistantships were awarded; career-related internships or fieldwork, health care benefits, unspecified assistantships, and project assistantships also available. Support available to part-time students. Financial award application deadline: 4/15; financial award applicants required to submit FAFSA. *Total annual research expenditures:* $128,142. *Unit head:* Deborah Padgett, Department Chair, 414-229-6452, E-mail: dpadgett@uwm.edu. *Application contact:* General Information Contact, 414-229-4982, Fax: 414-229-6967, E-mail: gradschool@uwm.edu. Web site: http://www.uwm.edu/Dept/SSW/sw/.

University of Wisconsin–Milwaukee, Graduate School, Sheldon B. Lubar School of Business, Program in Nonprofit Management and Leadership, Milwaukee, WI 53201-0413. Offers MS, Certificate. *Students:* 9 full-time (7 women), 38 part-time (30 women); includes 17 minority (7 Black or African American, non-Hispanic/Latino; 2 American Indian or Alaska Native, non-Hispanic/Latino; 1 Hispanic/Latino; 7 Two or more races, non-Hispanic/Latino). Average age 34. 14 applicants, 71% accepted, 7 enrolled. In 2011, 14 degrees awarded. *Entrance requirements:* For master's, GRE/GMAT. Additional exam requirements/recommendations for international students: Required—TOEFL (minimum score 550 paper-based; 213 computer-based; 79 iBT), IELTS (minimum score 6.5). *Application deadline:* Applications are processed on a rolling basis. Application fee: $56 ($96 for international students). Electronic applications accepted. One-time fee: $506.10 full-time. Tuition and fees vary according to course load and reciprocity agreements. *Financial support:* Fellowships, research assistantships, teaching assistantships, health care benefits, and unspecified assistantships available. Financial award applicants required to submit FAFSA. *Unit head:* Douglas Ihrke, Representative, 414-229-3176, E-mail: dihrke@uwm.edu. *Application contact:* Matthew Jensen, 414-229-5403, E-mail: mba-ms@uwm.edu.

Virginia Commonwealth University, Graduate School, College of Humanities and Sciences, Program in Nonprofit Management, Richmond, VA 23284-9005. Offers Graduate Certificate. Part-time programs available. *Students:* 1 full-time (0 women), 6 part-time (3 women); includes 4 minority (3 Black or African American, non-Hispanic/Latino; 1 Two or more races, non-Hispanic/Latino). 14 applicants, 71% accepted, 7 enrolled. In 2011, 6 Graduate Certificates awarded. *Entrance requirements:* Additional exam requirements/recommendations for international students: Required—TOEFL (minimum score 600 paper-based; 250 computer-based; 100 iBT); Recommended—IELTS (minimum score 6.5). *Application deadline:* Applications are processed on a rolling basis. Application fee: $50. Electronic applications accepted. *Expenses:* Tuition, state resident: full-time $9133; part-time $507 per credit. Tuition, nonresident: full-time $18,777; part-time $1043 per credit. *Required fees:* $77 per credit. Tuition and fees vary according to degree level, campus/location, program and student level. *Unit head:* Dr. Niraj Verma, Director of the L. Douglas Wilder School of Government and Public Affairs, 804-828-2292. *Application contact:* Dr. Nancy B. Stutts, Interim Chair, 804-827-2164, E-mail: nbstutts@vcu.edu.

Virginia Commonwealth University, Graduate School, College of Humanities and Sciences, Wilder School of Government and Public Affairs, Department of Political Science and Public Administration, Richmond, VA 23284-9005. Offers nonprofit management (CPM); public administration (MPA); public management (CPM). *Accreditation:* NASPAA (one or more programs are accredited). Part-time programs available. *Students:* 54 full-time (29 women), 134 part-time (86 women); includes 58 minority (51 Black or African American, non-Hispanic/Latino; 1 American Indian or Alaska Native, non-Hispanic/Latino; 2 Asian, non-Hispanic/Latino; 3 Hispanic/Latino; 1 Two or more races, non-Hispanic/Latino), 14 international. 143 applicants, 57% accepted, 59 enrolled. In 2011, 34 master's, 5 other advanced degrees awarded. *Entrance requirements:* For master's, GRE, GMAT or LSAT. Additional exam requirements/recommendations for international students: Required—TOEFL (minimum score 600 paper-based; 250 computer-based; 100 iBT); Recommended—IELTS (minimum score 6.5). *Application deadline:* For fall admission, 4/1 for domestic students; for spring admission, 10/1 for domestic students. Applications are processed on a rolling basis. Application fee: $50. Electronic applications accepted. *Expenses:* Tuition, state resident: full-time $9133; part-time $507 per credit. Tuition, nonresident: full-time $18,777; part-time $1043 per credit. *Required fees:* $77 per credit. Tuition and fees vary according to degree level, campus/location, program and student level. *Financial support:* Fellowships, career-related internships or fieldwork, Federal Work-Study, institutionally sponsored loans, and tuition waivers (full and partial) available. Support available to part-time students. Financial award application deadline: 3/1. *Faculty research:* Environmental policy, executive leadership, human resource management, local government management, nonprofit management, public financial management, public policy analysis and evaluation. *Unit head:* Dr. Niraj Verma, Director, L. Douglas Wilder School of Government and Public Affairs, 804-828-2292. *Application contact:* Richard R. Huff, Director of Graduate Advising, 804-827-1430, E-mail: rrhuff@vcu.edu. Web site: http://www.wilder.vcu.edu/academic/pubadmin.html.

Virginia Polytechnic Institute and State University, Graduate School, College of Architecture and Urban Studies, School of Public and International Affairs, Blacksburg, VA 24061. Offers economic development (Certificate); government and international affairs (MPIA); homeland security policy (Certificate); local government management (Certificate); nonprofit and nongovernmental organization management (Certificate); planning, governance and globalization (PhD); public administration and public affairs (MPA, PhD); urban and regional planning (MURPL). *Accreditation:* ACSP. *Degree requirements:* For master's, comprehensive exam (for some programs), thesis (for some programs); for doctorate, comprehensive exam (for some programs), thesis/dissertation (for some programs). *Entrance requirements:* For master's and doctorate, GRE. Additional exam requirements/recommendations for international students: Required—TOEFL (minimum score 550 paper-based; 213 computer-based). *Application deadline:* For fall admission, 7/1 for domestic and international students; for spring admission, 12/1 for domestic and international students. Applications are processed on a rolling basis. Application fee: $65. Electronic applications accepted. *Expenses:* Tuition, state resident: full-time $10,048; part-time $558.25 per credit hour. Tuition, nonresident: full-time $19,497; part-time $1083.25 per credit hour. *Required fees:* $405 per semester. Tuition and fees vary according to course load, campus/location and program. *Financial support:* Teaching assistantships with full tuition reimbursements, career-related internships or fieldwork, Federal Work-Study, scholarships/grants, health care benefits, and unspecified assistantships available. Financial award application deadline: 1/15. *Faculty research:* Design theory, environmental planning, town planning, transportation planning. *Unit head:* Dr. Karen M. Hult, Unit Head, 540-231-5351, Fax: 540-231-9938, E-mail: khult@vt.edu. *Application contact:* Krystal D. Wright, Information Contact, 540-231-2291, Fax: 540-231-9938, E-mail: garch@vt.edu. Web site: http://www.spia.vt.edu/.

Virginia Polytechnic Institute and State University, VT Online, Blacksburg, VA 24061. Offers advanced transportation systems (Certificate); aerospace engineering (MS); agricultural and life sciences (MSLFS); business information systems (Graduate Certificate); career and technical education (MS); civil engineering (MS); computer engineering (M Eng, MS); decision support systems (Graduate Certificate); eLearning leadership (MA); electrical engineering (M Eng, MS); engineering administration (MEA); environmental engineering (Certificate); environmental politics and policy (Graduate Certificate); environmental sciences and engineering (MS); foundations of political analysis (Graduate Certificate); health product risk management (Graduate Certificate); industrial and systems engineering (MS); information policy and society (Graduate Certificate); information security (Graduate Certificate); information technology (MIT); instructional technology (MA); integrative STEM education (MA Ed); liberal arts (Graduate Certificate); life sciences: health product risk management (MS); natural resources (MNR, Graduate Certificate); networking (Graduate Certificate); nonprofit and nongovernmental organization management (Graduate Certificate); ocean engineering (MS); political science (MA); security studies (Graduate Certificate); software development (Graduate Certificate). *Expenses:* Tuition, state resident: full-time $10,048; part-time $558.25 per credit hour. Tuition, nonresident: full-time $19,497; part-time $1083.25 per credit hour. *Required fees:* $405 per semester. Tuition and fees vary according to course load, campus/location and program. *Application contact:* Graduate School Applications General Assistance, 540-231-8636, Fax: 540-231-2039, E-mail: gradappl@vt.edu. Web site: http://www.vto.vt.edu/.

Walden University, Graduate Programs, School of Counseling and Social Service, Minneapolis, MN 55401. Offers career counseling (MS); counselor education and supervision (PhD), including consultation, counseling and social change, forensic mental health counseling, general program, nonprofit management and leadership, trauma and crisis; human services (PhD), including clinical social work, criminal justice, disaster, crisis and intervention, family studies and intervention strategies, general program, human services administration, public health, social policy analysis and planning; marriage, couple, and family counseling (MS), including forensic counseling, trauma and crisis counseling; mental health counseling (MS), including forensic counseling, trauma and crisis counseling. Part-time and evening/weekend programs available. Postbaccalaureate distance learning degree programs offered (minimal on-campus study). *Faculty:* 26 full-time (19 women), 252 part-time/adjunct (178 women). *Students:* 3,089 full-time (2,614 women), 1,044 part-time (907 women); includes 2,109 minority (1,718 Black or African American, non-Hispanic/Latino; 31 American Indian or Alaska Native, non-Hispanic/Latino; 43 Asian, non-Hispanic/Latino; 236 Hispanic/Latino; 2 Native Hawaiian or other Pacific Islander, non-Hispanic/Latino; 79 Two or more races, non-Hispanic/Latino), 55 international. Average age 39. In 2011, 180 master's, 15 doctorates awarded. *Degree requirements:* For master's, residency (for some programs); for doctorate, thesis/dissertation, residency. *Entrance requirements:* For master's, bachelor's degree or equivalent in related field, minimum GPA of 2.5; for doctorate, master's degree or equivalent in related field; minimum GPA of 3.0; official transcripts; three years' related professional/academic experience (preferred); access to computer and Internet. Additional exam requirements/recommendations for international students: Required—TOEFL (minimum score 550 paper-based; 213 computer-based), IELTS (minimum score 6.5), or Michigan English Language Assessment Battery (minimum score 82). *Application deadline:* Applications are processed on a rolling basis. Application fee: $50. Electronic applications accepted. *Financial support:* Federal Work-Study, scholarships/grants, unspecified assistantships, and family tuition reduction, active duty/veteran tuition reduction, group tuition reduction, interest-free payment plans, employee tuition reduction available. Support available to part-time students. Financial award applicants required to submit FAFSA. *Unit head:* Dr. Savitri Dixon-Saxon, Associate Dean, 800-925-3368. *Application contact:* Jennifer Hall, Vice President of Enrollment Management, 866-4-WALDEN, E-mail: info@waldenu.edu. Web site: http://www.waldenu.edu/Colleges-and-Schools/College-of-Social-and-Behavioral-Sciences/School-of-Counseling-and-Social-Service.htm.

Walden University, Graduate Programs, School of Psychology, Minneapolis, MN 55401. Offers clinical psychology (MS), including counseling; forensic psychology (MS), including forensic psychology in the community, general program, mental health applications, program planning and evaluation in forensic settings, psychology and legal systems; organizational psychology and development (Postbaccalaureate Certificate); psychology (MS, PhD), including applied psychology (MS), clinical psychology (PhD), counseling psychology (PhD), crisis management and response (MS), educational psychology, general psychology, health psychology, leadership development and coaching (MS), media psychology (MS), organizational psychology, organizational psychology and nonprofit management (MS), program evaluation and research (MS), psychology of culture (MS), psychology, public administration, and social change (MS), social psychology, terrorism and security (MS); teaching online (Post-Master's Certificate). Part-time and evening/weekend programs available. Postbaccalaureate distance learning degree programs offered (minimal on-campus study). *Faculty:* 35 full-time (23 women), 237 part-time/adjunct (124 women). *Students:* 3,206 full-time (2,508 women), 1,510 part-time (1,240 women); includes 2,028 minority (1,483 Black or African American, non-Hispanic/Latino; 43 American Indian or Alaska Native, non-Hispanic/Latino; 99 Asian, non-Hispanic/Latino; 308 Hispanic/Latino; 4 Native Hawaiian or other Pacific Islander, non-Hispanic/Latino; 91 Two or more races, non-Hispanic/Latino), 158 international. Average age 40. In 2011, 645 master's, 113 doctorates, 30 other advanced degrees awarded. Terminal master's awarded for partial completion of doctoral program. *Degree requirements:* For master's, thesis optional; for doctorate, thesis/dissertation, residency. *Entrance requirements:* For master's, bachelor's degree or equivalent in related field; minimum GPA of 2.5; official transcripts; goal statement; access to computer and Internet; for doctorate, master's degree or equivalent in related field; minimum GPA of 3.0; 3 years of related professional/academic experience (preferred). Additional exam requirements/recommendations for international students: Required—TOEFL (minimum score 550 paper-based; 213 computer-based), IELTS (minimum score 6.5), or Michigan English Language Assessment Battery (minimum score 82). *Application deadline:* Applications are processed on a rolling basis. Application fee: $50. Electronic applications accepted. *Financial support:* Federal Work-Study, scholarships/grants, unspecified assistantships, and family tuition reduction, active duty/veteran tuition reduction, group tuition reduction, interest-free payment plans, employee tuition reduction available. Support available to part-time students. Financial award applicants required to submit FAFSA. *Unit head:* Dr. Melanie Storms, Vice President, 800-925-3368. *Application contact:* Jennifer Hall, Vice President of Enrollment Management, 866-4-WALDEN, E-mail: info@waldenu.edu. Web site: http://www.waldenu.edu/Colleges-and-Schools/College-of-Social-and-Behavioral-Sciences/School-of%20-Psychology.htm.

Walden University, Graduate Programs, School of Public Policy and Administration, Minneapolis, MN 55401. Offers criminal justice (MPA, MPP, MS), including emergency management (MS, PhD), homeland security policy (MS, PhD), homeland security policy and coordination (MS, PhD), law and public policy (MS, PhD), policy analysis (MS, PhD), public management and leadership (MS, PhD), self-designed (MS), terrorism, mediation, and peace (MS, PhD); criminal justice leadership and executive management (MS), including emergency management (MS, PhD), homeland security policy (MS, PhD), homeland security policy and coordination (MS, PhD), law and public policy (MS, PhD), policy analysis (MS, PhD), public management and leadership (MS, PhD), self-designed, terrorism, mediation, and peace (MS, PhD); emergency management (MPA, MPP, MS), including criminal justice (MS, PhD), homeland security (MS), public management and leadership (MS, PhD), terrorism and emergency management (MS); government management (Postbaccalaureate Certificate); health policy (MPA); homeland security policy (MPA, MPP); homeland security policy and coordination (MPA, MPP); interdisciplinary policy studies (MPA, MPP); international nongovernmental organizations (MPA, MPP); law and public policy (MPA, MPP); local government management for sustainable communities (MPA, MPP); nonprofit management (Postbaccalaureate Certificate); nonprofit management and leadership (MPA, MPP, MS); policy analysis (MPA); public management and leadership (MPA, MPP); public policy and administration (PhD), including criminal justice (MS, PhD), emergency management (MS, PhD), health policy, homeland security policy (MS, PhD), homeland security policy and coordination (MS, PhD), interdisciplinary policy studies, international nongovernmental organizations, law and public policy (MS, PhD), local government management for sustainable communities, nonprofit management and leadership, policy analysis (MS, PhD), public management and leadership (MS, PhD), terrorism, mediation, and peace (MS, PhD); terrorism, mediation, and peace (MPA, MPP). Part-time and evening/weekend programs available. Postbaccalaureate distance learning degree programs offered (minimal on-campus study). *Faculty:* 9 full-time (3 women), 90 part-time/adjunct (41 women). *Students:* 1,396 full-time (886 women), 902 part-time (581 women); includes 1,392 minority (1,205 Black or African American, non-Hispanic/Latino; 11 American Indian or Alaska Native, non-Hispanic/Latino; 35 Asian, non-Hispanic/Latino; 95 Hispanic/Latino; 2 Native Hawaiian or other Pacific Islander, non-Hispanic/Latino; 44 Two or more races, non-Hispanic/Latino), 82 international. Average age 41. In 2011, 265 master's, 34 doctorates, 13 other advanced degrees awarded. *Degree requirements:* For doctorate, thesis/dissertation, residency. *Entrance requirements:* For master's, bachelor's degree or equivalent in related field, minimum GPA of 2.5; for doctorate, master's degree or equivalent in related field; minimum GPA of 3.0; official transcripts; three years of related professional/academic experience (preferred); access to computer and Internet. Additional exam requirements/recommendations for international students: Required—TOEFL (minimum score 550 paper-based; 213 computer-based), IELTS (minimum score 6.5), or Michigan English Language Assessment Battery (minimum score 82). *Application deadline:* Applications are processed on a rolling basis. Application fee: $50. Electronic applications accepted. *Financial support:* Federal Work-Study, scholarships/grants, unspecified assistantships, and family tuition reduction, active duty/veteran tuition reduction, group tuition reduction, interest-free payment plans, employee tuition reduction available. Support available to part-time students. Financial award applicants required to submit FAFSA. *Unit head:* Dr. Mark Gordon, Associate Dean, 800-925-3368. *Application contact:* Jennifer Hall, Vice President of Enrollment Management, 866-4-WALDEN, E-mail: info@waldenu.edu. Web site: http://www.waldenu.edu/Colleges-and-Schools/College-of-Social-and-Behavioral-Sciences/School-of-Public-Policy-and-Administration.htm.

Wayne State University, College of Liberal Arts and Sciences, Department of Political Science, Program in Public Administration, Detroit, MI 48202. Offers aging policy and management (MPA); criminal justice policy and management (MPA); economic development policy and management (MPA); health services policy and management (MPA); human resources management (MPA); information technology management (MPA); non-profit management (MPA); organizational behavior and management (MPA); public budgeting and financial management (MPA); public policy analysis and program evaluation (MPA); social welfare policy and management (MPA); urban policy and management (MPA). *Accreditation:* NASPAA. Evening/weekend programs available. *Students:* 22 full-time (17 women), 45 part-time (33 women); includes 19 minority (16 Black or African American, non-Hispanic/Latino; 1 American Indian or Alaska Native, non-Hispanic/Latino; 2 Hispanic/Latino), 1 international. Average age 31. 75 applicants, 28% accepted, 11 enrolled. In 2011, 20 master's awarded. *Degree requirements:* For master's, comprehensive exam. *Entrance requirements:* For master's, GRE General Test. Additional exam requirements/recommendations for international students: Required—TOEFL (minimum score 550 paper-based; 213 computer-based); Recommended—TWE (minimum score 5.5). *Application deadline:* For fall admission, 6/1 priority date for domestic students, 5/1 for international students; for winter admission, 10/1 priority date for domestic students, 9/1 for international students; for spring admission, 2/1 priority date for domestic students, 1/1 for international students. Applications are processed on a rolling basis. Application fee: $50. Electronic applications accepted. *Expenses:* Tuition, state resident: part-time $512.85 per credit. Tuition, nonresident: part-time $1132.65 per credit. *Required fees:* $26.60 per credit. $199.65 per semester. Tuition and fees vary according to course load and program. *Financial support:* In 2011–12, 7 students received support. Scholarships/grants available. *Faculty research:* Urban politics, urban education, state administration. *Unit head:* Dr. Brady Baybeck, Director, 313-577-2630, E-mail: mpa@wayne.edu. Web site: http://clasweb.clas.wayne.edu/mapa.

Webster University, George Herbert Walker School of Business and Technology, Department of Management, St. Louis, MO 63119-3194. Offers business and organizational security management (MA); computer resources and information management (MA); environmental management (MS); government contracting (Certificate); health care management (MA); health services management (MA); human resources development (MA); human resources management (MA); management (DM); management and leadership (MA); marketing (MA); nonprofit management (Certificate); procurement and acquisitions management (MA); public administration (MA); quality management (MA); space systems operations management (MS); telecommunications management (MA). *Accreditation:* ACBSP. Part-time and evening/weekend programs available. Postbaccalaureate distance learning degree programs offered (no on-campus study). *Degree requirements:* For master's, thesis (for some programs); for doctorate, thesis/dissertation, written exam. *Entrance requirements:* For doctorate, GMAT, 3 years of work experience, MBA. Additional exam requirements/recommendations for international students: Required—TOEFL. *Expenses: Tuition:* Full-time $10,890; part-time $605 per credit hour. Tuition and fees vary according to campus/location and program.

West Chester University of Pennsylvania, College of Business and Public Affairs, Department of Political Science, West Chester, PA 19383. Offers general public administration (MPA); human resource management (MPA, Certificate); non profit administration (Certificate); nonprofit administration (MPA); public administration (Certificate); training and development (MPA). Part-time and evening/weekend programs available. *Faculty:* 1 (woman) full-time, 6 part-time/adjunct (3 women). *Students:* 49 full-time (27 women), 57 part-time (37 women); includes 42 minority (38 Black or African American, non-Hispanic/Latino; 4 Hispanic/Latino), 2 international. Average age 29. 72 applicants, 65% accepted, 39 enrolled. In 2011, 100 degrees awarded. *Degree requirements:* For master's, capstone project. *Entrance requirements:* For master's and Certificate, statement of professional goals, resume, two letters of reference. Additional exam requirements/recommendations for international students: Required—TOEFL (minimum score 550 paper-based; 213 computer-based; 80 iBT). *Application deadline:* For fall admission, 4/15 priority date for domestic students, 3/15 for international students; for spring admission, 10/15 priority date for domestic students, 9/1 for international students. Applications are processed on a rolling basis. Application fee: $45. Electronic applications accepted. *Expenses:* Tuition, state resident: full-time $7488; part-time $416 per credit. Tuition, nonresident: full-time $11,232; part-time $624 per credit. *Required fees:* $1784.64; $67.59 per credit. Tuition and fees vary according to program. *Financial support:* Unspecified assistantships available. Support available to part-time students. Financial award application deadline: 2/15; financial award applicants required to submit FAFSA. *Faculty research:* Public policy, economic development, public opinion, urban politics, public administration . *Unit head:* Dr. Christopher Fiorentino, Dean, College of Business and Public Affairs, 610-436-2930, Fax: 610-436-3170, E-mail: cfiorentino@wcupa.edu. *Application contact:* Dr. Lorraine Bernotsky, Graduate Coordinator, 610-436-2438, Fax: 610-436-3047, E-mail: lbernotsky@wcupa.edu.

Western Michigan University, Graduate College, College of Arts and Sciences, School of Public Affairs and Administration, Kalamazoo, MI 49008. Offers health care administration (Graduate Certificate); nonprofit leadership and administration (Graduate Certificate); public administration (MPA, PhD). *Accreditation:* NASPAA (one or more programs are accredited). *Degree requirements:* For doctorate, thesis/dissertation, oral exams. *Entrance requirements:* For doctorate, GRE General Test.

Worcester State University, Graduate Studies, Program in Non-Profit Management, Worcester, MA 01602-2597. Offers MS. Part-time and evening/weekend programs available. *Faculty:* 1 (woman) full-time, 1 part-time/adjunct (0 women). *Students:* 5 full-time (3 women), 21 part-time (13 women); includes 4 minority (2 Black or African American, non-Hispanic/Latino; 1 Asian, non-Hispanic/Latino; 1 Hispanic/Latino), 1 international. Average age 35. 21 applicants, 62% accepted, 4 enrolled. In 2011, 6 master's awarded. *Degree requirements:* For master's, comprehensive exam (for some programs), thesis optional. *Entrance requirements:* For master's, GRE General Test or MAT. Additional exam requirements/recommendations for international students: Required—TOEFL (minimum score 500 paper-based; 61 iBT). *Application deadline:* For fall admission, 6/15 for domestic and international students; for spring admission, 4/1 for domestic and international students. Applications are processed on a rolling basis. Application fee: $40. Electronic applications accepted. *Expenses:* Tuition, state resident: full-time $2700; part-time $150 per credit. Tuition, nonresident: full-time $2700; part-time $150 per credit. *Required fees:* $2016; $112 per credit. *Financial support:* In 2011–12, 2 students received support, including 2 research assistantships with full tuition reimbursements available (averaging $4,800 per year); career-related internships or fieldwork, scholarships/grants, and unspecified assistantships also available. Financial award application deadline: 3/1; financial award applicants required to submit FAFSA. *Faculty research:* Politics of human services, models of supervision. *Unit head:* Dr. Shiko Gathuo, Coordinator, 508-929-8892, Fax: 508-929-8144, E-mail: agathuo@worcester.edu. *Application contact:* Sara Grady, Assistant Dean of Continuing Education, 508-929-8787, Fax: 508-929-8100, E-mail: sara.grady@worcester.edu.

Section 16
Organizational Studies

This section contains a directory of institutions offering graduate work in organizational studies, followed by an in-depth entry submitted by an institution that chose to prepare a detailed program description. Additional information about programs listed in the directory but not augmented by an in-depth entry may be obtained by writing directly to the dean of a graduate school or chair of a department at the address given in the directory.

For programs offering related work, see also in this book *Business Administration and Management, Human Resources,* and *Industrial and Manufacturing Management.* In another guide in this series:

Graduate Programs in the Humanities, Arts & Social Sciences

See *Communication and Media* and *Public, Regional, and Industrial Affairs*

CONTENTS

Program Directories

Displays and Close-Ups

See also:

Organizational Behavior

Amridge University, Graduate and Professional Programs, Montgomery, AL 36117. Offers behavioral leadership and management (MA); Biblical exposition (MA); biblical studies (MA, PhD); family therapy (D Min); historical and theological studies (MA); leadership and management (MS); marriage and family therapy (M Div, MA, PhD); ministerial leadership (M Div, MS); pastoral counseling (M Div, MS); practical ministry (MA); professional counseling (M Div, MA, PhD); theology (M Div, D Min). Part-time and evening/weekend programs available. Postbaccalaureate distance learning degree programs offered (no on-campus study). *Faculty:* 48 full-time (9 women), 27 part-time/adjunct (12 women). *Students:* 161 full-time (79 women), 258 part-time (147 women); includes 160 minority (153 Black or African American, non-Hispanic/Latino; 1 Asian, non-Hispanic/Latino; 6 Hispanic/Latino). Average age 35. *Degree requirements:* For master's, one foreign language, comprehensive exam (for some programs), thesis (for some programs); for doctorate, comprehensive exam (for some programs), thesis/dissertation. *Entrance requirements:* For master's and doctorate, GRE General Test or MAT. Additional exam requirements/recommendations for international students: Required—TOEFL. *Application deadline:* For fall admission, 9/1 priority date for domestic students; for spring admission, 1/1 priority date for domestic students. Applications are processed on a rolling basis. Application fee: $75. Electronic applications accepted. *Expenses: Tuition:* Full-time $10,680; part-time $610 per semester hour. *Required fees:* $600 per semester. *Financial support:* Federal Work-Study and scholarships/grants available. Support available to part-time students. Financial award applicants required to submit FAFSA. *Faculty research:* Homiletics, hermeneutics, ancient Near Eastern history. *Unit head:* Director of Enrollment Management, 800-351-4040 Ext. 7513, Fax: 334-387-3878. *Application contact:* Ora Davis, Admissions Officer, 334-387-3877 Ext. 7524, Fax: 334-387-3878, E-mail: admissions@amridgeuniversity.edu.

Argosy University, Chicago, College of Psychology and Behavioral Sciences, Doctoral Program in Clinical Psychology, Chicago, IL 60601. Offers child and adolescent psychology (Psy D); client-centered and experiential psychotherapies (Psy D); diversity and multicultural psychology (Psy D); family psychology (Psy D); forensic psychology (Psy D); health psychology (Psy D); neuropsychology (Psy D); organizational consulting (Psy D); psychoanalytic psychology (Psy D); psychology and spirituality (Psy D). *Accreditation:* APA.

Benedictine University, Graduate Programs, Program in Management and Organizational Behavior, Lisle, IL 60532-0900. Offers MS, MBA/MS, MPH/MS. Part-time and evening/weekend programs available. *Faculty:* 1 full-time (0 women), 15 part-time/adjunct (7 women). *Students:* 50 full-time (34 women), 137 part-time (104 women); includes 51 minority (38 Black or African American, non-Hispanic/Latino; 2 American Indian or Alaska Native, non-Hispanic/Latino; 5 Asian, non-Hispanic/Latino; 6 Hispanic/Latino), 5 international. Average age 40. 60 applicants, 87% accepted, 44 enrolled. In 2011, 49 master's awarded. *Entrance requirements:* For master's, GMAT. Additional exam requirements/recommendations for international students: Required—TOEFL (minimum score 550 paper-based; 213 computer-based). *Application deadline:* For fall admission, 9/1 for domestic students; for winter admission, 12/1 for domestic students; for spring admission, 2/15 for domestic students. Applications are processed on a rolling basis. Application fee: $40. Electronic applications accepted. *Financial support:* Career-related internships or fieldwork and health care benefits available. Support available to part-time students. *Faculty research:* Organizational change, transformation, development, learning organizations, career transitions for academics. *Unit head:* Dr. Peter F. Sorensen, Director, 630-829-6220, Fax: 630-960-1126, E-mail: psorensen@ben.edu. *Application contact:* Kari Gibbons, Associate Vice President, Enrollment Center, 630-829-6200, Fax: 630-829-6584, E-mail: kgibbons@ben.edu.

Benedictine University at Springfield, Program in Management and Organizational Behavior, Springfield, IL 62702. Offers MS. Evening/weekend programs available. *Entrance requirements:* For master's, official transcripts, 2 letters of reference, essay, resume, interview.

Bernard M. Baruch College of the City University of New York, Zicklin School of Business, Department of Management, New York, NY 10010-5585. Offers entrepreneurship (MBA); management (PhD); operations management (MBA); organizational behavior/human resources management (MBA); sustainable business (MBA). PhD offered jointly with Graduate School and University Center of the City University of New York. Part-time and evening/weekend programs available. *Degree requirements:* For doctorate, comprehensive exam, thesis/dissertation. *Entrance requirements:* For master's, GMAT, 2 letters of recommendation, resume, 2 years of work experience; for doctorate, GMAT. Additional exam requirements/recommendations for international students: Required—TOEFL (minimum score 590 paper-based; 243 computer-based), TWE.

Boston College, Carroll School of Management, Department of Organization Studies, Chestnut Hill, MA 02467-3800. Offers PhD. *Faculty:* 12 full-time (6 women), 11 part-time/adjunct (3 women). *Students:* 19 full-time (13 women); includes 3 minority (1 Black or African American, non-Hispanic/Latino; 2 Hispanic/Latino), 7 international. Average age 32. 86 applicants, 5% accepted, 3 enrolled. In 2011, 2 doctorates awarded. *Degree requirements:* For doctorate, comprehensive exam, thesis/dissertation, teaching experience. *Entrance requirements:* For doctorate, GMAT or GRE, letters of recommendation, resume, transcripts. Additional exam requirements/recommendations for international students: Required—TOEFL. *Application deadline:* For spring admission, 2/1 for domestic and international students. Application fee: $100. *Financial support:* In 2011–12, 19 fellowships, 19 research assistantships with full tuition reimbursements were awarded. Financial award application deadline: 3/1; financial award applicants required to submit FAFSA. *Faculty research:* Organizational transformation, mergers and acquisitions, managerial effectiveness, organizational change, organizational structure. *Unit head:* Dr. Jeffrey L. Ringuest, Associate Dean, Graduate Programs, 617-552-9100, Fax: 617-552-0514, E-mail: gsomdean@bc.edu. *Application contact:* Shelley A. Burt, Director of Graduate Enrollment, 617-552-3920, Fax: 617-552-8078, E-mail: bcmba@bc.edu. Web site: http://www.bc.edu/csom/.

Brooklyn College of the City University of New York, Division of Graduate Studies, Department of Psychology, Program in Industrial and Organizational Psychology, Brooklyn, NY 11210-2889. Offers human relations (MA); organizational behavior (MA). *Degree requirements:* For master's, comprehensive exam, thesis. *Entrance requirements:* For master's, 2 letters of recommendation. Additional exam requirements/recommendations for international students: Required—TOEFL (minimum score 520 paper-based; 190 computer-based; 69 iBT). Electronic applications accepted.

California Lutheran University, Graduate Studies, School of Management, Thousand Oaks, CA 91360-2787. Offers business (IMBA); computer science (MS); econometrics (MBA); economics (MS); entrepreneurship (MBA, Certificate); finance (MBA, Certificate); financial planning (MBA, Certificate); information systems and technology (MS); information technology management (MBA, Certificate); international business (MBA, Certificate); management and organization behavior (MBA); management and organizational behavior (Certificate); marketing (MBA, Certificate); microeconomics (MBA); nonprofit and social enterprise (MBA). Part-time and evening/weekend programs available. Postbaccalaureate distance learning degree programs offered (no on-campus study). *Entrance requirements:* For master's, GMAT, interview, minimum GPA of 3.0. *Expenses:* Contact institution.

Carnegie Mellon University, College of Humanities and Social Sciences, Department of Social and Decision Sciences, Pittsburgh, PA 15213-3891. Offers behavioral decision research (PhD); behavioral decision research and psychology (PhD); social and decision science (PhD); strategy, entrepreneurship, and technological change (PhD). Terminal master's awarded for partial completion of doctoral program. *Degree requirements:* For doctorate, comprehensive exam, thesis/dissertation, research paper. *Entrance requirements:* For doctorate, GRE General Test. Additional exam requirements/recommendations for international students: Required—TOEFL. Electronic applications accepted. *Faculty research:* Organization theory, political science, sociology, technology studies.

Carnegie Mellon University, Tepper School of Business, Organizational Behavior and Theory Program, Pittsburgh, PA 15213-3891. Offers PhD. *Degree requirements:* For doctorate, thesis/dissertation. *Entrance requirements:* For doctorate, GMAT or GRE General Test. Additional exam requirements/recommendations for international students: Required—TOEFL. *Faculty research:* Negotiation, organizational learning, interorganizational relations and strategy, group process and performance, communication process and electronic media, group goal setting, uncertainty in organizations, creation and effect of institutions and psychological contracts.

Case Western Reserve University, Weatherhead School of Management, Department of Organizational Behavior and Analysis, Cleveland, OH 44106. Offers MBA, MPOD, MS. Part-time and evening/weekend programs available. *Entrance requirements:* For master's, GMAT. *Faculty research:* Social innovation in global management, competency-based learning, life-long learning, organizational theory, organizational change.

Columbia College, Graduate Programs, Department of Human Relations, Columbia, SC 29203-5998. Offers interpersonal relations/conflict management (Certificate); organizational behavior/conflict management (Certificate); organizational change and leadership (MA). Part-time and evening/weekend programs available. Postbaccalaureate distance learning degree programs offered (minimal on-campus study). *Faculty:* 3 part-time/adjunct (2 women). *Students:* 26 full-time (all women), 11 part-time (all women); includes 20 minority (all Black or African American, non-Hispanic/Latino). Average age 29. 39 applicants, 92% accepted, 27 enrolled. In 2011, 7 master's awarded. *Degree requirements:* For master's, thesis, practicum. *Entrance requirements:* For master's, GRE General Test, MAT, 2 letters of recommendation, minimum GPA of 3.2. Additional exam requirements/recommendations for international students: Required—TOEFL. *Application deadline:* For fall admission, 7/15 priority date for domestic students, 7/15 for international students. Applications are processed on a rolling basis. Application fee: $50. Electronic applications accepted. *Expenses:* Contact institution. *Financial support:* Available to part-time students. Application deadline: 7/1; applicants required to submit FAFSA. *Faculty research:* Envisioning and the resolution of conflict, environmental conflict resolution, crisis negotiation. *Unit head:* Dr. Elaine Ferraro, Chair, 803-786-3687, Fax: 803-786-3790, E-mail: eferraro@colacoll.edu. *Application contact:* Carolyn Emeneker, Director of Graduate School and Evening College Admissions, 803-786-3766, Fax: 803-786-3674, E-mail: emeneker@colacoll.edu.

Cornell University, Graduate School, Graduate Field of Management, Ithaca, NY 14853-0001. Offers accounting (PhD); behavioral decision theory (PhD); finance (PhD); marketing (PhD); organizational behavior (PhD); production and operations management (PhD). *Accreditation:* AACSB. *Faculty:* 53 full-time (8 women). *Students:* 39 full-time (11 women); includes 2 minority (both Asian, non-Hispanic/Latino), 23 international. Average age 29. 424 applicants, 3% accepted, 8 enrolled. In 2011, 6 doctorates awarded. *Degree requirements:* For doctorate, comprehensive exam, thesis/dissertation. *Entrance requirements:* For doctorate, GMAT or GRE General Test. Additional exam requirements/recommendations for international students: Required—TOEFL (minimum score 600 paper-based; 250 computer-based; 77 iBT). *Application deadline:* For fall admission, 1/3 for domestic students. Application fee: $95. Electronic applications accepted. *Expenses:* Contact institution. *Financial support:* In 2011–12, 38 students received support, including 4 fellowships with full tuition reimbursements available, 33 research assistantships with full tuition reimbursements available, 2 teaching assistantships with full tuition reimbursements available; institutionally sponsored loans, scholarships/grants, health care benefits, tuition waivers (full and partial), and unspecified assistantships also available. Financial award applicants required to submit FAFSA. *Faculty research:* Operations and manufacturing. *Unit head:* Director of Graduate Studies, 607-255-3669. *Application contact:* Graduate Field Assistant, 607-255-9431, E-mail: js_phd@cornell.edu. Web site: http://www.gradschool.cornell.edu/fields.php?id-91&a-2.

Cornell University, Graduate School, Graduate Fields of Industrial and Labor Relations, Ithaca, NY 14853. Offers collective bargaining, labor law and labor history (MILR, MPS, MS, PhD); economic and social statistics (MILR); human resource studies (MILR, MPS, MS, PhD); industrial and labor relations problems (MILR, MPS, MS, PhD); international and comparative labor (MILR, MPS, MS, PhD); labor economics (MILR, MPS, MS, PhD); organizational behavior (MILR, MPS, MS, PhD). *Faculty:* 55 full-time (14 women). *Students:* 164 full-time (97 women); includes 37 minority (13 Black or African American, non-Hispanic/Latino; 2 American Indian or Alaska Native, non-Hispanic/Latino; 15 Asian, non-Hispanic/Latino; 7 Hispanic/Latino), 60 international. Average age 31. 335 applicants, 27% accepted, 63 enrolled. In 2011, 67 master's, 4 doctorates awarded. *Degree requirements:* For master's, thesis (MS); for doctorate, comprehensive exam, thesis/dissertation, teaching experience. *Entrance requirements:* For master's and doctorate, GMAT or GRE General Test, 2 academic recommendations. Additional exam requirements/recommendations for international students: Required—TOEFL (minimum score 550 paper-based; 213 computer-based; 77 iBT). Application fee: $95. Electronic applications accepted. *Expenses:* Contact institution. *Financial support:* In 2011–12, 73 students received support, including 23 fellowships with full tuition reimbursements available, 30 research assistantships with full tuition reimbursements available, 24 teaching assistantships with full tuition reimbursements available; institutionally sponsored loans, scholarships/grants, health care benefits, tuition waivers (full and partial), and unspecified assistantships also available. Financial award applicants required to submit FAFSA. *Unit head:* Director of Graduate Studies, 607-255-1522. *Application contact:* Graduate Field Assistant, 607-255-1522, E-mail: ilrgradapplicant@cornell.edu. Web site: http://www.gradschool.cornell.edu/fields.php?id-85&a-2.

Drexel University, LeBow College of Business, Program in Business Administration, Philadelphia, PA 19104-2875. Offers business administration (MBA, PhD, APC), including accounting (MBA, PhD), decision sciences (PhD), economics (MBA, PhD), finance (MBA, PhD), legal studies (MBA), management (MBA), marketing (MBA, PhD), organizational sciences (PhD), quantitative methods (MBA), strategic management (PhD). *Accreditation:* AACSB. Part-time and evening/weekend programs available. Postbaccalaureate distance learning degree programs offered (minimal on-campus study). Terminal master's awarded for partial completion of doctoral program. *Entrance requirements:* For master's, GMAT, minimum GPA of 2.75; for doctorate, GMAT. Additional exam requirements/recommendations for international students: Required—TOEFL. Electronic applications accepted. *Faculty research:* Decision support systems, individual and group behavior, operations research, techniques and strategy.

Fairleigh Dickinson University, College at Florham, Maxwell Becton College of Arts and Sciences, Department of Psychology, Program in Organizational Behavior, Madison, NJ 07940-1099. Offers organizational behavior (MA); organizational leadership (Certificate).

Florida Institute of Technology, Graduate Programs, College of Psychology and Liberal Arts, School of Psychology, Melbourne, FL 32901-6975. Offers applied behavior analysis (MS); applied behavior analysis and organizational behavior management (MS); behavior analysis (PhD); clinical psychology (Psy D); industrial/organizational psychology (MS, PhD); organizational behavior management (MS); psychology (MS). *Accreditation:* APA (one or more programs are accredited). Part-time programs available. *Faculty:* 24 full-time (13 women), 6 part-time/adjunct (1 woman). *Students:* 218 full-time (166 women), 11 part-time (7 women); includes 38 minority (6 Black or African American, non-Hispanic/Latino; 5 Asian, non-Hispanic/Latino; 26 Hispanic/Latino; 1 Two or more races, non-Hispanic/Latino), 18 international. Average age 27. 452 applicants, 36% accepted, 72 enrolled. In 2011, 38 master's, 12 doctorates awarded. Terminal master's awarded for partial completion of doctoral program. *Degree requirements:* For master's, comprehensive exam (for some programs), thesis (for some programs), BCBA certification, final exam; for doctorate, comprehensive exam, thesis/dissertation, internship, full-time resident of school for 4 years (8 semesters, 3 summers). *Entrance requirements:* For master's, GRE General Test, 3 letters of recommendation, minimum GPA of 3.0, resume, statement of objectives; for doctorate, GRE General Test, GRE Subject Test (psychology), 3 letters of recommendation, minimum GPA of 3.2, resume, statement of objectives. Additional exam requirements/recommendations for international students: Required—TOEFL (minimum score 550 paper-based; 213 computer-based; 79 iBT). *Application deadline:* For fall admission, 4/1 for international students; for spring admission, 9/30 for international students. Applications are processed on a rolling basis. Application fee: $0. Electronic applications accepted. *Expenses: Tuition:* Full-time $19,620; part-time $1090 per credit hour. Tuition and fees vary according to campus/location. *Financial support:* In 2011–12, 4 fellowships with full and partial tuition reimbursements (averaging $3,775 per year), 42 research assistantships with full and partial tuition reimbursements (averaging $4,945 per year), 8 teaching assistantships with full and partial tuition reimbursements (averaging $5,105 per year) were awarded; career-related internships or fieldwork, institutionally sponsored loans, tuition waivers (partial), unspecified assistantships, and tuition remissions also available. Support available to part-time students. Financial award application deadline: 3/1; financial award applicants required to submit FAFSA. *Faculty research:* Addictions, neuropsychology, child abuse, assessment, psychological trauma. *Total annual research expenditures:* $367,448. *Unit head:* Dr. Mary Beth Kenkel, Dean, 321-674-8142, Fax: 321-674-7105, E-mail: mkenkel@fit.edu. *Application contact:* Cheryl A. Brown, Associate Director of Graduate Admissions, 321-674-7581, Fax: 321-723-9468, E-mail: cbrown@fit.edu. Web site: http://cpla.fit.edu/psych/.

Florida State University, The Graduate School, College of Business, Tallahassee, FL 32306-1110. Offers accounting (M Acc), including accounting information services, assurance services, corporate accounting, taxation; business administration (MBA, PhD), including accounting (PhD), finance (PhD), management information systems (PhD), marketing (PhD), organizational behavior (PhD), risk management and insurance (PhD), strategic management (PhD); finance (MS); insurance (MSM); management information systems (MS); marketing (MS); JD/MBA; MSW/MBA. *Accreditation:* AACSB. Part-time programs available. Postbaccalaureate distance learning degree programs offered (no on-campus study). *Faculty:* 107 full-time (31 women). *Students:* 196 full-time (76 women), 310 part-time (109 women); includes 89 minority (27 Black or African American, non-Hispanic/Latino; 1 American Indian or Alaska Native, non-Hispanic/Latino; 31 Asian, non-Hispanic/Latino; 30 Hispanic/Latino). Average age 30. 702 applicants, 33% accepted, 205 enrolled. In 2011, 268 master's, 17 doctorates awarded. Terminal master's awarded for partial completion of doctoral program. *Degree requirements:* For doctorate, comprehensive exam, thesis/dissertation. *Entrance requirements:* For master's, GMAT, work experience (MBA, MS), minimum GPA of 3.0, letters of recommendation; for doctorate, GMAT, minimum graduate GPA of 3.5, letters of recommendation. Additional exam requirements/recommendations for international students: Required—TOEFL (minimum score 600 paper-based; 80 computer-based); Recommended—IELTS (minimum score 6.5). *Application deadline:* For fall admission, 6/1 for domestic students, 5/1 for international students; for spring admission, 10/1 for domestic students, 9/1 for international students. Applications are processed on a rolling basis. Application fee: $30. Electronic applications accepted. *Expenses:* Tuition, state resident: full-time $9474; part-time $350.88 per credit hour. Tuition, nonresident: full-time $16,236; part-time $601.34 per credit hour. *Required fees:* $630 per semester. One-time fee: $20. Tuition and fees vary according to course load and campus/location. *Financial support:* In 2011–12, 86 students received support, including 12 fellowships with full tuition reimbursements available (averaging $7,161 per year), 30 research assistantships with full tuition reimbursements available (averaging $6,000 per year), 43 teaching assistantships with full tuition reimbursements available (averaging $15,000 per year); career-related internships or fieldwork, scholarships/grants, health care benefits, tuition waivers (full and partial), and unspecified assistantships also available. Support available to part-time students. Financial award application deadline: 1/1. *Unit head:* Dr. Caryn Beck-Dudley, Dean, 850-644-3090, Fax: 850-644-0915. *Application contact:* Lisa Beverly, Director, Graduate Programs Admissions, 850-644-6458, Fax: 850-644-0588, E-mail: lbeverly@cob.fsu.edu. Web site: http://www.cob.fsu.edu/grad/.

Georgia Institute of Technology, Graduate Studies and Research, College of Management, Program in Business Administration, Atlanta, GA 30332-0001. Offers accounting (MBA); e-commerce (Certificate); engineering entrepreneurship (MBA); entrepreneurship (Certificate); finance (MBA); information technology management (MBA); international business (MBA, Certificate); management of technology (Certificate); marketing (MBA); operations management (MBA); organizational behavior (MBA); strategic management (MBA). *Accreditation:* AACSB.

Georgia Institute of Technology, Graduate Studies and Research, College of Management, Program in Management, Atlanta, GA 30332-0001. Offers accounting (PhD); finance (PhD); information technology management (PhD); marketing (PhD); operations management (PhD); organizational behavior (PhD); quantitative and computational finance (MS); strategic management (PhD). *Accreditation:* AACSB. *Degree requirements:* For doctorate, comprehensive exam, thesis/dissertation, oral exams. *Entrance requirements:* For master's and doctorate, GMAT. Additional exam requirements/recommendations for international students: Required—TOEFL. *Faculty research:* MIS, management of technology, international business, entrepreneurship, operations management.

Graduate School and University Center of the City University of New York, Graduate Studies, Program in Business, New York, NY 10016-4039. Offers accounting (PhD); behavioral science (PhD); finance (PhD); management planning systems (PhD). *Degree requirements:* For doctorate, thesis/dissertation. *Entrance requirements:* For doctorate, GMAT, writing sample (15 pages). Additional exam requirements/recommendations for international students: Required—TOEFL. Electronic applications accepted.

Harvard University, Graduate School of Arts and Sciences and Doctoral Programs in Management, Committee on Organizational Behavior, Cambridge, MA 02138. Offers PhD. *Entrance requirements:* For doctorate, GRE General Test or GMAT, major in psychology or sociology, course work in statistics or mathematics. Additional exam requirements/recommendations for international students: Required—TOEFL. *Expenses: Tuition:* Full-time $36,304. *Required fees:* $1186. Full-time tuition and fees vary according to program.

Harvard University, Harvard Business School, Doctoral Programs in Management, Boston, MA 02163. Offers accounting and management (DBA); business economics (PhD); health policy management (PhD); management (DBA); marketing (DBA); organizational behavior (PhD); science, technology and management (PhD); strategy (DBA); technology and operations management (DBA). *Degree requirements:* For doctorate, comprehensive exam (for some programs), thesis/dissertation. *Entrance requirements:* For doctorate, GRE General Test or GMAT. Additional exam requirements/recommendations for international students: Required—TOEFL. *Expenses: Tuition:* Full-time $36,304. *Required fees:* $1186. Full-time tuition and fees vary according to program.

John Jay College of Criminal Justice of the City University of New York, Graduate Studies, Programs in Criminal Justice, New York, NY 10019-1093. Offers criminal justice (MA, PhD); criminology and deviance (PhD); forensic psychology (PhD); forensic science (PhD); law and philosophy (PhD); organizational behavior (PhD); public policy (PhD). Part-time and evening/weekend programs available. Terminal master's awarded for partial completion of doctoral program. *Degree requirements:* For master's, thesis or alternative; for doctorate, one foreign language, thesis/dissertation. *Entrance requirements:* For master's, GRE General Test, minimum B average; for doctorate, GRE General Test. Additional exam requirements/recommendations for international students: Required—TOEFL (minimum score 500 paper-based; 173 computer-based).

Lake Forest Graduate School of Management, The Leadership MBA Program (LMBA), Lake Forest, IL 60045. Offers finance (MBA); global business (MBA); healthcare management (MBA); management (MBA); marketing (MBA); organizational behavior (MBA). Part-time and evening/weekend programs available. *Faculty:* 136 part-time/adjunct (41 women). *Students:* 734 part-time (306 women); includes 161 minority (34 Black or African American, non-Hispanic/Latino; 4 American Indian or Alaska Native, non-Hispanic/Latino; 87 Asian, non-Hispanic/Latino; 14 Hispanic/Latino; 4 Native Hawaiian or other Pacific Islander, non-Hispanic/Latino; 18 Two or more races, non-Hispanic/Latino). Average age 38. In 2011, 213 master's awarded. *Entrance requirements:* For master's, 4 years of work experience in field, interview, 2 letters of recommendation. *Application deadline:* For fall admission, 7/1 for domestic students; for winter admission, 1/5 for domestic students; for spring admission, 3/1 for domestic students. Applications are processed on a rolling basis. Application fee: $75. Electronic applications accepted. *Expenses: Tuition:* Part-time $2932 per unit. *Required fees:* $50 per unit. *Financial support:* Scholarships/grants available. Support available to part-time students. Financial award applicants required to submit FAFSA. *Unit head:* Chris Multhauf, Executive Vice President of Educational Programs and Solutions, 847-574-5270, Fax: 847-295-3656, E-mail: cmulthauf@lfgsm.edu. *Application contact:* Carolyn Brune, Director of Admissions, 800-737-4MBA, Fax: 847-295-3656, E-mail: admiss@lfgsm.edu. Web site: http://www.lakeforestmba.edu/lake_forest_mba_program/LFGSM-Leadership-MBA.aspx.

Marylhurst University, Department of Business Administration, Marylhurst, OR 97036-0261. Offers finance (MBA); general management (MBA); government policy and administration (MBA); green development (MBA); health care management (MBA); marketing (MBA); natural and organic resources (MBA); nonprofit management (MBA); organizational behavior (MBA); real estate (MBA); renewable energy (MBA); sustainable business (MBA). Part-time and evening/weekend programs available. Postbaccalaureate distance learning degree programs offered (no on-campus study). *Faculty:* 3 full-time (0 women), 36 part-time/adjunct (6 women). *Students:* 29 full-time (15 women), 675 part-time (373 women); includes 178 minority (59 Black or African American, non-Hispanic/Latino; 6 American Indian or Alaska Native, non-Hispanic/Latino; 34 Asian, non-Hispanic/Latino; 46 Hispanic/Latino; 4 Native Hawaiian or other Pacific Islander, non-Hispanic/Latino; 29 Two or more races, non-Hispanic/Latino), 14 international. Average age 37. 262 applicants, 91% accepted, 194 enrolled. In 2011, 352 master's awarded. *Degree requirements:* For master's, comprehensive exam, capstone course. *Entrance requirements:* For master's, GMAT (if GPA less than 3.0 and fewer than 5 years of work experience), interview, resume, 2 letters of recommendation. Additional exam requirements/recommendations for international students: Recommended—TOEFL (minimum score 550 paper-based; 213 computer-based; 80 iBT). *Application deadline:* For fall admission, 9/11 priority date for domestic students, 9/11 for international students; for winter admission, 12/15 priority date for domestic students, 12/15 for international students; for spring admission, 3/15 priority date for domestic students, 3/17 for international students. Applications are processed on a rolling basis. Application fee: $50. Electronic applications accepted. *Expenses: Tuition:* Full-time $14,796; part-time $548 per quarter hour. Tuition and fees vary according to program. *Financial support:* Scholarships/grants available. Support available to part-time students. Financial award applicants required to submit FAFSA. *Unit head:* David McNamee, Interim Chair, 503-636-8141, Fax: 503-697-5597, E-mail: mba@marylhurst.edu. *Application contact:* Maruska Lynch, Graduate Admissions Specialist, 800-634-9982 Ext. 6322, Fax: 503-699-6320, E-mail: admissions@marylhurst.edu. Web site: http://www.marylhurst.edu/.

New York University, Leonard N. Stern School of Business, Department of Management and Organizations, New York, NY 10012-1019. Offers management organizations (MBA); organization theory (PhD); organizational behavior (PhD); strategy (PhD). *Faculty research:* Strategic management, managerial cognition, interpersonal processes, conflict and negotiation.

Northwestern University, The Graduate School, Interdepartmental Programs and Kellogg School of Management, Program in Management and Organizations and Sociology, Evanston, IL 60208. Offers PhD. Program requires admission to both The Graduate School and the Kellogg School of Management. *Degree requirements:* For doctorate, comprehensive exam, thesis/dissertation. *Entrance requirements:* For doctorate, GRE General Test. Additional exam requirements/recommendations for international students: Required—TOEFL. Electronic applications accepted. *Faculty research:* Strategic alliances and organizational competitiveness, institutional change and the information of industries, social capital and the creation of financial capital, negotiation, organizational networks, diversity.

Northwestern University, The Graduate School, School of Education and Social Policy, Program in Learning and Organizational Change, Evanston, IL 60208. Offers MS. Part-time and evening/weekend programs available. Postbaccalaureate distance learning degree programs offered (minimal on-campus study). *Degree requirements:* For master's, thesis, practicum. *Entrance requirements:* For master's, GRE or GMAT (recommended), letters of recommendation. Additional exam requirements/ recommendations for international students: Required—TOEFL (minimum score 600 paper-based; 250 computer-based; 100 iBT); Recommended—IELTS (minimum score 7). Electronic applications accepted. *Faculty research:* Strategic change, learning and performance, workplace learning, leadership development, cognitive design, knowledge management.

Phillips Graduate Institute, Program in Organizational Management and Consulting, Encino, CA 91316-1509. Offers Psy D. Evening/weekend programs available. *Degree requirements:* For doctorate, thesis/dissertation. *Entrance requirements:* For doctorate, minimum GPA of 3.0, interview. *Application deadline:* For fall admission, 1/29 priority date for domestic students. Applications are processed on a rolling basis. Application fee: $75. Electronic applications accepted. *Expenses: Tuition:* Full-time $20,746; part-time $820 per unit. *Required fees:* $300 per semester. *Financial support:* Tuition waivers (full and partial) available. *Application contact:* Kim Bell, Admissions Advisor, 818-386-5639, Fax: 818-386-5699, E-mail: kbell@pgi.edu.

Polytechnic Institute of New York University, Department of Finance and Risk Engineering, Brooklyn, NY 11201-2990. Offers financial engineering (MS, Advanced Certificate), including capital markets (MS), computational finance (MS), financial technology (MS); financial technology management (Advanced Certificate); organizational behavior (Advanced Certificate); risk management (Advanced Certificate); technology management (Advanced Certificate). Part-time and evening/ weekend programs available. *Faculty:* 6 full-time (2 women), 23 part-time/adjunct (5 women). *Students:* 149 full-time (49 women), 44 part-time (8 women); includes 30 minority (6 Black or African American, non-Hispanic/Latino; 22 Asian, non-Hispanic/ Latino; 2 Hispanic/Latino), 135 international. Average age 27. 515 applicants, 36% accepted, 102 enrolled. In 2011, 95 degrees awarded. *Degree requirements:* For master's, comprehensive exam (for some programs), thesis (for some programs). *Entrance requirements:* For master's, GMAT, minimum B average in undergraduate course work. Additional exam requirements/recommendations for international students: Required—TOEFL (minimum score 550 paper-based; 213 computer-based; 80 iBT); Recommended—IELTS (minimum score 6.5). *Application deadline:* For fall admission, 7/31 priority date for domestic students, 4/30 for international students; for spring admission, 12/31 priority date for domestic students, 11/30 for international students. Applications are processed on a rolling basis. Application fee: $75. Electronic applications accepted. *Expenses: Tuition:* Full-time $22,464; part-time $1248 per credit. *Required fees:* $501 per semester. *Financial support:* Institutionally sponsored loans, scholarships/grants, and unspecified assistantships available. Support available to part-time students. Financial award applicants required to submit FAFSA. *Unit head:* Prof. Charles S. Tapiero, Academic Director, 718-260-3653, Fax: 718-260-3874, E-mail: ctapiero@poly.edu. *Application contact:* JeanCarlo Bonilla, Director, Graduate Enrollment Management, 718-260-3182, Fax: 718-260-3624.

Polytechnic Institute of New York University, Department of Technology Management, Major in Organizational Behavior, Brooklyn, NY 11201-2990. Offers MS. Part-time and evening/weekend programs available. *Students:* 27 full-time (18 women), 22 part-time (16 women); includes 17 minority (8 Black or African American, non-Hispanic/Latino; 5 Asian, non-Hispanic/Latino; 4 Hispanic/Latino), 13 international. Average age 29. 60 applicants, 65% accepted, 17 enrolled. In 2011, 25 master's awarded. *Degree requirements:* For master's, comprehensive exam (for some programs), thesis (for some programs). *Entrance requirements:* For master's, GMAT, minimum B average in undergraduate course work. Additional exam requirements/ recommendations for international students: Required—TOEFL (minimum score 550 paper-based; 213 computer-based; 80 iBT); Recommended—IELTS (minimum score 6.5). *Application deadline:* For fall admission, 7/31 priority date for domestic students, 4/ 30 for international students; for spring admission, 12/31 priority date for domestic students, 11/30 for international students. Applications are processed on a rolling basis. Application fee: $75. Electronic applications accepted. *Expenses: Tuition:* Full-time $22,464; part-time $1248 per credit. *Required fees:* $501 per semester. *Financial support:* Applicants required to submit FAFSA. *Unit head:* Prof. Bharadwaj Rao, Head, 718-260-3617, Fax: 718-260-3874, E-mail: brao@poly.edu. *Application contact:* JeanCarlo Bonilla, Director of Graduate Enrollment Management, 718-260-3182, Fax: 718-260-3624.

Purdue University, Graduate School, Krannert School of Management, Doctoral Program in Organizational Behavior and Human Resource Management, West Lafayette, IN 47907-2056. Offers PhD. *Students:* 6 full-time (3 women); includes 2 minority (1 Black or African American, non-Hispanic/Latino; 1 Asian, non-Hispanic/ Latino). Average age 32. 80 applicants, 0% accepted, 0 enrolled. In 2011, 3 doctorates awarded. *Degree requirements:* For doctorate, comprehensive exam, thesis/ dissertation, dissertation proposal, dissertation defense. *Entrance requirements:* For doctorate, GMAT or GRE, bachelor's degree, two semesters of calculus, one semester each of linear algebra and statistics. Additional exam requirements/recommendations for international students: Required—TOEFL (minimum score 575 paper-based; 233 computer-based); Recommended—TWE. *Application deadline:* For fall admission, 1/15 priority date for domestic students, 1/15 for international students. Application fee: $55. Electronic applications accepted. *Financial support:* In 2011–12, 1 fellowship with full tuition reimbursement (averaging $25,000 per year), research assistantships with partial tuition reimbursements (averaging $18,000 per year), teaching assistantships with partial tuition reimbursements (averaging $18,000 per year) were awarded; scholarships/grants, health care benefits, tuition waivers (full and partial), unspecified assistantships, and travel funds to present at a major conference also available. Support available to part-time students. Financial award application deadline: 1/15. *Faculty research:* Human resource management, organizational behavior. *Unit head:* Dr. P. Christopher Earley, Dean/Professor, 765-494-4366. *Application contact:* Krannert PhD Admissions, 765-494-4375, Fax: 765-494-0136, E-mail: krannertphd@purdue.edu. Web site: http://www.krannert.purdue.edu/programs/phd/.

Saybrook University, Graduate College of Psychology and Humanistic Studies, San Francisco, CA 94111-1920. Offers clinical psychology (Psy D); human science (MA, PhD), including consciousness and spirituality, humanistic and transpersonal psychology, integrative health studies, organizational systems, social transformation; organizational systems (MA, PhD), including consciousness and spirituality, humanistic and transpersonal psychology, integrative health studies, leadership of sustainable systems (MA), organizational systems, social transformation; psychology (MA, PhD), including clinical psychology (PhD), consciousness and spirituality, creativity studies (MA), humanistic and transpersonal psychology, integrative health studies, Jungian studies, marriage and family therapy (MA), organizational systems, social transformation. Postbaccalaureate distance learning degree programs offered (minimal on-campus study). *Faculty:* 11 full-time (3 women), 83 part-time/adjunct (34 women). *Students:* 479 full-time (333 women); includes 62 minority (30 Black or African American, non-Hispanic/Latino; 1 American Indian or Alaska Native, non-Hispanic/ Latino; 13 Asian, non-Hispanic/Latino; 18 Hispanic/Latino), 18 international. Average age 43. 280 applicants, 52% accepted, 105 enrolled. In 2011, 28 master's, 43 doctorates awarded. Terminal master's awarded for partial completion of doctoral program. *Degree requirements:* For master's, thesis or alternative; for doctorate, thesis/ dissertation. *Entrance requirements:* Additional exam requirements/recommendations for international students: Required—TOEFL (minimum score 580 paper-based; 237 computer-based; 93 iBT). *Application deadline:* For fall admission, 6/1 priority date for domestic students; for spring admission, 12/16 priority date for domestic students. Application fee: $50. Electronic applications accepted. *Financial support:* In 2011–12, 335 students received support. Scholarships/grants available. Financial award applicants required to submit FAFSA. *Faculty research:* Humanistic theory, health studies, organizational systems, consciousness and spirituality, social transformation. *Total annual research expenditures:* $90,000. *Unit head:* Mark Schulman, President, 800-825-4480, Fax: 415-433-9271. *Application contact:* Director of Admissions, 800-825-4480, Fax: 415-433-9271, E-mail: admissions@saybrook.edu. Web site: http:// www.saybrook.edu/phs.

Saybrook University, LIOS Graduate College, Leadership and Organization Development Track, San Francisco, CA 94111-1920. Offers MA. Program offered jointly with Bastyr University. *Faculty:* 10 full-time (6 women), 5 part-time/adjunct (2 women). *Students:* 48 full-time. Average age 40. 50 applicants, 98% accepted, 40 enrolled. In 2011, 19 master's awarded. *Degree requirements:* For master's, thesis (for some programs), oral exams. *Entrance requirements:* For master's, bachelor's degree from an accredited college or university. *Application deadline:* Applications are processed on a rolling basis. Application fee: $65. *Financial support:* In 2011–12, 32 students received support. Career-related internships or fieldwork, Federal Work-Study, and scholarships/ grants available. Financial award applicants required to submit FAFSA. *Faculty research:* Cross-functional work teams, communication, management authority, employee influence, systems theory. *Unit head:* Dr. Cynthia FitzGerald, Dean, 425-968-3410, Fax: 425-968-3409, E-mail: cfitzgerald@lios.saybroo.edu. *Application contact:* Rhys Clark, Director, Academic Admissions, 425-968-3400, Fax: 425-968-3410.

Silver Lake College of the Holy Family, Division of Graduate Studies, Program in Management and Organizational Behavior, Manitowoc, WI 54220-9319. Offers MS. Part-time and evening/weekend programs available. Postbaccalaureate distance learning degree programs offered (minimal on-campus study). *Degree requirements:* For master's, thesis optional. *Entrance requirements:* For master's, minimum undergraduate GPA of 3.0, statement of purpose, three letters of recommendation, professional resume. Additional exam requirements/recommendations for international students: Required—TOEFL. Electronic applications accepted.

Suffolk University, Sawyer Business School, Master of Business Administration Program, Boston, MA 02108-2770. Offers accounting (MBA); business administration (APC); corporate financial executive track (MBA); entrepreneurship (MBA); executive business administration (EMBA); finance (MBA); global business administration (GMBA); health administration (MBA); international business (MBA); marketing (MBA); organizational behavior (MBA); strategic management (MBA); taxation (MBA); JD/MBA; MBA/GDPA; MBA/MHA; MBA/MSA; MBA/MSF; MBA/MST. *Accreditation:* AACSB. Part-time and evening/weekend programs available. Postbaccalaureate distance learning degree programs offered (no on-campus study). *Faculty:* 98 full-time (30 women), 14 part-time/adjunct (3 women). *Students:* 139 full-time (49 women), 321 part-time (138 women); includes 53 minority (17 Black or African American, non-Hispanic/Latino; 1 American Indian or Alaska Native, non-Hispanic/Latino; 21 Asian, non-Hispanic/Latino; 11 Hispanic/Latino; 1 Native Hawaiian or other Pacific Islander, non-Hispanic/Latino; 2 Two or more races, non-Hispanic/Latino), 64 international. Average age 30. 437 applicants, 61% accepted, 121 enrolled. In 2011, 283 master's awarded. *Entrance requirements:* For master's, GMAT, minimum undergraduate GPA of 2.75 (MBA), 5 years of managerial experience (EMBA). Additional exam requirements/ recommendations for international students: Required—TOEFL (minimum score 550 paper-based; 213 computer-based). *Application deadline:* For fall admission, 6/15 priority date for domestic students, 6/15 for international students; for spring admission, 11/1 priority date for domestic students, 11/1 for international students. Applications are processed on a rolling basis. Application fee: $50. Electronic applications accepted. Tuition and fees vary according to program. *Financial support:* In 2011–12, 273 students received support, including 73 fellowships with full and partial tuition reimbursements available (averaging $12,415 per year); career-related internships or fieldwork, Federal Work-Study, and institutionally sponsored loans also available. Support available to part-time students. Financial award application deadline: 4/1; financial award applicants required to submit FAFSA. *Faculty research:* Foreign investments; career strategies and boundaryless careers; corporate ethics codes; interest rates, inflation, and growth options; innovation and product development performance. *Unit head:* Lillian Hallberg, Assistant Dean of Graduate Programs/Director of MBA Programs, 617-573-8306, E-mail: lhallber@suffolk.edu. *Application contact:* Ellen Driscoll, Director of Graduate Admissions, 617-573-8302, Fax: 617-305-1733, E-mail: grad.admission@suffolk.edu. Web site: http://www.suffolk.edu/mba.

Syracuse University, Martin J. Whitman School of Management, PhD Program in Business Administration, Syracuse, NY 13244. Offers accounting (PhD); finance (PhD); management information systems (PhD); managerial statistics (PhD); marketing (PhD); operations management (PhD); organizational behavior (PhD); strategy and human resources (PhD); supply chain management (PhD). *Faculty:* 79 full-time (20 women), 25 part-time/adjunct (6 women). *Students:* 32 full-time (10 women); includes 6 minority (3 Black or African American, non-Hispanic/Latino; 2 Asian, non-Hispanic/Latino; 1 Hispanic/Latino), 18 international. Average age 32. 260 applicants, 8% accepted, 12 enrolled. In 2011, 2 doctorates awarded. *Degree requirements:* For doctorate, comprehensive exam, thesis/dissertation, summer research paper. *Entrance requirements:* For doctorate, GMAT or GRE General Test, 3 recommendations. Additional exam requirements/recommendations for international students: Required—TOEFL (minimum score 600 paper-based; 250 computer-based; 100 iBT). *Application deadline:* For fall admission, 2/15 priority date for domestic students, 2/15 for international students. Applications are processed on a rolling basis. Application fee: $65. Electronic applications accepted. *Expenses: Tuition:* Part-time $1206 per credit. *Financial support:* In 2011–12, 1 fellowship with full tuition reimbursement (averaging $19,570 per year), 30 teaching assistantships with full tuition reimbursements (averaging $17,000 per year) were awarded; research assistantships with full tuition reimbursements, health care benefits, and unspecified assistantships also available. Financial award application deadline: 1/30. *Faculty research:* Marketing models, market microstructure, supply chain, auditing, corporate governance. *Unit head:* Dr. Eunkyu Lee, Director of the PhD Program, 315-443-3429, E-mail: elee06@syr.edu. *Application contact:* Carol Hilleges, Administrative Specialist, 315-443-9601, Fax: 315-443-3671, E-mail: clhilleg@syr.edu. Web site: http://whitman.syr.edu/phd/.

Towson University, Program in Organizational Change, Towson, MD 21252-0001. Offers CAS. *Students:* 16 full-time (12 women), 83 part-time (61 women); includes 21 minority (19 Black or African American, non-Hispanic/Latino; 1 Hispanic/Latino; 1 Two or more races, non-Hispanic/Latino), 1 international. *Entrance requirements:* For degree,

GRE or MAT, 2 letters of recommendation, minimum GPA of 3.5. Additional exam requirements/recommendations for international students: Required—TOEFL (minimum score 550 paper-based; 213 computer-based). *Application deadline:* Applications are processed on a rolling basis. Application fee: $50. Electronic applications accepted. *Expenses:* Tuition, state resident: part-time $337 per credit. Tuition, nonresident: part-time $709 per credit. *Required fees:* $99 per credit. *Unit head:* Diane Wood, Program Director, 410-704-2685, E-mail: dwood@towson.edu.

Universidad de las Americas, A.C., Program in International Organizations and Institutions, Mexico City, Mexico. Offers MA.

Université de Sherbrooke, Faculty of Administration, Program in Organizational Change and Intervention, Sherbrooke, QC J1K 2R1, Canada. Offers M Sc. *Faculty:* 8 full-time (2 women), 5 part-time/adjunct (2 women). *Students:* 42 full-time (27 women), 12 part-time (7 women). Average age 27. 86 applicants, 70% accepted, 22 enrolled. In 2011, 14 master's awarded. *Degree requirements:* For master's, one foreign language, thesis. *Entrance requirements:* For master's, bachelor's degree in related field, minimum GPA of 3.0 (on 4.3 scale). *Application deadline:* For fall admission, 4/30 for domestic students, 1/15 for international students. Applications are processed on a rolling basis. Application fee: $70. Electronic applications accepted. *Faculty research:* Organizational change, organizational communication, process approaches and qualitative research, organizational behavior. *Unit head:* Prof. Julien Bilodeau, Director, Graduate Programs in Business, 819-821-8000 Ext. 62355. *Application contact:* Marie-Claude Drouin, Programs Assistant Director, 819-821-8000 Ext. 63301.

The University of British Columbia, Sauder School of Business, Doctoral Program in Commerce and Business Administration, Vancouver, BC V6T 1Z1, Canada. Offers accounting (PhD); finance (PhD); international business (PhD); management information systems (PhD); management science (PhD); marketing (PhD); organizational behavior (PhD); strategy and business economics (PhD); transportation and logistics (PhD); urban land economics (PhD). *Degree requirements:* For doctorate, comprehensive exam, thesis/dissertation. *Entrance requirements:* For doctorate, GMAT or GRE. Additional exam requirements/recommendations for international students: Required—TOEFL (minimum score 600 paper-based; 250 computer-based; 100 iBT). Electronic applications accepted.

University of California, Berkeley, Graduate Division, Haas School of Business, PhD in Business Administration Program, Berkeley, CA 94720-1500. Offers accounting (PhD); business and public policy (PhD); finance (PhD); management of organizations (PhD); marketing (PhD); operations management (PhD); real estate (PhD). *Accreditation:* AACSB. *Faculty:* 77 full-time (18 women), 152 part-time/adjunct (24 women). *Students:* 79 full-time (25 women); includes 13 minority (12 Asian, non-Hispanic/Latino; 1 Hispanic/Latino), 34 international. Average age 30. 547 applicants, 5% accepted, 15 enrolled. In 2011, 14 doctorates awarded. *Degree requirements:* For doctorate, comprehensive exam, thesis/dissertation, written preliminary exams, oral qualifying exam. *Entrance requirements:* For doctorate, GMAT or GRE, minimum GPA of 3.0 in undergraduate and graduate coursework. Additional exam requirements/recommendations for international students: Required—TOEFL (minimum score 570 paper-based; 230 computer-based; 70 iBT), IELTS (minimum score 7). *Application deadline:* For fall admission, 12/10 for domestic and international students. Application fee: $80 ($100 for international students). Electronic applications accepted. *Financial support:* In 2011–12, 66 students received support, including 58 fellowships with full and partial tuition reimbursements available (averaging $29,000 per year), 77 teaching assistantships with full and partial tuition reimbursements available; research assistantships with full and partial tuition reimbursements available, scholarships/grants, health care benefits, tuition waivers (full), unspecified assistantships, and transit pass, travel grants also available. Financial award application deadline: 12/10; financial award applicants required to submit FAFSA. *Faculty research:* Accounting, business and public policy, finance, management of organizations, marketing, operations and information technology management, real estate. *Unit head:* Dr. Sunil Dutta, Director, 510-642-1229, Fax: 510-643-4255, E-mail: kimg@haas.berkeley.edu. *Application contact:* Kim Guilfoyle, Director, Student Affairs, 510-642-3944, Fax: 510-643-4255, E-mail: kimg@haas.berkeley.edu. Web site: http://www.haas.berkeley.edu/Phd/.

University of California, Los Angeles, Graduate Division, UCLA Anderson School of Management, Los Angeles, CA 90095-1481. Offers accounting (PhD); Asia Pacific (EMBA); business administration (EMBA, MBA); decisions, operations and technology management (PhD); finance (PhD); financial engineering (MFE); global economics and management (PhD); Latin America (EMBA); management and organizations (PhD); marketing (PhD); strategy (PhD); DDS/MBA; MBA/JD; MBA/MD; MBA/MLAS; MBA/MLIS; MBA/MPH; MBA/MPP; MBA/MSCS; MBA/MSN; MBA/MUP. *Accreditation:* AACSB. Part-time programs available. *Faculty:* 90 full-time (14 women), 62 part-time/adjunct (14 women). *Students:* 1,103 full-time (312 women), 842 part-time (223 women); includes 663 minority (18 Black or African American, non-Hispanic/Latino; 510 Asian, non-Hispanic/Latino; 46 Hispanic/Latino; 2 Native Hawaiian or other Pacific Islander, non-Hispanic/Latino; 87 Two or more races, non-Hispanic/Latino), 469 international. 4,737 applicants, 32% accepted, 875 enrolled. In 2011, 759 master's, 6 doctorates awarded. *Degree requirements:* For master's, comprehensive exam, field study consulting project (for MBA); thesis/dissertation (for MFE); for doctorate, comprehensive exam, thesis/dissertation, oral and written qualifying exams. *Entrance requirements:* For master's, GMAT (for MBA); GMAT or GRE General Test (for MFE), 4-year bachelor's degree or equivalent; for doctorate, GMAT or GRE General Test, 4-year bachelor's degree from regionally-accredited institution; minimum GPA of 3.0. Additional exam requirements/recommendations for international students: Required—TOEFL (minimum score 560 paper-based; 220 computer-based; 87 iBT), IELTS (minimum score 7). *Application deadline:* For fall admission, 10/26 for domestic and international students; for winter admission, 1/11 for domestic and international students; for spring admission, 4/18 for domestic and international students. Application fee: $200. Electronic applications accepted. *Expenses:* Contact institution. *Financial support:* In 2011–12, 600 students received support. Fellowships, research assistantships, teaching assistantships, career-related internships or fieldwork, institutionally sponsored loans, scholarships/grants, health care benefits, and tuition waivers (partial) available. Financial award application deadline: 4/15; financial award applicants required to submit FAFSA. *Unit head:* Judy D. Olian, Dean, 310-825-7982, Fax: 310-206-2073, E-mail: judy.olian@anderson.ucla.edu. *Application contact:* Robert Weiler, Assistant Dean, Director of MBA Admissions and Financial Aid, 310-825-6944, Fax: 310-825-8582, E-mail: mba.admissions@anderson.ucla.edu. Web site: http://www.anderson.ucla.edu/.

See Display on page 141 and Close-Up on page 249.

University of Chicago, Booth School of Business, Full-Time MBA Program, Chicago, IL 60637. Offers accounting (MBA); analytic finance (MBA); analytic management (MBA); business administration (PhD); econometrics and statistics (MBA); economics (MBA); entrepreneurship (MBA); finance (MBA); general management (MBA); health administration and policy (Certificate); human resource management (MBA); international business (IMBA, MBA); managerial and organizational behavior (MBA); marketing management (MBA); operations management (MBA); strategic management (MBA); MBA/AM; MBA/JD; MBA/MA; MBA/MD; MBA/MPP. *Accreditation:* AACSB. Part-time and evening/weekend programs available. *Faculty:* 166 full-time, 32 part-time/adjunct. *Students:* 1,160 full-time (412 women); includes 316 minority (61 Black or African American, non-Hispanic/Latino; 173 Asian, non-Hispanic/Latino; 63 Hispanic/Latino; 19 Two or more races, non-Hispanic/Latino), 378 international. Average age 28. 4,169 applicants, 575 enrolled. In 2011, 1,423 master's, 19 doctorates awarded. Terminal master's awarded for partial completion of doctoral program. *Entrance requirements:* For master's, GMAT, 2 letters of recommendation, 3 essays, resume, interview. Additional exam requirements/recommendations for international students: Required—TOEFL (minimum score 600 paper-based; 250 computer-based; 104 iBT), IELTS. *Application deadline:* For fall admission, 10/12 priority date for domestic students, 10/12 for international students; for winter admission, 1/4 for domestic and international students; for spring admission, 4/4 for domestic and international students. Application fee: $200. Electronic applications accepted. *Expenses:* Contact institution. *Financial support:* Fellowships available. Financial award applicants required to submit FAFSA. *Faculty research:* Finance, marketing, economics, entrepreneurship, strategy, management. *Unit head:* Stacey Kole, Deputy Dean, 773-702-7121. *Application contact:* Kurt Ahlm, Associate Dean of Student Recruitment and Admissions, 773-702-7369, Fax: 773-702-9085, E-mail: admissions@chicagobooth.edu. Web site: http://chicagobooth.edu/.

University of Hartford, College of Arts and Sciences, Department of Psychology, Program in Organizational Behavior, West Hartford, CT 06117-1599. Offers MS. Part-time and evening/weekend programs available. *Entrance requirements:* Additional exam requirements/recommendations for international students: Required—TOEFL (minimum score 550 paper-based; 213 computer-based). Electronic applications accepted.

University of Hawaii at Manoa, Graduate Division, Shidler College of Business, Program in Business Administration, Honolulu, HI 96822. Offers Asian business studies (MBA); Chinese business studies (MBA); decision sciences (MBA); entrepreneurship (MBA); finance (MBA); finance and banking (MBA); human resources management (MBA); information management (MBA); information technology (MBA); international business (MBA); Japanese business studies (MBA); marketing (MBA); organizational behavior (MBA); organizational management (MBA); real estate (MBA); student-designed track (MBA). *Accreditation:* AACSB. Part-time and evening/weekend programs available. *Degree requirements:* For master's, thesis optional. *Entrance requirements:* For master's, GMAT, minimum GPA of 3.0. Additional exam requirements/recommendations for international students: Required—TOEFL (minimum score 600 paper-based; 250 computer-based; 100 iBT), IELTS (minimum score 7). *Expenses:* Contact institution.

The University of North Carolina at Chapel Hill, Kenan-Flagler Business School, Doctoral Program in Business Administration, Chapel Hill, NC 27599. Offers accounting (PhD); finance (PhD); marketing (PhD); operations management (PhD); organizational behavior (PhD); strategy (PhD). *Accreditation:* AACSB. *Degree requirements:* For doctorate, thesis/dissertation. *Entrance requirements:* For doctorate, GMAT or GRE General Test. Electronic applications accepted. *Expenses:* Contact institution.

University of Oklahoma, College of Arts and Sciences, Department of Psychology, Program in Organizational Dynamics, Tulsa, OK 74135. Offers organizational dynamics (MA), including human resource management, organizational dynamics, technical project management. Part-time and evening/weekend programs available. *Students:* 13 full-time (8 women), 21 part-time (10 women); includes 11 minority (2 Black or African American, non-Hispanic/Latino; 1 American Indian or Alaska Native, non-Hispanic/Latino; 2 Asian, non-Hispanic/Latino; 4 Hispanic/Latino; 1 Native Hawaiian or other Pacific Islander, non-Hispanic/Latino; 1 Two or more races, non-Hispanic/Latino), 1 international. Average age 36. 8 applicants, 75% accepted, 4 enrolled. In 2011, 14 degrees awarded. *Entrance requirements:* For master's, minimum GPA of 3.0 in last 60 hours of undergraduate course work. Additional exam requirements/recommendations for international students: Required—TOEFL (minimum score 550 paper-based; 79 iBT). *Application deadline:* For fall admission, 4/15 priority date for domestic students, 3/1 for international students; for spring admission, 11/1 for domestic students, 9/1 for international students. Applications are processed on a rolling basis. Application fee: $40 ($90 for international students). Electronic applications accepted. *Expenses:* Tuition, state resident: full-time $4087; part-time $170.30 per credit hour. Tuition, nonresident: full-time $14,875; part-time $619.80 per credit hour. *Required fees:* $2659; $100.25 per credit hour. Tuition and fees vary according to course load and degree level. *Financial support:* In 2011–12, 7 students received support. Scholarships/grants, health care benefits, and unspecified assistantships available. Financial award application deadline: 3/1; financial award applicants required to submit FAFSA. *Faculty research:* Academic integrity, organizational behavior, interdisciplinary teams, shared leadership. *Unit head:* Dr. Jorge Mendoza, Chair, 405-325-4511, Fax: 405-325-4737, E-mail: jmendoza@ou.edu. *Application contact:* Jennifer Kisamore, Graduate Liaison, 918-660-3603, Fax: 918-660-3383, E-mail: jkisamore@ou.edu. Web site: http://tulsagrad.ou.edu/odyn/.

University of Pittsburgh, Katz Graduate School of Business, Doctoral Program in Business Administration, Pittsburgh, PA 15260. Offers accounting (PhD); finance (PhD); information systems (PhD); marketing (PhD); operations/decision sciences/artificial intelligence (PhD); organizational behavior and human resource management (PhD); strategic planning (PhD). *Accreditation:* AACSB. *Faculty:* 54 full-time (16 women). *Students:* 51 full-time (21 women); includes 9 minority (4 Black or African American, non-Hispanic/Latino; 4 Asian, non-Hispanic/Latino; 1 Hispanic/Latino), 23 international. 373 applicants, 7% accepted, 10 enrolled. In 2011, 6 doctorates awarded. *Degree requirements:* For doctorate, comprehensive exam, thesis/dissertation. *Entrance requirements:* For doctorate, GMAT or GRE. Additional exam requirements/recommendations for international students: Required—TOEFL. *Application deadline:* For fall admission, 2/1 priority date for domestic students, 2/1 for international students. Applications are processed on a rolling basis. Application fee: $50. Electronic applications accepted. *Expenses:* Tuition, state resident: full-time $18,774; part-time $760 per credit. Tuition, nonresident: full-time $30,736; part-time $1258 per credit. *Required fees:* $740; $200 per term. Tuition and fees vary according to program. *Financial support:* In 2011–12, 38 students received support, including 29 research assistantships with full tuition reimbursements available (averaging $19,400 per year), 10 teaching assistantships with full tuition reimbursements available (averaging $24,700 per year); fellowships, Federal Work-Study, scholarships/grants, health care benefits, and unspecified assistantships also available. Financial award application deadline: 2/1. *Faculty research:* Accounting statements and reporting, corporate finance, information systems processes, structures and decision-making, consumer behavior and marketing models. *Total annual research expenditures:* $254,031. *Unit head:* Dr. Dennis Galletta, Director, 412-648-1699, Fax: 412-624-3633, E-mail: galletta@katz.pitt.edu. *Application contact:* Carrie Woods, Assistant Director, 412-648-1525, Fax: 412-624-3633, E-mail: cawoods@katz.pitt.edu. Web site: http://www.business.pitt.edu/katz/phd/.

University of Pittsburgh, Katz Graduate School of Business, Master of Business Administration Programs, Pittsburgh , PA 15260. Offers finance (MBA); information systems (MBA); marketing (MBA); operations management (MBA); organizational behavior and human resource management (MBA); organizational leadership (Certificate); strategy, environment and organizations (MBA); technology, innovation and entrepreneurship (Certificate); MBA/JD; MBA/MIB; MBA/MPIA; MBA/MSE; MBA/

MSIS; MID/MBA. *Accreditation:* AACSB. Part-time and evening/weekend programs available. *Faculty:* 62 full-time (17 women), 21 part-time/adjunct (4 women). *Students:* 179 full-time (63 women), 572 part-time (373 women); includes 69 minority (29 Black or African American, non-Hispanic/Latino; 24 Asian, non-Hispanic/Latino; 16 Hispanic/Latino), 83 international. Average age 29. 391 applicants, 42% accepted, 78 enrolled. *Degree requirements:* For master's, minimum GPA of 3.0. *Entrance requirements:* For master's, GMAT, recommendations, undergraduate transcripts, essay, resume, interview, bachelor's degree. Additional exam requirements/recommendations for international students: Required—TOEFL (minimum score 600 paper, 250 computer, 100 iBT) or IELTS. *Application deadline:* For fall admission, 4/1 priority date for domestic students, 2/1 for international students. Application fee: $50. Electronic applications accepted. *Expenses:* Tuition, state resident: full-time $18,774; part-time $760 per credit. Tuition, nonresident: full-time $30,736; part-time $1258 per credit. *Required fees:* $740; $200 per term. Tuition and fees vary according to program. *Financial support:* In 2011–12, 58 students received support. Career-related internships or fieldwork and scholarships/grants available. Financial award application deadline: 3/1; financial award applicants required to submit FAFSA. *Faculty research:* Accounting statements and reporting, corporate finance, information systems processes, structures and decision-making, consumer behavior and marketing models. *Unit head:* William T. Valenta, Assistant Dean/Director, 412-648-1610, Fax: 412-648-1659, E-mail: wtvalenta@katz.pitt.edu. *Application contact:* Thomas Keller, Director of MBA Admissions, 412-648-1700, Fax: 412-648-1659, E-mail: mba@katz.pitt.edu. Web site: http://www.business.pitt.edu/katz/mba/.

Wayne State University, College of Liberal Arts and Sciences, Department of Political Science, Program in Public Administration, Detroit, MI 48202. Offers aging policy and management (MPA); criminal justice policy and management (MPA); economic development policy and management (MPA); health services policy and management (MPA); human resources management (MPA); information technology management (MPA); non-profit management (MPA); organizational behavior and management (MPA); public budgeting and financial management (MPA); public policy analysis and program evaluation (MPA); social welfare policy and management (MPA); urban policy and management (MPA). *Accreditation:* NASPAA. Evening/weekend programs available. *Students:* 22 full-time (17 women), 45 part-time (33 women); includes 19 minority (16 Black or African American, non-Hispanic/Latino; 1 American Indian or Alaska Native, non-Hispanic/Latino; 2 Hispanic/Latino), 1 international. Average age 31. 75 applicants, 28% accepted, 11 enrolled. In 2011, 20 master's awarded. *Degree requirements:* For master's, comprehensive exam. *Entrance requirements:* For master's, GRE General Test. Additional exam requirements/recommendations for international students: Required—TOEFL (minimum score 550 paper-based; 213 computer-based); Recommended—TWE (minimum score 5.5). *Application deadline:* For fall admission, 6/1 priority date for domestic students, 5/1 for international students; for winter admission, 10/1 priority date for domestic students, 9/1 for international students; for spring admission, 2/1 priority date for domestic students, 1/1 for international students. Applications are processed on a rolling basis. Application fee: $50. Electronic applications accepted. *Expenses:* Tuition, state resident: part-time $512.85 per credit. Tuition, nonresident: part-time $1132.65 per credit. *Required fees:* $26.60 per credit. $199.65 per semester. Tuition and fees vary according to course load and program. *Financial support:* In 2011–12, 7 students received support. Scholarships/grants available. *Faculty research:* Urban politics, urban education, state administration. *Unit head:* Dr. Brady Baybeck, Director, 313-577-2630, E-mail: mpa@wayne.edu. Web site: http://clasweb.clas.wayne.edu/mapa.

Western International University, Graduate Programs in Business, Program in Human Dynamics, Phoenix, AZ 85021-2718. Offers MA. Evening/weekend programs available. Postbaccalaureate distance learning degree programs offered (no on-campus study). *Entrance requirements:* Additional exam requirements/recommendations for international students: Required—TOEFL (minimum score 550 paper-based; 213 computer-based; 79 iBT).

Wilfrid Laurier University, Faculty of Graduate and Postdoctoral Studies, School of Business and Economics, Department of Business, Waterloo, ON N2L 3C5, Canada. Offers accounting (PhD); finance (M Fin); financial economics (PhD); marketing (PhD); operations and supply chain management (PhD); organizational behavior and human resource management (M Sc); organizational behaviour and human resource management (PhD); supply chain management (M Sc); technology management (EMTM). Part-time and evening/weekend programs available. *Degree requirements:* For master's, thesis optional; for doctorate, comprehensive exam, thesis/dissertation. *Entrance requirements:* For master's, GMAT, 4-year honors degree with minimum B+ average; for doctorate, GMAT, master's degree, minimum B+ average. Additional exam requirements/recommendations for international students: Required—TOEFL (minimum score 89 iBT). Electronic applications accepted. *Faculty research:* Financial economics, management and organizational behavior, operations and supply chain management.

Organizational Management

Alvernia University, Graduate Studies, Program in Leadership, Reading, PA 19607-1799. Offers PhD. *Degree requirements:* For doctorate, comprehensive exam, thesis/dissertation (for some programs). *Entrance requirements:* For doctorate, GRE, GMAT, or MAT, minimum GPA of 3.3, 3 letters of recommendation, resume, interview.

The American College, Graduate Programs, Bryn Mawr, PA 19010-2105. Offers financial services (MSFS); leadership (MSM). Part-time and evening/weekend programs available. Postbaccalaureate distance learning degree programs offered (minimal on-campus study). Electronic applications accepted. *Faculty research:* Retirement counseling, social security, aging, family composition, inflation.

American International College, School of Business Administration, Program in Organization Development, Springfield, MA 01109-3189. Offers MS. Part-time and evening/weekend programs available. *Degree requirements:* For master's, comprehensive exam (for some programs), thesis (for some programs), project or research report. *Entrance requirements:* Additional exam requirements/recommendations for international students: Required—TOEFL. Electronic applications accepted.

American Public University System, AMU/APU Graduate Programs, Charles Town, WV 25414. Offers accounting (MBA, MS); administration and supervision (M Ed); criminal justice (MA); emergency and disaster management (MA); entrepreneurship (MBA); environmental policy and management (MS), including environmental planning, environmental sustainability, fish and wildlife management, general (MA, MS), global environmental management; finance (MBA); general (MBA); global business management (MBA); guidance and counseling (M Ed); history (MA), including American history, ancient and classical history, European history, global history, military and diplomatic history, public history; homeland security (MA); homeland security resource allocation (MBA); humanities (MA); information technology (MS), including digital forensics, enterprise software development, information assurance and security, IT project management; information technology management (MBA); intelligence studies (MA), including criminal intelligence, general (MA, MS), homeland security, intelligence analysis, intelligence collection, intelligence operations, terrorism studies; international relations and conflict resolution (MA), including comparative and security issues, conflict resolution, international and transnational security issues, peacekeeping; legal studies (MA); management (MA), including defense management, general (MA, MS), human resource management, organizational leadership, public administration, reverse logistics, strategic consulting; marketing (MBA); military history (MA), including American military history, American revolution, civil war, war since 1946, World War II; military studies (MA), including air warfare, asymmetrical warfare, joint warfare, land warfare, naval warfare, strategic leadership; national security studies (MA), including general (MA, MS), homeland security, regional security studies, security and intelligence analysis, terrorism studies; nonprofit management (MBA); political science (MA), including American politics and government, comparative government and development, public policy; psychology (MA); public administration (MA, MPA), including disaster management (MPA), environmental policy (MA), health policy (MPA), human resources (MPA), national security (MPA), organizational management (MPA), security management (MPA); public health (MA, MPH), including emergency management (MPH), environmental health (MPH), public administration (MA); reverse logistics management (MA); security management (MA); space studies (MS), including aerospace science, planetary science; sports and health sciences (MS); sports management (MS), including coaching theory and strategy, sports administration; teaching (M Ed), including curriculum and instruction for elementary teachers, elementary, elementary reading, English language learners, instructional leadership, online learning, secondary social sciences, special education; transportation and logistics management (MA), including maritime engineering management. Programs offered via distance learning only. Part-time and evening/weekend programs available. Postbaccalaureate distance learning degree programs offered (no on-campus study). *Faculty:* 445 full-time (241 women), 1,360 part-time/adjunct (617 women). *Students:* 688 full-time (338 women), 10,168 part-time (3,706 women); includes 3,130 minority (1,007 Black or African American, non-Hispanic/Latino; 103 American Indian or Alaska Native, non-Hispanic/Latino; 825 Asian, non-Hispanic/Latino; 810 Hispanic/Latino; 51 Native Hawaiian or other Pacific Islander, non-Hispanic/Latino; 334 Two or more races, non-Hispanic/Latino), 134 international. Average age 35. In 2011, 2,386 master's awarded. *Degree requirements:* For master's, comprehensive exam or practicum. *Entrance requirements:* For master's, official transcript showing earned bachelor's degree from institution accredited by recognized accrediting body. Additional exam requirements/recommendations for international students: Required—TOEFL (minimum score 550 paper-based; 213 computer-based), IELTS (minimum score 6.5). *Application deadline:* Applications are processed on a rolling basis. Application fee: $0. Electronic applications accepted. *Expenses: Tuition:* Part-time $325 per credit hour. *Financial support:* Applicants required to submit FAFSA. *Faculty research:* Military history, criminal justice, management performance, national security. *Unit head:* Dr. Karan Powell, Executive Vice President and Provost, 877-468-6268, Fax: 304-724-3780. *Application contact:* Terry Grant, Vice President of Enrollment Management, 877-468-6268, Fax: 304-724-3780, E-mail: info@apus.edu. Web site: http://www.apus.edu.

American University, School of Public Affairs, Department of Public Administration, Program in Organization Development, Washington, DC 20016-8070. Offers MSOD. *Students:* 59 part-time (43 women); includes 18 minority (11 Black or African American, non-Hispanic/Latino; 1 American Indian or Alaska Native, non-Hispanic/Latino; 4 Asian, non-Hispanic/Latino; 2 Hispanic/Latino), 4 international. Average age 37. 27 applicants, 67% accepted, 15 enrolled. In 2011, 28 master's awarded. *Degree requirements:* For master's, comprehensive exam. *Entrance requirements:* For master's, GRE, 2 years of related professional experience, 2 recommendations, 2 writing samples, resume/curriculum vitae, list of personal growth workshops and other laboratory trainings attended, interview. Additional exam requirements/recommendations for international students: Required—TOEFL. *Application deadline:* For fall admission, 2/1 for domestic students; for spring admission, 11/1 for domestic students. Application fee: $55. *Expenses: Tuition:* Full-time $24,264; part-time $1348 per credit hour. *Required fees:* $430. Tuition and fees vary according to course load and program. *Financial support:* Application deadline: 2/1. *Unit head:* Dr. Jocelyn Johnston, Chair, 202-885-2608, Fax: 202-885-2347, E-mail: johnston@american.edu. *Application contact:* Brenda Manley, Admissions and Financial Aid Manager, 202-885-6202, Fax: 202-885-2355, E-mail: bmanley@american.edu. Web site: http://www.american.edu/spa/dpap/.

Amridge University, Graduate and Professional Programs, Montgomery, AL 36117. Offers behavioral leadership and management (MA); Biblical exposition (MA); biblical studies (MA, PhD); family therapy (D Min); historical and theological studies (MA); leadership and management (MS); marriage and family therapy (M Div, MA, PhD); ministerial leadership (M Div, MS); pastoral counseling (M Div, MS); practical ministry (MA); professional counseling (M Div, MA, PhD); theology (M Div, D Min). Part-time and evening/weekend programs available. Postbaccalaureate distance learning degree programs offered (no on-campus study). *Faculty:* 48 full-time (9 women), 27 part-time/adjunct (12 women). *Students:* 161 full-time (79 women), 258 part-time (147 women); includes 160 minority (153 Black or African American, non-Hispanic/Latino; 1 Asian, non-Hispanic/Latino; 6 Hispanic/Latino). Average age 35. *Degree requirements:* For master's, one foreign language, comprehensive exam (for some programs), thesis (for some programs); for doctorate, comprehensive exam (for some programs), thesis/dissertation. *Entrance requirements:* For master's and doctorate, GRE General Test or MAT. Additional exam requirements/recommendations for international students: Required—TOEFL. *Application deadline:* For fall admission, 9/1 priority date for domestic students; for spring admission, 1/1 priority date for domestic students. Applications are processed on a rolling basis. Application fee: $75. Electronic applications accepted. *Expenses: Tuition:* Full-time $10,680; part-time $610 per semester hour. *Required fees:* $600 per semester. *Financial support:* Federal Work-Study and scholarships/grants available. Support available to part-time students. Financial award applicants required to submit FAFSA. *Faculty research:* Homiletics, hermeneutics, ancient Near Eastern history. *Unit head:* Director of Enrollment Management, 800-351-4040 Ext. 7513, Fax: 334-387-3878. *Application contact:* Ora

Davis, Admissions Officer, 334-387-3877 Ext. 7524, Fax: 334-387-3878, E-mail: admissions@amridgeuniversity.edu.

Antioch University Los Angeles, Graduate Programs, Program in Organizational Management, Culver City, CA 90230. Offers human resource development (MA); leadership (MA); organizational development (MA). Part-time and evening/weekend programs available. *Entrance requirements:* For master's, interview. Additional exam requirements/recommendations for international students: Required—TOEFL. *Faculty research:* Systems thinking and chaos theory, technology and organizational structure, nonprofit management, power and empowerment.

Antioch University New England, Graduate School, Department of Organization and Management, Program in Organizational Development, Keene, NH 03431-3552. Offers Certificate.

Antioch University New England, Graduate School, Department of Organization and Management, Program in Organizational Leadership and Management, Keene, NH 03431-3552. Offers MS. *Degree requirements:* For master's, practicum. *Entrance requirements:* For master's, previous course work and work experience in organization and management. Additional exam requirements/recommendations for international students: Required—TOEFL (minimum score 600 paper-based; 250 computer-based). Electronic applications accepted. *Expenses:* Contact institution. *Faculty research:* Developing a collaborative CEO performance evaluation process, search conference process as change mechanism, implementing workflow designs to increase organizational competitiveness.

Antioch University Santa Barbara, Program in Organizational Management, Santa Barbara, CA 93101-1581. Offers MA. Part-time and evening/weekend programs available. Postbaccalaureate distance learning degree programs offered (minimal on-campus study). Electronic applications accepted. *Faculty research:* Multicultural communication, organizational change.

Antioch University Seattle, Graduate Programs, Center for Creative Change, Seattle, WA 98121-1814. Offers environment and community (MA); management (MS); organizational psychology (MA); strategic communications (MA); whole system design (MA). Evening/weekend programs available. Electronic applications accepted. *Expenses:* Contact institution.

Aquinas College, School of Management, Grand Rapids, MI 49506-1799. Offers health care administration (M Mgt); marketing management (M Mgt); organizational leadership (M Min); sustainable business (M Mgt, MSB). Part-time and evening/weekend programs available. *Faculty:* 11 full-time (3 women), 7 part-time/adjunct (0 women). *Students:* 12 full-time (6 women), 56 part-time (32 women); includes 7 minority (3 Black or African American, non-Hispanic/Latino; 1 Asian, non-Hispanic/Latino; 3 Hispanic/Latino). *Entrance requirements:* For master's, GMAT, minimum undergraduate GPA of 2.75, 2 years of work experience. Additional exam requirements/recommendations for international students: Required—TOEFL (minimum score 550 paper-based; 213 computer-based). *Application deadline:* Applications are processed on a rolling basis. *Expenses:* Contact institution. *Financial support:* Scholarships/grants available. Support available to part-time students. Financial award application deadline: 3/15; financial award applicants required to submit FAFSA. *Unit head:* Brian DiVita, Director, 616-632-2922, Fax: 616-732-4489. *Application contact:* Lynn Atkins-Rykert, Administrative Assistant, 616-632-2924, Fax: 616-732-4489, E-mail: atkinlyn@aquinas.edu.

Argosy University, Chicago, College of Business, Program in Organizational Leadership, Chicago, IL 60601. Offers Ed D.

Argosy University, Denver, College of Business, Denver, CO 80231. Offers accounting (DBA); corporate compliance (MBA); customized professional concentration (MBA, DBA); finance (MBA); fraud examination (MBA); global business sustainability (DBA); healthcare administration (MBA); information systems (DBA); information systems management (MBA); international business (MBA, DBA); management (MBA, MSM, DBA); marketing (MBA, DBA); organizational leadership (Ed D); public administration (MBA); sustainable management (MBA).

See Close-Up on page 185.

Argosy University, Hawai`i, College of Business, Program in Organizational Leadership, Honolulu, HI 96813. Offers Ed D.

Argosy University, Inland Empire, College of Business, San Bernardino, CA 92408. Offers accounting (DBA); corporate compliance (MBA); customized professional concentration (MBA, DBA); finance (MBA); fraud examination (MBA); global business sustainability (DBA); healthcare administration (MBA); information systems (DBA); information systems management (MBA); international business (MBA, DBA); management (MBA, MSM, DBA); marketing (MBA, DBA); organizational leadership (Ed D); public administration (MBA); sustainable management (MBA).

See Close-Up on page 189.

Argosy University, Los Angeles, College of Business, Santa Monica, CA 90045. Offers accounting (DBA); corporate compliance (MBA); customized professional concentration (MBA, DBA); finance (MBA); fraud examination (MBA); global business sustainability (DBA); healthcare administration (MBA); information systems (DBA); information systems management (MBA); international business (MBA, DBA); management (MBA, MSM, DBA); marketing (MBA, DBA); organizational leadership (Ed D); public administration (MBA); sustainable management (MBA).

See Close-Up on page 191.

Argosy University, Orange County, College of Business, Program in Organizational Leadership, Orange, CA 92868. Offers Ed D.

Argosy University, San Diego, College of Business, San Diego, CA 92108. Offers accounting (DBA); corporate compliance (MBA); customized professional concentration (MBA, DBA); finance (MBA); fraud examination (MBA); global business sustainability (DBA); information systems (DBA); information systems management (MBA); international business (MBA, DBA); management (MBA, MSM, DBA); marketing (MBA, DBA); organizational leadership (Ed D); public administration (MBA).

See Close-Up on page 201.

Argosy University, San Francisco Bay Area, College of Business, Alameda, CA 94501. Offers accounting (DBA); corporate compliance (MBA); customized professional concentration (MBA, DBA); finance (MBA); fraud examination (MBA); global business sustainability (DBA); healthcare administration (MBA); information systems (DBA); information systems management (MBA); international business (MBA, DBA); management (MBA, MSM, DBA); marketing (MBA, DBA); organizational leadership (Ed D); public administration (MBA); sustainable management (MBA).

See Close-Up on page 203.

Argosy University, Sarasota, College of Business, Sarasota, FL 34235. Offers accounting (DBA, Adv C); corporate compliance (MBA, DBA, Certificate); customized professional concentration (MBA, DBA); finance (MBA, Certificate); fraud examination (MBA, Certificate); global business sustainability (DBA, Adv C); healthcare administration (MBA, Certificate); information systems (DBA, Adv C, Certificate); information systems management (MBA); international business (MBA, DBA, Adv C, Certificate); management (MBA, MSM, DBA, Adv C, Certificate); marketing (MBA, DBA, Adv C, Certificate); organizational leadership (Ed D); public administration (MBA, Certificate); sustainable management (MBA, Certificate).

See Close-Up on page 205.

Argosy University, Seattle, College of Business, Seattle, WA 98121. Offers accounting (DBA); corporate compliance (MBA); customized professional concentration (MBA, DBA); finance (MBA); fraud examination (MBA); global business sustainability (DBA); healthcare administration (MBA); information systems (DBA); information systems management (MBA); international business (MBA, DBA); management (MBA, MSM, DBA); marketing (MBA, DBA); organizational leadership (Ed D); public administration (MBA); sustainable management (MBA).

See Close-Up on page 209.

Argosy University, Tampa, College of Business, Tampa, FL 33607. Offers accounting (DBA); corporate compliance (MBA); customized professional concentration (MBA, DBA); finance (MBA); fraud examination (MBA); global business sustainability (DBA); healthcare administration (MBA); information systems (DBA); information systems management (MBA); international business (MBA, DBA); management (MBA, MSM, DBA); marketing (MBA, DBA); organizational leadership (Ed D); public administration (MBA); sustainable management (MBA).

See Close-Up on page 211.

Argosy University, Twin Cities, College of Business, Eagan, MN 55121. Offers accounting (DBA); customized professional concentration (MBA, DBA); finance (MBA); fraud examination (MBA); global business sustainability (DBA); healthcare administration (MBA); information systems (DBA); information systems management (MBA); international business (MBA, DBA); management (MBA, MSM, DBA); marketing (MBA, DBA); organizational leadership (Ed D); public administration (MBA); sustainable management (MBA).

See Close-Up on page 213.

Argosy University, Washington DC, College of Business, Arlington, VA 22209. Offers accounting (DBA); customized professional concentration (MBA, DBA); finance (MBA); fraud examination (MBA); global business sustainability (DBA); healthcare administration (MBA); information systems (DBA); information systems management (MBA); international business (MBA, DBA, Certificate); management (MBA, MSM, DBA); marketing (MBA, DBA, Certificate); organizational leadership (Ed D); public administration (MBA); sustainable management (MBA).

See Close-Up on page 215.

Athabasca University, Centre for Integrated Studies, Athabasca, AB T9S 3A3, Canada. Offers adult education (MA); community studies (MA); cultural studies (MA); educational studies (MA); global change (MA); work, organization, and leadership (MA). Part-time and evening/weekend programs available. Postbaccalaureate distance learning degree programs offered (no on-campus study). *Degree requirements:* For master's, project. *Entrance requirements:* Additional exam requirements/recommendations for international students: Required—TOEFL (minimum score 560 paper-based; 220 computer-based). Electronic applications accepted. *Faculty research:* Women's history, literature and culture studies, sustainable development, labor and education.

Augsburg College, Program in Leadership, Minneapolis, MN 55454-1351. Offers MA. Part-time and evening/weekend programs available. *Degree requirements:* For master's, thesis or alternative. *Entrance requirements:* For master's, MAT, minimum GPA of 3.0. Additional exam requirements/recommendations for international students: Required—TOEFL (minimum score 600 paper-based; 250 computer-based). *Faculty research:* Soviet leaders, artificial intelligence, homelessness.

Avila University, Program in Organizational Development, Kansas City, MO 64145-1698. Offers MS. Part-time and evening/weekend programs available. Postbaccalaureate distance learning degree programs offered (no on-campus study). *Faculty:* 2 full-time (1 woman), 10 part-time/adjunct (7 women). *Students:* 74 full-time (58 women), 49 part-time (34 women); includes 33 minority (24 Black or African American, non-Hispanic/Latino; 2 American Indian or Alaska Native, non-Hispanic/Latino; 2 Asian, non-Hispanic/Latino; 4 Hispanic/Latino; 1 Native Hawaiian or other Pacific Islander, non-Hispanic/Latino), 11 international. Average age 35. 47 applicants, 64% accepted, 27 enrolled. In 2011, 24 master's awarded. *Degree requirements:* For master's, thesis optional. *Entrance requirements:* For master's, 2 letters of recommendation, minimum GPA of 3.25 during last 60 hours, resume. Additional exam requirements/recommendations for international students: Required—TOEFL. *Application deadline:* Applications are processed on a rolling basis. Application fee: $0. Electronic applications accepted. *Expenses: Tuition:* Full-time $8190; part-time $455 per credit hour. *Required fees:* $540. *Financial support:* In 2011–12, 69 students received support. Unspecified assistantships available. Support available to part-time students. Financial award applicants required to submit FAFSA. *Unit head:* Dr. Steve Iliff, Dean, 816-501-3737, Fax: 816-941-4650, E-mail: advantage@avila.edu. *Application contact:* Linda Dubar, School of Professional Studies, 816-501-3737, Fax: 816-941-4650, E-mail: advantage@avila.edu.

Azusa Pacific University, Center for Adult and Professional Studies, Azusa, CA 91702-7000. Offers leadership and organizational studies (MA). Postbaccalaureate distance learning degree programs offered.

Azusa Pacific University, School of Behavioral and Applied Sciences, Department of Higher Education and Organizational Leadership, Program in Organizational Leadership, Azusa, CA 91702-7000. Offers MA.

Azusa Pacific University, School of Business and Management, Azusa, CA 91702-7000. Offers business administration (MBA); diversity for strategic advantage (MA); entrepreneurship (MBA); finance (MBA); human and organizational development (MA); human resources and organizational development (MBA); human resources management (MA); international business (MBA); marketing (MBA); non-profit management (MA); organizational development and change (MA); performance improvement (MA); public administration (MA); strategic management (MBA). Part-time and evening/weekend programs available. *Degree requirements:* For master's, thesis (for some programs), final project. *Entrance requirements:* For master's, GMAT, minimum GPA of 3.0. Additional exam requirements/recommendations for international students: Required—TOEFL (minimum score 600 paper-based). *Expenses:* Contact institution. *Faculty research:* Gender issues, financial risk, leadership and ethics, marketing strategy.

Bellevue University, Graduate School, College of Professional Studies, Bellevue, NE 68005-3098. Offers instructional design and development (MS); justice administration and criminal management (MS); leadership (MA); organizational performance (MS); public administration (MPA); security management (MS).

Benedictine University, Graduate Programs, Program in Business Administration, Lisle, IL 60532-0900. Offers accounting (MBA); entrepreneurship and managing innovation (MBA); financial management (MBA); health administration (MBA); human resource management (MBA); information systems security (MBA); international business (MBA); management consulting (MBA); management information systems (MBA); marketing management (MBA); operations management and logistics (MBA); organizational leadership (MBA); MBA/MPH; MBA/MS. Part-time and evening/weekend programs available. Postbaccalaureate distance learning degree programs offered (minimal on-campus study). *Faculty:* 4 full-time (2 women), 24 part-time/adjunct (3 women). *Students:* 165 full-time (101 women), 766 part-time (381 women); includes 201 minority (118 Black or African American, non-Hispanic/Latino; 4 American Indian or Alaska Native, non-Hispanic/Latino; 37 Asian, non-Hispanic/Latino; 40 Hispanic/Latino; 2 Native Hawaiian or other Pacific Islander, non-Hispanic/Latino), 14 international. Average age 34. 313 applicants, 73% accepted, 166 enrolled. In 2011, 379 master's awarded. *Entrance requirements:* For master's, GMAT. Additional exam requirements/recommendations for international students: Required—TOEFL (minimum score 550 paper-based; 213 computer-based). *Application deadline:* For fall admission, 9/1 for domestic students; for winter admission, 12/1 for domestic students; for spring admission, 2/15 for domestic students. Applications are processed on a rolling basis. Application fee: $40. Electronic applications accepted. *Financial support:* Career-related internships or fieldwork and health care benefits available. Support available to part-time students. *Faculty research:* Strategic leadership in professional organizations, sociology of professions, organizational change, social identity theory, applications to change management. *Unit head:* Dr. Sharon Borowicz, Director, 630-829-6219, E-mail: sborowicz@ben.edu. *Application contact:* Kari Gibbons, Director, Admissions, 630-829-6200, Fax: 630-829-6584, E-mail: kgibbons@ben.edu.

Benedictine University, Graduate Programs, Program in Organizational Development, Lisle, IL 60532-0900. Offers PhD. Evening/weekend programs available. *Faculty:* 2 full-time (0 women), 2 part-time/adjunct (1 woman). *Students:* 35 full-time (23 women); includes 10 minority (8 Black or African American, non-Hispanic/Latino; 1 Asian, non-Hispanic/Latino; 1 Hispanic/Latino), 3 international. Average age 44. In 2011, 28 doctorates awarded. *Degree requirements:* For doctorate, thesis/dissertation. *Entrance requirements:* Additional exam requirements/recommendations for international students: Required—TOEFL (minimum score 550 paper-based). *Application deadline:* For fall admission, 9/1 for domestic students; for winter admission, 12/1 for domestic students; for spring admission, 2/15 for domestic students. Application fee: $40. Electronic applications accepted. *Financial support:* Career-related internships or fieldwork and health care benefits available. *Faculty research:* Change management, appreciative inquiry, innovation and organization design, global and international organization development, organization renewal. *Unit head:* Dr. Peter F. Sorensen, Director, 630-829-6220, Fax: 630-960-1126, E-mail: psorensen@ben.edu. *Application contact:* Kari Gibbons, Associate Vice President, Enrollment Center, 630-829-6200, Fax: 630-829-6584, E-mail: kgibbons@ben.edu.

Benedictine University at Springfield, Program in Business Administration, Springfield, IL 62702. Offers health administration (MBA); organizational leadership (MBA). Part-time and evening/weekend programs available. *Entrance requirements:* For master's, GMAT.

Benedictine University at Springfield, Program in Organization Development, Springfield, IL 62702. Offers PhD. Evening/weekend programs available. *Degree requirements:* For doctorate, thesis/dissertation.

Bethel University, Graduate School, St. Paul, MN 55112-6999. Offers autism spectrum disorders (Certificate); business administration (MBA); communication (MA); counseling psychology (MA); education (M Ed); educational leadership (Ed D); gerontology (MA, Certificate); international baccalaureate education (Certificate); K-12 education (MA); literacy education (MA); nursing (MA); nursing education (Certificate); nursing leadership (Certificate); organizational leadership (MA); postsecondary teaching (Certificate); special education (MA); teaching (MA). Part-time and evening/weekend programs available. Postbaccalaureate distance learning degree programs offered (minimal on-campus study). *Faculty:* 8 full-time (3 women), 98 part-time/adjunct (46 women). *Students:* 651 full-time (419 women), 312 part-time (212 women); includes 79 minority (35 Black or African American, non-Hispanic/Latino; 2 American Indian or Alaska Native, non-Hispanic/Latino; 19 Asian, non-Hispanic/Latino; 17 Hispanic/Latino; 6 Two or more races, non-Hispanic/Latino), 6 international. Average age 36. In 2011, 245 master's, 4 doctorates, 32 other advanced degrees awarded. *Degree requirements:* For master's, comprehensive exam (for some programs), thesis (for some programs); for doctorate, comprehensive exam, thesis/dissertation. *Entrance requirements:* Additional exam requirements/recommendations for international students: Required—TOEFL (minimum score 550 paper-based; 213 computer-based; 80 iBT). *Application deadline:* Applications are processed on a rolling basis. Electronic applications accepted. Tuition and fees vary according to course load, degree level and program. *Financial support:* Applicants required to submit FAFSA. *Unit head:* Dick Crombie, Vice-President/Dean, 651-635-8000, Fax: 651-635-8004, E-mail: gs@bethel.edu. *Application contact:* Paul Ives, Director of Admissions, 651-635-8000, Fax: 651-635-8004, E-mail: gs@bethel.edu. Web site: http://gs.bethel.edu/.

Bluffton University, Programs in Business, Bluffton, OH 45817. Offers business administration (MBA); organizational management (MA). Evening/weekend programs available. *Entrance requirements:* Additional exam requirements/recommendations for international students: Required—TOEFL. Electronic applications accepted.

Boston College, Carroll School of Management, Department of Organization Studies, Chestnut Hill, MA 02467-3800. Offers PhD. *Faculty:* 12 full-time (6 women), 11 part-time/adjunct (3 women). *Students:* 19 full-time (13 women); includes 3 minority (1 Black or African American, non-Hispanic/Latino; 2 Hispanic/Latino), 7 international. Average age 32. 86 applicants, 5% accepted, 3 enrolled. In 2011, 2 doctorates awarded. *Degree requirements:* For doctorate, comprehensive exam, thesis/dissertation, teaching experience. *Entrance requirements:* For doctorate, GMAT or GRE, letters of recommendation, resume, transcripts. Additional exam requirements/recommendations for international students: Required—TOEFL. *Application deadline:* For spring admission, 2/1 for domestic and international students. Application fee: $100. *Financial support:* In 2011–12, 19 fellowships, 19 research assistantships with full tuition reimbursements were awarded. Financial award application deadline: 3/1; financial award applicants required to submit FAFSA. *Faculty research:* Organizational transformation, mergers and acquisitions, managerial effectiveness, organizational change, organizational structure. *Unit head:* Dr. Jeffrey L. Ringuest, Associate Dean, Graduate Programs, 617-552-9100, Fax: 617-552-0514, E-mail: gsomdean@bc.edu. *Application contact:* Shelley A. Burt, Director of Graduate Enrollment, 617-552-3920, Fax: 617-552-8078, E-mail: bcmba@bc.edu. Web site: http://www.bc.edu/csom/.

Bowling Green State University, Graduate College, College of Business Administration, Program in Organization Development, Bowling Green, OH 43403. Offers MOD. Part-time and evening/weekend programs available. *Degree requirements:* For master's, thesis or alternative, internship. *Entrance requirements:* For master's, GMAT or GRE General Test. Additional exam requirements/recommendations for international students: Required—TOEFL. Electronic applications accepted. *Faculty research:* Charismatic leadership, self-managing work teams, knowledge workers, stress, effects of change processes.

Brandman University, School of Business and Professional Studies, Irvine, CA 92618. Offers business administration (MBA); human resources (MS); organizational leadership (MA); public administration (MPA).

Brenau University, Sydney O. Smith Graduate School, School of Business and Mass Communication, Gainesville, GA 30501. Offers accounting (MBA); business administration (MBA); healthcare management (MBA); organizational leadership (MS); project management (MBA). Part-time and evening/weekend programs available. Postbaccalaureate distance learning degree programs offered (no on-campus study). *Degree requirements:* For master's, comprehensive exam (for some programs). *Entrance requirements:* For master's, resume, minimum undergraduate GPA of 2.5. Additional exam requirements/recommendations for international students: Required—TOEFL (minimum score 500 paper-based; 173 computer-based; 61 iBT); Recommended—IELTS (minimum score 5). Electronic applications accepted. *Expenses:* Contact institution.

Briercrest Seminary, Graduate Programs, Program in Leadership and Management, Caronport, SK S0H 0S0, Canada. Offers organizational leadership (MA). Part-time programs available. *Degree requirements:* For master's, comprehensive exam, thesis optional. *Entrance requirements:* Additional exam requirements/recommendations for international students: Required—TOEFL (minimum score 550 paper-based; 213 computer-based).

Cabrini College, Graduate and Professional Studies, Radnor, PA 19087-3698. Offers education (M Ed); organization leadership (MS). Part-time and evening/weekend programs available. *Faculty:* 5 full-time (all women), 134 part-time/adjunct (76 women). *Students:* 157 full-time (111 women), 1,768 part-time (1,357 women); includes 247 minority (169 Black or African American, non-Hispanic/Latino; 1 American Indian or Alaska Native, non-Hispanic/Latino; 25 Asian, non-Hispanic/Latino; 44 Hispanic/Latino; 2 Native Hawaiian or other Pacific Islander, non-Hispanic/Latino; 6 Two or more races, non-Hispanic/Latino), 3 international. Average age 34. 509 applicants, 80% accepted, 405 enrolled. In 2011, 727 master's awarded. *Degree requirements:* For master's, thesis optional. *Entrance requirements:* For master's, GRE and/or MAT (in some cases), letter of recommendation, minimum GPA of 2.5. *Application deadline:* For fall admission, 7/29 priority date for domestic students, 7/29 for international students; for spring admission, 12/9 for domestic and international students. Applications are processed on a rolling basis. Application fee: $50. Electronic applications accepted. *Expenses: Tuition:* Part-time $595 per credit. *Financial support:* Career-related internships or fieldwork and unspecified assistantships available. Support available to part-time students. Financial award applicants required to submit FAFSA. *Unit head:* Dr. Martha Combs, Dean of Graduate and Professional Studies, 610-902-8502, Fax: 610-902-8522, E-mail: martha.w.combs@cabrini.edu. *Application contact:* Bruce D. Bryde, Director of Enrollment and Recruiting, 610-902-8291, Fax: 610-902-8522, E-mail: bruce.d.bryde@cabrini.edu. Web site: http://www.cabrini.edu/GPS.

Cairn University, School of Business and Leadership, Langhorne, PA 19047-2990. Offers organizational leadership (MSOL). Part-time and evening/weekend programs available. *Faculty:* 2 full-time (0 women), 1 part-time/adjunct (0 women). *Students:* 3 full-time (2 women), 18 part-time (9 women); includes 9 minority (7 Black or African American, non-Hispanic/Latino; 1 Asian, non-Hispanic/Latino; 1 Hispanic/Latino). Average age 37. 15 applicants, 33% accepted, 3 enrolled. In 2011, 8 master's awarded. *Entrance requirements:* Additional exam requirements/recommendations for international students: Required—TOEFL (minimum score 550 paper-based; 213 computer-based). *Application deadline:* Applications are processed on a rolling basis. Application fee: $25. Electronic applications accepted. *Expenses: Tuition:* Part-time $475 per credit hour. Tuition and fees vary according to program. *Financial support:* Scholarships/grants available. Support available to part-time students. Financial award applicants required to submit FAFSA. *Unit head:* Dr. William Bowles, Chair, Graduate Programs, 215-702-4871, Fax: 215-702-4248, E-mail: wbowles@pbu.edu. *Application contact:* Timothy Nessler, Assistant Director, Graduate Admissions, 800-572-2472, Fax: 215-702-4248, E-mail: tnessler@pbu.edu. Web site: http://pbu.edu/academics/business/index.cfm.

California Coast University, School of Education, Santa Ana, CA 92701. Offers administration (M Ed); curriculum and instruction (M Ed); educational administration (Ed D); educational psychology (Ed D); organizational leadership (Ed D). Postbaccalaureate distance learning degree programs offered (no on-campus study).

California College of the Arts, Graduate Programs, Program in Design Strategy, San Francisco, CA 94107. Offers MBA. *Accreditation:* NASAD. *Degree requirements:* For master's, thesis. *Entrance requirements:* Additional exam requirements/recommendations for international students: Required—TOEFL (minimum score 600 paper-based; 250 computer-based; 100 iBT).

California Intercontinental University, School of Business, Diamond Bar, CA 91765. Offers banking and finance (MBA); entrepreneurship and business management (DBA); global business leadership (DBA); international management and marketing (MBA); organizational management and human resource management (MBA).

California State University, East Bay, Office of Academic Programs and Graduate Studies, College of Business and Economics, Business Administration, MBA Program, Hayward, CA 94542-3000. Offers entrepreneurship (MBA); finance (MBA); global innovators (MBA); human resources and organizational behavior (MBA); information technology management (MBA); marketing management (MBA); operations and supply chain management (MBA); strategy and international business (MBA). Part-time and evening/weekend programs available. *Faculty:* 11 full-time (3 women). *Students:* 80 full-time (42 women), 141 part-time (61 women); includes 70 minority (5 Black or African American, non-Hispanic/Latino; 46 Asian, non-Hispanic/Latino; 13 Hispanic/Latino; 1 Native Hawaiian or other Pacific Islander, non-Hispanic/Latino; 5 Two or more races, non-Hispanic/Latino), 69 international. Average age 31. 371 applicants, 36% accepted, 79 enrolled. In 2011, 254 master's awarded. *Degree requirements:* For master's, comprehensive exam or thesis. *Entrance requirements:* For master's, GMAT (minimum 20th percentile verbal and quantitative section), bachelor's degree, minimum GPA of 2.75. Additional exam requirements/recommendations for international students: Required—TOEFL (minimum score 550 paper-based; 213 computer-based; 79 iBT). *Application deadline:* For fall admission, 6/30 for domestic and international students. Applications are processed on a rolling basis. Application fee: $55. Electronic applications accepted. *Expenses:* Contact institution. *Financial support:* Career-related internships or fieldwork, Federal Work-Study, institutionally sponsored loans, and scholarships/grants available. Support available to part-time students. Financial award application deadline: 3/2; financial award applicants required to submit FAFSA. *Unit head:* Dr. Terri Swartz, Dean, 510-885-3291, Fax: 510-885-4884, E-mail: terri.swartz@csueastbay.edu. *Application contact:* Prof. Joanna Lee, Director, CBE Graduate Programs, 510-885-3517, Fax: 510-885-2176, E-mail: joanna.lee@csueastbay.edu. Web site: http://www20.csueastbay.edu/ecat/graduate-chapters/g-buad.html#mba.

Cambridge College, School of Management, Cambridge, MA 02138-5304. Offers business negotiation and conflict resolution (M Mgt); general business (M Mgt); health care informatics (M Mgt); health care management (M Mgt); leadership in human and organizational dynamics (M Mgt); non-profit and public organization management (M Mgt); small business development (M Mgt); technology management (M Mgt). Part-time and evening/weekend programs available. *Degree requirements:* For master's, thesis, seminars. *Entrance requirements:* For master's, resume, 2 professional references. Additional exam requirements/recommendations for international students: Required—TOEFL (minimum score 550 paper-based; 213 computer-based; 79 iBT); Recommended—IELTS (minimum score 6). Electronic applications accepted. *Expenses:* Contact institution. *Faculty research:* Negotiation, mediation and conflict resolution; leadership; management of diverse organizations; case studies and simulation methodologies for management education, digital as a second language: social networking for digital immigrants, non-profit and public management.

Campbellsville University, School of Business and Economics, Campbellsville, KY 42718-2799. Offers business administration (MBA); business organizational management (MAOL). Part-time and evening/weekend programs available. *Students:* 74 full-time (39 women), 34 part-time (13 women); includes 6 minority (4 Black or African American, non-Hispanic/Latino; 2 Asian, non-Hispanic/Latino), 25 international. Average age 28. In 2011, 22 master's awarded. *Entrance requirements:* For master's, GRE or GMAT. Additional exam requirements/recommendations for international students: Required—TOEFL (minimum score 550 paper-based; 213 computer-based). *Application deadline:* For fall admission, 9/14 priority date for domestic students, 9/14 for international students; for winter admission, 1/18 priority date for domestic students, 1/18 for international students; for spring admission, 4/4 priority date for domestic students, 4/4 for international students. Applications are processed on a rolling basis. Application fee: $25. Electronic applications accepted. *Expenses:* Contact institution. *Financial support:* In 2011–12, 11 students received support. Tuition waivers (full) and unspecified assistantships available. Financial award application deadline: 6/1; financial award applicants required to submit FAFSA. *Unit head:* Dr. Patricia H. Cowherd, Dean, 270-789-5553, Fax: 270-789-5066, E-mail: phcowherd@campbellsville.edu. *Application contact:* Monica Bamwine, Assistant Director of Admissions, 270-789-5221, Fax: 270-789-5071, E-mail: mkbamwine@campbellsville.edu. Web site: http://www.campbellsville.edu.

Capella University, Harold Abel School of Psychology, Minneapolis, MN 55402. Offers child and adolescent development (MS); clinical psychology (MS, Psy D); counseling psychology (MS); educational psychology (MS, PhD); evaluation, research, and measurement (MS); general psychology (MS, PhD); industrial/organizational psychology (MS, PhD); leadership coaching psychology (MS); organizational leader development (MS); school psychology (MS); sport psychology (MS). Part-time and evening/weekend programs available. Postbaccalaureate distance learning degree programs offered (minimal on-campus study). Terminal master's awarded for partial completion of doctoral program. *Degree requirements:* For master's, thesis optional, project; for doctorate, thesis/dissertation. *Entrance requirements:* For degree, master's degree in school psychology. Additional exam requirements/recommendations for international students: Required—TOEFL (minimum score 550 paper-based; 213 computer-based), TWE (minimum score 4); Recommended—IELTS. Electronic applications accepted.

Capella University, School of Business and Technology, Minneapolis, MN 55402. Offers accounting (MBA), including system design and programming; business (Certificate), including human resource management (MS, PhD, Certificate), information technology management (MS, PhD, Certificate), leadership (MBA, MS, PhD, Certificate); finance (MBA); general business (MBA); health care management (MBA); information technology (MS, Certificate), including general information technology (MS), information security, network architecture and design (MS), professional projects management (Certificate), project management and leadership (MS), system design and development (MS),); information technology management (MBA); marketing (MBA); organization and management (MBA, MS, PhD), including general business (PhD), general organization and management (MBA, MS), human resource management (MS, PhD, Certificate), information technology management (MS, PhD, Certificate), leadership (MBA, MS, PhD, Certificate); project management (MBA). Part-time and evening/weekend programs available. Postbaccalaureate distance learning degree programs offered (minimal on-campus study). Terminal master's awarded for partial completion of doctoral program. *Degree requirements:* For master's, thesis optional, integrative project; for doctorate, comprehensive exam, thesis/dissertation. *Entrance requirements:* Additional exam requirements/recommendations for international students: Required—TOEFL (minimum score 550 paper-based; 213 computer-based), TWE (minimum score 4). Electronic applications accepted. *Faculty research:* Business policies: strategic, corporate, and financial management; interplay of technological, organizational and social change.

Carlos Albizu University, Miami Campus, Graduate Programs, Miami, FL 33172-2209. Offers clinical psychology (Psy D); entrepreneurship (MBA); exceptional student education (MS); industrial/organizational psychology (MS); marriage and family therapy (MS); mental health counseling (MS); nonprofit management (MBA); organizational management (MBA); psychology (MS); school counseling (MS); teaching English as a second language (MS). *Accreditation:* APA. Part-time and evening/weekend programs available. *Faculty:* 19 full-time (12 women), 53 part-time/adjunct (27 women). *Students:* 524 full-time (431 women), 216 part-time (169 women); includes 563 minority (50 Black or African American, non-Hispanic/Latino; 1 American Indian or Alaska Native, non-Hispanic/Latino; 4 Asian, non-Hispanic/Latino; 492 Hispanic/Latino; 16 Native Hawaiian or other Pacific Islander, non-Hispanic/Latino), 17 international. Average age 31. 174 applicants, 67% accepted, 116 enrolled. In 2011, 157 master's, 21 doctorates awarded. Terminal master's awarded for partial completion of doctoral program. *Degree requirements:* For master's, one foreign language, comprehensive exam, integrative project (MBA), research project (exceptional student education, teaching English as a second language); for doctorate, one foreign language, comprehensive exam, internship, project. *Entrance requirements:* For master's, 3 letters of recommendation, interview, minimum GPA of 3.0, resume, statement of purpose, official transcripts; for doctorate, 3 letters of recommendation, minimum GPA of 3.0, resume, interview, statement of purpose, official transcripts. Additional exam requirements/recommendations for international students: Required—Michigan Test of English Language Proficiency. *Application deadline:* For fall admission, 4/1 priority date for domestic students, 5/1 for international students; for spring admission, 11/1 priority date for domestic students, 9/1 for international students. Applications are processed on a rolling basis. Application fee: $50. Electronic applications accepted. *Expenses: Tuition:* Full-time $9360; part-time $520 per credit. *Required fees:* $298 per term. Tuition and fees vary according to course load, degree level and program. *Financial support:* In 2011–12, 106 students received support. Federal Work-Study, scholarships/grants, and tuition discounts available. Financial award application deadline: 6/1; financial award applicants required to submit FAFSA. *Faculty research:* Psychotherapy, forensic psychology, neuropsychology, marketing strategy, entrepreneurship, special education. *Unit head:* Dr. Carmen S. Roca, Chancellor, 305-593-1223 Ext. 120, Fax: 305-629-8052, E-mail: croca@albizu.edu. *Application contact:* Vanessa Almendarez, Administrative Assistant, 305-593-1223 Ext. 137, Fax: 305-593-1854, E-mail: valmendarez@albizu.edu.

Carlow University, School for Social Change, Pittsburgh, PA 15213-3165. Offers counseling psychology (Psy D); professional counseling (MS), including professional counseling, professional counseling/school counseling. *Accreditation:* APA. Part-time and evening/weekend programs available. *Students:* 204 full-time (177 women), 26 part-time (23 women); includes 35 minority (29 Black or African American, non-Hispanic/Latino; 1 Asian, non-Hispanic/Latino; 4 Hispanic/Latino; 1 Two or more races, non-Hispanic/Latino). Average age 30. 221 applicants, 45% accepted, 64 enrolled. In 2011, 46 master's, 8 doctorates awarded. *Degree requirements:* For doctorate, thesis/dissertation, internship. *Entrance requirements:* For master's, personal essay; resume or curriculum vitae; three recommendations; official transcripts; interview; minimum undergraduate GPA of 3.0; undergraduate courses in statistics, abnormal psychology, and personality theory; undergraduate work or work experience in the helping professions; for doctorate, GRE, resume or curriculum vitae; personal essay; reflective essay; official transcripts from all previous undergraduate and graduate institutions; three letters of recommendation; master's degree in closely-related field. Additional exam requirements/recommendations for international students: Required—TOEFL (minimum score 550 paper-based; 213 computer-based). *Application deadline:* For fall admission, 6/15 priority date for domestic students, 6/15 for international students; for spring admission, 11/15 priority date for domestic students, 11/15 for international students. Applications are processed on a rolling basis. Application fee: $20. Electronic applications accepted. Application fee is waived when completed online. *Expenses: Tuition:* Full-time $10,290; part-time $686 per credit. Tuition and fees vary according to course load, degree level and program. *Financial support:* Federal Work-Study available. Financial award application deadline: 4/1; financial award applicants required to submit FAFSA. *Unit head:* Dr. Robert A. Reed, Chair, Department of Psychology and Counseling, 412-575-6349, E-mail: reedra@carlow.edu. *Application contact:* Dr. Kathleen A. Chrisman, Associate Director, Graduate Admissions, 412-578-8812, Fax: 412-578-6321, E-mail: kachrisman@carlow.edu. Web site: http://www.carlow.edu.

Charleston Southern University, Program in Business, Charleston, SC 29423-8087. Offers accounting (MBA); finance (MBA); health care administration (MBA); information systems (MBA); organizational development (MBA). Part-time and evening/weekend programs available. *Degree requirements:* For master's, thesis optional. *Entrance requirements:* For master's, GMAT. Additional exam requirements/recommendations for international students: Required—TOEFL (minimum score 550 paper-based; 213 computer-based; 79 iBT).

City University of Seattle, Graduate Division, Albright School of Education, Bellevue, WA 98005. Offers administrator certification (Certificate); curriculum and instruction (M Ed); educational leadership (Ed D); elementary education (MIT); guidance and counseling (M Ed); higher education leadership (Ed D); leadership (M Ed); leadership and school counseling (M Ed); organizational leadership (Ed D); reading and literacy (M Ed); special education (MIT); superintendent certification (Certificate). Part-time and evening/weekend programs available. Postbaccalaureate distance learning degree programs offered (no on-campus study). *Faculty:* 23 full-time (15 women), 123 part-time/adjunct (82 women). *Students:* 353 full-time (263 women), 75 part-time (50 women); includes 40 minority (12 Black or African American, non-Hispanic/Latino; 5 American Indian or Alaska Native, non-Hispanic/Latino; 7 Asian, non-Hispanic/Latino; 8 Hispanic/Latino; 5 Native Hawaiian or other Pacific Islander, non-Hispanic/Latino; 3 Two or more races, non-Hispanic/Latino). Average age 36. 129 applicants, 98% accepted, 126 enrolled. In 2011, 351 master's, 30 Certificates awarded. *Degree requirements:* For master's, comprehensive exam (for some programs), thesis (for some programs); for doctorate, comprehensive exam, thesis/dissertation. *Entrance requirements:* Additional exam requirements/recommendations for international students: Required—TOEFL (minimum score 567 paper-based; 227 computer-based; 87 iBT); Recommended—IELTS. *Application deadline:* For fall admission, 9/1 for international students; for winter admission, 12/1 for international students; for spring admission, 3/1 for international students. Applications are processed on a rolling basis. Application fee: $50. Electronic applications accepted. *Expenses:* Contact institution. *Financial support:* In 2011–12, 40 students received support. Federal Work-Study and scholarships/grants available. Support available to part-time students. Financial award applicants required to submit FAFSA. *Unit head:* Craig Schieber, Dean, 425-637-101 Ext. 5460, Fax: 425-709-5363, E-mail: schieber@cityu.edu. *Application contact:* Alysa Borelli, 888-422-4898, Fax: 425-709-5363, E-mail: info@cityu.edu. Web site: http://www.cityu.edu/programs/soe/index.aspx.

City University of Seattle, Graduate Division, School of Management, Bellevue, WA 98005. Offers accounting (Certificate); change leadership (MBA, Certificate); computer systems (MS); finance (Certificate); financial management (MBA); general management (MBA); general management-Europe (MBA); global marketing (MBA); human resources management (Certificate); individualized study (MBA); information security (MS); information systems (MBA); leadership (MA); marketing (MBA, Certificate); project management (MBA, MS, Certificate); sustainable business (Certificate); technology management (MBA, Certificate). Part-time and evening/weekend programs available. Postbaccalaureate distance learning degree programs offered (no on-campus study). *Faculty:* 6 full-time (2 women), 95 part-time/adjunct (33 women). *Students:* 397 full-time (193 women), 283 part-time (137 women); includes 127 minority (67 Black or African American, non-Hispanic/Latino; 5 American Indian or Alaska Native, non-Hispanic/Latino; 33 Asian, non-Hispanic/Latino; 15 Hispanic/Latino; 1 Native Hawaiian or other Pacific Islander, non-Hispanic/Latino; 6 Two or more races, non-Hispanic/Latino), 117 international. Average age 36. 151 applicants, 100% accepted, 151 enrolled. In 2011, 369 master's, 32 other advanced degrees awarded. *Degree requirements:* For master's, comprehensive exam (for some programs), thesis (for some programs). *Entrance requirements:* Additional exam requirements/recommendations for international students: Required—TOEFL (minimum score 567 paper-based; 227 computer-based; 87 iBT); Recommended—IELTS. *Application deadline:* For fall admission, 9/1 for international students; for winter admission, 12/1 for international students; for spring admission, 3/1 for international students. Applications are processed on a rolling basis. Application fee: $50. Electronic applications accepted. *Financial support:* Federal Work-Study and scholarships/grants available. Support available to part-time students. Financial award applicants required to submit FAFSA. *Unit head:* Dr. Kurt Kirstein, Dean, 425-637-1010 Ext. 5456, Fax: 425-709-5363, E-mail: kdkirstein@cityu.edu. *Application contact:* Alysa Borelli, Director, Recruiting, 888-422-4898, Fax: 425-709-5363, E-mail: info@cityu.edu. Web site: http://www.cityu.edu/programs/som/index.aspx.

Cleary University, Online Program in Business Administration, Ann Arbor, MI 48105-2659. Offers financial planning (MBA); financial planning (Graduate Certificate); green business strategy (MBA, Graduate Certificate); management (MBA); nonprofit management (MBA, Graduate Certificate); organizational leadership (MBA); public accounting (MBA). Part-time and evening/weekend programs available. Postbaccalaureate distance learning degree programs offered (no on-campus study). *Degree requirements:* For master's, thesis. *Entrance requirements:* For master's, bachelor's degree; minimum GPA of 2.5; professional resume indicating minimum 2 years management or related experience; undergraduate degree from an accredited college or university with at least 18 quarter hours (or 12 semester hours) of accounting study (for MBA in accounting). Additional exam requirements/recommendations for international students: Required—TOEFL (minimum score 550 paper-based; 213 computer-based; 79 iBT), Michigan English Language Assessment Battery (minimum score: 75). Electronic applications accepted.

Organizational Management

Cleveland State University, College of Graduate Studies, College of Education and Human Services, Department of Counseling, Administration, Supervision and Adult Learning (CASAL), Cleveland, OH 44115. Offers accelerated degree in adult learning and development (M Ed); adult learning and development (M Ed); chemical dependency counseling (Certificate); clinical mental health counseling (M Ed); early childhood mental health counseling (Certificate); educational administration and supervision (M Ed); organizational leadership (M Ed); school administration (Ed S); school counseling (M Ed). *Accreditation:* ACA (one or more programs are accredited). Part-time and evening/weekend programs available. *Faculty:* 15 full-time (8 women), 19 part-time/adjunct (10 women). *Students:* 58 full-time (49 women), 273 part-time (221 women); includes 121 minority (106 Black or African American, non-Hispanic/Latino; 2 Asian, non-Hispanic/Latino; 9 Hispanic/Latino; 4 Two or more races, non-Hispanic/Latino), 1 international. Average age 35. 192 applicants, 86% accepted, 105 enrolled. In 2011, 151 master's, 23 Certificates awarded. *Degree requirements:* For master's, comprehensive exam (for some programs), thesis optional, internship. *Entrance requirements:* For master's, GRE General Test or MAT, letter of recommendation and minimum GPA of 2.75 (for counseling); 2 letters of recommendation and interviews (for organizational leadership). Additional exam requirements/recommendations for international students: Required—TOEFL (minimum score 525 paper-based; 197 computer-based), IELTS (minimum score 6). *Application deadline:* For fall admission, 6/21 for domestic students, 5/15 for international students; for spring admission, 8/31 for domestic students, 11/1 for international students. Application fee: $30. Electronic applications accepted. *Expenses:* Tuition, state resident: full-time $6416; part-time $494 per credit hour. Tuition, nonresident: full-time $12,074; part-time $929 per credit hour. *Financial support:* In 2011–12, 19 students received support, including 10 research assistantships with full and partial tuition reimbursements available (averaging $11,882 per year), 5 teaching assistantships with full and partial tuition reimbursements available (averaging $11,882 per year); scholarships/grants and unspecified assistantships also available. Support available to part-time students. *Faculty research:* Education law, career development, bullying, psychopharmacology, counseling and spirituality. *Total annual research expenditures:* $225,821. *Unit head:* Dr. Ann L. Bauer, Chairperson, 216-687-4582, Fax: 216-687-5378, E-mail: a.l.bauer@csuohio.edu. *Application contact:* Deborah L. Brown, Interim Assistant Director, Graduate Admissions, 216-523-7572, Fax: 216-687-5400, E-mail: d.l.brown@csuohio.edu. Web site: http://www.csuohio.edu/cehs/departments/casal/.

College of Mount St. Joseph, Master of Science in Organizational Leadership Program, Cincinnati, OH 45233-1670. Offers MS. Part-time and evening/weekend programs available. *Faculty:* 8 full-time (2 women). *Students:* 1 (woman) full-time, 78 part-time (53 women); includes 11 minority (9 Black or African American, non-Hispanic/Latino; 1 American Indian or Alaska Native, non-Hispanic/Latino; 1 Asian, non-Hispanic/Latino). Average age 42. 47 applicants, 64% accepted, 10 enrolled. In 2011, 11 master's awarded. *Degree requirements:* For master's, integrative project. *Entrance requirements:* For master's, minimum GPA of 3.0, interview, 3 years of work experience, 3 letters of reference, resume, letter of intent, essay. Additional exam requirements/recommendations for international students: Required—TOEFL (minimum score 560 paper-based; 220 computer-based; 83 iBT). *Application deadline:* Applications are processed on a rolling basis. Application fee: $50. Electronic applications accepted. *Expenses:* Contact institution. *Financial support:* In 2011–12, 2 students received support. Application deadline: 6/1; applicants required to submit FAFSA. *Faculty research:* Gender and cultural effects on management education, group identity formation, leadership skill development, methods for improving instructional effectiveness, technology-based productivity improvement. *Unit head:* Daryl Smith, Chair, 513-244-4920, Fax: 513-244-4270, E-mail: daryl_smith@mail.msj.edu. *Application contact:* Marilyn Hoskins, Assistant Director of Graduate Recruitment, 513-244-4723, Fax: 513-244-4629, E-mail: marilyn_hoskins@mail.msj.edu. Web site: http://www.msj.edu/view/academics/graduate-programs/organizational-leadership.aspx.

College of Saint Mary, Program in Organizational Leadership, Omaha, NE 68106. Offers MOL. Part-time and evening/weekend programs available. *Entrance requirements:* For master's, resume. Electronic applications accepted.

Colorado State University, Graduate School, College of Business, Program in Management Practice, Fort Collins, CO 80523-1201. Offers MMP. *Students:* 32 full-time (17 women), 12 part-time (8 women); includes 5 minority (1 Black or African American, non-Hispanic/Latino; 4 Hispanic/Latino), 7 international. Average age 27. 40 applicants, 90% accepted, 27 enrolled. In 2011, 37 master's awarded. *Entrance requirements:* For master's, GMAT or GRE, minimum cumulative GPA of 3.0, current resume, 3 recommendations. Additional exam requirements/recommendations for international students: Required—TOEFL (minimum score 565 paper-based; 227 computer-based; 86 iBT) or IELTS (minimum score 6.5). *Application deadline:* For fall admission, 7/15 for domestic students, 6/1 for international students; for spring admission, 12/5 for domestic students, 11/1 for international students. Applications are processed on a rolling basis. Application fee: $50. Electronic applications accepted. *Expenses:* Tuition, state resident: full-time $7992. Tuition, nonresident: full-time $19,592. *Required fees:* $1735; $58 per credit. *Financial support:* Fellowships with partial tuition reimbursements, research assistantships with partial tuition reimbursements, teaching assistantships, and unspecified assistantships available. Financial award application deadline: 4/1; financial award applicants required to submit FAFSA. *Faculty research:* Ethical behavior in the marketplace, sustainable entrepreneurship, corporate entrepreneurship, logistics in market orientation, organizational communication. *Total annual research expenditures:* $49,411. *Unit head:* Dr. John Hoxmeier, Associate Dean, 970-491-2142, Fax: 970-491-0269, E-mail: john.hoxmeier@colostate.edu. *Application contact:* Tonja Rosales, Admissions Coordinator, 970-491-4661, Fax: 970-491-3481, E-mail: tonja.rosales@colostate.edu. Web site: http://www.biz.colostate.edu/mmp/.

Colorado Technical University Sioux Falls, Programs in Business Administration and Management, Sioux Falls, SD 57108. Offers business administration (MBA); business management (MSM); health science management (MSM); human resources management (MSM); information technology (MSM); organizational leadership (MSM); project management (MBA); technology management (MBA). Evening/weekend programs available. *Degree requirements:* For master's, thesis optional. *Entrance requirements:* For master's, minimum 2 years work experience, resume.

Columbus State University, Graduate Studies, D. Abbott Turner College of Business and Computer Science, Columbus, GA 31907-5645. Offers applied computer science (MS); business administration (MBA); modeling and simulation (Certificate); organizational leadership (MS). *Accreditation:* AACSB. *Entrance requirements:* For master's, GMAT, GRE. Additional exam requirements/recommendations for international students: Required—TOEFL (minimum score 550 paper-based; 213 computer-based; 79 iBT). Electronic applications accepted.

Concordia University, School of Graduate Studies, Faculty of Arts and Science, Department of Applied Human Sciences, Montréal, QC H3G 1M8, Canada. Offers human systems intervention (MA). *Degree requirements:* For master's, 2 week residential laboratory. *Entrance requirements:* For master's, 1 week residential laboratory, 2 full years of work experience. *Faculty research:* Health promotion, adult learning and transitions, applications of group development and small group leadership, adolescent development, generational issues in immigrant families.

Concordia University Ann Arbor, Graduate Programs, Ann Arbor, MI 48105-2797. Offers curriculum and instruction (MS); educational leadership (MS); organizational leadership and administration (MS). Part-time and evening/weekend programs available. *Faculty:* 3 full-time (2 women), 24 part-time/adjunct (10 women). *Students:* 123 full-time (79 women), 46 part-time (24 women); includes 26 minority (19 Black or African American, non-Hispanic/Latino; 2 American Indian or Alaska Native, non-Hispanic/Latino; 3 Asian, non-Hispanic/Latino; 1 Hispanic/Latino; 1 Two or more races, non-Hispanic/Latino), 1 international. Average age 37. 45 applicants, 84% accepted, 37 enrolled. In 2011, 74 degrees awarded. *Degree requirements:* For master's, thesis. *Entrance requirements:* Additional exam requirements/recommendations for international students: Required—TOEFL (minimum score 80 iBT); Recommended—IELTS (minimum score 6.5). *Application deadline:* For fall admission, 7/1 priority date for domestic students, 6/1 for international students; for spring admission, 8/26 priority date for domestic students, 7/26 for international students. Applications are processed on a rolling basis. Electronic applications accepted. *Financial support:* Applicants required to submit FAFSA. *Unit head:* Dr. Ross Stueber, Vice President of Academics, 734-995-7586, Fax: 734-995-7448, E-mail: stuebr@cuaa.edu. *Application contact:* Caroline Harris, Graduate Admission Coordinator, 734-995-7521, Fax: 734-995-7530, E-mail: harrica@cuaa.edu. Web site: http://www.cuaa.edu/graduate.

Concordia University, St. Paul, College of Business and Organizational Leadership, St. Paul, MN 55104-5494. Offers business and organizational leadership (MBA); criminal justice leadership (MA); health care management (MBA); human resources management (MA); leadership and management (MA). *Accreditation:* ACBSP. Evening/weekend programs available. Postbaccalaureate distance learning degree programs offered (minimal on-campus study). *Faculty:* 16 full-time (6 women), 31 part-time/adjunct (12 women). *Students:* 417 full-time (230 women), 11 part-time (5 women); includes 83 minority (40 Black or African American, non-Hispanic/Latino; 2 American Indian or Alaska Native, non-Hispanic/Latino; 25 Asian, non-Hispanic/Latino; 5 Hispanic/Latino; 1 Native Hawaiian or other Pacific Islander, non-Hispanic/Latino; 10 Two or more races, non-Hispanic/Latino), 5 international. Average age 35. 316 applicants, 74% accepted, 198 enrolled. In 2011, 204 master's awarded. *Application deadline:* Applications are processed on a rolling basis. Application fee: $50. Electronic applications accepted. *Expenses: Tuition:* Full-time $8100; part-time $435 per credit. Tuition and fees vary according to program. *Financial support:* Applicants required to submit FAFSA. *Unit head:* Dr. Bruce Corrie, Dean, 651-641-8226, Fax: 651-641-8807, E-mail: corrie@csp.edu. *Application contact:* Kimberly Craig, Director of Graduate and Cohort Admission, 651-603-6223, Fax: 651-603-6320, E-mail: craig@csp.edu.

Dominican University, School of Professional and Continuing Studies, River Forest, IL 60305-1099. Offers conflict resolution (MA); family ministry (MA). Part-time and evening/weekend programs available. Postbaccalaureate distance learning degree programs offered. *Faculty:* 5 part-time/adjunct (1 woman). *Students:* 4 full-time (all women), 14 part-time (10 women); includes 6 minority (5 Black or African American, non-Hispanic/Latino; 1 Hispanic/Latino). Average age 42. In 2011, 28 master's awarded. *Entrance requirements:* Additional exam requirements/recommendations for international students: Required—TOEFL (minimum score 550 paper-based; 213 computer-based; 79 iBT). *Application deadline:* Applications are processed on a rolling basis. Application fee: $25. *Expenses:* Contact institution. *Unit head:* Dr. Matthew Hlinak, Assistant Provost for Continuing Studies and Special Initiatives, 708-714-9056, E-mail: mhlinak@dom.edu. *Application contact:* Monica Halloran, Associate Director of Academic Advising, 708-714-9007, Fax: 708-714-9126, E-mail: mhallora@dom.edu. Web site: http://www.dom.edu/spcs.

Duquesne University, School of Leadership and Professional Advancement, Pittsburgh, PA 15282-0001. Offers leadership (MS), including business ethics, community leadership, global leadership, information technology, leadership, liberal studies, professional administration, sports leadership. Part-time and evening/weekend programs available. Postbaccalaureate distance learning degree programs offered (no on-campus study). *Faculty:* 1 full-time (0 women), 88 part-time/adjunct (39 women). *Students:* 311 full-time (134 women), 151 part-time (68 women); includes 109 minority (69 Black or African American, non-Hispanic/Latino; 3 American Indian or Alaska Native, non-Hispanic/Latino; 11 Asian, non-Hispanic/Latino; 19 Hispanic/Latino; 1 Native Hawaiian or other Pacific Islander, non-Hispanic/Latino; 6 Two or more races, non-Hispanic/Latino), 9 international. Average age 35. 172 applicants, 73% accepted, 107 enrolled. In 2011, 67 degrees awarded. *Degree requirements:* For master's, capstone course. *Entrance requirements:* For master's, professional work experience, 500-word essay, resume, interview. Additional exam requirements/recommendations for international students: Required—TOEFL (minimum score 80 iBT). *Application deadline:* Applications are processed on a rolling basis. Application fee: $0. Electronic applications accepted. Application fee is waived when completed online. *Expenses: Tuition:* Full-time $16,596; part-time $922 per credit. *Required fees:* $1584; $88 per credit. Tuition and fees vary according to program. *Financial support:* Applicants required to submit FAFSA. *Unit head:* Dr. Dorothy Bassett, Dean, 412-396-2141, Fax: 412-396-4711, E-mail: bassettd@duq.edu. *Application contact:* Marianne Leister, Director of Student Services, 412-396-4933, Fax: 412-396-5072, E-mail: leister@duq.edu. Web site: http://www.duq.edu/leadership.

Eastern Connecticut State University, School of Education and Professional Studies/Graduate Division, Program in Organizational Management, Willimantic, CT 06226-2295. Offers MS. Part-time and evening/weekend programs available. *Degree requirements:* For master's, comprehensive exam or thesis. *Entrance requirements:* For master's, minimum GPA of 2.7. Additional exam requirements/recommendations for international students: Required—TOEFL (minimum score 550 paper-based; 213 computer-based).

Eastern Michigan University, Graduate School, College of Business, Department of Management, Program in Human Resources Management and Organizational Development, Ypsilanti, MI 48197. Offers MSHROD. Part-time and evening/weekend programs available. Postbaccalaureate distance learning degree programs offered (minimal on-campus study). *Students:* 30 full-time (22 women), 52 part-time (39 women); includes 18 minority (12 Black or African American, non-Hispanic/Latino; 4 Asian, non-Hispanic/Latino; 1 Hispanic/Latino; 1 Two or more races, non-Hispanic/Latino), 26 international. Average age 30. 50 applicants, 58% accepted, 10 enrolled. In 2011, 64 degrees awarded. *Degree requirements:* For master's, thesis optional. *Entrance requirements:* For master's, GMAT. Additional exam requirements/recommendations for international students: Required—TOEFL. *Application deadline:* Applications are processed on a rolling basis. Application fee: $35. *Expenses:* Tuition, state resident: full-time $10,367; part-time $432 per credit hour. Tuition, nonresident: full-time $20,435; part-time $851 per credit hour. *Required fees:* $39 per credit hour. $46 per semester. One-time fee: $100. Tuition and fees vary according to course level, degree level and reciprocity agreements. *Financial support:* Fellowships, research assistantships with full tuition reimbursements, teaching assistantships with full tuition reimbursements, career-related internships or fieldwork, Federal Work-Study, institutionally sponsored loans, scholarships/grants, tuition waivers (partial), and unspecified assistantships available. Support available to part-time students. Financial award applicants required to submit FAFSA. *Unit head:* Dr. Fraya Wagner-Marsh, Advisor, 734-787-3240, Fax: 734-487-4100, E-mail: fraya.wagner@emich.edu.

Application contact: K. Michelle Henry, Director, Academic Services, 734-487-4444, Fax: 734-483-1316, E-mail: mhenry1@emich.edu. Web site: http://www.emich.edu/public/cob/management/mshrod.

Eastern Michigan University, Graduate School, College of Business, Programs in Business Administration, Ypsilanti, MI 48197. Offers business administration (MBA, Graduate Certificate); computer information systems (Graduate Certificate); e-business (MBA, Graduate Certificate); enterprise business intelligence (MBA); entrepreneurship (MBA, Graduate Certificate); finance (MBA, Graduate Certificate); human resources (MBA); human resources management (Graduate Certificate); information systems (MBA); internal auditing (MBA); international business (MBA, Graduate Certificate); marketing management (Graduate Certificate); nonprofit management (MBA); organizational development (Graduate Certificate); supply chain management (MBA, Graduate Certificate). *Accreditation:* AACSB. Part-time programs available. Postbaccalaureate distance learning degree programs offered (no on-campus study). *Students:* 79 full-time (39 women), 287 part-time (143 women); includes 55 minority (22 Black or African American, non-Hispanic/Latino; 24 Asian, non-Hispanic/Latino; 6 Hispanic/Latino; 3 Two or more races, non-Hispanic/Latino), 238 international. Average age 32. 317 applicants, 62% accepted, 89 enrolled. In 2011, 102 master's, 58 other advanced degrees awarded. *Entrance requirements:* For master's, GMAT (minimum score 450), minimum cumulative undergraduate GPA of 2.75. Additional exam requirements/recommendations for international students: Required—TOEFL. *Application deadline:* For fall admission, 5/15 for domestic students, 5/1 for international students; for winter admission, 10/15 for domestic students, 10/1 for international students; for spring admission, 3/15 for domestic students, 3/1 for international students. Applications are processed on a rolling basis. Application fee: $35. *Expenses:* Tuition, state resident: full-time $10,367; part-time $432 per credit hour. Tuition, nonresident: full-time $20,435; part-time $851 per credit hour. *Required fees:* $39 per credit hour. $46 per semester. One-time fee: $100. Tuition and fees vary according to course level, degree level and reciprocity agreements. *Financial support:* Fellowships, research assistantships with full tuition reimbursements, teaching assistantships with full tuition reimbursements, career-related internships or fieldwork, Federal Work-Study, institutionally sponsored loans, scholarships/grants, tuition waivers (partial), and unspecified assistantships available. Support available to part-time students. Financial award applicants required to submit FAFSA. *Unit head:* K. Michelle Henry, Director, Academic Services, 734-487-4444, Fax: 734-483-1316, E-mail: mhenry1@emich.edu. *Application contact:* Beste Windes, Advisor, 734-487-4444, Fax: 734-483-1316, E-mail: bwindes@emich.edu. Web site: http://www.emich.edu/public/cob/gr/grad.html.

Eastern University, Office of Interdisciplinary Programs, Program in Organizational Leadership, St. Davids, PA 19087-3696. Offers PhD.

Eastern University, School of Leadership and Development, St. Davids, PA 19087-3696. Offers economic development (MBA), including international development, urban development (MA, MBA); international development (MA), including global development, urban development (MA, MBA); nonprofit management (MS); organizational leadership (MA); M Div/MBA. Part-time and evening/weekend programs available. *Degree requirements:* For master's, thesis (for some programs). *Entrance requirements:* For master's, GMAT (MBA), minimum GPA of 2.5. *Expenses:* Contact institution. *Faculty research:* Micro-level economic development, China welfare and economic development, macroethics, micro- and macro-level economic development in transitional economics, organizational effectiveness.

Edgewood College, Program in Organization Development, Madison, WI 53711-1997. Offers MS. Part-time and evening/weekend programs available. Postbaccalaureate distance learning degree programs offered (minimal on-campus study). *Students:* 15 part-time (13 women); includes 4 minority (2 Black or African American, non-Hispanic/Latino; 1 Hispanic/Latino; 1 Two or more races, non-Hispanic/Latino). Average age 39. *Degree requirements:* For master's, research project. *Application deadline:* For fall admission, 8/15 for domestic students, 5/1 for international students; for spring admission, 1/8 for domestic students, 11/1 for international students. Electronic applications accepted. *Expenses: Tuition:* Part-time $747 per credit. Part-time tuition and fees vary according to program. *Unit head:* Dr. Daniel A. Schroeder, Coordinator, 608-663-4255, E-mail: schroeder@edgewood.edu. *Application contact:* Jenna Alsteen, Program Representative, 608-663-4255, Fax: 608-663-3496, E-mail: jalsteen@edgewood.edu. Web site: http://www.edgewood.edu/Academics/Graduate/OrganizationalDevelopment.aspx.

Emory & Henry College, Graduate Programs, Emory, VA 24327-0947. Offers American history (MA Ed); organizational leadership (MCOL); professional studies (M Ed); reading specialist (MA Ed). Part-time and evening/weekend programs available. *Faculty:* 7 full-time (3 women). *Students:* 11 full-time (8 women), 32 part-time (22 women); includes 1 minority (Black or African American, non-Hispanic/Latino). Average age 36. 34 applicants, 85% accepted, 28 enrolled. In 2011, 36 master's awarded. *Entrance requirements:* For master's, GRE or PRAXIS I, recommendations, writing sample. Additional exam requirements/recommendations for international students: Recommended—TOEFL. *Application deadline:* Applications are processed on a rolling basis. Application fee: $30. *Expenses: Tuition:* Full-time $8370; part-time $465 per credit hour. *Financial support:* Applicants required to submit FAFSA. *Unit head:* Dr. Jack Roper, Director of Graduate Studies, 276-944-6188, Fax: 276-944-5223, E-mail: jroper@ehc.edu. *Application contact:* Dr. Jack Roper, Director of Graduate Studies, 276-944-6188, Fax: 276-944-5223, E-mail: jroper@ehc.edu.

Emory University, Goizueta Business School, Doctoral Program in Business, Atlanta, GA 30322-1100. Offers accounting (PhD); finance (PhD); information systems (PhD); marketing (PhD); organization and management (PhD). *Faculty:* 56 full-time (13 women). *Students:* 37 full-time (17 women); includes 21 minority (20 Asian, non-Hispanic/Latino; 1 Hispanic/Latino). Average age 29. 240 applicants, 6% accepted, 11 enrolled. In 2011, 5 doctorates awarded. *Degree requirements:* For doctorate, comprehensive exam, thesis/dissertation. *Entrance requirements:* For doctorate, GMAT (strongly preferred) or GRE. Additional exam requirements/recommendations for international students: Required—TOEFL (minimum score 250 computer-based). *Application deadline:* For fall admission, 1/3 priority date for domestic students, 1/1 for international students. Application fee: $50. Electronic applications accepted. *Expenses: Tuition:* Full-time $34,800. *Required fees:* $1300. *Financial support:* In 2011–12, 37 students received support. *Unit head:* Dr. Lawrence Benveniste, Dean, 404-727-6377, Fax: 404-727-0868, E-mail: larry_benveniste@bus.emory.edu. *Application contact:* Allison Gilmore, Director of Admissions and Student Services, 404-727-6353, Fax: 404-727-5337, E-mail: phd@bus.emory.edu.

Endicott College, Apicius International School of Hospitality, Florence, MA 50122, Italy. Offers organizational management (M Ed). Program held entirely in Florence, Italy. *Degree requirements:* For master's, thesis. *Entrance requirements:* For master's, MAT or GRE, 250-500 word essay explaining professional goals, official transcripts of all academic work, bachelor's degree, two letters of recommendation, personal interview. *Application deadline:* For fall admission, 6/30 for domestic and international students. Application fee: $50. Tuition and fees vary according to degree level and program. *Financial support:* Applicants required to submit FAFSA. *Application contact:* Dr. Mary Huegel, Dean of Graduate and Professional Studies, 978-232-2084, Fax: 978-232-3000, E-mail: mhuegel@endicott.edu. Web site: http://www.apicius.it.

Endicott College, Van Loan School of Graduate and Professional Studies, Program in Organizational Management, Beverly, MA 01915-2096. Offers M Ed. Part-time and evening/weekend programs available. *Faculty:* 2 full-time (0 women), 6 part-time/adjunct (2 women). *Students:* 48 full-time (27 women), 11 part-time (7 women); includes 6 minority (5 Black or African American, non-Hispanic/Latino; 1 Hispanic/Latino). Average age 38. 3 applicants, 100% accepted, 1 enrolled. In 2011, 38 master's awarded. *Degree requirements:* For master's, thesis. *Entrance requirements:* For master's, GRE or MAT, letters of recommendation. Additional exam requirements/recommendations for international students: Required—TOEFL. *Application deadline:* Applications are processed on a rolling basis. Application fee: $50. Electronic applications accepted. *Expenses:* Contact institution. *Financial support:* Career-related internships or fieldwork, Federal Work-Study, institutionally sponsored loans, and tuition waivers (partial) available. Financial award applicants required to submit FAFSA. *Unit head:* Richard Benedetto, Associate Dean of Graduate School, 978-232-2744, Fax: 978-232-3000, E-mail: rbenedet@endicott.edu.

Evangel University, Organizational Leadership Program, Springfield, MO 65802. Offers MOL. Part-time and evening/weekend programs available. Postbaccalaureate distance learning degree programs offered (minimal on-campus study). *Faculty:* 4 full-time (1 woman), 2 part-time/adjunct (0 women). *Students:* 56 full-time (28 women), 8 part-time (1 woman); includes 3 minority (1 Black or African American, non-Hispanic/Latino; 2 Asian, non-Hispanic/Latino). Average age 37. 20 applicants, 60% accepted, 8 enrolled. In 2011, 40 master's awarded. *Degree requirements:* For master's, comprehensive exam, thesis, capstone project. *Entrance requirements:* For master's, GMAT or GRE. Additional exam requirements/recommendations for international students: Required—TOEFL (minimum score 550 paper-based; 213 computer-based). *Application deadline:* For fall admission, 7/15 priority date for domestic students, 7/15 for international students; for spring admission, 11/15 priority date for domestic students, 11/15 for international students. Applications are processed on a rolling basis. Application fee: $25. Electronic applications accepted. *Financial support:* In 2011–12, 9 students received support. Career-related internships or fieldwork and scholarships/grants available. Support available to part-time students. Financial award application deadline: 3/1; financial award applicants required to submit FAFSA. *Unit head:* Dr. Jeff Fulks, Director of Graduate Studies, 417-865-2815 Ext. 8260, Fax: 417-575-5484, E-mail: fulksj@evangel.edu. *Application contact:* Micah Hildreth, Admissions Representative, Graduate and Professional Studies, 417-865-2815 Ext. 7227, Fax: 417-575-5484, E-mail: hildrethm@evangel.edu. Web site: http://www.evangel.edu/post/programs/master-of-organizational-leadership/.

Fairleigh Dickinson University, College at Florham, Maxwell Becton College of Arts and Sciences, Department of Psychology, Program in Organizational Behavior, Madison, NJ 07940-1099. Offers organizational behavior (MA); organizational leadership (Certificate).

Fielding Graduate University, Graduate Programs, School of Human and Organization Development, Santa Barbara, CA 93105-3538. Offers evidence-based coaching (Certificate); human and organizational systems (PhD), including aging, culture and society, information society and knowledge organizations, transformative learning for social justice; human development (PhD), including aging, culture and society, information society and knowledge organizations, transformative learning for social justice; integral studies (Certificate); organization management and development (MA, Certificate). Postbaccalaureate distance learning degree programs offered (minimal on-campus study). *Faculty:* 25 full-time (11 women), 11 part-time/adjunct (4 women). *Students:* 422 full-time (304 women), 130 part-time (91 women); includes 119 minority (67 Black or African American, non-Hispanic/Latino; 5 American Indian or Alaska Native, non-Hispanic/Latino; 14 Asian, non-Hispanic/Latino; 22 Hispanic/Latino; 11 Two or more races, non-Hispanic/Latino), 63 international. Average age 49. 133 applicants, 97% accepted, 85 enrolled. In 2011, 46 master's, 34 doctorates, 69 other advanced degrees awarded. Terminal master's awarded for partial completion of doctoral program. *Degree requirements:* For master's, thesis or alternative; for doctorate, comprehensive exam, thesis/dissertation. *Entrance requirements:* For master's, minimum GPA of 2.5, letter of recommendation; for doctorate, 2 letters of recommendation, writing sample, resume, self-assessment statement. *Application deadline:* For fall admission, 3/1 for domestic and international students; for spring admission, 9/1 for domestic and international students. Application fee: $75. Electronic applications accepted. *Expenses:* Contact institution. *Financial support:* In 2011–12, 38 students received support. Scholarships/grants and health care benefits available. Support available to part-time students. Financial award applicants required to submit FAFSA. *Unit head:* Dr. Charles McClintock, Dean, 805-898-2930, Fax: 805-687-4590, E-mail: cmcclintock@fielding.edu. *Application contact:* Carmen Kuchera, Admission Counselor, 800-340-1099 Ext. 4098, Fax: 805-687-9793, E-mail: hodadmissions@fielding.edu. Web site: http://www.fielding.edu/programs/hod/default.aspx.

Gannon University, School of Graduate Studies, College of Engineering and Business, School of Business, Program in Organizational Leadership, Erie, PA 16541-0001. Offers Certificate. Part-time and evening/weekend programs available. *Students:* 2 part-time (both women), 1 international. Average age 32. 1 applicant, 100% accepted, 0 enrolled. *Entrance requirements:* Additional exam requirements/recommendations for international students: Required—TOEFL (minimum score 79 iBT). Application fee: $25. *Financial support:* Application deadline: 7/1; applicants required to submit FAFSA. *Unit head:* Dr. Melanie Hatch, Dean, College of Engineering and Business, 814-871-7582, E-mail: hatch004@gannon.edu. *Application contact:* Kara Morgan, Director of Graduate Admissions, 814-871-5831, Fax: 814-871-5827, E-mail: graduate@gannon.edu.

Gannon University, School of Graduate Studies, College of Humanities, Education, and Social Sciences, School of Humanities, Program in Organizational Learning and Leadership, Erie, PA 16541-0001. Offers PhD. Part-time and evening/weekend programs available. *Students:* 2 full-time (1 woman), 59 part-time (33 women); includes 2 minority (both Black or African American, non-Hispanic/Latino). Average age 42. 41 applicants, 68% accepted, 20 enrolled. In 2011, 1 doctorate awarded. *Degree requirements:* For doctorate, thesis/dissertation. *Entrance requirements:* For doctorate, GRE (verbal, quantitative and written sections taken within the last 3 years), minimum graduate GPA of 3.5, 2 years post-baccalaureate work experience, letters of recommendation, statement of purpose. Additional exam requirements/recommendations for international students: Required—TOEFL (minimum score 79 iBT). *Application deadline:* For spring admission, 2/1 for domestic students. Application fee: $50. Electronic applications accepted. *Financial support:* Scholarships/grants and unspecified assistantships available. Financial award applicants required to submit FAFSA. *Unit head:* Dr. David B. Barker, Director, 814-871-7700, E-mail: barker002@gannon.edu. *Application contact:* Kara Morgan, Director of Graduate Admissions, 814-871-5831, Fax: 814-871-5827, E-mail: graduate@gannon.edu.

Geneva College, Program in Organizational Leadership, Beaver Falls, PA 15010-3599. Offers MS. Evening/weekend programs available. *Faculty:* 3 full-time (2 women), 17 part-time/adjunct (4 women). *Students:* 109 full-time (65 women); includes 20 minority (14 Black or African American, non-Hispanic/Latino; 1 American Indian or Alaska Native, non-Hispanic/Latino; 2 Asian, non-Hispanic/Latino; 1 Hispanic/Latino; 2 Two or more races, non-Hispanic/Latino). 21 applicants, 100% accepted, 13 enrolled. In 2011, 60 master's awarded. *Degree requirements:* For master's, thesis. *Entrance requirements:*

Organizational Management

For master's, 3-5 years of professional experience, minimum GPA of 3.0 (preferred), resume, writing sample, interview. Additional exam requirements/recommendations for international students: Required—TOEFL. *Application deadline:* Applications are processed on a rolling basis. Application fee: $15. Electronic applications accepted. *Expenses:* Contact institution. *Financial support:* In 2011–12, 21 students received support. Scholarships/grants available. Financial award applicants required to submit FAFSA. *Faculty research:* Servant leadership. *Unit head:* Dr. James K. Dittmar, Chair, 724-847-6853, Fax: 724-847-4198, E-mail: jkd@geneva.edu. *Application contact:* Linda Roundtree, Enrollment Counselor, 724-847-6856, Fax: 724-847-4198, E-mail: lroundtr@geneva.edu. Web site: http://www.geneva.edu/.

George Fox University, School of Business, Newberg, OR 97132-2697. Offers finance (MBA); management (DBA); management/general (MBA); marketing (DBA); organizational strategy (MBA); strategic human resource management (MBA). MBA offered part-time and full-time in Newberg, OR, and in Portland, OR. Part-time and evening/weekend programs available. Postbaccalaureate distance learning degree programs offered (minimal on-campus study). *Faculty:* 9 full-time (2 women), 6 part-time/adjunct (0 women). *Students:* 24 full-time (11 women), 239 part-time (81 women); includes 33 minority (4 Black or African American, non-Hispanic/Latino; 1 American Indian or Alaska Native, non-Hispanic/Latino; 14 Asian, non-Hispanic/Latino; 10 Hispanic/Latino; 4 Two or more races, non-Hispanic/Latino), 13 international. Average age 37. In 2011, 101 master's, 6 doctorates awarded. *Degree requirements:* For master's, capstone project; for doctorate, credit-applied research project. *Entrance requirements:* For master's, resume (5 years professional experience); 3 professional references; interview; financial e-learning course, official transcripts; for doctorate, GRE or GMAT, resume; personal mission statement; academic research writing sample; official transcript from each college/university attended; three professional references. Additional exam requirements/recommendations for international students: Required—TOEFL (minimum score 577 paper-based; 233 computer-based; 90 iBT) or IELTS (minimum score 7). *Application deadline:* For fall admission, 8/1 for domestic and international students; for spring admission, 12/1 for domestic and international students. Applications are processed on a rolling basis. Application fee: $40. Electronic applications accepted. *Expenses:* Contact institution. *Financial support:* Applicants required to submit FAFSA. *Unit head:* Dr. Dirk Barram, Professor/Dean, 800-631-0921. *Application contact:* Robin Halverson, Admissions Counselor, 800-493-4937, Fax: 503-554-6111, E-mail: mba@georgefox.edu. Web site: http://www.georgefox.edu/business/index.html.

George Mason University, School of Public Policy, Program in Organization Development and Knowledge Management, Arlington, VA 22201. Offers MS. *Faculty:* 54 full-time (18 women), 20 part-time/adjunct (8 women). *Students:* 59 full-time (38 women), 17 part-time (15 women); includes 21 minority (9 Black or African American, non-Hispanic/Latino; 1 American Indian or Alaska Native, non-Hispanic/Latino; 4 Asian, non-Hispanic/Latino; 6 Hispanic/Latino; 1 Two or more races, non-Hispanic/Latino), 3 international. Average age 37. 60 applicants, 58% accepted, 29 enrolled. In 2011, 39 master's awarded. *Degree requirements:* For master's, thesis or alternative. *Entrance requirements:* For master's, GRE (for students seeking merit-based scholarships), bachelor's degree with minimum GPA of 3.0, current resume, 2 letters of recommendation, expanded goals statement, 2 copies of official transcripts. Additional exam requirements/recommendations for international students: Required—TOEFL (minimum score 575 paper-based; 230 computer-based; 88 iBT), IELTS, Pearson Test of English. *Application deadline:* For fall admission, 6/1 priority date for domestic students, 5/1 for international students; for spring admission, 12/1 priority date for domestic students, 11/1 for international students. Applications are processed on a rolling basis. Application fee: $65 ($80 for international students). Electronic applications accepted. *Expenses:* Contact institution. *Financial support:* Career-related internships or fieldwork, Federal Work-Study, scholarships/grants, unspecified assistantships, and health care benefits (full-time research or teaching assistantship recipients) available. Financial award application deadline: 3/1; financial award applicants required to submit FAFSA. *Unit head:* Tojo Joseph Thatchenkery, Director, 703-993-3808, Fax: 703-993-8215, E-mail: thatchen@gmu.edu. *Application contact:* Tennille Haegele, Director, Graduate Admissions, 703-993-8099, Fax: 703-993-4876, E-mail: spp@gmu.edu. Web site: http://policy.gmu.edu/Home/AcademicProfessionalPrograms/MastersPrograms/OrganizationDevelopmentKnowledgeManagement/tabid/106/Default.aspx.

The George Washington University, Columbian College of Arts and Sciences, Department of Organizational Sciences and Communication, Washington, DC 20052. Offers human resources management (MA); industrial/organizational psychology (PhD); organizational management (MA). Part-time and evening/weekend programs available. *Faculty:* 9 full-time (6 women), 25 part-time/adjunct (16 women). *Students:* 28 full-time (22 women), 39 part-time (32 women); includes 15 minority (5 Black or African American, non-Hispanic/Latino; 2 Asian, non-Hispanic/Latino; 7 Hispanic/Latino; 1 Native Hawaiian or other Pacific Islander, non-Hispanic/Latino), 4 international. Average age 28. 80 applicants, 95% accepted, 37 enrolled. In 2011, 29 master's awarded. *Degree requirements:* For master's, comprehensive exam. *Entrance requirements:* For master's, GRE General Test, minimum GPA of 3.0. Additional exam requirements/recommendations for international students: Required—TOEFL (minimum score 500 paper-based; 213 computer-based; 80 iBT). *Application deadline:* For fall admission, 1/15 priority date for domestic students, 1/15 for international students; for spring admission, 10/1 priority date for domestic students, 9/1 for international students. Applications are processed on a rolling basis. Application fee: $75. Electronic applications accepted. *Financial support:* Federal Work-Study and institutionally sponsored loans available. *Unit head:* Dr. David Costanza, Acting Director, 202-994-1875, Fax: 202-994-1881, E-mail: dconstanz@gwu.edu. *Application contact:* Information Contact, 202-994-1880, Fax: 202-994-1881. Web site: http://www.gwu.edu/~orgsci/.

The George Washington University, Graduate School of Education and Human Development, Department of Human and Organizational Learning, Program in Organizational Learning and Change, Washington, DC 20052. Offers Graduate Certificate. *Entrance requirements:* For degree, two letters of recommendation, resume, statement of purpose.

Georgia State University, J. Mack Robinson College of Business, Department of Managerial Sciences, Atlanta, GA 30302-3083. Offers business analysis (MBA, MS); decision sciences (PhD); entrepreneurship (MBA); human resources management (MBA, MS); management (MBA, PhD); operations management (MBA, MS); organization change (MS); personnel employee relations (PhD); strategic management (PhD). *Accreditation:* AACSB. Part-time and evening/weekend programs available. *Degree requirements:* For doctorate, thesis/dissertation. *Entrance requirements:* For master's and doctorate, GMAT. Additional exam requirements/recommendations for international students: Required—TOEFL (minimum score 610 paper-based; 255 computer-based; 101 iBT). Electronic applications accepted. *Faculty research:* Abusive supervision, entrepreneurship, time series and neural networks, organizational controls, inventory control systems.

Gonzaga University, School of Professional Studies, Program in Organizational Leadership, Spokane, WA 99258. Offers MOL. Postbaccalaureate distance learning degree programs offered. *Entrance requirements:* For master's, GRE General Test or MAT, minimum B average in undergraduate course work. Additional exam requirements/recommendations for international students: Required—TOEFL.

Grand Canyon University, College of Doctoral Studies, Phoenix, AZ 85017-1097. Offers business administration (DBA); general psychology (PhD), including cognition and instruction, industrial and organizational psychology; organizational leadership (Ed D, PhD), including behavioral health (PhD), education and effective schools (PhD), higher education (PhD), instructional leadership (PhD), organizational development (Ed D). *Degree requirements:* For doctorate, comprehensive exam, thesis/dissertation. *Entrance requirements:* For doctorate, minimum GPA of 3.4 on earned advanced degree from regionally-accredited institution; transcripts; goals statement.

Grand View University, Master of Science in Innovative Leadership Program, Des Moines, IA 50316-1599. Offers business (MS); education (MS); nursing (MS). Part-time and evening/weekend programs available. *Faculty:* 7 full-time (3 women). *Students:* 31 part-time (23 women). Average age 32. In 2011, 16 master's awarded. *Degree requirements:* For master's, completion of all required coursework in common core and selected track with minimum cumulative GPA of 3.0 and no more than two grades of C. *Entrance requirements:* For master's, GRE, GMAT, or essay, minimum undergraduate GPA of 3.0, professional resume, 3 letters of recommendation, interview. Additional exam requirements/recommendations for international students: Required—TOEFL (minimum score 550 paper-based; 210 computer-based). *Application deadline:* Applications are processed on a rolling basis. Application fee: $40. Electronic applications accepted. *Expenses: Tuition:* Part-time $501 per credit. *Required fees:* $115 per semester. *Unit head:* Dr. Patricia Rinke, Dean of Graduate and Adult Programs, 515-263-2912, E-mail: prinke@grandview.edu. *Application contact:* Michael Norris, Director of Graduate Admissions, 515-263-2830, E-mail: gradadmissions@grandview.edu. Web site: http://www.grandview.edu.

Grantham University, College of Arts and Sciences, Kansas City, MO 64153. Offers case management (MSN); health systems management (MS); healthcare administration (MHA); nursing (MSN); nursing education (MSN); nursing informatics (MSN); nursing management and organizational leadership (MSN). Part-time and evening/weekend programs available. Postbaccalaureate distance learning degree programs offered (no on-campus study). *Degree requirements:* For master's, thesis (for some programs), capstone project. *Entrance requirements:* For master's, bachelor's degree from accredited degree-granting institution. Additional exam requirements/recommendations for international students: Required—TOEFL (minimum score 500 paper-based; 213 computer-based; 61 iBT). Electronic applications accepted.

Harding University, Paul R. Carter College of Business Administration, Searcy, AR 72149-0001. Offers health care management (MBA); information technology management (MBA); international business (MBA); leadership and organizational management (MBA). *Accreditation:* ACBSP. Part-time and evening/weekend programs available. Postbaccalaureate distance learning degree programs offered (no on-campus study). *Faculty:* 30 part-time/adjunct (6 women). *Students:* 60 full-time (25 women), 140 part-time (63 women); includes 33 minority (26 Black or African American, non-Hispanic/Latino; 1 American Indian or Alaska Native, non-Hispanic/Latino; 3 Asian, non-Hispanic/Latino; 1 Hispanic/Latino; 2 Two or more races, non-Hispanic/Latino), 24 international. Average age 30. 65 applicants, 98% accepted, 64 enrolled. In 2011, 120 master's awarded. *Degree requirements:* For master's, portfolio. *Entrance requirements:* For master's, GMAT (minimum score of 500) or GRE (minimum score of 300), minimum GPA of 3.0, 2 letters of recommendation, resume, 3 essays, all official transcripts. Additional exam requirements/recommendations for international students: Required—TOEFL (minimum score 550 paper-based; 213 computer-based; 79 iBT). *Application deadline:* For fall admission, 8/1 priority date for domestic students, 8/1 for international students; for spring admission, 12/1 priority date for domestic students, 12/1 for international students. Applications are processed on a rolling basis. Application fee: $40. *Expenses: Tuition:* Full-time $10,512; part-time $584 per credit hour. *Required fees:* $500; $25 per credit hour. Tuition and fees vary according to course load, degree level and program. *Financial support:* In 2011–12, 19 students received support. Unspecified assistantships available. Financial award application deadline: 7/30; financial award applicants required to submit FAFSA. *Unit head:* Glen Metheny, Director of Graduate Studies, 501-279-5851, Fax: 501-279-4805, E-mail: gmetheny@harding.edu. *Application contact:* Melanie Kiihnl, Recruiting Manager/Director of Marketing, 501-279-4523, Fax: 501-279-4805, E-mail: mba@harding.edu. Web site: http://www.harding.edu/mba.

Hawai`i Pacific University, College of Business Administration, Program in Organizational Change, Honolulu, HI 96813. Offers MA. Part-time and evening/weekend programs available. *Faculty:* 3 full-time (0 women), 1 (woman) part-time/adjunct. *Students:* 10 full-time (7 women), 9 part-time (5 women); includes 8 minority (1 Black or African American, non-Hispanic/Latino; 1 Asian, non-Hispanic/Latino; 3 Hispanic/Latino; 1 Native Hawaiian or other Pacific Islander, non-Hispanic/Latino; 2 Two or more races, non-Hispanic/Latino). Average age 34. 24 applicants, 75% accepted, 6 enrolled. In 2011, 17 master's awarded. *Expenses: Tuition:* Full-time $13,230; part-time $735 per credit. Tuition and fees vary according to course load and program. *Financial support:* In 2011–12, 1 student received support. Career-related internships or fieldwork, Federal Work-Study, scholarships/grants, tuition waivers, and unspecified assistantships available. *Unit head:* Dr. Gordon Jones, Dean, 808-544-1181, Fax: 808-544-0247, E-mail: gjones@hpu.edu. *Application contact:* Chad Schempp, Director of Graduate Admissions, 808-543-8035, Fax: 808-544-0280, E-mail: graduate@hpu.edu.

See Display on next page and Close-Up on page 625.

HEC Montreal, School of Business Administration, Master of Science Programs in Administration, Program in Cultural Enterprises, Montréal, QC H3T 2A7, Canada. Offers MM. Program offered in French only. Part-time programs available. *Degree requirements:* For master's, one foreign language. *Application deadline:* For fall admission, 4/1 for domestic and international students. Application fee: $80. Electronic applications accepted. Application fee is waived when completed online. *Expenses:* Tuition, state resident: full-time $2601.36. Tuition, nonresident: full-time $7030. *International tuition:* $17,474.04 full-time. *Required fees:* $1381.77. Tuition and fees vary according to degree level and program. *Financial support:* Research assistantships and teaching assistantships available. Financial award application deadline: 9/2. *Unit head:* Renaud Legoux, Director, 514-340-6997, Fax: 514-340-5631, E-mail: renaud.legoux@hec.ca. *Application contact:* Jo Anne Audet, Administrative Director, 514-340-1315, Fax: 514-340-6411, E-mail: joanne.audet@hec.ca. Web site: http://www.hec.ca/programmes_formations/des/maitrises_professionnelles/mmec/index.html.

HEC Montreal, School of Business Administration, Master of Science Programs in Administration, Program in Organizational Development, Montréal, QC H3T 2A7, Canada. Offers M Sc. All courses are given in French. Part-time programs available. *Students:* 47 full-time (33 women), 17 part-time (14 women). 32 applicants, 75% accepted, 17 enrolled. In 2011, 10 master's awarded. *Degree requirements:* For master's, one foreign language, thesis. *Entrance requirements:* For master's, Test de francais international (TFI) with minimum score of 850 (for those who have never studied in French), BBA, undergraduate degree in another field, degree deemed equivalent by program director and minimum GPA of 3.0 on 4.3 scale. *Application deadline:* For fall admission, 3/15 for domestic and international students; for winter admission, 9/15 for domestic and international students. Application fee: $80. Electronic applications accepted. Application fee is waived when completed online. *Expenses:* Contact institution. *Financial support:* Research assistantships, teaching assistantships, and scholarships/grants available. Financial award application deadline: 9/2. *Unit head:* Claude Laurin, Director, 514-340-6485, Fax: 514-340-6880, E-mail: claude.laurin@hec.ca. *Application contact:* Virginie Lefebvre, Administrative Director, 514-340-6112, Fax: 514-340-6411, E-mail: virginie.lefebvre@hec.ca. Web site: http://www.hec.ca/en/programs_training/executiveeducation/seminars/pido.html.

HEC Montreal, School of Business Administration, Master of Science Programs in Administration, Program in Organizational Studies, Montréal, QC H3T 2A7, Canada. Offers M Sc. All courses are given in French. Part-time programs available. *Students:* 5 full-time (3 women), 1 part-time (0 women). 5 applicants, 80% accepted, 3 enrolled. *Degree requirements:* For master's, one foreign language, thesis. *Entrance requirements:* For master's, Test de francais international (TFI) with minimum score of 850 (for those who have never studied in French), BBA, undergraduate degree in another field, degree deemed equivalent by program director and minimum GPA of 3.0 on 4.3 scale. *Application deadline:* For fall admission, 3/15 for domestic and international students; for winter admission, 9/15 for domestic and international students. Application fee: $80. Electronic applications accepted. Application fee is waived when completed online. *Expenses:* Tuition, state resident: full-time $2601.36. Tuition, nonresident: full-time $7030. *International tuition:* $17,474.04 full-time. *Required fees:* $1381.77. Tuition and fees vary according to degree level and program. *Financial support:* Research assistantships, teaching assistantships, and scholarships/grants available. Financial award application deadline: 9/2. *Unit head:* Claude Laurin, Director, 514-340-6485, Fax: 514-340-6880, E-mail: claude.laurin@hec.ca. *Application contact:* Virginie Lefebvre, Administrative Director, 514-340-6112, Fax: 514-340-6411, E-mail: virginie.lefebvre@hec.ca.

Immaculata University, College of Graduate Studies, Program in Organization Studies, Immaculata, PA 19345. Offers MA. Part-time and evening/weekend programs available. *Degree requirements:* For master's, comprehensive exam, thesis optional. *Entrance requirements:* For master's, GMAT, GRE General Test, MAT, minimum GPA of 3.0. Additional exam requirements/recommendations for international students: Required—TOEFL, IELTS. Electronic applications accepted.

Indiana Tech, Program in Organizational Leadership, Fort Wayne, IN 46803-1297. Offers MS. Part-time and evening/weekend programs available. Postbaccalaureate distance learning degree programs offered (minimal on-campus study). *Entrance requirements:* For master's, 3 years work experience with an increasing level of supervisory responsibilities, bachelor's degree transcript from accredited institution with minimum cumulative GPA of 2.5, 3 letters of recommendation, essay, current resume. Electronic applications accepted.

Indiana University Bloomington, School of Public and Environmental Affairs, Public Affairs Programs, Bloomington, IN 47405. Offers comparative and international affairs (MPA); economic development (MPA); energy (MPA); environmental policy (PhD); environmental policy and natural resource management (MPA); hazardous materials management (Certificate); information systems (MPA); international development (MPA); local government management (MPA); nonprofit management (MPA, Certificate); policy analysis (MPA); public budgeting and financial management (Certificate); public finance (PhD); public financial administration (MPA); public management (MPA, PhD, Certificate); public policy analysis (PhD); social entrepreneurship (Certificate); specialized public affairs (MPA); sustainability and sustainable development (MPA); JD/MPA; MPA/MA; MPA/MIS; MPA/MLS; MSES/MPA. *Accreditation:* NASPAA (one or more programs are accredited). Part-time programs available. *Faculty:* 80 full-time (30 women), 102 part-time/adjunct (43 women). *Students:* 338 full-time, 30 part-time; includes 27 minority (7 Black or African American, non-Hispanic/Latino; 2 American Indian or Alaska Native, non-Hispanic/Latino; 10 Asian, non-Hispanic/Latino; 8 Hispanic/Latino), 56 international. Average age 24. 501 applicants, 148 enrolled. In 2011, 172 master's, 7 doctorates awarded. *Degree requirements:* For master's, core classes, capstone, internship; for doctorate, comprehensive exam, thesis/dissertation. *Entrance requirements:* For master's, GRE General Test or GMAT, official transcripts, 3 letters of recommendation, resume, personal statement; for doctorate, GRE General Test or LSAT, official transcripts, 3 letters of recommendation, resume or curriculum vitae, statement of purpose. Additional exam requirements/recommendations for international students: Required—TOEFL (minimum score 600 paper-based; 96 iBT); Recommended—IELTS (minimum score 7). *Application deadline:* For fall admission, 2/1 priority date for domestic students, 12/1 for international students. Applications are processed on a rolling basis. Application fee: $55 ($65 for international students). Electronic applications accepted. *Financial support:* Fellowships with partial tuition reimbursements, research assistantships with partial tuition reimbursements, teaching assistantships with partial tuition reimbursements, career-related internships or fieldwork, Federal Work-Study, scholarships/grants, health care benefits, unspecified assistantships, and Service Corps programs available. Financial award application deadline: 2/1; financial award applicants required to submit FAFSA. *Faculty research:* Comparative and international affairs, environmental policy and resource management, policy analysis, public finance, public management, urban management, nonprofit management, energy policy, social policy, public finance. *Unit head:* Jennifer Forney, Director of Graduate Student Services, 812-855-9485, Fax: 812-856-3665, E-mail: speampo@indiana.edu. *Application contact:* Admissions Assistant, 812-855-2840, E-mail: speaapps@indiana.edu. Web site: http://www.indiana.edu/~spea/prospective_students/masters/.

Indiana University–Purdue University Fort Wayne, College of Engineering, Technology, and Computer Science, Department of Organizational Leadership and Supervision, Fort Wayne, IN 46805-1499. Offers human resources (MS); leadership (MS); organizational leadership and supervision (Certificate). Part-time programs available. *Faculty:* 7 full-time (1 woman). *Students:* 3 full-time (all women), 33 part-time (19 women); includes 9 minority (6 Black or African American, non-Hispanic/Latino; 2 Asian, non-Hispanic/Latino; 1 Hispanic/Latino). Average age 38. 9 applicants, 78% accepted, 4 enrolled. In 2011, 3 master's awarded. *Entrance requirements:* For master's, GRE or GMAT (if undergraduate GPA is below 3.0), current resume, 2 recent letters of recommendation, essay. Additional exam requirements/recommendations for international students: Required—TOEFL (minimum score 550 paper-based; 213 computer-based; 77 iBT); Recommended—TWE. *Application deadline:* For fall admission, 5/15 for domestic students, 4/1 for international students; for spring admission, 11/15 for domestic students, 10/1 for international students. Applications are processed on a rolling basis. Application fee: $55 ($60 for international students). Electronic applications accepted. *Financial support:* In 2011–12, 2 teaching assistantships with partial tuition reimbursements (averaging $12,930 per year) were awarded; scholarships/grants also available. Support available to part-time students. Financial award application deadline: 3/1; financial award applicants required to submit FAFSA. *Faculty research:* Diversity education, HRD curriculum and diversity. *Unit head:* Dr. Linda Hite, Chair, 260-481-6416, Fax: 260-481-6417, E-mail: hitel@ipfw.edu. *Application contact:* Dr. Linda Hite, Director of Graduate Studies, 260-481-6416, Fax: 260-481-6417, E-mail: hitel@ipfw.edu. Web site: http://www.ipfw.edu/ols/.

Indiana University–Purdue University Indianapolis, School of Public and Environmental Affairs, Indianapolis, IN 46202. Offers criminal justice and public safety (MS); homeland security and emergency management (Graduate Certificate); library management (Graduate Certificate); nonprofit management (Graduate Certificate); public affairs (MPA); public management (Graduate Certificate); social entrepreneurship: nonprofit and public benefit organizations (Graduate Certificate); JD/ MPA; MLS/NMC; MLS/PMC; MPA/MA. *Accreditation:* CAHME (one or more programs are accredited); NASPAA. Part-time and evening/weekend programs available. Postbaccalaureate distance learning degree programs offered (no on-campus study). *Faculty:* 24 full-time (8 women), 10 part-time/adjunct (2 women). *Students:* 204 full-time (124 women), 109 part-time (74 women); includes 61 minority (45 Black or African American, non-Hispanic/Latino; 1 American Indian or Alaska Native, non-Hispanic/ Latino; 7 Asian, non-Hispanic/Latino; 8 Hispanic/Latino), 11 international. Average age 31. 214 applicants, 83% accepted, 147 enrolled. In 2011, 55 master's, 43 other advanced degrees awarded. *Entrance requirements:* For master's, GRE General Test, GMAT or LSAT, minimum GPA of 3.0 (preferred). *Application deadline:* For fall admission, 5/15 priority date for domestic students, 2/1 for international students; for spring admission, 2/15 priority date for domestic students, 9/15 for international students. Applications are processed on a rolling basis. Application fee: $60. Electronic applications accepted. *Financial support:* In 2011–12, 12 research assistantships with full tuition reimbursements (averaging $12,000 per year) were awarded; fellowships, teaching assistantships, career-related internships or fieldwork, Federal Work-Study, institutionally sponsored loans, and scholarships/grants also available. Support available to part-time students. Financial award application deadline: 3/1; financial award applicants required to submit FAFSA. *Faculty research:* Nonprofit and public management, public policy, urban policy, sustainability policy, disaster preparedness and recovery, vehicular safety, homicide, offender rehabilitation and re-entry. *Total annual research expenditures:* $1.6 million. *Unit head:* Dr. Terry L. Baumer, Executive Associate Dean, 317-274-2016, Fax: 317-274-5153, E-mail: tebaumer@iupui.edu. *Application contact:* Luke Bickel, Director of Graduate Programs, 317-274-4656, Fax: 317-278-9668, E-mail: lbickel@iupui.edu. Web site: http://www.spea.iupui.edu/.

Indiana Wesleyan University, College of Adult and Professional Studies, Graduate Studies in Leadership, Marion, IN 46953. Offers organizational leadership (Ed D). Part-time programs available. Postbaccalaureate distance learning degree programs offered (minimal on-campus study). *Degree requirements:* For doctorate, comprehensive exam, thesis/dissertation, applied field project. *Entrance requirements:* For doctorate, GRE, GMAT. Additional exam requirements/recommendations for international students: Required—TOEFL. *Faculty research:* Organizational leadership as a new structural model for research and teaching, wisdom and its application for leaders, stewardship and its application for leaders, followership and its application for leaders, the importance of a world view in establishing authenticity for leaders.

Instituto Tecnologico de Santo Domingo, Graduate School, Area of Business, Santo Domingo, Dominican Republic. Offers banking and securities markets (M Mgmt); corporate finance (M Mgmt); human resources management (M Mgmt, Certificate); international trade management (M Mgmt); marketing (M Mgmt); organizational development (M Mgmt); quality and productivity management (Certificate); tax management and planning (M Mgmt); upper management (M Mgmt).

Jacksonville University, School of Education, Jacksonville, FL 32211. Offers educational leadership (M Ed); instructional leadership and organizational development (M Ed); sport management and leadership (M Ed). Part-time and evening/weekend programs available. *Degree requirements:* For master's, comprehensive exam. *Entrance requirements:* For master's, GRE General Test, minimum GPA of 3.0. Additional exam requirements/recommendations for international students: Required—TOEFL (minimum score 550 paper-based), TWE. *Expenses:* Contact institution.

John F. Kennedy University, School of Management, Program in Business Administration, Pleasant Hill, CA 94523-4817. Offers business administration (MBA); organizational leadership (Certificate). Part-time and evening/weekend programs available. *Degree requirements:* For master's, thesis or alternative. *Entrance requirements:* For master's, interview. Additional exam requirements/recommendations for international students: Required—TOEFL.

Jones International University, School of Education, Centennial, CO 80112. Offers adult education (M Ed); corporate training and knowledge management (M Ed); curriculum and instruction (M Ed), including elementary teacher licensure, secondary teacher licensure; e-learning technology and design (M Ed); educational leadership and administration (M Ed); educational leadership and administration: principal and administrator licensure (M Ed); elementary curriculum instruction and assessment (M Ed); higher education leadership and administration (M Ed); K-12 instructional technology (M Ed); K-12 instructional technology: teacher licensure (M Ed); secondary curriculum instruction and assessment (M Ed); technology and design (M Ed). Part-time and evening/weekend programs available. Postbaccalaureate distance learning degree programs offered (no on-campus study). *Entrance requirements:* For master's, minimum cumulative GPA of 2.5. Additional exam requirements/recommendations for international students: Recommended—TOEFL (minimum score 550 paper-based; 213 computer-based). Electronic applications accepted.

Judson University, Graduate Programs, Program in Organizational Leadership, Elgin, IL 60123-1498. Offers MA. Part-time and evening/weekend programs available. Postbaccalaureate distance learning degree programs offered (no on-campus study). In 2011, 24 master's awarded. *Degree requirements:* For master's, thesis optional. *Entrance requirements:* For master's, bachelor's degree from regionally-accredited college or university with minimum GPA of 3.0; employment verification form; two letters of reference; essay. Additional exam requirements/recommendations for international students: Required—TOEFL (minimum score 550 paper-based; 213 computer-based). *Application deadline:* Applications are processed on a rolling basis. Application fee: $35. Electronic applications accepted. *Expenses: Tuition:* Full-time $9500. *Required fees:* $350. Tuition and fees vary according to course load and program. *Financial support:* Institutionally sponsored loans and scholarships/grants available. Financial award applicants required to submit FAFSA. *Faculty research:* Leadership, human resource management, public affairs, international marketing. *Unit head:* Dr. David Cook, Director, 847-6281518, E-mail: dcook@judsonu.edu. *Application contact:* Maria Aguirre, Assistant to the Registrar for Graduate Programs, 847-628-1160, E-mail: maguirre@ judsonu.edu. Web site: http://www.judsonu.edu/maol/.

Kaplan University, Davenport Campus, School of Business, Davenport, IA 52807-2095. Offers business administration (MBA); change leadership (MS); entrepreneurship (MBA); finance (MBA); health care management (MBA, MS); human resource (MBA); international business (MBA); management (MS); marketing (MBA); project management (MBA, MS); supply chain management and logistics (MBA, MS). Part-time and evening/weekend programs available. Postbaccalaureate distance learning degree programs offered (no on-campus study). *Entrance requirements:* Additional exam requirements/recommendations for international students: Required—TOEFL (minimum score 550 paper-based; 218 computer-based; 80 iBT). Electronic applications accepted.

Keiser University, Doctor of Business Administration Program, Fort Lauderdale, FL 33309. Offers global business (DBA); global organizational leadership (DBA); marketing (DBA).

LaGrange College, Graduate Programs, Program in Organizational Leadership, LaGrange, GA 30240-2999. Offers MA. Program is held on Albany campus. Evening/ weekend programs available. *Entrance requirements:* For master's, GRE or MAT, minimum GPA of 2.5, 3 letters of reference. Additional exam requirements/ recommendations for international students: Required—TOEFL (minimum score 500 paper-based; 173 computer-based; 61 iBT). Electronic applications accepted.

Lewis University, College of Arts and Sciences, Program in Organizational Leadership, Romeoville, IL 60446. Offers higher education/student services (MA); non-for-profit management (MA); organizational management (MA); public administration (MA); training and development (MA). Part-time and evening/weekend programs available. Postbaccalaureate distance learning degree programs offered (no on-campus study). *Faculty:* 2 full-time (0 women), 9 part-time/adjunct (2 women). *Students:* 15 full-time (14 women), 193 part-time (143 women); includes 61 minority (50 Black or African American, non-Hispanic/Latino; 2 Asian, non-Hispanic/Latino; 9 Hispanic/Latino). Average age 36. In 2011, 46 master's awarded. *Entrance requirements:* For master's, bachelor's degree, at least 25 years of age, minimum of 3 years of work experience, minimum GPA of 3.0, letter of recommendation, interview. Additional exam requirements/recommendations for international students: Required—TOEFL (minimum score 550 paper-based; 213 computer-based). *Application deadline:* For fall admission, 5/1 for international students; for spring admission, 11/15 for international students. Applications are processed on a rolling basis. Application fee: $40. Electronic applications accepted. *Financial support:* Federal Work-Study, scholarships/grants, tuition waivers, and unspecified assistantships available. Financial award application deadline: 5/1; financial award applicants required to submit FAFSA. *Unit head:* Dr. Rich Walsh, Director, 815-838-0500, E-mail: walshri@lewisu.edu. *Application contact:* Julie Branchaw, Assistant Director, Graduate and Adult Admission, 815-836-5574, Fax: 815-836-5578, E-mail: branchju@lewisu.edu.

Lipscomb University, Nelson and Sue Andrews Institute for Civic Leadership, Nashville, TN 37204-3951. Offers MA. Evening/weekend programs available. *Faculty:* 1 (woman) full-time. *Students:* 24 full-time (15 women); includes 7 minority (all Black or African American, non-Hispanic/Latino). Average age 39. 48 applicants, 52% accepted, 24 enrolled. *Entrance requirements:* For master's, GRE, GMAT or MAT, 2 references, essay, resume. Additional exam requirements/recommendations for international students: Required—TOEFL (minimum score 570 paper-based; 230 computer-based). *Application deadline:* Applications are processed on a rolling basis. Application fee: $50 ($75 for international students). Electronic applications accepted. *Expenses: Tuition:* Full-time $16,830; part-time $935 per credit hour. Tuition and fees vary according to degree level and program. *Financial support:* Applicants required to submit FAFSA. *Unit head:* Linda Peek Schacht, Executive Director, 615-966-1341, E-mail: linda.schacht@ lipscomb.edu. *Application contact:* Leah Davis, Program Coordinator, 615-966-6155, E-mail: leah.davis@lipscomb.edu. Web site: http://leadingvoices.lipscomb.edu.

Lourdes University, Graduate School, Program in Organizational Leadership, Sylvania, OH 43560-2898. Offers MOL. Evening/weekend programs available. *Entrance requirements:* Additional exam requirements/recommendations for international students: Required—TOEFL.

Malone University, Graduate Program in Organizational Leadership, Canton, OH 44709. Offers MAOL. Part-time and evening/weekend programs available. *Faculty:* 7 full-time (6 women), 3 part-time/adjunct (1 woman). *Students:* 19 full-time (11 women), 53 part-time (31 women); includes 13 minority (all Black or African American, non-Hispanic/Latino). Average age 39. 56 applicants, 73% accepted, 19 enrolled. *Entrance requirements:* For master's, minimum GPA of 3.0. Additional exam requirements/ recommendations for international students: Required—TOEFL (minimum score 550 paper-based; 213 computer-based; 79 iBT). *Expenses:* Contact institution. *Financial support:* Tuition waivers (partial) available. Support available to part-time students. Financial award application deadline: 6/30. *Faculty research:* Graduates' perceptions of the impact of a Christian higher education. *Unit head:* Dr. Mary E. Quinn, Director, 330-471-8556, Fax: 330-471-8343, E-mail: mquinn@malone.edu. *Application contact:* Mona J. McAuliffe, Graduate Recruiter, 330-471-8623, Fax: 330-471-8343, E-mail: mmcauliffe@malone.edu. Web site: http://www.malone.edu/admissions/graduate/ organizational-leadership/.

Manhattanville College, Graduate Studies, Humanities and Social Sciences Programs, Program in Organizational Management and Human Resource Development, Purchase, NY 10577-2132. Offers MS. Part-time and evening/weekend programs available. *Degree requirements:* For master's, thesis. *Entrance requirements:* For master's, interview, 2 letters of recommendation. Additional exam requirements/recommendations for international students: Required—TOEFL.

Mansfield University of Pennsylvania, Graduate Studies, Program in Organizational Leadership, Mansfield, PA 16933. Offers MA. Postbaccalaureate distance learning degree programs offered. *Expenses:* Tuition, state resident: full-time $7488; part-time $416 per credit. Tuition, nonresident: full-time $11,232; part-time $624 per credit.

Marian University, Business Division, Fond du Lac, WI 54935-4699. Offers organizational leadership and quality (MS). Part-time and evening/weekend programs available. *Faculty:* 1 full-time (0 women), 14 part-time/adjunct (4 women). *Students:* 7 full-time (5 women), 94 part-time (58 women); includes 14 minority (8 Black or African American, non-Hispanic/Latino; 2 Asian, non-Hispanic/Latino; 4 Hispanic/Latino). Average age 41. 50 applicants, 94% accepted, 46 enrolled. In 2011, 44 master's awarded. *Degree requirements:* For master's, comprehensive group project. *Entrance requirements:* For master's, 3 years of managerial experience, minimum GPA of 2.75, letters of professional reference. Additional exam requirements/recommendations for international students: Required—TOEFL (minimum score 525 paper-based; 193 computer-based; 70 iBT). *Application deadline:* Applications are processed on a rolling basis. Application fee: $25. Electronic applications accepted. *Expenses:* Contact institution. *Financial support:* In 2011–12, 1 student received support. Institutionally sponsored loans available. Financial award application deadline: 3/1; financial award applicants required to submit FAFSA. *Faculty research:* Organizational values, statistical decision-making, learning organization, quality planning, customer research. *Unit head:* Dr. Jeffrey G. Reed, Dean, Marian School of Business, 920-923-8759, Fax: 920-923-7167, E-mail: jreed@marianuniversity.edu. *Application contact:* Tracy Qualman, Director of Marketing and Admission, 920-923-7159, Fax: 920-923-7167, E-mail: tqualmann@ marianuniversity.edu. Web site: http://www.marianuniversity.edu/interior.aspx?id-220.

Marymount University, Educational Partnerships Program, Arlington, VA 22207-4299. Offers business administration (MBA); health care management (MS); management studies (Certificate); organization development (Certificate). Part-time and evening/ weekend programs available. *Faculty:* 1 full-time (0 women), 4 part-time/adjunct (2 women). *Students:* 1 (woman) full-time, 26 part-time (16 women); includes 11 minority (9 Black or African American, non-Hispanic/Latino; 2 Asian, non-Hispanic/Latino), 1 international. Average age 42. *Entrance requirements:* For master's, GRE General Test or GMAT, resume; for Certificate, resume. Additional exam requirements/ recommendations for international students: Required—TOEFL (minimum score 600 paper-based; 250 computer-based; 96 iBT), IELTS (minimum score 6.5). *Application deadline:* For fall admission, 7/1 for international students; for spring admission, 11/15 for international students. Applications are processed on a rolling basis. Application fee: $40. Electronic applications accepted. *Expenses: Tuition:* Part-time $770 per credit hour. *Required fees:* $8 per credit hour. One-time fee: $180 full-time. *Financial support:* Career-related internships or fieldwork, Federal Work-Study, scholarships/grants, and unspecified assistantships available. Support available to part-time students. Financial award applicants required to submit FAFSA. *Unit head:* Dr. Sherri Hughes, Vice President for Academic Affairs and Provost, 703-284-1550, E-mail: sherri.hughes@marymount.edu. *Application contact:* Francesca Reed, Director, Graduate Admissions, 703-284-5901, Fax: 703-527-3815, E-mail: grad.admissions@marymount.edu.

Maryville University of Saint Louis, College of Arts and Sciences, St. Louis, MO 63141-7299. Offers actuarial science (MS); organizational leadership (MA); strategic communication and leadership (MA). Part-time and evening/weekend programs available. *Faculty:* 8 full-time (7 women). *Students:* 16 full-time (9 women), 24 part-time (19 women); includes 6 minority (3 Black or African American, non-Hispanic/Latino; 1 American Indian or Alaska Native, non-Hispanic/Latino; 1 Asian, non-Hispanic/Latino; 1 Two or more races, non-Hispanic/Latino), 5 international. Average age 31. In 2011, 8 master's awarded. *Entrance requirements:* For master's, GRE with minimum score of 600 (MS), strong mathematics background, 2 letters of recommendation, and personal statement (MS). Additional exam requirements/recommendations for international students: Required—TOEFL (minimum score 550 paper-based; 213 computer-based; 80 iBT). *Application deadline:* Applications are processed on a rolling basis. Application fee: $40 ($60 for international students). Electronic applications accepted. *Expenses: Tuition:* Full-time $21,922; part-time $675 per credit hour. *Required fees:* $233.75 per semester. *Financial support:* Application deadline: 3/1; applicants required to submit FAFSA. *Unit head:* Dr. Dan Sparling, Dean, 314-529-9436, Fax: 314-529-9965, E-mail: dsparling@maryville.edu. *Application contact:* Dr. Donna Payne, Vice President, Adult and Online Education, 314-529-9676, Fax: 314-529-9927, E-mail: dpayne@maryville.edu. Web site: http://www.maryville.edu/academics-as-actuarialscience-master.

Medaille College, Program in Business Administration - Amherst, Amherst, NY 14221. Offers business administration (MBA); organizational leadership (MA). Evening/weekend programs available. *Students:* 187 full-time (106 women), 10 part-time (3 women); includes 104 minority (24 Black or African American, non-Hispanic/Latino; 21 Asian, non-Hispanic/Latino; 6 Hispanic/Latino; 53 Native Hawaiian or other Pacific Islander, non-Hispanic/Latino). Average age 34. 65 applicants, 88% accepted, 33 enrolled. In 2011, 94 master's awarded. *Degree requirements:* For master's, thesis or alternative. *Entrance requirements:* For master's, GMAT, minimum undergraduate GPA of 2.7, 3 years of work experience. Additional exam requirements/recommendations for international students: Required—TOEFL (minimum score 550 paper-based; 213 computer-based). *Application deadline:* Applications are processed on a rolling basis. Application fee: $35. Electronic applications accepted. *Expenses:* Contact institution. *Financial support:* Federal Work-Study available. Financial award applicants required to submit FAFSA. *Unit head:* Jennifer Bavifard, Associate Dean for Special Programs, 716-631-1061 Ext. 150, Fax: 716-631-1380, E-mail: jbavifar@medaille.edu. *Application contact:* Jacqueline Matheny, Executive Director of Marketing and Enrollment, 716-932-2541, Fax: 716-632-1811, E-mail: jmatheny@medaille.edu. Web site: http://www.medaille.edu/.

Medaille College, Program in Business Administration - Rochester, Rochester, NY 14623. Offers business administration (MBA); organizational leadership (MA). Evening/weekend programs available. *Students:* 17 full-time (11 women), 2 part-time (both women); includes 11 minority (5 Black or African American, non-Hispanic/Latino; 3 Asian, non-Hispanic/Latino; 1 Hispanic/Latino; 2 Native Hawaiian or other Pacific Islander, non-Hispanic/Latino). Average age 36. 31 applicants, 90% accepted, 19 enrolled. In 2011, 8 master's awarded. *Degree requirements:* For master's, thesis or alternative. *Entrance requirements:* For master's, GMAT, 3 years of work experience, minimum undergraduate GPA of 2.7. Additional exam requirements/recommendations for international students: Required—TOEFL (minimum score 550 paper-based; 213 computer-based). *Application deadline:* Applications are processed on a rolling basis. Application fee: $35. *Expenses:* Contact institution. *Financial support:* Federal Work-Study available. Financial award applicants required to submit FAFSA. *Unit head:* Jennifer Bavifard, Branch Campus Director, 716-932-2591, Fax: 716-631-1380, E-mail: jbavifard@medaille.edu. *Application contact:* Jane Rowlands, Marketing Support, 585-272-0030, Fax: 585-272-0057, E-mail: jrowlands@medaille.edu. Web site: http://www.medaille.edu/.

Mercy College, School of Business, Program in Organizational Leadership, Dobbs Ferry, NY 10522-1189. Offers MS. Part-time and evening/weekend programs available. Postbaccalaureate distance learning degree programs offered (no on-campus study). *Entrance requirements:* For master's, assessment by program director, resume, 2 letters of reference, interview. Additional exam requirements/recommendations for international students: Required—TOEFL (minimum score 600 paper-based; 250 computer-based; 100 iBT), IELTS (minimum score 8). Electronic applications accepted. *Expenses:* Contact institution. *Faculty research:* Organizational behavior, strategic management, collaborative relationship.

Mercyhurst College, Graduate Studies, Program in Organizational Leadership, Erie, PA 16546. Offers accounting (MS); entrepreneurship (MS); higher education administration (MS); human resources (MS); nonprofit management (MS); organizational leadership (Certificate); sports leadership (MS). Part-time and evening/weekend programs available. *Faculty:* 1 full-time (0 women), 11 part-time/adjunct (4 women). *Students:* 42 full-time (16 women), 22 part-time (15 women); includes 5 minority (3 Black or African American, non-Hispanic/Latino; 1 American Indian or Alaska Native, non-Hispanic/Latino; 1 Hispanic/Latino), 9 international. Average age 30. 60 applicants, 62% accepted, 25 enrolled. In 2011, 27 master's, 2 other advanced degrees awarded. *Degree requirements:* For master's, thesis. *Entrance requirements:* For master's, GRE General Test or MAT, interview, resume, essay, three professional references, transcripts. Additional exam requirements/recommendations for international students: Required—TOEFL. *Application deadline:* For fall admission, 8/1 priority date for domestic students, 7/1 for international students; for winter admission, 11/1 for domestic students, 10/1 for international students; for spring admission, 2/1 for domestic students, 1/1 for international students. Applications are processed on a rolling basis. Application fee: $35. Electronic applications accepted. *Expenses: Tuition:* Part-time $570 per credit. *Required fees:* $90 per term. Tuition and fees vary according to program. *Financial support:* In 2011–12, 16 students received support, including 112 research assistantships with full and partial tuition reimbursements available (averaging $6,000 per year); career-related internships or fieldwork and unspecified assistantships also available. Support available to part-time students. Financial award application deadline: 5/1; financial award applicants required to submit FAFSA. *Faculty research:* Leadership training, organizational communication, leadership pedagogy. *Unit head:* Dr. Gilbert Jacobs, Director, 814-824-2390, E-mail: gjacobs@mercyhurst.edu. *Application contact:* Sarah Murphy, Academic Coordinator, 814-824-2297, Fax: 814-824-2055, E-mail: smurphy@mercyhurst.edu.

Mid-America Christian University, Program in Leadership, Oklahoma City, OK 73170-4504. Offers MA. *Entrance requirements:* For master's, bachelor's degree from a regionally accredited college or university, minimum overall cumulative GPA of 2.75 of bachelor course work. Additional exam requirements/recommendations for international students: Required—TOEFL (minimum score 550 paper-based; 213 computer-based).

MidAmerica Nazarene University, Graduate Studies in Management, Olathe, KS 66062-1899. Offers management (MBA); organizational administration (MA), including finance, international business, leadership, non-profit. Evening/weekend programs available. *Entrance requirements:* For master's, mathematical assessment, minimum undergraduate GPA of 3.0, letters of recommendation. Additional exam requirements/recommendations for international students: Required—TOEFL. Electronic applications accepted. *Faculty research:* Economic development, international finance, business development, employee evaluation.

Midway College, Leadership MBA Program, Midway, KY 40347-1120. Offers MBA. *Degree requirements:* For master's, capstone course. *Entrance requirements:* For master's, GMAT, bachelor's degree, minimum GPA of 3.0, 3 years of professional work experience, interview. Additional exam requirements/recommendations for international students: Required—TOEFL (minimum score 550 paper-based; 213 computer-based; 80 iBT).

Misericordia University, College of Professional Studies and Social Sciences, Program in Organizational Management, Dallas, PA 18612-1098. Offers MS. Part-time and evening/weekend programs available. Postbaccalaureate distance learning degree programs offered. *Faculty:* 3 full-time (1 woman), 7 part-time/adjunct (1 woman). *Students:* 69 part-time (45 women); includes 2 minority (1 Black or African American, non-Hispanic/Latino; 1 Asian, non-Hispanic/Latino). Average age 35. 37 applicants, 76% accepted, 14 enrolled. In 2011, 27 master's awarded. *Entrance requirements:* For master's, GRE General Test, MAT (35th percentile or higher), or minimum undergraduate GPA of 2.79. *Application deadline:* Applications are processed on a rolling basis. Application fee: $25. Electronic applications accepted. *Expenses:* Contact institution. *Financial support:* In 2011–12, 39 students received support. Career-related internships or fieldwork and scholarships/grants available. Support available to part-time students. Financial award application deadline: 6/30; financial award applicants required to submit FAFSA. *Unit head:* Dr. Fred Croop, Dean, College of Professional Studies and Social Sciences, 570-674-6327, E-mail: fcroop@misericordia.edu. *Application contact:* Larree Brown, Assistant Director of Admissions, Part-Time Undergraduate and Graduate Programs, 570-674-6451, Fax: 570-674-6232, E-mail: lbrown@misericordia.edu. Web site: http://www.misericordia.edu/om.

Mountain State University, School of Graduate Studies, Program in Executive Leadership, Beckley, WV 25802-9003. Offers DEL. *Faculty:* 4 full-time (1 woman), 5 part-time/adjunct (3 women). *Students:* 42 full-time (19 women); includes 15 minority (13 Black or African American, non-Hispanic/Latino; 1 American Indian or Alaska Native, non-Hispanic/Latino; 1 Hispanic/Latino). Average age 45. 17 applicants, 53% accepted, 8 enrolled. *Entrance requirements:* For doctorate, discussion paper, resume, official transcripts from all colleges/universities attended, master's degree, 2 professional references. Application fee: $75. *Unit head:* Dr. William White, Dean, School of Leadership and Professional Development/Interim Dean, School of Graduate Studies, 304-929-1658, E-mail: wwhite@mountainstate.edu.

Mount St. Mary's College, Graduate Division, Program in Business Administration, Los Angeles, CA 90049-1599. Offers entrepreneurship (MBA); nonprofit management (MBA); organizational leadership (MBA); project management (MBA). Evening/weekend programs available. *Entrance requirements:* Additional exam requirements/recommendations for international students: Required—TOEFL. *Application deadline:* For fall admission, 6/30 for domestic students. Electronic applications accepted. *Expenses:* Contact institution. *Financial support:* Scholarships/grants available. Financial award application deadline: 3/15; financial award applicants required to submit FAFSA. *Unit head:* Dr. Janet Robinson, Director, 310-954-4153, E-mail: jrobinson@msmc.la.edu. Web site: http://www.msmc.la.edu/graduate-programs/mba.asp.

National University, Academic Affairs, School of Business and Management, Department of Leadership and Human Resource Management, La Jolla, CA 92037-1011. Offers human resources management (MA); management information systems (MS); organizational leadership (MS). Part-time and evening/weekend programs available. Postbaccalaureate distance learning degree programs offered (no on-campus study). *Degree requirements:* For master's, thesis. *Entrance requirements:* For master's, interview, minimum GPA of 2.5. Additional exam requirements/recommendations for international students: Required—TOEFL (minimum score 550 paper-based; 213 computer-based; 79 iBT), IELTS (minimum score 6). *Application deadline:* Applications are processed on a rolling basis. Application fee: $60 ($65 for international students). Electronic applications accepted. *Financial support:* Career-related internships or fieldwork, institutionally sponsored loans, scholarships/grants, and tuition waivers (partial) available. Support available to part-time students. Financial award application deadline: 6/30; financial award applicants required to submit FAFSA. *Unit head:* Dr. Bruce Buchowicz, Chair, 858-642-8439, Fax: 858-642-8740, E-mail: bbuchowicz@nu.edu. *Application contact:* Dominick Giovanniello, Associate Regional Dean, 800-NAT-UNIV, Fax: 858-541-7792, E-mail: dgiovann@nu.edu. Web site: http://www.nu.edu/OurPrograms/SchoolOfBusinessAndManagement/LeadershipAndHumanResourceManagement.html.

Newman University, MBA Program, Wichita, KS 67213-2097. Offers finance (MBA); international business (MBA); leadership (MBA); management (MBA); technology (MBA). Part-time programs available. *Faculty:* 4 full-time (1 woman), 7 part-time/adjunct (2 women). *Students:* 28 full-time (7 women), 83 part-time (28 women); includes 31 minority (8 Black or African American, non-Hispanic/Latino; 1 American Indian or Alaska Native, non-Hispanic/Latino; 9 Asian, non-Hispanic/Latino; 9 Hispanic/Latino; 1 Native Hawaiian or other Pacific Islander, non-Hispanic/Latino; 3 Two or more races, non-Hispanic/Latino), 23 international. Average age 31. 63 applicants, 70% accepted, 38 enrolled. In 2011, 49 master's awarded. *Degree requirements:* For master's, thesis optional. *Entrance requirements:* For master's, interview; minimum GPA of 3.0; 3 letters of recommendation; course work in algebra, statistics, macroeconomics, and financial accounting. Additional exam requirements/recommendations for international students: Required—TOEFL (minimum score 600 paper-based; 250 computer-based; 100 iBT). *Application deadline:* For fall admission, 8/1 priority date for domestic students, 7/15 for international students; for winter admission, 1/1 priority date for domestic students; for spring admission, 1/1 priority date for domestic students, 11/15 for international students. Applications are processed on a rolling basis. Application fee: $25 ($40 for international students). Electronic applications accepted. *Expenses:* Contact institution. *Financial support:* In 2011–12, 18 students received support. Federal Work-Study available. Financial award application deadline: 8/15; financial award applicants required to submit FAFSA. *Unit head:* Dr. Wendy Munday, Director of MBA Program, 316-942-4291 Ext. 2296, Fax: 316-942-4483, E-mail: mundayw@newmanu.edu. *Application contact:* Linda Kay Sabala, Director of Graduate Admissions, 316-942-4291 Ext. 2230, Fax: 316-942-4483, E-mail: sabalal@newmanu.edu. Web site: http://www.newmanu.edu.

The New School, Milano The New School for Management and Urban Policy, Program in Organizational Change Management, New York, NY 10011. Offers MS. Part-time and evening/weekend programs available. *Degree requirements:* For master's, thesis. *Entrance requirements:* For master's, 3 years of work experience, interview. Additional exam requirements/recommendations for international students: Required—TOEFL (minimum score 600 paper-based; 250 computer-based; 100 iBT). Electronic applications accepted.

New York University, Leonard N. Stern School of Business, Department of Management and Organizations, New York, NY 10012-1019. Offers management organizations (MBA); organization theory (PhD); organizational behavior (PhD); strategy (PhD). *Faculty research:* Strategic management, managerial cognition, interpersonal processes, conflict and negotiation.

North Central College, Graduate and Continuing Education Programs, Program in Leadership Studies, Naperville, IL 60566-7063. Offers higher education leadership (MLS); professional leadership (MLS); social entrepreneurship (MLS); sports leadership (MLS). Part-time and evening/weekend programs available. *Faculty:* 9 full-time (1 woman), 11 part-time/adjunct (5 women). *Students:* 44 full-time (28 women), 32 part-time (20 women); includes 16 minority (9 Black or African American, non-Hispanic/Latino; 6 Hispanic/Latino; 1 Two or more races, non-Hispanic/Latino), 1 international. Average age 29. 69 applicants, 74% accepted, 32 enrolled. In 2011, 20 master's awarded. *Degree requirements:* For master's, thesis optional, project. *Entrance requirements:* For master's, interview. Additional exam requirements/recommendations for international students: Required—TOEFL (minimum score 570 paper-based; 233 computer-based; 90 iBT). *Application deadline:* For fall admission, 8/15 for domestic students; for winter admission, 12/1 for domestic students; for spring admission, 2/1 for domestic students. Applications are processed on a rolling basis. Application fee: $25. *Expenses:* Contact institution. *Financial support:* In 2011–12, 1 student received support. Scholarships/grants available. Support available to part-time students. *Unit head:* Dr. Thomas Cavenagh, Program Coordinator, Leadership Studies, 630-637-5285. *Application contact:* Wendy Kulpinski, Director of Graduate and Continuing Education Admission, 630-637-5808, Fax: 630-637-5844, E-mail: wekulpinski@noctrl.edu.

Northern Kentucky University, Office of Graduate Programs, College of Business, Program in Executive Leadership and Organizational Change, Highland Heights, KY 41099. Offers MS. Part-time and evening/weekend programs available. *Students:* 47 part-time (28 women); includes 6 minority (5 Black or African American, non-Hispanic/Latino; 1 Hispanic/Latino), 1 international. Average age 39. 36 applicants, 69% accepted, 25 enrolled. In 2011, 20 master's awarded. *Degree requirements:* For master's, field research project. *Entrance requirements:* For master's, minimum GPA of 2.5; essay on professional career objective; 3 letters of recommendation, 1 from a current organization; 3 years of professional or managerial work experience; full-time employment at time of entry. Additional exam requirements/recommendations for international students: Required—TOEFL (minimum score 600 paper-based; 213 computer-based; 79 iBT); Recommended—IELTS (minimum score 6.5). *Application deadline:* For fall admission, 6/15 for domestic students, 6/1 for international students. Applications are processed on a rolling basis. Application fee: $40. Electronic applications accepted. *Expenses:* Contact institution. *Financial support:* Unspecified assistantships available. Financial award applicants required to submit FAFSA. *Faculty research:* Leadership and development, organizational change, field research, team and conflict management, strategy development and systems thinking. *Unit head:* Dr. Kenneth Rhee, Program Director, 859-572-6310, Fax: 859-572-5150, E-mail: rhee@nku.edu. *Application contact:* Amberly Hurst-Nutini, Coordinator, 859-572-5947, Fax: 859-572-5150, E-mail: hurstam@nku.edu. Web site: http://cob.nku.edu/graduatedegrees/eloc.html.

Northwestern College, Program in Organizational Leadership, St. Paul, MN 55113-1598. Offers MOL. Evening/weekend programs available.

Northwestern University, The Graduate School, Kellogg School of Management, Department of Management and Organizations, Evanston, IL 60208. Offers PhD. Admissions and degree offered through The Graduate School. *Degree requirements:* For doctorate, comprehensive exam, thesis/dissertation. *Entrance requirements:* For doctorate, GMAT or GRE General Test. Additional exam requirements/recommendations for international students: Required—TOEFL. Electronic applications accepted. *Faculty research:* Bargaining and negotiation, organizational design, decision making, organizational change, strategic alliances.

Northwestern University, The Graduate School, School of Education and Social Policy, Program in Learning and Organizational Change, Evanston, IL 60208. Offers MS. Part-time and evening/weekend programs available. Postbaccalaureate distance learning degree programs offered (minimal on-campus study). *Degree requirements:* For master's, thesis, practicum. *Entrance requirements:* For master's, GRE or GMAT (recommended), letters of recommendation. Additional exam requirements/recommendations for international students: Required—TOEFL (minimum score 600 paper-based; 250 computer-based; 100 iBT); Recommended—IELTS (minimum score 7). Electronic applications accepted. *Faculty research:* Strategic change, learning and performance, workplace learning, leadership development, cognitive design, knowledge management.

Northwest University, School of Business and Management, Kirkland, WA 98033. Offers business administration (MBA); social entrepreneurship (MA). Part-time and evening/weekend programs available. *Faculty:* 6 full-time (1 woman), 7 part-time/adjunct (3 women). *Students:* 41 full-time (20 women), 3 part-time (1 woman); includes 10 minority (5 Black or African American, non-Hispanic/Latino; 3 Asian, non-Hispanic/Latino; 2 Hispanic/Latino), 9 international. Average age 34. 21 applicants, 86% accepted, 18 enrolled. In 2011, 2 master's awarded. *Degree requirements:* For master's, formalized research. *Entrance requirements:* For master's, GMAT. Additional exam requirements/recommendations for international students: Required—TOEFL (minimum score 550 paper-based; 237 computer-based; 75 iBT). *Application deadline:* For fall admission, 8/1 for domestic and international students; for spring admission, 12/1 for domestic and international students. Application fee: $75. Electronic applications accepted. *Expenses:* Contact institution. *Financial support:* Federal Work-Study, scholarships/grants, health care benefits, and tuition waivers (full and partial) available. Financial award applicants required to submit FAFSA. *Unit head:* Dr. Teresa Gillespie, Dean, 425-889-5290, E-mail: teresa.gillespie@northwestu.edu. *Application contact:* Aaron Oosterwyk, Director of Graduate and Professional Studies Enrollment, 425-889-7792, Fax: 425-803-3059, E-mail: aaron.oosterwyk@northwestu.edu. Web site: http://www.northwestu.edu/business/.

Norwich University, College of Graduate and Continuing Studies, Master of Business Administration Program, Northfield, VT 05663. Offers finance (MBA); organizational leadership (MBA); project management (MBA). *Accreditation:* ACBSP. Evening/weekend programs available. *Faculty:* 19 part-time/adjunct (5 women). *Students:* 100 full-time (34 women); includes 16 minority (4 Black or African American, non-Hispanic/Latino; 1 American Indian or Alaska Native, non-Hispanic/Latino; 5 Asian, non-Hispanic/Latino; 4 Hispanic/Latino; 2 Two or more races, non-Hispanic/Latino). Average age 36. 67 applicants, 69% accepted, 46 enrolled. In 2011, 103 master's awarded. *Degree requirements:* For master's, comprehensive exam (for some programs), thesis optional. *Entrance requirements:* For master's, minimum undergraduate GPA of 2.75. Additional exam requirements/recommendations for international students: Required—TOEFL (minimum score 550 paper-based; 213 computer-based; 83 iBT). *Application deadline:* For fall admission, 8/10 for domestic and international students; for winter admission, 11/7 for domestic and international students; for spring admission, 2/6 for domestic and international students. Applications are processed on a rolling basis. Application fee: $50. Electronic applications accepted. *Expenses: Tuition:* Full-time $16,174. *Required fees:* $2130. Full-time tuition and fees vary according to program. *Financial support:* In 2011–12, 58 students received support. Scholarships/grants available. Financial award applicants required to submit FAFSA. *Unit head:* Dr. Jose Cordova, Faculty Director, 802-485-2567, Fax: 802-485-2533, E-mail: jcordova@norwich.edu. *Application contact:* Kerri Murnyack, Associate Program Director, 802-485-3304, Fax: 802-485-2533, E-mail: kmurnyuac@norwich.edu. Web site: http://mba.norwich.edu.

Norwich University, College of Graduate and Continuing Studies, Master of Public Administration Program, Northfield, VT 05663. Offers continuity of government operations (MPA); criminal justice studies (MPA); fiscal management (MPA); international development and influence (MPA); leadership (MPA); organizational leadership (MPA); public works administration (MPA). Evening/weekend programs available. *Faculty:* 9 part-time/adjunct (5 women). *Students:* 62 full-time (22 women); includes 7 minority (1 Black or African American, non-Hispanic/Latino; 2 American Indian or Alaska Native, non-Hispanic/Latino; 1 Asian, non-Hispanic/Latino; 3 Hispanic/Latino). Average age 39. 68 applicants, 44% accepted, 30 enrolled. In 2011, 79 master's awarded. *Entrance requirements:* Additional exam requirements/recommendations for international students: Required—TOEFL (minimum score 550 paper-based; 212 computer-based; 83 iBT). *Application deadline:* For fall admission, 8/10 for domestic and international students; for winter admission, 11/7 for domestic and international students; for spring admission, 2/6 for domestic and international students. Applications are processed on a rolling basis. Application fee: $50. Electronic applications accepted. *Expenses: Tuition:* Full-time $16,174. *Required fees:* $2130. Full-time tuition and fees vary according to program. *Financial support:* In 2011–12, 40 students received support. Scholarships/grants available. Financial award applicants required to submit FAFSA. *Faculty research:* Pre-employment investigations for public safety professionals, sustainability programs and policy implementation, online curriculum design "Best Practice," innovative voting procedures. *Unit head:* Donal Hartman, Program Director, 802-485-2567, Fax: 802-485-2533, E-mail: dhartman@norwich.edu. *Application contact:* Christopher Ormsby, Associate Program Director, 802-485-2567, Fax: 802-485-2533, E-mail: cormsby@norwich.edu. Web site: http://publicadmin.norwich.edu/.

Norwich University, College of Graduate and Continuing Studies, Master of Science in Organizational Leadership Program, Northfield, VT 05663. Offers MSOL. Evening/weekend programs available. *Faculty:* 7 part-time/adjunct (2 women). *Students:* 42 full-time (20 women); includes 4 minority (1 Black or African American, non-Hispanic/Latino; 1 American Indian or Alaska Native, non-Hispanic/Latino; 1 Hispanic/Latino; 1 Native Hawaiian or other Pacific Islander, non-Hispanic/Latino). Average age 39. 23 applicants, 100% accepted, 23 enrolled. In 2011, 34 master's awarded. *Entrance requirements:* Additional exam requirements/recommendations for international students: Required—TOEFL (minimum score 550 paper-based; 212 computer-based; 83 iBT). *Application deadline:* For fall admission, 8/10 for domestic and international students; for winter admission, 11/7 for domestic and international students; for spring admission, 2/6 for domestic and international students. Applications are processed on a rolling basis. Application fee: $50. Electronic applications accepted. *Expenses: Tuition:* Full-time $16,174. *Required fees:* $2130. Full-time tuition and fees vary according to program. *Financial support:* In 2011–12, 27 students received support. Scholarships/grants available. Financial award applicants required to submit FAFSA. *Faculty research:* Portable computing in high risk team dynamics. *Unit head:* Donal Hartman, Program Director, 802-485-2767, Fax: 802-485-2533, E-mail: hartmand@norwich.edu. *Application contact:* Christopher Ormsby, Associate Program Director, 802-485-2567, Fax: 802-485-2533, E-mail: corsmby@norwich.edu. Web site: http://leadership.norwich.edu/.

Nyack College, School of Business and Leadership, Nyack, NY 10960-3698. Offers business administration (MBA); organizational leadership (MS). Evening/weekend programs available. *Students:* 114 full-time (73 women), 60 part-time (44 women); includes 140 minority (108 Black or African American, non-Hispanic/Latino; 3 Asian, non-Hispanic/Latino; 22 Hispanic/Latino; 7 Two or more races, non-Hispanic/Latino), 9 international. Average age 40. In 2011, 75 master's awarded. *Degree requirements:* For master's, thesis (for some programs). *Entrance requirements:* For master's, GMAT (for MBA only), transcripts, personal goals statement, recommendations, resume, interview. Additional exam requirements/recommendations for international students: Required—TOEFL (minimum score 550 paper-based; 220 computer-based; 83 iBT). *Application deadline:* Applications are processed on a rolling basis. Application fee: $50. Electronic applications accepted. *Expenses:* Contact institution. *Financial support:* Applicants required to submit FAFSA. *Unit head:* Dr. Anita Underwood, Dean, 845-675-4511, Fax: 845-353-5812. *Application contact:* Traci Piescki, Director of Admissions, 800-541-6891, Fax: 845-348-3912, E-mail: admissions.grad@nyack.edu. Web site: http://www.nyack.edu/sbl.

Olivet Nazarene University, Program in Organizational Leadership, Bourbonnais, IL 60914. Offers MOL.

Our Lady of the Lake University of San Antonio, School of Business and Leadership, Program in Leadership Studies, San Antonio, TX 78207-4689. Offers PhD. *Degree requirements:* For doctorate, thesis/dissertation, internship, qualifying exam. *Entrance requirements:* For doctorate, GRE General Test or MAT, interview.

Our Lady of the Lake University of San Antonio, School of Business and Leadership, Program in Organizational Leadership, San Antonio, TX 78207-4689. Offers MS.

Oxford Graduate School, Graduate Programs, Dayton, TN 37321-6736. Offers family life education (M Litt); organizational leadership (M Litt); sociological integration of religion and society (D Phil).

Palm Beach Atlantic University, MacArthur School of Leadership, West Palm Beach, FL 33416-4708. Offers MS. Part-time and evening/weekend programs available. *Faculty:* 5 full-time (2 women). *Students:* 2 full-time (1 woman), 82 part-time (50 women); includes 45 minority (31 Black or African American, non-Hispanic/Latino; 1 American Indian or Alaska Native, non-Hispanic/Latino; 1 Asian, non-Hispanic/Latino; 12 Hispanic/Latino), 2 international. Average age 39. 42 applicants, 81% accepted, 17 enrolled. In 2011, 36 master's awarded. *Entrance requirements:* For master's, minimum GPA of 3.0. Additional exam requirements/recommendations for international students: Required—TOEFL (minimum score 550 paper-based; 213 computer-based; 79 iBT). *Application deadline:* For fall admission, 7/15 priority date for domestic students; for spring admission, 11/15 priority date for domestic students. Applications are processed on a rolling basis. Application fee: $45. Electronic applications accepted. *Expenses: Tuition:* Full-time $11,478; part-time $470 per credit hour. *Required fees:* $99 per semester. Tuition and fees vary according to course load, degree level and campus/location. *Financial support:* Scholarships/grants available. Financial award applicants required to submit FAFSA. *Unit head:* Dr. Jim Laub, Dean, 561-803-2302, E-mail: jim_laub@pba.edu. *Application contact:* Graduate Admissions, 888-468-6722, E-mail: grad@pba.edu. Web site: http://www.pba.edu/.

Pepperdine University, Graduate School of Education and Psychology, Division of Education, MA Program in Social Entrepreneurship and Change, Malibu, CA 90263. Offers MA. *Entrance requirements:* For master's, two letters of recommendation, one- to two-page statement of educational purpose. Additional exam requirements/recommendations for international students: Required—TOEFL.

Pepperdine University, Graziadio School of Business and Management, MS in Organization Development Program, Malibu, CA 90263. Offers MSOD. Program consists of four week-long sessions per year at different locations in Northern California,

Southern California and abroad. Part-time programs available. *Entrance requirements:* For master's, GMAT or GRE, two letters of recommendation. Additional exam requirements/recommendations for international students: Required—TOEFL.

Peru State College, Graduate Programs, Program in Organizational Management, Peru, NE 68421. Offers MS. Program offered online only. Part-time programs available. *Degree requirements:* For master's, thesis (for some programs). *Expenses:* Contact institution. *Faculty research:* Emotional intelligence.

Pfeiffer University, Program in Leadership and Organizational Change, Misenheimer, NC 28109-0960. Offers MS, MBA/MS. *Entrance requirements:* For master's, GRE or GMAT.

Point Park University, School of Business, Pittsburgh, PA 15222-1984. Offers business (MBA); organizational leadership (MA). Part-time and evening/weekend programs available. *Faculty:* 11 full-time, 14 part-time/adjunct. *Students:* 110 full-time (71 women), 240 part-time (127 women); includes 87 minority (62 Black or African American, non-Hispanic/Latino; 1 American Indian or Alaska Native, non-Hispanic/Latino; 5 Asian, non-Hispanic/Latino; 9 Hispanic/Latino; 1 Native Hawaiian or other Pacific Islander, non-Hispanic/Latino; 9 Two or more races, non-Hispanic/Latino), 21 international. Average age 32. 328 applicants, 73% accepted, 146 enrolled. In 2011, 183 master's awarded. *Degree requirements:* For master's, comprehensive exam (for some programs), thesis or alternative. *Entrance requirements:* For master's, minimum QPA of 2.75; 2 letters of recommendation; resume (MA). Additional exam requirements/recommendations for international students: Required—TOEFL (minimum score 550 paper-based; 79 iBT). *Application deadline:* Applications are processed on a rolling basis. Application fee: $30. Electronic applications accepted. *Expenses: Tuition:* Full-time $13,050; part-time $725 per credit. *Required fees:* $720; $40 per credit. *Financial support:* In 2011–12, 284 students received support, including 8 teaching assistantships with full tuition reimbursements available (averaging $6,400 per year); scholarships/grants also available. Financial award application deadline: 4/15; financial award applicants required to submit FAFSA. *Faculty research:* Technology issues, foreign direct investment, multinational corporate issues, cross-cultural international organizations/administrations, regional integration issues. *Unit head:* Dr. Dimitrius Kraniou, Chair, Deptartment of Global Management and Organization, 412-392-3447, Fax: 412-392-8048, E-mail: dkraniou@pointpark.edu. *Application contact:* Michael Powell, Assistant Director, Graduate and Adult Enrollment, 412-392-3807, Fax: 412-392-6164, E-mail: mpowell@pointpark.edu. Web site: http://www.pointpark.edu.

Quinnipiac University, School of Business, Program in Organizational Leadership, Hamden, CT 06518-1940. Offers MS. Part-time and evening/weekend programs available. *Faculty:* 3 full-time (1 woman), 2 part-time/adjunct (1 woman). *Students:* 2 full-time (both women), 147 part-time (95 women); includes 27 minority (18 Black or African American, non-Hispanic/Latino; 2 Asian, non-Hispanic/Latino; 6 Hispanic/Latino; 1 Two or more races, non-Hispanic/Latino). 69 applicants, 75% accepted, 48 enrolled. In 2011, 56 master's awarded. *Entrance requirements:* Additional exam requirements/recommendations for international students: Required—TOEFL (minimum score 575 paper-based; 233 computer-based; 90 iBT), IELTS (minimum score 6.5). *Application deadline:* Applications are processed on a rolling basis. Application fee: $45. Electronic applications accepted. *Expenses: Tuition:* Part-time $855 per credit. *Required fees:* $35 per credit. *Financial support:* In 2011–12, 21 students received support. *Unit head:* Lisa Braiewa, Director of Online Master's Programs, School of Business, 203-582-3710, Fax: 203-582-8664, E-mail: lisa.braiewa@quinnipiac.edu. *Application contact:* Valerie Schlesinger, Director of Admissions for QU Online, 203-582-8949, Fax: 203-582-3443, E-mail: valerie.schlesinger@quinnipiac.edu. Web site: http://www.quinnipiac.edu/msol.xml.

Regent University, Graduate School, School of Global Leadership and Entrepreneurship, Virginia Beach, VA 23464-9800. Offers business administration (MBA), including management general; leadership (Certificate); management (MA); organizational leadership (MA, PhD), including ecclesial leadership (PhD), entrepreneurial leadership (PhD), human resource development (PhD); strategic foresight (MA); strategic leadership (DSL), including global consulting, leadership coaching, strategic foresight. Part-time and evening/weekend programs available. Postbaccalaureate distance learning degree programs offered (minimal on-campus study). *Faculty:* 13 full-time (3 women), 4 part-time/adjunct (1 woman). *Students:* 27 full-time (11 women), 589 part-time (241 women); includes 183 minority (143 Black or African American, non-Hispanic/Latino; 3 American Indian or Alaska Native, non-Hispanic/Latino; 15 Asian, non-Hispanic/Latino; 22 Hispanic/Latino), 128 international. Average age 41. 225 applicants, 57% accepted, 85 enrolled. In 2011, 80 master's, 38 doctorates awarded. *Degree requirements:* For master's, thesis or alternative, 3 credit hour culminating experience; for doctorate, thesis/dissertation. *Entrance requirements:* For master's, GRE, GMAT, minimum undergraduate GPA of 2.75, computer literacy survey, 2 recommendations, resume, transcripts, essay; for doctorate, GRE, GMAT, sample of writing, minimum 3 years of relevant experience, computer literacy survey, 2 recommendations, resume, essay, transcripts; for Certificate, writing sample, resume, transcripts. Additional exam requirements/recommendations for international students: Required—TOEFL (minimum score 577 paper-based; 233 computer-based). *Application deadline:* For fall admission, 5/1 priority date for domestic students; for spring admission, 10/1 priority date for domestic students. Applications are processed on a rolling basis. Application fee: $50. Electronic applications accepted. *Expenses:* Contact institution. *Financial support:* Career-related internships or fieldwork, scholarships/grants, and tuition waivers (full and partial) available. Support available to part-time students. Financial award application deadline: 9/1. *Faculty research:* Servant leadership, ethics and values, telecommuting and family values, organizational communications, distance education. *Unit head:* Dr. Bruce Winston, Dean, 757-352-4306, Fax: 757-352-4634, E-mail: brucwin@regent.edu. *Application contact:* Matthew Chadwick, Director of Enrollment Support Services, 800-373-5504, Fax: 757-352-4381, E-mail: admissions@regent.edu.

Regis University, College for Professional Studies, School of Management, Denver, CO 80221-1099. Offers accounting (MS, Certificate); executive international management (Certificate); executive leadership (Certificate); executive project management (Certificate); finance and accounting (MBA); general business administration (MBA); health care management (MBA); human resource management and leadership (MSOL); information technology leadership and management (MSOL); international business (MBA); marketing (MBA); operations management (MBA); organizational leadership and management (MSOL); project leadership and management (MSOL); project management (Certificate); strategic business management (Certificate); strategic human resource management (Certificate); strategic management (MBA). Offered at Colorado Springs Campus, Northwest Denver Campus, Southeast Denver Campus, Fort Collins Campus, Broomfield Campus, Henderson (Nevada) Campus, and Summerlin (Nevada) Campus and online. Part-time and evening/weekend programs available. Postbaccalaureate distance learning degree programs offered (no on-campus study). *Degree requirements:* For master's, thesis optional, capstone project. *Entrance requirements:* For master's, GMAT or essays, interview, 2 years of full-time business work experience, resume; for Certificate, GMAT. Additional exam requirements/recommendations for international students: Required—TOEFL, TWE (minimum score 5) or university-based test. Electronic applications accepted. *Faculty research:* Impact of information technology on small business regulation of accounting, international project financing, mineral development, delivery of healthcare to rural indigenous communities.

Rider University, Department of Graduate Education, Leadership and Counseling, Program in Organizational Leadership, Lawrenceville, NJ 08648-3001. Offers MA. *Entrance requirements:* For master's, resume. *Expenses: Tuition:* Full-time $32,820; part-time $710 per credit. *Required fees:* $350; $35 per course. Tuition and fees vary according to campus/location and program.

Robert Morris University, Graduate Studies, School of Communications and Information Systems, Moon Township, PA 15108-1189. Offers communication and information systems (MS); competitive intelligence systems (MS); information security and assurance (MS); information systems and communications (D Sc); information systems management (MS); information technology project management (MS); Internet information systems (MS); organizational leadership (MS). Part-time and evening/weekend programs available. Postbaccalaureate distance learning degree programs offered (no on-campus study). *Faculty:* 28 full-time (9 women), 9 part-time/adjunct (3 women). *Students:* 231 part-time (68 women); includes 41 minority (31 Black or African American, non-Hispanic/Latino; 8 Asian, non-Hispanic/Latino; 2 Hispanic/Latino), 16 international. *Degree requirements:* For doctorate, thesis/dissertation. *Entrance requirements:* For doctorate, employer letter of endorsement, interview. Additional exam requirements/recommendations for international students: Required—TOEFL (minimum score 550 paper-based; 213 computer-based; 79 iBT). *Application deadline:* For fall admission, 7/1 priority date for domestic students, 7/1 for international students; for spring admission, 11/1 priority date for domestic students, 11/1 for international students. Applications are processed on a rolling basis. Application fee: $35. Electronic applications accepted. *Expenses:* Contact institution. *Financial support:* Research assistantships with partial tuition reimbursements, institutionally sponsored loans, and unspecified assistantships available. Support available to part-time students. Financial award application deadline: 5/1. *Unit head:* Dr. Barbara J. Levine, Dean, 412-397-2591, Fax: 412-397-2481, E-mail: levine@rmu.edu. *Application contact:* Deborah Roach, Assistant Dean, Graduate Admissions, 412-397-5200, Fax: 412-397-2425, E-mail: graduateadmissions@rmu.edu. Web site: http://www.rmu.edu/web/cms/schools/scis/.

Roosevelt University, Graduate Division, College of Education, Program in Educational Leadership, Chicago, IL 60605. Offers MA, Ed D.

Rutgers, The State University of New Jersey, Newark, Rutgers Business School–Newark and New Brunswick, Doctoral Programs in Management, Newark, NJ 07102. Offers accounting (PhD); accounting information systems (PhD); economics (PhD); finance (PhD); individualized study (PhD); information technology (PhD); international business (PhD); management science (PhD); marketing science (PhD); organizational management (PhD); science, technology and management (PhD); supply chain management (PhD). *Degree requirements:* For doctorate, comprehensive exam, thesis/dissertation. *Entrance requirements:* For doctorate, GRE or GMAT. Additional exam requirements/recommendations for international students: Required—TOEFL (minimum score 550 paper-based; 213 computer-based; 79 iBT). Electronic applications accepted.

Sage Graduate School, School of Management, Program in Organization Management, Troy, NY 12180-4115. Offers organization management (MS); public administration (MS). Part-time and evening/weekend programs available. *Faculty:* 2 full-time (both women), 8 part-time/adjunct (1 woman). *Students:* 5 full-time (2 women), 47 part-time (31 women); includes 16 minority (12 Black or African American, non-Hispanic/Latino; 3 Asian, non-Hispanic/Latino; 1 Hispanic/Latino), 1 international. Average age 33. 26 applicants, 50% accepted, 12 enrolled. In 2011, 18 master's awarded. *Degree requirements:* For master's, capstone seminar. *Entrance requirements:* For master's, minimum GPA of 2.75. Additional exam requirements/recommendations for international students: Required—TOEFL (minimum score 550 paper-based; 213 computer-based). *Application deadline:* Applications are processed on a rolling basis. Application fee: $40. *Expenses: Tuition:* Full-time $11,880; part-time $660 per credit hour. Tuition and fees vary according to program. *Financial support:* Fellowships, research assistantships, Federal Work-Study, scholarships/grants, tuition waivers (partial), and unspecified assistantships available. Support available to part-time students. Financial award application deadline: 3/1; financial award applicants required to submit FAFSA. *Unit head:* Dr. Daniel Robeson, Dean, School of Management, 518-292-8637, Fax: 518-292-1964, E-mail: robesd@sage.edu. *Application contact:* Wendy D. Diefendorf, Director of Graduate and Adult Admission, 518-244-2443, Fax: 518-244-6880, E-mail: diefew@sage.edu. Web site: http://www.sage.edu/academics/management/programs/organization_management/.

St. Ambrose University, College of Business, Program in Organizational Leadership, Davenport, IA 52801. Offers MOL. Part-time and evening/weekend programs available. *Faculty:* 4 full-time (1 woman), 5 part-time/adjunct (2 women). *Students:* 18 full-time (14 women), 69 part-time (40 women); includes 15 minority (9 Black or African American, non-Hispanic/Latino; 1 Asian, non-Hispanic/Latino; 4 Hispanic/Latino; 1 Native Hawaiian or other Pacific Islander, non-Hispanic/Latino). Average age 37. 40 applicants, 90% accepted, 27 enrolled. In 2011, 43 master's awarded. *Degree requirements:* For master's, comprehensive exam (for some programs), thesis or alternative, integration projects. *Entrance requirements:* Additional exam requirements/recommendations for international students: Required—TOEFL. *Application deadline:* For fall admission, 8/15 priority date for domestic students; for winter admission, 12/15 priority date for domestic students; for spring admission, 1/1 priority date for domestic students. Applications are processed on a rolling basis. Application fee: $25. Electronic applications accepted. *Expenses:* Contact institution. *Financial support:* In 2011–12, 50 students received support, including 10 research assistantships (averaging $3,343 per year); scholarships/grants, tuition waivers (partial), and unspecified assistantships also available. Financial award application deadline: 3/15; financial award applicants required to submit FAFSA. *Unit head:* Dr. Ron O. Wastyn, Director, 563-322-1014, Fax: 563-324-0842, E-mail: wastynronaldo@sau.edu. *Application contact:* Megan M. Gisi, Program Coordinator, 563-322-1051, Fax: 563-324-0842, E-mail: gisimeganm@sau.edu. Web site: http://web.sau.edu/mol/.

St. Catharine College, School of Graduate Studies, St. Catharine, KY 40061-9499. Offers leadership (MA), including community and regional studies, health promotion and leadership. *Entrance requirements:* For master's, GRE, LSAT, MCAT or GMAT, official transcripts. Additional exam requirements/recommendations for international students: Required—TOEFL, IELTS, or Michigan English Language Assessment Battery. Electronic applications accepted.

St. Catherine University, Graduate Programs, Program in Organizational Leadership, St. Paul, MN 55105. Offers MA. Part-time and evening/weekend programs available. *Degree requirements:* For master's, thesis. *Entrance requirements:* For master's, GMAT, GRE General Test or MAT, 2 years of work experience, minimum GPA of 3.0. Additional exam requirements/recommendations for international students: Required—TOEFL (minimum score 600 paper-based; 250 computer-based; 100 iBT). *Expenses: Required fees:* $30 per semester. Tuition and fees vary according to program. *Faculty research:* Ethics.

St. Edward's University, School of Management and Business, Program in Organizational Leadership and Ethics, Austin, TX 78704. Offers MS. Part-time and evening/weekend programs available. *Students:* 41 part-time (23 women); includes 22 minority (5 Black or African American, non-Hispanic/Latino; 1 American Indian or Alaska Native, non-Hispanic/Latino; 1 Asian, non-Hispanic/Latino; 14 Hispanic/Latino; 1 Two or more races, non-Hispanic/Latino). Average age 37. 17 applicants, 94% accepted, 14 enrolled. In 2011, 24 master's awarded. *Degree requirements:* For master's, minimum of 24 hours in residence. *Entrance requirements:* For master's, GMAT or GRE General Test, minimum GPA of 2.75 in last 60 hours of course work. Additional exam requirements/recommendations for international students: Required—TOEFL (minimum score 550 paper-based; 213 computer-based; 79 iBT) or IELTS (minimum score 6). *Application deadline:* For fall admission, 7/1 for domestic and international students; for spring admission, 11/1 for domestic and international students. Applications are processed on a rolling basis. Application fee: $45 ($50 for international students). Electronic applications accepted. *Expenses: Tuition:* Full-time $17,550; part-time $975 per credit hour. *Required fees:* $50 per trimester. Full-time tuition and fees vary according to course load and program. *Unit head:* Dr. Tom Sechrest, Director, 512-637-1954, Fax: 512-448-8492, E-mail: thomasl@stedwards.edu. *Application contact:* Derrick Mueller, Graduate Admission Coordinator, 512-448-8600, Fax: 512-428-1032, E-mail: derrickm@stedwards.edu. Web site: http://www.stedwards.edu.

St. Edward's University, School of Management and Business, Program in Organization Development, Austin, TX 78704. Offers MA. Part-time and evening/weekend programs available. *Students:* 11 part-time (8 women); includes 7 minority (3 Black or African American, non-Hispanic/Latino; 4 Hispanic/Latino), 1 international. Average age 34. 16 applicants, 100% accepted, 11 enrolled. *Degree requirements:* For master's, minimum of 24 hours in residence. *Entrance requirements:* For master's, GMAT or GRE General Test, minimum GPA of 2.75 in last 60 hours of course work. Additional exam requirements/recommendations for international students: Required—TOEFL (minimum score 550 paper-based; 213 computer-based; 79 iBT) or IELTS (minimum score 6). *Application deadline:* For fall admission, 7/1 for domestic and international students. Applications are processed on a rolling basis. Application fee: $45 ($50 for international students). Electronic applications accepted. *Expenses: Tuition:* Full-time $17,550; part-time $975 per credit hour. *Required fees:* $50 per trimester. Full-time tuition and fees vary according to course load and program. *Unit head:* Connie Porter, Director, 512-416-5827, Fax: 512-448-8492, E-mail: constanp@stedwards.edu. *Application contact:* Derrick Mueller, Graduate Admissions Coordinator, 512-448-8600, Fax: 512-428-1032, E-mail: derrickm@stedwards.edu. Web site: http://www.stedwards.edu.

St. Joseph's College, Long Island Campus, Program in Management, Patchogue, NY 11772-2399. Offers health care (AC); health care management (MS); human resource management (AC); human resources management (MS); organizational management (MS).

Saint Joseph's University, College of Arts and Sciences, Organization Development and Leadership Programs, Philadelphia, PA 19131-1395. Offers adult learning and training (MS, Certificate); organization dynamics and leadership (MS, Certificate); organizational psychology and development (MS, Certificate). Part-time and evening/weekend programs available. Postbaccalaureate distance learning degree programs offered (no on-campus study). *Faculty:* 2 full-time (both women), 3 part-time/adjunct (1 woman). *Students:* 8 full-time (all women), 159 part-time (111 women); includes 50 minority (35 Black or African American, non-Hispanic/Latino; 1 American Indian or Alaska Native, non-Hispanic/Latino; 5 Asian, non-Hispanic/Latino; 7 Hispanic/Latino; 1 Native Hawaiian or other Pacific Islander, non-Hispanic/Latino; 1 Two or more races, non-Hispanic/Latino), 5 international. Average age 37. 57 applicants, 84% accepted, 42 enrolled. In 2011, 41 master's awarded. *Entrance requirements:* For master's, GRE (if GPA less than 2.7), minimum GPA of 2.7, 2 letters of recommendation, resume. Additional exam requirements/recommendations for international students: Required—TOEFL (minimum score 550 paper-based; 213 computer-based; 79 iBT). *Application deadline:* For fall admission, 7/15 priority date for domestic students, 4/15 for international students; for winter admission, 1/15 for international students; for spring admission, 11/15 priority date for domestic students, 10/15 for international students. Applications are processed on a rolling basis. Application fee: $35. Electronic applications accepted. *Expenses: Tuition:* Part-time $735 per credit hour. Tuition and fees vary according to degree level and program. *Financial support:* Applicants required to submit FAFSA. *Unit head:* Dr. Felice Tilin, Director, 610-660-1575, E-mail: ftilin@sju.edu. *Application contact:* Kate McConnell, Director, Graduate College of Arts and Sciences Admissions and Retention, 610-660-3184, Fax: 610-660-3230, E-mail: kate.mcconnell@sju.edu. Web site: http://www.sju.edu/academics/cas/grad/odl/index.html.

Saint Louis University, Graduate Education, College of Education and Public Service, Department of Public Policy Studies, St. Louis, MO 63103-2097. Offers geographic information systems (Certificate); organizational development (Certificate); public administration (MAPA); public policy analysis (PhD); urban affairs (MAUA); urban planning and real estate development (MUPRED). *Accreditation:* NASPAA. Part-time programs available. *Degree requirements:* For master's, comprehensive exam (for some programs), thesis (for some programs); for doctorate, comprehensive exam, thesis/dissertation, preliminary exams. *Entrance requirements:* For master's, GMAT, GRE General Test, or LSAT, letters of recommendation, resume; for doctorate, GMAT, GRE General Test, or LSAT, letters of recommendation, resumé, interview, transcripts, goal statement. Additional exam requirements/recommendations for international students: Required—TOEFL (minimum score 525 paper-based; 194 computer-based). Electronic applications accepted. *Faculty research:* Urban politics, brown fields, e-government, and administration, evaluation research, community development, electronic government and governance.

Saint Mary's University of Minnesota, Schools of Graduate and Professional Programs, Graduate School of Business and Technology, Organizational Leadership Program, Winona, MN 55987-1399. Offers MA. *Unit head:* Diana-Christine Teodorescu, Director, 507-238-4510, E-mail: dteodore@smumn.edu. *Application contact:* Yasin Alsaidi, Director of Admissions for Graduate and Professional Programs, 612-728-5207, Fax: 612-728-5121, E-mail: yalsaidi@smumn.edu. Web site: http://www.smumn.edu/graduate-home/areas-of-study/graduate-school-of-business-technology/ma-in-organizational-leadership.

Salve Regina University, Program in Management, Newport, RI 02840-4192. Offers business studies (Certificate); holistic leadership and management (Certificate); human resources management (Certificate); law enforcement leadership (MS); leadership and change management (Certificate); management (Certificate); organizational development (Certificate). Part-time and evening/weekend programs available. Postbaccalaureate distance learning degree programs offered (minimal on-campus study). *Faculty:* 2 full-time (1 woman), 15 part-time/adjunct (6 women). *Students:* 9 full-time (6 women), 40 part-time (20 women); includes 2 minority (both Black or African American, non-Hispanic/Latino). *Entrance requirements:* For master's, GMAT, GRE General Test, or MAT. Additional exam requirements/recommendations for international students: Required—TOEFL (minimum score 600 paper-based; 250 computer-based; 100 iBT). *Application deadline:* For fall admission, 3/15 priority date for domestic students, 3/5 for international students; for spring admission, 3/15 priority date for domestic students, 9/15 for international students. Applications are processed on a rolling basis. Application fee: $60. Electronic applications accepted. *Expenses: Tuition:* Full-time $7740; part-time $430 per credit. *Required fees:* $40 per semester. Tuition and fees vary according to program. *Financial support:* Career-related internships or fieldwork and Federal Work-Study available. Support available to part-time students. Financial award application deadline: 3/1; financial award applicants required to submit FAFSA. *Unit head:* Dr. Arlene Nicholas, Director, 401-341-3280, E-mail: arlene.nicholas@salve.edu. *Application contact:* Kelly Alverson, Associate Director of Graduate Admissions, 401-341-2153, Fax: 401-341-2973, E-mail: kelly.alverson@salve.edu. Web site: http://www.salve.edu/graduatestudies/programs/mgt/.

Santa Clara University, Leavey School of Business, Program in Business Administration, Santa Clara, CA 95053. Offers accounting (MBA); entrepreneurship (MBA); executive business administration (EMBA); finance (MBA); food and agribusiness (MBA); international business (MBA); leading people and organizations (MBA); managing technology and innovation (MBA); marketing management (MBA); supply chain management (MBA). *Accreditation:* AACSB. Part-time and evening/weekend programs available. *Students:* 196 full-time (80 women), 669 part-time (224 women); includes 302 minority (12 Black or African American, non-Hispanic/Latino; 246 Asian, non-Hispanic/Latino; 35 Hispanic/Latino; 6 Native Hawaiian or other Pacific Islander, non-Hispanic/Latino; 3 Two or more races, non-Hispanic/Latino), 186 international. Average age 32. 365 applicants, 74% accepted, 199 enrolled. In 2011, 366 degrees awarded. *Degree requirements:* For master's, thesis or alternative. *Entrance requirements:* For master's, GMAT, GRE. Additional exam requirements/recommendations for international students: Required—TOEFL (minimum score 600 paper-based; 250 computer-based; 100 iBT). *Application deadline:* For fall admission, 6/1 for domestic and international students; for spring admission, 1/19 for domestic students, 1/17 for international students. Applications are processed on a rolling basis. Application fee: $75 ($100 for international students). Electronic applications accepted. *Expenses:* Contact institution. *Financial support:* In 2011–12, 350 students received support. Fellowships with partial tuition reimbursements available, research assistantships with partial tuition reimbursements available, career-related internships or fieldwork, Federal Work-Study, institutionally sponsored loans, scholarships/grants, health care benefits, and unspecified assistantships available. Support available to part-time students. Financial award application deadline: 6/1; financial award applicants required to submit FAFSA. *Unit head:* Elizabeth B. Ford, Senior Assistant Dean, 408-554-2752, Fax: 408-554-4571, E-mail: eford@scu.edu. *Application contact:* Tammy Fox, Assistant Director, Graduate Business Admissions, 408-554-7858, E-mail: tkfox@scu.edu.

Saybrook University, Graduate College of Psychology and Humanistic Studies, San Francisco, CA 94111-1920. Offers clinical psychology (Psy D); human science (MA, PhD), including consciousness and spirituality, humanistic and transpersonal psychology, integrative health studies, organizational systems, social transformation; organizational systems (MA, PhD), including consciousness and spirituality, humanistic and transpersonal psychology, integrative health studies, leadership of sustainable systems (MA), organizational systems, social transformation; psychology (MA, PhD), including clinical psychology (PhD), consciousness and spirituality, creativity studies (MA), humanistic and transpersonal psychology, integrative health studies, Jungian studies, marriage and family therapy (MA), organizational systems, social transformation. Postbaccalaureate distance learning degree programs offered (minimal on-campus study). *Faculty:* 11 full-time (3 women), 83 part-time/adjunct (34 women). *Students:* 479 full-time (333 women); includes 62 minority (30 Black or African American, non-Hispanic/Latino; 1 American Indian or Alaska Native, non-Hispanic/Latino; 13 Asian, non-Hispanic/Latino; 18 Hispanic/Latino), 18 international. Average age 43. 280 applicants, 52% accepted, 105 enrolled. In 2011, 28 master's, 43 doctorates awarded. Terminal master's awarded for partial completion of doctoral program. *Degree requirements:* For master's, thesis or alternative; for doctorate, thesis/dissertation. *Entrance requirements:* Additional exam requirements/recommendations for international students: Required—TOEFL (minimum score 580 paper-based; 237 computer-based; 93 iBT). *Application deadline:* For fall admission, 6/1 priority date for domestic students; for spring admission, 12/16 priority date for domestic students. Application fee: $50. Electronic applications accepted. *Financial support:* In 2011–12, 335 students received support. Scholarships/grants available. Financial award applicants required to submit FAFSA. *Faculty research:* Humanistic theory, health studies, organizational systems, consciousness and spirituality, social transformation. *Total annual research expenditures:* $90,000. *Unit head:* Mark Schulman, President, 800-825-4480, Fax: 415-433-9271. *Application contact:* Director of Admissions, 800-825-4480, Fax: 415-433-9271, E-mail: admissions@saybrook.edu. Web site: http://www.saybrook.edu/phs.

Saybrook University, LIOS Graduate College, Leadership and Organization Development Track, San Francisco, CA 94111-1920. Offers MA. Program offered jointly with Bastyr University. *Faculty:* 10 full-time (6 women), 5 part-time/adjunct (2 women). *Students:* 48 full-time. Average age 40. 50 applicants, 98% accepted, 40 enrolled. In 2011, 19 master's awarded. *Degree requirements:* For master's, thesis (for some programs), oral exams. *Entrance requirements:* For master's, bachelor's degree from an accredited college or university. *Application deadline:* Applications are processed on a rolling basis. Application fee: $65. *Financial support:* In 2011–12, 32 students received support. Career-related internships or fieldwork, Federal Work-Study, and scholarships/grants available. Financial award applicants required to submit FAFSA. *Faculty research:* Cross-functional work teams, communication, management authority, employee influence, systems theory. *Unit head:* Dr. Cynthia FitzGerald, Dean, 425-968-3410, Fax: 425-968-3409, E-mail: cfitzgerald@lios.saybroo.edu. *Application contact:* Rhys Clark, Director, Academic Admissions, 425-968-3400, Fax: 425-968-3410.

Seattle University, Albers School of Business and Economics, Center for Leadership Formation, Seattle, WA 98122-1090. Offers leadership (Certificate). Evening/weekend programs available. *Faculty:* 18 full-time (6 women), 8 part-time/adjunct (7 women). *Students:* 51 full-time (24 women); includes 7 minority (2 Black or African American, non-Hispanic/Latino; 2 American Indian or Alaska Native, non-Hispanic/Latino; 2 Asian, non-Hispanic/Latino; 1 Two or more races, non-Hispanic/Latino), 3 international. Average age 42. 44 applicants, 91% accepted, 27 enrolled. In 2011, 17 master's awarded. *Entrance requirements:* For master's, GMAT, 7 years continuous professional experience, undergraduate degree with minimum GPA of 3.0; for Certificate, 7 years continuous professional experience, undergraduate degree with minimum GPA of 3.0. *Application deadline:* Applications are processed on a rolling basis. Application fee: $55. Electronic applications accepted. *Expenses:* Contact institution. *Unit head:* Dr. Marilyn Gist, Executive Director, 206-296-5374, E-mail: gistm@seattleu.edu. *Application contact:* Sommer Harrison, Recruiting Coordinator, 206-296-2529, Fax: 206-296-2374, E-mail: emba@seattleu.edu. Web site: http://www.seattleu.edu/albers/executiveeducation/.

Shippensburg University of Pennsylvania, School of Graduate Studies, College of Arts and Sciences, Department of Sociology and Anthropology, Shippensburg, PA 17257-2299. Offers organizational development and leadership (MS), including business, communications, environmental management, higher education structure and policy, historical administration, individual and organizational development, management information systems, public organizations, social structures and organizations. Part-time and evening/weekend programs available. *Faculty:* 3 full-time (all women). *Students:* 12 full-time (6 women), 40 part-time (34 women); includes 6 minority (3 Black or African American, non-Hispanic/Latino; 2 Asian, non-Hispanic/Latino; 1 Two or more races, non-Hispanic/Latino), 2 international. Average age 33. 52 applicants, 46% accepted, 16 enrolled. In 2011, 34 master's awarded. *Degree requirements:* For master's, capstone experience including internship. *Entrance requirements:* For master's, interview (if GPA less than 2.75), resume, personal goals statement. Additional exam requirements/recommendations for international students: Required—TOEFL (minimum score 580 paper-based; 237 computer-based); Recommended—IELTS (minimum score 6). *Application deadline:* For fall admission, 4/30 for international students; for spring admission, 9/30 for international students. Applications are processed on a rolling basis. Application fee: $30. Electronic applications accepted. *Expenses: Tuition, area resident:* Part-time $416 per credit. Tuition, state resident: part-time $416 per credit. Tuition, nonresident: part-time $624 per credit. *Required fees:* $119 per credit. *Financial support:* In 2011–12, 9 research assistantships with full tuition reimbursements (averaging $5,000 per year) were awarded; career-related internships or fieldwork, scholarships/grants, unspecified assistantships, and resident hall director and student payroll positions also available. Support available to part-time students. Financial award applicants required to submit FAFSA. *Unit head:* Dr. Barbara Denison, Program Coordinator, 717-477-1735, Fax: 717-477-4011, E-mail: bjdeni@ship.edu. *Application contact:* Jeremy R. Goshorn, Assistant Dean of Graduate Admissions, 717-477-1231, Fax: 717-477-4016, E-mail: jrgoshorn@ship.edu. Web site: http://www.ship.edu/odl/.

Southern New Hampshire University, School of Business, Manchester, NH 03106-1045. Offers accounting (MS); business administration (MBA, Certificate), including accounting (Certificate), business administration (MBA), finance (Certificate), forensic accounting (Certificate), human resources management (Certificate), international business (Certificate), international sport management (Certificate), leadership of not for profit organizations (Certificate), marketing (Certificate), operations management (Certificate), sport management (Certificate), taxation (Certificate); finance (MS); hospitality and tourism leadership (Certificate); information technology (MS, Certificate); information technology/international business (Certificate); integrated marketing communications (Certificate); international business (MS, DBA); marketing (MS); operations and project management (MS); organizational leadership (MS); project management (Certificate); sport management (MS); MBA/Certificate. *Accreditation:* ACBSP. Part-time and evening/weekend programs available. Postbaccalaureate distance learning degree programs offered (no on-campus study). Terminal master's awarded for partial completion of doctoral program. *Degree requirements:* For master's, one foreign language, comprehensive exam (for some programs), thesis or alternative; for doctorate, one foreign language, comprehensive exam, thesis/dissertation. *Entrance requirements:* For master's, minimum GPA of 2.5; for doctorate, GMAT. Additional exam requirements/recommendations for international students: Required—TOEFL (minimum score 500 paper-based). Electronic applications accepted.

Southwestern College, Fifth-Year Graduate Programs, Winfield, KS 67156-2499. Offers leadership (MS); management (MBA); music (MA), including education, performance. Part-time programs available. *Faculty:* 3 full-time (1 woman), 12 part-time/adjunct (4 women). *Students:* 13 full-time (5 women), 8 part-time (4 women); includes 3 minority (2 Black or African American, non-Hispanic/Latino; 1 American Indian or Alaska Native, non-Hispanic/Latino), 5 international. Average age 25. 21 applicants, 90% accepted, 16 enrolled. In 2011, 8 master's awarded. *Entrance requirements:* For master's, baccalaureate degree, minimum GPA of 3.0. Additional exam requirements/recommendations for international students: Required—TOEFL (minimum score 550 paper-based; 213 computer-based). *Application deadline:* For fall admission, 4/1 priority date for domestic students; for spring admission, 12/1 priority date for domestic students. Applications are processed on a rolling basis. Electronic applications accepted. Tuition and fees vary according to program. *Financial support:* In 2011–12, 8 students received support. Federal Work-Study, tuition waivers (partial), and unspecified assistantships available. Financial award application deadline: 4/1; financial award applicants required to submit FAFSA. *Unit head:* Dr. James Sheppard, Vice President for Academic Affairs, 620-229-6227, Fax: 620-229-6224, E-mail: james.sheppard@sckans.edu. *Application contact:* Marla Sexson, Director of Admissions, 800-846-1543 Ext. 6364, Fax: 620-229-6344, E-mail: marla.sexson@sckans.edu. Web site: http://www.sckans.edu/graduate.

Southwest University, MBA Program, Kenner, LA 70062. Offers business administration (MBA); management (MBA); organizational management (MBA).

Southwest University, Program in Organizational Management, Kenner, LA 70062. Offers MA.

Spring Arbor University, School of Graduate and Professional Studies, Spring Arbor, MI 49283-9799. Offers counseling (MAC); family studies (MAFS); nursing (MSN); organizational management (MSM). Part-time and evening/weekend programs available. Postbaccalaureate distance learning degree programs offered (no on-campus study). *Faculty:* 12 full-time (5 women), 113 part-time/adjunct (67 women). *Students:* 363 full-time (300 women), 344 part-time (265 women); includes 166 minority (142 Black or African American, non-Hispanic/Latino; 4 American Indian or Alaska Native, non-Hispanic/Latino; 5 Asian, non-Hispanic/Latino; 13 Hispanic/Latino; 2 Two or more races, non-Hispanic/Latino), 1 international. Average age 40. In 2011, 276 master's awarded. *Entrance requirements:* For master's, bachelor's degree from regionally-accredited college or university, minimum GPA of 3.0 for at least the last two years of the bachelor's degree, at least two recommendations from professional/academic individuals. Additional exam requirements/recommendations for international students: Required—TOEFL (minimum score 600 paper-based; 220 computer-based). *Application deadline:* Applications are processed on a rolling basis. Application fee: $40. Electronic applications accepted. *Expenses: Tuition:* Full-time $5500; part-time $490 per credit hour. *Required fees:* $240; $120 per term. Tuition and fees vary according to program. *Financial support:* Scholarships/grants available. Support available to part-time students. Financial award applicants required to submit FAFSA. *Unit head:* Natalie Gianetti, Dean, 517-750-1200 Ext. 1343, Fax: 517-750-6602, E-mail: gianetti@arbor.edu. *Application contact:* Greg Bentle, Coordinator of Graduate Recruitment, 517-750-6763, Fax: 517-750-6624, E-mail: gbentle@arbor.edu. Web site: http://www.arbor.edu/.

Springfield College, Graduate Programs, Program in Human Services, Springfield, MA 01109-3797. Offers human services (MS), including community counseling psychology, mental health counseling, organizational management and leadership. Part-time programs available. *Degree requirements:* For master's, comprehensive exam, thesis (for some programs), research project. *Entrance requirements:* For master's, GRE. Additional exam requirements/recommendations for international students: Required—TOEFL (minimum score 550 paper-based; 213 computer-based). Electronic applications accepted. *Expenses:* Contact institution.

State University of New York at Plattsburgh, Division of Education, Health, and Human Services, Program in Leadership, Plattsburgh, NY 12901-2681. Offers MS. Part-time and evening/weekend programs available. *Students:* 20 full-time (7 women), 17 part-time (10 women); includes 6 minority (3 Black or African American, non-Hispanic/Latino; 1 Asian, non-Hispanic/Latino; 1 Hispanic/Latino; 1 Two or more races, non-Hispanic/Latino), 5 international. Average age 31. *Entrance requirements:* For master's, GRE, GMAT, or MAT. Additional exam requirements/recommendations for international students: Required—TOEFL. *Application deadline:* For fall admission, 2/15 priority date for domestic students; for spring admission, 10/15 priority date for domestic students. Applications are processed on a rolling basis. Application fee: $75. *Financial support:* Application deadline: 4/15; applicants required to submit FAFSA. *Unit head:* Dr. Suzanne Catana, Coordinator, 518-696-2710, E-mail: catanasl@plattsburgh.edu. *Application contact:* Marguerite Adelman, Assistant Director, Graduate Admissions, 518-564-4723, Fax: 518-564-4722, E-mail: adelmaml@plattsburgh.edu. Web site: http://web.plattsburgh.edu/academics/leadership/.

State University of New York College at Potsdam, School of Education and Professional Studies, Program in Information and Communication Technology, Potsdam, NY 13676. Offers educational technology specialist (MS Ed); organizational performance, leadership and technology (MS Ed). Part-time and evening/weekend programs available. *Faculty:* 3 full-time (0 women), 2 part-time/adjunct (1 woman). *Students:* 22 full-time (12 women), 41 part-time (24 women); includes 3 minority (all Black or African American, non-Hispanic/Latino), 7 international. 31 applicants, 100% accepted, 25 enrolled. In 2011, 31 master's awarded. *Degree requirements:* For master's, culminating experience. *Entrance requirements:* For master's, minimum GPA of 3.0 in last 60 hours of course work. Additional exam requirements/recommendations for international students: Required—TOEFL (minimum score 550 paper-based; 213 computer-based; 80 iBT), IELTS (minimum score 6). *Application deadline:* For fall admission, 4/1 for domestic and international students; for winter admission, 10/15 for domestic and international students; for spring admission, 3/1 for domestic and international students. Applications are processed on a rolling basis. Application fee: $50. *Expenses:* Tuition, state resident: full-time $8870; part-time $370 per credit hour. Tuition, nonresident: full-time $15,160; part-time $632 per credit hour. *Required fees:* $1066; $44.10 per credit hour. One-time fee: $3. *Financial support:* Fellowships, teaching assistantships, career-related internships or fieldwork, Federal Work-Study, scholarships/grants, and unspecified assistantships available. Support available to part-time students. Financial award application deadline: 3/1; financial award applicants required to submit FAFSA. *Unit head:* Dr. Timothy V. Fossum, Chairperson, 315-267-2056, Fax: 315-267-3207, E-mail: fossumtv@potsdam.edu. *Application contact:* Peter Cutler, Graduate Admissions Counselor, 315-267-2165, Fax: 315-267-4802, E-mail: graduate@potsdam.edu.

Suffolk University, College of Arts and Sciences, Department of Education and Human Services, Boston, MA 02108-2770. Offers administration of higher education (M Ed, CAGS), including administration of higher education (M Ed), leadership (CAGS); human resource, learning and performance (MS, CAGS, Graduate Certificate), including global human resources (Graduate Certificate), human resources (MS, Graduate Certificate), organizational development (CAGS, Graduate Certificate), organizational learning and development (MS, Graduate Certificate); mental health counseling (MS, CAGS); school counseling (M Ed, CAGS); school teaching (M Ed, CAGS), including foundations of education (M Ed), middle school teaching (M Ed), secondary school teaching (M Ed); MPA/MSMHC; MS/Certificate. Part-time and evening/weekend programs available. *Faculty:* 10 full-time (6 women), 7 part-time/adjunct (3 women). *Students:* 53 full-time (39 women), 131 part-time (112 women); includes 21 minority (7 Black or African American, non-Hispanic/Latino; 2 American Indian or Alaska Native, non-Hispanic/Latino; 5 Asian, non-Hispanic/Latino; 5 Hispanic/Latino; 2 Two or more races, non-Hispanic/Latino), 9 international. Average age 28. 158 applicants, 73% accepted, 60 enrolled. In 2011, 72 master's, 8 other advanced degrees awarded. *Entrance requirements:* For master's, GRE General Test or MAT, 2 letters of recommendation, resume. Additional exam requirements/recommendations for international students: Required—TOEFL (minimum score 550 paper-based; 213 computer-based; 80 iBT). *Application deadline:* For fall admission, 6/15 priority date for domestic students, 6/15 for international students; for spring admission, 11/1 priority date for domestic students, 11/1 for international students. Applications are processed on a rolling basis. Application fee: $50. Electronic applications accepted. *Expenses:* Contact institution. *Financial support:* In 2011–12, 102 students received support, including 30 fellowships with full and partial tuition reimbursements available (averaging $10,664 per year); career-related internships or fieldwork, Federal Work-Study, and institutionally sponsored loans also available. Support available to part-time students. Financial award application deadline: 4/1; financial award applicants required to submit FAFSA. *Faculty research:* Predicting competent Head Start preschools, cultural differences. *Unit head:* Dr. Krisanne Bursik, Associate Dean and Acting Chair, 617-573-8261, Fax: 617-305-1743, E-mail: kbursik@suffolk.edu. *Application contact:* Ellen Driscoll, Director of Graduate Admissions, 617-573-8302, Fax: 617-305-1733, E-mail: grad.admission@suffolk.edu. Web site: http://www.suffolk.edu/college/9785.html.

Syracuse University, Maxwell School of Citizenship and Public Affairs, Program in Leadership of International and Non-governmental Organizations, Syracuse, NY 13244. Offers CAS. Part-time programs available. *Students:* 4 applicants, 100% accepted, 0 enrolled. In 2011, 10 degrees awarded. *Degree requirements:* For CAS, seminar. *Entrance requirements:* Additional exam requirements/recommendations for international students: Required—TOEFL (minimum score 100 iBT). *Application deadline:* For fall admission, 2/1 for domestic and international students. Application fee: $75. Electronic applications accepted. *Expenses: Tuition:* Part-time $1206 per credit. *Application contact:* Tammy Salisbury, 315-443-3159, E-mail: mtsalisb@maxwell.syr.edu. Web site: http://www.maxwell.syr.edu/.

Teachers College, Columbia University, Graduate Faculty of Education, Department of Organization and Leadership, Program in Social and Organizational Psychology, New York, NY 10027-6696. Offers change leadership (MA); social-organizational psychology (MA). *Faculty:* 8 full-time (5 women), 22 part-time/adjunct (10 women). *Students:* 156 full-time (94 women), 126 part-time (92 women); includes 80 minority (19 Black or African American, non-Hispanic/Latino; 32 Asian, non-Hispanic/Latino; 25 Hispanic/Latino; 4 Two or more races, non-Hispanic/Latino), 49 international. Average age 28. 225 applicants, 60% accepted, 81 enrolled. In 2011, 109 master's awarded. Terminal master's awarded for partial completion of doctoral program. *Degree requirements:* For master's, comprehensive exam. *Entrance requirements:* For master's, GRE, MAT, or GMAT, minimum GPA of 3.0. *Application deadline:* For fall admission, 1/15 priority date for domestic students. Application fee: $65. Electronic applications accepted. *Financial support:* Fellowships, research assistantships, career-related internships or fieldwork, Federal Work-Study, institutionally sponsored loans, and tuition waivers (full and partial) available. Support available to part-time students. Financial award application deadline: 2/1. *Faculty research:* Conflict resolution, human resource and organization development, management competence, organizational culture, leadership. *Unit head:* Dr. W. Warner Burke, Director, 212-678-3831, E-mail: wwb3@columbia.edu. *Application contact:* Lynda Hallmark, Program Manager, 212-678-3273, Fax: 212-678-3273, E-mail: hallmark@tc.edu.

Thomas Edison State College, School of Business and Management, Program in Organizational Leadership, Trenton, NJ 08608-1176. Offers Graduate Certificate. Part-time programs available. Postbaccalaureate distance learning degree programs offered (no on-campus study). *Students:* 43 part-time (22 women); includes 14 minority (9 Black or African American, non-Hispanic/Latino; 1 American Indian or Alaska Native, non-

Hispanic/Latino; 1 Asian, non-Hispanic/Latino; 3 Hispanic/Latino), 1 international. Average age 39. In 2011, 12 Graduate Certificates awarded. *Entrance requirements:* Additional exam requirements/recommendations for international students: Required—TOEFL (minimum score 550 paper-based; 213 computer-based; 79 iBT). *Application deadline:* For fall admission, 8/15 priority date for domestic students, 8/15 for international students; for winter admission, 11/15 priority date for domestic students, 11/15 for international students; for spring admission, 2/15 priority date for domestic students, 2/15 for international students. Applications are processed on a rolling basis. Application fee: $75. Electronic applications accepted. *Financial support:* Applicants required to submit FAFSA. *Unit head:* Dr. Susan Gilbert, Dean, School of Business and Management, 609-984-1130, Fax: 609-984-3898, E-mail: info@tesc.edu. *Application contact:* David Hoftiezer, Director of Admissions, 888-442-8372, Fax: 609-984-8447, E-mail: admissions@tesc.edu. Web site: http://www.tesc.edu/business/msm/Organizational-Leadership.cfm.

Trevecca Nazarene University, College of Lifelong Learning, Graduate Business Programs, Major in Management, Nashville, TN 37210-2877. Offers MSM. Evening/weekend programs available. *Students:* 31 full-time (19 women), 38 part-time (20 women); includes 20 minority (18 Black or African American, non-Hispanic/Latino; 1 Hispanic/Latino; 1 Two or more races, non-Hispanic/Latino). In 2011, 8 degrees awarded. *Entrance requirements:* For master's, GMAT, proficiency exam (quantitative skills), minimum GPA of 2.5, resume, 2 letters of recommendation, employer letter of recommendation, written business analysis. Additional exam requirements/recommendations for international students: Required—TOEFL (minimum score 550 paper-based; 213 computer-based). *Application deadline:* Applications are processed on a rolling basis. Application fee: $25. *Expenses:* Contact institution. *Financial support:* Applicants required to submit FAFSA. *Unit head:* Dr. Ed Anthony, Director of Graduate and Professional Programs (School of Business), 615-248-1529, E-mail: management@trevecca.edu. *Application contact:* Marcus Lackey, Enrollment Manager, 615-248-1427, E-mail: cll@trevecca.edu. Web site: http://www.trevecca.edu/mba/index.html.

Trevecca Nazarene University, College of Lifelong Learning, Organizational Leadership Program, Nashville, TN 37210-2877. Offers MOL. Postbaccalaureate distance learning degree programs offered (no on-campus study). *Students:* 29 full-time (15 women); includes 5 minority (4 Black or African American, non-Hispanic/Latino; 1 Native Hawaiian or other Pacific Islander, non-Hispanic/Latino). Average age 36. *Degree requirements:* For master's, capstone course. *Entrance requirements:* For master's, resume, writing sample (selected topics), minimum undergraduate GPA of 2.5. Additional exam requirements/recommendations for international students: Required—TOEFL (minimum score 550 paper-based; 213 computer-based). Tuition and fees vary according to course level and program. *Financial support:* Applicants required to submit FAFSA. *Unit head:* Dr. David Phillips, Dean, College of Lifelong Learning, 615-248-1259, E-mail: cll@trevecca.edu. *Application contact:* Marcus Lackey, Enrollment Manager, 615-248-1427, E-mail: cll@trevecca.edu. Web site: http://www.trevecca.edu/mol/home.

Trinity Washington University, School of Professional Studies, Washington, DC 20017-1094. Offers business administration (MBA); communication (MA); international security studies (MA); organizational management (MSA), including federal program management, human resource management, nonprofit management, organizational development, public and community health. Part-time and evening/weekend programs available. *Degree requirements:* For master's, thesis (for some programs), capstone project (MSA). *Entrance requirements:* For master's, minimum GPA of 2.5. Additional exam requirements/recommendations for international students: Required—TOEFL (minimum score 550 paper-based; 213 computer-based).

Trinity Western University, School of Graduate Studies, Program in Leadership, Langley, BC V2Y 1Y1, Canada. Offers business (MA, Certificate); Christian ministry (MA); education (MA, Certificate); healthcare (MA, Certificate); non-profit (MA, Certificate). Postbaccalaureate distance learning degree programs offered (minimal on-campus study). *Degree requirements:* For master's, major project. *Entrance requirements:* For master's, minimum GPA of 2.7. Additional exam requirements/recommendations for international students: Required—TOEFL (minimum score 620 paper-based; 260 computer-based; 105 iBT). Electronic applications accepted. *Expenses:* Contact institution. *Faculty research:* Servant leadership.

Troy University, Graduate School, College of Business, Program in Management, Troy, AL 36082. Offers applied management (MSM); healthcare management (MSM); human resources management (MSM); information systems (MSM); international hospitality management (MSM); international management (MSM); leadership and organizational effectiveness (MSM); public management (MS, MSM). *Accreditation:* ACBSP. Evening/weekend programs available. *Faculty:* 21 full-time (6 women), 7 part-time/adjunct (2 women). *Students:* 52 full-time (33 women), 284 part-time (183 women); includes 222 minority (186 Black or African American, non-Hispanic/Latino; 5 American Indian or Alaska Native, non-Hispanic/Latino; 11 Asian, non-Hispanic/Latino; 13 Hispanic/Latino; 1 Native Hawaiian or other Pacific Islander, non-Hispanic/Latino; 6 Two or more races, non-Hispanic/Latino). Average age 35. 157 applicants, 76% accepted, 55 enrolled. In 2011, 234 master's awarded. *Degree requirements:* For master's, Graduate Educational Testing Service Major Field Test, capstone exam, minimum GPA of 3.0. *Entrance requirements:* For master's, GMAT (minimum score 500) or GRE General Test (minimum score 900), minimum GPA of 2.5, bachelor's degree, letter of recommendation. Additional exam requirements/recommendations for international students: Required—TOEFL (minimum score 523 paper-based; 193 computer-based; 70 iBT), IELTS (minimum score 6), or ACT COMPASS ESL (minimum listening, reading, and grammar score 270). *Application deadline:* Applications are processed on a rolling basis. Application fee: $50. Electronic applications accepted. *Expenses:* Contact institution. *Unit head:* Dr. Edward Merkel, Director, Graduate Business Programs, 334-670-3194, Fax: 334-670-3599, E-mail: emerkel@troy.edu. *Application contact:* Brenda K. Campbell, Director of Graduate Admissions, 334-670-3178, Fax: 334-670-3733, E-mail: bcamp@troy.edu.

Tusculum College, Graduate School, Program in Organizational Management, Greeneville, TN 37743-9997. Offers MAOM. *Degree requirements:* For master's, thesis or alternative. *Entrance requirements:* For master's, GMAT, GRE Subject Test, MAT, 3 years of work experience, minimum GPA of 2.75.

United States International University, School of Business Administration, Nairobi, Kenya. Offers business administration (GEMBA); entrepreneurship (MBA); finance (MBA); human resource management (MBA); information technology management (MBA); integrated studies (MBA); international business administration (MBA); management and organizational development (MS); marketing (MBA); organizational development (EMS); strategic management (MBA). Part-time and evening/weekend programs available. *Degree requirements:* For master's, thesis. *Entrance requirements:* For master's, GMAT, 2 letters of reference, resume. Additional exam requirements/recommendations for international students: Required—TOEFL (minimum score 550 paper-based; 213 computer-based). *Faculty research:* Marketing in small business enterprises, total quality management in Kenya.

Université Laval, Faculty of Administrative Sciences, Programs in Business Administration, Québec, QC G1K 7P4, Canada. Offers accounting (MBA); agri-food management (MBA); electronic business (MBA, Diploma); factory management and logistics (MBA); finance (MBA); firm management (MBA); geomatic management (MBA); information technology management (MBA); international management (MBA); management (MBA); management accounting (MBA, Diploma); marketing (MBA); modeling and organizational decision (MBA); occupational health and safety management (MBA); pharmacy management (MBA); social and environmental responsibility (MBA); technological entrepreneurship (Diploma). *Accreditation:* AACSB. Part-time and evening/weekend programs available. Postbaccalaureate distance learning degree programs offered (no on-campus study). *Entrance requirements:* For master's and Diploma, knowledge of French and English. Electronic applications accepted.

University of Alberta, Faculty of Graduate Studies and Research, Doctoral Program in Business, Edmonton, AB T6G 2E1, Canada. Offers accounting (PhD); finance (PhD); human resources/industrial relations (PhD); management science (PhD); marketing (PhD); organizational analysis (PhD); MBA/PhD. *Accreditation:* AACSB. Part-time programs available. *Degree requirements:* For doctorate, comprehensive exam, thesis/dissertation. *Entrance requirements:* For doctorate, GMAT. Additional exam requirements/recommendations for international students: Required—TOEFL (minimum score 550 paper-based; 213 computer-based). Electronic applications accepted. *Faculty research:* Accounting, capital markets and corporate finance, organizational change and human resource management, marketing, strategic management.

University of Central Arkansas, Graduate School, Interdisciplinary PhD Program in Leadership Studies, Conway, AR 72035-0001. Offers PhD. Part-time programs available. *Faculty:* 14 full-time (7 women). *Students:* 4 full-time (1 woman), 14 part-time (6 women); includes 5 minority (all Black or African American, non-Hispanic/Latino). Average age 40. 22 applicants, 82% accepted, 17 enrolled. *Degree requirements:* For doctorate, thesis/dissertation. *Entrance requirements:* For doctorate, GRE. Additional exam requirements/recommendations for international students: Required—TOEFL. *Application deadline:* For fall admission, 3/1 for domestic students. Application fee: $25 ($50 for international students). *Expenses:* Tuition, state resident: full-time $4834; part-time $398.35 per credit hour. Tuition, nonresident: full-time $8686. *Financial support:* In 2011–12, 5 research assistantships were awarded; teaching assistantships, scholarships/grants, and unspecified assistantships also available. Financial award applicants required to submit FAFSA. *Unit head:* Dr. Rhonda McClellan, Director, 501-450-3124, Fax: 501-450-5678, E-mail: rmcclellan@uca.edu. *Application contact:* Sandy Burks, Administrative Specialist, 501-450-3124, Fax: 501-450-5678, E-mail: slburks@uca.edu. Web site: http://uca.edu/phdleadership/.

University of Cincinnati, Graduate School, McMicken College of Arts and Sciences, Center for Organizational Leadership, Cincinnati, OH 45221. Offers MALER. Part-time and evening/weekend programs available. *Entrance requirements:* For master's, GRE or GMAT. Additional exam requirements/recommendations for international students: Required—TOEFL (minimum score 520 paper-based; 190 computer-based; 68 iBT). Electronic applications accepted. *Faculty research:* Leadership and diversity.

University of Colorado Boulder, Leeds School of Business, Division of Business Administration, Boulder, CO 80309. Offers accounting (MS, PhD); finance (PhD); information systems (PhD); marketing (PhD); operations (PhD); strategic, organizational, and entrepreneurial studies (PhD). *Students:* 129 full-time (65 women), 6 part-time (0 women); includes 15 minority (1 Black or African American, non-Hispanic/Latino; 8 Asian, non-Hispanic/Latino; 5 Hispanic/Latino; 1 Two or more races, non-Hispanic/Latino), 21 international. Average age 27. 332 applicants, 9% accepted, 13 enrolled. In 2011, 53 master's, 6 doctorates awarded. *Entrance requirements:* For master's, GMAT, minimum undergraduate GPA of 3.0. *Application deadline:* For fall admission, 3/31 for domestic and international students; for spring admission, 10/31 for domestic and international students. Application fee: $50 ($60 for international students). Electronic applications accepted. *Financial support:* In 2011–12, 61 students received support, including 24 fellowships (averaging $3,398 per year), 19 research assistantships with full and partial tuition reimbursements available (averaging $27,830 per year), 15 teaching assistantships with full and partial tuition reimbursements available (averaging $25,615 per year); institutionally sponsored loans, scholarships/grants, health care benefits, and unspecified assistantships also available. Financial award applicants required to submit FAFSA. *Application contact:* E-mail: leedsphd@colorado.edu. Web site: http://leeds.colorado.edu/phdprog.

University of Dallas, Graduate School of Management, Irving, TX 75062-4736. Offers accounting (MBA, MM, MS); business management (MBA, MM); corporate finance (MBA, MM); financial services (MBA); global business (MBA, MM); health services management (MBA, MM); human resource management (MBA, MM); information assurance (MBA, MM, MS); information technology (MBA, MM, MS); information technology service management (MBA, MM, MS); marketing management (MBA, MM); organization development (MBA, MM); project management (MBA, MM); sports and entertainment management (MBA, MM); strategic leadership (MBA, MM); supply chain management (MBA); supply chain management and market logistics (MM). *Accreditation:* ACBSP. Part-time and evening/weekend programs available. Postbaccalaureate distance learning degree programs offered (no on-campus study). *Entrance requirements:* Additional exam requirements/recommendations for international students: Required—TOEFL. Electronic applications accepted. *Expenses:* Contact institution.

University of Denver, University College, Denver, CO 80208. Offers arts and culture (MLS, Certificate), including art, literature, and culture, arts development and program management (Certificate), creative writing; environmental policy and management (MAS, Certificate), including energy and sustainability (Certificate), environmental assessment of nuclear power (Certificate), environmental health and safety (Certificate), environmental management, natural resource management (Certificate); geographic information systems (MAS, Certificate); global affairs (MLS, Certificate), including translation studies, world history and culture; healthcare leadership (MPH, Certificate), including healthcare policy, law, and ethics, medical and healthcare information technologies, strategic management of healthcare; information and communications technology (MCIS, Certificate), including database design and administration (Certificate), geographic information systems (MCIS), information security systems security (Certificate), information systems security (MCIS), project management (MCIS, MPS, Certificate), software design and administration (Certificate), software design and programming (MCIS), technology management, telecommunications technology (MCIS), Web design and development; leadership and organizations (MPS, Certificate), including human capital in organizations, philanthropic leadership, project management (MCIS, MPS, Certificate), strategic innovation and change; organizational and professional communication (MPS, Certificate), including alternative dispute resolution, organizational communication, organizational development and training, public relations and marketing; security management (MAS, Certificate), including emergency planning and response, information security (MAS), organizational security; strategic human resource management (MPS, Certificate), including global human resources (MPS), human resource management and development (MPS). Part-time and evening/weekend programs available. Postbaccalaureate distance learning degree programs offered (no on-campus study). *Faculty:* 204 part-time/adjunct (80 women). *Students:* 56 full-time (26 women), 1,096 part-time (647 women); includes 196 minority (81 Black or African American, non-Hispanic/Latino; 7 American Indian or Alaska Native, non-Hispanic/Latino; 30 Asian, non-Hispanic/Latino; 66 Hispanic/Latino; 3 Native Hawaiian or other Pacific Islander, non-Hispanic/Latino; 9 Two or more races, non-Hispanic/Latino), 76 international. Average age 36. 572 applicants, 95% accepted, 410 enrolled. In 2011, 404 master's, 123 other advanced degrees awarded. *Degree requirements:* For master's, capstone project. *Entrance requirements:* For master's, two letters of recommendation, personal statement, resume. Additional exam requirements/recommendations for international students: Required—TOEFL (minimum score 550 paper-based; 80 iBT). *Application deadline:* For fall admission, 7/20 priority date for domestic students, 6/8 for international students; for winter admission, 10/26 priority date for domestic students, 9/14 for international students; for spring admission, 2/1 priority date for domestic students, 12/14 for international students. Applications are processed on a rolling basis. Application fee: $75. Electronic applications accepted. *Expenses:* Contact institution. *Financial support:* Applicants required to submit FAFSA. *Unit head:* Dr. James Davis, Dean, 303-871-2291, Fax: 303-871-4047, E-mail: jdavis@du.edu. *Application contact:* Information Contact, 303-871-3155, Fax: 303-871-4047, E-mail: ucolinfo@du.edu. Web site: http://www.universitycollege.du.edu/.

The University of Findlay, Graduate and Professional Studies, College of Business, Findlay, OH 45840-3653. Offers health care management (MBA); hospitality management (MBA); organizational leadership (MBA); public management (MBA). Part-time and evening/weekend programs available. Postbaccalaureate distance learning degree programs offered (no on-campus study). *Faculty:* 18 full-time (5 women), 1 part-time/adjunct (0 women). *Students:* 25 full-time (15 women), 184 part-time (100 women); includes 13 minority (3 Black or African American, non-Hispanic/Latino; 7 Asian, non-Hispanic/Latino; 3 Hispanic/Latino), 78 international. Average age 25. 72 applicants, 82% accepted, 24 enrolled. In 2011, 168 master's awarded. *Degree requirements:* For master's, thesis, cumulative project. *Entrance requirements:* For master's, GMAT or GRE, bachelor's degree from accredited institution, minimum undergraduate GPA of 3.0. Additional exam requirements/recommendations for international students: Required—TOEFL (minimum score 550 paper-based; 213 computer-based; 80 iBT). *Application deadline:* Applications are processed on a rolling basis. Application fee: $25. Electronic applications accepted. *Expenses:* Contact institution. *Financial support:* In 2011–12, 5 research assistantships with full and partial tuition reimbursements (averaging $4,200 per year) were awarded; career-related internships or fieldwork, Federal Work-Study, health care benefits, and unspecified assistantships also available. Financial award application deadline: 4/1; financial award applicants required to submit FAFSA. *Faculty research:* Health care management, operations and logistics management. *Unit head:* Dr. Paul Sears, Dean, 419-434-4704, Fax: 419-434-4822. *Application contact:* Heather Riffle, Assistant Director, Graduate and Professional Studies, 419-434-4640, Fax: 419-434-5517, E-mail: riffle@findlay.edu. Web site: http://www.findlay.edu/.

University of Guelph, Graduate Studies, College of Management and Economics, MA (Leadership) Program, Guelph, ON N1G 2W1, Canada. Offers MA. Part-time and evening/weekend programs available. Postbaccalaureate distance learning degree programs offered (minimal on-campus study). *Entrance requirements:* For master's, minimum B-average, minimum 5 years of relevant work experience. Additional exam requirements/recommendations for international students: Required—TOEFL (minimum score 550 paper-based; 213 computer-based). Electronic applications accepted. *Faculty research:* Theories of leadership, organizational change, ethics in leadership, decision making, politics of organizations.

University of Hawaii at Manoa, Graduate Division, Shidler College of Business, Program in Business Administration, Honolulu, HI 96822. Offers Asian business studies (MBA); Chinese business studies (MBA); decision sciences (MBA); entrepreneurship (MBA); finance (MBA); finance and banking (MBA); human resources management (MBA); information management (MBA); information technology (MBA); international business (MBA); Japanese business studies (MBA); marketing (MBA); organizational behavior (MBA); organizational management (MBA); real estate (MBA); student-designed track (MBA). *Accreditation:* AACSB. Part-time and evening/weekend programs available. *Degree requirements:* For master's, thesis optional. *Entrance requirements:* For master's, GMAT, minimum GPA of 3.0. Additional exam requirements/recommendations for international students: Required—TOEFL (minimum score 600 paper-based; 250 computer-based; 100 iBT), IELTS (minimum score 7). *Expenses:* Contact institution.

University of Hawaii at Manoa, Graduate Division, Shidler College of Business, Program in International Management, Honolulu, HI 96822. Offers Asian finance (PhD); global information technology management (PhD); international accounting (PhD); international marketing (PhD); international organization and strategy (PhD). Part-time programs available. *Degree requirements:* For doctorate, comprehensive exam, thesis/dissertation. *Entrance requirements:* For doctorate, GMAT or GRE General Test, minimum GPA of 3.0. Additional exam requirements/recommendations for international students: Required—TOEFL (minimum score 600 paper-based; 250 computer-based; 100 iBT), IELTS (minimum score 7). *Expenses:* Contact institution.

The University of Kansas, University of Kansas Medical Center, School of Nursing, Kansas City, KS 66160. Offers adult/gerontological clinical nurse specialist (PMC); adult/gerontological nurse practitioner (PMC); clinical research management (PMC); family nurse practitioner (PMC); health care informatics (PMC); health professions educator (PMC); nurse midwife (PMC); nursing (MS, DNP, PhD); organizational leadership (PMC); psychiatric/mental health nurse practitioner (PMC); public health nursing (PMC). *Accreditation:* AACN; ACNM/ACME. Part-time programs available. Postbaccalaureate distance learning degree programs offered (minimal on-campus study). *Faculty:* 80. *Students:* 79 full-time (71 women), 336 part-time (317 women); includes 63 minority (24 Black or African American, non-Hispanic/Latino; 2 American Indian or Alaska Native, non-Hispanic/Latino; 18 Asian, non-Hispanic/Latino; 15 Hispanic/Latino; 4 Two or more races, non-Hispanic/Latino), 6 international. Average age 37. 155 applicants, 82% accepted, 127 enrolled. In 2011, 79 master's, 15 doctorates, 12 other advanced degrees awarded. Terminal master's awarded for partial completion of doctoral program. *Degree requirements:* For master's, comprehensive exam, thesis optional, general oral exam; for doctorate, variable foreign language requirement, thesis/dissertation, comprehensive oral exam (for DNP); comprehensive written and oral exam (for PhD). *Entrance requirements:* For master's, bachelor's degree in nursing, minimum GPA of 3.0, RN license, 1 year of clinical experience, RN license in KS and MO; for doctorate, GRE General Test, master's degree in nursing, minimum GPA of 3.5, RN license in KS and MO; national certification (for some specialties). Additional exam requirements/recommendations for international students: Required—TOEFL. *Application deadline:* For fall admission, 4/1 for domestic and international students; for spring admission, 9/1 for domestic and international students. Application fee: $60. Electronic applications accepted. Tuition and fees vary according to course load, campus/location, program and reciprocity agreements. *Financial support:* Research assistantships with full and partial tuition reimbursements, teaching assistantships with full and partial tuition reimbursements, and traineeships available. Financial award application deadline: 2/14; financial award applicants required to submit FAFSA. *Faculty research:* Breastfeeding practices of teen mothers, national database of nursing quality indicators, caregiving of families of patients using technology in the home, simulation in nursing education, diaphragm fatigue. *Total annual research expenditures:* $6.1 million. *Unit head:* Dr. Karen L. Miller, Dean, 913-588-1601, Fax: 913-588-1660, E-mail: kmiller@kumc.edu. *Application contact:* Dr. Debra J. Ford, Associate Dean, Student Affairs, 913-588-1619, Fax: 913-588-1615, E-mail: dford@kumc.edu. Web site: http://nursing.kumc.edu.

University of La Verne, College of Business and Public Management, Program in Organizational Management and Leadership, La Verne, CA 91750-4443. Offers nonprofit management (Certificate); organizational leadership (Certificate); organizational management and leadership (MS). Part-time programs available. *Faculty:* 34 full-time (15 women), 38 part-time/adjunct (13 women). *Students:* 87 full-time (44 women), 78 part-time (56 women); includes 70 minority (13 Black or African American, non-Hispanic/Latino; 12 Asian, non-Hispanic/Latino; 43 Hispanic/Latino; 2 Two or more races, non-Hispanic/Latino), 48 international. Average age 33. In 2011, 138 master's awarded. *Degree requirements:* For master's, thesis or research project. *Entrance requirements:* For master's, minimum undergraduate GPA of 2.75, 2 letters of recommendation, interview, resume. Additional exam requirements/recommendations for international students: Required—TOEFL (minimum score 550 paper-based; 213 computer-based). *Application deadline:* Applications are processed on a rolling basis. Application fee: $50. *Expenses:* Contact institution. *Financial support:* Institutionally sponsored loans available. Financial award application deadline: 3/2; financial award applicants required to submit FAFSA. *Unit head:* Dr. Kathy Duncan, Program Director, 909-593-3511 Ext. 4415, E-mail: kduncan2@laverne.edu. *Application contact:* Program and Admissions Specialist, 909-593-3511 Ext. 4819, Fax: 909-392-2761, E-mail: cbpm@laverne.edu. Web site: http://laverne.edu/catalog/program/ms-leadership-and-management/.

University of La Verne, College of Education and Organizational Leadership, Doctoral Program in Organizational Leadership, La Verne, CA 91750-4443. Offers Ed D. Part-time programs available. *Faculty:* 19 full-time (12 women), 28 part-time/adjunct (22 women). *Students:* 130 full-time (79 women), 97 part-time (74 women); includes 104 minority (41 Black or African American, non-Hispanic/Latino; 2 American Indian or Alaska Native, non-Hispanic/Latino; 12 Asian, non-Hispanic/Latino; 48 Hispanic/Latino; 1 Native Hawaiian or other Pacific Islander, non-Hispanic/Latino), 2 international. Average age 45. In 2011, 42 doctorates awarded. *Degree requirements:* For doctorate, thesis/dissertation. *Entrance requirements:* For doctorate, GRE or MAT, minimum graduate GPA of 3.0, resume, 2 endorsement forms. Additional exam requirements/recommendations for international students: Required—TOEFL (minimum score 550 paper-based; 213 computer-based). *Application deadline:* Applications are processed on a rolling basis. Application fee: $75. *Expenses:* Contact institution. *Financial support:* Institutionally sponsored loans available. Financial award application deadline: 3/2; financial award applicants required to submit FAFSA. *Unit head:* Dr. Hyatt Laura, Chairperson, 909-593-3511 Ext. 4583, Fax: 909-392-2700, E-mail: lhyatt@laverne.edu. *Application contact:* Christy Ranells, Program and Admission Specialist, 909-593-3511 Ext. 4644, Fax: 909-392-2761, E-mail: cranells@laverne.edu. Web site: http://laverne.edu/education/.

University of La Verne, Regional Campus Administration, Graduate Programs, Central Coast/Vandenberg Air Force Base Campuses, La Verne, CA 91750-4443. Offers business (MBA-EP), including health services management, information technology; health administration (MHA); leadership and management (MS). *Entrance requirements:* For master's, 2 letters of recommendation, resume. *Expenses:* Contact institution.

University of La Verne, Regional Campus Administration, Graduate Programs, Inland Empire Campus, Rancho Cucamonga, CA 91730. Offers business (MBA-EP), including health services management, information technology, management, marketing; leadership and management (MS). *Entrance requirements:* For master's, 2 letters of recommendation, resume. *Expenses:* Contact institution.

University of La Verne, Regional Campus Administration, Graduate Programs, Kern County Campus, Bakersfield, CA 93301. Offers business (MBA-EP); health administration (MHA); leadership and management (MS). *Entrance requirements:* For master's, 2 letters of recommendation, resume. *Expenses:* Contact institution.

University of Maryland Eastern Shore, Graduate Programs, Program in Organizational Leadership, Princess Anne, MD 21853-1299. Offers PhD. Evening/weekend programs available. *Degree requirements:* For doctorate, comprehensive exam, thesis/dissertation, internship. *Entrance requirements:* For doctorate, interview, writing sample, successful record of employment or career in organization/profession. Additional exam requirements/recommendations for international students: Required—TOEFL (minimum score 213 computer-based; 80 iBT). Electronic applications accepted.

University of Massachusetts Amherst, Graduate School, Isenberg School of Management, Program in Management, Amherst, MA 01003. Offers accounting (PhD); business administration (MBA); business administration/sport management (MBA/MS); finance (PhD); hospitality and tourism management (PhD); management science (PhD); marketing (PhD); organization studies (PhD); sport management (PhD); strategic management (PhD); MBA/MS; MPH/MPPA. *Accreditation:* AACSB. Part-time programs available. *Faculty:* 61 full-time (14 women). *Students:* 92 full-time (34 women), 9 part-time (3 women); includes 8 minority (1 Black or African American, non-Hispanic/Latino; 4 Asian, non-Hispanic/Latino; 3 Hispanic/Latino), 47 international. Average age 33. 340 applicants, 15% accepted, 29 enrolled. In 2011, 31 master's, 13 doctorates awarded. Terminal master's awarded for partial completion of doctoral program. *Degree requirements:* For doctorate, comprehensive exam, thesis/dissertation. *Entrance requirements:* For master's and doctorate, GMAT. Additional exam requirements/recommendations for international students: Required—TOEFL (minimum score 550 paper-based; 213 computer-based; 80 iBT), IELTS (minimum score 6.5). *Application deadline:* For fall admission, 1/20 for domestic and international students. Applications are processed on a rolling basis. Application fee: $50 ($65 for international students). Electronic applications accepted. Tuition and fees vary according to course load, campus/location and program. *Financial support:* Fellowships with full and partial tuition reimbursements, research assistantships with full and partial tuition reimbursements, teaching assistantships with full and partial tuition reimbursements, career-related internships or fieldwork, Federal Work-Study, scholarships/grants, traineeships, health care benefits, tuition waivers (full and partial), and unspecified assistantships available. Support available to part-time students. Financial award application deadline: 1/20. *Unit head:* Dr. William Woodridge, Chair, 413-545-5675, Fax: 413-577-2234. *Application contact:* Lindsay DeSantis, Interim Supervisor of Admissions, 413-545-0722, Fax: 413-577-0010, E-mail: gradadm@grad.umass.edu. Web site: http://www.isenberg.umass.edu/.

University of Massachusetts Dartmouth, Graduate School, Charlton College of Business, Program in Business Administration, North Dartmouth, MA 02747-2300. Offers accounting (Postbaccalaureate Certificate); business administration (MBA); business foundation (online) (Graduate Certificate); finance (PMC); international business (online) (Graduate Certificate); leadership (online) (Graduate Certificate); management (Postbaccalaureate Certificate); marketing (Postbaccalaureate Certificate); supply chain management (PMC). *Accreditation:* AACSB. Part-time programs available. *Faculty:* 35 full-time (11 women), 26 part-time/adjunct (7 women). *Students:* 81 full-time (29 women), 119 part-time (56 women); includes 17 minority (6 Black or African American, non-Hispanic/Latino; 1 American Indian or Alaska Native, non-Hispanic/Latino; 3 Asian, non-Hispanic/Latino; 5 Hispanic/Latino; 2 Two or more races, non-Hispanic/Latino), 42 international. Average age 31. 132 applicants, 92% accepted, 68 enrolled. In 2011, 91 master's, 18 other advanced degrees awarded. *Entrance requirements:* For master's, GMAT, statement of intent, resume, 3 letters of recommendation; for other advanced degree, statement of intent, resume, 3 letters of recommendation. Additional exam requirements/recommendations for international students: Required—TOEFL (minimum score 500 paper-based; 200 computer-based; 72 iBT). *Application deadline:* For fall admission, 3/1 for domestic students, 2/1 for international students; for spring admission, 11/1 for domestic students, 10/15 for international students. Application fee: $40 ($60 for international students). Electronic applications accepted. *Expenses:* Tuition, state resident: full-time $2071; part-time $86.29 per credit. Tuition, nonresident: full-time $8099; part-time $337.46 per credit. *Required fees:* $438.58 per credit. Part-time tuition and fees vary according to class time, course load, degree level and reciprocity agreements. *Financial support:* Research assistantships, teaching assistantships, Federal Work-Study, and unspecified assistantships available. Support available to part-time students. Financial award application deadline: 3/1; financial award applicants required to submit FAFSA. *Faculty research:* Global business environment, e-commerce, managing diversity, agile manufacturing, green business. *Total annual research expenditures:* $8,653. *Unit head:* Stephanie Jacobsen, Program Coordinator, 508-999-8543, Fax: 508-999-8646, E-mail: s.jacobsen@umassd.edu. *Application contact:* Elan Turcotte-Shamski, Graduate Admissions Officer, 508-999-8604, Fax: 508-999-8183, E-mail: graduate@umassd.edu. Web site: http://www.umassd.edu/charlton/.

University of Missouri, Graduate School, Harry S Truman School of Public Affairs, Columbia, MO 65211. Offers grantsmanship (Graduate Certificate); nonprofit management (Graduate Certificate); organizational change (Graduate Certificate); public affairs (MPA, PhD); public management (Graduate Certificate); science and public policy (Graduate Certificate). *Accreditation:* NASPAA. *Faculty:* 12 full-time (5 women). *Students:* 83 full-time (46 women), 70 part-time (36 women); includes 10 minority (3 Black or African American, non-Hispanic/Latino; 3 Asian, non-Hispanic/Latino; 2 Hispanic/Latino; 2 Two or more races, non-Hispanic/Latino), 40 international. Average age 31. 122 applicants, 61% accepted, 51 enrolled. In 2011, 54 master's, 22 other advanced degrees awarded. *Entrance requirements:* For master's, GRE General Test, minimum GPA of 3.0. Additional exam requirements/recommendations for international students: Required—TOEFL (minimum score 550 paper-based; 213 computer-based; 79 iBT). *Application deadline:* For fall admission, 2/15 priority date for domestic students. Applications are processed on a rolling basis. Application fee: $55 ($75 for international students). *Expenses:* Tuition, state resident: full-time $5881. Tuition, nonresident: full-time $15,183. *Required fees:* $952. Tuition and fees vary according to campus/location and program. *Financial support:* Fellowships, research assistantships, teaching assistantships, and institutionally sponsored loans available. *Faculty research:* Public service ethics, history and theory, organizational symbolism and culture; program evaluation and social policy, with special emphasis on child development, education and health policies; organization theory and applied psychoanalytic theory; foreign policy and international political economy; health care delivery for persons with disabilities and health policy; survival strategies employed by low-income households; rural economic development, fiscal and economic impact analysis. *Unit head:* Dr. Bart Wechsler, Director, E-mail: wechslerb@missouri.edu. *Application contact:* Jessica Hosey, 573-882-3471, E-mail: hoseyj@missouri.edu. Web site: http://truman.missouri.edu/.

University of Nevada, Las Vegas, Graduate College, Greenspun College of Urban Affairs, School of Environmental and Public Affairs, Las Vegas, NV 89154-4030. Offers crisis and emergency management (MS); environmental science (MS, PhD); non-profit management (Certificate); public administration (MPA); public affairs (PhD); public management (Certificate); solar and renewabale energy (Certificate); urban leadership (MA); workforce development and organizational leadership (PhD). Part-time programs available. *Faculty:* 28 full-time (10 women), 53 part-time/adjunct (11 women). *Students:* 49 full-time (19 women), 117 part-time (57 women); includes 62 minority (31 Black or African American, non-Hispanic/Latino; 1 American Indian or Alaska Native, non-Hispanic/Latino; 4 Asian, non-Hispanic/Latino; 21 Hispanic/Latino; 5 Two or more races, non-Hispanic/Latino), 5 international. Average age 36. 94 applicants, 66% accepted, 47 enrolled. In 2011, 46 master's, 4 doctorates, 4 other advanced degrees awarded. *Degree requirements:* For master's, comprehensive exam (for some programs), thesis; for doctorate, comprehensive exam (for some programs), thesis/dissertation. *Entrance requirements:* Additional exam requirements/recommendations for international students: Required—TOEFL (minimum score 550 paper-based; 213 computer-based; 80 iBT), IELTS (minimum score 7). *Application deadline:* For fall admission, 2/15 priority date for domestic students, 5/1 for international students; for spring admission, 11/15 priority date for domestic students, 10/1 for international students. Applications are processed on a rolling basis. Application fee: $60 ($95 for international students). Electronic applications accepted. *Financial support:* In 2011–12, 33 students received support, including 20 research assistantships with partial tuition reimbursements available (averaging $11,193 per year), 13 teaching assistantships with partial tuition reimbursements available (averaging $10,928 per year); institutionally sponsored loans, scholarships/grants, health care benefits, and unspecified assistantships also available. Financial award application deadline: 3/1. *Faculty research:* Community and organizational resilience; environmental decision-making and management; budgeting and human resource/workforce management; urban design, sustainability and governance; public and non-profit management. *Total annual research expenditures:* $1.3 million. *Unit head:* Dr. Christopher Stream, Chair/Associate Professor, 702-895-5120, Fax: 702-895-4436, E-mail: chris.stream@unlv.edu. *Application contact:* Graduate College Admissions Evaluator, 702-895-3320, Fax: 702-895-4180, E-mail: gradcollege@unlv.edu. Web site: http://sepa.unlv.edu/.

University of New Haven, Graduate School, College of Arts and Sciences, Program in Industrial and Organizational Psychology, West Haven, CT 06516-1916. Offers conflict management (MA); human resource management (MA); industrial organizational psychology (MA); organizational development (MA); psychology of conflict management (Certificate). Part-time and evening/weekend programs available. *Students:* 93 full-time (66 women), 25 part-time (19 women); includes 20 minority (12 Black or African American, non-Hispanic/Latino; 1 Asian, non-Hispanic/Latino; 5 Hispanic/Latino; 2 Two or more races, non-Hispanic/Latino), 13 international. 67 applicants, 97% accepted, 50 enrolled. In 2011, 56 master's awarded. *Degree requirements:* For master's, thesis or alternative. *Entrance requirements:* Additional exam requirements/recommendations for international students: Required—TOEFL (minimum score 520 paper-based; 190 computer-based; 70 iBT); Recommended—IELTS (minimum score 5.5). *Application deadline:* For fall admission, 5/31 for international students; for winter admission, 10/15 for international students; for spring admission, 1/15 for international students. Applications are processed on a rolling basis. Application fee: $50. Electronic applications accepted. *Expenses:* Contact institution. *Financial support:* Research assistantships with partial tuition reimbursements, teaching assistantships with partial tuition reimbursements, career-related internships or fieldwork, Federal Work-Study, scholarships/grants, tuition waivers, and unspecified assistantships available. Support available to part-time students. Financial award applicants required to submit FAFSA. *Unit head:* Dr. Stuart D. Sidle, Coordinator, 203-932-7341. *Application contact:* Eloise Gormley, Information Contact, 203-932-7449. Web site: http://www.newhaven.edu/4730/.

University of New Mexico, Robert O. Anderson Graduate School of Management, Department of Organizational Studies, Albuquerque, NM 87131. Offers human resources management (MBA); policy and planning (MBA). Part-time and evening/weekend programs available. *Faculty:* 12 full-time (6 women), 16 part-time/adjunct (10 women). In 2011, 74 master's awarded. *Degree requirements:* For master's, minimum GPA of 3.0. *Entrance requirements:* For master's, GMAT or GRE. Additional exam requirements/recommendations for international students: Required—TOEFL (minimum score 550 paper-based; 213 computer-based; 79 iBT). *Application deadline:* For fall admission, 4/1 priority date for domestic students, 4/1 for international students; for spring admission, 10/1 priority date for domestic students, 10/1 for international students. Applications are processed on a rolling basis. Application fee: $50. Electronic applications accepted. *Financial support:* Fellowships, research assistantships, career-related internships or fieldwork, Federal Work-Study, scholarships/grants, and unspecified assistantships available. Support available to part-time students. Financial award application deadline: 6/1. *Faculty research:* Business ethics and social corporate responsibility, diversity, human resources, organizational strategy, organizational behavior. *Unit head:* Dr. Jacqueline Hood, Chair, 505-277-6471, Fax: 505-277-7108. *Application contact:* Megan Conner, Director, Student Services, 505-277-3290, Fax: 505-277-8436, E-mail: mconner@mgt.unm.edu.

University of Phoenix–Bay Area Campus, College of Information Systems and Technology, San Jose, CA 95134-1805. Offers information systems (MIS); organizational leadership/information systems and technology (DM). Evening/weekend programs available. *Degree requirements:* For master's, thesis (for some programs). *Entrance requirements:* For master's, minimum undergraduate GPA of 3.0, 3 years of work experience. Additional exam requirements/recommendations for international students: Required—TOEFL (minimum score 550 paper-based; 213 computer-based; 79 iBT). Electronic applications accepted.

University of Phoenix–Bay Area Campus, School of Business, San Jose, CA 95134-1805. Offers accountancy (MS); accounting (MBA); business administration (MBA, DBA); energy management (MBA); global management (MBA); health care management (MBA); human resource management (MBA); human resources management (MM); management (MM); marketing (MBA); organizational leadership (DM); project management (MBA); public administration (MPA); technology management (MBA). Evening/weekend programs available. Postbaccalaureate distance learning degree programs offered (no on-campus study). *Degree requirements:* For master's, thesis (for some programs). *Entrance requirements:* For master's, minimum undergraduate GPA of 3.0, 3 years of work experience. Additional exam requirements/recommendations for international students: Required—TOEFL (minimum score 550 paper-based; 213 computer-based; 79 iBT). Electronic applications accepted.

University of Phoenix–Milwaukee Campus, College of Information Systems and Technology, Milwaukee, WI 53045. Offers information systems (MIS); organziational leadership/information systems and technology (DM).

University of Phoenix–Milwaukee Campus, School of Business, Milwaukee, WI 53045. Offers accounting (MS); business administration (MBA, DBA); human resources management (MM); management (MM); organizational leadership (DM); public administration (MPA).

University of Phoenix–Online Campus, School of Advanced Studies, Phoenix, AZ 85034-7209. Offers business administration (DBA); education (Ed S); educational leadership (Ed D), including curriculum and instruction, education technology, educational leadership; health administration (DHA); higher education administration (PhD); industrial/organizational psychology (PhD); nursing (PhD); organizational leadership (DM), including information systems and technology, organizational leadership. Evening/weekend programs available. Postbaccalaureate distance learning degree programs offered. *Students:* 7,581 full-time (5,042 women); includes 3,199 minority (2,505 Black or African American, non-Hispanic/Latino; 68 American Indian or Alaska Native, non-Hispanic/Latino; 158 Asian, non-Hispanic/Latino; 395 Hispanic/Latino; 46 Native Hawaiian or other Pacific Islander, non-Hispanic/Latino; 27 Two or more races, non-Hispanic/Latino), 397 international. Average age 44. *Degree requirements:* For doctorate, thesis/dissertation. *Entrance requirements:* Additional exam requirements/recommendations for international students: Required—TOEFL, TOEIC (Test of English as an International Communication), Berlitz Online English Proficiency Exam, Pearson Test of English, or IELTS. *Application deadline:* Applications are processed on a rolling basis. Application fee: $45. Electronic applications accepted. *Expenses:* Contact institution. *Financial support:* Scholarships/grants available. Financial award applicants required to submit FAFSA. *Unit head:* Dr. Jeremy Moreland, Executive Dean. *Application contact:* 866-766-0766. Web site: http://www.phoenix.edu/colleges_divisions/doctoral.html.

University of Phoenix–Online Campus, School of Business, Phoenix, AZ 85034-7209. Offers accountancy (MS); accounting (MBA); business administration (MBA); energy management (MBA); global management (MBA); health care management (MBA); human resource management (MBA); human resources management (MM); international (MM); management (MM); marketing (MBA, Graduate Certificate); organizational management (MA); project management (MBA, Graduate Certificate); public administration (MBA, MM, MPA); technology management (MBA). Evening/weekend programs available. Postbaccalaureate distance learning degree programs offered. *Students:* 18,883 full-time (11,868 women); includes 6,302 minority (4,182 Black or African American, non-Hispanic/Latino; 121 American Indian or Alaska Native, non-Hispanic/Latino; 478 Asian, non-Hispanic/Latino; 1,252 Hispanic/Latino; 121 Native Hawaiian or other Pacific Islander, non-Hispanic/Latino; 148 Two or more races, non-Hispanic/Latino), 1,000 international. Average age 37. *Entrance requirements:* Additional exam requirements/recommendations for international students: Required—TOEFL, TOEIC (Test of English as an International Communication), Berlitz Online English Proficiency Exam, Pearson Test of English, or IELTS. *Application deadline:* Applications are processed on a rolling basis. Application fee: $45. Electronic applications accepted. *Expenses: Tuition:* Full-time $17,160. *Required fees:* $920. One-time fee: $45 full-time. Full-time tuition and fees vary according to course load, degree level, campus/location and program. *Financial support:* Scholarships/grants available. Financial award applicants required to submit FAFSA. *Application contact:* 866-766-0766. Web site: http://www.phoenix.edu/colleges_divisions/business.html.

University of Phoenix–Washington D.C. Campus, College of Information Systems and Technology, Washington, DC 20001. Offers information systems (MIS); organizational leadership/information systems and technology (DM).

University of Phoenix–Washington D.C. Campus, School of Business, Washington, DC 20001. Offers accountancy (MS); business administration (MBA, DBA); human resources management (MM); management (MM); organizational leadership (DM); public administration (MPA).

University of Regina, Faculty of Graduate Studies and Research, Kenneth Levene Graduate School of Business, Program in Business Administration, Regina, SK S4S 0A2, Canada. Offers business (Master's Certificate); business administration (MBA); executive business administration (MBA); international business (MBA); leadership (M Admin); organizational leadership (Master's Certificate); project management (Master's Certificate). Part-time and evening/weekend programs available. *Faculty:* 32 full-time (12 women), 10 part-time/adjunct (0 women). *Students:* 83 full-time (32 women), 51 part-time (26 women). 117 applicants, 75% accepted. In 2011, 35 master's awarded. *Degree requirements:* For master's, project. *Entrance requirements:* For master's, GMAT, two years relevant work experience. Additional exam requirements/ recommendations for international students: Required—TOEFL (minimum score 580 paper-based; 80 iBT), IELTS (minimum score 6.5). *Application deadline:* Applications are processed on a rolling basis. Application fee: $100. Electronic applications accepted. *Expenses:* Contact institution. *Financial support:* In 2011–12, 6 fellowships (averaging $6,000 per year), 9 teaching assistantships (averaging $2,298 per year) were awarded; research assistantships and scholarships/grants also available. Financial award application deadline: 6/15. *Faculty research:* Business policy and strategy, production and operations management, human behavior in organizations, financial management, social issues in business. *Unit head:* Dr. Morina Rennie, Dean, 306-585-4162, Fax: 306-585-4805, E-mail: morina.rennie@uregina.ca. *Application contact:* Steve Wield, Manager, Graduate Programs, 306-337-8463, Fax: 306-585-5361, E-mail: steve.wield@uregina.ca.

University of St. Thomas, Graduate Studies, School of Education, Program in Organization Learning and Development, St. Paul, MN 55105-1096. Offers e-learning (Certificate); human resource management (Certificate); learning technology (MA); organization development (Ed D, Certificate); strategic resources and change leadership (MA). Part-time and evening/weekend programs available. Postbaccalaureate distance learning degree programs offered (minimal on-campus study). *Faculty:* 6 full-time (4 women), 15 part-time/adjunct (8 women). *Students:* 6 full-time (all women), 125 part-time (96 women); includes 26 minority (13 Black or African American, non-Hispanic/Latino; 5 Asian, non-Hispanic/Latino; 4 Hispanic/Latino; 1 Native Hawaiian or other Pacific Islander, non-Hispanic/Latino; 3 Two or more races, non-Hispanic/Latino), 9 international. Average age 38. 40 applicants, 85% accepted, 28 enrolled. In 2011, 31 master's, 9 doctorates awarded. *Degree requirements:* For master's, practicum; for doctorate, comprehensive exam, thesis/dissertation. *Entrance requirements:* For master's, minimum GPA of 3.0, 2 letters of reference, personal statement, 2-5 years of organization experience; for doctorate, minimum GPA of 3.5, interview, 5-7 years of OD or leadership experience; for Certificate, minimum graduate GPA of 3.25. Additional exam requirements/recommendations for international students: Required—TOEFL (minimum score 550 paper-based; 213 computer-based). *Application deadline:* For fall admission, 8/1 priority date for domestic students, 8/1 for international students; for winter admission, 12/1 priority date for domestic students, 12/1 for international students; for spring admission, 12/1 priority date for domestic students, 12/1 for international students. Applications are processed on a rolling basis. Application fee: $50. Electronic applications accepted. *Expenses:* Contact institution. *Financial support:* In 2011–12, 1 student received support. Fellowships, research assistantships, institutionally sponsored loans, and scholarships/grants available. Support available to part-time students. Financial award applicants required to submit FAFSA. *Faculty research:* Workplace conflict, physician leaders, virtual teams, technology use in schools/workplace, developing masterful practitioners. *Unit head:* Dr. David W. Jamieson, Department Chair, 651-962-4387, Fax: 651-962-4169, E-mail: djamieson@stthomas.edu. *Application contact:* Liz G. Knight, Program Manager, 651-962-4459, Fax: 651-962-4169, E-mail: egknight@stthomas.edu. Web site: http://www.stthomas.edu/education.

University of San Francisco, School of Management, Program in Organization Development, San Francisco, CA 94117-1080. Offers MS. Part-time and evening/weekend programs available. *Faculty:* 2 full-time (0 women), 5 part-time/adjunct (3 women). *Students:* 130 full-time (98 women); includes 74 minority (17 Black or African American, non-Hispanic/Latino; 1 American Indian or Alaska Native, non-Hispanic/Latino; 29 Asian, non-Hispanic/Latino; 17 Hispanic/Latino; 2 Native Hawaiian or other Pacific Islander, non-Hispanic/Latino; 8 Two or more races, non-Hispanic/Latino), 4 international. Average age 37. 85 applicants, 74% accepted, 42 enrolled. In 2011, 57 master's awarded. *Degree requirements:* For master's, thesis. *Entrance requirements:* For master's, minimum GPA of 3.0. Application fee: $55 ($65 for international students). *Expenses: Tuition:* Full-time $20,070; part-time $1115 per unit. Tuition and fees vary according to course load, campus/location and program. *Financial support:* In 2011–12, 3 students received support. Application deadline: 3/2; applicants required to submit FAFSA. *Unit head:* Dr. Sharon Wagner, Head, 415-422-6886. *Application contact:* 415-422-6000, E-mail: graduate@usfca.edu.

The University of Scranton, College of Graduate and Continuing Education, Department of Health Administration and Human Resources, Program in Human Resources Administration, Scranton, PA 18510. Offers human resources (MS); human resources development (MS); organizational leadership (MS). Part-time and evening/weekend programs available. *Students:* 3 full-time (all women). Average age 36. 70 applicants, 80% accepted. In 2011, 5 master's awarded. *Degree requirements:* For master's, capstone experience. *Entrance requirements:* For master's, minimum GPA of 2.75. Additional exam requirements/recommendations for international students: Required—TOEFL (minimum score 500 paper-based; 173 computer-based), IELTS (minimum score 5.5). *Application deadline:* Applications are processed on a rolling basis. Application fee: $0. *Financial support:* Fellowships, teaching assistantships, career-related internships or fieldwork, Federal Work-Study, and unspecified assistantships available. Support available to part-time students. Financial award application deadline: 3/1. *Unit head:* Dr. Daniel West, Director, 570-941-6218, E-mail: westd1@scranton.edu. *Application contact:* Joseph M. Roback, Director of Admissions, 570-941-4385, Fax: 570-941-5928, E-mail: robackj2@scranton.edu.

University of Southern California, Graduate School, School of Policy, Planning, and Development, Executive Master of Leadership Program, Los Angeles, CA 90089. Offers EML. Part-time and evening/weekend programs available. *Entrance requirements:* Additional exam requirements/recommendations for international students: Required—TOEFL (minimum score 600 paper-based; 250 computer-based; 100 iBT). Electronic applications accepted. *Expenses:* Contact institution. *Faculty research:* Strategic planning, organizational transformation, strategic management, leadership.

The University of Texas at Dallas, Naveen Jindal School of Management, Program in Management and Administrative Sciences, Richardson, TX 75080. Offers electronic commerce (MS); finance (MS); healthcare administration (MS); information systems (MS); innovation and entrepreneurship (MS); international management (MS); leadership in organizations (MS); marketing (MS); operations (MS); organizations (MS); real estate (MS); strategy (MS). *Accreditation:* AACSB. Part-time and evening/weekend programs available. *Faculty:* 26 full-time (6 women), 9 part-time/adjunct (2 women). *Students:* 128 full-time (69 women), 169 part-time (95 women); includes 76 minority (18 Black or African American, non-Hispanic/Latino; 1 American Indian or Alaska Native, non-Hispanic/Latino; 37 Asian, non-Hispanic/Latino; 15 Hispanic/Latino; 1 Native Hawaiian or other Pacific Islander, non-Hispanic/Latino; 4 Two or more races, non-Hispanic/Latino), 77 international. Average age 34. 220 applicants, 63% accepted, 68 enrolled. In 2011, 58 master's awarded. *Degree requirements:* For master's, thesis optional. *Entrance requirements:* For master's, GMAT. Additional exam requirements/ recommendations for international students: Required—TOEFL (minimum score 550 paper-based; 215 computer-based). *Application deadline:* For fall admission, 7/15 for domestic students, 5/1 for international students; for spring admission, 11/15 for domestic students, 9/1 for international students. Applications are processed on a rolling basis. Application fee: $50 ($100 for international students). Electronic applications accepted. *Expenses:* Tuition, state resident: full-time $11,170; part-time $620.56 per credit hour. Tuition, nonresident: full-time $20,212; part-time $1122.89 per credit hour. *Financial support:* In 2011–12, 68 students received support, including 7 teaching assistantships with partial tuition reimbursements available (averaging $16,200 per year); research assistantships with partial tuition reimbursements available, career-related internships or fieldwork, Federal Work-Study, institutionally sponsored loans, scholarships/grants, and unspecified assistantships also available. Support available to part-time students. Financial award application deadline: 4/30; financial award applicants required to submit FAFSA. *Faculty research:* Integrated and detailed knowledge of functional areas of management, analytical tools for effective appraisal and decision-making. *Unit head:* Dr. Gregory Dess, Area Coordinator, 972-883-4439, E-mail: gdess@utdallas.edu. *Application contact:* James Parker, Assistant Director, 972-883-5842, E-mail: jparker@utdallas.edu. Web site: http://jindal.utdallas.edu/academic-areas/organizations-strategy-and-international-management/.

The University of Texas at San Antonio, College of Business, General Business Program, San Antonio, TX 78249-0617. Offers business (MBA); business administration (PhD), including accounting, business administration, finance, information technology, management and organization studies, marketing; information systems (MBA); international business (MBA); management accounting (MBA); management of technology (MBA); marketing management (MBA); taxation (MBA). *Students:* 170 full-time (52 women), 120 part-time (49 women); includes 90 minority (14 Black or African American, non-Hispanic/Latino; 2 American Indian or Alaska Native, non-Hispanic/Latino; 15 Asian, non-Hispanic/Latino; 55 Hispanic/Latino; 1 Native Hawaiian or other Pacific Islander, non-Hispanic/Latino; 3 Two or more races, non-Hispanic/Latino), 37 international. Average age 32. 395 applicants, 45% accepted, 133 enrolled. In 2011, 95 master's, 8 doctorates awarded. *Entrance requirements:* Additional exam requirements/ recommendations for international students: Required—TOEFL (minimum score 500 paper-based; 61 iBT), IELTS (minimum score 5). *Application deadline:* For fall admission, 7/1 for domestic students, 4/1 for international students; for spring admission, 11/1 for domestic students, 9/1 for international students. Application fee: $45 ($85 for international students). *Expenses:* Tuition, state resident: full-time $3148; part-time $2176 per semester. Tuition, nonresident: full-time $8782; part-time $5932 per semester. *Required fees:* $719 per semester. *Financial support:* In 2011–12, fellowships (averaging $22,000 per year), research assistantships (averaging $10,000 per year), teaching assistantships (averaging $10,000 per year) were awarded. *Unit head:* Dr. Lynda Y. de la Vinna, Dean, 210-458-4317, Fax: 210-458-4308, E-mail: lynda.delavina@utsa.edu. *Application contact:* Katherine Pope, Director of Graduate Student Services, 210-458-7316, Fax: 210-458-4398, E-mail: katherine.pope@utsa.edu. Web site: http://business.utsa.edu.

University of the Incarnate Word, School of Graduate Studies and Research, Dreeben School of Education, Programs in Education, San Antonio, TX 78209-6397. Offers adult education (M Ed, MA); cross-cultural education (M Ed, MA); early childhood literacy (M Ed, MA); general education (M Ed, MA); higher education (PhD); instructional technology (M Ed, MA); international education and entrepreneurship (PhD); kinesiology (M Ed, MA); literacy (M Ed, MA); organizational leadership (PhD); organizational learning and learning (M Ed, MA); reading (M Ed, MA); special education (M Ed, MA); teacher leadership (M Ed, MA). Part-time and evening/weekend programs available. *Faculty:* 14 full-time (8 women), 10 part-time/adjunct (9 women). *Students:* 13 full-time (7 women), 197 part-time (129 women); includes 111 minority (23 Black or African American, non-Hispanic/Latino; 2 American Indian or Alaska Native, non-Hispanic/Latino; 1 Asian, non-Hispanic/Latino; 85 Hispanic/Latino), 26 international. Average age 41. 78 applicants, 79% accepted, 34 enrolled. In 2011, 21 master's, 12 doctorates awarded. *Degree requirements:* For master's, capstone; for doctorate, thesis/dissertation, qualifying exam. *Entrance requirements:* For master's, baccalaureate degree; minimum foundation GPA of 2.5; interview; for doctorate, master's degree; interview; supervised writing sample. Additional exam requirements/recommendations for international students: Required—TOEFL (minimum score 560 paper-based; 220 computer-based; 83 iBT). *Application deadline:* Applications are processed on a rolling basis. Application fee: $20. Electronic applications accepted. *Expenses: Tuition:* Part-time $725 per credit hour. Tuition and fees vary according to degree level. *Financial support:* In 2011–12, 5 research assistantships were awarded; Federal Work-Study and scholarships/grants also available. Financial award applicants required to submit FAFSA. *Unit head:* Dr. Denise Staudt, Dean, Dreeben School of Education, 210-829-2762, E-mail: staudt@uiwtx.edu. *Application contact:* Andrea Cyterski-Acosta, Dean of Enrollment, 210-829-6005, Fax: 210-829-3921, E-mail: admis@uiwtx.edu. Web site: http://www.uiw.edu/education/index.htm.

University of the Incarnate Word, School of Graduate Studies and Research, H-E-B School of Business and Administration, Programs in Administration, San Antonio, TX 78209-6397. Offers adult education (MAA); applied administration (MAA); communication arts (MAA); healthcare administration (MAA); instructional technology (MAA); international business (Certificate); nutrition (MAA); organizational development (MAA, Certificate); project management (Certificate); sports management (MAA). Part-time and evening/weekend programs available. Postbaccalaureate distance learning degree programs offered (no on-campus study). *Faculty:* 23 full-time (10 women), 26 part-time/adjunct (12 women). *Students:* 25 full-time (18 women), 54 part-time (33 women); includes 50 minority (10 Black or African American, non-Hispanic/Latino; 40 Hispanic/Latino), 5 international. Average age 34. 35 applicants, 94% accepted, 19 enrolled. In 2011, 38 master's awarded. *Degree requirements:* For master's, capstone. *Entrance requirements:* For master's, GRE, GMAT, undergraduate degree, minimum GPA of 2.5. Additional exam requirements/recommendations for international students: Required—TOEFL (minimum score 560 paper-based; 220 computer-based; 83 iBT). *Application deadline:* Applications are processed on a rolling basis. Application fee: $20. Electronic applications accepted. *Expenses: Tuition:* Part-time $725 per credit hour. Tuition and fees vary according to degree level. *Financial support:* Federal Work-Study and scholarships/grants available. Financial award applicants required to submit FAFSA. *Unit head:* Dr. Mark Teachout, MAA Programs Director, 210-829-3177, Fax: 210-805-3564, E-mail: teachout@uiwtx.edu. *Application contact:* Andrea Cyterski-Acosta, Dean of Enrollment, 210-829-6005, Fax: 210-829-3921, E-mail: admis@uiwtx.edu. Web site: http://www.uiw.edu/maa/index.htm and http://www.uiw.edu/maa/admissions.html.

Upper Iowa University, Online Master's Programs, Fayette, IA 52142-1857. Offers accounting (MBA); corporate financial management (MBA); global business (MBA); health and human services (MPA); higher education administration (MHEA); homeland security (MPA); human resources management (MBA); justice administration (MPA); organizational development (MBA); public personnel management (MPA); quality management (MBA). MBA also available at Madison, WI campus. Part-time programs available. Postbaccalaureate distance learning degree programs offered (no on-campus study). *Degree requirements:* For master's, research project. *Entrance requirements:* For master's, GMAT, GRE, or minimum GPA of 2.7 during last 60 hours. Additional exam requirements/recommendations for international students: Required—TOEFL (minimum score 570 paper-based; 230 computer-based). Electronic applications accepted. *Faculty research:* Total quality management, CQI, teams, organization culture and climate, management.

Vanderbilt University, Peabody College, Department of Leadership, Policy, and Organizations, Nashville, TN 37240-1001. Offers education policy (MPP); educational leadership and policy (Ed D); higher education (M Ed); higher education, leadership and policy (Ed D); international education policy and management (M Ed); leadership and organizational performance (M Ed). Part-time and evening/weekend programs available. *Faculty:* 27 full-time (12 women), 10 part-time/adjunct (3 women). *Students:* 165 full-time (117 women), 98 part-time (46 women); includes 35 minority (15 Black or African American, non-Hispanic/Latino; 4 Asian, non-Hispanic/Latino; 10 Hispanic/Latino; 6 Two or more races, non-Hispanic/Latino), 30 international. Average age 28. 465 applicants, 54% accepted, 87 enrolled. In 2011, 102 master's, 25 doctorates awarded. *Degree requirements:* For master's, comprehensive exam, thesis optional; for doctorate, thesis/dissertation, qualifying exams, residency. *Entrance requirements:* For master's and doctorate, GRE General Test. Additional exam requirements/recommendations for international students: Required—TOEFL (minimum score 550 paper-based; 213 computer-based). *Application deadline:* For fall admission, 12/31 priority date for domestic students, 12/31 for international students; for spring admission, 11/1 priority date for domestic students, 11/1 for international students. Applications are processed on a rolling basis. Application fee: $0. Electronic applications accepted. *Financial support:* Fellowships with full and partial tuition reimbursements, research assistantships with full and partial tuition reimbursements, teaching assistantships with full and partial tuition reimbursements, Federal Work-Study, institutionally sponsored loans, scholarships/grants, tuition waivers (partial), and unspecified assistantships available. Support available to part-time students. Financial award application deadline: 2/1; financial award applicants required to submit FAFSA. *Faculty research:* Education policy, education reform, school choice, equity and diversity, higher education. *Unit head:* Dr. Ellen B. Goldring, Chair, 615-322-8000, Fax: 615-343-7094, E-mail: ellen.b.goldring@vanderbilt.edu. *Application contact:* Rosie Moody, Educational Coordinator, 615-322-8019, Fax: 615-343-7094, E-mail: rosie.moody@vanderbilt.edu.

Walden University, Graduate Programs, School of Management, Minneapolis, MN 55401. Offers accounting (MS, DBA), including accounting for the professional (MS), CPA (MS), self-designed (MS); accounting and management (MS), including accounting for strategic managers, self-designed; accounting for managers (MBA); advanced project management (Post-Graduate Certificate); applied project management (Post-Graduate Certificate); corporate finance (MBA); entrepreneurship (MBA, DBA); finance (DBA); global management (MS); global supply chain management (DBA); healthcare management (MBA, DBA); healthcare system improvement (MBA); human resource management (MBA, MS, PhD), including functional human resource management (MS), integrating functional and strategic human resource management (MS), organizational strategy (MS); information systems management (DBA); international business (MBA, DBA); leadership (MBA, MS, DBA), including entrepreneurship (MS), general management (MS), human resources leadership (MS), innovation and technology (MS), leader development (MS), leading sustainability (MS), project management (MS), self-designed (MS); management (MS), including healthcare management; managers as leaders (MS); marketing (MBA, DBA); project management (MBA, MS, DBA); research strategies (MS); risk management (MBA); self-designed (MBA, DBA, PhD); social impact management (DBA); strategies for sustainability (MBA); strategy and operations (MS); sustainable management (MS); technology (MBA); technology entrepreneurship (DBA); technology management (MS). Part-time and evening/weekend programs available. Postbaccalaureate distance learning degree programs offered (minimal on-campus study). *Faculty:* 32 full-time (14 women), 275 part-time/adjunct (98 women). *Students:* 3,962 full-time (2,095 women), 1,557 part-time (959 women); includes 3,003 minority (2,510 Black or African American, non-Hispanic/Latino; 25 American Indian or Alaska Native, non-Hispanic/Latino; 140 Asian, non-Hispanic/Latino; 240 Hispanic/Latino; 9 Native Hawaiian or other Pacific Islander, non-Hispanic/Latino; 79 Two or more races, non-Hispanic/Latino), 395 international. Average age 41. In 2011, 586 master's, 87 doctorates, 4 other advanced degrees awarded. *Degree requirements:* For doctorate, thesis/dissertation (for some programs), residency. *Entrance requirements:* For master's, bachelor's degree or equivalent in related field; minimum GPA of 2.5; official transcripts; goal statement; access to computer and Internet; for doctorate, master's degree or equivalent in related field; minimum GPA of 3.0; 3 years of related professional/academic experience (preferred). Additional exam requirements/recommendations for international students: Required—TOEFL (minimum score 550 paper-based; 213 computer-based), IELTS (minimum score 6.5), Michigan English Language Assessment Battery (minimum score 82). *Application deadline:* Applications are processed on a rolling basis. Application fee: $50. Electronic applications accepted. *Financial support:* Federal Work-Study, scholarships/grants, unspecified assistantships, and family tuition reduction, active duty/veteran tuition reduction, group tuition reduction, interest-free payment plans, employee tuition reduction available. Support available to part-time students. Financial award applicants required to submit FAFSA. *Unit head:* Dr. William Schulz, III, Associate Dean, 800-925-3368. *Application contact:* Jennifer Hall, Vice President of Enrollment Management, 866-4-WALDEN, E-mail: info@waldenu.edu. Web site: http://www.waldenu.edu/Colleges-and-Schools/College-of-Management-and-Technology.htm.

Walden University, Graduate Programs, School of Public Policy and Administration, Minneapolis, MN 55401. Offers criminal justice (MPA, MPP, MS), including emergency management (MS, PhD), homeland security policy (MS, PhD), homeland security policy and coordination (MS, PhD), law and public policy (MS, PhD), policy analysis (MS, PhD), public management and leadership (MS, PhD), self-designed (MS), terrorism, mediation, and peace (MS, PhD); criminal justice leadership and executive management (MS), including emergency management (MS, PhD), homeland security policy (MS, PhD), homeland security policy and coordination (MS, PhD), law and public policy (MS, PhD), policy analysis (MS, PhD), public management and leadership (MS, PhD), self-designed, terrorism, mediation, and peace (MS, PhD); emergency management (MPA, MPP, MS), including criminal justice (MS, PhD), homeland security (MS), public management and leadership (MS, PhD), terrorism and emergency management (MS); government management (Postbaccalaureate Certificate); health policy (MPA); homeland security policy (MPA, MPP); homeland security policy and coordination (MPA, MPP); interdisciplinary policy studies (MPA, MPP); international nongovernmental organizations (MPA, MPP); law and public policy (MPA, MPP); local government management for sustainable communities (MPA, MPP); nonprofit management (Postbaccalaureate Certificate); nonprofit management and leadership (MPA, MPP, MS); policy analysis (MPA); public management and leadership (MPA, MPP); public policy and administration (PhD), including criminal justice (MS, PhD), emergency management (MS, PhD), health policy, homeland security policy (MS, PhD), homeland security policy and coordination (MS, PhD), interdisciplinary policy studies, international nongovernmental organizations, law and public policy (MS, PhD), local government management for sustainable communities, nonprofit management and leadership, policy analysis (MS, PhD), public management and leadership (MS, PhD), terrorism, mediation, and peace (MS, PhD); terrorism, mediation, and peace (MPA, MPP). Part-time and evening/weekend programs available. Postbaccalaureate distance learning degree programs offered (minimal on-campus study). *Faculty:* 9 full-time (3 women), 90 part-time/adjunct (41 women). *Students:* 1,396 full-time (886 women), 902 part-time (581 women); includes 1,392 minority (1,205 Black or African American, non-Hispanic/Latino; 11 American Indian or Alaska Native, non-Hispanic/Latino; 35 Asian, non-Hispanic/Latino; 95 Hispanic/Latino; 2 Native Hawaiian or other Pacific Islander, non-Hispanic/Latino; 44 Two or more races, non-Hispanic/Latino), 82 international. Average age 41. In 2011, 265 master's, 34 doctorates, 13 other advanced degrees awarded. *Degree requirements:* For doctorate, thesis/dissertation, residency. *Entrance requirements:* For master's, bachelor's degree or equivalent in related field, minimum GPA of 2.5; for doctorate, master's degree or equivalent in related field; minimum GPA of 3.0; official transcripts; three years of related professional/academic experience (preferred); access to computer and Internet. Additional exam requirements/recommendations for international students: Required—TOEFL (minimum score 550 paper-based; 213 computer-based), IELTS (minimum score 6.5), or Michigan English Language Assessment Battery (minimum score 82). *Application deadline:* Applications are processed on a rolling basis. Application fee: $50. Electronic applications accepted. *Financial support:* Federal Work-Study, scholarships/grants, unspecified assistantships, and family tuition reduction, active duty/veteran tuition reduction, group tuition reduction, interest-free payment plans, employee tuition reduction available. Support available to part-time students. Financial award applicants required to submit FAFSA. *Unit head:* Dr. Mark Gordon, Associate Dean, 800-925-3368. *Application contact:* Jennifer Hall, Vice President of Enrollment Management, 866-4-WALDEN, E-mail: info@waldenu.edu. Web site: http://www.waldenu.edu/Colleges-and-Schools/College-of-Social-and-Behavioral-Sciences/School-of-Public-Policy-and-Administration.htm.

Warner Pacific College, Graduate Programs, Portland, OR 97215-4099. Offers biblical and theological studies (MA); biblical studies (M Rel); education (M Ed); management/organizational leadership (MS); pastoral ministries (M Rel); religion and ethics (M Rel); teaching (MA); theology (M Rel). Part-time programs available. *Degree requirements:* For master's, thesis or alternative, presentation of defense. *Entrance requirements:* For master's, interview, minimum GPA of 2.5, letters of recommendations. *Faculty research:* New Testament studies, nineteenth-century Wesleyan theology, preaching and church growth, Christian ethics.

Wayland Baptist University, Graduate Programs, Programs in Business Administration/Management, Plainview, TX 79072-6998. Offers general business (MBA); health care administration (MBA); human resource management (MBA); international management (MBA); management (MA, MBA), including health care administration (MA), human resource management (MA), organization management (MA); management information systems (MBA). Part-time and evening/weekend programs available. Postbaccalaureate distance learning degree programs offered (no on-campus study). *Degree requirements:* For master's, capstone course. *Entrance requirements:* For master's, GMAT, GRE or MAT. Additional exam requirements/recommendations for international students: Required—TOEFL (minimum score 500 paper-based; 173 computer-based; 61 iBT). Electronic applications accepted.

Waynesburg University, Graduate and Professional Studies, Waynesburg, PA 15370-1222. Offers business (MBA), including finance, health systems, human resources, leadership, market development; counseling (MA), including addictions counseling, clinical mental health; education (MAT); nursing (MSN), including administration, education, informatics, palliative care; nursing practice (DNP); special education (M Ed); technology (M Ed); MSN/MBA. *Accreditation:* AACN. Part-time and evening/weekend programs available. *Degree requirements:* For doctorate, thesis/dissertation. *Entrance requirements:* Additional exam requirements/recommendations for international students: Required—TOEFL. Electronic applications accepted.

Wayne State College, Department of Health, Human Performance and Sport, Wayne, NE 68787. Offers exercise science (MSE); organizational management (MS), including sport management. Part-time and evening/weekend programs available. *Degree requirements:* For master's, comprehensive exam, thesis optional. *Entrance requirements:* For master's, GRE General Test, minimum GPA of 3.0. Additional exam requirements/recommendations for international students: Required—TOEFL (minimum score 550 paper-based; 213 computer-based). Electronic applications accepted.

Wayne State University, College of Liberal Arts and Sciences, Department of Political Science, Program in Public Administration, Detroit, MI 48202. Offers aging policy and management (MPA); criminal justice policy and management (MPA); economic development policy and management (MPA); health services policy and management (MPA); human resources management (MPA); information technology management (MPA); non-profit management (MPA); organizational behavior and management (MPA); public budgeting and financial management (MPA); public policy analysis and program evaluation (MPA); social welfare policy and management (MPA); urban policy and management (MPA). *Accreditation:* NASPAA. Evening/weekend programs available. *Students:* 22 full-time (17 women), 45 part-time (33 women); includes 19 minority (16 Black or African American, non-Hispanic/Latino; 1 American Indian or Alaska Native, non-Hispanic/Latino; 2 Hispanic/Latino), 1 international. Average age 31. 75 applicants, 28% accepted, 11 enrolled. In 2011, 20 master's awarded. *Degree requirements:* For master's, comprehensive exam. *Entrance requirements:* For master's, GRE General Test. Additional exam requirements/recommendations for international students: Required—TOEFL (minimum score 550 paper-based; 213 computer-based); Recommended—TWE (minimum score 5.5). *Application deadline:* For fall admission, 6/1 priority date for domestic students, 5/1 for international students; for winter admission, 10/1 priority date for domestic students, 9/1 for international students; for spring admission, 2/1 priority date for domestic students, 1/1 for international students. Applications are processed on a rolling basis. Application fee: $50. Electronic applications accepted. *Expenses:* Tuition, state resident: part-time $512.85 per credit. Tuition, nonresident: part-time $1132.65 per credit. *Required fees:* $26.60 per credit. $199.65 per semester. Tuition and fees vary according to course load and program. *Financial support:* In 2011–12, 7 students received support. Scholarships/grants available. *Faculty research:* Urban politics, urban education, state administration. *Unit head:* Dr. Brady Baybeck, Director, 313-577-2630, E-mail: mpa@wayne.edu. Web site: http://clasweb.clas.wayne.edu/mapa.

Webster University, College of Arts and Sciences, Department of History, Politics and International Relations, Program in International Nongovernmental Organizations, St. Louis, MO 63119-3194. Offers MA. *Expenses: Tuition:* Full-time $10,890; part-time $605 per credit hour. Tuition and fees vary according to campus/location and program.

Western International University, Graduate Programs in Business, Program in Organization Development, Phoenix, AZ 85021-2718. Offers MBA. *Entrance requirements:* For master's, minimum GPA of 2.75.

Wheeling Jesuit University, Department of Social Sciences, Wheeling, WV 26003-6295. Offers MSOL. Part-time and evening/weekend programs available. *Faculty:* 10 full-time (3 women), 27 part-time/adjunct (7 women). *Students:* 13 part-time (3 women), 1 international. Average age 35. 21 applicants, 100% accepted, 0 enrolled. In 2011, 9 master's awarded. *Degree requirements:* For master's, thesis. *Entrance requirements:*

For master's, MAT, minimum GPA of 2.75, minimum of three years full-time professional work experience. Additional exam requirements/recommendations for international students: Required—TOEFL (minimum score 600 paper-based; 250 computer-based; 100 iBT). *Application deadline:* For fall admission, 8/1 priority date for domestic students, 8/1 for international students; for spring admission, 12/15 priority date for domestic students, 12/1 for international students. Applications are processed on a rolling basis. Application fee: $25. Electronic applications accepted. Application fee is waived when completed online. *Expenses: Tuition:* Full-time $9720; part-time $540 per credit hour. *Required fees:* $250. *Financial support:* In 2011–12, 6 students received support. Unspecified assistantships available. Financial award application deadline: 8/1; financial award applicants required to submit FAFSA. *Faculty research:* History, theory and philosophy of leadership; gender roles and leadership; spirituality and leadership. *Unit head:* Dr. Robert E. Phillips, Associate Professor and Chair, 304-243-2006, Fax: 304-243-6246, E-mail: phillips@wju.edu. *Application contact:* Melissa Rataiczak, Associate Director of Enrollment for Leadership Programs, 304-243-2236, Fax: 304-243-2397, E-mail: mrataiczak@wju.edu. Web site: http://www.wju.edu/adulted/msol.asp.

Wilfrid Laurier University, Faculty of Graduate and Postdoctoral Studies, Lyle S. Hallman Faculty of Social Work, Waterloo, ON N2L 3C5, Canada. Offers Aboriginal studies (MSW); community, policy, planning and organizations (MSW); critical social policy and organizational studies (PhD); individuals, families and groups (MSW); social work practice (individuals, families, groups and communities) (PhD); social work practice: individuals, families, groups and communities (PhD). Part-time programs available. *Degree requirements:* For master's, thesis optional; for doctorate, thesis/dissertation. *Entrance requirements:* For master's, course work in social science, research methodology, and statistics; honors BA with a minimum B average; for doctorate, master's degree in social work, minimum A- average. Additional exam requirements/recommendations for international students: Required—TOEFL (minimum score 89 iBT). Electronic applications accepted. *Expenses:* Contact institution.

Wilkes University, College of Graduate and Professional Studies, Jay S. Sidhu School of Business and Leadership, Wilkes-Barre, PA 18766-0002. Offers accounting (MBA); entrepreneurship (MBA); finance (MBA); health care administration (MBA); human resource management (MBA); international business (MBA); marketing (MBA); operations management (MBA); organizational leadership and development (MBA). *Accreditation:* ACBSP. Part-time and evening/weekend programs available. *Students:* 48 full-time (20 women), 134 part-time (62 women); includes 12 minority (2 Black or African American, non-Hispanic/Latino; 5 Asian, non-Hispanic/Latino; 2 Hispanic/Latino; 3 Two or more races, non-Hispanic/Latino), 9 international. Average age 30. In 2011, 69 master's awarded. *Entrance requirements:* For master's, GMAT. Additional exam requirements/recommendations for international students: Required—TOEFL (minimum score 550 paper-based; 213 computer-based; 79 iBT). *Application deadline:* Applications are processed on a rolling basis. Application fee: $45 ($65 for international students). Electronic applications accepted. *Expenses:* Contact institution. *Financial support:* Federal Work-Study and unspecified assistantships available. Financial award application deadline: 3/1; financial award applicants required to submit FAFSA. *Unit head:* Dr. Jeffrey Alves, Dean, 570-408-4702, Fax: 570-408-7846, E-mail: jeffrey.alves@wilkes.edu. *Application contact:* Erin Sutzko, Director of Extended Learning, 570-408-4253, Fax: 570-408-7846, E-mail: erin.sutzko@wilkes.edu. Web site: http://www.wilkes.edu/pages/457.asp.

Wilmington University, College of Business, New Castle, DE 19720-6491. Offers accounting (MBA, MS); business administration (MBA, DBA); environmental stewardship (MBA); finance (MBA); health care administration (MBA, MSM); homeland security (MBA, MSM); human resource management (MSM); management information systems (MBA, MSN); marketing (MSM); marketing management (MBA); military leadership (MSM); organizational leadership (MBA, MSM); public administration (MSM). Part-time and evening/weekend programs available. *Faculty:* 4 full-time (0 women). *Students:* 266 full-time (121 women), 700 part-time (505 women). Average age 34. *Entrance requirements:* Additional exam requirements/recommendations for international students: Required—TOEFL (minimum score 500 paper-based; 173 computer-based). *Application deadline:* Applications are processed on a rolling basis. Application fee: $35. Electronic applications accepted. *Expenses: Tuition:* Part-time $534 per credit hour. *Required fees:* $25 per term. *Financial support:* Applicants required to submit FAFSA. *Unit head:* Dr. Donald W. Durandetta, Dean, 302-356-6780, E-mail: donald.w.durandetta@wilmu.edu. *Application contact:* Chris Ferguson, Director of Admissions, 302-356-4636 Ext. 256, Fax: 302-328-5164, E-mail: inquire@wilmcoll.edu. Web site: http://www.wilmu.edu/business/.

Woodbury University, School of Business and Management, Program in Organizational Leadership, Burbank, CA 91504-1099. Offers MA. Evening/weekend programs available. *Faculty:* 1 (woman) full-time, 8 part-time/adjunct (4 women). *Students:* 81 full-time (46 women), 2 part-time (both women); includes 40 minority (11 Black or African American, non-Hispanic/Latino; 4 Asian, non-Hispanic/Latino; 24 Hispanic/Latino; 1 Native Hawaiian or other Pacific Islander, non-Hispanic/Latino), 4 international. Average age 37. 51 applicants, 76% accepted, 36 enrolled. In 2011, 54 master's awarded. *Entrance requirements:* For master's, GRE General Test (if GPA less than 2.5), 3 recommendations, essay, resume, academic transcripts. Additional exam requirements/recommendations for international students: Required—TOEFL (minimum score 550 paper-based; 220 computer-based; 83 iBT), IELTS (minimum score 6.5). *Application deadline:* For fall admission, 8/1 priority date for domestic students; for spring admission, 12/1 priority date for domestic students. Applications are processed on a rolling basis. Application fee: $35. *Expenses: Tuition:* Full-time $24,921; part-time $923 per unit. *Required fees:* $8 per unit. $50 per term. One-time fee: $110. Tuition and fees vary according to program. *Financial support:* Scholarships/grants available. *Unit head:* Paul Decker, Director of the Institute for Excellence in Teaching and Learning, 818-252-5267, E-mail: paul.decker@woodbury.edu. *Application contact:* Ruth Lorenzana, Director of Admissions, 800-784-9663, Fax: 818-767-7520, E-mail: admissions@woodbury.edu.

Worcester Polytechnic Institute, Graduate Studies and Research, School of Business, Worcester, MA 01609-2280. Offers information technology (MS), including information security management; management (Graduate Certificate); marketing and technological innovation (MS); operations design and leadership (MS); technology (MBA, MS). *Accreditation:* AACSB. Part-time and evening/weekend programs available. Postbaccalaureate distance learning degree programs offered (minimal on-campus study). *Faculty:* 12 full-time (7 women), 12 part-time/adjunct (2 women). *Students:* 108 full-time (64 women), 206 part-time (55 women); includes 27 minority (4 Black or African American, non-Hispanic/Latino; 12 Asian, non-Hispanic/Latino; 4 Hispanic/Latino; 7 Two or more races, non-Hispanic/Latino), 131 international. 596 applicants, 48% accepted, 131 enrolled. In 2011, 75 master's awarded. *Degree requirements:* For master's, thesis optional. *Entrance requirements:* For master's, GMAT (MBA), GMAT or GRE General Test (MS), resume; for Graduate Certificate, GMAT or GRE General Test, statement of purpose, 3 letters of recommendation. Additional exam requirements/recommendations for international students: Required—TOEFL (minimum score 563 paper-based; 223 computer-based; 84 iBT), IELTS (minimum score 7). *Application deadline:* For fall admission, 6/1 priority date for domestic students, 6/1 for international students; for spring admission, 11/1 priority date for domestic students, 10/1 for international students. Applications are processed on a rolling basis. Application fee: $70. Electronic applications accepted. *Financial support:* Career-related internships or fieldwork, institutionally sponsored loans, scholarships/grants, and unspecified assistantships available. Financial award application deadline: 6/1; financial award applicants required to submit FAFSA. *Faculty research:* Organizational aesthetics, resistance in organizations, dynamics of product innovation, economic approaches to productivity, corporate earnings forecasts and value relevance, ERP implementation, improving Web accessibility, information quality assessment, measuring strategic and transactional IT, website quality, service operations modeling, healthcare operations and performance analysis, entrepreneurship, leadership and change. *Unit head:* Dr. Mark Rice, Dean, 508-831-4665, Fax: 508-831-5218, E-mail: rice@wpi.edu. *Application contact:* Peggy Caisse, Recruiting Operations Coordinator, 508-831-4665, Fax: 508-831-5720, E-mail: mcaisse@wpi.edu. Web site: http://www.biz.wpi.edu/Graduate/.

Worcester State University, Graduate Studies, Program in Management, Worcester, MA 01602-2597. Offers accounting (MS); managerial leadership (MS). Part-time and evening/weekend programs available. *Faculty:* 1 full-time (0 women), 2 part-time/adjunct (1 woman). *Students:* 10 full-time (5 women), 18 part-time (7 women); includes 6 minority (2 Black or African American, non-Hispanic/Latino; 1 Asian, non-Hispanic/Latino; 2 Hispanic/Latino; 1 Two or more races, non-Hispanic/Latino), 3 international. Average age 31. 26 applicants, 62% accepted, 8 enrolled. In 2011, 5 master's awarded. *Degree requirements:* For master's, comprehensive exam (for some programs), thesis optional. *Entrance requirements:* For master's, GMAT. Additional exam requirements/recommendations for international students: Required—TOEFL (minimum score 500 paper-based; 61 iBT). *Application deadline:* For fall admission, 6/15 for domestic and international students; for spring admission, 4/1 for domestic and international students. Applications are processed on a rolling basis. Application fee: $40. Electronic applications accepted. *Expenses:* Tuition, state resident: full-time $2700; part-time $150 per credit. Tuition, nonresident: full-time $2700; part-time $150 per credit. *Required fees:* $2016; $112 per credit. *Financial support:* In 2011–12, 3 students received support, including 3 research assistantships with full tuition reimbursements available (averaging $4,800 per year); career-related internships or fieldwork, scholarships/grants, and unspecified assistantships also available. Financial award application deadline: 3/1; financial award applicants required to submit FAFSA. *Unit head:* Dr. Laurie Dahlin, Coordinator, 508-929-8084, Fax: 508-929-8048, E-mail: ldahlin@worcester.edu. *Application contact:* Sara Grady, Assistant Dean of Continuing Education, 508-929-8787, Fax: 508-929-8100, E-mail: sara.grady@worcester.edu.

Yale University, Yale School of Management and Graduate School of Arts and Sciences, Doctoral Program in Management, New Haven, CT 06520. Offers accounting (PhD); financial economics (PhD); marketing (PhD); organizations and management (PhD). *Accreditation:* AACSB. *Faculty:* 42 full-time (8 women). *Students:* 33 full-time (9 women); includes 4 minority (all Asian, non-Hispanic/Latino), 16 international. 439 applicants, 3% accepted, 4 enrolled. In 2011, 2 doctorates awarded. *Degree requirements:* For doctorate, comprehensive exam, thesis/dissertation. *Entrance requirements:* For doctorate, GMAT or GRE General Test. Additional exam requirements/recommendations for international students: Required—TOEFL or IELTS. *Application deadline:* For fall admission, 1/2 for domestic and international students. Application fee: $100. Electronic applications accepted. *Expenses:* Contact institution. *Financial support:* In 2011–12, 31 students received support, including 31 fellowships with full tuition reimbursements available, 31 research assistantships with full tuition reimbursements available, 31 teaching assistantships with full tuition reimbursements available; institutionally sponsored loans, scholarships/grants, and health care benefits also available. Financial award application deadline: 1/2. *Faculty research:* Pricing of options and futures, term structure of interest rates, use of accounting numbers in debt contracts, product differentiation, e-commerce and marketing, behavioral finance. *Unit head:* Carla Mills, Registrar, 203-432-3955, Fax: 203-432-0342.

HAWAI'I PACIFIC UNIVERSITY

Master of Arts in Organizational Change

Programs of Study

Today's leaders discover that they must continually realign their organizations to develop strategic visions, missions, and goals critical to short-term performance. Simultaneously, they are faced with the complex task of adapting their organization to compete in competitive, rapidly changing markets. They must also address diverse workforce needs, government regulations, new technologies, and deteriorating environments and resources. The Master of Arts in Organizational Change (MAOC) program takes a multidisciplinary perspective, using concepts and methods from such fields as organizational development, management, sociology, anthropology, communication, information systems, psychology, and comparative economics to address the issues faced by today's businesses.

The MAOC program emphasizes the management, design, implementation, and application of change methods to improve performance, management, and organizational culture. Students learn how to design and implement an actual program of change in an organization. The program is accredited by the Accrediting Commission for Senior Colleges of the Western Association of Schools and Colleges (WASC).

The MAOC program requires a minimum of 42 semester credits of graduate work. The 42 semester hours are divided into 36 semester hours of core courses and 6 semester hours of capstone courses. The program may be completed online from any location in the world.

The learning objectives of the MAOC online program are the same as the on-campus program. Students attain a solid foundation in the theory and practice of organizational design and behavior. They use this foundation to achieve competency in recognizing and reconciling cultural differences that effect change and development. Students will learn to understand change and development theories and practices from a systemic, holistic perspective. Upon completion of the program, graduates will be able to critically evaluate the effectiveness of various change and development models and methods in both global and local contexts. They will understand the dynamics of change—in particular, innovation diffusion, change leadership, knowledge management, problem solving, and technology transfer. They will also understand the global-wide change and development profession, including the roles of consultants, change agents, educators, political leaders, nonprofit administrators, and corporate executives; and they will be prepared to work with various stakeholders to design and implement effective and sustainable change and development initiatives.

Students who complete the MAOC program at Hawai'i Pacific University are given priority in the application process for a Ph.D. in Organizational Change and Development at Southern Cross University.

The joint Master of Arts in Organizational Change and Communication program (MAOC/MACOM) is designed for students who wish to develop skills in change leadership and organizational development, while acquiring a broad and thorough understanding of communication.

Research Facilities

To support graduate studies, HPU's Meader and Atherton Libraries offer more than 110,000 bound volumes, 350,000 microfiche items, and periodical subscriptions to 1,500 print titles and 30,000 electronic journals. Databases of public and state university libraries, legislative information, and business-oriented statistical data are also available in the library or online. Students can access HPU's library databases, course information, their academic information, and an e-mail account through Pipeline, the university's internal Web site for students. The University's accessible on-campus computer center houses more than 420 computers with specialized software to support graduate academic programs. HPU also provides free Wi-Fi so students can have wireless access to Pipeline resources anywhere on campus using laptops. A significant number of online courses are available.

Financial Aid

The University participates in all federal financial aid programs designated for graduate students. These programs provide aid in the form of subsidized (need-based) and unsubsidized (non-need-based) Federal Stafford Student Loans. Through these loans, funds may be available to cover the student's entire cost of education. To apply for aid, students must submit the Free Application for Federal Student Aid (FAFSA) beginning January 1.

The University also offers several types of institutional graduate scholarships to new full-time, degree-seeking students. U.S. citizens, permanent residents, and international students who have a demonstrated financial need may apply. HPU's graduate scholarships include the Graduate Trustee Scholarship of $6000 ($3000 for two semesters), the Graduate Dean Scholarship of $4000 ($2000 for two semesters), and the Graduate Kokua Scholarship of $2000 ($1000 for two semesters). Factors that may be considered when evaluating requests are previous academic record, community involvement and service, and professional work experience and achievement.

In order to be eligible for the best award package, students should apply by HPU's priority deadline of March 1. Applications received after the priority deadline will be awarded on a funds-available basis. Mailing of student award letters usually begins by the end of March. Applicants will be notified by mail as decisions are made.

Cost of Study

Tuition for graduate students enrolled in fall and spring semesters is determined on a per-credit basis; full-time status for a graduate student is 9 credits. Tuition for the optional winter and summer sessions is also determined on a per-credit basis. For the 2012–13 academic year, full-time tuition is $13,590 for most graduate degree programs, including the M.A.O.C. program. Other expenses, including books, personal expenses, fees, and a student bus pass are estimated at $3285.

Living and Housing Costs

The University has off-campus housing for graduate students and an apartment referral service. The cost of living in off-campus housing is approximately $12,482 for a double-occupancy room. Additional housing information is available online at www.hpu.edu/housing.

Student Group

University enrollment currently stands at more than 8,200. HPU is one of the most culturally diverse universities in America with students from all fifty U.S. states and more than 100 countries.

Location

Hawai'i Pacific University combines the excitement of an urban, downtown campus with the serenity of a residential campus. The urban campus is ideally located in downtown Honolulu, the business and financial center of the Pacific. The downtown campus is composed of seven buildings in the center of Honolulu's business district and is home to the College of Business Administration and the College of Humanities and Social Sciences.

Eight miles away, situated on 135 acres in Kaneohe, the windward Hawai'i Loa campus is the site of the College of Nursing and Health Sciences and the College of Natural and Computational Sciences. The Hawai'i Loa campus has residence halls; dining commons; the Educational Technology Center; a student center; and outdoor recreational facilities including a soccer field, tennis courts, a softball field, and an exercise room.

HPU is affiliated with the Oceanic Institute, an aquaculture research facility located on a 56-acre site at Makapu'u Point on the windward coast of Oahu, Hawaii. All three sites are linked by HPU shuttle and easily accessible by public transportation as well.

Notably, the downtown campus location is within walking distance of shopping and dining. Iolani Palace, the only royal palace in the United States, is a few blocks away, as are the State Capitol, City Hall, and the Blaisdell Concert Hall. The Honolulu Academy of Arts, Museum of Contemporary Art, Waikiki Aquarium, Honolulu Zoo, and many other cultural attractions are located nearby.

The University

HPU is a private, nonprofit university with approximately 8,200 students. Founded in 1965, HPU prides itself on maintaining strong academic programs, small class sizes, individual attention to students, and a diverse faculty and student population. Students may choose from more than fifty acclaimed undergraduate programs and fourteen distinguished graduate programs.

HPU is recognized as a Best in the West college by The Princeton Review and *U.S. News & World Report* and a Best Buy by *Barron's* business magazine.

HPU boasts more than 500 full- and part-time faculty members from around the world with outstanding academic and professional credentials. HPU's student-centered approach and low student-to-faculty ratio of 15:1 results in personal attention and one-on-one guidance. The average class size is under 25.

A wide range of counseling and other student support services are available. There are more than fifty student organizations on campus, including the Graduate Student Organization.

Applying

Students must have a baccalaureate degree from an accredited college or university in the United States or an equivalent degree from another country. Applicants should complete and forward a graduate admissions application, send in the $50 nonrefundable application fee, have official transcripts sent from all colleges or universities previously attended, and forward two letters of recommendation. A personal statement about the applicant's academic and career goals is required; submitting a resume is optional. Applicants who have taken the Graduate Record Examination (GRE) should have their scores sent directly to the Graduate Admissions Office. International students should submit scores of a recognized English proficiency test such as TOEFL. Admissions decisions are made on a rolling basis and applicants are notified between one and two weeks after all documents have been submitted. Applicants are encouraged to submit their applications online.

Correspondence and Information

Graduate Admissions
Hawai'i Pacific University
1164 Bishop Street, Suite 911
Honolulu, Hawai'i 96813
Phone: 808-544-1135
800-500-5565 (toll-free)
Fax: 808-544-0280
E-mail: graduate@hpu.edu
Web site: http://www.hpu.edu/hpumaoc

THE FACULTY AND THEIR RESEARCH

Hawai'i Pacific University's faculty members are known not only as outstanding teachers, but also as scholars in their respective fields. Faculty members in the Master of Arts in Organizational Change program have conducted extensive research in such areas as government, military, health care, and corporate networks. With stellar academic backgrounds and wide-ranging experiences in public service, HPU's faculty members bring a balance of theory and practical insight to the classroom. With an emphasis on meaningful faculty-student interaction, most courses are taught in a seminar format, where faculty members work one-on-one with graduate students.

W. Gerald Glover, Affiliate Professor of Management and Marketing; Ph.D., Florida.

Stewart Hase, Adjunct Faculty in Management and Marketing

Gordon Jones, Professor of Computer Science and Information Systems; Ph.D., New Mexico.

Margo Poole, Adjunct Faculty in Management and Marketing; Ph.D., Newcastle (Australia).

Richard Ward, Associate Professor in Management; Ed.D., USC.

Arthur Whatley, Professor in Management; Ph.D., North Texas State.

Larry Zimmerman, Assistant Professor in Management; Ph.D., Nebraska–Lincoln.

Section 17
Project Management

This section contains a directory of institutions offering graduate work in project management. Additional information about programs listed in the directory but not augmented by an in-depth entry may be obtained by writing directly to the dean of a graduate school or chair of a department at the address given in the directory.

For programs offering related work, see also in this book *Business Administration and Management.*

CONTENTS

Program Directory

Project Management

American Graduate University, Program in Project Management, Covina, CA 91724. Offers MPM, Certificate. Part-time programs available. Postbaccalaureate distance learning degree programs offered (no on-campus study). *Faculty:* 2 full-time (1 woman), 15 part-time/adjunct (2 women). *Students:* 125 part-time. In 2011, 8 master's awarded. *Entrance requirements:* For master's, undergraduate degree from institution accredited by accrediting agency recognized by the U.S. Department of Education. Additional exam requirements/recommendations for international students: Required—TOEFL. *Application deadline:* Applications are processed on a rolling basis. Application fee: $50. Electronic applications accepted. *Expenses: Tuition:* Part-time $275 per credit. *Unit head:* Paul McDonald, President, 626-966-4576 Ext. 1006, E-mail: paulmcdonald@agu.edu. *Application contact:* Marie Sirney, Director of Admissions, 626-966-4576 Ext. 1003, Fax: 626-915-1709, E-mail: mariesirney@agu.edu.

American InterContinental University Online, Program in Business Administration, Hoffman Estates, IL 60192. Offers accounting and finance (MBA); finance (MBA); healthcare management (MBA); human resource management (MBA); international business (MBA); management (MBA); marketing (MBA); operations management (MBA); organizational psychology and development (MBA); project management (MBA). Evening/weekend programs available. Postbaccalaureate distance learning degree programs offered (no on-campus study). *Entrance requirements:* Additional exam requirements/recommendations for international students: Required—TOEFL (minimum score 550 paper-based; 213 computer-based). Electronic applications accepted.

American InterContinental University Online, Program in Information Technology, Hoffman Estates, IL 60192. Offers Internet security (MIT); IT project management (MIT). Evening/weekend programs available. Postbaccalaureate distance learning degree programs offered (no on-campus study). *Entrance requirements:* Additional exam requirements/recommendations for international students: Required—TOEFL (minimum score 550 paper-based; 213 computer-based). Electronic applications accepted.

American Public University System, AMU/APU Graduate Programs, Charles Town, WV 25414. Offers accounting (MBA, MS); administration and supervision (M Ed); criminal justice (MA); emergency and disaster management (MA); entrepreneurship (MBA); environmental policy and management (MS), including environmental planning, environmental sustainability, fish and wildlife management, general (MA, MS), global environmental management; finance (MBA); general (MBA); global business management (MBA); guidance and counseling (M Ed); history (MA), including American history, ancient and classical history, European history, global history, military and diplomatic history, public history; homeland security (MA); homeland security resource allocation (MBA); humanities (MA); information technology (MS), including digital forensics, enterprise software development, information assurance and security, IT project management; information technology management (MBA); intelligence studies (MA), including criminal intelligence, general (MA, MS), homeland security, intelligence analysis, intelligence collection, intelligence operations, terrorism studies; international relations and conflict resolution (MA), including comparative and security issues, conflict resolution, international and transnational security issues, peacekeeping; legal studies (MA); management (MA), including defense management, general (MA, MS), human resource management, organizational leadership, public administration, reverse logistics, strategic consulting; marketing (MBA); military history (MA), including American military history, American revolution, civil war, war since 1946, World War II; military studies (MA), including air warfare, asymmetrical warfare, joint warfare, land warfare, naval warfare, strategic leadership; national security studies (MA), including general (MA, MS), homeland security, regional security studies, security and intelligence analysis, terrorism studies; nonprofit management (MBA); political science (MA), including American politics and government, comparative government and development, public policy; psychology (MA); public administration (MA, MPA), including disaster management (MPA), environmental policy (MA), health policy (MPA), human resources (MPA), national security (MPA), organizational management (MPA), security management (MPA); public health (MA, MPH), including emergency management (MPH), environmental health (MPH), public administration (MA); reverse logistics management (MA); security management (MA); space studies (MS), including aerospace science, planetary science; sports and health sciences (MS); sports management (MS), including coaching theory and strategy, sports administration; teaching (M Ed), including curriculum and instruction for elementary teachers, elementary, elementary reading, English language learners, instructional leadership, online learning, secondary social sciences, special education; transportation and logistics management (MA), including maritime engineering management. Programs offered via distance learning only. Part-time and evening/weekend programs available. Postbaccalaureate distance learning degree programs offered (no on-campus study). *Faculty:* 445 full-time (241 women), 1,360 part-time/adjunct (617 women). *Students:* 688 full-time (338 women), 10,168 part-time (3,706 women); includes 3,130 minority (1,007 Black or African American, non-Hispanic/Latino; 103 American Indian or Alaska Native, non-Hispanic/Latino; 825 Asian, non-Hispanic/Latino; 810 Hispanic/Latino; 51 Native Hawaiian or other Pacific Islander, non-Hispanic/Latino; 334 Two or more races, non-Hispanic/Latino), 134 international. Average age 35. In 2011, 2,386 master's awarded. *Degree requirements:* For master's, comprehensive exam or practicum. *Entrance requirements:* For master's, official transcript showing earned bachelor's degree from institution accredited by recognized accrediting body. Additional exam requirements/recommendations for international students: Required—TOEFL (minimum score 550 paper-based; 213 computer-based), IELTS (minimum score 6.5). *Application deadline:* Applications are processed on a rolling basis. Application fee: $0. Electronic applications accepted. *Expenses: Tuition:* Part-time $325 per credit hour. *Financial support:* Applicants required to submit FAFSA. *Faculty research:* Military history, criminal justice, management performance, national security. *Unit head:* Dr. Karan Powell, Executive Vice President and Provost, 877-468-6268, Fax: 304-724-3780. *Application contact:* Terry Grant, Vice President of Enrollment Management, 877-468-6268, Fax: 304-724-3780, E-mail: info@apus.edu. Web site: http://www.apus.edu.

Aspen University, Program in Business Administration, Denver, CO 80246. Offers business administration (MBA); finance (MBA); information management (MBA); project management (MBA, Certificate). Part-time and evening/weekend programs available. Postbaccalaureate distance learning degree programs offered (no on-campus study). *Entrance requirements:* Additional exam requirements/recommendations for international students: Required—TOEFL (minimum score 530 paper-based; 71 computer-based). Electronic applications accepted.

Athabasca University, Centre for Innovative Management, St. Albert, AB T8N 1B4, Canada. Offers business administration (MBA); information technology management (MBA), including policing concentration; management (GDM); project management (MBA, GDM). Part-time and evening/weekend programs available. Postbaccalaureate distance learning degree programs offered (no on-campus study). *Degree requirements:* For master's, thesis or alternative, applied project. *Entrance requirements:* For master's, 3-8 years of managerial experience, 3 years with undergraduate degree, 5 years managerial experience with professional designation, 8-10 years management experience (on exception). Electronic applications accepted. *Expenses:* Contact institution. *Faculty research:* Human resources, project management, operations research, information technology management, corporate stewardship, energy management.

Bellevue University, Graduate School, College of Information Technology, Bellevue, NE 68005-3098. Offers computer information systems (MS); cybersecurity (MS); management of information systems (MS); project management (MPM).

Boston University, Metropolitan College, Department of Administrative Sciences, Boston, MA 02215. Offers banking and financial management (MSM); business continuity in emergency management (MSM); economics development and tourism management (MSAS); electronic commerce, systems, and technology (MSAS); financial economics (MSAS); innovation and technology (MSAS); insurance management (MSM); international market management (MSM); multinational commerce (MSAS); project management (MSM). *Accreditation:* AACSB. Part-time and evening/weekend programs available. Postbaccalaureate distance learning degree programs offered (no on-campus study). *Faculty:* 14 full-time (2 women), 21 part-time/adjunct (2 women). *Students:* 151 full-time (75 women), 106 part-time (51 women); includes 27 minority (6 Black or African American, non-Hispanic/Latino; 14 Asian, non-Hispanic/Latino; 7 Hispanic/Latino), 173 international. Average age 28. 500 applicants, 65% accepted, 194 enrolled. In 2011, 154 master's awarded. *Degree requirements:* For master's, thesis optional. *Entrance requirements:* For master's, 1 year of work experience, minimum GPA of 3.0. Additional exam requirements/recommendations for international students: Required—TOEFL (minimum score 560 paper-based; 220 computer-based; 84 iBT). *Application deadline:* Applications are processed on a rolling basis. Application fee: $70. Electronic applications accepted. *Expenses: Tuition:* Full-time $40,848; part-time $1276 per credit hour. *Required fees:* $572; $286 per semester. *Financial support:* In 2011–12, 15 students received support, including 7 research assistantships (averaging $10,000 per year); career-related internships or fieldwork, Federal Work-Study, and unspecified assistantships also available. *Faculty research:* International business, innovative process. *Unit head:* Dr. Kip Becker, Chairman, 617-353-3016, E-mail: adminsc@bu.edu. *Application contact:* Lucille Dicker, Administrative Sciences Department, 617-353-3016, E-mail: adminsc@bu.edu. Web site: http://www.bu.edu/met/programs/.

Boston University, Metropolitan College, Department of Computer Science, Boston, MA 02215. Offers computer information systems (MS), including computer networks, database management and business intelligence, health informatics, IT project management, security, Web application development; computer science (MS), including computer networks, security; telecommunications (MS), including security. Evening/weekend programs available. Postbaccalaureate distance learning degree programs offered. *Faculty:* 12 full-time (2 women), 28 part-time/adjunct (2 women). *Students:* 25 full-time (6 women), 732 part-time (167 women); includes 208 minority (51 Black or African American, non-Hispanic/Latino; 1 American Indian or Alaska Native, non-Hispanic/Latino; 104 Asian, non-Hispanic/Latino; 43 Hispanic/Latino; 1 Native Hawaiian or other Pacific Islander, non-Hispanic/Latino; 8 Two or more races, non-Hispanic/Latino), 86 international. Average age 35. 260 applicants, 67% accepted, 143 enrolled. In 2011, 143 master's awarded. *Degree requirements:* For master's, thesis optional. *Entrance requirements:* For master's, 3 letters of recommendation, professional resume. Additional exam requirements/recommendations for international students: Required—TOEFL (minimum score 550 paper-based; 213 computer-based; 80 iBT). *Application deadline:* For fall admission, 6/1 for international students; for spring admission, 10/1 for international students. Applications are processed on a rolling basis. Application fee: $70. Electronic applications accepted. *Expenses: Tuition:* Full-time $40,848; part-time $1276 per credit hour. *Required fees:* $572; $286 per semester. *Financial support:* In 2011–12, 9 research assistantships (averaging $5,000 per year) were awarded; career-related internships or fieldwork and unspecified assistantships also available. Support available to part-time students. Financial award applicants required to submit FAFSA. *Faculty research:* Medical informatics, Web technologies, telecom and networks, security and forensics, software engineering, programming languages, multimedia and AI, information systems and IT project management. *Unit head:* Dr. Lubomir Chitkushev, Chairman, 617-353-2566, Fax: 617-353-2367, E-mail: csinfo@bu.edu. *Application contact:* Kim Richards, Program Coordinator, 617-353-2566, Fax: 617-353-2367, E-mail: kimrich@bu.edu. Web site: http://www.bu.edu/csmet/.

Brandeis University, Rabb School of Continuing Studies, Division of Graduate Professional Studies, Program in Management of Projects and Programs, Waltham, MA 02454-9110. Offers MS. Part-time programs available. Postbaccalaureate distance learning degree programs offered (no on-campus study). *Faculty:* 2 full-time (both women), 34 part-time/adjunct (8 women). *Students:* 69 part-time (31 women); includes 14 minority (5 Black or African American, non-Hispanic/Latino; 1 American Indian or Alaska Native, non-Hispanic/Latino; 4 Asian, non-Hispanic/Latino; 3 Hispanic/Latino; 1 Native Hawaiian or other Pacific Islander, non-Hispanic/Latino). Average age 35. 29 applicants, 100% accepted, 24 enrolled. In 2011, 15 master's awarded. *Entrance requirements:* For master's, resume, official transcripts, recommendations, goal statements. Additional exam requirements/recommendations for international students: Recommended—TOEFL (minimum score 600 paper-based; 250 computer-based; 100 iBT). *Application deadline:* For fall admission, 6/15 priority date for domestic students; for winter admission, 10/15 priority date for domestic students; for spring admission, 2/15 priority date for domestic students. Applications are processed on a rolling basis. Application fee: $50. Electronic applications accepted. *Unit head:* Leanne Bateman, Program Chair, 781-736-8787, Fax: 781-736-3420, E-mail: lbateman@brandeis.edu. *Application contact:* Frances Stearns, Associate Director of Admissions and Student Services, 781-736-8785, Fax: 781-736-3420, E-mail: fstearns@brandeis.edu. Web site: http://www.brandeis.edu/gps.

Brandeis University, Rabb School of Continuing Studies, Division of Graduate Professional Studies, Virtual Team Management and Communication Program, Waltham, MA 02454-9110. Offers MS. Part-time programs available. Postbaccalaureate distance learning degree programs offered (no on-campus study). *Faculty:* 2 full-time (both women), 34 part-time/adjunct (8 women). *Students:* 6 part-time (2 women); includes 1 minority (Black or African American, non-Hispanic/Latino). Average age 35. In 2011, 1 degree awarded. *Entrance requirements:* For master's, resume, official transcripts, recommendations, goal statements. Additional exam requirements/recommendations for international students: Recommended—TOEFL (minimum score 600 paper-based; 250 computer-based; 100 iBT). *Application deadline:* For fall admission, 6/15 priority date for domestic students; for winter admission, 10/15 priority date for domestic students; for spring admission, 2/15 priority date for domestic students. Applications are processed on a rolling basis. Application fee: $50. Electronic applications accepted. *Unit head:* Dr. Aline Yurik, Program Chair, 781-736-8787, Fax: 781-736-3420, E-mail: ayurik@brandeis.edu. *Application contact:* Frances Stearns,

Associate Director of Admissions and Student Services, 781-736-8785, Fax: 781-736-3420, E-mail: fstearns@brandeis.edu. Web site: http://www.brandeis.edu/gps.

Brenau University, Sydney O. Smith Graduate School, School of Business and Mass Communication, Gainesville, GA 30501. Offers accounting (MBA); business administration (MBA); healthcare management (MBA); organizational leadership (MS); project management (MBA). Part-time and evening/weekend programs available. Postbaccalaureate distance learning degree programs offered (no on-campus study). *Degree requirements:* For master's, comprehensive exam (for some programs). *Entrance requirements:* For master's, resume, minimum undergraduate GPA of 2.5. Additional exam requirements/recommendations for international students: Required—TOEFL (minimum score 500 paper-based; 173 computer-based; 61 iBT); Recommended—IELTS (minimum score 5). Electronic applications accepted. *Expenses:* Contact institution.

California Intercontinental University, School of Information Technology, Diamond Bar, CA 91765. Offers information systems and enterprise resource management (DBA); information systems and knowledge management (MBA); project and quality management (MBA).

Capella University, School of Business and Technology, Minneapolis, MN 55402. Offers accounting (MBA), including system design and programming; business (Certificate), including human resource management (MS, PhD, Certificate), information technology management (MS, PhD, Certificate), leadership (MBA, MS, PhD, Certificate); finance (MBA); general business (MBA); health care management (MBA); information technology (MS, Certificate), including general information technology (MS), information security, network architecture and design (MS), professional projects management (Certificate), project management and leadership (MS), system design and development (MS),); information technology management (MBA); marketing (MBA); organization and management (MBA, MS, PhD), including general business (PhD), general organization and management (MBA, MS), human resource management (MS, PhD, Certificate), information technology management (MS, PhD, Certificate), leadership (MBA, MS, PhD, Certificate); project management (MBA). Part-time and evening/weekend programs available. Postbaccalaureate distance learning degree programs offered (minimal on-campus study). Terminal master's awarded for partial completion of doctoral program. *Degree requirements:* For master's, thesis optional, integrative project; for doctorate, comprehensive exam, thesis/dissertation. *Entrance requirements:* Additional exam requirements/recommendations for international students: Required—TOEFL (minimum score 550 paper-based; 213 computer-based), TWE (minimum score 4). Electronic applications accepted. *Faculty research:* Business policies: strategic, corporate, and financial management; interplay of technological, organizational and social change.

Christian Brothers University, School of Business, Memphis, TN 38104-5581. Offers business (MBA); financial planning (Certificate); project management (Certificate). Part-time and evening/weekend programs available. *Entrance requirements:* For master's, GMAT, GRE. Additional exam requirements/recommendations for international students: Required—TOEFL.

The Citadel, The Military College of South Carolina, Citadel Graduate College, Department of Civil Engineering, Charleston, SC 29409. Offers technical project management (MS). Part-time and evening/weekend programs available. *Faculty:* 2 full-time, 3 part-time/adjunct. *Students:* 4 full-time (1 woman), 30 part-time (9 women); includes 4 minority (3 Black or African American, non-Hispanic/Latino; 1 Hispanic/Latino). Average age 37. In 2011, 8 master's awarded. *Entrance requirements:* For master's, GRE or GMAT, evidence of a minimum of one year of professional experience, or permission from department head; two letters of reference; resume detailing previous work. Additional exam requirements/recommendations for international students: Required—TOEFL (minimum score 550 paper-based; 213 computer-based; 79 iBT). *Application deadline:* For fall admission, 8/1 priority date for domestic students. Applications are processed on a rolling basis. Application fee: $30. Electronic applications accepted. *Expenses: Tuition, area resident:* Part-time $501 per credit hour. Tuition, state resident: part-time $501 per credit hour. Tuition, nonresident: part-time $824 per credit hour. *Required fees:* $40 per term. One-time fee: $30. *Financial support:* Health care benefits available. Support available to part-time students. Financial award application deadline: 7/1; financial award applicants required to submit FAFSA. *Unit head:* Dr. Kenneth P. Brannan, Department Head, 843-953-5007, Fax: 843-953-6328, E-mail: ken.brannan@citadel.edu. *Application contact:* Maj. Keith Plemmons, Program Director, 843-953-7677, Fax: 843-953-6328, E-mail: keith.plemmons@citadel.edu. Web site: http://www.citadel.edu/pmgt/.

City University of Seattle, Graduate Division, School of Management, Bellevue, WA 98005. Offers accounting (Certificate); change leadership (MBA, Certificate); computer systems (MS); finance (Certificate); financial management (MBA); general management (MBA); general management-Europe (MBA); global marketing (MBA); human resources management (Certificate); individualized study (MBA); information security (MS); information systems (MBA); leadership (MA); marketing (MBA, Certificate); project management (MBA, MS, Certificate); sustainable business (Certificate); technology management (MBA, Certificate). Part-time and evening/weekend programs available. Postbaccalaureate distance learning degree programs offered (no on-campus study). *Faculty:* 6 full-time (2 women), 95 part-time/adjunct (33 women). *Students:* 397 full-time (193 women), 283 part-time (137 women); includes 127 minority (67 Black or African American, non-Hispanic/Latino; 5 American Indian or Alaska Native, non-Hispanic/Latino; 33 Asian, non-Hispanic/Latino; 15 Hispanic/Latino; 1 Native Hawaiian or other Pacific Islander, non-Hispanic/Latino; 6 Two or more races, non-Hispanic/Latino), 117 international. Average age 36. 151 applicants, 100% accepted, 151 enrolled. In 2011, 369 master's, 32 other advanced degrees awarded. *Degree requirements:* For master's, comprehensive exam (for some programs), thesis (for some programs). *Entrance requirements:* Additional exam requirements/recommendations for international students: Required—TOEFL (minimum score 567 paper-based; 227 computer-based; 87 iBT); Recommended—IELTS. *Application deadline:* For fall admission, 9/1 for international students; for winter admission, 12/1 for international students; for spring admission, 3/1 for international students. Applications are processed on a rolling basis. Application fee: $50. Electronic applications accepted. *Financial support:* Federal Work-Study and scholarships/grants available. Support available to part-time students. Financial award applicants required to submit FAFSA. *Unit head:* Dr. Kurt Kirstein, Dean, 425-637-1010 Ext. 5456, Fax: 425-709-5363, E-mail: kdkirstein@cityu.edu. *Application contact:* Alysa Borelli, Director, Recruiting, 888-422-4898, Fax: 425-709-5363, E-mail: info@cityu.edu. Web site: http://www.cityu.edu/programs/som/index.aspx.

Colorado Christian University, Program in Business Administration, Lakewood, CO 80226. Offers corporate training (MBA); information security (MA); leadership (MBA); project management (MBA). Part-time and evening/weekend programs available. Postbaccalaureate distance learning degree programs offered (minimal on-campus study). *Degree requirements:* For master's, thesis optional. *Entrance requirements:* For master's, GMAT, 2 letters of recommendation, resume. Additional exam requirements/recommendations for international students: Required—TOEFL. Electronic applications accepted. *Expenses:* Contact institution.

Colorado Technical University Colorado Springs, Graduate Studies, Program in Management, Colorado Springs, CO 80907-3896. Offers accounting (MBA, MSA); business administration (MBA); finance (MBA); human resources management (MBA); logistics/supply chain management (MBA); management (DM); marketing (MBA); mediation and dispute resolution (MBA); operations management (MBA); project management (MBA); technology management (MBA). Part-time and evening/weekend programs available. Postbaccalaureate distance learning degree programs offered. *Degree requirements:* For master's, thesis or alternative; for doctorate, thesis/dissertation. *Entrance requirements:* For doctorate, minimum graduate GPA of 3.0, 5 years of related work experience. *Faculty research:* Sexual harassment, performance evaluation, critical thinking.

Colorado Technical University Denver South, Programs in Business Administration and Management, Aurora, CO 80014. Offers accounting (MBA); business administration (MBA); business administration and management (EMBA); finance (MBA); human resource management (MBA); marketing (MBA); mediation and dispute resolution (MBA); operations management (MBA); project management (MBA); technology management (MBA). Part-time and evening/weekend programs available. *Degree requirements:* For master's, thesis or alternative. *Entrance requirements:* For master's, minimum undergraduate GPA of 3.0, resume.

Colorado Technical University Sioux Falls, Programs in Business Administration and Management, Sioux Falls, SD 57108. Offers business administration (MBA); business management (MSM); health science management (MSM); human resources management (MSM); information technology (MSM); organizational leadership (MSM); project management (MBA); technology management (MBA). Evening/weekend programs available. *Degree requirements:* For master's, thesis optional. *Entrance requirements:* For master's, minimum 2 years work experience, resume.

Dallas Baptist University, College of Business, Business Administration Program, Dallas, TX 75211-9299. Offers accounting (MBA); business communication (MBA); conflict resolution management (MBA); entrepreneurship (MBA); finance (MBA); health care management (MBA); international business (MBA); leading the non-profit organization (MBA); management (MBA); management information systems (MBA); marketing (MBA); project management (MBA); technology and engineering management (MBA). *Accreditation:* ACBSP. Part-time and evening/weekend programs available. *Entrance requirements:* For master's, GMAT, minimum GPA of 3.0. Additional exam requirements/recommendations for international students: Required—TOEFL, IELTS. *Application deadline:* Applications are processed on a rolling basis. Application fee: $25. Electronic applications accepted. *Expenses: Tuition:* Full-time $12,060; part-time $670 per credit hour. *Required fees:* $100; $50 per semester. *Financial support:* Federal Work-Study, institutionally sponsored loans, scholarships/grants, and tuition waivers (full and partial) available. Support available to part-time students. Financial award applicants required to submit FAFSA. *Faculty research:* Sports management, services marketing, retailing, strategic management, financial planning/investments. *Unit head:* Dr. Sandra S. Reid, Director, 214-333-5280, Fax: 214-333-5293, E-mail: graduate@dbu.edu. *Application contact:* Kit P. Montgomery, Director of Graduate Programs, 214-333-5242, Fax: 214-333-5579, E-mail: graduate@dbu.edu. Web site: http://www3.dbu.edu/graduate/mba.asp.

DeSales University, Graduate Division, MBA Program, Center Valley, PA 18034-9568. Offers accounting (MBA); computer information systems (MBA); finance (MBA); health care systems management (MBA); human resources management (MBA); management (MBA); marketing (MBA); project management (MBA); self-design (MBA). *Accreditation:* ACBSP. Part-time programs available. Postbaccalaureate distance learning degree programs offered (no on-campus study). *Entrance requirements:* For master's, GMAT, minimum GPA of 3.0, 2 years of work experience. Additional exam requirements/recommendations for international students: Required—TOEFL. *Application deadline:* Applications are processed on a rolling basis. Electronic applications accepted. Tuition and fees vary according to degree level. *Faculty research:* Quality improvement, executive development, productivity, cross-cultural managerial differences, leadership. *Unit head:* Dr. David Gilfoil, Director, 610-282-1100 Ext. 1828, Fax: 610-282-2869, E-mail: david.gilfoil@desales.edu. *Application contact:* Caryn Stopper, Director of Graduate Admissions, 610-282-1100 Ext. 1768, Fax: 610-282-0525, E-mail: caryn.stopper@desales.edu.

DeVry University, Keller Graduate School of Management, Downers Grove, IL 60515. Offers accounting and financial management (MAFM); business administration (MBA); human resources management (MHRM); information systems management (MISM); network and communications management (MNCM); project management (MPM); public administration (MPA).

Dowling College, School of Business, Oakdale, NY 11769-1999. Offers aviation management (MBA, Certificate); banking and finance (MBA, Certificate); corporate finance (MBA); financial planning (Certificate); health care management (MBA, Certificate); human resource management (Certificate); information systems management (MBA); management and leadership (MBA); marketing (Certificate); project management (Certificate); public management (MBA, Certificate); sport, event and entertainment management (Certificate); JD/MBA. Part-time and evening/weekend programs available. Postbaccalaureate distance learning degree programs offered (minimal on-campus study). *Faculty:* 10 full-time (4 women), 54 part-time/adjunct (6 women). *Students:* 237 full-time (99 women), 403 part-time (199 women); includes 186 minority (95 Black or African American, non-Hispanic/Latino; 62 Asian, non-Hispanic/Latino; 28 Hispanic/Latino; 1 Native Hawaiian or other Pacific Islander, non-Hispanic/Latino), 1 international. Average age 35. 345 applicants, 83% accepted, 193 enrolled. In 2011, 350 master's, 7 other advanced degrees awarded. *Degree requirements:* For master's, comprehensive exam, thesis optional. *Entrance requirements:* For master's, minimum GPA of 2.8, 2 letters of recommendation, courses or seminar in accounting and finance, resume. Additional exam requirements/recommendations for international students: Required—TOEFL (minimum score 550 paper-based). *Application deadline:* For fall admission, 9/1 priority date for domestic students; for winter admission, 1/1 priority date for domestic students; for spring admission, 2/1 priority date for domestic students. Applications are processed on a rolling basis. Application fee: $50. Electronic applications accepted. *Expenses: Tuition:* Full-time $19,162; part-time $933 per credit. *Required fees:* $1330; $700 per year. Tuition and fees vary according to course load. *Financial support:* Career-related internships or fieldwork and Federal Work-Study available. Support available to part-time students. Financial award application deadline: 6/30; financial award applicants required to submit FAFSA. *Faculty research:* International finance, computer applications, labor relations, executive development. *Unit head:* Antonia Loschiavo, Assistant Dean, 631-244-3266, Fax: 631-244-1018, E-mail: loschiat@dowling.edu. *Application contact:* Ronnie S. Macdonald, Assistant Vice President for Enrollment Services/Dean of Admissions, 631-244-3357, Fax: 631-244-1059, E-mail: macdonar@dowling.edu.

Drexel University, Goodwin College of Professional Studies, School of Technology and Professional Studies, Philadelphia, PA 19104-2875. Offers construction management (MS); engineering technology (MS); food science (MS); hospitality management (MS); professional studies: creativity studies (MS); professional studies: e-learning leadership (MS); professional studies: homeland security management (MS); project management

(MS); property management (MS); sport management (MS). Postbaccalaureate distance learning degree programs offered.

Ellis University, MBA Program, Chicago, IL 60606-7204. Offers e-commerce (MBA); finance (MBA); general business (MBA); global management (MBA); health care administration (MBA); leadership (MBA); management of information systems (MBA); marketing (MBA); professional accounting (MBA); project management (MBA); public accounting (MBA); risk management (MBA).

Embry-Riddle Aeronautical University–Worldwide, Worldwide Headquarters - Graduate Degrees and Programs, Program in Project Management, Daytona Beach, FL 32114-3900. Offers MSPM, Graduate Certificate, MSPM/MBAA. Part-time and evening/weekend programs available. Postbaccalaureate distance learning degree programs offered. *Faculty:* 4 full-time (1 woman), 50 part-time/adjunct (15 women). *Students:* 192 full-time (43 women), 110 part-time (27 women); includes 63 minority (30 Black or African American, non-Hispanic/Latino; 1 American Indian or Alaska Native, non-Hispanic/Latino; 8 Asian, non-Hispanic/Latino; 21 Hispanic/Latino; 3 Two or more races, non-Hispanic/Latino). Average age 35. 118 applicants, 77% accepted, 69 enrolled. In 2011, 51 master's awarded. *Degree requirements:* For master's, thesis (for some programs). *Application deadline:* Applications are processed on a rolling basis. Application fee: $50. Electronic applications accepted. *Expenses: Tuition:* Part-time $395 per credit hour. Tuition and fees vary according to degree level and program. *Financial support:* In 2011–12, 74 students received support. *Unit head:* Dr. Kees Rietsema, Chair, 602-904-1285, E-mail: rietsd37@erau.edu. *Application contact:* Linda Dammer, Director of Admissions, 386-226-6396 Ext. 1, Fax: 386-226-6984, E-mail: worldwide@erau.edu.

Ferris State University, College of Business, Big Rapids, MI 49307. Offers business intelligence (MBA); design and innovation management (MBA); incident response (MBA); information security and intelligence (MS, MSISM), including business intelligence (MS), incident response (MSISM), project management (MSISM); management tools and concepts (MBA); project management (MBA). *Accreditation:* ACBSP. Part-time and evening/weekend programs available. Postbaccalaureate distance learning degree programs offered (minimal on-campus study). *Faculty:* 9 full-time (3 women), 2 part-time/adjunct (both women). *Students:* 22 full-time (7 women), 98 part-time (50 women); includes 14 minority (3 Black or African American, non-Hispanic/Latino; 4 American Indian or Alaska Native, non-Hispanic/Latino; 2 Asian, non-Hispanic/Latino; 2 Hispanic/Latino; 3 Two or more races, non-Hispanic/Latino), 3 international. Average age 34. 58 applicants, 79% accepted, 10 enrolled. In 2011, 56 master's awarded. *Degree requirements:* For master's, comprehensive exam, thesis (for MSISM). *Entrance requirements:* For master's, GRE or GMAT (waived if GPA is 3.5 or better), minimum GPA of 3.0 in junior/senior level classes, 2.75 overall; writing sample; 3 letters of reference; resume. Additional exam requirements/recommendations for international students: Required—TOEFL (minimum score 500 paper-based; 173 computer-based; 67 iBT). *Application deadline:* For fall admission, 7/1 priority date for domestic students, 6/15 for international students; for winter admission, 11/1 priority date for domestic students, 10/15 for international students; for spring admission, 3/1 priority date for domestic students, 2/15 for international students. Applications are processed on a rolling basis. Application fee: $30. Electronic applications accepted. Application fee is waived when completed online. *Financial support:* Career-related internships or fieldwork, Federal Work-Study, scholarships/grants, and unspecified assistantships available. Support available to part-time students. Financial award application deadline: 3/15; financial award applicants required to submit FAFSA. *Faculty research:* Quality improvement, client/server end-user computing, information management and policy, security, digital forensics. *Unit head:* Dr. David Steenstra, Department Chair, 231-591-2168, Fax: 231-591-3548, E-mail: yosts@ferris.edu. *Application contact:* Shannon Yost, Department Secretary, 231-591-2168, Fax: 231-591-3548, E-mail: yosts@ferris.edu. Web site: http://cbgp.ferris.edu/.

Florida Institute of Technology, Graduate Programs, Extended Studies Division, Melbourne, FL 32901-6975. Offers acquisition and contract management (MS); aerospace engineering (MS); business administration (MBA); computer information systems (MS); computer science (MS); electrical engineering (MS); engineering management (MS); human resources management (MS); logistics management (MS), including humanitarian and disaster relief logistics; management (MS), including acquisition and contract management, e-business, human resources management, information systems, logistics management, management, transportation management; material acquisition management (MS); mechanical engineering (MS); operations research (MS); project management (MS), including information systems, operations research; public administration (MPA); quality management (MS); software engineering (MS); space systems (MS); space systems management (MS); supply chain management (MS); systems management (MS), including information systems, operations research. Part-time and evening/weekend programs available. Postbaccalaureate distance learning degree programs offered (no on-campus study). *Faculty:* 9 full-time (2 women), 105 part-time/adjunct (24 women). *Students:* 113 full-time (52 women), 1,150 part-time (484 women); includes 496 minority (332 Black or African American, non-Hispanic/Latino; 11 American Indian or Alaska Native, non-Hispanic/Latino; 42 Asian, non-Hispanic/Latino; 71 Hispanic/Latino; 2 Native Hawaiian or other Pacific Islander, non-Hispanic/Latino; 38 Two or more races, non-Hispanic/Latino), 11 international. Average age 35. 568 applicants, 56% accepted, 296 enrolled. In 2011, 471 master's awarded. *Degree requirements:* For master's, comprehensive exam (for some programs), capstone course. *Entrance requirements:* For master's, GMAT or resume showing 8 years of supervised experience, minimum GPA of 3.0, 2 letters of recommendation, resume. Additional exam requirements/recommendations for international students: Required—TOEFL (minimum score 550 paper-based; 213 computer-based; 79 iBT). *Application deadline:* For fall admission, 4/1 for international students; for spring admission, 9/30 for international students. Applications are processed on a rolling basis. Application fee: $0. Electronic applications accepted. *Expenses:* Contact institution. *Financial support:* Application deadline: 3/1; applicants required to submit FAFSA. *Unit head:* Dr. Theodore R. Richardson, III, Senior Associate Dean, 321-674-8123, Fax: 321-674-7597, E-mail: trichardson@fit.edu. *Application contact:* Carolyn Farrior, Director of Graduate Admissions, Online Learning and Off-Campus Programs, 321-674-7118, Fax: 321-674-8216, E-mail: cfarrior@fit.edu. Web site: http://es.fit.edu.

Florida Institute of Technology, Graduate Programs, Nathan M. Bisk College of Business, Online Programs, Melbourne, FL 32901-6975. Offers accounting (MBA); accounting and finance (MBA); business administration (MBA); finance (MBA); healthcare management (MBA); information technology (MS); information technology cybersecurity (MS); information technology management (MBA); international business (MBA); Internet marketing (MBA); management (MBA); marketing (MBA); project management (MBA). Part-time and evening/weekend programs available. Postbaccalaureate distance learning degree programs offered (no on-campus study). *Faculty:* 47 part-time/adjunct (15 women). *Students:* 8 full-time (4 women), 1,122 part-time (547 women); includes 418 minority (271 Black or African American, non-Hispanic/Latino; 5 American Indian or Alaska Native, non-Hispanic/Latino; 55 Asian, non-Hispanic/Latino; 81 Hispanic/Latino; 6 Native Hawaiian or other Pacific Islander, non-Hispanic/Latino), 23 international. Average age 36. In 2011, 329 master's awarded. *Entrance requirements:* For master's, GMAT or resume showing 8 years of supervised experience, 2 letters of recommendation, resume, competency in math past college algebra. Additional exam requirements/recommendations for international students: Required—TOEFL (minimum score 550 paper-based; 213 computer-based; 79 iBT). *Application deadline:* For fall admission, 4/1 for international students; for spring admission, 9/30 for international students. Applications are processed on a rolling basis. Electronic applications accepted. *Expenses:* Contact institution. *Financial support:* Available to part-time students. Application deadline: 3/1; applicants required to submit FAFSA. *Unit head:* Dr. Mary S. Bonhomme, Dean, Florida Tech Online/Associate Provost for Online Learning, 321-674-8202, Fax: 321-674-8216, E-mail: bonhomme@fit.edu. *Application contact:* Carolyn Farrior, Director of Graduate Admissions, Online Learning and Off-Campus Programs, 321-674-7118, Fax: 321-674-8216, E-mail: cfarrior@fit.edu. Web site: http://online.fit.edu.

George Mason University, College of Visual and Performing Arts, Program in Arts Management, Fairfax, VA 22030. Offers arts management (MA); entrepreneurship (Certificate); fund-raising and development in the arts (Certificate); marketing and public relations in the arts (Certificate); programming and project management (Certificate). *Accreditation:* NASAD. *Faculty:* 2 full-time (both women), 8 part-time/adjunct (3 women). *Students:* 48 full-time (40 women), 37 part-time (34 women); includes 17 minority (6 Black or African American, non-Hispanic/Latino; 4 Asian, non-Hispanic/Latino; 3 Hispanic/Latino; 4 Two or more races, non-Hispanic/Latino), 9 international. Average age 29. 105 applicants, 54% accepted, 22 enrolled. In 2011, 44 master's, 21 other advanced degrees awarded. *Degree requirements:* For master's, internship. *Entrance requirements:* For master's and Certificate, GRE (recommended), undergraduate degree with minimum GPA of 3.0, official transcripts, 2 letters of recommendation, statement of purpose, resume. Additional exam requirements/recommendations for international students: Required—TOEFL (minimum score 570 paper-based; 230 computer-based; 88 iBT), IELTS, Pearson Test of English. *Application deadline:* For fall admission, 3/1 for domestic students, 2/15 for international students; for spring admission, 10/15 for domestic students, 9/15 for international students. Application fee: $65 ($80 for international students). Electronic applications accepted. *Expenses:* Tuition, state resident: full-time $8750; part-time $364.58 per credit. Tuition, nonresident: full-time $24,092; part-time $1003.83 per credit. *Required fees:* $2514; $104.75 per credit. *Financial support:* In 2011–12, 2 students received support, including 2 teaching assistantships with full and partial tuition reimbursements available (averaging $8,649 per year); career-related internships or fieldwork, Federal Work-Study, scholarships/grants, unspecified assistantships, and health care benefits (full-time research and teaching assistantship recipient) also available. Financial award application deadline: 3/1; financial award applicants required to submit FAFSA. *Faculty research:* Information technology for arts managers, special topics in arts management, directions in gallery management, arts in society, public relations/marketing strategies for art organizations. *Unit head:* Richard Kamenitzer, Director, 703-993-9194, Fax: 703-993-9829, E-mail: rkamenit@gmu.edu. *Application contact:* Mathilde Speier, Information Contact, 703-993-8926, Fax: 703-993-9829, E-mail: mspeier@gmu.edu. Web site: http://artsmanagement.gmu.edu/arts-management-ma/.

The George Washington University, School of Business, Department of Decision Sciences, Washington, DC 20052. Offers project management (MS). *Faculty:* 16 full-time (1 woman), 1 part-time/adjunct (0 women). *Students:* 16 full-time (5 women), 205 part-time (84 women); includes 63 minority (30 Black or African American, non-Hispanic/Latino; 1 American Indian or Alaska Native, non-Hispanic/Latino; 12 Asian, non-Hispanic/Latino; 20 Hispanic/Latino), 19 international. Average age 39. 101 applicants, 89% accepted. In 2011, 69 master's awarded. Application fee: $75. *Financial support:* Tuition waivers available. *Unit head:* Srinivas Prasad, Chair, 202-994-2078, Fax: 202-994-6382, E-mail: prasad@gwu.edu. *Application contact:* Kristin Williams, Assistant Vice President for Graduate and Special Enrollment Management, 202-994-0467, Fax: 202-994-0371, E-mail: ksw@gwu.edu. Web site: http://business.gwu.edu/decisionsciences/.

The George Washington University, School of Business, Department of Information Systems and Technology Management, Washington, DC 20052. Offers information and decision systems (PhD); information systems (MSIST); information systems development (MSIST); information systems management (MBA); information systems project management (MSIST); management information systems (MSIST); management of science, technology, and innovation (MBA, PhD). Programs also offered in Ashburn and Arlington, VA. Part-time and evening/weekend programs available. *Faculty:* 12 full-time (4 women), 5 part-time/adjunct (2 women). *Students:* 111 full-time (37 women), 144 part-time (47 women); includes 87 minority (36 Black or African American, non-Hispanic/Latino; 1 American Indian or Alaska Native, non-Hispanic/Latino; 30 Asian, non-Hispanic/Latino; 19 Hispanic/Latino; 1 Two or more races, non-Hispanic/Latino), 45 international. Average age 33. 231 applicants, 72% accepted, 93 enrolled. In 2011, 86 master's, 3 doctorates awarded. *Entrance requirements:* For master's, GMAT. Additional exam requirements/recommendations for international students: Required—TOEFL. *Application deadline:* For fall admission, 4/1 priority date for domestic students; for spring admission, 10/1 for domestic students. Applications are processed on a rolling basis. Application fee: $75. *Financial support:* In 2011–12, 35 students received support. Fellowships, teaching assistantships, career-related internships or fieldwork, Federal Work-Study, institutionally sponsored loans, and tuition waivers available. Financial award application deadline: 4/1. *Faculty research:* Expert systems, decision support systems. *Unit head:* Richard G. Donnelly, Chair, 202-994-4364, E-mail: rgd@gwu.edu. *Application contact:* Kristin Williams, Assistant Vice President for Graduate and Special Enrollment Management, 202-994-0467, Fax: 202-994-0371, E-mail: ksw@gwu.edu.

Granite State College, Program in Project Management, Concord, NH 03301. Offers MS. *Degree requirements:* For master's, capstone.

Grantham University, Mark Skousen School of Business, Kansas City, MO 64153. Offers business administration (MBA); business intelligence (MS); information management (MBA); information management technology (MS); information technology (MS); performance improvement (MS); project management (MBA, MSIM). Part-time and evening/weekend programs available. Postbaccalaureate distance learning degree programs offered (no on-campus study). *Degree requirements:* For master's, capstone project. *Entrance requirements:* For master's, bachelor's degree from accredited degree-granting institution. Additional exam requirements/recommendations for international students: Required—TOEFL (minimum score 500 paper-based; 213 computer-based; 61 iBT). Electronic applications accepted.

Harrisburg University of Science and Technology, Program in Project Management, Harrisburg, PA 17101. Offers construction services (MS); governmental services (MS); information technology (MS). Part-time and evening/weekend programs available. *Entrance requirements:* For master's, BS, BBA. Additional exam requirements/recommendations for international students: Required—TOEFL (minimum score 520 paper-based; 200 computer-based; 80 iBT). Electronic applications accepted.

Herzing University Online, Program in Business Administration, Milwaukee, WI 53203. Offers accounting (MBA); business administration (MBA); business management (MBA); healthcare management (MBA); human resources (MBA); marketing (MBA);

project management (MBA); technology management (MBA). Postbaccalaureate distance learning degree programs offered (no on-campus study).

Jones International University, School of Business, Centennial, CO 80112. Offers accounting (MBA); business communication (MABC); entrepreneurship (MABC, MBA); finance (MBA); global enterprise management (MBA); health care management (MBA); information security management (MBA); information technology management (MBA); leadership and influence (MABC); leading the customer-driven organization (MABC); negotiation and conflict management (MBA); project management (MABC, MBA). Program only offered online. Part-time and evening/weekend programs available. Postbaccalaureate distance learning degree programs offered (no on-campus study). *Degree requirements:* For master's, capstone project. *Entrance requirements:* For master's, minimum cumulative GPA of 2.5. Additional exam requirements/recommendations for international students: Recommended—TOEFL (minimum score 550 paper-based; 213 computer-based). Electronic applications accepted.

Kaplan University, Davenport Campus, School of Business, Davenport, IA 52807-2095. Offers business administration (MBA); change leadership (MS); entrepreneurship (MBA); finance (MBA); health care management (MBA, MS); human resource (MBA); international business (MBA); management (MS); marketing (MBA); project management (MBA, MS); supply chain management and logistics (MBA, MS). Part-time and evening/weekend programs available. Postbaccalaureate distance learning degree programs offered (no on-campus study). *Entrance requirements:* Additional exam requirements/recommendations for international students: Required—TOEFL (minimum score 550 paper-based; 218 computer-based; 80 iBT). Electronic applications accepted.

Lakeland College, Graduate Studies Division, Program in Business Administration, Sheboygan, WI 53082-0359. Offers accounting (MBA); finance (MBA); healthcare management (MBA); project management (MBA). *Entrance requirements:* For master's, GMAT. *Expenses:* Contact institution.

Lasell College, Graduate and Professional Studies in Management, Newton, MA 02466-2709. Offers elder care administration (MSM, Graduate Certificate); elder care marketing (MSM, Graduate Certificate); fundraising management (MSM, Graduate Certificate); human resource management (Graduate Certificate); human resources management (MSM); integrated marketing communication (Graduate Certificate); management (MSM, Graduate Certificate); marketing (MSM, Graduate Certificate); non-profit management (MSM, Graduate Certificate); project management (MSM, Graduate Certificate); public relations (Graduate Certificate). Part-time and evening/weekend programs available. Postbaccalaureate distance learning degree programs offered (no on-campus study). *Faculty:* 9 full-time (7 women), 20 part-time/adjunct (13 women). *Students:* 23 full-time (16 women), 92 part-time (65 women); includes 74 minority (8 Black or African American, non-Hispanic/Latino; 4 American Indian or Alaska Native, non-Hispanic/Latino; 53 Asian, non-Hispanic/Latino; 9 Hispanic/Latino), 14 international. Average age 30. 78 applicants, 67% accepted, 31 enrolled. In 2011, 49 master's, 7 other advanced degrees awarded. *Entrance requirements:* For master's and Graduate Certificate, bachelor's degree from an accredited institution. Additional exam requirements/recommendations for international students: Required—TOEFL (minimum score 550 paper-based; 213 computer-based; 79 iBT). *Application deadline:* For fall admission, 8/31 priority date for domestic students, 6/30 for international students; for spring admission, 12/31 priority date for domestic students, 10/31 for international students. Applications are processed on a rolling basis. Electronic applications accepted. *Expenses: Tuition:* Part-time $575 per credit. *Required fees:* $70 per semester. *Financial support:* Available to part-time students. Application deadline: 8/31; applicants required to submit FAFSA. *Unit head:* Dr. Joan Dolamore, Dean of Graduate and Professional Studies, 617-243-2485, Fax: 617-243-2450, E-mail: gradinfo@lasell.edu. *Application contact:* Adrienne Franciosi, Director of Graduate Admission, 617-243-2214, Fax: 617-243-2450, E-mail: gradinfo@lasell.edu. Web site: http://www.lasell.edu/Academics/Graduate-and-Professional-Studies/MS-in-Management.html.

Lawrence Technological University, College of Management, Southfield, MI 48075-1058. Offers business administration (MBA, DBA); business administration international (MBA); global leadership and management (MS); global operations and project management (MS); information systems (MS); information technology (DM); operations management (MS). *Accreditation:* ACBSP. Part-time and evening/weekend programs available. *Faculty:* 12 full-time (6 women), 39 part-time/adjunct (11 women). *Students:* 10 full-time (4 women), 518 part-time (228 women); includes 183 minority (123 Black or African American, non-Hispanic/Latino; 2 American Indian or Alaska Native, non-Hispanic/Latino; 44 Asian, non-Hispanic/Latino; 11 Hispanic/Latino; 3 Two or more races, non-Hispanic/Latino), 50 international. Average age 36. 420 applicants, 45% accepted, 97 enrolled. In 2011, 177 master's, 14 doctorates awarded. *Degree requirements:* For master's, thesis (for some programs). *Entrance requirements:* For master's, GMAT. Additional exam requirements/recommendations for international students: Required—TOEFL (minimum score 550 paper-based; 213 computer-based; 79 iBT). *Application deadline:* For fall admission, 7/27 priority date for domestic students, 5/23 for international students; for spring admission, 11/15 priority date for domestic students, 11/15 for international students. Applications are processed on a rolling basis. Application fee: $50. Electronic applications accepted. *Financial support:* In 2011–12, 122 students received support. Federal Work-Study and institutionally sponsored loans available. Support available to part-time students. Financial award application deadline: 4/1; financial award applicants required to submit FAFSA. *Unit head:* Dr. Alan McCord, Interim Dean, 248-204-3050, E-mail: mgtdean@ltu.edu. *Application contact:* Jane Rohrback, Director of Admissions, 248-204-3160, Fax: 248-204-2228, E-mail: admissions@ltu.edu. Web site: http://www.ltu.edu/management/index.asp.

Lehigh University, College of Business and Economics, Bethlehem, PA 18015. Offers accounting (MS), including accounting and information analysis; business administration (MBA); economics (MS, PhD); entrepreneurship (Certificate); finance (MS), including analytical finance; project management (Certificate); supply chain management (Certificate); MBA/E; MBA/M Ed. *Accreditation:* AACSB. Part-time and evening/weekend programs available. Postbaccalaureate distance learning degree programs offered (minimal on-campus study). *Faculty:* 40 full-time (10 women), 13 part-time/adjunct (0 women). *Students:* 159 full-time (85 women), 242 part-time (85 women); includes 40 minority (5 Black or African American, non-Hispanic/Latino; 27 Asian, non-Hispanic/Latino; 7 Hispanic/Latino; 1 Native Hawaiian or other Pacific Islander, non-Hispanic/Latino), 139 international. Average age 29. 890 applicants, 40% accepted, 89 enrolled. In 2011, 166 master's, 2 doctorates awarded. Terminal master's awarded for partial completion of doctoral program. *Degree requirements:* For master's, thesis optional; for doctorate, comprehensive exam, thesis/dissertation, proposal defense. *Entrance requirements:* For master's, GMAT, GRE General Test; for doctorate, GMAT or GRE General Test. Additional exam requirements/recommendations for international students: Required—TOEFL (minimum score 600 paper-based; 250 computer-based; 94 iBT). *Application deadline:* For fall admission, 7/15 for domestic students, 5/1 for international students; for spring admission, 12/1 for domestic and international students. Applications are processed on a rolling basis. Application fee: $100. Electronic applications accepted. *Expenses:* Contact institution. *Financial support:* In 2011–12, 93 students received support, including 2 fellowships with full tuition reimbursements available (averaging $16,000 per year), 39 research assistantships with full and partial tuition reimbursements available (averaging $2,269 per year), 17 teaching assistantships with full tuition reimbursements available (averaging $13,840 per year); career-related internships or fieldwork, scholarships/grants, health care benefits, tuition waivers (full and partial), and unspecified assistantships also available. Support available to part-time students. Financial award application deadline: 1/15. *Faculty research:* Public finance, energy, investments, activity-based costing, management information systems. *Unit head:* Paul R. Brown, Dean, 610-758-6725, Fax: 610-758-4499, E-mail: prb207@lehigh.edu. *Application contact:* Corinn McBride, Director of Recruitment and Admissions, 610-758-3418, Fax: 610-758-5283, E-mail: com207@lehigh.edu. Web site: http://www.lehigh.edu/business.

Lewis University, College of Business, Graduate School of Management, Program in Business Administration, Romeoville, IL 60446. Offers accounting (MBA); custom elective option (MBA); e-business (MBA); finance (MBA); healthcare management (MBA); human resources management (MBA); information security (MBA); international business (MBA); management information systems (MBA); marketing (MBA); project management (MBA); technology and operations management (MBA). Part-time and evening/weekend programs available. *Students:* 112 full-time (60 women), 232 part-time (118 women); includes 104 minority (62 Black or African American, non-Hispanic/Latino; 1 American Indian or Alaska Native, non-Hispanic/Latino; 7 Asian, non-Hispanic/Latino; 33 Hispanic/Latino; 1 Native Hawaiian or other Pacific Islander, non-Hispanic/Latino), 9 international. Average age 28. In 2011, 99 master's awarded. *Entrance requirements:* For master's, interview, bachelor's degree, resume, 2 recommendations. Additional exam requirements/recommendations for international students: Required—TOEFL (minimum score 550 paper-based; 213 computer-based). *Application deadline:* For fall admission, 8/15 priority date for domestic students, 5/1 for international students; for spring admission, 11/15 for international students. Applications are processed on a rolling basis. Application fee: $40. Electronic applications accepted. *Financial support:* Career-related internships or fieldwork, Federal Work-Study, scholarships/grants, and unspecified assistantships available. Financial award application deadline: 5/1; financial award applicants required to submit FAFSA. *Unit head:* Dr. Maureen Culleeney, Academic Program Director, 815-838-0500 Ext. 5631, E-mail: culleema@lewisu.edu. *Application contact:* Michele Ryan, Director of Admission, 815-838-0500 Ext. 5384, E-mail: gsm@lewisu.edu.

Lewis University, College of Business, Graduate School of Management, Program in Project Management, Romeoville, IL 60446. Offers MS. Part-time and evening/weekend programs available. *Students:* 1 (woman) full-time, 6 part-time (1 woman); includes 2 minority (both Black or African American, non-Hispanic/Latino). Average age 36. In 2011, 5 master's awarded. *Entrance requirements:* For master's, bachelor's degree, interview, resume, statement of purpose, 2 letters of recommendation, minimum GPA of 2.75. Additional exam requirements/recommendations for international students: Required—TOEFL (minimum score 550 paper-based; 213 computer-based). *Application deadline:* For fall admission, 5/1 for international students; for spring admission, 11/15 for international students. Applications are processed on a rolling basis. Application fee: $40. Electronic applications accepted. *Financial support:* Federal Work-Study and unspecified assistantships available. Support available to part-time students. Financial award application deadline: 5/1; financial award applicants required to submit FAFSA. *Unit head:* Rev. Dr. Kevin Spiess, Academic Program Director, 815-838-0500 Ext. 5399, E-mail: spiesske@lewisu.edu. *Application contact:* Michele Ryan, Director of Admission, 815-838-0500 Ext. 5384, E-mail: gsm@lewisu.edu.

Marlboro College, Graduate School, Program in Information Technologies, Marlboro, VT 05344. Offers information technologies (MS); open source Web development (Certificate); project management (Certificate). Part-time and evening/weekend programs available. Postbaccalaureate distance learning degree programs offered (minimal on-campus study). *Degree requirements:* For master's, 30 credits including capstone project. *Entrance requirements:* For master's, letter of intent, 2 letters of recommendation, transcripts. Electronic applications accepted.

Marymount University, School of Business Administration, Program in Information Technology, Arlington, VA 22207-4299. Offers computer security and information assurance (Certificate); health care informatics (Certificate); information technology (MS, Certificate); information technology project management: technology leadership (Certificate). Part-time and evening/weekend programs available. *Faculty:* 6 full-time (2 women), 9 part-time/adjunct (0 women). *Students:* 37 full-time (14 women), 32 part-time (13 women); includes 19 minority (9 Black or African American, non-Hispanic/Latino; 6 Asian, non-Hispanic/Latino; 3 Hispanic/Latino; 1 Two or more races, non-Hispanic/Latino), 30 international. Average age 30. 47 applicants, 98% accepted, 36 enrolled. In 2011, 28 master's, 10 other advanced degrees awarded. *Degree requirements:* For master's, thesis or alternative. *Entrance requirements:* For master's, GMAT or GRE General Test, interview, resume, bachelor's degree in computer-related field or degree in another subject with a post-baccalaureate certificate in a computer-related field; for Certificate, resume. Additional exam requirements/recommendations for international students: Required—TOEFL (minimum score 600 paper-based; 250 computer-based; 96 iBT), IELTS (minimum score 6.5). *Application deadline:* For fall admission, 7/1 priority date for domestic students, 7/1 for international students; for spring admission, 11/15 for domestic students, 11/16 for international students. Applications are processed on a rolling basis. Application fee: $40. Electronic applications accepted. *Expenses: Tuition:* Part-time $770 per credit hour. *Required fees:* $8 per credit hour. One-time fee: $180 full-time. *Financial support:* In 2011–12, 7 students received support. Research assistantships with full tuition reimbursements available, career-related internships or fieldwork, Federal Work-Study, scholarships/grants, and unspecified assistantships available. Support available to part-time students. Financial award applicants required to submit FAFSA. *Unit head:* Dr. Diane Murphy, Chair, 703-284-5958, Fax: 703-527-3830, E-mail: diane.murphy@marymount.edu. *Application contact:* Francesca Reed, Director, Graduate Admissions, 703-284-5901, Fax: 703-527-3815, E-mail: grad.admissions@marymount.edu. Web site: http://www.marymount.edu/academics/programs/infoTechMS.

Marymount University, School of Business Administration, Program in Management, Arlington, VA 22207-4299. Offers leadership (Certificate); management (MS); project management (Certificate). Part-time and evening/weekend programs available. *Faculty:* 8 full-time (6 women), 7 part-time/adjunct (3 women). *Students:* 2 full-time (0 women), 17 part-time (14 women); includes 6 minority (2 Black or African American, non-Hispanic/Latino; 1 Asian, non-Hispanic/Latino; 2 Hispanic/Latino; 1 Two or more races, non-Hispanic/Latino). Average age 42. 10 applicants, 40% accepted, 4 enrolled. In 2011, 11 master's, 1 other advanced degree awarded. *Degree requirements:* For master's, thesis or alternative. *Entrance requirements:* For master's, GMAT or GRE General Test, resume, at least 3 years of managerial experience, essay; for Certificate, resume, at least 3 years of managerial experience. Additional exam requirements/recommendations for international students: Required—TOEFL (minimum score 600 paper-based; 250 computer-based; 96 iBT), IELTS (minimum score 6.5). *Application deadline:* For fall admission, 7/1 priority date for domestic students, 7/1 for international students; for spring admission, 11/15 for domestic students, 11/16 for international students. Applications are processed on a rolling basis. Application fee: $40. Electronic applications accepted. *Expenses: Tuition:* Part-time $770 per credit hour. *Required fees:*

$8 per credit hour. One-time fee: $180 full-time. *Financial support:* In 2011–12, 1 student received support. Research assistantships with full tuition reimbursements available, career-related internships or fieldwork, Federal Work-Study, scholarships/grants, and unspecified assistantships available. Support available to part-time students. Financial award applicants required to submit FAFSA. *Unit head:* Dr. Lorri Cooper, Director, Master's in Management Program, 703-284-5950, Fax: 703-527-3830, E-mail: lorri.cooper@marymount.edu. *Application contact:* Francesca Reed, Director, Graduate Admissions, 703-284-5901, Fax: 703-527-3815, E-mail: grad.admissions@marymount.edu.

Maryville University of Saint Louis, The John E. Simon School of Business, St. Louis, MO 63141-7299. Offers accounting (MBA, PGC); business studies (PGC); management (MBA, PGC); marketing (MBA, PGC); process and project management (MBA, PGC); sport and entertainment management (MBA, PGC). *Accreditation:* ACBSP. Part-time and evening/weekend programs available. *Faculty:* 8 full-time (3 women), 14 part-time/adjunct (5 women). *Students:* 19 full-time (10 women), 114 part-time (56 women); includes 13 minority (7 Black or African American, non-Hispanic/Latino; 3 Asian, non-Hispanic/Latino; 2 Hispanic/Latino; 1 Two or more races, non-Hispanic/Latino), 3 international. Average age 31. In 2011, 56 master's awarded. *Entrance requirements:* For master's, GMAT (unless applicant possesses undergraduate business degree with minimum cumulative GPA of 3.0, or has completed master's degree from accredited university or one early access course prior to undergraduate degree). Additional exam requirements/recommendations for international students: Required—TOEFL (minimum score 85 iBT). *Application deadline:* Applications are processed on a rolling basis. Application fee: $40 ($60 for international students). Electronic applications accepted. *Expenses: Tuition:* Full-time $21,922; part-time $675 per credit hour. *Required fees:* $233.75 per semester. *Financial support:* Career-related internships or fieldwork, Federal Work-Study, tuition waivers (partial), and campus employment available. Financial award application deadline: 3/1; financial award applicants required to submit FAFSA. *Faculty research:* International business, e-marketing, strategic planning, interpersonal management skills, financial analysis. *Unit head:* Dr. Pamela Horwitz, Dean, 314-529-9418, Fax: 314-529-9975, E-mail: horwitz@maryville.edu. *Application contact:* Kathy Dougherty, Director of MBA Programs, 314-529-9382, Fax: 314-529-9975, E-mail: business@maryville.edu. Web site: http://www.maryville.edu/academics-bu-mba.

Metropolitan State University, College of Management, St. Paul, MN 55106-5000. Offers business administration (MBA, DBA); database administration (Graduate Certificate); healthcare information technology management (Graduate Certificate); information assurance security (Graduate Certificate); management information systems (MMIS); MIS generalist (Graduate Certificate); MIS systems analysis and design (Graduate Certificate); project management (Graduate Certificate); public and nonprofit administration (MPNA). Part-time and evening/weekend programs available. *Students:* 63 full-time (41 women), 409 part-time (192 women); includes 94 minority (38 Black or African American, non-Hispanic/Latino; 33 Asian, non-Hispanic/Latino; 14 Hispanic/Latino; 9 Two or more races, non-Hispanic/Latino), 61 international. Average age 35. *Degree requirements:* For master's, thesis optional, computer language (MMIS). *Entrance requirements:* For master's, GMAT (MBA), resume. Additional exam requirements/recommendations for international students: Required—TOEFL (minimum score 550 paper-based; 213 computer-based). *Application deadline:* For fall admission, 7/15 for international students; for winter admission, 11/15 for international students; for spring admission, 3/15 for international students. Applications are processed on a rolling basis. Application fee: $20. Electronic applications accepted. *Expenses:* Tuition, state resident: full-time $5799.06; part-time $322.17 per credit. Tuition, nonresident: full-time $11,411; part-time $633.92 per credit. Tuition and fees vary according to degree level, program and reciprocity agreements. *Financial support:* Research assistantships with partial tuition reimbursements, career-related internships or fieldwork, and Federal Work-Study available. Support available to part-time students. Financial award applicants required to submit FAFSA. *Faculty research:* Yugoslav economic system, workers' cooperatives, participative management and job enrichment, global business systems. *Unit head:* Dr. Paul Huo, Dean, 612-659-7271, Fax: 612-659-7268, E-mail: paul.huo@metrostate.edu. Web site: http://choose.metrostate.edu/comgradprograms.

Mississippi State University, College of Business, Graduate Studies in Business, Mississippi State, MS 39762. Offers business administration (MBA); project management (MBA). *Accreditation:* AACSB. Part-time and evening/weekend programs available. Postbaccalaureate distance learning degree programs offered (no on-campus study). *Students:* 95 full-time (41 women), 259 part-time (84 women); includes 36 minority (13 Black or African American, non-Hispanic/Latino; 5 American Indian or Alaska Native, non-Hispanic/Latino; 3 Asian, non-Hispanic/Latino; 9 Hispanic/Latino; 1 Native Hawaiian or other Pacific Islander, non-Hispanic/Latino; 5 Two or more races, non-Hispanic/Latino), 16 international. Average age 30. 219 applicants, 58% accepted, 95 enrolled. In 2011, 170 degrees awarded. Terminal master's awarded for partial completion of doctoral program. *Degree requirements:* For master's, comprehensive exam (for some programs), thesis optional. *Entrance requirements:* For master's, GMAT, minimum GPA of 3.0 in last 60 hours of course work. Additional exam requirements/recommendations for international students: Required—TOEFL (minimum score 575 paper-based; 233 computer-based; 90 iBT); Recommended—IELTS (minimum score 6.5). *Application deadline:* For fall admission, 7/1 for domestic students, 5/1 for international students; for spring admission, 11/1 for domestic students, 9/1 for international students. Applications are processed on a rolling basis. Application fee: $40. Electronic applications accepted. *Expenses:* Tuition, state resident: full-time $5805; part-time $322.50 per credit hour. Tuition, nonresident: full-time $14,670; part-time $815 per credit hour. *Financial support:* In 2011–12, 21 research assistantships with full tuition reimbursements (averaging $11,043 per year), 28 teaching assistantships with full tuition reimbursements (averaging $9,543 per year) were awarded; Federal Work-Study, institutionally sponsored loans, scholarships/grants, and unspecified assistantships also available. Financial award application deadline: 4/1; financial award applicants required to submit FAFSA. *Unit head:* Dr. Barbara Spencer, Director, 662-325-1891, Fax: 662-325-8161, E-mail: gsbi@cobilan.msstate.edu. Web site: http://business.msstate.edu/gsb/.

Missouri State University, Graduate College, Interdisciplinary Program in Administrative Studies, Springfield, MO 65897. Offers applied communication (MS); criminal justice (MS); environmental management (MS); homeland security (MS); project management (MS); sports management (MS). Part-time and evening/weekend programs available. Postbaccalaureate distance learning degree programs offered (no on-campus study). *Students:* 22 full-time (12 women), 61 part-time (28 women); includes 14 minority (5 Black or African American, non-Hispanic/Latino; 2 Asian, non-Hispanic/Latino; 4 Hispanic/Latino; 3 Two or more races, non-Hispanic/Latino). Average age 32. 31 applicants, 97% accepted, 18 enrolled. In 2011, 31 master's awarded. *Degree requirements:* For master's, comprehensive exam, thesis or alternative. *Entrance requirements:* For master's, GRE, GMAT, 3 years of work experience. Additional exam requirements/recommendations for international students: Required—TOEFL (minimum score 550 paper-based; 213 computer-based; 79 iBT). *Application deadline:* For fall admission, 7/20 priority date for domestic students; for spring admission, 12/20 priority date for domestic students. Applications are processed on a rolling basis. Application fee: $35 ($50 for international students). Electronic applications accepted. *Expenses:* Tuition, state resident: full-time $4086; part-time $227 per credit hour. Tuition, nonresident: full-time $8172; part-time $454 per credit hour. *Required fees:* $275 per semester. Tuition and fees vary according to course load, campus/location and program. *Financial support:* Career-related internships or fieldwork, Federal Work-Study, institutionally sponsored loans, scholarships/grants, and unspecified assistantships available. Support available to part-time students. Financial award application deadline: 3/31; financial award applicants required to submit FAFSA. *Unit head:* Dr. Thomas Tomasi, Interim Program Director, 417-836-5335, Fax: 417-836-6888, E-mail: tomtomasi@missouristate.edu. *Application contact:* Misty Stewart, Coordinator of Graduate Recruitment, 417-836-6079, Fax: 417-836-6200, E-mail: mistystewart@missouristate.edu. Web site: http://msas.missouristate.edu.

Montana Tech of The University of Montana, Graduate School, Project Engineering and Management Program, Butte, MT 59701-8997. Offers MPEM. Part-time and evening/weekend programs available. Postbaccalaureate distance learning degree programs offered (no on-campus study). *Faculty:* 1 full-time (0 women), 7 part-time/adjunct (1 woman). *Students:* 2 full-time (0 women), 10 part-time (6 women), 1 international. 4 applicants, 100% accepted, 4 enrolled. In 2011, 4 master's awarded. *Degree requirements:* For master's, comprehensive exam, final project presentation. *Entrance requirements:* For master's, minimum GPA of 3.0. Additional exam requirements/recommendations for international students: Required—TOEFL (minimum score 550 paper-based; 213 computer-based; 71 iBT). *Application deadline:* For fall admission, 4/1 priority date for domestic students, 3/1 for international students; for spring admission, 10/1 priority date for domestic students, 7/1 for international students. Applications are processed on a rolling basis. Application fee: $30. Electronic applications accepted. *Financial support:* Application deadline: 4/1; applicants required to submit FAFSA. *Unit head:* Dr. Kumar Ganesan, Director, 406-496-4239, Fax: 406-496-4650, E-mail: kganesan@mtech.edu. *Application contact:* Fred Sullivan, Administrator, Graduate School, 406-496-4304, Fax: 406-496-4710, E-mail: fsullivan@mtech.edu. Web site: http://www.mtech.edu/academics/gradschool/distancelearning/distancelearning-pem.htm.

Mount St. Mary's College, Graduate Division, Program in Business Administration, Los Angeles, CA 90049-1599. Offers entrepreneurship (MBA); nonprofit management (MBA); organizational leadership (MBA); project management (MBA). Evening/weekend programs available. *Entrance requirements:* Additional exam requirements/recommendations for international students: Required—TOEFL. *Application deadline:* For fall admission, 6/30 for domestic students. Electronic applications accepted. *Expenses:* Contact institution. *Financial support:* Scholarships/grants available. Financial award application deadline: 3/15; financial award applicants required to submit FAFSA. *Unit head:* Dr. Janet Robinson, Director, 310-954-4153, E-mail: jrobinson@msmc.la.edu. Web site: http://www.msmc.la.edu/graduate-programs/mba.asp.

National University, Academic Affairs, School of Engineering, Technology and Media, Department of Applied Engineering, La Jolla, CA 92037-1011. Offers engineering management (MS); environmental engineering (MS); homeland security and safety engineering (MS); project management (Certificate); security and safety engineering (Certificate); sustainability management (MS); wireless communications (MS). Part-time and evening/weekend programs available. Postbaccalaureate distance learning degree programs offered (no on-campus study). *Degree requirements:* For master's, thesis. *Entrance requirements:* For master's, interview, minimum GPA of 2.5. Additional exam requirements/recommendations for international students: Required—TOEFL (minimum score 550 paper-based; 213 computer-based; 79 iBT), IELTS (minimum score 6). *Application deadline:* Applications are processed on a rolling basis. Application fee: $60 ($65 for international students). Electronic applications accepted. *Financial support:* Career-related internships or fieldwork, institutionally sponsored loans, scholarships/grants, and tuition waivers (partial) available. Support available to part-time students. Financial award application deadline: 6/30; financial award applicants required to submit FAFSA. *Unit head:* Dr. Shekar Viswanathan, Chair and Associate Professor, 858-309-3416, Fax: 858-309-3420, E-mail: sviswana@nu.edu. *Application contact:* Dominick Giovanniello, Associate Regional Dean, 800-NAT-UNIV, Fax: 858-541-7792, E-mail: dgiovann@nu.edu. Web site: http://www.nu.edu/OurPrograms/SchoolOfEngineeringAndTechnology/AppliedEngineering.html.

New England College, Program in Management, Henniker, NH 03242-3293. Offers accounting (MSA); healthcare administration (MS); international relations (MA); marketing management (MS); nonprofit leadership (MS); project management (MS); strategic leadership (MS). Part-time and evening/weekend programs available. *Degree requirements:* For master's, independent research project. Electronic applications accepted.

Northwestern University, McCormick School of Engineering and Applied Science, Department of Civil and Environmental Engineering, Program in Project Management, Evanston, IL 60208. Offers MS. Part-time programs available. *Degree requirements:* For master's, capstone report. *Entrance requirements:* Additional exam requirements/recommendations for international students: Required—TOEFL (minimum score 560 paper-based; 220 computer-based). Electronic applications accepted. *Faculty research:* Construction management, environmental management, infrastructure management.

Northwestern University, School of Continuing Studies, Program in Information Systems, Evanston, IL 60208. Offers database and Internet technologies (MS); information systems management (MS); information systems security (MS); software project management and development (MS).

Norwich University, College of Graduate and Continuing Studies, Master of Business Administration Program, Northfield, VT 05663. Offers finance (MBA); organizational leadership (MBA); project management (MBA). *Accreditation:* ACBSP. Evening/weekend programs available. *Faculty:* 19 part-time/adjunct (5 women). *Students:* 100 full-time (34 women); includes 16 minority (4 Black or African American, non-Hispanic/Latino; 1 American Indian or Alaska Native, non-Hispanic/Latino; 5 Asian, non-Hispanic/Latino; 4 Hispanic/Latino; 2 Two or more races, non-Hispanic/Latino). Average age 36. 67 applicants, 69% accepted, 46 enrolled. In 2011, 103 master's awarded. *Degree requirements:* For master's, comprehensive exam (for some programs), thesis optional. *Entrance requirements:* For master's, minimum undergraduate GPA of 2.75. Additional exam requirements/recommendations for international students: Required—TOEFL (minimum score 550 paper-based; 213 computer-based; 83 iBT). *Application deadline:* For fall admission, 8/10 for domestic and international students; for winter admission, 11/7 for domestic and international students; for spring admission, 2/6 for domestic and international students. Applications are processed on a rolling basis. Application fee: $50. Electronic applications accepted. *Expenses: Tuition:* Full-time $16,174. *Required fees:* $2130. Full-time tuition and fees vary according to program. *Financial support:* In 2011–12, 58 students received support. Scholarships/grants available. Financial award applicants required to submit FAFSA. *Unit head:* Dr. Jose Cordova, Faculty Director, 802-485-2567, Fax: 802-485-2533, E-mail: jcordova@norwich.edu. *Application contact:* Kerri Murnyack, Associate Program Director, 802-485-3304, Fax: 802-485-2533, E-mail: kmurnyuac@norwich.edu. Web site: http://mba.norwich.edu.

Penn State Erie, The Behrend College, Graduate School, Erie, PA 16563-0001. Offers business administration (MBA); project management (MPM). *Accreditation:* AACSB. Part-time programs available. *Students:* 34 full-time (8 women), 57 part-time (14 women). Average age 28. 46 applicants, 63% accepted, 22 enrolled. In 2011, 86 master's awarded. *Entrance requirements:* Additional exam requirements/recommendations for international students: Required—TOEFL (minimum score 550 paper-based; 213 computer-based; 80 iBT). *Application deadline:* Applications are processed on a rolling basis. Application fee: $65. Electronic applications accepted. *Financial support:* Federal Work-Study available. Financial award application deadline: 2/15; financial award applicants required to submit FAFSA. *Unit head:* Dr. Donald L. Birx, Chancellor, 814-898-6160, Fax: 814-898-6461, E-mail: dlb69@psu.edu. *Application contact:* Ann M. Burbules, Graduate Admissions Counselor, 814-898-7255, Fax: 814-898-6044, E-mail: amb29@psu.edu. Web site: http://psbehrend.psu.edu/.

Polytechnic Institute of New York University, Department of Technology Management, Brooklyn, NY 11201-2990. Offers construction management (Advanced Certificate); electronic business management (Advanced Certificate); entrepreneurship (Advanced Certificate); human resources management (Advanced Certificate); information management (Advanced Certificate); management (MS); management of technology (MS); organizational behavior (MS, Advanced Certificate); project management (Advanced Certificate); technology management (MBA, PhD, Advanced Certificate); telecommunications and information management (MS); telecommunications management (Advanced Certificate). Part-time and evening/weekend programs available. *Faculty:* 6 full-time (1 woman), 32 part-time/adjunct (4 women). *Students:* 185 full-time (84 women), 94 part-time (41 women); includes 56 minority (15 Black or African American, non-Hispanic/Latino; 31 Asian, non-Hispanic/Latino; 10 Hispanic/Latino), 143 international. Average age 30. 467 applicants, 48% accepted, 123 enrolled. In 2011, 174 master's, 1 doctorate awarded. *Degree requirements:* For master's, comprehensive exam (for some programs), thesis (for some programs); for doctorate, comprehensive exam, thesis/dissertation. *Entrance requirements:* For master's, GMAT, minimum B average in undergraduate course work. Additional exam requirements/recommendations for international students: Required—TOEFL (minimum score 550 paper-based; 213 computer-based; 80 iBT); Recommended—IELTS (minimum score 6.5). *Application deadline:* For fall admission, 7/31 priority date for domestic students, 4/30 for international students; for spring admission, 12/31 priority date for domestic students, 11/30 for international students. Applications are processed on a rolling basis. Application fee: $75. Electronic applications accepted. *Expenses: Tuition:* Full-time $22,464; part-time $1248 per credit. *Required fees:* $501 per semester. *Financial support:* In 2011–12, 1 fellowship (averaging $26,400 per year) was awarded; research assistantships, teaching assistantships, institutionally sponsored loans, scholarships/grants, and unspecified assistantships also available. Support available to part-time students. *Unit head:* Prof. Bharadwaj Rao, Head, 718-260-3617, Fax: 718-260-3874, E-mail: brao@poly.edu. *Application contact:* JeanCarlo Bonilla, Director of Graduate Enrollment Management, 718-260-3182, Fax: 718-260-3624, E-mail: gradinfo@poly.edu. Web site: http://www.managementdept.poly.edu.

Polytechnic University of Puerto Rico, Miami Campus, Graduate School, Miami, FL 33166. Offers accounting (MBA); business administration (MBA); construction management (MEM); environmental management (MEM); finance (MBA); human resources management (MBA); logistics and supply chain management (MBA); management of international enterprises (MBA); manufacturing management (MEM); marketing management (MBA); project management (MBA). Part-time and evening/weekend programs available. Postbaccalaureate distance learning degree programs offered (no on-campus study). *Entrance requirements:* For master's, minimum GPA of 3.0. Electronic applications accepted.

Queen's University at Kingston, Queens School of Business, Program in Business Administration, Kingston, ON K7L 3N6, Canada. Offers consulting and project management (MBA); finance (MBA); innovation and entrepreneurship (MBA); marketing (MBA). *Accreditation:* AACSB. *Degree requirements:* For master's, thesis optional, research project. *Entrance requirements:* For master's, GMAT, minimum B+ average. Additional exam requirements/recommendations for international students: Required—TOEFL. Electronic applications accepted. *Faculty research:* Management fundamentals, strategic thinking, global business, innovation and change, leadership.

Regis University, College for Professional Studies, School of Management, Denver, CO 80221-1099. Offers accounting (MS, Certificate); executive international management (Certificate); executive leadership (Certificate); executive project management (Certificate); finance and accounting (MBA); general business administration (MBA); health care management (MBA); human resource management and leadership (MSOL); information technology leadership and management (MSOL); international business (MBA); marketing (MBA); operations management (MBA); organizational leadership and management (MSOL); project leadership and management (MSOL); project management (Certificate); strategic business management (Certificate); strategic human resource management (Certificate); strategic management (MBA). Offered at Colorado Springs Campus, Northwest Denver Campus, Southeast Denver Campus, Fort Collins Campus, Broomfield Campus, Henderson (Nevada) Campus, and Summerlin (Nevada) Campus and online. Part-time and evening/weekend programs available. Postbaccalaureate distance learning degree programs offered (no on-campus study). *Degree requirements:* For master's, thesis optional, capstone project. *Entrance requirements:* For master's, GMAT or essays, interview, 2 years of full-time business work experience, resume; for Certificate, GMAT. Additional exam requirements/recommendations for international students: Required—TOEFL, TWE (minimum score 5) or university-based test. Electronic applications accepted. *Faculty research:* Impact of information technology on small business regulation of accounting, international project financing, mineral development, delivery of healthcare to rural indigenous communities.

Robert Morris University, Graduate Studies, School of Communications and Information Systems, Moon Township, PA 15108-1189. Offers communication and information systems (MS); competitive intelligence systems (MS); information security and assurance (MS); information systems and communications (D Sc); information systems management (MS); information technology project management (MS); Internet information systems (MS); organizational leadership (MS). Part-time and evening/weekend programs available. Postbaccalaureate distance learning degree programs offered (no on-campus study). *Faculty:* 28 full-time (9 women), 9 part-time/adjunct (3 women). *Students:* 231 part-time (68 women); includes 41 minority (31 Black or African American, non-Hispanic/Latino; 8 Asian, non-Hispanic/Latino; 2 Hispanic/Latino), 16 international. *Degree requirements:* For doctorate, thesis/dissertation. *Entrance requirements:* For doctorate, employer letter of endorsement, interview. Additional exam requirements/recommendations for international students: Required—TOEFL (minimum score 550 paper-based; 213 computer-based; 79 iBT). *Application deadline:* For fall admission, 7/1 priority date for domestic students, 7/1 for international students; for spring admission, 11/1 priority date for domestic students, 11/1 for international students. Applications are processed on a rolling basis. Application fee: $35. Electronic applications accepted. *Expenses:* Contact institution. *Financial support:* Research assistantships with partial tuition reimbursements, institutionally sponsored loans, and unspecified assistantships available. Support available to part-time students. Financial award application deadline: 5/1. *Unit head:* Dr. Barbara J. Levine, Dean, 412-397-2591, Fax: 412-397-2481, E-mail: levine@rmu.edu. *Application contact:* Deborah Roach, Assistant Dean, Graduate Admissions, 412-397-5200, Fax: 412-397-2425, E-mail: graduateadmissions@rmu.edu. Web site: http://www.rmu.edu/web/cms/schools/scis/.

Rochester Institute of Technology, Graduate Enrollment Services, Center for Multidisciplinary Studies, Program in Project Management, Rochester, NY 14623-5603. Offers Certificate. Part-time programs available. Postbaccalaureate distance learning degree programs offered (no on-campus study). *Students:* 9 part-time (6 women); includes 2 minority (1 Black or African American, non-Hispanic/Latino; 1 Asian, non-Hispanic/Latino), 1 international. Average age 44. 10 applicants, 60% accepted, 6 enrolled. In 2011, 29 degrees awarded. *Entrance requirements:* Additional exam requirements/recommendations for international students: Required—TOEFL (minimum score 560 paper-based; 213 computer-based; 79 iBT) or IELTS (minimum score 6). *Application deadline:* Applications are processed on a rolling basis. Application fee: $50. Electronic applications accepted. *Expenses: Tuition:* Full-time $34,659; part-time $963 per credit hour. *Required fees:* $228; $76 per quarter. *Unit head:* Mary Boyd, Graduate Program Director, 585-475-2234, E-mail: mcbcms@rit.edu. *Application contact:* Diane Ellison, Assistant Vice President, Graduate Enrollment Services, 585-475-2229, Fax: 585-475-7164, E-mail: gradinfo@rit.edu.

Rowan University, Graduate School, College of Engineering, Department of Civil and Environmental Engineering, Program in Project Management, Glassboro, NJ 08028-1701. Offers MS. *Entrance requirements:* For master's, GRE General Test. Additional exam requirements/recommendations for international students: Required—TOEFL. Electronic applications accepted.

Royal Roads University, Graduate Studies, Applied Leadership and Management Program, Victoria, BC V9B 5Y2, Canada. Offers executive coaching (Graduate Certificate); health systems leadership (Graduate Certificate); project management (Graduate Certificate); public relations management (Graduate Certificate); strategic human resources management (Graduate Certificate).

St. Edward's University, School of Management and Business, Program in Project Management, Austin, TX 78704. Offers MS. Part-time and evening/weekend programs available. *Students:* 2 full-time (0 women), 32 part-time (15 women); includes 12 minority (3 Black or African American, non-Hispanic/Latino; 1 American Indian or Alaska Native, non-Hispanic/Latino; 8 Hispanic/Latino), 1 international. Average age 36. 22 applicants, 82% accepted, 12 enrolled. In 2011, 12 master's awarded. *Degree requirements:* For master's, minimum of 24 resident hours. *Entrance requirements:* For master's, GMAT or GRE General Test, minimum GPA of 2.75 in last 60 hours of course work. Additional exam requirements/recommendations for international students: Required—TOEFL (minimum score 550 paper-based; 213 computer-based; 79 iBT) or IELTS (minimum score 6). *Application deadline:* For fall admission, 7/1 for domestic and international students; for spring admission, 11/1 for domestic and international students. Applications are processed on a rolling basis. Application fee: $45 ($50 for international students). Electronic applications accepted. *Expenses: Tuition:* Full-time $17,550; part-time $975 per credit hour. *Required fees:* $50 per trimester. Full-time tuition and fees vary according to course load and program. *Financial support:* Scholarships/grants available. *Unit head:* Dr. John S. Loucks, Director, 512-448-8630, Fax: 512-448-8492, E-mail: johnsl@stedwards.edu. *Application contact:* Sarah Hennes, Graduate Admission Coordinator, 512-448-8600, Fax: 512-428-1032, E-mail: sarahhe@stedwards.edu. Web site: http://www.stedwards.edu.

Saint Mary's University of Minnesota, Schools of Graduate and Professional Programs, Graduate School of Business and Technology, Project Management Program, Winona, MN 55987-1399. Offers MS, Certificate. *Unit head:* Dr. Gerald Ellis, Director, 612-728-5178, E-mail: gellis@smumn.edu. *Application contact:* Yasin Alsaidi, Director of Admissions for Graduate and Professional Programs, 612-728-5207, Fax: 612-728-5121, E-mail: yalsaidi@smumn.edu. Web site: http://www.smumn.edu/graduate-home/areas-of-study/graduate-school-of-business-technology/ms-in-project-management.

Saint Xavier University, Graduate Studies, Graham School of Management, Chicago, IL 60655-3105. Offers employee health benefits (Certificate); finance (MBA); financial fraud examination and management (MBA, Certificate); financial planning (MBA, Certificate); generalist/individualized (MBA); health administration (MBA); managed care (Certificate); management (MBA); marketing (MBA); project management (MBA, Certificate); MBA/MS. *Accreditation:* ACBSP. Part-time and evening/weekend programs available. *Entrance requirements:* For master's, GMAT, minimum GPA of 3.0, 2 years of work experience. *Application deadline:* For fall admission, 8/15 for domestic students. Applications are processed on a rolling basis. Application fee: $35. Electronic applications accepted. *Expenses:* Contact institution. *Financial support:* Career-related internships or fieldwork available. Support available to part-time students. Financial award applicants required to submit FAFSA. *Unit head:* Dr. John E. Eber, Dean, 773-298-3601, Fax: 773-298-3601, E-mail: eber@sxu.edu. *Application contact:* Beth Gierach, Managing Director of Admission, 773-298-3053, Fax: 773-298-3076, E-mail: gierach@sxu.edu. Web site: http://www.sxu.edu/academics/colleges_schools/gsm/.

Sam Houston State University, College of Business Administration, Department of General Business and Finance, Huntsville, TX 77341. Offers banking and financial institutions (EMBA); business administration (MBA, MS); project management (MS). *Faculty:* 14 full-time (3 women). *Students:* 85 full-time (36 women), 233 part-time (103 women); includes 82 minority (31 Black or African American, non-Hispanic/Latino; 3 American Indian or Alaska Native, non-Hispanic/Latino; 11 Asian, non-Hispanic/Latino; 37 Hispanic/Latino), 11 international. Average age 31. 300 applicants, 52% accepted, 135 enrolled. In 2011, 74 master's awarded. *Entrance requirements:* For master's, GMAT. Additional exam requirements/recommendations for international students: Required—TOEFL (minimum score 550 paper-based; 213 computer-based; 79 iBT). *Application deadline:* For fall admission, 8/1 for domestic students, 6/25 for international students; for spring admission, 12/1 for domestic students, 11/12 for international students. Applications are processed on a rolling basis. Application fee: $45 ($75 for international students). Electronic applications accepted. *Expenses:* Tuition, state resident: full-time $4420; part-time $221 per credit hour. Tuition, nonresident: full-time $10,680; part-time $534 per credit hour. *Required fees:* $329 per credit hour. *Financial support:* Application deadline: 5/31; applicants required to submit FAFSA. *Unit head:* Dr. Kurt Jesswein, Chair, 936-294-4582, E-mail: kurt.jesswein@shsu.edu. *Application contact:* Dr. Leroy Ashorn, Advisor, 936-294-4040, Fax: 936-294-3612, E-mail: busgrad@shsu.edu. Web site: http://www.shsu.edu/~gba_www/.

Southern Illinois University Edwardsville, Graduate School, School of Business, Program in Business Administration, Edwardsville, IL 62026. Offers management information systems (MBA); project management (MBA). *Accreditation:* AACSB. Part-time and evening/weekend programs available. *Students:* 17 full-time (4 women), 119 part-time (39 women); includes 10 minority (3 Black or African American, non-Hispanic/Latino; 1 Asian, non-Hispanic/Latino; 1 Hispanic/Latino; 1 Native Hawaiian or other Pacific Islander, non-Hispanic/Latino; 4 Two or more races, non-Hispanic/Latino), 8 international. 101 applicants, 40% accepted. In 2011, 69 master's awarded. *Degree requirements:* For master's, comprehensive exam. *Entrance requirements:* For master's, GMAT. Additional exam requirements/recommendations for international students: Required—TOEFL (minimum score 550 paper-based; 213 computer-based; 79 iBT), IELTS (minimum score 6.5). *Application deadline:* For fall admission, 7/22 for domestic students, 6/1 for international students; for spring admission, 12/10 for domestic students, 10/1 for international students. Applications are processed on a rolling basis. Application fee: $30. Electronic applications accepted. Tuition and fees vary according to course load and program. *Financial support:* In 2011–12, 1 fellowship with full tuition reimbursement (averaging $8,370 per year), 1 research assistantship with full tuition reimbursement (averaging $9,927 per year) were awarded; teaching assistantships with full tuition reimbursements, institutionally sponsored loans, scholarships/grants, and unspecified assistantships also available. Financial award application deadline: 3/1; financial award applicants required to submit FAFSA. *Unit head:* Dr. Janice Joplin, Director, 618-650-2485, E-mail: jjoplin@siue.edu. *Application contact:* Michelle Robinson, Coordinator of Graduate Recruitment, 618-650-2811, Fax: 618-650-3523, E-mail: michero@siue.edu. Web site: http://www.siue.edu/business/mba.

Southern New Hampshire University, School of Business, Manchester, NH 03106-1045. Offers accounting (MS); business administration (MBA, Certificate), including accounting (Certificate), business administration (MBA), finance (Certificate), forensic accounting (Certificate), human resources management (Certificate), international business (Certificate), international sport management (Certificate), leadership of not for profit organizations (Certificate), marketing (Certificate), operations management (Certificate), sport management (Certificate), taxation (Certificate); finance (MS); hospitality and tourism leadership (Certificate); information technology (MS, Certificate); information technology/international business (Certificate); integrated marketing communications (Certificate); international business (MS, DBA); marketing (MS); operations and project management (MS); organizational leadership (MS); project management (Certificate); sport management (MS); MBA/Certificate. *Accreditation:* ACBSP. Part-time and evening/weekend programs available. Postbaccalaureate distance learning degree programs offered (no on-campus study). Terminal master's awarded for partial completion of doctoral program. *Degree requirements:* For master's, one foreign language, comprehensive exam (for some programs), thesis or alternative; for doctorate, one foreign language, comprehensive exam, thesis/dissertation. *Entrance requirements:* For master's, minimum GPA of 2.5; for doctorate, GMAT. Additional exam requirements/recommendations for international students: Required—TOEFL (minimum score 500 paper-based). Electronic applications accepted.

Stevens Institute of Technology, Graduate School, Wesley J. Howe School of Technology Management, Program in Business Administration, Hoboken, NJ 07030. Offers engineering management (MBA); financial engineering (MBA); information management (MBA); information technology in financial services (MBA); information technology in the pharmaceutical industry (MBA); information technology outsourcing (MBA); pharmaceutical management (MBA); project management (MBA); technology management (MBA); telecommunications management (MBA).

Stevens Institute of Technology, Graduate School, Wesley J. Howe School of Technology Management, Program in Information Systems, Hoboken, NJ 07030. Offers computer science (MS); e-commerce (MS); enterprise systems (MS); entrepreneurial information technology (MS); information architecture (MS); information management (MS, Certificate); information security (MS); information technology in financial services industry (MS); information technology in the pharmaceutical industry (MS); information technology outsourcing management (MS); project management (MS, Certificate); software engineering (MS); telecommunications (MS). *Degree requirements:* For master's, thesis optional. *Entrance requirements:* For master's, GMAT, GRE General Test. Additional exam requirements/recommendations for international students: Required—TOEFL. Electronic applications accepted.

Stevens Institute of Technology, Graduate School, Wesley J. Howe School of Technology Management, Program in Management, Hoboken, NJ 07030. Offers general management (MS); global innovation management (MS); human resource management (MS); information management (MS); project management (MS); technology commercialization (MS); technology management (MS). Part-time programs available. *Degree requirements:* For master's, thesis optional. *Entrance requirements:* For master's, GMAT, GRE General Test. Additional exam requirements/recommendations for international students: Required—TOEFL. Electronic applications accepted. *Faculty research:* Industrial economics.

Texas A&M University–San Antonio, School of Business, San Antonio, TX 78224. Offers business administration (MBA); enterprise resource planning systems (MBA); finance (MBA); healthcare management (MBA); human resources management (MBA); information assurance and security (MBA); international business (MBA); professional accounting (MPA); project management (MBA); supply chain management (MBA). Part-time and evening/weekend programs available. *Faculty:* 18 full-time (6 women), 1 part-time/adjunct (0 women). *Students:* 91 full-time (45 women), 278 part-time (150 women). Average age 33. In 2011, 20 master's awarded. *Entrance requirements:* For master's, GMAT. Additional exam requirements/recommendations for international students: Required—TOEFL (minimum score 550 paper-based; 213 computer-based; 80 iBT), IELTS (minimum score 6). *Application deadline:* For fall admission, 7/1 priority date for domestic students, 6/1 for international students; for spring admission, 11/15 priority date for domestic students, 10/1 for international students. Applications are processed on a rolling basis. Application fee: $35 ($50 for international students). Electronic applications accepted. *Expenses:* Tuition, state resident: part-time $691.11 per course. Tuition, nonresident: part-time $1621.11 per course. *Financial support:* Application deadline: 3/31; applicants required to submit FAFSA. *Unit head:* Dr. Tracy Hurley, MBA Coordinator, 210-932-6200, E-mail: tracy.hurley@tamusa.tamus.edu. *Application contact:* Melissa A. Villanueva, Graduate Admissions Specialist, 210-932-6200, Fax: 210-932-6209, E-mail: melissa.villanueva@tamusa.tamus.edu. Web site: http://www.tamusa.tamus.edu.

Trident University International, College of Business Administration, Program in Business Administration, Cypress, CA 90630. Offers business administration (PhD); conflict and negotiation management (MBA); criminal justice administration (MBA); entrepreneurship (MBA); finance (MBA); general management (MBA); government accounting (MBA); human resource management (MBA); information security and digital assurance management (MBA); information technology management (MBA); international business (MBA); logistics management (MBA); marketing (MBA); project management (MBA); public management (MBA); quality management (MBA); strategic leadership (MBA). Part-time and evening/weekend programs available. Postbaccalaureate distance learning degree programs offered (no on-campus study). *Degree requirements:* For doctorate, comprehensive exam, thesis/dissertation, defense of dissertation. *Entrance requirements:* For master's, minimum GPA of 2.5 (students with GPA 3.0 or greater may transfer up to 30% of graduate level credits); for doctorate, minimum GPA of 3.4, curriculum vitae, course work in research methods or statistics. Additional exam requirements/recommendations for international students: Required—TOEFL. Electronic applications accepted.

Universidad del Turabo, Graduate Programs, School in Business Administration, Program in Project Management, Gurabo, PR 00778-3030. Offers MBA. *Students:* 50 full-time (29 women), 29 part-time (12 women); includes 71 minority (all Hispanic/Latino). Average age 31. 46 applicants, 87% accepted, 33 enrolled. In 2011, 35 master's awarded. *Unit head:* Marcelino Rivera, Dean, 787-743-7979 Ext. 4117. *Application contact:* Virginia Gonzalez, Admissions Officer, 787-746-3009.

Universidad Nacional Pedro Henriquez Urena, Graduate School, Santo Domingo, Dominican Republic. Offers agricultural diversity (MS), including horticultural/fruit production, tropical animal production; conservation of monuments and cultural assets (M Arch); ecology and environment (MS); environmental engineering (MEE); international relations (MA); natural resource management (MS); political science (MA); project optimization (MPM); project feasibility (MPM); project management (MPM); sanitation engineering (ME); science for teachers (MS); tropical Caribbean architecture (M Arch).

Université du Québec à Chicoutimi, Graduate Programs, Program in Project Management, Chicoutimi, QC G7H 2B1, Canada. Offers M Sc. Part-time programs available. *Entrance requirements:* For master's, appropriate bachelor's degree, proficiency in French.

Université du Québec à Montréal, Graduate Programs, Program in Project Management, Montréal, QC H3C 3P8, Canada. Offers MGP, Diploma. Part-time programs available. *Entrance requirements:* For master's and Diploma, appropriate bachelor's degree or equivalent, proficiency in French.

Université du Québec à Rimouski, Graduate Programs, Program in Project Management, Rimouski, QC G5L 3A1, Canada. Offers M Sc, Diploma. Programs offered jointly with Université du Québec à Chicoutimi, Université du Québec à Trois-Rivières, Université du Québec en Outaouais, Université du Québec en Abitibi-Témiscamingue, and Université du Québec à Montréal. Part-time programs available. *Entrance requirements:* For master's, proficiency in French, appropriate bachelor's degree.

Université du Québec en Abitibi-Témiscamingue, Graduate Programs, Program in Project Management, Rouyn-Noranda, QC J9X 5E4, Canada. Offers M Sc, DESS. M Sc offered jointly with Université du Québec à Chicoutimi, Université du Québec à Rimouski, Université du Québec à Trois-Rivières, Université du Québec en Outaouais, and Université du Québec à Montréal. Part-time programs available. *Entrance requirements:* For master's, appropriate bachelor's degree, proficiency in French.

Université du Québec en Outaouais, Graduate Programs, Program in Project Management, Gatineau, QC J8X 3X7, Canada. Offers M Sc, MA, DESS, Diploma. Programs offered jointly with Université du Québec à Chicoutimi, Université du Québec à Rimouski, Université du Québec à Trois-Rivières, Université du Québec en Abitibi-T'miscamingue, and Université du Québec à Montral. Part-time and evening/weekend programs available. *Students:* 76 full-time, 201 part-time, 9 international. *Degree requirements:* For master's, thesis (for some programs). *Entrance requirements:* For master's, appropriate bachelor's degree, proficiency in French. *Application deadline:* For fall admission, 6/1 priority date for domestic students, 3/1 for international students; for winter admission, 11/1 priority date for domestic students, 10/1 for international students. Application fee: $30 Canadian dollars. *Financial support:* Fellowships, research assistantships, and teaching assistantships available. *Unit head:* Sebastien Azondekon, Director, 819-595-3900 Ext. 1936, Fax: 819-773-1747, E-mail: sebastien.azondekon@uqo.ca. *Application contact:* Registrar's Office, 819-773-1850, Fax: 819-773-1835, E-mail: registraire@ugo.ca.

The University of Alabama in Huntsville, School of Graduate Studies, College of Business Administration, Department of Management and Marketing, Huntsville, AL 35899. Offers federal contract procurement (Certificate); management (MBA), including acquisition management, entrepreneurship, federal contract accounting, finance, human resource management, logistics and supply chain management, marketing, project management; supply chain management (Certificate); technology and innovation management (Certificate). *Accreditation:* AACSB. Part-time and evening/weekend programs available. *Faculty:* 11 full-time (2 women), 3 part-time/adjunct (0 women). *Students:* 52 full-time (25 women), 145 part-time (68 women); includes 28 minority (14 Black or African American, non-Hispanic/Latino; 4 American Indian or Alaska Native, non-Hispanic/Latino; 7 Asian, non-Hispanic/Latino; 2 Hispanic/Latino; 1 Two or more races, non-Hispanic/Latino), 15 international. Average age 31. 103 applicants, 73% accepted, 65 enrolled. In 2011, 76 master's awarded. *Degree requirements:* For master's, comprehensive exam, thesis or alternative. *Entrance requirements:* For master's, GMAT (minimum score 500), minimum AACSB index of 1080. Additional exam requirements/recommendations for international students: Required—TOEFL (minimum score 550 paper-based; 213 computer-based; 62 iBT). *Application deadline:* For fall admission, 8/1 for domestic students, 4/1 for international students; for spring admission, 12/1 for domestic students, 9/1 for international students. Applications are processed on a rolling basis. Application fee: $40 ($50 for international students). Electronic applications accepted. *Expenses:* Tuition, state resident: full-time $7830; part-time $473.50 per credit. Tuition, nonresident: full-time $18,748; part-time $1128.33 per credit. Tuition and fees vary according to course load and program. *Financial support:* In 2011–12, 12 students received support, including 7 research assistantships with full tuition reimbursements available (averaging $9,829 per year), 4 teaching assistantships with full tuition reimbursements available (averaging $8,000 per year); career-related internships or fieldwork, Federal Work-Study, institutionally sponsored loans, scholarships/grants, health care benefits, and unspecified assistantships also available. Support available to part-time students. Financial award application deadline: 4/1; financial award applicants required to submit FAFSA. *Faculty research:* Strategic human resources, corporate governance, cross-function integration and the management of research and development, determinants of team performance. *Total annual research expenditures:* $3.4 million. *Unit head:* Dr. Cynthia Gramm, Chair, 256-824-6913, Fax: 256-824-6328, E-mail: cynthia.gramm@uah.edu. *Application contact:* Jennifer Pettitt, Director of Graduate Programs, 256-824-6681, Fax: 256-824-7571, E-mail: jennifer.pettitt@uah.edu.

University of Alaska Anchorage, School of Engineering, Program in Project Management, Anchorage, AK 99508. Offers MS. Part-time and evening/weekend programs available. Postbaccalaureate distance learning degree programs offered (no on-campus study). *Degree requirements:* For master's, thesis or alternative, case study and research project. *Entrance requirements:* For master's, two years of project management experience. Additional exam requirements/recommendations for international students: Required—TOEFL (minimum score 550 paper-based; 213 computer-based). *Expenses:* Contact institution.

University of Atlanta, Graduate Programs, Atlanta, GA 30360. Offers business (MS); business administration (Exec MBA, MBA); computer science (MS); educational leadership (MS, Ed D); healthcare administration (MS, D Sc, Graduate Certificate); information technology for management (Graduate Certificate); international project management (Graduate Certificate); law (JD); managerial science (DBA); project management (Graduate Certificate); social science (MS). Postbaccalaureate distance learning degree programs offered. *Entrance requirements:* For master's, minimum cumulative GPA of 2.5.

University of California, Berkeley, UC Berkeley Extension, Certificate Programs in Business, Berkeley, CA 94720-1500. Offers accounting (Certificate); business administration (Certificate); finance (Certificate); human resource management (Certificate); management (Certificate); marketing (Certificate); project management (Certificate). *Accreditation:* AACSB. Postbaccalaureate distance learning degree programs offered.

University of California, Berkeley, UC Berkeley Extension, International Diploma Programs, Berkeley, CA 94720-1500. Offers business administration (Certificate); finance (Certificate); global business management (Certificate); marketing (Certificate); project management (Certificate). *Accreditation:* AACSB.

University of Dallas, Graduate School of Management, Irving, TX 75062-4736. Offers accounting (MBA, MM, MS); business management (MBA, MM); corporate finance (MBA, MM); financial services (MBA); global business (MBA, MM); health services management (MBA, MM); human resource management (MBA, MM); information assurance (MBA, MM, MS); information technology (MBA, MM, MS); information technology service management (MBA, MM, MS); marketing management (MBA, MM); organization development (MBA, MM); project management (MBA, MM); sports and entertainment management (MBA, MM); strategic leadership (MBA, MM); supply chain management (MBA); supply chain management and market logistics (MM). *Accreditation:* ACBSP. Part-time and evening/weekend programs available. Postbaccalaureate distance learning degree programs offered (no on-campus study). *Entrance requirements:* Additional exam requirements/recommendations for international students: Required—TOEFL. Electronic applications accepted. *Expenses:* Contact institution.

University of Denver, University College, Denver, CO 80208. Offers arts and culture (MLS, Certificate), including art, literature, and culture, arts development and program management (Certificate), creative writing; environmental policy and management (MAS, Certificate), including energy and sustainability (Certificate), environmental assessment of nuclear power (Certificate), environmental health and safety (Certificate), environmental management, natural resource management (Certificate); geographic information systems (MAS, Certificate); global affairs (MLS, Certificate), including translation studies, world history and culture; healthcare leadership (MPH, Certificate), including healthcare policy, law, and ethics, medical and healthcare information technologies, strategic management of healthcare; information and communications technology (MCIS, Certificate), including database design and administration (Certificate), geographic information systems (MCIS), information security systems security (Certificate), information systems security (MCIS), project management (MCIS, MPS, Certificate), software design and administration (Certificate), software design and programming (MCIS), technology management, telecommunications technology (MCIS), Web design and development; leadership and organizations (MPS, Certificate), including human capital in organizations, philanthropic leadership, project management (MCIS, MPS, Certificate), strategic innovation and change; organizational and professional communication (MPS, Certificate), including alternative dispute resolution, organizational communication, organizational development and training, public relations and marketing; security management (MAS, Certificate), including emergency planning and response, information security (MAS), organizational security; strategic human resource management (MPS, Certificate), including global human resources (MPS), human resource management and development (MPS). Part-time and evening/weekend programs available. Postbaccalaureate distance learning degree programs offered (no on-campus study). *Faculty:* 204 part-time/adjunct (80 women). *Students:* 56 full-time (26 women), 1,096 part-time (647 women); includes 196 minority (81 Black or African American, non-Hispanic/Latino; 7 American Indian or Alaska Native, non-Hispanic/Latino; 30 Asian, non-Hispanic/Latino; 66 Hispanic/Latino; 3 Native Hawaiian or other Pacific Islander, non-Hispanic/Latino; 9 Two or more races, non-Hispanic/Latino), 76 international. Average age 36. 572 applicants, 95% accepted, 410 enrolled. In 2011, 404 master's, 123 other advanced degrees awarded. *Degree requirements:* For master's, capstone project. *Entrance requirements:* For master's, two letters of recommendation, personal statement, resume. Additional exam requirements/recommendations for international students: Required—TOEFL (minimum score 550 paper-based; 80 iBT). *Application deadline:* For fall admission, 7/20 priority date for domestic students, 6/8 for international students; for winter admission, 10/26 priority date for domestic students, 9/14 for international students; for spring admission, 2/1 priority date for domestic students, 12/14 for international students. Applications are processed on a rolling basis. Application fee: $75. Electronic applications accepted. *Expenses:* Contact institution. *Financial support:* Applicants required to submit FAFSA. *Unit head:* Dr. James Davis, Dean, 303-871-2291, Fax: 303-871-4047, E-mail: jdavis@du.edu. *Application contact:* Information Contact, 303-871-3155, Fax: 303-871-4047, E-mail: ucolinfo@du.edu. Web site: http://www.universitycollege.du.edu/.

University of Houston, College of Technology, Department of Information and Logistics Technology, Houston, TX 77204. Offers information security (MS); supply chain and logistics technology (MS); technology project management (MS). Part-time programs available. *Degree requirements:* For master's, project or thesis (most programs). *Entrance requirements:* For master's, GMAT. Additional exam requirements/recommendations for international students: Required—TOEFL (minimum score 550 paper-based; 79 iBT). Electronic applications accepted.

University of Management and Technology, Program in Business Administration, Arlington, VA 22209. Offers acquisition management (DBA); general management (MBA, DBA); project management (MBA, DBA). Part-time and evening/weekend programs available. Postbaccalaureate distance learning degree programs offered (no on-campus study). *Degree requirements:* For master's, comprehensive exam. *Entrance requirements:* For master's, 3 recommendations, resume. Additional exam requirements/recommendations for international students: Required—TOEFL (minimum score 550 paper-based; 213 computer-based). Electronic applications accepted.

University of Management and Technology, Program in Computer Science and Information Technology, Arlington, VA 22209. Offers computer science (MS); information technology (AC); information technology project management (MS); management information systems (MS); project management (AC); software engineering (MS). Part-time and evening/weekend programs available. Postbaccalaureate distance learning degree programs offered (no on-campus study). *Entrance requirements:* For master's, 3 recommendations, resume. Additional exam requirements/recommendations for international students: Required—TOEFL (minimum score 550 paper-based; 213 computer-based). Electronic applications accepted.

University of Management and Technology, Program in Management, Arlington, VA 22209. Offers acquisition management (MS, AC); general management (MS); project management (MS, AC); public administration (MPA, MS, AC). Part-time and evening/weekend programs available. Postbaccalaureate distance learning degree programs offered (no on-campus study). *Entrance requirements:* For master's, 3 recommendations, resume. Additional exam requirements/recommendations for international students: Required—TOEFL (minimum score 550 paper-based; 213 computer-based). Electronic applications accepted.

University of Mary, Gary Tharaldson School of Business, Bismarck, ND 58504-9652. Offers accountancy (MBA); business administration (MBA); health care (MBA); human resource management (MBA); management (MBA); project management (MPM); strategic leadership (MSSL). Part-time and evening/weekend programs available. *Faculty:* 8 full-time (5 women), 66 part-time/adjunct (22 women). *Students:* 340 full-time (190 women), 189 part-time (91 women); includes 69 minority (28 Black or African American, non-Hispanic/Latino; 25 American Indian or Alaska Native, non-Hispanic/Latino; 7 Asian, non-Hispanic/Latino; 7 Hispanic/Latino; 1 Native Hawaiian or other Pacific Islander, non-Hispanic/Latino; 1 Two or more races, non-Hispanic/Latino), 14 international. Average age 35. 207 applicants, 95% accepted, 148 enrolled. In 2011, 265 master's awarded. *Degree requirements:* For master's, strategic planning seminar. *Entrance requirements:* For master's, minimum GPA of 2.5. Additional exam requirements/recommendations for international students: Required—TOEFL (minimum score 500 paper-based; 197 computer-based; 71 iBT). *Application deadline:* Applications are processed on a rolling basis. Application fee: $40. *Financial support:* Application deadline: 8/1; applicants required to submit FAFSA. *Unit head:* Dr. Shanda Traiser, Director of the School of Accelerated and Distance Education, 701-355-8160, Fax: 701-255-7687, E-mail: straiser@umary.edu. *Application contact:* Wayne G. Maruska, Graduate Program Advisor, 701-355-8134, Fax: 701-255-7687, E-mail: wmaruska@umary.edu.

University of Michigan–Dearborn, College of Engineering and Computer Science, Department of Industrial and Manufacturing Systems Engineering, Dearborn, MI 48128-1491. Offers program and project management (MS); MBA/MSE. Part-time and evening/weekend programs available. *Faculty:* 13 full-time (0 women), 3 part-time/adjunct (0 women). *Students:* 18 full-time (6 women), 147 part-time (32 women); includes 49 minority (7 Black or African American, non-Hispanic/Latino; 1 American Indian or Alaska Native, non-Hispanic/Latino; 34 Asian, non-Hispanic/Latino; 7 Hispanic/Latino), 20 international. Average age 31. 98 applicants, 51% accepted, 45 enrolled. In 2011, 38 master's awarded. *Degree requirements:* For master's, thesis optional. *Entrance requirements:* For master's, bachelor's degree in applied mathematics, computer science, engineering, or physical science; minimum GPA of 3.0. Additional exam requirements/recommendations for international students: Required—TOEFL (minimum score 560 paper-based; 220 computer-based; 84 iBT). *Application deadline:* For fall admission, 8/1 priority date for domestic students, 4/1 for international students; for winter admission, 12/1 priority date for domestic students, 8/1 for international students; for spring admission, 4/1 for domestic students, 12/1 for international students. Applications are processed on a rolling basis. Application fee: $60. *Financial support:* Fellowships, research assistantships, teaching assistantships, and Federal Work-Study available. Financial award application deadline: 4/1; financial award applicants required to submit FAFSA. *Faculty research:* Health care systems, data and knowledge management, human factors engineering, machine diagnostics, precision machining. *Unit head:* Dr. Armen Zakarian, Chair, 313-593-5361, Fax: 313-593-3692, E-mail: zakarian@umd.umich.edu. *Application contact:* Joey W. Woods, Graduate Program Assistant, 313-593-5361, Fax: 313-593-3692, E-mail: jwwoods@umd.umich.edu. Web site: http://www.engin.umd.umich.edu/IMSE/.

University of Nebraska at Omaha, Graduate Studies, College of Information Science and Technology, Department of Information Systems and Quantitative Analysis, Omaha, NE 68182. Offers information assurance (Certificate); information technology (PhD); management information systems (MS); project management (Certificate); systems analysis and design (Certificate). Part-time and evening/weekend programs available. *Faculty:* 14 full-time (7 women). *Students:* 69 full-time (23 women), 87 part-time (26 women); includes 17 minority (4 Black or African American, non-Hispanic/Latino; 7 Asian, non-Hispanic/Latino; 4 Hispanic/Latino; 2 Two or more races, non-Hispanic/Latino), 75 international. Average age 32. 142 applicants, 43% accepted, 49 enrolled. In 2011, 38 master's, 3 doctorates, 29 other advanced degrees awarded. *Degree requirements:* For master's, comprehensive exam, thesis (for some programs); for doctorate, comprehensive exam, thesis/dissertation. *Entrance requirements:* For master's, GMAT or GRE General Test; for doctorate, GMAT or GRE General Test, letters of recommendation, writing sample, resume. Additional exam requirements/recommendations for international students: Required—TOEFL (minimum score 575 paper-based; 230 computer-based; 89 iBT). *Application deadline:* For fall admission, 2/15 for domestic students; for spring admission, 9/15 for domestic students. Applications are processed on a rolling basis. Application fee: $45. Electronic applications accepted. *Financial support:* In 2011–12, 31 students received support, including 25 research assistantships with tuition reimbursements available, 3 teaching assistantships with tuition reimbursements available; fellowships, career-related internships or fieldwork, Federal Work-Study, scholarships/grants, tuition waivers (partial), and unspecified assistantships also available. Financial award application deadline: 3/1; financial award applicants required to submit FAFSA. *Unit head:* Dr. Ilze Zigurs, Chairperson, 402-554-3770. *Application contact:* Carla Frakes, Information Contact, 402-554-2423.

University of Oklahoma, College of Arts and Sciences, Department of Psychology, Program in Organizational Dynamics, Tulsa, OK 74135. Offers organizational dynamics (MA), including human resource management, organizational dynamics, technical project management. Part-time and evening/weekend programs available. *Students:* 13 full-time (8 women), 21 part-time (10 women); includes 11 minority (2 Black or African American, non-Hispanic/Latino; 1 American Indian or Alaska Native, non-Hispanic/Latino; 2 Asian, non-Hispanic/Latino; 4 Hispanic/Latino; 1 Native Hawaiian or other Pacific Islander, non-Hispanic/Latino; 1 Two or more races, non-Hispanic/Latino), 1 international. Average age 36. 8 applicants, 75% accepted, 4 enrolled. In 2011, 14 degrees awarded. *Entrance requirements:* For master's, minimum GPA of 3.0 in last 60 hours of undergraduate course work. Additional exam requirements/recommendations for international students: Required—TOEFL (minimum score 550 paper-based; 79 iBT). *Application deadline:* For fall admission, 4/15 priority date for domestic students, 3/1 for international students; for spring admission, 11/1 for domestic students, 9/1 for international students. Applications are processed on a rolling basis. Application fee: $40 ($90 for international students). Electronic applications accepted. *Expenses:* Tuition, state resident: full-time $4087; part-time $170.30 per credit hour. Tuition, nonresident: full-time $14,875; part-time $619.80 per credit hour. *Required fees:* $2659; $100.25 per credit hour. Tuition and fees vary according to course load and degree level. *Financial support:* In 2011–12, 7 students received support. Scholarships/grants, health care benefits, and unspecified assistantships available. Financial award application deadline: 3/1; financial award applicants required to submit FAFSA. *Faculty research:* Academic integrity, organizational behavior, interdisciplinary teams, shared leadership. *Unit head:* Dr. Jorge Mendoza, Chair, 405-325-4511, Fax: 405-325-4737, E-mail: jmendoza@ou.edu. *Application contact:* Jennifer Kisamore, Graduate Liaison, 918-660-3603, Fax: 918-660-3383, E-mail: jkisamore@ou.edu. Web site: http://tulsagrad.ou.edu/odyn/.

University of Ottawa, Faculty of Graduate and Postdoctoral Studies, Faculty of Engineering, Engineering Management Program, Ottawa, ON K1N 6N5, Canada. Offers engineering management (M Eng); information technology (Certificate); project management (Certificate). *Degree requirements:* For master's, thesis or alternative. *Entrance requirements:* For master's and Certificate, honors degree or equivalent, minimum B average. Electronic applications accepted.

University of Phoenix–Bay Area Campus, School of Business, San Jose, CA 95134-1805. Offers accountancy (MS); accounting (MBA); business administration (MBA, DBA); energy management (MBA); global management (MBA); health care management (MBA); human resource management (MBA); human resources management (MM); management (MM); marketing (MBA); organizational leadership (DM); project management (MBA); public administration (MPA); technology management (MBA). Evening/weekend programs available. Postbaccalaureate distance learning degree programs offered (no on-campus study). *Degree requirements:* For master's, thesis (for some programs). *Entrance requirements:* For master's, minimum undergraduate GPA of 3.0, 3 years of work experience. Additional exam requirements/recommendations for international students: Required—TOEFL (minimum score 550 paper-based; 213 computer-based; 79 iBT). Electronic applications accepted.

University of Phoenix–Online Campus, School of Business, Phoenix, AZ 85034-7209. Offers accountancy (MS); accounting (MBA); business administration (MBA); energy management (MBA); global management (MBA); health care management (MBA); human resource management (MBA); human resources management (MM); international (MM); management (MM); marketing (MBA, Graduate Certificate); organizational management (MA); project management (MBA, Graduate Certificate); public administration (MBA, MM, MPA); technology management (MBA). Evening/weekend programs available. Postbaccalaureate distance learning degree programs offered. *Students:* 18,883 full-time (11,868 women); includes 6,302 minority (4,182 Black or African American, non-Hispanic/Latino; 121 American Indian or Alaska Native, non-Hispanic/Latino; 478 Asian, non-Hispanic/Latino; 1,252 Hispanic/Latino; 121 Native Hawaiian or other Pacific Islander, non-Hispanic/Latino; 148 Two or more races, non-Hispanic/Latino), 1,000 international. Average age 37. *Entrance requirements:* Additional exam requirements/recommendations for international students: Required—TOEFL, TOEIC (Test of English as an International Communication), Berlitz Online English Proficiency Exam, Pearson Test of English, or IELTS. *Application deadline:* Applications are processed on a rolling basis. Application fee: $45. Electronic applications accepted. *Expenses: Tuition:* Full-time $17,160. *Required fees:* $920. One-time fee: $45 full-time. Full-time tuition and fees vary according to course load, degree level, campus/location and program. *Financial support:* Scholarships/grants available. Financial award applicants required to submit FAFSA. *Application contact:* 866-766-0766. Web site: http://www.phoenix.edu/colleges_divisions/business.html.

University of Phoenix–Phoenix Main Campus, School of Business, Tempe, AZ 85282-2371. Offers accounting (MBA, MS); business administration (MBA); energy management (MBA); global management (MBA); health care management (MBA); human resource management (MBA); management (MM); marketing (MBA); project management (MBA); public administration (MPA); technology management (MBA). Evening/weekend programs available. Postbaccalaureate distance learning degree programs offered. *Students:* 1,151 full-time (531 women); includes 310 minority (99 Black or African American, non-Hispanic/Latino; 10 American Indian or Alaska Native, non-Hispanic/Latino; 39 Asian, non-Hispanic/Latino; 130 Hispanic/Latino; 15 Native Hawaiian or other Pacific Islander, non-Hispanic/Latino; 17 Two or more races, non-Hispanic/Latino), 63 international. Average age 34. *Entrance requirements:* Additional exam requirements/recommendations for international students: Required—TOEFL, TOEIC (Test of English as an International Communication), Berlitz Online English Proficiency Exam, Pearson Test of English, or IELTS. *Application deadline:* Applications are processed on a rolling basis. Application fee: $45. Electronic applications accepted. *Expenses:* Contact institution. *Financial support:* Scholarships/grants available. Financial award applicants required to submit FAFSA. *Application contact:* 866-766-0766. Web site: http://www.phoenix.edu/colleges_divisions/business.html.

University of Phoenix–Puerto Rico Campus, School of Business, Guaynabo, PR 00968. Offers accounting (MBA); energy management (MBA); global management (MBA); human resource management (MBA); marketing (MBA); project management (MBA); small business administration (MBA). Evening/weekend programs available. *Degree requirements:* For master's, thesis (for some programs). *Entrance requirements:* For master's, minimum undergraduate GPA of 3.0, 3 years work experience. Additional exam requirements/recommendations for international students: Required—TOEFL (minimum score 550 paper-based; 213 computer-based; 79 iBT). Electronic applications accepted.

University of Phoenix–Southern California Campus, School of Business, Costa Mesa, CA 92626. Offers accounting (MIS); business administration (MBA); energy management (MBA); global management (MBA); health care management (MBA); human resource management (MBA); management (MM); marketing (MBA); project management (MBA); public administration (MPA); technology management (MBA). Evening/weekend programs available. Postbaccalaureate distance learning degree programs offered. *Students:* 699 full-time (341 women); includes 318 minority (124 Black or African American, non-Hispanic/Latino; 4 American Indian or Alaska Native, non-Hispanic/Latino; 44 Asian, non-Hispanic/Latino; 124 Hispanic/Latino; 15 Native Hawaiian or other Pacific Islander, non-Hispanic/Latino; 7 Two or more races, non-Hispanic/Latino), 29 international. Average age 38. *Entrance requirements:* Additional exam requirements/recommendations for international students: Required—TOEFL, TOEIC (Test of English as an International Communication), Berlitz Online English Proficiency Exam, Pearson Test of English, or IELTS. *Application deadline:* Applications are processed on a rolling basis. Application fee: $45. Electronic applications accepted. *Expenses:* Contact institution. *Financial support:* Scholarships/grants available. Financial award applicants required to submit FAFSA. *Application contact:* 866-766-0766. Web site: http://www.phoenix.edu/colleges_divisions/business.html.

University of Regina, Faculty of Graduate Studies and Research, Kenneth Levene Graduate School of Business, Program in Business Administration, Regina, SK S4S 0A2, Canada. Offers business (Master's Certificate); business administration (MBA); executive business administration (MBA); international business (MBA); leadership (M Admin); organizational leadership (Master's Certificate); project management (Master's Certificate). Part-time and evening/weekend programs available. *Faculty:* 32 full-time (12 women), 10 part-time/adjunct (0 women). *Students:* 83 full-time (32 women), 51 part-time (26 women). 117 applicants, 75% accepted. In 2011, 35 master's awarded. *Degree requirements:* For master's, project. *Entrance requirements:* For master's, GMAT, two years relevant work experience. Additional exam requirements/recommendations for international students: Required—TOEFL (minimum score 580 paper-based; 80 iBT), IELTS (minimum score 6.5). *Application deadline:* Applications are processed on a rolling basis. Application fee: $100. Electronic applications accepted. *Expenses:* Contact institution. *Financial support:* In 2011–12, 6 fellowships (averaging $6,000 per year), 9 teaching assistantships (averaging $2,298 per year) were awarded; research assistantships and scholarships/grants also available. Financial award application deadline: 6/15. *Faculty research:* Business policy and strategy, production and operations management, human behavior in organizations, financial management, social issues in business. *Unit head:* Dr. Morina Rennie, Dean, 306-585-4162, Fax: 306-585-4805, E-mail: morina.rennie@uregina.ca. *Application contact:* Steve Wield, Manager, Graduate Programs, 306-337-8463, Fax: 306-585-5361, E-mail: steve.wield@uregina.ca.

University of San Francisco, School of Management, Program in Project Management, San Francisco, CA 94117-1080. Offers MS. *Faculty:* 1 (woman) full-time, 5 part-time/adjunct (3 women). *Students:* 9 full-time (8 women); includes 5 minority (1 Black or African American, non-Hispanic/Latino; 2 Asian, non-Hispanic/Latino; 2 Two or more races, non-Hispanic/Latino). Average age 33. 1 applicant, 100% accepted, 0 enrolled. *Expenses: Tuition:* Full-time $20,070; part-time $1115 per unit. Tuition and fees vary according to course load, campus/location and program. *Unit head:* Dr. Linda Henderson, Director, 415-422-2592. *Application contact:* 415-422-6000, E-mail: graduate@usfca.edu.

The University of Tennessee at Chattanooga, Graduate School, College of Engineering and Computer Science, Program in Engineering Management, Chattanooga, TN 37403. Offers engineering management (MS); fundamentals of engineering management (Graduate Certificate); power systems management (Graduate Certificate); project and value management (Graduate Certificate); quality management (Graduate Certificate). Postbaccalaureate distance learning degree programs offered (no on-campus study). *Faculty:* 5 full-time (1 woman), 2 part-time/adjunct (1 woman). *Students:* 14 full-time (2 women), 72 part-time (14 women); includes 17 minority (13 Black or African American, non-Hispanic/Latino; 2 Asian, non-Hispanic/Latino; 2 Hispanic/Latino). Average age 32. 52 applicants, 52% accepted, 14 enrolled. In 2011, 37 master's, 4 other advanced degrees awarded. *Degree requirements:* For master's, thesis. *Entrance requirements:* For master's, GRE General Test, letters of recommendation; minimum undergraduate GPA of 2.5 overall or 3.0 in senior year. Additional exam requirements/recommendations for international students: Required—TOEFL (minimum score 550 paper-based; 213 computer-based; 79 iBT), IELTS (minimum score 6). *Application deadline:* For fall admission, 8/1 priority date for domestic students, 6/1 for international students; for spring admission, 12/1 priority date for domestic students, 10/1 for international students. Applications are processed on a rolling basis. Application fee: $35. Electronic applications accepted. *Expenses:* Tuition, state resident: full-time $6472; part-time $359 per credit hour. Tuition, nonresident: full-time $20,006; part-time $1111 per credit hour. *Required fees:* $1320; $160 per credit hour. *Financial support:* Career-related internships or fieldwork, scholarships/grants, and unspecified assistantships available. Support available to part-time students. Financial award applicants required to submit FAFSA. *Faculty research:* Plant layout design, lean manufacturing, six sigma, value management, product development. *Unit head:* Dr. Neslihan Alp, Director, 423-425-4032, Fax: 423-425-5229, E-mail: neslihan-alp@utc.edu. *Application contact:* Dr. Jerald Ainsworth, Dean of Graduate Studies, 423-425-4478, Fax: 423-425-5223, E-mail: jerald-ainsworth@utc.edu. Web site: http://www.utc.edu/Departments/engrcs/engm/index.php.

The University of Texas at Dallas, Naveen Jindal School of Management, Program in Business Administration, Richardson, TX 75080. Offers cohort (MBA); executive business administration (EMBA); global leadership (EMBA); global online (MBA); healthcare management (EMBA); product lifecycle and supply chain management (EMBA); professional business administration (MBA); project management (EMBA). *Accreditation:* AACSB. Part-time and evening/weekend programs available. Postbaccalaureate distance learning degree programs offered (no on-campus study). *Faculty:* 88 full-time (16 women), 52 part-time/adjunct (13 women). *Students:* 390 full-time (129 women), 658 part-time (207 women); includes 291 minority (42 Black or African American, non-Hispanic/Latino; 4 American Indian or Alaska Native, non-Hispanic/Latino; 168 Asian, non-Hispanic/Latino; 66 Hispanic/Latino; 11 Two or more races, non-Hispanic/Latino), 161 international. Average age 32. 872 applicants, 51% accepted, 323 enrolled. In 2011, 471 master's awarded. *Degree requirements:* For master's, thesis optional. *Entrance requirements:* For master's, GMAT, 10 years of business experience (EMBA), minimum GPA of 3.0. Additional exam requirements/recommendations for international students: Required—TOEFL (minimum score 550 paper-based; 215 computer-based). *Application deadline:* For fall admission, 7/15 for domestic students, 5/1 for international students; for spring admission, 11/15 for domestic students, 9/1 for international students. Applications are processed on a rolling basis. Application fee: $50 ($100 for international students). Electronic applications accepted. *Expenses:* Contact institution. *Financial support:* In 2011–12, 223 students received support, including 1 research assistantship with partial tuition reimbursement available (averaging $13,400 per year), 24 teaching assistantships with partial tuition reimbursements available (averaging $10,050 per year); career-related internships or fieldwork, Federal Work-Study, institutionally sponsored loans, scholarships/grants, and unspecified assistantships also available. Support available to part-time students. Financial award application deadline: 4/30; financial award applicants required to submit FAFSA. *Faculty research:* Production scheduling, trade and finance, organizational decision-making, life/work planning. *Unit head:* Lisa Shatz, Director, Full-time MBA Program, 972-883-6191, E-mail: lisa.shatz@utdallas.edu. *Application contact:* James Parker, Assistant Director, 972-883-5842, E-mail: jparker@utdallas.edu. Web site: http://jindal.utdallas.edu/academic-programs/mba-programs/.

University of the Incarnate Word, School of Graduate Studies and Research, H-E-B School of Business and Administration, Programs in Administration, San Antonio, TX 78209-6397. Offers adult education (MAA); applied administration (MAA); communication arts (MAA); healthcare administration (MAA); instructional technology (MAA); international business (Certificate); nutrition (MAA); organizational development (MAA, Certificate); project management (Certificate); sports management (MAA). Part-time and evening/weekend programs available. Postbaccalaureate distance learning degree programs offered (no on-campus study). *Faculty:* 23 full-time (10 women), 26 part-time/adjunct (12 women). *Students:* 25 full-time (18 women), 54 part-time (33 women); includes 50 minority (10 Black or African American, non-Hispanic/Latino; 40 Hispanic/Latino), 5 international. Average age 34. 35 applicants, 94% accepted, 19 enrolled. In 2011, 38 master's awarded. *Degree requirements:* For master's, capstone. *Entrance requirements:* For master's, GRE, GMAT, undergraduate degree, minimum GPA of 2.5. Additional exam requirements/recommendations for international students: Required—TOEFL (minimum score 560 paper-based; 220 computer-based; 83 iBT). *Application deadline:* Applications are processed on a rolling basis. Application fee: $20. Electronic applications accepted. *Expenses: Tuition:* Part-time $725 per credit hour. Tuition and fees vary according to degree level. *Financial support:* Federal Work-Study and scholarships/grants available. Financial award applicants required to submit FAFSA. *Unit head:* Dr. Mark Teachout, MAA Programs Director, 210-829-3177, Fax: 210-805-3564, E-mail: teachout@uiwtx.edu. *Application contact:* Andrea Cyterski-Acosta, Dean of Enrollment, 210-829-6005, Fax: 210-829-3921, E-mail: admis@uiwtx.edu. Web site: http://www.uiw.edu/maa/index.htm and http://www.uiw.edu/maa/admissions.html.

University of Wisconsin–Platteville, School of Graduate Studies, Distance Learning Center, Online Master of Science in Project Management Program, Platteville, WI 53818-3099. Offers MS. Part-time and evening/weekend programs available. Postbaccalaureate distance learning degree programs offered (no on-campus study). *Students:* 4 full-time (3 women), 242 part-time (91 women); includes 27 minority (11 Black or African American, non-Hispanic/Latino; 3 American Indian or Alaska Native, non-Hispanic/Latino; 4 Asian, non-Hispanic/Latino; 7 Hispanic/Latino; 2 Native Hawaiian or other Pacific Islander, non-Hispanic/Latino), 26 international. 62 applicants, 82% accepted, 38 enrolled. In 2011, 50 master's awarded. *Degree requirements:* For master's, thesis or alternative. *Entrance requirements:* Additional exam requirements/recommendations for international students: Required—TOEFL (minimum score 500 paper-based; 61 iBT), IELTS (minimum score 6). *Application deadline:* For fall admission, 7/1 priority date for domestic students; for spring admission, 11/1 priority date for domestic students. Applications are processed on a rolling basis. Application fee: $56. Electronic applications accepted. *Unit head:* William Haskins, Coordinator, 608-342-1961, Fax: 608-342-1466, E-mail: haskinsd@uwplatt.edu. *Application contact:* William Haskins, Coordinator, 800-362-5460, Fax: 608-342-1071, E-mail: disted@uwplatt.edu.

Walden University, Graduate Programs, School of Management, Minneapolis, MN 55401. Offers accounting (MS, DBA), including accounting for the professional (MS), CPA (MS), self-designed (MS); accounting and management (MS), including accounting for strategic managers, self-designed; accounting for managers (MBA); advanced project management (Post-Graduate Certificate); applied project management (Post-Graduate Certificate); corporate finance (MBA); entrepreneurship (MBA, DBA); finance (DBA); global management (MS); global supply chain management (DBA); healthcare management (MBA, DBA); healthcare system improvement (MBA); human resource management (MBA, MS, PhD), including functional human resource management (MS), integrating functional and strategic human resource management (MS), organizational strategy (MS); information systems management (DBA); international business (MBA, DBA); leadership (MBA, MS, DBA), including entrepreneurship (MS), general management (MS), human resources leadership (MS), innovation and technology (MS), leader development (MS), leading sustainability (MS), project management (MS), self-designed (MS); management (MS), including healthcare management; managers as leaders (MS); marketing (MBA, DBA); project management (MBA, MS, DBA); research strategies (MS); risk management (MBA); self-designed (MBA, DBA, PhD); social impact management (DBA); strategies for sustainability (MBA); strategy and operations (MS); sustainable management (MS); technology (MBA); technology entrepreneurship (DBA); technology management (MS). Part-time and evening/weekend programs available. Postbaccalaureate distance learning degree programs offered (minimal on-campus study). *Faculty:* 32 full-time (14 women), 275 part-time/adjunct (98 women). *Students:* 3,962 full-time (2,095 women), 1,557 part-time (959 women); includes 3,003 minority (2,510 Black or African American, non-Hispanic/Latino; 25 American Indian or Alaska Native, non-Hispanic/Latino; 140 Asian, non-Hispanic/Latino; 240 Hispanic/Latino; 9 Native Hawaiian or other Pacific Islander, non-Hispanic/Latino; 79 Two or more races, non-Hispanic/Latino), 395 international. Average age 41. In 2011, 586 master's, 87 doctorates, 4 other advanced degrees awarded. *Degree requirements:* For doctorate, thesis/dissertation (for some programs), residency. *Entrance requirements:* For master's, bachelor's degree or equivalent in related field; minimum GPA of 2.5; official transcripts; goal statement; access to computer and Internet; for doctorate, master's degree or equivalent in related field; minimum GPA of 3.0; 3 years of related professional/academic experience (preferred). Additional exam requirements/recommendations for international students: Required—TOEFL (minimum score 550 paper-based; 213 computer-based), IELTS (minimum score 6.5), Michigan English Language Assessment Battery (minimum score 82). *Application deadline:* Applications are processed on a rolling basis. Application fee: $50. Electronic applications accepted. *Financial support:* Federal Work-Study, scholarships/grants, unspecified assistantships, and family tuition reduction, active duty/veteran tuition reduction, group tuition reduction, interest-free payment plans, employee tuition reduction available. Support available to part-time students. Financial award applicants required to submit FAFSA. *Unit head:* Dr. William Schulz, III, Associate Dean, 800-925-3368. *Application contact:* Jennifer Hall, Vice President of Enrollment Management, 866-4-WALDEN, E-mail: info@waldenu.edu. Web site: http://www.waldenu.edu/Colleges-and-Schools/College-of-Management-and-Technology.htm.

Western Carolina University, Graduate School, College of Business, Program in Project Management, Cullowhee, NC 28723. Offers MPM. Part-time and evening/weekend programs available. Postbaccalaureate distance learning degree programs offered (no on-campus study). *Students:* 1 (woman) full-time, 61 part-time (19 women); includes 18 minority (10 Black or African American, non-Hispanic/Latino; 1 American Indian or Alaska Native, non-Hispanic/Latino; 4 Asian, non-Hispanic/Latino; 2 Hispanic/Latino; 1 Two or more races, non-Hispanic/Latino), 2 international. Average age 37. 54 applicants, 91% accepted, 32 enrolled. In 2011, 53 master's awarded. *Entrance requirements:* For master's, GMAT or GRE, work experience in project management, appropriate undergraduate degree with minimum GPA of 3.0, employer recommendation, resume. Additional exam requirements/recommendations for international students: Required—TOEFL (minimum score 550 paper-based; 270 computer-based; 79 iBT). *Application deadline:* For fall admission, 5/1 priority date for domestic students; for spring admission, 9/1 priority date for domestic students. Applications are processed on a rolling basis. Application fee: $50. *Expenses:* Tuition, state resident: full-time $3348. Tuition, nonresident: full-time $12,933. *Required fees:* $3155. *Financial support:* Fellowships, research assistantships with full and partial tuition reimbursements, teaching assistantships with full and partial tuition reimbursements, institutionally sponsored loans, scholarships/grants, and unspecified assistantships available. Financial award application deadline: 3/31; financial award applicants required to submit FAFSA. *Unit head:* Dr. Vittal Anantatmula, Director, 828-828-668-2295, Fax: 828-227-7414, E-mail: vittal@email.wcu.edu. *Application contact:* Admissions Specialist for Project Management, 828-227-7398, Fax: 828-227-7480, E-mail: gradsch@email.wcu.edu. Web site: http://www.wcu.edu/1345.asp.

Winthrop University, College of Business Administration, Program in Software Project Management, Rock Hill, SC 29733. Offers software development (MS); software project management (Certificate). *Entrance requirements:* For master's, GMAT.

Wright State University, School of Graduate Studies, Raj Soin College of Business, Department of Management, Dayton, OH 45435. Offers flexible business (MBA); health care management (MBA); international business (MBA); management, innovation and change (MBA); project management (MBA); supply chain management (MBA); MBA/MS. *Entrance requirements:* For master's, GMAT, minimum AACSB index of 1000. Additional exam requirements/recommendations for international students: Required—TOEFL.

Section 18
Quality Management

This section contains a directory of institutions offering graduate work in quality management. Additional information about programs listed in the directory but not augmented by an in-depth entry may be obtained by writing directly to the dean of a graduate school or chair of a department at the address given in the directory.

For programs offering related work, see also in this book *Business Administration and Management.*

CONTENTS

Program Directory

Quality Management

California Intercontinental University, School of Information Technology, Diamond Bar, CA 91765. Offers information systems and enterprise resource management (DBA); information systems and knowledge management (MBA); project and quality management (MBA).

California State University, Dominguez Hills, College of Extended and International Education, Program in Quality Assurance, Carson, CA 90747-0001. Offers MS. Part-time and evening/weekend programs available. Postbaccalaureate distance learning degree programs offered (no on-campus study). *Faculty:* 1 full-time (0 women), 15 part-time/adjunct (3 women). *Students:* 5 full-time (2 women), 257 part-time (142 women); includes 102 minority (31 Black or African American, non-Hispanic/Latino; 42 Asian, non-Hispanic/Latino; 12 Hispanic/Latino; 17 Two or more races, non-Hispanic/Latino), 25 international. Average age 41. 226 applicants, 89% accepted, 67 enrolled. In 2011, 23 master's awarded. *Degree requirements:* For master's, thesis. *Entrance requirements:* For master's, minimum GPA of 2.75. Additional exam requirements/recommendations for international students: Required—TOEFL. *Application deadline:* For fall admission, 6/1 priority date for domestic students, 6/1 for international students; for spring admission, 10/1 priority date for domestic students, 10/1 for international students. Application fee: $55. Electronic applications accepted. *Expenses:* Contact institution. *Faculty research:* Six Sigma, lean thinking, risk management, quality management. *Unit head:* Dr. Milton Krivokuca, Coordinator, 310-243-, Fax: 310-516-4423, E-mail: mkrivokuca@csudh.edu. *Application contact:* Rodger Hamrick, Program Assistant, 310-243-3880, Fax: 310-516 4423, E-mail: rhamrick@csudh.edu. Web site: http://www.csudh.edu/msqa.

Calumet College of Saint Joseph, Program in Quality Assurance, Whiting, IN 46394-2195. Offers MS.

Case Western Reserve University, Weatherhead School of Management, Department of Operations, Cleveland, OH 44106. Offers management (MS, MSM), including finance (MS), information systems (MS), marketing (MS), operations research, quality management (MS), supply chain (MSM); management for liberal arts graduates (MSM); operations research (PhD); MBA/MSM. Part-time programs available. *Degree requirements:* For doctorate, thesis/dissertation. *Entrance requirements:* For master's, GRE General Test; for doctorate, GMAT, GRE General Test. *Faculty research:* Mathematical finance, mathematical programming, scheduling, stochastic optimization, environmental/energy models.

East Carolina University, Graduate School, College of Technology and Computer Science, Department of Technology Systems, Greenville, NC 27858-4353. Offers computer network professional (Certificate); industrial technology (MS), including computer networking management, digital communications, industrial distribution and logistics, information security, manufacturing, performance improvement, quality systems; information assurance (Certificate); Lean Six Sigma Black Belt (Certificate); occupational safety (MS); technology management (PhD); Website developer (Certificate). *Entrance requirements:* For master's and Certificate, GRE General Test or MAT, minimum GPA of 2.5; for doctorate, GRE General Test, related work experience. *Application deadline:* For fall admission, 6/1 priority date for domestic students. Applications are processed on a rolling basis. Application fee: $50. *Expenses:* Tuition, state resident: full-time $3557; part-time $444.63 per semester hour. Tuition, nonresident: full-time $14,351; part-time $1793.88 per semester hour. *Required fees:* $2016; $252 per semester hour. Part-time tuition and fees vary according to course load, campus/location and program. *Financial support:* Application deadline: 6/1. *Unit head:* Dr. Tijjani Mohammed, Interim Chair, 252-328-9668, E-mail: mohammedt@ecu.edu. Web site: http://www.ecu.edu/cs-tecs/techsystems/.

Eastern Michigan University, Graduate School, College of Technology, School of Engineering Technology, Program in Quality Management, Ypsilanti, MI 48197. Offers quality (MS, Graduate Certificate); quality management (MS). Part-time and evening/weekend programs available. Postbaccalaureate distance learning degree programs offered (minimal on-campus study). *Students:* 2 full-time (1 woman), 96 part-time (39 women); includes 20 minority (12 Black or African American, non-Hispanic/Latino; 3 American Indian or Alaska Native, non-Hispanic/Latino; 1 Asian, non-Hispanic/Latino; 3 Hispanic/Latino; 1 Two or more races, non-Hispanic/Latino), 3 international. Average age 42. 43 applicants, 74% accepted, 18 enrolled. In 2011, 37 master's, 5 other advanced degrees awarded. *Entrance requirements:* Additional exam requirements/recommendations for international students: Required—TOEFL. *Application deadline:* Applications are processed on a rolling basis. Application fee: $35. *Expenses:* Tuition, state resident: full-time $10,367; part-time $432 per credit hour. Tuition, nonresident: full-time $20,435; part-time $851 per credit hour. *Required fees:* $39 per credit hour. $46 per semester. One-time fee: $100. Tuition and fees vary according to course level, degree level and reciprocity agreements. *Financial support:* Fellowships, research assistantships with full tuition reimbursements, teaching assistantships with full tuition reimbursements, career-related internships or fieldwork, Federal Work-Study, institutionally sponsored loans, scholarships/grants, tuition waivers (partial), and unspecified assistantships available. Support available to part-time students. Financial award applicants required to submit FAFSA. *Unit head:* Dr. Walter Tucker, Program Coordinator, 734-487-2040, Fax: 734-487-8755, E-mail: walter.tucker@emich.edu. *Application contact:* Graduate Admissions, 734-487-2400, Fax: 734-487-6559, E-mail: graduate.admissions@emich.edu.

Florida Institute of Technology, Graduate Programs, Extended Studies Division, Melbourne, FL 32901-6975. Offers acquisition and contract management (MS); aerospace engineering (MS); business administration (MBA); computer information systems (MS); computer science (MS); electrical engineering (MS); engineering management (MS); human resources management (MS); logistics management (MS), including humanitarian and disaster relief logistics; management (MS), including acquisition and contract management, e-business, human resources management, information systems, logistics management, management, transportation management; material acquisition management (MS); mechanical engineering (MS); operations research (MS); project management (MS), including information systems, operations research; public administration (MPA); quality management (MS); software engineering (MS); space systems (MS); space systems management (MS); supply chain management (MS); systems management (MS), including information systems, operations research. Part-time and evening/weekend programs available. Postbaccalaureate distance learning degree programs offered (no on-campus study). *Faculty:* 9 full-time (2 women), 105 part-time/adjunct (24 women). *Students:* 113 full-time (52 women), 1,150 part-time (484 women); includes 496 minority (332 Black or African American, non-Hispanic/Latino; 11 American Indian or Alaska Native, non-Hispanic/Latino; 42 Asian, non-Hispanic/Latino; 71 Hispanic/Latino; 2 Native Hawaiian or other Pacific Islander, non-Hispanic/Latino; 38 Two or more races, non-Hispanic/Latino), 11 international. Average age 35. 568 applicants, 56% accepted, 296 enrolled. In 2011, 471 master's awarded. *Degree requirements:* For master's, comprehensive exam (for some programs), capstone course. *Entrance requirements:* For master's, GMAT or resume showing 8 years of supervised experience, minimum GPA of 3.0, 2 letters of recommendation, resume. Additional exam requirements/recommendations for international students: Required—TOEFL (minimum score 550 paper-based; 213 computer-based; 79 iBT). *Application deadline:* For fall admission, 4/1 for international students; for spring admission, 9/30 for international students. Applications are processed on a rolling basis. Application fee: $0. Electronic applications accepted. *Expenses:* Contact institution. *Financial support:* Application deadline: 3/1; applicants required to submit FAFSA. *Unit head:* Dr. Theodore R. Richardson, III, Senior Associate Dean, 321-674-8123, Fax: 321-674-7597, E-mail: trichardson@fit.edu. *Application contact:* Carolyn Farrior, Director of Graduate Admissions, Online Learning and Off-Campus Programs, 321-674-7118, Fax: 321-674-8216, E-mail: cfarrior@fit.edu. Web site: http://es.fit.edu.

Hofstra University, Frank G. Zarb School of Business, Department of Information Technology and Quantitative Methods, Hempstead, NY 11549. Offers business administration (MBA), including information technology, quality management; information technology (MS, Advanced Certificate). Part-time and evening/weekend programs available. *Faculty:* 9 full-time (2 women), 2 part-time/adjunct (0 women). *Students:* 16 full-time (3 women), 14 part-time (3 women); includes 6 minority (2 Black or African American, non-Hispanic/Latino; 3 Asian, non-Hispanic/Latino; 1 Hispanic/Latino), 8 international. Average age 29. 42 applicants, 76% accepted, 9 enrolled. In 2011, 4 master's awarded. *Degree requirements:* For master's, capstone course (for MBA); thesis (for MS); minimum GPA of 3.0. *Entrance requirements:* For master's, GMAT/GRE, 2 letters of recommendation; resume; essay; for Advanced Certificate, GMAT/GRE, 2 letters of recommendation; resume. Additional exam requirements/recommendations for international students: Required—TOEFL (minimum score 550 paper-based; 213 computer-based; 80 iBT); Recommended—IELTS (minimum score 6). *Application deadline:* Applications are processed on a rolling basis. Application fee: $70 ($75 for international students). Electronic applications accepted. *Expenses:* Contact institution. *Financial support:* In 2011–12, 5 students received support, including 5 fellowships with full and partial tuition reimbursements available (averaging $6,680 per year); research assistantships with full and partial tuition reimbursements available, career-related internships or fieldwork, Federal Work-Study, institutionally sponsored loans, scholarships/grants, tuition waivers (full and partial), and unspecified assistantships also available. Support available to part-time students. Financial award applicants required to submit FAFSA. *Faculty research:* IT Outsourcing, IT Strategy, SAP and enterprise systems, data mining/electronic medical records, IT and crisis management, inventory theory and modeling, forecasting. *Unit head:* Dr. Mohammed H. Tafti, Chairperson, 516-463-5720, E-mail: acsmht@hofstra.edu. *Application contact:* Carol Drummer, Dean of Graduate Admissions, 516-463-4876, Fax: 516-463-4664, E-mail: gradstudent@hofstra.edu. Web site: http://www.hofsta.edu/business/.

Instituto Tecnologico de Santo Domingo, Graduate School, Area of Business, Santo Domingo, Dominican Republic. Offers banking and securities markets (M Mgmt); corporate finance (M Mgmt); human resources management (M Mgmt, Certificate); international trade management (M Mgmt); marketing (M Mgmt); organizational development (M Mgmt); quality and productivity management (Certificate); tax management and planning (M Mgmt); upper management (M Mgmt).

Instituto Tecnológico y de Estudios Superiores de Monterrey, Campus Ciudad de México, Virtual University Division, Ciudad de Mexico, Mexico. Offers administration of information technologies (MA); computer sciences (MA); education (MA, PhD); educational technology (MA); environmental engineering (MA); environmental systems (MA); humanistic studies (MA); industrial engineering (MA); international business for Latin America (MA); quality systems (MA); quality systems and productivity (MA). Part-time and evening/weekend programs available. Postbaccalaureate distance learning degree programs offered (minimal on-campus study). *Entrance requirements:* For master's and doctorate, Instituto entrance exam. Additional exam requirements/recommendations for international students: Required—TOEFL.

Instituto Tecnológico y de Estudios Superiores de Monterrey, Campus Ciudad Juárez, Program in Quality Management, Ciudad Juárez, Mexico. Offers MQM.

Instituto Tecnológico y de Estudios Superiores de Monterrey, Campus Estado de México, Professional and Graduate Division, Estado de Mexico, Mexico. Offers administration of information technologies (MITA); architecture (M Arch); business administration (GMBA, MBA); computer sciences (MCS, PhD); education (M Ed); educational institution administration (MAD); educational technology and innovation (PhD); electronic commerce (MEC); environmental systems (MS); finance (MAF); humanistic studies (MHS); information sciences and knowledge management (MISKM); information systems (MS); manufacturing systems (MS); marketing (MEM); quality systems and productivity (MS); science and materials engineering (PhD); telecommunications management (MTM). Part-time programs available. Postbaccalaureate distance learning degree programs offered (minimal on-campus study). *Degree requirements:* For master's, one foreign language, thesis (for some programs); for doctorate, one foreign language, thesis/dissertation. *Entrance requirements:* For master's, E-PAEP 500, interview; for doctorate, E-PAEP 500, research proposal. Additional exam requirements/recommendations for international students: Required—TOEFL (minimum score 550 paper-based). *Faculty research:* Surface treatments by plasmas, mechanical properties, robotics, graphical computing, mechatronics security protocols.

Instituto Tecnológico y de Estudios Superiores de Monterrey, Campus Irapuato, Graduate Programs, Irapuato, Mexico. Offers administration (MBA); administration of information technology (MAIT); administration of telecommunications (MAT); architecture (M Arch); computer science (MCS); education (M Ed); educational administration (MEA); educational innovation and technology (DEIT); educational technology (MET); electronic commerce (MBA); environmental administration and planning (MEAP); environmental systems (MES); finances (MBA); humanistic studies (MHS); international management for Latin American executives (MIMLAE); library and information science (MLIS); manufacturing quality management (MMQM); marketing research (MBA).

Madonna University, School of Business, Livonia, MI 48150-1173. Offers business administration (MBA); international business (MSBA); leadership studies (MSBA); leadership studies in criminal justice (MSBA); quality and operations management (MSBA). Part-time and evening/weekend programs available. Postbaccalaureate distance learning degree programs offered (minimal on-campus study). *Degree requirements:* For master's, thesis (for some programs), foreign language proficiency (international business). *Entrance requirements:* For master's, GMAT, GRE General

Test, minimum GPA of 3.0. Electronic applications accepted. *Faculty research:* Management, women in management, future studies.

Marian University, Business Division, Fond du Lac, WI 54935-4699. Offers organizational leadership and quality (MS). Part-time and evening/weekend programs available. *Faculty:* 1 full-time (0 women), 14 part-time/adjunct (4 women). *Students:* 7 full-time (5 women), 94 part-time (58 women); includes 14 minority (8 Black or African American, non-Hispanic/Latino; 2 Asian, non-Hispanic/Latino; 4 Hispanic/Latino). Average age 41. 50 applicants, 94% accepted, 46 enrolled. In 2011, 44 master's awarded. *Degree requirements:* For master's, comprehensive group project. *Entrance requirements:* For master's, 3 years of managerial experience, minimum GPA of 2.75, letters of professional reference. Additional exam requirements/recommendations for international students: Required—TOEFL (minimum score 525 paper-based; 193 computer-based; 70 iBT). *Application deadline:* Applications are processed on a rolling basis. Application fee: $25. Electronic applications accepted. *Expenses:* Contact institution. *Financial support:* In 2011–12, 1 student received support. Institutionally sponsored loans available. Financial award application deadline: 3/1; financial award applicants required to submit FAFSA. *Faculty research:* Organizational values, statistical decision-making, learning organization, quality planning, customer research. *Unit head:* Dr. Jeffrey G. Reed, Dean, Marian School of Business, 920-923-8759, Fax: 920-923-7167, E-mail: jreed@marianuniversity.edu. *Application contact:* Tracy Qualman, Director of Marketing and Admission, 920-923-7159, Fax: 920-923-7167, E-mail: tqualmann@marianuniversity.edu. Web site: http://www.marianuniversity.edu/interior.aspx?id-220.

The National Graduate School of Quality Management, Graduate Programs, Falmouth, MA 02541. Offers homeland security (MS); quality systems management (MS, DBA).

Penn State University Park, Graduate School, Intercollege Graduate Programs, Intercollege Program in Quality and Manufacturing Management, State College, University Park, PA 16802-1503. Offers MMM. *Unit head:* Dr. Jose A. Ventura, Co-Director, 814-865-5802, Fax: 814-863-4745, E-mail: jav1@psu.edu. *Application contact:* Cynthia E. Nicosia, Director, Graduate Enrollment Services, 814-865-1795, Fax: 814-865-4627, E-mail: cey1@psu.edu.

Regis College, Program in Regulatory and Clinical Research Management, Weston, MA 02493. Offers MS. Part-time and evening/weekend programs available. *Degree requirements:* For master's, thesis optional, internship. *Entrance requirements:* For master's, GRE or MAT. Additional exam requirements/recommendations for international students: Required—TOEFL (minimum score 550 paper-based; 213 computer-based). *Expenses:* Contact institution. *Faculty research:* FDA regulatory affairs medical device.

Rutgers, The State University of New Jersey, New Brunswick, Graduate School-New Brunswick, Program in Statistics, Piscataway, NJ 08854-8097. Offers applied statistics (MS); biostatistics (MS); data mining (MS); quality and productivity management (MS); statistics (MS, PhD). Part-time programs available. Terminal master's awarded for partial completion of doctoral program. *Degree requirements:* For master's, comprehensive exam, essay, exam, non-thesis essay paper; for doctorate, one foreign language, thesis/dissertation, qualifying oral and written exams. *Entrance requirements:* For master's, GRE General Test; for doctorate, GRE General Test, GRE Subject Test (recommended). Additional exam requirements/recommendations for international students: Required—TOEFL (minimum score 550 paper-based; 213 computer-based). Electronic applications accepted. *Faculty research:* Probability, decision theory, linear models, multivariate statistics, statistical computing.

San Jose State University, Graduate Studies and Research, Charles W. Davidson College of Engineering, Department of Aviation and Technology, San Jose, CA 95192-0001. Offers quality assurance (MS). *Entrance requirements:* For master's, GRE. Electronic applications accepted.

Southern Polytechnic State University, School of Engineering Technology and Management, Department of Industrial Engineering Technology, Marietta, GA 30060-2896. Offers quality assurance (MS, Graduate Certificate). Part-time and evening/weekend programs available. Postbaccalaureate distance learning degree programs offered (no on-campus study). *Faculty:* 3 full-time (2 women), 6 part-time/adjunct (4 women). *Students:* 13 full-time (6 women), 61 part-time (22 women); includes 30 minority (22 Black or African American, non-Hispanic/Latino; 2 Asian, non-Hispanic/Latino; 5 Hispanic/Latino; 1 Two or more races, non-Hispanic/Latino), 4 international. Average age 39. 24 applicants, 92% accepted, 15 enrolled. In 2011, 19 master's awarded. *Degree requirements:* For master's and Graduate Certificate, comprehensive exam (for some programs). *Entrance requirements:* For master's, 3 reference forms, minimum GPA of 2.7, statement of purpose; for Graduate Certificate, minimum GPA of 2.7, statement of purpose. Additional exam requirements/recommendations for international students: Required—TOEFL (minimum score 550 paper-based; 213 computer-based; 79 iBT), IELTS (minimum score 6.5). *Application deadline:* For fall admission, 7/1 priority date for domestic students, 5/1 for international students; for spring admission, 11/1 priority date for domestic students, 9/1 for international students. Applications are processed on a rolling basis. Application fee: $50. Electronic applications accepted. *Expenses:* Tuition, state resident: full-time $2592; part-time $216 per semester hour. Tuition, nonresident: full-time $9408; part-time $784 per semester hour. *Required fees:* $698 per term. *Financial support:* In 2011–12, 1 research assistantship with partial tuition reimbursement (averaging $1,500 per year) was awarded; career-related internships or fieldwork and unspecified assistantships also available. Support available to part-time students. Financial award application deadline: 5/1; financial award applicants required to submit FAFSA. *Faculty research:* Application on industrial engineering to public sector, investigation of the response model method in robust design, effectiveness of online education, learning community, physical and mechanical properties of shape-wear garments to their functional performance, the advantage of tablet computer technology in a distance learning format, health care, BRIGE: Optimization Models for Public Health Policy. *Unit head:* Thomas Ball, Chair, 678-915-7162, Fax: 678-915-4991, E-mail: tball@spsu.edu. *Application contact:* Nikki Palamiotis, Director of Graduate Studies, 678-915-4276, Fax: 678-915-7292, E-mail: npalamio@spsu.edu. Web site: http://www.spsu.edu/iet/index.htm.

Stevens Institute of Technology, Graduate School, Charles V. Schaefer Jr. School of Engineering, Department of Civil, Environmental, and Ocean Engineering, Program in Construction Management, Hoboken, NJ 07030. Offers construction accounting/estimating (Certificate); construction engineering (Certificate); construction law/disputes (Certificate); construction management (MS); construction/quality management (Certificate). *Degree requirements:* For master's, thesis optional. *Entrance requirements:* For master's, GMAT, GRE General Test. Additional exam requirements/recommendations for international students: Required—TOEFL. Electronic applications accepted.

Trident University International, College of Business Administration, Program in Business Administration, Cypress, CA 90630. Offers business administration (PhD); conflict and negotiation management (MBA); criminal justice administration (MBA); entrepreneurship (MBA); finance (MBA); general management (MBA); government accounting (MBA); human resource management (MBA); information security and digital assurance management (MBA); information technology management (MBA); international business (MBA); logistics management (MBA); marketing (MBA); project management (MBA); public management (MBA); quality management (MBA); strategic leadership (MBA). Part-time and evening/weekend programs available. Postbaccalaureate distance learning degree programs offered (no on-campus study). *Degree requirements:* For doctorate, comprehensive exam, thesis/dissertation, defense of dissertation. *Entrance requirements:* For master's, minimum GPA of 2.5 (students with GPA 3.0 or greater may transfer up to 30% of graduate level credits); for doctorate, minimum GPA of 3.4, curriculum vitae, course work in research methods or statistics. Additional exam requirements/recommendations for international students: Required—TOEFL. Electronic applications accepted.

Trident University International, College of Health Sciences, Program in Health Sciences, Cypress, CA 90630. Offers clinical research administration (MS, Certificate); emergency and disaster management (MS, Certificate); environmental health science (Certificate); health care administration (PhD); health care management (MS), including health informatics; health education (MS, Certificate); health informatics (Certificate); health sciences (PhD); international health (MS); international health: educator or researcher option (PhD); international health: practitioner option (PhD); law and expert witness studies (MS, Certificate); public health (MS); quality assurance (Certificate). Part-time and evening/weekend programs available. Postbaccalaureate distance learning degree programs offered (no on-campus study). *Degree requirements:* For doctorate, comprehensive exam, thesis/dissertation, defense of dissertation. *Entrance requirements:* For master's, minimum GPA of 2.5 (students with GPA 3.0 or greater may transfer up to 30% of graduate level credits); for doctorate, minimum GPA of 3.4, curriculum vitae, course work in research methods or statistics. Additional exam requirements/recommendations for international students: Required—TOEFL. Electronic applications accepted.

Universidad de las Americas, A.C., Program in Business Administration, Mexico City, Mexico. Offers finance (MBA); marketing research (MBA); production and quality (MBA).

Universidad del Turabo, Graduate Programs, School in Business Administration, Program in Quality Management, Gurabo, PR 00778-3030. Offers MBA. *Students:* 25 full-time (16 women), 35 part-time (25 women); includes 58 minority (all Hispanic/Latino). Average age 34. 31 applicants, 71% accepted, 19 enrolled. In 2011, 26 master's awarded. *Unit head:* Marcelino Rivera, Dean, 787-743-7979 Ext. 4117. *Application contact:* Virginia Gonzalez, Admissions Officer, 787-746-3009.

The University of Alabama, Graduate School, College of Human Environmental Sciences, Program in Human Environmental Science, Tuscaloosa, AL 35487. Offers family financial planning and counseling (MS); interactive technology (MS); quality management (MS); restaurant and meeting management (MS); rural community health (MS); sport management (MS). *Faculty:* 1 full-time (0 women). *Students:* 80 full-time (53 women), 93 part-time (55 women); includes 51 minority (42 Black or African American, non-Hispanic/Latino; 3 American Indian or Alaska Native, non-Hispanic/Latino; 3 Hispanic/Latino; 3 Two or more races, non-Hispanic/Latino), 1 international. Average age 33. 118 applicants, 79% accepted, 75 enrolled. In 2011, 83 degrees awarded. *Degree requirements:* For master's, comprehensive exam. *Entrance requirements:* For master's, GRE (for some specializations), minimum GPA of 3.0. Additional exam requirements/recommendations for international students: Required—TOEFL. *Application deadline:* Applications are processed on a rolling basis. Application fee: $50 ($60 for international students). Electronic applications accepted. *Expenses:* Tuition, state resident: full-time $8600. Tuition, nonresident: full-time $21,900. *Faculty research:* Hospitality management, sports medicine education, technology and education. *Unit head:* Dr. Milla D. Boschung, Dean, 205-348-6250, Fax: 205-348-1786, E-mail: mboschun@ches.ua.edu. *Application contact:* Dr. Stuart Usdan, Associate Dean, 205-348-6150, Fax: 205-348-3789, E-mail: susdan@ches.ua.edu.

The University of Tennessee at Chattanooga, Graduate School, College of Engineering and Computer Science, Program in Engineering Management, Chattanooga, TN 37403. Offers engineering management (MS); fundamentals of engineering management (Graduate Certificate); power systems management (Graduate Certificate); project and value management (Graduate Certificate); quality management (Graduate Certificate). Postbaccalaureate distance learning degree programs offered (no on-campus study). *Faculty:* 5 full-time (1 woman), 2 part-time/adjunct (1 woman). *Students:* 14 full-time (2 women), 72 part-time (14 women); includes 17 minority (13 Black or African American, non-Hispanic/Latino; 2 Asian, non-Hispanic/Latino; 2 Hispanic/Latino). Average age 32. 52 applicants, 52% accepted, 14 enrolled. In 2011, 37 master's, 4 other advanced degrees awarded. *Degree requirements:* For master's, thesis. *Entrance requirements:* For master's, GRE General Test, letters of recommendation; minimum undergraduate GPA of 2.5 overall or 3.0 in senior year. Additional exam requirements/recommendations for international students: Required—TOEFL (minimum score 550 paper-based; 213 computer-based; 79 iBT), IELTS (minimum score 6). *Application deadline:* For fall admission, 8/1 priority date for domestic students, 6/1 for international students; for spring admission, 12/1 priority date for domestic students, 10/1 for international students. Applications are processed on a rolling basis. Application fee: $35. Electronic applications accepted. *Expenses:* Tuition, state resident: full-time $6472; part-time $359 per credit hour. Tuition, nonresident: full-time $20,006; part-time $1111 per credit hour. *Required fees:* $1320; $160 per credit hour. *Financial support:* Career-related internships or fieldwork, scholarships/grants, and unspecified assistantships available. Support available to part-time students. Financial award applicants required to submit FAFSA. *Faculty research:* Plant layout design, lean manufacturing, six sigma, value management, product development. *Unit head:* Dr. Neslihan Alp, Director, 423-425-4032, Fax: 423-425-5229, E-mail: neslihan-alp@utc.edu. *Application contact:* Dr. Jerald Ainsworth, Dean of Graduate Studies, 423-425-4478, Fax: 423-425-5223, E-mail: jerald-ainsworth@utc.edu. Web site: http://www.utc.edu/Departments/engrcs/engm/index.php.

Upper Iowa University, Online Master's Programs, Fayette, IA 52142-1857. Offers accounting (MBA); corporate financial management (MBA); global business (MBA); health and human services (MPA); higher education administration (MHEA); homeland security (MPA); human resources management (MBA); justice administration (MPA); organizational development (MBA); public personnel management (MPA); quality management (MBA). MBA also available at Madison, WI campus. Part-time programs available. Postbaccalaureate distance learning degree programs offered (no on-campus study). *Degree requirements:* For master's, research project. *Entrance requirements:* For master's, GMAT, GRE, or minimum GPA of 2.7 during last 60 hours. Additional exam requirements/recommendations for international students: Required—TOEFL (minimum score 570 paper-based; 230 computer-based). Electronic applications accepted. *Faculty research:* Total quality management, CQI, teams, organization culture and climate, management.

Webster University, George Herbert Walker School of Business and Technology, Department of Management, St. Louis, MO 63119-3194. Offers business and organizational security management (MA); computer resources and information management (MA); environmental management (MS); government contracting (Certificate); health care management (MA); health services management (MA); human resources development (MA); human resources management (MA); management (DM); management and leadership (MA); marketing (MA); nonprofit management (Certificate); procurement and acquisitions management (MA); public administration (MA); quality management (MA); space systems operations management (MS); telecommunications management (MA). *Accreditation:* ACBSP. Part-time and evening/weekend programs available. Postbaccalaureate distance learning degree programs offered (no on-campus study). *Degree requirements:* For master's, thesis (for some programs); for doctorate, thesis/dissertation, written exam. *Entrance requirements:* For doctorate, GMAT, 3 years of work experience, MBA. Additional exam requirements/recommendations for international students: Required—TOEFL. *Expenses: Tuition:* Full-time $10,890; part-time $605 per credit hour. Tuition and fees vary according to campus/location and program.

Section 19
Quantitative Analysis

This section contains a directory of institutions offering graduate work in quantitative analysis. Additional information about programs listed in the directory but not augmented by an in-depth entry may be obtained by writing directly to the dean of a graduate school or chair of a department at the address given in the directory.

For programs offering related work, see also in this book *Business Administration and Management.*

CONTENTS

Program Directory

Quantitative Analysis

Bernard M. Baruch College of the City University of New York, Zicklin School of Business, Department of Operations Research and Quantitative Methods, New York, NY 10010-5585. Offers quantitative methods and modeling (MBA, MS). Part-time programs available.

Bernard M. Baruch College of the City University of New York, Zicklin School of Business, Department of Statistics and Computer Information Systems, Program in Decision Sciences, New York, NY 10010-5585. Offers MBA. Part-time and evening/weekend programs available. *Entrance requirements:* For master's, GMAT, 2 letters of recommendation, resume, 2 years of work experience. Additional exam requirements/recommendations for international students: Required—TOEFL (minimum score 590 paper-based; 243 computer-based), TWE (minimum score 5).

Drexel University, LeBow College of Business, Program in Business Administration, Philadelphia, PA 19104-2875. Offers business administration (MBA, PhD, APC), including accounting (MBA, PhD), decision sciences (PhD), economics (MBA, PhD), finance (MBA, PhD), legal studies (MBA), management (MBA), marketing (MBA, PhD), organizational sciences (PhD), quantitative methods (MBA), strategic management (PhD). *Accreditation:* AACSB. Part-time and evening/weekend programs available. Postbaccalaureate distance learning degree programs offered (minimal on-campus study). Terminal master's awarded for partial completion of doctoral program. *Entrance requirements:* For master's, GMAT, minimum GPA of 2.75; for doctorate, GMAT. Additional exam requirements/recommendations for international students: Required—TOEFL. Electronic applications accepted. *Faculty research:* Decision support systems, individual and group behavior, operations research, techniques and strategy.

Georgia State University, J. Mack Robinson College of Business, Department of Managerial Sciences, Atlanta, GA 30302-3083. Offers business analysis (MBA, MS); decision sciences (PhD); entrepreneurship (MBA); human resources management (MBA, MS); management (MBA, PhD); operations management (MBA, MS); organization change (MS); personnel employee relations (PhD); strategic management (PhD). *Accreditation:* AACSB. Part-time and evening/weekend programs available. *Degree requirements:* For doctorate, thesis/dissertation. *Entrance requirements:* For master's and doctorate, GMAT. Additional exam requirements/recommendations for international students: Required—TOEFL (minimum score 610 paper-based; 255 computer-based; 101 iBT). Electronic applications accepted. *Faculty research:* Abusive supervision, entrepreneurship, time series and neural networks, organizational controls, inventory control systems.

Instituto Tecnologico de Santo Domingo, Graduate School, Area of Engineering, Santo Domingo, Dominican Republic. Offers construction administration (MS, Certificate); data telecommunications (M Eng, MS, Certificate); industrial engineering (M Eng, Certificate); industrial management (M Mgmt); information technology (Certificate); maintenance engineering (M Eng); occupational hazard prevention (M Mgmt); production management (Certificate); quantitative methods (Certificate); sanitary and environmental engineering (M Eng); structural engineering (M Eng); systems engineering and electronic data processing (Certificate); transportation (Certificate).

Lehigh University, College of Business and Economics, Department of Finance, Bethlehem, PA 18015. Offers analytical finance (MS). *Faculty:* 6 full-time (1 woman), 1 part-time/adjunct (0 women). *Students:* 56 full-time (31 women), 33 part-time (10 women); includes 9 minority (6 Asian, non-Hispanic/Latino; 2 Hispanic/Latino; 1 Native Hawaiian or other Pacific Islander, non-Hispanic/Latino), 51 international. Average age 26. 508 applicants, 22% accepted, 37 enrolled. In 2011, 55 master's awarded. *Degree requirements:* For master's, capstone project. *Entrance requirements:* For master's, GMAT or GRE, bachelor's degree from a mathematically rigorous program, minimum GPA of 3.0. Additional exam requirements/recommendations for international students: Required—TOEFL (minimum score 600 paper-based; 250 computer-based; 94 iBT). *Application deadline:* For fall admission, 7/15 for domestic students, 2/15 for international students. Applications are processed on a rolling basis. Application fee: $100. Electronic applications accepted. *Expenses:* Contact institution. *Unit head:* Richard Kish, Department Chair, 610-758-4205, E-mail: rjk7@lehigh.edu. *Application contact:* Corinn McBride, Director of Recruitment and Admissions, 610-758-3418, Fax: 610-758-5283, E-mail: com207@lehigh.edu. Web site: http://www4.lehigh.edu/business/academics/depts/finance.

New York University, Robert F. Wagner Graduate School of Public Service, Program in Public Administration, New York, NY 10012. Offers public administration (PhD); public and nonprofit management and policy (MPA, Advanced Certificate), including developmental administration (Advanced Certificate), financial management and public finance, human resources management (Advanced Certificate), international administration (Advanced Certificate), management (MPA), management for public and nonprofit organizations (Advanced Certificate), public policy analysis, quantitative analysis and computer applications (Advanced Certificate), urban public policy (Advanced Certificate); JD/MPA; MBA/MPA; MPA/MA. *Accreditation:* NASPAA (one or more programs are accredited). Part-time programs available. *Faculty:* 32 full-time (13 women), 41 part-time/adjunct (22 women). *Students:* 431 full-time (323 women), 131 part-time (98 women); includes 148 minority (35 Black or African American, non-Hispanic/Latino; 53 Asian, non-Hispanic/Latino; 38 Hispanic/Latino; 1 Native Hawaiian or other Pacific Islander, non-Hispanic/Latino; 21 Two or more races, non-Hispanic/Latino), 62 international. Average age 28. 1,063 applicants, 58% accepted, 205 enrolled. In 2011, 213 master's, 8 doctorates awarded. *Degree requirements:* For master's, thesis or alternative, capstone end event; for doctorate, one foreign language, thesis/dissertation. *Entrance requirements:* Additional exam requirements/recommendations for international students: Required—TOEFL, IELTS, TWE. *Application deadline:* For fall admission, 1/15 for domestic students, 1/5 for international students; for spring admission, 10/15 for domestic students, 9/15 for international students. Application fee: $85. Electronic applications accepted. *Expenses:* Contact institution. *Financial support:* In 2011–12, 118 students received support, including 117 fellowships (averaging $13,500 per year); career-related internships or fieldwork, Federal Work-Study, scholarships/grants, health care benefits, and unspecified assistantships also available. Support available to part-time students. Financial award application deadline: 1/5; financial award applicants required to submit FAFSA. *Unit head:* Katty Jones, Director, Program Services, 212-998-7411, Fax: 212-995-4164, E-mail: katty.jones@nyu.edu. *Application contact:* Christopher Alexander, Communications Coordinator, 212-998-7414, Fax: 212-995-4611, E-mail: wagner.admissions@nyu.edu. Web site: http://www.nyu.edu.wagner/.

Oklahoma State University, Spears School of Business, Department of Finance, Stillwater, OK 74078. Offers finance (PhD); quantitative financial economics (MS). Part-time programs available. *Faculty:* 13 full-time (1 woman), 5 part-time/adjunct (0 women). *Students:* 19 full-time (9 women), 9 part-time (3 women); includes 2 minority (1 Black or African American, non-Hispanic/Latino; 1 Asian, non-Hispanic/Latino), 12 international. Average age 29. 47 applicants, 13% accepted, 4 enrolled. In 2011, 9 master's, 2 doctorates awarded. *Degree requirements:* For master's, thesis or alternative; for doctorate, comprehensive exam, thesis/dissertation. *Entrance requirements:* For master's and doctorate, GRE or GMAT. Additional exam requirements/recommendations for international students: Required—TOEFL (minimum score 550 paper-based; 79 iBT). *Application deadline:* For fall admission, 3/1 for international students; for spring admission, 8/1 for international students. Applications are processed on a rolling basis. Application fee: $40 ($75 for international students). Electronic applications accepted. *Expenses:* Tuition, state resident: full-time $4044; part-time $168.50 per credit hour. Tuition, nonresident: full-time $16,008; part-time $667 per credit hour. *Required fees:* $2122; $88.45 per credit hour. One-time fee: $50. Tuition and fees vary according to course load and campus/location. *Financial support:* In 2011–12, 12 research assistantships (averaging $10,710 per year), 5 teaching assistantships (averaging $24,252 per year) were awarded; career-related internships or fieldwork, Federal Work-Study, scholarships/grants, health care benefits, tuition waivers (partial), and unspecified assistantships also available. Support available to part-time students. Financial award application deadline: 3/1; financial award applicants required to submit FAFSA. *Faculty research:* Corporate risk management, derivatives banking, investments and securities issuance, corporate governance, banking. *Unit head:* Dr. John Polonchek, Head, 405-744-5199, Fax: 405-744-5180. *Application contact:* Dr. Sheryl Tucker, Dean, 405-744-6368, Fax: 405-744-0355, E-mail: grad-i@okstate.edu. Web site: http://spears.okstate.edu/finance/.

Purdue University, Graduate School, College of Agriculture, Department of Forestry and Natural Resources, West Lafayette, IN 47907. Offers fisheries and aquatic sciences (MS, MSF, PhD); forest biology (MS, MSF, PhD); natural resource social science (MS, PhD); natural resources social science (MSF); quantitative ecology (MS, MSF, PhD); wildlife science (MS, MSF, PhD); wood products and wood products manufacturing (MS, MSF, PhD). *Faculty:* 26 full-time (3 women), 9 part-time/adjunct (1 woman). *Students:* 67 full-time (31 women), 8 part-time (3 women); includes 3 minority (2 Hispanic/Latino; 1 Two or more races, non-Hispanic/Latino), 17 international. Average age 29. 58 applicants, 16% accepted, 8 enrolled. In 2011, 9 master's, 11 doctorates awarded. *Degree requirements:* For master's, thesis; for doctorate, thesis/dissertation. *Entrance requirements:* For master's and doctorate, GRE General Test with minimum score required: verbal >=50th percentile; Quantitative >= 50th percentile; Analytical writing = 4.0 or greater, minimum undergraduate GPA of 3.2 or equivalent. Additional exam requirements/recommendations for international students: Required—TOEFL (minimum score 550 paper-based; 77 iBT). *Application deadline:* For fall admission, 1/5 for domestic students, 1/15 for international students; for spring admission, 9/15 for domestic and international students. Applications are processed on a rolling basis. Application fee: $60 ($75 for international students). Electronic applications accepted. *Financial support:* In 2011–12, 10 research assistantships (averaging $15,259 per year) were awarded; fellowships, teaching assistantships, career-related internships or fieldwork, and scholarships/grants also available. Support available to part-time students. Financial award application deadline: 1/5; financial award applicants required to submit FAFSA. *Faculty research:* Wildlife management, forest management, forest ecology, forest soils, limnology. *Unit head:* Dr. Robert K. Swihart, Interim Head, 765-494-3590, Fax: 765-494-9461, E-mail: rswihart@purdue.edu. *Application contact:* Kelly J. Garrett, Graduate Secretary, 765-494-3572, Fax: 765-494-9461, E-mail: kgarrett@purdue.edu. Web site: http://www.fnr.purdue.edu/.

St. John's University, The Peter J. Tobin College of Business, Department of Computer Information Systems and Decision Sciences, Queens, NY 11439. Offers business analytics (MBA); computer information systems for managers (Adv C). Part-time and evening/weekend programs available. *Students:* 6 full-time (3 women), 8 part-time (0 women); includes 4 minority (1 Black or African American, non-Hispanic/Latino; 2 Asian, non-Hispanic/Latino; 1 Hispanic/Latino), 1 international. Average age 26. 8 applicants, 75% accepted, 4 enrolled. In 2011, 5 master's awarded. *Degree requirements:* For master's, comprehensive exam (for some programs), thesis optional. *Entrance requirements:* For master's, GMAT, 2 letters of recommendation, resume, transcripts, essay. Additional exam requirements/recommendations for international students: Required—TOEFL (minimum score 600 paper-based; 250 computer-based; 100 iBT), IELTS (minimum score 7). *Application deadline:* For fall admission, 5/1 priority date for domestic students, 5/1 for international students; for spring admission, 11/1 priority date for domestic students, 11/1 for international students. Applications are processed on a rolling basis. Application fee: $50. Electronic applications accepted. *Expenses:* Contact institution. *Financial support:* Research assistantships, scholarships/grants, and unspecified assistantships available. Support available to part-time students. Financial award application deadline: 3/1; financial award applicants required to submit FAFSA. *Unit head:* Dr. Victor Lu, Chair. *Application contact:* Carol J. Swanberg, Assistant Dean/Director of Graduate Admissions, 718-990-1345, Fax: 718-990-5242, E-mail: tobingradnyc@stjohns.edu.

Syracuse University, Martin J. Whitman School of Management, PhD Program in Business Administration, Syracuse, NY 13244. Offers accounting (PhD); finance (PhD); management information systems (PhD); managerial statistics (PhD); marketing (PhD); operations management (PhD); organizational behavior (PhD); strategy and human resources (PhD); supply chain management (PhD). *Faculty:* 79 full-time (20 women), 25 part-time/adjunct (6 women). *Students:* 32 full-time (10 women); includes 6 minority (3 Black or African American, non-Hispanic/Latino; 2 Asian, non-Hispanic/Latino; 1 Hispanic/Latino), 18 international. Average age 32. 260 applicants, 8% accepted, 12 enrolled. In 2011, 2 doctorates awarded. *Degree requirements:* For doctorate, comprehensive exam, thesis/dissertation, summer research paper. *Entrance requirements:* For doctorate, GMAT or GRE General Test, 3 recommendations. Additional exam requirements/recommendations for international students: Required—TOEFL (minimum score 600 paper-based; 250 computer-based; 100 iBT). *Application deadline:* For fall admission, 2/15 priority date for domestic students, 2/15 for international students. Applications are processed on a rolling basis. Application fee: $65. Electronic applications accepted. *Expenses: Tuition:* Part-time $1206 per credit. *Financial support:* In 2011–12, 1 fellowship with full tuition reimbursement (averaging $19,570 per year), 30 teaching assistantships with full tuition reimbursements (averaging $17,000 per year) were awarded; research assistantships with full tuition reimbursements, health care benefits, and unspecified assistantships also available. Financial award application deadline: 1/30. *Faculty research:* Marketing models, market microstructure, supply chain, auditing, corporate governance. *Unit head:* Dr. Eunkyu Lee, Director of the PhD Program, 315-443-3429, E-mail: elee06@syr.edu. *Application contact:* Carol Hilleges, Administrative Specialist, 315-443-9601, Fax: 315-443-3671, E-mail: clhilleg@syr.edu. Web site: http://whitman.syr.edu/phd/.

Texas Tech University, Graduate School, Rawls College of Business Administration, Area of Information Systems and Quantitative Sciences, Lubbock, TX 79409. Offers business statistics (MS, PhD); healthcare management (MS); management information systems (MS, PhD); production and operations management (MS, PhD); risk management (MS). Part-time programs available. *Faculty:* 15 full-time (0 women). *Students:* 46 full-time (13 women), 8 part-time (0 women); includes 4 minority (1 American Indian or Alaska Native, non-Hispanic/Latino; 1 Asian, non-Hispanic/Latino; 2 Hispanic/Latino), 38 international. Average age 27. 101 applicants, 65% accepted, 18 enrolled. In 2011, 35 master's, 2 doctorates awarded. Terminal master's awarded for partial completion of doctoral program. *Degree requirements:* For master's, comprehensive exam or capstone course; for doctorate, thesis/dissertation, qualifying exams. *Entrance requirements:* For master's and doctorate, GMAT, holistic profile of academic credentials. Additional exam requirements/recommendations for international students: Required—TOEFL (minimum score 550 paper-based; 213 computer-based; 79 iBT). *Application deadline:* For fall admission, 4/1 priority date for domestic students, 1/15 for international students; for spring admission, 9/1 priority date for domestic students, 6/15 for international students. Applications are processed on a rolling basis. Application fee: $50 ($75 for international students). Electronic applications accepted. *Expenses:* Tuition, state resident: full-time $5899; part-time $245.80 per credit hour. Tuition, nonresident: full-time $13,411; part-time $558.80 per credit hour. *Required fees:* $2680.60; $86.50 per credit hour. $920.30 per semester. *Financial support:* In 2011–12, 5 research assistantships (averaging $16,160 per year), 5 teaching assistantships (averaging $18,000 per year) were awarded; Federal Work-Study, scholarships/grants, and unspecified assistantships also available. *Faculty research:* Database management systems, systems management and engineering, expert systems and adaptive knowledge-based sciences, statistical analysis and design. *Unit head:* Dr. Glenn Browne, Area Coordinator, 806-834-0969, Fax: 806-742-3193, E-mail: glenn.browne@ttu.edu. *Application contact:* Elizabeth Stuart, Director, Graduate Services Center, 806-742-3184, Fax: 806-742-3958, E-mail: ba_grad@ttu.edu. Web site: http://is.ba.ttu.edu.

The University of British Columbia, Faculty of Arts and Faculty of Graduate Studies, Department of Psychology, Vancouver, BC V6T 1Z4, Canada. Offers behavioral neuroscience (MA, PhD); clinical psychology (MA, PhD); cognitive science (MA, PhD); developmental psychology (MA, PhD); health psychology (MA, PhD); quantitative methods (MA, PhD); social/personality psychology (MA, PhD). *Accreditation:* APA (one or more programs are accredited). Terminal master's awarded for partial completion of doctoral program. *Degree requirements:* For master's, thesis; for doctorate, comprehensive exam, thesis/dissertation. *Entrance requirements:* For master's and doctorate, GRE General Test. Additional exam requirements/recommendations for international students: Required—TOEFL (minimum score 550 paper-based; 230 computer-based; 80 iBT). Electronic applications accepted. *Faculty research:* Clinical, developmental, social/personality, cognition, behavioral neuroscience.

University of California, Santa Barbara, Graduate Division, College of Letters and Sciences, Division of Mathematics, Life, and Physical Sciences, Department of Geography, Santa Barbara, CA 93106-4060. Offers cognitive science (PhD); geography (MA, PhD); quantitative methods in the social sciences (PhD); transportation (PhD); MA/PhD. *Faculty:* 23 full-time (4 women), 13 part-time/adjunct (4 women). *Students:* 68 full-time (29 women); includes 13 minority (3 Black or African American, non-Hispanic/Latino; 5 Asian, non-Hispanic/Latino; 4 Hispanic/Latino; 1 Two or more races, non-Hispanic/Latino), 13 international. Average age 31. 128 applicants, 26% accepted, 19 enrolled. In 2011, 6 master's, 11 doctorates awarded. Terminal master's awarded for partial completion of doctoral program. *Median time to degree:* Of those who began their doctoral program in fall 2003, 54% received their degree in 8 years or less. *Degree requirements:* For master's, comprehensive exam (for some programs), thesis or alternative; for doctorate, comprehensive exam, thesis/dissertation, 1 quarter of teaching assistantship. *Entrance requirements:* For master's and doctorate, GRE (minimum verbal and quantitative scores of 1100 in old scoring system). Additional exam requirements/recommendations for international students: Required—TOEFL (minimum score 550 paper-based; 80 iBT), IELTS (minimum score 7). *Application deadline:* For fall admission, 12/15 for domestic and international students. Application fee: $80 ($100 for international students). Electronic applications accepted. *Expenses:* Tuition, state resident: full-time $12,192. Tuition, nonresident: full-time $27,294. *Required fees:* $764.13. *Financial support:* In 2011–12, 61 students received support, including 49 fellowships with full and partial tuition reimbursements available (averaging $6,971 per year), 35 research assistantships with full and partial tuition reimbursements available (averaging $17,231 per year), 28 teaching assistantships with partial tuition reimbursements available (averaging $9,887 per year). Financial award applicants required to submit FAFSA. *Faculty research:* Earth system science, human environment relations, modeling, measurement and computation. *Total annual research expenditures:* $4.6 million. *Unit head:* Dr. Dar Alexander Roberts, Professor/Chair, 805-880-2531, Fax: 805-893-2578, E-mail: dar@geog.ucsb.edu. *Application contact:* Jose Luis Saleta, Student Programs Manager, 805-456-2829, Fax: 805-893-2578, E-mail: saleta@geog.ucsb.edu. Web site: http://www.geog.ucsb.edu/.

University of California, Santa Barbara, Graduate Division, College of Letters and Sciences, Division of Mathematics, Life, and Physical Sciences, Department of Statistics and Applied Probability, Santa Barbara, CA 93106-3110. Offers financial mathematics and statistics (PhD); quantitative methods in the social sciences (PhD); statistics (MA), including applied statistics, mathematical statistics; statistics and applied probability (PhD); MA/PhD. *Faculty:* 11 full-time (3 women). *Students:* 49 full-time (20 women); includes 9 minority (7 Asian, non-Hispanic/Latino; 1 Hispanic/Latino; 1 Two or more races, non-Hispanic/Latino), 31 international. Average age 29. 272 applicants, 19% accepted, 12 enrolled. In 2011, 14 master's, 5 doctorates awarded. Terminal master's awarded for partial completion of doctoral program. *Median time to degree:* Of those who began their doctoral program in fall 2003, 57% received their degree in 8 years or less. *Degree requirements:* For master's, comprehensive exam, thesis optional; for doctorate, comprehensive exam, thesis/dissertation. *Entrance requirements:* For master's and doctorate, GRE General Test. Additional exam requirements/recommendations for international students: Required—TOEFL (minimum score 550 paper-based; 80 iBT), IELTS (minimum score 7). *Application deadline:* For fall admission, 1/1 priority date for domestic students, 1/1 for international students; for winter admission, 11/1 priority date for domestic students, 11/1 for international students; for spring admission, 2/1 priority date for domestic students, 2/1 for international students. Application fee: $80 ($100 for international students). Electronic applications accepted. *Expenses:* Tuition, state resident: full-time $12,192. Tuition, nonresident: full-time $27,294. *Required fees:* $764.13. *Financial support:* In 2011–12, 23 students received support, including 6 fellowships with full tuition reimbursements available (averaging $11,285 per year), 1 research assistantship with full and partial tuition reimbursement available (averaging $2,790 per year), 28 teaching assistantships with partial tuition reimbursements available (averaging $14,557 per year); Federal Work-Study, scholarships/grants, and health care benefits also available. Financial award application deadline: 1/1; financial award applicants required to submit FAFSA. *Faculty research:* Bayesian inference, financial mathematics, stochastic processes, environmental statistics, biostatistical modeling. *Total annual research expenditures:* $139,480. *Unit head:* Dr. Yuedong Wang, Chair, 805-893-4870, E-mail: yeudong@pstat.ucsb.edu. *Application contact:* Dolly J. Cook, Graduate Program Assistant, 805-893-2129, Fax: 805-893-2334, E-mail: cook@pstat.ucsb.edu. Web site: http://www.pstat.ucsb.edu/.

University of California, Santa Barbara, Graduate Division, College of Letters and Sciences, Division of Social Sciences, Department of Communication, Santa Barbara, CA 93106-4020. Offers cognitive science (PhD); communication (PhD); feminist studies (PhD); quantitative methods in the social sciences (PhD); society and technology (PhD); MA/PhD. *Faculty:* 20 full-time (9 women). *Students:* 37 full-time (26 women); includes 11 minority (3 Black or African American, non-Hispanic/Latino; 3 Asian, non-Hispanic/Latino; 5 Hispanic/Latino), 2 international. Average age 30. 98 applicants, 11% accepted, 7 enrolled. In 2011, 3 doctorates awarded. Terminal master's awarded for partial completion of doctoral program. *Median time to degree:* Of those who began their doctoral program in fall 2003, 98% received their degree in 8 years or less. *Degree requirements:* For doctorate, comprehensive exam, thesis/dissertation. *Entrance requirements:* For doctorate, GRE. Additional exam requirements/recommendations for international students: Required—TOEFL (minimum score 80 iBT), IELTS (minimum score 7). *Application deadline:* For fall admission, 12/1 for domestic and international students. Application fee: $80 ($100 for international students). Electronic applications accepted. *Expenses:* Tuition, state resident: full-time $12,192. Tuition, nonresident: full-time $27,294. *Required fees:* $764.13. *Financial support:* In 2011–12, 37 students received support, including 37 fellowships with full and partial tuition reimbursements available (averaging $6,045 per year), 5 research assistantships with full and partial tuition reimbursements available (averaging $9,646 per year), 29 teaching assistantships with partial tuition reimbursements available (averaging $17,600 per year); career-related internships or fieldwork, health care benefits, and tuition waivers (full and partial) also available. Support available to part-time students. Financial award application deadline: 12/1. *Faculty research:* Interpersonal, intercultural, organizational, health, media. *Unit head:* Prof. Linda L. Putnam, Professor, 805-893-7935, Fax: 805-893-7102, E-mail: lputnam@comm.ucsb.edu. *Application contact:* N. J. Kittle, Business Officer, 805-893-4517, Fax: 805-893-7102, E-mail: kittle@comm.ucsb.edu. Web site: http://www.comm.ucsb.edu/.

University of Cincinnati, Graduate School, Carl H. Lindner College of Business, MS Program, Cincinnati, OH 45221. Offers accounting (MS); information systems (MS); marketing (MS); quantitative analysis (MS). Part-time and evening/weekend programs available. *Faculty:* 79 full-time (22 women), 71 part-time/adjunct (24 women). *Students:* 171 full-time (75 women), 106 part-time (46 women); includes 19 minority (6 Black or African American, non-Hispanic/Latino; 1 American Indian or Alaska Native, non-Hispanic/Latino; 7 Asian, non-Hispanic/Latino; 2 Hispanic/Latino; 3 Two or more races, non-Hispanic/Latino), 114 international. 404 applicants, 77% accepted, 125 enrolled. *Degree requirements:* For master's, thesis (for some programs). *Entrance requirements:* For master's, GMAT, GRE, resume, transcripts, essays, letters of recommendation. Additional exam requirements/recommendations for international students: Required—TOEFL (minimum score 600 paper-based; 250 computer-based; 100 iBT). *Application deadline:* For fall admission, 1/15 priority date for domestic students, 4/1 for international students. Applications are processed on a rolling basis. Application fee: $65 ($70 for international students). Electronic applications accepted. *Expenses:* Contact institution. *Financial support:* In 2011–12, 10 teaching assistantships with full and partial tuition reimbursements (averaging $5,400 per year) were awarded; scholarships/grants, tuition waivers (full and partial), and unspecified assistantships also available. Financial award application deadline: 2/1; financial award applicants required to submit FAFSA. *Unit head:* Dr. David Szymanski, Dean, 513-556-7001, Fax: 513-556-4891, E-mail: will.mcintosh@uc.edu. *Application contact:* Dona Clary, Director, Graduate Programs Office, 513-556-3546, Fax: 513-558-7006, E-mail: dona.clary@uc.edu.

University of Cincinnati, Graduate School, Carl H. Lindner College of Business, PhD Programs, Cincinnati, OH 45221. Offers accounting (PhD); finance (PhD); information systems (PhD); management (PhD); marketing (PhD); quantitative analysis and operations management (PhD). *Faculty:* 56 full-time (13 women). *Students:* 34 full-time (12 women), 12 part-time (4 women); includes 2 minority (1 Asian, non-Hispanic/Latino; 1 Hispanic/Latino), 25 international. Average age 29. 120 applicants, 13% accepted, 10 enrolled. In 2011, 8 degrees awarded. *Median time to degree:* Of those who began their doctoral program in fall 2003, 65% received their degree in 8 years or less. *Degree requirements:* For doctorate, comprehensive exam, thesis/dissertation. *Entrance requirements:* For doctorate, GMAT, GRE, transcripts, essays, resume, letters of recommendation. Additional exam requirements/recommendations for international students: Required—TOEFL (minimum score 600 paper-based; 250 computer-based; 100 iBT). *Application deadline:* For fall admission, 2/1 for domestic and international students. Application fee: $65 ($70 for international students). Electronic applications accepted. *Expenses:* Contact institution. *Financial support:* In 2011–12, 39 students received support, including 30 research assistantships with full and partial tuition reimbursements available (averaging $14,640 per year); scholarships/grants, tuition waivers (full and partial), and unspecified assistantships also available. Financial award application deadline: 2/1; financial award applicants required to submit FAFSA. *Unit head:* Dr. Suzanne Masterson, Director, 513-556-7125, Fax: 513-556-5499, E-mail: suzanne.masterson@uc.edu. *Application contact:* Deborah Schildknecht, Assistant Director, 513-556-7190, Fax: 513-558-7006, E-mail: deborah.schildknecht@uc.edu. Web site: http://www.business.uc.edu/phd.

University of Colorado Denver, Business School, Program in Decision Sciences, Denver, CO 80217. Offers MS, MS/MBA. Part-time and evening/weekend programs available. *Students:* 4 full-time (3 women), 4 part-time (2 women); includes 1 minority (Hispanic/Latino). Average age 35. 1 applicant, 0% accepted, 0 enrolled. In 2011, 1 master's awarded. *Degree requirements:* For master's, 30 semester hours (18 of required courses and 12 of electives). *Entrance requirements:* For master's, GMAT, essay, resume, two letters of recommendation; financial statements (for international students). Additional exam requirements/recommendations for international students: Required—TOEFL (minimum score 525 paper-based; 197 computer-based; 71 iBT), IELTS (minimum score 6). *Application deadline:* For fall admission, 4/15 priority date for domestic students, 3/15 for international students; for spring admission, 10/15 priority date for domestic students, 10/1 for international students. Applications are processed on a rolling basis. Application fee: $50 ($75 for international students). Electronic applications accepted. *Expenses:* Contact institution. *Financial support:* Federal Work-Study and scholarships/grants available. Support available to part-time students. Financial award application deadline: 4/1; financial award applicants required to submit FAFSA. *Faculty research:* Quantitative business analysis, quantitative methods and modeling, business intelligence, forecasting, quality and Six Sigma, optimization, project management, data mining, supply chain management. *Unit head:* Marlene Smith, Associate Professor/Director, 303-315-8421, E-mail: ma.smith@ucdenver.edu. *Application contact:* Shelly Townley, Admissions Coordinator, 303-556-5956, Fax: 303-556-5904, E-mail: shelly.townley@ucdenver.edu. Web site: http://www.ucdenver.edu/academics/colleges/business/degrees/ms/decision-sciences/Pages/default.aspx.

University of Connecticut, Graduate School, College of Liberal Arts and Sciences, Department of Public Policy, Field of Survey Research, Storrs, CT 06269. Offers quantitative research methods (Graduate Certificate); survey research (MA). *Degree requirements:* For master's, comprehensive exam. *Entrance requirements:* For master's, GRE General Test. Additional exam requirements/recommendations for international students: Required—TOEFL (minimum score 550 paper-based; 213 computer-based). Electronic applications accepted.

Quantitative Analysis

University of Florida, Graduate School, Warrington College of Business Administration, Hough Graduate School of Business, Programs in Business Administration, Gainesville, FL 32611. Offers accounting (MBA); arts administration (MBA); business strategy and public policy (MBA); competitive strategy (MBA); decision and information sciences (MBA); electronic commerce (MBA); finance (MBA); general business (MBA); global management (MBA); Graham-Buffett security analysis (MBA); health administration (MBA); human resources management (MBA); international studies (MBA); Latin American business (MBA); management (MBA); marketing (MBA); sports administration (MBA); JD/MBA; MBA/MS; MBA/PhD; MBA/Pharm D; MD/MBA. *Accreditation:* AACSB. Part-time and evening/weekend programs available. *Faculty:* 71 full-time (10 women). *Students:* 412 full-time (111 women), 467 part-time (135 women); includes 235 minority (39 Black or African American, non-Hispanic/Latino; 7 American Indian or Alaska Native, non-Hispanic/Latino; 79 Asian, non-Hispanic/Latino; 109 Hispanic/Latino; 1 Native Hawaiian or other Pacific Islander, non-Hispanic/Latino), 44 international. Average age 32. 589 applicants, 52% accepted, 247 enrolled. In 2011, 505 master's awarded. *Degree requirements:* For master's, capstone course. *Entrance requirements:* For master's, GMAT, minimum GPA of 3.0, interview. Additional exam requirements/recommendations for international students: Required—TOEFL (minimum score 550 paper-based; 213 computer-based; 80 iBT), IELTS (minimum score 6). *Application deadline:* For fall admission, 7/1 for domestic students, 1/1 for international students; for spring admission, 12/1 for domestic and international students. Applications are processed on a rolling basis. Application fee: $30. Electronic applications accepted. *Financial support:* Teaching assistantships, career-related internships or fieldwork, scholarships/grants, and unspecified assistantships available. Support available to part-time students. Financial award applicants required to submit FAFSA. *Faculty research:* Accounting, finance, insurance, management, real estate, urban analysis marketing. *Unit head:* Prof. Alexander D. Sevilla, Assistant Dean/ Director, 352-273-3252 Ext. 1206, E-mail: alex.sevilla@warrington.ufl.edu. *Application contact:* Prof. Kelli Gust, Associate Director, 352-273-3255, Fax: 352-392-8791, E-mail: kelly.gust@warrington.ufl.edu. Web site: http://www.floridamba.ufl.edu/.

University of Illinois at Chicago, Graduate College, School of Public Health, Biostatistics Section, Chicago, IL 60607-7128. Offers biostatistics (MS, PhD); quantitative methods (MPH). Part-time programs available. Terminal master's awarded for partial completion of doctoral program. *Degree requirements:* For master's, thesis, field practicum; for doctorate, thesis/dissertation, independent research, internship. *Entrance requirements:* For master's and doctorate, GRE General Test, minimum GPA of 2.75. Additional exam requirements/recommendations for international students: Required—TOEFL. Electronic applications accepted.

University of Medicine and Dentistry of New Jersey, UMDNJ–School of Public Health (UMDNJ, Rutgers, NJIT) Newark Campus, Newark, NJ 07107-1709. Offers clinical epidemiology (Certificate); dental public health (MPH); general public health (Certificate); public policy and oral health services administration (Certificate); quantitative methods (MPH); urban health (MPH); DMD/MPH; MD/MPH; MS/MPH. *Accreditation:* CEPH. Part-time and evening/weekend programs available. *Degree requirements:* For master's, thesis, internship. *Entrance requirements:* For master's, GRE General Test. Additional exam requirements/recommendations for international students: Required—TOEFL. Electronic applications accepted.

University of Minnesota, Twin Cities Campus, College of Science and Engineering, School of Mathematics, Minneapolis, MN 55455-0213. Offers mathematics (MS, PhD); quantitative finance (Certificate). Part-time programs available. *Faculty:* 63 full-time (3 women). *Students:* 224 (65 women); includes 23 minority (7 Black or African American, non-Hispanic/Latino; 1 American Indian or Alaska Native, non-Hispanic/Latino; 13 Asian, non-Hispanic/Latino; 2 Hispanic/Latino), 108 international. Terminal master's awarded for partial completion of doctoral program. *Degree requirements:* For master's, thesis (for some programs); for doctorate, 2 foreign languages, thesis/dissertation. *Entrance requirements:* For master's, GRE Subject Test (recommended); for doctorate, GRE Subject Test. Additional exam requirements/recommendations for international students: Required—TOEFL. *Application deadline:* For fall admission, 12/15 for domestic and international students. Applications are processed on a rolling basis. Application fee: $75 ($95 for international students). Electronic applications accepted. *Financial support:* Fellowships and teaching assistantships available. *Faculty research:* Partial and ordinary differential equations, algebra and number theory, geometry, combinatorics, numerical analysis, probability. *Application contact:* Mathematics Graduate Program, E-mail: gradprog@math.umn.edu. Web site: http:// www.math.umn.edu.

University of North Texas, Toulouse Graduate School, College of Business, Department of Information Technology and Decision Sciences, Denton, TX 76203. Offers business computer information systems (PhD); decision technologies (MS); information technology (MS); management science (PhD). Part-time and evening/ weekend programs available. *Degree requirements:* For doctorate, comprehensive exam, thesis/dissertation. *Entrance requirements:* For master's, GMAT; for doctorate, GMAT or GRE General Test. Additional exam requirements/recommendations for international students: Recommended—TOEFL (minimum score 550 paper-based; 213 computer-based; 79 iBT). Electronic applications accepted. *Expenses:* Tuition, state resident: part-time $100 per credit hour. Tuition, nonresident: part-time $413 per credit hour. *Faculty research:* Large scale IS, business intelligence, security, applied statistics, quality and reliability management.

University of Oregon, Graduate School, Charles H. Lundquist College of Business, Department of Decision Sciences, Eugene, OR 97403. Offers MA, MS. *Entrance requirements:* For master's, GMAT. *Faculty research:* Time-series analysis, production scheduling, nonparametric methods, decision theory.

University of Pittsburgh, Katz Graduate School of Business, Doctoral Program in Business Administration, Pittsburgh, PA 15260. Offers accounting (PhD); finance (PhD); information systems (PhD); marketing (PhD); operations/decision sciences/artificial intelligence (PhD); organizational behavior and human resource management (PhD); strategic planning (PhD). *Accreditation:* AACSB. *Faculty:* 54 full-time (16 women). *Students:* 51 full-time (21 women); includes 9 minority (4 Black or African American, non-Hispanic/Latino; 4 Asian, non-Hispanic/Latino; 1 Hispanic/Latino), 23 international. 373 applicants, 7% accepted, 10 enrolled. In 2011, 6 doctorates awarded. *Degree requirements:* For doctorate, comprehensive exam, thesis/dissertation. *Entrance requirements:* For doctorate, GMAT or GRE. Additional exam requirements/ recommendations for international students: Required—TOEFL. *Application deadline:* For fall admission, 2/1 priority date for domestic students, 2/1 for international students. Applications are processed on a rolling basis. Application fee: $50. Electronic applications accepted. *Expenses:* Tuition, state resident: full-time $18,774; part-time $760 per credit. Tuition, nonresident: full-time $30,736; part-time $1258 per credit. *Required fees:* $740; $200 per term. Tuition and fees vary according to program. *Financial support:* In 2011–12, 38 students received support, including 29 research assistantships with full tuition reimbursements available (averaging $19,400 per year), 10 teaching assistantships with full tuition reimbursements available (averaging $24,700 per year); fellowships, Federal Work-Study, scholarships/grants, health care benefits, and unspecified assistantships also available. Financial award application deadline: 2/1. *Faculty research:* Accounting statements and reporting, corporate finance, information systems processes, structures and decision-making, consumer behavior and marketing models. *Total annual research expenditures:* $254,031. *Unit head:* Dr. Dennis Galletta, Director, 412-648-1699, Fax: 412-624-3633, E-mail: galletta@katz.pitt.edu. *Application contact:* Carrie Woods, Assistant Director, 412-648-1525, Fax: 412-624-3633, E-mail: cawoods@katz.pitt.edu. Web site: http://www.business.pitt.edu/katz/phd/.

University of Puerto Rico, Río Piedras, College of Business Administration, San Juan, PR 00931-3300. Offers accounting (MBA); finance (MBA, PhD); general business (MBA); human resources management (MBA); international trade and business (MBA, PhD); marketing (MBA); operations management (MBA); quantitative methods (MBA). *Accreditation:* ACBSP. Part-time programs available. *Degree requirements:* For master's, comprehensive exam, thesis or alternative, research project. *Entrance requirements:* For master's, GMAT or PAEG, minimum GPA of 3.0, letter of recommendation; for doctorate, GMAT, PAEG, minimum GPA of 3.0, master degree. *Faculty research:* Management.

University of South Africa, College of Economic and Management Sciences, Pretoria, South Africa. Offers accounting (D Admin, D Com); accounting science (DA); auditing (D Admin, D Com); business administration (M Tech); business economics (D Admin); business leadership (DBL); business management (D Admin, D Com); economic management analysis (M Tech); economics (D Admin, D Com, PhD); human resource development (M Tech); industrial psychology (D Admin, D Com, PhD); logistics (D Com); marketing (M Tech); public administration (D Admin, D Com, DPA, PhD); public management (M Tech); quantitative management (D Admin, D Com); real estate (M Tech); statistics (D Admin, PhD); tourism management (D Admin, D Com); transport economics (D Admin, D Com).

University of Southern California, Graduate School, Dana and David Dornsife College of Letters, Arts and Sciences, Department of Psychology, Los Angeles, CA 90089. Offers brain and cognitive science (PhD); clinical science (PhD); developmental psychology (PhD); human behavior (MHB); quantitative methods (PhD); social psychology (PhD). *Accreditation:* APA. *Degree requirements:* For doctorate, comprehensive exam, thesis/dissertation, one-year internship (for clinical science students). *Entrance requirements:* For doctorate, GRE. Additional exam requirements/ recommendations for international students: Recommended—TOEFL (minimum score 600 paper-based; 250 computer-based; 100 iBT). Electronic applications accepted. *Faculty research:* Affective neuroscience; children and families; vision, culture and ethnicity; intergroup relations; aggression and violence; language and reading development; substance abuse.

The University of Texas at Arlington, Graduate School, College of Business, Department of Finance and Real Estate, Arlington, TX 76019. Offers finance (PhD); quantitative finance (MS); real estate (MS). Part-time and evening/weekend programs available. *Faculty:* 7 full-time (0 women), 1 (woman) part-time/adjunct. *Students:* 23 full-time (8 women), 40 part-time (11 women); includes 19 minority (5 Black or African American, non-Hispanic/Latino; 7 Asian, non-Hispanic/Latino; 6 Hispanic/Latino; 1 Two or more races, non-Hispanic/Latino), 15 international. 47 applicants, 57% accepted, 13 enrolled. In 2011, 42 degrees awarded. *Degree requirements:* For master's, thesis optional; for doctorate, comprehensive exam, thesis/dissertation. *Entrance requirements:* For master's, GMAT/GRE, minimum GPA of 3.0; for doctorate, GMAT/ GRE. Additional exam requirements/recommendations for international students: Required—TOEFL (minimum score 550 paper-based; 213 computer-based; 79 iBT). *Application deadline:* For fall admission, 6/1 priority date for domestic students, 4/1 for international students; for spring admission, 10/15 for domestic students, 9/15 for international students. Applications are processed on a rolling basis. Application fee: $40 ($70 for international students). *Financial support:* In 2011–12, 7 teaching assistantships (averaging $16,857 per year) were awarded; career-related internships or fieldwork, Federal Work-Study, institutionally sponsored loans, and unspecified assistantships also available. Financial award application deadline: 6/1; financial award applicants required to submit FAFSA. *Unit head:* Dr. David Diltz, Chair, 817-272-3705, Fax: 817-272-2252, E-mail: diltz@uta.edu. *Application contact:* Dr. Fred Forgey, Graduate Advisor, 817-272-0359, Fax: 817-272-2252, E-mail: realestate@uta.edu. Web site: http://wweb.uta.edu/finance/.

The University of Texas at Arlington, Graduate School, College of Business, Program in Business Administration, Arlington, TX 76019. Offers accounting (PhD); business statistics (PhD); finance (MBA, PhD); information systems (MBA, PhD); management (MBA, PhD); marketing (MBA, PhD); operations management (MBA, PhD); real estate (MBA). *Accreditation:* AACSB. Part-time and evening/weekend programs available. *Students:* 505 full-time (189 women), 369 part-time (140 women); includes 199 minority (58 Black or African American, non-Hispanic/Latino; 2 American Indian or Alaska Native, non-Hispanic/Latino; 70 Asian, non-Hispanic/Latino; 56 Hispanic/Latino; 1 Native Hawaiian or other Pacific Islander, non-Hispanic/Latino; 12 Two or more races, non-Hispanic/Latino), 306 international. 416 applicants, 81% accepted, 234 enrolled. In 2011, 495 master's, 3 doctorates awarded. *Degree requirements:* For master's, thesis optional; for doctorate, comprehensive exam, thesis/dissertation. *Entrance requirements:* For master's, GMAT or GRE; for doctorate, GMAT, minimum GPA of 3.0 (undergraduate), 3.4 (graduate); 30 hours of graduate course work. Additional exam requirements/recommendations for international students: Required—TOEFL (minimum score 550 paper-based; 213 computer-based; 79 iBT). *Application deadline:* For fall admission, 6/1 for domestic students, 4/1 for international students; for spring admission, 10/15 for domestic students, 9/15 for international students. Applications are processed on a rolling basis. Application fee: $40 ($70 for international students). Electronic applications accepted. *Financial support:* Career-related internships or fieldwork, scholarships/grants, and unspecified assistantships available. Support available to part-time students. Financial award application deadline: 6/1; financial award applicants required to submit FAFSA. *Unit head:* Dr. Edmund Prater, Director of PhD Programs, 817-272-2131, Fax: 817-272-5799. *Application contact:* Melanie McGee, Director of MBA Program, 817-272-3005, Fax: 817-272-5799, E-mail: mwmcgee@uta.edu.

The University of Texas at Austin, Graduate School, College of Education, Department of Educational Psychology, Austin, TX 78712-1111. Offers academic educational psychology (M Ed, MA); counseling psychology (PhD); counselor education (M Ed); human development, culture and learning sciences (PhD); program evaluation (MA); quantitative methods (M Ed, MA, PhD); school psychology (MA, PhD). *Accreditation:* APA (one or more programs are accredited). *Degree requirements:* For master's, thesis optional; for doctorate, thesis/dissertation. *Entrance requirements:* For master's and doctorate, GRE General Test, 3 letters of recommendation. Additional exam requirements/recommendations for international students: Required—TOEFL. *Application deadline:* For fall admission, 1/15 priority date for domestic students, 1/15 for international students; for spring admission, 10/1 priority date for domestic students, 10/ 1 for international students. Applications are processed on a rolling basis. Application fee: $50 ($75 for international students). *Financial support:* Fellowships with full and partial tuition reimbursements, research assistantships with partial tuition reimbursements, teaching assistantships with partial tuition reimbursements, career-related internships or fieldwork, Federal Work-Study, institutionally sponsored loans, scholarships/grants, tuition waivers (full and partial), and unspecified assistantships available. Financial award application deadline: 1/15. *Unit head:* Dr. Cindy Carlson,

Chair, 512-471-0276, Fax: 512-471-1288, E-mail: ccarlson@austin.utexas.edu. *Application contact:* Diane Schallert, Graduate Adviser, 512-232-4835, E-mail: dschallert@mail.utexas.edu. Web site: http://www.edb.utexas.edu/coe/depts/edp/edp.html.

Virginia Commonwealth University, Graduate School, School of Business, Program in Decision Sciences and Business Analytics, Richmond, VA 23284-9005. Offers MBA, MS. *Entrance requirements:* For master's, GMAT. Additional exam requirements/recommendations for international students: Required—TOEFL (minimum score 600 paper-based; 250 computer-based; 100 iBT). *Application deadline:* For fall admission, 7/1 for domestic students; for spring admission, 11/1 for domestic students. Applications are processed on a rolling basis. Application fee: $50. Electronic applications accepted. *Expenses:* Tuition, state resident: full-time $9133; part-time $507 per credit. Tuition, nonresident: full-time $18,777; part-time $1043 per credit. *Required fees:* $77 per credit. Tuition and fees vary according to degree level, campus/location, program and student level. *Financial support:* Fellowships, research assistantships, teaching assistantships, Federal Work-Study, institutionally sponsored loans, and tuition waivers (full and partial) available. Financial award application deadline: 3/15; financial award applicants required to submit FAFSA. *Unit head:* Dr. E. G. Miller, Interim Chair, Department of Management, 804-827-7404, Fax: 804-828-8884, E-mail: egmiller@vcu.edu. *Application contact:* Jana P. McQuaid, Assistant Dean, Master's Programs, 804-828-4622, Fax: 804-828-7174, E-mail: jpmcquaid@vcu.edu. Web site: http://www.business.vcu.edu/graduate/dsba.html.

Virginia Polytechnic Institute and State University, Graduate School, Intercollege, Certificate Program, Blacksburg, VA 24061. Offers collaborative community leadership (Certificate); future professoriate (Certificate); geospatial information technology (Certificate); international research and development (Certificate); macromolecular interfaces with life sciences (Certificate); quantitative resource assessment (Certificate). *Entrance requirements:* Additional exam requirements/recommendations for international students: Required—TOEFL (minimum score 550 paper-based; 213 computer-based). *Application deadline:* For fall admission, 7/1 for domestic and international students; for spring admission, 12/1 for domestic and international students. Application fee: $65. *Expenses:* Tuition, state resident: full-time $10,048; part-time $558.25 per credit hour. Tuition, nonresident: full-time $19,497; part-time $1083.25 per credit hour. *Required fees:* $405 per semester. Tuition and fees vary according to course load, campus/location and program. *Financial support:* Career-related internships or fieldwork, Federal Work-Study, scholarships/grants, health care benefits, and unspecified assistantships available. *Unit head:* Dr. Karen P. DePauw, Vice President and Dean for Graduate Education, 540-231-7581, Fax: 540-231-1670, E-mail: kpdepauw@vt.edu. *Application contact:* Jacqueline Nottingham, Director of Graduate Admissions and Academic Progress, 540-231-3092, Fax: 540-231-3750, E-mail: ntnghm@vt.edu. Web site: http://graduateschool.vt.edu/.

Virginia Polytechnic Institute and State University, VT Online, Blacksburg, VA 24061. Offers advanced transportation systems (Certificate); aerospace engineering (MS); agricultural and life sciences (MSLFS); business information systems (Graduate Certificate); career and technical education (MS); civil engineering (MS); computer engineering (M Eng, MS); decision support systems (Graduate Certificate); eLearning leadership (MA); electrical engineering (M Eng, MS); engineering administration (MEA); environmental engineering (Certificate); environmental politics and policy (Graduate Certificate); environmental sciences and engineering (MS); foundations of political analysis (Graduate Certificate); health product risk management (Graduate Certificate); industrial and systems engineering (MS); information policy and society (Graduate Certificate); information security (Graduate Certificate); information technology (MIT); instructional technology (MA); integrative STEM education (MA Ed); liberal arts (Graduate Certificate); life sciences: health product risk management (MS); natural resources (MNR, Graduate Certificate); networking (Graduate Certificate); nonprofit and nongovernmental organization management (Graduate Certificate); ocean engineering (MS); political science (MA); security studies (Graduate Certificate); software development (Graduate Certificate). *Expenses:* Tuition, state resident: full-time $10,048; part-time $558.25 per credit hour. Tuition, nonresident: full-time $19,497; part-time $1083.25 per credit hour. *Required fees:* $405 per semester. Tuition and fees vary according to course load, campus/location and program. *Application contact:* Graduate School Applications General Assistance, 540-231-8636, Fax: 540-231-2039, E-mail: gradappl@vt.edu. Web site: http://www.vto.vt.edu/.

Section 20
Real Estate

This section contains a directory of institutions offering graduate work in real estate. Additional information about programs listed in the directory but not augmented by an in-depth entry may be obtained by writing directly to the dean of a graduate school or chair of a department at the address given in the directory.

For programs offering related work, see also in this book *Business Administration and Management.*

CONTENTS

Program Directory

Real Estate

American University, Kogod School of Business, Department of Finance, Program in Real Estate, Washington, DC 20016-8044. Offers MS, Certificate. Part-time and evening/weekend programs available. *Students:* 10 full-time (4 women), 9 part-time (4 women); includes 3 minority (1 Black or African American, non-Hispanic/Latino; 2 Asian, non-Hispanic/Latino), 2 international. Average age 29. 26 applicants, 65% accepted, 9 enrolled. In 2011, 3 master's, 2 other advanced degrees awarded. *Entrance requirements:* For master's, GMAT, resume, personal statement, interview. Additional exam requirements/recommendations for international students: Required—TOEFL. *Application deadline:* For fall admission, 2/1 priority date for domestic students; for spring admission, 10/1 priority date for domestic students. Applications are processed on a rolling basis. Application fee: $100. *Expenses: Tuition:* Full-time $24,264; part-time $1348 per credit hour. *Required fees:* $430. Tuition and fees vary according to course load and program. *Financial support:* Fellowships, career-related internships or fieldwork, Federal Work-Study, and institutionally sponsored loans available. Support available to part-time students. Financial award application deadline: 2/1. *Unit head:* Dr. Ronald Anderson, Chair, 202-885-2199, Fax: 202-885-1946, E-mail: randers@american.edu. *Application contact:* Shannon Demko, Director of Admissions, 202-885-1968, Fax: 202-885-11078, E-mail: demko@american.edu. Web site: http://www.american.edu/kogod/.

American University, Kogod School of Business, Master of Business Administration Program, Washington, DC 20016-8044. Offers accounting (MBA); consulting (MBA), including business systems consulting, management consulting; entrepreneurship (MBA); entrepreneurship (Certificate); finance (MBA); global emerging markets (MBA); leadership and strategic human capital management (MBA); marketing (MBA); real estate (MBA); MBA/JD; MBA/LL M; MBA/MA. Part-time and evening/weekend programs available. *Faculty:* 13 full-time (6 women). *Students:* 96 full-time (43 women), 104 part-time (35 women); includes 49 minority (14 Black or African American, non-Hispanic/Latino; 16 Asian, non-Hispanic/Latino; 16 Hispanic/Latino; 1 Native Hawaiian or other Pacific Islander, non-Hispanic/Latino; 2 Two or more races, non-Hispanic/Latino), 22 international. Average age 29. 340 applicants, 52% accepted, 52 enrolled. In 2011, 124 master's awarded. *Entrance requirements:* For master's, GMAT, resume, personal statement, interview. Additional exam requirements/recommendations for international students: Required—TOEFL. *Application deadline:* For fall admission, 2/1 priority date for domestic students; for spring admission, 10/1 priority date for domestic students. Applications are processed on a rolling basis. Application fee: $100. *Expenses:* Contact institution. *Financial support:* In 2011–12, 19 students received support. Fellowships, research assistantships with partial tuition reimbursements available, career-related internships or fieldwork, Federal Work-Study, and institutionally sponsored loans available. Support available to part-time students. Financial award application deadline: 2/1. *Faculty research:* Information technology, decision-aiding methodology, negotiation. *Unit head:* Dr. Stevan R. Holmberg, Chair, 202-885-1921, Fax: 202-885-1916, E-mail: sholmbe@american.edu. *Application contact:* Shannon Demko, Director of Admissions, 202-885-1968, Fax: 202-885-1078, E-mail: demko@american.edu. Web site: http://www.american.edu/kogod/.

Arizona State University, W. P. Carey School of Business, Department of Marketing, Tempe, AZ 85287-4106. Offers business administration (marketing) (PhD); real estate development (MRED). Part-time and evening/weekend programs available. Postbaccalaureate distance learning degree programs offered. *Degree requirements:* For master's, thesis or alternative, capstone project, interactive Program of Study (iPOS) submitted before completing 50 percent of required credit hours; for doctorate, comprehensive exam, thesis/dissertation, interactive Program of Study (iPOS) submitted before completing 50 percent of required credit hours. *Entrance requirements:* For master's, GMAT, GRE, or LSAT, minimum GPA of 3.0 in last 2 years of work leading to bachelor's degree, 3 personal references, resume, official transcripts, personal statement; for doctorate, GMAT, minimum GPA of 3.0 in last 2 years of work leading to bachelor's degree, 3 letters of recommendation, personal statement/essay. Additional exam requirements/recommendations for international students: Required—TOEFL (minimum score 550 paper-based; 213 computer-based; 80 iBT), IELTS (minimum score 6.5). Electronic applications accepted. *Expenses:* Contact institution. *Faculty research:* Service marketing and management, strategic marketing, customer portfolio management, characteristics and skills of high-performing managers, market orientation, market segmentation, consumer behavior, marketing strategy, new product development, management of innovation, social influences on consumption, e-commerce, market research methodology.

Auburn University, Graduate School, Interdepartmental Programs, Program in Real Estate Development, Auburn University, AL 36849. Offers MRED. *Faculty:* 10 full-time (1 woman). *Students:* 30 part-time (2 women); includes 5 minority (4 Black or African American, non-Hispanic/Latino; 1 Asian, non-Hispanic/Latino). Average age 34. 27 applicants, 74% accepted, 14 enrolled. *Expenses:* Tuition, state resident: full-time $7290; part-time $405 per credit hour. Tuition, nonresident: full-time $21,870; part-time $1215 per credit hour. *International tuition:* $22,000 full-time. *Required fees:* $1402. *Unit head:* Jana Smith, Assistant Director, 334-844-5078, E-mail: mred.info@auburn.edu. *Application contact:* Dr. George Flowers, Dean of the Graduate School, 334-844-2125. Web site: http://mred.auburn.edu/.

Bernard M. Baruch College of the City University of New York, Zicklin School of Business, Department of Real Estate, New York, NY 10010-5585. Offers MBA, MS.

California State University, Sacramento, Office of Graduate Studies, College of Business Administration, Sacramento, CA 95819-6088. Offers accountancy (MS); business administration (MBA); human resources (MBA); urban land development (MBA). *Accreditation:* AACSB. Part-time and evening/weekend programs available. *Faculty:* 61 full-time (19 women), 28 part-time/adjunct (7 women). *Students:* 39 full-time, 91 part-time; includes 40 minority (6 Black or African American, non-Hispanic/Latino; 2 American Indian or Alaska Native, non-Hispanic/Latino; 12 Asian, non-Hispanic/Latino; 11 Hispanic/Latino; 4 Native Hawaiian or other Pacific Islander, non-Hispanic/Latino; 5 Two or more races, non-Hispanic/Latino), 16 international. Average age 29. 330 applicants, 64% accepted, 54 enrolled. In 2011, 212 master's awarded. *Degree requirements:* For master's, thesis or alternative, writing proficiency exam. *Entrance requirements:* For master's, GMAT. Additional exam requirements/recommendations for international students: Required—TOEFL. *Application deadline:* For fall admission, 2/1 for domestic students, 3/1 for international students; for spring admission, 9/15 for domestic students, 9/30 for international students. Applications are processed on a rolling basis. Application fee: $55. Electronic applications accepted. *Financial support:* Research assistantships, teaching assistantships, career-related internships or fieldwork, and Federal Work-Study available. Support available to part-time students. Financial award applicants required to submit FAFSA. *Unit head:* Dr. Sanjay Varshney, Dean, 916-278-6942, Fax: 916-278-5793, E-mail: cba@csus.edu. *Application contact:* Jose Martinez, Outreach and Graduate Diversity Coordinator, 916-278-6470, Fax: 916-278-5669, E-mail: martinj@skymail.csus.edu. Web site: http://www.cba.csus.edu.

Central European University, CEU Business School, Budapest, Hungary. Offers executive business administration (EMBA); finance (MBA); general management (MBA); information technology management (MBA); marketing (MBA); real estate management (MBA). Part-time and evening/weekend programs available. *Faculty:* 17 full-time (4 women), 12 part-time/adjunct (1 woman). *Students:* 31 full-time (12 women), 84 part-time (16 women). Average age 34. 162 applicants, 35% accepted, 31 enrolled. In 2011, 83 degrees awarded. *Degree requirements:* For master's, one foreign language. *Entrance requirements:* For master's, GMAT. Additional exam requirements/recommendations for international students: Required—TOEFL (minimum score 570 paper-based; 230 computer-based); Recommended—IELTS (minimum score 6.5). *Application deadline:* For fall admission, 5/15 priority date for domestic students, 5/22 for international students; for winter admission, 11/15 priority date for domestic students, 11/10 for international students. Applications are processed on a rolling basis. Application fee: $0. Electronic applications accepted. Tuition charges are reported in euros. *Expenses: Tuition:* Full-time 11,000 euros. *Financial support:* Tuition waivers (partial) available. *Faculty research:* Social and ethical business, marketing, international business. *Unit head:* Dr. Mel Horwitch, Dean and Managing Director, 361-887-5050, E-mail: mhorwitch@ceubusiness.com. *Application contact:* Agnes Schram, Admissions Manager, 361-887-5111, Fax: 361-887-5133, E-mail: mba@ceubusiness.com. Web site: http://www.ceubusiness.com.

Clemson University, Graduate School, College of Architecture, Arts, and Humanities, Department of Planning and Landscape Architecture and College of Business and Behavioral Science, Program in Real Estate Development, Clemson, SC 29634. Offers MRED. *Students:* 34 full-time (7 women); includes 2 minority (1 Black or African American, non-Hispanic/Latino; 1 Hispanic/Latino), 2 international. Average age 27. 31 applicants, 81% accepted, 14 enrolled. In 2011, 19 master's awarded. *Entrance requirements:* For master's, GRE or GMAT, 3 letters of recommendation, resume, personal statement. Additional exam requirements/recommendations for international students: Required—TOEFL (minimum score 600 paper-based). *Application deadline:* For fall admission, 2/15 priority date for domestic students, 2/15 for international students. Applications are processed on a rolling basis. Application fee: $70 ($80 for international students). Electronic applications accepted. *Financial support:* In 2011–12, 5 students received support, including 1 fellowship with partial tuition reimbursement available (averaging $5,000 per year); research assistantships with partial tuition reimbursements available, teaching assistantships with partial tuition reimbursements available, career-related internships or fieldwork, scholarships/grants, health care benefits, and unspecified assistantships also available. *Faculty research:* Real estate education, real estate investment/finance, sustainability, public private partnership, historic preservation. *Unit head:* Dr. Elaine M. Worzala, Interim Director, 864-656-4258, Fax: 864-656-7519, E-mail: eworzal@clemson.edu. *Application contact:* Amy Matthews, Program Coordinator, 864-656-4257, Fax: 864-656-7519, E-mail: matthe3@clemson.edu.

Cleveland State University, College of Graduate Studies, Maxine Goodman Levin College of Urban Affairs, Program in Environmental Studies, Cleveland, OH 44115. Offers environmental nonprofit management (MAES); environmental planning (MAES); geographic information systems (Certificate); policy and administration (MAES); sustainable economic development (MAES); urban economic development (Certificate); urban real estate development and finance (Certificate); JD/MAES. Part-time and evening/weekend programs available. *Faculty:* 26 full-time (10 women), 3 part-time/adjunct (0 women). *Students:* 12 full-time (5 women), 23 part-time (12 women); includes 1 minority (Asian, non-Hispanic/Latino), 4 international. 18 applicants, 61% accepted, 6 enrolled. In 2011, 9 master's awarded. *Degree requirements:* For master's, thesis or alternative, exit project. *Entrance requirements:* For master's, GRE General Test (minimum score: verbal and quantitative in 40th percentile, analytical writing 4.0), minimum GPA of 3.0. Additional exam requirements/recommendations for international students: Required—TOEFL (minimum score 525 paper-based; 197 computer-based; 65 iBT). *Application deadline:* For fall admission, 7/15 priority date for domestic students, 5/15 for international students; for spring admission, 11/1 for international students. Applications are processed on a rolling basis. Application fee: $30. Electronic applications accepted. *Expenses:* Tuition, state resident: full-time $6416; part-time $494 per credit hour. Tuition, nonresident: full-time $12,074; part-time $929 per credit hour. *Financial support:* In 2011–12, 6 students received support, including 2 research assistantships with full and partial tuition reimbursements available (averaging $7,200 per year), 4 teaching assistantships with full and partial tuition reimbursements available (averaging $2,400 per year); career-related internships or fieldwork, scholarships/grants, traineeships, and unspecified assistantships also available. Support available to part-time students. Financial award application deadline: 3/1; financial award applicants required to submit FAFSA. *Faculty research:* Environmental policy and administration, environmental planning, geographic information systems (GIS), urban sustainability planning and management, energy policy, land re-use. *Unit head:* Dr. Sanda Kaufman, Director, 216-687-2367, Fax: 216-687-9342, E-mail: s.kaufman@csuohio.edu. *Application contact:* Joan Demko, Graduate Academic Program Specialist, 216-523-7522, Fax: 216-687-5398, E-mail: urbanprograms@csuohio.edu. Web site: http://urban.csuohio.edu/academics/graduate/maes/.

Cleveland State University, College of Graduate Studies, Maxine Goodman Levin College of Urban Affairs, Program in Urban Planning, Design, and Development, Cleveland, OH 44115. Offers economic development (MUPDD); environmental sustainability (MUPDD); geographic information systems (Certificate); historic preservation (MUPDD); housing and neighborhood development (MUPDD); urban economic development (Certificate); urban real estate development and finance (MUPDD, Certificate); JD/MUPDD. *Accreditation:* ACSP. Part-time and evening/weekend programs available. *Faculty:* 32 full-time (19 women), 8 part-time/adjunct (4 women). *Students:* 30 full-time (10 women), 28 part-time (17 women); includes 9 minority (6 Black or African American, non-Hispanic/Latino; 3 Hispanic/Latino), 5 international. Average age 38. 91 applicants, 45% accepted, 21 enrolled. In 2011, 24 master's awarded. *Degree requirements:* For master's, thesis or alternative, capstone seminar. *Entrance requirements:* For master's, GRE General Test (minimum score in 50th percentile verbal and quantitative, 4.0 analytical writing), minimum GPA of 3.0. Additional exam requirements/recommendations for international students: Required—TOEFL (minimum score 525 paper-based; 197 computer-based; 65 iBT). *Application deadline:* For fall admission, 7/15 priority date for domestic students, 5/15 for international students; for spring admission, 11/1 for international students. Applications are processed on a rolling basis. Application fee: $30. Electronic applications accepted. *Expenses:* Tuition, state resident: full-time $6416; part-time $494 per credit hour. Tuition, nonresident: full-time $12,074; part-time $929 per credit hour. *Financial support:* In 2011–12, 15 students received support, including 10 research assistantships with full and partial tuition reimbursements available (averaging $6,960 per year), 5 teaching assistantships with full and partial tuition reimbursements available (averaging $6,960 per year); career-related internships or fieldwork, Federal Work-Study, scholarships/grants, tuition waivers, and unspecified assistantships also available. Support available to part-time students. Financial award application deadline: 3/1; financial award applicants required to submit FAFSA. *Faculty research:* Housing and neighborhood development, urban housing policy, environmental sustainability, economic development, GIS and planning decision support. *Unit head:* Dr. William Dennis Keating, Director, 216-687-2298, Fax: 216-687-2013, E-mail: w.keating@csuohio.edu. *Application contact:* Joan Demko, Graduate Program Coordinator, 216-523-7522, Fax: 216-687-5398, E-mail: urbanprograms@csuohio.edu. Web site: http://urban.csuohio.edu/academics/graduate/mupdd/.

Cleveland State University, College of Graduate Studies, Maxine Goodman Levin College of Urban Affairs, Program in Urban Studies, Cleveland, OH 44115. Offers law and public policy (MS); public finance (MS); urban economic development (Certificate); urban policy analysis (MS); urban real estate development (MS); urban real estate development and finance (Certificate). PhD program offered jointly with The University of Akron. Part-time and evening/weekend programs available. *Faculty:* 26 full-time (10 women), 20 part-time/adjunct (11 women). *Students:* 16 full-time (10 women), 35 part-time (18 women); includes 7 minority (all Black or African American, non-Hispanic/Latino), 17 international. Average age 37. 63 applicants, 49% accepted, 18 enrolled. In 2011, 7 master's, 5 doctorates, 6 other advanced degrees awarded. *Degree requirements:* For master's, thesis or alternative, exit project; for doctorate, comprehensive exam, thesis/dissertation. *Entrance requirements:* For master's, GRE General Test, minimum GPA of 3.0; for doctorate, GRE General Test, minimum GPA of 3.5. Additional exam requirements/recommendations for international students: Required—TOEFL (minimum score 525 paper-based; 197 computer-based; 65 iBT). *Application deadline:* For fall admission, 1/15 priority date for domestic students, 1/15 for international students. Applications are processed on a rolling basis. Application fee: $30. Electronic applications accepted. *Expenses:* Tuition, state resident: full-time $6416; part-time $494 per credit hour. Tuition, nonresident: full-time $12,074; part-time $929 per credit hour. *Financial support:* In 2011–12, 15 students received support, including 8 research assistantships with full and partial tuition reimbursements available (averaging $9,000 per year), 7 teaching assistantships with full and partial tuition reimbursements available (averaging $2,400 per year); career-related internships or fieldwork, scholarships/grants, traineeships, and unspecified assistantships also available. Support available to part-time students. Financial award application deadline: 3/1; financial award applicants required to submit FAFSA. *Faculty research:* Environmental issues, economic development, urban and public policy, public management. *Unit head:* Dr. Mittie Davis Jones, Director, 216-687-3861, Fax: 216-687-9342, E-mail: m.d.jones97@csuohio.edu. *Application contact:* Joan Demko, Graduate Academic Program Specialist, 216-523-7522, Fax: 216-687-5398, E-mail: urbanprograms@csuohio.edu. Web site: http://urban.csuohio.edu/academics/graduate/msus/.

Columbia University, Graduate School of Architecture, Planning, and Preservation, Program in Real Estate Development, New York, NY 10027. Offers MS. *Degree requirements:* For master's, thesis. *Entrance requirements:* For master's, GRE General Test.

Columbia University, Graduate School of Business, MBA Program, New York, NY 10027. Offers accounting (MBA); decision, risk, and operations (MBA); entrepreneurship (MBA); finance and economics (MBA); healthcare and pharmaceutical management (MBA); human resource management (MBA); international business (MBA); leadership and ethics (MBA); management (MBA); marketing (MBA); media (MBA); private equity (MBA); real estate (MBA); social enterprise (MBA); value investing (MBA); DDS/MBA; JD/MBA; MBA/MIA; MBA/MPH; MBA/MS; MD/MBA. *Entrance requirements:* For master's, GMAT, 2 letters of recommendation. Additional exam requirements/recommendations for international students: Required—TOEFL. Electronic applications accepted. *Expenses:* Contact institution. *Faculty research:* Human decision making and behavioral research; real estate market and mortgage defaults; financial crisis and corporate governance; international business; security analysis and accounting.

Cornell University, Graduate School, Graduate Fields of Architecture, Art and Planning, Field of Real Estate, Ithaca, NY 14853-0001. Offers MPSRE. *Faculty:* 18 full-time (0 women). *Students:* 42 full-time (9 women); includes 13 minority (4 Black or African American, non-Hispanic/Latino; 6 Asian, non-Hispanic/Latino; 3 Hispanic/Latino), 17 international. Average age 28. 90 applicants, 48% accepted, 25 enrolled. In 2011, 24 master's awarded. *Degree requirements:* For master's, project paper. *Entrance requirements:* For master's, GMAT, 2 letters of recommendation, resume. Additional exam requirements/recommendations for international students: Required—TOEFL (minimum score 600 paper-based; 250 computer-based; 77 iBT). *Application deadline:* For fall admission, 1/15 for domestic students. Application fee: $95. Electronic applications accepted. *Financial support:* In 2011–12, 1 fellowship with full tuition reimbursement was awarded; research assistantships with full tuition reimbursements, teaching assistantships with full tuition reimbursements, institutionally sponsored loans, scholarships/grants, health care benefits, and unspecified assistantships also available. Financial award applicants required to submit FAFSA. *Faculty research:* Smart growth, economic development, urban redevelopment, development financing, securitization of real estate. *Unit head:* Director of Graduate Studies, 607-255-7110, Fax: 607-255-0242. *Application contact:* Graduate Field Assistant, 607-255-7110, Fax: 607-255-0242, E-mail: real_estate@cornell.edu. Web site: http://www.gradschool.cornell.edu/fields.php?id-96&a-2.

DePaul University, Charles H. Kellstadt Graduate School of Business, Department of Finance, Chicago, IL 60604-2287. Offers behavioral finance (MBA); computational finance (MS); finance (MBA, MSF); financial analysis (MBA); financial management and control (MBA); international marketing and finance (MBA); managerial finance (MBA); real estate (MS); real estate finance and investment (MBA); strategy, execution and valuation (MBA). Part-time and evening/weekend programs available. *Faculty:* 26 full-time (5 women), 31 part-time/adjunct (4 women). *Students:* 454 full-time (138 women), 190 part-time (41 women); includes 85 minority (13 Black or African American, non-Hispanic/Latino; 53 Asian, non-Hispanic/Latino; 17 Hispanic/Latino; 2 Two or more races, non-Hispanic/Latino), 129 international. In 2011, 239 master's awarded. *Entrance requirements:* For master's, GMAT, 2 letters of recommendation, resume. Additional exam requirements/recommendations for international students: Required—TOEFL (minimum score 550 paper-based; 213 computer-based; 80 iBT). *Application deadline:* For fall admission, 7/1 for domestic students, 6/1 for international students; for winter admission, 10/1 for domestic students, 9/1 for international students; for spring admission, 2/1 for domestic students, 1/1 for international students. Applications are processed on a rolling basis. Application fee: $60. Electronic applications accepted. *Financial support:* In 2011–12, 10 students received support, including 10 research assistantships (averaging $15,120 per year); scholarships/grants and unspecified assistantships also available. Financial award application deadline: 6/1; financial award applicants required to submit FAFSA. *Faculty research:* Derivatives, valuation, international finance, real estate, corporate finance, behavioral finance. *Unit head:* Ali M. Fatemi, Professor and Chair, 312-362-8826, Fax: 312-362-6566, E-mail: afatemi@depaul.edu. *Application contact:* Melissa Booth, Director of Admission and Recruitment, 312-362-6353, Fax: 312-362-6677, E-mail: kgsb@depaul.edu. Web site: http://www.fin.depaul.edu/.

DePaul University, Charles H. Kellstadt Graduate School of Business, Department of Real Estate, Chicago, IL 60604-2287. Offers real estate (MS); real estate finance and investment (MBA). Part-time and evening/weekend programs available. *Faculty:* 6 full-time (1 woman), 10 part-time/adjunct (1 woman). *Students:* 44 full-time (13 women), 22 part-time (4 women); includes 8 minority (2 Black or African American, non-Hispanic/Latino; 3 Asian, non-Hispanic/Latino; 2 Hispanic/Latino; 1 Two or more races, non-Hispanic/Latino), 4 international. Average age 29. *Entrance requirements:* For master's, essay, 3 letters of recommendation. Additional exam requirements/recommendations for international students: Required—TOEFL; Recommended—IELTS. *Financial support:* In 2011–12, 2 teaching assistantships with full and partial tuition reimbursements were awarded; career-related internships or fieldwork and scholarships/grants also available. Financial award applicants required to submit FAFSA. *Unit head:* Susanne Cannon, Chairman/Director, 312-362-5905, Fax: 312-362-5907, E-mail: scannon@depaul.edu. *Application contact:* Melissa Carnwell, Director of Recruiting and Admission, 312-362-8810, Fax: 312-362-6677, E-mail: kgsb@depaul.edu.

Drexel University, Goodwin College of Professional Studies, School of Technology and Professional Studies, Philadelphia, PA 19104-2875. Offers construction management (MS); engineering technology (MS); food science (MS); hospitality management (MS); professional studies: creativity studies (MS); professional studies: e-learning leadership (MS); professional studies: homeland security management (MS); project management (MS); property management (MS); sport management (MS). Postbaccalaureate distance learning degree programs offered.

Florida International University, Alvah H. Chapman, Jr. Graduate School of Business, Department of Finance and Real Estate, Miami, FL 33199. Offers finance (MSF); international real estate (MS); real estate (MS). Part-time and evening/weekend programs available. *Entrance requirements:* For master's, GMAT or GRE, minimum GPA of 3.0 (upper-level coursework); letter of intent; resume. Additional exam requirements/recommendations for international students: Required—TOEFL (minimum score 550 paper-based; 213 computer-based; 80 iBT) or IELTS (minimum score 6.5). Electronic applications accepted. *Expenses:* Contact institution. *Faculty research:* Investment, corporate and international finance, commercial real estate.

Florida International University, Alvah H. Chapman, Jr. Graduate School of Business, Program in Real Estate, Miami, FL 33199. Offers international real estate (MS); real estate (MS). Part-time and evening/weekend programs available. *Entrance requirements:* For master's, GMAT or GRE, letter of intent; resume. Additional exam requirements/recommendations for international students: Required—TOEFL (minimum score 550 paper-based; 213 computer-based; 80 iBT) or IELTS (minimum score 6.5). Electronic applications accepted. *Expenses:* Contact institution. *Faculty research:* International real estate, real estate investments, commercial real estate.

George Mason University, School of Management, Fairfax, VA 22030. Offers accounting (MS); business administration (EMBA, MBA); management of secure information systems (MS); real estate development (MS); technology management (MS). Part-time and evening/weekend programs available. Postbaccalaureate distance learning degree programs offered. *Faculty:* 79 full-time (25 women), 49 part-time/adjunct (14 women). *Students:* 170 full-time (65 women), 349 part-time (113 women); includes 116 minority (30 Black or African American, non-Hispanic/Latino; 1 American Indian or Alaska Native, non-Hispanic/Latino; 64 Asian, non-Hispanic/Latino; 15 Hispanic/Latino; 1 Native Hawaiian or other Pacific Islander, non-Hispanic/Latino; 5 Two or more races, non-Hispanic/Latino), 49 international. Average age 30. 408 applicants, 58% accepted, 152 enrolled. In 2011, 273 master's awarded. *Entrance requirements:* For master's, GMAT. Additional exam requirements/recommendations for international students: Required—TOEFL (minimum score 570 paper-based; 230 computer-based; 88 iBT), IELTS, Pearson Test of English. *Application deadline:* Applications are processed on a rolling basis. Application fee: $65 ($80 for international students). Electronic applications accepted. *Expenses:* Tuition, state resident: full-time $8750; part-time $364.58 per credit. Tuition, nonresident: full-time $24,092; part-time $1003.83 per credit. *Required fees:* $2514; $104.75 per credit. *Financial support:* In 2011–12, 50 students received support, including 35 research assistantships with full and partial tuition reimbursements available (averaging $9,267 per year), 19 teaching assistantships with full and partial tuition reimbursements available (averaging $8,253 per year); career-related internships or fieldwork, Federal Work-Study, scholarships/grants, unspecified assistantships, and health care benefits (full-time research or teaching assistantship recipients) also available. Financial award application deadline: 3/1; financial award applicants required to submit FAFSA. *Faculty research:* Current leading global issues: offshore outsourcing, international financial risk, comparative systems of innovation. *Total annual research expenditures:* $382,706. *Unit head:* Jorge Haddock, Dean, 703-993-1875, E-mail: jhaddock@gmu.edu. *Application contact:* Melanie Pflugshaupt, Administrative Coordinator to Dean's Office, 703-993-3638, E-mail: mpflugsh@gmu.edu. Web site: http://som.gmu.edu/.

Georgetown University, Graduate School of Arts and Sciences, School of Continuing Studies, Washington, DC 20057. Offers American studies (MALS); Catholic studies (MALS); classical civilizations (MALS); disability studies (MPS); ethics and the professions (MALS); human resources management (MPS); humanities (MALS); individualized study (MALS); international affairs (MALS); Islam and Muslim-Christian relations (MALS); journalism (MPS); liberal studies (DLS); literature and society (MALS); medieval and early modern European studies (MALS); public relations and corporate communications (MPS); real estate (MPS); religious studies (MALS); social and public policy (MALS); sports industry management (MPS); the theory and practice of American democracy (MALS); visual culture (MALS). *Entrance requirements:* Additional exam requirements/recommendations for international students: Required—TOEFL.

The George Washington University, School of Business, Department of Finance, Washington, DC 20052. Offers finance (MSF, PhD); finance and investments (MBA); real estate and urban development (MBA). Part-time and evening/weekend programs available. *Faculty:* 17 full-time (4 women), 4 part-time/adjunct (1 woman). *Students:* 106 full-time (41 women), 45 part-time (11 women); includes 33 minority (7 Black or African American, non-Hispanic/Latino; 11 Asian, non-Hispanic/Latino; 10 Hispanic/Latino; 5 Two or more races, non-Hispanic/Latino), 87 international. Average age 29. 728 applicants, 25% accepted, 93 enrolled. In 2011, 48 master's awarded. *Degree requirements:* For doctorate, thesis/dissertation. *Entrance requirements:* For master's, GMAT; for doctorate, GMAT or GRE. Additional exam requirements/recommendations for international students: Required—TOEFL. *Application deadline:* For fall admission, 4/1 priority date for domestic students; for spring admission, 10/1 for domestic students. Applications are processed on a rolling basis. Application fee: $75. *Financial support:* In 2011–12, 38 students received support. Fellowships, teaching assistantships, career-related internships or fieldwork, Federal Work-Study, and institutionally sponsored loans available. Financial award application deadline: 4/1. *Unit head:* Mark S. Klock, Chair, 202-994-5996, E-mail: klock@gwu.edu. *Application contact:* Kristin Williams, Assistant Vice President for Graduate and Special Enrollment Management, 202-994-0467, Fax: 202-994-0371, E-mail: ksw@gwu.edu.

Georgia State University, J. Mack Robinson College of Business, Department of Real Estate, Atlanta, GA 30302-3083. Offers MBA, MSRE, PhD, Certificate. Part-time and evening/weekend programs available. Terminal master's awarded for partial completion of doctoral program. *Degree requirements:* For doctorate, comprehensive exam, thesis/dissertation. *Entrance requirements:* For master's and doctorate, GMAT. Additional exam requirements/recommendations for international students: Required—TOEFL (minimum score 610 paper-based; 255 computer-based; 101 iBT). Electronic applications accepted.

Hofstra University, Frank G. Zarb School of Business, Department of Finance, Hempstead, NY 11549. Offers banking (Advanced Certificate); business administration (MBA), including finance, real estate management (MBA, MS); corporate finance (Advanced Certificate); finance (MS), including investment analysis; investment management (Advanced Certificate); quantitative finance (MS), including real estate management (MBA, MS). Part-time and evening/weekend programs available. *Faculty:* 13 full-time (2 women), 4 part-time/adjunct (2 women). *Students:* 222 full-time (91 women), 98 part-time (23 women); includes 24 minority (6 Black or African American, non-Hispanic/Latino; 15 Asian, non-Hispanic/Latino; 3 Hispanic/Latino), 198 international. Average age 26. 666 applicants, 63% accepted, 106 enrolled. In 2011, 124 master's awarded. *Degree requirements:* For master's, capstone course (for MBA); thesis (for MS); minimum GPA of 3.0. *Entrance requirements:* For master's, GMAT/GRE, 2 letters of recommendation; resume; essay. Additional exam requirements/recommendations for international students: Required—TOEFL (minimum score 550 paper-based; 213 computer-based; 80 iBT); Recommended—IELTS (minimum score 6). *Application deadline:* Applications are processed on a rolling basis. Application fee: $70 ($75 for international students). Electronic applications accepted. *Expenses:* Contact institution. *Financial support:* In 2011–12, 32 students received support, including 26 fellowships with full and partial tuition reimbursements available (averaging $8,389 per year), 1 research assistantship with full and partial tuition reimbursement available (averaging $4,925 per year); Federal Work-Study, institutionally sponsored loans, scholarships/grants, and tuition waivers (full and partial) also available. Support available to part-time students. Financial award applicants required to submit FAFSA. *Faculty research:* International finance; investments; banking, corporate finance; real estate; derivatives. *Unit head:* Dr. K. G. Viswanathan, Chairperson, 516-463-5699, Fax: 516-463-4834, E-mail: finkgv@hofstra.edu. *Application contact:* Carol Drummer, Dean of Graduate Admissions, 516-463-4876, Fax: 516-463-4664, E-mail: gradstudent@hofstra.edu. Web site: http://www.hofstra.edu/business/.

Instituto Centroamericano de Administración de Empresas, Graduate Programs, La Garita, Costa Rica. Offers agribusiness management (MIAM); business administration (EMBA); finance (MBA); real estate management (MGREM); sustainable development (MBA); technology (MBA). *Degree requirements:* For master's, comprehensive exam, essay. *Entrance requirements:* For master's, GMAT or GRE General Test, fluency in Spanish, interview, letters of recommendation, minimum 1 year of work experience. Additional exam requirements/recommendations for international students: Recommended—TOEFL. Electronic applications accepted. *Faculty research:* Competitiveness, production.

John Marshall Law School, Graduate and Professional Programs, Chicago, IL 60604-3968. Offers employee benefits (LL M, MS); global legal studies (LL M); information technology (MS); information technology and privacy law (LL M); intellectual property (LL M, MS); international business and trade (LL M); law (JD); real estate (LL M, MS); taxation (LL M, MS); trial advocacy (LL M); JD/LL M; JD/MA; JD/MBA; JD/MPA. JD/MBA offered jointly with Dominican University; JD/MA and JD/MPA with Roosevelt University. *Accreditation:* ABA. Part-time and evening/weekend programs available. *Faculty:* 69 full-time (22 women), 133 part-time/adjunct (40 women). *Students:* 1,305 full-time (598 women), 368 part-time (180 women); includes 385 minority (148 Black or African American, non-Hispanic/Latino; 15 American Indian or Alaska Native, non-Hispanic/Latino; 108 Asian, non-Hispanic/Latino; 110 Hispanic/Latino; 2 Native Hawaiian or other Pacific Islander, non-Hispanic/Latino; 2 Two or more races, non-Hispanic/Latino), 40 international. Average age 27. 3,513 applicants, 48% accepted, 365 enrolled. In 2011, 86 master's, 403 doctorates awarded. *Degree requirements:* For master's, 24 credits; for doctorate, 90 credits. *Entrance requirements:* For master's, JD; for doctorate, LSAT. Additional exam requirements/recommendations for international students: Required—TOEFL. *Application deadline:* For fall admission, 3/1 priority date for domestic students, 3/1 for international students; for spring admission, 10/15 priority date for domestic students, 10/15 for international students. Applications are processed on a rolling basis. Application fee: $0. Electronic applications accepted. *Expenses:* Contact institution. *Financial support:* In 2011–12, 1,350 students received support. Scholarships/grants and tuition waivers (full and partial) available. Support available to part-time students. Financial award application deadline: 6/1; financial award applicants required to submit FAFSA. *Unit head:* John Corkery, Dean, 312-427-2737. *Application contact:* William B. Powers, Associate Dean of Admission and Student Affairs, 800-537-4280, Fax: 312-427-5136, E-mail: admission@jmls.edu.

The Johns Hopkins University, Carey Business School, The Edward St. John Department of Real Estate, Baltimore, MD 21218-2699. Offers MS. Part-time and evening/weekend programs available. *Degree requirements:* For master's, 36 credits including final project. *Entrance requirements:* For master's, GMAT, GRE, or LSAT (full-time only), minimum GPA of 3.0, resume, work experience, two letters of recommendation. Additional exam requirements/recommendations for international students: Required—TOEFL (minimum score 600 paper-based; 250 computer-based; 100 iBT). Electronic applications accepted.

Marquette University, Graduate School of Management, Department of Economics, Milwaukee, WI 53201-1881. Offers business economics (MSAE); financial economics (MSAE); international economics (MSAE); marketing research (MSAE); real estate economics (MSAE). Part-time and evening/weekend programs available. *Faculty:* 14 full-time (5 women), 3 part-time/adjunct (0 women). *Students:* 36 full-time (8 women), 37 part-time (13 women); includes 5 minority (2 Black or African American, non-Hispanic/Latino; 2 Hispanic/Latino; 1 Two or more races, non-Hispanic/Latino), 18 international. Average age 26. 120 applicants, 62% accepted, 27 enrolled. In 2011, 22 master's awarded. *Degree requirements:* For master's, comprehensive exam, professional project. *Entrance requirements:* For master's, GMAT or GRE General Test. Additional exam requirements/recommendations for international students: Required—TOEFL (minimum score 550 paper-based; 85 computer-based; 88 iBT), IELTS (minimum score 6.5), Pearson Test of English. *Application deadline:* For fall admission, 2/15 for domestic and international students. Applications are processed on a rolling basis. Application fee: $50. Electronic applications accepted. *Expenses: Tuition:* Full-time $17,010; part-time $945 per credit hour. Tuition and fees vary according to program. *Financial support:* In 2011–12, 2 fellowships, 7 teaching assistantships were awarded; research assistantships, Federal Work-Study, institutionally sponsored loans, scholarships/grants, and tuition waivers (full and partial) also available. Support available to part-time students. Financial award application deadline: 2/15. *Faculty research:* Monetary and fiscal policy in open economy, housing and regional migration, political economy of taxation and state/local government. *Total annual research expenditures:* $16,889. *Unit head:* Dr. Abdur Chowdhury, Chair, 414-288-6915, Fax: 414-288-5757. *Application contact:* Farrokh Nourzad, Information Contact, 414-288-3570. Web site: http://business.marquette.edu/academics/msae.

Marylhurst University, Department of Business Administration, Marylhurst, OR 97036-0261. Offers finance (MBA); general management (MBA); government policy and administration (MBA); green development (MBA); health care management (MBA); marketing (MBA); natural and organic resources (MBA); nonprofit management (MBA); organizational behavior (MBA); real estate (MBA); renewable energy (MBA); sustainable business (MBA). Part-time and evening/weekend programs available. Postbaccalaureate distance learning degree programs offered (no on-campus study). *Faculty:* 3 full-time (0 women), 36 part-time/adjunct (6 women). *Students:* 29 full-time (15 women), 675 part-time (373 women); includes 178 minority (59 Black or African American, non-Hispanic/Latino; 6 American Indian or Alaska Native, non-Hispanic/Latino; 34 Asian, non-Hispanic/Latino; 46 Hispanic/Latino; 4 Native Hawaiian or other Pacific Islander, non-Hispanic/Latino; 29 Two or more races, non-Hispanic/Latino), 14 international. Average age 37. 262 applicants, 91% accepted, 194 enrolled. In 2011, 352 master's awarded. *Degree requirements:* For master's, comprehensive exam, capstone course. *Entrance requirements:* For master's, GMAT (if GPA less than 3.0 and fewer than 5 years of work experience), interview, resume, 2 letters of recommendation. Additional exam requirements/recommendations for international students: Recommended—TOEFL (minimum score 550 paper-based; 213 computer-based; 80 iBT). *Application deadline:* For fall admission, 9/11 priority date for domestic students, 9/11 for international students; for winter admission, 12/15 priority date for domestic students, 12/15 for international students; for spring admission, 3/15 priority date for domestic students, 3/17 for international students. Applications are processed on a rolling basis. Application fee: $50. Electronic applications accepted. *Expenses: Tuition:* Full-time $14,796; part-time $548 per quarter hour. Tuition and fees vary according to program. *Financial support:* Scholarships/grants available. Support available to part-time students. Financial award applicants required to submit FAFSA. *Unit head:* David McNamee, Interim Chair, 503-636-8141, Fax: 503-697-5597, E-mail: mba@marylhurst.edu. *Application contact:* Maruska Lynch, Graduate Admissions Specialist, 800-634-9982 Ext. 6322, Fax: 503-699-6320, E-mail: admissions@marylhurst.edu. Web site: http://www.marylhurst.edu/.

Massachusetts Institute of Technology, School of Architecture and Planning, Center for Real Estate, Cambridge, MA 02139. Offers real estate development (MSRED). *Faculty:* 4 full-time (0 women), 4 part-time/adjunct (1 woman). *Students:* 23 full-time (6 women); includes 5 minority (all Asian, non-Hispanic/Latino), 8 international. Average age 31. 84 applicants, 40% accepted, 21 enrolled. In 2011, 14 master's awarded. *Degree requirements:* For master's, thesis. *Entrance requirements:* For master's, GMAT. Additional exam requirements/recommendations for international students: Required—TOEFL (minimum score 600 paper-based; 250 computer-based), IELTS (minimum score 7.5). *Application deadline:* For fall admission, 1/5 for domestic and international students. Application fee: $75. Electronic applications accepted. *Expenses: Tuition:* Full-time $40,460; part-time $630 per credit hour. *Required fees:* $272. *Financial support:* In 2011–12, 21 students received support. Fellowships, Federal Work-Study, institutionally sponsored loans, scholarships/grants, and health care benefits available. *Faculty research:* Real estate finance and investment, real estate development, urban design, planning, project management, infrastructure delivery methods, urban economics, entrepreneurship, strategic planning, housing, leadership development. *Unit head:* Prof. Brian A. Ciochetti, Chairman and Academic Director, 617-253-4373, Fax: 617-258-6991, E-mail: mit-cre@mit.edu. Web site: http://web.mit.edu/cre/.

Monmouth University, The Graduate School, Leon Hess Business School, West Long Branch, NJ 07764-1898. Offers accounting (MBA, Post-Master's Certificate); business (MBA); finance (MBA); healthcare management (MBA, Post-Master's Certificate); real estate (MBA). *Accreditation:* AACSB. Part-time and evening/weekend programs available. *Faculty:* 29 full-time (10 women), 8 part-time/adjunct (2 women). *Students:* 107 full-time (44 women), 161 part-time (61 women); includes 42 minority (8 Black or African American, non-Hispanic/Latino; 19 Asian, non-Hispanic/Latino; 12 Hispanic/Latino; 3 Two or more races, non-Hispanic/Latino), 23 international. Average age 28. 193 applicants, 84% accepted, 111 enrolled. In 2011, 87 master's awarded. *Degree requirements:* For master's, capstone course. *Entrance requirements:* For master's, GMAT, minimum GPA of 3.0 in major, 2.75 overall. Additional exam requirements/recommendations for international students: Required—TOEFL (minimum score 550 paper-based; 213 computer-based; 79 iBT), IELTS (minimum score 5), Michigan English Language Assessment Battery (minimum score 77), Cambridge A, B, C. *Application deadline:* For fall admission, 7/15 priority date for domestic students, 6/1 for international students; for spring admission, 11/15 priority date for domestic students, 11/1 for international students. Applications are processed on a rolling basis. Application fee: $50. Electronic applications accepted. *Financial support:* In 2011–12, 190 students received support, including 183 fellowships (averaging $1,638 per year), 21 research assistantships (averaging $9,311 per year); career-related internships or fieldwork, scholarships/grants, and unspecified assistantships also available. Support available to part-time students. Financial award applicants required to submit FAFSA. *Faculty research:* Information technology and marketing, behavioral research in accounting, human resources, management of technology. *Unit head:* Douglas Stives, MBA Program Director, 732-263-5894, Fax: 732-263-5517, E-mail: dstives@monmouth.edu. *Application contact:* Kevin Roane, Director, Office of Graduate Admission, 732-571-3452, Fax: 732-263-5123, E-mail: gradadm@monmouth.edu. Web site: http://www.monmouth.edu/mba.

New York University, School of Continuing and Professional Studies, Schack Institute of Real Estate, New York, NY 10012-1019. Offers construction management (MS, Advanced Certificate), including construction management; real estate (MS, Advanced Certificate), including real estate, real estate development. Part-time and evening/weekend programs available. *Faculty:* 14 full-time (4 women), 117 part-time/adjunct (19 women). *Students:* 127 full-time (41 women), 424 part-time (90 women); includes 43 minority (12 Black or African American, non-Hispanic/Latino; 1 American Indian or Alaska Native, non-Hispanic/Latino; 22 Asian, non-Hispanic/Latino; 8 Hispanic/Latino), 58 international. Average age 32. 352 applicants, 64% accepted, 129 enrolled. In 2011, 222 master's, 28 other advanced degrees awarded. *Degree requirements:* For master's, thesis. *Entrance requirements:* For master's, GRE/GMAT only upon request, relevant professional work, internship or volunteer experience. Additional exam requirements/recommendations for international students: Required—TOEFL (minimum score 600 paper-based; 250 computer-based; 100 iBT), IELTS (minimum score 7). *Application deadline:* For fall admission, 2/1 priority date for domestic students, 2/1 for international students; for spring admission, 10/15 priority date for domestic students, 8/15 for international students. Applications are processed on a rolling basis. Application fee: $150. Electronic applications accepted. *Financial support:* In 2011–12, 246 students received support, including 246 fellowships (averaging $2,171 per year); scholarships/grants also available. Support available to part-time students. Financial award application deadline: 3/1; financial award applicants required to submit FAFSA. *Faculty research:* Project financial management, sustainable design, impact of large-scale development projects, economics and market cycles, international property rights, comparative metropolitan economies, current market trends. *Unit head:* Rosemary Scanlon, Divisional Dean. *Application contact:* Office of Admissions, 212-998-7100, E-mail: scps.gradadmissions@nyu.edu. Web site: http://www.scps.nyu.edu/areas-of-study/real-estate/.

Nova Southeastern University, H. Wayne Huizenga School of Business and Entrepreneurship, Fort Lauderdale, FL 33314-7796. Offers accounting (M Acc); business administration (MBA, DBA); human resource management (MSHRM); international business administration (MIBA); leadership (MS); public administration (MPA, DPA); real estate development (MS); taxation (M Tax); JD/MBA; Pharm D/MBA. Part-time and evening/weekend programs available. Postbaccalaureate distance learning degree programs offered (minimal on-campus study). *Students:* 229 full-time (112 women), 3,506 part-time (2,109 women); includes 2,506 minority (1,256 Black or African American, non-Hispanic/Latino; 8 American Indian or Alaska Native, non-Hispanic/Latino; 146 Asian, non-Hispanic/Latino; 1,058 Hispanic/Latino; 4 Native Hawaiian or other Pacific Islander, non-Hispanic/Latino; 34 Two or more races, non-Hispanic/Latino), 174 international. Average age 33. In 2011, 1,252 master's, 17 doctorates awarded. *Degree requirements:* For master's, thesis optional; for doctorate, comprehensive exam, thesis/dissertation. *Entrance requirements:* For doctorate, GMAT. Additional exam requirements/recommendations for international students: Required—TOEFL (minimum score 550 paper-based; 213 computer-based; 79 iBT), IELTS (minimum score 6). *Application deadline:* Applications are processed on a rolling basis. Application fee: $50. Electronic applications accepted. *Financial support:* In 2011–12, 2 students received support. Federal Work-Study and scholarships/grants available. Support available to part-time students. Financial award applicants required to submit FAFSA. *Faculty research:* Reputation management, call centers, international social capital, corporate earnings guidance, corporate governance. *Unit head:* Dr. D. Michael Fields, Dean, 954-262-5005, E-mail: fieldsm@nova.edu. *Application contact:* Karen Goldberg, Associate Director of Recruitment and Special Events, 954-262-5039, Fax: 954-262-3822, E-mail: karen@nova.edu. Web site: http://www.huizenga.nova.edu.

Pacific States University, College of Business, Los Angeles, CA 90006. Offers accounting (MBA); finance (MBA); international business (MBA, DBA); management of information technology (MBA); real estate management (MBA). Part-time and evening/weekend programs available. Postbaccalaureate distance learning degree programs offered (no on-campus study). *Faculty:* 6 full-time (2 women), 14 part-time/adjunct (0 women). *Students:* 157 full-time (70 women); includes 13 minority (2 Black or African American, non-Hispanic/Latino; 8 Asian, non-Hispanic/Latino; 3 Native Hawaiian or other Pacific Islander, non-Hispanic/Latino), 140 international. Average age 31. 42 applicants, 83% accepted, 33 enrolled. *Degree requirements:* For doctorate, comprehensive exam, thesis/dissertation. *Entrance requirements:* For master's, minimum undergraduate GPA of 2.5 during last 90 hours of course work. Additional exam requirements/recommendations for international students: Required—TOEFL (minimum score 133 computer-based; 45 iBT), IELTS (minimum score 4.5). *Application deadline:* For fall admission, 8/15 priority date for domestic students; for winter admission, 10/15 priority date for domestic students; for spring admission, 1/15 priority date for domestic students. Applications are processed on a rolling basis. Application fee: $100. *Expenses: Tuition:* Full-time $11,040; part-time $345 per credit hour. *Required fees:* $150 per quarter. *Financial support:* Scholarships/grants available. Financial award applicants required to submit FAFSA. *Application contact:* Zolzaya Enkhbayar, Interim Registrar, 323-731-2383, Fax: 323-731-7276, E-mail: registrar@psuca.edu.

Pontificia Universidad Catolica Madre y Maestra, Graduate School, Faculty of Social and Administrative Sciences, Santiago, Dominican Republic. Offers business administration (MBA), including business development, finance, international business, management skills (M Mgmt, MBA), marketing, operations, strategic cost management, strategy, tourist destination planning and management; law (LL M), including civil law, corporate business law, criminal law, international relations, real estate law; management (M Mgmt), including higher financial management, insurance program administration, management skills (M Mgmt, MBA); psychology (MA), including clinical child and adolescent psychology, forensic psychology; strategic human resources (EMBA).

Roosevelt University, Graduate Division, Walter E. Heller College of Business Administration, School of Finance and Real Estate, Chicago, IL 60605. Offers commercial real estate development (Certificate); real estate (MBA, MS).

Southern Methodist University, Cox School of Business, MBA Program, Dallas, TX 75275. Offers accounting (MBA); finance (MBA); financial consulting (MBA); general business (MBA); information technology and operations management (MBA); management (MBA); marketing (MBA); real estate (MBA); strategy and entrepreneurship (MBA). Part-time and evening/weekend programs available. *Entrance requirements:* For master's, GMAT. Additional exam requirements/recommendations for international students: Required—TOEFL. Electronic applications accepted. *Expenses:* Contact institution. *Faculty research:* Corporate finance, financial reporting, modeling consumer decision-making, competition between national brands and store brands, institutional determinants of firms' strategy.

Texas Tech University, Graduate School, Rawls College of Business Administration, Programs in Business Administration, Lubbock, TX 79409. Offers agricultural business (MBA); business administration (IMBA); business statistics (MBA); entrepreneurship and innovation (MBA); general business (MBA); health organization management (MBA); international business (MBA); management and leadership skills (MBA); management information systems (MBA); marketing (MBA); real estate (MBA); JD/MBA; MBA/M Arch; MBA/MA; MBA/MD; MBA/MS; MBA/Pharm D. Part-time and evening/weekend programs available. *Faculty:* 49 full-time (8 women), 2 part-time/adjunct (0 women). *Students:* 195 full-time (55 women), 397 part-time (101 women); includes 123 minority (27 Black or African American, non-Hispanic/Latino; 4 American Indian or Alaska Native, non-Hispanic/Latino; 31 Asian, non-Hispanic/Latino; 61 Hispanic/Latino), 38 international. Average age 31. 374 applicants, 83% accepted, 255 enrolled. In 2011, 256 degrees awarded. *Degree requirements:* For master's, capstone course. *Entrance requirements:* For master's, GMAT, holistic review of academic credentials. Additional exam requirements/recommendations for international students: Required—TOEFL (minimum score 550 paper-based; 213 computer-based; 79 iBT). *Application deadline:* For fall admission, 4/1 priority date for domestic students, 1/15 for international students; for spring admission, 9/1 priority date for domestic students, 6/15 for international students. Applications are processed on a rolling basis. Application fee: $50 ($75 for international students). Electronic applications accepted. *Expenses:* Tuition, state resident: full-time $5899; part-time $245.80 per credit hour. Tuition, nonresident: full-time $13,411; part-time $558.80 per credit hour. *Required fees:* $2680.60; $86.50 per credit hour. $920.30 per semester. *Financial support:* In 2011–12, 22 research assistantships (averaging $8,800 per year) were awarded; teaching assistantships, career-related internships or fieldwork, Federal Work-Study, scholarships/grants, health care benefits, and unspecified assistantships also available. Support available to part-time students. Financial award applicants required to submit FAFSA. *Unit head:* Dr. W. Jay Conover, Director, 806-742-1546, Fax: 806-742-3958, E-mail: jay.conover@ttu.edu. *Application contact:* Elizabeth Stuart, Director, Graduate Services Center, 806-742-3184, Fax: 806-742-3958, E-mail: ba_grad@ttu.edu. Web site: http://mba.ba.ttu.edu/.

Universidad Iberoamericana, Graduate School, Santo Domingo D.N., Dominican Republic. Offers business administration (MBA, PMBA); constitutional law (LL M); dentistry (DMD); educational management (MA); integrated marketing communication (MA); psychopedagogical intervention (M Ed); real estate law (LL M); strategic management of human talent (MM).

University of California, Berkeley, Graduate Division, Haas School of Business, PhD in Business Administration Program, Berkeley, CA 94720-1500. Offers accounting (PhD); business and public policy (PhD); finance (PhD); management of organizations (PhD); marketing (PhD); operations management (PhD); real estate (PhD). *Accreditation:* AACSB. *Faculty:* 77 full-time (18 women), 152 part-time/adjunct (24 women). *Students:* 79 full-time (25 women); includes 13 minority (12 Asian, non-Hispanic/Latino; 1 Hispanic/Latino), 34 international. Average age 30. 547 applicants, 5% accepted, 15 enrolled. In 2011, 14 doctorates awarded. *Degree requirements:* For doctorate, comprehensive exam, thesis/dissertation, written preliminary exams, oral qualifying exam. *Entrance requirements:* For doctorate, GMAT or GRE, minimum GPA of 3.0 in undergraduate and graduate coursework. Additional exam requirements/recommendations for international students: Required—TOEFL (minimum score 570 paper-based; 230 computer-based; 70 iBT), IELTS (minimum score 7). *Application deadline:* For fall admission, 12/10 for domestic and international students. Application fee: $80 ($100 for international students). Electronic applications accepted. *Financial support:* In 2011–12, 66 students received support, including 58 fellowships with full and partial tuition reimbursements available (averaging $29,000 per year), 77 teaching assistantships with full and partial tuition reimbursements available; research assistantships with full and partial tuition reimbursements available, scholarships/grants, health care benefits, tuition waivers (full), unspecified assistantships, and transit pass, travel grants also available. Financial award application deadline: 12/10; financial award applicants required to submit FAFSA. *Faculty research:* Accounting, business and public policy, finance, management of organizations, marketing, operations and information technology management, real estate. *Unit head:* Dr. Sunil Dutta, Director, 510-642-1229, Fax: 510-643-4255, E-mail: kimg@haas.berkeley.edu. *Application contact:* Kim Guilfoyle, Director, Student Affairs, 510-642-3944, Fax: 510-643-4255, E-mail: kimg@haas.berkeley.edu. Web site: http://www.haas.berkeley.edu/Phd/.

University of Denver, Daniels College of Business, Franklin L. Burns School of Real Estate and Construction Management, Denver, CO 80208. Offers construction management (IMBA, MS); real estate (IMBA, MBA, MS). Part-time and evening/weekend programs available. *Faculty:* 7 full-time (0 women). *Students:* 24 full-time (3 women), 61 part-time (14 women); includes 9 minority (2 Black or African American, non-Hispanic/Latino; 1 Asian, non-Hispanic/Latino; 3 Hispanic/Latino; 3 Two or more races, non-Hispanic/Latino), 16 international. Average age 33. 84 applicants, 85% accepted, 42 enrolled. In 2011, 64 degrees awarded. *Entrance requirements:* For master's, GRE General Test or GMAT, essay, two letters of recommendation. Additional exam requirements/recommendations for international students: Required—TOEFL (minimum score 570 paper-based; 88 iBT). *Application deadline:* For fall admission, 11/15 priority date for domestic students; for spring admission, 10/15 priority date for domestic students. Applications are processed on a rolling basis. Application fee: $100. Electronic applications accepted. *Financial support:* In 2011–12, 2 teaching assistantships with full and partial tuition reimbursements (averaging $1,987 per year) were awarded; career-related internships or fieldwork, Federal Work-Study, institutionally sponsored loans, scholarships/grants, and unspecified assistantships also available. Support available to part-time students. Financial award application deadline: 2/15; financial award applicants required to submit FAFSA. *Unit head:* Dr. Mark Levine, Director, 303-871-2142, E-mail: mark.levine@du.edu. *Application contact:* Victoria Chen, Graduate Admissions Manager, 303-871-3826, E-mail: victoria.chen@du.edu. Web site: http://www.daniels.du.edu/schoolsdepartments/realestate/.

University of Florida, Graduate School, Warrington College of Business Administration, Hough Graduate School of Business, Department of Finance, Insurance and Real Estate, Gainesville, FL 32611. Offers finance (MS, PhD); financial services (Certificate); insurance (PhD); real estate and urban analysis (MS, PhD); JD/MBA. *Faculty:* 13 full-time (0 women). *Students:* 107 full-time (28 women), 10 part-time (2 women); includes 20 minority (6 Black or African American, non-Hispanic/Latino; 8 Asian, non-Hispanic/Latino; 6 Hispanic/Latino), 31 international. Average age 26. 245 applicants, 2% accepted, 3 enrolled. In 2011, 103 master's, 2 doctorates awarded. Terminal master's awarded for partial completion of doctoral program. *Degree requirements:* For master's, comprehensive exam, thesis; for doctorate, comprehensive exam, thesis/dissertation. *Entrance requirements:* For master's, GMAT or GRE General Test, minimum GPA of 3.0 for last 60 hours of undergraduate degree, work experience (preferred); for doctorate, GMAT or GRE General Test, minimum GPA of 3.0. Additional exam requirements/recommendations for international students: Required—TOEFL (minimum score 550 paper-based; 213 computer-based; 80 iBT), IELTS (minimum score 6). *Application deadline:* For fall admission, 1/15 priority date for domestic students, 1/15 for international students. Applications are processed on a rolling basis. Application fee: $30. Electronic applications accepted. *Financial support:* Fellowships, research assistantships, teaching assistantships, career-related internships or fieldwork, scholarships/grants, and unspecified assistantships available. Financial award application deadline: 1/15; financial award applicants required to submit FAFSA. *Faculty research:* Banking, empirical corporate finance, hedge funds. *Unit head:* Dr. Mahendrarajah Nimalendran, Chair, 352-392-9526, Fax: 352-392-0301, E-mail: nimal@ufl.edu. *Application contact:* Mark J. Flannery, Graduate Coordinator, 352-392-3184, Fax: 352-392-0301, E-mail: flannery@ufl.edu. Web site: http://www.cba.ufl.edu/fire/.

University of Hawaii at Manoa, Graduate Division, Shidler College of Business, Program in Business Administration, Honolulu, HI 96822. Offers Asian business studies (MBA); Chinese business studies (MBA); decision sciences (MBA); entrepreneurship (MBA); finance (MBA); finance and banking (MBA); human resources management (MBA); information management (MBA); information technology (MBA); international business (MBA); Japanese business studies (MBA); marketing (MBA); organizational behavior (MBA); organizational management (MBA); real estate (MBA); student-designed track (MBA). *Accreditation:* AACSB. Part-time and evening/weekend programs available. *Degree requirements:* For master's, thesis optional. *Entrance requirements:* For master's, GMAT, minimum GPA of 3.0. Additional exam requirements/recommendations for international students: Required—TOEFL (minimum score 600 paper-based; 250 computer-based; 100 iBT), IELTS (minimum score 7). *Expenses:* Contact institution.

University of Illinois at Chicago, Graduate College, Liautaud Graduate School of Business, Center for Urban Real Estate, Chicago, IL 60607-7128. Offers real estate (MA).

University of Maryland, College Park, Academic Affairs, School of Architecture, Planning and Preservation, Program in Real Estate Development, College Park, MD 20742. Offers MRED. *Students:* 27 full-time (14 women), 58 part-time (12 women); includes 22 minority (15 Black or African American, non-Hispanic/Latino; 2 Asian, non-Hispanic/Latino; 3 Hispanic/Latino; 2 Two or more races, non-Hispanic/Latino), 5 international. 87 applicants, 55% accepted, 19 enrolled. In 2011, 30 master's awarded. *Application deadline:* For fall admission, 8/1 for domestic students, 2/1 for international students; for spring admission, 10/15 for domestic students, 6/1 for international students. Application fee: $75. *Expenses: Tuition, area resident:* Part-time $525 per credit hour. Tuition, state resident: part-time $525 per credit hour. Tuition, nonresident: part-time $1131 per credit hour. *Required fees:* $386.31 per term. Tuition and fees vary according to program. *Financial support:* In 2011–12, 1 fellowship (averaging $11,480 per year), 5 teaching assistantships (averaging $15,387 per year) were awarded. *Unit head:* Dr. Margaret McFarland, Director, 301-405-6709, E-mail: mmcf@umd.edu. *Application contact:* Dr. Charles A. Caramello, Dean of Graduate School, 301-405-0358, Fax: 301-314-9305. Web site: http://www.arch.umd.edu/real_estate_development/.

University of Memphis, Graduate School, Fogelman College of Business and Economics, Program in Business Administration, Memphis, TN 38152. Offers accounting (MBA, PhD); economics (MBA, PhD); executive business administration (MBA); finance (PhD); finance, insurance, and real estate (MBA, MS); international business administration (IMBA); management (MBA, MS, PhD); management information systems (MBA, MS, PhD); management science (MBA); marketing (MBA, MS); marketing and supply chain management (PhD); real estate development (MS); JD/MBA. *Accreditation:* AACSB. *Degree requirements:* For master's, comprehensive exam; for doctorate, comprehensive exam, thesis/dissertation. *Entrance requirements:* For master's, GMAT, resume; for doctorate, GMAT, interview, minimum GPA of 3.4, resume, letter of recommendation. Additional exam requirements/recommendations for international students: Required—TOEFL (minimum score 550 paper-based; 220 computer-based). *Faculty research:* Competitive business strategy, finance microstructures, supply chain management innovations, health care economics, litigation risks and corporate audits.

University of Miami, Graduate School, School of Law, Coral Gables, FL 33124-8087. Offers business and financial law (Certificate); employment, labor and immigration law (JD); estate planning (LL M); international law (LL M), including general international law, inter-American law, international arbitration, U.S. transnational law for foreign lawyers; law (JD); ocean and coastal law (LL M); real property development (real estate) (LL M); taxation (LL M); JD/LL M; JD/LL M/MBA; JD/MA; JD/MBA; JD/MD; JD/MM; JD/MPH; JD/MPS. *Accreditation:* ABA. *Faculty:* 82 full-time (37 women), 107 part-time/adjunct (41 women). *Students:* 1,348 full-time (588 women), 135 part-time (58 women); includes 395 minority (90 Black or African American, non-Hispanic/Latino; 9 American Indian or Alaska Native, non-Hispanic/Latino; 49 Asian, non-Hispanic/Latino; 236 Hispanic/Latino; 1 Native Hawaiian or other Pacific Islander, non-Hispanic/Latino; 10 Two or more races, non-Hispanic/Latino), 56 international. Average age 24. 4,729 applicants, 46% accepted, 447 enrolled. In 2011, 96 master's, 385 doctorates awarded. *Entrance requirements:* For doctorate, LSAT, 2 letters of recommendation. Additional exam requirements/recommendations for international students: Required—TOEFL (minimum score 580 paper-based; 237 computer-based; 92 iBT). *Application deadline:* For fall admission, 1/6 priority date for domestic students, 1/6 for international students. Applications are processed on a rolling basis. Application fee: $60. Electronic applications accepted. *Expenses:* Contact institution. *Financial support:* Fellowships, research assistantships, career-related internships or fieldwork, Federal Work-Study, institutionally sponsored loans, scholarships/grants, and unspecified assistantships available. Financial award application deadline: 3/1; financial award applicants required to submit FAFSA. *Faculty research:* National security law, international finance, Internet law/law of electronic commerce, law of the seas, art law/cultural heritage law. *Unit head:* Michael Goodnight, Associate Dean of Admissions and Enrollment Management, 305-284-2527, Fax: 305-284-3084, E-mail: mgoodnig@law.miami.edu. *Application contact:* Therese Lambert, Director of Student Recruitment, 305-284-6746, Fax: 305-284-3084, E-mail: tlambert@law.miami.edu. Web site: http://www.law.miami.edu/.

University of Michigan, Taubman College of Architecture and Urban Planning, Urban and Regional Planning Program, Ann Arbor, MI 48109. Offers real estate development (Certificate); urban planning (MUP); JD/MUP; M Arch/MUP; MBA/MUP; MLA/MUP; MPP/MUP. Offered through the Horace H. Rackham School of Graduate Studies; students in the Certificate program must either be currently enrolled in a graduate program or have earned a master's or PhD degree within the last five years. *Accreditation:* ACSP (one or more programs are accredited). Part-time programs available. *Degree requirements:* For master's, thesis or alternative, professional project, capstone studio. *Entrance requirements:* For master's, GRE General Test, LSAT or GMAT. Additional exam requirements/recommendations for international students: Required—TOEFL (minimum score 600 paper-based; 250 computer-based; 100 iBT). Electronic applications accepted. *Faculty research:* Housing community and economic development; transportation planning; physical planning and urban design; planning in developing countries; land use and environmental planning.

University of Missouri–Kansas City, Henry W. Bloch School of Management, Kansas City, MO 64110-2499. Offers accounting (MS); business administration (MBA); entrepreneurial real estate (MERE); entrepreneurship and innovation (PhD); finance (MS); public affairs (MPA, PhD); JD/MBA; LL M/MPA. PhD (interdisciplinary) offered through the School of Graduate Studies. *Accreditation:* AACSB; NASPAA. Part-time and evening/weekend programs available. *Faculty:* 51 full-time (14 women), 29 part-time/adjunct (9 women). *Students:* 272 full-time (126 women), 407 part-time (180 women); includes 91 minority (43 Black or African American, non-Hispanic/Latino; 20 Asian, non-Hispanic/Latino; 19 Hispanic/Latino; 9 Two or more races, non-Hispanic/Latino), 49 international. Average age 30. 397 applicants, 63% accepted, 202 enrolled. In 2011, 257 master's awarded. Terminal master's awarded for partial completion of doctoral program. *Entrance requirements:* For master's, GMAT, GRE, 2 writing essays, 2 references; support of employer; for doctorate, GRE, minimum GPA of 3.0. Additional exam requirements/recommendations for international students: Required—TOEFL (minimum score 550 paper-based; 213 computer-based; 80 iBT). *Application deadline:* For fall admission, 5/1 priority date for domestic students, 5/1 for international students; for spring admission, 10/1 priority date for domestic students, 10/1 for international students. Applications are processed on a rolling basis. Application fee: $45 ($50 for international students). Electronic applications accepted. *Expenses:* Tuition, state resident: full-time $5798; part-time $322.10 per credit hour. Tuition, nonresident: full-time $14,969; part-time $831.60 per credit hour. *Required fees:* $93.51 per credit hour. *Financial support:* In 2011–12, 29 research assistantships with partial tuition reimbursements (averaging $11,490 per year), 3 teaching assistantships with partial tuition reimbursements (averaging $11,600 per year) were awarded; career-related internships or fieldwork, Federal Work-Study, institutionally sponsored loans, scholarships/grants, tuition waivers (full and partial), and unspecified assistantships also available. Support available to part-time students. Financial award application deadline: 3/1; financial award applicants required to submit FAFSA. *Faculty research:* Entrepreneurship, finance, non-profit, risk management. *Unit head:* Dr. Teng-Kee Tan, Dean, 816-235-2215, Fax: 816-235-2206. *Application contact:* 816-235-1111, E-mail: admit@umkc.edu. Web site: http://www.bloch.umkc.edu.

The University of North Carolina at Charlotte, Graduate School, Belk College of Business, Department of Management, Charlotte, NC 28223-0001. Offers business administration (MBA); real estate finance and development (Certificate). *Faculty:* 13 full-time (4 women). *Students:* 148 full-time (59 women), 280 part-time (87 women); includes 60 minority (24 Black or African American, non-Hispanic/Latino; 3 American Indian or Alaska Native, non-Hispanic/Latino; 20 Asian, non-Hispanic/Latino; 8 Hispanic/Latino; 5 Two or more races, non-Hispanic/Latino), 145 international. Average age 30. 289 applicants, 68% accepted, 127 enrolled. In 2011, 198 master's, 3 other advanced degrees awarded. *Degree requirements:* For master's, thesis or alternative. *Entrance requirements:* Additional exam requirements/recommendations for international students: Required—TOEFL (minimum score 557 paper-based; 220 computer-based; 83 iBT). Application fee: $65 ($75 for international students). *Expenses:* Tuition, state resident: full-time $3689. Tuition, nonresident: full-time $15,226. *Required fees:* $2198. Tuition and fees vary according to course load and program. *Financial support:* In 2011–12, 66 teaching assistantships (averaging $12,286 per year) were awarded; career-related internships or fieldwork, institutionally sponsored loans, and scholarships/grants also available. Financial award application deadline: 4/1. *Unit head:* Dr. Joe Mazzola, Interim Dean, 704-687-7577, Fax: 704-687-4014, E-mail: jmazzola@uncc.edu. *Application contact:* Kathy B. Giddings, Director of Graduate Admissions, 704-687-5503, Fax: 704-687-3279, E-mail: gradadm@uncc.edu. Web site: http://belkcollege.uncc.edu/about-college/departments/management.

University of North Texas, Toulouse Graduate School, College of Business, Department of Finance, Insurance, Real Estate, and Law, Denton, TX 76203. Offers finance (PhD); finance, insurance, real estate, and law (MS); real estate (MS). Part-time programs available. *Degree requirements:* For master's, thesis optional; for doctorate, comprehensive exam, thesis/dissertation. *Entrance requirements:* For master's, GMAT; for doctorate, GMAT or GRE General Test. Additional exam requirements/recommendations for international students: Recommended—TOEFL (minimum score 550 paper-based; 213 computer-based; 79 iBT). *Expenses:* Tuition, state resident: part-time $100 per credit hour. Tuition, nonresident: part-time $413 per credit hour. *Faculty research:* Financial impact of regulation, risk management, taxes and valuation, bankruptcy, real financial options.

University of Pennsylvania, Wharton School, Real Estate Department, Philadelphia, PA 19104. Offers MBA, PhD. Terminal master's awarded for partial completion of doctoral program. *Degree requirements:* For doctorate, thesis/dissertation. *Entrance requirements:* For master's, GMAT; for doctorate, GRE General Test. *Expenses: Tuition:* Full-time $26,660; part-time $4944 per course. *Required fees:* $2318; $291 per course. Tuition and fees vary according to course load, degree level and program. *Faculty research:* Public economics and taxation economics and finance of real estate markets, economics of housing markets, real estate development.

University of St. Thomas, Graduate Studies, Opus College of Business, Master of Science in Real Estate Program, Minneapolis, MN 55403. Offers MS. Part-time and evening/weekend programs available. *Students:* 30 part-time (9 women); includes 2 minority (1 Black or African American, non-Hispanic/Latino; 1 American Indian or Alaska Native, non-Hispanic/Latino), 1 international. Average age 32. In 2011, 5 master's awarded. *Entrance requirements:* For master's, GMAT. Additional exam requirements/recommendations for international students: Required—TOEFL (minimum score 80 iBT), IELTS (minimum score 6.5), or Michigan English Language Assessment Battery. *Application deadline:* For fall admission, 5/1 for domestic students, 4/15 for international students; for spring admission, 10/1 for domestic and international students. Applications are processed on a rolling basis. Application fee: $40. Electronic applications accepted. *Unit head:* Herb Tousley, Program Director, 651-962-4289, E-mail: msrealestate@stthomas.edu. *Application contact:* Susan Eckstein, Program Manager, 651-962-4289, Fax: 651-962-4410, E-mail: msrealestate@stthomas.edu. Web site: http://www.stthomas.edu/realestate.

University of San Diego, School of Business Administration, Program in Real Estate, San Diego, CA 92110-2492. Offers MS, MBA/MSRE. Part-time and evening/weekend programs available. *Students:* 16 full-time (3 women), 10 part-time (4 women); includes 6 minority (1 Black or African American, non-Hispanic/Latino; 1 Asian, non-Hispanic/Latino; 4 Hispanic/Latino), 2 international. Average age 29. In 2011, 22 master's awarded. *Degree requirements:* For master's, capstone course. *Entrance requirements:* For master's, GMAT (minimum score of 550), minimum GPA of 3, minimum 2 years relevant work experience. Additional exam requirements/recommendations for international students: Required—TOEFL (minimum score 580 paper-based; 237 computer-based; 92 iBT), TWE. *Application deadline:* For fall admission, 3/15 priority date for domestic students. Application fee: $80. Electronic applications accepted. *Expenses: Tuition:* Full-time $22,482; part-time $1249 per unit. *Required fees:* $224. Full-time tuition and fees vary according to course load and degree level. *Financial support:* In 2011–12, 17 students received support. Career-related internships or fieldwork, Federal Work-Study, institutionally sponsored loans, scholarships/grants, and unspecified assistantships available. Support available to part-time students. Financial award application deadline: 4/1; financial award applicants required to submit FAFSA. *Unit head:* Dr. Charles Tu, Academic Director, Real Estate Program, 619-260-5942, E-mail: realestate@sandiego.edu. *Application contact:* Monica Mahon, Associate Director of Graduate Admissions, 619-260-4524, Fax: 619-260-4158, E-mail: grads@sandiego.edu. Web site: http://www.sandiego.edu/realestate.

University of South Africa, College of Economic and Management Sciences, Pretoria, South Africa. Offers accounting (D Admin, D Com); accounting science (DA); auditing (D Admin, D Com); business administration (M Tech); business economics (D Admin); business leadership (DBL); business management (D Admin, D Com); economic management analysis (M Tech); economics (D Admin, D Com, PhD); human resource development (M Tech); industrial psychology (D Admin, D Com, PhD); logistics (D Com); marketing (M Tech); public administration (D Admin, D Com, DPA, PhD); public management (M Tech); quantitative management (D Admin, D Com); real estate (M Tech); statistics (D Admin, PhD); tourism management (D Admin, D Com); transport economics (D Admin, D Com).

University of Southern California, Graduate School, School of Policy, Planning, and Development, Master of Real Estate Development Program, Los Angeles, CA 90089. Offers MRED, JD/MRED, M Pl/MRED, MBA/MRED. Part-time programs available. *Degree requirements:* For master's, comprehensive exam. *Entrance requirements:* For master's, GRE, GMAT. Additional exam requirements/recommendations for international students: Required—TOEFL (minimum score 600 paper-based; 250 computer-based; 100 iBT). Electronic applications accepted. *Expenses:* Contact institution. *Faculty research:* Urban development, urban economics, real estate finance, housing markets.

University of South Florida, Graduate School, College of Business, Department of Finance, Tampa, FL 33620-9951. Offers finance (MS, PhD); real estate (MSRE). Part-time and evening/weekend programs available. *Faculty:* 14 full-time (3 women), 11 part-time/adjunct (2 women). *Students:* 48 full-time (16 women), 11 part-time (2 women); includes 6 minority (2 Black or African American, non-Hispanic/Latino; 3 Asian, non-Hispanic/Latino; 1 Hispanic/Latino), 28 international. Average age 26. 102 applicants, 53% accepted, 28 enrolled. In 2011, 14 master's, 1 doctorate awarded. Terminal master's awarded for partial completion of doctoral program. *Degree requirements:* For master's, thesis or alternative; for doctorate, comprehensive exam, thesis/dissertation. *Entrance requirements:* For master's, GMAT (minimum score of 550), minimum GPA of 3.0 in last 30 hours; for doctorate, GMAT or GRE, at least two letters of recommendation, personal statement, interview. Additional exam requirements/recommendations for international students: Required—TOEFL (minimum score 550 paper-based; 213 computer-based; 79 iBT) or IELTS (minimum score 6.5). *Application deadline:* For fall admission, 6/1 for domestic students, 1/2 for international students; for spring admission, 10/15 for domestic students, 6/1 for international students. Application fee: $30. Electronic applications accepted. *Financial support:* In 2011–12, 17 students received support, including 8 research assistantships (averaging $14,357 per year), 9 teaching assistantships with tuition reimbursements available (averaging $11,972 per year); scholarships/grants, health care benefits, and unspecified assistantships also available. Financial award application deadline: 6/30. *Faculty research:* Corporate governance, international finance, asset pricing models, risk management, market efficiency. *Total annual research expenditures:* $332,885. *Unit head:* Dr. Scott Besley, Chairperson, 813-974-2081, Fax: 813-974-3084, E-mail: sbesley@coba.usf.edu. *Application contact:* Wendy Baker, Assistant Director, Graduate Studies, 813-974-3335, Fax: 813-974-4518, E-mail: wbaker@usf.edu.

The University of Texas at Arlington, Graduate School, College of Business, Department of Finance and Real Estate, Arlington, TX 76019. Offers finance (PhD); quantitative finance (MS); real estate (MS). Part-time and evening/weekend programs available. *Faculty:* 7 full-time (0 women), 1 (woman) part-time/adjunct. *Students:* 23 full-time (8 women), 40 part-time (11 women); includes 19 minority (5 Black or African American, non-Hispanic/Latino; 7 Asian, non-Hispanic/Latino; 6 Hispanic/Latino; 1 Two or more races, non-Hispanic/Latino), 15 international. 47 applicants, 57% accepted, 13 enrolled. In 2011, 42 degrees awarded. *Degree requirements:* For master's, thesis optional; for doctorate, comprehensive exam, thesis/dissertation. *Entrance requirements:* For master's, GMAT/GRE, minimum GPA of 3.0; for doctorate, GMAT/GRE. Additional exam requirements/recommendations for international students: Required—TOEFL (minimum score 550 paper-based; 213 computer-based; 79 iBT). *Application deadline:* For fall admission, 6/1 priority date for domestic students, 4/1 for international students; for spring admission, 10/15 for domestic students, 9/15 for international students. Applications are processed on a rolling basis. Application fee: $40 ($70 for international students). *Financial support:* In 2011–12, 7 teaching assistantships (averaging $16,857 per year) were awarded; career-related internships or fieldwork, Federal Work-Study, institutionally sponsored loans, and unspecified assistantships also available. Financial award application deadline: 6/1; financial award applicants required to submit FAFSA. *Unit head:* Dr. David Diltz, Chair, 817-272-3705, Fax: 817-272-2252, E-mail: diltz@uta.edu. *Application contact:* Dr. Fred Forgey, Graduate Advisor, 817-272-0359, Fax: 817-272-2252, E-mail: realestate@uta.edu. Web site: http://wweb.uta.edu/finance/.

The University of Texas at Arlington, Graduate School, College of Business, Program in Business Administration, Arlington, TX 76019. Offers accounting (PhD); business statistics (PhD); finance (MBA, PhD); information systems (MBA, PhD); management (MBA, PhD); marketing (MBA, PhD); operations management (MBA, PhD); real estate (MBA). *Accreditation:* AACSB. Part-time and evening/weekend programs available. *Students:* 505 full-time (189 women), 369 part-time (140 women); includes 199 minority (58 Black or African American, non-Hispanic/Latino; 2 American Indian or Alaska Native, non-Hispanic/Latino; 70 Asian, non-Hispanic/Latino; 56 Hispanic/Latino; 1 Native Hawaiian or other Pacific Islander, non-Hispanic/Latino; 12 Two or more races, non-Hispanic/Latino), 306 international. 416 applicants, 81% accepted, 234 enrolled. In 2011, 495 master's, 3 doctorates awarded. *Degree requirements:* For master's, thesis optional; for doctorate, comprehensive exam, thesis/dissertation. *Entrance requirements:* For master's, GMAT or GRE; for doctorate, GMAT, minimum GPA of 3.0 (undergraduate), 3.4 (graduate); 30 hours of graduate course work. Additional exam requirements/recommendations for international students: Required—TOEFL (minimum score 550 paper-based; 213 computer-based; 79 iBT). *Application deadline:* For fall admission, 6/1 for domestic students, 4/1 for international students; for spring admission, 10/15 for domestic students, 9/15 for international students. Applications are processed on a rolling basis. Application fee: $40 ($70 for international students). Electronic applications accepted. *Financial support:* Career-related internships or fieldwork, scholarships/grants, and unspecified assistantships available. Support available to part-time students. Financial award application deadline: 6/1; financial award applicants required to submit FAFSA. *Unit head:* Dr. Edmund Prater, Director of PhD Programs, 817-272-2131, Fax: 817-272-5799. *Application contact:* Melanie McGee, Director of MBA Program, 817-272-3005, Fax: 817-272-5799, E-mail: mwmcgee@uta.edu.

The University of Texas at Dallas, Naveen Jindal School of Management, Program in Management and Administrative Sciences, Richardson, TX 75080. Offers electronic commerce (MS); finance (MS); healthcare administration (MS); information systems (MS); innovation and entrepreneurship (MS); international management (MS); leadership in organizations (MS); marketing (MS); operations (MS); organizations (MS); real estate (MS); strategy (MS). *Accreditation:* AACSB. Part-time and evening/weekend programs available. *Faculty:* 26 full-time (6 women), 9 part-time/adjunct (2 women). *Students:* 128 full-time (69 women), 169 part-time (95 women); includes 76 minority (18 Black or African American, non-Hispanic/Latino; 1 American Indian or Alaska Native, non-Hispanic/Latino; 37 Asian, non-Hispanic/Latino; 15 Hispanic/Latino; 1 Native Hawaiian or other Pacific Islander, non-Hispanic/Latino; 4 Two or more races, non-Hispanic/Latino), 77 international. Average age 34. 220 applicants, 63% accepted, 68 enrolled. In 2011, 58 master's awarded. *Degree requirements:* For master's, thesis optional. *Entrance requirements:* For master's, GMAT. Additional exam requirements/recommendations for international students: Required—TOEFL (minimum score 550 paper-based; 215 computer-based). *Application deadline:* For fall admission, 7/15 for domestic students, 5/1 for international students; for spring admission, 11/15 for domestic students, 9/1 for international students. Applications are processed on a rolling basis. Application fee: $50 ($100 for international students). Electronic applications accepted. *Expenses:* Tuition, state resident: full-time $11,170; part-time $620.56 per credit hour. Tuition, nonresident: full-time $20,212; part-time $1122.89 per credit hour. *Financial support:* In 2011–12, 68 students received support, including 7 teaching assistantships with partial tuition reimbursements available (averaging $16,200 per year); research assistantships with partial tuition reimbursements available, career-related internships or fieldwork, Federal Work-Study, institutionally sponsored loans, scholarships/grants, and unspecified assistantships also available. Support available to part-time students. Financial award application deadline: 4/30; financial award applicants required to submit FAFSA. *Faculty research:* Integrated and detailed knowledge of functional areas of management, analytical tools for effective appraisal and decision-making. *Unit head:* Dr. Gregory Dess, Area Coordinator, 972-883-4439, E-mail: gdess@utdallas.edu. *Application contact:* James Parker, Assistant Director, 972-883-5842, E-mail: jparker@utdallas.edu. Web site: http://jindal.utdallas.edu/academic-areas/organizations-strategy-and-international-management/.

University of Utah, Graduate School, David Eccles School of Business, Program in Real Estate Development, Salt Lake City, UT 84112-1107. Offers MRED. *Students:* 14 full-time (1 woman), 10 part-time (0 women); includes 2 minority (both Hispanic/Latino). Average age 33. 30 applicants, 53% accepted, 15 enrolled. In 2011, 20 degrees awarded. *Entrance requirements:* For master's, GMAT or GRE, minimum undergraduate GPA of 3.0. Additional exam requirements/recommendations for international students: Required—TOEFL (minimum score 600 paper-based; 250 computer-based; 100 iBT), IELTS (minimum score 7). *Application deadline:* For fall admission, 4/1 priority date for domestic students, 4/1 for international students. Applications are processed on a rolling basis. Application fee: $55 ($65 for international students). Electronic applications accepted. *Expenses:* Contact institution. *Financial support:* Scholarships/grants and unspecified assistantships available. *Unit head:* Buzz Welch, Program Director, 801-581-7463, E-mail: buzz.welch@utah.edu. *Application contact:* Carly Brisbay, Senior Admissions Coordinator, 801-581-7785, Fax: 801-581-3666, E-mail: mredsadmissions@business.utah.edu.

University of Wisconsin–Madison, Graduate School, Wisconsin School of Business, Doctoral Program in Real Estate and Urban Land Economics, Madison, WI 53706-1380. Offers PhD. *Faculty:* 6 full-time (0 women), 7 part-time/adjunct (1 woman). *Students:* 1 (woman) full-time, all international. Average age 28. 21 applicants, 0% accepted. In 2011, 2 doctorates awarded. *Degree requirements:* For doctorate, comprehensive exam, thesis/dissertation. *Entrance requirements:* For doctorate, GMAT or GRE. Additional exam requirements/recommendations for international students: Recommended—TOEFL (minimum score 623 paper-based; 263 computer-based; 106 iBT), IELTS (minimum score 7.5). *Application deadline:* For fall admission, 12/15 priority date for domestic students, 12/15 for international students. Application fee: $56. Electronic applications accepted. *Expenses:* Tuition, state resident: full-time $10,296; part-time $643.51 per credit. Tuition, nonresident: full-time $24,054; part-time $1503.40 per credit. *Required fees:* $70.06 per credit. Tuition and fees vary according to course load, campus/location, program and reciprocity agreements. *Financial support:* In 2011–12, 1 student received support, including fellowships with full tuition reimbursements available (averaging $18,756 per year), research assistantships with full tuition reimbursements available (averaging $16,506 per year), 1 teaching assistantship with full tuition reimbursement available (averaging $14,088 per year); career-related internships or fieldwork, Federal Work-Study, institutionally sponsored loans, scholarships/grants, health care benefits, and unspecified assistantships also available. Financial award application deadline: 2/1; financial award applicants required to submit FAFSA. *Faculty research:* Real estate finance, real estate equity investments, zoning restructurings, home ownership, international real estate and public policy. *Unit head:* Prof. Stephen Malpezzi, Chair, 608-262-6006, Fax: 608-265-2738, E-mail: smalpezzi@bus.wisc.edu. *Application contact:* Belle Heberling, Assistant Director for Research Programs, 608-262-3749, Fax: 608-890-0180, E-mail: phd@bus.wisc.edu. Web site: http://www.bus.wisc.edu/phd.

University of Wisconsin–Madison, Graduate School, Wisconsin School of Business, Wisconsin Full-Time MBA Program, Madison, WI 53706-1380. Offers applied security analysis (MBA); arts administration (MBA); brand and product management (MBA); corporate finance and investment banking (MBA); marketing research (MBA); operations and technology management (MBA); real estate (MBA); risk management and insurance (MBA); strategic human resource management (MBA); supply chain management (MBA). *Faculty:* 32 full-time (6 women), 27 part-time/adjunct (7 women). *Students:* 228 full-time (75 women); includes 53 minority (16 Black or African American, non-Hispanic/Latino; 25 Asian, non-Hispanic/Latino; 10 Hispanic/Latino; 2 Native Hawaiian or other Pacific Islander, non-Hispanic/Latino), 28 international. Average age 28. 509 applicants, 30% accepted, 111 enrolled. In 2011, 120 master's awarded. *Degree requirements:* For master's, thesis (for arts administration). *Entrance requirements:* For master's, GMAT, bachelor's or equivalent degree, 2 years of work experience, letters of recommendation. Additional exam requirements/recommendations for international students: Required—TOEFL (minimum score 600 paper-based; 250 computer-based; 100 iBT), IELTS. *Application deadline:* For fall admission, 11/4 for domestic and international students; for winter admission, 2/3 for domestic and international students; for spring admission, 4/27 for domestic and international students. Applications are processed on a rolling basis. Application fee: $56. Electronic applications accepted. *Expenses:* Tuition, state resident: full-time $10,296; part-time $643.51 per credit. Tuition, nonresident: full-time $24,054; part-time $1503.40 per credit. *Required fees:* $70.06 per credit. Tuition and fees vary according to course load, campus/location, program and reciprocity agreements. *Financial support:* In 2011–12, 176 students received support, including 20 fellowships with full and partial tuition reimbursements available (averaging $18,756 per year), 128 research assistantships with full tuition reimbursements available (averaging $25,185 per year), 28 teaching assistantships with full tuition reimbursements available (averaging $25,097 per year); scholarships/grants, health care benefits, and unspecified assistantships also available. Financial award application deadline: 4/27; financial award applicants required to submit FAFSA. *Faculty research:* Market consequences of International Financial Reporting Standards (IFRS), inter-firm relationships and strategic partnerships, application of Bayesian statistical methods and applied probability models to understanding individuals' behaviors in the context of customer relationship management (CRM) applications, liquidity provision and the structure of financial markets, strategic management of global startups. *Unit head:* Dr. Larry "Chip" W. Hunter, Associate Dean of Master's Programs, 608-265-3494, Fax: 608-265-4192, E-mail: lhunter@bus.wisc.edu. *Application contact:* Maria Reis, Assistant Director of MBA Marketing and Recruiting, 608-262-4000, Fax: 608-265-4192, E-mail: mreis@bus.wisc.edu. Web site: http://www.bus.wisc.edu/mba.

University of Wisconsin–Milwaukee, Graduate School, School of Architecture and Urban Planning, Department of Urban Planning, Milwaukee, WI 53201-0413. Offers geographic information systems (Certificate); real estate development (Certificate); urban planning (MUP); M Arch/MUP; MPA/MUP; MUP/MS. *Accreditation:* ACSP. Part-time programs available. *Faculty:* 4 full-time (2 women), 1 part-time/adjunct (0 women). *Students:* 42 full-time (15 women), 30 part-time (10 women); includes 9 minority (2 Black or African American, non-Hispanic/Latino; 1 American Indian or Alaska Native, non-Hispanic/Latino; 1 Asian, non-Hispanic/Latino; 1 Hispanic/Latino; 4 Two or more races, non-Hispanic/Latino), 1 international. Average age 30. 70 applicants, 74% accepted, 26 enrolled. In 2011, 15 degrees awarded. *Degree requirements:* For master's, comprehensive exam, thesis or alternative. *Entrance requirements:* For master's, GRE General Test. Additional exam requirements/recommendations for international students: Required—TOEFL (minimum score 550 paper-based; 213 computer-based; 79 iBT), IELTS (minimum score 6.5). *Application deadline:* For fall admission, 1/1 priority date for domestic students; for spring admission, 9/1 for domestic students. Applications are processed on a rolling basis. Application fee: $56 ($96 for international students). Electronic applications accepted. One-time fee: $506.10 full-time. Tuition and fees vary according to course load and reciprocity agreements. *Financial support:* Fellowships, research assistantships, teaching assistantships, career-related internships or fieldwork, health care benefits, and unspecified assistantships available. Support available to part-time students. Financial award application deadline: 4/15; financial award applicants required to submit FAFSA. *Unit head:* Nancy Frank, Department Chair, 414-229-5372, E-mail: frankn@uwm.edu. *Application contact:* General Information Contact, 414-229-4982, Fax: 414-229-6967, E-mail: gradschool@uwm.edu. Web site: http://www4.uwm.edu/sarup/program/planning/.

Villanova University, Villanova School of Business, MBA - The Fast Track Program, Villanova, PA 19085. Offers finance (MBA); health care management (MBA); international business (MBA); management information systems (MBA); marketing (MBA); real estate (MBA); strategic management (MBA). *Accreditation:* AACSB. Part-time and evening/weekend programs available. *Faculty:* 101 full-time (32 women), 38 part-time/adjunct (8 women). *Students:* 123 part-time (46 women); includes 14 minority (1 Black or African American, non-Hispanic/Latino; 3 American Indian or Alaska Native, non-Hispanic/Latino; 5 Asian, non-Hispanic/Latino; 1 Hispanic/Latino; 4 Two or more races, non-Hispanic/Latino). Average age 29. In 2011, 53 master's awarded. *Degree requirements:* For master's, minimum GPA of 3.0. *Entrance requirements:* For master's, GMAT, work experience. Additional exam requirements/recommendations for international students: Required—TOEFL (minimum score 550 paper-based; 213 computer-based; 80 iBT). *Application deadline:* For fall admission, 6/30 for domestic and international students. Application fee: $50. Electronic applications accepted. *Expenses: Tuition:* Part-time $675 per credit. Part-time tuition and fees vary according to degree level and program. *Financial support:* Scholarships/grants available. Financial award application deadline: 6/30; financial award applicants required to submit FAFSA. *Faculty research:* Business analytics; creativity, innovation and entrepreneurship; global leadership; marketing and public policy; real estate; church management. *Unit head:* Kristy Irwin, Director of Recruitment and Marketing, 610-519-6288, Fax: 610-519-6273, E-mail: kristy.irwin@villanova.edu. *Application contact:* Meredith L. Lockyer, Assistant Director, 610-519-7016, Fax: 610-519-6273, E-mail: meredith.lockyer@villanova.edu. Web site: http://www.mba.villanova.edu.

Villanova University, Villanova School of Business, MBA - The Flex Track Program, Villanova, PA 19085. Offers finance (MBA); health care management (MBA); international business (MBA); management information systems (MBA); marketing (MBA); real estate (MBA); strategic management (MBA); JD/MBA. *Accreditation:* AACSB. Part-time and evening/weekend programs available. Postbaccalaureate distance learning degree programs offered (minimal on-campus study). *Faculty:* 101 full-time (32 women), 38 part-time/adjunct (8 women). *Students:* 18 full-time (9 women), 412 part-time (127 women); includes 45 minority (7 Black or African American, non-Hispanic/Latino; 1 American Indian or Alaska Native, non-Hispanic/Latino; 25 Asian, non-Hispanic/Latino; 4 Hispanic/Latino; 1 Native Hawaiian or other Pacific Islander, non-Hispanic/Latino; 7 Two or more races, non-Hispanic/Latino). Average age 30. In 2011, 150 master's awarded. *Degree requirements:* For master's, minimum GPA of 3.0. *Entrance requirements:* For master's, GMAT, work experience. Additional exam requirements/recommendations for international students: Required—TOEFL (minimum score 550 paper-based; 213 computer-based; 80 iBT). *Application deadline:* For fall admission, 6/30 for domestic and international students; for winter admission, 11/15 for domestic and international students; for spring admission, 3/30 for domestic students, 3/31 for international students. Applications are processed on a rolling basis. Application fee: $50. Electronic applications accepted. *Expenses: Tuition:* Part-time $675 per credit. Part-time tuition and fees vary according to degree level and program. *Financial support:* In 2011–12, 18 research assistantships with full tuition reimbursements (averaging $13,100 per year) were awarded; scholarships/grants and unspecified assistantships also available. Financial award application deadline: 6/30; financial award applicants required to submit FAFSA. *Faculty research:* Business analytics; creativity, innovation and entrepreneurship; global leadership; marketing and public policy; real estate; church management. *Unit head:* Kristy Irwin, Director of Recruitment and Marketing, 610-610-6288, Fax: 610-519-6273, E-mail: kristy.irwin@villanova.edu. *Application contact:* Meredity L. Lockyer, Assistant Director, 610-519-7016, Fax: 610-519-6273, E-mail: meredith.lockyer@villanova.edu. Web site: http://www.mba.villanova.edu.

Virginia Commonwealth University, Graduate School, School of Business, Program in Finance, Insurance, and Real Estate, Richmond, VA 23284-9005. Offers MS. *Faculty:* 11 full-time (0 women). *Entrance requirements:* For master's, GMAT. Additional exam requirements/recommendations for international students: Required—TOEFL (minimum score 600 paper-based; 250 computer-based; 100 iBT); Recommended—IELTS (minimum score 6.5). *Application deadline:* For fall admission, 6/1 for domestic students; for spring admission, 11/1 for domestic students. Applications are processed on a rolling basis. Application fee: $50. Electronic applications accepted. *Expenses:* Tuition, state resident: full-time $9133; part-time $507 per credit. Tuition, nonresident: full-time $18,777; part-time $1043 per credit. *Required fees:* $77 per credit. Tuition and fees vary according to degree level, campus/location, program and student level. *Financial support:* Fellowships, research assistantships, teaching assistantships, Federal Work-Study, institutionally sponsored loans, and tuition waivers (full and partial) available. Financial award application deadline: 3/15; financial award applicants required to submit FAFSA. *Unit head:* Dr. Nanda Rangan, Chair, 804-828-6002, Fax: 804-828-7174, E-mail: nkrangan@vcu.edu. *Application contact:* Jana P. McQuaid, Assistant Dean, Master's Programs, 804-828-4622, Fax: 804-828-7174, E-mail: jpmcquaid@vcu.edu. Web site: http://www.business.vcu.edu/graduate.html.

Virginia Commonwealth University, Graduate School, School of Business, Program in Real Estate and Urban Land Development, Richmond, VA 23284-9005. Offers Certificate. *Entrance requirements:* Additional exam requirements/recommendations for international students: Required—TOEFL (minimum score 600 paper-based; 250 computer-based; 100 iBT); Recommended—IELTS (minimum score 6.5). Electronic applications accepted. *Expenses:* Tuition, state resident: full-time $9133; part-time $507 per credit. Tuition, nonresident: full-time $18,777; part-time $1043 per credit. *Required fees:* $77 per credit. Tuition and fees vary according to degree level, campus/location, program and student level.

Section 21
Transportation Management, Logistics, and Supply Chain Management

This section contains a directory of institutions offering graduate work in real estate, followed by an in-depth entry submitted by an institution that chose to prepare a detailed program description. Additional information about programs listed in the directory but not augmented by an in-depth entry may be obtained by writing directly to the dean of a graduate school or chair of a department at the address given in the directory.

For programs offering related work, see also in this book *Business Administration and Management.*

CONTENTS

Program Directories

Displays and Close-Ups

See also:

Aviation Management

Arizona State University, College of Technology and Innovation, Department of Technology Management, Mesa, AZ 85212. Offers technology (aviation management and human factors) (MS); technology (environmental technology management) (MS); technology (global technology and development) (MS); technology (graphic information technology) (MS); technology (management of technology) (MS). Part-time and evening/weekend programs available. Postbaccalaureate distance learning degree programs offered (minimal on-campus study). *Degree requirements:* For master's, thesis or applied project and oral defense; interactive Program of Study (iPOS) submitted before completing 50 percent of required credit hours. *Entrance requirements:* For master's, GRE, minimum GPA of 3.0 or equivalent in last 2 years of work leading to bachelor's degree. Additional exam requirements/recommendations for international students: Required—TOEFL (minimum score 83 iBT), TOEFL, IELTS, or Pearson Test of English. Electronic applications accepted. *Faculty research:* Digital imaging, digital publishing, Internet development/e-commerce, information aviation human factors, pilot selection, databases, multimedia, commercial digital photography, digital workflow, computer graphics modeling and animation, information design, sociotechnology, visual and technical literacy, environmental management, quality management, project management, industrial ethics, hazardous materials, environmental chemistry.

Concordia University, School of Graduate Studies, John Molson School of Business, Montréal, QC H3G 1M8, Canada. Offers administration (M Sc, Diploma); aviation management (Certificate, Diploma); business administration (MBA, UA Undergraduate Associate, PhD), including international aviation (UA Undergraduate Associate); chartered accountancy (Diploma); community organizational development (Certificate); event management and fundraising (Certificate); executive business administration (EMBA); investment management (Diploma); investment management option (MBA); management accounting (Certificate); management of healthcare organizations (Certificate); sport administration (Diploma). PhD program offered jointly with HEC Montreal, McGill University, and Université du Québec à Montréal. *Accreditation:* AACSB. Part-time and evening/weekend programs available. *Degree requirements:* For master's, one foreign language, thesis (for some programs), research project; for doctorate, one foreign language, thesis/dissertation; for other advanced degree, one foreign language. *Entrance requirements:* For master's and doctorate, GMAT. Additional exam requirements/recommendations for international students: Required—TOEFL. *Expenses:* Contact institution. *Faculty research:* General business, capital markets, international business.

Daniel Webster College, MBA Program for Aviation Professionals, Nashua, NH 03063-1300. Offers MBA. Part-time and evening/weekend programs available. *Degree requirements:* For master's, capstone research project. *Entrance requirements:* Additional exam requirements/recommendations for international students: Required—TOEFL (minimum score 550 paper-based; 213 computer-based; 79 iBT). Electronic applications accepted.

Delta State University, Graduate Programs, College of Business, Department of Commercial Aviation, Cleveland, MS 38733-0001. Offers MCA. Part-time and evening/weekend programs available. Postbaccalaureate distance learning degree programs offered (minimal on-campus study). *Degree requirements:* For master's, thesis or alternative. *Entrance requirements:* For master's, GMAT. *Expenses:* Tuition, state resident: full-time $4702; part-time $294 per credit hour. Tuition, nonresident: full-time $12,516; part-time $760 per credit hour. *Required fees:* $586.

Dowling College, School of Business, Oakdale, NY 11769-1999. Offers aviation management (MBA, Certificate); banking and finance (MBA, Certificate); corporate finance (MBA); financial planning (Certificate); health care management (MBA, Certificate); human resource management (Certificate); information systems management (MBA); management and leadership (MBA); marketing (Certificate); project management (Certificate); public management (MBA, Certificate); sport, event and entertainment management (Certificate); JD/MBA. Part-time and evening/weekend programs available. Postbaccalaureate distance learning degree programs offered (minimal on-campus study). *Faculty:* 10 full-time (4 women), 54 part-time/adjunct (6 women). *Students:* 237 full-time (99 women), 403 part-time (199 women); includes 186 minority (95 Black or African American, non-Hispanic/Latino; 62 Asian, non-Hispanic/Latino; 28 Hispanic/Latino; 1 Native Hawaiian or other Pacific Islander, non-Hispanic/Latino), 1 international. Average age 35. 345 applicants, 83% accepted, 193 enrolled. In 2011, 350 master's, 7 other advanced degrees awarded. *Degree requirements:* For master's, comprehensive exam, thesis optional. *Entrance requirements:* For master's, minimum GPA of 2.8, 2 letters of recommendation, courses or seminar in accounting and finance, resume. Additional exam requirements/recommendations for international students: Required—TOEFL (minimum score 550 paper-based). *Application deadline:* For fall admission, 9/1 priority date for domestic students; for winter admission, 1/1 priority date for domestic students; for spring admission, 2/1 priority date for domestic students. Applications are processed on a rolling basis. Application fee: $50. Electronic applications accepted. *Expenses: Tuition:* Full-time $19,162; part-time $933 per credit. *Required fees:* $1330; $700 per year. Tuition and fees vary according to course load. *Financial support:* Career-related internships or fieldwork and Federal Work-Study available. Support available to part-time students. Financial award application deadline: 6/30; financial award applicants required to submit FAFSA. *Faculty research:* International finance, computer applications, labor relations, executive development. *Unit head:* Antonia Loschiavo, Assistant Dean, 631-244-3266, Fax: 631-244-1018, E-mail: loschiat@dowling.edu. *Application contact:* Ronnie S. Macdonald, Assistant Vice President for Enrollment Services/Dean of Admissions, 631-244-3357, Fax: 631-244-1059, E-mail: macdonar@dowling.edu.

Embry-Riddle Aeronautical University–Daytona, Daytona Beach Campus Graduate Program, Department of Business Administration, Daytona Beach, FL 32114-3900. Offers MBA, MBA-AM. *Accreditation:* ACBSP. Part-time programs available. *Faculty:* 5 full-time (0 women), 5 part-time/adjunct (2 women). *Students:* 87 full-time (26 women), 43 part-time (15 women); includes 22 minority (5 Black or African American, non-Hispanic/Latino; 7 Asian, non-Hispanic/Latino; 10 Hispanic/Latino), 45 international. Average age 29. 84 applicants, 55% accepted, 32 enrolled. In 2011, 60 master's awarded. *Degree requirements:* For master's, thesis or alternative. *Entrance requirements:* For master's, GMAT, minimum GPA of 2.5. Additional exam requirements/recommendations for international students: Required—TOEFL (minimum score 550 paper-based; 213 computer-based; 79 iBT). *Application deadline:* For fall admission, 6/1 priority date for domestic students, 6/1 for international students; for spring admission, 11/1 priority date for domestic students, 10/1 for international students. Applications are processed on a rolling basis. Application fee: $50. Electronic applications accepted. *Expenses: Tuition:* Full-time $14,340; part-time $1195 per credit hour. *Financial support:* In 2011–12, 21 students received support, including 7 research assistantships with partial tuition reimbursements available (averaging $2,873 per year); teaching assistantships, career-related internships or fieldwork, Federal Work-Study, and unspecified assistantships also available. Support available to part-time students. Financial award application deadline: 4/15; financial award applicants required to submit FAFSA. *Faculty research:* Aircraft safety operations analysis, energy consumption analysis, statistical analysis of general aviation accidents, airport funding strategies, industry assessment and marketing analysis for ENAER aerospace. *Unit head:* Dr. Dawna Rhoades, MBA Program Coordinator, 386-226-7756, E-mail: dawna.rhoades@erau.edu. *Application contact:* Flavia Carreiro, Assistant Director, International and Graduate Admissions, 800-388-3728, Fax: 386-226-7070, E-mail: graduate.admissions@erau.edu. Web site: http://daytonabeach.erau.edu/cob/departments/graduate-degrees/master-business-administration/index.html.

See Display on next page and Close-Up on page 675.

Embry-Riddle Aeronautical University–Worldwide, Worldwide Headquarters - Graduate Degrees and Programs, Program in Aeronautics, Daytona Beach, FL 32114-3900. Offers aeronautical science (MAS); air transportation management (Graduate Certificate); airport planning design and development (Graduate Certificate); aviation/aerospace industrial management (Graduate Certificate); aviation/aerospace safety (Graduate Certificate); instructional system design (Graduate Certificate). Part-time and evening/weekend programs available. Postbaccalaureate distance learning degree programs offered (minimal on-campus study). *Faculty:* 24 full-time (2 women), 177 part-time/adjunct (20 women). *Students:* 1,684 full-time (248 women), 1,771 part-time (239 women); includes 497 minority (154 Black or African American, non-Hispanic/Latino; 20 American Indian or Alaska Native, non-Hispanic/Latino; 58 Asian, non-Hispanic/Latino; 251 Hispanic/Latino; 3 Native Hawaiian or other Pacific Islander, non-Hispanic/Latino; 11 Two or more races, non-Hispanic/Latino), 32 international. Average age 36. 913 applicants, 77% accepted, 330 enrolled. In 2011, 1032 degrees awarded. *Degree requirements:* For master's, comprehensive exam (for some programs), thesis optional. *Entrance requirements:* Additional exam requirements/recommendations for international students: Recommended—TOEFL (minimum score 550 paper-based; 213 computer-based; 79 iBT). *Application deadline:* Applications are processed on a rolling basis. Application fee: $50. Electronic applications accepted. *Expenses: Tuition:* Part-time $395 per credit hour. Tuition and fees vary according to degree level and program. *Financial support:* In 2011–12, 570 students received support. Available to part-time students. Applicants required to submit FAFSA. *Faculty research:* Unmanned aircraft system (UAS) operations, human factors, crash investigation, reliability and hazard analysis, aviation security. *Unit head:* Dr. Katherine A. Moran, Department Chair, 360-597-4560, E-mail: morank@erau.edu. *Application contact:* Linda Dammer, Director of Admissions, 386-226-6396 Ext. 1, Fax: 386-226-6984, E-mail: worldwide@erau.edu.

Embry-Riddle Aeronautical University–Worldwide, Worldwide Headquarters - Graduate Degrees and Programs, Program in Management, Daytona Beach, FL 32114-3900. Offers MSM, MSM/MBAA. Part-time and evening/weekend programs available. Postbaccalaureate distance learning degree programs offered. *Faculty:* 4 full-time (1 woman), 50 part-time/adjunct (15 women). *Students:* 409 full-time (103 women), 328 part-time (89 women); includes 196 minority (91 Black or African American, non-Hispanic/Latino; 5 American Indian or Alaska Native, non-Hispanic/Latino; 34 Asian, non-Hispanic/Latino; 52 Hispanic/Latino; 3 Native Hawaiian or other Pacific Islander, non-Hispanic/Latino; 11 Two or more races, non-Hispanic/Latino), 2 international. Average age 34. 173 applicants, 77% accepted, 100 enrolled. In 2011, 104 master's awarded. *Degree requirements:* For master's, thesis optional. *Entrance requirements:* For master's, GMAT. *Application deadline:* Applications are processed on a rolling basis. Application fee: $50. Electronic applications accepted. *Expenses: Tuition:* Part-time $395 per credit hour. Tuition and fees vary according to degree level and program. *Financial support:* In 2011–12, 188 students received support. Applicants required to submit FAFSA. *Unit head:* Dr. Kees Rietsema, Chair, 602-904-1285, E-mail: rietsd37@erau.edu. *Application contact:* Linda Dammer, Director of Admissions, 386-226-6396 Ext. 1, Fax: 386-226-6984, E-mail: worldwide@erau.edu. Web site: http://www.embryriddle.edu/.

Lewis University, College of Arts and Sciences, Program in Aviation and Transportation, Romeoville, IL 60446. Offers administration (MS); safety and security (MS). Part-time and evening/weekend programs available. Postbaccalaureate distance learning degree programs offered (no on-campus study). *Faculty:* 2 full-time (0 women), 1 part-time/adjunct (0 women). *Students:* 10 full-time (2 women), 14 part-time (4 women); includes 12 minority (4 Black or African American, non-Hispanic/Latino; 6 Hispanic/Latino; 2 Two or more races, non-Hispanic/Latino). Average age 37. In 2011, 4 degrees awarded. *Entrance requirements:* For master's, bachelor's degree, minimum GPA of 3.0, personal statement, 3 letters of recommendation. Additional exam requirements/recommendations for international students: Required—TOEFL (minimum score 550 paper-based; 213 computer-based; 80 iBT). *Application deadline:* For fall admission, 5/1 for international students; for spring admission, 11/15 for international students. Applications are processed on a rolling basis. Application fee: $40. Electronic applications accepted. *Financial support:* Application deadline: 5/1; applicants required to submit FAFSA. *Unit head:* Dr. Randal DeMik, Program Chair, 815-838-0500 Ext. 5559, E-mail: demikra@lewisu.edu. *Application contact:* Julie Branchaw, Assistant Director, Graduate and Adult Admission, 815-836-5574, E-mail: branchju@lewisu.edu.

Lynn University, College of Business and Management, Boca Raton, FL 33431-5598. Offers aviation management (MBA); financial valuation and investment management (MBA); hospitality management (MBA); international business (MBA); marketing (MBA); mass communication and media management (MBA); sports and athletics administration (MBA). Part-time and evening/weekend programs available. Postbaccalaureate distance learning degree programs offered. *Degree requirements:* For master's, project. *Entrance requirements:* For master's, GMAT or GRE, minimum undergraduate GPA of 3.0, resume, 2 letters of recommendation. Additional exam requirements/recommendations for international students: Required—TOEFL (minimum score 550 paper-based; 213 computer-based). Electronic applications accepted. *Faculty research:* Labor relations, dynamic balance in leisure-time skills, ethics in athletics, hotel development.

Middle Tennessee State University, College of Graduate Studies, College of Basic and Applied Sciences, Department of Aerospace, Program in Aviation Administration, Murfreesboro, TN 37132. Offers MS. Part-time and evening/weekend programs available. Postbaccalaureate distance learning degree programs offered. *Students:* 10 full-time (2 women), 21 part-time (4 women); includes 6 minority (5 Black or African American, non-Hispanic/Latino; 1 Hispanic/Latino). 34 applicants, 71% accepted. In 2011, 8 master's awarded. *Degree requirements:* For master's, comprehensive exam, thesis optional. *Entrance requirements:* For master's, GRE or MAT. Additional exam requirements/recommendations for international students: Required—TOEFL (minimum score 525 paper-based; 195 computer-based; 71 iBT) or IELTS (minimum score 6). *Application deadline:* For fall admission, 6/1 for domestic and international students. Applications are processed on a rolling basis. Application fee: $25 ($30 for international students). *Expenses:* Tuition, state resident: full-time $10,008. Tuition, nonresident:

full-time $25,056. *Financial support:* In 2011–12, 4 students received support. Tuition waivers available. Support available to part-time students. Financial award application deadline: 5/1. *Unit head:* Dr. Ron Ferrara, Chair, 615-898-2788, Fax: 615-904-8273, E-mail: ron.ferrara@mtsu.edu. *Application contact:* Dr. Michael D. Allen, Dean and Vice Provost for Research, 615-898-2840, Fax: 615-904-8020, E-mail: michael.allen@mtsu.edu.

Southeastern Oklahoma State University, Department of Aviation Science, Durant, OK 74701-0609. Offers aerospace administration and logistics (MS). Part-time and evening/weekend programs available. *Students:* 57 full-time (10 women), 68 part-time (11 women); includes 28 minority (10 Black or African American, non-Hispanic/Latino; 4 American Indian or Alaska Native, non-Hispanic/Latino; 7 Asian, non-Hispanic/Latino; 7 Hispanic/Latino), 1 international. Average age 30. 23 applicants, 96% accepted, 22 enrolled. *Entrance requirements:* For master's, minimum GPA of 3.0 in last 60 hours or 2.75 overall. Additional exam requirements/recommendations for international students: Required—TOEFL (minimum score 550 paper-based; 213 computer-based; 79 iBT). *Application deadline:* For fall admission, 8/1 for domestic students, 6/1 for international students; for spring admission, 1/5 for domestic students, 11/1 for international students. Application fee: $20 ($55 for international students). Electronic applications accepted. *Expenses:* Tuition, state resident: full-time $3537; part-time $173.95 per credit hour. Tuition, nonresident: full-time $8673; part-time $459.30 per credit hour. *Required fees:* $22.55 per credit hour. *Financial support:* Federal Work-Study and institutionally sponsored loans available. Support available to part-time students. Financial award application deadline: 6/15. *Unit head:* Dr. David Conway, Director, 580-745-3240, Fax: 580-924-0741, E-mail: dconway@se.edu. *Application contact:* Carrie Williamson, Administrative Assistant, Graduate Office, 580-745-2220, Fax: 580-745-7474, E-mail: cwilliamson@se.edu. Web site: http://aviation.se.edu/.

Vaughn College of Aeronautics and Technology, Graduate Programs, Flushing, NY 11369. Offers airport management (MS). *Degree requirements:* For master's, project or thesis.

Logistics

Air Force Institute of Technology, Graduate School of Engineering and Management, Department of Operational Sciences, Dayton, OH 45433-7765. Offers logistics management (MS); operations research (MS, PhD); space operations (MS). Part-time programs available. *Degree requirements:* For master's, thesis; for doctorate, thesis/dissertation. *Entrance requirements:* For doctorate, GRE General Test, minimum GPA of 3.0, U.S. citizenship. *Faculty research:* Optimization, simulation, combat modeling and analysis, reliability and maintainability, resource scheduling.

American Public University System, AMU/APU Graduate Programs, Charles Town, WV 25414. Offers accounting (MBA, MS); administration and supervision (M Ed); criminal justice (MA); emergency and disaster management (MA); entrepreneurship (MBA); environmental policy and management (MS), including environmental planning, environmental sustainability, fish and wildlife management, general (MA, MS), global environmental management; finance (MBA); general (MBA); global business management (MBA); guidance and counseling (M Ed); history (MA), including American history, ancient and classical history, European history, global history, military and diplomatic history, public history; homeland security (MA); homeland security resource allocation (MBA); humanities (MA); information technology (MS), including digital forensics, enterprise software development, information assurance and security, IT project management; information technology management (MBA); intelligence studies (MA), including criminal intelligence, general (MA, MS), homeland security, intelligence analysis, intelligence collection, intelligence operations, terrorism studies; international relations and conflict resolution (MA), including comparative and security issues, conflict resolution, international and transnational security issues, peacekeeping; legal studies (MA); management (MA), including defense management, general (MA, MS), human resource management, organizational leadership, public administration, reverse logistics, strategic consulting; marketing (MBA); military history (MA), including American military history, American revolution, civil war, war since 1946, World War II; military studies (MA), including air warfare, asymmetrical warfare, joint warfare, land warfare, naval warfare, strategic leadership; national security studies (MA), including general (MA, MS), homeland security, regional security studies, security and intelligence analysis, terrorism studies; nonprofit management (MBA); political science (MA), including American politics and government, comparative government and development, public policy; psychology (MA); public administration (MA, MPA), including disaster management (MPA), environmental policy (MA), health policy (MPA), human resources (MPA), national security (MPA), organizational management (MPA), security management (MPA); public health (MA, MPH), including emergency management (MPH), environmental health (MPH), public administration (MA); reverse logistics management (MA); security management (MA); space studies (MS), including aerospace science, planetary science; sports and health sciences (MS); sports management (MS), including coaching theory and strategy, sports administration; teaching (M Ed), including curriculum and instruction for elementary teachers, elementary, elementary reading, English language learners, instructional leadership, online learning, secondary social sciences, special education; transportation and logistics management (MA), including maritime engineering management. Programs offered via distance learning only. Part-time and evening/weekend programs available. Postbaccalaureate distance learning degree programs offered (no on-campus study). *Faculty:* 445 full-time (241 women), 1,360 part-time/adjunct (617 women). *Students:* 688 full-time (338 women), 10,168 part-time (3,706 women); includes 3,130 minority (1,007 Black or African American, non-Hispanic/Latino; 103 American Indian or Alaska Native, non-Hispanic/Latino; 825 Asian, non-Hispanic/Latino; 810 Hispanic/Latino; 51 Native Hawaiian or other Pacific Islander, non-Hispanic/Latino; 334 Two or more races, non-Hispanic/Latino), 134 international. Average age 35. In 2011, 2,386 master's awarded. *Degree requirements:* For master's, comprehensive exam or practicum. *Entrance requirements:* For master's, official transcript showing earned bachelor's degree from institution accredited by recognized accrediting body. Additional exam requirements/recommendations for international students: Required—TOEFL (minimum score 550 paper-based; 213 computer-based), IELTS (minimum score 6.5). *Application deadline:* Applications are processed on a rolling basis. Application fee: $0. Electronic applications accepted. *Expenses: Tuition:* Part-time $325 per credit hour. *Financial support:* Applicants required to submit FAFSA. *Faculty research:* Military history, criminal justice, management performance, national security. *Unit head:* Dr. Karan Powell, Executive Vice President and Provost, 877-468-6268, Fax: 304-724-3780. *Application contact:* Terry Grant, Vice President of Enrollment Management, 877-468-6268, Fax: 304-724-3780, E-mail: info@apus.edu. Web site: http://www.apus.edu.

Benedictine University, Graduate Programs, Program in Business Administration, Lisle, IL 60532-0900. Offers accounting (MBA); entrepreneurship and managing innovation (MBA); financial management (MBA); health administration (MBA); human resource management (MBA); information systems security (MBA); international business (MBA); management consulting (MBA); management information systems (MBA); marketing management (MBA); operations management and logistics (MBA); organizational leadership (MBA); MBA/MPH; MBA/MS. Part-time and evening/weekend programs available. Postbaccalaureate distance learning degree programs offered (minimal on-campus study). *Faculty:* 4 full-time (2 women), 24 part-time/adjunct (3 women). *Students:* 165 full-time (101 women), 766 part-time (381 women); includes 201 minority (118 Black or African American, non-Hispanic/Latino; 4 American Indian or Alaska Native, non-Hispanic/Latino; 37 Asian, non-Hispanic/Latino; 40 Hispanic/Latino; 2 Native Hawaiian or other Pacific Islander, non-Hispanic/Latino), 14 international. Average age 34. 313 applicants, 73% accepted, 166 enrolled. In 2011, 379 master's awarded. *Entrance requirements:* For master's, GMAT. Additional exam requirements/recommendations for international students: Required—TOEFL (minimum score 550 paper-based; 213 computer-based). *Application deadline:* For fall admission, 9/1 for domestic students; for winter admission, 12/1 for domestic students; for spring admission, 2/15 for domestic students. Applications are processed on a rolling basis. Application fee: $40. Electronic applications accepted. *Financial support:* Career-related internships or fieldwork and health care benefits available. Support available to part-time students. *Faculty research:* Strategic leadership in professional organizations, sociology of professions, organizational change, social identity theory, applications to change management. *Unit head:* Dr. Sharon Borowicz, Director, 630-829-6219, E-mail: sborowicz@ben.edu. *Application contact:* Kari Gibbons, Director, Admissions, 630-829-6200, Fax: 630-829-6584, E-mail: kgibbons@ben.edu.

California State University, Long Beach, Graduate Studies, College of Liberal Arts, Department of Economics, Long Beach, CA 90840. Offers economics (MA); global logistics (MA). Part-time programs available. *Faculty:* 7 full-time (3 women), 1 part-time/adjunct (0 women). *Students:* 17 full-time (9 women), 11 part-time (4 women); includes 13 minority (2 Black or African American, non-Hispanic/Latino; 5 Asian, non-Hispanic/Latino; 5 Hispanic/Latino; 1 Two or more races, non-Hispanic/Latino), 8 international. Average age 27. 91 applicants, 46% accepted, 14 enrolled. In 2011, 14 master's awarded. *Degree requirements:* For master's, comprehensive exam or thesis. *Entrance requirements:* For master's, GRE General Test, GRE Subject Test, minimum GPA of 3.0. *Application deadline:* For fall admission, 4/1 for domestic students. Applications are processed on a rolling basis. Application fee: $55. Electronic applications accepted. *Financial support:* Federal Work-Study, institutionally sponsored loans, and scholarships/grants available. Financial award application deadline: 3/2. *Faculty research:* Trade and development, economic forecasting, resource economics. *Unit head:* Dr. Joseph P. Magaddino, Chair, 562-985-5061, Fax: 562-985-5804, E-mail: magaddin@csulb.edu. *Application contact:* Dr. Alejandra C. Edwards, Graduate Advisor, 562-985-5969, Fax: 562-985-5804, E-mail: acoxedwa@csulb.edu.

Case Western Reserve University, School of Graduate Studies, Case School of Engineering, Department of Electrical Engineering and Computer Science, Cleveland, OH 44106. Offers computer engineering (MS, PhD); computing and information sciences (MS, PhD); electrical engineering (MS, PhD); systems and control engineering (MS, PhD). Part-time and evening/weekend programs available. Postbaccalaureate distance learning degree programs offered (minimal on-campus study). *Faculty:* 33 full-time (3 women). *Students:* 188 full-time (34 women), 22 part-time (4 women); includes 6 minority (3 Black or African American, non-Hispanic/Latino; 3 Asian, non-Hispanic/Latino), 132 international. In 2011, 30 master's, 22 doctorates awarded. Terminal master's awarded for partial completion of doctoral program. *Degree requirements:* For master's, thesis; for doctorate, thesis/dissertation, qualifying exam, teaching experience. *Entrance requirements:* For master's and doctorate, GRE General Test. Additional exam requirements/recommendations for international students: Required—TOEFL. *Application deadline:* For fall admission, 2/1 for domestic students; for spring admission, 11/1 for domestic students. Applications are processed on a rolling basis. Application fee: $50. *Financial support:* Fellowships with full and partial tuition reimbursements, research assistantships with full and partial tuition reimbursements, teaching assistantships, career-related internships or fieldwork, Federal Work-Study, and institutionally sponsored loans available. Support available to part-time students. Financial award application deadline: 3/1; financial award applicants required to submit FAFSA. *Faculty research:* Applied artificial intelligence, automation, computer-aided design and testing of digital systems. *Total annual research expenditures:* $6 million. *Unit head:* Dr. Michael Branicky, Department Chair, 216-368-6888, E-mail: branicky@case.edu. *Application contact:* David Easler, Student Affairs Coordinator, 216-368-4080, Fax: 216-368-2801, E-mail: david.easler@case.edu. Web site: http://eecs.cwru.edu/.

Central Connecticut State University, School of Graduate Studies, School of Technology, Department of Manufacturing and Construction Management, New Britain, CT 06050-4010. Offers construction management (MS, Certificate); lean manufacturing and Six Sigma (Certificate); supply chain and logistics (Certificate); technology management (MS). Part-time and evening/weekend programs available. *Faculty:* 18 full-time (4 women), 26 part-time/adjunct (2 women). *Students:* 23 full-time (5 women), 89 part-time (22 women); includes 18 minority (10 Black or African American, non-Hispanic/Latino; 7 Asian, non-Hispanic/Latino; 1 Hispanic/Latino), 7 international. Average age 36. 68 applicants, 78% accepted, 39 enrolled. In 2011, 25 master's, 1 other advanced degree awarded. *Degree requirements:* For master's, comprehensive exam, thesis or alternative; for Certificate, qualifying exam. *Entrance requirements:* For master's, minimum undergraduate GPA of 2.7. Additional exam requirements/recommendations for international students: Required—TOEFL (minimum score 550 paper-based; 213 computer-based). *Application deadline:* For fall admission, 6/1 for domestic students, 5/1 for international students; for spring admission, 11/1 for domestic and international students. Applications are processed on a rolling basis. Application fee: $50. Electronic applications accepted. *Expenses: Tuition, area resident:* Full-time $5137; part-time $482 per credit. Tuition, state resident: full-time $7707; part-time $494 per credit. Tuition, nonresident: full-time $14,311; part-time $494 per credit. *Required fees:* $3865. One-time fee: $62 part-time. *Financial support:* In 2011–12, 9 students received support, including 7 research assistantships; career-related internships or fieldwork, Federal Work-Study, scholarships/grants, and unspecified assistantships also available. Support available to part-time students. Financial award application deadline: 4/15; financial award applicants required to submit FAFSA. *Faculty research:* All aspects of middle management, technical supervision in the workplace. *Unit head:* Dr. Jacob Kovel, Chair, 860-832-1830, E-mail: kovelj@ccsu.edu. *Application contact:* Patricia Gardner, Associate Director of Graduate Studies, 860-832-2350, Fax: 860-832-2352, E-mail: graduateadmissions@ccsu.edu. Web site: http://www.ccsu.edu/page.cfm?p=6497.

Central Michigan University, Central Michigan University Global Campus, Program in Business Administration, Mount Pleasant, MI 48859. Offers enterprise resource planning (MBA, Certificate); logistics management (MBA, Certificate); value-driven organization (MBA). Part-time and evening/weekend programs available. *Entrance requirements:* For master's, GMAT. *Financial support:* Scholarships/grants available. Support available to part-time students. *Unit head:* Dr. Debasish Chakraborty, 989-774-3678, E-mail: chakt1d@cmich.edu. *Application contact:* Global Campus Student Services Call Center, 877-268-4636, E-mail: cmuglobal@cmich.edu.

Colorado Technical University Colorado Springs, Graduate Studies, Program in Management, Colorado Springs, CO 80907-3896. Offers accounting (MBA, MSA); business administration (MBA); finance (MBA); human resources management (MBA); logistics/supply chain management (MBA); management (DM); marketing (MBA); mediation and dispute resolution (MBA); operations management (MBA); project management (MBA); technology management (MBA). Part-time and evening/weekend programs available. Postbaccalaureate distance learning degree programs offered. *Degree requirements:* For master's, thesis or alternative; for doctorate, thesis/dissertation. *Entrance requirements:* For doctorate, minimum graduate GPA of 3.0, 5 years of related work experience. *Faculty research:* Sexual harassment, performance evaluation, critical thinking.

Copenhagen Business School, Graduate Programs, Copenhagen, Denmark. Offers business administration (Exec MBA, MBA, PhD); business administration and information systems (M Sc); business, language and culture (M Sc); economics and business administration (M Sc); health management (MHM); international business and politics (M Sc); public administration (MPA); shipping and logistics (Exec MBA); technology, market and organization (MBA).

East Carolina University, Graduate School, College of Technology and Computer Science, Department of Technology Systems, Greenville, NC 27858-4353. Offers computer network professional (Certificate); industrial technology (MS), including computer networking management, digital communications, industrial distribution and logistics, information security, manufacturing, performance improvement, quality systems; information assurance (Certificate); Lean Six Sigma Black Belt (Certificate); occupational safety (MS); technology management (PhD); Website developer (Certificate). *Entrance requirements:* For master's and Certificate, GRE General Test or MAT, minimum GPA of 2.5; for doctorate, GRE General Test, related work experience. *Application deadline:* For fall admission, 6/1 priority date for domestic students.

Applications are processed on a rolling basis. Application fee: $50. *Expenses:* Tuition, state resident: full-time $3557; part-time $444.63 per semester hour. Tuition, nonresident: full-time $14,351; part-time $1793.88 per semester hour. *Required fees:* $2016; $252 per semester hour. Part-time tuition and fees vary according to course load, campus/location and program. *Financial support:* Application deadline: 6/1. *Unit head:* Dr. Tijjani Mohammed, Interim Chair, 252-328-9668, E-mail: mohammedt@ecu.edu. Web site: http://www.ecu.edu/cs-tecs/techsystems/.

Embry-Riddle Aeronautical University–Worldwide, Worldwide Headquarters - Graduate Degrees and Programs, Program in Logistics and Supply Chain Management, Daytona Beach, FL 32114-3900. Offers integrated logistics management (Graduate Certificate); logistics and supply chain management (MSLSCM). *Faculty:* 4 full-time (1 woman), 50 part-time/adjunct (15 women). *Students:* 44 full-time (14 women), 57 part-time (21 women); includes 42 minority (21 Black or African American, non-Hispanic/Latino; 2 American Indian or Alaska Native, non-Hispanic/Latino; 5 Asian, non-Hispanic/Latino; 11 Hispanic/Latino; 3 Two or more races, non-Hispanic/Latino). Average age 35. 86 applicants, 66% accepted, 28 enrolled. In 2011, 1 master's awarded. *Degree requirements:* For master's, thesis (for some programs). Application fee: $50. *Expenses: Tuition:* Part-time $395 per credit hour. Tuition and fees vary according to degree level and program. *Financial support:* In 2011–12, 27 students received support. *Unit head:* Dr. Kees Rietsema, Chair, 602-904-1285, E-mail: rietsd37@erau.edu. *Application contact:* Linda Dammer, Director of Admissions, 386-226-6396 Ext. 1, Fax: 386-226-6984, E-mail: worldwide@erau.edu.

Florida Institute of Technology, Graduate Programs, Extended Studies Division, Melbourne, FL 32901-6975. Offers acquisition and contract management (MS); aerospace engineering (MS); business administration (MBA); computer information systems (MS); computer science (MS); electrical engineering (MS); engineering management (MS); human resources management (MS); logistics management (MS), including humanitarian and disaster relief logistics; management (MS), including acquisition and contract management, e-business, human resources management, information systems, logistics management, management, transportation management; material acquisition management (MS); mechanical engineering (MS); operations research (MS); project management (MS), including information systems, operations research; public administration (MPA); quality management (MS); software engineering (MS); space systems (MS); space systems management (MS); supply chain management (MS); systems management (MS), including information systems, operations research. Part-time and evening/weekend programs available. Postbaccalaureate distance learning degree programs offered (no on-campus study). *Faculty:* 9 full-time (2 women), 105 part-time/adjunct (24 women). *Students:* 113 full-time (52 women), 1,150 part-time (484 women); includes 496 minority (332 Black or African American, non-Hispanic/Latino; 11 American Indian or Alaska Native, non-Hispanic/Latino; 42 Asian, non-Hispanic/Latino; 71 Hispanic/Latino; 2 Native Hawaiian or other Pacific Islander, non-Hispanic/Latino; 38 Two or more races, non-Hispanic/Latino), 11 international. Average age 35. 568 applicants, 56% accepted, 296 enrolled. In 2011, 471 master's awarded. *Degree requirements:* For master's, comprehensive exam (for some programs), capstone course. *Entrance requirements:* For master's, GMAT or resume showing 8 years of supervised experience, minimum GPA of 3.0, 2 letters of recommendation, resume. Additional exam requirements/recommendations for international students: Required—TOEFL (minimum score 550 paper-based; 213 computer-based; 79 iBT). *Application deadline:* For fall admission, 4/1 for international students; for spring admission, 9/30 for international students. Applications are processed on a rolling basis. Application fee: $0. Electronic applications accepted. *Expenses:* Contact institution. *Financial support:* Application deadline: 3/1; applicants required to submit FAFSA. *Unit head:* Dr. Theodore R. Richardson, III, Senior Associate Dean, 321-674-8123, Fax: 321-674-7597, E-mail: trichardson@fit.edu. *Application contact:* Carolyn Farrior, Director of Graduate Admissions, Online Learning and Off-Campus Programs, 321-674-7118, Fax: 321-674-8216, E-mail: cfarrior@fit.edu. Web site: http://es.fit.edu.

George Mason University, School of Public Policy, Program in Transportation Policy, Operations and Logistics, Arlington, VA 22201. Offers MA, Certificate. *Faculty:* 54 full-time (18 women), 20 part-time/adjunct (8 women). *Students:* 8 full-time (1 woman), 24 part-time (7 women); includes 9 minority (4 Black or African American, non-Hispanic/Latino; 2 Hispanic/Latino; 1 Native Hawaiian or other Pacific Islander, non-Hispanic/Latino; 2 Two or more races, non-Hispanic/Latino), 2 international. Average age 32. 31 applicants, 65% accepted, 11 enrolled. In 2011, 18 master's awarded. *Degree requirements:* For master's, thesis or alternative. *Entrance requirements:* For master's, GRE (for students seeking merit-based scholarships), bachelor's degree with minimum GPA of 3.0, current resume, 2 letters of recommendation, expanded goals statement, 2 copies of official transcripts. Additional exam requirements/recommendations for international students: Required—TOEFL (minimum score 575 paper-based; 230 computer-based; 88 iBT), IELTS, Pearson Test of English. *Application deadline:* For fall admission, 6/1 priority date for domestic students, 5/1 for international students; for spring admission, 12/1 priority date for domestic students, 11/1 for international students. Applications are processed on a rolling basis. Application fee: $65 ($80 for international students). Electronic applications accepted. *Expenses:* Contact institution. *Financial support:* Career-related internships or fieldwork, Federal Work-Study, scholarships/grants, unspecified assistantships, and health care benefits (full-time research or teaching assistantship recipients) available. Financial award application deadline: 3/1; financial award applicants required to submit FAFSA. *Unit head:* Dr. Jonathan Gifford, Director, 703-993-2275, Fax: 703-993-9198, E-mail: jgifford@gmu.edu. *Application contact:* Tennille Haegele, Director, Graduate Admissions, 703-993-8099, Fax: 703-993-4876, E-mail: spp@gmu.edu. Web site: http://policy.gmu.edu/Home/AcademicProfessionalPrograms/MastersPrograms/TransportationPolicyOperationsLogistics/tabid/108/Default.aspx.

Georgia College & State University, Graduate School, College of Arts and Sciences, Department of Government and Sociology, Logistics Education Center, Milledgeville, GA 31061. Offers logistics management (MSA). Part-time and evening/weekend programs available. *Students:* 10 full-time (6 women), 67 part-time (28 women); includes 22 minority (18 Black or African American, non-Hispanic/Latino; 1 Hispanic/Latino; 3 Two or more races, non-Hispanic/Latino). Average age 36. 22 applicants, 59% accepted, 9 enrolled. In 2011, 29 master's awarded. *Entrance requirements:* For master's, MAT, GRE, GMAT, immunization record, transcripts. Additional exam requirements/recommendations for international students: Recommended—TOEFL (minimum score 550 paper-based; 213 computer-based; 79 iBT). *Application deadline:* For fall admission, 7/1 priority date for domestic students, 4/1 for international students; for spring admission, 11/15 priority date for domestic students, 9/1 for international students. Applications are processed on a rolling basis. Application fee: $40. Electronic applications accepted. *Expenses:* Tuition, state resident: full-time $4806; part-time $267 per credit hour. Tuition, nonresident: full-time $17,802; part-time $989 per credit hour. *Required fees:* $936 per semester. Tuition and fees vary according to course load and campus/location. *Financial support:* Application deadline: 3/1; applicants required to submit FAFSA. *Unit head:* Glen Easterly, Director of Robins Center/Coordinator of Logistics Program, 478-327-7376, Fax: 478-926-2468, E-mail: glenn.easterly@gcsu.edu. *Application contact:* Kate Marshall, Graduate Admissions Coordinator, 478-445-1184, Fax: 478-445-1336, E-mail: grad-admit@gcsu.edu.

Georgia Southern University, Jack N. Averitt College of Graduate Studies, College of Business Administration, Program in Logistics/Supply Chain Management, Statesboro, GA 30460. Offers PhD. *Students:* 13 full-time (5 women); includes 2 minority (1 Hispanic/Latino; 1 Two or more races, non-Hispanic/Latino), 5 international. Average age 35. 23 applicants, 35% accepted, 7 enrolled. *Degree requirements:* For doctorate, comprehensive exam, thesis/dissertation. *Entrance requirements:* For doctorate, GMAT or GRE, letters of reference. Additional exam requirements/recommendations for international students: Required—TOEFL (minimum score 550 paper-based; 213 computer-based; 80 iBT). *Application deadline:* For fall admission, 3/15 priority date for domestic students, 3/15 for international students. Application fee: $50. Electronic applications accepted. *Expenses:* Tuition, state resident: full-time $6300; part-time $263 per semester hour. Tuition, nonresident: full-time $25,174; part-time $1049 per semester hour. *Required fees:* $1872. *Financial support:* In 2011–12, 10 students received support. Career-related internships or fieldwork, Federal Work-Study, scholarships/grants, traineeships, and unspecified assistantships available. Support available to part-time students. Financial award application deadline: 4/15; financial award applicants required to submit FAFSA. *Faculty research:* Buyer-supplier relationships, retail supply chain management, military logistics/transportation/SCM, strategic sourcing/outsourcing, supply chain metrics. *Unit head:* Dr. Ron Shiffler, Dean, 912-478-5106, Fax: 912-478-0292, E-mail: shiffler@georgiasouthern.edu. *Application contact:* Dr. Stephen Rutner, Graduate Program Director, 912-478-0511, Fax: 912-478-1523, E-mail: srutner@georgiasouthern.edu. Web site: http://coba.georgiasouthern.edu/phd/.

HEC Montreal, School of Business Administration, Master of Science Programs in Administration, Program in International Logistics, Montréal, QC H3T 2A7, Canada. Offers M Sc. Part-time programs available. *Students:* 22 full-time (10 women), 6 part-time (3 women). 25 applicants, 44% accepted, 7 enrolled. In 2011, 5 master's awarded. *Degree requirements:* For master's, one foreign language, thesis. *Entrance requirements:* For master's, Test de francais international (TFI) with minimum score of 850 (for those who have never studied in French), BBA, undergraduate degree in another field, degree deemed equivalent by program director and minimum GPA of 3.0 on 4.3 scale. *Application deadline:* For fall admission, 3/15 for domestic and international students; for winter admission, 9/15 for domestic and international students. Application fee: $80 Canadian dollars. Electronic applications accepted. Application fee is waived when completed online. *Expenses:* Tuition, state resident: full-time $2601.36. Tuition, nonresident: full-time $7030. *International tuition:* $17,474.04 full-time. *Required fees:* $1381.77. Tuition and fees vary according to degree level and program. *Financial support:* Fellowships, research assistantships, teaching assistantships, and scholarships/grants available. Financial award application deadline: 9/2. *Unit head:* Dr. Claude Laurin, Director, 514-340-6485, Fax: 514-340-6880, E-mail: claude.laurin@hec.ca. *Application contact:* Virginie Lefebvre, Administrative Director, 514-340-6112, Fax: 514-340-6411, E-mail: virginie.lefebvre@hec.ca. Web site: http://www.hec.ca/en/programs_training/msc/options/logistics/.

Kaplan University, Davenport Campus, School of Business, Davenport, IA 52807-2095. Offers business administration (MBA); change leadership (MS); entrepreneurship (MBA); finance (MBA); health care management (MBA, MS); human resource (MBA); international business (MBA); management (MS); marketing (MBA); project management (MBA, MS); supply chain management and logistics (MBA, MS). Part-time and evening/weekend programs available. Postbaccalaureate distance learning degree programs offered (no on-campus study). *Entrance requirements:* Additional exam requirements/recommendations for international students: Required—TOEFL (minimum score 550 paper-based; 218 computer-based; 80 iBT). Electronic applications accepted.

Maine Maritime Academy, Department of Graduate Studies, Program in Maritime Management, Castine, ME 04420. Offers MS, Certificate, Diploma. Part-time programs available. *Degree requirements:* For master's, thesis optional, capstone course. *Entrance requirements:* For master's, GMAT or GRE General Test, letters of recommendation. Additional exam requirements/recommendations for international students: Required—TOEFL. *Faculty research:* Human resources in maritime environment, management of organization change, economic analysis and maritime law.

Massachusetts Institute of Technology, School of Engineering, Engineering Systems Division, Cambridge, MA 02139. Offers engineering and management (SM); engineering systems (SM, PhD); logistics (M Eng); technology and policy (SM); technology, management and policy (PhD); SM/MBA. *Faculty:* 22 full-time (7 women). *Students:* 296 full-time (88 women); includes 36 minority (3 Black or African American, non-Hispanic/Latino; 22 Asian, non-Hispanic/Latino; 6 Hispanic/Latino; 5 Two or more races, non-Hispanic/Latino), 132 international. Average age 31. 909 applicants, 26% accepted, 181 enrolled. In 2011, 143 master's, 13 doctorates awarded. *Degree requirements:* For master's, thesis; for doctorate, comprehensive exam, thesis/dissertation. *Entrance requirements:* For master's, GRE General Test (or GMAT for some programs); for doctorate, GRE General Test. Additional exam requirements/recommendations for international students: Required—IELTS (minimum score 7.5). Application fee: $75. Electronic applications accepted. *Expenses:* Contact institution. *Financial support:* In 2011–12, 223 students received support, including 44 fellowships (averaging $30,600 per year), 96 research assistantships (averaging $29,000 per year), 16 teaching assistantships (averaging $29,800 per year); career-related internships or fieldwork, Federal Work-Study, institutionally sponsored loans, scholarships/grants, health care benefits, and unspecified assistantships also available. *Faculty research:* Critical infrastructures, extended enterprises, energy and sustainability, health care delivery, humans and technology, uncertainty and dynamics, design and implementation, networks and flows, policy and standards. *Total annual research expenditures:* $13.7 million. *Unit head:* Prof. Joseph M. Sussman, Interim Director, 617-253-1764, E-mail: esdinquiries@mit.edu. *Application contact:* Graduate Admissions, 617-253-1182, E-mail: esdgrad@mit.edu. Web site: http://esd.mit.edu/.

Naval Postgraduate School, Departments and Academic Groups, School of Business and Public Policy, Monterey, CA 93943. Offers acquisitions and contract management (MBA); business administration (EMBA, MBA); contract management (MS); defense business management (MBA); defense systems analysis (MS), including management; defense systems management (international) (MBA); executive management (MBA); financial management (MBA); information systems management (MBA); manpower systems analysis (MS); material logistics support management (MBA); program management (MS); resource planning/management for international defense (MBA); supply chain management (MBA); systems acquisition management (MBA); transportation management (MBA). Program only open to commissioned officers of the United States and friendly nations and selected United States federal civilian employees. *Accreditation:* AACSB; NASPAA. Part-time programs available. Postbaccalaureate distance learning degree programs offered (minimal on-campus study). *Faculty:* 67 full-time (15 women), 32 part-time/adjunct (12 women). *Students:* 307 full-time (29 women), 327 part-time (71 women); includes 149 minority (55 Black or African American, non-Hispanic/Latino; 5 American Indian or Alaska Native, non-Hispanic/Latino; 46 Asian, non-Hispanic/Latino; 43 Hispanic/Latino), 44 international. Average age 42. In 2011, 295 master's awarded. *Degree requirements:* For master's, thesis (for some programs), terminal project/capstone (for some programs). *Faculty* *research:* U. S. and European public procurement policies for small and medium-sized enterprises, examining external validity criticisms in the choice of students as subjects in accounting experiment studies, assurance of learning in contract management education, contracting for cloud computing: opportunities and risks, NPS, Apple App Store as a business model supporting U. S. Navy requirements. *Total annual research expenditures:* $9 million. *Unit head:* Raymond Franck, Department Chair, 831-656-3614, E-mail: refranck@nps.edu. *Application contact:* Acting Director of Admissions. Web site: http://www.nps.edu/Academics/Schools/GSBPP/index.html.

North Dakota State University, College of Graduate and Interdisciplinary Studies, College of Engineering and Architecture, Department of Civil Engineering, Fargo, ND 58108. Offers civil engineering (MS, PhD); environmental engineering (MS, PhD); transportation and logistics (PhD). PhD in transportation and logistics offered jointly with Upper Great Plains Transportation Institute. Part-time programs available. Postbaccalaureate distance learning degree programs offered (minimal on-campus study). *Faculty:* 13 full-time (1 woman). *Students:* 25 full-time (2 women), 19 part-time (3 women); includes 3 minority (1 American Indian or Alaska Native, non-Hispanic/Latino; 2 Two or more races, non-Hispanic/Latino), 21 international. 46 applicants, 48% accepted, 8 enrolled. In 2011, 8 master's, 3 doctorates awarded. *Degree requirements:* For master's, thesis; for doctorate, comprehensive exam, thesis/dissertation. *Entrance requirements:* Additional exam requirements/recommendations for international students: Required—TOEFL (minimum score 525 paper-based; 197 computer-based; 71 iBT). *Application deadline:* For fall admission, 2/15 priority date for domestic students, 2/15 for international students; for spring admission, 9/15 priority date for domestic students, 9/15 for international students. Applications are processed on a rolling basis. Application fee: $35. Electronic applications accepted. *Financial support:* Fellowships with full tuition reimbursements, research assistantships with full tuition reimbursements, teaching assistantships with full tuition reimbursements, career-related internships or fieldwork, Federal Work-Study, and institutionally sponsored loans available. Support available to part-time students. Financial award application deadline: 1/15. *Faculty research:* Wastewater, solid waste, composites, nanotechnology. *Unit head:* Dr. Eakalak Khan, Chair, 701-231-7244, Fax: 701-231-6185, E-mail: eakalak.khan@ndsu.edu. *Application contact:* Dr. Kalpana Katti, Professor and Graduate Program Coordinator, 701-231-9504, Fax: 701-231-6185, E-mail: kalpana.katti@ndsu.edu. Web site: http://www.ce.ndsu.nodak.edu/.

North Dakota State University, College of Graduate and Interdisciplinary Studies, Interdisciplinary Program in Transportation and Logistics, Fargo, ND 58108. Offers PhD. *Students:* 28 full-time (6 women), 10 part-time (0 women); includes 7 minority (2 Black or African American, non-Hispanic/Latino; 2 Asian, non-Hispanic/Latino; 3 Two or more races, non-Hispanic/Latino), 12 international. 27 applicants, 74% accepted, 13 enrolled. In 2011, 7 doctorates awarded. *Entrance requirements:* For doctorate, 1 year of calculus, statistics and probability, minimum GPA of 3.0. Additional exam requirements/recommendations for international students: Required—TOEFL (minimum score 550 paper-based; 213 computer-based; 79 iBT). *Application deadline:* For fall admission, 5/1 priority date for domestic students. Applications are processed on a rolling basis. Application fee: $35. *Financial support:* Research assistantships with full tuition reimbursements available. *Faculty research:* Supply chain optimization, spatial analysis of transportation networks, advanced traffic analysis, transportation demand, railroad/intermodal freight. *Unit head:* Dr. Denver Tolliver, Director, 701-231-7938, Fax: 701-231-1945, E-mail: denver.tolliver@ndsu.nodak.edu. *Application contact:* Sonya Goergen, Marketing, Recruitment, and Public Relations Coordinator, 701-231-7033, Fax: 701-231-6524. Web site: http://www.mountain-plains.org/education/tlprogram/.

The Ohio State University, Graduate School, Max M. Fisher College of Business, Program in Business Logistics Engineering, Columbus, OH 43210. Offers MBLE. *Faculty:* 16. *Students:* 47 full-time (22 women), 19 part-time (12 women); includes 1 minority (Asian, non-Hispanic/Latino), 63 international. Average age 24. In 2011, 29 master's awarded. *Entrance requirements:* For master's, GRE or GMAT. Additional exam requirements/recommendations for international students: Required—TOEFL (minimum score 550 paper-based; 79 iBT), Michigan English Language Assessment Battery (minimum score 82). *Application deadline:* Applications are processed on a rolling basis. Application fee: $40 ($50 for international students). Electronic applications accepted. *Expenses:* Tuition, state resident: full-time $11,400. Tuition, nonresident: full-time $28,125. Tuition and fees vary according to course load, degree level, campus/location and program. *Unit head:* Walter Zinn, Chair, 614-292-0797, E-mail: zinn.13@osu.edu. *Application contact:* Graduate Admissions, 614-292-6031, Fax: 614-292-3656, E-mail: gradadmissions@osu.edu. Web site: http://fisher.osu.edu/mble.

Polytechnic University of Puerto Rico, Miami Campus, Graduate School, Miami, FL 33166. Offers accounting (MBA); business administration (MBA); construction management (MEM); environmental management (MEM); finance (MBA); human resources management (MBA); logistics and supply chain management (MBA); management of international enterprises (MBA); manufacturing management (MEM); marketing management (MBA); project management (MBA). Part-time and evening/weekend programs available. Postbaccalaureate distance learning degree programs offered (no on-campus study). *Entrance requirements:* For master's, minimum GPA of 3.0. Electronic applications accepted.

Pontifical Catholic University of Puerto Rico, College of Business Administration, Program in Maritime Logistics and Transportation, Ponce, PR 00717-0777. Offers Professional Certificate.

Pontificia Universidad Catolica Madre y Maestra, Graduate School, Faculty of Engineering Sciences, Santiago, Dominican Republic. Offers earthquake engineering (ME); logistics management (ME).

Stevens Institute of Technology, Graduate School, School of Systems and Enterprises, Program in Systems Design and Operational Effectiveness, Hoboken, NJ 07030. Offers M Eng.

Stevens Institute of Technology, Graduate School, School of Systems and Enterprises, Program in Systems Engineering, Hoboken, NJ 07030. Offers agile systems and enterprises (Certificate); systems and supportability engineering (Certificate); systems engineering (M Eng, PhD); systems engineering management (Certificate).

Trident University International, College of Business Administration, Program in Business Administration, Cypress, CA 90630. Offers business administration (PhD); conflict and negotiation management (MBA); criminal justice administration (MBA); entrepreneurship (MBA); finance (MBA); general management (MBA); government accounting (MBA); human resource management (MBA); information security and digital assurance management (MBA); information technology management (MBA); international business (MBA); logistics management (MBA); marketing (MBA); project management (MBA); public management (MBA); quality management (MBA); strategic leadership (MBA). Part-time and evening/weekend programs available. Postbaccalaureate distance learning degree programs offered (no on-campus study). *Degree requirements:* For doctorate, comprehensive exam, thesis/dissertation, defense of dissertation. *Entrance requirements:* For master's, minimum GPA of 2.5 (students with GPA 3.0 or greater may transfer up to 30% of graduate level credits); for doctorate, minimum GPA of 3.4, curriculum vitae, course work in research methods or statistics. Additional exam requirements/recommendations for international students: Required—TOEFL. Electronic applications accepted.

Universidad del Turabo, Graduate Programs, School in Business Administration, Program in Logistics and Materials Management, Gurabo, PR 00778-3030. Offers MBA. Part-time and evening/weekend programs available. *Faculty:* 4 full-time (2 women), 21 part-time/adjunct (3 women). *Students:* 17 full-time (7 women), 29 part-time (18 women); includes 41 minority (all Hispanic/Latino). Average age 36. 28 applicants, 93% accepted, 13 enrolled. In 2011, 30 master's awarded. *Entrance requirements:* For master's, GRE, EXADEP, interview. *Application deadline:* For fall admission, 8/5 for domestic students. Application fee: $25. *Unit head:* Marcelino Rivera, Dean, 787-743-7979 Ext. 4117. *Application contact:* Virginia Gonzalez, Admissions Officer, 787-746-3009.

University at Buffalo, the State University of New York, Graduate School, School of Management, Buffalo, NY 14260. Offers accounting (MS); business administration (EMBA, MBA, PMBA); finance (MS), including financial engineering, financial management; management (PhD); management information systems (MS); supply chains and operations management (MS); Au D/MBA; JD/MBA; M Arch/MBA; MA/MBA; MD/MBA; MPH/MBA; MSW/MBA; Pharm D/MBA. *Accreditation:* AACSB. Part-time and evening/weekend programs available. *Degree requirements:* For master's, thesis (for some programs); for doctorate, comprehensive exam, thesis/dissertation. *Entrance requirements:* For master's, GMAT (MBA, MS in accounting), GRE or GMAT (for all other MS concentrations); for doctorate, GMAT or GRE. Additional exam requirements/recommendations for international students: Required—TOEFL (minimum score 230 computer-based; 95 iBT). Electronic applications accepted. *Expenses:* Contact institution. *Faculty research:* Earnings management and electronic information assurance, supply chains and operations management, corporate financing and asset pricing, consumer behavior and quantitative modeling of marketing behavior, leadership and politics in organizations.

The University of Alabama in Huntsville, School of Graduate Studies, College of Business Administration, Department of Management and Marketing, Huntsville, AL 35899. Offers federal contract procurement (Certificate); management (MBA), including acquisition management, entrepreneurship, federal contract accounting, finance, human resource management, logistics and supply chain management, marketing, project management; supply chain management (Certificate); technology and innovation management (Certificate). *Accreditation:* AACSB. Part-time and evening/weekend programs available. *Faculty:* 11 full-time (2 women), 3 part-time/adjunct (0 women). *Students:* 52 full-time (25 women), 145 part-time (68 women); includes 28 minority (14 Black or African American, non-Hispanic/Latino; 4 American Indian or Alaska Native, non-Hispanic/Latino; 7 Asian, non-Hispanic/Latino; 2 Hispanic/Latino; 1 Two or more races, non-Hispanic/Latino), 15 international. Average age 31. 103 applicants, 73% accepted, 65 enrolled. In 2011, 76 master's awarded. *Degree requirements:* For master's, comprehensive exam, thesis or alternative. *Entrance requirements:* For master's, GMAT (minimum score 500), minimum AACSB index of 1080. Additional exam requirements/recommendations for international students: Required—TOEFL (minimum score 550 paper-based; 213 computer-based; 62 iBT). *Application deadline:* For fall admission, 8/1 for domestic students, 4/1 for international students; for spring admission, 12/1 for domestic students, 9/1 for international students. Applications are processed on a rolling basis. Application fee: $40 ($50 for international students). Electronic applications accepted. *Expenses:* Tuition, state resident: full-time $7830; part-time $473.50 per credit. Tuition, nonresident: full-time $18,748; part-time $1128.33 per credit. Tuition and fees vary according to course load and program. *Financial support:* In 2011–12, 12 students received support, including 7 research assistantships with full tuition reimbursements available (averaging $9,829 per year), 4 teaching assistantships with full tuition reimbursements available (averaging $8,000 per year); career-related internships or fieldwork, Federal Work-Study, institutionally sponsored loans, scholarships/grants, health care benefits, and unspecified assistantships also available. Support available to part-time students. Financial award application deadline: 4/1; financial award applicants required to submit FAFSA. *Faculty research:* Strategic human resources, corporate governance, cross-function integration and the management of research and development, determinants of team performance. *Total annual research expenditures:* $3.4 million. *Unit head:* Dr. Cynthia Gramm, Chair, 256-824-6913, Fax: 256-824-6328, E-mail: cynthia.gramm@uah.edu. *Application contact:* Jennifer Pettitt, Director of Graduate Programs, 256-824-6681, Fax: 256-824-7571, E-mail: jennifer.pettitt@uah.edu.

University of Alaska Anchorage, College of Business and Public Policy, Program in Logistics, Anchorage, AK 99508. Offers global supply chain management (MS); supply chain management (Certificate). Part-time and evening/weekend programs available. Postbaccalaureate distance learning degree programs offered (no on-campus study). *Degree requirements:* For master's, thesis or alternative, research project. *Entrance requirements:* Additional exam requirements/recommendations for international students: Required—TOEFL (minimum score 550 paper-based; 213 computer-based).

University of Dallas, Graduate School of Management, Irving, TX 75062-4736. Offers accounting (MBA, MM, MS); business management (MBA, MM); corporate finance (MBA, MM); financial services (MBA); global business (MBA, MM); health services management (MBA, MM); human resource management (MBA, MM); information assurance (MBA, MM, MS); information technology (MBA, MM, MS); information technology service management (MBA, MM, MS); marketing management (MBA, MM); organization development (MBA, MM); project management (MBA, MM); sports and entertainment management (MBA, MM); strategic leadership (MBA, MM); supply chain management (MBA); supply chain management and market logistics (MM). *Accreditation:* ACBSP. Part-time and evening/weekend programs available. Postbaccalaureate distance learning degree programs offered (no on-campus study). *Entrance requirements:* Additional exam requirements/recommendations for international students: Required—TOEFL. Electronic applications accepted. *Expenses:* Contact institution.

University of Houston, College of Technology, Department of Information and Logistics Technology, Houston, TX 77204. Offers information security (MS); supply chain and logistics technology (MS); technology project management (MS). Part-time programs available. *Degree requirements:* For master's, project or thesis (most programs). *Entrance requirements:* For master's, GMAT. Additional exam requirements/recommendations for international students: Required—TOEFL (minimum score 550 paper-based; 79 iBT). Electronic applications accepted.

University of Louisville, J. B. Speed School of Engineering, Department of Industrial Engineering, Louisville, KY 40292-0001. Offers engineering management (M Eng); industrial engineering (M Eng, MS, PhD); logistics and distribution (Certificate). *Accreditation:* ABET (one or more programs are accredited). Part-time programs available. *Faculty:* 10 full-time (1 woman). *Students:* 42 full-time (13 women), 11 part-time (6 women); includes 5 minority (4 Black or African American, non-Hispanic/Latino; 1 Hispanic/Latino), 21 international. Average age 28. 52 applicants, 33% accepted, 11 enrolled. In 2011, 43 master's, 3 doctorates awarded. Terminal master's awarded for partial completion of doctoral program. *Degree requirements:* For master's, comprehensive exam (for some programs), thesis or alternative; for doctorate, comprehensive exam, thesis/dissertation, minimum GPA of 3.0. *Entrance requirements:* For master's and doctorate, GRE General Test. Additional exam requirements/

recommendations for international students: Required—TOEFL (minimum score 550 paper-based; 213 computer-based; 80 iBT), IELTS (minimum score 6.5). *Application deadline:* For fall admission, 5/1 priority date for domestic students, 5/1 for international students; for spring admission, 11/1 priority date for domestic students, 11/1 for international students. Applications are processed on a rolling basis. Application fee: $50. Electronic applications accepted. *Expenses:* Tuition, state resident: full-time $9692; part-time $539 per credit hour. Tuition, nonresident: full-time $20,168; part-time $1121 per credit hour. Tuition and fees vary according to program and reciprocity agreements. *Financial support:* In 2011–12, 15 students received support, including 7 fellowships with full tuition reimbursements available (averaging $20,000 per year), 2 research assistantships with full tuition reimbursements available (averaging $20,000 per year), 6 teaching assistantships with full tuition reimbursements available (averaging $20,000 per year). Financial award application deadline: 1/25; financial award applicants required to submit FAFSA. *Faculty research:* Optimization, computer simulation, logistics and distribution, ergonomics and human factors, advanced manufacturing process. *Total annual research expenditures:* $748,000. *Unit head:* Dr. John S. Usher, Chair, 502-852-6342, Fax: 502-852-5633, E-mail: usher@louisville.edu. *Application contact:* Dr. Michael Day, Associate Dean, 502-852-6195, Fax: 502-852-7294, E-mail: day@louisville.edu. Web site: http://www.louisville.edu/speed/industrial/.

University of Missouri–St. Louis, College of Business Administration, Program in Business Administration, St. Louis, MO 63121. Offers accounting (MBA); business administration (Certificate); finance (MBA); human resource management (Certificate); information systems (MBA); logistics and supply chain management (MBA, Certificate); marketing (MBA); marketing management (Certificate); operations management (MBA). *Accreditation:* AACSB. Part-time and evening/weekend programs available. *Faculty:* 32 full-time (7 women), 10 part-time/adjunct (2 women). *Students:* 126 full-time (48 women), 305 part-time (141 women); includes 61 minority (25 Black or African American, non-Hispanic/Latino; 23 Asian, non-Hispanic/Latino; 9 Hispanic/Latino; 1 Native Hawaiian or other Pacific Islander, non-Hispanic/Latino; 3 Two or more races, non-Hispanic/Latino), 47 international. Average age 30. 241 applicants, 70% accepted, 134 enrolled. In 2011, 150 master's, 1 doctorate, 19 other advanced degrees awarded. *Entrance requirements:* For master's, GMAT, 2 letters of recommendation. Additional exam requirements/recommendations for international students: Required—TOEFL (minimum score 550 paper-based; 213 computer-based). *Application deadline:* For fall admission, 7/1 for domestic and international students; for spring admission, 12/1 for domestic and international students. Applications are processed on a rolling basis. Application fee: $35 ($40 for international students). Electronic applications accepted. *Expenses:* Tuition, state resident: full-time $6273; part-time $3866 per year. Tuition, nonresident: full-time $14,969; part-time $9980 per year. *Required fees:* $315 per year. *Financial support:* In 2011–12, 32 research assistantships with full and partial tuition reimbursements (averaging $6,000 per year), 6 teaching assistantships with full and partial tuition reimbursements (averaging $12,276 per year) were awarded; career-related internships or fieldwork, Federal Work-Study, and institutionally sponsored loans also available. Support available to part-time students. Financial award application deadline: 4/1; financial award applicants required to submit FAFSA. *Faculty research:* Human resources, strategic management, marketing strategy, consumer behavior product development, advertising. *Unit head:* Karl Kottemann, Assistant Director, 314-516-5885, Fax: 314-516-6420, E-mail: mba@umsl.edu. *Application contact:* 314-516-5458, Fax: 314-516-6996, E-mail: gradadm@umsl.edu. Web site: http://www.umsl.edu/divisions/business/mbaonline/mbaprog.htm.

University of Missouri–St. Louis, College of Business Administration, Program in Information Systems, St. Louis, MO 63121. Offers information systems (MS); logistics and supply chain management (PhD). Part-time and evening/weekend programs available. *Faculty:* 6 full-time (2 women), 4 part-time/adjunct (0 women). *Students:* 2 full-time (0 women), 18 part-time (2 women); includes 2 minority (both Asian, non-Hispanic/Latino), 3 international. Average age 33. 14 applicants, 57% accepted, 2 enrolled. In 2011, 11 degrees awarded. *Entrance requirements:* For master's, GMAT, 2 letters of recommendation. Additional exam requirements/recommendations for international students: Required—TOEFL (minimum score 550 paper-based; 213 computer-based). *Application deadline:* For fall admission, 7/1 priority date for domestic students, 7/1 for international students; for spring admission, 12/1 priority date for domestic students, 12/1 for international students. Applications are processed on a rolling basis. Application fee: $35 ($40 for international students). Electronic applications accepted. *Expenses:* Tuition, state resident: full-time $6273; part-time $3866 per year. Tuition, nonresident: full-time $14,969; part-time $9980 per year. *Required fees:* $315 per year. *Financial support:* Career-related internships or fieldwork, Federal Work-Study, and institutionally sponsored loans available. Support available to part-time students. Financial award application deadline: 4/1; financial award applicants required to submit FAFSA. *Faculty research:* International information systems, telecommunications, systems development, information systems sourcing. *Unit head:* Karl Kottemann, Assistant Director, 314-516-5885, Fax: 314-516-6420, E-mail: mba@umsl.edu. *Application contact:* 314-516-5458, Fax: 314-516-6996, E-mail: gradadm@umsl.edu. Web site: http://www.umsl.edu/divisions/business/mis/ms_req_mis.html.

University of New Hampshire, Graduate School, College of Engineering and Physical Sciences, Department of Mechanical Engineering, Durham, NH 03824. Offers mechanical engineering (MS, PhD); systems design (PhD). Part-time programs available. *Faculty:* 14 full-time (1 woman). *Students:* 29 full-time (3 women), 24 part-time (0 women); includes 2 minority (1 Black or African American, non-Hispanic/Latino; 1 Two or more races, non-Hispanic/Latino), 13 international. Average age 25. 50 applicants, 68% accepted, 18 enrolled. In 2011, 15 master's, 2 doctorates awarded. *Degree requirements:* For master's, thesis or alternative; for doctorate, thesis/dissertation. *Entrance requirements:* For master's and doctorate, GRE. Additional exam requirements/recommendations for international students: Required—TOEFL (minimum score 550 paper-based; 213 computer-based; 80 iBT). *Application deadline:* For fall admission, 4/1 priority date for domestic students, 4/1 for international students; for spring admission, 12/1 for domestic students. Applications are processed on a rolling basis. Application fee: $65. Electronic applications accepted. *Expenses:* Tuition, state resident: full-time $12,360; part-time $687 per credit hour. Tuition, nonresident: full-time $25,680; part-time $1058 per credit hour. *International tuition:* $29,550 full-time. *Required fees:* $1666; $833 per course. $416.50 per semester. Tuition and fees vary according to course load and degree level. *Financial support:* In 2011–12, 36 students received support, including 2 fellowships, 16 research assistantships, 17 teaching assistantships; Federal Work-Study, scholarships/grants, and tuition waivers (full and partial) also available. Support available to part-time students. Financial award application deadline: 2/15. *Faculty research:* Solid mechanics, dynamics, materials science, dynamic systems, automatic control. *Unit head:* Dr. Todd Gross, Chairperson, 603-862-2445. *Application contact:* Tracey Harvey, Administrative Assistant, 603-862-1353, E-mail: mechanical.engineering@unh.edu. Web site: http://www.unh.edu/mechanical-engineering/.

University of North Florida, Coggin College of Business, MBA Program, Jacksonville, FL 32224. Offers accounting (MBA); construction management (MBA); e-commerce (MBA); economics (MBA); finance (MBA); human resource management (MBA); international business (MBA); logistics (MBA); management applications (MBA). *Accreditation:* AACSB. Part-time and evening/weekend programs available. *Faculty:* 19 full-time (6 women), 1 part-time/adjunct (0 women). *Students:* 145 full-time (57 women), 277 part-time (108 women); includes 67 minority (19 Black or African American, non-Hispanic/Latino; 21 Asian, non-Hispanic/Latino; 20 Hispanic/Latino; 7 Two or more races, non-Hispanic/Latino), 34 international. Average age 29. 200 applicants, 48% accepted, 70 enrolled. In 2011, 153 master's awarded. *Entrance requirements:* For master's, GMAT or GRE, U.S. bachelor's degree from regionally-accredited university or equivalent foreign degree. Additional exam requirements/recommendations for international students: Required—TOEFL (minimum score 550 paper-based; 213 computer-based; 79 iBT). *Application deadline:* For fall admission, 7/1 priority date for domestic students, 5/1 for international students; for spring admission, 11/1 priority date for domestic students, 10/1 for international students. Applications are processed on a rolling basis. Application fee: $30. *Expenses:* Tuition, state resident: full-time $8793; part-time $366.38 per credit hour. Tuition, nonresident: full-time $23,502; part-time $979.24 per credit hour. *Required fees:* $1384; $57.66 per credit hour. Tuition and fees vary according to course load and program. *Financial support:* In 2011–12, 55 students received support, including 1 teaching assistantship (averaging $5,333 per year); research assistantships, Federal Work-Study, and tuition waivers (partial) also available. Support available to part-time students. Financial award application deadline: 4/1; financial award applicants required to submit FAFSA. *Faculty research:* Performance measures, costing, and inventory issues in logistics and supply chain management; inter-organizational systems; international management and marketing practices; e-commerce; organizational learning and socialization processes. *Total annual research expenditures:* $7,686. *Unit head:* Dr. C. Bruce Kavan, Chair, 904-620-2780, Fax: 904-620-2832. *Application contact:* Cheryl Campbell, Graduate Advisor, 904-620-2575, Fax: 904-620-2832, E-mail: ccampbell@unf.edu. Web site: http://www.unf.edu/coggin/academics/graduate/mba.aspx.

University of South Africa, College of Economic and Management Sciences, Pretoria, South Africa. Offers accounting (D Admin, D Com); accounting science (DA); auditing (D Admin, D Com); business administration (M Tech); business economics (D Admin); business leadership (DBL); business management (D Admin, D Com); economic management analysis (M Tech); economics (D Admin, D Com, PhD); human resource development (M Tech); industrial psychology (D Admin, D Com, PhD); logistics (D Com); marketing (M Tech); public administration (D Admin, D Com, DPA, PhD); public management (M Tech); quantitative management (D Admin, D Com); real estate (M Tech); statistics (D Admin, PhD); tourism management (D Admin, D Com); transport economics (D Admin, D Com).

The University of Tennessee, Graduate School, College of Business Administration, Program in Business Administration, Knoxville, TN 37996. Offers accounting (PhD); finance (MBA, PhD); logistics and transportation (MBA, PhD); management (PhD); marketing (MBA, PhD); operations management (MBA); professional business administration (MBA); statistics (PhD); JD/MBA; MS/MBA; Pharm D/MBA. Pharm D/MBA offered jointly with The University of Tennessee Health Science Center. *Accreditation:* AACSB. Postbaccalaureate distance learning degree programs offered. *Degree requirements:* For master's, thesis or alternative; for doctorate, thesis/dissertation. *Entrance requirements:* For master's and doctorate, GMAT, minimum GPA of 2.7. Additional exam requirements/recommendations for international students: Required—TOEFL. Electronic applications accepted. *Expenses:* Tuition, state resident: full-time $8332; part-time $464 per credit hour. Tuition, nonresident: full-time $25,174; part-time $1400 per credit hour. *Required fees:* $1162; $56 per credit hour. Tuition and fees vary according to program.

The University of Texas at Arlington, Graduate School, College of Engineering, Department of Industrial and Manufacturing Systems Engineering, Program in Logistics, Arlington, TX 76019. Offers MS. *Students:* 10 full-time (3 women), 6 part-time (3 women); includes 2 minority (1 Black or African American, non-Hispanic/Latino; 1 Asian, non-Hispanic/Latino), 11 international. 17 applicants, 88% accepted, 3 enrolled. In 2011, 4 degrees awarded. *Degree requirements:* For master's, comprehensive exam, thesis optional. *Entrance requirements:* For master's, GRE, GMAT, minimum GPA of 3.0. Additional exam requirements/recommendations for international students: Required—TOEFL (minimum score 550 paper-based; 213 computer-based). *Application deadline:* For fall admission, 6/6 for domestic students, 4/4 for international students; for spring admission, 10/15 for domestic students, 9/5 for international students. Application fee: $35 ($50 for international students). *Financial support:* Fellowships, research assistantships, teaching assistantships, career-related internships or fieldwork, Federal Work-Study, institutionally sponsored loans, scholarships/grants, and unspecified assistantships available. Financial award application deadline: 6/1; financial award applicants required to submit FAFSA. *Unit head:* Dr. Donald H. Liles, Chair, 817-272-3092, Fax: 817-272-3406, E-mail: dliles@uta.edu. *Application contact:* Dr. Jamie Rogers, Graduate Advisor, 817-272-2495, Fax: 817-272-3406, E-mail: jrogers@uta.edu. Web site: http://www.ie.uta.edu/.

University of Washington, Graduate School, College of Engineering, Department of Aeronautics and Astronautics, Seattle, WA 98195-2400. Offers aeronautics and astronautics (MS, PhD); aerospace engineering (MAE), including composite materials and structures; global trade, transportation and logistics (MS). Part-time programs available. Postbaccalaureate distance learning degree programs offered (no on-campus study). *Faculty:* 24 full-time (1 woman), 9 part-time/adjunct (1 woman). *Students:* 76 full-time (16 women), 115 part-time (17 women); includes 43 minority (5 Black or African American, non-Hispanic/Latino; 1 American Indian or Alaska Native, non-Hispanic/Latino; 21 Asian, non-Hispanic/Latino; 16 Hispanic/Latino), 28 international. Average age 27. 297 applicants, 52% accepted, 74 enrolled. In 2011, 24 master's, 5 doctorates awarded. *Degree requirements:* For master's, thesis optional; for doctorate, comprehensive exam, thesis/dissertation, qualifying, general and final exams; completion of all work toward degree within 10 years. *Entrance requirements:* For master's and doctorate, GRE General Test, minimum GPA of 3.0, letters of recommendation, statement of objectives, undergraduate degree in aerospace or mechanical engineering. Additional exam requirements/recommendations for international students: Required—TOEFL (minimum score 580 paper-based; 237 computer-based; 92 iBT); Recommended—IELTS (minimum score 7). *Application deadline:* For fall admission, 1/15 priority date for domestic students, 1/15 for international students. Applications are processed on a rolling basis. Application fee: $75. Electronic applications accepted. *Expenses:* Contact institution. *Financial support:* In 2011–12, 57 students received support, including 15 fellowships (averaging $9,540 per year), 26 research assistantships with full tuition reimbursements available (averaging $17,172 per year), 11 teaching assistantships with full tuition reimbursements available (averaging $13,725 per year); career-related internships or fieldwork, Federal Work-Study, health care benefits, tuition waivers (full), and unspecified assistantships also available. Financial award application deadline: 1/15; financial award applicants required to submit FAFSA. *Faculty research:* Space systems, aircraft systems, energy systems, composites/structures, fluid dynamics, controls. *Total annual research expenditures:* $7.8 million. *Unit head:* Dr. James Hermanson, Professor and Chair, 206-543-1950, Fax: 206-543-0217, E-mail: jherm@aa.washington.edu. *Application contact:* Wanda Frederick, Manager of Graduate Programs and External Relations, 206-616-1113, Fax: 206-543-0217, E-mail: wanda@aa.washington.edu. Web site: http://www.aa.washington.edu/.

Logistics

University of Washington, Graduate School, College of Engineering, Department of Civil and Environmental Engineering, Seattle, WA 98195-2700. Offers civil engineering (MS, MSE, PhD); construction engineering (MSCE); environmental engineering (MS, MSCE, MSE, PhD); global trade, transportation and logistics (MS); hydrology, water resources, and environmental fluid mechanics (MS, MSCE, MSE, PhD); structural and geotechnical engineering and mechanics (MS, MSCE, MSE, PhD); transportation and construction engineering (MS, MSE, PhD); transportation engineering (MSCE). Part-time programs available. Postbaccalaureate distance learning degree programs offered (no on-campus study). *Faculty:* 47 full-time (11 women), 9 part-time/adjunct (1 woman). *Students:* 195 full-time (67 women), 72 part-time (19 women); includes 37 minority (4 Black or African American, non-Hispanic/Latino; 27 Asian, non-Hispanic/Latino; 6 Hispanic/Latino), 65 international. 654 applicants, 57% accepted, 100 enrolled. In 2011, 88 master's, 7 doctorates awarded. Terminal master's awarded for partial completion of doctoral program. *Degree requirements:* For master's, thesis (for some programs); for doctorate, comprehensive exam, thesis/dissertation, general, qualifying, and final exams; completion of degree within 10 years. *Entrance requirements:* For master's, GRE General Test, minimum GPA of 3.0, statement of purpose, letters of recommendation, transcripts; for doctorate, GRE General Test, minimum GPA of 3.5, statement of purpose, letters of recommendation, transcripts. Additional exam requirements/recommendations for international students: Required—TOEFL (minimum score 580 paper-based; 237 computer-based; 92 iBT); Recommended—IELTS (minimum score 7). *Application deadline:* For fall admission, 1/10 priority date for domestic students, 1/10 for international students. Applications are processed on a rolling basis. Application fee: $75. Electronic applications accepted. *Expenses:* Contact institution. *Financial support:* In 2011–12, 99 students received support, including 16 fellowships with full and partial tuition reimbursements available (averaging $16,173 per year), 71 research assistantships with full tuition reimbursements available (averaging $16,380 per year), 10 teaching assistantships with full tuition reimbursements available (averaging $16,380 per year); scholarships/grants also available. Financial award application deadline: 1/10; financial award applicants required to submit FAFSA. *Faculty research:* Environmental/water resources, hydrology; construction/transportation; structures/ geotechnical. *Total annual research expenditures:* $13.6 million. *Unit head:* Dr. Gregory R. Miller, Professor/Chair, 206-543-0350, Fax: 206-543-1543, E-mail: gmiller@uw.edu. *Application contact:* Lorna Latal, Graduate Adviser, 206-543-2574, Fax: 206-543-1543, E-mail: llatal@u.washington.edu. Web site: http://www.ce.washington.edu/programs/prospective/grad/applying/gen_admission.html.

University of Washington, Graduate School, Interdisciplinary Program in Global Trade, Transportation and Logistics Studies, Seattle, WA 98195. Offers Certificate.

Virginia International University, School of Business, Fairfax, VA 22030. Offers accounting (MBA); executive management (Graduate Certificate); global logistics (MBA); health care management (MBA); human resources management (MBA); international business management (MBA); international finance (MBA); marketing management (MBA). Part-time programs available. *Entrance requirements:* For master's and Graduate Certificate, bachelor's degree. Additional exam requirements/recommendations for international students: Required—TOEFL (minimum score 550 paper-based; 213 computer-based; 80 iBT), IELTS (minimum score 6). Electronic applications accepted.

Wright State University, School of Graduate Studies, Raj Soin College of Business, Department of Information Systems and Operations Management, Logistics and Supply Chain Management Program, Dayton, OH 45435. Offers MS.

Supply Chain Management

Arizona State University, W. P. Carey School of Business, Program in Business Administration, Tempe, AZ 85287-4906. Offers accountancy (PhD); agribusiness (PhD); business administration (MBA); finance (PhD); financial management and markets (MBA); information management (MBA); information systems (PhD); management (PhD); marketing (PhD); strategic marketing and services leadership (MBA); supply chain financial management (MBA); supply chain management (MBA, PhD); JD/MBA; MBA/M Acc; MBA/M Arch. *Accreditation:* AACSB. Part-time and evening/weekend programs available. Postbaccalaureate distance learning degree programs offered (minimal on-campus study). Terminal master's awarded for partial completion of doctoral program. *Degree requirements:* For master's, thesis or alternative, internship, interactive Program of Study (iPOS) submitted before completing 50 percent of required credit hours; for doctorate, comprehensive exam, thesis/dissertation, interactive Program of Study (iPOS) submitted before completing 50 percent of required credit hours. *Entrance requirements:* For master's, GMAT, minimum GPA of 3.0 in last 2 years of work leading to bachelor's degree, 2 letters of recommendation, professional resume, official transcripts, 3 essays; for doctorate, GMAT or GRE, minimum GPA of 3.0 in last 2 years of work leading to bachelor's degree, 3 letters of recommendation, resume, personal statement/essay. Additional exam requirements/recommendations for international students: Required—TOEFL (minimum score 550 paper-based; 213 computer-based; 80 iBT), IELTS (minimum score 6.5). Electronic applications accepted. *Expenses:* Contact institution.

California State University, East Bay, Office of Academic Programs and Graduate Studies, College of Business and Economics, Business Administration, MBA Program, Hayward, CA 94542-3000. Offers entrepreneurship (MBA); finance (MBA); global innovators (MBA); human resources and organizational behavior (MBA); information technology management (MBA); marketing management (MBA); operations and supply chain management (MBA); strategy and international business (MBA). Part-time and evening/weekend programs available. *Faculty:* 11 full-time (3 women). *Students:* 80 full-time (42 women), 141 part-time (61 women); includes 70 minority (5 Black or African American, non-Hispanic/Latino; 46 Asian, non-Hispanic/Latino; 13 Hispanic/Latino; 1 Native Hawaiian or other Pacific Islander, non-Hispanic/Latino; 5 Two or more races, non-Hispanic/Latino), 69 international. Average age 31. 371 applicants, 36% accepted, 79 enrolled. In 2011, 254 master's awarded. *Degree requirements:* For master's, comprehensive exam or thesis. *Entrance requirements:* For master's, GMAT (minimum 20th percentile verbal and quantitative section), bachelor's degree, minimum GPA of 2.75. Additional exam requirements/recommendations for international students: Required—TOEFL (minimum score 550 paper-based; 213 computer-based; 79 iBT). *Application deadline:* For fall admission, 6/30 for domestic and international students. Applications are processed on a rolling basis. Application fee: $55. Electronic applications accepted. *Expenses:* Contact institution. *Financial support:* Career-related internships or fieldwork, Federal Work-Study, institutionally sponsored loans, and scholarships/grants available. Support available to part-time students. Financial award application deadline: 3/2; financial award applicants required to submit FAFSA. *Unit head:* Dr. Terri Swartz, Dean, 510-885-3291, Fax: 510-885-4884, E-mail: terri.swartz@csueastbay.edu. *Application contact:* Prof. Joanna Lee, Director, CBE Graduate Programs, 510-885-3517, Fax: 510-885-2176, E-mail: joanna.lee@csueastbay.edu. Web site: http://www20.csueastbay.edu/ecat/graduate-chapters/g-buad.html#mba.

California State University, East Bay, Office of Academic Programs and Graduate Studies, College of Business and Economics, Program in Information Technology Management, Option in Operations and Supply Chain Management, Hayward, CA 94542-3000. Offers MBA. *Degree requirements:* For master's, comprehensive exam or thesis. *Entrance requirements:* For master's, GMAT, minimum GPA of 2.75. Additional exam requirements/recommendations for international students: Required—TOEFL (minimum score 550 paper-based; 213 computer-based). *Application deadline:* For fall admission, 6/30 for domestic and international students. Application fee: $55. Electronic applications accepted. *Expenses:* Tuition, state resident: full-time $6738; part-time $1302 per quarter. Tuition, nonresident: full-time $12,690; part-time $2294 per quarter. *Required fees:* $449 per quarter. Tuition and fees vary according to degree level, program and reciprocity agreements. *Financial support:* Fellowships, career-related internships or fieldwork, Federal Work-Study, institutionally sponsored loans, and scholarships/grants available. Support available to part-time students. Financial award application deadline: 3/1; financial award applicants required to submit FAFSA. *Unit head:* Prof. Xinjian Lu, Chair, 510-885-3307, E-mail: xinjian.lu@csueastbay.edu. *Application contact:* Donna Wiley, Interim Associate Director, 510-885-2928, Fax: 510-885-4777, E-mail: donna.wiley@csueastbay.edu.

California State University, San Bernardino, Graduate Studies, College of Business and Public Administration, Master in Business Administration Program, San Bernardino, CA 92407. Offers accounting (MBA); entrepreneurship (MBA); executives (MBA); finance (MBA); global business (MBA); information assurance and security management (MBA); information management (MBA); management (MBA); marketing (MBA); professionals (MBA); supply chain management (MBA). *Accreditation:* AACSB. Part-time and evening/weekend programs available. Postbaccalaureate distance learning degree programs offered (no on-campus study). *Faculty:* 58 full-time (11 women), 26 part-time/adjunct (9 women). *Students:* 80 full-time (31 women), 137 part-time (56 women); includes 82 minority (19 Black or African American, non-Hispanic/Latino; 3 American Indian or Alaska Native, non-Hispanic/Latino; 20 Asian, non-Hispanic/Latino; 37 Hispanic/Latino; 3 Two or more races, non-Hispanic/Latino), 65 international. Average age 30. 217 applicants, 65% accepted, 79 enrolled. In 2011, 120 master's awarded. *Degree requirements:* For master's, comprehensive exam, thesis optional, portfolio, 48 units, minimum GPA of 3.0. *Entrance requirements:* For master's, GMAT, minimum GPA of 2.5. Additional exam requirements/recommendations for international students: Required—TOEFL (minimum score 550 paper-based; 213 computer-based; 79 iBT). *Application deadline:* For fall admission, 7/12 priority date for domestic students, 7/12 for international students; for winter admission, 10/26 priority date for domestic students, 10/26 for international students; for spring admission, 1/25 priority date for domestic students, 1/25 for international students. Applications are processed on a rolling basis. Application fee: $55. Electronic applications accepted. *Expenses:* Contact institution. *Financial support:* In 2011–12, 56 students received support, including 34 fellowships (averaging $3,732 per year), 18 research assistantships (averaging $2,193 per year), 4 teaching assistantships (averaging $2,606 per year); career-related internships or fieldwork, Federal Work-Study, institutionally sponsored loans, scholarships/grants, and unspecified assistantships also available. Support available to part-time students. Financial award application deadline: 3/1; financial award applicants required to submit FAFSA. *Faculty research:* Fraud, Stock Exchange, small business, logistics, job analysis. *Total annual research expenditures:* $4.8 million. *Unit head:* Dr. Lawrence C. Rose, Dean, 909-537-3703, Fax: 909-537-7026, E-mail: lrose@csusb.edu. *Application contact:* Dr. Sandra Kamusikiri, Associate Vice-President/ Dean of Graduate Studies, 909-537-7058, Fax: 909-537-5078, E-mail: skamusik@csusb.edu. Web site: http://mba.csusb.edu/.

Case Western Reserve University, Weatherhead School of Management, Department of Operations, Management Program, Cleveland, OH 44106. Offers operations research (MSM); supply chain (MSM); MBA/MSM. *Accreditation:* AACSB. Part-time and evening/weekend programs available. *Entrance requirements:* For master's, GMAT or GRE, 3 letters of recommendation, resume. Additional exam requirements/recommendations for international students: Required—TOEFL (minimum score 600 paper-based; 250 computer-based). *Faculty research:* Supply chain management, operations management, operations/finance interface optimization, scheduling.

Central Connecticut State University, School of Graduate Studies, School of Technology, Department of Manufacturing and Construction Management, New Britain, CT 06050-4010. Offers construction management (MS, Certificate); lean manufacturing and Six Sigma (Certificate); supply chain and logistics (Certificate); technology management (MS). Part-time and evening/weekend programs available. *Faculty:* 18 full-time (4 women), 26 part-time/adjunct (2 women). *Students:* 23 full-time (5 women), 89 part-time (22 women); includes 18 minority (10 Black or African American, non-Hispanic/Latino; 7 Asian, non-Hispanic/Latino; 1 Hispanic/Latino), 7 international. Average age 36. 68 applicants, 78% accepted, 39 enrolled. In 2011, 25 master's, 1 other advanced degree awarded. *Degree requirements:* For master's, comprehensive exam, thesis or alternative; for Certificate, qualifying exam. *Entrance requirements:* For master's, minimum undergraduate GPA of 2.7. Additional exam requirements/recommendations for international students: Required—TOEFL (minimum score 550 paper-based; 213 computer-based). *Application deadline:* For fall admission, 6/1 for domestic students, 5/1 for international students; for spring admission, 11/1 for domestic and international students. Applications are processed on a rolling basis. Application fee: $50. Electronic applications accepted. *Expenses: Tuition, area resident:* Full-time $5137; part-time $482 per credit. Tuition, state resident: full-time $7707; part-time $494 per credit. Tuition, nonresident: full-time $14,311; part-time $494 per credit. *Required fees:* $3865. One-time fee: $62 part-time. *Financial support:* In 2011–12, 9 students received support, including 7 research assistantships; career-related internships or fieldwork, Federal Work-Study, scholarships/grants, and unspecified assistantships also available. Support available to part-time students. Financial award application deadline: 4/15; financial award applicants required to submit FAFSA. *Faculty research:* All aspects of middle management, technical supervision in the workplace. *Unit head:* Dr. Jacob Kovel, Chair, 860-832-1830, E-mail: kovelj@ccsu.edu. *Application contact:* Patricia Gardner, Associate Director of Graduate Studies, 860-832-2350, Fax: 860-832-2352, E-mail: graduateadmissions@ccsu.edu. Web site: http://www.ccsu.edu/page.cfm?p=6497.

Clayton State University, School of Graduate Studies, Program in Business Administration, Morrow, GA 30260-0285. Offers accounting (MBA); international business (MBA); supply chain management (MBA). *Accreditation:* AACSB. Part-time and evening/weekend programs available. *Faculty:* 12 full-time (3 women). *Students:* 35 full-time (13 women), 85 part-time (25 women); includes 85 minority (78 Black or African American, non-Hispanic/Latino; 1 American Indian or Alaska Native, non-Hispanic/Latino; 3 Asian, non-Hispanic/Latino; 2 Hispanic/Latino; 1 Two or more races, non-Hispanic/Latino), 3 international. Average age 36. 62 applicants, 87% accepted, 47 enrolled. In 2011, 38 master's awarded. *Degree requirements:* For master's, thesis. *Entrance requirements:* For master's, GMAT, 3 letters of recommendation; statement of purpose; 2 official transcripts. Additional exam requirements/recommendations for international students: Required—TOEFL (minimum score 550 paper-based; 213 computer-based; 80 iBT). *Application deadline:* For fall admission, 6/15 priority date for domestic students, 5/1 for international students; for spring admission, 11/15 priority date for domestic students, 9/1 for international students. Applications are processed on a rolling basis. Application fee: $75. Electronic applications accepted. *Expenses:* Contact institution. *Financial support:* Application deadline: 7/1; applicants required to submit FAFSA. *Unit head:* Dr. Judith Ogden, Graduate Program Director, Master of Business Administration, 678-466-4509, E-mail: judithogden@clayton.edu. *Application contact:* Michelle Terrell, Program Manager, 678-466-4500, Fax: 648-466-4599, E-mail: michelleterrell@clayton.edu. Web site: http://business.clayton.edu/MBA/.

Eastern Michigan University, Graduate School, College of Business, Programs in Business Administration, Ypsilanti, MI 48197. Offers business administration (MBA, Graduate Certificate); computer information systems (Graduate Certificate); e-business (MBA, Graduate Certificate); enterprise business intelligence (MBA); entrepreneurship (MBA, Graduate Certificate); finance (MBA, Graduate Certificate); human resources (MBA); human resources management (Graduate Certificate); information systems (MBA); internal auditing (MBA); international business (MBA, Graduate Certificate); marketing management (Graduate Certificate); nonprofit management (MBA); organizational development (Graduate Certificate); supply chain management (MBA, Graduate Certificate). *Accreditation:* AACSB. Part-time programs available. Postbaccalaureate distance learning degree programs offered (no on-campus study). *Students:* 79 full-time (39 women), 287 part-time (143 women); includes 55 minority (22 Black or African American, non-Hispanic/Latino; 24 Asian, non-Hispanic/Latino; 6 Hispanic/Latino; 3 Two or more races, non-Hispanic/Latino), 238 international. Average age 32. 317 applicants, 62% accepted, 89 enrolled. In 2011, 102 master's, 58 other advanced degrees awarded. *Entrance requirements:* For master's, GMAT (minimum score 450), minimum cumulative undergraduate GPA of 2.75. Additional exam requirements/recommendations for international students: Required—TOEFL. *Application deadline:* For fall admission, 5/15 for domestic students, 5/1 for international students; for winter admission, 10/15 for domestic students, 10/1 for international students; for spring admission, 3/15 for domestic students, 3/1 for international students. Applications are processed on a rolling basis. Application fee: $35. *Expenses:* Tuition, state resident: full-time $10,367; part-time $432 per credit hour. Tuition, nonresident: full-time $20,435; part-time $851 per credit hour. *Required fees:* $39 per credit hour. $46 per semester. One-time fee: $100. Tuition and fees vary according to course level, degree level and reciprocity agreements. *Financial support:* Fellowships, research assistantships with full tuition reimbursements, teaching assistantships with full tuition reimbursements, career-related internships or fieldwork, Federal Work-Study, institutionally sponsored loans, scholarships/grants, tuition waivers (partial), and unspecified assistantships available. Support available to part-time students. Financial award applicants required to submit FAFSA. *Unit head:* K. Michelle Henry, Director, Academic Services, 734-487-4444, Fax: 734-483-1316, E-mail: mhenry1@emich.edu. *Application contact:* Beste Windes, Advisor, 734-487-4444, Fax: 734-483-1316, E-mail: bwindes@emich.edu. Web site: http://www.emich.edu/public/cob/gr/grad.html.

Elmhurst College, Graduate Programs, Program in Supply Chain Management, Elmhurst, IL 60126-3296. Offers MS. Part-time and evening/weekend programs available. *Faculty:* 2 full-time (0 women), 3 part-time/adjunct (0 women). *Students:* 35 part-time (11 women); includes 8 minority (5 Black or African American, non-Hispanic/Latino; 3 Asian, non-Hispanic/Latino). Average age 36. 41 applicants, 59% accepted, 20 enrolled. In 2011, 19 master's awarded. *Entrance requirements:* For master's, 3 recommendations, resume, statement of purpose. Additional exam requirements/recommendations for international students: Required—TOEFL (minimum score 550 paper-based; 213 computer-based). *Application deadline:* Applications are processed on a rolling basis. Application fee: $0. Electronic applications accepted. *Expenses:* Contact institution. *Financial support:* In 2011–12, 4 students received support. Federal Work-Study and scholarships/grants available. Support available to part-time students. Financial award application deadline: 6/1; financial award applicants required to submit FAFSA. *Unit head:* Elizabeth D. Kuebler, Director of Adult and Graduate Admission, 630-617-3300, Fax: 630-617-5501, E-mail: oaga@elmhurst.edu. *Application contact:* Elizabeth D. Kuebler, Director of Adult and Graduate Admission, 630-617-3300, Fax: 630-617-5501, E-mail: oaga@elmhurst.edu.

Embry-Riddle Aeronautical University–Worldwide, Worldwide Headquarters - Graduate Degrees and Programs, Program in Logistics and Supply Chain Management, Daytona Beach, FL 32114-3900. Offers integrated logistics management (Graduate Certificate); logistics and supply chain management (MSLSCM). *Faculty:* 4 full-time (1 woman), 50 part-time/adjunct (15 women). *Students:* 44 full-time (14 women), 57 part-time (21 women); includes 42 minority (21 Black or African American, non-Hispanic/Latino; 2 American Indian or Alaska Native, non-Hispanic/Latino; 5 Asian, non-Hispanic/Latino; 11 Hispanic/Latino; 3 Two or more races, non-Hispanic/Latino). Average age 35. 86 applicants, 66% accepted, 28 enrolled. In 2011, 1 master's awarded. *Degree requirements:* For master's, thesis (for some programs). Application fee: $50. *Expenses:* *Tuition:* Part-time $395 per credit hour. Tuition and fees vary according to degree level and program. *Financial support:* In 2011–12, 27 students received support. *Unit head:* Dr. Kees Rietsema, Chair, 602-904-1285, E-mail: rietsd37@erau.edu. *Application contact:* Linda Dammer, Director of Admissions, 386-226-6396 Ext. 1, Fax: 386-226-6984, E-mail: worldwide@erau.edu.

Florida Institute of Technology, Graduate Programs, Extended Studies Division, Melbourne, FL 32901-6975. Offers acquisition and contract management (MS); aerospace engineering (MS); business administration (MBA); computer information systems (MS); computer science (MS); electrical engineering (MS); engineering management (MS); human resources management (MS); logistics management (MS), including humanitarian and disaster relief logistics; management (MS), including acquisition and contract management, e-business, human resources management, information systems, logistics management, management, transportation management; material acquisition management (MS); mechanical engineering (MS); operations research (MS); project management (MS), including information systems, operations research; public administration (MPA); quality management (MS); software engineering (MS); space systems (MS); space systems management (MS); supply chain management (MS); systems management (MS), including information systems, operations research. Part-time and evening/weekend programs available. Postbaccalaureate distance learning degree programs offered (no on-campus study). *Faculty:* 9 full-time (2 women), 105 part-time/adjunct (24 women). *Students:* 113 full-time (52 women), 1,150 part-time (484 women); includes 496 minority (332 Black or African American, non-Hispanic/Latino; 11 American Indian or Alaska Native, non-Hispanic/Latino; 42 Asian, non-Hispanic/Latino; 71 Hispanic/Latino; 2 Native Hawaiian or other Pacific Islander, non-Hispanic/Latino; 38 Two or more races, non-Hispanic/Latino), 11 international. Average age 35. 568 applicants, 56% accepted, 296 enrolled. In 2011, 471 master's awarded. *Degree requirements:* For master's, comprehensive exam (for some programs), capstone course. *Entrance requirements:* For master's, GMAT or resume showing 8 years of supervised experience, minimum GPA of 3.0, 2 letters of recommendation, resume. Additional exam requirements/recommendations for international students: Required—TOEFL (minimum score 550 paper-based; 213 computer-based; 79 iBT). *Application deadline:* For fall admission, 4/1 for international students; for spring admission, 9/30 for international students. Applications are processed on a rolling basis. Application fee: $0. Electronic applications accepted. *Expenses:* Contact institution. *Financial support:* Application deadline: 3/1; applicants required to submit FAFSA. *Unit head:* Dr. Theodore R. Richardson, III, Senior Associate Dean, 321-674-8123, Fax: 321-674-7597, E-mail: trichardson@fit.edu. *Application contact:* Carolyn Farrior, Director of Graduate Admissions, Online Learning and Off-Campus Programs, 321-674-7118, Fax: 321-674-8216, E-mail: cfarrior@fit.edu. Web site: http://es.fit.edu.

Georgia Southern University, Jack N. Averitt College of Graduate Studies, College of Business Administration, Program in Logistics/Supply Chain Management, Statesboro, GA 30460. Offers PhD. *Students:* 13 full-time (5 women); includes 2 minority (1 Hispanic/Latino; 1 Two or more races, non-Hispanic/Latino), 5 international. Average age 35. 23 applicants, 35% accepted, 7 enrolled. *Degree requirements:* For doctorate, comprehensive exam, thesis/dissertation. *Entrance requirements:* For doctorate, GMAT or GRE, letters of reference. Additional exam requirements/recommendations for international students: Required—TOEFL (minimum score 550 paper-based; 213 computer-based; 80 iBT). *Application deadline:* For fall admission, 3/15 priority date for domestic students, 3/15 for international students. Application fee: $50. Electronic applications accepted. *Expenses:* Tuition, state resident: full-time $6300; part-time $263 per semester hour. Tuition, nonresident: full-time $25,174; part-time $1049 per semester hour. *Required fees:* $1872. *Financial support:* In 2011–12, 10 students received support. Career-related internships or fieldwork, Federal Work-Study, scholarships/grants, traineeships, and unspecified assistantships available. Support available to part-time students. Financial award application deadline: 4/15; financial award applicants required to submit FAFSA. *Faculty research:* Buyer-supplier relationships, retail supply chain management, military logistics/transportation/SCM, strategic sourcing/outsourcing, supply chain metrics. *Unit head:* Dr. Ron Shiffler, Dean, 912-478-5106, Fax: 912-478-0292, E-mail: shiffler@georgiasouthern.edu. *Application contact:* Dr. Stephen Rutner, Graduate Program Director, 912-478-0511, Fax: 912-478-1523, E-mail: srutner@georgiasouthern.edu. Web site: http://coba.georgiasouthern.edu/phd/.

Golden Gate University, Ageno School of Business, San Francisco, CA 94105-2968. Offers accounting (MBA); business administration (EMBA, MBA, PMBA, DBA); finance (MBA, MS, Certificate); financial planning (MS, Certificate); healthcare information systems (Certificate); human resource management (MBA, MS); human resources management (Certificate); information systems (MS); information technology (MBA); information technology management (Certificate); integrated marketing and communications (MS, Certificate); international business (MBA); management (MBA); marketing (MBA, MS, Certificate); operations supply chain management (Certificate); psychology (MA, Certificate); public administration (EMPA); public relations (MS, Certificate); technical market analysis (Certificate); JD/MBA. Part-time and evening/weekend programs available. *Faculty:* 19 full-time (6 women), 241 part-time/adjunct (72 women). *Students:* 397 full-time (230 women), 779 part-time (432 women); includes 376 minority (105 Black or African American, non-Hispanic/Latino; 5 American Indian or Alaska Native, non-Hispanic/Latino; 161 Asian, non-Hispanic/Latino; 77 Hispanic/Latino; 12 Native Hawaiian or other Pacific Islander, non-Hispanic/Latino; 16 Two or more races, non-Hispanic/Latino), 265 international. Average age 34. 871 applicants, 64% accepted, 271 enrolled. In 2011, 550 master's, 13 doctorates awarded. *Degree requirements:* For doctorate, thesis/dissertation, qualifying examination. *Entrance requirements:* For master's, GMAT (MBA), minimum GPA of 2.5 (MS). Additional exam requirements/recommendations for international students: Required—TOEFL (minimum score 550 paper-based; 213 computer-based; 79 iBT). *Application deadline:* For fall admission, 5/15 for domestic and international students; for winter admission, 1/15 for domestic and international students; for spring admission, 9/15 for domestic and international students. Applications are processed on a rolling basis. Application fee: $70 ($110 for international students). Electronic applications accepted. *Expenses:* Contact institution. *Financial support:* Career-related internships or fieldwork, Federal Work-Study, institutionally sponsored loans, and scholarships/grants available. Support available to part-time students. Financial award applicants required to submit FAFSA. *Unit head:* Dr. Paul Fouts, Dean, 415-442-7026, Fax: 415-442-6579. *Application contact:* Angela Melero, Enrollment Services, 415-442-7800, Fax: 415-442-7807, E-mail: info@ggu.edu. Web site: http://www.ggu.edu/programs/business-and-management.

HEC Montreal, School of Business Administration, Graduate Diplomas Programs in Administration, Program in Supply Chain Management, Montréal, QC H3T 2A7, Canada. Offers Graduate Diploma. Part-time programs available. *Students:* 23 full-time (9 women), 87 part-time (24 women). 54 applicants, 61% accepted, 26 enrolled. In 2011, 42 Graduate Diplomas awarded. *Degree requirements:* For Graduate Diploma, one foreign language. *Entrance requirements:* For degree, bachelor's degree, two years of working experience, letters of recommendation. *Application deadline:* For fall admission, 4/15 for domestic and international students; for winter admission, 9/15 for domestic and international students. Application fee: $80 Canadian dollars. Electronic applications accepted. Application fee is waived when completed online. *Expenses:* Contact institution. *Financial support:* Research assistantships and teaching assistantships available. Financial award application deadline: 9/2. *Unit head:* Silvia Ponce, Director, 514-340-6393, Fax: 514-340-6915, E-mail: silvia.ponce@hec.ca. *Application contact:* Jo Anne Audet, Administrative Director, 514-340-1315, Fax: 514-340-6411, E-mail: joanne.audet@hec.ca. Web site: http://www.hec.ca/programmes_formations/des/dess/dess_logistique/index.html.

HEC Montreal, School of Business Administration, Master of Science Programs in Administration, Program in Global Supply Chain Management, Montréal, QC H3T 2A7, Canada. Offers M Sc. Part-time programs available. *Degree requirements:* For master's, one foreign language, thesis. *Entrance requirements:* For master's, BBA, undergraduate degree in another field, degree deemed equivalent by program director and minimum GPA of 3.0 on 4.3 scale. Additional exam requirements/recommendations for international students: Required—HEC Montreal's Test of Proficiency in English (HECTOPE), TOEFL, or IELTS. *Application deadline:* For fall admission, 3/15 for domestic and international students; for winter admission, 9/15 for domestic and international students. Application fee: $80. Electronic applications accepted. Application fee is waived when completed online. *Expenses:* Tuition, state resident: full-time $2601.36. Tuition, nonresident: full-time $7030. *International tuition:* $17,474.04 full-time. *Required fees:* $1381.77. Tuition and fees vary according to degree level and program. *Financial support:* Fellowships, research assistantships, teaching assistantships, and scholarships/grants available. Financial award application deadline:

9/2. *Unit head:* Jean-Francois Cordeau, Academic Supervisor, 514-340-6278, Fax: 514-340-6834, E-mail: jean-francois.cordeau@hec.ca. *Application contact:* Virginie Lefebvre, Administrative Director, 514-340-6112, Fax: 514-340-6411, E-mail: virginie.lefebvre@hec.ca. Web site: http://www.hec.ca/en/programs_training/msc/options/global_supply_chain_management/global_supply_chain_management.html.

Howard University, School of Business, Graduate Programs in Business, Washington, DC 20059-0002. Offers accounting (MBA); entrepreneurship (MBA); finance (MBA); general management (MBA); human resources management (MBA); information systems (MBA); international business (MBA); marketing (MBA); supply chain management (MBA); JD/MBA. *Accreditation:* AACSB. Part-time and evening/weekend programs available. Postbaccalaureate distance learning degree programs offered (no on-campus study). *Entrance requirements:* For master's, GMAT, minimum 1 year post undergraduate work experience, resume, 3 letters of recommendation, advanced college algebra. Additional exam requirements/recommendations for international students: Required—TOEFL. *Faculty research:* Marketing research in multi-ethnic populations, U.S. trade policies and international relations, risk management (finance).

Kaplan University, Davenport Campus, School of Business, Davenport, IA 52807-2095. Offers business administration (MBA); change leadership (MS); entrepreneurship (MBA); finance (MBA); health care management (MBA, MS); human resource (MBA); international business (MBA); management (MS); marketing (MBA); project management (MBA, MS); supply chain management and logistics (MBA, MS). Part-time and evening/weekend programs available. Postbaccalaureate distance learning degree programs offered (no on-campus study). *Entrance requirements:* Additional exam requirements/recommendations for international students: Required—TOEFL (minimum score 550 paper-based; 218 computer-based; 80 iBT). Electronic applications accepted.

Lehigh University, College of Business and Economics, Bethlehem, PA 18015. Offers accounting (MS), including accounting and information analysis; business administration (MBA); economics (MS, PhD); entrepreneurship (Certificate); finance (MS), including analytical finance; project management (Certificate); supply chain management (Certificate); MBA/E; MBA/M Ed. *Accreditation:* AACSB. Part-time and evening/weekend programs available. Postbaccalaureate distance learning degree programs offered (minimal on-campus study). *Faculty:* 40 full-time (10 women), 13 part-time/adjunct (0 women). *Students:* 159 full-time (85 women), 242 part-time (85 women); includes 40 minority (5 Black or African American, non-Hispanic/Latino; 27 Asian, non-Hispanic/Latino; 7 Hispanic/Latino; 1 Native Hawaiian or other Pacific Islander, non-Hispanic/Latino), 139 international. Average age 29. 890 applicants, 40% accepted, 89 enrolled. In 2011, 166 master's, 2 doctorates awarded. Terminal master's awarded for partial completion of doctoral program. *Degree requirements:* For master's, thesis optional; for doctorate, comprehensive exam, thesis/dissertation, proposal defense. *Entrance requirements:* For master's, GMAT, GRE General Test; for doctorate, GMAT or GRE General Test. Additional exam requirements/recommendations for international students: Required—TOEFL (minimum score 600 paper-based; 250 computer-based; 94 iBT). *Application deadline:* For fall admission, 7/15 for domestic students, 5/1 for international students; for spring admission, 12/1 for domestic and international students. Applications are processed on a rolling basis. Application fee: $100. Electronic applications accepted. *Expenses:* Contact institution. *Financial support:* In 2011–12, 93 students received support, including 2 fellowships with full tuition reimbursements available (averaging $16,000 per year), 39 research assistantships with full and partial tuition reimbursements available (averaging $2,269 per year), 17 teaching assistantships with full tuition reimbursements available (averaging $13,840 per year); career-related internships or fieldwork, scholarships/grants, health care benefits, tuition waivers (full and partial), and unspecified assistantships also available. Support available to part-time students. Financial award application deadline: 1/15. *Faculty research:* Public finance, energy, investments, activity-based costing, management information systems. *Unit head:* Paul R. Brown, Dean, 610-758-6725, Fax: 610-758-4499, E-mail: prb207@lehigh.edu. *Application contact:* Corinn McBride, Director of Recruitment and Admissions, 610-758-3418, Fax: 610-758-5283, E-mail: com207@lehigh.edu. Web site: http://www.lehigh.edu/business.

Lindenwood University, Graduate Programs, School of Business and Entrepreneurship, St. Charles, MO 63301-1695. Offers accounting (MBA, MS); business administration (MBA); entrepreneurial studies (MBA, MS); finance (MBA, MS); human resource management (MBA); human resources (MS); international business (MBA, MS); management (MBA, MS); management information systems (MBA, MS); marketing (MBA, MS); public management (MBA, MS); sport management (MA); supply chain management (MBA). *Accreditation:* ACBSP. Part-time and evening/weekend programs available. *Faculty:* 20 full-time (8 women), 17 part-time/adjunct (5 women). *Students:* 165 full-time (66 women), 223 part-time (100 women); includes 59 minority (48 Black or African American, non-Hispanic/Latino; 4 Asian, non-Hispanic/Latino; 2 Native Hawaiian or other Pacific Islander, non-Hispanic/Latino; 5 Two or more races, non-Hispanic/Latino), 140 international. Average age 29. 156 applicants, 76% accepted, 103 enrolled. In 2011, 205 degrees awarded. *Degree requirements:* For master's, comprehensive exam (for some programs), thesis (for some programs). *Entrance requirements:* For master's, interview, minimum GPA of 3.0, letter of recommendation. Additional exam requirements/recommendations for international students: Required—TOEFL (minimum score 550 paper-based; 213 computer-based; 80 iBT). *Application deadline:* For fall admission, 8/15 priority date for domestic students, 8/15 for international students; for winter admission, 1/9 priority date for domestic students, 1/9 for international students; for spring admission, 3/12 priority date for domestic students, 3/12 for international students. Applications are processed on a rolling basis. Application fee: $30 ($100 for international students). Electronic applications accepted. *Expenses: Tuition:* Full-time $13,650; part-time $395 per credit hour. *Required fees:* $150 per semester. Tuition and fees vary according to course level and course load. *Financial support:* In 2011–12, 206 students received support. Career-related internships or fieldwork, Federal Work-Study, institutionally sponsored loans, and tuition waivers (partial) available. Financial award application deadline: 6/30; financial award applicants required to submit FAFSA. *Unit head:* Roger Ellis, Dean, 636-949-4839, E-mail: rellis@lindenwood.edu. *Application contact:* Brett Barger, Dean of Evening Admissions and Extension Campuses, 636-949-4934, Fax: 636-949-4109, E-mail: adultadmissions@lindenwood.edu. Web site: http://www.lindenwood.edu.

Maine Maritime Academy, Department of Graduate Studies, Program in Global Supply Chain Management, Castine, ME 04420. Offers MS, Certificate, Diploma. Part-time programs available. *Degree requirements:* For master's, capstone course. *Entrance requirements:* For master's, GMAT or GRE, letters of recommendation. Additional exam requirements/recommendations for international students: Required—TOEFL.

Marquette University, Graduate School of Management, Executive MBA Program, Milwaukee, WI 53201-1881. Offers economics (MBA); finance (MBA); human resources (MBA); international business (MBA); management information systems (MBA); marketing (MBA); operations and supply chain management (MBA); sports business (MBA). *Accreditation:* AACSB. *Students:* 50 full-time (15 women); includes 4 minority (1 Black or African American, non-Hispanic/Latino; 3 Asian, non-Hispanic/Latino), 3 international. Average age 37. 37 applicants, 81% accepted, 29 enrolled. In 2011, 36 master's awarded. *Degree requirements:* For master's, international trip. *Entrance requirements:* For master's, GMAT or GRE, two letters of recommendation, official transcripts from current and previous colleges/universities. Additional exam requirements/recommendations for international students: Required—TOEFL (minimum score 550 paper-based; 85 computer-based; 88 iBT), IELTS (minimum score 6.5), Pearson Test of English. *Application deadline:* For fall admission, 2/15 for domestic and international students. Application fee: $50. Electronic applications accepted. *Expenses:* Contact institution. *Financial support:* Application deadline: 2/15. *Faculty research:* International trade and finance, customer relationship management, consumer satisfaction, customer service . *Unit head:* Dr. Jeanne Simmons, Graduate Director, 414-288-7145, Fax: 414-288-1660, E-mail: jeanne.simmons@marquette.edu. *Application contact:* Debra Leutermann, Admissions Coordinator, 414-288-7145, Fax: 414-288-8078, E-mail: debra.leutermann@marquette.edu. Web site: http://www.busadm.mu.edu/emba/.

Marquette University, Graduate School of Management, Program in Business Administration, Milwaukee, WI 53201-1881. Offers business administration (MBA); economics (MBA); entrepreneurship (Certificate); finance (MBA); human resources (MBA); international business (MBA); management information systems (MBA); marketing (MBA); operations and supply chain management (MBA); sports business (MBA); JD/MBA; MBA/MA; MBA/MSN. *Accreditation:* AACSB. Part-time and evening/weekend programs available. *Students:* 42 full-time (14 women), 335 part-time (94 women); includes 24 minority (5 Black or African American, non-Hispanic/Latino; 1 American Indian or Alaska Native, non-Hispanic/Latino; 15 Asian, non-Hispanic/Latino; 3 Hispanic/Latino), 29 international. Average age 31. 182 applicants, 59% accepted, 103 enrolled. In 2011, 128 master's awarded. *Degree requirements:* For Certificate, business plan. *Entrance requirements:* For master's, GMAT or GRE, letters of recommendation. Additional exam requirements/recommendations for international students: Required—TOEFL (minimum score 550 paper-based; 85 computer-based; 88 iBT), IELTS (minimum score 6.5), Pearson Test of English. *Application deadline:* For fall admission, 2/15 for domestic and international students. Applications are processed on a rolling basis. Application fee: $50. Electronic applications accepted. *Expenses: Tuition:* Full-time $17,010; part-time $945 per credit hour. Tuition and fees vary according to program. *Financial support:* In 2011–12, 4 fellowships, 11 teaching assistantships were awarded; research assistantships, Federal Work-Study, institutionally sponsored loans, scholarships/grants, and tuition waivers (full and partial) also available. Support available to part-time students. Financial award application deadline: 2/15. *Faculty research:* Ethics in the professions, services marketing, technology impact on decision-making, mentoring. *Unit head:* Dr. Jeanne Simmons, Graduate Director, 414-288-7145, Fax: 414-288-1660, E-mail: jeanne.simmons@marquette.edu. *Application contact:* Debra Leutermann, Admissions Coordinator, 414-288-8064, Fax: 414-288-1902, E-mail: debra.leutermann@marquette.edu. Web site: http://business.marquette.edu/academics/mba.

Michigan State University, The Graduate School, Eli Broad Graduate School of Management, Department of Supply Chain Management, East Lansing, MI 48824. Offers business administration (PhD); supply chain management (MS). Part-time programs available. *Degree requirements:* For master's, field study, research project; for doctorate, comprehensive exam, thesis/dissertation, oral defense of dissertation proposal and dissertation. *Entrance requirements:* For master's, GMAT, bachelor's degree in related field, letters of recommendation, 2-3 years of work experience, minimum GPA of 3.0 in last 2 years of undergraduate course work; for doctorate, GMAT or GRE, letters of recommendation. Additional exam requirements/recommendations for international students: Required—TOEFL. Electronic applications accepted. *Expenses:* Contact institution.

Moravian College, Moravian College Comenius Center, Business and Management Programs, Bethlehem, PA 18018-6650. Offers accounting (MBA); general management (MBA); health care management (MBA); human resource management (MBA); leadership (MSHRM); learning and performance management (MSHRM); supply chain management (MBA). Part-time and evening/weekend programs available. *Entrance requirements:* For master's, GMAT. Additional exam requirements/recommendations for international students: Required—TOEFL (minimum score 550 paper-based; 260 computer-based; 90 iBT). *Expenses:* Contact institution. *Faculty research:* Leadership, change management, human resources.

Naval Postgraduate School, Departments and Academic Groups, School of Business and Public Policy, Monterey, CA 93943. Offers acquisitions and contract management (MBA); business administration (EMBA, MBA); contract management (MS); defense business management (MBA); defense systems analysis (MS), including management; defense systems management (international) (MBA); executive management (MBA); financial management (MBA); information systems management (MBA); manpower systems analysis (MS); material logistics support management (MBA); program management (MS); resource planning/management for international defense (MBA); supply chain management (MBA); systems acquisition management (MBA); transportation management (MBA). Program only open to commissioned officers of the United States and friendly nations and selected United States federal civilian employees. *Accreditation:* AACSB; NASPAA. Part-time programs available. Postbaccalaureate distance learning degree programs offered (minimal on-campus study). *Faculty:* 67 full-time (15 women), 32 part-time/adjunct (12 women). *Students:* 307 full-time (29 women), 327 part-time (71 women); includes 149 minority (55 Black or African American, non-Hispanic/Latino; 5 American Indian or Alaska Native, non-Hispanic/Latino; 46 Asian, non-Hispanic/Latino; 43 Hispanic/Latino), 44 international. Average age 42. In 2011, 295 master's awarded. *Degree requirements:* For master's, thesis (for some programs), terminal project/capstone (for some programs). *Faculty research:* U. S. and European public procurement policies for small and medium-sized enterprises, examining external validity criticisms in the choice of students as subjects in accounting experiment studies, assurance of learning in contract management education, contracting for cloud computing: opportunities and risks, NPS, Apple App Store as a business model supporting U. S. Navy requirements. *Total annual research expenditures:* $9 million. *Unit head:* Raymond Franck, Department Chair, 831-656-3614, E-mail: refranck@nps.edu. *Application contact:* Acting Director of Admissions. Web site: http://www.nps.edu/Academics/Schools/GSBPP/index.html.

North Carolina State University, Graduate School, Poole College of Management, Program in Business Administration, Raleigh, NC 27695. Offers biosciences management (MBA); entrepreneurship and technology commercialization (MBA); financial management (MBA); innovation management (MBA); marketing management (MBA); services management (MBA); supply chain management (MBA). *Accreditation:* AACSB. Part-time programs available. *Degree requirements:* For master's, thesis optional. *Entrance requirements:* For master's, GMAT, interview, 3 letters of recommendation. Additional exam requirements/recommendations for international students: Required—TOEFL (minimum score 600 paper-based; 250 computer-based; 100 iBT). Electronic applications accepted. *Faculty research:* Manufacturing strategy, information systems, technology commercialization, managing research and development, historical stock returns.

See Display on page 116 and Close-Up on page 225.

Polytechnic University of Puerto Rico, Miami Campus, Graduate School, Miami, FL 33166. Offers accounting (MBA); business administration (MBA); construction management (MEM); environmental management (MEM); finance (MBA); human resources management (MBA); logistics and supply chain management (MBA); management of international enterprises (MBA); manufacturing management (MEM); marketing management (MBA); project management (MBA). Part-time and evening/weekend programs available. Postbaccalaureate distance learning degree programs offered (no on-campus study). *Entrance requirements:* For master's, minimum GPA of 3.0. Electronic applications accepted.

Quinnipiac University, School of Business, Program in Business Administration, Hamden, CT 06518-1940. Offers chartered financial analyst (MBA); finance (MBA); healthcare management (MBA); information systems management (MBA); marketing (MBA); supply chain management (MBA); JD/MBA. *Accreditation:* AACSB. Part-time and evening/weekend programs available. Postbaccalaureate distance learning degree programs offered (no on-campus study). *Faculty:* 19 full-time (4 women), 2 part-time/adjunct (1 woman). *Students:* 89 full-time (36 women), 129 part-time (50 women); includes 16 minority (5 Black or African American, non-Hispanic/Latino; 5 Asian, non-Hispanic/Latino; 6 Hispanic/Latino), 19 international. Average age 29. 206 applicants, 81% accepted, 139 enrolled. In 2011, 95 master's awarded. *Entrance requirements:* For master's, GMAT or GRE, minimum GPA of 3.0. Additional exam requirements/recommendations for international students: Required—TOEFL (minimum score 575 paper-based; 233 computer-based; 90 iBT), IELTS (minimum score 6.5). *Application deadline:* For fall admission, 7/30 priority date for domestic students, 4/30 for international students; for spring admission, 12/15 priority date for domestic students, 9/15 for international students. Applications are processed on a rolling basis. Application fee: $45. Electronic applications accepted. *Expenses: Tuition:* Part-time $855 per credit. *Required fees:* $35 per credit. *Financial support:* In 2011–12, 23 students received support. Career-related internships or fieldwork, Federal Work-Study, scholarships/grants, tuition waivers (partial), and unspecified assistantships available. Support available to part-time students. Financial award application deadline: 4/15; financial award applicants required to submit FAFSA. *Faculty research:* Financial markets and investments, international business, supply chain management, health care management, corporate governance. *Unit head:* Lisa Braiewa, MBA Program Director, 203-582-3710, Fax: 203-582-8664, E-mail: lisa.braiewa@quinnipiac.edu. *Application contact:* Katie Ludovico, 800-462-1944, Fax: 203-582-3443, E-mail: katie.ludovico@quinnipiac.edu. Web site: http://www.quinnipiac.edu/mba.

Rutgers, The State University of New Jersey, Newark, Rutgers Business School–Newark and New Brunswick, Doctoral Programs in Management, Newark, NJ 07102. Offers accounting (PhD); accounting information systems (PhD); economics (PhD); finance (PhD); individualized study (PhD); information technology (PhD); international business (PhD); management science (PhD); marketing science (PhD); organizational management (PhD); science, technology and management (PhD); supply chain management (PhD). *Degree requirements:* For doctorate, comprehensive exam, thesis/dissertation. *Entrance requirements:* For doctorate, GRE or GMAT. Additional exam requirements/recommendations for international students: Required—TOEFL (minimum score 550 paper-based; 213 computer-based; 79 iBT). Electronic applications accepted.

Santa Clara University, Leavey School of Business, Program in Business Administration, Santa Clara, CA 95053. Offers accounting (MBA); entrepreneurship (MBA); executive business administration (EMBA); finance (MBA); food and agribusiness (MBA); international business (MBA); leading people and organizations (MBA); managing technology and innovation (MBA); marketing management (MBA); supply chain management (MBA). *Accreditation:* AACSB. Part-time and evening/weekend programs available. *Students:* 196 full-time (80 women), 669 part-time (224 women); includes 302 minority (12 Black or African American, non-Hispanic/Latino; 246 Asian, non-Hispanic/Latino; 35 Hispanic/Latino; 6 Native Hawaiian or other Pacific Islander, non-Hispanic/Latino; 3 Two or more races, non-Hispanic/Latino), 186 international. Average age 32. 365 applicants, 74% accepted, 199 enrolled. In 2011, 366 degrees awarded. *Degree requirements:* For master's, thesis or alternative. *Entrance requirements:* For master's, GMAT, GRE. Additional exam requirements/recommendations for international students: Required—TOEFL (minimum score 600 paper-based; 250 computer-based; 100 iBT). *Application deadline:* For fall admission, 6/1 for domestic and international students; for spring admission, 1/19 for domestic students, 1/17 for international students. Applications are processed on a rolling basis. Application fee: $75 ($100 for international students). Electronic applications accepted. *Expenses:* Contact institution. *Financial support:* In 2011–12, 350 students received support. Fellowships with partial tuition reimbursements available, research assistantships with partial tuition reimbursements available, career-related internships or fieldwork, Federal Work-Study, institutionally sponsored loans, scholarships/grants, health care benefits, and unspecified assistantships available. Support available to part-time students. Financial award application deadline: 6/1; financial award applicants required to submit FAFSA. *Unit head:* Elizabeth B. Ford, Senior Assistant Dean, 408-554-2752, Fax: 408-554-4571, E-mail: eford@scu.edu. *Application contact:* Tammy Fox, Assistant Director, Graduate Business Admissions, 408-554-7858, E-mail: tkfox@scu.edu.

Seton Hall University, Stillman School of Business, Programs in Business Administration, South Orange, NJ 07079-2697. Offers accounting (MBA); finance (MBA); information technology management (MBA); international business (MBA); management (MBA); marketing (MBA); sport management (MBA); supply chain management (MBA). Part-time and evening/weekend programs available. *Faculty:* 37 full-time (9 women), 19 part-time/adjunct (1 woman). *Students:* 166 full-time (65 women), 284 part-time (131 women); includes 113 minority (21 Black or African American, non-Hispanic/Latino; 81 Asian, non-Hispanic/Latino; 9 Hispanic/Latino; 2 Native Hawaiian or other Pacific Islander, non-Hispanic/Latino). Average age 29. 459 applicants, 59% accepted, 208 enrolled. In 2011, 210 master's awarded. *Degree requirements:* For master's, 20 hours of community service (Social Responsibility Project). *Entrance requirements:* For master's, GMAT, GRE or CPA, advanced degree from AACSB institution, MS in a business discipline, professional degree (MD, JD, PhD, DVM, DDS, etc.), minimum undergraduate GPA of 3.0. Additional exam requirements/recommendations for international students: Required—TOEFL (minimum score 102 iBT), IELTS or Pearson Test of English. *Application deadline:* For fall admission, 5/31 priority date for domestic students, 3/31 for international students; for spring admission, 10/31 priority date for domestic students, 9/30 for international students. Applications are processed on a rolling basis. Application fee: $75. Electronic applications accepted. *Expenses: Tuition:* Part-time $1033 per credit hour. *Required fees:* $85 per semester. *Financial support:* In 2011–12, research assistantships with full tuition reimbursements (averaging $35,610 per year) were awarded; career-related internships or fieldwork, Federal Work-Study, scholarships/grants, and unspecified assistantships also available. Support available to part-time students. Financial award application deadline: 6/30; financial award applicants required to submit FAFSA. *Faculty research:* Financial, hedge funds, international business, legal issues, disclosure and branding. *Unit head:* Dr. Joyce A. Strawser, Dean, 973-761-9013, Fax: 973-761-9217, E-mail: joyce.strawser@shu.edu. *Application contact:* Catherine Bianchi, Director of Graduate Admissions, 973-761-9262, Fax: 973-761-9208, E-mail: catherine.bianchi@shu.edu. Web site: http://www.shu.edu/academics/business.

Strayer University, Graduate Studies, Washington, DC 20005-2603. Offers accounting (MS); acquisition (MBA); business administration (MBA); communications technology (MS); educational management (M Ed); finance (MBA); health services administration (MHSA); hospitality and tourism management (MBA); human resource management (MBA); information systems (MS), including computer security management, decision support system management, enterprise resource management, network management, software engineering management, systems development management; management (MBA); management information systems (MS); marketing (MBA); professional accounting (MS), including accounting information systems, controllership, taxation; public administration (MPA); supply chain management (MBA); technology in education (M Ed). Programs also offered at campus locations in Birmingham, AL; Chamblee, GA; Cobb County, GA; Morrow, GA; White Marsh, MD; Charleston, SC; Columbia, SC; Greensboro, NC; Greenville, SC; Lexington, KY; Louisville, KY; Nashville, TN; North Raleigh, NC; Washington, DC. Part-time and evening/weekend programs available. Postbaccalaureate distance learning degree programs offered (minimal on-campus study). *Degree requirements:* For master's, thesis. *Entrance requirements:* For master's, GMAT, GRE General Test, bachelor's degree from an accredited college or university, minimum undergraduate GPA of 2.75. Electronic applications accepted.

Syracuse University, Martin J. Whitman School of Management, PhD Program in Business Administration, Syracuse, NY 13244. Offers accounting (PhD); finance (PhD); management information systems (PhD); managerial statistics (PhD); marketing (PhD); operations management (PhD); organizational behavior (PhD); strategy and human resources (PhD); supply chain management (PhD). *Faculty:* 79 full-time (20 women), 25 part-time/adjunct (6 women). *Students:* 32 full-time (10 women); includes 6 minority (3 Black or African American, non-Hispanic/Latino; 2 Asian, non-Hispanic/Latino; 1 Hispanic/Latino), 18 international. Average age 32. 260 applicants, 8% accepted, 12 enrolled. In 2011, 2 doctorates awarded. *Degree requirements:* For doctorate, comprehensive exam, thesis/dissertation, summer research paper. *Entrance requirements:* For doctorate, GMAT or GRE General Test, 3 recommendations. Additional exam requirements/recommendations for international students: Required—TOEFL (minimum score 600 paper-based; 250 computer-based; 100 iBT). *Application deadline:* For fall admission, 2/15 priority date for domestic students, 2/15 for international students. Applications are processed on a rolling basis. Application fee: $65. Electronic applications accepted. *Expenses: Tuition:* Part-time $1206 per credit. *Financial support:* In 2011–12, 1 fellowship with full tuition reimbursement (averaging $19,570 per year), 30 teaching assistantships with full tuition reimbursements (averaging $17,000 per year) were awarded; research assistantships with full tuition reimbursements, health care benefits, and unspecified assistantships also available. Financial award application deadline: 1/30. *Faculty research:* Marketing models, market microstructure, supply chain, auditing, corporate governance. *Unit head:* Dr. Eunkyu Lee, Director of the PhD Program, 315-443-3429, E-mail: elee06@syr.edu. *Application contact:* Carol Hilleges, Administrative Specialist, 315-443-9601, Fax: 315-443-3671, E-mail: clhilleg@syr.edu. Web site: http://whitman.syr.edu/phd/.

Syracuse University, Martin J. Whitman School of Management, Program in Business Administration, Syracuse, NY 13244. Offers accounting (MBA); entrepreneurship (MBA); finance (MBA); marketing (MBA); supply chain management (MBA). Postbaccalaureate distance learning degree programs offered (minimal on-campus study). *Faculty:* 79 full-time (20 women), 25 part-time/adjunct (6 women). *Students:* 116 full-time (43 women), 188 part-time (58 women); includes 62 minority (33 Black or African American, non-Hispanic/Latino; 1 American Indian or Alaska Native, non-Hispanic/Latino; 13 Asian, non-Hispanic/Latino; 9 Hispanic/Latino; 1 Native Hawaiian or other Pacific Islander, non-Hispanic/Latino; 5 Two or more races, non-Hispanic/Latino), 44 international. Average age 33. 276 applicants, 49% accepted, 77 enrolled. In 2011, 132 master's awarded. *Entrance requirements:* For master's, GMAT, 2 letters of recommendation. Additional exam requirements/recommendations for international students: Required—TOEFL (minimum score 600 paper-based; 250 computer-based; 100 iBT). *Application deadline:* For fall admission, 1/15 priority date for domestic students, 1/15 for international students. Applications are processed on a rolling basis. Application fee: $75. Electronic applications accepted. *Expenses: Tuition:* Part-time $1206 per credit. *Financial support:* In 2011–12, 17 students received support. Fellowships with full and partial tuition reimbursements available, teaching assistantships with partial tuition reimbursements available, career-related internships or fieldwork, scholarships/grants, tuition waivers (partial), unspecified assistantships, and paid hourly positions available. Support available to part-time students. Financial award application deadline: 3/1. *Unit head:* Prof. Dennis Gillen, Chair and Associate Professor of Management, 315-443-3432, Fax: 315-443-9517, E-mail: dgillen@syr.edu. *Application contact:* Josh LaFave, Director, Graduate Enrollment, 315-443-3497, Fax: 315-443-9517, E-mail: mbainfo@syr.edu. Web site: http://whitman.syr.edu/ftmba/.

Syracuse University, Martin J. Whitman School of Management, Program in Supply Chain Management, Syracuse, NY 13244. Offers MBA, PhD. Part-time programs available. Postbaccalaureate distance learning degree programs offered (minimal on-campus study). *Students:* 28 part-time (8 women); includes 3 minority (all Hispanic/Latino). Average age 32. 19 applicants, 74% accepted, 13 enrolled. *Entrance requirements:* For master's, GMAT. *Application deadline:* For fall admission, 1/1 priority date for domestic students, 1/1 for international students. Application fee: $75. Electronic applications accepted. *Expenses: Tuition:* Part-time $1206 per credit. *Application contact:* Josh LaFave, Director of Graduate Enrollment, 315-443-3497, Fax: 315-443-9517, E-mail: mbainfo@syr.edu. Web site: http://whitman.syr.edu/Academics/Marketing/SupplyChain/.

Texas A&M University–San Antonio, School of Business, San Antonio, TX 78224. Offers business administration (MBA); enterprise resource planning systems (MBA); finance (MBA); healthcare management (MBA); human resources management (MBA); information assurance and security (MBA); international business (MBA); professional accounting (MPA); project management (MBA); supply chain management (MBA). Part-time and evening/weekend programs available. *Faculty:* 18 full-time (6 women), 1 part-time/adjunct (0 women). *Students:* 91 full-time (45 women), 278 part-time (150 women). Average age 33. In 2011, 20 master's awarded. *Entrance requirements:* For master's, GMAT. Additional exam requirements/recommendations for international students: Required—TOEFL (minimum score 550 paper-based; 213 computer-based; 80 iBT), IELTS (minimum score 6). *Application deadline:* For fall admission, 7/1 priority date for domestic students, 6/1 for international students; for spring admission, 11/15 priority date for domestic students, 10/1 for international students. Applications are processed on a rolling basis. Application fee: $35 ($50 for international students). Electronic applications accepted. *Expenses:* Tuition, state resident: part-time $691.11 per course. Tuition, nonresident: part-time $1621.11 per course. *Financial support:* Application deadline: 3/31; applicants required to submit FAFSA. *Unit head:* Dr. Tracy Hurley, MBA Coordinator, 210-932-6200, E-mail: tracy.hurley@tamusa.tamus.edu. *Application contact:* Melissa A. Villanueva, Graduate Admissions Specialist, 210-932-6200, Fax: 210-932-6209, E-mail: melissa.villanueva@tamusa.tamus.edu. Web site: http://www.tamusa.tamus.edu.

The University of Akron, Graduate School, College of Business Administration, Department of Management, Program in Supply Chain Management, Akron, OH 44325. Offers MSM. *Students:* 6 full-time (2 women), 13 part-time (3 women), 6 international.

Supply Chain Management

Average age 30. 19 applicants, 53% accepted, 9 enrolled. In 2011, 7 master's awarded. *Entrance requirements:* For master's, GMAT, minimum GPA of 2.75, two letters of recommendation, statement of purpose, resume. Additional exam requirements/recommendations for international students: Required—TOEFL (minimum score 550 paper-based; 213 computer-based; 79 iBT). *Application deadline:* For fall admission, 7/15 for domestic and international students; for spring admission, 11/15 for domestic and international students. Application fee: $30 ($40 for international students). Electronic applications accepted. *Expenses:* Tuition, state resident: full-time $7038; part-time $391 per credit hour. Tuition, nonresident: full-time $12,051; part-time $670 per credit hour. *Required fees:* $1274; $34 per credit hour. *Unit head:* Chair. *Application contact:* Dr. Susan Hanlon, Director of Graduate Business Programs, 330-972-7043, Fax: 330-972-6588, E-mail: shanlon@uakron.edu.

The University of Alabama in Huntsville, School of Graduate Studies, College of Business Administration, Department of Management and Marketing, Huntsville, AL 35899. Offers federal contract procurement (Certificate); management (MBA), including acquisition management, entrepreneurship, federal contract accounting, finance, human resource management, logistics and supply chain management, marketing, project management; supply chain management (Certificate); technology and innovation management (Certificate). *Accreditation:* AACSB. Part-time and evening/weekend programs available. *Faculty:* 11 full-time (2 women), 3 part-time/adjunct (0 women). *Students:* 52 full-time (25 women), 145 part-time (68 women); includes 28 minority (14 Black or African American, non-Hispanic/Latino; 4 American Indian or Alaska Native, non-Hispanic/Latino; 7 Asian, non-Hispanic/Latino; 2 Hispanic/Latino; 1 Two or more races, non-Hispanic/Latino), 15 international. Average age 31. 103 applicants, 73% accepted, 65 enrolled. In 2011, 76 master's awarded. *Degree requirements:* For master's, comprehensive exam, thesis or alternative. *Entrance requirements:* For master's, GMAT (minimum score 500), minimum AACSB index of 1080. Additional exam requirements/recommendations for international students: Required—TOEFL (minimum score 550 paper-based; 213 computer-based; 62 iBT). *Application deadline:* For fall admission, 8/1 for domestic students, 4/1 for international students; for spring admission, 12/1 for domestic students, 9/1 for international students. Applications are processed on a rolling basis. Application fee: $40 ($50 for international students). Electronic applications accepted. *Expenses:* Tuition, state resident: full-time $7830; part-time $473.50 per credit. Tuition, nonresident: full-time $18,748; part-time $1128.33 per credit. Tuition and fees vary according to course load and program. *Financial support:* In 2011–12, 12 students received support, including 7 research assistantships with full tuition reimbursements available (averaging $9,829 per year), 4 teaching assistantships with full tuition reimbursements available (averaging $8,000 per year); career-related internships or fieldwork, Federal Work-Study, institutionally sponsored loans, scholarships/grants, health care benefits, and unspecified assistantships also available. Support available to part-time students. Financial award application deadline: 4/1; financial award applicants required to submit FAFSA. *Faculty research:* Strategic human resources, corporate governance, cross-function integration and the management of research and development, determinants of team performance. *Total annual research expenditures:* $3.4 million. *Unit head:* Dr. Cynthia Gramm, Chair, 256-824-6913, Fax: 256-824-6328, E-mail: cynthia.gramm@uah.edu. *Application contact:* Jennifer Pettitt, Director of Graduate Programs, 256-824-6681, Fax: 256-824-7571, E-mail: jennifer.pettitt@uah.edu.

University of Dallas, Graduate School of Management, Irving, TX 75062-4736. Offers accounting (MBA, MM, MS); business management (MBA, MM); corporate finance (MBA, MM); financial services (MBA); global business (MBA, MM); health services management (MBA, MM); human resource management (MBA, MM); information assurance (MBA, MM, MS); information technology (MBA, MM, MS); information technology service management (MBA, MM, MS); marketing management (MBA, MM); organization development (MBA, MM); project management (MBA, MM); sports and entertainment management (MBA, MM); strategic leadership (MBA, MM); supply chain management (MBA); supply chain management and market logistics (MM). *Accreditation:* ACBSP. Part-time and evening/weekend programs available. Postbaccalaureate distance learning degree programs offered (no on-campus study). *Entrance requirements:* Additional exam requirements/recommendations for international students: Required—TOEFL. Electronic applications accepted. *Expenses:* Contact institution.

University of Florida, Graduate School, Warrington College of Business Administration, Hough Graduate School of Business, Department of Information Systems and Operations Management, Gainesville, FL 32611. Offers information systems and operations management (MS, PhD); supply chain management (MS). *Faculty:* 13 full-time (2 women). *Students:* 203 full-time (77 women), 27 part-time (5 women); includes 31 minority (6 Black or African American, non-Hispanic/Latino; 13 Asian, non-Hispanic/Latino; 12 Hispanic/Latino), 148 international. Average age 25. 383 applicants, 79% accepted, 77 enrolled. In 2011, 89 master's, 2 doctorates awarded. Terminal master's awarded for partial completion of doctoral program. *Degree requirements:* For doctorate, thesis/dissertation. *Entrance requirements:* For master's, GMAT or GRE General Test, minimum GPA of 3.0; for doctorate, GMAT (minimum score 650) or GRE General Test (minimum score 1350 verbal and quantitative combined), minimum GPA of 3.0. Additional exam requirements/recommendations for international students: Required—TOEFL (minimum score 550 paper-based; 213 computer-based; 80 iBT), IELTS (minimum score 6), IELTS (minimum score 6) or Michigan English Language Assessment Battery (minimum score 77) also required for some. *Application deadline:* For fall admission, 4/1 priority date for domestic students, 3/1 for international students; for spring admission, 10/15 for domestic students, 10/1 for international students. Applications are processed on a rolling basis. Application fee: $30. *Financial support:* Fellowships, research assistantships, teaching assistantships, and unspecified assistantships available. Financial award application deadline: 2/1; financial award applicants required to submit FAFSA. *Faculty research:* Expert systems, nonconvex optimization, manufacturing management, production and operation management, telecommunication. *Unit head:* Dr. Gary J. Koehler, Chair, 352-846-2090, Fax: 352-392-5438, E-mail: koehler@ufl.edu. *Application contact:* Dr. Anand A. Paul, Graduate Coordinator for PhD Program, 352-392-9600, Fax: 352-392-5438, E-mail: paulaa@ufl.edu. Web site: http://www.cba.ufl.edu/isom/.

University of Houston, College of Technology, Department of Information and Logistics Technology, Houston, TX 77204. Offers information security (MS); supply chain and logistics technology (MS); technology project management (MS). Part-time programs available. *Degree requirements:* For master's, project or thesis (most programs). *Entrance requirements:* For master's, GMAT. Additional exam requirements/recommendations for international students: Required—TOEFL (minimum score 550 paper-based; 79 iBT). Electronic applications accepted.

University of Louisville, J. B. Speed School of Engineering, Department of Industrial Engineering, Louisville, KY 40292-0001. Offers engineering management (M Eng); industrial engineering (M Eng, MS, PhD); logistics and distribution (Certificate). *Accreditation:* ABET (one or more programs are accredited). Part-time programs available. *Faculty:* 10 full-time (1 woman). *Students:* 42 full-time (13 women), 11 part-time (6 women); includes 5 minority (4 Black or African American, non-Hispanic/Latino; 1 Hispanic/Latino), 21 international. Average age 28. 52 applicants, 33% accepted, 11 enrolled. In 2011, 43 master's, 3 doctorates awarded. Terminal master's awarded for partial completion of doctoral program. *Degree requirements:* For master's, comprehensive exam (for some programs), thesis or alternative; for doctorate, comprehensive exam, thesis/dissertation, minimum GPA of 3.0. *Entrance requirements:* For master's and doctorate, GRE General Test. Additional exam requirements/recommendations for international students: Required—TOEFL (minimum score 550 paper-based; 213 computer-based; 80 iBT), IELTS (minimum score 6.5). *Application deadline:* For fall admission, 5/1 priority date for domestic students, 5/1 for international students; for spring admission, 11/1 priority date for domestic students, 11/1 for international students. Applications are processed on a rolling basis. Application fee: $50. Electronic applications accepted. *Expenses:* Tuition, state resident: full-time $9692; part-time $539 per credit hour. Tuition, nonresident: full-time $20,168; part-time $1121 per credit hour. Tuition and fees vary according to program and reciprocity agreements. *Financial support:* In 2011–12, 15 students received support, including 7 fellowships with full tuition reimbursements available (averaging $20,000 per year), 2 research assistantships with full tuition reimbursements available (averaging $20,000 per year), 6 teaching assistantships with full tuition reimbursements available (averaging $20,000 per year). Financial award application deadline: 1/25; financial award applicants required to submit FAFSA. *Faculty research:* Optimization, computer simulation, logistics and distribution, ergonomics and human factors, advanced manufacturing process. *Total annual research expenditures:* $748,000. *Unit head:* Dr. John S. Usher, Chair, 502-852-6342, Fax: 502-852-5633, E-mail: usher@louisville.edu. *Application contact:* Dr. Michael Day, Associate Dean, 502-852-6195, Fax: 502-852-7294, E-mail: day@louisville.edu. Web site: http://www.louisville.edu/speed/industrial/.

University of Massachusetts Dartmouth, Graduate School, Charlton College of Business, Program in Business Administration, North Dartmouth, MA 02747-2300. Offers accounting (Postbaccalaureate Certificate); business administration (MBA); business foundation (online) (Graduate Certificate); finance (PMC); international business (online) (Graduate Certificate); leadership (online) (Graduate Certificate); management (Postbaccalaureate Certificate); marketing (Postbaccalaureate Certificate); supply chain management (PMC). *Accreditation:* AACSB. Part-time programs available. *Faculty:* 35 full-time (11 women), 26 part-time/adjunct (7 women). *Students:* 81 full-time (29 women), 119 part-time (56 women); includes 17 minority (6 Black or African American, non-Hispanic/Latino; 1 American Indian or Alaska Native, non-Hispanic/Latino; 3 Asian, non-Hispanic/Latino; 5 Hispanic/Latino; 2 Two or more races, non-Hispanic/Latino), 42 international. Average age 31. 132 applicants, 92% accepted, 68 enrolled. In 2011, 91 master's, 18 other advanced degrees awarded. *Entrance requirements:* For master's, GMAT, statement of intent, resume, 3 letters of recommendation; for other advanced degree, statement of intent, resume, 3 letters of recommendation. Additional exam requirements/recommendations for international students: Required—TOEFL (minimum score 500 paper-based; 200 computer-based; 72 iBT). *Application deadline:* For fall admission, 3/1 for domestic students, 2/1 for international students; for spring admission, 11/1 for domestic students, 10/15 for international students. Application fee: $40 ($60 for international students). Electronic applications accepted. *Expenses:* Tuition, state resident: full-time $2071; part-time $86.29 per credit. Tuition, nonresident: full-time $8099; part-time $337.46 per credit. *Required fees:* $438.58 per credit. Part-time tuition and fees vary according to class time, course load, degree level and reciprocity agreements. *Financial support:* Research assistantships, teaching assistantships, Federal Work-Study, and unspecified assistantships available. Support available to part-time students. Financial award application deadline: 3/1; financial award applicants required to submit FAFSA. *Faculty research:* Global business environment, e-commerce, managing diversity, agile manufacturing, green business. *Total annual research expenditures:* $8,653. *Unit head:* Stephanie Jacobsen, Program Coordinator, 508-999-8543, Fax: 508-999-8646, E-mail: s.jacobsen@umassd.edu. *Application contact:* Elan Turcotte-Shamski, Graduate Admissions Officer, 508-999-8604, Fax: 508-999-8183, E-mail: graduate@umassd.edu. Web site: http://www.umassd.edu/charlton/.

University of Memphis, Graduate School, Fogelman College of Business and Economics, Program in Business Administration, Memphis, TN 38152. Offers accounting (MBA, PhD); economics (MBA, PhD); executive business administration (MBA); finance (PhD); finance, insurance, and real estate (MBA, MS); international business administration (IMBA); management (MBA, MS, PhD); management information systems (MBA, MS, PhD); management science (MBA); marketing (MBA, MS); marketing and supply chain management (PhD); real estate development (MS); JD/MBA. *Accreditation:* AACSB. *Degree requirements:* For master's, comprehensive exam; for doctorate, comprehensive exam, thesis/dissertation. *Entrance requirements:* For master's, GMAT, resume; for doctorate, GMAT, interview, minimum GPA of 3.4, resume, letter of recommendation. Additional exam requirements/recommendations for international students: Required—TOEFL (minimum score 550 paper-based; 220 computer-based). *Faculty research:* Competitive business strategy, finance microstructures, supply chain management innovations, health care economics, litigation risks and corporate audits.

University of Michigan–Dearborn, College of Business, Dearborn, MI 48128-1491. Offers accounting (MBA, MS); business analytics (MS); finance (MBA, MS); information systems (MS); international business (MBA); management (MBA); management information systems (MBA); marketing (MBA); supply chain management (MBA, MS); MBA/MHSA; MBA/MSE; MBA/MSF; MBA/MSIS; MSF/MSA. *Accreditation:* AACSB. Part-time and evening/weekend programs available. Postbaccalaureate distance learning degree programs offered (no on-campus study). *Faculty:* 50 full-time (6 women), 32 part-time/adjunct (18 women). *Students:* 65 full-time (29 women), 356 part-time (121 women); includes 79 minority (19 Black or African American, non-Hispanic/Latino; 36 American Indian or Alaska Native, non-Hispanic/Latino; 15 Hispanic/Latino; 1 Native Hawaiian or other Pacific Islander, non-Hispanic/Latino; 8 Two or more races, non-Hispanic/Latino), 80 international. Average age 28. 175 applicants, 53% accepted, 68 enrolled. In 2011, 173 master's awarded. *Entrance requirements:* For master's, GMAT or GRE, 2 years of work experience (MBA); course work in computer applications, statistics, and pre-calculus or finite mathematics; 18 credits of accounting course work beyond introductory courses (MS in accounting). Additional exam requirements/recommendations for international students: Required—TOEFL (minimum score 560 paper-based; 220 computer-based; 84 iBT), IELTS. *Application deadline:* For fall admission, 8/1 priority date for domestic students, 6/1 for international students; for winter admission, 12/1 priority date for domestic students, 10/1 for international students; for spring admission, 4/1 priority date for domestic students, 2/1 for international students. Applications are processed on a rolling basis. Application fee: $60. Electronic applications accepted. *Expenses:* Contact institution. *Financial support:* Career-related internships or fieldwork, Federal Work-Study, and scholarships/grants available. Support available to part-time students. Financial award application deadline: 9/1; financial award applicants required to submit FAFSA. *Faculty research:* Cultural diversity, buyer-supplier relations, error detection in data, economic evolution. *Unit head:* Dr. Lee Redding, Interim Dean, 313-593-5248, Fax: 313-271-9835, E-mail: lredding@umd.umich.edu. *Application contact:* Joan Doherty, Academic Advisor/Counselor, 313-593-5460, Fax: 313-271-9838, E-mail: gradbusiness@umd.umich.edu. Web site: http://www.cob.umd.umich.edu.

University of Minnesota, Twin Cities Campus, Carlson School of Management, Carlson Full-Time MBA Program, Minneapolis, MN 55455. Offers finance (MBA); information technology (MBA); management (MBA); marketing (MBA); medical industry orientation (MBA); supply chain and operations (MBA); JD/MBA; MBA/MPP; MD/MBA; MHA/MBA; Pharm D/MBA. *Accreditation:* AACSB. *Faculty:* 58 full-time (17 women), 23 part-time/adjunct (5 women). *Students:* 172 full-time (54 women); includes 16 minority (4 Black or African American, non-Hispanic/Latino; 10 Asian, non-Hispanic/Latino; 2 Two or more races, non-Hispanic/Latino), 41 international. Average age 28. 538 applicants, 41% accepted, 99 enrolled. In 2011, 97 master's awarded. *Entrance requirements:* For master's, GMAT or GRE. Additional exam requirements/recommendations for international students: Required—TOEFL (minimum score 580 paper-based; 240 computer-based; 84 iBT), IELTS (minimum score 7), or Pearson Test of English. *Application deadline:* For fall admission, 4/1 for domestic students, 2/1 for international students. Application fee: $60 ($90 for international students). Electronic applications accepted. *Expenses:* Contact institution. *Financial support:* In 2011–12, 116 students received support, including 116 fellowships with full and partial tuition reimbursements available (averaging $18,702 per year); research assistantships with partial tuition reimbursements available, teaching assistantships with partial tuition reimbursements available, career-related internships or fieldwork, Federal Work-Study, institutionally sponsored loans, scholarships/grants, health care benefits, and unspecified assistantships also available. Financial award application deadline: 4/1; financial award applicants required to submit FAFSA. *Faculty research:* Finance and accounting: financial reporting, asset pricing models and corporate finance; information and decision sciences: on-line auctions, information transparency and recommender systems; marketing: psychological influences on consumer behavior, brand equity, pricing and marketing channels; operations: lean manufacturing, quality management and global supply chains; strategic management and organization: global strategy, networks, entrepreneurship and innovation, sustainability. *Unit head:* Philip J. Miller, Assistant Dean, MBA Programs and Graduate Business Career Center, 612-625-5555, Fax: 612-625-1012, E-mail: mba@umn.edu. *Application contact:* Linh Gilles, Director of Admissions and Recruiting, 612-625-5555, Fax: 612-625-1012, E-mail: ftmba@umn.edu. Web site: http://www.csom.umn.edu/MBA/full-time/.

University of Minnesota, Twin Cities Campus, Carlson School of Management, Carlson Part-Time MBA Program, Minneapolis, MN 55455. Offers finance (MBA); information technology (MBA); management (MBA); marketing (MBA); supply chain and operations (MBA). Part-time and evening/weekend programs available. *Faculty:* 63 full-time (16 women), 27 part-time/adjunct (4 women). *Students:* 1,459 part-time (463 women); includes 94 minority (11 Black or African American, non-Hispanic/Latino; 3 American Indian or Alaska Native, non-Hispanic/Latino; 68 Asian, non-Hispanic/Latino; 10 Hispanic/Latino; 2 Two or more races, non-Hispanic/Latino), 72 international. Average age 28. 336 applicants, 86% accepted, 256 enrolled. In 2011, 479 master's awarded. *Entrance requirements:* For master's, GMAT or GRE. Additional exam requirements/recommendations for international students: Required—TOEFL (minimum score 580 paper-based; 240 computer-based; 84 iBT), IELTS (minimum score 7), or Pearson Test of English. *Application deadline:* For fall admission, 5/1 priority date for domestic students, 5/1 for international students; for spring admission, 10/1 priority date for domestic students, 10/1 for international students. Applications are processed on a rolling basis. Application fee: $60 ($90 for international students). Electronic applications accepted. *Expenses:* Contact institution. *Financial support:* Applicants required to submit FAFSA. *Faculty research:* Finance and accounting: financial reporting, asset pricing models and corporate finance; information and decision sciences: on-line auctions, information transparency and recommender systems; marketing: psychological influences on consumer behavior, brand equity, pricing and marketing channels; operations: lean manufacturing, quality management and global supply chains; strategic management and organization: global strategy, networks, entrepreneurship and innovation, sustainability. *Unit head:* Philip J. Miller, Assistant Dean, MBA Programs and Graduate Business Career Center, 612-624-2039, Fax: 612-625-1012, E-mail: mba@umn.edu. *Application contact:* Linh Gilles, Director of Admissions and Recruiting, 612-625-5555, Fax: 612-625-1012, E-mail: ptmba@umn.edu. Web site: http://www.carlsonschool.umn.edu/ptmba.

University of Missouri–St. Louis, College of Business Administration, Program in Business Administration, St. Louis, MO 63121. Offers accounting (MBA); business administration (Certificate); finance (MBA); human resource management (Certificate); information systems (MBA); logistics and supply chain management (MBA, Certificate); marketing (MBA); marketing management (Certificate); operations management (MBA). *Accreditation:* AACSB. Part-time and evening/weekend programs available. *Faculty:* 32 full-time (7 women), 10 part-time/adjunct (2 women). *Students:* 126 full-time (48 women), 305 part-time (141 women); includes 61 minority (25 Black or African American, non-Hispanic/Latino; 23 Asian, non-Hispanic/Latino; 9 Hispanic/Latino; 1 Native Hawaiian or other Pacific Islander, non-Hispanic/Latino; 3 Two or more races, non-Hispanic/Latino), 47 international. Average age 30. 241 applicants, 70% accepted, 134 enrolled. In 2011, 150 master's, 1 doctorate, 19 other advanced degrees awarded. *Entrance requirements:* For master's, GMAT, 2 letters of recommendation. Additional exam requirements/recommendations for international students: Required—TOEFL (minimum score 550 paper-based; 213 computer-based). *Application deadline:* For fall admission, 7/1 for domestic and international students; for spring admission, 12/1 for domestic and international students. Applications are processed on a rolling basis. Application fee: $35 ($40 for international students). Electronic applications accepted. *Expenses:* Tuition, state resident: full-time $6273; part-time $3866 per year. Tuition, nonresident: full-time $14,969; part-time $9980 per year. *Required fees:* $315 per year. *Financial support:* In 2011–12, 32 research assistantships with full and partial tuition reimbursements (averaging $6,000 per year), 6 teaching assistantships with full and partial tuition reimbursements (averaging $12,276 per year) were awarded; career-related internships or fieldwork, Federal Work-Study, and institutionally sponsored loans also available. Support available to part-time students. Financial award application deadline: 4/1; financial award applicants required to submit FAFSA. *Faculty research:* Human resources, strategic management, marketing strategy, consumer behavior product development, advertising. *Unit head:* Karl Kottemann, Assistant Director, 314-516-5885, Fax: 314-516-6420, E-mail: mba@umsl.edu. *Application contact:* 314-516-5458, Fax: 314-516-6996, E-mail: gradadm@umsl.edu. Web site: http://www.umsl.edu/divisions/business/mbaonline/mbaprog.htm.

University of Missouri–St. Louis, College of Business Administration, Program in Information Systems, St. Louis, MO 63121. Offers information systems (MS); logistics and supply chain management (PhD). Part-time and evening/weekend programs available. *Faculty:* 6 full-time (2 women), 4 part-time/adjunct (0 women). *Students:* 2 full-time (0 women), 18 part-time (2 women); includes 2 minority (both Asian, non-Hispanic/Latino), 3 international. Average age 33. 14 applicants, 57% accepted, 2 enrolled. In 2011, 11 degrees awarded. *Entrance requirements:* For master's, GMAT, 2 letters of recommendation. Additional exam requirements/recommendations for international students: Required—TOEFL (minimum score 550 paper-based; 213 computer-based). *Application deadline:* For fall admission, 7/1 priority date for domestic students, 7/1 for international students; for spring admission, 12/1 priority date for domestic students, 12/1 for international students. Applications are processed on a rolling basis. Application fee: $35 ($40 for international students). Electronic applications accepted. *Expenses:* Tuition, state resident: full-time $6273; part-time $3866 per year. Tuition, nonresident: full-time $14,969; part-time $9980 per year. *Required fees:* $315 per year. *Financial support:* Career-related internships or fieldwork, Federal Work-Study, and institutionally sponsored loans available. Support available to part-time students. Financial award application deadline: 4/1; financial award applicants required to submit FAFSA. *Faculty research:* International information systems, telecommunications, systems development, information systems sourcing. *Unit head:* Karl Kottemann, Assistant Director, 314-516-5885, Fax: 314-516-6420, E-mail: mba@umsl.edu. *Application contact:* 314-516-5458, Fax: 314-516-6996, E-mail: gradadm@umsl.edu. Web site: http://www.umsl.edu/divisions/business/mis/ms_req_mis.html.

The University of North Carolina at Charlotte, Graduate School, Belk College of Business, Department of Business Information Systems and Operation Management, Charlotte, NC 28223-0001. Offers information and technology management (MBA); supply chain management (MBA). *Faculty:* 14 full-time (5 women). *Expenses:* Tuition, state resident: full-time $3689. Tuition, nonresident: full-time $15,226. *Required fees:* $2198. Tuition and fees vary according to course load and program. *Unit head:* Dr. Joe Mazzola, Interim Dean, 704-687-7577, Fax: 704-687-4014, E-mail: jmazzola@uncc.edu. *Application contact:* Kathy B. Giddings, Director of Graduate Admissions, 704-687-5503, Fax: 704-687-3279, E-mail: gradadm@uncc.edu. Web site: http://belkcollege.uncc.edu/about-college/departments/bisom.

The University of North Carolina at Greensboro, Graduate School, Bryan School of Business and Economics, Department of Information Systems and Operations Management, Greensboro, NC 27412-5001. Offers information systems (PhD); information technology (Certificate); information technology and management (MS); supply chain management (Certificate). *Entrance requirements:* For master's, GMAT, GRE General Test. Additional exam requirements/recommendations for international students: Required—TOEFL. Electronic applications accepted.

University of Rhode Island, Graduate School, College of Business Administration, Kingston, RI 02881. Offers accounting (MS); business administration (MBA, PhD), including finance and insurance (PhD), management (PhD), marketing (PhD), operations and supply chain management (MBA); finance (MBA); general business (MBA); management (MBA); marketing (MBA); supply chain management (MBA). *Accreditation:* AACSB. Part-time and evening/weekend programs available. *Faculty:* 56 full-time (15 women), 8 part-time/adjunct (4 women). *Students:* 93 full-time (40 women), 226 part-time (90 women); includes 35 minority (7 Black or African American, non-Hispanic/Latino; 1 American Indian or Alaska Native, non-Hispanic/Latino; 15 Asian, non-Hispanic/Latino; 11 Hispanic/Latino; 1 Two or more races, non-Hispanic/Latino), 24 international. In 2011, 78 master's, 3 doctorates awarded. *Degree requirements:* For master's, comprehensive exam (for some programs), thesis optional; for doctorate, comprehensive exam, thesis/dissertation. *Entrance requirements:* For master's, GMAT or GRE, 2 letters of recommendation, resume; for doctorate, GMAT or GRE, 3 letters of recommendation, resume. Additional exam requirements/recommendations for international students: Required—TOEFL (minimum score 575 paper-based; 233 computer-based; 91 iBT). Application fee: $65. Electronic applications accepted. *Expenses:* Tuition, state resident: full-time $10,432; part-time $580 per credit hour. Tuition, nonresident: full-time $23,130; part-time $1285 per credit hour. *Required fees:* $1362; $36 per credit hour. $35 per semester. One-time fee: $130. *Financial support:* In 2011–12, 13 teaching assistantships with full and partial tuition reimbursements (averaging $13,020 per year) were awarded. Financial award applicants required to submit FAFSA. *Unit head:* Dr. Mark Higgins, Dean, 401-874-4244, Fax: 401-874-4312, E-mail: markhiggins@uri.edu. *Application contact:* Lisa Lancellotta, Coordinator, MBA Programs, 401-874-4241, Fax: 401-874-4312, E-mail: mba@uri.edu. Web site: http://www.cba.uri.edu/.

University of San Diego, School of Business Administration, Program in Supply Chain Management, San Diego, CA 92110-2492. Offers MS, Certificate. Postbaccalaureate distance learning degree programs offered (minimal on-campus study). *Students:* 18 full-time (9 women), 53 part-time (16 women); includes 16 minority (7 Black or African American, non-Hispanic/Latino; 2 Asian, non-Hispanic/Latino; 6 Hispanic/Latino; 1 Two or more races, non-Hispanic/Latino), 3 international. Average age 36. In 2011, 20 master's, 28 other advanced degrees awarded. *Degree requirements:* For master's, capstone course. *Entrance requirements:* Additional exam requirements/recommendations for international students: Required—TOEFL (minimum score 580 paper-based; 237 computer-based; 92 iBT), TWE. Application fee: $80. *Expenses: Tuition:* Full-time $22,482; part-time $1249 per unit. *Required fees:* $224. Full-time tuition and fees vary according to course load and degree level. *Financial support:* In 2011–12, 11 students received support. Scholarships/grants available. Financial award application deadline: 4/1; financial award applicants required to submit FAFSA. *Unit head:* Lauren Lukens, Director, MS Program, 619-260-7901, E-mail: msscm@sandiego.edu. *Application contact:* Monica Mahon, Associate Director of Graduate Admissions, 619-260-4524, Fax: 619-260-4158, E-mail: grads@sandiego.edu. Web site: http://www.sandiego.edu/business/centers/supply_chain_management/MS-SCM/.

University of Southern California, Graduate School, Viterbi School of Engineering, Daniel J. Epstein Department of Industrial and Systems Engineering, Los Angeles, CA 90089. Offers digital supply chain management (MS); engineering management (MS); engineering technology communication (Graduate Certificate); health systems operations (Graduate Certificate); industrial and systems engineering (MS, PhD, Engr); manufacturing engineering (MS); operations research engineering (MS); optimization and supply chain management (Graduate Certificate); product development engineering (MS); safety systems and security (MS); systems architecting and engineering (MS, Graduate Certificate); systems safety and security (Graduate Certificate); transportation systems (Graduate Certificate); MS/MBA. Part-time and evening/weekend programs available. Postbaccalaureate distance learning degree programs offered (no on-campus study). Terminal master's awarded for partial completion of doctoral program. *Degree requirements:* For master's, thesis optional; for doctorate, thesis/dissertation. *Entrance requirements:* For master's and doctorate, GRE General Test. Additional exam requirements/recommendations for international students: Recommended—TOEFL. Electronic applications accepted. *Faculty research:* Health systems, music cognition and retrieval, transportation and logistics, manufacturing and automation, engineering systems design, risk and economic analysis.

The University of Texas at Austin, Graduate School, McCombs School of Business, Department of Information, Risk, and Operations Management, Austin, TX 78712-1111. Offers information management (MBA); information systems (PhD); risk analysis and decision making (PhD); risk management (MBA); supply chain and operations management (MBA, PhD). *Degree requirements:* For doctorate, thesis/dissertation. *Entrance requirements:* For doctorate, GMAT or GRE. *Application deadline:* For fall admission, 1/2 for domestic students. Applications are processed on a rolling basis. Application fee: $50 ($75 for international students). Electronic applications accepted. *Financial support:* Fellowships with full and partial tuition reimbursements, research assistantships, and teaching assistantships with partial tuition reimbursements available. Financial award application deadline: 1/2. *Faculty research:* Stochastic processing and queuing, discrete nonlinear and large-scale optimization simulation, quality assurance logistics, distributed artificial intelligence, organizational modeling.

Supply Chain Management

Unit head: Dr. Prabhudev Konana, Chair, 512-471-5219, E-mail: prabhudev.konana@mccombs.utexas.edu. Web site: http://www.mccombs.utexas.edu/dept/irom/.

The University of Texas at Dallas, Naveen Jindal School of Management, Program in Business Administration, Richardson, TX 75080. Offers cohort (MBA); executive business administration (EMBA); global leadership (EMBA); global online (MBA); healthcare management (EMBA); product lifecycle and supply chain management (EMBA); professional business administration (MBA); project management (EMBA). *Accreditation:* AACSB. Part-time and evening/weekend programs available. Postbaccalaureate distance learning degree programs offered (no on-campus study). *Faculty:* 88 full-time (16 women), 52 part-time/adjunct (13 women). *Students:* 390 full-time (129 women), 658 part-time (207 women); includes 291 minority (42 Black or African American, non-Hispanic/Latino; 4 American Indian or Alaska Native, non-Hispanic/Latino; 168 Asian, non-Hispanic/Latino; 66 Hispanic/Latino; 11 Two or more races, non-Hispanic/Latino), 161 international. Average age 32. 872 applicants, 51% accepted, 323 enrolled. In 2011, 471 master's awarded. *Degree requirements:* For master's, thesis optional. *Entrance requirements:* For master's, GMAT, 10 years of business experience (EMBA), minimum GPA of 3.0. Additional exam requirements/recommendations for international students: Required—TOEFL (minimum score 550 paper-based; 215 computer-based). *Application deadline:* For fall admission, 7/15 for domestic students, 5/1 for international students; for spring admission, 11/15 for domestic students, 9/1 for international students. Applications are processed on a rolling basis. Application fee: $50 ($100 for international students). Electronic applications accepted. *Expenses:* Contact institution. *Financial support:* In 2011–12, 223 students received support, including 1 research assistantship with partial tuition reimbursement available (averaging $13,400 per year), 24 teaching assistantships with partial tuition reimbursements available (averaging $10,050 per year); career-related internships or fieldwork, Federal Work-Study, institutionally sponsored loans, scholarships/grants, and unspecified assistantships also available. Support available to part-time students. Financial award application deadline: 4/30; financial award applicants required to submit FAFSA. *Faculty research:* Production scheduling, trade and finance, organizational decision-making, life/work planning. *Unit head:* Lisa Shatz, Director, Full-time MBA Program, 972-883-6191, E-mail: lisa.shatz@utdallas.edu. *Application contact:* James Parker, Assistant Director, 972-883-5842, E-mail: jparker@utdallas.edu. Web site: http://jindal.utdallas.edu/academic-programs/mba-programs/.

The University of Texas at Dallas, Naveen Jindal School of Management, Program in Supply Chain Management, Richardson, TX 75080. Offers MS. Part-time and evening/weekend programs available. *Faculty:* 14 full-time (0 women), 6 part-time/adjunct (1 woman). *Students:* 153 full-time (70 women), 31 part-time (15 women); includes 15 minority (2 Black or African American, non-Hispanic/Latino; 6 Asian, non-Hispanic/Latino; 5 Hispanic/Latino; 2 Two or more races, non-Hispanic/Latino), 145 international. Average age 27. 220 applicants, 75% accepted, 96 enrolled. In 2011, 29 master's awarded. *Degree requirements:* For master's, thesis optional. *Entrance requirements:* For master's, GMAT, minimum GPA of 3.0 in upper-level coursework in field. Additional exam requirements/recommendations for international students: Required—TOEFL (minimum score 550 paper-based; 215 computer-based). *Application deadline:* For fall admission, 7/15 for domestic students, 5/1 for international students; for spring admission, 11/15 for domestic students, 9/1 for international students. Applications are processed on a rolling basis. Application fee: $50 ($100 for international students). Electronic applications accepted. *Expenses:* Tuition, state resident: full-time $11,170; part-time $620.56 per credit hour. Tuition, nonresident: full-time $20,212; part-time $1122.89 per credit hour. *Financial support:* In 2011–12, 55 students received support, including 1 teaching assistantship with partial tuition reimbursement available (averaging $10,050 per year); research assistantships with partial tuition reimbursements available, career-related internships or fieldwork, Federal Work-Study, institutionally sponsored loans, scholarships/grants, and unspecified assistantships also available. Support available to part-time students. Financial award application deadline: 4/30; financial award applicants required to submit FAFSA. *Faculty research:* Inventory control and risk management. *Unit head:* Dr. Shawn Alborz, Director, 972-883-6455, E-mail: salborz@utdallas.edu. *Application contact:* David B. Ritchey, Director of Advising, 972-883-2750, Fax: 972-883-6425, E-mail: davidr@utdallas.edu. Web site: http://jindal.utdallas.edu/academic-areas/information-systems-and-operations-management/operationssupply-chain-management-programs.

The University of Toledo, College of Graduate Studies, College of Business and Innovation, Department of Information Operations and Technology Management, Toledo, OH 43606-3390. Offers information systems (MBA); manufacturing management (PhD); operations management (MBA); supply chain management (Certificate). Part-time and evening/weekend programs available. *Faculty:* 11. *Students:* 16 full-time (5 women), 36 part-time (9 women); includes 7 minority (5 Black or African American, non-Hispanic/Latino; 1 Asian, non-Hispanic/Latino; 1 Hispanic/Latino), 20 international. Average age 33. 41 applicants, 51% accepted, 10 enrolled. In 2011, 15 master's, 5 doctorates awarded. *Degree requirements:* For doctorate, thesis/dissertation. *Entrance requirements:* For master's, doctorate, and Certificate, GMAT, minimum GPA of 2.7 for all prior academic work, three letters of recommendation, statement of purpose, transcripts from all prior institutions attended. Additional exam requirements/recommendations for international students: Required—TOEFL (minimum score 550 paper-based; 213 computer-based; 80 iBT), IELTS (minimum score 6.5). *Application deadline:* For fall admission, 1/15 priority date for domestic students, 1/15 for international students. Applications are processed on a rolling basis. Application fee: $45 ($75 for international students). Electronic applications accepted. *Financial support:* In 2011–12, 23 research assistantships with full and partial tuition reimbursements (averaging $9,500 per year) were awarded; career-related internships or fieldwork, Federal Work-Study, institutionally sponsored loans, scholarships/grants, tuition waivers (full and partial), unspecified assistantships, and administrative assistantships also available. Support available to part-time students. *Unit head:* Dr. T. S. Ragu-Nathan, Chair, 419-530-2420. *Application contact:* Graduate School Office, 419-530-4723, Fax: 419-530-4724, E-mail: grdsch@utnet.utoledo.edu. Web site: http://www.utoledo.edu/business/index.html.

University of Wisconsin–Madison, Graduate School, Wisconsin School of Business, Wisconsin Full-Time MBA Program, Madison, WI 53706-1380. Offers applied security analysis (MBA); arts administration (MBA); brand and product management (MBA); corporate finance and investment banking (MBA); marketing research (MBA); operations and technology management (MBA); real estate (MBA); risk management and insurance (MBA); strategic human resource management (MBA); supply chain management (MBA). *Faculty:* 32 full-time (6 women), 27 part-time/adjunct (7 women). *Students:* 228 full-time (75 women); includes 53 minority (16 Black or African American, non-Hispanic/Latino; 25 Asian, non-Hispanic/Latino; 10 Hispanic/Latino; 2 Native Hawaiian or other Pacific Islander, non-Hispanic/Latino), 28 international. Average age 28. 509 applicants, 30% accepted, 111 enrolled. In 2011, 120 master's awarded. *Degree requirements:* For master's, thesis (for arts administration). *Entrance requirements:* For master's, GMAT, bachelor's or equivalent degree, 2 years of work experience, letters of recommendation. Additional exam requirements/recommendations for international students: Required—TOEFL (minimum score 600 paper-based; 250 computer-based; 100 iBT), IELTS. *Application deadline:* For fall admission, 11/4 for domestic and international students; for winter admission, 2/3 for domestic and international students; for spring admission, 4/27 for domestic and international students. Applications are processed on a rolling basis. Application fee: $56. Electronic applications accepted. *Expenses:* Tuition, state resident: full-time $10,296; part-time $643.51 per credit. Tuition, nonresident: full-time $24,054; part-time $1503.40 per credit. *Required fees:* $70.06 per credit. Tuition and fees vary according to course load, campus/location, program and reciprocity agreements. *Financial support:* In 2011–12, 176 students received support, including 20 fellowships with full and partial tuition reimbursements available (averaging $18,756 per year), 128 research assistantships with full tuition reimbursements available (averaging $25,185 per year), 28 teaching assistantships with full tuition reimbursements available (averaging $25,097 per year); scholarships/grants, health care benefits, and unspecified assistantships also available. Financial award application deadline: 4/27; financial award applicants required to submit FAFSA. *Faculty research:* Market consequences of International Financial Reporting Standards (IFRS), inter-firm relationships and strategic partnerships, application of Bayesian statistical methods and applied probability models to understanding individuals' behaviors in the context of customer relationship management (CRM) applications, liquidity provision and the structure of financial markets, strategic management of global startups. *Unit head:* Dr. Larry "Chip" W. Hunter, Associate Dean of Master's Programs, 608-265-3494, Fax: 608-265-4192, E-mail: lhunter@bus.wisc.edu. *Application contact:* Maria Reis, Assistant Director of MBA Marketing and Recruiting, 608-262-4000, Fax: 608-265-4192, E-mail: mreis@bus.wisc.edu. Web site: http://www.bus.wisc.edu/mba.

University of Wisconsin–Whitewater, School of Graduate Studies, College of Business and Economics, Program in Business Administration, Whitewater, WI 53190-1790. Offers finance (MBA); human resource management (MBA); information technology management (MBA); international business (MBA); management (MBA); marketing (MBA); operations and supply chain management (MBA). *Accreditation:* AACSB. Part-time and evening/weekend programs available. Postbaccalaureate distance learning degree programs offered (no on-campus study). *Students:* 170 full-time (53 women), 538 part-time (213 women); includes 130 minority (28 Black or African American, non-Hispanic/Latino; 87 Asian, non-Hispanic/Latino; 15 Hispanic/Latino). Average age 31. 448 applicants, 33% accepted, 120 enrolled. In 2011, 304 master's awarded. *Entrance requirements:* For master's, GMAT or GRE, minimum AACSB index of 1000, minimum GPA of 2.75. Additional exam requirements/recommendations for international students: Required—TOEFL (minimum score 550 paper-based; 213 computer-based; 80 iBT), IELTS (minimum score 6). *Application deadline:* For fall admission, 7/15 for domestic and international students; for spring admission, 12/1 for domestic and international students. Applications are processed on a rolling basis. Application fee: $56. Electronic applications accepted. *Expenses:* Tuition, state resident: full-time $4088. Tuition, nonresident: full-time $8817. Tuition and fees vary according to program. *Financial support:* In 2011–12, research assistantships (averaging $7,245 per year) were awarded; Federal Work-Study, unspecified assistantships, and out-of-state fee waivers also available. Support available to part-time students. Financial award application deadline: 3/15; financial award applicants required to submit FAFSA. *Faculty research:* Interface between social institutions and individual behavior, technology and innovation management, occupational mental health, workplace deviance and workplace romance. *Unit head:* Dr. John Chenoweth, Associate Dean, 262-472-1945, Fax: 262-472-4863, E-mail: chenowej@uww.edu.

Walden University, Graduate Programs, School of Management, Minneapolis, MN 55401. Offers accounting (MS, DBA), including accounting for the professional (MS), CPA (MS), self-designed (MS); accounting and management (MS), including accounting for strategic managers, self-designed; accounting for managers (MBA); advanced project management (Post-Graduate Certificate); applied project management (Post-Graduate Certificate); corporate finance (MBA); entrepreneurship (MBA, DBA); finance (DBA); global management (MS); global supply chain management (DBA); healthcare management (MBA, DBA); healthcare system improvement (MBA); human resource management (MBA, MS, PhD), including functional human resource management (MS), integrating functional and strategic human resource management (MS), organizational strategy (MS); information systems management (DBA); international business (MBA, DBA); leadership (MBA, MS, DBA), including entrepreneurship (MS), general management (MS), human resources leadership (MS), innovation and technology (MS), leader development (MS), leading sustainability (MS), project management (MS), self-designed (MS); management (MS), including healthcare management; managers as leaders (MS); marketing (MBA, DBA); project management (MBA, MS, DBA); research strategies (MS); risk management (MBA); self-designed (MBA, DBA, PhD); social impact management (DBA); strategies for sustainability (MBA); strategy and operations (MS); sustainable management (MS); technology (MBA); technology entrepreneurship (DBA); technology management (MS). Part-time and evening/weekend programs available. Postbaccalaureate distance learning degree programs offered (minimal on-campus study). *Faculty:* 32 full-time (14 women), 275 part-time/adjunct (98 women). *Students:* 3,962 full-time (2,095 women), 1,557 part-time (959 women); includes 3,003 minority (2,510 Black or African American, non-Hispanic/Latino; 25 American Indian or Alaska Native, non-Hispanic/Latino; 140 Asian, non-Hispanic/Latino; 240 Hispanic/Latino; 9 Native Hawaiian or other Pacific Islander, non-Hispanic/Latino; 79 Two or more races, non-Hispanic/Latino), 395 international. Average age 41. In 2011, 586 master's, 87 doctorates, 4 other advanced degrees awarded. *Degree requirements:* For doctorate, thesis/dissertation (for some programs), residency. *Entrance requirements:* For master's, bachelor's degree or equivalent in related field; minimum GPA of 2.5; official transcripts; goal statement; access to computer and Internet; for doctorate, master's degree or equivalent in related field; minimum GPA of 3.0; 3 years of related professional/academic experience (preferred). Additional exam requirements/recommendations for international students: Required—TOEFL (minimum score 550 paper-based; 213 computer-based), IELTS (minimum score 6.5), Michigan English Language Assessment Battery (minimum score 82). *Application deadline:* Applications are processed on a rolling basis. Application fee: $50. Electronic applications accepted. *Financial support:* Federal Work-Study, scholarships/grants, unspecified assistantships, and family tuition reduction, active duty/veteran tuition reduction, group tuition reduction, interest-free payment plans, employee tuition reduction available. Support available to part-time students. Financial award applicants required to submit FAFSA. *Unit head:* Dr. William Schulz, III, Associate Dean, 800-925-3368. *Application contact:* Jennifer Hall, Vice President of Enrollment Management, 866-4-WALDEN, E-mail: info@waldenu.edu. Web site: http://www.waldenu.edu/Colleges-and-Schools/College-of-Management-and-Technology.htm.

Washington University in St. Louis, Olin Business School, Program in Supply Chain Management, St. Louis, MO 63130-4899. Offers MS. Part-time programs available. *Faculty:* 88 full-time (29 women), 47 part-time/adjunct (10 women). *Students:* 18 full-time (8 women), 7 part-time (3 women), 17 international. Average age 26. 123 applicants, 31% accepted, 14 enrolled. In 2011, 13 master's awarded. *Entrance requirements:* For master's, GMAT or GRE. Additional exam requirements/recommendations for international students: Required—TOEFL. *Application deadline:* For fall admission, 11/1 for domestic and international students; for winter admission, 1/31 for domestic and international students; for spring admission, 2/28 for domestic students. Application fee: $100. Electronic applications accepted. *Financial support:* Applicants required to submit FAFSA. *Unit head:* Joseph Peter Fox, Associate Dean and Director of MBA Programs,

314-935-6322, Fax: 314-935-4464, E-mail: fox@wustl.edu. *Application contact:* Dr. Gary Hochberg, Director, Specialized Master's Programs, 314-935-6380, Fax: 314-935-4464, E-mail: hochberg@wustl.edu. Web site: http://www.olin.wustl.edu/academicprograms/MSSCM/Pages/default.aspx.

Wilfrid Laurier University, Faculty of Graduate and Postdoctoral Studies, School of Business and Economics, Department of Business, Waterloo, ON N2L 3C5, Canada. Offers accounting (PhD); finance (M Fin); financial economics (PhD); marketing (PhD); operations and supply chain management (PhD); organizational behavior and human resource management (M Sc); organizational behaviour and human resource management (PhD); supply chain management (M Sc); technology management (EMTM). Part-time and evening/weekend programs available. *Degree requirements:* For master's, thesis optional; for doctorate, comprehensive exam, thesis/dissertation. *Entrance requirements:* For master's, GMAT, 4-year honors degree with minimum B+ average; for doctorate, GMAT, master's degree, minimum B+ average. Additional exam requirements/recommendations for international students: Required—TOEFL (minimum score 89 iBT). Electronic applications accepted. *Faculty research:* Financial economics, management and organizational behavior, operations and supply chain management.

Wright State University, School of Graduate Studies, Raj Soin College of Business, Department of Information Systems and Operations Management, Logistics and Supply Chain Management Program, Dayton, OH 45435. Offers MS.

Wright State University, School of Graduate Studies, Raj Soin College of Business, Department of Management, Dayton, OH 45435. Offers flexible business (MBA); health care management (MBA); international business (MBA); management, innovation and change (MBA); project management (MBA); supply chain management (MBA); MBA/MS. *Entrance requirements:* For master's, GMAT, minimum AACSB index of 1000. Additional exam requirements/recommendations for international students: Required—TOEFL.

Transportation Management

American Public University System, AMU/APU Graduate Programs, Charles Town, WV 25414. Offers accounting (MBA, MS); administration and supervision (M Ed); criminal justice (MA); emergency and disaster management (MA); entrepreneurship (MBA); environmental policy and management (MS), including environmental planning, environmental sustainability, fish and wildlife management, general (MA, MS), global environmental management; finance (MBA); general (MBA); global business management (MBA); guidance and counseling (M Ed); history (MA), including American history, ancient and classical history, European history, global history, military and diplomatic history, public history; homeland security (MA); homeland security resource allocation (MBA); humanities (MA); information technology (MS), including digital forensics, enterprise software development, information assurance and security, IT project management; information technology management (MBA); intelligence studies (MA), including criminal intelligence, general (MA, MS), homeland security, intelligence analysis, intelligence collection, intelligence operations, terrorism studies; international relations and conflict resolution (MA), including comparative and security issues, conflict resolution, international and transnational security issues, peacekeeping; legal studies (MA); management (MA), including defense management, general (MA, MS), human resource management, organizational leadership, public administration, reverse logistics, strategic consulting; marketing (MBA); military history (MA), including American military history, American revolution, civil war, war since 1946, World War II; military studies (MA), including air warfare, asymmetrical warfare, joint warfare, land warfare, naval warfare, strategic leadership; national security studies (MA), including general (MA, MS), homeland security, regional security studies, security and intelligence analysis, terrorism studies; nonprofit management (MBA); political science (MA), including American politics and government, comparative government and development, public policy; psychology (MA); public administration (MA, MPA), including disaster management (MPA), environmental policy (MA), health policy (MPA), human resources (MPA), national security (MPA), organizational management (MPA), security management (MPA); public health (MA, MPH), including emergency management (MPH), environmental health (MPH), public administration (MA); reverse logistics management (MA); security management (MA); space studies (MS), including aerospace science, planetary science; sports and health sciences (MS); sports management (MS), including coaching theory and strategy, sports administration; teaching (M Ed), including curriculum and instruction for elementary teachers, elementary, elementary reading, English language learners, instructional leadership, online learning, secondary social sciences, special education; transportation and logistics management (MA), including maritime engineering management. Programs offered via distance learning only. Part-time and evening/weekend programs available. Postbaccalaureate distance learning degree programs offered (no on-campus study). *Faculty:* 445 full-time (241 women), 1,360 part-time/adjunct (617 women). *Students:* 688 full-time (338 women), 10,168 part-time (3,706 women); includes 3,130 minority (1,007 Black or African American, non-Hispanic/Latino; 103 American Indian or Alaska Native, non-Hispanic/Latino; 825 Asian, non-Hispanic/Latino; 810 Hispanic/Latino; 51 Native Hawaiian or other Pacific Islander, non-Hispanic/Latino; 334 Two or more races, non-Hispanic/Latino), 134 international. Average age 35. In 2011, 2,386 master's awarded. *Degree requirements:* For master's, comprehensive exam or practicum. *Entrance requirements:* For master's, official transcript showing earned bachelor's degree from institution accredited by recognized accrediting body. Additional exam requirements/recommendations for international students: Required—TOEFL (minimum score 550 paper-based; 213 computer-based), IELTS (minimum score 6.5). *Application deadline:* Applications are processed on a rolling basis. Application fee: $0. Electronic applications accepted. *Expenses: Tuition:* Part-time $325 per credit hour. *Financial support:* Applicants required to submit FAFSA. *Faculty research:* Military history, criminal justice, management performance, national security. *Unit head:* Dr. Karan Powell, Executive Vice President and Provost, 877-468-6268, Fax: 304-724-3780. *Application contact:* Terry Grant, Vice President of Enrollment Management, 877-468-6268, Fax: 304-724-3780, E-mail: info@apus.edu. Web site: http://www.apus.edu.

California Maritime Academy, Graduate Studies, Vallejo, CA 94590. Offers transportation and engineering management (MS). Postbaccalaureate distance learning degree programs offered (no on-campus study). *Faculty:* 7 part-time/adjunct (1 woman). *Students:* 20 full-time (3 women). *Degree requirements:* For master's, capstone course. *Entrance requirements:* For master's, equivalent of four-year U.S. bachelor's degree with minimum GPA of 2.5 during last two years (60 semester units or 90 quarter units) of coursework in degree program; five years of professional experience or GMAT/GRE. Additional exam requirements/recommendations for international students: Required—TOEFL (minimum score 550 paper-based; 213 computer-based). Application fee: $55. *Application contact:* Kathy Arnold, Coordinator, Graduate Studies, 707-654-1271, Fax: 707-654-1158, E-mail: karnold@csum.edu. Web site: http://www.csum.edu/web/industry/graduate-studies.

Concordia University, School of Graduate Studies, John Molson School of Business, Montréal, QC H3G 1M8, Canada. Offers administration (M Sc, Diploma); aviation management (Certificate, Diploma); business administration (MBA, UA Undergraduate Associate, PhD), including international aviation (UA Undergraduate Associate); chartered accountancy (Diploma); community organizational development (Certificate); event management and fundraising (Certificate); executive business administration (EMBA); investment management (Diploma); investment management option (MBA); management accounting (Certificate); management of healthcare organizations (Certificate); sport administration (Diploma). PhD program offered jointly with HEC Montreal, McGill University, and Université du Québec à Montréal. *Accreditation:* AACSB. Part-time and evening/weekend programs available. *Degree requirements:* For master's, one foreign language, thesis (for some programs), research project; for doctorate, one foreign language, thesis/dissertation; for other advanced degree, one foreign language. *Entrance requirements:* For master's and doctorate, GMAT. Additional exam requirements/recommendations for international students: Required—TOEFL. *Expenses:* Contact institution. *Faculty research:* General business, capital markets, international business.

Embry-Riddle Aeronautical University–Worldwide, Worldwide Headquarters - Graduate Degrees and Programs, Program in Aeronautics, Daytona Beach, FL 32114-3900. Offers aeronautical science (MAS); air transportation management (Graduate Certificate); airport planning design and development (Graduate Certificate); aviation/aerospace industrial management (Graduate Certificate); aviation/aerospace safety (Graduate Certificate); instructional system design (Graduate Certificate). Part-time and evening/weekend programs available. Postbaccalaureate distance learning degree programs offered (minimal on-campus study). *Faculty:* 24 full-time (2 women), 177 part-time/adjunct (20 women). *Students:* 1,684 full-time (248 women), 1,771 part-time (239 women); includes 497 minority (154 Black or African American, non-Hispanic/Latino; 20 American Indian or Alaska Native, non-Hispanic/Latino; 58 Asian, non-Hispanic/Latino; 251 Hispanic/Latino; 3 Native Hawaiian or other Pacific Islander, non-Hispanic/Latino; 11 Two or more races, non-Hispanic/Latino), 32 international. Average age 36. 913 applicants, 77% accepted, 330 enrolled. In 2011, 1032 degrees awarded. *Degree requirements:* For master's, comprehensive exam (for some programs), thesis optional. *Entrance requirements:* Additional exam requirements/recommendations for international students: Recommended—TOEFL (minimum score 550 paper-based; 213 computer-based; 79 iBT). *Application deadline:* Applications are processed on a rolling basis. Application fee: $50. Electronic applications accepted. *Expenses: Tuition:* Part-time $395 per credit hour. Tuition and fees vary according to degree level and program. *Financial support:* In 2011–12, 570 students received support. Available to part-time students. Applicants required to submit FAFSA. *Faculty research:* Unmanned aircraft system (UAS) operations, human factors, crash investigation, reliability and hazard analysis, aviation security. *Unit head:* Dr. Katherine A. Moran, Department Chair, 360-597-4560, E-mail: morank@erau.edu. *Application contact:* Linda Dammer, Director of Admissions, 386-226-6396 Ext. 1, Fax: 386-226-6984, E-mail: worldwide@erau.edu.

Florida Institute of Technology, Graduate Programs, Extended Studies Division, Melbourne, FL 32901-6975. Offers acquisition and contract management (MS); aerospace engineering (MS); business administration (MBA); computer information systems (MS); computer science (MS); electrical engineering (MS); engineering management (MS); human resources management (MS); logistics management (MS), including humanitarian and disaster relief logistics; management (MS), including acquisition and contract management, e-business, human resources management, information systems, logistics management, management, transportation management; material acquisition management (MS); mechanical engineering (MS); operations research (MS); project management (MS), including information systems, operations research; public administration (MPA); quality management (MS); software engineering (MS); space systems (MS); space systems management (MS); supply chain management (MS); systems management (MS), including information systems, operations research. Part-time and evening/weekend programs available. Postbaccalaureate distance learning degree programs offered (no on-campus study). *Faculty:* 9 full-time (2 women), 105 part-time/adjunct (24 women). *Students:* 113 full-time (52 women), 1,150 part-time (484 women); includes 496 minority (332 Black or African American, non-Hispanic/Latino; 11 American Indian or Alaska Native, non-Hispanic/Latino; 42 Asian, non-Hispanic/Latino; 71 Hispanic/Latino; 2 Native Hawaiian or other Pacific Islander, non-Hispanic/Latino; 38 Two or more races, non-Hispanic/Latino), 11 international. Average age 35. 568 applicants, 56% accepted, 296 enrolled. In 2011, 471 master's awarded. *Degree requirements:* For master's, comprehensive exam (for some programs), capstone course. *Entrance requirements:* For master's, GMAT or resume showing 8 years of supervised experience, minimum GPA of 3.0, 2 letters of recommendation, resume. Additional exam requirements/recommendations for international students: Required—TOEFL (minimum score 550 paper-based; 213 computer-based; 79 iBT). *Application deadline:* For fall admission, 4/1 for international students; for spring admission, 9/30 for international students. Applications are processed on a rolling basis. Application fee: $0. Electronic applications accepted. *Expenses:* Contact institution. *Financial support:* Application deadline: 3/1; applicants required to submit FAFSA. *Unit head:* Dr. Theodore R. Richardson, III, Senior Associate Dean, 321-674-8123, Fax: 321-674-7597, E-mail: trichardson@fit.edu. *Application contact:* Carolyn Farrior, Director of Graduate Admissions, Online Learning and Off-Campus Programs, 321-674-7118, Fax: 321-674-8216, E-mail: cfarrior@fit.edu. Web site: http://es.fit.edu.

George Mason University, School of Public Policy, Program in Transportation Policy, Operations and Logistics, Arlington, VA 22201. Offers MA, Certificate. *Faculty:* 54 full-time (18 women), 20 part-time/adjunct (8 women). *Students:* 8 full-time (1 woman), 24 part-time (7 women); includes 9 minority (4 Black or African American, non-Hispanic/Latino; 2 Hispanic/Latino; 1 Native Hawaiian or other Pacific Islander, non-Hispanic/Latino; 2 Two or more races, non-Hispanic/Latino), 2 international. Average age 32. 31 applicants, 65% accepted, 11 enrolled. In 2011, 18 master's awarded. *Degree requirements:* For master's, thesis or alternative. *Entrance requirements:* For master's, GRE (for students seeking merit-based scholarships), bachelor's degree with minimum GPA of 3.0, current resume, 2 letters of recommendation, expanded goals statement, 2 copies of official transcripts. Additional exam requirements/recommendations for international students: Required—TOEFL (minimum score 575 paper-based; 230

computer-based; 88 iBT), IELTS, Pearson Test of English. *Application deadline:* For fall admission, 6/1 priority date for domestic students, 5/1 for international students; for spring admission, 12/1 priority date for domestic students, 11/1 for international students. Applications are processed on a rolling basis. Application fee: $65 ($80 for international students). Electronic applications accepted. *Expenses:* Contact institution. *Financial support:* Career-related internships or fieldwork, Federal Work-Study, scholarships/grants, unspecified assistantships, and health care benefits (full-time research or teaching assistantship recipients) available. Financial award application deadline: 3/1; financial award applicants required to submit FAFSA. *Unit head:* Dr. Jonathan Gifford, Director, 703-993-2275, Fax: 703-993-9198, E-mail: jgifford@gmu.edu. *Application contact:* Tennille Haegele, Director, Graduate Admissions, 703-993-8099, Fax: 703-993-4876, E-mail: spp@gmu.edu. Web site: http://policy.gmu.edu/Home/AcademicProfessionalPrograms/MastersPrograms/TransportationPolicyOperationsLogistics/tabid/108/Default.aspx.

Instituto Tecnologico de Santo Domingo, Graduate School, Area of Engineering, Santo Domingo, Dominican Republic. Offers construction administration (MS, Certificate); data telecommunications (M Eng, MS, Certificate); industrial engineering (M Eng, Certificate); industrial management (M Mgmt); information technology (Certificate); maintenance engineering (M Eng); occupational hazard prevention (M Mgmt); production management (Certificate); quantitative methods (Certificate); sanitary and environmental engineering (M Eng); structural engineering (M Eng); systems engineering and electronic data processing (Certificate); transportation (Certificate).

Iowa State University of Science and Technology, Department of Community and Regional Planning, Ames, IA 50011-3094. Offers community and regional planning (MCRP); transportation (MS); M Arch/MCRP; MBA/MCRP; MCRP/MLA; MCRP/MPA. *Accreditation:* ACSP (one or more programs are accredited). *Degree requirements:* For master's, thesis or alternative. *Entrance requirements:* For master's, GRE General Test. Additional exam requirements/recommendations for international students: Required—TOEFL (minimum score 550 paper-based; 79 iBT), IELTS (minimum score 6.5). *Application deadline:* For fall admission, 1/1 priority date for domestic students, 1/1 for international students. Applications are processed on a rolling basis. Application fee: $40 ($90 for international students). Electronic applications accepted. *Financial support:* Tuition waivers (partial) available. Financial award applicants required to submit FAFSA. *Faculty research:* Economic development, housing, land use, geographic information systems planning in developing nations, regional and community revitalization, transportation planning in developing countries. *Unit head:* Dr. Francis Owusu, Director of Graduate Education, 515-294-8913, Fax: 515-294-2348, E-mail: crp@iastate.edu. *Application contact:* Rachel Hohenshell, Director of Graduate Education, 515-294-8913, E-mail: crp@iastate.edu. Web site: http://www.design.iastate.edu/communityplanning/.

Iowa State University of Science and Technology, Program in Transportation, Ames, IA 50011-8664. Offers MS. *Entrance requirements:* For master's, GMAT or GRE General Test. Additional exam requirements/recommendations for international students: Required—TOEFL (minimum score 550 paper-based; 82 iBT), IELTS (minimum score 6.5). *Application deadline:* For fall admission, 7/15 priority date for domestic students, 2/15 for international students. Application fee: $40 ($90 for international students). Electronic applications accepted. *Unit head:* Dr. Nadia Gkritza, Director of Graduate Education, 515-294-2343, Fax: 515-294-0467, E-mail: nadia@iastate.edu. *Application contact:* Nadia Gkritza, Information Contact, 515-294-2343, Fax: 515-294-0467, E-mail: grad_admissions@iastate.edu.

Maine Maritime Academy, Department of Graduate Studies, Program in Maritime Management, Castine, ME 04420. Offers MS, Certificate, Diploma. Part-time programs available. *Degree requirements:* For master's, thesis optional, capstone course. *Entrance requirements:* For master's, GMAT or GRE General Test, letters of recommendation. Additional exam requirements/recommendations for international students: Required—TOEFL. *Faculty research:* Human resources in maritime environment, management of organization change, economic analysis and maritime law.

McGill University, Faculty of Graduate and Postdoctoral Studies, Faculty of Engineering, School of Urban Planning, Montréal, QC H3A 2T5, Canada. Offers environmental planning (MUP); housing (MUP); transportation (MUP); urban design (MUP); urban planning, policy and design (PhD).

Morgan State University, School of Graduate Studies, Clarence M. Mitchell, Jr. School of Engineering, Department of Transportation, Baltimore, MD 21251. Offers MS. Part-time and evening/weekend programs available. *Degree requirements:* For master's, thesis optional, comprehensive exam or equivalent. *Entrance requirements:* For master's, minimum undergraduate GPA of 2.5. Additional exam requirements/recommendations for international students: Required—TOEFL (minimum score 550 paper-based; 213 computer-based). *Faculty research:* Distributional impacts of congestion, pricing education and training for intelligent vehicle highway systems.

Naval Postgraduate School, Departments and Academic Groups, School of Business and Public Policy, Monterey, CA 93943. Offers acquisitions and contract management (MBA); business administration (EMBA, MBA); contract management (MS); defense business management (MBA); defense systems analysis (MS), including management; defense systems management (international) (MBA); executive management (MBA); financial management (MBA); information systems management (MBA); manpower systems analysis (MS); material logistics support management (MBA); program management (MS); resource planning/management for international defense (MBA); supply chain management (MBA); systems acquisition management (MBA); transportation management (MBA). Program only open to commissioned officers of the United States and friendly nations and selected United States federal civilian employees. *Accreditation:* AACSB; NASPAA. Part-time programs available. Postbaccalaureate distance learning degree programs offered (minimal on-campus study). *Faculty:* 67 full-time (15 women), 32 part-time/adjunct (12 women). *Students:* 307 full-time (29 women), 327 part-time (71 women); includes 149 minority (55 Black or African American, non-Hispanic/Latino; 5 American Indian or Alaska Native, non-Hispanic/Latino; 46 Asian, non-Hispanic/Latino; 43 Hispanic/Latino), 44 international. Average age 42. In 2011, 295 master's awarded. *Degree requirements:* For master's, thesis (for some programs), terminal project/capstone (for some programs). *Faculty research:* U. S. and European public procurement policies for small and medium-sized enterprises, examining external validity criticisms in the choice of students as subjects in accounting experiment studies, assurance of learning in contract management education, contracting for cloud computing: opportunities and risks, NPS, Apple App Store as a business model supporting U. S. Navy requirements. *Total annual research expenditures:* $9 million. *Unit head:* Raymond Franck, Department Chair, 831-656-3614, E-mail: refranck@nps.edu. *Application contact:* Acting Director of Admissions. Web site: http://www.nps.edu/Academics/Schools/GSBPP/index.html.

New Jersey Institute of Technology, Office of Graduate Studies, Newark College of Engineering, Interdisciplinary Program in Transportation, Newark, NJ 07102. Offers MS, PhD. Part-time and evening/weekend programs available. *Students:* 17 full-time (3 women), 21 part-time (5 women); includes 16 minority (4 Black or African American, non-Hispanic/Latino; 8 Asian, non-Hispanic/Latino; 4 Hispanic/Latino), 11 international. Average age 34. 37 applicants, 81% accepted, 6 enrolled. In 2011, 6 degrees awarded. Terminal master's awarded for partial completion of doctoral program. *Degree requirements:* For master's, thesis or alternative; for doctorate, thesis/dissertation, residency. *Entrance requirements:* For master's, GRE General Test; for doctorate, GRE General Test, minimum graduate GPA of 3.5. Additional exam requirements/recommendations for international students: Required—TOEFL (minimum score 550 paper-based; 213 computer-based; 79 iBT). *Application deadline:* For fall admission, 6/1 priority date for domestic students, 5/1 for international students; for spring admission, 11/15 for domestic and international students. Applications are processed on a rolling basis. Application fee: $65. Electronic applications accepted. *Expenses:* Tuition, state resident: full-time $7980; part-time $867 per credit. Tuition, nonresident: full-time $11,336; part-time $1196 per credit. *Required fees:* $230 per credit. *Financial support:* Fellowships with full and partial tuition reimbursements, research assistantships with full and partial tuition reimbursements, teaching assistantships with full and partial tuition reimbursements, career-related internships or fieldwork, Federal Work-Study, institutionally sponsored loans, and unspecified assistantships available. Financial award application deadline: 1/15. *Faculty research:* Transportation planning, administration, and policy; intelligent vehicle highway systems; bridge maintenance. *Unit head:* Dr. Athanassios Bladikas, Director, 973-596-3653, E-mail: athanassios.bladikas@njit.edu. *Application contact:* Kathryn Kelly, Director of Admissions, 973-596-3300, Fax: 973-596-3461, E-mail: admissions@njit.edu. Web site: http://nce.njit.edu/departments/trans.php.

North Dakota State University, College of Graduate and Interdisciplinary Studies, College of Engineering and Architecture, Department of Civil Engineering, Fargo, ND 58108. Offers civil engineering (MS, PhD); environmental engineering (MS, PhD); transportation and logistics (PhD). PhD in transportation and logistics offered jointly with Upper Great Plains Transportation Institute. Part-time programs available. Postbaccalaureate distance learning degree programs offered (minimal on-campus study). *Faculty:* 13 full-time (1 woman). *Students:* 25 full-time (2 women), 19 part-time (3 women); includes 3 minority (1 American Indian or Alaska Native, non-Hispanic/Latino; 2 Two or more races, non-Hispanic/Latino), 21 international. 46 applicants, 48% accepted, 8 enrolled. In 2011, 8 master's, 3 doctorates awarded. *Degree requirements:* For master's, thesis; for doctorate, comprehensive exam, thesis/dissertation. *Entrance requirements:* Additional exam requirements/recommendations for international students: Required—TOEFL (minimum score 525 paper-based; 197 computer-based; 71 iBT). *Application deadline:* For fall admission, 2/15 priority date for domestic students, 2/15 for international students; for spring admission, 9/15 priority date for domestic students, 9/15 for international students. Applications are processed on a rolling basis. Application fee: $35. Electronic applications accepted. *Financial support:* Fellowships with full tuition reimbursements, research assistantships with full tuition reimbursements, teaching assistantships with full tuition reimbursements, career-related internships or fieldwork, Federal Work-Study, and institutionally sponsored loans available. Support available to part-time students. Financial award application deadline: 1/15. *Faculty research:* Wastewater, solid waste, composites, nanotechnology. *Unit head:* Dr. Eakalak Khan, Chair, 701-231-7244, Fax: 701-231-6185, E-mail: eakalak.khan@ndsu.edu. *Application contact:* Dr. Kalpana Katti, Professor and Graduate Program Coordinator, 701-231-9504, Fax: 701-231-6185, E-mail: kalpana.katti@ndsu.edu. Web site: http://www.ce.ndsu.nodak.edu/.

North Dakota State University, College of Graduate and Interdisciplinary Studies, Interdisciplinary Program in Transportation and Logistics, Fargo, ND 58108. Offers PhD. *Students:* 28 full-time (6 women), 10 part-time (0 women); includes 7 minority (2 Black or African American, non-Hispanic/Latino; 2 Asian, non-Hispanic/Latino; 3 Two or more races, non-Hispanic/Latino), 12 international. 27 applicants, 74% accepted, 13 enrolled. In 2011, 7 doctorates awarded. *Entrance requirements:* For doctorate, 1 year of calculus, statistics and probability, minimum GPA of 3.0. Additional exam requirements/recommendations for international students: Required—TOEFL (minimum score 550 paper-based; 213 computer-based; 79 iBT). *Application deadline:* For fall admission, 5/1 priority date for domestic students. Applications are processed on a rolling basis. Application fee: $35. *Financial support:* Research assistantships with full tuition reimbursements available. *Faculty research:* Supply chain optimization, spatial analysis of transportation networks, advanced traffic analysis, transportation demand, railroad/intermodal freight. *Unit head:* Dr. Denver Tolliver, Director, 701-231-7938, Fax: 701-231-1945, E-mail: denver.tolliver@ndsu.nodak.edu. *Application contact:* Sonya Goergen, Marketing, Recruitment, and Public Relations Coordinator, 701-231-7033, Fax: 701-231-6524. Web site: http://www.mountain-plains.org/education/tlprogram/.

Polytechnic Institute of New York University, Department of Civil Engineering, Major in Transportation Management, Brooklyn, NY 11201-2990. Offers MS. Part-time and evening/weekend programs available. *Students:* 3 full-time (1 woman), 14 part-time (5 women); includes 11 minority (8 Black or African American, non-Hispanic/Latino; 2 Asian, non-Hispanic/Latino; 1 Hispanic/Latino), 2 international. Average age 39. 10 applicants, 70% accepted, 3 enrolled. In 2011, 12 degrees awarded. *Degree requirements:* For master's, comprehensive exam (for some programs), thesis (for some programs). *Entrance requirements:* Additional exam requirements/recommendations for international students: Required—TOEFL (minimum score 550 paper-based; 213 computer-based; 80 iBT); Recommended—IELTS (minimum score 6.5). *Application deadline:* For fall admission, 7/31 priority date for domestic students, 4/30 for international students; for spring admission, 12/31 priority date for domestic students, 10/30 for international students. Applications are processed on a rolling basis. Application fee: $75. Electronic applications accepted. *Expenses: Tuition:* Full-time $22,464; part-time $1248 per credit. *Required fees:* $501 per semester. *Financial support:* Fellowships, research assistantships, teaching assistantships, institutionally sponsored loans, scholarships/grants, and unspecified assistantships available. Support available to part-time students. Financial award applicants required to submit FAFSA. *Unit head:* Dr. Lawrence Chiarelli, Head, 718-260-4040, Fax: 718-260-3433, E-mail: lchiarel@poly.edu. *Application contact:* JeanCarlo Bonilla, Director, Graduate Enrollment Management, 718-260-3182, Fax: 718-260-3624, E-mail: gradinfo@poly.edu.

Pontifical Catholic University of Puerto Rico, College of Business Administration, Program in Maritime Logistics and Transportation, Ponce, PR 00717-0777. Offers Professional Certificate.

San Jose State University, Graduate Studies and Research, Lucas Graduate School of Business, Program in Transportation Management, San Jose, CA 95192-0001. Offers MS. Part-time and evening/weekend programs available. Postbaccalaureate distance learning degree programs offered (minimal on-campus study). *Degree requirements:* For master's, comprehensive exam, thesis or alternative. *Entrance requirements:* For master's, GMAT, minimum GPA of 3.0. Electronic applications accepted. *Faculty research:* Surface intermodal transportation, economics, security.

State University of New York Maritime College, Program in International Transportation Management, Throggs Neck, NY 10465-4198. Offers MS. Part-time and evening/weekend programs available. *Degree requirements:* For master's, thesis. *Entrance requirements:* For master's, minimum GPA of 2.5. Additional exam requirements/recommendations for international students: Required—TOEFL. *Faculty research:* Ports, intermodal, shipping, logistics, port tax.

Texas A&M University at Galveston, Department of Maritime Administration, Galveston, TX 77553-1675. Offers maritime administration and logistics (MMAL). Part-time and evening/weekend programs available. *Faculty:* 5 full-time (2 women), 3 part-time/adjunct (0 women). *Students:* 4 full-time (0 women), 5 part-time (2 women); includes 2 minority (both Hispanic/Latino), 1 international. Average age 32. 9 applicants, 100% accepted, 8 enrolled. *Degree requirements:* For master's, thesis optional. *Entrance requirements:* For master's, GMAT, statistics, microeconomics, organizational behavior, financial and managerial accounting, management information systems. Additional exam requirements/recommendations for international students: Required—TOEFL (minimum score 550 paper-based; 80 iBT), IELTS (minimum score 6). *Application deadline:* For fall admission, 6/15 for domestic students, 5/1 for international students; for spring admission, 10/15 for domestic students, 10/1 for international students. Application fee: $75 ($90 for international students). Electronic applications accepted. *Expenses:* Tuition, state resident: full-time $2087; part-time $231.85 per contact hour. Tuition, nonresident: full-time $4904; part-time $545 per contact hour. *Required fees:* $65 per contact hour. $110 per semester. One-time fee: $50. *Financial support:* In 2011–12, 3 students received support, including 3 teaching assistantships; scholarships/grants and unspecified assistantships also available. Financial award applicants required to submit FAFSA. *Faculty research:* International trade, inland waterways management, brokerage and chartering, organizational behavior, transportation economics, port and terminal management . *Unit head:* Dr. Joan P. Mileski, Interim Head of Maritime Administration, 409-740-4978, E-mail: mileskij@tamug.edu. *Application contact:* Nicole Wilkins, Administrative Coordinator for Graduate Studies, 409-740-4937, Fax: 409-740-4754, E-mail: wilkinsn@tamug.edu. Web site: http://www.tamug.edu/mara/.

Texas Southern University, School of Science and Technology, Program in Transportation, Planning and Management, Houston, TX 77004-4584. Offers MS. Part-time and evening/weekend programs available. *Degree requirements:* For master's, comprehensive exam, thesis optional. *Entrance requirements:* For master's, GRE General Test, minimum GPA of 2.5. Additional exam requirements/recommendations for international students: Required—TOEFL. Electronic applications accepted. *Faculty research:* Highway traffic operations, transportation and policy planning, air quality in transportation, transportation modeling.

The University of British Columbia, Sauder School of Business, Doctoral Program in Commerce and Business Administration, Vancouver, BC V6T 1Z1, Canada. Offers accounting (PhD); finance (PhD); international business (PhD); management information systems (PhD); management science (PhD); marketing (PhD); organizational behavior (PhD); strategy and business economics (PhD); transportation and logistics (PhD); urban land economics (PhD). *Degree requirements:* For doctorate, comprehensive exam, thesis/dissertation. *Entrance requirements:* For doctorate, GMAT or GRE. Additional exam requirements/recommendations for international students: Required—TOEFL (minimum score 600 paper-based; 250 computer-based; 100 iBT). Electronic applications accepted.

University of California, Davis, College of Engineering, Graduate Group in Transportation Technology and Policy, Davis, CA 95616. Offers MS, PhD. Terminal master's awarded for partial completion of doctoral program. *Degree requirements:* For master's, comprehensive exam (for some programs), thesis (for some programs); for doctorate, thesis/dissertation. *Entrance requirements:* For master's, GRE General Test, minimum GPA of 3.0; for doctorate, GRE General Test, minimum GPA of 3.5. Additional exam requirements/recommendations for international students: Required—TOEFL (minimum score 550 paper-based; 213 computer-based). Electronic applications accepted.

University of California, Santa Barbara, Graduate Division, College of Letters and Sciences, Division of Mathematics, Life, and Physical Sciences, Department of Geography, Santa Barbara, CA 93106-4060. Offers cognitive science (PhD); geography (MA, PhD); quantitative methods in the social sciences (PhD); transportation (PhD); MA/PhD. *Faculty:* 23 full-time (4 women), 13 part-time/adjunct (4 women). *Students:* 68 full-time (29 women); includes 13 minority (3 Black or African American, non-Hispanic/Latino; 5 Asian, non-Hispanic/Latino; 4 Hispanic/Latino; 1 Two or more races, non-Hispanic/Latino), 13 international. Average age 31. 128 applicants, 26% accepted, 19 enrolled. In 2011, 6 master's, 11 doctorates awarded. Terminal master's awarded for partial completion of doctoral program. *Median time to degree:* Of those who began their doctoral program in fall 2003, 54% received their degree in 8 years or less. *Degree requirements:* For master's, comprehensive exam (for some programs), thesis or alternative; for doctorate, comprehensive exam, thesis/dissertation, 1 quarter of teaching assistantship. *Entrance requirements:* For master's and doctorate, GRE (minimum verbal and quantitative scores of 1100 in old scoring system). Additional exam requirements/recommendations for international students: Required—TOEFL (minimum score 550 paper-based; 80 iBT), IELTS (minimum score 7). *Application deadline:* For fall admission, 12/15 for domestic and international students. Application fee: $80 ($100 for international students). Electronic applications accepted. *Expenses:* Tuition, state resident: full-time $12,192. Tuition, nonresident: full-time $27,294. *Required fees:* $764.13. *Financial support:* In 2011–12, 61 students received support, including 49 fellowships with full and partial tuition reimbursements available (averaging $6,971 per year), 35 research assistantships with full and partial tuition reimbursements available (averaging $17,231 per year), 28 teaching assistantships with partial tuition reimbursements available (averaging $9,887 per year). Financial award applicants required to submit FAFSA. *Faculty research:* Earth system science, human environment relations, modeling, measurement and computation. *Total annual research expenditures:* $4.6 million. *Unit head:* Dr. Dar Alexander Roberts, Professor/Chair, 805-880-2531, Fax: 805-893-2578, E-mail: dar@geog.ucsb.edu. *Application contact:* Jose Luis Saleta, Student Programs Manager, 805-456-2829, Fax: 805-893-2578, E-mail: saleta@geog.ucsb.edu. Web site: http://www.geog.ucsb.edu/.

The University of Tennessee, Graduate School, College of Business Administration, Program in Business Administration, Knoxville, TN 37996. Offers accounting (PhD); finance (MBA, PhD); logistics and transportation (MBA, PhD); management (PhD); marketing (MBA, PhD); operations management (MBA); professional business administration (MBA); statistics (PhD); JD/MBA; MS/MBA; Pharm D/MBA. Pharm D/MBA offered jointly with The University of Tennessee Health Science Center. *Accreditation:* AACSB. Postbaccalaureate distance learning degree programs offered. *Degree requirements:* For master's, thesis or alternative; for doctorate, thesis/dissertation. *Entrance requirements:* For master's and doctorate, GMAT, minimum GPA of 2.7. Additional exam requirements/recommendations for international students: Required—TOEFL. Electronic applications accepted. *Expenses:* Tuition, state resident: full-time $8332; part-time $464 per credit hour. Tuition, nonresident: full-time $25,174; part-time $1400 per credit hour. *Required fees:* $1162; $56 per credit hour. Tuition and fees vary according to program.

University of Washington, Graduate School, College of Engineering, Department of Aeronautics and Astronautics, Seattle, WA 98195-2400. Offers aeronautics and astronautics (MS, PhD); aerospace engineering (MAE), including composite materials and structures; global trade, transportation and logistics (MS). Part-time programs available. Postbaccalaureate distance learning degree programs offered (no on-campus study). *Faculty:* 24 full-time (1 woman), 9 part-time/adjunct (1 woman). *Students:* 76 full-time (16 women), 115 part-time (17 women); includes 43 minority (5 Black or African American, non-Hispanic/Latino; 1 American Indian or Alaska Native, non-Hispanic/Latino; 21 Asian, non-Hispanic/Latino; 16 Hispanic/Latino), 28 international. Average age 27. 297 applicants, 52% accepted, 74 enrolled. In 2011, 24 master's, 5 doctorates awarded. *Degree requirements:* For master's, thesis optional; for doctorate, comprehensive exam, thesis/dissertation, qualifying, general and final exams; completion of all work toward degree within 10 years. *Entrance requirements:* For master's and doctorate, GRE General Test, minimum GPA of 3.0, letters of recommendation, statement of objectives, undergraduate degree in aerospace or mechanical engineering. Additional exam requirements/recommendations for international students: Required—TOEFL (minimum score 580 paper-based; 237 computer-based; 92 iBT); Recommended—IELTS (minimum score 7). *Application deadline:* For fall admission, 1/15 priority date for domestic students, 1/15 for international students. Applications are processed on a rolling basis. Application fee: $75. Electronic applications accepted. *Expenses:* Contact institution. *Financial support:* In 2011–12, 57 students received support, including 15 fellowships (averaging $9,540 per year), 26 research assistantships with full tuition reimbursements available (averaging $17,172 per year), 11 teaching assistantships with full tuition reimbursements available (averaging $13,725 per year); career-related internships or fieldwork, Federal Work-Study, health care benefits, tuition waivers (full), and unspecified assistantships also available. Financial award application deadline: 1/15; financial award applicants required to submit FAFSA. *Faculty research:* Space systems, aircraft systems, energy systems, composites/structures, fluid dynamics, controls. *Total annual research expenditures:* $7.8 million. *Unit head:* Dr. James Hermanson, Professor and Chair, 206-543-1950, Fax: 206-543-0217, E-mail: jherm@aa.washington.edu. *Application contact:* Wanda Frederick, Manager of Graduate Programs and External Relations, 206-616-1113, Fax: 206-543-0217, E-mail: wanda@aa.washington.edu. Web site: http://www.aa.washington.edu/.

University of Washington, Graduate School, College of Engineering, Department of Civil and Environmental Engineering, Seattle, WA 98195-2700. Offers civil engineering (MS, MSE, PhD); construction engineering (MSCE); environmental engineering (MS, MSCE, MSE, PhD); global trade, transportation and logistics (MS); hydrology, water resources, and environmental fluid mechanics (MS, MSCE, MSE, PhD); structural and geotechnical engineering and mechanics (MS, MSCE, MSE, PhD); transportation and construction engineering (MS, MSE, PhD); transportation engineering (MSCE). Part-time programs available. Postbaccalaureate distance learning degree programs offered (no on-campus study). *Faculty:* 47 full-time (11 women), 9 part-time/adjunct (1 woman). *Students:* 195 full-time (67 women), 72 part-time (19 women); includes 37 minority (4 Black or African American, non-Hispanic/Latino; 27 Asian, non-Hispanic/Latino; 6 Hispanic/Latino), 65 international. 654 applicants, 57% accepted, 100 enrolled. In 2011, 88 master's, 7 doctorates awarded. Terminal master's awarded for partial completion of doctoral program. *Degree requirements:* For master's, thesis (for some programs); for doctorate, comprehensive exam, thesis/dissertation, general, qualifying, and final exams; completion of degree within 10 years. *Entrance requirements:* For master's, GRE General Test, minimum GPA of 3.0, statement of purpose, letters of recommendation, transcripts; for doctorate, GRE General Test, minimum GPA of 3.5, statement of purpose, letters of recommendation, transcripts. Additional exam requirements/recommendations for international students: Required—TOEFL (minimum score 580 paper-based; 237 computer-based; 92 iBT); Recommended—IELTS (minimum score 7). *Application deadline:* For fall admission, 1/10 priority date for domestic students, 1/10 for international students. Applications are processed on a rolling basis. Application fee: $75. Electronic applications accepted. *Expenses:* Contact institution. *Financial support:* In 2011–12, 99 students received support, including 16 fellowships with full and partial tuition reimbursements available (averaging $16,173 per year), 71 research assistantships with full tuition reimbursements available (averaging $16,380 per year), 10 teaching assistantships with full tuition reimbursements available (averaging $16,380 per year); scholarships/grants also available. Financial award application deadline: 1/10; financial award applicants required to submit FAFSA. *Faculty research:* Environmental/water resources, hydrology; construction/transportation; structures/ geotechnical. *Total annual research expenditures:* $13.6 million. *Unit head:* Dr. Gregory R. Miller, Professor/Chair, 206-543-0350, Fax: 206-543-1543, E-mail: gmiller@uw.edu. *Application contact:* Lorna Latal, Graduate Adviser, 206-543-2574, Fax: 206-543-1543, E-mail: llatal@u.washington.edu. Web site: http://www.ce.washington.edu/programs/prospective/grad/applying/gen_admission.html.

University of Washington, Graduate School, Interdisciplinary Program in Global Trade, Transportation and Logistics Studies, Seattle, WA 98195. Offers Certificate.

EMBRY-RIDDLE AERONAUTICAL UNIVERSITY

College of Business–Daytona Beach

EMBRY-RIDDLE
Aeronautical University
DAYTONA BEACH, FLORIDA
COLLEGE OF BUSINESS

Program of Study

The Embry-Riddle M.B.A. provides graduates with a cutting-edge management education in an aviation/aerospace context. Professional managers who have earned their M.B.A. at Embry-Riddle Aeronautical University (ERAU) understand the imperatives of change, globalization, technological innovation, and increasingly sophisticated and demanding customers that mark the strategic and operational environments of today's airlines, airports, and aerospace firms. The M.B.A. is offered as a full-time residential program on the Daytona Beach campus. The curriculum combines a strong traditional business core with specializations in airport management, airline management, finance, aviation human resources, and aviation system management. The development of versatility and analytical resourcefulness are two of the key aims of the M.B.A. program. The program is fashioned to stress pragmatic solutions to the managerial, technical, and operational problems likely to arise in the aviation/aerospace industry as a result of the frequent and sweeping changes that occur in technology as well as in the domestic and international regulations with which the industry must abide. For those seeking a broader view of the global challenges airlines and airports face, the M.B.A. in Aviation Management is also offered on the Daytona Beach campus.

M.B.A. degree candidates in both degree programs must complete a minimum of 33 credit hours of course work consisting of 21 hours of core curriculum and 12 hours of specified electives. Three hours of elective credit may be awarded for an internship, which is strongly advised for all students. The employer-supported Business Eagles program is open to M.B.A. students and provides special access to development and placement activities. The M.B.A. program can usually be completed in sixteen to twenty-four months based on how the student progresses through the curriculum and whether an internship is taken.

Research Facilities

A cluster of servers (UNIX and IBM) and PCs supported by a telecommunications network provide the faculty and students with the latest advances in information management and computing facilities. These are augmented by academic student labs, the Applied Aviation Simulation Lab, and the Total Airspace and Airport Modeler (TAMM) Research Lab. Extensive modern computer facilities and Internet access are available to all students.

Financial Aid

Scholarships are awarded to outstanding graduate students during the admissions process. Assistantships are also available on a limited basis. Students may apply for financial aid by calling 800-943-6279 (toll-free). All graduate programs are approved for U.S. Veterans Administration education benefits.

Cost of Study

In 2012–13 tuition costs for the residential M.B.A. program are $1230 per credit hour. The estimated cost of books and supplies is $1400 per semester.

Living and Housing Costs

On-campus housing is available on a limited basis to graduate students on the Daytona Beach campus. Single students who share rent and utility expenses can expect off-campus room and board expenses of $4000 per semester.

Student Group

ERAU's graduate programs on the Daytona Beach campus currently enroll approximately 600 students. The students in the programs on the Daytona Beach campus possess various cultural origins—many are from other countries, 25 percent are women, and 23 percent are members of U.S. minority groups. The M.B.A. program attracts students with diverse academic backgrounds and common scholastic abilities that enrich the program. The majority of incoming students have business degrees, although all degrees are welcomed with many engineers and air science students currently enrolled. The average age of incoming students is 28.

Student Outcomes

In addition to contacts gained from internships with leading airlines, airports, and aerospace firms, the M.B.A. degree program conducts placement activities for its graduates. Years of research and consulting have allowed the faculty to cultivate contacts within the aviation industry, and its network provides job opportunities for graduates. The Career Services Office sponsors an annual industry Career Expo, which attracts more than 100 major companies such as Boeing, Federal Express, Delta, and United Airlines. In addition, the Career Resource Center offers corporate profiles, job postings, and development information. The office also assists with resume development and interview preparation.

Location

The Daytona Beach, Florida, campus is located next to the Daytona Beach International Airport and 10 minutes from the Daytona beaches. Within an hour's drive of Orlando and destinations such as Disney World, EPCOT, Universal Studios, SeaWorld, Kennedy Space Center, and St. Augustine.

The University

Since its founding in 1926, Embry-Riddle Aeronautical University has built a reputation for high-quality education within the field of aviation and has become a world leader in aerospace higher education. The University is comprised of the eastern campus in Daytona Beach, Florida; the western campus in Prescott, Arizona; and the WorldWide Campus, with off-campus programs.

Applying

A desired minimum bachelor degree cumulative GPA of 3.0 (4.0 scale) and a minimum score of 500 on the GMAT are the requirements for full admission consideration for the M.B.A. program. GRE scores may be submitted in lieu of the GMAT. Applications not meeting these qualifications may be considered for conditional admission with enhanced student oversight as an applicant matriculates into the program. Applications are accepted on a rolling basis and should be completed sixty days prior to the start of a semester for U.S. citizens, resident aliens, and international students. For international applicants the required minimum IELTS score is 6.0, or a TOEFL score of 550 or 79 on the TOFEL-IBT.

Correspondence and Information

Office of International and Graduate Admissions
Embry-Riddle Aeronautical University
600 South Clyde Morris Boulevard
Daytona Beach, Florida 32114-3900
United States
Phone: 386-226-6176 (outside the United States)
800-388-3728 (toll-free within the United States)
Fax: 386-226-7070
E-mail: graduate.admissions@erau.edu
Web site: http://www.embryriddle.edu/graduate

THE FACULTY

The College of Business faculty takes pride in bringing relevant, real-world problems, issues, and experiences into the classrooms. Faculty members give a high priority to preparing students for the leadership roles they will eventually assume. The faculty members accomplish this not only by excellence in teaching but also by advising students on their business research and consulting projects. Many members of the faculty serve as consultants to a variety of industries, and their diverse backgrounds provide a rich, multicultural teaching field, with an emphasis on global standards and practices.

In addition, the Embry-Riddle faculty members are the go-to references for print and broadcast journalists on questions of aviation. When the question concerns aviation business, the savvy journalist calls the experts at the Embry-Riddle College of Business. For issues such as airline mergers, acquisitions, bankruptcies, or the general state of the aviation business, members of the COB faculty have provided information to scores of journalists for countless articles and broadcasts. Such is the reputation of the faculty of the College of Business.

On the subject of aviation business, Embry-Riddle faculty members have written some of the leading textbooks in the field, such as the following from five COB professors.

Ahmed Abdelghany, Ph.D., Assistant Professor. *Modeling Applications in the Airline Industry.*

Massoud Bazargan, Ph.D., Professor, *Airline Operations and Scheduling.*

Bruce D. Chadbourne, Ed.D., Professor, *Introduction to Aviation and Risk Management.*

Dawna Rhoades, Ph.D., Professor, *Evolution of International Aviation: Phoenix Rising.*

Bijan Vasigh, Ph.D., Professor, *Introduction to Air Transport Economics, From Theory to Applications* and *Foundations of Airline Finance.*

The other faculty members of the college whom students may have as instructors in the M.B.A. program are:

Anke Arnaud, Ph.D., Assistant Professor, Organizational Behavior.

Tamilla Curtis, Ph.D., Assistant Professor, Marketing.

Vitaly Guzhva, Ph.D., Professor, Finance.

Lee Hays, D.B.A., Assistant Professor, Management.

Jenny Hinebaugh, M.B.A., Assistant Professor, Management.

John Ledgerwood, CPA, MSA, Associate Professor, Accounting.

Vedapuri Raghavan, Ph.D., Professor, Finance.

Rosemarie Reynolds, Ph.D., Associate Professor, Organizational Behavior.

Thomas Tacker, Ph.D., Professor, Economics. Co-author of *Introduction to Air Transport Economics, From Theory to Applications.*

Janet Tinoco, Ph.D., Assistant Professor, Marketing and Management.

Blaise Waguespack, Ph.D., Professor, Marketing.

Michael J. Williams, Ph.D., Dean, Professor, Management Information Systems.

Chunyan Yu, Ph.D., Associate Professor of Transport Management.

Bert Zarb, D.B.A., CPA, Associate Professor, Accounting.

Li Zou, Ph.D., Assistant Professor, Marketing.

The recently opened College of Business building on the Daytona Beach campus, part of a major infrastructure program bringing new academic and student facilities across the campus.

Students at work in the Applied Aviation Simulation Lab, which contains multiple servers to aid students in completing research projects for airlines and airports across the globe.

ACADEMIC AND PROFESSIONAL PROGRAMS IN EDUCATION

Section 22
Education

This section contains a directory of institutions offering graduate work in education, followed by in-depth entries submitted by institutions that chose to prepare detailed program descriptions. Additional information about programs listed in the directory but not augmented by an in-depth entry may be obtained by writing directly to the dean of a graduate school or chair of a department at the address given in the directory.

For programs offering related work, see also in this book *Administration, Instruction, and Theory; Instructional Levels; Leisure Studies and Recreation; Physical Education and Kinesiology; Special Focus;* and *Subject Areas.* In other guides in this series:

Graduate Programs in the Humanities, Arts & Social Sciences
See *Psychology and Counseling (School Psychology)*

Graduate Programs in the Biological/Biomedical Sciences & Health-Related Medical Professions
See *Health-Related Professions*

CONTENTS

Program Directory

Displays and Close-Ups

See also:

Education—General

Abilene Christian University, Graduate School, College of Education and Human Services, Abilene, TX 79699-9100. Offers M Ed, MS, MSSW, Certificate, Post-Master's Certificate. *Faculty:* 5 full-time (1 woman), 14 part-time/adjunct (7 women). *Students:* 77 full-time (67 women), 182 part-time (127 women); includes 70 minority (37 Black or African American, non-Hispanic/Latino; 2 Asian, non-Hispanic/Latino; 27 Hispanic/Latino; 4 Two or more races, non-Hispanic/Latino), 6 international. 221 applicants, 44% accepted, 64 enrolled. In 2011, 125 master's awarded. *Degree requirements:* For master's, comprehensive exam (for some programs), thesis (for some programs), practicum. *Entrance requirements:* For master's, GRE. Additional exam requirements/recommendations for international students: Required—TOEFL (minimum score 550 paper-based; 213 computer-based; 80 iBT), IELTS (minimum score 6). *Application deadline:* For fall admission, 8/15 priority date for domestic students; for winter admission, 10/1 priority date for domestic students; for spring admission, 12/15 priority date for domestic students. Applications are processed on a rolling basis. Application fee: $50. Electronic applications accepted. *Expenses: Tuition:* Full-time $14,168; part-time $787 per hour. *Required fees:* $82 per hour. $10 per term. *Financial support:* In 2011–12, 46 students received support. Career-related internships or fieldwork and scholarships/grants available. Financial award application deadline: 4/1; financial award applicants required to submit FAFSA. *Total annual research expenditures:* $154. *Unit head:* Dr. Donnie Snider, Interim Dean, 325-674-2700, E-mail: dcs03b@acu.edu. *Application contact:* David Pittman, Graduate Admissions Counselor, 325-674-2656, Fax: 325-674-6717, E-mail: gradinfo@acu.edu.

Acadia University, Faculty of Professional Studies, School of Education, Wolfville, NS B4P 2R6, Canada. Offers counseling (M Ed); curriculum studies (M Ed), including cultural and media studies, learning and technology, science, math and technology; inclusive education (M Ed); leadership (M Ed). *Degree requirements:* For master's, thesis optional. *Entrance requirements:* For master's, B Ed or the equivalent, 2 years of teaching or related experience. Additional exam requirements/recommendations for international students: Required—TOEFL (minimum score 580 paper-based; 237 computer-based; 93 iBT), IELTS (minimum score 6.5).

Adams State University, The Graduate School, Department of Teacher Education, Alamosa, CO 81102. Offers education (MA); special education (MA). *Accreditation:* Teacher Education Accreditation Council. Part-time programs available. Postbaccalaureate distance learning degree programs offered. *Degree requirements:* For master's, qualifying exam. *Entrance requirements:* For master's, GRE General Test or MAT, minimum undergraduate GPA of 3.0.

Adelphi University, Ruth S. Ammon School of Education, Garden City, NY 11530-0701. Offers MA, MS, DA, Certificate. *Accreditation:* NCATE. Part-time and evening/weekend programs available. *Faculty:* 68 full-time (45 women), 147 part-time/adjunct (103 women). *Students:* 596 full-time (490 women), 445 part-time (351 women); includes 235 minority (89 Black or African American, non-Hispanic/Latino; 29 Asian, non-Hispanic/Latino; 103 Hispanic/Latino; 2 Native Hawaiian or other Pacific Islander, non-Hispanic/Latino; 12 Two or more races, non-Hispanic/Latino), 27 international. Average age 28. 1,286 applicants, 51% accepted, 389 enrolled. In 2011, 513 master's, 4 doctorates, 93 other advanced degrees awarded. *Degree requirements:* For doctorate, one foreign language, comprehensive exam, thesis/dissertation. *Entrance requirements:* For master's, resume, letters of recommendation, minimum cumulative GPA of 2.75; for doctorate, GRE General Test, 3 letters of recommendation, interview. Additional exam requirements/recommendations for international students: Required—TOEFL (minimum score 550 paper-based; 213 computer-based; 80 iBT). *Application deadline:* For fall admission, 4/1 for international students; for spring admission, 11/1 for international students. Applications are processed on a rolling basis. Application fee: $50. Electronic applications accepted. *Expenses: Tuition:* Full-time $29,600; part-time $930 per credit. *Required fees:* $1100. *Financial support:* In 2011–12, 127 teaching assistantships (averaging $7,112 per year) were awarded; career-related internships or fieldwork, Federal Work-Study, institutionally sponsored loans, tuition waivers (full), and unspecified assistantships also available. Support available to part-time students. Financial award application deadline: 2/15; financial award applicants required to submit FAFSA. *Faculty research:* Multicultural and gender issues, psychometric assessment, quantitative research methods. *Unit head:* Dr. Jane Ashdown, Dean, 516-877-4065, E-mail: jashdown@adelphi.edu. *Application contact:* Christine Murphy, Director of Admissions, 516-877-3050, Fax: 516-877-3039, E-mail: graduateadmissions@adelphi.edu. Web site: http://education.adelphi.edu/.

See Display below and Close-Up on page 767.

Alabama Agricultural and Mechanical University, School of Graduate Studies, School of Education, Huntsville, AL 35811. Offers M Ed, MS, MS Ed, Ed S. *Accreditation:* NCATE. Part-time and evening/weekend programs available. *Degree requirements:* For master's, comprehensive exam. *Entrance requirements:* For master's, GRE General Test. Additional exam requirements/recommendations for international students: Required—TOEFL (minimum score 500 paper-based; 173 computer-based; 61 iBT). Electronic applications accepted. *Faculty research:* Speech defects, aging, blindness, multicultural education, learning styles.

Alaska Pacific University, Graduate Programs, Education Department, Program in Teaching, Anchorage, AK 99508-4672. Offers teaching (K-8) (MAT). *Degree requirements:* For master's, research project. *Entrance requirements:* For master's, GRE or MAT, PRAXIS, minimum GPA of 3.0.

Albany State University, College of Education, Albany, GA 31705-2717. Offers early childhood education (M Ed); education specialist (Ed S); educational leadership and administration (M Ed); health, physical education and recreation (M Ed); middle grades education (M Ed); school counseling (M Ed); special education (M Ed). *Accreditation:* NCATE. Part-time and evening/weekend programs available. Postbaccalaureate distance learning degree programs offered (minimal on-campus study). *Faculty:* 19 full-time (13 women), 7 part-time/adjunct (5 women). *Students:* 90 full-time (69 women), 118 part-time (92 women); includes 152 minority (151 Black or African American, non-Hispanic/Latino; 1 American Indian or Alaska Native, non-Hispanic/Latino), 1 international. Average age 35. 93 applicants, 78% accepted, 38 enrolled. In 2011, 43 master's, 8 Ed Ss awarded. *Degree requirements:* For master's, comprehensive exam, internship, GACE Content Exam. *Entrance requirements:* For master's, GRE or MAT. *Application deadline:* For fall admission, 6/1 for domestic students, 5/1 for international students; for spring admission, 11/1 for domestic students, 10/1 for international students. Applications are processed on a rolling basis. Application fee: $20. Electronic applications accepted. *Expenses:* Tuition, state resident: full-time $3204; part-time $178 per credit hour. Tuition, nonresident: full-time $12,816; part-time $712 per credit hour. *Required fees:* $379 per semester. *Financial support:* Scholarships/grants available. Financial award application deadline: 4/15; financial award applicants required to submit FAFSA. *Faculty research:* GACE preparation, STEM (science, technology, engineering, and mathematics), technology education, special education, professional teacher development, health implications liberation philosophy, NET-Q, learning community, disabled or at-risk students. *Total annual research expenditures:* $252,502. *Unit head:* Dr. Kimberly King-Jupiter, Dean, 229-430-1718, Fax: 229-430-4993, E-mail: kimberly.king-jupiter@asurams.edu. *Application contact:* Jeffrey Pierce, II, Graduate Admissions Counselor, 229-430-4646, Fax: 229-430-4105, E-mail: jeffrey.pierce@asurams.edu. Web site: http://asu-sacs.asurams.edu/ASUCatalog/Graduate/index.html.

Albertus Magnus College, Master of Science in Education Program, New Haven, CT 06511-1189. Offers MS Ed. *Faculty:* 3 full-time (1 woman), 9 part-time/adjunct (4 women). *Students:* 8 full-time (4 women), 15 part-time (14 women); includes 5 minority (2 Black or African American, non-Hispanic/Latino; 1 American Indian or Alaska Native, non-Hispanic/Latino; 1 Asian, non-Hispanic/Latino; 1 Hispanic/Latino). 4 applicants, 100% accepted, 4 enrolled. In 2011, 8 master's awarded. *Degree requirements:* For master's, thesis, capstone. *Entrance requirements:* For master's, bachelor's degree, official transcripts of all undergraduate work, three letters of recommendation, resume, essay, valid Connecticut Initial teacher certificate (preferred). *Application deadline:* For fall admission, 8/15 for domestic students; for spring admission, 1/15 for domestic students. Application fee: $50. *Faculty research:* Assessment, learning theory, educational leadership, differentiated instruction, multiculturalism. *Unit head:* Dr. Joan Venditto, Director, Education Programs, 203-773-8087, Fax: 203-773-4422, E-mail: jvenditto@albertus.edu. *Application contact:* Dr. Irene Rios, Dean of New Dimensions, 203-777-7100, Fax: 203-777-9906, E-mail: irios@albertus.edu. Web site: http://www.albertus.edu/masters-degrees/education/.

Albright College, Graduate Division, Reading, PA 19612-5234. Offers early childhood education (MS); elementary education (MS); English as a second language (MA); general education (MA); special education (MS). Part-time and evening/weekend programs available. *Degree requirements:* For master's, thesis. *Entrance requirements:* For master's, GRE General Test or MAT, minimum undergraduate GPA of 3.0, 2 letters of recommendation, interview. Additional exam requirements/recommendations for international students: Recommended—TOEFL (minimum score 525 paper-based; 197 computer-based). Electronic applications accepted.

Alcorn State University, School of Graduate Studies, School of Psychology and Education, Alcorn State, MS 39096-7500. Offers agricultural education (MS Ed); elementary education (MS Ed, Ed S); guidance and counseling (MS Ed); industrial education (MS Ed); secondary education (MS Ed), including health and physical education; special education (MS Ed). *Accreditation:* NCATE. *Degree requirements:* For master's, thesis optional.

Alfred University, Graduate School, Division of Education, Alfred, NY 14802-1205. Offers literacy teacher (MS Ed); numeracy (MS). *Accreditation:* Teacher Education Accreditation Council. Part-time programs available. *Entrance requirements:* For master's, LAST, Assessment of Teaching Skills (written), Content Specialty Test. Additional exam requirements/recommendations for international students: Required—TOEFL (minimum score 590 paper-based; 243 computer-based; 90 iBT), IELTS (minimum score 6.5). Electronic applications accepted. *Faculty research:* Whole language, ethics in counseling and psychotherapy.

Alliant International University–Fresno, Shirley M. Hufstedler School of Education, Teacher Education and Preparation Programs, Fresno, CA 93727. Offers MA. Part-time programs available. *Entrance requirements:* For master's, CBEST, CSET, interview; offer of employment as a teacher of record in a California school; minimum GPA of 2.5, 2 letters of recommendation. *Application deadline:* Applications are processed on a rolling basis. Electronic applications accepted. Tuition and fees vary according to course load. *Unit head:* Dr. Trudy Day, Systemwide Director, Education Policy and Practice, 415-955-2102, Fax: 415-955-2179, E-mail: admissions@alliant.edu. *Application contact:* Alliant International University Central Contact Center, 866-U-ALLIANT, Fax: 858-635-4555, E-mail: admissions@alliant.edu.

Alliant International University–Irvine, Shirley M. Hufstedler School of Education, Teacher Education Programs, Irvine, CA 92612. Offers auditory oral education (Certificate); CLAD (Certificate); preliminary multiple subject (Credential); preliminary multiple subject with BCLAD (Credential); preliminary single subject (Credential); professional clear multiple subject (Credential); professional clear single subject (Credential); teaching (MA, Credential); technology and learning (MA). Part-time and evening/weekend programs available. *Students:* 4. In 2011, 6 master's awarded. *Entrance requirements:* For degree, California Basic Educational Skills Test, minimum GPA of 2.5. Additional exam requirements/recommendations for international students: Required—TOEFL (minimum score 550 paper-based; 213 computer-based), TWE. *Application deadline:* For fall admission, 7/1 priority date for domestic students, 7/1 for international students; for spring admission, 12/1 priority date for domestic students, 12/1 for international students. Applications are processed on a rolling basis. Application fee: $55. Electronic applications accepted. *Financial support:* Career-related internships or fieldwork, Federal Work-Study, institutionally sponsored loans, and scholarships/grants available. Financial award applicants required to submit FAFSA. *Unit head:* Dr. Trudy Day, Assistant Dean, 866-825-5426, Fax: 949-833-3507, E-mail: admissions@alliant.edu. *Application contact:* Alliant International University Central Contact Center, 866-U-ALLIANT, Fax: 858-635-4555, E-mail: admissions@alliant.edu. Web site: http://www.alliant.edu/gsoe.

Alliant International University–Los Angeles, Shirley M. Hufstedler School of Education, TeachersCHOICE Preparation Programs, Alhambra, CA 91803-1360. Offers MA, Credential. Part-time programs available. *Faculty:* 10 part-time/adjunct (8 women). *Students:* 9 full-time, 10 part-time. Average age 30. In 2011, 2 master's awarded. *Entrance requirements:* For master's, CBEST, CSET, interview; offer of employment as a teacher of record in a California school; minimum GPA of 2.5; 2 letters of recommendation. *Application deadline:* For fall admission, 8/1 priority date for domestic students, 8/1 for international students. Application fee: $45. *Faculty research:* Multicultural and bilingual education pedagogy, teacher training pedagogy, curriculum development, instructional strategies. *Unit head:* Dr. Trudy Day, Program Director, Educational Policy and Practice, 415-955-2087, Fax: 415-955-2179, E-mail: admissions@alliant.edu. *Application contact:* Alliant International University Central Contact Center, 866-U-ALLIANT, Fax: 858-635-4555, E-mail: admissions@alliant.edu.

Alliant International University–México City, Shirley M. Hufstedler School of Education, Mexico City, Mexico. Offers educational administration (MA); teaching (MA). Part-time and evening/weekend programs available. Postbaccalaureate distance learning degree programs offered (no on-campus study). *Faculty:* 2 part-time/adjunct (both women). *Students:* Average age 38. In 2011, 5 master's awarded. *Entrance requirements:* For master's, minimum GPA of 2.5, letters of recommendation. Additional exam requirements/recommendations for international students: Required—TOEFL (minimum score 550 paper-based; 213 computer-based), TWE (minimum score 5). *Application deadline:* For fall admission, 8/1 priority date for domestic students, 8/1 for international students; for spring admission, 12/1 priority date for domestic students, 12/1 for international students. Application fee: $50. *Financial support:* Career-related internships or fieldwork, Federal Work-Study, institutionally sponsored loans, and scholarships/grants available. Financial award application deadline: 2/15; financial award applicants required to submit FAFSA. *Unit head:* Dr. Karen Schuster Webb, Systemwide Dean, 415-955-2051, E-mail: contacto@alliantmexico.com. *Application contact:* Lesly Gutierrez Garcia, Coordinator of Admissions and Student Services, (+5255) 5525-7651, E-mail: contacto@alliantmexico.com. Web site: http://www.alliantmexico.com/.

Alliant International University–Sacramento, Shirley M. Hufstedler School of Education, TeachersCHOICE Preparation Programs, Sacramento, CA 95825. Offers MA, Credential. *Faculty:* 1 (woman) full-time. *Students:* 5. Average age 35. *Entrance requirements:* For master's, CBEST, CSET, interview; offer of employment as a teacher of record in a California school; minimum GPA of 3.0; 2 letters of recommendation. *Application deadline:* For fall admission, 8/1 priority date for domestic students, 8/1 for international students. Applications are processed on a rolling basis. Application fee: $45. Electronic applications accepted. Tuition and fees vary according to program. *Financial support:* Application deadline: 2/1; applicants required to submit FAFSA. *Faculty research:* Innovative teacher education, educational leadership, cross-cultural education. *Unit head:* Dr. Karen Webb, Dean, 415-955-2051, Fax: 415-955-2179, E-mail: admissions@alliant.edu. *Application contact:* Alliant International University Central Contact Center, 866-U-ALLIANT, Fax: 858-635-4555, E-mail: admissions@alliant.edu.

Alliant International University–San Diego, Shirley M. Hufstedler School of Education, Teacher Education Programs, San Diego, CA 92131-1799. Offers preliminary single subject (Credential); professional clear multiple subject (Credential); professional clear single subject (Credential); teacher education (MA). Part-time and evening/weekend programs available. *Faculty:* 1 full-time, 4 part-time/adjunct (3 women). *Students:* 10 (5 women). In 2011, 11 master's awarded. *Entrance requirements:* For degree, California Basic Educational Skills Test, minimum GPA of 2.5. Additional exam requirements/recommendations for international students: Required—TOEFL (minimum score 550 paper-based; 213 computer-based), TWE. *Application deadline:* For fall admission, 7/1 priority date for domestic students, 7/1 for international students; for spring admission, 12/1 priority date for domestic students, 12/1 for international students. Applications are processed on a rolling basis. Application fee: $45. Electronic applications accepted. Tuition and fees vary according to degree level and program. *Financial support:* Career-related internships or fieldwork, Federal Work-Study, institutionally sponsored loans, and scholarships/grants available. Financial award application deadline: 2/15; financial award applicants required to submit FAFSA. *Faculty research:* Curriculum and instructional planning. *Unit head:* Dr. Trudy Day, Educational Policy and Practice Program Director, 415-955-2102, Fax: 858-435-4739, E-mail: admissions@alliant.edu. *Application contact:* Alliant International University Central Contact Center, 866-U-ALLIANT, Fax: 858-635-4555, E-mail: admissions@alliant.edu.

Alliant International University–San Francisco, Shirley M. Hufstedler School of Education, Teacher Education Programs, San Francisco, CA 94133-1221. Offers auditory oral education (Certificate); CLAD (Certificate); education specialist: mild/moderate disabilities (Credential); preliminary multiple subject (Credential); preliminary single subject (Credential); professional clear multiple subject (Credential); professional clear single subject (Credential); special education (MA); teaching (MA). Part-time and evening/weekend programs available. *Faculty:* 6 full-time (4 women), 10 part-time/adjunct (8 women). *Students:* 46 full-time (30 women), 79 part-time (54 women); includes 35 minority (9 Black or African American, non-Hispanic/Latino; 15 Asian, non-Hispanic/Latino; 11 Hispanic/Latino). Average age 38. In 2011, 20 master's awarded. *Degree requirements:* For master's, thesis. *Entrance requirements:* For degree, California Basic Educational Skills Test, minimum GPA of 2.5. Additional exam requirements/recommendations for international students: Required—TOEFL (minimum score 550 paper-based; 213 computer-based), TWE (minimum score 5). *Application deadline:* For fall admission, 7/1 priority date for domestic students, 7/1 for international students; for spring admission, 12/1 priority date for domestic students, 12/1 for international students. Applications are processed on a rolling basis. Application fee: $55. Electronic applications accepted. *Financial support:* Career-related internships or fieldwork, Federal Work-Study, institutionally sponsored loans, and scholarships/grants available. Financial award application deadline: 2/15; financial award applicants required to submit FAFSA. *Faculty research:* Curriculum development, first year teachers, cross-cultural issues in teaching, biliteracy. *Unit head:* Dr. Trudy Day, Program Director, 415-955-2102, Fax: 415-955-2179, E-mail: admissions@alliant.edu. *Application contact:* Alliant International University Central Contact Center, 866-U-ALLIANT, Fax: 858-635-4555, E-mail: admissions@alliant.edu. Web site: http://www.alliant.edu/.

Alvernia University, Graduate Studies, Program in Education, Reading, PA 19607-1799. Offers urban education (M Ed). Part-time and evening/weekend programs available. *Degree requirements:* For master's, thesis optional. *Entrance requirements:* For master's, GRE or MAT (alumni excluded). Electronic applications accepted.

Alverno College, School of Education, Milwaukee, WI 53234-3922. Offers adaptive education (MA); administrative leadership (MA); adult education and organizational development (MA); adult educational and instructional design (MA); adult educational and instructional technology (MA); global connections in the humanities (MA); instructional leadership (MA); instructional technology for K-12 settings (MA); professional development (MA); reading education (MA); reading education with adaptive education (MA); science education (MA); teaching in alternative schools (MA). *Accreditation:* NCATE. Part-time and evening/weekend programs available. *Faculty:* 22 full-time (18 women), 13 part-time/adjunct (all women). *Students:* 63 full-time (58 women), 91 part-time (81 women); includes 36 minority (29 Black or African American, non-Hispanic/Latino; 1 Asian, non-Hispanic/Latino; 4 Hispanic/Latino; 1 Native Hawaiian or other Pacific Islander, non-Hispanic/Latino; 1 Two or more races, non-Hispanic/Latino), 2 international. Average age 38. 151 applicants, 60% accepted, 62 enrolled. In 2011, 52 master's awarded. *Degree requirements:* For master's, presentation/defense of proposal, conference presentation of inquiry projects. *Entrance requirements:* For master's, bachelor's degree in related field, communication samples from work setting, 3 letters of recommendation. Additional exam requirements/recommendations for international students: Required—TOEFL. *Application deadline:* For fall admission, 7/15 priority date for domestic students, 7/15 for international students; for spring admission, 12/15 priority date for domestic students, 12/15 for international students. Applications are processed on a rolling basis. Application fee: $0. Electronic applications accepted. Application fee is waived when completed online. Tuition and fees vary according to program. *Financial support:* In 2011–12, 1 student received support. Federal Work-Study available. Support available to part-time students. Financial award application deadline: 4/15; financial award applicants required to submit FAFSA. *Faculty research:* Student self-assessment, self-reflection, integration of curriculum, identifying needs of students in strategic situations and designing appropriate classroom strategies. *Unit head:* Dr. Desiree Pointer-Mace, Associate Dean, Graduate Program, 414-382-6345, Fax: 414-382-6332, E-mail: desiree.pointer-mace@alverno.edu. *Application contact:* Mary Claire Jones, Graduate Recruiter, 414-382-6106, Fax: 414-382-6354, E-mail: maryclaire.jones@alverno.edu.

American College of Education, Graduate Programs, Chicago, IL 60606. Offers curriculum and instruction (M Ed), including bilingual, ESL; educational leadership (M Ed); educational technology (M Ed).

Education—General

American InterContinental University Online, Program in Education, Hoffman Estates, IL 60192. Offers curriculum and instruction (M Ed); educational assessment and evaluation (M Ed); instructional technology (M Ed); leadership of educational organizations (M Ed). Evening/weekend programs available. Postbaccalaureate distance learning degree programs offered (no on-campus study). *Entrance requirements:* Additional exam requirements/recommendations for international students: Required—TOEFL (minimum score 550 paper-based; 213 computer-based). Electronic applications accepted.

American International College, School of Arts, Education and Sciences, Department of Education, Springfield, MA 01109-3189. Offers early childhood education (M Ed, CAGS); educational leadership and supervision (Ed D); elementary education (M Ed, CAGS); middle/secondary education (M Ed, CAGS); moderate disabilities (M Ed, CAGS); reading (M Ed, CAGS); school adjustment counseling (MA, CAGS); school administration (M Ed, CAGS); school guidance counseling (MA, CAGS); teaching (MA, MS); teaching and learning (Ed D). Part-time and evening/weekend programs available. Terminal master's awarded for partial completion of doctoral program. *Degree requirements:* For master's, comprehensive exam (for some programs), thesis (for some programs), practicum; for doctorate, comprehensive exam (for some programs), thesis/dissertation; for CAGS, practicum. *Entrance requirements:* For master's, minimum B-average in undergraduate course work; for doctorate, GRE General Test, interview. Additional exam requirements/recommendations for international students: Required—TOEFL. Electronic applications accepted.

American Jewish University, Graduate School of Education, Program in Education, Bel Air, CA 90077-1599. Offers MA Ed. *Degree requirements:* For master's, one foreign language. *Entrance requirements:* For master's, GRE General Test, interview, minimum GPA of 3.0. Additional exam requirements/recommendations for international students: Required—TOEFL. *Faculty research:* Philosophy of education, curriculum development, teacher training.

American Jewish University, Graduate School of Education, Program in Education for Working Professionals, Bel Air, CA 90077-1599. Offers MA Ed. *Degree requirements:* For master's, comprehensive exam, internships. *Entrance requirements:* For master's, GRE General Test, interview. Additional exam requirements/recommendations for international students: Required—TOEFL.

American Public University System, AMU/APU Graduate Programs, Charles Town, WV 25414. Offers accounting (MBA, MS); administration and supervision (M Ed); criminal justice (MA); emergency and disaster management (MA); entrepreneurship (MBA); environmental policy and management (MS), including environmental planning, environmental sustainability, fish and wildlife management, general (MA, MS), global environmental management; finance (MBA); general (MBA); global business management (MBA); guidance and counseling (M Ed); history (MA), including American history, ancient and classical history, European history, global history, military and diplomatic history, public history; homeland security (MA); homeland security resource allocation (MBA); humanities (MA); information technology (MS), including digital forensics, enterprise software development, information assurance and security, IT project management; information technology management (MBA); intelligence studies (MA), including criminal intelligence, general (MA, MS), homeland security, intelligence analysis, intelligence collection, intelligence operations, terrorism studies; international relations and conflict resolution (MA), including comparative and security issues, conflict resolution, international and transnational security issues, peacekeeping; legal studies (MA); management (MA), including defense management, general (MA, MS), human resource management, organizational leadership, public administration, reverse logistics, strategic consulting; marketing (MBA); military history (MA), including American military history, American revolution, civil war, war since 1946, World War II; military studies (MA), including air warfare, asymmetrical warfare, joint warfare, land warfare, naval warfare, strategic leadership; national security studies (MA), including general (MA, MS), homeland security, regional security studies, security and intelligence analysis, terrorism studies; nonprofit management (MBA); political science (MA), including American politics and government, comparative government and development, public policy; psychology (MA); public administration (MA, MPA), including disaster management (MPA), environmental policy (MA), health policy (MPA), human resources (MPA), national security (MPA), organizational management (MPA), security management (MPA); public health (MA, MPH), including emergency management (MPH), environmental health (MPH), public administration (MA); reverse logistics management (MA); security management (MA); space studies (MS), including aerospace science, planetary science; sports and health sciences (MS); sports management (MS), including coaching theory and strategy, sports administration; teaching (M Ed), including curriculum and instruction for elementary teachers, elementary, elementary reading, English language learners, instructional leadership, online learning, secondary social sciences, special education; transportation and logistics management (MA), including maritime engineering management. Programs offered via distance learning only. Part-time and evening/weekend programs available. Postbaccalaureate distance learning degree programs offered (no on-campus study). *Faculty:* 445 full-time (241 women), 1,360 part-time/adjunct (617 women). *Students:* 688 full-time (338 women), 10,168 part-time (3,706 women); includes 3,130 minority (1,007 Black or African American, non-Hispanic/Latino; 103 American Indian or Alaska Native, non-Hispanic/Latino; 825 Asian, non-Hispanic/Latino; 810 Hispanic/Latino; 51 Native Hawaiian or other Pacific Islander, non-Hispanic/Latino; 334 Two or more races, non-Hispanic/Latino), 134 international. Average age 35. In 2011, 2,386 master's awarded. *Degree requirements:* For master's, comprehensive exam or practicum. *Entrance requirements:* For master's, official transcript showing earned bachelor's degree from institution accredited by recognized accrediting body. Additional exam requirements/recommendations for international students: Required—TOEFL (minimum score 550 paper-based; 213 computer-based), IELTS (minimum score 6.5). *Application deadline:* Applications are processed on a rolling basis. Application fee: $0. Electronic applications accepted. *Expenses: Tuition:* Part-time $325 per credit hour. *Financial support:* Applicants required to submit FAFSA. *Faculty research:* Military history, criminal justice, management performance, national security. *Unit head:* Dr. Karan Powell, Executive Vice President and Provost, 877-468-6268, Fax: 304-724-3780. *Application contact:* Terry Grant, Vice President of Enrollment Management, 877-468-6268, Fax: 304-724-3780, E-mail: info@apus.edu. Web site: http://www.apus.edu.

American University, College of Arts and Sciences, School of Education, Teaching, and Health, Washington, DC 20016-8030. Offers curriculum and instruction (M Ed, Certificate); early childhood education (MAT, Certificate); elementary education (MAT); English for speakers of other languages (MAT, Certificate); health promotion management (MS, Certificate); international training and education (MA, MAT); nutrition education (Certificate); secondary teaching (MAT, Certificate); special education (MA), including special education: learning disabilities; MAT/MA. *Accreditation:* NCATE. Part-time and evening/weekend programs available. *Faculty:* 14 full-time (10 women), 58 part-time/adjunct (41 women). *Students:* 69 full-time (61 women), 257 part-time (188 women); includes 55 minority (35 Black or African American, non-Hispanic/Latino; 2 American Indian or Alaska Native, non-Hispanic/Latino; 5 Asian, non-Hispanic/Latino; 10 Hispanic/Latino; 3 Two or more races, non-Hispanic/Latino), 4 international. Average age 28. 221 applicants, 81% accepted, 96 enrolled. In 2011, 226 master's, 5 other advanced degrees awarded. *Degree requirements:* For master's, comprehensive exam, thesis or alternative, PRAXIS II. *Entrance requirements:* For master's, GRE General Test, two letters of recommendation; for Certificate, bachelor's degree. Additional exam requirements/recommendations for international students: Required—TOEFL. *Application deadline:* For fall admission, 2/1 priority date for domestic students; for spring admission, 10/1 priority date for domestic students. Applications are processed on a rolling basis. Application fee: $80. *Expenses: Tuition:* Full-time $24,264; part-time $1348 per credit hour. *Required fees:* $430. Tuition and fees vary according to course load and program. *Financial support:* Fellowships, research assistantships with full and partial tuition reimbursements, teaching assistantships with full and partial tuition reimbursements, career-related internships or fieldwork, Federal Work-Study, and institutionally sponsored loans available. Support available to part-time students. Financial award application deadline: 2/1; financial award applicants required to submit FAFSA. *Faculty research:* Gender equity, socioeconomic technology, learning disabilities, gifted and talented education. *Unit head:* Dr. Sarah Irvine-Belson, Dean, 202-885-3714, Fax: 202-885-1187, E-mail: educate@american.edu. *Application contact:* Kathleen Clowery, Director, Graduate Admissions, 202-885-3621, Fax: 202-885-1505, E-mail: clowery@american.edu. Web site: http://www.american.edu/cas/seth/.

American University of Beirut, Graduate Programs, Faculty of Arts and Sciences, Beirut, Lebanon. Offers anthropology (MA); Arabic language and literature (MA); archaeology (MA); biology (MS); chemistry (MS); computational science (MS); computer science (MS); economics (MA); education (MA); English language (MA); English literature (MA); environmental policy planning (MSES); financial economics (MAFE); geology (MS); history (MA); mathematics (MA, MS); Middle Eastern studies (MA); philosophy (MA); physics (MS); political studies (MA); psychology (MA); public administration (MA); sociology (MA); statistics (MA, MS). Part-time programs available. *Faculty:* 154 full-time (44 women), 12 part-time/adjunct (2 women). *Students:* 180 full-time (122 women), 240 part-time (158 women). Average age 25. 336 applicants, 47% accepted, 86 enrolled. In 2011, 57 master's awarded. *Degree requirements:* For master's, one foreign language, comprehensive exam, thesis (for some programs). *Entrance requirements:* For master's, GRE, letter of recommendation. Additional exam requirements/recommendations for international students: Required—TOEFL (minimum score 600 paper-based; 250 computer-based; 97 iBT), IELTS (minimum score 7). *Application deadline:* For fall admission, 4/30 for domestic and international students; for spring admission, 11/1 for domestic and international students. Application fee: $50. *Expenses: Tuition:* Full-time $12,780; part-time $710 per credit. Tuition and fees vary according to course load and program. *Financial support:* In 2011–12, 33 students received support. Career-related internships or fieldwork, institutionally sponsored loans, scholarships/grants, health care benefits, and unspecified assistantships available. Financial award application deadline: 2/4; financial award applicants required to submit FAFSA. *Faculty research:* History of composition studies, syntax of Arabic dialects, Oscar Wilde, decadence, Middle Eastern and international politics, neural mechanisms of creativity and consciousness, personality and psycho-socio-cultural-spiritual correlates of negative and positive mental health, philosophy of mind, metaphysics, micropaleontology and stratigraphy, geochemistry, mineralogy and petrology, tectonophysics, Abbasid, Ottoman and Russian history, landscape, Bronze and Iron Age archaeology. *Unit head:* Dr. Patrick McGreevy, Dean, 961-1374374 Ext. 3800, Fax: 961-1744461, E-mail: pm07@aub.edu.lb. *Application contact:* Dr. Salim Kanaan, Director, Admissions Office, 961-1350000 Ext. 2594, Fax: 961-1750775, E-mail: sk00@aub.edu.lb. Web site: http://staff.aub.edu.lb/~webfas.

American University of Puerto Rico, Program in Education, Bayamón, PR 00960-2037. Offers art education (M Ed); elementary education 4-6 (M Ed); elementary education K-3 (M Ed); general science education (M Ed); physical education (M Ed); special education (M Ed). *Entrance requirements:* For master's, EXADEP, GRE, or MAT, 2 letters of recommendation, minimum GPA of 2.5. *Application deadline:* For fall admission, 8/1 for domestic students; for winter admission, 10/18 for domestic students; for spring admission, 3/15 for domestic students. Applications are processed on a rolling basis. Application fee: $50. *Expenses: Tuition:* Part-time $190 per credit. *Required fees:* $48.33 per credit. Tuition and fees vary according to course load and program. *Application contact:* Information Contact, 787-620-2040, E-mail: oficnaadmisiones@aupr.edu.

Anderson University, College of Education, Anderson, SC 29621-4035. Offers M Ed. *Accreditation:* NCATE.

Anderson University, School of Education, Anderson, IN 46012-3495. Offers M Ed. *Accreditation:* NCATE.

Andrews University, School of Graduate Studies, School of Education, Berrien Springs, MI 49104. Offers MA, MAT, MS, Ed D, PhD, Ed S. *Accreditation:* NCATE. Part-time programs available. *Faculty:* 22 full-time (8 women), 1 (woman) part-time/adjunct. *Students:* 68 full-time (49 women), 193 part-time (102 women); includes 82 minority (45 Black or African American, non-Hispanic/Latino; 1 American Indian or Alaska Native, non-Hispanic/Latino; 6 Asian, non-Hispanic/Latino; 26 Hispanic/Latino; 1 Native Hawaiian or other Pacific Islander, non-Hispanic/Latino; 3 Two or more races, non-Hispanic/Latino), 51 international. Average age 42. 190 applicants, 48% accepted, 50 enrolled. In 2011, 35 master's, 15 doctorates, 5 other advanced degrees awarded. Terminal master's awarded for partial completion of doctoral program. *Degree requirements:* For doctorate, thesis/dissertation. *Entrance requirements:* For master's, GRE Subject Test. Additional exam requirements/recommendations for international students: Required—TOEFL (minimum score 550 paper-based). *Application deadline:* Applications are processed on a rolling basis. Application fee: $40. *Financial support:* Fellowships, research assistantships, teaching assistantships, career-related internships or fieldwork, Federal Work-Study, institutionally sponsored loans, and tuition waivers (partial) available. Support available to part-time students. *Unit head:* Dr. James R. Jeffery, Dean, 269-471-3464. *Application contact:* Carolyn Hurst, Supervisor of Graduate Admission, 800-253-2874, Fax: 269-471-6321, E-mail: graduate@andrews.edu.

Angelo State University, College of Graduate Studies, College of Education, Department of Teacher Education, San Angelo, TX 76909. Offers professional education (M Ed); special education (M Ed). *Faculty:* 17 full-time (12 women). *Students:* 6 full-time (all women), 36 part-time (31 women); includes 8 minority (1 Black or African American, non-Hispanic/Latino; 1 American Indian or Alaska Native, non-Hispanic/Latino; 6 Hispanic/Latino), 1 international. Average age 39. 16 applicants, 81% accepted, 8 enrolled. In 2011, 6 master's awarded. *Application deadline:* For fall admission, 7/15 priority date for domestic students, 6/10 for international students; for spring admission, 12/1 priority date for domestic students, 11/1 for international students. Application fee: $40 ($50 for international students). *Unit head:* Dr. Linda Lucksinger, Department Head, 325-942-2052 Ext. 266, E-mail: linda.lucksinger@angelo.edu. *Application contact:* Aly Hunter, Graduate Admissions Assistant, 325-942-2169, Fax: 325-942-2194, E-mail: aly.hunter@angelo.edu.

Anna Maria College, Graduate Division, Program in Education, Paxton, MA 01612. Offers early childhood education (M Ed); education (CAGS); elementary education (M Ed); English language arts (M Ed); visual arts (M Ed). Part-time and evening/weekend programs available. *Entrance requirements:* For master's, bachelor's degree in liberal arts or sciences, minimum GPA of 3.0. Additional exam requirements/ recommendations for international students: Required—TOEFL (minimum score 500 paper-based). Electronic applications accepted.

Antioch University Los Angeles, Graduate Programs, Program in Education, Culver City, CA 90230. Offers MA. Evening/weekend programs available. *Entrance requirements:* Additional exam requirements/recommendations for international students: Required—TOEFL.

Antioch University Midwest, Graduate Programs, Individualized Liberal and Professional Studies Program, Yellow Springs, OH 45387-1609. Offers liberal and professional studies (MA), including counseling, creative writing, education, liberal studies, management, modern literature, psychology, visual arts. Part-time and evening/ weekend programs available. Postbaccalaureate distance learning degree programs offered (minimal on-campus study). *Faculty:* 2 full-time (1 woman), 2 part-time/adjunct (both women). *Students:* 25 full-time (16 women), 38 part-time (30 women); includes 17 minority (15 Black or African American, non-Hispanic/Latino; 2 Hispanic/Latino). Average age 38. 13 applicants, 69% accepted, 5 enrolled. In 2011, 17 master's awarded. *Degree requirements:* For master's, thesis or alternative. *Entrance requirements:* For master's, resume, goal statement, interview. *Application deadline:* For fall admission, 8/1 for domestic students; for winter admission, 12/1 for domestic students; for spring admission, 3/10 for domestic students. Applications are processed on a rolling basis. Application fee: $50. Electronic applications accepted. *Expenses:* Contact institution. *Financial support:* Federal Work-Study available. Financial award applicants required to submit FAFSA. *Unit head:* Dr. Joseph Cronin, Chair, 937-769-1894, Fax: 937-769-1807, E-mail: jcronin@antioch.edu. *Application contact:* Deena Kent-Hummel, Director of Admissions, 937-769-1800, Fax: 937-769-1804, E-mail: dkent@antioch.edu.

Antioch University Midwest, Graduate Programs, School of Education, Yellow Springs, OH 45387-1609. Offers M Ed. *Accreditation:* NCATE. Part-time and evening/ weekend programs available. *Faculty:* 11 full-time (8 women), 5 part-time/adjunct (3 women). *Students:* 183 full-time (132 women), 73 part-time (57 women); includes 85 minority (79 Black or African American, non-Hispanic/Latino; 2 Asian, non-Hispanic/ Latino; 4 Hispanic/Latino). Average age 32. 143 applicants, 70% accepted, 85 enrolled. In 2011, 171 master's awarded. *Degree requirements:* For master's, thesis or alternative. *Entrance requirements:* For master's, resume, goal statement, interview. *Application deadline:* For fall admission, 9/7 for domestic students; for winter admission, 12/10 for domestic students; for spring admission, 3/10 for domestic students. Applications are processed on a rolling basis. Application fee: $50. Electronic applications accepted. *Expenses:* Contact institution. *Financial support:* Federal Work-Study available. Financial award applicants required to submit FAFSA. *Unit head:* Dr. Marian Glancy, Director, 937-769-1880, Fax: 937-769-1805, E-mail: mglancy@ antioch.edu. *Application contact:* Deena Kent-Hummel, Director of Admissions, 937-769-1823, Fax: 937-769-1804, E-mail: dkent@antioch.edu. Web site: http:// midwest.antioch.edu.

Antioch University New England, Graduate School, Department of Education, Keene, NH 03431-3552. Offers experienced educators (M Ed); integrated learning (M Ed), including early childhood education, elementary education; Waldorf teacher training (M Ed). *Degree requirements:* For master's, thesis (for some programs), internship. *Entrance requirements:* Additional exam requirements/recommendations for international students: Required—TOEFL (minimum score 600 paper-based; 250 computer-based). *Expenses:* Contact institution. *Faculty research:* Classroom and school restructuring, problem-based learning, Waldorf collaborative leadership, ecological literacy.

Antioch University Santa Barbara, Program in Education/Teacher Credentialing, Santa Barbara, CA 93101-1581. Offers MA. Part-time programs available. *Entrance requirements:* Additional exam requirements/recommendations for international students: Required—TOEFL (minimum score 550 paper-based; 213 computer-based). Electronic applications accepted.

Antioch University Seattle, Graduate Programs, Program in Education, Seattle, WA 98121-1814. Offers MA. Part-time and evening/weekend programs available. *Expenses:* Contact institution. *Faculty research:* Transformative learning, intercultural studies, gay and lesbian studies.

Aquinas College, School of Education, Grand Rapids, MI 49506-1799. Offers M Ed, MAT, MSE. Part-time and evening/weekend programs available. *Faculty:* 16 full-time (12 women), 16 part-time/adjunct (13 women). *Students:* 12 full-time (9 women), 133 part-time (105 women); includes 18 minority (2 Black or African American, non-Hispanic/ Latino; 3 Asian, non-Hispanic/Latino; 13 Hispanic/Latino). *Degree requirements:* For master's, teaching project. *Entrance requirements:* For master's, Michigan Basic Skills Test, minimum undergraduate GPA of 3.0, teaching certificate. Additional exam requirements/recommendations for international students: Required—TOEFL (minimum score 550 paper-based; 213 computer-based). *Application deadline:* Applications are processed on a rolling basis. Application fee: $0. *Expenses:* Contact institution. *Financial support:* Scholarships/grants available. Support available to part-time students. Financial award application deadline: 3/15; financial award applicants required to submit FAFSA. *Unit head:* Nanette Clatterbuck, Associate Provost, 616-632-2973, Fax: 616-732-4465, E-mail: clattnan@aquinas.edu. *Application contact:* Michele Polega, Assistant to the Director of Field Placement, 616-632-2440, E-mail: polegmic@ aquinas.edu. Web site: http://www.aquinas.edu/education/.

Arcadia University, Graduate Studies, Department of Education, Glenside, PA 19038-3295. Offers art education (M Ed); computer education (CAS); curriculum (CAS); curriculum studies (M Ed); early childhood education (M Ed, CAS), including individualized (M Ed), master teacher (M Ed), research in child development (M Ed); educational leadership (M Ed, Ed D, CAS); elementary education (M Ed, CAS); English education (MA Ed); environmental education (MA Ed, CAS); history education (MA Ed); instructional technology (M Ed); language arts (M Ed, CAS); library science (M Ed); mathematics education (M Ed, MA Ed, CAS); music education (MA Ed); psychology (MA Ed); reading (M Ed, CAS); science education (M Ed, CAS); secondary education (M Ed, CAS); special education (M Ed, Ed D, CAS); theater arts (MA Ed); written communication (MA Ed). *Accreditation:* NASAD. Part-time and evening/weekend programs available. Postbaccalaureate distance learning degree programs offered (minimal on-campus study). *Faculty:* 12 full-time (8 women), 38 part-time/adjunct (26 women). *Students:* 66 full-time (48 women), 590 part-time (477 women); includes 65 minority (53 Black or African American, non-Hispanic/Latino; 6 Asian, non-Hispanic/ Latino; 3 Hispanic/Latino; 3 Two or more races, non-Hispanic/Latino), 4 international. Average age 36. In 2011, 229 master's, 5 doctorates awarded. *Application deadline:* Applications are processed on a rolling basis. Application fee: $50. Electronic applications accepted. *Expenses:* Contact institution. *Financial support:* Career-related internships or fieldwork, tuition waivers (partial), and unspecified assistantships available. *Unit head:* Dr. Steven P. Gulkus, Associate Professor, 215-572-2120, E-mail: gulkus@arcadia.edu. *Application contact:* 215-572-2925, Fax: 215-572-2126, E-mail: grad@arcadia.edu.

Argosy University, Atlanta, College of Education, Atlanta, GA 30328. Offers educational leadership (MAEd, Ed D, Ed S), including higher education administration (Ed D), K-12 education (Ed D); teaching and learning (MAEd, Ed D, Ed S), including education technology (Ed D), higher education (Ed D), K-12 education (Ed D).

See Close-Up on page 1017.

Argosy University, Chicago, College of Education, Chicago, IL 60601. Offers adult education and training (MA Ed); community college executive leadership (Ed D); educational leadership (MA Ed, Ed D, Ed S), including district leadership (Ed D), higher education administration (Ed D), K-12 education (Ed D); instructional leadership (Ed D, Ed S), including higher education (Ed D), K-12 education (Ed D). Postbaccalaureate distance learning degree programs offered (minimal on-campus study).

See Close-Up on page 769.

Argosy University, Dallas, College of Education, Farmers Branch, TX 75244. Offers educational administration (MA Ed); educational leadership (Ed D); higher and postsecondary education (MA Ed); instructional leadership (MA Ed); school psychology (MA).

See Close-Up on page 771.

Argosy University, Denver, College of Education, Denver, CO 80231. Offers community college executive leadership (Ed D); educational leadership (MA Ed, Ed D), including higher education (Ed D), K-12 education (Ed D); instructional leadership (MA Ed, Ed D), including higher education administration (Ed D), K-12 education (Ed D).

See Close-Up on page 773.

Argosy University, Hawai`i, College of Education, Honolulu, HI 96813. Offers adult education and training (MAEd); educational leadership (Ed D), including higher education administration, K-12 education; instructional leadership (Ed D), including higher education, K-12 education; school psychology (MA).

See Close-Up on page 775.

Argosy University, Inland Empire, College of Education, San Bernardino, CA 92408. Offers community college executive leadership (Ed D); educational leadership (MA Ed, Ed D), including higher education administration (Ed D), K-12 education (Ed D); instructional leadership (MA Ed, Ed D), including higher education (Ed D), K-12 education (Ed D), multiple subject teacher preparation (MA Ed), single subject teacher preparation (MA Ed).

See Close-Up on page 1019.

Argosy University, Los Angeles, College of Education, Santa Monica, CA 90045. Offers community college executive leadership (Ed D); educational leadership (MA Ed, Ed D), including higher education administration (Ed D), K-12 education (Ed D); instructional leadership (MA Ed, Ed D), including higher education (Ed D), K-12 education (Ed D), multiple subject teacher preparation (MA Ed), single subject teacher preparation (MA Ed).

See Close-Up on page 777.

Argosy University, Nashville, College of Education, Nashville, TN 37214. Offers MA Ed, Ed D, Ed S.

See Close-Up on page 1021.

Argosy University, Orange County, College of Education, Orange, CA 92868. Offers community college executive leadership (Ed D); educational leadership (MA Ed, Ed D), including higher education administration (Ed D), K-12 education (Ed D); instructional leadership (MA Ed, Ed D), including education technology (Ed D), higher education (Ed D), K-12 education (Ed D), multiple subject teacher preparation (MA Ed), single subject teacher preparation (MA Ed).

See Close-Up on page 779.

Argosy University, Phoenix, College of Education, Phoenix, AZ 85021. Offers adult education and training (MA Ed); advanced educational administration (Ed D, Ed S); community college executive leadership (Ed D); educational administration (MA Ed); educational leadership (MA Ed, Ed D, Ed S), including education technology (Ed D), higher education administration (Ed D), K-12 education (Ed D); higher and postsecondary education (MA Ed); initial educational administration (Ed D, Ed S); school psychology (MA); teaching and learning (MA Ed, Ed D, Ed S), including education technology (Ed D), higher education (Ed D), K-12 education (Ed D).

See Close-Up on page 781.

Argosy University, Salt Lake City, College of Education, Draper, UT 84020. Offers educational leadership (MA Ed, Ed D).

See Close-Up on page 783.

Argosy University, San Diego, College of Education, San Diego, CA 92108. Offers community college executive leadership (Ed D); educational leadership (MA Ed, Ed D), including higher education administration (Ed D), K-12 education (Ed D); instructional leadership (MA Ed, Ed D), including higher education (Ed D), K-12 education (Ed D).

See Close-Up on page 785.

Argosy University, San Francisco Bay Area, College of Education, Alameda, CA 94501. Offers community college executive leadership (Ed D); educational leadership (MA Ed, Ed D), including education technology (Ed D), higher education administration (Ed D), K-12 education (Ed D); instructional leadership (MA Ed, Ed D), including education technology (Ed D), higher education (Ed D), K-12 education (Ed D), multiple subject teacher preparation (MA Ed), single subject teacher preparation (MA Ed).

See Close-Up on page 787.

Argosy University, Sarasota, College of Education, Sarasota, FL 34235. Offers community college executive leadership (Ed D); educational leadership (MA Ed, Ed D, Ed S), including higher education administration (Ed D), K-12 education (Ed D); school counseling (MA, Ed S); school psychology (MA); teaching and learning (MA Ed, Ed D, Ed S), including education technology (Ed D), higher education (Ed D), K-12 education (Ed D).

See Close-Up on page 789.

Argosy University, Schaumburg, College of Education, Schaumburg, IL 60173-5403. Offers community college executive leadership (Ed D); educational leadership (MA Ed, Ed D, Ed S), including district leadership (Ed D), higher education administration (Ed D), K-12 education (Ed D); instructional leadership (Ed D, Ed S), including higher education (Ed D), K-12 education (Ed D).

See Close-Up on page 791.

Argosy University, Seattle, College of Education, Seattle, WA 98121. Offers adult education and training (MA Ed); community college executive leadership (Ed D); educational leadership (MA Ed, Ed D), including higher education administration (Ed D), K-12 education (Ed D); higher and postsecondary education (MA Ed); instructional leadership (MA Ed, Ed D), including education technology (Ed D), higher education (Ed D), K-12 education (Ed D).

See Close-Up on page 793.

Argosy University, Tampa, College of Education, Tampa, FL 33607. Offers community college executive leadership (Ed D); educational leadership (MA Ed, Ed D, Ed S), including higher education administration (Ed D), K-12 education (Ed D); school counseling (MA); teaching and learning (MA Ed, Ed D, Ed S), including higher education (Ed D), K-12 education (Ed D).

See Close-Up on page 795.

Argosy University, Twin Cities, College of Education, Eagan, MN 55121. Offers advanced educational administration (Ed D, Ed S); educational leadership (MA Ed, Ed D, Ed S), including higher education administration (Ed D), K-12 education (Ed D); higher and postsecondary education (MA Ed); initial educational administration (Ed D, Ed S); instructional leadership (MA Ed, Ed D, Ed S), including education technology (Ed D), higher education (Ed D), K-12 education (Ed D).

See Close-Up on page 797.

Argosy University, Washington DC, College of Education, Arlington, VA 22209. Offers community college executive leadership (Ed D); educational leadership (MA Ed, Ed D, Ed S), including higher education administration (Ed D), K-12 education (Ed D); instructional leadership (MA Ed, Ed D, Ed S), including higher education (Ed D), K-12 education (Ed D).

See Close-Up on page 799.

Arizona State University, Mary Lou Fulton Teachers College, Phoenix, AZ 85069. Offers M Ed, MA, MC, MPE, Ed D, PhD, Graduate Certificate. Part-time and evening/weekend programs available. Postbaccalaureate distance learning degree programs offered (minimal on-campus study). *Degree requirements:* For master's, comprehensive exam (for some programs), thesis (for some programs), interactive Program of Study (iPOS) submitted before completing 50 percent of required credit hours; for doctorate, comprehensive exam, thesis/dissertation, interactive Program of Study (iPOS) submitted before completing 50 percent of required credit hours. *Entrance requirements:* For master's and doctorate, GRE General Test or GMAT, minimum GPA of 3.0 or equivalent in last 2 years of work leading to bachelor's degree. Additional exam requirements/recommendations for international students: Required—TOEFL (minimum score 80 iBT), TOEFL, IELTS, or Pearson Test of English. Electronic applications accepted. *Expenses:* Contact institution.

Arkansas State University, Graduate School, College of Education, Jonesboro, State University, AR 72467. Offers MAT, MRC, MS, MSE, Ed D, PhD, Certificate, Ed S, SCCT. *Accreditation:* NCATE. Part-time programs available. Postbaccalaureate distance learning degree programs offered (no on-campus study). *Faculty:* 52 full-time (28 women). *Students:* 125 full-time (90 women), 2,434 part-time (1,844 women); includes 470 minority (370 Black or African American, non-Hispanic/Latino; 14 American Indian or Alaska Native, non-Hispanic/Latino; 12 Asian, non-Hispanic/Latino; 48 Hispanic/Latino; 2 Native Hawaiian or other Pacific Islander, non-Hispanic/Latino; 24 Two or more races, non-Hispanic/Latino), 13 international. Average age 36. 1,752 applicants, 74% accepted, 907 enrolled. In 2011, 887 master's, 8 doctorates, 50 other advanced degrees awarded. *Degree requirements:* For master's and other advanced degree, comprehensive exam, thesis or alternative; for doctorate, comprehensive exam, thesis/dissertation. *Entrance requirements:* For master's, GRE General Test or MAT, appropriate bachelor's degree, interview, letters of reference, official transcripts, immunization records; for doctorate, GRE General Test or MAT, interview, master's degree, letters of reference, official transcript, personal statement, immunization records, writing sample; for other advanced degree, GRE General Test, MAT, interview, master's degree, letters of reference, official transcript, 3 years teaching experience, mentor, teaching license, immunization records. Additional exam requirements/recommendations for international students: Required—TOEFL (minimum score 550 paper-based; 213 computer-based; 79 iBT), IELTS (minimum score 6), Pearson Test of English Academic (minimum score 56). *Application deadline:* Applications are processed on a rolling basis. Application fee: $50. Electronic applications accepted. *Expenses:* Tuition, state resident: full-time $4044; part-time $225 per credit hour. Tuition, nonresident: full-time $8087; part-time $449 per credit hour. *Required fees:* $936; $52 per credit hour. $25 per term. One-time fee: $30. Tuition and fees vary according to course load and program. *Financial support:* In 2011–12, 58 students received support. Fellowships, teaching assistantships, career-related internships or fieldwork, scholarships/grants, and unspecified assistantships available. Financial award application deadline: 7/1; financial award applicants required to submit FAFSA. *Unit head:* Dr. Gregory Meeks, Interim Dean, 870-972-3057, Fax: 870-972-3828, E-mail: gmeeks@astate.edu. *Application contact:* Dr. Andrew Sustich, Dean of the Graduate School, 870-972-3029, Fax: 870-972-3857, E-mail: sustich@astate.edu. Web site: http://www.astate.edu/a/education/.

Arkansas Tech University, Center for Leadership and Learning, College of Education, Russellville, AR 72801. Offers college student personnel (MS); educational leadership (Ed S); elementary education (M Ed); instructional improvement (M Ed); instructional technology (M Ed); physical education (M Ed); school counseling and leadership (M Ed); teaching (MAT). *Accreditation:* NCATE. Part-time and evening/weekend programs available. Postbaccalaureate distance learning degree programs offered (no on-campus study). *Students:* 70 full-time (44 women), 247 part-time (189 women); includes 57 minority (38 Black or African American, non-Hispanic/Latino; 1 American Indian or Alaska Native, non-Hispanic/Latino; 8 Asian, non-Hispanic/Latino; 4 Hispanic/Latino; 6 Two or more races, non-Hispanic/Latino), 3 international. Average age 31. In 2011, 58 master's awarded. *Degree requirements:* For master's, comprehensive exam, thesis optional, action research project. *Entrance requirements:* Additional exam requirements/recommendations for international students: Required—TOEFL (minimum score 550 paper-based; 213 computer-based; 79 iBT), IELTS (minimum score 6.5). *Application deadline:* For fall admission, 3/1 priority date for domestic students, 5/1 for international students; for spring admission, 10/1 priority date for domestic students, 10/1 for international students. Applications are processed on a rolling basis. Application fee: $25 ($75 for international students). Electronic applications accepted. *Expenses:* Tuition, state resident: full-time $4968; part-time $207 per credit hour. Tuition, nonresident: full-time $9936; part-time $414 per credit hour. *Required fees:* $375 per semester. Tuition and fees vary according to course load. *Financial support:* In 2011–12, teaching assistantships with full tuition reimbursements (averaging $4,800 per year) were awarded; research assistantships with full tuition reimbursements, career-related internships or fieldwork, Federal Work-Study, scholarships/grants, health care benefits, and unspecified assistantships also available. Support available to part-time students. Financial award application deadline: 4/15; financial award applicants required to submit FAFSA. *Unit head:* Dr. Eldon G. Clary, Jr., Dean, 479-968-0350, Fax: 479-968-0350, E-mail: eclary@atu.edu. *Application contact:* Dr. Mary B. Gunter, Dean of Graduate College, 479-968-0398, Fax: 479-964-0542, E-mail: gradcollege@atu.edu. Web site: http://www.atu.edu/education/.

Armstrong Atlantic State University, School of Graduate Studies, Program in Education, Savannah, GA 31419-1997. Offers adult education (M Ed); curriculum and instruction (M Ed); early childhood education (M Ed); education (M Ed); elementary education (M Ed); middle grades education (M Ed); secondary education (M Ed), including business education, English education, mathematics education, science education, social science education; special education (M Ed), including behavioral disorders, learning disabilities, speech-language pathology. *Accreditation:* NCATE. Part-time and evening/weekend programs available. Postbaccalaureate distance learning degree programs offered (minimal on-campus study). *Faculty:* 33 full-time (23 women), 3 part-time/adjunct (2 women). *Students:* 97 full-time (91 women), 262 part-time (227 women); includes 83 minority (70 Black or African American, non-Hispanic/Latino; 3 Asian, non-Hispanic/Latino; 8 Hispanic/Latino; 2 Two or more races, non-Hispanic/Latino), 5 international. Average age 34. 169 applicants, 69% accepted, 102 enrolled. In 2011, 227 master's awarded. *Degree requirements:* For master's, comprehensive exam, portfolio. *Entrance requirements:* For master's, GRE General Test or MAT, minimum GPA of 2.5, letters of recommendation. Additional exam requirements/recommendations for international students: Required—TOEFL (minimum score 523 paper-based; 193 computer-based). *Application deadline:* For fall admission, 7/1 priority date for domestic students, 5/1 for international students; for spring admission, 11/15 priority date for domestic students, 9/15 for international students. Applications are processed on a rolling basis. Application fee: $30. Electronic applications accepted. *Expenses:* Tuition, state resident: full-time $3402. Tuition, nonresident: full-time $12,636. *Financial support:* In 2011–12, research assistantships with full tuition reimbursements (averaging $5,000 per year) were awarded; career-related internships or fieldwork, Federal Work-Study, scholarships/grants, and unspecified assistantships also available. Support available to part-time students. Financial award applicants required to submit FAFSA. *Unit head:* Dr. Patricia Wachholz, Dean, College of Education, 912-344-2797, E-mail: patricia.wachholz@armstrong.edu. *Application contact:* Jill Bell, Director, Graduate Enrollment Services, 912-344-2798, Fax: 912-344-3488, E-mail: graduate@armstrong.edu. Web site: http://www.armstrong.edu/Education/coe_deans_office/coe_education_welcome.

Ashland University, Dwight Schar College of Education, Ashland, OH 44805-3702. Offers M Ed, Ed D. *Accreditation:* NCATE. Part-time and evening/weekend programs available. *Faculty:* 66 full-time (44 women), 130 part-time/adjunct (77 women). *Students:* 282 full-time (198 women), 576 part-time (395 women); includes 76 minority (57 Black or African American, non-Hispanic/Latino; 3 American Indian or Alaska Native, non-Hispanic/Latino; 2 Asian, non-Hispanic/Latino; 9 Hispanic/Latino; 5 Two or more races, non-Hispanic/Latino), 13 international. Average age 34. 190 applicants, 100% accepted, 167 enrolled. In 2011, 507 master's, 5 doctorates awarded. *Degree requirements:* For master's, thesis optional, capstone project; for doctorate, comprehensive exam, thesis/dissertation. *Entrance requirements:* For master's, GRE General Test or MAT, teaching certificate, minimum GPA of 2.75; for doctorate, GRE, master's degree, minimum GPA of 3.3, writing sample, letters of recommendation. Additional exam requirements/recommendations for international students: Required—TOEFL. *Application deadline:* For fall admission, 8/27 for domestic students; for spring admission, 1/14 for domestic students. Applications are processed on a rolling basis. Application fee: $30. *Expenses: Tuition:* Full-time $5580; part-time $465 per credit hour. *Financial support:* In 2011–12, 3 students received support. Teaching assistantships with partial tuition reimbursements available and scholarships/grants available. Financial award application deadline: 4/15. *Faculty research:* Teacher performance, administrative performance, collaborative learning groups, talent development, environmental education. *Total annual research expenditures:* $180,000. *Unit head:* Dr. James P. Van Keuren, Dean, 419-289-5377, E-mail: jvankeu1@ashland.edu. *Application contact:* Dr. Linda Billman, Associate Dean, 419-289-5369, Fax: 419-289-5331, E-mail: lbillman@ashland.edu.

Athabasca University, Centre for Distance Education, Athabasca, AB T9S 3A3, Canada. Offers distance education (MDE); distance education technology (Advanced Diploma). Part-time programs available. Postbaccalaureate distance learning degree programs offered (no on-campus study). *Degree requirements:* For master's, thesis optional. *Entrance requirements:* For master's, 3 or 4 year baccalaureate degree. Electronic applications accepted. *Expenses:* Contact institution. *Faculty research:* Role development, interaction, educational technology, and communities of practice in distance education; instructional design.

Athabasca University, Centre for Integrated Studies, Athabasca, AB T9S 3A3, Canada. Offers adult education (MA); community studies (MA); cultural studies (MA); educational studies (MA); global change (MA); work, organization, and leadership (MA). Part-time and evening/weekend programs available. Postbaccalaureate distance learning degree programs offered (no on-campus study). *Degree requirements:* For master's, project. *Entrance requirements:* Additional exam requirements/recommendations for international students: Required—TOEFL (minimum score 560 paper-based; 220 computer-based). Electronic applications accepted. *Faculty research:* Women's history, literature and culture studies, sustainable development, labor and education.

Auburn University, Graduate School, College of Education, Auburn University, AL 36849. Offers M Ed, MS, Ed D, PhD, Ed S, Graduate Certificate. *Accreditation:* NCATE. Part-time programs available. *Faculty:* 84 full-time (55 women), 11 part-time/adjunct (9 women). *Students:* 351 full-time (242 women), 530 part-time (354 women); includes 215 minority (184 Black or African American, non-Hispanic/Latino; 3 American Indian or Alaska Native, non-Hispanic/Latino; 14 Asian, non-Hispanic/Latino; 14 Hispanic/Latino), 23 international. Average age 33. 662 applicants, 55% accepted, 246 enrolled. In 2011, 237 master's, 56 doctorates, 57 other advanced degrees awarded. *Degree requirements:* For master's, thesis (for some programs); for doctorate, thesis/dissertation. *Entrance requirements:* For master's, doctorate, and other advanced degree, GRE General Test. Application fee: $50 ($60 for international students). Electronic applications accepted. *Expenses:* Tuition, state resident: full-time $7290; part-time $405 per credit hour. Tuition, nonresident: full-time $21,870; part-time $1215 per credit hour. *International tuition:* $22,000 full-time. *Required fees:* $1402. *Financial support:* Fellowships, research assistantships, teaching assistantships, career-related internships or fieldwork, and Federal Work-Study available. Support available to part-time students. Financial award application deadline: 3/15; financial award applicants required to submit FAFSA. *Faculty research:* Dropout phenomena, high school students and substance use and abuse. *Unit head:* Dr. Betty Lou Whitford, Dean, 334-844-4446. *Application contact:* Dr. George Flowers, Dean of the Graduate School, 334-844-2125. Web site: http://www.education.auburn.edu/.

Auburn University Montgomery, School of Education, Montgomery, AL 36124-4023. Offers M Ed, Ed S. *Accreditation:* NCATE. Part-time and evening/weekend programs available. *Degree requirements:* For master's and Ed S, comprehensive exam. *Entrance requirements:* For master's, GRE General Test or MAT, BS in teaching, certification; for Ed S, GRE General Test or MAT, certification. Electronic applications accepted. *Expenses:* Tuition, state resident: full-time $5076. Tuition, nonresident: full-time $15,228.

Augsburg College, Program in Education, Minneapolis, MN 55454-1351. Offers MAE. *Accreditation:* NCATE. Part-time and evening/weekend programs available. *Degree requirements:* For master's, comprehensive exam, final project. *Entrance requirements:* For master's, minimum GPA of 3.0. Additional exam requirements/recommendations for

international students: Required—TOEFL (minimum score 600 paper-based; 250 computer-based). Electronic applications accepted.

Augustana College, Department of Education, Sioux Falls, SD 57197. Offers MA. *Accreditation:* NCATE. Part-time and evening/weekend programs available. Postbaccalaureate distance learning degree programs offered (no on-campus study). *Faculty:* 6 full-time (4 women), 3 part-time/adjunct (2 women). *Students:* 15 part-time (11 women). 24 applicants, 67% accepted, 15 enrolled. In 2011, 1 master's awarded. *Degree requirements:* For master's, thesis, synthesis portfolio, paper, oral exam. *Entrance requirements:* For master's, appropriate bachelor's degree, minimum GPA of 3.0, teaching certificate. Additional exam requirements/recommendations for international students: Required—TOEFL. *Application deadline:* For spring admission, 5/11 priority date for domestic students, 5/11 for international students. Applications are processed on a rolling basis. Application fee: $50. Electronic applications accepted. *Expenses:* Contact institution. *Financial support:* Career-related internships or fieldwork, Federal Work-Study, institutionally sponsored loans, scholarships/grants, tuition waivers (partial), and unspecified assistantships available. Financial award application deadline: 3/1; financial award applicants required to submit FAFSA. *Faculty research:* Classroom management, stress management, youth at-risk. *Unit head:* Dr. Sheryl Feinstein, Education Master's Program Director, 605-274-5211, E-mail: sheryl.feinstein@augie.edu. *Application contact:* Nancy Wright, Graduate Coordinator, 605-274-4043, Fax: 605-274-4450, E-mail: graduate@augie.edu. Web site: http://www.augie.edu/academics/graduate-education/master-arts-education.

Augusta State University, Graduate Studies, College of Education, Augusta, GA 30904-2200. Offers M Ed, MAT, Ed S. *Accreditation:* NCATE. Part-time and evening/weekend programs available. *Faculty:* 31 full-time (16 women), 28 part-time/adjunct (23 women). *Students:* 356 full-time (294 women), 389 part-time (307 women); includes 259 minority (233 Black or African American, non-Hispanic/Latino; 2 American Indian or Alaska Native, non-Hispanic/Latino; 9 Asian, non-Hispanic/Latino; 15 Hispanic/Latino). Average age 36. 239 applicants, 82% accepted, 168 enrolled. In 2011, 72 master's, 97 other advanced degrees awarded. *Entrance requirements:* For master's, GRE, MAT, minimum GPA of 2.5. *Application deadline:* For fall admission, 7/16 priority date for domestic students. Applications are processed on a rolling basis. Application fee: $20. *Financial support:* Career-related internships or fieldwork, Federal Work-Study, institutionally sponsored loans, and unspecified assistantships available. Support available to part-time students. Financial award application deadline: 4/15; financial award applicants required to submit FAFSA. *Unit head:* Dr. Richard Harrison, Dean, 706-737-1499, Fax: 706-667-4706, E-mail: vharriso@aug.edu. *Application contact:* Andrea M. Scott, Secretary to the Dean, 706-737-1499, Fax: 706-667-4706, E-mail: ascott1@aug.edu.

Aurora University, College of Education, Aurora, IL 60506-4892. Offers curriculum and instruction (MA, Ed D); early childhood and special education (MA); education (MAT), including elementary certification; education and administration (Ed D); educational leadership (MEL); educational technology (MATL); reading instruction (MA); special education (MA). *Accreditation:* NCATE. Part-time and evening/weekend programs available. *Degree requirements:* For doctorate, comprehensive exam, thesis/dissertation. *Entrance requirements:* For master's, 2 years of teaching experience, valid teaching certificate. Additional exam requirements/recommendations for international students: Required—TOEFL (minimum score 550 paper-based; 213 computer-based). Electronic applications accepted. *Expenses:* Contact institution.

Austin College, Program in Education, Sherman, TX 75090-4400. Offers art education (MA); elementary education (MA); middle school education (MA); music education (MA); physical education and coaching (MA); secondary education (MA); theatre education (MA). Part-time programs available. *Faculty:* 5 full-time (4 women). *Students:* 21 full-time (13 women), 2 part-time (both women). Average age 23. In 2011, 24 master's awarded. *Degree requirements:* For master's, one foreign language, thesis or alternative. *Entrance requirements:* For master's, Texas Academic Skills Program Test. *Application deadline:* For fall admission, 5/1 priority date for domestic students; for spring admission, 1/15 priority date for domestic students. Applications are processed on a rolling basis. Application fee: $35. Electronic applications accepted. *Expenses: Tuition:* Full-time $38,445. *Required fees:* $160. *Financial support:* Career-related internships or fieldwork, Federal Work-Study, scholarships/grants, and unspecified assistantships available. Support available to part-time students. Financial award application deadline: 4/1; financial award applicants required to submit FAFSA. *Unit head:* Dr. Barbara Sylvester, Director of Teaching Program, 903-813-2327, E-mail: bsylvester@austincollege.edu. *Application contact:* Dr. Barbara Sylvester, Director of Teaching Program, 903-813-2327, E-mail: bsylvester@austincollege.edu. Web site: http://www.austincollege.edu/.

Austin Peay State University, College of Graduate Studies, College of Education, Clarksville, TN 37044. Offers MA Ed, MAT, Ed S. *Accreditation:* NCATE. Part-time and evening/weekend programs available. Postbaccalaureate distance learning degree programs offered. *Faculty:* 21 full-time (15 women), 7 part-time/adjunct (5 women). *Students:* 90 full-time (71 women), 183 part-time (147 women); includes 38 minority (18 Black or African American, non-Hispanic/Latino; 3 American Indian or Alaska Native, non-Hispanic/Latino; 2 Asian, non-Hispanic/Latino; 8 Hispanic/Latino; 1 Native Hawaiian or other Pacific Islander, non-Hispanic/Latino; 6 Two or more races, non-Hispanic/Latino). Average age 34. 94 applicants, 99% accepted, 74 enrolled. In 2011, 87 master's, 7 other advanced degrees awarded. *Degree requirements:* For master's, comprehensive exam, thesis optional. *Entrance requirements:* For master's, GRE General Test, 3 letters of recommendation, minimum undergraduate GPA of 2.75; for Ed S, GRE General Test, master's degree, minimum graduate GPA of 3.0, 3 letters of recommendation. Additional exam requirements/recommendations for international students: Required—TOEFL (minimum score 500 paper-based; 173 computer-based). *Application deadline:* For fall admission, 8/1 priority date for domestic students. Applications are processed on a rolling basis. Application fee: $25. Electronic applications accepted. *Expenses:* Tuition, state resident: part-time $350 per credit hour. Tuition, nonresident: full-time $20,644; part-time $971 per credit hour. *Required fees:* $1224; $61.20 per credit hour. *Financial support:* In 2011–12, research assistantships with full tuition reimbursements (averaging $5,184 per year) were awarded; career-related internships or fieldwork, Federal Work-Study, institutionally sponsored loans, scholarships/grants, and unspecified assistantships also available. Support available to part-time students. Financial award application deadline: 3/1; financial award applicants required to submit FAFSA. *Unit head:* Dr. Carlette Hardin, Director, 931-221-7696, Fax: 931-221-1292, E-mail: hardinc@apsu.edu. *Application contact:* Kendra Bryant, Graduate Admissions, 800-844-2778, Fax: 931-221-6188, E-mail: admissionsweb@apsu.edu. Web site: http://www.apsu.edu/educ/.

Averett University, Master in Education Program, Danville, VA 24541-3692. Offers curriculum and instruction (M Ed); English (M Ed). Program offered at Richmond, VA regional campus location. Part-time and evening/weekend programs available. *Faculty:* 9 full-time (2 women). *Students:* 234 full-time (165 women), 403 part-time (241 women); includes 168 minority (149 Black or African American, non-Hispanic/Latino; 1 American Indian or Alaska Native, non-Hispanic/Latino; 9 Asian, non-Hispanic/Latino; 9 Hispanic/Latino), 1 international. Average age 32. 59 applicants, 59% accepted, 21 enrolled. *Degree requirements:* For master's, 30-credit core curriculum, minimum GPA of 3.0 throughout program, completion of degree requirements within six years from start of program. *Entrance requirements:* For master's, minimum cumulative GPA of 3.0 over the last 60 semester hours of undergraduate study toward a baccalaureate degree. Additional exam requirements/recommendations for international students: Required—TOEFL (minimum score 600 paper-based; 250 computer-based; 100 iBT). *Application deadline:* Applications are processed on a rolling basis. Application fee: $100. *Expenses:* Contact institution. *Financial support:* Career-related internships or fieldwork, Federal Work-Study, and scholarships/grants available. Financial award application deadline: 4/1; financial award applicants required to submit FAFSA. *Unit head:* Dr. Nick Kalafatis, Director of Graduate Education Program, 804-720-4661, E-mail: nkalafat@averett.edu. Web site: http://www.averett.edu/adultprograms/admissions/forms/AVT%20Med_Insert_2-18-11.pdf.

Avila University, School of Education, Kansas City, MO 64145-1698. Offers education (MA); English for speakers of other languages (Advanced Certificate). Part-time and evening/weekend programs available. *Faculty:* 6 full-time (5 women), 5 part-time/adjunct (3 women). *Students:* 113 full-time (84 women), 33 part-time (28 women); includes 25 minority (15 Black or African American, non-Hispanic/Latino; 4 American Indian or Alaska Native, non-Hispanic/Latino; 4 Hispanic/Latino; 2 Two or more races, non-Hispanic/Latino), 2 international. Average age 34. 66 applicants, 79% accepted, 47 enrolled. In 2011, 20 master's awarded. *Entrance requirements:* For master's, minimum GPA of 3.0, writing sample, recommendation, interview; for Advanced Certificate, foreign language. Additional exam requirements/recommendations for international students: Required—TOEFL (minimum score 580 paper-based; 237 computer-based; 92 iBT). *Application deadline:* Applications are processed on a rolling basis. Electronic applications accepted. *Expenses:* Contact institution. *Financial support:* In 2011–12, 64 students received support, including 1 research assistantship; career-related internships or fieldwork also available. Support available to part-time students. Financial award applicants required to submit FAFSA. *Unit head:* Deana Angotti, Director of Graduate Education, 816-501-2446, Fax: 816-501-2915, E-mail: deana.angotti@avila.edu. *Application contact:* Margaret Longstreet, 816-501-2464, E-mail: margaret.longstreet@avila.edu.

Azusa Pacific University, School of Education, Azusa, CA 91702-7000. Offers M Ed, MA, MA Ed, Ed D, Credential. Part-time and evening/weekend programs available. *Degree requirements:* For doctorate, oral defense of dissertation, qualifying exam. *Entrance requirements:* For master's, minimum GPA of 3.0; for doctorate, GRE General Test or MAT, 5 years of experience, writing sample. Additional exam requirements/recommendations for international students: Required—TOEFL.

Baker University, School of Education, Baldwin City, KS 66006-0065. Offers MA Ed, MSSE, MSSL, MST, Ed D. Master-level programs also offered in Wichita, KS. *Accreditation:* NCATE. Part-time and evening/weekend programs available. Postbaccalaureate distance learning degree programs offered (minimal on-campus study). *Students:* 70 full-time (59 women), 535 part-time (390 women); includes 53 minority (33 Black or African American, non-Hispanic/Latino; 2 American Indian or Alaska Native, non-Hispanic/Latino; 1 Asian, non-Hispanic/Latino; 12 Hispanic/Latino; 5 Two or more races, non-Hispanic/Latino). Average age 35. In 2011, 407 master's, 8 doctorates awarded. *Degree requirements:* For master's, portfolio of learning; for doctorate, thesis/dissertation, portfolio of learning. *Entrance requirements:* For master's, 2 years full-time work experience, teaching certificate; for doctorate, interview. Additional exam requirements/recommendations for international students: Required—TOEFL (minimum score 600 paper-based; 250 computer-based; 100 iBT). *Application deadline:* Applications are processed on a rolling basis. *Expenses:* Contact institution. *Financial support:* Applicants required to submit FAFSA. *Unit head:* Dr. Peggy Harris, Vice President and Dean, 785-594-8492, Fax: 785-594-8363, E-mail: peggy.harris@bakeru.edu. *Application contact:* Judy Favor, Director of Graduate Program, 913-491-4432, Fax: 913-491-0470, E-mail: jfavor@bakeru.edu. Web site: http://www.bakeru.edu/soe-home.

Baldwin Wallace University, Graduate Programs, Division of Education, Berea, OH 44017-2088. Offers educational technology (MA Ed); leadership in higher education (MA Ed); literacy (MA Ed); mild/moderate educational needs (MA Ed); school leadership (MA Ed); teaching and learning (MA Ed). *Accreditation:* NCATE. Part-time and evening/weekend programs available. Postbaccalaureate distance learning degree programs offered. *Faculty:* 9 full-time (4 women), 7 part-time/adjunct (4 women). *Students:* 94 full-time (71 women), 71 part-time (55 women); includes 20 minority (15 Black or African American, non-Hispanic/Latino; 3 Hispanic/Latino; 2 Two or more races, non-Hispanic/Latino). Average age 31. 114 applicants, 50% accepted, 33 enrolled. In 2011, 97 master's awarded. *Degree requirements:* For master's, comprehensive exam. *Entrance requirements:* For master's, bachelor's degree in field, MAT or minimum GPA of 2.75. Additional exam requirements/recommendations for international students: Required—TOEFL (minimum score 523 paper-based; 193 computer-based; 70 iBT). *Application deadline:* For fall admission, 8/15 priority date for domestic students; for spring admission, 12/15 priority date for domestic students. Applications are processed on a rolling basis. Application fee: $25. Electronic applications accepted. Application fee is waived when completed online. *Expenses:* Contact institution. *Financial support:* Career-related internships or fieldwork available. Support available to part-time students. Financial award application deadline: 5/1; financial award applicants required to submit FAFSA. *Faculty research:* Literacy, technology and literacy, diversity in education, assessment, special education, research methodology, leadership. *Unit head:* Dr. Karen Kaye, Chair, 440-826-2168, Fax: 440-826-3779, E-mail: kkaye@bw.edu. *Application contact:* Winifred W. Gerhardt, Director of Admission for the Evening and Weekend College, 440-826-2222, Fax: 440-826-3830, E-mail: admission@bw.edu. Web site: http://www.bw.edu/academics/mae/programs/.

Ball State University, Graduate School, Teachers College, Muncie, IN 47306-1099. Offers MA, MAE, Ed D, PhD, Ed S, Graduate Certificate. *Accreditation:* NCATE. Part-time and evening/weekend programs available. Postbaccalaureate distance learning degree programs offered (no on-campus study). *Faculty:* 123. *Students:* 590 full-time (418 women), 1,956 part-time (1,539 women); includes 171 minority (109 Black or African American, non-Hispanic/Latino; 4 American Indian or Alaska Native, non-Hispanic/Latino; 17 Asian, non-Hispanic/Latino; 24 Hispanic/Latino; 17 Two or more races, non-Hispanic/Latino), 46 international. Average age 28. 1,394 applicants, 59% accepted, 590 enrolled. In 2011, 482 master's, 36 doctorates, 16 other advanced degrees awarded. Terminal master's awarded for partial completion of doctoral program. *Degree requirements:* For doctorate, comprehensive exam, thesis/dissertation; for other advanced degree, comprehensive exam, thesis. *Entrance requirements:* For master's, minimum undergraduate GPA of 2.75 (for most programs); for doctorate, GRE General Test, minimum graduate GPA of 3.2; for other advanced degree, GRE General Test. Additional exam requirements/recommendations for international students: Required—TOEFL (minimum score 550 paper-based; 213 computer-based), IELTS (minimum score 6.5). *Application deadline:* For fall admission, 1/1 for international students. Application fee: $50. Tuition and fees vary according to program and reciprocity agreements. *Financial support:* In 2011–12, 287 students received support, including 205 teaching assistantships with full tuition reimbursements available (averaging $11,947 per year); research assistantships with full tuition reimbursements available, career-related internships or fieldwork, and Federal Work-

Study also available. Support available to part-time students. Financial award application deadline: 3/1. *Unit head:* Dr. John E. Jacobson, Dean, 765-285-5251, Fax: 765-285-5455, E-mail: jejacobson@bsu.edu. *Application contact:* Dr. Robert Morris, Associate Provost for Research and Dean of the Graduate School, 765-285-1300, E-mail: rmorris@bsu.edu. Web site: http://www.bsu.edu/teachers/.

Bank Street College of Education, Graduate School, New York, NY 10025. Offers Ed M, MS, MS Ed. *Faculty:* 72 full-time (61 women), 56 part-time/adjunct (47 women). *Students:* 372 full-time (329 women), 526 part-time (461 women); includes 231 minority (85 Black or African American, non-Hispanic/Latino; 3 American Indian or Alaska Native, non-Hispanic/Latino; 39 Asian, non-Hispanic/Latino; 77 Hispanic/Latino; 2 Native Hawaiian or other Pacific Islander, non-Hispanic/Latino; 25 Two or more races, non-Hispanic/Latino), 11 international. Average age 30. 638 applicants, 79% accepted, 352 enrolled. In 2011, 325 master's awarded. *Degree requirements:* For master's, thesis. *Entrance requirements:* For master's, interview, essays. Additional exam requirements/recommendations for international students: Required—TOEFL (minimum score 600 paper-based; 250 computer-based; 100 iBT), IELTS (minimum score 7). *Application deadline:* For fall admission, 2/15 priority date for domestic students, 2/15 for international students; for spring admission, 11/1 priority date for domestic students, 11/1 for international students. Applications are processed on a rolling basis. Application fee: $65. Electronic applications accepted. *Expenses: Required fees:* $1240 per credit. $100 per term. One-time fee: $250 part-time. *Financial support:* In 2011–12, 674 students received support. Career-related internships or fieldwork, Federal Work-Study, scholarships/grants, and unspecified assistantships available. Support available to part-time students. Financial award application deadline: 4/15; financial award applicants required to submit FAFSA. *Faculty research:* Understanding developmental variations in inclusive classrooms, urban teacher education and technology, learner-centered education, improving teacher preparation. *Unit head:* Dr. Virginia Roach, Dean, 212-875-4668, Fax: 212-875-4753, E-mail: vroach@bankstreet.edu. *Application contact:* Ann Morgan, Director of Graduate Admissions, 212-875-4403, Fax: 212-875-4678, E-mail: amorgan@bankstreet.edu. Web site: http://www.bankstreet.edu/graduate-school.

Baptist Bible College of Pennsylvania, Graduate School, Clarks Summit, PA 18411-1297. Offers Bible (MA); counseling (MS); education (MS). Part-time and evening/weekend programs available. Postbaccalaureate distance learning degree programs offered (no on-campus study). *Entrance requirements:* Additional exam requirements/recommendations for international students: Required—TOEFL (minimum score 500 paper-based; 173 computer-based).

Bard College, Master of Arts in Teaching Program, Annandale-on-Hudson, NY 12504. Offers MAT. *Degree requirements:* For master's, 2 research projects, field work. *Entrance requirements:* For master's, resume, 3 letters of recommendation. Additional exam requirements/recommendations for international students: Required—TOEFL. Electronic applications accepted.

Barry University, School of Education, Miami Shores, FL 33161-6695. Offers MS, Ed D, PhD, Certificate, Ed S. Part-time and evening/weekend programs available. Postbaccalaureate distance learning degree programs offered. *Degree requirements:* For master's, comprehensive exam; for doctorate, thesis/dissertation. *Entrance requirements:* For master's, GRE General Test or MAT, minimum GPA of 3.0; for doctorate, GRE General Test, minimum GPA of 3.25; for other advanced degree, GRE General Test, minimum GPA of 3.0. Additional exam requirements/recommendations for international students: Required—TOEFL (minimum score 550 paper-based; 213 computer-based). Electronic applications accepted.

Bayamón Central University, Graduate Programs, Program in Education, Bayamón, PR 00960-1725. Offers administration and supervision (MA Ed); commercial education (MA Ed); elementary education (K–3) (MA Ed); family counseling (Graduate Certificate); guidance and counseling (MA Ed); pre-elementary teacher (MA Ed); rehabilitation counseling (MA Ed); special education (MA Ed), including attention deficit disorder, education of the autistic, learning disabilities. Part-time and evening/weekend programs available. *Degree requirements:* For master's, comprehensive exam. *Entrance requirements:* For master's, EXADEP, bachelor's degree in education or related field.

Baylor University, Graduate School, School of Education, Waco, TX 76798. Offers MA, MS Ed, Ed D, PhD, Ed S. *Accreditation:* NCATE. Part-time programs available. Postbaccalaureate distance learning degree programs offered (minimal on-campus study). *Students:* 165 full-time (119 women), 66 part-time (34 women); includes 37 minority (11 Black or African American, non-Hispanic/Latino; 7 Asian, non-Hispanic/Latino; 14 Hispanic/Latino; 5 Two or more races, non-Hispanic/Latino), 13 international. 248 applicants, 35% accepted, 28 enrolled. In 2011, 83 master's, 4 doctorates, 10 other advanced degrees awarded. *Degree requirements:* For doctorate, thesis/dissertation. *Application deadline:* Applications are processed on a rolling basis. Application fee: $25. Electronic applications accepted. *Financial support:* Research assistantships, teaching assistantships, career-related internships or fieldwork, Federal Work-Study, institutionally sponsored loans, scholarships/grants, and tuition waivers (partial) available. *Unit head:* Dr. Jon Engelhardt, Dean, 254-710-3111, Fax: 254-710-3987. *Application contact:* Julie Baker, Administrative Assistant, 254-710-3050, Fax: 254-710-3870, E-mail: julie_baker@baylor.edu. Web site: http://www.baylor.edu/soe/.

Belhaven University, School of Education, Jackson, MS 39202-1789. Offers elementary education (M Ed, MAT); secondary education (M Ed, MAT). Part-time and evening/weekend programs available. *Faculty:* 7 full-time (6 women), 15 part-time/adjunct (10 women). *Students:* 167 full-time (133 women), 124 part-time (97 women); includes 205 minority (193 Black or African American, non-Hispanic/Latino; 7 Hispanic/Latino; 5 Two or more races, non-Hispanic/Latino). Average age 33. 446 applicants, 64% accepted, 210 enrolled. In 2011, 94 master's awarded. *Degree requirements:* For master's, comprehensive exam, portfolio. *Entrance requirements:* For master's, PRAXIS I and II, minimum GPA of 2.8. *Application deadline:* Applications are processed on a rolling basis. Application fee: $25. Electronic applications accepted. *Expenses: Tuition:* Part-time $545 per contact hour. *Financial support:* Federal Work-Study, scholarships/grants, tuition waivers (full), and unspecified assistantships available. Support available to part-time students. Financial award applicants required to submit FAFSA. *Unit head:* Dr. Sandra L. Rasberry, Dean, 601-968-8703, Fax: 601-974-6461, E-mail: srasberry@belhaven.edu. *Application contact:* Jenny Mixon, Director of Graduate and Online Admission, 601-968-8947, Fax: 601-968-5953, E-mail: gradadmission@belhaven.edu. Web site: http://graduateed.belhaven.edu.

Bellarmine University, Annsley Frazier Thornton School of Education, Louisville, KY 40205-0671. Offers early elementary education (MA Ed, MAT); education and social change (PhD); learning and behavior disorders (MA Ed, MAT); middle school education (MA Ed, MAT); principalship (Ed S); reading and writing endorsement (MA Ed); secondary school education (MAT); teacher leadership, grades P-12 (MA Ed). *Accreditation:* NCATE. Part-time and evening/weekend programs available. *Faculty:* 13 full-time (6 women), 12 part-time/adjunct (10 women). *Students:* 85 full-time (65 women), 186 part-time (144 women); includes 30 minority (22 Black or African American, non-Hispanic/Latino; 1 American Indian or Alaska Native, non-Hispanic/Latino; 6 Asian, non-Hispanic/Latino; 1 Hispanic/Latino). Average age 33. In 2011, 105 master's awarded. *Degree requirements:* For master's, comprehensive exam, thesis (for some programs); for doctorate, comprehensive exam, thesis/dissertation. *Entrance requirements:* For master's, GRE, baccalaureate degree from accredited institution; minimum overall GPA of 2.75, 3.0 in major; letters of recommendation; valid Kentucky provisional or professional certificate; for doctorate, GRE, minimum GPA of 3.5 in all graduate coursework completed at time of application; baccalaureate and master's degrees in education (MA, MS) or fields directly relevant to education; three letters of recommendation; two essays (no more than 1,000 words each); interview. Additional exam requirements/recommendations for international students: Required—TOEFL (minimum score 550 paper-based; 213 computer-based; 80 iBT). *Application deadline:* Applications are processed on a rolling basis. Application fee: $25. *Expenses:* Contact institution. *Financial support:* Scholarships/grants available. Financial award applicants required to submit FAFSA. *Faculty research:* Literacy, service-learning, dispositions, educational technology, special education. *Unit head:* Dr. Robert Cooter, Dean, 502-272-8191, Fax: 502-272-8189, E-mail: rcooter@bellarmine.edu. *Application contact:* Theresa Klapheke, Administrative Director of Graduate Programs, 502-272-8271, Fax: 502-272-8002, E-mail: tklapheke@bellarmine.edu. Web site: http://www.bellarmine.edu/education/graduate.

Belmont University, College of Arts and Sciences, Department of Education, Nashville, TN 37212-3757. Offers education (M Ed); elementary education (MAT), including early childhood education, elementary education, language arts education; English (MAT); history (MAT); mathematics (MAT); middle grade education (MAT); science (MAT); secondary education (MAT); special education (MAT); sports administration (MSA). *Accreditation:* NCATE. Part-time and evening/weekend programs available. *Faculty:* 11 full-time (8 women), 23 part-time/adjunct (12 women). *Students:* 83 full-time (77 women), 205 part-time (162 women); includes 50 minority (36 Black or African American, non-Hispanic/Latino; 1 American Indian or Alaska Native, non-Hispanic/Latino; 1 Asian, non-Hispanic/Latino; 7 Hispanic/Latino; 5 Two or more races, non-Hispanic/Latino), 2 international. Average age 30. 83 applicants, 67% accepted, 35 enrolled. In 2011, 169 master's awarded. *Degree requirements:* For master's, thesis (for some programs). *Entrance requirements:* For master's, MAT or GRE and/or GMAT, minimum GPA of 2.75. Additional exam requirements/recommendations for international students: Required—TOEFL. *Application deadline:* For fall admission, 8/1 priority date for domestic students, 6/1 for international students; for spring admission, 12/1 priority date for domestic students, 10/1 for international students. Applications are processed on a rolling basis. Application fee: $50. *Expenses:* Contact institution. *Financial support:* In 2011–12, 30 students received support. Fellowships with partial tuition reimbursements available, teaching assistantships with partial tuition reimbursements available, institutionally sponsored loans, tuition waivers (partial), and unspecified assistantships available. Financial award application deadline: 4/15; financial award applicants required to submit FAFSA. *Faculty research:* Improving secondary literacy, Montessori, classroom management strategies, teacher residency programs, online professional development, mentoring, leadership, faculty development. *Total annual research expenditures:* $2,500. *Unit head:* Dr. Cynthia R. Watkins, Associate Dean, 615-460-6053, Fax: 615-460-5556, E-mail: cynthia.watkins@belmont.edu. *Application contact:* Andrea McClain, Admission/Licensure Officer, 615-460-5483, Fax: 615-460-5556, E-mail: andrea.mcclain@belmont.edu.

Bemidji State University, School of Graduate Studies, Bemidji, MN 56601-2699. Offers biology (MS); counseling psychology (MS); education (M Ed, MS); English (MA, MS); environmental studies (MS); mathematics (MS); mathematics (elementary and middle level education) (MS); special education (M Sp Ed, MS). Part-time programs available. Postbaccalaureate distance learning degree programs offered (no on-campus study). *Faculty:* 114 full-time (47 women), 22 part-time/adjunct (16 women). *Students:* 68 full-time (45 women), 311 part-time (198 women); includes 21 minority (4 Black or African American, non-Hispanic/Latino; 2 American Indian or Alaska Native, non-Hispanic/Latino; 5 Asian, non-Hispanic/Latino; 5 Hispanic/Latino; 5 Two or more races, non-Hispanic/Latino), 5 international. Average age 34. 82 applicants, 98% accepted, 37 enrolled. In 2011, 72 master's awarded. *Degree requirements:* For master's, comprehensive exam, thesis (for some programs). *Entrance requirements:* For master's, GRE, letters of recommendation, letters of interest. Additional exam requirements/recommendations for international students: Required—TOEFL (minimum score 550 paper-based; 213 computer-based; 80 iBT). *Application deadline:* Applications are processed on a rolling basis. Application fee: $20. Electronic applications accepted. *Expenses:* Tuition, state resident: full-time $6182; part-time $343.45 per credit. Tuition, nonresident: full-time $6182; part-time $343.45 per credit. *Required fees:* $954. *Financial support:* In 2011–12, 253 students received support, including 36 research assistantships with partial tuition reimbursements available (averaging $7,441 per year), 36 teaching assistantships with partial tuition reimbursements available (averaging $7,441 per year); career-related internships or fieldwork, scholarships/grants, health care benefits, and unspecified assistantships also available. Support available to part-time students. Financial award application deadline: 4/15; financial award applicants required to submit FAFSA. *Unit head:* Dr. Patricia Rogers, Dean of Health Sciences and Human Ecology, 218-755-2027, Fax: 218-755-2258, E-mail: progers@bemidjistate.edu. *Application contact:* Joan Miller, Senior Office and Administrative Specialist, 218-755-2027, Fax: 218-755-2258, E-mail: jmiller@bemidjistate.edu. Web site: http://www.bemidjistate.edu/academics/graduate_studies/.

Benedictine University, Graduate Programs, Program in Education, Lisle, IL 60532-0900. Offers curriculum and instruction and collaborative teaching (M Ed); elementary education (MA Ed); leadership and administration (M Ed); reading and literacy (M Ed); secondary education (MA Ed); special education (MA Ed). Part-time and evening/weekend programs available. *Faculty:* 4 full-time (2 women), 52 part-time/adjunct (30 women). *Students:* 178 full-time (157 women), 239 part-time (211 women); includes 41 minority (29 Black or African American, non-Hispanic/Latino; 4 Asian, non-Hispanic/Latino; 8 Hispanic/Latino), 2 international. Average age 33. 177 applicants, 44% accepted, 68 enrolled. In 2011, 278 master's awarded. *Degree requirements:* For master's, comprehensive exam, thesis (for some programs). *Entrance requirements:* For master's, GRE or MAT. Additional exam requirements/recommendations for international students: Required—TOEFL (minimum score 550 paper-based; 213 computer-based). *Application deadline:* For fall admission, 9/1 for domestic students; for winter admission, 12/1 for domestic students; for spring admission, 2/15 for domestic students. Applications are processed on a rolling basis. Application fee: $40. Electronic applications accepted. *Expenses:* Contact institution. *Financial support:* Career-related internships or fieldwork and health care benefits available. Support available to part-time students. *Unit head:* MeShelda Jackson, Director, 630-829-6282, E-mail: mjackson@ben.edu. *Application contact:* Kari Gibbons, Associate Vice President, Enrollment Center, 630-829-6200, Fax: 630-829-6584, E-mail: kgibbons@ben.edu.

Bennington College, Graduate Programs, MA in Teaching a Second Language Program, Bennington, VT 05201. Offers education (MATSL); foreign language education (MATSL); French (MATSL); Spanish (MATSL). Part-time programs available. *Faculty:* 2 full-time (both women), 5 part-time/adjunct (3 women). *Students:* 19 part-time (all women); includes 3 minority (1 Black or African American, non-Hispanic/Latino; 2 Hispanic/Latino). Average age 42. 13 applicants, 92% accepted, 9 enrolled. In 2011, 5 master's awarded. *Degree requirements:* For master's, one foreign language, 2 major projects and presentations. *Entrance requirements:* For master's, Oral Proficiency Interview (OPI). Additional exam requirements/recommendations for international students: Required—TOEFL (minimum score 577 paper-based; 233 computer-based; 91 iBT). *Application deadline:* For spring admission, 4/1 priority date for domestic students, 4/1 for international students. Applications are processed on a rolling basis. Application fee: $60. *Expenses:* Contact institution. *Financial support:* In 2011–12, 4 students received support. Scholarships/grants available. Financial award application deadline: 4/1; financial award applicants required to submit FAFSA. *Faculty research:* Acquisition, evaluation, assessment, conceptual teaching and learning, content-driven communication, applied linguistics. *Unit head:* Carol Meyer, Director, 802-440-4375, E-mail: cmeyer@bennington.edu. *Application contact:* Nancy Pearlman, Assistant Director, 802-440-4710, E-mail: matsl@bennington.edu. Web site: http://www.bennington.edu/Academics/GraduateCertificatePrograms/MATSL.aspx.

Berry College, Graduate Programs, Graduate Programs in Education, Mount Berry, GA 30149-0159. Offers early childhood education (M Ed, MAT); leadership in curriculum and instruction (Ed S), including curriculum and instruction, educational leadership; middle grades education and reading (M Ed, MAT), including middle grades education (MAT), middle grades education and reading (M Ed); secondary education (M Ed, MAT). *Accreditation:* NCATE. Part-time programs available. *Faculty:* 19 part-time/adjunct (12 women). *Students:* 12 full-time (9 women), 111 part-time (77 women). Average age 34. In 2011, 28 master's, 10 other advanced degrees awarded. *Degree requirements:* For master's, thesis optional, oral exams; for Ed S, thesis, portfolio, oral exams. *Entrance requirements:* For master's, GRE General Test, MAT, or NTE, minimum GPA of 2.5; for Ed S, M Ed from NCATE-accredited school, minimum GPA of 3.25. Additional exam requirements/recommendations for international students: Required—TOEFL (minimum score 550 paper-based; 213 computer-based). *Application deadline:* For fall admission, 5/1 for domestic and international students; for spring admission, 10/1 for domestic and international students. Applications are processed on a rolling basis. Application fee: $25 ($30 for international students). *Expenses:* Contact institution. *Financial support:* In 2011–12, 22 students received support, including 13 research assistantships with full tuition reimbursements available (averaging $4,275 per year); scholarships/grants, tuition waivers (partial), and unspecified assistantships also available. Support available to part-time students. Financial award application deadline: 3/1; financial award applicants required to submit FAFSA. *Faculty research:* Curriculum development, teaching strategies, teacher training, math education, kinesiology. *Unit head:* Dr. Jacqueline McDowell, Dean, Charter School of Education and Human Sciences, 706-236-1717, Fax: 706-238-5827, E-mail: jmcdowell@berry.edu. *Application contact:* Brett Kennedy, Director of Admissions, 706-236-2215, Fax: 706-290-2178, E-mail: admissions@berry.edu. Web site: http://www.berry.edu/academics/education/graduate/.

Bethel College, Division of Graduate Studies, Program in Education, Mishawaka, IN 46545-5591. Offers M Ed, MAT. *Accreditation:* NCATE. Part-time programs available. *Faculty:* 13 part-time/adjunct (9 women). *Students:* 9 full-time (7 women), 52 part-time (30 women); includes 5 minority (3 Black or African American, non-Hispanic/Latino; 2 Hispanic/Latino), 1 international. 82 applicants, 83% accepted, 51 enrolled. In 2011, 16 master's awarded. *Entrance requirements:* Additional exam requirements/recommendations for international students: Required—TOEFL (minimum score 540 paper-based; 207 computer-based). *Application deadline:* For fall admission, 5/1 for international students; for spring admission, 10/1 for international students. Application fee: $25. Electronic applications accepted. *Financial support:* Career-related internships or fieldwork available. Financial award applicants required to submit FAFSA. *Unit head:* Dr. Ralph Stutzman, Director, 574-257-3493, E-mail: stutzmr@bethelcollege.edu.

Bethel University, Graduate School, St. Paul, MN 55112-6999. Offers autism spectrum disorders (Certificate); business administration (MBA); communication (MA); counseling psychology (MA); education (M Ed); educational leadership (Ed D); gerontology (MA, Certificate); international baccalaureate education (Certificate); K-12 education (MA); literacy education (MA); nursing (MA); nursing education (Certificate); nursing leadership (Certificate); organizational leadership (MA); postsecondary teaching (Certificate); special education (MA); teaching (MA). Part-time and evening/weekend programs available. Postbaccalaureate distance learning degree programs offered (minimal on-campus study). *Faculty:* 8 full-time (3 women), 98 part-time/adjunct (46 women). *Students:* 651 full-time (419 women), 312 part-time (212 women); includes 79 minority (35 Black or African American, non-Hispanic/Latino; 2 American Indian or Alaska Native, non-Hispanic/Latino; 19 Asian, non-Hispanic/Latino; 17 Hispanic/Latino; 6 Two or more races, non-Hispanic/Latino), 6 international. Average age 36. In 2011, 245 master's, 4 doctorates, 32 other advanced degrees awarded. *Degree requirements:* For master's, comprehensive exam (for some programs), thesis (for some programs); for doctorate, comprehensive exam, thesis/dissertation. *Entrance requirements:* Additional exam requirements/recommendations for international students: Required—TOEFL (minimum score 550 paper-based; 213 computer-based; 80 iBT). *Application deadline:* Applications are processed on a rolling basis. Electronic applications accepted. Tuition and fees vary according to course load, degree level and program. *Financial support:* Applicants required to submit FAFSA. *Unit head:* Dick Crombie, Vice-President/Dean, 651-635-8000, Fax: 651-635-8004, E-mail: gs@bethel.edu. *Application contact:* Paul Ives, Director of Admissions, 651-635-8000, Fax: 651-635-8004, E-mail: gs@bethel.edu. Web site: http://gs.bethel.edu/.

Biola University, School of Education, La Mirada, CA 90639-0001. Offers special education (Certificate). Part-time programs available. Postbaccalaureate distance learning degree programs offered. *Faculty:* 14. *Students:* 40 full-time (35 women), 100 part-time (83 women); includes 34 minority (2 Black or African American, non-Hispanic/Latino; 1 American Indian or Alaska Native, non-Hispanic/Latino; 28 Asian, non-Hispanic/Latino; 3 Two or more races, non-Hispanic/Latino), 2 international. *Entrance requirements:* Additional exam requirements/recommendations for international students: Required—TOEFL (minimum score 100 iBT). *Application deadline:* For fall admission, 7/1 for domestic students, 6/1 for international students; for spring admission, 12/1 for domestic students. Applications are processed on a rolling basis. Application fee: $55. Electronic applications accepted. *Financial support:* Institutionally sponsored loans, scholarships/grants, and unspecified assistantships available. Financial award applicants required to submit FAFSA. *Faculty research:* Early childhood education, elementary education, special education, curriculum development, teacher preparation. *Unit head:* Dr. June Hetzel, Dean, 562-903-4715. *Application contact:* Graduate Admissions Office, 562-903-4752, E-mail: graduate.admissions@biola.edu. Web site: http://education.biola.edu/.

Bishop's University, School of Education, Sherbrooke, QC J1M 0C8, Canada. Offers advanced studies in education (Diploma); education (M Ed, MA); teaching English as a second language (Certificate). Part-time programs available. Postbaccalaureate distance learning degree programs offered (minimal on-campus study). *Degree requirements:* For master's, thesis (for some programs). *Entrance requirements:* For master's, teaching license, 2 years of teaching experience. *Faculty research:* Integration of special needs students, multigrade classes/small schools, leadership in organizational development, second language acquisition.

Bloomsburg University of Pennsylvania, School of Graduate Studies, College of Education, Bloomsburg, PA 17815-1301. Offers M Ed, MS. *Accreditation:* NCATE. *Entrance requirements:* For master's, minimum QPA of 3.0. Additional exam requirements/recommendations for international students: Required—TOEFL. Electronic applications accepted.

Bluffton University, Program in Education, Bluffton, OH 45817. Offers MA Ed. *Accreditation:* NCATE. Part-time programs available. *Degree requirements:* For master's, action research project, public presentation. *Entrance requirements:* Additional exam requirements/recommendations for international students: Required—TOEFL. Electronic applications accepted. *Faculty research:* Mentoring.

Boise State University, Graduate College, College of Education, Boise, ID 83725-0399. Offers M Ed, MA, MET, MPE, MS, MS Ed, Ed D. *Accreditation:* NCATE. Part-time programs available. *Degree requirements:* For doctorate, thesis/dissertation. *Entrance requirements:* For master's, minimum GPA of 3.0; for doctorate, GRE General Test, minimum GPA of 3.0. Electronic applications accepted.

Boston College, Lynch Graduate School of Education, Chestnut Hill, MA 02467-3800. Offers M Ed, MA, MAT, MST, Ed D, PhD, CAES, JD/M Ed, JD/MA, M Ed/MA, MA/MA, MBA/MA. *Accreditation:* Teacher Education Accreditation Council. *Faculty:* 56 full-time (33 women), 46 part-time/adjunct (31 women). *Students:* 671 full-time (527 women), 253 part-time (165 women); includes 172 minority (56 Black or African American, non-Hispanic/Latino; 2 American Indian or Alaska Native, non-Hispanic/Latino; 43 Asian, non-Hispanic/Latino; 55 Hispanic/Latino; 16 Two or more races, non-Hispanic/Latino), 87 international. 1,970 applicants, 46% accepted, 448 enrolled. In 2011, 365 master's, 39 doctorates, 10 other advanced degrees awarded. *Entrance requirements:* Additional exam requirements/recommendations for international students: Required—TOEFL (minimum score 550 paper-based; 213 computer-based; 79 iBT). Application fee: $65. Electronic applications accepted. *Unit head:* Dr. Maureen Kenny, Interim Dean, 617-552-4200, Fax: 617-552-0812. *Application contact:* Adam Poluzzi, Director, Graduate Admission and Financial Aid, 617-552-4214, Fax: 617-552-0398, E-mail: poluzzi@bc.edu. Web site: http://www.bc.edu/education/.

Boston University, School of Education, Boston, MA 02215. Offers Ed M, MAT, Ed D, CAGS. Part-time programs available. *Faculty:* 57 full-time, 39 part-time/adjunct. *Students:* 253 full-time (197 women), 371 part-time (280 women); includes 76 minority (12 Black or African American, non-Hispanic/Latino; 3 American Indian or Alaska Native, non-Hispanic/Latino; 22 Asian, non-Hispanic/Latino; 29 Hispanic/Latino; 10 Two or more races, non-Hispanic/Latino), 74 international. Average age 30. 1,270 applicants, 66% accepted, 292 enrolled. In 2011, 223 master's, 17 doctorates, 9 other advanced degrees awarded. Terminal master's awarded for partial completion of doctoral program. *Degree requirements:* For master's, thesis (for some programs); for doctorate, comprehensive exam, thesis/dissertation; for CAGS, comprehensive exam. *Entrance requirements:* For master's and CAGS, GRE General Test or MAT; for doctorate, GRE General Test. Additional exam requirements/recommendations for international students: Required—TOEFL, IELTS. *Application deadline:* For fall admission, 1/15 priority date for domestic students, 1/15 for international students; for spring admission, 9/15 priority date for domestic students, 9/15 for international students. Applications are processed on a rolling basis. Application fee: $70. Electronic applications accepted. *Expenses: Tuition:* Full-time $40,848; part-time $1276 per credit hour. *Required fees:* $572; $286 per semester. *Financial support:* In 2011–12, 276 students received support, including 31 fellowships with full tuition reimbursements available, 16 research assistantships, 26 teaching assistantships with partial tuition reimbursements available; career-related internships or fieldwork, Federal Work-Study, and scholarships/grants also available. Support available to part-time students. Financial award applicants required to submit FAFSA. *Faculty research:* Deaf studies, social emotional learning, civic engagement and education, STEM education, pre-college educational pipelines. *Total annual research expenditures:* $2.6 million. *Unit head:* Dr. Hardin Coleman, Dean, 617-353-3213. *Application contact:* Katherine Nelson, Director of Enrollment, 617-353-4237, Fax: 617-353-8937, E-mail: sedgrad@bu.edu. Web site: http://www.bu.edu/sed.

Bowie State University, Graduate Programs, Program in Teaching, Bowie, MD 20715-9465. Offers MAT. *Accreditation:* NCATE. Part-time and evening/weekend programs available. *Students:* 6 full-time (all women), 24 part-time (21 women); includes 20 minority (all Black or African American, non-Hispanic/Latino). Average age 32. 34 applicants, 88% accepted, 18 enrolled. In 2011, 12 master's awarded. *Entrance requirements:* For master's, PRAXIS I. *Application deadline:* For fall admission, 4/1 priority date for domestic students, 4/1 for international students; for spring admission, 11/1 priority date for domestic students, 11/1 for international students. Applications are processed on a rolling basis. Electronic applications accepted. *Expenses:* Tuition, state resident: full-time $4140; part-time $3105 per semester. Tuition, nonresident: full-time $7836; part-time $5877 per semester. *Required fees:* $1715; $648 per semester. *Unit head:* Dr. Constance Brooks, Program Coordinator, 301-860-3133, E-mail: cebrooks@bowiestate.edu. *Application contact:* Angela Issac, Information Contact, 301-860-4000.

Bradley University, Graduate School, College of Education and Health Sciences, Peoria, IL 61625-0002. Offers MA, MSN, DPT, Certificate. *Accreditation:* NCATE. Part-time and evening/weekend programs available. *Degree requirements:* For master's, comprehensive exam, thesis optional. *Entrance requirements:* For master's, GRE General Test or MAT, letters of recommendation; for doctorate, GRE, letters of recommendation. Additional exam requirements/recommendations for international students: Required—TOEFL (minimum score 550 paper-based; 213 computer-based; 79 iBT). *Faculty research:* Health care, professional nurse traineeship, gifted education.

Brandman University, School of Education, Irvine, CA 92618. Offers education (MA); educational leadership (MA); school counseling (MA); special education (MA); teaching (MA).

Brandon University, Faculty of Education, Brandon, MB R7A 6A9, Canada. Offers curriculum and instruction (M Ed, Diploma); educational administration (M Ed, Diploma); guidance and counseling (M Ed, Diploma); special education (M Ed, Diploma). *Degree requirements:* For master's, thesis. *Entrance requirements:* For master's, minimum GPA of 3.0, teaching certificate or equivalent. Additional exam requirements/recommendations for international students: Required—TOEFL. *Faculty research:* Comparative education, environmental studies, parent/school council.

Brenau University, Sydney O. Smith Graduate School, School of Education, Gainesville, GA 30501. Offers early childhood (Ed S); early childhood education (M Ed, MAT); middle grades (Ed S); middle grades education (M Ed, MAT); secondary education (MAT); special education (M Ed, MAT). *Accreditation:* NCATE. Part-time and evening/weekend programs available. Postbaccalaureate distance learning degree programs offered (no on-campus study). *Degree requirements:* For master's, thesis optional, comprehensive exam or applied research project, effective portfolio; for Ed S, thesis, applied research project. *Entrance requirements:* For master's, GRE, MAT, interview, minimum GPA of 3.0, 3 references, writing samples; for Ed S, GRE, MAT, master's degree, minimum GPA of 3.0, writing sample, letters of reference. Additional exam requirements/recommendations for international students: Required—TOEFL (minimum score 500 paper-based; 173 computer-based; 61 iBT); Recommended—IELTS (minimum score 5). Electronic applications accepted. *Expenses:* Contact institution.

Bridgewater State University, School of Graduate Studies, School of Education and Allied Studies, Bridgewater, MA 02325-0001. Offers M Ed, MAT, MS, CAGS. *Accreditation:* NCATE. Part-time and evening/weekend programs available. *Degree* *requirements:* For CAGS, comprehensive exam. *Entrance requirements:* For master's, GRE General Test or Massachusetts Test for Educator Licensure; for CAGS, master's degree. Additional exam requirements/recommendations for international students: Required—TOEFL (minimum score 215 computer-based).

Brigham Young University, Graduate Studies, David O. McKay School of Education, Provo, UT 84602. Offers M Ed, MA, MS, Ed D, PhD, Ed S. *Accreditation:* Teacher Education Accreditation Council. Part-time programs available. *Faculty:* 61 full-time (26 women), 14 part-time/adjunct (5 women). *Students:* 64 full-time (46 women), 269 part-time (158 women); includes 26 minority (9 Asian, non-Hispanic/Latino; 12 Hispanic/Latino; 5 Two or more races, non-Hispanic/Latino). Average age 31. 203 applicants, 44% accepted, 85 enrolled. In 2011, 56 master's, 22 doctorates, 9 other advanced degrees awarded. *Degree requirements:* For master's, comprehensive exam, thesis; for doctorate, comprehensive exam, thesis/dissertation; for Ed S, comprehensive exam (for some programs). *Entrance requirements:* For master's, GRE, MAT, LSAT, minimum GPA of 3.25, minimum 1 year of teaching experience, letters of recommendation; for doctorate, GRE, MAT, LSAT, minimum GPA of 3.0 in last 60 hours of undergraduate coursework. Additional exam requirements/recommendations for international students: Required—TOEFL (minimum score 580 paper-based; 237 computer-based). *Application deadline:* For fall admission, 2/1 for domestic and international students; for winter admission, 2/1 for domestic and international students; for spring admission, 2/15 for domestic and international students. Application fee: $50. Electronic applications accepted. *Expenses: Tuition:* Full-time $5760; part-time $320 per credit. Tuition and fees vary according to student's religious affiliation. *Financial support:* In 2011–12, 150 students received support, including 85 research assistantships with full and partial tuition reimbursements available (averaging $4,754 per year), 34 teaching assistantships with full and partial tuition reimbursements available (averaging $4,649 per year); fellowships, career-related internships or fieldwork, institutionally sponsored loans, scholarships/grants, tuition waivers (partial), and unspecified assistantships also available. Support available to part-time students. Financial award applicants required to submit FAFSA. *Faculty research:* Reading, learning, teacher education, assessment and evaluation, speech-language pathology. *Unit head:* Dr. K. Richard Young, Dean, 801-422-3695, Fax: 801-422-0200, E-mail: richard_young@byu.edu. *Application contact:* Jay Oliver, Director, Education Student Services, 801-422-1202, Fax: 801-422-0195. Web site: http://education.byu.edu/.

Brock University, Faculty of Graduate Studies, Faculty of Education, St. Catharines, ON L2S 3A1, Canada. Offers M Ed, PhD. Part-time and evening/weekend programs available. *Degree requirements:* For master's, thesis optional; for doctorate, thesis/dissertation. *Entrance requirements:* For master's, 1 year of teaching experience, honors degree; for doctorate, master's degree. Additional exam requirements/recommendations for international students: Required—TOEFL (minimum score 550 paper-based; 213 computer-based; 80 iBT), IELTS (minimum score 6.5), TWE (minimum score 4). Electronic applications accepted. *Expenses:* Contact institution. *Faculty research:* International and comparative education, early childhood education, educational leadership, adult education.

Brooklyn College of the City University of New York, Division of Graduate Studies, School of Education, Brooklyn, NY 11210-2889. Offers MA, MAT, MS Ed, CAS. *Accreditation:* NCATE. Part-time and evening/weekend programs available. *Entrance requirements:* For master's, LAST, 2 letters of recommendation, essay, resume, state teaching certificate; for CAS, master's degree. Additional exam requirements/recommendations for international students: Required—TOEFL (minimum score 500 paper-based; 173 computer-based; 61 iBT). Electronic applications accepted.

Brown University, Graduate School, Department of Education, Providence, RI 02912. Offers teaching (MAT), including biology, elementary education, English, history/social studies; urban education policy (AM). *Degree requirements:* For master's, student teaching, portfolio. *Entrance requirements:* For master's, GRE General Test, letters of recommendation, interview. Additional exam requirements/recommendations for international students: Recommended—TOEFL.

Bucknell University, Graduate Studies, College of Arts and Sciences, Department of Education, Lewisburg, PA 17837. Offers college student personnel (MS Ed). Part-time programs available. *Faculty:* 12 full-time (9 women), 4 part-time/adjunct (2 women). *Students:* 10 full-time (6 women), 7 part-time (6 women). 5 applicants, 60% accepted, 3 enrolled. In 2011, 18 master's awarded. *Degree requirements:* For master's, comprehensive exam (for some programs), thesis or alternative. *Entrance requirements:* For master's, GRE General Test, minimum GPA of 3.0. Additional exam requirements/recommendations for international students: Required—TOEFL (minimum score 600 paper-based). *Application deadline:* For fall admission, 2/1 priority date for domestic students, 1/1 for international students. Application fee: $25. *Financial support:* In 2011–12, 10 students received support, including 2 fellowships with full and partial tuition reimbursements available (averaging $20,000 per year); scholarships/grants and tuition waivers (full and partial) also available. Financial award application deadline: 2/1. *Unit head:* Dr. Joe Murray, Head, 717-577-1324. *Application contact:* Gretchen H. Fegley, Coordinator, 570-577-3655, Fax: 570-577-3760, E-mail: gfegley@bucknell.edu. Web site: http://www.bucknell.edu/education.

Buena Vista University, School of Education, Storm Lake, IA 50588. Offers curriculum and instruction (M Ed), including effective teaching, TESL; school guidance and counseling (MS Ed). Program offered in summer only. Part-time and evening/weekend programs available. Postbaccalaureate distance learning degree programs offered (minimal on-campus study). *Degree requirements:* For master's, thesis, fieldwork/practicum, capstone portfolio. *Entrance requirements:* For master's, Analytical Writing Assessment (in-house), minimum undergraduate GPA of 2.75. Electronic applications accepted. *Faculty research:* Reading, curriculum, educational psychology, special education.

Butler University, College of Education, Indianapolis, IN 46208-3485. Offers administration (MS); elementary education (MS); reading (MS); school counseling (MS); secondary education (MS); special education (MS). *Accreditation:* ACA; NCATE. Part-time and evening/weekend programs available. *Faculty:* 7 full-time (4 women), 5 part-time/adjunct (all women). *Students:* 9 full-time (6 women), 136 part-time (105 women); includes 21 minority (14 Black or African American, non-Hispanic/Latino; 5 Asian, non-Hispanic/Latino; 1 Hispanic/Latino; 1 Two or more races, non-Hispanic/Latino), 1 international. Average age 31. 69 applicants, 94% accepted, 24 enrolled. In 2011, 66 master's awarded. *Entrance requirements:* For master's, GRE General Test, MAT, interview. *Application deadline:* For fall admission, 8/15 priority date for domestic students. Applications are processed on a rolling basis. Application fee: $35. Electronic applications accepted. *Expenses: Tuition:* Part-time $466 per credit. *Financial support:* Institutionally sponsored loans available. Support available to part-time students. Financial award application deadline: 7/15; financial award applicants required to submit FAFSA. *Faculty research:* Ethics in cybercounseling, history of sports for disabled, effect of fetal alcohol syndrome on perceptual learning, reading recovery's theoretical framework in teacher education. *Unit head:* Dr. Ena Shelley, Dean, 317-940-9752, Fax: 317-940-6481. *Application contact:* Karen Farrell, Department Secretary, 317-940-9220, E-mail: kfarrell@butler.edu.

Cabrini College, Graduate and Professional Studies, Radnor, PA 19087-3698. Offers education (M Ed); organization leadership (MS). Part-time and evening/weekend programs available. *Faculty:* 5 full-time (all women), 134 part-time/adjunct (76 women). *Students:* 157 full-time (111 women), 1,768 part-time (1,357 women); includes 247 minority (169 Black or African American, non-Hispanic/Latino; 1 American Indian or Alaska Native, non-Hispanic/Latino; 25 Asian, non-Hispanic/Latino; 44 Hispanic/Latino; 2 Native Hawaiian or other Pacific Islander, non-Hispanic/Latino; 6 Two or more races, non-Hispanic/Latino), 3 international. Average age 34. 509 applicants, 80% accepted, 405 enrolled. In 2011, 727 master's awarded. *Degree requirements:* For master's, thesis optional. *Entrance requirements:* For master's, GRE and/or MAT (in some cases), letter of recommendation, minimum GPA of 2.5. *Application deadline:* For fall admission, 7/29 priority date for domestic students, 7/29 for international students; for spring admission, 12/9 for domestic and international students. Applications are processed on a rolling basis. Application fee: $50. Electronic applications accepted. *Expenses: Tuition:* Part-time $595 per credit. *Financial support:* Career-related internships or fieldwork and unspecified assistantships available. Support available to part-time students. Financial award applicants required to submit FAFSA. *Unit head:* Dr. Martha Combs, Dean of Graduate and Professional Studies, 610-902-8502, Fax: 610-902-8522, E-mail: martha.w.combs@cabrini.edu. *Application contact:* Bruce D. Bryde, Director of Enrollment and Recruiting, 610-902-8291, Fax: 610-902-8522, E-mail: bruce.d.bryde@cabrini.edu. Web site: http://www.cabrini.edu/GPS.

Cairn University, School of Education, Langhorne, PA 19047-2990. Offers educational leadership and administration (MS El); teacher education (MS Ed). Part-time and evening/weekend programs available. *Faculty:* 3 full-time (2 women), 3 part-time/adjunct (all women). *Students:* 12 full-time (7 women), 41 part-time (30 women); includes 12 minority (7 Black or African American, non-Hispanic/Latino; 3 Asian, non-Hispanic/Latino; 1 Native Hawaiian or other Pacific Islander, non-Hispanic/Latino; 1 Two or more races, non-Hispanic/Latino), 3 international. Average age 35. 21 applicants, 71% accepted, 10 enrolled. In 2011, 22 master's awarded. *Entrance requirements:* Additional exam requirements/recommendations for international students: Required—TOEFL (minimum score 550 paper-based; 213 computer-based). *Application deadline:* Applications are processed on a rolling basis. Application fee: $25. Electronic applications accepted. *Expenses: Tuition:* Part-time $475 per credit hour. Tuition and fees vary according to program. *Financial support:* Scholarships/grants available. Support available to part-time students. Financial award applicants required to submit FAFSA. *Unit head:* Dr. Deborah MacCullough, Dean, 215-702-4360, E-mail: teacher.ed@pbu.edu. *Application contact:* Caitlin Lenker, Enrollment Counselor, Graduate Education, 800-572-2472, Fax: 215-702-4248, E-mail: clenker@pbu.edu.

Caldwell College, Graduate Studies, Division of Education, Caldwell, NJ 07006-6195. Offers curriculum and instruction (MA); educational administration (MA); learning disabilities teacher-consultant (Post-Master's Certificate); literacy instruction (MA); principal (Post-Master's Certificate); reading specialist (Post-Master's Certificate); special education (MA), including special education, teaching of students with disabilities, teaching of students with disabilities and learning disabilities teacher-consultant; superintendent (Post-Master's Certificate); supervisor (Post-Master's Certificate). Part-time and evening/weekend programs available. *Students:* 66 full-time (41 women), 230 part-time (188 women); includes 24 minority (14 Black or African American, non-Hispanic/Latino; 1 Asian, non-Hispanic/Latino; 9 Hispanic/Latino). *Entrance requirements:* Additional exam requirements/recommendations for international students: Required—TOEFL (minimum score 580 paper-based; 237 computer-based). *Application deadline:* Applications are processed on a rolling basis. Application fee: $40. Electronic applications accepted. *Expenses: Tuition:* Full-time $14,400; part-time $800 per credit. *Required fees:* $200; $100 per semester. *Financial support:* Applicants required to submit FAFSA. *Unit head:* Dr. Janice Stewart, Coordinator, 973-618-3626, E-mail: jstewart@caldwell.edu. *Application contact:* Vilma Mueller, Director of Graduate Studies, 973-618-3544, E-mail: graduate@caldwell.edu.

California Baptist University, Program in Education, Riverside, CA 92504-3206. Offers educational leadership for faith-based instruction (MS); educational leadership for public institutions (MS); educational technology (MS); instructional computer applications (MS); international education (MS); reading (MS); school counseling (MS); school psychology (MS); special education (MS); special education in mild/moderate disabilities (MS); special education in moderate/severe disabilities (MS); teaching (MS); teaching and learning with induction program (MS Ed). Part-time and evening/weekend programs available. *Faculty:* 16 full-time (10 women), 1 (woman) part-time/adjunct. *Students:* 380 full-time (323 women); includes 149 minority (28 Black or African American, non-Hispanic/Latino; 2 American Indian or Alaska Native, non-Hispanic/Latino; 13 Asian, non-Hispanic/Latino; 100 Hispanic/Latino; 2 Native Hawaiian or other Pacific Islander, non-Hispanic/Latino; 4 Two or more races, non-Hispanic/Latino). Average age 32. 181 applicants, 70% accepted, 111 enrolled. In 2011, 82 master's awarded. *Degree requirements:* For master's, comprehensive exam or thesis. *Entrance requirements:* For master's, minimum undergraduate GPA of 3.0; 18 semester units of prerequisite course work in education; three recommendations; essay; interview. Additional exam requirements/recommendations for international students: Required—TOEFL (minimum score 575 paper-based; 230 computer-based; 89 iBT). *Application deadline:* For fall admission, 8/1 priority date for domestic students, 7/1 for international students; for spring admission, 12/1 priority date for domestic students, 11/1 for international students. Applications are processed on a rolling basis. Application fee: $45. Electronic applications accepted. *Expenses:* Contact institution. *Financial support:* In 2011–12, 4 students received support. Federal Work-Study and institutionally sponsored loans available. Financial award applicants required to submit FAFSA. *Faculty research:* Special education, neurosciences and education, cultural influences on behavior, faith-based school leadership, social and philosophical contexts of education. *Unit head:* Dr. John Shoup, Dean, School of Education, 951-343-4205, Fax: 951-343-4516, E-mail: jshoup@calbaptist.edu. *Application contact:* Dr. James Heyman, Director, Master of Science Program in Education, 951-343-4243, Fax: 951-343-5095, E-mail: jheyman@calbaptist.edu. Web site: http://www.calbaptist.edu/mastersined/.

California Coast University, School of Education, Santa Ana, CA 92701. Offers administration (M Ed); curriculum and instruction (M Ed); educational administration (Ed D); educational psychology (Ed D); organizational leadership (Ed D). Postbaccalaureate distance learning degree programs offered (no on-campus study).

California Lutheran University, Graduate Studies, Graduate School of Education, Thousand Oaks, CA 91360-2787. Offers counseling and guidance (MS), including college student personnel, counseling and guidance; educational leadership (MA, Ed D), including educational leadership (K-12) (Ed D), higher education leadership (Ed D); special education (MS); teacher leadership (M Ed); teaching (M Ed). *Accreditation:* NCATE. Part-time and evening/weekend programs available. *Entrance requirements:* For master's, GRE General Test, interview, minimum GPA of 3.0.

California Polytechnic State University, San Luis Obispo, College of Science and Mathematics, School of Education, San Luis Obispo, CA 93407. Offers MA. Part-time and evening/weekend programs available. *Faculty:* 6 full-time (3 women), 8 part-time/adjunct (6 women). *Students:* 74 full-time (52 women), 4 part-time (3 women); includes 16 minority (2 Asian, non-Hispanic/Latino; 12 Hispanic/Latino; 2 Two or more races, non-Hispanic/Latino), 1 international. Average age 29. 130 applicants, 52% accepted,

59 enrolled. In 2011, 52 master's awarded. *Degree requirements:* For master's, comprehensive exam (for some programs), thesis (for some programs). *Entrance requirements:* For master's, minimum GPA of 3.0 in last 90 quarter units, letters of recommendation. Additional exam requirements/recommendations for international students: Required—TOEFL (minimum score 550 paper-based; 213 computer-based) or IELTS (minimum score 6). *Application deadline:* For fall admission, 2/1 priority date for domestic students, 11/30 for international students. Application fee: $55. *Expenses:* Tuition, state resident: full-time $6738. Tuition, nonresident: full-time $17,898. *Required fees:* $2449. *Financial support:* Fellowships, research assistantships, career-related internships or fieldwork, Federal Work-Study, and institutionally sponsored loans available. Support available to part-time students. Financial award application deadline: 3/2; financial award applicants required to submit FAFSA. *Faculty research:* Rural school counseling, partner school effectiveness, college student affairs, special education, educational leadership and administration. *Unit head:* Dr. Robert Detweiler, Interim Dean, 805-756-6585, Fax: 805-756-7430, E-mail: rdetweil@calpoly.edu. *Application contact:* Dr. James Maraviglia, Associate Vice Provost for Marketing and Enrollment Development, 805-756-2311, Fax: 805-756-5400, E-mail: admissions@calpoly.edu. Web site: http://soe.calpoly.edu/.

California State Polytechnic University, Pomona, Academic Affairs, College of Education and Integrative Studies, Pomona, CA 91768-2557. Offers MA. Part-time programs available. *Faculty:* 39 full-time (27 women), 39 part-time/adjunct (22 women). *Students:* 51 full-time (40 women), 176 part-time (122 women); includes 107 minority (9 Black or African American, non-Hispanic/Latino; 1 American Indian or Alaska Native, non-Hispanic/Latino; 28 Asian, non-Hispanic/Latino; 65 Hispanic/Latino; 4 Two or more races, non-Hispanic/Latino), 3 international. Average age 36. 90 applicants, 64% accepted, 42 enrolled. In 2011, 84 master's awarded. *Degree requirements:* For master's, thesis or alternative. *Application deadline:* For fall admission, 5/1 priority date for domestic students; for winter admission, 10/15 priority date for domestic students; for spring admission, 1/20 priority date for domestic students. Applications are processed on a rolling basis. Application fee: $55. Electronic applications accepted. *Expenses:* Tuition, state resident: full-time $6738. Tuition, nonresident: full-time $12,300. *Required fees:* $657. Tuition and fees vary according to course load and program. *Financial support:* Career-related internships or fieldwork, Federal Work-Study, and institutionally sponsored loans available. Support available to part-time students. Financial award application deadline: 3/2; financial award applicants required to submit FAFSA. *Faculty research:* Cognitive style, human factors, learning-handicapped children, teaching and learning, severely handicapped children. *Unit head:* Dr. Peggy Kelly, Dean, 909-869-2307, E-mail: pkelly@csupomona.edu. *Application contact:* Dr. Dorothy MacNevin, Co-Chair, Graduate Education Department, 909-869-2311, Fax: 909-869-4822, E-mail: dmacnevin@csupomona.edu. Web site: http://www.csupomona.edu/~ceis/.

California State University, Bakersfield, Division of Graduate Studies, School of Social Sciences and Education, Bakersfield, CA 93311. Offers MA, MS, MSW, Certificate. *Accreditation:* NCATE. *Degree requirements:* For master's, thesis or alternative, culminating projects. *Application deadline:* Applications are processed on a rolling basis. Application fee: $55. *Expenses: Required fees:* $1302 per unit. Part-time tuition and fees vary according to course load and program. *Unit head:* Dr. Kathleen M. Knutzen, Dean, 661-664-2219, Fax: 661-664-2016, E-mail: kknutzen@csub.edu. Web site: http://www.csub.edu/sse/.

California State University, Dominguez Hills, College of Professional Studies, School of Education, Division of Graduate Education, Carson, CA 90747-0001. Offers counseling (MA); curriculum and instruction (MA); curriculum and instruction: science education (MA); educational administration (MA); individualized education (MA); multicultural education (MA); technology-based education (MA, Certificate). Part-time and evening/weekend programs available. *Faculty:* 16 full-time (10 women), 12 part-time/adjunct (7 women). *Students:* 224 full-time (155 women), 187 part-time (123 women); includes 292 minority (79 Black or African American, non-Hispanic/Latino; 2 American Indian or Alaska Native, non-Hispanic/Latino; 32 Asian, non-Hispanic/Latino; 167 Hispanic/Latino; 1 Native Hawaiian or other Pacific Islander, non-Hispanic/Latino; 11 Two or more races, non-Hispanic/Latino), 3 international. Average age 36. 282 applicants, 73% accepted, 143 enrolled. In 2011, 227 master's awarded. *Entrance requirements:* For master's, minimum GPA of 2.75. *Application deadline:* For fall admission, 6/1 for domestic students. Application fee: $55. *Unit head:* Dr. Cynthia Grutzik, Acting Director, 310-243-3510, E-mail: cgrutzik@csudh.edu. *Application contact:* Admissions Office, 310-243-3530. Web site: http://www.csudh.edu/cps/soe/programsdegrees/graduate-programs.shtml.

California State University, East Bay, Office of Academic Programs and Graduate Studies, College of Education and Allied Studies, Department of Teacher Education, Hayward, CA 94542-3000. Offers education (MS), including curriculum, early childhood education, educational technology leadership, online teaching and learning, reading instruction. Postbaccalaureate distance learning degree programs offered. *Faculty:* 5 full-time (4 women), 2 part-time/adjunct (both women). *Students:* 64 full-time (53 women), 55 part-time (39 women); includes 50 minority (14 Black or African American, non-Hispanic/Latino; 17 Asian, non-Hispanic/Latino; 15 Hispanic/Latino; 4 Two or more races, non-Hispanic/Latino), 3 international. Average age 35. 98 applicants, 69% accepted, 30 enrolled. In 2011, 149 master's awarded. *Degree requirements:* For master's, project or thesis. *Entrance requirements:* For master's, minimum GPA of 3.0 in field, 2.5 overall; teaching experience; baccalaureate degree; 3 letters of recommendation. Additional exam requirements/recommendations for international students: Required—TOEFL (minimum score 550 paper-based; 213 computer-based), IELTS. *Application deadline:* For fall admission, 6/30 for domestic and international students. Application fee: $55. Electronic applications accepted. *Expenses:* Tuition, state resident: full-time $6738; part-time $1302 per quarter. Tuition, nonresident: full-time $12,690; part-time $2294 per quarter. *Required fees:* $449 per quarter. Tuition and fees vary according to degree level, program and reciprocity agreements. *Financial support:* Career-related internships or fieldwork, Federal Work-Study, and institutionally sponsored loans available. Support available to part-time students. Financial award application deadline: 3/2; financial award applicants required to submit FAFSA. *Faculty research:* Online, pedagogy, writing, learning, teaching. *Unit head:* Dr. Jeanette Bicais, Chair, 510-885-3027, Fax: 510-885-4632, E-mail: jeanette.bicais@csueastbay.edu. *Application contact:* Prof. Valerie Helgren-Lempesis, Education Graduate Advisor, 510-885-3006, Fax: 510-885-4632, E-mail: valerie.lempesis@csueastbay.edu. Web site: http://www20.csueastbay.edu/ceas/departments/ted/index.html.

California State University, Fresno, Division of Graduate Studies, School of Education and Human Development, Fresno, CA 93740-8027. Offers MA, MS, Ed D. *Accreditation:* NCATE. Part-time and evening/weekend programs available. *Degree requirements:* For master's, thesis or alternative; for doctorate, thesis/dissertation. *Entrance requirements:* For master's, GRE General Test, MAT; for doctorate, GRE or MAT, minimum GPA of 3.2, master's degree. Additional exam requirements/recommendations for international students: Required—TOEFL. Electronic applications accepted. *Faculty research:* Adult community education, parenting, gifted and talented curriculum and instruction, peer mediation and conflict resolution.

California State University, Long Beach, Graduate Studies, College of Education, Long Beach, CA 90840. Offers MA, MS, Ed D. *Accreditation:* NCATE. Part-time and evening/weekend programs available. *Faculty:* 46 full-time (30 women), 24 part-time/adjunct (16 women). *Students:* 252 full-time (193 women), 510 part-time (401 women); includes 470 minority (61 Black or African American, non-Hispanic/Latino; 30 American Indian or Alaska Native, non-Hispanic/Latino; 86 Asian, non-Hispanic/Latino; 257 Hispanic/Latino; 15 Native Hawaiian or other Pacific Islander, non-Hispanic/Latino; 21 Two or more races, non-Hispanic/Latino), 17 international. Average age 33. 880 applicants, 34% accepted, 249 enrolled. In 2011, 289 master's, 26 doctorates awarded. *Entrance requirements:* For master's, GRE General Test, minimum GPA of 2.75. *Application deadline:* For fall admission, 3/1 for domestic students. Applications are processed on a rolling basis. Application fee: $55. Electronic applications accepted. *Financial support:* Federal Work-Study, institutionally sponsored loans, and scholarships/grants available. Financial award application deadline: 3/2. *Faculty research:* K-16 educational reform and partnership, gender issues related to teaching and learning, urban education (poverty, diversity, language), assessment and standards-based education. *Unit head:* Dr. Marquita Grenot-Scheyer, Dean, 562-985-1609, Fax: 562-985-4951, E-mail: cedinfo@csulb.edu. *Application contact:* Nancy L. McGlothin, Coordinator for Graduate Studies and Research, 562-985-8476, Fax: 562-985-4951, E-mail: nmcgloth@csulb.edu.

California State University, Los Angeles, Graduate Studies, Charter College of Education, Los Angeles, CA 90032-8530. Offers MA, MS, PhD. *Accreditation:* NCATE. Part-time and evening/weekend programs available. *Faculty:* 47 full-time (29 women), 37 part-time/adjunct (24 women). *Students:* 697 full-time (527 women), 704 part-time (518 women); includes 1,035 minority (78 Black or African American, non-Hispanic/Latino; 3 American Indian or Alaska Native, non-Hispanic/Latino; 179 Asian, non-Hispanic/Latino; 749 Hispanic/Latino; 26 Two or more races, non-Hispanic/Latino), 45 international. Average age 34. 754 applicants, 51% accepted, 176 enrolled. In 2011, 465 master's awarded. *Degree requirements:* For doctorate, thesis/dissertation. *Entrance requirements:* For master's, minimum GPA of 2.75 in last 90 units of course work, teaching certificate; for doctorate, GRE General Test, master's degree; minimum undergraduate GPA of 3.0, graduate 3.5. Additional exam requirements/recommendations for international students: Required—TOEFL (minimum score 500 paper-based; 173 computer-based). *Application deadline:* For fall admission, 5/1 for domestic and international students. Applications are processed on a rolling basis. Application fee: $55. Electronic applications accepted. *Expenses:* Tuition, state resident: full-time $8225. *Financial support:* Career-related internships or fieldwork and Federal Work-Study available. Support available to part-time students. Financial award application deadline: 3/1. *Unit head:* Dr. Mary Falvey, Dean, 323-343-4300, Fax: 323-343-4318, E-mail: mfalvey@calstatela.edu. *Application contact:* Dr. Alan Muchlinski, Dean of Graduate Studies, 323-343-3820, Fax: 323-343-5653, E-mail: amuchli@exchange.calstatela.edu. Web site: http://www.calstatela.edu/academic/ccoe/index.htm.

California State University, Monterey Bay, College of Professional Studies, Institute for Advanced Studies in Education, Seaside, CA 93955-8001. Offers MA. *Accreditation:* NCATE. Part-time and evening/weekend programs available. *Degree requirements:* For master's, one foreign language, thesis, 2 years of teaching experience. *Entrance requirements:* For master's, recommendations, verification of U. S. Constitution requirement. Additional exam requirements/recommendations for international students: Required—TOEFL (minimum score 550 paper-based; 213 computer-based; 71 iBT). Electronic applications accepted. *Faculty research:* Multicultural education, linguistic diversity, behavior analysis.

California State University, Northridge, Graduate Studies, College of Education, Northridge, CA 91330. Offers MA, MA Ed, MS, Ed D. *Accreditation:* NCATE. Part-time and evening/weekend programs available. *Entrance requirements:* Additional exam requirements/recommendations for international students: Required—TOEFL. *Faculty research:* Federal teacher center support, bilingual teacher training.

California State University, Sacramento, Office of Graduate Studies, College of Education, Sacramento, CA 95819-6079. Offers MA, MS. Part-time programs available. *Faculty:* 76 full-time (48 women), 67 part-time/adjunct (52 women). *Students:* 909 full-time, 317 part-time; includes 402 minority (70 Black or African American, non-Hispanic/Latino; 14 American Indian or Alaska Native, non-Hispanic/Latino; 71 Asian, non-Hispanic/Latino; 182 Hispanic/Latino; 35 Native Hawaiian or other Pacific Islander, non-Hispanic/Latino; 30 Two or more races, non-Hispanic/Latino), 7 international. Average age 35. 924 applicants, 82% accepted, 580 enrolled. In 2011, 408 master's awarded. *Degree requirements:* For master's, thesis or alternative, writing proficiency exam. *Entrance requirements:* Additional exam requirements/recommendations for international students: Required—TOEFL. *Application deadline:* For fall admission, 3/1 for international students; for spring admission, 9/30 for international students. Applications are processed on a rolling basis. Application fee: $55. Electronic applications accepted. *Financial support:* Research assistantships, teaching assistantships, career-related internships or fieldwork, and Federal Work-Study available. Support available to part-time students. Financial award application deadline: 3/1; financial award applicants required to submit FAFSA. *Unit head:* Dr. Vanessa Sheared, Dean, 916-278-5883, Fax: 916-278-5904, E-mail: vsheared@saclink.csus.edu. *Application contact:* Jose Martinez, Outreach and Graduate Diversity Coordinator, 916-278-6470, Fax: 916-278-5669, E-mail: martinj@skymail.csus.edu. Web site: http://www.edweb.csus.edu.

California State University, San Bernardino, Graduate Studies, College of Education, San Bernardino, CA 92407-2397. Offers bilingual/cross-cultural education (MA); curriculum and instruction (MA); educational administration (MA); educational leadership and curriculum (Ed D); educational psychology and counseling (MA, MS), including correctional and alternative education (MA), counseling and guidance (MS), rehabilitation counseling (MA); English as a second language (MA); general education (MA); history and English for secondary teachers (MA); instructional technology (MA); reading (MA); secondary education (MA); special education and rehabilitation counseling (MA), including rehabilitation counseling, special education; teaching of science (MA); vocational and career education (MA). *Accreditation:* NCATE. Part-time and evening/weekend programs available. *Students:* 434 full-time (335 women), 188 part-time (139 women); includes 271 minority (54 Black or African American, non-Hispanic/Latino; 2 American Indian or Alaska Native, non-Hispanic/Latino; 29 Asian, non-Hispanic/Latino; 172 Hispanic/Latino; 2 Native Hawaiian or other Pacific Islander, non-Hispanic/Latino; 12 Two or more races, non-Hispanic/Latino), 28 international. Average age 32. 382 applicants, 61% accepted, 186 enrolled. In 2011, 279 master's awarded. *Degree requirements:* For master's, comprehensive exam (for some programs), thesis (for some programs), advancement to candidacy. *Entrance requirements:* For master's, minimum GPA of 3.0 in education. *Application deadline:* For fall admission, 8/31 priority date for domestic students. Application fee: $55. *Expenses:* Tuition, state resident: full-time $7356. Tuition, nonresident: full-time $7356. *Required fees:* $1077. Tuition and fees vary according to program. *Financial support:* Career-related internships or fieldwork and Federal Work-Study available. Support available to part-time students. *Faculty research:* Multicultural education, brain-based learning, science education, social studies/global education. *Unit head:* Dr. Patricia Arlin, Dean, 909-537-5600, Fax: 909-537-7011, E-mail: parlin@csusb.edu. *Application contact:*

Olivia Rosas, Director of Admissions, 909-537-7577, Fax: 909-537-7034, E-mail: orosas@csusb.edu.

California State University, San Marcos, College of Education, San Marcos, CA 92096-0001. Offers MA. *Accreditation:* NCATE. Part-time and evening/weekend programs available. *Degree requirements:* For master's, thesis. *Entrance requirements:* For master's, minimum GPA of 3.0, teaching credentials, 1 year of teaching experience. *Faculty research:* Multicultural literature, art as knowledge, poetry and second language acquisition, restructuring K–12 education and improving the training of K–8 science teachers.

California State University, Stanislaus, College of Education, Turlock, CA 95382. Offers MA, Ed D, Graduate Certificate. *Accreditation:* NCATE. Part-time and evening/weekend programs available. *Degree requirements:* For master's, thesis. *Entrance requirements:* For master's, MAT, minimum GPA of 3.0. Additional exam requirements/recommendations for international students: Required—TOEFL (minimum score 550 paper-based; 213 computer-based). *Application deadline:* For fall admission, 6/30 for domestic students; for winter admission, 11/30 for domestic students; for spring admission, 11/30 for domestic students. Application fee: $55. *Expenses: Required fees:* $4616 per year. *Financial support:* Fellowships, career-related internships or fieldwork, and Federal Work-Study available. Financial award application deadline: 3/1; financial award applicants required to submit FAFSA. *Unit head:* Dr. Carl Brown, Dean, 209-667-3652. *Application contact:* Graduate School, 209-667-3129, Fax: 209-664-7025, E-mail: graduate_school@csustan.edu.

California University of Pennsylvania, School of Graduate Studies and Research, College of Education and Human Services, California, PA 15419-1394. Offers M Ed, MAT, MS, MSW. *Accreditation:* NCATE. Part-time and evening/weekend programs available. Postbaccalaureate distance learning degree programs offered (minimal on-campus study). *Degree requirements:* For master's, comprehensive exam, thesis optional. *Entrance requirements:* For master's, PRAXIS, MAT, minimum QPA of 3.0. Additional exam requirements/recommendations for international students: Required—TOEFL (minimum score 550 paper-based; 213 computer-based; 80 iBT). Electronic applications accepted. *Faculty research:* Autism counseling, injury and education, early childhood education, National Board certification.

Calvin College, Graduate Programs in Education, Grand Rapids, MI 49546-4388. Offers curriculum and instruction (M Ed); educational leadership (M Ed); learning disabilities (M Ed); literacy (M Ed). Part-time programs available. *Degree requirements:* For master's, thesis or seminar. *Entrance requirements:* For master's, teaching certificate. Additional exam requirements/recommendations for international students: Required—TOEFL (minimum score 550 paper-based; 213 computer-based; 80 iBT). Electronic applications accepted. *Faculty research:* Literacy, racialized gender and gendered identity, teacher learning, learning disabilities identification.

Cambridge College, School of Education, Cambridge, MA 02138-5304. Offers autism specialist (M Ed); autism/behavior analyst (M Ed); behavior analyst (Post-Master's Certificate); behavioral management (M Ed); early childhood teacher (M Ed); education specialist in curriculum and instruction (CAGS); educational leadership (Ed D); elementary teacher (M Ed); English as a second language (M Ed, Certificate); general science (M Ed); health education (Post-Master's Certificate); health/family and consumer sciences (M Ed); history (M Ed); individualized (M Ed); information technology literacy (M Ed); instructional technology (M Ed); interdisciplinary studies (M Ed); library teacher (M Ed); literacy education (M Ed); mathematics (M Ed); mathematics specialist (Certificate); middle school mathematics and science (M Ed); school administration (M Ed, CAGS); school guidance counselor (M Ed); school nurse education (M Ed); school social worker/school adjustment counselor (M Ed); special education administrator (CAGS); special education/moderate disabilities (M Ed); teaching skills and methodologies (M Ed). Part-time and evening/weekend programs available. Postbaccalaureate distance learning degree programs offered (minimal on-campus study). *Degree requirements:* For master's, thesis, internship/practicum (licensure program only); for doctorate, thesis/dissertation; for other advanced degree, thesis. *Entrance requirements:* For master's, interview, resume, documentation of licensure, 2 professional references; for doctorate, official transcripts, interview, resume, documentation of licensure (if any), written personal statement/essay, portfolio of scholarly and professional work, qualifying assessment, 2 professional references, health insurance, immunizations form; for other advanced degree, official transcripts, interview, resume, documentation of licensure (if any), written personal statement/essay, 2 professional references, health insurance, immunizations form. Additional exam requirements/recommendations for international students: Required—TOEFL (minimum score 550 paper-based; 213 computer-based; 79 iBT); Recommended—IELTS (minimum score 6). Electronic applications accepted. *Expenses:* Contact institution. *Faculty research:* Adult education, accelerated learning, mathematics education, brain compatible learning, special education and law.

Cameron University, Office of Graduate Studies, Program in Education, Lawton, OK 73505-6377. Offers M Ed. *Accreditation:* NCATE. Part-time and evening/weekend programs available. *Degree requirements:* For master's, portfolio. *Entrance requirements:* Additional exam requirements/recommendations for international students: Required—TOEFL (minimum score 550 paper-based; 213 computer-based). Electronic applications accepted. *Faculty research:* Motivation, computer learning, special education mathematics, inquiry-based learning.

Cameron University, Office of Graduate Studies, Program in Teaching, Lawton, OK 73505-6377. Offers MAT. *Accreditation:* NCATE. *Degree requirements:* For master's, portfolio. *Entrance requirements:* Additional exam requirements/recommendations for international students: Required—TOEFL (minimum score 550 paper-based; 213 computer-based). Electronic applications accepted. *Faculty research:* Teacher retention/attrition, teacher education.

Campbellsville University, School of Education, Campbellsville, KY 42718-2799. Offers curriculum and instruction (MAE); special education (MASE). *Accreditation:* NCATE. Part-time and evening/weekend programs available. Postbaccalaureate distance learning degree programs offered (minimal on-campus study). *Students:* 232 full-time (159 women), 45 part-time (36 women); includes 34 minority (all Black or African American, non-Hispanic/Latino), 8 international. In 2011, 79 master's awarded. *Degree requirements:* For master's, thesis, research paper. *Entrance requirements:* For master's, GRE or PRAXIS, minimum undergraduate GPA of 2.75, teaching certificate, professional growth plan, letters of recommendation, disposition assessment, interview. *Application deadline:* For fall admission, 6/1 priority date for domestic students, 5/1 for international students; for spring admission, 11/1 priority date for domestic students, 10/1 for international students. Applications are processed on a rolling basis. Application fee: $25. Electronic applications accepted. *Expenses: Tuition:* Full-time $6030; part-time $335 per credit hour. *Financial support:* In 2011–12, 250 students received support. Institutionally sponsored loans, scholarships/grants, and unspecified assistantships available. Support available to part-time students. Financial award application deadline: 6/1; financial award applicants required to submit FAFSA. *Faculty research:* Professional development, curriculum development, school governance, assessment, special education. *Unit head:* Dr. Brenda A. Priddy, Dean, 270-789-5344, Fax: 270-789-5206, E-mail: bapriddy@campbellsville.edu. *Application contact:* Monica Bamwine, Assistant Director of Admissions, 270-789-5221, Fax: 270-789-5071, E-mail: redeaton@campbellsville.edu.

Campbell University, Graduate and Professional Programs, School of Education, Buies Creek, NC 27506. Offers administration (MSA); community counseling (MA); elementary education (M Ed); English education (M Ed); interdisciplinary studies (M Ed); mathematics education (M Ed); middle grades education (M Ed); physical education (M Ed); school counseling (M Ed); secondary education (M Ed); social science education (M Ed). *Accreditation:* NCATE. Part-time and evening/weekend programs available. *Degree requirements:* For master's, comprehensive exam. *Entrance requirements:* For master's, GRE General Test, minimum GPA of 2.7. *Faculty research:* Spiritual values and wellness issues in counseling, stress and professional burnout among counselors, thinking strategies, leadership, adaptive technology.

Canisius College, Graduate Division, School of Education and Human Services, Buffalo, NY 14208-1098. Offers MS, MS Ed, Certificate. Part-time and evening/weekend programs available. Postbaccalaureate distance learning degree programs offered (minimal on-campus study). *Faculty:* 53 full-time (31 women), 126 part-time/adjunct (66 women). *Students:* 648 full-time (414 women), 673 part-time (388 women); includes 130 minority (84 Black or African American, non-Hispanic/Latino; 6 American Indian or Alaska Native, non-Hispanic/Latino; 11 Asian, non-Hispanic/Latino; 14 Hispanic/Latino; 15 Two or more races, non-Hispanic/Latino), 133 international. Average age 29. 802 applicants, 80% accepted, 375 enrolled. In 2011, 567 master's awarded. *Degree requirements:* For master's, thesis (for some programs). *Entrance requirements:* For master's, GRE if cumulative GPA less than 2.7, transcripts. Additional exam requirements/recommendations for international students: Required—TOEFL. *Application deadline:* Applications are processed on a rolling basis. Application fee: $25. Electronic applications accepted. *Financial support:* Career-related internships or fieldwork, Federal Work-Study, scholarships/grants, tuition waivers (partial), and unspecified assistantships available. Support available to part-time students. Financial award application deadline: 4/30; financial award applicants required to submit FAFSA. *Faculty research:* Asperger's disease, autism, culturally congruent pedagogy in physical education, family as faculty, impact of trauma on adults, information processing and perceptual styles of athletes, integrating digital technologies in the classroom, long term psych-social impact on police officers, private higher education, qualities of effective coaches, reading strategies, student perceptions of online courses, teaching effectiveness, teaching methods, tutorial experiences in modern math. *Unit head:* Dr. Michael J. Pardales, Dean, 716-888-3294, E-mail: pardalem@canisius.edu. *Application contact:* Jim Bagwell, Director of Graduate Recruitment and Admissions, 716-888-2544, E-mail: bagwellj@canisius.edu. Web site: http://www.canisius.edu/education/graduate.asp.

Capella University, School of Education, Minneapolis, MN 55402. Offers college teaching (Certificate); curriculum and instruction (MS, PhD); education (MS); enrollment management (MS); instructional design for online learning (MS, PhD); k-12 studies in education (MS, PhD); leadership for higher education (MS, PhD); leadership in education administration (Certificate); leadership in educational administration (MS, PhD); postsecondary and adult education (MS, PhD); professional studies in education (MS, PhD); reading and literacy (MS); training and performance improvement (MS, PhD). Part-time and evening/weekend programs available. Postbaccalaureate distance learning degree programs offered (minimal on-campus study). Terminal master's awarded for partial completion of doctoral program. *Degree requirements:* For master's, thesis optional, integrative project; for doctorate, comprehensive exam, thesis/dissertation. *Entrance requirements:* Additional exam requirements/recommendations for international students: Required—TOEFL (minimum score 550 paper-based; 213 computer-based), TWE (minimum score 4). Electronic applications accepted. *Faculty research:* Higher education administration, distance learning, adult education, training and curriculum design.

Cardinal Stritch University, College of Education, Milwaukee, WI 53217-3985. Offers MA, MAT, ME, MS, Ed D, PhD. *Accreditation:* NCATE. Part-time and evening/weekend programs available. *Degree requirements:* For master's, comprehensive exam, thesis (for some programs); for doctorate, thesis/dissertation, practica/field experience. *Entrance requirements:* For doctorate, minimum GPA of 3.5 in master's coursework, portfolio, interview, letters of recommendation (3).

Caribbean University, Graduate School, Bayamón, PR 00960-0493. Offers administration and supervision (MA Ed); criminal justice (MA); curriculum and instruction (MA Ed, PhD), including elementary education (MA Ed), English education (MA Ed), history education (MA Ed), mathematics education (MA Ed), primary education (MA Ed), science education (MA Ed), Spanish education (MA Ed); educational technology in instructional systems (MA Ed); gerontology (MSN); human resources (MBA); museology, archiving and art history (MA Ed); neonatal pediatrics (MSN); physical education (MA Ed); special education (MA Ed). *Entrance requirements:* For master's, interview, minimum GPA of 2.5.

Carlow University, School of Education, Pittsburgh, PA 15213-3165. Offers art education (M Ed); early childhood education (M Ed); early childhood supervision (M Ed); education (M Ed), including art education, early childhood education, instructional technology specialist, middle level education, secondary education, special education. Part-time and evening/weekend programs available. *Students:* 120 full-time (100 women), 49 part-time (45 women); includes 30 minority (28 Black or African American, non-Hispanic/Latino; 2 Hispanic/Latino). Average age 34. 93 applicants, 48% accepted, 32 enrolled. In 2011, 64 master's awarded. *Entrance requirements:* Additional exam requirements/recommendations for international students: Required—TOEFL (minimum score 550 paper-based; 213 computer-based). *Application deadline:* For fall admission, 6/15 priority date for domestic students, 6/15 for international students; for spring admission, 11/15 priority date for domestic students, 11/15 for international students. Applications are processed on a rolling basis. Application fee: $20. Electronic applications accepted. *Expenses: Tuition:* Full-time $10,290; part-time $686 per credit. Tuition and fees vary according to course load, degree level and program. *Financial support:* Application deadline: 4/1; applicants required to submit FAFSA. *Unit head:* Dr. Roberta Schomburg, Associate Dean and Director, 412-578-6312, Fax: 412-578-8816, E-mail: schomburgrl@carlow.edu. *Application contact:* Jo Danhires, Administrative Assistant of Admissions, 412-578-6059, Fax: 412-578-6321, E-mail: gradstudies@carlow.edu. Web site: http://www.carlow.edu/.

Carnegie Mellon University, College of Humanities and Social Sciences, Center for Innovation in Learning, Pittsburgh, PA 15213-3891. Offers instructional science (PhD). *Faculty research:* Improvement of undergraduate education, teaching and learning at the college level.

Carroll University, Graduate Program in Education, Waukesha, WI 53186-5593. Offers education (M Ed); learning and teaching (M Ed). Part-time and evening/weekend programs available. *Degree requirements:* For master's, thesis. *Entrance requirements:* For master's, minimum undergraduate GPA of 2.5 in related field. Additional exam requirements/recommendations for international students: Required—TOEFL. Electronic applications accepted. *Faculty research:* Qualitative research methods, whole language approaches to teaching, the writing process, multicultural education, gifted/talented learners.

Carson-Newman College, Graduate Program in Education, Jefferson City, TN 37760. Offers curriculum and instruction (M Ed); educational leadership (M Ed); elementary education (MAT); school counseling (MS); secondary education (MAT); teaching English as a second language (MATESL). *Accreditation:* NCATE. Part-time and evening/weekend programs available. *Faculty:* 5 full-time (2 women), 10 part-time/adjunct (3 women). *Students:* 85 full-time (55 women), 76 part-time (53 women); includes 8 minority (5 Black or African American, non-Hispanic/Latino; 2 Asian, non-Hispanic/Latino; 1 Two or more races, non-Hispanic/Latino), 23 international. Average age 32. 80 applicants, 96% accepted. In 2011, 90 master's awarded. *Degree requirements:* For master's, thesis or alternative. *Entrance requirements:* For master's, NTE, minimum GPA of 3.0 in major, 2.5 overall. *Application deadline:* For fall admission, 7/15 priority date for domestic students. Applications are processed on a rolling basis. Application fee: $25 ($50 for international students). *Expenses: Tuition:* Full-time $6750; part-time $375 per credit hour. *Required fees:* $200. *Financial support:* In 2011–12, 41 students received support. Federal Work-Study and unspecified assistantships available. Financial award application deadline: 4/1; financial award applicants required to submit FAFSA. *Unit head:* Dr. Sharon Teets, Chair, 865-471-3461. *Application contact:* Graduate Admissions and Services Adviser, 865-471-3460, Fax: 865-471-3875.

Carthage College, Division of Teacher Education, Kenosha, WI 53140. Offers classroom guidance and counseling (M Ed); creative arts (M Ed); gifted and talented children (M Ed); language arts (M Ed); modern language (M Ed); natural sciences (M Ed); reading (M Ed, Certificate); social sciences (M Ed); teacher leadership (M Ed). Part-time and evening/weekend programs available. *Degree requirements:* For master's, thesis optional. *Entrance requirements:* For master's, MAT, minimum B average, letters of reference.

Castleton State College, Division of Graduate Studies, Department of Education, Castleton, VT 05735. Offers curriculum and instruction (MA Ed); educational leadership (MA Ed, CAGS); language arts and reading (MA Ed, CAGS); special education (MA Ed, CAGS). Part-time and evening/weekend programs available. *Degree requirements:* For master's, thesis or alternative; for CAGS, publishable paper. *Entrance requirements:* For master's, GRE General Test, MAT, interview, minimum undergraduate GPA of 3.0; for CAGS, educational research, master's degree, minimum undergraduate GPA of 3.0. *Faculty research:* Assessment, narrative.

Catawba College, Program in Education, Salisbury, NC 28144-2488. Offers elementary education (M Ed). *Accreditation:* NCATE. Part-time and evening/weekend programs available. *Faculty:* 4 full-time (3 women). *Students:* 35 part-time (34 women). Average age 36. In 2011, 17 master's awarded. *Degree requirements:* For master's, portfolio. *Entrance requirements:* For master's, NTE, PRAXIS II, minimum undergraduate GPA of 3.0, valid teaching license, official transcripts, 3 references, essay, interview, practicing teacher. *Application deadline:* For fall admission, 7/1 for domestic students; for spring admission, 12/1 for domestic students. Applications are processed on a rolling basis. Application fee: $25. *Expenses: Tuition:* Part-time $160 per credit hour. *Financial support:* Scholarships/grants available. Financial award applicants required to submit FAFSA. *Unit head:* Dr. Rhonda Truitt, Chair, Department of Teacher Education, 704-637-4468, Fax: 704-637-4732, E-mail: rltruitt@catawba.edu. *Application contact:* Dr. Lou W. Kasias, Director, Graduate Program, 704-637-4462, Fax: 704-637-4732, E-mail: lakasias@catawba.edu. Web site: http://www.catawba.edu/academic/teachereducation/grad/.

The Catholic University of America, School of Arts and Sciences, Department of Education, Washington, DC 20064. Offers Catholic educational leadership and policy studies (PhD); Catholic school leadership (MA); education (Certificate); educational psychology (PhD); secondary education (MA); special education (MA). *Accreditation:* NCATE. Part-time programs available. *Faculty:* 10 full-time (8 women), 10 part-time/adjunct (8 women). *Students:* 4 full-time (all women), 44 part-time (34 women); includes 12 minority (6 Black or African American, non-Hispanic/Latino; 4 Hispanic/Latino; 2 Two or more races, non-Hispanic/Latino). Average age 39. 38 applicants, 24% accepted, 2 enrolled. In 2011, 5 master's, 4 doctorates, 3 other advanced degrees awarded. *Degree requirements:* For master's, comprehensive exam, thesis or alternative; for doctorate, comprehensive exam, thesis/dissertation; for Certificate, action research project. *Entrance requirements:* For master's and doctorate, GRE General Test or MAT, statement of purpose, official copies of academic transcripts, three letters of recommendation, interview; for Certificate, PRAXIS I, statement of purpose, official copies of academic transcripts, three letters of recommendation, interview. Additional exam requirements/recommendations for international students: Required—TOEFL (minimum score 580 paper-based; 237 computer-based). *Application deadline:* For fall admission, 8/1 priority date for domestic students, 7/15 for international students; for spring admission, 12/1 priority date for domestic students, 10/15 for international students. Applications are processed on a rolling basis. Application fee: $55. Electronic applications accepted. *Expenses: Tuition:* Full-time $35,260; part-time $1380 per credit. *Required fees:* $80; $40 per semester hour. One-time fee: $425. *Financial support:* Fellowships, research assistantships, teaching assistantships, Federal Work-Study, scholarships/grants, tuition waivers (full and partial), and unspecified assistantships available. Financial award application deadline: 2/1; financial award applicants required to submit FAFSA. *Faculty research:* Special education, early childhood education, educational psychology, Catholic school administration, leadership and policy studies, counseling, curriculum and instruction. *Total annual research expenditures:* $36,210. *Unit head:* Dr. Merylann J. Schuttloffel, Chair, 202-319-5805, Fax: 202-319-5815, E-mail: schuttloffel@cua.edu. *Application contact:* Andrew Woodall, Director of Graduate Admissions, 202-319-5057, Fax: 202-319-6533, E-mail: cua-admissions@cua.edu. Web site: http://education.cua.edu/.

Cedar Crest College, Department of Education, Allentown, PA 18104-6196. Offers M Ed. Part-time and evening/weekend programs available. *Faculty:* 7 full-time (3 women), 3 part-time/adjunct (1 woman). *Students:* 42 full-time (37 women), 96 part-time (90 women). In 2011, 40 master's awarded. *Entrance requirements:* Additional exam requirements/recommendations for international students: Required—TOEFL. *Application deadline:* For fall admission, 8/7 priority date for domestic students, 8/7 for international students; for winter admission, 11/7 priority date for domestic students, 11/7 for international students; for spring admission, 1/8 priority date for domestic students, 1/8 for international students. Applications are processed on a rolling basis. *Expenses: Tuition:* Part-time $590 per credit. Tuition and fees vary according to program. *Financial support:* In 2011–12, 60 students received support. Available to part-time students. Applicants required to submit FAFSA. *Faculty research:* Science education, reading, history of Pennsylvania, math education. *Unit head:* Dr. Jill Purdy, Graduate Program Director, 610-606-4666 Ext. 3419, E-mail: jepurdy@cedarcrest.edu. *Application contact:* Bonnie Soffarelli, Director of School of Adult and Graduate Education, 610-606-4666, E-mail: sage@cedarcrest.edu.

Cedarville University, Graduate Programs, Cedarville, OH 45314-0601. Offers family nurse practitioner (MSN); global health nursing (MSN); nurse educator (MSN); teacher leader (M Ed). Part-time programs available. *Faculty:* 27 part-time/adjunct (14 women). *Students:* 13 full-time (11 women), 66 part-time (51 women), 2 international. Average age 33. 65 applicants, 83% accepted, 38 enrolled. In 2011, 2 master's awarded. *Degree requirements:* For master's, thesis. *Entrance requirements:* For master's, GRE, 2 professional recommendations. Additional exam requirements/recommendations for international students: Required—TOEFL (minimum score 550 paper-based; 80 iBT). *Application deadline:* For fall admission, 5/1 priority date for domestic students, 5/1 for international students; for spring admission, 11/1 priority date for domestic students, 11/1 for international students. Applications are processed on a rolling basis. Application fee: $30. Electronic applications accepted. *Financial support:* Scholarships/grants and unspecified assistantships available. Support available to part-time students. Financial award applicants required to submit FAFSA. *Unit head:* Dr. Andrew A. Runyan, Senior Associate Academic Vice-President/Dean of Graduate Studies, 937-766-3840, E-mail: arunyan@cedarville.edu. *Application contact:* Roscoe F. Smith, Associate Vice-President of Enrollment, 937-766-7700, Fax: 937-766-7575, E-mail: smithr@cedarville.edu. Web site: http://www.cedarville.edu/academics/graduate/.

Centenary College, Program in Education, Hackettstown, NJ 07840-2100. Offers educational leadership (MA); instructional leadership (MA); special education (MA). *Accreditation:* Teacher Education Accreditation Council. Part-time and evening/weekend programs available. Postbaccalaureate distance learning degree programs offered (minimal on-campus study). *Degree requirements:* For master's, thesis. *Entrance requirements:* For master's, interview, minimum undergraduate GPA of 2.8.

Centenary College of Louisiana, Graduate Programs, Department of Education, Shreveport, LA 71104. Offers administration (M Ed); elementary education (MAT); secondary education (MAT); supervision of instruction (M Ed). Part-time and evening/weekend programs available. *Degree requirements:* For master's, comprehensive exam. *Entrance requirements:* For master's, GRE General Test (M Ed), PRAXIS I and PRAXIS II (MAT), teacher certification (M Ed), minimum GPA of 2.5. *Expenses:* Contact institution. *Faculty research:* Teachers as advocates for teachers, portfolio assessment, disabled readers.

Central Connecticut State University, School of Graduate Studies, School of Education and Professional Studies, New Britain, CT 06050-4010. Offers MAT, MS, Ed D, Certificate, Sixth Year Certificate. *Accreditation:* NCATE. Part-time and evening/weekend programs available. *Faculty:* 66 full-time (34 women), 105 part-time/adjunct (64 women). *Students:* 247 full-time (192 women), 875 part-time (659 women); includes 168 minority (80 Black or African American, non-Hispanic/Latino; 2 American Indian or Alaska Native, non-Hispanic/Latino; 13 Asian, non-Hispanic/Latino; 62 Hispanic/Latino; 1 Native Hawaiian or other Pacific Islander, non-Hispanic/Latino; 10 Two or more races, non-Hispanic/Latino), 3 international. Average age 32. 548 applicants, 59% accepted, 228 enrolled. In 2011, 344 master's, 6 doctorates, 70 other advanced degrees awarded. *Degree requirements:* For master's, comprehensive exam, thesis or alternative; for doctorate, thesis/dissertation; for other advanced degree, qualifying exam. *Entrance requirements:* For master's, minimum undergraduate GPA of 2.7; for doctorate, GRE. Additional exam requirements/recommendations for international students: Required—TOEFL (minimum score 550 paper-based; 213 computer-based). *Application deadline:* For fall admission, 6/1 for domestic students, 5/1 for international students; for spring admission, 11/1 for domestic and international students. Applications are processed on a rolling basis. Application fee: $50. Electronic applications accepted. *Expenses: Tuition, area resident:* Full-time $5137; part-time $482 per credit. Tuition, state resident: full-time $7707; part-time $494 per credit. Tuition, nonresident: full-time $14,311; part-time $494 per credit. *Required fees:* $3865. One-time fee: $62 part-time. *Financial support:* In 2011–12, 77 students received support, including 21 research assistantships; career-related internships or fieldwork, Federal Work-Study, scholarships/grants, and unspecified assistantships also available. Support available to part-time students. Financial award application deadline: 4/15; financial award applicants required to submit FAFSA. *Unit head:* Dr. Mitchell Sakofs, Dean, 860-832-2100, E-mail: sakofsm@ccsu.edu. *Application contact:* Patricia Gardner, Associate Director of Graduate Studies, 860-832-2350, Fax: 860-832-2352, E-mail: graduateadmissions@ccsu.edu. Web site: http://www.education.ccsu.edu/.

Central Methodist University, College of Graduate and Extended Studies, Fayette, MO 65248-1198. Offers clinical counseling (MS); clinical nurse leader (MSN); education (M Ed). Part-time and evening/weekend programs available. Postbaccalaureate distance learning degree programs offered (no on-campus study). *Degree requirements:* For master's, thesis. *Entrance requirements:* For master's, GRE General Test, minimum GPA of 2.75. Electronic applications accepted.

Central Michigan University, Central Michigan University Global Campus, Program in Education, Mount Pleasant, MI 48859. Offers adult education (MA); college teaching (Graduate Certificate); community college (MA); educational leadership (MA), including charter school leadership; educational technology (MA); guidance and development (MA); instruction (MA); reading and literacy K-12 (MA); school principalship (MA); teacher leadership (MA). *Accreditation:* Teacher Education Accreditation Council. Part-time and evening/weekend programs available. *Entrance requirements:* For master's, minimum GPA of 2.7 in major. Additional exam requirements/recommendations for international students: Required—TOEFL. *Application deadline:* Applications are processed on a rolling basis. Application fee: $50. Electronic applications accepted. *Financial support:* Scholarships/grants available. Support available to part-time students. *Unit head:* Dr. Peter Ross, Director, 989-774-4456, E-mail: ross1pg@cmich.edu. *Application contact:* 877-268-4636, E-mail: cmuglobal@cmich.edu.

Central Michigan University, College of Graduate Studies, College of Education and Human Services, Mount Pleasant, MI 48859. Offers MA, MS, Ed D, Ed S, Graduate Certificate. *Accreditation:* Teacher Education Accreditation Council. Part-time and evening/weekend programs available. *Degree requirements:* For master's and other advanced degree, thesis or alternative; for doctorate, thesis/dissertation. Electronic applications accepted.

Central State University, Program in Education, Wilberforce, OH 45384. Offers M Ed. *Accreditation:* NCATE. Part-time and evening/weekend programs available. *Degree requirements:* For master's, thesis or alternative. *Entrance requirements:* For master's, GRE.

Central Washington University, Graduate Studies and Research, College of Education and Professional Studies, Department of Language, Literacy and Special Education, Ellensburg, WA 98926. Offers reading education (M Ed); special education (M Ed). Part-time programs available. *Faculty:* 11 full-time (8 women). *Students:* 1 (woman) full-time, 3 part-time (2 women). 5 applicants, 100% accepted, 3 enrolled. In 2011, 2 master's awarded. *Degree requirements:* For master's, thesis or alternative. *Entrance requirements:* For master's, minimum GPA of 3.0. Additional exam requirements/recommendations for international students: Required—TOEFL (minimum score 550 paper-based; 213 computer-based; 79 iBT), IELTS (minimum score 6.5). *Application deadline:* For fall admission, 2/1 priority date for domestic students; for winter admission, 10/1 for domestic students; for spring admission, 1/1 for domestic students. Applications are processed on a rolling basis. Application fee: $50. Electronic applications accepted. *Expenses:* Tuition, state resident: full-time $8112; part-time $270 per credit. Tuition, nonresident: full-time $18,069; part-time $602 per credit. *Required fees:* $924. *Financial support:* In 2011–12, teaching assistantships with partial tuition reimbursements (averaging $9,234 per year) were awarded; Federal Work-Study, health care benefits, and unspecified assistantships also available. Financial award application deadline: 3/1; financial award applicants required to submit FAFSA. *Unit head:* Dr. Dan Fennerty, Co-Chair, 509-963-2737. *Application contact:* Justine Eason, Admissions

Program Coordinator, 509-963-3103, Fax: 509-963-1799, E-mail: masters@cwu.edu. Web site: http://www.cwu.edu/~llse/.

Chadron State College, School of Professional and Graduate Studies, Department of Education, Chadron, NE 69337. Offers business (MA Ed); community counseling (MA Ed); educational administration (MS Ed, Sp Ed); elementary education (MS Ed); history (MA Ed); language and literature (MA Ed); secondary administration (MS Ed); secondary education (MS Ed). *Accreditation:* NCATE. Part-time and evening/weekend programs available. Postbaccalaureate distance learning degree programs offered. *Degree requirements:* For master's, thesis optional. *Entrance requirements:* For master's, GRE General Test, GRE Writing Test, minimum GPA of 2.75 or 12 graduate hours at CSC with minimum GPA of 3.25. Additional exam requirements/ recommendations for international students: Required—TOEFL. Electronic applications accepted. *Faculty research:* Rural education, technology, mental health.

Chaminade University of Honolulu, Graduate Services, Program in Education, Honolulu, HI 96816-1578. Offers child development (M Ed); educational leadership (M Ed); elementary education with licensure (MAT); instructional leadership (M Ed); Montessori credential (M Ed); Montessori emphasis (M Ed); secondary education with licensure (MAT), including English, math, science, social studies; special education with licensure (MAT). Part-time and evening/weekend programs available. Postbaccalaureate distance learning degree programs offered (minimal on-campus study). *Faculty:* 2 full-time (both women), 32 part-time/adjunct (25 women). *Students:* 53 full-time (38 women), 88 part-time (67 women); includes 77 minority (6 Black or African American, non-Hispanic/Latino; 1 American Indian or Alaska Native, non-Hispanic/ Latino; 44 Asian, non-Hispanic/Latino; 5 Hispanic/Latino; 17 Native Hawaiian or other Pacific Islander, non-Hispanic/Latino; 4 Two or more races, non-Hispanic/Latino), 1 international. Average age 35. 40 applicants, 88% accepted, 30 enrolled. In 2011, 105 master's awarded. *Degree requirements:* For master's, thesis or alternative. *Entrance requirements:* For master's, PRAXIS (for MAT only), minimum GPA of 2.75, 3 letters of recommendation. Additional exam requirements/recommendations for international students: Required—TOEFL (minimum score 550 paper-based). *Application deadline:* For fall admission, 9/1 priority date for domestic students, 9/1 for international students; for winter admission, 12/1 priority date for domestic students, 12/1 for international students; for spring admission, 3/1 priority date for domestic students, 3/1 for international students. Applications are processed on a rolling basis. Application fee: $50. Electronic applications accepted. *Expenses: Required fees:* $600 per credit hour. One-time fee: $93 part-time. *Financial support:* In 2011–12, 172 students received support. Career-related internships or fieldwork, Federal Work-Study, institutionally sponsored loans, scholarships/grants, and tuition waivers (partial) available. Support available to part-time students. Financial award application deadline: 3/1; financial award applicants required to submit FAFSA. *Faculty research:* Peace and curriculum education. *Unit head:* Dr. Joseph Peters, Dean, 808-440-4251, Fax: 808-739-4607, E-mail: joseph.peters@chaminade.edu. *Application contact:* 808-739-4663, Fax: 808-739-8329, E-mail: gradserv@chaminade.edu. Web site: http://www.chaminade.edu/ education/grad.php.

Champlain College, Graduate Studies, Burlington, VT 05402-0670. Offers business (MBA); digital forensic management (MS); education (M Ed); emergent media (MFA); health care management (MS); law (MS); managing innovation and information technology (MS); mediation and applied conflict studies (MS). Part-time programs available. Postbaccalaureate distance learning degree programs offered (no on-campus study). *Faculty:* 11 full-time (1 woman), 26 part-time/adjunct (11 women). *Students:* 328 full-time (213 women), 66 part-time (36 women); includes 17 minority (11 Black or African American, non-Hispanic/Latino; 1 Asian, non-Hispanic/Latino; 4 Hispanic/Latino; 1 Two or more races, non-Hispanic/Latino). Average age 37. 132 applicants, 90% accepted, 102 enrolled. In 2011, 8 master's awarded. *Degree requirements:* For master's, capstone project. *Entrance requirements:* Additional exam requirements/ recommendations for international students: Required—TOEFL. *Application deadline:* For fall admission, 8/1 priority date for domestic students, 8/1 for international students; for spring admission, 1/1 priority date for domestic students, 1/1 for international students. Applications are processed on a rolling basis. Application fee: $50. Electronic applications accepted. *Expenses: Tuition:* Part-time $746 per credit. Tuition and fees vary according to program. *Financial support:* Applicants required to submit FAFSA. *Unit head:* Dr. Donald Haggerty, Associate Provost, 802-865-6403, Fax: 802-865-6447. *Application contact:* Jon Walsh, Assistant Vice President, Graduate Admission, 800-570-5858, E-mail: walsh@champlain.edu. Web site: http://www.champlain.edu/master/.

Chapman University, College of Educational Studies, Orange, CA 92866. Offers communication sciences and disorders (MS); counseling (MA), including school counseling (MA, Credential); education (MA, PhD), including cultural and curricular studies (PhD), disability studies (PhD), school psychology (PhD, Credential); educational psychology (MA); professional clear (Credential); pupil personnel services (Credential), including school counseling (MA, Credential), school psychology (PhD, Credential); school psychology (Ed S); single subject (Credential); special education (MA); special education (level ii) (Credential), including mild/moderate, moderate/ severe; special education (preliminary) (Credential), including mild/moderate, moderate/ severe; speech language pathology (Credential); teaching (MA), including elementary education, secondary education. *Accreditation:* Teacher Education Accreditation Council. Part-time and evening/weekend programs available. *Faculty:* 27 full-time (18 women), 35 part-time/adjunct (24 women). *Students:* 220 full-time (188 women), 164 part-time (128 women); includes 140 minority (12 Black or African American, non-Hispanic/Latino; 1 American Indian or Alaska Native, non-Hispanic/Latino; 44 Asian, non-Hispanic/Latino; 73 Hispanic/Latino; 4 Native Hawaiian or other Pacific Islander, non-Hispanic/Latino; 6 Two or more races, non-Hispanic/Latino), 1 international. Average age 29. 436 applicants, 38% accepted, 126 enrolled. In 2011, 130 master's, 5 doctorates awarded. *Entrance requirements:* Additional exam requirements/ recommendations for international students: Required—TOEFL (minimum score 550 paper-based; 213 computer-based; 80 iBT). *Application deadline:* Applications are processed on a rolling basis. Application fee: $60. Electronic applications accepted. Tuition and fees vary according to degree level and program. *Financial support:* Fellowships and scholarships/grants available. Financial award application deadline: 6/ 30; financial award applicants required to submit FAFSA. *Unit head:* Dr. Don Cardinal, Dean, 714-997-6781, E-mail: cardinal@chapman.edu. *Application contact:* Admissions Coordinator, 714-997-6714. Web site: http://www.chapman.edu/CES/.

Charleston Southern University, School of Education, Charleston, SC 29423-8087. Offers administration and supervision (M Ed), including elementary, secondary; elementary education (M Ed); secondary education (M Ed). *Accreditation:* NCATE. Part-time and evening/weekend programs available. *Degree requirements:* For master's, thesis optional. *Entrance requirements:* For master's, GRE or MAT. Additional exam requirements/recommendations for international students: Required—TOEFL (minimum score 550 paper-based; 213 computer-based; 79 iBT). *Expenses:* Contact institution.

Chatham University, Program in Education, Pittsburgh, PA 15232-2826. Offers early childhood education (MAT); elementary education (MAT); environmental education (K-12) (MAT); secondary art (MAT); secondary biology education (MAT); secondary chemistry education (MAT); secondary English education (MAT); secondary math education (MAT); secondary physics education (MAT); secondary social studies education (MAT); special education (MAT). *Students:* 52 full-time (42 women), 17 part-time (16 women); includes 2 minority (1 Black or African American, non-Hispanic/Latino; 1 Hispanic/Latino). Average age 29. 39 applicants, 82% accepted, 23 enrolled. In 2011, 37 master's awarded. *Degree requirements:* For master's, thesis, teaching experience. *Entrance requirements:* For master's, minimum GPA of 3.0, sample of written work, recommendation letters. Additional exam requirements/recommendations for international students: Required—TOEFL (minimum score 600 paper-based; 250 computer-based; 100 iBT), IELTS (minimum score 7), TWE. *Application deadline:* For fall admission, 4/1 priority date for domestic students, 4/1 for international students; for spring admission, 11/1 priority date for domestic students, 10/1 for international students. Applications are processed on a rolling basis. Application fee: $45. Electronic applications accepted. Application fee is waived when completed online. *Expenses: Tuition:* Full-time $13,896. Tuition and fees vary according to program. *Financial support:* Career-related internships or fieldwork available. Financial award applicants required to submit FAFSA. *Faculty research:* Gifted education, environmental education, technology in education, writing as learning, class size and achievement. *Unit head:* Dr. Elvira Sanatullova-Allison, Director of Education Programs, 412-365-2773, E-mail: esanatullovaallison@chatham.edu. *Application contact:* Dory Perry, Associate Director of Graduate Admission, 412-365-2758, Fax: 412-365-1609, E-mail: gradadmissions@ chatham.edu. Web site: http://www.chatham.edu/mat.

Chestnut Hill College, School of Graduate Studies, Department of Education, Philadelphia, PA 19118-2693. Offers early education (M Ed); educational leadership (M Ed); middle education (M Ed); secondary education (M Ed). Part-time and evening/ weekend programs available. *Faculty:* 6 full-time (4 women), 50 part-time/adjunct (33 women). *Students:* 42 full-time (30 women), 246 part-time (201 women); includes 50 minority (35 Black or African American, non-Hispanic/Latino; 5 Asian, non-Hispanic/ Latino; 8 Hispanic/Latino; 2 Two or more races, non-Hispanic/Latino). Average age 32. 77 applicants, 99% accepted. In 2011, 138 master's awarded. *Degree requirements:* For master's, thesis optional. *Entrance requirements:* For master's, PRAXIS I or proof of teaching certification, letters of recommendation, writing sample, 6 graduate credits with minimum B grade if undergraduate GPA less than 3.0. Additional exam requirements/ recommendations for international students: Required—TOEFL (minimum score 500 paper-based; 213 computer-based). *Application deadline:* For fall admission, 7/17 priority date for domestic students, 7/15 for international students; for spring admission, 12/15 priority date for domestic students, 12/15 for international students. Applications are processed on a rolling basis. Application fee: $55. *Expenses: Tuition:* Part-time $555 per credit hour. One-time fee: $55 part-time. Part-time tuition and fees vary according to degree level and program. *Financial support:* Unspecified assistantships available. *Faculty research:* Culturally responsive pedagogy, gender issues, autism, inclusive education, mentoring and induction programs. *Unit head:* Dr. Carol Pate, Department Chair, 215-248-7127, Fax: 215-248-7155, E-mail: cpate@chc.edu. *Application contact:* Amy Boorse, Administrative Assistant, School of Graduate Studies Office, 215-248-7170, Fax: 215-248-7161, E-mail: gradadmissions@chc.edu. Web site: http:// www.chc.edu/Graduate/Programs/Masters/Education/.

Cheyney University of Pennsylvania, School of Education and Professional Studies, Cheyney, PA 19319. Offers M Ed, MAT, MPA, MS, Certificate. *Accreditation:* NCATE. Part-time and evening/weekend programs available. *Degree requirements:* For master's and Certificate, thesis or alternative. *Entrance requirements:* For master's and Certificate, GRE General Test, MAT, minimum GPA of 2.75. Electronic applications accepted. *Faculty research:* Teacher motivation, critical thinking.

Chicago State University, School of Graduate and Professional Studies, College of Education, Chicago, IL 60628. Offers M Ed, MA, MAT, MS Ed, Ed D. *Accreditation:* NCATE. Part-time programs available. *Degree requirements:* For master's, thesis optional. *Entrance requirements:* For master's, minimum GPA of 2.75.

Chowan University, School of Graduate Studies, Murfreesboro, NC 27855. Offers education (M Ed). Electronic applications accepted.

Christian Brothers University, School of Arts, Memphis, TN 38104-5581. Offers Catholic studies (MACS); educational leadership (MSEL); teacher-leadership (M Ed); teaching (MAT). Part-time and evening/weekend programs available. *Entrance requirements:* For master's, GRE, GMAT, PRAXIS II. *Expenses:* Contact institution.

Christopher Newport University, Graduate Studies, Department of Teacher Preparation, Newport News, VA 23606-2998. Offers art (PK-12) (MAT); biology (6-12) (MAT); chemistry (6-12) (MAT); computer science (6-12) (MAT); elementary (PK-6) (MAT); English (6-12) (MAT); English as second language (PK-12) (MAT); French (PK-12) (MAT); history and social science (6-12) (MAT); mathematics (6-12) (MAT); music (PK-12) (MAT), including choral, instrumental; physics (6-12) (MAT); Spanish (PK-12) (MAT). Part-time and evening/weekend programs available. *Degree requirements:* For master's, comprehensive exam, thesis or alternative. *Entrance requirements:* For master's, PRAXIS I, minimum GPA of 3.0. Additional exam requirements/ recommendations for international students: Required—TOEFL (minimum score 580 paper-based; 237 computer-based; 92 iBT). Electronic applications accepted. *Faculty research:* Early literacy development, instructional innovations, professional teaching standards, multicultural issues, aesthetic education.

The Citadel, The Military College of South Carolina, Citadel Graduate College, School of Education, Charleston, SC 29409. Offers M Ed, MAE, MAT, Ed S. *Accreditation:* NCATE. Part-time and evening/weekend programs available. *Faculty:* 12 full-time (8 women), 9 part-time/adjunct (4 women). *Students:* 45 full-time (33 women), 191 part-time (138 women); includes 35 minority (26 Black or African American, non-Hispanic/Latino; 1 American Indian or Alaska Native, non-Hispanic/Latino; 4 Asian, non-Hispanic/Latino; 4 Hispanic/Latino). Average age 32. In 2011, 92 master's, 3 other advanced degrees awarded. *Degree requirements:* For master's and Ed S, comprehensive exam (for some programs), thesis (for some programs), internship. *Entrance requirements:* For master's, GRE (minimum score 900) or MAT (minimum score 396), minimum undergraduate GPA of 2.5, 2.7 for last 60 undergraduate semester hours; for Ed S, GRE (minimum score 900) or MAT (minimum score 396), minimum GPA of 3.5; SC State Professional Certificate with school administrator endorsement and two years in an administrative position equivalent to assistant principal or higher in education. Additional exam requirements/recommendations for international students: Required—TOEFL (minimum score 550 paper-based; 213 computer-based; 79 iBT). *Application deadline:* Applications are processed on a rolling basis. Application fee: $30. Electronic applications accepted. *Expenses: Tuition, area resident:* Part-time $501 per credit hour. Tuition, state resident: part-time $501 per credit hour. Tuition, nonresident: part-time $824 per credit hour. *Required fees:* $40 per term. One-time fee: $30. *Financial support:* Fellowships, career-related internships or fieldwork, health care benefits, and unspecified assistantships available. Support available to part-time students. Financial award application deadline: 7/1; financial award applicants required to submit FAFSA. *Unit head:* Dr. Tony W. Johnson, Dean, 843-953-5871, Fax: 843-953-7258, E-mail: tony.johnson@citadel.edu. *Application contact:* Dr. Steve A. Nida, Associate Provost, The Citadel Graduate College, 843-953-5089, Fax: 843-953-7630, E-mail: cgc@citadel.edu. Web site: http://www.citadel.edu/education/.

City College of the City University of New York, Graduate School, School of Education, New York, NY 10031-9198. Offers MA, MS, AC. *Accreditation:* NCATE. Part-time and evening/weekend programs available. *Entrance requirements:* For master's, Liberal Arts and Sciences Test (LAST), Content Specialty Test (CST). Additional exam requirements/recommendations for international students: Required—TOEFL.

City University of Seattle, Graduate Division, Albright School of Education, Bellevue, WA 98005. Offers administrator certification (Certificate); curriculum and instruction (M Ed); educational leadership (Ed D); elementary education (MIT); guidance and counseling (M Ed); higher education leadership (Ed D); leadership (M Ed); leadership and school counseling (M Ed); organizational leadership (Ed D); reading and literacy (M Ed); special education (MIT); superintendent certification (Certificate). Part-time and evening/weekend programs available. Postbaccalaureate distance learning degree programs offered (no on-campus study). *Faculty:* 23 full-time (15 women), 123 part-time/adjunct (82 women). *Students:* 353 full-time (263 women), 75 part-time (50 women); includes 40 minority (12 Black or African American, non-Hispanic/Latino; 5 American Indian or Alaska Native, non-Hispanic/Latino; 7 Asian, non-Hispanic/Latino; 8 Hispanic/Latino; 5 Native Hawaiian or other Pacific Islander, non-Hispanic/Latino; 3 Two or more races, non-Hispanic/Latino). Average age 36. 129 applicants, 98% accepted, 126 enrolled. In 2011, 351 master's, 30 Certificates awarded. *Degree requirements:* For master's, comprehensive exam (for some programs), thesis (for some programs); for doctorate, comprehensive exam, thesis/dissertation. *Entrance requirements:* Additional exam requirements/recommendations for international students: Required—TOEFL (minimum score 567 paper-based; 227 computer-based; 87 iBT); Recommended—IELTS. *Application deadline:* For fall admission, 9/1 for international students; for winter admission, 12/1 for international students; for spring admission, 3/1 for international students. Applications are processed on a rolling basis. Application fee: $50. Electronic applications accepted. *Expenses:* Contact institution. *Financial support:* In 2011–12, 40 students received support. Federal Work-Study and scholarships/grants available. Support available to part-time students. Financial award applicants required to submit FAFSA. *Unit head:* Craig Schieber, Dean, 425-637-101 Ext. 5460, Fax: 425-709-5363, E-mail: schieber@cityu.edu. *Application contact:* Alysa Borelli, 888-422-4898, Fax: 425-709-5363, E-mail: info@cityu.edu. Web site: http://www.cityu.edu/programs/soe/index.aspx.

Claremont Graduate University, Graduate Programs, School of Educational Studies, Claremont, CA 91711-6160. Offers Africana education (Certificate); education and policy (MA, PhD); higher education/student affairs (MA, PhD); human development (MA, PhD); public school administration (MA, PhD); quantitative evaluation (MA, PhD); special education (MA, PhD); teacher education (MA); teaching and learning (MA, PhD); urban leadership (PhD); MBA/PhD: PhD program offered jointly with San Diego State University. Part-time programs available. *Faculty:* 18 full-time (10 women), 2 part-time/adjunct (1 woman). *Students:* 307 full-time (220 women), 134 part-time (96 women); includes 228 minority (59 Black or African American, non-Hispanic/Latino; 3 American Indian or Alaska Native, non-Hispanic/Latino; 37 Asian, non-Hispanic/Latino; 110 Hispanic/Latino; 2 Native Hawaiian or other Pacific Islander, non-Hispanic/Latino; 17 Two or more races, non-Hispanic/Latino), 13 international. Average age 38. In 2011, 93 master's, 23 doctorates, 10 other advanced degrees awarded. Terminal master's awarded for partial completion of doctoral program. *Entrance requirements:* For master's and doctorate, GRE General Test. Additional exam requirements/recommendations for international students: Required—TOEFL (minimum score 550 paper-based; 213 computer-based; 80 iBT). *Application deadline:* For fall admission, 2/1 priority date for domestic students. Applications are processed on a rolling basis. Application fee: $60. Electronic applications accepted. *Expenses: Tuition:* Full-time $36,374; part-time $1581 per unit. *Required fees:* $165 per semester. *Financial support:* Fellowships, research assistantships, Federal Work-Study, institutionally sponsored loans, and scholarships/grants available. Support available to part-time students. Financial award application deadline: 2/15; financial award applicants required to submit FAFSA. *Faculty research:* Education administration, K-12 and higher education, multicultural education, education policy, diversity in higher education, faculty issues. *Unit head:* Margaret Grogan, Dean, 909-621-8075, Fax: 909-621-8734, E-mail: margaret.grogan@cgu.edu. *Application contact:* Julia Evans, Director of Central Recruitment, 909-607-3689, Fax: 909-607-7285, E-mail: admiss@cgu.edu. Web site: http://www.cgu.edu/pages/267.asp.

Clarion University of Pennsylvania, Office of Graduate Programs, Master of Education Program, Clarion, PA 16214. Offers curriculum and instruction (M Ed); early childhood (M Ed, Certificate); English (M Ed); instructional technology specialist (K-12) (Certificate); literacy (M Ed); mathematics education (M Ed); reading specialist (M Ed, Certificate); science education (M Ed); special education (M Ed); technology (M Ed); world language (M Ed). *Accreditation:* NCATE. Part-time programs available. *Students:* 14 full-time (11 women), 207 part-time (163 women); includes 3 minority (1 Black or African American, non-Hispanic/Latino; 2 Hispanic/Latino). Average age 31. In 2011, 96 master's awarded. *Degree requirements:* For master's, thesis or alternative. *Entrance requirements:* For master's, minimum QPA of 3.0. *Application deadline:* Applications are processed on a rolling basis. *Expenses:* Tuition, state resident: part-time $429 per credit. Tuition, nonresident: part-time $644 per credit. *Financial support:* Research assistantships with full and partial tuition reimbursements and career-related internships or fieldwork available. Support available to part-time students. Financial award application deadline: 3/1. *Unit head:* Dr. John Groves, Dean, 814-393-2146, Fax: 514-393-2446. *Application contact:* Dr. Brenda Sanders Dede, Assistant Vice President for Academic Affairs, 814-393-2337, Fax: 814-393-2030, E-mail: bdede@clarion.edu. Web site: http://www.clarion.edu/25887/.

Clark Atlanta University, School of Education, Atlanta, GA 30314. Offers MA, MAT, Ed D, Ed S. *Accreditation:* NCATE. Part-time and evening/weekend programs available. *Faculty:* 10 full-time (7 women), 13 part-time/adjunct (9 women). *Students:* 53 full-time (35 women), 74 part-time (44 women); includes 120 minority (119 Black or African American, non-Hispanic/Latino; 1 Asian, non-Hispanic/Latino), 1 international. Average age 33. 71 applicants, 92% accepted, 31 enrolled. In 2011, 40 master's, 10 doctorates, 1 other advanced degree awarded. *Degree requirements:* For master's, comprehensive exam; for doctorate, comprehensive exam, thesis/dissertation. *Entrance requirements:* For master's, GRE General Test, minimum undergraduate GPA of 2.6; for doctorate, GRE General Test, minimum graduate GPA of 3.0. Additional exam requirements/recommendations for international students: Required—TOEFL (minimum score 500 paper-based; 173 computer-based; 61 iBT). *Application deadline:* For fall admission, 4/1 for domestic and international students; for spring admission, 11/1 for domestic and international students. Applications are processed on a rolling basis. Application fee: $40 ($55 for international students). Electronic applications accepted. *Expenses: Tuition:* Full-time $13,572; part-time $754 per credit hour. *Required fees:* $806; $403 per semester. *Financial support:* Career-related internships or fieldwork, Federal Work-Study, scholarships/grants, and unspecified assistantships available. Support available to part-time students. Financial award application deadline: 4/30; financial award applicants required to submit FAFSA. *Unit head:* Dr. Sean Warner, Interim Dean, 404-880-8504, E-mail: swarner@cau.edu. *Application contact:* Michelle Clark-Davis, Graduate Program Admissions, 404-880-6605, E-mail: cauadmissions@cau.edu.

Clarke University, Program in Education, Dubuque, IA 52001-3198. Offers early childhood/special education (MAE); educational administration: elementary and secondary (MAE); educational media: elementary and secondary (MAE); multi-categorical resource k-12 (MAE); multidisciplinary studies (MAE); reading: elementary (MAE); technology in education (MAE). Part-time and evening/weekend programs available. Postbaccalaureate distance learning degree programs offered (minimal on-campus study). *Faculty:* 4 full-time (3 women), 2 part-time/adjunct (1 woman). *Students:* 7 full-time (all women), 43 part-time (40 women). Average age 31. In 2011, 11 master's awarded. *Degree requirements:* For master's, comprehensive exam, thesis optional. *Entrance requirements:* For master's, GRE General Test or MAT, minimum GPA of 2.75. *Application deadline:* Applications are processed on a rolling basis. Application fee: $25. Electronic applications accepted. *Expenses: Tuition:* Part-time $690 per credit hour. *Required fees:* $35 per credit hour. Tuition and fees vary according to program and student level. *Financial support:* Career-related internships or fieldwork available. Financial award applicants required to submit FAFSA. *Unit head:* Dr. Larry Bice, Chair, 319-588-6397, Fax: 319-584-8604. *Application contact:* Joan Coates, Information Contact, 563-588-6354, Fax: 563-588-6789, E-mail: graduate@clarke.edu.

Clark University, Graduate School, Department of Education, Worcester, MA 01610-1477. Offers MAT. *Faculty:* 6 full-time (5 women), 5 part-time/adjunct (2 women). *Students:* 38 full-time (28 women), 5 part-time (4 women); includes 4 minority (all Hispanic/Latino). Average age 24. 57 applicants, 82% accepted, 42 enrolled. In 2011, 48 master's awarded. *Degree requirements:* For master's, thesis or alternative, oral exam. *Entrance requirements:* For master's, GRE General Test, minimum GPA of 3.0, professional experience. Additional exam requirements/recommendations for international students: Required—TOEFL. *Application deadline:* For fall admission, 2/1 priority date for domestic students. Applications are processed on a rolling basis. Application fee: $50. *Expenses: Tuition:* Full-time $37,000; part-time $1156 per credit hour. *Financial support:* Fellowships with full and partial tuition reimbursements, research assistantships with full and partial tuition reimbursements, teaching assistantships with full and partial tuition reimbursements, institutionally sponsored loans, and tuition waivers (partial) available. Financial award application deadline: 5/1. *Faculty research:* Developmental learning, instructional theory, educational program management, special education, urban education. *Total annual research expenditures:* $360,000. *Unit head:* Dr. Thomas DelPrete, Chair, 508-793-7222. *Application contact:* Marlene Shepard, Program Coordinator, 508-793-7222, Fax: 508-793-8864, E-mail: education@clarku.edu. Web site: http://www.clarku.edu/departments/education/graduate/mat_grad.cfm.

Clayton State University, School of Graduate Studies, Program in Education, Morrow, GA 30260-0285. Offers English (MAT); mathematics (MAT). *Accreditation:* NCATE. *Faculty:* 12 full-time (7 women). *Students:* 11 full-time (8 women), 11 part-time (4 women); includes 10 minority (all Black or African American, non-Hispanic/Latino). Average age 33. 11 applicants, 100% accepted, 8 enrolled. In 2011, 9 master's awarded. *Entrance requirements:* For master's, GRE, GACE, 2 official copies of transcripts, 3 recommendation letters, statement of purpose. Additional exam requirements/recommendations for international students: Required—TOEFL (minimum score 550 paper-based; 213 computer-based). *Application deadline:* For fall admission, 6/15 priority date for domestic students, 5/1 for international students; for spring admission, 10/15 priority date for domestic students. Applications are processed on a rolling basis. Application fee: $75. Electronic applications accepted. *Expenses:* Tuition, state resident: full-time $3528; part-time $196 per credit hour. Tuition, nonresident: full-time $13,176; part-time $732 per credit hour. *Required fees:* $1404; $552 per semester. Tuition and fees vary according to course load and campus/location. *Unit head:* Dr. Mari Ann Roberts, Program Director, Master of Arts in Teaching (Education), 678-466-4720, E-mail: mariroberts@clayton.edu. *Application contact:* Melanie Nolan, Administrative Assistant, Master of Arts in Teaching English, 678-466-4735, Fax: 678-466-4899, E-mail: melanienolan@clayton.edu.

Clemson University, Graduate School, College of Health, Education, and Human Development, Eugene T. Moore School of Education, Clemson, SC 29634. Offers administration and supervision (K-12) (M Ed, Ed S); counselor education (M Ed), including clinical mental health counseling, community mental health, school counseling (K-12), student affairs (higher education); curriculum and instruction (PhD); early childhood education (M Ed), including early childhood education, elementary education, secondary English, secondary math, secondary science; early childhood education (M Ed), including secondary social studies; educational leadership (PhD), including higher education, K-12; human resource development (MHRD); middle grades education (MAT); reading literacy (M Ed); secondary education: math and science (MAT); special education (M Ed); teaching and learning (M Ed), including elementary education, English education, mathematics education, science education, social studies education. Part-time programs available. *Faculty:* 65 full-time (39 women), 4 part-time/adjunct (2 women). *Students:* 255 full-time (179 women), 284 part-time (188 women); includes 92 minority (67 Black or African American, non-Hispanic/Latino; 1 American Indian or Alaska Native, non-Hispanic/Latino; 4 Asian, non-Hispanic/Latino; 12 Hispanic/Latino; 1 Native Hawaiian or other Pacific Islander, non-Hispanic/Latino; 7 Two or more races, non-Hispanic/Latino), 7 international. Average age 33. 957 applicants, 32% accepted, 166 enrolled. In 2011, 213 master's, 21 doctorates, 1 other advanced degree awarded. *Degree requirements:* For doctorate, thesis/dissertation. *Entrance requirements:* For master's and doctorate, GRE General Test; for Ed S, GRE General Test, PRAXIS II, 1 year of teaching experience. Additional exam requirements/recommendations for international students: Required—TOEFL. *Application deadline:* Applications are processed on a rolling basis. Application fee: $70 ($80 for international students). Electronic applications accepted. *Expenses:* Contact institution. *Financial support:* In 2011–12, 129 students received support, including 8 fellowships with full and partial tuition reimbursements available (averaging $18,475 per year), 29 research assistantships with partial tuition reimbursements available (averaging $48,547 per year), 28 teaching assistantships with partial tuition reimbursements available (averaging $61,077 per year); career-related internships or fieldwork, institutionally sponsored loans, scholarships/grants, health care benefits, tuition waivers (full), and unspecified assistantships also available. Support available to part-time students. Financial award application deadline: 6/1; financial award applicants required to submit FAFSA. *Total annual research expenditures:* $2.4 million. *Unit head:* Dr. Michael J. Padilla, Director/Associate Dean, 864-656-4444, Fax: 864-656-0311, E-mail: padilla@clemson.edu. *Application contact:* Dr. David Fleming, Graduate Programs Coordinator, 864-656-1881, Fax: 864-656-0311, E-mail: dflemin@clemson.edu. Web site: http://www.clemson.edu/hehd/departments/education/index.html.

Cleveland State University, College of Graduate Studies, College of Education and Human Services, Cleveland, OH 44115. Offers M Ed, MPH, PhD, Certificate, Ed S. *Accreditation:* NCATE. Part-time and evening/weekend programs available. Postbaccalaureate distance learning degree programs offered (minimal on-campus study). *Faculty:* 86 full-time (60 women), 106 part-time/adjunct (81 women). *Students:* 239 full-time (175 women), 839 part-time (634 women); includes 303 minority (253 Black or African American, non-Hispanic/Latino; 15 Asian, non-Hispanic/Latino; 28 Hispanic/Latino; 1 Native Hawaiian or other Pacific Islander, non-Hispanic/Latino; 6 Two or more races, non-Hispanic/Latino), 51 international. Average age 34. 809 applicants, 61% accepted, 368 enrolled. In 2011, 409 master's, 18 doctorates, 20 other advanced degrees awarded. *Degree requirements:* For master's, comprehensive exam (for some programs), thesis optional; for doctorate, one foreign language, comprehensive exam, thesis/dissertation; for other advanced degree, comprehensive exam (for some programs), thesis optional, internship. *Entrance requirements:* For master's, GRE General Test or MAT, minimum undergraduate GPA of 2.75, 3.0 if undergraduate degree is 6 or more years old; for doctorate, GRE General Test, master's degree, minimum graduate GPA of 3.25; for other advanced degree, GRE General Test or MAT, master's degree, minimum graduate GPA of 3.0. Additional exam requirements/recommendations for international students: Required—TOEFL (minimum score 525 paper-based; 197 computer-based; 65 iBT). *Application deadline:* For fall admission, 7/15 priority date for domestic students, 5/15 for international students; for spring admission, 12/8 priority date for domestic students, 11/1 for international students. Applications are processed on a rolling basis. Application fee: $30. Electronic applications accepted. *Expenses:* Tuition, state resident: full-time $6416; part-time $494 per credit hour. Tuition, nonresident: full-time $12,074; part-time $929 per credit hour. *Financial support:* In 2011–12, 64 students received support, including 38 research assistantships with full tuition reimbursements available (averaging $6,960 per year), 2 teaching assistantships with full tuition reimbursements available (averaging $7,800 per year); career-related internships or fieldwork, Federal Work-Study, scholarships/grants, tuition waivers (partial), and unspecified assistantships also available. Support available to part-time students. Financial award application deadline: 8/1; financial award applicants required to submit FAFSA. *Faculty research:* Adult learning and development, counseling theory and practice, equity issues in education (race, ethnicity, gender, socioeconomics), health care and health education, population nursing, urban educational leadership, curriculum and instruction. *Total annual research expenditures:* $7.5 million. *Unit head:* Dr. James A. McLoughlin, Dean, 216-687-3737, Fax: 216-687-5415, E-mail: j.mcloughlin@csuohio.edu. *Application contact:* Deborah L. Brown, Interim Assistant Director of Graduate Admissions, 216-687-5599, Fax: 216-687-5400, E-mail: d.l.brown@csuohio.edu. Web site: http://www.csuohio.edu/cehs/.

Coastal Carolina University, William L. Spadoni College of Education, Conway, SC 29528-6054. Offers education (MAT); educational leadership (M Ed); learning and teaching (M Ed). *Accreditation:* NCATE. Part-time and evening/weekend programs available. *Faculty:* 15 full-time (7 women), 4 part-time/adjunct (1 woman). *Students:* 67 full-time (40 women), 190 part-time (143 women); includes 34 minority (27 Black or African American, non-Hispanic/Latino; 1 American Indian or Alaska Native, non-Hispanic/Latino; 2 Hispanic/Latino; 2 Native Hawaiian or other Pacific Islander, non-Hispanic/Latino; 2 Two or more races, non-Hispanic/Latino), 4 international. Average age 33. 171 applicants, 89% accepted, 119 enrolled. In 2011, 112 master's awarded. *Degree requirements:* For master's, comprehensive exam. *Entrance requirements:* For master's, GRE, MAT, 2 letters of recommendation, copy of teaching credential. Additional exam requirements/recommendations for international students: Required—TOEFL (minimum score 550 paper-based; 213 computer-based; 79 iBT). *Application deadline:* For fall admission, 7/1 priority date for domestic students, 7/1 for international students; for spring admission, 11/1 priority date for domestic students, 11/1 for international students. Applications are processed on a rolling basis. Application fee: $45. Electronic applications accepted. *Expenses:* Tuition, state resident: full-time $11,040; part-time $460 per credit hour. Tuition, nonresident: full-time $16,560; part-time $690 per credit hour. *Required fees:* $80; $40 per term. *Financial support:* Fellowships, research assistantships, and unspecified assistantships available. Support available to part-time students. Financial award application deadline: 3/1; financial award applicants required to submit FAFSA. *Unit head:* Dr. Edward Jadallah, Dean, 843-349-2773, Fax: 843-349-2106, E-mail: ejadalla@coastal.edu. *Application contact:* Dr. James O. Luken, Associate Provost/Director of Graduate Studies, 843-349-2235, Fax: 843-349-6444, E-mail: joluken@coastal.edu. Web site: http://www.coastal.edu/education/.

Coe College, Department of Education, Cedar Rapids, IA 52402-5092. Offers MAT. Part-time programs available. *Entrance requirements:* For master's, minimum undergraduate GPA of 2.75, letters of reference. *Faculty research:* Math education, international and multicultural education.

The College at Brockport, State University of New York, School of Education and Human Services, Department of Education and Human Development, Brockport, NY 14420-2997. Offers adolescence education (MS Ed), including adolescence biology education, adolescence chemistry education, adolescence earth science education, adolescence English education, adolescence mathematics education, adolescence physics education, adolescence social studies education; adolescence inclusive education (MS Ed), including English, mathematics, science, social studies; bilingual education (MS Ed, AGC), including bilingual education, Spanish (AGC); childhood curriculum specialist (MS Ed); childhood literacy (MS Ed). *Accreditation:* NCATE. *Students:* 63 full-time (39 women), 215 part-time (149 women); includes 23 minority (6 Black or African American, non-Hispanic/Latino; 1 American Indian or Alaska Native, non-Hispanic/Latino; 5 Asian, non-Hispanic/Latino; 10 Hispanic/Latino; 1 Native Hawaiian or other Pacific Islander, non-Hispanic/Latino). 133 applicants, 75% accepted, 63 enrolled. In 2011, 97 master's awarded. *Degree requirements:* For master's, thesis or alternative. *Entrance requirements:* For master's, minimum GPA of 3.0, letters of recommendation, interview (for some programs); statement of objectives, current resume. Additional exam requirements/recommendations for international students: Required—TOEFL (minimum score 550 paper-based; 213 computer-based; 79 iBT). *Application deadline:* For fall admission, 2/15 priority date for domestic students, 2/15 for international students; for spring admission, 9/15 priority date for domestic students, 9/15 for international students. Application fee: $80. Electronic applications accepted. *Financial support:* In 2011–12, 2 teaching assistantships with full tuition reimbursements (averaging $6,000 per year) were awarded; Federal Work-Study, scholarships/grants, and unspecified assistantships also available. Support available to part-time students. Financial award application deadline: 3/15; financial award applicants required to submit FAFSA. *Faculty research:* Educational assessment, literacy education, inclusive education, teacher preparation, qualitative methodology. *Unit head:* Dr. Donald Halquist, Chairperson, 585-395-5550, Fax: 585-395-2172, E-mail: snovinge@brockport.edu. *Application contact:* Michael Harrison, Coordinator of Certification and Graduate Advisement, 585-395-2326, Fax: 585-395-2172, E-mail: mharriso@brockport.edu. Web site: http://www.brockport.edu/graduate/.

College of Charleston, Graduate School, School of Education, Health, and Human Performance, Charleston, SC 29424-0001. Offers M Ed, MAT, Certificate. *Accreditation:* NCATE. Part-time and evening/weekend programs available. *Faculty:* 34 full-time (25 women), 9 part-time/adjunct (all women). *Students:* 117 full-time (94 women), 96 part-time (83 women); includes 26 minority (14 Black or African American, non-Hispanic/Latino; 3 Asian, non-Hispanic/Latino; 5 Hispanic/Latino; 1 Native Hawaiian or other Pacific Islander, non-Hispanic/Latino; 3 Two or more races, non-Hispanic/Latino), 1 international. Average age 29. 133 applicants, 56% accepted, 67 enrolled. In 2011, 75 master's awarded. *Degree requirements:* For master's, thesis or alternative, written qualifying exam, student teaching experience (MAT). *Entrance requirements:* For master's, teaching certificate (M Ed). Additional exam requirements/recommendations for international students: Required—TOEFL (minimum score 81 iBT). *Application deadline:* For fall admission, 4/1 for domestic students; for spring admission, 11/1 for domestic students. Applications are processed on a rolling basis. Application fee: $45. Electronic applications accepted. *Expenses:* Tuition, state resident: full-time $5455; part-time $455 per credit. Tuition, nonresident: full-time $13,917; part-time $1160 per credit. *Financial support:* In 2011–12, research assistantships (averaging $19,000 per year), teaching assistantships (averaging $13,300 per year) were awarded; career-related internships or fieldwork, Federal Work-Study, scholarships/grants, and unspecified assistantships also available. Support available to part-time students. Financial award application deadline: 4/1; financial award applicants required to submit FAFSA. *Faculty research:* Computer-assisted instruction, higher education, faculty development, teaching study skills to college students. *Unit head:* Dr. Frances Welch, Dean, 843-953-5613, Fax: 843-953-5407, E-mail: welchf@cofc.edu. *Application contact:* Susan Hallatt, Director of Graduate Admissions, 843-953-5614, Fax: 843-953-1434, E-mail: hallatts@cofc.edu. Web site: http://www.cofc.edu/schoolofeducation/.

The College of Idaho, Program in Teacher Education, Caldwell, ID 83605. Offers MAT. *Degree requirements:* For master's, thesis. *Entrance requirements:* For master's, GRE, portfolio, minimum undergraduate GPA of 3.0, interview. *Faculty research:* Discourse analysis, at-risk youth, children's literature, research design, program evaluation.

College of Mount St. Joseph, Graduate Education Program, Cincinnati, OH 45233-1670. Offers adolescent young adult education (MA); art (MA); inclusive early childhood education (MA); instructional leadership (MA); middle childhood education (MA); multi-age education (MA); multicultural special education (MA); music (MA); reading (MA). *Accreditation:* Teacher Education Accreditation Council. Part-time and evening/weekend programs available. *Faculty:* 22 full-time (12 women), 11 part-time/adjunct (8 women). *Students:* 51 full-time (40 women), 92 part-time (72 women); includes 17 minority (14 Black or African American, non-Hispanic/Latino; 1 American Indian or Alaska Native, non-Hispanic/Latino; 1 Asian, non-Hispanic/Latino; 1 Hispanic/Latino). Average age 34. 87 applicants, 44% accepted, 29 enrolled. In 2011, 61 master's awarded. *Degree requirements:* For master's, research project, student teaching, clinical and field-based experiences. *Entrance requirements:* For master's, GRE, PRAXIS II in teaching content area (math or science), 2 letters of recommendation, interview, resume. Additional exam requirements/recommendations for international students: Required—TOEFL (minimum score 560 paper-based; 220 computer-based; 83 iBT). *Application deadline:* Applications are processed on a rolling basis. Application fee: $50. Electronic applications accepted. *Expenses: Tuition:* Full-time $24,200; part-time $540 per credit hour. *Required fees:* $112.50 per semester. One-time fee: $200. *Financial support:* In 2011–12, 22 students received support. Scholarships/grants available. Financial award applicants required to submit FAFSA. *Faculty research:* Foreign and second language learning problems/reading disabilities/hyperlexia, multicultural/bilingual special education, alternative educator licensure, science education, pedagogical content knowledge. *Unit head:* Dr. Mary West, Chair, 513-244-3263, Fax: 513-244-4867, E-mail: mary_west@mail.msj.edu. *Application contact:* Marilyn Hoskins, Assistant Director of Graduate Recruitment, 513-244-4723, Fax: 513-244-4629, E-mail: marilyn_hoskins@mail.msj.edu. Web site: http://www.msj.edu/view/academics/graduate-programs/education.aspx.

College of Mount Saint Vincent, School of Professional and Continuing Studies, Department of Teacher Education, Riverdale, NY 10471-1093. Offers instructional technology and global perspectives (Certificate); middle level education (Certificate); multicultural studies (Certificate); urban and multicultural education (MS Ed). *Accreditation:* Teacher Education Accreditation Council. Part-time programs available. *Degree requirements:* For master's, comprehensive exam. *Entrance requirements:* For master's, interview, New York teaching certificate. Additional exam requirements/recommendations for international students: Required—TOEFL.

The College of New Jersey, Graduate Studies, School of Education, Ewing, NJ 08628. Offers M Ed, MA, MAT, Certificate, Ed S. *Accreditation:* NCATE. Part-time and evening/weekend programs available. *Degree requirements:* For master's, comprehensive exam. *Entrance requirements:* For master's, GRE, minimum GPA of 3.0 in field or 2.75 overall; for other advanced degree, previous master's degree or higher. Additional exam requirements/recommendations for international students: Required—TOEFL. Electronic applications accepted.

The College of New Rochelle, Graduate School, Division of Education, New Rochelle, NY 10805-2308. Offers creative teaching and learning (MS Ed, Certificate); elementary education/early childhood education (MS Ed); literacy education (MS Ed); school administration and supervision (MS, Advanced Certificate, Advanced Diploma), including dual certification: school building leader/school district leader (MS), school building leader (MS, Advanced Certificate), school district leader (MS, Advanced Diploma); special education (MS Ed); teaching English as a second language and multilingual/multicultural education (MS Ed, Certificate), including bilingual education (Certificate), teaching English as a second language (MS Ed). Part-time and evening/weekend programs available. *Degree requirements:* For master's, comprehensive exam (for some programs), thesis (for some programs). *Entrance requirements:* For master's, interview, minimum GPA of 3.0 in field, 2.7 overall.

College of Saint Elizabeth, Department of Education, Morristown, NJ 07960-6989. Offers accelerated certification for teachers (Certificate); assistive technology (Certificate); education: human services leadership (MA); educational leadership (MA, Ed D); educational technology (MA). Part-time and evening/weekend programs available. *Faculty:* 10 full-time (3 women), 12 part-time/adjunct (6 women). *Students:* 69 full-time (50 women), 203 part-time (175 women); includes 43 minority (26 Black or African American, non-Hispanic/Latino; 1 Asian, non-Hispanic/Latino; 16 Hispanic/Latino). Average age 36. 114 applicants, 72% accepted, 70 enrolled. In 2011, 84 master's, 14 doctorates, 119 other advanced degrees awarded. *Degree requirements:* For master's, thesis or alternative, portfolio; for doctorate, thesis/dissertation. *Entrance requirements:* For master's, interview, minimum undergraduate GPA of 3.0; for doctorate, master's degree. *Application deadline:* For fall admission, 6/30 priority date for domestic students; for spring admission, 11/30 for domestic students. Applications are processed on a rolling basis. Application fee: $35. Electronic applications accepted. *Expenses: Tuition:* Part-time $899 per credit. *Required fees:* $73 per credit. *Financial support:* Career-related internships or fieldwork, tuition waivers (partial), and unspecified assistantships available. Support available to part-time students. Financial award application deadline: 3/15; financial award applicants required to submit FAFSA. *Faculty research:* Developmental stages for teaching and human services professionals, effectiveness of humanities core curriculum. *Unit head:* Dr. Alan H. Markowitz, Director of Graduate Education Programs, 973-290-4374, Fax: 973-290-4389, E-mail: amarkowitz@cse.edu. *Application contact:* Donna Tatarka, Dean of Admission, 973-290-4705, Fax: 973-290-4710, E-mail: dtatarka@cse.edu. Web site: http://www.cse.edu/academics/academic-areas/human-social-dev/education/?tabID-tabGraduate&divID-progGraduate.

College of St. Joseph, Graduate Programs, Division of Education, Rutland, VT 05701-3899. Offers elementary education (M Ed); general education (M Ed); reading (M Ed); secondary education (M Ed), including English, social studies; special education (M Ed). Part-time and evening/weekend programs available. *Faculty:* 2 full-time (both women), 7 part-time/adjunct (3 women). *Students:* 7 full-time (4 women), 36 part-time (29 women). Average age 31. 17 applicants, 82% accepted, 12 enrolled. In 2011, 24 master's awarded. *Degree requirements:* For master's, comprehensive exam. *Entrance requirements:* For master's, PRAXIS I, essay; two letters of reference from academic or professional sources; official transcripts of all graduate and undergraduate study. Additional exam requirements/recommendations for international students: Required—TOEFL (minimum score 550 paper-based). *Application deadline:* Applications are processed on a rolling basis. Application fee: $35. Electronic applications accepted. *Expenses: Tuition:* Full-time $15,200; part-time $400 per credit. *Required fees:* $45 per semester. *Financial support:* Career-related internships or fieldwork, Federal Work-Study, and unspecified assistantships available. Support available to part-time students. Financial award application deadline: 3/1. *Faculty research:* Co-teaching, Response to Intervention (RTI). *Unit head:* Dr. Maria Bove, Chair, 802-773-5900 Ext. 3243, Fax: 802-776-5258, E-mail: mbove@csj.edu. *Application contact:* Alan Young, Dean of Admissions, 802-773-5900 Ext. 3227, Fax: 802-776-5310, E-mail: alanyoung@csj.edu. Web site: http://www.csj.edu/.

College of Saint Mary, Program in Teaching, Omaha, NE 68106. Offers MAT. Evening/weekend programs available. *Entrance requirements:* For master's, Pre-Professional Skills Tests (PPST), minimum cumulative GPA of 2.5, background check.

The College of Saint Rose, Graduate Studies, School of Education, Albany, NY 12203-1419. Offers MS, MS Ed, Certificate. *Accreditation:* NCATE. Part-time and evening/weekend programs available. *Degree requirements:* For master's, thesis or alternative. *Entrance requirements:* For master's, minimum undergraduate GPA of 3.0. Additional exam requirements/recommendations for international students: Required—TOEFL (minimum score 550 paper-based; 213 computer-based). Electronic applications accepted.

The College of St. Scholastica, Graduate Studies, Program in Teaching, Duluth, MN 55811-4199. Offers M Ed, Certificate. *Accreditation:* Teacher Education Accreditation Council. Part-time programs available. Postbaccalaureate distance learning degree programs offered (minimal on-campus study). *Faculty:* 4 full-time (2 women), 6 part-time/adjunct (5 women). *Students:* 105 full-time (72 women), 61 part-time (44 women); includes 13 minority (7 Black or African American, non-Hispanic/Latino; 1 American Indian or Alaska Native, non-Hispanic/Latino; 1 Asian, non-Hispanic/Latino; 1 Hispanic/Latino; 3 Two or more races, non-Hispanic/Latino). Average age 34. 29 applicants, 48% accepted, 14 enrolled. In 2011, 14 master's awarded. *Entrance requirements:* For master's and Certificate, minimum undergraduate cumulative GPA of 2.8. Additional exam requirements/recommendations for international students: Required—TOEFL (minimum score 550 paper-based; 213 computer-based; 79 iBT). *Application deadline:* For fall admission, 8/1 priority date for domestic students, 8/1 for international students; for spring admission, 11/15 priority date for domestic students, 11/15 for international students. Applications are processed on a rolling basis. Application fee: $50. Electronic applications accepted. *Financial support:* In 2011–12, 10 students received support. Applicants required to submit FAFSA. *Unit head:* Chery Takkunen, Director, 218-723-7052, Fax: 218-723-2275. *Application contact:* Lindsay Lahti, Director of Graduate and Extended Studies Recruitment, 218-733-2240, Fax: 218-733-2275, E-mail: llahti@css.edu.

College of Staten Island of the City University of New York, Graduate Programs, Department of Education, Staten Island, NY 10314-6600. Offers adolescence education (MS Ed); childhood education (MS Ed); school building and district leadership (6th Year Certificate); special education (MS Ed). *Accreditation:* NCATE. *Students:* 46 full-time (40 women), 558 part-time (453 women). Average age 29. 333 applicants, 74% accepted, 197 enrolled. In 2011, 171 master's, 19 6th Year Certificates awarded. Application fee: $125. *Expenses:* Tuition, state resident: full-time $8210; part-time $345 per credit. Tuition, nonresident: part-time $640 per credit. *Required fees:* $128 per semester. *Financial support:* In 2011–12, 2 students received support. Applicants required to submit FAFSA. *Unit head:* Dr. Kenneth Gold, Chairperson, 718-982-3737, Fax: 718-982-3743, E-mail: kenneth.gold@csi.cuny.edu. *Application contact:* Sasha Spence, Assistant Director for Graduate Admissions, 718-982-2699, Fax: 718-982-2500, E-mail: sasha.spence@csi.cuny.edu. Web site: http://www.library.csi.cuny.edu/~education/programs.html.

The College of William and Mary, School of Education, Williamsburg, VA 23187-8795. Offers M Ed, MA Ed, Ed D, PhD, Ed S. *Accreditation:* NCATE. Part-time and evening/weekend programs available. *Faculty:* 39 full-time (22 women), 60 part-time/adjunct (48 women). *Students:* 223 full-time (187 women), 174 part-time (127 women); includes 72 minority (42 Black or African American, non-Hispanic/Latino; 2 American Indian or Alaska Native, non-Hispanic/Latino; 3 Asian, non-Hispanic/Latino; 10 Hispanic/Latino; 15 Two or more races, non-Hispanic/Latino), 7 international. Average age 32. 634 applicants, 53% accepted, 218 enrolled. In 2011, 139 master's, 15 doctorates, 11 other advanced degrees awarded. *Degree requirements:* For master's, project; for doctorate, comprehensive exam, thesis/dissertation; for Ed S, internship. *Entrance requirements:* For master's, GRE or MAT, minimum GPA of 2.5; for doctorate, GRE or MAT, minimum GPA of 3.5; for Ed S, GRE, minimum GPA of 3.0. Additional exam requirements/recommendations for international students: Required—TOEFL. *Application deadline:* For fall admission, 1/15 for domestic and international students; for spring admission, 10/1 for domestic and international students. Application fee: $50. Electronic applications accepted. *Expenses:* Tuition, state resident: full-time $6400; part-time $365 per credit hour. Tuition, nonresident: full-time $19,720; part-time $985 per credit hour. *Required fees:* $4562. *Financial support:* In 2011–12, 174 students received support, including 1 fellowship with full tuition reimbursement available (averaging $20,000 per year), 112 research assistantships with full and partial tuition reimbursements available (averaging $13,000 per year); career-related internships or fieldwork, Federal Work-Study, institutionally sponsored loans, scholarships/grants, and unspecified assistantships also available. Financial award application deadline: 1/15; financial award applicants required to submit FAFSA. *Faculty research:* Writing, gifted education, curriculum and instruction, special education, leadership, faculty development, cultural diversity. *Total annual research expenditures:* $6.5 million. *Unit head:* Dr. Virginia McLaughlin, Dean, 757-221-2317, E-mail: vamcla@wm.edu. *Application contact:* Dorothy Smith Osborne, Assistant Dean for Admission, 757-221-2317, Fax: 757-221-2293, E-mail: dsosbo@wm.edu. Web site: http://education.wm.edu.

Collège universitaire de Saint-Boniface, Department of Education, Saint-Boniface, MB R2H 0H7, Canada. Offers M Ed.

Colorado Christian University, Program in Curriculum and Instruction, Lakewood, CO 80226. Offers corporate education (MACI); early childhood educator (MACI); elementary educator (MACI); instructional technology (MACI); master educator (MACI); online course developer (MACI); online teaching and learning (MACI); special education generalist (MACI). Part-time and evening/weekend programs available. *Degree requirements:* For master's, thesis optional, practicum. *Entrance requirements:* For master's, interviews, letters of recommendation. Additional exam requirements/recommendations for international students: Required—TOEFL. Electronic applications accepted. *Expenses:* Contact institution.

The Colorado College, Education Department, Colorado Springs, CO 80903-3294. Offers elementary education (MAT), including elementary school teaching; secondary education (MAT), including art teaching (K-12), English teaching, foreign language teaching, mathematics teaching, music teaching, science teaching, social studies teaching. *Faculty:* 5 full-time (3 women), 13 part-time/adjunct (10 women). *Students:* 20 full-time (15 women); includes 3 minority (1 Asian, non-Hispanic/Latino; 2 Hispanic/Latino). Average age 25. 38 applicants, 84% accepted, 20 enrolled. In 2011, 24 master's awarded. *Degree requirements:* For master's, thesis, internship. *Application deadline:* For fall admission, 12/1 priority date for domestic students, 12/1 for international students. Applications are processed on a rolling basis. Application fee: $50. Electronic applications accepted. *Expenses: Tuition:* Full-time $29,313. *Required fees:* $2000. *Financial support:* In 2011–12, 18 students received support. Institutionally sponsored loans, scholarships/grants, and health care benefits available. Financial award application deadline: 2/15; financial award applicants required to submit FAFSA. *Faculty research:* Geology, environmental resources, urban education, educational psychology, arts integration in the classroom, literacy/early childhood. *Total annual research expenditures:* $42,783. *Unit head:* Mike Taber, Chair, 719-389-6026, Fax: 719-389-6473, E-mail: mike.taber@coloradocollege.edu. *Application contact:* Debra Yazulla Mortenson, Education Services Manager, 719-389-6472, Fax: 719-389-6473, E-mail: debra.mortenson@coloradocollege.edu. Web site: http://www2.coloradocollege.edu/dept/ED/.

Colorado Mesa University, Center for Teacher Education, Grand Junction, CO 81501-3122. Offers educational leadership (MAEd); English for speakers of other languages (MAEd). *Accreditation:* NCATE. Part-time programs available. Postbaccalaureate distance learning degree programs offered (minimal on-campus study). *Degree requirements:* For master's, comprehensive exam, capstone presentation. *Entrance requirements:* For master's, GRE, 2 professional letters of recommendation. Additional exam requirements/recommendations for international students: Required—TOEFL (minimum score 550 paper-based; 207 computer-based). Electronic applications accepted.

Colorado State University, Graduate School, College of Applied Human Sciences, School of Education, Fort Collins, CO 80523-1588. Offers adult education and training (M Ed); community college leadership (PhD); counseling and career development (M Ed); education and human resource studies (M Ed, PhD); educational leadership (M Ed, PhD); interdisciplinary studies (PhD); organizational performance and change (M Ed, PhD); student affairs in higher education (MS). *Accreditation:* ACA; Teacher Education Accreditation Council. Part-time and evening/weekend programs available. *Faculty:* 18 full-time (11 women), 1 part-time/adjunct (0 women). *Students:* 161 full-time (106 women), 491 part-time (291 women); includes 130 minority (28 Black or African American, non-Hispanic/Latino; 5 American Indian or Alaska Native, non-Hispanic/Latino; 12 Asian, non-Hispanic/Latino; 68 Hispanic/Latino; 3 Native Hawaiian or other Pacific Islander, non-Hispanic/Latino; 14 Two or more races, non-Hispanic/Latino), 29 international. Average age 38. 468 applicants, 31% accepted, 112 enrolled. In 2011, 192 master's, 30 doctorates awarded. *Degree requirements:* For master's, comprehensive exam (for some programs), thesis optional; for doctorate, comprehensive exam, thesis/dissertation, minimum of 60 credits. *Entrance requirements:* For master's, GRE, minimum undergraduate GPA of 3.0, 3 letters of recommendation, curriculum vitae/resume; for doctorate, minimum GPA of 3.0, 3 letters of recommendation, curriculum vitae. Additional exam requirements/recommendations for international students: Required—TOEFL (minimum score 550 paper-based; 213 computer-based; 80 iBT). *Application deadline:* For fall admission, 2/15 priority date for domestic students, 2/15 for international students; for spring admission, 9/1 priority date for domestic students, 9/1 for international students. Applications are processed on a rolling basis. Application fee: $50. Electronic applications accepted. *Expenses:* Tuition, state resident: full-time $7992. Tuition, nonresident: full-time $19,592. *Required fees:* $1735; $58 per credit. *Financial support:* In 2011–12, 11 students received support, including 1 fellowship (averaging $37,500 per year), 3 research assistantships with full tuition reimbursements available (averaging $8,911 per year), 7 teaching assistantships with full tuition reimbursements available (averaging $12,691 per year); Federal Work-Study, scholarships/grants, and unspecified assistantships also available. Financial award application deadline: 2/15; financial award applicants required to submit FAFSA. *Faculty research:* Innovative instruction, diverse learners, transition, scientifically-based evaluation methods, leadership and organizational development, research methodology. *Total annual research expenditures:* $455,133. *Unit head:* Dr. Kevin Oltjenbruns, Interim Director, 970-491-6316, Fax: 970-491-1317, E-mail: kevin.oltjenbruns@colostate.edu. *Application contact:* Kathy Lucas, Graduate Contact, 970-491-1963, Fax: 970-491-1317, E-mail: kplucas@cahs.colostate.edu. Web site: http://www.soe.cahs.colostate.edu/.

Colorado State University–Pueblo, College of Education, Engineering and Professional Studies, Education Program, Pueblo, CO 81001-4901. Offers art education (M Ed); foreign language education (M Ed); health and physical education (M Ed); instructional technology (M Ed); linguistically diverse education (M Ed); music education (M Ed); special education (M Ed). *Accreditation:* Teacher Education Accreditation Council. Part-time programs available. *Degree requirements:* For master's, portfolio. *Entrance requirements:* For master's, 3 recommendations, teaching license. Additional exam requirements/recommendations for international students: Required—TOEFL (minimum score 500 paper-based; 173 computer-based). Electronic applications accepted. *Faculty research:* Portfolio assessment, math education, science education.

Columbia College, Graduate Programs, Department of Education, Columbia, SC 29203-5998. Offers divergent learning (M Ed). *Accreditation:* NCATE. Part-time and evening/weekend programs available. Postbaccalaureate distance learning degree programs offered (minimal on-campus study). *Faculty:* 3 full-time (1 woman), 18 part-time/adjunct (10 women). *Students:* 93 full-time (89 women), 18 part-time (16 women); includes 33 minority (32 Black or African American, non-Hispanic/Latino; 1 Asian, non-Hispanic/Latino). Average age 27. 53 applicants, 96% accepted, 43 enrolled. In 2011, 197 master's awarded. *Degree requirements:* For master's, thesis. *Entrance requirements:* For master's, GRE General Test, MAT, 2 recommendations, current South Carolina teaching certificate, minimum GPA of 3.2. *Application deadline:* For fall admission, 8/22 for domestic students. Application fee: $50. *Expenses:* Contact institution. *Financial support:* Available to part-time students. Application deadline: 7/1; applicants required to submit FAFSA. *Unit head:* Dr. Mary Steppling, Chair, 803-786-3782, Fax: 803-786-3034, E-mail: msteppling@colacoll.edu. *Application contact:* Carolyn Emeneker, Director of Graduate School and Evening College Admissions, 803-786-3766, Fax: 803-786-3674, E-mail: emeneker@colacoll.edu.

Columbia College, Master of Arts in Teaching Program, Columbia, MO 65216-0002. Offers MAT. Evening/weekend programs available. Postbaccalaureate distance learning degree programs offered (no on-campus study). *Faculty:* 18 full-time (14 women), 7 part-time/adjunct (5 women). *Students:* 5 full-time (4 women), 53 part-time (48 women); includes 10 minority (6 Black or African American, non-Hispanic/Latino; 2 American Indian or Alaska Native, non-Hispanic/Latino; 1 Asian, non-Hispanic/Latino; 1 Hispanic/Latino), 2 international. Average age 33. 59 applicants, 66% accepted, 35 enrolled. In 2011, 54 master's awarded. *Degree requirements:* For master's, culminating experience. *Entrance requirements:* For master's, 3 letters of recommendation, minimum cumulative undergraduate GPA of 3.0, resume, goal statement. Additional exam requirements/recommendations for international students: Required—TOEFL (minimum score 500 paper-based; 61 iBT). *Application deadline:* For fall admission, 8/9 priority date for domestic students, 8/9 for international students; for spring admission, 12/27 priority date for domestic students, 12/27 for international students. Applications are processed on a rolling basis. Application fee: $55. Electronic applications accepted. *Expenses: Tuition:* Part-time $315 per credit hour. *Financial support:* In 2011–12, 10 students received support. Career-related internships or fieldwork, Federal Work-Study, and scholarships/grants available. Financial award application deadline: 3/15; financial award applicants required to submit FAFSA. *Faculty research:* K-12 teaching and schools around the world. *Total annual research expenditures:* $2,250. *Unit head:* Dr. Kristina Miller, Graduate Program Coordinator, 573-875-7590, Fax: 573-876-4493, E-mail: kmiller@ccis.edu. *Application contact:* Samantha White, Director of Admissions, 573-875-7352, Fax: 573-875-7506, E-mail: sjwhite@ccis.edu. Web site: http://www.ccis.edu/graduate/academics/degrees.asp?MAT.

Columbia College Chicago, Graduate School, Department of Educational Studies, Chicago, IL 60605-1996. Offers elementary education (MAT); English (MAT); interdisciplinary arts (MAT); multicultural education (MA); urban teaching (MA). Part-time and evening/weekend programs available. *Degree requirements:* For master's, thesis, student teaching experience, 100 pre-clinical hours. *Entrance requirements:* For master's, supplemental recommendation form. Additional exam requirements/recommendations for international students: Required—TOEFL (minimum score 550 paper-based; 213 computer-based). Electronic applications accepted.

Columbia International University, Columbia Graduate School, Columbia, SC 29230-3122. Offers Bible teaching (MABT); Christian higher education leadership (Ed D); Christian school educational leadership (Ed D); counseling (MACN); curriculum and instruction (M Ed), including Christian school guidance, English as a second language, learning disabilities, school technology; early childhood and elementary education (MAT); educational administration (M Ed); teaching English as a foreign language (Certificate); teaching English as a foreign language and intercultural studies (MATF). Part-time and evening/weekend programs available. *Degree requirements:* For master's, internships, professional project. *Entrance requirements:* For master's, Minnesota Multiphasic Personality Inventory, MAT, minimum GPA of 2.7. Additional exam requirements/recommendations for international students: Required—TOEFL. Electronic applications accepted.

Columbus State University, Graduate Studies, College of Education and Health Professions, Columbus, GA 31907-5645. Offers M Ed, MAT, MPA, MS, Ed D, Ed S. *Accreditation:* ACA (one or more programs are accredited); NCATE. Part-time and evening/weekend programs available. Postbaccalaureate distance learning degree programs offered (minimal on-campus study). *Degree requirements:* For master's, thesis, exit exam; for Ed S, thesis or alternative. *Entrance requirements:* For master's, GRE General Test, minimum GPA of 2.75; for Ed S, GRE General Test. Additional exam requirements/recommendations for international students: Required—TOEFL (minimum score 550 paper-based; 213 computer-based; 79 iBT). Electronic applications accepted.

Concordia College, Program in Education, Moorhead, MN 56562. Offers world language instruction (M Ed). *Degree requirements:* For master's, thesis/seminar. *Entrance requirements:* For master's, 2 professional references, 1 personal reference.

Concordia University, College of Education, Portland, OR 97211-6099. Offers curriculum and instruction (elementary) (M Ed); educational administration (M Ed); elementary education (MAT); secondary education (MAT). Part-time programs available. Postbaccalaureate distance learning degree programs offered (no on-campus study). *Degree requirements:* For master's, comprehensive exam, work samples/portfolio. *Entrance requirements:* For master's, California Basic Educational Skills Test or PRAXIS I, minimum undergraduate GPA of 2.8, graduate 3.0; 2 letters of recommendation. Additional exam requirements/recommendations for international students: Required—TOEFL (minimum score 525 paper-based; 195 computer-based). Electronic applications accepted. *Faculty research:* Learner centered classroom, brain-based learning future of on-line learning.

Concordia University, School of Education, Irvine, CA 92612-3299. Offers curriculum and instruction (MA); education and preliminary teaching credential (M Ed); educational administration and preliminary administrative services credential (MA); school counseling with pupil personnel services credential (MA). Part-time and evening/weekend programs available. Postbaccalaureate distance learning degree programs offered (no on-campus study). *Faculty:* 16 full-time (11 women), 68 part-time/adjunct (32 women). *Students:* 556 full-time (434 women), 277 part-time (211 women); includes 278 minority (42 Black or African American, non-Hispanic/Latino; 1 American Indian or Alaska Native, non-Hispanic/Latino; 51 Asian, non-Hispanic/Latino; 172 Hispanic/Latino; 12 Two or more races, non-Hispanic/Latino), 1 international. Average age 39. 296 applicants, 96% accepted, 256 enrolled. In 2011, 378 master's awarded. *Degree requirements:* For master's, action research project. *Entrance requirements:* For master's, California Basic Educational Skills Test, California Subject Examinations for Teachers (M Ed and MA in educational administration and preliminary administrative services credential), official college transcript(s), signed statement of intent, two references, copy of credential. Additional exam requirements/recommendations for international students: Required—TOEFL. *Application deadline:* For fall admission, 7/15 priority date for domestic students, 6/1 for international students; for spring admission, 11/30 priority date for domestic students, 10/1 for international students. Applications are processed on a rolling basis. Application fee: $50 ($125 for international students). Electronic applications accepted. *Expenses:* Contact institution. *Financial support:* In 2011–12, 17 students received support. Scholarships/grants and unspecified assistantships available. Financial award applicants required to submit FAFSA. *Unit head:* Dr. Janice Nelson, Dean, 949-214-3334, E-mail: janice.nelson@cui.edu. *Application contact:* Scott Eskelson, 949-214-3362, Fax: 949-854-6894, E-mail: scott.eskelson@cui.edu.

Concordia University, School of Graduate Studies, Faculty of Arts and Science, Department of Education, Montréal, QC H3G 1M8, Canada. Offers adult education (Diploma); applied linguistics (MA); child study (MA); educational studies (MA); educational technology (MA, PhD); instructional technology (Diploma); teaching English as a second language (Certificate). *Degree requirements:* For master's, one foreign language, thesis optional; for doctorate, comprehensive exam, thesis/dissertation. *Entrance requirements:* For doctorate, MA in educational technology or equivalent.

Concordia University Chicago, College of Education, Program in Teaching, River Forest, IL 60305-1499. Offers early childhood education (MAT); elementary education (MAT); secondary education (MAT). *Degree requirements:* For master's, thesis or alternative. *Entrance requirements:* For master's, minimum GPA of 2.9. Additional exam requirements/recommendations for international students: Required—TOEFL (minimum score 550 paper-based; 195 computer-based). Electronic applications accepted.

Concordia University, Nebraska, Graduate Programs in Education, Seward, NE 68434-1599. Offers M Ed, MPE, MS. *Accreditation:* NCATE. Part-time and evening/weekend programs available. *Degree requirements:* For master's, comprehensive exam, thesis or alternative. *Entrance requirements:* For master's, GRE, MAT, or NTE, minimum GPA of 3.0, BS in education or equivalent. Additional exam requirements/recommendations for international students: Required—TOEFL. Electronic applications accepted.

Concordia University, St. Paul, College of Education, St. Paul, MN 55104-5494. Offers curriculum and instruction (MA Ed), including K-12 reading endorsement; differentiated instruction (MA Ed); early childhood education (MA Ed); educational leadership (MA Ed); educational technology (MA Ed); family life education (MA); K-12 reading endorsement (Certificate); special education (Certificate); sports management (MA). *Accreditation:* NCATE. Evening/weekend programs available. Postbaccalaureate distance learning degree programs offered (minimal on-campus study). *Faculty:* 7 full-time (3 women), 64 part-time/adjunct (42 women). *Students:* 617 full-time (495 women), 9 part-time (6 women); includes 57 minority (30 Black or African American, non-Hispanic/Latino; 2 American Indian or Alaska Native, non-Hispanic/Latino; 17 Asian, non-Hispanic/Latino; 5 Hispanic/Latino; 1 Native Hawaiian or other Pacific Islander, non-Hispanic/Latino; 2 Two or more races, non-Hispanic/Latino). Average age 36. 302 applicants, 83% accepted, 210 enrolled. In 2011, 320 master's, 68 other advanced degrees awarded. *Application deadline:* Applications are processed on a rolling basis. Application fee: $50. Electronic applications accepted. *Expenses: Tuition:* Full-time $8100; part-time $435 per credit. Tuition and fees vary according to program. *Financial support:* Applicants required to submit FAFSA. *Unit head:* Dr. Donald Helmstetter, Dean, 651-641-8227, Fax: 651-641-8807, E-mail: helmstetter@csp.edu. *Application contact:* Kimberly Craig, Director of Graduate and Cohort Admission, 651-603-6223, Fax: 651-603-6320, E-mail: craig@csp.edu.

Concordia University Texas, College of Education, Austin, TX 78726. Offers M Ed. Part-time and evening/weekend programs available. *Degree requirements:* For master's, thesis (for some programs), portfolio presentation.

Concordia University Wisconsin, Graduate Programs, Department of Education, Mequon, WI 53097-2402. Offers art education (MS Ed); curriculum and instruction (MS Ed); early childhood (MS Ed); educational administration (MS Ed); environmental education (MS Ed); family studies (MS Ed); reading (MS Ed); school counseling (MS Ed); special education (MS Ed). Part-time and evening/weekend programs available. Postbaccalaureate distance learning degree programs offered (minimal on-campus study). *Faculty:* 30. *Students:* 386 full-time (279 women), 808 part-time (598 women); includes 84 minority (42 Black or African American, non-Hispanic/Latino; 4 American Indian or Alaska Native, non-Hispanic/Latino; 9 Asian, non-Hispanic/Latino; 13 Hispanic/Latino; 16 Two or more races, non-Hispanic/Latino), 5 international. Average age 37. In 2011, 51 master's awarded. *Degree requirements:* For master's, comprehensive exam, thesis or alternative. *Entrance requirements:* For master's, minimum GPA of 3.0, teaching license. Additional exam requirements/recommendations for international students: Required—TOEFL. Application fee: $35. *Financial support:* Career-related internships or fieldwork and tuition waivers (partial) available. Financial award application deadline: 8/1. *Faculty research:* Motivation, developmental learning, learning styles. *Unit head:* Dr. James Juergensen, Director, 262-243-4214, E-mail: james.juergensen@cuw.edu. *Application contact:* Graduate Admissions, 262-243-4248, Fax: 262-243-4428.

Converse College, School of Education and Graduate Studies, Spartanburg, SC 29302-0006. Offers art education (M Ed); early childhood education (MAT); education (Ed S), including administration and supervision, curriculum and instruction, marriage and family therapy; elementary education (M Ed, MAT); gifted education (M Ed); leadership (M Ed); liberal arts (MLA), including English (M Ed, MAT, MLA), history, political science; secondary education (M Ed, MAT), including biology (MAT), chemistry (MAT), English (M Ed, MAT, MLA), mathematics, natural sciences (M Ed), social sciences; special education (M Ed, MAT), including learning disabilities (MAT), mental disabilities (MAT), special education (M Ed). *Accreditation:* NASAD; NCATE. Part-time and evening/weekend programs available. *Entrance requirements:* For master's, PRAXIS II (M Ed), minimum GPA of 2.75; for Ed S, GRE or MAT, minimum GPA of 3.0. Electronic applications accepted. *Faculty research:* Motivation, classroom management, predictors of success in classroom teaching, sex equity in public education, gifted research.

Coppin State University, Division of Graduate Studies, Division of Education, Department of Curriculum and Instruction, Program in Teaching, Baltimore, MD 21216-3698. Offers teacher education (MAT). Part-time and evening/weekend programs available. Postbaccalaureate distance learning degree programs offered. *Degree requirements:* For master's, thesis, exit portfolio. *Entrance requirements:* For master's, GRE, resume, references.

Corban University, Graduate School, Education Program, Salem, OR 97301-9392. Offers MS Ed.

Cornell University, Graduate School, Graduate Fields of Agriculture and Life Sciences, Field of Education, Ithaca, NY 14853-0001. Offers agricultural education (MAT); biology (7-12) (MAT); chemistry (7-12) (MAT); curriculum and instruction (MPS, MS, PhD); earth science (7-12) (MAT); extension, and adult education (MPS, MS, PhD); mathematics (7-12) (MAT); physics (7-12) (MAT). *Faculty:* 23 full-time (10 women). *Students:* 32 full-time (18 women); includes 6 minority (4 Asian, non-Hispanic/Latino; 2 Hispanic/Latino), 1 international. Average age 30. 60 applicants, 33% accepted, 12 enrolled. In 2011, 22 master's, 7 doctorates awarded. Terminal master's awarded for partial completion of doctoral program. *Degree requirements:* For master's, thesis (MS); for doctorate, comprehensive exam, thesis/dissertation. *Entrance requirements:* For master's and doctorate, GRE General Test, sample of written work (recommended), 2 letters of recommendation. Additional exam requirements/recommendations for international students: Required—TOEFL (minimum score 550 paper-based; 213 computer-based; 77 iBT). *Application deadline:* For fall admission, 2/15 for domestic students. Application fee: $95. Electronic applications accepted. *Financial support:* In 2011–12, 2 fellowships with full tuition reimbursements, 4 research assistantships with full tuition reimbursements, 12 teaching assistantships with full tuition reimbursements were awarded; institutionally sponsored loans, scholarships/grants, health care benefits, tuition waivers (full and partial), and unspecified assistantships also available. Financial award applicants required to submit FAFSA. *Faculty research:* Moral development and professional ethics, public issues education and community development, socio/political issues in public education, teacher education and curriculum in agricultural science and mathematics, extension research. *Unit head:* Director of Graduate Studies, 607-255-4278, Fax: 607-255-7905. *Application contact:* Graduate Field Assistant, 607-255-4278, Fax: 607-255-7905, E-mail: rh22@cornell.edu. Web site: http://www.gradschool.cornell.edu/fields.php?id-80&a-2.

Cornerstone University, Graduate Programs, Grand Rapids, MI 49525-5897. Offers business administration (MBA); education (MA Ed); management (MSM); teaching English to speakers of other languages (MA, Graduate Certificate). Programs also offered at Holland, Kalamazoo, and Troy, MI campuses. Part-time programs available. Postbaccalaureate distance learning degree programs offered. *Degree requirements:* For master's, comprehensive exam (for some programs), thesis (for some programs). *Entrance requirements:* For master's, minimum GPA of 2.5, 2 letters of reference. Additional exam requirements/recommendations for international students: Required—TOEFL (minimum score 575 paper-based; 235 computer-based). Electronic applications accepted.

Covenant College, Program in Education, Lookout Mountain, GA 30750. Offers M Ed. Part-time programs available. *Degree requirements:* For master's, comprehensive exam, special project. *Entrance requirements:* For master's, GRE General Test, 2 professional recommendations, minimum GPA of 3.0, writing sample.

Creighton University, Graduate School, College of Arts and Sciences, Department of Education, Omaha, NE 68178-0001. Offers counselor education (MS), including college student affairs, community counseling, elementary school guidance, secondary school guidance; educational leadership (MS, Ed D), including elementary school administration (MS), leadership (Ed D), secondary school administration (MS), teacher leadership (MS); special populations in education (MS); teaching (M Ed), including elementary teaching, secondary teaching. *Accreditation:* NCATE. Part-time and evening/weekend programs available. *Faculty:* 14 full-time (8 women). *Students:* 12 full-time (5 women), 111 part-time (75 women); includes 10 minority (2 Black or African American, non-Hispanic/Latino; 2 American Indian or Alaska Native, non-Hispanic/Latino; 5 Hispanic/Latino; 1 Two or more races, non-Hispanic/Latino), 3 international. Average age 33. 20 applicants, 80% accepted, 15 enrolled. In 2011, 37 master's awarded. *Degree requirements:* For master's, comprehensive exam (for some programs), portfolio. *Entrance requirements:* For master's, GRE General Test, PPST, 3 letters of recommendation; writing samples, resume. Additional exam requirements/recommendations for international students: Required—TOEFL (minimum score 550 paper-based; 213 computer-based; 80 iBT). *Application deadline:* For fall admission, 7/1 priority date for domestic students, 3/1 for international students; for winter admission, 12/1 for domestic students, 7/1 for international students; for spring admission, 4/1 for domestic students, 10/1 for international students. Applications are processed on a rolling basis. Application fee: $50. Electronic applications accepted. *Expenses: Tuition:* Full-time $12,672; part-time $704 per credit hour. *Required fees:* $1410; $136 per semester. Tuition and fees vary according to campus/location and reciprocity agreements. *Financial support:* Scholarships/grants and tuition waivers (partial) available. Support available to part-time students. Financial award applicants required to submit FAFSA. *Unit head:* Dr. Debra Ponec, Chair, 402-280-2557, E-mail: dlponec@creighton.edu. *Application contact:* Taunya Plater, Senior Program Coordinator, 402-280-2870, Fax: 402-280-2423, E-mail: taunyaplater@creighton.edu.

Cumberland University, Program in Education, Lebanon, TN 37087. Offers MAE. Part-time and evening/weekend programs available. Postbaccalaureate distance learning degree programs offered (no on-campus study). *Degree requirements:* For master's, comprehensive exam. *Entrance requirements:* For master's, GRE General Test, MAT, or NTE, 3 letters of recommendation. Additional exam requirements/recommendations for international students: Required—TOEFL (minimum score 500 paper-based; 173 computer-based).

Curry College, Graduate Studies, Program in Education, Milton, MA 02186-9984. Offers elementary education (M Ed); foundations (non-license) (M Ed); reading (M Ed, Certificate); special education (M Ed). Part-time and evening/weekend programs available. *Degree requirements:* For master's, project or thesis. *Entrance requirements:* For master's, interview, recommendations, resume, written statement. Additional exam requirements/recommendations for international students: Required—TOEFL (minimum score 550 paper-based; 213 computer-based; 80 iBT). *Expenses:* Contact institution. *Faculty research:* Classroom trauma, therapeutic writing, inclusionary practices.

Daemen College, Education Department, Amherst, NY 14226-3592. Offers adolescence education (MS); childhood education (MS); childhood special education (MS); childhood special-alternative certification (MS); early childhood special-alternative certification (MS). Part-time programs available. *Degree requirements:* For master's, thesis optional, research thesis in lieu of comprehensive exam; completion of degree within 5 years. *Entrance requirements:* For master's, 2 letters of recommendation (professional and character), proof of initial certificate of license for professional programs, resume. Additional exam requirements/recommendations for international students: Required—TOEFL (minimum score 500 paper-based; 173 computer-based; 63 iBT), IELTS (minimum score 5.5). Electronic applications accepted. *Faculty research:* Transition for students with disabilities, early childhood special education, traumatic brain injury (TBI), reading assessment.

Dakota State University, College of Education, Madison, SD 57042-1799. Offers instructional technology (MSET). *Accreditation:* NCATE. Part-time and evening/weekend programs available. Postbaccalaureate distance learning degree programs offered (minimal on-campus study). *Faculty:* 6 full-time (3 women), 2 part-time/adjunct (0 women). *Students:* 1 full-time (0 women), 24 part-time (15 women); includes 3 minority (all Hispanic/Latino), 1 international. Average age 33. 5 applicants, 100% accepted, 5 enrolled. In 2011, 9 master's awarded. *Degree requirements:* For master's, thesis, portfolio. *Entrance requirements:* For master's, GRE General Test, demonstration of technology skills, minimum GPA of 2.7. Additional exam requirements/recommendations for international students: Required—TOEFL (minimum score 550 paper-based; 213 computer-based; 78 iBT). *Application deadline:* For fall admission, 6/15 for domestic and international students; for spring admission, 11/15 for domestic and international students. Applications are processed on a rolling basis. Application fee: $35 ($85 for international students). *Financial support:* In 2011–12, 14 students received support, including 3 research assistantships with partial tuition reimbursements available (averaging $11,116 per year); teaching assistantships, Federal Work-Study, scholarships/grants, tuition waivers (partial), unspecified assistantships, and administrative assistantships also available. Support available to part-time students. Financial award applicants required to submit FAFSA. *Faculty research:* Educational technology evaluation, computer-supported collaborative learning, cognitive theory and visual representation of the effects of ambiquitous wireless computing on student learning and productivity. *Unit head:* Dr. Judy Dittman, Dean, 605-256-5177, Fax: 605-256-7300, E-mail: judy.dittman@dsu.edu. *Application contact:* Erin Blankespoor, Secretary, Office of Graduate Studies and Research, 605-256-5799, Fax: 605-256-5093, E-mail: erin.blankespoor@dsu.edu. Web site: http://www.dsu.edu/educate/index.aspx.

Dakota Wesleyan University, Program in Education, Mitchell, SD 57301-4398. Offers curriculum and instruction (MA Ed); educational policy and administration (MA Ed); preK-12 principal certification (MA Ed); secondary certification (MA Ed). Part-time and evening/weekend programs available. *Degree requirements:* For master's, comprehensive exam, thesis optional, electronic portfolio. *Entrance requirements:* For master's, minimum GPA of 2.7, elementary statistics course, statement of purpose, official transcripts, resume, three letters of recommendation. Additional exam requirements/recommendations for international students: Required—TOEFL (minimum score 500 paper-based; 71 computer-based), IELTS (minimum score 6.5). Electronic applications accepted. *Faculty research:* Math, political policy, technology in the classroom.

Dallas Baptist University, Dorothy M. Bush College of Education, Teaching Program, Dallas, TX 75211-9299. Offers all-level (MAT); distance learning (MAT); elementary (MAT); English as a second language (MAT); Montessori (MAT); multisensory (MAT); secondary (MAT). Part-time and evening/weekend programs available. *Entrance requirements:* For master's, GRE General Test, minimum GPA of 3.0. Additional exam requirements/recommendations for international students: Required—TOEFL, IELTS. *Application deadline:* Applications are processed on a rolling basis. Application fee: $25. Electronic applications accepted. *Expenses: Tuition:* Full-time $12,060; part-time $670 per credit hour. *Required fees:* $100; $50 per semester. *Financial support:* Federal Work-Study, institutionally sponsored loans, scholarships/grants, and tuition waivers (full and partial) available. Support available to part-time students. Financial award applicants required to submit FAFSA. *Unit head:* Dara Owen, Acting Director, 214-333-5413, Fax: 214-333-5551, E-mail: graduate@dbu.edu. *Application contact:* Kit P. Montgomery, Director of Graduate Programs, 214-333-5242, Fax: 214-333-5579, E-mail: graduate@dbu.edu. Web site: http://www3.dbu.edu/graduate/mat.asp.

Defiance College, Program in Education, Defiance, OH 43512-1610. Offers adolescent and young adult licensure (MA); mild and moderate intervention specialist (MA). Part-time programs available. *Faculty:* 7 full-time (4 women), 1 part-time/adjunct (0 women). *Students:* 34 part-time (25 women). *Degree requirements:* For master's, thesis (for some programs). *Entrance requirements:* For master's, teaching certificate. *Application deadline:* For fall admission, 8/1 for domestic students. Applications are processed on a rolling basis. Application fee: $25. *Expenses: Tuition:* Full-time $10,800; part-time $450 per credit hour. *Required fees:* $95; $35 per semester. *Unit head:* Dr. Suzanne McFarland, Coordinator, 419-783-2315, Fax: 419-784-0426, E-mail: smcfarland@defiance.edu. *Application contact:* Sally Bissell, Director of Continuing Education, 419-783-2350, Fax: 419-784-0426, E-mail: sbissell@defiance.edu.

Delaware State University, Graduate Programs, College of Education, Health and Public Policy, Dover, DE 19901-2277. Offers MA, MS, MSW, Ed D. *Accreditation:* NCATE. Part-time and evening/weekend programs available. *Degree requirements:* For master's, comprehensive exam, thesis optional. *Entrance requirements:* For master's, GRE General Test, minimum GPA of 3.0 in major, 2.75 overall. Additional exam requirements/recommendations for international students: Required—TOEFL (minimum score 500 paper-based). Electronic applications accepted.

Delta State University, Graduate Programs, College of Education, Cleveland, MS 38733-0001. Offers M Ed, MAT, MS, Ed D, Ed S. *Accreditation:* NCATE. Part-time and evening/weekend programs available. *Degree requirements:* For master's, thesis optional; for doctorate, thesis/dissertation. *Entrance requirements:* For doctorate, GRE General Test; for Ed S, master's degree, teaching certificate. *Expenses:* Tuition, state resident: full-time $4702; part-time $294 per credit hour. Tuition, nonresident: full-time $12,516; part-time $760 per credit hour. *Required fees:* $586.

DePaul University, College of Education, Chicago, IL 60106. Offers bilingual bicultural education (M Ed, MA); counseling (M Ed, MA), including college student development, community counseling, school counseling; curriculum studies (M Ed, MA, Ed D); early childhood education (M Ed, MA); educational leadership (M Ed, MA, Ed D), including administration and supervision (M Ed, MA), physical education (M Ed, MA); middle school mathematics education (MS); reading specialist (M Ed, MA); social and cultural foundations in education (M Ed, MA), including curriculum studies/development (MA); special education (M Ed, MA); teaching and learning (M Ed, MA), including elementary education, secondary education; world languages education (M Ed, MA). Part-time and evening/weekend programs available. *Faculty:* 49 full-time (28 women), 94 part-time/adjunct (60 women). *Students:* 894 full-time (707 women), 473 part-time (361 women); includes 349 minority (159 Black or African American, non-Hispanic/Latino; 3 American Indian or Alaska Native, non-Hispanic/Latino; 45 Asian, non-Hispanic/Latino; 115 Hispanic/Latino; 2 Native Hawaiian or other Pacific Islander, non-Hispanic/Latino; 25 Two or more races, non-Hispanic/Latino), 21 international. Average age 30. 872 applicants, 64% accepted, 325 enrolled. In 2011, 499 master's, 10 doctorates awarded. *Median time to degree:* Of those who began their doctoral program in fall 2003, 32% received their degree in 8 years or less. *Degree requirements:* For master's, thesis/dissertation (for MA); capstone course or paper (for M Ed); for doctorate, thesis/dissertation. *Entrance requirements:* For master's, interview, minimum GPA of 2.75, 2 letters of recommendation, bachelor's degree conferred by accredited college or university; for doctorate, interview, master's degree, writing sample, 3 letters of recommendation. Additional exam requirements/recommendations for international students: Required—TOEFL (minimum score 550 paper-based; 213 computer-based; 80 iBT). *Application deadline:* For fall admission, 8/15 priority date for domestic students; for winter admission, 12/1 priority date for domestic students; for spring admission, 3/1 priority date for domestic students. Applications are processed on a rolling basis. Application fee: $40. Electronic applications accepted. *Financial support:* In 2011–12, 163 students received support, including 15 research assistantships with full tuition reimbursements available (averaging $6,375 per year); career-related internships or fieldwork, Federal Work-Study, scholarships/grants, and unspecified assistantships also available. Support available to part-time students. Financial award application deadline: 12/31; financial award applicants required to submit FAFSA. *Faculty research:* Reflective teaching, children at risk, loss, ethnicity, urban education. *Total annual research expenditures:* $916,310. *Unit head:* Dr. Paul Zionts, Dean, 773-325-7581, Fax: 773-325-7713, E-mail: pzionts@depaul.edu. *Application contact:* Brandon Washington, Enrollment Management Coordinator, 773-325-1152, Fax: 773-325-2270, E-mail: bwashin3@depaul.edu. Web site: http://education.depaul.edu.

DePaul University, School for New Learning, Chicago, IL 60604. Offers applied professional studies (MA); applied technology (MS); educating adults (MA). Part-time and evening/weekend programs available. *Faculty:* 11 full-time (6 women), 12 part-time/adjunct (8 women). *Students:* 8 full-time (2 women), 160 part-time (119 women); includes 87 minority (64 Black or African American, non-Hispanic/Latino; 4 Asian, non-Hispanic/Latino; 15 Hispanic/Latino; 4 Two or more races, non-Hispanic/Latino). Average age 44. 53 applicants, 60% accepted, 29 enrolled. In 2011, 20 master's awarded. *Degree requirements:* For master's, thesis or alternative. *Entrance requirements:* For master's, 3 years of work experience, current related employment. *Application deadline:* For fall admission, 9/1 priority date for domestic students; for spring admission, 3/1 priority date for domestic students. Applications are processed on a rolling basis. Application fee: $25. Electronic applications accepted. *Financial support:* In 2011–12, 7 students received support. Scholarships/grants and tuition waivers (partial) available. Financial award applicants required to submit FAFSA. *Faculty research:* Interactive problem-based learning, liberal learning and professional competence, effective instructional practice. *Unit head:* Dr. Russ Rogers, Program Director, 312-362-8512, Fax: 312-362-8809, E-mail: rrogers@depaul.edu. *Application contact:* Sarah Hellstrom, Assistant Director, 312-362-5744, Fax: 312-362-8809, E-mail: shellstr@depaul.edu. Web site: http://snl.depaul.edu/.

DeSales University, Graduate Division, Program in Education, Center Valley, PA 18034-9568. Offers academic standards and reform (M Ed); academic standards for K-6 (M Ed); English as a second language (M Ed); instructional technology for K-12 (M Ed); special education (M Ed); teaching English to speakers of other languages (M Ed). Part-time and evening/weekend programs available. Postbaccalaureate distance learning degree programs offered (no on-campus study). *Degree requirements:* For master's, thesis project. *Entrance requirements:* Additional exam requirements/recommendations for international students: Required—TOEFL. *Application deadline:* Applications are processed on a rolling basis. Electronic applications accepted. Tuition and fees vary according to degree level. *Financial support:* Application deadline: 5/1. *Unit head:* Dr. Judith Rance-Roney, Interim Director, 610-282-1100 Ext. 1323, E-mail: judith.rance-roney@desales.edu. *Application contact:* Caryn Stopper, Director of Graduate Admissions, 610-282-1100 Ext. 1768, Fax: 610-282-0525, E-mail: caryn.stopper@desales.edu.

Doane College, Program in Education, Crete, NE 68333-2430. Offers curriculum and instruction (M Ed); educational leadership (M Ed). *Accreditation:* NCATE. Part-time and evening/weekend programs available. *Students:* 126 full-time (103 women), 381 part-time (284 women); includes 20 minority (8 Black or African American, non-Hispanic/Latino; 2 American Indian or Alaska Native, non-Hispanic/Latino; 9 Hispanic/Latino; 1 Two or more races, non-Hispanic/Latino). Average age 33. In 2011, 312 master's awarded. *Degree requirements:* For master's, thesis. *Entrance requirements:* For master's, minimum GPA of 2.5. Additional exam requirements/recommendations for international students: Required—TOEFL. *Application deadline:* Applications are processed on a rolling basis. Electronic applications accepted. *Expenses:* Contact institution. *Financial support:* Applicants required to submit FAFSA. *Unit head:* Lyn C. Forester, Dean, 402-826-8604, Fax: 402-826-8278. *Application contact:* Wilma Daddario, Assistant Dean, 402-464-1223, Fax: 402-466-4228, E-mail: wdaddario@doane.edu. Web site: http://www.doane.edu/Admission/Graduate_Admission/Master_Of_Education/.

Dominican College, Division of Teacher Education, Department of Teacher Education, Orangeburg, NY 10962-1210. Offers childhood education (MS Ed); teacher of students with disabilities (MS Ed); teacher of visually impaired (MS Ed). *Accreditation:* Teacher Education Accreditation Council. Part-time and evening/weekend programs available. Postbaccalaureate distance learning degree programs offered (minimal on-campus study). *Degree requirements:* For master's, practicum, research project. *Entrance requirements:* For master's, interview, 3 letters of recommendation, minimum undergraduate GPA of 3.0. Additional exam requirements/recommendations for international students: Required—TOEFL (minimum score 550 paper-based; 213 computer-based).

Dominican University, School of Education, River Forest, IL 60305-1099. Offers curriculum and instruction (MA Ed); early childhood education (MS); education (MAT); educational administration (MA); elementary (online) (MS); English as a second language (online) (MS); reading (online) (MS); special education (MS). Part-time and evening/weekend programs available. Postbaccalaureate distance learning degree programs offered (no on-campus study). *Faculty:* 19 full-time (13 women), 53 part-time/adjunct (41 women). *Students:* 24 full-time (19 women), 434 part-time (357 women); includes 95 minority (27 Black or African American, non-Hispanic/Latino; 1 American Indian or Alaska Native, non-Hispanic/Latino; 12 Asian, non-Hispanic/Latino; 48 Hispanic/Latino; 7 Two or more races, non-Hispanic/Latino), 1 international. Average age 33. 92 applicants, 99% accepted, 91 enrolled. In 2011, 267 master's awarded. *Entrance requirements:* For master's, Illinois certification test of basic skills. Additional exam requirements/recommendations for international students: Required—TOEFL (minimum score 550 paper-based; 213 computer-based; 79 iBT). *Application deadline:* Applications are processed on a rolling basis. Application fee: $25. *Expenses:* Contact institution. *Financial support:* Career-related internships or fieldwork, scholarships/grants, and tuition waivers (partial) available. Support available to part-time students. Financial award application deadline: 8/15; financial award applicants required to submit FAFSA. *Faculty research:* Governance of private education institutions, reading and language arts, inclusion, organizational planning, leadership and vision. *Unit head:* Dr. Colleen Reardon, Dean, 718-524-6643, Fax: 708-524-6665, E-mail: creardon@dom.edu. *Application contact:* Keven Hansen, Coordinator of Recruitment and Admissions, 708-524-6921, Fax: 708-524-6665, E-mail: educate@dom.edu. Web site: http://www.dom.edu/soe.

Dominican University of California, Graduate Programs, School of Education and Counseling Psychology, Multiple Subject Teaching Program, San Rafael, CA 94901-2298. Offers MS, Credential. Program also offered in Ukiah, CA. *Faculty:* 4 full-time (all women), 13 part-time/adjunct (11 women). *Students:* 29 full-time (22 women), 21 part-time (15 women); includes 11 minority (1 Black or African American, non-Hispanic/Latino; 1 Asian, non-Hispanic/Latino; 6 Hispanic/Latino; 1 Native Hawaiian or other Pacific Islander, non-Hispanic/Latino; 2 Two or more races, non-Hispanic/Latino). Average age 34. 42 applicants, 60% accepted, 21 enrolled. In 2011, 15 master's, 42 other advanced degrees awarded. *Entrance requirements:* For master's, CBEST and/or CSET; for Credential, California Basic Educational Skills Test, PRAXIS, 48 units of course work in education, bachelor's degree in area other than education, minimum GPA of 2.7. Additional exam requirements/recommendations for international students: Required—TOEFL (minimum score 550 paper-based; 213 computer-based), IELTS (minimum score 7). *Application deadline:* For fall admission, 6/15 priority date for domestic students, 6/15 for international students; for spring admission, 11/15 priority date for domestic students, 11/15 for international students. Applications are processed on a rolling basis. Application fee: $40. Electronic applications accepted. *Expenses: Tuition:* Full-time $15,660. *Required fees:* $300. Tuition and fees vary according to program. *Financial support:* In 2011–12, 18 students received support. Application deadline: 3/2; applicants required to submit FAFSA. *Unit head:* Dr. Mary Crosby, Chair, 415-485-3288, Fax: 415-458-3790, E-mail: crosby@dominican.edu. *Application contact:* Moriah Dunning, Associate Director, 415-485-3246, Fax: 415-485-3214, E-mail: moriah.dunning@dominican.edu. Web site: http://www.dominican.edu/.

Dominican University of California, Graduate Programs, School of Education and Counseling Psychology, Program in Education, San Rafael, CA 94901-2298. Offers MS. *Faculty:* 1 (woman) full-time, 4 part-time/adjunct (3 women). *Students:* 9 full-time (8 women), 17 part-time (13 women); includes 4 minority (1 Black or African American, non-Hispanic/Latino; 3 Hispanic/Latino), 2 international. Average age 42. 26 applicants, 77% accepted, 12 enrolled. In 2011, 14 master's awarded. *Entrance requirements:* For master's, minimum GPA of 3.0, research project. Additional exam requirements/recommendations for international students: Required—TOEFL (minimum score 550 paper-based; 213 computer-based). *Application deadline:* For fall admission, 6/15 priority date for domestic students, 6/15 for international students; for spring admission, 11/15 priority date for domestic students, 11/15 for international students. Applications are processed on a rolling basis. Application fee: $40. Electronic applications accepted. *Expenses: Tuition:* Full-time $15,660. *Required fees:* $300. Tuition and fees vary according to program. *Financial support:* In 2011–12, 5 students received support. Application deadline: 3/2; applicants required to submit FAFSA. *Unit head:* Dr. Madalienne Peters, Professor, 415-485-3285, Fax: 415-458-3790, E-mail: peters@dominican.edu. *Application contact:* Moriah Dunning, Director, 415-458-3246, Fax: 415-485-3214, E-mail: moriah.dunning@dominican.edu.

Dominican University of California, Graduate Programs, School of Education and Counseling Psychology, Single Subject Teaching Program, San Rafael, CA 94901-2298. Offers MS, Credential. *Faculty:* 3 full-time (2 women), 18 part-time/adjunct (10 women). *Students:* 39 full-time (27 women), 11 part-time (8 women); includes 7 minority (2 Asian, non-Hispanic/Latino; 3 Hispanic/Latino; 2 Two or more races, non-Hispanic/Latino). Average age 37. 46 applicants, 59% accepted, 19 enrolled. In 2011, 4 master's, 28 other advanced degrees awarded. *Entrance requirements:* For master's, CBEST and/or CSET; for Credential, California Basic Educational Skills Test, PRAXIS, minimum GPA of 2.7, bachelor's degree in area other than education, 48 units of course work in education. Additional exam requirements/recommendations for international students: Required—TOEFL (minimum score 550 paper-based; 213 computer-based). *Application deadline:* For fall admission, 6/15 priority date for domestic students, 6/15 for international students; for spring admission, 11/15 priority date for domestic students, 11/15 for international students. Applications are processed on a rolling basis. Application fee: $40. Electronic applications accepted. *Expenses: Tuition:* Full-time $15,660. *Required fees:* $300. Tuition and fees vary according to program. *Financial support:* In 2011–12, 22 students received support. Application deadline: 3/2; applicants required to submit FAFSA. *Unit head:* Dr. Margaret Golden, Associate Professor, 415-482-3593, Fax: 415-458-3790, E-mail: margaret.golden@dominican.edu. *Application contact:* Moriah Dunning, Associate Director, 415-485-3246, Fax: 415-485-3214, E-mail: moriah.dunning@dominican.edu. Web site: http://www.dominican.edu/.

Dordt College, Program in Education, Sioux Center, IA 51250-1697. Offers M Ed. Part-time programs available. Postbaccalaureate distance learning degree programs offered (minimal on-campus study). *Degree requirements:* For master's, comprehensive exam, thesis. *Entrance requirements:* For master's, GRE or MAT. Additional exam requirements/recommendations for international students: Required—TOEFL. Electronic applications accepted.

Dowling College, Graduate Programs in Education, Oakdale, NY 11769-1999. Offers adolescence education with middle childhood extension (MS); advanced certificate in gifted education (AC); childhood and early childhood education (MS); childhood and gifted education (MS); computers in education (AC); early childhood education (MS); educational administration (Ed D); educational technology leadership (MS); educational technology specialist (AC); literacy education (MS); literary education (AC); school building leader (AC); school district business leader (MBA, AC); school district leader (AC); special education (MS); sports management (MS). *Accreditation:* NCATE. Part-time and evening/weekend programs available. Postbaccalaureate distance learning degree programs offered (minimal on-campus study). *Faculty:* 23 full-time (12 women), 70 part-time/adjunct (44 women). *Students:* 336 full-time (245 women), 631 part-time (485 women); includes 83 minority (29 Black or African American, non-Hispanic/Latino; 2 American Indian or Alaska Native, non-Hispanic/Latino; 7 Asian, non-Hispanic/Latino; 45 Hispanic/Latino). Average age 32. 280 applicants, 85% accepted, 167 enrolled. In 2011, 425 master's, 27 doctorates, 40 other advanced degrees awarded. *Degree requirements:* For master's and AC, comprehensive exam; for doctorate, thesis/dissertation. *Entrance requirements:* For master's, minimum GPA of 3.0; for doctorate, GRE, master's degree; for AC, teaching certificate. Additional exam requirements/recommendations for international students: Required—TOEFL (minimum score 550 paper-based). *Application deadline:* For fall admission, 9/1 priority date for domestic students; for winter admission, 1/1 priority date for domestic students; for spring admission, 2/1 priority date for domestic students. Applications are processed on a rolling basis. Application fee: $50. Electronic applications accepted. *Expenses: Tuition:* Full-time $19,162; part-time $933 per credit. *Required fees:* $1330; $700 per year. Tuition and fees vary according to course load. *Financial support:* Career-related internships or fieldwork and Federal Work-Study available. Support available to part-time students. Financial award application deadline: 6/30; financial award applicants required to submit FAFSA. *Faculty research:* Natural readers, Korean styles and learning strategies, mothers of children with disabilities, computers in instruction, cultural background and organizational roadblocks to problem solving. *Unit head:* Carol Pulsonetti, Director of Operations, School of Education, 631-244-3243, E-mail: pulsonec@dowling.edu. *Application contact:* Ronnie S. Macdonald, Assistant Vice President for Enrollment Services/Dean of Admissions, 631-244-3357, Fax: 631-244-1059, E-mail: macdonar@dowling.edu.

Drake University, School of Education, Des Moines, IA 50311-4516. Offers MAT, MS, MSE, MST, Ed D, Ed S. Part-time and evening/weekend programs available. *Faculty:* 21 full-time (12 women), 38 part-time/adjunct (25 women). *Students:* 92 full-time (66 women), 545 part-time (415 women); includes 40 minority (17 Black or African American, non-Hispanic/Latino; 4 Asian, non-Hispanic/Latino; 13 Hispanic/Latino; 1 Native Hawaiian or other Pacific Islander, non-Hispanic/Latino; 5 Two or more races, non-Hispanic/Latino), 1 international. Average age 34. 227 applicants, 74% accepted, 110 enrolled. In 2011, 178 master's, 4 doctorates, 29 other advanced degrees awarded. *Degree requirements:* For master's and Ed S, comprehensive exam, internships (for some programs); for doctorate, comprehensive exam, thesis/dissertation, internships (for some programs). *Entrance requirements:* For master's, GRE General Test, MAT, or Drake Writing Assessment, resume, 2 letters of recommendation; for doctorate, GRE General Test or MAT, master's degree, 3 letters of recommendation; for Ed S, GRE General Test or MAT. Additional exam requirements/recommendations for international students: Required—TOEFL (minimum score 550 paper-based; 213 computer-based). *Application deadline:* For fall admission, 7/1 priority date for domestic students, 6/1 for international students; for spring admission, 11/1 priority date for domestic students, 10/1 for international students. Applications are processed on a rolling basis. Application fee: $25. Electronic applications accepted. *Expenses:* Contact institution. *Financial support:* In 2011–12, 14 research assistantships were awarded; career-related internships or fieldwork and unspecified assistantships also available. Support available to part-time students. *Faculty research:* Counseling and rehabilitation, behavioral supports, inquiry-based science methods, teacher quality enhancement. *Total annual research expenditures:* $1.5 million. *Unit head:* Dr. Janet McMahill, Dean, 515-271-3829, E-mail: janet.mcmahill@drake.edu. *Application contact:* Ann J. Martin, Graduate Coordinator, 515-271-2034, Fax: 515-271-2831, E-mail: ann.martin@drake.edu.

Drew University, Caspersen School of Graduate Studies, Program in Education, Madison, NJ 07940-1493. Offers biology (MAT); chemistry (MAT); English (MAT); French (MAT); Italian (MAT); math (MAT); physics (MAT); social studies (MAT); Spanish (MAT); theatre arts (MAT). Part-time programs available. *Entrance requirements:* For master's, transcripts, personal statement, recommendations. Additional exam requirements/recommendations for international students: Required—TOEFL, TWE. *Expenses:* Contact institution.

Drexel University, Goodwin College of Professional Studies, School of Education, Philadelphia, PA 19104-2875. Offers educational administration: collaborative leadership (MS); educational leadership and management (Ed D); educational leadership development and learning technologies (PhD); global and international education (MS); higher education (MS); human resources development (MS); learning technologies (MS); mathematics, learning and teaching (MS); special education (MS); teaching, learning and curriculum (MS). Part-time and evening/weekend programs available. Postbaccalaureate distance learning degree programs offered. *Degree requirements:* For doctorate, thesis/dissertation. *Entrance requirements:* Additional exam requirements/recommendations for international students: Required—TOEFL. Electronic applications accepted. *Expenses:* Contact institution.

Drury University, Graduate Programs in Education, Springfield, MO 65802. Offers elementary education (M Ed); gifted education (M Ed); human services (M Ed); instructional mathematics K-8 (M Ed); instructional technology (M Ed); middle school teaching (M Ed); secondary education (M Ed); special education (M Ed); special reading (M Ed). *Accreditation:* NCATE. Part-time and evening/weekend programs available. *Degree requirements:* For master's, thesis. *Entrance requirements:* For master's, GRE or MAT, minimum GPA of 2.75. Additional exam requirements/recommendations for international students: Required—TOEFL. Electronic applications accepted. *Faculty research:* Cultural enrichment, research skills, parental involvement relating to reading skills, reading strategies for mainstreaming children.

Duke University, Graduate School, Program in Teaching, Durham, NC 27708. Offers MAT, MAT/MEM. *Accreditation:* NCATE. *Students:* 13 full-time (8 women); includes 5 minority (2 Black or African American, non-Hispanic/Latino; 2 Asian, non-Hispanic/Latino; 1 Hispanic/Latino). 72 applicants, 40% accepted, 13 enrolled. In 2011, 14 degrees awarded. *Entrance requirements:* For master's, GRE General Test. Additional exam requirements/recommendations for international students: Required—TOEFL (minimum score 550 paper-based; 213 computer-based; 83 iBT), IELTS (minimum score 7). *Application deadline:* For fall admission, 1/30 priority date for domestic students, 1/30 for international students. Application fee: $75. Electronic applications accepted. *Expenses: Tuition:* Full-time $40,720. *Required fees:* $3107. *Financial support:* Application deadline: 2/15. *Unit head:* Ginny Buckner, Director, 919-684-4353, Fax: 919-684-4483, E-mail: fns@duke.edu. *Application contact:* Elizabeth Hutton, Director of Admissions, 919-684-3913, E-mail: grad-admissions@duke.edu. Web site: http://www.duke.edu/web/MAT/.

Duquesne University, School of Education, Pittsburgh, PA 15282-0001. Offers MS Ed, Ed D, PhD, CAGS, Post-Master's Certificate. *Accreditation:* NCATE. Part-time and evening/weekend programs available. Postbaccalaureate distance learning degree programs offered (minimal on-campus study). *Faculty:* 50 full-time (27 women). *Students:* 585 full-time (427 women), 110 part-time (94 women); includes 82 minority (56 Black or African American, non-Hispanic/Latino; 10 Asian, non-Hispanic/Latino; 11 Hispanic/Latino; 5 Two or more races, non-Hispanic/Latino), 33 international. Average age 31. 656 applicants, 44% accepted, 162 enrolled. In 2011, 248 master's, 22 doctorates, 9 other advanced degrees awarded. *Degree requirements:* For master's, comprehensive exam (for some programs); for doctorate, comprehensive exam (for some programs), thesis/dissertation (for some programs); for other advanced degree, comprehensive exam (for some programs), thesis (for some programs). *Entrance requirements:* For master's, letters of recommendation, essay, personal statement, interview, bachelor's degree; for doctorate, GRE, letters of recommendation, essay, personal statement, interview, master's degree; for other advanced degree, GRE, letters of recommendation, essay, personal statement, interview, bachelor's/master's degree. Additional exam requirements/recommendations for international students: Required—TOEFL (minimum score 550 paper-based; 80 computer-based), IELTS (minimum score 7). *Application deadline:* For fall admission, 3/1 for domestic students; for spring admission, 9/1 for domestic students. Applications are processed on a rolling basis. Application fee: $0. Electronic applications accepted. Application fee is waived when completed online. *Expenses: Tuition:* Full-time $16,596; part-time $922 per credit. *Required fees:* $1584; $88 per credit. Tuition and fees vary according to program. *Financial support:* Research assistantships, teaching assistantships with tuition reimbursements, career-related internships or fieldwork, Federal Work-Study, institutionally sponsored loans, and tuition waivers available. Support available to part-time students. *Total annual research expenditures:* $40,000. *Unit head:* Dr. Olga Welch, Dean, 412-396-6102, Fax: 412-396-5585. *Application contact:* Michael Dolinger, Director of Student and Academic Services, 412-396-6647, Fax: 412-396-5585, E-mail: dolingerm@duq.edu. Web site: http://www.education.duq.edu.

D'Youville College, Department of Education, Buffalo, NY 14201-1084. Offers elementary education (MS Ed, Teaching Certificate); secondary education (MS Ed, Teaching Certificate); special education (MS Ed). Part-time and evening/weekend programs available. *Faculty:* 29 full-time (18 women), 29 part-time/adjunct (17 women). *Students:* 198 full-time (133 women), 52 part-time (41 women); includes 12 minority (7 Black or African American, non-Hispanic/Latino; 1 American Indian or Alaska Native, non-Hispanic/Latino; 1 Asian, non-Hispanic/Latino; 3 Hispanic/Latino), 161 international. Average age 29. 245 applicants, 46% accepted, 57 enrolled. In 2011, 235 master's awarded. *Degree requirements:* For master's, one foreign language, comprehensive exam, project or thesis. *Entrance requirements:* For master's, GRE (if GPA less than 2.75), minimum GPA of 3.0. Additional exam requirements/recommendations for international students: Required—TOEFL (minimum score 500 paper-based; 173 computer-based). *Application deadline:* For fall admission, 5/1 for international students; for spring admission, 9/1 for international students. Applications are processed on a rolling basis. Application fee: $25. Electronic applications accepted. *Expenses: Tuition:* Full-time $18,960; part-time $790 per credit hour. *Required fees:* $310. Tuition and fees vary according to degree level and program. *Financial support:* In 2011–12, 1 research assistantship with partial tuition reimbursement (averaging $3,000 per year) was awarded; career-related internships or fieldwork, Federal Work-Study, institutionally sponsored loans, scholarships/grants, tuition waivers (full and partial), and unspecified assistantships also available. Support available to part-time students. Financial award application deadline: 3/1; financial award applicants required to submit FAFSA. *Faculty research:* Developmental disabilities, multiculturalism, early childhood education. *Unit head:* Dr. Hilary Lochte, Chair, 716-829-8110, Fax: 716-829-7660. *Application contact:* Linda Fisher, Graduate Admissions Director, 716-829-8400, Fax: 716-829-7900, E-mail: graduateadmissions@dyc.edu.

Earlham College, Graduate Programs, Richmond, IN 47374-4095. Offers M Ed, MAT. *Entrance requirements:* For master's, GRE, PRAXIS I, PRAXIS II.

East Carolina University, Graduate School, College of Education, Greenville, NC 27858-4353. Offers MA, MA Ed, MAT, MLS, MS, MSA, Ed D, Certificate, Ed S. *Accreditation:* NCATE. Part-time and evening/weekend programs available. Postbaccalaureate distance learning degree programs offered (no on-campus study). *Degree requirements:* For master's, comprehensive exam, thesis optional; for doctorate, thesis/dissertation. *Entrance requirements:* For master's, GRE or MAT, bachelor's degree in related field, minimum GPA of 2.5; for doctorate, GRE or MAT, interview, minimum GPA of 3.5. Additional exam requirements/recommendations for international students: Required—TOEFL. *Application deadline:* For fall admission, 6/1 priority date for domestic students. Applications are processed on a rolling basis. Application fee: $50. *Expenses:* Tuition, state resident: full-time $3557; part-time $444.63 per semester hour. Tuition, nonresident: full-time $14,351; part-time $1793.88 per semester hour. *Required fees:* $2016; $252 per semester hour. Part-time tuition and fees vary according to course load, campus/location and program. *Financial support:* Research assistantships with partial tuition reimbursements, teaching assistantships with partial tuition reimbursements, and Federal Work-Study available. Support available to part-time students. Financial award application deadline: 6/1. *Unit head:* Dr. Linda Ann Patriarca, Dean, 252-328-1000, Fax: 252-328-4219, E-mail: patriarcal@ecu.edu. *Application contact:* Dean of Graduate School, 252-328-6012, Fax: 252-328-6071, E-mail: gradschool@ecu.edu. Web site: http://www.ecu.edu/cs-educ/.

East Central University, School of Graduate Studies, Department of Education, Ada, OK 74820-6899. Offers M Ed. *Accreditation:* NCATE. Part-time and evening/weekend programs available. *Entrance requirements:* For master's, minimum GPA of 2.5. Electronic applications accepted.

Eastern Connecticut State University, School of Education and Professional Studies/Graduate Division, Willimantic, CT 06226-2295. Offers MS. *Accreditation:* NCATE. Part-time and evening/weekend programs available. *Degree requirements:* For master's, comprehensive exam, thesis optional. *Entrance requirements:* For master's, minimum GPA of 2.7. Additional exam requirements/recommendations for international students: Required—TOEFL (minimum score 550 paper-based; 213 computer-based).

Eastern Illinois University, Graduate School, College of Education and Professional Studies, Charleston, IL 61920-3099. Offers MS, MS Ed, Ed S. *Accreditation:* NCATE. Part-time and evening/weekend programs available. *Faculty:* 114 full-time. In 2011, 273 master's, 47 other advanced degrees awarded. *Degree requirements:* For Ed S, thesis. *Application deadline:* For fall admission, 3/31 priority date for domestic students. Applications are processed on a rolling basis. Application fee: $30. *Expenses:* Tuition, state resident: part-time $279 per credit hour. Tuition, nonresident: part-time $670 per credit hour. *Required fees:* $179.07 per credit hour. $1253 per semester. *Financial support:* In 2011–12, 12 research assistantships with full tuition reimbursements (averaging $8,100 per year), 13 teaching assistantships with full tuition reimbursements (averaging $8,100 per year) were awarded; career-related internships or fieldwork and Federal Work-Study also available. Support available to part-time students. *Unit head:* Dr. Diane Jackman, Dean, 217-581-2524, Fax: 217-581-2518, E-mail: dhjackman@eiu.edu. *Application contact:* Bill Elliott, Director of Graduate Admissions, 217-581-7489, Fax: 217-581-6020, E-mail: wjelliott@eiu.edu.

Eastern Kentucky University, The Graduate School, College of Education, Richmond, KY 40475-3102. Offers MA, MA Ed, MAT. *Accreditation:* NCATE. Part-time programs available. Postbaccalaureate distance learning degree programs offered (minimal on-campus study). *Entrance requirements:* For master's, GRE General Test, minimum GPA of 2.5. *Faculty research:* Dispositions to teach, technology in education, distance learning.

Eastern Mennonite University, Program in Education, Harrisonburg, VA 22802-2462. Offers MA. *Accreditation:* NCATE. Part-time programs available. *Degree requirements:* For master's, portfolio, research projects. *Entrance requirements:* For master's, 1 year of teaching experience, interview, minimum undergraduate GPA of 2.75. Additional exam requirements/recommendations for international students: Required—TOEFL (minimum score 550 paper-based; 213 computer-based). *Expenses:* Contact institution. *Faculty research:* Effective literacy instruction for middle school English language learners, beginning teacher's emotional experiences, constructivist learning environments, restorative discipline.

Eastern Michigan University, Graduate School, College of Education, Ypsilanti, MI 48197. Offers MA, Ed D, PhD, Graduate Certificate, Post Master's Certificate, SPA. *Accreditation:* NCATE. Part-time and evening/weekend programs available. Postbaccalaureate distance learning degree programs offered (minimal on-campus study). *Faculty:* 88 full-time (62 women). *Students:* 178 full-time (144 women), 1,155 part-time (885 women); includes 255 minority (191 Black or African American, non-Hispanic/Latino; 5 American Indian or Alaska Native, non-Hispanic/Latino; 23 Asian, non-Hispanic/Latino; 25 Hispanic/Latino; 1 Native Hawaiian or other Pacific Islander, non-Hispanic/Latino; 10 Two or more races, non-Hispanic/Latino), 22 international. Average age 35. 842 applicants, 51% accepted, 266 enrolled. In 2011, 285 master's, 11 doctorates, 490 other advanced degrees awarded. *Degree requirements:* For doctorate, thesis/dissertation. *Entrance requirements:* For master's, GRE; for doctorate, GRE General Test. Additional exam requirements/recommendations for international students: Required—TOEFL. *Application deadline:* Applications are processed on a rolling basis. Application fee: $35. *Expenses:* Tuition, state resident: full-time $10,367; part-time $432 per credit hour. Tuition, nonresident: full-time $20,435; part-time $851 per credit hour. *Required fees:* $39 per credit hour. $46 per semester. One-time fee: $100. Tuition and fees vary according to course level, degree level and reciprocity agreements. *Financial support:* Fellowships, research assistantships with full tuition reimbursements, teaching assistantships with full tuition reimbursements, career-related internships or fieldwork, Federal Work-Study, institutionally sponsored loans, scholarships/grants, tuition waivers (partial), and unspecified assistantships available. Support available to part-time students. Financial award applicants required to submit FAFSA. *Unit head:* Dr. Jann Joseph, Dean, 734-487-1414, Fax: 734-484-6471, E-mail: jann.joseph@emich.edu. *Application contact:* Graduate Admissions, 734-487-2400, Fax: 734-487-6559, E-mail: graduate.admissions@emich.edu. Web site: http://www.emich.edu/coe/.

Eastern Nazarene College, Adult and Graduate Studies, Division of Teacher Education, Quincy, MA 02170. Offers administration (M Ed); early childhood education (M Ed, Certificate); elementary education (M Ed, Certificate); English as a second language (Certificate); instructional enrichment and development (Certificate); middle school education (M Ed, Certificate); moderate special needs education (Certificate); principal (Certificate); program development and supervision (Certificate); secondary education (M Ed, Certificate); special education administrator (Certificate); special needs (M Ed); supervisor (Certificate); teacher of reading (M Ed, Certificate). M Ed also available through weekend program for administration, special needs, and teacher of reading only. Part-time and evening/weekend programs available. *Entrance requirements:* Additional exam requirements/recommendations for international students: Required—TOEFL (minimum score 550 paper-based).

Eastern New Mexico University, Graduate School, College of Education and Technology, Department of Educational Studies, Portales, NM 88130. Offers counseling (MA); education (M Ed), including educational adminstration, secondary education; school counseling (M Ed); special education (M Sp Ed), including early childhood special education, general. *Accreditation:* NCATE. Part-time and evening/weekend programs available. Postbaccalaureate distance learning degree programs offered (minimal on-campus study). *Degree requirements:* For master's, comprehensive exam, thesis optional. *Entrance requirements:* For master's, minimum GPA of 3.0, letter of recommendation, photocopy of teaching license, writing assessment, Level II teaching license (for M Ed in educational administration). Additional exam requirements/recommendations for international students: Required—TOEFL (minimum score 550 paper-based; 213 computer-based; 79 iBT), IELTS (minimum score 6). Electronic applications accepted.

Eastern Oregon University, Master of Science Program, La Grande, OR 97850-2899. Offers MS. Part-time programs available. Postbaccalaureate distance learning degree programs offered (no on-campus study). *Degree requirements:* For master's, thesis. *Entrance requirements:* For master's, GRE General Test.

Eastern University, Graduate Education Programs, St. Davids, PA 19087-3696. Offers multicultural education (M Ed); school health services (M Ed); school nurse (Certificate). Part-time programs available. *Entrance requirements:* For master's, minimum GPA of 2.5. Additional exam requirements/recommendations for international students: Required—TOEFL.

Eastern Washington University, Graduate Studies, College of Arts, Letters and Education, Department of Education, Cheney, WA 99004-2431. Offers adult education (M Ed); curriculum development (M Ed); early childhood education (M Ed); education (M Ed); educational leadership (M Ed); elementary teaching (M Ed); foundations of education (M Ed); instructional media and technology (M Ed); literacy (M Ed); secondary teaching (M Ed); teaching K-8 (M Ed). Part-time programs available. *Faculty:* 25 full-time (16 women). *Students:* 40 full-time (27 women), 39 part-time (31 women); includes 4 minority (1 American Indian or Alaska Native, non-Hispanic/Latino; 3 Hispanic/Latino), 4 international. Average age 38. 48 applicants, 21% accepted, 8 enrolled. In 2011, 44 master's awarded. *Degree requirements:* For master's, comprehensive exam. *Entrance requirements:* For master's, minimum GPA of 3.0. *Application deadline:* For fall admission, 4/1 priority date for domestic students; for spring admission, 1/15 for domestic students. Applications are processed on a rolling basis. Application fee: $50. *Financial support:* In 2011–12, 2 teaching assistantships with partial tuition reimbursements (averaging $7,000 per year) were awarded; career-related internships or fieldwork, Federal Work-Study, institutionally sponsored loans, scholarships/grants, health care benefits, tuition waivers (partial), and unspecified assistantships also available. Support available to part-time students. Financial award application deadline: 2/1; financial award applicants required to submit FAFSA. *Unit head:* Dr. Kevin Pyatt, Assistant Professor, Science and Technology, 509-359-2831, E-mail: kpyatt@ewu.edu. *Application contact:* Dr. Robin Showalter, Graduate Program Coordinator, 509-359-

6492, E-mail: rshowalter@ewu.edu. Web site: http://www.ewu.edu/CALE/Programs/Education.xml.

East Stroudsburg University of Pennsylvania, Graduate School, College of Education, East Stroudsburg, PA 18301-2999. Offers M Ed. Part-time and evening/weekend programs available. *Degree requirements:* For master's, comprehensive exam, thesis (for some programs). *Entrance requirements:* Additional exam requirements/recommendations for international students: Required—TOEFL (minimum score 560 paper-based; 220 computer-based; 83 iBT).

East Tennessee State University, School of Graduate Studies, College of Education, Johnson City, TN 37614. Offers M Ed, MA, MAT, Ed D, PhD, Ed S, Post-Master's Certificate, Postbaccalaureate Certificate. *Accreditation:* NCATE. *Faculty:* 69 full-time (41 women), 11 part-time/adjunct (9 women). *Students:* 327 full-time (208 women), 319 part-time (246 women); includes 51 minority (29 Black or African American, non-Hispanic/Latino; 1 American Indian or Alaska Native, non-Hispanic/Latino; 6 Asian, non-Hispanic/Latino; 6 Hispanic/Latino; 9 Two or more races, non-Hispanic/Latino), 15 international. Average age 34. 457 applicants, 46% accepted, 206 enrolled. In 2011, 194 master's, 38 doctorates, 6 other advanced degrees awarded. *Entrance requirements:* Additional exam requirements/recommendations for international students: Required—TOEFL (minimum score 550 paper-based; 213 computer-based; 79 iBT). *Expenses:* Tuition, state resident: full-time $7312; part-time $350 per credit hour. Tuition, nonresident: full-time $18,490; part-time $621 per credit hour. *Required fees:* $63 per credit hour. Tuition and fees vary according to course load and program. *Financial support:* In 2011–12, 213 students received support, including 19 fellowships with full tuition reimbursements available, 39 research assistantships with full tuition reimbursements available, 36 teaching assistantships with full tuition reimbursements available; career-related internships or fieldwork, institutionally sponsored loans, scholarships/grants, and unspecified assistantships also available. Financial award application deadline: 7/1; financial award applicants required to submit FAFSA. *Total annual research expenditures:* $3,100. *Unit head:* Dr. Hal Knight, Dean, 423-439-7626, Fax: 423-439-7560, E-mail: knighth@etsu.edu. *Application contact:* School of Graduate Studies, 423-439-4221, Fax: 423-439-5624, E-mail: gradsch@etsu.edu.

Edgewood College, Program in Education, Madison, WI 53711-1997. Offers adult learning (MA Ed); bilingual teaching and learning (MA Ed); director of instruction (Certificate); director of special education and pupil services (Certificate); education (MA Ed); educational administration (MA Ed); educational leadership (Ed D); professional studies (MA Ed); program coordinator (Certificate); reading administration (MA Ed); school business administration (Certificate); school principalship K-12 (Certificate); special education (MA Ed); sustainability leadership (MA Ed); teaching and learning (MA Ed); teaching English to speakers of other languages (TESOL) (MA Ed). *Accreditation:* NCATE (one or more programs are accredited). Part-time and evening/weekend programs available. *Students:* 155 full-time (93 women), 152 part-time (116 women); includes 39 minority (13 Black or African American, non-Hispanic/Latino; 5 Asian, non-Hispanic/Latino; 17 Hispanic/Latino; 4 Two or more races, non-Hispanic/Latino), 9 international. Average age 36. In 2011, 39 master's, 32 doctorates awarded. *Degree requirements:* For master's, practicum, research project; for doctorate, comprehensive exam, thesis/dissertation. *Entrance requirements:* For master's, minimum GPA of 2.75, 2 letters of recommendation, personal statement; for doctorate, resume, letter of intent, 2 letters of recommendation, interview, writing sample. Additional exam requirements/recommendations for international students: Required—TOEFL (minimum score 525 paper-based; 197 computer-based; 72 iBT). *Application deadline:* For fall admission, 8/15 for domestic students, 5/1 for international students; for spring admission, 1/8 for domestic students, 11/1 for international students. Applications are processed on a rolling basis. Application fee: $25. Electronic applications accepted. *Expenses: Tuition:* Part-time $747 per credit. Part-time tuition and fees vary according to program. *Unit head:* Dr. Jane Belmore, Dean, 608-663-8336, Fax: 608-663-3291, E-mail: jbelmore@edgewood.edu. *Application contact:* Joann Eastman, Admissions Counselor, 608-663-3250, Fax: 608-663-2214, E-mail: gps@edgewood.edu. Web site: http://education.edgewood.edu/graduate.html.

Edinboro University of Pennsylvania, School of Education, Edinboro, PA 16444. Offers M Ed, MA, MS, Certificate. *Accreditation:* NCATE. Part-time and evening/weekend programs available. *Faculty:* 22 full-time (15 women). *Students:* 297 full-time (211 women), 848 part-time (665 women); includes 35 minority (26 Black or African American, non-Hispanic/Latino; 1 American Indian or Alaska Native, non-Hispanic/Latino; 1 Asian, non-Hispanic/Latino; 6 Hispanic/Latino; 1 Two or more races, non-Hispanic/Latino). Average age 31. In 2011, 405 master's, 54 other advanced degrees awarded. *Degree requirements:* For master's and Certificate, competency exam. *Entrance requirements:* For master's and Certificate, GRE or MAT, minimum QPA of 2.5. *Application deadline:* Applications are processed on a rolling basis. Application fee: $30. Electronic applications accepted. *Financial support:* In 2011–12, 78 research assistantships with full and partial tuition reimbursements (averaging $4,050 per year) were awarded; career-related internships or fieldwork, Federal Work-Study, institutionally sponsored loans, scholarships/grants, and unspecified assistantships also available. Support available to part-time students. Financial award application deadline: 2/15; financial award applicants required to submit FAFSA. *Unit head:* Dr. Nomsa Geleta, Dean, 814-732-2724, Fax: 814-732-2268, E-mail: ngeleta@edinboro.edu. *Application contact:* Dr. Alan Biel, Dean of Graduate Studies and Research, 814-732-2856, Fax: 814-732-2611, E-mail: abiel@edinboro.edu.

Elizabeth City State University, School of Education and Psychology, Elizabeth City, NC 27909-7806. Offers M Ed, MSA. Part-time and evening/weekend programs available. *Degree requirements:* For master's, comprehensive exam (for some programs), thesis. Electronic applications accepted.

Ellis University, Program in Education, Chicago, IL 60606-7204. Offers early childhood education (MA Ed); education (MA Ed); teacher as a leader (MA Ed). *Degree requirements:* For master's, thesis or capstone.

Elms College, Division of Education, Chicopee, MA 01013-2839. Offers early childhood education (MAT); education (M Ed, CAGS); elementary education (MAT); English as a second language (MAT); reading (MAT); secondary education (MAT), including biology education, English education, Spanish education; special education (MAT). Part-time and evening/weekend programs available. *Degree requirements:* For master's, thesis (for some programs). *Entrance requirements:* For master's, Massachusetts Educators Certification Test, minimum GPA of 3.0; for CAGS, master's degree in education. Additional exam requirements/recommendations for international students: Required—TOEFL.

Elon University, Program in Education, Elon, NC 27244-2010. Offers elementary education (M Ed); gifted education (M Ed); special education (M Ed). *Accreditation:* NCATE. Part-time programs available. *Faculty:* 19 full-time (15 women). *Students:* 47 part-time (41 women); includes 8 minority (7 Black or African American, non-Hispanic/Latino; 1 Asian, non-Hispanic/Latino). Average age 33. 29 applicants, 86% accepted, 22 enrolled. In 2011, 39 master's awarded. *Entrance requirements:* For master's, GRE, MAT. Additional exam requirements/recommendations for international students: Required—TOEFL (minimum score 550 paper-based; 213 computer-based; 79 iBT). *Application deadline:* For winter admission, 6/1 priority date for domestic students. Applications are processed on a rolling basis. Application fee: $50. Electronic applications accepted. *Expenses:* Contact institution. *Financial support:* In 2011–12, 5 students received support. Federal Work-Study and scholarships/grants available. Support available to part-time students. Financial award application deadline: 6/1; financial award applicants required to submit FAFSA. *Faculty research:* Teaching reading to low-achieving second and third graders, pre- and post-student teaching attitudes , children's writing, whole language methodology, critical creative thinking. *Unit head:* Dr. Angela Owusu-Ansah, Director and Associate Dean of Education, 336-278-5885, Fax: 336-278-5919, E-mail: aansah@elon.edu. *Application contact:* Art Fadde, Director of Graduate Admissions, 800-334-8448 Ext. 3, Fax: 336-278-7699, E-mail: afadde@elon.edu. Web site: http://www.elon.edu/med/.

Embry-Riddle Aeronautical University–Worldwide, Worldwide Headquarters - Graduate Degrees and Programs, Program in Space Education, Daytona Beach, FL 32114-3900. Offers MSSE. *Faculty:* 4 full-time (1 woman), 50 part-time/adjunct (15 women). *Students:* 5 full-time (2 women), 12 part-time (5 women); includes 2 minority (both Hispanic/Latino). Average age 31. 14 applicants, 64% accepted, 7 enrolled. *Degree requirements:* For master's, thesis (for some programs). Application fee: $50. *Expenses: Tuition:* Part-time $395 per credit hour. Tuition and fees vary according to degree level and program. *Financial support:* In 2011–12, 4 students received support. Applicants required to submit FAFSA. *Unit head:* Dr. Kees Rietsema, Chair, 602-904-1285, E-mail: rietsd37@erau.edu. *Application contact:* Linda Dammer, Director of Admissions, 386-226-6396 Ext. 1, Fax: 386-226-6984, E-mail: worldwide@erau.edu.

Emmanuel College, Graduate and Professional Programs, Graduate Programs in Education, Boston, MA 02115. Offers educational leadership (CAGS); elementary education (MAT); school administration (M Ed); secondary education (MAT). Part-time and evening/weekend programs available. *Faculty:* 3 full-time (all women), 11 part-time/adjunct (3 women). *Students:* 12 full-time (11 women), 28 part-time (21 women); includes 9 minority (6 Black or African American, non-Hispanic/Latino; 1 American Indian or Alaska Native, non-Hispanic/Latino; 2 Hispanic/Latino). Average age 30. 9 applicants, 78% accepted, 6 enrolled. In 2011, 14 degrees awarded. *Degree requirements:* For master's, 36 credits, including 6-credit practicum. *Entrance requirements:* For master's and CAGS, transcripts from all regionally-accredited institutions attended (showing proof of bachelor's degree completion), 2 letters of recommendation, essay, resume, interview. Additional exam requirements/recommendations for international students: Required—TOEFL (minimum score 600 paper-based; 250 computer-based; 106 iBT) or IELTS (minimum score 6.5). *Application deadline:* For fall admission, 7/31 priority date for domestic students; for spring admission, 11/30 priority date for domestic students. Applications are processed on a rolling basis. Application fee: $0. Electronic applications accepted. *Expenses: Tuition:* Part-time $2139 per course. Tuition and fees vary according to program and reciprocity agreements. *Financial support:* Applicants required to submit FAFSA. *Faculty research:* Literature/reading, history of education, multicultural education, special education. *Unit head:* Dr. Joyce DeLeo, Vice President of Academic Affairs, 617-735-9700, Fax: 617-507-0434, E-mail: gpp@emmanuel.edu. *Application contact:* Enrollment Counselor, 617-735-9700, Fax: 617-507-0434, E-mail: gpp@emmanuel.edu. Web site: http://gpp.emmanuel.edu.

Emory & Henry College, Graduate Programs, Emory, VA 24327-0947. Offers American history (MA Ed); organizational leadership (MCOL); professional studies (M Ed); reading specialist (MA Ed). Part-time and evening/weekend programs available. *Faculty:* 7 full-time (3 women). *Students:* 11 full-time (8 women), 32 part-time (22 women); includes 1 minority (Black or African American, non-Hispanic/Latino). Average age 36. 34 applicants, 85% accepted, 28 enrolled. In 2011, 36 master's awarded. *Entrance requirements:* For master's, GRE or PRAXIS I, recommendations, writing sample. Additional exam requirements/recommendations for international students: Recommended—TOEFL. *Application deadline:* Applications are processed on a rolling basis. Application fee: $30. *Expenses: Tuition:* Full-time $8370; part-time $465 per credit hour. *Financial support:* Applicants required to submit FAFSA. *Unit head:* Dr. Jack Roper, Director of Graduate Studies, 276-944-6188, Fax: 276-944-5223, E-mail: jroper@ehc.edu. *Application contact:* Dr. Jack Roper, Director of Graduate Studies, 276-944-6188, Fax: 276-944-5223, E-mail: jroper@ehc.edu.

Emory University, Laney Graduate School, Division of Educational Studies, Atlanta, GA 30322-1100. Offers educational studies (MA, PhD); middle grades teaching (MAT); secondary teaching (MAT). *Accreditation:* NCATE. *Faculty:* 10 full-time (4 women), 3 part-time/adjunct (2 women). *Students:* 56 full-time (48 women); includes 20 minority (18 Black or African American, non-Hispanic/Latino; 2 Asian, non-Hispanic/Latino), 2 international. 86 applicants, 42% accepted, 26 enrolled. In 2011, 16 master's, 4 doctorates awarded. Terminal master's awarded for partial completion of doctoral program. *Degree requirements:* For master's, thesis; for doctorate, comprehensive exam, thesis/dissertation. *Entrance requirements:* For master's and doctorate, GRE General Test, minimum GPA of 3.0. Additional exam requirements/recommendations for international students: Required—TOEFL. *Application deadline:* For fall admission, 1/3 for domestic students. Application fee: $45. Electronic applications accepted. *Expenses: Tuition:* Full-time $34,800. *Required fees:* $1300. *Financial support:* In 2011–12, 50 students received support, including 10 fellowships; research assistantships, teaching assistantships, career-related internships or fieldwork, scholarships/grants, tuition waivers (full and partial), and unspecified assistantships also available. Financial award application deadline: 1/3. *Faculty research:* Educational policy, educational measurement, urban and multicultural education, mathematics and science education, comparative education. *Total annual research expenditures:* $130,000. *Unit head:* Prof. George Engelhard, Director of Graduate Studies, 404-727-0607, E-mail: gengelh@emory.edu. *Application contact:* Dr. Glen Avant, Graduate Program Administrator, 404-727-0612, E-mail: gavant@emory.edu. Web site: http://des.emory.edu/.

Emporia State University, Graduate School, Teachers College, Emporia, KS 66801-5087. Offers M Ed, MS, Ed S. *Accreditation:* NCATE. Part-time programs available. Postbaccalaureate distance learning degree programs offered (no on-campus study). *Faculty:* 83 full-time (50 women), 5 part-time/adjunct (2 women). *Students:* 210 full-time (139 women), 923 part-time (648 women); includes 106 minority (33 Black or African American, non-Hispanic/Latino; 4 American Indian or Alaska Native, non-Hispanic/Latino; 10 Asian, non-Hispanic/Latino; 41 Hispanic/Latino; 6 Native Hawaiian or other Pacific Islander, non-Hispanic/Latino; 12 Two or more races, non-Hispanic/Latino), 30 international. 314 applicants, 82% accepted, 182 enrolled. In 2011, 403 master's, 10 other advanced degrees awarded. *Degree requirements:* For master's, comprehensive exam or thesis; for Ed S, comprehensive exam, thesis or alternative, internship. *Entrance requirements:* For master's, appropriate bachelor's degree; for Ed S, GRE, graduate essay exam, letters of recommendation, teacher certification. *Application deadline:* Applications are processed on a rolling basis. Application fee: $30 ($75 for international students). Electronic applications accepted. *Expenses:* Tuition, state resident: full-time $2342; part-time $195 per credit hour. Tuition, nonresident: full-time $7254; part-time $605 per credit hour. *Required fees:* $66 per credit hour. Tuition and fees vary according to campus/location. *Financial support:* In 2011–12, 2 research assistantships with full tuition reimbursements (averaging $7,059 per year), 29 teaching assistantships with full tuition reimbursements (averaging $6,453 per year) were awarded; career-related internships or fieldwork, Federal Work-Study, institutionally sponsored loans, health care benefits, and unspecified assistantships also available. Financial award application deadline: 3/15; financial award applicants required to submit FAFSA. *Unit head:* Dr. J. Phillip Bennett, Dean, 620-341-5367, Fax: 620-341-5785, E-mail: pbennett@emporia.edu. *Application contact:* Mary Sewell, Admissions Coordinator, 800-950-GRAD, Fax: 620-341-5909, E-mail: msewell@emporia.edu. Web site: http://www.emporia.edu/teach/.

Emporia State University, Graduate School, Teachers College, Department of School Leadership and Middle/Secondary Education, Program in Teaching, Emporia, KS 66801-5087. Offers M Ed. Postbaccalaureate distance learning degree programs offered (no on-campus study). *Students:* 4 full-time (3 women), 17 part-time (11 women); includes 3 minority (1 American Indian or Alaska Native, non-Hispanic/Latino; 2 Hispanic/Latino). 9 applicants, 78% accepted, 3 enrolled. In 2011, 1 master's awarded. *Entrance requirements:* For master's, GRE or MAT, minimum GPA of 2.5 on last 60 undergraduate hours; two personal references. *Expenses:* Tuition, state resident: full-time $2342; part-time $195 per credit hour. Tuition, nonresident: full-time $7254; part-time $605 per credit hour. *Required fees:* $66 per credit hour. Tuition and fees vary according to campus/location. *Unit head:* Dr. Jerry Will, Chair, 620-341-5777, E-mail: jwill@emporia.edu. *Application contact:* Mary Sewell, Admissions Coordinator, 800-950-GRAD, Fax: 620-341-5909, E-mail: msewell@emporia.edu.

Evangel University, Department of Education, Springfield, MO 65802. Offers educational leadership (M Ed); reading education (M Ed); secondary teaching (M Ed); teaching (MA). *Accreditation:* NCATE. Part-time and evening/weekend programs available. *Faculty:* 4 full-time (1 woman), 2 part-time/adjunct (1 woman). *Students:* 10 full-time (5 women), 39 part-time (25 women). Average age 33. 14 applicants, 86% accepted, 11 enrolled. In 2011, 21 master's awarded. *Degree requirements:* For master's, comprehensive exam, thesis optional. *Entrance requirements:* For master's, PRAXIS II (preferred) or GRE. Additional exam requirements/recommendations for international students: Required—TOEFL (minimum score 550 paper-based; 213 computer-based). *Application deadline:* For fall admission, 7/15 priority date for domestic students; for spring admission, 11/15 priority date for domestic students. Applications are processed on a rolling basis. Application fee: $25. *Financial support:* In 2011–12, 3 students received support. Career-related internships or fieldwork, institutionally sponsored loans, and scholarships/grants available. Support available to part-time students. Financial award application deadline: 3/1; financial award applicants required to submit FAFSA. *Unit head:* Dr. Matt Stringer, Program Coordinator, 417-865-2815 Ext. 8563, E-mail: stringerm@evangel.edu. *Application contact:* Micah Hildreth, Admissions Representative, Graduate and Professional Studies, 417-865-2811 Ext. 7227, Fax: 417-865-9599, E-mail: hildrethm@evangel.edu. Web site: http://www.evangel.edu/departments/education/about-the-department/.

The Evergreen State College, Graduate Programs, Program in Teaching, Olympia, WA 98505. Offers MIT. *Faculty:* 8 full-time (4 women). *Students:* 84 full-time (58 women); includes 14 minority (3 Black or African American, non-Hispanic/Latino; 4 American Indian or Alaska Native, non-Hispanic/Latino; 3 Asian, non-Hispanic/Latino; 4 Hispanic/Latino). 64 applicants, 80% accepted, 45 enrolled. In 2011, 36 master's awarded. *Degree requirements:* For master's, project, 20-week teaching internship. *Entrance requirements:* For master's, Washington Educator Skills Test-Basic, Washington Educator Skills Test-Endorsements, minimum undergraduate GPA of 3.0 for last 90 quarter hours, official transcript, resume, endorsement worksheets, 3 letters of recommendation, personal statement, essay. Additional exam requirements/recommendations for international students: Required—TOEFL (minimum score 600 paper-based; 250 computer-based; 100 iBT). *Application deadline:* For fall admission, 4/30 for domestic and international students. Application fee: $50. Electronic applications accepted. *Expenses:* Contact institution. *Financial support:* In 2011–12, 76 students received support, including 11 fellowships with partial tuition reimbursements available (averaging $993 per year); career-related internships or fieldwork, Federal Work-Study, institutionally sponsored loans, scholarships/grants, and tuition waivers (partial) also available. Financial award application deadline: 3/1; financial award applicants required to submit FAFSA. *Faculty research:* Mathematics teaching and learning and preservice and in-service teacher education, systematic and creative design of instruction and the psychological health of teachers, language and literacy development, teaching for social justice, and promoting democratic classrooms, literacy education, multicultural education, curriculum integration, technology, qualitative research methods and critical pedagogy, math for social justice. *Unit head:* Dr. Sherry Walton, Director, 360-867-6753, E-mail: waltonsl@evergreen.edu. *Application contact:* Maggie Foran, Associate Director, 360-867-6559, Fax: 360-867-6575, E-mail: foranm@evergreen.edu. Web site: http://www.evergreen.edu/mit/.

Fairfield University, Graduate School of Education and Allied Professions, Fairfield, CT 06824-5195. Offers applied psychology (MA); bilingual education (CAS); clinical mental health counseling (MA, CAS); educational technology (MA); elementary education (MA); family studies (MA); marriage and family therapy (MA); school counseling (MA, CAS); school psychology (MA, CAS); special education (MA); teaching (Certificate); teaching and foundations (MA, CAS); TESOL foreign language and bilingual/multicultural education (MA, CAS). *Accreditation:* NCATE. Part-time and evening/weekend programs available. *Faculty:* 24 full-time (19 women). *Students:* 147 full-time (120 women), 391 part-time (321 women); includes 60 minority (13 Black or African American, non-Hispanic/Latino; 8 Asian, non-Hispanic/Latino; 35 Hispanic/Latino; 4 Two or more races, non-Hispanic/Latino), 1 international. Average age 34. 319 applicants, 48% accepted, 80 enrolled. In 2011, 185 master's, 20 other advanced degrees awarded. *Degree requirements:* For master's, comprehensive exam. *Entrance requirements:* For master's, PRAXIS I (for certification programs), minimum QPA of 3.0, 2 recommendations, resume. Additional exam requirements/recommendations for international students: Required—TOEFL (minimum score 550 paper-based; 213 computer-based; 84 iBT) or IELTS (minimum score 7.5). *Application deadline:* For fall admission, 2/15 for international students; for spring admission, 10/1 for international students. Application fee: $60. Electronic applications accepted. *Expenses: Tuition:* Part-time $600 per credit hour. *Required fees:* $25 per term. *Financial support:* In 2011–12, 45 students received support. Career-related internships or fieldwork and unspecified assistantships available. Financial award applicants required to submit FAFSA. *Faculty research:* Literacy, adolescent psychology, special education, early childhood education, teaching development. *Unit head:* Dr. Susan D. Franzosa, Dean, 203-254-4000 Ext. 4250, Fax: 203-254-4241, E-mail: sfranzosa@fairfield.edu. *Application contact:* Marianne Gumpper, Director of Graduate and Continuing Studies Admission, 203-254-4184, Fax: 203-254-4073, E-mail: gradadmis@fairfield.edu. Web site: http://www.fairfield.edu/gseap/gseap_grad_1.html.

Fairleigh Dickinson University, College at Florham, Maxwell Becton College of Arts and Sciences, Department of English, Communication and Philosophy, Program in Creative Writing and Literature for Educators, Madison, NJ 07940-1099. Offers MA.

Fairleigh Dickinson University, College at Florham, University College: Arts, Sciences, and Professional Studies, Peter Sammartino School of Education, Madison, NJ 07940-1099. Offers education for certified teachers (MA, Certificate); educational leadership (MA); instructional technology (Certificate); literacy/reading (Certificate); teaching (MAT).

Fairleigh Dickinson University, Metropolitan Campus, University College: Arts, Sciences, and Professional Studies, Peter Sammartino School of Education, Teaneck, NJ 07666-1914. Offers dyslexia specialist (Certificate); education for certified teachers (MA); educational leadership (MA); instructional technology (Certificate); learning disabilities (MA); literacy/reading (Certificate); multilingual education (MA); teacher of the handicapped (Certificate); teaching (MAT). *Accreditation:* Teacher Education Accreditation Council. Part-time programs available. *Degree requirements:* For master's, research project (MAT).

Fairmont State University, Programs in Education, Fairmont, WV 26554. Offers digital media, new literacies and learning (M Ed); education (MAT); exercise science, fitness and wellness (M Ed); leadership studies (M Ed); online learning (M Ed); professional studies (M Ed); reading (M Ed); special education (M Ed). *Accreditation:* NCATE. Part-time and evening/weekend programs available. Postbaccalaureate distance learning degree programs offered. *Faculty:* 16 part-time/adjunct (10 women). *Students:* 103 full-time (72 women), 142 part-time (103 women); includes 11 minority (2 Black or African American, non-Hispanic/Latino; 1 American Indian or Alaska Native, non-Hispanic/Latino; 6 Hispanic/Latino; 2 Two or more races, non-Hispanic/Latino), 2 international. Average age 33. 71 applicants, 85% accepted. In 2011, 58 master's awarded. *Entrance requirements:* For master's, GRE. *Application deadline:* For fall admission, 5/1 for domestic and international students. Applications are processed on a rolling basis. Application fee: $40. *Expenses:* Tuition, state resident: full-time $5900. Tuition, nonresident: full-time $12,596. *Unit head:* Dr. Van O. Dempsey, III, Dean, School of Education, 304-367-4241, Fax: 304-367-4599, E-mail: vdempsey@fairmontstate.edu. Web site: http://www.fairmontstate.edu/graduatestudies/default.asp.

Faulkner University, College of Education, Montgomery, AL 36109-3398. Offers M Ed.

Felician College, Program in Education, Lodi, NJ 07644-2117. Offers education (MA); educational leadership (principal/supervision) (MA); educational supervision (PMC); principal (PMC); school nursing and health education (MA, Certificate). *Accreditation:* Teacher Education Accreditation Council. Part-time and evening/weekend programs available. *Students:* 12 full-time (9 women), 93 part-time (83 women); includes 15 minority (5 Black or African American, non-Hispanic/Latino; 1 Asian, non-Hispanic/Latino; 9 Hispanic/Latino), 3 international. Average age 37. 18 applicants, 50% accepted, 9 enrolled. *Degree requirements:* For master's, project. *Entrance requirements:* For master's, MAT, minimum GPA of 3.0, 3 letters of recommendation. Additional exam requirements/recommendations for international students: Recommended—TOEFL (minimum score 550 paper-based; 213 computer-based). *Application deadline:* Applications are processed on a rolling basis. Application fee: $40. *Expenses: Tuition:* Part-time $925 per credit. *Required fees:* $262.50 per semester. Part-time tuition and fees vary according to class time and student level. *Financial support:* Federal Work-Study available. *Unit head:* Dr. Rosemarie Liebmann, Associate Dean, 201-559-3537, E-mail: liebmannr@felician.edu. *Application contact:* Dr. Margaret Smolin, Associate Director, Graduate Admissions, 201-559-6077, Fax: 201-559-6138, E-mail: graduate@felician.edu.

See Display on next page and Close-Up on page 801.

Ferris State University, College of Education and Human Services, School of Education, Big Rapids, MI 49307. Offers administration (MSCTE); curriculum and instruction (M Ed), including administration, elementary education, experiential education, philanthropic education, reading, secondary education, special education, subject matter option; education technology (MSCTE); instructor (MSCTE); post-secondary administration (MSCTE); training and development (MSCTE). Part-time and evening/weekend programs available. Postbaccalaureate distance learning degree programs offered (minimal on-campus study). *Faculty:* 9 full-time (7 women), 9 part-time/adjunct (6 women). *Students:* 8 full-time (7 women), 132 part-time (75 women); includes 13 minority (11 Black or African American, non-Hispanic/Latino; 1 American Indian or Alaska Native, non-Hispanic/Latino; 1 Hispanic/Latino), 5 international. Average age 36. 20 applicants, 100% accepted, 8 enrolled. In 2011, 51 master's awarded. *Degree requirements:* For master's, thesis, research paper. *Entrance requirements:* For master's, 2 years of work experience for vocational setting, minimum GPA of 2.75. Additional exam requirements/recommendations for international students: Recommended—TOEFL (minimum score 500 paper-based; 173 computer-based; 61 iBT). *Application deadline:* For fall admission, 7/1 priority date for domestic students, 7/1 for international students; for spring admission, 11/1 priority date for domestic students, 11/1 for international students. Applications are processed on a rolling basis. Application fee: $30. Electronic applications accepted. Application fee is waived when completed online. *Financial support:* Career-related internships or fieldwork and scholarships/grants available. Support available to part-time students. Financial award applicants required to submit FAFSA. *Faculty research:* Suicide prevention, reading, women in education, special needs, administration. *Unit head:* Dr. James Powell, Director, 231-591-5362, Fax: 231-591-2043, E-mail: powelj20@ferris.edu. *Application contact:* Kimisue Worrall, Secretary, 231-591-5361, Fax: 231-591-2043. Web site: http://www.ferris.edu/education/education/.

Florida Agricultural and Mechanical University, Division of Graduate Studies, Research, and Continuing Education, College of Education, Tallahassee, FL 32307-3200. Offers M Ed, MBE, MS Ed, PhD. *Accreditation:* NCATE. Part-time and evening/weekend programs available. *Degree requirements:* For master's, thesis (for some programs); for doctorate, thesis/dissertation. *Entrance requirements:* For master's, GRE General Test, minimum GPA of 3.0. Additional exam requirements/recommendations for international students: Required—TOEFL.

Florida Atlantic University, College of Education, Boca Raton, FL 33431-0991. Offers M Ed, MS, Ed D, PhD, Ed S. *Accreditation:* NCATE. Part-time and evening/weekend programs available. *Faculty:* 104 full-time (66 women), 173 part-time/adjunct (126 women). *Students:* 330 full-time (248 women), 646 part-time (508 women); includes 284 minority (122 Black or African American, non-Hispanic/Latino; 1 American Indian or Alaska Native, non-Hispanic/Latino; 30 Asian, non-Hispanic/Latino; 118 Hispanic/Latino; 13 Two or more races, non-Hispanic/Latino), 16 international. Average age 33. 930 applicants, 43% accepted, 166 enrolled. In 2011, 315 master's, 14 doctorates awarded. *Degree requirements:* For doctorate, comprehensive exam, thesis/dissertation; for Ed S, departmental qualifying exam. *Entrance requirements:* For master's, doctorate, and Ed S, GRE General Test. *Application deadline:* For fall admission, 5/1 for domestic students. Applications are processed on a rolling basis. Application fee: $30. Electronic applications accepted. *Expenses: Tuition, area resident:* Part-time $343.02 per credit hour. Tuition, state resident: full-time $8232. Tuition, nonresident: full-time $23,931; part-time $997.14 per credit hour. *Financial support:* Fellowships with partial tuition reimbursements, research assistantships with partial tuition reimbursements, teaching assistantships with partial tuition reimbursements, career-related internships or fieldwork, Federal Work-Study, and unspecified assistantships available. *Faculty research:* Marriage and family counseling, multicultural education, self-directed learning, assessment, reading. *Unit head:* Dr. Valerie J. Bristor, Dean, 561-297-3564, E-mail: bristor@fau.edu. *Application contact:* Dr. Eliah Watlington, Associate Dean, 561-296-8520, Fax: 261-297-2991, E-mail: ewatling@fau.edu. Web site: http://www.coe.fau.edu/.

Education—General

Florida Gulf Coast University, College of Education, Fort Myers, FL 33965-6565. Offers M Ed, MA, Ed D, Ed S. Part-time and evening/weekend programs available. Postbaccalaureate distance learning degree programs offered (minimal on-campus study). *Faculty:* 34 full-time (26 women), 57 part-time/adjunct (40 women). *Students:* 203 full-time (169 women), 67 part-time (58 women); includes 53 minority (14 Black or African American, non-Hispanic/Latino; 1 American Indian or Alaska Native, non-Hispanic/Latino; 5 Asian, non-Hispanic/Latino; 29 Hispanic/Latino; 1 Native Hawaiian or other Pacific Islander, non-Hispanic/Latino; 3 Two or more races, non-Hispanic/Latino), 1 international. Average age 34. 142 applicants, 86% accepted, 98 enrolled. In 2011, 115 master's, 5 other advanced degrees awarded. *Entrance requirements:* For master's, GRE General Test, MAT, minimum GPA of 3.0. Additional exam requirements/recommendations for international students: Required—TOEFL (minimum score 550 paper-based; 213 computer-based). *Application deadline:* For fall admission, 7/1 priority date for domestic students; for spring admission, 10/15 for domestic students. Applications are processed on a rolling basis. Application fee: $30. Electronic applications accepted. *Expenses:* Tuition, state resident: full-time $8289. Tuition, nonresident: full-time $28,895. *Required fees:* $1831. One-time fee: $30 full-time. *Faculty research:* Inclusion, emergent literacy, pre-service and in-service teacher education, education policy. *Unit head:* Dr. Marci Greene, Dean, 239-590-7781, Fax: 239-590-7801, E-mail: mgreene@fgcu.edu. Web site: http://coe.fgcu.edu/.

Florida International University, College of Education, Miami, FL 33199. Offers MAT, MS, Ed D, PhD, Certificate, Ed S. *Accreditation:* NCATE. Part-time and evening/weekend programs available. *Degree requirements:* For doctorate, comprehensive exam, thesis/dissertation. *Entrance requirements:* For master's and other advanced degree, GRE General Test (for some programs); for doctorate, GRE General Test. Additional exam requirements/recommendations for international students: Required—TOEFL (minimum score 550 paper-based; 213 computer-based; 80 iBT), IELTS (minimum score 6.3). Electronic applications accepted. *Faculty research:* School improvement, cognitive processes, international development, urban education, multicultural/multilingual education.

Florida Memorial University, School of Education, Miami-Dade, FL 33054. Offers elementary education (MS); exceptional student education (MS); reading (MS). *Degree requirements:* For master's, comprehensive exam or thesis, field and clinical experiences, exit exam. *Entrance requirements:* For master's, GRE, CLAST, PRAXIS I, baccalaureate or graduate degree with minimum GPA of 3.0 in last 60 hours, 3 recommendations. Additional exam requirements/recommendations for international students: Recommended—TOEFL.

Florida Southern College, Programs in Teaching, Lakeland, FL 33801-5698. Offers M Ed, MAT. Part-time and evening/weekend programs available. *Degree requirements:* For master's, FICE General Knowledge test and professional education exam (MAT), eligibility for the Florida Professional Teacher Certificate (M Ed). *Entrance requirements:* For master's, Florida Teacher Certification exam (MAT). Additional exam requirements/recommendations for international students: Required—TOEFL (minimum score 550 paper-based).

Florida State University, The Graduate School, College of Education, Tallahassee, FL 32306. Offers MS, Ed D, PhD, Certificate, Ed S, MS/Ed S. *Accreditation:* NCATE. Part-time and evening/weekend programs available. Postbaccalaureate distance learning degree programs offered. *Faculty:* 85 full-time (47 women), 86 part-time/adjunct (61 women). *Students:* 671 full-time (452 women), 452 part-time (305 women); includes 237 minority (136 Black or African American, non-Hispanic/Latino; 10 American Indian or Alaska Native, non-Hispanic/Latino; 26 Asian, non-Hispanic/Latino; 64 Hispanic/Latino; 1 Two or more races, non-Hispanic/Latino), 180 international. Average age 31. 1,042 applicants, 53% accepted, 252 enrolled. In 2011, 348 master's, 62 doctorates, 51 other advanced degrees awarded. Terminal master's awarded for partial completion of doctoral program. *Degree requirements:* For master's and other advanced degree, comprehensive exam, thesis optional; for doctorate, comprehensive exam, thesis/dissertation, preliminary exam, prospectus defense. *Entrance requirements:* For master's, doctorate, and other advanced degree, GRE General Test, minimum GPA of 3.0. Additional exam requirements/recommendations for international students: Required—TOEFL (minimum score 550 paper-based; 213 computer-based; 80 iBT). *Application deadline:* For fall admission, 7/1 for domestic and international students; for winter admission, 11/1 for domestic and international students; for spring admission, 3/1 for domestic and international students. Applications are processed on a rolling basis. Application fee: $30. Electronic applications accepted. *Expenses:* Tuition, state resident: full-time $9474; part-time $350.88 per credit hour. Tuition, nonresident: full-time $16,236; part-time $601.34 per credit hour. *Required fees:* $630 per semester. One-time fee: $20. Tuition and fees vary according to course load and campus/location. *Financial support:* In 2011–12, 86 students received support, including 13 fellowships with full and partial tuition reimbursements available, 174 research assistantships with full and partial tuition reimbursements available, 182 teaching assistantships with full and partial tuition reimbursements available; career-related internships or fieldwork, scholarships/grants, traineeships, health care benefits, and unspecified assistantships also available. Financial award application deadline: 1/15; financial award applicants required to submit FAFSA. *Faculty research:* Educational policy, higher education, sport administration, reading research, preparing school leaders. *Total annual research expenditures:* $5.3 million. *Unit head:* Dr. Marcy P. Driscoll, Dean, 850-644-6885, Fax: 850-644-2725, E-mail: mdriscoll@fsu.edu. *Application contact:* Dr. Pamela S. Carroll, Academic Dean, 850-644-0372, Fax: 850-644-1258, E-mail: pcarroll@fsu.edu. Web site: http://www.coe.fsu.edu/.

Fontbonne University, Graduate Programs, Department of Education, St. Louis, MO 63105-3098. Offers MA. *Accreditation:* NCATE. Part-time and evening/weekend programs available. Postbaccalaureate distance learning degree programs offered (minimal on-campus study). *Entrance requirements:* For master's, minimum GPA of 3.0.

Fordham University, Graduate School of Education, New York, NY 10023. Offers MAT, MS, MSE, MST, Ed D, PhD, Adv C. *Accreditation:* NCATE. Part-time and evening/weekend programs available. *Degree requirements:* For master's and Adv C, comprehensive exam (for some programs); for doctorate, thesis/dissertation. *Entrance requirements:* For master's and Adv C, minimum GPA of 3.0; for doctorate, GRE or MAT. *Expenses:* Contact institution.

Fort Hays State University, Graduate School, College of Education and Technology, Hays, KS 67601-4099. Offers MS, MSE, Ed S. *Accreditation:* NCATE. Part-time programs available. *Degree requirements:* For master's, comprehensive exam, thesis or alternative. *Entrance requirements:* Additional exam requirements/recommendations for international students: Required—TOEFL (minimum score 550 paper-based; 213 computer-based). Electronic applications accepted.

Franciscan University of Steubenville, Graduate Programs, Department of Education, Steubenville, OH 43952-1763. Offers administration (MS Ed); teaching (MS Ed). Part-time and evening/weekend programs available. *Degree requirements:* For master's, project. *Entrance requirements:* For master's, minimum undergraduate GPA of 2.5 or written exam. *Expenses:* Contact institution.

Francis Marion University, Graduate Programs, School of Education, Florence, SC 29502-0547. Offers early childhood education (M Ed); elementary education (M Ed); learning disabilities (M Ed, MAT); remedial education (M Ed); secondary education (M Ed). *Accreditation:* NCATE. Part-time programs available. *Faculty:* 20 full-time (16 women), 1 (woman) part-time/adjunct. *Students:* 10 full-time (8 women), 115 part-time (88 women); includes 30 minority (26 Black or African American, non-Hispanic/Latino; 3

Asian, non-Hispanic/Latino; 1 Hispanic/Latino), 1 international. Average age 32. 249 applicants, 33% accepted, 77 enrolled. In 2011, 41 master's awarded. *Degree requirements:* For master's, comprehensive exam. *Entrance requirements:* For master's, GRE General Test, MAT, NTE, or PRAXIS II. *Application deadline:* For fall admission, 3/15 priority date for domestic students; for spring admission, 10/15 priority date for domestic students. Applications are processed on a rolling basis. Application fee: $31. *Expenses:* Tuition, state resident: full-time $8467; part-time $443.35 per credit hour. Tuition, nonresident: full-time $16,934; part-time $866.70 per credit hour. *Required fees:* $335; $12.25 per credit hour. $30 per semester. *Financial support:* In 2011–12, 3 research assistantships (averaging $6,000 per year) were awarded; scholarships/grants and unspecified assistantships also available. Support available to part-time students. Financial award application deadline: 3/1; financial award applicants required to submit FAFSA. *Faculty research:* Identification and alternate assessment of at-risk students. *Unit head:* Dr. James R. Faulkenberry, Dean, 843-661-1460, Fax: 843-661-4647. *Application contact:* Rannie Gamble, Administrative Manager, 843-661-1286, Fax: 843-661-4688, E-mail: rgamble@fmarion.edu.

Freed-Hardeman University, Program in Education, Henderson, TN 38340-2399. Offers curriculum and instruction (M Ed); school counseling (M Ed), including administration and supervision, special education; school leadership (Ed S). *Accreditation:* NCATE. Part-time and evening/weekend programs available. *Degree requirements:* For master's, comprehensive exam, thesis optional; for Ed S, thesis. *Entrance requirements:* For master's, GRE General Test or NTE; for Ed S, 3 years of teaching experience. Additional exam requirements/recommendations for international students: Required—TOEFL (minimum score 500 paper-based; 173 computer-based).

Fresno Pacific University, Graduate Programs, School of Education, Fresno, CA 93702-4709. Offers administration (MA Ed), including administrative services; foundations, curriculum and teaching (MA Ed), including curriculum and teaching, school library and information technology; language, literacy, and culture (MA Ed), including bilingual/cross-cultural education, language development, multilingual contexts, reading; mathematics/science/computer education (MA Ed), including educational technology, integrated mathematics/science education, mathematics education; pupil personnel services (MA Ed), including school counseling, school psychology; special education (MA Ed), including mild/moderate, moderate/severe, physical and health impairments. Part-time and evening/weekend programs available. *Degree requirements:* For master's, thesis (for some programs). *Entrance requirements:* For master's, interview; GMAT, GRE, MAT, or 6 units of course work with a faculty recommendation. Additional exam requirements/recommendations for international students: Required—TOEFL (minimum score 550 paper-based; 213 computer-based). Electronic applications accepted.

Friends University, Graduate School, Wichita, KS 67213. Offers accounting (MBA); business administration (MBA); business law (MBL); Christian ministry (MACM); environment science (MSES); family therapy (MSFT); global leadership and management (MA); health care leadership (MHCL); management information systems (MMIS); operations management (MSOM); organization development (MSOD); teaching (MAT). Part-time and evening/weekend programs available. Postbaccalaureate distance learning degree programs offered (no on-campus study). *Faculty:* 14 full-time (5 women), 2 part-time/adjunct (1 woman). *Students:* 158 full-time (114 women), 616 part-time (367 women); includes 159 minority (83 Black or African American, non-Hispanic/Latino; 12 American Indian or Alaska Native, non-Hispanic/Latino; 26 Asian, non-Hispanic/Latino; 22 Hispanic/Latino; 2 Native Hawaiian or other Pacific Islander, non-Hispanic/Latino; 14 Two or more races, non-Hispanic/Latino). Average age 36. 497 applicants, 68% accepted, 256 enrolled. In 2011, 341 degrees awarded. *Degree requirements:* For master's, research project. *Entrance requirements:* For master's, bachelor's degree from accredited institution, official transcripts from institution granting bachelor's degree, interview with program director, letter(s) of recommendation. Additional exam requirements/recommendations for international students: Required—TOEFL (minimum score 560 paper-based; 220 computer-based). *Application deadline:* Applications are processed on a rolling basis. Application fee: $45 ($65 for international students). Electronic applications accepted. *Expenses: Tuition:* Part-time $601 per credit hour. One-time fee: $45 full-time. Tuition and fees vary according to campus/location and program. *Financial support:* Applicants required to submit FAFSA. *Unit head:* Dr. Evelyn Hume, Dean, 800-794-6945 Ext. 5859, Fax: 316-295-5040, E-mail: evelyn_hume@friends.edu. *Application contact:* Jeanette Hanson, Executive Director of Adult Recruitment, 800-794-6945, Fax: 316-295-5050, E-mail: jeanette@friends.edu. Web site: http://www.friends.edu.

Frostburg State University, Graduate School, College of Education, Frostburg, MD 21532-1099. Offers M Ed, MAT, MS. *Accreditation:* NCATE. Part-time and evening/weekend programs available. *Entrance requirements:* Additional exam requirements/recommendations for international students: Required—TOEFL. Electronic applications accepted.

Furman University, Graduate Division, Department of Education, Greenville, SC 29613. Offers curriculum and instruction (MA); early childhood education (MA); educational leadership (Ed S); English as a second language (MA); literacy (MA); school leadership (MA); special education (MA). *Accreditation:* NCATE. Part-time programs available. Postbaccalaureate distance learning degree programs offered (minimal on-campus study). *Faculty:* 14 full-time (8 women), 6 part-time/adjunct (4 women). *Students:* 237 part-time (188 women); includes 27 minority (22 Black or African American, non-Hispanic/Latino; 1 Asian, non-Hispanic/Latino; 3 Hispanic/Latino; 1 Native Hawaiian or other Pacific Islander, non-Hispanic/Latino). Average age 29. 97 applicants, 100% accepted, 90 enrolled. In 2011, 34 master's awarded. *Degree requirements:* For master's, comprehensive exam (for some programs), thesis or alternative. *Entrance requirements:* For master's, PRAXIS II. *Application deadline:* For fall admission, 8/1 priority date for domestic students, 7/15 for international students; for spring admission, 12/1 priority date for domestic students, 12/1 for international students. Applications are processed on a rolling basis. Application fee: $50. *Financial support:* Scholarships/grants available. Financial award application deadline: 5/15; financial award applicants required to submit FAFSA. *Faculty research:* Literacy, pedagogy and practice, social justice, advanced leadership, achievement in high poverty schools. *Unit head:* Dr. Nelly Hecker, Head, 864-294-3385. *Application contact:* Helen Reynolds, Department Assistant, 864-294-2213, Fax: 864-294-3579, E-mail: helen.reynolds@furman.edu. Web site: http://www.furman.edu/gradstudies/.

Gallaudet University, The Graduate School, Washington, DC 20002-3625. Offers audiology (Au D); clinical psychology (PhD); critical studies in the education of deaf learners (PhD); deaf and hard of hearing infants, toddlers, and their families (Certificate); deaf education (Ed S); deaf education: advanced studies (MA); deaf education: special programs in deaf education (MA); deaf history (Certificate); deaf studies (MA, Certificate); education deaf students with disabilities (Certificate); education: teacher preparation (MA), including deaf education, early childhood education and deaf education, elementary education and deaf education, secondary education and deaf education; hearing, speech and language sciences (MS, PhD); international development (MA); interpretation (MA, PhD); linguistics (MA, PhD); mental health counseling (MA); public administration (MA); school counseling (MA); school psychology (Psy S); sign language teaching (MA); social work (MSW); speech-language pathology (MS). Part-time programs available. *Faculty:* 62 full-time (44 women). *Students:* 300 full-time (246 women), 110 part-time (82 women); includes 80 minority (27 Black or African American, non-Hispanic/Latino; 1 American Indian or Alaska Native, non-Hispanic/Latino; 11 Asian, non-Hispanic/Latino; 25 Hispanic/Latino; 1 Native Hawaiian or other Pacific Islander, non-Hispanic/Latino; 15 Two or more races, non-Hispanic/Latino), 24 international. Average age 30. 498 applicants, 45% accepted, 168 enrolled. In 2011, 129 master's, 24 doctorates, 19 other advanced degrees awarded. Terminal master's awarded for partial completion of doctoral program. *Degree requirements:* For master's, comprehensive exam (for some programs), thesis optional; for doctorate, comprehensive exam, thesis/dissertation. *Entrance requirements:* For master's and doctorate, GRE General Test or MAT, letters of recommendation, interviews, goals statement, ASL proficiency interview, written English competency. Additional exam requirements/recommendations for international students: Required—TOEFL. *Application deadline:* For fall admission, 2/15 for domestic students. Applications are processed on a rolling basis. Application fee: $50. Electronic applications accepted. *Expenses: Tuition:* Full-time $12,770; part-time $710 per credit. *Required fees:* $376. *Financial support:* In 2011–12, 287 students received support. Fellowships, research assistantships, teaching assistantships, career-related internships or fieldwork, Federal Work-Study, scholarships/grants, tuition waivers (partial), and unspecified assistantships available. Support available to part-time students. Financial award applicants required to submit FAFSA. *Faculty research:* Bimodal bilingualism development, audiology, telecommunications access, early childhood education, linguistics, visual language and visual learning, rehabilitation and hearing enhancement. *Unit head:* Dr. Carol J. Erting, Dean, 202-651-5520, Fax: 202-651-5027, E-mail: carol.erting@gallaudet.edu. *Application contact:* Wednesday Luria, Coordinator of Prospective Graduate Student Services, 202-651-5400, Fax: 202-651-5295, E-mail: graduate.school@gallaudet.edu. Web site: http://www.gallaudet.edu/x26696.xml.

Gannon University, School of Graduate Studies, College of Humanities, Education, and Social Sciences, School of Education, Erie, PA 16541-0001. Offers M Ed, MS, PhD, Certificate. Part-time and evening/weekend programs available. Postbaccalaureate distance learning degree programs offered (no on-campus study). *Faculty:* 7 full-time (5 women), 28 part-time/adjunct (15 women). *Students:* 24 full-time (17 women), 293 part-time (217 women); includes 15 minority (10 Black or African American, non-Hispanic/Latino; 2 Asian, non-Hispanic/Latino; 2 Hispanic/Latino; 1 Native Hawaiian or other Pacific Islander, non-Hispanic/Latino), 1 international. Average age 32. 149 applicants, 91% accepted, 69 enrolled. In 2011, 217 master's awarded. *Degree requirements:* For master's, thesis (for some programs), portfolio project. *Entrance requirements:* For master's, bachelor's degree, minimum GPA of 3.0. Additional exam requirements/recommendations for international students: Required—TOEFL (minimum score 79 iBT). *Application deadline:* Applications are processed on a rolling basis. Application fee: $25. Electronic applications accepted. *Expenses:* Contact institution. *Financial support:* In 2011–12, 6 fellowships (averaging $6,558 per year) were awarded; career-related internships or fieldwork, scholarships/grants, and unspecified assistantships also available. Financial award application deadline: 7/1; financial award applicants required to submit FAFSA. *Faculty research:* Program evaluation, international educational models, international teacher training, online teaching and learning, qualitative research and design. *Unit head:* Dr. Kathleen Kingston, Director, Graduate Education Programs, 814-871-5626, E-mail: kingston002@gannon.edu. *Application contact:* Kara Morgan, Director of Graduate Admissions, 814-871-5831, Fax: 814-871-5827, E-mail: graduate@gannon.edu.

Gardner-Webb University, Graduate School, School of Education, Boiling Springs, NC 28017. Offers curriculum and instruction (Ed D); educational leadership (Ed D); elementary education (MA); middle grades education (MA); school administration (MA). *Accreditation:* NCATE. Part-time and evening/weekend programs available. *Faculty:* 10 full-time (4 women), 20 part-time/adjunct (7 women). *Students:* 11 full-time (7 women), 1,001 part-time (779 women); includes 275 minority (253 Black or African American, non-Hispanic/Latino; 5 American Indian or Alaska Native, non-Hispanic/Latino; 10 Asian, non-Hispanic/Latino; 7 Hispanic/Latino). Average age 37. In 2011, 116 master's, 10 doctorates awarded. *Degree requirements:* For master's, comprehensive exam. *Entrance requirements:* For master's, GRE General Test or NTE, PRAXIS, minimum GPA of 2.5. *Application deadline:* For fall admission, 8/1 priority date for domestic students. Applications are processed on a rolling basis. Application fee: $40. Electronic applications accepted. *Expenses: Tuition:* Full-time $6300; part-time $350 per credit hour. *Financial support:* Unspecified assistantships available. *Unit head:* Dr. Alan D. Eury, Dean, 704-406-4402, Fax: 704-406-3921, E-mail: dsimmons@gardner-webb.edu. *Application contact:* Office of Graduate Admissions, 877-498-4723, Fax: 704-406-3895, E-mail: gradinfo@gardner-webb.edu.

Geneva College, Master of Arts in Higher Education Program, Beaver Falls, PA 15010-3599. Offers campus ministry (MA); college teaching (MA); educational leadership (MA); student affairs administration (MA). Part-time and evening/weekend programs available. Postbaccalaureate distance learning degree programs offered (minimal on-campus study). *Faculty:* 1 full-time (0 women), 4 part-time/adjunct (0 women). *Students:* 30 full-time (13 women), 34 part-time (21 women); includes 5 minority (3 Black or African American, non-Hispanic/Latino; 1 Native Hawaiian or other Pacific Islander, non-Hispanic/Latino; 1 Two or more races, non-Hispanic/Latino). Average age 25. 39 applicants, 90% accepted, 24 enrolled. In 2011, 23 master's awarded. *Degree requirements:* For master's, 36 hours (27 in core courses) including a capstone research project. *Entrance requirements:* For master's, minimum GPA of 3.0, writing sample, 3 letters of recommendation, essay on motivation for participation in the HED program. Additional exam requirements/recommendations for international students: Required—TOEFL. *Application deadline:* For fall admission, 9/1 priority date for domestic students; for winter admission, 1/2 priority date for domestic students; for spring admission, 3/11 priority date for domestic students. Applications are processed on a rolling basis. Electronic applications accepted. *Expenses: Tuition:* Part-time $625 per credit hour. Tuition and fees vary according to program. *Financial support:* In 2011–12, 45 students received support. Unspecified assistantships available. Financial award application deadline: 8/1; financial award applicants required to submit FAFSA. *Faculty research:* Student development, learning theories, church-related higher education, assessment, organizational culture. *Unit head:* Dr. David Guthrie, Program Director, 724-847-5565, Fax: 724-847-6107, E-mail: hed@geneva.edu. *Application contact:* Jerryn S. Carson, Program Coordinator, 724-847-6510, Fax: 724-847-6696, E-mail: hed@geneva.edu. Web site: http://www.geneva.edu/.

George Fox University, School of Education, Newberg, OR 97132-2697. Offers M Ed, MA, MAT, MS, Ed D, Certificate, Ed S. *Application contact:* Bonnie Nakashimada, Director for Graduate and SPS Admissions and Regional Sites, 503-554-6149, Fax: 503-554-3110, E-mail: bnakashimada@georgefox.edu.

George Mason University, College of Education and Human Development, Fairfax, VA 22030. Offers M Ed, MA, MS, PhD, Certificate. *Accreditation:* NCATE. Part-time and evening/weekend programs available. Postbaccalaureate distance learning degree programs offered. *Faculty:* 126 full-time (83 women), 214 part-time/adjunct (164 women). *Students:* 474 full-time (395 women), 2,130 part-time (1,730 women); includes 495 minority (192 Black or African American, non-Hispanic/Latino; 7 American Indian or Alaska Native, non-Hispanic/Latino; 116 Asian, non-Hispanic/Latino; 131 Hispanic/

Education—General

Latino; 3 Native Hawaiian or other Pacific Islander, non-Hispanic/Latino; 46 Two or more races, non-Hispanic/Latino), 44 international. Average age 33. 1,553 applicants, 73% accepted, 832 enrolled. In 2011, 1,002 master's, 16 doctorates, 226 other advanced degrees awarded. *Degree requirements:* For doctorate, comprehensive exam, final project, internship. *Entrance requirements:* For master's, PRAXIS I, minimum GPA of 3.0 in last 60 hours of course work, goals statement and/or interview; for doctorate, GRE or MAT, appropriate master's degree, interview. Additional exam requirements/recommendations for international students: Required—TOEFL (minimum score 570 paper-based; 230 computer-based; 88 iBT), IELTS, Pearson Test of English. Application fee: $65 ($80 for international students). Electronic applications accepted. *Expenses:* Tuition, state resident: full-time $8750; part-time $364.58 per credit. Tuition, nonresident: full-time $24,092; part-time $1003.83 per credit. *Required fees:* $2514; $104.75 per credit. *Financial support:* In 2011–12, 124 students received support, including 3 fellowships with full tuition reimbursements available (averaging $18,000 per year), 99 research assistantships with full and partial tuition reimbursements available (averaging $9,194 per year), 30 teaching assistantships with full and partial tuition reimbursements available (averaging $6,939 per year); career-related internships or fieldwork, Federal Work-Study, scholarships/grants, unspecified assistantships, and health care benefits (full-time research or teaching assistantship recipients) also available. Support available to part-time students. Financial award application deadline: 3/1; financial award applicants required to submit FAFSA. *Faculty research:* Special education/human disabilities, mathematics/science/technology education, education leadership, school/community/agency/higher education, counseling and administration. *Total annual research expenditures:* $9.6 million. *Unit head:* Mark Ginsberg, Dean, 703-993-2004, Fax: 703-993-2001, E-mail: mginsber@gmu.edu. *Application contact:* Angela Swadley, Academic Services Specialist, 703-993-2079, Fax: 703-993-2082, E-mail: aswadley@gmu.edu. Web site: http://cehd.gmu.edu/.

Georgetown College, Department of Education, Georgetown, KY 40324-1696. Offers reading and writing (MA Ed); special education (MA Ed); teaching (MA Ed). *Accreditation:* NCATE. Part-time programs available. *Degree requirements:* For master's, portfolio. *Entrance requirements:* For master's, teaching certificate, minimum GPA of 2.7 or GRE General Test.

The George Washington University, Graduate School of Education and Human Development, Washington, DC 20052. Offers M Ed, MA Ed, MAT, Ed D, PhD, Certificate, Ed S, Graduate Certificate. *Accreditation:* NCATE. Part-time and evening/weekend programs available. Postbaccalaureate distance learning degree programs offered (no on-campus study). *Faculty:* 78 full-time (49 women), 85 part-time/adjunct (57 women). *Students:* 426 full-time (319 women), 1,190 part-time (890 women); includes 516 minority (343 Black or African American, non-Hispanic/Latino; 5 American Indian or Alaska Native, non-Hispanic/Latino; 63 Asian, non-Hispanic/Latino; 87 Hispanic/Latino; 3 Native Hawaiian or other Pacific Islander, non-Hispanic/Latino; 15 Two or more races, non-Hispanic/Latino), 70 international. Average age 37. 1,487 applicants, 89% accepted, 604 enrolled. In 2011, 448 master's, 46 doctorates, 166 other advanced degrees awarded. *Degree requirements:* For master's and other advanced degree, comprehensive exam; for doctorate, comprehensive exam, thesis/dissertation. *Entrance requirements:* For master's, GRE General Test or MAT, minimum GPA of 2.75; for doctorate, GRE General Test or MAT, interview, minimum GPA of 3.3; for other advanced degree, GRE General Test or MAT, minimum GPA of 3.3. *Application deadline:* For fall admission, 1/15 priority date for domestic students; for spring admission, 10/1 for domestic students. Applications are processed on a rolling basis. Application fee: $75. Electronic applications accepted. *Financial support:* In 2011–12, 279 students received support. Fellowships with tuition reimbursements available, research assistantships with tuition reimbursements available, teaching assistantships with tuition reimbursements available, career-related internships or fieldwork, Federal Work-Study, and tuition waivers (full and partial) available. Support available to part-time students. Financial award application deadline: 1/15. *Faculty research:* Policy, special education, bilingual education, counseling, human resource development. *Total annual research expenditures:* $4.6 million. *Unit head:* Dr. Mary Hatwood Futrell, Dean, 202-994-6161, Fax: 202-994-7207, E-mail: mfutrell@gwu.edu. *Application contact:* Sarah Lang, Director of Graduate Admissions, 202-994-1447, Fax: 202-994-7207, E-mail: slang@gwu.edu. Web site: http://gsehd.gwu.edu/.

Georgia College & State University, Graduate School, The John H. Lounsbury College of Education, Milledgeville, GA 31061. Offers M Ed, MAT, Ed S. *Accreditation:* NCATE. Part-time programs available. *Students:* 178 full-time (109 women), 204 part-time (175 women); includes 112 minority (98 Black or African American, non-Hispanic/Latino; 3 Asian, non-Hispanic/Latino; 7 Hispanic/Latino; 4 Two or more races, non-Hispanic/Latino), 1 international. Average age 33. 197 applicants, 56% accepted, 96 enrolled. In 2011, 162 master's, 41 other advanced degrees awarded. *Degree requirements:* For master's and Ed S, comprehensive exam. *Entrance requirements:* For master's, on-site writing assessment, 2 professional recommendations, level 4 teaching certificate; for Ed S, on-site writing assessment, master's degree, 2 years of teaching experience, 2 professional recommendations, level 5 GA teacher certification. Additional exam requirements/recommendations for international students: Recommended—TOEFL (minimum score 550 paper-based; 213 computer-based; 79 iBT). *Application deadline:* For fall admission, 7/1 priority date for domestic students; for spring admission, 11/15 priority date for domestic students. Applications are processed on a rolling basis. Application fee: $40. Electronic applications accepted. *Expenses:* Tuition, state resident: full-time $4806; part-time $267 per credit hour. Tuition, nonresident: full-time $17,802; part-time $989 per credit hour. *Required fees:* $936 per semester. Tuition and fees vary according to course load and campus/location. *Financial support:* In 2011–12, 17 research assistantships were awarded; career-related internships or fieldwork, Federal Work-Study, and unspecified assistantships also available. Support available to part-time students. Financial award application deadline: 3/1; financial award applicants required to submit FAFSA. *Unit head:* Dr. Jane Hinson, Dean, 478-445-4546, E-mail: jane.hinson@gcsu.edu. *Application contact:* Shanda Brand, Graduate Coordinator, 478-445-1383, Fax: 478-445-6582, E-mail: shanda.brand@gcsu.edu. Web site: http://www.gcsu.edu/education/graduate/index.htm.

Georgian Court University, School of Education, Lakewood, NJ 08701-2697. Offers administration and leadership (MA); education (MA). *Accreditation:* Teacher Education Accreditation Council. Part-time and evening/weekend programs available. *Faculty:* 23 full-time (15 women), 25 part-time/adjunct (16 women). *Students:* 107 full-time (80 women), 365 part-time (321 women); includes 51 minority (8 Black or African American, non-Hispanic/Latino; 2 American Indian or Alaska Native, non-Hispanic/Latino; 2 Asian, non-Hispanic/Latino; 34 Hispanic/Latino; 1 Native Hawaiian or other Pacific Islander, non-Hispanic/Latino; 4 Two or more races, non-Hispanic/Latino). Average age 32. 537 applicants, 68% accepted, 197 enrolled. In 2011, 118 master's awarded. *Degree requirements:* For master's, comprehensive exam (for some programs), thesis (for some programs). *Entrance requirements:* For master's, GRE, MAT or NTE/PRAXIS, 3 letters of recommendation. Additional exam requirements/recommendations for international students: Required—TOEFL (minimum score 550 paper-based; 213 computer-based). *Application deadline:* For fall admission, 8/1 priority date for domestic students, 4/1 for international students; for spring admission, 1/1 priority date for domestic students, 7/1 for international students. Applications are processed on a rolling basis. Application fee: $40. Electronic applications accepted. *Expenses: Tuition:* Full-time $13,410; part-time $745 per credit. *Required fees:* $450 per year. Tuition and fees vary according to campus/location and program. *Financial support:* Scholarships/grants, health care benefits, and unspecified assistantships available. Financial award application deadline: 4/15; financial award applicants required to submit FAFSA. *Unit head:* Dr. Jacqueline Kress, Dean, 732-987-2729. *Application contact:* Patrick Givens, Assistant Director of Graduate Admissions, 732-987-2736, Fax: 732-987-2084, E-mail: graduateadmissions@georgian.edu. Web site: http://www.georgian.edu/education/index.htm.

Georgia Southern University, Jack N. Averitt College of Graduate Studies, College of Education, Statesboro, GA 30460. Offers M Ed, MAT, Ed D, Ed S. *Accreditation:* NCATE. Part-time and evening/weekend programs available. Postbaccalaureate distance learning degree programs offered (no on-campus study). *Faculty:* 71 full-time (48 women), 11 part-time/adjunct (8 women). *Students:* 323 full-time (247 women), 1,081 part-time (859 women); includes 433 minority (374 Black or African American, non-Hispanic/Latino; 3 American Indian or Alaska Native, non-Hispanic/Latino; 8 Asian, non-Hispanic/Latino; 31 Hispanic/Latino; 1 Native Hawaiian or other Pacific Islander, non-Hispanic/Latino; 16 Two or more races, non-Hispanic/Latino), 10 international. Average age 35. 375 applicants, 94% accepted, 187 enrolled. In 2011, 278 master's, 58 doctorates, 96 other advanced degrees awarded. *Degree requirements:* For master's, comprehensive exam (for some programs), portfolio or assessments; for doctorate, comprehensive exam, thesis/dissertation, exams; for Ed S, assessments. *Entrance requirements:* For master's, GRE General Test or MAT, minimum GPA of 2.5; for doctorate, GRE General Test or MAT, minimum GPA of 3.5, letters of reference, writing sample; for Ed S, GRE General Test or MAT, minimum graduate GPA of 3.25. Additional exam requirements/recommendations for international students: Required—TOEFL (minimum score 550 paper-based; 213 computer-based; 80 iBT). *Application deadline:* For fall admission, 3/1 priority date for domestic students, 3/1 for international students; for spring admission, 10/1 priority date for domestic students, 10/1 for international students. Applications are processed on a rolling basis. Application fee: $50. Electronic applications accepted. *Expenses:* Tuition, state resident: full-time $6300; part-time $263 per semester hour. Tuition, nonresident: full-time $25,174; part-time $1049 per semester hour. *Required fees:* $1872. *Financial support:* In 2011–12, 92 students received support, including 26 research assistantships with partial tuition reimbursements available (averaging $7,200 per year), teaching assistantships with partial tuition reimbursements available (averaging $7,200 per year); career-related internships or fieldwork, Federal Work-Study, scholarships/grants, tuition waivers (partial), unspecified assistantships, and doctoral stipends also available. Support available to part-time students. Financial award application deadline: 4/15; financial award applicants required to submit FAFSA. *Faculty research:* Teacher preparation, literacy education, curriculum issues, technology-enhanced teaching and learning, school reform, assessment of teaching and learning. *Total annual research expenditures:* $324,536. *Unit head:* Dr. Thomas Koballa, Dean, 912-478-5648, Fax: 912-478-5093, E-mail: tkoballa@georgiasouthern.edu. *Application contact:* Amanda Gilliland, Coordinator of Graduate Student Recruitment, 912-478-5384, Fax: 912-478-0740, E-mail: gradadmissions@georgiasouthern.edu. Web site: http://coe.georgiasouthern.edu/.

Georgia Southwestern State University, Graduate Studies, School of Education, Americus, GA 31709-4693. Offers early childhood education (M Ed, Ed S); health and physical education (M Ed); middle grades education (M Ed, Ed S); reading (M Ed); secondary education (M Ed); special education (M Ed). *Accreditation:* NCATE. *Degree requirements:* For master's, comprehensive exam. *Entrance requirements:* For master's, GRE General Test or MAT, minimum GPA of 2.5; for Ed S, GRE General Test or MAT, minimum graduate GPA of 3.25, M Ed from accredited college or university, 3 years teaching experience. Electronic applications accepted.

Georgia State University, College of Education, Atlanta, GA 30302-3083. Offers M Ed, MAT, MLM, MS, PhD, Ed S. *Accreditation:* NCATE. Part-time and evening/weekend programs available. Postbaccalaureate distance learning degree programs offered (no on-campus study). *Degree requirements:* For master's, comprehensive exam, portfolio (for some programs); for doctorate, comprehensive exam, thesis/dissertation; for Ed S, portfolio. *Entrance requirements:* For master's, GRE General Test; for doctorate and Ed S, GRE General Test, MAT. Additional exam requirements/recommendations for international students: Required—TOEFL (minimum score 550 paper-based; 213 computer-based). Electronic applications accepted. *Faculty research:* Evaluation and test development; teacher/school administration effectiveness; curriculum strategies and interventions; school safety, climate, and classroom management; policies and best practices in urban education.

Goddard College, Graduate Division, Master of Arts in Education and Licensure Program, Plainfield, VT 05667-9432. Offers community education (MA); teacher licensure (MA). Part-time programs available. Postbaccalaureate distance learning degree programs offered (minimal on-campus study). *Degree requirements:* For master's, thesis. *Entrance requirements:* For master's, 3 letters of recommendation, interview. Electronic applications accepted. *Faculty research:* Democratic curriculum leadership, service learning and academic achievement, middle grades curriculum, community education.

Gonzaga University, School of Education, Spokane, WA 99258. Offers M Anesth Ed, M Ed, MA Ed Ad, MAA, MAC, MAP, MASPAA, MAT, MES, MIT. *Accreditation:* NCATE. Part-time and evening/weekend programs available. *Degree requirements:* For master's, comprehensive exam. *Entrance requirements:* Additional exam requirements/recommendations for international students: Required—TOEFL.

Gordon College, Graduate Education, Wenham, MA 01984-1899. Offers education (M Ed, MAT); music education (MME). Part-time and evening/weekend programs available. *Entrance requirements:* For master's, GRE or MAT, references. Additional exam requirements/recommendations for international students: Required—TOEFL (minimum score 550 paper-based; 213 computer-based). *Faculty research:* Reading, early childhood development, ELL (English Language Learners).

Goucher College, Graduate Programs in Education, Baltimore, MD 21204-2794. Offers M Ed, MAT. Part-time and evening/weekend programs available. *Faculty:* 3 full-time (all women), 118 part-time/adjunct (28 women). *Students:* 47 full-time (33 women), 234 part-time (184 women); includes 47 minority (41 Black or African American, non-Hispanic/Latino; 1 American Indian or Alaska Native, non-Hispanic/Latino; 1 Asian, non-Hispanic/Latino; 3 Hispanic/Latino; 1 Two or more races, non-Hispanic/Latino). Average age 34. 40 applicants, 88% accepted, 25 enrolled. In 2011, 96 master's awarded. *Degree requirements:* For master's, thesis (M Ed), final presentation (MAT). *Entrance requirements:* For master's, minimum GPA of 3.0. Additional exam requirements/recommendations for international students: Required—TOEFL (minimum score 560 paper-based). *Application deadline:* For fall admission, 9/1 priority date for domestic students; for spring admission, 1/15 for domestic students. Applications are processed on a rolling basis. Application fee: $25. *Financial support:* In 2011–12, 3 research assistantships with tuition reimbursements (averaging $4,500 per year) were awarded; career-related internships or fieldwork and need-based awards also available. Support available to part-time students. Financial award application deadline: 8/15; financial award applicants required to submit FAFSA. *Faculty research:* Urban education, middle school, school improvement, teacher education, at-risk student achievement. *Unit head:* Dr. Phyllis Sunshine, Director, 410-337-6047, Fax: 410-337-6394, E-mail: psunshin@goucher.edu. *Application contact:* Megan Cornett, Associate Director, Administrative Student Services, 410-337-6200, Fax: 410-337-6394, E-mail: mcornett@goucher.edu. Web site: http://www.goucher.edu/gped/.

Governors State University, College of Education, Program in Education, University Park, IL 60484. Offers MA. Part-time and evening/weekend programs available. *Students:* 16 full-time (13 women), 44 part-time (36 women); includes 19 minority (7 Black or African American, non-Hispanic/Latino; 12 Hispanic/Latino), 1 international. Average age 34. *Degree requirements:* For master's, comprehensive exam, thesis or alternative, practicum. *Entrance requirements:* For master's, minimum GPA of 2.75 in last 60 hours of undergraduate course work, 3.0 graduate. *Application deadline:* For fall admission, 7/15 priority date for domestic students; for spring admission, 11/10 for domestic students. Applications are processed on a rolling basis. Application fee: $25. *Financial support:* Career-related internships or fieldwork, Federal Work-Study, institutionally sponsored loans, tuition waivers (full and partial), and unspecified assistantships available. Support available to part-time students. Financial award application deadline: 5/1. *Faculty research:* Teaching problem-solving microcomputer use in special education, science, and mathematics. *Unit head:* Dr. Deborah Bordelon, Dean, 708-534-4050.

Graceland University, Gleazer School of Education, Lamoni, IA 50140. Offers collaborative learning and teaching (M Ed); differentiated instruction (M Ed); management in the inclusive classroom (M Ed); mild/moderate special education (M Ed); technology integration (M Ed). *Accreditation:* NCATE. Part-time and evening/weekend programs available. Postbaccalaureate distance learning degree programs offered (no on-campus study). *Faculty:* 12 full-time (11 women), 18 part-time/adjunct (14 women). *Students:* 315 full-time (256 women), 69 part-time (51 women); includes 11 minority (4 Black or African American, non-Hispanic/Latino; 1 American Indian or Alaska Native, non-Hispanic/Latino; 2 Asian, non-Hispanic/Latino; 4 Hispanic/Latino), 8 international. *Degree requirements:* For master's, action research project. *Entrance requirements:* For master's, minimum GPA of 3.0, teaching certificate, current teaching contract. *Application deadline:* For fall admission, 7/15 for domestic students; for winter admission, 10/15 for domestic students; for spring admission, 1/15 priority date for domestic students. Application fee: $50. Electronic applications accepted. *Financial support:* Institutionally sponsored loans and scholarships/grants available. Financial award application deadline: 12/15; financial award applicants required to submit FAFSA. *Unit head:* Dr. Tammy Everett, Dean, 641-784-5000 Ext. 5226, E-mail: teverett@graceland.edu. *Application contact:* Cathy Porter, Program Consultant, 816-833-0524 Ext. 4516, E-mail: cgporter@graceland.edu. Web site: http://www.graceland.edu/education.

Grambling State University, School of Graduate Studies and Research, College of Education, Grambling, LA 71245. Offers MS, Ed D. *Accreditation:* NCATE. Part-time and evening/weekend programs available. *Degree requirements:* For master's, comprehensive exam, thesis (for some programs); for doctorate, comprehensive exam, thesis/dissertation. *Entrance requirements:* For master's, GRE; for doctorate, GRE (minimum 1000, 500 on Verbal), master's degree, minimum GPA of 3.0 on last degree. Additional exam requirements/recommendations for international students: Required—TOEFL (minimum score 500 paper-based; 173 computer-based; 61 iBT). Electronic applications accepted. *Expenses:* Tuition, state resident: full-time $3546; part-time $192 per credit hour. Tuition, nonresident: full-time $3456; part-time $192 per credit hour. *Required fees:* $1829; $1829 per semester hour.

Grand Canyon University, College of Doctoral Studies, Phoenix, AZ 85017-1097. Offers business administration (DBA); general psychology (PhD), including cognition and instruction, industrial and organizational psychology; organizational leadership (Ed D, PhD), including behavioral health (PhD), education and effective schools (PhD), higher education (PhD), instructional leadership (PhD), organizational development (Ed D). *Degree requirements:* For doctorate, comprehensive exam, thesis/dissertation. *Entrance requirements:* For doctorate, minimum GPA of 3.4 on earned advanced degree from regionally-accredited institution; transcripts; goals statement.

Grand Canyon University, College of Education, Phoenix, AZ 85017-1097. Offers curriculum and instruction (M Ed); education administration (M Ed); elementary education (M Ed); secondary education (M Ed); special education (M Ed); teaching (MA). Part-time and evening/weekend programs available. Postbaccalaureate distance learning degree programs offered (no on-campus study). *Degree requirements:* For master's, publishable research paper (M Ed), e-portfolio. *Entrance requirements:* For master's, undergraduate degree from accredited, GCU-approved college, university, or program with minimum GPA 2.8. Additional exam requirements/recommendations for international students: Required—TOEFL (minimum score 550 paper-based; 213 computer-based; 79 iBT), IELTS (minimum score 6). Electronic applications accepted.

Grand Valley State University, College of Education, Programs in General Education, Allendale, MI 49401-9403. Offers adult and higher education (M Ed); early childhood education (M Ed); educational differentiation (M Ed); educational leadership (M Ed); educational technology integration (M Ed); elementary education (M Ed); middle level education (M Ed); school library media services (M Ed); secondary level education (M Ed); teaching English to speakers of other languages (M Ed). Part-time and evening/weekend programs available. Postbaccalaureate distance learning degree programs offered (minimal on-campus study). *Degree requirements:* For master's, thesis. *Entrance requirements:* For master's, GRE General Test or minimum GPA of 3.0. Additional exam requirements/recommendations for international students: Required—TOEFL. Electronic applications accepted. *Faculty research:* Effectiveness of technology in education, parental involvement, effective teaching, effective schools research.

Grand View University, Master of Science in Innovative Leadership Program, Des Moines, IA 50316-1599. Offers business (MS); education (MS); nursing (MS). Part-time and evening/weekend programs available. *Faculty:* 7 full-time (3 women). *Students:* 31 part-time (23 women). Average age 32. In 2011, 16 master's awarded. *Degree requirements:* For master's, completion of all required coursework in common core and selected track with minimum cumulative GPA of 3.0 and no more than two grades of C. *Entrance requirements:* For master's, GRE, GMAT, or essay, minimum undergraduate GPA of 3.0, professional resume, 3 letters of recommendation, interview. Additional exam requirements/recommendations for international students: Required—TOEFL (minimum score 550 paper-based; 210 computer-based). *Application deadline:* Applications are processed on a rolling basis. Application fee: $40. Electronic applications accepted. *Expenses: Tuition:* Part-time $501 per credit. *Required fees:* $115 per semester. *Unit head:* Dr. Patricia Rinke, Dean of Graduate and Adult Programs, 515-263-2912, E-mail: prinke@grandview.edu. *Application contact:* Michael Norris, Director of Graduate Admissions, 515-263-2830, E-mail: gradadmissions@grandview.edu. Web site: http://www.grandview.edu.

Gratz College, Graduate Programs, Program in Education, Melrose Park, PA 19027. Offers MA. Part-time programs available. *Faculty:* 116 part-time/adjunct (93 women). *Students:* 588 part-time (453 women); includes 38 minority (26 Black or African American, non-Hispanic/Latino; 5 Asian, non-Hispanic/Latino; 7 Hispanic/Latino). Average age 35. 90 applicants, 96% accepted. In 2011, 105 master's awarded. *Degree requirements:* For master's, one foreign language, project. *Entrance requirements:* For master's, teaching certificate. *Application deadline:* Applications are processed on a rolling basis. Application fee: $50. *Financial support:* Application deadline: 4/1. *Unit head:* Joyce Ness, Director, 215-635-7300 Ext. 134, E-mail: jness@gratz.edu. *Application contact:* Roz Weinstein, Admissions Coordinator, 215-635-7300 Ext. 129, Fax: 215-635-7320, E-mail: rweinstein@gratz.edu.

Greensboro College, Program in Education, Greensboro, NC 27401-1875. Offers elementary education (M Ed); special education (M Ed). Part-time and evening/weekend programs available. *Degree requirements:* For master's, thesis. *Entrance requirements:* For master's, GRE, teacher license, 2 years of teaching experience, 2 letters of recommendation. Additional exam requirements/recommendations for international students: Required—TOEFL (minimum score 550 paper-based; 213 computer-based). Electronic applications accepted.

Greenville College, Program in Education, Greenville, IL 62246-0159. Offers education (MAT); elementary education (MAE); secondary education (MAE). *Degree requirements:* For master's, thesis (for some programs). *Entrance requirements:* For master's, GRE, Illinois Basic Skills Test, teacher certification. Electronic applications accepted.

Gwynedd-Mercy College, School of Education, Gwynedd Valley, PA 19437-0901. Offers educational administration (MS); master teacher (MS); reading (MS); school counseling (MS); special education (MS). Part-time and evening/weekend programs available. *Faculty:* 8 full-time (5 women), 38 part-time/adjunct (24 women). *Students:* 33 full-time (22 women), 157 part-time (116 women); includes 33 minority (22 Black or African American, non-Hispanic/Latino; 6 Asian, non-Hispanic/Latino; 5 Hispanic/Latino), 1 international. Average age 33. In 2011, 186 master's awarded. *Degree requirements:* For master's, thesis, internship, practicum. *Entrance requirements:* For master's, GRE or MAT; PRAXIS I, minimum GPA of 3.0. *Application deadline:* Applications are processed on a rolling basis. Application fee: $25. *Expenses: Tuition:* Part-time $630 per credit hour. *Financial support:* In 2011–12, 2 research assistantships were awarded; career-related internships or fieldwork, Federal Work-Study, tuition waivers (full and partial), unspecified assistantships, and Federal Stafford loans, Federal work study, alternative loans, graduate assistantships also available. Financial award applicants required to submit FAFSA. *Faculty research:* Learning and the brain, reading literacy, ethics and moral judgment, leadership, teaching and multicultural education. *Unit head:* Dr. Sandra Mangano, Dean, 215-641-5549, Fax: 215-542-4695, E-mail: mangano.s@gmc.edu. *Application contact:* Graduate Program Coordinator. Web site: http://www.gmc.edu/academics/education/.

Hamline University, School of Education, St. Paul, MN 55104-1284. Offers education (MA Ed, Ed D); English as a second language (MA); literacy education (MA); natural science and environmental education (MA Ed); teaching (MAT). *Accreditation:* NCATE (one or more programs are accredited). Part-time and evening/weekend programs available. Postbaccalaureate distance learning degree programs offered (no on-campus study). *Faculty:* 33 full-time (24 women), 106 part-time/adjunct (77 women). *Students:* 319 full-time (221 women), 717 part-time (524 women); includes 88 minority (30 Black or African American, non-Hispanic/Latino; 2 American Indian or Alaska Native, non-Hispanic/Latino; 26 Asian, non-Hispanic/Latino; 27 Hispanic/Latino; 3 Two or more races, non-Hispanic/Latino), 21 international. Average age 32. 468 applicants, 76% accepted, 259 enrolled. In 2011, 197 master's, 10 doctorates awarded. *Degree requirements:* For master's, thesis, foreign language (for MA in English as a second language only); for doctorate, comprehensive exam, thesis/dissertation. *Entrance requirements:* For master's, written essay, official transcripts, 2 letters of recommendation, minimum GPA of 2.5 from bachelor's work; for doctorate, personal statement, master's degree, 3 years experience, 3 letters of recommendation, writing sample, interview. Additional exam requirements/recommendations for international students: Required—TOEFL (minimum score 625 paper-based; 107 computer-based; 75 iBT) or IELTS. *Application deadline:* Applications are processed on a rolling basis. Application fee: $0 ($100 for international students). Electronic applications accepted. *Expenses: Tuition:* Full-time $3720; part-time $465 per credit. *Required fees:* $28 per year. Tuition and fees vary according to degree level, campus/location and program. *Financial support:* Federal Work-Study and scholarships/grants available. Support available to part-time students. Financial award applicants required to submit FAFSA. *Faculty research:* Adult basic education, service-learning, teacher dispositions, diversity, technology. *Unit head:* Dr. Larry Harris, Interim Dean, 651-523-2600, Fax: 651-523-2489, E-mail: lharris02@gw.hamline.edu. *Application contact:* Michael Hand, Assistant Director, Graduate Admission, 651-523-2900, Fax: 651-523-3058, E-mail: mhand01@gw.hamline.edu. Web site: http://www.hamline.edu/education.

Hampton University, Graduate College, College of Education and Continuing Studies, Hampton, VA 23668. Offers counseling (MA), including college student development, community agency counseling, pastoral counseling, school counseling; educational leadership (MA); elementary education (MA); gifted education (MA); Montessori education (MA); teaching (MT), including early childhood education, middle school education, music education, secondary education, special education. *Accreditation:* NCATE. Part-time and evening/weekend programs available. *Entrance requirements:* For master's, GRE General Test.

Hannibal-LaGrange University, Program in Education, Hannibal, MO 63401-1999. Offers literacy (MS Ed); teaching and learning (MS Ed). Part-time and evening/weekend programs available. *Degree requirements:* For master's, thesis, portfolio, documenting of program outcomes, public sharing of research. *Entrance requirements:* For master's, copy of current teaching certificate; minimum GPA of 2.75. *Faculty research:* Reading assessment, reading remediation, handwriting instruction, early childhood intervention.

Harding University, College of Education, Searcy, AR 72149-0001. Offers advanced studies in teaching and learning (M Ed); art (MSE); behavioral science (MSE); counseling (MS, Ed S); early childhood special education (M Ed, MSE); education (MSE); educational leadership (M Ed, Ed S); elementary education (M Ed); English (MSE); French (MSE); history/social science (MSE); kinesiology (MSE); math (MSE); reading (M Ed); secondary education (M Ed); Spanish (MSE); teaching (MAT); teaching English as a second language (MSE). *Accreditation:* NCATE. Part-time and evening/weekend programs available. *Faculty:* 9 full-time (2 women), 48 part-time/adjunct (26 women). *Students:* 100 full-time (77 women), 333 part-time (239 women); includes 76 minority (59 Black or African American, non-Hispanic/Latino; 1 Asian, non-Hispanic/Latino; 10 Hispanic/Latino; 6 Two or more races, non-Hispanic/Latino), 2 international. Average age 36. 93 applicants, 91% accepted, 83 enrolled. In 2011, 159 master's, 10 other advanced degrees awarded. *Degree requirements:* For master's, comprehensive exam (for some programs), thesis optional, portfolio(s); for Ed S, comprehensive exam, portfolio, project. *Entrance requirements:* For master's, GRE, MAT, PRAXIS; for Ed S, MAT or GRE. Additional exam requirements/recommendations for international students: Required—TOEFL (minimum score 550 paper-based; 79 iBT). *Application deadline:* For fall admission, 8/1 for domestic and international students; for spring admission, 1/1 for domestic and international students. Applications are processed on a rolling basis. Application fee: $35. *Expenses: Tuition:* Full-time $10,512; part-time $584 per credit hour. *Required fees:* $500; $25 per credit hour. Tuition and fees vary according to course load, degree level and program. *Financial support:* In 2011–12, 37 students received support. Unspecified assistantships available. *Faculty research:*

Education—General

Reading, comprehension, school violence, educational technology, behavior, college choice, differentiated instruction, brain-based teaching. *Unit head:* Dr. Clara Carroll, Chair, 501-279-4501, Fax: 501-279-4083, E-mail: ccarroll@harding.edu. *Application contact:* Information Contact, 501-279-4315, E-mail: gradstudiesedu@harding.edu. Web site: http://www.harding.edu/education/grad.html.

Hardin-Simmons University, Graduate School, Irvin School of Education, Abilene, TX 79698-0001. Offers M Ed. Part-time programs available. *Faculty:* 16 full-time (11 women), 6 part-time/adjunct (3 women). *Students:* 53 full-time (34 women), 77 part-time (60 women); includes 23 minority (9 Black or African American, non-Hispanic/Latino; 1 American Indian or Alaska Native, non-Hispanic/Latino; 1 Asian, non-Hispanic/Latino; 12 Hispanic/Latino), 2 international. Average age 31. 68 applicants, 91% accepted, 49 enrolled. In 2011, 42 master's awarded. *Degree requirements:* For master's, comprehensive exam. *Entrance requirements:* For master's, minimum undergraduate GPA of 3.0 in major, 2.7 overall. Additional exam requirements/recommendations for international students: Required—TOEFL (minimum score 550 paper-based; 213 computer-based; 75 iBT). *Application deadline:* For fall admission, 8/15 priority date for domestic students, 4/1 for international students; for spring admission, 1/5 priority date for domestic students, 9/1 for international students. Applications are processed on a rolling basis. Application fee: $50. *Expenses: Tuition:* Full-time $12,870; part-time $715 per credit hour. *Required fees:* $650; $110 per semester. Tuition and fees vary according to degree level. *Financial support:* In 2011–12, 102 students received support, including 22 fellowships (averaging $1,680 per year); career-related internships or fieldwork, scholarships/grants, and coaching assistantships also available. Support available to part-time students. Financial award application deadline: 6/30; financial award applicants required to submit FAFSA. *Unit head:* Dr. Pam Williford, Dean, 325-670-1352, Fax: 325-670-5859, E-mail: pwilliford@hsutx.edu. *Application contact:* Dr. Nancy Kucinski, Dean of Graduate Studies, 325-670-1298, Fax: 325-670-1564, E-mail: gradoff@hsutx.edu. Web site: http://www.hsutx.edu/academics/irvin.

Harrison Middleton University, Graduate Program, Tempe, AZ 85282. Offers education (MA, Ed D); humanities (MA); imaginative literature (MA); interdisciplinary studies (DA); jurisprudence (MA); natural science (MA); philosophy and religion (MA); social science (MA). Part-time and evening/weekend programs available. Postbaccalaureate distance learning degree programs offered (no on-campus study). *Faculty:* 18 full-time (7 women), 14 part-time/adjunct (6 women). *Students:* 53 full-time (20 women). 4 applicants, 100% accepted, 4 enrolled. In 2011, 4 master's awarded. *Degree requirements:* For master's and doctorate, capstone project. *Entrance requirements:* For doctorate, 2 academic letters of reference, interview. Additional exam requirements/recommendations for international students: Required—TOEFL (minimum score 550 paper-based; 80 iBT). *Application deadline:* Applications are processed on a rolling basis. Application fee: $50. Electronic applications accepted. One-time fee: $400 full-time. Full-time tuition and fees vary according to course load and degree level. *Faculty research:* Japanese animation, educational leadership, war art, John Muir's wilderness. *Unit head:* Susan Chiaramonte, Director of Accreditation and Licensure, 877-248-6724, Fax: 800-762-1622, E-mail: schiaramonte@hmu.edu. *Application contact:* Dr. Deborah Deacon, Dean of Graduate Studies, 877-248-6724, Fax: 800-762-1622, E-mail: ddeacon@hmu.edu. Web site: http://www.hmu.edu.

Harvard University, Harvard Graduate School of Education, Cambridge, MA 02138. Offers Ed M, Ed D, Ed L D. Part-time programs available. *Faculty:* 83 full-time (44 women), 67 part-time/adjunct (29 women). *Students:* 893 full-time (636 women), 91 part-time (61 women); includes 310 minority (86 Black or African American, non-Hispanic/Latino; 5 American Indian or Alaska Native, non-Hispanic/Latino; 106 Asian, non-Hispanic/Latino; 77 Hispanic/Latino; 3 Native Hawaiian or other Pacific Islander, non-Hispanic/Latino; 33 Two or more races, non-Hispanic/Latino), 125 international. Average age 30. 2,744 applicants, 35% accepted, 680 enrolled. In 2011, 653 master's, 47 doctorates awarded. *Degree requirements:* For doctorate, thesis/dissertation (for some programs), capstone project in lieu of thesis (for Ed.L.D.). *Entrance requirements:* For master's, GRE General Test, statement of purpose, 3 letters of recommendation, resume, official transcripts; for doctorate, GRE General Test or GMAT (for Ed.L.D. only), statement of purpose, 3 letters of recommendation, resume, official transcripts, 2 short essay questions (for Ed.L.D. only). Additional exam requirements/recommendations for international students: Required—TOEFL (minimum score 613 paper-based; 104 computer-based; 100 iBT), TWE (minimum score 5). *Application deadline:* For fall admission, 12/14 for domestic and international students. Application fee: $85. Electronic applications accepted. *Expenses:* Contact institution. *Financial support:* In 2011–12, 672 students received support, including 126 fellowships with full and partial tuition reimbursements available (averaging $16,766 per year), 35 research assistantships (averaging $9,534 per year), 212 teaching assistantships (averaging $8,806 per year); career-related internships or fieldwork, Federal Work-Study, institutionally sponsored loans, scholarships/grants, health care benefits, tuition waivers (full and partial), and unspecified assistantships also available. Support available to part-time students. Financial award application deadline: 2/1; financial award applicants required to submit FAFSA. *Faculty research:* Learning and development, educational leadership and organizations, education policy analysis. *Total annual research expenditures:* $26 million. *Unit head:* Dr. Kathleen McCartney, Dean, 617-495-3401. *Application contact:* Information Contact, 617-495-3414, Fax: 617-496-3577, E-mail: gseadmissions@harvard.edu. Web site: http://www.gse.harvard.edu/.

Hastings College, Department of Teacher Education, Hastings, NE 68901-7696. Offers MAT. *Accreditation:* NCATE. Part-time programs available. *Degree requirements:* For master's, comprehensive exam, thesis, or oral teaching presentation; digital portfolio. *Entrance requirements:* For master's, minimum GPA of 2.5, 2 letters of reference, interview. Additional exam requirements/recommendations for international students: Required—TOEFL. Electronic applications accepted. *Faculty research:* Assessments, performance competencies.

Hebrew College, Shoolman Graduate School of Jewish Education, Newton Centre, MA 02459. Offers early childhood Jewish education (Certificate); Jewish day school education (Certificate); Jewish education (MJ Ed); Jewish family education (Certificate); Jewish special education (Certificate); Jewish youth education, informal education and camping (Certificate). Part-time and evening/weekend programs available. Postbaccalaureate distance learning degree programs offered. *Degree requirements:* For master's, one foreign language. *Entrance requirements:* For master's, GRE, interview. Additional exam requirements/recommendations for international students: Required—TOEFL.

Hebrew Union College–Jewish Institute of Religion, School of Education, New York, NY 10012-1186. Offers MARE. Part-time programs available. *Degree requirements:* For master's, one foreign language, thesis. *Entrance requirements:* For master's, GRE, minimum 2 years of college-level Hebrew.

Heidelberg University, Program in Education, Tiffin, OH 44883-2462. Offers MAE. Part-time and evening/weekend programs available. *Degree requirements:* For master's, thesis or alternative, internship, practicum. *Entrance requirements:* For master's, minimum cumulative GPA of 2.75, 3 recommendations, bachelor's degree. Additional exam requirements/recommendations for international students: Required—TOEFL (minimum score 550 paper-based).

Henderson State University, Graduate Studies, Teachers College, Arkadelphia, AR 71999-0001. Offers MAT, MS, MSE, Ed S, Graduate Certificate. *Accreditation:* NCATE. Part-time programs available. *Entrance requirements:* For master's, GRE General Test or MAT, minimum GPA of 2.7, teacher certification. Additional exam requirements/recommendations for international students: Required—TOEFL (minimum score 550 paper-based; 213 computer-based); Recommended—IELTS (minimum score 6). Electronic applications accepted.

Heritage University, Graduate Programs in Education, Toppenish, WA 98948-9599. Offers counseling (M Ed); educational administration (M Ed); professional studies (M Ed), including bilingual education/ESL, biology, English and literature, reading/literacy, special education; teaching (MIT). Part-time and evening/weekend programs available. *Degree requirements:* For master's, comprehensive exam, thesis (for some programs). *Entrance requirements:* For master's, interview, letters of recommendation, teaching certificate. Additional exam requirements/recommendations for international students: Recommended—TOEFL (minimum score 550 paper-based; 213 computer-based).

High Point University, Norcross Graduate School, High Point, NC 27262-3598. Offers business administration (MBA); educational leadership (M Ed); elementary education (M Ed); history (MA); nonprofit management (MA); secondary math (M Ed); special education (M Ed); strategic communication (MA); teaching elementary education k-6 (MAT); teaching secondary mathematics 9-12 (MAT). *Accreditation:* ACBSP; NCATE. Part-time and evening/weekend programs available. *Degree requirements:* For master's, comprehensive exam (for some programs), thesis (for some programs). *Entrance requirements:* For master's, GMAT (MBA), GRE, MAT, minimum GPA of 3.0. Additional exam requirements/recommendations for international students: Required—TOEFL (minimum score 550 paper-based). Electronic applications accepted.

Hodges University, Graduate Programs, Naples, FL 34119. Offers business administration (MBA); criminal justice (MS); education (MPS); information systems management (MIS); legal studies (MS); management (MSM); mental health counseling (MS); public administration (MPA). Part-time and evening/weekend programs available. Postbaccalaureate distance learning degree programs offered (no on-campus study). *Faculty:* 22 full-time (9 women), 3 part-time/adjunct (2 women). *Students:* 28 full-time (21 women), 237 part-time (156 women); includes 76 minority (35 Black or African American, non-Hispanic/Latino; 5 Asian, non-Hispanic/Latino; 36 Hispanic/Latino). Average age 36. 92 applicants, 91% accepted, 81 enrolled. *Degree requirements:* For master's, comprehensive exam (for some programs), thesis (for some programs). *Entrance requirements:* For master's, in-house entrance exam. Additional exam requirements/recommendations for international students: Recommended—TOEFL. *Application deadline:* Applications are processed on a rolling basis. Application fee: $50. Electronic applications accepted. *Expenses: Tuition:* Full-time $11,340; part-time $630 per credit hour. *Required fees:* $250 per term. *Financial support:* In 2011–12, 200 students received support. Federal Work-Study and scholarships/grants available. Financial award application deadline: 7/9; financial award applicants required to submit FAFSA. *Unit head:* Terry McMahan, President, 239-513-1122, Fax: 239-598-6253, E-mail: tmcmahan@hodges.edu. *Application contact:* Rita Lampus, Vice President of Student Enrollment Management, 239-513-1122, Fax: 239-598-6253, E-mail: rlampus@hodges.edu.

Hofstra University, School of Education, Health, and Human Services, Hempstead, NY 11549. Offers MA, MHA, MPH, MS, MS Ed, Ed D, PhD, Advanced Certificate, PD, Advanced Certificate/Advanced Certificate. *Accreditation:* Teacher Education Accreditation Council. Part-time and evening/weekend programs available. Postbaccalaureate distance learning degree programs offered (minimal on-campus study). *Faculty:* 70 full-time (49 women), 78 part-time/adjunct (44 women). *Students:* 660 full-time (517 women), 645 part-time (493 women); includes 279 minority (157 Black or African American, non-Hispanic/Latino; 2 American Indian or Alaska Native, non-Hispanic/Latino; 40 Asian, non-Hispanic/Latino; 74 Hispanic/Latino; 1 Native Hawaiian or other Pacific Islander, non-Hispanic/Latino; 5 Two or more races, non-Hispanic/Latino), 32 international. Average age 30. 870 applicants, 80% accepted, 391 enrolled. In 2011, 574 master's, 8 doctorates, 99 other advanced degrees awarded. *Degree requirements:* For master's, one foreign language, comprehensive exam (for some programs), thesis (for some programs), capstone, electronic portfolio, student teaching, practicum, internship, seminars, field work, curriculum project, clinical hours, minimum GPA of 3.0; for doctorate, variable foreign language requirement, comprehensive exam (for some programs), thesis/dissertation, qualifying hearing, minimum GPA of 3.0; for other advanced degree, comprehensive exam (for some programs), thesis optional, electronic portfolio, fieldwork, internship, state exams, exit project, minimum GPA of 3.0. *Entrance requirements:* For master's, GRE, letters of recommendation, interview, portfolio, resume, essay, certification; for doctorate, GRE, 3 letters of recommendation, essay, interview, 2 years full-time teaching. Additional exam requirements/recommendations for international students: Required—TOEFL (minimum score 550 paper-based; 213 computer-based; 80 iBT). *Application deadline:* Applications are processed on a rolling basis. Application fee: $70 ($75 for international students). Electronic applications accepted. *Expenses: Tuition:* Full-time $18,990; part-time $1055 per credit hour. *Required fees:* $970. Tuition and fees vary according to program. *Financial support:* In 2011–12, 647 students received support, including 230 fellowships with full and partial tuition reimbursements available (averaging $3,645 per year), 12 research assistantships with full and partial tuition reimbursements available (averaging $13,630 per year); career-related internships or fieldwork, Federal Work-Study, institutionally sponsored loans, scholarships/grants, tuition waivers (full and partial), and unspecified assistantships also available. Support available to part-time students. Financial award applicants required to submit FAFSA. *Faculty research:* School management, childhood obesity, inclusive schooling and universal design for learning (UDL), multicultural education, applied linguistics. *Total annual research expenditures:* $1.3 million. *Unit head:* Dr. Nancy E. Halliday, Interim Dean, 516-463-5811, Fax: 516-463-6461, E-mail: hprneh@hofstra.edu. *Application contact:* Carol Drummer, Dean of Graduate Admissions, 516-463-4876, Fax: 516-463-4664, E-mail: gradstudent@hofstra.edu. Web site: http://www.hofstra.edu/education/.

Hollins University, Graduate Programs, Program in Teaching, Roanoke, VA 24020-1603. Offers MAT. *Accreditation:* Teacher Education Accreditation Council. Part-time and evening/weekend programs available. *Degree requirements:* For master's, thesis. *Entrance requirements:* For master's, PRAXIS I, letters of recommendation, writing sample. Additional exam requirements/recommendations for international students: Required—TOEFL (minimum score 550 paper-based; 213 computer-based; 79 iBT). Electronic applications accepted. *Faculty research:* Television violence and its effect on the developing brain, phonological/phonemic awareness, technology in the classroom.

Holy Family University, Graduate School, School of Education, Philadelphia, PA 19114. Offers education (M Ed); education leadership (M Ed); elementary education (M Ed); reading specialist (M Ed); secondary education (M Ed); special education (M Ed). Part-time and evening/weekend programs available. *Degree requirements:* For master's, thesis optional. *Entrance requirements:* For master's, GRE or MAT, interview. Electronic applications accepted. *Faculty research:* Cognition, developmental issues, sociological issues in education.

See Display on next page and Close-Up on page 803.

Holy Names University, Graduate Division, Department of Education, Oakland, CA 94619-1699. Offers educational therapy (Certificate); level 1 education specialist mild/moderate disabilities (Credential); level 2 education specialist mild/moderate disabilities (Credential); multiple subject teaching credential (Credential); single subject teaching credential (Credential); teaching English as a second language (TESL) (M Ed); urban education: educational therapy (M Ed); urban education: K-12 education (M Ed); urban education: special education (M Ed). Part-time programs available. *Degree requirements:* For master's, comprehensive exam, research paper, thesis or project. *Entrance requirements:* For master's, minimum undergraduate GPA of 2.6 overall, 3.0 in major. Additional exam requirements/recommendations for international students: Required—TOEFL (minimum score 550 paper-based; 213 computer-based; 80 iBT). *Faculty research:* Cognitive development, language development, learning handicaps.

Hood College, Graduate School, Department of Education, Frederick, MD 21701-8575. Offers curriculum and instruction (MS), including early childhood education, elementary education, elementary school science and mathematics, secondary education, special education; educational leadership (MS, Certificate); reading specialization (MS). Part-time and evening/weekend programs available. *Degree requirements:* For master's, action research project, portfolio (reading). *Entrance requirements:* For master's, minimum GPA of 2.75, teaching certification. Additional exam requirements/recommendations for international students: Required—TOEFL (minimum score 575 paper-based; 231 computer-based; 89 iBT). Electronic applications accepted. *Faculty research:* Leadership, action research, brain research, learning styles.

Hope International University, School of Graduate and Professional Studies, Program in Education, Fullerton, CA 92831-3138. Offers education administration (MA); elementary education (ME); secondary education (ME). Part-time and evening/weekend programs available. *Degree requirements:* For master's, comprehensive exam (for some programs), thesis. *Entrance requirements:* For master's, minimum GPA of 3.0, 2 references. Additional exam requirements/recommendations for international students: Required—TOEFL (minimum score 550 paper-based; 213 computer-based; 86 iBT); Recommended—IELTS (minimum score 6.5). Electronic applications accepted. *Expenses:* Contact institution. *Faculty research:* Distance education.

Houston Baptist University, College of Education and Behavioral Sciences, Programs in Education, Houston, TX 77074-3298. Offers bilingual education (M Ed); counselor education (M Ed); curriculum and instruction (M Ed); educational administration (M Ed); educational diagnostician (M Ed); reading education (M Ed). Part-time programs available. *Entrance requirements:* For master's, GRE General Test or MAT. Additional exam requirements/recommendations for international students: Required—TOEFL (minimum score 550 paper-based; 213 computer-based).

Howard University, School of Education, Washington, DC 20059. Offers M Ed, Ed D, PhD. *Accreditation:* NCATE. *Faculty:* 27 full-time (15 women), 7 part-time/adjunct (5 women). *Students:* 191 full-time (148 women), 111 part-time (73 women); includes 262 minority (257 Black or African American, non-Hispanic/Latino; 1 Asian, non-Hispanic/Latino; 3 Hispanic/Latino; 1 Two or more races, non-Hispanic/Latino), 26 international. Average age 32. 232 applicants, 63% accepted, 109 enrolled. In 2011, 45 master's, 6 doctorates awarded. *Degree requirements:* For master's, comprehensive exam, expository writing exam; for doctorate, one foreign language, comprehensive exam, thesis/dissertation, expository writing exam, internship. *Entrance requirements:* For master's, minimum GPA of 2.7; for doctorate, GRE General Test, minimum GPA of 3.4. Additional exam requirements/recommendations for international students: Required—TOEFL (minimum score 550 paper-based). *Application deadline:* For fall admission, 2/15 priority date for domestic students; for spring admission, 11/1 for domestic students. Applications are processed on a rolling basis. Application fee: $45. Electronic applications accepted. *Financial support:* In 2011–12, 37 students received support, including 26 fellowships with full and partial tuition reimbursements available (averaging $16,000 per year), 8 research assistantships (averaging $3,000 per year); career-related internships or fieldwork, Federal Work-Study, institutionally sponsored loans, scholarships/grants, and unspecified assistantships also available. Financial award application deadline: 3/15; financial award applicants required to submit FAFSA. *Faculty research:* Policy affecting education for African-Americans; information technology use in underserved school populations; increasing literacy skills for public school students; violence intervention and prevention; successes, problems, and needs of disabled African-Americans. *Total annual research expenditures:* $3.6 million. *Unit head:* Dr. Leslie T. Fenwick, Dean, School of Education, 202-806-7334, Fax: 202-806-5302, E-mail: lfenwick@howard.edu. *Application contact:* Dr. Melanie Carter, Senior Associate Dean for Academic Programs and Student Affairs, 202-806-7340, Fax: 202-806-5302, E-mail: melcarter@howard.edu. Web site: http://www.howard.edu/schooleducation/.

Humboldt State University, Academic Programs, College of Professional Studies, School of Education, Arcata, CA 95521-8299. Offers MA. Part-time and evening/weekend programs available. *Students:* 8 full-time (5 women), 23 part-time (14 women); includes 1 minority (Hispanic/Latino), 3 international. Average age 38. 21 applicants, 67% accepted, 9 enrolled. In 2011, 4 master's awarded. *Degree requirements:* For master's, thesis or alternative. *Entrance requirements:* For master's, minimum GPA of 3.0, 3 letters of recommendation. Additional exam requirements/recommendations for international students: Required—TOEFL (minimum score 500 paper-based; 173 computer-based). *Application deadline:* For fall admission, 4/1 for domestic and international students. Applications are processed on a rolling basis. Application fee: $55. *Expenses:* Tuition, state resident: full-time $6734. Tuition, nonresident: full-time $15,662; part-time $372 per credit. *Required fees:* $903. Tuition and fees vary according to program. *Financial support:* Application deadline: 3/1; applicants required to submit FAFSA. *Unit head:* Dr. Ann Diver-Stamnes, Chair, 707-826-5822, Fax: 707-826-5868, E-mail: ann.diver-stamnes@humboldt.edu. *Application contact:* Dr. Eric Van Duzer, Coordinator, 707-826-3726, Fax: 707-826-5868, E-mail: evv1@humboldt.edu. Web site: http://www.humboldt.edu/~educ/masters.html.

Hunter College of the City University of New York, Graduate School, School of Education, New York, NY 10021-5085. Offers MA, MS, MS Ed, AC. *Accreditation:* NCATE. *Faculty:* 105 full-time (63 women), 242 part-time/adjunct (175 women). *Students:* 281 full-time (228 women), 1,721 part-time (1,408 women); includes 698 minority (163 Black or African American, non-Hispanic/Latino; 13 American Indian or Alaska Native, non-Hispanic/Latino; 164 Asian, non-Hispanic/Latino; 358 Hispanic/Latino), 34 international. Average age 29. 2,061 applicants, 44% accepted, 346 enrolled. In 2011, 798 master's, 39 other advanced degrees awarded. *Degree requirements:* For master's, thesis; for AC, portfolio review. *Entrance requirements:* For degree, minimum B average in graduate course work, teaching certificate, minimum 3 years of full-time teaching experience, interview, 2 letters of support. Additional exam requirements/recommendations for international students: Required—TOEFL. *Application deadline:* For fall admission, 4/1 for domestic students, 2/1 for international students; for spring admission, 11/1 for domestic students, 9/1 for international students. Applications are processed on a rolling basis. Application fee: $125. *Expenses:* Tuition, state resident: full-time $8210; part-time $345 per credit. Tuition, nonresident: full-time $15,360; part-time $640 per credit. *Required fees:* $280 per semester. One-time fee: $125. Tuition and fees vary according to class time, campus/location and program. *Financial support:* Fellowships, career-related internships or fieldwork, Federal Work-Study, institutionally sponsored loans, and tuition waivers (full and partial) available. Support available to part-time students. *Faculty research:* Multicultural and multiracial urban education; mentoring new teachers; mathematics and science education; bilingual, bicultural, and special education. *Unit head:* Dr. David Steiner, Dean, 212-772-4622, E-mail: david.steiner@hunter.cuny.edu. *Application contact:* Milena Solo, Director for Graduate

Admissions, 212-772-4482, Fax: 212-650-3336, E-mail: milena.solo@hunter.cuny.edu. Web site: http://www.hunter.cuny.edu/school-of-education/programs/graduate.

Huntington University, Graduate School, Huntington, IN 46750-1299. Offers counseling (MA), including licensed mental health counselor; education (M Ed); youth ministry leadership (MA). Part-time programs available. Postbaccalaureate distance learning degree programs offered (minimal on-campus study). *Degree requirements:* For master's, thesis. *Entrance requirements:* For master's, GRE (for counseling and education students only). Additional exam requirements/recommendations for international students: Required—TOEFL. Electronic applications accepted. *Faculty research:* Leadership, educational technology trends, evangelism, youth ministry, mental health.

Idaho State University, Office of Graduate Studies, College of Education, Pocatello, ID 83209-8059. Offers M Ed, MPE, Ed D, PhD, 5th Year Certificate, 6th Year Certificate, Ed S. *Accreditation:* NCATE. Part-time programs available. *Degree requirements:* For master's, comprehensive exam, thesis optional, oral exam, written exam; for doctorate, comprehensive exam, thesis/dissertation, written exam; for other advanced degree, comprehensive exam, oral exam, written exam, practicum or field project. *Entrance requirements:* For master's, GRE General Test or MAT, minimum undergraduate GPA of 3.0, interview, bachelor's degree or equivalent; for doctorate, GRE General Test or MAT, minimum undergraduate GPA of 3.0, 3.5 graduate; departmental interview; current curriculum vitae, computer skill competency checklist; for other advanced degree, GRE General Test, minimum graduate GPA of 3.0, master's degree, letter from supervisor attesting to school administration potential. Additional exam requirements/recommendations for international students: Required—TOEFL (minimum score 550 paper-based; 213 computer-based; 80 iBT). Electronic applications accepted. *Faculty research:* School reform, inclusion, students at risk, teacher education standards, teaching cases, education leadership.

Illinois State University, Graduate School, College of Education, Normal, IL 61790-2200. Offers MS, MS Ed, Ed D, PhD. *Accreditation:* NCATE. Part-time programs available. *Degree requirements:* For doctorate, thesis/dissertation, 2 terms of residency. *Entrance requirements:* For master's and doctorate, GRE General Test.

Indiana State University, College of Graduate and Professional Studies, College of Education, Terre Haute, IN 47809. Offers M Ed, MS, PhD, Ed S, MA/MS. *Accreditation:* NCATE. Part-time and evening/weekend programs available. *Degree requirements:* For doctorate, thesis/dissertation. *Entrance requirements:* For master's, minimum undergraduate GPA of 2.5; for doctorate, GRE General Test; for Ed S, GRE General Test, minimum graduate GPA of 3.25. Electronic applications accepted.

Indiana University Bloomington, School of Education, Bloomington, IN 47405-7000. Offers MS, Ed D, PhD, Ed S. *Accreditation:* NCATE. Part-time programs available. Postbaccalaureate distance learning degree programs offered. Terminal master's awarded for partial completion of doctoral program. *Degree requirements:* For master's, thesis optional; for doctorate, comprehensive exam, thesis/dissertation; for Ed S, comprehensive exam (for some programs), thesis (for some programs), comprehensive exam or project. *Entrance requirements:* For master's and Ed S, GRE General Test, minimum GPA of 3.0 (recommended), 3 letters of recommendation; for doctorate, GRE General Test, minimum GPA of 3.0, 3 letters of recommendation. Additional exam requirements/recommendations for international students: Required—TOEFL (minimum score 550 paper-based; 213 computer-based; 79 iBT). Electronic applications accepted.

Indiana University East, School of Education, Richmond, IN 47374-1289. Offers MS Ed. *Accreditation:* NCATE. *Entrance requirements:* For master's, 3 letters of recommendation, interview.

Indiana University Kokomo, Division of Education, Kokomo, IN 46904-9003. Offers elementary education (MS Ed). *Accreditation:* NCATE. Part-time and evening/weekend programs available. *Faculty:* 1 full-time (0 women). *Students:* 13 full-time (10 women), 6 part-time (4 women); includes 1 minority (Hispanic/Latino). Average age 36. 9 applicants, 100% accepted, 8 enrolled. In 2011, 14 master's awarded. *Degree requirements:* For master's, thesis optional, research project. *Entrance requirements:* For master's, GRE General Test, minimum GPA of 2.5. *Application deadline:* For fall admission, 8/1 for domestic students; for spring admission, 12/1 for domestic students. Applications are processed on a rolling basis. Application fee: $40 ($50 for international students). *Financial support:* In 2011–12, 2 fellowships (averaging $375 per year) were awarded; minority teacher scholarships also available. *Faculty research:* Reading, teaching effectiveness, portfolio, curriculum development. *Unit head:* D. Antonio Cantu, Dean, 765-455-9441, Fax: 765-455-9503. *Application contact:* Charlotte Miller, Coordinator, Educational and Student Resources, 765-455-9367, Fax: 765-455-9503, E-mail: cmiller@iuk.edu.

Indiana University Northwest, School of Education, Gary, IN 46408-1197. Offers elementary education (MS Ed); secondary education (MS Ed). *Accreditation:* NCATE. Part-time and evening/weekend programs available. *Faculty:* 5 full-time (2 women). *Students:* 49 full-time (37 women), 204 part-time (164 women); includes 119 minority (84 Black or African American, non-Hispanic/Latino; 1 American Indian or Alaska Native, non-Hispanic/Latino; 1 Asian, non-Hispanic/Latino; 30 Hispanic/Latino; 3 Two or more races, non-Hispanic/Latino). Average age 37. 32 applicants, 100% accepted, 25 enrolled. In 2011, 44 master's awarded. *Entrance requirements:* For master's, GRE General Test or MAT, minimum GPA of 3.0. *Application deadline:* For fall admission, 7/15 priority date for domestic students; for spring admission, 11/15 for domestic students. Application fee: $25. *Unit head:* Dr. Stanley E. Wigle, Dean, 219-980-6510, Fax: 219-981-4208, E-mail: amsanche@iun.edu. *Application contact:* Admissions Counselor, 219-980-6760, Fax: 219-980-7103. Web site: http://www.iun.edu/~edu/.

Indiana University of Pennsylvania, School of Graduate Studies and Research, College of Education and Educational Technology, Indiana, PA 15705. Offers M Ed, MA, MS, D Ed, PhD, Certificate. *Accreditation:* NCATE. Part-time and evening/weekend programs available. *Faculty:* 62 full-time (36 women), 13 part-time/adjunct (10 women). *Students:* 295 full-time (225 women), 484 part-time (344 women); includes 53 minority (38 Black or African American, non-Hispanic/Latino; 1 American Indian or Alaska Native, non-Hispanic/Latino; 6 Asian, non-Hispanic/Latino; 3 Hispanic/Latino; 5 Two or more races, non-Hispanic/Latino), 16 international. Average age 29. 1,010 applicants, 46% accepted, 312 enrolled. In 2011, 196 master's, 33 doctorates, 10 other advanced degrees awarded. Terminal master's awarded for partial completion of doctoral program. *Degree requirements:* For master's, thesis optional; for doctorate, comprehensive exam, thesis/dissertation. *Entrance requirements:* For master's and doctorate, 2 letters of recommendation. Additional exam requirements/recommendations for international students: Required—TOEFL (minimum score 540 paper-based; 207 computer-based). *Application deadline:* Applications are processed on a rolling basis. Application fee: $50. Electronic applications accepted. *Expenses:* Tuition, state resident: full-time $7488; part-time $416 per credit. Tuition, nonresident: full-time $11,232; part-time $624 per credit. *Required fees:* $2070; $192.20 per credit. $90 per semester. *Financial support:* In 2011–12, 16 fellowships (averaging $6,085 per year), 115 research assistantships (averaging $4,541 per year), 10 teaching assistantships with partial tuition reimbursements (averaging $16,525 per year) were awarded; career-related internships or fieldwork and Federal Work-Study also available. Support available to part-time students. Financial award application deadline: 4/15; financial award applicants required to submit FAFSA. *Unit head:* Dr. A. Keith Dils, Dean, 724-357-2482, Fax: 724-357-5595, E-mail: kdils@iup.edu. *Application contact:* Dr. Edward Nardi, Associate Dean, 724-357-2480, Fax: 724-357-5595, E-mail: ewnardi@iup.edu. Web site: http://www.iup.edu/education.

Indiana University–Purdue University Fort Wayne, College of Education and Public Policy, Fort Wayne, IN 46805-1499. Offers MPA, MPM, MS Ed, Certificate. *Accreditation:* NCATE. Part-time programs available. *Faculty:* 28 full-time (14 women), 1 (woman) part-time/adjunct. *Students:* 17 full-time (14 women), 221 part-time (171 women); includes 29 minority (18 Black or African American, non-Hispanic/Latino; 2 Asian, non-Hispanic/Latino; 7 Hispanic/Latino; 2 Two or more races, non-Hispanic/Latino), 2 international. Average age 33. 82 applicants, 66% accepted, 46 enrolled. In 2011, 82 master's, 1 Certificate awarded. *Entrance requirements:* For master's, minimum GPA of 2.5, 3 professional letters of recommendation. Additional exam requirements/recommendations for international students: Required—TOEFL (minimum score 550 paper-based; 213 computer-based; 77 iBT). *Application deadline:* For fall admission, 4/1 priority date for domestic students, 4/1 for international students. Applications are processed on a rolling basis. Application fee: $55. *Financial support:* In 2011–12, 1 teaching assistantship with partial tuition reimbursement (averaging $12,930 per year) was awarded; scholarships/grants also available. Support available to part-time students. Financial award application deadline: 3/1; financial award applicants required to submit FAFSA. *Faculty research:* Ethnic minority education, hospital care and patient education, Holocaust education. *Total annual research expenditures:* $77,627. *Unit head:* Dr. Barry Kanpol, Dean, 260-481-6456, Fax: 260-481-5408, E-mail: kanpolb@ipfw.edu. *Application contact:* Vicky L. Schmidt, Graduate Recorder, 260-481-6450, Fax: 260-481-5408, E-mail: schmidt@ipfw.edu. Web site: http://www.ipfw.edu/cepp.

Indiana University–Purdue University Indianapolis, School of Education, Indianapolis, IN 46202-2896. Offers computer education (Certificate); curriculum and instruction (MS); early childhood (MS); educational leadership (MS, Certificate); English as a second language (Certificate); higher education and student affairs (MS); kindergarten (Certificate); language education (MS); reading (Certificate); school counseling (MS); special education (MS, Certificate). Part-time and evening/weekend programs available. *Faculty:* 41 full-time, 80 part-time/adjunct. *Students:* 67 full-time (52 women), 467 part-time (360 women); includes 82 minority (44 Black or African American, non-Hispanic/Latino; 3 American Indian or Alaska Native, non-Hispanic/Latino; 8 Asian, non-Hispanic/Latino; 13 Hispanic/Latino; 14 Two or more races, non-Hispanic/Latino), 10 international. Average age 33. 63 applicants, 57% accepted, 29 enrolled. In 2011, 167 master's awarded. *Degree requirements:* For master's, thesis optional. *Entrance requirements:* For master's, GRE General Test, minimum GPA of 3.0. Additional exam requirements/recommendations for international students: Required—TOEFL. *Application deadline:* For fall admission, 5/1 priority date for domestic students; for spring admission, 11/1 for domestic students. Application fee: $55 ($65 for international students). *Financial support:* Fellowships, research assistantships with partial tuition reimbursements, teaching assistantships, Federal Work-Study, institutionally sponsored loans, scholarships/grants, and tuition waivers (partial) available. Support available to part-time students. *Faculty research:* Teachers in the process of change, learning cycles, children's concepts of science. *Total annual research expenditures:* $614,458. *Unit head:* Dr. Chris Leland, Interim Executive Associate Dean, 317-274-6801, Fax: 317-274-6864. *Application contact:* Sarah Brandenburg, Graduate Advisor, 317-274-6801, Fax: 317-274-6864, E-mail: edugrad@iupui.edu. Web site: http://education.iupui.edu/.

Indiana University South Bend, School of Education, South Bend, IN 46634-7111. Offers counseling and human services (MS Ed); elementary education (MS Ed); secondary education (MS Ed); special education (MS Ed). *Accreditation:* NCATE. Part-time and evening/weekend programs available. *Faculty:* 21 full-time (11 women), 9 part-time/adjunct (3 women). *Students:* 70 full-time (45 women), 262 part-time (206 women); includes 39 minority (15 Black or African American, non-Hispanic/Latino; 3 American Indian or Alaska Native, non-Hispanic/Latino; 5 Asian, non-Hispanic/Latino; 14 Hispanic/Latino; 2 Two or more races, non-Hispanic/Latino), 15 international. Average age 36. 52 applicants, 75% accepted, 28 enrolled. In 2011, 75 master's awarded. *Degree requirements:* For master's, thesis or alternative, exit project. *Entrance requirements:* For master's, letters of recommendation, GRE or minimum GPA of 3.0. Additional exam requirements/recommendations for international students: Required—TOEFL. *Application deadline:* For fall admission, 7/1 for domestic students; for spring admission, 11/1 for domestic students. Applications are processed on a rolling basis. Application fee: $50 ($60 for international students). Electronic applications accepted. *Financial support:* Career-related internships or fieldwork available. Support available to part-time students. Financial award application deadline: 3/1; financial award applicants required to submit FAFSA. *Faculty research:* Professional dispositions, early childhood literacy, online learning, program assessments, problem-based learning. *Unit head:* Dr. Michael Horvath, Professor/Dean, 574-520-4339, Fax: 574-520-4550. *Application contact:* Dr. Todd Norris, Director of Education Student Services, 574-520-4845, E-mail: toanorri@iusb.edu. Web site: http://www.iusb.edu/~edud/.

Indiana University Southeast, School of Education, New Albany, IN 47150-6405. Offers counselor education (MS Ed); elementary education (MS Ed); secondary education (MS Ed). *Accreditation:* NCATE. Part-time and evening/weekend programs available. *Students:* 31 full-time (24 women), 622 part-time (497 women); includes 83 minority (63 Black or African American, non-Hispanic/Latino; 2 American Indian or Alaska Native, non-Hispanic/Latino; 5 Asian, non-Hispanic/Latino; 8 Hispanic/Latino; 5 Two or more races, non-Hispanic/Latino). Average age 33. 99 applicants, 93% accepted, 75 enrolled. In 2011, 143 master's awarded. *Entrance requirements:* For master's, minimum undergraduate GPA of 2.5, graduate 3.0. *Application deadline:* Applications are processed on a rolling basis. Application fee: $35. *Financial support:* Career-related internships or fieldwork, Federal Work-Study, and institutionally sponsored loans available. Support available to part-time students. Financial award applicants required to submit FAFSA. *Faculty research:* Learning styles, technology, constructivism, group process, innovative math strategies. *Unit head:* Dr. Gloria Murray, Dean, 812-941-2169, Fax: 812-941-2667, E-mail: soeinfo@ius.edu. *Application contact:* Admissions Counselor, 812-941-2212, Fax: 812-941-2595, E-mail: admissions@ius.edu. Web site: http://www.ius.edu/education/.

Institute for Christian Studies, Graduate Programs, Toronto, ON M5T 1R4, Canada. Offers education (M Phil F, PhD); history of philosophy (M Phil F, PhD); philosophical aesthetics (M Phil F, PhD); philosophy of religion (M Phil F, PhD); political theory (M Phil F, PhD); systematic philosophy (M Phil F, PhD); theology (M Phil F, PhD); worldview studies (MWS). Part-time programs available. Postbaccalaureate distance learning degree programs offered (minimal on-campus study). *Degree requirements:* For master's, one foreign language, thesis; for doctorate, 2 foreign languages, thesis/dissertation. *Entrance requirements:* For master's and doctorate, philosophy background. Additional exam requirements/recommendations for international students: Required—TOEFL (minimum score 600 paper-based; 250 computer-based). *Faculty research:* Human rights, anthropology of self, medieval discourse, gender and body, post-modern thought; biblical hermeneutics, creational aesthetics, ecumenism, epistemology, political theory and public policy, relational psychotherapy.

Instituto Tecnologico de Santo Domingo, Graduate School, Area of Humanities and Social Sciences, Santo Domingo, Dominican Republic. Offers accounting (Certificate); adult education (Certificate); applied linguistics (MA); economics (MA); education (M Ed); educational psychology (MA, Certificate); gender and development (MA, Certificate); humanistic studies (MA); international marketing management (Certificate); international relations in the Caribbean basin (Certificate); intervention systems in family therapy (MA); linguistic and literary communication (Certificate); pedagogical support (MA); social science education (M Ed); sustainable human development (MA); terminal illness and death psychology (Certificate); youth and adult education (M Ed).

Instituto Tecnológico y de Estudios Superiores de Monterrey, Campus Central de Veracruz, Graduate Programs, Córdoba, Mexico. Offers administration (MA); administration of information technologies (MTI); computer sciences (MCC); education (MEE); educational institution administration (MAD); educational technology (MTE); electronic commerce (MCE); finance (MAF); humanistic studies (MEH); international business for Latin America (MNL); marketing (MMT); science (MCP). Part-time and evening/weekend programs available. Postbaccalaureate distance learning degree programs offered (minimal on-campus study). *Degree requirements:* For master's, thesis (for some programs). *Entrance requirements:* For master's, PAEP College Board. Electronic applications accepted.

Instituto Tecnológico y de Estudios Superiores de Monterrey, Campus Ciudad de México, Virtual University Division, Ciudad de Mexico, Mexico. Offers administration of information technologies (MA); computer sciences (MA); education (MA, PhD); educational technology (MA); environmental engineering (MA); environmental systems (MA); humanistic studies (MA); industrial engineering (MA); international business for Latin America (MA); quality systems (MA); quality systems and productivity (MA). Part-time and evening/weekend programs available. Postbaccalaureate distance learning degree programs offered (minimal on-campus study). *Entrance requirements:* For master's and doctorate, Instituto entrance exam. Additional exam requirements/recommendations for international students: Required—TOEFL.

Instituto Tecnológico y de Estudios Superiores de Monterrey, Campus Ciudad Juárez, Program in Education, Ciudad Juárez, Mexico. Offers M Ed.

Instituto Tecnológico y de Estudios Superiores de Monterrey, Campus Ciudad Obregón, Programs in Education, Ciudad Obregón, Mexico. Offers cognitive development (ME); communications (ME); mathematics (ME).

Instituto Tecnológico y de Estudios Superiores de Monterrey, Campus Estado de México, Professional and Graduate Division, Estado de Mexico, Mexico. Offers administration of information technologies (MITA); architecture (M Arch); business administration (GMBA, MBA); computer sciences (MCS, PhD); education (M Ed); educational institution administration (MAD); educational technology and innovation (PhD); electronic commerce (MEC); environmental systems (MS); finance (MAF); humanistic studies (MHS); information sciences and knowledge management (MISKM); information systems (MS); manufacturing systems (MS); marketing (MEM); quality systems and productivity (MS); science and materials engineering (PhD); telecommunications management (MTM). Part-time programs available. Postbaccalaureate distance learning degree programs offered (minimal on-campus study). *Degree requirements:* For master's, one foreign language, thesis (for some programs); for doctorate, one foreign language, thesis/dissertation. *Entrance requirements:* For master's, E-PAEP 500, interview; for doctorate, E-PAEP 500, research proposal. Additional exam requirements/recommendations for international students: Required—TOEFL (minimum score 550 paper-based). *Faculty research:* Surface treatments by plasmas, mechanical properties, robotics, graphical computing, mechatronics security protocols.

Instituto Tecnológico y de Estudios Superiores de Monterrey, Campus Irapuato, Graduate Programs, Irapuato, Mexico. Offers administration (MBA); administration of information technology (MAIT); administration of telecommunications (MAT); architecture (M Arch); computer science (MCS); education (M Ed); educational administration (MEA); educational innovation and technology (DEIT); educational technology (MET); electronic commerce (MBA); environmental administration and planning (MEAP); environmental systems (MES); finances (MBA); humanistic studies (MHS); international management for Latin American executives (MIMLAE); library and information science (MLIS); manufacturing quality management (MMQM); marketing research (MBA).

Instituto Tecnológico y de Estudios Superiores de Monterrey, Campus Sonora Norte, Program in Education, Hermosillo, Mexico. Offers MA. *Entrance requirements:* For master's, MAT.

Inter American University of Puerto Rico, Arecibo Campus, Programs in Education, Arecibo, PR 00614-4050. Offers administration and educational supervision (MA Ed); counseling and guidance (MA Ed); curriculum and teaching (MA Ed), including biology education, English as a second language, history education, math education, Spanish; elementary education (MA Ed). *Degree requirements:* For master's, comprehensive exam, thesis optional. *Entrance requirements:* For master's, GRE, EXADEP, bachelor's degree in education or teaching license (administration and supervision) or courses in education and psychology (counseling and guidance), minimum GPA of 2.5 in last 60 credits.

Inter American University of Puerto Rico, Barranquitas Campus, Program in Education, Barranquitas, PR 00794. Offers curriculum and teaching (M Ed), including biology education, English as a second language, history education, mathematics education, Spanish; educational leadership and management (MA); elementary education (M Ed); information and library service technology (M Ed); special education (MA). *Degree requirements:* For master's, comprehensive exam, thesis optional. *Entrance requirements:* For master's, EXADEP, letter of recommendation. Electronic applications accepted.

Inter American University of Puerto Rico, Metropolitan Campus, Graduate Programs, Program in Education, San Juan, PR 00919-1293. Offers curriculum and instruction (Ed D); educational administration (Ed D); guidance and counseling (MA, Ed D); special education administration (Ed D). *Degree requirements:* For doctorate, comprehensive exam, thesis/dissertation. *Entrance requirements:* For doctorate, GRE, MAT, or EXADEP. Electronic applications accepted.

International Baptist College, Program in Education, Chandler, AZ 85286. Offers M Ed. *Degree requirements:* For master's, research paper/thesis. *Entrance requirements:* For master's, letter of recommendation.

Iona College, School of Arts and Science, Program in Education, New Rochelle, NY 10801-1890. Offers adolescence education: biology (MS Ed, MST); adolescence education: English (MS Ed, MST); adolescence education: Italian (MS Ed, MST); adolescence education: mathematics (MS Ed, MST); adolescence education: social studies (MS Ed, MST); adolescence education: Spanish (MS Ed, MST); adolescence special education 5-12 (MST); adolescence special education/literacy 5-12 (MS Ed); childhood 1-6/special education 1-6 (MST); childhood education (MST); early childhood/childhood (MST); educational leadership (MS Ed); literacy birth-grade 6/special education 1-6 (MS Ed); literacy education: birth-grade 6 (MS Ed). *Accreditation:* NCATE. Part-time and evening/weekend programs available. *Faculty:* 21 full-time (13 women), 13 part-time/adjunct (8 women). *Students:* 59 full-time (45 women), 101 part-time (78 women); includes 11 minority (2 Black or African American, non-Hispanic/Latino; 2 Asian, non-Hispanic/Latino; 7 Hispanic/Latino). Average age 26. 74 applicants, 66% accepted, 35 enrolled. In 2011, 46 master's awarded. *Degree requirements:* For master's, thesis or alternative. *Entrance requirements:* For master's, minimum GPA of 2.5 (MST), New York teaching certificate (MS Ed). Additional exam requirements/recommendations for international students: Required—TOEFL (minimum score 550 paper-based; 213 computer-based). *Application deadline:* Applications are processed on a rolling basis. Application fee: $50. Electronic applications accepted. *Expenses: Tuition:* Part-time $872 per credit. *Required fees:* $225 per term. *Financial support:* Unspecified assistantships available. Support available to part-time students. Financial award application deadline: 4/15; financial award applicants required to submit FAFSA. *Faculty research:* Reading/writing, educational technology, administration, early literacy assessment, literacy development. *Unit head:* Dr. Catherine O'Callaghan, Chair, 914-633-2210, Fax: 914-633-2608, E-mail: cocallaghan@iona.edu. *Application contact:* Dr. Jeanne Zaino, Interim Dean, School of Arts and Science, 914-633-2112, Fax: 914-633-2023, E-mail: jzaino@iona.edu.

Jackson State University, Graduate School, College of Education and Human Development, Jackson, MS 39217. Offers MS, MS Ed, Ed D, PhD, Ed S. *Accreditation:* NCATE. Part-time and evening/weekend programs available. Terminal master's awarded for partial completion of doctoral program. *Degree requirements:* For master's, comprehensive exam; for doctorate, comprehensive exam, thesis/dissertation. *Entrance requirements:* For master's, GRE General Test; for doctorate, MAT, teaching experience. Additional exam requirements/recommendations for international students: Required—TOEFL (minimum score 520 paper-based; 195 computer-based; 67 iBT).

Jacksonville State University, College of Graduate Studies and Continuing Education, College of Education and Professional Studies, Jacksonville, AL 36265-1602. Offers MS, MS Ed, Ed S. *Accreditation:* NCATE. Part-time and evening/weekend programs available. *Degree requirements:* For master's, comprehensive exam, thesis (for some programs). *Entrance requirements:* For master's, GRE General Test or MAT. Additional exam requirements/recommendations for international students: Required—TOEFL (minimum score 500 paper-based; 173 computer-based; 61 iBT). Electronic applications accepted. *Expenses:* Tuition, state resident: part-time $336 per hour. Tuition, nonresident: part-time $672 per hour. Part-time tuition and fees vary according to degree level.

Jacksonville University, School of Education, Jacksonville, FL 32211. Offers educational leadership (M Ed); instructional leadership and organizational development (M Ed); sport management and leadership (M Ed). Part-time and evening/weekend programs available. *Degree requirements:* For master's, comprehensive exam. *Entrance requirements:* For master's, GRE General Test, minimum GPA of 3.0. Additional exam requirements/recommendations for international students: Required—TOEFL (minimum score 550 paper-based), TWE. *Expenses:* Contact institution.

John Carroll University, Graduate School, Department of Education and Allied Studies, University Heights, OH 44118-4581. Offers administration (M Ed, MA); educational and school psychology (M Ed, MA); professional teacher education (M Ed, MA); school based adolescent-young adult education (M Ed); school based early childhood education (M Ed); school based middle childhood education (M Ed); school based multi-age education (M Ed); school counseling (M Ed, MA). *Accreditation:* NCATE. Part-time and evening/weekend programs available. *Degree requirements:* For master's, comprehensive exam, research essay or thesis (MA only). *Entrance requirements:* For master's, GRE General Test or MAT, minimum GPA of 2.75. *Faculty research:* Children's literacy, diversity issues, teaching development, impact of technology.

John F. Kennedy University, School of Education and Liberal Arts, Department of Education, Pleasant Hill, CA 94523-4817. Offers MAT. Part-time and evening/weekend programs available. *Degree requirements:* For master's, thesis. *Entrance requirements:* For master's, California Basic Educational Skills Test, NTE, interview. Additional exam requirements/recommendations for international students: Required—TOEFL.

The Johns Hopkins University, School of Education, Department of Interdisciplinary Studies in Education, Baltimore, MD 21218. Offers earth/space science (Certificate); education (MS), including educational studies; health care education (MEHP); mind, brain, and teaching (Certificate); teaching the adult learner (Certificate); urban education (Certificate). Part-time and evening/weekend programs available. Postbaccalaureate distance learning degree programs offered (minimal on-campus study). *Degree requirements:* For master's, capstone course. *Entrance requirements:* For master's and Certificate, minimum undergraduate GPA of 3.0. Additional exam requirements/recommendations for international students: Required—TOEFL (minimum score 600 paper-based; 250 computer-based; 100 iBT). Electronic applications accepted. *Faculty research:* Neuro-education, urban school reform, leadership development, teacher leadership, charter schools, techniques for teaching reading to adolescents with delayed reading skills, school culture.

The Johns Hopkins University, School of Education, Department of Teacher Development and Leadership, Baltimore, MD 21218-2699. Offers adolescent literacy education (Certificate); data-based decision making and organizational improvement (Certificate); education (MS), including reading, school administration and supervision, technology for educators; educational leadership for independent schools (Certificate); effective teaching of reading (Certificate); emergent literacy education (Certificate); English as a second language instruction (Certificate); gifted education (Certificate); leadership for school, family, and community collaboration (Certificate); leadership in technology integration (Certificate); school administration and supervision (Certificate); teacher development and leadership (Ed D); teacher leadership (Certificate). Part-time and evening/weekend programs available. Postbaccalaureate distance learning degree programs offered (minimal on-campus study). *Degree requirements:* For master's and Certificate, portfolio; for doctorate, comprehensive exam (for some programs), thesis/dissertation, portfolio or comprehensive exam. *Entrance requirements:* For master's and Certificate, bachelor's degree; minimum undergraduate GPA of 3.0; essay/statement of goals; for doctorate, GRE, essay/statement of goals; three letters of recommendation; curriculum vitae/resume; K-12 professional experience; interview; writing assessment. Additional exam requirements/recommendations for international students: Required—TOEFL (minimum score 600 paper-based; 250 computer-based; 100 iBT). Electronic applications accepted. *Faculty research:* Application of psychoanalytic concepts to teaching, schools, and education reform; adolescent literacies; use of emerging technologies for teaching, learning, and school leadership; quantitative analyses of the social contexts of education; school, family, and community collaboration; program evaluation methodologies.

The Johns Hopkins University, School of Education, Department of Teacher Preparation, Baltimore, MD 21218. Offers early childhood education (MAT); education (MS), including educational studies; elementary education (MAT); English for speakers of other languages (MAT); K-8 mathematics lead-teacher (Certificate); K-8 science lead-teacher (Certificate); secondary education (MAT), including biology, chemistry, earth/space/environmental science, English, French, mathematics, physics, social studies, Spanish. Part-time and evening/weekend programs available. *Degree requirements:* For master's, portfolio, PRAXIS II, internship. *Entrance requirements:* For master's, PRAXIS I, SAT, ACT, or GRE (MAT), minimum undergraduate GPA of 3.0, interview, 1 letter of recommendation, curriculum vitae/resume; for Certificate, bachelor's degree, minimum undergraduate GPA of 3.0, essay/statement of goals, interview. Additional exam requirements/recommendations for international students: Required—TOEFL (minimum score 600 paper-based; 250 computer-based; 100 iBT). Electronic applications accepted. *Faculty research:* Teacher retention, STEM education reform, alternative certification programs, school-university partnerships, urban education, action research/data-informed instruction, family engagement.

Johnson & Wales University, The Alan Shawn Feinstein Graduate School, MAT Program in Teacher Education, Providence, RI 02903-3703. Offers business education and secondary special education (MAT); elementary education and elementary special education (MAT); elementary education and elementary/secondary special education (MAT); elementary education and secondary special education (MAT); food service education (MAT). Part-time and evening/weekend programs available. *Entrance requirements:* For master's, MAT, minimum GPA of 2.75. Additional exam requirements/recommendations for international students: Required—TOEFL (minimum score 550 paper-based; 210 computer-based) or IELTS (recommended). *Faculty research:* Secondary education, student teaching, educational reform, evaluation procedures.

Johnson & Wales University, The Alan Shawn Feinstein Graduate School, M Ed Program in Teaching and Learning, Providence, RI 02903-3703. Offers M Ed. Evening/weekend programs available. *Entrance requirements:* For master's, bachelor's degree with minimum GPA of 2.75 from accredited institution of higher education, valid teaching license. Additional exam requirements/recommendations for international students: Required—TOEFL (minimum score 80 iBT), TOEFL (minimum score 550 paper-based; 210 computer-based) or Michigan English Language Assessment Battery (minimum score 77).

Johnson State College, Graduate Program in Education, Johnson, VT 05656. Offers applied behavior analysis (MA Ed), including applied behavior analysis, autism, children's mental health; curriculum and instruction (MA Ed); gifted and talented (MA Ed); literacy (MA Ed); science education (MA Ed); secondary education (MA Ed); special education (MA Ed). Part-time programs available. *Degree requirements:* For master's, comprehensive exam, thesis or alternative. *Entrance requirements:* For master's, interview. Additional exam requirements/recommendations for international students: Required—TOEFL. *Application deadline:* For fall admission, 7/15 priority date for domestic students, 4/15 for international students; for spring admission, 11/1 priority date for domestic students, 8/15 for international students. Applications are processed on a rolling basis. Application fee: $35. *Expenses: Tuition, area resident:* Part-time $459 per credit hour. Tuition, nonresident: part-time $990 per credit hour. *Financial support:* Career-related internships or fieldwork, Federal Work-Study, institutionally sponsored loans, and unspecified assistantships available. Support available to part-time students. Financial award application deadline: 3/1; financial award applicants required to submit FAFSA. *Application contact:* Catherine H. Higley, Administrative Assistant, 800-635-2356 Ext. 1244, Fax: 802-635-1248, E-mail: catherine.higley@jsc.edu.

Johnson University, Teacher Education Program, Knoxville, TN 37998-1001. Offers Bible and educational technology (MA); holistic education (MA). Part-time programs available. *Degree requirements:* For master's, multimedia action research presentation. *Entrance requirements:* For master's, interview, minimum GPA of 3.0, portfolio, teaching license. Additional exam requirements/recommendations for international students: Required—TOEFL. *Faculty research:* Instructional technology.

Jones International University, School of Education, Centennial, CO 80112. Offers adult education (M Ed); corporate training and knowledge management (M Ed); curriculum and instruction (M Ed), including elementary teacher licensure, secondary teacher licensure; e-learning technology and design (M Ed); educational leadership and administration (M Ed); educational leadership and administration: principal and administrator licensure (M Ed); elementary curriculum instruction and assessment (M Ed); higher education leadership and administration (M Ed); K-12 instructional technology (M Ed); K-12 instructional technology: teacher licensure (M Ed); secondary curriculum instruction and assessment (M Ed); technology and design (M Ed). Part-time and evening/weekend programs available. Postbaccalaureate distance learning degree programs offered (no on-campus study). *Entrance requirements:* For master's, minimum cumulative GPA of 2.5. Additional exam requirements/recommendations for international students: Recommended—TOEFL (minimum score 550 paper-based; 213 computer-based). Electronic applications accepted.

Judson University, Graduate Programs, Program in Education with ESL/Bilingual Endorsement, Elgin, IL 60123-1498. Offers M Ed. Part-time programs available. *Degree requirements:* For master's, thesis, portfolio. *Entrance requirements:* For master's, bachelor's degree with minimum GPA of 3.0; letters of reference. Additional exam requirements/recommendations for international students: Required—TOEFL (minimum score 550 paper-based; 213 computer-based). Application fee: $40. Electronic applications accepted. *Expenses: Tuition:* Full-time $9500. *Required fees:* $350. Tuition and fees vary according to course load and program. *Financial support:* Partial tuition reimbursement from some school districts available. Financial award applicants required to submit FAFSA. *Faculty research:* Bilingual education, multicultural policies and subject integration, legal issues in the classroom, curriculum planning and design, differentiated instruction, inclusive classrooms, cross-curricular integration. *Unit head:* Dr. Kathy Miller, Dean, School of Education, 847-628-1088, E-mail: dsimmons@judsonu.edu. *Application contact:* Maria Aguirre, Assistant to the Registrar for Graduate Programs, 847-628-1160, E-mail: maguirre@judsonu.edu. Web site: http://www.judsonu.edu/MEDESLBilingual/.

Kansas State University, Graduate School, College of Education, Manhattan, KS 66506. Offers MS, Ed D, PhD. *Accreditation:* NCATE. Part-time and evening/weekend programs available. Postbaccalaureate distance learning degree programs offered. *Faculty:* 40 full-time (25 women), 15 part-time/adjunct (6 women). *Students:* 179 full-time (123 women), 629 part-time (441 women); includes 115 minority (45 Black or African American, non-Hispanic/Latino; 6 American Indian or Alaska Native, non-Hispanic/Latino; 10 Asian, non-Hispanic/Latino; 44 Hispanic/Latino; 2 Native Hawaiian or other Pacific Islander, non-Hispanic/Latino; 8 Two or more races, non-Hispanic/Latino), 20 international. Average age 36. 410 applicants, 64% accepted, 131 enrolled. In 2011, 233 master's, 24 doctorates awarded. Terminal master's awarded for partial completion of doctoral program. *Degree requirements:* For master's, thesis or alternative, oral or comprehensive exam; for doctorate, thesis/dissertation, residency. *Entrance requirements:* For master's and doctorate, GRE or MAT. Additional exam requirements/recommendations for international students: Required—GRE General Test or TOEFL. *Application deadline:* For fall admission, 2/1 priority date for domestic students, 2/1 for international students; for spring admission, 8/1 priority date for domestic students, 8/1 for international students. Applications are processed on a rolling basis. Application fee: $40 ($55 for international students). Electronic applications accepted. *Financial support:* In 2011–12, 11 research assistantships (averaging $17,781 per year), 17 teaching assistantships with full tuition reimbursements (averaging $13,213 per year) were awarded; career-related internships or fieldwork, Federal Work-Study, institutionally sponsored loans, and scholarships/grants also available. Support available to part-time students. Financial award application deadline: 3/1; financial award applicants required to submit FAFSA. *Faculty research:* Teacher preparation, program evaluation, science education, ESL-bilingual education, rural issues in education. *Total annual research expenditures:* $6 million. *Unit head:* Michael Holen, Dean, 785-532-5525, Fax: 785-532-7304, E-mail: mholen@ksu.edu. *Application contact:* Paul R. Burden, Assistant Dean, 785-532-5595, Fax: 785-532-7304, E-mail: burden@ksu.edu. Web site: http://www.coe.k-state.edu/.

Kaplan University, Davenport Campus, School of Teacher Education, Davenport, IA 52807-2095. Offers education (M Ed); secondary education (M Ed); teaching and learning (MA); teaching literacy and language: grades 6-12 (MA); teaching literacy and language: grades K-6 (MA); teaching mathematics: grades 6-8 (MA); teaching mathematics: grades 9-12 (MA); teaching mathematics: grades K-5 (MA); teaching science: grades 6-12 (MA); teaching science: grades K-6 (MA); teaching students with special needs (MA); teaching with technology (MA). Part-time and evening/weekend programs available. Postbaccalaureate distance learning degree programs offered (no on-campus study). *Entrance requirements:* Additional exam requirements/recommendations for international students: Required—TOEFL (minimum score 550 paper-based; 218 computer-based; 80 iBT).

Kean University, College of Education, Union, NJ 07083. Offers MA, MS. *Accreditation:* NCATE. *Faculty:* 57 full-time (39 women). *Students:* 254 full-time (215 women), 544 part-time (452 women); includes 221 minority (73 Black or African American, non-Hispanic/Latino; 2 American Indian or Alaska Native, non-Hispanic/Latino; 26 Asian, non-Hispanic/Latino; 117 Hispanic/Latino; 3 Two or more races, non-Hispanic/Latino), 8 international. Average age 32. 626 applicants, 58% accepted, 265 enrolled. In 2011, 200 master's awarded. *Degree requirements:* For master's, comprehensive exam, thesis, practicum, portfolio, field experience. *Entrance requirements:* Additional exam requirements/recommendations for international students: Required—TOEFL (minimum score 79 iBT). *Application deadline:* For fall admission, 6/1 for domestic and international students; for spring admission, 12/1 for domestic and international students. Applications are processed on a rolling basis. Application fee: $75 ($150 for international students). Electronic applications accepted. *Expenses:* Tuition, state resident: full-time $11,302; part-time $550 per credit. Tuition, nonresident: full-time $15,318; part-time $674 per credit. *Required fees:* $2849; $130 per credit. Tuition and fees vary according to degree level. *Financial support:* In 2011–12, 25 research assistantships with full tuition reimbursements (averaging $3,263 per year) were awarded; unspecified assistantships also available. Financial award applicants required to submit FAFSA. *Unit head:* Dr. Susan Polirstok, Dean, 908-737-3750, Fax: 908-737-3760, E-mail: fpolirsts@kean.edu. *Application contact:* Ann-Marie Kay, Assistant Director of Graduate Admissions, 908-737-5922, Fax: 908-737-5925, E-mail: akay@kean.edu. Web site: http://www.kean.edu/KU/College-of-Education.

Keene State College, School of Professional and Graduate Studies, Keene, NH 03435. Offers curriculum and instruction (M Ed); education leadership (PMC); educational leadership (M Ed); safety and occupational health applied science (MS); school counselor (M Ed, PMC); special education (M Ed); teacher certification (Postbaccalaureate Certificate). *Accreditation:* NCATE. Part-time and evening/weekend programs available. *Faculty:* 11 full-time (7 women), 15 part-time/adjunct (8 women). *Students:* 36 full-time (32 women), 69 part-time (54 women); includes 1 minority (American Indian or Alaska Native, non-Hispanic/Latino), 1 international. Average age 33. 48 applicants, 83% accepted, 32 enrolled. In 2011, 39 master's, 12 other advanced degrees awarded. *Entrance requirements:* For master's, PRAXIS I, resume; minimum GPA of 2.5. Additional exam requirements/recommendations for international students: Required—TOEFL (minimum score 550 paper-based; 173 computer-based; 61 iBT). *Application deadline:* For fall admission, 4/1 for domestic students; for spring admission, 12/1 for domestic students. Applications are processed on a rolling basis. Application fee: $50. Electronic applications accepted. *Expenses:* Tuition, state resident: part-time $420 per credit. Tuition, nonresident: part-time $460 per credit. Tuition and fees vary according to course load. *Financial support:* Research assistantships, career-related internships or fieldwork, Federal Work-Study, institutionally sponsored loans, and unspecified assistantships available. Support available to part-time students. Financial award application deadline: 3/1; financial award applicants required to submit FAFSA. *Unit head:* Dr. Melinda Treadwell, Dean, 603-358-2220, E-mail: mtreadwe@keene.edu. *Application contact:* Peggy Richmond, Director of Admissions, 603-358-2276, Fax: 603-358-2767, E-mail: admissions@keene.edu. Web site: http://www.keene.edu/ps/.

Keiser University, Master of Science in Education Program, Fort Lauderdale, FL 33309. Offers college administration (MS Ed); leadership (MS Ed); teaching and learning (MS Ed). Part-time programs available. Postbaccalaureate distance learning degree programs offered (no on-campus study). *Entrance requirements:* For master's, minimum GPA of 2.7 from an accredited institution. Additional exam requirements/recommendations for international students: Required—TOEFL. Electronic applications accepted.

Kennesaw State University, Leland and Clarice C. Bagwell College of Education, Kennesaw, GA 30144-5591. Offers M Ed, MAT, Ed D, Ed S. *Accreditation:* NCATE. Part-time programs available. *Students:* 162 full-time (121 women), 257 part-time (202 women); includes 88 minority (58 Black or African American, non-Hispanic/Latino; 12 Asian, non-Hispanic/Latino; 12 Hispanic/Latino; 6 Two or more races, non-Hispanic/Latino), 3 international. Average age 36. 86 applicants, 80% accepted, 51 enrolled. In 2011, 198 master's, 16 doctorates, 31 other advanced degrees awarded. *Degree requirements:* For master's, thesis or alternative. *Entrance requirements:* For master's, GRE General Test, minimum GPA of 2.75, renewable teaching certificate. Additional exam requirements/recommendations for international students: Required—TOEFL (minimum score 550 paper-based; 213 computer-based; 80 iBT), IELTS (minimum score 6). *Application deadline:* For fall admission, 7/1 for domestic and international students; for spring admission, 10/1 for domestic and international students. Application fee: $60. Electronic applications accepted. *Expenses:* Tuition, state resident: full-time $3000; part-time $250 per semester hour. Tuition, nonresident: full-time $10,836; part-time $903 per semester hour. *Required fees:* $774 per semester. *Financial support:* Federal Work-Study available. Support available to part-time students. Financial award application deadline: 4/1; financial award applicants required to submit FAFSA. *Unit head:* Dr. Arlinda Eaton, Dean, 770-423-6117, Fax: 770-423-6567. *Application contact:* Alisha Bello, Administrative Coordinator, 770-423-6043, Fax: 770-420-4435, E-mail: abello2@kennesaw.edu. Web site: http://www.kennesaw.edu/education/.

Kent State University, Graduate School of Education, Health, and Human Services, Kent, OH 44242-0001. Offers M Ed, MA, MAT, MPH, MS, Au D, PhD, Ed S. *Accreditation:* NCATE. Part-time and evening/weekend programs available. Postbaccalaureate distance learning degree programs offered. *Faculty:* 271 full-time (165 women), 220 part-time/adjunct (160 women). *Students:* 981 full-time (754 women), 671 part-time (514 women); includes 152 minority (94 Black or African American, non-Hispanic/Latino; 1 American Indian or Alaska Native, non-Hispanic/Latino; 35 Asian, non-Hispanic/Latino; 21 Hispanic/Latino; 1 Native Hawaiian or other Pacific Islander, non-Hispanic/Latino). 1,343 applicants, 44% accepted. In 2011, 543 master's, 35 doctorates, 35 other advanced degrees awarded. *Degree requirements:* For master's, thesis (for some programs); for doctorate, comprehensive exam, thesis/dissertation. *Entrance requirements:* For doctorate and Ed S, GRE General Test. Additional exam requirements/recommendations for international students: Required—TOEFL (minimum score 525 paper-based; 197 computer-based; 65 iBT). *Application deadline:* Applications are processed on a rolling basis. Application fee: $30 ($60 for international students). Electronic applications accepted. *Expenses:* Tuition, state resident: full-time $8136; part-time $452 per credit hour. Tuition, nonresident: full-time $14,292; part-time $794 per credit hour. *Financial support:* In 2011–12, 32 fellowships with full tuition reimbursements (averaging $11,219 per year), 92 research assistantships with full tuition reimbursements (averaging $10,701 per year) were awarded; teaching assistantships, Federal Work-Study, scholarships/grants, unspecified assistantships, and 24 administrative assistantships (averaging $9,229 per year) also available. Financial award application deadline: 4/1; financial award applicants required to submit FAFSA. *Unit head:* Dr. Daniel Mahony, Dean, 330-672-2202, Fax: 330-672-3407, E-mail: dmahony@kent.edu. *Application contact:* Nancy Miller, Academic Program Coordinator, Office of Graduate Student Services, 330-672-2576, Fax: 330-672-9162, E-mail: nmiller1@kent.edu. Web site: http://www.educ.kent.edu/.

Kent State University at Stark, Graduate School of Education, Health and Human Services, Canton, OH 44720-7599. Offers curriculum and instruction studies (M Ed, MA).

Kutztown University of Pennsylvania, College of Education, Kutztown, PA 19530-0730. Offers M Ed, MA, MLS. *Accreditation:* NCATE. Part-time and evening/weekend programs available. *Faculty:* 32 full-time (21 women), 1 (woman) part-time/adjunct. *Students:* 120 full-time (81 women), 307 part-time (233 women); includes 21 minority (10 Black or African American, non-Hispanic/Latino; 1 American Indian or Alaska Native, non-Hispanic/Latino; 3 Asian, non-Hispanic/Latino; 6 Hispanic/Latino; 1 Two or more races, non-Hispanic/Latino). Average age 29. 113 applicants, 78% accepted, 54 enrolled. In 2011, 155 master's awarded. *Degree requirements:* For master's, comprehensive exam. *Entrance requirements:* For master's, GRE. Additional exam requirements/recommendations for international students: Required—TOEFL (minimum score 550 paper-based; 79 iBT). *Application deadline:* For fall admission, 8/1 priority date for domestic students, 8/1 for international students; for spring admission, 12/1 priority date for domestic students, 12/1 for international students. Applications are processed on a rolling basis. Application fee: $35. Electronic applications accepted. *Expenses:* Tuition, state resident: full-time $7488; part-time $416 per credit. Tuition, nonresident: full-time $11,232; part-time $624 per credit. *Financial support:* Career-related internships or fieldwork, Federal Work-Study, scholarships/grants, and unspecified assistantships available. Financial award application deadline: 3/1; financial award applicants required to submit FAFSA. *Unit head:* Dr. Darrell Garber, Dean, 610-683-4253, Fax: 610-683-4255, E-mail: garber@kutztown.edu. *Application contact:* Kelly D. Burr, Associate Director, Graduate Admissions, 610-683-4200, Fax: 610-683-1393, E-mail: graduate@kutztown.edu. Web site: http://www.kutztown.edu/academics/education.

LaGrange College, Graduate Programs, Department of Education, LaGrange, GA 30240-2999. Offers curriculum and instruction (M Ed, Ed S); middle grades (MAT); secondary education (MAT). Part-time and evening/weekend programs available. *Degree requirements:* For master's, comprehensive exam. *Entrance requirements:* For master's, GRE, MAT, minimum GPA of 2.5. Additional exam requirements/recommendations for international students: Required—TOEFL (minimum score 550 paper-based).

Lake Erie College, School of Professional and Innovative Studies, Painesville, OH 44077-3389. Offers curriculum and instruction (MS Ed); education (MS Ed); educational leadership (MS Ed); reading (MS Ed). Part-time and evening/weekend programs available. *Faculty:* 3 full-time (all women), 1 part-time/adjunct (0 women). *Students:* 20 part-time (15 women); includes 14 minority (all American Indian or Alaska Native, non-Hispanic/Latino). Average age 35. 5 applicants, 100% accepted, 1 enrolled. In 2011, 7 master's awarded. *Degree requirements:* For master's, comprehensive exam (for some programs), thesis optional, applied research project. *Entrance requirements:* For master's, GRE General Test (minimum score of 440 verbal or 500 quantitative) or minimum GPA of 2.75; bachelor's degree from accredited 4-year institution; references; essay. Additional exam requirements/recommendations for international students: Required—TOEFL (minimum score 550 paper-based; 79 computer-based). *Application deadline:* For fall admission, 8/1 priority date for domestic students, 6/1 for international students; for spring admission, 12/15 for domestic students, 10/1 for international students. Applications are processed on a rolling basis. Application fee: $30. Electronic applications accepted. Application fee is waived when completed online. *Expenses:* Contact institution. *Financial support:* Teaching assistantships, tuition waivers, and unspecified assistantships available. Financial award applicants required to submit FAFSA. *Faculty research:* Cooperative learning, portfolio assessment, education systems abroad, Web-based instruction. *Unit head:* Prof. Dale Sheptak, Interim Dean of the School of Professional and Innovative Studies/Assistant Professor, 440-375-7131, E-mail: dsheptak@lec.edu. *Application contact:* Christopher Harris, Dean of Admissions and Financial Aid, 800-916-0904, Fax: 440-375-7000, E-mail: admissions@lec.edu. Web site: http://www.lec.edu/med.

Lake Forest College, Graduate Program in Teaching, Lake Forest, IL 60045. Offers MAT.

Lakehead University, Graduate Studies, Faculty of Education, Thunder Bay, ON P7B 5E1, Canada. Offers educational studies (PhD); gerontology (M Ed); women's studies (M Ed). Part-time and evening/weekend programs available. *Degree requirements:* For master's, project or thesis. *Entrance requirements:* For master's, minimum B average. Additional exam requirements/recommendations for international students: Required—TOEFL. *Faculty research:* Art education, AIDS education, language arts education, gerontology, women's studies.

Lakeland College, Graduate Studies Division, Program in Education, Sheboygan, WI 53082-0359. Offers M Ed. *Accreditation:* Teacher Education Accreditation Council. *Degree requirements:* For master's, thesis. *Expenses:* Contact institution.

Lamar University, College of Graduate Studies, College of Education and Human Development, Beaumont, TX 77710. Offers M Ed, MS, DE, Ed D, Certificate. *Accreditation:* NCATE. Part-time and evening/weekend programs available. Postbaccalaureate distance learning degree programs offered. *Faculty:* 49 full-time (29 women), 3 part-time/adjunct (2 women). *Students:* 79 full-time (50 women), 2,586 part-time (1,908 women); includes 799 minority (438 Black or African American, non-Hispanic/Latino; 25 American Indian or Alaska Native, non-Hispanic/Latino; 34 Asian, non-Hispanic/Latino; 300 Hispanic/Latino; 2 Two or more races, non-Hispanic/Latino), 10 international. Average age 36. 1,584 applicants, 97% accepted, 592 enrolled. In 2011, 1,865 master's, 16 doctorates awarded. *Degree requirements:* For master's, comprehensive exam, thesis optional; for doctorate, comprehensive exam, thesis/dissertation. *Entrance requirements:* For master's, GRE General Test, minimum GPA of 2.5; for doctorate, GRE, interview. Additional exam requirements/recommendations for international students: Required—TOEFL. *Application deadline:* For fall admission, 8/1 for domestic students; for spring admission, 12/1 for domestic students. Applications are processed on a rolling basis. Application fee: $25 ($50 for international students). *Expenses:* Tuition, state resident: full-time $5430; part-time $272 per credit hour. Tuition, nonresident: full-time $11,540; part-time $577 per credit hour. *Required fees:* $1916. *Financial support:* Fellowships, research assistantships, teaching assistantships, career-related internships or fieldwork, Federal Work-Study, institutionally sponsored loans, and scholarships/grants available. Support available to part-time students. Financial award application deadline: 4/1. *Faculty research:* School dropouts, suicide prevention in public school students, school climate and gifted performance, teacher evaluation. *Unit head:* Dr. H. Lowery-Moore, Dean, 409-880-8661. *Application contact:* Dr. Lula Henry, Director of Professional Service, 409-880-8218.

Lander University, School of Education, Greenwood, SC 29649-2099. Offers elementary education (M Ed); teaching (MAT). *Accreditation:* NCATE. Part-time programs available. *Degree requirements:* For master's, comprehensive exam, thesis or alternative. *Entrance requirements:* For master's, GRE General Test. Additional exam requirements/recommendations for international students: Required—TOEFL (minimum score 550 paper-based; 213 computer-based). Electronic applications accepted.

Langston University, School of Education and Behavioral Sciences, Langston, OK 73050. Offers bilingual/multicultural (M Ed); elementary education (M Ed); English as a second language (M Ed); rehabilitation counseling (M Sc); urban education (M Ed). *Accreditation:* CORE; NCATE (one or more programs are accredited). Part-time programs available. *Degree requirements:* For master's, comprehensive exam, thesis optional. *Entrance requirements:* For master's, GRE, writing skills test, minimum GPA of 2.5, 3 letters of recommendation. Additional exam requirements/recommendations for international students: Required—TOEFL, TWE. *Faculty research:* Bilingual/multicultural education, financing post-secondary education.

La Salle University, School of Arts and Sciences, Program in Education, Philadelphia, PA 19141-1199. Offers MA. Part-time and evening/weekend programs available. *Degree requirements:* For master's, comprehensive exam. *Entrance requirements:* For master's, MAT. *Expenses:* Contact institution. *Faculty research:* Educational reform and social realities, adult development, curriculum design for special needs children, developmentally-based schooling.

Lasell College, Graduate and Professional Studies in Education, Newton, MA 02466-2709. Offers elementary education - grades 1-6 (M Ed); special education: moderate disabilities (pre-K-8) (M Ed). Part-time and evening/weekend programs available. Postbaccalaureate distance learning degree programs offered. *Faculty:* 2 full-time (both women). *Students:* 9 part-time (8 women); includes 2 minority (1 Black or African American, non-Hispanic/Latino; 1 Hispanic/Latino). Average age 26. 12 applicants, 42% accepted, 5 enrolled. *Degree requirements:* For master's, 18 credits in licensure requirements for initial licensure; 12 in licensure requirements plus 6 credits selected with advisor and department approval for professional licensure. *Entrance requirements:* For master's, bachelor's degree from an accredited institution. Additional exam requirements/recommendations for international students: Required—TOEFL (minimum score 550 paper-based; 213 computer-based; 79 iBT), IELTS. *Application deadline:* For fall admission, 8/31 priority date for domestic students, 6/30 for international students; for spring admission, 12/31 priority date for domestic students, 10/31 for international students. Applications are processed on a rolling basis. Electronic applications accepted. *Expenses: Tuition:* Part-time $575 per credit. *Required fees:* $70 per semester. *Financial support:* Available to part-time students. Application deadline: 8/31; applicants required to submit FAFSA. *Unit head:* Dr. Joan Dolamore, Dean of Graduate and Professional Studies, 617-243-2485, Fax: 617-243-2450, E-mail: gradinfo@lasell.edu. *Application contact:* Adrienne Franciosi, Director of Graduate Admission, 617-243-2214, Fax: 617-243-2450, E-mail: gradinfo@lasell.edu. Web site: http://www.lasell.edu/Academics/Graduate-and-Professional-Studies/Master-of-Education.html.

La Sierra University, School of Education, Riverside, CA 92515. Offers MA, MAT, Ed D, Ed S. Part-time and evening/weekend programs available. Terminal master's awarded for partial completion of doctoral program. *Degree requirements:* For doctorate, thesis/dissertation; for Ed S, thesis optional. *Entrance requirements:* For master's, minimum GPA of 3.0; for doctorate, GRE General Test, GRE Subject Test, minimum GPA of 3.3; for Ed S, minimum GPA of 3.3.

Lee University, Program in Education, Cleveland, TN 37320-3450. Offers classroom teaching (M Ed, Ed S); educational leadership (M Ed, Ed S); elementary/secondary education (MAT); secondary education (MAT); special education (M Ed); special education (secondary) (MAT). Part-time programs available. *Faculty:* 14 full-time (6 women), 5 part-time/adjunct (3 women). *Students:* 43 full-time (27 women), 176 part-time (107 women); includes 19 minority (4 Black or African American, non-Hispanic/Latino; 3 American Indian or Alaska Native, non-Hispanic/Latino; 1 Asian, non-Hispanic/Latino; 8 Hispanic/Latino; 3 Two or more races, non-Hispanic/Latino), 4 international. Average age 33. 52 applicants, 100% accepted, 38 enrolled. In 2011, 90 master's, 14 other advanced degrees awarded. *Degree requirements:* For master's, variable foreign language requirement, comprehensive exam, thesis, internship. *Entrance requirements:* For master's, MAT or GRE General Test, minimum GPA of 2.75, 3 letters of recommendation, interview, writing sample. Additional exam requirements/recommendations for international students: Required—TOEFL (minimum score 450 paper-based; 45 computer-based). *Application deadline:* For fall admission, 4/1 priority date for domestic students; for spring admission, 10/1 priority date for domestic students. Applications are processed on a rolling basis. Application fee: $25. *Expenses: Tuition:* Full-time $12,120; part-time $506 per credit hour. *Required fees:* $560; $305 per term. Part-time tuition and fees vary according to course load. *Financial support:* In 2011–12, 18 teaching assistantships (averaging $1,966 per year) were awarded; career-related internships or fieldwork, Federal Work-Study, institutionally sponsored loans, scholarships/grants, and unspecified assistantships also available. Financial award application deadline: 3/1; financial award applicants required to submit FAFSA. *Unit head:* Dr. Gary Riggins, Director, 423-614-8193. *Application contact:* Vicki Glasscock, Graduate Admissions Director, 423-614-8059, E-mail: vglasscock@leeuniversity.edu. Web site: http://www.leeuniversity.edu/academics/graduate/education.

Lehigh University, College of Education, Bethlehem, PA 18015. Offers M Ed, MA, MS, Ed D, PhD, Certificate, Ed S, Graduate Certificate, M Ed/MA, MBA/M Ed. Part-time and evening/weekend programs available. Postbaccalaureate distance learning degree programs offered (minimal on-campus study). *Faculty:* 31 full-time (18 women), 36 part-time/adjunct (25 women). *Students:* 181 full-time (138 women), 356 part-time (230 women); includes 44 minority (14 Black or African American, non-Hispanic/Latino; 21 Asian, non-Hispanic/Latino; 8 Hispanic/Latino; 1 Native Hawaiian or other Pacific Islander, non-Hispanic/Latino), 47 international. Average age 32. 511 applicants, 46% accepted, 85 enrolled. In 2011, 152 master's, 22 doctorates awarded. Terminal master's awarded for partial completion of doctoral program. *Degree requirements:* For master's, thesis (for some programs), internship; for doctorate, comprehensive exam, thesis/dissertation, internship. *Entrance requirements:* For doctorate, GRE and/or MAT. Additional exam requirements/recommendations for international students: Required—TOEFL (minimum score 600 paper-based; 250 computer-based; 93 iBT). *Application deadline:* For fall admission, 1/1 for domestic and international students; for spring admission, 11/1 for domestic and international students. Applications are processed on a rolling basis. Application fee: $65. Electronic applications accepted. *Expenses:* Contact institution. *Financial support:* In 2011–12, 118 students received support, including 6 fellowships with full and partial tuition reimbursements available (averaging $25,000 per year), 36 research assistantships with full and partial tuition reimbursements available (averaging $16,000 per year); teaching assistantships with full and partial tuition reimbursements available, career-related internships or fieldwork, Federal Work-Study, institutionally sponsored loans, scholarships/grants, tuition waivers (full and partial), and unspecified assistantships also available. Financial award application deadline: 3/1; financial award applicants required to submit FAFSA. *Faculty research:* Urban educational leadership, special education, instructional technology, school and counseling psychology, international education. *Unit head:* Dr. Gary M. Sasso, Dean, 610-758-3221, Fax: 610-758-6223, E-mail: gary.sasso@lehigh.edu. *Application contact:* Donna M. Johnson, Manager of Admissions and Recruitment, 610-758-3231, Fax: 610-758-6223, E-mail: dmj4@lehigh.edu. Web site: http://www.lehigh.edu/education.

Lehman College of the City University of New York, Division of Education, Bronx, NY 10468-1589. Offers MA, MS Ed. *Accreditation:* NCATE. Part-time and evening/weekend programs available.

Le Moyne College, Department of Education, Syracuse, NY 13214. Offers adolescent education (MS Ed, MST); adolescent education/special education (MS Ed, MST); adolescent English (grades 7-12) (MST); adolescent history (grades 7-12) (MST); childhood education (MS Ed); childhood education/special education (MS Ed); elementary education (MS Ed); general professional education (MS Ed); inclusive childhood education (MST); literacy education (birth to grade 6) (MS Ed); literacy education (grades 5-12) (MS Ed); school building leadership (MS Ed, CAS); school district business leader (MS Ed, CAS); school district leadership (MS Ed, CAS); secondary education (MS Ed); special education (MS Ed); students with disabilities-generalist (grades 7-12) (MS Ed); TESOL (teaching English to speakers of other languages) (MS Ed); urban studies (MS Ed). *Accreditation:* Teacher Education Accreditation Council. Part-time and evening/weekend programs available. *Faculty:* 9 full-time (6 women), 51 part-time/adjunct (28 women). *Students:* 61 full-time (47 women), 311 part-time (222 women); includes 31 minority (19 Black or African American, non-Hispanic/Latino; 3 American Indian or Alaska Native, non-Hispanic/Latino; 4 Asian, non-Hispanic/Latino; 5 Hispanic/Latino), 2 international. Average age 30. 242 applicants, 90% accepted, 180 enrolled. In 2011, 168 master's, 23 CASs awarded. *Degree requirements:* For master's, thesis. *Entrance requirements:* For master's, GRE General Test, bachelor's degree, 2 letters of recommendation, written statement, transcripts. Additional exam requirements/recommendations for international students: Required—TOEFL (minimum score 550 paper-based; 213 computer-based; 79 iBT). *Application deadline:* For fall admission, 4/1 priority date for domestic students, 4/1 for international students; for spring admission, 10/1 priority date for domestic students, 10/1 for international students. Applications are processed on a rolling basis. Application fee: $50. *Expenses:* Contact institution. *Financial support:* In 2011–12, 32 students received support. Career-related internships or fieldwork and health care benefits available. Support available to part-time students. Financial award applicants required to submit FAFSA. *Faculty research:* Minority teachers, special education, multiculturalism, literacy, technology, video games learning, autism, school district organization, service-learning, higher level problem solving, teacher leadership. *Unit head:* Dr. Suzanne L. Gilmour, Chair, Department of Education and Director of Graduate Education Programs, 315-445-4376, Fax: 315-445-4744, E-mail: gilmous@lemoyne.edu. *Application contact:* Kristen P. Trapasso, Director of Graduate Admission, 315-445-4265, Fax: 315-445-6027, E-mail: trapaskp@lemoyne.edu. Web site: http://www.lemoyne.edu/education.

Lenoir-Rhyne University, Graduate Programs, School of Education, Hickory, NC 28601. Offers MA. *Accreditation:* NCATE. Part-time and evening/weekend programs available. *Degree requirements:* For master's, comprehensive exam, thesis optional. *Entrance requirements:* For master's, GRE General Test or MAT, minimum undergraduate GPA of 2.7, graduate 3.0. Additional exam requirements/recommendations for international students: Required—TOEFL (minimum score 600 paper-based). Electronic applications accepted.

Lesley University, School of Education, Cambridge, MA 02138-2790. Offers curriculum and instruction (M Ed, CAGS); early childhood education (M Ed); educational studies (PhD); elementary education (M Ed); individually designed (M Ed); middle school education (M Ed); moderate special needs (M Ed); reading (M Ed, CAGS); science in education (M Ed); severe special needs (M Ed); special needs (CAGS); technology in education (M Ed, CAGS). *Accreditation:* Teacher Education Accreditation Council. Part-time and evening/weekend programs available. Postbaccalaureate distance learning degree programs offered (no on-campus study). *Faculty:* 36 full-time (27 women), 170 part-time/adjunct (129 women). *Students:* 552 full-time (437 women), 1,971 part-time (1,697 women); includes 364 minority (189 Black or African American, non-Hispanic/Latino; 19 American Indian or Alaska Native, non-Hispanic/Latino; 45 Asian, non-Hispanic/Latino; 83 Hispanic/Latino; 2 Native Hawaiian or other Pacific Islander, non-Hispanic/Latino; 26 Two or more races, non-Hispanic/Latino), 28 international. Average age 37. In 2011, 1,390 master's, 8 doctorates, 42 other advanced degrees awarded. *Degree requirements:* For master's, practicum; for doctorate, thesis/dissertation. *Entrance requirements:* For doctorate, GRE General Test or MAT, interview, master's degree, resume; for CAGS, interview, master's degree. Additional exam requirements/recommendations for international students: Required—TOEFL (minimum score 550 paper-based; 213 computer-based; 80 iBT). *Application deadline:* Applications are processed on a rolling basis. Application fee: $50. Electronic applications accepted. *Financial support:* In 2011–12, research assistantships (averaging $3,400 per year), teaching assistantships (averaging $3,400 per year) were awarded; career-related internships or fieldwork, Federal Work-Study, scholarships/grants, and unspecified assistantships also available. Support available to part-time students. Financial award application deadline: 4/15; financial award applicants required to submit FAFSA. *Faculty research:* Assessment in literacy, mathematics and science; autism spectrum disorders; instructional technology and online learning; multicultural education and ELL. *Unit head:* Dr. Mario Borunda, Dean, 617-349-8375, Fax: 617-349-8607, E-mail: mborunda@lesley.edu. *Application contact:* Rosie Davis, Senior Assistant Director of Admissions, 617-349-8851, Fax: 617-349-8313, E-mail: rdavis4@lesley.edu. Web site: http://www.lesley.edu/soe.html.

LeTourneau University, School of Graduate and Professional Studies, Longview, TX 75607-7001. Offers business administration (MBA); counseling (MA); education (M Ed); engineering (M Sc); health care administration (MS); psychology (MA); strategic leadership (MSL). Part-time and evening/weekend programs available. Postbaccalaureate distance learning degree programs offered (no on-campus study). *Faculty:* 19 full-time (5 women), 62 part-time/adjunct (25 women). *Students:* 12 full-time (6 women), 347 part-time (273 women); includes 191 minority (162 Black or African American, non-Hispanic/Latino; 2 American Indian or Alaska Native, non-Hispanic/Latino; 3 Asian, non-Hispanic/Latino; 20 Hispanic/Latino; 1 Native Hawaiian or other Pacific Islander, non-Hispanic/Latino; 3 Two or more races, non-Hispanic/Latino), 1 international. Average age 37. 138 applicants, 90% accepted, 120 enrolled. In 2011, 129 master's awarded. *Degree requirements:* For master's, thesis (for some programs). *Entrance requirements:* For master's, GRE (for counseling and engineering programs), minimum GPA of 2.8 (3.0 for counseling and engineering programs). Additional exam requirements/recommendations for international students: Required—TOEFL. *Application deadline:* Applications are processed on a rolling basis. Electronic applications accepted. *Expenses: Tuition:* Full-time $13,020; part-time $620 per credit hour. *Financial support:* In 2011–12, 15 students received support, including 5 research assistantships (averaging $9,600 per year); institutionally sponsored loans and unspecified assistantships also available. *Unit head:* Dr. Carol Green, Vice President, 903-233-4010, Fax: 903-233-3227, E-mail: carolgreen@letu.edu. *Application contact:* Chris Fontaine, Assistant Vice President for Enrollment Management and Marketing, 903-233-4071, Fax: 903-233-3227, E-mail: chrisfontaine@letu.edu. Web site: http://www.adults.letu.edu/.

Lewis University, College of Education, Romeoville, IL 60446. Offers advanced study in education (CAS), including general administrative, superintendent endorsement; curriculum and instruction: instructional technology (M Ed); early childhood education (MA); educational leadership (M Ed, MA); educational leadership for teaching and learning (Ed D); elementary education (MA); English as a second language (M Ed); instructional technology (M Ed); reading and literacy (M Ed, MA); secondary education (MA), including biology, chemistry, English, history, math, physics, psychology and social science; special education (MA). *Accreditation:* NCATE. Part-time and evening/weekend programs available. *Faculty:* 23 full-time (16 women), 40 part-time/adjunct (25 women). *Students:* 76 full-time (55 women), 388 part-time (312 women); includes 101 minority (56 Black or African American, non-Hispanic/Latino; 7 Asian, non-Hispanic/Latino; 36 Hispanic/Latino; 1 Native Hawaiian or other Pacific Islander, non-Hispanic/Latino; 1 Two or more races, non-Hispanic/Latino), 1 international. Average age 34. In 2011, 111 master's, 7 doctorates awarded. *Degree requirements:* For master's, thesis optional; for doctorate, thesis/dissertation. *Entrance requirements:* For master's, departmental qualifying exam, writing exam, minimum GPA of 2.75, 3 letters of recommendation, interview. Additional exam requirements/recommendations for international students: Required—TOEFL (minimum score 550 paper-based; 213 computer-based; 80 iBT). *Application deadline:* For fall admission, 5/1 for international students; for spring admission, 11/15 for international students. Applications are processed on a rolling basis. Application fee: $40. Electronic applications accepted. *Financial support:* Federal Work-Study, scholarships/grants, tuition waivers (partial), and unspecified assistantships available. Financial award application deadline: 5/1; financial award applicants required to submit FAFSA. *Unit head:* Dr. Jeanette Mines, Dean, 815-838-0500 Ext. 5316, Fax: 815-836-5879, E-mail: minesje@lewisu.edu. *Application contact:* Kelly Lofgren, Graduate Admission Counselor, 815-836-5704, Fax: 815-836-5578, E-mail: lofgreke@lewisu.edu.

Liberty University, School of Education, Lynchburg, VA 24502. Offers administration and supervision (M Ed); curriculum and instruction (M Ed); early childhood education (M Ed); educational leadership (Ed D, Ed S); educational technology and online instruction (M Ed); elementary education (M Ed, MAT); gifted education (M Ed); math specialist (M Ed); middle grades (M Ed); outdoor adventure sport (MS); reading specialist (M Ed); school counseling (M Ed); secondary education (M Ed, MAT); special education (M Ed, MAT); sports administration (MS); teaching and learning (Ed D, Ed S). *Accreditation:* NCATE. Part-time programs available. Postbaccalaureate distance learning degree programs offered (minimal on-campus study). *Students:* 2,245 full-time (1,572 women), 3,500 part-time (2,558 women); includes 1,141 minority (888 Black or African American, non-Hispanic/Latino; 19 American Indian or Alaska Native, non-Hispanic/Latino; 21 Asian, non-Hispanic/Latino; 123 Hispanic/Latino; 9 Native Hawaiian or other Pacific Islander, non-Hispanic/Latino; 81 Two or more races, non-Hispanic/Latino), 76 international. Average age 37. In 2011, 760 master's, 48 doctorates, 321 other advanced degrees awarded. *Degree requirements:* For doctorate, comprehensive exam, thesis/dissertation. *Entrance requirements:* For master's, GRE General Test or MAT (if taken in or before 1999), 2 letters of recommendation, minimum undergraduate GPA of 3.0, curriculum vitae; for doctorate, GRE General Test or MAT (if taken before 1999), minimum master's GPA of 3.0, 3 years of teacher experience; for Ed S, GRE General Test or MAT (if taken before 1999), minimum master's GPA of 3.0, 3 years of teaching experience. Additional exam requirements/recommendations for international students: Required—TOEFL (minimum score 600 paper-based; 250 computer-based). *Application deadline:* For fall admission, 6/1 priority date for domestic students; for spring admission, 11/1 for domestic students. Applications are processed on a rolling basis. Application fee: $50. Electronic applications accepted. *Expenses:* Contact institution. *Financial support:* Federal Work-Study and tuition waivers (partial) available. *Faculty research:* Self-determination, character education, bibliotherapy, learning styles, distance education. *Unit head:* Dr. Karen L. Parker, Dean, 434-582-2195, Fax: 434-582-2468, E-mail: kparker@liberty.edu. *Application contact:* Jay Bridge, Director of Graduate Admissions, 800-424-9595, Fax: 800-628-7977, E-mail: gradadmissions@liberty.edu. Web site: http://www.liberty.edu/academics/education/graduate/.

Lincoln Memorial University, Carter and Moyers School of Education, Harrogate, TN 37752-1901. Offers administration and supervision (M Ed, Ed S); counseling and guidance (M Ed); curriculum and instruction (M Ed, Ed D, Ed S); English (M Ed); executive leadership (Ed D); higher education administration (Ed D); human resource development (Ed D); leadership and administration (Ed D). Part-time and evening/weekend programs available. Postbaccalaureate distance learning degree programs offered. *Degree requirements:* For master's, comprehensive exam, thesis optional; for Ed S, comprehensive exam. *Entrance requirements:* For master's, PRAXIS, NTE, GRE, MAT, letters of recommendation; for Ed S, graduate transcripts. Additional exam requirements/recommendations for international students: Recommended—TOEFL. *Faculty research:* Brain compatible teaching and learning; poverty in Appalachia; leadership for change; ethics, moral responsibility and social justice; human and organizational learning.

Lindenwood University, Graduate Programs, School of Education, St. Charles, MO 63301-1695. Offers education (MA); educational administration (MA, Ed D, Ed S); human performance (MS); instructional leadership (Ed D, Ed S); library media (MA); professional and school counseling (MA); professional counseling (MA); school administration (Ed S); school counseling (MA); teaching (MA); teaching English to speakers of other languages (MA). Part-time and evening/weekend programs available. *Faculty:* 33 full-time (13 women), 176 part-time/adjunct (83 women). *Students:* 472 full-time (353 women), 1,772 part-time (1,373 women); includes 666 minority (605 Black or African American, non-Hispanic/Latino; 15 American Indian or Alaska Native, non-Hispanic/Latino; 5 Asian, non-Hispanic/Latino; 2 Hispanic/Latino; 4 Native Hawaiian or other Pacific Islander, non-Hispanic/Latino; 35 Two or more races, non-Hispanic/Latino), 24 international. Average age 36. 472 applicants, 87% accepted, 366 enrolled. In 2011, 747 master's, 42 doctorates, 69 other advanced degrees awarded. *Degree requirements:* For master's, thesis (for some programs), minimum GPA of 3.0; for doctorate, thesis/dissertation, minimum GPA of 3.0; for Ed S, comprehensive exam, project, minimum GPA of 3.0. *Entrance requirements:* For master's, interview, minimum GPA of 3.0, writing sample, letter of recommendation; for doctorate, GRE, minimum graduate GPA of 3.4, resume, interview, writing sample, 4 letters of recommendation; for Ed S, master's degree in education, relevant work experience. Additional exam requirements/recommendations for international students: Required—TOEFL (minimum score 550 paper-based; 213 computer-based; 80 iBT). *Application deadline:* For fall admission, 8/26 priority date for domestic students, 8/26 for international students; for spring admission, 1/27 priority date for domestic students, 1/27 for international students. Applications are processed on a rolling basis. Application fee: $30 ($100 for international students). Electronic applications accepted. *Expenses: Tuition:* Full-time $13,650; part-time $395 per credit hour. *Required fees:* $150 per semester. Tuition and fees vary according to course level and course load. *Financial support:* In 2011–12, 153 students received support. Career-related internships or fieldwork, institutionally sponsored loans, tuition waivers (partial), and unspecified assistantships available. Financial award application deadline: 6/30; financial award applicants required to submit FAFSA. *Unit head:* Dr. Cynthia Bice, Dean, 636-949-4618, Fax: 636-949-4197, E-mail: cbice@lindenwood.edu. *Application contact:* Brett Barger, Dean of Evening Admissions and Extension Campuses, 636-949-4934, Fax: 636-949-4109, E-mail: adultadmissions@lindenwood.edu.

Lipscomb University, Program in Education, Nashville, TN 37204-3951. Offers educational leadership (M Ed); English language learning (M Ed); instructional practice (M Ed); instructional technology (M Ed); learning organizations and strategic change (Ed D); math specialty (M Ed); special education (M Ed); teaching, learning, and leading (M Ed). *Accreditation:* NCATE. Part-time and evening/weekend programs available. *Faculty:* 18 full-time (10 women), 23 part-time/adjunct (16 women). *Students:* 377 full-time (281 women), 117 part-time (85 women); includes 55 minority (39 Black or African American, non-Hispanic/Latino; 4 American Indian or Alaska Native, non-Hispanic/Latino; 5 Asian, non-Hispanic/Latino; 7 Hispanic/Latino). Average age 32. 300 applicants, 66% accepted, 142 enrolled. In 2011, 190 master's awarded. *Degree requirements:* For master's, comprehensive exam, portfolio, research project and presentation; for doctorate, practical capstone project in experiential setting. *Entrance requirements:* For master's, MAT or GRE General Test, 2 reference letters, goals statement, writing sample, interview; for doctorate, MAT or GRE General Test, 3 reference letters, artifact of demonstrated academic excellence, written personal statements, interview. Additional exam requirements/recommendations for international students: Required—TOEFL (minimum score 570 paper-based; 230 computer-based). *Application deadline:* For fall admission, 8/29 priority date for domestic students; for spring admission, 1/15 priority date for domestic students. Applications are processed on a rolling basis. Application fee: $50 ($75 for international students). *Expenses: Tuition:* Full-time $16,830; part-time $935 per credit hour. Tuition and fees vary according to degree level and program. *Financial support:* In 2011–12, 67 students received support. Scholarships/grants and tuition waivers (partial) available. Financial award applicants required to submit FAFSA. *Faculty research:* Facilitative learning styles, leadership, student assessment, interactive multimedia inclusion, learning organizations and strategic change. *Unit head:* Dr. Deborah Boyd, Director, 615-966-6263, E-mail: deborah.boyd@lipscomb.edu. *Application contact:* Kristin Baese, Assistant Director of Enrollment and Outreach, 615-966-7628 Ext. 6081, Fax: 615-966-5173, E-mail: kristin.baese@lipscomb.edu. Web site: http://graduateeducation.lipscomb.edu/.

Lock Haven University of Pennsylvania, Department of Education, Lock Haven, PA 17745-2390. Offers alternative education (M Ed); teaching and learning (M Ed). *Accreditation:* NCATE. Part-time and evening/weekend programs available. Postbaccalaureate distance learning degree programs offered. *Degree requirements:* For master's, thesis. *Entrance requirements:* For master's, minimum undergraduate GPA of 3.0. Additional exam requirements/recommendations for international students: Required—TOEFL. Electronic applications accepted.

Long Island University–Brentwood Campus, School of Education, Brentwood, NY 11717. Offers childhood education (MS); early childhood education (MS); literacy (MS); mental health counseling (MS); school counseling (MS); special education (MS). Part-time and evening/weekend programs available.

Long Island University–Brooklyn Campus, School of Education, Brooklyn, NY 11201-8423. Offers MS, MS Ed, Certificate. *Accreditation:* Teacher Education Accreditation Council. Part-time and evening/weekend programs available. *Degree requirements:* For master's, thesis optional. *Entrance requirements:* For master's, 2 letters of recommendation. Additional exam requirements/recommendations for international students: Required—TOEFL (minimum score 500 paper-based; 173 computer-based). Electronic applications accepted.

Long Island University–C. W. Post Campus, School of Education, Brookville, NY 11548-1300. Offers MA, MS, MS Ed, Ed D, AC. *Accreditation:* Teacher Education Accreditation Council. Part-time and evening/weekend programs available. *Degree requirements:* For AC, internship. Electronic applications accepted.

Long Island University–Hudson at Westchester, Programs in Education-Teaching, Purchase, NY 10577. Offers early childhood education (MS Ed, Advanced Certificate); elementary education (MS Ed, Advanced Certificate); literacy education (MS Ed, Advanced Certificate); second language, TESOL, bilingual education (MS Ed, Advanced Certificate); special education and secondary education (MS Ed, Advanced Certificate). *Accreditation:* Teacher Education Accreditation Council. Part-time and evening/weekend programs available. *Degree requirements:* For master's, comprehensive exam.

Long Island University–Riverhead, Education Division, Riverhead, NY 11901. Offers applied behavior analysis (Advanced Certificate); childhood education (MS Ed), including childhood education, elementary education; literacy education (MS Ed); teaching students with disabilities (MS Ed). *Accreditation:* Teacher Education Accreditation Council. Part-time and evening/weekend programs available. *Faculty:* 1 full-time (0 women), 11 part-time/adjunct (7 women). *Students:* 25 full-time (23 women), 58 part-time (50 women); includes 6 minority (4 Black or African American, non-Hispanic/Latino; 2 Hispanic/Latino). Average age 30. In 2011, 38 master's awarded. *Degree requirements:* For master's, thesis (for some programs); for Advanced Certificate, comprehensive exam (for some programs). *Entrance requirements:* For master's, minimum GPA of 2.75, writing sample, letter of reference, interview, official college transcripts. Additional exam requirements/recommendations for international students: Required—TOEFL (minimum score 550 paper-based; 250 computer-based). *Application deadline:* Applications are processed on a rolling basis. Electronic applications accepted. Application fee is waived when completed online. *Expenses: Tuition:* Part-time $1028 per credit. *Financial support:* Scholarships/grants and tuition waivers (partial) available. Support available to part-time students. Financial award applicants required to submit FAFSA. *Unit head:* Dr. R. Lawrence McCann, Director, 631-287-8211, E-mail: admissions@southampton.liu.edu. *Application contact:* Andrea Borra, Director of Graduate Admissions and Program Administration, 631-287-8010 Ext. 8326, Fax: 631-287-8253, E-mail: andrea.borra@liu.edu.

Longwood University, Office of Graduate Studies, College of Education and Human Services, Farmville, VA 23909. Offers communication sciences and disorders (MS); community and college counseling (MS); curriculum and instruction specialist-elementary (MS), including mild disabilities, modern languages; curriculum and instruction specialist-secondary (MS), including English, mild disabilities, modern languages; educational leadership (MS); guidance and counseling (MS); literacy and culture (MS); school library media (MS). *Accreditation:* NCATE. Part-time and evening/weekend programs available. *Degree requirements:* For master's, comprehensive exam, thesis optional. *Entrance requirements:* For master's, GRE (communication sciences and disorders), minimum GPA of 2.75. Additional exam requirements/recommendations for international students: Required—TOEFL (minimum score 550 paper-based; 213 computer-based).

Louisiana State University and Agricultural and Mechanical College, Graduate School, College of Education, Baton Rouge, LA 70803. Offers M Ed, MA, MAT, MS, PhD, Ed S. *Accreditation:* NCATE. Part-time and evening/weekend programs available. *Students:* 261 full-time (179 women), 189 part-time (144 women); includes 117 minority (100 Black or African American, non-Hispanic/Latino; 1 American Indian or Alaska Native, non-Hispanic/Latino; 6 Asian, non-Hispanic/Latino; 6 Hispanic/Latino; 4 Two or more races, non-Hispanic/Latino), 14 international. Average age 31. 247 applicants, 62% accepted, 93 enrolled. In 2011, 171 master's, 23 doctorates, 11 other advanced degrees awarded. Terminal master's awarded for partial completion of doctoral program. *Degree requirements:* For doctorate, thesis/dissertation; for Ed S, thesis optional. *Entrance requirements:* For master's and doctorate, GRE General Test, minimum GPA of 3.0. Additional exam requirements/recommendations for international students: Required—TOEFL (minimum score 550 paper-based; 213 computer-based; 79 iBT) or IELTS (minimum score 6.5). *Application deadline:* For fall admission, 1/25 priority date for domestic students, 5/15 for international students; for spring admission, 10/15 for international students. Applications are processed on a rolling basis. Application fee: $50 ($70 for international students). Electronic applications accepted. *Financial support:* In 2011–12, 310 students received support, including 5 fellowships (averaging $19,653 per year), 24 research assistantships with partial tuition reimbursements available (averaging $10,052 per year), 78 teaching assistantships with partial tuition reimbursements available (averaging $11,473 per year); career-related internships or fieldwork, Federal Work-Study, institutionally sponsored loans, health care benefits, tuition waivers (partial), and unspecified assistantships also available. Support available to part-time students. Financial award applicants required to submit FAFSA. *Faculty research:* Instructional learning, educational administration, exercise physiology, sports psychology, literacy education curriculum and instruction. *Total annual research expenditures:* $1.1 million. *Unit head:* Dr. Laura F. Lindsay, Dean, 225-578-1258, Fax: 225-578-2267, E-mail: aclind@lsu.edu. *Application contact:* Dr. Patricia Exner, Associate Dean, 225-578-2208, Fax: 225-578-2267, E-mail: pexner@lsu.edu. Web site: http://chse.lsu.edu/.

Louisiana State University in Shreveport, College of Business, Education, and Human Development, Program in Education, Shreveport, LA 71115-2399. Offers education curriculum and instruction (M Ed); educational leadership (M Ed); school counseling (M Ed). Part-time programs available. *Students:* 6 full-time (all women), 55 part-time (40 women); includes 14 minority (12 Black or African American, non-Hispanic/Latino; 1 Asian, non-Hispanic/Latino; 1 Hispanic/Latino). Average age 35. 34 applicants, 97% accepted, 13 enrolled. In 2011, 14 master's awarded. *Degree requirements:* For master's, orally-presented project, 200-hour internship (educational leadership). *Entrance requirements:* For master's, GRE, minimum GPA of 2.5; teacher certification; recommendations and interview (for educational leadership). Additional exam requirements/recommendations for international students: Required—TOEFL (minimum score 550 paper-based; 213 computer-based; 80 iBT). *Application deadline:* For fall admission, 6/30 for domestic and international students; for spring admission, 11/30 for domestic and international students. Applications are processed on a rolling basis. Application fee: $10 ($20 for international students). *Financial support:* In 2011–12, 5 research assistantships (averaging $2,150 per year) were awarded. *Unit head:* Dr. Julie Bergeron, Coordinator, 318-797-5033, Fax: 318-798-4144, E-mail: julie.bergeron@lsus.edu. *Application contact:* Christianne Wojcik, Director of Academic Services, 318-797-5247, Fax: 318-798-4120, E-mail: christianne.wojcik@lsus.edu.

Louisiana Tech University, Graduate School, College of Education, Ruston, LA 71272. Offers M Ed, MA, MS, Ed D, PhD. *Accreditation:* NCATE. Part-time programs available. *Degree requirements:* For doctorate, thesis/dissertation. *Entrance requirements:* For master's and doctorate, GRE General Test.

Lourdes University, Graduate School, Program in Education, Sylvania, OH 43560-2898. Offers endorsement in computer technology (M Ed). *Accreditation:* Teacher Education Accreditation Council. Evening/weekend programs available. *Entrance requirements:* Additional exam requirements/recommendations for international students: Required—TOEFL.

Loyola Marymount University, School of Education, Los Angeles, CA 90045. Offers MA, Ed D. *Accreditation:* NCATE. *Unit head:* Dr. Shane Martin, Dean, 310-338-7301, E-mail: smartin@lmu.edu. *Application contact:* Chake H. Kouyoumjian, Associate Dean of the Graduate Division, 310-338-2721, E-mail: ckouyoum@lmu.edu. Web site: http://soe.lmu.edu.

Loyola University Chicago, School of Education, Chicago, IL 60660. Offers M Ed, MA, Ed D, PhD, Certificate, Ed S. *Accreditation:* NCATE. Part-time and evening/weekend programs available. *Faculty:* 53 full-time (36 women), 53 part-time/adjunct (37 women). *Students:* 479 full-time (361 women), 247 part-time (176 women); includes 171 minority (67 Black or African American, non-Hispanic/Latino; 1 American Indian or Alaska Native, non-Hispanic/Latino; 34 Asian, non-Hispanic/Latino; 60 Hispanic/Latino; 1 Native Hawaiian or other Pacific Islander, non-Hispanic/Latino; 8 Two or more races, non-Hispanic/Latino), 23 international. Average age 36. 744 applicants, 61% accepted, 187 enrolled. In 2011, 259 master's, 58 doctorates, 24 other advanced degrees awarded. *Degree requirements:* For master's, comprehensive exam (for some programs), thesis (for some programs); for doctorate, comprehensive exam, thesis/dissertation; for other advanced degree, comprehensive exam. *Entrance requirements:* For master's, minimum GPA of 3.0, 3 letters of recommendation, resume, transcripts; for doctorate, GRE, interview, minimum GPA of 3.0, 3 letters of recommendation, resume; for other advanced degree, GRE, interview, minimum GPA of 3.0, letters of recommendation, resume, transcripts. Additional exam requirements/recommendations for international students: Required—TOEFL (minimum score 550 paper-based; 213 computer-based; 79 iBT). Application fee: $50. Electronic applications accepted. Application fee is waived when completed online. *Expenses: Tuition:* Full-time $15,660; part-time $870 per credit hour. *Required fees:* $125 per semester. Tuition and fees vary according to course load and program. *Financial support:* In 2011–12, 113 fellowships with full tuition reimbursements (averaging $12,000 per year), 53 research assistantships with full tuition reimbursements (averaging $12,000 per year), 126 teaching assistantships (averaging $4,000 per year) were awarded; career-related internships or fieldwork, Federal Work-Study, institutionally sponsored loans, scholarships/grants, traineeships, health care benefits, tuition waivers (partial), and unspecified assistantships also available. Support available to part-time students. Financial award application deadline: 2/1; financial award applicants required to submit FAFSA. *Faculty research:* Policy studies, historical foundations, teacher education, research methodologies, comparative education. *Total annual research expenditures:* $2.1 million. *Unit head:* Dr. David Prasse, Dean, 312-915-6992, Fax: 312-915-6980, E-mail: dprasse@luc.edu. *Application contact:* Marie Rosin-Dittmar, Information Contact, 312-915-6800, E-mail: schleduc@luc.edu. Web site: http://www.luc.edu/education.

Loyola University Maryland, Graduate Programs, Department of Education, Baltimore, MD 21210-2699. Offers M Ed, MA, MAT, CAS, Certificate. *Accreditation:* NCATE. Part-time and evening/weekend programs available. *Faculty:* 93 full-time (64 women), 35 part-time/adjunct (21 women). *Students:* 135 full-time (114 women), 474 part-time (402 women); includes 90 minority (49 Black or African American, non-Hispanic/Latino; 1 American Indian or Alaska Native, non-Hispanic/Latino; 10 Asian, non-Hispanic/Latino; 16 Hispanic/Latino; 14 Two or more races, non-Hispanic/Latino), 8 international. Average age 30. In 2011, 273 master's, 2 other advanced degrees awarded. *Degree requirements:* For master's, thesis. *Entrance requirements:* Additional exam requirements/recommendations for international students: Required—TOEFL (minimum score 550 paper-based; 213 computer-based). *Application deadline:* For fall admission, 6/15 priority date for domestic students; for spring admission, 11/1 priority date for domestic students. Application fee: $50. Electronic applications accepted. *Financial support:* Research assistantships and unspecified assistantships available. Financial award application deadline: 4/15; financial award applicants required to submit FAFSA. *Unit head:* Dr. L. Mickey Fenzel, Interim Dean, 410-617-5343, E-mail: lfenzel@loyola.edu. *Application contact:* Maureen Faux, Executive Director, Graduate Admissions, 410-617-5020, Fax: 410-617-2002, E-mail: graduate@loyola.edu. Web site: http://www.loyola.edu/education/.

Lynchburg College, Graduate Studies, School of Education and Human Development, Lynchburg, VA 24501-3199. Offers clinical mental health counseling (M Ed); curriculum and instruction (M Ed), including instructional leadership, teacher licensure; educational leadership (M Ed); leadership studies (Ed D); reading (M Ed), including reading instruction, reading specialist; school counseling (M Ed); science education (M Ed); special education (M Ed). Part-time and evening/weekend programs available. *Faculty:* 28 full-time (14 women), 13 part-time/adjunct (8 women). *Students:* 85 full-time (59 women), 165 part-time (122 women); includes 33 minority (25 Black or African American, non-Hispanic/Latino; 1 American Indian or Alaska Native, non-Hispanic/Latino; 2 Asian, non-Hispanic/Latino; 4 Hispanic/Latino; 1 Two or more races, non-Hispanic/Latino), 8 international. Average age 34. In 2011, 46 master's awarded. *Degree requirements:* For master's, comprehensive exam (for some programs). *Entrance requirements:* For master's, GRE, minimum GPA of 3.0 (preferred), three letters of recommendation, official transcript (bachelor's, others as relevant), career goals statement. Additional exam requirements/recommendations for international students: Required—TOEFL (minimum score 550 paper-based; 213 computer-based; 79 iBT), IELTS (minimum score 6.5). *Application deadline:* For fall admission, 7/31 for domestic students, 6/1 for international students; for spring admission, 11/30 for domestic students, 10/15 for international students. Applications are processed on a rolling basis. Application fee: $30. Electronic applications accepted. Application fee is waived when completed online. *Expenses: Tuition:* Full-time $7740; part-time $430 per credit hour. *Financial support:* Career-related internships or fieldwork, scholarships/grants, and unspecified assistantships available. Financial award application deadline: 7/31; financial award applicants required to submit FAFSA. *Unit head:* Dr. Jan Stenette, Dean, School of Education and Human Development, 434-544-8662, Fax: 434-544-8483, E-mail: stennette@lynchburg.edu. *Application contact:* Anne Pingstock, Executive Assistant, Graduate Studies, 434-544-8383, Fax: 434-544-8483, E-mail: gradstudies@lynchburg.edu. Web site: http://www.lynchburg.edu/med.xml.

Lyndon State College, Graduate Programs in Education, Lyndonville, VT 05851-0919. Offers education (M Ed), including curriculum and instruction, reading specialist, special education, teaching and counseling; natural sciences (MST), including science education. Part-time and evening/weekend programs available. *Degree requirements:* For master's, exam or major field project. *Entrance requirements:* Additional exam requirements/recommendations for international students: Recommended—TOEFL (minimum score 500 paper-based; 173 computer-based). *Faculty research:* Impaired reading, cognitive style, counseling relationship.

Lynn University, Donald and Helen Ross College of Education, Boca Raton, FL 33431-5598. Offers educational leadership (M Ed, PhD); exceptional student education (M Ed); teacher preparation (PhD). Part-time and evening/weekend programs available. *Degree requirements:* For master's, thesis (for some programs); for doctorate, thesis/dissertation, qualifying paper. *Entrance requirements:* For master's, GRE, minimum undergraduate GPA of 3.0, resume, 2 letters of recommendation; for doctorate, GRE or GMAT, minimum GPA of 3.25, resume, 2 letters of recommendation. Additional exam requirements/recommendations for international students: Required—TOEFL (minimum score 550 paper-based; 213 computer-based). Electronic applications accepted. *Faculty research:* Non-traditional education, innovative curricula, multicultural education, simulation games.

Madonna University, Programs in Education, Livonia, MI 48150-1173. Offers Catholic school leadership (MSA); educational leadership (MSA); learning disabilities (MAT); literacy education (MAT); teaching and learning (MAT). *Accreditation:* NCATE. Part-time and evening/weekend programs available. *Degree requirements:* For master's, thesis or alternative. Electronic applications accepted.

Maharishi University of Management, Graduate Studies, Department of Education, Fairfield, IA 52557. Offers teaching elementary education (MA); teaching secondary education (MA). *Degree requirements:* For master's, thesis or alternative. *Entrance requirements:* For master's, GRE, minimum GPA of 3.0. Additional exam requirements/recommendations for international students: Required—TOEFL. *Faculty research:* Unified field-based approach to education, moral climate, scientific study of teaching.

Malone University, Graduate Program in Education, Canton, OH 44709. Offers curriculum and instruction (MA), including teacher leader endorsement; curriculum, instruction, and professional development (MA); educational leadership (MA), including principal license; intervention specialist (MA); reading (MA). Part-time and evening/weekend programs available. *Faculty:* 9 full-time (5 women), 8 part-time/adjunct (6 women). *Students:* 2 full-time (both women), 43 part-time (33 women); includes 2 minority (both Black or African American, non-Hispanic/Latino). Average age 36. 35 applicants, 91% accepted, 12 enrolled. In 2011, 11 master's awarded. *Degree requirements:* For master's, research project. *Entrance requirements:* For master's, minimum GPA of 3.0, teaching license. Additional exam requirements/recommendations for international students: Required—TOEFL (minimum score 550 paper-based; 213 computer-based; 79 iBT). *Application deadline:* Applications are processed on a rolling basis. *Expenses: Tuition:* Part-time $625 per semester hour. Part-time tuition and fees vary according to program. *Financial support:* Tuition waivers (partial) available. Support available to part-time students. Financial award application deadline: 6/30. *Faculty research:* Educational leadership styles: Jesus as master teacher, assessment accommodations for English language learners, preparing culturally proficient teachers, using naturally occurring text in the classroom to meet the syntactic needs of students with learning disabilities, using iPad instructional technology to meet the needs of students with disabilities. *Unit head:* Dr. Alice E. Christie, Director, 330-478-8541, Fax: 330-471-8563, E-mail: achristie@malone.edu. *Application contact:* Dan DePasquale, Senior Recruiter, 330-471-8381, Fax: 330-471-8343, E-mail: depasquale@malone.edu. Web site: http://www.malone.edu/admissions/graduate/education/.

Manchester College, Graduate Programs, Program in Education, North Manchester, IN 46962-1225. Offers M Ed. Part-time and evening/weekend programs available. Postbaccalaureate distance learning degree programs offered (minimal on-campus study). *Faculty:* 4 full-time (2 women). *Students:* 15 part-time (12 women). 24 applicants, 67% accepted, 15 enrolled. *Degree requirements:* For master's, 33 credits with minimum GPA of 3.0; culminating action research project or curriculum development project; final portfolio. *Entrance requirements:* For master's, baccalaureate degree from regionally-accredited institution; minimum cumulative undergraduate GPA of 3.0 or minimum of 9 semester hours of graduate coursework in the M Ed with minimum B average. Additional exam requirements/recommendations for international students: Required—TOEFL (minimum score 550 paper-based; 213 computer-based; 79 iBT). *Application deadline:* Applications are processed on a rolling basis. Application fee: $25. Electronic applications accepted. Application fee is waived when completed online. *Expenses:* Contact institution. *Financial support:* Application deadline: 5/1; applicants required to submit FAFSA. *Unit head:* Dr. Michael Slavkin, Director of Teacher Education, 260-982-5056, E-mail: mlslavkin@manchester.edu. Web site: http://graduateprograms.manchester.edu/ED/index.htm.

Manhattan College, Graduate Division, School of Education, Riverdale, NY 10471. Offers counseling (MA, MS, Advanced Certificate, Diploma), including bilingual pupil personnel services (Advanced Certificate), mental health counseling (MS, Advanced Certificate), school counseling (MA, Diploma); school building leadership (MS Ed, Professional Diploma); special education (MS Ed, Certificate, Professional Diploma), including autism spectrum disorder (Professional Diploma), bilingual special education (Certificate), dual childhood/special education (MS Ed), special education (MS Ed). *Accreditation:* Teacher Education Accreditation Council. Part-time and evening/weekend programs available. *Faculty:* 12 full-time (8 women), 47 part-time/adjunct (35 women). *Students:* 97 full-time (83 women), 172 part-time (142 women). 284 applicants, 91% accepted, 131 enrolled. In 2011, 69 master's, 17 other advanced degrees awarded. *Degree requirements:* For master's, thesis, internship. *Entrance requirements:* For master's, minimum GPA of 3.0. *Application deadline:* For fall admission, 8/10 priority date for domestic students; for spring admission, 1/7 priority date for domestic students. Applications are processed on a rolling basis. *Expenses: Tuition:* Full-time $14,850; part-time $825 per credit. *Required fees:* $390; $150. *Financial support:* In 2011–12, 1 research assistantship was awarded; Federal Work-Study, scholarships/grants, tuition waivers (partial), and unspecified assistantships also available. Financial award application deadline: 2/1. *Faculty research:* Adapted physical education, cross-training of preschool regular and special education teachers. *Unit head:* Dr. William Merriman, Dean, 718-862-7373, Fax: 718-862-8011. *Application contact:* William Bisset, Vice President for Enrollment, 718-862-7199, Fax: 718-862-8019, E-mail: william.bisset@manhattan.edu.

Manhattanville College, Graduate Studies, School of Education, Purchase, NY 10577-2132. Offers M Ed, MAT, MPS, Ed D. *Accreditation:* NCATE. Part-time and evening/weekend programs available. *Entrance requirements:* For master's, minimum undergraduate GPA of 3.0, 2 letters of recommendation. Additional exam requirements/recommendations for international students: Required—TOEFL (minimum score 550 paper-based; 213 computer-based). Electronic applications accepted.

See Display on next page and Close-Up on page 805.

Mansfield University of Pennsylvania, Graduate Studies, Department of Education and Special Education, Mansfield, PA 16933. Offers elementary education (M Ed); secondary education (MS); special education (M Ed). *Accreditation:* NCATE (one or more programs are accredited). Part-time and evening/weekend programs available. Postbaccalaureate distance learning degree programs offered (no on-campus study). *Degree requirements:* For master's, comprehensive exam, thesis optional. *Entrance requirements:* For master's, minimum GPA of 3.0. Additional exam requirements/recommendations for international students: Required—TOEFL (minimum score 550 paper-based; 220 computer-based). Electronic applications accepted. *Expenses:* Tuition, state resident: full-time $7488; part-time $416 per credit. Tuition, nonresident: full-time $11,232; part-time $624 per credit.

Marian University, School of Education, Indianapolis, IN 46222-1997. Offers MAT. *Accreditation:* NCATE. Part-time and evening/weekend programs available. *Entrance requirements:* For master's, PRAXIS I and/or PRAXIS II.

Marian University, School of Education, Fond du Lac, WI 54935-4699. Offers educational leadership (MAE, PhD); leadership studies (PhD); teacher development (MAE). PhD in leadership studies offered with Business Division. *Accreditation:* NCATE. Part-time programs available. *Faculty:* 20 full-time (11 women), 40 part-time/adjunct (23 women). *Students:* 29 full-time (23 women), 398 part-time (274 women); includes 18 minority (6 Black or African American, non-Hispanic/Latino; 3 American Indian or Alaska Native, non-Hispanic/Latino; 3 Asian, non-Hispanic/Latino; 6 Hispanic/Latino). Average age 36. 105 applicants, 80% accepted, 80 enrolled. In 2011, 227 master's, 7 doctorates awarded. *Degree requirements:* For master's, exam, field-based experience project, portfolio; for doctorate, comprehensive exam, thesis/dissertation, field-based experience. *Entrance requirements:* For master's, minimum GPA of 3.0, BA in education or related field, teaching license; for doctorate, GRE, MAT, resume, 2 writing samples, interview. Additional exam requirements/recommendations for international students: Required—TOEFL (minimum score 525 paper-based; 193 computer-based; 70 iBT). *Application deadline:* Applications are processed on a rolling basis. Application fee: $50. *Expenses: Tuition:* Part-time $428 per credit. Tuition and fees vary according to degree level and program. *Financial support:* Federal Work-Study and institutionally sponsored loans available. Support available to part-time students. Financial award application deadline: 3/1; financial award applicants required to submit FAFSA. *Faculty research:* At-risk youth, multicultural issues, values in education, teaching/learning strategies. *Unit head:* Sue Stoddart, Dean, 920-923-8099, Fax: 920-923-7663, E-mail: sstoddart@marianuniversity.edu. *Application contact:* Robert Bohnsack, Graduate Education Admissions, 920-923-8100, Fax: 920-923-7154, E-mail: bbohnsack@marianuniversity.edu. Web site: http://soe.marianuniversity.edu/.

Marietta College, Program in Education, Marietta, OH 45750-4000. Offers MA. *Accreditation:* NCATE. Part-time and evening/weekend programs available. *Degree requirements:* For master's, writing portfolio. *Entrance requirements:* For master's, MAT. *Faculty research:* Teaching of reading.

Marist College, Graduate Programs, School of Social and Behavioral Sciences, Poughkeepsie, NY 12601-1387. Offers education (M Ed, MA); mental health counseling (MA); school psychology (MA, Adv C). Part-time and evening/weekend programs available. *Degree requirements:* For master's, thesis optional. *Entrance requirements:* For master's, GRE General Test, letters of recommendation, minimum undergraduate GPA of 3.0, interview. Additional exam requirements/recommendations for international students: Required—TOEFL (minimum score 550 paper-based; 213 computer-based; 80 iBT); Recommended—IELTS (minimum score 6.5). Electronic applications accepted. *Faculty research:* AIDS prevention, educational intervention, humanistic counseling research, aging and development, neuroimaging.

Marlboro College, Graduate School, Program in Teaching with Technology, Marlboro, VT 05344. Offers MAT. Part-time and evening/weekend programs available. Postbaccalaureate distance learning degree programs offered (minimal on-campus study). *Degree requirements:* For master's, 30 credits including capstone project. *Entrance requirements:* For master's, letter of intent, 2 letters of recommendation, transcripts. Electronic applications accepted.

Marquette University, Graduate School, College of Education, Milwaukee, WI 53201-1881. Offers M Ed, MA, MS, PhD, Certificate. *Accreditation:* NCATE. Part-time programs available. *Faculty:* 24 full-time (15 women), 35 part-time/adjunct (26 women). *Students:* 107 full-time (80 women), 172 part-time (105 women); includes 45 minority (20 Black or African American, non-Hispanic/Latino; 1 American Indian or Alaska Native, non-Hispanic/Latino; 5 Asian, non-Hispanic/Latino; 14 Hispanic/Latino; 5 Two or more races, non-Hispanic/Latino), 5 international. Average age 30. 309 applicants, 50% accepted, 99 enrolled. In 2011, 74 master's, 14 doctorates, 5 other advanced degrees awarded. Terminal master's awarded for partial completion of doctoral program. *Degree requirements:* For master's, comprehensive exam, thesis (for some programs); for doctorate, thesis/dissertation, qualifying exam, supporting minor. *Entrance requirements:* For master's, GRE General Test or MAT, official transcripts from all current and previous colleges/universities except Marquette, three letters of recommendation, statement of purpose; for doctorate, GRE General Test, MAT, sample of written work, official transcripts from all current and previous colleges/universities except Marquette, three letters of recommendation, statement of purpose, resume/curriculum vitae; for Certificate, GRE General Test or MAT, master's degree. Additional exam requirements/recommendations for international students: Required—TOEFL (minimum score 530 paper-based; 78 computer-based). *Application deadline:* For fall admission, 1/15 for domestic and international students. Application fee: $50. *Expenses:* Contact institution. *Financial support:* In 2011–12, 155 students received support, including 2 fellowships with full and partial tuition reimbursements available, 11 research assistantships with full tuition reimbursements available; scholarships/grants, health care benefits, tuition waivers (partial), and unspecified assistantships also available. Support available to part-time students. Financial award application deadline: 2/15. *Faculty research:* Parenting, psychology of motivation, reading assessment, socialization of educational administrators, education philosophy of Cardinal Newman. *Total annual research expenditures:* $254,520. *Unit head:* Dr. Bill Henk, Dean, 414-288-7376. *Application contact:* Craig Pierce, Director of Graduate Admissions, 414-288-5740, Fax: 414-288-1902, E-mail: craig.pierce@marquette.edu. Web site: http://www.marquette.edu/education/.

Marshall University, Academic Affairs Division, Graduate School of Education and Professional Development, Huntington, WV 25755. Offers MA, MS, Ed D, Certificate, Ed S. *Accreditation:* NCATE. Part-time and evening/weekend programs available. *Faculty:* 46 full-time (23 women), 26 part-time/adjunct (18 women). *Students:* 359 full-time (274 women), 888 part-time (702 women); includes 60 minority (38 Black or African American, non-Hispanic/Latino; 2 American Indian or Alaska Native, non-Hispanic/Latino; 8 Asian, non-Hispanic/Latino; 10 Hispanic/Latino; 2 Two or more races, non-Hispanic/Latino), 12 international. Average age 34. In 2011, 305 master's, 19 doctorates, 21 other advanced degrees awarded. *Degree requirements:* For master's, thesis optional, comprehensive or oral assessment. *Entrance requirements:* Additional exam requirements/recommendations for international students: Required—TOEFL. *Application deadline:* For fall admission, 5/1 for domestic students; for spring admission, 12/1 for domestic students. Applications are processed on a rolling basis. Application fee: $40. Electronic applications accepted. *Financial support:* Career-related internships or fieldwork, Federal Work-Study, tuition waivers (full and partial), and unspecified assistantships available. Support available to part-time students. Financial award applicants required to submit FAFSA. *Unit head:* Dr. Teresa Eagle, Dean, 304-746-8924, E-mail: thardman@marshall.edu. *Application contact:* Information Contact, 304-746-1900, Fax: 304-746-1902, E-mail: services@marshall.edu. Web site: http://www.marshall.edu/gsepd/.

Martin Luther College, Graduate Studies, New Ulm, MN 56073. Offers instruction (MS Ed); leadership (MS Ed); special education (MS Ed). Part-time programs available. Postbaccalaureate distance learning degree programs offered. *Degree requirements:* For master's, capstone project or comprehensive exam. *Entrance requirements:* For master's, undergraduate degree in education from an accredited college or university, minimum undergraduate GPA of 3.0. Electronic applications accepted.

Mary Baldwin College, Graduate Studies, Program in Teaching, Staunton, VA 24401-3610. Offers elementary education (MAT); middle grades education (MAT). *Accreditation:* Teacher Education Accreditation Council.

Marygrove College, Graduate Division, Program in the Art of Teaching, Detroit, MI 48221-2599. Offers MAT. Postbaccalaureate distance learning degree programs offered (no on-campus study). *Degree requirements:* For master's, portfolio. *Entrance requirements:* For master's, MAT, interview, minimum undergraduate GPA of 3.0, teaching certificate.

Marylhurst University, Department of Education, Marylhurst, OR 97036-0261. Offers M Ed, MA. Part-time programs available. *Faculty:* 5 full-time (3 women), 25 part-time/adjunct (20 women). *Students:* 47 full-time (36 women), 36 part-time (29 women); includes 14 minority (1 Black or African American, non-Hispanic/Latino; 1 American Indian or Alaska Native, non-Hispanic/Latino; 4 Asian, non-Hispanic/Latino; 4 Hispanic/Latino; 4 Two or more races, non-Hispanic/Latino). Average age 35. 58 applicants, 81% accepted, 40 enrolled. In 2011, 54 master's awarded. *Degree requirements:* For master's, comprehensive exam. *Entrance requirements:* For master's, PRAXIS I or CBEST, resume, writing sample, fingerprint verification. Additional exam requirements/recommendations for international students: Required—TOEFL (minimum score 550 paper-based; 213 computer-based; 80 iBT). *Application deadline:* For fall admission, 3/1 priority date for domestic students, 3/1 for international students. Applications are processed on a rolling basis. Application fee: $50. *Expenses: Tuition:* Full-time $14,796; part-time $548 per quarter hour. Tuition and fees vary according to program. *Financial support:* Federal Work-Study and scholarships/grants available. Support available to part-time students. Financial award applicants required to submit FAFSA. *Unit head:* Dr. Jan Carpenter, Chair, 503-636-8141, Fax: 503-636-9526, E-mail: jcarpenter@marylhurst.edu. *Application contact:* Maruska Lynch, Graduate Admissions Specialist, 800-634-9982 Ext. 6322, Fax: 503-699-6320, E-mail: admissions@marylhurst.edu.

Marymount University, School of Education and Human Services, Program in Education, Arlington, VA 22207-4299. Offers elementary education (M Ed); English as a second language (M Ed); professional studies (M Ed); secondary education (M Ed); special education, general curriculum (M Ed). *Accreditation:* NCATE. Part-time and evening/weekend programs available. *Faculty:* 9 full-time (7 women), 7 part-time/adjunct (5 women). *Students:* 62 full-time (57 women), 103 part-time (86 women); includes 22 minority (3 Black or African American, non-Hispanic/Latino; 4 Asian, non-Hispanic/Latino; 10 Hispanic/Latino; 5 Two or more races, non-Hispanic/Latino), 13 international. Average age 31. 69 applicants, 100% accepted, 52 enrolled. In 2011, 79 master's awarded. *Degree requirements:* For master's, thesis or alternative. *Entrance requirements:* For master's, GRE or MAT and PRAXIS I or SAT/ACT and VCLA, 2 letters of recommendation, resume, interview. Additional exam requirements/recommendations for international students: Required—TOEFL (minimum score 600 paper-based; 250 computer-based; 96 iBT), IELTS (minimum score 6.5). *Application deadline:* For fall admission, 7/1 for international students. Applications are processed on a rolling basis. Application fee: $40. Electronic applications accepted. *Expenses: Tuition:* Part-time $770 per credit hour. *Required fees:* $8 per credit hour. One-time fee: $180 full-time. *Financial support:* In 2011–12, 27 students received support. Research assistantships with full tuition reimbursements available, career-related internships or fieldwork, Federal Work-Study, scholarships/grants, and unspecified assistantships available. Support available to part-time students. Financial award applicants required to submit FAFSA. *Unit head:* Dr. Shelly Haser, Chair, 703-526-6855, Fax: 703-284-1631, E-mail: shelly.haser@marymount.edu. *Application contact:* Francesca Reed, Director, Graduate Admissions, 703-284-5901, Fax: 703-527-3815, E-mail: grad.admissions@marymount.edu. Web site: http://www.marymount.edu/academics/schools/sehs/grad.aspx.

Maryville University of Saint Louis, School of Education, St. Louis, MO 63141-7299. Offers art education (MA Ed); early childhood education (MA Ed); educational leadership (Ed D); educational leadership: principal certification (MA Ed); elementary education (MA Ed); gifted education (MA Ed); higher education leadership (Ed D);

literacy specialist (MA Ed); middle grades education (MA Ed); secondary teaching and inquiry (MA Ed); teacher as leader (MA Ed). *Accreditation:* NCATE. Part-time and evening/weekend programs available. *Faculty:* 10 full-time (6 women), 19 part-time/adjunct (15 women). *Students:* 33 full-time (25 women), 251 part-time (190 women); includes 42 minority (32 Black or African American, non-Hispanic/Latino; 1 American Indian or Alaska Native, non-Hispanic/Latino; 4 Asian, non-Hispanic/Latino; 2 Hispanic/Latino; 3 Two or more races, non-Hispanic/Latino). Average age 38. In 2011, 69 master's, 43 doctorates awarded. *Degree requirements:* For master's, thesis, project. *Entrance requirements:* For master's, minimum cumulative GPA of 3.0, 3 professional recommendations, essays, interview with program faculty; for doctorate, minimum GPA of 3.0, 3 professional recommendations, essay, interview, on-site writing sample. Additional exam requirements/recommendations for international students: Required—TOEFL (minimum score 550 paper-based). *Application deadline:* Applications are processed on a rolling basis. Application fee: $40 ($60 for international students). Electronic applications accepted. *Expenses: Tuition:* Full-time $21,922; part-time $675 per credit hour. *Required fees:* $233.75 per semester. *Financial support:* Career-related internships or fieldwork, Federal Work-Study, tuition waivers (partial), and professional educator discounts available. Financial award application deadline: 3/1; financial award applicants required to submit FAFSA. *Faculty research:* Collaboration with public schools, pre-service program development, mathematics, diversity, literacy. *Unit head:* Dr. Sam Hausfather, Dean, 314-529-9466, Fax: 314-529-9921, E-mail: shausfather@maryville.edu. *Application contact:* Holly Stanwich, Graduate Admissions Coordinator, 314-529-9542, Fax: 314-529-9921, E-mail: teachered@maryville.edu. Web site: http://www.maryville.edu/academics-ed-graduate.

Marywood University, Academic Affairs, Reap College of Education and Human Development, Department of Education, Scranton, PA 18509-1598. Offers early childhood intervention (MS); elementary education (MAT); higher education administration (MS); instructional leadership (M Ed); reading education (MS); school leadership (MS); secondary/k-12 education (MAT); special education (MS); special education administration and supervision (MS). *Accreditation:* NCATE. *Entrance requirements:* Additional exam requirements/recommendations for international students: Required—TOEFL (minimum score 550 paper-based; 213 computer-based; 79 iBT). Application fee: $35. Electronic applications accepted. *Financial support:* Career-related internships or fieldwork, scholarships/grants, and unspecified assistantships available. Support available to part-time students. Financial award application deadline: 6/30; financial award applicants required to submit FAFSA. *Faculty research:* Catholic identity in higher education, school reading programs, teacher practice enhancement, cooperative learning, institutional and instructional leadership. *Unit head:* Dr. Patricia S. Arter, Chairperson, 570-348-6211 Ext. 2511, E-mail: psarter@marywood.edu. *Application contact:* Tammy Manka, Assistant Director of Graduate Admissions, 570-348-6211 Ext. 2322, E-mail: tmanka@marywood.edu. Web site: http://www.marywood.edu/education/.

Massachusetts College of Art and Design, Graduate Programs, Program in Teaching, Boston, MA 02115-5882. Offers MAT. *Faculty:* 5 full-time (2 women), 7 part-time/adjunct (4 women). *Students:* 26 full-time (21 women); includes 1 minority (Black or African American, non-Hispanic/Latino), 4 international. Average age 24. 34 applicants, 68% accepted, 16 enrolled. In 2011, 6 master's awarded. *Entrance requirements:* For master's, portfolio, resume, college transcripts, statement of purpose, letters of reference, interview. Additional exam requirements/recommendations for international students: Required—TOEFL (minimum score 563 paper-based; 223 computer-based; 85 iBT); Recommended—IELTS (minimum score 6.5). *Application deadline:* For fall admission, 1/15 for domestic and international students. Application fee: $85. Electronic applications accepted. *Expenses:* Tuition, state resident: full-time $21,600; part-time $720 per credit. Tuition, nonresident: full-time $21,600; part-time $720 per credit. Tuition and fees vary according to course load and degree level. *Financial support:* In 2011–12, 7 research assistantships (averaging $2,000 per year), 1 teaching assistantship (averaging $2,000 per year) were awarded; travel scholarships also available. *Unit head:* George Creamer, Director, 617-879-7163, Fax: 617-879-7171, E-mail: creamer@massart.edu. *Application contact:* 617-879-7166, E-mail: gradprograms@massart.edu. Web site: http://www.massart.edu/Academic_Programs/Art_Education/Master_of_Arts_in_Teaching.html.

Massachusetts College of Liberal Arts, Program in Education, North Adams, MA 01247-4100. Offers curriculum (M Ed); educational administration (M Ed); reading (M Ed); special education (M Ed). Part-time and evening/weekend programs available. *Degree requirements:* For master's, thesis. *Entrance requirements:* For master's, writing sample.

McGill University, Faculty of Graduate and Postdoctoral Studies, Faculty of Education, Department of Integrated Studies in Education, Montréal, QC H3A 2T5, Canada. Offers culture and values in education (MA, PhD); curriculum studies (MA); educational leadership (MA, Certificate); educational studies (PhD); integrated studies in education (M Ed); second language education (MA, PhD).

McKendree University, Graduate Programs, Master of Arts in Education Program, Lebanon, IL 62254-1299. Offers certification (MA Ed); educational administration and leadership (MA Ed); educational studies (MA Ed); higher education administrative services (MA Ed); music education (MA Ed); special education (MA Ed); teacher leadership (MA Ed); transition to teaching (MA Ed). *Accreditation:* NCATE. Part-time and evening/weekend programs available. Postbaccalaureate distance learning degree programs offered (no on-campus study). *Entrance requirements:* For master's, official transcripts from institutions attended, minimum GPA of 3.0, resume, references. Additional exam requirements/recommendations for international students: Required—TOEFL. Electronic applications accepted.

Medaille College, Program in Education, Buffalo, NY 14214-2695. Offers adolescent education (MS Ed); curriculum and instruction (MS Ed); education preparation (MS Ed); literacy (MS Ed); special education (MS). *Accreditation:* Teacher Education Accreditation Council. Part-time and evening/weekend programs available. *Faculty:* 15 full-time (11 women), 31 part-time/adjunct (21 women). *Students:* 371 full-time (281 women), 37 part-time (29 women); includes 75 minority (11 Black or African American, non-Hispanic/Latino; 6 Asian, non-Hispanic/Latino; 3 Hispanic/Latino; 55 Native Hawaiian or other Pacific Islander, non-Hispanic/Latino), 264 international. Average age 29. 354 applicants, 99% accepted, 163 enrolled. In 2011, 457 master's awarded. *Degree requirements:* For master's, comprehensive exam (for some programs), thesis or alternative. *Entrance requirements:* For master's, minimum undergraduate GPA of 2.7. Additional exam requirements/recommendations for international students: Required—TOEFL (minimum score 550 paper-based; 213 computer-based). *Application deadline:* For fall admission, 8/15 priority date for domestic students; for spring admission, 1/15 priority date for domestic students. Applications are processed on a rolling basis. Application fee: $35. Electronic applications accepted. Tuition and fees vary according to program. *Financial support:* Federal Work-Study available. Financial award applicants required to submit FAFSA. *Faculty research:* Curriculum planning, truancy, tracking minority students, curriculum design, mentoring students. *Unit head:* Dr. Robert DiSibio, Director of Graduate Programs, 716-932-2548, Fax: 716-631-1380, E-mail: rdisibio@medaille.edu. *Application contact:* Jacqueline Matheny, Executive Director of Marketing and Enrollment, 716-932-2541, Fax: 716-632-1811, E-mail: jmatheny@medaille.edu. Web site: http://www.medaille.edu.

Memorial University of Newfoundland, School of Graduate Studies, Faculty of Education, St. John's, NL A1C 5S7, Canada. Offers counseling psychology (M Ed); curriculum, teaching, and learning studies (M Ed); education (PhD); educational leadership studies (M Ed); information technology (M Ed); post-secondary studies (M Ed, Diploma), including health professional education (Diploma). Part-time programs available. *Degree requirements:* For master's, thesis optional, internship, paper folio, project; for doctorate, comprehensive exam, thesis/dissertation, thesis seminar, oral defense of thesis. *Entrance requirements:* For master's, undergraduate degree with at least 2nd class standing, 1-2 years work experience; for doctorate, minimum A average in graduate course work, MA in education, 2 years professional experience; for Diploma, 2nd class degree, 2 years of work experience with adult learners, appropriate academic qualifications and work experience in a health-related field. Electronic applications accepted. *Faculty research:* Critical thinking, literacy, cognitive studies and counseling, educational change, technology in instruction.

Mercer University, Graduate Studies, Cecil B. Day Campus, Tift College of Education (Atlanta), Macon, GA 31207-0003. Offers curriculum and instruction (PhD); early childhood education (M Ed, MAT); educational leadership (PhD, Ed S); higher education leadership (M Ed); middle grades education (M Ed, MAT); reading education (M Ed); school counseling (Ed S); secondary education (M Ed, MAT); teacher leadership (Ed S). *Accreditation:* NCATE. Part-time and evening/weekend programs available. *Faculty:* 31 full-time (17 women), 6 part-time/adjunct (3 women). *Students:* 249 full-time (207 women), 413 part-time (326 women); includes 349 minority (322 Black or African American, non-Hispanic/Latino; 1 American Indian or Alaska Native, non-Hispanic/Latino; 18 Asian, non-Hispanic/Latino; 6 Hispanic/Latino; 2 Two or more races, non-Hispanic/Latino), 6 international. Average age 34. 204 applicants, 76% accepted, 125 enrolled. In 2011, 235 master's, 8 doctorates, 27 other advanced degrees awarded. *Degree requirements:* For master's and Ed S, research project; for doctorate, thesis/dissertation. *Entrance requirements:* For master's, GRE or MAT, minimum undergraduate GPA of 2.75; for doctorate, GRE; for Ed S, GRE or MAT, minimum GPA of 3.25, 3 years of teaching experience. Additional exam requirements/recommendations for international students: Required—TOEFL. *Application deadline:* For fall admission, 8/1 for domestic and international students; for spring admission, 12/1 for domestic and international students. Applications are processed on a rolling basis. Application fee: $25. *Expenses:* Contact institution. *Financial support:* Federal Work-Study available. Support available to part-time students. Financial award application deadline: 5/1. *Faculty research:* Educational technology, multicultural and minority issues in education, educational leadership (P-12 and higher education), school discipline and school bullying, standards-based mathematics education. *Unit head:* Dr. Carl R. Martray, Dean, 478-301-5397, Fax: 478-301-2280, E-mail: martray_cr@mercer.edu. *Application contact:* Dr. Allison Gilmore, Associate Dean for Graduate Teacher Education, 678-547-6333, Fax: 678-547-6055, E-mail: gilmore_a@mercer.edu. Web site: http://www.mercer.edu/education/.

Mercer University, Graduate Studies, Macon Campus, Tift College of Education (Macon), Macon, GA 31207-0003. Offers curriculum and instruction (PhD); early childhood education (M Ed); education leadership (PhD), including higher education, P-12; educational leadership (Ed S); higher education (M Ed); teacher leadership (Ed S). *Accreditation:* NCATE. Part-time and evening/weekend programs available. Postbaccalaureate distance learning degree programs offered (minimal on-campus study). *Faculty:* 26 full-time (17 women), 2 part-time/adjunct (0 women). *Students:* 87 full-time (78 women), 147 part-time (124 women); includes 92 minority (83 Black or African American, non-Hispanic/Latino; 3 American Indian or Alaska Native, non-Hispanic/Latino; 3 Asian, non-Hispanic/Latino; 3 Hispanic/Latino), 1 international. Average age 36. 122 applicants, 66% accepted, 72 enrolled. In 2011, 51 master's, 5 doctorates, 37 other advanced degrees awarded. *Degree requirements:* For master's, research project report; for doctorate, comprehensive exam, thesis/dissertation. *Entrance requirements:* For master's, GRE or MAT, minimum GPA of 2.75; for doctorate, GRE, minimum GPA of 3.5; interview; writing sample; 3 recommendations; for Ed S, GRE or MAT, minimum GPA of 3.5 (for Ed S in teacher leadership), 3.0 (for Ed S in educational leadership). Additional exam requirements/recommendations for international students: Required—TOEFL. *Application deadline:* For fall admission, 8/1 for domestic students; for spring admission, 12/1 for domestic students. Applications are processed on a rolling basis. Application fee: $35. *Expenses:* Contact institution. *Financial support:* Federal Work-Study and institutionally sponsored loans available. Support available to part-time students. Financial award application deadline: 5/1. *Faculty research:* Teacher effectiveness, specific learning disabilities, inclusion. *Unit head:* Dr. Carl R. Martray, Dean, 478-301-5397, Fax: 478-301-2280, E-mail: martray_cr@mercer.edu. *Application contact:* Tracey Wofford, Associate Director of Admissions, 678-547-6422, Fax: 678-547-6367, E-mail: wofford_tm@mercer.edu. Web site: http://education.mercer.edu.

Mercy College, School of Education, Dobbs Ferry, NY 10522-1189. Offers adolescence education, grades 7-12 (MS); applied behavior analysis (Post Master's Certificate); bilingual education (MS); childhood education, grade 1-6 (MS); early childhood education, birth-grade 2 (MS); early childhood education/students with disabilities (MS); individualized certification plan for teachers (ICPT) (MS); middle childhood education, grades 5-9 (MS); school building leadership (MS, Advanced Certificate); teaching English to speakers of other languages (TESOL) (MS, Advanced Certificate); teaching literacy, birth-6 (MS); teaching literacy/birth-grade 12 (MS); teaching literacy/grades 5-12 (MS); urban education (MS). Postbaccalaureate distance learning degree programs offered (minimal on-campus study). *Degree requirements:* For master's, comprehensive exam, thesis (for some programs). *Entrance requirements:* For master's, interview, resume, minimum undergraduate GPA of 3.0. Additional exam requirements/recommendations for international students: Required—TOEFL (minimum score 600 paper-based; 250 computer-based; 100 iBT), IELTS (minimum score 8). Electronic applications accepted. *Expenses:* Contact institution. *Faculty research:* Teaching, literacy, educational evaluation.

Meredith College, John E. Weems Graduate School, School of Education, Raleigh, NC 27607-5298. Offers M Ed, MAT. *Accreditation:* NCATE. Part-time and evening/weekend programs available. *Faculty:* 8 full-time (all women), 5 part-time/adjunct (all women). *Students:* 38 full-time (33 women), 80 part-time (76 women); includes 14 minority (10 Black or African American, non-Hispanic/Latino; 1 Asian, non-Hispanic/Latino; 2 Hispanic/Latino; 1 Native Hawaiian or other Pacific Islander, non-Hispanic/Latino). Average age 36. 88 applicants, 78% accepted, 49 enrolled. In 2011, 55 master's awarded. *Degree requirements:* For master's, thesis optional. *Entrance requirements:* For master's, GRE General Test or MAT, minimum GPA of 2.5, teaching license, recommendations. Additional exam requirements/recommendations for international students: Required—TOEFL. *Application deadline:* For fall admission, 7/1 priority date for domestic students; for spring admission, 11/1 priority date for domestic students. Applications are processed on a rolling basis. Application fee: $50. Electronic applications accepted. *Expenses:* Contact institution. *Financial support:* Career-related internships or fieldwork, institutionally sponsored loans, and tuition waivers (partial) available. Support available to part-time students. Financial award application deadline:

2/15; financial award applicants required to submit FAFSA. *Unit head:* Erin Barrow, Graduate Program Manager, 919-760-8316, Fax: 919-760-2303, E-mail: barrower@meredith.edu. *Application contact:* Dr. Ellen Graden, Coordinator, 919-760-8077, Fax: 919-760-2303, E-mail: gradene@meredith.edu.

Merrimack College, School of Education, North Andover, MA 01845-5800. Offers community engagement (M Ed); early childhood education (M Ed); elementary education (M Ed); elementary education plus moderate disabilities-dual license (M Ed); English as a second language (M Ed); general studies (M Ed); higher education (M Ed); middle (M Ed); moderate disabilities (preK-8) (M Ed); reading (M Ed); secondary (M Ed); teacher leadership (CAGS). Part-time and evening/weekend programs available. *Faculty:* 4 full-time (all women), 9 part-time/adjunct (7 women). *Students:* 70 full-time (60 women), 39 part-time (33 women); includes 2 minority (1 Asian, non-Hispanic/Latino; 1 Hispanic/Latino). Average age 27. In 2011, 26 master's awarded. *Degree requirements:* For master's, portfolio. *Entrance requirements:* Additional exam requirements/recommendations for international students: Required—TOEFL (minimum score 80 iBT). *Application deadline:* For fall admission, 8/1 priority date for domestic students, 7/15 for international students; for winter admission, 12/1 priority date for domestic students, 11/15 for international students; for spring admission, 3/1 priority date for domestic students, 2/15 for international students. Applications are processed on a rolling basis. Electronic applications accepted. *Expenses: Tuition:* Part-time $475 per credit. *Required fees:* $62.50 per semester. *Financial support:* In 2011–12, 50 fellowships were awarded; career-related internships or fieldwork and scholarships/grants also available. Financial award applicants required to submit FAFSA. *Faculty research:* Higher education, community engagement, literacy, leadership. *Unit head:* Dr. Theresa Kirk, Chair, 978-837-5436, E-mail: kirkt@merrimack.edu. *Application contact:* Jessica McCarthy, Program Coordinator, 978-837-5443, E-mail: mccarthyj@merrimack.edu. Web site: http://www.merrimack.edu/academics/education/med/.

Miami University, School of Education and Allied Professions, Oxford, OH 45056. Offers M Ed, MA, MAT, MS, Ed D, PhD, Ed S. *Accreditation:* NCATE. *Entrance requirements:* For master's, minimum undergraduate GPA of 3.0 during previous 2 years or 2.75 overall; for doctorate, minimum undergraduate GPA of 2.75, graduate 3.0. Application fee: $50. *Expenses:* Tuition, state resident: full-time $12,023; part-time $501 per credit hour. Tuition, nonresident: full-time $26,554; part-time $1107 per credit hour. *Required fees:* $528. *Unit head:* Dr. Carine M. Feyten, Dean, 513-529-6317, Fax: 513-529-7270. *Application contact:* Graduate Admission Coordinator, 513-529-3734, Fax: 513-529-3762, E-mail: gradschool@muohio.edu. Web site: http://www.units.muohio.edu/eap/.

Michigan State University, The Graduate School, College of Education, East Lansing, MI 48824. Offers MA, MS, PhD, Ed S. *Accreditation:* Teacher Education Accreditation Council. *Entrance requirements:* Additional exam requirements/recommendations for international students: Required—TOEFL. Electronic applications accepted.

MidAmerica Nazarene University, Graduate Studies in Education, Olathe, KS 66062-1899. Offers ESOL (M Ed); professional teaching (M Ed); special education (MA); technology enhanced teaching (M Ed). *Accreditation:* NCATE. Part-time and evening/weekend programs available. Postbaccalaureate distance learning degree programs offered (no on-campus study). *Degree requirements:* For master's, thesis or alternative, creative project, technology leadership practicum. *Entrance requirements:* For master's, minimum undergraduate GPA of 2.8, 2 years of teaching experience. *Expenses:* Contact institution.

Middle Tennessee State University, College of Graduate Studies, College of Education, Murfreesboro, TN 37132. Offers M Ed, PhD, Ed S. *Accreditation:* NCATE. Part-time and evening/weekend programs available. Postbaccalaureate distance learning degree programs offered. *Faculty:* 36 full-time (20 women), 29 part-time/adjunct (19 women). *Students:* 33 full-time (24 women), 807 part-time (674 women); includes 131 minority (100 Black or African American, non-Hispanic/Latino; 14 Asian, non-Hispanic/Latino; 7 Hispanic/Latino; 1 Native Hawaiian or other Pacific Islander, non-Hispanic/Latino; 9 Two or more races, non-Hispanic/Latino). 615 applicants, 88% accepted. In 2011, 298 master's, 99 other advanced degrees awarded. *Degree requirements:* For master's, comprehensive exam, thesis (for some programs); for doctorate, comprehensive exam, thesis/dissertation; for Ed S, comprehensive exam, thesis or alternative. *Entrance requirements:* For master's, doctorate, and Ed S, GRE, MAT, current teaching license or PRAXIS. Additional exam requirements/recommendations for international students: Required—TOEFL (minimum score 525 paper-based; 195 computer-based; 71 iBT) or IELTS (minimum score 6). *Application deadline:* For fall admission, 6/1 for domestic and international students. Applications are processed on a rolling basis. Application fee: $25 ($30 for international students). Electronic applications accepted. *Expenses:* Tuition, state resident: full-time $10,008. Tuition, nonresident: full-time $25,056. *Financial support:* In 2011–12, 21 students received support. Tuition waivers available. Support available to part-time students. Financial award application deadline: 5/1; financial award applicants required to submit FAFSA. *Unit head:* Dr. Lana Seivers, Dean, 615-898-2874, Fax: 615-898-5188, E-mail: lana.seivers@mtsu.edu. *Application contact:* Dr. Michael D. Allen, Dean and Vice Provost for Research, 615-898-2840, Fax: 615-904-8020, E-mail: michael.allen@mtsu.edu.

Midwestern State University, Graduate Studies, College of Education, Wichita Falls, TX 76308. Offers M Ed, MA, ME. Part-time and evening/weekend programs available. *Degree requirements:* For master's, comprehensive exam, thesis (for some programs). *Entrance requirements:* For master's, GRE General Test or MAT. Additional exam requirements/recommendations for international students: Required—TOEFL (minimum score 550 paper-based; 213 computer-based). Electronic applications accepted. *Faculty research:* Assessment, reading education, vocabulary instruction, current role of the principal, educational research methodology.

Millersville University of Pennsylvania, College of Graduate and Professional Studies, School of Education, Millersville, PA 17551-0302. Offers M Ed, MS. *Accreditation:* NCATE. Part-time and evening/weekend programs available. *Faculty:* 76 full-time (42 women), 39 part-time/adjunct (17 women). *Students:* 101 full-time (76 women), 297 part-time (230 women); includes 20 minority (9 Black or African American, non-Hispanic/Latino; 5 Asian, non-Hispanic/Latino; 5 Hispanic/Latino; 1 Two or more races, non-Hispanic/Latino), 2 international. Average age 29. 153 applicants, 79% accepted, 79 enrolled. In 2011, 171 master's awarded. *Degree requirements:* For master's, comprehensive exam (for some programs), thesis optional, graded portfolio (educational foundations). *Entrance requirements:* For master's, GRE or MAT, 3 letters of recommendation, copy of teaching certificate. Additional exam requirements/recommendations for international students: Required—TOEFL (minimum score 500 paper-based; 183 computer-based; 65 iBT). *Application deadline:* For fall admission, 1/15 priority date for domestic students, 1/15 for international students; for winter admission, 10/1 priority date for domestic students, 10/1 for international students; for spring admission, 10/1 priority date for domestic students, 10/1 for international students. Applications are processed on a rolling basis. Application fee: $40 ($50 for international students). Electronic applications accepted. *Expenses:* Tuition, state resident: full-time $3744; part-time $416 per credit. Tuition, nonresident: full-time $5616; part-time $624 per credit. *Required fees:* $1130; $125.50 per credit. Tuition and fees vary according to course load. *Financial support:* In 2011–12, 69 students received support, including 78 research assistantships with full tuition reimbursements available (averaging $3,425 per year); institutionally sponsored loans and unspecified assistantships also available. Support available to part-time students. Financial award application deadline: 3/15; financial award applicants required to submit FAFSA. *Faculty research:* Professional development schools, English language learners, early childhood education, bullying in the classroom, teaching mathematics and science. *Unit head:* Dr. Jane S. Bray, Dean of School of Education, 717-872-3379, Fax: 717-872-3856, E-mail: jane.bray@millersville.edu. *Application contact:* Dr. Victor S. DeSantis, Dean, College of Graduate and Professional Studies, 717-872-3099, Fax: 717-872-3453, E-mail: victor.desantis@millersville.edu. Web site: http://www.millersville.edu/education/.

Milligan College, Area of Teacher Education, Milligan College, TN 37682. Offers M Ed. *Accreditation:* NCATE. Part-time programs available. *Degree requirements:* For master's, thesis, portfolio, research project. *Entrance requirements:* For master's, MAT or GRE General Test, interview. Electronic applications accepted. *Expenses:* Contact institution. *Faculty research:* Teacher education evaluation, professional development centers, internship, early childhood, technology.

Mills College, Graduate Studies, School of Education, Oakland, CA 94613-1000. Offers child life in hospitals (MA); early childhood education (MA); education (MA), including art education, curriculum and instruction, elementary education, English education, foreign language education, mathematics education, science education, secondary education, social studies education, teaching; educational leadership (MA, Ed D). Part-time and evening/weekend programs available. *Faculty:* 13 full-time (10 women), 14 part-time/adjunct (10 women). *Students:* 149 full-time (133 women), 69 part-time (61 women); includes 85 minority (32 Black or African American, non-Hispanic/Latino; 1 American Indian or Alaska Native, non-Hispanic/Latino; 16 Asian, non-Hispanic/Latino; 24 Hispanic/Latino; 1 Native Hawaiian or other Pacific Islander, non-Hispanic/Latino; 11 Two or more races, non-Hispanic/Latino), 3 international. Average age 28. 238 applicants, 84% accepted, 106 enrolled. In 2011, 41 master's, 2 doctorates awarded. Terminal master's awarded for partial completion of doctoral program. *Degree requirements:* For master's, comprehensive exam. *Entrance requirements:* For master's, statement of purpose, official transcript, 3 recommendations; for doctorate, GRE General Test. Additional exam requirements/recommendations for international students: Required—TOEFL (minimum score 550 paper-based; 80 iBT) or IELTS (minimum score 6). *Application deadline:* For fall admission, 12/31 priority date for domestic students, 12/15 for international students; for spring admission, 11/1 priority date for domestic students, 10/1 for international students. Applications are processed on a rolling basis. Application fee: $50. Electronic applications accepted. *Expenses: Tuition:* Full-time $28,280; part-time $15,640 per year. *Required fees:* $958. Tuition and fees vary according to program. *Financial support:* In 2011–12, 43 students received support, including 225 fellowships with full and partial tuition reimbursements available (averaging $6,020 per year), 43 teaching assistantships with full and partial tuition reimbursements available (averaging $6,782 per year); career-related internships or fieldwork and scholarships/grants also available. Support available to part-time students. Financial award application deadline: 2/1; financial award applicants required to submit FAFSA. *Faculty research:* Early childhood education, teacher preparation, educational leadership. *Total annual research expenditures:* $2.3 million. *Unit head:* Katherine Schultz, Chairperson, 510-430-3170, Fax: 510-430-3379, E-mail: grad-studies@mills.edu. *Application contact:* Tiana Kozoil, Graduate Admission Specialist, 510-430-3305, Fax: 510-430-2159, E-mail: grad-studies@mills.edu. Web site: http://www.mills.edu/education.

Minnesota State University Mankato, College of Graduate Studies, College of Education, Mankato, MN 56001. Offers MAT, MS, Ed D, Certificate, SP. *Accreditation:* NCATE. Part-time and evening/weekend programs available. *Students:* 177 full-time (122 women), 481 part-time (335 women). In 2011, 46 other advanced degrees awarded. *Degree requirements:* For master's, comprehensive exam, thesis or alternative; for other advanced degree, thesis. *Entrance requirements:* For master's, GRE or MAT, minimum GPA of 3.0 during previous 2 years; for other advanced degree, minimum GPA of 3.0. Additional exam requirements/recommendations for international students: Required—TOEFL. *Application deadline:* Applications are processed on a rolling basis. Application fee: $40. Electronic applications accepted. *Financial support:* Fellowships with partial tuition reimbursements, research assistantships with full tuition reimbursements, teaching assistantships with full tuition reimbursements, career-related internships or fieldwork, Federal Work-Study, institutionally sponsored loans, and unspecified assistantships available. Support available to part-time students. Financial award application deadline: 3/15; financial award applicants required to submit FAFSA. *Faculty research:* Longitudinal studies of alternative education graduates, student achievement scores. *Unit head:* Dr. Jean Haar, Interim Dean, 507-389-5445. *Application contact:* 507-389-2321, E-mail: grad@mnsu.edu.

Minnesota State University Moorhead, Graduate Studies, College of Education and Human Services, Moorhead, MN 56563-0002. Offers counseling and student affairs (MS); curriculum and instruction (MS); educational leadership (MS, Ed S); nursing (MS); reading (MS); special education (MS); speech-language pathology (MS). *Accreditation:* NCATE. Part-time and evening/weekend programs available. *Degree requirements:* For master's, comprehensive exam, final oral exam, project or thesis. *Entrance requirements:* Additional exam requirements/recommendations for international students: Required—TOEFL. Electronic applications accepted.

Misericordia University, College of Professional Studies and Social Sciences, Program in Education/Curriculum, Dallas, PA 18612-1098. Offers MS. Part-time and evening/weekend programs available. Postbaccalaureate distance learning degree programs offered. *Faculty:* 4 full-time (2 women), 11 part-time/adjunct (5 women). *Students:* 48 part-time (35 women); includes 4 minority (1 Black or African American, non-Hispanic/Latino; 1 American Indian or Alaska Native, non-Hispanic/Latino; 2 Hispanic/Latino). Average age 34. 20 applicants, 75% accepted, 11 enrolled. In 2011, 8 master's awarded. *Entrance requirements:* For master's, minimum undergraduate GPA of 3.0. *Application deadline:* Applications are processed on a rolling basis. Application fee: $25. Electronic applications accepted. *Expenses: Tuition:* Full-time $25,700; part-time $575 per credit. *Financial support:* In 2011–12, 17 students received support. Scholarships/grants available. Support available to part-time students. Financial award application deadline: 6/30; financial award applicants required to submit FAFSA. *Unit head:* Dr. Kingsley Banya, Chair of Education Department, 570-674-1488, E-mail: kbanya@misericordia.edu. *Application contact:* Larree Brown, Assistant Director of Admissions, Part-Time Undergraduate and Graduate Programs, 570-674-6451, Fax: 570-674-6232, E-mail: lbrown@misericordia.edu.

Mississippi College, Graduate School, School of Education, Clinton, MS 39058. Offers M Ed, MS, Ed D, Ed S. *Accreditation:* NCATE. Part-time and evening/weekend programs available. Postbaccalaureate distance learning degree programs offered (no on-campus study). *Degree requirements:* For master's, comprehensive exam, thesis optional. *Entrance requirements:* For master's, GRE or NTE, minimum GPA of 2.5, Class A Certificate (for some programs); for Ed S, NTE, minimum GPA of 3.0. Additional exam requirements/recommendations for international students: Recommended—TOEFL, IELTS. Electronic applications accepted.

Mississippi State University, College of Education, Mississippi State, MS 39762. Offers MAT, MS, MSIT, Ed D, PhD, Ed S. *Accreditation:* NCATE. Part-time and evening/

weekend programs available. Postbaccalaureate distance learning degree programs offered (minimal on-campus study). *Faculty:* 55 full-time (34 women), 5 part-time/adjunct (3 women). *Students:* 364 full-time (242 women), 457 part-time (345 women); includes 329 minority (304 Black or African American, non-Hispanic/Latino; 5 American Indian or Alaska Native, non-Hispanic/Latino; 6 Asian, non-Hispanic/Latino; 6 Hispanic/Latino; 2 Native Hawaiian or other Pacific Islander, non-Hispanic/Latino; 6 Two or more races, non-Hispanic/Latino), 11 international. Average age 34. 483 applicants, 51% accepted, 192 enrolled. In 2011, 172 master's, 25 doctorates, 25 other advanced degrees awarded. Terminal master's awarded for partial completion of doctoral program. *Degree requirements:* For master's, thesis optional, comprehensive oral or written exam; for doctorate, thesis/dissertation; for Ed S, thesis or alternative, final written or oral exam. *Entrance requirements:* For master's, doctorate, and Ed S, GRE. Additional exam requirements/recommendations for international students: Required—TOEFL (minimum score 550 paper-based; 213 computer-based; 79 iBT); Recommended—IELTS (minimum score 6.5). *Application deadline:* For fall admission, 7/1 for domestic students, 5/1 for international students; for spring admission, 11/1 for domestic students, 9/1 for international students. Applications are processed on a rolling basis. Application fee: $40. Electronic applications accepted. *Expenses:* Tuition, state resident: full-time $5805; part-time $322.50 per credit hour. Tuition, nonresident: full-time $14,670; part-time $815 per credit hour. *Financial support:* In 2011–12, 18 research assistantships (averaging $10,259 per year), 16 teaching assistantships (averaging $9,457 per year) were awarded; career-related internships or fieldwork, Federal Work-Study, institutionally sponsored loans, scholarships/grants, and unspecified assistantships also available. Financial award applicants required to submit FAFSA. *Faculty research:* Leadership behavior, creativity measures, early childhood education, employability of the blind, quality indicators of professional educators. *Total annual research expenditures:* $2.5 million. *Unit head:* Dr. Richard Blackbourn, Dean, 662-325-3717, Fax: 662-325-8784, E-mail: rlb277@msstate.edu. *Application contact:* Forest Sparks, Admissions Manager, 662-325-7403, Fax: 662-325-1967, E-mail: grad@grad.msstate.edu. Web site: http://www.educ.msstate.edu/.

Mississippi University for Women, Graduate School, College of Education and Human Sciences, Columbus, MS 39701-9998. Offers differentiated instruction (M Ed); educational leadership (M Ed); gifted studies (M Ed); reading/literacy (M Ed); teaching (MAT). *Accreditation:* ASHA; NCATE. Part-time programs available. *Degree requirements:* For master's, comprehensive exam, thesis optional. *Entrance requirements:* For master's, GRE General Test or NTE (M Ed in gifted education or MS in speech/language pathology), MAT (M Ed in instructional management), minimum QPA of 3.0.

Mississippi Valley State University, Department of Education, Itta Bena, MS 38941-1400. Offers education (MAT); elementary education (MA). *Accreditation:* NCATE.

Missouri Baptist University, Graduate Programs, St. Louis, MO 63141-8660. Offers business administration (MBA); Christian ministries (MACM); counseling (MAC); education (MSE); education administration (MEA); educational leadership (MSE, Ed S); teaching (MAT).

Missouri Southern State University, Program in Teaching, Joplin, MO 64801-1595. Offers MAT. Program offered jointly with Missouri State University. *Accreditation:* NCATE. *Degree requirements:* For master's, research seminar.

Molloy College, Graduate Education Program, Rockville Centre, NY 11571-5002. Offers MS Ed, Certificate. *Accreditation:* NCATE. *Faculty:* 22 full-time (16 women), 6 part-time/adjunct (4 women). *Students:* 101 full-time (77 women), 190 part-time (150 women); includes 41 minority (13 Black or African American, non-Hispanic/Latino; 1 American Indian or Alaska Native, non-Hispanic/Latino; 3 Asian, non-Hispanic/Latino; 23 Hispanic/Latino; 1 Two or more races, non-Hispanic/Latino). Average age 29. 129 applicants, 78% accepted, 54 enrolled. In 2011, 139 master's awarded. *Application deadline:* Applications are processed on a rolling basis. *Faculty research:* Teaching English to students of other languages, learning needs of students with disabilities, diverse classrooms/multicultural education, multiple intelligences/emotional intelligences, learning styles. *Unit head:* Joanne O'Brien, Associate Dean/Director, 516-678-5000 Ext. 6280. *Application contact:* Alina Haitz, Assistant Director of Graduate Admissions, 516-678-5000 Ext. 6399, Fax: 516-256-2247, E-mail: ahaitz@molloy.edu.

Monmouth University, The Graduate School, School of Education, West Long Branch, NJ 07764-1898. Offers education (M Ed); initial certification (MAT), including elementary level, K-12, secondary level; learning disabilities-teacher consultant (Certificate); principal (MS Ed); principal/school administrator (MS Ed); reading specialist (MS Ed, Certificate); school counseling (MS Ed); special education (MS Ed), including autism, learning disabilities teacher consultant, teacher of students with disabilities, teaching in inclusive settings; supervisor (Certificate); teacher of the handicapped (Certificate); teaching English to speakers of other languages (TESOL) (Certificate). *Accreditation:* NCATE. Part-time and evening/weekend programs available. *Faculty:* 16 full-time (12 women), 24 part-time/adjunct (17 women). *Students:* 134 full-time (104 women), 293 part-time (246 women); includes 34 minority (11 Black or African American, non-Hispanic/Latino; 2 Asian, non-Hispanic/Latino; 18 Hispanic/Latino; 3 Two or more races, non-Hispanic/Latino), 2 international. Average age 29. 288 applicants, 92% accepted, 182 enrolled. In 2011, 173 master's awarded. *Entrance requirements:* For master's, minimum GPA of 3.0 in major, 2.75 overall; 2 letters of recommendation (for some programs). Additional exam requirements/recommendations for international students: Required—TOEFL (minimum score 550 paper-based; 213 computer-based; 79 iBT), IELTS (minimum score 5), Michigan English Language Assessment Battery (minimum score 77), Cambridge A, B, C. *Application deadline:* For fall admission, 7/15 priority date for domestic students, 7/1 for international students; for spring admission, 11/15 priority date for domestic students, 11/1 for international students. Applications are processed on a rolling basis. Application fee: $50. Electronic applications accepted. *Financial support:* In 2011–12, 274 students received support, including 291 fellowships (averaging $1,783 per year), 21 research assistantships (averaging $8,792 per year); career-related internships or fieldwork, scholarships/grants, and unspecified assistantships also available. Support available to part-time students. Financial award applicants required to submit FAFSA. *Faculty research:* Multicultural literacy, science and mathematics teaching strategies, teacher as reflective practitioner, children with disabilities. *Unit head:* Dr. Jason Barr, Program Director, 732-263-5238, Fax: 732-263-5277, E-mail: jbarr@monmouth.edu. *Application contact:* Kevin Roane, Director, Office of Graduate Admission, 732-571-3452, Fax: 732-263-5123, E-mail: gradadm@monmouth.edu. Web site: http://www.monmouth.edu/academics/schools/education/default.asp.

Montana State University, College of Graduate Studies, College of Education, Health, and Human Development, Department of Education, Bozeman, MT 59717. Offers adult and higher education (Ed D); curriculum and instruction (M Ed, Ed D), including professional educator (M Ed), technology education (M Ed); education (M Ed), including adult and higher education, educational leadership, school counseling; educational leadership (Ed D, Ed S). *Accreditation:* Teacher Education Accreditation Council. Part-time programs available. Postbaccalaureate distance learning degree programs offered (minimal on-campus study). *Degree requirements:* For master's, comprehensive exam; for doctorate, comprehensive exam, thesis/dissertation. *Entrance requirements:* For master's, GRE, 3 letters of reference, essays, BA transcripts; for doctorate, GRE, MAT, 3 letters of reference, essay, BA and M Ed transcripts; for Ed S, PRAXIS. Additional exam requirements/recommendations for international students: Required—TOEFL (minimum score 550 paper-based; 213 computer-based). Electronic applications accepted. *Faculty research:* Critical literacy; standards-based education; school Improvement, organizational change, leadership in rural education, leadership in Indian education; student Learning; multicultural/culturally responsive education for social justice Native American indigenous education, community-centered education teacher preparation.

Montana State University Billings, College of Education, Billings, MT 59101-0298. Offers M Ed, MS Sp Ed, Certificate. *Accreditation:* NCATE. Part-time programs available. Postbaccalaureate distance learning degree programs offered (minimal on-campus study). *Degree requirements:* For master's, thesis optional. *Entrance requirements:* For master's, GRE General Test. *Faculty research:* Social studies education, science education.

Montana State University–Northern, Graduate Programs, Havre, MT 59501-7751. Offers counselor education (M Ed); learning development (M Ed). Part-time and evening/weekend programs available. Postbaccalaureate distance learning degree programs offered (minimal on-campus study). *Degree requirements:* For master's, comprehensive exam, oral exams or thesis. *Entrance requirements:* For master's, GRE General Test or MAT, minimum GPA of 3.0. Electronic applications accepted.

Montclair State University, The Graduate School, College of Education and Human Services, Montclair, NJ 07043-1624. Offers M Ed, MA, MAT, MPH, MS, Ed D, PhD, Certificate, Post-Master's Certificate, Postbaccalaureate Certificate. *Accreditation:* NCATE. Part-time and evening/weekend programs available. *Faculty:* 116 full-time (79 women), 202 part-time/adjunct (150 women). *Students:* 543 full-time (391 women), 1,269 part-time (1,024 women); includes 400 minority (132 Black or African American, non-Hispanic/Latino; 2 American Indian or Alaska Native, non-Hispanic/Latino; 69 Asian, non-Hispanic/Latino; 185 Hispanic/Latino; 3 Native Hawaiian or other Pacific Islander, non-Hispanic/Latino; 9 Two or more races, non-Hispanic/Latino), 22 international. Average age 31. 1,431 applicants, 57% accepted, 650 enrolled. In 2011, 537 master's, 32 other advanced degrees awarded. *Degree requirements:* For master's, comprehensive exam (for some programs), thesis (for some programs); for doctorate, comprehensive exam, thesis/dissertation. *Entrance requirements:* For master's, GRE, GMAT, MAT, 2 letters of recommendation; for doctorate, GRE General Test, 3 letters of recommendation. Additional exam requirements/recommendations for international students: Required—TOEFL (minimum score 83 iBT) or IELTS. *Application deadline:* For fall admission, 6/1 for international students; for spring admission, 10/1 for international students. Applications are processed on a rolling basis. Application fee: $60. Electronic applications accepted. *Financial support:* In 2011–12, 78 research assistantships with full tuition reimbursements (averaging $7,727 per year), 1 teaching assistantship with full tuition reimbursement (averaging $7,000 per year) were awarded; Federal Work-Study, scholarships/grants, and unspecified assistantships also available. Support available to part-time students. Financial award application deadline: 3/1; financial award applicants required to submit FAFSA. *Faculty research:* Key factors in the preparation of teachers for urban schools, factors affecting upper extremity motion patterns and injuries, implementation fidelity of instructional interventions. data-based decision-making in educational contexts, nutrition and physical activity of the aging population in the U. S.. *Total annual research expenditures:* $850,549. *Unit head:* Dr. Ada Beth Cutler, Dean, 973-655-5167, E-mail: cutler@mail.montclair.edu. *Application contact:* Amy Aiello, Executive Director of The Graduate School, 973-655-5147, E-mail: graduate.school@montclair.edu. Web site: http://cehs.montclair.edu/.

Morehead State University, Graduate Programs, College of Education, Morehead, KY 40351. Offers MA, MA Ed, MAT, Ed S. *Accreditation:* NCATE. Part-time and evening/weekend programs available. *Degree requirements:* For master's, comprehensive exam, thesis or alternative; for Ed S, thesis. *Entrance requirements:* For master's, GRE General Test or PRAXIS, minimum overall undergraduate GPA of 2.5; for Ed S, GRE General Test, interview, master's degree, minimum GPA of 3.5, work experience. Additional exam requirements/recommendations for international students: Required—TOEFL (minimum score 500 paper-based; 173 computer-based). Electronic applications accepted. *Faculty research:* Regional economic development, computer applications for school administrators, effectiveness of teacher interns, perceptual processes, alcoholism.

Morgan State University, School of Graduate Studies, School of Education and Urban Studies, Baltimore, MD 21251. Offers MAT, MS, MSW, Ed D, PhD. Part-time programs available. *Degree requirements:* For master's, comprehensive exam; for doctorate, comprehensive exam, thesis/dissertation. *Entrance requirements:* For doctorate, GRE General Test or MAT. Additional exam requirements/recommendations for international students: Required—TOEFL (minimum score 550 paper-based; 213 computer-based). *Faculty research:* Multicultural education, cooperative learning, psychology of cognition.

Morningside College, Graduate Division, Department of Education, Sioux City, IA 51106. Offers professional educator (MAT); special education: instructional strategist I: mild/moderate elementary (K-6) (MAT); special education: instructional strategist II-mild/moderate secondary (7-12) (MAT); special education: K-12 instructional strategist II-behavior disorders/learning disabilities (MAT); special education: K-12 instructional strategist II-mental disabilities (MAT). Part-time and evening/weekend programs available. *Entrance requirements:* For master's, MAT, writing sample.

Mount Aloysius College, Program in Education, Cresson, PA 16630-1999. Offers MS. Part-time programs available.

Mount Mary College, Graduate Programs, Programs in Education, Milwaukee, WI 53222-4597. Offers education (MA); professional development (MA). Part-time and evening/weekend programs available. *Faculty:* 5 full-time (all women), 10 part-time/adjunct (7 women). *Students:* 18 full-time (14 women), 45 part-time (40 women); includes 9 minority (4 Black or African American, non-Hispanic/Latino; 1 Asian, non-Hispanic/Latino; 2 Hispanic/Latino; 1 Native Hawaiian or other Pacific Islander, non-Hispanic/Latino; 1 Two or more races, non-Hispanic/Latino). Average age 37. 8 applicants, 63% accepted, 4 enrolled. In 2011, 24 master's awarded. *Degree requirements:* For master's, action research project. *Entrance requirements:* For master's, minimum GPA of 2.75, teaching license. Additional exam requirements/recommendations for international students: Required—TOEFL (minimum score 500 paper-based; 173 computer-based). *Application deadline:* For fall admission, 8/29 priority date for domestic students, 8/29 for international students; for spring admission, 1/20 for domestic and international students. Applications are processed on a rolling basis. Application fee: $45 ($100 for international students). *Financial support:* In 2011–12, 1 student received support. Federal Work-Study available. Support available to part-time students. Financial award application deadline: 5/1; financial award applicants required to submit FAFSA. *Faculty research:* Staff development, writing across the curriculum, effective schools, critical thinking skills, mathematics education. *Unit head:* Dr. Deb Dosemagen, Director, 414-256-1214, E-mail: dosemagd@mtmary.edu. *Application contact:* Dr. Douglas J. Mickelson, Associate Dean for Graduate and Continuing Education, 414-256-1252, Fax: 414-256-0167, E-mail: mickelsd@mtmary.edu.

Mount Mercy University, Program in Education, Cedar Rapids, IA 52402-4797. Offers reading (MA Ed); special education (MA Ed). *Entrance requirements:* For master's, minimum cumulative GPA of 3.0, 2 letters of recommendation, resume, valid teaching license. Additional exam requirements/recommendations for international students: Required—TOEFL (minimum score 570 paper-based; 88 iBT). Electronic applications accepted.

Mount Saint Mary College, Division of Education, Newburgh, NY 12550-3494. Offers adolescence and special education (MS Ed); adolescence education (MS Ed); childhood and special education (MS Ed); childhood education (MS Ed); literacy (5-12) (Advanced Certificate); literacy (birth-6) (Advanced Certificate); literacy and special education (MS Ed); literacy/childhood (MS Ed); middle school (5-6) (MS Ed); middle school (7-9) (MS Ed); special education (1-6) (MS Ed); special education (7-12) (MS Ed). *Accreditation:* NCATE. Part-time and evening/weekend programs available. *Faculty:* 14 full-time (12 women), 14 part-time/adjunct (8 women). *Students:* 55 full-time (42 women), 158 part-time (125 women); includes 23 minority (4 Black or African American, non-Hispanic/Latino; 1 Asian, non-Hispanic/Latino; 18 Hispanic/Latino). Average age 29. 119 applicants, 45% accepted, 24 enrolled. In 2011, 107 master's awarded. *Application deadline:* Applications are processed on a rolling basis. Application fee: $45. Application fee is waived when completed online. *Expenses: Tuition:* Full-time $13,356; part-time $742 per credit. *Required fees:* $70 per semester. *Financial support:* In 2011–12, 99 students received support. Unspecified assistantships available. Financial award application deadline: 4/15; financial award applicants required to submit FAFSA. *Faculty research:* Learning and teaching styles, computers in special education, language development. *Unit head:* Dr. Theresa Lewis, Coordinator, 845-569-3149, Fax: 845-569-3535, E-mail: tlewis@msmc.edu. *Application contact:* Courtney McDermott, Graduate Recruiter, 845-569-3402, Fax: 845-569-3450, E-mail: courtney.mcdermott@msmc.edu. Web site: http://www.msmc.edu/Academics/Graduate_Programs/Master_of_Science_in_Education.

Mount St. Mary's College, Graduate Division, Department of Education, Los Angeles, CA 90049-1599. Offers elementary education (MS); instructional leadership (MS, Certificate); secondary education (MS); special education (MS, Ed S). Part-time and evening/weekend programs available. *Degree requirements:* For master's, thesis, research project. *Entrance requirements:* For master's, minimum GPA of 2.5; for other advanced degree, CBEST, CSET. Additional exam requirements/recommendations for international students: Required—TOEFL (minimum score 550 paper-based). *Application deadline:* For fall admission, 7/15 priority date for domestic students; for spring admission, 11/15 priority date for domestic students. Electronic applications accepted. *Expenses: Tuition:* Part-time $752 per unit. Part-time tuition and fees vary according to degree level and program. *Financial support:* Career-related internships or fieldwork, institutionally sponsored loans, scholarships/grants, and tuition waivers (full and partial) available. Support available to part-time students. Financial award application deadline: 3/15; financial award applicants required to submit FAFSA. *Unit head:* Dr. Shelly Tochluk, Chair, 213-477-2623, E-mail: stochluk@msmc.la.edu. Web site: http://www.msmc.la.edu/graduate-programs/education.asp.

Mount St. Mary's University, Program in Education, Emmitsburg, MD 21727-7799. Offers M Ed, MAT. *Accreditation:* NCATE. Part-time and evening/weekend programs available. *Faculty:* 7 full-time (6 women), 4 part-time/adjunct (1 woman). *Students:* 34 full-time (23 women), 51 part-time (38 women); includes 4 minority (2 Black or African American, non-Hispanic/Latino; 2 Hispanic/Latino), 1 international. Average age 34. 16 applicants, 100% accepted, 16 enrolled. In 2011, 26 master's awarded. *Degree requirements:* For master's, thesis (for some programs), exit portfolio/presentation. *Entrance requirements:* For master's, PRAXIS I, PRAXIS II. Additional exam requirements/recommendations for international students: Required—TOEFL (minimum score 550 paper-based; 83 computer-based). *Application deadline:* For fall admission, 8/15 for domestic and international students. Applications are processed on a rolling basis. Application fee: $35. *Expenses:* Contact institution. *Financial support:* Career-related internships or fieldwork and unspecified assistantships available. Financial award applicants required to submit FAFSA. *Faculty research:* Distance education, reading motivation, inclusive education in Catholic schools, historical foundations of American education, preparing new teachers for high poverty/high minority schools. *Unit head:* Dr. Barbara Martin-Palmer, Dean of School of Education and Human Services, 301-447-5371, Fax: 301-447-5250, E-mail: palmer@msmary.edu. Web site: http://www.msmary.edu/School_of_education_and_human_services/graduate_programs/.

Mount Saint Vincent University, Graduate Programs, Faculty of Education, Halifax, NS B3M 2J6, Canada. Offers adult education (M Ed, MA Ed, MA-R); curriculum studies (M Ed, MA Ed, MA-R), including education of young adolescents, general studies, teaching English as a second language; educational foundations (M Ed, MA Ed, MA-R); educational psychology (M Ed, MA Ed, MA-R), including education of the blind or visually impaired (M Ed, MA Ed), education of the deaf or hard of hearing (M Ed, MA Ed), educational psychology (MA-R), human relations (M Ed, MA Ed); elementary education (M Ed, MA Ed, MA-R); literacy education (M Ed, MA Ed, MA-R); school psychology (MASP). Part-time and evening/weekend programs available. Postbaccalaureate distance learning degree programs offered (minimal on-campus study). *Degree requirements:* For master's, thesis (for some programs), practicum. *Entrance requirements:* For master's, bachelor's degree in related field. Electronic applications accepted.

Mount Vernon Nazarene University, Department of Education, Mount Vernon, OH 43050-9500. Offers education (MA Ed); professional educator's license (MA Ed). *Accreditation:* NCATE. Part-time and evening/weekend programs available. *Degree requirements:* For master's, project.

Multnomah University, Multnomah Bible College Graduate Degree Programs, Portland, OR 97220-5898. Offers counseling (MA); teaching (MA); TESOL (MA). *Faculty:* 5 full-time (all women), 25 part-time/adjunct (12 women). *Students:* 126 full-time (84 women), 21 part-time (13 women); includes 24 minority (5 Black or African American, non-Hispanic/Latino; 1 American Indian or Alaska Native, non-Hispanic/Latino; 8 Asian, non-Hispanic/Latino; 7 Hispanic/Latino; 3 Two or more races, non-Hispanic/Latino). Average age 35. 73 applicants, 81% accepted, 45 enrolled. In 2011, 13 master's awarded. *Degree requirements:* For master's, variable foreign language requirement, comprehensive exam (for some programs), thesis optional. *Entrance requirements:* For master's, CBEST or WEST-B (for MAT), interview; references (4 for teaching); writing sample (for counseling). Additional exam requirements/recommendations for international students: Required—TOEFL (minimum score 550 paper-based; 213 computer-based). *Application deadline:* For fall admission, 8/1 for domestic students, 12/1 for international students; for spring admission, 12/1 for domestic and international students. Application fee: $40. *Expenses: Tuition:* Part-time $485 per credit hour. *Required fees:* $25 per semester. Tuition and fees vary according to campus/location and program. *Financial support:* Career-related internships or fieldwork and scholarships/grants available. Support available to part-time students. Financial award application deadline: 7/1; financial award applicants required to submit FAFSA. *Unit head:* Dr. Rex Koivisto, Academic Dean, 503-251-6401. *Application contact:* Jennifer Hancock, Assistant Director of Graduate and Seminary Admissions, 503-251-6481, Fax: 503-254-1268, E-mail: admiss@multnomah.edu.

Murray State University, College of Education, Murray, KY 42071. Offers MA Ed, MS, Ed D, PhD, Ed S. PhD, Ed D offered jointly with University of Kentucky. *Accreditation:* NCATE. Part-time programs available.

Muskingum University, Graduate Programs in Education, New Concord, OH 43762. Offers MAE, MAT. *Accreditation:* NCATE. Part-time programs available. *Entrance requirements:* For master's, minimum GPA of 2.7, teaching license. *Faculty research:* Brain behavior relationships, school partnerships, staff development, school law, proficiency testing, multi-age groupings.

Naropa University, Graduate Programs, Program in Contemplative Education, Boulder, CO 80302-6697. Offers MA. Part-time and evening/weekend programs available. Postbaccalaureate distance learning degree programs offered (minimal on-campus study). *Faculty:* 1 full-time (0 women), 3 part-time/adjunct (all women). *Students:* 14 part-time (10 women); includes 1 minority (Hispanic/Latino), 1 international. Average age 40. 23 applicants, 52% accepted, 6 enrolled. In 2011, 12 master's awarded. *Degree requirements:* For master's, thesis. *Entrance requirements:* For master's, interview (by phone or in-person), 3 letters of recommendation, resume, statement of interest. Additional exam requirements/recommendations for international students: Required—TOEFL (minimum score 600 paper-based; 250 computer-based). *Application deadline:* For fall admission, 1/15 priority date for domestic students, 1/15 for international students. Applications are processed on a rolling basis. Application fee: $60. Electronic applications accepted. *Expenses: Tuition:* Full-time $20,400; part-time $850 per credit. *Required fees:* $660; $250 per semester. *Financial support:* In 2011–12, 5 students received support. Career-related internships or fieldwork, Federal Work-Study, scholarships/grants, health care benefits, tuition waivers (partial), and unspecified assistantships available. Support available to part-time students. Financial award application deadline: 3/1; financial award applicants required to submit FAFSA. *Unit head:* Dr. Jeanine Canty, Director, School of Natural and Social Sciences, 303-245-4735, E-mail: jcanty@naropa.edu. *Application contact:* Office of Admissions, 303-546-3572, Fax: 303-546-3583, E-mail: admissions@naropa.edu. Web site: http://www.naropa.edu/academics/snss/grad/contemplative-education-low-residency-ma/index.php.

National Louis University, National College of Education, Chicago, IL 60603. Offers administration and supervision (M Ed, Ed D, CAS, Ed S); curriculum and instruction (M Ed, MS Ed, CAS); early childhood administration (M Ed, CAS); early childhood education (M Ed, MAT, MS Ed, CAS); education (Ed D); educational psychology/human learning and development (M Ed, MS Ed, CAS, Ed S); elementary education (MAT); interdisciplinary curriculum and instruction (M Ed); mathematics education (M Ed, MS Ed, CAS); reading and language (M Ed, MS Ed, CAS); school psychology (M Ed, Ed S); science education (M Ed, MS Ed, CAS); secondary education (MAT); special education (M Ed, MAT, CAS); technology in education (M Ed, CAS). *Accreditation:* NCATE. Part-time and evening/weekend programs available. *Students:* 224 full-time (162 women), 2,336 part-time (1,767 women); includes 677 minority (366 Black or African American, non-Hispanic/Latino; 8 American Indian or Alaska Native, non-Hispanic/Latino; 68 Asian, non-Hispanic/Latino; 218 Hispanic/Latino; 2 Native Hawaiian or other Pacific Islander, non-Hispanic/Latino; 15 Two or more races, non-Hispanic/Latino), 2 international. Average age 34. In 2011, 1,711 master's, 76 doctorates, 86 other advanced degrees awarded. *Degree requirements:* For doctorate, comprehensive exam, thesis/dissertation. *Entrance requirements:* For master's, MAT or GRE, minimum GPA of 3.0; for doctorate, GRE General Test, minimum GPA of 3.25, interview, resume, writing sample, 4 recommendations. Additional exam requirements/recommendations for international students: Required—TOEFL (minimum score 550 paper-based; 213 computer-based; 79 iBT). *Application deadline:* Applications are processed on a rolling basis. Application fee: $40. *Financial support:* Fellowships, research assistantships, teaching assistantships, career-related internships or fieldwork, Federal Work-Study, institutionally sponsored loans, and scholarships/grants available. Support available to part-time students. Financial award applicants required to submit FAFSA. *Unit head:* Dr. Alison Hilsabeck, Dean, 312-361-3580, Fax: 312-261-2580, E-mail: ahilsabeck@nl.edu. *Application contact:* Ken Kasprzak, Director of Admission, 888-658-8632, Fax: 847-947-5575, E-mail: kkasprzak@nl.edu.

National University, Academic Affairs, School of Education, La Jolla, CA 92037-1011. Offers M Ed, MA, MS, Certificate. Part-time and evening/weekend programs available. Postbaccalaureate distance learning degree programs offered (no on-campus study). *Degree requirements:* For master's, thesis (for some programs). *Entrance requirements:* For master's, interview, minimum GPA of 2.5. Additional exam requirements/recommendations for international students: Required—TOEFL (minimum score 550 paper-based; 213 computer-based; 79 iBT), IELTS (minimum score 6). *Application deadline:* Applications are processed on a rolling basis. Application fee: $60 ($65 for international students). Electronic applications accepted. *Financial support:* Career-related internships or fieldwork, institutionally sponsored loans, scholarships/grants, and tuition waivers (partial) available. Support available to part-time students. Financial award application deadline: 6/30. *Faculty research:* Teacher education, special education, educational effectiveness, teaching abroad, school counseling. *Unit head:* School of Education, 858-642-8320, Fax: 858-642-8724, E-mail: soe@nu.edu. *Application contact:* Dominick Giovanniello, Associate Regional Dean, 800-NAT-UNIV, Fax: 858-541-7792, E-mail: dgiovann@nu.edu. Web site: http://www.nu.edu/OurPrograms/SchoolOfEducation.html.

Nazareth College of Rochester, Graduate Studies, Department of Education, Rochester, NY 14618-3790. Offers educational technology/computer education (MS Ed); inclusive education-adolescence level (MS Ed); inclusive education-childhood level (MS Ed); inclusive education-early childhood level (MS Ed); literacy education (MS Ed); teaching English to speakers of other languages (MS Ed). *Accreditation:* Teacher Education Accreditation Council. Part-time and evening/weekend programs available. *Entrance requirements:* For master's, minimum GPA of 3.0.

Neumann University, Program in Education, Aston, PA 19014-1298. Offers MS. Part-time programs available. *Entrance requirements:* For master's, GRE, MAT, or PRAXIS. Additional exam requirements/recommendations for international students: Required—TOEFL.

New England College, Program in Education, Henniker, NH 03242-3293. Offers higher education administration (MS, Ed D); K-12 leadership (Ed D); literacy and language arts (M Ed); meeting the needs of all learners/special education (M Ed); teacher leadership/school reform (M Ed). Part-time and evening/weekend programs available.

Newman University, Master of Education Program, Wichita, KS 67213-2097. Offers building leadership (MS Ed); curriculum and instruction (MS Ed), including accountability, English as a second language, reading specialist. *Accreditation:* NCATE. Part-time and evening/weekend programs available. Postbaccalaureate distance learning degree programs offered (no on-campus study). *Faculty:* 4 full-time (2 women), 38 part-time/adjunct (all women). *Students:* 47 full-time (40 women), 414 part-time (318 women); includes 62 minority (20 Black or African American, non-Hispanic/Latino; 8 Asian, non-Hispanic/Latino; 30 Hispanic/Latino; 3 Native Hawaiian or other Pacific Islander, non-Hispanic/Latino; 1 Two or more races, non-Hispanic/Latino), 3 international. Average age 35. 42 applicants, 76% accepted, 27 enrolled. In 2011, 46 master's awarded. *Degree requirements:* For master's, thesis optional. *Entrance* *requirements:* For master's, interview, minimum GPA of 3.0, writing sample, 2 letters of recommendation, evidence of teaching certification. Additional exam requirements/ recommendations for international students: Required—TOEFL (minimum score 600 paper-based; 250 computer-based; 100 iBT). *Application deadline:* For fall admission, 8/ 15 priority date for domestic students, 7/15 for international students; for spring admission, 1/10 priority date for domestic students, 11/15 for international students. Applications are processed on a rolling basis. Application fee: $25 ($40 for international students). Electronic applications accepted. *Expenses:* Contact institution. *Financial support:* In 2011–12, 18 students received support. Federal Work-Study available. Financial award application deadline: 8/15; financial award applicants required to submit FAFSA. *Unit head:* Dr. Guy Glidden, Director, Graduate Education, 316-942-4291 Ext. 2331, Fax: 316-942-4483, E-mail: gliddeng@newmanu.edu. *Application contact:* Linda Kay Sabala, Director of Graduate Admissions, 316-942-4291 Ext. 2230, Fax: 316-942-4483, E-mail: sabalal@newmanu.edu.

New Mexico Highlands University, Graduate Studies, School of Education, Las Vegas, NM 87701. Offers curriculum and instruction (MA); education (MA), including counseling, school counseling; educational leadership (MA); exercise and sport sciences (MA), including human performance and sport, sports administration, teacher education; guidance and counseling (MA), including professional counseling, rehabilitation counseling, school counseling; special education (MA), including). Part-time programs available. *Faculty:* 29 full-time (18 women). *Students:* 136 full-time (100 women), 275 part-time (219 women); includes 231 minority (8 Black or African American, non-Hispanic/Latino; 22 American Indian or Alaska Native, non-Hispanic/ Latino; 2 Asian, non-Hispanic/Latino; 194 Hispanic/Latino; 1 Native Hawaiian or other Pacific Islander, non-Hispanic/Latino; 4 Two or more races, non-Hispanic/Latino), 14 international. Average age 39. 117 applicants, 82% accepted, 91 enrolled. In 2011, 105 master's awarded. *Degree requirements:* For master's, comprehensive exam, thesis or alternative. *Entrance requirements:* For master's, minimum undergraduate GPA of 3.0. Additional exam requirements/recommendations for international students: Required—TOEFL (minimum score 540 paper-based; 207 computer-based). *Application deadline:* For fall admission, 8/1 priority date for domestic students. Applications are processed on a rolling basis. Application fee: $15. *Expenses:* Tuition, state resident: full-time $2767; part-time $146 per credit hour. Tuition, nonresident: full-time $4879; part-time $234 per credit hour. *International tuition:* $5436 full-time. *Required fees:* $737. *Financial support:* In 2011–12, 12 students received support. Career-related internships or fieldwork, Federal Work-Study, institutionally sponsored loans, scholarships/grants, traineeships, tuition waivers (partial), and unspecified assistantships available. Support available to part-time students. Financial award application deadline: 3/1; financial award applicants required to submit FAFSA. *Faculty research:* Teaching the United States Constitution, middle school curriculum, integrated computer applications for pre-service classroom teachers, adolescent literacy, narrative cognitive modes in NM multicultural setting. *Unit head:* Dr. Michael Anderson, Interim Dean, 505-454-3213, E-mail: mfanderson@nmhu.edu. *Application contact:* Diane Trujillo, Administrative Assistant for Graduate Studies, 505-454-3266, Fax: 505-426-2117, E-mail: dtrujillo@nmhu.edu.

New Mexico State University, Graduate School, College of Education, Las Cruces, NM 88003-8001. Offers MA, MAT, Ed D, PhD, Ed S. *Accreditation:* NCATE. Part-time and evening/weekend programs available. Postbaccalaureate distance learning degree programs offered (minimal on-campus study). *Faculty:* 57 full-time (38 women), 4 part-time/adjunct (0 women). *Students:* 305 full-time (244 women), 506 part-time (388 women); includes 406 minority (14 Black or African American, non-Hispanic/Latino; 25 American Indian or Alaska Native, non-Hispanic/Latino; 13 Asian, non-Hispanic/Latino; 347 Hispanic/Latino; 7 Two or more races, non-Hispanic/Latino), 38 international. Average age 37. 387 applicants, 48% accepted, 142 enrolled. In 2011, 188 master's, 34 doctorates, 11 other advanced degrees awarded. *Degree requirements:* For doctorate, thesis/dissertation. *Entrance requirements:* Additional exam requirements/ recommendations for international students: Required—TOEFL (minimum score 550 paper-based; 79 iBT), IELTS (minimum score 6.5). *Application deadline:* Applications are processed on a rolling basis. Application fee: $40 ($50 for international students). Electronic applications accepted. *Expenses:* Tuition, state resident: full-time $5004; part-time $208.50 per credit. Tuition, nonresident: full-time $17,446; part-time $726.90 per credit. *Financial support:* In 2011–12, 30 students received support, including 5 fellowships (averaging $4,876 per year), 40 research assistantships (averaging $16,898 per year), 76 teaching assistantships (averaging $15,935 per year); career-related internships or fieldwork, Federal Work-Study, and health care benefits also available. Support available to part-time students. Financial award application deadline: 3/1. *Faculty research:* Bilingual special education, early childhood education/Head Start, leadership in border settings, exercise physiology, school-based mental health. *Unit head:* Dr. Michael Morehead, Dean, 575-646-3404, Fax: 575-646-6032, E-mail: mmorehea@nmsu.edu. *Application contact:* Coordinator, 575-646-2736, Fax: 575-646-7721, E-mail: gradinfo@nmsu.edu. Web site: http://education.nmsu.edu/.

New Mexico State University, Graduate School, College of Extended Learning, Online Teaching and Learning Program, Las Cruces, NM 88003-8001. Offers Graduate Certificate. *Students:* 4 full-time (all women), 12 part-time (9 women); includes 4 minority (1 Black or African American, non-Hispanic/Latino; 2 Hispanic/Latino; 1 Two or more races, non-Hispanic/Latino). Average age 41. 5 applicants, 20% accepted, 1 enrolled. In 2011, 13 Graduate Certificates awarded. *Degree requirements:* For Graduate Certificate, practicum. *Entrance requirements:* Additional exam requirements/ recommendations for international students: Required—TOEFL (minimum score 550 paper-based; 79 iBT), IELTS (minimum score 6.5). Application fee: $40 ($50 for international students). *Expenses:* Tuition, state resident: full-time $5004; part-time $208.50 per credit. Tuition, nonresident: full-time $17,446; part-time $726.90 per credit. *Unit head:* Dr. Roberta Derlin, Associate Vice Provost, 575-646-8231. *Application contact:* Coordinator, 575-646-2736, Fax: 575-646-7721, E-mail: gradinfo@nmsu.edu. Web site: http://extended.nmsu.edu/academics/otl/index.html.

New York Institute of Technology, Graduate Division, School of Education, Old Westbury, NY 11568-8000. Offers MS, Advanced Certificate, Professional Diploma. *Accreditation:* NCATE. Part-time and evening/weekend programs available. Postbaccalaureate distance learning degree programs offered. *Students:* 35 full-time (23 women), 370 part-time (261 women); includes 107 minority (43 Black or African American, non-Hispanic/Latino; 6 American Indian or Alaska Native, non-Hispanic/ Latino; 17 Asian, non-Hispanic/Latino; 39 Hispanic/Latino; 2 Two or more races, non-Hispanic/Latino), 4 international. Average age 33. In 2011, 115 master's, 12 other advanced degrees awarded. *Entrance requirements:* For master's, minimum QPA of 3.0. Additional exam requirements/recommendations for international students: Required—TOEFL (minimum score 550 paper-based; 213 computer-based). *Application deadline:* For fall admission, 7/1 priority date for domestic students; for spring admission, 12/1 priority date for domestic students. Applications are processed on a rolling basis. Application fee: $50. Electronic applications accepted. *Expenses:* Tuition: Part-time $930 per credit hour. *Financial support:* Research assistantships with partial tuition reimbursements, career-related internships or fieldwork, institutionally sponsored loans, and tuition waivers (full and partial) available. Support available to part-time students. Financial award applicants required to submit FAFSA. *Faculty research:* Distance learning, instructional uses of the World Wide Web, telecommunication technologies, emotional intelligence. *Unit head:* Dr. Michael Uttendorfer, Dean, 516-686-7706, Fax: 516-686-7655, E-mail: muttendo@nyit.edu. *Application contact:* Dr. Jacquelyn Nealon, Vice President for Enrollment Services, 516-686-7925, Fax: 516-686-7597, E-mail: jnealon@nyit.edu.

New York University, Steinhardt School of Culture, Education, and Human Development, New York, NY 10003. Offers MA, MFA, MM, MS, DPS, DPT, Ed D, PhD, Advanced Certificate, MA/MA, MM/Advanced Certificate. *Accreditation:* Teacher Education Accreditation Council. Part-time programs available. *Degree requirements:* For master's, thesis (for some programs); for doctorate, comprehensive exam (for some programs), thesis/dissertation. *Entrance requirements:* For doctorate, GRE General Test, interview. Additional exam requirements/recommendations for international students: Required—TOEFL. Electronic applications accepted. *Expenses:* Contact institution. *Faculty research:* Equity, urban adolescents, arts in education, globalization, community and public health.

Niagara University, Graduate Division of Education, Niagara Falls, Niagara University, NY 14109. Offers educational leadership (MS Ed, Certificate), including administration/ supervision (Certificate), educational administration/supervision (MS Ed), educational leadership school district building (MS Ed), school business administration (Certificate), school business leadership (MS Ed), school district administration (Certificate); foundations of teaching (MA, MS Ed); leadership and policy (PhD); literacy instruction (MS Ed); mental health counseling (MS, Certificate); school counseling (MS Ed, Certificate); school psychology (MS, Certificate); teacher education (Certificate), including early childhood and childhood education, middle and adolescence education, special education (grades 1-12). *Accreditation:* NCATE (one or more programs are accredited). Part-time and evening/weekend programs available. *Faculty:* 19 full-time (10 women), 36 part-time/adjunct (17 women). *Students:* 370 full-time (256 women), 228 part-time (166 women); includes 23 minority (11 Black or African American, non-Hispanic/Latino; 1 American Indian or Alaska Native, non-Hispanic/Latino; 2 Asian, non-Hispanic/Latino; 4 Hispanic/Latino; 1 Native Hawaiian or other Pacific Islander, non-Hispanic/Latino; 4 Two or more races, non-Hispanic/Latino), 225 international. Average age 28. 382 applicants, 75% accepted, 154 enrolled. In 2011, 341 master's, 57 other advanced degrees awarded. *Entrance requirements:* For master's, GRE General Test or MAT. *Application deadline:* For fall admission, 8/1 for domestic students. Applications are processed on a rolling basis. Application fee: $30. *Expenses:* Contact institution. *Financial support:* In 2011–12, 2 fellowships, 3 research assistantships were awarded; career-related internships or fieldwork, Federal Work-Study, scholarships/grants, and unspecified assistantships also available. Support available to part-time students. Financial award application deadline: 3/15; financial award applicants required to submit FAFSA. *Faculty research:* Instructional supervision, appraisal and evaluation, career opportunities. *Unit head:* Dr. Debra A. Colley, Dean, 716-286-8560, Fax: 716-286-8561, E-mail: dcolley@niagara.edu. *Application contact:* Carlos Tejada, Associate Dean for Graduate Recruitment, 716-286-8769, Fax: 716-286-8170.

Nicholls State University, Graduate Studies, College of Education, Department of Teacher Education, Thibodaux, LA 70310. Offers administration and supervision (M Ed); counselor education (M Ed); curriculum and instruction (M Ed). *Accreditation:* NCATE. Part-time and evening/weekend programs available. *Degree requirements:* For master's, comprehensive exam, portfolio. *Entrance requirements:* For master's, GRE General Test, teaching license. Electronic applications accepted.

Nipissing University, Faculty of Education, North Bay, ON P1B 8L7, Canada. Offers M Ed, Certificate. Part-time and evening/weekend programs available. *Degree requirements:* For master's, comprehensive exam (for some programs), thesis (for some programs). *Entrance requirements:* For master's, 1 year of experience, letters of recommendation, minimum undergraduate GPA of 3.0. Additional exam requirements/ recommendations for international students: Required—TOEFL (minimum score 600 paper-based; 250 computer-based), IELTS (minimum score 7), TWE (minimum score 5).

Norfolk State University, School of Graduate Studies, School of Education, Norfolk, VA 23504. Offers MA, MAT. *Accreditation:* NCATE. Part-time programs available. *Degree requirements:* For master's, comprehensive exam. *Entrance requirements:* For master's, PRAXIS, GRE/GMAT, interview, teacher license. *Faculty research:* Urban, pre-elementary, and special education.

North Carolina Agricultural and Technical State University, School of Graduate Studies, School of Education, Greensboro, NC 27411. Offers MA Ed, MAT, MS. *Accreditation:* NCATE. Part-time and evening/weekend programs available. *Degree requirements:* For master's, comprehensive exam, qualifying exam. *Entrance requirements:* For master's, GRE General Test.

North Carolina Central University, Division of Academic Affairs, School of Education, Durham, NC 27707-3129. Offers M Ed, MA, MAT, MSA. *Accreditation:* NCATE. Part-time and evening/weekend programs available. *Degree requirements:* For master's, comprehensive exam, thesis or alternative. *Entrance requirements:* For master's, minimum GPA of 3.0 in major, 2.5 overall. Additional exam requirements/ recommendations for international students: Required—TOEFL.

North Carolina State University, Graduate School, College of Education, Raleigh, NC 27695. Offers M Ed, MS, MS Ed, MSA, Ed D, PhD, Certificate. *Accreditation:* NCATE. Part-time programs available. *Degree requirements:* For doctorate, thesis/dissertation. *Entrance requirements:* For master's, doctorate, and Certificate, GRE General Test or MAT, minimum GPA of 3.0 in major. Electronic applications accepted. *Faculty research:* Moral/ethical development, financial policy analysis, middle years education, adult education.

North Central College, Graduate and Continuing Education Programs, Department of Education, Naperville, IL 60566-7063. Offers curriculum and instruction (MA Ed); leadership and administration (MA Ed). Part-time and evening/weekend programs available. *Faculty:* 10 full-time (6 women), 6 part-time/adjunct (3 women). *Students:* 7 full-time (all women), 23 part-time (16 women); includes 3 minority (all Hispanic/Latino). Average age 30. 25 applicants, 56% accepted, 12 enrolled. In 2011, 39 master's awarded. *Degree requirements:* For master's, thesis optional, clinical practicum, project. *Entrance requirements:* For master's, interview. Additional exam requirements/ recommendations for international students: Required—TOEFL (minimum score 577 paper-based; 233 computer-based; 90 iBT). *Application deadline:* For fall admission, 8/ 15 for domestic students; for winter admission, 12/1 for domestic students; for spring admission, 2/1 for domestic students. Applications are processed on a rolling basis. Application fee: $25. *Expenses:* Contact institution. *Financial support:* In 2011–12, 4 students received support. Available to part-time students. *Unit head:* Dr. Kristine Servais, Graduate Program Coordinator, Education, 630-637-5739, Fax: 630-637-5844. *Application contact:* Wendy Kulpinski, Director of Graduate and Continuing Education Admission, 630-637-5808, Fax: 630-637-5844, E-mail: wekulpinski@noctrl.edu.

Northcentral University, Graduate Studies, Prescott Valley, AZ 86314. Offers business (MBA, DBA, PhD, CAGS); education (M Ed, Ed D, PhD, CAGS); marriage and family therapy (MA, PhD); psychology (MA, PhD, CAGS). Evening/weekend programs available. Postbaccalaureate distance learning degree programs offered (no on-campus study). *Faculty:* 41 full-time (21 women), 615 part-time/adjunct (284 women). *Students:* 3,005 full-time (1,743 women), 6,198 part-time (3,248 women); includes 834 minority (577 Black or African American, non-Hispanic/Latino; 28 American Indian or Alaska

Native, non-Hispanic/Latino; 81 Asian, non-Hispanic/Latino; 132 Hispanic/Latino; 16 Native Hawaiian or other Pacific Islander, non-Hispanic/Latino). Average age 44. In 2011, 367 master's, 150 doctorates, 33 other advanced degrees awarded. *Entrance requirements:* For master's, bachelor's degree from regionally-accredited institution, current resume; for doctorate and CAGS, master's degree from regionally-accredited university. Additional exam requirements/recommendations for international students: Required—TOEFL (minimum score 95 computer-based), IELTS (minimum score 7), Pearson Test of English (minimum score 60). *Application deadline:* Applications are processed on a rolling basis. Application fee: $75. *Expenses: Tuition:* Full-time $11,178. *Financial support:* Scholarships/grants available. *Unit head:* Dr. Clinton D. Gardner, President and Provost, 888-327-2877, Fax: 928-759-6381, E-mail: president@ncu.edu. *Application contact:* Marina Swedberg, Senior Director of Admissions, 480-253-3537, Fax: 928-515-5690, E-mail: swedberg@ncu.edu.

North Dakota State University, College of Graduate and Interdisciplinary Studies, College of Human Development and Education, School of Education, Fargo, ND 58108. Offers agricultural education (M Ed, MS), including agricultural education, agricultural extension education (MS); counseling (M Ed, MS, PhD); curriculum and instruction (M Ed, MS), including pedagogy, physical education and athletic administration; education (PhD); educational leadership (M Ed, MS, Ed S); family and consumer sciences education (M Ed, MS); history education (M Ed, MS); institutional analysis (Ed D); mathematics education (M Ed, MS); music education (M Ed, MS); occupational and adult education (Ed D); science education (M Ed, MS). *Accreditation:* NCATE. Part-time and evening/weekend programs available. Postbaccalaureate distance learning degree programs offered (minimal on-campus study). *Faculty:* 24 full-time (10 women), 2 part-time/adjunct (1 woman). *Students:* 91 full-time (64 women), 114 part-time (78 women); includes 13 minority (4 Black or African American, non-Hispanic/Latino; 5 American Indian or Alaska Native, non-Hispanic/Latino; 1 Hispanic/Latino; 3 Two or more races, non-Hispanic/Latino), 8 international. 88 applicants, 67% accepted, 56 enrolled. In 2011, 43 master's, 12 doctorates awarded. *Degree requirements:* For master's, comprehensive exam; for doctorate, thesis/dissertation; for Ed S, thesis. *Entrance requirements:* For degree, GRE General Test, master's degree, minimum GPA of 3.25. Additional exam requirements/recommendations for international students: Required—TOEFL. *Application deadline:* Applications are processed on a rolling basis. Application fee: $45 ($60 for international students). *Financial support:* Research assistantships, teaching assistantships, career-related internships or fieldwork, Federal Work-Study, institutionally sponsored loans, and tuition waivers (full) available. Financial award application deadline: 4/15. *Unit head:* Dr. William Martin, Chair, 701-231-7202, Fax: 701-231-7416, E-mail: william.martin@ndsu.edu. *Application contact:* Sonya Goergen, Marketing, Recruitment, and Public Relations Coordinator, 701-231-7033, Fax: 701-231-6524. Web site: http://www.ndsu.nodak.edu/school_of_education/.

Northeastern Illinois University, Graduate College, College of Education, Chicago, IL 60625-4699. Offers MA, MAT, MS, MSI. Part-time and evening/weekend programs available. *Degree requirements:* For master's, comprehensive exam (for some programs), thesis (for some programs). *Entrance requirements:* For master's, minimum GPA of 2.75. Additional exam requirements/recommendations for international students: Required—TOEFL (minimum score 550 paper-based; 213 computer-based; 79 iBT). Electronic applications accepted. *Faculty research:* Leadership, problem-based learning strategies, school improvement, bilingual education, use of technology.

Northeastern State University, Graduate College, College of Education, Tahlequah, OK 74464-2399. Offers M Ed, MS, MS Ed. *Accreditation:* NCATE. Part-time and evening/weekend programs available. *Faculty:* 26 full-time (11 women). *Students:* 143 full-time (108 women), 457 part-time (385 women); includes 146 minority (21 Black or African American, non-Hispanic/Latino; 111 American Indian or Alaska Native, non-Hispanic/Latino; 3 Asian, non-Hispanic/Latino; 11 Hispanic/Latino), 6 international. In 2011, 212 master's awarded. *Degree requirements:* For master's, thesis. *Entrance requirements:* For master's, GRE or MAT. Additional exam requirements/recommendations for international students: Required—TOEFL (minimum score 213 computer-based). *Application deadline:* For fall admission, 6/1 priority date for domestic students. Applications are processed on a rolling basis. Application fee: $25. Electronic applications accepted. *Financial support:* Teaching assistantships, career-related internships or fieldwork, and Federal Work-Study available. Financial award application deadline: 3/1. *Unit head:* Dr. Kay Grant, Head, 918-456-5511 Ext. 3700. *Application contact:* Margie Railey, Administrative Assistant, 918-456-5511 Ext. 2093, Fax: 918-458-2061, E-mail: railey@nsouk.edu.

Northern Arizona University, Graduate College, College of Education, Flagstaff, AZ 86011. Offers M Ed, MA, Ed D, PhD, Certificate, Ed S. *Accreditation:* NCATE. Part-time and evening/weekend programs available. Postbaccalaureate distance learning degree programs offered (minimal on-campus study). *Faculty:* 96 full-time (58 women). *Students:* 953 full-time (697 women), 1,552 part-time (1,149 women); includes 782 minority (104 Black or African American, non-Hispanic/Latino; 162 American Indian or Alaska Native, non-Hispanic/Latino; 39 Asian, non-Hispanic/Latino; 426 Hispanic/Latino; 5 Native Hawaiian or other Pacific Islander, non-Hispanic/Latino; 46 Two or more races, non-Hispanic/Latino), 14 international. Average age 36. 848 applicants, 85% accepted, 531 enrolled. In 2011, 1,110 master's, 22 doctorates, 81 other advanced degrees awarded. *Degree requirements:* For master's, comprehensive exam, thesis (for some programs); for doctorate, comprehensive exam, thesis/dissertation. *Entrance requirements:* For master's, minimum GPA of 3.0; for doctorate, GRE or MAT. Additional exam requirements/recommendations for international students: Required—TOEFL (minimum score 550 paper-based; 213 computer-based; 80 iBT), IELTS (minimum score 7). *Application deadline:* Applications are processed on a rolling basis. Application fee: $65. Electronic applications accepted. *Expenses:* Tuition, state resident: full-time $7190; part-time $355 per credit hour. Tuition, nonresident: full-time $18,092; part-time $1005 per credit hour. *Required fees:* $818; $328 per semester. *Financial support:* In 2011–12, 2 research assistantships with partial tuition reimbursements (averaging $10,000 per year), 15 teaching assistantships with partial tuition reimbursements (averaging $10,000 per year) were awarded; career-related internships or fieldwork, Federal Work-Study, scholarships/grants, health care benefits, tuition waivers (full and partial), and unspecified assistantships also available. Financial award applicants required to submit FAFSA. *Unit head:* Dr. Gypsy Denzine, Dean, 928-523-9211, Fax: 928-523-1929, E-mail: gypsy.denzine@nau.edu. *Application contact:* April Sandoval, Coordinator, 928-523-4348, Fax: 928-523-8950, E-mail: april.sandoval@nau.edu. Web site: http://nau.edu/coe/.

Northern Illinois University, Graduate School, College of Education, De Kalb, IL 60115-2854. Offers MS, MS Ed, Ed D, Ed S. *Accreditation:* NCATE. Part-time and evening/weekend programs available. Postbaccalaureate distance learning degree programs offered (minimal on-campus study). *Faculty:* 110 full-time (66 women), 5 part-time/adjunct (3 women). *Students:* 299 full-time (195 women), 1,104 part-time (776 women); includes 305 minority (177 Black or African American, non-Hispanic/Latino; 2 American Indian or Alaska Native, non-Hispanic/Latino; 43 Asian, non-Hispanic/Latino; 69 Hispanic/Latino; 14 Two or more races, non-Hispanic/Latino), 45 international. Average age 34. 428 applicants, 67% accepted, 160 enrolled. In 2011, 519 master's, 50 doctorates, 39 other advanced degrees awarded. Terminal master's awarded for partial completion of doctoral program. *Degree requirements:* For master's and Ed S, comprehensive exam, thesis optional; for doctorate, thesis/dissertation, candidacy exam, dissertation defense. *Entrance requirements:* For master's, GRE General Test or MAT, minimum GPA of 2.75; for doctorate, GRE General Test or MAT, minimum GPA of 2.75 (undergraduate), 3.2 (graduate); for Ed S, GRE General Test, master's degree; minimum undergraduate GPA of 2.75, graduate 3.2. Additional exam requirements/recommendations for international students: Required—TOEFL (minimum score 550 paper-based; 213 computer-based). *Application deadline:* For fall admission, 6/1 for domestic students, 5/1 for international students; for spring admission, 11/1 for domestic students, 10/1 for international students. Applications are processed on a rolling basis. Application fee: $40. Electronic applications accepted. *Financial support:* In 2011–12, 6 teaching assistantships with full tuition reimbursements were awarded; fellowships with full tuition reimbursements, research assistantships with full tuition reimbursements, career-related internships or fieldwork, Federal Work-Study, scholarships/grants, tuition waivers (full), and staff assistantships also available. Support available to part-time students. Financial award applicants required to submit FAFSA. *Unit head:* Dr. La Vonne I. Neal, Dean, 815-753-1949, Fax: 851-753-2100. *Application contact:* Graduate School Office, 815-753-0395, E-mail: gradsch@niu.edu. Web site: http://www.cedu.niu.edu/.

Northern Kentucky University, Office of Graduate Programs, College of Education and Human Services, Highland Heights, KY 41099. Offers MA, MS, MSW, Ed D, Certificate, Ed S. *Accreditation:* NCATE. Part-time and evening/weekend programs available. *Faculty:* 44 full-time (28 women), 9 part-time/adjunct (6 women). *Students:* 156 full-time (128 women), 374 part-time (273 women); includes 38 minority (29 Black or African American, non-Hispanic/Latino; 2 Asian, non-Hispanic/Latino; 6 Hispanic/Latino; 1 Native Hawaiian or other Pacific Islander, non-Hispanic/Latino), 1 international. Average age 34. 300 applicants, 56% accepted, 149 enrolled. In 2011, 192 master's, 2 doctorates, 11 other advanced degrees awarded. *Degree requirements:* For master's, comprehensive exam (for some programs), thesis (for some programs). *Entrance requirements:* For master's, GRE. Additional exam requirements/recommendations for international students: Required—TOEFL (minimum score 550 paper-based; 213 computer-based; 79 iBT); Recommended—IELTS (minimum score 6.5). *Application deadline:* For fall admission, 6/1 for international students; for spring admission, 10/1 for international students. Application fee: $40. Electronic applications accepted. *Expenses:* Tuition, state resident: full-time $7614; part-time $423 per credit hour. Tuition, nonresident: full-time $13,104; part-time $728 per credit hour. Tuition and fees vary according to degree level and reciprocity agreements. *Financial support:* Unspecified assistantships available. Financial award applicants required to submit FAFSA. *Unit head:* Dr. Mark Wasicsko, Dean, 859-572-5229, Fax: 859-572-6623, E-mail: wasicskom1@nku.edu. *Application contact:* Dr. Peg Griffin, Director of Graduate Programs, 859-572-6934, Fax: 859-572-6670, E-mail: griffinp@nku.edu. Web site: http://www.nku.edu/~education/.

Northern Michigan University, College of Graduate Studies, College of Professional Studies, School of Education, Marquette, MI 49855-5301. Offers administration and supervision (MA Ed, Ed S); elementary education (MA Ed); learning disabilities (MA Ed); reading education (MA Ed, Ed S), including literacy leadership (Ed S), reading (MA Ed), reading specialist (MA Ed); school guidance counseling (MA Ed); science education (MS); secondary education (MA Ed). *Accreditation:* Teacher Education Accreditation Council. Part-time programs available. *Degree requirements:* For master's, thesis or alternative. *Entrance requirements:* For master's, minimum GPA of 3.0.

Northern State University, Division of Graduate Studies in Education, Aberdeen, SD 57401-7198. Offers MS, MS Ed. *Accreditation:* NCATE. Part-time and evening/weekend programs available. *Degree requirements:* For master's, thesis optional. *Entrance requirements:* For master's, minimum GPA of 2.75. Additional exam requirements/recommendations for international students: Required—TOEFL (minimum score 550 paper-based; 213 computer-based; 78 iBT), IELTS (minimum score 6). Electronic applications accepted.

North Georgia College & State University, School of Education, Dahlonega, GA 30597. Offers art education (MAT); early childhood education (M Ed); English education (MAT); history education (MAT); math education (MAT); middle grades education (M Ed, MAT); physical education (MS); school leadership (Ed S); secondary education (M Ed), including English education, history education, mathematics education, physical education; teacher education (MAT). *Accreditation:* NCATE. Part-time and evening/weekend programs available. Postbaccalaureate distance learning degree programs offered (no on-campus study). *Faculty:* 23 full-time (14 women), 16 part-time/adjunct (11 women). *Students:* 19 full-time (17 women), 199 part-time (147 women); includes 7 minority (3 Black or African American, non-Hispanic/Latino; 1 Asian, non-Hispanic/Latino; 3 Hispanic/Latino), 1 international. Average age 34. 259 applicants, 66% accepted, 112 enrolled. In 2011, 100 master's, 16 other advanced degrees awarded. *Degree requirements:* For master's, comprehensive exam, thesis optional. *Entrance requirements:* For master's, GRE or MAT, GACE, minimum GPA of 2.75; for Ed S, GRE General Test or MAT, 3 years of teaching experience, master's degree, minimum graduate GPA of 3.25, leadership position in the school. Additional exam requirements/recommendations for international students: Required—TOEFL (minimum score 550 paper-based; 213 computer-based; 79 iBT), IELTS (minimum score 6.5). *Application deadline:* For fall admission, 8/1 priority date for domestic students, 7/1 for international students; for spring admission, 12/1 priority date for domestic students, 11/1 for international students. Applications are processed on a rolling basis. Application fee: $40. Electronic applications accepted. *Expenses:* Tuition, state resident: full-time $3528; part-time $196 per credit hour. Tuition, nonresident: full-time $14,094; part-time $783 per credit hour. *Required fees:* $1718; $859 per semester. Tuition and fees vary according to course load, campus/location and program. *Financial support:* Teaching assistantships, career-related internships or fieldwork, scholarships/grants, and unspecified assistantships available. Financial award application deadline: 5/1; financial award applicants required to submit CSS PROFILE or FAFSA. *Faculty research:* Identification of professional development school structures supporting P-12 student achievement, impact of diverse field placement settings in teacher belief development among preservice teachers, use of inquiry methodology in social studies teaching with English language learners, use of instructional differentiation in the middle grades classroom, effects of international school placements on preservice teacher beliefs and attitudes. *Unit head:* Dr. Bob Michael, Dean, School of Education, 706-864-1998, Fax: 706-867-2850, E-mail: bmichael@northgeorgia.edu. *Application contact:* Susan L. Perry, Graduate Admissions Coordinator, 706-864-1543, Fax: 706-867-2795, E-mail: slperry@northgeorgia.edu. Web site: http://www.northgeorgia.edu/soe/.

North Greenville University, T. Walter Brashier Graduate School, Greer, SC 29651. Offers Christian ministry (MCM, D Min); education (M Ed); financial planning (MBA); human resources (MBA). Part-time and evening/weekend programs available. Postbaccalaureate distance learning degree programs offered (no on-campus study). *Faculty:* 8 full-time (3 women), 15 part-time/adjunct (0 women). *Students:* 55 full-time (33 women), 148 part-time (53 women); includes 48 minority (37 Black or African American, non-Hispanic/Latino; 1 American Indian or Alaska Native, non-Hispanic/Latino; 3 Asian, non-Hispanic/Latino; 5 Hispanic/Latino; 2 Two or more races, non-Hispanic/Latino). Average age 32. 180 applicants, 98% accepted, 170 enrolled. In 2011, 58 master's awarded. *Degree requirements:* For master's, comprehensive exam (for some programs), thesis or alternative, capstone course. *Entrance requirements:* For master's, minimum GPA of 2.25 overall, 2.5 in major; for doctorate, MAT. Additional exam requirements/recommendations for international students: Required—TOEFL (minimum score 550 paper-based; 213 computer-based). *Application deadline:* For fall admission, 8/1 for domestic students, 6/1 for international students; for winter admission, 1/1 for domestic students, 10/1 for international students; for spring admission, 3/1 for domestic students, 1/1 for international students. Applications are processed on a rolling basis. Application fee: $30. Electronic applications accepted. *Financial support:* In 2011–12, 112 students received support, including 1 research assistantship (averaging $2,000 per year); Federal Work-Study, institutionally sponsored loans, scholarships/grants, tuition waivers (partial), and unspecified assistantships also available. Support available to part-time students. Financial award applicants required to submit FAFSA. *Faculty research:* Organizational behavior, church growth, homiletics, human resources, business strategy. *Unit head:* Dr. Joseph Samuel Isgett, Jr., Vice President for Graduate Studies, 864-877-3052, Fax: 864-877-1653, E-mail: sisgett@ngu.edu. *Application contact:* Tawana P. Scott, Dean of Graduate Enrollment, 864-877-1598, Fax: 864-877-1653, E-mail: tscott@ngu.edu. Web site: http://www.ngu.edu/gradschool.php.

North Park University, School of Education, Chicago, IL 60625-4895. Offers MA. *Degree requirements:* For master's, thesis. *Entrance requirements:* For master's, GRE General Test. *Faculty research:* Teacher leadership, research design, teacher education.

Northwest Christian University, School of Education and Counseling, Eugene, OR 97401-3745. Offers community counseling (MA); education (M Ed); school counseling (MA). Part-time and evening/weekend programs available. *Entrance requirements:* For master's, MAT, interview, minimum GPA of 3.0. Electronic applications accepted.

Northwestern Oklahoma State University, School of Professional Studies, Alva, OK 73717-2799. Offers adult education management and administration (M Ed); counseling psychology (MCP); curriculum and instruction (M Ed); educational leadership (M Ed); elementary education (M Ed); non-certificate (M Ed); reading specialist (M Ed); school counseling (M Ed); secondary education (M Ed). *Accreditation:* NCATE (one or more programs are accredited). Part-time programs available. *Faculty:* 29 full-time (14 women), 27 part-time/adjunct (18 women). *Students:* 47 full-time (35 women), 77 part-time (56 women); includes 14 minority (2 Black or African American, non-Hispanic/Latino; 11 American Indian or Alaska Native, non-Hispanic/Latino; 1 Hispanic/Latino), 1 international. Average age 31. 43 applicants, 86% accepted, 37 enrolled. In 2011, 66 master's awarded. *Degree requirements:* For master's, comprehensive exam (for some programs), thesis optional, portfolio. *Entrance requirements:* For master's, GRE General Test or MAT, minimum GPA of 2.75. *Application deadline:* Applications are processed on a rolling basis. Application fee: $15. *Financial support:* Federal Work-Study available. Support available to part-time students. Financial award application deadline: 5/1; financial award applicants required to submit FAFSA. *Unit head:* Dr. Shawn Holliday, Associate Dean of Graduate Studies, 580-327-8451, E-mail: spholliday@nwosu.edu. *Application contact:* Sabrina Watson, Coordinator of Graduate Studies, 580-327-8410, E-mail: sdwatson@nwosu.edu. Web site: http://www.nwosu.edu/professional-studies.

Northwestern State University of Louisiana, Graduate Studies and Research, College of Education and Human Development, Natchitoches, LA 71497. Offers M Ed, MA, MAT, Ed S. *Accreditation:* ACA (one or more programs are accredited); NCATE. *Faculty:* 18 full-time (13 women), 8 part-time/adjunct (6 women). *Students:* 100 full-time (79 women), 486 part-time (395 women); includes 122 minority (99 Black or African American, non-Hispanic/Latino; 5 American Indian or Alaska Native, non-Hispanic/Latino; 4 Asian, non-Hispanic/Latino; 9 Hispanic/Latino; 5 Two or more races, non-Hispanic/Latino), 3 international. Average age 34. 195 applicants, 98% accepted, 140 enrolled. In 2011, 141 master's, 12 other advanced degrees awarded. *Degree requirements:* For master's, comprehensive exam, thesis (for some programs); for Ed S, comprehensive exam, thesis. *Entrance requirements:* For master's, GRE General Test, GRE Subject Test, minimum undergraduate GPA of 2.5; for Ed S, GRE General Test. Additional exam requirements/recommendations for international students: Required—TOEFL. *Application deadline:* For fall admission, 3/15 priority date for domestic students; for spring admission, 10/15 priority date for domestic students. Applications are processed on a rolling basis. Application fee: $20 ($30 for international students). Electronic applications accepted. *Expenses:* Tuition, state resident: full-time $3440. Tuition, nonresident: full-time $12,010. *Financial support:* Career-related internships or fieldwork and Federal Work-Study available. Financial award application deadline: 5/1; financial award applicants required to submit FAFSA. *Faculty research:* Teacher-parent-child-friendly physical activities for young children, Net generation and social media, positive emotion and multimedia learning, the effects of Web-based mathematics resources on the motivation and achievement of high school students with learning disabilities, educational leadership. *Unit head:* Dr. Vickie Gentry, Chair, 318-357-6288, Fax: 318-357-6275, E-mail: education@nsula.edu. *Application contact:* Dr. Steven G. Horton, Associate Provost/Dean, Graduate Studies, Research, and Information Systems, 318-357-5851, Fax: 318-357-5019, E-mail: grad_school@nsula.edu. Web site: http://www.nsula.edu/education/.

Northwestern University, The Graduate School, School of Education and Social Policy, Evanston, IL 60208. Offers education (MS), including advanced teaching, elementary teaching, higher education administration, secondary teaching; human development and social policy (PhD); learning and organizational change (MS); learning sciences (MA, PhD). MA and PhD admissions and degrees offered through The Graduate School. Part-time and evening/weekend programs available. *Degree requirements:* For doctorate, comprehensive exam, thesis/dissertation. *Entrance requirements:* For master's and doctorate, GRE General Test. Electronic applications accepted. *Expenses:* Contact institution. *Faculty research:* Technology, curriculum design, welfare, education reform, learning.

See Display below and Close-Up on page 807.

Northwest Missouri State University, Graduate School, College of Education and Human Services, Maryville, MO 64468-6001. Offers MS, MS Ed, Certificate, Ed S. *Accreditation:* NCATE. Part-time programs available. *Faculty:* 45 full-time (29 women). *Students:* 68 full-time (42 women), 221 part-time (170 women); includes 55 minority (9 Black or African American, non-Hispanic/Latino; 35 American Indian or Alaska Native, non-Hispanic/Latino; 2 Asian, non-Hispanic/Latino; 7 Hispanic/Latino; 2 Two or more races, non-Hispanic/Latino), 3 international. 103 applicants, 100% accepted, 62 enrolled. In 2011, 143 master's, 15 other advanced degrees awarded. *Degree requirements:* For master's, comprehensive exam; for other advanced degree, comprehensive exam, thesis. *Entrance requirements:* For master's, GRE General Test, writing sample; for other advanced degree, minimum graduate GPA of 3.25. Additional exam requirements/recommendations for international students: Required—TOEFL (minimum score 550 paper-based; 213 computer-based). *Application deadline:* For fall admission, 7/1 for domestic and international students; for spring admission, 11/15 for domestic and international students. Application fee: $0 ($50 for international students). Electronic applications accepted. *Financial support:* In 2011–12, 4 research assistantships with full tuition reimbursements (averaging $6,000 per year), 49 teaching assistantships with full tuition reimbursements (averaging $6,000 per year) were awarded; unspecified assistantships also available. Financial award application deadline: 4/1; financial award applicants required to submit FAFSA. *Faculty research:* Great books of educational administration. *Unit head:* Dr. Joyce Piveral, Dean, 660-562-

1778. *Application contact:* Dr. Gregory Haddock, Dean of Graduate School, 660-562-1145, Fax: 660-562-1096, E-mail: gradsch@nwmissouri.edu.

Northwest Nazarene University, Graduate Studies, Program in Teacher Education, Nampa, ID 83686-5897. Offers curriculum and instruction (M Ed); educational leadership (M Ed, Ed D, Ed S); exceptional child (M Ed); reading education (M Ed). *Accreditation:* ACA (one or more programs are accredited); NCATE. Part-time programs available. Postbaccalaureate distance learning degree programs offered (no on-campus study). *Faculty:* 15 full-time (9 women), 36 part-time/adjunct (21 women). *Students:* 80 full-time (54 women), 119 part-time (98 women); includes 13 minority (1 American Indian or Alaska Native, non-Hispanic/Latino; 10 Hispanic/Latino; 1 Native Hawaiian or other Pacific Islander, non-Hispanic/Latino; 1 Two or more races, non-Hispanic/Latino), 8 international. Average age 36. 60 applicants, 95% accepted, 39 enrolled. In 2011, 43 master's, 24 other advanced degrees awarded. *Degree requirements:* For master's, comprehensive exam (for some programs), action research project. *Entrance requirements:* For master's, minimum undergraduate GPA of 2.8 overall or 3.0 during final 30 semester credits. *Application deadline:* For fall admission, 9/1 for domestic students. Applications are processed on a rolling basis. Application fee: $25. *Faculty research:* Action research, cooperative learning, accountability, institutional accreditation. *Unit head:* Dr. Paula Kellerer, Chair, 208-467-8729, Fax: 208-467-8562. *Application contact:* Jackie Schober, 208-467-8341, Fax: 208-467-8786, E-mail: jsschober@nnu.edu. Web site: http://www.nnu.edu/graded/.

Northwest University, School of Education, Kirkland, WA 98033. Offers education (M Ed); teaching (MIT). Part-time and evening/weekend programs available. *Faculty:* 6 full-time (3 women), 6 part-time/adjunct (3 women). *Students:* 24 full-time (19 women), 18 part-time (14 women); includes 4 minority (1 Black or African American, non-Hispanic/Latino; 3 Asian, non-Hispanic/Latino). 38 applicants, 100% accepted, 30 enrolled. In 2011, 41 master's awarded. *Degree requirements:* For master's, action research project. *Entrance requirements:* For master's, (WEST-B) Washington Educator Skills Test-Basic/(WEST-E) Washington Educator Skills Test-Endorsements, minimum GPA of 3.3. Additional exam requirements/recommendations for international students: Recommended—TOEFL. *Application deadline:* For fall admission, 4/1 priority date for domestic students. Application fee: $75. Electronic applications accepted. *Expenses:* Contact institution. *Financial support:* Federal Work-Study, health care benefits, and tuition waivers (full and partial) available. *Unit head:* Dr. Ron Jacobson, Dean, 425-889-5304, E-mail: ron.jacobson@northwestu.edu. *Application contact:* Aaron Oosterwyk, Director of Graduate and Professional Studies Enrollment, 425-889-7792, Fax: 425-803-3059, E-mail: aaron.oosterwyk@northwestu.edu. Web site: http://www.northwestu.edu/education/.

Notre Dame de Namur University, Division of Academic Affairs, School of Education and Leadership, Program in Teacher Education, Belmont, CA 94002-1908. Offers curriculum and instruction (MA); disciplinary studies (MA); educational technology (MA); multiple subject teaching credential (Certificate); single subject teaching credential (Certificate). Part-time and evening/weekend programs available. *Students:* 93 full-time (71 women), 128 part-time (89 women); includes 40 minority (3 Black or African American, non-Hispanic/Latino; 2 American Indian or Alaska Native, non-Hispanic/Latino; 14 Asian, non-Hispanic/Latino; 19 Hispanic/Latino; 1 Native Hawaiian or other Pacific Islander, non-Hispanic/Latino; 1 Two or more races, non-Hispanic/Latino), 2 international. In 2011, 18 master's awarded. *Entrance requirements:* Additional exam requirements/recommendations for international students: Required—TOEFL (minimum score 550 paper-based; 213 computer-based; 79 iBT). Application fee: $60. *Expenses: Tuition:* Full-time $14,220; part-time $790 per credit. *Required fees:* $35 per semester. Tuition and fees vary according to program. *Financial support:* Career-related internships or fieldwork available. Support available to part-time students. Financial award applicants required to submit FAFSA. *Unit head:* Dr. Kim Tolley, Director, 650-508-3464, E-mail: ktolley@ndnu.edu. *Application contact:* Candace Hallmark, Associate Director of Admissions, 650-508-3592, Fax: 650-508-3426, E-mail: grad.admit@ndnu.edu.

Notre Dame of Maryland University, Graduate Studies, Program in Teaching, Baltimore, MD 21210-2476. Offers MA. *Accreditation:* NCATE. *Entrance requirements:* For master's, Watson-Glaser Critical Thinking Appraisal, writing test, grammar test, interview. Additional exam requirements/recommendations for international students: Required—TOEFL (minimum score 500 paper-based; 173 computer-based; 61 iBT). Electronic applications accepted.

Nova Southeastern University, Abraham S. Fischler School of Education, Fort Lauderdale, FL 33314-7796. Offers education (MS, Ed D, Ed S); instructional design and diversity education (MS); instructional technology and distance education (MS); speech language pathology (MS, SLPD); teaching and learning (MA). Part-time and evening/weekend programs available. *Students:* 3,832 full-time (3,039 women), 4,222 part-time (3,452 women); includes 4,795 minority (3,209 Black or African American, non-Hispanic/Latino; 27 American Indian or Alaska Native, non-Hispanic/Latino; 97 Asian, non-Hispanic/Latino; 1,394 Hispanic/Latino; 16 Native Hawaiian or other Pacific Islander, non-Hispanic/Latino; 52 Two or more races, non-Hispanic/Latino), 54 international. Average age 40. In 2011, 1,669 master's, 383 doctorates, 402 other advanced degrees awarded. *Degree requirements:* For master's, practicum, internship; for doctorate, thesis/dissertation; for Ed S, thesis, practicum, internship. *Entrance requirements:* For master's, MAT or GRE (for some programs), CLAST, PRAXIS I, CBEST, General Knowledge Test, teaching certification, minimum GPA of 2.5, verification of teaching, BS; for doctorate, MAT or GRE, master's degree, minimum cumulative GPA of 3.0; for Ed S, MAT or GRE, master's degree, teaching certificate; minimum GPA of 3.0. Additional exam requirements/recommendations for international students: Recommended—TOEFL (minimum score 550 paper-based; 213 computer-based; 80 iBT), IELTS (minimum score 6). *Application deadline:* Applications are processed on a rolling basis. Application fee: $50. Electronic applications accepted. *Financial support:* In 2011–12, 2 fellowships with full tuition reimbursements (averaging $30,000 per year) were awarded; career-related internships or fieldwork, Federal Work-Study, and tuition waivers (full) also available. Support available to part-time students. Financial award application deadline: 4/15; financial award applicants required to submit FAFSA. *Unit head:* Dr. H. Wells Singleton, Provost/Dean, 954-262-8730, Fax: 954-262-3894, E-mail: singlew@nova.edu. *Application contact:* Dr. Jennifer Quinones Nottingham, Dean of Student Affairs, 800-986-3223 Ext. 8500, E-mail: jlquinon@nova.edu. Web site: http://www.fischlerschool.nova.edu/.

Oakland City University, School of Education, Oakland City, IN 47660-1099. Offers educational leadership (Ed D); teaching (MA). *Accreditation:* NCATE. *Faculty:* 4 full-time (1 woman), 16 part-time/adjunct (8 women). *Students:* 39 full-time (23 women), 65 part-time (38 women); includes 9 minority (all Black or African American, non-Hispanic/Latino). Average age 32. 46 applicants, 91% accepted, 40 enrolled. In 2011, 64 master's, 8 doctorates awarded. Terminal master's awarded for partial completion of doctoral program. *Degree requirements:* For master's, thesis; for doctorate, comprehensive exam, thesis/dissertation. *Entrance requirements:* For master's, MAT, minimum GPA of 3.0, interview, resume, letters of recommendation; for doctorate, MAT, GRE, minimum GPA of 3.2, interview, resume, letters of recommendation. *Application deadline:* For spring admission, 5/1 for domestic students. Applications are processed on a rolling basis. Application fee: $35. *Expenses:* Contact institution. *Financial support:* Unspecified assistantships available. Financial award applicants required to submit FAFSA. *Faculty research:* Assessment, cultural diversity, teacher education, education leadership. *Unit head:* Dr. Mary Jo Beauchamp, Dean, 812-749-1399, Fax: 812-749-1511, E-mail: mbeauchamp@oak.edu. *Application contact:* Kim Heldt, Director of Admissions, 812-749-1218, E-mail: kheldt@oak.edu. Web site: http://www.oak.edu/.

Oakland University, Graduate Study and Lifelong Learning, School of Education and Human Services, Rochester, MI 48309-4401. Offers M Ed, MA, MAT, MTD, PhD, Certificate, Ed S. *Accreditation:* Teacher Education Accreditation Council. Part-time and evening/weekend programs available. *Degree requirements:* For doctorate, thesis/dissertation. *Entrance requirements:* For master's and doctorate, minimum GPA of 3.0 for unconditional admission. Additional exam requirements/recommendations for international students: Required—TOEFL (minimum score 550 paper-based; 213 computer-based). Electronic applications accepted. *Faculty research:* Earth science for middle and high school teachers.

Occidental College, Graduate Studies, Department of Education, Los Angeles, CA 90041-3314. Offers elementary education (MAT), including liberal studies; secondary education (MAT), including English and comparative literary studies, history, life science, mathematics, physical science, social science, Spanish. Part-time programs available. *Degree requirements:* For master's, comprehensive exam, graduate synthesis paper. *Entrance requirements:* For master's, GRE General Test, minimum GPA of 3.0. Additional exam requirements/recommendations for international students: Required—TOEFL (minimum score 625 paper-based; 263 computer-based). *Expenses:* Contact institution. *Faculty research:* Preparing teacher-leaders, curriculum development.

Oglethorpe University, Division of Education, Atlanta, GA 30319-2797. Offers early childhood education (MAT). Part-time programs available. *Degree requirements:* For master's, comprehensive exam. *Entrance requirements:* For master's, GRE General Test, PRAXIS, minimum GPA of 2.8, 3 recommendations.

Ohio Dominican University, Graduate Programs, Division of Education, Columbus, OH 43219-2099. Offers M Ed. *Accreditation:* NCATE. Part-time and evening/weekend programs available. Postbaccalaureate distance learning degree programs offered. *Degree requirements:* For master's, thesis or alternative. *Entrance requirements:* For master's, minimum undergraduate GPA of 3.0, teaching certificate, teaching experience, 3 letters of recommendation. Additional exam requirements/recommendations for international students: Required—TOEFL (minimum score 550 paper-based; 213 computer-based), IELTS (minimum score 6.5).

The Ohio State University, Graduate School, College of Education and Human Ecology, Columbus, OH 43210. Offers M Ed, MA, MS, PhD. *Accreditation:* NCATE. *Faculty:* 154. *Students:* 648 full-time (463 women), 545 part-time (397 women); includes 157 minority (77 Black or African American, non-Hispanic/Latino; 4 American Indian or Alaska Native, non-Hispanic/Latino; 31 Asian, non-Hispanic/Latino; 33 Hispanic/Latino; 12 Two or more races, non-Hispanic/Latino), 191 international. Average age 32. In 2011, 136 master's, 100 doctorates awarded. Terminal master's awarded for partial completion of doctoral program. *Degree requirements:* For master's, comprehensive exam (for some programs), thesis optional; for doctorate, comprehensive exam, thesis/dissertation. *Entrance requirements:* For doctorate, GRE. Additional exam requirements/recommendations for international students: Required—TOEFL (minimum score 600 paper-based; 250 computer-based; 79 iBT), Michigan English Language Assessment Battery (minimum score 82). *Application deadline:* For fall admission, 8/15 priority date for domestic students, 7/1 for international students; for winter admission, 12/1 priority date for domestic students, 11/1 for international students; for spring admission, 3/1 priority date for domestic students, 2/1 for international students. Applications are processed on a rolling basis. Application fee: $40 ($50 for international students). Electronic applications accepted. *Expenses:* Tuition, state resident: full-time $11,400. Tuition, nonresident: full-time $28,125. Tuition and fees vary according to course load, degree level, campus/location and program. *Financial support:* Fellowships with tuition reimbursements, research assistantships with tuition reimbursements, teaching assistantships with tuition reimbursements, career-related internships or fieldwork, Federal Work-Study, institutionally sponsored loans, scholarships/grants, traineeships, health care benefits, and unspecified assistantships available. Support available to part-time students. *Faculty research:* Math and science education; teaching professional development; issues related to urban education; health, well-being, and sports; literacy education. *Total annual research expenditures:* $19 million. *Unit head:* Cheryl Achterberg, Dean, 614-292-6691, E-mail: cachterberg@ehe.osu.edu. *Application contact:* Graduate Admissions, 614-292-6031, Fax: 614-292-3656, E-mail: gradadmissions@osu.edu. Web site: http://ehe.osu.edu/.

The Ohio State University at Lima, Graduate Programs, Lima, OH 45804. Offers early childhood education (M Ed); education (MA); middle childhood education (M Ed); social work (MSW). Part-time programs available. *Faculty:* 41. *Students:* 27 full-time (13 women), 39 part-time (33 women); includes 3 minority (1 Black or African American, non-Hispanic/Latino; 2 Two or more races, non-Hispanic/Latino). Average age 34. Terminal master's awarded for partial completion of doctoral program. *Degree requirements:* For master's, comprehensive exam (for some programs), thesis (for some programs). *Entrance requirements:* For master's, GRE, minimum GPA of 3.0. Additional exam requirements/recommendations for international students: Required—TOEFL (minimum score 550 paper-based; 79 iBT), Michigan English Language Assessment Battery (minimum score 82); Recommended—IELTS (minimum score 7), TWE. *Application deadline:* For fall admission, 6/1 priority date for domestic students, 6/1 for international students; for spring admission, 10/15 priority date for domestic students, 10/15 for international students. Applications are processed on a rolling basis. Application fee: $40 ($50 for international students). Electronic applications accepted. *Expenses:* Tuition, state resident: full-time $11,130. Tuition, nonresident: full-time $27,855. *Financial support:* Application deadline: 2/1. *Unit head:* Dr. John Snyder, Dean/Director, 419-995-8481, E-mail: snyder.4@osu.edu. *Application contact:* Graduate Admissions, 614-292-9444, Fax: 614-292-3895, E-mail: domestic.grad@osu.edu.

The Ohio State University at Marion, Graduate Programs, Marion, OH 43302-5695. Offers early childhood education (pre-K to grade 3) (M Ed); education - teaching and learning (MA); middle childhood education (grades 4-9) (M Ed). Part-time programs available. *Faculty:* 38. *Students:* 67 full-time (49 women), 13 part-time (9 women); includes 2 minority (1 American Indian or Alaska Native, non-Hispanic/Latino; 1 Hispanic/Latino). Average age 32. *Degree requirements:* For master's, comprehensive exam (for some programs), thesis (for some programs). *Entrance requirements:* For master's, GRE, minimum undergraduate GPA of 3.0. Additional exam requirements/recommendations for international students: Required—Michigan English Language Assessment Battery (minimum score 82); Recommended—TOEFL (minimum score 650 paper-based; 79 iBT), IELTS (minimum score 7). *Application deadline:* For fall admission, 6/1 priority date for domestic students, 6/1 for international students; for spring admission, 10/15 priority date for domestic students, 10/15 for international students. Applications are processed on a rolling basis. Application fee: $40 ($50 for international students). Electronic applications accepted. *Expenses:* Tuition, state resident: full-time $11,130. Tuition, nonresident: full-time $27,855. Tuition and fees vary according to course load. *Financial support:* Application deadline: 1/15; applicants required to submit FAFSA. *Unit head:* Dr. Gregory S. Rose, Dean/Director, 740-389-

6786 Ext. 6218, E-mail: rose.9@osu.edu. *Application contact:* Graduate Admissions, 614-292-9444, Fax: 614-292-3895, E-mail: domestic.grad@osu.edu.

The Ohio State University–Mansfield Campus, Graduate Programs, Mansfield, OH 44906-1599. Offers early childhood education (M Ed); education (MA); middle childhood education (M Ed); social work (MSW). Part-time programs available. *Faculty:* 41. *Students:* 21 full-time (15 women), 57 part-time (48 women); includes 5 minority (2 Black or African American, non-Hispanic/Latino; 1 Asian, non-Hispanic/Latino; 1 Hispanic/Latino; 1 Two or more races, non-Hispanic/Latino), 1 international. Average age 33. *Degree requirements:* For master's, comprehensive exam (for some programs), thesis (for some programs). *Entrance requirements:* For master's, GRE, minimum GPA of 3.0. Additional exam requirements/recommendations for international students: Required—TOEFL (minimum score 550 paper-based; 79 iBT), Michigan English Language Assessment Battery (minimum score 82); Recommended—IELTS (minimum score 7). *Application deadline:* For fall admission, 6/1 priority date for domestic students, 6/1 for international students; for spring admission, 10/15 priority date for domestic students, 10/15 for international students. Applications are processed on a rolling basis. Application fee: $40 ($50 for international students). Electronic applications accepted. *Expenses:* Tuition, state resident: full-time $11,130. Tuition, nonresident: full-time $27,855. Tuition and fees vary according to course load. *Financial support:* Teaching assistantships with full tuition reimbursements, Federal Work-Study, and scholarships/grants available. Support available to part-time students. Financial award application deadline: 2/1. *Unit head:* Dr. Stephen M. Gavazzi, Dean and Director, 419-755-4221, Fax: 419-755-4241, E-mail: gavazzi.1@osu.edu. *Application contact:* Graduate Admissions, 614-292-9444, Fax: 614-292-3895, E-mail: domestic.grad@osu.edu.

The Ohio State University–Newark Campus, Graduate Programs, Newark, OH 43055-1797. Offers early/middle childhood education (M Ed); education - teaching and learning (MA); social work (MSW). Part-time programs available. *Faculty:* 56. *Students:* 63 full-time (55 women), 46 part-time (39 women); includes 6 minority (1 Black or African American, non-Hispanic/Latino; 1 Asian, non-Hispanic/Latino; 3 Hispanic/Latino; 1 Two or more races, non-Hispanic/Latino). Average age 31. Terminal master's awarded for partial completion of doctoral program. *Degree requirements:* For master's, comprehensive exam (for some programs), thesis (for some programs). *Entrance requirements:* For master's, GRE, minimum GPA of 3.0. Additional exam requirements/recommendations for international students: Required—Michigan English Language Assessment Battery (minimum score 82); Recommended—TOEFL (minimum score 550 paper-based; 79 iBT), IELTS (minimum score 7). *Application deadline:* For fall admission, 6/1 priority date for domestic students, 6/1 for international students; for spring admission, 10/15 priority date for domestic students, 2/1 for international students. Applications are processed on a rolling basis. Application fee: $40 ($50 for international students). Electronic applications accepted. *Unit head:* Dr. William L. MacDonald, Dean/Director, 740-366-9333 Ext. 330, E-mail: macdonald.24@osu.edu. *Application contact:* Graduate Admissions, 614-292-9444, Fax: 614-292-3985, E-mail: domestic.grad@osu.edu.

Ohio University, Graduate College, Gladys W. and David H. Patton College of Education and Human Services, Athens, OH 45701-2979. Offers M Ed, MS, MSA, Ed D, PhD. *Accreditation:* NCATE. Part-time and evening/weekend programs available. *Faculty:* 60 full-time (30 women), 48 part-time/adjunct (25 women). *Students:* 460 full-time (314 women), 437 part-time (176 women); includes 119 minority (73 Black or African American, non-Hispanic/Latino; 6 American Indian or Alaska Native, non-Hispanic/Latino; 4 Asian, non-Hispanic/Latino; 23 Hispanic/Latino; 13 Two or more races, non-Hispanic/Latino), 68 international. 488 applicants, 68% accepted, 259 enrolled. In 2011, 217 master's, 30 doctorates awarded. *Degree requirements:* For master's, comprehensive exam (for some programs), thesis or alternative; for doctorate, comprehensive exam, thesis/dissertation. *Entrance requirements:* For master's, GRE General Test or MAT; for doctorate, GRE General Test, MAT, master's degree. Additional exam requirements/recommendations for international students: Required—TOEFL (minimum score 550 paper-based; 80 iBT) or IELTS (minimum score 6.5). *Application deadline:* Applications are processed on a rolling basis. Application fee: $50 ($55 for international students). Electronic applications accepted. *Financial support:* Research assistantships with full and partial tuition reimbursements, teaching assistantships with full and partial tuition reimbursements, Federal Work-Study, institutionally sponsored loans, tuition waivers (full and partial), and unspecified assistantships available. Financial award application deadline: 3/15. *Faculty research:* School improvement, partnerships, literacy, rural education. *Total annual research expenditures:* $2.2 million. *Unit head:* Dr. Renee A. Middleton, Dean, 740-593-4403, E-mail: middletonr@ohio.edu. *Application contact:* Floyd J. Doney, Director of Student Affairs, 740-593-4400, Fax: 740-593-9310, E-mail: doney@ohio.edu. Web site: http://www.cehs.ohio.edu/.

Ohio Valley University, School of Graduate Education, Vienna, WV 26105-8000. Offers M Ed. Postbaccalaureate distance learning degree programs offered. *Faculty:* 2 full-time (1 woman), 4 part-time/adjunct (3 women). *Students:* 12 full-time (7 women), 29 part-time (24 women). *Entrance requirements:* For master's, 2 letters of recommendation, official transcripts from all previous institutions, essay. Application fee: $30. *Unit head:* Dr. Toni DeVore, Chair, 304-865-6149, E-mail: toni.devore@ovu.edu. *Application contact:* Brad Wilson, Coordinator of Recruiting and Retention, 304-865-6177, E-mail: brad.wilson@ovu.edu.

Oklahoma State University, College of Education, Stillwater, OK 74078. Offers MS, Ed D, PhD, Ed S. *Accreditation:* NCATE. Part-time programs available. Postbaccalaureate distance learning degree programs offered. *Faculty:* 100 full-time (58 women), 65 part-time/adjunct (35 women). *Students:* 290 full-time (194 women), 639 part-time (432 women); includes 200 minority (62 Black or African American, non-Hispanic/Latino; 56 American Indian or Alaska Native, non-Hispanic/Latino; 10 Asian, non-Hispanic/Latino; 31 Hispanic/Latino; 41 Two or more races, non-Hispanic/Latino), 50 international. Average age 35. 444 applicants, 40% accepted, 130 enrolled. In 2011, 195 master's, 62 doctorates awarded. *Degree requirements:* For master's, thesis or alternative; for doctorate, comprehensive exam, thesis/dissertation. *Entrance requirements:* For master's and doctorate, GRE or GMAT. Additional exam requirements/recommendations for international students: Required—TOEFL (minimum score 550 paper-based; 79 iBT). *Application deadline:* For fall admission, 3/1 for international students; for spring admission, 8/1 for international students. Applications are processed on a rolling basis. Application fee: $40 ($75 for international students). Electronic applications accepted. *Expenses:* Tuition, state resident: full-time $4044; part-time $168.50 per credit hour. Tuition, nonresident: full-time $16,008; part-time $667 per credit hour. *Required fees:* $2122; $88.45 per credit hour. One-time fee: $50. Tuition and fees vary according to course load and campus/location. *Financial support:* In 2011–12, 47 research assistantships (averaging $9,632 per year), 86 teaching assistantships (averaging $9,055 per year) were awarded; career-related internships or fieldwork, Federal Work-Study, scholarships/grants, health care benefits, tuition waivers (partial), and unspecified assistantships also available. Support available to part-time students. Financial award application deadline: 3/1; financial award applicants required to submit FAFSA. *Unit head:* Dr. Pamela Fry, Interim Dean, 405-744-3373, Fax: 405-744-6399. *Application contact:* Dr. Sheryl Tucker, Dean, 405-744-7099, Fax: 405-744-0355, E-mail: grad-i@okstate.edu. Web site: http://education.okstate.edu/.

Old Dominion University, Darden College of Education, Norfolk, VA 23529. Offers MS, MS Ed, PhD, Ed S. Part-time and evening/weekend programs available. Postbaccalaureate distance learning degree programs offered (no on-campus study). *Faculty:* 94 full-time (55 women), 62 part-time/adjunct (40 women). *Students:* 647 full-time (519 women), 840 part-time (618 women); includes 370 minority (257 Black or African American, non-Hispanic/Latino; 5 American Indian or Alaska Native, non-Hispanic/Latino; 23 Asian, non-Hispanic/Latino; 42 Hispanic/Latino; 7 Native Hawaiian or other Pacific Islander, non-Hispanic/Latino; 36 Two or more races, non-Hispanic/Latino), 13 international. Average age 33. 1,125 applicants, 72% accepted. In 2011, 529 master's, 39 doctorates, 20 other advanced degrees awarded. *Degree requirements:* For master's, thesis (for some programs), exam; for doctorate, comprehensive exam, thesis/dissertation; for Ed S, comprehensive exam. *Entrance requirements:* For doctorate, GRE General Test, master's degree, minimum GPA of 3.25; for Ed S, GRE General Test or MAT. Additional exam requirements/recommendations for international students: Required—TOEFL (minimum score 550 paper-based). *Application deadline:* For fall admission, 6/1 priority date for domestic students, 6/1 for international students; for spring admission, 11/1 priority date for domestic students, 11/1 for international students. Applications are processed on a rolling basis. Application fee: $50. Electronic applications accepted. *Expenses:* Tuition, state resident: full-time $9096; part-time $379 per credit. Tuition, nonresident: full-time $23,064; part-time $961 per credit. *Required fees:* $127 per semester. One-time fee: $50. *Financial support:* In 2011–12, 141 students received support, including 4 fellowships with full and partial tuition reimbursements available (averaging $15,000 per year), 60 research assistantships with full and partial tuition reimbursements available (averaging $15,000 per year), 72 teaching assistantships with full and partial tuition reimbursements available (averaging $15,000 per year); career-related internships or fieldwork, Federal Work-Study, institutionally sponsored loans, scholarships/grants, tuition waivers (partial), and unspecified assistantships also available. Support available to part-time students. Financial award application deadline: 2/15; financial award applicants required to submit CSS PROFILE or FAFSA. *Faculty research:* Effective urban teaching practices, curriculum theory, clinical practices, special education, instructional technology. *Total annual research expenditures:* $8.1 million. *Unit head:* Dr. Linda Irwin-DeVitis, Dean, 757-683-3938, Fax: 757-683-5083, E-mail: ldevitis@odu.edu. *Application contact:* Nechell Bonds, Director of Admissions, 757-683-3685, Fax: 757-683-3255, E-mail: gradadmit@odu.edu. Web site: http://education.odu.edu/.

Olivet College, Program in Education, Olivet, MI 49076-9701. Offers MAT. *Degree requirements:* For master's, portfolio. *Entrance requirements:* For master's, current K-12 teacher certification. Electronic applications accepted.

Olivet Nazarene University, Graduate School, Division of Education, Bourbonnais, IL 60914. Offers curriculum and instruction (MAE); elementary education (MAT); library information specialist (MAE); reading specialist (MAE); school leadership (MAE); secondary education (MAT). *Accreditation:* NCATE. Evening/weekend programs available. *Degree requirements:* For master's, thesis or alternative.

Oral Roberts University, School of Education, Tulsa, OK 74171. Offers Christian school administration (K-12) (MA Ed, Ed D); Christian school curriculum development (MA Ed); college and higher education administration (Ed D); public school administration (K-12) (MA Ed, Ed D); public school teaching (MA Ed). *Accreditation:* NCATE. Part-time programs available. Postbaccalaureate distance learning degree programs offered (minimal on-campus study). *Degree requirements:* For master's, comprehensive exam, thesis optional; for doctorate, comprehensive exam, thesis/dissertation. *Entrance requirements:* For master's, GRE General Test or MAT, minimum GPA of 3.0; for doctorate, minimum GPA of 3.0. Additional exam requirements/recommendations for international students: Required—TOEFL (minimum score 500 paper-based; 173 computer-based). *Expenses:* Contact institution. *Faculty research:* Teacher effectiveness, college success in high achieving African-Americans, professional development practices.

Oregon State University, Graduate School, College of Education, Program in General Education, Corvallis, OR 97331. Offers Ed M, MAIS, MS, Ed D, PhD. Part-time programs available. Terminal master's awarded for partial completion of doctoral program. *Degree requirements:* For master's, variable foreign language requirement, thesis (for some programs); for doctorate, variable foreign language requirement, thesis/dissertation. *Entrance requirements:* For master's, California Basic Educational Skills Test, NTE, minimum GPA of 3.0 in last 90 hours of course work; for doctorate, GRE or MAT, master's degree, minimum GPA of 3.0 in last 90 hours of course work. Additional exam requirements/recommendations for international students: Required—TOEFL. *Faculty research:* School administration, educational foundations, research methodology, education policy development, higher education administration.

Oregon State University–Cascades, Program in Education, Bend, OR 97701. Offers MAT.

Ottawa University, Graduate Studies-Arizona, Program in Education, Ottawa, KS 66067-3399. Offers community college counseling (MA); curriculum and instruction (MA); early childhood (MA); education intervention (MA); education leadership (MA); education technology (MA); Montessori early childhood education (MA); Montessori elementary education (MA); professional development (MA); school guidance counseling (MA); special education - cross categorical (MA). Programs offered in Mesa, Phoenix, Tempe and West Valley, AZ. *Accreditation:* NCATE. Part-time programs available. *Degree requirements:* For master's, thesis or alternative. *Entrance requirements:* For master's, minimum undergraduate GPA of 3.0, copy of current state certification or teaching license. Additional exam requirements/recommendations for international students: Required—TOEFL (minimum score 550 paper-based; 213 computer-based). Electronic applications accepted. *Expenses:* Contact institution.

Otterbein University, Department of Education, Westerville, OH 43081. Offers MAE, MAT. *Accreditation:* NCATE. *Degree requirements:* For master's, capstone project. *Entrance requirements:* For master's, 2 reference forms, essay, interview. Additional exam requirements/recommendations for international students: Required—TOEFL (minimum score 550 paper-based; 213 computer-based; 79 iBT). *Faculty research:* Computer technology middle level education, assessment, teacher leadership, multicultural education.

Our Lady of Holy Cross College, Program in Education and Counseling, New Orleans, LA 70131-7399. Offers administration and supervision (M Ed); curriculum and instruction (M Ed); marriage and family counseling (MA); school counseling (M Ed, MA). *Accreditation:* ACA; NCATE. Part-time and evening/weekend programs available. *Degree requirements:* For master's, thesis. *Entrance requirements:* For master's, GRE General Test, minimum GPA of 2.7.

Our Lady of the Lake University of San Antonio, School of Professional Studies, San Antonio, TX 78207-4689. Offers communication and learning disorders (MA); curriculum and instruction (M Ed), including bilingual, early childhood education, English as a second language, integrated math teaching, integrated science teaching, master reading teacher, master technology teacher, reading specialist; early elementary education (M Ed); generic special education (M Ed), including elementary education; human sciences (MA); intermediate education (M Ed), including math/science education, professional studies; learning resources specialist (M Ed); principal (M Ed);

psychology (MS, Psy D), including counseling psychology, marriage and family therapy (MS), school psychology (MS); school counseling (M Ed); secondary education (M Ed). Part-time and evening/weekend programs available. *Degree requirements:* For master's, comprehensive exam; for doctorate, thesis/dissertation, internship, qualifying exam. *Entrance requirements:* For master's, GRE General Test or MAT; for doctorate, GRE General Test or MAT, interview. Additional exam requirements/recommendations for international students: Required—TOEFL. Electronic applications accepted.

Pace University, School of Education, New York, NY 10038. Offers adolescent education (MST); childhood education (MST); educational leadership (MS Ed); educational technology studies (MS); literacy (MSE); school business management (Certificate); special education (MS Ed); teaching students with disabilities (MSE). *Accreditation:* NCATE. Part-time and evening/weekend programs available. *Students:* 164 full-time (131 women), 533 part-time (396 women); includes 157 minority (59 Black or African American, non-Hispanic/Latino; 2 American Indian or Alaska Native, non-Hispanic/Latino; 26 Asian, non-Hispanic/Latino; 54 Hispanic/Latino; 1 Native Hawaiian or other Pacific Islander, non-Hispanic/Latino; 15 Two or more races, non-Hispanic/ Latino), 10 international. Average age 29. 256 applicants, 79% accepted, 114 enrolled. In 2011, 334 master's, 34 other advanced degrees awarded. *Degree requirements:* For master's, internship. *Entrance requirements:* For master's, interview, teaching certificate. Additional exam requirements/recommendations for international students: Required—TOEFL. *Application deadline:* For fall admission, 7/31 priority date for domestic students; for spring admission, 11/30 for domestic students. Applications are processed on a rolling basis. Application fee: $70. Electronic applications accepted. *Expenses:* Contact institution. *Financial support:* Research assistantships, career-related internships or fieldwork, and Federal Work-Study available. Support available to part-time students. Financial award applicants required to submit FAFSA. *Unit head:* Dr. Andrea M. Spencer, Dean, 212-346-1345, E-mail: aspencer@pace.edu. *Application contact:* Susan Ford-Goldschein, Director of Admissions, 212-346-1660, Fax: 212-346-1585, E-mail: gradnyc@pace.edu. Web site: http://www.pace.edu/.

Pacific Lutheran University, Division of Graduate Studies, School of Education, Tacoma, WA 98447. Offers MAE. *Accreditation:* NCATE. Part-time and evening/ weekend programs available. *Faculty:* 8 full-time (2 women), 6 part-time/adjunct (3 women). *Students:* 29 full-time (20 women), 10 part-time (6 women); includes 5 minority (1 Black or African American, non-Hispanic/Latino; 1 American Indian or Alaska Native, non-Hispanic/Latino; 1 Asian, non-Hispanic/Latino; 1 Native Hawaiian or other Pacific Islander, non-Hispanic/Latino; 1 Two or more races, non-Hispanic/Latino). Average age 31. In 2011, 37 master's awarded. *Degree requirements:* For master's, comprehensive exam, thesis optional. *Entrance requirements:* For master's, GRE General Test or MAT, interview. Additional exam requirements/recommendations for international students: Required—TOEFL (minimum score 550 paper-based; 213 computer-based). *Application deadline:* For winter admission, 1/31 priority date for domestic students, 1/31 for international students. Applications are processed on a rolling basis. Application fee: $40. *Expenses:* Contact institution. *Financial support:* Fellowships, Federal Work-Study, scholarships/grants, and unspecified assistantships available. Financial award application deadline: 3/1. *Unit head:* Dr. Frank Kline, Dean, School of Education and Movement Studies, 253-535-7272. *Application contact:* Rachel Christopherson, Director of Graduate Admission, 253-535-8570, Fax: 253-536-5136, E-mail: admissions@ plu.edu.

Pacific Union College, Education Department, Angwin, CA 94508-9707. Offers education (M Ed); elementary teaching (MAT); secondary teaching (MAT). Part-time programs available. *Faculty:* 3 full-time (1 woman), 3 part-time/adjunct (all women). *Students:* 14 part-time (9 women). *Degree requirements:* For master's, thesis, action research project, field experiences. *Entrance requirements:* For master's, GRE, two interviews, teaching credential, letters of recommendation. *Application deadline:* Applications are processed on a rolling basis. Application fee: $0. *Expenses: Tuition:* Full-time $25,740; part-time $750 per quarter hour. Tuition and fees vary according to student's religious affiliation. *Financial support:* Available to part-time students. *Unit head:* Prof. Thomas Lee, Chair, 707-965-6646, Fax: 707-965-6645, E-mail: tdlee@ puc.edu. *Application contact:* Marsha Crow, Assistant Chair/Accreditation and Certification Specialist, 707-965-6643, Fax: 707-965-6645, E-mail: mcrow@puc.edu. Web site: http://www.puc.edu/academics/departments/education/.

Pacific University, College of Education, Forest Grove, OR 97116-1797. Offers early childhood education (MAT); education (MAE); elementary education (MAT); high school education (MAT); middle school education (MAT); special education (MAT); visual function in learning (M Ed). *Accreditation:* NCATE. Part-time and evening/weekend programs available. *Degree requirements:* For master's, research project. *Entrance requirements:* For master's, California Basic Educational Skills Test, PRAXIS II, minimum undergraduate GPA of 2.75, 3.0 graduate. Additional exam requirements/ recommendations for international students: Required—TOEFL. Electronic applications accepted. *Expenses:* Contact institution. *Faculty research:* Defining a culturally competent classroom, technology in the k-12 classroom, Socratic seminars, social studies education.

Palm Beach Atlantic University, School of Education and Behavioral Studies, West Palm Beach, FL 33416-4708. Offers counseling psychology (MS), including addictions/ mental health, marriage and family therapy, mental health counseling, school guidance counseling. Part-time and evening/weekend programs available. *Faculty:* 13 full-time (4 women), 11 part-time/adjunct (6 women). *Students:* 251 full-time (213 women), 53 part-time (46 women); includes 118 minority (65 Black or African American, non-Hispanic/ Latino; 4 Asian, non-Hispanic/Latino; 47 Hispanic/Latino; 2 Native Hawaiian or other Pacific Islander, non-Hispanic/Latino), 5 international. Average age 35. 135 applicants, 64% accepted, 72 enrolled. In 2011, 101 master's awarded. *Entrance requirements:* For master's, GRE, minimum GPA of 3.0. Additional exam requirements/recommendations for international students: Required—TOEFL (minimum score 550 paper-based; 213 computer-based; 79 iBT). *Application deadline:* For fall admission, 7/15 priority date for domestic students; for spring admission, 11/15 priority date for domestic students. Applications are processed on a rolling basis. Application fee: $45. Electronic applications accepted. *Expenses: Tuition:* Full-time $11,478; part-time $470 per credit hour. *Required fees:* $99 per semester. Tuition and fees vary according to course load, degree level and campus/location. *Financial support:* Applicants required to submit FAFSA. *Unit head:* Dr. Lisa Stubbs, Program Director, 561-803-2286. *Application contact:* Graduate Admissions, 888-468-6722, E-mail: grad@pba.edu. Web site: http:// www.pba.edu/.

Park University, College of Graduate and Professional Studies, Kansas City, MO 54105. Offers adult education (M Ed); at-risk students (M Ed); disaster and emergency management (MPA); educational administration (M Ed); entrepreneurship (MBA); general business (MBA); general education (M Ed); government/business relations (MPA); healthcare/services management (MBA, MPA); international business (MBA); K-12 certification (MAT); management information systems (MBA); management of information systems (MPA); middle school certification (MAT); multi-cultural education (M Ed); nonprofit management (MPA); public management (MPA); school law (M Ed); secondary school certification (MAT); special education (M Ed). Part-time and evening/ weekend programs available. Postbaccalaureate distance learning degree programs offered (no on-campus study). *Degree requirements:* For master's, comprehensive exam, thesis (for some programs). *Entrance requirements:* For master's, GRE, GMAT, teacher certification (M Ed). Additional exam requirements/recommendations for international students: Required—TOEFL (minimum score 550 paper-based). Electronic applications accepted. *Faculty research:* Literacy, leadership, brain based research, multicultural education, diversity.

Penn State Great Valley, Graduate Studies, Education Division, Malvern, PA 19355-1488. Offers education (M Ed); special education (MS). *Unit head:* Dr. Roy Clariana, Division Head, 610-648-3253, Fax: 610-725-5253, E-mail: rbc4@psu.edu. *Application contact:* 610-648-3242, Fax: 610-889-1334. Web site: http://www.sgps.psu.edu/ Level3.aspx?id=512.

Penn State Harrisburg, Graduate School, School of Behavioral Sciences and Education, Middletown, PA 17057-4898. Offers applied behavior analysis (MA); applied clinical psychology (MA); applied psychological research (MA); community psychology and social change (MA); health education (M Ed); literacy education (M Ed); teaching and curriculum (M Ed); training and development (M Ed). Part-time and evening/ weekend programs available. *Financial support:* Career-related internships or fieldwork available. *Unit head:* Dr. Catherine A. Surra, Director, 717-948-6205, Fax: 717-948-6209, E-mail: cas87@psu.edu. *Application contact:* Robert Coffman, Director of Admissions, 717-948-6214, E-mail: rwc11@psu.edu. Web site: http:// harrisburg.psu.edu/behavioral-sciences-and-education/.

Penn State University Park, Graduate School, College of Education, State College, University Park, PA 16802-1503. Offers M Ed, MA, MS, D Ed, PhD, Certificate. *Accreditation:* NCATE. *Students:* 512 full-time (357 women), 273 part-time (165 women). Average age 35. 869 applicants, 46% accepted, 216 enrolled. In 2011, 223 master's, 79 doctorates awarded. *Entrance requirements:* Additional exam requirements/recommendations for international students: Required—TOEFL (minimum score 550 paper-based; 213 computer-based; 80 iBT). *Application deadline:* Applications are processed on a rolling basis. Application fee: $65. Electronic applications accepted. *Financial support:* Fellowships, research assistantships, and teaching assistantships available. Financial award applicants required to submit FAFSA. *Unit head:* Dr. David H. Monk, Dean, 814-865-2526, Fax: 814-865-0555, E-mail: dhm6@psu.edu. *Application contact:* Cynthia E. Nicosia, Director, Graduate Enrollment Services, 814-865-1834, E-mail: cey1@psu.edu. Web site: http://www.ed.psu.edu/ educ/.

Pepperdine University, Graduate School of Education and Psychology, Division of Education, Malibu, CA 90263. Offers administration and preliminary administrative services credential (MS); education (MA); educational leadership, administration, and policy (Ed D); learning technologies (MA, Ed D); organization change (Ed D); organizational leadership (Ed D); social entrepreneurship and change (MA). Part-time and evening/weekend programs available. Postbaccalaureate distance learning degree programs offered (minimal on-campus study). *Degree requirements:* For doctorate, thesis/dissertation. *Entrance requirements:* For master's, GRE General Test; for doctorate, GRE General Test, MAT. Additional exam requirements/recommendations for international students: Required—TOEFL. *Expenses:* Contact institution.

Peru State College, Graduate Programs, Program in Education, Peru, NE 68421. Offers curriculum and instruction (MS Ed). *Accreditation:* NCATE. Part-time programs available. *Degree requirements:* For master's, comprehensive exam (for some programs), thesis optional.

Piedmont College, School of Education, Demorest, GA 30535-0010. Offers early childhood education (MA, MAT); middle grades education (MA); secondary education (MA, MAT); special education (MA, MAT); teacher leadership (Ed S). Part-time and evening/weekend programs available. *Students:* 546 full-time (433 women), 809 part-time (698 women); includes 172 minority (139 Black or African American, non-Hispanic/ Latino; 2 American Indian or Alaska Native, non-Hispanic/Latino; 6 Asian, non-Hispanic/ Latino; 18 Hispanic/Latino; 7 Two or more races, non-Hispanic/Latino), 17 international. Average age 37. 342 applicants, 83% accepted, 234 enrolled. In 2011, 444 master's, 510 other advanced degrees awarded. *Degree requirements:* For master's, thesis, field experience in the classroom teaching ; for doctorate, thesis/dissertation. *Entrance requirements:* For master's, GRE General Test, MAT, minimum undergraduate GPA of 2.5; for Ed S, minimum graduate GPA of 3.5, valid teaching certificate. Additional exam requirements/recommendations for international students: Required—TOEFL (minimum score 550 paper-based; 213 computer-based). *Application deadline:* For fall admission, 7/15 for domestic students; for spring admission, 12/1 for domestic students. Applications are processed on a rolling basis. Application fee: $0. Electronic applications accepted. *Expenses: Tuition:* Part-time $407 per credit hour. Tuition and fees vary according to program. *Financial support:* Career-related internships or fieldwork, Federal Work-Study, and unspecified assistantships available. Support available to part-time students. Financial award applicants required to submit FAFSA. *Unit head:* Dr. Bob Cummings, Dean, 706-778-3000 Ext. 1201, Fax: 706-776-9608, E-mail: bcummings@ piedmont.edu. *Application contact:* Penny Loggins, Director of Graduate Admissions, 706-778-8500 Ext. 1181, Fax: 706-778-0150, E-mail: ploggins@piedmont.edu.

Pittsburg State University, Graduate School, College of Education, Pittsburg, KS 66762. Offers MAT, MS, Ed S. *Accreditation:* NCATE. *Degree requirements:* For master's, thesis or alternative.

Plymouth State University, College of Graduate Studies, Graduate Studies in Education, Program in Certificate of Advanced Graduate Studies, Plymouth, NH 03264-1595. Offers CAGS. Part-time and evening/weekend programs available.

Point Loma Nazarene University, Program in Education, San Diego, CA 92106-2899. Offers MA, MAT, Ed S. Part-time and evening/weekend programs available. *Degree requirements:* For master's, thesis optional. *Entrance requirements:* For master's, GRE General Test or MAT, portfolio, letters of recommendation; for Ed S, GRE General Test or MAT, portfolio.

Point Park University, School of Arts and Sciences, Department of Education, Pittsburgh, PA 15222-1984. Offers curriculum and instruction (MA); educational administration (MA); special education (M Ed); teaching and leadership (M Ed). Part-time and evening/weekend programs available. *Faculty:* 5 full-time, 9 part-time/adjunct. *Students:* 12 full-time (8 women), 40 part-time (31 women); includes 12 minority (11 Black or African American, non-Hispanic/Latino; 1 Asian, non-Hispanic/Latino), 2 international. Average age 33. 46 applicants, 61% accepted, 18 enrolled. In 2011, 15 master's awarded. *Degree requirements:* For master's, comprehensive exam (for some programs), thesis or alternative. *Entrance requirements:* For master's, minimum GPA of 3.0, resume, 2 letters of recommendation. Additional exam requirements/ recommendations for international students: Required—TOEFL. *Application deadline:* Applications are processed on a rolling basis. Application fee: $30. Electronic applications accepted. *Expenses: Tuition:* Full-time $13,050; part-time $725 per credit. *Required fees:* $720; $40 per credit. *Financial support:* In 2011–12, 42 students received support, including 2 teaching assistantships with full tuition reimbursements available (averaging $6,400 per year); scholarships/grants also available. Financial award application deadline: 4/15; financial award applicants required to submit FAFSA. *Unit head:* Dr. Darlene Marnich, Chair, 412-392-3474, Fax: 412-392-3927, E-mail: dmarnich@pointpark.edu. *Application contact:* Lynn C. Ribar, Associate Director,

Graduate and Adult Enrollment, 412-392-3908, Fax: 412-392-6164, E-mail: lribar@pointpark.edu.

Pontifical Catholic University of Puerto Rico, College of Education, Ponce, PR 00717-0777. Offers M Ed, MA Ed, MRE, PhD. Part-time and evening/weekend programs available. *Degree requirements:* For master's, comprehensive exam, thesis (for some programs). *Entrance requirements:* For master's, GRE General Test, 2 letters of recommendation, interview, minimum GPA of 2.75; for doctorate, EXADEP, GRE or MAT, 3 letters of recommendation. *Faculty research:* Teaching English as a second language, learning styles, leadership styles.

Portland State University, Graduate Studies, School of Education, Portland, OR 97207-0751. Offers M Ed, MA, MAT, MS, MST, Ed D. *Accreditation:* NCATE. Part-time and evening/weekend programs available. *Degree requirements:* For doctorate, thesis/dissertation. *Entrance requirements:* For master's, minimum GPA of 3.0 in upper-division course work or 2.75 overall. Additional exam requirements/recommendations for international students: Required—TOEFL (minimum score 550 paper-based; 213 computer-based).

Post University, Program in Education, Waterbury, CT 06723-2540. Offers education (M Ed); instructional design and technology (M Ed); teaching and learning (M Ed). Postbaccalaureate distance learning degree programs offered.

Prairie View A&M University, College of Education, Prairie View, TX 77446-0519. Offers M Ed, MA, MS, MS Ed, PhD. *Accreditation:* NCATE. Part-time and evening/weekend programs available. Postbaccalaureate distance learning degree programs offered (no on-campus study). *Degree requirements:* For master's, thesis optional, minimum GPA of 3.0; for doctorate, comprehensive exam, thesis/dissertation. *Entrance requirements:* For master's, 3 letters of reference, minimum undergraduate GPA of 2.5; for doctorate, GRE General Test, 3 letters of reference, minimum undergraduate GPA of 3.0, essay. Additional exam requirements/recommendations for international students: Required—TOEFL (minimum score 550 paper-based). Electronic applications accepted. *Faculty research:* Mentoring, assessment, humanistic education, diversity, literacy education, recruitment, student retention, school collaboration, leadership skills, structural equations.

Prescott College, Graduate Programs, Program in Education, Prescott, AZ 86301. Offers early childhood education (MA); early childhood special education (MA); education (MA); elementary education (MA); environmental education leadership and administration (MA); equine-assisted experiential learning (MA); school guidance counseling (MA); secondary education (MA); special education, learning disability (MA); special education, mental retardation (MA); special education, serious emotional disability (MA); student-directed independent study (MA); sustainability education (PhD). Part-time programs available. Postbaccalaureate distance learning degree programs offered (minimal on-campus study). *Faculty:* 2 full-time (both women), 47 part-time/adjunct (31 women). *Students:* 59 full-time (36 women), 48 part-time (30 women); includes 16 minority (3 Black or African American, non-Hispanic/Latino; 1 American Indian or Alaska Native, non-Hispanic/Latino; 1 Asian, non-Hispanic/Latino; 8 Hispanic/Latino; 3 Two or more races, non-Hispanic/Latino), 2 international. Average age 40. 75 applicants, 76% accepted, 36 enrolled. In 2011, 14 master's, 8 doctorates awarded. *Degree requirements:* For master's, thesis, fieldwork or internship, practicum; for doctorate, thesis/dissertation. *Entrance requirements:* For master's, 2 letters of recommendation, resume; for doctorate, 3 letters of recommendation, resume, official transcripts, personal statement, program proposal. Additional exam requirements/recommendations for international students: Required—TOEFL (minimum score 500 paper-based; 173 computer-based). *Application deadline:* For fall admission, 4/15 priority date for domestic students, 4/15 for international students; for spring admission, 9/15 priority date for domestic students, 9/15 for international students. Applications are processed on a rolling basis. Application fee: $40. Electronic applications accepted. *Expenses: Tuition:* Full-time $16,440; part-time $685 per credit. *Required fees:* $150 per semester. One-time fee: $350. *Financial support:* Career-related internships or fieldwork and Federal Work-Study available. Financial award applicants required to submit FAFSA. *Unit head:* Noel Caniglia, Chair, 928-358-3201, Fax: 928-776-5151, E-mail: ncaniglia@prescott.edu. *Application contact:* Kerstin Alicki, Admissions Counselor, 928-350-2100, Fax: 928-776-5242, E-mail: admissions@prescott.edu.

Purdue University, Graduate School, College of Education, West Lafayette, IN 47907. Offers MS, MS Ed, PhD, Ed S. *Accreditation:* NCATE. Part-time and evening/weekend programs available. *Faculty:* 30 full-time (21 women), 1 (woman) part-time/adjunct. *Students:* 89 full-time (64 women), 134 part-time (84 women); includes 31 minority (12 Black or African American, non-Hispanic/Latino; 3 American Indian or Alaska Native, non-Hispanic/Latino; 7 Asian, non-Hispanic/Latino; 9 Hispanic/Latino), 49 international. Average age 36. 153 applicants. In 2011, 26 master's, 13 doctorates awarded. *Degree requirements:* For master's, thesis optional; for doctorate, thesis/dissertation, oral and written exams; for Ed S, oral presentation, project. *Entrance requirements:* For master's, GRE general test is required if undergraduate GPA is below 3.0, minimum undergraduate GPA of 3.0 or equivalent; for doctorate, GRE General Test, a combined GRE verbal and quantitative score of 1000 (300 for revised GRE Test) or more is expected, minimum undergraduate GPA of 3.0 or equivalent; master's degree with minimum GPA of 3.0 or equivalent; for Ed S, GRE general test, a combined GRE verbal and quantitative score of 1000 (300 for revised GRE Test) or more is expected, minimum undergraduate GPA of 3.0 or equivalent; master's degree. Additional exam requirements/recommendations for international students: Required—TOEFL (minimum score 550 paper-based; 77 iBT); Recommended—TWE. *Application deadline:* For fall admission, 12/15 for domestic students, 3/1 for international students; for spring admission, 9/15 for domestic students, 8/1 for international students. Application fee: $60 ($75 for international students). Electronic applications accepted. *Financial support:* Fellowships with full tuition reimbursements, research assistantships with full tuition reimbursements, teaching assistantships with full tuition reimbursements, career-related internships or fieldwork, and tuition waivers (full) available. Support available to part-time students. Financial award application deadline: 3/1; financial award applicants required to submit FAFSA. *Unit head:* Dr. Phillip J. VanFossen, Head, 765-494-7935, E-mail: vanfoss@purdue.edu. *Application contact:* Sarah N. Prater, Graduate Contact, 765-494-2345, E-mail: prater0@purdue.edu. Web site: http://www.education.purdue.edu/.

Purdue University Calumet, Graduate Studies Office, School of Education, Hammond, IN 46323-2094. Offers counseling (MS Ed), including human services, mental health counseling, school counseling; educational administration (MS Ed); instructional technology (MS Ed); special education (MS Ed). *Accreditation:* NCATE. *Entrance requirements:* Additional exam requirements/recommendations for international students: Required—TOEFL.

Purdue University North Central, Program in Education, Westville, IN 46391-9542. Offers elementary education (MS Ed). *Accreditation:* NCATE. Part-time and evening/weekend programs available. *Degree requirements:* For master's, one foreign language. *Entrance requirements:* For master's, GRE, minimum GPA of 3.0. Electronic applications accepted. *Faculty research:* Diversity, integration.

Queens College of the City University of New York, Division of Graduate Studies, Division of Education, Flushing, NY 11367-1597. Offers MA, MS Ed, AC. *Accreditation:* NCATE. Part-time and evening/weekend programs available. *Faculty:* 73 full-time (50 women). *Students:* 234 full-time (191 women), 1,869 part-time (1,451 women); includes 627 minority (135 Black or African American, non-Hispanic/Latino; 187 Asian, non-Hispanic/Latino; 305 Hispanic/Latino), 13 international. 1,603 applicants, 58% accepted, 709 enrolled. In 2011, 612 master's, 58 other advanced degrees awarded. *Degree requirements:* For master's, research project; for AC, thesis optional. *Entrance requirements:* For master's, minimum GPA of 3.0. Additional exam requirements/recommendations for international students: Required—TOEFL. *Application deadline:* For fall admission, 4/1 for domestic students; for spring admission, 11/1 for domestic students. Applications are processed on a rolling basis. Application fee: $125. *Expenses:* Tuition, state resident: part-time $345 per credit. Tuition, nonresident: part-time $640 per credit. *Required fees:* $145.25 per semester. *Financial support:* Career-related internships or fieldwork, Federal Work-Study, institutionally sponsored loans, and tuition waivers (partial) available. Support available to part-time students. Financial award application deadline: 4/1; financial award applicants required to submit FAFSA. *Unit head:* Dr. Penny Hammrich, Dean, 718-997-5220. *Application contact:* Mario Caruso, Director of Graduate Admissions, 718-997-5200, Fax: 718-997-5193, E-mail: graduate_admissions@qc.edu.

Queen's University at Kingston, School of Graduate Studies and Research, Faculty of Education, Kingston, ON K7L 3N6, Canada. Offers M Ed, PhD. Part-time programs available. *Degree requirements:* For master's, thesis optional; for doctorate, comprehensive exam, thesis/dissertation. *Entrance requirements:* Additional exam requirements/recommendations for international students: Required—TOEFL (minimum score 580 paper-based; 237 computer-based); Recommended—TWE (minimum score 4). *Faculty research:* Literacy, assessment and evaluation, special needs, mathematics, science and technology education.

Queens University of Charlotte, Wayland H. Cato, Jr. School of Education, Charlotte, NC 28274-0002. Offers education in literacy (M Ed); elementary education (MAT); school administration (MSA). *Accreditation:* NCATE. Part-time and evening/weekend programs available. *Degree requirements:* For master's, comprehensive exam. *Entrance requirements:* For master's, GRE General Test. *Expenses:* Contact institution.

Quincy University, Program in Education, Quincy, IL 62301-2699. Offers alternative certification (MS Ed); curriculum and instruction (MS Ed); leadership (MS Ed); reading education (MS Ed); school administration (MS Ed); special education (MS Ed); teacher leader in reading (MS Ed); teaching certification (MS Ed). Part-time and evening/weekend programs available. Postbaccalaureate distance learning degree programs offered. *Students:* 221 full-time (168 women), 100 part-time (69 women); includes 104 minority (69 Black or African American, non-Hispanic/Latino; 1 American Indian or Alaska Native, non-Hispanic/Latino; 5 Asian, non-Hispanic/Latino; 27 Hispanic/Latino; 2 Two or more races, non-Hispanic/Latino). In 2011, 132 master's awarded. *Degree requirements:* For master's, comprehensive exam (for some programs), thesis or alternative. *Entrance requirements:* For master's, MAT or GRE. Additional exam requirements/recommendations for international students: Required—TOEFL (minimum score 550 paper-based; 79 iBT). *Application deadline:* Applications are processed on a rolling basis. Application fee: $25. Electronic applications accepted. *Expenses: Tuition:* Full-time $9120; part-time $380 per semester hour. *Required fees:* $360; $15 per semester hour. Tuition and fees vary according to course load, campus/location and program. *Financial support:* Applicants required to submit FAFSA. *Unit head:* Kristen Anguiano, Director, 217-228-5432 Ext. 3119, E-mail: anguikr@quincy.edu. *Application contact:* Office of Admissions, 217-228-5210, Fax: 217-228-5479, E-mail: admissions@quincy.edu. Web site: http://www.quincy.edu/academics/graduate-programs/education.

Quinnipiac University, School of Education, Hamden, CT 06518-1940. Offers MAT, MS, Diploma. *Accreditation:* NCATE. *Faculty:* 16 full-time (11 women), 52 part-time/adjunct (29 women). *Students:* 130 full-time (105 women), 86 part-time (68 women); includes 19 minority (4 Black or African American, non-Hispanic/Latino; 3 Asian, non-Hispanic/Latino; 12 Hispanic/Latino). Average age 24. 177 applicants, 91% accepted, 147 enrolled. In 2011, 108 master's, 25 other advanced degrees awarded. *Entrance requirements:* For master's, PRAXIS I, minimum GPA of 2.67, interview. *Application deadline:* For fall admission, 3/31 priority date for domestic students. Applications are processed on a rolling basis. Application fee: $45. Electronic applications accepted. *Expenses: Tuition:* Part-time $855 per credit. *Required fees:* $35 per credit. *Financial support:* In 2011–12, 16 students received support. Career-related internships or fieldwork, Federal Work-Study, scholarships/grants, tuition waivers (partial), and unspecified assistantships available. Financial award application deadline: 4/30; financial award applicants required to submit FAFSA. *Faculty research:* Equity and excellence in education. *Unit head:* Dr. Gary Alger, Interim Dean, School of Education, 203-582-3289, Fax: 203-582-8709, E-mail: gary.alger@quinnipiac.edu. *Application contact:* Jennifer Boutin, Associate Director of Graduate Admissions, 800-462-1944, Fax: 203-582-3443, E-mail: jennifer.boutin@quinnipiac.edu. Web site: http://www.quinnipiac.edu/academics/colleges-schools-and-departments/school-of-education/graduate-programs.

Radford University, College of Graduate and Professional Studies, College of Education and Human Development, Radford, VA 24142. Offers MS. *Accreditation:* NCATE. Part-time programs available. *Faculty:* 41 full-time (29 women), 23 part-time/adjunct (18 women). *Students:* 136 full-time (111 women), 243 part-time (193 women); includes 25 minority (17 Black or African American, non-Hispanic/Latino; 2 American Indian or Alaska Native, non-Hispanic/Latino; 3 Asian, non-Hispanic/Latino; 1 Hispanic/Latino; 2 Two or more races, non-Hispanic/Latino). Average age 32. 175 applicants, 92% accepted, 114 enrolled. In 2011, 189 master's awarded. *Degree requirements:* For master's, comprehensive exam, thesis optional. *Entrance requirements:* For master's, GRE or MAT, minimum GPA of 2.75; 2 letters of reference. Additional exam requirements/recommendations for international students: Required—TOEFL (minimum score 550 paper-based; 213 computer-based; 79 iBT). *Application deadline:* For fall admission, 2/15 priority date for domestic students, 12/1 for international students; for spring admission, 7/1 for international students. Applications are processed on a rolling basis. Application fee: $50. Electronic applications accepted. *Expenses:* Tuition, state resident: full-time $6262; part-time $261 per credit hour. Tuition, nonresident: full-time $14,540; part-time $606 per credit hour. *Required fees:* $2812; $117 per credit hour. Tuition and fees vary according to program. *Financial support:* In 2011–12, 95 students received support, including 22 research assistantships (averaging $7,415 per year), 6 teaching assistantships with partial tuition reimbursements available (averaging $8,908 per year); career-related internships or fieldwork, Federal Work-Study, institutionally sponsored loans, scholarships/grants, and unspecified assistantships also available. Financial award application deadline: 3/1; financial award applicants required to submit FAFSA. *Unit head:* Dr. Patricia Shoemaker, Dean, 540-831-5439, Fax: 540-831-5440, E-mail: pshoemak@radford.edu. *Application contact:* Rebecca Conner, Graduate Admissions, 540-831-5431, Fax: 540-831-6061, E-mail: gradcollege@radford.edu. Web site: http://www.radford.edu/content/cehd/home.html.

Randolph College, Programs in Education, Lynchburg, VA 24503. Offers curriculum and instruction (MAT); special education-learning disabilities (M Ed, MAT). *Accreditation:* Teacher Education Accreditation Council. *Entrance requirements:* For master's, minimum GPA of 3.0 in prerequisite education coursework, 2.7 in major or field of interest (MAT); teaching license (M Ed); 2 recommendations; interview.

Regent University, Graduate School, School of Education, Virginia Beach, VA 23464-9800. Offers adult education (Ed D); adult/staff development (Ed D, PhD); career switcher with licensure (M Ed), including alternative licensure; character education (Ed D, PhD); Christian education leadership (Ed D, PhD); Christian education specialist (Ed S); Christian school program (M Ed), including ACSI licensure; distance education (Ed D, PhD); education licensure (M Ed), including preK-6th grade; educational leadership (M Ed, PhD); educational leadership - special education (Ed S), including administration and supervision; educational psychology (Ed D, PhD), including learning and development, research and evaluation, special education; higher education (Ed D, PhD), including administration, research and institutional planning, teaching; higher education leadership (Ed D); individualized degree plan (M Ed), including behavior disorders, learning disabilities, mental retardation, reading specialist; K-12 school leadership (Ed D, PhD); leadership in character education (M Ed); master teacher (M Ed), including TESOL; mathematics education (M Ed); special education (PhD); student affairs (M Ed); TESOL (M Ed), including adult education, ESL: preK-12. *Accreditation:* Teacher Education Accreditation Council. Part-time and evening/weekend programs available. Postbaccalaureate distance learning degree programs offered (minimal on-campus study). *Faculty:* 26 full-time (13 women), 54 part-time/adjunct (34 women). *Students:* 140 full-time (109 women), 786 part-time (626 women); includes 218 minority (189 Black or African American, non-Hispanic/Latino; 2 American Indian or Alaska Native, non-Hispanic/Latino; 11 Asian, non-Hispanic/Latino; 16 Hispanic/Latino), 42 international. Average age 39. 673 applicants, 57% accepted, 298 enrolled. In 2011, 178 master's, 15 doctorates awarded. *Degree requirements:* For master's, thesis or alternative; for doctorate, comprehensive exam, thesis/dissertation. *Entrance requirements:* For master's, MAT, minimum undergraduate GPA of 2.75, writing sample, resume, recommendations, interview; for doctorate, GRE, writing sample, 3 years of relevant professional experience, master's-level paper, copies of published work, resume, transcripts, interview, recommendations. Additional exam requirements/recommendations for international students: Required—TOEFL (minimum score 577 paper-based; 233 computer-based). *Application deadline:* For fall admission, 4/1 priority date for domestic students; for spring admission, 10/15 priority date for domestic students. Applications are processed on a rolling basis. Application fee: $50. Electronic applications accepted. *Expenses:* Contact institution. *Financial support:* Fellowships, career-related internships or fieldwork, scholarships/grants, tuition waivers (full and partial), and unspecified assistantships available. Support available to part-time students. Financial award application deadline: 4/1; financial award applicants required to submit FAFSA. *Faculty research:* Character development and discipline for children, education leadership development, diversity in schools, classroom management, technology in education settings. *Unit head:* Dr. Alan A. Arroyo, Dean, 757-352-4261, Fax: 757-352-4318, E-mail: alanarr@regent.edu. *Application contact:* Matthew Chadwick, Director of Enrollment Support Services, 800-373-5504, Fax: 757-352-4381, E-mail: admissions@regent.edu. Web site: http://www.regent.edu/education/.

Regis College, Programs in Education, Weston, MA 02493. Offers elementary teacher (MAT); reading (MAT); special education (MAT). Part-time and evening/weekend programs available. *Degree requirements:* For master's, thesis. *Entrance requirements:* For master's, GRE or MAT. Additional exam requirements/recommendations for international students: Required—TOEFL. Electronic applications accepted. *Faculty research:* Reflective teaching, gender-based education, integrated teaching.

Regis University, College for Professional Studies, School of Education and Counseling, Department of Education, Denver, CO 80221-1099. Offers adult learning, training, and development (M Ed, Certificate); autism (Certificate); curriculum, instruction, and assessment (M Ed); educational leadership (Certificate); educational technology (Certificate); instructional technology (M Ed); literacy (Certificate); professional leadership (M Ed); reading (M Ed); self-designed (M Ed); space studies (M Ed). Program also offered in Henderson and Las Vegas (Summerlin), NV. *Accreditation:* Teacher Education Accreditation Council. Part-time and evening/weekend programs available. Postbaccalaureate distance learning degree programs offered (no on-campus study). *Degree requirements:* For master's, thesis. *Entrance requirements:* For master's, resume, minimum GPA of 2.75, criminal background check. Additional exam requirements/recommendations for international students: Required—TOEFL (minimum score 213 computer-based), TWE (minimum score 5). Electronic applications accepted. *Faculty research:* Issues of equity in the middle school classroom, professional learning communities, school reform, socialinguistic and discursive obstacles to student integration, inclusive language arts curriculum.

Regis University, Regis College, Denver, CO 80221-1099. Offers education (MA). Offered at Northwest Denver Campus. *Accreditation:* Teacher Education Accreditation Council. Part-time and evening/weekend programs available. *Degree requirements:* For master's, capstone presentation. *Entrance requirements:* For master's, 1 year of teaching experience, Colorado teaching certificate, videotape sample of teaching. *Expenses:* Contact institution.

Reinhardt University, Program in Early Childhood Education, Waleska, GA 30183-2981. Offers M Ed, MAT. Part-time and evening/weekend programs available. Postbaccalaureate distance learning degree programs offered. *Faculty:* 12 full-time (8 women), 6 part-time/adjunct (5 women). *Degree requirements:* For master's, comprehensive exam. *Entrance requirements:* For master's, GACE, background check. Additional exam requirements/recommendations for international students: Required—TOEFL. *Application deadline:* For fall admission, 5/7 for domestic and international students. Applications are processed on a rolling basis. Application fee: $25. Electronic applications accepted. *Expenses: Tuition:* Full-time $7020; part-time $390 per credit hour. *Required fees:* $70 per semester hour. *Financial support:* Application deadline: 5/1; applicants required to submit FAFSA. *Unit head:* Nancy Carter, Director of Graduate Studies, 770-720-5948, Fax: 770-720-9173, E-mail: ntc@reinhardt.edu. *Application contact:* Ray Schumacher, Admissions Counselor, 770-993-6971, Fax: 770-475-0263, E-mail: res@reinhardt.edu.

Rhode Island College, School of Graduate Studies, Feinstein School of Education and Human Development, Program in Education, Providence, RI 02908-1991. Offers PhD. Program offered jointly with University of Rhode Island. *Accreditation:* NCATE. Part-time and evening/weekend programs available. *Faculty:* 6 part-time/adjunct (3 women). *Students:* 58 part-time (41 women); includes 6 minority (1 Black or African American, non-Hispanic/Latino; 2 Asian, non-Hispanic/Latino; 3 Hispanic/Latino). Average age 40. In 2011, 6 doctorates awarded. *Degree requirements:* For doctorate, comprehensive exam, thesis/dissertation. *Entrance requirements:* For doctorate, GRE, two official transcripts from all colleges and universities attended, 3 letters of recommendation, personal statement, professional resume. Additional exam requirements/recommendations for international students: Recommended—TOEFL (minimum score 550 paper-based; 213 computer-based; 79 iBT). *Application deadline:* For fall admission, 1/29 for domestic students. Applications are processed on a rolling basis. Application fee: $65. *Expenses:* Tuition, state resident: full-time $8592; part-time $358 per credit hour. Tuition, nonresident: full-time $16,800; part-time $700 per credit hour. *Required fees:* $602; $22 per credit. $72 per term. *Financial support:* Health care benefits available. Support available to part-time students. Financial award application deadline: 5/15; financial award applicants required to submit FAFSA. *Unit head:* Karen Castagno, Co-Director, 401-456-8594. *Application contact:* Graduate Studies, 401-456-8700. Web site: http://www.ric.edu/feinsteinschooleducationhumandevelopment/jointPHD.php.

Rice University, Graduate Programs, Programs in Education Certification, Houston, TX 77251-1892. Offers MAT. *Entrance requirements:* For master's, GRE General Test, minimum GPA of 3.0. Additional exam requirements/recommendations for international students: Required—TOEFL (minimum score 600 paper-based; 250 computer-based; 90 iBT). Electronic applications accepted. *Faculty research:* Assessment, integration of math and science.

The Richard Stockton College of New Jersey, School of Graduate and Continuing Studies, Program in Education, Pomona, NJ 08240-0195. Offers MA. *Accreditation:* Teacher Education Accreditation Council. Part-time and evening/weekend programs available. *Faculty:* 8 full-time (4 women), 10 part-time/adjunct (6 women). *Students:* 10 full-time (all women), 182 part-time (156 women); includes 32 minority (9 Black or African American, non-Hispanic/Latino; 1 American Indian or Alaska Native, non-Hispanic/Latino; 2 Asian, non-Hispanic/Latino; 19 Hispanic/Latino; 1 Two or more races, non-Hispanic/Latino). Average age 36. 113 applicants, 87% accepted, 71 enrolled. In 2011, 37 master's awarded. *Degree requirements:* For master's, comprehensive exam (for some programs), project. *Entrance requirements:* For master's, GRE, MAT, minimum GPA of 2.75, teaching certificate. *Application deadline:* For fall admission, 7/1 for domestic students; for spring admission, 12/1 for domestic students. Applications are processed on a rolling basis. Application fee: $50. Electronic applications accepted. *Expenses:* Tuition, state resident: full-time $13,035; part-time $543 per credit. Tuition, nonresident: full-time $20,065; part-time $836 per credit. *Required fees:* $3920; $163 per credit. Tuition and fees vary according to degree level. *Financial support:* In 2011–12, 7 students received support, including 11 research assistantships with partial tuition reimbursements available; fellowships, career-related internships or fieldwork, Federal Work-Study, scholarships/grants, and unspecified assistantships also available. Support available to part-time students. Financial award application deadline: 3/1; financial award applicants required to submit FAFSA. *Faculty research:* Curriculum instruction, math, science, special education, language arts, literacy. *Unit head:* Dr. Kim LeBak, Program Director, 609-626-3640, E-mail: gradschool@stockton.edu. *Application contact:* Tara Williams, Assistant Director of Graduate Enrollment Management, 609-626-3640, Fax: 609-626-6050, E-mail: gradschool@stockton.edu.

Rider University, Department of Graduate Education, Leadership and Counseling, Lawrenceville, NJ 08648-3001. Offers counseling services (MA, Certificate, Ed S), including counseling services (MA, Ed S), director of school counseling (Certificate), school counseling services (Certificate); curriculum, instruction and supervision (MA, Certificate), including curriculum, instruction and supervision (MA), supervisor (Certificate); educational administration (MA, Certificate), including educational administration (MA), principal (Certificate), school administrator (Certificate); organizational leadership (MA); reading/language arts (MA, Certificate), including reading specialist (Certificate), reading/language arts (MA); school psychology (Certificate, Ed S); special education (MA, Certificate), including alternative route in special education (Certificate), special education (MA), teacher of students with disabilities (Certificate), teacher of the handicapped (Certificate); teacher certification (Certificate), including business education, elementary education, English as a second language, English education, mathematics education, preschool to grade 3, science education, social studies education, world languages; teaching (MA). *Accreditation:* NCATE. Part-time and evening/weekend programs available. *Degree requirements:* For master's, comprehensive exam (for some programs), thesis or alternative, internship, portfolios; for other advanced degree, internship, professional portfolio. *Entrance requirements:* For master's, GRE (counseling, school psychology), MAT, interview, resume, letters of recommendation; for other advanced degree, PRAXIS. Additional exam requirements/recommendations for international students: Required—TOEFL (minimum score 550 paper-based; 213 computer-based). Electronic applications accepted. *Expenses: Tuition:* Full-time $32,820; part-time $710 per credit. *Required fees:* $350; $35 per course. Tuition and fees vary according to campus/location and program. *Faculty research:* Gifted students, self-esteem, hope and mental health, conflicts in group work, cultural diversity and counseling assessment of special needs in children.

Rivier University, School of Graduate Studies, Department of Education, Nashua, NH 03060. Offers curriculum and instruction (M Ed); early childhood education (M Ed); educational administration (M Ed); educational studies (M Ed); elementary education (M Ed); elementary education and general special education (M Ed); emotional and behavioral disorders (M Ed); general social education (M Ed); leadership and learning (Ed D, CAGS); learning disabilities (M Ed); learning disabilities and reading (M Ed); mental health counseling (MA); reading (M Ed); school counseling (M Ed). Part-time and evening/weekend programs available. *Degree requirements:* For master's, comprehensive exam (for some programs), internships. *Entrance requirements:* For master's, GRE General Test or MAT.

Robert Morris University, Graduate Studies, School of Education and Social Sciences, Moon Township, PA 15108-1189. Offers business education (MS); education (Postbaccalaureate Certificate); instructional leadership (MS), including education, sport management; instructional management and leadership (PhD). *Accreditation:* Teacher Education Accreditation Council. Part-time and evening/weekend programs available. Postbaccalaureate distance learning degree programs offered (no on-campus study). *Faculty:* 14 full-time (3 women), 11 part-time/adjunct (6 women). *Students:* 326 part-time (217 women); includes 24 minority (21 Black or African American, non-Hispanic/Latino; 1 Asian, non-Hispanic/Latino; 2 Hispanic/Latino), 1 international. *Degree requirements:* For doctorate, thesis/dissertation. *Entrance requirements:* Additional exam requirements/recommendations for international students: Required—TOEFL (minimum score 550 paper-based; 213 computer-based; 79 iBT). *Application deadline:* For fall admission, 7/1 priority date for domestic students, 7/1 for international students; for spring admission, 11/1 priority date for domestic students, 11/1 for international students. Applications are processed on a rolling basis. Application fee: $35. Electronic applications accepted. *Expenses:* Contact institution. *Unit head:* Dr. John E. Graham, Dean, 412-397-6022, Fax: 412-397-2524, E-mail: graham@rmu.edu. *Application contact:* Debra Roach, Assistant Dean, Graduate Admissions, 412-397-5200, Fax: 412-397-2425, E-mail: graduateadmissions@rmu.edu. Web site: http://www.rmu.edu/web/cms/schools/sess/.

Roberts Wesleyan College, Division of Teacher Education, Rochester, NY 14624-1997. Offers adolescence education (M Ed); childhood and special education (M Ed); literacy education (M Ed); urban education (M Ed). Part-time and evening/weekend programs available. *Degree requirements:* For master's, thesis.

Rockford College, Graduate Studies, Department of Education, Rockford, IL 61108-2393. Offers early childhood education (MAT); elementary education (MAT); instructional strategies (MAT); reading (MAT); secondary education (MAT); special education (MAT). Part-time and evening/weekend programs available. *Degree requirements:* For master's, thesis optional, professional portfolio (for instructional strategies program). *Entrance requirements:* For master's, GRE General Test, basic skills test (for students seeking certification), 3 letters of recommendation. Additional exam requirements/recommendations for international students: Required—TOEFL (minimum score 550 paper-based; 213 computer-based; 79 iBT). *Application deadline:*

Education—General

Applications are processed on a rolling basis. Application fee: $50. Electronic applications accepted. *Expenses: Tuition:* Full-time $16,200; part-time $675 per credit. *Required fees:* $80; $40 per semester. Tuition and fees vary according to class time, course level, course load, degree level, campus/location and program. *Financial support:* Scholarships/grants and unspecified assistantships available. Support available to part-time students. Financial award application deadline: 3/1; financial award applicants required to submit FAFSA. *Unit head:* Dr. Michelle McReynolds, MAT Director, 815-226-3390, Fax: 815-394-3706, E-mail: mmcreynolds@rockford.edu. *Application contact:* Michele Mehren, Office Manager for Graduate Studies, 815-226-4041, Fax: 815-394-3706, E-mail: mmehren@rockford.edu. Web site: http://www.rockford.edu/?page=Education.

Rockhurst University, School of Graduate and Professional Studies, Program in Education, Kansas City, MO 64110-2561. Offers M Ed. *Accreditation:* Teacher Education Accreditation Council. Part-time and evening/weekend programs available. *Faculty:* 9 full-time (8 women), 12 part-time/adjunct (10 women). *Students:* 56 full-time (36 women), 120 part-time (84 women); includes 29 minority (18 Black or African American, non-Hispanic/Latino; 2 Asian, non-Hispanic/Latino; 6 Hispanic/Latino; 1 Native Hawaiian or other Pacific Islander, non-Hispanic/Latino; 2 Two or more races, non-Hispanic/Latino). Average age 31. 55 applicants, 67% accepted, 30 enrolled. In 2011, 103 master's awarded. *Entrance requirements:* For master's, minimum GPA of 2.5, 2 letters of recommendation. Additional exam requirements/recommendations for international students: Required—TOEFL (minimum score 550 paper-based; 213 computer-based; 79 iBT). *Application deadline:* Applications are processed on a rolling basis. Application fee: $25. Electronic applications accepted. Application fee is waived when completed online. *Expenses:* Contact institution. *Financial support:* Applicants required to submit FAFSA. *Faculty research:* English language learners, urban literacy, on-line discussions, character education, teaching K-12 students about math and literacy. *Unit head:* Mary Pat Shelledy, Chair, 816-501-3538, E-mail: marypat.shelledy@rockhurst.edu. *Application contact:* Cheryl Hooper, Director of Graduate Recruitment and Admission, 816-501-4097, Fax: 816-501-4241, E-mail: cheryl.hooper@rockhurst.edu. Web site: http://www.rockhurst.edu/academic/education/index.asp.

Roger Williams University, School of Education, Bristol, RI 02809. Offers MA, MAT. Part-time and evening/weekend programs available. *Entrance requirements:* For master's, resume, 3 letters of recommendation. Additional exam requirements/recommendations for international students: Recommended—TOEFL, IELTS. Electronic applications accepted. *Expenses:* Contact institution.

Rollins College, Hamilton Holt School, Graduate Studies in Education, Winter Park, FL 32789. Offers elementary education (M Ed, MAT). Part-time and evening/weekend programs available. *Faculty:* 6 full-time (3 women), 5 part-time/adjunct (2 women). *Students:* 9 full-time (7 women), 19 part-time (18 women); includes 4 minority (1 Black or African American, non-Hispanic/Latino; 3 Hispanic/Latino), 2 international. Average age 33. 10 applicants, 70% accepted, 7 enrolled. In 2011, 10 master's awarded. *Degree requirements:* For master's, comprehensive exam, Professional Education Test (PED) and Subject Area Examination (SAE) of the Florida Teacher Certification Examinations (FTCE), successful review of the Expanded Teacher Education Portfolio (ETEP), successful completion of all required coursework. *Entrance requirements:* For master's, General Knowledge Test of the Florida Teacher Certification Examination (FTCE), official transcripts, letter(s) of recommendation, essay. Additional exam requirements/recommendations for international students: Required—TOEFL (minimum score 550 paper-based; 213 computer-based; 80 iBT). *Application deadline:* For fall admission, 8/11 for domestic students; for spring admission, 12/10 for domestic students. Applications are processed on a rolling basis. Application fee: $50. *Expenses:* Contact institution. *Financial support:* In 2011–12, 12 students received support. Federal Work-Study, scholarships/grants, and unspecified assistantships available. Support available to part-time students. Financial award applicants required to submit FAFSA. *Unit head:* Dr. J. Scott Hewit, Faculty Director, 407-646-2300, E-mail: shewit@rollins.edu. *Application contact:* Rebecca Cordray, Coordinator of Records and Registration, 407-646-1568, Fax: 407-975-6430, E-mail: rcordray@rollins.edu. Web site: http://www.rollins.edu/holt/graduate/gse.html.

Roosevelt University, Graduate Division, College of Education, Chicago, IL 60605. Offers MA, Ed D. *Accreditation:* ACA; NCATE. Part-time and evening/weekend programs available. *Degree requirements:* For doctorate, thesis/dissertation. *Entrance requirements:* For doctorate, GRE or MAT.

Rosemont College, Schools of Graduate and Professional Studies, Graduate Education Program, Rosemont, PA 19010-1699. Offers elementary certification (MA). Part-time and evening/weekend programs available. *Faculty:* 8 part-time/adjunct (4 women). *Students:* 9 full-time (7 women), 13 part-time (10 women); includes 3 minority (all Black or African American, non-Hispanic/Latino). Average age 29. 18 applicants, 89% accepted, 16 enrolled. In 2011, 36 master's awarded. *Degree requirements:* For master's, thesis optional. *Entrance requirements:* For master's, minimum college GPA of 3.0, 3 letters of recommendation. Additional exam requirements/recommendations for international students: Required—TOEFL. *Application deadline:* Applications are processed on a rolling basis. Application fee: $50. Electronic applications accepted. Application fee is waived when completed online. *Expenses: Tuition:* Part-time $650 per credit. *Financial support:* Career-related internships or fieldwork, institutionally sponsored loans, and unspecified assistantships available. Support available to part-time students. Financial award applicants required to submit FAFSA. *Unit head:* Dr. Ann S. Hartsock, Director, 610-527-0200 Ext. 3108, E-mail: ahartsock@rosemont.edu. *Application contact:* Meghan Mellinger, Director, Enrollment and Student Services, 610-527-0200 Ext. 2596, Fax: 610-520-4399, E-mail: gpsadmissions@rosemont.edu. Web site: http://www.rosemont.edu/.

Rowan University, Graduate School, College of Education, Glassboro, NJ 08028-1701. Offers M Ed, MA, MST, MST, Ed D, Ed S. *Accreditation:* NCATE. Part-time and evening/weekend programs available. *Degree requirements:* For master's, comprehensive exam, thesis; for doctorate, thesis/dissertation. *Entrance requirements:* For master's, GRE General Test, PRAXIS I, PRAXIS II; for doctorate, GRE, master's degree. Additional exam requirements/recommendations for international students: Required—TOEFL. Electronic applications accepted.

Rutgers, The State University of New Jersey, New Brunswick, Graduate School of Education, New Brunswick, NJ 08901. Offers Ed M, Ed D, PhD. *Accreditation:* Teacher Education Accreditation Council. Part-time and evening/weekend programs available. Terminal master's awarded for partial completion of doctoral program. *Degree requirements:* For master's, comprehensive exam (for some programs); for doctorate, thesis/dissertation. *Entrance requirements:* For master's and doctorate, GRE General Test. Additional exam requirements/recommendations for international students: Required—TOEFL (minimum score 575 paper-based; 233 computer-based; 83 iBT). Electronic applications accepted.

Sacred Heart University, Graduate Programs, Isabelle Farrington College of Education, Fairfield, CT 06825-1000. Offers administration (CAS); educational technology (MAT); elementary education (MAT); reading (CAS); secondary education (MAT); teaching (CAS). Part-time and evening/weekend programs available. Postbaccalaureate distance learning degree programs offered (minimal on-campus study). *Degree requirements:* For master's, thesis or alternative. *Entrance requirements:* For master's, PRAXIS (teacher certification/MAT); for CAS, PRAXIS I. Additional exam requirements/recommendations for international students: Required—TOEFL (minimum score 550 paper-based; 213 computer-based). Electronic applications accepted. *Expenses:* Contact institution. *Faculty research:* Reading education, learning theory, teacher preparation, education of underachievers.

Sage Graduate School, Esteves School of Education, Troy, NY 12180-4115. Offers MAT, MS, MS Ed, Ed D, Post Master's Certificate. *Accreditation:* NCATE. Part-time and evening/weekend programs available. *Faculty:* 10 full-time (6 women), 24 part-time/adjunct (18 women). *Students:* 138 full-time (123 women), 310 part-time (247 women); includes 44 minority (14 Black or African American, non-Hispanic/Latino; 2 American Indian or Alaska Native, non-Hispanic/Latino; 6 Asian, non-Hispanic/Latino; 18 Hispanic/Latino; 4 Two or more races, non-Hispanic/Latino). Average age 29. 417 applicants, 49% accepted, 136 enrolled. In 2011, 174 master's, 11 doctorates, 5 other advanced degrees awarded. *Entrance requirements:* Additional exam requirements/recommendations for international students: Required—TOEFL (minimum score 550 paper-based; 213 computer-based). *Application deadline:* Applications are processed on a rolling basis. Application fee: $40. *Expenses: Tuition:* Full-time $11,880; part-time $660 per credit hour. Tuition and fees vary according to program. *Financial support:* Fellowships, research assistantships, Federal Work-Study, scholarships/grants, tuition waivers (partial), and unspecified assistantships available. Support available to part-time students. Financial award application deadline: 3/1; financial award applicants required to submit FAFSA. *Faculty research:* Literacy development in at-risk children, effective behavior strategies for class instruction. *Unit head:* Dr. Lori Quigley, Dean, Esteves School of Education, 518-244-2326, Fax: 518-244-4571, E-mail: l.quigley@sage.edu. *Application contact:* Wendy D. Diefendorf, Director of Graduate and Adult Admission, 518-244-2443, Fax: 518-244-6880, E-mail: diefew@sage.edu.

Saginaw Valley State University, College of Education, University Center, MI 48710. Offers M Ed, MA, MAT, Ed S. *Accreditation:* NCATE. Part-time and evening/weekend programs available. *Faculty:* 94 full-time (69 women), 53 part-time/adjunct (36 women). *Students:* 57 full-time (40 women), 763 part-time (577 women); includes 44 minority (20 Black or African American, non-Hispanic/Latino; 5 American Indian or Alaska Native, non-Hispanic/Latino; 5 Asian, non-Hispanic/Latino; 8 Hispanic/Latino; 6 Two or more races, non-Hispanic/Latino), 176 international. Average age 34. 180 applicants, 99% accepted, 124 enrolled. In 2011, 358 master's, 37 other advanced degrees awarded. *Entrance requirements:* For master's, minimum GPA of 3.0, teaching certificate. Additional exam requirements/recommendations for international students: Required—TOEFL (minimum score 525 paper-based; 197 computer-based; 71 iBT). *Application deadline:* Applications are processed on a rolling basis. Application fee: $25. Electronic applications accepted. *Expenses:* Tuition, state resident: full-time $8300; part-time $5333 per year. Tuition, nonresident: full-time $15,613; part-time $10,209 per year. *International tuition:* $15,631 full-time. *Financial support:* Federal Work-Study and scholarships/grants available. Support available to part-time students. Financial award applicants required to submit FAFSA. *Unit head:* Dr. Steve P. Barbus, Jr., Dean, 989-964-6067, Fax: 989-790-4385, E-mail: barbus@svsu.edu. *Application contact:* Kathy Lopez, Certification Officer, 989-964-4661, Fax: 989-964-4385, E-mail: klopez@svsu.edu. Web site: http://www.svsu.edu/coe.

St. Ambrose University, College of Education and Health Sciences, Program in Education, Davenport, IA 52803-2898. Offers special education (M Ed); teaching (M Ed). *Accreditation:* Teacher Education Accreditation Council. Part-time and evening/weekend programs available. Postbaccalaureate distance learning degree programs offered (no on-campus study). *Faculty:* 2 full-time (1 woman), 1 part-time/adjunct (0 women). *Students:* 25 part-time (21 women); includes 5 minority (1 Asian, non-Hispanic/Latino; 2 Hispanic/Latino; 2 Two or more races, non-Hispanic/Latino). Average age 31. 9 applicants, 89% accepted, 8 enrolled. In 2011, 10 master's awarded. *Degree requirements:* For master's, comprehensive exam. *Entrance requirements:* For master's, GRE General Test or MAT, minimum GPA of 2.75. Additional exam requirements/recommendations for international students: Required—TOEFL. *Application deadline:* For fall admission, 8/15 priority date for domestic students; for spring admission, 11/1 for domestic students. Applications are processed on a rolling basis. Application fee: $25. Electronic applications accepted. *Expenses: Tuition:* Full-time $13,770; part-time $765 per credit hour. *Required fees:* $60 per semester. Tuition and fees vary according to degree level, program and reciprocity agreements. *Financial support:* In 2011–12, 13 students received support, including 1 research assistantship with partial tuition reimbursement available (averaging $3,600 per year); career-related internships or fieldwork, scholarships/grants, tuition waivers (full and partial), and unspecified assistantships also available. Financial award application deadline: 3/15; financial award applicants required to submit FAFSA. *Faculty research:* Disabilities and postsecondary career avenues, self-determination. *Unit head:* Marguerite K. Woods, Head, 563-388-7653, Fax: 563-388-7662, E-mail: woodsmargueritek@sau.edu. *Application contact:* Penny L. McCulloch, Administrative Assistant, 563-322-1034, Fax: 563-388-7662, E-mail: mccullochpennyl@sau.edu.

St. Bonaventure University, School of Graduate Studies, School of Education, St. Bonaventure, NY 14778-2284. Offers MS Ed, Adv C. *Accreditation:* NCATE. Part-time and evening/weekend programs available. *Faculty:* 16 full-time (11 women), 19 part-time/adjunct (13 women). *Students:* 192 full-time (155 women), 96 part-time (71 women); includes 13 minority (4 Black or African American, non-Hispanic/Latino; 1 American Indian or Alaska Native, non-Hispanic/Latino; 7 Hispanic/Latino; 1 Two or more races, non-Hispanic/Latino), 2 international. Average age 28. 203 applicants, 76% accepted, 105 enrolled. In 2011, 104 master's, 8 Adv Cs awarded. *Entrance requirements:* For master's, teaching certificate, interview, references, writing sample, transcripts, bachelor's degree. Additional exam requirements/recommendations for international students: Required—TOEFL (minimum score 550 paper-based; 213 computer-based; 80 iBT). *Application deadline:* For fall admission, 6/15 priority date for domestic students, 2/1 for international students; for spring admission, 11/15 priority date for domestic students, 7/1 for international students. Applications are processed on a rolling basis. Application fee: $30. Electronic applications accepted. *Expenses: Tuition:* Part-time $670 per credit. *Financial support:* In 2011–12, 12 research assistantships with full and partial tuition reimbursements were awarded; career-related internships or fieldwork, Federal Work-Study, scholarships/grants, health care benefits, tuition waivers (partial), and unspecified assistantships also available. Support available to part-time students. Financial award application deadline: 4/15; financial award applicants required to submit FAFSA. *Unit head:* Dr. Joseph E. Zimmer, Dean, 716-375-2388, E-mail: jezimmer@sbu.edu. *Application contact:* Bruce Campbell, Director of Graduate Admissions, 716-375-2429, E-mail: gradsch@sbu.edu.

St. Catherine University, Graduate Programs, Program in Education–Curriculum and Instruction, St. Paul, MN 55105. Offers MA. Part-time and evening/weekend programs available. Postbaccalaureate distance learning degree programs offered (minimal on-campus study). *Degree requirements:* For master's, thesis. *Entrance requirements:* For master's, current teaching license, classroom experience, minimum GPA of 3.0. Additional exam requirements/recommendations for international students: Required—Michigan English Language Assessment Battery or TOEFL (minimum score 600 paper-based; 250 computer-based; 100 iBT). *Expenses:* Contact institution.

St. Catherine University, Graduate Programs, Program in Education - Initial Licensure, St. Paul, MN 55105. Offers MA. Part-time and evening/weekend programs available. *Expenses: Required fees:* $30 per semester. Tuition and fees vary according to program.

St. Cloud State University, School of Graduate Studies, School of Education, St. Cloud, MN 56301-4498. Offers MS, Ed D. *Accreditation:* NCATE. Part-time and evening/weekend programs available. Postbaccalaureate distance learning degree programs offered (no on-campus study). *Faculty:* 96 full-time (52 women), 18 part-time/adjunct (14 women). *Students:* 297 full-time (226 women), 560 part-time (409 women); includes 78 minority (28 Black or African American, non-Hispanic/Latino; 8 American Indian or Alaska Native, non-Hispanic/Latino; 35 Asian, non-Hispanic/Latino; 7 Hispanic/Latino), 50 international. 293 applicants, 74% accepted. In 2011, 128 master's awarded. *Degree requirements:* For master's, comprehensive exam (for some programs), thesis or alternative; for doctorate, comprehensive exam, thesis/dissertation. *Entrance requirements:* For master's, GRE General Test (for some programs), minimum GPA of 2.75; for doctorate, GRE. Additional exam requirements/recommendations for international students: Required—Michigan English Language Assessment Battery; Recommended—TOEFL (minimum score 550 paper-based; 213 computer-based), IELTS (minimum score 6.5). *Application deadline:* Applications are processed on a rolling basis. Application fee: $35. *Financial support:* Career-related internships or fieldwork, Federal Work-Study, scholarships/grants, and unspecified assistantships available. Financial award application deadline: 3/1. *Unit head:* Dr. Osman Alawiye, Dean, 320-308-3023, Fax: 320-308-4237, E-mail: olalawiye@stcloudstate.edu. *Application contact:* Linda Lou Krueger, School of Graduate Studies, 320-308-2113, Fax: 320-308-5371, E-mail: lekrueger@stcloudstate.edu. Web site: http://www.stcloudstate.edu/soe.

St. Edward's University, School of Education, Austin, TX 78704. Offers MA, Certificate. Part-time and evening/weekend programs available. *Students:* 1 full-time (0 women), 32 part-time (22 women); includes 14 minority (2 Black or African American, non-Hispanic/Latino; 1 Asian, non-Hispanic/Latino; 10 Hispanic/Latino; 1 Two or more races, non-Hispanic/Latino), 1 international. Average age 32. 8 applicants, 75% accepted, 6 enrolled. In 2011, 13 master's awarded. *Degree requirements:* For master's, minimum of 24 resident hours. *Entrance requirements:* For master's, GRE General Test, minimum GPA of 3.0 in last 60 hours or 2.75 overall. Additional exam requirements/recommendations for international students: Required—TOEFL (minimum score 550 paper-based; 213 computer-based; 79 iBT) or IELTS (minimum score 6). *Application deadline:* For fall admission, 7/1 for domestic and international students; for spring admission, 11/1 for domestic and international students. Applications are processed on a rolling basis. Application fee: $45 ($50 for international students). Electronic applications accepted. *Expenses: Tuition:* Full-time $17,550; part-time $975 per credit hour. *Required fees:* $50 per trimester. Full-time tuition and fees vary according to course load and program. *Unit head:* Dr. Grant Simpson, Dean, 512-448-8655, Fax: 512-428-1372, E-mail: grants@stedwards.edu. *Application contact:* Sarah Hennes, Graduate Admission Coordinator, 512-448-8600, Fax: 512-428-1032, E-mail: sarahhe@stedwards.edu. Web site: http://www.stedwards.edu.

Saint Francis University, Graduate Education Program, Loretto, PA 15940-0600. Offers education (M Ed); leadership (M Ed); reading (M Ed). Part-time and evening/weekend programs available. *Faculty:* 22 part-time/adjunct (9 women). *Students:* 130 part-time (95 women); includes 1 minority (Hispanic/Latino). Average age 30. 30 applicants, 100% accepted, 30 enrolled. In 2011, 53 master's awarded. *Degree requirements:* For master's, comprehensive exam, thesis optional. *Entrance requirements:* For master's, GRE or MAT (if undergraduate GPA less than 2.8), minimum undergraduate QPA of 2.5. *Application deadline:* Applications are processed on a rolling basis. Application fee: $30. *Expenses:* Contact institution. *Financial support:* Applicants required to submit FAFSA. *Unit head:* Dr. Janette D. Kelly, Director, 814-472-3068, Fax: 814-472-3864, E-mail: jkelly@francis.edu. *Application contact:* Sherri L. Toth, Coordinator, 814-472-3058, Fax: 814-472-3864, E-mail: stoth@francis.edu. Web site: http://www.francis.edu/medhome.htm.

St. Francis Xavier University, Graduate Studies, Graduate Studies in Education, Antigonish, NS B2G 2W5, Canada. Offers curriculum and instruction (M Ed); educational administration and leadership (M Ed). Part-time programs available. Postbaccalaureate distance learning degree programs offered (minimal on-campus study). *Degree requirements:* For master's, thesis. *Entrance requirements:* For master's, minimum undergraduate B average, 2 years of teaching experience. *Faculty research:* Inclusive education, qualitative research.

St. John Fisher College, Ralph C. Wilson Jr. School of Education, Rochester, NY 14618-3597. Offers MS, MS Ed, Ed D, Certificate. *Accreditation:* NCATE. Part-time and evening/weekend programs available. *Faculty:* 23 full-time (13 women), 20 part-time/adjunct (15 women). *Students:* 187 full-time (130 women), 168 part-time (131 women); includes 87 minority (62 Black or African American, non-Hispanic/Latino; 5 Asian, non-Hispanic/Latino; 19 Hispanic/Latino; 1 Two or more races, non-Hispanic/Latino). Average age 34. 248 applicants, 83% accepted, 134 enrolled. In 2011, 139 master's, 22 doctorates awarded. *Degree requirements:* For doctorate, thesis/dissertation. *Entrance requirements:* For master's and doctorate, 2 letters of recommendation, current resume. Additional exam requirements/recommendations for international students: Required—TOEFL (minimum score 575 paper-based; 233 computer-based; 80 iBT). *Application deadline:* Applications are processed on a rolling basis. Application fee: $30. Electronic applications accepted. *Expenses: Tuition:* Part-time $735 per credit. One-time fee: $50 part-time. Tuition and fees vary according to course load, degree level and program. *Financial support:* In 2011–12, 70 students received support. Scholarships/grants available. Financial award applicants required to submit FAFSA. *Unit head:* Dr. Wendy A. Paterson, Dean, 585-385-3813, E-mail: jadams@sjfc.edu. *Application contact:* Jose Perales, Director of Graduate Admissions, 585-385-8067, E-mail: jperales@sjfc.edu.

St. John's University, The School of Education, Queens, NY 11439. Offers MS Ed, Ed D, PhD, Adv C. *Accreditation:* Teacher Education Accreditation Council. Part-time and evening/weekend programs available. Postbaccalaureate distance learning degree programs offered (no on-campus study). *Faculty:* 41 full-time (30 women), 135 part-time/adjunct (67 women). *Students:* 408 full-time (338 women), 1,192 part-time (895 women); includes 529 minority (188 Black or African American, non-Hispanic/Latino; 1 American Indian or Alaska Native, non-Hispanic/Latino; 84 Asian, non-Hispanic/Latino; 236 Hispanic/Latino; 2 Native Hawaiian or other Pacific Islander, non-Hispanic/Latino; 18 Two or more races, non-Hispanic/Latino), 60 international. Average age 33. 979 applicants, 84% accepted, 467 enrolled. In 2011, 409 master's, 29 doctorates, 24 other advanced degrees awarded. *Degree requirements:* For master's, comprehensive exam (for some programs), thesis (for some programs), residency; for doctorate, comprehensive exam, thesis/dissertation. *Entrance requirements:* For master's, 2 letters of recommendation, official transcript, minimum GPA of 3.0, personal statement; for doctorate, GRE General Test, MAT (PhD in literacy), interview, writing sample, 2 years of teaching experience, resume (PhD in literacy only); for Adv C, 2 letters of recommendation, master's degree from accredited college or university. Additional exam requirements/recommendations for international students: Required—TOEFL (minimum score 600 paper-based; 250 computer-based; 100 iBT), IELTS (minimum score 5.5). *Application deadline:* For fall admission, 4/1 priority date for domestic students, 5/1 for international students; for spring admission, 11/1 priority date for domestic students, 11/1 for international students. Applications are processed on a rolling basis. Application fee: $70. Electronic applications accepted. *Expenses: Tuition:* Full-time $18,000; part-time $1000 per credit. *Required fees:* $170 per semester. Tuition and fees vary according to program. *Financial support:* In 2011–12, 96 fellowships with full and partial tuition reimbursements (averaging $20,078 per year), 9 research assistantships with full and partial tuition reimbursements (averaging $14,333 per year), 1 teaching assistantship with full and partial tuition reimbursement (averaging $24,000 per year) were awarded; career-related internships or fieldwork, scholarships/grants, and unspecified assistantships also available. Support available to part-time students. Financial award application deadline: 3/1; financial award applicants required to submit FAFSA. *Faculty research:* Results of school partnerships, effective means of working with recent immigrant populations, results of graduates who participated in programs leading to alternative certification routes, resolution of issues surrounding middle schools, identifying means of supporting children at both ends of the academic continuum. *Unit head:* Dr. Jerrold Ross, Dean, 718-990-1305, Fax: 718-990-6096, E-mail: rossj@stjohns.edu. *Application contact:* Dr. Kelly K. Ronayne, Associate Dean for Graduate Admissions, 718-990-2304, Fax: 718-990-2343, E-mail: graded@stjohns.edu. Web site: http://www.stjohns.edu/academics/graduate/education.

St. Joseph's College, New York, Graduate Programs, Program in Education, Brooklyn, NY 11205-3688. Offers infant/toddler early childhood special education (MA); literacy and cognition (MA); special education (MA), including severe and multiple disabilities.

See Display on next page and Close-Up on page 809.

Saint Joseph's College of Maine, Master of Science in Education Program, Standish, ME 04084. Offers adult education and training (MS Ed); Catholic school leadership (MS Ed); health care educator (MS Ed); school educator (MS Ed). Program available by correspondence. Part-time programs available. Postbaccalaureate distance learning degree programs offered (minimal on-campus study). *Faculty:* 20 part-time/adjunct (13 women). *Students:* 273 part-time (190 women); includes 21 minority (14 Black or African American, non-Hispanic/Latino; 1 American Indian or Alaska Native, non-Hispanic/Latino; 2 Asian, non-Hispanic/Latino; 4 Hispanic/Latino). Average age 43. In 2011, 25 master's awarded. *Application deadline:* Applications are processed on a rolling basis. Application fee: $50. Electronic applications accepted. One-time fee: $50. *Financial support:* Institutionally sponsored loans available. Support available to part-time students. Financial award applicants required to submit FAFSA. *Unit head:* Dr. Thomas Hancock, Director, 207-893-7841, Fax: 207-892-7987, E-mail: thancock@sjcme.edu. *Application contact:* Lynne Robinson, Director of Admissions, 800-752-4723, Fax: 207-892-7480, E-mail: info@sjcme.edu. Web site: http://online.sjcme.edu/master-science-education.php.

Saint Joseph's University, College of Arts and Sciences, Department of Education, Philadelphia, PA 19131-1395. Offers curriculum supervisor of instruction (Certificate); educational leadership (MS, Ed D); elementary education (MS, Certificate); elementary/middle years (Certificate); English second language specialist online (Certificate); hearing impaired: N-12th grade (Certificate); instructional technology (MS, Certificate); principal certification (Certificate); professional education (MS); reading specialist (MS, Certificate); reading supervisory (Certificate); secondary education (MS, Certificate); special education (MS, Certificate); superintendent's letter of eligibility (Certificate); supervisor of special education (Certificate); Wilson reading certificate online (Certificate). Part-time and evening/weekend programs available. Postbaccalaureate distance learning degree programs offered (no on-campus study). *Faculty:* 26 full-time (24 women), 83 part-time/adjunct (52 women). *Students:* 112 full-time (92 women), 923 part-time (709 women); includes 147 minority (92 Black or African American, non-Hispanic/Latino; 4 American Indian or Alaska Native, non-Hispanic/Latino; 19 Asian, non-Hispanic/Latino; 28 Hispanic/Latino; 4 Two or more races, non-Hispanic/Latino), 8 international. Average age 31. 285 applicants, 77% accepted, 176 enrolled. In 2011, 276 master's, 13 doctorates, 2 other advanced degrees awarded. *Entrance requirements:* For master's, 2 letters of recommendation, minimum GPA of 3.0, official transcripts, personal statement; for doctorate, GRE, master's degree from accredited institution, minimum graduate GPA of 3.5, computer competence, commitment to participate in cohort, interview with program director. Additional exam requirements/recommendations for international students: Required—TOEFL (minimum score 550 paper-based; 213 computer-based; 79 iBT). *Application deadline:* For fall admission, 7/15 priority date for domestic students, 4/15 for international students; for winter admission, 11/15 for domestic students, 1/15 for international students; for spring admission, 11/15 priority date for domestic students, 10/15 for international students. Applications are processed on a rolling basis. Application fee: $35. Electronic applications accepted. *Expenses:* Contact institution. *Financial support:* Unspecified assistantships available. Financial award applicants required to submit FAFSA. *Faculty research:* Public education professional development, factors predicting early mathematics skills for low income children. *Total annual research expenditures:* $92,975. *Unit head:* Dr. Jeanne Brady, Associate Dean, Education, 610-660-1580, E-mail: jebrady@sju.edu. *Application contact:* Kate McConnell, Director, Graduate College of Arts and Sciences Admissions and Retention, 610-660-3184, Fax: 610-660-3230, E-mail: kate.mcconnell@sju.edu.

St. Lawrence University, Department of Education, Canton, NY 13617-1455. Offers counseling and human development (M Ed, MS, CAS), including mental health counseling (MS), school counseling (M Ed, CAS); educational leadership (M Ed, CAS), including combined school building leadership/school district leadership (CAS), educational leadership (M Ed), school building leadership (M Ed), school district leadership (CAS); general studies in education (M Ed). *Accreditation:* Teacher Education Accreditation Council. Part-time and evening/weekend programs available. *Degree requirements:* For master's, thesis optional. *Entrance requirements:* For master's, GRE General Test. *Faculty research:* Defense mechanisms, conflict negotiations and mediation, teacher education policy.

Saint Leo University, Graduate Studies in Education, Saint Leo, FL 33574-6665. Offers educational leadership (M Ed); exceptional student education (M Ed); higher education leadership (Ed S); instructional design (MS); instructional leadership (M Ed); reading (M Ed); school leadership (Ed S). Part-time and evening/weekend programs available. Postbaccalaureate distance learning degree programs offered (minimal on-campus study). *Faculty:* 14 full-time (10 women), 21 part-time/adjunct (16 women). *Students:* 523 full-time (427 women), 20 part-time (17 women); includes 65 minority (43 Black or African American, non-Hispanic/Latino; 2 Asian, non-Hispanic/Latino; 16 Hispanic/Latino; 4 Two or more races, non-Hispanic/Latino), 3 international. Average age 37. In 2011, 153 master's, 18 other advanced degrees awarded. *Degree requirements:* For master's, comprehensive exam, appropriate State of Florida certification tests. *Entrance requirements:* For master's, GRE (minimum score of 1000) or MAT (minimum score of 410) if undergraduate GPA for last 60 hours of coursework was below 3.0 (for M Ed), bachelor's degree with minimum GPA of 3.0 for last 60 hours of coursework from regionally-accredited college or university, 2 recommendations, resume, statement of professional goals, copy of valid teaching certificate (for M Ed); for Ed S, GRE (minimum score 1000) or MAT (minimum score 410) if undergraduate GPA for last 60 hours of coursework less than 3.0, bachelor's degree with minimum GPA of 3.0 for last 60 hours of coursework from regionally-accredited college or university, 2 recommendations, resume, valid teaching certificate. Additional exam requirements/recommendations for international students: Required—TOEFL (minimum score 550 paper-based; 213 computer-based; 80 iBT). *Application deadline:* For fall admission, 7/1 priority date for domestic students, 7/1 for international students; for winter admission, 7/1 for international students; for spring admission, 11/1 priority date for domestic students. Applications are processed on a rolling basis. Application fee: $80. Electronic applications accepted. *Expenses:* Contact institution. *Financial support:* In 2011–12, 20 students received support. Career-related internships or fieldwork, Federal Work-Study, scholarships/grants, and health care benefits available. Financial award application deadline: 3/1; financial award applicants required to submit FAFSA. *Faculty research:* The role of the school leader in data analysis of student achievement, teacher recruitment, teacher effectiveness. *Unit head:* Dr. Sharyn Disabato, Director, 352-588-8309, Fax: 352-588-8861, E-mail: med@saintleo.edu. *Application contact:* Jared Welling, Director of Graduate Admission, 800-707-8846, Fax: 352-588-7873, E-mail: grad.admissions@saintleo.edu. Web site: http://www.saintleo.edu/Academics/School-of-Education-Social-Services/Graduate-Degree-Programs.

Saint Louis University, Graduate Education, College of Education and Public Service, Department of Educational Studies, St. Louis, MO 63103-2097. Offers curriculum and instruction (MA, Ed D, PhD); educational foundations (MA, Ed D, PhD); special education (MA); teaching (MAT). *Accreditation:* NCATE. Part-time programs available. *Degree requirements:* For master's, comprehensive exam; for doctorate, comprehensive exam, thesis/dissertation, preliminary oral and written exams. *Entrance requirements:* For master's, GRE General Test or MAT, letters of recommendation, resume; for doctorate, GRE General Test, letters of recommendation, resumé, goal statement, transcripts. Additional exam requirements/recommendations for international students: Required—TOEFL (minimum score 525 paper-based; 194 computer-based). Electronic applications accepted. *Faculty research:* Teacher preparation, multicultural issues, children with special needs, qualitative research in education, inclusion.

Saint Martin's University, Graduate Programs, College of Education, Lacey, WA 98503. Offers administration (M Ed); English as a second language (M Ed); guidance and counseling (M Ed); reading (M Ed); special education (M Ed); teaching (MIT). *Accreditation:* Teacher Education Accreditation Council. Part-time and evening/weekend programs available. *Faculty:* 12 full-time (8 women), 9 part-time/adjunct (7 women). *Students:* 68 full-time (38 women), 28 part-time (20 women); includes 15 minority (2 Black or African American, non-Hispanic/Latino; 2 American Indian or Alaska Native, non-Hispanic/Latino; 7 Asian, non-Hispanic/Latino; 2 Hispanic/Latino; 2 Two or more races, non-Hispanic/Latino), 4 international. Average age 35. 17 applicants, 94% accepted, 15 enrolled. In 2011, 12 master's awarded. *Degree requirements:* For master's, comprehensive exam (for some programs), thesis or alternative, project or comprehensives. *Entrance requirements:* For master's, GRE General Test or MAT, resume. Additional exam requirements/recommendations for international students: Required—TOEFL (minimum score 560 paper-based; 220 computer-based; 83 iBT). *Application deadline:* For fall admission, 6/1 priority date for domestic students, 6/1 for international students; for spring admission, 10/1 priority date for domestic students, 10/1 for international students. Applications are processed on a rolling basis. Application fee: $35. *Expenses: Tuition:* Part-time $910 per credit hour. Tuition and fees vary according to course level, campus/location and program. *Financial support:* Career-related internships or fieldwork, Federal Work-Study, institutionally sponsored loans, and unspecified assistantships available. Support available to part-time students. Financial award application deadline: 3/1; financial award applicants required to submit FAFSA. *Faculty research:* Reader's theatre and reader/writer workshops, curriculum and assessment integration, gender and equity, classroom evaluations, organizational leadership. *Unit head:* Dr. Joyce Westgard, Dean, College of Education and Professional Psychology, 360-438-4509, Fax: 360-438-4486, E-mail: westgard@stmartin.edu. *Application contact:* Ryan M. Smith, Administrative Assistant, 360-438-4333, Fax: 360-438-4486, E-mail: ryan.smith@stmartin.edu. Web site: http://www.stmartin.edu/CEPP/.

Saint Mary's College of California, Kalmanovitz School of Education, Moraga, CA 94556. Offers M Ed, MA, MAT, Ed D. Part-time and evening/weekend programs available. *Students:* 202 full-time (168 women), 423 part-time (344 women); includes 163 minority (47 Black or African American, non-Hispanic/Latino; 5 American Indian or Alaska Native, non-Hispanic/Latino; 39 Asian, non-Hispanic/Latino; 65 Hispanic/Latino; 6 Native Hawaiian or other Pacific Islander, non-Hispanic/Latino; 1 Two or more races, non-Hispanic/Latino), 1 international. Average age 36. 617 applicants, 71% accepted, 366 enrolled. In 2011, 160 master's, 7 doctorates awarded. *Degree requirements:* For master's, thesis or alternative; for doctorate, thesis/dissertation. *Entrance requirements:* For master's, interview, minimum GPA of 3.0; for doctorate, GRE or MAT, interview, MA, minimum GPA of 3.0. *Application deadline:* Applications are processed on a rolling basis. Application fee: $50. *Expenses:* Contact institution. *Financial support:* Career-related internships or fieldwork and tuition waivers (partial) available. Support available to part-time students. Financial award application deadline: 2/15; financial award applicants required to submit FAFSA. *Faculty research:* Teacher effectiveness, school-based management, multicultural teaching, language and literacy development. *Unit head:* Dr. Phyllis Metcalf-Turner, Dean, 925-631-4309, Fax: 925-376-8379. *Application contact:* Jane Joyce, Coordinator, Recruitment and Admissions, 925-631-4700, Fax: 925-376-8379, E-mail: soereq@stmarys-ca.edu. Web site: http://www.stmarys-ca.edu/node/6631.

St. Mary's College of Maryland, Department of Educational Studies, St. Mary's City, MD 20686-3001. Offers MAT. *Faculty:* 8 full-time (7 women). *Students:* 30 full-time (25 women); includes 5 minority (2 Black or African American, non-Hispanic/Latino; 1 Asian, non-Hispanic/Latino; 1 Hispanic/Latino; 1 Two or more races, non-Hispanic/Latino). Average age 23. 42 applicants, 95% accepted, 30 enrolled. In 2011, 34 master's awarded. *Degree requirements:* For master's, internship, electronic portfolio, research projects, PRAXIS II. *Entrance requirements:* For master's, SAT, ACT, GRE or PRAXIS I, 2 letters of recommendation. Additional exam requirements/recommendations for international students: Required—TOEFL. *Application deadline:* For fall admission, 10/1 for domestic students. Application fee: $50. *Expenses:* Tuition, state resident: full-time $13,190. *Required fees:* $2440. One-time fee: $1330 full-time. *Financial support:* Application deadline: 3/1; applicants required to submit FAFSA. *Faculty research:* Supporting English language learners across the curriculum, supporting women and minorities in math and science, instructional technology, multicultural young adult literature, educating teachers to be advocates for equity and social justice. *Unit head:* Dr. Lois T. Stover, Chair, 240-895-2187, Fax: 240-895-4436, E-mail: ltstover@smcm.edu. Web site: http://www.smcm.edu/educationstudies/.

St. Mary's University, Graduate School, Department of Teacher Education, San Antonio, TX 78228-8507. Offers Catholic principalship (Certificate); Catholic school leadership (MA, Certificate), including Catholic school administrators (Certificate), Catholic school leadership (MA), Catholic school teachers (Certificate); educational leadership (MA, Certificate), including educational leadership (MA), principalship (mid-management) (Certificate); reading (MA). Part-time and evening/weekend programs available. *Degree requirements:* For master's, comprehensive exam. *Entrance requirements:* For master's, GRE General Test. Additional exam requirements/recommendations for international students: Required—TOEFL (minimum score 550 paper-based; 213 computer-based; 80 iBT). Electronic applications accepted.

Saint Mary's University of Minnesota, Schools of Graduate and Professional Programs, Graduate School of Education, Education Program, Winona, MN 55987-1399. Offers education (MA); gifted and talented instruction (Certificate). *Unit head:*

Sandra Nicholson, Director, 612-728-5179, Fax: 612-728-5121, E-mail: snichols@smumn.edu. *Application contact:* Yasin Alsaidi, Director of Admissions for Graduate and Professional Programs, 612-728-5207, Fax: 612-728-5121, E-mail: yalsaidi@smumn.edu. Web site: http://www.smumn.edu/graduate-home/areas-of-study/graduate-school-of-education/ma-in-education.

Saint Mary's University of Minnesota, Schools of Graduate and Professional Programs, Graduate School of Education, Education-Wisconsin Program, Winona, MN 55987-1399. Offers MA. *Unit head:* Lynda Sullivan, Director, 877-442-4020, E-mail: lsulliva@smumn.edu. *Application contact:* Yasin Alsaidi, Director of Admissions for Graduate and Professional Programs, 612-728-5207, Fax: 612-728-5121, E-mail: yalsaidi@smumn.edu. Web site: http://www.smumn.edu/graduate-home/areas-of-study/graduate-school-of-education/ma-in-education-wisconsin.

Saint Mary's University of Minnesota, Schools of Graduate and Professional Programs, Graduate School of Education, Teaching and Learning Program, Winona, MN 55987-1399. Offers M Ed. *Unit head:* Suzanne Peterson, Director, 952-891-3792, E-mail: speterso@smumn.edu. *Application contact:* Jana Korder, Director of Admissions for Graduate and Professional Programs, 507-457-6615, E-mail: jkorder@smumn.edu. Web site: http://www.smumn.edu/graduate-home/areas-of-study/graduate-school-of-education/med-in-teaching-learning.

Saint Michael's College, Graduate Programs, Program in Education, Colchester, VT 05439. Offers administration (M Ed, CAGS); arts in education (CAGS); curriculum and instruction (M Ed, CAGS); information technology (CAGS); reading (M Ed); special education (M Ed, CAGS); technology (M Ed). Part-time and evening/weekend programs available. *Degree requirements:* For master's, thesis. *Entrance requirements:* For master's, minimum GPA of 3.0. Electronic applications accepted. *Faculty research:* Integrative curriculum, moral and spiritual dimensions of education, learning styles, multiple intelligences, integrating technology into the curriculum.

St. Norbert College, Program in Education, De Pere, WI 54115-2099. Offers MS. Part-time and evening/weekend programs available. *Faculty:* 4 full-time (1 woman), 3 part-time/adjunct (2 women). *Students:* 8 part-time (7 women). 12 applicants, 100% accepted, 8 enrolled. In 2011, 8 master's awarded. *Degree requirements:* For master's, advocacy project. *Entrance requirements:* For master's, minimum undergraduate GPA of 3.0, graduate 3.25; 2 years of teaching experience; state teacher certification or proof of teaching experience. *Application deadline:* For spring admission, 4/20 for domestic students. Application fee: $35. Electronic applications accepted. *Expenses: Tuition:* Part-time $390 per credit hour. *Faculty research:* Literacy, portfolios, integrated curriculum, technology. *Unit head:* Dr. Susan M. Landt, Director/Professor, 920-403-1328, Fax: 920-403-4078, E-mail: susan.landt@snc.edu. *Application contact:* Dr. Susan Landt, Director/Professor, 920-403-1328, Fax: 920-403-4078, E-mail: joanne.wilson@snc.edu. Web site: http://www.snc.edu/mse/.

Saint Peter's University, Graduate Programs in Education, Jersey City, NJ 07306-5997. Offers director of school counseling services (Certificate); educational leadership (MA Ed, Ed D); middle school mathematics (Certificate); professional/associate counselor (Certificate); reading (MA Ed); school business administrator (Certificate); school counseling (MA, Certificate); special education (MA Ed, Certificate), including applied behavioral analysis (MA Ed), literacy (MA Ed), teacher of students with disabilities (Certificate); teaching (MA Ed, Certificate), including 6-8 middle school education, K-12 secondary education, K-5 elementary education. *Accreditation:* Teacher Education Accreditation Council. Part-time and evening/weekend programs available. *Degree requirements:* For master's, comprehensive exam; for doctorate, comprehensive exam, thesis/dissertation. *Entrance requirements:* For master's and doctorate, GRE or MAT. Additional exam requirements/recommendations for international students: Required—TOEFL (minimum score 79 computer-based). Electronic applications accepted.

St. Thomas Aquinas College, Division of Teacher Education, Sparkill, NY 10976. Offers adolescence education (MST); childhood and special education (MST); childhood education (MST); educational leadership (MS Ed); reading (MS Ed, PMC); special education (MS Ed, PMC); teaching (MS Ed), including elementary education, middle school education, secondary education. *Accreditation:* NCATE. Part-time and evening/weekend programs available. *Degree requirements:* For master's, comprehensive exam, comprehensive professional portfolio; for PMC, action research project. *Entrance requirements:* For master's, New York State Qualifying Exam, GRE General Test or minimum GPA of 3.0, teaching certificate; for PMC, GRE General Test or minimum GPA of 3.0. Electronic applications accepted. *Faculty research:* Computer applications in education, adolescent special education students, literacy development, inclusive practices for special education students.

St. Thomas University, School of Leadership Studies, Institute for Education, Miami Gardens, FL 33054-6459. Offers earth/space science (Certificate); educational administration (MS, Certificate); educational leadership (Ed D); elementary education (MS); ESOL (Certificate); gifted education (Certificate); instructional technology (MS, Certificate); professional/studies (Certificate); reading (MS, Certificate); special education (MS). Part-time and evening/weekend programs available. *Degree requirements:* For master's, comprehensive exam; for doctorate, comprehensive exam, thesis/dissertation. *Entrance requirements:* For master's, interview, minimum GPA of 3.0 or GRE; for doctorate, GRE or MAT. Additional exam requirements/recommendations for international students: Required—TOEFL (minimum score 550 paper-based; 213 computer-based; 79 iBT). Electronic applications accepted.

Saint Vincent College, Program in Education, Latrobe, PA 15650-2690. Offers curriculum and instruction (MS); educational media and technology (MS); environmental education (MS); school administration and supervision (MS); special education (MS). Part-time and evening/weekend programs available. *Degree requirements:* For master's, comprehensive exam. *Entrance requirements:* For master's, GRE (if undergraduate GPA less than 3.0). Additional exam requirements/recommendations for international students: Required—TOEFL (minimum score 550 paper-based; 213 computer-based). *Faculty research:* Assessment and instructional technology.

Saint Xavier University, Graduate Studies, School of Education, Chicago, IL 60655-3105. Offers counseling (MA); curriculum and instruction (MA); early childhood education (MA); educational administration (MA); elementary education (MA); individualized studies (MA), including educational technology, English as a second language (ESL), ISTEM (integrative science, technology, engineering, and math), science education; music education (MA); reading (MA); secondary education (MA); Spanish education (MA); special education (MA); teaching and leadership (MA). *Accreditation:* NCATE. Part-time and evening/weekend programs available. *Degree requirements:* For master's, thesis or project. *Entrance requirements:* For master's, minimum GPA of 3.0. *Application deadline:* For fall admission, 8/15 priority date for domestic students. Applications are processed on a rolling basis. Application fee: $35. *Expenses:* Contact institution. *Financial support:* Career-related internships or fieldwork available. Support available to part-time students. Financial award applicants required to submit FAFSA. *Unit head:* Dr. Beverly Gulley, Dean, 773-298-3221, Fax: 773-779-9061, E-mail: gulley@sxu.edu. *Application contact:* Beth Gierach, Managing Director of Admission, 773-298-3053, Fax: 773-298-3076, E-mail: gierach@sxu.edu.

Salem College, Department of Teacher Education, Winston-Salem, NC 27101. Offers art education (MAT); elementary education (M Ed, MAT); language and literacy (M Ed); middle school education (MAT); music education (MAT); school counseling (M Ed); second language studies (MAT); secondary education (MAT); special education (M Ed, MAT). *Accreditation:* NCATE. Part-time and evening/weekend programs available. Postbaccalaureate distance learning degree programs offered (minimal on-campus study). *Degree requirements:* For master's, comprehensive exam, practicum (MAT), project (M Ed), oral and written comprehensive exams. *Entrance requirements:* For master's, GRE, minimum GPA of 2.5. *Faculty research:* Content area reading strategies, literacy development, brain compatible instruction.

Salem International University, School of Education, Salem, WV 26426-0500. Offers curriculum and instruction (M Ed); educational leadership (M Ed). Part-time and evening/weekend programs available. Postbaccalaureate distance learning degree programs offered. *Degree requirements:* For master's, comprehensive exam (for some programs), thesis (for some programs). *Entrance requirements:* For master's, GRE, MAT, NTE, 3 letters of recommendation. Additional exam requirements/recommendations for international students: Required—TOEFL (minimum score 550 paper-based; 213 computer-based). Electronic applications accepted. *Expenses:* Contact institution. *Faculty research:* Improved classroom effectiveness.

Salisbury University, Graduate Division, Department of Education, Master of Arts in Teaching Program, Salisbury, MD 21801-6837. Offers MAT. Part-time programs available. *Students:* 11 full-time (9 women), 5 part-time (3 women); includes 1 minority (Black or African American, non-Hispanic/Latino). Average age 30. 1 applicant, 100% accepted, 1 enrolled. In 2011, 12 master's awarded. *Degree requirements:* For master's, comprehensive exam, internship, seminar. *Entrance requirements:* For master's, PRAXIS I, GRE, SAT, or ACT, minimum undergraduate GPA of 3.0 or prior graduate degree, 3 recommendations, interview. Additional exam requirements/recommendations for international students: Required—TOEFL (minimum score 550 paper-based; 79 iBT). *Application deadline:* For winter admission, 10/1 for domestic students. Applications are processed on a rolling basis. Application fee: $45. Electronic applications accepted. *Expenses: Tuition, area resident:* Part-time $306 per credit hour. Tuition, state resident: part-time $306 per credit hour. Tuition, nonresident: part-time $595 per credit hour. *Required fees:* $68 per credit hour. *Financial support:* In 2011–12, 11 students received support. Career-related internships or fieldwork, institutionally sponsored loans, scholarships/grants, and unspecified assistantships available. Support available to part-time students. Financial award application deadline: 3/1; financial award applicants required to submit FAFSA. *Unit head:* Dr. Regina Royer, Program Management Specialist, 410-543-6379, Fax: 410-677-0249, E-mail: rdroyer@salisbury.edu. Web site: http://www.salisbury.edu/educationspecialties/mat.html.

Samford University, Orlean Bullard Beeson School of Education and Professional Studies, Birmingham, AL 35229. Offers early childhood education (Ed S); early childhood/elementary education (MS Ed); educational administration (Ed S); educational leadership (Ed D); elementary education (Ed S); gifted education (MS Ed); instructional leadership (MS Ed); secondary collaboration (MS Ed); M Div/MS Ed. *Accreditation:* NCATE. Part-time programs available. *Faculty:* 11 full-time (7 women), 9 part-time/adjunct (7 women). *Students:* 20 full-time (16 women), 169 part-time (122 women); includes 30 minority (26 Black or African American, non-Hispanic/Latino; 1 American Indian or Alaska Native, non-Hispanic/Latino; 1 Asian, non-Hispanic/Latino; 2 Hispanic/Latino), 1 international. Average age 39. 51 applicants, 92% accepted, 44 enrolled. In 2011, 57 master's, 9 doctorates, 35 other advanced degrees awarded. *Degree requirements:* For master's, comprehensive exam; for doctorate, comprehensive exam, thesis/dissertation. *Entrance requirements:* For master's, GRE or MAT, minimum GPA of 3.0; for doctorate, minimum GPA of 3.7; for Ed S, GRE, master's degree, teaching certificate, minimum GPA of 3.25. Additional exam requirements/recommendations for international students: Required—TOEFL (minimum score 550 paper-based; 213 computer-based). *Application deadline:* For fall admission, 7/15 for domestic students; for winter admission, 4/5 for domestic students; for spring admission, 12/4 for domestic students. Applications are processed on a rolling basis. Application fee: $25. *Expenses: Tuition:* Full-time $29,934; part-time $655 per credit. *Required fees:* $705. *Financial support:* Research assistantships, career-related internships or fieldwork, Federal Work-Study, scholarships/grants, and tuition waivers (partial) available. Support available to part-time students. Financial award applicants required to submit FAFSA. *Faculty research:* School law, the characteristics of beginning teachers, the nature of school reform, school culture, quality improvement in education, K-12 student achievement. *Unit head:* Dr. Jean Ann Box, Dean, 205-726-2565, E-mail: jabox@samford.edu. *Application contact:* Dr. Maurice Persall, Director, Graduate Office, 205-726-2019, E-mail: jmpersal@samford.edu. Web site: http://dlserver.samford.edu.

Sam Houston State University, College of Education, Huntsville, TX 77341. Offers M Ed, MA, MLS, Ed D, PhD. *Accreditation:* NCATE. Part-time and evening/weekend programs available. *Faculty:* 80 full-time (55 women), 37 part-time/adjunct (22 women). *Students:* 161 full-time (113 women), 1,046 part-time (886 women); includes 397 minority (182 Black or African American, non-Hispanic/Latino; 20 American Indian or Alaska Native, non-Hispanic/Latino; 14 Asian, non-Hispanic/Latino; 180 Hispanic/Latino; 1 Native Hawaiian or other Pacific Islander, non-Hispanic/Latino), 13 international. Average age 35. 980 applicants, 58% accepted, 384 enrolled. In 2011, 443 master's, 30 doctorates awarded. *Degree requirements:* For doctorate, comprehensive exam (for some programs). *Entrance requirements:* For master's, GRE General Test. Additional exam requirements/recommendations for international students: Required—TOEFL (minimum score 550 paper-based; 213 computer-based; 79 iBT). *Application deadline:* For fall admission, 8/1 for domestic students, 6/25 for international students; for spring admission, 12/1 for domestic students, 11/12 for international students. Applications are processed on a rolling basis. Application fee: $45 ($75 for international students). Electronic applications accepted. *Expenses:* Tuition, state resident: full-time $4420; part-time $221 per credit hour. Tuition, nonresident: full-time $10,680; part-time $534 per credit hour. *Required fees:* $329 per credit hour. *Financial support:* Research assistantships, teaching assistantships, career-related internships or fieldwork, Federal Work-Study, institutionally sponsored loans, and tuition waivers (partial) available. Support available to part-time students. Financial award application deadline: 5/31; financial award applicants required to submit FAFSA. *Unit head:* Dr. Genevieve Brown, Dean, 936-294-1101, Fax: 936-294-1102, E-mail: edu_gxb@shsu.edu. *Application contact:* Beverly Irby, Associate Dean, 936-294-1105, E-mail: edu_mxd@shsu.edu. Web site: http://www.shsu.edu/~edu_www.

San Diego State University, Graduate and Research Affairs, College of Education, San Diego, CA 92182. Offers MA, MS, Ed D, PhD. *Accreditation:* NCATE. Part-time and evening/weekend programs available. *Degree requirements:* For master's, thesis optional; for doctorate, thesis/dissertation. *Entrance requirements:* For master's, GRE General Test, letters of reference; for doctorate, GRE General Test, 3 letters of reference, resumé. Additional exam requirements/recommendations for international students: Required—TOEFL. Electronic applications accepted. *Faculty research:* Special education, rehabilitation counseling, educational psychology.

San Francisco State University, Division of Graduate Studies, College of Education, San Francisco, CA 94132-1722. Offers MA, MS, Ed D, PhD, AC, Credential. *Accreditation:* NCATE. *Unit head:* Dr. Jacob Perea, Dean, 415-338-2687, E-mail:

pjoost@sfsu.edu. *Application contact:* Dr. David Hemphill, Associate Dean, 415-338-2689, E-mail: hemphill@sfsu.edu. Web site: http://www.coe.sfsu.edu.

San Jose State University, Graduate Studies and Research, Connie L. Lurie College of Education, San Jose, CA 95192-0001. Offers MA, Certificate. *Accreditation:* NCATE. Evening/weekend programs available. Electronic applications accepted.

Santa Clara University, School of Education and Counseling Psychology, Department of Education, Santa Clara, CA 95053. Offers educational administration (MA, Certificate); interdisciplinary education (MA); teacher education (Certificate), including multiple subject teaching, single subject teaching. Part-time and evening/weekend programs available. *Students:* 50 full-time (39 women), 187 part-time (148 women); includes 62 minority (4 Black or African American, non-Hispanic/Latino; 2 American Indian or Alaska Native, non-Hispanic/Latino; 19 Asian, non-Hispanic/Latino; 32 Hispanic/Latino; 3 Native Hawaiian or other Pacific Islander, non-Hispanic/Latino; 2 Two or more races, non-Hispanic/Latino), 5 international. Average age 33. 132 applicants, 64% accepted, 70 enrolled. In 2011, 86 master's, 124 other advanced degrees awarded. *Degree requirements:* For master's, comprehensive exam (for some programs), thesis (for some programs). *Entrance requirements:* For master's, statement of purpose, letters of recommendation, transcripts. Additional exam requirements/recommendations for international students: Required—TOEFL (minimum score 600 paper-based; 100 computer-based; 100 iBT). *Application deadline:* For fall admission, 6/15 for domestic and international students; for winter admission, 10/15 for domestic and international students; for spring admission, 1/31 for domestic and international students. Applications are processed on a rolling basis. Application fee: $50. Electronic applications accepted. *Expenses:* Contact institution. *Financial support:* In 2011–12, 66 students received support, including 66 fellowships (averaging $3,695 per year); Federal Work-Study, institutionally sponsored loans, and scholarships/grants also available. Support available to part-time students. Financial award application deadline: 5/15; financial award applicants required to submit FAFSA. *Faculty research:* Predispositions toward teaching science to diverse learners, environmental education, teacher practices and student motivation, critical thinking pedagogy and assessment, early childhood and elementary education, teacher technology integration. *Total annual research expenditures:* $396,365. *Unit head:* Dr. Atom Yee, Interim Dean, 408-554-4455, Fax: 408-554-5038, E-mail: ayee@scu.edu. *Application contact:* ECP Admissions, 408-554-4355, E-mail: ecpadmissions@scu.edu.

Santa Fe University of Art and Design, Program in Education, Santa Fe, NM 87505-7634. Offers MA. Part-time and evening/weekend programs available. *Entrance requirements:* For master's, minimum GPA of 3.0. *Faculty research:* Integrated curriculum, child development, brain research, learning styles, systemic issues in education.

Sarah Lawrence College, Graduate Studies, Program in Art of Teaching, Bronxville, NY 10708-5999. Offers MS Ed. Part-time programs available. *Degree requirements:* For master's, thesis, fieldwork, oral presentation. *Entrance requirements:* For master's, minimum B average in undergraduate coursework. Additional exam requirements/recommendations for international students: Required—TOEFL (minimum score 600 paper-based). *Expenses:* Contact institution.

Savannah College of Art and Design, Graduate School, Program in Professional Education, Savannah, GA 31402-3146. Offers art (MAT); drama (MAT). *Faculty:* 1 (woman) full-time, 4 part-time/adjunct (all women). *Students:* 21 full-time (19 women); includes 1 minority (Black or African American, non-Hispanic/Latino). Average age 27. 4 applicants, 0% accepted, 0 enrolled. In 2011, 16 master's awarded. *Degree requirements:* For master's, comprehensive exam, student teaching. *Entrance requirements:* For master's, research paper; portfolio (for MAT in art); audition and interview (for MAT in drama). Additional exam requirements/recommendations for international students: Required—TOEFL (minimum score 400 paper-based; 50 computer-based). *Application deadline:* For fall admission, 4/1 priority date for domestic students, 4/1 for international students. Applications are processed on a rolling basis. Application fee: $35. Electronic applications accepted. *Expenses: Tuition:* Full-time $30,960; part-time $6880 per quarter. One-time fee: $500. *Financial support:* Fellowships, career-related internships or fieldwork, Federal Work-Study, and scholarships/grants available. Financial award application deadline: 4/1; financial award applicants required to submit FAFSA. *Unit head:* Robert Eisinger, Dean/Acting Chair, 912-525-4834, E-mail: aprice@scad.edu. *Application contact:* Elizabeth Mathis, Director of Graduate Recruitment, 912-525-5965, Fax: 912-525-5985, E-mail: emathis@scad.edu. Web site: http://www.sead.edu/.

Schreiner University, Department of Education, Kerrville, TX 78028-5697. Offers M Ed. Evening/weekend programs available. Postbaccalaureate distance learning degree programs offered (minimal on-campus study). *Faculty:* 2 full-time (1 woman), 1 (woman) part-time/adjunct. *Students:* 44 full-time (35 women); includes 15 minority (1 Black or African American, non-Hispanic/Latino; 14 Hispanic/Latino). Average age 31. 29 applicants, 72% accepted, 16 enrolled. In 2011, 28 master's awarded. *Degree requirements:* For master's, thesis or 2 additional courses. *Entrance requirements:* For master's, GRE (waived if undergraduate cumulative GPA is 3.0 or above), 3 references; transcripts. *Application deadline:* For fall admission, 7/1 priority date for domestic students. Applications are processed on a rolling basis. Application fee: $25. Electronic applications accepted. *Expenses: Tuition:* Full-time $16,200; part-time $450 per credit hour. *Financial support:* Institutionally sponsored loans available. Financial award application deadline: 8/1; financial award applicants required to submit FAFSA. *Unit head:* Dr. Neva Cramer, Director, Teacher Education, 830-792-7266, Fax: 830-792-7382, E-mail: nvcramer@schreiner.edu. *Application contact:* Betty Lavonne Miller, Administrative Assistant, 830-792-7455, Fax: 830-792-7382, E-mail: lmiller@schreiner.edu. Web site: http://www.schreiner.edu/academics/graduate/index.html.

Seattle University, College of Education, Seattle, WA 98122-1090. Offers M Ed, MA, MIT, Ed D, Certificate, Ed S, Post-Master's Certificate. *Accreditation:* NCATE. Part-time and evening/weekend programs available. *Faculty:* 29 full-time (16 women), 13 part-time/adjunct (9 women). *Students:* 198 full-time (143 women), 369 part-time (281 women); includes 147 minority (33 Black or African American, non-Hispanic/Latino; 3 American Indian or Alaska Native, non-Hispanic/Latino; 46 Asian, non-Hispanic/Latino; 41 Hispanic/Latino; 2 Native Hawaiian or other Pacific Islander, non-Hispanic/Latino; 22 Two or more races, non-Hispanic/Latino), 19 international. Average age 31. 550 applicants, 49% accepted, 150 enrolled. In 2011, 215 master's, 16 doctorates, 29 other advanced degrees awarded. *Degree requirements:* For master's and other advanced degree, comprehensive exam; for doctorate, comprehensive exam, thesis/dissertation. *Entrance requirements:* For doctorate, GRE General Test, MAT, interview, MA, minimum GPA of 3.5, 3 years of related experience. Additional exam requirements/recommendations for international students: Required—TOEFL. Application fee: $55. *Expenses:* Contact institution. *Financial support:* Career-related internships or fieldwork, Federal Work-Study, and unspecified assistantships available. Support available to part-time students. Financial award applicants required to submit FAFSA. *Faculty research:* Service-learning, learning and technology, assessment models of professional education, alternative delivery systems. *Unit head:* Dr. Sue Schmitt, Dean, 206-296-5760, E-mail: sschmitt@seattleu.edu. *Application contact:* Janet Shandley, Associate Dean of Graduate Admissions, 206-296-5900, Fax: 206-298-5656, E-mail: grad_admissions@seattleu.edu. Web site: http://www.seattleu.edu/soe/.

Seton Hall University, College of Education and Human Services, South Orange, NJ 07079-2697. Offers MA, MS, Ed D, Exec Ed D, PhD, Ed S, Professional Diploma. *Accreditation:* NCATE. Part-time and evening/weekend programs available. *Faculty:* 43 full-time (28 women), 85 part-time/adjunct (47 women). *Students:* 270 full-time (178 women), 870 part-time (516 women); includes 285 minority (163 Black or African American, non-Hispanic/Latino; 3 American Indian or Alaska Native, non-Hispanic/Latino; 27 Asian, non-Hispanic/Latino; 89 Hispanic/Latino; 1 Native Hawaiian or other Pacific Islander, non-Hispanic/Latino; 2 Two or more races, non-Hispanic/Latino), 26 international. Average age 35. 548 applicants, 67% accepted, 252 enrolled. In 2011, 282 master's, 41 doctorates, 80 other advanced degrees awarded. *Degree requirements:* For master's, comprehensive exam (for some programs), internship; for doctorate, comprehensive exam, thesis/dissertation, internship. *Entrance requirements:* For master's, GRE or MAT, PRAXIS, letters of recommendation, interview, personal statement, curriculum vitae, transcript; for doctorate, GRE, interview, letters of recommendation, personal statement, curriculum vitae, transcript; for other advanced degree, GRE or MAT, PRAXIS, interview, letters of recommendation, personal statement, curriculum vitae, transcript. *Application deadline:* Applications are processed on a rolling basis. Application fee: $50. Electronic applications accepted. *Expenses: Tuition:* Part-time $1033 per credit hour. *Required fees:* $85 per semester. *Financial support:* In 2011–12, 13 students received support. Fellowships, research assistantships, career-related internships or fieldwork, institutionally sponsored loans, and unspecified assistantships available. Financial award application deadline: 2/1; financial award applicants required to submit FAFSA. *Faculty research:* Information technology and classrooms, adult development including career family systems, therapy effectiveness, management systems, principal effectiveness. *Total annual research expenditures:* $30,000. *Unit head:* Dr. Joseph V. De Pierro, Dean, 973-761-9025, E-mail: joseph.depierro@shu.edu. *Application contact:* Dr. Manina Urgolo Huckvale, Associate Dean, 973-761-9668, Fax: 973-275-2187, E-mail: manina.urgolo-huckvale@shu.edu. Web site: http://education.shu.edu/.

Seton Hill University, Program in Inclusive Education, Greensburg, PA 15601. Offers MA. *Accreditation:* Teacher Education Accreditation Council. Part-time and evening/weekend programs available. Postbaccalaureate distance learning degree programs offered (no on-campus study). *Faculty:* 3 full-time (2 women), 5 part-time/adjunct (3 women). *Students:* 4 full-time (all women), 15 part-time (13 women). In 2011, 8 degrees awarded. *Entrance requirements:* For master's, 3 letters of recommendation, transcripts. Additional exam requirements/recommendations for international students: Required—TOEFL (minimum score 600 paper-based; 250 computer-based; 100 iBT), IELTS (minimum score 6.5). *Application deadline:* Applications are processed on a rolling basis. Application fee: $0. Electronic applications accepted. *Expenses: Tuition:* Full-time $13,446; part-time $747 per credit. *Required fees:* $700; $25 per credit. $50 per term. *Financial support:* Tuition discounts available. *Faculty research:* Autism, integrating technology into instruction. *Unit head:* Dr. Sondra Lettrich, Director, 724-830-1010, E-mail: lettrich@setonhill.edu. *Application contact:* Laurel Komarny, Program Counselor, 724-838-4209, E-mail: komarny@setonhill.edu.

Shawnee State University, Program in Curriculum and Instruction, Portsmouth, OH 45662-4344. Offers M Ed. *Accreditation:* NCATE.

Shenandoah University, School of Education and Human Development, Winchester, VA 22601-5195. Offers MS, MSE, D Ed, D Prof, Certificate. *Accreditation:* Teacher Education Accreditation Council. Part-time and evening/weekend programs available. Postbaccalaureate distance learning degree programs offered (minimal on-campus study). *Faculty:* 10 full-time (6 women), 19 part-time/adjunct (13 women). *Students:* 35 full-time (22 women), 324 part-time (247 women); includes 35 minority (14 Black or African American, non-Hispanic/Latino; 1 American Indian or Alaska Native, non-Hispanic/Latino; 8 Asian, non-Hispanic/Latino; 11 Hispanic/Latino; 1 Two or more races, non-Hispanic/Latino), 9 international. Average age 38. 182 applicants, 91% accepted, 132 enrolled. In 2011, 111 master's, 15 doctorates, 25 other advanced degrees awarded. *Degree requirements:* For master's, comprehensive exam (for some programs), thesis (for some programs), internship; for doctorate, comprehensive exam, thesis/dissertation; for Certificate, full-time teaching in area for 1 year. *Entrance requirements:* For master's, minimum GPA of 3.0 or satisfactory GRE, 3 letters of recommendation, valid teaching license, writing sample; for doctorate, minimum graduate GPA of 3.5, 3 years of teaching experience, 3 letters of recommendation, writing samples, interview, resume; for Certificate, minimum undergraduate GPA of 3.0, essay, 3 letters of recommendation. Additional exam requirements/recommendations for international students: Required—TOEFL (minimum score 550 paper-based; 213 computer-based; 79 iBT), IELTS (minimum score 6.5), Sakae Institute of Study Abroad (minimum score 550). *Application deadline:* For fall admission, 7/1 for domestic and international students; for spring admission, 10/15 for domestic and international students. Application fee: $30. Electronic applications accepted. *Expenses: Tuition:* Full-time $17,952; part-time $748 per credit. *Required fees:* $500 per term. Tuition and fees vary according to course level, course load and program. *Financial support:* In 2011–12, 6 students received support. Career-related internships or fieldwork, institutionally sponsored loans, scholarships/grants, and federal loans, alternative loans available. Support available to part-time students. Financial award application deadline: 3/15; financial award applicants required to submit FAFSA. *Unit head:* Dr. Steven E. Humphries, Director, 540-535-3574, E-mail: shumphri@su.edu. *Application contact:* David Anthony, Dean of Admissions, 540-665-4581, Fax: 540-665-4627, E-mail: admit@su.edu. Web site: http://www.su.edu/education/A343D5EBA23B4C7BA98D91428652383C.asp.

Shippensburg University of Pennsylvania, School of Graduate Studies, College of Education and Human Services, Shippensburg, PA 17257-2299. Offers M Ed, MS, MSW, Certificate. *Accreditation:* NCATE. Part-time and evening/weekend programs available. *Faculty:* 46 full-time (26 women), 19 part-time/adjunct (12 women). *Students:* 148 full-time (126 women), 393 part-time (307 women); includes 49 minority (26 Black or African American, non-Hispanic/Latino; 1 American Indian or Alaska Native, non-Hispanic/Latino; 5 Asian, non-Hispanic/Latino; 10 Hispanic/Latino; 7 Two or more races, non-Hispanic/Latino), 5 international. Average age 30. 336 applicants, 54% accepted, 131 enrolled. In 2011, 240 master's awarded. *Entrance requirements:* Additional exam requirements/recommendations for international students: Required—TOEFL (minimum score 580 paper-based; 237 computer-based); Recommended—IELTS (minimum score 6). *Application deadline:* For fall admission, 4/30 for international students; for spring admission, 9/30 for international students. Applications are processed on a rolling basis. Application fee: $30. Electronic applications accepted. *Expenses: Tuition, area resident:* Part-time $416 per credit. Tuition, state resident: part-time $416 per credit. Tuition, nonresident: part-time $624 per credit. *Required fees:* $119 per credit. *Financial support:* In 2011–12, 72 research assistantships with full tuition reimbursements (averaging $5,000 per year) were awarded; career-related internships or fieldwork, scholarships/grants, unspecified assistantships, and resident hall director and student payroll positions also available. Support available to part-time students. Financial award application deadline: 3/1; financial award applicants required to submit FAFSA. *Unit head:* Dr. James R. Johnson, Dean, 717-477-1373, Fax: 717-477-4012, E-mail: jrjohnson@ship.edu. *Application contact:* Jeremy R. Goshorn, Assistant Dean of Graduate Admissions, 717-477-1231, Fax: 717-477-4016, E-mail: jrgoshorn@ship.edu. Web site: http://www.ship.edu/COEHS/.

Siena Heights University, Graduate College, Program in Teacher Education, Adrian, MI 49221-1796. Offers early childhood education (MA), including Montessori education; elementary education (MA), including elementary education/reading; mathematics education (MA); middle school education (MA); secondary education (MA), including secondary education/reading. Part-time programs available. *Degree requirements:* For master's, thesis, presentation. *Entrance requirements:* For master's, minimum GPA of 3.0, interview. *Expenses: Tuition:* Full-time $11,400; part-time $475 per credit hour. *Required fees:* $1000; $500 $125 per term. Tuition and fees vary according to degree level. *Faculty research:* Teaching/learning styles, outcomes-based teaching, multiple intelligences, assessment.

Sierra Nevada College, Teacher Education Program, Incline Village, NV 89451. Offers advanced teaching and leadership (M Ed); elementary education (MAT); secondary education (MAT). Part-time and evening/weekend programs available. Postbaccalaureate distance learning degree programs offered (minimal on-campus study). *Faculty:* 2 full-time (both women), 26 part-time/adjunct (16 women). *Students:* 247 full-time (192 women), 240 part-time (162 women); includes 234 minority (44 Black or African American, non-Hispanic/Latino; 8 American Indian or Alaska Native, non-Hispanic/Latino; 132 Asian, non-Hispanic/Latino; 38 Hispanic/Latino; 12 Native Hawaiian or other Pacific Islander, non-Hispanic/Latino). Average age 35. 147 applicants, 84% accepted, 124 enrolled. In 2011, 146 master's awarded. *Degree requirements:* For master's, comprehensive exam, thesis, PRAXIS I and II. *Entrance requirements:* For master's, 2 letters of recommendation, minimum GPA of 3.0. *Application deadline:* For fall admission, 8/6 priority date for domestic students; for winter admission, 1/7 priority date for domestic students; for spring admission, 5/6 priority date for domestic students. Applications are processed on a rolling basis. Application fee: $50. Electronic applications accepted. *Expenses: Tuition:* Full-time $7138; part-time $397 per credit. *Required fees:* $100 per semester. *Financial support:* In 2011–12, 334 students received support. Federal Work-Study available. Support available to part-time students. Financial award application deadline: 8/15; financial award applicants required to submit FAFSA. *Unit head:* Beth Bouchard, Chair of Education Department, 775-831-1314, Fax: 775-832-1686, E-mail: bbouchard@sierranevada.edu. *Application contact:* Katrina Midgley, Director of Graduate Admission, 775-831-1314 Ext. 7517, Fax: 775-832-1686, E-mail: kmidgley@sierranevada.edu. Web site: http://www.sierranevada.edu/.

Silver Lake College of the Holy Family, Division of Graduate Studies, Program in Education, Manitowoc, WI 54220-9319. Offers administrative leadership (MA Ed); teacher leadership (MA Ed). Part-time and evening/weekend programs available. Postbaccalaureate distance learning degree programs offered (no on-campus study). *Degree requirements:* For master's, comprehensive exam, thesis or alternative, public presentation of culminating project. *Entrance requirements:* For master's, minimum undergraduate GPA of 3.0, writing sample, 3 letters of recommendation. Additional exam requirements/recommendations for international students: Required—TOEFL. Electronic applications accepted.

Simmons College, College of Arts and Sciences Graduate Studies, Boston, MA 02115. Offers applied behavior analysis (PhD); behavior analysis (MS, Ed S); children's literature (MA); education (MS, CAGS, Ed S); educational leadership (PhD, CAGS); English (MA); gender and cultural studies (MA); health professions education (PhD); history (MA); Spanish (MA); special education moderate licensure (Certificate); special needs administration (Ed D); special needs education (Ed S); teaching (MAT); teaching English as a second language (MA, CAGS); urban education (CAGS); writing for children (MFA); MA/MA; MA/MS; MAT/MA. *Unit head:* Renee White, Dean. *Application contact:* Kristen Haack, Director, Graduate Studies Admission, 617-521-2917, Fax: 617-521-3058, E-mail: gsa@simmons.edu. Web site: http://www.simmons.edu/gradstudies/.

Simon Fraser University, Graduate Studies, Faculty of Education, Burnaby, BC V5A 1S6, Canada. Offers M Ed, M Sc, MA, Ed D, PhD. *Degree requirements:* For master's, project or thesis; for doctorate, thesis/dissertation. *Entrance requirements:* For master's, minimum GPA of 3.0; for doctorate, GRE, master's degree or exceptional record in a bachelor's degree, minimum GPA of 3.5. Additional exam requirements/recommendations for international students: Required—TOEFL or IELTS. *Faculty research:* Drama education, gender equity, children's literature, theory and curriculum development, counseling psychology.

Simpson College, Department of Education, Indianola, IA 50125-1297. Offers secondary education (MAT). *Degree requirements:* For master's, PRAXIS II, electronic portfolio. *Entrance requirements:* For master's, bachelor's degree; minimum cumulative GPA of 2.75, 3.0 in major; 3 letters of recommendation.

Simpson University, School of Education, Redding, CA 96003-8606. Offers education (MA); education and preliminary administrative services (MA); education and preliminary teaching (MA); teaching (MA). Part-time and evening/weekend programs available. *Faculty:* 4 full-time (2 women), 16 part-time/adjunct (7 women). *Students:* 71 full-time (51 women), 84 part-time (57 women); includes 20 minority (1 Black or African American, non-Hispanic/Latino; 10 Asian, non-Hispanic/Latino; 9 Hispanic/Latino). Average age 33. 109 applicants, 83% accepted, 75 enrolled. In 2011, 42 master's awarded. *Degree requirements:* For master's, thesis optional. *Entrance requirements:* For master's, California Basic Educational Skills Test, CSET, 2 letters of reference. Additional exam requirements/recommendations for international students: Required—TOEFL (minimum score 550 paper-based; 180 computer-based). *Application deadline:* Applications are processed on a rolling basis. Application fee: $25. Electronic applications accepted. *Expenses: Tuition:* Full-time $5400; part-time $600 per unit. Tuition and fees vary according to program. *Financial support:* Scholarships/grants available. Financial award applicants required to submit FAFSA. *Unit head:* Dr. Glee Brooks, Dean, 530-226-4606, Fax: 530-226-4861, E-mail: edadmissions@simpsonu.edu. *Application contact:* Kendell Kluttz, Director of Enrollment Management, 530-226-4770, Fax: 530-226-4861, E-mail: edadmissions@simpsonu.edu.

Sinte Gleska University, Graduate Education Program, Mission, SD 57555. Offers elementary education (M Ed). Part-time and evening/weekend programs available. *Degree requirements:* For master's, thesis. *Entrance requirements:* For master's, 2 years of experience in elementary education, minimum GPA of 2.5, South Dakota elementary education certification. *Faculty research:* American Indian graduate education, teaching of Native American students.

Slippery Rock University of Pennsylvania, Graduate Studies (Recruitment), College of Education, Slippery Rock, PA 16057-1383. Offers M Ed, MA, MS. *Accreditation:* NCATE. Part-time and evening/weekend programs available. Postbaccalaureate distance learning degree programs offered. *Faculty:* 35 full-time (17 women), 4 part-time/adjunct (1 woman). *Students:* 180 full-time (115 women), 186 part-time (155 women); includes 19 minority (8 Black or African American, non-Hispanic/Latino; 2 American Indian or Alaska Native, non-Hispanic/Latino; 4 Asian, non-Hispanic/Latino; 2 Hispanic/Latino; 3 Two or more races, non-Hispanic/Latino), 1 international. Average age 29. 411 applicants, 64% accepted, 138 enrolled. In 2011, 225 degrees awarded. *Degree requirements:* For master's, comprehensive exam (for some programs), thesis (for some programs), internship, portfolio (depending on program). *Entrance requirements:* For master's, GRE General Test, MAT, minimum GPA of 2.75 (depending on program). Additional exam requirements/recommendations for international students: Required—TOEFL (minimum score 550 paper-based; 213 computer-based; 80 iBT). *Application deadline:* For fall admission, 3/1 priority date for domestic students, 5/1 for international students; for spring admission, 10/1 priority date for domestic students, 9/1 for international students. Applications are processed on a rolling basis. Application fee: $25 ($30 for international students). Electronic applications accepted. *Expenses:* Contact institution. *Financial support:* Career-related internships or fieldwork, Federal Work-Study, institutionally sponsored loans, scholarships/grants, tuition waivers (partial), and unspecified assistantships available. Support available to part-time students. Financial award application deadline: 5/1; financial award applicants required to submit FAFSA. *Unit head:* Dr. Kathleen Strickland, Interim Dean, 724-738-2007, Fax: 724-738-2880, E-mail: kathleen.strickland@sru.edu. *Application contact:* Angela Barrett, Director of Graduate Admissions, 724-738-2051, Fax: 724-738-2146, E-mail: graduate.admissions@sru.edu.

Smith College, Graduate and Special Programs, Department of Education and Child Study, Northampton, MA 01063. Offers education of the deaf (MED); elementary education (MAT); middle school education (MAT); secondary education (MAT), including biological sciences education, chemistry education, English education, French education, geology education, government education, history education, mathematics education, physics education, Spanish education. Part-time programs available. *Faculty:* 6 full-time (4 women), 3 part-time/adjunct (2 women). *Students:* 34 full-time (28 women), 7 part-time (all women); includes 3 minority (2 Asian, non-Hispanic/Latino; 1 Hispanic/Latino). Average age 29. 72 applicants, 64% accepted, 34 enrolled. In 2011, 30 master's awarded. *Entrance requirements:* For master's, GRE. Additional exam requirements/recommendations for international students: Required—TOEFL (minimum score 590 paper-based; 243 computer-based; 97 iBT). *Application deadline:* For fall admission, 4/1 for domestic students, 1/15 for international students; for spring admission, 12/1 for domestic students. Application fee: $60. *Expenses: Tuition:* Full-time $14,925; part-time $1245 per credit. *Financial support:* In 2011–12, 38 students received support, including 7 fellowships; career-related internships or fieldwork, institutionally sponsored loans, and scholarships/grants also available. Support available to part-time students. Financial award application deadline: 1/15; financial award applicants required to submit CSS PROFILE or FAFSA. *Unit head:* Sam Intrator, Chair, 413-585-3242, Fax: 413-585-3268, E-mail: sintrato@smith.edu. *Application contact:* Ruth Morgan, Administrative Assistant, 413-585-3050, Fax: 413-585-3054, E-mail: gradstdy@smith.edu.

Sonoma State University, School of Education, Rohnert Park, CA 94928-3609. Offers education (MA, Ed D); multiple subject (Credential); single subject (Credential); special education (Credential). *Accreditation:* NCATE. Part-time and evening/weekend programs available. *Faculty:* 12 full-time (9 women), 4 part-time/adjunct (1 woman). *Students:* 226 full-time (175 women), 181 part-time (137 women); includes 70 minority (3 Black or African American, non-Hispanic/Latino; 3 American Indian or Alaska Native, non-Hispanic/Latino; 10 Asian, non-Hispanic/Latino; 28 Hispanic/Latino; 1 Native Hawaiian or other Pacific Islander, non-Hispanic/Latino; 25 Two or more races, non-Hispanic/Latino), 4 international. Average age 31. 336 applicants, 61% accepted, 95 enrolled. In 2011, 54 master's, 478 other advanced degrees awarded. *Degree requirements:* For master's, thesis or alternative. *Entrance requirements:* For master's, minimum GPA of 2.5. Additional exam requirements/recommendations for international students: Required—TOEFL (minimum score 500 paper-based; 173 computer-based). Application fee: $55. *Financial support:* Fellowships, career-related internships or fieldwork, and Federal Work-Study available. Support available to part-time students. Financial award application deadline: 3/2; financial award applicants required to submit FAFSA. *Unit head:* Dr. Carlos Ayala, Dean, 707-664-4412, E-mail: carlos.ayala@sonoma.edu. *Application contact:* Dr. Jennifer Mahdavi, Coordinator of Graduate Studies, 707-664-3311, E-mail: jennifer.mahdavi@sonoma.edu. Web site: http://www.sonoma.edu/education/.

South Carolina State University, School of Graduate Studies, Department of Education, Orangeburg, SC 29117-0001. Offers counseling education (M Ed); early childhood and special education (M Ed); early childhood education (MAT); educational leadership (Ed D, Ed S); elementary education (M Ed, MAT); engineering (MAT); general science (MAT); mathematics (MAT); secondary education (M Ed), including biology education, business education, counselor education, English education, home economics education, industrial education, mathematics education, science education, social studies education; special education (M Ed), including emotionally handicapped, learning disabilities, mentally handicapped. *Accreditation:* NCATE. Part-time and evening/weekend programs available. *Faculty:* 9 full-time (6 women), 6 part-time/adjunct (2 women). *Students:* 34 full-time (29 women), 50 part-time (40 women); includes 74 minority (72 Black or African American, non-Hispanic/Latino; 1 Asian, non-Hispanic/Latino; 1 Hispanic/Latino). Average age 34. 23 applicants, 91% accepted, 14 enrolled. In 2011, 11 master's awarded. *Degree requirements:* For master's, thesis optional, departmental qualifying exam. *Entrance requirements:* For master's, GRE General Test, NTE, interview, teaching certificate. *Application deadline:* For fall admission, 6/15 priority date for domestic students, 6/15 for international students; for spring admission, 11/1 for domestic and international students. Applications are processed on a rolling basis. Application fee: $25. Electronic applications accepted. *Expenses:* Tuition, state resident: full-time $8688; part-time $514 per credit hour. Tuition, nonresident: full-time $17,600; part-time $1009 per credit hour. *Required fees:* $570. *Financial support:* In 2011–12, 3 fellowships (averaging $5,020 per year) were awarded; career-related internships or fieldwork, Federal Work-Study, and institutionally sponsored loans also available. Financial award application deadline: 6/1. *Faculty research:* Critical thinking, child abuse, stress, test-taking skills, conflict resolution, mainstreaming. *Unit head:* Dr. Charlie Spell, Interim Chair, 803-536-7098, Fax: 803-516-4568, E-mail: cspell@scsu.edu. *Application contact:* Annette Hazzard-Jones, Program Coordinator II, 803-536-8809, Fax: 803-536-8812, E-mail: zs_ahazzard@scsu.edu.

South Dakota State University, Graduate School, College of Education and Human Sciences, Brookings, SD 57007. Offers M Ed, MFCS, MS, PhD. *Degree requirements:* For master's, thesis, oral exam. *Entrance requirements:* Additional exam requirements/recommendations for international students: Required—TOEFL.

Southeastern Louisiana University, College of Education and Human Development, Hammond, LA 70402. Offers M Ed, MAT, Ed D. *Accreditation:* NCATE. Part-time programs available. *Faculty:* 36 full-time (22 women), 1 (woman) part-time/adjunct. *Students:* 103 full-time (92 women), 365 part-time (308 women); includes 122 minority (102 Black or African American, non-Hispanic/Latino; 4 Asian, non-Hispanic/Latino; 11 Hispanic/Latino; 5 Two or more races, non-Hispanic/Latino). Average age 34. 77 applicants, 100% accepted, 49 enrolled. In 2011, 174 master's, 19 doctorates awarded. *Degree requirements:* For master's, comprehensive exam (for some programs), thesis optional; for doctorate, thesis/dissertation. *Entrance requirements:* For doctorate, GRE (minimum combined score for verbal and quantitative sections of 900), master's degree from an accredited university; minimum GPA of 3.0 on the last 60 undergraduate hours, 3.25 on all graduate-level course work. Additional exam requirements/recommendations for international students: Required—TOEFL (minimum score 500 paper-based; 173 computer-based; 61 iBT). *Application deadline:* For fall admission, 7/15 priority date for domestic students, 6/1 for international students; for spring admission, 12/1 priority date for domestic students, 10/1 for international students. Applications are processed on a rolling basis. Application fee: $20 ($30 for international students). Electronic applications accepted. *Expenses:* Tuition, state resident: full-time $3977; part-time $283 per semester hour. Tuition, nonresident: full-time $13,482; part-time $811 per semester hour. *Financial support:* Career-related internships or fieldwork, Federal Work-Study, institutionally sponsored loans, scholarships/grants, and unspecified assistantships available. Support available to part-time students. Financial award application deadline: 5/1; financial award applicants required to submit FAFSA. *Total annual research expenditures:* $1.3 million. *Unit head:* Dr. John Fischetti, Dean, 985-549-2217, Fax: 985-549-2070, E-mail: jfischetti@selu.edu. *Application contact:* Sandra Meyers, Graduate Admissions Analyst, 985-549-5620, Fax: 985-549-5632, E-mail: admissions@selu.edu. Web site: http://www.selu.edu/acad_research/colleges/edu_hd/index.html.

Southeastern Oklahoma State University, School of Education, Durant, OK 74701-0609. Offers math specialist (M Ed); reading specialist (M Ed); school administration (M Ed); school counseling (M Ed); special education (M Ed). *Accreditation:* NCATE. Part-time and evening/weekend programs available. *Faculty:* 52 full-time (19 women), 1 (woman) part-time/adjunct. *Students:* 15 full-time (11 women), 54 part-time (40 women); includes 24 minority (2 Black or African American, non-Hispanic/Latino; 16 American Indian or Alaska Native, non-Hispanic/Latino; 6 Hispanic/Latino). Average age 34. 31 applicants, 94% accepted, 29 enrolled. *Degree requirements:* For master's, comprehensive exam, thesis optional, portfolio (M Ed). *Entrance requirements:* For master's, GRE General Test (MBS), minimum GPA of 3.0 in last 60 hours or 2.75 overall. Additional exam requirements/recommendations for international students: Required—TOEFL (minimum score 550 paper-based; 213 computer-based; 79 iBT). *Application deadline:* For fall admission, 8/1 for domestic students, 6/1 for international students; for spring admission, 1/5 for domestic students, 11/1 for international students. Application fee: $20 ($55 for international students). Electronic applications accepted. *Expenses:* Tuition, state resident: full-time $3537; part-time $173.95 per credit hour. Tuition, nonresident: full-time $8673; part-time $459.30 per credit hour. *Required fees:* $22.55 per credit hour. *Financial support:* In 2011–12, 1 teaching assistantship with full tuition reimbursement (averaging $5,000 per year) was awarded; Federal Work-Study, institutionally sponsored loans, and tuition waivers (partial) also available. Support available to part-time students. Financial award application deadline: 6/15; financial award applicants required to submit FAFSA. *Unit head:* Dr. John Love, M Ed Coordinator, 580-745-2226, Fax: 580-745-7508, E-mail: jlove@se.edu. *Application contact:* Carrie Williamson, Graduate Secretary, 580-745-2220, Fax: 580-745-7474, E-mail: cwilliamson@se.edu. Web site: http://www.se.edu/graduate-programs/master-of-education/.

Southeastern University, College of Education, Lakeland, FL 33801-6099. Offers educational leadership (M Ed); elementary education (M Ed); teaching and learning (M Ed).

Southern Adventist University, School of Education and Psychology, Collegedale, TN 37315-0370. Offers clinical mental health counseling (MS); inclusive education (MS Ed); instructional leadership (MS Ed); literacy education (MS Ed); outdoor teacher education (MS Ed); school counseling (MS). *Accreditation:* NCATE. Part-time and evening/weekend programs available. *Degree requirements:* For master's, comprehensive exam (for some programs), thesis optional, position paper (MS), portfolio (MS Ed in outdoor teacher education). *Entrance requirements:* For master's, interview (MS); 9 semester hours of upper division course work in psychology or related field, including 1 course in psychology research or statistics; 9 semester hours of education (MS Ed). Additional exam requirements/recommendations for international students: Required—TOEFL (minimum score 600 paper-based; 250 computer-based; 100 iBT). Electronic applications accepted.

Southern Arkansas University–Magnolia, Graduate Programs, Magnolia, AR 71754. Offers agriculture (MS); business administration (MBA); computer and information sciences (MS); education (M Ed), including counseling and development, curriculum and instruction, educational administration and supervision, elementary education, middle level, reading, secondary education, TESOL; kinesiology (M Ed); library media and information specialist (M Ed); mental health and clinical counseling (MS); public administration (MPA); school counseling (M Ed); teaching (MAT). *Accreditation:* NCATE. Part-time and evening/weekend programs available. Postbaccalaureate distance learning degree programs offered. *Faculty:* 34 full-time (15 women), 8 part-time/adjunct (5 women). *Students:* 87 full-time (62 women), 320 part-time (224 women); includes 116 minority (111 Black or African American, non-Hispanic/Latino; 2 American Indian or Alaska Native, non-Hispanic/Latino; 2 Asian, non-Hispanic/Latino; 1 Hispanic/Latino), 25 international. Average age 33. 201 applicants, 98% accepted, 156 enrolled. In 2011, 162 master's awarded. *Degree requirements:* For master's, comprehensive exam (for some programs), thesis optional. *Entrance requirements:* For master's, GRE, MAT or GMAT, minimum GPA of 2.5. Additional exam requirements/recommendations for international students: Required—TOEFL (minimum score 173 computer-based). *Application deadline:* For fall admission, 7/15 for domestic and international students; for winter admission, 12/1 for domestic and international students; for spring admission, 12/1 for domestic and international students. Applications are processed on a rolling basis. Application fee: $25 ($35 for international students). Electronic applications accepted. *Expenses:* Tuition, state resident: part-time $232 per credit. Tuition, nonresident: part-time $339 per credit. *Required fees:* $44 per credit. Part-time tuition and fees vary according to course load. *Financial support:* Career-related internships or fieldwork, Federal Work-Study, scholarships/grants, tuition waivers (full), and unspecified assistantships available. Financial award applicants required to submit FAFSA. *Faculty research:* Alternative certification for teachers, supervision of instruction, instructional leadership, counseling. *Unit head:* Dr. Kim Bloss, Dean, School of Graduate Studies, 870-235-4150, Fax: 870-235-5227, E-mail: kkbloss@saumag.edu. *Application contact:* Gaye Calhoun, Admissions Specialist, 870-235-4150, Fax: 870-235-5227, E-mail: glcalhoun@saumag.edu. Web site: http://www.saumag.edu/graduate.

Southern Connecticut State University, School of Graduate Studies, School of Education, New Haven, CT 06515-1355. Offers MLS, MS, MS Ed, Ed D, Diploma, JD/MLS, MLS/MA, MLS/MS. *Accreditation:* NCATE. Part-time programs available. *Faculty:* 61 full-time (38 women), 37 part-time/adjunct (23 women). *Students:* 343 full-time (279 women), 808 part-time (644 women); includes 113 minority (51 Black or African American, non-Hispanic/Latino; 14 Asian, non-Hispanic/Latino; 38 Hispanic/Latino; 10 Two or more races, non-Hispanic/Latino), 3 international. 2,204 applicants, 16% accepted, 288 enrolled. In 2011, 358 master's, 3 doctorates, 172 other advanced degrees awarded. *Degree requirements:* For doctorate, comprehensive exam, thesis/dissertation. *Entrance requirements:* For degree, master's degree. Application fee: $50. Electronic applications accepted. *Expenses:* Tuition, state resident: full-time $5137; part-time $413 per credit. *Required fees:* $4008; $55 per term. *Financial support:* Research assistantships, teaching assistantships, and career-related internships or fieldwork available. *Unit head:* Dr. Michael R. Sampson, Dean, 203-392-5900, E-mail: misasis1@southernct.edu. *Application contact:* Lisa Galvin, Assistant Dean of Graduate Studies, 203-392-5240, Fax: 203-392-5235, E-mail: galvinl1@southernct.edu.

Southern Illinois University Carbondale, Graduate School, College of Education and Human Services, Carbondale, IL 62901-4701. Offers MPH, MS, MS Ed, MSW, PhD, Rh D, JD/MSW. *Accreditation:* NCATE. Part-time programs available. *Faculty:* 175 full-time (74 women), 25 part-time/adjunct (6 women). *Students:* 523 full-time (346 women), 589 part-time (407 women); includes 249 minority (193 Black or African American, non-Hispanic/Latino; 6 American Indian or Alaska Native, non-Hispanic/Latino; 20 Asian, non-Hispanic/Latino; 30 Hispanic/Latino), 84 international. Average age 34. 565 applicants, 50% accepted, 156 enrolled. In 2011, 309 master's, 25 doctorates awarded. Terminal master's awarded for partial completion of doctoral program. *Degree requirements:* For doctorate, thesis/dissertation. *Entrance requirements:* For master's, minimum GPA of 2.7. Additional exam requirements/recommendations for international students: Required—TOEFL. Application fee: $20. *Financial support:* In 2011–12, 306 students received support, including 8 fellowships, 115 research assistantships, 166 teaching assistantships; career-related internships or fieldwork, Federal Work-Study, institutionally sponsored loans, traineeships, tuition waivers (full), and unspecified assistantships also available. Support available to part-time students. *Faculty research:* Safety education, community health, curriculum development, gifted, effective schools. *Unit head:* Dr. John Koropchak, Dean, 618-536-7791. *Application contact:* Lu Lyons, Supervisor, Admissions, 618-453-4512, E-mail: llyons@siu.edu. Web site: http://web.coehs.siu.edu/.

Southern Illinois University Edwardsville, Graduate School, School of Education, Edwardsville, IL 62062. Offers MA, MAT, MS, MS Ed, Ed D, Ed S, Post-Master's Certificate, Postbaccalaureate Certificate, SD. *Accreditation:* NCATE. Part-time programs available. *Faculty:* 82 full-time (43 women). *Students:* 141 full-time (102 women), 570 part-time (430 women); includes 100 minority (64 Black or African American, non-Hispanic/Latino; 7 Asian, non-Hispanic/Latino; 20 Hispanic/Latino; 9 Two or more races, non-Hispanic/Latino), 9 international. 566 applicants, 27% accepted. In 2011, 227 master's, 36 other advanced degrees awarded. *Degree requirements:* For master's, comprehensive exam (for some programs), thesis (for some programs), final exam, portfolio. *Entrance requirements:* For master's, GRE. Additional exam requirements/recommendations for international students: Required—TOEFL (minimum score 550 paper-based; 213 computer-based; 79 iBT), IELTS (minimum score 6.5). *Application deadline:* For fall admission, 7/22 for domestic students, 6/1 for international students; for spring admission, 12/10 for domestic students, 10/1 for international students. Applications are processed on a rolling basis. Application fee: $30. Electronic applications accepted. Tuition and fees vary according to course load and program. *Financial support:* In 2011–12, 3 fellowships with full tuition reimbursements (averaging $8,370 per year), 18 research assistantships with full tuition reimbursements (averaging $9,927 per year), 36 teaching assistantships with full tuition reimbursements (averaging $9,927 per year) were awarded; institutionally sponsored loans, scholarships/grants, and unspecified assistantships also available. Financial award application deadline: 3/1; financial award applicants required to submit FAFSA. *Unit head:* Dr. Bette Bergeron, Interim Dean, 618-650-3350, E-mail: bberger@siue.edu. *Application contact:* Michelle Robinson, Coordinator of Graduate Recruitment, 618-650-2811, Fax: 618-650-3523, E-mail: michero@siue.edu. Web site: http://www.siue.edu/education.

Southern Methodist University, Annette Caldwell Simmons School of Education and Human Development, Department of Teaching and Learning, Dallas, TX 75275. Offers bilingual/ESL education (MBE); education (M Ed, PhD); educational preparation (Certificate); gifted and talented focus (MBE); learning therapist (Certificate). Part-time and evening/weekend programs available. Terminal master's awarded for partial completion of doctoral program. *Degree requirements:* For master's, comprehensive exam, minimum GPA of 3.0; for doctorate, thesis/dissertation, qualifying exams, major area paper, evidence of teaching competency, dissemination of research (e.g., conference presentation), professional portfolio. *Entrance requirements:* For master's, minimum GPA of 3.0 or GRE, 3 letters of recommendation; for doctorate, GRE, minimum GPA of 3.3, 3 years of full-time teaching, 3 letters of recommendation, interview. Additional exam requirements/recommendations for international students: Required—TOEFL. Electronic applications accepted. *Faculty research:* Reading intervention, mathematics intervention, bilingual education, new literacies.

Southern New Hampshire University, School of Education, Manchester, NH 03106-1045. Offers business education (MS); child development (M Ed); computer technology education (Certificate); curriculum and instruction (M Ed); education (M Ed, CAS); elementary education (M Ed); general special education (Certificate); school business administrator (Certificate); secondary education (M Ed); training and development (Certificate). Part-time and evening/weekend programs available. Postbaccalaureate distance learning degree programs offered (no on-campus study). *Degree requirements:* For master's, comprehensive exam (for some programs), thesis or alternative. *Entrance requirements:* For master's, PRAXIS I, minimum GPA of 2.75. Additional exam requirements/recommendations for international students: Required—TOEFL (minimum score 550 paper-based; 213 computer-based). Electronic applications accepted. *Expenses:* Contact institution.

Southern Oregon University, Graduate Studies, School of Education, Ashland, OR 97520. Offers elementary education (MA Ed, MS Ed), including classroom teacher, early childhood, handicapped learner, reading, supervision; secondary education (MA Ed, MS Ed), including classroom teacher, handicapped learner, reading, supervision; teaching (MAT). *Faculty:* 18 full-time (10 women), 10 part-time/adjunct (all women). *Students:* 128 full-time (88 women), 145 part-time (103 women); includes 32 minority (1 Black or African American, non-Hispanic/Latino; 3 American Indian or Alaska Native, non-Hispanic/Latino; 5 Asian, non-Hispanic/Latino; 13 Hispanic/Latino; 3 Native Hawaiian or other Pacific Islander, non-Hispanic/Latino; 7 Two or more races, non-Hispanic/Latino), 1 international. Average age 35. 48 applicants, 60% accepted, 23 enrolled. In 2011, 102 degrees awarded. *Degree requirements:* For master's, thesis optional. *Entrance requirements:* For master's, GRE General Test, minimum GPA of 3.0. *Application deadline:* For fall admission, 2/1 for domestic students. Application fee: $50. Electronic applications accepted. *Expenses:* Tuition, state resident: full-time $12,600; part-time $350 per credit. Tuition, nonresident: full-time $16,200; part-time $450 per credit. *Required fees:* $1590. *Financial support:* Research assistantships with partial tuition reimbursements available. *Unit head:* Dr. Geoff Mills, Dean, 541-552-6920, E-mail: mills@sou.edu. *Application contact:* Mark Bottorff, Director of Admissions, 541-552-6411, Fax: 541-552-8403, E-mail: admissions@sou.edu. Web site: http://www.sou.edu/education/.

Southern University and Agricultural and Mechanical College, Graduate School, College of Education, Baton Rouge, LA 70813. Offers M Ed, MA, MS, PhD. *Accreditation:* NCATE. *Degree requirements:* For master's, comprehensive exam, thesis optional. *Entrance requirements:* For master's and doctorate, GRE General Test. Additional exam requirements/recommendations for international students: Required—TOEFL (minimum score 525 paper-based; 193 computer-based).

Southern Utah University, Program in Education, Cedar City, UT 84720-2498. Offers M Ed. *Accreditation:* Teacher Education Accreditation Council. *Students:* 3 full-time (all women), 315 part-time (222 women); includes 17 minority (1 Black or African American, non-Hispanic/Latino; 2 Asian, non-Hispanic/Latino; 11 Hispanic/Latino; 3 Native Hawaiian or other Pacific Islander, non-Hispanic/Latino). 29 applicants, 97% accepted, 25 enrolled. In 2011, 256 master's awarded. *Application deadline:* For fall admission, 7/15 for domestic students; for spring admission, 11/15 for domestic students. Applications are processed on a rolling basis. Application fee: $50 ($65 for international students). Electronic applications accepted. *Financial support:* Career-related internships or fieldwork, scholarships/grants, and tuition waivers (partial) available. Support available to part-time students. *Unit head:* Dr. Bart Reynolds, Department

Chair, 435-865-8125, Fax: 435-865-8485, E-mail: reynolds@suu.edu. *Application contact:* Bobbie Jensen, Administrative Assistant, 435-865-8383, Fax: 435-865-8485, E-mail: jensenb@suu.edu.

Southern Wesleyan University, Program in Education, Central, SC 29630-1020. Offers M Ed. Program also offered at Greenville, S. C. site. *Accreditation:* NCATE. Evening/weekend programs available. *Entrance requirements:* For master's, GRE General Test or MAT, 1 year teaching experience, minimum undergraduate GPA of 3.0, teacher certification. Additional exam requirements/recommendations for international students: Required—TOEFL (minimum score 500 paper-based; 173 computer-based).

Southwest Baptist University, Program in Education, Bolivar, MO 65613-2597. Offers education (MS); educational administration (MS, Ed S). Part-time programs available. *Degree requirements:* For master's, comprehensive exam, thesis optional, 6-hour residency; for Ed S, comprehensive exam, 5-hour residency. *Entrance requirements:* For master's, GRE or PRAXIS II, interviews, minimum GPA of 2.75; for Ed S, master's degree. Additional exam requirements/recommendations for international students: Required—TOEFL (minimum score 550 paper-based; 213 computer-based). *Faculty research:* At-risk programs, principal retention, mentoring beginning principals.

Southwestern Adventist University, Education Department, Keene, TX 76059. Offers curriculum and instruction with reading emphasis (M Ed); educational leadership (M Ed). Part-time and evening/weekend programs available. *Degree requirements:* For master's, thesis or alternative, professional paper. *Entrance requirements:* For master's, GRE General Test.

Southwestern Assemblies of God University, Thomas F. Harrison School of Graduate Studies, Program in Education, Waxahachie, TX 75165-5735. Offers Christian school administration (MS); curriculum development (MS); early education administration (M Ed); middle and secondary education (M Ed). *Degree requirements:* For master's, comprehensive written and oral exams. *Entrance requirements:* For master's, GRE General Test, minimum GPA of 2.5. Electronic applications accepted.

Southwestern College, Education Programs, Winfield, KS 67156-2499. Offers curriculum and instruction (M Ed); education (Ed D); special education (M Ed); teaching (MA). *Accreditation:* NCATE. Part-time and evening/weekend programs available. Postbaccalaureate distance learning degree programs offered (minimal on-campus study). *Faculty:* 6 full-time (3 women), 6 part-time/adjunct (all women). *Students:* 9 full-time (7 women), 94 part-time (73 women); includes 12 minority (4 Black or African American, non-Hispanic/Latino; 2 Asian, non-Hispanic/Latino; 3 Hispanic/Latino; 3 Two or more races, non-Hispanic/Latino), 9 international. Average age 35. 77 applicants, 60% accepted, 34 enrolled. In 2011, 56 master's awarded. *Degree requirements:* For master's, practicum, portfolio. *Entrance requirements:* For master's, baccalaureate degree, minimum GPA of 2.5, valid teaching certificate (for special education). Additional exam requirements/recommendations for international students: Required—TOEFL (minimum score 550 paper-based; 213 computer-based). *Application deadline:* For fall admission, 8/1 for domestic students; for spring admission, 12/1 for domestic students. Applications are processed on a rolling basis. Application fee: $0. Electronic applications accepted. *Expenses:* Contact institution. *Financial support:* In 2011–12, 4 students received support. Federal Work-Study, tuition waivers (partial), and unspecified assistantships available. Financial award application deadline: 4/1; financial award applicants required to submit FAFSA. *Unit head:* Dr. David Hofmeister, Director of Teacher Education, 800-846-1543 Ext. 6115, Fax: 620-229-6341, E-mail: david.hofmeister@sckans.edu. Web site: http://www.sckans.edu/graduate/education-med/.

Southwestern Oklahoma State University, College of Professional and Graduate Studies, School of Behavioral Sciences and Education, Weatherford, OK 73096-3098. Offers community counseling (M Ed); early childhood education (M Ed); educational administration (M Ed); elementary education (M Ed); health sciences and microbiology (M Ed); kinesiology (M Ed); parks and recreation management (M Ed); school counseling (M Ed); school psychology (MS); school psychometry (M Ed); secondary education (M Ed); special education (M Ed). *Accreditation:* NCATE. Part-time and evening/weekend programs available. Postbaccalaureate distance learning degree programs offered (minimal on-campus study). *Degree requirements:* For master's, exam. *Entrance requirements:* For master's, GRE General Test or minimum undergraduate GPA of 3.0. Additional exam requirements/recommendations for international students: Required—TOEFL.

Southwest Minnesota State University, Department of Education, Marshall, MN 56258. Offers ESL (MS); math (MS); reading (MS); special education (MS), including developmental disabilities, early childhood education, emotional behavioral disorders, learning disabilities; teaching, learning and leadership (MS). Part-time and evening/weekend programs available. Postbaccalaureate distance learning degree programs offered (no on-campus study). *Entrance requirements:* Additional exam requirements/recommendations for international students: Required—TOEFL or IELTS; Recommended—TOEFL (minimum score 550 paper-based; 213 computer-based; 80 iBT), IELTS.

Spalding University, Graduate Studies, College of Education, Louisville, KY 40203-2188. Offers M Ed, MA, MAT, Ed D. *Accreditation:* NCATE. Part-time and evening/weekend programs available. *Faculty:* 11 full-time (9 women), 47 part-time/adjunct (30 women). *Students:* 169 full-time (117 women), 114 part-time (85 women); includes 105 minority (93 Black or African American, non-Hispanic/Latino; 1 American Indian or Alaska Native, non-Hispanic/Latino; 1 Asian, non-Hispanic/Latino; 6 Hispanic/Latino; 4 Two or more races, non-Hispanic/Latino), 6 international. Average age 37. 124 applicants, 44% accepted, 52 enrolled. In 2011, 69 master's, 19 doctorates awarded. *Degree requirements:* For master's, portfolio, final project, clinical experience; for doctorate, comprehensive exam, thesis/dissertation. *Entrance requirements:* For master's and doctorate, GRE General Test or MAT, interview, resume, recommendations. Additional exam requirements/recommendations for international students: Required—TOEFL (minimum score 535 paper-based; 203 computer-based). *Application deadline:* Applications are processed on a rolling basis. Application fee: $30. Electronic applications accepted. *Expenses: Tuition:* Full-time $12,438. Tuition and fees vary according to course load, degree level and program. *Financial support:* In 2011–12, 91 students received support, including 3 research assistantships with partial tuition reimbursements available (averaging $4,490 per year); scholarships/grants, traineeships, and unspecified assistantships also available. Financial award application deadline: 3/15; financial award applicants required to submit FAFSA. *Faculty research:* School leadership, assessment of student learning, classroom management. *Unit head:* Dr. Beverly Keepers, Dean, 502-873-4268, E-mail: bkeepers@spalding.edu. *Application contact:* Bonnie Caughron, Admissions Office, 502-873-4262, E-mail: bcaughron@spalding.edu.

Spring Arbor University, School of Education, Spring Arbor, MI 49283-9799. Offers education (MAE); reading (MAR); special education (MSE). Part-time and evening/weekend programs available. Postbaccalaureate distance learning degree programs offered (minimal on-campus study). *Faculty:* 6 full-time (5 women), 13 part-time/adjunct (8 women). *Students:* 43 full-time (33 women), 188 part-time (158 women); includes 13 minority (10 Black or African American, non-Hispanic/Latino; 1 Asian, non-Hispanic/Latino; 2 Hispanic/Latino). Average age 36. In 2011, 54 master's awarded. *Degree requirements:* For master's, thesis. *Entrance requirements:* For master's, official transcripts from all institutions attended, including evidence of an earned bachelor's degree from regionally-accredited college or university with minimum cumulative GPA of 3.0 for the last two years of the bachelor's degree; two professional letters of recommendation. Additional exam requirements/recommendations for international students: Required—TOEFL (minimum score 600 paper-based; 220 computer-based). *Application deadline:* For fall admission, 9/1 priority date for domestic students; for winter admission, 2/1 priority date for domestic students; for spring admission, 2/1 priority date for domestic students. Applications are processed on a rolling basis. Application fee: $40. Electronic applications accepted. *Expenses: Tuition:* Full-time $5500; part-time $490 per credit hour. *Required fees:* $240; $120 per term. Tuition and fees vary according to program. *Financial support:* Applicants required to submit FAFSA. *Unit head:* Dr. Linda Sherrill, Dean, 517-750-1200 Ext. 1562, Fax: 517-750-6629, E-mail: lsherril@arbor.edu. *Application contact:* James R. Weidman, Coordinator of Graduate Recruitment, 517-750-6523, Fax: 517-750-6629, E-mail: jimw@arbor.edu. Web site: http://www.arbor.edu/Master-Arts-Education/Graduate/index.aspx.

Springfield College, Graduate Programs, Program in Education, Springfield, MA 01109-3797. Offers counseling and secondary education (M Ed, MS); early childhood education (M Ed, MS); education (M Ed, MS); educational administration (M Ed, MS); educational studies (M Ed, MS); elementary education (M Ed, MS); secondary education (M Ed, MS); special education (M Ed, MS). Part-time and evening/weekend programs available. *Entrance requirements:* Additional exam requirements/recommendations for international students: Required—TOEFL (minimum score 550 paper-based; 213 computer-based). Electronic applications accepted.

Spring Hill College, Graduate Programs, Program in Education, Mobile, AL 36608-1791. Offers early childhood education (MAT, MS Ed); educational theory (MS Ed); elementary education (MAT, MS Ed); secondary education (MAT, MS Ed). Part-time programs available. *Faculty:* 3 full-time (2 women), 3 part-time/adjunct (all women). *Students:* 7 full-time (6 women), 21 part-time (18 women); includes 7 minority (6 Black or African American, non-Hispanic/Latino; 1 Asian, non-Hispanic/Latino). Average age 31. In 2011, 13 master's awarded. *Degree requirements:* For master's, comprehensive exam, completion of program within 6 calendar years of entrance into graduate studies at Spring Hill; documentation of course field assignments (MS) or completion of internship (MAT). *Entrance requirements:* For master's, GRE, MAT, or PRAXIS (varies by program), bachelor's degree with minimum undergraduate GPA of 3.0; class B certificate (MS) or minimum number of hours in specific fields (MAT). Additional exam requirements/recommendations for international students: Required—TOEFL (minimum score 550 paper-based; 213 computer-based; 80 iBT), IELTS (minimum score 6.5), CPE or CAE (minimum score C),Michigan English Language Assessment Battery (minimum score 90). *Application deadline:* For fall admission, 8/1 priority date for domestic students, 8/1 for international students; for spring admission, 12/1 priority date for domestic students, 12/1 for international students. Applications are processed on a rolling basis. Application fee: $25 ($35 for international students). Electronic applications accepted. *Expenses:* Contact institution. *Financial support:* Applicants required to submit FAFSA. *Unit head:* Dr. Ann A. Adams, Chair of Teacher Education, 251-380-3479, Fax: 251-460-2184, E-mail: aadams@shc.edu. *Application contact:* Donna B. Tarasavage, Director of Admissions, Graduate and Continuing Studies, 251-380-3067, Fax: 251-460-2190, E-mail: dtarasavage@shc.edu. Web site: http://www.shc.edu/grad/academics/teaching.

Stanford University, School of Education, Stanford, CA 94305-9991. Offers MA, Ed D, PhD. *Accreditation:* NCATE. *Degree requirements:* For doctorate, thesis/dissertation. *Entrance requirements:* For master's and doctorate, GRE General Test. Electronic applications accepted. *Expenses: Tuition:* Full-time $40,050; part-time $890 per credit.

State University of New York at Binghamton, Graduate School, School of Education, Binghamton, NY 13902-6000. Offers MAT, MS Ed, MST, Ed D. *Accreditation:* Teacher Education Accreditation Council. Part-time and evening/weekend programs available. *Faculty:* 18 full-time (12 women), 17 part-time/adjunct (15 women). *Students:* 148 full-time (113 women), 140 part-time (112 women); includes 17 minority (9 Black or African American, non-Hispanic/Latino; 2 American Indian or Alaska Native, non-Hispanic/Latino; 2 Asian, non-Hispanic/Latino; 3 Hispanic/Latino; 1 Native Hawaiian or other Pacific Islander, non-Hispanic/Latino), 7 international. Average age 31. 190 applicants, 74% accepted, 102 enrolled. In 2011, 127 master's, 3 doctorates awarded. *Degree requirements:* For doctorate, thesis/dissertation. *Entrance requirements:* For master's, GRE General Test; for doctorate, GRE General Test, writing sample. Additional exam requirements/recommendations for international students: Required—TOEFL (minimum score 550 paper-based; 213 computer-based; 80 iBT). *Application deadline:* For fall admission, 2/1 priority date for domestic students, 2/1 for international students; for spring admission, 10/15 priority date for domestic students, 10/15 for international students. Applications are processed on a rolling basis. Application fee: $60. Electronic applications accepted. *Financial support:* In 2011–12, 30 students received support, including 5 fellowships with full tuition reimbursements available (averaging $12,000 per year), 2 research assistantships with full tuition reimbursements available (averaging $12,000 per year), 3 teaching assistantships with full tuition reimbursements available (averaging $12,000 per year); career-related internships or fieldwork, Federal Work-Study, institutionally sponsored loans, scholarships/grants, health care benefits, tuition waivers (full and partial), and unspecified assistantships also available. Financial award application deadline: 2/15; financial award applicants required to submit FAFSA. *Unit head:* Dr. S. S. Grant, Dean, 607-777-7329, E-mail: ssgrant@binghamton.edu. *Application contact:* Catherine Smith, Recruiting and Admissions Coordinator, 607-777-2151, Fax: 607-777-2501, E-mail: cmsmith@binghamton.edu. Web site: http://sehd.binghamton.edu/.

State University of New York at Fredonia, Graduate Studies, College of Education, Fredonia, NY 14063-1136. Offers educational administration (CAS); elementary education (MS Ed); literacy (MS Ed); secondary education (MS Ed); teaching English to speakers of other languages (MS Ed). *Accreditation:* NCATE. Part-time and evening/weekend programs available. *Degree requirements:* For master's, thesis optional; for CAS, thesis or alternative. *Expenses:* Tuition, state resident: full-time $6666; part-time $370 per credit hour. Tuition, nonresident: full-time $11,376; part-time $632 per credit hour. *Required fees:* $1059.30; $58.85 per credit hour. Tuition and fees vary according to course load.

State University of New York at New Paltz, Graduate School, School of Education, New Paltz, NY 12561. Offers MAT, MPS, MS Ed, MST, CAS. *Accreditation:* NCATE. Part-time and evening/weekend programs available. *Faculty:* 41 full-time (27 women), 20 part-time/adjunct (16 women). *Students:* 201 full-time (156 women), 380 part-time (294 women); includes 89 minority (28 Black or African American, non-Hispanic/Latino; 1 American Indian or Alaska Native, non-Hispanic/Latino; 11 Asian, non-Hispanic/Latino; 37 Hispanic/Latino; 1 Native Hawaiian or other Pacific Islander, non-Hispanic/Latino; 11 Two or more races, non-Hispanic/Latino), 3 international. Average age 31. 401 applicants, 69% accepted, 203 enrolled. In 2011, 232 master's, 66 other advanced degrees awarded. *Degree requirements:* For master's, comprehensive exam (for some programs), portfolio; for CAS, internship. *Entrance requirements:* For master's, GRE, MAT, minimum GPA of 3.0, New York State Teaching Certificate; for CAS, minimum GPA of 3.0. Additional exam requirements/recommendations for international students:

Education—General

Required—TOEFL (minimum score 550 paper-based; 213 computer-based; 80 iBT), IELTS (minimum score 6.5). *Application deadline:* For fall admission, 3/1 priority date for domestic students, 3/1 for international students; for spring admission, 10/1 priority date for domestic students, 10/1 for international students. Applications are processed on a rolling basis. Application fee: $50. Electronic applications accepted. *Expenses:* Tuition, state resident: full-time $8870; part-time $370 per credit. Tuition, nonresident: full-time $15,160; part-time $632 per credit. *Required fees:* $1188; $34 per credit. $184 per semester. *Financial support:* In 2011–12, 12 students received support, including 4 fellowships (averaging $5,000 per year); career-related internships or fieldwork, Federal Work-Study, institutionally sponsored loans, scholarships/grants, and tuition waivers (full) also available. Financial award application deadline: 8/1; financial award applicants required to submit FAFSA. *Faculty research:* Kindergarten readiness, translation learning experiences, assessment in mathematics education, long and short term outcomes of delayed school entry, parental involvement in children's education. *Unit head:* Dr. Karen Bell, Interim Dean, 845-257-2800, E-mail: schoolofed@newpaltz.edu. *Application contact:* Caroline Murphy, Graduate Admissions Advisor, 845-257-3285, Fax: 845-257-3284, E-mail: gradschool@newpaltz.edu.

State University of New York at Oswego, Graduate Studies, School of Education, Oswego, NY 13126. Offers MAT, MS, MS Ed, MST, CAS, MS/CAS. *Accreditation:* NCATE. Part-time programs available. *Degree requirements:* For master's, comprehensive exam (for some programs), thesis optional. *Entrance requirements:* For degree, GRE General Test, interview, MA or MS, minimum GPA of 3.0. Additional exam requirements/recommendations for international students: Required—TOEFL (minimum score 560 paper-based; 220 computer-based).

State University of New York College at Cortland, Graduate Studies, School of Education, Cortland, NY 13045. Offers childhood/early child education (MS Ed, MST); educational leadership (CAS); literacy (MS Ed); teaching students with disabilities (MS Ed). *Accreditation:* NCATE. Part-time and evening/weekend programs available. *Entrance requirements:* Additional exam requirements/recommendations for international students: Required—TOEFL.

State University of New York College at Geneseo, Graduate Studies, School of Education, Geneseo, NY 14454-1401. Offers childhood multicultural education (1-6) (MS Ed); early childhood education (MS Ed); elementary education (MS Ed); reading (MS Ed); secondary education (MS Ed). *Accreditation:* NCATE. Part-time and evening/weekend programs available. *Degree requirements:* For master's, thesis optional.

State University of New York College at Oneonta, Graduate Education, Division of Education, Oneonta, NY 13820-4015. Offers educational psychology and counseling (MS Ed, CAS), including school counselor K-12; educational technology specialist (MS Ed); elementary education and reading (MS Ed), including childhood education, literacy education; secondary education (MS Ed), including adolescence education, family and consumer science education; special education (MS Ed), including adolescence, childhood. *Accreditation:* NCATE. Part-time and evening/weekend programs available. *Entrance requirements:* For master's, GRE General Test.

State University of New York Empire State College, Graduate Studies, Program in Teaching, Saratoga Springs, NY 12866-4391. Offers MA.

Stephen F. Austin State University, Graduate School, College of Education, Nacogdoches, TX 75962. Offers M Ed, MA, MS, Ed D. *Accreditation:* NCATE. Part-time and evening/weekend programs available. *Degree requirements:* For master's, comprehensive exam; for doctorate, thesis/dissertation. *Entrance requirements:* For master's, GRE General Test; for doctorate, GRE General Test, interview, writing sample. Additional exam requirements/recommendations for international students: Required—TOEFL.

Stetson University, College of Arts and Sciences, Division of Education, DeLand, FL 32723. Offers M Ed, MS, Ed S. *Accreditation:* NCATE (one or more programs are accredited). Part-time and evening/weekend programs available. *Students:* 140 full-time (115 women), 14 part-time (13 women); includes 38 minority (17 Black or African American, non-Hispanic/Latino; 3 Asian, non-Hispanic/Latino; 17 Hispanic/Latino; 1 Two or more races, non-Hispanic/Latino), 4 international. Average age 33. In 2011, 99 master's awarded. *Entrance requirements:* For master's and Ed S, GRE General Test or MAT. *Application deadline:* For fall admission, 3/1 priority date for domestic students; for spring admission, 11/1 for domestic students. Applications are processed on a rolling basis. Application fee: $25. *Financial support:* Career-related internships or fieldwork, institutionally sponsored loans, scholarships/grants, and tuition waivers (partial) available. Support available to part-time students. *Faculty research:* Values, cultural diversity, cooperative learning, reading. *Unit head:* Dr. Karen Ryan, Dean, 386-822-7515. *Application contact:* Diana Belian, Office of Graduate Studies, 386-822-7075, Fax: 386-822-7388, E-mail: dbelian@stetson.edu.

Strayer University, Graduate Studies, Washington, DC 20005-2603. Offers accounting (MS); acquisition (MBA); business administration (MBA); communications technology (MS); educational management (M Ed); finance (MBA); health services administration (MHSA); hospitality and tourism management (MBA); human resource management (MBA); information systems (MS), including computer security management, decision support system management, enterprise resource management, network management, software engineering management, systems development management; management (MBA); management information systems (MS); marketing (MBA); professional accounting (MS), including accounting information systems, controllership, taxation; public administration (MPA); supply chain management (MBA); technology in education (M Ed). Programs also offered at campus locations in Birmingham, AL; Chamblee, GA; Cobb County, GA; Morrow, GA; White Marsh, MD; Charleston, SC; Columbia, SC; Greensboro, NC; Greenville, SC; Lexington, KY; Louisville, KY; Nashville, TN; North Raleigh, NC; Washington, DC. Part-time and evening/weekend programs available. Postbaccalaureate distance learning degree programs offered (minimal on-campus study). *Degree requirements:* For master's, thesis. *Entrance requirements:* For master's, GMAT, GRE General Test, bachelor's degree from an accredited college or university, minimum undergraduate GPA of 2.75. Electronic applications accepted.

Suffolk University, College of Arts and Sciences, Department of Education and Human Services, Boston, MA 02108-2770. Offers administration of higher education (M Ed, CAGS), including administration of higher education (M Ed), leadership (CAGS); human resource, learning and performance (MS, CAGS, Graduate Certificate), including global human resources (Graduate Certificate), human resources (MS, Graduate Certificate), organizational development (CAGS, Graduate Certificate), organizational learning and development (MS, Graduate Certificate); mental health counseling (MS, CAGS); school counseling (M Ed, CAGS); school teaching (M Ed, CAGS), including foundations of education (M Ed), middle school teaching (M Ed), secondary school teaching (M Ed); MPA/MSMHC; MS/Certificate. Part-time and evening/weekend programs available. *Faculty:* 10 full-time (6 women), 7 part-time/adjunct (3 women). *Students:* 53 full-time (39 women), 131 part-time (112 women); includes 21 minority (7 Black or African American, non-Hispanic/Latino; 2 American Indian or Alaska Native, non-Hispanic/Latino; 5 Asian, non-Hispanic/Latino; 5 Hispanic/Latino; 2 Two or more races, non-Hispanic/Latino), 9 international. Average age 28. 158 applicants, 73% accepted, 60 enrolled. In 2011, 72 master's, 8 other advanced degrees awarded. *Entrance requirements:* For master's, GRE General Test or MAT, 2 letters of recommendation, resume. Additional exam requirements/recommendations for international students: Required—TOEFL (minimum score 550 paper-based; 213 computer-based; 80 iBT). *Application deadline:* For fall admission, 6/15 priority date for domestic students, 6/15 for international students; for spring admission, 11/1 priority date for domestic students, 11/1 for international students. Applications are processed on a rolling basis. Application fee: $50. Electronic applications accepted. *Expenses:* Contact institution. *Financial support:* In 2011–12, 102 students received support, including 30 fellowships with full and partial tuition reimbursements available (averaging $10,664 per year); career-related internships or fieldwork, Federal Work-Study, and institutionally sponsored loans also available. Support available to part-time students. Financial award application deadline: 4/1; financial award applicants required to submit FAFSA. *Faculty research:* Predicting competent Head Start preschools, cultural differences. *Unit head:* Dr. Krisanne Bursik, Associate Dean and Acting Chair, 617-573-8261, Fax: 617-305-1743, E-mail: kbursik@suffolk.edu. *Application contact:* Ellen Driscoll, Director of Graduate Admissions, 617-573-8302, Fax: 617-305-1733, E-mail: grad.admission@suffolk.edu. Web site: http://www.suffolk.edu/college/9785.html.

Sul Ross State University, Rio Grande College of Sul Ross State University, Alpine, TX 79832. Offers business administration (MBA); teacher education (M Ed), including bilingual education, counseling, educational diagnostics, elementary education, general education, reading, school administration, secondary education. Part-time and evening/weekend programs available. Postbaccalaureate distance learning degree programs offered (no on-campus study). *Faculty:* 11 full-time (3 women), 4 part-time/adjunct (3 women). *Students:* 45 full-time (36 women), 255 part-time (168 women); includes 218 minority (2 Black or African American, non-Hispanic/Latino; 1 American Indian or Alaska Native, non-Hispanic/Latino; 215 Hispanic/Latino), 1 international. Average age 36. In 2011, 47 master's awarded. *Degree requirements:* For master's, comprehensive exam, thesis optional, minimum GPA of 3.0. *Entrance requirements:* For master's, GMAT or GRE General Test, minimum GPA of 2.5 in last 60 hours of undergraduate work. Additional exam requirements/recommendations for international students: Required—TOEFL. *Application deadline:* Applications are processed on a rolling basis. Application fee: $0 ($50 for international students). *Financial support:* Career-related internships or fieldwork, Federal Work-Study, and institutionally sponsored loans available. Support available to part-time students. Financial award application deadline: 5/1; financial award applicants required to submit FAFSA. *Unit head:* Dr. Paul Sorrels, Associate Provost/Dean, 512-278-3339, Fax: 512-278-3330. *Application contact:* Claudia R. Wright, Director of Admissions and Records, 915-837-8050, Fax: 915-837-8431, E-mail: rcullins@sulross.edu.

Sul Ross State University, School of Professional Studies, Department of Teacher Education, Alpine, TX 79832. Offers bilingual education (M Ed); counseling (M Ed); educational diagnostics (M Ed); elementary education (M Ed); reading specialist (M Ed); school administration (M Ed); secondary education (M Ed); supervision (M Ed). Part-time and evening/weekend programs available. *Degree requirements:* For master's, thesis optional. *Entrance requirements:* For master's, GMAT or GRE General Test, minimum GPA of 2.5 in last 60 hours of undergraduate work. *Faculty research:* Critical thinking skills, adolescent eating disorders, reading-based study skills, cross-cultural adaptations, educational leadership.

Sweet Briar College, Department of Education, Sweet Briar, VA 24595. Offers M Ed, MAT. Part-time programs available. *Faculty:* 3 full-time (1 woman), 4 part-time/adjunct (all women). *Students:* 11 full-time (all women), 1 (woman) part-time. Average age 30. 13 applicants, 85% accepted, 11 enrolled. In 2011, 8 master's awarded. *Degree requirements:* For master's, comprehensive exam (for some programs), thesis. *Entrance requirements:* For master's, PRAXIS I and II; Virginia Communication and Literacy Assessment, Virginia Reading Assessment (MAT); GRE (M Ed), current teaching license (M Ed). Additional exam requirements/recommendations for international students: Required—TOEFL (minimum score 550 paper-based; 213 computer-based; 79 iBT), IELTS (minimum score 6.5). *Application deadline:* For fall admission, 2/1 for domestic and international students. Application fee: $40. Electronic applications accepted. *Expenses: Tuition:* Full-time $13,950; part-time $310 per credit hour. *Financial support:* Available to part-time students. Applicants required to submit FAFSA. *Faculty research:* Differentiation of K-12 student achievement, mentoring and teacher retention, teaching science by inquiry. *Unit head:* Dr. James L. Alouf, Director of Graduate Program, 434-381-6130, E-mail: alouf@sbc.edu. *Application contact:* Savannah Oxner, Assistant Director of Admissions, 434-381-6142, Fax: 434-381-6152, E-mail: soxner@sbc.edu. Web site: http://sbc.edu/education.

Syracuse University, School of Education, Syracuse, NY 13244. Offers M Mus, MS, Ed D, PhD, CAS, Certificate, Ed D/PhD. *Accreditation:* NCATE. Part-time programs available. *Faculty:* 54 full-time (33 women), 66 part-time/adjunct (47 women). *Students:* 374 full-time (278 women), 265 part-time (195 women); includes 87 minority (39 Black or African American, non-Hispanic/Latino; 4 American Indian or Alaska Native, non-Hispanic/Latino; 16 Asian, non-Hispanic/Latino; 17 Hispanic/Latino; 3 Native Hawaiian or other Pacific Islander, non-Hispanic/Latino; 8 Two or more races, non-Hispanic/Latino), 68 international. Average age 33. 490 applicants, 65% accepted, 170 enrolled. In 2011, 188 master's, 12 doctorates, 38 other advanced degrees awarded. *Degree requirements:* For master's, thesis or alternative; for doctorate, thesis/dissertation; for other advanced degree, thesis. *Entrance requirements:* For master's, GRE (for some programs); for doctorate and other advanced degree, GRE. Additional exam requirements/recommendations for international students: Required—TOEFL (minimum score 100 iBT). *Application deadline:* For fall admission, 2/1 priority date for domestic students, 2/1 for international students; for spring admission, 10/15 priority date for domestic students, 10/15 for international students. Applications are processed on a rolling basis. Application fee: $75. Electronic applications accepted. *Expenses: Tuition:* Part-time $1206 per credit. *Financial support:* Fellowships with full tuition reimbursements, research assistantships with full and partial tuition reimbursements, teaching assistantships with full and partial tuition reimbursements, career-related internships or fieldwork, institutionally sponsored loans, scholarships/grants, health care benefits, tuition waivers (partial), and unspecified assistantships available. Support available to part-time students. Financial award application deadline: 1/1; financial award applicants required to submit FAFSA. *Faculty research:* Teaching and curriculum, reading and language arts, literacy, inclusive education, communication sciences and disorders. *Unit head:* Dr. Douglas Biklen, Dean, 315-443-4751. *Application contact:* Laurie Deyo, Graduate Recruiter, School of Education, 315-443-2505, E-mail: e-gradrcrt@syr.edu. Web site: http://soeweb.syr.edu/.

Tarleton State University, College of Graduate Studies, College of Education, Stephenville, TX 76402. Offers M Ed, Ed D, Certificate. Part-time and evening/weekend programs available. Postbaccalaureate distance learning degree programs offered (minimal on-campus study). *Faculty:* 38 full-time (21 women), 24 part-time/adjunct (14 women). *Students:* 101 full-time (81 women), 580 part-time (431 women); includes 153 minority (72 Black or African American, non-Hispanic/Latino; 6 American Indian or Alaska Native, non-Hispanic/Latino; 1 Asian, non-Hispanic/Latino; 61 Hispanic/Latino; 1 Native Hawaiian or other Pacific Islander, non-Hispanic/Latino; 12 Two or more races, non-Hispanic/Latino), 1 international. Average age 35. 183 applicants, 93% accepted, 126 enrolled. In 2011, 153 master's, 12 doctorates awarded. *Degree requirements:* For master's, comprehensive exam, thesis (for some programs); for doctorate, thesis/

dissertation. *Entrance requirements:* For master's, GRE General Test, minimum GPA of 3.0; for doctorate, GRE, 4 letters of reference, leadership portfolio. Additional exam requirements/recommendations for international students: Required—TOEFL (minimum score 550 paper-based; 213 computer-based; 80 iBT). *Application deadline:* For fall admission, 8/5 priority date for domestic students; for spring admission, 12/1 for domestic students. Applications are processed on a rolling basis. Application fee: $30 ($130 for international students). Electronic applications accepted. *Expenses:* Tuition, state resident: full-time $3131.46; part-time $174 per credit hour. Tuition, nonresident: full-time $8225; part-time $457 per credit hour. *Required fees:* $1446. Tuition and fees vary according to course load and campus/location. *Financial support:* Research assistantships, teaching assistantships with partial tuition reimbursements, career-related internships or fieldwork, Federal Work-Study, institutionally sponsored loans, and tuition waivers (partial) available. Support available to part-time students. Financial award application deadline: 5/1; financial award applicants required to submit FAFSA. *Unit head:* Dr. Jill Burk, Dean, 254-968-9089, Fax: 254-968-9525, E-mail: burk@tarleton.edu. *Application contact:* Information Contact, 254-968-9104, Fax: 254-968-9670, E-mail: gradoffice@tarleton.edu. Web site: http://www.tarleton.edu/~coe.

Teacher Education University, Graduate Programs, Winter Park, FL 32789. Offers educational leadership (MA); educational technology (MA); elementary education K-6 (MA); instructional strategies (MA Ed); school guidance and counseling (MA).

Teachers College, Columbia University, Graduate Faculty of Education, New York, NY 10027-6696. Offers Ed M, MA, MS, Ed D, Ed DCT, PhD, Certificate, MBA/Ed D. *Accreditation:* NCATE. Part-time and evening/weekend programs available. *Students:* 1,704 full-time (1,330 women), 3,593 part-time (2,740 women); includes 1,545 minority (478 Black or African American, non-Hispanic/Latino; 9 American Indian or Alaska Native, non-Hispanic/Latino; 587 Asian, non-Hispanic/Latino; 471 Hispanic/Latino), 801 international. Average age 31. 5,417 applicants, 55% accepted, 1370 enrolled. In 2011, 1,990 master's, 229 doctorates awarded. *Degree requirements:* For doctorate, comprehensive exam, thesis/dissertation. Application fee: $65. Electronic applications accepted. *Financial support:* Fellowships, research assistantships, teaching assistantships, career-related internships or fieldwork, Federal Work-Study, institutionally sponsored loans, traineeships, tuition waivers (full and partial), and unspecified assistantships available. Support available to part-time students. Financial award application deadline: 2/1. *Faculty research:* Education and the economy, postsecondary governance and finance, career success, dropout prevention evaluation, education across the lifespan. *Unit head:* Susan Furhman, President, 212-678-3050. *Application contact:* Thomas P. Rock, Director of Admissions, 212-678-3083, Fax: 212-678-4171, E-mail: rock@tc.edu. Web site: http://www.tc.columbia.edu/.

Temple University, College of Education, Philadelphia, PA 19122-6096. Offers Ed M, MS Ed, Ed D, PhD. *Accreditation:* Teacher Education Accreditation Council. Part-time and evening/weekend programs available. *Faculty:* 45 full-time (25 women). *Students:* 254 full-time (178 women), 332 part-time (219 women); includes 116 minority (76 Black or African American, non-Hispanic/Latino; 14 Asian, non-Hispanic/Latino; 18 Hispanic/Latino; 8 Two or more races, non-Hispanic/Latino), 11 international. Average age 33. 351 applicants, 64% accepted, 163 enrolled. In 2011, 256 master's, 51 doctorates awarded. Terminal master's awarded for partial completion of doctoral program. *Degree requirements:* For doctorate, thesis/dissertation. *Entrance requirements:* For master's, GRE General Test or MAT, minimum GPA of 3.0. Additional exam requirements/recommendations for international students: Required—TOEFL (minimum score 550 paper-based; 213 computer-based; 79 iBT). *Application deadline:* For fall admission, 12/15 for international students; for spring admission, 8/1 for international students. Applications are processed on a rolling basis. Application fee: $50. Electronic applications accepted. *Expenses:* Tuition, state resident: full-time $12,366; part-time $687 per credit hour. Tuition, nonresident: full-time $17,298; part-time $961 per credit hour. *Required fees:* $590; $213 per year. *Financial support:* Fellowships, research assistantships, teaching assistantships, career-related internships or fieldwork, and Federal Work-Study available. Financial award application deadline: 1/15; financial award applicants required to submit FAFSA. *Faculty research:* School improvement in city schools, teaching strategies, student motivation, individual differences in learning, educational leadership and policy studies. *Unit head:* Dr. James Earl Davis, Interim Dean, 215-204-8017, Fax: 215-204-5622, E-mail: dean.ed@temple.edu. *Application contact:* Tara Schumacher, Coordinator of Outreach, 215-204-6575, Fax: 215-204-8781, E-mail: tara.schumacher@temple.edu. Web site: http://www.temple.edu/education/.

Tennessee State University, The School of Graduate Studies and Research, College of Education, Nashville, TN 37209-1561. Offers M Ed, MA Ed, MS, Ed D, PhD, Ed S. *Accreditation:* NCATE. Part-time and evening/weekend programs available. *Degree requirements:* For doctorate, thesis/dissertation. *Entrance requirements:* For doctorate, minimum GPA of 3.25. *Faculty research:* Class size, biobehavioral research, equity, dropout rate, K–12 teachers: first 5 years of employment.

Tennessee Technological University, Graduate School, College of Education, Cookeville, TN 38505. Offers M Ed, MA, PhD, Ed S. *Accreditation:* NCATE. Part-time and evening/weekend programs available. *Faculty:* 58 full-time (16 women). *Students:* 210 full-time (155 women), 407 part-time (298 women); includes 30 minority (21 Black or African American, non-Hispanic/Latino; 2 American Indian or Alaska Native, non-Hispanic/Latino; 1 Asian, non-Hispanic/Latino; 5 Hispanic/Latino; 1 Native Hawaiian or other Pacific Islander, non-Hispanic/Latino), 3 international. Average age 27. 271 applicants, 76% accepted, 151 enrolled. In 2011, 222 master's, 7 doctorates, 89 other advanced degrees awarded. *Degree requirements:* For master's and Ed S, comprehensive exam, thesis or alternative; for doctorate, comprehensive exam, thesis/dissertation. *Entrance requirements:* For master's, GRE or MAT; for doctorate, GRE; for Ed S, MAT or GRE. Additional exam requirements/recommendations for international students: Required—TOEFL (minimum score 527 paper-based; 71 iBT), IELTS (minimum score 5.5), Pearson Test of English Academic. *Application deadline:* For fall admission, 8/1 for domestic students, 5/1 for international students; for spring admission, 12/1 for domestic students, 10/1 for international students. Application fee: $25 ($30 for international students). Electronic applications accepted. *Expenses:* Tuition, state resident: full-time $8094; part-time $422 per credit hour. Tuition, nonresident: full-time $20,574; part-time $1046 per credit hour. *Financial support:* In 2011–12, 42 fellowships (averaging $8,000 per year), 33 research assistantships (averaging $4,000 per year), 26 teaching assistantships (averaging $4,000 per year) were awarded; career-related internships or fieldwork also available. Support available to part-time students. Financial award application deadline: 4/1. *Faculty research:* Teacher evaluation. *Unit head:* Dr. Matthew R. Smith, Dean, 931-372-3124, Fax: 931-372-6319, E-mail: mrsmith@tntech.edu. *Application contact:* Shelia K. Kendrick, Coordinator of Graduate Admissions, 931-372-3808, Fax: 931-372-3497, E-mail: skendrick@tntech.edu.

Tennessee Temple University, Graduate Studies in Education, Chattanooga, TN 37404. Offers M Ed. Part-time programs available. *Degree requirements:* For master's, comprehensive exam, thesis or alternative. *Entrance requirements:* For master's, GRE, minimum GPA of 3.0.

Texas A&M International University, Office of Graduate Studies and Research, College of Education, Laredo, TX 78041-1900. Offers MS, MS Ed. Part-time and evening/weekend programs available. *Faculty:* 17 full-time (10 women), 2 part-time/adjunct (1 woman). *Students:* 26 full-time (19 women), 335 part-time (277 women); includes 347 minority (2 Black or African American, non-Hispanic/Latino; 1 Asian, non-Hispanic/Latino; 344 Hispanic/Latino), 2 international. Average age 34. 154 applicants, 69% accepted, 62 enrolled. In 2011, 72 degrees awarded. *Degree requirements:* For master's, thesis (for some programs). *Entrance requirements:* For master's, GRE General Test. Additional exam requirements/recommendations for international students: Required—TOEFL (minimum score 550 paper-based; 213 computer-based; 79 iBT). *Application deadline:* For fall admission, 4/30 priority date for domestic students, 4/30 for international students; for spring admission, 11/30 for domestic students, 10/1 for international students. Applications are processed on a rolling basis. Application fee: $35 ($50 for international students). *Expenses:* Tuition, state resident: full-time $5063. *Financial support:* In 2011–12, 7 students received support, including 4 fellowships, 3 research assistantships; Federal Work-Study and institutionally sponsored loans also available. Support available to part-time students. Financial award application deadline: 4/1; financial award applicants required to submit FAFSA. *Unit head:* Dr. Catheryn Weitman, Dean, 956-326-2420, E-mail: catheryn.weitman@tamiu.edu. *Application contact:* Suzanne Hansen-Alford, Director of Graduate Recruiting, 956-326-3023, Fax: 956-326-3021, E-mail: graduateschool@tamiu.edu. Web site: http://www.tamiu.edu/coedu/.

Texas A&M University, College of Education and Human Development, College Station, TX 77843. Offers M Ed, MS, Ed D, PhD. Part-time and evening/weekend programs available. Postbaccalaureate distance learning degree programs offered (no on-campus study). *Faculty:* 144. *Students:* 611 full-time (411 women), 657 part-time (464 women); includes 427 minority (162 Black or African American, non-Hispanic/Latino; 4 American Indian or Alaska Native, non-Hispanic/Latino; 40 Asian, non-Hispanic/Latino; 202 Hispanic/Latino; 19 Two or more races, non-Hispanic/Latino), 170 international. Average age 36. In 2011, 310 master's, 124 doctorates awarded. *Degree requirements:* For doctorate, thesis/dissertation. *Entrance requirements:* For master's and doctorate, GRE General Test. Additional exam requirements/recommendations for international students: Required—TOEFL. Application fee: $50 ($75 for international students). Electronic applications accepted. *Expenses:* Tuition, state resident: full-time $5437; part-time $226.55 per credit hour. Tuition, nonresident: full-time $12,949; part-time $539.55 per credit hour. *Required fees:* $2741. *Financial support:* In 2011–12, fellowships with partial tuition reimbursements (averaging $12,000 per year), research assistantships with partial tuition reimbursements (averaging $10,000 per year), teaching assistantships with partial tuition reimbursements (averaging $10,000 per year) were awarded; career-related internships or fieldwork, Federal Work-Study, institutionally sponsored loans, scholarships/grants, tuition waivers (partial), and unspecified assistantships also available. Financial award applicants required to submit FAFSA. *Unit head:* Dr. Doug Palmer, Dean, 979-862-6649, E-mail: dpalmer@tamu.edu. *Application contact:* Dr. Becky Carr, Assistant Dean for Administrative Services, 979-862-1342, Fax: 979-845-6129, E-mail: bcarr@tamu.edu. Web site: http://education.tamu.edu/.

Texas A&M University–Commerce, Graduate School, College of Education and Human Services, Commerce, TX 75429-3011. Offers M Ed, MA, MS, MSW, Ed D, PhD. Part-time programs available. Terminal master's awarded for partial completion of doctoral program. *Degree requirements:* For master's, comprehensive exam; for doctorate, thesis/dissertation, departmental qualifying exam. *Entrance requirements:* For master's and doctorate, GRE General Test. Electronic applications accepted. *Faculty research:* Reading, early childhood, deviance, migration, physical fitness.

Texas A&M University–Corpus Christi, Graduate Studies and Research, College of Education, Corpus Christi, TX 78412-5503. Offers counseling (MS, PhD), including counseling (MS), counselor education (PhD); curriculum and instruction (MS, Ed D); early childhood education (MS); educational administration (MS); educational leadership (Ed D); educational technology (MS); elementary education (MS); kinesiology (MS); reading (MS); secondary education (MS); special education (MS). Part-time and evening/weekend programs available. *Degree requirements:* For master's, comprehensive exam, thesis (for some programs); for doctorate, comprehensive exam, thesis/dissertation. *Entrance requirements:* For master's, GRE General Test. Additional exam requirements/recommendations for international students: Required—TOEFL. Electronic applications accepted.

Texas A&M University–Kingsville, College of Graduate Studies, College of Education, Kingsville, TX 78363. Offers M Ed, MA, MS, Ed D, PhD. Part-time and evening/weekend programs available. *Degree requirements:* For master's, comprehensive exam; for doctorate, one foreign language, comprehensive exam, thesis/dissertation. *Entrance requirements:* For master's, GRE General Test, minimum GPA of 3.0; for doctorate, GRE General Test, MAT, minimum GPA of 3.25. *Faculty research:* Rural schools, facilities planning, linguistics.

Texas A&M University–Texarkana, Graduate Studies and Research, College of Education and Liberal Arts, Texarkana, TX 75505-5518. Offers adult education (MS); curriculum and instruction (M Ed); education (MS); educational administration (M Ed); English (MA); instructional technology (MS); interdisciplinary studies (MA, MS); special education (MS). Part-time and evening/weekend programs available. *Degree requirements:* For master's, comprehensive exam (for some programs), thesis optional. *Entrance requirements:* For master's, minimum GPA of 2.5 on last 60 hours of bachelor's degree. Additional exam requirements/recommendations for international students: Required—TOEFL. Electronic applications accepted.

Texas Christian University, College of Education, Fort Worth, TX 76129-0002. Offers M Ed, Ed D, PhD, Certificate, MBA/Ed D. Part-time and evening/weekend programs available. *Faculty:* 27 full-time (21 women), 1 part-time/adjunct. *Students:* 81 full-time (68 women), 99 part-time (68 women); includes 42 minority (20 Black or African American, non-Hispanic/Latino; 2 American Indian or Alaska Native, non-Hispanic/Latino; 4 Asian, non-Hispanic/Latino; 15 Hispanic/Latino; 1 Two or more races, non-Hispanic/Latino), 6 international. Average age 30. 114 applicants, 82% accepted, 76 enrolled. In 2011, 68 master's, 9 doctorates awarded. *Degree requirements:* For master's, paper/thesis; for doctorate, comprehensive exam, thesis/dissertation. *Entrance requirements:* For master's, GRE (counseling and educational leadership only); for doctorate, GRE or MAT. Additional exam requirements/recommendations for international students: Required—TOEFL (minimum score 550 paper-based; 213 computer-based; 80 iBT). *Application deadline:* For fall admission, 11/15 for domestic and international students; for spring admission, 3/1 for domestic and international students. Application fee: $60. Electronic applications accepted. *Expenses: Tuition:* Full-time $20,250; part-time $1125 per credit hour. Part-time tuition and fees vary according to course load and program. *Financial support:* Teaching assistantships with full tuition reimbursements, career-related internships or fieldwork, scholarships/grants, and unspecified assistantships available. Financial award application deadline: 3/1. *Unit head:* Dr. Jan Lacina, Associate Dean, 817-257-6786, E-mail: j.lacina@tcu.edu. *Application contact:* Patricia Garcia, Academic Program Specialist, 817-257-7661, E-mail: p.m.garcia@tcu.edu. Web site: http://www.coe.tcu.edu/graduateprograms.asp.

Texas Southern University, College of Education, Houston, TX 77004-4584. Offers M Ed, MS, Ed D. Part-time and evening/weekend programs available. *Degree requirements:* For master's, comprehensive exam; for doctorate, comprehensive exam, thesis/dissertation. *Entrance requirements:* For master's, GRE General Test, minimum GPA of 2.5; for doctorate, GRE General Test or MAT, master's degree, minimum B+ average. Additional exam requirements/recommendations for international students: Required—TOEFL. Electronic applications accepted.

Texas State University–San Marcos, Graduate School, College of Education, San Marcos, TX 78666. Offers M Ed, MA, MSRLS, PhD, SSP. Part-time and evening/weekend programs available. *Faculty:* 92 full-time (56 women), 46 part-time/adjunct (33 women). *Students:* 559 full-time (413 women), 760 part-time (591 women); includes 435 minority (90 Black or African American, non-Hispanic/Latino; 4 American Indian or Alaska Native, non-Hispanic/Latino; 27 Asian, non-Hispanic/Latino; 292 Hispanic/Latino; 1 Native Hawaiian or other Pacific Islander, non-Hispanic/Latino; 21 Two or more races, non-Hispanic/Latino), 11 international. Average age 32. 764 applicants, 60% accepted, 289 enrolled. In 2011, 550 master's, 9 doctorates awarded. *Degree requirements:* For master's, comprehensive exam, thesis (for some programs). *Entrance requirements:* For master's, GRE (for some programs). Additional exam requirements/recommendations for international students: Required—TOEFL (minimum score 550 paper-based; 213 computer-based; 78 iBT). *Application deadline:* For fall admission, 6/15 priority date for domestic students, 6/1 for international students; for spring admission, 10/15 priority date for domestic students, 10/1 for international students. Applications are processed on a rolling basis. Application fee: $40 ($90 for international students). Electronic applications accepted. *Expenses:* Tuition, state resident: full-time $6408; part-time $3204 per semester. Tuition, nonresident: full-time $14,832; part-time $7416 per semester. *Required fees:* $1824; $912 per semester. Tuition and fees vary according to course load. *Financial support:* In 2011–12, 756 students received support, including 90 research assistantships (averaging $12,564 per year), 72 teaching assistantships (averaging $10,980 per year); fellowships, career-related internships or fieldwork, Federal Work-Study, and institutionally sponsored loans also available. Support available to part-time students. Financial award application deadline: 4/1; financial award applicants required to submit FAFSA. *Faculty research:* Texas Family Literacy Resource Center, Adult Education Credential project, P-16 Infrastructure, novice teacher induction, science for ELL, Sexual ABCs, teacher quality. *Total annual research expenditures:* $4.3 million. *Unit head:* Dr. Stan Carpenter, Dean, 512-245-2150, Fax: 512-245-3158, E-mail: sc33@txstate.edu. *Application contact:* Dr. J. Michael Willoughby, Dean of Graduate School, 512-245-2581, Fax: 512-245-8365, E-mail: gradcollege@txstate.edu. Web site: http://www.education.txstate.edu/.

Texas Tech University, Graduate School, College of Education, Lubbock, TX 79409. Offers M Ed, MS, Ed D, PhD. *Accreditation:* NCATE. Part-time programs available. *Faculty:* 72 full-time (43 women), 1 (woman) part-time/adjunct. *Students:* 338 full-time (257 women), 726 part-time (541 women); includes 258 minority (56 Black or African American, non-Hispanic/Latino; 3 American Indian or Alaska Native, non-Hispanic/Latino; 11 Asian, non-Hispanic/Latino; 177 Hispanic/Latino; 11 Two or more races, non-Hispanic/Latino), 68 international. Average age 36. 757 applicants, 44% accepted, 248 enrolled. In 2011, 207 master's, 39 doctorates awarded. *Degree requirements:* For master's, thesis or alternative; for doctorate, thesis/dissertation. *Entrance requirements:* For master's and doctorate, GRE General Test. Additional exam requirements/recommendations for international students: Required—TOEFL (minimum score 550 paper-based; 213 computer-based; 79 iBT). *Application deadline:* For fall admission, 6/1 priority date for domestic students, 1/15 for international students; for spring admission, 9/1 priority date for domestic students, 6/15 for international students. Applications are processed on a rolling basis. Application fee: $50 ($75 for international students). Electronic applications accepted. *Expenses:* Contact institution. *Financial support:* In 2011–12, 357 students received support. Career-related internships or fieldwork, Federal Work-Study, institutionally sponsored loans, scholarships/grants, traineeships, health care benefits, and unspecified assistantships available. Support available to part-time students. Financial award application deadline: 4/15; financial award applicants required to submit FAFSA. *Faculty research:* Multicultural foundations of education, teacher education, psychological processes of teaching and learning, teaching populations with special needs, institutional technology. *Total annual research expenditures:* $2.4 million. *Unit head:* Dr. Charles Ruch, Interim Dean, 806-742-1998 Ext. 450, Fax: 806-742-2179, E-mail: charles.ruch@ttu.edu. *Application contact:* Stephenie Allyn McDaniel, Administrative Assistant, 806-742-1988 Ext. 434, Fax: 806-742-2179, E-mail: stephenie.mcdaniel@ttu.edu. Web site: http://www.educ.ttu.edu/.

Texas Wesleyan University, Graduate Programs, Programs in Education, Fort Worth, TX 76105-1536. Offers education (M Ed, Ed D); marriage and family therapy (MSMFT); professional counseling (MA); school counseling (MS). Part-time and evening/weekend programs available. Postbaccalaureate distance learning degree programs offered (no on-campus study). *Faculty:* 11 full-time (7 women), 3 part-time/adjunct (2 women). *Students:* 47 full-time (36 women), 193 part-time (159 women); includes 97 minority (52 Black or African American, non-Hispanic/Latino; 2 American Indian or Alaska Native, non-Hispanic/Latino; 6 Asian, non-Hispanic/Latino; 37 Hispanic/Latino), 4 international. Average age 35. 116 applicants, 72% accepted, 76 enrolled. In 2011, 179 master's awarded. *Entrance requirements:* For master's, GRE General Test, minimum GPA of 3.0 in final 60 hours of undergraduate course work, interview. *Application deadline:* For fall admission, 6/15 priority date for domestic students; for spring admission, 10/15 priority date for domestic students. Applications are processed on a rolling basis. Application fee: $40 ($50 for international students). Tuition and fees vary according to course level, course load, degree level and program. *Financial support:* Career-related internships or fieldwork, Federal Work-Study, scholarships/grants, and tuition waivers (full and partial) available. Support available to part-time students. Financial award application deadline: 3/15; financial award applicants required to submit FAFSA. *Faculty research:* Teacher effectiveness, bilingual education, analytic teaching. *Unit head:* Dr. Carlos Martinez, Dean, School of Education, 817-531-4940, Fax: 817-531-4943. *Application contact:* Beth Hargrove, Coordinator of Graduate Programs, 817-531-4498, Fax: 817-531-4261, E-mail: bhargrove@txwes.edu. Web site: http://www.txwes.edu/academics/education.

Texas Woman's University, Graduate School, College of Professional Education, Denton, TX 76201. Offers M Ed, MA, MAT, MLS, MS, Ed D, PhD. Part-time and evening/weekend programs available. *Faculty:* 77 full-time (59 women), 7 part-time/adjunct (6 women). *Students:* 281 full-time (261 women), 1,033 part-time (953 women); includes 441 minority (235 Black or African American, non-Hispanic/Latino; 4 American Indian or Alaska Native, non-Hispanic/Latino; 41 Asian, non-Hispanic/Latino; 161 Hispanic/Latino), 17 international. Average age 37. 456 applicants, 69% accepted, 262 enrolled. In 2011, 416 master's, 33 doctorates awarded. Terminal master's awarded for partial completion of doctoral program. *Degree requirements:* For master's, comprehensive exam (for some programs), thesis (for some programs); for doctorate, comprehensive exam, thesis/dissertation. *Entrance requirements:* For master's and doctorate, minimum GPA of 3.0. Additional exam requirements/recommendations for international students: Required—TOEFL (minimum score 550 paper-based; 213 computer-based; 79 iBT). *Application deadline:* For fall admission, 7/1 priority date for domestic students, 3/1 for international students; for spring admission, 12/1 priority date for domestic students, 7/1 for international students. Applications are processed on a rolling basis. Application fee: $50 ($75 for international students). Electronic applications accepted. *Expenses:* Tuition, state resident: full-time $3834; part-time $213 per credit hour. Tuition, nonresident: full-time $9468; part-time $526 per credit hour. *Required fees:* $213 per credit hour. Tuition and fees vary according to course load. *Financial support:* In 2011–12, 332 students received support, including 40 research assistantships (averaging $12,164 per year), 8 teaching assistantships (averaging $12,164 per year); career-related internships or fieldwork, Federal Work-Study, institutionally sponsored loans, scholarships/grants, traineeships, health care benefits, and unspecified assistantships also available. Support available to part-time students. Financial award application deadline: 3/1; financial award applicants required to submit FAFSA. *Total annual research expenditures:* $254,752. *Unit head:* Dr. Nan L. Restine, Dean, 940-898-2202, Fax: 940-898-2209, E-mail: cope@twu.edu. *Application contact:* Dr. Samuel Wheeler, Assistant Director of Admissions, 940-898-3188, Fax: 940-898-3081, E-mail: wheelersr@twu.edu. Web site: http://www.twu.edu/college-professional-education/.

Thomas More College, Program in Teaching, Crestview Hills, KY 41017-3495. Offers MAT. *Faculty:* 4 full-time (3 women), 5 part-time/adjunct (4 women). *Students:* 34 part-time (22 women); includes 3 minority (2 Asian, non-Hispanic/Latino; 1 Hispanic/Latino). Average age 33. 15 applicants, 80% accepted, 11 enrolled. In 2011, 15 master's awarded. *Degree requirements:* For master's, comprehensive exam. *Entrance requirements:* For master's, GRE (minimum combined score of 1200 if GPA less than 2.7), PRAXIS II in content area, minimum undergraduate content GPA of 2.7, interview. Additional exam requirements/recommendations for international students: Required—TOEFL (minimum score 600 paper-based; 250 computer-based; 100 iBT). *Application deadline:* For fall admission, 6/1 for domestic students. Applications are processed on a rolling basis. Application fee: $0. Electronic applications accepted. *Expenses: Tuition:* Full-time $13,057; part-time $570 per credit hour. Tuition and fees vary according to program. *Financial support:* In 2011–12, 7 students received support. Federal Work-Study, institutionally sponsored loans, and scholarships/grants available. Financial award application deadline: 3/15; financial award applicants required to submit FAFSA. *Unit head:* Joyce Hamberg, Director, 859-344-3404, Fax: 859-344-3345, E-mail: joyce.hamberg@thomasmore.edu. *Application contact:* Joyce Hamberg, 859-344-3404, Fax: 859-344-3345, E-mail: joyce.hamberg@thomasmore.edu.

Thomas University, Department of Education, Thomasville, GA 31792-7499. Offers M Ed. Part-time programs available. *Entrance requirements:* For master's, resume, 3 academic/professional references. Additional exam requirements/recommendations for international students: Required—TOEFL (minimum score 600 paper-based; 250 computer-based). Electronic applications accepted.

Thompson Rivers University, Program in Education, Kamloops, BC V2C 5N3, Canada. Offers M Ed. Part-time programs available. *Entrance requirements:* For master's, 2 letters of reference, minimum GPA of 3.0 in final 2 years of undergraduate degree.

Touro College, Graduate School of Education, New York, NY 10010. Offers bilingual programs (Advanced Certificate); education and special education (MS); gifted and talented education (Advanced Certificate); instructional technology (MS); mathematics education (MS); school leadership (MS); teaching children with autism and other severe or multiple disabilities (Advanced Certificate); teaching English to speakers of other languages (MS, Advanced Certificate); teaching literacy (MS). Part-time and evening/weekend programs available. Postbaccalaureate distance learning degree programs offered (no on-campus study). *Faculty:* 75 full-time, 131 part-time/adjunct. *Students:* 382 full-time (324 women), 3,790 part-time (3,196 women); includes 1,211 minority (537 Black or African American, non-Hispanic/Latino; 4 American Indian or Alaska Native, non-Hispanic/Latino; 187 Asian, non-Hispanic/Latino; 472 Hispanic/Latino; 3 Native Hawaiian or other Pacific Islander, non-Hispanic/Latino; 8 Two or more races, non-Hispanic/Latino), 1 international. 1,422 applicants, 50% accepted, 675 enrolled. In 2011, 6 master's, 4 other advanced degrees awarded. *Application deadline:* For fall admission, 8/26 for domestic students, 7/15 for international students; for spring admission, 12/31 for domestic students, 12/15 for international students. Applications are processed on a rolling basis. Application fee: $50. *Financial support:* Federal Work-Study available. Financial award applicants required to submit FAFSA. *Faculty research:* Equity assistance, language development, scholar communications, Latin American studies and cultural sensitivity, behavior management techniques and strategies in special education. *Unit head:* Dr. LaMar Miller, Dean, 212-463-0400 Ext. 5561, Fax: 212-462-4889, E-mail: lpmiller@touro.edu. *Application contact:* Natalie Arroyo, Admissions Assistant, 212-463-0400 Ext. 5119, E-mail: natalie.arroyo@touro.edu.

Touro University, Graduate Programs, Vallejo, CA 94592. Offers education (MA); medical health sciences (MS); osteopathic medicine (DO); pharmacy (Pharm D); public health (MPH). *Accreditation:* AOsA; ARC-PA. Part-time and evening/weekend programs available. *Faculty:* 93 full-time (52 women), 55 part-time/adjunct (28 women). *Students:* 1,402 full-time (851 women). 6,914 applicants, 12% accepted, 503 enrolled. *Degree requirements:* For master's, comprehensive exam, thesis; for doctorate, comprehensive exam. *Entrance requirements:* For doctorate, BS/BA. *Application deadline:* For fall admission, 3/15 for domestic students; for winter admission, 12/1 for domestic students. Applications are processed on a rolling basis. Application fee: $100. Electronic applications accepted. *Expenses: Tuition:* Full-time $25,000; part-time $575 per credit. *Required fees:* $250 per year. Tuition and fees vary according to course level, course load, degree level and program. *Financial support:* Fellowships, research assistantships, teaching assistantships, Federal Work-Study, and scholarships/grants available. Support available to part-time students. Financial award applicants required to submit FAFSA. *Faculty research:* Cancer, heart disease. *Application contact:* Steve Davis, Associate Director of Admissions, 707-638-5270, Fax: 707-638-5250, E-mail: steven.davis@tu.edu.

Towson University, Program in Teaching, Towson, MD 21252-0001. Offers MAT. *Students:* 127 full-time (93 women), 93 part-time (71 women); includes 25 minority (15 Black or African American, non-Hispanic/Latino; 1 American Indian or Alaska Native, non-Hispanic/Latino; 3 Asian, non-Hispanic/Latino; 3 Hispanic/Latino; 3 Two or more races, non-Hispanic/Latino), 7 international. *Degree requirements:* For master's, portfolio. *Entrance requirements:* For master's, PRAXIS I, 2 letters of reference, resume. Additional exam requirements/recommendations for international students: Required—TOEFL (minimum score 550 paper-based). *Application deadline:* For fall admission, 6/15 priority date for domestic students, 6/15 for international students; for spring admission, 10/15 priority date for domestic students, 10/15 for international students. Applications are processed on a rolling basis. Application fee: $50. Electronic applications accepted. *Expenses:* Tuition, state resident: part-time $337 per credit. Tuition, nonresident: part-time $709 per credit. *Required fees:* $99 per credit. *Financial support:* Application deadline: 4/1; applicants required to submit FAFSA. *Unit head:* Judy Reber, Graduate Program Director, 410-704-4935, Fax: 410-704-2733, E-mail: jreber@towson.edu. Web site: http://www.towson.edu/col/programs/mat/mat.htm.

Trevecca Nazarene University, College of Lifelong Learning, School of Education, Nashville, TN 37210-2877. Offers curriculum, assessment, and instruction K-12 (M Ed); educational leadership (M Ed); English language learners (PreK-12) (M Ed); leadership and professional practice (Ed D); leading instructional improvement for teachers PreK-12 (M Ed); library and information science (MLI Sc); teaching (MAT), including teaching 7-12, teaching K-6; visual impairment special education (M Ed). *Accreditation:* NCATE. Part-time and evening/weekend programs available. Postbaccalaureate distance learning degree programs offered. *Faculty:* 17 full-time (15 women), 22 part-time/adjunct

(14 women). *Students:* 379 full-time (283 women), 77 part-time (60 women); includes 87 minority (78 Black or African American, non-Hispanic/Latino; 2 Asian, non-Hispanic/Latino; 3 Hispanic/Latino; 4 Two or more races, non-Hispanic/Latino), 3 international. Average age 36. In 2011, 188 master's, 23 doctorates awarded. *Degree requirements:* For master's, exit assessment; for doctorate, thesis/dissertation, proposal study, symposium presentation. *Entrance requirements:* For master's, GRE General Test, MAT, minimum GPA of 2.7, 2 reference forms; for doctorate, GMAT, GRE, MAT, or NTE, minimum GPA of 3.4, resume, writing sample, interview, reference forms. Additional exam requirements/recommendations for international students: Required—TOEFL (minimum score 550 paper-based; 213 computer-based). *Application deadline:* Applications are processed on a rolling basis. Application fee: $25. *Expenses:* Contact institution. *Financial support:* Applicants required to submit FAFSA. *Unit head:* Dr. Esther Swink, Dean/Director of Graduate Education Programs, 615-248-1201, Fax: 615-248-1597, E-mail: eswink@trevecca.edu. *Application contact:* Melanie Eaton, Admissions, 615-248-1498, E-mail: admissions_ged@trevecca.edu. Web site: http://www.trevecca.edu/academics/schools-colleges/education/.

Trident University International, College of Education, Cypress, CA 90630. Offers MA Ed, PhD. Part-time and evening/weekend programs available. Postbaccalaureate distance learning degree programs offered (no on-campus study). *Degree requirements:* For doctorate, comprehensive exam, thesis/dissertation, defense of dissertation. *Entrance requirements:* For master's, minimum GPA of 2.5 (students with GPA 3.0 or greater may transfer up to 30% of graduate level credits); for doctorate, minimum GPA of 3.4, curriculum vitae, course work in research methods or statistics. Additional exam requirements/recommendations for international students: Required—TOEFL (minimum score 525 paper-based). Electronic applications accepted.

Trinity International University, Trinity Graduate School, Deerfield, IL 60015-1284. Offers bioethics (MA); communication and culture (MA); counseling psychology (MA); instructional leadership (M Ed); teaching (MA). Part-time and evening/weekend programs available. Postbaccalaureate distance learning degree programs offered (minimal on-campus study). *Degree requirements:* For master's, comprehensive exam. *Entrance requirements:* For master's, GRE General Test or MAT, minimum undergraduate GPA of 3.0. Additional exam requirements/recommendations for international students: Required—TOEFL (minimum score 580 paper-based; 237 computer-based), TWE (minimum score 4). Electronic applications accepted.

Trinity University, Department of Education, San Antonio, TX 78212-7200. Offers school administration (M Ed); school psychology (MA); teacher education (MAT). *Accreditation:* NCATE. Part-time and evening/weekend programs available. *Entrance requirements:* For master's, GRE General Test, minimum GPA of 3.0, interview.

Trinity Washington University, School of Education, Washington, DC 20017-1094. Offers counseling (MA); early childhood education (MAT); educating for change (M Ed); educational administration (MSA); elementary education (MAT); school counseling (MA); secondary education (MAT), including English, social studies; special education (MAT); teaching English as a second language (MAT); teaching English to speakers of other languages (M Ed); the teaching of reading (M Ed). *Accreditation:* NCATE. Part-time and evening/weekend programs available. *Degree requirements:* For master's, thesis (for some programs), capstone project(s). *Entrance requirements:* For master's, PRAXIS I, minimum GPA of 2.8. Additional exam requirements/recommendations for international students: Required—TOEFL (minimum score 550 paper-based; 213 computer-based). *Faculty research:* Technology, literacy, special education, organizations, inclusion models.

Troy University, Graduate School, College of Arts and Sciences, Program in Public Administration, Troy, AL 36082. Offers education (MPA); environmental management (MPA); government contracting (MPA); health care administration (MPA); justice administration (MPA); national security affairs (MPA); nonprofit management (MPA); public human resources management (MPA); public management (MPA). *Accreditation:* NASPAA. Part-time and evening/weekend programs available. Postbaccalaureate distance learning degree programs offered (no on-campus study). *Faculty:* 17 full-time (10 women), 10 part-time/adjunct (3 women). *Students:* 97 full-time (71 women), 400 part-time (259 women); includes 298 minority (264 Black or African American, non-Hispanic/Latino; 5 American Indian or Alaska Native, non-Hispanic/Latino; 15 Asian, non-Hispanic/Latino; 11 Hispanic/Latino; 3 Two or more races, non-Hispanic/Latino). Average age 33. 323 applicants, 63% accepted, 97 enrolled. In 2011, 249 master's awarded. *Degree requirements:* For master's, capstone course, minimum GPA of 3.0, admission to candidacy. *Entrance requirements:* For master's, GRE (minimum score of 920), MAT (minimum score of 400) or GMAT (minimum score of 490), minimum undergraduate GPA of 2.5, letter of recommendation, essay. Additional exam requirements/recommendations for international students: Required—TOEFL (minimum score 523 paper-based; 193 computer-based; 70 iBT), IELTS (minimum score 6). *Application deadline:* Applications are processed on a rolling basis. Application fee: $50. Electronic applications accepted. *Expenses:* Tuition, state resident: full-time $6960; part-time $290 per credit hour. Tuition, nonresident: full-time $13,920; part-time $580 per credit hour. *Required fees:* $386 per term. *Financial support:* Available to part-time students. Applicants required to submit FAFSA. *Unit head:* Dr. Charles Kruprick, Chairman, 334-670-5968, Fax: 334-670-5647, E-mail: ckrupnickl@troy.edu. *Application contact:* Brenda K. Campbell, Director of Graduate Admissions, 334-670-3178, Fax: 334-670-3733, E-mail: bcamp@troy.edu.

Troy University, Graduate School, College of Education, Troy, AL 36082. Offers M Ed, MS, Ed S. *Accreditation:* NCATE. Part-time and evening/weekend programs available. *Faculty:* 120 full-time (56 women), 85 part-time/adjunct (49 women). *Students:* 534 full-time (422 women), 1,207 part-time (975 women); includes 992 minority (721 Black or African American, non-Hispanic/Latino; 5 American Indian or Alaska Native, non-Hispanic/Latino; 191 Asian, non-Hispanic/Latino; 60 Hispanic/Latino; 1 Native Hawaiian or other Pacific Islander, non-Hispanic/Latino; 14 Two or more races, non-Hispanic/Latino). Average age 34. 798 applicants, 83% accepted, 376 enrolled. In 2011, 695 master's, 26 other advanced degrees awarded. *Degree requirements:* For master's, comprehensive exam, thesis. *Entrance requirements:* For master's, GRE General Test, MAT or GMAT, minimum GPA of 2.5; for Ed S, GRE General Test, MAT or GMAT, Alabama Class A certificate or equivalent, minimum graduate GPA of 3.0. Additional exam requirements/recommendations for international students: Required—TOEFL (minimum score 523 paper-based; 193 computer-based; 70 iBT), IELTS (minimum score 6). *Application deadline:* For fall admission, 6/1 for international students; for spring admission, 10/15 for international students. Applications are processed on a rolling basis. Application fee: $50. Electronic applications accepted. *Expenses:* Tuition, state resident: full-time $6960; part-time $290 per credit hour. Tuition, nonresident: full-time $13,920; part-time $580 per credit hour. *Required fees:* $386 per term. *Financial support:* Career-related internships or fieldwork available. Support available to part-time students. Financial award applicants required to submit FAFSA. *Unit head:* Dr. Sib Jeffrey, Dean, 334-670-3712, Fax: 334-670-3474, E-mail: djeffr@troy.edu. *Application contact:* Brenda K. Campbell, Director of Graduate Admissions, 334-670-3178, Fax: 334-670-3733, E-mail: bcamp@troy.edu.

Truman State University, Graduate School, School of Health Sciences and Education, Program in Education, Kirksville, MO 63501-4221. Offers MAE. *Accreditation:* NCATE. *Degree requirements:* For master's, comprehensive exam, thesis or alternative. *Entrance requirements:* For master's, GRE, minimum GPA of 2.75. Additional exam requirements/recommendations for international students: Required—TOEFL (minimum score 550 paper-based; 213 computer-based). Electronic applications accepted.

Tufts University, Graduate School of Arts and Sciences, Department of Education, Medford, MA 02155. Offers education (MA, MAT, MS, PhD), including education (MS, PhD), middle and secondary education (MA, MAT), secondary education (MA); school psychology (MA, Ed S). *Faculty:* 13 full-time, 9 part-time/adjunct. *Students:* 166 (132 women); includes 31 minority (10 Black or African American, non-Hispanic/Latino; 4 American Indian or Alaska Native, non-Hispanic/Latino; 8 Asian, non-Hispanic/Latino; 9 Hispanic/Latino), 4 international. Average age 27. 272 applicants, 66% accepted, 105 enrolled. In 2011, 97 master's, 7 doctorates, 11 other advanced degrees awarded. *Degree requirements:* For doctorate, thesis/dissertation. *Entrance requirements:* For master's and doctorate, GRE General Test. Additional exam requirements/recommendations for international students: Required—TOEFL (minimum score 550 paper-based; 213 computer-based; 80 iBT). *Application deadline:* For fall admission, 2/1 for domestic students, 12/15 for international students; for spring admission, 10/15 for domestic students, 9/15 for international students. Applications are processed on a rolling basis. Application fee: $75. Electronic applications accepted. *Expenses:* Tuition: Full-time $41,208; part-time $1030 per credit hour. Full-time tuition and fees vary according to degree level, program and student level. Part-time tuition and fees vary according to course load. *Financial support:* Teaching assistantships with full and partial tuition reimbursements, Federal Work-Study, scholarships/grants, and tuition waivers (partial) available. Support available to part-time students. Financial award application deadline: 2/1; financial award applicants required to submit FAFSA. *Unit head:* Barbara Brizuela, Chair, 617-627-3244, Fax: 617-627-3901. *Application contact:* Patricia Romeo, Department Administrator, 617-627-3244. Web site: http://www.ase.tufts.edu/education/.

Tusculum College, Graduate School, Program in Education, Greeneville, TN 37743-9997. Offers adult education (MA Ed); K–12 (MA Ed). Evening/weekend programs available. *Degree requirements:* For master's, thesis or alternative. *Entrance requirements:* For master's, 3 years of work experience, minimum GPA of 2.75.

Union College, Graduate Programs, Department of Education, Barbourville, KY 40906-1499. Offers elementary education (MA); health and physical education (MA); middle grades (MA); music education (MA); principalship (MA); reading specialist (MA); secondary education (MA); special education (MA). *Degree requirements:* For master's, thesis optional. *Entrance requirements:* For master's, GRE General Test, NTE.

Union Graduate College, School of Education, Schenectady, NY 12308-3107. Offers biology (MAT, MS); chemistry (MAT); Chinese (MAT); earth science (MAT); English (MAT); French (MAT); general science (MAT); German (MAT); Greek (MAT); languages (MAT); Latin (MAT); mathematics (MAT); mathematics and technology (MS); mentoring and teacher leadership (AC); middle childhood extension (AC); national board certificate and teacher leadership (AC); physical science (MS); physics (MAT); social studies (MAT); Spanish (MAT). *Accreditation:* Teacher Education Accreditation Council. *Faculty:* 3 full-time (1 woman), 51 part-time/adjunct (24 women). *Students:* 37 full-time (26 women), 25 part-time (16 women); includes 4 minority (3 Asian, non-Hispanic/Latino; 1 Hispanic/Latino). Average age 32. 66 applicants, 83% accepted, 41 enrolled. In 2011, 47 master's, 29 other advanced degrees awarded. *Degree requirements:* For master's, thesis or project. *Entrance requirements:* For master's, minimum GPA of 3.0, letters of recommendation. Additional exam requirements/recommendations for international students: Required—TOEFL (minimum score 550 paper-based; 213 computer-based). *Application deadline:* Applications are processed on a rolling basis. Application fee: $60. Electronic applications accepted. *Expenses:* Contact institution. *Financial support:* In 2011–12, 22 students received support. Career-related internships or fieldwork, Federal Work-Study, scholarships/grants, health care benefits, and tuition waivers (partial) available. Support available to part-time students. Financial award applicants required to submit FAFSA. *Faculty research:* Transformative learning, science education, National Board Certification, teacher leadership, teacher quality. *Unit head:* Dr. Patrick Allen, Dean, 518-631-9870, Fax: 518-631-9901. *Application contact:* Christine Angley, Assistant, 518-631-9871, Fax: 518-631-9903, E-mail: angleyc@uniongraduatecollege.edu.

Union Institute & University, Education Programs, Cincinnati, OH 45206-1925. Offers adult and higher education (M Ed); curriculum and instruction (M Ed); educational leadership (M Ed, Ed D); guidance and counseling (Ed S); higher education (Ed D); issues in education (M Ed); reading (Ed S). M Ed offered online and in Vermont and Florida, concentrations vary by location; Ed S offered in Florida; Ed D program is a hybrid (online with limited residency) offered in Ohio. Postbaccalaureate distance learning degree programs offered (minimal on-campus study). *Degree requirements:* For master's, comprehensive exam (for some programs), thesis (for some programs), electronic portfolio; for doctorate, comprehensive exam, thesis/dissertation, electronic portfolio.

Union Institute & University, Master of Arts Program–Online, Montpelier, VT 05602. Offers creativity studies (MA); education (MA); health and wellness (MA); history and culture (MA); leadership, public policy, and social issues (MA); literature and writing (MA); psychology (MA). Part-time programs available. Postbaccalaureate distance learning degree programs offered (no on-campus study). *Degree requirements:* For master's, thesis. Electronic applications accepted.

Union University, School of Education, Jackson, TN 38305-3697. Offers education (M Ed, MA Ed); education administration generalist (Ed S); educational leadership (Ed D); educational supervision (Ed S); higher education (Ed D). M Ed also available at Germantown campus. *Accreditation:* NCATE. Part-time and evening/weekend programs available. *Degree requirements:* For master's, thesis (for some programs), capstone research course; for doctorate, comprehensive exam, thesis/dissertation; for Ed S, thesis or alternative. *Entrance requirements:* For master's, MAT, PRAXIS II or GRE, minimum GPA of 3.0, teaching license, writing sample; for doctorate, GRE, minimum graduate GPA of 3.2, writing sample; for Ed S, PRAXIS II, minimum graduate GPA of 3.2, writing sample. *Faculty research:* Mathematics education, direct instruction, language disorders and special education, brain compatible learning, empathy and school leadership.

United States University, School of Education, Cypress, CA 90630. Offers administration (MA Ed); early childhood education (MA Ed); general (MA Ed); higher education administration (MA Ed); Spanish language education (MA Ed); special education (MA Ed). *Degree requirements:* For master's, portfolio. *Entrance requirements:* For master's, minimum undergraduate GPA of 2.5. Additional exam requirements/recommendations for international students: Required—TOEFL (minimum score 500 paper-based; 173 computer-based; 61 iBT).

Universidad Autonoma de Guadalajara, Graduate Programs, Guadalajara, Mexico. Offers administrative law and justice (LL M); advertising and corporate communications (MA); architecture (M Arch); business (MBA); computational science (MCC); education (Ed M, Ed D); English-Spanish translation (MA); entrepreneurship and management (MBA); integrated management of digital animation (MA); international business (MIB); international corporate law (LL M); internet technologies (MS); manufacturing systems (MMS); occupational health (MS); philosophy (MA, PhD); power electronics (MS);

quality systems (MQS); renewable energy (MS); social evaluation of projects (MBA); strategic market research (MBA); tax law (MA); teaching mathematics (MA).

Universidad de las Americas, A.C., Program in Education, Mexico City, Mexico. Offers M Ed. *Entrance requirements:* For master's, 2 years of professional experience; undergraduate degree in early childhood education, human communication, psychology, science of education, special education or related fields.

Universidad de las Américas–Puebla, Division of Graduate Studies, School of Social Sciences, Program in Education, Puebla, Mexico. Offers MA. Part-time and evening/weekend programs available. *Degree requirements:* For master's, one foreign language, thesis. *Faculty research:* Curriculum development, curriculum evaluation, instructional technology, critical thinking.

Universidad del Turabo, Graduate Programs, Programs in Education, Gurabo, PR 00778-3030. Offers administration of school libraries (M Ed, Certificate); athletic training (MPHE); coaching (MPHE); curriculum and instruction and appropriate environment (D Ed); curriculum and teaching (M Ed); educational administration (M Ed); educational leadership (D Ed); guidance counseling (M Ed); library service and information technology (M Ed); special education (M Ed); teaching at primary level (M Ed); teaching English as a second language (M Ed); teaching of fine arts (M Ed); wellness (MPHE). Part-time and evening/weekend programs available. *Students:* 311 full-time (223 women), 468 part-time (366 women); includes 643 minority (all Hispanic/Latino). Average age 36. 449 applicants, 88% accepted, 295 enrolled. In 2011, 268 master's, 14 doctorates awarded. *Entrance requirements:* For master's, GRE, EXADEP, interview. *Application deadline:* For fall admission, 8/5 for domestic students. Application fee: $25. *Financial support:* Institutionally sponsored loans available. *Unit head:* Angela Candelario, Dean, 787-743-7979 Ext. 4126. *Application contact:* Virginia Gonzalez, Admissions Officer, 787-746-3009.

Universidad FLET, Department of Graduate Studies, Miami, FL 33186. Offers education (M Ed); theological studies (MTS). *Degree requirements:* For master's, thesis or project. *Entrance requirements:* For master's, letter of recommendation.

Universidad Metropolitana, School of Education, San Juan, PR 00928-1150. Offers administration and supervision (M Ed); curriculum and teaching (M Ed); educational administration and supervision (M Ed); managing recreation and sports services (M Ed); pre-school centers administration (M Ed); special education (M Ed); teaching of physical education (M Ed), including teaching of adult physical education, teaching of elementary physical education, teaching of secondary physical education. Part-time and evening/weekend programs available. *Degree requirements:* For master's, thesis or alternative. Electronic applications accepted.

Université de Moncton, Faculty of Education, Graduate Studies in Education, Moncton, NB E1A 3E9, Canada. Offers educational psychology (M Ed, MA Ed); guidance (M Ed, MA Ed); school administration (M Ed, MA Ed); teaching (M Ed, MA Ed). Part-time programs available. *Degree requirements:* For master's, proficiency in English and French. *Entrance requirements:* For master's, minimum GPA of 3.0. *Faculty research:* Guidance, ethnolinguistic vitality, children's rights, ecological education, entrepreneurship.

Université de Montréal, Faculty of Education, Montréal, QC H3C 3J7, Canada. Offers M Ed, MA, PhD, DESS. Part-time and evening/weekend programs available. *Degree requirements:* For doctorate, thesis/dissertation, general exam. Electronic applications accepted.

Université de Sherbrooke, Faculty of Education, Sherbrooke, QC J1K 2R1, Canada. Offers M Ed, MA, Diploma. Part-time and evening/weekend programs available. *Degree requirements:* For master's, thesis. *Faculty research:* Career education, teaching, professional instruction.

Université du Québec à Chicoutimi, Graduate Programs, Program in Education, Chicoutimi, QC G7H 2B1, Canada. Offers M Ed, MA, PhD. PhD offered jointly with Université du Québec à Rimouski, Université du Québec à Trois-Rivières, Université du Québec èn Outaouais, Université du Québec en Abitibi-Témiscamingue. and Université du Québec à Montréal. Part-time programs available. *Degree requirements:* For doctorate, thesis/dissertation. *Entrance requirements:* For master's, appropriate bachelor's degree, proficiency in French; for doctorate, appropriate master's degree, proficiency in French.

Université du Québec à Montréal, Graduate Programs, Program in Education, Montréal, QC H3C 3P8, Canada. Offers education (M Ed, MA, PhD); education of the environmental sciences (Diploma). PhD offered jointly with Université du Québec à Chicoutimi, Université du Québec à Rimouski, Université du Québec à Trois-Rivières, Université du Québec en Outaouais, and Université du Québec en Abitibi-Témiscamingue. Part-time programs available. *Degree requirements:* For master's, thesis (for some programs); for doctorate, thesis/dissertation. *Entrance requirements:* For master's and Diploma, appropriate bachelor's degree or equivalent, proficiency in French; for doctorate, appropriate master's degree or equivalent, proficiency in French.

Université du Québec à Rimouski, Graduate Programs, Program in Education, Rimouski, QC G5L 3A1, Canada. Offers M Ed, MA, PhD, Diploma. M Ed and MA offered jointly with Université du Québec en Outaouais and Université du Québec en Abitibi-Témiscamingue; PhD with Université du Québec à Chicoutimi, Université du Québec à Trois-Rivières, Université du Québec en Outaouais, and Université du Québec en Abitibi-Témiscamingue. Part-time programs available. *Degree requirements:* For master's, thesis optional; for doctorate, thesis/dissertation. *Entrance requirements:* For master's, appropriate bachelor's degree, proficiency in French; for doctorate, appropriate master's degree, proficiency in French.

Université du Québec à Trois-Rivières, Graduate Programs, Program in Education, Trois-Rivières, QC G9A 5H7, Canada. Offers M Ed, PhD. Part-time programs available. *Degree requirements:* For master's, research report. *Entrance requirements:* For master's, appropriate bachelor's degree, proficiency in French.

Université du Québec en Abitibi-Témiscamingue, Graduate Programs, Program in Education, Rouyn-Noranda, QC J9X 5E4, Canada. Offers M Ed, MA, PhD, DESS. M Ed and MA offered jointly with Université du Québec à Rimouski and Université du Québec en Outaouais; PhD with Université du Québec à Chicoutimi, Université du Québec à Rimouski, Université du Québec à Trois-Rivières, Université du Québec en Outaouais, and Université du Québec à Montréal. Part-time programs available. *Degree requirements:* For master's, thesis optional; for doctorate, thesis/dissertation. *Entrance requirements:* For master's, appropriate bachelor's degree, proficiency in French; for doctorate, appropriate master's degree, proficiency in French.

Université du Québec en Outaouais, Graduate Programs, Program in Education, Gatineau, QC J8X 3X7, Canada. Offers M Ed, MA, PhD, Diploma. Part-time programs available. *Students:* 42 full-time, 104 part-time. *Degree requirements:* For master's, thesis optional; for doctorate, thesis/dissertation. *Entrance requirements:* For master's, appropriate bachelor's degree, proficiency in French; for doctorate, appropriate master's degree, proficiency in French. *Application deadline:* For fall admission, 6/1 priority date for domestic students, 3/1 for international students; for winter admission, 11/1 priority date for domestic students, 10/1 for international students. Application fee: $30 Canadian dollars. *Financial support:* Fellowships, research assistantships, and teaching assistantships available. *Unit head:* Francine Sinclair, Director, 819-595-4415, Fax: 819-595-4459, E-mail: francine.sinclair@uqo.ca. *Application contact:* Registrar's Office, 819-773-1850, Fax: 819-773-1835, E-mail: registraire@ugo.ca.

Université Laval, Faculty of Education, Québec, QC G1K 7P4, Canada. Offers MA, PhD, Diploma. Part-time programs available. *Degree requirements:* For doctorate, comprehensive exam, thesis/dissertation. Electronic applications accepted.

University at Albany, State University of New York, School of Education, Albany, NY 12222-0001. Offers MA, MS, Ed D, PhD, Psy D, CAS. *Accreditation:* Teacher Education Accreditation Council. Part-time and evening/weekend programs available. *Degree requirements:* For doctorate, thesis/dissertation. *Entrance requirements:* For doctorate, GRE General Test. Additional exam requirements/recommendations for international students: Required—TOEFL (minimum score 550 paper-based; 213 computer-based). Electronic applications accepted.

University at Buffalo, the State University of New York, Graduate School, Graduate School of Education, Buffalo, NY 14260. Offers Ed M, MA, MLS, MS, Ed D, PhD, Advanced Certificate, Certificate, Certificate/Ed M. *Accreditation:* Teacher Education Accreditation Council. Part-time programs available. Postbaccalaureate distance learning degree programs offered (no on-campus study). *Faculty:* 77 full-time (52 women), 119 part-time/adjunct (90 women). *Students:* 642 full-time (484 women), 820 part-time (596 women); includes 198 minority (82 Black or African American, non-Hispanic/Latino; 11 American Indian or Alaska Native, non-Hispanic/Latino; 66 Asian, non-Hispanic/Latino; 39 Hispanic/Latino), 122 international. Average age 31. 1,336 applicants, 46% accepted, 561 enrolled. In 2011, 438 master's, 48 doctorates, 85 other advanced degrees awarded. Terminal master's awarded for partial completion of doctoral program. *Degree requirements:* For master's, comprehensive exam; for doctorate, thesis/dissertation. *Entrance requirements:* For master's, GRE General Test; for doctorate, GRE, MAT. Additional exam requirements/recommendations for international students: Required—TOEFL (minimum score 79 iBT). *Application deadline:* Applications are processed on a rolling basis. Application fee: $50. Electronic applications accepted. *Financial support:* In 2011–12, 100 fellowships (averaging $10,157 per year), 88 research assistantships (averaging $10,409 per year) were awarded; teaching assistantships with full tuition reimbursements, career-related internships or fieldwork, Federal Work-Study, institutionally sponsored loans, and unspecified assistantships also available. Financial award applicants required to submit FAFSA. *Faculty research:* Early childhood mathematics education, finance and management of higher education, curricular policy, practice and reform, student behavior in small classes, psychological measurement and assessment. *Unit head:* Dr. Mary H. Gresham, Dean, 716-645-6640, Fax: 716-645-2479, E-mail: gse-info@buffalo.edu. *Application contact:* Dr. Radhika Suresh, Director of Graduate Admissions and Student Services, 716-645-2110, Fax: 716-645-7937, E-mail: gse-info@buffalo.edu. Web site: http://www.gse.buffalo.edu/.

The University of Akron, Graduate School, College of Education, Akron, OH 44325. Offers MA, MS, Ed D, PhD. *Accreditation:* NCATE. Part-time programs available. *Faculty:* 59 full-time (41 women), 178 part-time/adjunct (108 women). *Students:* 490 full-time (310 women), 747 part-time (555 women); includes 180 minority (128 Black or African American, non-Hispanic/Latino; 12 Asian, non-Hispanic/Latino; 20 Hispanic/Latino; 1 Native Hawaiian or other Pacific Islander, non-Hispanic/Latino; 19 Two or more races, non-Hispanic/Latino), 33 international. Average age 33. 601 applicants, 54% accepted, 228 enrolled. In 2011, 429 master's, 7 doctorates awarded. Terminal master's awarded for partial completion of doctoral program. *Degree requirements:* For master's, comprehensive exam, thesis optional; for doctorate, one foreign language, comprehensive exam, thesis/dissertation, written and oral exams. *Entrance requirements:* For master's, letters of recommendation, resume, statement of purpose; for doctorate, GRE or MAT, minimum GPA of 3.25, writing sample, interview, letters of recommendation, curriculum vitae/resume, statement of purpose indicating nature of interest in the program and future career goals. Additional exam requirements/recommendations for international students: Required—TOEFL (minimum score 550 paper-based; 213 computer-based; 79 iBT). *Application deadline:* For fall admission, 3/1 for domestic and international students; for spring admission, 10/15 for domestic and international students. Applications are processed on a rolling basis. Application fee: $30 ($40 for international students). Electronic applications accepted. *Expenses:* Tuition, state resident: full-time $7038; part-time $391 per credit hour. Tuition, nonresident: full-time $12,051; part-time $670 per credit hour. *Required fees:* $1274; $34 per credit hour. *Financial support:* In 2011–12, 24 research assistantships with full tuition reimbursements, 97 teaching assistantships with full tuition reimbursements were awarded. *Faculty research:* History, philosophy of education, ethnographic research in education, case study methodology in education, multiple linear regression. *Total annual research expenditures:* $2.7 million. *Unit head:* Dr. Mark Shermis, Dean, 330-972-7680, E-mail: shermis@uakron.edu. *Application contact:* Dr. Evonn Welton, Associate Dean, 330-972-6742, E-mail: ewelton@uakron.edu. Web site: http://www.uakron.edu/education/.

The University of Alabama at Birmingham, College of Arts and Sciences, School of Education, Birmingham, AL 35294. Offers MA, MA Ed, Ed D, PhD, Ed S. *Accreditation:* NCATE. Part-time and evening/weekend programs available. *Degree requirements:* For master's, thesis optional; for doctorate, thesis/dissertation; for Ed S, comprehensive exam, thesis optional. *Entrance requirements:* For master's, GRE General Test, MAT, or NTE, minimum GPA of 3.0; for doctorate, GRE General Test, MAT, minimum GPA of 3.25; for Ed S, GRE General Test, MAT, minimum GPA of 3.0, master's degree. *Application deadline:* Applications are processed on a rolling basis. Electronic applications accepted. *Expenses:* Tuition, state resident: full-time $5922; part-time $309 per hour. Tuition, nonresident: full-time $13,428; part-time $726 per hour. Tuition and fees vary according to program. *Financial support:* Fellowships, career-related internships or fieldwork, and Federal Work-Study available. Support available to part-time students. *Unit head:* Dean's Office, 205-934-5332. Web site: http://www.uab.edu/educ/.

University of Alaska Anchorage, College of Education, Anchorage, AK 99508. Offers M Ed, MAT, Certificate. *Accreditation:* NCATE. Part-time programs available. *Degree requirements:* For master's, comprehensive exam, thesis or alternative, portfolio. *Entrance requirements:* For master's, interview, minimum GPA of 3.0. Additional exam requirements/recommendations for international students: Required—TOEFL (minimum score 550 paper-based; 213 computer-based).

University of Alaska Fairbanks, School of Education, Fairbanks, AK 99775. Offers counseling (M Ed), including counseling; education (M Ed, Graduate Certificate), including cross-cultural education (M Ed), curriculum and instruction (M Ed), education (M Ed), elementary education (M Ed), language and literacy (M Ed), reading (M Ed), secondary education (M Ed), special education (M Ed); guidance and counseling (M Ed). *Accreditation:* NCATE. Postbaccalaureate distance learning degree programs offered. *Faculty:* 26 full-time (15 women). *Students:* 61 full-time (46 women), 120 part-time (89 women); includes 35 minority (6 Black or African American, non-Hispanic/Latino; 10 American Indian or Alaska Native, non-Hispanic/Latino; 1 Asian, non-Hispanic/Latino; 8 Hispanic/Latino; 1 Native Hawaiian or other Pacific Islander, non-Hispanic/Latino; 9 Two or more races, non-Hispanic/Latino), 3 international. Average age 34. 111 applicants, 71% accepted, 62 enrolled. In 2011, 34 master's, 23 other advanced degrees awarded. *Degree requirements:* For master's, comprehensive exam, thesis or alternative, student teaching. *Entrance requirements:* For master's, GRE General Test, PRAXIS I, PRAXIS II, writing sample, evidence of technology competence, criminal background check. Additional exam requirements/ recommendations for international students: Required—TOEFL (minimum score 550 paper-based; 213 computer-based; 80 iBT). *Application deadline:* For fall admission, 3/1 for domestic and international students; for spring admission, 10/15 for domestic students, 9/1 for international students. Application fee: $60. Electronic applications accepted. *Expenses:* Tuition, state resident: full-time $6696; part-time $372 per credit. Tuition, nonresident: full-time $13,680; part-time $760 per credit. Tuition and fees vary according to course load and reciprocity agreements. *Financial support:* In 2011–12, 4 teaching assistantships with tuition reimbursements (averaging $13,330 per year) were awarded; fellowships with tuition reimbursements, research assistantships with tuition reimbursements, career-related internships or fieldwork, Federal Work-Study, scholarships/grants, health care benefits, and unspecified assistantships also available. Support available to part-time students. Financial award application deadline: 2/15; financial award applicants required to submit FAFSA. *Faculty research:* Native ways of knowing, classroom research in methods of literacy instruction, multiple intelligence theory, geometry concept development, mathematics and science curriculum development. *Total annual research expenditures:* $6,000. *Unit head:* Allan Morotti, Dean, 907-474-7341, Fax: 907-474-5451, E-mail: uaf-soe-school@alaska.edu. *Application contact:* Mike Earnest, Director of Admissions, 907-474-7500, Fax: 907-474-5379, E-mail: admissions@uaf.edu. Web site: http://www.uaf.edu/educ/.

University of Alaska Southeast, Graduate Programs, Program in Education, Juneau, AK 99801. Offers early childhood education (M Ed, MAT); educational technology (M Ed); elementary education (MAT); reading (M Ed); secondary education (MAT). *Accreditation:* NCATE. Part-time and evening/weekend programs available. Postbaccalaureate distance learning degree programs offered (minimal on-campus study). *Degree requirements:* For master's, comprehensive exam or project, portfolio. *Entrance requirements:* For master's, PRAXIS, minimum GPA of 3.0, writing sample, letters of recommendation. Electronic applications accepted. *Faculty research:* Applied classroom research, culturally responsive practices, action research, teaching effectiveness.

The University of Arizona, College of Education, Tucson, AZ 85721. Offers M Ed, MA, MS, Ed D, PhD, Ed S. Part-time programs available. Postbaccalaureate distance learning degree programs offered (no on-campus study). *Faculty:* 46 full-time (29 women), 1 (woman) part-time/adjunct. *Students:* 403 full-time (282 women), 210 part-time (158 women); includes 185 minority (28 Black or African American, non-Hispanic/ Latino; 7 American Indian or Alaska Native, non-Hispanic/Latino; 7 Asian, non-Hispanic/ Latino; 93 Hispanic/Latino; 2 Native Hawaiian or other Pacific Islander, non-Hispanic/ Latino; 48 Two or more races, non-Hispanic/Latino), 39 international. Average age 35. 399 applicants, 66% accepted, 177 enrolled. In 2011, 211 master's, 35 doctorates awarded. Terminal master's awarded for partial completion of doctoral program. *Degree requirements:* For master's, comprehensive exam, thesis (for some programs); for doctorate, comprehensive exam, thesis/dissertation. *Entrance requirements:* For doctorate, GRE. Additional exam requirements/recommendations for international students: Required—TOEFL (minimum score 550 paper-based; 213 computer-based; 79 iBT). *Application deadline:* For fall admission, 2/1 priority date for domestic students, 2/1 for international students; for spring admission, 10/1 priority date for domestic students, 9/1 for international students. Applications are processed on a rolling basis. Application fee: $75. Electronic applications accepted. *Expenses:* Tuition, state resident: full-time $10,840. Tuition, nonresident: full-time $25,802. *Financial support:* In 2011–12, 48 research assistantships with full tuition reimbursements (averaging $18,347 per year), 37 teaching assistantships with full tuition reimbursements (averaging $18,081 per year) were awarded; career-related internships or fieldwork, Federal Work-Study, institutionally sponsored loans, scholarships/grants, health care benefits, tuition waivers (full and partial), and unspecified assistantships also available. Support available to part-time students. Financial award application deadline: 3/1. *Faculty research:* Teacher effectiveness, pupil achievement, learning skills, program evaluation, instructional method effects. *Total annual research expenditures:* $13.6 million. *Unit head:* Dr. Ronald Marx, Dean, 520-621-1081, Fax: 520-621-9271, E-mail: ronmarx@email.arizona.edu. *Application contact:* General Information Contact, 520-621-3471, Fax: 520-621-4101, E-mail: gradadm@grad.arizona.edu. Web site: http://www.coe.arizona.edu.

University of Arkansas, Graduate School, College of Education and Health Professions, Fayetteville, AR 72701-1201. Offers M Ed, MAT, MAT, MS, MSN, Ed D, PhD, Ed S. *Accreditation:* NCATE. *Students:* 456 full-time (337 women), 568 part-time (390 women); includes 179 minority (104 Black or African American, non-Hispanic/ Latino; 14 American Indian or Alaska Native, non-Hispanic/Latino; 9 Asian, non-Hispanic/Latino; 28 Hispanic/Latino; 24 Two or more races, non-Hispanic/Latino), 41 international. In 2011, 330 master's, 47 doctorates, 5 other advanced degrees awarded. *Degree requirements:* For doctorate, thesis/dissertation. *Application deadline:* For fall admission, 4/1 for international students; for spring admission, 10/1 for international students. Applications are processed on a rolling basis. Application fee: $40 ($50 for international students). Electronic applications accepted. *Financial support:* In 2011–12, 110 research assistantships, 15 teaching assistantships were awarded; fellowships with tuition reimbursements, career-related internships or fieldwork, and Federal Work-Study also available. Support available to part-time students. Financial award application deadline: 4/1; financial award applicants required to submit FAFSA. *Unit head:* Dr. Thomas E. Smith, Dean, 479-575-3208, Fax: 479-575-3119, E-mail: tecsmith@uark.edu. *Application contact:* Graduate Admissions, 479-575-6246, Fax: 479-575-5908, E-mail: gradinfo@uark.edu. Web site: http://coehp.uark.edu/.

University of Arkansas at Little Rock, Graduate School, College of Education, Little Rock, AR 72204-1099. Offers M Ed, MA, Ed D, Ed S, Graduate Certificate. *Accreditation:* CORE; NCATE (one or more programs are accredited). Part-time and evening/weekend programs available. *Degree requirements:* For doctorate, comprehensive exam, oral defense of dissertation, residency; for other advanced degree, comprehensive exam. *Entrance requirements:* For master's, minimum GPA of 2.75; for doctorate, GRE General Test or MAT, minimum graduate GPA of 3.0, teaching certificate, work experience; for other advanced degree, GRE General Test or MAT, teaching certificate.

University of Arkansas at Monticello, School of Education, Monticello, AR 71656. Offers education (M Ed, MAT); educational leadership (M Ed). *Accreditation:* NCATE. Part-time and evening/weekend programs available. Postbaccalaureate distance learning degree programs offered (minimal on-campus study). *Degree requirements:* For master's, comprehensive exam. *Entrance requirements:* For master's, minimum GPA of 3.0. Additional exam requirements/recommendations for international students: Required—TOEFL (minimum score 550 paper-based; 213 computer-based). Electronic applications accepted.

University of Arkansas at Pine Bluff, School of Education, Pine Bluff, AR 71601-2799. Offers early childhood education (M Ed); secondary education (M Ed), including English education, mathematics education, physical education, science education, social studies education; teaching (MAT). *Accreditation:* NCATE. Part-time and evening/weekend programs available. *Degree requirements:* For master's, comprehensive exam. *Entrance requirements:* For master's, GRE, minimum GPA of 2.75, NTE or Standard Arkansas Teaching Certificate. *Faculty research:* Teacher certification, accreditation, assessment, standards, portfolio development, rehabilitation, technology.

University of Bridgeport, School of Education, Department of Education, Bridgeport, CT 06604. Offers education (MS); educational management (Ed D, Diploma), including intermediate administrator or supervisor (Diploma), leadership (Ed D); elementary education (MS, Diploma), including early childhood education, elementary education; middle school education (MS); music education (MS); remedial reading and language arts (Diploma); secondary education (MS, Diploma), including computer specialist (Diploma), international education (Diploma), reading specialist, secondary education. Part-time and evening/weekend programs available. *Faculty:* 12 full-time (5 women), 108 part-time/adjunct (60 women). *Students:* 232 full-time (161 women), 216 part-time (160 women); includes 61 minority (21 Black or African American, non-Hispanic/Latino; 8 Asian, non-Hispanic/Latino; 22 Hispanic/Latino; 10 Two or more races, non-Hispanic/ Latino), 34 international. Average age 30. 412 applicants, 63% accepted, 147 enrolled. In 2011, 216 master's, 7 other advanced degrees awarded. *Degree requirements:* For master's, final exam, final project, or thesis; for doctorate, comprehensive exam, thesis/ dissertation; for Diploma, thesis or alternative, final project. *Entrance requirements:* For master's, minimum undergraduate QPA of 2.67; for doctorate, GRE, MAT; for Diploma, GRE General Test or MAT, minimum graduate QPA of 3.0. Additional exam requirements/recommendations for international students: Recommended—TOEFL (minimum score 550 paper-based; 213 computer-based; 80 iBT), IELTS (minimum score 6.5). *Application deadline:* For fall admission, 8/1 priority date for domestic students, 8/1 for international students; for spring admission, 12/1 priority date for domestic students, 12/1 for international students. Applications are processed on a rolling basis. Application fee: $50. Electronic applications accepted. *Expenses: Tuition:* Full-time $22,880; part-time $700 per credit. *Required fees:* $1870; $95 per semester. Tuition and fees vary according to course load and program. *Financial support:* In 2011–12, 120 students received support. Fellowships, research assistantships, teaching assistantships, career-related internships or fieldwork, Federal Work-Study, and institutionally sponsored loans available. Support available to part-time students. Financial award application deadline: 6/1; financial award applicants required to submit FAFSA. *Faculty research:* Self-concept, internship assessment, stress and situational development, follow-up of graduation, trend analysis. *Unit head:* Dr. Allen P. Cook, Dean, 203-576-4192, Fax: 203-576-4200, E-mail: acook@bridgeport.edu. *Application contact:* Karissa Peckham, Dean of Admissions, 203-576-4552, Fax: 203-576-4941, E-mail: admit@bridgeport.edu.

The University of British Columbia, Faculty of Education, Vancouver, BC V6T1Z4, Canada. Offers M Ed, M Sc, MA, MET, MHK, Ed D, PhD, Diploma. Part-time and evening/weekend programs available. Postbaccalaureate distance learning degree programs offered (no on-campus study). Terminal master's awarded for partial completion of doctoral program. *Degree requirements:* For master's, thesis (for some programs); for doctorate, comprehensive exam, thesis/dissertation. *Entrance requirements:* Additional exam requirements/recommendations for international students: Required—TOEFL. Electronic applications accepted. *Expenses:* Contact institution. *Faculty research:* Curriculum and pedagogy; school counseling psychology; educational administration; human kinetics; language and literacy education.

University of California, Berkeley, Graduate Division, School of Education, Berkeley, CA 94720-1500. Offers MA, PhD, MA/Credential, PhD/Credential, PhD/MA. Terminal master's awarded for partial completion of doctoral program. *Degree requirements:* For master's, exam or thesis; for doctorate, thesis/dissertation, oral qualifying exam (PhD). *Entrance requirements:* For master's and doctorate, GRE General Test, minimum undergraduate GPA of 3.0 during last 2 years, 3 letters of recommendation. *Faculty research:* Cognition and development; language, literacy and culture.

University of California, Berkeley, UC Berkeley Extension, Certificate Programs in Education, Berkeley, CA 94720-1500. Offers college admissions and career planning (Certificate); teaching English as a second language (Certificate).

University of California, Davis, Graduate Studies, Graduate Group in Education, Davis, CA 95616. Offers education (MA, Ed D); instructional studies (PhD); psychological studies (PhD); sociocultural studies (PhD). Ed D offered jointly with California State University, Fresno. Terminal master's awarded for partial completion of doctoral program. *Degree requirements:* For master's, comprehensive exam (for some programs), thesis (for some programs); for doctorate, thesis/dissertation. *Entrance requirements:* For master's and doctorate, GRE. Additional exam requirements/ recommendations for international students: Required—TOEFL (minimum score 550 paper-based; 213 computer-based). Electronic applications accepted. *Faculty research:* Language and literacy, mathematics education, science education, teacher development, school psychology.

University of California, Irvine, Department of Education, Irvine, CA 92697. Offers educational administration (Ed D); educational administration and leadership (Ed D); elementary and secondary education (MAT). Part-time and evening/weekend programs available. *Students:* 246 full-time (185 women), 8 part-time (5 women); includes 121 minority (4 Black or African American, non-Hispanic/Latino; 1 American Indian or Alaska Native, non-Hispanic/Latino; 65 Asian, non-Hispanic/Latino; 37 Hispanic/Latino; 2 Native Hawaiian or other Pacific Islander, non-Hispanic/Latino; 12 Two or more races, non-Hispanic/Latino), 7 international. Average age 28. 455 applicants, 75% accepted, 185 enrolled. In 2011, 146 master's, 12 doctorates awarded. *Degree requirements:* For doctorate, thesis/dissertation. *Entrance requirements:* For master's, GRE, minimum GPA of 3.0; for doctorate, GRE General Test, minimum GPA of 3.0. Additional exam requirements/recommendations for international students: Required—TOEFL (minimum score 550 paper-based; 213 computer-based). *Application deadline:* For fall admission, 1/2 priority date for domestic students, 1/2 for international students. Application fee: $80 ($100 for international students). Electronic applications accepted. *Financial support:* Fellowships, research assistantships with full tuition reimbursements, institutionally sponsored loans, traineeships, health care benefits, and unspecified assistantships available. Financial award application deadline: 3/1; financial award applicants required to submit FAFSA. *Faculty research:* Education technology, learning theory, social theory, cultural diversity, postmodernism. *Unit head:* Deborah L. Vandell, Chair, 949-824-8026, Fax: 949-824-3968, E-mail: dvandell@uci.edu. *Application contact:* Sarah K. Singh, Credential Program Counselor, 949-824-6673, Fax: 949-824-9103, E-mail: sksingh@uci.edu. Web site: http://www.gse.uci.edu/.

University of California, Los Angeles, Graduate Division, Graduate School of Education and Information Studies, Department of Education, Los Angeles, CA 90095. Offers M Ed, MA, Ed D, PhD. Evening/weekend programs available. *Degree requirements:* For master's, comprehensive exam; for doctorate, thesis/dissertation, oral and written qualifying exams. *Entrance requirements:* For master's, GRE General Test, minimum GPA of 3.0; for doctorate, GRE General Test, minimum undergraduate GPA of 3.0. Additional exam requirements/recommendations for international students: Required—TOEFL (minimum score 560 paper-based; 220 computer-based; 87 iBT). Electronic applications accepted.

Education—General

University of California, Riverside, Graduate Division, Graduate School of Education, Riverside, CA 92521-0102. Offers autism (M Ed); diversity and equity (M Ed); education, society and culture (MA, PhD); educational psychology (MA, PhD); general education (M Ed); higher education administration and policy (M Ed, PhD); reading (M Ed); school psychology (PhD); special education (M Ed, MA, PhD). *Faculty:* 19 full-time (9 women), 9 part-time/adjunct (6 women). *Students:* 181 full-time (128 women); includes 79 minority (8 Black or African American, non-Hispanic/Latino; 1 American Indian or Alaska Native, non-Hispanic/Latino; 26 Asian, non-Hispanic/Latino; 34 Hispanic/Latino; 10 Two or more races, non-Hispanic/Latino), 5 international. Average age 31. 200 applicants, 48% accepted, 76 enrolled. In 2011, 67 master's, 12 doctorates awarded. Terminal master's awarded for partial completion of doctoral program. *Degree requirements:* For master's, thesis optional, comprehensive exams or thesis (MA), case study or analytical report (M Ed); for doctorate, thesis/dissertation, written and oral qualifying exams, college teaching practicum. *Entrance requirements:* For master's, GRE General Test, CBEST, CSET, minimum GPA of 3.2; for doctorate, GRE General Test, master's degree (desirable), minimum GPA of 3.2. Additional exam requirements/recommendations for international students: Required—TOEFL (minimum score 550 paper-based; 213 computer-based; 80 iBT), IELTS (minimum score 7). *Application deadline:* For fall admission, 9/1 for domestic students, 4/1 for international students; for winter admission, 12/1 for domestic students, 7/1 for international students; for spring admission, 3/1 for domestic students, 10/1 for international students. Applications are processed on a rolling basis. Application fee: $80 ($100 for international students). Electronic applications accepted. *Financial support:* In 2011–12, 59 students received support, including 9 fellowships with full and partial tuition reimbursements available (averaging $26,587 per year), 21 research assistantships with full and partial tuition reimbursements available (averaging $14,517 per year), 1 teaching assistantship with full and partial tuition reimbursement available (averaging $17,307 per year); career-related internships or fieldwork, Federal Work-Study, institutionally sponsored loans, scholarships/grants, and unspecified assistantships also available. Financial award application deadline: 1/5. *Faculty research:* Responsiveness to intervention, faculty core, response to intervention of English language learners, advanced modeling techniques, study on social capital, trust, and motivation. *Total annual research expenditures:* $2.8 million. *Unit head:* Prof. Douglas Mitchell, Interim Dean, 951-827-5802, Fax: 951-827-3942, E-mail: douglas.mitchell@ucr.edu. *Application contact:* Prof. Robert Ream, Graduate Advisor for Admission, 951-827-6362, Fax: 951-827-3291, E-mail: edgrad@ucr.edu. Web site: http://www.education.ucr.edu/.

University of California, San Diego, Office of Graduate Studies, Program in Teacher Education, La Jolla, CA 92093. Offers bilingual education (MA); curriculum design (MA); teacher education (M Ed); teaching and learning (Ed D). *Entrance requirements:* For master's, GRE General Test. Electronic applications accepted.

University of California, Santa Barbara, Graduate Division, Gevirtz Graduate School of Education, Santa Barbara, CA 93106-9490. Offers counseling, clinical and school psychology (M Ed, MA, PhD, Credential), including clinical psychology (PhD), counseling psychology (MA, PhD), school psychology (M Ed, PhD), school psychology: pupil personnel services (Credential); education (M Ed, MA, PhD, Credential), including child and adolescent development (MA, PhD), cultural perspectives and comparative education (MA, PhD), educational leadership and organizations (MA, PhD), multiple subject teaching (Credential), research methodology (MA, PhD), single subject teaching (Credential), special education (Credential), special education disabilities and risk studies (MA), special education, disabilities and risk studies (PhD), teaching (M Ed), teaching and learning (MA, PhD); MA/PhD. *Accreditation:* APA (one or more programs are accredited). *Faculty:* 40 full-time (21 women), 2 part-time/adjunct (both women). *Students:* 389 full-time (301 women); includes 131 minority (14 Black or African American, non-Hispanic/Latino; 2 American Indian or Alaska Native, non-Hispanic/Latino; 41 Asian, non-Hispanic/Latino; 69 Hispanic/Latino; 1 Native Hawaiian or other Pacific Islander, non-Hispanic/Latino; 4 Two or more races, non-Hispanic/Latino), 25 international. Average age 28. 691 applicants, 35% accepted, 154 enrolled. In 2011, 145 master's, 45 doctorates, 118 other advanced degrees awarded. Terminal master's awarded for partial completion of doctoral program. *Degree requirements:* For master's, comprehensive exam (for some programs), thesis (for some programs); for doctorate, comprehensive exam (for some programs), thesis/dissertation; for Credential, CA state requirements (varies by credential). *Entrance requirements:* For master's and doctorate, GRE; for Credential, GRE or MAT, CSET and CBEST. Additional exam requirements/recommendations for international students: Required—TOEFL (minimum score 550 paper-based; 80 iBT), IELTS (minimum score 7). Application fee: $80 ($100 for international students). Electronic applications accepted. *Expenses:* Tuition, state resident: full-time $12,192. Tuition, nonresident: full-time $27,294. *Required fees:* $764.13. *Financial support:* In 2011–12, 301 students received support, including 429 fellowships with partial tuition reimbursements available (averaging $5,017 per year), 83 research assistantships with full and partial tuition reimbursements available (averaging $6,262 per year), 55 teaching assistantships with partial tuition reimbursements available (averaging $8,655 per year); career-related internships or fieldwork also available. Financial award applicants required to submit FAFSA. *Faculty research:* Needs of diverse students, school accountability and leadership, school violence, language learning and literacy, science/math education. *Total annual research expenditures:* $3 million. *Unit head:* Arlis Markel, Assistant Dean, 805-893-5492, Fax: 805-893-2588, E-mail: arlis@education.ucsb.edu. *Application contact:* Kathryn Marie Tucciarone, Student Affairs Officer, 805-893-2137, Fax: 805-893-2588, E-mail: katiet@education.ucsb.edu. Web site: http://www.education.ucsb.edu/.

University of California, Santa Cruz, Division of Graduate Studies, Division of Social Sciences, Department of Education, Santa Cruz, CA 95064. Offers MA, PhD. Terminal master's awarded for partial completion of doctoral program. *Degree requirements:* For master's, thesis; for doctorate, thesis/dissertation. *Entrance requirements:* Additional exam requirements/recommendations for international students: Required—TOEFL (minimum score 550 paper-based; 220 computer-based; 83 iBT); Recommended—IELTS (minimum score 8). Electronic applications accepted. *Faculty research:* Bilingual/multicultural education, special education, curriculum and instruction, child development, gaps in the learning opportunities of underserved students, discovery of more effective practices.

University of Central Arkansas, Graduate School, College of Education, Conway, AR 72035-0001. Offers MAT, MS, MSE, Ed S. *Accreditation:* NCATE. Part-time programs available. *Students:* 104 full-time (74 women), 428 part-time (348 women); includes 89 minority (58 Black or African American, non-Hispanic/Latino; 8 American Indian or Alaska Native, non-Hispanic/Latino; 5 Asian, non-Hispanic/Latino; 11 Hispanic/Latino; 7 Two or more races, non-Hispanic/Latino), 5 international. Average age 33. 173 applicants, 98% accepted, 131 enrolled. In 2011, 2,138 master's awarded. Terminal master's awarded for partial completion of doctoral program. *Degree requirements:* For master's, comprehensive exam, thesis optional, portfolio. *Entrance requirements:* For master's, GRE General Test, minimum GPA of 2.7. Additional exam requirements/recommendations for international students: Required—TOEFL (minimum score 550 paper-based; 213 computer-based). *Application deadline:* For fall admission, 3/1 priority date for domestic students, 3/1 for international students; for spring admission, 10/1 priority date for domestic students, 10/1 for international students. Applications are processed on a rolling basis. Application fee: $25 ($50 for international students). *Expenses:* Tuition, state resident: full-time $4834; part-time $398.35 per credit hour. Tuition, nonresident: full-time $8686. *Financial support:* Career-related internships or fieldwork, Federal Work-Study, scholarships/grants, tuition waivers (partial), and unspecified assistantships available. Financial award application deadline: 2/15; financial award applicants required to submit FAFSA. *Unit head:* Dr. Diana Pounder, Interim Dean, 501-450-5401, Fax: 501-450-5424, E-mail: dpounder@uca.edu. *Application contact:* Susan Wood, Administrative Specialist, 501-450-3124, Fax: 501-450-5678, E-mail: swood@uca.edu.

University of Central Arkansas, Graduate School, College of Education, Department of Teaching and Learning, Graduate Program in Teaching, Conway, AR 72035-0001. Offers MAT. Part-time programs available. Postbaccalaureate distance learning degree programs offered (minimal on-campus study). *Students:* 54 full-time (41 women), 210 part-time (161 women); includes 42 minority (27 Black or African American, non-Hispanic/Latino; 2 American Indian or Alaska Native, non-Hispanic/Latino; 3 Asian, non-Hispanic/Latino; 6 Hispanic/Latino; 4 Two or more races, non-Hispanic/Latino), 1 international. Average age 31. 78 applicants, 97% accepted, 56 enrolled. In 2011, 83 master's awarded. *Degree requirements:* For master's, comprehensive exam, thesis optional. *Entrance requirements:* For master's, GRE General Test, minimum GPA of 2.7. Additional exam requirements/recommendations for international students: Required—TOEFL (minimum score 550 paper-based; 213 computer-based). *Application deadline:* For fall admission, 3/1 priority date for domestic students, 3/1 for international students; for spring admission, 10/1 priority date for domestic students, 10/1 for international students. Applications are processed on a rolling basis. Application fee: $25 ($50 for international students). *Expenses:* Tuition, state resident: full-time $4834; part-time $398.35 per credit hour. Tuition, nonresident: full-time $8686. *Financial support:* Federal Work-Study, scholarships/grants, and unspecified assistantships available. Financial award application deadline: 2/15; financial award applicants required to submit FAFSA. *Unit head:* Tammy Benson, Unit Head, 501-450-5462. *Application contact:* Sandy Burks, Administrative Specialist, 501-450-3124, Fax: 501-450-5678, E-mail: slburks@uca.edu.

University of Central Arkansas, Graduate School, College of Education, Department of Teaching and Learning, Program in Advanced Studies of Teaching and Learning, Conway, AR 72035-0001. Offers MSE. *Students:* 11 part-time (all women); includes 4 minority (all Black or African American, non-Hispanic/Latino). Average age 29. 5 applicants, 80% accepted, 2 enrolled. In 2011, 13 master's awarded. *Entrance requirements:* For master's, GRE General Test, minimum GPA of 2.7. Additional exam requirements/recommendations for international students: Required—TOEFL (minimum score 550 paper-based; 213 computer-based). *Application deadline:* For fall admission, 3/1 priority date for domestic students, 3/1 for international students; for spring admission, 10/1 priority date for domestic students, 10/1 for international students. Applications are processed on a rolling basis. Application fee: $25 ($50 for international students). *Expenses:* Tuition, state resident: full-time $4834; part-time $398.35 per credit hour. Tuition, nonresident: full-time $8686. *Financial support:* Federal Work-Study, scholarships/grants, and unspecified assistantships available. Financial award application deadline: 2/15; financial award applicants required to submit FAFSA. *Unit head:* Jeff Whittingham, 501-450-5445, E-mail: jwhittingham@uca.edu. *Application contact:* Sandy Burks, Admissions Assistant, 501-450-3124, Fax: 501-450-5678, E-mail: slburks@uca.edu.

University of Central Missouri, The Graduate School, College of Education, Warrensburg, MO 64093. Offers career and technical education administration (MS); career and technical education industry training (MS); career and technical education leadership/teaching (MS); college student personnel administration (MS); counseling (MS); curriculum and instruction (Ed S); educational leadership (Ed D); educational technology (MS); elementary education/educational foundations and literacy (MSE); elementary school administration (MSE); elementary school principalship (Ed S); human services/learning resources (Ed S); human services/professional counseling (Ed S); human services/special education (Ed S); human services/technology and occupational education (Ed S); K-12 education/educational foundations and literacy (MSE); K-12 special education (MSE); library science and information services (MS); literacy education (MSE); secondary education/educational foundations & literacy (MSE); secondary school administration (MSE); secondary school principalship (Ed S); superintendency (Ed S); teaching (MAT). Ed D offered jointly with University of Missouri. Part-time programs available. Postbaccalaureate distance learning degree programs offered. *Entrance requirements:* Additional exam requirements/recommendations for international students: Required—TOEFL (minimum score 550 paper-based; 79 computer-based). Electronic applications accepted.

University of Central Oklahoma, College of Graduate Studies and Research, College of Education and Professional Studies, Edmond, OK 73034-5209. Offers M Ed, MA, MS. *Accreditation:* NCATE. Part-time programs available. *Faculty:* 69 full-time (45 women), 48 part-time/adjunct (30 women). *Students:* 283 full-time (228 women), 671 part-time (562 women); includes 213 minority (95 Black or African American, non-Hispanic/Latino; 31 American Indian or Alaska Native, non-Hispanic/Latino; 10 Asian, non-Hispanic/Latino; 43 Hispanic/Latino; 2 Native Hawaiian or other Pacific Islander, non-Hispanic/Latino; 32 Two or more races, non-Hispanic/Latino), 68 international. Average age 36. In 2011, 312 master's awarded. *Entrance requirements:* For master's, GRE General Test. Additional exam requirements/recommendations for international students: Required—TOEFL (minimum score 550 paper-based; 213 computer-based). *Application deadline:* For fall admission, 7/1 for international students; for spring admission, 11/1 for international students. Applications are processed on a rolling basis. Application fee: $50. Electronic applications accepted. *Expenses:* Tuition, state resident: full-time $3901; part-time $218.30 per credit hour. Tuition, nonresident: full-time $9198; part-time $511.20 per credit hour. Tuition and fees vary according to program. *Financial support:* Career-related internships or fieldwork and unspecified assistantships available. Financial award application deadline: 3/31; financial award applicants required to submit FAFSA. *Unit head:* Dr. James Machell, Dean, 405-974-5701, Fax: 405-974-3851. *Application contact:* Dr. Richard Bernard, Dean, Jackson College of Graduate Studies, 405-974-3493, Fax: 405-974-3852, E-mail: gradcoll@uco.edu. Web site: http://www.uco.edu/ceps/.

University of Cincinnati, Graduate School, College of Education, Criminal Justice, and Human Services, Cincinnati, OH 45221. Offers M Ed, MA, MS, Ed D, PhD, CAGS, Certificate, Ed S. *Accreditation:* NCATE. Part-time programs available. Postbaccalaureate distance learning degree programs offered (no on-campus study). *Degree requirements:* For master's, comprehensive exam (for some programs), thesis (for some programs); for doctorate, comprehensive exam, thesis/dissertation. *Entrance requirements:* For master's and doctorate, GRE. Additional exam requirements/recommendations for international students: Required—TOEFL (minimum score 550 paper-based), OEPT 3. Electronic applications accepted. *Faculty research:* Alcohol and drug prevention, family-based prevention, criminal justice, literacy, urban education.

University of Colorado at Colorado Springs, College of Education, Colorado Springs, CO 80933-7150. Offers counseling and human services (MA); curriculum and instruction (MA); educational administration (MA); educational leadership (MA, PhD); special education (MA). *Accreditation:* ACA; NCATE. Part-time and evening/weekend programs available. Postbaccalaureate distance learning degree programs offered (minimal on-campus study). *Faculty:* 26 full-time (16 women), 9 part-time/adjunct (5 women). *Students:* 307 full-time (203 women), 115 part-time (92 women); includes 82 minority (24 Black or African American, non-Hispanic/Latino; 3 American Indian or Alaska Native, non-Hispanic/Latino; 12 Asian, non-Hispanic/Latino; 36 Hispanic/Latino; 1 Native Hawaiian or other Pacific Islander, non-Hispanic/Latino; 6 Two or more races, non-Hispanic/Latino), 1 international. Average age 36. 99 applicants, 86% accepted, 61 enrolled. In 2011, 165 master's, 6 doctorates awarded. *Degree requirements:* For master's, comprehensive exam, thesis or alternative, microcomputer proficiency; for doctorate, comprehensive exam, thesis/dissertation, research lab. *Entrance requirements:* For master's, GRE General Test. Additional exam requirements/recommendations for international students: Recommended—TOEFL. *Application deadline:* For fall admission, 2/28 priority date for domestic students, 2/28 for international students; for spring admission, 10/15 for domestic and international students. Applications are processed on a rolling basis. Application fee: $60 ($75 for international students). *Expenses:* Tuition, state resident: part-time $660 per credit hour. Tuition, nonresident: part-time $1133 per credit hour. Tuition and fees vary according to degree level, program and student level. *Financial support:* In 2011–12, 57 students received support. Career-related internships or fieldwork, Federal Work-Study, and scholarships/grants available. Support available to part-time students. Financial award application deadline: 3/1; financial award applicants required to submit FAFSA. *Faculty research:* Job training for special populations, materials development for classroom. *Total annual research expenditures:* $1.6 million. *Unit head:* Dr. Mary Snyder, Dean, 719-255-3701, Fax: 719-262-4133, E-mail: msnyder3@uccs.edu. *Application contact:* Juliane Field, Director, 719-255-4526, Fax: 719-255-4110, E-mail: jfield@uccs.edu. Web site: http://www.uccs.edu/coe.

University of Colorado Boulder, Graduate School, School of Education, Boulder, CO 80309. Offers MA, PhD. *Accreditation:* NCATE. *Faculty:* 28 full-time (15 women). *Students:* 204 full-time (143 women), 136 part-time (114 women); includes 85 minority (7 Black or African American, non-Hispanic/Latino; 2 American Indian or Alaska Native, non-Hispanic/Latino; 14 Asian, non-Hispanic/Latino; 58 Hispanic/Latino; 4 Two or more races, non-Hispanic/Latino), 4 international. Average age 33. 268 applicants, 52% accepted, 74 enrolled. In 2011, 161 master's, 17 doctorates awarded. Terminal master's awarded for partial completion of doctoral program. *Degree requirements:* For master's, comprehensive exam, thesis or alternative; for doctorate, one foreign language, comprehensive exam, thesis/dissertation. *Entrance requirements:* For master's, GRE General Test or MAT, minimum undergraduate GPA of 2.75; for doctorate, GRE General Test. *Application deadline:* For fall admission, 2/1 priority date for domestic students, 12/1 for international students; for spring admission, 9/1 for domestic students, 12/1 for international students. Application fee: $50 ($60 for international students). Electronic applications accepted. *Financial support:* In 2011–12, 298 students received support, including 188 fellowships (averaging $5,021 per year), 56 research assistantships with full and partial tuition reimbursements available (averaging $16,283 per year), 62 teaching assistantships with full and partial tuition reimbursements available (averaging $13,770 per year); institutionally sponsored loans, scholarships/grants, health care benefits, and unspecified assistantships also available. Financial award applicants required to submit FAFSA. *Total annual research expenditures:* $6.7 million. *Application contact:* E-mail: gradinfo@colorado.edu. Web site: http://www.colorado.edu/education/.

University of Colorado Denver, School of Education and Human Development, Denver, CO 80217. Offers MA, Ed D, PhD, Ed S. *Accreditation:* NCATE. Part-time and evening/weekend programs available. Postbaccalaureate distance learning degree programs offered (no on-campus study). *Faculty:* 63 full-time (44 women), 97 part-time/adjunct (73 women). *Students:* 1,003 full-time (803 women), 453 part-time (383 women); includes 168 minority (29 Black or African American, non-Hispanic/Latino; 3 American Indian or Alaska Native, non-Hispanic/Latino; 35 Asian, non-Hispanic/Latino; 97 Hispanic/Latino; 4 Two or more races, non-Hispanic/Latino), 22 international. Average age 34. 455 applicants, 78% accepted, 203 enrolled. In 2011, 533 master's, 11 doctorates, 45 other advanced degrees awarded. *Degree requirements:* For master's and Ed S, comprehensive exam (for some programs); for doctorate, comprehensive exam, thesis/dissertation. *Entrance requirements:* Additional exam requirements/recommendations for international students: Required—TOEFL (minimum score 525 paper-based; 197 computer-based). Application fee: $50 ($75 for international students). Electronic applications accepted. *Expenses:* Contact institution. *Financial support:* In 2011–12, 49 students received support. Fellowships, research assistantships, teaching assistantships, Federal Work-Study, scholarships/grants, and unspecified assistantships available. Support available to part-time students. Financial award application deadline: 4/1; financial award applicants required to submit FAFSA. *Faculty research:* Educational equity: race, class, culture, power and privilege; analytic approaches to educational program effectiveness and measuring student learning; early childhood special education/early intervention policies; recruiting and retention of African-American teachers; secondary and postsecondary institutions; accountability systems to improve public education. *Total annual research expenditures:* $4.8 million. *Unit head:* Rebecca Kantor, Dean, 303-315-6343, E-mail: rebecca.kantor@ucdenver.edu. *Application contact:* Student Services Center, 303-315-6300, Fax: 303-315-6311, E-mail: education@ucdenver.edu. Web site: http://www.ucdenver.edu/academics/colleges/SchoolOfEducation/Pages/Home.aspx.

University of Connecticut, Graduate School, Neag School of Education, Storrs, CT 06269. Offers MA, DPT, Ed D, PhD, Post-Master's Certificate. *Accreditation:* NCATE. Terminal master's awarded for partial completion of doctoral program. *Degree requirements:* For master's, comprehensive exam, thesis or alternative; for doctorate, thesis/dissertation. *Entrance requirements:* For doctorate, GRE General Test. Additional exam requirements/recommendations for international students: Required—TOEFL (minimum score 550 paper-based; 213 computer-based). Electronic applications accepted.

University of Delaware, College of Education and Human Development, School of Education, Newark, DE 19716. Offers education (PhD); educational leadership (Ed D); higher education (M Ed); instruction (MI); reading (M Ed); school leadership (M Ed); school psychology (MA, Ed S); teaching English as a second language (TESL) (MA). *Accreditation:* NCATE. Part-time and evening/weekend programs available. Terminal master's awarded for partial completion of doctoral program. *Degree requirements:* For master's, comprehensive exam (for some programs), thesis (for some programs); for doctorate, comprehensive exam (for some programs), thesis/dissertation. *Entrance requirements:* For master's and doctorate, GRE, 3 letters of recommendation. Additional exam requirements/recommendations for international students: Required—TOEFL (minimum score 600 paper-based; 250 computer-based). Electronic applications accepted. *Faculty research:* Teacher education; curriculum theory and development; community based education models, educational leadership.

University of Denver, Morgridge College of Education, Denver, CO 80208. Offers advanced study in law librarianship (Certificate); child and family studies (MA, PhD); counseling psychology (MA, PhD); curriculum and instruction (MA, PhD, Certificate); educational leadership (Ed D, PhD); educational leadership and policy studies (MA, Certificate); higher education (MA, PhD); library and information science (MLIS); research methods and statistics (MA, PhD); school administration (PhD); school psychology (Ed S). *Accreditation:* ALA; APA (one or more programs are accredited). Part-time and evening/weekend programs available. Postbaccalaureate distance learning degree programs offered (no on-campus study). *Faculty:* 34 full-time (25 women), 70 part-time/adjunct (54 women). *Students:* 385 full-time (289 women), 386 part-time (303 women); includes 168 minority (49 Black or African American, non-Hispanic/Latino; 8 American Indian or Alaska Native, non-Hispanic/Latino; 25 Asian, non-Hispanic/Latino; 71 Hispanic/Latino; 1 Native Hawaiian or other Pacific Islander, non-Hispanic/Latino; 14 Two or more races, non-Hispanic/Latino), 17 international. Average age 33. 668 applicants, 72% accepted, 256 enrolled. In 2011, 308 master's, 43 doctorates, 55 other advanced degrees awarded. Terminal master's awarded for partial completion of doctoral program. *Degree requirements:* For master's, comprehensive exam; for doctorate, 2 foreign languages, comprehensive exam, thesis/dissertation. *Entrance requirements:* For master's and doctorate, GRE General Test or GMAT. Additional exam requirements/recommendations for international students: Required—TOEFL (minimum score 550 paper-based; 80 iBT). *Application deadline:* Applications are processed on a rolling basis. Application fee: $60. Electronic applications accepted. *Financial support:* In 2011–12, 72 teaching assistantships with full and partial tuition reimbursements (averaging $9,049 per year) were awarded; career-related internships or fieldwork, Federal Work-Study, institutionally sponsored loans, scholarships/grants, and unspecified assistantships also available. Support available to part-time students. Financial award application deadline: 2/15; financial award applicants required to submit FAFSA. *Faculty research:* Parkinson's disease, personnel training, development and assessments, gifted education, service-learning, transportation, public schools. *Unit head:* Dr. Gregory M. Anderson, Dean, 303-871-3665, E-mail: gregory.m.anderson@du.edu. *Application contact:* Chris Dowen, Director, MCE Admission Office, 303-871-2783, E-mail: chris.dowen@du.edu. Web site: http://www.du.edu/education/.

University of Detroit Mercy, College of Liberal Arts and Education, Department of Education, Detroit, MI 48221. Offers curriculum and instruction (MA); educational administration (MA); special education (MA), including emotionally impaired, learning disabilities. Part-time and evening/weekend programs available.

University of Evansville, College of Education and Health Sciences, School of Education, Evansville, IN 47722. Offers MS Ed. Postbaccalaureate distance learning degree programs offered (minimal on-campus study). *Degree requirements:* For master's, thesis, research/inquiry project. *Entrance requirements:* For master's, GRE (minimum combined score of 1,000) or MAT (minimum scaled score of 400), bachelor's degree from regionally-accredited college or university; 500-word statement of educational purpose; minimum undergraduate GPA of 3.0; current valid teaching license; interview. *Expenses:* Contact institution.

The University of Findlay, Graduate and Professional Studies, College of Education, Findlay, OH 45840-3653. Offers administration (MA Ed); children's literature (MA Ed); early childhood (MA Ed); human resource development (MA Ed); reading endorsement (MA Ed); science (MA Ed); special education (MA Ed); technology (MA Ed). *Accreditation:* NCATE. Part-time and evening/weekend programs available. Postbaccalaureate distance learning degree programs offered (no on-campus study). *Faculty:* 16 full-time (12 women), 5 part-time/adjunct (2 women). *Students:* 72 full-time (49 women), 198 part-time (119 women); includes 10 minority (7 Black or African American, non-Hispanic/Latino; 1 Asian, non-Hispanic/Latino; 2 Hispanic/Latino), 16 international. Average age 30. 75 applicants, 88% accepted, 36 enrolled. In 2011, 76 master's awarded. *Degree requirements:* For master's, thesis, cumulative project. *Entrance requirements:* For master's, bachelor's degree from accredited institution, minimum undergraduate GPA of 2.75 in last 62 hours of course work. Additional exam requirements/recommendations for international students: Required—TOEFL (minimum score 550 paper-based; 213 computer-based; 80 iBT). *Application deadline:* Applications are processed on a rolling basis. Application fee: $25. Electronic applications accepted. *Expenses:* Contact institution. *Financial support:* In 2011–12, 5 research assistantships with full and partial tuition reimbursements (averaging $4,200 per year) were awarded; Federal Work-Study, health care benefits, and unspecified assistantships also available. Financial award application deadline: 4/1; financial award applicants required to submit FAFSA. *Faculty research:* Children's literature, books and artwork, educational technology, professional development. *Unit head:* Dr. Julie McIntosh, Dean, 419-434-4862, Fax: 419-434-4822. *Application contact:* Heather Riffle, Assistant Director, Graduate and Professional Studies, 419-434-4640, Fax: 419-434-5517, E-mail: riffle@findlay.edu. Web site: http://www.findlay.edu.

University of Florida, Graduate School, College of Education, Gainesville, FL 32611. Offers M Ed, MAE, Ed D, PhD, Ed S, PhD/JD. *Accreditation:* NCATE. Part-time and evening/weekend programs available. Postbaccalaureate distance learning degree programs offered (minimal on-campus study). *Faculty:* 72 full-time (49 women). *Students:* 775 full-time (646 women), 652 part-time (545 women); includes 360 minority (131 Black or African American, non-Hispanic/Latino; 6 American Indian or Alaska Native, non-Hispanic/Latino; 42 Asian, non-Hispanic/Latino; 181 Hispanic/Latino), 82 international. Average age 32. 734 applicants, 49% accepted, 221 enrolled. In 2011, 420 master's, 68 doctorates, 84 other advanced degrees awarded. Terminal master's awarded for partial completion of doctoral program. *Degree requirements:* For master's, comprehensive exam (for some programs), thesis (for some programs); for doctorate, comprehensive exam (for some programs), thesis/dissertation (for some programs), capstone project (for professional practice). *Entrance requirements:* For master's and doctorate, GRE General Test, minimum GPA of 3.0; for Ed S, GRE General Test. Additional exam requirements/recommendations for international students: Required—TOEFL (minimum score 550 paper-based; 213 computer-based; 80 iBT), IELTS (minimum score 6). *Application deadline:* For fall admission, 2/15 for domestic students, 12/1 for international students; for spring admission, 9/15 for domestic students, 3/1 for international students. Applications are processed on a rolling basis. Application fee: $30. Electronic applications accepted. *Financial support:* In 2011–12, 259 students received support, including 32 fellowships with tuition reimbursements available, 106 research assistantships with tuition reimbursements available, 121 teaching assistantships with tuition reimbursements available; career-related internships or fieldwork, Federal Work-Study, and unspecified assistantships also available. Support available to part-time students. Financial award applicants required to submit FAFSA. *Faculty research:* Early childhood, child and adolescents, diverse learners, race/ethnicity issues, teacher education, professional development, language and literacy development, policy development. *Total annual research expenditures:* $8.9 million. *Unit head:* Glenn E. Good, PhD, Dean and Professor, 352-273-4135, E-mail: ggood@ufl.edu. Web site: http://www.coe.ufl.edu/index.php.

University of Georgia, College of Education, Athens, GA 30602. Offers M Ed, MA, MA Ed, MAT, MM Ed, MS, Ed D, PhD, Ed S. *Accreditation:* NCATE. *Faculty:* 177 full-time (95 women), 2 part-time/adjunct (1 woman). *Students:* 974 full-time (693 women), 1,025 part-time (719 women); includes 422 minority (323 Black or African American, non-Hispanic/Latino; 3 American Indian or Alaska Native, non-Hispanic/Latino; 37 Asian, non-Hispanic/Latino; 40 Hispanic/Latino; 2 Native Hawaiian or other Pacific Islander, non-Hispanic/Latino; 17 Two or more races, non-Hispanic/Latino), 166 international. Average age 33. 1,534 applicants, 44% accepted, 329 enrolled. In 2011, 449 master's, 179 doctorates, 91 other advanced degrees awarded. *Degree requirements:* For doctorate, thesis/dissertation. *Entrance requirements:* For doctorate,

GRE General Test. *Application deadline:* For fall admission, 7/1 priority date for domestic students; for spring admission, 11/15 for domestic students. Application fee: $50. Electronic applications accepted. *Financial support:* Fellowships, research assistantships, teaching assistantships, and unspecified assistantships available. *Unit head:* Dr. Arthur M. Horne, Interim Dean, 706-542-6446, Fax: 706-542-0360, E-mail: ahorne@uga.edu. *Application contact:* Director of Enrolled Student Services. Web site: http://www.coe.uga.edu/.

University of Great Falls, Graduate Studies, Program in Education, Great Falls, MT 59405. Offers M Ed. Part-time and evening/weekend programs available. *Degree requirements:* For master's, thesis, extensive portfolio. *Entrance requirements:* For master's, GRE General Test or MAT, 3 letters of recommendation, BA or BS from accredited college, teacher certification, interview. Additional exam requirements/recommendations for international students: Required—TOEFL (minimum score 500 paper-based; 205 computer-based). Electronic applications accepted. *Faculty research:* Native American attitudinal research.

University of Guam, Office of Graduate Studies, School of Education, Mangilao, GU 96923. Offers M Ed, MA. *Accreditation:* NCATE. Part-time programs available. *Degree requirements:* For master's, comprehensive oral and written exams. *Entrance requirements:* For master's, GRE General Test. Additional exam requirements/recommendations for international students: Required—TOEFL. *Faculty research:* Multicultural issues, computerized student advising.

University of Hartford, College of Education, Nursing, and Health Professions, West Hartford, CT 06117-1599. Offers M Ed, MS, MSN, MSPT, DPT, Ed D, CAGS, Sixth Year Certificate. *Accreditation:* NCATE. Part-time and evening/weekend programs available. *Degree requirements:* For doctorate, thesis/dissertation; for other advanced degree, comprehensive exam or research project. *Entrance requirements:* For doctorate, MAT. Additional exam requirements/recommendations for international students: Required—TOEFL (minimum score 550 paper-based; 213 computer-based). Electronic applications accepted. *Expenses:* Contact institution.

University of Hawaii at Hilo, Program in Education, Hilo, HI 96720-4091. Offers M Ed. Part-time and evening/weekend programs available. Electronic applications accepted.

University of Hawaii at Manoa, Graduate Division, College of Education, Honolulu, HI 96822. Offers M Ed, M Ed T, MS, Ed D, PhD, Graduate Certificate. *Accreditation:* NCATE. Part-time and evening/weekend programs available. *Entrance requirements:* Additional exam requirements/recommendations for international students: Required—TOEFL or IELTS.

University of Houston, College of Education, Houston, TX 77204. Offers M Ed, Ed D, PhD. *Accreditation:* NCATE. Part-time programs available. *Degree requirements:* For master's, comprehensive exam or thesis; for doctorate, comprehensive exam, thesis/dissertation. *Entrance requirements:* For master's, GRE General Test, transcripts, 3 letters of recommendation, curriculum vita, goal statement; for doctorate, GRE General Test, transcripts, 3 letters of recommendation, curriculum vita, goal statement, writing sample, interview. Additional exam requirements/recommendations for international students: Required—TOEFL (minimum score 550 paper-based). Electronic applications accepted.

University of Houston–Clear Lake, School of Education, Houston, TX 77058-1098. Offers MS, Ed D. *Accreditation:* NCATE. Part-time and evening/weekend programs available. *Degree requirements:* For master's, thesis optional; for doctorate, comprehensive exam, thesis/dissertation. *Entrance requirements:* For master's, GRE or minimum GPA of 3.0 in last 60 hours; for doctorate, GRE, master's degree, letters of reference. Additional exam requirements/recommendations for international students: Required—TOEFL (minimum score 550 paper-based; 213 computer-based). Electronic applications accepted.

University of Houston–Victoria, School of Education and Human Development, Victoria, TX 77901-4450. Offers administration and supervision (M Ed); counseling (M Ed); curriculum and instruction (M Ed); special education (M Ed). Part-time and evening/weekend programs available. Postbaccalaureate distance learning degree programs offered (minimal on-campus study). *Degree requirements:* For master's, comprehensive exam, project or thesis. *Entrance requirements:* For master's, GRE General Test. Additional exam requirements/recommendations for international students: Required—TOEFL. Electronic applications accepted. *Faculty research:* Reading and language arts education, evaluation and diagnosis of special children's abilities.

University of Idaho, College of Graduate Studies, College of Education, Moscow, ID 83844-3080. Offers M Ed, MS, DAT, Ed D, PhD, Ed S. *Accreditation:* NCATE. *Faculty:* 47 full-time (25 women), 11 part-time/adjunct (6 women). *Students:* 144 full-time (89 women), 417 part-time (256 women). Average age 40. In 2011, 181 master's, 26 doctorates, 43 other advanced degrees awarded. *Degree requirements:* For doctorate, thesis/dissertation. *Entrance requirements:* For master's, minimum GPA of 2.8; for doctorate, minimum undergraduate GPA of 2.8, 3.0 graduate. *Application deadline:* For fall admission, 8/1 for domestic students; for spring admission, 12/15 for domestic students. Applications are processed on a rolling basis. Application fee: $60. Electronic applications accepted. *Expenses:* Tuition, state resident: full-time $3874; part-time $334 per credit hour. Tuition, nonresident: full-time $16,394; part-time $861 per credit hour. *Required fees:* $2808; $99 per credit hour. Tuition and fees vary according to program. *Financial support:* Teaching assistantships and Federal Work-Study available. Support available to part-time students. Financial award applicants required to submit FAFSA. *Faculty research:* Technology integration, curricular development for cooperative environments, increasing science literacy, best practices for online pedagogy. *Unit head:* Dr. Corinne Mantle-Bromley, Dean, 208-885-6772, E-mail: coe@uidaho.edu. *Application contact:* Erick Larson, Director of Graduate Admissions, 208-885-4723, E-mail: gadms@uidaho.edu. Web site: http://www.uidaho.edu/ed/.

University of Illinois at Chicago, Graduate College, College of Education, Chicago, IL 60607-7128. Offers M Ed, Ed D, PhD. Part-time and evening/weekend programs available. Terminal master's awarded for partial completion of doctoral program. *Degree requirements:* For doctorate, thesis/dissertation. *Entrance requirements:* For master's, minimum GPA of 2.75; for doctorate, GRE General Test, minimum GPA of 2.75. Additional exam requirements/recommendations for international students: Required—TOEFL. Electronic applications accepted. *Faculty research:* Teaching and learning, program design, school and classroom organization with emphasis on urban settings.

University of Illinois at Springfield, Graduate Programs, College of Education and Human Services, Springfield, IL 62703-5407. Offers MA. Part-time and evening/weekend programs available. Postbaccalaureate distance learning degree programs offered (no on-campus study). *Faculty:* 19 full-time (8 women), 17 part-time/adjunct (7 women). *Students:* 69 full-time (58 women), 320 part-time (262 women); includes 59 minority (41 Black or African American, non-Hispanic/Latino; 1 American Indian or Alaska Native, non-Hispanic/Latino; 5 Asian, non-Hispanic/Latino; 9 Hispanic/Latino; 3 Two or more races, non-Hispanic/Latino). Average age 33. 182 applicants, 49% accepted, 71 enrolled. In 2011, 132 master's awarded. *Entrance requirements:* Additional exam requirements/recommendations for international students: Required—TOEFL (minimum score 500 paper-based; 176 computer-based; 61 iBT). Application fee: $50 ($60 for international students). Electronic applications accepted. *Expenses:* Tuition, state resident: full-time $6978; part-time $290.75 per credit hour. Tuition, nonresident: full-time $15,282; part-time $636.75 per credit hour. *Required fees:* $2106; $87.75 per credit hour. *Financial support:* In 2011–12, fellowships with full tuition reimbursements (averaging $8,550 per year), research assistantships with full tuition reimbursements (averaging $8,550 per year), teaching assistantships with full tuition reimbursements (averaging $8,550 per year) were awarded; career-related internships or fieldwork, Federal Work-Study, scholarships/grants, health care benefits, and unspecified assistantships also available. Support available to part-time students. Financial award application deadline: 11/15; financial award applicants required to submit FAFSA. *Unit head:* Dr. James Ermatinger, Interim Dean, 217-206-6784, Fax: 217-206-6775, E-mail: jerma2@uis.edu. *Application contact:* Dr. Lynn Pardie, Office of Graduate Studies, 800-252-8533, Fax: 217-206-7623, E-mail: lpard1@uis.edu.

University of Illinois at Urbana–Champaign, Graduate College, College of Education, Champaign, IL 61820. Offers Ed M, MA, MS, Ed D, PhD, CAS, MBA/M Ed. *Faculty:* 79 full-time (46 women), 3 part-time/adjunct (2 women). *Students:* 383 full-time (277 women), 544 part-time (376 women); includes 278 minority (137 Black or African American, non-Hispanic/Latino; 4 American Indian or Alaska Native, non-Hispanic/Latino; 45 Asian, non-Hispanic/Latino; 74 Hispanic/Latino; 18 Two or more races, non-Hispanic/Latino), 137 international. 582 applicants, 57% accepted, 173 enrolled. In 2011, 304 master's, 75 doctorates, 6 other advanced degrees awarded. *Application deadline:* Applications are processed on a rolling basis. Application fee: $75 ($90 for international students). Electronic applications accepted. *Financial support:* In 2011–12, 85 fellowships, 150 research assistantships, 162 teaching assistantships were awarded; tuition waivers (full and partial) also available. *Unit head:* Mary A. Kalantzis, Dean, 217-333-0960, Fax: 217-333-5847, E-mail: kalantzi@illinois.edu. *Application contact:* Gregory S. Harman, Admissions Support Staff, 217-244-4637. Web site: http://education.illinois.edu/.

University of Indianapolis, Graduate Programs, School of Education, Indianapolis, IN 46227-3697. Offers art education (MAT); biology (MAT); chemistry (MAT); curriculum and instruction (MA); earth sciences (MAT); education (MA, MAT); educational leadership (MA); elementary education (MA); English (MAT); French (MAT); math (MAT); physical education (MAT); physics (MAT); secondary education (MA), including art education, education, English education, social studies education; social studies (MAT); Spanish (MAT). *Accreditation:* NCATE. Part-time and evening/weekend programs available. *Faculty:* 3 full-time (2 women), 3 part-time/adjunct (2 women). *Students:* 32 full-time (18 women), 97 part-time (56 women); includes 22 minority (20 Black or African American, non-Hispanic/Latino; 1 Asian, non-Hispanic/Latino; 1 Hispanic/Latino), 3 international. Average age 33. In 2011, 78 master's awarded. *Entrance requirements:* For master's, GRE Subject Test, PRAXIS I, minimum GPA of 2.5, 3 letters of recommendation, interview, writing exercise. Additional exam requirements/recommendations for international students: Required—TOEFL (minimum score 550 paper-based; 213 computer-based). *Application deadline:* Applications are processed on a rolling basis. Application fee: $50. Tuition and fees vary according to degree level and program. *Financial support:* Federal Work-Study available. Financial award application deadline: 5/1; financial award applicants required to submit FAFSA. *Faculty research:* Assessment of teacher education, perceptions of prospective teachers by parents. *Unit head:* Dr. Kathy Moran, Dean, 317-788-3285, Fax: 317-788-3300, E-mail: kmoran@uindy.edu. *Application contact:* Jeni Kirby, 317-788-2113, E-mail: kirbyj@uindy.edu. Web site: http://education.uindy.edu/.

The University of Iowa, Graduate College, College of Education, Iowa City, IA 52242-1316. Offers MA, MAT, PhD, Ed S, JD/PhD. *Degree requirements:* For master's and Ed S, exam; for doctorate, comprehensive exam, thesis/dissertation. *Entrance requirements:* For master's, doctorate, and Ed S, GRE General Test, minimum GPA of 3.0. Additional exam requirements/recommendations for international students: Required—TOEFL (minimum score 550 paper-based; 213 computer-based; 81 iBT). Electronic applications accepted. *Faculty research:* Computer-assisted instrumentation, testing and measurement, instructional design.

The University of Kansas, Graduate Studies, School of Education, Lawrence, KS 66045-3101. Offers MA, MS, MS Ed, Ed D, PhD, Ed S. *Accreditation:* NCATE. Part-time programs available. *Students:* 687 full-time (484 women), 368 part-time (277 women); includes 121 minority (32 Black or African American, non-Hispanic/Latino; 9 American Indian or Alaska Native, non-Hispanic/Latino; 33 Asian, non-Hispanic/Latino; 32 Hispanic/Latino; 15 Two or more races, non-Hispanic/Latino), 121 international. Average age 32. 687 applicants, 62% accepted, 317 enrolled. In 2011, 261 master's, 66 doctorates, 10 other advanced degrees awarded. *Degree requirements:* For doctorate, thesis/dissertation. *Entrance requirements:* For master's and Ed S, minimum GPA of 3.0; for doctorate, GRE General Test. Additional exam requirements/recommendations for international students: Required—TOEFL. Application fee: $55 ($65 for international students). Electronic applications accepted. Tuition and fees vary according to course load, campus/location, program and reciprocity agreements. *Financial support:* Fellowships, research assistantships with partial tuition reimbursements, teaching assistantships with full and partial tuition reimbursements, career-related internships or fieldwork, scholarships/grants, and unspecified assistantships available. Financial award application deadline: 2/1. *Unit head:* Dr. Rick Ginsberg, Dean, 785-864-4297. *Application contact:* Mary Ann Williams, Graduate Admissions Coordinator, 785-864-4510, E-mail: mwilliams@ku.edu. Web site: http://www.soe.ku.edu/.

University of Kentucky, Graduate School, College of Education, Lexington, KY 40506-0032. Offers M Ed, MA Ed, MRC, MS, MS Ed, Ed D, PhD, Ed S. *Accreditation:* NCATE. Part-time and evening/weekend programs available. Terminal master's awarded for partial completion of doctoral program. *Degree requirements:* For master's and Ed S, comprehensive exam; for doctorate, comprehensive exam, thesis/dissertation. *Entrance requirements:* For master's, GRE General Test, minimum undergraduate GPA of 2.75; for doctorate, GRE General Test, minimum graduate GPA of 3.0; for Ed S, GRE General Test. Additional exam requirements/recommendations for international students: Required—TOEFL (minimum score 550 paper-based; 213 computer-based). Electronic applications accepted.

University of La Verne, College of Education and Organizational Leadership, Credential Program in Teacher Education, La Verne, CA 91750-4443. Offers multiple subject (Credential); single subject (Credential). Part-time programs available. *Faculty:* 19 full-time (12 women), 28 part-time/adjunct (22 women). *Students:* 43 full-time (34 women), 114 part-time (77 women); includes 82 minority (5 Black or African American, non-Hispanic/Latino; 6 Asian, non-Hispanic/Latino; 66 Hispanic/Latino; 1 Native Hawaiian or other Pacific Islander, non-Hispanic/Latino; 4 Two or more races, non-Hispanic/Latino). Average age 29. *Entrance requirements:* For degree, California Basic Educational Skills Test, minimum GPA of 3.0, interview, writing sample. Additional exam requirements/recommendations for international students: Required—TOEFL (minimum score 550 paper-based; 213 computer-based). *Application deadline:* Applications are processed on a rolling basis. Application fee: $50. *Expenses:* Contact institution. *Financial support:* Institutionally sponsored loans, scholarships/grants, and unspecified assistantships available. Financial award application deadline: 3/2; financial award applicants required to submit FAFSA. *Unit head:* Dr. Anita Flemington, Chairperson, 909-593-3511 Ext. 4623, E-mail: aflemington@laverne.edu. *Application contact:* Christy

Ranells, Program and Admission Specialist, 909-593-3511 Ext. 4644, Fax: 909-392-2761, E-mail: cranells@laverne.edu. Web site: http://laverne.edu/education/.

University of La Verne, College of Education and Organizational Leadership, Master's Program in Education, La Verne, CA 91750-4443. Offers M Ed. Part-time programs available. *Faculty:* 31 full-time (22 women), 39 part-time/adjunct (30 women). *Students:* 28 full-time (21 women), 118 part-time (99 women); includes 65 minority (6 Black or African American, non-Hispanic/Latino; 2 American Indian or Alaska Native, non-Hispanic/Latino; 5 Asian, non-Hispanic/Latino; 48 Hispanic/Latino; 4 Two or more races, non-Hispanic/Latino), 2 international. Average age 30. In 2011, 135 master's awarded. *Degree requirements:* For master's, thesis optional. *Entrance requirements:* For master's, California Basic Educational Skills Test, interview, writing sample, minimum GPA of 3.0, 3 letters of recommendation. Additional exam requirements/recommendations for international students: Required—TOEFL (minimum score 550 paper-based; 213 computer-based). *Application deadline:* Applications are processed on a rolling basis. Application fee: $50. *Expenses:* Contact institution. *Financial support:* Institutionally sponsored loans and unspecified assistantships available. Financial award application deadline: 3/2; financial award applicants required to submit FAFSA. *Unit head:* Valerie Beltran, Chair, 909-593-3511 Ext. 4659, E-mail: vbeltran@laverne.edu. *Application contact:* Christy Ranells, Program and Admission Specialist, 909-593-3511 Ext. 4644, Fax: 909-392-2761, E-mail: cranells@ulv.edu.

University of La Verne, Regional Campus Administration, Graduate Credential Program in Education, California Statewide Campus, La Verne, CA 91750-4443. Offers cross cultural language and academic development (Credential); multiple subject (Credential); single subject (Credential). *Entrance requirements:* For degree, California Basic Educational Skills Test, minimum undergraduate GPA of 2.75, 3 letters of recommendation, interview. *Expenses:* Contact institution.

University of La Verne, Regional Campus Administration, Master's Programs in Education, California Statewide Campus, La Verne, CA 91750-4443. Offers educational management (M Ed), including preliminary administrative services credential; multiple or single subject teaching credential (M Ed); school counseling (MS), including public personnel services credential. *Entrance requirements:* For master's, California Basic Educational Skills Test, 3 letters of recommendation, teaching credential. *Expenses:* Contact institution.

University of Lethbridge, School of Graduate Studies, Lethbridge, AB T1K 3M4, Canada. Offers accounting (MScM); addictions counseling (M Sc); agricultural biotechnology (M Sc); agricultural studies (M Sc, MA); anthropology (MA); archaeology (MA); art (MA, MFA); biochemistry (M Sc); biological sciences (M Sc); biomolecular science (PhD); biosystems and biodiversity (PhD); Canadian studies (MA); chemistry (M Sc); computer science (M Sc); computer science and geographical information science (M Sc); counseling psychology (M Ed); dramatic arts (MA); earth, space, and physical science (PhD); economics (MA); educational leadership (M Ed); English (MA); environmental science (M Sc); evolution and behavior (PhD); exercise science (M Sc); finance (MScM); French (MA); French/German (MA); French/Spanish (MA); general education (M Ed); general management (MScM); geography (M Sc, MA); German (MA); health science (M Sc); history (MA); human resource management and labour relations (MScM); individualized multidisciplinary (M Sc, MA); information systems (MScM); international management (MScM); kinesiology (M Sc, MA); management (M Sc, MA); marketing (MScM); mathematics (M Sc); music (M Mus, MA); Native American studies (MA); neuroscience (M Sc, PhD); new media (MA); nursing (M Sc); philosophy (MA); physics (M Sc); policy and strategy (MScM); political science (MA); psychology (M Sc, MA); religious studies (MA); social sciences (MA); sociology (MA); theatre and dramatic arts (MFA); theoretical and computational science (PhD); urban and regional studies (MA); women's studies (MA). Part-time and evening/weekend programs available. *Degree requirements:* For doctorate, comprehensive exam, thesis/dissertation. *Entrance requirements:* For master's, GMAT (M Sc in management), bachelor's degree in related field, minimum GPA of 3.0 during previous 20 graded semester courses, 2 years teaching or related experience (M Ed); for doctorate, master's degree, minimum graduate GPA of 3.5. Additional exam requirements/recommendations for international students: Required—TOEFL. *Faculty research:* Movement and brain plasticity, gibberellin physiology, photosynthesis, carbon cycling, molecular properties of main-group ring components.

University of Louisiana at Lafayette, College of Education, Lafayette, LA 70504. Offers M Ed, Ed D. *Accreditation:* NCATE. Part-time programs available. *Degree requirements:* For master's, thesis or alternative. *Entrance requirements:* For master's, GRE General Test, teaching certificate. Additional exam requirements/recommendations for international students: Required—TOEFL (minimum score 550 paper-based; 213 computer-based). Electronic applications accepted.

University of Louisiana at Monroe, Graduate School, College of Education and Human Development, Monroe, LA 71209-0001. Offers M Ed, MA, MAT, MS, Ed D, PhD, SSP. *Accreditation:* NCATE. Part-time and evening/weekend programs available. Postbaccalaureate distance learning degree programs offered. *Faculty:* 27 full-time (14 women). *Students:* 235 full-time (170 women), 278 part-time (199 women); includes 146 minority (129 Black or African American, non-Hispanic/Latino; 2 American Indian or Alaska Native, non-Hispanic/Latino; 5 Asian, non-Hispanic/Latino; 4 Hispanic/Latino; 6 Two or more races, non-Hispanic/Latino), 20 international. Average age 33. 207 applicants, 76% accepted, 133 enrolled. In 2011, 173 master's, 9 doctorates, 5 other advanced degrees awarded. *Degree requirements:* For master's, thesis; for doctorate, thesis/dissertation. *Entrance requirements:* For master's, GRE General Test, minimum cumulative GPA of 2.75; for doctorate, GRE General Test (minimum score of 1000 Verbal and Quantitative or 1500 Verbal, Quantitative and Analytic), minimum cumulative GPA of 2.75; for SSP, GRE General Test, minimum cumulative GPA of 3.0. Additional exam requirements/recommendations for international students: Required—TOEFL (minimum score 500 paper-based; 173 computer-based; 61 iBT). *Application deadline:* For fall admission, 8/24 priority date for domestic students, 7/1 for international students; for winter admission, 12/14 priority date for domestic students; for spring admission, 1/19 priority date for domestic students, 11/1 for international students. Applications are processed on a rolling basis. Application fee: $20 ($30 for international students). Electronic applications accepted. *Expenses:* Tuition, state resident: full-time $3436; part-time $240 per credit hour. Tuition, nonresident: full-time $3436; part-time $240 per credit hour. *International tuition:* $10,733 full-time. *Required fees:* $1460.90. *Financial support:* In 2011–12, 48 research assistantships (averaging $3,099 per year) were awarded; career-related internships or fieldwork, Federal Work-Study, institutionally sponsored loans, and unspecified assistantships also available. Financial award application deadline: 4/1; financial award applicants required to submit FAFSA. *Unit head:* Dr. Sandra M. Lemoine, Dean, 318-342-1235, Fax: 318-342-1240, E-mail: slemoine@ulm.edu. *Application contact:* Dr. Jack Palmer, Director of Graduate Studies, 318-342-1250, Fax: 318-342-1240, E-mail: palmer@ulm.edu. Web site: http://www.ulm.edu/cehd/.

University of Louisville, Graduate School, College of Education and Human Development, Louisville, KY 40292-0001. Offers M Ed, MA, MAT, MS, Ed D, PhD, Ed S. *Accreditation:* NCATE. Part-time and evening/weekend programs available. Postbaccalaureate distance learning degree programs offered. Terminal master's awarded for partial completion of doctoral program. *Entrance requirements:* For master's, doctorate, and Ed S, GRE General Test. Additional exam requirements/recommendations for international students: Required—TOEFL (minimum score 560 paper-based; 210 computer-based; 83 iBT). Electronic applications accepted. *Expenses:* Tuition, state resident: full-time $9692; part-time $539 per credit hour. Tuition, nonresident: full-time $20,168; part-time $1121 per credit hour. Tuition and fees vary according to program and reciprocity agreements. *Faculty research:* Mathematics and science education, early childhood development, literacy acquisition and development, culturally-responsive education, health promotion, sports administration, exercise physiology, prevention science, counseling psychology, mental health counseling, school counseling, college student personnel, art therapy, educational leadership, school reform, evaluation, P-12 and higher education administration, organizational development, instructional technology development.

University of Maine, Graduate School, College of Education and Human Development, Orono, ME 04469. Offers counselor education (M Ed, MA, MS, Ed D, CAS); curriculum, assessment, and instruction (M Ed), including elementary and secondary education; educational leadership (M Ed, Ed D, CAS); elementary education (M Ed, MAT, MS, CAS); higher education (M Ed, MA, MS, Ed D, CAS); human development and family relations (MS), including human development; instructional technology (M Ed); kinesiology and physical education (M Ed, MS), including curriculum and instruction (M Ed), exercise science (MS); literacy education (M Ed, MA, MS, Ed D, CAS); science education (M Ed, MS, CAS); secondary education (M Ed, MA, MAT, MS, CAS); social studies education (M Ed, MA, MS, CAS); special education (M Ed, CAS); teaching (MST), including earth sciences, generalist, mathematics, physics and astronomy. *Accreditation:* NCATE. Part-time and evening/weekend programs available. *Faculty:* 36 full-time (16 women), 73 part-time/adjunct (60 women). *Students:* 205 full-time (153 women), 283 part-time (214 women); includes 19 minority (3 Black or African American, non-Hispanic/Latino; 7 American Indian or Alaska Native, non-Hispanic/Latino; 2 Asian, non-Hispanic/Latino; 4 Hispanic/Latino; 3 Two or more races, non-Hispanic/Latino), 8 international. Average age 37. 194 applicants, 70% accepted, 125 enrolled. In 2011, 152 master's, 8 doctorates, 36 other advanced degrees awarded. *Degree requirements:* For doctorate, thesis/dissertation. *Entrance requirements:* For doctorate, GRE General Test; for CAS, MA, M Ed, or MS. Additional exam requirements/recommendations for international students: Required—TOEFL. *Application deadline:* For fall admission, 2/1 priority date for domestic students. Applications are processed on a rolling basis. Application fee: $65. Electronic applications accepted. *Expenses:* Tuition, state resident: full-time $5016. Tuition, nonresident: full-time $14,424. *Financial support:* In 2011–12, 21 teaching assistantships with full tuition reimbursements (averaging $13,600 per year) were awarded; career-related internships or fieldwork, Federal Work-Study, institutionally sponsored loans, and unspecified assistantships also available. Support available to part-time students. Financial award application deadline: 3/1. *Faculty research:* Development of training models for the severely handicapped, marine education, counselor training models. *Total annual research expenditures:* $412,103. *Unit head:* Dr. Ann Pooler, Dean, 207-581-2441, Fax: 207-581-2423. *Application contact:* Scott G. Delcourt, Associate Dean of the Graduate School, 207-581-3291, Fax: 207-581-3232, E-mail: graduate@maine.edu. Web site: http://www2.umaine.edu/graduate/.

University of Maine at Farmington, Program in Education, Farmington, ME 04938-1990. Offers early childhood education (MS Ed); educational leadership (MS Ed). *Accreditation:* NCATE. Part-time and evening/weekend programs available. Postbaccalaureate distance learning degree programs offered (minimal on-campus study). *Degree requirements:* For master's, capstone project (for educational leadership). *Entrance requirements:* For master's, baccalaureate degree from accredited institution, valid teaching certificate or professional experience in education, professional employment by school district or other educational institution (exceptions may be made by the Assistant Dean), minimum of two years experience in professional education. *Faculty research:* School improvement strategies, technology integration.

The University of Manchester, School of Education, Manchester, United Kingdom. Offers counseling (D Couns); counseling psychology (D Couns); education (M Phil, Ed D, PhD); educational and child psychology (Ed D); educational psychology (Ed D).

University of Manitoba, Faculty of Graduate Studies, College Universitaire de Saint Boniface, Education Program?Saint-Boniface, Winnipeg, MB R3T 2N2, Canada. Offers M Ed.

University of Manitoba, Faculty of Graduate Studies, Faculty of Education, Winnipeg, MB R3T 2N2, Canada. Offers M Ed, PhD. *Degree requirements:* For master's, thesis or alternative.

University of Mary, School of Education and Behavioral Sciences, Department of Education, Bismarck, ND 58504-9652. Offers college teaching (M Ed); curriculum, instruction and assessment (M Ed); early childhood education (M Ed); early childhood special education (M Ed); elementary administration (M Ed); emotional disorders (M Ed); learning disabilities (M Ed); reading (M Ed); secondary administration (M Ed); special education strategist (M Ed). Part-time programs available. *Faculty:* 6 full-time (5 women), 12 part-time/adjunct (8 women). *Students:* 5 full-time (4 women), 77 part-time (56 women); includes 9 minority (1 Black or African American, non-Hispanic/Latino; 4 American Indian or Alaska Native, non-Hispanic/Latino; 1 Asian, non-Hispanic/Latino; 3 Hispanic/Latino), 1 international. Average age 30. 58 applicants, 55% accepted, 29 enrolled. In 2011, 16 master's awarded. *Degree requirements:* For master's, portfolio or thesis. *Entrance requirements:* For master's, interview, letters of reference, minimum GPA of 2.5. Additional exam requirements/recommendations for international students: Required—TOEFL (minimum score 500 paper-based; 197 computer-based; 71 iBT). *Application deadline:* Applications are processed on a rolling basis. Application fee: $40. Electronic applications accepted. *Financial support:* In 2011–12, 1 teaching assistantship with full tuition reimbursement was awarded; career-related internships or fieldwork also available. Financial award application deadline: 8/1; financial award applicants required to submit FAFSA. *Faculty research:* Innovative pedagogy in higher education, technology in education, content standards, children of poverty, children with diverse learning needs. *Unit head:* Dr. Rebecca Yunker Salveson, Director, 701-355-8186, E-mail: rysalves@umary.edu. *Application contact:* Leona Friedig, Administrative Secretary, 701-355-8058, E-mail: lfriedig@umary.edu.

University of Mary Hardin-Baylor, Graduate Studies in Education, Belton, TX 76513. Offers administration of intervention programs (M Ed); curriculum and instruction (M Ed); educational administration (M Ed, Ed D). Part-time and evening/weekend programs available. *Faculty:* 17 full-time (9 women), 3 part-time/adjunct (2 women). *Students:* 39 full-time (21 women), 88 part-time (51 women); includes 43 minority (24 Black or African American, non-Hispanic/Latino; 2 Asian, non-Hispanic/Latino; 17 Hispanic/Latino), 3 international. Average age 37. 32 applicants, 66% accepted, 12 enrolled. In 2011, 20 master's, 14 doctorates awarded. *Degree requirements:* For master's, comprehensive exam; for doctorate, thesis/dissertation. *Entrance requirements:* For master's, GRE General Test, minimum GPA of 2.75, Texas teaching certificate; for doctorate, GRE, minimum GPA of 3.5, interview, essay. *Application deadline:* For fall admission, 6/1 priority date for domestic students; for spring admission, 11/1 for domestic students. Applications are processed on a rolling basis. Application fee: $35 ($135 for international students). Electronic applications accepted. *Expenses: Tuition:* Full-time $12,780. *Required fees:* $2350. *Financial support:* Federal Work-Study and scholarships (for some active duty military personnel only) available. Support available to part-time students. Financial award application deadline: 6/1; financial award applicants required to submit FAFSA. *Unit head:* Dr. Austin Vasek, Program Director, 254-295-4185, Fax: 254-295-4480, E-mail: austin.vasek@umhb.edu. *Application contact:* Melissa Ford, Director of Graduate Admissions, 254-295-4020, Fax: 254-295-5301, E-mail: mford@umhb.edu.

University of Maryland, Baltimore County, Graduate School, College of Arts, Humanities and Social Sciences, Department of Education, Baltimore, MD 21250. Offers distance education (Postbaccalaureate Certificate); education (MA), including education; instructional systems development (MA, Graduate Certificate), including distance education (Graduate Certificate), instructional design for e-learning (Graduate Certificate), instructional systems development, instructional technology (Graduate Certificate); mathematics education (Postbaccalaureate Certificate); mathematics instructional leadership (K-8) (Postbaccalaureate Certificate); teaching (MAT), including early childhood education, elementary education, secondary education; teaching English for speakers of other languages (MA); teaching English to speakers of other languages (Postbaccalaureate Certificate). *Accreditation:* NCATE. Part-time and evening/weekend programs available. Postbaccalaureate distance learning degree programs offered (no on-campus study). *Faculty:* 21 full-time (15 women), 25 part-time/adjunct (19 women). *Students:* 102 full-time (70 women), 263 part-time (202 women); includes 83 minority (42 Black or African American, non-Hispanic/Latino; 1 American Indian or Alaska Native, non-Hispanic/Latino; 18 Asian, non-Hispanic/Latino; 15 Hispanic/Latino; 2 Native Hawaiian or other Pacific Islander, non-Hispanic/Latino; 5 Two or more races, non-Hispanic/Latino), 17 international. Average age 34. 90 applicants, 94% accepted, 80 enrolled. In 2011, 100 master's awarded. *Degree requirements:* For master's, comprehensive exam (for some programs), thesis (for some programs). *Entrance requirements:* For master's, GRE General Test, GRE Subject Test (MA in TESOL), PRAXIS I (MAT), minimum GPA of 3.0. Additional exam requirements/recommendations for international students: Required—TOEFL. *Application deadline:* For fall admission, 6/1 for domestic students; for spring admission, 11/1 for domestic students. Applications are processed on a rolling basis. Application fee: $50. Electronic applications accepted. *Financial support:* In 2011–12, 12 students received support, including teaching assistantships with full tuition reimbursements available (averaging $12,000 per year); fellowships, career-related internships or fieldwork, Federal Work-Study, scholarships/grants, tuition waivers (partial), and unspecified assistantships also available. Financial award application deadline: 3/1. *Faculty research:* Teacher leadership; STEM education; ESOL/bilingual education; early childhood education; language, literacy and culture. *Total annual research expenditures:* $1.3 million. *Unit head:* Dr. Eugene Schaffer, Department Chair, 410-455-2465, Fax: 410-455-3986, E-mail: schaffer@umbc.edu. *Application contact:* Dr. Susan M. Blunck, Graduate Program Director, 410-455-2869, Fax: 410-455-3986, E-mail: blunck@umbc.edu. Web site: http://www.umbc.edu/education/.

University of Maryland, College Park, Academic Affairs, College of Education, College Park, MD 20742. Offers M Ed, MA, Ed D, PhD, AGSC, CAGS. *Accreditation:* NCATE. Part-time and evening/weekend programs available. Postbaccalaureate distance learning degree programs offered. *Faculty:* 193 full-time (136 women), 77 part-time/adjunct (62 women). *Students:* 698 full-time (531 women), 342 part-time (257 women); includes 307 minority (136 Black or African American, non-Hispanic/Latino; 1 American Indian or Alaska Native, non-Hispanic/Latino; 84 Asian, non-Hispanic/Latino; 67 Hispanic/Latino; 19 Two or more races, non-Hispanic/Latino), 104 international. 1,123 applicants, 29% accepted, 211 enrolled. In 2011, 325 master's, 72 doctorates awarded. *Degree requirements:* For doctorate, thesis/dissertation. *Entrance requirements:* For master's, GRE General Test or MAT, minimum GPA of 3.0. *Application deadline:* For fall admission, 3/1 for domestic students, 2/1 for international students; for spring admission, 9/1 for domestic students, 6/1 for international students. Applications are processed on a rolling basis. Application fee: $75. Electronic applications accepted. *Expenses: Tuition, area resident:* Part-time $525 per credit hour. Tuition, state resident: part-time $525 per credit hour. Tuition, nonresident: part-time $1131 per credit hour. *Required fees:* $386.31 per term. Tuition and fees vary according to program. *Financial support:* In 2011–12, 50 fellowships with full and partial tuition reimbursements (averaging $16,030 per year), 17 research assistantships (averaging $17,276 per year), 279 teaching assistantships (averaging $16,701 per year) were awarded; career-related internships or fieldwork, Federal Work-Study, and scholarships/grants also available. Support available to part-time students. Financial award applicants required to submit FAFSA. *Total annual research expenditures:* $14.2 million. *Unit head:* Donna L. Wiseman, Dean, 301-405-2336, Fax: 301-314-9890, E-mail: dlwise@umd.edu. *Application contact:* Dean of Graduate School, 301-405-0376, Fax: 301-314-9305.

University of Maryland Eastern Shore, Graduate Programs, Department of Education, Program in Teaching, Princess Anne, MD 21853-1299. Offers MAT. Program offered jointly with Salisbury University. *Accreditation:* NCATE. *Degree requirements:* For master's, comprehensive exam, internship, seminar paper, PRAXIS II. *Entrance requirements:* For master's, PRAXIS I, interview, minimum GPA of 3.0, writing sample. Additional exam requirements/recommendations for international students: Required—TOEFL (minimum score 213 computer-based; 80 iBT). Electronic applications accepted.

University of Maryland University College, Graduate School of Management and Technology, Master of Arts in Teaching Program, Adelphi, MD 20783. Offers MAT. Part-time and evening/weekend programs available. *Students:* 14 full-time (8 women), 112 part-time (81 women); includes 30 minority (18 Black or African American, non-Hispanic/Latino; 5 Asian, non-Hispanic/Latino; 3 Hispanic/Latino; 4 Two or more races, non-Hispanic/Latino). Average age 34. 84 applicants, 100% accepted, 20 enrolled. In 2011, 6 degrees awarded. *Degree requirements:* For master's, comprehensive exam, thesis or alternative. *Application deadline:* Applications are processed on a rolling basis. Application fee: $50. Electronic applications accepted. *Financial support:* Application deadline: 6/1; applicants required to submit FAFSA. *Unit head:* Dr. Virginia Pilato, Chair, Education Department, 240-684-2400, Fax: 240-684-2401, E-mail: virginia.pilato@umuc.edu. *Application contact:* Coordinator, Graduate Admissions, 800-888-8682, Fax: 240-684-2151, E-mail: newgrad@umuc.edu. Web site: http://www.umuc.edu/programs/grad/mat/mat.shtml.

University of Maryland University College, Graduate School of Management and Technology, Program in Education, Adelphi, MD 20783. Offers M Ed. Part-time and evening/weekend programs available. Postbaccalaureate distance learning degree programs offered (no on-campus study). *Students:* 3 full-time (all women), 259 part-time (199 women); includes 101 minority (75 Black or African American, non-Hispanic/Latino; 1 American Indian or Alaska Native, non-Hispanic/Latino; 6 Asian, non-Hispanic/Latino; 15 Hispanic/Latino; 1 Native Hawaiian or other Pacific Islander, non-Hispanic/Latino; 3 Two or more races, non-Hispanic/Latino), 3 international. Average age 35. 52 applicants, 100% accepted, 52 enrolled. In 2011, 58 master's awarded. *Degree requirements:* For master's, thesis or alternative. *Application deadline:* Applications are processed on a rolling basis. Application fee: $50. Electronic applications accepted. *Financial support:* Federal Work-Study and scholarships/grants available. Support available to part-time students. Financial award application deadline: 6/1; financial award applicants required to submit FAFSA. *Unit head:* Dr. Katherine Woodward, Director, 240-684-2400, Fax: 240-684-2401, E-mail: katherine.woodward@umuc.edu. *Application contact:* Coordinator, Graduate Admissions, 800-888-8682, Fax: 240-684-2151, E-mail: newgrad@umuc.edu.

University of Mary Washington, College of Education, Fredericksburg, VA 22401-5358. Offers M Ed, MS. Part-time and evening/weekend programs available. *Faculty:* 19 full-time (17 women), 13 part-time/adjunct (11 women). *Students:* 31 full-time (28 women), 307 part-time (253 women); includes 57 minority (27 Black or African American, non-Hispanic/Latino; 2 American Indian or Alaska Native, non-Hispanic/Latino; 3 Asian, non-Hispanic/Latino; 18 Hispanic/Latino; 7 Two or more races, non-Hispanic/Latino). Average age 31. 122 applicants, 79% accepted, 73 enrolled. In 2011, 136 master's awarded. *Degree requirements:* For master's, one foreign language, comprehensive exam (for some programs). *Entrance requirements:* For master's, PRAXIS I or Virginia Department of Education accepted equivalent. Additional exam requirements/recommendations for international students: Required—TOEFL (minimum score 570 paper-based; 230 computer-based; 88 iBT), IELTS (minimum score 6.5). *Application deadline:* For fall admission, 4/15 for domestic and international students; for spring admission, 9/15 for domestic and international students. Application fee: $50. Electronic applications accepted. Application fee is waived when completed online. *Financial support:* In 2011–12, 13 students received support. Scholarships/grants available. Financial award application deadline: 7/30; financial award applicants required to submit FAFSA. *Unit head:* Dr. Mary L. Gendernalik-Cooper, Dean, 540-654-1290. *Application contact:* Matthew E. Mejia, Associate Dean of Admissions, 540-286-8088, Fax: 540-286-8085, E-mail: mmejia@umw.edu. Web site: http://www.umw.edu/education/.

University of Massachusetts Amherst, Graduate School, School of Education, Amherst, MA 01003. Offers M Ed, Ed D, PhD, CAGS. *Accreditation:* NCATE. Part-time programs available. Postbaccalaureate distance learning degree programs offered (minimal on-campus study). *Faculty:* 81 full-time (46 women). *Students:* 370 full-time (266 women), 334 part-time (227 women); includes 114 minority (36 Black or African American, non-Hispanic/Latino; 1 American Indian or Alaska Native, non-Hispanic/Latino; 15 Asian, non-Hispanic/Latino; 51 Hispanic/Latino; 1 Native Hawaiian or other Pacific Islander, non-Hispanic/Latino; 10 Two or more races, non-Hispanic/Latino), 99 international. Average age 35. 823 applicants, 54% accepted, 213 enrolled. In 2011, 179 master's, 36 doctorates, 44 other advanced degrees awarded. Terminal master's awarded for partial completion of doctoral program. *Degree requirements:* For doctorate, comprehensive exam, thesis/dissertation. *Entrance requirements:* Additional exam requirements/recommendations for international students: Required—TOEFL (minimum score 550 paper-based; 213 computer-based; 80 iBT), IELTS (minimum score 6.5). *Application deadline:* For fall admission, 1/15 for domestic and international students. Applications are processed on a rolling basis. Application fee: $50 ($65 for international students). Electronic applications accepted. Tuition and fees vary according to course load, campus/location and program. *Financial support:* Fellowships with full and partial tuition reimbursements, research assistantships with full and partial tuition reimbursements, teaching assistantships with full and partial tuition reimbursements, career-related internships or fieldwork, Federal Work-Study, scholarships/grants, traineeships, health care benefits, tuition waivers (full and partial), and unspecified assistantships available. Support available to part-time students. Financial award application deadline: 1/15. *Unit head:* Dr. Christine B. McCormick, Dean, 413-545-6984, Fax: 413-545-4240. *Application contact:* Lindsay DeSantis, Interim Supervisor of Admissions, 413-545-0722, Fax: 413-577-0010, E-mail: gradadm@grad.umass.edu. Web site: http://www.umass.edu/education/.

University of Massachusetts Boston, Office of Graduate Studies, Graduate College of Education, Boston, MA 02125-3393. Offers M Ed, MA, Ed D, CAGS, Certificate. Part-time and evening/weekend programs available. *Degree requirements:* For master's, comprehensive exam; for doctorate, comprehensive exam, thesis/dissertation. *Entrance requirements:* For master's, GRE General Test or MAT; for doctorate, GRE General Test or MAT, minimum GPA of 2.75; for other advanced degree, minimum GPA of 2.75. *Faculty research:* Effects of ethnicity on applied psychology and education, enhancing equity and excellence in public schools, diversity and change in higher education, improving the functioning of individuals with disabilities.

University of Massachusetts Dartmouth, Graduate School, School of Education, Public Policy, and Civic Engagement, Department of Teaching and Learning, North Dartmouth, MA 02747-2300. Offers elementary education (MAT, Postbaccalaureate Certificate); middle school education (MAT); principal initial licensure (Postbaccalaureate Certificate); secondary school education (MAT). *Faculty:* 5 full-time (4 women), 9 part-time/adjunct (4 women). *Students:* 15 full-time (10 women), 180 part-time (119 women); includes 17 minority (7 Black or African American, non-Hispanic/Latino; 1 Asian, non-Hispanic/Latino; 5 Hispanic/Latino; 4 Two or more races, non-Hispanic/Latino). Average age 34. 110 applicants, 98% accepted, 85 enrolled. In 2011, 88 master's, 28 other advanced degrees awarded. *Degree requirements:* For master's, thesis or alternative. *Entrance requirements:* For master's, Massachusetts Tests for Educator Licensure (MTEL), minimum undergraduate GPA of 2.7, teacher certification, 3 letters of recommendation, resume, statement of intent; for Postbaccalaureate Certificate, Massachusetts Tests for Educator Licensure (MTEL), 3 letters of recommendation, resume, statement of intent. Additional exam requirements/recommendations for international students: Required—TOEFL (minimum score 533 paper-based; 200 computer-based; 72 iBT). *Application deadline:* For fall admission, 7/15 priority date for domestic students, 6/15 for international students; for spring admission, 12/15 priority date for domestic students, 11/15 for international students. Applications are processed on a rolling basis. Application fee: $40 ($60 for international students). *Expenses:* Tuition, state resident: full-time $2071; part-time $86.29 per credit. Tuition, nonresident: full-time $8099; part-time $337.46 per credit. *Required fees:* $438.58 per credit. Part-time tuition and fees vary according to class time, course load, degree level and reciprocity agreements. *Financial support:* Federal Work-Study available. Financial award application deadline: 3/1. *Total annual research expenditures:* $92,694. *Unit head:* Sheila Macrine, Graduate Program Director, 508-999-9234, Fax: 508-910-6916, E-mail: smacrine@umassd.edu. *Application contact:* Elan Turcotte-Shamski, Graduate Admissions Officer, 508-999-8604, Fax: 508-999-8183, E-mail: graduate@umassd.edu. Web site: http://www.umassd.edu/seppce/teachingandlearning/index.html.

University of Massachusetts Lowell, Graduate School of Education, Lowell, MA 01854-2881. Offers administration, planning, and policy (CAGS); curriculum and instruction (M Ed, CAGS); educational administration (M Ed); language arts and literacy (Ed D); leadership in schooling (Ed D); math and science education (Ed D); reading and language (M Ed, CAGS). *Accreditation:* NCATE. Part-time and evening/weekend programs available. Postbaccalaureate distance learning degree programs offered (no on-campus study). Terminal master's awarded for partial completion of doctoral program. *Degree requirements:* For doctorate, thesis/dissertation. *Entrance requirements:* For master's, doctorate, and CAGS, GRE General Test. Additional exam requirements/recommendations for international students: Required—TOEFL. Electronic applications accepted.

University of Memphis, Graduate School, College of Education, Memphis, TN 38152. Offers M Ed, MAT, MS, Ed D, PhD, Graduate Certificate. *Accreditation:* NCATE. Part-time and evening/weekend programs available. Terminal master's awarded for partial completion of doctoral program. *Degree requirements:* For master's, comprehensive exam; for doctorate, comprehensive exam, thesis/dissertation. *Entrance requirements:* For master's, GRE General Test or MAT; for doctorate, GRE General Test. *Faculty research:* Urban school effectiveness, literacy development, teacher effectiveness, exercise physiology, crisis counseling.

University of Miami, Graduate School, School of Education and Human Development, Coral Gables, FL 33124. Offers MS Ed, Ed D, PhD, Certificate, Ed S. *Faculty:* 36 full-time (18 women). *Students:* 208 full-time (140 women), 67 part-time (46 women); includes 116 minority (31 Black or African American, non-Hispanic/Latino; 6 Asian, non-Hispanic/Latino; 74 Hispanic/Latino; 5 Two or more races, non-Hispanic/Latino), 29 international. Average age 29. 524 applicants, 40% accepted, 96 enrolled. In 2011, 99 master's, 20 doctorates, 3 other advanced degrees awarded. Terminal master's awarded for partial completion of doctoral program. *Degree requirements:* For master's, comprehensive exam (for some programs), thesis optional, electronic portfolio, special project, personal growth experience; for doctorate, thesis/dissertation, qualifying exam. *Entrance requirements:* For master's and doctorate, GRE General Test. Additional exam requirements/recommendations for international students: Required—TOEFL (minimum score 550 paper-based; 80 iBT); Recommended—IELTS (minimum score 6.5). *Application deadline:* For fall admission, 10/15 for international students. Application fee: $65. Electronic applications accepted. *Financial support:* In 2011–12, 141 students received support, including 9 fellowships with full tuition reimbursements available (averaging $28,800 per year), 46 research assistantships with full and partial tuition reimbursements available (averaging $28,800 per year), 9 teaching assistantships with full and partial tuition reimbursements available (averaging $28,800 per year); career-related internships or fieldwork, institutionally sponsored loans, scholarships/grants, traineeships, health care benefits, tuition waivers (full and partial), and unspecified assistantships also available. Support available to part-time students. Financial award application deadline: 3/1; financial award applicants required to submit FAFSA. *Faculty research:* Social skills and learning disabilities, planning for mainstreamed pupils, alcohol and drug abuse, restructuring education for all learners. *Unit head:* Dr. Walter Secada, Senior Associate Dean, 305-284-2102, Fax: 305-284-9395, E-mail: wsecada@miami.edu. *Application contact:* Lois Heffernan, Graduate Admissions Coordinator, 305-284-2167, Fax: 305-284-9395, E-mail: lheffernan@miami.edu. Web site: http://www.education.miami.edu/department/departments_List.asp.

University of Michigan, Horace H. Rackham School of Graduate Studies, Combined Program in Education and Psychology, Ann Arbor, MI 48109-1259. Offers PhD. *Accreditation:* Teacher Education Accreditation Council. *Faculty:* 17 part-time/adjunct (8 women). *Students:* 36 full-time (27 women); includes 18 minority (11 Black or African American, non-Hispanic/Latino; 2 Asian, non-Hispanic/Latino; 5 Hispanic/Latino), 5 international. Average age 27. 64 applicants, 19% accepted, 7 enrolled. In 2011, 1 doctorate awarded. *Degree requirements:* For doctorate, thesis/dissertation, independent research project, preliminary exam, oral defense of dissertation. *Entrance requirements:* For doctorate, GRE General Test with Analytical Writing Test. Additional exam requirements/recommendations for international students: Required—TOEFL (minimum score 600 paper-based; 250 computer-based; 100 iBT). *Application deadline:* For fall admission, 12/1 for domestic and international students. Application fee: $65 ($75 for international students). Electronic applications accepted. *Financial support:* In 2011–12, 36 students received support, including 20 fellowships with full tuition reimbursements available (averaging $27,664 per year), 5 research assistantships with full tuition reimbursements available (averaging $28,728 per year), 9 teaching assistantships with full tuition reimbursements available (averaging $30,109 per year); institutionally sponsored loans, scholarships/grants, traineeships, tuition waivers (full and partial), and unspecified assistantships also available. Financial award application deadline: 12/1. *Faculty research:* Human development in context of schools, families, communities; cognitive and learning sciences; motivation and self-regulated learning; culture, ethnicity, social and class influences on learning and motivation. *Unit head:* Dr. Robert J. Jagers, Director, 734-647-0626, Fax: 734-615-2164, E-mail: rjagers@umich.edu. *Application contact:* Janie Knieper, Administrative Specialist, 734-647-0626, Fax: 734-763-0680, E-mail: cpep@umich.edu. Web site: http://www.soe.umich.edu/academics/doctoral_programs/ep/.

University of Michigan–Dearborn, School of Education, Doctoral Program in Education, Dearborn, MI 48126. Offers curriculum and practice (Ed D); educational leadership (Ed D); educational psychology/special education (Ed D); metropolitan education (Ed D). Part-time and evening/weekend programs available. *Faculty:* 8 full-time (6 women), 2 part-time/adjunct (0 women). *Students:* 47 part-time (34 women); includes 12 minority (6 Black or African American, non-Hispanic/Latino; 3 Asian, non-Hispanic/Latino; 1 Hispanic/Latino; 2 Two or more races, non-Hispanic/Latino). Average age 40. 55 applicants, 35% accepted, 17 enrolled. *Degree requirements:* For doctorate, comprehensive exam, thesis/dissertation. *Entrance requirements:* For doctorate, GRE (taken within the last 5 years), master's degree with minimum GPA of 3.3, 3 letters of recommendation (1 from faculty), 3 years' professional and/or teaching experience. Additional exam requirements/recommendations for international students: Required—TOEFL (minimum score 550 paper-based). *Application deadline:* For fall admission, 3/1 for domestic and international students. Application fee: $60 ($75 for international students). *Financial support:* Scholarships/grants available. *Faculty research:* Educational leadership, metropolitan education, curriculum and practice, educational psychology, special education, assessment. *Unit head:* Bonnie Beyer, Coordinator, 313-593-5583, E-mail: beyer@umd.umich.edu. *Application contact:* Catherine Parkins, Customer Service Assistant, 313-583-6349, Fax: 313-593-4748, E-mail: cparkins@umd.umich.edu. Web site: http://www.soe.umd.umich.edu/soe_edd/.

University of Michigan–Dearborn, School of Education, Master of Arts in Teaching Program, Dearborn, MI 48126-2638. Offers MAT. Part-time and evening/weekend programs available. Postbaccalaureate distance learning degree programs offered (minimal on-campus study). *Faculty:* 14 full-time (8 women), 37 part-time/adjunct (all women). *Students:* 16 full-time (11 women), 9 part-time (5 women); includes 11 minority (3 Black or African American, non-Hispanic/Latino; 5 Asian, non-Hispanic/Latino; 3 Hispanic/Latino). Average age 34. 5 applicants, 100% accepted, 5 enrolled. In 2011, 28 master's awarded. *Entrance requirements:* For master's, Michigan Test for Teacher Certification (Basic Skills Test and Subject Area Test in teaching), minimum cumulative GPA of 3.0, interview, 3 letters of recommendation. *Application deadline:* For fall admission, 9/5 for domestic students; for winter admission, 12/22 for domestic students; for spring admission, 5/5 for domestic students. Applications are processed on a rolling basis. Application fee: $60. Electronic applications accepted. *Financial support:* Career-related internships or fieldwork available. Support available to part-time students. Financial award application deadline: 4/1; financial award applicants required to submit FAFSA. *Unit head:* Dr. Paul R. Fossum, Coordinator, 313-593-0982, Fax: 313-593-9961, E-mail: pfossum@umich.edu. *Application contact:* Judy Garfield, Customer Service Assistant, 313-593-5090, Fax: 313-593-4748, E-mail: jlgarfie@umd.umich.edu. Web site: http://www.soe.umd.umich.edu/soe_mat/.

University of Michigan–Dearborn, School of Education, Program in Education, Dearborn, MI 48126-2638. Offers MAT. Part-time and evening/weekend programs available. Postbaccalaureate distance learning degree programs offered (minimal on-campus study). *Faculty:* 14 full-time (8 women), 37 part-time/adjunct (all women). *Students:* 52 full-time (47 women), 21 part-time (19 women); includes 7 minority (1 Black or African American, non-Hispanic/Latino; 3 Asian, non-Hispanic/Latino; 2 Hispanic/Latino; 1 Two or more races, non-Hispanic/Latino). Average age 34. 14 applicants, 100% accepted, 14 enrolled. In 2011, 28 master's awarded. *Entrance requirements:* For master's, minimum GPA of 3.0, teaching certificate, 3 letters of recommendation, statement of purpose. *Application deadline:* For fall admission, 9/5 for domestic students; for winter admission, 12/22 for domestic students; for spring admission, 5/5 for domestic students. Applications are processed on a rolling basis. Application fee: $60. *Financial support:* Career-related internships or fieldwork available. Support available to part-time students. Financial award application deadline: 4/1; financial award applicants required to submit FAFSA. *Unit head:* Dr. Martha A. Adler, Program Coordinator, 313-583-6418, E-mail: maadler@umich.edu. *Application contact:* Elizabeth Morden, Customer Service Assistant, 313-583-6333, Fax: 313-593-4748, E-mail: emorden@umd.umich.edu. Web site: http://www.soe.umd.umich.edu/soe_masters/.

University of Michigan–Flint, School of Education and Human Services, Flint, MI 48502-1950. Offers MA. Part-time programs available. *Entrance requirements:* For master's, BS with minimum GPA of 3.0. Additional exam requirements/recommendations for international students: Required—TOEFL (minimum score 560 paper-based; 220 computer-based; 84 iBT), IELTS (minimum score 6.5). *Expenses:* Contact institution.

University of Minnesota, Duluth, Graduate School, College of Education and Human Service Professions, Department of Education, Duluth, MN 55812-2496. Offers Ed D. Part-time and evening/weekend programs available. *Degree requirements:* For doctorate, comprehensive exam. *Entrance requirements:* For doctorate, GRE, MA (preferred) minimum GPA of 3.0, 3 letters of recommendation, 3 work samples. Additional exam requirements/recommendations for international students: Required—TOEFL (minimum score 550 paper-based; 213 computer-based).

University of Minnesota, Twin Cities Campus, Graduate School, College of Education and Human Development, Minneapolis, MN 55455-0213. Offers M Ed, MA, MSW, Ed D, PhD, Certificate, Ed S. *Accreditation:* NCATE. Part-time programs available. *Faculty:* 179 full-time (95 women). *Students:* 1,520 full-time (1,120 women), 963 part-time (675 women); includes 355 minority (138 Black or African American, non-Hispanic/Latino; 28 American Indian or Alaska Native, non-Hispanic/Latino; 121 Asian, non-Hispanic/Latino; 66 Hispanic/Latino; 2 Native Hawaiian or other Pacific Islander, non-Hispanic/Latino), 227 international. Average age 33. 2,331 applicants, 54% accepted, 956 enrolled. In 2011, 1,035 master's, 118 doctorates, 207 other advanced degrees awarded. Application fee: $55. *Financial support:* In 2011–12, 67 fellowships (averaging $17,043 per year), 347 research assistantships with full tuition reimbursements (averaging $9,209 per year), 212 teaching assistantships with full tuition reimbursements (averaging $9,701 per year) were awarded; scholarships/grants and tuition waivers (partial) also available. Financial award applicants required to submit FAFSA. *Faculty research:* Learning technologies, literacy, violence prevention, exercise science and movement, assessment and accountability, aging, science and mathematics education, curriculum-based measurement and student assessment. *Total annual research expenditures:* $32.7 million. *Unit head:* Dr. Jean K. Quam, Dean, 612-626-9252, Fax: 612-626-7496, E-mail: jquam@umn.edu. *Application contact:* Dr. Jennifer Engler, Assistant Dean for Student Services, 612-626-2887, Fax: 612-626-7496, E-mail: engle009@umn.edu. Web site: http://www.cehd.umn.edu.

University of Mississippi, Graduate School, School of Education, Oxford, University, MS 38677. Offers M Ed, MA, Ed D, PhD, Ed S, Specialist. *Accreditation:* NCATE. *Students:* 225 full-time (163 women), 374 part-time (276 women); includes 175 minority (158 Black or African American, non-Hispanic/Latino; 3 Asian, non-Hispanic/Latino; 8 Hispanic/Latino; 6 Two or more races, non-Hispanic/Latino), 11 international. In 2011, 227 master's, 24 doctorates awarded. *Degree requirements:* For doctorate, thesis/dissertation. *Entrance requirements:* For master's, GRE General Test, minimum GPA of 3.0; for doctorate, GRE General Test. Additional exam requirements/recommendations for international students: Required—TOEFL. *Application deadline:* For fall admission, 4/1 for domestic students; for spring admission, 10/1 for domestic students. Applications are processed on a rolling basis. Application fee: $25. Electronic applications accepted. *Financial support:* Scholarships/grants available. Financial award application deadline: 3/1; financial award applicants required to submit FAFSA. *Unit head:* Dr. David Rock, Interim Dean, 662-915-7063, Fax: 662-915-7249, E-mail: soe@olemiss.edu. *Application contact:* Dr. Christy M. Wyandt, Associate Dean, 662-915-7474, Fax: 662-915-7577, E-mail: cwyandt@olemiss.edu.

University of Missouri, Graduate School, College of Education, Columbia, MO 65211. Offers M Ed, MA, Ed D, PhD, Ed S. Part-time and evening/weekend programs available. *Faculty:* 111 full-time (66 women), 98 part-time/adjunct (80 women). *Students:* 635 full-time (466 women), 964 part-time (687 women); includes 144 minority (71 Black or African American, non-Hispanic/Latino; 4 American Indian or Alaska Native, non-Hispanic/Latino; 18 Asian, non-Hispanic/Latino; 35 Hispanic/Latino; 16 Two or more races, non-Hispanic/Latino), 115 international. Average age 34. 1,019 applicants, 63% accepted, 458 enrolled. In 2011, 495 master's, 84 doctorates, 57 other advanced degrees awarded. Terminal master's awarded for partial completion of doctoral program. *Degree requirements:* For master's, variable foreign language requirement, thesis (for some programs); for doctorate, variable foreign language requirement, comprehensive exam (for some programs), thesis/dissertation. *Entrance requirements:* For master's, minimum GPA of 3.0; for doctorate, GRE General Test. *Application deadline:* Applications are processed on a rolling basis. Application fee: $55 ($75 for international students). *Expenses:* Tuition, state resident: full-time $5881. Tuition, nonresident: full-time $15,183. *Required fees:* $952. Tuition and fees vary according to campus/location and program. *Financial support:* Fellowships, research assistantships, teaching assistantships, institutionally sponsored loans, and scholarships/grants available. *Unit head:* Dr. Rose Porter, Interim Dean, 573-882-8524, E-mail: porterr@missouri.edu. *Application contact:* Adrienne Vaughn, Recruitment Coordinator, E-mail: alvhcd@mizzou.edu. Web site: http://education.missouri.edu/.

University of Missouri–Kansas City, School of Education, Kansas City, MO 64110-2499. Offers administration (Ed D); counseling and guidance (MA, Ed S); counseling psychology (PhD); curriculum and instruction (MA, Ed S); education (PhD); educational administration (MA, Ed S); reading education (MA, Ed S); special education (MA). PhD in education offered through the School of Graduate Studies. *Accreditation:* NCATE. Part-time and evening/weekend programs available. *Faculty:* 59 full-time (47 women), 57 part-time/adjunct (42 women). *Students:* 221 full-time (155 women), 379 part-time (271 women); includes 140 minority (95 Black or African American, non-Hispanic/Latino; 1 American Indian or Alaska Native, non-Hispanic/Latino; 15 Asian, non-Hispanic/Latino; 27 Hispanic/Latino; 2 Two or more races, non-Hispanic/Latino), 16 international. Average age 33. 332 applicants, 51% accepted, 136 enrolled. In 2011, 131 master's, 4 doctorates, 25 other advanced degrees awarded. *Degree requirements:* For doctorate, thesis/dissertation, internship, practicum. *Entrance requirements:* For master's, GRE, minimum GPA of 2.75, 2 letters of reference, written statement of purpose; for doctorate, GRE, minimum GPA of 3.0; for Ed S, minimum GPA of 3.0. Additional exam requirements/recommendations for international students: Required—TOEFL (minimum score 550 paper-based; 213 computer-based; 80 iBT). *Application deadline:* For fall admission, 4/1 priority date for domestic students, 4/1 for international students; for spring admission, 11/1 priority date for domestic students, 11/1 for international students. Applications are processed on a rolling basis. Application fee: $45 ($50 for international students). *Expenses:* Tuition, state resident: full-time $5798; part-time $322.10 per credit hour. Tuition, nonresident: full-time $14,969; part-time $831.60 per credit hour. *Required fees:* $93.51 per credit hour. *Financial support:* In 2011–12, 15 research assistantships with partial tuition reimbursements (averaging $10,720 per year) were awarded; career-related internships or fieldwork, Federal Work-Study, institutionally sponsored loans, and tuition waivers (full and partial) also available. Support available to part-time students. Financial award application deadline: 3/1; financial award applicants required to submit FAFSA. *Faculty research:* Urban education, inquiry-based field study, theories of counseling and psychotherapy, school literacy, educational technology. *Unit head:* Dr. Wanda Blanchett, Dean, 816-235-2234, Fax: 816-235-5270, E-mail: education@umkc.edu. *Application contact:* Erica Hernandez-Scott, Student Recruiter, 816-235-1295, Fax: 816-235-5270, E-mail: hernandeze@umkc.edu. Web site: http://education.umkc.edu.

University of Missouri–St. Louis, College of Education, St. Louis, MO 63121. Offers M Ed, Ed D, PhD, Certificate, Ed S. *Accreditation:* NCATE. Part-time and evening/weekend programs available. *Faculty:* 65 full-time (31 women), 79 part-time/adjunct (52 women). *Students:* 232 full-time (168 women), 1,257 part-time (954 women); includes 402 minority (317 Black or African American, non-Hispanic/Latino; 4 American Indian or Alaska Native, non-Hispanic/Latino; 27 Asian, non-Hispanic/Latino; 43 Hispanic/Latino; 11 Two or more races, non-Hispanic/Latino), 23 international. Average age 33. 662 applicants, 77% accepted, 391 enrolled. In 2011, 307 master's, 27 doctorates, 35 other advanced degrees awarded. *Degree requirements:* For master's, comprehensive exam, thesis optional; for doctorate, thesis/dissertation. *Entrance requirements:* For doctorate, GRE General Test, 3 letters of recommendation. Additional exam requirements/recommendations for international students: Recommended—TOEFL (minimum score 550 paper-based; 213 computer-based). *Application deadline:* For fall admission, 7/1 priority date for domestic students, 7/1 for international students; for spring admission, 12/1 priority date for domestic students, 12/1 for international students. Applications are processed on a rolling basis. Application fee: $35 ($40 for international students). Electronic applications accepted. *Expenses:* Tuition, state resident: full-time $6273; part-time $3866 per year. Tuition, nonresident: full-time $14,969; part-time $9980 per year. *Required fees:* $315 per year. *Financial support:* In 2011–12, 30 research assistantships with full and partial tuition reimbursements (averaging $11,565 per year), 13 teaching assistantships with full and partial tuition reimbursements (averaging $12,400 per year) were awarded. Financial award application deadline: 4/1; financial award applicants required to submit FAFSA. *Faculty research:* Remedial reading, literacy, educational policy and research, science education. *Unit head:* Dr. Kathleen Haywood, Director of Graduate Studies, 314-516-5483, Fax: 314-516-5227, E-mail: kathleen_haywood@umsl.edu. *Application contact:* 314-516-5458, Fax: 314-516-6996, E-mail: gradadm@umsl.edu. Web site: http://coe.umsl.edu/.

University of Mobile, Graduate Programs, Program in Education, Mobile, AL 36613. Offers MA. Part-time programs available. *Faculty:* 6 full-time (3 women), 4 part-time/adjunct (all women). *Students:* 28 full-time (24 women), 91 part-time (83 women); includes 72 minority (70 Black or African American, non-Hispanic/Latino; 1 American Indian or Alaska Native, non-Hispanic/Latino; 1 Two or more races, non-Hispanic/Latino), 1 international. Average age 34. 28 applicants, 100% accepted, 14 enrolled. In 2011, 25 master's awarded. *Degree requirements:* For master's, comprehensive exam, thesis optional. *Entrance requirements:* For master's, GRE, Alabama teaching certificate. Additional exam requirements/recommendations for international students: Required—TOEFL (minimum score 550 paper-based; 213 computer-based; 80 iBT). *Application deadline:* For fall admission, 8/3 priority date for domestic students; for spring admission, 12/23 for domestic students. Applications are processed on a rolling basis. Application fee: $40 ($50 for international students). *Expenses: Tuition:* Full-time $8262; part-time $459 per credit hour. *Required fees:* $110 per term. *Financial support:* Application deadline: 8/1. *Faculty research:* Retention, writing across the curriculum. *Unit head:* Dr. Peter Kingsford, Dean, School of Education, 251-442-2355, Fax: 251-442-2523, E-mail: pkingsford@umobile.edu. *Application contact:* Tammy C. Eubanks, Administrative Assistant to Dean of Graduate Programs, 251-442-2270, Fax: 251-442-2523, E-mail: teubanks@umobile.edu. Web site: http://www.umobile.edu/Academics/AcademicAreas/SchoolofEducation/MasterofArtsinEducation.aspx.

The University of Montana, Graduate School, College of Visual and Performing Arts, School of Art, Missoula, MT 59812-0002. Offers fine arts (MA, MFA), including art (MA), art history (MA), ceramics (MFA), integrated arts and education (MA), media arts (MFA), painting and drawing (MFA), photography (MFA), printmaking (MFA), sculpture (MFA). *Accreditation:* NASAD (one or more programs are accredited). *Degree requirements:* For master's, thesis exhibit. *Entrance requirements:* For master's, GRE General Test, portfolio.

The University of Montana, Graduate School, College of Visual and Performing Arts, School of Theatre and Dance, Missoula, MT 59812-0002. Offers fine arts (MA, MFA), including acting (MFA), design/technology (MFA), directing (MFA), drama (MA), integrated arts and education (MA), media arts (MFA). *Accreditation:* NAST (one or more programs are accredited). *Degree requirements:* For master's, thesis or alternative. *Entrance requirements:* For master's, GRE General Test, audition, portfolio, production notebook.

The University of Montana, Graduate School, Phyllis J. Washington College of Education and Human Sciences, Missoula, MT 59812-0002. Offers M Ed, MA, MS, Ed D, Ed S. *Accreditation:* NCATE. Part-time programs available. *Degree requirements:* For Ed S, thesis. *Entrance requirements:* For master's, GRE General Test, minimum GPA of 3.0; for Ed S, GRE General Test. Additional exam requirements/recommendations for international students: Required—TOEFL. *Faculty research:* Cooperative learning, administrative styles.

University of Montevallo, College of Education, Montevallo, AL 35115. Offers M Ed, Ed S. *Accreditation:* NCATE. Part-time and evening/weekend programs available. *Students:* 134 full-time (109 women), 253 part-time (182 women); includes 82 minority (76 Black or African American, non-Hispanic/Latino; 3 American Indian or Alaska Native, non-Hispanic/Latino; 2 Hispanic/Latino; 1 Two or more races, non-Hispanic/Latino), 1 international. In 2011, 123 master's, 32 Ed Ss awarded. *Degree requirements:* For master's, comprehensive exam. *Entrance requirements:* For master's, GRE General Test, MAT, minimum undergraduate GPA of 2.5. Additional exam requirements/recommendations for international students: Required—TOEFL (minimum score 550 paper-based). *Application deadline:* For fall admission, 7/15 for domestic students; for spring admission, 11/15 for domestic students. Application fee: $25. *Financial support:* Federal Work-Study, scholarships/grants, and unspecified assistantships available. *Unit head:* Dr. Anna E. McEwan, Dean, 205-665-6360, E-mail: mcewanae@montevallo.edu. *Application contact:* E-mail: hartleyrs@montevallo.edu. Web site: http://www.montevallo.edu/coe/.

University of Nebraska at Kearney, Graduate Studies, College of Education, Kearney, NE 68849-0001. Offers MA Ed, MS Ed, Ed S. *Accreditation:* NCATE. Part-time and evening/weekend programs available. *Degree requirements:* For master's, thesis optional. *Entrance requirements:* For degree, GRE General Test. Electronic applications accepted.

University of Nebraska at Omaha, Graduate Studies, College of Education, Omaha, NE 68182. Offers MA, MS, Ed D, Certificate, Ed S. *Accreditation:* NCATE. Part-time and evening/weekend programs available. *Faculty:* 53 full-time (27 women). *Students:* 137 full-time (100 women), 592 part-time (460 women); includes 36 minority (16 Black or African American, non-Hispanic/Latino; 4 American Indian or Alaska Native, non-Hispanic/Latino; 4 Asian, non-Hispanic/Latino; 10 Hispanic/Latino; 2 Two or more races, non-Hispanic/Latino), 4 international. Average age 33. 196 applicants, 76% accepted, 108 enrolled. In 2011, 231 master's, 15 doctorates, 3 other advanced degrees awarded. *Degree requirements:* For master's, comprehensive exam (for some programs), thesis (for some programs); for doctorate, comprehensive exam, thesis/dissertation. *Entrance requirements:* For master's, minimum GPA of 3.0; for doctorate, GRE General Test, resume, 3 samples of research/written work, statement of purpose, letters of recommendation. Additional exam requirements/recommendations for international students: Required—TOEFL. *Application deadline:* Applications are processed on a rolling basis. Application fee: $45. Electronic applications accepted. *Financial support:* In 2011–12, 98 students received support, including 43 research assistantships with tuition reimbursements available, 13 teaching assistantships with tuition reimbursements available; fellowships, career-related internships or fieldwork, Federal Work-Study, institutionally sponsored loans, scholarships/grants, tuition waivers (full), and unspecified assistantships also available. Support available to part-time students. Financial award application deadline: 3/1; financial award applicants required to submit FAFSA. *Unit head:* Dr. Nancy Edick, Chairperson, 402-554-2212. *Application contact:* Fax: 402-554-3143, E-mail: graduate@unomaha.edu.

University of Nevada, Las Vegas, Graduate College, College of Education, Las Vegas, NV 89154-3001. Offers M Ed, MS, Ed D, PhD, Advanced Certificate, Ed S, PhD/JD. *Accreditation:* NCATE. Part-time and evening/weekend programs available. *Faculty:* 81 full-time (40 women), 47 part-time/adjunct (29 women). *Students:* 387 full-time (273 women), 672 part-time (482 women); includes 287 minority (96 Black or African American, non-Hispanic/Latino; 4 American Indian or Alaska Native, non-Hispanic/Latino; 30 Asian, non-Hispanic/Latino; 113 Hispanic/Latino; 6 Native Hawaiian or other Pacific Islander, non-Hispanic/Latino; 38 Two or more races, non-Hispanic/Latino), 27 international. Average age 35. 500 applicants, 76% accepted, 329 enrolled. In 2011, 534 master's, 32 doctorates, 14 other advanced degrees awarded. *Degree requirements:* For master's, comprehensive exam (for some programs), thesis optional; for doctorate, comprehensive exam, thesis/dissertation. *Entrance requirements:* Additional exam requirements/recommendations for international students: Required—TOEFL (minimum score 550 paper-based; 213 computer-based; 80 iBT), IELTS (minimum score 7). *Application deadline:* For fall admission, 5/1 for international students; for spring admission, 10/1 for international students. Application fee: $60 ($95 for international students). Electronic applications accepted. *Financial support:* In 2011–12, 141 students received support, including 1 fellowship with full tuition reimbursement available (averaging $25,000 per year), 49 research assistantships with partial tuition reimbursements available (averaging $8,845 per year), 91 teaching assistantships with partial tuition reimbursements available (averaging $10,967 per year); institutionally sponsored loans, scholarships/grants, health care benefits, and unspecified assistantships also available. Financial award application deadline: 3/1. *Total annual research expenditures:* $1.7 million. *Unit head:* Dr. William Speer, Interim Dean, 702-895-3375, Fax: 702-895-4068, E-mail: william.speer@unlv.edu. *Application contact:* Graduate College Admissions Evaluator, 702-895-3320, Fax: 702-895-4180, E-mail: gradcollege@unlv.edu. Web site: http://education.unlv.edu/.

University of Nevada, Reno, Graduate School, College of Education, Reno, NV 89557. Offers M Ed, MA, MS, Ed D, PhD, Ed S. *Accreditation:* NCATE. Terminal master's awarded for partial completion of doctoral program. *Degree requirements:* For master's, thesis optional; for doctorate, thesis/dissertation. *Entrance requirements:* For master's, GRE, minimum GPA of 2.75; for doctorate, GRE, minimum GPA of 3.0. Additional exam requirements/recommendations for international students: Required—TOEFL (minimum score 500 paper-based; 173 computer-based; 61 iBT), IELTS (minimum score 6). Electronic applications accepted.

University of New Brunswick Fredericton, School of Graduate Studies, Faculty of Education, Fredericton, NB E3B 5A3, Canada. Offers M Ed, PhD. Part-time programs available. Postbaccalaureate distance learning degree programs offered. *Faculty:* 33 full-time (18 women), 21 part-time/adjunct (13 women). *Students:* 84 full-time (65 women), 355 part-time (263 women). In 2011, 174 master's, 1 doctorate awarded. *Degree requirements:* For master's, variable foreign language requirement, thesis optional; for doctorate, variable foreign language requirement, comprehensive exam, thesis/dissertation. *Entrance requirements:* For master's, minimum GPA of 3.0. Additional exam requirements/recommendations for international students: Required—TOEFL (minimum score 650 paper-based; 280 computer-based); Recommended—TWE (minimum score 5.5). *Application deadline:* For fall admission, 1/31 priority date for domestic students, 1/31 for international students; for winter admission, 1/31 priority date for domestic students, 1/31 for international students; for spring admission, 1/31 priority date for domestic students, 1/31 for international students. Application fee: $50 Canadian dollars. Electronic applications accepted. *Financial support:* Fellowships, research assistantships, teaching assistantships, and tuition waivers available. *Faculty research:* Second language research; health and education research; social policy; youth, science, teaching and learning; early childhood. *Unit head:* Dr. David Wagner, Associate Dean, 506-447-3294, Fax: 506-453-3569, E-mail: dwagner@unb.ca. *Application contact:* Carolyn King, Graduate Secretary, 506-458-7147, Fax: 506-453-3569, E-mail: kingc@unb.ca. Web site: http://www.unbf.ca/education.

University of New England, College of Arts and Sciences, Program in Education, Biddeford, ME 04005-9526. Offers advanced educational leadership (CAGS); curriculum and instruction strategies (CAGS); curriculum and instruction strategy (MS Ed); educational leadership (MS Ed, CAGS); general studies (MS Ed); inclusion education (MS Ed); leadership, ethics and change (CAGS); literacy K-12 (MS Ed, CAGS); teaching methodologies (MS Ed). Part-time programs available. Postbaccalaureate distance learning degree programs offered (minimal on-campus study). *Faculty:* 20 part-time/adjunct. *Students:* 514 full-time (417 women), 218 part-time (165 women). In 2011, 307 master's, 86 CAGSs awarded. *Degree requirements:* For master's, collaborative action research project, integrative seminar portfolio. *Entrance requirements:* For master's, teaching certificate, 2 years of teaching experience. Additional exam requirements/recommendations for international students: Required—TOEFL. *Application deadline:* For fall admission, 9/15 for domestic students; for spring admission, 1/15 for domestic students. Applications are processed on a rolling basis. Application fee: $40. Electronic applications accepted. *Expenses:* Contact institution. *Financial support:* Application deadline: 5/1; applicants required to submit FAFSA. *Faculty research:* Distance learning, effective teaching, transition planning, adult learning. *Unit head:* Dr. Doug Lynch, Chair of Education Department, 207-283-0171 Ext. 2888, E-mail: dlynch@une.edu. *Application contact:* Stacy Gato, Assistant Director of Graduate Admissions, 207-221-4225, Fax: 207-221-4898, E-mail: gradadmissions@une.edu.

University of New Hampshire, Graduate School, College of Liberal Arts, Department of Education, Durham, NH 03824. Offers counseling (M Ed); early childhood education (M Ed), including early childhood education, special needs; education (PhD); educational administration (M Ed, Ed S); elementary education (M Ed, MAT); secondary education (M Ed, MAT); special education (M Ed, Postbaccalaureate Certificate); teacher leadership (M Ed, Postbaccalaureate Certificate). *Accreditation:* Teacher Education Accreditation Council. Part-time programs available. *Faculty:* 29 full-time (19 women). *Students:* 150 full-time (110 women), 225 part-time (167 women); includes 14 minority (3 Black or African American, non-Hispanic/Latino; 7 Asian, non-Hispanic/Latino; 3 Hispanic/Latino; 1 Two or more races, non-Hispanic/Latino), 3 international. Average age 31. 183 applicants, 64% accepted, 69 enrolled. In 2011, 213 master's, 11 doctorates, 5 other advanced degrees awarded. *Degree requirements:* For doctorate, thesis/dissertation. *Entrance requirements:* For master's, doctorate, and other advanced degree, GRE General Test. Additional exam requirements/recommendations for international students: Required—TOEFL (minimum score 550 paper-based; 213 computer-based; 80 iBT). *Application deadline:* For fall admission, 4/1 priority date for domestic students, 4/1 for international students; for spring admission, 12/1 priority date for domestic students. Applications are processed on a rolling basis. Application fee: $65. Electronic applications accepted. *Expenses:* Tuition, state resident: full-time $12,360; part-time $687 per credit hour. Tuition, nonresident: full-time $25,680; part-time $1058 per credit hour. *International tuition:* $29,550 full-time. *Required fees:* $1666; $833 per course. $416.50 per semester. Tuition and fees vary according to course load and degree level. *Financial support:* In 2011–12, 56 students received support, including 1 fellowship, 17 teaching assistantships; research assistantships, career-related internships or fieldwork, Federal Work-Study, scholarships/grants, and tuition waivers (full and partial) also available. Support available to part-time students. Financial award application deadline: 2/15. *Unit head:* Dr. Michael Middleton, Chairperson, 603-862-7054, E-mail: education.department@unh.edu. *Application contact:* Lisa Wilder, Graduate Coordinator, 603-862-2310, E-mail: education.department@unh.edu. Web site: http://www.unh.edu/education/.

University of New Hampshire, Graduate School Manchester Campus, Manchester, NH 03101. Offers business administration (MBA); counseling (M Ed); education (M Ed, MAT); educational administration and supervision (M Ed, Ed S); information technology (MS); management of technology (MS); public administration (MPA); public health (MPH, Certificate); social work (MSW); software systems engineering (Certificate). Part-time and evening/weekend programs available. *Students:* 78 full-time (50 women), 130 part-time (65 women); includes 62 minority (2 Black or African American, non-Hispanic/Latino; 56 Asian, non-Hispanic/Latino; 4 Hispanic/Latino), 4 international. Average age 34. 132 applicants, 55% accepted, 57 enrolled. In 2011, 66 master's, 9 other advanced degrees awarded. *Degree requirements:* For master's, thesis or alternative. *Entrance requirements:* Additional exam requirements/recommendations for international students: Required—TOEFL (minimum score 550 paper-based; 213 computer-based; 80 iBT). *Application deadline:* For fall admission, 6/1 for domestic students, 4/1 for international students; for spring admission, 12/1 for domestic students. Applications are processed on a rolling basis. Application fee: $65. Electronic applications accepted. *Expenses:* Tuition, state resident: full-time $12,360; part-time $687 per credit hour. Tuition, nonresident: full-time $25,680; part-time $1058 per credit hour. *International tuition:* $29,550 full-time. *Required fees:* $1666; $833 per course. $416.50 per semester. Tuition and fees vary according to course load and degree level. *Financial support:* In 2011–12, 11 students received support, including 2 teaching assistantships; fellowships, research assistantships, Federal Work-Study, scholarships/grants, health care benefits, and unspecified assistantships also available. Support available to part-time students. Financial award application deadline: 3/1; financial award applicants required to submit FAFSA. *Unit head:* Candice Brown, Director, 603-641-4313, E-mail: unhm.gradcenter@unh.edu. *Application contact:* Graduate Admissions Office, 603-862-3000, Fax: 603-862-0275, E-mail: grad.school@unh.edu. Web site: http://www.gradschool.unh.edu/manchester/.

University of New Haven, Graduate School, College of Arts and Sciences, Programs in Education, West Haven, CT 06516-1916. Offers professional education (MS); teacher certification (MS). Part-time and evening/weekend programs available. *Students:* 121 full-time (88 women), 113 part-time (84 women); includes 15 minority (6 Black or African American, non-Hispanic/Latino; 1 Asian, non-Hispanic/Latino; 5 Hispanic/Latino; 3 Two or more races, non-Hispanic/Latino). 97 applicants, 89% accepted, 82 enrolled. In 2011, 201 master's awarded. *Entrance requirements:* For master's, PRAXIS I. Additional exam requirements/recommendations for international students: Required—TOEFL (minimum score 520 paper-based; 190 computer-based; 70 iBT); Recommended—IELTS (minimum score 5.5). *Application deadline:* For fall admission, 5/31 for international students; for winter admission, 10/15 for international students; for spring admission, 1/15 for international students. Applications are processed on a rolling basis. Application fee: $50. Electronic applications accepted. *Expenses: Tuition:* Part-time $750 per credit. *Financial support:* Research assistantships with partial tuition reimbursements, teaching assistantships with partial tuition reimbursements, career-related internships or fieldwork, Federal Work-Study, scholarships/grants, tuition waivers, and unspecified assistantships available. Financial award applicants required to submit FAFSA. *Unit head:* Dr. Nancy Neimi, Chair, 203-932-932-7466, E-mail: nniemi@newhaven.edu. *Application contact:* Eloise Gormley, Director of Graduate Admissions, 203-932-7449, Fax: 203-932-7137, E-mail: gradinfo@newhaven.edu. Web site: http://www.newhaven.edu/4601/Education/.

University of New Mexico, Graduate School, College of Education, Department of Teacher Education, Albuquerque, NM 87131-2039. Offers curriculum and instruction (Ed S); elementary education (MA), including math, science, environmental and technology education; multicultural teacher and childhood education (Ed D, PhD); secondary education (MA), including mathematics, science, and educational technology education. Part-time and evening/weekend programs available. *Faculty:* 26 full-time (21 women), 1 part-time/adjunct (0 women). *Students:* 76 full-time (55 women), 233 part-time (182 women); includes 116 minority (7 Black or African American, non-Hispanic/Latino; 17 American Indian or Alaska Native, non-Hispanic/Latino; 12 Asian, non-Hispanic/Latino; 74 Hispanic/Latino; 1 Native Hawaiian or other Pacific Islander, non-Hispanic/Latino; 5 Two or more races, non-Hispanic/Latino), 4 international. Average age 35. 123 applicants, 64% accepted, 63 enrolled. In 2011, 145 degrees awarded. *Degree requirements:* For master's, comprehensive exam, thesis optional; for Ed S, comprehensive exam. *Entrance requirements:* For master's, minimum overall GPA of 3.0, some experience working with students; for Ed S, master's degree, minimum overall GPA of 3.0, experience working with students. Additional exam requirements/recommendations for international students: Required—TOEFL (minimum score 550 paper-based; 213 computer-based). *Application deadline:* For fall admission, 3/1 for domestic students; for spring admission, 10/1 for domestic students. Applications are processed on a rolling basis. Application fee: $50. Electronic applications accepted. *Financial support:* In 2011–12, 211 students received support, including 1 fellowship (averaging $2,000 per year), 2 research assistantships (averaging $22,000 per year), 5 teaching assistantships with partial tuition reimbursements available (averaging $8,662 per year); career-related internships or fieldwork, scholarships/grants, and unspecified assistantships also available. Financial award applicants required to submit FAFSA. *Total annual research expenditures:* $15,147. *Unit head:* Dr. Rosalita Mitchell, Department Chair, 505-277-9611, Fax: 505-277-0455, E-mail: ted@unm.edu. *Application contact:* Sarah Valles, Administrator, 505-277-0504, Fax: 505-277-0455, E-mail: ted@unm.edu. Web site: http://ted.unm.edu/.

University of New Orleans, Graduate School, College of Education and Human Development, New Orleans, LA 70148. Offers M Ed, MAT, PhD, GCE. *Accreditation:* NCATE. Part-time programs available. Postbaccalaureate distance learning degree programs offered. *Degree requirements:* For master's, comprehensive exam, thesis optional; for doctorate, comprehensive exam, thesis/dissertation. *Entrance requirements:* For master's and doctorate, GRE General Test. Additional exam requirements/recommendations for international students: Required—TOEFL (minimum score 550 paper-based; 213 computer-based; 79 iBT). Electronic applications accepted. *Faculty research:* Special education and habilitation, educational administration, exercise physiology, wellness, effective school instruction.

University of North Alabama, College of Education, Florence, AL 35632-0001. Offers MA, MA Ed, MS, Ed S. *Accreditation:* NCATE. Part-time and evening/weekend programs available. *Faculty:* 9 full-time (4 women), 19 part-time/adjunct (14 women). *Students:* 120 full-time (76 women), 181 part-time (139 women); includes 34 minority (22 Black or African American, non-Hispanic/Latino; 3 American Indian or Alaska Native, non-Hispanic/Latino; 2 Asian, non-Hispanic/Latino; 3 Hispanic/Latino; 4 Two or more races, non-Hispanic/Latino), 4 international. Average age 32. In 2011, 81 master's, 8 other advanced degrees awarded. *Degree requirements:* For master's, comprehensive exam. *Entrance requirements:* For master's, GRE, MAT, or NTE, minimum GPA of 2.5, Alabama Class B Certificate or equivalent, teaching experience. *Application deadline:* For fall admission, 7/1 priority date for domestic students; for spring admission, 12/1 for domestic students. Applications are processed on a rolling basis. Application fee: $25. Electronic applications accepted. *Financial support:* Federal Work-Study available. Support available to part-time students. Financial award application deadline: 4/1. *Unit head:* Dr. Donna Jacobs, Dean, 256-765-4252, Fax: 256-765-4664, E-mail: dpjacobs@una.edu. *Application contact:* Kim Mauldin, Director of Admissions, 256-765-4608, Fax: 256-765-4960, E-mail: komauldin@una.edu. Web site: http://www.una.edu/education/.

The University of North Carolina at Chapel Hill, Graduate School, School of Education, Chapel Hill, NC 27514-3500. Offers M Ed, MA, MAT, MSA, Ed D, PhD. *Accreditation:* NCATE. Part-time programs available. *Degree requirements:* For master's, comprehensive exam, thesis (for some programs); for doctorate, comprehensive exam, thesis/dissertation. *Entrance requirements:* For master's and doctorate, GRE General Test, minimum GPA of 3.0 during last 2 years of undergraduate course work. Additional exam requirements/recommendations for international students: Required—TOEFL (minimum score 550 paper-based; 79 computer-based). Electronic applications accepted. *Faculty research:* Curriculum development; school success and intervention; professional development, recruitment and retention; service-learning; evaluation.

The University of North Carolina at Greensboro, Graduate School, School of Education, Greensboro, NC 27412-5001. Offers M Ed, MLIS, MS, MSA, Ed D, PhD, Certificate, Ed S, PMC, MS/Ed S, MS/PhD. *Accreditation:* NCATE. Part-time and evening/weekend programs available. *Degree requirements:* For doctorate, thesis/dissertation. *Entrance requirements:* For master's, doctorate, and other advanced degree, GRE General Test. Additional exam requirements/recommendations for international students: Required—TOEFL. Electronic applications accepted. *Faculty research:* Effects of homogeneous grouping, women in higher education, assessment of student achievement.

The University of North Carolina at Pembroke, Graduate Studies, School of Education, Pembroke, NC 28372-1510. Offers elementary education (MA Ed); middle grades education (MA Ed, MAT); reading education (MA Ed); school administration (MSA); school counseling (MA Ed). *Accreditation:* NCATE. Part-time and evening/weekend programs available. *Degree requirements:* For master's, comprehensive exam (for some programs), thesis optional. *Entrance requirements:* For master's, GRE General Test or MAT, minimum GPA of 3.0 in major, 2.5 overall. Additional exam requirements/recommendations for international students: Required—TOEFL.

The University of North Carolina Wilmington, Watson School of Education, Wilmington, NC 28403-3297. Offers M Ed, MAT, MS, MSA, Ed D. *Accreditation:* NCATE. Part-time and evening/weekend programs available. *Degree requirements:* For master's, comprehensive exam, thesis (for some programs); for doctorate, comprehensive exam, thesis/dissertation. *Entrance requirements:* For master's, GRE General Test, MAT, minimum B average in upper-division undergraduate course work. Additional exam requirements/recommendations for international students: Required—TOEFL (minimum score 550 paper-based; 217 computer-based; 79 iBT), IELTS (minimum score 6.5).

University of North Dakota, Graduate School, College of Education and Human Development, Grand Forks, ND 58202. Offers M Ed, MA, MS, MSW, Ed D, PhD, Specialist. *Accreditation:* NCATE. Part-time and evening/weekend programs available. Postbaccalaureate distance learning degree programs offered (minimal on-campus study). *Degree requirements:* For master's, comprehensive exam, thesis or alternative; for doctorate, comprehensive exam, thesis/dissertation; for Specialist, comprehensive exam (for some programs), thesis (for some programs). *Entrance requirements:* For master's, GRE General Test, MAT, GRE Subject Test, minimum GPA of 3.0; for doctorate, GRE Subject Test, minimum GPA of 3.5. Additional exam requirements/recommendations for international students: Required—TOEFL (minimum score 550 paper-based; 213 computer-based; 79 iBT), IELTS (minimum score 6.5). Electronic applications accepted.

University of Northern British Columbia, Office of Graduate Studies, Prince George, BC V2N 4Z9, Canada. Offers business administration (Diploma); community health science (M Sc); disability management (MA); education (M Ed); first nations studies (MA); gender studies (MA); history (MA); interdisciplinary studies (MA); international studies (MA); mathematical, computer and physical sciences (M Sc); natural resources and environmental studies (M Sc, MA, MNRES, PhD); political science (MA); psychology (M Sc, PhD); social work (MSW). Part-time and evening/weekend programs available. Postbaccalaureate distance learning degree programs offered (no on-campus study). *Degree requirements:* For master's, thesis; for doctorate, thesis/dissertation. *Entrance requirements:* For master's, GRE, minimum B average in undergraduate course work; for doctorate, candidacy exam, minimum A average in graduate course work.

University of Northern Colorado, Graduate School, College of Education and Behavioral Sciences, Greeley, CO 80639. Offers MA, MAT, MS, Ed D, PhD, Ed S. *Accreditation:* NCATE. Part-time programs available. Postbaccalaureate distance learning degree programs offered. *Degree requirements:* For master's, comprehensive exam, thesis optional; for doctorate, comprehensive exam, thesis/dissertation; for Ed S, comprehensive exam, thesis. *Entrance requirements:* For doctorate, GRE General Test.

University of Northern Iowa, Graduate College, College of Education, Cedar Falls, IA 50614. Offers MA, MAE, MS, Ed D, Ed S. Part-time and evening/weekend programs available. *Students:* 157 full-time (98 women), 347 part-time (261 women); includes 52 minority (31 Black or African American, non-Hispanic/Latino; 6 Asian, non-Hispanic/Latino; 14 Hispanic/Latino; 1 Two or more races, non-Hispanic/Latino), 27 international.

372 applicants, 60% accepted, 157 enrolled. In 2011, 182 master's, 12 doctorates, 5 other advanced degrees awarded. *Degree requirements:* For Ed S, thesis or alternative. *Entrance requirements:* For master's, minimum GPA of 3.0; for doctorate, GRE, master's degree, minimum GPA of 3.5; for Ed S, GRE General Test, GRE Subject Test. Additional exam requirements/recommendations for international students: Required—TOEFL (minimum score 500 paper-based; 180 computer-based; 61 iBT). *Application deadline:* For fall admission, 8/1 priority date for domestic students. Applications are processed on a rolling basis. Application fee: $50 ($70 for international students). Electronic applications accepted. *Expenses:* Tuition, state resident: full-time $7476. Tuition, nonresident: full-time $16,410. *Required fees:* $942. *Financial support:* Career-related internships or fieldwork, Federal Work-Study, institutionally sponsored loans, scholarships/grants, and tuition waivers (full and partial) available. Support available to part-time students. Financial award application deadline: 2/1. *Unit head:* Dr. Dwight Watson, Dean, 319-273-2717, Fax: 319-273-2607, E-mail: dwight.watson@uni.edu. *Application contact:* Laurie S. Russell, Record Analyst, 319-273-2623, Fax: 319-273-2885, E-mail: laurie.russell@uni.edu. Web site: http://www.uni.edu/coe/.

University of North Florida, College of Education and Human Services, Jacksonville, FL 32224. Offers M Ed, Ed D. *Accreditation:* NCATE. Part-time and evening/weekend programs available. *Faculty:* 52 full-time (33 women), 4 part-time/adjunct (3 women). *Students:* 122 full-time (104 women), 303 part-time (226 women); includes 98 minority (61 Black or African American, non-Hispanic/Latino; 3 American Indian or Alaska Native, non-Hispanic/Latino; 9 Asian, non-Hispanic/Latino; 21 Hispanic/Latino; 4 Two or more races, non-Hispanic/Latino), 10 international. Average age 34. 181 applicants, 54% accepted, 78 enrolled. In 2011, 146 master's, 6 doctorates awarded. Terminal master's awarded for partial completion of doctoral program. *Degree requirements:* For doctorate, thesis/dissertation. *Entrance requirements:* For master's, GRE General Test, minimum GPA of 3.0 in last 60 hours, interview, 3 letters of recommendation; for doctorate, GRE General Test, master's degree, interview, writing sample, 3 letters of recommendation. Additional exam requirements/recommendations for international students: Required—TOEFL (minimum score 500 paper-based; 173 computer-based). *Application deadline:* For fall admission, 7/1 priority date for domestic students, 5/1 for international students; for spring admission, 11/1 priority date for domestic students, 10/1 for international students. Applications are processed on a rolling basis. Application fee: $30. Electronic applications accepted. *Expenses:* Tuition, state resident: full-time $8793; part-time $366.38 per credit hour. Tuition, nonresident: full-time $23,502; part-time $979.24 per credit hour. *Required fees:* $1384; $57.66 per credit hour. Tuition and fees vary according to course load and program. *Financial support:* In 2011–12, 110 students received support, including 5 research assistantships (averaging $5,540 per year), 2 teaching assistantships (averaging $6,250 per year); career-related internships or fieldwork, Federal Work-Study, scholarships/grants, and tuition waivers (partial) also available. Support available to part-time students. Financial award application deadline: 4/1; financial award applicants required to submit FAFSA. *Faculty research:* Effective instruction, technology education, exceptional student education, multiculturalism. *Total annual research expenditures:* $1.1 million. *Unit head:* Dr. Larry Daniel, Dean, 904-620-2520, E-mail: ldaniel@unf.edu. *Application contact:* Dr. John Kemppainen, Director, Office of Student Services, 904-620-2530, Fax: 904-620-1135, E-mail: jkemppai@unf.edu. Web site: http://www.unf.edu/coehs/.

University of North Texas, Toulouse Graduate School, College of Education, Denton, TX 76203. Offers M Ed, MS, Ed D, PhD, Certificate. *Accreditation:* NCATE. Part-time and evening/weekend programs available. Terminal master's awarded for partial completion of doctoral program. *Degree requirements:* For master's, thesis or alternative; for doctorate, thesis/dissertation. *Entrance requirements:* For master's and doctorate, GRE General Test. Additional exam requirements/recommendations for international students: Recommended—TOEFL (minimum score 550 paper-based; 213 computer-based). *Expenses:* Tuition, state resident: part-time $100 per credit hour. Tuition, nonresident: part-time $413 per credit hour. *Faculty research:* Teacher competency, educational measurement, higher education, biological and chemical bases of learning, technology in the classroom.

University of Notre Dame, Graduate School, College of Arts and Letters, Division of Social Science, Institute for Educational Initiatives, Notre Dame, IN 46556. Offers M Ed, MA. Enrollment restricted to participants in the Alliance for Catholic Education (ACE) program. *Entrance requirements:* For master's, GRE General Test, acceptance into the Alliance for Catholic Education program. Electronic applications accepted. *Faculty research:* Effective teaching, motivation, social and ethical development, literacy.

University of Oklahoma, Jeannine Rainbolt College of Education, Norman, OK 73019. Offers M Ed, Ed D, PhD, Graduate Certificate. *Accreditation:* NCATE. Evening/weekend programs available. Postbaccalaureate distance learning degree programs offered (no on-campus study). *Faculty:* 75 full-time (48 women), 2 part-time/adjunct (1 woman). *Students:* 372 full-time (258 women), 443 part-time (304 women); includes 192 minority (81 Black or African American, non-Hispanic/Latino; 51 American Indian or Alaska Native, non-Hispanic/Latino; 14 Asian, non-Hispanic/Latino; 22 Hispanic/Latino; 2 Native Hawaiian or other Pacific Islander, non-Hispanic/Latino; 22 Two or more races, non-Hispanic/Latino), 29 international. Average age 33. 402 applicants, 70% accepted, 227 enrolled. In 2011, 186 master's, 33 doctorates awarded. *Degree requirements:* For doctorate, thesis/dissertation. *Entrance requirements:* For master's, minimum GPA of 3.0 in last 60 hours of undergraduate course work, BS in education; for doctorate, GRE General Test, master's degree. Additional exam requirements/recommendations for international students: Required—TOEFL (minimum score 550 paper-based; 79 iBT). *Application deadline:* For fall admission, 6/1 for domestic students, 3/1 for international students; for spring admission, 11/1 for domestic students, 9/1 for international students. Applications are processed on a rolling basis. Application fee: $40 ($90 for international students). Electronic applications accepted. *Expenses:* Tuition, state resident: full-time $4087; part-time $170.30 per credit hour. Tuition, nonresident: full-time $14,875; part-time $619.80 per credit hour. *Required fees:* $2659; $100.25 per credit hour. Tuition and fees vary according to course load and degree level. *Financial support:* In 2011–12, 534 students received support, including 4 fellowships with full tuition reimbursements available (averaging $5,000 per year), 59 research assistantships with partial tuition reimbursements available (averaging $14,316 per year), 29 teaching assistantships with partial tuition reimbursements available (averaging $10,866 per year); career-related internships or fieldwork, Federal Work-Study, institutionally sponsored loans, scholarships/grants, tuition waivers (full and partial), and unspecified assistantships also available. Support available to part-time students. Financial award applicants required to submit FAFSA. *Total annual research expenditures:* $5.9 million. *Unit head:* Dr. Joan Karen Smith, Dean, 405-325-1081, Fax: 405-325-7390, E-mail: jksmith@ou.edu. *Application contact:* Mark McMasters, Director of Admissions, 405-325-2252, Fax: 405-325-7124, E-mail: mmcmasters@ou.edu. Web site: http://www.ou.edu/education/.

University of Oregon, Graduate School, College of Education, Eugene, OR 97403. Offers M Ed, MA, MS, D Ed, PhD. Part-time programs available. Terminal master's awarded for partial completion of doctoral program. *Degree requirements:* For master's, exam, paper, or project; for doctorate, comprehensive exam, thesis/dissertation. *Entrance requirements:* Additional exam requirements/recommendations for international students: Required—TOEFL. *Faculty research:* Basic and applied research in teaching, learning and habilitation in all settings, schooling effectiveness.

University of Ottawa, Faculty of Graduate and Postdoctoral Studies, Faculty of Education, Ottawa, ON K1N 6N5, Canada. Offers M Ed, MA Ed, PhD, Certificate. Postbaccalaureate distance learning degree programs offered (minimal on-campus study). *Degree requirements:* For master's, thesis or alternative; for doctorate, comprehensive exam, thesis/dissertation, seminar. *Entrance requirements:* For master's, honors degree or equivalent, minimum B average; for doctorate, master's degree, minimum B+ average. Electronic applications accepted. *Faculty research:* Teaching, learning and evaluation; second language education; organizational studies in education; society, culture and literacies; educational counseling.

University of Pennsylvania, Graduate School of Education, Philadelphia, PA 19104. Offers M Phil, MS Ed, Ed D, PhD, DMD/MS Ed. *Faculty:* 58 full-time (22 women), 40 part-time/adjunct (18 women). *Students:* 1,206 full-time (868 women), 198 part-time (141 women); includes 350 minority (184 Black or African American, non-Hispanic/Latino; 3 American Indian or Alaska Native, non-Hispanic/Latino; 70 Asian, non-Hispanic/Latino; 59 Hispanic/Latino; 34 Two or more races, non-Hispanic/Latino), 241 international. 2,574 applicants, 51% accepted, 786 enrolled. In 2011, 543 master's, 91 doctorates awarded. Terminal master's awarded for partial completion of doctoral program. *Degree requirements:* For master's, exam; for doctorate, thesis/dissertation, exam. *Entrance requirements:* For master's, GRE. *Application deadline:* For fall admission, 12/15 priority date for domestic students. Applications are processed on a rolling basis. Application fee: $70. Electronic applications accepted. *Expenses:* Contact institution. *Financial support:* In 2011–12, 101 students received support. Fellowships, research assistantships, teaching assistantships, institutionally sponsored loans, scholarships/grants, traineeships, health care benefits, and unspecified assistantships available. Financial award application deadline: 12/15. *Unit head:* Dr. Andrew Porter, Dean, 215-898-7014. *Application contact:* Alyssa D'Alconzo, Associate Director, Admissions, 215-898-6415, Fax: 215-746-6884, E-mail: admissions@gse.upenn.edu. Web site: http://www.gse.upenn.edu/.

See Display on next page and Close-Up on page 811.

University of Phoenix–Austin Campus, College of Education, Austin, TX 78759. Offers curriculum and instruction (MA Ed).

University of Phoenix–Bay Area Campus, College of Education, San Jose, CA 95134-1805. Offers administration and supervision (MA Ed); adult education and training (MA Ed); early childhood education (MA Ed); education (Ed S); educational leadership (Ed D); elementary teacher education (MA Ed); higher education administration (PhD); secondary teacher education (MA Ed); special education (MA Ed); teacher leadership (MA Ed). Evening/weekend programs available. Postbaccalaureate distance learning degree programs offered (no on-campus study). *Degree requirements:* For master's, thesis (for some programs). *Entrance requirements:* For master's, minimum undergraduate GPA of 2.5, 3 years of work experience. Additional exam requirements/recommendations for international students: Required—TOEFL (minimum score 550 paper-based; 213 computer-based; 79 iBT). Electronic applications accepted.

University of Phoenix–Central Florida Campus, College of Education, Maitland, FL 32751-7057. Offers administration and supervision (MA Ed); curriculum and instruction (MA Ed); curriculum and instruction-computer education (MA Ed); curriculum and instruction-mathematics education (MA Ed); early childhood education (MA Ed); elementary teacher education (MA Ed); secondary teacher education (MA Ed). Evening/weekend programs available. *Degree requirements:* For master's, thesis (for some programs). *Entrance requirements:* For master's, 3 years of work experience, minimum undergraduate GPA of 2.5. Additional exam requirements/recommendations for international students: Required—TOEFL (minimum score 550 paper-based; 213 computer-based; 79 iBT). Electronic applications accepted.

University of Phoenix–Central Massachusetts Campus, College of Education, Westborough, MA 01581-3906. Offers MA Ed. Evening/weekend programs available. *Degree requirements:* For master's, thesis (for some programs). *Entrance requirements:* For master's, minimum undergraduate GPA of 2.5, 3 years of work experience. Additional exam requirements/recommendations for international students: Required—TOEFL (minimum score 550 paper-based; 213 computer-based; 79 iBT). Electronic applications accepted.

University of Phoenix–Central Valley Campus, College of Education, Fresno, CA 93720-1562. Offers curriculum and instruction (MA Ed); curriculum and instruction-computer education (MA Ed); elementary teacher education (MA Ed); secondary teacher education (MA Ed).

University of Phoenix–Chattanooga Campus, College of Education, Chattanooga, TN 37421-3707. Offers administration and supervision (MA Ed); curriculum and instruction (MA Ed); elementary teacher education (MA Ed); secondary teacher education (MA Ed).

University of Phoenix–Dallas Campus, College of Education, Dallas, TX 75251-2009. Offers curriculum and instruction (MA Ed).

University of Phoenix–Denver Campus, College of Education, Lone Tree, CO 80124-5453. Offers administration and supervision (MAEd); curriculum instruction (MAEd); elementary teacher education (MAEd); school counseling (MSC); secondary teacher education (MAEd). Evening/weekend programs available. *Degree requirements:* For master's, thesis (for some programs). *Entrance requirements:* For master's, minimum undergraduate GPA of 2.5, 3 years work experience. Additional exam requirements/recommendations for international students: Required—TOEFL (minimum score 550 paper-based; 213 computer-based; 79 iBT). Electronic applications accepted.

University of Phoenix–Hawaii Campus, College of Education, Honolulu, HI 96813-4317. Offers administration and supervision (MA Ed); curriculum and instruction (MA Ed); elementary education (MA Ed); secondary education (MA Ed); special education (MA Ed); teacher education for elementary licensure (MA Ed). Evening/weekend programs available. *Degree requirements:* For master's, thesis (for some programs). *Entrance requirements:* For master's, minimum undergraduate GPA of 2.5, 3 years of work experience. Additional exam requirements/recommendations for international students: Required—TOEFL (minimum score 550 paper-based; 213 computer-based; 79 iBT). Electronic applications accepted.

University of Phoenix–Houston Campus, College of Education, Houston, TX 77079-2004. Offers curriculum and instruction (MA Ed).

University of Phoenix–Idaho Campus, College of Education, Meridian, ID 83642-5114. Offers administration and supervision (MA Ed); curriculum and instruction (MA Ed); elementary teacher education (MA Ed); secondary teacher education (MA Ed). Evening/weekend programs available. *Degree requirements:* For master's, thesis (for some programs). *Entrance requirements:* For master's, minimum undergraduate GPA of 2.5, 3 years of work experience. Additional exam requirements/recommendations for international students: Required—TOEFL (minimum score 550 paper-based; 213 computer-based). Electronic applications accepted.

University of Phoenix–Indianapolis Campus, College of Education, Indianapolis, IN 46250-932. Offers elementary teacher education (MA Ed); secondary teacher education (MA Ed).

University of Phoenix–Kansas City Campus, College of Education, Kansas City, MO 64131-4517. Offers administration and supervision (MA Ed). Postbaccalaureate distance learning degree programs offered.

University of Phoenix–Las Vegas Campus, College of Education, Las Vegas, NV 89128. Offers administration and supervision (MA Ed); curriculum and instruction (MA Ed); school counseling (MSC); teacher education-elementary licensure (MA Ed). Evening/weekend programs available. *Degree requirements:* For master's, thesis (for some programs). *Entrance requirements:* For master's, minimum undergraduate GPA of 2.5, 3 years of work experience. Additional exam requirements/recommendations for international students: Required—TOEFL (minimum score 550 paper-based; 213 computer-based; 79 iBT). Electronic applications accepted.

University of Phoenix–Louisiana Campus, College of Education, Metairie, LA 70001-2082. Offers curriculum and instruction (MA Ed); early childhood education (MA Ed). Postbaccalaureate distance learning degree programs offered. *Degree requirements:* For master's, thesis. *Entrance requirements:* For master's, minimum undergraduate GPA of 2.5, 3 years work experience. Additional exam requirements/recommendations for international students: Required—TOEFL (minimum score 550 paper-based; 213 computer-based; 79 iBT).

University of Phoenix–Madison Campus, College of Education, Madison, WI 53718-2416. Offers education (Ed S); educational leadership (Ed D); educational leadership: curriculum and instruction (Ed D); higher education administration (PhD).

University of Phoenix–Memphis Campus, College of Education, Cordova, TN 38018. Offers administration and supervision (MA Ed); curriculum and instruction (MA Ed); elementary teacher education (MA Ed); secondary teacher education (MA Ed).

University of Phoenix–Metro Detroit Campus, College of Education, Troy, MI 48098-2623. Offers administration and supervision (MA Ed); elementary teacher education (MA Ed); secondary teacher education (MA Ed); special education (MA Ed). Evening/weekend programs available. *Degree requirements:* For master's, thesis (for some programs). *Entrance requirements:* For master's, 3 years of work experience, minimum undergraduate GPA of 2.5. Additional exam requirements/recommendations for international students: Required—TOEFL (minimum score 550 paper-based; 213 computer-based; 79 iBT). Electronic applications accepted.

University of Phoenix–Milwaukee Campus, College of Education, Milwaukee, WI 53045. Offers curriculum and instruction (MA Ed, Ed D); education (Ed S); educational leadership (Ed D); English as a second language (MA Ed); higher education administration (PhD).

University of Phoenix–Nashville Campus, College of Education, Nashville, TN 37214-5048. Offers administration and supervision (MA Ed); curriculum and instruction (MA Ed); elementary teacher education (MA Ed); secondary teacher education (MA Ed). Evening/weekend programs available. *Degree requirements:* For master's, thesis (for some programs). *Entrance requirements:* For master's, minimum undergraduate GPA of 2.5, 3 years work experience. Additional exam requirements/recommendations for international students: Required—TOEFL (minimum score 500 paper-based; 213 computer-based; 79 iBT). Electronic applications accepted.

University of Phoenix–New Mexico Campus, College of Education, Albuquerque, NM 87113-1570. Offers administration and supervision (MAEd); curriculum and instruction (MAEd); elementary teacher education (MAEd); school counseling (MSC); secondary teacher education (MAEd). Evening/weekend programs available. *Degree requirements:* For master's, thesis (for some programs). *Entrance requirements:* For master's, minimum undergraduate GPA of 2.5, 3 years of work experience. Additional exam requirements/recommendations for international students: Required—TOEFL (minimum score 550 paper-based; 213 computer-based; 79 iBT). Electronic applications accepted.

University of Phoenix–Northern Nevada Campus, College of Education, Reno, NV 89521-5862. Offers administration and supervision (MA Ed); curriculum and instruction (MA Ed); elementary teacher education (MA Ed); secondary teacher education (MA Ed).

University of Phoenix–Northern Virginia Campus, College of Education, Reston, VA 20190. Offers administration and supervision (MA Ed).

University of Phoenix–North Florida Campus, College of Education, Jacksonville, FL 32216-0959. Offers administration and supervision (MA Ed); curriculum and instruction (MA Ed), including computer education, mathematics education; early childhood education (MA Ed); elementary teacher education (MA Ed); secondary teacher education (MA Ed). Evening/weekend programs available. *Degree requirements:* For master's, thesis (for some programs). *Entrance requirements:* For master's, 3 years of work experience, minimum undergraduate GPA of 2.5. Additional exam requirements/recommendations for international students: Required—TOEFL (minimum score 550 paper-based; 213 computer-based; 49 iBT). Electronic applications accepted.

University of Phoenix–Omaha Campus, College of Education, Omaha, NE 68154-5240. Offers administration and supervision (MA Ed); curriculum and instruction (MA Ed), including adult education, computer education, curriculum and instruction, English and language arts education, English as a second language, mathematics education; elementary teacher education (MA Ed); secondary teacher education (MA Ed); special education (MA Ed).

University of Phoenix–Online Campus, College of Education, Phoenix, AZ 85034-7209. Offers administration and supervision (MAEd, Graduate Certificate); adult education and training (MAEd); curriculum and instruction (MAEd); curriculum and instruction reading (MAEd); curriculum and instruction-computer education (MAEd); curriculum and instruction-language arts (MAEd); curriculum and instruction-mathematics (MAEd); early childhood education (MAEd); educational studies (MAEd); elementary teacher education (MAEd); elementary teacher education-early childhood (MAEd); secondary teacher education (MAEd); special education (MAEd); teacher education - elementary/middle level (MAEd); teacher education middle level generalist (MAEd); teacher education middle level mathematics (MAEd); teacher education middle level science (MAEd); teacher education secondary mathematics (MAEd); teacher education secondary science (MAEd); teacher leadership (MAEd). *Accreditation:* Teacher Education Accreditation Council. Evening/weekend programs available. Postbaccalaureate distance learning degree programs offered. *Students:* 9,180 full-time (7,178 women); includes 2,913 minority (2,069 Black or African American, non-Hispanic/Latino; 50 American Indian or Alaska Native, non-Hispanic/Latino; 100 Asian, non-Hispanic/Latino; 542 Hispanic/Latino; 48 Native Hawaiian or other Pacific Islander, non-Hispanic/Latino; 104 Two or more races, non-Hispanic/Latino), 147 international. Average age 36. *Entrance requirements:* Additional exam requirements/recommendations for international students: Required—TOEFL, TOEIC (Test of English as an International Communication), Berlitz Online English Proficiency Exam, Pearson Test of English, or IELTS. *Application deadline:* Applications are processed on a rolling basis. Application fee: $45. Electronic applications accepted. *Expenses:* Contact institution. *Financial support:* Scholarships/grants available. Financial award applicants required to submit FAFSA. *Application contact:* 866-766-0766. Web site: http://www.phoenix.edu/colleges_divisions/education.html.

University of Phoenix–Oregon Campus, College of Education, Tigard, OR 97223. Offers curriculum and instruction (MA Ed); early childhood education (MA Ed); elementary education (MA Ed), including early childhood specialization, middle level specialization; secondary education (MA Ed), including middle level specialization. Evening/weekend programs available. *Degree requirements:* For master's, thesis (for some programs). *Entrance requirements:* For master's, minimum undergraduate GPA of 2.5, 3 years work experience. Additional exam requirements/recommendations for international students: Required—TOEFL (minimum score 550 paper-based; 213 computer-based; 79 iBT). Electronic applications accepted.

University of Phoenix–Phoenix Main Campus, College of Education, Tempe, AZ 85282-2371. Offers administration and supervision (MA Ed); adult education and training (MA Ed); curriculum and instruction reading (MA Ed); curriculum instruction (MA Ed); early childhood education (MA Ed); education studies (MA Ed); elementary teacher education (MA Ed); secondary teacher education (MA Ed); special education (MA Ed); teacher leadership (MA Ed). Evening/weekend programs available. Postbaccalaureate distance learning degree programs offered. *Students:* 297 full-time (203 women); includes 53 minority (19 Black or African American, non-Hispanic/Latino; 1 American Indian or Alaska Native, non-Hispanic/Latino; 6 Asian, non-Hispanic/Latino; 21 Hispanic/Latino; 2 Native Hawaiian or other Pacific Islander, non-Hispanic/Latino; 4 Two or more races, non-Hispanic/Latino), 3 international. Average age 35. *Entrance requirements:* Additional exam requirements/recommendations for international students: Required—TOEFL, TOEIC (Test of English as an International Communication), Berlitz Online English Proficiency Exam, Pearson Test of English, or IELTS. *Application deadline:* Applications are processed on a rolling basis. Application fee: $45. Electronic applications accepted. *Expenses:* Contact institution. *Financial support:* Scholarships/grants available. Financial award applicants required to submit FAFSA. *Application contact:* 866-766-0766. Web site: http://www.phoenix.edu/colleges_divisions/education.html.

University of Phoenix–Puerto Rico Campus, College of Education, Guaynabo, PR 00968. Offers administration and supervision (MA Ed); early childhood education (MA Ed); school counselor (MSC). Evening/weekend programs available. *Degree requirements:* For master's, thesis (for some programs). *Entrance requirements:* For master's, minimum undergraduate GPA of 2.5, 3 years work experience. Additional exam requirements/recommendations for international students: Required—TOEFL (minimum score 550 paper-based; 213 computer-based; 79 iBT). Electronic applications accepted.

University of Phoenix–Richmond Campus, College of Education, Richmond, VA 23230. Offers administration and supervision (MA Ed); curriculum and instruction (MA Ed).

University of Phoenix–Sacramento Valley Campus, College of Education, Sacramento, CA 95833-3632. Offers adult education (MA Ed); curriculum instruction (MA Ed); elementary teacher education (MA Ed); secondary teacher education (MA Ed); teacher education (Certificate). Evening/weekend programs available. *Degree requirements:* For master's, thesis (for some programs). *Entrance requirements:* For master's, 3 years of work experience, minimum undergraduate GPA of 2.5. Additional exam requirements/recommendations for international students: Required—TOEFL (minimum score 550 paper-based; 213 computer-based; 79 iBT). Electronic applications accepted.

University of Phoenix–San Diego Campus, College of Education, San Diego, CA 92123. Offers curriculum and instruction (MA Ed), including computer education, curriculum and instruction, English as a second language; elementary teacher education (MA Ed); secondary teacher education (MA Ed). Evening/weekend programs available. *Degree requirements:* For master's, thesis (for some programs). *Entrance requirements:* For master's, 3 years of work experience, minimum undergraduate GPA of 3.0. Additional exam requirements/recommendations for international students: Required—TOEFL (minimum score 550 paper-based; 213 computer-based; 79 iBT). Electronic applications accepted.

University of Phoenix–Southern Arizona Campus, College of Education, Tucson, AZ 85711. Offers administration and supervision (MA Ed); adult education and training (MA Ed); curriculum instruction (MA Ed); educational counseling (MA Ed); elementary teacher education (MA Ed); school counseling (MSC); secondary teacher education (MA Ed); special education (MA Ed, Certificate). Evening/weekend programs available. *Degree requirements:* For master's, thesis (for some programs). *Entrance requirements:* For master's, minimum undergraduate GPA of 2.5, 3 years of work experience. Additional exam requirements/recommendations for international students: Required—TOEFL (minimum score 550 paper-based; 213 computer-based; 79 iBT). Electronic applications accepted.

University of Phoenix–Southern California Campus, College of Education, Costa Mesa, CA 92626. Offers administration and supervision (MA Ed); adult education and training (MA Ed); educational studies (MA Ed); teacher leadership (MA Ed). Evening/weekend programs available. Postbaccalaureate distance learning degree programs offered. *Students:* 190 full-time (132 women); includes 82 minority (25 Black or African American, non-Hispanic/Latino; 5 Asian, non-Hispanic/Latino; 46 Hispanic/Latino; 4 Native Hawaiian or other Pacific Islander, non-Hispanic/Latino; 2 Two or more races, non-Hispanic/Latino), 3 international. Average age 35. *Entrance requirements:* Additional exam requirements/recommendations for international students: Required—TOEFL, TOEIC (Test of English as an International Communication), Berlitz Online English Proficiency Exam, Pearson Test of English, or IELTS. *Application deadline:* Applications are processed on a rolling basis. Application fee: $45. Electronic applications accepted. *Expenses:* Contact institution. *Financial support:* Scholarships/grants available. Financial award applicants required to submit FAFSA. *Application contact:* 866-766-0766. Web site: http://www.phoenix.edu/colleges_divisions/education.html.

University of Phoenix–Southern Colorado Campus, College of Education, Colorado Springs, CO 80919-2335. Offers administration and supervision (MA Ed); curriculum and instruction (MA Ed); elementary teacher education (MA Ed); principal licensure certification (Certificate); school counseling (MSC); secondary teacher education (MA Ed). Evening/weekend programs available. *Degree requirements:* For master's, thesis (for some programs). *Entrance requirements:* For master's, minimum undergraduate GPA of 2.5, 3 years of work experience. Additional exam requirements/recommendations for international students: Required—TOEFL (minimum score 550 paper-based; 213 computer-based; 79 iBT). Electronic applications accepted.

University of Phoenix–South Florida Campus, College of Education, Fort Lauderdale, FL 33309. Offers administration and supervision (MA Ed); curriculum and instruction (MA Ed), including computer education, curriculum and instruction, mathematics education; early childhood education (MA Ed); elementary teacher education (MA Ed); secondary teacher education (MA Ed). Evening/weekend programs available. *Degree requirements:* For master's, thesis (for some programs). *Entrance requirements:* For master's, 3 years of work experience, minimum undergraduate GPA of 2.5. Additional exam requirements/recommendations for international students: Required—TOEFL (minimum score 550 paper-based; 213 computer-based; 79 iBT). Electronic applications accepted.

University of Phoenix–Springfield Campus, College of Education, Springfield, MO 65804-7211. Offers administration and supervision (MA Ed); curriculum and instruction (MA Ed), including computer education, curriculum and instruction, English and language arts education, English as a second language, mathematics education; English and language arts education (MA Ed).

University of Phoenix–Utah Campus, College of Education, Salt Lake City, UT 84123-4617. Offers administration and supervision (MA Ed); curriculum and instruction (MA Ed); elementary teacher education (MA Ed); school counseling (MSC); secondary teacher education (MA Ed); special education (MA Ed). Evening/weekend programs available. *Degree requirements:* For master's, thesis (for some programs). *Entrance requirements:* For master's, minimum undergraduate GPA of 2.5, 3 years work experience. Additional exam requirements/recommendations for international students: Required—TOEFL (minimum score 550 paper-based; 213 computer-based; 79 iBT). Electronic applications accepted.

University of Phoenix–Vancouver Campus, The Artemis School, College of Education, Burnaby, BC V5C 6G9, Canada. Offers administration and supervision (MA Ed); curriculum and instruction (MA Ed), including computer education, curriculum and instruction. Evening/weekend programs available. *Degree requirements:* For master's, thesis (for some programs). *Entrance requirements:* For master's, minimum undergraduate GPA of 2.5, 3 years work experience. Additional exam requirements/recommendations for international students: Required—TOEFL (minimum score 550 paper-based; 213 computer-based; 79 iBT). Electronic applications accepted.

University of Phoenix–Washington D.C. Campus, College of Education, Washington, DC 20001. Offers administration and supervision (MA Ed); adult education and training (MA Ed); computer education (MA Ed); curriculum and instruction (MA Ed, Ed D); early childhood education (MA Ed); education (Ed S); educational leadership (Ed D); educational technology (Ed D); elementary teacher education (MA Ed); English and language arts education (MA Ed); English as a second language (MA Ed); higher education administration (PhD); mathematics education (MA Ed); secondary teacher education (MA Ed); special education (MA Ed); teacher leadership (MA Ed).

University of Phoenix–West Florida Campus, College of Education, Temple Terrace, FL 33637. Offers administration and supervision (MA Ed); curriculum and instruction (MA Ed), including computer education, curriculum and instruction, mathematics education; curriculum and technology (MA Ed); early childhood education (MA Ed); elementary teacher education (MA Ed); secondary teacher education (MA Ed). Evening/weekend programs available. *Degree requirements:* For master's, thesis (for some programs). *Entrance requirements:* For master's, 3 years of work experience, minimum undergraduate GPA of 2.5. Additional exam requirements/recommendations for international students: Required—TOEFL (minimum score 550 paper-based; 213 computer-based; 79 iBT).

University of Pittsburgh, School of Education, Pittsburgh, PA 15260. Offers M Ed, MA, MAT, MS, Ed D, PhD. Part-time and evening/weekend programs available. Postbaccalaureate distance learning degree programs offered (minimal on-campus study). *Faculty:* 98 full-time (55 women), 115 part-time/adjunct (74 women). *Students:* 560 full-time (398 women), 538 part-time (393 women); includes 102 minority (56 Black or African American, non-Hispanic/Latino; 15 Asian, non-Hispanic/Latino; 21 Hispanic/Latino; 10 Two or more races, non-Hispanic/Latino), 79 international. Average age 32. 765 applicants, 68% accepted, 377 enrolled. In 2011, 387 master's, 51 doctorates awarded. Terminal master's awarded for partial completion of doctoral program. *Degree requirements:* For master's, comprehensive exam, thesis (for some programs); for doctorate, comprehensive exam, thesis/dissertation. *Entrance requirements:* For doctorate, GRE. Additional exam requirements/recommendations for international students: Required—TOEFL (minimum score 550 paper-based; 213 computer-based; 80 iBT). *Application deadline:* For fall admission, 2/1 priority date for domestic students, 2/1 for international students; for spring admission, 11/15 priority date for domestic students, 7/1 for international students. Applications are processed on a rolling basis. Application fee: $50. Electronic applications accepted. *Expenses:* Tuition, state resident: full-time $18,774; part-time $760 per credit. Tuition, nonresident: full-time $30,736; part-time $1258 per credit. *Required fees:* $740; $200 per term. Tuition and fees vary according to program. *Financial support:* In 2011–12, 18 fellowships with full and partial tuition reimbursements (averaging $16,462 per year), 86 research assistantships with full and partial tuition reimbursements (averaging $16,000 per year), 50 teaching assistantships with full and partial tuition reimbursements (averaging $14,862 per year) were awarded; career-related internships or fieldwork, Federal Work-Study, institutionally sponsored loans, scholarships/grants, traineeships, tuition waivers (partial), and unspecified assistantships also available. Support available to part-time students. Financial award applicants required to submit FAFSA. *Total annual research expenditures:* $15.3 million. *Unit head:* Dr. Alan Lesgold, Dean, 412-648-1773, Fax: 412-648-1825, E-mail: al@pitt.edu. *Application contact:* Marianne L. Budziszewski, Director of Admissions and Enrollment Services, 412-648-7056, Fax: 412-648-1899, E-mail: soeinfo@pitt.edu. Web site: http://www.education.pitt.edu/.

University of Portland, School of Education, Portland, OR 97203-5798. Offers M Ed, MA, MAT. M Ed also available through the Graduate Outreach Program for teachers residing in the Oregon and Washington state areas. *Accreditation:* NCATE. Part-time and evening/weekend programs available. *Faculty:* 17 full-time (10 women), 12 part-time/adjunct (4 women). *Students:* 54 full-time (35 women), 211 part-time (154 women); includes 43 minority (1 Black or African American, non-Hispanic/Latino; 1 American Indian or Alaska Native, non-Hispanic/Latino; 6 Asian, non-Hispanic/Latino; 10 Hispanic/Latino; 19 Native Hawaiian or other Pacific Islander, non-Hispanic/Latino; 6 Two or more races, non-Hispanic/Latino), 44 international. Average age 33. In 2011, 125 master's awarded. *Entrance requirements:* For master's, minimum GPA of 3.0, teaching certificate, letters of recommendation, resume, statement of goals, official transcripts. Additional exam requirements/recommendations for international students: Required—TOEFL (minimum score 550 paper-based; 80 iBT), IELTS (minimum score 7). *Application deadline:* For fall admission, 7/15 priority date for domestic students, 7/15 for international students; for spring admission, 12/15 priority date for domestic students, 12/15 for international students. Applications are processed on a rolling basis. Application fee: $50. *Expenses: Tuition:* Part-time $980 per credit hour. Tuition and fees vary according to program. *Financial support:* Federal Work-Study and scholarships/grants available. Support available to part-time students. Financial award application deadline: 3/1; financial award applicants required to submit FAFSA. *Faculty research:* Multicultural education, supervision/leadership. *Unit head:* Dr. Bruce Weitzel, Associate Dean, 503-943-7208, Fax: 503-943-8042, E-mail: weitzel@up.edu. *Application contact:* Dr. Bruce Weitzel, Associate Dean, 503-943-7135, E-mail: weitzel@up.edu.

University of Prince Edward Island, Faculty of Education, Charlottetown, PE C1A 4P3, Canada. Offers leadership and learning (M Ed). Part-time programs available. *Degree requirements:* For master's, thesis. *Entrance requirements:* For master's, 2 years of professional experience, bachelor of education, professional certificate. Additional exam requirements/recommendations for international students: Required—TOEFL (minimum score 550 paper-based; 213 computer-based; 80 iBT), Canadian Academic English Language Assessment, Michigan English Language Assessment Battery, Canadian Test of English for Scholars and Trainees. *Faculty research:* Distance learning, aboriginal communities and education leadership development, international development, immersion language learning.

University of Puerto Rico, Río Piedras, College of Education, San Juan, PR 00931-3300. Offers M Ed, MS, Ed D. *Accreditation:* NCATE. Part-time programs available. *Degree requirements:* For master's, thesis; for doctorate, thesis/dissertation, internship. *Entrance requirements:* For master's, GRE or PAEG, minimum GPA of 3.0, letter of recommendation; for doctorate, GRE or PAEG, master's degree, minimum GPA of 3.0, letter of recommendation (2), interview. *Faculty research:* Curriculum, math teaching.

University of Puget Sound, Graduate Studies, School of Education, Tacoma, WA 98416. Offers M Ed, MAT. *Accreditation:* NCATE. *Faculty:* 8 full-time (5 women). *Students:* 30 full-time (19 women), 27 part-time (23 women); includes 7 minority (1 Black or African American, non-Hispanic/Latino; 1 Asian, non-Hispanic/Latino; 3 Hispanic/Latino; 2 Two or more races, non-Hispanic/Latino). Average age 28. 86 applicants, 70% accepted, 44 enrolled. In 2011, 45 master's awarded. *Degree requirements:* For master's, capstone course. *Entrance requirements:* For master's, GRE General Test, minimum GPA of 3.0. Additional exam requirements/recommendations for international students: Required—TOEFL (minimum score 550 paper-based; 213 computer-based; 80 iBT). *Application deadline:* For fall admission, 3/1 priority date for domestic students, 3/1 for international students. Applications are processed on a rolling basis. Application fee: $60. Electronic applications accepted. *Financial support:* In 2011–12, 24 students received support. Teaching assistantships, career-related internships or fieldwork, and scholarships/grants available. Financial award application deadline: 3/31; financial award applicants required to submit FAFSA. *Unit head:* Dr. John Woodward, Dean, 253-879-3375, E-mail: woodward@pugetsound.edu. *Application contact:* Dr. George H. Mills, Jr., Vice President for Enrollment, 253-879-3211, Fax: 253-879-3993, E-mail: admission@pugetsound.edu. Web site: http://www.pugetsound.edu/academics/departments-and-programs/graduate/school-of-education/.

University of Redlands, School of Education, Redlands, CA 92373-0999. Offers MA, Ed D, Certificate. Part-time and evening/weekend programs available. *Entrance requirements:* For master's, minimum undergraduate GPA of 3.0, 2 letters of recommendation. Additional exam requirements/recommendations for international students: Required—TOEFL (minimum score 550 paper-based; 213 computer-based). *Expenses:* Contact institution.

University of Regina, Faculty of Graduate Studies and Research, Faculty of Education, Regina, SK S4S 0A2, Canada. Offers M Ed, MA Ed, MHRD, PhD, Master's Certificate. Part-time programs available. *Faculty:* 46 full-time (24 women), 2 part-time/adjunct (0 women). *Students:* 75 full-time (59 women), 239 part-time (182 women). 171 applicants, 29% accepted. In 2011, 65 master's, 6 doctorates awarded. *Degree requirements:* For master's, thesis (for some programs), practicum, project, or thesis; for doctorate, thesis/dissertation. *Entrance requirements:* For master's, 4-year B Ed or equivalent, two years of teaching experience. Additional exam requirements/recommendations for international students: Required—TOEFL (minimum score 580 paper-based; 80 iBT), IELTS (minimum score 6.5). *Application deadline:* 2/15 for domestic and international students. Application fee: $100. Electronic applications accepted. *Expenses:* Contact institution. *Financial support:* In 2011–12, 11 fellowships (averaging $6,400 per year), 16 teaching assistantships (averaging $2,298 per year) were awarded; research assistantships, career-related internships or fieldwork, and scholarships/grants also available. Financial award application deadline: 6/15. *Faculty research:* Curriculum and instruction, educational administration, educational psychology, human resource development; adult education. *Unit head:* Dr. Rod Dolmage, Associate Dean, Research and Graduate Programs, 306-585-4816, Fax: 306-585-5387, E-mail: rod.dolmage@uregina.ca. *Application contact:* Tania Gates, Graduate Program Coordinator, 306-585-4506, Fax: 306-585-5387, E-mail: edgrad@uregina.ca.

University of Rhode Island, Graduate School, College of Human Science and Services, School of Education, Kingston, RI 02881. Offers adult education (MA); education (PhD); elementary education (MA); music education (MM); reading education (MA); secondary education (MA); special education (MA); MS/PhD. *Accreditation:* NCATE. Part-time and evening/weekend programs available. *Faculty:* 21 full-time (13 women), 3 part-time/adjunct (1 woman). *Students:* 54 full-time (48 women), 108 part-time (86 women); includes 14 minority (3 Black or African American, non-Hispanic/Latino; 4 Asian, non-Hispanic/Latino; 7 Hispanic/Latino), 4 international. In 2011, 56 master's, 8 doctorates awarded. *Degree requirements:* For master's, comprehensive exam (for some programs), thesis optional; for doctorate, comprehensive exam, thesis/dissertation. *Entrance requirements:* For master's, 2 letters of recommendation; interview (for special education applicants); for doctorate, GRE, 3 letters of recommendation, resume. Additional exam requirements/recommendations for international students: Required—TOEFL (minimum score 600 paper-based; 250 computer-based; 100 iBT). *Application deadline:* For fall admission, 1/31 for international students. Application fee: $65. Electronic applications accepted. *Expenses:* Tuition, state resident: full-time $10,432; part-time $580 per credit hour. Tuition, nonresident: full-time $23,130; part-time $1285 per credit hour. *Required fees:* $1362; $36 per credit hour. $35 per semester. One-time fee: $130. *Financial support:* In 2011–12, 4 teaching assistantships with full and partial tuition reimbursements (averaging $12,157 per year) were awarded; career-related internships or fieldwork also available. Financial award applicants required to submit FAFSA. *Unit head:* Dr. David Byrd, Director, 401-874-5484, Fax: 401-874-5471, E-mail: dbyrd@uri.edu. *Application contact:* Dr. John Boulmetis, Coordinator of Graduate Studies, 401-874-4159, Fax: 401-874-7610, E-mail: johnb@uri.edu. Web site: http://www.uri.edu/hss/education/.

University of Rio Grande, Graduate School, Rio Grande, OH 45674. Offers classroom teaching (M Ed), including fine arts, learning disabilities, mathematics, reading education. *Accreditation:* NCATE. Part-time and evening/weekend programs available. *Degree requirements:* For master's, final research project, portfolio. *Entrance requirements:* For master's, minimum GPA of 2.7 in major, 2.5 overall. Additional exam requirements/recommendations for international students: Required—TOEFL. *Faculty research:* Interagency collaboration, reading and mathematics, learning styles, college access, literacy.

University of Rochester, Margaret Warner Graduate School of Education and Human Development, Rochester, NY 14627. Offers MS, Ed D, PhD. *Accreditation:* ACA (one or more programs are accredited); NCATE. Part-time and evening/weekend programs available. Terminal master's awarded for partial completion of doctoral program. *Degree requirements:* For master's, thesis (for some programs); for doctorate, thesis/dissertation, qualifying exam. *Expenses: Tuition:* Full-time $41,040.

University of St. Francis, College of Education, Joliet, IL 60435-6169. Offers educational leadership (MS, Ed D); elementary education certification (M Ed); reading (MS); secondary education certification (M Ed), including English education, math education, science education, social studies education, visual arts education; special education (M Ed); teaching and learning (MS). *Accreditation:* NCATE. Part-time and evening/weekend programs available. Postbaccalaureate distance learning degree programs offered (no on-campus study). *Faculty:* 7 full-time (5 women), 21 part-time/adjunct (14 women). *Students:* 32 full-time (21 women), 230 part-time (175 women); includes 23 minority (7 Black or African American, non-Hispanic/Latino; 2 Asian, non-Hispanic/Latino; 13 Hispanic/Latino; 1 Two or more races, non-Hispanic/Latino), 1 international. Average age 32. 147 applicants, 60% accepted, 57 enrolled. In 2011, 156 master's awarded. *Entrance requirements:* For doctorate, master's degree, IL Type 75 or Principal's endorsement, interview. Additional exam requirements/recommendations for international students: Required—TOEFL (minimum score 550 paper-based; 213 computer-based). *Application deadline:* Applications are processed on a rolling basis. Application fee: $30. Electronic applications accepted. *Expenses:* Contact institution. *Financial support:* In 2011–12, 23 students received support. Federal Work-Study, scholarships/grants, tuition waivers (partial), and unspecified assistantships available. Support available to part-time students. Financial award applicants required to submit FAFSA. *Unit head:* Dr. John Gambro, Dean, 815-740-3829, Fax: 815-740-2264, E-mail: jgambro@stfrancis.edu. *Application contact:* Sandra Sloka, Director of Admissions for Graduate and Degree Completion Programs, 800-735-7500, Fax: 815-740-5032, E-mail: ssloka@stfrancis.edu. Web site: http://www.stfrancis.edu/academics/college-of-education/.

University of Saint Francis, Graduate School, Department of Education, Fort Wayne, IN 46808-3994. Offers special education (MS Ed). *Accreditation:* NCATE. Part-time and evening/weekend programs available. Postbaccalaureate distance learning degree programs offered (no on-campus study). *Faculty:* 3 full-time (all women), 4 part-time/adjunct (all women). *Students:* 4 full-time (all women), 15 part-time (12 women); includes 1 minority (Asian, non-Hispanic/Latino). In 2011, 9 master's awarded. *Degree requirements:* For master's, comprehensive exam. *Entrance requirements:* For master's, MAT, PRAXIS, minimum GPA of 2.5. *Application deadline:* For fall admission, 7/1 priority date for domestic students; for spring admission, 11/1 for domestic students. Applications are processed on a rolling basis. Application fee: $20. Application fee is waived when completed online. *Financial support:* Federal Work-Study, scholarships/grants, tuition waivers (full and partial), and unspecified assistantships available. Support available to part-time students. Financial award applicants required to submit FAFSA. *Unit head:* Dr. Jane Swiss, Dean, 260-399-7700 Ext. 8414, Fax: 260-399-8170, E-mail: jswiss@sf.edu. *Application contact:* Kyna Steury-Johnson, Admissions Counselor, 260-399-7700 Ext. 6316, Fax: 260-399-8152, E-mail: ksteury@sf.edu.

University of Saint Joseph, Department of Education, West Hartford, CT 06117-2700. Offers education (MA); special education (MA). Part-time and evening/weekend programs available. *Students:* 61 full-time (53 women), 792 part-time (688 women); includes 68 minority (30 Black or African American, non-Hispanic/Latino; 7 Asian, non-Hispanic/Latino; 28 Hispanic/Latino; 3 Two or more races, non-Hispanic/Latino). Average age 33. *Degree requirements:* For master's, comprehensive exam, thesis or alternative. *Entrance requirements:* For master's, 2 letters of recommendation. *Application deadline:* Applications are processed on a rolling basis. Application fee: $50. Electronic applications accepted. Application fee is waived when completed online. *Expenses: Tuition:* Part-time $670 per credit. *Required fees:* $40 per credit. Tuition and fees vary according to course load, degree level, campus/location and program. *Financial support:* Career-related internships or fieldwork and unspecified assistantships available. Support available to part-time students. Financial award applicants required to submit FAFSA. *Application contact:* Graduate Admissions Office, 860-231-5261, E-mail: graduate@usj.edu.

University of Saint Mary, Graduate Programs, Program in Education, Leavenworth, KS 66048-5082. Offers curriculum and instruction (MAT). *Accreditation:* NCATE. Part-time and evening/weekend programs available. Postbaccalaureate distance learning degree programs offered (no on-campus study). *Degree requirements:* For master's, thesis, oral presentation. *Entrance requirements:* For master's, minimum undergraduate GPA of 2.75. *Faculty research:* Curriculum and instruction.

University of Saint Mary, Graduate Programs, Program in Teaching, Leavenworth, KS 66048-5082. Offers education (MA). Part-time and evening/weekend programs available. *Degree requirements:* For master's, thesis. *Entrance requirements:* For master's, minimum undergraduate GPA of 2.75.

University of St. Thomas, Graduate Studies, School of Education, St. Paul, MN 55105-1096. Offers MA, MAT, Ed D, Certificate, Ed S. Part-time and evening/weekend programs available. *Faculty:* 28 full-time (16 women), 89 part-time/adjunct (60 women). *Students:* 95 full-time (73 women), 864 part-time (586 women); includes 139 minority (59 Black or African American, non-Hispanic/Latino; 10 American Indian or Alaska Native, non-Hispanic/Latino; 28 Asian, non-Hispanic/Latino; 25 Hispanic/Latino; 3 Native Hawaiian or other Pacific Islander, non-Hispanic/Latino; 14 Two or more races, non-Hispanic/Latino), 27 international. Average age 36. 483 applicants, 82% accepted, 307 enrolled. In 2011, 243 master's, 28 doctorates, 41 other advanced degrees awarded. *Entrance requirements:* For master's, minimum GPA of 3.0 or MAT. Additional exam requirements/recommendations for international students: Required—TOEFL (minimum score 550 paper-based; 213 computer-based; 80 iBT). *Application deadline:* For fall admission, 6/1 priority date for domestic students; for spring admission, 11/1 priority date for domestic students. Applications are processed on a rolling basis. Application fee: $50. *Expenses:* Contact institution. *Financial support:* Fellowships, research assistantships, career-related internships or fieldwork, institutionally sponsored loans, and scholarships/grants available. Support available to part-time students. Financial award applicants required to submit FAFSA. *Unit head:* Dr. Bruce H. Kramer, Dean, 651-962-4435, Fax: 651-962-4169, E-mail: bhkramer@stthomas.edu. *Application contact:* Vicky L. Rasmusson, Admissions Coordinator, 651-962-4430, Fax: 651-962-4169, E-mail: vlrasmusson@stthomas.edu. Web site: http://www.stthomas.edu/education/.

University of St. Thomas, School of Education, Houston, TX 77006-4696. Offers all level teaching (M Ed); bilingual/dual language (M Ed); Catholic school teaching (M Ed); Catholic/private school leadership (M Ed); counselor education (M Ed); curriculum and instruction (M Ed); educational leadership (M Ed); elementary teaching (M Ed); English as a second language (M Ed); exceptionality/ educational diagnostician (M Ed); exceptionality/special education (M Ed); generalist (M Ed); reading (M Ed); secondary teaching (M Ed). Part-time and evening/weekend programs available. Postbaccalaureate distance learning degree programs offered (no on-campus study). *Faculty:* 30 full-time (17 women), 54 part-time/adjunct (37 women). *Students:* 66 full-time (43 women), 1,178 part-time (1,044 women); includes 777 minority (313 Black or African American, non-Hispanic/Latino; 5 American Indian or Alaska Native, non-Hispanic/Latino; 29 Asian, non-Hispanic/Latino; 395 Hispanic/Latino; 2 Native Hawaiian or other Pacific Islander, non-Hispanic/Latino; 33 Two or more races, non-Hispanic/Latino), 26 international. Average age 36. 551 applicants, 94% accepted, 416 enrolled. In 2011, 72 master's awarded. *Degree requirements:* For master's, thesis, field experience. *Entrance requirements:* For master's, GRE or MAT if GPA is below 3.0, bachelor's degree; minimum GPA of 2.75 in bachelor's degree or last 60 credit hours; official transcripts from all institutions; goal statement of 250-300 words; 1 reference. Additional exam requirements/recommendations for international students: Required—TOEFL. *Application deadline:* Applications are processed on a rolling basis. Application fee: $35. Electronic applications accepted. *Expenses:* Contact institution. *Financial support:* In 2011–12, 9 students received support. Federal Work-Study, scholarships/grants, and state work-study, institutional employment available. Support available to part-time students. Financial award application deadline: 4/15; financial award applicants required to submit FAFSA. *Faculty research:* Leadership, diversity, personality traits, second language acquisition. *Unit head:* Dr. Nora Hutto, Dean, 713-525-3540, Fax: 713-525-3871, E-mail: education@stthom.edu. *Application contact:* Paula C. Hollis, Administrative Assistant, 713-525-3540, Fax: 713-525-3871, E-mail: education@stthom.edu. Web site: http://www.stthom.edu/Schools_Centers_of_Excellence/Schools_of_Study/School_of_Education/Index.aqf.

University of San Diego, School of Leadership and Education Sciences, San Diego, CA 92110-2492. Offers M Ed, MA, MAT, PhD, Certificate. *Accreditation:* NCATE. Part-time and evening/weekend programs available. *Faculty:* 32 full-time (18 women), 72 part-time/adjunct (48 women). *Students:* 221 full-time (178 women), 311 part-time (235 women); includes 183 minority (30 Black or African American, non-Hispanic/Latino; 1 American Indian or Alaska Native, non-Hispanic/Latino; 32 Asian, non-Hispanic/Latino; 86 Hispanic/Latino; 4 Native Hawaiian or other Pacific Islander, non-Hispanic/Latino; 30 Two or more races, non-Hispanic/Latino), 23 international. Average age 31. In 2011, 208 master's, 15 doctorates awarded. *Degree requirements:* For doctorate, comprehensive exam (for some programs), thesis/dissertation (for some programs). *Entrance requirements:* For doctorate, GRE General Test, master's degree. Additional exam requirements/recommendations for international students: Required—TOEFL (minimum score 580 paper-based; 237 computer-based; 83 iBT), TWE. Application fee: $45. *Expenses: Tuition:* Full-time $22,482; part-time $1249 per unit. *Required fees:* $224. Full-time tuition and fees vary according to course load and degree level. *Financial support:* In 2011–12, 366 students received support. Career-related internships or fieldwork, Federal Work-Study, institutionally sponsored loans, unspecified assistantships, and stipends available. Support available to part-time students. Financial award application deadline: 4/1; financial award applicants required to submit FAFSA. *Unit head:* Dr. Paula A. Cordeiro, Dean, 619-260-4540, Fax: 619-260-6835, E-mail: cordeiro@sandiego.edu. *Application contact:* Monica Mahon, Associate Director of Graduate Admissions, 619-260-4524, Fax: 619-260-4158, E-mail: grads@sandiego.edu. Web site: http://www.sandiego.edu/soles/.

University of San Francisco, School of Education, San Francisco, CA 94117-1080. Offers MA, Ed D. Part-time and evening/weekend programs available. *Faculty:* 26 full-time (17 women), 110 part-time/adjunct (74 women). *Students:* 807 full-time (621 women), 197 part-time (139 women); includes 376 minority (55 Black or African American, non-Hispanic/Latino; 5 American Indian or Alaska Native, non-Hispanic/Latino; 109 Asian, non-Hispanic/Latino; 155 Hispanic/Latino; 2 Native Hawaiian or other Pacific Islander, non-Hispanic/Latino; 50 Two or more races, non-Hispanic/Latino), 44 international. Average age 33. 1,009 applicants, 64% accepted, 351 enrolled. In 2011, 331 master's, 47 doctorates awarded. *Degree requirements:* For doctorate, thesis/dissertation. Application fee: $55 ($65 for international students). *Expenses: Tuition:* Full-time $20,070; part-time $1115 per unit. Tuition and fees vary according to course load, campus/location and program. *Financial support:* In 2011–12, 103 students received support. Fellowships, research assistantships, and teaching assistantships available. Financial award application deadline: 3/2; financial award applicants required to submit FAFSA. *Unit head:* Dr. Walter Gmelch, Dean, 415-422-6525. *Application contact:* Beth Teabue, Associate Director of Graduate Outreach, 415-422-5467, E-mail: schoolofeducation@usfca.edu.

University of Saskatchewan, College of Graduate Studies and Research, College of Education, Saskatoon, SK S7N 5A2, Canada. Offers M Ed, MC Ed, PhD, Diploma. Part-time programs available. *Degree requirements:* For master's, thesis (for some programs); for doctorate, comprehensive exam (for some programs), thesis/dissertation. *Entrance requirements:* Additional exam requirements/recommendations for international students: Required—TOEFL (minimum score 80 iBT); Recommended—IELTS (minimum score 6.5). Electronic applications accepted.

The University of Scranton, College of Graduate and Continuing Education, Department of Education, Scranton, PA 18510. Offers curriculum and instruction (MA, MS); early childhood education (MA, MS); educational administration (MS); elementary education (MS); English as a second language (MS); reading education (MS); secondary education (MS); special education (MS). *Accreditation:* NCATE. Part-time and evening/weekend programs available. Postbaccalaureate distance learning degree programs offered (no on-campus study). *Faculty:* 17 full-time (11 women), 47 part-time/adjunct (18 women). *Students:* 249 full-time (166 women), 365 part-time (233 women); includes 37 minority (23 Black or African American, non-Hispanic/Latino; 2 American Indian or Alaska Native, non-Hispanic/Latino; 5 Asian, non-Hispanic/Latino; 7 Hispanic/Latino), 9 international. Average age 28. 143 applicants, 95% accepted. In 2011, 395 master's awarded. *Degree requirements:* For master's, comprehensive exam, thesis (for some programs), capstone experience. *Entrance requirements:* For master's, minimum GPA of 2.75. Additional exam requirements/recommendations for international students: Required—TOEFL (minimum score 500 paper-based; 173 computer-based), IELTS (minimum score 5.5). *Application deadline:* Applications are processed on a rolling basis. Application fee: $0. *Financial support:* In 2011–12, 18 students received support, including 18 teaching assistantships with full and partial tuition reimbursements available (averaging $5,378 per year); fellowships, career-related internships or fieldwork, Federal Work-Study, and unspecified assistantships also available. Support available to part-time students. Financial award application deadline: 3/1. *Faculty research:* Meta-analysis as a research tool, family involvement in school activities, effect of curriculum integration on student learning and attitude, the effects of inclusion on students, development of emotional intelligence of young children. *Unit head:* Dr. Art Chambers, Chair, 570-941-4668, Fax: 570-941-5515, E-mail: lchambersa2@scranton.edu. *Application contact:* Joseph M. Roback, Director of Admissions, 570-941-4385, Fax: 570-941-5928, E-mail: robackj2@scranton.edu. Web site: http://matrix.scranton.edu/academics/pcps/education/.

University of Sioux Falls, Fredrikson School of Education, Sioux Falls, SD 57105-1699. Offers educational administration (Ed S), including principal leadership, superintendent and district leadership; leadership in reading (M Ed); leadership in schools (M Ed); leadership in technology (M Ed); teaching (M Ed). Admission in summer only. *Accreditation:* NCATE. Part-time and evening/weekend programs available. *Faculty:* 9 full-time (8 women), 10 part-time/adjunct (7 women). *Students:* 196 part-time (144 women); includes 2 minority (1 Black or African American, non-Hispanic/Latino; 1 American Indian or Alaska Native, non-Hispanic/Latino). 55 applicants, 100% accepted, 47 enrolled. *Degree requirements:* For master's, comprehensive exam (for some programs), research application project; for Ed S, comprehensive exam, portfolio. *Entrance requirements:* For master's, minimum GPA of 3.0, 1 year of teaching experience; for Ed S, minimum 3 years of teaching experience, minimum cumulative GPA of 3.5, 1 year of administrative experience. Additional exam requirements/recommendations for international students: Required—TOEFL. *Application deadline:* Applications are processed on a rolling basis. Application fee: $25. *Expenses: Tuition:* Part-time $345 per semester hour. *Required fees:* $35 per term. Part-time tuition and fees vary according to degree level and program. *Financial support:* Available to part-time students. Applicants required to submit FAFSA. *Faculty research:* Reading, literacy, leadership. *Unit head:* Dawn Olson, Director of Graduate Programs in Education, 605-575-2083, Fax: 605-575-2079, E-mail: dawn.olson@usiouxfalls.edu. *Application contact:* Student Contact, 605-331-5000.

University of South Africa, College of Human Sciences, Pretoria, South Africa. Offers adult education (M Ed); African languages (MA, PhD); African politics (MA, PhD); Afrikaans (MA, PhD); ancient history (MA, PhD); ancient Near Eastern studies (MA, PhD); anthropology (MA, PhD); applied linguistics (MA); Arabic (MA, PhD); archaeology (MA); art history (MA); Biblical archaeology (MA); Biblical studies (M Th, D Th, PhD); Christian spirituality (M Th, D Th); church history (M Th, D Th); classical studies (MA, PhD); clinical psychology (MA); communication (MA, PhD); comparative education (M Ed, Ed D); consulting psychology (D Admin, D Com, PhD); curriculum studies (M Ed, Ed D); development studies (M Admin, MA, D Admin, PhD); didactics (M Ed, Ed D); education (M Tech); education management (M Ed, Ed D); educational psychology (M Ed); English (MA); environmental education (M Ed); French (MA, PhD); German (MA, PhD); Greek (MA); guidance and counseling (M Ed); health studies (MA, PhD), including health sciences education (MA), health services management (MA), medical and surgical nursing science (critical care general) (MA), midwifery and neonatal nursing science (MA), trauma and emergency care (MA); history (MA, PhD); history of education (Ed D); inclusive education (M Ed, Ed D); information and communications technology policy and regulation (MA); information science (MA, MIS, PhD); international politics (MA, PhD); Islamic studies (MA, PhD); Italian (MA, PhD); Judaica (MA, PhD); linguistics (MA, PhD); mathematical education (M Ed); mathematics education (MA); missiology (M Th, D Th); modern Hebrew (MA, PhD); musicology (MA, MMus, D Mus, PhD); natural science education (M Ed); New Testament (M Th, D Th); Old Testament (D Th); pastoral therapy (M Th, D Th); philosophy (MA); philosophy of education (M Ed, Ed D); politics (MA, PhD); Portuguese (MA, PhD); practical theology (M Th, D Th); psychology (MA, MS, PhD); psychology of education (M Ed, Ed D); public health (MA); religious studies (MA, D Th, PhD); Romance languages (MA); Russian (MA, PhD); Semitic languages (MA, PhD); social behavior studies in HIV/AIDS (MA); social science (mental health) (MA); social science in development studies (MA); social science in psychology (MA); social science in social work (MA); social science in sociology (MA); social work (MSW, DSW, PhD); socio-education (M Ed, Ed D); sociolinguistics (MA); sociology (MA, PhD); Spanish (MA, PhD); systematic theology (M Th, D Th); TESOL (teaching English to speakers of other languages) (MA); theological ethics (M Th, D Th); theory of literature (MA, PhD); urban ministries (D Th); urban ministry (M Th).

University of South Alabama, Graduate School, College of Education, Mobile, AL 36688-0002. Offers M Ed, MS, PhD, Ed S. *Accreditation:* NCATE. Part-time programs available. *Faculty:* 44 full-time (23 women). *Students:* 252 full-time (192 women), 198 part-time (164 women); includes 101 minority (85 Black or African American, non-Hispanic/Latino; 4 American Indian or Alaska Native, non-Hispanic/Latino; 5 Asian, non-Hispanic/Latino; 5 Hispanic/Latino; 2 Two or more races, non-Hispanic/Latino), 10 international. 171 applicants, 50% accepted, 73 enrolled. In 2011, 137 master's, 4 doctorates awarded. *Degree requirements:* For master's, comprehensive exam; for doctorate, comprehensive exam, thesis/dissertation. *Entrance requirements:* For master's, GRE General Test or MAT. Additional exam requirements/recommendations for international students: Required—TOEFL. *Application deadline:* For fall admission, 7/15 priority date for domestic students, 6/15 for international students; for spring admission, 12/1 priority date for domestic students, 11/1 for international students. Applications are processed on a rolling basis. Application fee: $35. *Expenses:* Tuition, state resident: full-time $7968; part-time $332 per credit hour. Tuition, nonresident: full-time $15,936; part-time $664 per credit hour. *Financial support:* In 2011–12, 23 research assistantships, 10 teaching assistantships were awarded; career-related internships or fieldwork also available. Support available to part-time students. Financial award application deadline: 4/1. *Unit head:* Dr. Richard Hayes, Dean, 251-380-2738. *Application contact:* Dr. Abigail Baxter, Director of Graduate Studies, 251-460-6310, Fax: 251-461-1513, E-mail: kharriso@usouthal.edu. Web site: http://www.southalabama.edu/coe.

University of South Carolina, The Graduate School, College of Education, Columbia, SC 29208. Offers IMA, M Ed, MAT, MS, MT, Ed D, PhD, Certificate, Ed S. *Accreditation:* NCATE. Part-time and evening/weekend programs available. Postbaccalaureate distance learning degree programs offered (minimal on-campus study). *Degree requirements:* For master's, comprehensive exam, thesis (for some programs), foreign language (MA); for doctorate, one foreign language, comprehensive exam, thesis/dissertation. *Entrance requirements:* For master's, GRE General Test or MAT, official transcripts, letters of recommendation, letter of intent; for doctorate, GRE General Test or MAT/qualifying exams, letters of recommendation, letters of intent, interview. Electronic applications accepted. *Faculty research:* Inquiry learning, assessment of student learning, equity issues in education, multicultural education, cultural diversity.

University of South Carolina Upstate, Graduate Programs, Spartanburg, SC 29303-4999. Offers early childhood education (M Ed); elementary education (M Ed); special education: visual impairment (M Ed). *Accreditation:* NCATE. Part-time and evening/weekend programs available. *Faculty:* 8 full-time (6 women), 4 part-time/adjunct (2 women). *Students:* 6 full-time (all women), 69 part-time (63 women); includes 16 minority (14 Black or African American, non-Hispanic/Latino; 2 Two or more races, non-Hispanic/Latino), 2 international. Average age 33. In 2011, 8 master's awarded. *Degree requirements:* For master's, professional portfolio. *Entrance requirements:* For master's, GRE General Test or MAT, interview, minimum undergraduate GPA of 2.5, teaching certificate, 2 letters of recommendation. *Application deadline:* Applications are processed on a rolling basis. Application fee: $40. *Expenses:* Tuition, state resident: full-time $10,916; part-time $455 per credit hour. Tuition, nonresident: full-time $23,444; part-time $977 per credit hour. *Required fees:* $450 per semester. Tuition and fees vary according to course load and program. *Financial support:* Institutionally sponsored loans and institutional work-study available. Financial award application deadline: 7/15; financial award applicants required to submit FAFSA. *Faculty research:* Rough and tumble play, social justice education, American Indian literatures and cultures, diversity and multicultural education, science teaching strategy. *Unit head:* Dr. Tina Herzberg, Director of Graduate Programs, 864-503-5572, Fax: 864-503-5573, E-mail: rstevens@uscupstate.edu. *Application contact:* Donette Stewart, Associate Vice Chancellor for Enrollment Services, 864-503-5280, E-mail: dstewart@uscupstate.edu. Web site: http://www.uscupstate.edu/graduate/.

The University of South Dakota, Graduate School, School of Education, Vermillion, SD 57069-2390. Offers MA, MS, Ed D, PhD, Ed S. *Accreditation:* NCATE. Part-time and evening/weekend programs available. Postbaccalaureate distance learning degree programs offered (no on-campus study). *Degree requirements:* For master's and Ed S, comprehensive exam, thesis or alternative; for doctorate, comprehensive exam, thesis/dissertation. *Entrance requirements:* For master's and doctorate, GRE General Test or Miller Analogies Test, minimum GPA of 2.7. Additional exam requirements/recommendations for international students: Required—TOEFL (minimum score 550 paper-based; 213 computer-based; 79 iBT). Electronic applications accepted. *Expenses:* Tuition, state resident: full-time $3118.50; part-time $173.25 per credit hour. Tuition, nonresident: full-time $6601; part-time $366.70 per credit hour. *Required fees:* $2268; $126 per credit hour. Tuition and fees vary according to program.

University of Southern California, Graduate School, Rossier School of Education, Los Angeles, CA 90089. Offers MAT, ME, MMFT, Ed D, PhD. *Degree requirements:* For master's, thesis optional; for doctorate, thesis/dissertation. *Entrance requirements:* For master's and doctorate, GRE. Additional exam requirements/recommendations for international students: Required—TOEFL (minimum score 250 computer-based; 100 iBT). Electronic applications accepted. *Faculty research:* Data-driven decision-making in K-12 schools and districts; examination of college and university leadership and management in U. S. and Asia; studies in facilitating student learning; organizational change and the role of leaders; leadership, diversity, learning and accountability.

University of Southern Indiana, Graduate Studies, College of Science, Engineering, and Education, Department of Teacher Education, Evansville, IN 47712-3590. Offers elementary education (MS); secondary education (MS). *Accreditation:* NCATE. Part-time and evening/weekend programs available. *Faculty:* 8 full-time (4 women), 1 part-time/adjunct (0 women). *Students:* 1 (woman) full-time, 135 part-time (100 women);

includes 7 minority (5 Black or African American, non-Hispanic/Latino; 1 Asian, non-Hispanic/Latino; 1 Hispanic/Latino), 2 international. Average age 32. 75 applicants, 99% accepted, 53 enrolled. In 2011, 36 master's awarded. *Entrance requirements:* For master's, GRE General Test, NTE or PRAXIS I, minimum GPA of 3.0, teaching license. Additional exam requirements/recommendations for international students: Required—TOEFL (minimum score 550 paper-based; 213 computer-based; 79 iBT), IELTS (minimum score 6). *Application deadline:* For fall admission, 7/1 priority date for domestic students, 1/1 for international students. Applications are processed on a rolling basis. Application fee: $35. Electronic applications accepted. *Expenses:* Tuition, state resident: full-time $5044; part-time $280.21 per credit hour. Tuition, nonresident: full-time $9949; part-time $552.71 per credit hour. *Required fees:* $240; $22.75 per term. Tuition and fees vary according to course load and reciprocity agreements. *Financial support:* In 2011–12, 4 students received support. Federal Work-Study, scholarships/grants, tuition waivers (full and partial), and unspecified assistantships available. Financial award application deadline: 3/1; financial award applicants required to submit FAFSA. *Unit head:* Dr. Vella Goebel, Director, 812-461-5306, E-mail: vgoebel@usi.edu. *Application contact:* Dr. Wes Durham, Interim Director, Graduate Studies, 812-465-7015, Fax: 812-464-1956, E-mail: wdurham@usi.edu.

University of Southern Maine, School of Education and Human Development, Gorham, ME 04038. Offers MS, MS Ed, Psy D, CAS, Certificate. *Accreditation:* Teacher Education Accreditation Council. Part-time and evening/weekend programs available. Postbaccalaureate distance learning degree programs offered (minimal on-campus study). Terminal master's awarded for partial completion of doctoral program. *Degree requirements:* For master's, comprehensive exam (for some programs), thesis or alternative; for doctorate, thesis/dissertation; for other advanced degree, thesis or alternative. *Entrance requirements:* For master's, GRE General Test or MAT, PRAXIS (extended teacher education), proof of teacher certification; for doctorate, GRE; for other advanced degree, master's degree. Additional exam requirements/recommendations for international students: Required—TOEFL (minimum score 550 paper-based; 213 computer-based; 79 iBT). Electronic applications accepted. *Faculty research:* Teacher development, library technology outreach, literacy through literature, college-bound, multicultural education, school psychology, education policy and evaluation.

University of Southern Mississippi, Graduate School, College of Education and Psychology, Hattiesburg, MS 39406-0001. Offers M Ed, MA, MAT, MLIS, MS, Ed D, PhD, Ed S, Graduate Certificate. *Accreditation:* NCATE. Part-time programs available. *Faculty:* 98 full-time (51 women), 13 part-time/adjunct (4 women). *Students:* 271 full-time (213 women), 699 part-time (541 women); includes 238 minority (205 Black or African American, non-Hispanic/Latino; 1 American Indian or Alaska Native, non-Hispanic/Latino; 5 Asian, non-Hispanic/Latino; 17 Hispanic/Latino; 10 Two or more races, non-Hispanic/Latino), 14 international. Average age 36. 455 applicants, 42% accepted, 157 enrolled. In 2011, 252 master's, 62 doctorates, 40 other advanced degrees awarded. Terminal master's awarded for partial completion of doctoral program. *Degree requirements:* For master's, comprehensive exam, thesis (for some programs); for doctorate, comprehensive exam, thesis/dissertation; for other advanced degree, comprehensive exam, thesis. *Entrance requirements:* For master's, GRE General Test, MAT, minimum GPA of 2.75 on last 60 hours; for doctorate, GRE General Test, minimum GPA of 3.5; for other advanced degree, GRE General Test. Additional exam requirements/recommendations for international students: Required—TOEFL, IELTS. *Application deadline:* For fall admission, 3/1 priority date for domestic students, 3/1 for international students; for spring admission, 11/1 priority date for domestic students, 11/1 for international students. Applications are processed on a rolling basis. Application fee: $50. Electronic applications accepted. *Financial support:* In 2011–12, 80 research assistantships with full tuition reimbursements (averaging $9,586 per year), 53 teaching assistantships with full tuition reimbursements (averaging $7,775 per year) were awarded; career-related internships or fieldwork, Federal Work-Study, institutionally sponsored loans, scholarships/grants, health care benefits, and unspecified assistantships also available. Financial award application deadline: 3/15; financial award applicants required to submit FAFSA. *Faculty research:* Reading, sleep, animal cognition. *Unit head:* Dr. Ann P. Blackwell, Dean, 601-266-4568, Fax: 601-266-4175. *Application contact:* Shonna Breland, Manager of Graduate Admissions, 601-266-6563, Fax: 601-266-5138. Web site: http://www.usm.edu/graduateschool/table.php.

University of South Florida, Graduate School, College of Education, Tampa, FL 33620-9951. Offers M Ed, MA, MAT, Ed D, PhD, Ed S. *Accreditation:* NCATE. Part-time and evening/weekend programs available. Postbaccalaureate distance learning degree programs offered (no on-campus study). *Faculty:* 134 full-time (82 women), 36 part-time/adjunct (21 women). *Students:* 591 full-time (434 women), 967 part-time (700 women); includes 395 minority (172 Black or African American, non-Hispanic/Latino; 6 American Indian or Alaska Native, non-Hispanic/Latino; 36 Asian, non-Hispanic/Latino; 158 Hispanic/Latino; 23 Two or more races, non-Hispanic/Latino), 64 international. Average age 36. 1,133 applicants, 64% accepted, 517 enrolled. In 2011, 446 master's, 69 doctorates, 16 other advanced degrees awarded. *Degree requirements:* For master's, comprehensive exam, thesis (for some programs), project (for some programs); for doctorate, comprehensive exam, thesis/dissertation, philosophies of inquiry; multiple research methods. *Entrance requirements:* For master's, GRE General Test, minimum GPA of 3.5 in last 60 hours of course work; for doctorate, GRE General Test, minimum GPA of 3.5; for Ed S, GRE General Test. Additional exam requirements/recommendations for international students: Required—TOEFL (minimum score 550 paper-based; 213 computer-based). *Application deadline:* For fall admission, 2/15 for domestic students, 1/2 for international students; for spring admission, 10/15 for domestic students, 6/1 for international students. Application fee: $30. Electronic applications accepted. *Financial support:* In 2011–12, 9 fellowships with full tuition reimbursements (averaging $15,000 per year), 2 research assistantships with full tuition reimbursements (averaging $15,000 per year) were awarded; career-related internships or fieldwork, Federal Work-Study, institutionally sponsored loans, scholarships/grants, health care benefits, and unspecified assistantships also available. Support available to part-time students. Financial award applicants required to submit FAFSA. *Faculty research:* Scholarship of teaching and learning, educator preparation, diversity issues as they relate to PK-20 education, urban education. *Total annual research expenditures:* $22 million. *Unit head:* Dr. Colleen S. Kennedy, Dean, 813-974-3400, Fax: 813-974-3826. *Application contact:* Dr. Diane Briscoe, Coordinator of Graduate Studies, 813-974-1804, Fax: 813-974-3391, E-mail: briscoe@usf.edu. Web site: http://www.coedu.usf.edu/.

University of South Florida–St. Petersburg Campus, College of Education, St. Petersburg, FL 33701. Offers educational leadership development (M Ed); elementary education (MA), including math/science; English education (MA); middle grades STEM education (MS); reading education (MA). Part-time programs available. *Students:* 30 full-time (27 women), 130 part-time (109 women); includes 28 minority (14 Black or African American, non-Hispanic/Latino; 4 Asian, non-Hispanic/Latino; 9 Hispanic/Latino; 1 Two or more races, non-Hispanic/Latino). Average age 34. 63 applicants, 70% accepted, 36 enrolled. In 2011, 74 master's awarded. *Degree requirements:* For master's, comprehensive exam, practicum, internship, comprehensive portfolio. *Entrance requirements:* For master's, State of Florida General Knowledge Test (GKT), Florida Teaching Certificate (for non-initial certification programs), letters of recommendation. Additional exam requirements/recommendations for international students: Required—TOEFL (minimum score 550 paper-based; 79 iBT); Recommended—IELTS. *Application deadline:* For fall admission, 6/1 priority date for domestic students, 6/1 for international students; for spring admission, 10/15 priority date for domestic students, 10/15 for international students. Applications are processed on a rolling basis. Application fee: $30. Electronic applications accepted. *Expenses:* Tuition, state resident: full-time $8847. Tuition, nonresident: full-time $18,423. One-time fee: $35 full-time. Full-time tuition and fees vary according to course load and program. *Financial support:* Applicants required to submit FAFSA. *Unit head:* Dr. Harold W. Heller, Dean, 727-873-4155, Fax: 727-873-4191, E-mail: hheller@usfsp.edu. *Application contact:* Eric Douthirt, Enrollment Management Specialist, 727-873-4450, E-mail: douthirt@usfsp.edu. Web site: http://www1.usfsp.edu/coe/index.asp.

University of South Florida Sarasota-Manatee, College of Education, Sarasota, FL 34243. Offers educational leadership (M Ed), including curriculum leadership, K-12, non-public/charter school leadership; elementary education K-6 (MA); K-6 with ESOL endorsement (MAT); reading education K-12 (MA); MAT/MA. Part-time and evening/weekend programs available. *Faculty:* 12 full-time (8 women), 4 part-time/adjunct (3 women). *Students:* 19 full-time (17 women), 64 part-time (50 women); includes 7 minority (1 Black or African American, non-Hispanic/Latino; 1 Asian, non-Hispanic/Latino; 4 Hispanic/Latino; 1 Two or more races, non-Hispanic/Latino). Average age 33. 50 applicants, 62% accepted, 21 enrolled. In 2011, 41 master's awarded. *Degree requirements:* For master's, comprehensive exam (for some programs). *Entrance requirements:* For master's, GRE. Additional exam requirements/recommendations for international students: Required—TOEFL (minimum score 213 computer-based; 79 iBT) or IELTS. *Application deadline:* For fall admission, 2/15 for domestic students, 1/2 for international students; for spring admission, 10/15 for domestic students, 6/1 for international students. Applications are processed on a rolling basis. Application fee: $30. Electronic applications accepted. *Expenses:* Tuition, state resident: full-time $9301; part-time $387.55 per credit hour. Tuition, nonresident: full-time $19,412; part-time $808.85 per credit hour. *Required fees:* $15; $5 per semester. One-time fee: $30. *Financial support:* Federal Work-Study, scholarships/grants, health care benefits, and unspecified assistantships available. Support available to part-time students. Financial award application deadline: 3/1; financial award applicants required to submit FAFSA. *Faculty research:* Child development, student achievement, intergenerational studies. *Unit head:* Dr. Terry A. Osborn, Dean, 941-359-4531, E-mail: terryosborn@sar.usf.edu. *Application contact:* Jo Lynn Raudebaugh, Graduate Admissions Advisor, 941-359-4587, E-mail: jraudeba@sar.usf.edu. Web site: http://www.sarasota.usf.edu/Academics/COE/.

The University of Tampa, Program in Teaching, Tampa, FL 33606-1490. Offers curricula and instructional leadership (M Ed); teaching (M Ed). Part-time and evening/weekend programs available. *Faculty:* 5 full-time (2 women), 7 part-time/adjunct (6 women). *Students:* 25 full-time (12 women), 2 part-time (both women); includes 6 minority (5 Hispanic/Latino; 1 Two or more races, non-Hispanic/Latino). Average age 30. 102 applicants, 38% accepted, 27 enrolled. In 2011, 43 master's awarded. *Entrance requirements:* For master's, Florida Teacher Certification Exam, PRAXIS, GRE, or GMAT, bachelor's degree in education or professional teaching certificate. Additional exam requirements/recommendations for international students: Required—TOEFL (minimum score 577 paper-based; 230 computer-based; 90 iBT), IELTS (minimum score 7). *Application deadline:* For fall admission, 5/1 for domestic students. Applications are processed on a rolling basis. Application fee: $40. Electronic applications accepted. *Expenses: Tuition:* Full-time $8320; part-time $520 per credit hour. *Required fees:* $40 per semester. Tuition and fees vary according to program. *Financial support:* In 2011–12, 8 students received support. Grants available. Financial award applicants required to submit FAFSA. *Faculty research:* Diversity in the classroom, technology integration, assessment methodologies, complex and ill-structured problem solving, and communities of practice.. *Unit head:* Dr. Anne Gormly, Dean, College of Social Sciences, Mathematics and Education, 813-253-3333 Ext. 6262, E-mail: agormly@ut.edu. *Application contact:* Charlene Tobie, Associate Director, Graduate and Continuing Studies, 813-258-7409, Fax: 813-258-7451, E-mail: ctobie@ut.edu. Web site: http://www.ut.edu/graduate.

The University of Tennessee, Graduate School, College of Education, Health and Human Sciences, Knoxville, TN 37996. Offers MPH, MS, Ed D, PhD, Ed S, MS/MPH. *Accreditation:* NCATE. Part-time and evening/weekend programs available. Postbaccalaureate distance learning degree programs offered (no on-campus study). Terminal master's awarded for partial completion of doctoral program. *Degree requirements:* For master's and Ed S, thesis optional; for doctorate, thesis/dissertation. *Entrance requirements:* For master's, minimum GPA of 2.7; for doctorate and Ed S, GRE General Test, minimum GPA of 2.7. Additional exam requirements/recommendations for international students: Required—TOEFL. Electronic applications accepted. *Expenses:* Tuition, state resident: full-time $8332; part-time $464 per credit hour. Tuition, nonresident: full-time $25,174; part-time $1400 per credit hour. *Required fees:* $1162; $56 per credit hour. Tuition and fees vary according to program.

The University of Tennessee at Chattanooga, Graduate School, College of Health, Education and Professional Studies, School of Education, Chattanooga, TN 37403-2598. Offers counseling (M Ed), including community counseling, school counseling; education (M Ed, Post-Master's Certificate), including elementary education (M Ed), school leadership, secondary education (M Ed), special education (M Ed); educational specialist (Ed S), including educational technology, school psychology; learning and leadership (Ed D), including educational leadership. *Accreditation:* ACA; NCATE. Part-time and evening/weekend programs available. Postbaccalaureate distance learning degree programs offered (no on-campus study). *Faculty:* 25 full-time (17 women), 10 part-time/adjunct (3 women). *Students:* 145 full-time (104 women), 319 part-time (236 women); includes 63 minority (43 Black or African American, non-Hispanic/Latino; 4 American Indian or Alaska Native, non-Hispanic/Latino; 2 Asian, non-Hispanic/Latino; 6 Hispanic/Latino; 8 Two or more races, non-Hispanic/Latino), 2 international. Average age 34. 226 applicants, 79% accepted, 111 enrolled. In 2011, 120 master's, 9 doctorates, 17 other advanced degrees awarded. *Degree requirements:* For master's, comprehensive exam, thesis optional, culminating experience; for doctorate, comprehensive exam, thesis/dissertation; for other advanced degree, internship. *Entrance requirements:* For master's, GRE General Test, PPST 1, teaching certificate; for doctorate, GRE General Test, master's degree, two years of practical work experience in organizational environment; for other advanced degree, GRE General Test, letters of reference. Additional exam requirements/recommendations for international students: Required—TOEFL (minimum score 550 paper-based; 213 computer-based; 79 iBT), IELTS (minimum score 6). *Application deadline:* For fall admission, 8/1 for domestic students, 6/1 for international students; for spring admission, 12/1 for domestic students, 10/1 for international students. Applications are processed on a rolling basis. Application fee: $35. Electronic applications accepted. *Expenses:* Tuition, state resident: full-time $6472; part-time $359 per credit hour. Tuition, nonresident: full-time $20,006; part-time $1111 per credit hour. *Required fees:* $1320; $160 per credit hour. *Financial support:* Career-related internships or fieldwork, institutionally sponsored loans, scholarships/grants, and unspecified assistantships available. Support available to part-time students. Financial award applicants required to submit FAFSA. *Faculty research:* School counseling, community counseling, elementary and secondary education, school leadership and administration. *Total annual research* *expenditures:* $675,479. *Unit head:* Dr. John Freeman, Head, 423-425-4133, Fax: 423-425-5380, E-mail: john-freeman@utc.edu. *Application contact:* Dr. Jerald Ainsworth, Dean of Graduate Studies, 423-425-4478, Fax: 423-425-5223, E-mail: jerald-ainsworth@utc.edu. Web site: http://www.utc.edu/Administration/HealthEducationAndProfessionalStudies/Graduate_Studies/graduate_studies.html.

The University of Tennessee at Martin, Graduate Programs, College of Education, Health, and Behavioral Sciences, Martin, TN 38238-1000. Offers MS Ed. *Accreditation:* NCATE. Part-time programs available. Postbaccalaureate distance learning degree programs offered (minimal on-campus study). *Faculty:* 61. *Students:* 221 (168 women); includes 20 minority (16 Black or African American, non-Hispanic/Latino; 1 American Indian or Alaska Native, non-Hispanic/Latino; 1 Hispanic/Latino; 2 Two or more races, non-Hispanic/Latino). 140 applicants, 59% accepted, 59 enrolled. In 2011, 67 master's awarded. *Degree requirements:* For master's, comprehensive exam. *Entrance requirements:* For master's, GRE General Test, minimum GPA of 2.5. Additional exam requirements/recommendations for international students: Required—TOEFL (minimum score 525 paper-based; 197 computer-based; 71 iBT). *Application deadline:* For fall admission, 8/1 priority date for domestic students, 7/15 for international students; for spring admission, 12/15 priority date for domestic students, 12/1 for international students. Applications are processed on a rolling basis. Application fee: $30 ($130 for international students). Electronic applications accepted. *Expenses:* Tuition, state resident: full-time $6726; part-time $374 per credit hour. Tuition, nonresident: full-time $19,136; part-time $1064 per credit hour. *Required fees:* $61 per credit hour. *Financial support:* In 2011–12, 16 students received support, including 13 research assistantships with full tuition reimbursements available (averaging $7,729 per year), 3 teaching assistantships with full tuition reimbursements available (averaging $6,283 per year); scholarships/grants and unspecified assistantships also available. Support available to part-time students. Financial award application deadline: 1/15; financial award applicants required to submit FAFSA. *Faculty research:* Environmental education, self-concept, science education, attention deficit disorder, special education. *Total annual research expenditures:* $1 million. *Unit head:* Dr. Mary Lee Hall, Dean, 731-881-7127, Fax: 731-881-7975, E-mail: mlhall@utm.edu. *Application contact:* Linda S. Arant, Student Services Specialist, 731-881-7012, Fax: 731-881-7499, E-mail: larant@utm.edu. Web site: http://www.utm.edu/departments/cehbs/.

The University of Texas at Arlington, Graduate School, College of Education and Health Professions, Arlington, TX 76019. Offers M Ed, MS, PhD. *Unit head:* Dr. Phil Cohen, Dean of Graduate Studies, 817-272-3186, Fax: 817-272-2625, E-mail: graduate.school@uta.edu. *Application contact:* Dr. Phil Cohen, Dean of Graduate Studies, 817-272-3186, Fax: 817-272-2625, E-mail: graduate.school@uta.edu.

The University of Texas at Arlington, Graduate School, Department of Curriculum and Instruction, Arlington, TX 76019. Offers curriculum and instruction (M Ed); teaching (with certification) (M Ed T). *Accreditation:* NCATE. Part-time and evening/weekend programs available. Postbaccalaureate distance learning degree programs offered (no on-campus study). *Faculty:* 19 full-time (13 women). *Students:* 68 full-time (50 women), 874 part-time (776 women); includes 324 minority (128 Black or African American, non-Hispanic/Latino; 2 American Indian or Alaska Native, non-Hispanic/Latino; 25 Asian, non-Hispanic/Latino; 144 Hispanic/Latino; 25 Two or more races, non-Hispanic/Latino), 18 international. Average age 35. 727 applicants, 88% accepted, 552 enrolled. In 2011, 318 degrees awarded. *Degree requirements:* For master's, comprehensive exam (for some programs), comprehensive activity, research project. *Entrance requirements:* For master's, GRE General Test, minimum undergraduate GPA of 3.0 in last 60 hours of course work, writing sample, 3 letters of recommendation. Additional exam requirements/recommendations for international students: Required—TOEFL (minimum score 550 paper-based; 213 computer-based). *Application deadline:* For fall admission, 6/1 priority date for domestic students, 4/1 for international students; for spring admission, 10/15 priority date for domestic students, 9/15 for international students. Applications are processed on a rolling basis. Application fee: $50. Electronic applications accepted. *Financial support:* In 2011–12, 85 students received support, including 4 research assistantships (averaging $3,000 per year), 4 teaching assistantships (averaging $3,000 per year); career-related internships or fieldwork, Federal Work-Study, scholarships/grants, and unspecified assistantships also available. Financial award application deadline: 6/1; financial award applicants required to submit FAFSA. *Unit head:* Dr. John A. Smith, Chair, 817-272-0116, Fax: 817-272-2618, E-mail: smithj@uta.edu. *Application contact:* Racine Reza, Graduate Advisor, 817-272-2956, Fax: 817-272-7624, E-mail: racine@uta.edu. Web site: http://www.uta.edu/coed.

The University of Texas at Austin, Graduate School, College of Education, Austin, TX 78712-1111. Offers M Ed, MA, MS, Ed D, PhD. Part-time programs available. *Entrance requirements:* For master's and doctorate, GRE General Test. Application fee: $50 ($75 for international students). Electronic applications accepted. *Financial support:* Fellowships, research assistantships, teaching assistantships with partial tuition reimbursements, career-related internships or fieldwork, and Federal Work-Study available. Financial award application deadline: 2/1; financial award applicants required to submit FAFSA. *Unit head:* Dr. Manuel J. Justiz, Dean, 512-471-7255, Fax: 512-471-0846, E-mail: mjustiz@mail.utexas.edu. *Application contact:* Dr. Sharon Evans, Director, 521-471-1511, E-mail: dr.sharonevans@mail.utexas.edu. Web site: http://www.edb.utexas.edu/education/.

The University of Texas at Brownsville, Graduate Studies, School of Education, Brownsville, TX 78520-4991. Offers bilingual education (M Ed); counseling and guidance (M Ed); curriculum and instruction (M Ed); early childhood education (M Ed); educational administration (M Ed); educational technology (M Ed); English as a second language (M Ed); reading specialist (M Ed); special education/educational diagnostician (M Ed). Part-time and evening/weekend programs available. Postbaccalaureate distance learning degree programs offered (minimal on-campus study). *Degree requirements:* For master's, thesis optional. *Entrance requirements:* For master's, GRE General Test. Additional exam requirements/recommendations for international students: Required—TOEFL.

The University of Texas at El Paso, Graduate School, College of Education, El Paso, TX 79968-0001. Offers M Ed, MA, Ed D, PhD. Part-time and evening/weekend programs available. Postbaccalaureate distance learning degree programs offered. *Students:* 1,101 (826 women); includes 900 minority (30 Black or African American, non-Hispanic/Latino; 3 American Indian or Alaska Native, non-Hispanic/Latino; 17 Asian, non-Hispanic/Latino; 847 Hispanic/Latino; 2 Native Hawaiian or other Pacific Islander, non-Hispanic/Latino; 1 Two or more races, non-Hispanic/Latino), 43 international. Average age 34. 301 applicants, 76% accepted, 190 enrolled. In 2011, 154 master's, 2 doctorates awarded. *Degree requirements:* For master's, thesis optional; for doctorate, thesis/dissertation. *Entrance requirements:* For master's, minimum GPA of 3.0, letter of intent, resume, letters of recommendation, copy of teaching certificate, district service record; for doctorate, GRE, resume, letters of recommendation, scholarly paper. Additional exam requirements/recommendations for international students: Required—TOEFL; Recommended—IELTS. *Application deadline:* For fall admission, 8/1 for domestic students, 3/1 for international students; for spring admission, 11/1 priority date for domestic students, 9/1 for international students. Applications are processed on a rolling basis. Application fee: $45 ($80 for international students). Electronic applications accepted. *Financial support:* In 2011–12, research assistantships with partial tuition reimbursements (averaging $16,642 per year), teaching assistantships with partial tuition reimbursements (averaging $13,314 per year) were awarded; fellowships with partial tuition reimbursements, institutionally sponsored loans, scholarships/grants, health care benefits, tuition waivers (partial), and unspecified assistantships also available. Support available to part-time students. Financial award application deadline: 3/15; financial award applicants required to submit FAFSA. *Unit head:* Dr. Josie V. Tinajero, Dean, 915-747-5572, Fax: 915-747-5755, E-mail: tinajero@utep.edu. *Application contact:* Dr. Benjamin Flores, Interim Dean of the Graduate School, 915-747-5491, Fax: 915-747-5788, E-mail: bflores@utep.edu.

The University of Texas of the Permian Basin, Office of Graduate Studies, School of Education, Odessa, TX 79762-0001. Offers MA. *Accreditation:* NCATE. *Entrance requirements:* For master's, GRE General Test. Additional exam requirements/recommendations for international students: Required—TOEFL (minimum score 550 paper-based; 213 computer-based).

The University of Texas–Pan American, College of Education, Edinburg, TX 78539. Offers M Ed, MA, MS, Ed D, PhD. Ed D offered jointly with The University of Texas at Austin. Part-time and evening/weekend programs available. *Degree requirements:* For master's, thesis optional. *Entrance requirements:* For master's, GRE General Test. *Application deadline:* For fall admission, 7/17 for domestic students; for spring admission, 11/16 for domestic students. Application fee: $0. Tuition and fees vary according to course load, program and student level. *Financial support:* Research assistantships, teaching assistantships, career-related internships or fieldwork, Federal Work-Study, and institutionally sponsored loans available. Support available to part-time students. Financial award application deadline: 4/15. *Faculty research:* Literacy development, bilingual education, brain mapping. *Unit head:* Dr. Hector Ochoa, Dean, 956-665-2530, E-mail: shochoa@utpa.edu. Web site: http://portal.utpa.edu/utpa_main/daa_home/coed_home.

University of the Cumberlands, Graduate Programs in Education, Williamsburg, KY 40769-1372. Offers all grades (P-12) (M Ed); business and marketing (MA Ed, MAT); director of pupil personnel (Certificate); director of special education (Certificate); educational administration and supervision (Ed S); educational leadership (Ed D); elementary education (MA Ed, MAT); instructional leadership - principalship (MA Ed); instructional leadership - school principal (Certificate); middle school education (MA Ed, MAT); reading and writing (MA Ed); school counseling (MA Ed); school superintendent (Certificate); secondary education (MA Ed, MAT); special education (MAT); supervisor of instruction (Certificate); teacher leader (MA Ed). Part-time and evening/weekend programs available. Postbaccalaureate distance learning degree programs offered. *Degree requirements:* For master's, comprehensive exam. Electronic applications accepted.

University of the District of Columbia, College of Arts and Sciences, Department of Education, Washington, DC 20008-1175. Offers early childhood education (MA); special education (MA). *Accreditation:* NCATE. Part-time programs available. *Degree requirements:* For master's, comprehensive exam, research paper. *Entrance requirements:* For master's, GRE General Test, writing proficiency exam. *Expenses: Tuition, area resident:* Full-time $7580; part-time $421 per credit hour. Tuition, state resident: full-time $8580; part-time $477 per credit hour. Tuition, nonresident: full-time $14,580; part-time $810 per credit hour. *Required fees:* $620; $30 per credit hour. $310 per semester.

University of the Incarnate Word, School of Graduate Studies and Research, Dreeben School of Education, Program in Teaching, San Antonio, TX 78209-6397. Offers all-level teaching (MAT); elementary teaching (MAT); secondary teaching (MAT). Part-time and evening/weekend programs available. *Faculty:* 14 full-time (8 women), 10 part-time/adjunct (9 women). *Students:* 2 full-time (1 woman), 29 part-time (25 women); includes 20 minority (2 Black or African American, non-Hispanic/Latino; 18 Hispanic/Latino). Average age 33. 11 applicants, 91% accepted, 7 enrolled. In 2011, 9 degrees awarded. *Degree requirements:* For master's, internship. *Entrance requirements:* For master's, GRE, Texas Higher Education Assessment test (THEA), interview. Additional exam requirements/recommendations for international students: Required—TOEFL (minimum score 560 paper-based; 220 computer-based; 83 iBT). *Application deadline:* Applications are processed on a rolling basis. Application fee: $20. Electronic applications accepted. *Expenses: Tuition:* Part-time $725 per credit hour. Tuition and fees vary according to degree level. *Financial support:* Federal Work-Study and scholarships/grants available. Financial award applicants required to submit FAFSA. *Unit head:* Dr. Elda Martinez, Director of Teacher Education, 210-832-3297, Fax: 210-829-3134, E-mail: eemartin@uiwtx.edu. *Application contact:* Andrea Cyterski-Acosta, Dean of Enrollment, 210-829-6005, Fax: 210-829-3921, E-mail: admis@uiwtx.edu. Web site: http://www.uiw.edu/education/graduate.html.

University of the Incarnate Word, School of Graduate Studies and Research, Dreeben School of Education, Programs in Education, San Antonio, TX 78209-6397. Offers adult education (M Ed, MA); cross-cultural education (M Ed, MA); early childhood literacy (M Ed, MA); general education (M Ed, MA); higher education (PhD); instructional technology (M Ed, MA); international education and entrepreneurship (PhD); kinesiology (M Ed, MA); literacy (M Ed, MA); organizational leadership (PhD); organizational learning and learning (M Ed, MA); reading (M Ed, MA); special education (M Ed, MA); teacher leadership (M Ed, MA). Part-time and evening/weekend programs available. *Faculty:* 14 full-time (8 women), 10 part-time/adjunct (9 women). *Students:* 13 full-time (7 women), 197 part-time (129 women); includes 111 minority (23 Black or African American, non-Hispanic/Latino; 2 American Indian or Alaska Native, non-Hispanic/Latino; 1 Asian, non-Hispanic/Latino; 85 Hispanic/Latino), 26 international. Average age 41. 78 applicants, 79% accepted, 34 enrolled. In 2011, 21 master's, 12 doctorates awarded. *Degree requirements:* For master's, capstone; for doctorate, thesis/dissertation, qualifying exam. *Entrance requirements:* For master's, baccalaureate degree; minimum foundation GPA of 2.5; interview; for doctorate, master's degree; interview; supervised writing sample. Additional exam requirements/recommendations for international students: Required—TOEFL (minimum score 560 paper-based; 220 computer-based; 83 iBT). *Application deadline:* Applications are processed on a rolling basis. Application fee: $20. Electronic applications accepted. *Expenses: Tuition:* Part-time $725 per credit hour. Tuition and fees vary according to degree level. *Financial support:* In 2011–12, 5 research assistantships were awarded; Federal Work-Study and scholarships/grants also available. Financial award applicants required to submit FAFSA. *Unit head:* Dr. Denise Staudt, Dean, Dreeben School of Education, 210-829-2762, E-mail: staudt@uiwtx.edu. *Application contact:* Andrea Cyterski-Acosta, Dean of Enrollment, 210-829-6005, Fax: 210-829-3921, E-mail: admis@uiwtx.edu. Web site: http://www.uiw.edu/education/index.htm.

University of the Pacific, School of Education, Stockton, CA 95211-0197. Offers M Ed, MA, Ed D, Ed S. *Accreditation:* NCATE. *Faculty:* 20 full-time (11 women), 6 part-time/adjunct (4 women). *Students:* 91 full-time (66 women), 211 part-time (159 women); includes 133 minority (17 Black or African American, non-Hispanic/Latino; 1 American Indian or Alaska Native, non-Hispanic/Latino; 83 Asian, non-Hispanic/Latino; 32 Hispanic/Latino), 12 international. Average age 33. 138 applicants, 75% accepted, 70 enrolled. In 2011, 109 master's, 26 doctorates awarded. *Degree requirements:* For doctorate, thesis/dissertation. *Entrance requirements:* For master's, GRE General Test; for doctorate, GRE General Test, GRE Subject Test. Additional exam requirements/

recommendations for international students: Required—TOEFL (minimum score 475 paper-based; 150 computer-based). *Application deadline:* For fall admission, 3/1 priority date for domestic students; for spring admission, 10/15 for domestic students. Applications are processed on a rolling basis. Application fee: $75. *Expenses: Tuition:* Full-time $18,900; part-time $1181 per unit. *Required fees:* $949. *Financial support:* In 2011–12, 13 teaching assistantships were awarded; institutionally sponsored loans also available. Support available to part-time students. Financial award application deadline: 3/1; financial award applicants required to submit FAFSA. *Unit head:* Dr. Lynn Beck, Dean, 209-946-2683, E-mail: lbeck@pacific.edu. *Application contact:* Office of Graduate Admissions, 209-946-2344.

University of the Sacred Heart, Graduate Programs, Department of Education, San Juan, PR 00914-0383. Offers early childhood education (M Ed); information technology and multimedia (Certificate); instruction systems and education technology (M Ed), including English, information technology and multimedia, instructional design, mathematics, Spanish. Part-time and evening/weekend programs available. *Degree requirements:* For master's, thesis. *Entrance requirements:* For master's, EXADEP, minimum undergraduate GPA of 2.75, interview.

University of the Southwest, Graduate Programs, Hobbs, NM 88240-9129. Offers business administration (MBA); curriculum and instruction (MSE); curriculum and instruction: bilingual (MSE); curriculum and instruction: TESOL (MSE); early childhood education (MSE); educational administration (MSE); mental health counseling (MSE); school counseling (MSE); special education (MSE); sports management (MBA). Part-time and evening/weekend programs available. Postbaccalaureate distance learning degree programs offered (no on-campus study). *Faculty:* 13 full-time (6 women), 28 part-time/adjunct (17 women). *Students:* 76 full-time (63 women), 229 part-time (194 women); includes 104 minority (50 Black or African American, non-Hispanic/Latino; 2 American Indian or Alaska Native, non-Hispanic/Latino; 8 Asian, non-Hispanic/Latino; 44 Hispanic/Latino). Average age 38. 173 applicants, 71% accepted, 101 enrolled. In 2011, 75 master's awarded. *Degree requirements:* For master's, comprehensive exam, thesis (for some programs). *Entrance requirements:* Additional exam requirements/recommendations for international students: Recommended—TOEFL. *Application deadline:* Applications are processed on a rolling basis. Application fee: $50. Electronic applications accepted. *Expenses: Tuition:* Full-time $12,288; part-time $512 per credit hour. One-time fee: $50. Tuition and fees vary according to course load. *Financial support:* In 2011–12, 47 students received support. Federal Work-Study available. Financial award application deadline: 4/1; financial award applicants required to submit FAFSA. *Unit head:* Dr. Mary Harris, Dean of Education, 575-492-2162, Fax: 575-392-6006, E-mail: mharris@usw.edu. *Application contact:* Melissa Mitchell, Senior Online Program Advisor, 575-492-2142, Fax: 575-392-6006, E-mail: mmitchell@usw.edu. Web site: http://www.usw.edu/admissions/graduate_admission/graduate_admissions.

University of the Virgin Islands, Graduate Programs, Division of Education, Saint Thomas, VI 00802-9990. Offers MAE. Part-time and evening/weekend programs available. *Degree requirements:* For master's, comprehensive exam, thesis or alternative. *Entrance requirements:* For master's, minimum GPA of 2.5, BA degree from accredited institution. Additional exam requirements/recommendations for international students: Required—TOEFL (minimum score 550 paper-based; 213 computer-based). *Faculty research:* Student self-concept and sense of futility.

The University of Toledo, College of Graduate Studies, Judith Herb College of Education, Health Science and Human Service, Toledo, OH 43606-3390. Offers MA, MAE, ME, MES, MME, MPH, MSW, MSX, DE, DPT, OTD, PhD, Certificate, Ed S, JD/MA. *Accreditation:* NCATE. Part-time and evening/weekend programs available. *Faculty:* 158. *Students:* 446 full-time (313 women), 791 part-time (575 women); includes 198 minority (135 Black or African American, non-Hispanic/Latino; 2 American Indian or Alaska Native, non-Hispanic/Latino; 20 Asian, non-Hispanic/Latino; 33 Hispanic/Latino; 8 Two or more races, non-Hispanic/Latino), 37 international. Average age 33. 1,022 applicants, 42% accepted, 332 enrolled. In 2011, 370 master's, 76 doctorates, 39 other advanced degrees awarded. Terminal master's awarded for partial completion of doctoral program. *Degree requirements:* For master's, thesis; for doctorate, comprehensive exam (for some programs), thesis/dissertation (for some programs); for other advanced degree, thesis optional. *Entrance requirements:* For master's and other advanced degree, minimum cumulative GPA of 2.7 for all previous academic work, letters of recommendation, statement of purpose, transcripts from all prior institutions attended; for doctorate, GRE, minimum cumulative GPA of 2.7 for all previous academic work, 3.0 for occupational therapy and physical therapy; letters of recommendation; statement of purpose; transcripts from all prior institutions attended. Additional exam requirements/recommendations for international students: Required—TOEFL (minimum score 550 paper-based; 213 computer-based; 80 iBT), IELTS (minimum score 6.5). *Application deadline:* For fall admission, 1/15 priority date for domestic students, 1/15 for international students. Applications are processed on a rolling basis. Application fee: $45 ($75 for international students). Electronic applications accepted. *Financial support:* In 2011–12, 32 research assistantships with full and partial tuition reimbursements (averaging $7,797 per year), 99 teaching assistantships with full and partial tuition reimbursements (averaging $8,750 per year) were awarded; career-related internships or fieldwork, Federal Work-Study, institutionally sponsored loans, scholarships/grants, tuition waivers (full and partial), unspecified assistantships, and administrative assistantships also available. Support available to part-time students. *Unit head:* Dr. Beverly Schmoll, Dean, 419-530-2495, E-mail: beverly.schmoll@utoledo.edu. *Application contact:* Graduate School Office, 419-530-4723, Fax: 419-530-4724, E-mail: grdsch@utnet.utoledo.edu. Web site: http://www.utoledo.edu/eduhshs/.

University of Toronto, School of Graduate Studies, Ontario Institute for Studies in Education, Toronto, ON M5S 1A1, Canada. Offers M Ed, MA, MT, Ed D, PhD. Part-time and evening/weekend programs available. *Degree requirements:* For master's, thesis (for some programs); for doctorate, thesis/dissertation. *Entrance requirements:* For master's, minimum B average in final year, 1 year of professional experience in field (MA, M Ed); for doctorate, minimum B+ average, professional experience in education or a relevant field (Ed D). Additional exam requirements/recommendations for international students: Required—TOEFL (minimum score 580 paper-based; 93 iBT), TWE (minimum score 5). *Expenses:* Contact institution.

University of Tulsa, Graduate School, College of Arts and Sciences, School of Education, Tulsa, OK 74104-3189. Offers education (M Ed, MA), including education (MA), elementary certification (M Ed), secondary certification (M Ed); mathematics and science education (MSMSE); teaching arts (MTA), including art, biology, English, history, mathematics, theatre. *Accreditation:* Teacher Education Accreditation Council. Part-time programs available. *Faculty:* 7 full-time (3 women). *Students:* 19 full-time (14 women), 4 part-time (3 women); includes 5 minority (1 Black or African American, non-Hispanic/Latino; 2 American Indian or Alaska Native, non-Hispanic/Latino; 1 Asian, non-Hispanic/Latino; 1 Hispanic/Latino), 3 international. Average age 28. 22 applicants, 68% accepted, 12 enrolled. In 2011, 8 master's awarded. *Degree requirements:* For master's, thesis optional. *Entrance requirements:* For master's, GRE General Test. Additional exam requirements/recommendations for international students: Required—TOEFL (minimum score 577 paper-based; 233 computer-based; 91 iBT), IELTS (minimum score 6.5). *Application deadline:* For fall admission, 2/1 priority date for domestic students. Applications are processed on a rolling basis. Application fee: $40. Electronic applications accepted. *Expenses: Tuition:* Full-time $17,748; part-time $986 per hour. *Required fees:* $5 per contact hour. $75 per semester. Tuition and fees vary according to program. *Financial support:* In 2011–12, 15 students received support, including 1 research assistantship with full and partial tuition reimbursement available (averaging $6,051 per year), 14 teaching assistantships with full and partial tuition reimbursements available (averaging $10,570 per year); fellowships with full and partial tuition reimbursements available, career-related internships or fieldwork, Federal Work-Study, scholarships/grants, health care benefits, tuition waivers (full and partial), and unspecified assistantships also available. Support available to part-time students. Financial award application deadline: 2/1; financial award applicants required to submit FAFSA. *Faculty research:* Elementary/secondary certification; math/science education; educational foundations; language, discourse, and development. *Total annual research expenditures:* $362,470. *Unit head:* Dr. Thomas Benediktson, Dean, 918-631-2541, Fax: 918-631-3721, E-mail: dale-benediktson@utulsa.edu. *Application contact:* Dr. David Brown, Advisor, 918-631-2719, Fax: 918-631-2133, E-mail: david-brown@utulsa.edu. Web site: http://www.cas.utulsa.edu/education/.

University of Utah, Graduate School, College of Education, Salt Lake City, UT 84112. Offers M Ed, M Phil, M Stat, MA, MAT, MS, PhD, MPA/PhD. Part-time and evening/weekend programs available. *Faculty:* 72 full-time (43 women), 12 part-time/adjunct (10 women). *Students:* 250 full-time (186 women), 259 part-time (185 women); includes 99 minority (6 Black or African American, non-Hispanic/Latino; 10 American Indian or Alaska Native, non-Hispanic/Latino; 11 Asian, non-Hispanic/Latino; 56 Hispanic/Latino; 6 Native Hawaiian or other Pacific Islander, non-Hispanic/Latino; 10 Two or more races, non-Hispanic/Latino), 15 international. Average age 34. 431 applicants, 35% accepted, 115 enrolled. In 2011, 121 master's, 22 doctorates awarded. *Median time to degree:* Of those who began their doctoral program in fall 2003, 56% received their degree in 8 years or less. *Degree requirements:* For master's, variable foreign language requirement, comprehensive exam, thesis (for some programs); for doctorate, variable foreign language requirement, thesis/dissertation. *Entrance requirements:* For master's, minimum undergraduate GPA of 3.0; for doctorate, minimum GPA of 3.0 (3.5 recommended). Additional exam requirements/recommendations for international students: Required—TOEFL (minimum score 600 paper-based; 250 computer-based; 100 iBT); Recommended—IELTS (minimum score 7). *Application deadline:* For fall admission, 2/15 priority date for domestic students, 2/15 for international students; for spring admission, 11/1 for domestic and international students. Applications are processed on a rolling basis. Application fee: $55 ($65 for international students). Electronic applications accepted. *Expenses:* Contact institution. *Financial support:* Fellowships with full tuition reimbursements, research assistantships with full tuition reimbursements, teaching assistantships with full and partial tuition reimbursements, career-related internships or fieldwork, Federal Work-Study, institutionally sponsored loans, scholarships/grants, tuition waivers (full and partial), and unspecified assistantships available. Support available to part-time students. Financial award application deadline: 2/1; financial award applicants required to submit FAFSA. *Faculty research:* Leadership, autism, reading instruction, mental retardation, diagnosis. *Total annual research expenditures:* $434,535. *Unit head:* Michael Hardman, Dean, 801-581-8121, Fax: 801-585-6476, E-mail: michael.hardman@utah.edu. *Application contact:* Mindy Jones, Executive Secretary, College Dean's Office, 801-581-8222, Fax: 801-581-5223, E-mail: mindy.jones@utah.edu. Web site: http://www.ed.utah.edu/.

University of Vermont, Graduate College, College of Education and Social Services, Burlington, VT 05405. Offers M Ed, MAT, MS, MSW, Ed D, PhD. *Accreditation:* NCATE. Part-time programs available. *Students:* 422 (325 women); includes 38 minority (14 Black or African American, non-Hispanic/Latino; 1 American Indian or Alaska Native, non-Hispanic/Latino; 7 Asian, non-Hispanic/Latino; 16 Hispanic/Latino), 6 international. 598 applicants, 56% accepted, 127 enrolled. In 2011, 182 master's, 18 doctorates awarded. *Degree requirements:* For doctorate, thesis/dissertation. *Entrance requirements:* Additional exam requirements/recommendations for international students: Required—TOEFL (minimum score 550 paper-based; 213 computer-based; 80 iBT). Application fee: $40. Electronic applications accepted. *Financial support:* Fellowships, research assistantships, teaching assistantships, career-related internships or fieldwork, and Federal Work-Study available. *Unit head:* Dr. Fayneese Miller, Dean, 802-656-3424. *Application contact:* Ralph Swenson, Director of Graduate Admissions, 802-656-2699, Fax: 802-656-0519, E-mail: graduate.admissions@uvm.edu.

University of Vermont, Graduate College, College of Education and Social Services, Department of Education, Program in Educational Studies, Burlington, VT 05405. Offers M Ed. *Students:* 5 applicants, 20% accepted, 0 enrolled. *Degree requirements:* For master's, thesis or alternative. *Entrance requirements:* Additional exam requirements/recommendations for international students: Required—TOEFL (minimum score 550 paper-based; 213 computer-based; 80 iBT). *Application deadline:* Applications are processed on a rolling basis. Application fee: $40. Electronic applications accepted. *Financial support:* Fellowships, research assistantships, and teaching assistantships available. Financial award application deadline: 3/1. *Application contact:* Ralph Swenson, Director of Graduate Admissions, 802-656-2699, Fax: 802-656-0519, E-mail: graduate.admissions@uvm.edu.

University of Victoria, Faculty of Graduate Studies, Faculty of Education, Victoria, BC V8W 2Y2, Canada. Offers M Ed, M Sc, MA, PhD.

University of Virginia, Curry School of Education, Charlottesville, VA 22903. Offers M Ed, MT, Ed D, PhD, Ed S. *Accreditation:* Teacher Education Accreditation Council. *Faculty:* 87 full-time (47 women), 3 part-time/adjunct (all women). *Students:* 517 full-time (390 women), 163 part-time (102 women); includes 78 minority (33 Black or African American, non-Hispanic/Latino; 23 Asian, non-Hispanic/Latino; 15 Hispanic/Latino; 7 Two or more races, non-Hispanic/Latino), 28 international. Average age 30. 877 applicants, 46% accepted, 242 enrolled. In 2011, 363 master's, 90 doctorates, 32 other advanced degrees awarded. *Degree requirements:* For master's, comprehensive exam (for some programs), thesis (for some programs); for doctorate, comprehensive exam (for some programs), thesis/dissertation. *Entrance requirements:* For master's, doctorate, and Ed S, GRE General Test, letters of recommendation. Additional exam requirements/recommendations for international students: Required—TOEFL (minimum score 600 paper-based; 250 computer-based; 90 iBT), IELTS (minimum score 7). *Application deadline:* Applications are processed on a rolling basis. Application fee: $60. Electronic applications accepted. *Financial support:* Fellowships, research assistantships, teaching assistantships, and Federal Work-Study available. Financial award application deadline: 1/5; financial award applicants required to submit FAFSA. *Unit head:* Robert C. Pianta, Dean, 434-924-3334. *Application contact:* Joanne McNergney, Assistant Dean for Admissions and Student Services, 434-924-3334, E-mail: curry-admissions@virginia.edu. Web site: http://curry.edschool.virginia.edu/.

University of Washington, Graduate School, College of Education, Seattle, WA 98195. Offers curriculum and instruction (M Ed, Ed D, PhD), including educational technology, general curriculum (Ed D, PhD), language, literacy, and culture, mathematics education, multicultural education, reading and language arts education (Ed D), science education, social studies education, teaching and curriculum (M Ed); educational leadership and policy studies (M Ed, Ed D, PhD), including administration (Ed D), educational policy, organization, and leadership (M Ed, PhD), higher education, leadership for learning

(Ed D), social and cultural foundations of education (M Ed, PhD); educational psychology (M Ed, PhD), including educational psychology (PhD), human development and cognition (M Ed), learning sciences, measurement, statistics and research design (M Ed), school psychology (M Ed); instructional leadership (M Ed); intercollegiate athletic leadership (M Ed); special education (M Ed, Ed D, PhD), including early childhood special education (M Ed), emotional and behavioral disabilities (M Ed), learning disabilities (M Ed), low-incidence disabilities (M Ed), severe disabilities (M Ed), special education (Ed D, PhD); teacher education (MIT). *Accreditation:* APA. Part-time and evening/weekend programs available. *Degree requirements:* For master's, thesis optional; for doctorate, thesis/dissertation. *Entrance requirements:* For master's and doctorate, GRE General Test, minimum GPA of 3.0. Additional exam requirements/recommendations for international students: Required—TOEFL. Electronic applications accepted. *Faculty research:* School restructuring/effective schools, special education interventions, literacy and writing, technology, school partnerships, teacher preparation.

University of Washington, Bothell, Program in Education, Bothell, WA 98011-8246. Offers education (M Ed); leadership development for educators (M Ed); secondary/middle level endorsement (M Ed). Part-time and evening/weekend programs available. *Faculty:* 14 full-time (10 women), 1 (woman) part-time/adjunct. *Students:* 52 full-time (40 women), 115 part-time (94 women); includes 19 minority (3 Black or African American, non-Hispanic/Latino; 9 Asian, non-Hispanic/Latino; 4 Hispanic/Latino; 3 Two or more races, non-Hispanic/Latino). Average age 35. 76 applicants, 80% accepted, 57 enrolled. In 2011, 74 master's awarded. *Degree requirements:* For master's, thesis. *Entrance requirements:* Additional exam requirements/recommendations for international students: Required—TOEFL. *Application deadline:* For fall admission, 8/14 priority date for domestic students, 8/14 for international students; for spring admission, 4/7 priority date for domestic students, 11/1 for international students. Applications are processed on a rolling basis. Application fee: $75. Electronic applications accepted. *Financial support:* In 2011–12, 2 students received support. Federal Work-Study and unspecified assistantships available. Financial award application deadline: 5/2. *Faculty research:* Multicultural education in citizenship education, intercultural education, knowledge and practice in the principalship, educational public policy, national board certification for teachers, teacher learning in literacy, technology and its impact on teaching and learning of mathematics, reading assessments, professional development in literacy education and mobility, digital media, education and class. *Unit head:* Dr. Bradley S. Portin, Director/Professor, 425-352-3482, Fax: 425-352-5234, E-mail: bportin@uwb.edu. *Application contact:* Nick Brownlee, Advisor, 425-352-5369, Fax: 425-352-5369, E-mail: nbrownlee@uwb.edu.

University of Washington, Tacoma, Graduate Programs, Program in Education, Tacoma, WA 98402-3100. Offers education (M Ed); educational administration (principal or program administrator certification) (M Ed); elementary education teacher certification (M Ed); elementary education/special education teacher certification (M Ed); secondary science or math teacher certification (M Ed). Part-time and evening/weekend programs available. *Degree requirements:* For master's, culminating project. *Entrance requirements:* For master's, WEST-B, WEST-E (teacher certification programs only), official sealed transcript from every college/university attended, personal goal statement, letters of recommendation, copy of valid teaching certificate. Additional exam requirements/recommendations for international students: Required—TOEFL (minimum score 580 paper-based; 237 computer-based; 92 iBT). Electronic applications accepted. *Faculty research:* Global learning communities for English/Chinese languages, evaluation of mathematics and reading intervention programs, response to intervention, school-wide behavioral and emotional support, mathematics education and culturally responsive mathematics education.

The University of West Alabama, School of Graduate Studies, College of Education, Livingston, AL 35470. Offers M Ed, MAT, MSCE. *Accreditation:* NCATE. Part-time and evening/weekend programs available. *Faculty:* 37 full-time (19 women), 80 part-time/adjunct (53 women). *Students:* 2,849 full-time (2,450 women), 333 part-time (267 women); includes 1,988 minority (1,947 Black or African American, non-Hispanic/Latino; 17 American Indian or Alaska Native, non-Hispanic/Latino; 3 Asian, non-Hispanic/Latino; 18 Hispanic/Latino; 3 Two or more races, non-Hispanic/Latino), 3 international. In 2011, 944 master's awarded. *Degree requirements:* For master's, comprehensive exam. *Entrance requirements:* For master's, GRE General Test, MAT, minimum GPA of 2.75. Additional exam requirements/recommendations for international students: Required—TOEFL (minimum score 61 computer-based). *Application deadline:* For fall admission, 9/10 priority date for domestic students; for spring admission, 3/24 for domestic students. Applications are processed on a rolling basis. Application fee: $25 ($50 for international students). *Expenses:* Tuition, state resident: full-time $5112; part-time $284 per credit hour. Tuition, nonresident: full-time $10,224; part-time $568 per credit hour. *Required fees:* $180; $40 per semester. One-time fee: $65. Tuition and fees vary according to class time, course load, campus/location and program. *Financial support:* In 2011–12, 35 students received support, including 35 teaching assistantships (averaging $9,600 per year); career-related internships or fieldwork, Federal Work-Study, scholarships/grants, and unspecified assistantships also available. Support available to part-time students. Financial award application deadline: 3/1. *Unit head:* Dr. Kathy Chandler, Dean, 205-652-3421, Fax: 205-652-3706, E-mail: kchandler@uwa.edu. Web site: http://www.uwa.edu/coe/.

The University of Western Ontario, Faculty of Graduate Studies, Social Sciences Division, Faculty of Education, London, ON N6A 5B8, Canada. Offers M Ed. Part-time programs available. *Entrance requirements:* For master's, minimum B average.

University of West Florida, College of Professional Studies, Ed D Programs, Specialization in Curriculum and Instruction: Teacher Education, Pensacola, FL 32514-5750. Offers Ed D. Part-time and evening/weekend programs available. *Students:* 1 (woman) full-time, 11 part-time (10 women); includes 3 minority (2 Black or African American, non-Hispanic/Latino; 1 Hispanic/Latino). Average age 43. 9 applicants, 22% accepted, 2 enrolled. In 2011, 5 doctorates awarded. *Degree requirements:* For doctorate, comprehensive exam, thesis/dissertation. *Entrance requirements:* For doctorate, GRE, MAT, or GMAT, letter of intent; writing sample; three letters of recommendation; two completed disposition assessment forms; written statement of goals; interview with admissions committee. Additional exam requirements/recommendations for international students: Required—TOEFL (minimum score 550 paper-based; 213 computer-based). *Application deadline:* For fall admission, 6/1 for domestic and international students; for spring admission, 10/1 for domestic students. Application fee: $30. *Expenses:* Tuition, state resident: full-time $5729; part-time $302 per credit hour. Tuition, nonresident: full-time $20,059; part-time $961 per credit hour. *Required fees:* $1509; $63 per credit hour. *Unit head:* Dr. Pam Northrup, Interim Dean, 850-474-2769, Fax: 850-474-3205. *Application contact:* Terry McCray, Assistant Director of Graduate Admissions, 850-473-7718, Fax: 850-473-7714, E-mail: gradadmissions@uwf.edu. Web site: http://uwf.edu/edd/teacher_ed.cfm.

University of West Georgia, College of Education, Carrollton, GA 30118. Offers M Ed, Ed D, Ed S. *Accreditation:* NCATE. Part-time and evening/weekend programs available. Postbaccalaureate distance learning degree programs offered (minimal on-campus study). *Faculty:* 64 full-time (38 women), 7 part-time/adjunct (5 women). *Students:* 298 full-time (233 women), 833 part-time (683 women); includes 506 minority (280 Black or African American, non-Hispanic/Latino; 4 Asian, non-Hispanic/Latino; 25 Hispanic/Latino; 197 Two or more races, non-Hispanic/Latino), 3 international. Average age 35. 532 applicants, 60% accepted, 109 enrolled. In 2011, 295 master's, 13 doctorates, 154 other advanced degrees awarded. *Degree requirements:* For master's, comprehensive exam, electronic portfolio; internship; for doctorate, comprehensive exam, thesis/dissertation, research paper; for Ed S, comprehensive exam, research paper/project. *Entrance requirements:* Additional exam requirements/recommendations for international students: Required—TOEFL (minimum score 523 paper-based; 193 computer-based; 69 iBT); Recommended—IELTS (minimum score 6). *Application deadline:* For fall admission, 7/21 for domestic students, 6/1 for international students; for spring admission, 11/30 for domestic students, 10/15 for international students. Applications are processed on a rolling basis. Application fee: $30. Electronic applications accepted. *Expenses:* Tuition, state resident: full-time $4336; part-time $181 per credit hour. Tuition, nonresident: full-time $17,362; part-time $724 per credit hour. Tuition and fees vary according to course load, degree level, campus/location and program. *Financial support:* In 2011–12, 9 research assistantships with full tuition reimbursements (averaging $3,000 per year) were awarded; career-related internships or fieldwork, scholarships/grants, and unspecified assistantships also available. Support available to part-time students. Financial award application deadline: 7/1; financial award applicants required to submit FAFSA. *Faculty research:* Distance education, technology integration, collaboration, e-books for children, instructional design, early childhood education, social justice. *Unit head:* Dr. Kim Metcalf, Dean, 678-839-6570, Fax: 678-839-6098, E-mail: kmetcalf@westga.edu. *Application contact:* Deanna Richards, Coordinator, Graduate Studies, 678-8395946, E-mail: drichard@westga.edu. Web site: http://coe.westga.edu/.

University of Windsor, Faculty of Graduate Studies, Faculty of Education, Windsor, ON N9B 3P4, Canada. Offers education (M Ed); educational studies (PhD). Part-time and evening/weekend programs available. *Degree requirements:* For master's, thesis or alternative; for doctorate, comprehensive exam, thesis/dissertation. *Entrance requirements:* For master's, minimum B average, teaching certificate; for doctorate, M Ed or MA in education, minimum A average, evidence of research competencies. Additional exam requirements/recommendations for international students: Required—TOEFL (minimum score 600 paper-based; 250 computer-based). Electronic applications accepted. *Faculty research:* School structures, teacher morale, cognitive deficits, new technologies in art education, internal and external factors that affect learning and teaching.

University of Wisconsin–Eau Claire, College of Education and Human Sciences, Eau Claire, WI 54702-4004. Offers MEPD, MS, MSE, MST. *Faculty:* 36 full-time (23 women). *Students:* 38 full-time (32 women), 50 part-time (44 women); includes 7 minority (2 American Indian or Alaska Native, non-Hispanic/Latino; 2 Asian, non-Hispanic/Latino; 2 Hispanic/Latino; 1 Two or more races, non-Hispanic/Latino). Average age 30. 203 applicants, 16% accepted, 28 enrolled. In 2011, 38 master's awarded. *Degree requirements:* For master's, comprehensive exam. *Entrance requirements:* For master's, GRE (MST, MSE, MS); GRE and pre-professional skills test (MAT), minimum undergraduate GPA of 2.75 or 3.0 in the last half of undergraduate work. Additional exam requirements/recommendations for international students: Required—TOEFL (minimum score 550 paper-based; 213 computer-based; 79 iBT); Recommended—IELTS (minimum score 7). *Application deadline:* For fall admission, 7/1 priority date for domestic students, 6/1 for international students; for spring admission, 12/1 priority date for domestic students, 11/1 for international students. Applications are processed on a rolling basis. Application fee: $56. Electronic applications accepted. *Expenses:* Tuition, state resident: full-time $7312; part-time $406 per credit. Tuition, nonresident: full-time $16,771; part-time $932 per credit. *Required fees:* $1101; $61 per credit. *Financial support:* In 2011–12, 23 students received support. Application deadline: 3/1; applicants required to submit FAFSA. *Unit head:* Dr. Gail Scukanec, Dean, 715-836-3264, Fax: 715-836-3245, E-mail: scukangp@uwec.edu. *Application contact:* Nancy Amdahl, Graduate Dean Assistant, 715-836-2721, Fax: 715-836-2902, E-mail: graduate@uwec.edu. Web site: http://www.uwec.edu/coehs.

University of Wisconsin–Green Bay, Graduate Studies, Program in Applied Leadership for Teaching and Learning, Green Bay, WI 54311-7001. Offers MS Ed. Part-time and evening/weekend programs available. *Faculty:* 5 full-time (1 woman), 1 (woman) part-time/adjunct. *Students:* 3 full-time (all women), 4 part-time (2 women); includes 3 minority (all American Indian or Alaska Native, non-Hispanic/Latino). Average age 37. 3 applicants, 100% accepted, 3 enrolled. In 2011, 24 master's awarded. *Degree requirements:* For master's, thesis or alternative. *Entrance requirements:* For master's, minimum GPA of 3.0. *Application deadline:* For fall admission, 8/1 for domestic students; for spring admission, 11/1 for domestic students. Applications are processed on a rolling basis. Application fee: $56. Electronic applications accepted. *Expenses:* Tuition, state resident: full-time $7312; part-time $406 per credit. Tuition, nonresident: full-time $16,771; part-time $932 per credit. *Required fees:* $1312; $55 per credit. Tuition and fees vary according to reciprocity agreements. *Financial support:* Application deadline: 7/15. *Faculty research:* Curriculum design, assessment. *Unit head:* Dr. Tim Kaufman, Director, 920-465-2964, E-mail: kaufmant@uwgb.edu. *Application contact:* Inga Zile, Graduate Studies Coordinator, 920-465-2123, Fax: 920-465-2043, E-mail: zilei@uwgb.edu. Web site: http://www.uwgb.edu/gradstu/.

University of Wisconsin–La Crosse, Office of University Graduate Studies, College of Liberal Studies, Department of Educational Studies, Master of Education-Professional Development Learning Community Program, La Crosse, WI 54601-3742. Offers MEPD. Part-time and evening/weekend programs available. Postbaccalaureate distance learning degree programs offered (minimal on-campus study). *Students:* 147 part-time (111 women); includes 2 minority (1 Black or African American, non-Hispanic/Latino; 1 Hispanic/Latino). Average age 34. 25 applicants, 92% accepted, 14 enrolled. In 2011, 137 master's awarded. *Degree requirements:* For master's, professional development plan and classroom action research. *Entrance requirements:* Additional exam requirements/recommendations for international students: Required—TOEFL (minimum score 550 paper-based; 213 computer-based; 79 iBT). *Application deadline:* Applications are processed on a rolling basis. Application fee: $56. Electronic applications accepted. *Expenses:* Tuition, state resident: full-time $8391; part-time $481.17 per credit. Tuition, nonresident: full-time $17,850; part-time $1006.68 per credit. *Required fees:* $2 per credit. $18.25 per semester. Tuition and fees vary according to course load, program, reciprocity agreements and student level. *Financial support:* Federal Work-Study, scholarships/grants, and health care benefits available. Support available to part-time students. Financial award application deadline: 3/15; financial award applicants required to submit FAFSA. *Faculty research:* Impact of learning community on student learning, constructivism in education, transformational learning, education of children who are homeless or at risk for homelessness. *Unit head:* Dr. Patricia A. Markos, Director, 608-785-5087, Fax: 608-785-6560, E-mail: lc@uwlax.edu. *Application contact:* Kathryn Kiefer, Director of Admissions, 608-785-8939, E-mail: admissions@uwlax.edu. Web site: http://www.masterteacherscommunity.org.

University of Wisconsin–Madison, Graduate School, School of Education, Madison, WI 53706-1380. Offers MA, MFA, MS, PhD, Certificate. *Faculty:* 134 full-time (65 women). *Students:* 770 full-time (521 women), 349 part-time (233 women). In 2011, 250 master's, 90 doctorates awarded. *Degree requirements:* For doctorate, thesis/dissertation. *Entrance requirements:* Additional exam requirements/recommendations for international students: Required—TOEFL (minimum score 550 paper-based; 213 computer-based; 80 iBT), IELTS (minimum score 6). Application fee: $56. *Expenses:* Tuition, state resident: full-time $10,296; part-time $643.51 per credit. Tuition, nonresident: full-time $24,054; part-time $1503.40 per credit. *Required fees:* $70.06 per credit. Tuition and fees vary according to course load, campus/location, program and reciprocity agreements. *Financial support:* In 2011–12, 45 fellowships with full tuition reimbursements, 21 research assistantships with full tuition reimbursements, 215 teaching assistantships with full tuition reimbursements were awarded; Federal Work-Study, scholarships/grants, traineeships, health care benefits, unspecified assistantships, and project assistantships also available. *Total annual research expenditures:* $28.5 million. *Unit head:* Dr. Julie K. Underwood, Dean, 608-262-1763. *Application contact:* 608-262-2433, Fax: 608-262-5134, E-mail: gradadmiss@mail.bascom.wisc.edu. Web site: http://www.education.wisc.edu.

University of Wisconsin–Milwaukee, Graduate School, School of Education, Milwaukee, WI 53201. Offers MS, PhD, Certificate, Ed S. Part-time programs available. *Faculty:* 61 full-time (40 women), 2 part-time/adjunct (1 woman). *Students:* 312 full-time (229 women), 348 part-time (266 women); includes 179 minority (89 Black or African American, non-Hispanic/Latino; 1 American Indian or Alaska Native, non-Hispanic/Latino; 26 Asian, non-Hispanic/Latino; 20 Hispanic/Latino; 43 Two or more races, non-Hispanic/Latino), 22 international. Average age 33. 450 applicants, 58% accepted, 125 enrolled. In 2011, 181 master's, 28 doctorates, 9 other advanced degrees awarded. *Degree requirements:* For doctorate, thesis/dissertation. *Entrance requirements:* For doctorate, GRE General Test. *Application deadline:* For fall admission, 1/1 priority date for domestic students; for spring admission, 9/1 for domestic students. Applications are processed on a rolling basis. Application fee: $56 ($96 for international students). Electronic applications accepted. One-time fee: $506.10 full-time. Tuition and fees vary according to course load and reciprocity agreements. *Financial support:* In 2011–12, 7 teaching assistantships were awarded; fellowships, career-related internships or fieldwork, Federal Work-Study, health care benefits, unspecified assistantships, and project assistantships also available. Support available to part-time students. Financial award application deadline: 4/15; financial award applicants required to submit FAFSA. *Total annual research expenditures:* $1.8 million. *Unit head:* Carol Colbeck, Dean, 414-229-4181, E-mail: colbeck@uwm.edu. *Application contact:* General Information Contact, 414-229-4982, Fax: 414-229-6967, E-mail: gradschool@uwm.edu. Web site: http://www.uwm.edu/SOE/.

University of Wisconsin–Oshkosh, Graduate Studies, College of Education and Human Services, Oshkosh, WI 54901. Offers MS, MSE. Part-time and evening/weekend programs available. *Degree requirements:* For master's, comprehensive exam (for some programs), thesis or alternative, field report, PPST, PRAXIS II. *Entrance requirements:* For master's, PPST, PRAXIS II, teaching license, letters of recommendation, interview. Additional exam requirements/recommendations for international students: Required—TOEFL (minimum score 550 paper-based; 213 computer-based; 79 iBT). Electronic applications accepted.

University of Wisconsin–Platteville, School of Graduate Studies, College of Liberal Arts and Education, School of Education, Platteville, WI 53818-3099. Offers adult education (MSE); elementary education (MSE); English education (MSE); middle school education (MSE); secondary education (MSE). *Accreditation:* NCATE. Part-time programs available. *Faculty:* 8 part-time/adjunct (3 women). *Students:* 62 full-time (47 women), 86 part-time (69 women); includes 22 minority (20 Black or African American, non-Hispanic/Latino; 2 Hispanic/Latino), 55 international. 17 applicants, 76% accepted. In 2011, 82 master's awarded. *Degree requirements:* For master's, comprehensive exam, thesis or alternative. *Entrance requirements:* Additional exam requirements/recommendations for international students: Required—TOEFL (minimum score 500 paper-based; 61 iBT), IELTS (minimum score 6). *Application deadline:* For fall admission, 7/1 priority date for domestic students; for spring admission, 11/1 for domestic students. Applications are processed on a rolling basis. Application fee: $56. Electronic applications accepted. *Financial support:* Research assistantships with partial tuition reimbursements, career-related internships or fieldwork, Federal Work-Study, institutionally sponsored loans, scholarships/grants, and unspecified assistantships available. Support available to part-time students. Financial award applicants required to submit FAFSA. *Unit head:* Dr. Karen Stinson, Director, 608-342-1131, Fax: 608-342-1133, E-mail: stinsonk@uwplatt.edu. *Application contact:* Lisa Popp, School of Graduate Studies, 608-342-1322, Fax: 608-342-1389, E-mail: poppl@uwplatt.edu. Web site: http://www.uwplatt.edu/.

University of Wisconsin–River Falls, Outreach and Graduate Studies, College of Education and Professional Studies, Department of Teacher Education, River Falls, WI 54022. Offers elementary education (MSE); professional development shared inquiry communities (MSE); reading (MSE). Part-time programs available. *Degree requirements:* For master's, comprehensive exam, thesis or alternative. *Entrance requirements:* For master's, minimum GPA of 2.75. Additional exam requirements/recommendations for international students: Required—TOEFL (minimum score 500 paper-based; 65 iBT), IELTS (minimum score 5.5). Electronic applications accepted.

University of Wisconsin–Stevens Point, College of Professional Studies, School of Education, Stevens Point, WI 54481-3897. Offers education—general/reading (MSE); education—general/special (MSE); educational administration (MSE); elementary education (MSE); guidance and counseling (MSE). Part-time programs available. *Degree requirements:* For master's, comprehensive exam, thesis or alternative. *Entrance requirements:* For master's, teacher certification, minimum undergraduate GPA of 3.0, 2 years of teaching experience, letters of recommendation. Additional exam requirements/recommendations for international students: Required—TOEFL (minimum score 523 paper-based; 193 computer-based). *Faculty research:* Gifted education early childhood, special education curriculum and instruction, standards-based education.

University of Wisconsin–Stout, Graduate School, School of Education, Menomonie, WI 54751. Offers MS, MS Ed, Ed S. *Accreditation:* NCATE. Part-time programs available. Postbaccalaureate distance learning degree programs offered (no on-campus study). *Degree requirements:* For master's and Ed S, thesis. *Entrance requirements:* For degree, minimum GPA of 3.25. Additional exam requirements/recommendations for international students: Required—TOEFL (minimum score 500 paper-based; 173 computer-based; 61 iBT). Electronic applications accepted.

University of Wisconsin–Superior, Graduate Division, Department of Teacher Education, Superior, WI 54880-4500. Offers instruction (MSE); special education (MSE), including emotional/behavior disabilities, learning disabilities; teaching reading (MSE). Part-time and evening/weekend programs available. Postbaccalaureate distance learning degree programs offered (minimal on-campus study). *Degree requirements:* For master's, research project. *Entrance requirements:* For master's, minimum GPA of 2.75, teaching certificate. *Faculty research:* Science teaching.

University of Wisconsin–Whitewater, School of Graduate Studies, College of Education and Professional Studies, Whitewater, WI 53190-1790. Offers MS, MS Ed, MSE. *Accreditation:* NCATE. Part-time and evening/weekend programs available. Postbaccalaureate distance learning degree programs offered (no on-campus study). *Students:* 104 full-time (76 women), 292 part-time (213 women); includes 32 minority (10 Black or African American, non-Hispanic/Latino; 2 Asian, non-Hispanic/Latino; 20 Hispanic/Latino). Average age 34. 133 applicants, 82% accepted, 62 enrolled. In 2011, 124 master's awarded. *Entrance requirements:* Additional exam requirements/recommendations for international students: Required—TOEFL (minimum score 550 paper-based; 213 computer-based). *Application deadline:* For fall admission, 7/15 priority date for domestic students; for spring admission, 12/1 priority date for domestic students. Applications are processed on a rolling basis. Application fee: $45. Electronic applications accepted. *Expenses:* Tuition, state resident: full-time $4088. Tuition, nonresident: full-time $8817. Tuition and fees vary according to program. *Financial support:* In 2011–12, 1 research assistantship (averaging $9,875 per year) was awarded; career-related internships or fieldwork, Federal Work-Study, unspecified assistantships, and out of state fee waiver also available. Support available to part-time students. Financial award application deadline: 3/15; financial award applicants required to submit FAFSA. *Unit head:* Dr. John Stone, Dean, 262-472-1006, Fax: 262-472-507, E-mail: stonej@uww.edu. *Application contact:* Sally A. Lange, School of Graduate Studies, 262-472-1006, Fax: 262-472-5027, E-mail: gradschl@uww.edu. Web site: http://www.uww.edu/coe/.

Upper Iowa University, Master of Education Program, Fayette, IA 52142-1857. Offers M Ed.

Urbana University, College of Education and Sports Studies, Urbana, OH 43078-2091. Offers classroom education (M Ed). Part-time and evening/weekend programs available. *Degree requirements:* For master's, comprehensive oral exam, capstone research project. *Entrance requirements:* For master's, minimum GPA of 2.7, teaching license. Additional exam requirements/recommendations for international students: Required—TOEFL (minimum score 550 paper-based; 213 computer-based). *Faculty research:* Best professional practices, reading/special education, classroom management, teaching models, school finance.

Ursuline College, School of Graduate Studies, Program for Advanced Study in Education (PASE), Pepper Pike, OH 44124-4398. Offers MA. Part-time programs available. *Faculty:* 3 part-time/adjunct (2 women). *Students:* 1 (woman) full-time, 18 part-time (17 women); includes 6 minority (5 Black or African American, non-Hispanic/Latino; 1 Asian, non-Hispanic/Latino). Average age 33. 11 applicants, 82% accepted, 8 enrolled. In 2011, 29 master's awarded. *Degree requirements:* For master's, comprehensive exam (for some programs), thesis (for some programs). *Entrance requirements:* Additional exam requirements/recommendations for international students: Required—TOEFL (minimum score 500 paper-based; 173 computer-based). *Application deadline:* Applications are processed on a rolling basis. Application fee: $25. Electronic applications accepted. *Expenses: Tuition:* Part-time $875 per credit hour. *Required fees:* $170 per semester. *Financial support:* Applicants required to submit FAFSA. *Unit head:* Joseph LaGuardia, Assistant Director, 440-646-6046, Fax: 440-684-6088, E-mail: jlaguardia@ursuline.edu. *Application contact:* Melanie Steele, Graduate Admission Assistant, 440-646-8199, Fax: 440-684-6138, E-mail: graduateadmissions@ursuline.edu.

Ursuline College, School of Graduate Studies, Program in Education, Pepper Pike, OH 44124-4398. Offers art education (MA); early childhood education (MA); language arts education (MA); life science education (MA); math education (MA); middle school education (MA); social studies education (MA); special education (MA). *Accreditation:* NCATE. *Faculty:* 3 full-time (all women), 8 part-time/adjunct (6 women). *Students:* 28 full-time (22 women), 1 (woman) part-time; includes 11 minority (7 Black or African American, non-Hispanic/Latino; 2 Asian, non-Hispanic/Latino; 1 Hispanic/Latino; 1 Native Hawaiian or other Pacific Islander, non-Hispanic/Latino). Average age 32. In 2011, 29 master's awarded. *Degree requirements:* For master's, comprehensive exam. *Entrance requirements:* For master's, minimum undergraduate GPA of 3.0. Additional exam requirements/recommendations for international students: Required—TOEFL (minimum score 500 paper-based; 173 computer-based). *Application deadline:* For fall admission, 8/1 priority date for domestic students. Applications are processed on a rolling basis. Application fee: $25. *Expenses:* Contact institution. *Financial support:* Federal Work-Study available. Financial award application deadline: 3/1. *Unit head:* Dr. Edna West, Director, Master's Apprentice Program, 440-646-6134, Fax: 440-684-6088, E-mail: ewest@ursuline.edu. *Application contact:* Melanie Steele, Graduate Admission Assistant, 440-646-8199, Fax: 440-684-6138, E-mail: graduateadmissions@ursuline.edu.

Utah State University, School of Graduate Studies, Emma Eccles Jones College of Education and Human Services, Logan, UT 84322. Offers M Ed, MA, MFHD, MRC, MS, Au D, Ed D, PhD, Ed S. Part-time and evening/weekend programs available. Postbaccalaureate distance learning degree programs offered (no on-campus study). *Degree requirements:* For doctorate, comprehensive exam, thesis/dissertation. *Entrance requirements:* For master's, GRE General Test, minimum GPA of 3.0; for doctorate, GRE General Test, master's degree; for Ed S, GRE General Test, GRE Subject Test. Additional exam requirements/recommendations for international students: Required—TOEFL (minimum score 550 paper-based; 213 computer-based). *Faculty research:* Literacy instruction, design and delivery of instruction, children at-risk and their families, hearing assessment and management, language and literacy development.

Utah Valley University, Program in Education, Orem, UT 84058-5999. Offers M Ed. *Accreditation:* Teacher Education Accreditation Council. Part-time programs available. *Faculty:* 4 full-time (2 women). *Students:* 5 full-time (all women), 68 part-time (42 women); includes 2 minority (1 Asian, non-Hispanic/Latino; 1 Hispanic/Latino). Average age 33. *Entrance requirements:* For master's, GRE, 3 letters of recommendation, interview. Additional exam requirements/recommendations for international students: Required—TOEFL (minimum score 83 iBT). *Application deadline:* For fall admission, 3/31 for domestic and international students. Application fee: $45 ($100 for international students). Electronic applications accepted. *Financial support:* Application deadline: 5/1; applicants required to submit FAFSA. *Unit head:* Maureen Andrade, Associate Vice President for Academic Programs, 801-863-6832. *Application contact:* Maggie Hewlett, Administrative Assistant III, 801-863-8270.

Utica College, Teacher Education Programs, Utica, NY 13502-4892. Offers MS, MS Ed, CAS. *Accreditation:* Teacher Education Accreditation Council. *Degree requirements:* For master's, comprehensive exam or thesis. *Entrance requirements:* For master's, CST, LAST, minimum GPA of 3.0. Additional exam requirements/recommendations for international students: Required—TOEFL (minimum score 525 paper-based; 195 computer-based). Electronic applications accepted. *Expenses:* Contact institution.

Valley City State University, Online Master of Education Program, Valley City, ND 58072. Offers library and information technologies (M Ed); teaching and technology (M Ed); teaching English language learners (ELL) (M Ed); technology education (M Ed). *Accreditation:* NCATE. Part-time and evening/weekend programs available. Postbaccalaureate distance learning degree programs offered (no on-campus study). *Faculty:* 25 full-time (18 women), 2 part-time/adjunct (both women). *Students:* 4 full-time (3 women), 147 part-time (99 women); includes 6 minority (1 Black or African American, non-Hispanic/Latino; 1 American Indian or Alaska Native, non-Hispanic/Latino; 2 Asian, non-Hispanic/Latino; 2 Hispanic/Latino). Average age 34. 40 applicants, 83% accepted, 30 enrolled. In 2011, 30 master's awarded. *Degree requirements:* For master's, action research report, comprehensive portfolio. *Entrance requirements:* For master's, GRE, MAT, PRAXIS II or National Teaching Board for Professional Standards (if GPA less than 3.0). Additional exam requirements/recommendations for international students: Required—TOEFL (minimum score 525 paper-based; 70 iBT). *Application deadline:* For fall admission, 5/23 priority date for domestic students, 5/23 for international students; for spring admission, 4/20 priority date for domestic students, 4/23 for international students. Applications are processed on a rolling basis. Application fee: $35. Electronic applications accepted. *Expenses:* Tuition, state resident: full-time $4533.30; part-time $251.85 per credit hour. Tuition, nonresident: full-time $4533; part-time $251.85 per credit hour. *Required fees:* $1239.48; $68.86 per credit hour. *Financial support:* In 2011–12, 27 students received support. Tuition waivers (full and partial) available. Financial award application deadline: 5/15; financial award applicants required to submit FAFSA. *Faculty research:* Academically at-risk students in higher education, communication pedagogy and technology, gender communication, computer-mediated communication, creativity in music. *Total annual research expenditures:* $26,000. *Unit head:* Dr. Gary Thompson, Dean, 701-845-7197, E-mail: gary.thompson@vcsu.edu. *Application contact:* Misty Lindgren, 701-845-7303, Fax: 701-845-7305, E-mail: misty.lindgren@vcsu.edu. Web site: http://www.vcsu.edu/graduate.

Valparaiso University, Graduate School, Department of Education, Valparaiso, IN 46383. Offers initial licensure (M Ed); instructional leadership (M Ed); teaching and learning (M Ed); M Ed/Ed S. *Accreditation:* NCATE. Part-time and evening/weekend programs available. Postbaccalaureate distance learning degree programs offered (minimal on-campus study). *Faculty:* 13 part-time/adjunct (11 women). *Students:* 48 full-time (36 women), 9 part-time (6 women); includes 6 minority (1 Asian, non-Hispanic/Latino; 3 Hispanic/Latino; 2 Two or more races, non-Hispanic/Latino), 2 international. Average age 28. In 2011, 38 master's awarded. *Entrance requirements:* For master's, GRE General Test, minimum GPA of 3.0. Additional exam requirements/recommendations for international students: Required—TOEFL (minimum score 550 paper-based; 213 computer-based; 80 iBT). *Application deadline:* Applications are processed on a rolling basis. Application fee: $30 ($50 for international students). Electronic applications accepted. *Expenses: Tuition:* Part-time $560 per credit hour. Tuition and fees vary according to course load and program. *Financial support:* Traineeships and unspecified assistantships available. Support available to part-time students. Financial award applicants required to submit FAFSA. *Unit head:* Dr. David L. Rowland, Dean, Graduate School and Continuing Education/Associate Provost, 219-464-5313, Fax: 219-464-5381, E-mail: david.rowland@valpo.edu. *Application contact:* Dustin Jesch, Coordinator, U.S. Student Engagement, 219-464-5313, Fax: 219-464-5381, E-mail: dustin.jesch@valpo.edu. Web site: http://valpo.edu/education/.

Vanderbilt University, Graduate School, Program in Learning, Teaching and Diversity, Nashville, TN 37240-1001. Offers MS, PhD. *Faculty:* 21 full-time (11 women), 1 (woman) part-time/adjunct. *Students:* 54 full-time (35 women), 3 part-time (1 woman); includes 7 minority (2 Black or African American, non-Hispanic/Latino; 4 Asian, non-Hispanic/Latino; 1 Two or more races, non-Hispanic/Latino), 6 international. Average age 34. 147 applicants, 5% accepted, 6 enrolled. In 2011, 1 master's, 1 doctorate awarded. *Degree requirements:* For doctorate, comprehensive exam, thesis/dissertation. *Entrance requirements:* For doctorate, GRE General Test. Additional exam requirements/recommendations for international students: Required—TOEFL (minimum score 570 paper-based; 230 computer-based; 88 iBT). *Application deadline:* For fall admission, 12/31 for domestic and international students. Application fee: $0. Electronic applications accepted. *Financial support:* Fellowships with full and partial tuition reimbursements, research assistantships with full tuition reimbursements, teaching assistantships with full tuition reimbursements, Federal Work-Study, institutionally sponsored loans, scholarships/grants, traineeships, and health care benefits available. Financial award application deadline: 1/15; financial award applicants required to submit CSS PROFILE or FAFSA. *Faculty research:* New pedagogies for math, science, and language; the support of English language learners; the uses of new technology and media in the classroom; middle school mathematics and the institutional setting of teaching. *Unit head:* Dr. Paul Cobb, Chair, 615-343-1492, Fax: 615-322-8999, E-mail: paul.cobb@vanderbilt.edu. *Application contact:* Dr. Clifford Hofwolt, Director of Graduate Studies, 615-322-8227, Fax: 615-322-8014, E-mail: clifford.hofwolt@vanderbilt.edu. Web site: http://peabody.vanderbilt.edu/Admissions_and_Programs/PhD_Programs/PhD_Program_Choices.xml.

Vanderbilt University, Peabody College, Nashville, TN 37240-1001. Offers M Ed, MPP, Ed D. *Accreditation:* APA (one or more programs are accredited); NCATE. Part-time programs available. *Faculty:* 145 full-time (84 women), 54 part-time/adjunct (32 women). *Students:* 464 full-time (374 women), 171 part-time (106 women); includes 93 minority (36 Black or African American, non-Hispanic/Latino; 15 Asian, non-Hispanic/Latino; 23 Hispanic/Latino; 19 Two or more races, non-Hispanic/Latino), 47 international. Average age 26. 1,051 applicants, 53% accepted, 238 enrolled. In 2011, 267 master's, 25 doctorates awarded. *Degree requirements:* For master's, comprehensive exam, thesis optional; for doctorate, thesis/dissertation, qualifying examinations, residency. *Entrance requirements:* For master's, GRE General Test, MAT; for doctorate, GRE General Test. Additional exam requirements/recommendations for international students: Required—TOEFL (minimum score 550 paper-based; 213 computer-based). *Application deadline:* For fall admission, 12/31 priority date for domestic students, 12/31 for international students; for spring admission, 11/1 priority date for domestic students, 11/1 for international students. Applications are processed on a rolling basis. Application fee: $0. Electronic applications accepted. *Expenses:* Contact institution. *Financial support:* In 2011–12, 509 students received support, including 5 fellowships with full and partial tuition reimbursements available, 172 research assistantships with full and partial tuition reimbursements available, 51 teaching assistantships with full and partial tuition reimbursements available; career-related internships or fieldwork, Federal Work-Study, institutionally sponsored loans, scholarships/grants, traineeships, tuition waivers (partial), and unspecified assistantships also available. Support available to part-time students. Financial award application deadline: 2/1; financial award applicants required to submit FAFSA. *Total annual research expenditures:* $38 million. *Unit head:* Dr. Camilla P. Benbow, Dean, 615-322-8407, Fax: 615-322-8501, E-mail: camilla.benbow@vanderbilt.edu. *Application contact:* Kimberly Tanner, Director of Graduate and Professional Admissions, 615-332-8410, Fax: 615-343-3474, E-mail: kim.tanner@vanderbilt.edu. Web site: http://peabody.vanderbilt.edu/.

See Display below and Close-Up on page 813.

Vanguard University of Southern California, Graduate Programs in Education, Costa Mesa, CA 92626-9601. Offers MA. Evening/weekend programs available. *Degree requirements:* For master's, thesis or alternative. *Entrance requirements:* For master's, California Basic Educational Skills Test, California Subject Examinations for Teachers, minimum GPA of 3.0. Additional exam requirements/recommendations for international students: Required—TOEFL (minimum score 550 paper-based; 213 computer-based; 79 iBT). Electronic applications accepted. *Expenses:* Contact institution. *Faculty research:* Reading, educational administration.

Villanova University, Graduate School of Liberal Arts and Sciences, Department of Education and Counseling, Villanova, PA 19085-1699. Offers clinical mental health counseling (MS), including counseling and human relations; elementary school counseling (MS), including counseling and human relations; graduate education (MA); secondary education (MA); secondary school counseling (MS), including counseling and human relations; teacher leadership (MA). Part-time and evening/weekend programs available. *Faculty:* 11 full-time (6 women), 15 part-time/adjunct (8 women). *Students:* 99

full-time (71 women), 34 part-time (23 women); includes 8 minority (2 Black or African American, non-Hispanic/Latino; 2 Asian, non-Hispanic/Latino; 2 Hispanic/Latino; 2 Two or more races, non-Hispanic/Latino), 2 international. Average age 29. 87 applicants, 92% accepted, 32 enrolled. In 2011, 94 master's awarded. *Degree requirements:* For master's, comprehensive exam. *Entrance requirements:* For master's, GRE or MAT, minimum GPA of 3.0. Additional exam requirements/recommendations for international students: Required—TOEFL. *Application deadline:* For fall admission, 5/1 for international students; for spring admission, 10/15 for international students. Applications are processed on a rolling basis. Application fee: $50. Electronic applications accepted. *Expenses: Tuition:* Part-time $675 per credit. Part-time tuition and fees vary according to degree level and program. *Financial support:* Research assistantships, teaching assistantships, career-related internships or fieldwork, Federal Work-Study, and unspecified assistantships available. Financial award applicants required to submit FAFSA. *Unit head:* Dr. Edward Fierros, Chairperson, 610-519-4625. *Application contact:* Dean, Graduate School of Liberal Arts and Sciences. Web site: http://www.education.villanova.edu/.

Virginia Commonwealth University, Graduate School, School of Education, Richmond, VA 23284-9005. Offers M Ed, MS, MSAT, MT, Ed D, PhD, Certificate. *Accreditation:* NCATE. Part-time programs available. *Students:* 365 full-time (286 women), 469 part-time (358 women). 457 applicants, 65% accepted, 214 enrolled. In 2011, 357 master's, 47 doctorates, 93 other advanced degrees awarded. *Degree requirements:* For doctorate, thesis/dissertation. *Entrance requirements:* For master's, GRE General Test or MAT; for doctorate, GRE (PhD only), MAT (EdD only), interview, master's degree. Additional exam requirements/recommendations for international students: Required—TOEFL (minimum score 600 paper-based; 250 computer-based; 100 iBT); Recommended—IELTS (minimum score 6.5). Application fee: $50. Electronic applications accepted. *Expenses:* Tuition, state resident: full-time $9133; part-time $507 per credit. Tuition, nonresident: full-time $18,777; part-time $1043 per credit. *Required fees:* $77 per credit. Tuition and fees vary according to degree level, campus/location, program and student level. *Financial support:* Fellowships, research assistantships, teaching assistantships, career-related internships or fieldwork, Federal Work-Study, institutionally sponsored loans, and tuition waivers (full and partial) available. Support available to part-time students. Financial award application deadline: 3/1; financial award applicants required to submit FAFSA. *Unit head:* Dr. Christine S. Walther-Thomas, Dean, 804-828-3382, E-mail: cswalthertho@vcu.edu. *Application contact:* Dr. Diane Simon, Associate Dean for Student Affairs, 804-828-3382, Fax: 804-828-1323, E-mail: dsimon@vcu.edu. Web site: http://www.vcu.edu/eduweb/.

Virginia Polytechnic Institute and State University, VT Online, Blacksburg, VA 24061. Offers advanced transportation systems (Certificate); aerospace engineering (MS); agricultural and life sciences (MSLFS); business information systems (Graduate Certificate); career and technical education (MS); civil engineering (MS); computer engineering (M Eng, MS); decision support systems (Graduate Certificate); eLearning leadership (MA); electrical engineering (M Eng, MS); engineering administration (MEA); environmental engineering (Certificate); environmental politics and policy (Graduate Certificate); environmental sciences and engineering (MS); foundations of political analysis (Graduate Certificate); health product risk management (Graduate Certificate); industrial and systems engineering (MS); information policy and society (Graduate Certificate); information security (Graduate Certificate); information technology (MIT); instructional technology (MA); integrative STEM education (MA Ed); liberal arts (Graduate Certificate); life sciences: health product risk management (MS); natural resources (MNR, Graduate Certificate); networking (Graduate Certificate); nonprofit and nongovernmental organization management (Graduate Certificate); ocean engineering (MS); political science (MA); security studies (Graduate Certificate); software development (Graduate Certificate). *Expenses:* Tuition, state resident: full-time $10,048; part-time $558.25 per credit hour. Tuition, nonresident: full-time $19,497; part-time $1083.25 per credit hour. *Required fees:* $405 per semester. Tuition and fees vary according to course load, campus/location and program. *Application contact:* Graduate School Applications General Assistance, 540-231-8636, Fax: 540-231-2039, E-mail: gradappl@vt.edu. Web site: http://www.vto.vt.edu/.

Virginia State University, School of Graduate Studies, Research, and Outreach, School of Liberal Arts and Education, Petersburg, VA 23806-0001. Offers M Ed, MA, MS, CAGS. *Accreditation:* NCATE. Part-time and evening/weekend programs available.

Viterbo University, Graduate Program in Education, La Crosse, WI 54601-4797. Offers MA. Courses held on weekends and during summer. *Accreditation:* NCATE. Part-time and evening/weekend programs available. *Degree requirements:* For master's, thesis. *Entrance requirements:* For master's, MAT, teaching certificate, 2 years of teaching experience.

Wagner College, Division of Graduate Studies, Department of Education, Staten Island, NY 10301-4495. Offers adolescent education (MS Ed); childhood education (MS Ed); early childhood education (birth-grade 2) (MS Ed); educational leadership (MS Ed), including school building leader; literacy (B-6) (MS Ed). *Accreditation:* NCATE. Part-time and evening/weekend programs available. *Faculty:* 6 full-time (4 women), 21 part-time/adjunct (14 women). *Students:* 74 full-time (55 women), 34 part-time (27 women); includes 11 minority (5 Black or African American, non-Hispanic/Latino; 3 Asian, non-Hispanic/Latino; 3 Hispanic/Latino), 1 international. Average age 25. 66 applicants, 92% accepted, 46 enrolled. In 2011, 56 master's awarded. *Degree requirements:* For master's, thesis (for some programs). *Entrance requirements:* For master's, Liberal Arts and Sciences Test (LAST), New York State Teacher Certification Examinations (NYSTCE), minimum GPA of 2.75. Additional exam requirements/recommendations for international students: Required—TOEFL (minimum score 550 paper-based; 217 computer-based; 79 iBT). *Application deadline:* For fall admission, 5/1 priority date for domestic students, 3/1 for international students; for spring admission, 11/1 priority date for domestic students, 10/1 for international students. Applications are processed on a rolling basis. Application fee: $50 ($85 for international students). *Expenses: Tuition:* Full-time $16,200; part-time $890 per credit. *Financial support:* Career-related internships or fieldwork, tuition waivers (partial), unspecified assistantships, and alumni fellowship grant available. Financial award applicants required to submit FAFSA. *Unit head:* Dr. Stephen Preskill, Chair, 718-420-4070, Fax: 718-390-3456, E-mail: stephen.preskill@wagner.edu. *Application contact:* Patricia Clancy, Administrative Assistant, Admissions, 718-420-4464, Fax: 718-390-3105, E-mail: patricia.clancy@wagner.edu. Web site: http://www.wagner.edu/dept/education/.

Wake Forest University, Graduate School of Arts and Sciences, Department of Education, Winston-Salem, NC 27109. Offers secondary education (MA Ed). *Accreditation:* ACA; NCATE. Part-time programs available. *Faculty:* 7 full-time (4 women), 6 part-time/adjunct (3 women). *Students:* 24 full-time (14 women), 17 part-time (14 women); includes 10 minority (3 Black or African American, non-Hispanic/Latino; 1 Asian, non-Hispanic/Latino; 6 Hispanic/Latino). Average age 26. 46 applicants, 59% accepted, 26 enrolled. In 2011, 36 master's awarded. *Degree requirements:* For master's, thesis optional. *Entrance requirements:* For master's, GRE General Test. Additional exam requirements/recommendations for international students: Required—TOEFL (minimum score 550 paper-based; 213 computer-based). *Application deadline:* For fall admission, 1/15 for domestic and international students. Application fee: $60. Electronic applications accepted. *Expenses:* Contact institution. *Financial support:* In 2011–12, 24 fellowships with full tuition reimbursements (averaging $48,000 per year) were awarded; teaching assistantships with full tuition reimbursements, scholarships/grants, and tuition waivers (full) also available. Support available to part-time students. Financial award application deadline: 2/15. *Faculty research:* Teaching and learning. *Unit head:* Dr. MaryLynn Redmond, Chair, 336-758-5341, Fax: 336-758-4591, E-mail: redmond@wfu.edu. *Application contact:* Dr. Leah McCoy, Program Director, 336-758-5998, Fax: 336-758-4591, E-mail: mccoy@wfu.edu. Web site: http://college.wfu.edu/education/graduate-program/overview-of-graduate-programs/.

Walden University, Graduate Programs, Richard W. Riley College of Education and Leadership, Minneapolis, MN 55401. Offers administrator leadership for teaching and learning (Ed D, Ed S); adult education (Ed D, Ed S); adult learning (MS, Postbaccalaureate Certificate), including developmental education (MS), online teaching (MS), teaching adults English as a second language (MS), training and performance management (MS); college teaching and learning (Ed D, Ed S, Postbaccalaureate Certificate); curriculum, instruction and assessment (Ed D, Postbaccalaureate Certificate); curriculum, instruction, and professional development (Ed S); developmental education (Postbaccalaureate Certificate); early childhood administration, management, and leadership (Postbaccalaureate Certificate); early childhood education (birth-grade 3) (MAT); early childhood public policy and advocacy (Postbaccalaureate Certificate); early childhood studies (MS), including administration, management and leadership, early childhood public policy and advocacy, teaching adults in the early childhood field, teaching and diversity; education (MS, PhD), including adolescent literacy and technology (grades 6-12) (MS), adult education leadership (PhD), assessment, evaluation, and accountability (PhD), community college leadership (PhD), curriculum, instruction, and assessment, early childhood education (PhD), educational technology (PhD), elementary reading and literacy (MS), elementary reading and mathematics (MS), general program, global and comparative education (PhD), higher education (PhD), integrating technology in the classroom (MS), K-12 educational leadership (PhD), leadership, policy and change (PhD), learning, instruction and innovation (PhD), literacy and learning in the content areas (MS), mathematics (grades 6-8) (MS), mathematics (grades K-5) (MS), middle level education (grades 5-8) (MS), professional development (MS), science (grades K-8) (MS), self-designed (PhD), special education (PhD), special education (non-licensure) (MS), teacher leadership (grades K-12) (MS), teaching English language learners (grades K-12) (MS); educational leadership and administration (principal preparation) (Ed S); educational technology (Ed S); elementary reading and literacy (Postbaccalaureate Certificate); engaging culturally diverse learners (Postbaccalaureate Certificate); enrollment management and institutional marketing (Postbaccalaureate Certificate); higher education (MS), including college teaching and learning, enrollment management and institutional planning, global higher education, leadership for student success, online and distance learning; higher education leadership (Ed D); instructional design (Postbaccalaureate Certificate); instructional design and technology (MS), including general program (MS, PhD), online learning, training and performance improvement; integrating technology in the classroom (Postbaccalaureate Certificate); online teaching for adult learners (Postbaccalaureate Certificate); professional development (Postbaccalaureate Certificate); reading and literacy leadership (Ed D); science K-8 (Postbaccalaureate Certificate); special education (Ed D, Ed S); special education: emotional/behavioral disorders (K-12) (MAT); special education: learning disabilities (K-12) (MAT); teacher leadership (Ed D, Ed S, Postbaccalaureate Certificate); training and performance management (Postbaccalaureate Certificate). Part-time and evening/weekend programs available. Postbaccalaureate distance learning degree programs offered (minimal on-campus study). *Faculty:* 71 full-time (48 women), 853 part-time/adjunct (585 women). *Students:* 11,326 full-time (9,212 women), 2,148 part-time (1,795 women); includes 5,346 minority (4,403 Black or African American, non-Hispanic/Latino; 76 American Indian or Alaska Native, non-Hispanic/Latino; 140 Asian, non-Hispanic/Latino; 561 Hispanic/Latino; 21 Native Hawaiian or other Pacific Islander, non-Hispanic/Latino; 145 Two or more races, non-Hispanic/Latino), 322 international. Average age 39. In 2011, 3,477 master's, 318 doctorates, 471 other advanced degrees awarded. *Degree requirements:* For doctorate, thesis/dissertation (for some programs), residency; for other advanced degree, residency (for some programs). *Entrance requirements:* For master's, bachelor's degree or equivalent in related field; minimum GPA of 2.5; official transcripts; goal statement; access to computer and Internet; for doctorate, master's degree or equivalent in related field; minimum GPA of 3.0; official transcripts; three years' related professional/academic experience (preferred); access to computer and Internet; for other advanced degree, master's degree or equivalent in related field; minimum GPA of 3.0; 3 years related professional/academic experience (preferred); access to computer and Internet (Ed S). Additional exam requirements/recommendations for international students: Required—TOEFL (minimum score 550 paper-based; 213 computer-based), IELTS (minimum score 6.5), or Michigan English Language Assessment Battery (minimum score 82). *Application deadline:* Applications are processed on a rolling basis. Application fee: $50. Electronic applications accepted. *Financial support:* Federal Work-Study, scholarships/grants, unspecified assistantships, and family tuition reduction, active duty/veteran tuition reduction, group tuition reduction, interest-free payment plans, employee tuition reduction available. Support available to part-time students. Financial award applicants required to submit FAFSA. *Unit head:* Dr. Kate Steffens, Dean, 800-925-3368. *Application contact:* Jennifer Hall, Vice President of Enrollment Management, 866-4-WALDEN, E-mail: info@waldenu.edu. Web site: http://www.waldenu.edu/Colleges-and-Schools/College-of-Education-and-Leadership.htm.

Walla Walla University, Graduate School, School of Education and Psychology, College Place, WA 99324-1198. Offers counseling psychology (MA); curriculum and instruction (M Ed, MA, MAT); educational leadership (M Ed, MA, MAT); literacy instruction (M Ed, MA, MAT); students at risk (M Ed, MA, MAT); teaching (MAT). Part-time programs available. *Entrance requirements:* For master's, GRE General Test, minimum GPA of 2.75. Additional exam requirements/recommendations for international students: Required—TOEFL (minimum score 550 paper-based; 213 computer-based; 79 iBT). Electronic applications accepted. *Faculty research:* Admissions/retention, instructional psychology, moral development, teaching of reading.

Walsh University, Graduate Studies, Program in Education, North Canton, OH 44720-3396. Offers MA. *Accreditation:* NCATE. Part-time and evening/weekend programs available. *Faculty:* 4 full-time (1 woman), 15 part-time/adjunct (9 women). *Students:* 19 full-time (11 women), 123 part-time (60 women); includes 3 minority (2 Black or African American, non-Hispanic/Latino; 1 Hispanic/Latino), 1 international. Average age 36. 18 applicants, 67% accepted, 12 enrolled. In 2011, 54 master's awarded. *Degree requirements:* For master's, comprehensive exam, thesis optional, teaching skills laboratory. *Entrance requirements:* For master's, MAT (minimum score 396) or GRE (minimum score 900), interview, minimum GPA of 3.0, writing sample, 3 recommendation forms, moral affidavit. Additional exam requirements/recommendations for international students: Required—TOEFL (minimum score 500 paper-based; 173 computer-based; 61 iBT). *Application deadline:* For fall admission, 7/15 priority date for domestic students. Applications are processed on a rolling basis. Application fee: $25. Electronic applications accepted. *Expenses: Tuition:* Full-time $10,170; part-time $565 per credit hour. *Financial support:* In 2011–12, 33 students received support, including 6 research assistantships with partial tuition reimbursements available (averaging $9,040 per year), 3 teaching assistantships (averaging $4,121 per year); tuition waivers (partial) and unspecified assistantships also available. Support available to part-time students. Financial award application deadline: 12/31. *Faculty research:* Technology in education, strategies for working with children with special needs, reading literacy, whole brain teaching, hybrid learning, online teaching. *Unit head:* Dr. Gary Jacobs, Director, 330-490-7336, Fax: 330-490-7326, E-mail: gjacobs@walsh.edu. *Application contact:* Vanessa Freiman, Graduate and Transfer Admissions Counselor, 330-490-7177, Fax: 330-244-4925, E-mail: vfreiman@walsh.edu.

Warner Pacific College, Graduate Programs, Portland, OR 97215-4099. Offers biblical and theological studies (MA); biblical studies (M Rel); education (M Ed); management/organizational leadership (MS); pastoral ministries (M Rel); religion and ethics (M Rel); teaching (MA); theology (M Rel). Part-time programs available. *Degree requirements:* For master's, thesis or alternative, presentation of defense. *Entrance requirements:* For master's, interview, minimum GPA of 2.5, letters of recommendations. *Faculty research:* New Testament studies, nineteenth-century Wesleyan theology, preaching and church growth, Christian ethics.

Warner University, Teacher Education Department, Lake Wales, FL 33859. Offers MAEd. Part-time and evening/weekend programs available. *Degree requirements:* For master's, thesis, accomplished practices portfolio. *Entrance requirements:* For master's, GRE or MAT, minimum GPA of 3.0 in last 60 hours of undergraduate coursework; documented teacher education certification; 2 letters of recommendation. Additional exam requirements/recommendations for international students: Required—TOEFL (minimum score 550 paper-based). Electronic applications accepted.

Washburn University, College of Arts and Sciences, Department of Education, Topeka, KS 66621. Offers curriculum and instruction (M Ed); educational leadership (M Ed); reading (M Ed); special education (M Ed). *Accreditation:* NCATE. Part-time programs available. *Faculty:* 6 full-time (3 women), 1 (woman) part-time/adjunct. *Students:* 2 full-time (both women), 26 part-time (16 women). Average age 36. In 2011, 17 master's awarded. *Degree requirements:* For master's, comprehensive exam, thesis or alternative, portfolio, comprehensive paper, or action research project. *Entrance requirements:* For master's, department graduate admissions test, GRE General Test, or MAT, minimum GPA of 3.0 in graduate coursework or last 60 hours of undergraduate coursework. Additional exam requirements/recommendations for international students: Required—TOEFL (minimum score 550 paper-based; 80 iBT). *Application deadline:* For fall admission, 8/1 for domestic and international students; for spring admission, 11/1 for domestic and international students. Applications are processed on a rolling basis. *Expenses:* Tuition, state resident: full-time $5346; part-time $297 per credit hour. Tuition, nonresident: full-time $10,908; part-time $606 per credit hour. *Required fees:* $86; $43 per semester. *Financial support:* Federal Work-Study, institutionally sponsored loans, and scholarships/grants available. Support available to part-time students. Financial award applicants required to submit FAFSA. *Faculty research:* Reading/literature/literacy, foundations, educational administration/leadership, special education, diversity. *Unit head:* Dr. Judith McConnell-Farmer, Interim Chairperson, 785-670-1472, Fax: 785-670-1046, E-mail: judy.mcconnell-farmer@washburn.edu. *Application contact:* Tara Porter, Licensure Officer, 785-670-1434, Fax: 785-670-1046, E-mail: tara.porter@washburn.edu. Web site: http://www.washburn.edu/academics/college-schools/arts-sciences/departments/education/index.html.

Washington State University, Graduate School, College of Education, Pullman, WA 99164. Offers Ed M, M Ed, MA, MIT, MS, Ed D, PhD, Certificate. *Accreditation:* NCATE. *Faculty:* 39. *Students:* 182 full-time (119 women), 89 part-time (60 women); includes 60 minority (9 Black or African American, non-Hispanic/Latino; 15 Asian, non-Hispanic/Latino; 29 Hispanic/Latino; 1 Native Hawaiian or other Pacific Islander, non-Hispanic/Latino; 6 Two or more races, non-Hispanic/Latino), 61 international. Average age 32. 350 applicants, 34% accepted, 88 enrolled. In 2011, 78 master's, 14 doctorates awarded. Terminal master's awarded for partial completion of doctoral program. *Degree requirements:* For master's, comprehensive exam (for some programs), thesis (for some programs), oral and written exams; for doctorate, comprehensive exam, thesis/dissertation, oral and written exams. *Entrance requirements:* For master's, GRE General Test, current resume, three letters of recommendation, transcripts of all past academic work; for doctorate, GRE General Test or MAT, current resume, three letters of recommendation, transcripts of all past academic work. Additional exam requirements/recommendations for international students: Required—TOEFL (minimum score 550 paper-based; 213 computer-based), IELTS. *Application deadline:* For fall admission, 1/10 for domestic and international students. Application fee: $75. Electronic applications accepted. *Financial support:* In 2011–12, 51 research assistantships with partial tuition reimbursements (averaging $18,204 per year), 32 teaching assistantships with partial tuition reimbursements (averaging $18,204 per year) were awarded; career-related internships or fieldwork, Federal Work-Study, institutionally sponsored loans, scholarships/grants, tuition waivers (partial), and staff assistantships, teaching associateships also available. Financial award application deadline: 2/15; financial award applicants required to submit FAFSA. *Faculty research:* At-risk; bilingual/multicultural, mathematics, special, and cross-cultural education. *Total annual research expenditures:* $935,000. *Unit head:* Dr. A. G. Rud, Dean, 509-335-4853, Fax: 509-335-2097, E-mail: ag.rud@wsu.edu. *Application contact:* Graduate School Admissions, 800-GRADWSU, Fax: 509-335-1949, E-mail: gradsch@wsu.edu. Web site: http://www.educ.wsu.edu/index.shtml.

Washington State University Spokane, Graduate Programs, Program in Education, Spokane, WA 99210. Offers educational leadership (Ed M, MA); principal (Certificate); professional certification for teachers (Certificate); program administrator (Certificate); school psychologist (Certificate); superintendent (Certificate); teaching (MIT). *Faculty:* 24. *Students:* 11 full-time (10 women), 25 part-time (17 women); includes 1 minority (Hispanic/Latino). Average age 37. 27 applicants, 67% accepted, 18 enrolled. In 2011, 8 degrees awarded. *Degree requirements:* For master's, comprehensive exam (for some programs), thesis (for some programs). *Entrance requirements:* For master's, GRE or GMAT, minimum GPA of 3.0, 3 letters of recommendation, resume. Additional exam requirements/recommendations for international students: Required—TOEFL (minimum score 550 paper-based; 213 computer-based). *Application deadline:* For fall admission, 1/10 priority date for domestic students, 1/10 for international students; for spring admission, 7/1 priority date for domestic students, 7/1 for international students. Application fee: $50. *Financial support:* In 2011–12, 33 students received support, including research assistantships (averaging $14,634 per year), teaching assistantships (averaging $13,383 per year). *Total annual research expenditures:* $16,557. *Unit head:* Dr. Joan Kingrey, Director, 509-358-7939, Fax: 509-358-7900, E-mail: kingrey@wsu.edu. *Application contact:* Graduate School Admissions, 800-GRADWSU, Fax: 509-335-1949, E-mail: gradsch@wsu.edu.

Washington State University Tri-Cities, Graduate Programs, Program in Education, Richland, WA 99352-1671. Offers counseling (Ed M); educational leadership (Ed M, Ed D); literacy (Ed M); secondary certification (Ed M); teaching (MIT). Part-time programs available. *Faculty:* 24. *Students:* 19 full-time (14 women), 73 part-time (46 women); includes 18 minority (1 Black or African American, non-Hispanic/Latino; 3 Asian, non-Hispanic/Latino; 14 Hispanic/Latino). Average age 34. 26 applicants, 69% accepted, 18 enrolled. In 2011, 31 master's awarded. *Degree requirements:* For master's, comprehensive exam, thesis or alternative; for doctorate, comprehensive exam, thesis/dissertation. *Entrance requirements:* For master's, GRE, minimum GPA of 3.0, Working with Youth form, Character and Fitness form, 3 letters of recommendation. Additional exam requirements/recommendations for international students: Required—TOEFL. *Application deadline:* For fall admission, 1/10 priority date for domestic students, 1/10 for international students; for spring admission, 7/1 priority date for domestic students, 7/1 for international students. Applications are processed on a rolling basis. Application fee: $75. Electronic applications accepted. *Financial support:* In 2011–12, 59 students received support, including research assistantships (averaging $14,634 per year), teaching assistantships (averaging $13,383 per year); Federal Work-Study, scholarships/grants, and unspecified assistantships also available. Financial award application deadline: 2/15. *Faculty research:* Multicultural counseling, socio-cultural influences in schools, diverse learners, teacher education, K-12 educational leadership. *Unit head:* Dr. Elizabeth Nagel, Director, 509-372-7398, E-mail: elizabeth_nagel@tricity.wsu.edu. *Application contact:* Helen Berry, Academic Coordinator, 800-GRADWSU, Fax: 509-372-3796, E-mail: hberry@tricity.wsu.edu. Web site: http://www.tricity.wsu.edu/education/graduate.html.

Washington State University Vancouver, Graduate Programs, Program in Education, Vancouver, WA 98686. Offers Ed M, MIT, Ed D. Part-time programs available. *Faculty:* 30. *Students:* 47 full-time (36 women), 95 part-time (63 women); includes 13 minority (1 Black or African American, non-Hispanic/Latino; 1 American Indian or Alaska Native, non-Hispanic/Latino; 2 Asian, non-Hispanic/Latino; 7 Hispanic/Latino; 2 Two or more races, non-Hispanic/Latino). Average age 37. 74 applicants, 76% accepted, 44 enrolled. In 2011, 47 degrees awarded. *Degree requirements:* For master's, comprehensive exam, thesis (for some programs); for doctorate, comprehensive exam, thesis/dissertation. *Entrance requirements:* For master's, WEST-B, PRAXIS II (MIT), minimum GPA of 3.0, 3 letters of recommendation. Additional exam requirements/recommendations for international students: Required—TOEFL (minimum score 550 paper-based; 213 computer-based). *Application deadline:* For fall admission, 1/10 priority date for domestic students, 1/10 for international students; for spring admission, 7/1 priority date for domestic students, 7/1 for international students. Application fee: $75. *Financial support:* In 2011–12, research assistantships (averaging $14,634 per year), teaching assistantships (averaging $13,383 per year) were awarded; Federal Work-Study, scholarships/grants, and unspecified assistantships also available. Financial award application deadline: 2/15. *Faculty research:* Language literacy and culture, developing learning community, developing teacher-mentors. *Total annual research expenditures:* $493,391. *Unit head:* Dr. June Canty, Academic Director, 360-546-9108, E-mail: canty@vancouver.wsu.edu. *Application contact:* Jillane Homme, Graduate Academic Coordinator, 360-546-9075, Fax: 360-546-9040, E-mail: jhomme22@vancouver.wsu.edu. Web site: http://education.vancouver.wsu.edu/master-education.

Washington University in St. Louis, Graduate School of Arts and Sciences, Department of Education, St. Louis, MO 63130-4899. Offers educational research (PhD); elementary education (MA Ed); secondary education (MA Ed, MAT). *Degree requirements:* For master's, thesis or alternative; for doctorate, thesis/dissertation. *Entrance requirements:* For master's, GRE General Test or MAT; for doctorate, GRE General Test. Electronic applications accepted.

Wayland Baptist University, Graduate Programs, Program in Education, Plainview, TX 79072-6998. Offers education administration (M Ed); higher education administration (M Ed); instructional leadership (M Ed); instructional technology (M Ed); special education (M Ed). Part-time and evening/weekend programs available. Postbaccalaureate distance learning degree programs offered (no on-campus study). *Degree requirements:* For master's, comprehensive exam, capstone course. *Entrance requirements:* For master's, GRE, GMAT or MAT. Additional exam requirements/recommendations for international students: Required—TOEFL (minimum score 500 paper-based; 173 computer-based; 61 iBT). Electronic applications accepted.

Waynesburg University, Graduate and Professional Studies, Waynesburg, PA 15370-1222. Offers business (MBA), including finance, health systems, human resources, leadership, market development; counseling (MA), including addictions counseling, clinical mental health; education (MAT); nursing (MSN), including administration, education, informatics, palliative care; nursing practice (DNP); special education (M Ed); technology (M Ed); MSN/MBA. *Accreditation:* AACN. Part-time and evening/weekend programs available. *Degree requirements:* For doctorate, thesis/dissertation. *Entrance requirements:* Additional exam requirements/recommendations for international students: Required—TOEFL. Electronic applications accepted.

Wayne State College, School of Education and Counseling, Wayne, NE 68787. Offers MSE, Ed S. *Accreditation:* NCATE. Part-time and evening/weekend programs available. *Degree requirements:* For master's, comprehensive exam, thesis (for some programs). *Entrance requirements:* For master's, GRE General Test, minimum cumulative GPA of 3.0; for Ed S, GRE General Test, minimum GPA of 3.2 in all program coursework. Additional exam requirements/recommendations for international students: Required—TOEFL (minimum score 550 paper-based; 213 computer-based).

Wayne State University, College of Education, Detroit, MI 48202. Offers M Ed, MA, MAT, Ed D, PhD, Certificate, Ed S, M Ed/MA. Evening/weekend programs available. *Students:* 540 full-time (395 women), 1,170 part-time (868 women); includes 658 minority (548 Black or African American, non-Hispanic/Latino; 6 American Indian or Alaska Native, non-Hispanic/Latino; 41 Asian, non-Hispanic/Latino; 43 Hispanic/Latino; 3 Native Hawaiian or other Pacific Islander, non-Hispanic/Latino; 17 Two or more races, non-Hispanic/Latino), 46 international. Average age 37. 823 applicants, 37% accepted, 212 enrolled. In 2011, 432 master's, 37 doctorates, 97 other advanced degrees awarded. Terminal master's awarded for partial completion of doctoral program. *Degree requirements:* For master's, thesis (for some programs); for doctorate, thesis/dissertation. *Entrance requirements:* Additional exam requirements/recommendations for international students: Required—TOEFL (minimum score 550 paper-based; 213 computer-based); Recommended—TWE (minimum score 5.5). *Application deadline:* For fall admission, 6/1 priority date for domestic students, 5/1 for international students; for winter admission, 10/1 priority date for domestic students, 9/1 for international students; for spring admission, 2/1 priority date for domestic students, 1/1 for international students. Applications are processed on a rolling basis. Application fee: $50. Electronic applications accepted. *Expenses:* Tuition, state resident: part-time $512.85 per credit. Tuition, nonresident: part-time $1132.65 per credit. *Required fees:* $26.60 per credit. $199.65 per semester. Tuition and fees vary according to course load and program. *Financial support:* In 2011–12, 192 students received support, including 4 fellowships with tuition reimbursements available (averaging $16,615 per year), 12 research assistantships (averaging $15,858 per year), 1 teaching assistantship with tuition reimbursement available (averaging $18,000 per year); career-related internships or fieldwork, Federal Work-Study, institutionally sponsored loans, scholarships/grants, health care benefits, and unspecified assistantships also available. Support available to part-time students. *Faculty research:* Alternative routes to teacher certification; innovations in science, mathematics and technology education; literacy; K-12 school reform, including special education and self-determination for special populations; adult workplace learning. *Total annual research expenditures:* $402,370. *Unit head:* Dr. Carolyn Shields, Dean, 313-577-1620, Fax: 313-577-3606, E-mail: cshields@wayne.edu. *Application contact:* Janice Green, Assistant Dean, 313-577-1605, E-mail: jwgreen@wayne.edu. Web site: http://coe.wayne.edu/.

Weber State University, Jerry and Vickie Moyes College of Education, Ogden, UT 84408-1001. Offers M Ed, MSAT. *Accreditation:* NCATE. Part-time and evening/weekend programs available. *Degree requirements:* For master's, project presentation and exam. *Entrance requirements:* Additional exam requirements/recommendations for international students: Required—TOEFL (minimum score 550 paper-based; 213 computer-based), American Council on the Teaching of Foreign Languages test.

Webster University, School of Education, St. Louis, MO 63119-3194. Offers MAT, Ed S. *Accreditation:* NCATE. Part-time programs available. Postbaccalaureate distance learning degree programs offered (no on-campus study). *Degree requirements:* For master's, thesis (for some programs). *Entrance requirements:* For master's, minimum GPA of 2.5. Additional exam requirements/recommendations for international students: Required—TOEFL. *Expenses: Tuition:* Full-time $10,890; part-time $605 per credit hour. Tuition and fees vary according to campus/location and program.

Wesleyan College, Department of Education, Macon, GA 31210-4462. Offers early childhood education (MA). Part-time programs available. *Degree requirements:* For master's, thesis or alternative, practicum, professional portfolio. *Entrance requirements:* For master's, GRE or MAT, interview, teaching certificate, 3 letters of recommendation. Additional exam requirements/recommendations for international students: Required—TOEFL. *Faculty research:* Neuroscience, gender bias in science and mathematics.

Wesley College, Education Program, Dover, DE 19901-3875. Offers M Ed, MA Ed, MAT. Part-time and evening/weekend programs available. *Degree requirements:* For master's, thesis optional. *Entrance requirements:* For master's, GRE. *Faculty research:* Learning styles, community-higher education partnerships, curriculum models, science learning and teaching, literacy development in early elementary.

West Chester University of Pennsylvania, College of Education, West Chester, PA 19383. Offers M Ed, MS, Certificate, Teaching Certificate. *Accreditation:* NCATE. Part-time and evening/weekend programs available. Postbaccalaureate distance learning degree programs offered (no on-campus study). *Faculty:* 8 full-time (3 women), 50 part-time/adjunct (38 women). *Students:* 202 full-time (174 women), 515 part-time (436 women); includes 64 minority (33 Black or African American, non-Hispanic/Latino; 8 Asian, non-Hispanic/Latino; 15 Hispanic/Latino; 8 Two or more races, non-Hispanic/Latino). Average age 29. 383 applicants, 64% accepted, 174 enrolled. In 2011, 95 master's, 6 other advanced degrees awarded. *Degree requirements:* For master's, comprehensive exam (for some programs), thesis (for some programs). *Entrance requirements:* Additional exam requirements/recommendations for international students: Required—TOEFL (minimum score 550 paper-based; 213 computer-based; 80 iBT). *Application deadline:* For fall admission, 4/15 priority date for domestic students, 3/15 for international students; for spring admission, 10/15 priority date for domestic students, 9/1 for international students. Applications are processed on a rolling basis. Application fee: $45. Electronic applications accepted. *Expenses:* Tuition, state resident: full-time $7488; part-time $416 per credit. Tuition, nonresident: full-time $11,232; part-time $624 per credit. *Required fees:* $1784.64; $67.59 per credit. Tuition and fees vary according to program. *Financial support:* Unspecified assistantships available. Support available to part-time students. Financial award application deadline: 2/15; financial award applicants required to submit FAFSA. *Unit head:* Dr. Kenneth D. Witmer, Jr., Dean, 610-436-2321, Fax: 610-436-3102, E-mail: kcrouse@wcupa.edu. *Application contact:* Office of Graduate Studies, 610-436-2943, Fax: 610-436-2763, E-mail: gradstudy@wcupa.edu. Web site: http://www.wcupa.edu/_academics/sch_sed/.

Western Carolina University, Graduate School, College of Education and Allied Professions, Cullowhee, NC 28723. Offers M Ed, MA, MA Ed, MAT, MS, MSA, Ed D, Ed S, PMC. *Accreditation:* NCATE. Part-time and evening/weekend programs available. Postbaccalaureate distance learning degree programs offered. *Students:* 211 full-time (148 women), 410 part-time (322 women); includes 56 minority (31 Black or African American, non-Hispanic/Latino; 4 American Indian or Alaska Native, non-Hispanic/Latino; 6 Asian, non-Hispanic/Latino; 12 Hispanic/Latino; 3 Two or more races, non-Hispanic/Latino), 17 international. Average age 33. 739 applicants, 53% accepted, 239 enrolled. In 2011, 295 master's, 14 doctorates, 5 other advanced degrees awarded. *Degree requirements:* For master's, comprehensive exam, thesis; for doctorate, comprehensive exam, thesis/dissertation. *Entrance requirements:* For master's, GRE, appropriate undergraduate degree with minimum GPA of 3.0, 3 recommendations, writing sample, resume, interview; for doctorate, GRE General Test, minimum graduate GPA of 3.5, appropriate master's degree; for other advanced degree, GRE General Test, minimum graduate GPA of 3.5, work experience, appropriate master's degree. Additional exam requirements/recommendations for international students: Required—TOEFL (minimum score 550 paper-based; 270 computer-based; 79 iBT). *Application deadline:* For fall admission, 2/1 for domestic students; for spring admission, 9/1 priority date for domestic students. Applications are processed on a rolling basis. Application fee: $50. *Expenses:* Tuition, state resident: full-time $3348. Tuition, nonresident: full-time $12,933. *Required fees:* $3155. *Financial support:* In 2011–12, 102 students received support. Fellowships, research assistantships with full and partial tuition reimbursements available, teaching assistantships with full and partial tuition reimbursements available, career-related internships or fieldwork, institutionally sponsored loans, scholarships/grants, and unspecified assistantships available. Financial award application deadline: 3/31; financial award applicants required to submit FAFSA. *Faculty research:* Evolutionary psychology, marital and family development, program evaluation, rural education, special education, educational leadership, employee recruitment/retention. *Unit head:* Dr. Perry Schoon, Dean, 828-227-7311, Fax: 828-227-7388, E-mail: pschoon@wcu.edu. *Application contact:* Admissions Specialist for Education and Allied Professions, 828-227-7398, Fax: 828-227-7480, E-mail: gradsch@email.wcu.edu. Web site: http://www.wcu.edu/3030.asp.

Western Connecticut State University, Division of Graduate Studies, School of Professional Studies, Department of Education and Educational Psychology, Danbury, CT 06810-6885. Offers community counseling (MS); counselor education (MS), including guidance and counseling; curriculum (MS); English education (MS); instructional leadership (Ed D); instructional technology (MS); mathematics education (MS); reading (MS); school counseling (MS); secondary education (MAT), including biology, mathematics; special education (MS). *Accreditation:* NCATE. Part-time programs available. *Faculty:* 15 full-time (9 women), 10 part-time/adjunct (7 women). *Students:* 23 full-time (13 women), 216 part-time (168 women); includes 22 minority (3 Black or African American, non-Hispanic/Latino; 2 American Indian or Alaska Native, non-Hispanic/Latino; 2 Asian, non-Hispanic/Latino; 12 Hispanic/Latino; 1 Native Hawaiian or other Pacific Islander, non-Hispanic/Latino; 2 Two or more races, non-Hispanic/Latino). Average age 35. 175 applicants, 45% accepted, 67 enrolled. In 2011, 102 master's, 2 doctorates awarded. *Degree requirements:* For master's, thesis or alternative, completion of program in 6 years. *Entrance requirements:* For master's, MAT (if GPA is below 2.8), valid teaching certificate, letters of reference; for doctorate, GRE or MAT, resume, three recommendations (one in a supervisory capacity in an educational setting), satisfactory interview with WCSU representatives from the EdD Admissions Committee. Additional exam requirements/recommendations for international students: Recommended—TOEFL (minimum score 550 paper-based; 213 computer-based; 79 iBT), IELTS (minimum score 6). *Application deadline:* For fall admission, 8/5 priority date for domestic students; for spring admission, 1/5 for domestic students. Applications are processed on a rolling basis. Application fee: $50. *Expenses:* Contact institution. *Financial support:* Scholarships/grants available. Financial award application deadline: 5/1; financial award applicants required to submit FAFSA. *Faculty research:* Cultural diversity in teacher and counselor education programs, African-American educational leaders, urban education and equity. *Unit head:* Dr. Theresa Canada, Chairperson, Department of Education and Educational Psychology, 203-837-8509, Fax: 203-837-8413, E-mail: canadat@wcsu.edu. *Application contact:* Chris Shankle, Associate Director of Graduate Studies, 203-837-9005, Fax: 203-837-8326, E-mail: shanklec@wcsu.edu. Web site: http://www.wcsu.edu/education/.

Western Governors University, Teachers College, Salt Lake City, UT 84107. Offers curriculum and instruction (MS); educational leadership (MS); educational studies (MA); educational studies (5-12) (MA), including mathematics; elementary education (k-8) (Postbaccalaureate Certificate); English language learning (K-12) (MA); instructional design (MAT); learning and technology (M Ed, MA); management and innovation (M Ed); mathematics (5-12) (Postbaccalaureate Certificate); mathematics (5-9) (Postbaccalaureate Certificate); mathematics education (5-12) (MA); mathematics education (5-9) (MA); mathematics education (K-6) (MA); measurement and evaluation (M Ed); science (5-12) (Postbaccalaureate Certificate); science (5-9) (Postbaccalaureate Certificate); science education (5-12) (MA), including biology, chemistry, geology, physics; science education (5-9) (MA); social science (5-12) (MAT); special education (MAT). *Accreditation:* NCATE. Evening/weekend programs available. Postbaccalaureate distance learning degree programs offered (no on-campus study). *Students:* 3,746 full-time (2,811 women); includes 652 minority (332 Black or African American, non-Hispanic/Latino; 37 American Indian or Alaska Native, non-Hispanic/Latino; 74 Asian, non-Hispanic/Latino; 139 Hispanic/Latino; 70 Two or more races, non-Hispanic/Latino), 12 international. Average age 37. In 2011, 1,080 master's, 242 other advanced degrees awarded. *Degree requirements:* For master's, capstone project. *Entrance requirements:* For master's and Postbaccalaureate Certificate, Readiness Assessment, commitment counseling discussion, transcript submissions, completion of orientation. Additional exam requirements/recommendations for international students: Required—TOEFL (minimum score 450 paper-based; 80 iBT). *Application deadline:* Applications are processed on a rolling basis. Application fee: $65. Electronic applications accepted. *Expenses:* Contact institution. *Financial support:* Scholarships/grants and tuition waivers (partial) available. Financial award applicants required to submit FAFSA. *Unit head:* Dr. Philip Schmidt, Dean of the Teachers College, 845-255-4656. *Application contact:* Enrollment Department, 866-225-5948, Fax: 801-274-3306, E-mail: info@wgu.edu.

Western Illinois University, School of Graduate Studies, College of Education and Human Services, Macomb, IL 61455-1390. Offers MA, MS, MS Ed, Ed D, Certificate, Ed S. *Accreditation:* NCATE. Part-time and evening/weekend programs available. Postbaccalaureate distance learning degree programs offered (no on-campus study). *Students:* 283 full-time (170 women), 666 part-time (463 women); includes 93 minority (51 Black or African American, non-Hispanic/Latino; 2 American Indian or Alaska Native, non-Hispanic/Latino; 9 Asian, non-Hispanic/Latino; 25 Hispanic/Latino; 6 Two or more races, non-Hispanic/Latino), 33 international. Average age 27. 408 applicants, 56% accepted. In 2011, 337 master's, 9 doctorates, 34 other advanced degrees awarded. *Degree requirements:* For master's, comprehensive exam (for some programs), thesis or alternative; for doctorate, comprehensive exam, thesis/dissertation, electronic portfolio. *Entrance requirements:* For master's, GRE and MAT (for selected programs); for doctorate, GRE. Additional exam requirements/recommendations for international students: Required—TOEFL. *Application deadline:* Applications are processed on a rolling basis. Application fee: $30. Electronic applications accepted. *Expenses:* Tuition, state resident: part-time $281.16 per credit hour. Tuition, nonresident: part-time $562.32 per credit hour. Part-time tuition and fees vary according to campus/location and reciprocity agreements. *Financial support:* In 2011–12, 152 students received support, including 140 research assistantships with full tuition reimbursements available (averaging $7,360 per year), 12 teaching assistantships with full tuition reimbursements available (averaging $8,480 per year). Financial award applicants required to submit FAFSA. *Unit head:* Dr. Sterling Saddler, Dean, 309-298-1690. *Application contact:* Dr. Nancy Parsons, Interim Associate Provost and Director of Graduate Studies, 309-298-1806, Fax: 309-298-2345, E-mail: grad-office@wiu.edu. Web site: http://wiu.edu/coehs.

Western Michigan University, Graduate College, College of Education and Human Development, Kalamazoo, MI 49008. Offers MA, MS, Ed D, PhD, Ed S, Graduate Certificate. *Accreditation:* NCATE. Part-time programs available. *Degree requirements:* For doctorate, thesis/dissertation; for other advanced degree, thesis, oral exams. *Entrance requirements:* For doctorate and other advanced degree, GRE General Test.

Western New Mexico University, Graduate Division, School of Education, Silver City, NM 88062-0680. Offers bilingual education (MAT); counseling (MA); educational leadership (MA); elementary education (MAT); reading (MAT); school psychology (MA); secondary education (MAT); special education (MAT); TESOL (teaching English to speakers of other languages) (MAT). *Accreditation:* NCATE. *Degree requirements:* For master's, comprehensive exam. *Entrance requirements:* For master's, GRE General Test, GRE Subject Test, minimum GPA of 3.2 in last 64 hours of undergraduate study. Additional exam requirements/recommendations for international students: Required—TOEFL (minimum score 550 paper-based; 213 computer-based). Electronic applications accepted.

Western Oregon University, Graduate Programs, College of Education, Monmouth, OR 97361-1394. Offers MAT, MS, MS Ed. *Accreditation:* NCATE. Part-time and evening/weekend programs available. Postbaccalaureate distance learning degree programs offered (minimal on-campus study). *Degree requirements:* For master's, comprehensive exam (for some programs), thesis optional, written exam. *Entrance requirements:* For master's, minimum GPA of 3.0. Additional exam requirements/recommendations for international students: Required—TOEFL (minimum score 550 paper-based; 213 computer-based; 79 iBT), IELTS (minimum score 6.5). *Faculty research:* Effectiveness of work, sample methodology, documentation of learning gains, appropriateness of advanced proficiency.

Western State College of Colorado, Graduate Programs in Education, Gunnison, CO 81231. Offers education administrator leadership (MA); reading leadership (MA); teacher leadership (MA). Postbaccalaureate distance learning degree programs offered (minimal on-campus study). *Degree requirements:* For master's, capstone.

Western Washington University, Graduate School, Woodring College of Education, Bellingham, WA 98225-5996. Offers M Ed, MA, MIT. *Accreditation:* NCATE. Part-time programs available. Postbaccalaureate distance learning degree programs offered (minimal on-campus study). *Degree requirements:* For master's, comprehensive exam, thesis optional. *Entrance requirements:* For master's, GRE General Test or MAT, minimum GPA of 3.0 in last 60 semester hours or last 90 quarter hours. Additional exam requirements/recommendations for international students: Required—TOEFL (minimum score 567 paper-based; 227 computer-based). Electronic applications accepted.

Westfield State University, Division of Graduate and Continuing Education, Department of Education, Westfield, MA 01086. Offers early childhood education (M Ed); elementary education (M Ed); occupational education (M Ed, CAGS); reading (M Ed); school administration (M Ed, CAGS); secondary education (M Ed); special education (M Ed); technology for educators (M Ed). *Accreditation:* NCATE. Part-time

Education—General

and evening/weekend programs available. *Degree requirements:* For master's, comprehensive exam; for CAGS, research-based field internship. *Entrance requirements:* For master's, GRE General Test or MAT, minimum undergraduate GPA of 2.7; for CAGS, master's degree. *Faculty research:* Collaborative teacher education, developmental early childhood education.

West Liberty University, School of Education, West Liberty, WV 26074. Offers MA Ed. *Accreditation:* NCATE. *Degree requirements:* For master's, capstone experience. *Entrance requirements:* For master's, GRE or MAT, minimum GPA of 2.5, teaching license, interview. Electronic applications accepted.

Westminster College, Programs in Education, New Wilmington, PA 16172-0001. Offers administration (M Ed, Certificate); general education (M Ed); guidance and counseling (M Ed, Certificate); reading (M Ed, Certificate). Part-time and evening/weekend programs available. *Degree requirements:* For master's, comprehensive exam, portfolio. *Entrance requirements:* For master's, GRE or MAT, minimum GPA of 3.0.

Westminster College, School of Education, Salt Lake City, UT 84105-3697. Offers community leadership (MA); education (M Ed); teaching (MAT). *Accreditation:* Teacher Education Accreditation Council. Part-time and evening/weekend programs available. *Faculty:* 13 full-time (10 women), 22 part-time/adjunct (17 women). *Students:* 117 full-time (83 women), 69 part-time (57 women); includes 9 minority (1 American Indian or Alaska Native, non-Hispanic/Latino; 3 Asian, non-Hispanic/Latino; 5 Hispanic/Latino). Average age 33. 137 applicants, 82% accepted, 96 enrolled. In 2011, 82 master's awarded. *Degree requirements:* For master's, project or thesis. *Entrance requirements:* For master's, personal resume, 2 letters of recommendation, minimum GPA of 3.0, copy of current teaching certificate, statement of purpose, official transcript. Additional exam requirements/recommendations for international students: Required—TOEFL (minimum score 600 paper-based; 100 iBT), IELTS (minimum score 7). *Application deadline:* Applications are processed on a rolling basis. Application fee: $50. Electronic applications accepted. *Expenses:* Contact institution. *Financial support:* In 2011–12, 12 students received support. Career-related internships or fieldwork and tuition reimbursement, tuition remission available. Support available to part-time students. Financial award applicants required to submit FAFSA. *Faculty research:* Early childhood literacy, English as a Second Language instruction, special education, instruction in teacher education, e-portfolios as assessment tools, funds of knowledge. *Unit head:* Robert Shaw, Dean, School of Education, 801-832-2470, Fax: 801-832-3105. *Application contact:* Dr. Gary Daynes, Vice President for Strategic Outreach and Enrollment, 801-832-2200, Fax: 801-832-3101, E-mail: admission@westminstercollege.edu. Web site: http://www.westminstercollege.edu/med.

West Texas A&M University, College of Education and Social Sciences, Division of Education, Canyon, TX 79016-0001. Offers administration (M Ed); counseling education (M Ed); curriculum and instruction (M Ed); educational diagnostician (M Ed); educational technology (M Ed); professional counseling (MA); reading (M Ed); special education (M Ed). Part-time and evening/weekend programs available. Postbaccalaureate distance learning degree programs offered (minimal on-campus study). *Degree requirements:* For master's, comprehensive exam, thesis optional. *Entrance requirements:* For master's, GRE General Test. Additional exam requirements/recommendations for international students: Required—TOEFL (minimum score 550 paper-based). Electronic applications accepted. *Faculty research:* Modified internship for novice teachers, effective instructional strategies, cognitive-relational group, community college, recruitment/retention.

West Virginia University, College of Human Resources and Education, Morgantown, WV 26506. Offers MA, MS, Au D, Ed D, PhD. *Accreditation:* NCATE. Part-time and evening/weekend programs available. Postbaccalaureate distance learning degree programs offered (no on-campus study). *Degree requirements:* For master's, content exams; for doctorate, comprehensive exam, thesis/dissertation. *Entrance requirements:* Additional exam requirements/recommendations for international students: Required—TOEFL. Electronic applications accepted. *Faculty research:* Internet training and integration for teachers, rural education, teacher preparation, organization of schools, evaluation of personnel.

West Virginia Wesleyan College, Department of Education, Buckhannon, WV 26201. Offers M Ed. *Accreditation:* NCATE.

Wheaton College, Graduate School, Department of Education, Wheaton, IL 60187-5593. Offers elementary level (MAT); secondary level (MAT). *Accreditation:* NCATE. *Students:* 17 full-time (12 women), 24 part-time (21 women); includes 5 minority (4 Asian, non-Hispanic/Latino; 1 Hispanic/Latino). Average age 24. 8 applicants, 100% accepted, 2 enrolled. In 2011, 4 master's awarded. *Degree requirements:* For master's, thesis or alternative. *Entrance requirements:* For master's, GRE General Test or MAT. Additional exam requirements/recommendations for international students: Required—TOEFL (minimum score 550 paper-based; 80 iBT), IELTS (minimum score 6.5). *Application deadline:* For fall admission, 5/1 for domestic students, 1/1 for international students; for spring admission, 11/1 for domestic students. Applications are processed on a rolling basis. Application fee: $30. Electronic applications accepted. *Expenses: Tuition:* Full-time $16,440; part-time $685 per credit hour. Tuition and fees vary according to degree level and program. *Financial support:* Career-related internships or fieldwork and Federal Work-Study available. Financial award application deadline: 3/1; financial award applicants required to submit FAFSA. *Unit head:* Dr. Jillian Lederhouse, Chair, 630-752-5764, E-mail: jillian.lederhouse@wheaton.edu. *Application contact:* Julie A. Huebner, Director of Graduate Admissions, 630-752-5195, Fax: 630-752-5935, E-mail: gradadm@wheaton.edu. Web site: http://www.wheaton.edu/academics/departments/education.

Wheelock College, Graduate Programs, Boston, MA 02215-4176. Offers MS, MSW. *Accreditation:* NCATE (one or more programs are accredited). Part-time and evening/weekend programs available. Postbaccalaureate distance learning degree programs offered (minimal on-campus study). *Entrance requirements:* For master's, interview. Additional exam requirements/recommendations for international students: Required—TOEFL (minimum score 550 paper-based; 260 computer-based). *Faculty research:* Teacher development and leadership, national standards science education, high academic achievement for students of color, cultural influences on development, media literacy.

Whittier College, Graduate Programs, Department of Education and Child Development, Whittier, CA 90608-0634. Offers educational administration (MA Ed); elementary education (MA Ed); secondary education (MA Ed). Part-time and evening/weekend programs available. *Degree requirements:* For master's, thesis. *Entrance requirements:* For master's, GRE General Test, MAT, minimum GPA of 3.5, academic writing sample.

Whitworth University, School of Education, Graduate Studies in Education, Spokane, WA 99251-0001. Offers administration (M Ed); counseling (M Ed), including school counselors, social agency/church setting; elementary education (M Ed); gifted and talented (MAT); secondary education (M Ed); special education (MAT); teaching (MIT). *Accreditation:* NCATE. Part-time and evening/weekend programs available. *Degree requirements:* For master's, comprehensive exam, thesis (for some programs). *Entrance requirements:* For master's, GRE General Test, MAT. Additional exam requirements/recommendations for international students: Required—TOEFL. Tuition and fees vary according to program. *Faculty research:* Rural program development, mainstreaming, special needs learners.

Wichita State University, Graduate School, College of Education, Wichita, KS 67260. Offers M Ed, MAT, Ed D, Ed S. *Accreditation:* NCATE. Part-time and evening/weekend programs available. *Expenses:* Tuition, state resident: full-time $4746; part-time $263.65 per credit. Tuition, nonresident: full-time $11,669; part-time $648.30 per credit. *Unit head:* Dr. Pearl Sharon Iorio, Dean, 316-978-3301, Fax: 316-978-3302, E-mail: sharon.iorio@wichita.edu. *Application contact:* Carrie C. Henderson, Admissions Coordinator, 316-978-3095, Fax: 316-978-3253, E-mail: carrie.henderson@wichita.edu. Web site: http://www.wichita.edu/.

Widener University, School of Human Service Professions, Center for Education, Chester, PA 19013-5792. Offers adult education (M Ed); counseling in higher education (M Ed); counselor education (M Ed); early childhood education (M Ed); educational foundations (M Ed); educational leadership (M Ed); educational psychology (M Ed); elementary education (M Ed); English and language arts (M Ed); health education (M Ed); higher education leadership (Ed D); home and school visitor (M Ed); human sexuality (M Ed, PhD); mathematics education (M Ed); middle school education (M Ed); principalship (M Ed); reading and language arts (Ed D); reading education (M Ed); school administration (Ed D); science education (M Ed); social studies education (M Ed); special education (M Ed); technology education (M Ed). *Accreditation:* NCATE. Part-time and evening/weekend programs available. Terminal master's awarded for partial completion of doctoral program. *Degree requirements:* For doctorate, thesis/dissertation. *Entrance requirements:* For master's, minimum GPA of 2.5; for doctorate, GRE or MAT, minimum GPA of 2.0 (undergraduate), 3.5 (graduate). Electronic applications accepted. *Expenses:* Contact institution. *Faculty research:* Reading and cognition, adult education, technology education, educational leadership, special education.

Wilkes University, College of Graduate and Professional Studies, School of Education, Wilkes-Barre, PA 18766-0002. Offers art and science of teaching (MS Ed); classroom technology (MS Ed); early childhood literacy (MS Ed); educational computing (MS Ed); educational development and strategies (MS Ed); educational leadership (MS Ed); educational technology (Ed D); higher education administration (Ed D); instructional media (MS Ed); instructional technology (MS Ed); K-12 administration (Ed D); online teaching (MS Ed); reading (MS Ed); school business leadership (MS Ed); secondary education (MS Ed), including biology, chemistry, English, history, mathematics; special education (MS Ed); teaching English as a second language (MS Ed); twenty-first century teaching and learning (MS Ed). Part-time and evening/weekend programs available. Postbaccalaureate distance learning degree programs offered (minimal on-campus study). *Students:* 92 full-time (63 women), 2,005 part-time (1,459 women); includes 89 minority (23 Black or African American, non-Hispanic/Latino; 1 American Indian or Alaska Native, non-Hispanic/Latino; 14 Asian, non-Hispanic/Latino; 33 Hispanic/Latino; 1 Native Hawaiian or other Pacific Islander, non-Hispanic/Latino; 17 Two or more races, non-Hispanic/Latino), 6 international. Average age 33. In 2011, 1,150 master's, 3 doctorates awarded. *Entrance requirements:* Additional exam requirements/recommendations for international students: Required—TOEFL (minimum score 550 paper-based; 213 computer-based; 79 iBT). *Application deadline:* Applications are processed on a rolling basis. Application fee: $45. Electronic applications accepted. *Expenses:* Contact institution. *Financial support:* Federal Work-Study and unspecified assistantships available. Financial award application deadline: 3/1; financial award applicants required to submit FAFSA. *Unit head:* Dr. Michael Speziale, Dean, 570-408-4679, Fax: 570-408-4905, E-mail: michael.speziale@wilkes.edu. *Application contact:* Erin Sutzko, Director of Extended Learning, 570-408-4253, Fax: 570-408-7846, E-mail: erin.sutzko@wilkes.edu. Web site: http://www.wilkes.edu/pages/383.asp.

Willamette University, Graduate School of Education, Salem, OR 97301-3931. Offers environmental literacy (M Ed); reading (M Ed); special education (M Ed); teaching (MAT). *Accreditation:* NCATE. Evening/weekend programs available. *Degree requirements:* For master's, leadership project (action research). *Entrance requirements:* For master's, California Basic Educational Skills Test, Multiple Subject Assessment for Teachers, PRAXIS, minimum GPA of 3.0, classroom experience, 2 letters of reference. Additional exam requirements/recommendations for international students: Recommended—TOEFL. Electronic applications accepted. *Expenses:* Contact institution. *Faculty research:* Educational leadership, multicultural education, middle school education, clinical supervision, educational technology.

William Carey University, School of Education, Hattiesburg, MS 39401-5499. Offers art education (M Ed); art of teaching (M Ed); elementary education (M Ed, Ed S); English education (M Ed); gifted education (M Ed); history and social science (M Ed); mild/moderate disabilities (M Ed); secondary education (M Ed). Part-time programs available. *Degree requirements:* For master's, comprehensive exam. *Entrance requirements:* For master's, GRE, MAT, minimum GPA of 2.5, Class A teacher's license. Additional exam requirements/recommendations for international students: Required—TOEFL (minimum score 550 paper-based; 213 computer-based).

William Howard Taft University, Graduate Programs, The Boyer Graduate School of Education, Santa Ana, CA 92704. Offers M Ed.

William Paterson University of New Jersey, College of Education, Wayne, NJ 07470-8420. Offers curriculum and learning (M Ed); educational leadership (M Ed); reading (M Ed); special education and counseling services (M Ed), including counseling services, special education; teaching (MAT). *Accreditation:* NCATE. Part-time and evening/weekend programs available. *Degree requirements:* For master's, comprehensive exam. *Entrance requirements:* For master's, GRE General Test, MAT, minimum GPA of 2.75, teaching certificate. Electronic applications accepted. *Faculty research:* Urban community service.

Wilmington College, Department of Education, Wilmington, OH 45177. Offers reading (M Ed); special education (M Ed). Part-time programs available. *Degree requirements:* For master's, comprehensive exam. *Entrance requirements:* For master's, GRE or MAT, minimum GPA of 3.0, 2 letters of recommendation. Additional exam requirements/recommendations for international students: Required—TOEFL. *Faculty research:* Reading instruction, special education practices, conflict resolution in the schools, models of higher education for teachers.

Wilmington University, College of Education, New Castle, DE 19720-6491. Offers applied technology in education (M Ed); career and technical education (M Ed); educational leadership (Ed D); elementary and secondary school counseling (M Ed); elementary studies (M Ed); ESOL literacy (M Ed); higher education leadership (Ed D); instruction: gifted and talented (M Ed); instruction: teacher of reading (M Ed); instruction: teaching and learning (M Ed); organizational leadership (Ed D); school leadership (M Ed); secondary education (MAT); special education (M Ed). *Accreditation:* NCATE. Part-time and evening/weekend programs available. *Faculty:* 7 full-time (4 women). *Students:* 638 full-time (425 women), 2,014 part-time (1,635 women). Average age 33. *Entrance requirements:* For master's, 2 letters of recommendation, interview. Additional exam requirements/recommendations for international students: Required—TOEFL (minimum score 500 paper-based; 173 computer-based). *Application deadline:* For fall admission, 4/30 for domestic students. Applications are processed on a rolling basis. Application fee: $35. Electronic applications accepted. *Expenses: Tuition:* Part-time $534 per credit hour. *Required fees:* $25 per term. *Financial support:* Applicants required to submit FAFSA. *Unit head:* Dr. John C. Gray, Dean, 302-295-1139. *Application contact:* Chris Ferguson, Director of Admissions, 302-356-4636 Ext. 256, Fax: 302-328-5164, E-mail: inquire@wilmcoll.edu. Web site: http://www.wilmu.edu/education/.

Wilson College, Program in Education, Chambersburg, PA 17201-1285. Offers M Ed. Evening/weekend programs available. *Degree requirements:* For master's, project. *Entrance requirements:* For master's, PRAXIS, minimum undergraduate cumulative GPA of 3.0, 2 letters of recommendation, current certification for eligibility to teach in grades K-12, resume, personal interview. Electronic applications accepted.

Wingate University, Thayer School of Education, Wingate, NC 28174-0159. Offers community college leadership (Ed D); educational leadership (MA Ed, Ed D); elementary education (MA Ed, MAT); health and physical education (MA Ed); sport administration (MA Ed). *Accreditation:* NCATE. Part-time and evening/weekend programs available. *Faculty:* 5 full-time (3 women), 10 part-time/adjunct (3 women). *Students:* 7 full-time (4 women), 251 part-time (152 women); includes 68 minority (63 Black or African American, non-Hispanic/Latino; 1 American Indian or Alaska Native, non-Hispanic/Latino; 1 Asian, non-Hispanic/Latino; 3 Hispanic/Latino), 2 international. Average age 35. In 2011, 29 master's awarded. *Degree requirements:* For master's, portfolio. *Entrance requirements:* For master's, GRE General Test or MAT, teaching certificate (MA Ed). *Application deadline:* For fall admission, 8/15 priority date for domestic students; for spring admission, 12/15 for domestic students. Applications are processed on a rolling basis. Application fee: $0. *Expenses: Tuition:* Part-time $455 per credit hour. Part-time tuition and fees vary according to degree level and program. *Financial support:* In 2011–12, 20 students received support. Scholarships/grants available. Support available to part-time students. Financial award applicants required to submit FAFSA. *Unit head:* Dr. Sarah Harrison-Burns, Dean, 704-233-8128, E-mail: shburns@wingate.edu. *Application contact:* Theresa Hopkins, Secretary, 704-321-1470, Fax: 704-233-8273, E-mail: t.hopkins@wingate.edu.

Winona State University, College of Education, Department of Education, Winona, MN 55987. Offers MS. *Accreditation:* NCATE. Part-time and evening/weekend programs available. *Students:* 33 full-time (19 women), 4 part-time (2 women), 1 international. Average age 28. In 2011, 26 master's awarded. *Degree requirements:* For master's, comprehensive exam, thesis (for some programs). *Entrance requirements:* For master's, minimum GPA of 2.75/teaching license. *Application deadline:* For fall admission, 9/1 priority date for domestic students; for spring admission, 1/1 priority date for domestic students. Applications are processed on a rolling basis. Application fee: $20. *Financial support:* Teaching assistantships and unspecified assistantships available. Financial award applicants required to submit FAFSA. *Unit head:* Dr. Melanie Reap, Chairperson, 507-457-2449, E-mail: mreap@winona.edu. *Application contact:* Sandra K. Hunter, Administrative Assistant, 507-457-5360, Fax: 507-457-5354, E-mail: shunter@winona.edu.

Winthrop University, College of Education, Rock Hill, SC 29733. Offers M Ed, MAT, MS. *Accreditation:* NCATE. Part-time programs available. *Entrance requirements:* Additional exam requirements/recommendations for international students: Required—TOEFL (minimum paper-based score of 520, computer-based 190, iBT 68) or IELTS (minimum score of 6). Electronic applications accepted.

Wittenberg University, Graduate Program, Springfield, OH 45501-0720. Offers education (MA). *Accreditation:* NCATE.

Worcester State University, Graduate Studies, Department of Education, Worcester, MA 01602-2597. Offers early childhood education (M Ed); elementary education (M Ed); health education (M Ed); leadership and administration (M Ed, CAGS); middle school education (M Ed, Postbaccalaureate Certificate); moderate special needs (M Ed, Postbaccalaureate Certificate); reading (M Ed, CAGS); school psychology (CAGS); secondary education (M Ed). Part-time and evening/weekend programs available. *Faculty:* 12 full-time (9 women), 22 part-time/adjunct (10 women). *Students:* 29 full-time (26 women), 261 part-time (184 women); includes 19 minority (4 Black or African American, non-Hispanic/Latino; 1 Asian, non-Hispanic/Latino; 9 Hispanic/Latino; 5 Two or more races, non-Hispanic/Latino), 1 international. Average age 34. 302 applicants, 73% accepted, 108 enrolled. In 2011, 78 master's, 154 CAGSs awarded. *Degree requirements:* For master's, comprehensive exam (for some programs), thesis optional. *Entrance requirements:* For master's, GRE General Test, MAT or GMAT, teaching certificate. Additional exam requirements/recommendations for international students: Required—TOEFL (minimum score 500 paper-based; 61 iBT). *Application deadline:* For fall admission, 6/15 for domestic and international students; for spring admission, 4/1 for domestic and international students. Applications are processed on a rolling basis. Application fee: $40. Electronic applications accepted. *Expenses:* Tuition, state resident: full-time $2700; part-time $150 per credit. Tuition, nonresident: full-time $2700; part-time $150 per credit. *Required fees:* $2016; $112 per credit. *Financial support:* In 2011–12, 4 students received support, including 4 research assistantships with full tuition reimbursements available (averaging $4,800 per year); career-related internships or fieldwork, scholarships/grants, and unspecified assistantships also available. Financial award application deadline: 3/1; financial award applicants required to submit FAFSA. *Unit head:* Dr. Elaine Tateronis, Coordinator, 508-929-8823, Fax: 508-929-8164, E-mail: etateronis@worcester.edu. *Application contact:* Sara Grady, Assistant Dean of Graduate and Continuing Education, 508-929-8787, Fax: 508-929-8100, E-mail: sara.grady@worcester.edu.

Wright State University, School of Graduate Studies, College of Education and Human Services, Dayton, OH 45435. Offers M Ed, MA, MRC, MS, MST, Ed S. *Accreditation:* NCATE. Part-time and evening/weekend programs available. *Degree requirements:* For Ed S, thesis. *Entrance requirements:* For master's, GRE General Test, MAT, PRAXIS II; for Ed S, GRE General Test, MAT. Additional exam requirements/recommendations for international students: Required—TOEFL.

Xavier University, College of Social Sciences, Health and Education, School of Education, Cincinnati, OH 45207. Offers M Ed, MA, MS. *Accreditation:* Teacher Education Accreditation Council. *Faculty:* 25 full-time (12 women), 60 part-time/adjunct (31 women). *Students:* 292 full-time (213 women), 487 part-time (363 women); includes 104 minority (74 Black or African American, non-Hispanic/Latino; 2 American Indian or Alaska Native, non-Hispanic/Latino; 14 Asian, non-Hispanic/Latino; 12 Hispanic/Latino; 2 Two or more races, non-Hispanic/Latino), 5 international. Average age 33. 177 applicants, 92% accepted, 125 enrolled. In 2011, 317 master's awarded. *Entrance requirements:* Additional exam requirements/recommendations for international students: Required—TOEFL (minimum score 550 paper-based; 213 computer-based; 79 iBT). *Application deadline:* Applications are processed on a rolling basis. Application fee: $35. Electronic applications accepted. *Expenses: Tuition:* Part-time $576 per credit hour. *Financial support:* In 2011–12, 454 students received support. Applicants required to submit FAFSA. *Faculty research:* Early childhood literacy, service-learning, family resiliency/special needs families, technology integration, leadership theory, Montessori methodology. *Unit head:* Dr. Mark Meyers, Dean of Social Sciences, Health, and Education, 513-745-3119, Fax: 513-745-1048, E-mail: meyersd3@xavier.edu. *Application contact:* Roger Bosse, Graduate Services Director, 513-745-3357, Fax: 513-745-1048, E-mail: bosse@xavier.edu. Web site: http://www.xavier.edu/education/.

Xavier University of Louisiana, Graduate School, Programs in Education, New Orleans, LA 70125-1098. Offers curriculum and instruction (MA); education administration and supervision (MA); guidance and counseling (MA). *Accreditation:* NCATE. Part-time and evening/weekend programs available. *Degree requirements:* For master's, comprehensive exam, thesis or alternative. *Entrance requirements:* For master's, GRE General Test, MAT, minimum GPA of 2.5. Additional exam requirements/recommendations for international students: Required—TOEFL.

York College of Pennsylvania, Department of Education, York, PA 17405-7199. Offers educational leadership (M Ed); reading specialist (M Ed). Part-time and evening/weekend programs available. *Faculty:* 3 full-time (2 women), 4 part-time/adjunct (2 women). *Students:* 82 part-time (65 women). 10 applicants, 60% accepted, 5 enrolled. In 2011, 17 master's awarded. *Degree requirements:* For master's, comprehensive exam, thesis optional, portfolio. *Entrance requirements:* For master's, GRE, MAT or PRAXIS, letters of recommendation, portfolio. *Application deadline:* For fall admission, 7/15 priority date for domestic students; for spring admission, 11/15 priority date for domestic students. Applications are processed on a rolling basis. Application fee: $50. Electronic applications accepted. *Expenses: Tuition:* Full-time $12,060; part-time $670 per credit hour. *Required fees:* $340 per semester. Tuition and fees vary according to degree level. *Faculty research:* Mentoring, principal development, principal retention. *Unit head:* Dr. Philip Monteith, Director, 717-815-6406, E-mail: med@ycp.edu. *Application contact:* Irene Z. Altland, Administrative Assistant, 717-815-6406, Fax: 717-849-1629, E-mail: med@ycp.edu. Web site: http://www.ycp.edu/academics/academic-departments/education/.

York University, Faculty of Graduate Studies, Faculty of Education, Toronto, ON M3J 1P3, Canada. Offers M Ed, PhD. Part-time programs available. *Degree requirements:* For master's, thesis or alternative; for doctorate, comprehensive exam, thesis/dissertation. Electronic applications accepted.

Youngstown State University, Graduate School, Beeghly College of Education, Youngstown, OH 44555-0001. Offers MS Ed, Ed D. *Accreditation:* NCATE. Part-time and evening/weekend programs available. *Degree requirements:* For master's, comprehensive exam; for doctorate, comprehensive exam, thesis/dissertation. *Entrance requirements:* For master's, minimum GPA of 2.7; for doctorate, GRE General Test, GRE Subject Test, interview, minimum GPA of 3.5. Additional exam requirements/recommendations for international students: Required—TOEFL. *Faculty research:* Euthanasia, psychometrics, ethical issues, community relations, educational law.

ADELPHI UNIVERSITY

Ruth S. Ammon School of Education

Programs of Study

The Ruth S. Ammon School of Education at Adelphi University offers a comprehensive array of graduate programs in three departments: curriculum and instruction; communication sciences and disorders; and exercise science, health studies, physical education, and sport management. Dedicated faculty members, mentoring programs, flexible scheduling, convenient off-campus centers in Hauppauge and Manhattan, extensive partnerships with community school districts and healthcare institutions, and a Professional Development Initiative help candidates achieve their academic and professional goals.

The Department of Curriculum and Instruction offers in-service and precertification degree programs in the Master of Arts and Post-Master's Certificate in Early Childhood Education; the Master of Science and Post-Master's Certificate in Early Childhood Special Education; the Master of Arts in Childhood Education; the Master of Science and Post-Master's Certificate in Childhood Special Education; the Master of Science in Bilingual Childhood Special Education; the Master of Arts in Adolescent Education (science, English, mathematics, and social studies); the Master of Science in Adolescent Special Education; the Master of Science in Literacy; the Master of Arts in Art Education; the Master of Arts and Post-Master's Certificate in TESOL; the Master of Arts and Post-Master's Certificate in Educational Leadership; the Master of Arts and Post-Master's Certificate in Educational Technology; the Post-Master's Certificate in Bilingual Education for Certified Teachers; and the Post-Master's Certificate in Bilingual Certification Extension for School Social Work.

The Department of Exercise Science, Health Studies, Physical Education, and Sport Management offers the Master of Science in Exercise Science; the Master of Science in Sport Management; the Master of Arts in Health Education; the Master of Arts and Graduate Certificate in Physical Education; and the Master of Arts and Post-Master's Certificate in Community Health Promotion.

The Department of Communication Sciences and Disorders offers the Master of Science in Speech-Language Pathology; the Master of Science in TSSLD; the Post-Master's Certificate in Bilingual Education for TSSLD-Certified Teachers; the Doctor of Philosophy in Speech-Language Pathology; and the Doctor of Audiology.

The Ammon School of Education prepares teachers to make a difference. Many of the distinguished faculty members are leaders in their fields. They share their passion for teaching in an environment that fosters creativity and excellence. Students have the opportunity to collaborate on faculty research and presentations at national and international conferences. Adelphi students engage in meaningful partnerships with local schools and service organizations. Through established mentoring programs, students learn from master teachers and clinical experts who set the standards for best practices in teaching. Students get invaluable firsthand experience with mentors and clinicians in community-based service programs.

Research Facilities

The University's primary research holdings are at Swirbul Library and include 600,000 volumes (including bound periodicals and government publications), 806,000 items in microformats, 33,000 audiovisual items, and online access to more than 61,000 electronic journal titles and 221 research databases.

Research, laboratory and clinical programs and facilities are offered in all departments of the Ammon School of Education. The Hy Weinberg Center, dedicated to research in communication disorders and clinical and therapeutic services, is equipped with state-of-the-art clinical audiometric instrumentation, as well as speech and hearing laboratories for the objective measurement of important parameters of speech and voice. Research conducted in the Human Performance Laboratory is showcased at the Annual Student Research Symposium. Its facilities include a multiple 12-lead ECG/exercise stress system, hydrostatic weighing, pulmonary-function testing, Cybex isokinetic muscle testing, an adult fitness and cardiopulmonary rehabilitation program, DEXA, and POLAR Heart Rate Training Center. The Center for Literacy and Learning offers a practicum in assessing and addressing literacy needs, and the new Alice Brown Early Learning Center provides field experience in child development and early childhood curriculum.

Financial Aid

Adelphi University offers financial aid counseling, federal and state aid programs, and scholarship and fellowship programs that include a limited number of graduate assistantships. Programs include the Federal Direct Stafford Loan; Federal Work-Study Program; Adelphi's Pathways to Teaching, scholarships for students seeking teacher certification in secondary mathematics and science that are funded by a grant from the U.S. Department of Education; Project BEST: Bilingual Educators in Science Technology for qualified bilingual candidates seeking a career in science education; SEA (Science Education Advancement) a program for graduate science education students; the New York State Tuition Assistance Program (TAP); New York State Scholarship Programs; Vietnam and Persian Gulf Veterans Tuition Awards; and Regents Professional Opportunity Scholarships. Students with outstanding undergraduate or graduate records in education can apply for paid graduate internships in adolescent education.

Cost of Study

For the 2012–13 academic year, the tuition rate is $965 per credit. University fees range from $315 to $550 per semester.

Living and Housing Costs

Living and housing costs vary considerably depending on personal circumstances. Most graduate students in the Ammon School of Education attend on a part-time basis and live off campus in established households. Information on residence hall fees can be found on the University's Web site.

Location

Located in Garden City, New York, 45 minutes from Manhattan and 20 minutes from Queens, Adelphi's 75-acre suburban campus is known for the beauty of its landscape and architecture. The campus is a short walk from the Long Island Rail Road and is convenient to New York's major airports and several major highways. Off-campus centers are located in Manhattan, Hauppauge, and Poughkeepsie.

Adelphi University

The University

Founded in 1896, Adelphi is a fully accredited, private university with nearly 8,000 undergraduate, graduate, and returning-adult students in the arts and sciences, business, clinical psychology, education, nursing, and social work. A visionary in the field of education, the Ammon School seeks to meet the personal needs and professional goals of its students through community partnerships and programs in education, communication disorders, and health sciences.

Applying

Candidates must possess a bachelor's degree from an accredited college or university and present evidence of their academic accomplishment. Admission is competitive, and requirements for specific programs in the Ammon School of Education vary considerably. Applications and admission requirements for specific programs can be found online at http://admissions.adelphi.edu/onlineapp.php.

Correspondence and Information

Ruth S. Ammon School of Education
Harvey Hall
Adelphi University
One South Avenue
Garden City, New York 11530-0701
Phone: 516-877-4100
Fax: 516-877-4097
Web site: http://education.adelphi.edu

Applications and inquiries:
Office of Graduate Admissions
Levermore Hall, Room 114
Adelphi University
One South Avenue
Garden City, New York 11530
Phone: 516-877-3050
800-ADELPHI (toll-free)
Fax: 516-877-3039
E-mail: graduateadmissions@adelphi.edu
Web site: http://admissions.adelphi.edu/graduate

Adelphi's campus is located in historic Garden City, Long Island, New York.

A registered arboretum, Adelphi is truly a green campus.

THE FACULTY

Full-time faculty members in the Ammon School of Education number more than 60 individuals in three departments. Prospective students should visit the Web site at http://academics.adelphi.edu/bulletin-index.php or www.adelphi.edu/faculty/profiles for complete faculty member information, including credentials and specific research projects.

Faculty members in the Department of Communication Sciences and Disorders specialize in research pertinent to assessing and developing intervention strategies for speech, language, and hearing disorders.

Faculty members in the Department of Curriculum and Instruction specialize in research pertaining to adolescent, childhood, and early childhood education; art education; bilingual/TESOL education; educational leadership; and special education.

Faculty members in the Department of Exercise Science, Health Studies, Physical Education, and Sport Management specialize in research pertinent to human nutrition, stress reduction, and physical activity for a diverse population in school settings, the community, and the workplace.

ARGOSY UNIVERSITY, CHICAGO

College of Education

Programs of Study

Argosy University, Chicago, offers Master of Arts in Education (M.A.Ed.) degrees in Adult Education and Training, Educational Administration, Higher and Postsecondary Education, Teaching and Learning: ELL/ESL, Teaching and Learning: Reading, and Teaching and Learning: Special Education; Education Specialist (Ed.S.) degrees in Advanced Educational Administration, Initial Educational Administration, and Teaching and Learning; and Doctor of Education (Ed.D.) degrees in Advanced Educational Administration, Community College Executive Leadership, Educational Leadership, Initial Educational Administration, and Teaching and Learning.

The Master of Arts in Education (M.A.Ed.) in Adult Education and Training program is designed for the working professional associated with adult learning, training, or staff development in business, government, or other private or public organizations. The program's goal is to enhance the knowledge and skills in the area of adult learning for employment and other organizational settings. Students will develop core practical and academic skills in analysis, oral and written communication, problem solving, critical thinking, team building, and computer technology, through courses that examine the practical, historical, philosophical, psychological, social, technical, and theoretical aspects of education.

The Master of Arts in Education (M.A.Ed.) in Educational Administration program prepares individuals to serve as school administrators. The program is designed for practicing educators who have already completed a bachelor's degree program from a regionally accredited institution and are seeking administrative credentialing. Based on state requirements, students may be required to complete additional experiences or course work.

The Master of Arts in Education (M.A.Ed.) in Higher and Postsecondary Education program is designed for individuals who seek administrative and other positions in noninstructional units at higher education and postsecondary institutions. Graduates of this program will have enhanced practical skills, knowledge, and experiences as professionals and leaders in universities, colleges, and postsecondary educational institutions. A bachelor's degree is required for admission to this program.

The Master of Arts in Education (M.A.Ed.) in Teaching and Learning: ELL/ESL is a 30-credit-hour degree program intended to prepare educators who work in the P–12 setting as change agents who engage actively in their communities, using appropriate pedagogy and technology to foster the development of global citizens. In addition to the core course requirements, students will complete a four-course sequence to strengthen knowledge and skills when working with students who are classified as English Language Learners (ELL) or English as a Second Language (ESL). This program does not lead to certification or credential endorsement.

The Master of Arts in Education (M.A.Ed.) in Teaching and Learning: Reading is a 30-credit program intended to prepare educators who work in the P–12 setting as change agents who engage actively in their communities, using appropriate pedagogy and technology to foster the development of global citizens. Students enrolled in this program will complete a four-course sequence in reading to strengthen knowledge and skills in this specific area. This program does not lead to certification or credential endorsement.

The Master of Arts in Education (M.A.Ed.) in Teaching and Learning: Special Education is a 30-credit program intended to prepare educators who work in the P–12 setting as change agents who engage actively in their communities, using appropriate pedagogy and technology to foster the development of global citizens. Students enrolled in this program will complete a four-course sequence designed to strengthen knowledge and skills when working with students with special learning needs. This program does not lead to certification or credential endorsement.

The Education Specialist (Ed.S.) in Advanced Educational Administration noncertification program is designed to prepare currently certified or licensed school administrators for advanced positions or increase professional expertise. Students must be practicing educators who have already completed a graduate-level program from a regionally accredited institution and currently hold principal or initial administrative licensure.

The Education Specialist (Ed.S.) in Initial Educational Administration program prepares individuals to serve as school principals and/or building-level administrators. The program is designed for practicing educators who have already completed a graduate level program from a regionally accredited institution or an appropriately certified foreign institution, and are seeking administrative licensure at the initial or K–12 level.

The Education Specialist (Ed.S.) in Teaching and Learning program is designed to prepare educators in P–12 settings as change agents and leaders who engage actively in their communities, using appropriate pedagogy and technology to foster the development of global citizens. This program does not lead to certification or any credential endorsement.

The Doctor of Education (Ed.D.) in Advanced Educational Administration program prepares individuals to serve as school administrators in advanced positions. The program is designed for practicing educators who have already completed a graduate level program from a regionally accredited institution and currently hold principal or initial administrative licensure. Completion of the program results in a terminal degree which includes a specific writing, research, and dissertation sequence.

The Doctor of Education (Ed.D.) in Community College Executive Leadership program is designed for community college administrators who seek to move into senior administrative positions (such as president, vice-president, dean, and director) at community colleges.

The Doctor of Education (Ed.D.) in Educational Leadership noncertification program is designed for students preparing for or advancing their careers as educational leaders in professional positions as school district, regional, state, or national administrators. Students much choose a concentration in either higher education administration or K–12 education.

The Doctor of Education (Ed.D.) in Initial Educational Administration program prepares individuals to serve as school principals and/or building-level administrators. The program is designed for practicing educators who have already completed a graduate-level program from a regionally accredited institution or an appropriately certified foreign institution, and are seeking administrative licensure at the initial or K–12 level. Completion of the program results in a terminal degree which includes a specific writing, research, and dissertation sequence.

The Doctor of Education (Ed.D.) in Teaching and Learning program is designed to prepare educators in P–12 settings to serve as change agents and leaders who engage actively in their communities, using appropriate pedagogy and technology to foster the development of global citizens. This program does not lead to certification or credential endorsement.

Research Facilities

Argosy University libraries provide curriculum support and educational resources, including current text materials, diagnostic training documents, reference materials and databases, journals and dissertations, and major and current titles in program areas. There is an online public-access catalog of library resources available throughout the Argosy University system. Students have remote access to the campus library database, enabling them to study and conduct research at home. Academic databases offer dissertation abstracts, academic journals, and professional periodicals. All library computers are Internet accessible. Software applications include Word, Excel, PowerPoint, SPSS, and various test-scoring programs.

Financial Aid

Financial aid is available to those who qualify. Argosy University, Chicago, offers access to federal and state aid programs, merit-based awards, grants, loans, and a work-study program. As a first step, students should complete the Free Application for Federal Student Aid (FAFSA). Prospective students can apply electronically at http://www.fafsa.ed.gov or at the campus.

Cost of Study

Tuition varies by program. Students should contact Argosy University, Chicago, for tuition information.

Living and Housing Costs

Students typically live in apartments in the metropolitan Chicago area. Living expenses vary according to each student's preferred standard of living, housing, and transportation. The University does not offer or operate student housing. Most of the students are full-time working professionals who live within driving distance of the campus. Several nearby hotels offer special rates for those who commute from long distances. The Admissions Department also maintains a list of housing options, including contact information for University students who wish to share housing. For more information, students should contact the Admissions Department.

Student Group

Admission to Argosy University, Chicago, is selective to ensure a dynamic and engaged student body. It encourages diversity in academic and employment backgrounds and promotes integration of the student body into professional life through established connections with local and national professional associations. Argosy University offers a professionally oriented education with rich opportunities to gain practical experience in class, field placements, and internships. Full-time students and working professionals gain the extensive knowledge and range of skills necessary for effective performance in their chosen fields.

Student Outcomes

Students can register with the University's online career-services system and use select services from a distance, such as degree-specific career e-mail lists, national job posts, and virtual job fairs. Students should contact the University for more information.

Location

Chicago is a city of world-class status and beauty, drawing visitors from around the globe. Argosy University, Chicago, sits in the heart of The Loop, the city's business and entertainment center. Located on the shores of Lake Michigan, Chicago is home to world-champion sports teams, an internationally acclaimed symphony orchestra, renowned architecture, and a variety of history and art museums. Recreational opportunities include hiking and cycling on miles of lakefront trails, golfing, and shopping.

Many educational institutions and agencies in the area provide excellent opportunities for student training. Chicago's business environment includes a broad array of companies, including Boeing and Pepsi America. The commercial banking headquarters of JPMorgan Chase is also located in Chicago.

The University

Argosy University is a private institution with nineteen locations across the nation. Argosy University, Chicago, provides a career resources office, an academic resources center, and extensive information access for research. It offers the resources of a large university, plus the friendliness and personal attention of a small campus. Argosy University, Chicago, is closely associated with the University's Schaumburg, Illinois campus, located 45 minutes from downtown Chicago.

The innovative programs feature dynamic, relevant, and practical curricula delivered in flexible class formats. Students enjoy scheduling options that make it easier to fit school into their busy lives, choosing from day and evening courses, on campus or online. Many students find a combination of class formats to be an ideal way of continuing their education while meeting family and professional demands.

Argosy University is accredited by the Accrediting Commission for Senior Colleges and Universities of the Western Association for Schools and Colleges (985 Atlantic Avenue, Suite 100, Alameda, California, 94501, http://www.wascsenior.org).

Applying

Argosy University, Chicago, accepts students year-round on a rolling admissions basis, depending on availability of required courses. Applications for admission are available online or by contacting the campus.

Correspondence and Information

Argosy University, Chicago
225 North Michigan Avenue, Suite 1300
Chicago, Illinois 60601
United States
Phone: 312-777-7600
800-626-4123 (toll-free)
Fax: 312-777-7748
E-mail: auadmissions@argosy.edu
Web site: http://www.argosy.edu/chicago

THE FACULTY

The Argosy University faculty comprises working professionals who are eager to help students succeed. Members bring real-world experience and the latest practice innovations to the academic setting. The diverse faculty members of the College of Education are widely recognized for contributions to the field. Most hold doctoral degrees. They provide a substantive education that combines comprehensive knowledge with critical skills and practical workplace relevance. Above all, faculty members are committed to their students' personal and professional development.

ARGOSY UNIVERSITY, DALLAS

College of Education

Programs of Study

Argosy University, Dallas, offers the Master of Arts in Education (M.A.Ed.) degrees in Adult Education & Training, Educational Administration, Higher and Postsecondary Education, Teaching and Learning: ELL/ESL, Teaching and Learning: Integrated Concentration, Teaching and Learning: Reading, and Teaching and Learning: Special Education; the Master of Arts (M.A.) in School Psychology; the Doctor of Education (Ed.D.) degrees in Higher and Postsecondary Education and Teaching and Learning; and the Education Specialist (Ed.S.) degree in School Psychology and Teaching and Learning.

The Master of Arts in Education (M.A.Ed.) in Adult Education and Training program is designed for the working professional associated with adult learning, training, or staff development in business, government, or other private or public organizations. The program's goal is to enhance the knowledge and skills in the area of adult learning for employment and other organizational settings. Students will develop core practical and academic skills in analysis, oral and written communication, problem solving, critical thinking, team building, and computer technology, through courses that examine the practical, historical, philosophical, psychological, social, technical, and theoretical aspects of education.

The Master of Arts in Education (M.A.Ed.) in Educational Administration program prepares individuals to serve as school administrators. The program is designed for practicing educators who have already completed a bachelor's degree program from a regionally accredited institution and are seeking administrative credentialing. Based on state requirements, students may be required to complete additional experiences or course work.

The Master of Arts in Education (M.A.Ed.) in Higher and Postsecondary Education program is designed for individuals who seek administrative and other positions in noninstructional units at higher education and postsecondary institutions. Graduates of this program will have enhanced practical skills, knowledge, and experiences as professionals and leaders in universities, colleges, and postsecondary educational institutions. A bachelor's degree is required for admission to this program.

The Master of Arts in Education (M.A.Ed.) in Teaching and Learning: ELL/ESL is a 30-credit-hour degree program intended to prepare educators who work in the P–12 setting as change agents who engage actively in their communities, using appropriate pedagogy and technology to foster the development of global citizens. In addition to the core course requirements, students will complete a four-course sequence to strengthen knowledge and skills when working with students who are classified as English Language Learners (ELL) or English as a Second Language (ESL). This program does not lead to certification or credential endorsement.

The Master of Arts in Education (M.A.Ed.) in Teaching and Learning: Integrated Concentration degree program is intended to prepare educators who work in the P–12 setting as change agents who engage actively in their communities, using appropriate pedagogy and technology to foster the development of global citizens. In addition to the core course requirements, students enrolled in this degree program will complete a four-course sequence designed to strengthen educators' knowledge and skills in order to work more effectively in the current classroom environment. This degree program does not lead to certification or credential endorsement.

The Master of Arts in Education (M.A.Ed.) in Teaching and Learning: Reading is a 30-credit program intended to prepare educators who work in the P–12 setting as change agents who engage actively in their communities, using appropriate pedagogy and technology to foster the development of global citizens. Students enrolled in this program will complete a four-course sequence in reading to strengthen knowledge and skills in this specific area. This program does not lead to certification or credential endorsement.

The Master of Arts in Education (M.A.Ed.) in Teaching and Learning: Special Education is a 30-credit program intended to prepare educators who work in the P–12 setting as change agents who engage actively in their communities, using appropriate pedagogy and technology to foster the development of global citizens. Students enrolled in this program will complete a four-course sequence designed to strengthen knowledge and skills when working with students with special learning needs. This program does not lead to certification or credential endorsement.

The Master of Arts (M.A.) in School Psychology degree program is designed to prepare ethical, responsible and competent school psychologists who are able to serve effectively in a number of professional roles. Students develop core competencies in psychological assessment, intervention, and consultation while working with diverse populations. This 66-credit degree program, based on standards developed by the National Association of School Psychologists (NASP), is designed for those seeking to be certified or licensed as school psychologists within the P–12 environment.

The Doctor of Education (Ed.D.) in Higher and Postsecondary Education program is designed for students to enhance their professional competence as educational leaders, instructors, or consultants in academic affairs, student affairs, or student services divisions within community colleges, technical schools and institutes, and four-year colleges and universities, as well as in government, military, religious, and profit or nonprofit postsecondary educational organizations and divisions. The program offers three concentrations: student affairs and services, teaching and learning, and interdisciplinary studies.

The Doctor of Education (Ed.D.) in Teaching and Learning is designed to prepare educators in P–12 settings to serve as change agents and leaders who engage actively in their communities, using appropriate pedagogy and technology to foster the development of global citizens. This program does not lead to certification or credential endorsement.

The Education Specialist (Ed.S.) in Teaching and Learning program is designed to prepare educators in P–12 settings as change agents and leaders who engage actively in their communities, using appropriate pedagogy and technology to foster the development of global citizens. This program does not lead to certification or any credential endorsement.

Research Facilities

Argosy University libraries provide curriculum support and educational resources, including current text materials, diagnostic training documents, reference materials and databases, journals and dissertations, and major and current titles in program areas. There is an online public-access catalog of library resources available throughout the Argosy University system. Students have remote access to the campus library database, enabling them to study and conduct research at home. Academic databases offer dissertation abstracts, academic journals, and professional periodicals. All library computers are Internet accessible. Software applications include Word, Excel, PowerPoint, SPSS, and various test-scoring programs.

Financial Aid

Financial aid is available to those who qualify. Argosy University, Dallas, offers access to federal and state aid programs, merit-based awards, grants, loans, and a work-study program. As a first step, students should complete the Free Application for Federal Student Aid (FAFSA). Prospective students can apply electronically at http://www.fafsa.ed.gov or at the campus.

Cost of Study

Tuition varies by program. Students should contact Argosy University, Dallas, for tuition information.

Living and Housing Costs

Students typically live in apartments in the metropolitan area. Living expenses vary according to each student's preferred standard of living, housing, and transportation. The University does not offer or operate student housing. Most of the students are full-time working professionals who live within driving distance of the campus. Several nearby hotels offer special rates for those who commute from long distances. The Admissions Department also maintains a list of housing options, including contact information for University students who wish to share housing. For more information, students should contact the Admissions Department.

Student Group

Admission to Argosy University, Dallas, is selective to ensure a dynamic and engaged student body. It encourages diversity in academic and employment backgrounds and promotes integration of the student body into professional life through established connections with local and national professional associations. Argosy University offers a professionally oriented education with rich opportunities to gain practical experience in class, field placements, and internships. Full-time students and working professionals gain the extensive knowledge and range of skills necessary for effective performance in their chosen fields.

Student Outcomes

Students can register with the University's online career-services system and use select services from a distance, such as degree-specific career e-mail lists, national job posts, and virtual job fairs. Students should contact the University for more information.

Location

Argosy University, Dallas, offers a north-central location in Dallas, with easy access to freeways, neighboring colleges and universities, libraries, shops, restaurants, theaters, art museums, and other tourist attractions.

Many educational institutions and agencies in the area provide varied opportunities for student training. The city is home to a broad array of companies, including Lockheed Martin Corporation, Baylor University Medical System, and Southwest Airlines.

The University

Argosy University is a private institution with nineteen locations across the nation. Argosy University, Dallas, provides students with a career resources office, an academic resources center, and extensive information access for research. It offers the resources of a large university, plus the friendliness and personal attention of a small campus.

The innovative programs feature dynamic, relevant, and practical curricula delivered in flexible class formats. Students enjoy scheduling options that make it easier to fit school into their busy lives, choosing from day and evening courses, on campus or online. Many students find a combination of class formats to be an ideal way of continuing their education while meeting family and professional demands.

Argosy University is accredited by the Accrediting Commission for Senior Colleges and Universities of the Western Association for Schools and Colleges (985 Atlantic Avenue, Suite 100, Alameda, California, 94501, http://www.wascsenior.org).

Applying

Argosy University, Dallas, accepts students year-round on a rolling admissions basis, depending on availability of required courses. Applications for admission are available online or by contacting the campus.

Correspondence and Information

Argosy University, Dallas
5001 Lyndon B. Johnson Freeway
Heritage Square
Farmers Branch, Texas 75244
United States
Phone: 214-890-9900
866-954-9900 (toll-free)
Fax: 214-378-8555
E-mail: auadmissions@argosy.edu
Web site: http://www.argosy.edu/dallas

THE FACULTY

The Argosy University faculty comprises working professionals who are eager to help students succeed. Members bring real-world experience and the latest practice innovations to the academic setting. The diverse faculty members of the College of Education are widely recognized for contributions to the field. Most hold doctoral degrees. They provide a substantive education that combines comprehensive knowledge with critical skills and practical workplace relevance. Above all, faculty members are committed to their students' personal and professional development.

ARGOSY UNIVERSITY, DENVER

College of Education

Program of Study

Argosy University, Denver, offers the Master of Arts in Education (M.A.Ed.) degrees in Higher and Postsecondary Education, Teaching and Learning: ELL/ESL, Teaching and Learning: Reading, and Teaching and Learning: Special Education; and the Doctor of Education (Ed.D.) degrees in Higher and Postsecondary Education and Teaching and Learning; and the Education Specialist (Ed.S.) degrees in Higher and Postsecondary Education and Teaching and Learning.

The Master of Arts in Education (M.A.Ed.) in Higher and Postsecondary Education program is designed for individuals who seek administrative and other positions in noninstructional units at higher education and postsecondary institutions. Graduates of this program will have enhanced practical skills, knowledge, and experiences as professionals and leaders in universities, colleges, and postsecondary educational institutions. A bachelor's degree is required for admission to this program.

The Master of Arts in Education (M.A.Ed.) in Teaching and Learning: ELL/ESL is a 30-credit-hour degree program intended to prepare educators who work in the P–12 setting as change agents who engage actively in their communities, using appropriate pedagogy and technology to foster the development of global citizens. In addition to the core course requirements, students will complete a four-course sequence to strengthen knowledge and skills when working with students who are classified as English Language Learners (ELL) or English as a Second Language (ESL). This program does not lead to certification or credential endorsement.

The Master of Arts in Education (M.A.Ed.) in Teaching and Learning: Reading is a 30-credit program intended to prepare educators who work in the P–12 setting as change agents who engage actively in their communities, using appropriate pedagogy and technology to foster the development of global citizens. Students enrolled in this program will complete a four-course sequence in reading to strengthen knowledge and skills in this specific area. This program does not lead to certification or credential endorsement.

The Master of Arts in Education (M.A.Ed.) in Teaching and Learning: Special Education is a 30-credit program intended to prepare educators who work in the P–12 setting as change agents who engage actively in their communities, using appropriate pedagogy and technology to foster the development of global citizens. Students enrolled in this program will complete a four-course sequence designed to strengthen knowledge and skills when working with students with special learning needs. This program does not lead to certification or credential endorsement.

The Doctor of Education (Ed.D.) in Higher and Postsecondary Education program is designed for students to enhance their professional competence as educational leaders, instructors, or consultants in academic affairs, student affairs, or student services divisions within community colleges, technical schools and institutes, and four-year colleges and universities, as well as in government, military, religious, and profit or nonprofit postsecondary educational organizations and divisions. The program offers three concentrations: student affairs and services, teaching and learning, and interdisciplinary studies.

The Doctor of Education (Ed.D.) in Teaching and Learning is designed to prepare educators in P–12 settings to serve as change agents and leaders who engage actively in their communities, using appropriate pedagogy and technology to foster the development of global citizens. This program does not lead to certification or credential endorsement.

The Education Specialist (Ed.S.) in Higher and Postsecondary Education program is designed for students to enhance their professional competence as educational leaders, instructors, or consultants in academic affairs, student affairs, or student services divisions within community colleges, technical schools and institutes, four-year colleges and universities, as well as in government, military, religious, profit or nonprofit postsecondary educational organizations and divisions. The program offers three concentrations: student affairs and services, teaching and learning, and interdisciplinary studies.

The Education Specialist (Ed.S.) in Teaching and Learning program is designed to prepare educators in P–12 settings as change agents and leaders who engage actively in their communities, using appropriate pedagogy and technology to foster the development of global citizens. This program does not lead to certification or any credential endorsement.

Research Facilities

Argosy University libraries provide curriculum support and educational resources, including current text materials, diagnostic training documents, reference materials and databases, journals and dissertations, and major and current titles in program areas. There is an online public access catalog of library resources available throughout the Argosy University system. Students have remote access to the campus library database, enabling them to study and conduct research at home. Academic databases offer dissertation abstracts, academic journals, and professional periodicals. All library computers are Internet accessible. Software applications include Word, Excel, PowerPoint, SPSS, and various test-scoring programs.

Financial Aid

Financial aid is available to those who qualify. Argosy University, Denver, offers access to federal and state aid programs, merit-based awards, grants, loans, and a work-study program. As a first step, students should complete the Free Application for Federal Student Aid (FAFSA). Prospective students can apply electronically at http://www.fafsa.ed.gov or at the campus.

Cost of Study

Tuition varies by program. Students should contact Argosy University, Denver, for tuition information.

Argosy University, Denver

Living and Housing Costs

Students typically live in apartments in the metropolitan Denver area. Living expenses vary according to each student's preferred standard of living, housing, and transportation. The University does not offer or operate student housing. Most of the students are full-time working professionals who live within driving distance of the campus. Several nearby hotels offer special rates for those who commute from long distances. The Admissions Department also maintains a list of housing options, including contact information for University students who wish to share housing. For more information, students should contact the Admissions Department.

Student Group

Admission to Argosy University, Denver, is selective to ensure a dynamic and engaged student body. The University encourages diversity in academic and employment backgrounds and promotes integration of the student body into professional life through established connections with local and national professional associations. Argosy University offers a professionally oriented education with rich opportunities to gain practical experience in class, field placements, and internships. Full-time students and working professionals gain the extensive knowledge and range of skills necessary for effective performance in their chosen fields.

Student Outcomes

Students can register with the University's online career-services system and use select services from a distance, such as degree-specific career e-mail lists, national job posts, and virtual job fairs. Students should contact the University for more information.

Location

Argosy University, Denver, is conveniently located at 7600 East Eastman Avenue in Denver, Colorado. The campus is close to a variety of local libraries, shops, restaurants, theaters, and art museums. Denver's thriving professional organizations, major corporations, high-tech companies, hospitals, schools, clinics, and social service agencies can also provide varied training opportunities for students.

The University

Argosy University is a private institution with nineteen locations across the nation. Argosy University, Denver, provides students with a network of resources found at larger universities and the friendliness and personal attention of a small campus.

The innovative programs feature dynamic, relevant, and practical curricula delivered in flexible class formats. Students enjoy scheduling options that make it easier to fit school into their busy lives, choosing from day and evening courses, on campus or online. Many students find a combination of class formats to be an ideal way of continuing their education while meeting family and professional demands.

Argosy University is accredited by the Accrediting Commission for Senior Colleges and Universities of the Western Association for Schools and Colleges (985 Atlantic Avenue, Suite 100, Alameda, California, 94501, http://www.wascsenior.org).

Applying

Argosy University, Denver, accepts students year-round on a rolling admissions basis, depending on availability of required courses. Applications for admission are available online or by contacting the campus.

Correspondence and Information

Argosy University, Denver
7600 East Eastman Avenue
Denver, Colorado 80231
United States
Phone: 303-923-4110
866-431-5981 (toll-free)
Fax: 303-923-4111
E-mail: auadmissions@argosy.edu
Web site: http://www.argosy.edu/denver

THE FACULTY

The Argosy University faculty comprises working professionals who are eager to help students succeed. Members bring real-world experience and the latest practice innovations to the academic setting. The diverse faculty members of the College of Education are widely recognized for contributions to the field. Most hold doctoral degrees. They provide a substantive education that combines comprehensive knowledge with critical skills and practical workplace relevance. Above all, faculty members are committed to their students' personal and professional development.

ARGOSY UNIVERSITY, HAWAI'I

College of Education

Program of Study

Argosy University, Hawai'i, offers the Master of Arts in Education (M.A.Ed.) degrees Educational Administration, Higher and Postsecondary Education, Teaching and Learning: ELL/ESL, Teaching and Learning: Reading, Teaching and Learning: Special Education; the Doctor of Education (Ed.D.) degrees in Advanced Educational Administration, Higher and Postsecondary Education, Initial Educational Administration, Teacher Leadership and Teaching and Learning; and the Education Specialist (Ed.S.) degrees in Teacher Leadership and Teaching and Learning.

The Master of Arts in Education (M.A.Ed.) in Educational Administration program prepares individuals to serve as school administrators. The program is designed for practicing educators who have already completed a bachelor's degree program from a regionally accredited institution and are seeking administrative credentialing. Based on state requirements, students may be required to complete additional experiences or course work.

The Master of Arts in Education (M.A.Ed.) in Higher and Postsecondary Education program is designed for individuals who seek administrative and other positions in noninstructional units at higher education and postsecondary institutions. Graduates of this program will have enhanced practical skills, knowledge, and experiences as professionals and leaders in universities, colleges, and postsecondary educational institutions. A bachelor's degree is required for admission to this program.

The Master of Arts in Education (M.A.Ed.) in Teaching and Learning: ELL/ESL is a 30-credit-hour degree program intended to prepare educators who work in the P–12 setting as change agents who engage actively in their communities, using appropriate pedagogy and technology to foster the development of global citizens. In addition to the core course requirements, students will complete a four-course sequence to strengthen knowledge and skills when working with students who are classified as English Language Learners (ELL) or English as a Second Language (ESL). This program does not lead to certification or credential endorsement.

The Master of Arts in Education (M.A.Ed.) in Teaching and Learning: Reading is a 30-credit program intended to prepare educators who work in the P–12 setting as change agents who engage actively in their communities, using appropriate pedagogy and technology to foster the development of global citizens. Students enrolled in this program will complete a four-course sequence in reading to strengthen knowledge and skills in this specific area. This program does not lead to certification or credential endorsement.

The Master of Arts in Education (M.A.Ed.) in Teaching and Learning: Special Education is a 30-credit program intended to prepare educators who work in the P–12 setting as change agents who engage actively in their communities, using appropriate pedagogy and technology to foster the development of global citizens. Students enrolled in this program will complete a four-course sequence designed to strengthen knowledge and skills when working with students with special learning needs. This program does not lead to certification or credential endorsement.

The Doctor of Education (Ed.D.) in Advanced Educational Administration program prepares individuals to serve as school administrators in advanced positions. The program is designed for practicing educators who have already completed a graduate level program from a regionally accredited institution and currently hold principal or initial administrative licensure. Completion of the program results in a terminal degree which includes a specific writing, research, and dissertation sequence.

The Doctor of Education (Ed.D.) in Higher and Postsecondary Education program is designed for students to enhance their professional competence as educational leaders, instructors, or consultants in academic affairs, student affairs, or student services divisions within community colleges, technical schools and institutes, and four-year colleges and universities, as well as in government, military, religious, and profit or nonprofit postsecondary educational organizations and divisions. The program offers three concentrations: student affairs and services, teaching and learning, and interdisciplinary studies.

The Doctor of Education (Ed.D.) in Initial Educational Administration program prepares individuals to serve as school principals and/or building-level administrators. The program is designed for practicing educators who have already completed a graduate-level program from a regionally accredited institution or an appropriately certified foreign institution, and are seeking administrative licensure at the initial or K–12 level. Completion of the program results in a terminal degree which includes a specific writing, research, and dissertation sequence.

The Doctor of Education (Ed.D.) in Teacher Leadership degree program is a 60 credit hour program designed for classroom teachers who are looking to expand their content knowledge, develop leadership skills, teach more effectively, and support the professional development of their peers. Candidates in this degree program will have the opportunity to become skillful in building collaborative relationships and learning communities that focus on student learning and support a strong positive climate in the school. Peer mentoring and coaching are modeled and practiced throughout the program in field experiences and the culminating research project. The program culminates in a dissertation related to teacher leadership and is designed to add knowledge to the field of teacher leadership. The Ed.D. in Teacher Leadership degree program does not prepare for or lead to teacher or school administrative certification/ licensure.

The Doctor of Education (Ed.D.) in Teaching and Learning program is designed to prepare educators in P–12 settings to serve as change agents and leaders who engage actively in their communities, using appropriate pedagogy and technology to foster the development of global citizens. This program does not lead to certification or credential endorsement.

The Education Specialist (Ed.S.) in Teacher Leadership degree program is a 33 credit hour program designed for classroom teachers who are looking to expand their content knowledge, develop leadership skills, teach more effectively, and support the professional development of their peers. Candidates in this degree program will have the opportunity to become skillful in building collaborative relationships and learning communities that focus on student learning and support a strong positive climate in the school. Peer mentoring and coaching are modeled and practiced throughout the program in field experiences and the culminating research project. The Ed.S. in Teacher Leadership degree program does not prepare for or lead to teacher or school administrative certification/ licensure.

The Education Specialist (Ed.S.) in Teaching and Learning program is designed to prepare educators in P–12 settings as change agents and leaders who engage actively in their communities, using appropriate pedagogy and technology to foster the development of global citizens. This program does not lead to certification or any credential endorsement.

Argosy University, Hawai'i

Research Facilities

Argosy University libraries provide curriculum support and educational resources, including current text materials, diagnostic training documents, reference materials and databases, journals and dissertations, and major and current titles in program areas. There is an online public-access catalog of library resources available throughout the Argosy University system. Students have remote access to the campus library database, enabling them to study and conduct research at home. Academic databases offer dissertation abstracts, academic journals, and professional periodicals. All library computers are Internet accessible. Software applications include Word, Excel, PowerPoint, SPSS, and various test-scoring programs.

Financial Aid

Financial aid is available to those who qualify. Argosy University, Hawai'i, offers access to federal and state aid programs, merit-based awards, grants, loans, and a work-study program. As a first step, students should complete the Free Application for Federal Student Aid (FAFSA). Prospective students can apply electronically at http://www.fafsa.ed.gov or at the campus.

Cost of Study

Tuition varies by program. Students should contact Argosy University, Hawai'i, for tuition information.

Living and Housing Costs

Students typically live in apartments in the metropolitan Honolulu area. Living expenses vary according to each student's preferred standard of living, housing, and transportation. The University does not offer or operate student housing. Most of the students are full-time working professionals who live within driving distance of the campus. Several nearby hotels offer special rates for those who commute from long distances. The Admissions Department also maintains a list of housing options, including contact information for University students who wish to share housing. For more information, students should contact the Admissions Department.

Student Group

Admission to Argosy University, Hawai'i, is selective to ensure a dynamic and engaged student body. The University encourages diversity in academic and employment backgrounds and promotes integration of the student body into professional life through established connections with local and national professional associations. Argosy University offers a professionally oriented education with rich opportunities to gain practical experience in class, field placements, and internships. Full-time students and working professionals gain the extensive knowledge and range of skills necessary for effective performance in their chosen fields.

Student Outcomes

Students can register with the University's online career-services system and use select services from a distance, such as degree-specific career e-mail lists, national job posts, and virtual job fairs. Students should contact the University for more information.

Location

Argosy University, Hawai'i, is located in downtown Honolulu on Oahu. Additional satellite locations on Maui and in Hilo on the island of Hawaii offer programs to communities on the neighbor islands. These locations connect the campus to Hawaii and to the local and native communities of the Pacific Islands and the Pacific Rim. Students enjoy the cultural and recreational opportunities that these locations provide. University faculty and staff members often work in cooperation with the Hawaiian community to create an educational focus on social issues, human diversity, and programs that make a difference to underserved populations.

Many educational institutions and agencies in the area provide excellent opportunities for student training. Honolulu's business environment includes a broad array of companies. The area's largest employers include Bank of Hawaii, Queens Medical Center, and the U.S. government.

The University

Argosy University is a private institution with nineteen locations across the nation. Argosy University, Hawai'i, provides students with a career resources office, an academic resources center, and extensive information access for research. It offers the resources of a large university, plus the friendliness and personal attention of a small campus.

The innovative programs feature dynamic, relevant, and practical curricula delivered in flexible class formats. Students enjoy scheduling options that make it easier to fit school into their busy lives, choosing from day and evening courses, on campus or online. Many students find a combination of class formats to be an ideal way of continuing their education while meeting family and professional demands.

Argosy University is accredited by the Accrediting Commission for Senior Colleges and Universities of the Western Association for Schools and Colleges (985 Atlantic Avenue, Suite 100, Alameda, California, 94501, http://www.wascsenior.org).

Applying

Argosy University, Hawai'i, accepts students year-round on a rolling admissions basis, depending on availability of required courses. Applications for admission are available online or by contacting the campus.

Correspondence and Information

Argosy University, Hawai'i
1001 Bishop Street, Suite 400
Honolulu, Hawaii 96813
United States
Phone: 808-536-5555
888-323-2777 (toll-free)
Fax: 808-536-5505
E-mail: auadmissions@argosy.edu
Web site: http://www.argosy.edu/hawaii

THE FACULTY

The Argosy University faculty comprises working professionals who are eager to help students succeed. Members bring real-world experience and the latest practice innovations to the academic setting. The diverse faculty members of the College of Education are widely recognized for contributions to the field. Most hold doctoral degrees. They provide a substantive education that combines comprehensive knowledge with critical skills and practical workplace relevance. Above all, faculty members are committed to their students' personal and professional development.

ARGOSY UNIVERSITY, LOS ANGELES

College of Education

Programs of Study

Argosy University, Los Angeles, offers the Master of Arts in Education (M.A.Ed.) degrees in Educational Administration, Higher and Postsecondary Education, Teaching and Learning: ELL/ESL, Teaching and Learning: Reading, and Teaching and Learning: Special Education; the Doctor of Education (Ed.D.) degrees in Higher and Postsecondary Education, Initial Educational Administration, and Teaching and Learning; and Education Specialist (Ed.S.) degrees in Higher and Postsecondary Education and Initial Educational Administration.

The Master of Arts in Education (M.A.Ed.) in Educational Administration program prepares individuals to serve as school administrators. The program is designed for practicing educators who have already completed a bachelor's degree program from a regionally accredited institution and are seeking administrative credentialing. Based on state requirements, students may be required to complete additional experiences or course work.

The Master of Arts in Education (M.A.Ed.) in Higher and Postsecondary Education program is designed for individuals who seek administrative and other positions in noninstructional units at higher education and postsecondary institutions. Graduates of this program will have enhanced practical skills, knowledge, and experiences as professionals and leaders in universities, colleges, and postsecondary educational institutions. A bachelor's degree is required for admission to this program.

The Master of Arts in Education (M.A.Ed.) in Teaching and Learning: ELL/ESL is a 30-credit-hour degree program intended to prepare educators who work in the P–12 setting as change agents who engage actively in their communities, using appropriate pedagogy and technology to foster the development of global citizens. In addition to the core course requirements, students will complete a four-course sequence to strengthen knowledge and skills when working with students who are classified as English Language Learners (ELL) or English as a Second Language (ESL). This program does not lead to certification or credential endorsement.

The Master of Arts in Education (M.A.Ed.) in Teaching and Learning: Reading is a 30-credit program intended to prepare educators who work in the P–12 setting as change agents who engage actively in their communities, using appropriate pedagogy and technology to foster the development of global citizens. Students enrolled in this program will complete a four-course sequence in reading to strengthen knowledge and skills in this specific area. This program does not lead to certification or credential endorsement.

The Master of Arts in Education (M.A.Ed.) in Teaching and Learning: Special Education is a 30-credit program intended to prepare educators who work in the P–12 setting as change agents who engage actively in their communities, using appropriate pedagogy and technology to foster the development of global citizens. Students enrolled in this program will complete a four-course sequence designed to strengthen knowledge and skills when working with students with special learning needs. This program does not lead to certification or credential endorsement.

The Doctor of Education (Ed.D.) in Higher and Postsecondary Education program is designed for students to enhance their professional competence as educational leaders, instructors, or consultants in academic affairs, student affairs, or student services divisions within community colleges, technical schools and institutes, and four-year colleges and universities, as well as in government, military, religious, and profit or nonprofit postsecondary educational organizations and divisions. The program offers three concentrations: student affairs and services, teaching and learning, and interdisciplinary studies.

The Doctor of Education (Ed.D.) in Initial Educational Administration program prepares individuals to serve as school principals and/or building-level administrators. The program is designed for practicing educators who have already completed a graduate-level program from a regionally accredited institution or an appropriately certified foreign institution, and are seeking administrative licensure at the initial or K–12 level. Completion of the program results in a terminal degree which includes a specific writing, research, and dissertation sequence.

The Doctor of Education (Ed.D.) in Teaching and Learning is designed to prepare educators in P–12 settings to serve as change agents and leaders who engage actively in their communities, using appropriate pedagogy and technology to foster the development of global citizens. This program does not lead to certification or credential endorsement.

The Education Specialist (Ed.S.) in Higher and Postsecondary Education program is designed for students to enhance their professional competence as educational leaders, instructors, or consultants in academic affairs, student affairs, or student services divisions within community colleges, technical schools and institutes, four-year colleges and universities, as well as in government, military, religious, profit or nonprofit postsecondary educational organizations and divisions. The program offers three concentrations: student affairs and services, teaching and learning, and interdisciplinary studies.

The Education Specialist (Ed.S.) in Initial Educational Administration program prepares individuals to serve as school administrators. The program is designed for practicing educators who have already completed a master's degree program from a regionally accredited institution and are seeking administrative credentialing. Based on state requirements, students may be required to complete additional experiences or course work.

Research Facilities

Argosy University libraries provide curriculum support and educational resources, including current text materials, diagnostic training documents, reference materials and databases, journals and dissertations, and major and current titles in program areas. There is an online public-access catalog of library resources available throughout the Argosy University system. Students have remote access to the campus library database, enabling them to study and conduct research at home.

Argosy University, Los Angeles

Academic databases offer dissertation abstracts, academic journals, and professional periodicals. All library computers are Internet accessible. Software applications include Word, Excel, PowerPoint, SPSS, and various test-scoring programs.

Financial Aid

Financial aid is available to those who qualify. Argosy University, Los Angeles, offers access to federal and state aid programs, merit-based awards, grants, loans, and a work-study program. As a first step, students should complete the Free Application for Federal Student Aid (FAFSA). Prospective students can apply electronically at http://www.fafsa.ed.gov or at the campus.

Cost of Study

Tuition varies by program. Students should contact Argosy University, Los Angeles, for tuition information.

Living and Housing Costs

Students typically live in apartments in the metropolitan Santa Monica area. Living expenses vary according to each student's preferred standard of living, housing, and transportation. The University does not offer or operate student housing. Most of the students are full-time working professionals who live within driving distance of the campus. Several nearby hotels offer special rates for those who commute from long distances. The Admissions Department also maintains a list of housing options, including contact information for University students who wish to share housing. For more information, students should contact the Admissions Department.

Student Group

Admission to Argosy University, Los Angeles, is selective to ensure a dynamic and engaged student body. It encourages diversity in academic and employment backgrounds and promotes integration of the student body into professional life through established connections with local and national professional associations. Argosy University offers a professionally oriented education with rich opportunities to gain practical experience in class, field placements, and internships. Full-time students and working professionals gain the extensive knowledge and range of skills necessary for effective performance in their chosen fields.

Student Outcomes

Students can register with the University's online career-services system and use select services from a distance, such as degree-specific career e-mail lists, national job posts, and virtual job fairs. Students should contact the University for more information.

Location

Argosy University, Los Angeles, is conveniently located near the interchange between I-405 and I-105, just minutes from Los Angeles International Airport and the Pacific coast. The business environment in the Los Angeles metropolitan area features a broad array of companies, including a proliferation of entertainment, technology, and software firms. Among the principal employers in the area are Yahoo!, MTV Networks, RAND Corporation, and Symantec Corporation. The many businesses in the area provide varied opportunities for student training.

The University

Argosy University is a private institution with nineteen locations across the nation. Argosy University, Los Angeles, provides students with a career resources office, an academic resources center, and extensive information access for research. It offers the resources of a large university plus the friendliness and personal attention of a small campus.

The innovative programs feature dynamic, relevant, and practical curricula delivered in flexible class formats. Students enjoy scheduling options that make it easier to fit school into their busy lives, choosing from day and evening courses, on campus or online. Many students find a combination of class formats to be an ideal way of continuing their education while meeting family and professional demands.

Argosy University is accredited by the Accrediting Commission for Senior Colleges and Universities of the Western Association for Schools and Colleges (985 Atlantic Avenue, Suite 100, Alameda, California, 94501, http://www.wascsenior.org).

Applying

Argosy University, Los Angeles, accepts students year-round on a rolling admissions basis, depending on availability of required courses. Applications for admission are available online or by contacting the campus.

Correspondence and Information

Argosy University, Los Angeles
5230 Pacific Concourse, Suite 200
Los Angeles, California 90045
United States
Phone: 310-531-9700
866-505-0332 (toll-free)
Fax: 310-531-9801
E-mail: auadmissions@argosy.edu
Web site: http://www.argosy.edu/losangeles

THE FACULTY

The Argosy University faculty comprises working professionals who are eager to help students succeed. Members bring real-world experience and the latest-practice innovations to the academic setting. The diverse faculty members of the College of Education are widely recognized for contributions to the field. Most hold doctoral degrees. They provide a substantive education that combines comprehensive knowledge with critical skills and practical workplace relevance. Above all, faculty members are committed to their students' personal and professional development.

ARGOSY UNIVERSITY, ORANGE COUNTY

College of Education

Programs of Study

Argosy University, Orange County, offers the Master of Arts in Education (M.A.Ed.) degrees in Educational Administration, Higher and Postsecondary Education, Teaching and Learning: ELL/ESL, Teaching and Learning: Reading, and Teaching and Learning: Special Education; the Doctor of Education (Ed.D.) degrees in Higher and Postsecondary Education, Initial Educational Administration, and Teaching and Learning; and the Education Specialist (Ed.S.) degree in Higher and Postsecondary Education and Initial Educational Administration.

The Master of Arts in Education (M.A.Ed.) in Educational Administration program prepares individuals to serve as school administrators. The program is designed for practicing educators who have already completed a bachelor's degree program from a regionally accredited institution and are seeking administrative credentialing. Based on state requirements, students may be required to complete additional experiences or course work.

The Master of Arts in Education (M.A.Ed.) in Higher and Postsecondary Education program is designed for individuals who seek administrative and other positions in noninstructional units at higher education and postsecondary institutions. Graduates of this program will have enhanced practical skills, knowledge, and experiences as professionals and leaders in universities, colleges, and postsecondary educational institutions. A bachelor's degree is required for admission to this program.

The Master of Arts in Education (M.A.Ed.) in Teaching and Learning: ELL/ESL is a 30-credit-hour degree program intended to prepare educators who work in the P–12 setting as change agents who engage actively in their communities, using appropriate pedagogy and technology to foster the development of global citizens. In addition to the core course requirements, students will complete a four-course sequence to strengthen knowledge and skills when working with students who are classified as English Language Learners (ELL) or English as a Second Language (ESL). This program does not lead to certification or credential endorsement.

The Master of Arts in Education (M.A.Ed.) in Teaching and Learning: Reading is a 30-credit program intended to prepare educators who work in the P–12 setting as change agents who engage actively in their communities, using appropriate pedagogy and technology to foster the development of global citizens. Students enrolled in this program will complete a four-course sequence in reading to strengthen knowledge and skills in this specific area. This program does not lead to certification or credential endorsement.

The Master of Arts in Education (M.A.Ed.) in Teaching and Learning: Special Education is a 30-credit program intended to prepare educators who work in the P–12 setting as change agents who engage actively in their communities, using appropriate pedagogy and technology to foster the development of global citizens. Students enrolled in this program will complete a four-course sequence designed to strengthen knowledge and skills when working with students with special learning needs. This program does not lead to certification or credential endorsement.

The Doctor of Education (Ed.D.) in Higher and Postsecondary Education program is designed for students to enhance their professional competence as educational leaders, instructors, or consultants in academic affairs, student affairs, or student services divisions within community colleges, technical schools and institutes, and four-year colleges and universities, as well as in government, military, religious, and profit or nonprofit postsecondary educational organizations and divisions. The program offers three concentrations: student affairs and services, teaching and learning, and interdisciplinary studies.

The Doctor of Education (Ed.D.) in Initial Educational Administration program prepares individuals to serve as school principals and/or building-level administrators. The program is designed for practicing educators who have already completed a graduate-level program from a regionally accredited institution or an appropriately certified foreign institution, and are seeking administrative licensure at the initial or K–12 level. Completion of the program results in a terminal degree which includes a specific writing, research, and dissertation sequence.

The Doctor of Education (Ed.D.) in Teaching and Learning is designed to prepare educators in P–12 settings to serve as change agents and leaders who engage actively in their communities, using appropriate pedagogy and technology to foster the development of global citizens. This program does not lead to certification or credential endorsement.

The Education Specialist (Ed.S.) in Higher and Postsecondary Education program is designed for students to enhance their professional competence as educational leaders, instructors, or consultants in academic affairs, student affairs, or student services divisions within community colleges, technical schools and institutes, four-year colleges and universities, as well as in government, military, religious, profit or nonprofit postsecondary educational organizations and divisions. The program offers three concentrations: student affairs and services, teaching and learning, and interdisciplinary studies.

The Education Specialist (Ed.S.) in Initial Educational Administration program prepares individuals to serve as school administrators. The program is designed for practicing educators who have already completed a master's degree program from a regionally accredited institution and are seeking administrative credentialing. Based on state requirements, students may be required to complete additional experiences or course work.

Research Facilities

Argosy University libraries provide curriculum support and educational resources, including current text materials, diagnostic training documents, reference materials and databases, journals and dissertations, and major and current titles in program areas. There is an online public-access catalog of library resources available throughout the Argosy University system. Students have remote access to the campus library database, enabling them to study and conduct research at home. Academic databases offer dissertation abstracts, academic journals, and professional periodicals. All library computers are Internet accessible. Software applications include Word, Excel, PowerPoint, SPSS, and various test-scoring programs.

Financial Aid

Financial aid is available to those who qualify. Argosy University, Orange County, offers access to federal and state aid programs, merit-based awards, grants, loans, and a work-study program. As a

Argosy University, Orange County

first step, students should complete the Free Application for Federal Student Aid (FAFSA). Prospective students can apply electronically at http://www.fafsa.ed.gov or at the campus.

Cost of Study

Tuition varies by program. Students should contact Argosy University, Orange County, for tuition information.

Living and Housing Costs

Students typically live in apartments in the metropolitan area. Living expenses vary according to each student's preferred standard of living, housing, and transportation. The University does not offer or operate student housing. Most of the students are full-time working professionals who live within driving distance of the campus. Several nearby hotels offer special rates for those who commute from long distances. The Admissions Department also maintains a list of housing options, including contact information for University students who wish to share housing. For more information, students should contact the Admissions Department.

Student Group

Admission to Argosy University, Orange County, is selective to ensure a dynamic and engaged student body. It encourages diversity in academic and employment backgrounds and promotes integration of the student body into professional life through established connections with local and national professional associations. Argosy University offers a professionally oriented education with rich opportunities to gain practical experience in class, field placements, and internships. Full-time students and working professionals gain the extensive knowledge and range of skills necessary for effective performance in their chosen fields.

Student Outcomes

Students can register with the University's online career-services system and use select services from a distance, such as degree-specific career e-mail lists, national job posts, and virtual job fairs. Students should contact the University for more information.

Location

Argosy University, Orange County, attracts students from Southern California, as well as from around the country and the world. Orange County features a temperate climate, sunny beaches, and a host of cultural and entertainment options. The campus is located approximately 30 miles south of downtown Los Angeles, 90 miles north of San Diego, and just minutes from one of the many freeways that connect the Southern California basin. Regional parks and preserved lands provide opportunities for hiking, biking, riding, and other recreational activities. Whether it's ultrachic Newport Beach, artsy Laguna Beach, or unspoiled Catalina Island, Orange County's ocean-side personalities are as varied as the people who visit the area.

Many educational institutions and agencies in the area provide varied opportunities for student training. Orange County's business environment includes an array of companies. The area's largest employers include Ingram Micro Inc., Orange County Register, ITT Industries, and OneSource.

The University

Argosy University is a private institution with nineteen locations across the nation. Argosy University, Orange County, provides students with a career resources office, an academic resources center, and extensive information access for research. It offers the resources of a large university, plus the friendliness and personal attention of a small campus.

The innovative programs feature dynamic, relevant, and practical curricula delivered in flexible class formats. Students enjoy scheduling options that make it easier to fit school into their busy lives, choosing from day and evening courses, on campus or online. Many students find a combination of class formats to be an ideal way of continuing their education while meeting family and professional demands.

Argosy University is accredited by the Accrediting Commission for Senior Colleges and Universities of the Western Association for Schools and Colleges (985 Atlantic Avenue, Suite 100, Alameda, California, 94501, http://www.wascsenior.org).

Applying

Argosy University, Orange County, accepts students year-round on a rolling admissions basis, depending on availability of required courses. Applications for admission are available online or by contacting the campus.

Correspondence and Information

Argosy University, Orange County
601 South Lewis Street
Orange, California 92868
United States
Phone: 714-620-3700
800-716-9598 (toll-free)
Fax: 714-620-3800
E-mail: auadmissions@argosy.edu
Web site: http://www.argosy.edu/orangecounty/

THE FACULTY

The Argosy University faculty comprises working professionals who are eager to help students succeed. Members bring real-world experience and the latest practice innovations to the academic setting. The diverse faculty members of the College of Education are widely recognized for contributions to the field. Most hold doctoral degrees. They provide a substantive education that combines comprehensive knowledge with critical skills and practical workplace relevance. Above all, faculty members are committed to their students' personal and professional development.

ARGOSY UNIVERSITY, PHOENIX

College of Education

Programs of Study

Argosy University, Phoenix, offers the Master of Arts (M.A.) degree in Education Psychology and School Psychology; the Master of Arts in Education (M.A.Ed.) degrees in Adult Education and Training, Curriculum and Instruction, Curriculum and Instruction: ELL/ESL. Curriculum and Instruction : Reading, Curriculum and Instruction: Special Education, Educational Administration, Higher and Postsecondary Education; the Doctor of Education (Ed.D.) degrees in Advanced Educational Administration, Curriculum and Instruction, Higher and Postsecondary Education, and Initial Educational Administration; the Doctor of Psychology (Psy.D.) degree for Practicing School Psychologists, School Psychology–certification program and School Psychology-Non-certification program; and the Education Specialist (Ed.S.) degrees in Advanced Educational Administration, Curriculum and Instruction, Higher and Postsecondary Education, Initial Educational Administration, and School Psychology.

The Master of Arts (M.A.) in Educational Psychology degree program is the foundational program for those interested in the field of school psychology. Based upon national standards for school psychologists, the curriculum reflects the most current information in the field. In many courses, students observe certified school psychologists at work and practice basic analytical skills under the close supervision.

Through the M.A. in School Psychology program, students develop core competencies in psychological assessment, intervention, and consultation/education, as well as cultural and individual diversity. Successful completion permits students to request a transcript review by the Florida Department of Education for certification as school psychologists in the state of Florida. Students may also apply to become Nationally Certified School Psychologists in a process designed for graduates of non-NASP-approved programs.

In the M.A.Ed. in Adult Education and Training program, students develop core practical and academic skills in analysis, oral and written communication, problem solving, critical thinking, team building, and computer technology through courses that examine the practical, historical, philosophical, psychological, social, technical, and theoretical aspects of education.

The M.A.Ed. in Curriculum and Instruction: ELL/ESL degree program is a 30-credit-hour degree program intended to prepare educators who work in the P–12 setting as change agents who engage actively in their communities, using appropriate pedagogy and technology to foster the development of global citizens. In addition to the core course requirements, students enrolled in this degree program will complete a four course sequence designed to strengthen educators' knowledge and skills when working with students who are classified as English Language Learners (ELL) or English as a Second Language (ESL). This degree program does not lead to certification or credential endorsement.

The M.A.Ed. in Curriculum and Instruction: Reading degree program is a 30 credit hour program intended to prepare educators who work in the P–12 setting as change agents who engage actively in their communities, using appropriate pedagogy and technology to foster the development of global citizens. Students enrolled in this program will complete a four course sequence in reading designed to strengthen educators' knowledge and skills in this specific area of focus. This program does not lead to certification or credential endorsement.

The M.A.Ed. in Curriculum and Instruction: Special Education degree program is a 30 credit hour program intended to prepare educators who work in the P–12 setting as change agents who engage actively in their communities, using appropriate pedagogy and technology to foster the development of global citizens. Students enrolled in this program will complete a four course sequence designed to strengthen educators' knowledge and skills when working with students with special learning needs. This program does not lead to certification or credential endorsement.

The M.A.Ed. in Educational Administration program prepares individuals to serve as school administrators. It is designed for practicing educators who have completed a bachelor's degree program from a regionally accredited institution and are seeking administrative credentialing.

The M.A.Ed. in Higher and Postsecondary Education program is designed for individuals who seek administrative and other positions in noninstructional units at higher education and postsecondary institutions. A bachelor's degree is required for admission to this program.

The Ed.D. in Advanced Educational Administration noncertification program prepares currently certified or licensed school administrators for advanced positions or to increase their professional expertise. The program is for practicing educators who have completed a graduate-level program from a regionally accredited institution and currently hold principal or initial administrative licensure. The program does not lead to certification or licensure for building and district administrative positions.

The Doctor of Education (Ed.D.) in Curriculum and Instruction degree program is designed to prepare educators as change agents and leaders in the P–12 setting who engage actively in their communities, using appropriate pedagogy and technology to foster the development of global citizens. This program does not lead to certification or credential endorsement.

The Ed.D. in Higher and Postsecondary Education program is designed for students to enhance their professional competence as educational leaders, instructors, or consultants in academic affairs, student affairs, or student services divisions. The three concentrations offered are student affairs and services, teaching and learning, and interdisciplinary studies.

The Ed.D. in Initial Educational Administration program prepares individuals to serve as school principals and/or building-level administrators. The program is designed for practicing educators who have completed a graduate-level program from a regionally accredited institution or an appropriately certified foreign institution, and are seeking administrative licensure at the initial or K–12 level. Program completion results in a terminal degree, which includes a specific writing, research, and dissertation sequence.

The Doctor of Psychology (Psy.D.) in for Practicing School Psychologists degree program is designed to respond to the National Association of School Psychology (NASP) recommendation to provide opportunities for doctoral study to practicing school psychologists. Enrollment in this 32 credit hour program is limited to school psychologists who have a minimum five years of experience.

The Psy.D. in School Psychology program prepares students to meet the criteria for state certification as school psychologists and to become nationally certified school psychologists in accordance with criteria developed by the National Association of School Psychologists (NASP). Through direct instruction, assessment, and supervision, students acquire competencies in psychological and educational foundations; cognitive, academic and personality assessment; psychoeducational interventions; statistics and research methodology; research initiatives, practicum experiences; and professional school psychology course work.

The Ed.S. in Advanced Educational Administration noncertification program prepares currently certified or licensed school administrators for advanced positions or increase professional expertise. Students must be practicing educators who have completed a graduate-level program from a regionally accredited institution and currently hold principal or initial administrative licensure. The program does not lead to certification or licensure for building and district administrative positions.

The Education Specialist (Ed.S.) in Curriculum and Instruction degree program is designed to prepare educators as change agents and leaders in the P–12 setting who engage actively in their communities, using appropriate pedagogy and technology to foster the development of global citizens. This program does not lead to certification or any credential endorsement.

The Ed.S. in Higher and Postsecondary Education program is designed for students to enhance their professional competence as educational leaders, instructors, or consultants. The program offers concentrations in student affairs and services, teaching and learning, and interdisciplinary studies.

The Ed.S. in Initial Educational Administration program prepares individuals to serve as school principals and/or building-level administrators. The program is designed for practicing educators who have already completed a graduate level program from a regionally accredited institution or an appropriately certified foreign institution, and are seeking administrative licensure at the initial or K–12 level.

Research Facilities

Argosy University libraries provide curriculum support and educational resources, including current text materials, diagnostic training documents, reference materials and databases, journals and dissertations, and major and current titles in program areas. There is an online public-access catalog of library resources available throughout the Argosy University system. Students have remote access to the campus library database, enabling them to study and conduct research at home. Academic databases offer dissertation abstracts, academic journals, and professional periodicals. All library computers are Internet accessible. Software applications include Word, Excel, PowerPoint, SPSS, and various test-scoring programs.

Financial Aid

Financial aid is available to those who qualify. Argosy University, Phoenix, offers access to federal and state aid programs, merit-based awards, grants, loans, and a work-study program. As a first step, students should complete the Free Application for Federal Student Aid (FAFSA). Prospective students can apply electronically at http://www.fafsa.ed.gov or at the campus.

Cost of Study

Tuition varies by program. Students should contact Argosy University, Phoenix, for tuition information.

Living and Housing Costs

Students typically live in apartments in the metropolitan Phoenix area. Living expenses vary according to each student's preferred standard of living, housing, and transportation. The University does not offer or operate student housing. Most students are full-time working professionals who live within driving distance of the campus. Several nearby hotels offer special rates for those who commute from long distances. The Admissions Department also maintains a list of housing options, including contact information for University students who wish to share housing. For more information, contact the Admissions Department.

Student Group

Admission to Argosy University, Phoenix, is selective to ensure a dynamic and engaged student body. It encourages diversity in academic and employment backgrounds and promotes integration of the student body into professional life through established connections with local and national professional associations. Argosy University offers a professionally oriented education with rich opportunities to gain practical experience in class, field placements, and internships. Full-time students and working professionals gain the extensive knowledge and range of skills necessary for effective performance in their chosen fields.

Student Outcomes

Students can register with the University's online career-services system and use select services from a distance, such as degree-specific career e-mail lists, national job posts, and virtual job fairs.

Location

The Argosy University, Phoenix, campus is located near I-17, close to shops, restaurants, and recreational areas. Phoenix is home to several major-league sports teams, and the city offers an array of cultural activities ranging from opera and theater to science museums. The multicultural environment of Arizona, coupled with the University's professional training affiliations, creates an exciting opportunity for students to work with urban, rural, and culturally diverse populations.

The University

Argosy University is a private institution with nineteen locations across the nation. Argosy University, Phoenix, provides students with a career resources office, an academic resources center, and extensive information access for research. It offers the resources of a large university, plus the friendliness and personal attention of a small campus. The innovative programs feature dynamic, relevant, and practical curricula delivered in flexible class formats. Students enjoy scheduling options that make it easier to fit school into their busy lives, choosing from day and evening courses, on campus or online.

Argosy University is accredited by the Accrediting Commission for Senior Colleges and Universities of the Western Association for Schools and Colleges (985 Atlantic Avenue, Suite 100, Alameda, California, 94501, http://www.wascsenior.org).

Applying

Argosy University, Phoenix, accepts students year-round on a rolling admissions basis, depending on availability of required courses. Applications for admission are available online or by contacting the campus.

Correspondence and Information

Argosy University, Phoenix
2233 West Dunlap Avenue
Phoenix, Arizona 85021
United States
Phone: 602-216-2600
866-216-2777 (toll-free)
Fax: 602-216-3151
E-mail: auadmissions@argosy.edu
Web site: http://argosy.edu/phoenix/

THE FACULTY

The Argosy University faculty comprises working professionals who are eager to help students succeed. Members bring real-world experience and the latest practice innovations to the academic setting. The diverse faculty members of the College of Education are widely recognized for contributions to the field. Most hold doctoral degrees. They provide a substantive education that combines comprehensive knowledge with critical skills and practical workplace relevance. Above all, faculty members are committed to their students' personal and professional development.

ARGOSY UNIVERSITY, SALT LAKE CITY

College of Education

Programs of Study

Argosy University, Salt Lake City, offers the Master of Arts in Education (M.A.Ed.) degrees in Educational Administration, Higher and Postsecondary Education, Teaching and Learning: ELL/ESL, Teaching and Learning: Reading, and Teaching and Learning: Special Education; the Doctor of Education (Ed.D.) degrees in Advanced Educational Administration, Higher and Postsecondary Education, Initial Educational Administration, and Teaching and Learning; and the Education Specialist (Ed.S.) degrees in Advanced Educational Administration, Higher and Postsecondary Education, Initial Educational Administration, and Teaching and Learning.

The Master of Arts in Education (M.A.Ed.) in Educational Administration program prepares individuals to serve as school administrators. The program is designed for practicing educators who have already completed a bachelor's degree program from a regionally accredited institution and are seeking administrative credentialing. Based on state requirements, students may be required to complete additional experiences or course work.

The Master of Arts in Education (M.A.Ed.) in Higher and Postsecondary Education program is designed for individuals who seek administrative and other positions in noninstructional units at higher education and postsecondary institutions. Graduates of this program will have enhanced practical skills, knowledge, and experiences as professionals and leaders in universities, colleges, and postsecondary educational institutions. A bachelor's degree is required for admission to this program.

The Master of Arts in Education (M.A.Ed.) in Teaching and Learning: ELL/ESL is a 30-credit-hour degree program intended to prepare educators who work in the P–12 setting as change agents who engage actively in their communities, using appropriate pedagogy and technology to foster the development of global citizens. In addition to the core course requirements, students will complete a four-course sequence to strengthen knowledge and skills when working with students who are classified as English Language Learners (ELL) or English as a Second Language (ESL). This program does not lead to certification or credential endorsement.

The Master of Arts in Education (M.A.Ed.) in Teaching and Learning: Reading is a 30-credit program intended to prepare educators who work in the P–12 setting as change agents who engage actively in their communities, using appropriate pedagogy and technology to foster the development of global citizens. Students enrolled in this program will complete a four-course sequence in reading to strengthen knowledge and skills in this specific area. This program does not lead to certification or credential endorsement.

The Master of Arts in Education (M.A.Ed.) in Teaching and Learning: Special Education is a 30-credit program intended to prepare educators who work in the P–12 setting as change agents who engage actively in their communities, using appropriate pedagogy and technology to foster the development of global citizens. Students enrolled in this program will complete a four-course sequence designed to strengthen knowledge and skills when working with students with special learning needs. This program does not lead to certification or credential endorsement.

The Doctor of Education (Ed.D.) in Advanced Educational Administration program prepares individuals to serve as school administrators in advanced positions. The program is designed for practicing educators who have already completed a graduate level program from a regionally accredited institution and currently hold principal or initial administrative licensure. Completion of the program results in a terminal degree which includes a specific writing, research, and dissertation sequence.

The Doctor of Education (Ed.D.) in Higher and Postsecondary Education program is designed for students to enhance their professional competence as educational leaders, instructors, or consultants in academic affairs, student affairs, or student services divisions within community colleges, technical schools and institutes, and four-year colleges and universities, as well as in government, military, religious, and profit or nonprofit postsecondary educational organizations and divisions. The program offers three concentrations: student affairs and services, teaching and learning, and interdisciplinary studies.

The Doctor of Education (Ed.D.) in Initial Educational Administration program prepares individuals to serve as school principals and/or building-level administrators. The program is designed for practicing educators who have already completed a graduate-level program from a regionally accredited institution or an appropriately certified foreign institution, and are seeking administrative licensure at the initial or K–12 level. Completion of the program results in a terminal degree which includes a specific writing, research, and dissertation sequence.

The Doctor of Education (Ed.D.) in Teaching and Learning is designed to prepare educators in P–12 settings to serve as change agents and leaders who engage actively in their communities, using appropriate pedagogy and technology to foster the development of global citizens. This program does not lead to certification or credential endorsement.

The Education Specialist (Ed.S.) in Advanced Educational Administration noncertification program is designed to prepare currently certified or licensed school administrators for advanced positions or increase professional expertise. Students must be practicing educators who have already completed a graduate-level program from a regionally accredited institution and currently hold principal or initial administrative licensure.

The Education Specialist (Ed.S.) in Higher and Postsecondary Education program is designed for students to enhance their professional competence as educational leaders, instructors, or consultants in academic affairs, student affairs, or student services divisions within community colleges, technical schools and institutes, four-year colleges and universities, as well as in government, military, religious, profit or nonprofit postsecondary educational organizations and divisions. The program offers three concentrations: student affairs and services, teaching and learning, and interdisciplinary studies.

The Education Specialist (Ed.S.) in Initial Educational Administration program prepares individuals to serve as school principals and/or building-level administrators. The program is designed for practicing educators who have already completed a graduate level program from a regionally accredited institution or an appropriately certified foreign institution, and are seeking administrative licensure at the initial or K–12 level.

The Education Specialist (Ed.S.) in Teaching and Learning program is designed to prepare educators in P–12 settings as change agents and leaders who engage actively in their communities, using appropriate pedagogy and technology to foster the development of global citizens. This program does not lead to certification or any credential endorsement.

Note: These programs do not lead to teacher or administrator certification, licensure, or endorsement in any state in the United States.

Argosy University, Salt Lake City

Research Facilities

Argosy University libraries provide curriculum support and educational resources, including current text materials, diagnostic training documents, reference materials and databases, journals and dissertations, and major and current titles in program areas. There is an online public access catalog of library resources available throughout the Argosy University system. Students have remote access to the campus library database, enabling them to study and conduct research at home. Academic databases offer dissertation abstracts, academic journals, and professional periodicals. All library computers are Internet accessible. Software applications include Word, Excel, PowerPoint, SPSS, and various test-scoring programs.

Financial Aid

Financial aid is available to those who qualify. Argosy University, Salt Lake City, offers access to federal and state aid programs, merit-based awards, grants, loans, and a work-study program. As a first step, students should complete the Free Application for Federal Student Aid (FAFSA). Prospective students can apply electronically at http://www.fafsa.ed.gov or at the campus.

Cost of Study

Tuition varies by program. Students should contact Argosy University, Salt Lake City, for tuition information.

Living and Housing Costs

Students typically live in apartments in the metropolitan Salt Lake City area. Living expenses vary according to each student's preferred standard of living, housing, and transportation. The University does not offer or operate student housing. Most of the students are full-time working professionals who live within driving distance of the campus. Several nearby hotels offer special rates for those who commute from long distances. The Admissions Department also maintains a list of housing options, including contact information for University students who wish to share housing. For more information, students should contact the Admissions Department.

Student Group

Admission to Argosy University, Salt Lake City, is selective to ensure a dynamic and engaged student body. It encourages diversity in academic and employment backgrounds and promotes integration of the student body into professional life through established connections with local and national professional associations. Argosy University offers a professionally oriented education with rich opportunities to gain practical experience in class, field placements, and internships. Full-time students and working professionals gain the extensive knowledge and range of skills necessary for effective performance in their chosen fields.

Student Outcomes

Students can register with the University's online career-services system and use select services from a distance, such as degree-specific career e-mail lists, national job posts, and virtual job fairs. Students should contact the University for more information.

Location

Argosy University, Salt Lake City, offers a high-quality education in an intimate, small-group setting. Argosy University, Salt Lake City, is conveniently located in Draper, Utah, nestled in the Wasatch Mountains about 20 miles south of Salt Lake City. The area's business climate and numerous hospitals, schools, clinics, and social service agencies can provide many exciting training opportunities for students.

The University

Argosy University is a private institution with nineteen locations across the nation. Argosy University, Salt Lake City, provides students with a career resources office, an academic resources center, and extensive information access for research. It offers the resources of a large university, plus the friendliness and personal attention of a small campus.

The innovative programs feature dynamic, relevant, and practical curricula delivered in flexible class formats. Students enjoy scheduling options that make it easier to fit school into their busy lives, choosing from day and evening courses, on campus or online. Many students find a combination of class formats to be an ideal way of continuing their education while meeting family and professional demands.

Argosy University is accredited by the Accrediting Commission for Senior Colleges and Universities of the Western Association for Schools and Colleges (985 Atlantic Avenue, Suite 100, Alameda, California, 94501, http://www.wascsenior.org).

Applying

Argosy University, Salt Lake City, accepts students year-round on a rolling admissions basis, depending on availability of required courses. Applications for admission are available online or by contacting the campus.

Correspondence and Information

Argosy University, Salt Lake City
121 Election Road, Suite 300
Draper, Utah 84020
United States
Phone: 801-601-5000
888-639-4756 (toll-free)
Fax: 801-601-4990
E-mail: auadmissions@argosy.edu
Web site: http://www.argosy.edu/saltlakecity

THE FACULTY

The Argosy University faculty comprises working professionals who are eager to help students succeed. Members bring real-world experience and the latest practice innovations to the academic setting. The diverse faculty members of the College of Education are widely recognized for contributions to their field. Most hold doctoral degrees. They provide a substantive education that combines comprehensive knowledge with critical skills and practical workplace relevance. Above all, faculty members are committed to their students' personal and professional development.

ARGOSY UNIVERSITY, SAN DIEGO

College of Education

Programs of Study

Argosy University, San Diego, offers Master of Arts in Education (M.A.Ed.) degrees in Educational Administration, Higher and Postsecondary Education, Teaching and Learning: ELL/ESL, Teaching and Learning: Reading, and Teaching and Learning: Special Education; Doctor of Education (Ed.D.) degrees in Higher and Postsecondary Education, Initial Educational Administration, and Teaching and Learning; and Education Specialist (Ed.S.) degrees in Higher and Postsecondary Education and Initial Educational Administration.

The Master of Arts in Education (M.A.Ed.) in Educational Administration program prepares individuals to serve as school administrators. The program is designed for practicing educators who have already completed a bachelor's degree program from a regionally accredited institution and are seeking administrative credentialing. Based on state requirements, students may be required to complete additional experiences or course work.

The Master of Arts in Education (M.A.Ed.) in Higher and Postsecondary Education program is designed for individuals who seek administrative and other positions in noninstructional units at higher education and postsecondary institutions. Graduates of this program will have enhanced practical skills, knowledge, and experiences as professionals and leaders in universities, colleges, and postsecondary educational institutions. A bachelor's degree is required for admission to this program.

The Master of Arts in Education (M.A.Ed.) in Teaching and Learning: ELL/ESL is a 30-credit-hour degree program intended to prepare educators who work in the P–12 setting as change agents who engage actively in their communities, using appropriate pedagogy and technology to foster the development of global citizens. In addition to the core course requirements, students will complete a four-course sequence to strengthen knowledge and skills when working with students who are classified as English Language Learners (ELL) or English as a Second Language (ESL). This program does not lead to certification or credential endorsement.

The Master of Arts in Education (M.A.Ed.) in Teaching and Learning: Reading is a 30-credit program intended to prepare educators who work in the P–12 setting as change agents who engage actively in their communities, using appropriate pedagogy and technology to foster the development of global citizens. Students enrolled in this program will complete a four-course sequence in reading to strengthen knowledge and skills in this specific area. This program does not lead to certification or credential endorsement.

The Master of Arts in Education (M.A.Ed.) in Teaching and Learning: Special Education is a 30-credit program intended to prepare educators who work in the P–12 setting as change agents who engage actively in their communities, using appropriate pedagogy and technology to foster the development of global citizens. Students enrolled in this program will complete a four-course sequence designed to strengthen knowledge and skills when working with students with special learning needs. This program does not lead to certification or credential endorsement.

The Doctor of Education (Ed.D.) in Higher and Postsecondary Education program is designed for students to enhance their professional competence as educational leaders, instructors, or consultants in academic affairs, student affairs, or student services divisions within community colleges, technical schools and institutes, and four-year colleges and universities, as well as in government, military, religious, and profit or nonprofit postsecondary educational organizations and divisions. The program offers three concentrations: student affairs and services, teaching and learning, and interdisciplinary studies.

The Doctor of Education (Ed.D.) in Initial Educational Administration program prepares individuals to serve as school principals and/or building-level administrators. The program is designed for practicing educators who have already completed a graduate-level program from a regionally accredited institution or an appropriately certified foreign institution, and are seeking administrative licensure at the initial or K–12 level. Completion of the program results in a terminal degree which includes a specific writing, research, and dissertation sequence.

The Doctor of Education (Ed.D.) in Teaching and Learning is designed to prepare educators in P–12 settings to serve as change agents and leaders who engage actively in their communities, using appropriate pedagogy and technology to foster the development of global citizens. This program does not lead to certification or credential endorsement.

The Education Specialist (Ed.S.) in Higher and Postsecondary Education program is designed for students to enhance their professional competence as educational leaders, instructors, or consultants in academic affairs, student affairs, or student services divisions within community colleges, technical schools and institutes, four-year colleges and universities, as well as in government, military, religious, profit or nonprofit postsecondary educational organizations and divisions. The program offers three concentrations: student affairs and services, teaching and learning, and interdisciplinary studies.

The Education Specialist (Ed.S.) in Initial Educational Administration program prepares individuals to serve as school principals and/or building-level administrators. The program is designed for practicing educators who have already completed a graduate level program from a regionally accredited institution or an appropriately certified foreign institution, and are seeking administrative licensure at the initial or K–12 level.

Note: Programs offered through the College of Education do not lead to teacher or administrator certification, licensure, or endorsement in any state in the United States. The programs offered through Argosy University online programs do not lead to teacher or administrator certification, licensure, or endorsement in any state in the United States regardless of the state in which the student resides.

Research Facilities

Argosy University libraries provide curriculum support and educational resources, including current text materials, diagnostic training documents, reference materials and databases, journals and dissertations, and major and current titles in program areas. There is an online public access catalog of library resources available throughout the Argosy University system. Students have remote access to the campus library database, enabling them to study and conduct research at home. Academic databases offer dissertation abstracts, academic journals, and professional periodicals. All library computers are Internet accessible. Software applications include Word, Excel, PowerPoint, SPSS, and various test-scoring programs.

Argosy University, San Diego

Financial Aid

Financial aid is available to those who qualify. Argosy University, San Diego, offers access to federal and state aid programs, merit-based awards, grants, loans, and a work-study program. As a first step, students should complete the Free Application for Federal Student Aid (FAFSA). Prospective students can apply electronically at http://www.fafsa.ed.gov or at the campus.

Cost of Study

Tuition varies by program. Students should contact Argosy University, San Diego, for tuition information.

Living and Housing Costs

Students typically live in apartments in the metropolitan San Diego area. Living expenses vary according to each student's preferred standard of living, housing, and transportation. The University does not offer or operate student housing. Most of the students are full-time working professionals who live within driving distance of the campus. Several nearby hotels offer special rates for those who commute from long distances. The Admissions Department also maintains a list of housing options, including contact information for University students who wish to share housing. For more information, students should contact the Admissions Department.

Student Group

Admission to Argosy University, San Diego, is selective to ensure a dynamic and engaged student body. It encourages diversity in academic and employment backgrounds and promotes integration of the student body into professional life through established connections with local and national professional associations. Argosy University offers a professionally oriented education with rich opportunities to gain practical experience in class, field placements, and internships. Full-time students and working professionals gain the extensive knowledge and range of skills necessary for effective performance in their chosen fields.

Student Outcomes

Students can register with the University's online career-services system and use select services from a distance, such as degree-specific career e-mail lists, national job posts, and virtual job fairs. Students should contact the University for more information.

Location

San Diego, southern California's second-largest city, offers an ideal climate year-round, 70 miles of beautiful beaches, colorful neighborhoods, and a dynamic downtown district. Argosy University, San Diego, offers classrooms, a library resource center, student lounge, staff and faculty offices, and other amenities. The area offers numerous attractions, including Sea World and the famous San Diego Zoo and Wild Animal Park.

San Diego's business environment includes several Fortune 500 companies such as QUALCOMM and Pfizer, Inc., and a concentration of high-tech companies. Many educational institutions and agencies in the area provide varied opportunities for student training.

The University

Argosy University is a private institution with nineteen locations across the nation. Argosy University, San Diego, provides a career resources office, an academic resources center, and extensive information access for research. It offers the resources of a large university plus the friendliness and personal attention of a small campus.

The innovative programs feature dynamic, relevant, and practical curricula delivered in flexible class formats. Students enjoy scheduling options that make it easier to fit school into their busy lives, choosing from day and evening courses, on campus or online. Many students find a combination of class formats to be an ideal way of continuing their education while meeting family and professional demands.

Argosy University is accredited by the Accrediting Commission for Senior Colleges and Universities of the Western Association for Schools and Colleges (985 Atlantic Avenue, Suite 100, Alameda, California, 94501, http://www.wascsenior.org).

Applying

Argosy University, San Diego, accepts students year-round on a rolling admissions basis, depending on availability of required courses. Applications for admission are available online or by contacting the campus.

Correspondence and Information

Argosy University, San Diego
1615 Murray Canyon Road, Suite 100
San Diego, California 92108
United States
Phone: 619-321-3000
866-505-0333 (toll-free)
Fax: 619-321-3005
E-mail: auadmissions@argosy.edu
Web site: http://argosy.edu/sandiego/

THE FACULTY

The Argosy University faculty comprises working professionals who are eager to help students succeed. Members bring real-world experience and the latest practice innovations to the academic setting. The diverse faculty members of the College of Education are widely recognized for contributions to their field. Many are published scholars, and most hold doctoral degrees. They provide a substantive education that combines comprehensive knowledge with critical skills and practical workplace relevance. Above all, faculty members are committed to their students' personal and professional development.

ARGOSY UNIVERSITY, SAN FRANCISCO BAY AREA

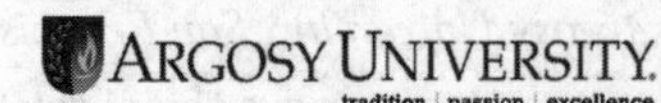

College of Education

Programs of Study

Argosy University, San Francisco Bay Area, offers Master of Arts in Education (M.A.Ed.) degrees in Educational Administration, Higher and Postsecondary Education, Teaching and Learning: ELL/ ESL, Teaching and Learning: Reading, and Teaching and Learning: Special Education; Doctor of Education (Ed.D.) degrees in Higher and Postsecondary Education, Initial Educational Administration, and Teaching and Learning; and Education Specialist (Ed.S.) degrees in Higher and Postsecondary Education and Initial Educational Administration.

The Master of Arts in Education (M.A.Ed.) in Educational Administration program prepares individuals to serve as school administrators. The program is designed for practicing educators who have already completed a bachelor's degree program from a regionally accredited institution and are seeking administrative credentialing. Based on state requirements, students may be required to complete additional experiences or course work.

The Master of Arts in Education (M.A.Ed.) in Higher and Postsecondary Education program is designed for individuals who seek administrative and other positions in noninstructional units at higher education and postsecondary institutions. Graduates of this program will have enhanced practical skills, knowledge, and experiences as professionals and leaders in universities, colleges, and postsecondary educational institutions. A bachelor's degree is required for admission to this program.

The Master of Arts in Education (M.A.Ed.) in Teaching and Learning: ELL/ESL is a 30-credit-hour degree program intended to prepare educators who work in the P–12 setting as change agents who engage actively in their communities, using appropriate pedagogy and technology to foster the development of global citizens. In addition to the core course requirements, students will complete a four-course sequence to strengthen knowledge and skills when working with students who are classified as English Language Learners (ELL) or English as a Second Language (ESL). This program does not lead to certification or credential endorsement.

The Master of Arts in Education (M.A.Ed.) in Teaching and Learning: Reading is a 30-credit program intended to prepare educators who work in the P–12 setting as change agents who engage actively in their communities, using appropriate pedagogy and technology to foster the development of global citizens. Students enrolled in this program will complete a four-course sequence in reading to strengthen knowledge and skills in this specific area. This program does not lead to certification or credential endorsement.

The Master of Arts in Education (M.A.Ed.) in Teaching and Learning: Special Education is a 30-credit program intended to prepare educators who work in the P–12 setting as change agents who engage actively in their communities, using appropriate pedagogy and technology to foster the development of global citizens. Students enrolled in this program will complete a four-course sequence designed to strengthen knowledge and skills when working with students with special learning needs. This program does not lead to certification or credential endorsement.

The Doctor of Education (Ed.D.) in Higher and Postsecondary Education program is designed for students to enhance their professional competence as educational leaders, instructors, or consultants in academic affairs, student affairs, or student services divisions within community colleges, technical schools and institutes, and four-year colleges and universities, as well as in government, military, religious, and profit or nonprofit postsecondary educational organizations and divisions. The program offers three concentrations: student affairs and services, teaching and learning, and interdisciplinary studies.

The Doctor of Education (Ed.D.) in Initial Educational Administration program prepares individuals to serve as school principals and/or building-level administrators. The program is designed for practicing educators who have already completed a graduate-level program from a regionally accredited institution or an appropriately certified foreign institution, and are seeking administrative licensure at the initial or K–12 level. Completion of the program results in a terminal degree which includes a specific writing, research, and dissertation sequence.

The Doctor of Education (Ed.D.) in Teaching and Learning is designed to prepare educators in P–12 settings to serve as change agents and leaders who engage actively in their communities, using appropriate pedagogy and technology to foster the development of global citizens. This program does not lead to certification or credential endorsement.

The Education Specialist (Ed.S.) in Higher and Postsecondary Education program is designed for students to enhance their professional competence as educational leaders, instructors, or consultants in academic affairs, student affairs, or student services divisions within community colleges, technical schools and institutes, four-year colleges and universities, as well as in government, military, religious, profit or nonprofit postsecondary educational organizations and divisions. The program offers three concentrations: student affairs and services, teaching and learning, and interdisciplinary studies.

The Education Specialist (Ed.S.) in Initial Educational Administration program prepares individuals to serve as school principals and/or building-level administrators. The program is designed for practicing educators who have already completed a graduate level program from a regionally accredited institution or an appropriately certified foreign institution, and are seeking administrative licensure at the initial or K–12 level.

Note: The M.A.Ed. in Instructional Leadership (multiple subject teacher credential prep) and the M.A.Ed. in Instructional Leadership (single subject teacher credential prep) programs can lead to multiple subject teaching credential or single subject teaching credential depending on the program concentration selected. All other programs offered through the College of Education do not lead to teacher or administrator certification, licensure, or endorsement in any state in the United States. The programs offered through Argosy University online programs do not lead to teacher or administrator certification, licensure, or endorsement in any state in the United States regardless of the state in which the student resides.

Research Facilities

Argosy University libraries provide curriculum support and educational resources, including current text materials, diagnostic training documents, reference materials and databases, journals and dissertations, and major and current titles in program areas. There is an online public-access catalog of library resources available throughout the Argosy University system. Students have remote

Argosy University, San Francisco Bay Area

access to the campus library database, enabling them to study and conduct research at home. Academic databases offer dissertation abstracts, academic journals, and professional periodicals. All library computers are Internet accessible. Software applications include Word, Excel, PowerPoint, SPSS, and various test-scoring programs.

Financial Aid

Financial aid is available to those who qualify. Argosy University, San Francisco Bay Area, offers access to federal and state aid programs, merit-based awards, grants, loans, and a work-study program. As a first step, students should complete the Free Application for Federal Student Aid (FAFSA). Prospective students can apply electronically at http://www.fafsa.ed.gov or at the campus.

Cost of Study

Tuition varies by program. Students should contact Argosy University, San Francisco Bay Area, for tuition information.

Living and Housing Costs

Students typically live in apartments in the metropolitan area. Living expenses vary according to each student's preferred standard of living, housing, and transportation. The University does not offer or operate student housing. Most of the students are full-time working professionals who live within driving distance of the campus. Several nearby hotels offer special rates for those who commute from long distances. The Admissions Department also maintains a list of housing options, including contact information for University students who wish to share housing. For more information, students should contact the Admissions Department.

Student Group

Admission to Argosy University, San Francisco Bay Area, is selective to ensure a dynamic and engaged student body. It encourages diversity in academic and employment backgrounds and promotes integration of the student body into professional life through established connections with local and national professional associations. Argosy University offers a professionally oriented education with rich opportunities to gain practical experience in class, field placements, and internships. Full-time students and working professionals gain the extensive knowledge and range of skills necessary for effective performance in their chosen fields.

Student Outcomes

Students can register with the University's online career-services system and use select services from a distance, such as degree-specific career e-mail lists, national job posts, and virtual job fairs. Students should contact the University for more information.

Location

Located in northern California, Argosy University, San Francisco Bay Area, attracts students from the immediate area as well as from around the country and the world. The energy in San Francisco is contagious. Numerous surveys rank San Francisco as one of the most wired cities in the world, thanks to its high concentration of computer-savvy citizens and businesses.

Many educational institutions and agencies in the area provide varied opportunities for student training. The Bay Area and nearby Silicon Valley are home to leading new media companies such as Pixar, ILM, and Sega. A who's who of technology companies call the Bay Area home, including Apple, Cisco, Hewlett-Packard, Intel, Oracle, and Sun Microsystems. The Bay Area also is the home of traditional companies such as BankAmerica, Chevron, Levi-Strauss, Safeway, and Wells Fargo.

The University

Argosy University is a private institution with nineteen locations across the nation. Argosy University, San Francisco Bay Area, provides students with a career resources office, an academic resources center, and extensive information access for research. It offers the resources of a large university plus the friendliness and personal attention of a small campus. The innovative programs feature dynamic, relevant, and practical curricula delivered in flexible class formats. Students enjoy scheduling options that make it easier to fit school into their busy lives, choosing from day and evening courses, on campus or online. Many students find a combination of class formats to be an ideal way of continuing their education while meeting family and professional demands.

Argosy University is accredited by the Accrediting Commission for Senior Colleges and Universities of the Western Association for Schools and Colleges (985 Atlantic Avenue, Suite 100, Alameda, California, 94501, http://www.wascsenior.org).

Applying

Argosy University, San Francisco Bay Area, accepts students year-round on a rolling admissions basis, depending on availability of required courses. Applications for admission are available online or by contacting the campus.

Correspondence and Information

Argosy University, San Francisco Bay Area
1005 Atlantic Avenue
Alameda, California 94501
United States
Phone: 510-215-4700
866-215-2777 (toll free)
Fax: 510-217-4806
E-mail: auadmissions@argosy.edu
Web site: http://www.argosy.edu/sanfrancisco

THE FACULTY

The Argosy University faculty comprises working professionals who are eager to help students succeed. Members bring real-world experience and the latest practice innovations to the academic setting. The diverse faculty members of the College of Education are widely recognized for contributions to the field. Most hold doctoral degrees. They provide a substantive education that combines comprehensive knowledge with critical skills and practical workplace relevance. Above all, faculty members are committed to their students' personal and professional development.

ARGOSY UNIVERSITY, SARASOTA

College of Education

Programs of Study

Argosy University, Sarasota, offers Master of Arts (M.A.) degrees in Education Psychology, School Counseling and School Psychology; Master of Arts in Education (M.A.Ed.) degrees in Curriculum and Instruction, Curriculum and Instruction: ELL/ESL, Curriculum and Instruction : Reading, Curriculum and Instruction: Special Education, Educational Administration, and Higher and Postsecondary Education; Doctor of Education (Ed.D.) degrees in Advanced Educational Administration, Community College Executive Leadership, Curriculum and Instruction, Educational Leadership, Higher and Postsecondary Education, Initial Educational Administration, and Teacher Leadership; the Doctor of Psychology (Psy.D.) degree for Practicing School Psychologist, and School Psychology; and Education Specialist (Ed.S.) degrees in Curriculum and Instruction , Educational Leadership and Initial Educational Administration.

The Master of Arts (M.A.) in Educational Psychology degree program is the foundational program for those interested in the field of school psychology. Based upon national standards for school psychologists, the curriculum reflects the most current information in the field. In many courses, students observe certified school psychologists at work and practice basic analytical skills under the close supervision.

The Master of Arts (M.A.) in School Counseling program educates and trains students to enter a professional career as master's-level practitioners with a demonstrated knowledge of social and cultural diversity, theoretical foundations of professional counseling, and field experience into appropriate client interaction and intervention skills for utilization in a school setting with diverse clients.

The Master of Arts (M.A.) in School Psychology program is dedicated to producing ethical, responsible, and competent school psychologists who are able to serve effectively in a number of professional roles. Students have the opportunity to develop core competencies in psychological assessment, intervention, and consultation/education, as well as cultural and individual diversity. The program focuses on student preparation and professional development. Successful completion will permit students to request a transcript review by the Florida Department of Education for certification as school psychologists in the state of Florida. Students are also eligible to apply to become Nationally Certified School Psychologists in a process designed for graduates of non-NASP-approved programs.

The Master of Arts in Education (M.A.Ed.) in Curriculum and Instruction degree program is intended to prepare educators who work in the P–12 setting as change agents who engage actively in their communities, using appropriate pedagogy and technology to foster the development of global citizens. In addition to the core course requirements, students enrolled in this degree program will complete a four course sequence designed to strengthen educators' knowledge and skills in order to work more effectively in the current classroom environment. This degree program does not lead to certification or credential endorsement.

The Master of Arts in Education (M.A.Ed.) in Curriculum and Instruction: ELL/ESL degree program is a 30-credit-hour degree program intended to prepare educators who work in the P–12 setting as change agents who engage actively in their communities, using appropriate pedagogy and technology to foster the development of global citizens. In addition to the core course requirements, students enrolled in this degree program will complete a four course sequence designed to strengthen educators' knowledge and skills when working with students who are classified as English Language Learners (ELL) or English as a Second Language (ESL). This degree program does not lead to certification or credential endorsement.

The Master of Arts in Education (M.A.Ed.) in Curriculum and Instruction: Reading degree program is a 30-credit-hour program intended to prepare educators who work in the P–12 setting as change agents who engage actively in their communities, using appropriate pedagogy and technology to foster the development of global citizens. Students enrolled in this program will complete a four course sequence in reading designed to strengthen educators' knowledge and skills in this specific area of focus. This program does not lead to certification or credential endorsement.

The Master of Arts in Education (M.A.Ed.) in Curriculum and Instruction: Special Education degree program is a 30-credit-hour program intended to prepare educators who work in the P–12 setting as change agents who engage actively in their communities, using appropriate pedagogy and technology to foster the development of global citizens. Students enrolled in this program will complete a four course sequence designed to strengthen educators' knowledge and skills when working with students with special learning needs. This program does not lead to certification or credential endorsement.

The Master of Arts in Education (M.A.Ed.) in Educational Administration program prepares individuals to serve as school administrators. The program is designed for practicing educators who have already completed a bachelor's degree program from a regionally accredited institution and are seeking administrative credentialing. Based on state requirements, students may be required to complete additional experiences or course work.

The Master of Arts in Education (M.A.Ed.) in Higher and Postsecondary Education program is designed for individuals who seek administrative and other positions in noninstructional units at higher education and postsecondary institutions. Graduates of this program will have enhanced practical skills, knowledge, and experiences as professionals and leaders in universities, colleges, and postsecondary educational institutions. A bachelor's degree is required for admission to this program.

The Doctor of Education (Ed.D.) in Advanced Educational Administration program prepares individuals to serve as school administrators in advanced positions. The program is designed for practicing educators who have already completed a graduate level program from a regionally accredited institution and currently hold principal or initial administrative licensure. Completion of the program results in a terminal degree which includes a specific writing, research, and dissertation sequence.

The Doctor of Education (Ed.D.) in Community College Executive Leadership program is designed for community college administrators who seek to move into senior administrative positions (such as president, vice-president, dean, and director) at community colleges.

The Doctor of Education (Ed.D.) in Curriculum and Instruction degree program is designed to prepare educators as change agents and leaders in the P-12 setting who engage actively in their communities, using appropriate pedagogy and technology to foster the development of global citizens. This program does not lead to certification or credential endorsement.

The Doctor of Education (Ed.D.) in Educational Leadership noncertification program is designed for students preparing for or advancing their careers as educational leaders in professional positions as school district, regional, state, or national administrators. Students much choose a concentration in either higher education administration or K–12 education.

The Doctor of Education (Ed.D.) in Higher and Postsecondary Education program is designed for students to enhance their professional competence as educational leaders, instructors, or consultants in academic affairs, student affairs, or student services divisions within community colleges, technical schools and institutes, and four-year colleges and universities, as well as in government, military, religious, and profit or nonprofit postsecondary educational organizations and divisions. The program offers three concentrations: student affairs and services, teaching and learning, and interdisciplinary studies.

The Doctor of Education (Ed.D.) in Initial Educational Administration program prepares individuals to serve as school principals and/or building-level administrators. The program is designed for practicing educators who have already completed a graduate-level program from a regionally accredited institution or an appropriately certified foreign institution, and are seeking administrative licensure at the initial or K–12 level. Completion of the program results in a terminal degree which includes a specific writing, research, and dissertation sequence.

The Doctor of Education (Ed.D.) in Teacher Leadership degree program is a 60-credit-hour program designed for classroom teachers who are looking to expand their content knowledge, develop leadership skills, teach more effectively, and support the professional development of their peers. Candidates in this degree program will have the opportunity to become skillful in building collaborative relationships and learning communities that focus on student learning and support a strong positive climate in the school. Peer mentoring and coaching are modeled and practiced throughout the program in field experiences and the culminating research project. The program culminates in a dissertation related to teacher leadership and is designed to add knowledge to the field of teacher leadership. The Ed.D. in Teacher Leadership degree program does not prepare for or lead to teacher or school administrative certification/ licensure.

The Doctor of Psychology (Psy.D.) in School Psychology program prepares students to meet the criteria for state certification as school psychologists and to become nationally certified school psychologists in accordance with criteria developed by the National Association of School Psychologists (NASP). The program focuses on student preparation and professional development. Students can apply to become nationally certified school psychologists in a process designed for graduates of non-NASP-approved programs. Through direct instruction, assessment, and supervision, students acquire competencies in psychological and educational foundations; cognitive, academic and personality assessment; psychoeducational interventions; statistics and research methodology; research initiatives, practicum experiences; and professional school psychology course work.

The Education Specialist (Ed.S.) in Curriculum and Instruction degree program is designed to prepare educators as change agents and leaders in the P–12 setting who engage actively in their communities, using appropriate pedagogy and technology to foster the development of global citizens. This program does not lead to certification or any credential endorsement.

The Education Specialist (Ed.S.) in Educational Leadership program concentrates on applied organizational theory within the context of educational organizations. This specialized program develops the competencies required to secure educational administrator positions at the elementary or secondary school level.

The Education Specialist (Ed.S.) in Initial Educational Administration program prepares individuals to serve as school principals and/or building-level administrators. The program is designed for practicing educators who have already completed a graduate level program from a regionally accredited institution or an appropriately certified foreign institution, and are seeking administrative licensure at the initial or K–12 level.

Note: These programs do not lead to teacher or administrator certification, licensure, or endorsement in any state in the United States.

Research Facilities

Argosy University libraries provide curriculum support and educational resources, including current text materials, diagnostic training documents, reference materials and databases, journals and dissertations, and major and current titles in program areas. There is an online public-access catalog of library resources available throughout the Argosy University system. Students have remote access to the campus library database, enabling them to study and conduct research at home. Academic databases offer dissertation abstracts, academic journals, and professional periodicals. All library computers are Internet accessible. Software applications include Word, Excel, PowerPoint, SPSS, and various test-scoring programs.

Financial Aid

Financial aid is available to those who qualify. Argosy University, Sarasota, offers access to federal and state aid programs, merit-based awards, grants, loans, and a work-study program. As a first step, students should complete the Free Application for Federal Student Aid (FAFSA). Prospective students can apply electronically at http://www.fafsa.ed.gov or at the campus.

Cost of Study

Tuition varies by program. Students should contact Argosy University, Sarasota, for tuition information.

Living and Housing Costs

Students typically live in apartments in the metropolitan Sarasota area. Living expenses vary according to each student's preferred standard of living, housing, and transportation. The University does not offer or operate student housing. Most of the students are full-time working professionals who live within driving distance of the campus. Several nearby hotels offer special rates for students when they attend one-week in-residence intersessions. The Admissions Department also maintains a list of housing options, including contact information for University students who wish to share housing. For more information, students should contact the Admissions Department.

Student Group

Admission to Argosy University, Sarasota, is selective to ensure a dynamic and engaged student body. It encourages diversity in academic and employment backgrounds and promotes integration of the student body into professional life through established connections with local and national professional associations. Argosy University offers a professionally oriented education with rich opportunities to gain practical experience in class, field placements, and internships. Full-time students and working professionals gain the extensive knowledge and range of skills necessary for effective performance in their chosen fields.

Student Outcomes

Students can register with the University's online career-services system and use select services from a distance, such as degree-specific career e-mail lists, national job posts, and virtual job fairs. Students should contact the University for more information.

Location

Located in northeast Sarasota, the campus is specifically designed for postsecondary and graduate-level instruction through a unique combination of in-residence course work, tutorials, and online study courses. Several of the programs are off-site tutorials and intensive one-week classroom sessions. Students may also complete up to 49 percent of the work of some degree programs via online courses that allow interaction with faculty members and classmates from any Internet connection.

Sarasota is recognized as Florida's cultural center and is home to a professional symphony, ballet, and opera as well as dozens of theaters and art galleries. Well-known vacation attractions such as Disney World, Busch Gardens–Tampa, and the city of Miami are within a few hours' drive. The area enjoys mild winters and endless summer beauty.

The business sector in the Gulf Coast community helps make it one of the top 20 places to live and work. ASO Corporation, Nelson Publishing, and Select Technology Group are among the numerous companies headquartered in Sarasota County. The area's top employers include Sarasota Memorial Hospital and Publix Supermarkets. Many educational institutions and agencies in the area provide varied opportunities for student training.

The University

Argosy University is a private institution with nineteen locations across the nation. Argosy University, Sarasota, provides students with a career resources office, an academic resources center, and extensive information access for research. It offers the resources of a large university plus the friendliness and personal attention of a small campus.

The innovative programs feature dynamic, relevant, and practical curricula delivered in flexible class formats. Students enjoy scheduling options that make it easier to fit school into their busy lives, choosing from day and evening courses, on campus or online. Many students find a combination of class formats to be an ideal way of continuing their education while meeting family and professional demands.

Argosy University is accredited by the Accrediting Commission for Senior Colleges and Universities of the Western Association for Schools and Colleges (985 Atlantic Avenue, Suite 100, Alameda, California, 94501, http://www.wascsenior.org).

Applying

Argosy University, Sarasota, accepts students year-round on a rolling admissions basis, depending on availability of required courses. Applications for admission are available online or by contacting the campus.

Correspondence and Information

Argosy University, Sarasota
5250 17th Street
Sarasota, Florida 34235
United States
Phone: 941-379-0404
800-331-5995 (toll-free)
Fax: 941-379-5964
E-mail: auadmissions@argosy.edu
Web site: http://www.argosy.edu/sarasota

THE FACULTY

The Argosy University faculty comprises working professionals who are eager to help students succeed. Members bring real-world experience and the latest practice innovations to the academic setting. The diverse faculty members of the College of Education are widely recognized for contributions to their field. Most hold doctoral degrees. They provide a substantive education that combines comprehensive knowledge with critical skills and practical workplace relevance. Above all, faculty members are committed to their students' personal and professional development.

ARGOSY UNIVERSITY, SCHAUMBURG

College of Education

Programs of Study

Argosy University, Schaumburg, offers Master of Arts in Education (M.A.Ed.) degrees in Educational Administration, Higher and Postsecondary Education, Teaching and learning: ELL/ESL, Teaching and Learning: Reading, and Teaching and Learning: Special Education; Doctor of Education (Ed.D.) degrees in Advanced Educational Administration, Community College Executive Leadership, Educational Leadership, Initial Educational Administration, and Teaching and Learning; and Education Specialist (Ed.S.) degrees in Advanced Educational Administration, Initial Educational Administration, and Teaching and Learning.

The Master of Arts in Education (M.A.Ed.) in Educational Administration program prepares individuals to serve as school administrators. The program is designed for practicing educators who have already completed a bachelor's degree program from a regionally accredited institution and are seeking administrative credentialing. Based on state requirements, students may be required to complete additional experiences or course work.

The Master of Arts in Education (M.A.Ed.) in Higher and Postsecondary Education program is designed for individuals who seek administrative and other positions in noninstructional units at higher education and postsecondary institutions. Graduates of this program will have enhanced practical skills, knowledge, and experiences as professionals and leaders in universities, colleges, and postsecondary educational institutions. A bachelor's degree is required for admission to this program.

The Master of Arts in Education (M.A.Ed.) in Teaching and Learning: ELL/ESL is a 30-credit-hour degree program intended to prepare educators who work in the P–12 setting as change agents who engage actively in their communities, using appropriate pedagogy and technology to foster the development of global citizens. In addition to the core course requirements, students will complete a four-course sequence to strengthen knowledge and skills when working with students who are classified as English Language Learners (ELL) or English as a Second Language (ESL). This program does not lead to certification or credential endorsement.

The Master of Arts in Education (M.A.Ed.) in Teaching and Learning: Reading is a 30-credit program intended to prepare educators who work in the P–12 setting as change agents who engage actively in their communities, using appropriate pedagogy and technology to foster the development of global citizens. Students enrolled in this program will complete a four-course sequence in reading to strengthen knowledge and skills in this specific area. This program does not lead to certification or credential endorsement.

The Master of Arts in Education (M.A.Ed.) in Teaching and Learning: Special Education is a 30-credit program intended to prepare educators who work in the P–12 setting as change agents who engage actively in their communities, using appropriate pedagogy and technology to foster the development of global citizens. Students enrolled in this program will complete a four-course sequence designed to strengthen knowledge and skills when working with students with special learning needs. This program does not lead to certification or credential endorsement.

The Doctor of Education (Ed.D.) in Advanced Educational Administration program prepares individuals to serve as school administrators in advanced positions. The program is designed for practicing educators who have already completed a graduate level program from a regionally accredited institution and currently hold principal or initial administrative licensure. Completion of the program results in a terminal degree which includes a specific writing, research, and dissertation sequence.

The Doctor of Education (Ed.D.) in Community College Executive Leadership program is designed for community college administrators who seek to move into senior administrative positions (such as president, vice-president, dean, and director) at community colleges.

The Doctor of Education (Ed.D.) in Educational Leadership program is designed to enhance educational leadership strengths. Students learn innovative and collaborative techniques to manage and govern educational institutions. The program prepares students for administrative leadership positions at the district, regional, state, or national level. Students must choose a concentration in higher education administration or K–12 education. The program now offers an optional concentration in district leadership.

The Doctor of Education (Ed.D.) in Initial Educational Administration program prepares individuals to serve as school principals and/or building-level administrators. The program is designed for practicing educators who have already completed a graduate-level program from a regionally accredited institution or an appropriately certified foreign institution, and are seeking administrative licensure at the initial or K–12 level. Completion of the program results in a terminal degree which includes a specific writing, research, and dissertation sequence.

The Doctor of Education (Ed.D.) in Teaching and Learning is designed to prepare educators in P–12 settings to serve as change agents and leaders who engage actively in their communities, using appropriate pedagogy and technology to foster the development of global citizens. This program does not lead to certification or credential endorsement.

The Education Specialist (Ed.S.) in Advanced Educational Administration program prepares individuals to serve as school administrators in advanced positions. The program is designed for practicing educators who have already completed a graduate level program from a regionally accredited institution and currently hold principal or initial administrative licensure.

The Education Specialist (Ed.S.) in Initial Educational Administration program prepares individuals to serve as school principals and/or building-level administrators. The program is designed for practicing educators who have already completed a graduate-level program from a regionally accredited institution or an appropriately certified foreign institution and are seeking administrative licensure at the initial or K–12 level.

The Education Specialist (Ed.S.) in Teaching and Learning program is designed to prepare educators in P–12 settings as change agents and leaders who engage actively in their communities, using appropriate pedagogy and technology to foster the development of global citizens. This program does not lead to certification or any credential endorsement.

Note: The Ed.S. in Educational Leadership–Illinois Type 75 certification/superintendent preparation track, certification of advanced studies in educational leadership–Illinois Type 75 certification/superintendent preparation track, and the Ed.D. in Educational Leadership–superintendent preparation track can lead to State of Illinois Type 75 superintendent's endorsement. All other programs offered through the College of Education do not lead to teacher or administrator certification, licensure, or endorsement in any state in the United States. The programs offered through Argosy University online programs do not lead to teacher or administrator certification, licensure, or endorsement in any state in the United States regardless of the state in which the student resides.

Argosy University, Schaumburg

Research Facilities

Argosy University libraries provide curriculum support and educational resources, including current text materials, diagnostic training documents, reference materials and databases, journals and dissertations, and major and current titles in program areas. There is an online public access catalog of library resources available throughout the Argosy University system. Students have remote access to the campus library database, enabling them to study and conduct research at home. Academic databases offer dissertation abstracts, academic journals, and professional periodicals. All library computers are Internet accessible. Software applications include Word, Excel, PowerPoint, SPSS, and various test-scoring programs.

Financial Aid

Financial aid is available to those who qualify. Argosy University, Schaumburg, offers access to federal and state aid programs, merit-based awards, grants, loans, and a work-study program. As a first step, students should complete the Free Application for Federal Student Aid (FAFSA). Prospective students can apply electronically at http://www.fafsa.ed.gov or at the campus.

Cost of Study

Tuition varies by program. Students should contact Argosy University, Schaumburg, for tuition information.

Living and Housing Costs

Students typically live in apartments in the metropolitan Schaumburg area. Living expenses vary according to each student's preferred standard of living, housing, and transportation. The University does not offer or operate student housing. Most of the students are full-time working professionals who live within driving distance of the campus. Several nearby hotels offer special rates for those who commute from long distances. The Admissions Department also maintains a list of housing options, including contact information for University students who wish to share housing. For more information, students should contact the Admissions Department.

Student Group

Admission to Argosy University, Schaumburg, is selective to ensure a dynamic and engaged student body. It encourages diversity in academic and employment backgrounds and promotes integration of the student body into professional life through established connections with local and national professional associations. Argosy University offers a professionally oriented education with rich opportunities to gain practical experience in class, field placements, and internships. Full-time students and working professionals gain the extensive knowledge and range of skills necessary for effective performance in their chosen fields.

Student Outcomes

Students can register with the University's online career-services system and use select services from a distance, such as degree-specific career e-mail lists, national job posts, and virtual job fairs. Students should contact the University for more information.

Location

Argosy University, Schaumburg, is conveniently located in the northwest suburban area, approximately 45 minutes from downtown Chicago. The University's small size offers a highly personal atmosphere and flexible programs tailored to students' needs. Visitors to Chicago experience a range of attractions to stimulate both intellectual and recreational pursuits. Located on the shores of Lake Michigan in the Midwest, Chicago is home to world-champion sports teams, an internationally acclaimed symphony orchestra, renowned architecture, and nearly 3 million residents. Among the variety of history and art museums in the city, the Chicago Cultural Center offers more than 600 art programs and exhibits each year. Recreational opportunities include hiking and cycling on miles of lakefront trails, golfing, and shopping.

Many educational institutions and agencies in the area provide varied opportunities for student training. Schaumburg's business environment includes 5,000 businesses that employ 80,000 people. The area's largest employers are Motorola, Experian, Cingular, and IBM.

The University

Argosy University is a private institution with nineteen locations across the nation. Argosy University, Schaumburg, provides students with a career resources office, an academic resources center, and extensive information access for research. It offers the resources of a large university, plus the friendliness and personal attention of a small campus.

The innovative programs feature dynamic, relevant, and practical curricula delivered in flexible class formats. Students enjoy scheduling options that make it easier to fit school into their busy lives, choosing from day and evening courses, on campus or online. Many students find a combination of class formats to be an ideal way of continuing their education while meeting family and professional demands.

Argosy University is accredited by the Accrediting Commission for Senior Colleges and Universities of the Western Association for Schools and Colleges (985 Atlantic Avenue, Suite 100, Alameda, California, 94501, http://www.wascsenior.org).

Applying

Argosy University, Schaumburg, accepts students year-round on a rolling admissions basis, depending on availability of required courses. Applications for admission are available online or by contacting the campus.

Correspondence and Information

Argosy University, Schaumburg
999 North Plaza Drive, Suite 111
Schaumburg, Illinois 60173-5403
United States
Phone: 847-969-4900
866-290-2777 (toll-free)
Fax: 847-969-4999
E-mail: auadmissions@argosy.edu
Web site: http://www.argosy.edu/schaumburg

THE FACULTY

The Argosy University faculty comprises working professionals who are eager to help students succeed. Members bring real-world experience and the latest practice innovations to the academic setting. The diverse faculty members of the College of Education are widely recognized for contributions to the field. Most hold doctoral degrees. They provide a substantive education that combines comprehensive knowledge with critical skills and practical workplace relevance. Above all, faculty members are committed to their students' personal and professional development.

ARGOSY UNIVERSITY, SEATTLE

College of Education

Programs of Study

Argosy University, Seattle, offers Master of Arts in Education (M.A.Ed.) degrees in Adult Education and Training, Higher and Postsecondary Education, Teaching and Learning: ELL/ESL, Teaching and Learning: Reading, and Teaching and Learning: Special Education; Doctor of Education (Ed.D.) degrees in Higher and Postsecondary Education, and Teaching and Learning; and Education Specialist (Ed.S.) degrees in Higher and Postsecondary Education and Teaching and Learning.

The Master of Arts in Education (M.A.Ed.) in Adult Education and Training program is designed for the working professional associated with adult learning, training, or staff development in business, government, or other private or public organizations. The program's goal is to enhance the knowledge and skills in the area of adult learning for employment and other organizational settings. Students will develop core practical and academic skills in analysis, oral and written communication, problem solving, critical thinking, team building, and computer technology, through courses that examine the practical, historical, philosophical, psychological, social, technical, and theoretical aspects of education.

The Master of Arts in Education (M.A.Ed.) in Higher and Postsecondary Education program is designed for individuals who seek administrative and other positions in noninstructional units at higher education and postsecondary institutions. Graduates of this program will have enhanced practical skills, knowledge, and experiences as professionals and leaders in universities, colleges, and postsecondary educational institutions. A bachelor's degree is required for admission to this program.

The Master of Arts in Education (M.A.Ed.) in Teaching and Learning: ELL/ESL is a 30-credit-hour degree program intended to prepare educators who work in the P–12 setting as change agents who engage actively in their communities, using appropriate pedagogy and technology to foster the development of global citizens. In addition to the core course requirements, students will complete a four-course sequence to strengthen knowledge and skills when working with students who are classified as English Language Learners (ELL) or English as a Second Language (ESL). This program does not lead to certification or credential endorsement.

The Master of Arts in Education (M.A.Ed.) in Teaching and Learning: Reading is a 30-credit program intended to prepare educators who work in the P–12 setting as change agents who engage actively in their communities, using appropriate pedagogy and technology to foster the development of global citizens. Students enrolled in this program will complete a four-course sequence in reading to strengthen knowledge and skills in this specific area. This program does not lead to certification or credential endorsement.

The Master of Arts in Education (M.A.Ed.) in Teaching and Learning: Special Education is a 30-credit program intended to prepare educators who work in the P–12 setting as change agents who engage actively in their communities, using appropriate pedagogy and technology to foster the development of global citizens. Students enrolled in this program will complete a four-course sequence designed to strengthen knowledge and skills when working with students with special learning needs. This program does not lead to certification or credential endorsement.

The Doctor of Education (Ed.D.) in Higher and Postsecondary Education program is designed for students to enhance their professional competence as educational leaders, instructors, or consultants in academic affairs, student affairs, or student services divisions within community colleges, technical schools and institutes, and four-year colleges and universities, as well as in government, military, religious, and profit or nonprofit postsecondary educational organizations and divisions. The program offers three concentrations: student affairs and services, teaching and learning, and interdisciplinary studies.

The Doctor of Education (Ed.D.) in Teaching and Learning is designed to prepare educators in P–12 settings to serve as change agents and leaders who engage actively in their communities, using appropriate pedagogy and technology to foster the development of global citizens. This program does not lead to certification or credential endorsement.

The Education Specialist (Ed.S.) in Higher and Postsecondary Education program is designed for students to enhance their professional competence as educational leaders, instructors, or consultants in academic affairs, student affairs, or student services divisions within community colleges, technical schools and institutes, four-year colleges and universities, as well as in government, military, religious, profit or nonprofit postsecondary educational organizations and divisions. The program offers three concentrations: student affairs and services, teaching and learning, and interdisciplinary studies.

The Education Specialist (Ed.S.) in Teaching and Learning program prepares educators to serve in the P–12 setting as change agents and leaders who engage actively in their communities, using appropriate pedagogy and technology to foster the development of global citizens. This program does not lead to certification or any credential endorsement.

Note: These programs do not lead to teacher or administrator certification, licensure, or endorsement in any state in the United States.

Research Facilities

Argosy University libraries provide curriculum support and educational resources, including current text materials, diagnostic training documents, reference materials and databases, journals and dissertations, and major and current titles in program areas. There is an online public-access catalog of library resources available throughout the Argosy University system. Students have remote access to the campus library database, enabling them to study and conduct research at home. Academic databases offer dissertation abstracts, academic journals, and professional periodicals. All library computers are

Internet accessible. Software applications include Word, Excel, PowerPoint, SPSS, and various test-scoring programs.

Financial Aid

Financial aid is available to those who qualify. Argosy University, Seattle, offers access to federal and state aid programs, merit-based awards, grants, loans, and a work-study program. As a first step, students should complete the Free Application for Federal Student Aid (FAFSA). Prospective students can apply electronically at http://www.fafsa.ed.gov or at the campus.

Cost of Study

Tuition varies by program. Students should contact Argosy University, Seattle, for tuition information.

Living and Housing Costs

Students typically live in apartments in the Seattle metropolitan area. Living expenses vary according to each student's preferred standard of living, housing, and transportation. The University does not offer or operate student housing. Most of the students are full-time working professionals who live within driving distance of the campus. Several nearby hotels offer special rates for those who commute from long distances. The Admissions Department also maintains a list of housing options, including contact information for University students who wish to share housing. For more information, students should contact the Admissions Department.

Student Group

Admission to Argosy University, Seattle, is selective to ensure a dynamic and engaged student body. It encourages diversity in academic and employment backgrounds and promotes integration of the student body into professional life through established connections with local and national professional associations. Argosy University offers a professionally oriented education with rich opportunities to gain practical experience in class, field placements, and internships. Full-time students and working professionals gain the extensive knowledge and range of skills necessary for effective performance in their chosen fields.

Student Outcomes

Students can register with the University's online career-services system and use select services from a distance, such as degree-specific career e-mail lists, national job posts, and virtual job fairs. Students should contact the University for more information.

Location

Argosy University, Seattle, aspires to provide a supportive, collaborative, engaging, yet challenging learning environment. Easily reached through the King County Public Transportation System, the campus offers convenient access to local libraries, shops, restaurants, theaters, and art museums. Seattle offers numerous historical and multicultural museums, a symphony, the ballet, and many theater companies. The city is home to several major-league sports teams and offers myriad outdoor recreational opportunities, such as camping, hiking, fishing, skiing, and rock-climbing.

Many educational institutions and agencies in the area provide varied opportunities for student training. Seattle's business environment encompasses a wide range of industries and features such giants as Microsoft, Boeing, and Alaska Air Group. The Port of Seattle and the University of Washington are also among the area's largest employers.

The University

Argosy University is a private institution with nineteen locations across the nation. Argosy University, Seattle, provides students with a career resources office, an academic resources center, and extensive information access for research. It offers the resources of a large university plus the friendliness and personal attention of a small campus. The innovative programs feature dynamic, relevant, and practical curricula delivered in flexible class formats. Students enjoy scheduling options that make it easier to fit school into their busy lives, choosing from day and evening courses, on campus or online. Many students find a combination of class formats to be an ideal way of continuing their education while meeting family and professional demands.

Argosy University is accredited by the Accrediting Commission for Senior Colleges and Universities of the Western Association for Schools and Colleges (985 Atlantic Avenue, Suite 100, Alameda, California, 94501, http://www.wascsenior.org).

Applying

Argosy University, Seattle, accepts students year-round on a rolling admissions basis, depending on availability of required courses. Applications for admission are available online or by contacting the campus.

Correspondence and Information

Argosy University, Seattle
2601-A Elliott Avenue
Seattle, Washington 98121
United States
Phone: 206-283-4500
888-283-2777 (toll-free)
Fax: 206-393-3592
E-mail: auadmissions@argosy.edu
Web site: http://www.argosy.edu/seattle

THE FACULTY

The Argosy University faculty comprises working professionals who are eager to help students succeed. Members bring real-world experience and the latest practice innovations to the academic setting. The diverse faculty members of the College of Education are widely recognized for contributions to the field. Most hold doctoral degrees. They provide a substantive education that combines comprehensive knowledge with critical skills and practical workplace relevance. Above all, faculty members of the College of Education are committed to their students' personal and professional development.

ARGOSY UNIVERSITY, TAMPA

College of Education

Programs of Study

Argosy University, Tampa, offers the Master of Arts (M.A.) degree in School Counseling, Master of Arts in Education (M.A.Ed.) degrees in Curriculum and Instruction, Curriculum and Instruction : ELL/ESL, Curriculum and Instruction : Reading, Curriculum and Instruction : Special Education, Educational Administration, and Higher and Postsecondary Education; Doctor of Education (Ed.D.) degrees in Advanced Educational Administration, Community College Executive Leadership, Curriculum and Instruction, Educational Leadership, Higher and Postsecondary Education, Initial Educational Administration, and Teacher Leadership; and Education Specialist (Ed.S.) degrees in Curriculum and Instruction, Educational Leadership and Initial Educational Administration.

The Master of Arts (M.A.) in School Counseling program introduces students to basic counseling skills that integrate individual and group theoretical foundations into appropriate client interaction and intervention skills. The program emphasizes development of attitudes, knowledge, and skills essential in the formation of school counselors who are committed to the ethical provision of quality services. The program educates and trainings students to enter a professional career as Master's-level practitioners with a demonstrated knowledge of social and cultural diversity, theoretical foundations of professional counseling, and field experience into appropriate client interaction and intervention skills for utilization in a school setting with diverse clients.

The Master of Arts in Education (M.A.Ed.) in Curriculum and Instruction degree program is intended to prepare educators who work in the P–12 setting as change agents who engage actively in their communities, using appropriate pedagogy and technology to foster the development of global citizens. In addition to the core course requirements, students enrolled in this degree program will complete a four course sequence designed to strengthen educators' knowledge and skills in order to work more effectively in the current classroom environment. This degree program does not lead to certification or credential endorsement.

The Master of Arts in Education (M.A.Ed.) in Curriculum and Instruction: ELL/ESL degree program is a 30-credit-hour degree program intended to prepare educators who work in the P–12 setting as change agents who engage actively in their communities, using appropriate pedagogy and technology to foster the development of global citizens. In addition to the core course requirements, students enrolled in this degree program will complete a four course sequence designed to strengthen educators' knowledge and skills when working with students who are classified as English Language Learners (ELL) or English as a Second Language (ESL). This degree program does not lead to certification or credential endorsement.

The Master of Arts in Education (M.A.Ed.) in Curriculum and Instruction: Reading degree program is a 30-credit-hour program intended to prepare educators who work in the P–12 setting as change agents who engage actively in their communities, using appropriate pedagogy and technology to foster the development of global citizens. Students enrolled in this program will complete a four course sequence in reading designed to strengthen educators' knowledge and skills in this specific area of focus. This program does not lead to certification or credential endorsement.

The Master of Arts in Education (M.A.Ed.) in Educational Administration program prepares individuals to serve as school administrators. The program is designed for practicing educators who have already completed a bachelor's degree program from a regionally accredited institution and are seeking administrative credentialing. Based on state requirements, students may be required to complete additional experiences or course work.

The Master of Arts in Education (M.A.Ed.) in Higher and Postsecondary Education program is designed for individuals who seek administrative and other positions in noninstructional units at higher education and postsecondary institutions. Graduates of this program will have enhanced practical skills, knowledge, and experiences as professionals and leaders in universities, colleges, and postsecondary educational institutions. A bachelor's degree is required for admission to this program.

The Doctor of Education (Ed.D.) in Advanced Educational Administration program prepares individuals to serve as school administrators in advanced positions. The program is designed for practicing educators who have already completed a graduate level program from a regionally accredited institution and currently hold principal or initial administrative licensure. Completion of the program results in a terminal degree which includes a specific writing, research, and dissertation sequence.

The Doctor of Education (Ed.D.) in Community College Executive Leadership program is designed for community college administrators who seek to move into senior administrative positions (such as president, vice-president, dean, and director) at community colleges.

The Doctor of Education (Ed.D.) in Curriculum and Instruction degree program is designed to prepare educators as change agents and leaders in the P–12 setting who engage actively in their communities, using appropriate pedagogy and technology to foster the development of global citizens. This program does not lead to certification or credential endorsement.

The Doctor of Education (Ed.D.) in Higher and Postsecondary Education program is designed for students to enhance their professional competence as educational leaders, instructors, or consultants in academic affairs, student affairs, or student services divisions within community colleges, technical schools and institutes, and four-year colleges and universities, as well as in government, military, religious, and profit or nonprofit postsecondary educational organizations and divisions. The program offers three concentrations: student affairs and services, teaching and learning, and interdisciplinary studies.

The Doctor of Education (Ed.D.) in Educational Leadership program is designed to enhance educational leadership strengths. Students learn innovative and collaborative techniques used to manage and govern educational institutions. The program prepares students for administrative leadership positions at the district, regional, state, or national level. Students must choose a concentration in higher education administration or K–12 education.

The Doctor of Education (Ed.D.) in Initial Educational Administration program prepares individuals to serve as school principals and/or building-level administrators. The program is designed for practicing educators who have already completed a graduate-level program from a regionally accredited institution or an appropriately certified foreign institution, and are seeking administrative licensure at the initial or K–12 level. Completion of the program results in a terminal degree which includes a specific writing, research, and dissertation sequence.

The Doctor of Education (Ed.D.) in Teacher Leadership degree program is a 60-credit-hour program designed for classroom teachers who are looking to expand their content knowledge, develop leadership skills, teach more effectively, and support the professional development of their peers. Candidates in this degree program will have the opportunity to become skillful in building collaborative relationships and learning communities that focus on student learning and support a strong positive climate in the school. Peer mentoring and coaching are modeled and practiced throughout the program in field experiences and the culminating research project. The program culminates in a dissertation related to teacher leadership and is designed to add knowledge to the field of teacher leadership. The Ed.D. in Teacher Leadership degree program does not prepare for or lead to teacher or school administrative certification/ licensure.

The Education Specialist (Ed.S.) in Curriculum and Instruction degree program is designed to prepare educators as change agents and leaders in the P–12 setting who engage actively in their communities, using appropriate pedagogy and technology to foster the development of global citizens. This program does not lead to certification or any credential endorsement.

The Education Specialist (Ed.S.) in Educational Leadership noncertification program provides students a focus on courses and curricula designed to parallel prevailing licensure and certification requirements. However, each student should check with the agency in the state in which they intend to teach.

The Education Specialist (Ed.S.) in Initial Educational Administration program prepares individuals to serve as school principals and/or building-level administrators. The program is designed for practicing educators who have already completed a graduate level program from a regionally accredited institution or an appropriately certified foreign institution, and are seeking administrative licensure at the initial or K–12 level.

Note: These programs do not lead to teacher or administrator certification, licensure, or endorsement in any state in the United States.

Research Facilities

Argosy University libraries provide curriculum support and educational resources, including current text materials, diagnostic training documents, reference materials and databases, journals and dissertations, and major and current titles in program areas. There is an online public-access catalog of library resources available throughout the Argosy University system. Students have remote access to the campus library database, enabling them to study and conduct research at home. Academic databases offer dissertation abstracts, academic journals, and professional periodicals. All library computers are Internet accessible. Software applications include Word, Excel, PowerPoint, SPSS, and various test-scoring programs.

Financial Aid

Financial aid is available to those who qualify. Argosy University, Tampa, offers access to federal and state aid programs, merit-based awards, grants, loans, and a work-study program. As a first step, students should complete the Free Application for Federal Student Aid (FAFSA). Prospective students can apply electronically at http://www.fafsa.ed.gov or at the campus.

Cost of Study

Tuition varies by program. Students should contact Argosy University, Tampa, for tuition information.

Living and Housing Costs

Students typically live in apartments in the metropolitan Tampa area. Living expenses vary according to each student's preferred standard of living, housing, and transportation. The University does not offer or operate student housing. Most of the students are full-time working professionals who live within driving distance of the campus. Several nearby hotels offer special rates for those who commute from long distances. The Admissions Department also maintains a list of housing options, including contact information, for University students who wish to share housing. For more information, students should contact the Admissions Department.

Student Group

Admission to Argosy University, Tampa, is selective to ensure a dynamic and engaged student body. It encourages diversity in academic and employment backgrounds and promotes integration of the student body into professional life through established connections with local and national professional associations. Argosy University offers a professionally oriented education with rich opportunities to gain practical experience in class, field placements, and internships. Full-time students and working professionals gain the extensive knowledge and range of skills necessary for effective performance in their chosen fields.

Student Outcomes

Students can register with the University's online career-services system and use select services from a distance, such as degree-specific career e-mail lists, national job posts, and virtual job fairs. Students should contact the University for more information.

Location

Located in sunny Florida, Argosy University, Tampa, attracts a diverse student population from throughout the United States, the Caribbean, Europe, Africa, and Asia. The school offers rigorous programs of study in a supportive, collaborative environment. The campus sits within an hour's drive of some of the most popular tourist destinations in the world, including the Disney theme parks, Busch Gardens, and the Florida Gulf Coast beaches. Major-league sporting events, concerts, theaters, world-renowned restaurants, recreational facilities, and a cosmopolitan social scene are all within easy reach. Tampa combines the opportunities of a large city with the friendliness of a small town with a strong sense of community.

Many educational institutions and agencies in the area provide varied opportunities for student training. The Tampa-St. Petersburg-Clearwater metropolitan area offers a diversified economic base fueled by an array of companies, including Verizon Communications and JP Morgan Chase.

The University

Argosy University is a private institution with nineteen locations across the nation. Argosy University, Tampa, provides students with a career resources office, an academic resources center, and extensive information access for research. It offers the resources of a large university, plus the friendliness and personal attention of a small campus. The innovative programs feature dynamic, relevant, and practical curricula delivered in flexible class formats. Students enjoy scheduling options that make it easier to fit school into their busy lives, choosing from day and evening courses, on campus or online. Many students find a combination of class formats to be an ideal way of continuing their education while meeting family and professional demands.

Argosy University is accredited by the Accrediting Commission for Senior Colleges and Universities of the Western Association for Schools and Colleges (985 Atlantic Avenue, Suite 100, Alameda, California, 94501, http://www.wascsenior.org). Licensed by the Commission for Independent Education, License No. 2610.

Applying

Argosy University, Tampa, accepts students year-round on a rolling admissions basis, depending on availability of required courses. Applications for admission are available online or by contacting the campus.

Correspondence and Information

Argosy University, Tampa
1403 North Howard Avenue
Tampa, Florida 33607
United States
Phone: 813-393-5290
800-850-6488 (toll-free)
Fax: 813-874-1989
E-mail: auadmissions@argosy.edu
Web site: http://www.argosy.edu/tampa

THE FACULTY

The Argosy University faculty comprises working professionals who are eager to help students succeed. Members bring real-world experience and the latest practice innovations to the academic setting. The diverse faculty members of the College of Education are widely recognized for contributions to the field. Most hold doctoral degrees. They provide a substantive education that combines comprehensive knowledge with critical skills and practical workplace relevance. Above all, faculty members are committed to their students' personal and professional development.

ARGOSY UNIVERSITY, TWIN CITIES

College of Education

Programs of Study

Argosy University, Twin Cities, offers Master of Arts in Education (M.A.Ed.) degrees in Higher and Postsecondary Education, Teaching and Learning: ELL/ESL, Teaching and Learning: Reading, and Teaching and Learning: Special Education; Doctor of Education (Ed.D.) degrees in Advanced Educational Administration, Higher and Postsecondary Education, Initial Educational Administration, and Teaching and Learning; and Education Specialist (Ed.S.) degrees in Advanced Educational Administration, Higher and Postsecondary Education, Initial Educational Administration, and Teaching and Learning.

The Master of Arts in Education (M.A.Ed.) in Higher and Postsecondary Education program is designed for individuals who seek administrative and other positions in noninstructional units at higher education and postsecondary institutions. Graduates of this program will have enhanced practical skills, knowledge, and experiences as professionals and leaders in universities, colleges, and postsecondary educational institutions. A bachelor's degree is required for admission to this program.

The Master of Arts in Education (M.A.Ed.) in Teaching and Learning: ELL/ESL is a 30-credit-hour degree program intended to prepare educators who work in the P–12 setting as change agents who engage actively in their communities, using appropriate pedagogy and technology to foster the development of global citizens. In addition to the core course requirements, students will complete a four-course sequence to strengthen knowledge and skills when working with students who are classified as English Language Learners (ELL) or English as a Second Language (ESL). This program does not lead to certification or credential endorsement.

The Master of Arts in Education (M.A.Ed.) in Teaching and Learning: Reading is a 30-credit program intended to prepare educators who work in the P–12 setting as change agents who engage actively in their communities, using appropriate pedagogy and technology to foster the development of global citizens. Students enrolled in this program will complete a four-course sequence in reading to strengthen knowledge and skills in this specific area. This program does not lead to certification or credential endorsement.

The Master of Arts in Education (M.A.Ed.) in Teaching and Learning: Special Education is a 30-credit program intended to prepare educators who work in the P–12 setting as change agents who engage actively in their communities, using appropriate pedagogy and technology to foster the development of global citizens. Students enrolled in this program will complete a four-course sequence designed to strengthen knowledge and skills when working with students with special learning needs. This program does not lead to certification or credential endorsement.

The Doctor of Education (Ed.D.) in Advanced Educational Administration program prepares individuals to serve as school administrators in advanced positions. The program is designed for practicing educators who have already completed a graduate level program from a regionally accredited institution and currently hold principal or initial administrative licensure. Completion of the program results in a terminal degree which includes a specific writing, research, and dissertation sequence.

The Doctor of Education (Ed.D.) in Higher and Postsecondary Education program is designed for students to enhance their professional competence as educational leaders, instructors, or consultants in academic affairs, student affairs, or student services divisions within community colleges, technical schools and institutes, and four-year colleges and universities, as well as in government, military, religious, and profit or nonprofit postsecondary educational organizations and divisions. The program offers three concentrations: student affairs and services, teaching and learning, and interdisciplinary studies.

The Doctor of Education (Ed.D.) in Initial Educational Administration program prepares individuals to serve as school principals and/or building-level administrators. The program is designed for practicing educators who have already completed a graduate-level program from a regionally accredited institution or an appropriately certified foreign institution, and are seeking administrative licensure at the initial or K–12 level. Completion of the program results in a terminal degree which includes a specific writing, research, and dissertation sequence.

The Doctor of Education (Ed.D.) in Teaching and Learning is designed to prepare educators in P–12 settings to serve as change agents and leaders who engage actively in their communities, using appropriate pedagogy and technology to foster the development of global citizens. This program does not lead to certification or credential endorsement.

The Education Specialist (Ed.S.) in Advanced Educational Administration program prepares individuals to serve as school administrators in advanced positions. The program is designed for practicing educators who have already completed a graduate-level program from a regionally accredited institution and currently hold principal or initial administrative licensure.

The Education Specialist (Ed.S.) in Higher and Postsecondary Education program is designed for students to enhance their professional competence as educational leaders, instructors, or consultants in academic affairs, student affairs, or student services divisions within community colleges, technical schools and institutes, four-year colleges and universities, as well as in government, military, religious, profit or nonprofit postsecondary educational organizations and divisions. The program offers three concentrations: student affairs and services, teaching and learning, and interdisciplinary studies.

The Education Specialist (Ed.S.) in Initial Educational Administration program prepares individuals to serve as school principals and/or building-level administrators. The program is designed for practicing educators who have already completed a graduate level program from a regionally accredited institution or an appropriately certified foreign institution, and are seeking administrative licensure at the initial or K–12 level.

The Education Specialist (Ed.S.) in Teaching and Learning program is designed to prepare educators in P–12 settings as change agents and leaders who engage actively in their communities, using appropriate pedagogy and technology to foster the development of global citizens. This program does not lead to certification or any credential endorsement.

Note: These programs do not lead to teacher or administrator certification, licensure, or endorsement in any state in the United States.

Argosy University, Twin Cities

Research Facilities

Argosy University libraries provide curriculum support and educational resources including current text materials, diagnostic training documents, reference materials and databases, journals and dissertations, and major and current titles in program areas. There is an online public-access catalog of library resources available throughout the Argosy University system. Students have remote access to the campus library database, enabling them to study and conduct research at home. Academic databases offer dissertation abstracts, academic journals, and professional periodicals. All library computers are Internet accessible. Software applications include Word, Excel, PowerPoint, SPSS, and various test-scoring programs.

Financial Aid

Financial aid is available to those who qualify. Argosy University, Twin Cities, offers access to federal and state aid programs, merit-based awards, grants, loans, and a work-study program. As a first step, students should complete the Free Application for Federal Student Aid (FAFSA). Prospective students can apply electronically at http://www.fafsa.ed.gov or at the campus.

Cost of Study

Tuition varies by program. Students should contact Argosy University, Twin Cities, for tuition information.

Living and Housing Costs

Students typically live in apartments in the metropolitan area. Living expenses vary according to each student's preferred standard of living, housing, and transportation. The University does not offer or operate student housing. Most of the students are full-time working professionals who live within driving distance of the campus. Several nearby hotels offer special rates for those who commute from long distances. The Admissions Department also maintains a list of housing options, including contact information for University students who wish to share housing. For more information, students should contact the Admissions Department.

Student Group

Admission to Argosy University, Twin Cities, is selective to ensure a dynamic and engaged student body. The University encourages diversity in academic and employment backgrounds and promotes integration of the student body into professional life through established connections with local and national professional associations. Argosy University offers a professionally oriented education with rich opportunities to gain practical experience in class, field placements, and internships. Full-time students and working professionals gain the extensive knowledge and range of skills necessary for effective performance in their chosen fields.

Student Outcomes

Students can register with the University's online career-services system and use select services from a distance, such as degree-specific career e-mail lists, national job posts, and virtual job fairs. Students should contact the University for more information.

Location

Argosy University, Twin Cities, offers rigorous academics in a supportive environment. The campus is nestled in a parklike suburban setting within 10 miles of the airport and the Mall of America. Students enjoy the convenience of nearby shops, restaurants, and housing and easy freeway access. The neighboring Eagan Community Center offers many amenities, including walking paths, a fitness center, meeting rooms, and an outdoor amphitheater. The Twin Cities of Minneapolis and St. Paul have been rated by popular magazines as one of the most livable metropolitan areas in the country. With a population of 2.5 million, the area offers an abundance of recreational activities. Year-round outdoor activities, nationally acclaimed venues for theater art and music, and professional sports teams attract residents and visitors alike.

Many educational institutions and agencies in the area provide varied opportunities for student training. The Minneapolis-St. Paul metropolitan area offers a diversified economic base fueled by an array of companies. Among the numerous publicly traded companies headquartered in the area are Target, UnitedHealth Group, 3M, General Mills, and U.S. Bancorp.

The University

Argosy University is a private institution with nineteen locations across the nation. Argosy University, Twin Cities, provides students with a career resources office, an academic resources center and extensive information access for research. It offers the resources of a large university plus the friendliness and personal attention of a small campus. The innovative programs feature dynamic, relevant, and practical curricula delivered in flexible class formats. Students enjoy scheduling options that make it easier to fit school into their busy lives, choosing from day and evening courses, on campus or online. Many students find a combination of class formats to be an ideal way of continuing their education while meeting family and professional demands.

Argosy University is accredited by the Accrediting Commission for Senior Colleges and Universities of the Western Association for Schools and Colleges (985 Atlantic Avenue, Suite 100, Alameda, California, 94501, http://www.wascsenior.org).

Applying

Argosy University, Twin Cities, accepts students year-round on a rolling admissions basis, depending on the availability of required courses. Applications for admission are available online or by contacting the campus.

Correspondence and Information

Argosy University, Twin Cities
1515 Central Parkway
Eagan, Minnesota 55121
United States
Phone: 651-846-2882
888-844-2004 (toll-free)
Fax: 651-994-7956
E-mail: auadmissions@argosy.edu
Web site: http://www.argosy.edu/twincities

THE FACULTY

The Argosy University faculty comprises working professionals who are eager to help students succeed. Members bring real-world experience and the latest practice innovations to the academic setting. The diverse faculty members of the College of Education are widely recognized for contributions to the field. Most hold doctoral degrees. They provide a substantive education that combines comprehensive knowledge with critical skills and practical workplace relevance. Above all, faculty members are committed to their students' personal and professional development.

ARGOSY UNIVERSITY, WASHINGTON DC

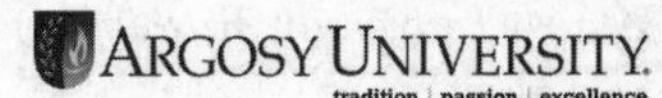

College of Education

Programs of Study

Argosy University, Washington DC, offers Master of Arts in Education (M.A.Ed.) degrees in Higher and Postsecondary Education and Teaching and Learning, Teaching and Learning: ELL/ESL, Teaching and Learning: Integrated Concentration, Teaching and Learning: Reading, and Teaching and Learning: Special Education; Education Specialist (Ed.S.) degrees in Educational Leadership and Teaching and Learning; and Doctor of Education (Ed.D.) degrees in Community College Executive Leadership, Higher and Postsecondary Education and Teaching and Learning.

The Master of Arts in Education (M.A.Ed.) in Higher and Postsecondary Education program is designed for individuals who seek administrative and other positions in noninstructional units at higher education and postsecondary institutions. Graduates of this program will have enhanced practical skills, knowledge, and experiences as professionals and leaders in universities, colleges, and postsecondary educational institutions. A bachelor's degree is required for admission to this program.

The Education Specialist (Ed.S.) in Educational Leadership program concentrates on applied organizational theory within the context of educational organizations. This specialized program develops the competencies required to secure educational administrator positions at the elementary or secondary school level.

The Doctor of Education (Ed.D.) in Educational Leadership program is designed to enhance educational leadership strengths. Students learn innovative and collaborative techniques to manage and govern educational institutions. The program prepares students for administrative leadership positions at the district, regional, state, or national level. Students must choose a concentration in higher education administration or K–12 education.

The Doctor of Education (Ed.D.) in Community College Executive Leadership program is designed for community college administrators who seek to move into senior administrative positions (such as president, vice-president, dean, and director) at community colleges.

Note: These programs do not lead to teacher or administrator certification, licensure, or endorsement in any state in the United States.

Research Facilities

Argosy University libraries provide curriculum support and educational resources, including current text materials, diagnostic training documents, reference materials and databases, journals and dissertations, and major and current titles in program areas. There is an online public-access catalog of library resources available throughout the Argosy University system. Students have remote access to the campus library database, enabling them to study and conduct research at home. Academic databases offer dissertation abstracts, academic journals, and professional periodicals. All library computers are Internet accessible. Software applications include Word, Excel, PowerPoint, SPSS, and various test-scoring programs.

Financial Aid

Financial aid is available to those who qualify. Argosy University, Washington DC, offers access to federal and state aid programs, merit-based awards, grants, loans, and a work-study program. As a first step, students should complete the Free Application for Federal Student Aid (FAFSA). Prospective students can apply electronically at http://www.fafsa.ed.gov or at the campus.

Cost of Study

Tuition varies by program. Students should contact Argosy University, Washington DC, for tuition information.

Living and Housing Costs

Students typically live in apartments in the metropolitan Washington, D.C., area. Living expenses vary according to each student's preferred standard of living, housing, and transportation. The University does not offer or operate student housing. Most of the students are full-time working professionals who live within driving distance of the campus. Several nearby hotels offer special rates for those who commute from long distances. The Admissions Department also maintains a list of housing options, including contact information for university students who wish to share housing. For more information, students should contact the Admissions Department.

Student Group

Admission to Argosy University, Washington DC, is selective to ensure a dynamic and engaged student body. It encourages diversity in academic and employment backgrounds and promotes integration of the student body into professional life through established connections with local and national professional associations. Argosy University offers a professionally oriented education with rich opportunities to gain practical experience in class, field placements, and internships. Full-time students and working professionals gain the extensive knowledge and range of skills necessary for effective performance in their chosen fields.

Student Outcomes

Students can register with the University's online career-services system and use select services from a distance, such as degree-specific career e-mail lists, national job posts, and virtual job fairs. Students should contact the University for more information.

Argosy University, Washington DC

Location

Argosy University, Washington DC, is located in suburban Arlington, Virginia. The University is conveniently situated to provide access to most major highways in the area and is easily accessible by public transportation. In proximity to Georgetown, students enjoy access to the many diverse attractions of the D.C. area. Additional campus space is located at The Art Institute of Washington Building (1820 Fort Myer Drive). The University houses administrative offices and seven classrooms at this location. Perhaps best known as the home of the Pentagon and Arlington National Cemetery, Arlington, Virginia, is one of the most highly educated areas in the nation. It is also one of the most diverse.

Many educational institutions and agencies in the area provide varied opportunities for student training. Major employers in the region include MCI Telecommunications Corporation, Bell Atlantic Network Services, and Gannett/USA Today Company, Inc.

The University

Argosy University is a private institution with nineteen locations across the nation. Argosy University, Washington DC, provides students with a career resources office, an academic resources center, and extensive information access for research. It offers the resources of a large university, plus the friendliness and personal attention of a small campus. The innovative programs feature dynamic, relevant, and practical curricula delivered in flexible class formats. Students enjoy scheduling options that make it easier to fit school into their busy lives, choosing from day and evening courses, on campus or online. Many students find a combination of class formats to be an ideal way of continuing their education while meeting family and professional demands.

Argosy University is accredited by the Accrediting Commission for Senior Colleges and Universities of the Western Association for Schools and Colleges (985 Atlantic Avenue, Suite 100, Alameda, California, 94501, http://www.wascsenior.org).

Applying

Argosy University, Washington DC, accepts students year-round on a rolling admissions basis, depending on availability of required courses. Applications for admission are available online or by contacting the campus.

Correspondence and Information

Argosy University, Washington DC
1550 Wilson Boulevard, Suite 600
Arlington, Virginia 22209
United States
Phone: 703-526-5800
866-703-2777 (toll-free)
Fax: 703-526-5850
E-mail: auadmissions@argosy.edu
Web site: http://www.argosy.edu/washingtondc

THE FACULTY

The Argosy University faculty comprises working professionals who are eager to help students succeed. Members bring real-world experience and the latest practice innovations to the academic setting. The diverse faculty members of the College of Education are widely recognized for contributions to the field. Most hold doctoral degrees. They provide a substantive education that combines comprehensive knowledge with critical skills and practical workplace relevance. Above all, faculty members are committed to their students' personal and professional development.

FELICIAN COLLEGE

Programs in Education

Programs of Study

Felician College is a coeducational liberal arts institution deeply rooted in the Catholic/Franciscan tradition. Felician College is dedicated to providing an academic environment that encourages its students to reach their highest potential while preparing them to meet the challenges of the twenty-first century with an informed mind and an understanding heart.

Felician College offers two master's degree programs in education, a Master of Arts in Education and a Master of Arts in Education: Leadership. Master's and certificate programs in school nursing/teacher of health education are also available.

The Master of Arts in Education program is for certified teachers looking to earn a master's degree and advance their career, or for students and career changers who seek to become certified teachers and want the advantage of a master's degree. The Master of Arts in Education program with a concentration in elementary education consists of 33 credits (37 for initial licensure); the concentration in teachers of students with disabilities consists 42 credits (46 for initial licensure).

The Master of Arts in Education: Leadership program offers experienced teachers the opportunity to earn a master's degree with principal and/or supervisory endorsements. It is designed for those who aspire to a leadership position in public or private schools and who want both the academic theory and hands-on, practical experience of educational leadership. Those who seek the Master of Arts in Education: Leadership program with principal and supervision endorsement are required to complete 36 credits, including 6 credits in an internship. Applicants to this program are required to have five years of educational experience under valid certification. Those who seek the Master of Arts in Education: Leadership program with supervision endorsement only are required to complete 33 credits. Three years of educational experience under valid certification is required of applicants to this program track.

The Master of Arts in Education: School Nursing, Master of Arts in Education: Health Education, and Master of Arts in Education: School Nursing and Health Education programs prepare registered nurses with a baccalaureate degree to obtain dual licensure as school nurses and/or teachers of health education, or for licensed school nurses to obtain a master's degree.

The School Nursing and Teacher of Health Education graduate certificate program prepares registered nurses with a baccalaureate degree to provide nursing service and health education in the K–12 school setting. The program is approved by the State of New Jersey Department of Education and consists of 19 credits (seven required courses). The certificate can be completed in either two or four semesters.

Research Facilities

The College Library is a two-story building that serves the needs of students, faculty and staff members, and alumni with more than 110,000 books and over 800 periodical subscriptions. This collection is enhanced by large holdings of materials in microform, which can be used on the library's reader/printer equipment. With its computers linked to information services such as Dialog and OCLC, and as a member of the New Jersey Library Network and VALE, the library locates and obtains information, journal articles, and books not available in its collection from sources all over the country. Computerized databases can also be accessed directly by users through the online FirstSearch workstation, where up-to-date information on 40 million books and an index of 15,000 periodicals is available. The library is also connected to the Internet and has several CD-ROM workstations. Through EBSCOhost, Bell & Howell's ProQuest, CINAHL, and other services, students and faculty and staff members have access to numerous online journal indexes—as well as articles from thousands of periodicals—from anywhere on the campus computer network or from their home computers. An experienced staff of professional librarians is available to assist users.

The College's computer facilities include an academic and administrative network, four computerized labs, a computerized learning center, and two computer centers that are available for students, with a total of about 200 computers available for student/faculty member use. All classrooms, offices, and facilities are wired for Internet and e-mail.

Financial Aid

To qualify for financial aid, a student must complete the Free Application for Federal Student Aid (FAFSA).

Cost of Study

In 2012–13, graduate tuition is $915 per credit. Fees are additional.

Living and Housing Costs

Students are housed in two residence halls on the Rutherford campus, Milton Court and Elliott Terrace. Both buildings have housing organized around student suites with semiprivate baths. On-campus room and board is approximately $11,400 per year. On-campus housing is not available to married students.

Student Group

Felician College enrolls approximately 2,300 students. In fall 2011, there were approximately 350 students enrolled in graduate programs.

Location

Felician College's Lodi campus is located on the banks of the Saddle River on a beautifully landscaped campus of 27 acres and offers a collegiate setting in suburban Bergen County, within easy driving distance of New York City. The Felician College Rutherford Campus is set on 10.5 beautifully landscaped acres in the heart of the historic community of Rutherford, New Jersey. Only 15 minutes from the Lodi campus, the Rutherford complex contains student residences, classroom buildings, a student

Felician College

center, and a gymnasium. The campus is a short distance from downtown Rutherford, where there are many shops and businesses of interest to students. Regular shuttle bus service between the two campuses is a quick 10-minute ride that turns two campuses into a one-campus home for the students.

The College

Felician College, a coeducational liberal arts college, is a Catholic, private, independent institution for students representing diverse religious, racial, and ethnic backgrounds. The College operates on two campuses in Lodi and Rutherford, New Jersey. The College is one of the institutions of higher learning sponsored by the Felician Franciscan Sisters. Its mission is to provide a values-oriented education based in the liberal arts while it prepares students for meaningful lives and careers in contemporary society. To meet the needs of students and to provide personal enrichment courses to matriculated and nonmatriculated students, Felician College offers day, evening, and weekend programs. The College is accredited by the Middle States Association of Colleges and Schools and carries program accreditation from the Commission on Collegiate Nursing Education, the International Assembly for Collegiate Business Education, and the Teacher Education Accreditation Council.

Applying

Applicants should complete the application for adult and graduate admission and submit it along with the $40 application fee; transcript(s) from all undergraduate and/or graduate institutions previously attended; a copy of New Jersey teacher certification, if currently certified; three letters of reference (one personal and two professional); and a personal statement. An interview and additional information may be required.

Correspondence and Information

Office of Graduate Admission
262 South Main Street
Lodi, New Jersey 07644-2117
United States
Phone: 201-559-6077
Fax: 201-559-6138
E-mail: graduate@felician.edu
Web site: http://www.felician.edu/

THE FACULTY

Specific information regarding the faculty of Felician College is available on the College's Web site at http://www.felician.edu.

HOLY FAMILY UNIVERSITY

School of Education
Graduate Programs

Programs of Study

Since its founding, Holy Family University has been a regional leader in education. Holy Family Education alumni hold teaching and leadership positions in school districts throughout the Greater Philadelphia area. Through its School of Education, the University has greatly expanded its offerings to include master's degrees, a variety of certifications, and a doctorate in educational leadership and professional studies.

Holy Family's graduate education programs are designed for individuals seeking initial teacher certification and for experienced teachers looking for an advanced degree and/ or additional certifications. Whether students are interested in elementary school or secondary school teaching, there is a degree program available to meet their needs.

Holy Family's programs include the general Master of Education (M.Ed.) degree as well as M.Ed. degrees with Pennsylvania certification in PK–4, 4–8, or secondary education; Pennsylvania reading specialist and supervisor certification; and certification in PK–8 or 7–12 special education. The University also offers the M.Ed. in TESOL and Literacy and certificates in education leadership and the principalship. Certificate programs are available in reading supervision, English as a second language, autism, and teacher internship. In addition, a new Doctor of Education in Educational Leadership and Professional Studies (Ed.D.) degree program is available.

Research Facilities

Holy Family's newest academic facility, the Education & Technology Center, is a 62,000-square-foot facility that contains eight general classrooms, four computer labs with 25 personal computers in each, and five classrooms specially designed to model primary and secondary classroom instruction for the University's education students. These model classrooms allow students with certain disabilities, such as vision or hearing impairment, to be integrated fully into a regular classroom, providing Holy Family's Education graduates with valuable experience using adaptive technology in a classroom environment. In addition, the facility contains a 200-seat auditorium, three conference rooms, a teacher resource room, a café, student and faculty lounges, and faculty and administrative offices for the School of Education. It also contains classroom, studio, and gallery space for the University's art and art education programs.

Financial Aid

Holy Family is committed to helping adults further their education by consistently maintaining competitive tuition rates. Most graduate students are eligible for Federal Stafford Loans when attending with a half-time enrollment status (6 graduate credits) or greater. For more information, students may contact the Financial Aid Office at finaid@holyfamily.edu or call 267-341-3233.

Cost of Study

Tuition for Holy Family's traditional graduate programs is $655 per credit hour.

Living and Housing Costs

Holy Family University has housing for full-time graduate students, pending availability. There are also numerous housing options available in the nearby area.

Student Group

Approximately 600 students, nearly all of them studying part-time, are enrolled in the graduate education programs. Student organizations include Alpha Upsilon Alpha, the Honor Society of the International Reading Association; the Education Connections Society; and Kappa Delta Pi International Honor Society. In addition, Holy Family is a candidate member of the Teacher Education Accreditation Council.

Student Outcomes

Whether students wish to work with preschoolers, elementary school students, adolescents, second language learners, or children with special needs, Holy Family University's School of Education offers a variety of study options to fit their career goals and interests. The University's state-approved graduate programs are ideal for experienced teachers seeking additional certification or career changers who wish to become teachers. Holy Family Education alumni hold teaching and leadership positions in school districts throughout the area.

Location

The School of Education is housed on Holy Family's Northeast Philadelphia campus. Located less than a mile from Bucks County, Holy Family offers the benefits of a big city in a quiet, park-like suburban setting. With easy access to regional rail lines, city bus routes, and nearby expressways, the University is conveniently located for students throughout Greater Philadelphia.

The University

It's easy to see why Holy Family graduates stand out. The difference is real-world. The difference is experience. The difference is preparedness and a focus on student outcomes.

Respect for the individual, the dignity of the human person—these values are at the very core of Holy Family University. They are values that are taught here; even more, they are values that are lived here. Holy Family's concern for moral values and social justice guides its programs and enriches everything that the University does

Applying

Admissions are rolling. Applicants must submit a statement of goals, official transcripts, two letters of reference (three letters for the Ed.D. program), and the application fee. Students who have an undergraduate GPA below 3.0 must take the GRE or MAT. Current teachers must submit copies of their teacher certification. Applicants to the Ed.D. program must submit copies of all certification documents, a current resume, two writing samples completed during the master's program or a copy of their master's thesis, and GRE or MAT scores.

Correspondence and Information

Graduate Admissions Office
Holy Family University
9801 Frankford Avenue
Philadelphia, Pennsylvania 19114
United States
Phone: 267-341-3327
Fax: 215-637-1478
E-mail: gradstudy@holyfamily.edu
Web site: http://www.holyfamily.edu

THE FACULTY AND THEIR RESEARCH

Maria Agnew, Assistant Professor; Ph.D., Temple. Research interests: autism and special education.

Anthony Applegate, Professor; Ph.D., Temple. Research interests: assessment and promotion of thoughtful literacy; link between thoughtful literacy and motivation to read; link between thoughtful literacy and fluency in reading; reading habits and attitudes of teachers.

Brian Berry, Professor; Ph.D., Temple. Research interests: inclusion/acceptance of children/individuals with disabilities; transition from school to adult life for students with disabilities; supported employment; personnel preparation reform.

Mary Kay Doran, Professor; Ph.D., North Carolina, Greensboro. Research interests: sociological issues of schooling/education.

Roger Gee, Associate Professor; Ph.D., Pennsylvania. Research interests: reading rate and comprehension, corpus linguistics.

Helen Hoffner, Professor; Ed.D., Widener; Research interests: ways in which closed-captioned and visually described television programs and films can be used to improve reading ability for children and adults.

Elizabeth Jones, Professor; Ph.D., Penn State. Research interest: assessment and curriculum reform.

Barry MacGibeny, Professor; Ph.D., Ed.D., Temple. Research interests: educational leadership and educational technology.

Kathleen Quinn, Professor; Ph.D., Temple. Research interests: preparation of reading specialists, impact of teaching and use of technology on children's reading and writing achievement, and assessment of reading and writing.

Donna Rafter, Associate Professor; Ph.D., Rutgers. Research interests: teachers' beliefs and practices in literacy, especially writing.

Claire Ann Sullivan, Professor; Ed.D., Rutgers. Research interests: special education (low incidence disabilities) and college teaching.

Roseanna Wright, Assistant Professor; Ph.D., Temple. Research interests: support of children and adults with significant disabilities in achieving and maintaining a quality lifestyle, and the transition from school to adult living for these individuals.

MANHATTANVILLE COLLEGE

School of Education

Programs of Study

The School of Education at Manhattanville College offers programs to prepare graduates for careers in education at all levels, from teaching to leadership and administration. Undergraduates often earn a double major in education and another liberal arts concentration, while the graduate program is geared to students interested in becoming teachers, often after having had other careers, and to classroom teachers who want to extend their teaching certifications or update their knowledge base. All programs are registered with and approved by the New York State Education Department. Education programs at Manhattanville are accredited by the National Council for Accreditation of Teacher Education (NCATE).

Manhattanville offers a graduate-level accelerated teacher certification program, Jump Start, which is especially popular with adults who are changing careers. Jump Start classes begin in February, and its students are in their own classrooms by September as well-prepared, fully paid teachers with full benefits while they finish the additional requirements for the master's degree.

Manhattanville offers three master's programs, the Master of Arts in Teaching (M.A.T.), the Master of Professional Studies (M.P.S.), and the Master in Educational Studies (M.Ed.), as well as a Doctor of Education (Ed.D.) degree in educational leadership. In addition, Manhattanville offers classes in more than sixty areas of concentration leading to eighteen different New York State certifications. Manhattanville also offers the Master of Professional Studies (M.P.S.), post-master's certifications, certificates of advanced study, and a professional diploma.

The Master of Arts in Teaching degree program is intended for strong liberal arts graduates with few or no prior courses in education. On completion of the program, the candidate is eligible for New York State certification as a teacher of childhood (grades 1–6), early childhood (birth–grade 2), early childhood and childhood (birth–grade 6), biology (grades 5–12), chemistry (grades 5–12), English (grades 5–12), French (grades 7–12), Italian (grades 7–12), Latin (grades 7–12), mathematics (grades 5–12), music (all grades), physical education and sports pedagogy (all grades), physics (grades 7–12), social studies (grades 5–12), Spanish (grades 7–12), or visual arts (all grades). Most M.A.T. programs range from 36 to 39 credits. The program in childhood/early childhood is 49 credits. All M.A.T. programs include one semester of full-time student teaching or supervised fieldwork. The accelerated Jump Start program leads to an M.A.T. degree and certification in eighteen months.

The Master of Professional Studies degree includes programs in educational leadership (SBL), literacy, special education, or teaching English to speakers of another language (all grades or adult and international settings). There are also dual-certification programs in childhood, secondary, or middle child/adolescence literacy and special education. On completion of the program, the candidate is eligible for either initial or professional certification. The classification is determined by the credentials presented at the time of matriculation into the selected program. M.P.S. programs require from 36 to 47 credits, depending on the program and the area in which certification is sought.

The Doctor of Education (Ed.D.) degree program in Educational Leadership is designed to meet the needs of midcareer professionals who have leadership experience in public or private schools, community programs, governmental agencies, or nongovernmental organizations with major education initiatives. This program builds on Manhattanville's educational leadership master's and professional diploma certification programs for building-level and/or district-level leadership.

The certification programs offer students who already hold a functionally related master's degree an opportunity to complete a program of 27 to 30 credits that makes them eligible for certification in a specific field and level of education. Manhattanville also offers a 15-credit Teacher Leader program for those interested in serving as leaders in their schools.

In addition there are several advanced certificate programs in the areas of bilingual education (childhood/Spanish), health and wellness, administration of physical education, athletics and sport pedagogy, and education for sustainability.

Research Facilities

Manhattanville's teaching library ranks among the foremost undergraduate teaching libraries in the country. The Manhattanville library provides a wide range of subscription databases, electronic journals, and electronic books to support teaching and learning at every level. The Educational Resource Center in the library building has curriculum materials to assist preservice and new teachers. Reference service is available both in person during the day and evening hours, and online at any time from anywhere in the world. Students and faculty members may also text questions to a librarian. A library mobile app delivers services to users on the go.

Manhattanville College supports instruction in French, Spanish, Russian, Italian, German, Chinese, Japanese, Hindi, Marathi, modern Hebrew, and English as a second language. The College provides tutoring in every academic subject, customized services for students with special needs, audiovisual facilities, and a leading Information Literacy instruction program. The library building is open 24 hours, 7 days a week through most of the fall and spring semesters, and it has computer labs, quiet study areas, group-study rooms, and a café where students and faculty members can meet informally. The Manhattanville College Library has a dedicated Education Librarian who works with the faculty members and undergraduate, graduate, and doctoral students to assist in any way with their research needs.

Manhattanville, which was named one of the top 100 wired colleges in the U.S., has state-of-the-art computers, computer labs, and campus networking for student use and instruction.

Financial Aid

Family Educational Loans are available to graduate students. A deferred payment plan is also available. There are a limited number of graduate assistantships, for which matriculated students work 200 hours to earn the cost of 6 credit hours. A maximum of three assistantships per student are possible, and courses must be taken concurrently with the assistantship. For further information, prospective students should contact the Office of Financial Aid, Reid Hall, Purchase, New York 10577 (telephone: 914-323-5357).

Cost of Study

Tuition is $895 per credit for 2012–13. There is a semester registration fee of $60 and there are some course fees.

Manhattanville College

Living and Housing Costs

Most School of Education graduate students live and work in their own homes and communities throughout Westchester and the surrounding counties. For campus housing information, students should call Residence Life at 914-323-5217.

Student Group

There are approximately 900 students in the School of Education at Manhattanville College. Fifty-five percent are career changers. Their average age is 30.

Location

Manhattanville's campus, 100 acres of suburban countryside, is located in New York's Westchester County, just minutes from White Plains to the west and Greenwich, Connecticut, to the east. It is 30 miles from Manhattan. The campus is accessible via public transportation.

The College

Manhattanville College is a coeducational, independent liberal arts college whose mission is to educate ethically and socially responsible leaders for the global community. Founded in 1841, the College has 1,600 undergraduate students and almost 1,200 graduate students. Of the graduate students, 820 are enrolled in the School of Education. Manhattanville offers bachelor's, master's, and doctoral degrees in more than fifty academic concentrations in the arts and sciences. Its curriculum nurtures intellectual curiosity and independent thinking.

Applying

Applications are reviewed on a continuing basis. Applicants are encouraged to apply at least sixty days in advance of the semester for which matriculation is sought (fall, spring, summer I, or summer II). Application requirements are the submission of a completed application form, a fee of $70, two recommendations, a two- to three-page typewritten essay on the applicant's background and philosophy of education, and official transcripts of all previous college work (both undergraduate and graduate). Limited study as a nonmatriculated student is permitted.

Correspondence and Information

Jeanine Pardey-Levine
Director of Admissions
School of Education
Manhattanville College
2900 Purchase Street
Purchase, New York 10577
Phone: 914-323-5142 (Admissions)
Fax: 914-694-1732
E-mail: edschool@mville.edu
Web site: http://www.mville.edu/graduate/academics/education.html

THE FACULTY

School of Education Administration

Shelley B. Wepner, Professor and Dean; Ed.D., Pennsylvania.
Elizabeth J. Johnston-O'Connor, Associate Dean of Accreditation and Technology; Ph.D., Rochester.
Laurence Krute, Associate Professor of ESL/Foreign Language and Associate Dean of Graduate Advising; Ph.D., Columbia.
Laura Bigaouette, Assistant Dean; M.B.A., Pace.
Danielle Wachter, Assistant to the Dean; B.S., LIU, Southampton.
Mikki Shaw, Director of Jump Start; Ed.D., Columbia Teachers College.
Jeanine Pardey-Levine, Director of Admissions; M.M., Hartford.
Gail Robinson, Director of Field Placement, Certification, and Community Outreach; M.S., CUNY, Hunter.

Curriculum and Instruction

JoAnne Ferrara, Associate Professor and Department Chair; Ed.D., Nova Southeastern.
Frederick Heckendorn III, Assistant Professor of Secondary/ Social Studies Education; Ed.D., Hofstra.
Joan Gujarti, Assistant Professor; Ed.D., Columbia Teachers College.
Sherie McClam, Assistant Professor; Ph.D., Colorado at Boulder.
Lynn Huber, Assistant Professor; Ph.D., Fordham.

Early Childhood

Patricia Vardin, Associate Professor and Department Chair; Ed.D., Columbia Teachers College.
Victoria Fantozzi, Assistant Professor for Early Childhood and Childhood, Ph.D., Virginia.

Educational Leadership and Special Subjects

Yiping Wan, Professor; Ph.D., Texas at Austin.
Lenora Boehlert, Assistant Professor; Ed.D., Vanderbilt.
Stephen Caldas, Professor; Ph.D., LSU.
Robert Monson, Associate Professor; Ph.D., St. Louis.
Robert Schmidlein, Assistant Professor; Ed.D., Georgia.
Rhonda Clements, Professor and Program Director of Physical Education and Sports Pedagogy; Ed.D., Columbia Teachers College.
Diane Gomez, Assistant Professor and Chair; Ph.D., Fordham.
Laurence Krute, Associate Professor of ESL/Foreign Language and Associate Dean of Graduate Advising; Ph.D., Columbia.
Joan Rudel Weinreich, Professor; Ph.D., Fordham.

Literacy

Ross Collin, Assistant Professor; Ph.D., Wisconsin–Madison.
Katherine Cunningham, Assistant Professor; Ed.D., Columbia Teachers College.
Kristin Rainville, Assistant Professor and Department Chair; Ed.D., Columbia Teachers College.
Courtney Ryan Kelly, Assistant Professor; Ph.D., Ohio State.

Special Education

Vance Austin, Associate Professor and Department Chair; Ph.D., Fordham.
Ellis I. Barowsky, Assistant Professor; Ph.D., CUNY Graduate Center.
Nikki Josephs, Ph.D., Georgia State.
Micheline S. Malow, Assistant Professor and Associate Department Chair; Ph.D., CUNY Graduate Center.

NORTHWESTERN UNIVERSITY

School of Education and Social Policy

Programs of Study

Northwestern University's School of Education and Social Policy offers programs leading to the M.S., M.A., and Ph.D. degrees. There are four program areas: Education (M.S.), Higher Education (M.S.), Learning and Organizational Change (M.S.), Learning Sciences (M.A. and Ph.D.), and Human Development and Social Policy (Ph.D.).

The Learning Sciences M.A. and Ph.D. programs are dedicated to the preparation of researchers, developers, and practitioners qualified to advance the scientific understanding and practice of teaching and learning. Both programs in the learning sciences are interdisciplinary, offering a synthesis of computational, educational, and social science research; linguistics; computer science; anthropology; and cognitive science.

The Human Development and Social Policy Ph.D. program prepares students to bridge human development, social science, and social policy. Graduates of this program assume positions as professors, researchers, and policy makers who can bring multidisciplinary knowledge about human development directly to bear upon policy.

Concentrations in the M.S. in Education program include public and private school teaching, advanced teaching, and higher education administration. Students enrolled full-time typically complete the program in twelve months, provided they matriculate with no course deficiencies; opportunities for part-time study toward a master's degree are also available.

Research Facilities

Northwestern's research libraries contain more than 5 million volumes, 4.6 million microfilm units, and 109,140 current periodical and serial publications. Research and teaching activities are supported by a state-of-the-art multimedia computing network with full Internet access. The School is actively involved with the Institute for Policy Research, a University-wide research center that promotes interdisciplinary urban policy research and training. Specialized research and service resources within the School include the Center for Talent Development, a nationally prominent center that identifies and provides programming for academically talented youth, their parents, and the professionals who work with them. The Tarry Center for Collaborative Teaching and Learning provides state-of-the-art facilities for innovative teaching with technology.

Financial Aid

Several forms of aid are available, including fellowships and scholarships. In addition, there are teaching assistantships awarded to doctoral students who work with the School's undergraduate programs. Special opportunities for research assistantships and other employment also exist within the School's and the University's many research centers. Arrangements for loans are also possible.

Cost of Study

Tuition for full-time study in the M.S. in Education program in 2012–13 is $43,212; part-time enrollment tuition is $2903 per course. Tuition for full-time study in the M.S. in Higher Education program in 2012–13 is $47,715; part-time enrollment tuition is $3181 per course. Tuition for full-time study in the M.S. in Learning and Organizational Change program is $58,455; part-time enrollment is $3897 per course. Tuition for full-time study (three courses per quarter) in pursuit of the M.A. or Ph.D. in 2011–12 was $46,995 for the academic year or $14,460 per quarter.

Living and Housing Costs

The University operates a residence in Evanston for the use of graduate students. For those Northwestern students interested in securing off-campus housing near the University, information and assistance are also available.

Student Group

Graduate study occurs within the context of individualized instruction, and enrollments are selective. Currently, 204 students are enrolled in master's programs, and 65 are enrolled in Ph.D. programs. Since an interdisciplinary perspective is valued, students with preparation in a wide range of disciplinary areas are encouraged to apply.

Student Outcomes

Graduates teach and conduct research in academic and nonacademic settings; occupy strategic policy positions in government, corporations, and institutions; and assume positions of responsibility in a wide range of service organizations. Potential professional settings for learning sciences graduates include University research and teaching as well as business, industry, or school system-based careers studying, designing, and/or implementing learning environments. Graduates of the Ph.D. in Human Development and Social Policy program assume positions as teachers, researchers, or policy makers who can bring multidisciplinary knowledge about human development directly to bear upon policy. Graduates of the Learning Sciences M.A. program are practitioners in the vanguard of teaching and learning systems development and instructional resource development. Most students in the M.S. in Education and Higher Education programs gain on-site experience through supervised internships for future careers as professional educators and administrators.

Location

The campus is located on Lake Michigan, 12 miles north of Chicago. The beautiful lakefront campus offers a rich cultural environment through a wealth of theatrical, musical, and athletic events. The extensive cultural resources of Chicago are readily accessible via public transportation.

The University and The School

Established in 1851, Northwestern has grown to become one of the most distinguished private universities in the country. The School of Education and Social Policy has developed from its origins as a department of pedagogy by continually broadening its scope to encompass those educative, learning, and socializing experiences that take place throughout the life span in families, schools, communities, and the workplace.

Applying

Applications for admission are reviewed and acted upon as they are received. Students should consult program brochures for specific application deadlines. Applicants planning to seek financial aid must meet early submission deadlines.

Correspondence and Information

School of Education and Social Policy
Northwestern University
2120 Campus Drive
Evanston, Illinois 60208-2610
Phone: 847-491-3790 (Office of Student Affairs)
847-467-1458 (M.S. in Education)
847-491-4620 (M.S. in Higher Education)
847-491-4329 (Human Development and Social Policy Ph.D.)
847-491-7376 (Learning and Organizational Change M.S.)
847-491-7494 (Learning Sciences M.A.)
847-491-7494 (Learning Sciences Ph.D.)
Web site: http://www.sesp.northwestern.edu

THE FACULTY AND THEIR RESEARCH

Emma Adam, Ph.D., Minnesota. Parent, child, and adolescent stress and emotion; attachment; health policy.
Linda Brazdil, Ph.D. Case Western Reserve. Urban science education, STEM research.
Lindsay Chase-Lansdale, Ph.D., Michigan. Child and adolescent development, family functioning, public policy, multidisciplinary research, poverty and welfare reform, family structure, risk and resilience.
Jeannette Colyvas, Ph.D., Stanford. Organizations and entrepreneurship; comparing public, private, and nonprofit forms of organizing; the study of networks.
Fay L. Cook, Ph.D., Chicago. Social welfare policy, public attitudes, policy issues in aging, family support systems.
Thomas D. Cook, Ph.D., Stanford. Social-psychological processes, measurement of attitudes, evaluation of social programs.
Mesmin Destin, Ph.D., Michigan. Academic motivation and achievement, small classroom-based interventions to improve school outcomes for low-income and minority youth.
Matthew Easterday, Ph.D., Carnegie Mellon. Human-computer interaction, constructionism, computer-based modeling.
David Figlio, Ph.D., Wisconsin–Madison. Accountability policy, economics of education, teacher quality, teacher labor markets, anti-poverty policy, intergenerational transmission of human capital, evaluation design.
Kenneth D. Forbus, Ph.D., MIT. Qualitative physics, cognitive simulation of analogy, intelligence tutoring systems and learning environments for science and engineering.
Wendi Gardner, Ph.D., Ohio State. Centrality of social inclusion to the self.
Dedre Gentner, Ph.D., Berkeley. Learning, reasoning, and conceptual change in adults and children; mental models; acquisition of meaning.
Elizabeth Gerber, Ph.D., Stanford. Design and innovation work practices.
Jonathan Guryan, Ph.D., MIT. Racial inequality, economics of education.
Sophie Haroutunian-Gordon, Ph.D., Chicago. Philosophy of education, philosophy of psychology, inquiry, interpretive discussion, teacher preparation.
Romana Hasnain-Wynia, Ph.D., Brandeis. Equity in health care, reducing disparities in health care, quality of care for diverse populations, health policy.
Larry Hedges, Ph.D., Stanford. Statistical methods for research in education, social sciences, and policy studies; social distribution of test scores.
Susan Hespos, Ph.D., Emory. Object representation, number and spatial relationships.
Barton J. Hirsch, Ph.D., Oregon. Community psychology, social networks, ecology of adolescent development, after-school programs.
Michael Horn, Ph.D., Tufts. Design of educational technology, learning in museums, computer programming, tangible interaction.
Simone Ispa-Landa, Ph.D., Harvard. Qualitative methods, race and ethnic rlations, social identity, American family, intersectionality theory, micro-macro links.
Kirabo Jackson, Ph.D., Harvard. Economics of education, labor economics, public finance, applied econometrics, development.
John Kretzmann, Ph.D., Northwestern. Sociology, community development, asset building in communities.
Eva Lam, Ph.D., Berkeley. Second language and literacy development, digital literacy and learning, language and identity, language socialization, globalization and English learning, multilingualism and cultural diversity in education.
Carol D. Lee, Ph.D., Chicago. Cultural contexts affecting learning broadly and literacy specifically, teacher preparation and development, classroom discourse, urban education.
Dan A. Lewis, Ph.D., California, Santa Cruz. Policy analysis, urban social problems, community organization, urban school reform.
Gregory Light, Ph.D., London. Student learning in higher and professional education, faculty development, faculty concepts and approaches to teaching, variation theory.
Regina Logan, Ph.D., Northwestern. Teaching and learning processes, adulthood and aging, gender studies.
Jelani Mandara, Ph.D., California, Riverside. Effects of parenting, fathers, and other home factors on child and adolescent academic and social development, achievement gap, and person-centered research methods.
Dan P. McAdams, Ph.D., Harvard. Personality development, identity and life stories, intimacy, adult development, narrative psychology, modernity and the self, autobiographical memory, psychological biography.
Thomas McDade, Ph.D., Emory. Human biology, biocultural perspectives on health and human development, medical anthropology and global health, ecological immunology, stress, health disparities.
Steven McGee, Ph.D., Northwestern. Science education, urban education reform, high school transformation, assessment, educational testing, science curriculum development.
Douglas L. Medin, Ph.D., South Dakota. Learning, reasoning, and conceptual change in adults and children; mental models; acquisition of meaning; culture and education.
Paula M. Olszewski-Kubilius, Ph.D., Northwestern. Gifted education, child development, minority gifted child development, accelerated educational programs, needs of special populations of gifted children.
Penelope L. Peterson, Ph.D., Stanford. Learning and teaching in schools and classrooms, particularly in mathematics and literacy; teacher learning in reform contexts; relations among educational research, policy, and practice.
Deborah Puntenney, Ph.D, Northwestern. Community development.
David Rapp, Ph.D., SUNY at Stony Brook. Experimental psychology, comprehension of texts, psychology of learning, multimedia learning, visualization and learning tools.
Brian J. Reiser, Ph.D., Yale. Intelligent tutoring systems, interactive learning environments for science and technology, scientific inquiry skills.
Christopher K. Riesbeck, Ph.D., Stanford. Natural language and analyzers, case-based reasoners, intelligent computational media.
James E. Rosenbaum, Ph.D., Harvard. Adolescent and adult development, poverty and housing, welfare reform, high school to work transition.
Diane Schanzenbach, Ph.D., Princeton. Early childhood education, accountability policy, economics of education, obesity, anti-poverty policy, education and health.
Kimberly Scott, Ph.D., Ohio State. Organizational effectiveness and change, organizational learning, job satisfaction.
Bruce Sherin, Ph.D., Berkeley. Science education, instructional technology, external representations in science and mathematical learning.
Miriam Sherin, Ph.D., Berkeley. Mathematics teaching and learning, teacher cognition, teacher education.
Sylvia Smith-Demuth, Ph.D., Chicago. Mathematics achievement, mathematics teaching, learning and cognition, social context of education, opportunity to learn.
Bruce D. Spencer, Ph.D., Yale. Social and educational measurement, statistics for policy analysis, demography, decision theory.
James P. Spillane, Ph.D., Michigan State. Educational policy, intergovernmental relations, school reform, relations between policy and local practice.
Reed Stevens, Ph.D., Berkeley. Curriculum design, learning in atypical settings, design of learning tools.
Linda Teplin, Ph.D., Northwestern. Epidemiologic studies of psychiatric disorders, juvenile justice, drug abuse, public health policy, HIV/AIDS risk behaviors, correlates of violence.
Lois Trautvetter, Ph.D., Michigan. Higher education, gender issues and females in science.
David H. Uttal, Ph.D., Michigan. Mental representation, cognitive development, spatial cognition, early symbolization.
Laurie Wakschlag, Ph.D., Chicago. Behavioral sciences.
Ellen Wartella, Ph.D., Minnesota. Effects of media on children and adolescents, impact of food marketing on childhood obesity.
Sandra R. Waxman, Ph.D., Pennsylvania. Language and conceptual development, early cognitive development, language and thought.
Uri Wilensky, Ph.D., MIT. Science and mathematics learning and technology, connected learning, constructionism, computer-based modeling, agent-based modeling, complex systems and education.
Michael Wolf, Ph.D., Illinois. Adult literacy, patient education, medication and safety adherence.

ST. JOSEPH'S COLLEGE, NEW YORK

Programs in Education

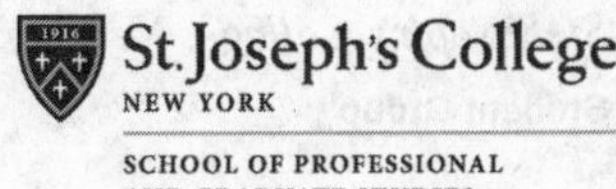

Programs of Study

St. Joseph's College (SJC) offers graduate education that balances in-depth research and theoretical study with hands-on professional training. This unique educational experience enables students to enter the workplace extremely well prepared and able to apply their knowledge with confidence born from experience.

The newest program is the Master of Arts in mathematics education, a 30-credit degree that can be earned in two years of part-time study. The purpose of the program is to prepare students to become accomplished mathematics teachers. It aims to extend the depth and breadth of mathematical skills previously learned on the undergraduate level and to enable teaching professionals to use these expanded skills to motivate and engage a diverse population of students with varying cognitive skills and learning styles. Completion of the program will satisfy the degree requirements for professional certification in New York State.

The Master of Arts in childhood or adolescence special education with an annotation in severe multiple disabilities program allows students to put the theories and principles of special education into practice by linking diagnosis, assessment, and instruction of special needs children.

Depending on initial certification, SJC graduate students are able to obtain additional certification in areas including childhood special education, biology special education, English special education, history special education, and mathematics special education. Each certificate also includes an annotation for several and multiple disabilities of children from birth to age 21.

The Master of Arts in literacy and cognition responds to the No Child Left Behind Act, providing students with basic core classes that link literacy instruction to the New York State Learning Standards. The program addresses the challenges teachers face in the area of literacy as they work with students and families of diverse cultures. The M.A. in literacy and cognition program grants certifications in literacy and cognition from birth through grade 6. Interested students may also choose to pursue additional literacy certifications in birth through grade 12 or grade 5 through grade 12, offered only at the Long Island campus.

The Master of Arts in infant/toddler early childhood special education at SJC is designed for students who already have a teaching certification and are interested in working with infants and young children or children with certain developmental delays.

This program focuses on fieldwork that presents solutions to current challenges in teaching and learning. The course work encourages students to combine classroom experience with sensitivity and effective teaching and learning processes for young age groups, which grants certifications in early childhood and early childhood special education, from birth to grade 2.

Research Facilities

The Dillon Child Study Center offers toddler, preschool, and kindergarten programs based on the child development approach to the education of young children. Located on SJC's Brooklyn campus, the center is historically one of the first college preschools on the East Coast.

The Callahan Library at the Long Island Campus is a modern, 25,000-square-foot, freestanding facility with seating for more than 300 readers. A curriculum library, seminar rooms, administrative offices, and two classrooms are housed in this building. Holdings include more than 105,000 volumes and 307 periodical titles, and they are supplemented by videos and other instructional aids. Patrons have access to the Internet and to several online academic databases. A fully automated library system, Endeavor, ensures the efficient retrieval and management of all library resources. Other resources include the library at St. Joseph's Brooklyn Campus, with more than 109,000 volumes, and membership in the Long Island Library Resources Council, which facilitates cooperative associations with the academic and special libraries on Long Island. Internet access, subscriptions to several online full-text databases, and membership in the international bibliographic utility, OCLC, allow almost limitless access to available information.

McEntegart Hall is a fully air-conditioned five-level structure. Three spacious reading areas with a capacity for 300 readers, including individual study carrels and shelf space for 200,000 volumes, provide an excellent environment for research. In addition, McEntegart Hall houses the college archives, a curriculum library, three computer laboratories, a nursing education laboratory, and a videoconference room. There are eight classrooms, a chapel, cafeteria, and faculty and student lounges.

A high-speed fiber-optic intracampus network connects all offices, instructional facilities, computer laboratories, and libraries on both the Brooklyn and Long Island campuses. The network provides Internet access to all students and faculty and staff members. An integrated online library system enables students to search for and check out books at either campus. Online databases and other electronic resources are available to students from either campus or from their home computers. Two wireless laptop classrooms with "smart classroom" features provide flexible instruction spaces with the latest technologies. Videoconferencing facilities connect the two campuses, allowing for real-time distance learning in a small-group setting.

Financial Aid

Financial aid is available in the form of federal and private loans. Students should contact the Financial Aid Office for more information (Brooklyn Campus, telephone: 718-940-5700; Long Island Campus, telephone: 631-687-2600).

Cost of Study

The 2012–13 tuition is $19,500 or $715 per credit for graduate programs. Per semester, the college and technology fees for 12 or more credits totaled $200.

Living and Housing Costs

Off-campus housing is available on the Brooklyn Campus at the St. George Hotel. New York's number-one resource for student housing, and St. Joseph's College have partnered to offer off-campus housing. Accommodations include cable TV, high-speed access, a completely furnished bedroom, a full bath, a closet, a kitchen on each floor, and 24-hour security. Housing applications are available online.

Student Group

The total enrollment for all graduate programs on both campuses is 740.

Location

St. Joseph's College has two campuses—the main campus in the residential Clinton Hill section of Brooklyn and the campus in Patchogue, New York. The main campus offers easy access to all transit lines; to the Long Island Expressway; to all bridges in Brooklyn, Manhattan, and Queens; and to the Verrazano-Narrows Bridge to Staten Island. Within the space of half an hour, students leaving St. Joseph's College may find themselves in the Metropolitan Museum of Art, the 42nd Street Library, Carnegie Hall and Lincoln Center, the Broadway theater district, Madison Square Garden, or Shea Stadium. The College itself stands in the center of one of the nation's most diversified academic communities, consisting of six colleges and universities within a 2-mile radius of each other. The 27-acre Long Island campus, adjacent to Great Patchogue Lake, is an ideal setting for studying, socializing, and partaking in extracurricular activities. Just off Sunrise Highway, the College is easily accessible from all parts of Long Island.

The College

St. Joseph's College is a fully accredited institution that has been dedicated to providing a diverse population of students in the New York metropolitan area with an affordable education rooted in the liberal arts tradition since 1916. Independent and coeducational, the College provides a strong academic and value-oriented education at the undergraduate and graduate levels. For over a decade, the College has consistently been ranked among America's best colleges by *U.S. News & World Report* and *Forbes*.

Building on the strength of the St. Joseph's College long-renowned teacher education program, the master's programs in infant/toddler early childhood special education and in literacy/cognition are designed to produce innovative teachers in the fields of early childhood, childhood, and special education and in literacy and English language arts.

Applying

Students should have a bachelor's degree from an accredited institution, with a minimum GPA of 3.0. Applicants must submit the completed application, the application fee, official transcripts, a current resume, copies of all teaching certificates, and two letters of recommendation. An interview is required.

Correspondence and Information

Brooklyn Campus
St. Joseph's College
245 Clinton Avenue
Brooklyn, New York 11205
Phone: 718-940-5800
E-mail: brooklynap@sjcny.edu
Web site: http://www.sjcny.edu/ Academics/Graduate-Programs/260

Long Island Campus
St. Joseph's College
155 West Roe Boulevard
Patchogue, New York 11772
Phone: 631-687-4500
E-mail: suffolkap@sjcny.edu

THE FACULTY

Esther Berkowitz, Assistant Professor of Child Study and Director of the M.A. in Literacy and Cognition; Ph.D., Fordham.

S. Elizabeth Calfapietra, Associate Professor of Child Study; Ed.D., Columbia.

S. Frances Carmody, Professor of Child Study Development; Ph.D., Syracuse.

Susan Straut Collard, Professor of Child Study, Co-Director of Child Study Department, and Director of Dillon Child Study Center; Ph.D., Columbia.

S. Miriam Honora Corr, Chairperson of the Child Study Department; Ed.D., Columbia.

Barry Friedman, Assistant Professor of Child Study; Ph.D., Hofstra.

Wendy P. Hope, Associate Professor of Child Study; Ph.D., NYU.

S. Helen Kearney, Assistant Professor of Child Study; Ph.D., NYU.

Claire Lenz, Assistant Professor of Child Study and Director of the Master of Arts in Literacy and Cognition, Suffolk Program; Ed.D., St. John's (New York).

Karen Russo, Assistant Professor of Child Study; St. John's (New York).

UNIVERSITY OF PENNSYLVANIA

Graduate School of Education

Programs of Study

The Penn Graduate School of Education (Penn GSE) offers programs leading to the Master of Science in Education (M.S.Ed.), the Master of Science (M.S.), the Master of Philosophy in Education (M.Phil.Ed.), the Doctor of Education (Ed.D.), and the Doctor of Philosophy (Ph.D.) degrees. The degree programs offer a range of professional preparation for those seeking to begin or advance a career in education.

GSE seeks students who are interested in promoting a deeper understanding of educational issues and contributing to societal change. The curriculum places a strong emphasis on the interactive relationship of theory, research, and practice, often focusing on urban education. Students engage in extensive fieldwork throughout their studies and are both learners and agents of change within the University and the surrounding Philadelphia neighborhoods.

For the working professional, Penn GSE offers executive programs in educational leadership, higher education management, school counseling, and corporate learning. In addition, many master's and Ed.D. programs may be completed part-time.

Research Facilities

Research centers at Penn GSE bring faculty members and students together to study the various intersections of education and society. This research includes international studies of cross-cultural and comparative education. The centers include the Center for Research and Evaluation in Social Policy, the Center for the Study of Race and Equity in Education, the Center for Urban Ethnography, the Consortium for Policy Research in Education, and the National Center on Fathers and Families. A full list is available online at http://www.gse.upenn.edu/faculty_research/centers.

Financial Aid

Financial aid for Penn GSE students is available through the School, private sources, and from the state and federal governments through loans and work-study jobs. Graduate assistantships, scholarships, fellowships, and research assistantships are awarded by the School based on academic merit.

Cost of Study

The most current tuition rates can be found online at http://www.gse.upenn.edu/admissions_financial/tuition.

Living and Housing Costs

University graduate housing is available on campus for single students as well as married students and their families. On-campus housing ranges from $746 per month for a single room to $1464 per month for an apartment. Off-campus apartment rents range upward from $575 per month.

Student Group

Penn GSE students range from recent college graduates to career changers and experienced practitioners. The approximately 500 students beginning course work in 2011 represented a broad demographic spectrum; 25 percent were international students from twenty-two countries. The age ranges for 2011–12 were as follows: master's students, 20–71; Ph.D. students, 21–30; and Ed.D. students, 24–67.

Student Outcomes

Penn GSE graduates pursue careers in a variety of fields, including schools, government agencies, universities, think tanks, foundations, and corporations. In these fields, they work in positions that include superintendents, principals, teachers, counselors, university professors, policy analysts, researchers, foundation officers, psychologists, and higher education administrators.

Location

Penn GSE's location in a major metropolitan area enhances the quality of its programs, research, and student life. Philadelphia is a thriving mix of ethnic neighborhoods, historic colonial streets, and contemporary architecture. With close to 100 institutions of higher learning, the city is a magnet for students from around the world. The city's cultural and recreational life has a world-class orchestra and opera, dozens of museums, four professional sports teams, art galleries, secondhand bookstores, jazz clubs, an Italian market, and a renowned international film festival. The city is conveniently located in the cradle of the metropolitan northeastern United States, within 2 hours of Baltimore, New York, and Washington, D.C.

The School

Penn GSE, one of the best graduate schools of education in the United States, is one of only three Ivy League schools of education. The School is noted for excellence in educational research in the areas of policy, evaluation, sociocultural foundations, and urban education. The student experience at Penn GSE is shaped by the small size of the School. Students find both the flexibility to pursue their own research interests and the support they need to do so. The interdisciplinary nature of educational programs means that Penn GSE students take courses across the University. Penn GSE also maintains community connections, which are an important resource for students, faculty members, and neighboring schools.

University of Pennsylvania

Applying

To apply and learn more about application deadlines, prospective students can visit http://www.gse.upenn.edu/admissions_financial/howtoapply.

Correspondence and Information

Admissions Office
Graduate School of Education
University of Pennsylvania
3700 Walnut Street
Philadelphia, Pennsylvania 19104-6216
Phone: 215-898-6415
E-mail: admissions@gse.upenn.edu
Web site: http://www.gse.upenn.edu

THE FACULTY

For a full list of all Penn GSE faculty members, including associated faculty members, students should visit http://www.gse.upenn.edu/node/419.

VANDERBILT UNIVERSITY

Peabody College

Programs of Study

Vanderbilt University's Peabody College of Education and Human Development offers programs leading to the Master of Education (M.Ed.), Master of Public Policy (M.P.P.), and Doctor of Education (Ed.D.) degrees. The Vanderbilt Graduate School, through Peabody departments, offers the Doctor of Philosophy degree. Peabody is committed to preparing students to become research scholars or innovative practitioners in the field of education and human development. Students may attend full- or part-time. Weekend courses are offered in several programs for working professionals who want to earn an advanced degree.

Students may pursue the Master of Education (M.Ed.) in child studies; community development and action; elementary education; English language learners; higher education administration (including specializations in administration, student life, and service learning); human development counseling (with specializations in school or community counseling and prevention science); international education policy and management; leadership and organizational performance; learning, diversity, and urban studies; learning and instruction (including specializations in teaching and learning; digital literacies; language, culture, and international studies; science and mathematics; or an individualized program); reading education; secondary education; and special education (including specializations in applied behavior analysis, early childhood, high-incidence disabilities, and low-incidence disabilities). A Master of Public Policy is available in education policy. Vanderbilt also offers a joint M.P.P./J.D. program.

Students interested in doctoral study may enroll in educational leadership and policy (Ed.D.); educational neuroscience (Ph.D); higher education leadership and policy (Ed.D.); community research and action (Ph.D.); leadership and policy studies (Ph.D., with specializations in educational leadership and policy, higher education leadership and policy, and international education policy and management); learning, teaching, and diversity (Ph.D., with specializations in development, learning, and diversity; language, literacy, and culture; mathematics and science; and science and learning environment design); psychological sciences (Ph.D., with specializations in clinical science, cognitive science, developmental science, and quantitative methods and evaluation); and special education (Ph.D., with specializations in early childhood, high-incidence disabilities, and severe disabilities).

Peabody's teacher education and advanced certification programs are approved by the National Council for Accreditation of Teacher Education (NCATE). Programs in psychology and counseling are accredited by the American Psychological Association and the Council on Accreditation of Counseling and Related Educational Programs (CACREP), respectively.

Research Opportunities

In addition to the Vanderbilt University Library System, which has more than 2.6 million volumes, excellent research facilities and opportunities to conduct research are available through the Vanderbilt Kennedy Center for Research on Human Development, the Learning Sciences Institute, the Peabody Research Institute, the Susan Gray School, the National Center on School Choice, the National Center on Performance Initiatives, and the Center for Community Studies. The many local field sites available for research include hospitals, Metropolitan Nashville Public Schools, private schools, rehabilitation centers, schools for people with disabilities, government agencies, corporations, and nonprofit organizations.

Financial Aid

More than 60 percent of new students at Peabody receive financial aid. The College sponsors several substantial scholarship programs with offerings that range from partial to full tuition, including several scholarships designated for outstanding students from minority groups. In addition, assistantships, traineeships, loans, and part-time employment are available. Awards are made annually, and every attempt is made to meet a student's financial need. Application for financial aid does not affect the admission decision.

Cost of Study

Tuition for study at Peabody College for the 2012–13 academic year is $1265 per semester credit hour for the M.Ed., M.P.P., and Ed.D. programs, and $1712 per semester credit hour for programs offered through the Graduate School.

Living and Housing Costs

Vanderbilt's location in Nashville offers students the advantage of a wide range of living choices. Costs for housing, food, and other living expenses are moderate when compared with other metropolitan areas nationwide.

Student Group

Vanderbilt has a diverse student body of about 12,000. Peabody has an enrollment of approximately 1,800 students, of whom about 700 are graduate students. Women make up about 65 percent of Peabody's graduate students, while students from minority groups make up about 20 percent. Students have a broad range of academic backgrounds and include recent graduates of baccalaureate programs as well as men and women who have many years of professional experience. The median age of current students is 27.

Student Outcomes

Graduates who earn a master's or doctoral degree from Peabody are prepared to work for educational, corporate, government, and service organizations in a variety of roles. More than 10,000 alumni are practicing teachers, more than 175 are school superintendents, and more than 50 are current or former college or university presidents.

Location

Nashville, the capital of Tennessee, is a cosmopolitan city with a metropolitan area population of 1.23 million. Vanderbilt University is one of more than a dozen institutions of higher learning located in Nashville and the surrounding area, leading Nashville to be called the "Athens of the South."

Nashville offers residents and visitors much in the way of music, art, and recreation. More than 100 local venues provide a wide variety of music, while classical and contemporary music is performed by the Nashville Symphony Orchestra and the Nashville Chamber Orchestra. The Tennessee Performing Arts Center (TPAC) is home to two theater companies, a ballet company, and an opera company. Vanderbilt's own Great Performances series frequently brings the best in chamber music, new music, theater, and all forms of dance to the Vanderbilt campus. Outstanding exhibitions of fine art can be seen at the Frist Center for the Visual Arts and at Cheekwood Botanical Garden and Museum of Art. There are more than 6,000 acres of public parks in the city, and the surrounding region of rolling hills and lakes is dotted with state parks and recreation areas.

Vanderbilt University

Nashville has been named one of the 15 best U.S. cities for work and family by *Fortune* magazine, was ranked as the most popular U.S. city for corporate relocations by *Expansion Management* magazine, and was named by *Forbes* magazine as one of the 25 cities most likely to have the country's highest job growth over the coming five years. More information on Nashville can be found online at http://www.vanderbilt.edu/nashville.

The University and The College

Vanderbilt University, founded in 1873, is a private nondenominational institution with a strong tradition of graduate and professional education. Peabody, recognized for more than a century as one of the nation's foremost independent colleges of education, merged with Vanderbilt University in 1979. The College is currently ranked the number one graduate school of education in the nation by *U.S. News & World Report.* Peabody seeks to create knowledge through research, to prepare leaders, to support practitioners, and to strengthen communities at all levels.

Applying

Admission to professional degree programs is based on an evaluation of the applicant's potential for academic success and professional service, with consideration given to transcripts of previous course work, GRE General Test or MAT scores, letters of reference, and a letter outlining personal goals. Additional supporting credentials, such as a sample of the applicant's scholarly writing or a personal interview, may also be required.

The application fee is waived for applicants who apply online at http://peabody.vanderbilt.edu/degrees-programs/admissions_and_programs.php. A nonrefundable $40 fee must accompany each paper application. Applicants who apply after the deadline should know that admission and financial assistance depend upon the availability of space and funds in the department in which they seek to study. Deadlines are December 1 for the Ph.D and Ed.D programs and December 31 for the M.Ed. and M.P.P. programs.

Correspondence and Information

Graduate Admissions
Peabody College of Vanderbilt University
Peabody Station, Box 227
Nashville, Tennessee 37203
United States
Phone: 615-322-8410
Fax: 615-322-4029
E-mail: peabody.admissions@vanderbilt.edu
Web site: http://peabody.vanderbilt.edu

THE FACULTY

Department of Human and Organizational Development
Sandra Barnes, Professor; Ph.D., Georgia State.
Kimberly D. Bess, Assistant Professor; Ph.D., Vanderbilt.
Vera Chatman, Professor of the Practice; Ph.D., George Peabody.
Victoria J. Davis, Clinical Assistant Professor; Ed.D., Vanderbilt.
Paul R. Dokecki, Professor; Ph.D., George Peabody.
James C. Fraser, Associate Professor; Ph.D., Georgia State.
Gina Frieden, Assistant Professor of the Practice; Ph.D., Memphis State.
Susan K. Friedman, Lecturer; M.B.A., Arizona State.
Brian Griffith, Assistant Clinical Professor; Ph.D., South Carolina.
Craig Anne Heflinger, Professor; Ph.D., Vanderbilt.
Linda Isaacs, Lecturer; Ed.D., Vanderbilt.
Torin Monahan, Associate Professor; Ph.D., Rensselaer.
Velma McBride Murry, Professor; Ph.D., Missouri–Columbia.
Maury Nation, Associate Professor; Ph.D., South Carolina.
Douglas Perkins, Associate Professor; Ph.D., NYU.
Sharon Shields, Professor of the Practice; Ph.D., George Peabody.
Marybeth Shinn, Professor; Ph.D., Michigan.
Heather Smith, Assistant Professor of the Practice; Ph.D., Central Florida.
Paul Speer, Associate Professor; Ph.D., Missouri–Kansas City.
William L. Turner, Professor; Ph.D., Virginia Tech.
Andrew Van Schaack, Assistant Professor; Ph.D., Utah State.

Department of Leadership, Policy, and Organizations
Robert Dale Ballou, Associate Professor; Ph.D., Yale.
John Braxton, Professor; D.Ed., Penn State.
Mark D. Cannon, Associate Professor; Ph.D., Harvard.
Robert L. Crowson, Professor; Ph.D., Chicago.
Corbette Doyle, Lecturer; M.B.A., Vanderbilt.
William R. Doyle, Assistant Professor; Ph.D., Stanford.
Mimi Engel, Assistant Professor; Ph.D., Northwestern.
Stella M. Flores, Assistant Professor; Ed.D., Harvard.
Ellen Goldring, Professor; Ph.D., Chicago.
Gary T. Henry, Professor; Ph.D., Wisconsin.
Stephen P. Heyneman, Professor; Ph.D., Chicago.
Catherine Gavin Loss, Lecturer; Ph.D., Virginia.
Christopher P. Loss, Assistant Professor; Ph.D., Virginia.
Joseph Murphy, Professor; Ph.D., Ohio State.
Pearl Sims, Senior Lecturer; Ed.D., Vanderbilt.
Thomas M. Smith, Associate Professor; Ph.D., Penn State.
Claire Smrekar, Associate Professor; Ph.D., Stanford.

Department of Psychology and Human Development
Camilla P. Benbow, Professor; Ed.D., Johns Hopkins.
Leonard Bickman, Professor; Ph.D., CUNY.
Sun-Joo Cho, Assistant Professor; Ph.D., Georgia.
David A. Cole, Professor; Ph.D., Houston.
Bruce E. Compas, Professor; Ph.D., UCLA.
David Cordray, Professor; Ph.D., Claremont.
Elizabeth May Dykens, Professor; Ph.D., Kansas.
Judy Garber, Associate Professor; Ph.D., Minnesota, Twin Cities.
Kathleen Hoover-Dempsey, Associate Professor; Ph.D., Michigan State.
Daniel T. Levin, Associate Professor; Ph.D., Cornell.
David Lubinski, Professor; Ph.D., Minnesota.
Bruce McCandliss, Professor; Ph.D., Oregon.
Joseph McLaughlin, Associate Professor; Ph.D., Vanderbilt.
Amy Needham, Professor; Ph.D., Illinois.
Laura R. Novick, Associate Professor; Ph.D., Stanford.
Gavin Price, Assistant Professor; Ph.D., Jyväskylä (Finland).
John R. Rieser, Professor; Ph.D., Minnesota, Twin Cities.
Bethany Rittle-Johnson, Assistant Professor; Ph.D., Carnegie Mellon.
Joseph Lee Rodgers III, Professor; Ph.D., North Carolina.
Howard M. Sandler, Professor; Ph.D., Northwestern.
Megan M. Saylor, Assistant Professor; Ph.D., Oregon.
Craig A. Smith, Associate Professor; Ph.D., Stanford.
James Steiger, Professor; Ph.D., Purdue.
Georgene Troseth, Associate Professor; Ph.D., Illinois at Urbana-Champaign.
Tedra Ann Walden, Professor; Ph.D., Florida.
Bahr Weiss, Associate Professor; Ph.D., North Carolina at Chapel Hill.

Department of Special Education
Andrea Capizzi, Assistant Professor of the Practice; Ph.D., Vanderbilt.
Laurie Cutting, Associate Professor; Ph.D., Northwestern.
Alex da Fonte, Assistant Professor; M.S., Purdue.
Donna Y. Ford, Professor; Ph.D., Cleveland State.
Deborah D. Hatton, Associate Professor; Ph.D., North Carolina.
Robert Hodapp, Professor; Ph.D., Boston University.
Ann Kaiser, Professor; Ph.D., Kansas.
Craig Kennedy, Professor; Ph.D., California, Santa Barbara.
Kim Paulsen, Associate Professor of the Practice; Ed.D., Nevada, Las Vegas.
Dan Reschly, Professor; Ph.D., Oregon.
Joseph H. Wehby, Associate Professor; Ph.D., Vanderbilt.
Mark Wolery, Professor; Ph.D., Washington (Seattle).
Ruth Wolery, Assistant Professor of the Practice; Ph.D., Pittsburgh.
Paul J. Yoder, Professor; Ph.D., North Carolina.

Department of Teaching and Learning
Paul A. Cobb, Professor; Ph.D., Georgia.
Douglas Clark, Associate Professor; Ph.D., Berkeley.
David Dickinson, Professor; Ed.D., Harvard.
Dale C. Farran, Professor; Ph.D., Bryn Mawr.
Melissa Sommerfield Gresalfi, Associate Professor; Ph.D., Stanford.
Andrew L. Hofstetler, Assistant Professor of the Practice; Ph.D., Illinois.
Clifford A. Hofwolt, Associate Professor; Ed.D., Northern Colorado.
Ilana Horn, Associate Professor; Ph.D., Berkeley.
Robert T. Jimenez, Professor; Ph.D., Illinois at Urbana-Champaign.
Kevin Leander, Associate Professor; Ph.D., Illinois.
Richard Lehrer, Professor; Ph.D., Chicago.
Henry Richard Milner, Associate Professor; M.A., Ohio State.
Ann M. Neely, Associate Professor of the Practice; Ed.D., Georgia.
Amy Palmeri, Assistant Professor of the Practice; Ph.D., Indiana Bloomington.
Lisa Pray, Associate Professor of the Practice; Ph.D., Arizona State.
Victoria J. Risko, Professor; Ed.D., West Virginia.
Deborah W. Rowe, Associate Professor; Ph.D., Indiana.
Leona Schauble, Professor; Ph.D., Columbia.
Pratim Sengupta, Assistant Professor; Ph.D., Northwestern.
Marcy Singer-Gabella, Professor of the Practice; Ph.D., Stanford.

Section 23
Administration, Instruction, and Theory

This section contains a directory of institutions offering graduate work in administration, instruction, and theory, followed by in-depth entries submitted by institutions that chose to prepare detailed program descriptions. Additional information about programs listed in the directory but not augmented by an in-depth entry may be obtained by writing directly to the dean of a graduate school or chair of a department at the address given in the directory.

For programs offering related work, see also in this book *Education, Instructional Levels, Leisure Studies and Recreation, Physical Education and Kinesiology, Special Focus,* and *Subject Areas.* In other guides in this series:

Graduate Programs in the Humanities, Arts & Social Sciences
See *Psychology and Counseling (School Psychology)*
Graduate Programs in the Biological/Biomedical Sciences & Health-Related Medical Professions
See *Health-Related Professions*

CONTENTS

Program Directories

Displays and Close-Ups

See also:

Curriculum and Instruction

Abilene Christian University, Graduate School, College of Education and Human Services, Graduate Studies in Education, Curriculum and Instruction Program, Abilene, TX 79699-9100. Offers M Ed. Part-time programs available. Postbaccalaureate distance learning degree programs offered (no on-campus study). *Faculty:* 4 full-time (1 woman). *Students:* 6 full-time (5 women), 48 part-time (41 women); includes 10 minority (4 Black or African American, non-Hispanic/Latino; 1 Asian, non-Hispanic/Latino; 5 Hispanic/Latino). 23 applicants, 39% accepted, 9 enrolled. In 2011, 34 master's awarded. *Degree requirements:* For master's, capstone. *Entrance requirements:* Additional exam requirements/recommendations for international students: Required—TOEFL (minimum score 550 paper-based; 213 computer-based; 80 iBT), IELTS (minimum score 6). *Application deadline:* For fall admission, 8/15 priority date for domestic students; for winter admission, 10/1 priority date for domestic students; for spring admission, 12/15 priority date for domestic students. Applications are processed on a rolling basis. Application fee: $50. Electronic applications accepted. *Expenses: Tuition:* Full-time $14,168; part-time $787 per hour. *Required fees:* $82 per hour. $10 per term. *Financial support:* In 2011–12, 2 students received support. Career-related internships or fieldwork and Federal Work-Study available. Support available to part-time students. Financial award application deadline: 4/1; financial award applicants required to submit FAFSA. *Unit head:* Dr. Lloyd Goldsmith, Graduate Director, 325-674-2946, Fax: 325-674-2123, E-mail: lloyd.goldsmith@acu.edu. *Application contact:* David Pittman, Graduate Admissions Counselor, 325-674-2656, Fax: 325-674-6717, E-mail: gradinfo@acu.edu.

Acadia University, Faculty of Professional Studies, School of Education, Program in Curriculum Studies, Wolfville, NS B4P 2R6, Canada. Offers cultural and media studies (M Ed); learning and technology (M Ed); science, math and technology (M Ed). Part-time programs available. *Degree requirements:* For master's, thesis optional. *Entrance requirements:* For master's, B Ed or the equivalent, minimum B average in undergraduate course work, 2 years of teaching experience. Additional exam requirements/recommendations for international students: Required—TOEFL (minimum score 580 paper-based; 237 computer-based; 93 iBT), IELTS (minimum score 6.5). *Faculty research:* Literacy development, postmodern philosophy and curriculum theory, historiography, philosophy of education, learning and technology.

American College of Education, Graduate Programs, Chicago, IL 60606. Offers curriculum and instruction (M Ed), including bilingual, ESL; educational leadership (M Ed); educational technology (M Ed).

American InterContinental University Online, Program in Education, Hoffman Estates, IL 60192. Offers curriculum and instruction (M Ed); educational assessment and evaluation (M Ed); instructional technology (M Ed); leadership of educational organizations (M Ed). Evening/weekend programs available. Postbaccalaureate distance learning degree programs offered (no on-campus study). *Entrance requirements:* Additional exam requirements/recommendations for international students: Required—TOEFL (minimum score 550 paper-based; 213 computer-based). Electronic applications accepted.

American Public University System, AMU/APU Graduate Programs, Charles Town, WV 25414. Offers accounting (MBA, MS); administration and supervision (M Ed); criminal justice (MA); emergency and disaster management (MA); entrepreneurship (MBA); environmental policy and management (MS), including environmental planning, environmental sustainability, fish and wildlife management, general (MA, MS), global environmental management; finance (MBA); general (MBA); global business management (MBA); guidance and counseling (M Ed); history (MA), including American history, ancient and classical history, European history, global history, military and diplomatic history, public history; homeland security (MA); homeland security resource allocation (MBA); humanities (MA); information technology (MS), including digital forensics, enterprise software development, information assurance and security, IT project management; information technology management (MBA); intelligence studies (MA), including criminal intelligence, general (MA, MS), homeland security, intelligence analysis, intelligence collection, intelligence operations, terrorism studies; international relations and conflict resolution (MA), including comparative and security issues, conflict resolution, international and transnational security issues, peacekeeping; legal studies (MA); management (MA), including defense management, general (MA, MS), human resource management, organizational leadership, public administration, reverse logistics, strategic consulting; marketing (MBA); military history (MA), including American military history, American revolution, civil war, war since 1946, World War II; military studies (MA), including air warfare, asymmetrical warfare, joint warfare, land warfare, naval warfare, strategic leadership; national security studies (MA), including general (MA, MS), homeland security, regional security studies, security and intelligence analysis, terrorism studies; nonprofit management (MBA); political science (MA), including American politics and government, comparative government and development, public policy; psychology (MA); public administration (MA, MPA), including disaster management (MPA), environmental policy (MA), health policy (MPA), human resources (MPA), national security (MPA), organizational management (MPA), security management (MPA); public health (MA, MPH), including emergency management (MPH), environmental health (MPH), public administration (MA); reverse logistics management (MA); security management (MA); space studies (MS), including aerospace science, planetary science; sports and health sciences (MS); sports management (MS), including coaching theory and strategy, sports administration; teaching (M Ed), including curriculum and instruction for elementary teachers, elementary, elementary reading, English language learners, instructional leadership, online learning, secondary social sciences, special education; transportation and logistics management (MA), including maritime engineering management. Programs offered via distance learning only. Part-time and evening/weekend programs available. Postbaccalaureate distance learning degree programs offered (no on-campus study). *Faculty:* 445 full-time (241 women), 1,360 part-time/adjunct (617 women). *Students:* 688 full-time (338 women), 10,168 part-time (3,706 women); includes 3,130 minority (1,007 Black or African American, non-Hispanic/Latino; 103 American Indian or Alaska Native, non-Hispanic/Latino; 825 Asian, non-Hispanic/Latino; 810 Hispanic/Latino; 51 Native Hawaiian or other Pacific Islander, non-Hispanic/Latino; 334 Two or more races, non-Hispanic/Latino), 134 international. Average age 35. In 2011, 2,386 master's awarded. *Degree requirements:* For master's, comprehensive exam or practicum. *Entrance requirements:* For master's, official transcript showing earned bachelor's degree from institution accredited by recognized accrediting body. Additional exam requirements/recommendations for international students: Required—TOEFL (minimum score 550 paper-based; 213 computer-based), IELTS (minimum score 6.5). *Application deadline:* Applications are processed on a rolling basis. Application fee: $0. Electronic applications accepted. *Expenses: Tuition:* Part-time $325 per credit hour. *Financial support:* Applicants required to submit FAFSA. *Faculty research:* Military history, criminal justice, management performance, national security. *Unit head:* Dr. Karan Powell, Executive Vice President and Provost, 877-468-6268, Fax: 304-724-3780. *Application contact:* Terry Grant, Vice President of Enrollment Management, 877-468-6268, Fax: 304-724-3780, E-mail: info@apus.edu. Web site: http://www.apus.edu.

American University, College of Arts and Sciences, School of Education, Teaching, and Health, Program in Curriculum and Instruction, Washington, DC 20016-8001. Offers M Ed, Certificate. *Students:* 33 part-time (26 women); includes 9 minority (6 Black or African American, non-Hispanic/Latino; 1 Asian, non-Hispanic/Latino; 2 Hispanic/Latino). Average age 28. 38 applicants, 87% accepted, 24 enrolled. In 2011, 3 master's awarded. *Degree requirements:* For master's, comprehensive exam, PRAXIS II. *Entrance requirements:* For master's, GRE, prior teaching experience (preferred). Application fee: $80. *Expenses: Tuition:* Full-time $24,264; part-time $1348 per credit hour. *Required fees:* $430. Tuition and fees vary according to course load and program. *Unit head:* Dr. Sarah Irvine-Belson, Dean, 202-885-3714, Fax: 202-885-1187, E-mail: educate@american.edu. *Application contact:* Kathleen Clowery, Director, Graduate Admissions, 202-885-3621, Fax: 202-885-1505, E-mail: clowery@american.edu.

Andrews University, School of Graduate Studies, School of Education, Department of Teaching, Learning, and Curriculum, Program in Curriculum and Instruction, Berrien Springs, MI 49104. Offers MA, Ed D, PhD, Ed S. *Faculty:* 5 full-time (1 woman). *Students:* 8 full-time (6 women), 23 part-time (19 women); includes 14 minority (9 Black or African American, non-Hispanic/Latino; 1 Asian, non-Hispanic/Latino; 3 Hispanic/Latino; 1 Native Hawaiian or other Pacific Islander, non-Hispanic/Latino), 8 international. Average age 45. 28 applicants, 46% accepted, 7 enrolled. In 2011, 2 doctorates, 2 other advanced degrees awarded. *Degree requirements:* For master's, thesis optional; for doctorate, thesis/dissertation. *Entrance requirements:* For master's, GRE Subject Test. Additional exam requirements/recommendations for international students: Required—TOEFL (minimum score 550 paper-based). *Application deadline:* Applications are processed on a rolling basis. Application fee: $40. *Financial support:* Fellowships, research assistantships, teaching assistantships, career-related internships or fieldwork, Federal Work-Study, institutionally sponsored loans, and tuition waivers (partial) available. Support available to part-time students. *Unit head:* Dr. Larry D. Burton, Coordinator, 269-971-6674. *Application contact:* Carolyn Hurst, Supervisor of Graduate Admission, 800-253-2874, Fax: 269-471-6321, E-mail: graduate@andrews.edu.

Angelo State University, College of Graduate Studies, College of Education, Department of Curriculum and Instruction, Program in Curriculum and Instruction, San Angelo, TX 76909. Offers MA. Part-time and evening/weekend programs available. *Faculty:* 17 full-time (12 women). *Students:* 23 full-time (17 women), 70 part-time (53 women); includes 25 minority (7 Black or African American, non-Hispanic/Latino; 2 Asian, non-Hispanic/Latino; 16 Hispanic/Latino). Average age 36. 29 applicants, 76% accepted, 18 enrolled. In 2011, 15 master's awarded. *Degree requirements:* For master's, comprehensive exam. *Entrance requirements:* Additional exam requirements/recommendations for international students: Required—TOEFL or IELTS. *Application deadline:* For fall admission, 7/15 priority date for domestic students, 6/10 for international students; for spring admission, 12/1 priority date for domestic students, 11/1 for international students. Applications are processed on a rolling basis. Application fee: $40 ($50 for international students). Electronic applications accepted. *Financial support:* In 2011–12, 6 students received support. Career-related internships or fieldwork, Federal Work-Study, scholarships/grants, and unspecified assistantships available. Support available to part-time students. Financial award application deadline: 3/1; financial award applicants required to submit FAFSA. *Unit head:* Dr. Kim Livengood, Graduate Advisor, 325-942-2647 Ext. 478, E-mail: kim.livengood@angelo.edu. *Application contact:* Aly Hunter, Graduate Admissions Assistant, 325-942-2169, Fax: 325-942-2039, E-mail: aly.hunter@angelo.edu. Web site: http://www.angelo.edu/dept/education/.

Appalachian State University, Cratis D. Williams Graduate School, Department of Curriculum and Instruction, Boone, NC 28608. Offers curriculum specialist (MA); educational media (MA); elementary education (MA); middle grades education (MA), including language arts, mathematics, science, social studies. *Accreditation:* NCATE. Part-time and evening/weekend programs available. Postbaccalaureate distance learning degree programs offered (no on-campus study). *Faculty:* 33 full-time (23 women), 5 part-time/adjunct (2 women). *Students:* 23 full-time (18 women), 110 part-time (90 women); includes 7 minority (4 Black or African American, non-Hispanic/Latino; 1 Asian, non-Hispanic/Latino; 2 Hispanic/Latino). 79 applicants, 94% accepted, 64 enrolled. In 2011, 87 master's awarded. *Degree requirements:* For master's, comprehensive exam, thesis or alternative. *Entrance requirements:* For master's, GRE General Test or MAT, 3 letters of recommendation. Additional exam requirements/recommendations for international students: Required—TOEFL (minimum score 570 paper-based; 230 computer-based; 79 iBT), IELTS (minimum score 6.5). *Application deadline:* For fall admission, 3/14 for domestic students, 2/1 for international students; for spring admission, 11/1 for domestic students, 7/1 for international students. Applications are processed on a rolling basis. Application fee: $55. Electronic applications accepted. *Expenses:* Tuition, state resident: full-time $4040; part-time $180 per semester hour. Tuition, nonresident: full-time $15,900; part-time $760 per semester hour. *Required fees:* $2500; $20 per semester hour. Tuition and fees vary according to campus/location. *Financial support:* In 2011–12, 6 teaching assistantships (averaging $8,000 per year) were awarded; fellowships, research assistantships, career-related internships or fieldwork, Federal Work-Study, scholarships/grants, and unspecified assistantships also available. Financial award application deadline: 4/1; financial award applicants required to submit FAFSA. *Faculty research:* Media literacy, elementary teaching, curriculum development, online learning environments. *Total annual research expenditures:* $480,000. *Unit head:* Dr. Michael Jacobson, Chairperson, 828-262-2224. *Application contact:* Sandy Krause, Director of Admissions and Recruiting, 828-262-2130, Fax: 828-262-2709, E-mail: krausesl@appstate.edu. Web site: http://www.ced.appstate.edu/departments/ci.

Arcadia University, Graduate Studies, Department of Education, Glenside, PA 19038-3295. Offers art education (M Ed); computer education (CAS); curriculum (CAS); curriculum studies (M Ed); early childhood education (M Ed, CAS), including individualized (M Ed), master teacher (M Ed), research in child development (M Ed); educational leadership (M Ed, Ed D, CAS); elementary education (M Ed, CAS); English education (MA Ed); environmental education (MA Ed, CAS); history education (MA Ed); instructional technology (M Ed); language arts (M Ed, CAS); library science (M Ed); mathematics education (M Ed, MA Ed, CAS); music education (MA Ed); psychology (MA Ed); reading (M Ed, CAS); science education (M Ed, CAS); secondary education (M Ed, CAS); special education (M Ed, Ed D, CAS); theater arts (MA Ed); written communication (MA Ed). *Accreditation:* NASAD. Part-time and evening/weekend programs available. Postbaccalaureate distance learning degree programs offered (minimal on-campus study). *Faculty:* 12 full-time (8 women), 38 part-time/adjunct (26 women). *Students:* 66 full-time (48 women), 590 part-time (477 women); includes 65 minority (53 Black or African American, non-Hispanic/Latino; 6 Asian, non-Hispanic/Latino; 3 Hispanic/Latino; 3 Two or more races, non-Hispanic/Latino), 4 international.

Average age 36. In 2011, 229 master's, 5 doctorates awarded. *Application deadline:* Applications are processed on a rolling basis. Application fee: $50. Electronic applications accepted. *Expenses:* Contact institution. *Financial support:* Career-related internships or fieldwork, tuition waivers (partial), and unspecified assistantships available. *Unit head:* Dr. Steven P. Gulkus, Associate Professor, 215-572-2120, E-mail: gulkus@arcadia.edu. *Application contact:* 215-572-2925, Fax: 215-572-2126, E-mail: grad@arcadia.edu.

Arizona State University, Mary Lou Fulton Teachers College, Program in Curriculum and Instruction, Phoenix, AZ 85069. Offers curriculum and instruction (M Ed, MA, PhD); elementary education (M Ed); physical education (MPE); secondary education (M Ed). Part-time and evening/weekend programs available. Postbaccalaureate distance learning degree programs offered (minimal on-campus study). Terminal master's awarded for partial completion of doctoral program. *Degree requirements:* For master's, thesis or alternative, applied project, interactive Program of Study (iPOS) submitted before completing 50 percent of required credit hours; for doctorate, comprehensive exam, thesis/dissertation, interactive Program of Study (iPOS) submitted before completing 50 percent of required credit hours. *Entrance requirements:* For master's, GRE or GMAT (for some programs), minimum GPA of 3.0 or equivalent in last 2 years of work leading to bachelor's degree, 3 letters of recommendation, personal statement describing research and career goals, curriculum vitae or resume, IVP fingerprint clearance card (for those seeking Arizona certification); for doctorate, GRE or GMAT (depending on program), minimum GPA of 3.0 or equivalent in last 2 years of work leading to bachelor's degree, 3 letters of recommendation, personal statement describing research and career goals, curriculum vitae or resume. Additional exam requirements/recommendations for international students: Required—TOEFL, IELTS, or Pearson Test of English. Electronic applications accepted. *Expenses:* Contact institution. *Faculty research:* Early childhood, media and computers, elementary education, secondary education, English education, bilingual education, language and literacy, science education, engineering education, exercise and wellness education.

Arkansas State University, Graduate School, College of Education, Department of Educational Leadership, Curriculum, and Special Education, Jonesboro, State University, AR 72467. Offers community college administration education (SCCT); curriculum and instruction (MSE); educational leadership (MSE, Ed D, PhD, Ed S), including curriculum and instruction (MSE, Ed S); special education (MSE), including gifted, talented, and creative, instructional specialist 4-12, instructional specialist P-4. *Accreditation:* NCATE. Part-time programs available. Postbaccalaureate distance learning degree programs offered (no on-campus study). *Faculty:* 12 full-time (5 women). *Students:* 11 full-time (6 women), 2,240 part-time (1,686 women); includes 374 minority (278 Black or African American, non-Hispanic/Latino; 14 American Indian or Alaska Native, non-Hispanic/Latino; 12 Asian, non-Hispanic/Latino; 46 Hispanic/Latino; 2 Native Hawaiian or other Pacific Islander, non-Hispanic/Latino; 22 Two or more races, non-Hispanic/Latino), 1 international. Average age 37. 1,519 applicants, 76% accepted, 790 enrolled. In 2011, 827 master's, 8 doctorates, 30 other advanced degrees awarded. *Degree requirements:* For master's, comprehensive exam, thesis or alternative; for doctorate, comprehensive exam, thesis/dissertation; for other advanced degree, comprehensive exam. *Entrance requirements:* For master's, GRE General Test or MAT, appropriate bachelor's degree, letters of reference, interview, official transcript, immunization records; for doctorate, GRE General Test or MAT, interview, master's degree, letters of reference, official transcript, personal statement, writing sample, immunization records; for other advanced degree, GRE General Test or MAT, interview, master's degree, letters of reference, official transcript, 3 years teaching experience, mentor, teaching license, immunization records. Additional exam requirements/recommendations for international students: Required—TOEFL (minimum score 550 paper-based; 213 computer-based; 79 iBT), IELTS (minimum score 6), Pearson Test of English Academic (minimum score 56). *Application deadline:* Applications are processed on a rolling basis. Application fee: $50. Electronic applications accepted. *Expenses:* Tuition, state resident: full-time $4044; part-time $225 per credit hour. Tuition, nonresident: full-time $8087; part-time $449 per credit hour. *Required fees:* $936; $52 per credit hour. $25 per term. One-time fee: $30. Tuition and fees vary according to course load and program. *Financial support:* In 2011–12, 6 students received support. Fellowships, teaching assistantships, career-related internships or fieldwork, scholarships/grants, and unspecified assistantships available. Financial award application deadline: 7/1; financial award applicants required to submit FAFSA. *Unit head:* Dr. Mitchell Holifield, Chair, 870-972-3062, Fax: 870-680-8130, E-mail: hfield@astate.edu. *Application contact:* Dr. Andrew Sustich, Dean of the Graduate School, 870-972-3029, Fax: 870-972-3857, E-mail: sustich@astate.edu. Web site: http://www.astate.edu/a/education/elcse/.

Arkansas Tech University, Center for Leadership and Learning, College of Education, Russellville, AR 72801. Offers college student personnel (MS); educational leadership (Ed S); elementary education (M Ed); instructional improvement (M Ed); instructional technology (M Ed); physical education (M Ed); school counseling and leadership (M Ed); teaching (MAT). *Accreditation:* NCATE. Part-time and evening/weekend programs available. Postbaccalaureate distance learning degree programs offered (no on-campus study). *Students:* 70 full-time (44 women), 247 part-time (189 women); includes 57 minority (38 Black or African American, non-Hispanic/Latino; 1 American Indian or Alaska Native, non-Hispanic/Latino; 8 Asian, non-Hispanic/Latino; 4 Hispanic/Latino; 6 Two or more races, non-Hispanic/Latino), 3 international. Average age 31. In 2011, 58 master's awarded. *Degree requirements:* For master's, comprehensive exam, thesis optional, action research project. *Entrance requirements:* Additional exam requirements/recommendations for international students: Required—TOEFL (minimum score 550 paper-based; 213 computer-based; 79 iBT), IELTS (minimum score 6.5). *Application deadline:* For fall admission, 3/1 priority date for domestic students, 5/1 for international students; for spring admission, 10/1 priority date for domestic students, 10/1 for international students. Applications are processed on a rolling basis. Application fee: $25 ($75 for international students). Electronic applications accepted. *Expenses:* Tuition, state resident: full-time $4968; part-time $207 per credit hour. Tuition, nonresident: full-time $9936; part-time $414 per credit hour. *Required fees:* $375 per semester. Tuition and fees vary according to course load. *Financial support:* In 2011–12, teaching assistantships with full tuition reimbursements (averaging $4,800 per year) were awarded; research assistantships with full tuition reimbursements, career-related internships or fieldwork, Federal Work-Study, scholarships/grants, health care benefits, and unspecified assistantships also available. Support available to part-time students. Financial award application deadline: 4/15; financial award applicants required to submit FAFSA. *Unit head:* Dr. Eldon G. Clary, Jr., Dean, 479-968-0350, Fax: 479-968-0350, E-mail: eclary@atu.edu. *Application contact:* Dr. Mary B. Gunter, Dean of Graduate College, 479-968-0398, Fax: 479-964-0542, E-mail: gradcollege@atu.edu. Web site: http://www.atu.edu/education/.

Armstrong Atlantic State University, School of Graduate Studies, Program in Education, Savannah, GA 31419-1997. Offers adult education (M Ed); curriculum and instruction (M Ed); early childhood education (M Ed); education (M Ed); elementary education (M Ed); middle grades education (M Ed); secondary education (M Ed), including business education, English education, mathematics education, science education, social science education; special education (M Ed), including behavioral disorders, learning disabilities, speech-language pathology. *Accreditation:* NCATE. Part-time and evening/weekend programs available. Postbaccalaureate distance learning degree programs offered (minimal on-campus study). *Faculty:* 33 full-time (23 women), 3 part-time/adjunct (2 women). *Students:* 97 full-time (91 women), 262 part-time (227 women); includes 83 minority (70 Black or African American, non-Hispanic/Latino; 3 Asian, non-Hispanic/Latino; 8 Hispanic/Latino; 2 Two or more races, non-Hispanic/Latino), 5 international. Average age 34. 169 applicants, 69% accepted, 102 enrolled. In 2011, 227 master's awarded. *Degree requirements:* For master's, comprehensive exam, portfolio. *Entrance requirements:* For master's, GRE General Test or MAT, minimum GPA of 2.5, letters of recommendation. Additional exam requirements/recommendations for international students: Required—TOEFL (minimum score 523 paper-based; 193 computer-based). *Application deadline:* For fall admission, 7/1 priority date for domestic students, 5/1 for international students; for spring admission, 11/15 priority date for domestic students, 9/15 for international students. Applications are processed on a rolling basis. Application fee: $30. Electronic applications accepted. *Expenses:* Tuition, state resident: full-time $3402. Tuition, nonresident: full-time $12,636. *Financial support:* In 2011–12, research assistantships with full tuition reimbursements (averaging $5,000 per year) were awarded; career-related internships or fieldwork, Federal Work-Study, scholarships/grants, and unspecified assistantships also available. Support available to part-time students. Financial award applicants required to submit FAFSA. *Unit head:* Dr. Patricia Wachholz, Dean, College of Education, 912-344-2797, E-mail: patricia.wachholz@armstrong.edu. *Application contact:* Jill Bell, Director, Graduate Enrollment Services, 912-344-2798, Fax: 912-344-3488, E-mail: graduate@armstrong.edu. Web site: http://www.armstrong.edu/Education/coe_deans_office/coe_education_welcome.

Ashland University, Dwight Schar College of Education, Department of Educational Administration, Ashland, OH 44805-3702. Offers curriculum specialist (M Ed); principalship (M Ed); pupil services (M Ed). Part-time programs available. *Faculty:* 7 full-time (3 women), 16 part-time/adjunct (4 women). *Students:* 108 full-time (72 women), 185 part-time (94 women); includes 34 minority (26 Black or African American, non-Hispanic/Latino; 2 American Indian or Alaska Native, non-Hispanic/Latino; 1 Asian, non-Hispanic/Latino; 2 Hispanic/Latino; 3 Two or more races, non-Hispanic/Latino), 2 international. Average age 33. 75 applicants, 100% accepted, 65 enrolled. In 2011, 143 master's awarded. *Degree requirements:* For master's, thesis or alternative, internship. *Entrance requirements:* For master's, teaching certificate or license, bachelor's degree, minimum cumulative GPA of 2.75. Additional exam requirements/recommendations for international students: Required—TOEFL. *Application deadline:* Applications are processed on a rolling basis. Application fee: $30. Electronic applications accepted. *Expenses: Tuition:* Full-time $5580; part-time $465 per credit hour. *Financial support:* Institutionally sponsored loans and scholarships/grants available. Financial award application deadline: 4/15. *Faculty research:* Gender and religious considerations in employment, ISLLC standards, adjunct faculty training, politics of school finance, ethnicity and employment. *Unit head:* Dr. Robert Thiede, Chair, 419-289-5258, Fax: 419-207-6702, E-mail: rthiede@ashland.edu. *Application contact:* Dr. Linda Billman, Director and Chair, Graduate Studies in Education/Associate Dean, 419-289-5369, Fax: 419-289-5331, E-mail: lbillman@ashland.edu.

Auburn University, Graduate School, College of Education, Department of Educational Foundations, Leadership, and Technology, Auburn University, AL 36849. Offers adult education (M Ed, MS, Ed D); curriculum and instruction (M Ed, MS, Ed D, Ed S); curriculum supervision (M Ed, MS, Ed D, Ed S); educational psychology (PhD); higher education administration (M Ed, MS, Ed D, Ed S); media instructional design (MS); media specialist (M Ed); school administration (M Ed, MS, Ed D, Ed S). *Accreditation:* NCATE. Part-time programs available. *Faculty:* 26 full-time (16 women), 3 part-time/adjunct (all women). *Students:* 58 full-time (28 women), 215 part-time (135 women); includes 89 minority (82 Black or African American, non-Hispanic/Latino; 1 American Indian or Alaska Native, non-Hispanic/Latino; 4 Asian, non-Hispanic/Latino; 2 Hispanic/Latino), 13 international. Average age 35. 140 applicants, 61% accepted, 56 enrolled. In 2011, 37 master's, 29 doctorates, 9 other advanced degrees awarded. *Degree requirements:* For master's, thesis (for some programs); for doctorate, thesis/dissertation; for Ed S, field project. *Entrance requirements:* For master's, doctorate, and Ed S, GRE General Test. *Application deadline:* For fall admission, 7/7 for domestic students; for spring admission, 11/24 for domestic students. Applications are processed on a rolling basis. Application fee: $50 ($60 for international students). Electronic applications accepted. *Expenses:* Tuition, state resident: full-time $7290; part-time $405 per credit hour. Tuition, nonresident: full-time $21,870; part-time $1215 per credit hour. *International tuition:* $22,000 full-time. *Required fees:* $1402. *Financial support:* Teaching assistantships and Federal Work-Study available. Support available to part-time students. Financial award application deadline: 3/15; financial award applicants required to submit FAFSA. *Unit head:* Dr. Sherida Downer, Head, 334-844-4460. *Application contact:* Dr. George Flowers, Dean of the Graduate School, 334-844-4700. Web site: http://www.education.auburn.edu/academic_departments/eflt/.

Augusta State University, Graduate Studies, College of Education, Program in Curriculum/Instruction, Augusta, GA 30904-2200. Offers M Ed. *Faculty:* 1 full-time (0 women), 4 part-time/adjunct (all women). *Students:* 33 full-time (31 women), 44 part-time (38 women); includes 16 minority (14 Black or African American, non-Hispanic/Latino; 2 Hispanic/Latino). 29 applicants, 86% accepted, 20 enrolled. In 2011, 28 master's awarded. *Degree requirements:* For master's, thesis, portfolio. *Entrance requirements:* For master's, GRE, MAT, minimum GPA of 2.5. Application fee: $20. *Financial support:* Career-related internships or fieldwork, Federal Work-Study, institutionally sponsored loans, and unspecified assistantships available. Support available to part-time students. Financial award application deadline: 4/15; financial award applicants required to submit FAFSA. *Unit head:* Dr. J. Gordon Eisenman, Chair, 706-737-1496, Fax: 706-667-4706, E-mail: geisenman@aug.edu. *Application contact:* Andrea M. Scott, Secretary to the Dean, 706-737-1499, Fax: 706-667-4706, E-mail: ascott1@aug.edu.

Aurora University, College of Education, Aurora, IL 60506-4892. Offers curriculum and instruction (MA, Ed D); early childhood and special education (MA); education (MAT), including elementary certification; education and administration (Ed D); educational leadership (MEL); educational technology (MATL); reading instruction (MA); special education (MA). *Accreditation:* NCATE. Part-time and evening/weekend programs available. *Degree requirements:* For doctorate, comprehensive exam, thesis/dissertation. *Entrance requirements:* For master's, 2 years of teaching experience, valid teaching certificate. Additional exam requirements/recommendations for international students: Required—TOEFL (minimum score 550 paper-based; 213 computer-based). Electronic applications accepted. *Expenses:* Contact institution.

Austin Peay State University, College of Graduate Studies, College of Education, Department of Educational Specialties, Clarksville, TN 37044. Offers administration and supervision (Ed S); curriculum and instruction (MA Ed); education leadership (MA Ed); elementary education (Ed S); secondary education (Ed S); special education (MA Ed). Part-time and evening/weekend programs available. Postbaccalaureate distance learning degree programs offered. *Faculty:* 7 full-time (4 women), 4 part-time/adjunct (3 women). *Students:* 6 full-time (4 women), 86 part-time (66 women); includes 11 minority (6 Black or African American, non-Hispanic/Latino; 1 American Indian or Alaska Native, non-Hispanic/Latino; 4 Hispanic/Latino). Average age 37. 33 applicants, 100%

accepted, 23 enrolled. In 2011, 32 master's, 7 Ed Ss awarded. *Degree requirements:* For master's, comprehensive exam, thesis optional. *Entrance requirements:* For master's, GRE General Test, 3 letters of recommendation, minimum undergraduate GPA of 2.75. Additional exam requirements/recommendations for international students: Required—TOEFL (minimum score 500 paper-based; 173 computer-based). *Application deadline:* For fall admission, 8/1 priority date for domestic students. Applications are processed on a rolling basis. Application fee: $25. Electronic applications accepted. *Expenses:* Tuition, state resident: part-time $350 per credit hour. Tuition, nonresident: full-time $20,644; part-time $971 per credit hour. *Required fees:* $1224; $61.20 per credit hour. *Financial support:* Career-related internships or fieldwork, Federal Work-Study, institutionally sponsored loans, scholarships/grants, and unspecified assistantships available. Support available to part-time students. Financial award application deadline: 3/1; financial award applicants required to submit FAFSA. *Unit head:* Dr. Moniqueka Gold, Chair, 931-221-7696, Fax: 931-221-1292, E-mail: goldm@apsu.edu. *Application contact:* Kendra Bryant, Graduate Admissions, 800-844-2778, Fax: 931-221-6188, E-mail: admissionsweb@apsu.edu.

Austin Peay State University, College of Graduate Studies, College of Education, Department of Teaching and Learning, Clarksville, TN 37044. Offers elementary education K-6 (MAT); reading (MA Ed); secondary education 7-12 (MAT); special education K-12 (MAT). Part-time and evening/weekend programs available. Postbaccalaureate distance learning degree programs offered. *Faculty:* 14 full-time (11 women), 3 part-time/adjunct (2 women). *Students:* 84 full-time (67 women), 97 part-time (81 women); includes 27 minority (12 Black or African American, non-Hispanic/Latino; 2 American Indian or Alaska Native, non-Hispanic/Latino; 2 Asian, non-Hispanic/Latino; 4 Hispanic/Latino; 1 Native Hawaiian or other Pacific Islander, non-Hispanic/Latino; 6 Two or more races, non-Hispanic/Latino). Average age 33. 61 applicants, 98% accepted, 51 enrolled. In 2011, 55 master's awarded. *Degree requirements:* For master's, comprehensive exam, thesis optional. *Entrance requirements:* For master's, GRE General Test, 3 letters of recommendation, minimum undergraduate GPA of 2.75. Additional exam requirements/recommendations for international students: Required—TOEFL (minimum score 500 paper-based; 173 computer-based). *Application deadline:* For fall admission, 8/1 priority date for domestic students. Applications are processed on a rolling basis. Application fee: $25. Electronic applications accepted. *Expenses:* Tuition, state resident: part-time $350 per credit hour. Tuition, nonresident: full-time $20,644; part-time $971 per credit hour. *Required fees:* $1224; $61.20 per credit hour. *Financial support:* Career-related internships or fieldwork, Federal Work-Study, institutionally sponsored loans, scholarships/grants, and unspecified assistantships available. Support available to part-time students. Financial award application deadline: 3/1; financial award applicants required to submit FAFSA. *Unit head:* Dr. Rebecca McMahan, Chair, 931-221-7513, Fax: 931-221-1292, E-mail: mcmahanb@apsu.edu. *Application contact:* Kendra Bryant, Graduate Admissions, 800-844-2778, Fax: 931-221-6188, E-mail: admissionsweb@apsu.edu.

Averett University, Master in Education Program, Danville, VA 24541-3692. Offers curriculum and instruction (M Ed); English (M Ed). Program offered at Richmond, VA regional campus location. Part-time and evening/weekend programs available. *Faculty:* 9 full-time (2 women). *Students:* 234 full-time (165 women), 403 part-time (241 women); includes 168 minority (149 Black or African American, non-Hispanic/Latino; 1 American Indian or Alaska Native, non-Hispanic/Latino; 9 Asian, non-Hispanic/Latino; 9 Hispanic/Latino), 1 international. Average age 32. 59 applicants, 59% accepted, 21 enrolled. *Degree requirements:* For master's, 30-credit core curriculum, minimum GPA of 3.0 throughout program, completion of degree requirements within six years from start of program. *Entrance requirements:* For master's, minimum cumulative GPA of 3.0 over the last 60 semester hours of undergraduate study toward a baccalaureate degree. Additional exam requirements/recommendations for international students: Required—TOEFL (minimum score 600 paper-based; 250 computer-based; 100 iBT). *Application deadline:* Applications are processed on a rolling basis. Application fee: $100. *Expenses:* Contact institution. *Financial support:* Career-related internships or fieldwork, Federal Work-Study, and scholarships/grants available. Financial award application deadline: 4/1; financial award applicants required to submit FAFSA. *Unit head:* Dr. Nick Kalafatis, Director of Graduate Education Program, 804-720-4661, E-mail: nkalafat@averett.edu. Web site: http://www.averett.edu/adultprograms/admissions/forms/AVT%20Med_Insert_2-18-11.pdf.

Azusa Pacific University, School of Education, Department of Foundations and Transdisciplinary Studies, Program in Curriculum and Instruction in Multicultural Contexts, Azusa, CA 91702-7000. Offers MA Ed. *Accreditation:* NCATE. Part-time and evening/weekend programs available. *Degree requirements:* For master's, core exams, oral presentation. *Entrance requirements:* For master's, 12 units of course work in education, minimum GPA of 3.0. *Faculty research:* Diversity in teacher education programs, teacher morale, student perception of school, case study instruction.

Azusa Pacific University, School of Education, Department of Foundations and Transdisciplinary Studies, Program in Teaching, Azusa, CA 91702-7000. Offers MA Ed.

Ball State University, Graduate School, Teachers College, Department of Educational Studies, Program in Curriculum, Muncie, IN 47306-1099. Offers MAE, Ed S. *Accreditation:* NCATE. *Students:* 9 full-time (8 women), 98 part-time (73 women); includes 8 minority (2 Black or African American, non-Hispanic/Latino; 2 Asian, non-Hispanic/Latino; 3 Hispanic/Latino; 1 Two or more races, non-Hispanic/Latino), 2 international. Average age 36. 21 applicants, 86% accepted, 12 enrolled. In 2011, 15 master's, 3 other advanced degrees awarded. *Degree requirements:* For Ed S, thesis. *Entrance requirements:* For degree, GRE General Test, interview. Application fee: $50. Tuition and fees vary according to program and reciprocity agreements. *Financial support:* In 2011–12, 5 students received support, including 1 teaching assistantship (averaging $5,966 per year). Financial award application deadline: 3/1. *Unit head:* Jayne Beilke, Head, 785-285-5460, Fax: 785-285-5489. *Application contact:* Dr. Jon Clausen, Associate Provost for Research and Dean of the Graduate School, 765-285-1300, E-mail: rmorris@bsu.edu. Web site: http://www.bsu.edu/teachers/departments/edstudies/.

Barry University, School of Education, Program in Curriculum and Instruction, Miami Shores, FL 33161-6695. Offers accomplished teacher (Ed S); culture, language and literacy (TESOL) (PhD); curriculum evaluation and research (PhD); early childhood (Ed S); early childhood education (PhD); elementary (Ed S); elementary education (PhD); ESOL (Ed S); gifted (Ed S); Montessori (Ed S); PKP/elementary (Ed S); reading (Ed S); reading, language and cognition (PhD). *Entrance requirements:* For doctorate, GRE, minimum GPA of 3.25.

Baylor University, Graduate School, School of Education, Department of Curriculum and Instruction, Waco, TX 76798. Offers MA, MS Ed, Ed D, PhD. *Accreditation:* NCATE. Part-time programs available. *Faculty:* 11 full-time (5 women), 2 part-time/adjunct (1 woman). *Students:* 35 full-time (27 women), 19 part-time (10 women); includes 7 minority (1 Asian, non-Hispanic/Latino; 6 Hispanic/Latino), 3 international. Average age 30. 33 applicants, 70% accepted, 21 enrolled. In 2011, 19 master's, 3 doctorates awarded. *Degree requirements:* For doctorate, thesis/dissertation. *Entrance requirements:* For master's and doctorate, GRE General Test (including Analytic Writing). Additional exam requirements/recommendations for international students: Required—TOEFL (minimum score 550 paper-based; 213 computer-based) or IELTS (minimum score 6.5). *Application deadline:* For fall admission, 3/15 priority date for domestic students, 3/15 for international students; for spring admission, 10/15 priority date for domestic students, 10/15 for international students. Applications are processed on a rolling basis. Application fee: $25. *Financial support:* In 2011–12, 7 research assistantships (averaging $17,500 per year), 6 teaching assistantships (averaging $6,600 per year) were awarded; Federal Work-Study and institutionally sponsored loans also available. Support available to part-time students. Financial award application deadline: 3/15. *Faculty research:* Teacher education, language and literacy. *Unit head:* Dr. Tony L. Talbert, Graduate Program Director, 254-710-4481, Fax: 254-710-3870, E-mail: tony_talbert@baylor.edu. *Application contact:* Amy Williams, Administrative Assistant, 254-710-4481, Fax: 254-710-3870, E-mail: amy_williams1@baylor.edu.

Benedictine University, Graduate Programs, Program in Education, Lisle, IL 60532-0900. Offers curriculum and instruction and collaborative teaching (M Ed); elementary education (MA Ed); leadership and administration (M Ed); reading and literacy (M Ed); secondary education (MA Ed); special education (MA Ed). Part-time and evening/weekend programs available. *Faculty:* 4 full-time (2 women), 52 part-time/adjunct (30 women). *Students:* 178 full-time (157 women), 239 part-time (211 women); includes 41 minority (29 Black or African American, non-Hispanic/Latino; 4 Asian, non-Hispanic/Latino; 8 Hispanic/Latino), 2 international. Average age 33. 177 applicants, 44% accepted, 68 enrolled. In 2011, 278 master's awarded. *Degree requirements:* For master's, comprehensive exam, thesis (for some programs). *Entrance requirements:* For master's, GRE or MAT. Additional exam requirements/recommendations for international students: Required—TOEFL (minimum score 550 paper-based; 213 computer-based). *Application deadline:* For fall admission, 9/1 for domestic students; for winter admission, 12/1 for domestic students; for spring admission, 2/15 for domestic students. Applications are processed on a rolling basis. Application fee: $40. Electronic applications accepted. *Expenses:* Contact institution. *Financial support:* Career-related internships or fieldwork and health care benefits available. Support available to part-time students. *Unit head:* MeShelda Jackson, Director, 630-829-6282, E-mail: mjackson@ben.edu. *Application contact:* Kari Gibbons, Associate Vice President, Enrollment Center, 630-829-6200, Fax: 630-829-6584, E-mail: kgibbons@ben.edu.

Berry College, Graduate Programs, Graduate Programs in Education, Program in Leadership in Curriculum and Instruction, Mount Berry, GA 30149-0159. Offers curriculum and instruction (Ed S); educational leadership (Ed S). *Accreditation:* NCATE. *Faculty:* 6 part-time/adjunct (3 women). *Students:* 49 part-time (33 women); includes 7 minority (4 Black or African American, non-Hispanic/Latino; 1 Asian, non-Hispanic/Latino; 2 Hispanic/Latino). Average age 37. In 2011, 10 Ed Ss awarded. *Degree requirements:* For Ed S, thesis, portfolio, oral exams. *Entrance requirements:* For degree, M Ed from NCATE-accredited school, minimum GPA of 3.25. Additional exam requirements/recommendations for international students: Required—TOEFL (minimum score 550 paper-based; 213 computer-based). *Application deadline:* For fall admission, 5/1 for domestic and international students; for spring admission, 10/1 for domestic and international students. Applications are processed on a rolling basis. Application fee: $25 ($30 for international students). Electronic applications accepted. *Expenses:* Contact institution. *Financial support:* In 2011–12, 1 student received support. Scholarships/grants available. Support available to part-time students. Financial award application deadline: 3/1; financial award applicants required to submit FAFSA. *Faculty research:* Curriculum development, teacher training, pedagogy. *Unit head:* Dr. Jacqueline McDowell, 706-236-1717, Fax: 706-238-5827, E-mail: jmcdowell@berry.edu. *Application contact:* Brett Kennedy, Director of Admissions, 706-236-2215, Fax: 706-290-2178, E-mail: admissions@berry.edu. Web site: http://www.berry.edu/academics/education/graduate/.

Black Hills State University, Graduate Studies, Program in Curriculum and Instruction, Spearfish, SD 57799. Offers MS. Part-time programs available. *Entrance requirements:* Additional exam requirements/recommendations for international students: Required—TOEFL (minimum score 500 paper-based; 171 computer-based; 60 iBT).

Bloomsburg University of Pennsylvania, School of Graduate Studies, College of Education, Department of Educational Studies and Secondary Education, Program in Curriculum and Instruction, Bloomsburg, PA 17815-1301. Offers M Ed. *Accreditation:* NCATE. *Degree requirements:* For master's, thesis. *Entrance requirements:* For master's, MAT or PRAXIS, minimum QPA of 3.0. Additional exam requirements/recommendations for international students: Required—TOEFL (minimum score 550 paper-based; 213 computer-based; 79 iBT). Electronic applications accepted. *Faculty research:* Administration.

Bob Jones University, Graduate Programs, Greenville, SC 29614. Offers accountancy (MS); Bible (MA); Bible translation (MA); Biblical studies (Certificate); broadcast management (MS); business administration (MBA); church history (MA, PhD); church ministries (MA); church music (MM); cinema and video production (MA); counseling (MS); curriculum and instruction (Ed D); divinity (M Div); dramatic production (MA); educational leadership (MS, Ed D, Ed S); elementary education (M Ed, MAT); English (M Ed, MA, MAT); fine arts (MA); graphic design (MA); history (M Ed, MA); illustration (MA); interpretative speech (MA); mathematics (M Ed, MAT); medical missions (Certificate); ministry (MM, D Min); multi-categorical special education (M Ed, MAT); music (M Ed); New Testament interpretation (PhD); Old Testament interpretation (PhD); orchestral instrument performance (MM); organ performance (MM); pastoral studies (MA); personnel services (MS, Ed S); piano pedagogy (MM); piano performance (MM); platform arts (MA); radio and television broadcasting (MS); rhetoric and public address (MA); secondary education (M Ed); studio art (MA); teaching Bible (MA); theology (MA, PhD); voice performance (MM); youth ministries (MA); M Div/MM.

Boise State University, Graduate College, College of Education, Department of Curriculum, Instruction and Foundational Studies, Doctoral Program in Curriculum and Instruction, Boise, ID 83725-0399. Offers Ed D. *Accreditation:* NCATE. Part-time programs available. *Degree requirements:* For doctorate, thesis/dissertation. *Entrance requirements:* For doctorate, GRE General Test, minimum GPA of 3.0. Electronic applications accepted.

Boston College, Lynch Graduate School of Education, Program in Curriculum and Instruction, Chestnut Hill, MA 02467-3800. Offers M Ed, PhD, CAES, JD/M Ed. Part-time and evening/weekend programs available. *Students:* 123 full-time (92 women), 26 part-time (16 women); includes 19 minority (4 Black or African American, non-Hispanic/Latino; 2 American Indian or Alaska Native, non-Hispanic/Latino; 7 Asian, non-Hispanic/Latino; 5 Hispanic/Latino; 1 Two or more races, non-Hispanic/Latino), 32 international. 216 applicants, 53% accepted, 68 enrolled. In 2011, 44 master's, 8 doctorates, 3 other advanced degrees awarded. Terminal master's awarded for partial completion of doctoral program. *Degree requirements:* For master's and CAES, comprehensive exam; for doctorate, comprehensive exam, thesis/dissertation. *Entrance requirements:* For master's and CAES, GRE General Test or MAT; for doctorate, GRE General Test. Additional exam requirements/recommendations for international students: Required—TOEFL (minimum score 550 paper-based; 213 computer-based; 79 iBT). Application fee: $65. Electronic applications accepted. *Financial support:* Fellowships with full and partial tuition reimbursements, research assistantships with full and partial tuition reimbursements, teaching assistantships with full and partial tuition reimbursements, career-related internships or fieldwork, Federal Work-Study, scholarships/grants, traineeships, health care benefits, tuition waivers (full and partial), and unspecified assistantships available. Support available to part-time students. Financial award applicants required to submit FAFSA. *Faculty research:* Literacy, bilingualism, urban education, technology and education, diversity and social justice in education. *Unit head:* Dr. Maria E. Brisk, Chairperson, 617-552-4214, Fax: 617-552-0398. *Application contact:* Adam Poluzzi, Director, Graduate Admission and Financial Aid, 617-552-4214, Fax: 617-552-0398, E-mail: poluzzi@bc.edu. Web site: http://www.bc.edu/schools/lsoe/academics/departments/teseci/graduate/curriculum.html.

Bowling Green State University, Graduate College, College of Education and Human Development, School of Education and Intervention Services, Teaching and Learning Division, Program in Curriculum and Teaching, Bowling Green, OH 43403. Offers curriculum (M Ed); master teaching (M Ed). Part-time and evening/weekend programs available. *Degree requirements:* For master's, thesis or alternative. *Entrance requirements:* For master's, GRE General Test or PRAXIS. Additional exam requirements/recommendations for international students: Required—TOEFL. Electronic applications accepted. *Faculty research:* Cognitive development in cultural context, sociocultural and activity theory, philosophy in education, performance assessment.

Bradley University, Graduate School, College of Education and Health Sciences, Department of Curriculum and Instruction, Peoria, IL 61625-0002. Offers MA, Certificate. *Accreditation:* NCATE. Part-time and evening/weekend programs available. *Degree requirements:* For master's, comprehensive exam, thesis optional. *Entrance requirements:* For master's, GRE General Test or MAT, 2 letters of recommendation. Additional exam requirements/recommendations for international students: Required—TOEFL (minimum score 550 paper-based; 213 computer-based; 79 iBT).

Brandon University, Faculty of Education, Brandon, MB R7A 6A9, Canada. Offers curriculum and instruction (M Ed, Diploma); educational administration (M Ed, Diploma); guidance and counseling (M Ed, Diploma); special education (M Ed, Diploma). *Degree requirements:* For master's, thesis. *Entrance requirements:* For master's, minimum GPA of 3.0, teaching certificate or equivalent. Additional exam requirements/recommendations for international students: Required—TOEFL. *Faculty research:* Comparative education, environmental studies, parent/school council.

Brescia University, Program in Curriculum and Instruction, Owensboro, KY 42301-3023. Offers MSCI. Part-time and evening/weekend programs available. *Degree requirements:* For master's, action research project, portfolio. *Entrance requirements:* For master's, PRAXIS II, interview, minimum GPA of 2.5. Electronic applications accepted.

Buena Vista University, School of Education, Storm Lake, IA 50588. Offers curriculum and instruction (M Ed), including effective teaching, TESL; school guidance and counseling (MS Ed). Program offered in summer only. Part-time and evening/weekend programs available. Postbaccalaureate distance learning degree programs offered (minimal on-campus study). *Degree requirements:* For master's, thesis, fieldwork/practicum, capstone portfolio. *Entrance requirements:* For master's, Analytical Writing Assessment (in-house), minimum undergraduate GPA of 2.75. Electronic applications accepted. *Faculty research:* Reading, curriculum, educational psychology, special education.

Caldwell College, Graduate Studies, Division of Education, Caldwell, NJ 07006-6195. Offers curriculum and instruction (MA); educational administration (MA); learning disabilities teacher-consultant (Post-Master's Certificate); literacy instruction (MA); principal (Post-Master's Certificate); reading specialist (Post-Master's Certificate); special education (MA), including special education, teaching of students with disabilities, teaching of students with disabilities and learning disabilities teacher-consultant; superintendent (Post-Master's Certificate); supervisor (Post-Master's Certificate). Part-time and evening/weekend programs available. *Students:* 66 full-time (41 women), 230 part-time (188 women); includes 24 minority (14 Black or African American, non-Hispanic/Latino; 1 Asian, non-Hispanic/Latino; 9 Hispanic/Latino). *Entrance requirements:* Additional exam requirements/recommendations for international students: Required—TOEFL (minimum score 580 paper-based; 237 computer-based). *Application deadline:* Applications are processed on a rolling basis. Application fee: $40. Electronic applications accepted. *Expenses: Tuition:* Full-time $14,400; part-time $800 per credit. *Required fees:* $200; $100 per semester. *Financial support:* Applicants required to submit FAFSA. *Unit head:* Dr. Janice Stewart, Coordinator, 973-618-3626, E-mail: jstewart@caldwell.edu. *Application contact:* Vilma Mueller, Director of Graduate Studies, 973-618-3544, E-mail: graduate@caldwell.edu.

California Baptist University, Program in Education, Riverside, CA 92504-3206. Offers educational leadership for faith-based instruction (MS); educational leadership for public institutions (MS); educational technology (MS); instructional computer applications (MS); international education (MS); reading (MS); school counseling (MS); school psychology (MS); special education (MS); special education in mild/moderate disabilities (MS); special education in moderate/severe disabilities (MS); teaching (MS); teaching and learning with induction program (MS Ed). Part-time and evening/weekend programs available. *Faculty:* 16 full-time (10 women), 1 (woman) part-time/adjunct. *Students:* 380 full-time (323 women); includes 149 minority (28 Black or African American, non-Hispanic/Latino; 2 American Indian or Alaska Native, non-Hispanic/Latino; 13 Asian, non-Hispanic/Latino; 100 Hispanic/Latino; 2 Native Hawaiian or other Pacific Islander, non-Hispanic/Latino; 4 Two or more races, non-Hispanic/Latino). Average age 32. 181 applicants, 70% accepted, 111 enrolled. In 2011, 82 master's awarded. *Degree requirements:* For master's, comprehensive exam or thesis. *Entrance requirements:* For master's, minimum undergraduate GPA of 3.0; 18 semester units of prerequisite course work in education; three recommendations; essay; interview. Additional exam requirements/recommendations for international students: Required—TOEFL (minimum score 575 paper-based; 230 computer-based; 89 iBT). *Application deadline:* For fall admission, 8/1 priority date for domestic students, 7/1 for international students; for spring admission, 12/1 priority date for domestic students, 11/1 for international students. Applications are processed on a rolling basis. Application fee: $45. Electronic applications accepted. *Expenses:* Contact institution. *Financial support:* In 2011–12, 4 students received support. Federal Work-Study and institutionally sponsored loans available. Financial award applicants required to submit FAFSA. *Faculty research:* Special education, neurosciences and education, cultural influences on behavior, faith-based school leadership, social and philosophical contexts of education. *Unit head:* Dr. John Shoup, Dean, School of Education, 951-343-4205, Fax: 951-343-4516, E-mail: jshoup@calbaptist.edu. *Application contact:* Dr. James Heyman, Director, Master of Science Program in Education, 951-343-4243, Fax: 951-343-5095, E-mail: jheyman@calbaptist.edu. Web site: http://www.calbaptist.edu/mastersined/.

California Coast University, School of Education, Santa Ana, CA 92701. Offers administration (M Ed); curriculum and instruction (M Ed); educational administration (Ed D); educational psychology (Ed D); organizational leadership (Ed D). Postbaccalaureate distance learning degree programs offered (no on-campus study).

California State University, Chico, Office of Graduate Studies, College of Communication and Education, School of Education, Option in Curriculum and Instruction, Chico, CA 95929-0722. Offers MA. *Degree requirements:* For master's, comprehensive exam, thesis or project. *Entrance requirements:* Additional exam requirements/recommendations for international students: Required—TOEFL (minimum score 550 paper-based; 213 computer-based; 80 iBT), IELTS (minimum score 6.5), Pearson Test of English (minimum score 59). *Application deadline:* For fall admission, 3/1 for domestic and international students; for spring admission, 9/15 for domestic and international students. Application fee: $55. Electronic applications accepted. Tuition and fees vary according to class time, course load and degree level. *Financial support:* Fellowships, career-related internships or fieldwork, scholarships/grants, and stipends available. *Unit head:* Dr. Deborah Summers, Chair, 530-898-6421, Fax: 530-898-6177, E-mail: educ@csuchico.edu. *Application contact:* Judy L. Rice, Graduate Admissions Coordinator, 530-898-5416, Fax: 530-898-5416, E-mail: jlrice@csuchico.edu. Web site: http://www.csuchico.edu/soe/advanced/education/curric-instruct.shtml.

California State University, Dominguez Hills, College of Professional Studies, School of Education, Division of Graduate Education, Program in Curriculum and Instruction, Carson, CA 90747-0001. Offers MA. Part-time and evening/weekend programs available. *Faculty:* 4 full-time (2 women), 1 part-time/adjunct (0 women). *Students:* 41 full-time (24 women), 57 part-time (36 women); includes 67 minority (23 Black or African American, non-Hispanic/Latino; 1 American Indian or Alaska Native, non-Hispanic/Latino; 9 Asian, non-Hispanic/Latino; 29 Hispanic/Latino; 5 Two or more races, non-Hispanic/Latino), 1 international. Average age 33. 54 applicants, 78% accepted, 31 enrolled. In 2011, 30 master's awarded. *Degree requirements:* For master's, comprehensive exam. *Entrance requirements:* For master's, minimum GPA of 2.75. Additional exam requirements/recommendations for international students: Required—TOEFL. *Application deadline:* For fall admission, 6/1 for domestic students. Applications are processed on a rolling basis. Application fee: $55. *Faculty research:* Cooperative learning, student engagement. *Unit head:* Dr. James L. Cooper, Professor, 310-243-3961, E-mail: jcooper@csudh.edu. *Application contact:* Admissions Office, 310-243-3530. Web site: http://www.csudh.edu/cps/soe/programsdegrees/graduate-programs-curriculum.shtml.

California State University, Fresno, Division of Graduate Studies, School of Education and Human Development, Department of Curriculum and Instruction, Fresno, CA 93740-8027. Offers education (MA), including curriculum and instruction. *Accreditation:* NCATE. Part-time and evening/weekend programs available. *Degree requirements:* For master's, thesis or alternative. *Entrance requirements:* For master's, GRE General Test, MAT, minimum GPA of 2.75. Additional exam requirements/recommendations for international students: Required—TOEFL. Electronic applications accepted. *Faculty research:* Teacher excellence, teacher quality improvement, online assessment.

California State University, Northridge, Graduate Studies, College of Education, Department of Elementary Education, Northridge, CA 91330. Offers curriculum and instruction (MA); language and literacy (MA); multilingual/multicultural education (MA); teaching and learning (MA). *Accreditation:* NCATE. Part-time and evening/weekend programs available. *Degree requirements:* For master's, comprehensive exam. *Entrance requirements:* For master's, GRE General Test or minimum GPA of 3.0. Additional exam requirements/recommendations for international students: Required—TOEFL.

California State University, Sacramento, Office of Graduate Studies, College of Education, Department of Teacher Education, Sacramento, CA 95819-6079. Offers curriculum and instruction (MA); early childhood education (MA); reading education (MA). Part-time programs available. *Faculty:* 30 full-time (19 women), 23 part-time/adjunct (21 women). *Students:* 116 full-time, 313 part-time; includes 116 minority (7 Black or African American, non-Hispanic/Latino; 4 American Indian or Alaska Native, non-Hispanic/Latino; 28 Asian, non-Hispanic/Latino; 51 Hispanic/Latino; 10 Native Hawaiian or other Pacific Islander, non-Hispanic/Latino; 16 Two or more races, non-Hispanic/Latino). Average age 37. 284 applicants, 96% accepted, 225 enrolled. In 2011, 49 master's awarded. *Entrance requirements:* Additional exam requirements/recommendations for international students: Required—TOEFL. *Application deadline:* For fall admission, 3/1 for domestic and international students; for spring admission, 9/15 for domestic students, 9/30 for international students. Applications are processed on a rolling basis. Application fee: $55. Electronic applications accepted. *Financial support:* Teaching assistantships, career-related internships or fieldwork, and Federal Work-Study available. Support available to part-time students. Financial award application deadline: 3/1; financial award applicants required to submit FAFSA. *Faculty research:* Technology integration and psychological implications for teaching and learning; inquiry-based research and learning in science and technology; uncovering the process of everyday creativity in teachers and other leaders; universal design as a foundation for inclusion; bullying, cyber-bullying and impact on school success; diversity, social justice in adult/vocational education. *Unit head:* Dr. Rita Johnson, Chair, 916-278-6155, Fax: 916-278-6643, E-mail: rjohnson@csus.edu. *Application contact:* Jose Martinez, Outreach and Graduate Diversity Coordinator, 916-278-6470, Fax: 916-278-5669, E-mail: martinj@skymail.csus.edu. Web site: http://www.edweb.csus.edu/edte.

California State University, San Bernardino, Graduate Studies, College of Education, Program in Curriculum and Instruction, San Bernardino, CA 92407-2397. Offers MA. *Students:* 20 full-time (17 women), 7 part-time (4 women); includes 14 minority (3 Black or African American, non-Hispanic/Latino; 1 Asian, non-Hispanic/Latino; 8 Hispanic/Latino; 2 Two or more races, non-Hispanic/Latino). Average age 29. 29 applicants, 66% accepted, 14 enrolled. In 2011, 15 master's awarded. *Degree requirements:* For master's, comprehensive exam (for some programs), thesis (for some programs). Application fee: $55. *Expenses:* Tuition, state resident: full-time $7356. Tuition, nonresident: full-time $7356. *Required fees:* $1077. Tuition and fees vary according to program. *Unit head:* Dr. Jay Fiene, Department Chair, 909-537-7621, Fax: 909-537-7510, E-mail: jfiene@csusb.edu. *Application contact:* Sandra Kamusikiri, Associate Vice-President/Dean of Graduate Studies, 909-537-5058, E-mail: skamusik@csusb.edu.

California State University, Stanislaus, College of Education, Program in Education (MA), Turlock, CA 95382. Offers curriculum and instruction (MA), including education technology, elementary education, multilingual education, physical education, reading, secondary education, special education; school administration (MA); school counseling (MA). Part-time and evening/weekend programs available. *Degree requirements:* For master's, comprehensive exam (for some programs), thesis (for some programs). *Entrance requirements:* For master's, MAT, GRE, or CBEST (varies by concentration), 3 letters of recommendation, personal statement. Additional exam requirements/recommendations for international students: Required—TOEFL (minimum score 550 paper-based; 213 computer-based). *Application deadline:* For fall admission, 5/1 for domestic students; for spring admission, 1/7 for domestic students. Application fee: $55. Electronic applications accepted. *Expenses: Required fees:* $4616 per year. *Financial support:* Federal Work-Study available. Financial award application deadline: 3/1; financial award applicants required to submit FAFSA. *Faculty research:* Children's perspectives on historical events, method elementary schools dual language education, K-12 reading and CYRM programs. *Unit head:* Dr. Kathy Norman, Dean, College of Education, 209-667-3652, Fax: 209-664-6613, E-mail: coe@csustan.edu. *Application contact:* Graduate School, 209-667-3129, Fax: 209-664-7025, E-mail: graduate_school@csustan.edu. Web site: http://www.csustan.edu/COE/.

Calvin College, Graduate Programs in Education, Grand Rapids, MI 49546-4388. Offers curriculum and instruction (M Ed); educational leadership (M Ed); learning disabilities (M Ed); literacy (M Ed). Part-time programs available. *Degree requirements:*

For master's, thesis or seminar. *Entrance requirements:* For master's, teaching certificate. Additional exam requirements/recommendations for international students: Required—TOEFL (minimum score 550 paper-based; 213 computer-based; 80 iBT). Electronic applications accepted. *Faculty research:* Literacy, racialized gender and gendered identity, teacher learning, learning disabilities identification.

Cambridge College, School of Education, Cambridge, MA 02138-5304. Offers autism specialist (M Ed); autism/behavior analyst (M Ed); behavior analyst (Post-Master's Certificate); behavioral management (M Ed); early childhood teacher (M Ed); education specialist in curriculum and instruction (CAGS); educational leadership (Ed D); elementary teacher (M Ed); English as a second language (M Ed, Certificate); general science (M Ed); health education (Post-Master's Certificate); health/family and consumer sciences (M Ed); history (M Ed); individualized (M Ed); information technology literacy (M Ed); instructional technology (M Ed); interdisciplinary studies (M Ed); library teacher (M Ed); literacy education (M Ed); mathematics (M Ed); mathematics specialist (Certificate); middle school mathematics and science (M Ed); school administration (M Ed, CAGS); school guidance counselor (M Ed); school nurse education (M Ed); school social worker/school adjustment counselor (M Ed); special education administrator (CAGS); special education/moderate disabilities (M Ed); teaching skills and methodologies (M Ed). Part-time and evening/weekend programs available. Postbaccalaureate distance learning degree programs offered (minimal on-campus study). *Degree requirements:* For master's, thesis, internship/practicum (licensure program only); for doctorate, thesis/dissertation; for other advanced degree, thesis. *Entrance requirements:* For master's, interview, resume, documentation of licensure, 2 professional references; for doctorate, official transcripts, interview, resume, documentation of licensure (if any), written personal statement/essay, portfolio of scholarly and professional work, qualifying assessment, 2 professional references, health insurance, immunizations form; for other advanced degree, official transcripts, interview, resume, documentation of licensure (if any), written personal statement/essay, 2 professional references, health insurance, immunizations form. Additional exam requirements/recommendations for international students: Required—TOEFL (minimum score 550 paper-based; 213 computer-based; 79 iBT); Recommended—IELTS (minimum score 6). Electronic applications accepted. *Expenses:* Contact institution. *Faculty research:* Adult education, accelerated learning, mathematics education, brain compatible learning, special education and law.

Campbellsville University, School of Education, Campbellsville, KY 42718-2799. Offers curriculum and instruction (MAE); special education (MASE). *Accreditation:* NCATE. Part-time and evening/weekend programs available. Postbaccalaureate distance learning degree programs offered (minimal on-campus study). *Students:* 232 full-time (159 women), 45 part-time (36 women); includes 34 minority (all Black or African American, non-Hispanic/Latino), 8 international. In 2011, 79 master's awarded. *Degree requirements:* For master's, thesis, research paper. *Entrance requirements:* For master's, GRE or PRAXIS, minimum undergraduate GPA of 2.75, teaching certificate, professional growth plan, letters of recommendation, disposition assessment, interview. *Application deadline:* For fall admission, 6/1 priority date for domestic students, 5/1 for international students; for spring admission, 11/1 priority date for domestic students, 10/1 for international students. Applications are processed on a rolling basis. Application fee: $25. Electronic applications accepted. *Expenses: Tuition:* Full-time $6030; part-time $335 per credit hour. *Financial support:* In 2011–12, 250 students received support. Institutionally sponsored loans, scholarships/grants, and unspecified assistantships available. Support available to part-time students. Financial award application deadline: 6/1; financial award applicants required to submit FAFSA. *Faculty research:* Professional development, curriculum development, school governance, assessment, special education. *Unit head:* Dr. Brenda A. Priddy, Dean, 270-789-5344, Fax: 270-789-5206, E-mail: bapriddy@campbellsville.edu. *Application contact:* Monica Bamwine, Assistant Director of Admissions, 270-789-5221, Fax: 270-789-5071, E-mail: redeaton@campbellsville.edu.

Capella University, School of Education, Minneapolis, MN 55402. Offers college teaching (Certificate); curriculum and instruction (MS, PhD); education (MS); enrollment management (MS); instructional design for online learning (MS, PhD); k-12 studies in education (MS, PhD); leadership for higher education (MS, PhD); leadership in education administration (Certificate); leadership in educational administration (MS, PhD); postsecondary and adult education (MS, PhD); professional studies in education (MS, PhD); reading and literacy (MS); training and performance improvement (MS, PhD). Part-time and evening/weekend programs available. Postbaccalaureate distance learning degree programs offered (minimal on-campus study). Terminal master's awarded for partial completion of doctoral program. *Degree requirements:* For master's, thesis optional, integrative project; for doctorate, comprehensive exam, thesis/dissertation. *Entrance requirements:* Additional exam requirements/recommendations for international students: Required—TOEFL (minimum score 550 paper-based; 213 computer-based), TWE (minimum score 4). Electronic applications accepted. *Faculty research:* Higher education administration, distance learning, adult education, training and curriculum design.

Caribbean University, Graduate School, Bayamón, PR 00960-0493. Offers administration and supervision (MA Ed); criminal justice (MA); curriculum and instruction (MA Ed, PhD), including elementary education (MA Ed), English education (MA Ed), history education (MA Ed), mathematics education (MA Ed), primary education (MA Ed), science education (MA Ed), Spanish education (MA Ed); educational technology in instructional systems (MA Ed); gerontology (MSN); human resources (MBA); museology, archiving and art history (MA Ed); neonatal pediatrics (MSN); physical education (MA Ed); special education (MA Ed). *Entrance requirements:* For master's, interview, minimum GPA of 2.5.

Carson-Newman College, Graduate Program in Education, Jefferson City, TN 37760. Offers curriculum and instruction (M Ed); educational leadership (M Ed); elementary education (MAT); school counseling (MS); secondary education (MAT); teaching English as a second language (MATESL). *Accreditation:* NCATE. Part-time and evening/weekend programs available. *Faculty:* 5 full-time (2 women), 10 part-time/adjunct (3 women). *Students:* 85 full-time (55 women), 76 part-time (53 women); includes 8 minority (5 Black or African American, non-Hispanic/Latino; 2 Asian, non-Hispanic/Latino; 1 Two or more races, non-Hispanic/Latino), 23 international. Average age 32. 80 applicants, 96% accepted. In 2011, 90 master's awarded. *Degree requirements:* For master's, thesis or alternative. *Entrance requirements:* For master's, NTE, minimum GPA of 3.0 in major, 2.5 overall. *Application deadline:* For fall admission, 7/15 priority date for domestic students. Applications are processed on a rolling basis. Application fee: $25 ($50 for international students). *Expenses: Tuition:* Full-time $6750; part-time $375 per credit hour. *Required fees:* $200. *Financial support:* In 2011–12, 41 students received support. Federal Work-Study and unspecified assistantships available. Financial award application deadline: 4/1; financial award applicants required to submit FAFSA. *Unit head:* Dr. Sharon Teets, Chair, 865-471-3461. *Application contact:* Graduate Admissions and Services Adviser, 865-471-3460, Fax: 865-471-3875.

Castleton State College, Division of Graduate Studies, Department of Education, Program in Curriculum and Instruction, Castleton, VT 05735. Offers MA Ed. Part-time and evening/weekend programs available. *Degree requirements:* For master's, thesis or alternative. *Entrance requirements:* For master's, GRE General Test, MAT, interview, minimum undergraduate GPA of 3.0.

Centenary College of Louisiana, Graduate Programs, Department of Education, Shreveport, LA 71104. Offers administration (M Ed); elementary education (MAT); secondary education (MAT); supervision of instruction (M Ed). Part-time and evening/weekend programs available. *Degree requirements:* For master's, comprehensive exam. *Entrance requirements:* For master's, GRE General Test (M Ed), PRAXIS I and PRAXIS II (MAT), teacher certification (M Ed), minimum GPA of 2.5. *Expenses:* Contact institution. *Faculty research:* Teachers as advocates for teachers, portfolio assessment, disabled readers.

Central Michigan University, College of Graduate Studies, College of Education and Human Services, Department of Educational Leadership, Mount Pleasant, MI 48859. Offers educational leadership (MA, Ed D), including charter school leadership (MA), educational technology (Ed D, Ed S), general educational leadership (MA), higher education administration (MA, Ed S), higher education leadership (Ed D), K-12 curriculum (Ed D), K-12 leadership (Ed D), student affairs administration (MA); general educational administration (Ed S), including administrative leadership K-12, educational technology (Ed D, Ed S), higher education administration (MA, Ed S), instructional leadership K-12; school principalship (MA); teacher leadership (MA). Part-time and evening/weekend programs available. *Degree requirements:* For master's and other advanced degree, thesis or alternative; for doctorate, thesis/dissertation. *Entrance requirements:* For doctorate, GRE or MAT, master's degree, minimum GPA of 3.5, 3 years of professional education experience. Electronic applications accepted. *Faculty research:* Elementary administration, secondary administration, student achievement, in-service training, internships in administration.

Central Washington University, Graduate Studies and Research, College of Education and Professional Studies, Department of Educational Foundations and Curriculum, Program in Master Teacher, Ellensburg, WA 98926. Offers M Ed. Part-time programs available. *Faculty:* 19 full-time (9 women). *Students:* 22 part-time (21 women). 14 applicants, 64% accepted, 9 enrolled. In 2011, 12 master's awarded. *Degree requirements:* For master's, comprehensive exam (for some programs), thesis or alternative. *Entrance requirements:* For master's, minimum GPA of 3.0, 1 year of contracted teaching experience. Additional exam requirements/recommendations for international students: Required—TOEFL (minimum score 550 paper-based; 213 computer-based; 79 iBT), IELTS (minimum score 6.5). *Application deadline:* For fall admission, 2/1 priority date for domestic students; for winter admission, 10/1 for domestic students; for spring admission, 1/1 for domestic students. Applications are processed on a rolling basis. Application fee: $50. Electronic applications accepted. *Expenses:* Tuition, state resident: full-time $8112; part-time $270 per credit. Tuition, nonresident: full-time $18,069; part-time $602 per credit. *Required fees:* $924. *Financial support:* In 2011–12, 1 teaching assistantship with full and partial tuition reimbursement (averaging $9,234 per year) was awarded; research assistantships with full and partial tuition reimbursements, Federal Work-Study, health care benefits, and unspecified assistantships also available. Financial award application deadline: 3/1; financial award applicants required to submit FAFSA. *Unit head:* Dr. Barry Donahue, Chair, 509-963-1448, Fax: 509-963-1162. *Application contact:* Justine Eason, Admissions Program Coordinator, 509-963-3103, Fax: 509-963-1799, E-mail: masters@cwu.edu. Web site: http://www.cwu.edu/~education/master.html.

Chapman University, College of Educational Studies, Orange, CA 92866. Offers communication sciences and disorders (MS); counseling (MA), including school counseling (MA, Credential); education (MA, PhD), including cultural and curricular studies (PhD), disability studies (PhD), school psychology (PhD, Credential); educational psychology (MA); professional clear (Credential); pupil personnel services (Credential), including school counseling (MA, Credential), school psychology (PhD, Credential); school psychology (Ed S); single subject (Credential); special education (MA); special education (level ii) (Credential), including mild/moderate, moderate/severe; special education (preliminary) (Credential), including mild/moderate, moderate/severe; speech language pathology (Credential); teaching (MA), including elementary education, secondary education. *Accreditation:* Teacher Education Accreditation Council. Part-time and evening/weekend programs available. *Faculty:* 27 full-time (18 women), 35 part-time/adjunct (24 women). *Students:* 220 full-time (188 women), 164 part-time (128 women); includes 140 minority (12 Black or African American, non-Hispanic/Latino; 1 American Indian or Alaska Native, non-Hispanic/Latino; 44 Asian, non-Hispanic/Latino; 73 Hispanic/Latino; 4 Native Hawaiian or other Pacific Islander, non-Hispanic/Latino; 6 Two or more races, non-Hispanic/Latino), 1 international. Average age 29. 436 applicants, 38% accepted, 126 enrolled. In 2011, 130 master's, 5 doctorates awarded. *Entrance requirements:* Additional exam requirements/recommendations for international students: Required—TOEFL (minimum score 550 paper-based; 213 computer-based; 80 iBT). *Application deadline:* Applications are processed on a rolling basis. Application fee: $60. Electronic applications accepted. Tuition and fees vary according to degree level and program. *Financial support:* Fellowships and scholarships/grants available. Financial award application deadline: 6/30; financial award applicants required to submit FAFSA. *Unit head:* Dr. Don Cardinal, Dean, 714-997-6781, E-mail: cardinal@chapman.edu. *Application contact:* Admissions Coordinator, 714-997-6714. Web site: http://www.chapman.edu/CES/.

City University of Seattle, Graduate Division, Albright School of Education, Bellevue, WA 98005. Offers administrator certification (Certificate); curriculum and instruction (M Ed); educational leadership (Ed D); elementary education (MIT); guidance and counseling (M Ed); higher education leadership (Ed D); leadership (M Ed); leadership and school counseling (M Ed); organizational leadership (Ed D); reading and literacy (M Ed); special education (MIT); superintendent certification (Certificate). Part-time and evening/weekend programs available. Postbaccalaureate distance learning degree programs offered (no on-campus study). *Faculty:* 23 full-time (15 women), 123 part-time/adjunct (82 women). *Students:* 353 full-time (263 women), 75 part-time (50 women); includes 40 minority (12 Black or African American, non-Hispanic/Latino; 5 American Indian or Alaska Native, non-Hispanic/Latino; 7 Asian, non-Hispanic/Latino; 8 Hispanic/Latino; 5 Native Hawaiian or other Pacific Islander, non-Hispanic/Latino; 3 Two or more races, non-Hispanic/Latino). Average age 36. 129 applicants, 98% accepted, 126 enrolled. In 2011, 351 master's, 30 Certificates awarded. *Degree requirements:* For master's, comprehensive exam (for some programs), thesis (for some programs); for doctorate, comprehensive exam, thesis/dissertation. *Entrance requirements:* Additional exam requirements/recommendations for international students: Required—TOEFL (minimum score 567 paper-based; 227 computer-based; 87 iBT); Recommended—IELTS. *Application deadline:* For fall admission, 9/1 for international students; for winter admission, 12/1 for international students; for spring admission, 3/1 for international students. Applications are processed on a rolling basis. Application fee: $50. Electronic applications accepted. *Expenses:* Contact institution. *Financial support:* In 2011–12, 40 students received support. Federal Work-Study and scholarships/grants available. Support available to part-time students. Financial award applicants required to submit FAFSA. *Unit head:* Craig Schieber, Dean, 425-637-101 Ext. 5460, Fax: 425-709-5363, E-mail: schieber@cityu.edu. *Application contact:* Alysa Borelli, 888-422-4898, Fax: 425-709-5363, E-mail: info@cityu.edu. Web site: http://www.cityu.edu/programs/soe/index.aspx.

Clarion University of Pennsylvania, Office of Graduate Programs, Master of Education Program, Clarion, PA 16214. Offers curriculum and instruction (M Ed); early childhood (M Ed, Certificate); English (M Ed); instructional technology specialist (K-12) (Certificate); literacy (M Ed); mathematics education (M Ed); reading specialist (M Ed, Certificate); science education (M Ed); special education (M Ed); technology (M Ed); world language (M Ed). *Accreditation:* NCATE. Part-time programs available. *Students:* 14 full-time (11 women), 207 part-time (163 women); includes 3 minority (1 Black or African American, non-Hispanic/Latino; 2 Hispanic/Latino). Average age 31. In 2011, 96 master's awarded. *Degree requirements:* For master's, thesis or alternative. *Entrance requirements:* For master's, minimum QPA of 3.0. *Application deadline:* Applications are processed on a rolling basis. *Expenses:* Tuition, state resident: part-time $429 per credit. Tuition, nonresident: part-time $644 per credit. *Financial support:* Research assistantships with full and partial tuition reimbursements and career-related internships or fieldwork available. Support available to part-time students. Financial award application deadline: 3/1. *Unit head:* Dr. John Groves, Dean, 814-393-2146, Fax: 514-393-2446. *Application contact:* Dr. Brenda Sanders Dede, Assistant Vice President for Academic Affairs, 814-393-2337, Fax: 814-393-2030, E-mail: bdede@clarion.edu. Web site: http://www.clarion.edu/25887/.

Clark Atlanta University, School of Education, Department of Curriculum, Atlanta, GA 30314. Offers special education general curriculum (MA); teaching math and science (MAT). Part-time programs available. *Faculty:* 4 full-time (all women), 4 part-time/adjunct (3 women). *Students:* 10 full-time (5 women), 9 part-time (7 women); includes 18 minority (all Black or African American, non-Hispanic/Latino). Average age 31. 13 applicants, 100% accepted, 9 enrolled. In 2011, 21 master's awarded. *Degree requirements:* For master's, one foreign language, comprehensive exam. *Entrance requirements:* For master's, GRE General Test, minimum undergraduate GPA of 2.6. Additional exam requirements/recommendations for international students: Required—TOEFL (minimum score 500 paper-based; 173 computer-based; 61 iBT). *Application deadline:* For fall admission, 4/1 for domestic and international students; for spring admission, 11/1 for domestic and international students. Applications are processed on a rolling basis. Application fee: $40 ($55 for international students). *Expenses: Tuition:* Full-time $13,572; part-time $754 per credit hour. *Required fees:* $806; $403 per semester. *Financial support:* Career-related internships or fieldwork, Federal Work-Study, scholarships/grants, and unspecified assistantships available. Support available to part-time students. Financial award application deadline: 4/30; financial award applicants required to submit FAFSA. *Unit head:* Dr. Doris Terrell, Chairperson, 404-880-6336, E-mail: dterrell@cau.edu. *Application contact:* Michelle Clark-Davis, Graduate Program Admissions, 404-880-6605, E-mail: cauadmissions@cau.edu. Web site: http://www.cau.edu/School_of_Education_curriculum_dept.aspx.

Clemson University, Graduate School, College of Health, Education, and Human Development, Eugene T. Moore School of Education, Program in Curriculum and Instruction, Clemson, SC 29634. Offers PhD. *Accreditation:* NCATE. Part-time and evening/weekend programs available. *Students:* 27 full-time (15 women), 15 part-time (10 women); includes 3 minority (all Black or African American, non-Hispanic/Latino), 3 international. Average age 38. 22 applicants, 45% accepted, 6 enrolled. In 2011, 11 doctorates awarded. *Degree requirements:* For doctorate, comprehensive exam, thesis/dissertation. *Entrance requirements:* For doctorate, GRE General Test, teaching certificate; 3 years of teaching experience. Additional exam requirements/recommendations for international students: Required—TOEFL; Recommended—IELTS. *Application deadline:* For fall admission, 3/1 for domestic and international students; for spring admission, 10/1 for domestic and international students. Applications are processed on a rolling basis. Application fee: $70 ($80 for international students). Electronic applications accepted. *Expenses:* Contact institution. *Financial support:* In 2011–12, 26 students received support, including 10 research assistantships with partial tuition reimbursements available (averaging $8,402 per year), 1 teaching assistantship with partial tuition reimbursement available (averaging $12,528 per year); fellowships with full and partial tuition reimbursements available, institutionally sponsored loans, health care benefits, and unspecified assistantships also available. Financial award application deadline: 3/1; financial award applicants required to submit FAFSA. *Faculty research:* Elementary and early childhood education, secondary education (English, math, social studies, and science), special education, reading and literacy. *Unit head:* Dr. Michael J. Padilla, Director/Associate Dean, 864-656-4444, Fax: 864-656-0311, E-mail: padilla@clemson.edu. *Application contact:* Dr. David Fleming, Graduate Coordinator, 864-656-1881, Fax: 864-656-0311, E-mail: dflemin@clemson.edu. Web site: http://www.grad.clemson.edu/programs/Curriculum-Instruction/.

The College at Brockport, State University of New York, School of Education and Human Services, Department of Education and Human Development, Program in Childhood Curriculum Specialist, Brockport, NY 14420-2997. Offers MS Ed. *Accreditation:* NCATE. Part-time programs available. *Students:* 3 full-time (all women), 30 part-time (20 women); includes 4 minority (2 Black or African American, non-Hispanic/Latino; 1 Asian, non-Hispanic/Latino; 1 Hispanic/Latino). 14 applicants, 71% accepted, 2 enrolled. In 2011, 25 master's awarded. *Degree requirements:* For master's, thesis or alternative. *Entrance requirements:* For master's, minimum GPA of 3.0, letters of recommendation; statement of objectives; current resume. Additional exam requirements/recommendations for international students: Required—TOEFL (minimum score 550 paper-based; 213 computer-based; 79 iBT). *Application deadline:* For fall admission, 2/15 priority date for domestic students, 2/15 for international students; for spring admission, 9/15 priority date for domestic students, 9/15 for international students. Application fee: $80. Electronic applications accepted. *Financial support:* Federal Work-Study, scholarships/grants, and unspecified assistantships available. Support available to part-time students. Financial award application deadline: 3/15; financial award applicants required to submit FAFSA. *Unit head:* Dr. Don Halquist, Chairperson, 585-395-5550, Fax: 585-395-2172, E-mail: snovinge@brockport.edu. *Application contact:* Michael Harrison, Coordinator of Certification and Graduate Advisement, 585-395-2326, Fax: 585-395-2172, E-mail: mharriso@brockport.edu. Web site: http://www.brockport.edu/graduate/.

The College of Saint Rose, Graduate Studies, School of Education, Teacher Education Department, Albany, NY 12203-1419. Offers business and marketing (MS Ed); childhood education (MS Ed); curriculum and instruction (MS Ed); early childhood education (MS Ed); elementary education (K-6) (MS Ed); secondary education (MS Ed, Certificate); teacher education (MS Ed, Certificate), including bilingual pupil personnel services (Certificate), teacher education (MS Ed). Part-time and evening/weekend programs available. *Entrance requirements:* For master's, minimum undergraduate GPA of 3.0. Additional exam requirements/recommendations for international students: Required—TOEFL (minimum score 550 paper-based; 213 computer-based). Electronic applications accepted.

The College of William and Mary, School of Education, Program in Curriculum and Instruction, Williamsburg, VA 23187-8795. Offers elementary education (MA Ed); gifted education (MA Ed); math specialist (MA Ed); reading education (MA Ed); secondary education (MA Ed), including English education, mathematics education, modern foreign languages education, science education, social studies education; special education (MA Ed), including collaborating master educator, general curriculum. *Accreditation:* NCATE. Part-time programs available. *Faculty:* 15 full-time (10 women), 39 part-time/adjunct (32 women). *Students:* 80 full-time (69 women), 13 part-time (11 women); includes 11 minority (3 Black or African American, non-Hispanic/Latino; 1 American Indian or Alaska Native, non-Hispanic/Latino; 2 Hispanic/Latino; 5 Two or more races, non-Hispanic/Latino), 1 international. Average age 25. 220 applicants, 56% accepted, 85 enrolled. In 2011, 78 master's awarded. *Degree requirements:* For master's, project. *Entrance requirements:* For master's, GRE or MAT, minimum GPA of 2.5. Additional exam requirements/recommendations for international students: Required—TOEFL. *Application deadline:* For fall admission, 1/15 for domestic and international students; for spring admission, 10/1 for domestic and international students. Application fee: $50. Electronic applications accepted. *Expenses:* Tuition, state resident: full-time $6400; part-time $365 per credit hour. Tuition, nonresident: full-time $19,720; part-time $985 per credit hour. *Required fees:* $4562. *Financial support:* In 2011–12, 53 students received support, including 10 research assistantships with full and partial tuition reimbursements available (averaging $7,000 per year); career-related internships or fieldwork, Federal Work-Study, institutionally sponsored loans, scholarships/grants, and unspecified assistantships also available. Financial award application deadline: 1/15; financial award applicants required to submit FAFSA. *Faculty research:* National Council of Teachers of Mathematics Standards, counseling, self-concept and self-esteem, special education, curriculum development. *Unit head:* Dr. Margie Mason, Area Coordinator, 757-221-2327, E-mail: mmmaso@wm.edu. *Application contact:* Dorothy Smith Osborne, Assistant Dean for Admission, 757-221-2317, Fax: 757-221-2293, E-mail: dsosbo@wm.edu. Web site: http://education.wm.edu.

The College of William and Mary, School of Education, Program in Education Policy, Planning, and Leadership, Williamsburg, VA 23187-8795. Offers curriculum and educational technology (Ed D, PhD); curriculum leadership (Ed D, PhD); educational leadership (M Ed), including higher education administration (M Ed, Ed D, PhD), K-12 administration and supervision; educational policy, planning, and leadership (Ed D, PhD), including general education administration, gifted education administration, higher education administration (M Ed, Ed D, PhD), special education administration; gifted education administration (M Ed). *Accreditation:* NCATE. Part-time and evening/weekend programs available. *Faculty:* 11 full-time (5 women), 11 part-time/adjunct (9 women). *Students:* 50 full-time (38 women), 145 part-time (104 women); includes 45 minority (35 Black or African American, non-Hispanic/Latino; 2 Asian, non-Hispanic/Latino; 4 Hispanic/Latino; 4 Two or more races, non-Hispanic/Latino), 5 international. Average age 38. 173 applicants, 62% accepted, 75 enrolled. In 2011, 21 master's, 10 doctorates awarded. *Degree requirements:* For doctorate, comprehensive exam, thesis/dissertation. *Entrance requirements:* For master's, GRE or MAT, minimum GPA of 2.5; for doctorate, GRE or MAT, minimum GPA of 3.0. Additional exam requirements/recommendations for international students: Required—TOEFL. *Application deadline:* For fall admission, 1/15 for domestic and international students. Application fee: $50. Electronic applications accepted. *Expenses:* Tuition, state resident: full-time $6400; part-time $365 per credit hour. Tuition, nonresident: full-time $19,720; part-time $985 per credit hour. *Required fees:* $4562. *Financial support:* In 2011–12, 54 students received support, including 1 fellowship (averaging $20,000 per year), 38 research assistantships with full and partial tuition reimbursements available (averaging $15,000 per year); career-related internships or fieldwork, Federal Work-Study, institutionally sponsored loans, scholarships/grants, and unspecified assistantships also available. Support available to part-time students. Financial award application deadline: 1/15; financial award applicants required to submit FAFSA. *Faculty research:* Higher education policy, faculty incentives, history of adversity, resilience, leadership. *Unit head:* Dr. Pamela Eddy, Area Coordinator, 757-221-2349, E-mail: peddy@wm.edu. *Application contact:* Dorothy Smith Osborne, Assistant Dean for Admission, 757-221-2317, Fax: 757-221-2293, E-mail: dsosbo@wm.edu. Web site: http://education.wm.edu.

Colorado Christian University, Program in Curriculum and Instruction, Lakewood, CO 80226. Offers corporate education (MACI); early childhood educator (MACI); elementary educator (MACI); instructional technology (MACI); master educator (MACI); online course developer (MACI); online teaching and learning (MACI); special education generalist (MACI). Part-time and evening/weekend programs available. *Degree requirements:* For master's, thesis optional, practicum. *Entrance requirements:* For master's, interviews, letters of recommendation. Additional exam requirements/recommendations for international students: Required—TOEFL. Electronic applications accepted. *Expenses:* Contact institution.

Columbia International University, Columbia Graduate School, Columbia, SC 29230-3122. Offers Bible teaching (MABT); Christian higher education leadership (Ed D); Christian school educational leadership (Ed D); counseling (MACN); curriculum and instruction (M Ed), including Christian school guidance, English as a second language, learning disabilities, school technology; early childhood and elementary education (MAT); educational administration (M Ed); teaching English as a foreign language (Certificate); teaching English as a foreign language and intercultural studies (MATF). Part-time and evening/weekend programs available. *Degree requirements:* For master's, internships, professional project. *Entrance requirements:* For master's, Minnesota Multiphasic Personality Inventory, MAT, minimum GPA of 2.7. Additional exam requirements/recommendations for international students: Required—TOEFL. Electronic applications accepted.

Columbus State University, Graduate Studies, College of Education and Health Professions, Department of Counseling, Foundations, and Leadership, Columbus, GA 31907-5645. Offers community counseling (MS); curriculum and leadership (Ed D); educational leadership (M Ed, Ed S); higher education (M Ed); school counseling (M Ed, Ed S). *Accreditation:* ACA; NCATE. Part-time and evening/weekend programs available. Postbaccalaureate distance learning degree programs offered (minimal on-campus study). *Degree requirements:* For master's, thesis, exit exam; for Ed S, thesis or alternative. *Entrance requirements:* For master's, GRE General Test, minimum GPA of 2.75; for doctorate, minimum graduate GPA of 3.5, four years of professional service; for Ed S, GRE General Test. Additional exam requirements/recommendations for international students: Required—TOEFL (minimum score 550 paper-based; 213 computer-based; 79 iBT). Electronic applications accepted.

Concordia University, College of Education, Portland, OR 97211-6099. Offers curriculum and instruction (elementary) (M Ed); educational administration (M Ed); elementary education (MAT); secondary education (MAT). Part-time programs available. Postbaccalaureate distance learning degree programs offered (no on-campus study). *Degree requirements:* For master's, comprehensive exam, work samples/portfolio. *Entrance requirements:* For master's, California Basic Educational Skills Test or PRAXIS I, minimum undergraduate GPA of 2.8, graduate 3.0; 2 letters of recommendation. Additional exam requirements/recommendations for international students: Required—TOEFL (minimum score 525 paper-based; 195 computer-based). Electronic applications accepted. *Faculty research:* Learner centered classroom, brain-based learning future of on-line learning.

Concordia University, School of Education, Irvine, CA 92612-3299. Offers curriculum and instruction (MA); education and preliminary teaching credential (M Ed); educational administration and preliminary administrative services credential (MA); school counseling with pupil personnel services credential (MA). Part-time and evening/weekend programs available. Postbaccalaureate distance learning degree programs offered (no on-campus study). *Faculty:* 16 full-time (11 women), 68 part-time/adjunct (32 women). *Students:* 556 full-time (434 women), 277 part-time (211 women); includes 278 minority (42 Black or African American, non-Hispanic/Latino; 1 American Indian or Alaska Native, non-Hispanic/Latino; 51 Asian, non-Hispanic/Latino; 172 Hispanic/Latino; 12 Two or more races, non-Hispanic/Latino), 1 international. Average age 39. 296 applicants, 96% accepted, 256 enrolled. In 2011, 378 master's awarded. *Degree requirements:* For master's, action research project. *Entrance requirements:* For master's, California Basic Educational Skills Test, California Subject Examinations for Teachers (M Ed and MA in educational administration and preliminary administrative services credential), official college transcript(s), signed statement of intent, two references, copy of credential. Additional exam requirements/recommendations for international students: Required—TOEFL. *Application deadline:* For fall admission, 7/15 priority date for domestic students, 6/1 for international students; for spring admission, 11/30 priority date for domestic students, 10/1 for international students. Applications are processed on a rolling basis. Application fee: $50 ($125 for international students). Electronic applications accepted. *Expenses:* Contact institution. *Financial support:* In 2011–12, 17 students received support. Scholarships/grants and unspecified assistantships available. Financial award applicants required to submit FAFSA. *Unit head:* Dr. Janice Nelson, Dean, 949-214-3334, E-mail: janice.nelson@cui.edu. *Application contact:* Scott Eskelson, 949-214-3362, Fax: 949-854-6894, E-mail: scott.eskelson@cui.edu.

Concordia University Ann Arbor, Graduate Programs, Ann Arbor, MI 48105-2797. Offers curriculum and instruction (MS); educational leadership (MS); organizational leadership and administration (MS). Part-time and evening/weekend programs available. *Faculty:* 3 full-time (2 women), 24 part-time/adjunct (10 women). *Students:* 123 full-time (79 women), 46 part-time (24 women); includes 26 minority (19 Black or African American, non-Hispanic/Latino; 2 American Indian or Alaska Native, non-Hispanic/Latino; 3 Asian, non-Hispanic/Latino; 1 Hispanic/Latino; 1 Two or more races, non-Hispanic/Latino), 1 international. Average age 37. 45 applicants, 84% accepted, 37 enrolled. In 2011, 74 degrees awarded. *Degree requirements:* For master's, thesis. *Entrance requirements:* Additional exam requirements/recommendations for international students: Required—TOEFL (minimum score 80 iBT); Recommended—IELTS (minimum score 6.5). *Application deadline:* For fall admission, 7/1 priority date for domestic students, 6/1 for international students; for spring admission, 8/26 priority date for domestic students, 7/26 for international students. Applications are processed on a rolling basis. Electronic applications accepted. *Financial support:* Applicants required to submit FAFSA. *Unit head:* Dr. Ross Stueber, Vice President of Academics, 734-995-7586, Fax: 734-995-7448, E-mail: stuebr@cuaa.edu. *Application contact:* Caroline Harris, Graduate Admission Coordinator, 734-995-7521, Fax: 734-995-7530, E-mail: harrica@cuaa.edu. Web site: http://www.cuaa.edu/graduate.

Concordia University Chicago, College of Education, Program in Curriculum and Instruction, River Forest, IL 60305-1499. Offers MA. MA offered jointly with the Chicago Consortium of Colleges and Universities. *Accreditation:* NCATE. Part-time and evening/weekend programs available. *Degree requirements:* For master's, comprehensive exam, thesis. *Entrance requirements:* For master's, minimum GPA of 2.9. Additional exam requirements/recommendations for international students: Required—TOEFL (minimum score 550 paper-based; 195 computer-based). Electronic applications accepted. *Faculty research:* School discipline, school improvement, leadership.

Concordia University, St. Paul, College of Education, St. Paul, MN 55104-5494. Offers curriculum and instruction (MA Ed), including K-12 reading endorsement; differentiated instruction (MA Ed); early childhood education (MA Ed); educational leadership (MA Ed); educational technology (MA Ed); family life education (MA); K-12 reading endorsement (Certificate); special education (Certificate); sports management (MA). *Accreditation:* NCATE. Evening/weekend programs available. Postbaccalaureate distance learning degree programs offered (minimal on-campus study). *Faculty:* 7 full-time (3 women), 64 part-time/adjunct (42 women). *Students:* 617 full-time (495 women), 9 part-time (6 women); includes 57 minority (30 Black or African American, non-Hispanic/Latino; 2 American Indian or Alaska Native, non-Hispanic/Latino; 17 Asian, non-Hispanic/Latino; 5 Hispanic/Latino; 1 Native Hawaiian or other Pacific Islander, non-Hispanic/Latino; 2 Two or more races, non-Hispanic/Latino). Average age 36. 302 applicants, 83% accepted, 210 enrolled. In 2011, 320 master's, 68 other advanced degrees awarded. *Application deadline:* Applications are processed on a rolling basis. Application fee: $50. Electronic applications accepted. *Expenses: Tuition:* Full-time $8100; part-time $435 per credit. Tuition and fees vary according to program. *Financial support:* Applicants required to submit FAFSA. *Unit head:* Dr. Donald Helmstetter, Dean, 651-641-8227, Fax: 651-641-8807, E-mail: helmstetter@csp.edu. *Application contact:* Kimberly Craig, Director of Graduate and Cohort Admission, 651-603-6223, Fax: 651-603-6320, E-mail: craig@csp.edu.

Concordia University Wisconsin, Graduate Programs, Department of Education, Program in Curriculum and Instruction, Mequon, WI 53097-2402. Offers MS Ed. Postbaccalaureate distance learning degree programs offered (minimal on-campus study). *Students:* 25 full-time (15 women), 67 part-time (53 women); includes 10 minority (7 Black or African American, non-Hispanic/Latino; 2 Asian, non-Hispanic/Latino; 1 Two or more races, non-Hispanic/Latino). Average age 37. In 2011, 30 master's awarded. *Degree requirements:* For master's, comprehensive exam, thesis or alternative. *Entrance requirements:* For master's, minimum GPA of 3.0, teaching license. Additional exam requirements/recommendations for international students: Required—TOEFL. Application fee: $35. *Financial support:* Application deadline: 8/1. *Unit head:* Dr. Ross Stueber, Head, 262-243-4285, Fax: 262-243-4428, E-mail: ross.stueber@cuw.edu. *Application contact:* Graduate Admissions, 262-243-4248, Fax: 262-243-4428, E-mail: ross.steuber@cuw.edu.

Converse College, School of Education and Graduate Studies, Education Specialist Program, Spartanburg, SC 29302-0006. Offers administration and supervision (Ed S); curriculum and instruction (Ed S); marriage and family therapy (Ed S). *Accreditation:* AAMFT/COAMFTE. Part-time programs available. *Entrance requirements:* For degree, GRE or MAT (marriage and family therapy), minimum GPA of 3.0. Electronic applications accepted.

Coppin State University, Division of Graduate Studies, Division of Education, Baltimore, MD 21216-3698. Offers adult and general education (MS); curriculum and instruction (M Ed, MAT, MS), including curriculum and instruction (M Ed), reading education (MS), teaching (MAT); special education (M Ed). *Accreditation:* NCATE. Part-time and evening/weekend programs available. Postbaccalaureate distance learning degree programs offered. *Degree requirements:* For master's, comprehensive exam (for some programs), thesis (for some programs).

Coppin State University, Division of Graduate Studies, Division of Education, Department of Curriculum and Instruction, Program in Curriculum and Instruction, Baltimore, MD 21216-3698. Offers M Ed. Part-time and evening/weekend programs available. Postbaccalaureate distance learning degree programs offered. *Degree requirements:* For master's, thesis. *Entrance requirements:* For master's, GRE or MAT, minimum GPA of 3.0, teacher certification.

Cornell University, Graduate School, Graduate Fields of Agriculture and Life Sciences, Field of Education, Ithaca, NY 14853-0001. Offers agricultural education (MAT); biology (7-12) (MAT); chemistry (7-12) (MAT); curriculum and instruction (MPS, MS, PhD); earth science (7-12) (MAT); extension, and adult education (MPS, MS, PhD); mathematics (7-12) (MAT); physics (7-12) (MAT). *Faculty:* 23 full-time (10 women). *Students:* 32 full-time (18 women); includes 6 minority (4 Asian, non-Hispanic/Latino; 2 Hispanic/Latino), 1 international. Average age 30. 60 applicants, 33% accepted, 12 enrolled. In 2011, 22 master's, 7 doctorates awarded. Terminal master's awarded for partial completion of doctoral program. *Degree requirements:* For master's, thesis (MS); for doctorate, comprehensive exam, thesis/dissertation. *Entrance requirements:* For master's and doctorate, GRE General Test, sample of written work (recommended), 2 letters of recommendation. Additional exam requirements/recommendations for international students: Required—TOEFL (minimum score 550 paper-based; 213 computer-based; 77 iBT). *Application deadline:* For fall admission, 2/15 for domestic students. Application fee: $95. Electronic applications accepted. *Financial support:* In 2011–12, 2 fellowships with full tuition reimbursements, 4 research assistantships with full tuition reimbursements, 12 teaching assistantships with full tuition reimbursements were awarded; institutionally sponsored loans, scholarships/grants, health care benefits, tuition waivers (full and partial), and unspecified assistantships also available. Financial award applicants required to submit FAFSA. *Faculty research:* Moral development and professional ethics, public issues education and community development, socio/political issues in public education, teacher education and curriculum in agricultural science and mathematics, extension research. *Unit head:* Director of Graduate Studies, 607-255-4278, Fax: 607-255-7905. *Application contact:* Graduate Field Assistant, 607-255-4278, Fax: 607-255-7905, E-mail: rh22@cornell.edu. Web site: http://www.gradschool.cornell.edu/fields.php?id-80&a-2.

Dakota Wesleyan University, Program in Education, Mitchell, SD 57301-4398. Offers curriculum and instruction (MA Ed); educational policy and administration (MA Ed); preK-12 principal certification (MA Ed); secondary certification (MA Ed). Part-time and evening/weekend programs available. *Degree requirements:* For master's, comprehensive exam, thesis optional, electronic portfolio. *Entrance requirements:* For master's, minimum GPA of 2.7, elementary statistics course, statement of purpose, official transcripts, resume, three letters of recommendation. Additional exam requirements/recommendations for international students: Required—TOEFL (minimum score 500 paper-based; 71 computer-based), IELTS (minimum score 6.5). Electronic applications accepted. *Faculty research:* Math, political policy, technology in the classroom.

Dallas Baptist University, Dorothy M. Bush College of Education, Program in Curriculum and Instruction, Dallas, TX 75211-9299. Offers M Ed. Part-time and evening/weekend programs available. *Entrance requirements:* For master's, GRE General Test, minimum GPA of 3.0. Additional exam requirements/recommendations for international students: Required—TOEFL, IELTS. Application fee: $25. *Expenses: Tuition:* Full-time $12,060; part-time $670 per credit hour. *Required fees:* $100; $50 per semester. *Financial support:* Federal Work-Study, institutionally sponsored loans, scholarships/grants, and tuition waivers (full and partial) available. Support available to part-time students. Financial award applicants required to submit FAFSA. *Unit head:* Dr. Sharon Lee, Director, 214-333-5894, Fax: 214-333-5551, E-mail: graduate@dbu.edu. *Application contact:* Kit P. Montgomery, Director of Graduate Programs, 214-333-5242, Fax: 214-333-5579, E-mail: graduate@dbu.edu. Web site: http://www3.dbu.edu/graduate/curriculum_instruction.asp.

Delaware State University, Graduate Programs, College of Education, Health and Public Policy, Program in Curriculum and Instruction, Dover, DE 19901-2277. Offers MA. Part-time and evening/weekend programs available. *Degree requirements:* For master's, comprehensive exam, thesis optional. *Entrance requirements:* For master's, GRE General Test, minimum GPA of 3.0 in major, 2.75 overall. Additional exam requirements/recommendations for international students: Required—TOEFL (minimum score 550 paper-based). Electronic applications accepted.

Delaware Valley College, Program in Educational Leadership, Doylestown, PA 18901-2697. Offers instruction, curriculum and technology (MS); school administration and leadership (MS). Part-time and evening/weekend programs available. *Entrance requirements:* For master's, minimum undergraduate GPA of 3.0.

DePaul University, College of Education, Chicago, IL 60106. Offers bilingual bicultural education (M Ed, MA); counseling (M Ed, MA), including college student development, community counseling, school counseling; curriculum studies (M Ed, MA, Ed D); early childhood education (M Ed, MA); educational leadership (M Ed, MA, Ed D), including administration and supervision (M Ed, MA), physical education (M Ed, MA); middle school mathematics education (MS); reading specialist (M Ed, MA); social and cultural foundations in education (M Ed, MA), including curriculum studies/development (MA); special education (M Ed, MA); teaching and learning (M Ed, MA), including elementary education, secondary education; world languages education (M Ed, MA). Part-time and evening/weekend programs available. *Faculty:* 49 full-time (28 women), 94 part-time/adjunct (60 women). *Students:* 894 full-time (707 women), 473 part-time (361 women); includes 349 minority (159 Black or African American, non-Hispanic/Latino; 3 American Indian or Alaska Native, non-Hispanic/Latino; 45 Asian, non-Hispanic/Latino; 115 Hispanic/Latino; 2 Native Hawaiian or other Pacific Islander, non-Hispanic/Latino; 25 Two or more races, non-Hispanic/Latino), 21 international. Average age 30. 872 applicants, 64% accepted, 325 enrolled. In 2011, 499 master's, 10 doctorates awarded. *Median time to degree:* Of those who began their doctoral program in fall 2003, 32% received their degree in 8 years or less. *Degree requirements:* For master's, thesis/dissertation (for MA); capstone course or paper (for M Ed); for doctorate, thesis/dissertation. *Entrance requirements:* For master's, interview, minimum GPA of 2.75, 2 letters of recommendation, bachelor's degree conferred by accredited college or university; for doctorate, interview, master's degree, writing sample, 3 letters of recommendation. Additional exam requirements/recommendations for international students: Required—TOEFL (minimum score 550 paper-based; 213 computer-based; 80 iBT). *Application deadline:* For fall admission, 8/15 priority date for domestic students; for winter admission, 12/1 priority date for domestic students; for spring admission, 3/1 priority date for domestic students. Applications are processed on a rolling basis. Application fee: $40. Electronic applications accepted. *Financial support:* In 2011–12, 163 students received support, including 15 research assistantships with full tuition reimbursements available (averaging $6,375 per year); career-related internships or fieldwork, Federal Work-Study, scholarships/grants, and unspecified assistantships also available. Support available to part-time students. Financial award application deadline: 12/31; financial award applicants required to submit FAFSA. *Faculty research:* Reflective teaching, children at risk, loss, ethnicity, urban education. *Total annual research expenditures:* $916,310. *Unit head:* Dr. Paul Zionts, Dean, 773-325-7581, Fax: 773-325-7713, E-mail: pzionts@depaul.edu. *Application contact:* Brandon Washington, Enrollment Management Coordinator, 773-325-1152, Fax: 773-325-2270, E-mail: bwashin3@depaul.edu. Web site: http://education.depaul.edu.

Doane College, Program in Education, Crete, NE 68333-2430. Offers curriculum and instruction (M Ed); educational leadership (M Ed). *Accreditation:* NCATE. Part-time and evening/weekend programs available. *Students:* 126 full-time (103 women), 381 part-time (284 women); includes 20 minority (8 Black or African American, non-Hispanic/

Latino; 2 American Indian or Alaska Native, non-Hispanic/Latino; 9 Hispanic/Latino; 1 Two or more races, non-Hispanic/Latino). Average age 33. In 2011, 312 master's awarded. *Degree requirements:* For master's, thesis. *Entrance requirements:* For master's, minimum GPA of 2.5. Additional exam requirements/recommendations for international students: Required—TOEFL. *Application deadline:* Applications are processed on a rolling basis. Electronic applications accepted. *Expenses:* Contact institution. *Financial support:* Applicants required to submit FAFSA. *Unit head:* Lyn C. Forester, Dean, 402-826-8604, Fax: 402-826-8278. *Application contact:* Wilma Daddario, Assistant Dean, 402-464-1223, Fax: 402-466-4228, E-mail: wdaddario@doane.edu. Web site: http://www.doane.edu/Admission/Graduate_Admission/Master_Of_Education/.

Dominican University, School of Education, River Forest, IL 60305-1099. Offers curriculum and instruction (MA Ed); early childhood education (MS); education (MAT); educational administration (MA); elementary (online) (MS); English as a second language (online) (MS); reading (online) (MS); special education (MS). Part-time and evening/weekend programs available. Postbaccalaureate distance learning degree programs offered (no on-campus study). *Faculty:* 19 full-time (13 women), 53 part-time/adjunct (41 women). *Students:* 24 full-time (19 women), 434 part-time (357 women); includes 95 minority (27 Black or African American, non-Hispanic/Latino; 1 American Indian or Alaska Native, non-Hispanic/Latino; 12 Asian, non-Hispanic/Latino; 48 Hispanic/Latino; 7 Two or more races, non-Hispanic/Latino), 1 international. Average age 33. 92 applicants, 99% accepted, 91 enrolled. In 2011, 267 master's awarded. *Entrance requirements:* For master's, Illinois certification test of basic skills. Additional exam requirements/recommendations for international students: Required—TOEFL (minimum score 550 paper-based; 213 computer-based; 79 iBT). *Application deadline:* Applications are processed on a rolling basis. Application fee: $25. *Expenses:* Contact institution. *Financial support:* Career-related internships or fieldwork, scholarships/grants, and tuition waivers (partial) available. Support available to part-time students. Financial award application deadline: 8/15; financial award applicants required to submit FAFSA. *Faculty research:* Governance of private education institutions, reading and language arts, inclusion, organizational planning, leadership and vision. *Unit head:* Dr. Colleen Reardon, Dean, 718-524-6643, Fax: 708-524-6665, E-mail: creardon@dom.edu. *Application contact:* Keven Hansen, Coordinator of Recruitment and Admissions, 708-524-6921, Fax: 708-524-6665, E-mail: educate@dom.edu. Web site: http://www.dom.edu/soe.

Drexel University, Goodwin College of Professional Studies, School of Education, Program in Science of Instruction, Philadelphia, PA 19104-2875. Offers MS. Part-time and evening/weekend programs available. *Entrance requirements:* For master's, GRE, bachelor's degree in related field. Additional exam requirements/recommendations for international students: Required—TOEFL. Electronic applications accepted.

Drexel University, Goodwin College of Professional Studies, School of Education, Program in Teaching, Learning and Curriculum, Philadelphia, PA 19104-2875. Offers MS.

Duquesne University, School of Education, Department of Foundations and Leadership, Program in School Administration and Supervision, Pittsburgh, PA 15282-0001. Offers curriculum and instruction (Post-Master's Certificate); school administration K-12 (MS Ed, Post-Master's Certificate); school supervision (MS Ed). Part-time and evening/weekend programs available. Postbaccalaureate distance learning degree programs offered (minimal on-campus study). *Faculty:* 3 full-time (1 woman). *Students:* 30 full-time (16 women), 17 part-time (15 women); includes 4 minority (2 Black or African American, non-Hispanic/Latino; 2 Hispanic/Latino). Average age 35. 11 applicants, 64% accepted, 4 enrolled. In 2011, 35 degrees awarded. *Degree requirements:* For master's, thesis optional. *Entrance requirements:* For master's and Post-Master's Certificate, bachelor's degree. Additional exam requirements/recommendations for international students: Required—TOEFL (minimum score 550 paper-based; 80 computer-based), IELTS (minimum score 7). *Application deadline:* For fall admission, 9/1 for domestic students; for spring admission, 1/1 for domestic students. Applications are processed on a rolling basis. Application fee: $0. Electronic applications accepted. Application fee is waived when completed online. *Expenses: Tuition:* Full-time $16,596; part-time $922 per credit. *Required fees:* $1584; $88 per credit. Tuition and fees vary according to program. *Financial support:* Research assistantships available. Support available to part-time students. *Unit head:* Dr. Robert Furman, Director, 412-396-5274, Fax: 412-396-1274, E-mail: furman@duq.edu. *Application contact:* Michael Dolinger, Director of Student and Academic Services, 412-396-6647, Fax: 412-396-5585, E-mail: dolingerm@duq.edu. Web site: http://www.duq.edu/education.

East Carolina University, Graduate School, College of Education, Department of Curriculum and Instruction, Greenville, NC 27858-4353. Offers assistive technology (Certificate); autism (Certificate); deaf/blindness (Certificate); elementary education (MA Ed); English education (MA Ed); history (MA Ed); middle grade education (MA Ed); reading education (MA Ed); special education (MA Ed); teaching (MAT). Part-time programs available. Postbaccalaureate distance learning degree programs offered. *Degree requirements:* For master's, comprehensive exam, thesis optional. *Entrance requirements:* For master's, GRE General Test or MAT, interview, bachelor's degree in related field, minimum GPA of 2.5, teaching license. Additional exam requirements/recommendations for international students: Required—TOEFL. *Application deadline:* For fall admission, 6/1 priority date for domestic students. Applications are processed on a rolling basis. Application fee: $50. *Expenses:* Tuition, state resident: full-time $3557; part-time $444.63 per semester hour. Tuition, nonresident: full-time $14,351; part-time $1793.88 per semester hour. *Required fees:* $2016; $252 per semester hour. Part-time tuition and fees vary according to course load, campus/location and program. *Financial support:* Research assistantships, teaching assistantships, and Federal Work-Study available. Support available to part-time students. Financial award application deadline: 6/1; financial award applicants required to submit FAFSA. *Unit head:* Carolyn C. Ledford, Interim Chair, 252-328-1100, E-mail: ledfordc@ecu.edu. *Application contact:* Dean of Graduate School, 252-328-6012, Fax: 252-328-6071, E-mail: gradschool@ecu.edu. Web site: http://www.ecu.edu/cs-educ/ci/Graduate.cfm.

Eastern Kentucky University, The Graduate School, College of Education, Department of Curriculum and Instruction, Richmond, KY 40475-3102. Offers elementary education (MA Ed), including early elementary education, reading; library science (MA Ed); music education (MA Ed); secondary and higher education (MA Ed), including secondary education; teaching (MAT). *Accreditation:* NCATE. Part-time programs available. *Degree requirements:* For master's, portfolio is part of exam. *Entrance requirements:* For master's, GRE General Test, PRAXIS II (KY), minimum GPA of 2.5. *Faculty research:* Technology in education, reading instruction, e-portfolios, induction to teacher education, dispositions of teachers.

Eastern Michigan University, Graduate School, College of Education, Department of Teacher Education, Program in Curriculum and Instruction, Ypsilanti, MI 48197. Offers MA. *Students:* 36 part-time (28 women); includes 5 minority (all Black or African American, non-Hispanic/Latino). Average age 35. 15 applicants, 93% accepted, 9 enrolled. In 2011, 20 degrees awarded. *Expenses:* Tuition, state resident: full-time $10,367; part-time $432 per credit hour. Tuition, nonresident: full-time $20,435; part-time $851 per credit hour. *Required fees:* $39 per credit hour. $46 per semester. One-time fee: $100. Tuition and fees vary according to course level, degree level and reciprocity agreements. *Unit head:* Dr. Donald Bennion, Department Head, 734-487-3260, Fax: 734-487-2101, E-mail: donald.bennion@emich.edu. *Application contact:* Dr. Ethan Lowenstein, Coordinator/Advisor, 734-487-7210 Ext. 2584, Fax: 734-487-2101, E-mail: ethan.lowenstein@emich.edu.

Eastern Michigan University, Graduate School, College of Education, Department of Teacher Education, Program in K–12 Education, Ypsilanti, MI 48197. Offers curriculum and instruction (MA); elementary education (MA); K-12 education (MA); middle school education (MA); secondary school education (MA). *Accreditation:* NCATE. Part-time and evening/weekend programs available. Postbaccalaureate distance learning degree programs offered (minimal on-campus study). *Students:* 14 full-time (9 women), 87 part-time (62 women); includes 12 minority (7 Black or African American, non-Hispanic/Latino; 1 American Indian or Alaska Native, non-Hispanic/Latino; 1 Asian, non-Hispanic/Latino; 2 Hispanic/Latino; 1 Two or more races, non-Hispanic/Latino). Average age 37. 57 applicants, 74% accepted, 25 enrolled. In 2011, 6 master's awarded. *Entrance requirements:* For master's, GRE. Additional exam requirements/recommendations for international students: Required—TOEFL. *Application deadline:* Applications are processed on a rolling basis. Application fee: $35. *Expenses:* Tuition, state resident: full-time $10,367; part-time $432 per credit hour. Tuition, nonresident: full-time $20,435; part-time $851 per credit hour. *Required fees:* $39 per credit hour. $46 per semester. One-time fee: $100. Tuition and fees vary according to course level, degree level and reciprocity agreements. *Financial support:* Fellowships, research assistantships with full tuition reimbursements, teaching assistantships with full tuition reimbursements, career-related internships or fieldwork, Federal Work-Study, institutionally sponsored loans, scholarships/grants, tuition waivers (partial), and unspecified assistantships available. Support available to part-time students. Financial award applicants required to submit FAFSA. *Unit head:* Dr. Wendy Burke, Coordinator, 734-487-3260, Fax: 734-487-2101, E-mail: wendy.burke@emich.edu. *Application contact:* Dr. Anne Bednar, Advisor, 734-487-3260, Fax: 734-487-2101, E-mail: anne.bednar@emich.edu.

Eastern New Mexico University, Graduate School, College of Education and Technology, Department of Curriculum and Instruction, Portales, NM 88130. Offers bilingual education (M Ed); educational technology (M Ed); elementary education (M Ed); English as a second language (M Ed); pedagogy and learning (M Ed); professional technical education (M Ed); reading/literacy (M Ed). Part-time programs available. Postbaccalaureate distance learning degree programs offered (minimal on-campus study). *Degree requirements:* For master's, comprehensive exam, thesis optional. *Entrance requirements:* For master's, minimum GPA of 3.0, photocopy of teaching license, writing assessment, letter of recommendation. Additional exam requirements/recommendations for international students: Required—TOEFL (minimum score 550 paper-based; 213 computer-based; 79 iBT), IELTS (minimum score 6). Electronic applications accepted.

Eastern Washington University, Graduate Studies, College of Arts, Letters and Education, Department of Education, Program in Curriculum Development, Cheney, WA 99004-2431. Offers M Ed. *Students:* 3 full-time (all women). Average age 34. 8 applicants, 38% accepted, 3 enrolled. In 2011, 14 master's awarded. *Degree requirements:* For master's, comprehensive exam. *Entrance requirements:* For master's, minimum GPA of 3.0. *Application deadline:* For fall admission, 4/1 priority date for domestic students; for spring admission, 1/15 for domestic students. Applications are processed on a rolling basis. Application fee: $50. *Financial support:* In 2011–12, teaching assistantships with partial tuition reimbursements (averaging $7,000 per year) were awarded; career-related internships or fieldwork, Federal Work-Study, institutionally sponsored loans, scholarships/grants, health care benefits, tuition waivers (partial), and unspecified assistantships also available. Support available to part-time students. Financial award application deadline: 2/1. *Unit head:* Robin Showalter, Program Coordinator, 509-359-6492, E-mail: rshowalter@mail.ewu.edu. *Application contact:* Dr. Kevin Pyatt, Graduate Program Coordinator, 509-359-6091, E-mail: kpyatt@ewu.edu.

East Tennessee State University, School of Graduate Studies, College of Education, Department of Curriculum and Instruction, Johnson City, TN 37614. Offers educational media/educational technology (M Ed), including educational communications and technology, school library media; elementary education (M Ed); reading (MA), including reading education, storytelling; school library professional (Post-Master's Certificate); secondary education (M Ed), including classroom technology, secondary education (M Ed, MAT); storytelling (Postbaccalaureate Certificate); teacher education with multiple levels (initial licensure) (MAT), including elementary education, middle grades education, secondary education (M Ed, MAT). *Accreditation:* NCATE. Part-time and evening/weekend programs available. Postbaccalaureate distance learning degree programs offered (no on-campus study). *Faculty:* 20 full-time (13 women), 3 part-time/adjunct (all women). *Students:* 108 full-time (76 women), 107 part-time (97 women); includes 9 minority (4 Black or African American, non-Hispanic/Latino; 1 Asian, non-Hispanic/Latino; 2 Hispanic/Latino; 2 Two or more races, non-Hispanic/Latino), 2 international. Average age 33. 141 applicants, 57% accepted, 79 enrolled. In 2011, 129 master's awarded. *Degree requirements:* For master's, comprehensive exam, thesis optional, student teaching, practicum; for other advanced degree, field work (school library); culminating experience (storytelling). *Entrance requirements:* For master's, GRE, SAT, ACT, PRAXIS, minimum GPA of 3.0; for other advanced degree, master's degree, TN teaching license (school library professional post-master's certificate); three letters of recommendation (storytelling certificate). Additional exam requirements/recommendations for international students: Required—TOEFL (minimum score 550 paper-based; 213 computer-based; 79 iBT). *Application deadline:* For fall admission, 6/1 for domestic students, 4/30 for international students; for spring admission, 11/1 for domestic students, 4/30 for international students. Application fee: $35 ($45 for international students). Electronic applications accepted. *Expenses:* Tuition, state resident: full-time $7312; part-time $350 per credit hour. Tuition, nonresident: full-time $18,490; part-time $621 per credit hour. *Required fees:* $63 per credit hour. Tuition and fees vary according to course load and program. *Financial support:* In 2011–12, 60 students received support, including 7 research assistantships with full tuition reimbursements available (averaging $6,000 per year), 11 teaching assistantships with full tuition reimbursements available (averaging $6,000 per year); career-related internships or fieldwork, institutionally sponsored loans, scholarships/grants, and unspecified assistantships also available. Financial award application deadline: 7/1; financial award applicants required to submit FAFSA. *Faculty research:* Critical thinking; curriculum development in reading, math, and science education; cultural diversity; cognitive processes; effective teaching strategies. *Unit head:* Dr. Rhona Hurwitz, Chair, 423-439-7598, Fax: 423-439-8362, E-mail: hurwitz@etsu.edu. *Application contact:* Fiona Goodyear, Graduate Specialist, 423-439-6148, Fax: 423-439-5624, E-mail: goodyear@etsu.edu.

Emporia State University, Graduate School, Teachers College, Department of School Leadership and Middle/Secondary Education, Program in Curriculum and Instruction, Emporia, KS 66801-5087. Offers curriculum leadership (MS); effective practitioner (MS); national board certification (MS). *Accreditation:* NCATE. Part-time programs available. *Students:* 1 (woman) full-time, 126 part-time (105 women); includes 11 minority (5 Black or African American, non-Hispanic/Latino; 1 American Indian or Alaska Native, non-Hispanic/Latino; 5 Hispanic/Latino). 31 applicants, 94% accepted, 23 enrolled. In 2011,

57 master's awarded. *Degree requirements:* For master's, comprehensive exam or thesis, practicum. *Entrance requirements:* For master's, GRE or MAT, appropriate bachelor's degree, teacher certification, 1 year of teaching experience, letters of recommendation. *Application deadline:* For fall admission, 8/15 priority date for domestic students. Applications are processed on a rolling basis. Application fee: $30 ($75 for international students). Electronic applications accepted. *Expenses:* Tuition, state resident: full-time $2342; part-time $195 per credit hour. Tuition, nonresident: full-time $7254; part-time $605 per credit hour. *Required fees:* $66 per credit hour. Tuition and fees vary according to campus/location. *Financial support:* Career-related internships or fieldwork, Federal Work-Study, institutionally sponsored loans, health care benefits, and unspecified assistantships available. Financial award application deadline: 3/15; financial award applicants required to submit FAFSA. *Unit head:* Dr. Jerry Will, Chair, 620-341-5777, E-mail: jwill@emporia.edu. *Application contact:* Mary Sewell, Admissions Coordinator, 800-950-GRAD, Fax: 620-341-5909, E-mail: msewell@emporia.edu.

Fairleigh Dickinson University, Metropolitan Campus, University College: Arts, Sciences, and Professional Studies, Peter Sammartino School of Education, Program in Teaching, Teaneck, NJ 07666-1914. Offers MAT.

Ferris State University, College of Education and Human Services, School of Education, Big Rapids, MI 49307. Offers administration (MSCTE); curriculum and instruction (M Ed), including administration, elementary education, experiential education, philanthropic education, reading, secondary education, special education, subject matter option; education technology (MSCTE); instructor (MSCTE); post-secondary administration (MSCTE); training and development (MSCTE). Part-time and evening/weekend programs available. Postbaccalaureate distance learning degree programs offered (minimal on-campus study). *Faculty:* 9 full-time (7 women), 9 part-time/adjunct (6 women). *Students:* 8 full-time (7 women), 132 part-time (75 women); includes 13 minority (11 Black or African American, non-Hispanic/Latino; 1 American Indian or Alaska Native, non-Hispanic/Latino; 1 Hispanic/Latino), 5 international. Average age 36. 20 applicants, 100% accepted, 8 enrolled. In 2011, 51 master's awarded. *Degree requirements:* For master's, thesis, research paper. *Entrance requirements:* For master's, 2 years of work experience for vocational setting, minimum GPA of 2.75. Additional exam requirements/recommendations for international students: Recommended—TOEFL (minimum score 500 paper-based; 173 computer-based; 61 iBT). *Application deadline:* For fall admission, 7/1 priority date for domestic students, 7/1 for international students; for spring admission, 11/1 priority date for domestic students, 11/1 for international students. Applications are processed on a rolling basis. Application fee: $30. Electronic applications accepted. Application fee is waived when completed online. *Financial support:* Career-related internships or fieldwork and scholarships/grants available. Support available to part-time students. Financial award applicants required to submit FAFSA. *Faculty research:* Suicide prevention, reading, women in education, special needs, administration. *Unit head:* Dr. James Powell, Director, 231-591-5362, Fax: 231-591-2043, E-mail: powelj20@ferris.edu. *Application contact:* Kimisue Worrall, Secretary, 231-591-5361, Fax: 231-591-2043. Web site: http://www.ferris.edu/education/education/.

Fitchburg State University, Division of Graduate and Continuing Education, Program in Curriculum and Teaching, Fitchburg, MA 01420-2697. Offers M Ed. Part-time and evening/weekend programs available. *Students:* 46 full-time (35 women), 127 part-time (94 women); includes 4 minority (all Hispanic/Latino), 1 international. Average age 37. 61 applicants, 98% accepted, 51 enrolled. In 2011, 203 master's awarded. *Entrance requirements:* Additional exam requirements/recommendations for international students: Required—TOEFL (minimum score 550 paper-based; 213 computer-based; 79 iBT). *Application deadline:* For fall admission, 7/15 for international students; for spring admission, 12/1 for international students. Applications are processed on a rolling basis. Application fee: $25 ($50 for international students). Electronic applications accepted. *Expenses:* Tuition, state resident: full-time $2700; part-time $150 per credit. Tuition, nonresident: full-time $2700; part-time $150 per credit. *Required fees:* $2286; $127 per credit. *Financial support:* In 2011–12, research assistantships with partial tuition reimbursements (averaging $5,500 per year) were awarded; Federal Work-Study, scholarships/grants, and unspecified assistantships also available. Support available to part-time students. Financial award application deadline: 3/1; financial award applicants required to submit FAFSA. *Unit head:* Dr. Elaine Francis, Chair, 978-665-3501, Fax: 978-665-3658, E-mail: gce@fitchburgstate.edu. *Application contact:* Kay Reynolds, Director of Admissions, 978-665-3144, Fax: 978-665-4540, E-mail: admissions@fitchburgstate.edu. Web site: http://www.fitchburgstate.edu.

Florida Atlantic University, College of Education, Department of Curriculum, Culture, and Educational Inquiry, Boca Raton, FL 33431-0991. Offers curriculum and instruction (Ed D, Ed S); early childhood education (M Ed); multicultural education (M Ed); teaching English to speakers of other languages (TESOL) (M Ed). *Faculty:* 14 full-time (11 women), 16 part-time/adjunct (13 women). *Students:* 28 full-time (21 women), 138 part-time (106 women); includes 46 minority (18 Black or African American, non-Hispanic/Latino; 1 American Indian or Alaska Native, non-Hispanic/Latino; 3 Asian, non-Hispanic/Latino; 23 Hispanic/Latino; 1 Two or more races, non-Hispanic/Latino), 7 international. Average age 36. 120 applicants, 53% accepted, 32 enrolled. In 2011, 33 master's, 2 doctorates awarded. *Application deadline:* For fall admission, 7/1 for domestic students, 2/15 for international students; for spring admission, 11/1 for domestic students, 7/15 for international students. *Expenses: Tuition, area resident:* Part-time $343.02 per credit hour. Tuition, state resident: full-time $8232. Tuition, nonresident: full-time $23,931; part-time $997.14 per credit hour. *Faculty research:* Multicultural education, early intervention strategies, family literacy, religious diversity in schools, early childhood curriculum. *Unit head:* Dr. James McLaughlin, Interim Chair, 561-297-3965, E-mail: jmclau17@fau.edu. *Application contact:* Dr. Eliah Watlington, Associate Dean, 561-296-8520, Fax: 261-297-2991, E-mail: ewatling@fau.edu. Web site: http://www.coe.fau.edu/academicdepartments/ccei/.

Florida Atlantic University, College of Education, Department of Teaching and Learning, Boca Raton, FL 33431-0991. Offers curriculum and instruction (M Ed); elementary education (M Ed); environmental education (M Ed); reading education (M Ed); social foundations of education (M Ed). *Accreditation:* NCATE. Part-time and evening/weekend programs available. *Faculty:* 32 full-time (25 women), 90 part-time/adjunct (68 women). *Students:* 34 full-time (30 women), 103 part-time (96 women); includes 29 minority (8 Black or African American, non-Hispanic/Latino; 7 Asian, non-Hispanic/Latino; 11 Hispanic/Latino; 3 Two or more races, non-Hispanic/Latino), 1 international. Average age 32. 96 applicants, 66% accepted, 24 enrolled. In 2011, 71 master's awarded. *Entrance requirements:* For master's, GRE General Test, minimum GPA of 3.0 in last 2 years of undergraduate course work. Additional exam requirements/recommendations for international students: Required—TOEFL. *Application deadline:* For fall admission, 7/1 for domestic students, 2/15 for international students; for spring admission, 11/1 for domestic students, 7/15 for international students. Applications are processed on a rolling basis. Application fee: $30. *Expenses: Tuition, area resident:* Part-time $343.02 per credit hour. Tuition, state resident: full-time $8232. Tuition, nonresident: full-time $23,931; part-time $997.14 per credit hour. *Financial support:* Fellowships with partial tuition reimbursements, research assistantships with partial tuition reimbursements, teaching assistantships with partial tuition reimbursements, career-related internships or fieldwork, scholarships/grants, and unspecified assistantships available. *Faculty research:* Technology, teaching English to speakers of other languages, math teaching, electronic portfolio assessment, global perspectives through social studies. *Unit head:* Dr. Barbara Ridener, Chairperson, 561-297-3588. *Application contact:* Dr. Eliah Watlington, Associate Dean, 561-296-8520, Fax: 261-297-2991, E-mail: ewatling@fau.edu. Web site: http://www.coe.fau.edu/academicdepartments/tl/.

Florida Gulf Coast University, College of Education, Program in Curriculum and Instruction, Fort Myers, FL 33965-6565. Offers curriculum and instruction (Ed D, Ed S); educational technology (M Ed, MA); English education (M Ed). Part-time and evening/weekend programs available. Postbaccalaureate distance learning degree programs offered (minimal on-campus study). *Faculty:* 34 full-time (26 women), 57 part-time/adjunct (40 women). *Students:* 19 full-time (18 women), 8 part-time (all women); includes 2 minority (both Hispanic/Latino). Average age 34. 13 applicants, 85% accepted, 10 enrolled. In 2011, 9 master's awarded. *Degree requirements:* For master's, final project or portfolio. *Entrance requirements:* For master's, GRE General Test, MAT, minimum undergraduate GPA of 3.0 in last 2 years. Additional exam requirements/recommendations for international students: Required—TOEFL (minimum score 550 paper-based; 213 computer-based). *Application deadline:* For fall admission, 7/1 priority date for domestic students; for spring admission, 10/15 for domestic students. Applications are processed on a rolling basis. Application fee: $30. Electronic applications accepted. *Expenses:* Tuition, state resident: full-time $8289. Tuition, nonresident: full-time $28,895. *Required fees:* $1831. One-time fee: $30 full-time. *Faculty research:* Internet in schools, technology in pre-service and in-service teacher training. *Unit head:* Dr. Diane Schmidt, Department Chair, 239-590-7741, Fax: 239-590-7801, E-mail: dschmidt@fgcu.edu. *Application contact:* Keiana Desmore, Adviser/Counselor, 239-590-7759, Fax: 239-590-7801, E-mail: kdesmore@fgcu.edu. Web site: http://edtech.fgcu.edu/.

Florida International University, College of Education, Department of Curriculum and Instruction, Miami, FL 33199. Offers art education (MAT, MS, Ed D); curriculum and instruction (Ed S); curriculum development (MS); curriculum studies (PhD); early childhood education (MS, Ed D); elementary education (MS, Ed D); English education (MAT, MS, Ed D); foreign language education - teaching English to speakers of other languages (TESOL) (MS, Certificate), including foreign language education (Certificate), teaching English (MS); French education - initial teacher preparation (MAT); international and intercultural development education (Ed D); international and intercultural developmental education (MS); language, literacy and culture (PhD); learning technologies (MS, Ed D, PhD); mathematics education (MAT, MS, Ed D, PhD); modern language education/bilingual education (MS, Ed D); physical education (MS); reading education (MS, Ed D); science education (MAT, MS, Ed D, PhD); social studies education (MAT, MS, Ed D); Spanish education - initial teacher preparation (MAT); special education (MS). Part-time and evening/weekend programs available. *Degree requirements:* For doctorate, comprehensive exam, thesis/dissertation. *Entrance requirements:* For master's, GRE General Test, Florida General Knowledge Test or Florida College Level Academic Skills Test; for doctorate and other advanced degree, GRE General Test. Additional exam requirements/recommendations for international students: Required—TOEFL (minimum score 550 paper-based; 213 computer-based; 80 iBT), IELTS (minimum score 6.3). Electronic applications accepted.

Fordham University, Graduate School of Education, Division of Curriculum and Teaching, New York, NY 10023. Offers adult education (MS, MSE); bilingual teacher education (MSE); curriculum and teaching (MSE); early childhood education (MSE); elementary education (MST); language, literacy, and learning (PhD); reading education (MSE, Adv C); secondary education (MAT, MSE); special education (MSE, Adv C); teaching English as a second language (MSE). *Accreditation:* NCATE. *Degree requirements:* For doctorate, thesis/dissertation; for Adv C, thesis. *Entrance requirements:* For doctorate, MAT, GRE General Test. *Expenses: Tuition:* Full-time $30,480; part-time $1270 per credit. *Required fees:* $586; $293 per semester.

Framingham State University, Division of Graduate and Continuing Education, Program in Curriculum and Instructional Technology, Framingham, MA 01701-9101. Offers M Ed. Postbaccalaureate distance learning degree programs offered.

Franciscan University of Steubenville, Graduate Programs, Department of Education, Steubenville, OH 43952-1763. Offers administration (MS Ed); teaching (MS Ed). Part-time and evening/weekend programs available. *Degree requirements:* For master's, project. *Entrance requirements:* For master's, minimum undergraduate GPA of 2.5 or written exam. *Expenses:* Contact institution.

Franklin Pierce University, Graduate Studies, Rindge, NH 03461-0060. Offers curriculum and instruction (M Ed); emerging network technologies (Graduate Certificate); energy and sustainability studies (MBA); health administration (MBA, Graduate Certificate); human resource management (MBA, Graduate Certificate); information technology (MBA); information technology management (MS); leadership (MBA, DA); nursing (MS); physical therapy (DPT); physician assistant studies (MPAS); special education (M Ed); sports management (MBA). *Accreditation:* APTA. Part-time programs available. Postbaccalaureate distance learning degree programs offered (no on-campus study). *Degree requirements:* For master's, concentrated original research projects; student teaching; fieldwork and/or internship; leadership project; PRAXIS I and II (for M Ed); for doctorate, concentrated original research projects, clinical fieldwork and/or internship, leadership project. *Entrance requirements:* For master's, minimum GPA of 2.5, 3 letters of recommendation; competencies in accounting, economics, statistics, and computer skills through life experience or undergraduate coursework (for MBA); certification/e-portfolio, minimum C grade in all education courses (for M Ed); license to practice as RN (for MS in nursing); for doctorate, GRE, BA/BS, 3 letters of recommendation, personal mission statement, interview, writing sample, minimum cumulative GPA of 2.8, master's degree (for DA); 80 hours of observation/work in PT settings, completion of anatomy, chemistry, physics, and statistics, minimum GPA of 3.0 (for DPT). Additional exam requirements/recommendations for international students: Required—TOEFL (minimum score 550 paper-based; 195 computer-based; 61 iBT). Electronic applications accepted. *Faculty research:* Evidence-based practice in sports physical therapy, human resource management in economic crisis, leadership in nursing, innovation in sports facility management, differentiated learning and understanding by design.

Freed-Hardeman University, Program in Education, Henderson, TN 38340-2399. Offers curriculum and instruction (M Ed); school counseling (M Ed), including administration and supervision, special education; school leadership (Ed S). *Accreditation:* NCATE. Part-time and evening/weekend programs available. *Degree requirements:* For master's, comprehensive exam, thesis optional; for Ed S, thesis. *Entrance requirements:* For master's, GRE General Test or NTE; for Ed S, 3 years of teaching experience. Additional exam requirements/recommendations for international students: Required—TOEFL (minimum score 500 paper-based; 173 computer-based).

Fresno Pacific University, Graduate Programs, School of Education, Fresno, CA 93702-4709. Offers administration (MA Ed), including administrative services; foundations, curriculum and teaching (MA Ed), including curriculum and teaching, school library and information technology; language, literacy, and culture (MA Ed), including bilingual/cross-cultural education, language development, multilingual contexts, reading; mathematics/science/computer education (MA Ed), including educational technology, integrated mathematics/science education, mathematics education; pupil personnel services (MA Ed), including school counseling, school psychology; special education (MA Ed), including mild/moderate, moderate/severe, physical and health impairments. Part-time and evening/weekend programs available. *Degree requirements:* For master's, thesis (for some programs). *Entrance requirements:* For master's, interview; GMAT, GRE, MAT, or 6 units of course work with a faculty recommendation. Additional exam requirements/recommendations for international students: Required—TOEFL (minimum score 550 paper-based; 213 computer-based). Electronic applications accepted.

Fresno Pacific University, Graduate Programs, School of Education, Division of Foundations, Curriculum and Teaching, Program in Curriculum and Teaching, Fresno, CA 93702-4709. Offers MA Ed. Part-time and evening/weekend programs available. Postbaccalaureate distance learning degree programs offered. *Degree requirements:* For master's, thesis or alternative. *Entrance requirements:* Additional exam requirements/recommendations for international students: Required—TOEFL (minimum score 550 paper-based; 213 computer-based). Electronic applications accepted.

Frostburg State University, Graduate School, College of Education, Department of Educational Professions, Program in Curriculum and Instruction, Frostburg, MD 21532-1099. Offers educational technology (M Ed); elementary education (M Ed); secondary education (M Ed). Part-time and evening/weekend programs available. *Degree requirements:* For master's, thesis or alternative. *Entrance requirements:* For master's, teaching certificate. Additional exam requirements/recommendations for international students: Required—TOEFL. Electronic applications accepted.

Furman University, Graduate Division, Department of Education, Greenville, SC 29613. Offers curriculum and instruction (MA); early childhood education (MA); educational leadership (Ed S); English as a second language (MA); literacy (MA); school leadership (MA); special education (MA). *Accreditation:* NCATE. Part-time programs available. Postbaccalaureate distance learning degree programs offered (minimal on-campus study). *Faculty:* 14 full-time (8 women), 6 part-time/adjunct (4 women). *Students:* 237 part-time (188 women); includes 27 minority (22 Black or African American, non-Hispanic/Latino; 1 Asian, non-Hispanic/Latino; 3 Hispanic/Latino; 1 Native Hawaiian or other Pacific Islander, non-Hispanic/Latino). Average age 29. 97 applicants, 100% accepted, 90 enrolled. In 2011, 34 master's awarded. *Degree requirements:* For master's, comprehensive exam (for some programs), thesis or alternative. *Entrance requirements:* For master's, PRAXIS II. *Application deadline:* For fall admission, 8/1 priority date for domestic students, 7/15 for international students; for spring admission, 12/1 priority date for domestic students, 12/1 for international students. Applications are processed on a rolling basis. Application fee: $50. *Financial support:* Scholarships/grants available. Financial award application deadline: 5/15; financial award applicants required to submit FAFSA. *Faculty research:* Literacy, pedagogy and practice, social justice, advanced leadership, achievement in high poverty schools. *Unit head:* Dr. Nelly Hecker, Head, 864-294-3385. *Application contact:* Helen Reynolds, Department Assistant, 864-294-2213, Fax: 864-294-3579, E-mail: helen.reynolds@furman.edu. Web site: http://www.furman.edu/gradstudies/.

Gannon University, School of Graduate Studies, College of Humanities, Education, and Social Sciences, School of Education, Program in Curriculum and Instruction, Erie, PA 16541-0001. Offers M Ed. Part-time and evening/weekend programs available. Postbaccalaureate distance learning degree programs offered (no on-campus study). *Students:* 18 full-time (12 women), 235 part-time (180 women); includes 13 minority (9 Black or African American, non-Hispanic/Latino; 2 Asian, non-Hispanic/Latino; 2 Hispanic/Latino), 1 international. Average age 36. 65 applicants, 89% accepted, 26 enrolled. In 2011, 212 master's awarded. *Degree requirements:* For master's, thesis or alternative, portfolio project. *Entrance requirements:* For master's, bachelor's degree, minimum GPA of 3.0; letters of recommendation; teacher certification. Additional exam requirements/recommendations for international students: Required—TOEFL (minimum score 79 iBT). *Application deadline:* Applications are processed on a rolling basis. Application fee: $25. Electronic applications accepted. *Expenses:* Contact institution. *Financial support:* Scholarships/grants available. Financial award application deadline: 7/1; financial award applicants required to submit FAFSA. *Faculty research:* Program evaluation, instructional leadership, organizational leadership, qualitative research and design, online teaching and learning. *Unit head:* Dr. Kathleen Kingston, Director, Graduate Education Programs, 814-871-5626, E-mail: kingston002@gannon.edu. *Application contact:* Kara Morgan, Director of Graduate Admissions, 814-871-5831, Fax: 814-871-5827, E-mail: graduate@gannon.edu.

Gardner-Webb University, Graduate School, School of Education, Program in Curriculum and Instruction, Boiling Springs, NC 28017. Offers Ed D. *Faculty:* 10 full-time (4 women), 20 part-time/adjunct (7 women). *Students:* 3 full-time (2 women), 95 part-time (78 women); includes 24 minority (20 Black or African American, non-Hispanic/Latino; 2 Asian, non-Hispanic/Latino; 2 Hispanic/Latino). Average age 38. In 2011, 3 doctorates awarded. *Expenses: Tuition:* Full-time $6300; part-time $350 per credit hour. *Unit head:* Dr. Alan D. Eury, Chair, 704-406-4402, Fax: 704-406-3921, E-mail: dsimmons@gardner-webb.edu. *Application contact:* Office of Graduate Admissions, 877-498-4723, Fax: 704-406-3895, E-mail: gradinfo@gardner-webb.edu.

George Fox University, School of Education, Educational Foundations and Leadership Program, Newberg, OR 97132-2697. Offers continuing administrator license (Certificate); curriculum and instruction (M Ed); educational leadership (M Ed, Ed D); ESOL (Certificate); higher education (M Ed); initial administrator license (Certificate); instructional leadership (Ed S); library media (M Ed, Certificate); literacy (M Ed); reading (M Ed); secondary education (M Ed). *Accreditation:* NCATE. Part-time and evening/weekend programs available. Postbaccalaureate distance learning degree programs offered (minimal on-campus study). *Faculty:* 10 full-time (3 women), 6 part-time/adjunct (3 women). *Students:* 2 full-time (both women), 111 part-time (83 women); includes 16 minority (2 American Indian or Alaska Native, non-Hispanic/Latino; 6 Asian, non-Hispanic/Latino; 7 Hispanic/Latino; 1 Native Hawaiian or other Pacific Islander, non-Hispanic/Latino), 3 international. Average age 39. 44 applicants, 98% accepted, 43 enrolled. In 2011, 34 master's, 7 doctorates, 76 Certificates awarded. *Degree requirements:* For master's, thesis (for some programs); for doctorate, comprehensive exam, thesis/dissertation, project. *Entrance requirements:* For master's, minimum undergraduate GPA of 3.0 during previous 2 years of course work, resume, 3 professional recommendations on university forms, official transcripts; for doctorate, GRE, master's degree with minimum GPA of 3.25, 3 years of relevant professional experience, interview, personal essay, scholarly work, 3 professional recommendations on university forms along with 3 written letters of recommendation, official transcripts. Additional exam requirements/recommendations for international students: Required—TOEFL (minimum score 577 paper-based; 233 computer-based; 90 iBT). *Application deadline:* For fall admission, 7/15 for domestic and international students; for winter admission, 11/1 for domestic and international students; for spring admission, 4/1 for domestic and international students. Applications are processed on a rolling basis. Application fee: $40. Electronic applications accepted. *Expenses:* Contact institution. *Financial support:* Career-related internships or fieldwork available. Financial award applicants required to submit FAFSA. *Unit head:* Dr. Scot Headley, Professor/Chair, 503-554-2836, E-mail: sheadley@georgefox.edu. *Application contact:* Alex Martin, Admissions Counselor, 800-631-0921, Fax: 503-554-3110, E-mail: amartin@georgefox.edu. Web site: http://www.georgefox.edu/education/index.html.

George Mason University, College of Education and Human Development, Programs in Curriculum and Instruction, Fairfax, VA 22030. Offers M Ed. *Faculty:* 43 full-time (34 women), 130 part-time/adjunct (118 women). *Students:* 203 full-time (174 women), 767 part-time (637 women); includes 172 minority (44 Black or African American, non-Hispanic/Latino; 3 American Indian or Alaska Native, non-Hispanic/Latino; 51 Asian, non-Hispanic/Latino; 50 Hispanic/Latino; 1 Native Hawaiian or other Pacific Islander, non-Hispanic/Latino; 23 Two or more races, non-Hispanic/Latino), 22 international. Average age 31. 571 applicants, 78% accepted, 337 enrolled. In 2011, 406 degrees awarded. *Degree requirements:* For master's, comprehensive exam, thesis (for some programs). *Entrance requirements:* For master's, PRAXIS I, PRAXIS II, Virginia Communication and Literacy Assessment Test (VCLA), minimum GPA of 3.0 in last 60 hours, licensed as teacher or educational administrator, 3 recommendation letters, interview. Additional exam requirements/recommendations for international students: Required—TOEFL (minimum score 570 paper-based; 230 computer-based; 88 iBT), IELTS, Pearson Test of English. *Application deadline:* Applications are processed on a rolling basis. Application fee: $65 ($80 for international students). Electronic applications accepted. *Expenses:* Tuition, state resident: full-time $8750; part-time $364.58 per credit. Tuition, nonresident: full-time $24,092; part-time $1003.83 per credit. *Required fees:* $2514; $104.75 per credit. *Financial support:* In 2011–12, 4 students received support, including 1 research assistantship with full and partial tuition reimbursement available (averaging $10,286 per year), 3 teaching assistantships with full and partial tuition reimbursements available (averaging $8,798 per year); career-related internships or fieldwork, Federal Work-Study, scholarships/grants, unspecified assistantships, and health care benefits (full-time research or teaching assistantship recipients) also available. Financial award application deadline: 3/1; financial award applicants required to submit FAFSA. *Unit head:* Rebecca Fox, Associate Professor, 703-993-4123, Fax: 703-993-9380, E-mail: rfox@gmu.edu. *Application contact:* Dolores Izer-Horn, Program Manager, 703-993-3640, Fax: 703-993-9380, E-mail: dhorn@gmu.edu. Web site: http://gse.gmu.edu/div_lt/.

The George Washington University, Graduate School of Education and Human Development, Department of Curriculum and Pedagogy, Program in Curriculum and Instruction, Washington, DC 20052. Offers MA Ed, Ed D, Ed S. *Accreditation:* NCATE. Evening/weekend programs available. *Students:* 16 full-time (15 women), 34 part-time (25 women); includes 12 minority (9 Black or African American, non-Hispanic/Latino; 3 Asian, non-Hispanic/Latino), 4 international. Average age 34. 39 applicants, 90% accepted, 10 enrolled. In 2011, 6 master's, 6 doctorates, 3 other advanced degrees awarded. *Degree requirements:* For master's and Ed S, comprehensive exam; for doctorate, comprehensive exam, thesis/dissertation. *Entrance requirements:* For master's, GRE General Test or MAT, minimum GPA of 2.75, resume; for doctorate and Ed S, GRE General Test or MAT, interview, minimum GPA of 3.3. *Application deadline:* For fall admission, 1/15 priority date for domestic students; for spring admission, 10/1 for domestic students. Applications are processed on a rolling basis. Application fee: $75. *Financial support:* In 2011–12, 25 students received support. Fellowships, research assistantships, career-related internships or fieldwork, Federal Work-Study, and tuition waivers (partial) available. Financial award application deadline: 1/15; financial award applicants required to submit FAFSA. *Faculty research:* Cognitive skills-teaching, metacognitive strategies, adult basic literacy. *Unit head:* Dr. Sharon Lynch, Faculty Coordinator, 202-994-6174, E-mail: slynch@gwu.edu. *Application contact:* Sarah Lang, Director of Graduate Admissions, 202-994-1447, Fax: 202-994-7207, E-mail: slang@gwu.edu.

Georgia College & State University, Graduate School, The John H. Lounsbury College of Education, Department of Foundations and Secondary Education, Milledgeville, GA 31061. Offers curriculum and instruction (Ed S), including secondary education; educational technology (M Ed), including library media; educational technology (M Ed), including instructional technology; secondary education (M Ed, MAT). *Accreditation:* NCATE. Part-time and evening/weekend programs available. *Students:* 84 full-time (47 women), 120 part-time (98 women); includes 51 minority (43 Black or African American, non-Hispanic/Latino; 2 Asian, non-Hispanic/Latino; 4 Hispanic/Latino; 2 Two or more races, non-Hispanic/Latino), 1 international. Average age 31. 69 applicants, 51% accepted, 28 enrolled. In 2011, 105 master's, 33 other advanced degrees awarded. *Degree requirements:* For master's, comprehensive exam; for Ed S, comprehensive exam, electronic portfolio presentation. *Entrance requirements:* For master's, on-site writing assessment, 2 letters of recommendation, level 4 teaching certificate; for Ed S, on-site writing assessment, master's degree, 2 letters of recommendation, 2 years of teaching experience, level 5 teacher certification. Additional exam requirements/recommendations for international students: Recommended—TOEFL (minimum score 550 paper-based; 213 computer-based; 79 iBT). *Application deadline:* For fall admission, 7/1 priority date for domestic students, 4/1 for international students; for spring admission, 11/15 priority date for domestic students, 9/1 for international students. Applications are processed on a rolling basis. Application fee: $40. Electronic applications accepted. *Expenses:* Tuition, state resident: full-time $4806; part-time $267 per credit hour. Tuition, nonresident: full-time $17,802; part-time $989 per credit hour. *Required fees:* $936 per semester. Tuition and fees vary according to course load and campus/location. *Financial support:* In 2011–12, 12 research assistantships with full tuition reimbursements were awarded; career-related internships or fieldwork and Federal Work-Study also available. Support available to part-time students. Financial award applicants required to submit FAFSA. *Unit head:* Dr. Brian Mumma, Interim Chair, 478-445-2517, E-mail: brian.mumma@gcsu.edu. *Application contact:* Shanda Brand, Graduate Advisor, 478-445-1383, E-mail: shanda.brand@gcsu.edu.

Georgia Southern University, Jack N. Averitt College of Graduate Studies, College of Education, Department of Curriculum, Foundations, and Reading, Program in Curriculum Studies, Statesboro, GA 30460. Offers Ed D. Part-time programs available. *Students:* 25 full-time (17 women), 174 part-time (144 women); includes 54 minority (44 Black or African American, non-Hispanic/Latino; 1 American Indian or Alaska Native, non-Hispanic/Latino; 3 Asian, non-Hispanic/Latino; 5 Hispanic/Latino; 1 Two or more races, non-Hispanic/Latino), 1 international. Average age 43. 1 applicant, 100% accepted, 0 enrolled. In 2011, 21 doctorates awarded. *Degree requirements:* For doctorate, thesis/dissertation, exams. *Entrance requirements:* For doctorate, GRE or MAT, letters of reference, minimum GPA of 3.5, writing sample. Additional exam requirements/recommendations for international students: Required—TOEFL (minimum score 550 paper-based; 213 computer-based; 80 iBT). Application fee: $50. Electronic applications accepted. *Expenses:* Tuition, state resident: full-time $6300; part-time $263 per semester hour. Tuition, nonresident: full-time $25,174; part-time $1049 per semester hour. *Required fees:* $1872. *Financial support:* In 2011–12, 4 students received support, including research assistantships with partial tuition reimbursements available (averaging $9,500 per year), teaching assistantships with partial tuition reimbursements available (averaging $9,500 per year); career-related internships or fieldwork, Federal Work-Study, scholarships/grants, and unspecified assistantships also available. Support available to part-time students. Financial award application deadline: 4/15; financial award applicants required to submit FAFSA. *Faculty research:* Curriculum theory; science studies; documentary film; race, class and gender; social justice. *Unit* *head:* Dr. John Weaver, Program Coordinator, 912-478-1709, E-mail: jweaver@georgiasouthern.edu. *Application contact:* Amanda Gilliland, Coordinator for Graduate Student Recruitment, 912-478-5384, Fax: 912-478-0740, E-mail: gradadmissions@georgiasouthern.edu. Web site: http://coe.georgiasouthern.edu/foundations/edd/.

Georgia Southern University, Jack N. Averitt College of Graduate Studies, College of Education, Department of Teaching and Learning, Program in Curriculum and Instruction - Accomplished Teaching, Statesboro, GA 30460. Offers M Ed. Part-time programs available. Postbaccalaureate distance learning degree programs offered (no on-campus study). *Students:* 8 full-time (7 women), 24 part-time (21 women); includes 7 minority (all Black or African American, non-Hispanic/Latino). Average age 31. 49 applicants, 100% accepted, 30 enrolled. *Entrance requirements:* For master's, current Georgia teaching certificate. *Expenses:* Tuition, state resident: full-time $6300; part-time $263 per semester hour. Tuition, nonresident: full-time $25,174; part-time $1049 per semester hour. *Required fees:* $1872. *Unit head:* Dr. Ronnie Sheppard, Chair, 912-478-0198, Fax: 912-478-0026, E-mail: sheppard@georgiasouthern.edu. *Application contact:* Amanda Gilliland, Coordinator for Graduate Student Recruitment, 912-478-5384, Fax: 912-478-0740, E-mail: gradschool@georgiasouthern.edu.

Grambling State University, School of Graduate Studies and Research, College of Education, Department of Educational Leadership, Grambling, LA 71245. Offers curriculum and instruction (Ed D); developmental education (MS, Ed D), including curriculum and instruction: reading (Ed D), English (MS), guidance and counseling (MS), higher education administration (Ed D), instructional systems and technology (Ed D), mathematics (MS), reading (MS), science (MS), student development and personnel services (Ed D); educational leadership (MS, Ed D). Part-time and evening/weekend programs available. *Degree requirements:* For master's, comprehensive exam, thesis (for some programs); for doctorate, comprehensive exam, thesis/dissertation. *Entrance requirements:* For master's, GRE, minimum GPA of 2.5 on last degree; for doctorate, GRE (minimum 1000, 500 on Verbal), master's degree, minimum GPA of 3.0 on last degree. Additional exam requirements/recommendations for international students: Required—TOEFL (minimum score 500 paper-based; 173 computer-based; 61 iBT). Electronic applications accepted. *Expenses:* Tuition, state resident: full-time $3546; part-time $192 per credit hour. Tuition, nonresident: full-time $3456; part-time $192 per credit hour. *Required fees:* $1829; $1829 per semester hour.

Grand Canyon University, College of Education, Phoenix, AZ 85017-1097. Offers curriculum and instruction (M Ed); education administration (M Ed); elementary education (M Ed); secondary education (M Ed); special education (M Ed); teaching (MA). Part-time and evening/weekend programs available. Postbaccalaureate distance learning degree programs offered (no on-campus study). *Degree requirements:* For master's, publishable research paper (M Ed), e-portfolio. *Entrance requirements:* For master's, undergraduate degree from accredited, GCU-approved college, university, or program with minimum GPA 2.8. Additional exam requirements/recommendations for international students: Required—TOEFL (minimum score 550 paper-based; 213 computer-based; 79 iBT), IELTS (minimum score 6). Electronic applications accepted.

Grand Valley State University, College of Education, Program in Instruction and Curriculum, Allendale, MI 49401-9403. Offers M Ed.

Harvard University, Harvard Graduate School of Education, Master's Programs in Education, Cambridge, MA 02138. Offers arts in education (Ed M); education policy and management (Ed M); higher education (Ed M); human development and psychology (Ed M); international education policy (Ed M); language and literacy (Ed M); learning and teaching (Ed M); mid-career mathematics and science (teaching certificate) (Ed M); mind brain and education (Ed M); prevention science and practice (Ed M); school leadership (Ed M); special studies (Ed M); teaching and curriculum (teaching certificate) (Ed M); technology innovation and education (Ed M). Part-time programs available. *Faculty:* 83 full-time (44 women), 67 part-time/adjunct (29 women). *Students:* 592 full-time (431 women), 75 part-time (54 women); includes 194 minority (41 Black or African American, non-Hispanic/Latino; 4 American Indian or Alaska Native, non-Hispanic/Latino; 75 Asian, non-Hispanic/Latino; 45 Hispanic/Latino; 2 Native Hawaiian or other Pacific Islander, non-Hispanic/Latino; 27 Two or more races, non-Hispanic/Latino), 95 international. Average age 28. 1,679 applicants, 52% accepted, 627 enrolled. In 2011, 653 master's awarded. *Entrance requirements:* For master's, GRE General Test, statement of purpose, 3 letters of recommendation, resume, official transcripts. Additional exam requirements/recommendations for international students: Required—TOEFL (minimum score 613 paper-based; 104 computer-based; 100 iBT), TWE (minimum score 5). *Application deadline:* For fall admission, 1/4 for domestic and international students. Application fee: $85. Electronic applications accepted. *Expenses:* Contact institution. *Financial support:* In 2011–12, 419 students received support, including 14 fellowships with full and partial tuition reimbursements available (averaging $12,831 per year); career-related internships or fieldwork, Federal Work-Study, institutionally sponsored loans, scholarships/grants, health care benefits, tuition waivers (full and partial), and unspecified assistantships also available. Support available to part-time students. Financial award application deadline: 2/1; financial award applicants required to submit FAFSA. *Faculty research:* Learning and development, educational leadership and organizations, educational policy analysis. *Total annual research expenditures:* $26 million. *Unit head:* Jennifer L. Petrallia, Assistant Dean, 617-495-8445. *Application contact:* Information Contact, 617-495-3414, Fax: 617-496-3577, E-mail: gseadmissions@harvard.edu. Web site: http://www.gse.harvard.edu/.

Henderson State University, Graduate Studies, Teachers College, Department of Advanced Instructional Studies, Arkadelphia, AR 71999-0001. Offers early childhood (P-4) (MSE); education (MAT); middle school (MSE); reading (MSE); special education (MSE). *Accreditation:* NCATE. Part-time programs available. *Entrance requirements:* For master's, GRE General Test or MAT, minimum GPA of 2.7, teacher certification. Additional exam requirements/recommendations for international students: Required—TOEFL (minimum score 550 paper-based; 213 computer-based); Recommended—IELTS (minimum score 6). Electronic applications accepted.

Hood College, Graduate School, Department of Education, Frederick, MD 21701-8575. Offers curriculum and instruction (MS), including early childhood education, elementary education, elementary school science and mathematics, secondary education, special education; educational leadership (MS, Certificate); reading specialization (MS). Part-time and evening/weekend programs available. *Degree requirements:* For master's, action research project, portfolio (reading). *Entrance requirements:* For master's, minimum GPA of 2.75, teaching certification. Additional exam requirements/recommendations for international students: Required—TOEFL (minimum score 575 paper-based; 231 computer-based; 89 iBT). Electronic applications accepted. *Faculty research:* Leadership, action research, brain research, learning styles.

Houston Baptist University, College of Education and Behavioral Sciences, Programs in Education, Houston, TX 77074-3298. Offers bilingual education (M Ed); counselor education (M Ed); curriculum and instruction (M Ed); educational administration (M Ed); educational diagnostician (M Ed); reading education (M Ed). Part-time programs available. *Entrance requirements:* For master's, GRE General Test or MAT. Additional exam requirements/recommendations for international students: Required—TOEFL (minimum score 550 paper-based; 213 computer-based).

Idaho State University, Office of Graduate Studies, College of Education, Department of Educational Foundations, Pocatello, ID 83209-8059. Offers child and family studies (M Ed); curriculum leadership (M Ed); education (M Ed); educational administration (M Ed); educational foundations (5th Year Certificate); elementary education (M Ed), including K-12 education, literacy, secondary education. Part-time programs available. *Degree requirements:* For master's, comprehensive exam, thesis optional, oral exam, written exam; for 5th Year Certificate, comprehensive exam, thesis (for some programs), oral exam, written exam. *Entrance requirements:* For master's, GRE General Test or MAT, minimum undergraduate GPA of 3.0; for 5th Year Certificate, GRE General Test, minimum undergraduate GPA of 3.0, master's degree. Additional exam requirements/recommendations for international students: Required—TOEFL (minimum score 550 paper-based; 213 computer-based; 80 iBT). Electronic applications accepted. *Faculty research:* Child and families studies; business education; special education; math, science, and technology education.

Illinois State University, Graduate School, College of Education, Department of Curriculum and Instruction, Normal, IL 61790-2200. Offers curriculum and instruction (MS, MS Ed, Ed D); educational policies (Ed D); postsecondary education (Ed D); reading (MS Ed); supervision (Ed D). *Accreditation:* NCATE. *Degree requirements:* For master's, variable foreign language requirement, thesis or alternative; for doctorate, variable foreign language requirement, thesis/dissertation, 2 terms of residency, internship. *Entrance requirements:* For master's, GRE General Test, minimum GPA of 3.0 in last 60 hours of course work; for doctorate, GRE General Test. *Faculty research:* In-service and pre-service teacher education for teachers of English language learners; teachers for all children: developing a model for alternative, bilingual elementary certification for paraprofessionals in Illinois; Illinois Geographic Alliance, Connections Project.

Indiana State University, College of Graduate and Professional Studies, College of Education, Department of Curriculum, Instruction, and Media Technology, Terre Haute, IN 47809. Offers curriculum and instruction (M Ed, PhD); educational technology (MS). *Accreditation:* NCATE. *Degree requirements:* For doctorate, thesis/dissertation. *Entrance requirements:* For doctorate, GRE General Test. Electronic applications accepted. *Faculty research:* Discipline FERPA reading, teacher strengths and needs.

Indiana University Bloomington, School of Education, Department of Curriculum and Instruction, Bloomington, IN 47405-7000. Offers art education (MS, Ed D, PhD); curriculum studies (Ed D, PhD); elementary education (MS, Ed D, PhD, Ed S); mathematics education (MS, Ed D, PhD); science education (MS, Ed D, PhD); secondary education (MS, Ed D, PhD); social studies education (MS, PhD); special education (PhD, Ed S). *Accreditation:* NCATE. Part-time and evening/weekend programs available. Terminal master's awarded for partial completion of doctoral program. *Degree requirements:* For doctorate, thesis/dissertation; for Ed S, comprehensive exam or project. *Entrance requirements:* For master's, doctorate, and Ed S, GRE General Test. Electronic applications accepted.

Indiana University of Pennsylvania, School of Graduate Studies and Research, College of Education and Educational Technology, Department of Professional Studies in Education, Program in Curriculum and Instruction, Indiana, PA 15705-1087. Offers M Ed, D Ed. D Ed offered jointly with Bloomsburg University of Pennsylvania and Edinboro University of Pennsylvania. *Accreditation:* NCATE. *Faculty:* 19 full-time (13 women), 1 (woman) part-time/adjunct. *Students:* 16 full-time (12 women), 98 part-time (79 women); includes 4 minority (all Black or African American, non-Hispanic/Latino), 7 international. Average age 39. 58 applicants, 59% accepted, 27 enrolled. In 2011, 11 doctorates awarded. *Degree requirements:* For doctorate, one foreign language, comprehensive exam, thesis/dissertation. *Entrance requirements:* For doctorate, 2 letters of recommendation. Additional exam requirements/recommendations for international students: Required—TOEFL (minimum score 540 paper-based; 207 computer-based). *Application deadline:* Applications are processed on a rolling basis. Application fee: $50. Electronic applications accepted. *Expenses:* Tuition, state resident: full-time $7488; part-time $416 per credit. Tuition, nonresident: full-time $11,232; part-time $624 per credit. *Required fees:* $2070; $192.20 per credit. $90 per semester. *Financial support:* In 2011–12, 3 fellowships (averaging $2,000 per year), 21 research assistantships with full and partial tuition reimbursements (averaging $4,209 per year), 4 teaching assistantships (averaging $18,665 per year) were awarded; career-related internships or fieldwork and Federal Work-Study also available. Support available to part-time students. Financial award application deadline: 4/15; financial award applicants required to submit FAFSA. *Unit head:* Dr. Mary R. Jalongo, Graduate Coordinator, 724-357-2417, E-mail: mjalongo@iup.edu. *Application contact:* Dr. Edward Nardi, Associate Dean, 724-357-2480, Fax: 724-357-5595, E-mail: ewnardi@iup.edu. Web site: http://www.iup.edu/grad/CandI/default.aspx.

Indiana University–Purdue University Indianapolis, School of Education, Indianapolis, IN 46202-2896. Offers computer education (Certificate); curriculum and instruction (MS); early childhood (MS); educational leadership (MS, Certificate); English as a second language (Certificate); higher education and student affairs (MS); kindergarten (Certificate); language education (MS); reading (Certificate); school counseling (MS); special education (MS, Certificate). Part-time and evening/weekend programs available. *Faculty:* 41 full-time, 80 part-time/adjunct. *Students:* 67 full-time (52 women), 467 part-time (360 women); includes 82 minority (44 Black or African American, non-Hispanic/Latino; 3 American Indian or Alaska Native, non-Hispanic/Latino; 8 Asian, non-Hispanic/Latino; 13 Hispanic/Latino; 14 Two or more races, non-Hispanic/Latino), 10 international. Average age 33. 63 applicants, 57% accepted, 29 enrolled. In 2011, 167 master's awarded. *Degree requirements:* For master's, thesis optional. *Entrance requirements:* For master's, GRE General Test, minimum GPA of 3.0. Additional exam requirements/recommendations for international students: Required—TOEFL. *Application deadline:* For fall admission, 5/1 priority date for domestic students; for spring admission, 11/1 for domestic students. Application fee: $55 ($65 for international students). *Financial support:* Fellowships, research assistantships with partial tuition reimbursements, teaching assistantships, Federal Work-Study, institutionally sponsored loans, scholarships/grants, and tuition waivers (partial) available. Support available to part-time students. *Faculty research:* Teachers in the process of change, learning cycles, children's concepts of science. *Total annual research expenditures:* $614,458. *Unit head:* Dr. Chris Leland, Interim Executive Associate Dean, 317-274-6801, Fax: 317-274-6864. *Application contact:* Sarah Brandenburg, Graduate Advisor, 317-274-6801, Fax: 317-274-6864, E-mail: edugrad@iupui.edu. Web site: http://education.iupui.edu/.

Inter American University of Puerto Rico, Arecibo Campus, Programs in Education, Arecibo, PR 00614-4050. Offers administration and educational supervision (MA Ed); counseling and guidance (MA Ed); curriculum and teaching (MA Ed), including biology education, English as a second language, history education, math education, Spanish; elementary education (MA Ed). *Degree requirements:* For master's, comprehensive exam, thesis optional. *Entrance requirements:* For master's, GRE, EXADEP, bachelor's degree in education or teaching license (administration and supervision) or courses in education and psychology (counseling and guidance), minimum GPA of 2.5 in last 60 credits.

Inter American University of Puerto Rico, Barranquitas Campus, Program in Education, Barranquitas, PR 00794. Offers curriculum and teaching (M Ed), including biology education, English as a second language, history education, mathematics education, Spanish; educational leadership and management (MA); elementary education (M Ed); information and library service technology (M Ed); special education (MA). *Degree requirements:* For master's, comprehensive exam, thesis optional. *Entrance requirements:* For master's, EXADEP, letter of recommendation. Electronic applications accepted.

Inter American University of Puerto Rico, Metropolitan Campus, Graduate Programs, Program in Education, San Juan, PR 00919-1293. Offers curriculum and instruction (Ed D); educational administration (Ed D); guidance and counseling (MA, Ed D); special education administration (Ed D). *Degree requirements:* For doctorate, comprehensive exam, thesis/dissertation. *Entrance requirements:* For doctorate, GRE, MAT, or EXADEP. Electronic applications accepted.

Inter American University of Puerto Rico, San Germán Campus, Graduate Studies Center, Program in Curriculum and Instruction, San Germán, PR 00683-5008. Offers Ed D. *Expenses: Required fees:* $213 per semester. *Unit head:* Dr. Elba T. Irizarry, Director of Graduate Studies Center, 787-264-1912 Ext. 7357, Fax: 787-892-6350, E-mail: elbat@sg.inter.edu.

Iowa State University of Science and Technology, Department of Curriculum and Instruction, Ames, IA 50011. Offers curriculum and instructional technology (M Ed, MS, PhD); elementary education (M Ed, MS); historical, philosophical, and comparative studies in education (M Ed, MS); special education (M Ed, MS, PhD). *Degree requirements:* For master's, thesis or alternative; for doctorate, thesis/dissertation. *Entrance requirements:* For master's and doctorate, GRE General Test. Additional exam requirements/recommendations for international students: Required—TOEFL (minimum score 560 paper-based; 83 iBT), IELTS (minimum score 6.5). *Application deadline:* For fall admission, 1/1 priority date for domestic students, 1/1 for international students; for spring admission, 9/1 for domestic and international students. Application fee: $40 ($90 for international students). Electronic applications accepted. *Unit head:* Dr. Anne Foegen, Director of Graduate Education, 515-294-7021, Fax: 515-294-6206, E-mail: cigrad@iastate.edu. *Application contact:* Phyllis Kendall, Director of Graduate Education, 515-294-7021, Fax: 515-294-6206, E-mail: cigrad@iastate.edu. Web site: http://www.ci.hs.iastate.edu.

The Johns Hopkins University, School of Education, Department of Teacher Preparation, Baltimore, MD 21218. Offers early childhood education (MAT); education (MS), including educational studies; elementary education (MAT); English for speakers of other languages (MAT); K-8 mathematics lead-teacher (Certificate); K-8 science lead-teacher (Certificate); secondary education (MAT), including biology, chemistry, earth/space/environmental science, English, French, mathematics, physics, social studies, Spanish. Part-time and evening/weekend programs available. *Degree requirements:* For master's, portfolio, PRAXIS II, internship. *Entrance requirements:* For master's, PRAXIS I, SAT, ACT, or GRE (MAT), minimum undergraduate GPA of 3.0, interview, 1 letter of recommendation, curriculum vitae/resume; for Certificate, bachelor's degree, minimum undergraduate GPA of 3.0, essay/statement of goals, interview. Additional exam requirements/recommendations for international students: Required—TOEFL (minimum score 600 paper-based; 250 computer-based; 100 iBT). Electronic applications accepted. *Faculty research:* Teacher retention, STEM education reform, alternative certification programs, school-university partnerships, urban education, action research/data-informed instruction, family engagement.

Johnson State College, Graduate Program in Education, Program in Curriculum and Instruction, Johnson, VT 05656. Offers MA Ed. Part-time programs available. *Degree requirements:* For master's, comprehensive exam, thesis or alternative, field-based experience. *Entrance requirements:* For master's, interview. Additional exam requirements/recommendations for international students: Required—TOEFL. *Application deadline:* For fall admission, 7/15 priority date for domestic students, 4/15 for international students; for spring admission, 11/1 priority date for domestic students, 8/15 for international students. Applications are processed on a rolling basis. Application fee: $35. *Expenses: Tuition, area resident:* Part-time $459 per credit hour. Tuition, nonresident: part-time $990 per credit hour. *Financial support:* Career-related internships or fieldwork, Federal Work-Study, and institutionally sponsored loans available. Support available to part-time students. Financial award application deadline: 3/1; financial award applicants required to submit FAFSA. *Unit head:* Dr. Darlene Witte-Townsend, Program Coordinator, 802-635-1322, E-mail: darlene.witte@jsc.edu. *Application contact:* Catherine H. Higley, Administrative Assistant, 800-635-2356 Ext. 1244, Fax: 802-635-1248, E-mail: catherine.higley@jsc.edu.

Jones International University, School of Education, Centennial, CO 80112. Offers adult education (M Ed); corporate training and knowledge management (M Ed); curriculum and instruction (M Ed), including elementary teacher licensure, secondary teacher licensure; e-learning technology and design (M Ed); educational leadership and administration (M Ed); educational leadership and administration: principal and administrator licensure (M Ed); elementary curriculum instruction and assessment (M Ed); higher education leadership and administration (M Ed); K-12 instructional technology (M Ed); K-12 instructional technology: teacher licensure (M Ed); secondary curriculum instruction and assessment (M Ed); technology and design (M Ed). Part-time and evening/weekend programs available. Postbaccalaureate distance learning degree programs offered (no on-campus study). *Entrance requirements:* For master's, minimum cumulative GPA of 2.5. Additional exam requirements/recommendations for international students: Recommended—TOEFL (minimum score 550 paper-based; 213 computer-based). Electronic applications accepted.

Kansas State University, Graduate School, College of Education, Department of Curriculum and Instruction, Manhattan, KS 66506. Offers career and technical education (Ed D, PhD); curriculum studies (Ed D, PhD); digital teaching and learning (MS); educational computing, design and online learning (MS); educational technology (Ed D, PhD); elementary/middle level (MS); English as a second language (MS); language/diversity education (Ed D, PhD); literacy education (Ed D, PhD); mathematics education (Ed D, PhD); middle level/secondary (MS); reading and language arts (MS); reading specialist endorsement (MS); science education (Ed D, PhD); social science education (Ed D, PhD); teacher education (Ed D, PhD); teacher leader/school improvement (MS, Ed D). *Accreditation:* NCATE. Part-time programs available. Postbaccalaureate distance learning degree programs offered (minimal on-campus study). *Faculty:* 15 full-time (12 women), 3 part-time/adjunct (2 women). *Students:* 37 full-time (30 women), 113 part-time (91 women); includes 14 minority (4 Black or African American, non-Hispanic/Latino; 1 American Indian or Alaska Native, non-Hispanic/Latino; 1 Asian, non-Hispanic/Latino; 7 Hispanic/Latino; 1 Two or more races, non-Hispanic/Latino), 15 international. Average age 37. 75 applicants, 51% accepted, 9 enrolled. In 2011, 48 master's, 14 doctorates awarded. *Degree requirements:* For master's, comprehensive exam, portfolio, project, report or thesis; for doctorate, comprehensive exam, thesis/dissertation, preliminary exam. *Entrance requirements:* For master's, minimum GPA of 3.0; for doctorate, GRE, minimum GPA of 3.0. Additional exam requirements/recommendations for international students: Required—TOEFL. *Application deadline:* For fall admission, 2/1 priority date for domestic students, 2/1 for international students; for spring admission, 8/1 priority date for domestic students, 8/1 for international students. Applications are processed on a rolling basis. Application fee: $40 ($55 for international students). Electronic applications accepted. *Financial support:* In 2011–12, 1 research assistantship (averaging $16,900 per year), 8 teaching assistantships (averaging $12,466 per year) were awarded; career-related internships or fieldwork, institutionally sponsored loans, and scholarships/grants also available. Support available to part-time students. Financial award application deadline: 3/1; financial award applicants required to submit FAFSA. *Faculty research:* Literacy and technology, critical race theory and diversity, achievement gaps, school improvement, teacher education. *Total annual research expenditures:* $510,907. *Unit head:* Dr. Gail Shroyer, Chair, 785-532-5550, Fax: 785-532-7304, E-mail: gshroyer@ksu.edu. *Application contact:* Dona Deam, Application Contact, 785-532-5595, Fax: 785-532-7304, E-mail: ddeam@ksu.edu. Web site: http://coe.k-state.edu/departments/currin/curringrad.htm.

Kean University, College of Education, Program in Early Childhood Education, Union, NJ 07083. Offers administration in early childhood and family studies (MA); advanced curriculum and teaching (MA); classroom instruction (MA), including preschool-third grade; education for family living (MA). *Accreditation:* NCATE. *Faculty:* 22 full-time (12 women). *Students:* 9 full-time (all women), 40 part-time (38 women); includes 15 minority (7 Black or African American, non-Hispanic/Latino; 1 American Indian or Alaska Native, non-Hispanic/Latino; 2 Asian, non-Hispanic/Latino; 5 Hispanic/Latino), 2 international. Average age 33. 26 applicants, 100% accepted, 19 enrolled. In 2011, 12 master's awarded. *Degree requirements:* For master's, portfolio. *Entrance requirements:* For master's, GRE General Test, minimum GPA of 3.0, 2 letters of recommendation, interview, teacher certification (for some programs), writing sample, official transcripts, resume. Additional exam requirements/recommendations for international students: Required—TOEFL (minimum score 79 iBT). *Application deadline:* For fall admission, 6/1 for domestic and international students; for spring admission, 12/1 for domestic and international students. Applications are processed on a rolling basis. Application fee: $75 ($150 for international students). Electronic applications accepted. *Expenses:* Tuition, state resident: full-time $11,302; part-time $550 per credit. Tuition, nonresident: full-time $15,318; part-time $674 per credit. *Required fees:* $2849; $130 per credit. Tuition and fees vary according to degree level. *Financial support:* In 2011–12, 1 research assistantship with full tuition reimbursement (averaging $3,263 per year) was awarded; unspecified assistantships also available. Financial award applicants required to submit FAFSA. *Unit head:* Dr. Jennifer Chen, Program Coordinator, 908-737-3809, E-mail: jchen@kean.edu. *Application contact:* Ann-Marie Kay, Assistant Director of Graduate Admissions, 908-737-5922, Fax: 908-737-5925, E-mail: akay@kean.edu. Web site: http://www.kean.edu/KU/Administration-in-Early-Childhood-Family-Studies.

Kean University, College of Education, Program in Instruction and Curriculum, Union, NJ 07083. Offers bilingual (MA); classroom instruction (MA); mathematics/science/computer education (MA); teaching (MA); teaching English as a second language (MA); teaching physics (MA); world languages (Spanish) (MA). *Accreditation:* NCATE. *Faculty:* 22 full-time (12 women). *Students:* 56 full-time (33 women), 139 part-time (103 women); includes 87 minority (27 Black or African American, non-Hispanic/Latino; 8 Asian, non-Hispanic/Latino; 52 Hispanic/Latino), 1 international. Average age 34. 85 applicants, 100% accepted, 72 enrolled. In 2011, 78 master's awarded. *Degree requirements:* For master's, comprehensive exam, two-semester advanced seminar. *Entrance requirements:* For master's, GRE General Test or MAT, PRAXIS, minimum GPA of 3.0, 2 letters of recommendation, interview, teacher certification (for some programs), transcripts, resume. Additional exam requirements/recommendations for international students: Required—TOEFL (minimum score 79 iBT). *Application deadline:* For fall admission, 6/1 for domestic and international students; for spring admission, 12/1 for domestic and international students. Applications are processed on a rolling basis. Application fee: $75 ($150 for international students). Electronic applications accepted. *Expenses:* Tuition, state resident: full-time $11,302; part-time $550 per credit. Tuition, nonresident: full-time $15,318; part-time $674 per credit. *Required fees:* $2849; $130 per credit. Tuition and fees vary according to degree level. *Financial support:* In 2011–12, 3 research assistantships with full tuition reimbursements (averaging $3,263 per year) were awarded; unspecified assistantships also available. Financial award applicants required to submit FAFSA. *Unit head:* Dr. Thomas Walsh, Program Coordinator, 908-737-4003, E-mail: tpwalsh@kean.edu. *Application contact:* Ann-Marie Kay, Assistant Director for Graduate Admissions, 908-737-5922, Fax: 908-737-5925, E-mail: akay@kean.edu. Web site: http://www.kean.edu/KU/Bilingual-Bicultural-Education-Instruction-and-Curriculum.

Keene State College, School of Professional and Graduate Studies, Keene, NH 03435. Offers curriculum and instruction (M Ed); education leadership (PMC); educational leadership (M Ed); safety and occupational health applied science (MS); school counselor (M Ed, PMC); special education (M Ed); teacher certification (Postbaccalaureate Certificate). *Accreditation:* NCATE. Part-time and evening/weekend programs available. *Faculty:* 11 full-time (7 women), 15 part-time/adjunct (8 women). *Students:* 36 full-time (32 women), 69 part-time (54 women); includes 1 minority (American Indian or Alaska Native, non-Hispanic/Latino), 1 international. Average age 33. 48 applicants, 83% accepted, 32 enrolled. In 2011, 39 master's, 12 other advanced degrees awarded. *Entrance requirements:* For master's, PRAXIS I, resume; minimum GPA of 2.5. Additional exam requirements/recommendations for international students: Required—TOEFL (minimum score 550 paper-based; 173 computer-based; 61 iBT). *Application deadline:* For fall admission, 4/1 for domestic students; for spring admission, 12/1 for domestic students. Applications are processed on a rolling basis. Application fee: $50. Electronic applications accepted. *Expenses:* Tuition, state resident: part-time $420 per credit. Tuition, nonresident: part-time $460 per credit. Tuition and fees vary according to course load. *Financial support:* Research assistantships, career-related internships or fieldwork, Federal Work-Study, institutionally sponsored loans, and unspecified assistantships available. Support available to part-time students. Financial award application deadline: 3/1; financial award applicants required to submit FAFSA. *Unit head:* Dr. Melinda Treadwell, Dean, 603-358-2220, E-mail: mtreadwe@keene.edu. *Application contact:* Peggy Richmond, Director of Admissions, 603-358-2276, Fax: 603-358-2767, E-mail: admissions@keene.edu. Web site: http://www.keene.edu/ps/.

Kent State University, Graduate School of Education, Health, and Human Services, School of Teaching, Learning and Curriculum Studies, Program in Curriculum and Instruction, Kent, OH 44242-0001. Offers M Ed, PhD, Ed S. *Accreditation:* NCATE. Part-time and evening/weekend programs available. *Faculty:* 25 full-time (16 women), 6 part-time/adjunct (5 women). *Students:* 95 full-time (68 women), 62 part-time (46 women); includes 12 minority (5 Black or African American, non-Hispanic/Latino; 6 Asian, non-Hispanic/Latino; 1 Hispanic/Latino). 52 applicants, 50% accepted. In 2011, 30 master's, 12 doctorates, 2 other advanced degrees awarded. *Degree requirements:* For doctorate, comprehensive exam, thesis/dissertation. *Entrance requirements:* For master's, 2 letters of reference, goals statement; for doctorate, GRE General Test, 2 letters of reference, goals statement, writing sample, resume; for Ed S, GRE General Test, 2 letters of reference, goals statement. Additional exam requirements/recommendations for international students: Required—TOEFL (minimum score 550 paper-based; 213 computer-based; 80 iBT). *Application deadline:* Applications are processed on a rolling basis. Application fee: $30 ($60 for international students). Electronic applications accepted. *Expenses:* Tuition, state resident: full-time $8136; part-time $452 per credit hour. Tuition, nonresident: full-time $14,292; part-time $794 per credit hour. *Financial support:* In 2011–12, 9 fellowships with full tuition reimbursements (averaging $13,500 per year), research assistantships with full tuition reimbursements (averaging $12,706 per year) were awarded; teaching assistantships with full tuition reimbursements,

Federal Work-Study, scholarships/grants, unspecified assistantships, and 2 administrative assistantships (averaging $13,500 per year) also available. Financial award application deadline: 4/1; financial award applicants required to submit FAFSA. *Faculty research:* Gender equity issues in teaching, learning math and science, teaching as inquiry artistry, curriculum studies for democratic humanism. *Unit head:* Dr. James Henderson, Coordinator, 330-672-0631, E-mail: jhenders@kent.edu. *Application contact:* Nancy Miller, Academic Program Coordinator, Office of Graduate Student Services, 330-672-2576, Fax: 330-672-9162, E-mail: ogs@kent.edu.

Kent State University at Stark, Graduate School of Education, Health and Human Services, Canton, OH 44720-7599. Offers curriculum and instruction studies (M Ed, MA).

Kutztown University of Pennsylvania, College of Education, Program in Secondary Education, Kutztown, PA 19530-0730. Offers biology (M Ed); curriculum and instruction (M Ed); English (M Ed); mathematics (M Ed); social studies (M Ed). *Accreditation:* NCATE. Part-time and evening/weekend programs available. *Faculty:* 7 full-time (2 women). *Students:* 29 full-time (12 women), 73 part-time (43 women); includes 3 minority (1 Black or African American, non-Hispanic/Latino; 1 Asian, non-Hispanic/Latino; 1 Hispanic/Latino). Average age 28. 12 applicants, 100% accepted, 12 enrolled. In 2011, 29 master's awarded. *Degree requirements:* For master's, comprehensive exam, thesis optional. *Entrance requirements:* For master's, GRE General Test. Additional exam requirements/recommendations for international students: Required—TOEFL (minimum score 550 paper-based; 79 iBT). *Application deadline:* For fall admission, 8/1 priority date for domestic students, 8/1 for international students; for spring admission, 12/1 priority date for domestic students, 12/1 for international students. Applications are processed on a rolling basis. Application fee: $35. Electronic applications accepted. *Expenses:* Tuition, state resident: full-time $7488; part-time $416 per credit. Tuition, nonresident: full-time $11,232; part-time $624 per credit. *Financial support:* Career-related internships or fieldwork, Federal Work-Study, scholarships/grants, and unspecified assistantships available. Financial award application deadline: 3/1; financial award applicants required to submit FAFSA. *Unit head:* Dr. Theresa Stahler, Chairperson, 610-683-4259, Fax: 610-683-1338, E-mail: stahler@kutztown.edu. *Application contact:* Kelly D. Burr, Associate Director, Graduate Admissions, 610-683-4200, Fax: 610-683-1393, E-mail: graduate@kutztown.edu.

LaGrange College, Graduate Programs, Department of Education, LaGrange, GA 30240-2999. Offers curriculum and instruction (M Ed, Ed S); middle grades (MAT); secondary education (MAT). Part-time and evening/weekend programs available. *Degree requirements:* For master's, comprehensive exam. *Entrance requirements:* For master's, GRE, MAT, minimum GPA of 2.5. Additional exam requirements/recommendations for international students: Required—TOEFL (minimum score 550 paper-based).

Lake Erie College, School of Professional and Innovative Studies, Painesville, OH 44077-3389. Offers curriculum and instruction (MS Ed); education (MS Ed); educational leadership (MS Ed); reading (MS Ed). Part-time and evening/weekend programs available. *Faculty:* 3 full-time (all women), 1 part-time/adjunct (0 women). *Students:* 20 part-time (15 women); includes 14 minority (all American Indian or Alaska Native, non-Hispanic/Latino). Average age 35. 5 applicants, 100% accepted, 1 enrolled. In 2011, 7 master's awarded. *Degree requirements:* For master's, comprehensive exam (for some programs), thesis optional, applied research project. *Entrance requirements:* For master's, GRE General Test (minimum score of 440 verbal or 500 quantitative) or minimum GPA of 2.75; bachelor's degree from accredited 4-year institution; references; essay. Additional exam requirements/recommendations for international students: Required—TOEFL (minimum score 550 paper-based; 79 computer-based). *Application deadline:* For fall admission, 8/1 priority date for domestic students, 6/1 for international students; for spring admission, 12/15 for domestic students, 10/1 for international students. Applications are processed on a rolling basis. Application fee: $30. Electronic applications accepted. Application fee is waived when completed online. *Expenses:* Contact institution. *Financial support:* Teaching assistantships, tuition waivers, and unspecified assistantships available. Financial award applicants required to submit FAFSA. *Faculty research:* Cooperative learning, portfolio assessment, education systems abroad, Web-based instruction. *Unit head:* Prof. Dale Sheptak, Interim Dean of the School of Professional and Innovative Studies/Assistant Professor, 440-375-7131, E-mail: dsheptak@lec.edu. *Application contact:* Christopher Harris, Dean of Admissions and Financial Aid, 800-916-0904, Fax: 440-375-7000, E-mail: admissions@lec.edu. Web site: http://www.lec.edu/med.

Lander University, School of Education, Greenwood, SC 29649-2099. Offers elementary education (M Ed); teaching (MAT). *Accreditation:* NCATE. Part-time programs available. *Degree requirements:* For master's, comprehensive exam, thesis or alternative. *Entrance requirements:* For master's, GRE General Test. Additional exam requirements/recommendations for international students: Required—TOEFL (minimum score 550 paper-based; 213 computer-based). Electronic applications accepted.

La Sierra University, School of Education, Department of Curriculum and Instruction, Riverside, CA 92515. Offers curriculum and instruction (MA, Ed D, Ed S); teaching (MAT). Part-time and evening/weekend programs available. *Degree requirements:* For doctorate, thesis/dissertation; for Ed S, thesis optional. *Entrance requirements:* For master's, minimum GPA of 3.0; for doctorate, GRE General Test, GRE Subject Test, minimum GPA of 3.3; for Ed S, minimum GPA of 3.3. *Faculty research:* New teacher success, politics of knowledge, computer-assisted instruction, diversity issues.

Lehigh University, College of Education, Program in Educational Leadership, Bethlehem, PA 18015. Offers educational leadership (M Ed, Ed D); principal certification K-12 (Certificate); pupil services (Certificate); special education (Certificate); superintendant certification (Certificate); supervisor of curriculum and instruction (Certificate); supervisor of pupil services (Certificate); MBA/M Ed. Part-time and evening/weekend programs available. Postbaccalaureate distance learning degree programs offered (minimal on-campus study). *Faculty:* 7 full-time (2 women), 8 part-time/adjunct (6 women). *Students:* 4 full-time (all women), 149 part-time (68 women); includes 6 minority (2 Black or African American, non-Hispanic/Latino; 2 Asian, non-Hispanic/Latino; 2 Hispanic/Latino), 19 international. Average age 38. 61 applicants, 52% accepted, 4 enrolled. In 2011, 36 master's, 5 doctorates awarded. *Degree requirements:* For doctorate, comprehensive exam, thesis/dissertation. *Entrance requirements:* For master's and Certificate, minimum undergraduate GPA of 3.0; for doctorate, GRE General Test or MAT, minimum graduate GPA of 3.6, 2 letters of recommendation, essay, transcript. Additional exam requirements/recommendations for international students: Required—TOEFL (minimum score 600 paper-based; 250 computer-based; 93 iBT). *Application deadline:* For fall admission, 1/15 for domestic and international students; for spring admission, 11/1 for domestic and international students. Applications are processed on a rolling basis. Application fee: $65. Electronic applications accepted. *Expenses:* Contact institution. *Financial support:* In 2011–12, 1 student received support, including 1 research assistantship with full and partial tuition reimbursement available (averaging $13,000 per year); fellowships with full and partial tuition reimbursements available, teaching assistantships with full and partial tuition reimbursements available, career-related internships or fieldwork, Federal Work-Study, institutionally sponsored loans, scholarships/grants, and tuition waivers (full and partial) also available. Financial award application deadline: 1/31. *Faculty research:* School finance and law, supervision of instruction, middle-level education, organizational change, leadership preparation and development, international school leadership, urban school leadership. *Unit head:* Dr. Floyd D. Beachum, Director, 610-758-5955, Fax: 610-758-3227, E-mail: fdb209@lehigh.edu. *Application contact:* Donna M. Johnson, Coordinator, 610-758-3231, Fax: 610-758-6223, E-mail: dmj4@lehigh.edu.

Lesley University, School of Education, Cambridge, MA 02138-2790. Offers curriculum and instruction (M Ed, CAGS); early childhood education (M Ed); educational studies (PhD); elementary education (M Ed); individually designed (M Ed); middle school education (M Ed); moderate special needs (M Ed); reading (M Ed, CAGS); science in education (M Ed); severe special needs (M Ed); special needs (CAGS); technology in education (M Ed, CAGS). *Accreditation:* Teacher Education Accreditation Council. Part-time and evening/weekend programs available. Postbaccalaureate distance learning degree programs offered (no on-campus study). *Faculty:* 36 full-time (27 women), 170 part-time/adjunct (129 women). *Students:* 552 full-time (437 women), 1,971 part-time (1,697 women); includes 364 minority (189 Black or African American, non-Hispanic/Latino; 19 American Indian or Alaska Native, non-Hispanic/Latino; 45 Asian, non-Hispanic/Latino; 83 Hispanic/Latino; 2 Native Hawaiian or other Pacific Islander, non-Hispanic/Latino; 26 Two or more races, non-Hispanic/Latino), 28 international. Average age 37. In 2011, 1,390 master's, 8 doctorates, 42 other advanced degrees awarded. *Degree requirements:* For master's, practicum; for doctorate, thesis/dissertation. *Entrance requirements:* For doctorate, GRE General Test or MAT, interview, master's degree, resume; for CAGS, interview, master's degree. Additional exam requirements/recommendations for international students: Required—TOEFL (minimum score 550 paper-based; 213 computer-based; 80 iBT). *Application deadline:* Applications are processed on a rolling basis. Application fee: $50. Electronic applications accepted. *Financial support:* In 2011–12, research assistantships (averaging $3,400 per year), teaching assistantships (averaging $3,400 per year) were awarded; career-related internships or fieldwork, Federal Work-Study, scholarships/grants, and unspecified assistantships also available. Support available to part-time students. Financial award application deadline: 4/15; financial award applicants required to submit FAFSA. *Faculty research:* Assessment in literacy, mathematics and science; autism spectrum disorders; instructional technology and online learning; multicultural education and ELL. *Unit head:* Dr. Mario Borunda, Dean, 617-349-8375, Fax: 617-349-8607, E-mail: mborunda@lesley.edu. *Application contact:* Rosie Davis, Senior Assistant Director of Admissions, 617-349-8851, Fax: 617-349-8313, E-mail: rdavis4@lesley.edu. Web site: http://www.lesley.edu/soe.html.

Lewis & Clark College, Graduate School of Education and Counseling, Department of Teacher Education, Program in Curriculum and Instruction, Portland, OR 97219-7899. Offers M Ed. Part-time and evening/weekend programs available. *Faculty:* 2 full-time (both women), 9 part-time/adjunct (8 women). *Students:* 7 full-time (all women), 22 part-time (19 women); includes 5 minority (all Hispanic/Latino), 1 international. Average age 34. 12 applicants, 92% accepted, 6 enrolled. In 2011, 10 master's awarded. *Entrance requirements:* For master's, minimum GPA of 2.75. Additional exam requirements/recommendations for international students: Required—TOEFL (minimum score 575 paper-based; 233 computer-based). *Application deadline:* Applications are processed on a rolling basis. Application fee: $50. Electronic applications accepted. *Expenses: Tuition:* Part-time $738 per semester hour. Tuition and fees vary according to course level and campus/location. *Financial support:* In 2011–12, 4 students received support. Career-related internships or fieldwork, Federal Work-Study, institutionally sponsored loans, scholarships/grants, health care benefits, and tuition waivers (partial) available. Support available to part-time students. Financial award application deadline: 3/1; financial award applicants required to submit FAFSA. *Unit head:* Dr. Vern Jones, Chair, 503-768-6100, Fax: 503-768-6115, E-mail: lcteach@lclark.edu. *Application contact:* Becky Haas, Director of Admissions, 503-768-6200, Fax: 503-768-6205, E-mail: gseadmit@lclark.edu. Web site: http://www.lclark.edu/graduate/departments/teacher_education/current_teachers/master_of_education/.

Liberty University, School of Education, Lynchburg, VA 24502. Offers administration and supervision (M Ed); curriculum and instruction (M Ed); early childhood education (M Ed); educational leadership (Ed D, Ed S); educational technology and online instruction (M Ed); elementary education (M Ed, MAT); gifted education (M Ed); math specialist (M Ed); middle grades (M Ed); outdoor adventure sport (MS); reading specialist (M Ed); school counseling (M Ed); secondary education (M Ed, MAT); special education (M Ed, MAT); sports administration (MS); teaching and learning (Ed D, Ed S). *Accreditation:* NCATE. Part-time programs available. Postbaccalaureate distance learning degree programs offered (minimal on-campus study). *Students:* 2,245 full-time (1,572 women), 3,500 part-time (2,558 women); includes 1,141 minority (888 Black or African American, non-Hispanic/Latino; 19 American Indian or Alaska Native, non-Hispanic/Latino; 21 Asian, non-Hispanic/Latino; 123 Hispanic/Latino; 9 Native Hawaiian or other Pacific Islander, non-Hispanic/Latino; 81 Two or more races, non-Hispanic/Latino), 76 international. Average age 37. In 2011, 760 master's, 48 doctorates, 321 other advanced degrees awarded. *Degree requirements:* For doctorate, comprehensive exam, thesis/dissertation. *Entrance requirements:* For master's, GRE General Test or MAT (if taken in or before 1999), 2 letters of recommendation, minimum undergraduate GPA of 3.0, curriculum vitae; for doctorate, GRE General Test or MAT (if taken before 1999), minimum master's GPA of 3.0, 3 years of teacher experience; for Ed S, GRE General Test or MAT (if taken before 1999), minimum master's GPA of 3.0, 3 years of teaching experience. Additional exam requirements/recommendations for international students: Required—TOEFL (minimum score 600 paper-based; 250 computer-based). *Application deadline:* For fall admission, 6/1 priority date for domestic students; for spring admission, 11/1 for domestic students. Applications are processed on a rolling basis. Application fee: $50. Electronic applications accepted. *Expenses:* Contact institution. *Financial support:* Federal Work-Study and tuition waivers (partial) available. *Faculty research:* Self-determination, character education, bibliotherapy, learning styles, distance education. *Unit head:* Dr. Karen L. Parker, Dean, 434-582-2195, Fax: 434-582-2468, E-mail: kparker@liberty.edu. *Application contact:* Jay Bridge, Director of Graduate Admissions, 800-424-9595, Fax: 800-628-7977, E-mail: gradadmissions@liberty.edu. Web site: http://www.liberty.edu/academics/education/graduate/.

Lincoln Memorial University, Carter and Moyers School of Education, Harrogate, TN 37752-1901. Offers administration and supervision (M Ed, Ed S); counseling and guidance (M Ed); curriculum and instruction (M Ed, Ed D, Ed S); English (M Ed); executive leadership (Ed D); higher education administration (Ed D); human resource development (Ed D); leadership and administration (Ed D). Part-time and evening/weekend programs available. Postbaccalaureate distance learning degree programs offered. *Degree requirements:* For master's, comprehensive exam, thesis optional; for Ed S, comprehensive exam. *Entrance requirements:* For master's, PRAXIS, NTE, GRE, MAT, letters of recommendation; for Ed S, graduate transcripts. Additional exam requirements/recommendations for international students: Recommended—TOEFL. *Faculty research:* Brain compatible teaching and learning; poverty in Appalachia; leadership for change; ethics, moral responsibility and social justice; human and organizational learning.

Louisiana State University in Shreveport, College of Business, Education, and Human Development, Program in Education, Shreveport, LA 71115-2399. Offers education curriculum and instruction (M Ed); educational leadership (M Ed); school counseling (M Ed). Part-time programs available. *Students:* 6 full-time (all women), 55 part-time (40 women); includes 14 minority (12 Black or African American, non-Hispanic/Latino; 1 Asian, non-Hispanic/Latino; 1 Hispanic/Latino). Average age 35. 34 applicants, 97% accepted, 13 enrolled. In 2011, 14 master's awarded. *Degree requirements:* For master's, orally-presented project, 200-hour internship (educational leadership). *Entrance requirements:* For master's, GRE, minimum GPA of 2.5; teacher certification; recommendations and interview (for educational leadership). Additional exam requirements/recommendations for international students: Required—TOEFL (minimum score 550 paper-based; 213 computer-based; 80 iBT). *Application deadline:* For fall admission, 6/30 for domestic and international students; for spring admission, 11/30 for domestic and international students. Applications are processed on a rolling basis. Application fee: $10 ($20 for international students). *Financial support:* In 2011–12, 5 research assistantships (averaging $2,150 per year) were awarded. *Unit head:* Dr. Julie Bergeron, Coordinator, 318-797-5033, Fax: 318-798-4144, E-mail: julie.bergeron@lsus.edu. *Application contact:* Christianne Wojcik, Director of Academic Services, 318-797-5247, Fax: 318-798-4120, E-mail: christianne.wojcik@lsus.edu.

Louisiana Tech University, Graduate School, College of Education, Department of Curriculum, Instruction and Leadership, Ruston, LA 71272. Offers curriculum and instruction (MS, Ed D); educational leadership (Ed D); secondary education (M Ed), including business education, English education, foreign language education, health and physical education, mathematics education, science education, social studies education, speech education. *Accreditation:* NCATE. Part-time programs available. *Degree requirements:* For doctorate, thesis/dissertation. *Entrance requirements:* For master's and doctorate, GRE General Test.

Loyola University Chicago, School of Education, Program in Curriculum and Instruction, Chicago, IL 60660. Offers M Ed, Ed D. Part-time and evening/weekend programs available. *Faculty:* 4 full-time (3 women), 2 part-time/adjunct (1 woman). *Students:* 77. Average age 35. 31 applicants, 48% accepted, 11 enrolled. In 2011, 8 master's, 17 doctorates awarded. Terminal master's awarded for partial completion of doctoral program. *Degree requirements:* For master's, comprehensive exam; for doctorate, comprehensive exam, thesis/dissertation. *Entrance requirements:* For master's, 3 references, minimum GPA of 3.0, resume; for doctorate, GRE, 3 references, interview, minimum GPA of 3.0, resume. Additional exam requirements/recommendations for international students: Required—TOEFL (minimum score 550 paper-based; 213 computer-based; 79 iBT). *Application deadline:* For fall admission, 2/15 for domestic and international students; for spring admission, 11/1 for domestic and international students. Applications are processed on a rolling basis. Application fee: $50. Electronic applications accepted. Application fee is waived when completed online. *Expenses: Tuition:* Full-time $15,660; part-time $870 per credit hour. *Required fees:* $125 per semester. Tuition and fees vary according to course load and program. *Financial support:* In 2011–12, 10 fellowships with full tuition reimbursements (averaging $5,000 per year), 6 research assistantships with full tuition reimbursements (averaging $12,000 per year) were awarded; institutionally sponsored loans, scholarships/grants, tuition waivers (partial), and unspecified assistantships also available. Support available to part-time students. Financial award application deadline: 2/1; financial award applicants required to submit FAFSA. *Faculty research:* School improvement, technology, change, reading. *Unit head:* Dr. Ann Marie Ryan, Director, 312-915-6232, E-mail: aryan3@luc.edu. *Application contact:* Marie Rosin-Dittmar, Information Contact, 312-915-6800, E-mail: schleduc@luc.edu.

Loyola University Maryland, Graduate Programs, Department of Education, Program in Curriculum and Instruction, Baltimore, MD 21210-2699. Offers M Ed, MA, CAS. Part-time programs available. *Faculty:* 57 full-time (32 women), 21 part-time/adjunct (10 women). *Students:* 3 full-time (1 woman), 63 part-time (57 women); includes 12 minority (7 Black or African American, non-Hispanic/Latino; 3 Hispanic/Latino; 2 Two or more races, non-Hispanic/Latino). Average age 31. In 2011, 26 master's awarded. *Degree requirements:* For master's, thesis. *Entrance requirements:* Additional exam requirements/recommendations for international students: Required—TOEFL (minimum score 550 paper-based; 213 computer-based). *Application deadline:* For fall admission, 6/15 priority date for domestic students; for spring admission, 11/1 priority date for domestic students. Application fee: $50. Electronic applications accepted. *Financial support:* Research assistantships and unspecified assistantships available. Financial award application deadline: 4/15; financial award applicants required to submit FAFSA. *Unit head:* Stephanie Flores-Koulish, Director, 410-617-5456, E-mail: sfloreskoulish@loyola.edu. *Application contact:* Maureen Faux, Executive Director, Graduate Admissions, 410-617-5020, Fax: 410-617-2002, E-mail: graduate@loyola.edu.

Lynchburg College, Graduate Studies, School of Education and Human Development, M Ed Program in Curriculum and Instruction, Lynchburg, VA 24501-3199. Offers instructional leadership (M Ed); teacher licensure (M Ed). Part-time and evening/weekend programs available. *Faculty:* 7 full-time (4 women), 3 part-time/adjunct (1 woman). *Students:* 4 full-time (3 women), 13 part-time (11 women); includes 2 minority (1 Black or African American, non-Hispanic/Latino; 1 Asian, non-Hispanic/Latino). Average age 30. In 2011, 5 master's awarded. *Degree requirements:* For master's, National Board Certification portfolio or comprehensive exam. *Entrance requirements:* For master's, GRE, minimum GPA of 3.0 (preferred), official transcripts (bachelor's, others as relevant), three letters of recommendation, career goals statement. Additional exam requirements/recommendations for international students: Required—TOEFL (minimum score 550 paper-based; 213 computer-based; 79 iBT), IELTS (minimum score 6.5). *Application deadline:* For fall admission, 7/31 for domestic students, 6/1 for international students; for spring admission, 11/30 for domestic students, 10/15 for international students. Applications are processed on a rolling basis. Application fee: $30. Electronic applications accepted. Application fee is waived when completed online. *Expenses: Tuition:* Full-time $7740; part-time $430 per credit hour. *Financial support:* Fellowships, research assistantships, Federal Work-Study, scholarships/grants, health care benefits, and unspecified assistantships available. Support available to part-time students. Financial award application deadline: 7/31; financial award applicants required to submit FAFSA. *Unit head:* Dr. John Walker, Associate Professor/Program Director, Curriculum and Instruction, 434-544-8032, Fax: 434-544-8483, E-mail: walker.jc@lynchburg.edu. *Application contact:* Anne Pingstock, Executive Assistant, Graduate Studies, 434-544-8383, Fax: 434-544-8483, E-mail: gradstudies@lynchburg.edu. Web site: http://www.lynchburg.edu/teachingandlearning.xml.

Lyndon State College, Graduate Programs in Education, Department of Education, Lyndonville, VT 05851-0919. Offers curriculum and instruction (M Ed); reading specialist (M Ed); special education (M Ed); teaching and counseling (M Ed). Part-time and evening/weekend programs available. *Degree requirements:* For master's, exam or major field project. *Entrance requirements:* Additional exam requirements/recommendations for international students: Recommended—TOEFL (minimum score 500 paper-based; 173 computer-based).

Malone University, Graduate Program in Education, Canton, OH 44709. Offers curriculum and instruction (MA), including teacher leader endorsement; curriculum, instruction, and professional development (MA); educational leadership (MA), including principal license; intervention specialist (MA); reading (MA). Part-time and evening/weekend programs available. *Faculty:* 9 full-time (5 women), 8 part-time/adjunct (6 women). *Students:* 2 full-time (both women), 43 part-time (33 women); includes 2 minority (both Black or African American, non-Hispanic/Latino). Average age 36. 35 applicants, 91% accepted, 12 enrolled. In 2011, 11 master's awarded. *Degree requirements:* For master's, research project. *Entrance requirements:* For master's, minimum GPA of 3.0, teaching license. Additional exam requirements/recommendations for international students: Required—TOEFL (minimum score 550 paper-based; 213 computer-based; 79 iBT). *Application deadline:* Applications are processed on a rolling basis. *Expenses: Tuition:* Part-time $625 per semester hour. Part-time tuition and fees vary according to program. *Financial support:* Tuition waivers (partial) available. Support available to part-time students. Financial award application deadline: 6/30. *Faculty research:* Educational leadership styles: Jesus as master teacher, assessment accommodations for English language learners, preparing culturally proficient teachers, using naturally occurring text in the classroom to meet the syntactic needs of students with learning disabilities, using iPad instructional technology to meet the needs of students with disabilities. *Unit head:* Dr. Alice E. Christie, Director, 330-478-8541, Fax: 330-471-8563, E-mail: achristie@malone.edu. *Application contact:* Dan DePasquale, Senior Recruiter, 330-471-8381, Fax: 330-471-8343, E-mail: depasquale@malone.edu. Web site: http://www.malone.edu/admissions/graduate/education/.

Marquette University, Graduate School, College of Education, Department of Educational Policy and Leadership, Milwaukee, WI 53201-1881. Offers college student personnel administration (M Ed); curriculum and instruction (MA); education (MA); educational administration (M Ed); educational policy and foundations (MA); elementary education (Certificate); literacy (MA); principal (Certificate); reading specialist (Certificate); reading teacher (Certificate); secondary education (Certificate); superintendent (Certificate). Part-time and evening/weekend programs available. *Faculty:* 14 full-time (9 women). *Students:* 40 full-time (34 women), 137 part-time (80 women); includes 25 minority (14 Black or African American, non-Hispanic/Latino; 1 American Indian or Alaska Native, non-Hispanic/Latino; 2 Asian, non-Hispanic/Latino; 8 Hispanic/Latino), 2 international. Average age 32. 132 applicants, 73% accepted, 67 enrolled. In 2011, 46 master's, 3 doctorates, 5 other advanced degrees awarded. Terminal master's awarded for partial completion of doctoral program. *Degree requirements:* For master's, comprehensive exam, thesis (for some programs); for doctorate, thesis/dissertation, qualifying exam, supporting minor. *Entrance requirements:* For master's, GRE General Test or MAT, official transcripts from all current and previous colleges/universities except Marquette, three letters of recommendation, statement of purpose; for doctorate, GRE General Test, MAT, sample of written work, official transcripts from all current and previous colleges/universities except Marquette, three letters of recommendation, statement of purpose, resume/curriculum vitae; for Certificate, GRE General Test or MAT, master's degree. Additional exam requirements/recommendations for international students: Required—TOEFL (minimum score 530 paper-based; 78 computer-based). *Application deadline:* For fall admission, 1/15 for domestic and international students. Application fee: $50. *Expenses:* Contact institution. *Financial support:* In 2011–12, 130 students received support, including 1 fellowship with full tuition reimbursement available (averaging $18,780 per year), 5 research assistantships with full tuition reimbursements available (averaging $13,404 per year); health care benefits, tuition waivers (partial), and unspecified assistantships also available. Support available to part-time students. Financial award application deadline: 2/15. *Faculty research:* Leadership; social justice in education; development of lifelong learners; race, class, and schooling in historical perspective; urban teacher education. *Unit head:* Dr. Ellen Eckman, Chair, 414-288-1561, E-mail: ellen.eckman@marquette.edu. *Application contact:* Craig Pierce, Assistant Dean of the Graduate School, 414-288-5740, Fax: 414-288-1902, E-mail: craig.pierce@marquette.edu.

Martin Luther College, Graduate Studies, New Ulm, MN 56073. Offers instruction (MS Ed); leadership (MS Ed); special education (MS Ed). Part-time programs available. Postbaccalaureate distance learning degree programs offered. *Degree requirements:* For master's, capstone project or comprehensive exam. *Entrance requirements:* For master's, undergraduate degree in education from an accredited college or university, minimum undergraduate GPA of 3.0. Electronic applications accepted.

Massachusetts College of Liberal Arts, Program in Education, North Adams, MA 01247-4100. Offers curriculum (M Ed); educational administration (M Ed); reading (M Ed); special education (M Ed). Part-time and evening/weekend programs available. *Degree requirements:* For master's, thesis. *Entrance requirements:* For master's, writing sample.

McDaniel College, Graduate and Professional Studies, Program in Curriculum and Instruction, Westminster, MD 21157-4390. Offers MS. *Degree requirements:* For master's, comprehensive exam (for some programs), thesis optional. *Entrance requirements:* For master's, letter of reference. Additional exam requirements/recommendations for international students: Required—TOEFL (minimum score 213 computer-based).

McGill University, Faculty of Graduate and Postdoctoral Studies, Faculty of Education, Department of Integrated Studies in Education, Montréal, QC H3A 2T5, Canada. Offers culture and values in education (MA, PhD); curriculum studies (MA); educational leadership (MA, Certificate); educational studies (PhD); integrated studies in education (M Ed); second language education (MA, PhD).

McNeese State University, Doré School of Graduate Studies, Burton College of Education, Department of Education Professions, Program in Curriculum and Instruction, Lake Charles, LA 70609. Offers early childhood education (M Ed); elementary education (M Ed); reading (M Ed); secondary education (M Ed). Evening/weekend programs available. *Faculty:* 10 full-time (5 women). *Students:* 8 full-time (7 women), 11 part-time (all women); includes 6 minority (all Black or African American, non-Hispanic/Latino), 1 international. In 2011, 6 master's awarded. *Entrance requirements:* For master's, GRE, teaching certificate. *Application deadline:* For fall admission, 5/15 priority date for domestic students, 5/15 for international students; for spring admission, 10/15 priority date for domestic students, 10/15 for international students. Applications are processed on a rolling basis. Application fee: $20 ($30 for international students). *Expenses:* Tuition, state resident: part-time $519 per credit hour. Tuition and fees vary according to course load. *Financial support:* Application deadline: 5/1. *Unit head:* Dr. Dustin M. Hebert, Director, 337-475-5424, Fax: 337-475-5272, E-mail: dhebert@mcneese.edu. *Application contact:* Dr. George F. Mead, Jr., Interim Dean of Dore' School of Graduate Studies, 337-475-5396, Fax: 337-475-5397, E-mail: admissions@mcneese.edu.

Medaille College, Program in Education, Buffalo, NY 14214-2695. Offers adolescent education (MS Ed); curriculum and instruction (MS Ed); education preparation (MS Ed); literacy (MS Ed); special education (MS). *Accreditation:* Teacher Education Accreditation Council. Part-time and evening/weekend programs available. *Faculty:* 15 full-time (11 women), 31 part-time/adjunct (21 women). *Students:* 371 full-time (281 women), 37 part-time (29 women); includes 75 minority (11 Black or African American, non-Hispanic/Latino; 6 Asian, non-Hispanic/Latino; 3 Hispanic/Latino; 55 Native Hawaiian or other Pacific Islander, non-Hispanic/Latino), 264 international. Average age 29. 354 applicants, 99% accepted, 163 enrolled. In 2011, 457 master's awarded. *Degree requirements:* For master's, comprehensive exam (for some programs), thesis or alternative. *Entrance requirements:* For master's, minimum undergraduate GPA of 2.7. Additional exam requirements/recommendations for international students:

Required—TOEFL (minimum score 550 paper-based; 213 computer-based). *Application deadline:* For fall admission, 8/15 priority date for domestic students; for spring admission, 1/15 priority date for domestic students. Applications are processed on a rolling basis. Application fee: $35. Electronic applications accepted. Tuition and fees vary according to program. *Financial support:* Federal Work-Study available. Financial award applicants required to submit FAFSA. *Faculty research:* Curriculum planning, truancy, tracking minority students, curriculum design, mentoring students. *Unit head:* Dr. Robert DiSibio, Director of Graduate Programs, 716-932-2548, Fax: 716-631-1380, E-mail: rdisibio@medaille.edu. *Application contact:* Jacqueline Matheny, Executive Director of Marketing and Enrollment, 716-932-2541, Fax: 716-632-1811, E-mail: jmatheny@medaille.edu. Web site: http://www.medaille.edu.

Memorial University of Newfoundland, School of Graduate Studies, Faculty of Education, St. John's, NL A1C 5S7, Canada. Offers counseling psychology (M Ed); curriculum, teaching, and learning studies (M Ed); education (PhD); educational leadership studies (M Ed); information technology (M Ed); post-secondary studies (M Ed, Diploma), including health professional education (Diploma). Part-time programs available. *Degree requirements:* For master's, thesis optional, internship, paper folio, project; for doctorate, comprehensive exam, thesis/dissertation, thesis seminar, oral defense of thesis. *Entrance requirements:* For master's, undergraduate degree with at least 2nd class standing, 1-2 years work experience; for doctorate, minimum A average in graduate course work, MA in education, 2 years professional experience; for Diploma, 2nd class degree, 2 years of work experience with adult learners, appropriate academic qualifications and work experience in a health-related field. Electronic applications accepted. *Faculty research:* Critical thinking, literacy, cognitive studies and counseling, educational change, technology in instruction.

Mercer University, Graduate Studies, Cecil B. Day Campus, Tift College of Education (Atlanta), Macon, GA 31207-0003. Offers curriculum and instruction (PhD); early childhood education (M Ed, MAT); educational leadership (PhD, Ed S); higher education leadership (M Ed); middle grades education (M Ed, MAT); reading education (M Ed); school counseling (Ed S); secondary education (M Ed, MAT); teacher leadership (Ed S). *Accreditation:* NCATE. Part-time and evening/weekend programs available. *Faculty:* 31 full-time (17 women), 6 part-time/adjunct (3 women). *Students:* 249 full-time (207 women), 413 part-time (326 women); includes 349 minority (322 Black or African American, non-Hispanic/Latino; 1 American Indian or Alaska Native, non-Hispanic/Latino; 18 Asian, non-Hispanic/Latino; 6 Hispanic/Latino; 2 Two or more races, non-Hispanic/Latino), 6 international. Average age 34. 204 applicants, 76% accepted, 125 enrolled. In 2011, 235 master's, 8 doctorates, 27 other advanced degrees awarded. *Degree requirements:* For master's and Ed S, research project; for doctorate, thesis/dissertation. *Entrance requirements:* For master's, GRE or MAT, minimum undergraduate GPA of 2.75; for doctorate, GRE; for Ed S, GRE or MAT, minimum GPA of 3.25, 3 years of teaching experience. Additional exam requirements/recommendations for international students: Required—TOEFL. *Application deadline:* For fall admission, 8/1 for domestic and international students; for spring admission, 12/1 for domestic and international students. Applications are processed on a rolling basis. Application fee: $25. *Expenses:* Contact institution. *Financial support:* Federal Work-Study available. Support available to part-time students. Financial award application deadline: 5/1. *Faculty research:* Educational technology, multicultural and minority issues in education, educational leadership (P-12 and higher education), school discipline and school bullying, standards-based mathematics education. *Unit head:* Dr. Carl R. Martray, Dean, 478-301-5397, Fax: 478-301-2280, E-mail: martray_cr@mercer.edu. *Application contact:* Dr. Allison Gilmore, Associate Dean for Graduate Teacher Education, 678-547-6333, Fax: 678-547-6055, E-mail: gilmore_a@mercer.edu. Web site: http://www.mercer.edu/education/.

Mercer University, Graduate Studies, Macon Campus, Tift College of Education (Macon), Macon, GA 31207-0003. Offers curriculum and instruction (PhD); early childhood education (M Ed); education leadership (PhD), including higher education, P-12; educational leadership (Ed S); higher education (M Ed); teacher leadership (Ed S). *Accreditation:* NCATE. Part-time and evening/weekend programs available. Postbaccalaureate distance learning degree programs offered (minimal on-campus study). *Faculty:* 26 full-time (17 women), 2 part-time/adjunct (0 women). *Students:* 87 full-time (78 women), 147 part-time (124 women); includes 92 minority (83 Black or African American, non-Hispanic/Latino; 3 American Indian or Alaska Native, non-Hispanic/Latino; 3 Asian, non-Hispanic/Latino; 3 Hispanic/Latino), 1 international. Average age 36. 122 applicants, 66% accepted, 72 enrolled. In 2011, 51 master's, 5 doctorates, 37 other advanced degrees awarded. *Degree requirements:* For master's, research project report; for doctorate, comprehensive exam, thesis/dissertation. *Entrance requirements:* For master's, GRE or MAT, minimum GPA of 2.75; for doctorate, GRE, minimum GPA of 3.5; interview; writing sample; 3 recommendations; for Ed S, GRE or MAT, minimum GPA of 3.5 (for Ed S in teacher leadership), 3.0 (for Ed S in educational leadership). Additional exam requirements/recommendations for international students: Required—TOEFL. *Application deadline:* For fall admission, 8/1 for domestic students; for spring admission, 12/1 for domestic students. Applications are processed on a rolling basis. Application fee: $35. *Expenses:* Contact institution. *Financial support:* Federal Work-Study and institutionally sponsored loans available. Support available to part-time students. Financial award application deadline: 5/1. *Faculty research:* Teacher effectiveness, specific learning disabilities, inclusion. *Unit head:* Dr. Carl R. Martray, Dean, 478-301-5397, Fax: 478-301-2280, E-mail: martray_cr@mercer.edu. *Application contact:* Tracey Wofford, Associate Director of Admissions, 678-547-6422, Fax: 678-547-6367, E-mail: wofford_tm@mercer.edu. Web site: http://education.mercer.edu.

Miami University, School of Education and Allied Professions, Department of Educational Leadership, Oxford, OH 45056. Offers curriculum and teacher leadership (M Ed); educational administration (Ed D, PhD); school leadership (MS); student affairs in higher education (MS, PhD). *Accreditation:* NCATE. Part-time programs available. *Students:* 102 full-time (63 women), 96 part-time (73 women); includes 45 minority (34 Black or African American, non-Hispanic/Latino; 1 American Indian or Alaska Native, non-Hispanic/Latino; 3 Asian, non-Hispanic/Latino; 2 Hispanic/Latino; 5 Two or more races, non-Hispanic/Latino), 7 international. Average age 32. In 2011, 52 master's, 7 doctorates awarded. *Entrance requirements:* For master's, MAT or GRE, minimum undergraduate GPA of 3.0 during previous 2 years or 2.75 overall; for doctorate, GRE, minimum GPA of 2.75 (undergraduate), 3.0 (graduate). Additional exam requirements/recommendations for international students: Required—TOEFL. Application fee: $50. *Expenses:* Tuition, state resident: full-time $12,023; part-time $501 per credit hour. Tuition, nonresident: full-time $26,554; part-time $1107 per credit hour. *Required fees:* $528. *Financial support:* Fellowships with full tuition reimbursements, research assistantships with full tuition reimbursements, teaching assistantships with full tuition reimbursements, career-related internships or fieldwork, Federal Work-Study, health care benefits, tuition waivers (full), and unspecified assistantships available. Financial award application deadline: 2/15; financial award applicants required to submit FAFSA. *Unit head:* Dr. Kate Rousmaniere, Chair, 513-529-6843, Fax: 513-529-1729, E-mail: rousmak@muohio.edu. Web site: http://www.units.muohio.edu/eap/edl/index.html.

Michigan State University, The Graduate School, College of Education, Department of Teacher Education, East Lansing, MI 48824. Offers curriculum, instruction and teacher education (PhD, Ed S); teaching and curriculum (MA). *Entrance requirements:* Additional exam requirements/recommendations for international students: Required—TOEFL. Electronic applications accepted.

Middle Tennessee State University, College of Graduate Studies, College of Education, Department of Educational Leadership, Program in Curriculum and Instruction, Murfreesboro, TN 37132. Offers curriculum and instruction (M Ed, Ed S); English as a second language (M Ed, Ed S); secondary education (M Ed); technology and curriculum design (Ed S). *Accreditation:* NCATE. Part-time and evening/weekend programs available. Postbaccalaureate distance learning degree programs offered. *Faculty:* 22 full-time (11 women), 22 part-time/adjunct (12 women). *Students:* 13 full-time (7 women), 208 part-time (167 women); includes 38 minority (29 Black or African American, non-Hispanic/Latino; 2 Asian, non-Hispanic/Latino; 2 Hispanic/Latino; 5 Two or more races, non-Hispanic/Latino). 154 applicants, 97% accepted. In 2011, 144 master's, 40 Ed Ss awarded. *Degree requirements:* For master's, comprehensive exam; for Ed S, comprehensive exam, thesis or alternative. *Entrance requirements:* For master's and Ed S, GRE, MAT or PRAXIS. Additional exam requirements/recommendations for international students: Required—TOEFL (minimum score 525 paper-based; 195 computer-based; 71 iBT) or IELTS (minimum score 6). *Application deadline:* For fall admission, 6/1 for domestic and international students. Applications are processed on a rolling basis. Application fee: $25 ($30 for international students). Electronic applications accepted. *Expenses:* Tuition, state resident: full-time $10,008. Tuition, nonresident: full-time $25,056. *Financial support:* Tuition waivers available. Support available to part-time students. Financial award application deadline: 5/1. *Unit head:* Dr. James Huffman, Chair, 615-898-2855, Fax: 615-898-2859. *Application contact:* Dr. Michael D. Allen, Dean and Vice Provost for Research, 615-898-2840, Fax: 615-904-8020, E-mail: michael.allen@mtsu.edu.

Midwestern State University, Graduate Studies, College of Education, Program in Curriculum and Instruction, Wichita Falls, TX 76308. Offers ME. Part-time and evening/weekend programs available. *Degree requirements:* For master's, comprehensive exam. *Entrance requirements:* For master's, GRE General Test, MAT, or GMAT. Additional exam requirements/recommendations for international students: Required—TOEFL (minimum score 550 paper-based; 213 computer-based). Electronic applications accepted. *Faculty research:* Role of the twenty-first century principal, instructional effectiveness, motivation, curriculum theory, educational research methodology.

Mills College, Graduate Studies, School of Education, Oakland, CA 94613-1000. Offers child life in hospitals (MA); early childhood education (MA); education (MA), including art education, curriculum and instruction, elementary education, English education, foreign language education, mathematics education, science education, secondary education, social studies education, teaching; educational leadership (MA, Ed D). Part-time and evening/weekend programs available. *Faculty:* 13 full-time (10 women), 14 part-time/adjunct (10 women). *Students:* 149 full-time (133 women), 69 part-time (61 women); includes 85 minority (32 Black or African American, non-Hispanic/Latino; 1 American Indian or Alaska Native, non-Hispanic/Latino; 16 Asian, non-Hispanic/Latino; 24 Hispanic/Latino; 1 Native Hawaiian or other Pacific Islander, non-Hispanic/Latino; 11 Two or more races, non-Hispanic/Latino), 3 international. Average age 28. 238 applicants, 84% accepted, 106 enrolled. In 2011, 41 master's, 2 doctorates awarded. Terminal master's awarded for partial completion of doctoral program. *Degree requirements:* For master's, comprehensive exam. *Entrance requirements:* For master's, statement of purpose, official transcript, 3 recommendations; for doctorate, GRE General Test. Additional exam requirements/recommendations for international students: Required—TOEFL (minimum score 550 paper-based; 80 iBT) or IELTS (minimum score 6). *Application deadline:* For fall admission, 12/31 priority date for domestic students, 12/15 for international students; for spring admission, 11/1 priority date for domestic students, 10/1 for international students. Applications are processed on a rolling basis. Application fee: $50. Electronic applications accepted. *Expenses: Tuition:* Full-time $28,280; part-time $15,640 per year. *Required fees:* $958. Tuition and fees vary according to program. *Financial support:* In 2011–12, 43 students received support, including 225 fellowships with full and partial tuition reimbursements available (averaging $6,020 per year), 43 teaching assistantships with full and partial tuition reimbursements available (averaging $6,782 per year); career-related internships or fieldwork and scholarships/grants also available. Support available to part-time students. Financial award application deadline: 2/1; financial award applicants required to submit FAFSA. *Faculty research:* Early childhood education, teacher preparation, educational leadership. *Total annual research expenditures:* $2.3 million. *Unit head:* Katherine Schultz, Chairperson, 510-430-3170, Fax: 510-430-3379, E-mail: grad-studies@mills.edu. *Application contact:* Tiana Kozoil, Graduate Admission Specialist, 510-430-3305, Fax: 510-430-2159, E-mail: grad-studies@mills.edu. Web site: http://www.mills.edu/education.

Minnesota State University Mankato, College of Graduate Studies, College of Education, Department of Educational Studies: K–12 and Secondary Programs, Mankato, MN 56001. Offers curriculum and instruction (SP); educational technology (MS); library media education (MS, Certificate); teacher licensure program (MAT); teaching and learning (MS, Certificate). *Accreditation:* NCATE. *Students:* 34 full-time (19 women), 93 part-time (62 women). *Degree requirements:* For master's, comprehensive exam, thesis or alternative; for other advanced degree, comprehensive exam, thesis. *Entrance requirements:* For master's, GRE General Test or MAT, minimum GPA of 3.0 during previous 2 years; for other advanced degree, GRE, minimum GPA of 3.0. Additional exam requirements/recommendations for international students: Required—TOEFL. *Application deadline:* For fall admission, 7/1 priority date for domestic students, 5/1 for international students; for spring admission, 11/1 for domestic students, 10/1 for international students. Applications are processed on a rolling basis. Application fee: $40. Electronic applications accepted. *Financial support:* Application deadline: 3/15. *Unit head:* Dr. Kitty Foord, Chairperson, 507-389-1965. *Application contact:* 507-389-2321, E-mail: grad@mnsu.edu. Web site: http://ed.mnsu.edu/ksp/.

Minnesota State University Moorhead, Graduate Studies, College of Education and Human Services, Program in Curriculum and Instruction, Moorhead, MN 56563-0002. Offers MS. *Accreditation:* NCATE. Part-time programs available. *Degree requirements:* For master's, comprehensive exam, final oral exam, project or thesis. *Entrance requirements:* For master's, MAT, bachelor's degree in education, minimum GPA of 2.75, one year teaching experience. Additional exam requirements/recommendations for international students: Required—TOEFL (minimum score 550 paper-based; 213 computer-based). Electronic applications accepted.

Misericordia University, College of Professional Studies and Social Sciences, Program in Education/Curriculum, Dallas, PA 18612-1098. Offers MS. Part-time and evening/weekend programs available. Postbaccalaureate distance learning degree programs offered. *Faculty:* 4 full-time (2 women), 11 part-time/adjunct (5 women). *Students:* 48 part-time (35 women); includes 4 minority (1 Black or African American, non-Hispanic/Latino; 1 American Indian or Alaska Native, non-Hispanic/Latino; 2 Hispanic/Latino). Average age 34. 20 applicants, 75% accepted, 11 enrolled. In 2011, 8 master's awarded. *Entrance requirements:* For master's, minimum undergraduate GPA of 3.0. *Application deadline:* Applications are processed on a rolling basis. Application fee: $25. Electronic applications accepted. *Expenses: Tuition:* Full-time $25,700; part-time $575 per credit. *Financial support:* In 2011–12, 17 students received support.

Scholarships/grants available. Support available to part-time students. Financial award application deadline: 6/30; financial award applicants required to submit FAFSA. *Unit head:* Dr. Kingsley Banya, Chair of Education Department, 570-674-1488, E-mail: kbanya@misericordia.edu. *Application contact:* Larree Brown, Assistant Director of Admissions, Part-Time Undergraduate and Graduate Programs, 570-674-6451, Fax: 570-674-6232, E-mail: lbrown@misericordia.edu.

Mississippi College, Graduate School, School of Education, Department of Teacher Education and Leadership, Clinton, MS 39058. Offers art (M Ed); biological science (M Ed); business education (M Ed); computer science (M Ed); dyslexia therapy (M Ed); educational leadership (M Ed, Ed D, Ed S); elementary education (M Ed, Ed S); English (M Ed); higher education administration (MS); mathematics (M Ed); secondary education (M Ed); social studies (history) (M Ed); teaching arts (M Ed). Part-time programs available. Postbaccalaureate distance learning degree programs offered (no on-campus study). *Degree requirements:* For master's, comprehensive exam, thesis optional. *Entrance requirements:* For master's, NTE. Additional exam requirements/recommendations for international students: Recommended—TOEFL, IELTS. Electronic applications accepted.

Mississippi State University, College of Education, Department of Curriculum, Instruction and Special Education, Mississippi State, MS 39762. Offers elementary education (MS, PhD, Ed S); middle level education (MAT); secondary education (MAT, MS, Ed S); special education (MS, Ed S). *Accreditation:* NCATE. Part-time and evening/weekend programs available. *Faculty:* 12 full-time (10 women), 2 part-time/adjunct (1 woman). *Students:* 57 full-time (41 women), 104 part-time (81 women); includes 54 minority (52 Black or African American, non-Hispanic/Latino; 1 Hispanic/Latino; 1 Two or more races, non-Hispanic/Latino). Average age 33. 100 applicants, 60% accepted, 48 enrolled. In 2011, 38 master's, 5 doctorates, 5 other advanced degrees awarded. *Degree requirements:* For master's, comprehensive exam; for doctorate, thesis/dissertation; for Ed S, comprehensive exam, thesis or alternative. *Entrance requirements:* For master's, GRE, minimum GPA of 2.75 in junior and senior year, eligibility for initial teacher certification; for doctorate, GRE, minimum graduate GPA of 3.4; for Ed S, GRE, minimum graduate GPA of 3.2. Additional exam requirements/recommendations for international students: Required—TOEFL (minimum score 600 paper-based; 250 computer-based; 100 iBT); Recommended—IELTS (minimum score 7.5). *Application deadline:* For fall admission, 3/1 priority date for domestic students, 5/1 for international students; for spring admission, 9/1 priority date for domestic students, 9/1 for international students. Applications are processed on a rolling basis. Application fee: $40. Electronic applications accepted. *Expenses:* Tuition, state resident: full-time $5805; part-time $322.50 per credit hour. Tuition, nonresident: full-time $14,670; part-time $815 per credit hour. *Financial support:* In 2011–12, 7 research assistantships with full and partial tuition reimbursements (averaging $9,264 per year), 4 teaching assistantships (averaging $8,937 per year) were awarded; Federal Work-Study, institutionally sponsored loans, scholarships/grants, and unspecified assistantships also available. Financial award application deadline: 4/1; financial award applicants required to submit FAFSA. *Faculty research:* Early childhood education, reading, rural schools, multicultural education, use of technology in instruction. *Unit head:* Dr. Devon Brenner, Professor and Interim Head, 662-325-7119, Fax: 662-325-7857, E-mail: devon@ra.msstate.edu. *Application contact:* Dr. C. Susie Burroughs, Professor and Graduate Coordinator, 662-325-3747, Fax: 662-325-7857, E-mail: susie.burroughs@msstate.edu. Web site: http://www.cise.msstate.edu/.

Mississippi University for Women, Graduate School, College of Education and Human Sciences, Columbus, MS 39701-9998. Offers differentiated instruction (M Ed); educational leadership (M Ed); gifted studies (M Ed); reading/literacy (M Ed); teaching (MAT). *Accreditation:* ASHA; NCATE. Part-time programs available. *Degree requirements:* For master's, comprehensive exam, thesis optional. *Entrance requirements:* For master's, GRE General Test or NTE (M Ed in gifted education or MS in speech/language pathology), MAT (M Ed in instructional management), minimum QPA of 3.0.

Missouri State University, Graduate College, College of Education, Department of Reading, Foundations, and Technology, Master of Arts in Teaching Program, Springfield, MO 65897. Offers MAT. Part-time programs available. *Students:* 35 full-time (19 women), 84 part-time (47 women); includes 14 minority (3 Black or African American, non-Hispanic/Latino; 1 American Indian or Alaska Native, non-Hispanic/Latino; 2 Asian, non-Hispanic/Latino; 5 Hispanic/Latino; 1 Native Hawaiian or other Pacific Islander, non-Hispanic/Latino; 2 Two or more races, non-Hispanic/Latino). Average age 35. 23 applicants, 83% accepted, 11 enrolled. In 2011, 39 master's awarded. *Degree requirements:* For master's, comprehensive exam, project. *Entrance requirements:* For master's, PRAXIS II. Additional exam requirements/recommendations for international students: Required—TOEFL (minimum score 550 paper-based; 213 computer-based; 79 iBT). *Application deadline:* For fall admission, 2/15 priority date for domestic students, 2/15 for international students. Application fee: $35 ($50 for international students). Electronic applications accepted. *Expenses:* Tuition, state resident: full-time $4086; part-time $227 per credit hour. Tuition, nonresident: full-time $8172; part-time $454 per credit hour. *Required fees:* $275 per semester. Tuition and fees vary according to course load, campus/location and program. *Financial support:* Federal Work-Study, institutionally sponsored loans, scholarships/grants, tuition waivers (full), and unspecified assistantships available. Financial award application deadline: 3/31; financial award applicants required to submit FAFSA. *Unit head:* Dr. Steven Hinch, Program Coordinator, 417-836-3170, E-mail: shinch@missouristate.edu. *Application contact:* Misty Stewart, Coordinator of Admissions and Recruitment, 417-836-6079, Fax: 417-836-6200, E-mail: mistystewart@missouristate.edu.

Montana State University, College of Graduate Studies, College of Education, Health, and Human Development, Department of Education, Bozeman, MT 59717. Offers adult and higher education (Ed D); curriculum and instruction (M Ed, Ed D), including professional educator (M Ed), technology education (M Ed); education (M Ed), including adult and higher education, educational leadership, school counseling; educational leadership (Ed D, Ed S). *Accreditation:* Teacher Education Accreditation Council. Part-time programs available. Postbaccalaureate distance learning degree programs offered (minimal on-campus study). *Degree requirements:* For master's, comprehensive exam; for doctorate, comprehensive exam, thesis/dissertation. *Entrance requirements:* For master's, GRE, 3 letters of reference, essays, BA transcripts; for doctorate, GRE, MAT, 3 letters of reference, essay, BA and M Ed transcripts; for Ed S, PRAXIS. Additional exam requirements/recommendations for international students: Required—TOEFL (minimum score 550 paper-based; 213 computer-based). Electronic applications accepted. *Faculty research:* Critical literacy; standards-based education; school Improvement, organizational change, leadership in rural education, leadership in Indian education; student Learning; multicultural/culturally responsive education for social justice Native American indigenous education, community-centered education teacher preparation.

Montana State University Billings, College of Education, Department of Educational Theory and Practice, Option in General Curriculum, Billings, MT 59101-0298. Offers M Ed. *Accreditation:* NCATE. Part-time programs available. *Degree requirements:* For master's, thesis or professional paper and/or field experience. *Entrance requirements:* For master's, GRE General Test or MAT, minimum GPA of 3.0 (undergraduate), 3.25 (graduate). *Faculty research:* Social studies education, science education.

Montclair State University, The Graduate School, College of Education and Human Services, Department of Curriculum and Teaching, Program in Teaching in Content Area, Montclair, NJ 07043-1624. Offers art (MAT); biology (MAT); chemistry (MAT); earth science (MAT); English (MAT); French (MAT); health and physical education (MAT); health education (MAT); mathematics (MAT); music (MAT); physical education (MAT); physical science (MAT); social studies (MAT); Spanish (MAT); teacher of English as a second language (MAT). *Students:* 162 full-time (90 women), 47 part-time (29 women); includes 37 minority (4 Black or African American, non-Hispanic/Latino; 11 Asian, non-Hispanic/Latino; 18 Hispanic/Latino; 4 Two or more races, non-Hispanic/Latino), 5 international. Average age 31. 145 applicants, 41% accepted, 56 enrolled. In 2011, 229 master's awarded. *Degree requirements:* For master's, comprehensive exam, thesis or alternative. *Entrance requirements:* For master's, GRE General Test, interview, 2 letters of recommendation. Additional exam requirements/recommendations for international students: Required—TOEFL (minimum score 83 iBT), IELTS (minimum score 6.5). *Application deadline:* Applications are processed on a rolling basis. Application fee: $60. Electronic applications accepted. *Financial support:* Federal Work-Study, scholarships/grants, and unspecified assistantships available. Support available to part-time students. Financial award application deadline: 3/1; financial award applicants required to submit FAFSA. *Unit head:* Dr. David Schwarzer, Chairperson, 973-655-5187. *Application contact:* Amy Aiello, Executive Director of The Graduate School, 973-655-5147, Fax: 973-655-7869, E-mail: graduate.school@montclair.edu.

Montclair State University, The Graduate School, College of Education and Human Services, Department of Educational Foundations, Montclair, NJ 07043-1624. Offers educational foundations (Certificate); pedagogy and philosophy (Ed D). Part-time and evening/weekend programs available. *Faculty:* 13 full-time (5 women), 10 part-time/adjunct (7 women). *Students:* 1 part-time (0 women); minority (Hispanic/Latino). Average age 31. *Entrance requirements:* For doctorate, GRE General Test, 3 years of classroom teaching experience, interview, writing sample. Additional exam requirements/recommendations for international students: Required—TOEFL (minimum score 83 iBT) or IELTS. *Application deadline:* For fall admission, 2/1 for domestic students, 2/15 for international students; for spring admission, 10/15 for domestic and international students. Applications are processed on a rolling basis. Application fee: $60. Electronic applications accepted. *Financial support:* In 2011–12, 3 research assistantships with full tuition reimbursements (averaging $7,000 per year) were awarded; Federal Work-Study and scholarships/grants also available. Support available to part-time students. Financial award application deadline: 3/1; financial award applicants required to submit FAFSA. *Faculty research:* Pragmatism and education: theoretical and practical, history of education, children and philosophy, academic development, developing theory and practice - transforming K-12 school pedagogy. *Unit head:* Dr. Jeremy Price, Chairperson, 973-655-7039. *Application contact:* Amy Aiello, Executive Director of The Graduate School, 973-655-5147, Fax: 973-655-7869, E-mail: graduate.school@montclair.edu. Web site: http://www.montclair.edu/cehs/academics/departments/educational-foundations/.

Moravian College, Moravian College Comenius Center, Education Programs, Bethlehem, PA 18018-6650. Offers curriculum and instruction (M Ed). Part-time and evening/weekend programs available. *Faculty:* 4 full-time (2 women), 4 part-time/adjunct (2 women). *Students:* 94 part-time (82 women). Average age 35. 23 applicants, 65% accepted, 13 enrolled. In 2011, 17 degrees awarded. *Degree requirements:* For master's, thesis. *Entrance requirements:* For master's, state teacher certification. Application fee: $40. *Unit head:* Dr. Joseph Shosh, Director, 610-861-1400, Fax: 610-861-1466, E-mail: comenius@moravian.edu. *Application contact:* Dr. William A. Kleintop, Associate Dean for Business and Management Programs, 610-625-7704, Fax: 610-861-1466, E-mail: comenius@moravian.edu.

Morehead State University, Graduate Programs, College of Education, Department of Curriculum and Instruction, Morehead, KY 40351. Offers curriculum and instruction (Ed S); elementary education (MA Ed), including elementary education, international education, middle school education, reading; secondary education (MA Ed); special education (MA Ed); teaching (MAT). Part-time and evening/weekend programs available. *Degree requirements:* For master's, comprehensive exam, thesis optional; for Ed S, thesis, oral exam. *Entrance requirements:* For master's, GRE General Test, minimum GPA of 2.75, teaching certificate; for Ed S, GRE General Test, interview, master's degree, minimum GPA of 3.5, work experience. Additional exam requirements/recommendations for international students: Required—TOEFL (minimum score 500 paper-based; 173 computer-based). Electronic applications accepted. *Faculty research:* Communicative competence of learning-disabled students, teaching social studies in elementary schools, ungraded primary school organization, study skills.

Morehead State University, Graduate Programs, College of Education, Department of Foundational and Graduate Studies in Education, Morehead, KY 40351. Offers adult and higher education (MA, Ed S); certified professional counselor (Ed S); counseling P-12 (MA); curriculum and instruction (Ed S); educational technology (MA Ed); instructional leadership (Ed S); school administration (MA); school counseling (Ed S); teacher leader business and marketing content (MA Ed); teacher leader business and marketing technology (MA Ed); teacher leader educational technology (MA Ed); teacher leader English (MA Ed); teacher leader gifted education (MA Ed); teacher leader IECE certification (MA Ed); teacher leader interdisciplinary education P-5 (MA Ed); teacher leader middle grades (MA Ed); teacher leader non IECE certification (MA Ed); teacher leader reading/writing - non-certification (MA Ed); teacher leader reading/writing certification (MA Ed); teacher leader school communication - certification (MA Ed); teacher leader school communication - non-certification (MA Ed); teacher leader social studies (MA Ed); teacher leader special education (MA Ed). *Accreditation:* NCATE. Part-time and evening/weekend programs available. *Degree requirements:* For master's, thesis optional, oral and/or written comprehensive exams; for Ed S, thesis, oral exam. *Entrance requirements:* For master's, GRE General Test, minimum overall undergraduate GPA of 2.5; for Ed S, GRE General Test, interview, master's degree, minimum GPA of 3.5, work experience. Additional exam requirements/recommendations for international students: Required—TOEFL (minimum score 500 paper-based; 173 computer-based). Electronic applications accepted. *Faculty research:* Character education, school accountability, computer applications for school administrators.

Mount Saint Vincent University, Graduate Programs, Faculty of Education, Program in Curriculum Studies, Halifax, NS B3M 2J6, Canada. Offers education of young adolescents (M Ed, MA Ed, MA-R); general studies (M Ed, MA Ed, MA-R); teaching English as a second language (M Ed, MA Ed, MA-R). Part-time and evening/weekend programs available. Postbaccalaureate distance learning degree programs offered (minimal on-campus study). *Degree requirements:* For master's, thesis (for some programs). *Entrance requirements:* For master's, bachelor's degree in related field, minimum B average, 1 year of teaching experience. Electronic applications accepted. *Faculty research:* Science education, cultural studies, international education, curriculum development.

National Louis University, National College of Education, Chicago, IL 60603. Offers administration and supervision (M Ed, Ed D, CAS, Ed S); curriculum and instruction

(M Ed, MS Ed, CAS); early childhood administration (M Ed, CAS); early childhood education (M Ed, MAT, MS Ed, CAS); education (Ed D); educational psychology/human learning and development (M Ed, MS Ed, CAS, Ed S); elementary education (MAT); interdisciplinary curriculum and instruction (M Ed); mathematics education (M Ed, MS Ed, CAS); reading and language (M Ed, MS Ed, CAS); school psychology (M Ed, Ed S); science education (M Ed, MS Ed, CAS); secondary education (MAT); special education (M Ed, MAT, CAS); technology in education (M Ed, CAS). *Accreditation:* NCATE. Part-time and evening/weekend programs available. *Students:* 224 full-time (162 women), 2,336 part-time (1,767 women); includes 677 minority (366 Black or African American, non-Hispanic/Latino; 8 American Indian or Alaska Native, non-Hispanic/Latino; 68 Asian, non-Hispanic/Latino; 218 Hispanic/Latino; 2 Native Hawaiian or other Pacific Islander, non-Hispanic/Latino; 15 Two or more races, non-Hispanic/Latino), 2 international. Average age 34. In 2011, 1,711 master's, 76 doctorates, 86 other advanced degrees awarded. *Degree requirements:* For doctorate, comprehensive exam, thesis/dissertation. *Entrance requirements:* For master's, MAT or GRE, minimum GPA of 3.0; for doctorate, GRE General Test, minimum GPA of 3.25, interview, resume, writing sample, 4 recommendations. Additional exam requirements/recommendations for international students: Required—TOEFL (minimum score 550 paper-based; 213 computer-based; 79 iBT). *Application deadline:* Applications are processed on a rolling basis. Application fee: $40. *Financial support:* Fellowships, research assistantships, teaching assistantships, career-related internships or fieldwork, Federal Work-Study, institutionally sponsored loans, and scholarships/grants available. Support available to part-time students. Financial award applicants required to submit FAFSA. *Unit head:* Dr. Alison Hilsabeck, Dean, 312-361-3580, Fax: 312-261-2580, E-mail: ahilsabeck@nl.edu. *Application contact:* Ken Kasprzak, Director of Admission, 888-658-8632, Fax: 847-947-5575, E-mail: kkasprzak@nl.edu.

Newman University, Master of Education Program, Wichita, KS 67213-2097. Offers building leadership (MS Ed); curriculum and instruction (MS Ed), including accountability, English as a second language, reading specialist. *Accreditation:* NCATE. Part-time and evening/weekend programs available. Postbaccalaureate distance learning degree programs offered (no on-campus study). *Faculty:* 4 full-time (2 women), 38 part-time/adjunct (all women). *Students:* 47 full-time (40 women), 414 part-time (318 women); includes 62 minority (20 Black or African American, non-Hispanic/Latino; 8 Asian, non-Hispanic/Latino; 30 Hispanic/Latino; 3 Native Hawaiian or other Pacific Islander, non-Hispanic/Latino; 1 Two or more races, non-Hispanic/Latino), 3 international. Average age 35. 42 applicants, 76% accepted, 27 enrolled. In 2011, 46 master's awarded. *Degree requirements:* For master's, thesis optional. *Entrance requirements:* For master's, interview, minimum GPA of 3.0, writing sample, 2 letters of recommendation, evidence of teaching certification. Additional exam requirements/recommendations for international students: Required—TOEFL (minimum score 600 paper-based; 250 computer-based; 100 iBT). *Application deadline:* For fall admission, 8/15 priority date for domestic students, 7/15 for international students; for spring admission, 1/10 priority date for domestic students, 11/15 for international students. Applications are processed on a rolling basis. Application fee: $25 ($40 for international students). Electronic applications accepted. *Expenses:* Contact institution. *Financial support:* In 2011–12, 18 students received support. Federal Work-Study available. Financial award application deadline: 8/15; financial award applicants required to submit FAFSA. *Unit head:* Dr. Guy Glidden, Director, Graduate Education, 316-942-4291 Ext. 2331, Fax: 316-942-4483, E-mail: gliddeng@newmanu.edu. *Application contact:* Linda Kay Sabala, Director of Graduate Admissions, 316-942-4291 Ext. 2230, Fax: 316-942-4483, E-mail: sabalal@newmanu.edu.

New Mexico Highlands University, Graduate Studies, School of Education, Las Vegas, NM 87701. Offers curriculum and instruction (MA); education (MA), including counseling, school counseling; educational leadership (MA); exercise and sport sciences (MA), including human performance and sport, sports administration, teacher education; guidance and counseling (MA), including professional counseling, rehabilitation counseling, school counseling; special education (MA), including). Part-time programs available. *Faculty:* 29 full-time (18 women). *Students:* 136 full-time (100 women), 275 part-time (219 women); includes 231 minority (8 Black or African American, non-Hispanic/Latino; 22 American Indian or Alaska Native, non-Hispanic/Latino; 2 Asian, non-Hispanic/Latino; 194 Hispanic/Latino; 1 Native Hawaiian or other Pacific Islander, non-Hispanic/Latino; 4 Two or more races, non-Hispanic/Latino), 14 international. Average age 39. 117 applicants, 82% accepted, 91 enrolled. In 2011, 105 master's awarded. *Degree requirements:* For master's, comprehensive exam, thesis or alternative. *Entrance requirements:* For master's, minimum undergraduate GPA of 3.0. Additional exam requirements/recommendations for international students: Required—TOEFL (minimum score 540 paper-based; 207 computer-based). *Application deadline:* For fall admission, 8/1 priority date for domestic students. Applications are processed on a rolling basis. Application fee: $15. *Expenses:* Tuition, state resident: full-time $2767; part-time $146 per credit hour. Tuition, nonresident: full-time $4879; part-time $234 per credit hour. *International tuition:* $5436 full-time. *Required fees:* $737. *Financial support:* In 2011–12, 12 students received support. Career-related internships or fieldwork, Federal Work-Study, institutionally sponsored loans, scholarships/grants, traineeships, tuition waivers (partial), and unspecified assistantships available. Support available to part-time students. Financial award application deadline: 3/1; financial award applicants required to submit FAFSA. *Faculty research:* Teaching the United States Constitution, middle school curriculum, integrated computer applications for pre-service classroom teachers, adolescent literacy, narrative cognitive modes in NM multicultural setting. *Unit head:* Dr. Michael Anderson, Interim Dean, 505-454-3213, E-mail: mfanderson@nmhu.edu. *Application contact:* Diane Trujillo, Administrative Assistant for Graduate Studies, 505-454-3266, Fax: 505-426-2117, E-mail: dtrujillo@nmhu.edu.

New Mexico State University, Graduate School, College of Education, Department of Curriculum and Instruction, Las Cruces, NM 88003-8001. Offers curriculum and instruction (MAT, Ed D, PhD); general education (MA). *Accreditation:* NCATE. Part-time and evening/weekend programs available. Postbaccalaureate distance learning degree programs offered (no on-campus study). *Faculty:* 26 full-time (14 women), 2 part-time/adjunct (0 women). *Students:* 145 full-time (115 women), 315 part-time (244 women); includes 215 minority (10 Black or African American, non-Hispanic/Latino; 6 American Indian or Alaska Native, non-Hispanic/Latino; 9 Asian, non-Hispanic/Latino; 186 Hispanic/Latino; 4 Two or more races, non-Hispanic/Latino), 33 international. Average age 37. 142 applicants, 70% accepted, 70 enrolled. In 2011, 116 master's, 15 doctorates awarded. *Median time to degree:* Of those who began their doctoral program in fall 2003, 32% received their degree in 8 years or less. *Degree requirements:* For master's, thesis optional; for doctorate, comprehensive exam, thesis/dissertation. *Entrance requirements:* For master's, minimum cumulative GPA of 3.0; for doctorate, portfolio. Additional exam requirements/recommendations for international students: Required—TOEFL (minimum score 550 paper-based; 213 computer-based; 79 iBT), IELTS (minimum score 6). *Application deadline:* For fall admission, 7/1 priority date for domestic students; for spring admission, 11/1 for domestic students. Applications are processed on a rolling basis. Application fee: $40 ($50 for international students). *Expenses:* Tuition, state resident: full-time $5004; part-time $208.50 per credit. Tuition, nonresident: full-time $17,446; part-time $726.90 per credit. *Financial support:* In 2011–12, 30 research assistantships (averaging $16,431 per year), 21 teaching assistantships (averaging $22,887 per year) were awarded; fellowships, career-related internships or fieldwork, Federal Work-Study, scholarships/grants, health care benefits, and unspecified assistantships also available. Support available to part-time students. Financial award application deadline: 3/1. *Faculty research:* Literacy/biliteracy education, bilingual and English as a second language education, critical pedagogy/multicultural education, educational learning technologies, early childhood education. *Unit head:* Dr. Jeanette Haynes Writer, Associate Department Head for Graduate Studies, 575-646-5411, Fax: 575-646-5436, E-mail: jeanette@nmsu.edu. *Application contact:* Coordinator, 575-646-2736, Fax: 575-646-7721, E-mail: gradinfo@nmsu.edu. Web site: http://education.nmsu.edu/ci/index.html.

New York University, Steinhardt School of Culture, Education, and Human Development, Department of Teaching and Learning, Program in English Education, New York, NY 10012-1019. Offers secondary and college (PhD), including applied linguistics, comparative education, curriculum, literature and reading, media education; teachers of English 7-12 (MA); teachers of English language and literature in college (Advanced Certificate). *Accreditation:* Teacher Education Accreditation Council. Part-time programs available. *Degree requirements:* For master's, thesis (for some programs); for doctorate, thesis/dissertation. *Entrance requirements:* For doctorate, GRE General Test, interview; for Advanced Certificate, master's degree. Additional exam requirements/recommendations for international students: Required—TOEFL. Electronic applications accepted. *Faculty research:* Making meaning of literature, teaching of literature, urban adolescent literacy and equity, literacy development and globalization, digital media and literacy .

Nicholls State University, Graduate Studies, College of Education, Department of Teacher Education, Thibodaux, LA 70310. Offers administration and supervision (M Ed); counselor education (M Ed); curriculum and instruction (M Ed). *Accreditation:* NCATE. Part-time and evening/weekend programs available. *Degree requirements:* For master's, comprehensive exam, portfolio. *Entrance requirements:* For master's, GRE General Test, teaching license. Electronic applications accepted.

North Carolina Central University, Division of Academic Affairs, School of Education, Department of Curriculum, Instruction and Professional Studies, Durham, NC 27707-3129. Offers curriculum and instruction (MA), including elementary education, middle grades education. *Accreditation:* NCATE. Part-time and evening/weekend programs available. *Degree requirements:* For master's, comprehensive exam, thesis or alternative. *Entrance requirements:* For master's, minimum GPA of 3.0 in major, 2.5 overall. Additional exam requirements/recommendations for international students: Required—TOEFL. *Faculty research:* Simulation of decision-making behavior of school boards.

North Carolina State University, Graduate School, College of Education, Department of Curriculum and Instruction, Program in Curriculum and Instruction, Raleigh, NC 27695. Offers M Ed, MS, PhD. *Accreditation:* NCATE. *Degree requirements:* For master's, thesis (for some programs); for doctorate, thesis/dissertation. *Entrance requirements:* For master's, GRE General Test or MAT, minimum GPA of 3.0 in major; for doctorate, GRE General Test, minimum GPA of 3.0 in major. Electronic applications accepted. *Faculty research:* Curriculum development, teacher development, intervention for exceptional children, literacy development.

North Central College, Graduate and Continuing Education Programs, Department of Education, Naperville, IL 60566-7063. Offers curriculum and instruction (MA Ed); leadership and administration (MA Ed). Part-time and evening/weekend programs available. *Faculty:* 10 full-time (6 women), 6 part-time/adjunct (3 women). *Students:* 7 full-time (all women), 23 part-time (16 women); includes 3 minority (all Hispanic/Latino). Average age 30. 25 applicants, 56% accepted, 12 enrolled. In 2011, 39 master's awarded. *Degree requirements:* For master's, thesis optional, clinical practicum, project. *Entrance requirements:* For master's, interview. Additional exam requirements/recommendations for international students: Required—TOEFL (minimum score 577 paper-based; 233 computer-based; 90 iBT). *Application deadline:* For fall admission, 8/15 for domestic students; for winter admission, 12/1 for domestic students; for spring admission, 2/1 for domestic students. Applications are processed on a rolling basis. Application fee: $25. *Expenses:* Contact institution. *Financial support:* In 2011–12, 4 students received support. Available to part-time students. *Unit head:* Dr. Kristine Servais, Graduate Program Coordinator, Education, 630-637-5739, Fax: 630-637-5844. *Application contact:* Wendy Kulpinski, Director of Graduate and Continuing Education Admission, 630-637-5808, Fax: 630-637-5844, E-mail: wekulpinski@noctrl.edu.

Northern Arizona University, Graduate College, College of Education, Department of Educational Specialties, Flagstaff , AZ 86011. Offers autism spectrum disorders (Certificate); bilingual/multicultural education (M Ed), including bilingual education, ESL education; career and technical education (M Ed, Certificate); curriculum and instruction (Ed D); early childhood special education (M Ed); early intervention (Certificate); educational technology (M Ed, Certificate); special education (M Ed). *Faculty:* 28 full-time (19 women). *Students:* 113 full-time (91 women), 206 part-time (158 women); includes 104 minority (8 Black or African American, non-Hispanic/Latino; 17 American Indian or Alaska Native, non-Hispanic/Latino; 6 Asian, non-Hispanic/Latino; 65 Hispanic/Latino; 2 Native Hawaiian or other Pacific Islander, non-Hispanic/Latino; 6 Two or more races, non-Hispanic/Latino), 3 international. Average age 30. 141 applicants, 75% accepted, 76 enrolled. In 2011, 167 master's, 7 Certificates awarded. *Degree requirements:* For master's, comprehensive exam (for some programs), thesis (for some programs). *Entrance requirements:* For master's, minimum GPA of 3.0. Additional exam requirements/recommendations for international students: Required—TOEFL (minimum score 550 paper-based; 213 computer-based; 80 iBT), IELTS (minimum score 7). *Application deadline:* For fall admission, 3/1 for international students; for spring admission, 9/15 for international students. Applications are processed on a rolling basis. Application fee: $65. Electronic applications accepted. *Expenses:* Tuition, state resident: full-time $7190; part-time $355 per credit hour. Tuition, nonresident: full-time $18,092; part-time $1005 per credit hour. *Required fees:* $818; $328 per semester. *Financial support:* Applicants required to submit FAFSA. *Unit head:* Dr. Jennifer Prior, Chair, 928-523-5064, Fax: 928-523-1929, E-mail: jennifer.prior@nau.edu. *Application contact:* Shirley Robinson, Coordinator, 928-523-4348, Fax: 928-523-8950, E-mail: shirley.robinson@nau.edu. Web site: http://nau.edu/coe/ed-specialties/.

Northern Illinois University, Graduate School, College of Education, Department of Special and Early Education, De Kalb, IL 60115-2854. Offers curriculum and instruction (MS Ed, Ed D), including curriculum leadership (Ed D), elementary education (Ed D), secondary education (Ed D); early childhood education (MS Ed); elementary education (MS Ed); special education (MS Ed). Part-time and evening/weekend programs available. *Faculty:* 22 full-time (14 women), 2 part-time/adjunct (both women). *Students:* 58 full-time (46 women), 241 part-time (189 women); includes 35 minority (17 Black or African American, non-Hispanic/Latino; 7 Asian, non-Hispanic/Latino; 9 Hispanic/Latino; 2 Two or more races, non-Hispanic/Latino), 3 international. Average age 35. 100 applicants, 65% accepted, 45 enrolled. In 2011, 186 master's, 7 doctorates awarded. *Degree requirements:* For master's, comprehensive exam, thesis optional; for doctorate, thesis/dissertation, candidacy exam, dissertation defense. *Entrance requirements:* For master's, GRE General Test or MAT, minimum undergraduate GPA of 2.75; for doctorate, GRE General Test or MAT, minimum undergraduate GPA of 2.75, graduate 3.2. Additional exam requirements/recommendations for international students: Required—TOEFL (minimum score 550 paper-based; 213 computer-based). *Application* *deadline:* For fall admission, 6/1 for domestic students, 5/1 for international students; for spring admission, 11/1 for domestic students, 10/1 for international students. Applications are processed on a rolling basis. Application fee: $40. Electronic applications accepted. *Financial support:* In 2011–12, 34 research assistantships with full tuition reimbursements were awarded; fellowships with full tuition reimbursements, teaching assistantships with full tuition reimbursements, career-related internships or fieldwork, Federal Work-Study, scholarships/grants, tuition waivers (full), and unspecified assistantships also available. Support available to part-time students. Financial award applicants required to submit FAFSA. *Faculty research:* Teacher certification, stress reduction during student teaching, teaching history, portfolios in student teaching. *Unit head:* Dr. Connie Fox, Interim Chair, 815-753-1619, E-mail: seed@niu.edu. *Application contact:* Gail Myers, 815-753-0381, E-mail: gmyers@niu.edu. Web site: http://www.cedu.niu.edu/seed/.

Northwestern Oklahoma State University, School of Professional Studies, Program in Curriculum and Instruction, Alva, OK 73717-2799. Offers M Ed. Part-time programs available. *Faculty:* 7 full-time (5 women). *Students:* 2 part-time (both women). 2 applicants, 100% accepted, 2 enrolled. *Degree requirements:* For master's, thesis optional, portfolio. *Entrance requirements:* For master's, GRE General Test or MAT, minimum GPA of 2.75. Application fee: $15. *Financial support:* Federal Work-Study available. Support available to part-time students. Financial award application deadline: 5/1; financial award applicants required to submit FAFSA. *Unit head:* Dr. Beverly Warden. *Application contact:* Sabrina Watson, Coordinator of Graduate Studies, 580-327-8410, E-mail: sdwatson@nwosu.edu.

Northwestern State University of Louisiana, Graduate Studies and Research, College of Education and Human Development, Program in Curriculum and Instruction, Natchitoches, LA 71497. Offers M Ed. *Students:* 4 full-time (3 women), 32 part-time (all women); includes 3 minority (all Black or African American, non-Hispanic/Latino), 2 international. Average age 37. 11 applicants, 100% accepted, 8 enrolled. In 2011, 3 master's awarded. *Entrance requirements:* Additional exam requirements/recommendations for international students: Required—TOEFL. *Application deadline:* For fall admission, 3/15 priority date for domestic students; for spring admission, 10/15 priority date for domestic students. Applications are processed on a rolling basis. Application fee: $20 ($30 for international students). Electronic applications accepted. *Expenses:* Tuition, state resident: full-time $3440. Tuition, nonresident: full-time $12,010. *Financial support:* Application deadline: 5/1; applicants required to submit FAFSA. *Unit head:* Dr. Steven G. Horton, Associate Provost/Dean, Graduate Studies, Research, and Information Systems, 318-357-5851, Fax: 318-357-5019, E-mail: grad_school@nsula.edu. *Application contact:* Dr. Steven G. Horton, Associate Provost/Dean, Graduate Studies, Research, and Information Systems, 318-357-5851, Fax: 318-357-5019, E-mail: grad_school@nsula.edu.

Northwest Nazarene University, Graduate Studies, Program in Teacher Education, Nampa, ID 83686-5897. Offers curriculum and instruction (M Ed); educational leadership (M Ed, Ed D, Ed S); exceptional child (M Ed); reading education (M Ed). *Accreditation:* ACA (one or more programs are accredited); NCATE. Part-time programs available. Postbaccalaureate distance learning degree programs offered (no on-campus study). *Faculty:* 15 full-time (9 women), 36 part-time/adjunct (21 women). *Students:* 80 full-time (54 women), 119 part-time (98 women); includes 13 minority (1 American Indian or Alaska Native, non-Hispanic/Latino; 10 Hispanic/Latino; 1 Native Hawaiian or other Pacific Islander, non-Hispanic/Latino; 1 Two or more races, non-Hispanic/Latino), 8 international. Average age 36. 60 applicants, 95% accepted, 39 enrolled. In 2011, 43 master's, 24 other advanced degrees awarded. *Degree requirements:* For master's, comprehensive exam (for some programs), action research project. *Entrance requirements:* For master's, minimum undergraduate GPA of 2.8 overall or 3.0 during final 30 semester credits. *Application deadline:* For fall admission, 9/1 for domestic students. Applications are processed on a rolling basis. Application fee: $25. *Faculty research:* Action research, cooperative learning, accountability, institutional accreditation. *Unit head:* Dr. Paula Kellerer, Chair, 208-467-8729, Fax: 208-467-8562. *Application contact:* Jackie Schober, 208-467-8341, Fax: 208-467-8786, E-mail: jsschober@nnu.edu. Web site: http://www.nnu.edu/graded/.

Notre Dame de Namur University, Division of Academic Affairs, School of Education and Leadership, Program in Teacher Education, Belmont, CA 94002-1908. Offers curriculum and instruction (MA); disciplinary studies (MA); educational technology (MA); multiple subject teaching credential (Certificate); single subject teaching credential (Certificate). Part-time and evening/weekend programs available. *Students:* 93 full-time (71 women), 128 part-time (89 women); includes 40 minority (3 Black or African American, non-Hispanic/Latino; 2 American Indian or Alaska Native, non-Hispanic/Latino; 14 Asian, non-Hispanic/Latino; 19 Hispanic/Latino; 1 Native Hawaiian or other Pacific Islander, non-Hispanic/Latino; 1 Two or more races, non-Hispanic/Latino), 2 international. In 2011, 18 master's awarded. *Entrance requirements:* Additional exam requirements/recommendations for international students: Required—TOEFL (minimum score 550 paper-based; 213 computer-based; 79 iBT). Application fee: $60. *Expenses: Tuition:* Full-time $14,220; part-time $790 per credit. *Required fees:* $35 per semester. Tuition and fees vary according to program. *Financial support:* Career-related internships or fieldwork available. Support available to part-time students. Financial award applicants required to submit FAFSA. *Unit head:* Dr. Kim Tolley, Director, 650-508-3464, E-mail: ktolley@ndnu.edu. *Application contact:* Candace Hallmark, Associate Director of Admissions, 650-508-3592, Fax: 650-508-3426, E-mail: grad.admit@ndnu.edu.

Ohio University, Graduate College, Gladys W. and David H. Patton College of Education and Human Services, Department of Teacher Education, Athens, OH 45701-2979. Offers adolescent to young adult education (M Ed); curriculum and instruction (M Ed, PhD); early childhood/special education (M Ed); intervention specialist/mild-moderate needs (M Ed); intervention specialist/moderate-intensive needs (M Ed); mathematics education (PhD); middle child education (M Ed); reading education (M Ed); social studies education (PhD). Part-time and evening/weekend programs available. *Students:* 131 full-time (92 women), 82 part-time (62 women); includes 9 minority (4 Black or African American, non-Hispanic/Latino; 2 American Indian or Alaska Native, non-Hispanic/Latino; 1 Asian, non-Hispanic/Latino; 1 Hispanic/Latino; 1 Two or more races, non-Hispanic/Latino), 11 international. 136 applicants, 70% accepted, 65 enrolled. In 2011, 58 master's, 8 doctorates awarded. *Degree requirements:* For master's, thesis or alternative; for doctorate, comprehensive exam, thesis/dissertation. *Entrance requirements:* For master's, GRE General Test or MAT (if GPA is below 2.9); for doctorate, GRE General Test, minimum GPA of 3.4, work experience. Additional exam requirements/recommendations for international students: Required—TOEFL (minimum score 550 paper-based; 80 iBT) or IELTS (minimum score 6.5). *Application deadline:* For fall admission, 5/1 priority date for domestic students, 4/1 for international students; for winter admission, 11/1 priority date for domestic students, 10/1 for international students; for spring admission, 2/15 priority date for domestic students, 1/1 for international students. Applications are processed on a rolling basis. Application fee: $50 ($55 for international students). Electronic applications accepted. *Financial support:* Research assistantships with full tuition reimbursements, teaching assistantships with full tuition reimbursements, Federal Work-Study, institutionally sponsored loans, tuition waivers (partial), and unspecified assistantships available. Financial award application deadline: 3/1. *Faculty research:* Cognition literacy, character education, teacher's education reform, disabilities. *Total annual research expenditures:* $46,933. *Unit head:* Dr. John Henning, Chair, 740-597-1830, Fax: 740-593-0477, E-mail: henningj@ohio.edu. *Application contact:* Floyd J. Doney, Director of Student Affairs, 740-593-4400, Fax: 740-593-9310, E-mail: doney@ohio.edu. Web site: http://www.cehs.ohio.edu/academics/te/index.htm.

Oklahoma State University, College of Education, School of Teaching and Curriculum Leadership, Stillwater, OK 74078. Offers MS, PhD. Part-time programs available. *Faculty:* 32 full-time (27 women), 21 part-time/adjunct (19 women). *Students:* 53 full-time (39 women), 219 part-time (165 women); includes 58 minority (22 Black or African American, non-Hispanic/Latino; 16 American Indian or Alaska Native, non-Hispanic/Latino; 1 Asian, non-Hispanic/Latino; 7 Hispanic/Latino; 12 Two or more races, non-Hispanic/Latino), 11 international. Average age 38. 134 applicants, 57% accepted, 54 enrolled. In 2011, 76 master's, 18 doctorates awarded. *Degree requirements:* For master's, thesis or alternative; for doctorate, comprehensive exam, thesis/dissertation. *Entrance requirements:* For master's and doctorate, GRE or GMAT. Additional exam requirements/recommendations for international students: Required—TOEFL (minimum score 550 paper-based; 79 iBT). *Application deadline:* For fall admission, 3/1 for international students; for spring admission, 8/1 for international students. Applications are processed on a rolling basis. Application fee: $40 ($75 for international students). Electronic applications accepted. *Expenses:* Tuition, state resident: full-time $4044; part-time $168.50 per credit hour. Tuition, nonresident: full-time $16,008; part-time $667 per credit hour. *Required fees:* $2122; $88.45 per credit hour. One-time fee: $50. Tuition and fees vary according to course load and campus/location. *Financial support:* In 2011–12, 15 research assistantships (averaging $9,475 per year), 8 teaching assistantships (averaging $14,925 per year) were awarded; career-related internships or fieldwork, Federal Work-Study, scholarships/grants, health care benefits, tuition waivers (partial), and unspecified assistantships also available. Support available to part-time students. Financial award application deadline: 3/1; financial award applicants required to submit FAFSA. *Unit head:* Dr. Pamela Brown, Interim Head, 405-744-7125, Fax: 405-744-6290. *Application contact:* Dr. Sheryl Tucker, Dean, 405-744-7099, Fax: 405-744-0355, E-mail: grad-i@okstate.edu. Web site: http://education.okstate.edu/index.php/academic-units/stcl.

Old Dominion University, Darden College of Education, Doctoral Program in Curriculum and Instruction, Norfolk, VA 23529. Offers PhD. Part-time and evening/weekend programs available. *Faculty:* 9 full-time (6 women). *Students:* 8 full-time (6 women), 14 part-time (10 women); includes 2 minority (1 Black or African American, non-Hispanic/Latino; 1 Hispanic/Latino). Average age 40. 8 applicants, 63% accepted, 3 enrolled. In 2011, 5 doctorates awarded. *Degree requirements:* For doctorate, comprehensive exam, thesis/dissertation. *Entrance requirements:* For doctorate, GRE, letters of recommendation; minimum undergraduate GPA of 2.8, graduate 3.2. Additional exam requirements/recommendations for international students: Required—TOEFL (minimum score 600 paper-based; 250 computer-based). *Application deadline:* For fall admission, 3/15 priority date for domestic students, 3/15 for international students; for spring admission, 11/15 for domestic and international students. Applications are processed on a rolling basis. Application fee: $50. Electronic applications accepted. *Expenses:* Tuition, state resident: full-time $9096; part-time $379 per credit. Tuition, nonresident: full-time $23,064; part-time $961 per credit. *Required fees:* $127 per semester. One-time fee: $50. *Financial support:* In 2011–12, fellowships with full tuition reimbursements (averaging $15,000 per year), 3 teaching assistantships with full tuition reimbursements (averaging $15,000 per year) were awarded; scholarships/grants and unspecified assistantships also available. Financial award application deadline: 4/15. *Faculty research:* Curriculum change, language arts, library science, multicultural education, foundations in education. *Unit head:* Dr. Charlene Fleener, Graduate Program Director, 757-683-4387, E-mail: cfleener@odu.edu. *Application contact:* William Heffelfinger, Director of Graduate Admissions, 757-683-5554, Fax: 757-683-3255, E-mail: gradadmit@odu.edu. Web site: http://education.odu.edu/eci/ciphd/.

Old Dominion University, Darden College of Education, Program in Physical Education, Curriculum and Instruction Emphasis, Norfolk, VA 23529. Offers MS Ed. Part-time and evening/weekend programs available. *Faculty:* 1 (woman) full-time, 1 (woman) part-time/adjunct. *Students:* 3 full-time (2 women), 3 part-time (0 women); includes 1 minority (Native Hawaiian or other Pacific Islander, non-Hispanic/Latino). Average age 28. 6 applicants, 83% accepted, 1 enrolled. In 2011, 6 master's awarded. *Degree requirements:* For master's, comprehensive exam (for some programs), thesis or alternative, internship, research project. *Entrance requirements:* For master's, GRE, PRAXIS I (for licensure only), minimum GPA of 2.8 overall, 3.0 in major. Additional exam requirements/recommendations for international students: Required—TOEFL (minimum score 500 paper-based; 200 computer-based). *Application deadline:* For fall admission, 7/1 priority date for domestic students; for spring admission, 11/1 priority date for domestic students. Applications are processed on a rolling basis. Application fee: $50. Electronic applications accepted. *Expenses:* Tuition, state resident: full-time $9096; part-time $379 per credit. Tuition, nonresident: full-time $23,064; part-time $961 per credit. *Required fees:* $127 per semester. One-time fee: $50. *Financial support:* In 2011–12, 1 teaching assistantship with partial tuition reimbursement (averaging $9,000 per year) was awarded; career-related internships or fieldwork and scholarships/grants also available. Financial award application deadline: 4/15. *Faculty research:* Motor development, physical education, health education. *Unit head:* Xihu Zhu, Graduate Program Director, 757-683-4995, E-mail: lgagen@odu.edu. *Application contact:* William Heffelfinger, Director of Graduate Admissions, 757-683-5554, Fax: 757-683-3255, E-mail: gradadmit@odu.edu. Web site: http://education.odu.edu/esper/academics/degrees/hpe/hpe.shtml.

Olivet Nazarene University, Graduate School, Division of Education, Program in Curriculum and Instruction, Bourbonnais, IL 60914. Offers MAE. Evening/weekend programs available. *Degree requirements:* For master's, thesis or alternative.

Oral Roberts University, School of Education, Tulsa, OK 74171. Offers Christian school administration (K-12) (MA Ed, Ed D); Christian school curriculum development (MA Ed); college and higher education administration (Ed D); public school administration (K-12) (MA Ed, Ed D); public school teaching (MA Ed). *Accreditation:* NCATE. Part-time programs available. Postbaccalaureate distance learning degree programs offered (minimal on-campus study). *Degree requirements:* For master's, comprehensive exam, thesis optional; for doctorate, comprehensive exam, thesis/dissertation. *Entrance requirements:* For master's, GRE General Test or MAT, minimum GPA of 3.0; for doctorate, minimum GPA of 3.0. Additional exam requirements/recommendations for international students: Required—TOEFL (minimum score 500 paper-based; 173 computer-based). *Expenses:* Contact institution. *Faculty research:* Teacher effectiveness, college success in high achieving African-Americans, professional development practices.

Ottawa University, Graduate Studies-Arizona, Program in Education, Ottawa, KS 66067-3399. Offers community college counseling (MA); curriculum and instruction (MA); early childhood (MA); education intervention (MA); education leadership (MA); education technology (MA); Montessori early childhood education (MA); Montessori elementary education (MA); professional development (MA); school guidance counseling (MA); special education - cross categorical (MA). Programs offered in Mesa, Phoenix, Tempe and West Valley, AZ. *Accreditation:* NCATE. Part-time programs available. *Degree requirements:* For master's, thesis or alternative. *Entrance requirements:* For master's, minimum undergraduate GPA of 3.0, copy of current state certification or teaching license. Additional exam requirements/recommendations for international students: Required—TOEFL (minimum score 550 paper-based; 213 computer-based). Electronic applications accepted. *Expenses:* Contact institution.

Our Lady of Holy Cross College, Program in Education and Counseling, New Orleans, LA 70131-7399. Offers administration and supervision (M Ed); curriculum and instruction (M Ed); marriage and family counseling (MA); school counseling (M Ed, MA). *Accreditation:* ACA; NCATE. Part-time and evening/weekend programs available. *Degree requirements:* For master's, thesis. *Entrance requirements:* For master's, GRE General Test, minimum GPA of 2.7.

Our Lady of the Lake University of San Antonio, School of Professional Studies, Program in Curriculum and Instruction, San Antonio, TX 78207-4689. Offers bilingual (M Ed); early childhood education (M Ed); English as a second language (M Ed); integrated math teaching (M Ed); integrated science teaching (M Ed); master reading teacher (M Ed); master technology teacher (M Ed); reading specialist (M Ed).

Pacific Lutheran University, Division of Graduate Studies, School of Education, Program in Initial Teaching Certification, Tacoma, WA 98447. Offers MAE. *Accreditation:* NCATE. *Faculty:* 10 full-time (5 women), 1 (woman) part-time/adjunct. *Students:* 41 full-time (24 women), 1 (woman) part-time; includes 5 minority (1 Black or African American, non-Hispanic/Latino; 1 American Indian or Alaska Native, non-Hispanic/Latino; 2 Asian, non-Hispanic/Latino; 1 Hispanic/Latino), 2 international. Average age 27. 60 applicants, 97% accepted, 41 enrolled. In 2011, 29 master's awarded. *Degree requirements:* For master's, comprehensive exam, thesis. *Entrance requirements:* For master's, GRE General Test or MAT, interview. Additional exam requirements/recommendations for international students: Required—TOEFL (minimum score 550 paper-based; 213 computer-based). *Application deadline:* For fall admission, 1/31 priority date for domestic students. Application fee: $40. *Expenses:* Contact institution. *Financial support:* In 2011–12, 34 students received support, including 10 fellowships (averaging $2,500 per year); Federal Work-Study, scholarships/grants, and unspecified assistantships also available. Financial award application deadline: 3/1. *Unit head:* Dr. Michael Hillis, Graduate Director, 253-535-7272, Fax: 253-535-7184, E-mail: hillis@plu.edu. *Application contact:* Linda DuBay, Senior Office Assistant, 253-535-7151, Fax: 253-536-5136, E-mail: admissions@plu.edu.

Penn State Harrisburg, Graduate School, School of Behavioral Sciences and Education, Middletown, PA 17057-4898. Offers applied behavior analysis (MA); applied clinical psychology (MA); applied psychological research (MA); community psychology and social change (MA); health education (M Ed); literacy education (M Ed); teaching and curriculum (M Ed); training and development (M Ed). Part-time and evening/weekend programs available. *Financial support:* Career-related internships or fieldwork available. *Unit head:* Dr. Catherine A. Surra, Director, 717-948-6205, Fax: 717-948-6209, E-mail: cas87@psu.edu. *Application contact:* Robert Coffman, Director of Admissions, 717-948-6214, E-mail: rwc11@psu.edu. Web site: http://harrisburg.psu.edu/behavioral-sciences-and-education/.

Penn State University Park, Graduate School, College of Education, Department of Curriculum and Instruction, State College, University Park, PA 16802-1503. Offers M Ed, MS, D Ed, PhD, Certificate. *Accreditation:* NCATE. *Unit head:* Dr. David H. Monk, Dean, 814-865-2526, Fax: 814-865-0555, E-mail: dhm6@psu.edu. *Application contact:* Cynthia E. Nicosia, Director, Graduate Enrollment Services, 814-865-1834, E-mail: cey1@psu.edu. Web site: http://www.ed.psu.edu/educ/c-and-i/.

Peru State College, Graduate Programs, Program in Education, Peru, NE 68421. Offers curriculum and instruction (MS Ed). *Accreditation:* NCATE. Part-time programs available. *Degree requirements:* For master's, comprehensive exam (for some programs), thesis optional.

Point Park University, School of Arts and Sciences, Department of Education, Pittsburgh, PA 15222-1984. Offers curriculum and instruction (MA); educational administration (MA); special education (M Ed); teaching and leadership (M Ed). Part-time and evening/weekend programs available. *Faculty:* 5 full-time, 9 part-time/adjunct. *Students:* 12 full-time (8 women), 40 part-time (31 women); includes 12 minority (11 Black or African American, non-Hispanic/Latino; 1 Asian, non-Hispanic/Latino), 2 international. Average age 33. 46 applicants, 61% accepted, 18 enrolled. In 2011, 15 master's awarded. *Degree requirements:* For master's, comprehensive exam (for some programs), thesis or alternative. *Entrance requirements:* For master's, minimum GPA of 3.0, resume, 2 letters of recommendation. Additional exam requirements/recommendations for international students: Required—TOEFL. *Application deadline:* Applications are processed on a rolling basis. Application fee: $30. Electronic applications accepted. *Expenses: Tuition:* Full-time $13,050; part-time $725 per credit. *Required fees:* $720; $40 per credit. *Financial support:* In 2011–12, 42 students received support, including 2 teaching assistantships with full tuition reimbursements available (averaging $6,400 per year); scholarships/grants also available. Financial award application deadline: 4/15; financial award applicants required to submit FAFSA. *Unit head:* Dr. Darlene Marnich, Chair, 412-392-3474, Fax: 412-392-3927, E-mail: dmarnich@pointpark.edu. *Application contact:* Lynn C. Ribar, Associate Director, Graduate and Adult Enrollment, 412-392-3908, Fax: 412-392-6164, E-mail: lribar@pointpark.edu.

Pontifical Catholic University of Puerto Rico, College of Education, Doctoral Program in Curriculum and Instruction, Ponce, PR 00717-0777. Offers PhD. *Degree requirements:* For doctorate, thesis/dissertation. *Entrance requirements:* For doctorate, EXADEP, GRE General Test or MAT, 3 letters of recommendation.

Pontifical Catholic University of Puerto Rico, College of Education, Master's Program in Curriculum and Instruction, Ponce, PR 00717-0777. Offers M Ed. *Degree requirements:* For master's, comprehensive exam, thesis (for some programs). *Entrance requirements:* For master's, GRE, 2 letters of recommendation, interview, minimum GPA of 2.75.

Portland State University, Graduate Studies, School of Education, Department of Curriculum and Instruction, Portland, OR 97207-0751. Offers early childhood education (MA, MS); education (M Ed, MA, MS); educational leadership: curriculum and instruction (Ed D); educational media/school librarianship (MA, MS); elementary education (M Ed, MAT, MST); reading (MA, MS); secondary education (M Ed, MAT, MST). *Accreditation:* NCATE. Part-time programs available. *Degree requirements:* For master's, comprehensive exam, thesis or alternative; for doctorate, thesis/dissertation. *Entrance requirements:* For master's, California Basic Educational Skills Test, minimum GPA of 3.0 in upper-division course work or 2.75 overall. Additional exam requirements/recommendations for international students: Required—TOEFL (minimum score 550 paper-based; 213 computer-based). *Faculty research:* Early literacy, characteristics of successful teachers of at-risk students, participation of women/minorities in technology courses, selection of cooperating teachers.

Prairie View A&M University, College of Education, Department of Curriculum and Instruction, Prairie View, TX 77446-0519. Offers curriculum and instruction (M Ed, MS Ed); special education (M Ed, MS Ed). *Accreditation:* NCATE. Part-time and evening/weekend programs available. *Degree requirements:* For master's, thesis optional. *Entrance requirements:* For master's, GRE, minimum GPA of 2.5, 3 references. Electronic applications accepted. *Faculty research:* Metacognitive strategies, emotionally disturbed, language arts, teachers recruit, diversity, recruitment, retention, school collaboration.

Purdue University, Graduate School, College of Education, Department of Curriculum and Instruction, West Lafayette, IN 47907. Offers agricultural and extension education (PhD, Ed S); agriculture and extension education (MS, MS Ed); art education (PhD); consumer and family sciences and extension education (MS Ed, PhD, Ed S); curriculum studies (MS Ed, PhD, Ed S); educational technology (MS Ed, PhD, Ed S); elementary education (MS Ed); foreign language education (MS Ed, PhD, Ed S); industrial technology (PhD, Ed S); language arts (MS Ed, PhD, Ed S); literacy (MS Ed, PhD, Ed S); mathematics/science education (MS, MS Ed, PhD, Ed S); social studies (MS Ed, PhD); social studies education (Ed S); vocational/industrial education (MS Ed, PhD, Ed S); vocational/technical education (MS Ed, PhD, Ed S). *Accreditation:* NCATE. Part-time and evening/weekend programs available. *Faculty:* 30 full-time (21 women), 1 (woman) part-time/adjunct. *Students:* 89 full-time (64 women), 134 part-time (84 women); includes 31 minority (12 Black or African American, non-Hispanic/Latino; 3 American Indian or Alaska Native, non-Hispanic/Latino; 7 Asian, non-Hispanic/Latino; 9 Hispanic/Latino), 49 international. Average age 36. 136 applicants, 83% accepted, 72 enrolled. In 2011, 26 master's, 13 doctorates awarded. *Degree requirements:* For master's, thesis optional; for doctorate, thesis/dissertation, oral and written exams; for Ed S, oral presentation, project. *Entrance requirements:* For master's, GRE general test is required if undergraduate GPA is below 3.0, minimum undergraduate GPA of 3.0 or equivalent; for doctorate, GRE General Test, a combined GRE verbal and quantitative score of 1000 (300 for revised GRE Test) or more is expected, minimum undergraduate GPA of 3.0 or equivalent; master's degree with minimum GPA of 3.0 or equivalent; for Ed S, GRE general test, a combined GRE verbal and quantitative score of 1000 (300 for revised GRE Test) or more is expected, minimum undergraduate GPA of 3.0 or equivalent; master's degree. Additional exam requirements/recommendations for international students: Required—TOEFL (minimum score 550 paper-based; 77 iBT). *Application deadline:* For fall admission, 12/15 priority date for domestic students, 3/1 for international students; for spring admission, 9/15 for domestic students, 8/1 for international students. Application fee: $60 ($75 for international students). Electronic applications accepted. *Financial support:* Fellowships with full tuition reimbursements, research assistantships with full tuition reimbursements, teaching assistantships with full tuition reimbursements, career-related internships or fieldwork, and tuition waivers (full) available. Support available to part-time students. Financial award application deadline: 3/1; financial award applicants required to submit FAFSA. *Faculty research:* Literacy acquisition and development, teacher beliefs and knowledge, recruitment and retention of underrepresented students, economic education, literacy discourse. *Unit head:* Dr. Philip J. VanFossen, Head, 765-494-7935, Fax: 765-496-1622, E-mail: vanfoss@purdue.edu. *Application contact:* Sarah N. Prater, Graduate Contact, 765-494-2345, Fax: 765-494-5832, E-mail: prater0@purdue.edu. Web site: http://www.edci.purdue.edu/.

Quincy University, Program in Education, Quincy, IL 62301-2699. Offers alternative certification (MS Ed); curriculum and instruction (MS Ed); leadership (MS Ed); reading education (MS Ed); school administration (MS Ed); special education (MS Ed); teacher leader in reading (MS Ed); teaching certification (MS Ed). Part-time and evening/weekend programs available. Postbaccalaureate distance learning degree programs offered. *Students:* 221 full-time (168 women), 100 part-time (69 women); includes 104 minority (69 Black or African American, non-Hispanic/Latino; 1 American Indian or Alaska Native, non-Hispanic/Latino; 5 Asian, non-Hispanic/Latino; 27 Hispanic/Latino; 2 Two or more races, non-Hispanic/Latino). In 2011, 132 master's awarded. *Degree requirements:* For master's, comprehensive exam (for some programs), thesis or alternative. *Entrance requirements:* For master's, MAT or GRE. Additional exam requirements/recommendations for international students: Required—TOEFL (minimum score 550 paper-based; 79 iBT). *Application deadline:* Applications are processed on a rolling basis. Application fee: $25. Electronic applications accepted. *Expenses: Tuition:* Full-time $9120; part-time $380 per semester hour. *Required fees:* $360; $15 per semester hour. Tuition and fees vary according to course load, campus/location and program. *Financial support:* Applicants required to submit FAFSA. *Unit head:* Kristen Anguiano, Director, 217-228-5432 Ext. 3119, E-mail: anguikr@quincy.edu. *Application contact:* Office of Admissions, 217-228-5210, Fax: 217-228-5479, E-mail: admissions@quincy.edu. Web site: http://www.quincy.edu/academics/graduate-programs/education.

Randolph College, Programs in Education, Lynchburg, VA 24503. Offers curriculum and instruction (MAT); special education-learning disabilities (M Ed, MAT). *Accreditation:* Teacher Education Accreditation Council. *Entrance requirements:* For master's, minimum GPA of 3.0 in prerequisite education coursework, 2.7 in major or field of interest (MAT); teaching license (M Ed); 2 recommendations; interview.

Regis University, College for Professional Studies, School of Education and Counseling, Department of Education, Denver, CO 80221-1099. Offers adult learning, training, and development (M Ed, Certificate); autism (Certificate); curriculum, instruction, and assessment (M Ed); educational leadership (Certificate); educational technology (Certificate); instructional technology (M Ed); literacy (Certificate); professional leadership (M Ed); reading (M Ed); self-designed (M Ed); space studies (M Ed). Program also offered in Henderson and Las Vegas (Summerlin), NV. *Accreditation:* Teacher Education Accreditation Council. Part-time and evening/weekend programs available. Postbaccalaureate distance learning degree programs offered (no on-campus study). *Degree requirements:* For master's, thesis. *Entrance requirements:* For master's, resume, minimum GPA of 2.75, criminal background check. Additional exam requirements/recommendations for international students: Required—TOEFL (minimum score 213 computer-based), TWE (minimum score 5). Electronic applications accepted. *Faculty research:* Issues of equity in the middle school classroom, professional learning communities, school reform, socialinguistic and discursive obstacles to student integration, inclusive language arts curriculum.

Rider University, Department of Graduate Education, Leadership and Counseling, Program in Curriculum, Instruction and Supervision, Lawrenceville, NJ 08648-3001. Offers curriculum, instruction and supervision (MA); supervisor (Certificate). *Accreditation:* NCATE. Part-time and evening/weekend programs available. *Degree requirements:* For master's, comprehensive exam, practicum project. *Entrance requirements:* For master's, interview, 2 letters of recommendation from current supervisors, resume. Additional exam requirements/recommendations for international students: Required—TOEFL (minimum score 550 paper-based; 213 computer-based). Electronic applications accepted. *Expenses: Tuition:* Full-time $32,820; part-time $710 per credit. *Required fees:* $350; $35 per course. Tuition and fees vary according to campus/location and program. *Faculty research:* Curriculum change, curriculum development, teacher evaluation.

Rivier University, School of Graduate Studies, Department of Education, Nashua, NH 03060. Offers curriculum and instruction (M Ed); early childhood education (M Ed); educational administration (M Ed); educational studies (M Ed); elementary education (M Ed); elementary education and general special education (M Ed); emotional and behavioral disorders (M Ed); general social education (M Ed); leadership and learning (Ed D, CAGS); learning disabilities (M Ed); learning disabilities and reading (M Ed); mental health counseling (MA); reading (M Ed); school counseling (M Ed). Part-time and evening/weekend programs available. *Degree requirements:* For master's, comprehensive exam (for some programs), internships. *Entrance requirements:* For master's, GRE General Test or MAT.

Rowan University, Graduate School, College of Education, Department of Educational Leadership, Program in Supervision and Curriculum Development, Glassboro, NJ 08028-1701. Offers MA. *Accreditation:* NCATE. Part-time and evening/weekend programs available. *Degree requirements:* For master's, comprehensive exam, thesis. *Entrance requirements:* For master's, GRE General Test, minimum GPA of 2.8, 2 years of teaching experience. Additional exam requirements/recommendations for international students: Required—TOEFL. Electronic applications accepted.

St. Catherine University, Graduate Programs, Program in Education–Curriculum and Instruction, St. Paul, MN 55105. Offers MA. Part-time and evening/weekend programs available. Postbaccalaureate distance learning degree programs offered (minimal on-campus study). *Degree requirements:* For master's, thesis. *Entrance requirements:* For master's, current teaching license, classroom experience, minimum GPA of 3.0. Additional exam requirements/recommendations for international students: Required—Michigan English Language Assessment Battery or TOEFL (minimum score 600 paper-based; 250 computer-based; 100 iBT). *Expenses:* Contact institution.

St. Cloud State University, School of Graduate Studies, School of Education, Department of Teacher Development, St. Cloud, MN 56301-4498. Offers curriculum and instruction (MS). *Degree requirements:* For master's, thesis or alternative. *Entrance requirements:* For master's, GRE General Test, minimum GPA of 2.75. Additional exam requirements/recommendations for international students: Required—Michigan English Language Assessment Battery; Recommended—TOEFL (minimum score 550 paper-based; 213 computer-based), IELTS (minimum score 6.5). Electronic applications accepted.

St. Francis Xavier University, Graduate Studies, Graduate Studies in Education, Antigonish, NS B2G 2W5, Canada. Offers curriculum and instruction (M Ed); educational administration and leadership (M Ed). Part-time programs available. Postbaccalaureate distance learning degree programs offered (minimal on-campus study). *Degree requirements:* For master's, thesis. *Entrance requirements:* For master's, minimum undergraduate B average, 2 years of teaching experience. *Faculty research:* Inclusive education, qualitative research.

Saint Joseph's University, College of Arts and Sciences, Department of Education, Philadelphia, PA 19131-1395. Offers curriculum supervisor of instruction (Certificate); educational leadership (MS, Ed D); elementary education (MS, Certificate); elementary/middle years (Certificate); English second language specialist online (Certificate); hearing impaired: N-12th grade (Certificate); instructional technology (MS, Certificate); principal certification (Certificate); professional education (MS); reading specialist (MS, Certificate); reading supervisory (Certificate); secondary education (MS, Certificate); special education (MS, Certificate); superintendent's letter of eligibility (Certificate); supervisor of special education (Certificate); Wilson reading certificate online (Certificate). Part-time and evening/weekend programs available. Postbaccalaureate distance learning degree programs offered (no on-campus study). *Faculty:* 26 full-time (24 women), 83 part-time/adjunct (52 women). *Students:* 112 full-time (92 women), 923 part-time (709 women); includes 147 minority (92 Black or African American, non-Hispanic/Latino; 4 American Indian or Alaska Native, non-Hispanic/Latino; 19 Asian, non-Hispanic/Latino; 28 Hispanic/Latino; 4 Two or more races, non-Hispanic/Latino), 8 international. Average age 31. 285 applicants, 77% accepted, 176 enrolled. In 2011, 276 master's, 13 doctorates, 2 other advanced degrees awarded. *Entrance requirements:* For master's, 2 letters of recommendation, minimum GPA of 3.0, official transcripts, personal statement; for doctorate, GRE, master's degree from accredited institution, minimum graduate GPA of 3.5, computer competence, commitment to participate in cohort, interview with program director. Additional exam requirements/recommendations for international students: Required—TOEFL (minimum score 550 paper-based; 213 computer-based; 79 iBT). *Application deadline:* For fall admission, 7/15 priority date for domestic students, 4/15 for international students; for winter admission, 11/15 for domestic students, 1/15 for international students; for spring admission, 11/15 priority date for domestic students, 10/15 for international students. Applications are processed on a rolling basis. Application fee: $35. Electronic applications accepted. *Expenses:* Contact institution. *Financial support:* Unspecified assistantships available. Financial award applicants required to submit FAFSA. *Faculty research:* Public education professional development, factors predicting early mathematics skills for low income children. *Total annual research expenditures:* $92,975. *Unit head:* Dr. Jeanne Brady, Associate Dean, Education, 610-660-1580, E-mail: jebrady@sju.edu. *Application contact:* Kate McConnell, Director, Graduate College of Arts and Sciences Admissions and Retention, 610-660-3184, Fax: 610-660-3230, E-mail: kate.mcconnell@sju.edu.

Saint Leo University, Graduate Studies in Education, Saint Leo, FL 33574-6665. Offers educational leadership (M Ed); exceptional student education (M Ed); higher education leadership (Ed S); instructional design (MS); instructional leadership (M Ed); reading (M Ed); school leadership (Ed S). Part-time and evening/weekend programs available. Postbaccalaureate distance learning degree programs offered (minimal on-campus study). *Faculty:* 14 full-time (10 women), 21 part-time/adjunct (16 women). *Students:* 523 full-time (427 women), 20 part-time (17 women); includes 65 minority (43 Black or African American, non-Hispanic/Latino; 2 Asian, non-Hispanic/Latino; 16 Hispanic/Latino; 4 Two or more races, non-Hispanic/Latino), 3 international. Average age 37. In 2011, 153 master's, 18 other advanced degrees awarded. *Degree requirements:* For master's, comprehensive exam, appropriate State of Florida certification tests. *Entrance requirements:* For master's, GRE (minimum score of 1000) or MAT (minimum score of 410) if undergraduate GPA for last 60 hours of coursework was below 3.0 (for M Ed), bachelor's degree with minimum GPA of 3.0 for last 60 hours of coursework from regionally-accredited college or university, 2 recommendations, resume, statement of professional goals, copy of valid teaching certificate (for M Ed); for Ed S, GRE (minimum score 1000) or MAT (minimum score 410) if undergraduate GPA for last 60 hours of coursework less than 3.0, bachelor's degree with minimum GPA of 3.0 for last 60 hours of coursework from regionally-accredited college or university, 2 recommendations, resume, valid teaching certificate. Additional exam requirements/recommendations for international students: Required—TOEFL (minimum score 550 paper-based; 213 computer-based; 80 iBT). *Application deadline:* For fall admission, 7/1 priority date for domestic students, 7/1 for international students; for winter admission, 7/1 for international students; for spring admission, 11/1 priority date for domestic students. Applications are processed on a rolling basis. Application fee: $80. Electronic applications accepted. *Expenses:* Contact institution. *Financial support:* In 2011–12, 20 students received support. Career-related internships or fieldwork, Federal Work-Study, scholarships/grants, and health care benefits available. Financial award application deadline: 3/1; financial award applicants required to submit FAFSA. *Faculty research:* The role of the school leader in data analysis of student achievement, teacher recruitment, teacher effectiveness. *Unit head:* Dr. Sharyn Disabato, Director, 352-588-8309, Fax: 352-588-8861, E-mail: med@saintleo.edu. *Application contact:* Jared Welling, Director of Graduate Admission, 800-707-8846, Fax: 352-588-7873, E-mail: grad.admissions@saintleo.edu. Web site: http://www.saintleo.edu/Academics/School-of-Education-Social-Services/Graduate-Degree-Programs.

Saint Louis University, Graduate Education, College of Education and Public Service, Department of Educational Studies, St. Louis, MO 63103-2097. Offers curriculum and instruction (MA, Ed D, PhD); educational foundations (MA, Ed D, PhD); special education (MA); teaching (MAT). *Accreditation:* NCATE. Part-time programs available. *Degree requirements:* For master's, comprehensive exam; for doctorate, comprehensive exam, thesis/dissertation, preliminary oral and written exams. *Entrance requirements:* For master's, GRE General Test or MAT, letters of recommendation, resume; for doctorate, GRE General Test, letters of recommendation, resumé, goal statement, transcripts. Additional exam requirements/recommendations for international students: Required—TOEFL (minimum score 525 paper-based; 194 computer-based). Electronic applications accepted. *Faculty research:* Teacher preparation, multicultural issues, children with special needs, qualitative research in education, inclusion.

Saint Mary's College of California, Kalmanovitz School of Education, Program in Early Childhood Education, Moraga, CA 94556. Offers curriculum and instruction (MA); supervision and leadership (MA). Part-time and evening/weekend programs available. *Students:* 9 part-time (all women); includes 1 minority (Black or African American, non-Hispanic/Latino). Average age 33. In 2011, 1 master's awarded. *Degree requirements:* For master's, thesis or alternative. *Entrance requirements:* For master's, interview, minimum GPA of 3.0. *Application deadline:* Applications are processed on a rolling basis. Application fee: $50. Tuition and fees vary according to course load, degree level and program. *Financial support:* Career-related internships or fieldwork available. Support available to part-time students. Financial award application deadline: 2/15. *Unit head:* Patricia Chambers, Coordinator, 925-631-4036, Fax: 925-376-8379, E-mail: pchambers@stmarys-ca.edu. *Application contact:* Jane Joyce, Coordinator, Recruitment and Admissions, 925-631-4700, Fax: 925-376-8379, E-mail: soereq@stmarys-ca.edu. Web site: http://www.stmarys-ca.edu/master-of-arts-degree-in-early-childhood-education.

Saint Mary's College of California, Kalmanovitz School of Education, Program in Instruction, Moraga, CA 94556. Offers M Ed. *Students:* 23 full-time (18 women), 21 part-time (13 women); includes 11 minority (2 Black or African American, non-Hispanic/Latino; 3 Asian, non-Hispanic/Latino; 6 Hispanic/Latino). Average age 33. In 2011, 16 master's awarded. Tuition and fees vary according to course load, degree level and program. *Unit head:* Dr. Mary Parish, Director, 925-631-4249, Fax: 925-376-8379, E-mail: mparish@stmarys-ca.edu. *Application contact:* Jane Joyce, Coordinator of Recruitment and Admissions, 925-631-4700, Fax: 925-376-8379, E-mail: soereq@stmarys-ca.edu.

Saint Michael's College, Graduate Programs, Program in Education, Colchester, VT 05439. Offers administration (M Ed, CAGS); arts in education (CAGS); curriculum and instruction (M Ed, CAGS); information technology (CAGS); reading (M Ed); special education (M Ed, CAGS); technology (M Ed). Part-time and evening/weekend programs available. *Degree requirements:* For master's, thesis. *Entrance requirements:* For master's, minimum GPA of 3.0. Electronic applications accepted. *Faculty research:* Integrative curriculum, moral and spiritual dimensions of education, learning styles, multiple intelligences, integrating technology into the curriculum.

Saint Vincent College, Program in Education, Latrobe, PA 15650-2690. Offers curriculum and instruction (MS); educational media and technology (MS); environmental education (MS); school administration and supervision (MS); special education (MS). Part-time and evening/weekend programs available. *Degree requirements:* For master's, comprehensive exam. *Entrance requirements:* For master's, GRE (if undergraduate GPA less than 3.0). Additional exam requirements/recommendations for international students: Required—TOEFL (minimum score 550 paper-based; 213 computer-based). *Faculty research:* Assessment and instructional technology.

Saint Xavier University, Graduate Studies, School of Education, Chicago, IL 60655-3105. Offers counseling (MA); curriculum and instruction (MA); early childhood education (MA); educational administration (MA); elementary education (MA); individualized studies (MA), including educational technology, English as a second language (ESL), ISTEM (integrative science, technology, engineering, and math), science education; music education (MA); reading (MA); secondary education (MA); Spanish education (MA); special education (MA); teaching and leadership (MA). *Accreditation:* NCATE. Part-time and evening/weekend programs available. *Degree requirements:* For master's, thesis or project. *Entrance requirements:* For master's, minimum GPA of 3.0. *Application deadline:* For fall admission, 8/15 priority date for domestic students. Applications are processed on a rolling basis. Application fee: $35. *Expenses:* Contact institution. *Financial support:* Career-related internships or fieldwork available. Support available to part-time students. Financial award applicants required to submit FAFSA. *Unit head:* Dr. Beverly Gulley, Dean, 773-298-3221, Fax: 773-779-9061, E-mail: gulley@sxu.edu. *Application contact:* Beth Gierach, Managing Director of Admission, 773-298-3053, Fax: 773-298-3076, E-mail: gierach@sxu.edu.

Salem International University, School of Education, Salem, WV 26426-0500. Offers curriculum and instruction (M Ed); educational leadership (M Ed). Part-time and evening/weekend programs available. Postbaccalaureate distance learning degree programs offered. *Degree requirements:* For master's, comprehensive exam (for some programs), thesis (for some programs). *Entrance requirements:* For master's, GRE, MAT, NTE, 3 letters of recommendation. Additional exam requirements/recommendations for international students: Required—TOEFL (minimum score 550 paper-based; 213 computer-based). Electronic applications accepted. *Expenses:* Contact institution. *Faculty research:* Improved classroom effectiveness.

Sam Houston State University, College of Education, Department of Curriculum and Instruction, Huntsville, TX 77341. Offers curriculum and instruction (M Ed, MA); instructional technology (M Ed). *Accreditation:* NCATE. Part-time and evening/weekend programs available. *Faculty:* 13 full-time (8 women), 1 part-time/adjunct (0 women). *Students:* 25 full-time (17 women), 192 part-time (156 women); includes 72 minority (37 Black or African American, non-Hispanic/Latino; 3 American Indian or Alaska Native, non-Hispanic/Latino; 4 Asian, non-Hispanic/Latino; 27 Hispanic/Latino; 1 Native Hawaiian or other Pacific Islander, non-Hispanic/Latino). Average age 33. 285 applicants, 51% accepted, 86 enrolled. In 2011, 53 master's awarded. *Entrance requirements:* For master's, GRE General Test. Additional exam requirements/recommendations for international students: Required—TOEFL (minimum score 550 paper-based; 213 computer-based; 79 iBT). *Application deadline:* For fall admission, 8/1 for domestic students, 6/25 for international students; for spring admission, 12/1 for domestic students, 11/12 for international students. Application fee: $45 ($75 for international students). *Expenses:* Tuition, state resident: full-time $4420; part-time $221 per credit hour. Tuition, nonresident: full-time $10,680; part-time $534 per credit hour. *Required fees:* $329 per credit hour. *Financial support:* Teaching assistantships and institutionally sponsored loans available. Financial award application deadline: 5/31; financial award applicants required to submit FAFSA. *Unit head:* Dr. Daphne Johnson, Chair, 936-294-3875, Fax: 936-294-1056, E-mail: edu_dxe@shsu.edu. *Application contact:* Dr. Eren Johnson, Advisor, 936-294-1140, E-mail: edu_mej@shsu.edu. Web site: http://www.shsu.edu/~cai_www/.

Curriculum and Instruction

San Diego State University, Graduate and Research Affairs, College of Education, School of Teacher Education, Program in Elementary Curriculum and Instruction, San Diego, CA 92182. Offers MA. *Accreditation:* NCATE. Evening/weekend programs available. *Entrance requirements:* For master's, GRE General Test, letters of reference. Additional exam requirements/recommendations for international students: Required—TOEFL. Electronic applications accepted.

San Diego State University, Graduate and Research Affairs, College of Education, School of Teacher Education, Program in Secondary Curriculum and Instruction, San Diego, CA 92182. Offers MA. *Accreditation:* NCATE. *Entrance requirements:* For master's, GRE General Test, letters of reference. Additional exam requirements/recommendations for international students: Required—TOEFL. Electronic applications accepted.

San Jose State University, Graduate Studies and Research, Connie L. Lurie College of Education, Department of Elementary Education, San Jose, CA 95192-0001. Offers curriculum and instruction (MA); reading (Certificate). *Accreditation:* NCATE. *Degree requirements:* For master's, thesis or alternative. Electronic applications accepted.

Seattle Pacific University, M Ed in Curriculum and Instruction Program, Seattle, WA 98119-1997. Offers reading/language arts education (M Ed). *Accreditation:* NCATE. Part-time and evening/weekend programs available. *Degree requirements:* For master's, comprehensive exam. *Entrance requirements:* For master's, GRE General Test or MAT, minimum GPA of 3.0. Additional exam requirements/recommendations for international students: Required—TOEFL (minimum score 550 paper-based). Electronic applications accepted. *Expenses:* Contact institution. *Faculty research:* Educational technology, classroom environments, character education.

Seattle University, College of Education, Program in Curriculum and Instruction, Seattle, WA 98122-1090. Offers M Ed, MA, Certificate. *Accreditation:* NCATE. Part-time and evening/weekend programs available. *Students:* 5 full-time (3 women), 23 part-time (18 women); includes 3 minority (2 Black or African American, non-Hispanic/Latino; 1 Hispanic/Latino), 2 international. Average age 29. 9 applicants, 89% accepted, 7 enrolled. In 2011, 25 master's, 1 other advanced degree awarded. *Degree requirements:* For master's, comprehensive exam. *Entrance requirements:* For master's, GRE, MAT, or minimum GPA of 3.0; 1 year of related experience. Additional exam requirements/recommendations for international students: Required—TOEFL. *Application deadline:* For fall admission, 8/20 for domestic students; for winter admission, 11/20 for domestic students; for spring admission, 2/20 for domestic students. Applications are processed on a rolling basis. Application fee: $55. *Financial support:* Career-related internships or fieldwork and Federal Work-Study available. Support available to part-time students. Financial award applicants required to submit FAFSA. *Unit head:* Dr. Katherine Schlick Noe, Director, 206-296-5768, E-mail: kschlnoe@seattleu.edu. *Application contact:* Janet Shandley, Associate Dean of Graduate Admissions, 206-296-5900, Fax: 206-298-5656, E-mail: grad_admissions@seattleu.edu.

Shawnee State University, Program in Curriculum and Instruction, Portsmouth, OH 45662-4344. Offers M Ed. *Accreditation:* NCATE.

Shaw University, Department of Education, Raleigh, NC 27601-2399. Offers curriculum and instruction (MS). Part-time and evening/weekend programs available. *Degree requirements:* For master's, comprehensive exam, thesis, practicum/internship, PRAXIS II. *Entrance requirements:* For master's, GRE General Test, letters of recommendation. Additional exam requirements/recommendations for international students: Required—TOEFL (minimum score 500 paper-based). Electronic applications accepted. *Faculty research:* Multicultural education, instructional technology.

Shepherd University, Program in Curriculum and Instruction, Shepherdstown, WV 25443. Offers MA. *Accreditation:* NCATE.

Shippensburg University of Pennsylvania, School of Graduate Studies, College of Education and Human Services, Department of Teacher Education, Shippensburg, PA 17257-2299. Offers curriculum and instruction (M Ed), including biology, early childhood education, elementary education, English, geography/earth science, history, mathematics, middle level education, modern languages; reading (M Ed). *Accreditation:* NCATE. Part-time and evening/weekend programs available. *Faculty:* 14 full-time (11 women), 8 part-time/adjunct (7 women). *Students:* 16 full-time (15 women), 143 part-time (130 women); includes 11 minority (4 Black or African American, non-Hispanic/Latino; 1 Asian, non-Hispanic/Latino; 4 Hispanic/Latino; 2 Two or more races, non-Hispanic/Latino), 1 international. Average age 30. 55 applicants, 55% accepted, 25 enrolled. In 2011, 76 master's awarded. *Degree requirements:* For master's, comprehensive exam (for some programs), thesis optional, practicum or internship; capstone seminar (for some programs). *Entrance requirements:* For master's, MAT (if GPA less than 2.75), interview, 3 letters of reference, questionnaire of teaching background and future goals. Additional exam requirements/recommendations for international students: Required—TOEFL (minimum score 580 paper-based; 237 computer-based); Recommended—IELTS (minimum score 6). *Application deadline:* For fall admission, 6/1 priority date for domestic students, 4/30 for international students; for spring admission, 9/1 priority date for domestic students, 9/30 for international students. Applications are processed on a rolling basis. Application fee: $30. Electronic applications accepted. *Expenses: Tuition, area resident:* Part-time $416 per credit. Tuition, state resident: part-time $416 per credit. Tuition, nonresident: part-time $624 per credit. *Required fees:* $119 per credit. *Financial support:* In 2011–12, 5 research assistantships with full tuition reimbursements (averaging $5,000 per year) were awarded; career-related internships or fieldwork, scholarships/grants, unspecified assistantships, and resident hall director and student payroll positions also available. Support available to part-time students. Financial award application deadline: 3/1; financial award applicants required to submit FAFSA. *Unit head:* Dr. Christine A. Royce, Chairperson, 717-477-1688, Fax: 717-477-4046, E-mail: caroyc@ship.edu. *Application contact:* Jeremy R. Goshorn, Assistant Dean of Graduate Admissions, 717-477-1231, Fax: 717-477-4016, E-mail: jrgoshorn@ship.edu. Web site: http://www.ship.edu/teacher/.

Shorter University, Professional Studies, Rome, GA 30165. Offers accountancy (MAC); business administration (MBA); curriculum and instruction (M Ed); leadership (MA). Evening/weekend programs available. *Degree requirements:* For master's, project. *Entrance requirements:* For master's, minimum undergraduate GPA of 2.75 in last 60 hours, 3 years of work experience. Additional exam requirements/recommendations for international students: Required—TOEFL (minimum score 550 paper-based; 213 computer-based; 79 iBT). *Faculty research:* Systems design, leadership, pedagogy using technology.

Simon Fraser University, Graduate Studies, Faculty of Education, Programs in Curriculum and Instruction, Burnaby, BC V5A 1S6, Canada. Offers curriculum theory and implementation (PhD); foundations (M Ed, MA); philosophy of education (PhD). *Degree requirements:* For master's, project or thesis; for doctorate, thesis/dissertation. *Entrance requirements:* For master's, minimum GPA of 3.0; for doctorate, GRE, master's degree or exceptional record in a bachelor's degree, minimum GPA of 3.5. Additional exam requirements/recommendations for international students: Required—TOEFL or IELTS.

South Dakota State University, Graduate School, College of Education and Human Sciences, Department of Educational Leadership, Brookings, SD 57007. Offers curriculum and instruction (M Ed); educational administration (M Ed). Part-time and evening/weekend programs available. Postbaccalaureate distance learning degree programs offered (minimal on-campus study). *Degree requirements:* For master's, portfolio, oral exam. *Entrance requirements:* For master's, minimum GPA of 2.75. Additional exam requirements/recommendations for international students: Required—TOEFL (minimum score 550 paper-based; 213 computer-based; 80 iBT). *Faculty research:* Inclusion school climate, K-12 reform and restructuring, rural development, ESL, leadership.

Southeastern Louisiana University, College of Education and Human Development, Department of Teaching and Learning, Hammond, LA 70402. Offers curriculum and instruction (M Ed); elementary education (MAT); special education (M Ed); special education: early interventionist (MAT). *Accreditation:* NCATE. Part-time and evening/weekend programs available. *Faculty:* 13 full-time (11 women). *Students:* 30 full-time (all women), 84 part-time (78 women); includes 15 minority (10 Black or African American, non-Hispanic/Latino; 2 Asian, non-Hispanic/Latino; 3 Hispanic/Latino). Average age 32. 20 applicants, 100% accepted, 14 enrolled. In 2011, 37 degrees awarded. *Degree requirements:* For master's, comprehensive exam (for some programs), thesis (for some programs), action research project, oral defense of research project, portfolio, teaching certificate, minimum cumulative GPA of 3.0. *Entrance requirements:* For master's, GRE (verbal and quantitative), PRAXIS (MAT). Additional exam requirements/recommendations for international students: Required—TOEFL (minimum score 500 paper-based; 173 computer-based; 61 iBT). *Application deadline:* For fall admission, 7/15 priority date for domestic students, 6/1 for international students; for spring admission, 12/1 priority date for domestic students, 10/1 for international students. Applications are processed on a rolling basis. Application fee: $20 ($30 for international students). Electronic applications accepted. *Expenses:* Tuition, state resident: full-time $3977; part-time $283 per semester hour. Tuition, nonresident: full-time $13,482; part-time $811 per semester hour. *Financial support:* Career-related internships or fieldwork, Federal Work-Study, institutionally sponsored loans, scholarships/grants, and unspecified assistantships available. Support available to part-time students. Financial award application deadline: 5/1; financial award applicants required to submit FAFSA. *Faculty research:* ESL, dyslexia, pre-service teachers, inclusion, early childhood education. *Total annual research expenditures:* $356,182. *Unit head:* Dr. Cynthia Elliott, Interim Department Head, 985-549-2221, Fax: 985-549-5009, E-mail: celliott@selu.edu. *Application contact:* Sandra Meyers, Graduate Admissions Analyst, 985-549-5620, Fax: 985-549-5632, E-mail: admissions@selu.edu. Web site: http://www.selu.edu/acad_research/depts/teach_lrn/index.html.

Southern Arkansas University–Magnolia, Graduate Programs, Magnolia, AR 71754. Offers agriculture (MS); business administration (MBA); computer and information sciences (MS); education (M Ed), including counseling and development, curriculum and instruction, educational administration and supervision, elementary education, middle level, reading, secondary education, TESOL; kinesiology (M Ed); library media and information specialist (M Ed); mental health and clinical counseling (MS); public administration (MPA); school counseling (M Ed); teaching (MAT). *Accreditation:* NCATE. Part-time and evening/weekend programs available. Postbaccalaureate distance learning degree programs offered. *Faculty:* 34 full-time (15 women), 8 part-time/adjunct (5 women). *Students:* 87 full-time (62 women), 320 part-time (224 women); includes 116 minority (111 Black or African American, non-Hispanic/Latino; 2 American Indian or Alaska Native, non-Hispanic/Latino; 2 Asian, non-Hispanic/Latino; 1 Hispanic/Latino), 25 international. Average age 33. 201 applicants, 98% accepted, 156 enrolled. In 2011, 162 master's awarded. *Degree requirements:* For master's, comprehensive exam (for some programs), thesis optional. *Entrance requirements:* For master's, GRE, MAT or GMAT, minimum GPA of 2.5. Additional exam requirements/recommendations for international students: Required—TOEFL (minimum score 173 computer-based). *Application deadline:* For fall admission, 7/15 for domestic and international students; for winter admission, 12/1 for domestic and international students; for spring admission, 12/1 for domestic and international students. Applications are processed on a rolling basis. Application fee: $25 ($35 for international students). Electronic applications accepted. *Expenses:* Tuition, state resident: part-time $232 per credit. Tuition, nonresident: part-time $339 per credit. *Required fees:* $44 per credit. Part-time tuition and fees vary according to course load. *Financial support:* Career-related internships or fieldwork, Federal Work-Study, scholarships/grants, tuition waivers (full), and unspecified assistantships available. Financial award applicants required to submit FAFSA. *Faculty research:* Alternative certification for teachers, supervision of instruction, instructional leadership, counseling. *Unit head:* Dr. Kim Bloss, Dean, School of Graduate Studies, 870-235-4150, Fax: 870-235-5227, E-mail: kkbloss@saumag.edu. *Application contact:* Gaye Calhoun, Admissions Specialist, 870-235-4150, Fax: 870-235-5227, E-mail: glcalhoun@saumag.edu. Web site: http://www.saumag.edu/graduate.

Southern Illinois University Carbondale, Graduate School, College of Education and Human Services, Department of Curriculum and Instruction, Carbondale, IL 62901-4701. Offers MS Ed, PhD. *Accreditation:* NCATE. Part-time programs available. *Faculty:* 30 full-time (12 women), 2 part-time/adjunct (0 women). *Students:* 56 full-time (24 women), 145 part-time (120 women); includes 30 minority (24 Black or African American, non-Hispanic/Latino; 1 American Indian or Alaska Native, non-Hispanic/Latino; 2 Asian, non-Hispanic/Latino; 3 Hispanic/Latino), 37 international. 57 applicants, 74% accepted, 13 enrolled. In 2011, 46 master's, 6 doctorates awarded. *Degree requirements:* For doctorate, variable foreign language requirement, thesis/dissertation. *Entrance requirements:* For master's, minimum GPA of 2.7; for doctorate, GRE or MAT, minimum GPA of 3.25. Additional exam requirements/recommendations for international students: Required—TOEFL. *Application deadline:* Applications are processed on a rolling basis. Application fee: $20. *Financial support:* In 2011–12, 4 fellowships with full tuition reimbursements, 10 research assistantships with full tuition reimbursements, 45 teaching assistantships with full tuition reimbursements were awarded; career-related internships or fieldwork, Federal Work-Study, institutionally sponsored loans, and tuition waivers (full) also available. Support available to part-time students. *Faculty research:* Early childhood, science/environmental education, teacher education, instructional development/technology, reading. *Total annual research expenditures:* $3 million. *Unit head:* Dr. Lynn C. Smith, Chair, 618-536-2441, E-mail: lcsmith@siu.edu. *Application contact:* Lois Cornett, Administrative Clerk, 618-453-4267, Fax: 618-453-4244, E-mail: lcorn@siu.edu.

Southern Illinois University Edwardsville, Graduate School, School of Education, Department of Curriculum and Instruction, Program in Curriculum and Instruction, Edwardsville, IL 62026. Offers MS Ed. *Accreditation:* NCATE. Part-time and evening/weekend programs available. *Faculty:* 19 full-time (12 women). *Students:* 4 full-time (all women), 106 part-time (92 women); includes 21 minority (17 Black or African American, non-Hispanic/Latino; 3 Asian, non-Hispanic/Latino; 1 Hispanic/Latino), 1 international. 21 applicants, 62% accepted. In 2011, 38 master's awarded. *Degree requirements:* For master's, thesis (for some programs), final exam/paper. *Entrance requirements:* For master's, teaching certificate. Additional exam requirements/recommendations for international students: Required—TOEFL (minimum score 550 paper-based; 213 computer-based; 79 iBT), IELTS (minimum score 6.5). *Application deadline:* For fall admission, 7/22 for domestic students, 6/1 for international students; for spring admission, 12/10 for domestic students, 10/1 for international students. Applications are processed on a rolling basis. Application fee: $30. Electronic applications accepted. Tuition and fees vary according to course load and program. *Financial support:* In 2011–12, 1 research assistantship (averaging $9,927 per year) was awarded; fellowships, teaching assistantships, institutionally sponsored loans, scholarships/grants, and unspecified assistantships also available. Financial award application deadline: 3/1; financial award applicants required to submit FAFSA. *Unit head:* Dr. Susan Breck, Director, 618-650-3444, E-mail: sbreck@siue.edu. *Application contact:* Dr. Michelle Robinson, Coordinator of Graduate Recruitment, 618-650-2811, Fax: 618-650-3523, E-mail: michero@siue.edu. Web site: http://www.siue.edu/education/ci/.

Southern New Hampshire University, School of Education, Manchester, NH 03106-1045. Offers business education (MS); child development (M Ed); computer technology education (Certificate); curriculum and instruction (M Ed); education (M Ed, CAS); elementary education (M Ed); general special education (Certificate); school business administrator (Certificate); secondary education (M Ed); training and development (Certificate). Part-time and evening/weekend programs available. Postbaccalaureate distance learning degree programs offered (no on-campus study). *Degree requirements:* For master's, comprehensive exam (for some programs), thesis or alternative. *Entrance requirements:* For master's, PRAXIS I, minimum GPA of 2.75. Additional exam requirements/recommendations for international students: Required—TOEFL (minimum score 550 paper-based; 213 computer-based). Electronic applications accepted. *Expenses:* Contact institution.

Southwestern Adventist University, Education Department, Keene, TX 76059. Offers curriculum and instruction with reading emphasis (M Ed); educational leadership (M Ed). Part-time and evening/weekend programs available. *Degree requirements:* For master's, thesis or alternative, professional paper. *Entrance requirements:* For master's, GRE General Test.

Southwestern Assemblies of God University, Thomas F. Harrison School of Graduate Studies, Program in Education, Waxahachie, TX 75165-5735. Offers Christian school administration (MS); curriculum development (MS); early education administration (M Ed); middle and secondary education (M Ed). *Degree requirements:* For master's, comprehensive written and oral exams. *Entrance requirements:* For master's, GRE General Test, minimum GPA of 2.5. Electronic applications accepted.

Southwestern College, Education Programs, Winfield, KS 67156-2499. Offers curriculum and instruction (M Ed); education (Ed D); special education (M Ed); teaching (MA). *Accreditation:* NCATE. Part-time and evening/weekend programs available. Postbaccalaureate distance learning degree programs offered (minimal on-campus study). *Faculty:* 6 full-time (3 women), 6 part-time/adjunct (all women). *Students:* 9 full-time (7 women), 94 part-time (73 women); includes 12 minority (4 Black or African American, non-Hispanic/Latino; 2 Asian, non-Hispanic/Latino; 3 Hispanic/Latino; 3 Two or more races, non-Hispanic/Latino), 9 international. Average age 35. 77 applicants, 60% accepted, 34 enrolled. In 2011, 56 master's awarded. *Degree requirements:* For master's, practicum, portfolio. *Entrance requirements:* For master's, baccalaureate degree, minimum GPA of 2.5, valid teaching certificate (for special education). Additional exam requirements/recommendations for international students: Required—TOEFL (minimum score 550 paper-based; 213 computer-based). *Application deadline:* For fall admission, 8/1 for domestic students; for spring admission, 12/1 for domestic students. Applications are processed on a rolling basis. Application fee: $0. Electronic applications accepted. *Expenses:* Contact institution. *Financial support:* In 2011–12, 4 students received support. Federal Work-Study, tuition waivers (partial), and unspecified assistantships available. Financial award application deadline: 4/1; financial award applicants required to submit FAFSA. *Unit head:* Dr. David Hofmeister, Director of Teacher Education, 800-846-1543 Ext. 6115, Fax: 620-229-6341, E-mail: david.hofmeister@sckans.edu. Web site: http://www.sckans.edu/graduate/education-med/.

Stanford University, School of Education, Program in Curriculum Studies and Teacher Education, Stanford, CA 94305-9991. Offers art education (MA, PhD); dance education (MA); English education (MA, PhD); general curriculum studies (MA, PhD); mathematics education (MA, PhD); science education (MA, PhD); social studies education (PhD); teacher education (MA, PhD). *Degree requirements:* For master's, thesis (for some programs); for doctorate, thesis/dissertation. *Entrance requirements:* For master's and doctorate, GRE General Test. Electronic applications accepted. *Expenses: Tuition:* Full-time $40,050; part-time $890 per credit.

State University of New York at Plattsburgh, Division of Education, Health, and Human Services, Program in Teacher Education: Teaching and Learning, Plattsburgh, NY 12901-2681. Offers MS Ed. Part-time and evening/weekend programs available. *Students:* 48 part-time (32 women); includes 1 minority (Two or more races, non-Hispanic/Latino). Average age 29. *Entrance requirements:* For master's, minimum GPA of 2.5. Additional exam requirements/recommendations for international students: Required—TOEFL. *Application deadline:* For fall admission, 2/15 priority date for domestic students; for spring admission, 10/15 priority date for domestic students. Applications are processed on a rolling basis. Application fee: $75. *Financial support:* Application deadline: 4/15; applicants required to submit FAFSA. *Unit head:* Dr. Heidi Schnackenberg, Coordinator, 518-564-5143, E-mail: schnachl@plattsburgh.edu. *Application contact:* Marguerite Adelman, Assistant Director, Graduate Admissions, 518-564-4723, Fax: 518-564-4722, E-mail: adelmaml@plattsburgh.edu.

State University of New York College at Potsdam, School of Education and Professional Studies, Program in Curriculum and Instruction, Potsdam, NY 13676. Offers childhood education (MST); curriculum and instruction (MS Ed). *Accreditation:* NCATE. Postbaccalaureate distance learning degree programs offered (minimal on-campus study). *Faculty:* 14 full-time (12 women), 8 part-time/adjunct (4 women). *Students:* 136 full-time (105 women), 44 part-time (34 women); includes 9 minority (5 Black or African American, non-Hispanic/Latino; 1 American Indian or Alaska Native, non-Hispanic/Latino; 3 Hispanic/Latino), 75 international. 100 applicants, 99% accepted, 69 enrolled. In 2011, 146 master's awarded. *Degree requirements:* For master's, thesis (for some programs). *Entrance requirements:* For master's, minimum GPA of 2.75 in last 60 credit hours of undergraduate study. Additional exam requirements/recommendations for international students: Required—TOEFL (minimum score 550 paper-based; 213 computer-based; 80 iBT), IELTS (minimum score 6). *Application deadline:* For fall admission, 4/1 for domestic and international students; for winter admission, 10/15 for domestic and international students; for spring admission, 3/1 for domestic and international students. Applications are processed on a rolling basis. Application fee: $50. *Expenses:* Tuition, state resident: full-time $8870; part-time $370 per credit hour. Tuition, nonresident: full-time $15,160; part-time $632 per credit hour. *Required fees:* $1066; $44.10 per credit hour. One-time fee: $3. *Financial support:* Federal Work-Study, scholarships/grants, and unspecified assistantships available. Support available to part-time students. Financial award application deadline: 3/1; financial award applicants required to submit FAFSA. *Unit head:* Dr. Sandy Chadwick, Chairperson, 315-267-2502, Fax: 315-267-4802, E-mail: chadwisc@potsdam.edu. *Application contact:* Peter Cutler, Graduate Admissions Counselor, 315-267-2165, Fax: 315-267-4802, E-mail: graduate@potsdam.edu. Web site: http://www.potsdam.edu/academics/SOEPS/Curriculum/.

Stephens College, Division of Graduate and Continuing Studies, Program in Curriculum and Instruction, Columbia, MO 65215-0002. Offers M Ed. Part-time programs available. Postbaccalaureate distance learning degree programs offered (minimal on-campus study). *Faculty:* 1 (woman) full-time, 2 part-time/adjunct (both women). *Students:* 10 full-time (all women); includes 1 minority (Black or African American, non-Hispanic/Latino). Average age 28. In 2011, 7 master's awarded. *Entrance requirements:* For master's, minimum GPA of 3.5 in last 60 hours. Additional exam requirements/recommendations for international students: Required—TOEFL (minimum score 213 computer-based). *Application deadline:* For fall admission, 7/25 priority date for domestic students, 7/25 for international students; for winter admission, 12/1 priority date for domestic students, 12/1 for international students; for spring admission, 4/25 priority date for domestic students, 4/25 for international students. Applications are processed on a rolling basis. Application fee: $40. *Expenses: Tuition:* Full-time $2220; part-time $370 per credit hour. *Required fees:* $228; $38 per credit hour. *Financial support:* In 2011–12, 3 students received support, including 3 fellowships (averaging $11,424 per year); scholarships/grants and unspecified assistantships also available. Financial award application deadline: 12/5; financial award applicants required to submit FAFSA. *Unit head:* Dr. Leslie Willey, Department Chair, 800-388-7579, E-mail: online@stephens.edu. *Application contact:* Pamela Beerup, Assistant Director of Marketing and Recruitment, 800-388-7579, E-mail: online@stephens.edu.

Syracuse University, School of Education, Program in Instructional Design, Development, and Evaluation, Syracuse, NY 13244. Offers MS, PhD, CAS. Part-time programs available. *Students:* 32 full-time (23 women), 21 part-time (11 women); includes 13 minority (6 Black or African American, non-Hispanic/Latino; 3 Asian, non-Hispanic/Latino; 4 Hispanic/Latino), 16 international. Average age 38. 28 applicants, 61% accepted, 8 enrolled. In 2011, 14 master's, 1 doctorate, 1 other advanced degree awarded. *Degree requirements:* For master's, thesis or alternative; for doctorate, thesis/dissertation. *Entrance requirements:* For doctorate, GRE, interview, master's degree; for CAS, GRE (recommended), interview. Additional exam requirements/recommendations for international students: Required—TOEFL (minimum score 100 iBT). *Application deadline:* For fall admission, 2/1 priority date for domestic students, 2/1 for international students; for spring admission, 10/15 priority date for domestic students, 10/15 for international students. Applications are processed on a rolling basis. Application fee: $75. Electronic applications accepted. *Expenses: Tuition:* Part-time $1206 per credit. *Financial support:* Fellowships with full tuition reimbursements, research assistantships with full and partial tuition reimbursements, and teaching assistantships with full and partial tuition reimbursements available. Financial award application deadline: 1/1; financial award applicants required to submit FAFSA. *Faculty research:* Cultural pluralism and instructional design, corrections training, aging and learning, the University and social change, investigative evaluation. *Unit head:* Dr. Nick Smith, Chair, 315-443-2685, E-mail: nlsmith@syr.edu. *Application contact:* Laurie Deyo, Graduate Recruiter, School of Education, 315-443-2505, E-mail: e-gradrcrt@syr.edu. Web site: http://soeweb.syr.edu/idde/instrucdesign.html.

Syracuse University, School of Education, Program in Teaching and Curriculum, Syracuse, NY 13244. Offers MS, PhD. Part-time programs available. *Students:* 31 full-time (18 women), 18 part-time (14 women); includes 3 minority (all Black or African American, non-Hispanic/Latino), 14 international. Average age 39. 22 applicants, 73% accepted, 14 enrolled. In 2011, 10 master's, 2 doctorates awarded. *Degree requirements:* For master's, thesis or alternative; for doctorate, thesis/dissertation. *Entrance requirements:* For doctorate, GRE, writing sample; master's degree; interview (recommended). Additional exam requirements/recommendations for international students: Required—TOEFL (minimum score 100 iBT). *Application deadline:* For fall admission, 2/1 priority date for domestic students, 2/1 for international students; for spring admission, 10/15 priority date for domestic students, 10/15 for international students. Applications are processed on a rolling basis. Application fee: $75. Electronic applications accepted. *Expenses: Tuition:* Part-time $1206 per credit. *Financial support:* Fellowships with full tuition reimbursements, teaching assistantships with full and partial tuition reimbursements, and tuition waivers available. Financial award application deadline: 1/1. *Unit head:* Dr. Gerald Mager, Program Coordinator, 315-443-2685, E-mail: gmmager@syr.edu. *Application contact:* Laurie Deyo, Graduate Recruiter, School of Education, 315-443-2505, E-mail: e-gradrcrt@syr.edu. Web site: http://soeweb.syr.edu/.

Tarleton State University, College of Graduate Studies, College of Education, Department of Curriculum and Instruction, Stephenville, TX 76402. Offers M Ed. Part-time and evening/weekend programs available. *Faculty:* 10 full-time (8 women), 6 part-time/adjunct (all women). *Students:* 6 full-time (all women), 111 part-time (94 women); includes 35 minority (19 Black or African American, non-Hispanic/Latino; 15 Hispanic/Latino; 1 Two or more races, non-Hispanic/Latino). Average age 35. 26 applicants, 92% accepted, 13 enrolled. In 2011, 22 master's awarded. *Degree requirements:* For master's, comprehensive exam. *Entrance requirements:* For master's, GRE General Test, minimum GPA of 3.0. Additional exam requirements/recommendations for international students: Required—TOEFL (minimum score 550 paper-based; 213 computer-based; 80 iBT). *Application deadline:* For fall admission, 8/5 priority date for domestic students; for spring admission, 12/1 for domestic students. Applications are processed on a rolling basis. Application fee: $30 ($130 for international students). Electronic applications accepted. *Expenses:* Tuition, state resident: full-time $3131.46; part-time $174 per credit hour. Tuition, nonresident: full-time $8225; part-time $457 per credit hour. *Required fees:* $1446. Tuition and fees vary according to course load and campus/location. *Financial support:* Research assistantships, teaching assistantships, career-related internships or fieldwork, Federal Work-Study, and institutionally sponsored loans available. Support available to part-time students. Financial award application deadline: 5/1; financial award applicants required to submit FAFSA. *Unit head:* Dr. Ann Calahan, Head, 254-968-9933, Fax: 254-968-9947, E-mail: acalahan@tarleton.edu. *Application contact:* Information Contact, 254-968-9104, Fax: 254-968-9670, E-mail: gradoffice@tarleton.edu. Web site: http://www.tarleton.edu/~teachered.

Teachers College, Columbia University, Graduate Faculty of Education, Department of Curriculum and Teaching, Program in Curriculum and Teaching, New York, NY 10027. Offers Ed M, MA, Ed D. *Faculty:* 20 full-time (15 women), 22 part-time/adjunct (20 women). *Students:* 65 full-time (51 women), 144 part-time (125 women); includes 61 minority (20 Black or African American, non-Hispanic/Latino; 20 Asian, non-Hispanic/Latino; 21 Hispanic/Latino), 24 international. Average age 34. 127 applicants, 61% accepted, 33 enrolled. In 2011, 26 master's, 10 doctorates awarded. *Degree requirements:* For master's, project; for doctorate, comprehensive exam, thesis/dissertation. *Entrance requirements:* For master's, resume and proof of initial New York state teacher certification (formerly provisional) or certification from another state, or proof of accredited teacher preparation/student program completion; minimum undergraduate GPA of 3.0 (for MA); for doctorate, GRE General Test or MAT, writing sample. Additional exam requirements/recommendations for international students: Required—TOEFL. *Application deadline:* For fall admission, 1/2 priority date for domestic students. Application fee: $65. *Financial support:* Career-related internships or fieldwork, Federal Work-Study, institutionally sponsored loans, and tuition waivers (full and partial) available. Support available to part-time students. Financial award application deadline: 2/1. *Faculty research:* Teacher education, reading education, curriculum development. *Unit head:* Prof. Thomas Hatch, Program Coordinator, 212-678-3765, E-mail: c&t_edd@tc.edu. *Application contact:* Peter Shon, Assistant Director of Admission, 212-678-3305, Fax: 212-678-4171, E-mail: shon@exchange.tc.columbia.edu. Web site: http://www.tc.edu/c&t/.

Tennessee State University, The School of Graduate Studies and Research, College of Education, Department of Teaching and Learning, Program in Curriculum and Instruction, Nashville, TN 37209-1561. Offers M Ed, Ed D. *Accreditation:* NCATE. *Degree requirements:* For master's, thesis optional; for doctorate, thesis/dissertation. *Entrance requirements:* For master's, GRE General Test, GRE Subject Test, or MAT, minimum GPA of 2.5; for doctorate, GRE General Test, GRE Subject Test, or MAT. Additional exam requirements/recommendations for international students: Required—TOEFL.

Tennessee Technological University, Graduate School, College of Education, Department of Curriculum and Instruction, Program in Curriculum, Cookeville, TN 38505. Offers MA, Ed S. *Accreditation:* NCATE. Part-time and evening/weekend programs available. *Faculty:* 2 full-time (1 woman). *Students:* 26 full-time (18 women), 71 part-time (45 women); includes 4 minority (3 Black or African American, non-Hispanic/Latino; 1 Hispanic/Latino). Average age 27. 40 applicants, 68% accepted, 23 enrolled. In 2011, 29 master's, 12 other advanced degrees awarded. *Degree requirements:* For master's and Ed S, comprehensive exam, thesis or alternative. *Entrance requirements:* For master's and Ed S, MAT or GRE. Additional exam requirements/recommendations for international students: Required—TOEFL (minimum score 550 paper-based; 71 iBT), IELTS (minimum score 5.5), Pearson Test of English Academic. *Application deadline:* For fall admission, 8/1 for domestic students, 5/1 for international students; for spring admission, 12/1 for domestic students, 10/1 for international students. Application fee: $25 ($30 for international students). Electronic applications accepted. *Expenses:* Tuition, state resident: full-time $8094; part-time $422 per credit hour. Tuition, nonresident: full-time $20,574; part-time $1046 per credit hour. *Financial support:* In 2011–12, 2 fellowships (averaging $8,000 per year), research assistantships (averaging $4,000 per year), 1 teaching assistantship (averaging $4,000 per year) were awarded. Financial award application deadline: 4/1. *Unit head:* Dr. Susan Gore, Interim Chairperson, 931-372-3181, Fax: 931-372-6270, E-mail: sgore@tntech.edu. *Application contact:* Shelia K. Kendrick, Coordinator of Graduate Admissions, 931-372-3808, Fax: 931-372-3497, E-mail: skendrick@tntech.edu.

Tennessee Temple University, Graduate Studies in Education, Program in Instructional Effectiveness, Chattanooga, TN 37404-3587. Offers M Ed. *Degree requirements:* For master's, comprehensive exam, thesis or alternative. *Entrance requirements:* For master's, GRE, minimum cumulative undergraduate GPA of 3.0, 3 references.

Texas A&M International University, Office of Graduate Studies and Research, College of Education, Department of Curriculum and Instruction, Laredo, TX 78041-1900. Offers MS. *Faculty:* 3 full-time (all women), 1 (woman) part-time/adjunct. *Students:* 7 full-time (3 women), 80 part-time (70 women); includes 78 minority (all Hispanic/Latino), 2 international. Average age 36. 24 applicants, 75% accepted, 11 enrolled. In 2011, 30 degrees awarded. *Degree requirements:* For master's, comprehensive exam. *Entrance requirements:* Additional exam requirements/recommendations for international students: Required—TOEFL (minimum score 550 paper-based; 213 computer-based; 79 iBT). *Application deadline:* For fall admission, 4/30 priority date for domestic students, 4/30 for international students; for spring admission, 11/30 for domestic students, 10/1 for international students. Applications are processed on a rolling basis. *Expenses:* Tuition, state resident: full-time $5063. *Financial support:* In 2011–12, 1 student received support, including 1 research assistantship; Federal Work-Study, scholarships/grants, and unspecified assistantships also available. Financial award application deadline: 4/1. *Unit head:* Dr. Cathy Guerra, Interim Chair, 956-326-2438, E-mail: cgsakta@tamiu.edu. *Application contact:* Suzanne Hansen-Alford, Director of Graduate Recruiting, 956-326-3023, E-mail: graduateschool@tamiu.edu. Web site: http://www.tamiu.edu/coedu/dept_cirr_ist.shtml.

Texas A&M University, College of Education and Human Development, Department of Teaching, Learning, and Culture, College Station, TX 77843. Offers culture and curriculum (M Ed, MS); curriculum and instruction (PhD); English as a second language (M Ed, MS, PhD); mathematics education (M Ed, MS, PhD); reading and language arts education (M Ed, MS, PhD); science education (M Ed, MS, PhD); urban education (M Ed, MS, PhD). Part-time programs available. *Faculty:* 30. *Students:* 163 full-time (119 women), 226 part-time (185 women); includes 108 minority (56 Black or African American, non-Hispanic/Latino; 2 American Indian or Alaska Native, non-Hispanic/Latino; 6 Asian, non-Hispanic/Latino; 37 Hispanic/Latino; 7 Two or more races, non-Hispanic/Latino), 62 international. Average age 36. In 2011, 107 master's, 44 doctorates awarded. *Degree requirements:* For master's, comprehensive exam, thesis (for some programs); for doctorate, comprehensive exam, thesis/dissertation. *Entrance requirements:* For master's, GRE General Test, minimum GPA of 3.0; for doctorate, GRE General Test, 3 years of teaching experience. Additional exam requirements/recommendations for international students: Required—TOEFL (minimum score 550 paper-based; 213 computer-based). *Application deadline:* For fall admission, 1/15 priority date for domestic students, 1/15 for international students; for spring admission, 9/15 priority date for domestic students, 9/15 for international students. Applications are processed on a rolling basis. Application fee: $50 ($75 for international students). Electronic applications accepted. *Expenses:* Tuition, state resident: full-time $5437; part-time $226.55 per credit hour. Tuition, nonresident: full-time $12,949; part-time $539.55 per credit hour. *Required fees:* $2741. *Financial support:* In 2011–12, fellowships with partial tuition reimbursements (averaging $3,000 per year), teaching assistantships with partial tuition reimbursements (averaging $7,200 per year) were awarded; research assistantships with partial tuition reimbursements, career-related internships or fieldwork, Federal Work-Study, institutionally sponsored loans, scholarships/grants, tuition waivers (partial), and unspecified assistantships also available. Support available to part-time students. Financial award application deadline: 4/1; financial award applicants required to submit FAFSA. *Unit head:* Dr. Yeping Li, Head, 979-845-8384, Fax: 979-845-9663, E-mail: yepingli@tamu.edu. *Application contact:* Kerri Smith, Senior Academic Advisor II, 979-845-8382, Fax: 979-845-9663, E-mail: krsmith@tamu.edu. Web site: http://tlac.tamu.edu.

Texas A&M University–Corpus Christi, Graduate Studies and Research, College of Education, Program in Curriculum and Instruction, Corpus Christi, TX 78412-5503. Offers MS, Ed D. Part-time and evening/weekend programs available. *Degree requirements:* For master's, comprehensive exam, thesis (for some programs). *Entrance requirements:* For master's, GRE General Test. Additional exam requirements/recommendations for international students: Required—TOEFL. Electronic applications accepted.

Texas A&M University–Texarkana, Graduate Studies and Research, College of Education and Liberal Arts, Texarkana, TX 75505-5518. Offers adult education (MS); curriculum and instruction (M Ed); education (MS); educational administration (M Ed); English (MA); instructional technology (MS); interdisciplinary studies (MA, MS); special education (MS). Part-time and evening/weekend programs available. *Degree requirements:* For master's, comprehensive exam (for some programs), thesis optional. *Entrance requirements:* For master's, minimum GPA of 2.5 on last 60 hours of bachelor's degree. Additional exam requirements/recommendations for international students: Required—TOEFL. Electronic applications accepted.

Texas Christian University, College of Education, Program in Curriculum Studies, Fort Worth, TX 76129-0002. Offers M Ed, PhD. Part-time and evening/weekend programs available. *Faculty:* 27 full-time (21 women), 1 part-time/adjunct. *Students:* 7 full-time (6 women), 2 part-time (both women); includes 4 minority (2 Black or African American, non-Hispanic/Latino; 2 Hispanic/Latino), 1 international. Average age 31. 4 applicants, 100% accepted, 2 enrolled. In 2011, 2 master's awarded. *Degree requirements:* For master's, comprehensive exam, thesis; for doctorate, comprehensive exam, thesis/dissertation. *Entrance requirements:* Additional exam requirements/recommendations for international students: Required—TOEFL (minimum score 550 paper-based; 213 computer-based; 80 iBT). *Application deadline:* For fall admission, 11/15 for domestic students, 11/16 for international students; for winter admission, 2/1 for domestic and international students; for spring admission, 3/1 for domestic and international students. Application fee: $60. Electronic applications accepted. *Expenses: Tuition:* Full-time $20,250; part-time $1125 per credit hour. Part-time tuition and fees vary according to course load and program. *Financial support:* Teaching assistantships with full tuition reimbursements, career-related internships or fieldwork, scholarships/grants, and unspecified assistantships available. Financial award application deadline: 3/1. *Unit head:* Dr. Jan Lacina, Associate Dean, 817-257-6786, E-mail: j.lacina@tcu.edu. *Application contact:* Patricia Garcia, Academic Program Specialist, 817-257-7661, E-mail: p.m.garcia@tcu.edu.

Texas Southern University, College of Education, Area of Curriculum and Instruction, Houston, TX 77004-4584. Offers bilingual education (M Ed); curriculum and instruction (Ed D); secondary education (M Ed). Part-time and evening/weekend programs available. *Degree requirements:* For master's, comprehensive exam; for doctorate, comprehensive exam, thesis/dissertation. *Entrance requirements:* For master's, GRE General Test, minimum GPA of 2.5; for doctorate, GRE General Test or MAT, master's degree, minimum B+ average. Additional exam requirements/recommendations for international students: Required—TOEFL. Electronic applications accepted.

Texas Tech University, Graduate School, College of Education, Department of Curriculum and Instruction, Lubbock, TX 79409. Offers bilingual education (M Ed); curriculum and instruction (M Ed, PhD); elementary education (M Ed); language/literacy education (M Ed); secondary education (M Ed). *Accreditation:* NCATE. Part-time programs available. *Students:* 69 full-time (50 women), 115 part-time (91 women); includes 62 minority (9 Black or African American, non-Hispanic/Latino; 3 Asian, non-Hispanic/Latino; 47 Hispanic/Latino; 3 Two or more races, non-Hispanic/Latino), 18 international. Average age 34. 95 applicants, 41% accepted, 26 enrolled. In 2011, 62 master's, 9 doctorates awarded. *Degree requirements:* For master's, comprehensive written exam with 36 hours of course credit or thesis (6 hours) with 30 hours of course credit; for doctorate, thesis/dissertation. *Entrance requirements:* For doctorate, GRE General Test. Additional exam requirements/recommendations for international students: Required—TOEFL (minimum score 550 paper-based; 213 computer-based; 79 iBT). *Application deadline:* For fall admission, 6/1 priority date for domestic students, 1/15 for international students; for spring admission, 9/1 priority date for domestic students, 6/15 for international students. Applications are processed on a rolling basis. Application fee: $50 ($75 for international students). Electronic applications accepted. *Expenses:* Tuition, state resident: full-time $5899; part-time $245.80 per credit hour. Tuition, nonresident: full-time $13,411; part-time $558.80 per credit hour. *Required fees:* $2680.60; $86.50 per credit hour. $920.30 per semester. *Financial support:* In 2011–12, 58 students received support. Application deadline: 4/15; applicants required to submit FAFSA. *Faculty research:* Multicultural foundations of education, teacher education, instruction and pedagogy in subject areas, curriculum theory, language and literary. *Total annual research expenditures:* $948,943. *Unit head:* Dr. Margaret A. Price, Interim Chair, 806-742-1997 Ext. 318, Fax: 806-742-2179, E-mail: peggie.price@ttu.edu. *Application contact:* Stephenie Allyn McDaniel, Administrative Assistant, 806-742-1988 Ext. 434, Fax: 806-742-2179, E-mail: stephenie.mcdaniel@ttu.edu.

Texas Woman's University, Graduate School, College of Professional Education, Department of Teacher Education, Denton, TX 76201. Offers administration (M Ed, MA); special education (M Ed, MA, PhD), including educational diagnostician (M Ed, MA); teaching, learning, and curriculum (M Ed). Part-time programs available. *Faculty:* 27 full-time (20 women), 2 part-time/adjunct (both women). *Students:* 14 full-time (12 women), 164 part-time (142 women); includes 68 minority (33 Black or African American, non-Hispanic/Latino; 1 American Indian or Alaska Native, non-Hispanic/Latino; 6 Asian, non-Hispanic/Latino; 28 Hispanic/Latino), 1 international. Average age 37. 38 applicants, 74% accepted, 24 enrolled. In 2011, 67 master's, 4 doctorates awarded. Terminal master's awarded for partial completion of doctoral program. *Degree requirements:* For master's, comprehensive exam, thesis, professional paper (M Ed); for doctorate, comprehensive exam, thesis/dissertation. *Entrance requirements:* For master's, minimum GPA of 3.0 on last 60 undergraduate hours, 2 letters of reference, resume, copy of certifications, teacher service record, statement of intent; for doctorate, GRE General Test, minimum GPA of 3.0, 3 letters of reference, resume, copy of certifications, teacher service record, statement of intent. Additional exam requirements/recommendations for international students: Required—TOEFL (minimum score 550 paper-based; 213 computer-based; 79 iBT). *Application deadline:* For fall admission, 7/1 priority date for domestic students, 3/1 for international students; for spring admission, 11/1 priority date for domestic students, 7/1 for international students. Applications are processed on a rolling basis. Application fee: $50 ($75 for international students). Electronic applications accepted. *Expenses:* Tuition, state resident: full-time $3834; part-time $213 per credit hour. Tuition, nonresident: full-time $9468; part-time $526 per credit hour. *Required fees:* $213 per credit hour. Tuition and fees vary according to course load. *Financial support:* In 2011–12, 42 students received support, including 8 research assistantships (averaging $12,942 per year); career-related internships or fieldwork, Federal Work-Study, institutionally sponsored loans, scholarships/grants, traineeships, health care benefits, and unspecified assistantships also available. Support available to part-time students. Financial award application deadline: 3/1; financial award applicants required to submit FAFSA. *Faculty research:* Language and literacy, classroom management, learning disabilities, staff and professional development, leadership preparation practice. *Unit head:* Dr. Jane Pemberton, Chair, 940-898-2271, Fax: 940-898-2270, E-mail: mrule1@twu.edu. *Application contact:* Dr. Samuel Wheeler, Assistant Director of Admissions, 940-898-3188, Fax: 940-898-3081, E-mail: wheelersr@twu.edu. Web site: http://www.twu.edu/teacher-education/.

Trevecca Nazarene University, College of Lifelong Learning, School of Education, Major in Curriculum, Assessment, and Instruction K-12, Nashville, TN 37210-2877. Offers M Ed. Part-time programs available. Postbaccalaureate distance learning degree programs offered. *Students:* 12 full-time (11 women), 1 (woman) part-time; includes 1 minority (Black or African American, non-Hispanic/Latino). *Degree requirements:* For master's, exit assessment. *Entrance requirements:* For master's, MAT; GRE, 2 references, interview, immunization. Additional exam requirements/recommendations for international students: Required—TOEFL (minimum score 550 paper-based; 213 computer-based). Application fee: $25. Tuition and fees vary according to course level and program. *Financial support:* Applicants required to submit FAFSA. *Unit head:* Dr. Esther Swink, Dean/Director of Graduate Education Programs, 615-248-1201, Fax: 615-

248-1597, E-mail: eswink@trevecca.edu. *Application contact:* Melanie Eaton, Admissions, 615-248-1498, E-mail: admissions_ged@trevecca.edu. Web site: http://www.trevecca.edu/soe/.

Trevecca Nazarene University, College of Lifelong Learning, School of Education, Major in Leading Instructional Improvement for Teachers PreK-12, Nashville, TN 37210-2877. Offers M Ed. Part-time and evening/weekend programs available. *Students:* 2 full-time (both women), 10 part-time (all women); includes 6 minority (all Black or African American, non-Hispanic/Latino). In 2011, 10 master's awarded. *Degree requirements:* For master's, exit assessment. *Entrance requirements:* For master's, MAT; GRE, 2 references, immunizations, interview, teaching experience. Additional exam requirements/recommendations for international students: Required—TOEFL (minimum score 550 paper-based; 213 computer-based). Application fee: $25. Tuition and fees vary according to course level and program. *Financial support:* Applicants required to submit FAFSA. *Unit head:* Dr. Esther Swink, Dean/Director of Graduate Education Programs, 615-248-1201, Fax: 615-248-1597, E-mail: eswink@trevecca.edu. *Application contact:* Melanie Eaton, Admissions, 615-248-1498, E-mail: admissions_ged@trevecca.edu. Web site: http://www.trevecca.edu/soe/.

Trinity Washington University, School of Education, Washington, DC 20017-1094. Offers counseling (MA); early childhood education (MAT); educating for change (M Ed); educational administration (MSA); elementary education (MAT); school counseling (MA); secondary education (MAT), including English, social studies; special education (MAT); teaching English as a second language (MAT); teaching English to speakers of other languages (M Ed); the teaching of reading (M Ed). *Accreditation:* NCATE. Part-time and evening/weekend programs available. *Degree requirements:* For master's, thesis (for some programs), capstone project(s). *Entrance requirements:* For master's, PRAXIS I, minimum GPA of 2.8. Additional exam requirements/recommendations for international students: Required—TOEFL (minimum score 550 paper-based; 213 computer-based). *Faculty research:* Technology, literacy, special education, organizations, inclusion models.

Union Institute & University, Education Programs, Cincinnati, OH 45206-1925. Offers adult and higher education (M Ed); curriculum and instruction (M Ed); educational leadership (M Ed, Ed D); guidance and counseling (Ed S); higher education (Ed D); issues in education (M Ed); reading (Ed S). M Ed offered online and in Vermont and Florida, concentrations vary by location; Ed S offered in Florida; Ed D program is a hybrid (online with limited residency) offered in Ohio. Postbaccalaureate distance learning degree programs offered (minimal on-campus study). *Degree requirements:* For master's, comprehensive exam (for some programs), thesis (for some programs), electronic portfolio; for doctorate, comprehensive exam, thesis/dissertation, electronic portfolio.

Universidad Adventista de las Antillas, EGECED Department, Mayagüez, PR 00681-0118. Offers curriculum and instruction (M Ed); health education (M Ed); medical surgical nursing (MN); pastoral theology (M Div); school administration and supervision (M Ed). *Degree requirements:* For master's, comprehensive exam (for some programs), thesis (for some programs). *Entrance requirements:* For master's, EXADEP or GRE General Test, recommendations. Electronic applications accepted.

Universidad del Turabo, Graduate Programs, Programs in Education, Program in Curriculum and Instruction and Appropriate Environment, Gurabo, PR 00778-3030. Offers D Ed. *Students:* 28 full-time (21 women), 82 part-time (66 women); includes 106 minority (all Hispanic/Latino). Average age 43. 34 applicants, 91% accepted, 30 enrolled. In 2011, 6 doctorates awarded. *Unit head:* Angela Candelario, Dean, 787-743-7979 Ext. 4126. *Application contact:* Virginia Gonzalez, Admissions Officer, 787-746-3009.

Universidad del Turabo, Graduate Programs, Programs in Education, Program in Curriculum and Teaching, Gurabo, PR 00778-3030. Offers M Ed. *Students:* 17 full-time (11 women), 26 part-time (22 women); includes 39 minority (all Hispanic/Latino). Average age 36. 44 applicants, 86% accepted, 25 enrolled. In 2011, 24 master's awarded. *Unit head:* Angela Candelario, Dean, 787-743-7979 Ext. 4126. *Application contact:* Virginia Gonzalez, Admissions Officer, 787-746-3009.

Universidad Metropolitana, School of Education, Program in Curriculum and Teaching, San Juan, PR 00928-1150. Offers M Ed. Part-time and evening/weekend programs available. *Degree requirements:* For master's, thesis or alternative. *Entrance requirements:* For master's, EXADEP, interview.

Université de Montréal, Faculty of Education, Department of Didactics, Montréal, QC H3C 3J7, Canada. Offers M Ed, MA, PhD, DESS. Terminal master's awarded for partial completion of doctoral program. *Degree requirements:* For master's, thesis (for some programs); for doctorate, thesis/dissertation, general exam. Electronic applications accepted. *Faculty research:* Teaching of French as a first or second language, teaching of science and technology, teaching of mathematics, teaching of arts.

Université Laval, Faculty of Education, Department of Teaching and Learning Studies, Programs in Didactics, Québec, QC G1K 7P4, Canada. Offers MA, PhD. Terminal master's awarded for partial completion of doctoral program. *Degree requirements:* For master's, thesis (for some programs); for doctorate, comprehensive exam, thesis/dissertation. *Entrance requirements:* For master's and doctorate, English exam (comprehension of written English), knowledge of French. Electronic applications accepted.

University at Albany, State University of New York, School of Education, Department of Educational Theory and Practice, Albany, NY 12222-0001. Offers curriculum and instruction (MS, Ed D, CAS); curriculum planning and development (MA); educational communications (MS, CAS). Evening/weekend programs available. *Degree requirements:* For doctorate, one foreign language, thesis/dissertation. *Entrance requirements:* For doctorate, GRE General Test. Additional exam requirements/recommendations for international students: Required—TOEFL (minimum score 550 paper-based; 213 computer-based). Electronic applications accepted.

The University of Alabama at Birmingham, College of Arts and Sciences, School of Education, Program in Curriculum Education, Birmingham, AL 35294. Offers Ed S. *Degree requirements:* For Ed S, comprehensive exam, thesis optional. *Entrance requirements:* For degree, GRE General Test, MAT, minimum GPA of 3.0, master's degree. *Expenses:* Tuition, state resident: full-time $5922; part-time $309 per hour. Tuition, nonresident: full-time $13,428; part-time $726 per hour. Tuition and fees vary according to program. *Unit head:* Dr. Kristi Menear, Chair, 205-975-7409, Fax: 205-975-8040, E-mail: kmenear@uab.edu.

University of Alaska Fairbanks, School of Education, Program in Education, Fairbanks, AK 99775. Offers curriculum and instruction (M Ed); education (M Ed, Graduate Certificate); elementary education (M Ed); language and literacy (M Ed); reading (M Ed); secondary education (M Ed); special education (M Ed). *Faculty:* 25 full-time (15 women). *Students:* 30 full-time (23 women), 69 part-time (50 women); includes 17 minority (7 American Indian or Alaska Native, non-Hispanic/Latino; 1 Asian, non-Hispanic/Latino; 2 Hispanic/Latino; 1 Native Hawaiian or other Pacific Islander, non-Hispanic/Latino; 6 Two or more races, non-Hispanic/Latino), 1 international. Average age 33. 68 applicants, 76% accepted, 37 enrolled. In 2011, 26 master's, 22 other advanced degrees awarded. *Degree requirements:* For master's, comprehensive exam, thesis, oral defense. *Entrance requirements:* Additional exam requirements/recommendations for international students: Required—TOEFL (minimum score 550 paper-based; 213 computer-based; 80 iBT). *Application deadline:* For fall admission, 5/1 for domestic students, 3/1 for international students; for spring admission, 10/15 for domestic students, 8/1 for international students. Applications are processed on a rolling basis. Application fee: $60. Electronic applications accepted. *Expenses:* Tuition, state resident: full-time $6696; part-time $372 per credit. Tuition, nonresident: full-time $13,680; part-time $760 per credit. Tuition and fees vary according to course load and reciprocity agreements. *Financial support:* Fellowships with tuition reimbursements, research assistantships with tuition reimbursements, teaching assistantships with tuition reimbursements, career-related internships or fieldwork, Federal Work-Study, scholarships/grants, health care benefits, and unspecified assistantships available. Support available to part-time students. Financial award application deadline: 6/1; financial award applicants required to submit FAFSA. *Unit head:* Allan Morotti, Interim Dean, 907-474-7341, Fax: 907-474-5451, E-mail: uaf-soe-school@alaska.edu. *Application contact:* Mike Earnest, Director of Admissions, 907-474-7500, Fax: 907-474-5379, E-mail: admissions@uaf.edu. Web site: http://www.uaf.edu/educ/graduate/counseling.html.

University of Arkansas, Graduate School, College of Education and Health Professions, Department of Curriculum and Instruction, Program in Curriculum and Instruction, Fayetteville, AR 72701-1201. Offers PhD. Part-time programs available. *Students:* 27 full-time (20 women), 40 part-time (33 women); includes 9 minority (4 Black or African American, non-Hispanic/Latino; 1 American Indian or Alaska Native, non-Hispanic/Latino; 3 Hispanic/Latino; 1 Two or more races, non-Hispanic/Latino), 12 international. In 2011, 9 doctorates awarded. *Degree requirements:* For doctorate, thesis/dissertation. *Entrance requirements:* For doctorate, GRE General Test. *Application deadline:* For fall admission, 4/1 for international students; for spring admission, 10/1 for international students. Applications are processed on a rolling basis. Application fee: $40 ($50 for international students). Electronic applications accepted. *Financial support:* In 2011–12, 12 research assistantships, 2 teaching assistantships were awarded; fellowships with tuition reimbursements also available. Financial award application deadline: 4/1. *Unit head:* Dr. Michael Daugherty, Unit Head, 479-575-4209, E-mail: mkd03@uark.edu. *Application contact:* Dr. Barbara Gartin, Graduate Coordinator, 479-575-7525, Fax: 479-575-6676, E-mail: bgartin@uark.edu. Web site: http://cied.uark.edu/.

The University of British Columbia, Faculty of Education, Centre for Cross-Faculty Inquiry in Education, Vancouver, BC V6T 1Z1, Canada. Offers curriculum and instruction (M Ed, MA, PhD); early childhood education (M Ed, MA). Part-time and evening/weekend programs available. Terminal master's awarded for partial completion of doctoral program. *Degree requirements:* For master's, thesis (MA); for doctorate, thesis/dissertation. *Entrance requirements:* Additional exam requirements/recommendations for international students: Required—TOEFL (minimum score 567 paper-based; 227 computer-based). Electronic applications accepted.

The University of British Columbia, Faculty of Education, Department of Curriculum and Pedagogy, Vancouver, BC V6T 1Z4, Canada. Offers art education (M Ed, MA); business education (MA); curriculum studies (M Ed, MA, PhD); home economics education (M Ed, MA); math education (M Ed, MA); music education (M Ed, MA); physical education (M Ed, MA); science education (M Ed, MA); social studies education (M Ed, MA); technology studies education (M Ed, MA). Part-time programs available. *Degree requirements:* For master's, thesis (MA); for doctorate, comprehensive exam, thesis/dissertation. *Entrance requirements:* Additional exam requirements/recommendations for international students: Required—TOEFL (minimum score 580 paper-based; 237 computer-based; 92 iBT). Electronic applications accepted. *Expenses:* Contact institution. *Faculty research:* School subjects, teaching and learning.

University of Calgary, Faculty of Graduate Studies, Faculty of Education, Graduate Division of Educational Research, Calgary, AB T2N 1N4, Canada. Offers community rehabilitation and disability studies (M Ed, M Sc, Ed D, PhD, Graduate Certificate, Graduate Diploma); curriculum, teaching and learning (M Ed, M Sc, MA, Ed D, PhD, Graduate Certificate, Graduate Diploma); educational contexts (M Ed, MA, Ed D, PhD, Graduate Certificate, Graduate Diploma); educational leadership (M Ed, MA, Ed D, PhD, Graduate Certificate, Graduate Diploma); educational technology (M Ed, M Sc, MA, Ed D, PhD, Graduate Certificate, Graduate Diploma); gifted education (M Sc, MA, Ed D, PhD, Graduate Certificate, Graduate Diploma); higher education administration (Ed D); interpretive studies in education (M Ed, M Sc, MA, Ed D, PhD, Graduate Certificate, Graduate Diploma); second language teaching (M Ed, Ed D, PhD, Graduate Certificate, Graduate Diploma); teaching English as a second language (M Ed, M Sc, MA, Ed D, PhD, Graduate Certificate, Graduate Diploma); workplace and adult learning (M Ed, MA, Ed D, PhD, Graduate Certificate, Graduate Diploma). Ed D in both higher education administration and educational leadership offered via distance delivery. Part-time and evening/weekend programs available. Postbaccalaureate distance learning degree programs offered (minimal on-campus study). *Degree requirements:* For master's, thesis (for some programs); for doctorate, thesis/dissertation, candidacy exam. *Entrance requirements:* For master's, minimum GPA of 3.0, 3 letters of reference; for doctorate, minimum GPA of 3.5, 3 letters of reference; for other advanced degree, minimum GPA of 3.0. Additional exam requirements/recommendations for international students: Required—TOEFL, IELTS. Electronic applications accepted. *Faculty research:* Curriculum, leadership, technology, contexts, gifted, second language teaching, work place and adult learning.

University of California, Davis, Graduate Studies, Graduate Group in Education, Davis, CA 95616. Offers education (MA, Ed D); instructional studies (PhD); psychological studies (PhD); sociocultural studies (PhD). Ed D offered jointly with California State University, Fresno. Terminal master's awarded for partial completion of doctoral program. *Degree requirements:* For master's, comprehensive exam (for some programs), thesis (for some programs); for doctorate, thesis/dissertation. *Entrance requirements:* For master's and doctorate, GRE. Additional exam requirements/recommendations for international students: Required—TOEFL (minimum score 550 paper-based; 213 computer-based). Electronic applications accepted. *Faculty research:* Language and literacy, mathematics education, science education, teacher development, school psychology.

University of Central Missouri, The Graduate School, College of Education, Warrensburg, MO 64093. Offers career and technical education administration (MS); career and technical education industry training (MS); career and technical education leadership/teaching (MS); college student personnel administration (MS); counseling (MS); curriculum and instruction (Ed S); educational leadership (Ed D); educational technology (MS); elementary education/educational foundations and literacy (MSE); elementary school administration (MSE); elementary school principalship (Ed S); human services/learning resources (Ed S); human services/professional counseling (Ed S); human services/special education (Ed S); human services/technology and occupational education (Ed S); K-12 education/educational foundations and literacy (MSE); K-12 special education (MSE); library science and information services (MS); literacy education (MSE); secondary education/educational foundations & literacy (MSE); secondary school administration (MSE); secondary school principalship (Ed S); superintendency (Ed S); teaching (MAT). Ed D offered jointly with University of Missouri.

Curriculum and Instruction

Part-time programs available. Postbaccalaureate distance learning degree programs offered. *Entrance requirements:* Additional exam requirements/recommendations for international students: Required—TOEFL (minimum score 550 paper-based; 79 computer-based). Electronic applications accepted.

University of Cincinnati, Graduate School, College of Education, Criminal Justice, and Human Services, Division of Teacher Education, Program in Curriculum and Instruction, Cincinnati, OH 45221. Offers M Ed, Ed D. *Accreditation:* NCATE. Part-time programs available. *Degree requirements:* For master's, thesis; for doctorate, thesis/dissertation. *Entrance requirements:* For master's, GRE General Test; for doctorate, GRE General Test, GRE Subject Test. Additional exam requirements/recommendations for international students: Required—TOEFL (minimum score 550 paper-based; 213 computer-based), TWE (minimum score 4.5), OEPT. Electronic applications accepted.

University of Colorado at Colorado Springs, College of Education, Colorado Springs, CO 80933-7150. Offers counseling and human services (MA); curriculum and instruction (MA); educational administration (MA); educational leadership (MA, PhD); special education (MA). *Accreditation:* ACA; NCATE. Part-time and evening/weekend programs available. Postbaccalaureate distance learning degree programs offered (minimal on-campus study). *Faculty:* 26 full-time (16 women), 9 part-time/adjunct (5 women). *Students:* 307 full-time (203 women), 115 part-time (92 women); includes 82 minority (24 Black or African American, non-Hispanic/Latino; 3 American Indian or Alaska Native, non-Hispanic/Latino; 12 Asian, non-Hispanic/Latino; 36 Hispanic/Latino; 1 Native Hawaiian or other Pacific Islander, non-Hispanic/Latino; 6 Two or more races, non-Hispanic/Latino), 1 international. Average age 36. 99 applicants, 86% accepted, 61 enrolled. In 2011, 165 master's, 6 doctorates awarded. *Degree requirements:* For master's, comprehensive exam, thesis or alternative, microcomputer proficiency; for doctorate, comprehensive exam, thesis/dissertation, research lab. *Entrance requirements:* For master's, GRE General Test. Additional exam requirements/recommendations for international students: Recommended—TOEFL. *Application deadline:* For fall admission, 2/28 priority date for domestic students, 2/28 for international students; for spring admission, 10/15 for domestic and international students. Applications are processed on a rolling basis. Application fee: $60 ($75 for international students). *Expenses:* Tuition, state resident: part-time $660 per credit hour. Tuition, nonresident: part-time $1133 per credit hour. Tuition and fees vary according to degree level, program and student level. *Financial support:* In 2011–12, 57 students received support. Career-related internships or fieldwork, Federal Work-Study, and scholarships/grants available. Support available to part-time students. Financial award application deadline: 3/1; financial award applicants required to submit FAFSA. *Faculty research:* Job training for special populations, materials development for classroom. *Total annual research expenditures:* $1.6 million. *Unit head:* Dr. Mary Snyder, Dean, 719-255-3701, Fax: 719-262-4133, E-mail: msnyder3@uccs.edu. *Application contact:* Juliane Field, Director, 719-255-4526, Fax: 719-255-4110, E-mail: jfield@uccs.edu. Web site: http://www.uccs.edu/coe.

University of Colorado Boulder, Graduate School, School of Education, Division of Instruction and Curriculum, Boulder, CO 80309. Offers MA, PhD. *Accreditation:* NCATE. *Students:* 78 full-time (44 women), 49 part-time (40 women); includes 12 minority (1 American Indian or Alaska Native, non-Hispanic/Latino; 3 Asian, non-Hispanic/Latino; 6 Hispanic/Latino; 2 Two or more races, non-Hispanic/Latino). Average age 30. 129 applicants, 60% accepted, 42 enrolled. In 2011, 51 master's, 3 doctorates awarded. Terminal master's awarded for partial completion of doctoral program. *Degree requirements:* For master's, comprehensive exam, thesis or alternative; for doctorate, one foreign language, comprehensive exam, thesis/dissertation. *Entrance requirements:* For master's, GRE General Test or MAT, minimum undergraduate GPA of 2.75; for doctorate, GRE General Test. *Application deadline:* For fall admission, 2/1 priority date for domestic students, 12/1 for international students; for spring admission, 9/1 for domestic students, 12/1 for international students. Application fee: $50 ($60 for international students). Electronic applications accepted. *Financial support:* In 2011–12, 118 students received support, including 53 fellowships (averaging $5,874 per year), 16 research assistantships with full and partial tuition reimbursements available (averaging $16,329 per year), 25 teaching assistantships with full and partial tuition reimbursements available (averaging $12,156 per year); institutionally sponsored loans, scholarships/grants, health care benefits, and unspecified assistantships also available. Financial award applicants required to submit FAFSA. *Application contact:* E-mail: edadvise@colorado.edu. Web site: http://www.colorado.edu/education/.

University of Delaware, College of Education and Human Development, School of Education, Newark, DE 19716. Offers education (PhD); educational leadership (Ed D); higher education (M Ed); instruction (MI); reading (M Ed); school leadership (M Ed); school psychology (MA, Ed S); teaching English as a second language (TESL) (MA). *Accreditation:* NCATE. Part-time and evening/weekend programs available. Terminal master's awarded for partial completion of doctoral program. *Degree requirements:* For master's, comprehensive exam (for some programs), thesis (for some programs); for doctorate, comprehensive exam (for some programs), thesis/dissertation. *Entrance requirements:* For master's and doctorate, GRE, 3 letters of recommendation. Additional exam requirements/recommendations for international students: Required—TOEFL (minimum score 600 paper-based; 250 computer-based). Electronic applications accepted. *Faculty research:* Teacher education; curriculum theory and development; community based education models, educational leadership.

University of Denver, Morgridge College of Education, Denver, CO 80208. Offers advanced study in law librarianship (Certificate); child and family studies (MA, PhD); counseling psychology (MA, PhD); curriculum and instruction (MA, PhD, Certificate); educational leadership (Ed D, PhD); educational leadership and policy studies (MA, Certificate); higher education (MA, PhD); library and information science (MLIS); research methods and statistics (MA, PhD); school administration (PhD); school psychology (Ed S). *Accreditation:* ALA; APA (one or more programs are accredited). Part-time and evening/weekend programs available. Postbaccalaureate distance learning degree programs offered (no on-campus study). *Faculty:* 34 full-time (25 women), 70 part-time/adjunct (54 women). *Students:* 385 full-time (289 women), 386 part-time (303 women); includes 168 minority (49 Black or African American, non-Hispanic/Latino; 8 American Indian or Alaska Native, non-Hispanic/Latino; 25 Asian, non-Hispanic/Latino; 71 Hispanic/Latino; 1 Native Hawaiian or other Pacific Islander, non-Hispanic/Latino; 14 Two or more races, non-Hispanic/Latino), 17 international. Average age 33. 668 applicants, 72% accepted, 256 enrolled. In 2011, 308 master's, 43 doctorates, 55 other advanced degrees awarded. Terminal master's awarded for partial completion of doctoral program. *Degree requirements:* For master's, comprehensive exam; for doctorate, 2 foreign languages, comprehensive exam, thesis/dissertation. *Entrance requirements:* For master's and doctorate, GRE General Test or GMAT. Additional exam requirements/recommendations for international students: Required—TOEFL (minimum score 550 paper-based; 80 iBT). *Application deadline:* Applications are processed on a rolling basis. Application fee: $60. Electronic applications accepted. *Financial support:* In 2011–12, 72 teaching assistantships with full and partial tuition reimbursements (averaging $9,049 per year) were awarded; career-related internships or fieldwork, Federal Work-Study, institutionally sponsored loans, scholarships/grants, and unspecified assistantships also available. Support available to part-time students. Financial award application deadline: 2/15; financial award applicants required to submit FAFSA. *Faculty research:* Parkinson's disease, personnel training, development and assessments, gifted education, service-learning, transportation, public schools. *Unit head:* Dr. Gregory M. Anderson, Dean, 303-871-3665, E-mail: gregory.m.anderson@du.edu. *Application contact:* Chris Dowen, Director, MCE Admission Office, 303-871-2783, E-mail: chris.dowen@du.edu. Web site: http://www.du.edu/education/.

University of Detroit Mercy, College of Liberal Arts and Education, Department of Education, Program in Curriculum and Instruction, Detroit, MI 48221. Offers MA. Part-time and evening/weekend programs available. *Degree requirements:* For master's, thesis or alternative. *Entrance requirements:* For master's, minimum GPA of 2.75. *Faculty research:* Integrative curriculum planning, curriculum planning for ethical and character education.

University of Florida, Graduate School, College of Education, Department of Educational Administration and Policy, Gainesville, FL 32611. Offers curriculum and instruction (Ed D, PhD); educational leadership (M Ed, MAE, Ed D, PhD, Ed S); higher education administration (Ed D, PhD, Ed S); student personnel in higher education (M Ed, MAE); PhD/JD. *Accreditation:* NCATE. Part-time and evening/weekend programs available. Postbaccalaureate distance learning degree programs offered. Terminal master's awarded for partial completion of doctoral program. *Degree requirements:* For master's, thesis (for some programs); for doctorate, comprehensive exam (for some programs), thesis/dissertation (for some programs). *Entrance requirements:* For master's, GRE General Test, minimum GPA of 3.0, teaching experience; for doctorate and Ed S, GRE General Test, minimum GPA of 3.0. Additional exam requirements/recommendations for international students: Required—TOEFL (minimum score 550 paper-based; 213 computer-based; 80 iBT), IELTS (minimum score 6). *Application deadline:* For fall admission, 2/15 for domestic students, 12/1 for international students; for spring admission, 9/15 for domestic students, 3/1 for international students. Applications are processed on a rolling basis. Application fee: $30. Electronic applications accepted. *Financial support:* Career-related internships or fieldwork and unspecified assistantships available. Financial award applicants required to submit FAFSA.

University of Florida, Graduate School, College of Education, School of Teaching and Learning, Gainesville, FL 32611. Offers bilingual/ESOL education (M Ed, MAE, Ed D, PhD, Ed S); curriculum and instruction (M Ed, MAE, Ed D, PhD, Ed S); elementary education (M Ed, MAE); English education (M Ed, MAE); mathematics education (M Ed, MAE); reading education (M Ed, MAE); science education (M Ed, MAE); social foundations of education (M Ed, MAE, Ed D, PhD); social studies education (M Ed, MAE). *Accreditation:* NCATE. Part-time and evening/weekend programs available. Postbaccalaureate distance learning degree programs offered (no on-campus study). *Faculty:* 26 full-time (19 women). *Students:* 247 full-time (201 women), 236 part-time (196 women); includes 100 minority (32 Black or African American, non-Hispanic/Latino; 2 American Indian or Alaska Native, non-Hispanic/Latino; 15 Asian, non-Hispanic/Latino; 51 Hispanic/Latino), 32 international. Average age 33. 290 applicants, 60% accepted, 122 enrolled. In 2011, 284 master's, 19 doctorates, 29 other advanced degrees awarded. Terminal master's awarded for partial completion of doctoral program. *Degree requirements:* For master's, comprehensive exam (for some programs), thesis (for some programs); for doctorate, comprehensive exam (for some programs), thesis/dissertation (for some programs). *Entrance requirements:* For master's and doctorate, GRE General Test, minimum GPA of 3.0; for Ed S, GRE General Test. Additional exam requirements/recommendations for international students: Required—TOEFL (minimum score 550 paper-based; 213 computer-based; 80 iBT), IELTS (minimum score 6). *Application deadline:* For fall admission, 2/15 for domestic students, 12/1 for international students; for spring admission, 9/15 for domestic students, 3/1 for international students. Applications are processed on a rolling basis. Application fee: $30. Electronic applications accepted. *Financial support:* Fellowships, research assistantships, teaching assistantships, career-related internships or fieldwork, and unspecified assistantships available. Financial award applicants required to submit FAFSA. *Faculty research:* Early childhood, child and adolescents, diverse learners, race/ethnicity issues, teacher education, professional development, language and literacy development, policy development. *Unit head:* Dr. Elizabeth Bondy, Chair, 352-273-4242, Fax: 352-392-9193, E-mail: bondy@coe.ufl.edu. *Application contact:* Wevan Terzian, Graduate Coordinator, 352-273-4216, Fax: 352-392-9193, E-mail: sterzian@coe.ufl.edu. Web site: http://education.ufl.edu/school-teaching-learning/.

University of Hawaii at Manoa, Graduate Division, College of Education, Department of Curriculum Studies, Honolulu, HI 96822. Offers curriculum studies (M Ed); early childhood education (M Ed). Part-time programs available. *Degree requirements:* For master's, thesis optional. *Entrance requirements:* Additional exam requirements/recommendations for international students: Required—TOEFL (minimum score 500 paper-based; 173 computer-based; 61 iBT), IELTS (minimum score 5).

University of Hawaii at Manoa, Graduate Division, College of Education, PhD in Education Program, Honolulu, HI 96822. Offers curriculum and instruction (PhD); educational administration (PhD); educational foundations (PhD); educational policy studies (PhD); educational technology (PhD); exceptionalities (PhD); kinesiology (PhD). Part-time and evening/weekend programs available. *Degree requirements:* For doctorate, thesis/dissertation. *Entrance requirements:* For doctorate, GRE General Test, sample of written work. Additional exam requirements/recommendations for international students: Required—TOEFL (minimum score 600 paper-based; 250 computer-based; 100 iBT), IELTS (minimum score 7).

University of Houston, College of Education, Department of Curriculum and Instruction, Houston, TX 77204. Offers administration and supervision (M Ed); curriculum and instruction (M Ed, Ed D); professional leadership (Ed D). *Accreditation:* NCATE. Part-time and evening/weekend programs available. *Degree requirements:* For master's, comprehensive exam, thesis optional; for doctorate, comprehensive exam, thesis/dissertation. *Entrance requirements:* For master's and doctorate, GRE, minimum cumulative undergraduate GPA of 2.6, 3 letters of recommendation, resume/vita, goal statement. Additional exam requirements/recommendations for international students: Required—TOEFL (minimum score 550 paper-based; 79 iBT). Electronic applications accepted. *Faculty research:* Teaching-learning process, instructional technology in schools, teacher education, classroom management, at-risk students.

University of Houston–Clear Lake, School of Education, Program in Curriculum and Instruction, Houston, TX 77058-1098. Offers curriculum and instruction (MS); early childhood education (MS); reading (MS); school library and information science (MS). Part-time and evening/weekend programs available. *Degree requirements:* For master's, thesis (for some programs). *Entrance requirements:* For master's, GRE or minimum GPA of 3.0 in last 60 hours. Additional exam requirements/recommendations for international students: Required—TOEFL (minimum score 550 paper-based; 213 computer-based). Electronic applications accepted.

University of Houston–Downtown, College of Public Service, Department of Urban Education, Houston, TX 77002. Offers bilingual education (MAT); curriculum and instruction (MAT); elementary education (MAT); secondary education (MAT). Part-time and evening/weekend programs available. *Faculty:* 12 full-time (8 women). *Students:* 13 full-time (10 women), 25 part-time (22 women); includes 30 minority (15 Black or African

American, non-Hispanic/Latino; 3 Asian, non-Hispanic/Latino; 11 Hispanic/Latino; 1 Two or more races, non-Hispanic/Latino). Average age 35. 17 applicants, 100% accepted, 16 enrolled. In 2011, 5 master's awarded. *Degree requirements:* For master's, capstone course with completed project, position paper, grant proposal, empirical study, curriculum development/revision, or advanced technology project presented at annual Graduate Project Exhibition. *Entrance requirements:* For master's, GRE, personal statement, 3 recommendation forms. Additional exam requirements/recommendations for international students: Required—TOEFL (minimum score 550 paper-based; 213 computer-based; 80 iBT). *Application deadline:* For fall admission, 7/15 for domestic and international students; for spring admission, 11/15 for domestic and international students. Applications are processed on a rolling basis. Application fee: $35 ($60 for international students). Electronic applications accepted. *Expenses:* Tuition, state resident: full-time $3420; part-time $2280 per year. Tuition, nonresident: full-time $8424; part-time $5616 per year. *Required fees:* $1018; $840 per year. Tuition and fees vary according to program. *Financial support:* Scholarships/grants available. Financial award applicants required to submit FAFSA. *Unit head:* Dr. Myrna Cohen, Department Chair, 713-221-2759, Fax: 713-226-5294, E-mail: cohenm@uhd.edu. *Application contact:* Traneshia Parker, Associate Director of International Student Services and Graduate Admissions, 713-221-8093, Fax: 713-221-8157, E-mail: parkert@uhd.edu. Web site: http://www.uhd.edu/academic/colleges/publicservice/urbaned/mat.htm.

University of Houston–Victoria, School of Education and Human Development, Victoria, TX 77901-4450. Offers administration and supervision (M Ed); counseling (M Ed); curriculum and instruction (M Ed); special education (M Ed). Part-time and evening/weekend programs available. Postbaccalaureate distance learning degree programs offered (minimal on-campus study). *Degree requirements:* For master's, comprehensive exam, project or thesis. *Entrance requirements:* For master's, GRE General Test. Additional exam requirements/recommendations for international students: Required—TOEFL. Electronic applications accepted. *Faculty research:* Reading and language arts education, evaluation and diagnosis of special children's abilities.

University of Idaho, College of Graduate Studies, College of Education, Department of Curriculum and Instruction, Moscow, ID 83844-3082. Offers curriculum and instruction (Ed S); special education (M Ed). *Faculty:* 22 full-time, 2 part-time/adjunct. *Students:* 17 full-time (9 women), 62 part-time (45 women). Average age 38. In 2011, 47 master's, 2 Ed Ss awarded. *Entrance requirements:* For master's, minimum GPA of 2.8. *Application deadline:* For fall admission, 8/1 for domestic students; for spring admission, 12/15 for domestic students. Applications are processed on a rolling basis. Application fee: $60. Electronic applications accepted. *Expenses:* Tuition, state resident: full-time $3874; part-time $334 per credit hour. Tuition, nonresident: full-time $16,394; part-time $861 per credit hour. *Required fees:* $2808; $99 per credit hour. Tuition and fees vary according to program. *Financial support:* Research assistantships and teaching assistantships available. Financial award applicants required to submit FAFSA. *Unit head:* Dr. Paul H. Gathercoal, Chair, 208-885-6587. *Application contact:* Erick Larson, Director of Graduate Admissions, 208-885-4723, E-mail: gadms@uidaho.edu. Web site: http://www.uidaho.edu/ed/ci.

University of Illinois at Chicago, Graduate College, College of Education, Department of Curriculum and Instruction, Chicago, IL 60607-7128. Offers curriculum studies (PhD); educational studies (M Ed); elementary education (M Ed); literacy, language and culture (M Ed, PhD); secondary education (M Ed). Part-time and evening/weekend programs available. *Degree requirements:* For doctorate, thesis/dissertation. *Entrance requirements:* For master's, minimum GPA of 2.75; for doctorate, GRE General Test, minimum GPA of 2.75. Additional exam requirements/recommendations for international students: Required—TOEFL. Electronic applications accepted. *Faculty research:* Curriculum theory, curriculum development, research on teaching, curriculum and context, reading/literacy.

University of Illinois at Urbana–Champaign, Graduate College, College of Education, Department of Curriculum and Instruction, Champaign, IL 61820. Offers curriculum and instruction (Ed M, MA, MS, Ed D, PhD, CAS); early childhood education (Ed M); elementary education (Ed M); secondary education (Ed M). Part-time programs available. Postbaccalaureate distance learning degree programs offered (minimal on-campus study). *Faculty:* 22 full-time (16 women). *Students:* 94 full-time (75 women), 94 part-time (79 women); includes 40 minority (13 Black or African American, non-Hispanic/Latino; 1 American Indian or Alaska Native, non-Hispanic/Latino; 14 Asian, non-Hispanic/Latino; 9 Hispanic/Latino; 3 Two or more races, non-Hispanic/Latino), 49 international. 161 applicants, 60% accepted, 45 enrolled. In 2011, 65 master's, 18 doctorates, 1 other advanced degree awarded. *Entrance requirements:* For master's, minimum GPA of 3.0; for doctorate, GRE General Test, writing sample. Additional exam requirements/recommendations for international students: Required—TOEFL (minimum score 550 paper-based; 213 computer-based; 79 iBT). *Application deadline:* Applications are processed on a rolling basis. Application fee: $75 ($90 for international students). Electronic applications accepted. *Financial support:* In 2011–12, 8 fellowships, 35 research assistantships, 56 teaching assistantships were awarded; tuition waivers (full and partial) also available. *Unit head:* Fouad Abd El Khalick, Head, 217-244-1221, Fax: 217-244-4572, E-mail: fouad@illinois.edu. *Application contact:* Myranda Lyons, Office Support Associate, 217-244-8286, Fax: 217-244-4572, E-mail: mjlyons@illinois.edu. Web site: http://www.education.illinois.edu/ci.

University of Indianapolis, Graduate Programs, School of Education, Indianapolis, IN 46227-3697. Offers art education (MAT); biology (MAT); chemistry (MAT); curriculum and instruction (MA); earth sciences (MAT); education (MA, MAT); educational leadership (MA); elementary education (MA); English (MAT); French (MAT); math (MAT); physical education (MAT); physics (MAT); secondary education (MA), including art education, education, English education, social studies education; social studies (MAT); Spanish (MAT). *Accreditation:* NCATE. Part-time and evening/weekend programs available. *Faculty:* 3 full-time (2 women), 3 part-time/adjunct (2 women). *Students:* 32 full-time (18 women), 97 part-time (56 women); includes 22 minority (20 Black or African American, non-Hispanic/Latino; 1 Asian, non-Hispanic/Latino; 1 Hispanic/Latino), 3 international. Average age 33. In 2011, 78 master's awarded. *Entrance requirements:* For master's, GRE Subject Test, PRAXIS I, minimum GPA of 2.5, 3 letters of recommendation, interview, writing exercise. Additional exam requirements/recommendations for international students: Required—TOEFL (minimum score 550 paper-based; 213 computer-based). *Application deadline:* Applications are processed on a rolling basis. Application fee: $50. Tuition and fees vary according to degree level and program. *Financial support:* Federal Work-Study available. Financial award application deadline: 5/1; financial award applicants required to submit FAFSA. *Faculty research:* Assessment of teacher education, perceptions of prospective teachers by parents. *Unit head:* Dr. Kathy Moran, Dean, 317-788-3285, Fax: 317-788-3300, E-mail: kmoran@uindy.edu. *Application contact:* Jeni Kirby, 317-788-2113, E-mail: kirbyj@uindy.edu. Web site: http://education.uindy.edu/.

The University of Iowa, Graduate College, College of Education, Department of Teaching and Learning, Program in Elementary Education, Iowa City, IA 52242-1316. Offers curriculum and supervision (MA, PhD); developmental reading (MA); early childhood education and care (MA); elementary education (MA, PhD); language, literature and culture (PhD). *Degree requirements:* For master's, thesis optional, exam; for doctorate, comprehensive exam, thesis/dissertation. *Entrance requirements:* For master's and doctorate, GRE General Test, minimum GPA of 3.0. Additional exam requirements/recommendations for international students: Required—TOEFL (minimum score 550 paper-based; 213 computer-based; 81 iBT). Electronic applications accepted.

The University of Iowa, Graduate College, College of Education, Department of Teaching and Learning, Program in Secondary Education, Iowa City, IA 52242-1316. Offers art education (PhD); curriculum and supervision (PhD); curriculum supervision (MA); developmental reading (MA); English education (MA, MAT); foreign language education (MA, MAT); foreign language/ESL education (PhD); language, literature and culture (PhD); math education (PhD); mathematics education (MA); social studies (MA, PhD). *Degree requirements:* For master's, thesis optional, exam; for doctorate, comprehensive exam, thesis/dissertation. *Entrance requirements:* For master's and doctorate, GRE General Test, minimum GPA of 3.0. Additional exam requirements/recommendations for international students: Required—TOEFL (minimum score 550 paper-based; 213 computer-based; 81 iBT). Electronic applications accepted.

The University of Kansas, Graduate Studies, School of Education, Department of Curriculum and Teaching, Lawrence, KS 66045-3101. Offers curriculum and instruction (MA, MS Ed, Ed D, PhD). Part-time and evening/weekend programs available. *Faculty:* 24 full-time (17 women). *Students:* 244 full-time (171 women), 113 part-time (92 women); includes 37 minority (4 Black or African American, non-Hispanic/Latino; 16 Asian, non-Hispanic/Latino; 11 Hispanic/Latino; 6 Two or more races, non-Hispanic/Latino), 44 international. Average age 31. 190 applicants, 77% accepted, 128 enrolled. In 2011, 107 master's, 15 doctorates awarded. *Degree requirements:* For master's, comprehensive exam (for some programs), thesis optional; for doctorate, comprehensive exam, thesis/dissertation. *Entrance requirements:* For master's, minimum GPA of 3.0; for doctorate, GRE General Test, minimum graduate GPA of 3.5. Additional exam requirements/recommendations for international students: Required—TOEFL (minimum score 590 paper-based; 243 computer-based; 96 iBT), IELTS (minimum score 7). *Application deadline:* For fall admission, 3/15 priority date for domestic students, 3/15 for international students; for spring admission, 10/15 priority date for domestic students, 10/15 for international students. Applications are processed on a rolling basis. Application fee: $55 ($65 for international students). Electronic applications accepted. Tuition and fees vary according to course load, campus/location, program and reciprocity agreements. *Financial support:* Fellowships, research assistantships with full and partial tuition reimbursements, teaching assistantships with full and partial tuition reimbursements, Federal Work-Study, scholarships/grants, and unspecified assistantships available. Financial award application deadline: 3/15; financial award applicants required to submit FAFSA. *Faculty research:* Literacy, curriculum studies, math education, science education, social studies education. *Unit head:* Dr. Steven Hugh White, Associate Professor and Chair, 785-864-9662, Fax: 785-864-5207, E-mail: s-white@ku.edu. *Application contact:* Susan M. McGee, Graduate Admissions Coordinator, 785-864-4437, Fax: 785-864-5207, E-mail: smmcgee@ku.edu. Web site: http://soe.ku.edu/ct/.

University of Kentucky, Graduate School, College of Education, Program in Curriculum and Instruction, Lexington, KY 40506-0032. Offers curriculum and instruction (MA Ed, Ed D); instruction and administration (Ed D); instruction system design (MS Ed); middle school education (MS Ed). *Accreditation:* NCATE. *Degree requirements:* For master's, comprehensive exam, thesis optional; for doctorate, comprehensive exam, thesis/dissertation. *Entrance requirements:* For master's, GRE General Test, minimum undergraduate GPA of 2.75; for doctorate, GRE General Test, minimum graduate GPA of 3.0. Additional exam requirements/recommendations for international students: Required—TOEFL (minimum score 550 paper-based; 213 computer-based). Electronic applications accepted. *Faculty research:* Educational reform, multicultural education, classroom instructional practices, performance based assessment, primary school programs.

University of Louisiana at Lafayette, College of Education, Graduate Studies and Research in Education, Program in Curriculum and Instruction, Lafayette, LA 70504. Offers M Ed. *Accreditation:* NCATE. *Degree requirements:* For master's, thesis or alternative. *Entrance requirements:* For master's, GRE General Test, teaching certificate. Additional exam requirements/recommendations for international students: Required—TOEFL (minimum score 550 paper-based; 213 computer-based). Electronic applications accepted.

University of Louisiana at Monroe, Graduate School, College of Education and Human Development, Department of Curriculum and Instruction, Program in Curriculum and Instruction, Monroe, LA 71209-0001. Offers curriculum and instruction (Ed D); elementary education (1-5) (M Ed); reading education (K-12) (M Ed); SPED-academically gifted education (K-12) (M Ed); SPED-early intervention education (birth-3) (M Ed); SPED-educational diagnostics education (PreK-12) (M Ed). *Accreditation:* NCATE. *Students:* 42 full-time (37 women), 54 part-time (47 women); includes 20 minority (18 Black or African American, non-Hispanic/Latino; 1 Asian, non-Hispanic/Latino; 1 Hispanic/Latino), 12 international. Average age 36. 55 applicants, 95% accepted, 38 enrolled. In 2011, 27 master's, 1 doctorate awarded. *Degree requirements:* For master's, comprehensive exam (for some programs), thesis; for doctorate, thesis/dissertation, internships. *Entrance requirements:* For master's, GRE General Test; for doctorate, GRE General Test, minimum undergraduate GPA of 2.75, graduate 3.25. Additional exam requirements/recommendations for international students: Required—TOEFL (minimum score 500 paper-based; 173 computer-based; 61 iBT). *Application deadline:* For fall admission, 8/24 priority date for domestic students, 7/1 for international students; for winter admission, 12/14 priority date for domestic students; for spring admission, 1/19 for domestic students, 11/1 for international students. Applications are processed on a rolling basis. Application fee: $20 ($30 for international students). Electronic applications accepted. *Expenses:* Tuition, state resident: full-time $3436; part-time $240 per credit hour. Tuition, nonresident: full-time $3436; part-time $240 per credit hour. *International tuition:* $10,733 full-time. *Required fees:* $1460.90. *Financial support:* In 2011–12, 12 research assistantships with full tuition reimbursements (averaging $2,500 per year) were awarded; career-related internships or fieldwork, Federal Work-Study, and unspecified assistantships also available. Financial award application deadline: 4/1; financial award applicants required to submit FAFSA. *Unit head:* Dr. Dorothy Schween, Coordinator, 318-342-1269, Fax: 318-342-3131, E-mail: schween@ulm.edu. *Application contact:* Whitney Sutherland, Administrative Assistant to the Department Head, 318-342-1266, Fax: 318-342-3131, E-mail: sutherland@ulm.edu. Web site: http://www.ulm.edu/ci/.

University of Louisville, Graduate School, College of Education and Human Development, Department of Teaching and Learning, Louisville, KY 40292-0001. Offers art education (MAT); curriculum and instruction (PhD); early elementary education (MAT); instructional technology (M Ed); interdisciplinary early childhood education (MAT); middle school education (MAT); music education (MAT); reading education (M Ed); secondary education (MAT); special education (M Ed, MAT); teacher leadership (M Ed). Part-time and evening/weekend programs available. *Degree requirements:* For doctorate, comprehensive exam, thesis/dissertation. *Entrance requirements:* For master's, GRE General Test, PRAXIS II (for some programs); for doctorate, GRE General Test. Additional exam requirements/recommendations for international students: Required—TOEFL (minimum score 560 paper-based; 210 computer-based;

83 iBT). Electronic applications accepted. *Expenses:* Tuition, state resident: full-time $9692; part-time $539 per credit hour. Tuition, nonresident: full-time $20,168; part-time $1121 per credit hour. Tuition and fees vary according to program and reciprocity agreements. *Faculty research:* Mathematics teacher education and ongoing professional development in pedagogy and content knowledge; development of literacy, including early literacy in science and mathematics and literacy development for English language learners; immersive visualizations for promoting STEM education from nanoscience to cosmic scales; evidence-based practices for students with disabilities; urban education, including teacher response to intervention systems in schools and cross-cultural competence.

University of Maine, Graduate School, College of Education and Human Development, Program in Curriculum, Assessment, and Instruction, Orono, ME 04469. Offers elementary and secondary education (M Ed). *Students:* 4 full-time (3 women), 20 part-time (16 women), 1 international. Average age 37. 10 applicants, 40% accepted, 4 enrolled. In 2011, 15 degrees awarded. Application fee: $65. *Expenses:* Tuition, state resident: full-time $5016. Tuition, nonresident: full-time $14,424. *Unit head:* Dr. Janet Spector, Dean, 207-581-2441, Fax: 207-581-2423. *Application contact:* Scott G. Delcourt, Associate Dean of the Graduate School, 207-581-3291, Fax: 207-581-3232, E-mail: graduate@maine.edu. Web site: http://www2.umaine.edu/graduate/.

University of Maine, Graduate School, College of Education and Human Development, Program in Kinesiology and Physical Education, Orono, ME 04469. Offers curriculum and instruction (M Ed); exercise science (MS). Part-time and evening/weekend programs available. *Students:* 10 full-time (3 women), 2 part-time (1 woman); includes 2 minority (1 Hispanic/Latino; 1 Two or more races, non-Hispanic/Latino). Average age 29. 16 applicants, 69% accepted, 9 enrolled. In 2011, 8 degrees awarded. *Degree requirements:* For master's, thesis or alternative. *Entrance requirements:* For master's, MAT. Additional exam requirements/recommendations for international students: Required—TOEFL. *Application deadline:* For fall admission, 2/1 priority date for domestic students. Applications are processed on a rolling basis. Application fee: $65. Electronic applications accepted. *Expenses:* Tuition, state resident: full-time $5016. Tuition, nonresident: full-time $14,424. *Financial support:* Career-related internships or fieldwork, Federal Work-Study, institutionally sponsored loans, tuition waivers (full and partial), and unspecified assistantships available. Support available to part-time students. Financial award application deadline: 3/1. *Unit head:* Dr. Janet Spector, Coordinator, 207-581-2444, Fax: 207-581-2423. *Application contact:* Scott G. Delcourt, Associate Dean of the Graduate School, 207-581-3291, Fax: 207-581-3232, E-mail: graduate@maine.edu. Web site: http://www2umaine.edu/graduate/.

University of Manitoba, Faculty of Graduate Studies, Faculty of Education, Department of Curriculum, Teaching and Learning, Winnipeg, MB R3T 2N2, Canada. Offers language and literacy (M Ed); second language education (M Ed); studies in curriculum, teaching and learning (M Ed). *Degree requirements:* For master's, thesis or alternative.

University of Mary, School of Education and Behavioral Sciences, Department of Education, Bismarck, ND 58504-9652. Offers college teaching (M Ed); curriculum, instruction and assessment (M Ed); early childhood education (M Ed); early childhood special education (M Ed); elementary administration (M Ed); emotional disorders (M Ed); learning disabilities (M Ed); reading (M Ed); secondary administration (M Ed); special education strategist (M Ed). Part-time programs available. *Faculty:* 6 full-time (5 women), 12 part-time/adjunct (8 women). *Students:* 5 full-time (4 women), 77 part-time (56 women); includes 9 minority (1 Black or African American, non-Hispanic/Latino; 4 American Indian or Alaska Native, non-Hispanic/Latino; 1 Asian, non-Hispanic/Latino; 3 Hispanic/Latino), 1 international. Average age 30. 58 applicants, 55% accepted, 29 enrolled. In 2011, 16 master's awarded. *Degree requirements:* For master's, portfolio or thesis. *Entrance requirements:* For master's, interview, letters of reference, minimum GPA of 2.5. Additional exam requirements/recommendations for international students: Required—TOEFL (minimum score 500 paper-based; 197 computer-based; 71 iBT). *Application deadline:* Applications are processed on a rolling basis. Application fee: $40. Electronic applications accepted. *Financial support:* In 2011–12, 1 teaching assistantship with full tuition reimbursement was awarded; career-related internships or fieldwork also available. Financial award application deadline: 8/1; financial award applicants required to submit FAFSA. *Faculty research:* Innovative pedagogy in higher education, technology in education, content standards, children of poverty, children with diverse learning needs. *Unit head:* Dr. Rebecca Yunker Salveson, Director, 701-355-8186, E-mail: rysalves@umary.edu. *Application contact:* Leona Friedig, Administrative Secretary, 701-355-8058, E-mail: lfriedig@umary.edu.

University of Mary Hardin-Baylor, Graduate Studies in Education, Belton, TX 76513. Offers administration of intervention programs (M Ed); curriculum and instruction (M Ed); educational administration (M Ed, Ed D). Part-time and evening/weekend programs available. *Faculty:* 17 full-time (9 women), 3 part-time/adjunct (2 women). *Students:* 39 full-time (21 women), 88 part-time (51 women); includes 43 minority (24 Black or African American, non-Hispanic/Latino; 2 Asian, non-Hispanic/Latino; 17 Hispanic/Latino), 3 international. Average age 37. 32 applicants, 66% accepted, 12 enrolled. In 2011, 20 master's, 14 doctorates awarded. *Degree requirements:* For master's, comprehensive exam; for doctorate, thesis/dissertation. *Entrance requirements:* For master's, GRE General Test, minimum GPA of 2.75, Texas teaching certificate; for doctorate, GRE, minimum GPA of 3.5, interview, essay. *Application deadline:* For fall admission, 6/1 priority date for domestic students; for spring admission, 11/1 for domestic students. Applications are processed on a rolling basis. Application fee: $35 ($135 for international students). Electronic applications accepted. *Expenses: Tuition:* Full-time $12,780. *Required fees:* $2350. *Financial support:* Federal Work-Study and scholarships (for some active duty military personnel only) available. Support available to part-time students. Financial award application deadline: 6/1; financial award applicants required to submit FAFSA. *Unit head:* Dr. Austin Vasek, Program Director, 254-295-4185, Fax: 254-295-4480, E-mail: austin.vasek@umhb.edu. *Application contact:* Melissa Ford, Director of Graduate Admissions, 254-295-4020, Fax: 254-295-5301, E-mail: mford@umhb.edu.

University of Maryland, Baltimore County, Graduate School, College of Arts, Humanities and Social Sciences, Department of Education, Baltimore, MD 21250. Offers distance education (Postbaccalaureate Certificate); education (MA), including education; instructional systems development (MA, Graduate Certificate), including distance education (Graduate Certificate), instructional design for e-learning (Graduate Certificate), instructional systems development, instructional technology (Graduate Certificate); mathematics education (Postbaccalaureate Certificate); mathematics instructional leadership (K-8) (Postbaccalaureate Certificate); teaching (MAT), including early childhood education, elementary education, secondary education; teaching English for speakers of other languages (MA); teaching English to speakers of other languages (Postbaccalaureate Certificate). *Accreditation:* NCATE. Part-time and evening/weekend programs available. Postbaccalaureate distance learning degree programs offered (no on-campus study). *Faculty:* 21 full-time (15 women), 25 part-time/adjunct (19 women). *Students:* 102 full-time (70 women), 263 part-time (202 women); includes 83 minority (42 Black or African American, non-Hispanic/Latino; 1 American Indian or Alaska Native, non-Hispanic/Latino; 18 Asian, non-Hispanic/Latino; 15 Hispanic/Latino; 2 Native Hawaiian or other Pacific Islander, non-Hispanic/Latino; 5 Two or more races, non-Hispanic/Latino), 17 international. Average age 34. 90 applicants, 94% accepted, 80 enrolled. In 2011, 100 master's awarded. *Degree requirements:* For master's, comprehensive exam (for some programs), thesis (for some programs). *Entrance requirements:* For master's, GRE General Test, GRE Subject Test (MA in TESOL), PRAXIS I (MAT), minimum GPA of 3.0. Additional exam requirements/recommendations for international students: Required—TOEFL. *Application deadline:* For fall admission, 6/1 for domestic students; for spring admission, 11/1 for domestic students. Applications are processed on a rolling basis. Application fee: $50. Electronic applications accepted. *Financial support:* In 2011–12, 12 students received support, including teaching assistantships with full tuition reimbursements available (averaging $12,000 per year); fellowships, career-related internships or fieldwork, Federal Work-Study, scholarships/grants, tuition waivers (partial), and unspecified assistantships also available. Financial award application deadline: 3/1. *Faculty research:* Teacher leadership; STEM education; ESOL/bilingual education; early childhood education; language, literacy and culture. *Total annual research expenditures:* $1.3 million. *Unit head:* Dr. Eugene Schaffer, Department Chair, 410-455-2465, Fax: 410-455-3986, E-mail: schaffer@umbc.edu. *Application contact:* Dr. Susan M. Blunck, Graduate Program Director, 410-455-2869, Fax: 410-455-3986, E-mail: blunck@umbc.edu. Web site: http://www.umbc.edu/education/.

University of Maryland, College Park, Academic Affairs, College of Education, Department of Curriculum and Instruction, College Park, MD 20742. Offers reading (M Ed, MA, PhD, CAGS); secondary education (M Ed, MA, Ed D, PhD, CAGS); teaching English to speakers of other languages (M Ed). *Accreditation:* NCATE. Part-time and evening/weekend programs available. Postbaccalaureate distance learning degree programs offered (no on-campus study). *Faculty:* 51 full-time (38 women), 23 part-time/adjunct (18 women). *Students:* 252 full-time (177 women), 178 part-time (134 women); includes 121 minority (51 Black or African American, non-Hispanic/Latino; 37 Asian, non-Hispanic/Latino; 24 Hispanic/Latino; 9 Two or more races, non-Hispanic/Latino), 41 international. 264 applicants, 48% accepted, 80 enrolled. In 2011, 176 master's, 17 doctorates awarded. *Degree requirements:* For master's, comprehensive exam, seminar paper; for doctorate, comprehensive exam, thesis/dissertation, published paper, oral exam. *Entrance requirements:* For master's, GRE General Test or MAT, minimum GPA of 3.0, 3 letters of recommendation; for doctorate, GRE General Test or MAT, minimum undergraduate GPA of 3.0, graduate 3.5; 3 letters of recommendation. *Application deadline:* For fall admission, 11/15 priority date for domestic students, 11/15 for international students. Applications are processed on a rolling basis. Application fee: $75. Electronic applications accepted. *Expenses: Tuition, area resident:* Part-time $525 per credit hour. Tuition, state resident: part-time $525 per credit hour. Tuition, nonresident: part-time $1131 per credit hour. *Required fees:* $386.31 per term. Tuition and fees vary according to program. *Financial support:* In 2011–12, 11 research assistantships (averaging $17,535 per year), 79 teaching assistantships (averaging $17,270 per year) were awarded; Federal Work-Study and scholarships/grants also available. Support available to part-time students. Financial award applicants required to submit FAFSA. *Faculty research:* Teacher preparation, curriculum study, in-service education. *Total annual research expenditures:* $3.6 million. *Unit head:* Francine Hultgren, Interim Chair, 301-405-3117, E-mail: fh@umd.edu. *Application contact:* Dr. Charles A. Caramello, Dean of Graduate School, 301-405-0358, Fax: 301-314-9305.

University of Massachusetts Boston, Office of Graduate Studies, Graduate College of Education, Program in Instructional Design, Boston, MA 02125-3393. Offers M Ed. Part-time and evening/weekend programs available. *Degree requirements:* For master's, comprehensive exam, thesis optional, practicum. *Entrance requirements:* For master's, MAT, minimum GPA of 2.75. *Faculty research:* Distance education, adult education.

University of Massachusetts Lowell, Graduate School of Education, Lowell, MA 01854-2881. Offers administration, planning, and policy (CAGS); curriculum and instruction (M Ed, CAGS); educational administration (M Ed); language arts and literacy (Ed D); leadership in schooling (Ed D); math and science education (Ed D); reading and language (M Ed, CAGS). *Accreditation:* NCATE. Part-time and evening/weekend programs available. Postbaccalaureate distance learning degree programs offered (no on-campus study). Terminal master's awarded for partial completion of doctoral program. *Degree requirements:* For doctorate, thesis/dissertation. *Entrance requirements:* For master's, doctorate, and CAGS, GRE General Test. Additional exam requirements/recommendations for international students: Required—TOEFL. Electronic applications accepted.

University of Memphis, Graduate School, College of Education, Department of Instruction and Curriculum Leadership, Memphis, TN 38152. Offers early childhood education (MAT, MS, Ed D); elementary education (MAT); instruction and curriculum (MS, Ed D); instruction design and technology (MS, Ed D); middle grades education (MAT); reading (MS, Ed D); secondary education (MAT); special education (MAT, MS, Ed D). *Accreditation:* NCATE (one or more programs are accredited). Part-time programs available. Terminal master's awarded for partial completion of doctoral program. *Degree requirements:* For master's, comprehensive exam, thesis or alternative; for doctorate, comprehensive exam, thesis/dissertation. *Entrance requirements:* For master's, GRE General Test, minimum GPA of 2.5; for doctorate, GRE General Test, GRE Subject Test, 2 years of teaching experience. Electronic applications accepted. *Faculty research:* Effective urban teachers, preparation and retention of urban teachers, technology utilization in schools, field-based teacher preparation programs, effective use of online instruction.

University of Michigan–Dearborn, School of Education, Doctoral Program in Education, Dearborn, MI 48126. Offers curriculum and practice (Ed D); educational leadership (Ed D); educational psychology/special education (Ed D); metropolitan education (Ed D). Part-time and evening/weekend programs available. *Faculty:* 8 full-time (6 women), 2 part-time/adjunct (0 women). *Students:* 47 part-time (34 women); includes 12 minority (6 Black or African American, non-Hispanic/Latino; 3 Asian, non-Hispanic/Latino; 1 Hispanic/Latino; 2 Two or more races, non-Hispanic/Latino). Average age 40. 55 applicants, 35% accepted, 17 enrolled. *Degree requirements:* For doctorate, comprehensive exam, thesis/dissertation. *Entrance requirements:* For doctorate, GRE (taken within the last 5 years), master's degree with minimum GPA of 3.3, 3 letters of recommendation (1 from faculty), 3 years' professional and/or teaching experience. Additional exam requirements/recommendations for international students: Required—TOEFL (minimum score 550 paper-based). *Application deadline:* For fall admission, 3/1 for domestic and international students. Application fee: $60 ($75 for international students). *Financial support:* Scholarships/grants available. *Faculty research:* Educational leadership, metropolitan education, curriculum and practice, educational psychology, special education, assessment. *Unit head:* Bonnie Beyer, Coordinator, 313-593-5583, E-mail: beyer@umd.umich.edu. *Application contact:* Catherine Parkins, Customer Service Assistant, 313-583-6349, Fax: 313-593-4748, E-mail: cparkins@umd.umich.edu. Web site: http://www.soe.umd.umich.edu/soe_edd/.

University of Minnesota, Twin Cities Campus, Graduate School, College of Education and Human Development, Department of Curriculum and Instruction, Minneapolis, MN 55455-0213. Offers art education (M Ed, MA, PhD); children's literature (M Ed, MA, PhD); curriculum and instruction (MA, PhD); early childhood education (M Ed, PhD); elementary education (M Ed, MA, PhD); English education (MA, PhD); environmental education (M Ed); family education (M Ed, MA, Ed D, PhD); instructional systems and technology (M Ed, MA, PhD); language arts (MA, PhD);

language immersion education (Certificate); literacy education (MA); mathematics education (MA, PhD); reading education (MA, PhD); science education (MA, PhD); second languages and cultures education (MA, PhD); social studies education (MA, PhD); teaching (M Ed), including Chinese, earth science, elementary special education, English, English as a second language, French, German, Hebrew, Japanese, life sciences, mathematics, middle school science, science, second languages and cultures, social studies, Spanish; technology enhanced learning (Certificate); writing education (M Ed, MA, PhD). *Faculty:* 34 full-time (22 women). *Students:* 433 full-time (319 women), 310 part-time (239 women); includes 97 minority (34 Black or African American, non-Hispanic/Latino; 6 American Indian or Alaska Native, non-Hispanic/Latino; 35 Asian, non-Hispanic/Latino; 22 Hispanic/Latino), 47 international. Average age 33. 660 applicants, 68% accepted, 395 enrolled. In 2011, 518 master's, 19 doctorates, 14 other advanced degrees awarded. Application fee: $55. *Financial support:* In 2011–12, 6 fellowships (averaging $9,308 per year), 39 research assistantships with full tuition reimbursements (averaging $8,301 per year), 61 teaching assistantships with full tuition reimbursements (averaging $9,206 per year) were awarded. *Faculty research:* Teaching and learning; quality of education; influence of cultural, linguistic, social, political, technological and economic factors on teaching, learning and educational research; relationship between educational practice and a democratic and just society. *Total annual research expenditures:* $943,365. *Unit head:* Dr. Nina Asher, Chair, 612-624-4772, Fax: 612-624-1357, E-mail: nasher@umn.edu. *Application contact:* Dr. Jennifer Engler, Assistant Dean, 612-626-2887, Fax: 612-626-7496, E-mail: engle009@umn.edu. Web site: http://www.cehd.umn.edu/ci.

University of Mississippi, Graduate School, School of Education, Department of Curriculum and Instruction, Oxford, University, MS 38677. Offers curriculum and instruction (M Ed, Ed D, Ed S); education (PhD). *Accreditation:* NCATE. *Students:* 70 full-time (57 women), 197 part-time (166 women); includes 75 minority (67 Black or African American, non-Hispanic/Latino; 2 Asian, non-Hispanic/Latino; 3 Hispanic/Latino; 3 Two or more races, non-Hispanic/Latino), 4 international. In 2011, 147 master's, 13 doctorates, 14 other advanced degrees awarded. *Degree requirements:* For master's, thesis (for some programs); for doctorate, one foreign language, thesis/dissertation. *Entrance requirements:* For master's, GRE General Test, minimum GPA of 3.0; for doctorate, GRE General Test. Additional exam requirements/recommendations for international students: Required—TOEFL. *Application deadline:* For fall admission, 7/1 for domestic students; for spring admission, 10/1 for domestic students. Applications are processed on a rolling basis. Application fee: $25. *Financial support:* Scholarships/grants available. Financial award application deadline: 3/1; financial award applicants required to submit FAFSA. *Unit head:* Dr. Kimberly Jeane Hartman, Chair, 662-915-5908, E-mail: khartman@olemiss.edu. *Application contact:* Dr. Christy M. Wyandt, Associate Dean, 662-915-7474, Fax: 662-915-7577, E-mail: cwyandt@olemiss.edu.

University of Missouri, Graduate School, College of Education, Department of Educational, School, and Counseling Psychology, Columbia, MO 65211. Offers counseling psychology (M Ed, MA, PhD, Ed S); educational psychology (M Ed, MA, PhD, Ed S); learning and instruction (M Ed); school psychology (M Ed, MA, PhD, Ed S). *Accreditation:* APA (one or more programs are accredited). Part-time programs available. *Faculty:* 25 full-time (13 women), 4 part-time/adjunct (2 women). *Students:* 161 full-time (124 women), 54 part-time (40 women); includes 29 minority (15 Black or African American, non-Hispanic/Latino; 1 American Indian or Alaska Native, non-Hispanic/Latino; 2 Asian, non-Hispanic/Latino; 9 Hispanic/Latino; 2 Two or more races, non-Hispanic/Latino), 41 international. Average age 28. 262 applicants, 53% accepted, 118 enrolled. In 2011, 59 master's, 14 doctorates, 17 other advanced degrees awarded. *Degree requirements:* For doctorate, thesis/dissertation. *Entrance requirements:* For master's, doctorate, and Ed S, GRE General Test, minimum GPA of 3.0. Additional exam requirements/recommendations for international students: Required—TOEFL (minimum score 580 paper-based; 237 computer-based; 92 iBT). *Application deadline:* For fall admission, 1/8 priority date for domestic students. Applications are processed on a rolling basis. Application fee: $55 ($75 for international students). *Expenses:* Tuition, state resident: full-time $5881. Tuition, nonresident: full-time $15,183. *Required fees:* $952. Tuition and fees vary according to campus/location and program. *Financial support:* Fellowships, research assistantships, teaching assistantships, and institutionally sponsored loans available. *Faculty research:* Out-of-school learning, social cognitive career theory, black psychology and the intersectionality of social identities, test session behavior. *Unit head:* Dr. Deborah Carr, Department Chair, 573-882-5081, E-mail: carrd@missouri.edu. *Application contact:* Latoya Owens, 573-882-7732, E-mail: owensla@missouri.edu. Web site: http://education.missouri.edu/ESCP/.

University of Missouri, Graduate School, College of Education, Department of Learning, Teaching and Curriculum, Columbia, MO 65211. Offers agricultural education (M Ed, PhD, Ed S); art education (M Ed, PhD, Ed S); business and office education (M Ed, PhD, Ed S); early childhood education (M Ed, PhD, Ed S); elementary education (M Ed, PhD, Ed S); English education (M Ed, PhD, Ed S); foreign language education (M Ed, PhD, Ed S); health education and promotion (M Ed, PhD); learning and instruction (M Ed); marketing education (M Ed, PhD, Ed S); mathematics education (M Ed, PhD, Ed S); music education (M Ed, PhD, Ed S); reading education (M Ed, PhD, Ed S); science education (M Ed, PhD, Ed S); social studies education (M Ed, PhD, Ed S); vocational education (M Ed, PhD, Ed S). Part-time programs available. *Faculty:* 26 full-time (16 women), 3 part-time/adjunct (2 women). *Students:* 184 full-time (145 women), 276 part-time (215 women); includes 34 minority (10 Black or African American, non-Hispanic/Latino; 1 American Indian or Alaska Native, non-Hispanic/Latino; 7 Asian, non-Hispanic/Latino; 8 Hispanic/Latino; 8 Two or more races, non-Hispanic/Latino), 39 international. Average age 32. 309 applicants, 76% accepted, 204 enrolled. In 2011, 232 master's, 8 doctorates, 2 other advanced degrees awarded. Terminal master's awarded for partial completion of doctoral program. *Degree requirements:* For doctorate, thesis/dissertation. *Entrance requirements:* For master's and Ed S, GRE General Test or MAT, minimum GPA of 3.0; for doctorate, GRE General Test, minimum GPA of 3.0. Additional exam requirements/recommendations for international students: Required—TOEFL (minimum score 600 paper-based; 250 computer-based; 100 iBT). Application fee: $55 ($75 for international students). Electronic applications accepted. *Expenses:* Tuition, state resident: full-time $5881. Tuition, nonresident: full-time $15,183. *Required fees:* $952. Tuition and fees vary according to campus/location and program. *Financial support:* Fellowships, research assistantships, teaching assistantships, and institutionally sponsored loans available. *Application contact:* Fran Colley, 573-882-6462, E-mail: colleyf@missouri.edu. Web site: http://education.missouri.edu/LTC/.

University of Missouri, Graduate School, College of Education, Department of Special Education, Columbia, MO 65211. Offers administration and supervision of special education (PhD); behavior disorders (M Ed, PhD); curriculum development of exceptional students (M Ed, PhD); early childhood special education (M Ed, PhD); general special education (M Ed, MA, PhD); learning and instruction (M Ed); learning disabilities (M Ed, PhD); mental retardation (M Ed, PhD). Part-time and evening/weekend programs available. Postbaccalaureate distance learning degree programs offered (no on-campus study). *Faculty:* 11 full-time (8 women), 1 (woman) part-time/adjunct. *Students:* 26 full-time (23 women), 65 part-time (60 women); includes 7 minority (2 Black or African American, non-Hispanic/Latino; 4 Hispanic/Latino; 1 Two or more races, non-Hispanic/Latino). Average age 33. 56 applicants, 64% accepted, 32 enrolled. In 2011, 31 master's, 3 doctorates awarded. *Degree requirements:* For master's, comprehensive exam, thesis or alternative; for doctorate, comprehensive exam, thesis/dissertation. *Entrance requirements:* For master's and doctorate, GRE General Test, letters of recommendation. Additional exam requirements/recommendations for international students: Required—TOEFL (minimum score 500 paper-based; 173 computer-based; 61 iBT). *Application deadline:* For fall admission, 7/1 priority date for domestic students, 7/1 for international students; for winter admission, 11/1 priority date for domestic students, 11/1 for international students; for spring admission, 4/1 priority date for domestic students, 4/1 for international students. Application fee: $55 ($75 for international students). Electronic applications accepted. *Expenses:* Tuition, state resident: full-time $5881. Tuition, nonresident: full-time $15,183. *Required fees:* $952. Tuition and fees vary according to campus/location and program. *Financial support:* Fellowships with full and partial tuition reimbursements, research assistantships with full and partial tuition reimbursements, teaching assistantships with full and partial tuition reimbursements, career-related internships or fieldwork, scholarships/grants, health care benefits, and unspecified assistantships available. *Faculty research:* Positive behavior support, applied behavior analysis, attention deficit disorder, pre-linguistic development, school discipline. *Total annual research expenditures:* $1.4 million. *Unit head:* Dr. Mike Pullis, Department Chair, E-mail: pullism@missouri.edu. *Application contact:* Glenda Rice, 573-882-4421, E-mail: riceg@missouri.edu. Web site: http://education.missouri.edu/SPED/.

University of Missouri–Kansas City, School of Education, Kansas City, MO 64110-2499. Offers administration (Ed D); counseling and guidance (MA, Ed S); counseling psychology (PhD); curriculum and instruction (MA, Ed S); education (PhD); educational administration (MA, Ed S); reading education (MA, Ed S); special education (MA). PhD in education offered through the School of Graduate Studies. *Accreditation:* NCATE. Part-time and evening/weekend programs available. *Faculty:* 59 full-time (47 women), 57 part-time/adjunct (42 women). *Students:* 221 full-time (155 women), 379 part-time (271 women); includes 140 minority (95 Black or African American, non-Hispanic/Latino; 1 American Indian or Alaska Native, non-Hispanic/Latino; 15 Asian, non-Hispanic/Latino; 27 Hispanic/Latino; 2 Two or more races, non-Hispanic/Latino), 16 international. Average age 33. 332 applicants, 51% accepted, 136 enrolled. In 2011, 131 master's, 4 doctorates, 25 other advanced degrees awarded. *Degree requirements:* For doctorate, thesis/dissertation, internship, practicum. *Entrance requirements:* For master's, GRE, minimum GPA of 2.75, 2 letters of reference, written statement of purpose; for doctorate, GRE, minimum GPA of 3.0; for Ed S, minimum GPA of 3.0. Additional exam requirements/recommendations for international students: Required—TOEFL (minimum score 550 paper-based; 213 computer-based; 80 iBT). *Application deadline:* For fall admission, 4/1 priority date for domestic students, 4/1 for international students; for spring admission, 11/1 priority date for domestic students, 11/1 for international students. Applications are processed on a rolling basis. Application fee: $45 ($50 for international students). *Expenses:* Tuition, state resident: full-time $5798; part-time $322.10 per credit hour. Tuition, nonresident: full-time $14,969; part-time $831.60 per credit hour. *Required fees:* $93.51 per credit hour. *Financial support:* In 2011–12, 15 research assistantships with partial tuition reimbursements (averaging $10,720 per year) were awarded; career-related internships or fieldwork, Federal Work-Study, institutionally sponsored loans, and tuition waivers (full and partial) also available. Support available to part-time students. Financial award application deadline: 3/1; financial award applicants required to submit FAFSA. *Faculty research:* Urban education, inquiry-based field study, theories of counseling and psychotherapy, school literacy, educational technology. *Unit head:* Dr. Wanda Blanchett, Dean, 816-235-2234, Fax: 816-235-5270, E-mail: education@umkc.edu. *Application contact:* Erica Hernandez-Scott, Student Recruiter, 816-235-1295, Fax: 816-235-5270, E-mail: hernandeze@umkc.edu. Web site: http://education.umkc.edu.

University of Missouri–St. Louis, College of Education, Division of Teaching and Learning, St. Louis, MO 63121. Offers autism studies (Certificate); elementary education (M Ed), including early childhood, general, reading; secondary education (M Ed), including curriculum and instruction, general, middle level education, reading, teaching English to speakers of other languages (TESOL); secondary school teaching (Certificate); special education (M Ed), including autism and developmental disabilities, early childhood special education, general; teaching English to speakers of other languages (Certificate). Part-time and evening/weekend programs available. *Faculty:* 32 full-time (16 women), 51 part-time/adjunct (36 women). *Students:* 95 full-time (63 women), 703 part-time (541 women); includes 176 minority (125 Black or African American, non-Hispanic/Latino; 1 American Indian or Alaska Native, non-Hispanic/Latino; 16 Asian, non-Hispanic/Latino; 26 Hispanic/Latino; 8 Two or more races, non-Hispanic/Latino), 11 international. Average age 29. 379 applicants, 90% accepted, 263 enrolled. In 2011, 190 master's, 9 Certificates awarded. *Degree requirements:* For master's, comprehensive exam. *Entrance requirements:* Additional exam requirements/recommendations for international students: Recommended—TOEFL (minimum score 550 paper-based; 213 computer-based). *Application deadline:* For fall admission, 7/1 priority date for domestic students, 7/1 for international students; for spring admission, 12/1 priority date for domestic students, 12/1 for international students. Application fee: $35 ($40 for international students). Electronic applications accepted. *Expenses:* Tuition, state resident: full-time $6273; part-time $3866 per year. Tuition, nonresident: full-time $14,969; part-time $9980 per year. *Required fees:* $315 per year. *Financial support:* In 2011–12, 6 research assistantships with full and partial tuition reimbursements (averaging $9,500 per year), 2 teaching assistantships with full and partial tuition reimbursements (averaging $10,500 per year) were awarded. Financial award application deadline: 4/1; financial award applicants required to submit FAFSA. *Unit head:* Dr. Joseph Polman, Chair, 314-516-5791. *Application contact:* 314-516-5458, Fax: 314-516-6996, E-mail: gadadm@umsl.edu. Web site: http://coe.umsl.edu/web/divisions/teach-learn/index.html.

The University of Montana, Graduate School, Phyllis J. Washington College of Education and Human Sciences, Department of Curriculum and Instruction, Missoula, MT 59812-0002. Offers M Ed, Ed D. Part-time programs available. *Degree requirements:* For doctorate, thesis/dissertation. *Entrance requirements:* For master's, GRE General Test. Additional exam requirements/recommendations for international students: Required—TOEFL.

University of Nebraska at Kearney, Graduate Studies, College of Education, Department of Teacher Education, Kearney, NE 68849-0001. Offers curriculum and instruction (MS Ed); instructional technology (MS Ed); reading education (MA Ed); special education (MA Ed). Part-time and evening/weekend programs available. *Degree requirements:* For master's, comprehensive exam, thesis optional. *Entrance requirements:* For master's, portfolio or GRE. Additional exam requirements/recommendations for international students: Required—TOEFL (minimum score 550 paper-based; 213 computer-based). Electronic applications accepted.

University of Nebraska–Lincoln, Graduate College, College of Education and Human Sciences, Department of Teaching, Learning and Teacher Education, Lincoln, NE 68588. Offers adult and continuing education (MA); educational studies (Ed D, PhD), including special education (Ed D); teaching, learning and teacher education (M Ed, MA, MST, Ed D, PhD); vocational and adult education (M Ed, MA). *Accreditation:* NCATE. *Degree requirements:* For master's, thesis optional. *Entrance requirements:* Additional exam requirements/recommendations for international students: Required—TOEFL (minimum score 550 paper-based; 213 computer-based). Electronic applications accepted. *Faculty research:* Teacher education, instructional leadership, literacy education, technology, improvement of school curriculum.

University of Nebraska–Lincoln, Graduate College, College of Education and Human Sciences, Interdepartmental Area of Administration, Curriculum and Instruction, Lincoln, NE 68588. Offers Ed D, PhD, JD/PhD. *Accreditation:* NCATE. Postbaccalaureate distance learning degree programs offered. *Degree requirements:* For doctorate, comprehensive exam, thesis/dissertation. *Entrance requirements:* For doctorate, GRE, curriculum vitae. Additional exam requirements/recommendations for international students: Required—TOEFL (minimum score 550 paper-based; 213 computer-based). Electronic applications accepted.

University of Nevada, Las Vegas, Graduate College, College of Education, Department of Curriculum and Instruction, Las Vegas, NV 89154-3005. Offers curriculum and instruction (M Ed, MS, Ed D, PhD, Ed S); teacher education (PhD). *Accreditation:* NCATE. Part-time and evening/weekend programs available. *Faculty:* 32 full-time (13 women), 14 part-time/adjunct (6 women). *Students:* 165 full-time (96 women), 272 part-time (191 women); includes 105 minority (23 Black or African American, non-Hispanic/Latino; 2 American Indian or Alaska Native, non-Hispanic/Latino; 15 Asian, non-Hispanic/Latino; 45 Hispanic/Latino; 3 Native Hawaiian or other Pacific Islander, non-Hispanic/Latino; 17 Two or more races, non-Hispanic/Latino), 16 international. Average age 34. 224 applicants, 85% accepted, 154 enrolled. In 2011, 159 master's, 6 doctorates awarded. *Degree requirements:* For master's, comprehensive exam (for some programs), thesis (for some programs); for doctorate, comprehensive exam, thesis/dissertation, defense of dissertation, article for publication (curriculum and instruction); for Ed S, comprehensive exam, oral presentation of special project or professional paper. *Entrance requirements:* For doctorate and Ed S, GRE General Test. Additional exam requirements/recommendations for international students: Required—TOEFL (minimum score 550 paper-based; 213 computer-based; 80 iBT), IELTS (minimum score 7). *Application deadline:* For fall admission, 3/15 priority date for domestic students, 5/1 for international students; for spring admission, 11/1 priority date for domestic students, 10/1 for international students. Applications are processed on a rolling basis. Application fee: $60 ($95 for international students). Electronic applications accepted. *Financial support:* In 2011–12, 45 students received support, including 14 research assistantships with partial tuition reimbursements available (averaging $8,649 per year), 31 teaching assistantships with partial tuition reimbursements available (averaging $11,828 per year); institutionally sponsored loans, scholarships/grants, health care benefits, and unspecified assistantships also available. Financial award application deadline: 3/1. *Faculty research:* Content area and critical literacy, education in content areas, teacher education, STEM education, technology education. *Total annual research expenditures:* $699,524. *Unit head:* Dr. Randall Boone, Chair/Professor, 702-895-3331, Fax: 702-895-4898, E-mail: randall.boone@unlv.edu. *Application contact:* Graduate College Admissions Evaluator, 702-895-3320, Fax: 702-895-4180, E-mail: gradcollege@unlv.edu. Web site: http://tl.unlv.edu/.

University of Nevada, Reno, Graduate School, College of Education, Department of Curriculum, Teaching and Learning, Program in Curriculum and Instruction, Reno, NV 89557. Offers PhD. *Degree requirements:* For doctorate, thesis/dissertation. *Entrance requirements:* For doctorate, GRE General Test, minimum GPA of 3.0. Additional exam requirements/recommendations for international students: Required—TOEFL (minimum score 500 paper-based; 179 computer-based; 61 iBT), IELTS (minimum score 6). Electronic applications accepted. *Faculty research:* Education, development, pedagogy.

University of Nevada, Reno, Graduate School, College of Education, Department of Curriculum, Teaching and Learning, Program in Curriculum, Teaching and Learning, Reno, NV 89557. Offers Ed D, PhD. *Degree requirements:* For doctorate, comprehensive exam, thesis/dissertation. *Entrance requirements:* For doctorate, GRE General Test, minimum GPA of 3.0. Additional exam requirements/recommendations for international students: Required—TOEFL (minimum score 500 paper-based; 173 computer-based; 61 iBT), IELTS (minimum score 6). Electronic applications accepted. *Faculty research:* Education, trends, pedagogy.

University of New England, College of Arts and Sciences, Program in Education, Biddeford, ME 04005-9526. Offers advanced educational leadership (CAGS); curriculum and instruction strategies (CAGS); curriculum and instruction strategy (MS Ed); educational leadership (MS Ed, CAGS); general studies (MS Ed); inclusion education (MS Ed); leadership, ethics and change (CAGS); literacy K-12 (MS Ed, CAGS); teaching methodologies (MS Ed). Part-time programs available. Postbaccalaureate distance learning degree programs offered (minimal on-campus study). *Faculty:* 20 part-time/adjunct. *Students:* 514 full-time (417 women), 218 part-time (165 women). In 2011, 307 master's, 86 CAGSs awarded. *Degree requirements:* For master's, collaborative action research project, integrative seminar portfolio. *Entrance requirements:* For master's, teaching certificate, 2 years of teaching experience. Additional exam requirements/recommendations for international students: Required—TOEFL. *Application deadline:* For fall admission, 9/15 for domestic students; for spring admission, 1/15 for domestic students. Applications are processed on a rolling basis. Application fee: $40. Electronic applications accepted. *Expenses:* Contact institution. *Financial support:* Application deadline: 5/1; applicants required to submit FAFSA. *Faculty research:* Distance learning, effective teaching, transition planning, adult learning. *Unit head:* Dr. Doug Lynch, Chair of Education Department, 207-283-0171 Ext. 2888, E-mail: dlynch@une.edu. *Application contact:* Stacy Gato, Assistant Director of Graduate Admissions, 207-221-4225, Fax: 207-221-4898, E-mail: gradadmissions@une.edu.

University of New Mexico, Graduate School, College of Education, Department of Teacher Education, Program in Curriculum and Instruction, Albuquerque, NM 87131-2039. Offers Ed S. *Students:* 1 applicant, 0% accepted, 0 enrolled. *Unit head:* Dr. Rosalita Mitchell. *Application contact:* Sarah Valles, Department Administrator, 505-277-0504, Fax: 505-277-0455, E-mail: ted@unm.edu.

University of New Orleans, Graduate School, College of Education and Human Development, Department of Curriculum and Instruction, New Orleans, LA 70148. Offers M Ed, PhD, GCE. *Accreditation:* NCATE. Evening/weekend programs available. *Degree requirements:* For doctorate, variable foreign language requirement, thesis/dissertation. *Entrance requirements:* For master's, GRE General Test; for doctorate, GRE General Test, GRE Subject Test. Additional exam requirements/recommendations for international students: Required—TOEFL (minimum score 550 paper-based; 213 computer-based; 79 iBT). Electronic applications accepted.

The University of North Carolina at Chapel Hill, Graduate School, School of Education, Program in Education, Chapel Hill, NC 27599. Offers culture, curriculum and change (MA, PhD); early childhood, intervention and literacy (MA, PhD); educational psychology, measurement and evaluation (MA, PhD). *Accreditation:* NCATE. *Degree requirements:* For master's, thesis; for doctorate, comprehensive exam, thesis/dissertation. *Entrance requirements:* For master's, GRE General Test, minimum GPA of 3.0 during last 2 years of undergraduates course work; for doctorate, GRE General Test, minimum GPA of 3.0 during last 2 years of undergraduate course work. Additional exam requirements/recommendations for international students: Required—TOEFL (minimum score 550 paper-based; 213 computer-based). Electronic applications accepted.

The University of North Carolina at Charlotte, Graduate School, College of Education, Department of Educational Leadership, Charlotte, NC 28223-0001. Offers curriculum and supervision (M Ed); educational leadership (Ed D); instructional systems technology (M Ed); school administration (MSA). Part-time and evening/weekend programs available. *Faculty:* 24 full-time (12 women), 2 part-time/adjunct (0 women). *Students:* 32 full-time (22 women), 180 part-time (120 women); includes 74 minority (68 Black or African American, non-Hispanic/Latino; 1 American Indian or Alaska Native, non-Hispanic/Latino; 2 Asian, non-Hispanic/Latino; 2 Hispanic/Latino; 1 Two or more races, non-Hispanic/Latino), 1 international. Average age 38. 26 applicants, 92% accepted, 21 enrolled. In 2011, 46 master's, 27 doctorates awarded. *Degree requirements:* For master's, thesis. *Entrance requirements:* For master's and doctorate, GRE or MAT. Additional exam requirements/recommendations for international students: Required—TOEFL (minimum score 550 paper-based; 220 computer-based; 83 iBT). *Application deadline:* For fall admission, 7/1 for domestic students, 5/1 for international students; for spring admission, 11/1 for domestic students, 10/1 for international students. Applications are processed on a rolling basis. Application fee: $65 ($75 for international students). Electronic applications accepted. *Expenses:* Tuition, state resident: full-time $3689. Tuition, nonresident: full-time $15,226. *Required fees:* $2198. Tuition and fees vary according to course load and program. *Financial support:* In 2011–12, 4 students received support, including 4 research assistantships (averaging $6,031 per year); career-related internships or fieldwork, institutionally sponsored loans, scholarships/grants, and unspecified assistantships also available. Support available to part-time students. Financial award application deadline: 4/1; financial award applicants required to submit FAFSA. *Faculty research:* Educational leadership theory and practice, instructional systems technology, educational research methodology, curriculum and supervision in the schools, school law and finance. *Total annual research expenditures:* $638,519. *Unit head:* Dr. Dawson R. Hancock, Chair, 704-687-8863, Fax: 704-687-3493, E-mail: dhancock@uncc.edu. *Application contact:* Kathy B. Giddings, Director of Graduate Admissions, 704-687-5503, Fax: 704-687-3279, E-mail: gradadm@uncc.edu. Web site: http://education.uncc.edu/eart/programs.htm.

The University of North Carolina at Greensboro, Graduate School, School of Education, Department of Curriculum and Instruction, Greensboro, NC 27412-5001. Offers college teaching and adult learning (Certificate); curriculum and instruction (M Ed), including chemistry education, elementary education, English as a second language, French education, instructional technology, mathematics education, middle grades education, reading education, science education, social studies education, Spanish education; curriculum and teaching (PhD), including higher education, teacher education and development; English as a second language (Certificate); higher education (M Ed); supervision (M Ed). *Accreditation:* NCATE. Part-time programs available. *Degree requirements:* For doctorate, thesis/dissertation. *Entrance requirements:* For master's and doctorate, GRE General Test. Additional exam requirements/recommendations for international students: Required—TOEFL. Electronic applications accepted. *Faculty research:* Community college literacy program, middle school mathematics/computer mathematics.

The University of North Carolina at Greensboro, Graduate School, School of Education, Department of Educational Leadership and Cultural Foundations, Greensboro, NC 27412-5001. Offers curriculum and teaching (PhD), including cultural studies; educational leadership (Ed D, Ed S); school administration (MSA). *Accreditation:* NCATE. *Degree requirements:* For doctorate, thesis/dissertation. *Entrance requirements:* For master's, doctorate, and Ed S, GRE General Test. Additional exam requirements/recommendations for international students: Required—TOEFL. Electronic applications accepted.

The University of North Carolina Wilmington, Watson School of Education, Department of Educational Leadership, Program in Curriculum, Instruction and Supervision, Wilmington, NC 28403-3297. Offers M Ed. *Degree requirements:* For master's, comprehensive exam.

University of Northern Iowa, Graduate College, College of Education, Department of Curriculum and Instruction, Program in Curriculum and Instruction, Cedar Falls, IA 50614. Offers Ed D. Part-time and evening/weekend programs available. *Students:* 5 full-time (2 women), 11 part-time (all women), 4 international. 5 applicants, 20% accepted, 1 enrolled. In 2011, 5 doctorates awarded. *Degree requirements:* For doctorate, thesis/dissertation. *Entrance requirements:* For doctorate, GRE, minimum GPA of 3.0, master's degree. Additional exam requirements/recommendations for international students: Required—TOEFL (minimum score 500 paper-based; 180 computer-based; 61 iBT). *Application deadline:* For fall admission, 8/1 priority date for domestic students. Applications are processed on a rolling basis. Application fee: $50 ($70 for international students). *Expenses:* Tuition, state resident: full-time $7476. Tuition, nonresident: full-time $16,410. *Required fees:* $942. *Financial support:* Career-related internships or fieldwork, Federal Work-Study, and tuition waivers (full and partial) available. Support available to part-time students. Financial award application deadline: 2/1. *Unit head:* Dr. Linda Fitzgerald, Coordinator, 319-273-2214, Fax: 319-273-5886, E-mail: linda.fitzgerald@uni.edu. *Application contact:* Laurie S. Russell, Record Analyst, 319-273-2623, Fax: 319-273-2885, E-mail: laurie.russell@uni.edu. Web site: http://www.uni.edu/coe/ci/.

University of North Texas, Toulouse Graduate School, College of Education, Department of Teacher Education and Administration, Program in Curriculum and Instruction, Denton, TX 76203. Offers M Ed, Ed D, PhD. *Accreditation:* NCATE. Part-time programs available. *Degree requirements:* For doctorate, thesis/dissertation. *Entrance requirements:* For doctorate, GRE General Test. Additional exam requirements/recommendations for international students: Recommended—TOEFL (minimum score 550 paper-based; 213 computer-based; 79 iBT). Electronic applications accepted. *Expenses:* Tuition, state resident: part-time $100 per credit hour. Tuition, nonresident: part-time $413 per credit hour. *Faculty research:* K-12 achievement gaps, early literacy, special action, GIs technologies and social studies, immigration.

University of Oklahoma, Jeannine Rainbolt College of Education, Department of Educational Leadership and Policy Studies, Program in Educational Administration, Curriculum and Supervision, Norman, OK 73019. Offers curriculum and supervision (M Ed); education administration (M Ed, Ed D, PhD); law and policy (M Ed); technology leadership (M Ed). *Accreditation:* NCATE. Part-time and evening/weekend programs available. *Students:* 35 full-time (19 women), 136 part-time (95 women); includes 42 minority (20 Black or African American, non-Hispanic/Latino; 14 American Indian or Alaska Native, non-Hispanic/Latino; 2 Asian, non-Hispanic/Latino; 3 Hispanic/Latino; 1 Native Hawaiian or other Pacific Islander, non-Hispanic/Latino; 2 Two or more races, non-Hispanic/Latino). Average age 39. 47 applicants, 79% accepted, 28 enrolled. In 2011, 38 master's, 9 doctorates awarded. Terminal master's awarded for partial completion of doctoral program. *Degree requirements:* For master's, thesis optional; for doctorate, variable foreign language requirement, thesis/dissertation, general exam. *Entrance requirements:* For master's, 12 hours of course work in education; for doctorate, GRE General Test, master's degree, 3 letters of reference, writing sample. Additional exam requirements/recommendations for international students: Required—

TOEFL (minimum score 550 paper-based; 79 iBT). *Application deadline:* For fall admission, 6/1 priority date for domestic students, 3/1 for international students; for spring admission, 10/1 for domestic students, 9/1 for international students. Application fee: $40 ($90 for international students). Electronic applications accepted. *Expenses:* Tuition, state resident: full-time $4087; part-time $170.30 per credit hour. Tuition, nonresident: full-time $14,875; part-time $619.80 per credit hour. *Required fees:* $2659; $100.25 per credit hour. Tuition and fees vary according to course load and degree level. *Financial support:* In 2011–12, 76 students received support. Unspecified assistantships available. Financial award applicants required to submit FAFSA. *Faculty research:* Collective and student trust, urban school district renewal and community revitalization, single gender education, female secondary school leaders, school-university social order. *Unit head:* David Tan, Chair, 405-325-4202, Fax: 405-325-2403, E-mail: dtan@ou.edu. *Application contact:* Geri Evans, Graduate Programs Representative, 405-325-5978, Fax: 405-325-2403, E-mail: gevans@ou.edu. Web site: http://education.ou.edu/departments_1/eacs_1/.

University of Oklahoma, Jeannine Rainbolt College of Education, Department of Instructional Leadership and Academic Curriculum, Norman, OK 73072. Offers communication, culture and pedagogy for Hispanic populations in educational settings (Graduate Certificate); instructional leadership and academic curriculum (M Ed, PhD), including bilingual education, early childhood education, elementary education, English education, instructional leadership, mathematics education, reading education, science education, science, technology, engineering and mathematics education (M Ed), secondary education, social studies education, teacher education (M Ed). *Accreditation:* NCATE. Part-time and evening/weekend programs available. *Faculty:* 19 full-time (13 women), 1 (woman) part-time/adjunct. *Students:* 73 full-time (63 women), 114 part-time (87 women); includes 29 minority (5 Black or African American, non-Hispanic/Latino; 12 American Indian or Alaska Native, non-Hispanic/Latino; 5 Asian, non-Hispanic/Latino; 3 Hispanic/Latino; 1 Native Hawaiian or other Pacific Islander, non-Hispanic/Latino; 3 Two or more races, non-Hispanic/Latino), 7 international. Average age 33. 87 applicants, 86% accepted, 68 enrolled. In 2011, 36 master's, 6 doctorates awarded. Terminal master's awarded for partial completion of doctoral program. *Degree requirements:* For doctorate, thesis/dissertation. *Entrance requirements:* For master's, 12 hours of course work in education; for doctorate, GRE General Test, master's degree, minimum graduate GPA of 3.0. Additional exam requirements/recommendations for international students: Required—TOEFL (minimum score 550 paper-based; 79 iBT). *Application deadline:* For fall admission, 6/1 priority date for domestic students, 3/1 for international students; for spring admission, 11/1 for domestic students, 9/1 for international students. Applications are processed on a rolling basis. Application fee: $40 ($90 for international students). Electronic applications accepted. *Expenses:* Tuition, state resident: full-time $4087; part-time $170.30 per credit hour. Tuition, nonresident: full-time $14,875; part-time $619.80 per credit hour. *Required fees:* $2659; $100.25 per credit hour. Tuition and fees vary according to course load and degree level. *Financial support:* In 2011–12, 128 students received support, including 2 research assistantships with partial tuition reimbursements available (averaging $12,431 per year), 12 teaching assistantships with partial tuition reimbursements available (averaging $10,161 per year); institutionally sponsored loans, scholarships/grants, and unspecified assistantships also available. Financial award applicants required to submit FAFSA. *Faculty research:* Engineering in practice for sustainable future, no child left behind (reading), early childhood learning games impact study, Educare randomized control startup, Oklahoma mentoring professional development. *Total annual research expenditures:* $1.1 million. *Unit head:* Lawrence Baines, Chair, 405-325-1498, Fax: 405-325-4061, E-mail: lbaines@ou.edu. *Application contact:* Lynn Crussel, Graduate Programs Officer, 405-325-4843, Fax: 405-325-4061, E-mail: lcrussel@ou.edu. Web site: http://education.ou.edu/departments/ilac.

University of Phoenix–Austin Campus, College of Education, Austin, TX 78759. Offers curriculum and instruction (MA Ed).

University of Phoenix–Central Florida Campus, College of Education, Maitland, FL 32751-7057. Offers administration and supervision (MA Ed); curriculum and instruction (MA Ed); curriculum and instruction-computer education (MA Ed); curriculum and instruction-mathematics education (MA Ed); early childhood education (MA Ed); elementary teacher education (MA Ed); secondary teacher education (MA Ed). Evening/weekend programs available. *Degree requirements:* For master's, thesis (for some programs). *Entrance requirements:* For master's, 3 years of work experience, minimum undergraduate GPA of 2.5. Additional exam requirements/recommendations for international students: Required—TOEFL (minimum score 550 paper-based; 213 computer-based; 79 iBT). Electronic applications accepted.

University of Phoenix–Central Valley Campus, College of Education, Fresno, CA 93720-1562. Offers curriculum and instruction (MA Ed); curriculum and instruction-computer education (MA Ed); elementary teacher education (MA Ed); secondary teacher education (MA Ed).

University of Phoenix–Chattanooga Campus, College of Education, Chattanooga, TN 37421-3707. Offers administration and supervision (MA Ed); curriculum and instruction (MA Ed); elementary teacher education (MA Ed); secondary teacher education (MA Ed).

University of Phoenix–Dallas Campus, College of Education, Dallas, TX 75251-2009. Offers curriculum and instruction (MA Ed).

University of Phoenix–Denver Campus, College of Education, Lone Tree, CO 80124-5453. Offers administration and supervision (MAEd); curriculum instruction (MAEd); elementary teacher education (MAEd); school counseling (MSC); secondary teacher education (MAEd). Evening/weekend programs available. *Degree requirements:* For master's, thesis (for some programs). *Entrance requirements:* For master's, minimum undergraduate GPA of 2.5, 3 years work experience. Additional exam requirements/recommendations for international students: Required—TOEFL (minimum score 550 paper-based; 213 computer-based; 79 iBT). Electronic applications accepted.

University of Phoenix–Hawaii Campus, College of Education, Honolulu, HI 96813-4317. Offers administration and supervision (MA Ed); curriculum and instruction (MA Ed); elementary education (MA Ed); secondary education (MA Ed); special education (MA Ed); teacher education for elementary licensure (MA Ed). Evening/weekend programs available. *Degree requirements:* For master's, thesis (for some programs). *Entrance requirements:* For master's, minimum undergraduate GPA of 2.5, 3 years of work experience. Additional exam requirements/recommendations for international students: Required—TOEFL (minimum score 550 paper-based; 213 computer-based; 79 iBT). Electronic applications accepted.

University of Phoenix–Houston Campus, College of Education, Houston, TX 77079-2004. Offers curriculum and instruction (MA Ed).

University of Phoenix–Idaho Campus, College of Education, Meridian, ID 83642-5114. Offers administration and supervision (MA Ed); curriculum and instruction (MA Ed); elementary teacher education (MA Ed); secondary teacher education (MA Ed). Evening/weekend programs available. *Degree requirements:* For master's, thesis (for some programs). *Entrance requirements:* For master's, minimum undergraduate GPA of 2.5, 3 years of work experience. Additional exam requirements/recommendations for international students: Required—TOEFL (minimum score 550 paper-based; 213 computer-based). Electronic applications accepted.

University of Phoenix–Las Vegas Campus, College of Education, Las Vegas, NV 89128. Offers administration and supervision (MA Ed); curriculum and instruction (MA Ed); school counseling (MSC); teacher education-elementary licensure (MA Ed). Evening/weekend programs available. *Degree requirements:* For master's, thesis (for some programs). *Entrance requirements:* For master's, minimum undergraduate GPA of 2.5, 3 years of work experience. Additional exam requirements/recommendations for international students: Required—TOEFL (minimum score 550 paper-based; 213 computer-based; 79 iBT). Electronic applications accepted.

University of Phoenix–Louisiana Campus, College of Education, Metairie, LA 70001-2082. Offers curriculum and instruction (MA Ed); early childhood education (MA Ed). Postbaccalaureate distance learning degree programs offered. *Degree requirements:* For master's, thesis. *Entrance requirements:* For master's, minimum undergraduate GPA of 2.5, 3 years work experience. Additional exam requirements/recommendations for international students: Required—TOEFL (minimum score 550 paper-based; 213 computer-based; 79 iBT).

University of Phoenix–Madison Campus, College of Education, Madison, WI 53718-2416. Offers education (Ed S); educational leadership (Ed D); educational leadership: curriculum and instruction (Ed D); higher education administration (PhD).

University of Phoenix–Memphis Campus, College of Education, Cordova, TN 38018. Offers administration and supervision (MA Ed); curriculum and instruction (MA Ed); elementary teacher education (MA Ed); secondary teacher education (MA Ed).

University of Phoenix–Milwaukee Campus, College of Education, Milwaukee, WI 53045. Offers curriculum and instruction (MA Ed, Ed D); education (Ed S); educational leadership (Ed D); English as a second language (MA Ed); higher education administration (PhD).

University of Phoenix–Nashville Campus, College of Education, Nashville, TN 37214-5048. Offers administration and supervision (MA Ed); curriculum and instruction (MA Ed); elementary teacher education (MA Ed); secondary teacher education (MA Ed). Evening/weekend programs available. *Degree requirements:* For master's, thesis (for some programs). *Entrance requirements:* For master's, minimum undergraduate GPA of 2.5, 3 years work experience. Additional exam requirements/recommendations for international students: Required—TOEFL (minimum score 500 paper-based; 213 computer-based; 79 iBT). Electronic applications accepted.

University of Phoenix–New Mexico Campus, College of Education, Albuquerque, NM 87113-1570. Offers administration and supervision (MAEd); curriculum and instruction (MAEd); elementary teacher education (MAEd); school counseling (MSC); secondary teacher education (MAEd). Evening/weekend programs available. *Degree requirements:* For master's, thesis (for some programs). *Entrance requirements:* For master's, minimum undergraduate GPA of 2.5, 3 years of work experience. Additional exam requirements/recommendations for international students: Required—TOEFL (minimum score 550 paper-based; 213 computer-based; 79 iBT). Electronic applications accepted.

University of Phoenix–Northern Nevada Campus, College of Education, Reno, NV 89521-5862. Offers administration and supervision (MA Ed); curriculum and instruction (MA Ed); elementary teacher education (MA Ed); secondary teacher education (MA Ed).

University of Phoenix–North Florida Campus, College of Education, Jacksonville, FL 32216-0959. Offers administration and supervision (MA Ed); curriculum and instruction (MA Ed), including computer education, mathematics education; early childhood education (MA Ed); elementary teacher education (MA Ed); secondary teacher education (MA Ed). Evening/weekend programs available. *Degree requirements:* For master's, thesis (for some programs). *Entrance requirements:* For master's, 3 years of work experience, minimum undergraduate GPA of 2.5. Additional exam requirements/recommendations for international students: Required—TOEFL (minimum score 550 paper-based; 213 computer-based; 49 iBT). Electronic applications accepted.

University of Phoenix–Omaha Campus, College of Education, Omaha, NE 68154-5240. Offers administration and supervision (MA Ed); curriculum and instruction (MA Ed), including adult education, computer education, curriculum and instruction, English and language arts education, English as a second language, mathematics education; elementary teacher education (MA Ed); secondary teacher education (MA Ed); special education (MA Ed).

University of Phoenix–Online Campus, College of Education, Phoenix, AZ 85034-7209. Offers administration and supervision (MAEd, Graduate Certificate); adult education and training (MAEd); curriculum and instruction (MAEd); curriculum and instruction reading (MAEd); curriculum and instruction-computer education (MAEd); curriculum and instruction-language arts (MAEd); curriculum and instruction-mathematics (MAEd); early childhood education (MAEd); educational studies (MAEd); elementary teacher education (MAEd); elementary teacher education-early childhood (MAEd); secondary teacher education (MAEd); special education (MAEd); teacher education - elementary/middle level (MAEd); teacher education middle level generalist (MAEd); teacher education middle level mathematics (MAEd); teacher education middle level science (MAEd); teacher education secondary mathematics (MAEd); teacher education secondary science (MAEd); teacher leadership (MAEd). *Accreditation:* Teacher Education Accreditation Council. Evening/weekend programs available. Postbaccalaureate distance learning degree programs offered. *Students:* 9,180 full-time (7,178 women); includes 2,913 minority (2,069 Black or African American, non-Hispanic/Latino; 50 American Indian or Alaska Native, non-Hispanic/Latino; 100 Asian, non-Hispanic/Latino; 542 Hispanic/Latino; 48 Native Hawaiian or other Pacific Islander, non-Hispanic/Latino; 104 Two or more races, non-Hispanic/Latino), 147 international. Average age 36. *Entrance requirements:* Additional exam requirements/recommendations for international students: Required—TOEFL, TOEIC (Test of English as an International Communication), Berlitz Online English Proficiency Exam, Pearson Test of English, or IELTS. *Application deadline:* Applications are processed on a rolling basis. Application fee: $45. Electronic applications accepted. *Expenses:* Contact institution. *Financial support:* Scholarships/grants available. Financial award applicants required to submit FAFSA. *Application contact:* 866-766-0766. Web site: http://www.phoenix.edu/colleges_divisions/education.html.

University of Phoenix–Online Campus, School of Advanced Studies, Phoenix, AZ 85034-7209. Offers business administration (DBA); education (Ed S); educational leadership (Ed D), including curriculum and instruction, education technology, educational leadership; health administration (DHA); higher education administration (PhD); industrial/organizational psychology (PhD); nursing (PhD); organizational leadership (DM), including information systems and technology, organizational leadership. Evening/weekend programs available. Postbaccalaureate distance learning degree programs offered. *Students:* 7,581 full-time (5,042 women); includes 3,199 minority (2,505 Black or African American, non-Hispanic/Latino; 68 American Indian or Alaska Native, non-Hispanic/Latino; 158 Asian, non-Hispanic/Latino; 395 Hispanic/Latino; 46 Native Hawaiian or other Pacific Islander, non-Hispanic/Latino; 27 Two or more races, non-Hispanic/Latino), 397 international. Average age 44. *Degree requirements:* For doctorate, thesis/dissertation. *Entrance requirements:* Additional exam requirements/recommendations for international students: Required—TOEFL, TOEIC (Test of English as an International Communication), Berlitz Online English Proficiency Exam, Pearson Test of English, or IELTS. *Application deadline:* Applications are processed on a rolling basis. Application fee: $45. Electronic applications accepted. *Expenses:* Contact institution. *Financial support:* Scholarships/grants available. Financial award applicants required to submit FAFSA. *Unit head:* Dr. Jeremy Moreland, Executive Dean. *Application contact:* 866-766-0766. Web site: http://www.phoenix.edu/colleges_divisions/doctoral.html.

University of Phoenix–Oregon Campus, College of Education, Tigard, OR 97223. Offers curriculum and instruction (MA Ed); early childhood education (MA Ed); elementary education (MA Ed), including early childhood specialization, middle level specialization; secondary education (MA Ed), including middle level specialization. Evening/weekend programs available. *Degree requirements:* For master's, thesis (for some programs). *Entrance requirements:* For master's, minimum undergraduate GPA of 2.5, 3 years work experience. Additional exam requirements/recommendations for international students: Required—TOEFL (minimum score 550 paper-based; 213 computer-based; 79 iBT). Electronic applications accepted.

University of Phoenix–Phoenix Main Campus, College of Education, Tempe, AZ 85282-2371. Offers administration and supervision (MA Ed); adult education and training (MA Ed); curriculum and instruction reading (MA Ed); curriculum instruction (MA Ed); early childhood education (MA Ed); education studies (MA Ed); elementary teacher education (MA Ed); secondary teacher education (MA Ed); special education (MA Ed); teacher leadership (MA Ed). Evening/weekend programs available. Postbaccalaureate distance learning degree programs offered. *Students:* 297 full-time (203 women); includes 53 minority (19 Black or African American, non-Hispanic/Latino; 1 American Indian or Alaska Native, non-Hispanic/Latino; 6 Asian, non-Hispanic/Latino; 21 Hispanic/Latino; 2 Native Hawaiian or other Pacific Islander, non-Hispanic/Latino; 4 Two or more races, non-Hispanic/Latino), 3 international. Average age 35. *Entrance requirements:* Additional exam requirements/recommendations for international students: Required—TOEFL, TOEIC (Test of English as an International Communication), Berlitz Online English Proficiency Exam, Pearson Test of English, or IELTS. *Application deadline:* Applications are processed on a rolling basis. Application fee: $45. Electronic applications accepted. *Expenses:* Contact institution. *Financial support:* Scholarships/grants available. Financial award applicants required to submit FAFSA. *Application contact:* 866-766-0766. Web site: http://www.phoenix.edu/colleges_divisions/education.html.

University of Phoenix–Richmond Campus, College of Education, Richmond, VA 23230. Offers administration and supervision (MA Ed); curriculum and instruction (MA Ed).

University of Phoenix–Sacramento Valley Campus, College of Education, Sacramento, CA 95833-3632. Offers adult education (MA Ed); curriculum instruction (MA Ed); elementary teacher education (MA Ed); secondary teacher education (MA Ed); teacher education (Certificate). Evening/weekend programs available. *Degree requirements:* For master's, thesis (for some programs). *Entrance requirements:* For master's, 3 years of work experience, minimum undergraduate GPA of 2.5. Additional exam requirements/recommendations for international students: Required—TOEFL (minimum score 550 paper-based; 213 computer-based; 79 iBT). Electronic applications accepted.

University of Phoenix–San Antonio Campus, College of Education, San Antonio, TX 78230. Offers curriculum and instruction (MA Ed).

University of Phoenix–San Diego Campus, College of Education, San Diego, CA 92123. Offers curriculum and instruction (MA Ed), including computer education, curriculum and instruction, English as a second language; elementary teacher education (MA Ed); secondary teacher education (MA Ed). Evening/weekend programs available. *Degree requirements:* For master's, thesis (for some programs). *Entrance requirements:* For master's, 3 years of work experience, minimum undergraduate GPA of 3.0. Additional exam requirements/recommendations for international students: Required—TOEFL (minimum score 550 paper-based; 213 computer-based; 79 iBT). Electronic applications accepted.

University of Phoenix–Southern Arizona Campus, College of Education, Tucson, AZ 85711. Offers administration and supervision (MA Ed); adult education and training (MA Ed); curriculum instruction (MA Ed); educational counseling (MA Ed); elementary teacher education (MA Ed); school counseling (MSC); secondary teacher education (MA Ed); special education (MA Ed, Certificate). Evening/weekend programs available. *Degree requirements:* For master's, thesis (for some programs). *Entrance requirements:* For master's, minimum undergraduate GPA of 2.5, 3 years of work experience. Additional exam requirements/recommendations for international students: Required—TOEFL (minimum score 550 paper-based; 213 computer-based; 79 iBT). Electronic applications accepted.

University of Phoenix–Southern Colorado Campus, College of Education, Colorado Springs, CO 80919-2335. Offers administration and supervision (MA Ed); curriculum and instruction (MA Ed); elementary teacher education (MA Ed); principal licensure certification (Certificate); school counseling (MSC); secondary teacher education (MA Ed). Evening/weekend programs available. *Degree requirements:* For master's, thesis (for some programs). *Entrance requirements:* For master's, minimum undergraduate GPA of 2.5, 3 years of work experience. Additional exam requirements/recommendations for international students: Required—TOEFL (minimum score 550 paper-based; 213 computer-based; 79 iBT). Electronic applications accepted.

University of Phoenix–South Florida Campus, College of Education, Fort Lauderdale, FL 33309. Offers administration and supervision (MA Ed); curriculum and instruction (MA Ed), including computer education, curriculum and instruction, mathematics education; early childhood education (MA Ed); elementary teacher education (MA Ed); secondary teacher education (MA Ed). Evening/weekend programs available. *Degree requirements:* For master's, thesis (for some programs). *Entrance requirements:* For master's, 3 years of work experience, minimum undergraduate GPA of 2.5. Additional exam requirements/recommendations for international students: Required—TOEFL (minimum score 550 paper-based; 213 computer-based; 79 iBT). Electronic applications accepted.

University of Phoenix–Springfield Campus, College of Education, Springfield, MO 65804-7211. Offers administration and supervision (MA Ed); curriculum and instruction (MA Ed), including computer education, curriculum and instruction, English and language arts education, English as a second language, mathematics education; English and language arts education (MA Ed).

University of Phoenix–Utah Campus, College of Education, Salt Lake City, UT 84123-4617. Offers administration and supervision (MA Ed); curriculum and instruction (MA Ed); elementary teacher education (MA Ed); school counseling (MSC); secondary teacher education (MA Ed); special education (MA Ed). Evening/weekend programs available. *Degree requirements:* For master's, thesis (for some programs). *Entrance requirements:* For master's, minimum undergraduate GPA of 2.5, 3 years work experience. Additional exam requirements/recommendations for international students: Required—TOEFL (minimum score 550 paper-based; 213 computer-based; 79 iBT). Electronic applications accepted.

University of Phoenix–Vancouver Campus, The Artemis School, College of Education, Burnaby, BC V5C 6G9, Canada. Offers administration and supervision (MA Ed); curriculum and instruction (MA Ed), including computer education, curriculum and instruction. Evening/weekend programs available. *Degree requirements:* For master's, thesis (for some programs). *Entrance requirements:* For master's, minimum undergraduate GPA of 2.5, 3 years work experience. Additional exam requirements/recommendations for international students: Required—TOEFL (minimum score 550 paper-based; 213 computer-based; 79 iBT). Electronic applications accepted.

University of Phoenix–Washington D.C. Campus, College of Education, Washington, DC 20001. Offers administration and supervision (MA Ed); adult education and training (MA Ed); computer education (MA Ed); curriculum and instruction (MA Ed, Ed D); early childhood education (MA Ed); education (Ed S); educational leadership (Ed D); educational technology (Ed D); elementary teacher education (MA Ed); English and language arts education (MA Ed); English as a second language (MA Ed); higher education administration (PhD); mathematics education (MA Ed); secondary teacher education (MA Ed); special education (MA Ed); teacher leadership (MA Ed).

University of Phoenix–West Florida Campus, College of Education, Temple Terrace, FL 33637. Offers administration and supervision (MA Ed); curriculum and instruction (MA Ed), including computer education, curriculum and instruction, mathematics education; curriculum and technology (MA Ed); early childhood education (MA Ed); elementary teacher education (MA Ed); secondary teacher education (MA Ed). Evening/weekend programs available. *Degree requirements:* For master's, thesis (for some programs). *Entrance requirements:* For master's, 3 years of work experience, minimum undergraduate GPA of 2.5. Additional exam requirements/recommendations for international students: Required—TOEFL (minimum score 550 paper-based; 213 computer-based; 79 iBT).

University of Puerto Rico, Río Piedras, College of Education, Program in Curriculum and Teaching, San Juan, PR 00931-3300. Offers biology education (M Ed); chemistry education (M Ed); curriculum and teaching (Ed D); history education (M Ed); mathematics education (M Ed); physics education (M Ed); Spanish education (M Ed). Part-time programs available. *Degree requirements:* For master's, thesis; for doctorate, thesis/dissertation, internship. *Entrance requirements:* For master's, PAEG or GRE, minimum GPA of 3.0, letter of recommendation; for doctorate, GRE or PAEG, master's degree, minimum GPA of 3.0, letter of recommendation (2), interview. *Faculty research:* Curriculum, math teaching.

University of Regina, Faculty of Graduate Studies and Research, Faculty of Education, Department of Curriculum and Instruction, Regina, SK S4S 0A2, Canada. Offers M Ed. Part-time programs available. *Faculty:* 26 full-time (16 women), 2 part-time/adjunct (0 women). *Students:* 10 full-time (7 women), 110 part-time (93 women). 48 applicants, 96% accepted. In 2011, 28 master's awarded. *Degree requirements:* For master's, thesis optional, practicum, project, or thesis. *Entrance requirements:* For master's, bachelor's degree in education, two years teaching experience. Additional exam requirements/recommendations for international students: Required—TOEFL (minimum score 580 paper-based; 80 iBT), IELTS (minimum score 6.5). *Application deadline:* For fall admission, 2/15 for domestic students; for winter admission, 2/15 for domestic students; for spring admission, 2/15 for domestic students. Application fee: $100. Electronic applications accepted. *Financial support:* In 2011–12, 1 fellowship (averaging $6,000 per year) was awarded; research assistantships, teaching assistantships, and scholarships/grants also available. Financial award application deadline: 6/15. *Faculty research:* Writing process and pedagogy: the Saskatchewan Writing Project; second language reading, writing, and spoken acquisition; assessing experiential learning; multicultural and anti-racist relations issues in curriculum; social media and open education. *Unit head:* Dr. Rod Dolmage, Associate Dean, Research and Graduate Programs, 306-585-4816, Fax: 306-585-5387, E-mail: rod.dolmage@uregina.ca. *Application contact:* Tania Gates, Graduate Program Coordinator, 306-585-4506, Fax: 306-585-5387, E-mail: edgrad@uregina.ca.

University of Rochester, Eastman School of Music, Program in Music Theory Pedagogy, Rochester, NY 14627. Offers MA. *Expenses: Tuition:* Full-time $41,040.

University of Rochester, Margaret Warner Graduate School of Education and Human Development, Doctoral Programs in Education, Rochester, NY 14627. Offers counseling (Ed D); educational administration (Ed D); educational policy and theory (PhD); higher education (PhD); human development in educational context (PhD); teaching, curriculum, and change (PhD). *Expenses: Tuition:* Full-time $41,040.

University of Rochester, Margaret Warner Graduate School of Education and Human Development, Master's Program in Teaching and Curriculum, Rochester, NY 14627. Offers MS. *Expenses: Tuition:* Full-time $41,040.

University of St. Francis, College of Education, Joliet, IL 60435-6169. Offers educational leadership (MS, Ed D); elementary education certification (M Ed); reading (MS); secondary education certification (M Ed), including English education, math education, science education, social studies education, visual arts education; special education (M Ed); teaching and learning (MS). *Accreditation:* NCATE. Part-time and evening/weekend programs available. Postbaccalaureate distance learning degree programs offered (no on-campus study). *Faculty:* 7 full-time (5 women), 21 part-time/adjunct (14 women). *Students:* 32 full-time (21 women), 230 part-time (175 women); includes 23 minority (7 Black or African American, non-Hispanic/Latino; 2 Asian, non-Hispanic/Latino; 13 Hispanic/Latino; 1 Two or more races, non-Hispanic/Latino), 1 international. Average age 32. 147 applicants, 60% accepted, 57 enrolled. In 2011, 156 master's awarded. *Entrance requirements:* For doctorate, master's degree, IL Type 75 or Principal's endorsement, interview. Additional exam requirements/recommendations for international students: Required—TOEFL (minimum score 550 paper-based; 213 computer-based). *Application deadline:* Applications are processed on a rolling basis. Application fee: $30. Electronic applications accepted. *Expenses:* Contact institution. *Financial support:* In 2011–12, 23 students received support. Federal Work-Study, scholarships/grants, tuition waivers (partial), and unspecified assistantships available. Support available to part-time students. Financial award applicants required to submit FAFSA. *Unit head:* Dr. John Gambro, Dean, 815-740-3829, Fax: 815-740-2264, E-mail: jgambro@stfrancis.edu. *Application contact:* Sandra Sloka, Director of Admissions for Graduate and Degree Completion Programs, 800-735-7500, Fax: 815-740-5032, E-mail: ssloka@stfrancis.edu. Web site: http://www.stfrancis.edu/academics/college-of-education/.

University of Saint Mary, Graduate Programs, Program in Education, Leavenworth, KS 66048-5082. Offers curriculum and instruction (MAT). *Accreditation:* NCATE. Part-time and evening/weekend programs available. Postbaccalaureate distance learning degree programs offered (no on-campus study). *Degree requirements:* For master's, thesis, oral presentation. *Entrance requirements:* For master's, minimum undergraduate GPA of 2.75. *Faculty research:* Curriculum and instruction.

University of St. Thomas, Graduate Studies, School of Education, Department of Teacher Education, St. Paul, MN 55105-1096. Offers curriculum and instruction (MA), including elementary, individualized, K-12, secondary; elementary (MAT); engineering education (Certificate); English as a second language (MA); math education (Certificate); multicultural education (Certificate); reading (MA, Certificate), including elementary (MA), K-12 (MA). *Accreditation:* NCATE. Part-time and evening/weekend programs available. *Faculty:* 7 full-time (4 women), 26 part-time/adjunct (20 women). *Students:* 19 full-time (14 women), 161 part-time (113 women); includes 28 minority (3

Black or African American, non-Hispanic/Latino; 7 American Indian or Alaska Native, non-Hispanic/Latino; 6 Asian, non-Hispanic/Latino; 9 Hispanic/Latino; 3 Two or more races, non-Hispanic/Latino), 5 international. Average age 35. 150 applicants, 79% accepted, 88 enrolled. In 2011, 83 master's awarded. *Entrance requirements:* For master's, minimum GPA of 3.0 or MAT. Additional exam requirements/recommendations for international students: Required—TOEFL (minimum score 550 paper-based; 210 computer-based; 80 iBT). *Application deadline:* For fall admission, 6/1 for domestic students; for spring admission, 11/1 for domestic students. Applications are processed on a rolling basis. Application fee: $50. *Financial support:* Fellowships, research assistantships, institutionally sponsored loans, and scholarships/grants available. Support available to part-time students. Financial award applicants required to submit FAFSA. *Unit head:* Dr. Jan L. H. Frank, Department Chair, 651-962-4446, Fax: 651-962-4169, E-mail: jlhfrank@stthomas.edu. *Application contact:* Rosemary R. Barreto, Department Assistant, 651-962-4420, Fax: 651-962-4169, E-mail: barr7879@stthomas.edu. Web site: http://www.stthomas.edu/education.

University of St. Thomas, School of Education, Houston, TX 77006-4696. Offers all level teaching (M Ed); bilingual/dual language (M Ed); Catholic school teaching (M Ed); Catholic/private school leadership (M Ed); counselor education (M Ed); curriculum and instruction (M Ed); educational leadership (M Ed); elementary teaching (M Ed); English as a second language (M Ed); exceptionality/ educational diagnostician (M Ed); exceptionality/special education (M Ed); generalist (M Ed); reading (M Ed); secondary teaching (M Ed). Part-time and evening/weekend programs available. Postbaccalaureate distance learning degree programs offered (no on-campus study). *Faculty:* 30 full-time (17 women), 54 part-time/adjunct (37 women). *Students:* 66 full-time (43 women), 1,178 part-time (1,044 women); includes 777 minority (313 Black or African American, non-Hispanic/Latino; 5 American Indian or Alaska Native, non-Hispanic/Latino; 29 Asian, non-Hispanic/Latino; 395 Hispanic/Latino; 2 Native Hawaiian or other Pacific Islander, non-Hispanic/Latino; 33 Two or more races, non-Hispanic/Latino), 26 international. Average age 36. 551 applicants, 94% accepted, 416 enrolled. In 2011, 72 master's awarded. *Degree requirements:* For master's, thesis, field experience. *Entrance requirements:* For master's, GRE or MAT if GPA is below 3.0, bachelor's degree; minimum GPA of 2.75 in bachelor's degree or last 60 credit hours; official transcripts from all institutions; goal statement of 250-300 words; 1 reference. Additional exam requirements/recommendations for international students: Required—TOEFL. *Application deadline:* Applications are processed on a rolling basis. Application fee: $35. Electronic applications accepted. *Expenses:* Contact institution. *Financial support:* In 2011–12, 9 students received support. Federal Work-Study, scholarships/grants, and state work-study, institutional employment available. Support available to part-time students. Financial award application deadline: 4/15; financial award applicants required to submit FAFSA. *Faculty research:* Leadership, diversity, personality traits, second language acquisition. *Unit head:* Dr. Nora Hutto, Dean, 713-525-3540, Fax: 713-525-3871, E-mail: education@stthom.edu. *Application contact:* Paula C. Hollis, Administrative Assistant, 713-525-3540, Fax: 713-525-3871, E-mail: education@stthom.edu. Web site: http://www.stthom.edu/Schools_Centers_of_Excellence/Schools_of_Study/School_of_Education/Index.aqf.

University of San Diego, School of Leadership and Education Sciences, Department of Learning and Teaching, San Diego, CA 92110-2492. Offers curriculum and instruction (M Ed); special education (M Ed); special education with deaf and hard of hearing (M Ed); teaching (MAT); TESOL, literacy and culture (M Ed). Part-time and evening/weekend programs available. *Faculty:* 11 full-time (8 women), 41 part-time/adjunct (32 women). *Students:* 86 full-time (69 women), 73 part-time (62 women); includes 54 minority (7 Black or African American, non-Hispanic/Latino; 1 American Indian or Alaska Native, non-Hispanic/Latino; 7 Asian, non-Hispanic/Latino; 27 Hispanic/Latino; 1 Native Hawaiian or other Pacific Islander, non-Hispanic/Latino; 11 Two or more races, non-Hispanic/Latino), 12 international. Average age 28. 177 applicants, 60% accepted, 61 enrolled. In 2011, 57 master's awarded. *Degree requirements:* For master's, thesis (for some programs). *Entrance requirements:* For master's, minimum GPA of 3.0. Additional exam requirements/recommendations for international students: Required—TOEFL (minimum score 580 paper-based; 237 computer-based; 83 iBT), TWE. *Application deadline:* For fall admission, 3/1 priority date for domestic students, 3/1 for international students; for spring admission, 10/15 priority date for domestic students, 10/15 for international students. Application fee: $45. Electronic applications accepted. *Expenses: Tuition:* Full-time $22,482; part-time $1249 per unit. *Required fees:* $224. Full-time tuition and fees vary according to course load and degree level. *Financial support:* In 2011–12, 77 students received support. Career-related internships or fieldwork, Federal Work-Study, institutionally sponsored loans, and stipends available. Support available to part-time students. Financial award application deadline: 4/1; financial award applicants required to submit FAFSA. *Faculty research:* Action research methodology, cultural studies, instructional theories and practices, second language acquisition, school reform. *Unit head:* Dr. Heather Lattimer, Director, 619-260-7616, Fax: 619-260-8159, E-mail: hlattimer@sandiego.edu. *Application contact:* Monica Mahon, Associate Director of Graduate Admissions, 619-260-4524, Fax: 619-260-4158, E-mail: grads@sandiego.edu. Web site: http://www.sandiego.edu/soles/programs/learning_and_teaching/.

University of San Francisco, School of Education, Department of Learning and Instruction, San Francisco, CA 94117-1080. Offers digital media and learning (MA); learning and instruction (MA, Ed D); teaching (MA); teaching reading (MA). *Faculty:* 10 full-time (6 women), 1 part-time/adjunct (0 women). *Students:* 275 full-time (201 women), 67 part-time (42 women); includes 97 minority (7 Black or African American, non-Hispanic/Latino; 3 American Indian or Alaska Native, non-Hispanic/Latino; 32 Asian, non-Hispanic/Latino; 34 Hispanic/Latino; 1 Native Hawaiian or other Pacific Islander, non-Hispanic/Latino; 20 Two or more races, non-Hispanic/Latino), 4 international. Average age 32. 310 applicants, 72% accepted, 135 enrolled. In 2011, 118 master's, 10 doctorates awarded. *Degree requirements:* For doctorate, thesis/dissertation. Application fee: $55 ($65 for international students). *Expenses: Tuition:* Full-time $20,070; part-time $1115 per unit. Tuition and fees vary according to course load, campus/location and program. *Financial support:* In 2011–12, 54 students received support. Fellowships, research assistantships, and teaching assistantships available. Financial award application deadline: 3/2; financial award applicants required to submit FAFSA. *Unit head:* Dr. Robert Burns, Chair, 415-422-6289. *Application contact:* Beth Teague, Associate Director of Graduate Outreach, 415-422-5467, E-mail: schoolofeducation@usfca.edu.

University of Saskatchewan, College of Graduate Studies and Research, College of Education, Department of Curriculum Studies, Saskatoon, SK S7N 5A2, Canada. Offers M Ed, PhD, Diploma. Part-time programs available. *Degree requirements:* For master's, thesis (for some programs); for doctorate, comprehensive exam (for some programs), thesis/dissertation. *Entrance requirements:* For master's, MAT. Additional exam requirements/recommendations for international students: Required—TOEFL (minimum score 80 iBT); Recommended—IELTS (minimum score 6.5). Electronic applications accepted.

The University of Scranton, College of Graduate and Continuing Education, Department of Education, Program in Curriculum and Instruction, Scranton, PA 18510. Offers MA, MS. Part-time and evening/weekend programs available. Postbaccalaureate distance learning degree programs offered (no on-campus study). *Students:* 107 full-time (87 women), 125 part-time (98 women); includes 16 minority (10 Black or African American, non-Hispanic/Latino; 1 American Indian or Alaska Native, non-Hispanic/Latino; 3 Asian, non-Hispanic/Latino; 2 Hispanic/Latino), 5 international. Average age 32. 46 applicants, 98% accepted. In 2011, 190 master's awarded. *Degree requirements:* For master's, comprehensive exam, thesis (for some programs), capstone experience. *Entrance requirements:* For master's, minimum GPA of 2.75. Additional exam requirements/recommendations for international students: Required—TOEFL (minimum score 500 paper-based; 173 computer-based), IELTS (minimum score 5.3). *Application deadline:* Applications are processed on a rolling basis. Application fee: $0. *Financial support:* Federal Work-Study and unspecified assistantships available. Financial award application deadline: 3/1. *Unit head:* Dr. Art Chambers, Director, 570-941-4668, Fax: 570-941-5515, E-mail: chambersa2@scranton.edu. *Application contact:* Joseph M. Roback, Director of Admissions, 570-941-4385, Fax: 570-941-5928, E-mail: robackj2@scranton.edu.

University of South Africa, College of Human Sciences, Pretoria, South Africa. Offers adult education (M Ed); African languages (MA, PhD); African politics (MA, PhD); Afrikaans (MA, PhD); ancient history (MA, PhD); ancient Near Eastern studies (MA, PhD); anthropology (MA, PhD); applied linguistics (MA); Arabic (MA, PhD); archaeology (MA); art history (MA); Biblical archaeology (MA); Biblical studies (M Th, D Th, PhD); Christian spirituality (M Th, D Th); church history (M Th, D Th); classical studies (MA, PhD); clinical psychology (MA); communication (MA, PhD); comparative education (M Ed, Ed D); consulting psychology (D Admin, D Com, PhD); curriculum studies (M Ed, Ed D); development studies (M Admin, MA, D Admin, PhD); didactics (M Ed, Ed D); education (M Tech); education management (M Ed, Ed D); educational psychology (M Ed); English (MA); environmental education (M Ed); French (MA, PhD); German (MA, PhD); Greek (MA); guidance and counseling (M Ed); health studies (MA, PhD), including health sciences education (MA), health services management (MA), medical and surgical nursing science (critical care general) (MA), midwifery and neonatal nursing science (MA), trauma and emergency care (MA); history (MA, PhD); history of education (Ed D); inclusive education (M Ed, Ed D); information and communications technology policy and regulation (MA); information science (MA, MIS, PhD); international politics (MA, PhD); Islamic studies (MA, PhD); Italian (MA, PhD); Judaica (MA, PhD); linguistics (MA, PhD); mathematical education (M Ed); mathematics education (MA); missiology (M Th, D Th); modern Hebrew (MA, PhD); musicology (MA, MMus, D Mus, PhD); natural science education (M Ed); New Testament (M Th, D Th); Old Testament (D Th); pastoral therapy (M Th, D Th); philosophy (MA); philosophy of education (M Ed, Ed D); politics (MA, PhD); Portuguese (MA, PhD); practical theology (M Th, D Th); psychology (MA, MS, PhD); psychology of education (M Ed, Ed D); public health (MA); religious studies (MA, D Th, PhD); Romance languages (MA); Russian (MA, PhD); Semitic languages (MA, PhD); social behavior studies in HIV/AIDS (MA); social science (mental health) (MA); social science in development studies (MA); social science in psychology (MA); social science in social work (MA); social science in sociology (MA); social work (MSW, DSW, PhD); socio-education (M Ed, Ed D); sociolinguistics (MA); sociology (MA, PhD); Spanish (MA, PhD); systematic theology (M Th, D Th); TESOL (teaching English to speakers of other languages) (MA); theological ethics (M Th, D Th); theory of literature (MA, PhD); urban ministries (D Th); urban ministry (M Th).

University of South Carolina, The Graduate School, College of Education, Department of Instruction and Teacher Education, Program in Curriculum and Instruction, Columbia, SC 29208. Offers Ed D. This degree cuts across two departments and represents 6 different concentrations. *Accreditation:* NCATE. Part-time and evening/weekend programs available. *Degree requirements:* For doctorate, comprehensive exam, thesis/dissertation. *Entrance requirements:* For doctorate, GRE General Test or MAT, interview, resume, letter of intent, letters of reference. Electronic applications accepted. *Faculty research:* Teacher education, historian recording project, curriculum development in international areas, human sexuality.

The University of South Dakota, Graduate School, School of Education, Division of Curriculum and Instruction, Vermillion, SD 57069-2390. Offers curriculum and instruction (Ed D, Ed S); elementary education (MA); secondary education (MA); special education (MA); technology for education and training (MS, Ed S). *Accreditation:* NCATE. Part-time programs available. Postbaccalaureate distance learning degree programs offered. *Degree requirements:* For master's and Ed S, comprehensive exam, thesis or alternative; for doctorate, comprehensive exam, thesis/dissertation. *Entrance requirements:* For master's, doctorate, and Ed S, GRE General Test, MAT, minimum GPA of 2.7. Additional exam requirements/recommendations for international students: Required—TOEFL (minimum score 550 paper-based; 213 computer-based; 79 iBT). Electronic applications accepted. *Expenses:* Tuition, state resident: full-time $3118.50; part-time $173.25 per credit hour. Tuition, nonresident: full-time $6601; part-time $366.70 per credit hour. *Required fees:* $2268; $126 per credit hour. Tuition and fees vary according to program.

University of Southern Mississippi, Graduate School, College of Education and Psychology, Department of Curriculum, Instruction, and Special Education, Hattiesburg, MS 39406-0001. Offers alternative secondary teacher education (MAT); early childhood education (M Ed, Ed S); education (Ed D); education of the gifted (M Ed, PhD, Ed S); elementary education (M Ed, PhD, Ed S); reading (M Ed, MS); secondary education (M Ed, MS, PhD); special education (M Ed, PhD, Ed S). Part-time programs available. *Faculty:* 23 full-time (17 women), 3 part-time/adjunct (2 women). *Students:* 39 full-time (34 women), 92 part-time (77 women); includes 36 minority (31 Black or African American, non-Hispanic/Latino; 3 Hispanic/Latino; 2 Two or more races, non-Hispanic/Latino), 3 international. Average age 37. 56 applicants, 55% accepted, 29 enrolled. In 2011, 45 master's, 5 doctorates awarded. *Degree requirements:* For master's and Ed S, comprehensive exam, thesis (for some programs); for doctorate, comprehensive exam, thesis/dissertation. *Entrance requirements:* For master's, GRE General Test, MAT, minimum GPA of 3.0; for doctorate, GRE General Test, minimum GPA of 3.5; for Ed S, GRE General Test, MAT, minimum GPA of 3.25. Additional exam requirements/recommendations for international students: Required—TOEFL, IELTS. *Application deadline:* For fall admission, 3/1 priority date for domestic students, 3/1 for international students; for spring admission, 1/10 priority date for domestic students, 1/10 for international students. Applications are processed on a rolling basis. Application fee: $50. *Financial support:* In 2011–12, 9 research assistantships with tuition reimbursements (averaging $18,316 per year), 2 teaching assistantships with full tuition reimbursements (averaging $8,500 per year) were awarded; Federal Work-Study, institutionally sponsored loans, scholarships/grants, health care benefits, tuition waivers (partial), and unspecified assistantships also available. Financial award application deadline: 3/15; financial award applicants required to submit FAFSA. *Faculty research:* Mathematical problem solving, integrative curriculum, writing process, teacher education models. *Total annual research expenditures:* $100,000. *Unit head:* Dr. David Daves, Chair, 601-266-4547, Fax: 601-266-4175, E-mail: david.daves@usm.edu. *Application contact:* Dr. Marie Crowe, Director of Graduate Studies, 601-266-6005, Fax: 601-266-4548, E-mail: margie.crowe@usm.edu. Web site: http://www.usm.edu/graduateschool/table.php.

University of South Florida, Graduate School, College of Education, Department of Secondary Education, Tampa, FL 33620-9951. Offers English education (M Ed, MA,

MAT, PhD); foreign language education/ESOL (M Ed, MA, MAT); instructional technology (M Ed, PhD, Ed S); mathematics education (M Ed, MA, MAT, PhD, Ed S); science education (M Ed, MA, MAT, PhD); second language acquisition/instructional technology (PhD); secondary education (M Ed, PhD); secondary education/TESOL (M Ed); social science education (M Ed, MA, MAT); teaching and learning in the content area (PhD). *Accreditation:* NCATE. Part-time and evening/weekend programs available. *Faculty:* 28 full-time (17 women), 3 part-time/adjunct (1 woman). *Students:* 174 full-time (116 women), 268 part-time (184 women); includes 103 minority (26 Black or African American, non-Hispanic/Latino; 10 Asian, non-Hispanic/Latino; 58 Hispanic/Latino; 9 Two or more races, non-Hispanic/Latino), 32 international. Average age 37. 229 applicants, 73% accepted, 141 enrolled. In 2011, 115 master's, 16 doctorates, 5 other advanced degrees awarded. *Degree requirements:* For master's, variable foreign language requirement, comprehensive exam, project (for some programs); for doctorate, variable foreign language requirement, comprehensive exam, thesis/dissertation, philosophies of inquiry; multiple research methods. *Entrance requirements:* For master's, GRE General Test or General Knowledge Test, minimum GPA of 3.0; for doctorate, GRE General Test, minimum GPA of 3.5; for Ed S, GRE General Test. Additional exam requirements/recommendations for international students: Required—TOEFL (minimum score 550 paper-based; 213 computer-based; 79 iBT). *Application deadline:* For fall admission, 2/15 for domestic students, 1/2 for international students; for spring admission, 10/15 for domestic students, 6/1 for international students. Application fee: $30. Electronic applications accepted. *Financial support:* In 2011–12, 7 students received support, including 1 research assistantship with full tuition reimbursement available (averaging $10,000 per year), 55 teaching assistantships with full and partial tuition reimbursements available (averaging $7,900 per year); scholarships/grants and unspecified assistantships also available. Financial award application deadline: 4/15; financial award applicants required to submit FAFSA. *Faculty research:* English language learners/multicultural, social science education, mathematics education, science education, instructional technology. *Total annual research expenditures:* $336,023. *Unit head:* Dr. Stephen Thornton, Chairperson, 813-974-3533, Fax: 813-974-3837, E-mail: thornton@usf.edu. *Application contact:* Dr. Diane Briscoe, Coordinator of Graduate Studies, 813-974-1804, Fax: 813-974-3391, E-mail: briscoe@usf.edu. Web site: http://www.coedu.usf.edu/main/departments/seced/seced.html.

University of South Florida Sarasota-Manatee, College of Education, Sarasota, FL 34243. Offers educational leadership (M Ed), including curriculum leadership, K-12, non-public/charter school leadership; elementary education K-6 (MA); K-6 with ESOL endorsement (MAT); reading education K-12 (MA); MAT/MA. Part-time and evening/weekend programs available. *Faculty:* 12 full-time (8 women), 4 part-time/adjunct (3 women). *Students:* 19 full-time (17 women), 64 part-time (50 women); includes 7 minority (1 Black or African American, non-Hispanic/Latino; 1 Asian, non-Hispanic/Latino; 4 Hispanic/Latino; 1 Two or more races, non-Hispanic/Latino). Average age 33. 50 applicants, 62% accepted, 21 enrolled. In 2011, 41 master's awarded. *Degree requirements:* For master's, comprehensive exam (for some programs). *Entrance requirements:* For master's, GRE. Additional exam requirements/recommendations for international students: Required—TOEFL (minimum score 213 computer-based; 79 iBT) or IELTS. *Application deadline:* For fall admission, 2/15 for domestic students, 1/2 for international students; for spring admission, 10/15 for domestic students, 6/1 for international students. Applications are processed on a rolling basis. Application fee: $30. Electronic applications accepted. *Expenses:* Tuition, state resident: full-time $9301; part-time $387.55 per credit hour. Tuition, nonresident: full-time $19,412; part-time $808.85 per credit hour. *Required fees:* $15; $5 per semester. One-time fee: $30. *Financial support:* Federal Work-Study, scholarships/grants, health care benefits, and unspecified assistantships available. Support available to part-time students. Financial award application deadline: 3/1; financial award applicants required to submit FAFSA. *Faculty research:* Child development, student achievement, intergenerational studies. *Unit head:* Dr. Terry A. Osborn, Dean, 941-359-4531, E-mail: terryosborn@sar.usf.edu. *Application contact:* Jo Lynn Raudebaugh, Graduate Admissions Advisor, 941-359-4587, E-mail: jraudeba@sar.usf.edu. Web site: http://www.sarasota.usf.edu/Academics/COE/.

The University of Tampa, Program in Teaching, Tampa, FL 33606-1490. Offers curricula and instructional leadership (M Ed); teaching (M Ed). Part-time and evening/weekend programs available. *Faculty:* 5 full-time (2 women), 7 part-time/adjunct (6 women). *Students:* 25 full-time (12 women), 2 part-time (both women); includes 6 minority (5 Hispanic/Latino; 1 Two or more races, non-Hispanic/Latino). Average age 30. 102 applicants, 38% accepted, 27 enrolled. In 2011, 43 master's awarded. *Entrance requirements:* For master's, Florida Teacher Certification Exam, PRAXIS, GRE, or GMAT, bachelor's degree in education or professional teaching certificate. Additional exam requirements/recommendations for international students: Required—TOEFL (minimum score 577 paper-based; 230 computer-based; 90 iBT), IELTS (minimum score 7). *Application deadline:* For fall admission, 5/1 for domestic students. Applications are processed on a rolling basis. Application fee: $40. Electronic applications accepted. *Expenses: Tuition:* Full-time $8320; part-time $520 per credit hour. *Required fees:* $40 per semester. Tuition and fees vary according to program. *Financial support:* In 2011–12, 8 students received support. Grants available. Financial award applicants required to submit FAFSA. *Faculty research:* Diversity in the classroom, technology integration, assessment methodologies, complex and ill-structured problem solving, and communities of practice.. *Unit head:* Dr. Anne Gormly, Dean, College of Social Sciences, Mathematics and Education, 813-253-3333 Ext. 6262, E-mail: agormly@ut.edu. *Application contact:* Charlene Tobie, Associate Director, Graduate and Continuing Studies, 813-258-7409, Fax: 813-258-7451, E-mail: ctobie@ut.edu. Web site: http://www.ut.edu/graduate.

The University of Tennessee, Graduate School, College of Education, Health and Human Sciences, Program in Education, Knoxville, TN 37996. Offers art education (MS); counseling education (PhD); cultural studies in education (PhD); curriculum (MS, Ed S); curriculum, educational research and evaluation (Ed D, PhD); early childhood education (PhD); early childhood special education (MS); education of deaf and hard of hearing (MS); educational administration and policy studies (Ed D, PhD); educational administration and supervision (Ed S); educational psychology (Ed D, PhD); elementary education (MS, Ed S); elementary teaching (MS); English education (MS, Ed S); exercise science (PhD); foreign language/ESL education (MS, Ed S); instructional technology (MS, Ed D, PhD, Ed S); literacy, language and ESL education (PhD); literacy, language education, and ESL education (Ed D); mathematics education (MS, Ed S); modified and comprehensive special education (MS); reading education (MS, Ed S); school counseling (Ed S); school psychology (PhD, Ed S); science education (MS, Ed S); secondary teaching (MS); social foundations (MS); social science education (MS, Ed S); socio-cultural foundations of sports and education (PhD); special education (Ed S); teacher education (Ed D, PhD). *Accreditation:* NCATE. Part-time and evening/weekend programs available. *Degree requirements:* For master's and Ed S, thesis optional; for doctorate, variable foreign language requirement, thesis/dissertation. *Entrance requirements:* For master's, minimum GPA of 2.7; for doctorate and Ed S, GRE General Test, minimum GPA of 2.7. Additional exam requirements/recommendations for international students: Required—TOEFL. Electronic applications accepted. *Expenses:* Tuition, state resident: full-time $8332; part-time $464 per credit hour. Tuition, nonresident: full-time $25,174; part-time $1400 per credit hour. *Required fees:* $1162; $56 per credit hour. Tuition and fees vary according to program.

The University of Texas at Arlington, Graduate School, Department of Curriculum and Instruction, Arlington, TX 76019. Offers curriculum and instruction (M Ed); teaching (with certification) (M Ed T). *Accreditation:* NCATE. Part-time and evening/weekend programs available. Postbaccalaureate distance learning degree programs offered (no on-campus study). *Faculty:* 19 full-time (13 women). *Students:* 68 full-time (50 women), 874 part-time (776 women); includes 324 minority (128 Black or African American, non-Hispanic/Latino; 2 American Indian or Alaska Native, non-Hispanic/Latino; 25 Asian, non-Hispanic/Latino; 144 Hispanic/Latino; 25 Two or more races, non-Hispanic/Latino), 18 international. Average age 35. 727 applicants, 88% accepted, 552 enrolled. In 2011, 318 degrees awarded. *Degree requirements:* For master's, comprehensive exam (for some programs), comprehensive activity, research project. *Entrance requirements:* For master's, GRE General Test, minimum undergraduate GPA of 3.0 in last 60 hours of course work, writing sample, 3 letters of recommendation. Additional exam requirements/recommendations for international students: Required—TOEFL (minimum score 550 paper-based; 213 computer-based). *Application deadline:* For fall admission, 6/1 priority date for domestic students, 4/1 for international students; for spring admission, 10/15 priority date for domestic students, 9/15 for international students. Applications are processed on a rolling basis. Application fee: $50. Electronic applications accepted. *Financial support:* In 2011–12, 85 students received support, including 4 research assistantships (averaging $3,000 per year), 4 teaching assistantships (averaging $3,000 per year); career-related internships or fieldwork, Federal Work-Study, scholarships/grants, and unspecified assistantships also available. Financial award application deadline: 6/1; financial award applicants required to submit FAFSA. *Unit head:* Dr. John A. Smith, Chair, 817-272-0116, Fax: 817-272-2618, E-mail: smithj@uta.edu. *Application contact:* Racine Reza, Graduate Advisor, 817-272-2956, Fax: 817-272-7624, E-mail: racine@uta.edu. Web site: http://www.uta.edu/coed.

The University of Texas at Austin, Graduate School, College of Education, Department of Curriculum and Instruction, Austin, TX 78712-1111. Offers bilingual/bicultural education (M Ed, MA, PhD); cultural studies in education (M Ed, MA, PhD); early childhood education (M Ed, MA, PhD); language and literacy studies (M Ed, PhD); learning technologies (M Ed, MA, PhD); physical education (M Ed, MA, PhD). Terminal master's awarded for partial completion of doctoral program. *Degree requirements:* For doctorate, thesis/dissertation. *Entrance requirements:* For master's and doctorate, GRE General Test. *Application deadline:* For fall admission, 3/1 for domestic students; for spring admission, 10/1 for domestic students. Applications are processed on a rolling basis. Application fee: $50 ($75 for international students). Electronic applications accepted. *Financial support:* Fellowships and teaching assistantships with partial tuition reimbursements available. Financial award application deadline: 2/1. *Unit head:* Betty Maloch, Chair, 512-232-4262, E-mail: bmaloch@austin.utexas.edu. *Application contact:* Stephen Flynn, Graduate Coordinator, 512-471-3747, E-mail: sflynn@austin.utexas.edu. Web site: http://www.edb.utexas.edu/coe/depts/ci/cti.html.

The University of Texas at Brownsville, Graduate Studies, School of Education, Brownsville, TX 78520-4991. Offers bilingual education (M Ed); counseling and guidance (M Ed); curriculum and instruction (M Ed); early childhood education (M Ed); educational administration (M Ed); educational technology (M Ed); English as a second language (M Ed); reading specialist (M Ed); special education/educational diagnostician (M Ed). Part-time and evening/weekend programs available. Postbaccalaureate distance learning degree programs offered (minimal on-campus study). *Degree requirements:* For master's, thesis optional. *Entrance requirements:* For master's, GRE General Test. Additional exam requirements/recommendations for international students: Required—TOEFL.

The University of Texas at El Paso, Graduate School, College of Education, Department of Teacher Education, El Paso, TX 79968-0001. Offers education (MA); instruction (M Ed); reading education (M Ed); teaching, learning, and culture (PhD). Part-time and evening/weekend programs available. *Students:* 595 (433 women); includes 473 minority (16 Black or African American, non-Hispanic/Latino; 2 American Indian or Alaska Native, non-Hispanic/Latino; 13 Asian, non-Hispanic/Latino; 439 Hispanic/Latino; 2 Native Hawaiian or other Pacific Islander, non-Hispanic/Latino; 1 Two or more races, non-Hispanic/Latino), 22 international. Average age 34. 168 applicants, 79% accepted, 108 enrolled. In 2011, 79 master's awarded. *Degree requirements:* For master's, thesis optional. *Entrance requirements:* For master's, GRE General Test, minimum GPA of 3.0. Additional exam requirements/recommendations for international students: Required—TOEFL. *Application deadline:* For fall admission, 7/1 priority date for domestic students, 3/1 for international students; for spring admission, 11/1 priority date for domestic students, 9/1 for international students. Applications are processed on a rolling basis. Application fee: $15 ($65 for international students). Electronic applications accepted. *Financial support:* In 2011–12, research assistantships with partial tuition reimbursements (averaging $16,642 per year), teaching assistantships with partial tuition reimbursements (averaging $13,134 per year) were awarded; Federal Work-Study, institutionally sponsored loans, scholarships/grants, and tuition waivers (partial) also available. Financial award application deadline: 3/15; financial award applicants required to submit FAFSA. *Unit head:* Dr. Elaine Hampton, Chair, 915-747-5426, E-mail: ehampton@utep.edu. *Application contact:* Dr. Benjamin Flores, Interim Dean of the Graduate School, 915-747-5491, Fax: 915-747-5788, E-mail: bflores@utep.edu.

The University of Texas at San Antonio, College of Education and Human Development, Department of Interdisciplinary Learning and Teaching, San Antonio, TX 78249-0617. Offers adult learning and teaching (MA); education (MA), including curriculum and instruction, early childhood and elementary education, educational psychology/special education, instructional technology, reading and literacy education; interdisciplinary learning and teaching (PhD). Part-time and evening/weekend programs available. *Faculty:* 26 full-time (21 women), 1 (woman) part-time/adjunct. *Students:* 131 full-time (100 women), 357 part-time (283 women); includes 275 minority (31 Black or African American, non-Hispanic/Latino; 9 Asian, non-Hispanic/Latino; 227 Hispanic/Latino; 8 Two or more races, non-Hispanic/Latino), 31 international. Average age 33. 239 applicants, 75% accepted, 120 enrolled. In 2011, 119 master's awarded. *Degree requirements:* For master's, comprehensive exam, thesis optional, 36 hours of course work without thesis (33 with thesis); for doctorate, comprehensive exam, thesis/dissertation, minimum of 60 semester credit hours. *Entrance requirements:* For master's, GRE General Test, bachelor's degree with minimum GPA of 3.0 in last 60 hours of coursework; resume; two letters of recommendation; statement of purpose; for doctorate, GRE, transcripts from all colleges and universities attended, professional vitae demonstrating experience in work environment where education was primary professional emphasis, 3 letters of recommendation, statement of purpose, master's degree transcript documenting minimum GPA of 3.5. Additional exam requirements/recommendations for international students: Required—TOEFL (minimum score 500 paper-based; 61 iBT), IELTS (minimum score 5). *Application deadline:* For fall admission, 7/1 for domestic students, 4/1 for international students; for spring admission, 11/1 for domestic students, 9/1 for international students. Application fee: $45 ($85 for international students). *Expenses:* Tuition, state resident: full-time $3148; part-time $2176 per semester. Tuition, nonresident: full-time $8782; part-time $5932 per semester. *Required fees:* $719 per semester. *Financial support:* In 2011–12, 9 fellowships with partial tuition reimbursements (averaging $27,000 per year) were awarded; career-related internships or fieldwork, Federal Work-Study, and scholarships/grants also available. Support available to part-time students. *Faculty research:* Explorations of science, learning and teaching, family Involvement in early childhood, culturally-responsive literacy instruction in diverse settings, STEM education, autism spectrum disorders. *Total annual research expenditures:* $5.9 million. *Unit head:* Dr. Maria R. Cortez, Department Chair, 210-458-5969, Fax: 210-458-7281, E-mail: mari.cortez@utsa.edu. *Application contact:* Erin Doran, Student Development Specialist, 210-458-7443, Fax: 210-458-7281, E-mail: erin.doran@utsa.edu.

University of the Pacific, School of Education, Department of Curriculum and Instruction, Stockton, CA 95211-0197. Offers curriculum and instruction (M Ed, MA, Ed D); education (M Ed); special education (MA). *Accreditation:* NCATE. *Faculty:* 10 full-time (6 women), 6 part-time/adjunct (4 women). *Students:* 48 full-time (36 women), 112 part-time (93 women); includes 78 minority (4 Black or African American, non-Hispanic/Latino; 59 Asian, non-Hispanic/Latino; 15 Hispanic/Latino), 4 international. Average age 33. 75 applicants, 85% accepted, 43 enrolled. In 2011, 38 master's awarded. *Degree requirements:* For master's, thesis (for some programs). *Entrance requirements:* For master's, GRE General Test. Additional exam requirements/recommendations for international students: Required—TOEFL (minimum score 475 paper-based; 150 computer-based). *Application deadline:* For fall admission, 3/1 priority date for domestic students; for spring admission, 10/1 priority date for domestic students. Applications are processed on a rolling basis. Application fee: $75. *Expenses: Tuition:* Full-time $18,900; part-time $1181 per unit. *Required fees:* $949. *Financial support:* In 2011–12, 7 teaching assistantships were awarded. Financial award application deadline: 3/1; financial award applicants required to submit FAFSA. *Unit head:* Dr. Marilyn Draheim, Chairperson, 209-946-2685, E-mail: mdraheim@pacific.edu. *Application contact:* Office of Graduate Admissions, 209-946-2344.

University of the Southwest, Graduate Programs, Hobbs, NM 88240-9129. Offers business administration (MBA); curriculum and instruction (MSE); curriculum and instruction: bilingual (MSE); curriculum and instruction: TESOL (MSE); early childhood education (MSE); educational administration (MSE); mental health counseling (MSE); school counseling (MSE); special education (MSE); sports management (MBA). Part-time and evening/weekend programs available. Postbaccalaureate distance learning degree programs offered (no on-campus study). *Faculty:* 13 full-time (6 women), 28 part-time/adjunct (17 women). *Students:* 76 full-time (63 women), 229 part-time (194 women); includes 104 minority (50 Black or African American, non-Hispanic/Latino; 2 American Indian or Alaska Native, non-Hispanic/Latino; 8 Asian, non-Hispanic/Latino; 44 Hispanic/Latino). Average age 38. 173 applicants, 71% accepted, 101 enrolled. In 2011, 75 master's awarded. *Degree requirements:* For master's, comprehensive exam, thesis (for some programs). *Entrance requirements:* Additional exam requirements/recommendations for international students: Recommended—TOEFL. *Application deadline:* Applications are processed on a rolling basis. Application fee: $50. Electronic applications accepted. *Expenses: Tuition:* Full-time $12,288; part-time $512 per credit hour. One-time fee: $50. Tuition and fees vary according to course load. *Financial support:* In 2011–12, 47 students received support. Federal Work-Study available. Financial award application deadline: 4/1; financial award applicants required to submit FAFSA. *Unit head:* Dr. Mary Harris, Dean of Education, 575-492-2162, Fax: 575-392-6006, E-mail: mharris@usw.edu. *Application contact:* Melissa Mitchell, Senior Online Program Advisor, 575-492-2142, Fax: 575-392-6006, E-mail: mmitchell@usw.edu. Web site: http://www.usw.edu/admissions/graduate_admission/graduate_admissions.

The University of Toledo, College of Graduate Studies, Judith Herb College of Education, Health Science and Human Service, Department of Curriculum and Instruction, Toledo, OH 43606-3390. Offers art education (ME); career and technical education (ME); curriculum and instruction (ME, PhD, Ed S); education and anthropology (MAE); education and biology (MES); education and chemistry (MES); education and classics (MAE); education and economics (MAE); education and English (MAE); education and French (MAE); education and geography (MAE); education and geology (MES); education and German (MAE); education and history (MAE); education and mathematics (MAE, MES); education and physics (MES); education and political science (MAE); education and sociology (MAE); education and Spanish (MAE); educational media (PhD); educational technology (ME); English as a second language (MAE); gifted and talented (PhD); middle childhood education licensure (ME); music education (MME); secondary education (PhD); secondary education licensure (ME). *Accreditation:* NCATE. Part-time and evening/weekend programs available. *Faculty:* 24. *Students:* 60 full-time (31 women), 211 part-time (161 women); includes 23 minority (21 Black or African American, non-Hispanic/Latino; 2 Hispanic/Latino), 20 international. Average age 35. 115 applicants, 73% accepted, 74 enrolled. In 2011, 105 master's, 3 doctorates, 4 other advanced degrees awarded. *Degree requirements:* For master's, comprehensive exam, thesis or alternative; for doctorate, comprehensive exam, thesis/dissertation; for Ed S, thesis optional. *Entrance requirements:* For master's, doctorate, and Ed S, minimum cumulative GPA of 2.7 for all previous academic work, letters of recommendation. Additional exam requirements/recommendations for international students: Required—TOEFL (minimum score 550 paper-based; 213 computer-based; 80 iBT), IELTS (minimum score 6.5). *Application deadline:* For fall admission, 1/15 priority date for domestic students, 1/15 for international students. Applications are processed on a rolling basis. Application fee: $45 ($75 for international students). Electronic applications accepted. *Financial support:* In 2011–12, 9 research assistantships with full and partial tuition reimbursements (averaging $7,184 per year), 12 teaching assistantships with full and partial tuition reimbursements (averaging $8,425 per year) were awarded; career-related internships or fieldwork, Federal Work-Study, institutionally sponsored loans, scholarships/grants, tuition waivers (full and partial), unspecified assistantships, and administrative assistantships also available. Support available to part-time students. *Unit head:* Dr. Leigh Chiarelott, Chair, 419-530-5371, E-mail: eigh.chiarelott@utoledo.edu. *Application contact:* Graduate School Office, 419-530-4723, Fax: 419-530-4724, E-mail: grdsch@utnet.utoledo.edu. Web site: http://www.utoledo.edu/eduhshs/.

University of Vermont, Graduate College, College of Education and Social Services, Department of Education, Program in Curriculum and Instruction, Burlington, VT 05405. Offers M Ed, MAT. *Accreditation:* NCATE. *Students:* 145 (108 women); includes 3 minority (all Hispanic/Latino). 139 applicants, 79% accepted, 21 enrolled. In 2011, 63 master's awarded. *Entrance requirements:* For master's, GRE (for M Ed), resume (for M Ed). Additional exam requirements/recommendations for international students: Required—TOEFL (minimum score 550 paper-based; 213 computer-based; 80 iBT). *Application deadline:* For fall admission, 3/15 priority date for domestic students, 3/15 for international students. Applications are processed on a rolling basis. Application fee: $40. Electronic applications accepted. *Financial support:* Fellowships, teaching assistantships, and career-related internships or fieldwork available. Financial award application deadline: 3/1. *Application contact:* Prof. Maureen Neumann, M Ed Coordinator, 802-656-3356.

University of Victoria, Faculty of Graduate Studies, Faculty of Education, Department of Curriculum and Instruction, Victoria, BC V8W 2Y2, Canada. Offers art education (M Ed, PhD); curriculum studies (M Ed, MA, PhD); early childhood education (M Ed, PhD); educational studies (PhD); language and literacy (M Ed, MA, PhD); mathematics (M Ed, MA, PhD); music education (M Ed, MA, PhD); science (M Ed, MA, PhD); social studies (M Ed, MA); social, cultural and foundational studies (MA, PhD); technology and environmental education (PhD). Part-time programs available. *Degree requirements:* For master's, thesis, project (M Ed); for doctorate, comprehensive exam, thesis/dissertation. *Entrance requirements:* For master's, minimum B average. Additional exam requirements/recommendations for international students: Required—TOEFL (minimum score 575 paper-based; 233 computer-based), IELTS (minimum score 7). Electronic applications accepted. *Faculty research:* Elementary and secondary English, language arts, curriculum theory and practice, educational media and technology, educational administration and leadership, history and philosophy of education.

University of Virginia, Curry School of Education, Department of Curriculum, Instruction, and Special Education, Program in Curriculum and Instruction, Charlottesville, VA 22903. Offers curriculum and instruction (M Ed, Ed S); elementary (M Ed, Ed D); English (M Ed, Ed D); foreign language (M Ed); mathematics (M Ed, Ed D); reading (M Ed, Ed D, Ed S); science (Ed D); social studies (M Ed). *Students:* 22 full-time (17 women), 29 part-time (27 women); includes 4 minority (1 Black or African American, non-Hispanic/Latino; 1 Asian, non-Hispanic/Latino; 2 Two or more races, non-Hispanic/Latino), 1 international. Average age 33. 67 applicants, 75% accepted, 33 enrolled. In 2011, 78 master's, 2 doctorates, 12 other advanced degrees awarded. *Degree requirements:* For master's, comprehensive exam (for some programs); for doctorate, comprehensive exam, thesis/dissertation; for Ed S, comprehensive exam. *Entrance requirements:* For master's, doctorate, and Ed S, GRE General Test, 2 letters of recommendation. Additional exam requirements/recommendations for international students: Required—TOEFL (minimum score 600 paper-based; 250 computer-based; 90 iBT), IELTS (minimum score 7). *Application deadline:* Applications are processed on a rolling basis. Application fee: $60. Electronic applications accepted. *Financial support:* Fellowships with tuition reimbursements, research assistantships with tuition reimbursements, and teaching assistantships with tuition reimbursements available. Financial award application deadline: 1/5; financial award applicants required to submit FAFSA. *Unit head:* Laura Smolkin, Chair, 434-924-0831. *Application contact:* Karen Dwier, Information Contact, 434-924-0831, E-mail: kgd9g@virginia.edu.

University of Virginia, Curry School of Education, Program in Education, Charlottesville, VA 22903. Offers administration and supervision (PhD); applied developmental science (PhD); counselor education (PhD); curriculum and instruction (PhD); early childhood-developmental risk (MT); education evaluation (PhD); educational psychology (PhD); educational research (PhD); elementary (MT, PhD); English education (MT, PhD); foreign language education (MT); higher education (PhD); instructional technology (PhD); kinesiology (MT, PhD); math education (PhD); reading education (PhD); research statistics and evaluation (PhD); school psychology (PhD); science education (PhD); social studies education (MT, PhD); special education (PhD); world languages education (MT). *Students:* 299 full-time (216 women), 60 part-time (33 women); includes 46 minority (18 Black or African American, non-Hispanic/Latino; 17 Asian, non-Hispanic/Latino; 7 Hispanic/Latino; 4 Two or more races, non-Hispanic/Latino), 23 international. Average age 30. 307 applicants, 42% accepted, 80 enrolled. In 2011, 113 master's, 62 doctorates awarded. *Degree requirements:* For master's, comprehensive exam (for some programs), field project; for doctorate, comprehensive exam, thesis/dissertation. *Entrance requirements:* For doctorate, GRE General Test. Additional exam requirements/recommendations for international students: Required—TOEFL (minimum score 600 paper-based; 250 computer-based; 90 iBT), IELTS (minimum score 7). *Application deadline:* Applications are processed on a rolling basis. Application fee: $60. Electronic applications accepted. *Financial support:* Fellowships, research assistantships, and teaching assistantships available. Financial award application deadline: 1/5; financial award applicants required to submit FAFSA. *Unit head:* Robert C. Pianta, Dean, 434-924-3334. *Application contact:* Joanne McNergney, Assistant Dean for Admissions and Student Services, 434-924-3334, E-mail: curry-admissions@virginia.edu.

University of Washington, Graduate School, College of Education, Seattle, WA 98195. Offers curriculum and instruction (M Ed, Ed D, PhD), including educational technology, general curriculum (Ed D, PhD), language, literacy, and culture, mathematics education, multicultural education, reading and language arts education (Ed D), science education, social studies education, teaching and curriculum (M Ed); educational leadership and policy studies (M Ed, Ed D, PhD), including administration (Ed D), educational policy, organization, and leadership (M Ed, PhD), higher education, leadership for learning (Ed D), social and cultural foundations of education (M Ed, PhD); educational psychology (M Ed, PhD), including educational psychology (PhD), human development and cognition (M Ed), learning sciences, measurement, statistics and research design (M Ed), school psychology (M Ed); instructional leadership (M Ed); intercollegiate athletic leadership (M Ed); special education (M Ed, Ed D, PhD), including early childhood special education (M Ed), emotional and behavioral disabilities (M Ed), learning disabilities (M Ed), low-incidence disabilities (M Ed), severe disabilities (M Ed), special education (Ed D, PhD); teacher education (MIT). *Accreditation:* APA. Part-time and evening/weekend programs available. *Degree requirements:* For master's, thesis optional; for doctorate, thesis/dissertation. *Entrance requirements:* For master's and doctorate, GRE General Test, minimum GPA of 3.0. Additional exam requirements/recommendations for international students: Required—TOEFL. Electronic applications accepted. *Faculty research:* School restructuring/effective schools, special education interventions, literacy and writing, technology, school partnerships, teacher preparation.

The University of West Alabama, School of Graduate Studies, College of Education, Departments of Instructional Leadership and Support/Curriculum and Instruction, Livinston, AL 35470. Offers college student development (MSCE); continuing education (MSCE); early childhood education (M Ed); elementary education (M Ed); guidance and counseling (M Ed, MSCE), including continuing education (MSCE), guidance and counseling (M Ed); instructional leadership (M Ed); library media (M Ed); secondary education (MAT); special education (M Ed). *Accreditation:* NCATE. Part-time and evening/weekend programs available. *Faculty:* 37 full-time (19 women), 80 part-time/adjunct (53 women). *Students:* 2,849 full-time (2,450 women), 333 part-time (267 women); includes 1,988 minority (1,947 Black or African American, non-Hispanic/Latino; 17 American Indian or Alaska Native, non-Hispanic/Latino; 3 Asian, non-Hispanic/Latino; 18 Hispanic/Latino; 3 Two or more races, non-Hispanic/Latino), 3 international. In 2011, 944 master's awarded. *Degree requirements:* For master's, comprehensive exam. *Entrance requirements:* For master's, GRE General Test, MAT, minimum GPA of 2.75. Additional exam requirements/recommendations for international students: Required—TOEFL (minimum score 61 computer-based). *Application deadline:* For fall admission, 9/10 priority date for domestic students; for spring admission, 3/24 for domestic students. Applications are processed on a rolling basis. Application fee: $25 ($50 for international students). *Expenses:* Tuition, state resident: full-time $5112; part-time $284 per credit hour. Tuition, nonresident: full-time $10,224; part-time $568 per credit hour. *Required fees:* $180; $40 per semester. One-time fee: $65. Tuition and fees vary according to class time, course load, campus/location and program. *Financial support:* In 2011–12, 35 students received support, including 35 teaching assistantships (averaging $9,600 per year); career-related internships or fieldwork, Federal Work-Study, scholarships/grants, and unspecified assistantships also available. Support available to part-time students. Financial award application deadline: 3/1. *Unit head:* Dr.

Jan Miller, Chair of Instructional Leadership and Support, 205-652-3445, Fax: 205-652-3706, E-mail: jmiller@uwa.edu. *Application contact:* Dr. Kathy Chandler, Dean of Graduate Studies, 205-652-3421, Fax: 205-652-3670, E-mail: kchandler@uwa.edu. Web site: http://www.uwa.edu/ils/.

The University of Western Ontario, Faculty of Graduate Studies, Social Sciences Division, Faculty of Education, Program in Educational Studies, London, ON N6A 5B8, Canada. Offers curriculum studies (M Ed); educational policy studies (M Ed); educational psychology/special education (M Ed). Part-time programs available. *Faculty research:* Reflective practice, gender and schooling, feminist pedagogy, narrative inquiry, second language, multiculturalism in Canada, education and law.

University of West Florida, College of Professional Studies, Department of Applied Science, Technology and Administration, Pensacola, FL 32514-5750. Offers career and technical education (M Ed); curriculum and instruction (Ed S); curriculum and instruction: instructional technology (Ed D); educational leadership (M Ed), including education and training management; instructional technology (M Ed), including educational leadership, instructional technology. *Faculty:* 10 full-time (4 women), 5 part-time/adjunct (2 women). *Students:* 44 full-time (33 women), 188 part-time (113 women); includes 72 minority (38 Black or African American, non-Hispanic/Latino; 4 American Indian or Alaska Native, non-Hispanic/Latino; 4 Asian, non-Hispanic/Latino; 19 Hispanic/Latino; 2 Native Hawaiian or other Pacific Islander, non-Hispanic/Latino; 5 Two or more races, non-Hispanic/Latino), 2 international. Average age 35. 126 applicants, 58% accepted, 49 enrolled. In 2011, 81 degrees awarded. *Entrance requirements:* For master's, GRE, GMAT, or MAT, letter of intent, names of references. Additional exam requirements/recommendations for international students: Required—TOEFL (minimum score 550 paper-based; 213 computer-based). *Application deadline:* For fall admission, 6/1 for domestic and international students; for spring admission, 10/1 for domestic and international students. Applications are processed on a rolling basis. Electronic applications accepted. *Expenses:* Tuition, state resident: full-time $5729; part-time $302 per credit hour. Tuition, nonresident: full-time $20,059; part-time $961 per credit hour. *Required fees:* $1509; $63 per credit hour. *Financial support:* In 2011–12, 17 fellowships (averaging $200 per year), 11 research assistantships with partial tuition reimbursements, 3 teaching assistantships with partial tuition reimbursements were awarded; unspecified assistantships also available. *Unit head:* Dr. Karen Rasmussen, Chair, 850-474-2300, E-mail: krasmuss@uwf.edu. *Application contact:* Terry McCray, Assistant Director of Graduate Admissions, 850-473-7718, Fax: 850-473-7714, E-mail: gradadmissions@uwf.edu. Web site: http://uwf.edu/ect/.

University of West Florida, College of Professional Studies, Department of Research and Applied Studies, Program in Curriculum and Instruction: Specialist in Education, Pensacola, FL 32514-5750. Offers Ed S. *Accreditation:* NCATE. Evening/weekend programs available. *Students:* 4 full-time (1 woman), 6 part-time (4 women); includes 3 minority (all Black or African American, non-Hispanic/Latino), 1 international. Average age 33. 16 applicants, 75% accepted, 5 enrolled. In 2011, 49 Ed Ss awarded. *Entrance requirements:* Additional exam requirements/recommendations for international students: Required—TOEFL (minimum score 550 paper-based; 213 computer-based). *Application deadline:* For fall admission, 6/1 for domestic and international students; for spring admission, 10/1 for domestic and international students. Applications are processed on a rolling basis. Application fee: $30. *Expenses:* Tuition, state resident: full-time $5729; part-time $302 per credit hour. Tuition, nonresident: full-time $20,059; part-time $961 per credit hour. *Required fees:* $1509; $63 per credit hour. *Financial support:* Fellowships, Federal Work-Study, institutionally sponsored loans, scholarships/grants, and tuition waivers (partial) available. Support available to part-time students. Financial award application deadline: 4/15; financial award applicants required to submit FAFSA. *Unit head:* Dr. Karen L. Rasmussen, Interim Chairperson, 850-474-2300, Fax: 850-857-6288, E-mail: krasmuss@uwf.edu. *Application contact:* Terry McCray, Assistant Director of Graduate Admissions, 850-473-7718, Fax: 850-473-7714, E-mail: gradadmissions@uwf.edu.

University of West Florida, College of Professional Studies, School of Education, Program in Curriculum and Instruction, Pensacola, FL 32514-5750. Offers curriculum and instruction: special education (M Ed); elementary education (M Ed); primary education (M Ed). Part-time and evening/weekend programs available. *Students:* 10 full-time (all women), 62 part-time (56 women); includes 16 minority (9 Black or African American, non-Hispanic/Latino; 1 American Indian or Alaska Native, non-Hispanic/Latino; 1 Asian, non-Hispanic/Latino; 3 Hispanic/Latino; 1 Native Hawaiian or other Pacific Islander, non-Hispanic/Latino; 1 Two or more races, non-Hispanic/Latino). Average age 35. 67 applicants, 70% accepted, 37 enrolled. In 2011, 62 master's awarded. *Entrance requirements:* For master's, GRE (minimum score 450 verbal) or MAT (minimum score 396) if bachelor's GPA less than 3.0, state teaching certification; letter of intent; two professional references. Additional exam requirements/recommendations for international students: Required—TOEFL (minimum score 550 paper-based; 213 computer-based). *Application deadline:* For fall admission, 6/1 for domestic and international students; for spring admission, 10/1 for domestic and international students. Applications are processed on a rolling basis. Application fee: $30. *Expenses:* Tuition, state resident: full-time $5729; part-time $302 per credit hour. Tuition, nonresident: full-time $20,059; part-time $961 per credit hour. *Required fees:* $1509; $63 per credit hour. *Financial support:* Career-related internships or fieldwork, Federal Work-Study, scholarships/grants, and tuition waivers (partial) available. Support available to part-time students. Financial award application deadline: 4/15; financial award applicants required to submit FAFSA. *Unit head:* Dr. William H. Evans, Acting Director, 850-474-2892, Fax: 850-474-2844, E-mail: wevans@uwf.edu. *Application contact:* Terry McCray, Assistant Director of Graduate Admissions, 850-473-7718, Fax: 850-473-7714, E-mail: gradadmissions@uwf.edu.

University of Wisconsin–Madison, Graduate School, School of Education, Department of Curriculum and Instruction, Madison, WI 53706-1380. Offers art education (MA); curriculum and instruction (MS, PhD); education and mathematics (MA); French education (MA); German education (MA); music education (MS); science education (MS); Spanish education (MA). *Accreditation:* NASM (one or more programs are accredited). *Degree requirements:* For doctorate, thesis/dissertation. Application fee: $56. *Expenses:* Tuition, state resident: full-time $10,296; part-time $643.51 per credit. Tuition, nonresident: full-time $24,054; part-time $1503.40 per credit. *Required fees:* $70.06 per credit. Tuition and fees vary according to course load, campus/location, program and reciprocity agreements. *Financial support:* Project assistantships available. *Unit head:* Dr. John Rudolph, Chair, 608-263-4600, E-mail: jlrudolp@wisc.edu. *Application contact:* 608-262-2433, Fax: 608-262-5134, E-mail: gradadmiss@mail.bascom.wisc.edu. Web site: http://www.education.wisc.edu/ci.

University of Wisconsin–Milwaukee, Graduate School, School of Education, Department of Curriculum and Instruction, Milwaukee, WI 53201-0413. Offers curriculum planning and instruction improvement (MS); early childhood education (MS); elementary education (MS); junior high/middle school education (MS); reading education (MS); secondary education (MS); teaching in an urban setting (MS). Part-time programs available. *Faculty:* 18 full-time (13 women). *Students:* 29 full-time (23 women), 54 part-time (44 women); includes 21 minority (10 Black or African American, non-Hispanic/Latino; 4 Asian, non-Hispanic/Latino; 3 Hispanic/Latino; 4 Two or more races, non-Hispanic/Latino). Average age 32. 43 applicants, 65% accepted, 13 enrolled. In 2011, 23 degrees awarded. *Degree requirements:* For master's, thesis or alternative. *Entrance requirements:* Additional exam requirements/recommendations for international students: Required—TOEFL (minimum score 550 paper-based; 79 iBT), IELTS (minimum score 6.5). *Application deadline:* For fall admission, 1/1 priority date for domestic students; for spring admission, 9/1 for domestic students. Applications are processed on a rolling basis. Application fee: $56 ($96 for international students). Electronic applications accepted. One-time fee: $506.10 full-time. Tuition and fees vary according to course load and reciprocity agreements. *Financial support:* In 2011–12, 1 fellowship was awarded; research assistantships, teaching assistantships, career-related internships or fieldwork, health care benefits, unspecified assistantships, and project assistantships also available. Support available to part-time students. Financial award application deadline: 4/15; financial award applicants required to submit FAFSA. *Total annual research expenditures:* $21,843. *Unit head:* Hope Longwell-Grice, Department Chair, 414-229-3059, Fax: 414-229-5571, E-mail: hope@uwm.edu. *Application contact:* General Information Contact, 414-229-4982, Fax: 414-229-6967, E-mail: gradschool@uwm.edu. Web site: http://www.uwm.edu/SOE/.

University of Wisconsin–Milwaukee, Graduate School, School of Education, Program in Urban Education, Milwaukee, WI 53201-0413. Offers adult and continuing education (PhD); curriculum and instruction (PhD); educational administration (PhD); educational and media technology (PhD); educational psychology (PhD); multicultural studies (PhD); social foundations of education (PhD). *Students:* 65 full-time (45 women), 37 part-time (25 women); includes 39 minority (18 Black or African American, non-Hispanic/Latino; 1 American Indian or Alaska Native, non-Hispanic/Latino; 6 Asian, non-Hispanic/Latino; 6 Hispanic/Latino; 8 Two or more races, non-Hispanic/Latino), 5 international. Average age 41. 26 applicants, 62% accepted, 2 enrolled. In 2011, 13 degrees awarded. *Degree requirements:* For doctorate, comprehensive exam, thesis/dissertation. *Entrance requirements:* For doctorate, GRE General Test, minimum undergraduate GPA of 2.85, graduate 3.5. Additional exam requirements/recommendations for international students: Required—TOEFL (minimum score 550 paper-based; 79 iBT), IELTS (minimum score 6.5). *Application deadline:* For fall admission, 1/1 priority date for domestic students; for spring admission, 9/1 for domestic students. Applications are processed on a rolling basis. Application fee: $56 ($96 for international students). Electronic applications accepted. One-time fee: $506.10 full-time. Tuition and fees vary according to course load and reciprocity agreements. *Financial support:* In 2011–12, 11 fellowships, 1 teaching assistantship were awarded; research assistantships, career-related internships or fieldwork, health care benefits, unspecified assistantships, and project assistantships also available. Support available to part-time students. Financial award application deadline: 4/15; financial award applicants required to submit FAFSA. *Unit head:* Larry Martin, Representative, 414-229-4729, Fax: 414-229-2920, E-mail: lmartin@uwm.edu. *Application contact:* General Information Contact, 414-229-4982, Fax: 414-229-6967, E-mail: gradschool@uwm.edu. Web site: http://www.uwm.edu/Dept/UrbanEd/.

University of Wisconsin–Oshkosh, Graduate Studies, College of Education and Human Services, Department of Curriculum and Instruction, Oshkosh, WI 54901. Offers MSE. Part-time and evening/weekend programs available. *Degree requirements:* For master's, thesis or alternative, seminar paper. *Entrance requirements:* For master's, teaching license, letters of recommendation. Additional exam requirements/recommendations for international students: Required—TOEFL (minimum score 550 paper-based; 213 computer-based; 79 iBT). Electronic applications accepted. *Faculty research:* Early childhood, middle school teaching, literacy, elementary teaching, bilingual education.

University of Wisconsin–Superior, Graduate Division, Department of Teacher Education, Program in Instruction, Superior, WI 54880-4500. Offers MSE. Part-time and evening/weekend programs available. *Degree requirements:* For master's, comprehensive exam, thesis or alternative, research project. *Entrance requirements:* For master's, minimum GPA of 2.75, teaching certificate.

University of Wisconsin–Whitewater, School of Graduate Studies, College of Education and Professional Studies, Department of Curriculum and Instruction, Whitewater, WI 53190-1790. Offers professional development (MS), including bilingual education, challenging advanced learners, curriculum and instruction, educational leadership, health, human performance and recreation, health, physical education and coaching, information technologies and libraries, reading. *Accreditation:* NCATE. Part-time and evening/weekend programs available. Postbaccalaureate distance learning degree programs offered. *Students:* 25 full-time (12 women), 68 part-time (51 women); includes 26 minority (15 Black or African American, non-Hispanic/Latino; 3 Asian, non-Hispanic/Latino; 8 Hispanic/Latino). Average age 33. 29 applicants, 86% accepted, 16 enrolled. In 2011, 44 master's awarded. *Degree requirements:* For master's, thesis or integrated project. *Entrance requirements:* Additional exam requirements/recommendations for international students: Required—TOEFL (minimum score 550 paper-based; 213 computer-based; 80 iBT), IELTS (minimum score 6). *Application deadline:* For fall admission, 7/15 priority date for domestic students, 7/15 for international students; for spring admission, 12/1 priority date for domestic students, 12/1 for international students. Applications are processed on a rolling basis. Application fee: $56. Electronic applications accepted. *Expenses:* Tuition, state resident: full-time $4088. Tuition, nonresident: full-time $8817. Tuition and fees vary according to program. *Financial support:* Research assistantships, Federal Work-Study, unspecified assistantships, and out-of-state fee waivers available. Support available to part-time students. Financial award application deadline: 3/15; financial award applicants required to submit FAFSA. *Faculty research:* Hybrid of exercise physiology and psychology; gender equity; education, pedagogy, and technology; comprehensive school health education. *Unit head:* Dr. John Zbikowski, Coordinator, 262-472-4860, Fax: 262-472-1988, E-mail: zbikowskij@uww.edu. *Application contact:* Sally A. Lange, School of Graduate Studies, 262-472-1006, Fax: 262-472-5027, E-mail: gradschl@uww.edu.

University of Wyoming, College of Education, Programs in Curriculum and Instruction, Laramie, WY 82070. Offers MA, Ed D, PhD. Part-time programs available. Postbaccalaureate distance learning degree programs offered. Terminal master's awarded for partial completion of doctoral program. *Degree requirements:* For master's, comprehensive exam, thesis; for doctorate, comprehensive exam, thesis/dissertation. *Entrance requirements:* For master's, minimum GPA of 3.0, 3 letters of reference, writing samples; for doctorate, accredited master's degree, 3 letters of reference, 3 years of teaching experience, writing sample. Additional exam requirements/recommendations for international students: Required—TOEFL (minimum score 525 paper-based). *Faculty research:* Teaching and learning teacher education, multi-cultural education, early childhood, discipline-specific pedagogy.

Utah State University, School of Graduate Studies, Emma Eccles Jones College of Education and Human Services, Doctoral Program in Education, Logan, UT 84322. Offers business information systems (Ed D, PhD); curriculum and instruction (Ed D, PhD); research and evaluation (PhD). *Degree requirements:* For doctorate, comprehensive exam, thesis/dissertation. *Entrance requirements:* For doctorate, GRE General Test, minimum GPA of 3.0, master's degree. Additional exam requirements/recommendations for international students: Required—TOEFL. Electronic applications accepted. *Faculty research:* Language and literacy development, math and science education, instructional technology, hearing problems/deafness, domestic violence and animal abuse.

Virginia Polytechnic Institute and State University, Graduate School, College of Liberal Arts and Human Sciences, School of Education, Department of Teaching and Learning, Blacksburg, VA 24061. Offers career and technical education (MS Ed, Ed D, PhD, Ed S); cognition and education (Certificate); counselor education (MA, PhD); curriculum and instruction (MA Ed, Ed D, PhD, Ed S); educational research, evaluation (PhD); higher education administration (Certificate); integrative STEM education (Certificate). *Accreditation:* NCATE. Postbaccalaureate distance learning degree programs offered (no on-campus study). Terminal master's awarded for partial completion of doctoral program. *Degree requirements:* For master's, comprehensive exam (for some programs), thesis (for some programs); for doctorate, comprehensive exam (for some programs), thesis/dissertation (for some programs). *Entrance requirements:* For master's and doctorate, GRE. Additional exam requirements/ recommendations for international students: Required—TOEFL (minimum score 550 paper-based; 213 computer-based). *Application deadline:* For fall admission, 7/1 for domestic and international students; for spring admission, 12/1 for domestic and international students. Applications are processed on a rolling basis. Application fee: $65. Electronic applications accepted. *Expenses:* Tuition, state resident: full-time $10,048; part-time $558.25 per credit hour. Tuition, nonresident: full-time $19,497; part-time $1083.25 per credit hour. *Required fees:* $405 per semester. Tuition and fees vary according to course load, campus/location and program. *Financial support:* Career-related internships or fieldwork, Federal Work-Study, scholarships/grants, health care benefits, and unspecified assistantships available. Financial award application deadline: 1/15. *Faculty research:* Instructional technology, teacher evaluation, school change, literacy, teaching strategies. *Unit head:* Dr. Daisy L. Stewart, Unit Head, 540-231-8180, Fax: 540-231-3717, E-mail: daisys@vt.edu. *Application contact:* Daisy Stewart, Contact, 540-231-8180, Fax: 540-231-3717, E-mail: daisys@vt.edu. Web site: http://www.soe.vt.edu/.

Walden University, Graduate Programs, Richard W. Riley College of Education and Leadership, Minneapolis, MN 55401. Offers administrator leadership for teaching and learning (Ed D, Ed S); adult education (Ed D, Ed S); adult learning (MS, Postbaccalaureate Certificate), including developmental education (MS), online teaching (MS), teaching adults English as a second language (MS), training and performance management (MS); college teaching and learning (Ed D, Ed S, Postbaccalaureate Certificate); curriculum, instruction and assessment (Ed D, Postbaccalaureate Certificate); curriculum, instruction, and professional development (Ed S); developmental education (Postbaccalaureate Certificate); early childhood administration, management, and leadership (Postbaccalaureate Certificate); early childhood education (birth-grade 3) (MAT); early childhood public policy and advocacy (Postbaccalaureate Certificate); early childhood studies (MS), including administration, management and leadership, early childhood public policy and advocacy, teaching adults in the early childhood field, teaching and diversity; education (MS, PhD), including adolescent literacy and technology (grades 6-12) (MS), adult education leadership (PhD), assessment, evaluation, and accountability (PhD), community college leadership (PhD), curriculum, instruction, and assessment, early childhood education (PhD), educational technology (PhD), elementary reading and literacy (MS), elementary reading and mathematics (MS), general program, global and comparative education (PhD), higher education (PhD), integrating technology in the classroom (MS), K-12 educational leadership (PhD), leadership, policy and change (PhD), learning, instruction and innovation (PhD), literacy and learning in the content areas (MS), mathematics (grades 6-8) (MS), mathematics (grades K-5) (MS), middle level education (grades 5-8) (MS), professional development (MS), science (grades K-8) (MS), self-designed (PhD), special education (PhD), special education (non-licensure) (MS), teacher leadership (grades K-12) (MS), teaching English language learners (grades K-12) (MS); educational leadership and administration (principal preparation) (Ed S); educational technology (Ed S); elementary reading and literacy (Postbaccalaureate Certificate); engaging culturally diverse learners (Postbaccalaureate Certificate); enrollment management and institutional marketing (Postbaccalaureate Certificate); higher education (MS), including college teaching and learning, enrollment management and institutional planning, global higher education, leadership for student success, online and distance learning; higher education leadership (Ed D); instructional design (Postbaccalaureate Certificate); instructional design and technology (MS), including general program (MS, PhD), online learning, training and performance improvement; integrating technology in the classroom (Postbaccalaureate Certificate); online teaching for adult learners (Postbaccalaureate Certificate); professional development (Postbaccalaureate Certificate); reading and literacy leadership (Ed D); science K-8 (Postbaccalaureate Certificate); special education (Ed D, Ed S); special education: emotional/behavioral disorders (K-12) (MAT); special education: learning disabilities (K-12) (MAT); teacher leadership (Ed D, Ed S, Postbaccalaureate Certificate); training and performance management (Postbaccalaureate Certificate). Part-time and evening/ weekend programs available. Postbaccalaureate distance learning degree programs offered (minimal on-campus study). *Faculty:* 71 full-time (48 women), 853 part-time/ adjunct (585 women). *Students:* 11,326 full-time (9,212 women), 2,148 part-time (1,795 women); includes 5,346 minority (4,403 Black or African American, non-Hispanic/Latino; 76 American Indian or Alaska Native, non-Hispanic/Latino; 140 Asian, non-Hispanic/ Latino; 561 Hispanic/Latino; 21 Native Hawaiian or other Pacific Islander, non-Hispanic/ Latino; 145 Two or more races, non-Hispanic/Latino), 322 international. Average age 39. In 2011, 3,477 master's, 318 doctorates, 471 other advanced degrees awarded. *Degree requirements:* For doctorate, thesis/dissertation (for some programs), residency; for other advanced degree, residency (for some programs). *Entrance requirements:* For master's, bachelor's degree or equivalent in related field; minimum GPA of 2.5; official transcripts; goal statement; access to computer and Internet; for doctorate, master's degree or equivalent in related field; minimum GPA of 3.0; official transcripts; three years' related professional/academic experience (preferred); access to computer and Internet; for other advanced degree, master's degree or equivalent in related field; minimum GPA of 3.0; 3 years related professional/academic experience (preferred); access to computer and Internet (Ed S). Additional exam requirements/ recommendations for international students: Required—TOEFL (minimum score 550 paper-based; 213 computer-based), IELTS (minimum score 6.5), or Michigan English Language Assessment Battery (minimum score 82). *Application deadline:* Applications are processed on a rolling basis. Application fee: $50. Electronic applications accepted. *Financial support:* Federal Work-Study, scholarships/grants, unspecified assistantships, and family tuition reduction, active duty/veteran tuition reduction, group tuition reduction, interest-free payment plans, employee tuition reduction available. Support available to part-time students. Financial award applicants required to submit FAFSA. *Unit head:* Dr. Kate Steffens, Dean, 800-925-3368. *Application contact:* Jennifer Hall, Vice President of Enrollment Management, 866-4-WALDEN, E-mail: info@waldenu.edu. Web site: http://www.waldenu.edu/Colleges-and-Schools/College-of-Education-and-Leadership.htm.

Walla Walla University, Graduate School, School of Education and Psychology, College Place, WA 99324-1198. Offers counseling psychology (MA); curriculum and instruction (M Ed, MA, MAT); educational leadership (M Ed, MA, MAT); literacy instruction (M Ed, MA, MAT); students at risk (M Ed, MA, MAT); teaching (MAT). Part-time programs available. *Entrance requirements:* For master's, GRE General Test, minimum GPA of 2.75. Additional exam requirements/recommendations for international students: Required—TOEFL (minimum score 550 paper-based; 213 computer-based; 79 iBT). Electronic applications accepted. *Faculty research:* Admissions/retention, instructional psychology, moral development, teaching of reading.

Washburn University, College of Arts and Sciences, Department of Education, Topeka, KS 66621. Offers curriculum and instruction (M Ed); educational leadership (M Ed); reading (M Ed); special education (M Ed). *Accreditation:* NCATE. Part-time programs available. *Faculty:* 6 full-time (3 women), 1 (woman) part-time/adjunct. *Students:* 2 full-time (both women), 26 part-time (16 women). Average age 36. In 2011, 17 master's awarded. *Degree requirements:* For master's, comprehensive exam, thesis or alternative, portfolio, comprehensive paper, or action research project. *Entrance requirements:* For master's, department graduate admissions test, GRE General Test, or MAT, minimum GPA of 3.0 in graduate coursework or last 60 hours of undergraduate coursework. Additional exam requirements/recommendations for international students: Required—TOEFL (minimum score 550 paper-based; 80 iBT). *Application deadline:* For fall admission, 8/1 for domestic and international students; for spring admission, 11/1 for domestic and international students. Applications are processed on a rolling basis. *Expenses:* Tuition, state resident: full-time $5346; part-time $297 per credit hour. Tuition, nonresident: full-time $10,908; part-time $606 per credit hour. *Required fees:* $86; $43 per semester. *Financial support:* Federal Work-Study, institutionally sponsored loans, and scholarships/grants available. Support available to part-time students. Financial award applicants required to submit FAFSA. *Faculty research:* Reading/literature/literacy, foundations, educational administration/leadership, special education, diversity. *Unit head:* Dr. Judith McConnell-Farmer, Interim Chairperson, 785-670-1472, Fax: 785-670-1046, E-mail: judy.mcconnell-farmer@washburn.edu. *Application contact:* Tara Porter, Licensure Officer, 785-670-1434, Fax: 785-670-1046, E-mail: tara.porter@washburn.edu. Web site: http://www.washburn.edu/academics/college-schools/arts-sciences/departments/education/index.html.

Washington State University, Graduate School, College of Education, Department of Teaching and Learning, Pullman, WA 99164. Offers curriculum and instruction (Ed D, PhD); diverse languages (M Ed, MA); elementary education (M Ed, MA, MIT); exercise science (MS); literacy education (M Ed, MA, PhD); math education (PhD); secondary education (M Ed, MA). *Accreditation:* NCATE. *Faculty:* 20. *Students:* 79 full-time (51 women), 40 part-time (31 women); includes 24 minority (3 Black or African American, non-Hispanic/Latino; 5 Asian, non-Hispanic/Latino; 13 Hispanic/Latino; 1 Native Hawaiian or other Pacific Islander, non-Hispanic/Latino; 2 Two or more races, non-Hispanic/Latino), 43 international. Average age 34. 106 applicants, 47% accepted, 43 enrolled. In 2011, 34 master's, 3 doctorates awarded. *Degree requirements:* For master's, comprehensive exam (for some programs), thesis (for some programs), oral or written exam; for doctorate, comprehensive exam, thesis/dissertation, oral and written exam. *Entrance requirements:* For master's and doctorate, GRE General Test, minimum GPA of 3.0, 3 letters of recommendation. Additional exam requirements/ recommendations for international students: Required—TOEFL. *Application deadline:* For fall admission, 2/1 for domestic students, 3/1 for international students; for spring admission, 9/1 for domestic students, 7/1 for international students. Applications are processed on a rolling basis. Application fee: $75. *Financial support:* In 2011–12, 130 teaching assistantships with partial tuition reimbursements (averaging $18,204 per year) were awarded; career-related internships or fieldwork, Federal Work-Study, institutionally sponsored loans, tuition waivers (partial), unspecified assistantships, and staff assistantships, teaching associateships also available. Financial award application deadline: 4/1. *Faculty research:* Evolution of middle school education, issues in special education, computer-assisted language learning. *Total annual research expenditures:* $324,000. *Unit head:* Dr. Dawn Shinew, Interim Chair, 509-335-5027, E-mail: dshinew@wsu.edu. *Application contact:* Graduate School Admissions, 800-GRADWSU, Fax: 509-335-1949, E-mail: gradsch@wsu.edu. Web site: http://www.educ.wsu.edu/TL/overview.htm.

Wayne State College, School of Education and Counseling, Department of Educational Foundations and Leadership, Program in Curriculum and Instruction, Wayne, NE 68787. Offers alternative education (MSE); business and information technology education (MSE); communication arts education (MSE); early childhood education (MSE); elementary education (MSE); English as a second language (MSE); English education (MSE); family and consumer sciences education (MSE); industrial technology and vocational education (MSE); learning communities (MSE); mathematics education (MSE); music education (MSE); science education (MSE); social science education (MSE). *Accreditation:* NCATE. Part-time and evening/weekend programs available. *Degree requirements:* For master's, comprehensive exam, thesis optional. *Entrance requirements:* For master's, GRE General Test. Additional exam requirements/ recommendations for international students: Required—TOEFL (minimum score 550 paper-based; 213 computer-based).

Wayne State University, College of Education, Division of Administrative and Organizational Studies, Detroit, MI 48202. Offers college and university teaching (Certificate); educational leadership (M Ed); educational leadership and policy studies (Ed D, PhD); general administration and supervision (Ed S); instructional technology (M Ed, Ed D, PhD, Ed S); online teaching (Certificate); secondary curriculum and instruction (Ed S). *Students:* 86 full-time (62 women), 261 part-time (172 women); includes 171 minority (145 Black or African American, non-Hispanic/Latino; 1 American Indian or Alaska Native, non-Hispanic/Latino; 8 Asian, non-Hispanic/Latino; 16 Hispanic/ Latino; 1 Two or more races, non-Hispanic/Latino), 8 international. Average age 39. 122 applicants, 40% accepted, 28 enrolled. In 2011, 73 master's, 9 doctorates, 50 other advanced degrees awarded. *Degree requirements:* For doctorate, thesis/dissertation. *Entrance requirements:* For doctorate, GRE or MAT, interview; autobiography or curriculum vitae; references; master's degree; minimum undergraduate GPA of 3.0, graduate 3.75; 3 years relevant experience; foundational course work; for other advanced degree, minimum GPA of 3.4. Additional exam requirements/ recommendations for international students: Required—TOEFL (minimum score 550 paper-based; 213 computer-based), TWE (minimum score 5.5). *Application deadline:* For fall admission, 6/1 priority date for domestic students, 5/1 for international students; for winter admission, 10/1 priority date for domestic students, 9/1 for international students; for spring admission, 2/1 priority date for domestic students, 1/1 for international students. Applications are processed on a rolling basis. Application fee: $50. Electronic applications accepted. *Expenses:* Tuition, state resident: part-time $512.85 per credit. Tuition, nonresident: part-time $1132.65 per credit. *Required fees:* $26.60 per credit. $199.65 per semester. Tuition and fees vary according to course load and program. *Financial support:* In 2011–12, 59 students received support, including 1 fellowship with tuition reimbursement available (averaging $17,347 per year), 4 research assistantships with tuition reimbursements available (averaging $15,713 per year); career-related internships or fieldwork, Federal Work-Study, institutionally sponsored loans, scholarships/grants, health care benefits, and unspecified assistantships also available. Support available to part-time students. *Faculty research:* Total quality management, participatory management, administering educational technology, school improvement, principalship. *Total annual research expenditures:* $22,232. *Unit head:* Dr. Alan Hoffman, Interim Assistant Dean, 313-577-5235, E-mail: alanhoffman@wayne.edu. *Application contact:* Janice Green, Assistant Dean, 313-577-1605, E-mail: jwgreen@wayne.edu. Web site: http://coe.wayne.edu/aos/index.php.

Curriculum and Instruction

Wayne State University, College of Education, Division of Teacher Education, Detroit, MI 48202. Offers art education (M Ed), including art therapy; bilingual/bicultural education (M Ed); career and technical education (M Ed); curriculum and instruction (Ed D, PhD, Ed S), including art education (PhD), bilingual education (Ed D, Ed S), bilingual-bicultural education (PhD), career and technical education (MAT, Ed D, PhD, Ed S), early childhood education (MAT, Ed D, PhD, Ed S), elementary education, English as a second language (MAT, Ed D, Ed S), English education (MAT, Ed D, PhD, Ed S), foreign language education (MAT, PhD), K-12 curriculum, mathematics education (MAT, Ed D, PhD, Ed S), science education (MAT, Ed D, PhD, Ed S), secondary education, social studies education (MAT, Ed S), social studies education: secondary (Ed D, PhD); elementary education (MAT), including special education; elementary education (M Ed, MAT), including children's literature (MAT), early childhood education (MAT, Ed D, PhD, Ed S), general elementary education (MAT); elementary or secondary education (MAT), including bilingual/bicultural education, English as a second language (MAT, Ed D, Ed S), mathematics education (MAT, Ed D, PhD, Ed S), science education (MAT, Ed D, PhD, Ed S), social studies education (MAT, Ed S); English education-secondary (M Ed); foreign language education (M Ed); mathematics education (M Ed); reading (M Ed, Ed S); reading, languages and literature (Ed D); science education (M Ed); secondary education (MAT), including art education (K-12), career and technical education (MAT, Ed D, PhD, Ed S), English education (MAT, Ed D, PhD, Ed S), foreign language education (MAT, PhD), kinesiology; social studies education secondary (M Ed); special education (M Ed, Ed D, PhD, Ed S). *Students:* 216 full-time (154 women), 626 part-time (478 women); includes 289 minority (227 Black or African American, non-Hispanic/Latino; 4 American Indian or Alaska Native, non-Hispanic/Latino; 27 Asian, non-Hispanic/Latino; 21 Hispanic/Latino; 1 Native Hawaiian or other Pacific Islander, non-Hispanic/Latino; 9 Two or more races, non-Hispanic/Latino), 14 international. Average age 37. 347 applicants, 37% accepted, 93 enrolled. In 2011, 226 master's, 12 doctorates, 46 other advanced degrees awarded. *Degree requirements:* For master's, thesis (for some programs), thesis, essay or project (for some M Ed programs), professional field experience (for MAT programs); for doctorate, thesis/dissertation. *Entrance requirements:* For master's, Michigan Basic Skills Test (MA in teaching); for doctorate, minimum undergraduate GPA of 3.0, graduate 3.5; interview, curriculum vitae; references. Additional exam requirements/recommendations for international students: Required—TOEFL (minimum score 550 paper-based; 213 computer-based), TWE (minimum score 5.5). *Application deadline:* For fall admission, 6/1 priority date for domestic students, 5/1 for international students; for winter admission, 10/1 priority date for domestic students, 9/1 for international students; for spring admission, 2/1 priority date for domestic students, 1/1 for international students. Applications are processed on a rolling basis. Application fee: $50. Electronic applications accepted. *Expenses:* Tuition, state resident: part-time $512.85 per credit. Tuition, nonresident: part-time $1132.65 per credit. *Required fees:* $26.60 per credit. $199.65 per semester. Tuition and fees vary according to course load and program. *Financial support:* In 2011–12, 42 students received support. Fellowships, research assistantships with tuition reimbursements available, teaching assistantships, scholarships/grants, and unspecified assistantships available. *Faculty research:* Reading and writing literacy and literature. *Total annual research expenditures:* $264,016. *Unit head:* Dr. Craig Roney, Assistant Dean, 313-577-0902, E-mail: rroney@wayne.edu. Web site: http://coe.wayne.edu/ted/index.php.

Weber State University, Jerry and Vickie Moyes College of Education, Program in Curriculum and Instruction, Ogden, UT 84408-1001. Offers M Ed. *Accreditation:* NCATE. Part-time and evening/weekend programs available. *Degree requirements:* For master's, thesis or alternative, project presentation and exam. *Entrance requirements:* For master's, MAT or GRE, minimum GPA of 3.0 in last 90 credits. Additional exam requirements/recommendations for international students: Required—TOEFL (minimum score 550 paper-based; 213 computer-based), American Council on the Teaching of Foreign Languages test. *Faculty research:* Special needs, best practices in education literacy, metacognition.

Western Connecticut State University, Division of Graduate Studies, School of Professional Studies, Department of Education and Educational Psychology, Curriculum Option, Danbury, CT 06810-6885. Offers MS. Part-time programs available. *Faculty:* 2 full-time (0 women). *Students:* 1 (woman) full-time, 20 part-time (15 women); includes 2 minority (both Hispanic/Latino). Average age 34. 11 applicants, 64% accepted, 6 enrolled. In 2011, 18 degrees awarded. *Degree requirements:* For master's, thesis or alternative, thesis research project or 3 extra classes and comprehensive exam, completion of program in 6 years. *Entrance requirements:* For master's, minimum GPA of 2.8 or MAT, teaching certificate in elementary or secondary education. Additional exam requirements/recommendations for international students: Recommended—TOEFL (minimum score 550 paper-based; 213 computer-based; 79 iBT), IELTS (minimum score 6). *Application deadline:* For fall admission, 8/5 priority date for domestic students; for spring admission, 1/5 priority date for domestic students. Applications are processed on a rolling basis. Application fee: $50. Tuition and fees vary according to course level, course load, degree level and program. *Financial support:* Application deadline: 5/1; applicants required to submit FAFSA. *Faculty research:* Instructing various methods of instruction that include class discussions, lectures, independent projects, cooperative learning, experiential learning and field studies, recitals, demonstrations, shows, group projects, and technology-enhanced instruction. *Unit head:* Dr. Adeline Merrill, Graduate Coordinator, 203-837-3267, Fax: 203-837-8413, E-mail: merrilla@wcsu.edu. *Application contact:* Chris Shankle, Associate Director of Graduate Studies, 203-837-9005, Fax: 203-837-8326, E-mail: shanklec@wcsu.edu.

West Texas A&M University, College of Education and Social Sciences, Division of Education, Program in Curriculum and Instruction, Canyon, TX 79016-0001. Offers M Ed. Part-time and evening/weekend programs available. Postbaccalaureate distance learning degree programs offered. *Degree requirements:* For master's, comprehensive exam, thesis optional. *Entrance requirements:* For master's, GRE General Test, 18 semester hours of education course work. Additional exam requirements/recommendations for international students: Required—TOEFL (minimum score 550 paper-based). Electronic applications accepted.

West Virginia University, College of Human Resources and Education, Department of Curriculum and Instruction/Literacy Studies, Morgantown, WV 26506. Offers curriculum and instruction (Ed D); elementary education (MA); reading (MA); secondary education (MA), including higher education curriculum and teaching, secondary education; special education (Ed D), including special education. *Accreditation:* NCATE. Part-time and evening/weekend programs available. *Degree requirements:* For doctorate, comprehensive exam, thesis/dissertation. *Entrance requirements:* For master's, minimum GPA of 2.75; for doctorate, GRE General Test or MAT, 3 letters of recommendation, curriculum vitae. Additional exam requirements/recommendations for international students: Required—TOEFL. *Faculty research:* Teacher education, curriculum development, educational technology, curriculum assessment.

Wichita State University, Graduate School, College of Education, Department of Curriculum and Instruction, Wichita, KS 67260. Offers curriculum and instruction (M Ed); special education (M Ed), including adaptive, early childhood unified (M Ed, MAT), functional, gifted; teaching (MAT), including curriculum and instruction, early childhood unified (M Ed, MAT). *Accreditation:* NCATE. Part-time and evening/weekend programs available. *Entrance requirements:* For master's, MAT, minimum GPA of 2.75. *Expenses:* Tuition, state resident: full-time $4746; part-time $263.65 per credit. Tuition, nonresident: full-time $11,669; part-time $648.30 per credit. *Unit head:* Dr. Janice Ewing, Chairperson, 316-978-3322, E-mail: janice.ewing@wichita.edu. *Application contact:* Dr. Kay Gibson, Graduate Coordinator, 316-978-3322, E-mail: kay.gibson@wichita.edu. Web site: http://www.wichita.edu/.

Wilkes University, College of Graduate and Professional Studies, School of Education, Wilkes-Barre, PA 18766-0002. Offers art and science of teaching (MS Ed); classroom technology (MS Ed); early childhood literacy (MS Ed); educational computing (MS Ed); educational development and strategies (MS Ed); educational leadership (MS Ed); educational technology (Ed D); higher education administration (Ed D); instructional media (MS Ed); instructional technology (MS Ed); K-12 administration (Ed D); online teaching (MS Ed); reading (MS Ed); school business leadership (MS Ed); secondary education (MS Ed), including biology, chemistry, English, history, mathematics; special education (MS Ed); teaching English as a second language (MS Ed); twenty-first century teaching and learning (MS Ed). Part-time and evening/weekend programs available. Postbaccalaureate distance learning degree programs offered (minimal on-campus study). *Students:* 92 full-time (63 women), 2,005 part-time (1,459 women); includes 89 minority (23 Black or African American, non-Hispanic/Latino; 1 American Indian or Alaska Native, non-Hispanic/Latino; 14 Asian, non-Hispanic/Latino; 33 Hispanic/Latino; 1 Native Hawaiian or other Pacific Islander, non-Hispanic/Latino; 17 Two or more races, non-Hispanic/Latino), 6 international. Average age 33. In 2011, 1,150 master's, 3 doctorates awarded. *Entrance requirements:* Additional exam requirements/recommendations for international students: Required—TOEFL (minimum score 550 paper-based; 213 computer-based; 79 iBT). *Application deadline:* Applications are processed on a rolling basis. Application fee: $45. Electronic applications accepted. *Expenses:* Contact institution. *Financial support:* Federal Work-Study and unspecified assistantships available. Financial award application deadline: 3/1; financial award applicants required to submit FAFSA. *Unit head:* Dr. Michael Speziale, Dean, 570-408-4679, Fax: 570-408-4905, E-mail: michael.speziale@wilkes.edu. *Application contact:* Erin Sutzko, Director of Extended Learning, 570-408-4253, Fax: 570-408-7846, E-mail: erin.sutzko@wilkes.edu. Web site: http://www.wilkes.edu/pages/383.asp.

William Woods University, Graduate and Adult Studies, Fulton, MO 65251-1098. Offers administration (Ed S); agriculture (MBA); athletic/activities administration (M Ed); curriculum and instruction (M Ed); curriculum leadership (Ed S); elementary administration (M Ed); health management (MBA); human resources (MBA); principalship (Ed S); secondary administration (M Ed); special education director (M Ed). Evening/weekend programs available. *Degree requirements:* For master's, capstone course (MBA), action research (M Ed); for Ed S, field experience. *Entrance requirements:* For master's, 2 recommendations, resumé, BA/BS; teaching certification (M Ed); course work in economics and accounting (MBA); for Ed S, M Ed, 2 letters of recommendation, resume, teaching certification. Additional exam requirements/recommendations for international students: Required—TOEFL (minimum score 550 paper-based). Electronic applications accepted.

Wright State University, School of Graduate Studies, College of Education and Human Services, Department of Educational Leadership, Program in Advanced Educational Leadership, Dayton, OH 45435. Offers advanced curriculum and instruction (Ed S); higher education-adult education (Ed S); superintendent (Ed S). *Accreditation:* NCATE. *Degree requirements:* For Ed S, thesis. *Entrance requirements:* For degree, GRE General Test, MAT. Additional exam requirements/recommendations for international students: Required—TOEFL.

Wright State University, School of Graduate Studies, College of Education and Human Services, Department of Educational Leadership, Programs in Educational Leadership, Dayton, OH 45435. Offers curriculum and instruction: teacher leader (MA); educational administrative specialist: teacher leader (M Ed); educational administrative specialist: vocational education administration (M Ed, MA); student affairs in higher education-administration (M Ed, MA). *Accreditation:* NCATE. *Degree requirements:* For master's, thesis (for some programs). *Entrance requirements:* For master's, GRE General Test, MAT. Additional exam requirements/recommendations for international students: Required—TOEFL.

Xavier University of Louisiana, Graduate School, Programs in Education, New Orleans, LA 70125-1098. Offers curriculum and instruction (MA); education administration and supervision (MA); guidance and counseling (MA). *Accreditation:* NCATE. Part-time and evening/weekend programs available. *Degree requirements:* For master's, comprehensive exam, thesis or alternative. *Entrance requirements:* For master's, GRE General Test, MAT, minimum GPA of 2.5. Additional exam requirements/recommendations for international students: Required—TOEFL.

Youngstown State University, Graduate School, Beeghly College of Education, Department of Teacher Education, Youngstown, OH 44555-0001. Offers adolescent/young adult education (MS Ed); content area concentration (MS Ed); early childhood education (MS Ed); educational technology (MS Ed); literacy (MS Ed); middle childhood education (MS Ed); special education (MS Ed), including gifted and talented education, special education. *Accreditation:* NCATE. Part-time and evening/weekend programs available. *Degree requirements:* For master's, comprehensive exam. *Entrance requirements:* For master's, GRE, MAT, or teaching certificate; minimum GPA of 2.7. Additional exam requirements/recommendations for international students: Required—TOEFL. *Faculty research:* Multicultural literacy, hands-on mathematics teaching, integrated instruction, reading comprehension, emergent curriculum.

Distance Education Development

American Public University System, AMU/APU Graduate Programs, Charles Town, WV 25414. Offers accounting (MBA, MS); administration and supervision (M Ed); criminal justice (MA); emergency and disaster management (MA); entrepreneurship (MBA); environmental policy and management (MS), including environmental planning, environmental sustainability, fish and wildlife management, general (MA, MS), global environmental management; finance (MBA); general (MBA); global business management (MBA); guidance and counseling (M Ed); history (MA), including American history, ancient and classical history, European history, global history, military and diplomatic history, public history; homeland security (MA); homeland security resource allocation (MBA); humanities (MA); information technology (MS), including digital forensics, enterprise software development, information assurance and security, IT project management; information technology management (MBA); intelligence studies (MA), including criminal intelligence, general (MA, MS), homeland security, intelligence analysis, intelligence collection, intelligence operations, terrorism studies; international relations and conflict resolution (MA), including comparative and security issues, conflict resolution, international and transnational security issues, peacekeeping; legal studies (MA); management (MA), including defense management, general (MA, MS), human resource management, organizational leadership, public administration, reverse logistics, strategic consulting; marketing (MBA); military history (MA), including American military history, American revolution, civil war, war since 1946, World War II; military studies (MA), including air warfare, asymmetrical warfare, joint warfare, land warfare, naval warfare, strategic leadership; national security studies (MA), including general (MA, MS), homeland security, regional security studies, security and intelligence analysis, terrorism studies; nonprofit management (MBA); political science (MA), including American politics and government, comparative government and development, public policy; psychology (MA); public administration (MA, MPA), including disaster management (MPA), environmental policy (MA), health policy (MPA), human resources (MPA), national security (MPA), organizational management (MPA), security management (MPA); public health (MA, MPH), including emergency management (MPH), environmental health (MPH), public administration (MA); reverse logistics management (MA); security management (MA); space studies (MS), including aerospace science, planetary science; sports and health sciences (MS); sports management (MS), including coaching theory and strategy, sports administration; teaching (M Ed), including curriculum and instruction for elementary teachers, elementary, elementary reading, English language learners, instructional leadership, online learning, secondary social sciences, special education; transportation and logistics management (MA), including maritime engineering management. Programs offered via distance learning only. Part-time and evening/weekend programs available. Postbaccalaureate distance learning degree programs offered (no on-campus study). *Faculty:* 445 full-time (241 women), 1,360 part-time/adjunct (617 women). *Students:* 688 full-time (338 women), 10,168 part-time (3,706 women); includes 3,130 minority (1,007 Black or African American, non-Hispanic/Latino; 103 American Indian or Alaska Native, non-Hispanic/Latino; 825 Asian, non-Hispanic/Latino; 810 Hispanic/Latino; 51 Native Hawaiian or other Pacific Islander, non-Hispanic/Latino; 334 Two or more races, non-Hispanic/Latino), 134 international. Average age 35. In 2011, 2,386 master's awarded. *Degree requirements:* For master's, comprehensive exam or practicum. *Entrance requirements:* For master's, official transcript showing earned bachelor's degree from institution accredited by recognized accrediting body. Additional exam requirements/recommendations for international students: Required—TOEFL (minimum score 550 paper-based; 213 computer-based), IELTS (minimum score 6.5). *Application deadline:* Applications are processed on a rolling basis. Application fee: $0. Electronic applications accepted. *Expenses: Tuition:* Part-time $325 per credit hour. *Financial support:* Applicants required to submit FAFSA. *Faculty research:* Military history, criminal justice, management performance, national security. *Unit head:* Dr. Karan Powell, Executive Vice President and Provost, 877-468-6268, Fax: 304-724-3780. *Application contact:* Terry Grant, Vice President of Enrollment Management, 877-468-6268, Fax: 304-724-3780, E-mail: info@apus.edu. Web site: http://www.apus.edu.

Athabasca University, Centre for Distance Education, Athabasca, AB T9S 3A3, Canada. Offers distance education (MDE); distance education technology (Advanced Diploma). Part-time programs available. Postbaccalaureate distance learning degree programs offered (no on-campus study). *Degree requirements:* For master's, thesis optional. *Entrance requirements:* For master's, 3 or 4 year baccalaureate degree. Electronic applications accepted. *Expenses:* Contact institution. *Faculty research:* Role development, interaction, educational technology, and communities of practice in distance education; instructional design.

Barry University, School of Education, Graduate Certificate Programs, Miami Shores, FL 33161-6695. Offers advanced teaching and learning with technology (Certificate); distance education (Certificate); higher education technology integration (Certificate); human resources: not for profit and religious organizations (Certificate); K-12 technology integration (Certificate).

California State University, East Bay, Office of Academic Programs and Graduate Studies, College of Education and Allied Studies, Department of Teacher Education, Hayward, CA 94542-3000. Offers education (MS), including curriculum, early childhood education, educational technology leadership, online teaching and learning, reading instruction. Postbaccalaureate distance learning degree programs offered. *Faculty:* 5 full-time (4 women), 2 part-time/adjunct (both women). *Students:* 64 full-time (53 women), 55 part-time (39 women); includes 50 minority (14 Black or African American, non-Hispanic/Latino; 17 Asian, non-Hispanic/Latino; 15 Hispanic/Latino; 4 Two or more races, non-Hispanic/Latino), 3 international. Average age 35. 98 applicants, 69% accepted, 30 enrolled. In 2011, 149 master's awarded. *Degree requirements:* For master's, project or thesis. *Entrance requirements:* For master's, minimum GPA of 3.0 in field, 2.5 overall; teaching experience; baccalaureate degree; 3 letters of recommendation. Additional exam requirements/recommendations for international students: Required—TOEFL (minimum score 550 paper-based; 213 computer-based), IELTS. *Application deadline:* For fall admission, 6/30 for domestic and international students. Application fee: $55. Electronic applications accepted. *Expenses:* Tuition, state resident: full-time $6738; part-time $1302 per quarter. Tuition, nonresident: full-time $12,690; part-time $2294 per quarter. *Required fees:* $449 per quarter. Tuition and fees vary according to degree level, program and reciprocity agreements. *Financial support:* Career-related internships or fieldwork, Federal Work-Study, and institutionally sponsored loans available. Support available to part-time students. Financial award application deadline: 3/2; financial award applicants required to submit FAFSA. *Faculty research:* Online, pedagogy, writing, learning, teaching. *Unit head:* Dr. Jeanette Bicais, Chair, 510-885-3027, Fax: 510-885-4632, E-mail: jeanette.bicais@csueastbay.edu. *Application contact:* Prof. Valerie Helgren-Lempesis, Education Graduate Advisor, 510-885-3006, Fax: 510-885-4632, E-mail: valerie.lempesis@csueastbay.edu. Web site: http://www20.csueastbay.edu/ceas/departments/ted/index.html.

Colorado Christian University, Program in Curriculum and Instruction, Lakewood, CO 80226. Offers corporate education (MACI); early childhood educator (MACI); elementary educator (MACI); instructional technology (MACI); master educator (MACI); online course developer (MACI); online teaching and learning (MACI); special education generalist (MACI). Part-time and evening/weekend programs available. *Degree requirements:* For master's, thesis optional, practicum. *Entrance requirements:* For master's, interviews, letters of recommendation. Additional exam requirements/recommendations for international students: Required—TOEFL. Electronic applications accepted. *Expenses:* Contact institution.

Dallas Baptist University, Dorothy M. Bush College of Education, Teaching Program, Dallas, TX 75211-9299. Offers all-level (MAT); distance learning (MAT); elementary (MAT); English as a second language (MAT); Montessori (MAT); multisensory (MAT); secondary (MAT). Part-time and evening/weekend programs available. *Entrance requirements:* For master's, GRE General Test, minimum GPA of 3.0. Additional exam requirements/recommendations for international students: Required—TOEFL, IELTS. *Application deadline:* Applications are processed on a rolling basis. Application fee: $25. Electronic applications accepted. *Expenses: Tuition:* Full-time $12,060; part-time $670 per credit hour. *Required fees:* $100; $50 per semester. *Financial support:* Federal Work-Study, institutionally sponsored loans, scholarships/grants, and tuition waivers (full and partial) available. Support available to part-time students. Financial award applicants required to submit FAFSA. *Unit head:* Dara Owen, Acting Director, 214-333-5413, Fax: 214-333-5551, E-mail: graduate@dbu.edu. *Application contact:* Kit P. Montgomery, Director of Graduate Programs, 214-333-5242, Fax: 214-333-5579, E-mail: graduate@dbu.edu. Web site: http://www3.dbu.edu/graduate/mat.asp.

East Carolina University, Graduate School, College of Education, Department of Mathematics, Science, and Instructional Technology Education, Greenville, NC 27858-4353. Offers computer-based instruction (Certificate); distance learning and administration (Certificate); instructional technology (MA Ed, MS); mathematics (MA Ed); performance improvement (Certificate); science education (MA, MA Ed); special endorsement in computer education (Certificate). Part-time and evening/weekend programs available. *Degree requirements:* For master's, comprehensive exam, thesis optional. *Entrance requirements:* For master's, GRE General Test or MAT, interview, minimum GPA of 2.5, bachelor's degree in related field, teaching license (MA Ed). Additional exam requirements/recommendations for international students: Required—TOEFL. *Application deadline:* For fall admission, 6/1 priority date for domestic students. Applications are processed on a rolling basis. Application fee: $50. *Expenses:* Tuition, state resident: full-time $3557; part-time $444.63 per semester hour. Tuition, nonresident: full-time $14,351; part-time $1793.88 per semester hour. *Required fees:* $2016; $252 per semester hour. Part-time tuition and fees vary according to course load, campus/location and program. *Financial support:* Research assistantships, teaching assistantships, and Federal Work-Study available. Support available to part-time students. Financial award application deadline: 6/1. *Unit head:* Susan Ganter, Chair, 252-328-9353, E-mail: ganters@ecu.edu. *Application contact:* Dean of Graduate School, 252-328-6012, Fax: 252-328-6071, E-mail: gradschool@ecu.edu.

Endicott College, Van Loan School of Graduate and Professional Studies, Program in Integrative Learning, Beverly, MA 01915-2096. Offers M Ed. Part-time and evening/weekend programs available. Postbaccalaureate distance learning degree programs offered. *Faculty:* 2 full-time (1 woman). *Students:* 8 full-time (5 women). Average age 40. 2 applicants, 100% accepted, 2 enrolled. In 2011, 5 master's awarded. *Degree requirements:* For master's, thesis. *Entrance requirements:* Additional exam requirements/recommendations for international students: Required—TOEFL. *Application deadline:* Applications are processed on a rolling basis. Application fee: $50. *Expenses:* Contact institution. *Financial support:* Tuition waivers (partial) available. Financial award applicants required to submit FAFSA. *Unit head:* Enid E. Larsen, Assistant Dean of Academic Programs, 978-232-2198, Fax: 978-232-3000, E-mail: elarsen@endicott.edu. *Application contact:* Dr. Phil Snow Gang, Dean, 406-387-5107, Fax: 413-778-9644, E-mail: ties@endicott.edu.

Fairmont State University, Programs in Education, Fairmont, WV 26554. Offers digital media, new literacies and learning (M Ed); education (MAT); exercise science, fitness and wellness (M Ed); leadership studies (M Ed); online learning (M Ed); professional studies (M Ed); reading (M Ed); special education (M Ed). *Accreditation:* NCATE. Part-time and evening/weekend programs available. Postbaccalaureate distance learning degree programs offered. *Faculty:* 16 part-time/adjunct (10 women). *Students:* 103 full-time (72 women), 142 part-time (103 women); includes 11 minority (2 Black or African American, non-Hispanic/Latino; 1 American Indian or Alaska Native, non-Hispanic/Latino; 6 Hispanic/Latino; 2 Two or more races, non-Hispanic/Latino), 2 international. Average age 33. 71 applicants, 85% accepted. In 2011, 58 master's awarded. *Entrance requirements:* For master's, GRE. *Application deadline:* For fall admission, 5/1 for domestic and international students. Applications are processed on a rolling basis. Application fee: $40. *Expenses:* Tuition, state resident: full-time $5900. Tuition, nonresident: full-time $12,596. *Unit head:* Dr. Van O. Dempsey, III, Dean, School of Education, 304-367-4241, Fax: 304-367-4599, E-mail: vdempsey@fairmontstate.edu. Web site: http://www.fairmontstate.edu/graduatestudies/default.asp.

Florida State University, The Graduate School, College of Education, Department of Educational Psychology and Learning Systems, Program in Instructional Systems, Tallahassee, FL 32306. Offers instructional systems (MS, PhD, Ed S); open and distance learning (MS); performance improvement and human resources (MS). *Faculty:* 6 full-time (4 women), 1 (woman) part-time/adjunct. *Students:* 68 full-time (47 women), 78 part-time (48 women); includes 19 minority (8 Black or African American, non-Hispanic/Latino; 1 American Indian or Alaska Native, non-Hispanic/Latino; 6 Asian, non-Hispanic/Latino; 4 Hispanic/Latino), 48 international. Average age 36. 60 applicants, 27% accepted, 7 enrolled. In 2011, 31 master's, 3 doctorates awarded. *Median time to degree:* Of those who began their doctoral program in fall 2003, 50% received their degree in 8 years or less. *Degree requirements:* For master's and Ed S, comprehensive exam, thesis optional; for doctorate, comprehensive exam, thesis/dissertation. *Entrance requirements:* For master's, doctorate, and Ed S, GRE General Test, minimum GPA of 3.0. Additional exam requirements/recommendations for international students: Required—TOEFL (minimum score 550 paper-based; 213 computer-based; 80 iBT). *Application deadline:* For fall admission, 7/1 for domestic and international students; for winter admission, 11/1 for domestic and international students; for spring admission, 3/1 for domestic and international students. Applications are processed on a rolling basis. Application fee: $30. Electronic applications accepted. *Expenses:* Tuition, state resident: full-time $9474; part-time $350.88 per credit hour. Tuition, nonresident: full-time $16,236; part-time $601.34 per credit hour. *Required fees:* $630 per semester. One-time fee: $20. Tuition and fees vary according to course load and campus/location. *Financial support:* Fellowships with full and partial tuition reimbursements, research assistantships with full and partial tuition reimbursements, teaching assistantships with

Distance Education Development

full and partial tuition reimbursements, career-related internships or fieldwork, scholarships/grants, health care benefits, and unspecified assistantships available. Financial award applicants required to submit FAFSA. *Faculty research:* Human performance improvement, educational semiotics, development of software tools to measure online interaction among learners. *Unit head:* Dr. Vanessa Dennen, Program Leader, 850-644-8783, Fax: 850-644-8776, E-mail: vdennen@fsu.edu. *Application contact:* Mary Kate McKee, Program Coordinator, 850-644-8792, Fax: 850-644-8776, E-mail: mmckee@campus.fsu.edu.

The George Washington University, Graduate School of Education and Human Development, Department of Educational Leadership, Program in E-Learning, Washington, DC 20052. Offers Graduate Certificate.

Jones International University, School of Education, Centennial, CO 80112. Offers adult education (M Ed); corporate training and knowledge management (M Ed); curriculum and instruction (M Ed), including elementary teacher licensure, secondary teacher licensure; e-learning technology and design (M Ed); educational leadership and administration (M Ed); educational leadership and administration: principal and administrator licensure (M Ed); elementary curriculum instruction and assessment (M Ed); higher education leadership and administration (M Ed); K-12 instructional technology (M Ed); K-12 instructional technology: teacher licensure (M Ed); secondary curriculum instruction and assessment (M Ed); technology and design (M Ed). Part-time and evening/weekend programs available. Postbaccalaureate distance learning degree programs offered (no on-campus study). *Entrance requirements:* For master's, minimum cumulative GPA of 2.5. Additional exam requirements/recommendations for international students: Recommended—TOEFL (minimum score 550 paper-based; 213 computer-based). Electronic applications accepted.

Liberty University, School of Education, Lynchburg, VA 24502. Offers administration and supervision (M Ed); curriculum and instruction (M Ed); early childhood education (M Ed); educational leadership (Ed D, Ed S); educational technology and online instruction (M Ed); elementary education (M Ed, MAT); gifted education (M Ed); math specialist (M Ed); middle grades (M Ed); outdoor adventure sport (MS); reading specialist (M Ed); school counseling (M Ed); secondary education (M Ed, MAT); special education (M Ed, MAT); sports administration (MS); teaching and learning (Ed D, Ed S). *Accreditation:* NCATE. Part-time programs available. Postbaccalaureate distance learning degree programs offered (minimal on-campus study). *Students:* 2,245 full-time (1,572 women), 3,500 part-time (2,558 women); includes 1,141 minority (888 Black or African American, non-Hispanic/Latino; 19 American Indian or Alaska Native, non-Hispanic/Latino; 21 Asian, non-Hispanic/Latino; 123 Hispanic/Latino; 9 Native Hawaiian or other Pacific Islander, non-Hispanic/Latino; 81 Two or more races, non-Hispanic/Latino), 76 international. Average age 37. In 2011, 760 master's, 48 doctorates, 321 other advanced degrees awarded. *Degree requirements:* For doctorate, comprehensive exam, thesis/dissertation. *Entrance requirements:* For master's, GRE General Test or MAT (if taken in or before 1999), 2 letters of recommendation, minimum undergraduate GPA of 3.0, curriculum vitae; for doctorate, GRE General Test or MAT (if taken before 1999), minimum master's GPA of 3.0, 3 years of teacher experience; for Ed S, GRE General Test or MAT (if taken before 1999), minimum master's GPA of 3.0, 3 years of teaching experience. Additional exam requirements/recommendations for international students: Required—TOEFL (minimum score 600 paper-based; 250 computer-based). *Application deadline:* For fall admission, 6/1 priority date for domestic students; for spring admission, 11/1 for domestic students. Applications are processed on a rolling basis. Application fee: $50. Electronic applications accepted. *Expenses:* Contact institution. *Financial support:* Federal Work-Study and tuition waivers (partial) available. *Faculty research:* Self-determination, character education, bibliotherapy, learning styles, distance education. *Unit head:* Dr. Karen L. Parker, Dean, 434-582-2195, Fax: 434-582-2468, E-mail: kparker@liberty.edu. *Application contact:* Jay Bridge, Director of Graduate Admissions, 800-424-9595, Fax: 800-628-7977, E-mail: gradadmissions@liberty.edu. Web site: http://www.liberty.edu/academics/education/graduate/.

New Mexico State University, Graduate School, College of Extended Learning, Online Teaching and Learning Program, Las Cruces, NM 88003-8001. Offers Graduate Certificate. *Students:* 4 full-time (all women), 12 part-time (9 women); includes 4 minority (1 Black or African American, non-Hispanic/Latino; 2 Hispanic/Latino; 1 Two or more races, non-Hispanic/Latino). Average age 41. 5 applicants, 20% accepted, 1 enrolled. In 2011, 13 Graduate Certificates awarded. *Degree requirements:* For Graduate Certificate, practicum. *Entrance requirements:* Additional exam requirements/recommendations for international students: Required—TOEFL (minimum score 550 paper-based; 79 iBT), IELTS (minimum score 6.5). Application fee: $40 ($50 for international students). *Expenses:* Tuition, state resident: full-time $5004; part-time $208.50 per credit. Tuition, nonresident: full-time $17,446; part-time $726.90 per credit. *Unit head:* Dr. Roberta Derlin, Associate Vice Provost, 575-646-8231. *Application contact:* Coordinator, 575-646-2736, Fax: 575-646-7721, E-mail: gradinfo@nmsu.edu. Web site: http://extended.nmsu.edu/academics/otl/index.html.

New York Institute of Technology, Graduate Division, School of Education, Program in Instructional Technology, Old Westbury, NY 11568-8000. Offers distance learning (Advanced Certificate); instructional technology (MS); multimedia (Advanced Certificate). Part-time and evening/weekend programs available. Postbaccalaureate distance learning degree programs offered. *Students:* 24 full-time (15 women), 251 part-time (166 women); includes 61 minority (28 Black or African American, non-Hispanic/Latino; 2 American Indian or Alaska Native, non-Hispanic/Latino; 11 Asian, non-Hispanic/Latino; 20 Hispanic/Latino), 3 international. Average age 33. In 2011, 93 master's, 4 other advanced degrees awarded. *Degree requirements:* For master's, thesis. *Entrance requirements:* For master's, minimum QPA of 3.0; for Advanced Certificate, master's degree, minimum GPA of 3.0, 3 years of teaching experience, New York teaching certificate, 2 letters of recommendation. Additional exam requirements/recommendations for international students: Required—TOEFL (minimum score 550 paper-based; 213 computer-based). *Application deadline:* For fall admission, 7/1 priority date for domestic students; for spring admission, 12/1 priority date for domestic students. Applications are processed on a rolling basis. Application fee: $50. Electronic applications accepted. *Expenses: Tuition:* Part-time $930 per credit hour. *Financial support:* Research assistantships with partial tuition reimbursements, career-related internships or fieldwork, institutionally sponsored loans, and tuition waivers (full and partial) available. Support available to part-time students. Financial award applicants required to submit FAFSA. *Faculty research:* Distance learning, teacher training resources and strategies. *Unit head:* Dr. Sarah McPherson, Department Chair, 516-686-1053, Fax: 516-686-7655, E-mail: smcphers@nyit.edu. *Application contact:* Dr. Jacquelyn Nealon, Vice President for Enrollment Services, 516-686-7925, Fax: 516-686-7597, E-mail: jnealon@nyit.edu.

Nova Southeastern University, Abraham S. Fischler School of Education, Fort Lauderdale, FL 33314-7796. Offers education (MS, Ed D, Ed S); instructional design and diversity education (MS); instructional technology and distance education (MS); speech language pathology (MS, SLPD); teaching and learning (MA). Part-time and evening/weekend programs available. *Students:* 3,832 full-time (3,039 women), 4,222 part-time (3,452 women); includes 4,795 minority (3,209 Black or African American, non-Hispanic/Latino; 27 American Indian or Alaska Native, non-Hispanic/Latino; 97 Asian, non-Hispanic/Latino; 1,394 Hispanic/Latino; 16 Native Hawaiian or other Pacific Islander, non-Hispanic/Latino; 52 Two or more races, non-Hispanic/Latino), 54 international. Average age 40. In 2011, 1,669 master's, 383 doctorates, 402 other advanced degrees awarded. *Degree requirements:* For master's, practicum, internship; for doctorate, thesis/dissertation; for Ed S, thesis, practicum, internship. *Entrance requirements:* For master's, MAT or GRE (for some programs), CLAST, PRAXIS I, CBEST, General Knowledge Test, teaching certification, minimum GPA of 2.5, verification of teaching, BS; for doctorate, MAT or GRE, master's degree, minimum cumulative GPA of 3.0; for Ed S, MAT or GRE, master's degree, teaching certificate; minimum GPA of 3.0. Additional exam requirements/recommendations for international students: Recommended—TOEFL (minimum score 550 paper-based; 213 computer-based; 80 iBT), IELTS (minimum score 6). *Application deadline:* Applications are processed on a rolling basis. Application fee: $50. Electronic applications accepted. *Financial support:* In 2011–12, 2 fellowships with full tuition reimbursements (averaging $30,000 per year) were awarded; career-related internships or fieldwork, Federal Work-Study, and tuition waivers (full) also available. Support available to part-time students. Financial award application deadline: 4/15; financial award applicants required to submit FAFSA. *Unit head:* Dr. H. Wells Singleton, Provost/Dean, 954-262-8730, Fax: 954-262-3894, E-mail: singlew@nova.edu. *Application contact:* Dr. Jennifer Quinones Nottingham, Dean of Student Affairs, 800-986-3223 Ext. 8500, E-mail: jlquinon@nova.edu. Web site: http://www.fischlerschool.nova.edu/.

Regent University, Graduate School, School of Education, Virginia Beach, VA 23464-9800. Offers adult education (Ed D); adult/staff development (Ed D, PhD); career switcher with licensure (M Ed), including alternative licensure; character education (Ed D, PhD); Christian education leadership (Ed D, PhD); Christian education specialist (Ed S); Christian school program (M Ed), including ACSI licensure; distance education (Ed D, PhD); education licensure (M Ed), including preK-6th grade; educational leadership (M Ed, PhD); educational leadership - special education (Ed S), including administration and supervision; educational psychology (Ed D, PhD), including learning and development, research and evaluation, special education; higher education (Ed D, PhD), including administration, research and institutional planning, teaching; higher education leadership (Ed D); individualized degree plan (M Ed), including behavior disorders, learning disabilities, mental retardation, reading specialist; K-12 school leadership (Ed D, PhD); leadership in character education (M Ed); master teacher (M Ed), including TESOL; mathematics education (M Ed); special education (PhD); student affairs (M Ed); TESOL (M Ed), including adult education, ESL: preK-12. *Accreditation:* Teacher Education Accreditation Council. Part-time and evening/weekend programs available. Postbaccalaureate distance learning degree programs offered (minimal on-campus study). *Faculty:* 26 full-time (13 women), 54 part-time/adjunct (34 women). *Students:* 140 full-time (109 women), 786 part-time (626 women); includes 218 minority (189 Black or African American, non-Hispanic/Latino; 2 American Indian or Alaska Native, non-Hispanic/Latino; 11 Asian, non-Hispanic/Latino; 16 Hispanic/Latino), 42 international. Average age 39. 673 applicants, 57% accepted, 298 enrolled. In 2011, 178 master's, 15 doctorates awarded. *Degree requirements:* For master's, thesis or alternative; for doctorate, comprehensive exam, thesis/dissertation. *Entrance requirements:* For master's, MAT, minimum undergraduate GPA of 2.75, writing sample, resume, recommendations, interview; for doctorate, GRE, writing sample, 3 years of relevant professional experience, master's-level paper, copies of published work, resume, transcripts, interview, recommendations. Additional exam requirements/recommendations for international students: Required—TOEFL (minimum score 577 paper-based; 233 computer-based). *Application deadline:* For fall admission, 4/1 priority date for domestic students; for spring admission, 10/15 priority date for domestic students. Applications are processed on a rolling basis. Application fee: $50. Electronic applications accepted. *Expenses:* Contact institution. *Financial support:* Fellowships, career-related internships or fieldwork, scholarships/grants, tuition waivers (full and partial), and unspecified assistantships available. Support available to part-time students. Financial award application deadline: 4/1; financial award applicants required to submit FAFSA. *Faculty research:* Character development and discipline for children, education leadership development, diversity in schools, classroom management, technology in education settings. *Unit head:* Dr. Alan A. Arroyo, Dean, 757-352-4261, Fax: 757-352-4318, E-mail: alanarr@regent.edu. *Application contact:* Matthew Chadwick, Director of Enrollment Support Services, 800-373-5504, Fax: 757-352-4381, E-mail: admissions@regent.edu. Web site: http://www.regent.edu/education/.

Saginaw Valley State University, College of Education, Program in E-Learning, University Center, MI 48710. Offers MA. *Students:* 5 full-time (all women), 11 part-time (7 women); includes 1 minority (American Indian or Alaska Native, non-Hispanic/Latino), 1 international. Average age 40. 43 applicants, 98% accepted, 16 enrolled. *Entrance requirements:* Additional exam requirements/recommendations for international students: Required—TOEFL (minimum score 525 paper-based; 197 computer-based; 71 iBT). *Expenses:* Tuition, state resident: full-time $8300; part-time $5333 per year. Tuition, nonresident: full-time $15,613; part-time $10,209 per year. *International tuition:* $15,631 full-time. *Financial support:* Federal Work-Study and scholarships/grants available. Support available to part-time students. *Unit head:* Dr. Steve P. Barbus, Jr., Dean, 989-964-6067, Fax: 989-790-4385, E-mail: barbus@svsu.edu. *Application contact:* Kathy Lopez, Certification Officer, 989-964-4661, Fax: 989-964-4385, E-mail: klopez@svsu.edu.

Télé-université, Graduate Programs, Québec, QC G1K 9H5, Canada. Offers computer science (PhD); corporate finance (MS); distance learning (MS). Part-time programs available.

Thomas Edison State College, Heavin School of Arts and Sciences, Program in Online Learning and Teaching, Trenton, NJ 08608-1176. Offers Graduate Certificate. Part-time programs available. Postbaccalaureate distance learning degree programs offered (no on-campus study). *Students:* 23 part-time (14 women); includes 10 minority (6 Black or African American, non-Hispanic/Latino; 4 Hispanic/Latino). Average age 48. In 2011, 10 Graduate Certificates awarded. *Entrance requirements:* Additional exam requirements/recommendations for international students: Required—TOEFL (minimum score 550 paper-based; 213 computer-based; 79 iBT). *Application deadline:* For fall admission, 8/15 priority date for domestic students, 8/15 for international students; for winter admission, 11/15 priority date for domestic students, 11/15 for international students; for spring admission, 2/15 priority date for domestic students, 2/15 for international students. Applications are processed on a rolling basis. Application fee: $75. Electronic applications accepted. *Financial support:* Applicants required to submit FAFSA. *Unit head:* Dr. Susan Davenport, Dean, Heavin School of Arts and Sciences, 609-984-1130, Fax: 609-984-0740, E-mail: info@tesc.edu. *Application contact:* David Hoftiezer, Director of Admissions, 888-442-8372, Fax: 609-984-8447, E-mail: admissions@tesc.edu. Web site: http://www.tesc.edu/1880.php.

University of Colorado Denver, School of Education and Human Development, Information and Learning Technologies Program, Denver, CO 80217-3364. Offers e-learning design and implementation (MA); instructional design and adult learning (MA); K-12 teaching (MA). Part-time and evening/weekend programs available. Postbaccalaureate distance learning degree programs offered (no on-campus study). *Students:* 82 full-time (65 women), 46 part-time (38 women); includes 13 minority (2 Black or African American, non-Hispanic/Latino; 3 Asian, non-Hispanic/Latino; 8 Hispanic/Latino), 3 international. Average age 38. 35 applicants, 89% accepted, 27 enrolled. In 2011, 79 master's awarded. *Degree requirements:* For master's, comprehensive exam (for some programs), comprehensive exam or online portfolio; 30 credit hours. *Entrance requirements:* For master's, GRE or MAT (if GPA is below 2.75), resume, statement of intent, three letters of recommendation. Additional exam requirements/recommendations for international students: Required—TOEFL (minimum score 525 paper-based; 197 computer-based). *Application deadline:* For fall admission, 5/15 for domestic students; for spring admission, 11/15 for domestic students. Application fee: $50 ($75 for international students). *Expenses:* Contact institution. *Financial support:* Scholarships/grants available. Financial award application deadline: 4/1; financial award applicants required to submit FAFSA. *Faculty research:* Technology for educational management, instructional design foundations, e-Learning, educational design. *Unit head:* Brent Wilson, Professor, 303-315-4963, E-mail: brent.wilson@ucdenver.edu. *Application contact:* Hans Broers, Academic Advisor, 303-315-6351, Fax: 303-315-6311, E-mail: hans.broers@ucdenver.edu. Web site: http://www.ucdenver.edu/ACADEMICS/COLLEGES/SCHOOLOFEDUCATION/ACADEMICS/Pages/AcademicPrograms.aspx.

University of Maryland, Baltimore County, Graduate School, College of Arts, Humanities and Social Sciences, Department of Education, Program in Instructional Systems Development, Baltimore, MD 21250. Offers distance education (Graduate Certificate); instructional design for e-learning (Graduate Certificate); instructional systems development (MA, Graduate Certificate); instructional technology (Graduate Certificate). Part-time and evening/weekend programs available. Postbaccalaureate distance learning degree programs offered (no on-campus study). *Faculty:* 2 full-time (0 women), 13 part-time/adjunct (4 women). *Students:* 5 full-time (3 women), 68 part-time (53 women); includes 51 minority (35 Black or African American, non-Hispanic/Latino; 1 American Indian or Alaska Native, non-Hispanic/Latino; 6 Asian, non-Hispanic/Latino; 7 Hispanic/Latino; 2 Two or more races, non-Hispanic/Latino), 4 international. Average age 44. 97 applicants, 85% accepted, 45 enrolled. In 2011, 38 master's, 47 other advanced degrees awarded. *Entrance requirements:* Additional exam requirements/recommendations for international students: Required—TOEFL (minimum score 550 paper-based; 213 computer-based; 80 iBT). *Application deadline:* For fall admission, 6/1 priority date for domestic students, 1/1 for international students; for spring admission, 11/1 priority date for domestic students, 6/1 for international students. Applications are processed on a rolling basis. Application fee: $50. Electronic applications accepted. *Financial support:* Applicants required to submit FAFSA. *Faculty research:* E-learning, distance education, instructional design. *Unit head:* Dr. Greg Williams, Director, 410-455-6773, Fax: 410-455-1344, E-mail: gregw@umbc.edu. *Application contact:* Sharese Essien, Program Coordinator, 410-455-8670, Fax: 410-455-1344, E-mail: sharese@umbc.edu. Web site: http://www.umbc.edu/isd.

University of Maryland University College, Graduate School of Management and Technology, Program in Distance Education, Adelphi, MD 20783. Offers MDE, Certificate. Part-time and evening/weekend programs available. Postbaccalaureate distance learning degree programs offered (no on-campus study). *Students:* 1 (woman) full-time, 165 part-time (122 women); includes 67 minority (54 Black or African American, non-Hispanic/Latino; 1 American Indian or Alaska Native, non-Hispanic/Latino; 4 Asian, non-Hispanic/Latino; 8 Hispanic/Latino), 4 international. Average age 42. 96 applicants, 100% accepted, 31 enrolled. In 2011, 23 master's, 34 other advanced degrees awarded. *Degree requirements:* For master's, thesis or alternative. *Application deadline:* Applications are processed on a rolling basis. Application fee: $50. Electronic applications accepted. *Financial support:* Federal Work-Study and scholarships/grants available. Support available to part-time students. Financial award application deadline: 6/1; financial award applicants required to submit FAFSA. *Unit head:* Dr. Stella Porto, Director, 240-684-2400, Fax: 240-684-2401, E-mail: sporto@umuc.edu. *Application contact:* Coordinator, Graduate Admissions, 800-888-8682, Fax: 240-684-2151, E-mail: newgrad@umuc.edu. Web site: http://www.umuc.edu/grad/mde/mde.shtml.

Virginia Polytechnic Institute and State University, VT Online, Blacksburg, VA 24061. Offers advanced transportation systems (Certificate); aerospace engineering (MS); agricultural and life sciences (MSLFS); business information systems (Graduate Certificate); career and technical education (MS); civil engineering (MS); computer engineering (M Eng, MS); decision support systems (Graduate Certificate); eLearning leadership (MA); electrical engineering (M Eng, MS); engineering administration (MEA); environmental engineering (Certificate); environmental politics and policy (Graduate Certificate); environmental sciences and engineering (MS); foundations of political analysis (Graduate Certificate); health product risk management (Graduate Certificate); industrial and systems engineering (MS); information policy and society (Graduate Certificate); information security (Graduate Certificate); information technology (MIT); instructional technology (MA); integrative STEM education (MA Ed); liberal arts (Graduate Certificate); life sciences: health product risk management (MS); natural resources (MNR, Graduate Certificate); networking (Graduate Certificate); nonprofit and nongovernmental organization management (Graduate Certificate); ocean engineering (MS); political science (MA); security studies (Graduate Certificate); software development (Graduate Certificate). *Expenses:* Tuition, state resident: full-time $10,048; part-time $558.25 per credit hour. Tuition, nonresident: full-time $19,497; part-time $1083.25 per credit hour. *Required fees:* $405 per semester. Tuition and fees vary according to course load, campus/location and program. *Application contact:* Graduate School Applications General Assistance, 540-231-8636, Fax: 540-231-2039, E-mail: gradappl@vt.edu. Web site: http://www.vto.vt.edu/.

Walden University, Graduate Programs, Richard W. Riley College of Education and Leadership, Minneapolis, MN 55401. Offers administrator leadership for teaching and learning (Ed D, Ed S); adult education (Ed D, Ed S); adult learning (MS, Postbaccalaureate Certificate), including developmental education (MS), online teaching (MS), teaching adults English as a second language (MS), training and performance management (MS); college teaching and learning (Ed D, Ed S, Postbaccalaureate Certificate); curriculum, instruction and assessment (Ed D, Postbaccalaureate Certificate); curriculum, instruction, and professional development (Ed S); developmental education (Postbaccalaureate Certificate); early childhood administration, management, and leadership (Postbaccalaureate Certificate); early childhood education (birth-grade 3) (MAT); early childhood public policy and advocacy (Postbaccalaureate Certificate); early childhood studies (MS), including administration, management and leadership, early childhood public policy and advocacy, teaching adults in the early childhood field, teaching and diversity; education (MS, PhD), including adolescent literacy and technology (grades 6-12) (MS), adult education leadership (PhD), assessment, evaluation, and accountability (PhD), community college leadership (PhD), curriculum, instruction, and assessment, early childhood education (PhD), educational technology (PhD), elementary reading and literacy (MS), elementary reading and mathematics (MS), general program, global and comparative education (PhD), higher education (PhD), integrating technology in the classroom (MS), K-12 educational leadership (PhD), leadership, policy and change (PhD), learning, instruction and innovation (PhD), literacy and learning in the content areas (MS), mathematics (grades 6-8) (MS), mathematics (grades K-5) (MS), middle level education (grades 5-8) (MS), professional development (MS), science (grades K-8) (MS), self-designed (PhD), special education (PhD), special education (non-licensure) (MS), teacher leadership (grades K-12) (MS), teaching English language learners (grades K-12) (MS); educational leadership and administration (principal preparation) (Ed S); educational technology (Ed S); elementary reading and literacy (Postbaccalaureate Certificate); engaging culturally diverse learners (Postbaccalaureate Certificate); enrollment management and institutional marketing (Postbaccalaureate Certificate); higher education (MS), including college teaching and learning, enrollment management and institutional planning, global higher education, leadership for student success, online and distance learning; higher education leadership (Ed D); instructional design (Postbaccalaureate Certificate); instructional design and technology (MS), including general program (MS, PhD), online learning, training and performance improvement; integrating technology in the classroom (Postbaccalaureate Certificate); online teaching for adult learners (Postbaccalaureate Certificate); professional development (Postbaccalaureate Certificate); reading and literacy leadership (Ed D); science K-8 (Postbaccalaureate Certificate); special education (Ed D, Ed S); special education: emotional/behavioral disorders (K-12) (MAT); special education: learning disabilities (K-12) (MAT); teacher leadership (Ed D, Ed S, Postbaccalaureate Certificate); training and performance management (Postbaccalaureate Certificate). Part-time and evening/weekend programs available. Postbaccalaureate distance learning degree programs offered (minimal on-campus study). *Faculty:* 71 full-time (48 women), 853 part-time/adjunct (585 women). *Students:* 11,326 full-time (9,212 women), 2,148 part-time (1,795 women); includes 5,346 minority (4,403 Black or African American, non-Hispanic/Latino; 76 American Indian or Alaska Native, non-Hispanic/Latino; 140 Asian, non-Hispanic/Latino; 561 Hispanic/Latino; 21 Native Hawaiian or other Pacific Islander, non-Hispanic/Latino; 145 Two or more races, non-Hispanic/Latino), 322 international. Average age 39. In 2011, 3,477 master's, 318 doctorates, 471 other advanced degrees awarded. *Degree requirements:* For doctorate, thesis/dissertation (for some programs), residency; for other advanced degree, residency (for some programs). *Entrance requirements:* For master's, bachelor's degree or equivalent in related field; minimum GPA of 2.5; official transcripts; goal statement; access to computer and Internet; for doctorate, master's degree or equivalent in related field; minimum GPA of 3.0; official transcripts; three years' related professional/academic experience (preferred); access to computer and Internet; for other advanced degree, master's degree or equivalent in related field; minimum GPA of 3.0; 3 years related professional/academic experience (preferred); access to computer and Internet (Ed S). Additional exam requirements/recommendations for international students: Required—TOEFL (minimum score 550 paper-based; 213 computer-based), IELTS (minimum score 6.5), or Michigan English Language Assessment Battery (minimum score 82). *Application deadline:* Applications are processed on a rolling basis. Application fee: $50. Electronic applications accepted. *Financial support:* Federal Work-Study, scholarships/grants, unspecified assistantships, and family tuition reduction, active duty/veteran tuition reduction, group tuition reduction, interest-free payment plans, employee tuition reduction available. Support available to part-time students. Financial award applicants required to submit FAFSA. *Unit head:* Dr. Kate Steffens, Dean, 800-925-3368. *Application contact:* Jennifer Hall, Vice President of Enrollment Management, 866-4-WALDEN, E-mail: info@waldenu.edu. Web site: http://www.waldenu.edu/Colleges-and-Schools/College-of-Education-and-Leadership.htm.

Wayne State University, College of Education, Division of Administrative and Organizational Studies, Detroit, MI 48202. Offers college and university teaching (Certificate); educational leadership (M Ed); educational leadership and policy studies (Ed D, PhD); general administration and supervision (Ed S); instructional technology (M Ed, Ed D, PhD, Ed S); online teaching (Certificate); secondary curriculum and instruction (Ed S). *Students:* 86 full-time (62 women), 261 part-time (172 women); includes 171 minority (145 Black or African American, non-Hispanic/Latino; 1 American Indian or Alaska Native, non-Hispanic/Latino; 8 Asian, non-Hispanic/Latino; 16 Hispanic/Latino; 1 Two or more races, non-Hispanic/Latino), 8 international. Average age 39. 122 applicants, 40% accepted, 28 enrolled. In 2011, 73 master's, 9 doctorates, 50 other advanced degrees awarded. *Degree requirements:* For doctorate, thesis/dissertation. *Entrance requirements:* For doctorate, GRE or MAT, interview; autobiography or curriculum vitae; references; master's degree; minimum undergraduate GPA of 3.0, graduate 3.75; 3 years relevant experience; foundational course work; for other advanced degree, minimum GPA of 3.4. Additional exam requirements/recommendations for international students: Required—TOEFL (minimum score 550 paper-based; 213 computer-based), TWE (minimum score 5.5). *Application deadline:* For fall admission, 6/1 priority date for domestic students, 5/1 for international students; for winter admission, 10/1 priority date for domestic students, 9/1 for international students; for spring admission, 2/1 priority date for domestic students, 1/1 for international students. Applications are processed on a rolling basis. Application fee: $50. Electronic applications accepted. *Expenses:* Tuition, state resident: part-time $512.85 per credit. Tuition, nonresident: part-time $1132.65 per credit. *Required fees:* $26.60 per credit. $199.65 per semester. Tuition and fees vary according to course load and program. *Financial support:* In 2011–12, 59 students received support, including 1 fellowship with tuition reimbursement available (averaging $17,347 per year), 4 research assistantships with tuition reimbursements available (averaging $15,713 per year); career-related internships or fieldwork, Federal Work-Study, institutionally sponsored loans, scholarships/grants, health care benefits, and unspecified assistantships also available. Support available to part-time students. *Faculty research:* Total quality management, participatory management, administering educational technology, school improvement, principalship. *Total annual research expenditures:* $22,232. *Unit head:* Dr. Alan Hoffman, Interim Assistant Dean, 313-577-5235, E-mail: alanhoffman@wayne.edu. *Application contact:* Janice Green, Assistant Dean, 313-577-1605, E-mail: jwgreen@wayne.edu. Web site: http://coe.wayne.edu/aos/index.php.

Western Illinois University, School of Graduate Studies, College of Education and Human Services, Department of Instructional Design and Technology, Macomb, IL 61455-1390. Offers distance learning (Certificate); educational technology specialist (Certificate); graphic applications (Certificate); instructional design and technology (MS); multimedia (Certificate); technology integration in education (Certificate); training development (Certificate). Part-time programs available. Postbaccalaureate distance learning degree programs offered (no on-campus study). *Students:* 23 full-time (16 women), 58 part-time (35 women); includes 15 minority (8 Black or African American, non-Hispanic/Latino; 1 American Indian or Alaska Native, non-Hispanic/Latino; 2 Asian, non-Hispanic/Latino; 4 Hispanic/Latino), 7 international. Average age 35. 25 applicants, 80% accepted. In 2011, 20 master's, 8 other advanced degrees awarded. *Degree requirements:* For master's, thesis or alternative. *Entrance requirements:* Additional exam requirements/recommendations for international students: Required—TOEFL (minimum score 550 paper-based; 213 computer-based; 80 iBT). *Application deadline:* Applications are processed on a rolling basis. Application fee: $30. Electronic applications accepted. *Expenses:* Tuition, state resident: part-time $281.16 per credit hour. Tuition, nonresident: part-time $562.32 per credit hour. Part-time tuition and fees vary according to campus/location and reciprocity agreements. *Financial support:* In 2011–12, 13 students received support, including 10 research assistantships with full tuition reimbursements available (averaging $7,360 per year), 3 teaching assistantships with full tuition reimbursements available (averaging $8,480 per year). Financial award applicants required to submit FAFSA. *Unit head:* Dr. Hoyet Hemphill, Chairperson, 309-298-1952. *Application contact:* Dr. Nancy Parsons, Interim Associate Provost and Director of Graduate Studies, 309-298-1806, Fax: 309-298-2345, E-mail: grad-office@wiu.edu. Web site: http://wiu.edu/idt.

Wilkes University, College of Graduate and Professional Studies, School of Education, Wilkes-Barre, PA 18766-0002. Offers art and science of teaching (MS Ed); classroom technology (MS Ed); early childhood literacy (MS Ed); educational computing (MS Ed); educational development and strategies (MS Ed); educational leadership (MS Ed); educational technology (Ed D); higher education administration (Ed D); instructional media (MS Ed); instructional technology (MS Ed); K-12 administration (Ed D); online teaching (MS Ed); reading (MS Ed); school business leadership (MS Ed); secondary education (MS Ed), including biology, chemistry, English, history, mathematics; special education (MS Ed); teaching English as a second language (MS Ed); twenty-first century teaching and learning (MS Ed). Part-time and evening/weekend programs available. Postbaccalaureate distance learning degree programs offered (minimal on-campus study). *Students:* 92 full-time (63 women), 2,005 part-time (1,459 women); includes 89 minority (23 Black or African American, non-Hispanic/Latino; 1 American Indian or Alaska Native, non-Hispanic/Latino; 14 Asian, non-Hispanic/Latino; 33 Hispanic/Latino; 1 Native Hawaiian or other Pacific Islander, non-Hispanic/Latino; 17 Two or more races, non-Hispanic/Latino), 6 international. Average age 33. In 2011, 1,150 master's, 3 doctorates awarded. *Entrance requirements:* Additional exam requirements/recommendations for international students: Required—TOEFL (minimum score 550 paper-based; 213 computer-based; 79 iBT). *Application deadline:* Applications are processed on a rolling basis. Application fee: $45. Electronic applications accepted. *Expenses:* Contact institution. *Financial support:* Federal Work-Study and unspecified assistantships available. Financial award application deadline: 3/1; financial award applicants required to submit FAFSA. *Unit head:* Dr. Michael Speziale, Dean, 570-408-4679, Fax: 570-408-4905, E-mail: michael.speziale@wilkes.edu. *Application contact:* Erin Sutzko, Director of Extended Learning, 570-408-4253, Fax: 570-408-7846, E-mail: erin.sutzko@wilkes.edu. Web site: http://www.wilkes.edu/pages/383.asp.

Educational Leadership and Administration

Abilene Christian University, Graduate School, College of Education and Human Services, Graduate Studies in Education, Leadership of Learning Program, Abilene, TX 79699-9100. Offers leadership of digital learning (Certificate); leadership of learning (M Ed). Part-time programs available. Postbaccalaureate distance learning degree programs offered (no on-campus study). *Faculty:* 4 full-time (1 woman). *Students:* 3 full-time (1 woman), 69 part-time (51 women); includes 15 minority (8 Black or African American, non-Hispanic/Latino; 1 Asian, non-Hispanic/Latino; 5 Hispanic/Latino; 1 Two or more races, non-Hispanic/Latino), 2 international. 41 applicants, 39% accepted, 12 enrolled. In 2011, 32 master's, 5 Certificates awarded. *Degree requirements:* For master's, comprehensive exam, practicum. *Entrance requirements:* Additional exam requirements/recommendations for international students: Required—TOEFL (minimum score 550 paper-based; 213 computer-based; 80 iBT), IELTS (minimum score 6). *Application deadline:* For fall admission, 8/15 priority date for domestic students; for winter admission, 10/1 priority date for domestic students; for spring admission, 12/15 priority date for domestic students. Applications are processed on a rolling basis. Application fee: $50. Electronic applications accepted. *Expenses: Tuition:* Full-time $14,168; part-time $787 per hour. *Required fees:* $82 per hour. $10 per term. *Financial support:* In 2011–12, 1 student received support. Application deadline: 4/1; applicants required to submit FAFSA. *Unit head:* Dr. Lloyd Goldsmith, Graduate Director, 325-674-2946, Fax: 325-674-2123, E-mail: lloyd.goldsmith@acu.edu. *Application contact:* David Pittman, Graduate Admissions Counselor, 325-674-2656, Fax: 325-674-6717, E-mail: gradinfo@acu.edu.

Abilene Christian University, Graduate School, College of Education and Human Services, Graduate Studies in Education, Superintendent Certification Program, Abilene, TX 79699-9100. Offers Post-Master's Certificate. *Faculty:* 4 full-time (1 woman). *Students:* 23 part-time (7 women); includes 10 minority (9 Black or African American, non-Hispanic/Latino; 1 Hispanic/Latino). 14 applicants, 14% accepted, 1 enrolled. In 2011, 8 Post-Master's Certificates awarded. *Entrance requirements:* Additional exam requirements/recommendations for international students: Required—TOEFL (minimum score 550 paper-based; 213 computer-based; 80 iBT), IELTS (minimum score 6). *Application deadline:* For fall admission, 8/15 priority date for domestic students; for winter admission, 10/1 priority date for domestic students; for spring admission, 11/15 priority date for domestic students. Applications are processed on a rolling basis. Application fee: $50. Electronic applications accepted. *Expenses: Tuition:* Full-time $14,168; part-time $787 per hour. *Required fees:* $82 per hour. $10 per term. *Financial support:* Applicants required to submit FAFSA. *Unit head:* Dr. Bruce Scott, Graduate Director, 325-674-2974, Fax: 325-674-2123, E-mail: bruce.scott@acu.edu. *Application contact:* David Pittman, Graduate Admissions Counselor, 325-674-2656, Fax: 325-674-6717, E-mail: gradinfo@acu.edu.

Acadia University, Faculty of Professional Studies, School of Education, Program in Leadership, Wolfville, NS B4P 2R6, Canada. Offers M Ed. Part-time programs available. *Degree requirements:* For master's, thesis optional. *Entrance requirements:* For master's, B Ed or the equivalent, 2 years teaching or related experience. Additional exam requirements/recommendations for international students: Required—TOEFL (minimum score 580 paper-based; 237 computer-based; 93 iBT), IELTS (minimum score 6.5). *Faculty research:* Organizational theory and structural change, professionalism, sexuality education.

Adelphi University, Ruth S. Ammon School of Education, Program in Educational Leadership and Technology, Garden City, NY 11530-0701. Offers MA, Certificate. *Students:* 1 (woman) full-time, 34 part-time (23 women); includes 17 minority (10 Black or African American, non-Hispanic/Latino; 5 Hispanic/Latino; 2 Two or more races, non-Hispanic/Latino). Average age 35. In 2011, 13 master's, 13 other advanced degrees awarded. *Entrance requirements:* For master's, 2 letters of recommendation, resume, letter attesting to teaching experience (3 years full-time K-12). Additional exam requirements/recommendations for international students: Required—TOEFL (minimum score 550 paper-based; 213 computer-based; 80 iBT). *Application deadline:* For fall admission, 8/15 priority date for domestic students, 4/1 for international students; for spring admission, 1/15 priority date for domestic students, 11/1 for international students. Applications are processed on a rolling basis. Application fee: $50. Electronic applications accepted. *Expenses: Tuition:* Full-time $29,600; part-time $930 per credit. *Required fees:* $1100. *Financial support:* Research assistantships with partial tuition reimbursements and institutionally sponsored loans available. Financial award application deadline: 2/15; financial award applicants required to submit FAFSA. *Faculty research:* Technology methodology focusing on in-service and pre-service curriculum. *Unit head:* Dr. Devin Thornburg, Director, 516-877-4026, E-mail: thornburg@adelphi.edu. *Application contact:* Christine Murphy, Director of Admissions, 516-877-3050, Fax: 516-877-3039, E-mail: graduateadmissions@adelphi.edu.

Alabama Agricultural and Mechanical University, School of Graduate Studies, School of Education, Area in Secondary Education, Huntsville, AL 35811. Offers education (M Ed, Ed S); higher administration (MS). *Accreditation:* NCATE. Evening/weekend programs available. *Degree requirements:* For master's, comprehensive exam; for Ed S, thesis. *Entrance requirements:* For master's, GRE General Test. Additional exam requirements/recommendations for international students: Required—TOEFL (minimum score 500 paper-based; 173 computer-based; 61 iBT). Electronic applications accepted. *Faculty research:* World peace through education, computer-assisted instruction.

Alabama State University, Department of Instructional Support, Program in Educational Administration, Montgomery, AL 36101-0271. Offers educational administration (M Ed, Ed S); educational leadership, policy and law (Ed D). Part-time programs available. *Students:* 30 full-time (17 women), 91 part-time (56 women); includes 91 minority (86 Black or African American, non-Hispanic/Latino; 3 Asian, non-Hispanic/Latino; 2 Hispanic/Latino). Average age 43. 48 applicants, 50% accepted, 8 enrolled. In 2011, 5 master's awarded. *Degree requirements:* For master's, comprehensive exam, thesis optional; for Ed S, thesis. *Entrance requirements:* For master's, GRE General Test, MAT, graduate writing competency test; for Ed S, graduate writing competency test, GRE, MAT. Additional exam requirements/recommendations for international students: Required—TOEFL (minimum score 500 paper-based; 173 computer-based). *Application deadline:* For fall admission, 7/15 for domestic students; for spring admission, 12/15 for domestic students. Applications are processed on a rolling basis. Application fee: $10. *Financial support:* In 2011–12, research assistantships (averaging $9,450 per year) were awarded. *Faculty research:* Nontraditional roles, computer applications for principals, women in educational administration. *Unit head:* Dr. Hyacinth Findlay, Coordinator, 334-229-4417, E-mail: hfindlay@alasu.edu. *Application contact:* Dr. Doris Screws, Dean of Graduate Studies, 334-229-4274, Fax: 334-229-4928, E-mail: dscrews@alasu.edu. Web site: http://www.alasu.edu/academics/colleges—departments/college-of-education/instructional-support-programs/instructional-leadership/eds-in-educational-a.

Albany State University, College of Education, Albany, GA 31705-2717. Offers early childhood education (M Ed); education specialist (Ed S); educational leadership and administration (M Ed); health, physical education and recreation (M Ed); middle grades education (M Ed); school counseling (M Ed); special education (M Ed). *Accreditation:* NCATE. Part-time and evening/weekend programs available. Postbaccalaureate distance learning degree programs offered (minimal on-campus study). *Faculty:* 19 full-time (13 women), 7 part-time/adjunct (5 women). *Students:* 90 full-time (69 women), 118 part-time (92 women); includes 152 minority (151 Black or African American, non-Hispanic/Latino; 1 American Indian or Alaska Native, non-Hispanic/Latino), 1 international. Average age 35. 93 applicants, 78% accepted, 38 enrolled. In 2011, 43 master's, 8 Ed Ss awarded. *Degree requirements:* For master's, comprehensive exam, internship, GACE Content Exam. *Entrance requirements:* For master's, GRE or MAT. *Application deadline:* For fall admission, 6/1 for domestic students, 5/1 for international students; for spring admission, 11/1 for domestic students, 10/1 for international students. Applications are processed on a rolling basis. Application fee: $20. Electronic applications accepted. *Expenses:* Tuition, state resident: full-time $3204; part-time $178 per credit hour. Tuition, nonresident: full-time $12,816; part-time $712 per credit hour. *Required fees:* $379 per semester. *Financial support:* Scholarships/grants available. Financial award application deadline: 4/15; financial award applicants required to submit FAFSA. *Faculty research:* GACE preparation, STEM (science, technology, engineering, and mathematics), technology education, special education, professional teacher development, health implications liberation philosophy, NET-Q, learning community, disabled or at-risk students. *Total annual research expenditures:* $252,502. *Unit head:* Dr. Kimberly King-Jupiter, Dean, 229-430-1718, Fax: 229-430-4993, E-mail: kimberly.king-jupiter@asurams.edu. *Application contact:* Jeffrey Pierce, II, Graduate Admissions Counselor, 229-430-4646, Fax: 229-430-4105, E-mail: jeffrey.pierce@asurams.edu. Web site: http://asu-sacs.asurams.edu/ASUCatalog/Graduate/index.html.

Alliant International University–Fresno, Shirley M. Hufstedler School of Education, Program in Educational Leadership, Fresno, CA 93727. Offers educational leadership and management (Ed D). Part-time programs available. *Students:* 1 (woman) full-time, 33 part-time (27 women); includes 19 minority (6 Black or African American, non-Hispanic/Latino; 1 American Indian or Alaska Native, non-Hispanic/Latino; 2 Asian, non-Hispanic/Latino; 10 Hispanic/Latino), 1 international. Average age 50. In 2011, 2 doctorates awarded. *Entrance requirements:* For doctorate, minimum GPA of 3.0, letters of recommendation. Additional exam requirements/recommendations for international students: Required—TOEFL (minimum score 550 paper-based; 213 computer-based), TWE (minimum score 5). *Application deadline:* For fall admission, 7/1 priority date for domestic students, 7/1 for international students; for spring admission, 12/1 priority date for domestic students, 12/1 for international students. Applications are processed on a rolling basis. Application fee: $55. Electronic applications accepted. Tuition and fees vary according to course load. *Financial support:* Federal Work-Study, institutionally sponsored loans, and scholarships/grants available. Financial award application deadline: 2/15; financial award applicants required to submit FAFSA. *Faculty research:* School administration, cross-cultural leadership. *Unit head:* Dr. Xuanning Fu, Program Coordinator, 866-825-8426, Fax: 559-253-2267, E-mail: admissions@alliant.edu. *Application contact:* Alliant International University Central Contact Center, 866-U-ALLIANT, Fax: 858-635-4555, E-mail: admissions@alliant.edu. Web site: http://www.alliant.edu/gsoe/.

Alliant International University–Irvine, Shirley M. Hufstedler School of Education, Educational Leadership Programs, Irvine, CA 92612. Offers educational administration (MA, Credential); educational leadership and management (K-12) (Ed D); higher education (Ed D); preliminary administrative services (Credential). Part-time programs available. *Students:* 11. In 2011, 8 master's, 4 doctorates awarded. *Entrance requirements:* For master's and doctorate, minimum GPA of 3.0, letters of recommendation. Additional exam requirements/recommendations for international students: Required—TOEFL (minimum score 550 paper-based; 213 computer-based), TWE (minimum score 5). *Application deadline:* For fall admission, 7/1 priority date for domestic students, 7/1 for international students; for spring admission, 12/1 priority date for domestic students, 12/1 for international students. Applications are processed on a rolling basis. Application fee: $55. Electronic applications accepted. *Financial support:* Federal Work-Study, institutionally sponsored loans, and scholarships/grants available.

Financial award application deadline: 2/15. *Unit head:* Dr. Suzanne Power, Acting Director, 866-825-5426, Fax: 949-833-3507, E-mail: admissions@alliant.edu. *Application contact:* Alliant International University Central Contact Center, 866-U-ALLIANT, Fax: 858-635-4555, E-mail: admissions@alliant.edu. Web site: http://www.alliant.edu/gsoe/.

Alliant International University–Los Angeles, Shirley M. Hufstedler School of Education, Educational Leadership Programs, Alhambra, CA 91803-1360. Offers educational administration (MA); preliminary administrative services (Credential). Part-time programs available. *Students:* 14 (9 women). *Entrance requirements:* For master's, minimum GPA of 3.0, letters of recommendation. Additional exam requirements/recommendations for international students: Required—TOEFL (minimum score 550 paper-based; 213 computer-based), TWE (minimum score 5). *Application deadline:* For fall admission, 7/1 priority date for domestic students, 7/1 for international students; for spring admission, 12/1 priority date for domestic students, 12/1 for international students. Application fee: $55. *Financial support:* Federal Work-Study, institutionally sponsored loans, and scholarships/grants available. Financial award application deadline: 2/15; financial award applicants required to submit FAFSA. *Unit head:* Dr. Suzanne Power, Acting Director, 866-825-5426, Fax: 620-284-0550, E-mail: admissions@alliant.edu. *Application contact:* Alliant International University Central Contact Center, 866-U-ALLIANT, Fax: 858-635-4555, E-mail: admissions@alliant.edu. Web site: http://www.alliant.edu/gsoe.

Alliant International University–México City, Shirley M. Hufstedler School of Education, Mexico City, Mexico. Offers educational administration (MA); teaching (MA). Part-time and evening/weekend programs available. Postbaccalaureate distance learning degree programs offered (no on-campus study). *Faculty:* 2 part-time/adjunct (both women). *Students:* Average age 38. In 2011, 5 master's awarded. *Entrance requirements:* For master's, minimum GPA of 2.5, letters of recommendation. Additional exam requirements/recommendations for international students: Required—TOEFL (minimum score 550 paper-based; 213 computer-based), TWE (minimum score 5). *Application deadline:* For fall admission, 8/1 priority date for domestic students, 8/1 for international students; for spring admission, 12/1 priority date for domestic students, 12/1 for international students. Application fee: $50. *Financial support:* Career-related internships or fieldwork, Federal Work-Study, institutionally sponsored loans, and scholarships/grants available. Financial award application deadline: 2/15; financial award applicants required to submit FAFSA. *Unit head:* Dr. Karen Schuster Webb, Systemwide Dean, 415-955-2051, E-mail: contacto@alliantmexico.com. *Application contact:* Lesly Gutierrez Garcia, Coordinator of Admissions and Student Services, (+5255) 5525-7651, E-mail: contacto@alliantmexico.com. Web site: http://www.alliantmexico.com/.

Alliant International University–San Diego, Shirley M. Hufstedler School of Education, Educational Leadership Programs, San Diego, CA 92131-1799. Offers educational administration (MA); educational leadership and management (K-12) (Ed D); higher education (Ed D, Certificate); preliminary administrative services (Credential). Part-time programs available. *Faculty:* 4 full-time (2 women), 3 part-time/adjunct (2 women). *Students:* 11 full-time (8 women), 32 part-time (21 women); includes 19 minority (10 Black or African American, non-Hispanic/Latino; 5 Asian, non-Hispanic/Latino; 4 Hispanic/Latino), 4 international. Average age 45. In 2011, 1 master's, 5 doctorates awarded. *Degree requirements:* For doctorate, comprehensive exam, thesis/dissertation. *Entrance requirements:* For master's, minimum GPA of 2.5, letters of recommendation; for doctorate, minimum GPA of 3.0, letters of recommendation. Additional exam requirements/recommendations for international students: Required—TOEFL (minimum score 550 paper-based; 213 computer-based), TWE (minimum score 5). *Application deadline:* For fall admission, 7/1 priority date for domestic students, 7/1 for international students; for spring admission, 12/1 priority date for domestic students, 12/1 for international students. Applications are processed on a rolling basis. Application fee: $55. Electronic applications accepted. Tuition and fees vary according to degree level and program. *Financial support:* Federal Work-Study, institutionally sponsored loans, and scholarships/grants available. Financial award application deadline: 2/15; financial award applicants required to submit FAFSA. *Faculty research:* Global education, women and international educational opportunities. *Unit head:* Dr. Trudy Day, Program Director, Educational Policy and Practice Programs, 415-955-2102, Fax: 415-955-2179, E-mail: admissions@alliant.edu. *Application contact:* Alliant International University Central Contact Center, 866-U-ALLIANT, Fax: 858-635-4555, E-mail: admissions@alliant.edu.

Alliant International University–San Francisco, Shirley M. Hufstedler School of Education, Educational Leadership Programs, San Francisco, CA 94133-1221. Offers community college administration (Ed D); educational administration (MA); educational leadership and management (K-12) (Ed D); higher education (Ed D); preliminary administrative services (Credential). Part-time programs available. *Faculty:* 5 full-time (2 women), 2 part-time/adjunct (both women). *Students:* 11 part-time (5 women). Average age 46. In 2011, 2 doctorates awarded. *Degree requirements:* For doctorate, comprehensive exam, thesis/dissertation. *Entrance requirements:* For master's and doctorate, minimum GPA of 3.0, letters of recommendation. Additional exam requirements/recommendations for international students: Required—TOEFL (minimum score 550 paper-based; 213 computer-based; 80 iBT), TWE (minimum score 5). *Application deadline:* For fall admission, 7/1 priority date for domestic students, 7/1 for international students; for spring admission, 12/1 priority date for domestic students, 12/1 for international students. Applications are processed on a rolling basis. Application fee: $65. Electronic applications accepted. *Financial support:* Federal Work-Study, institutionally sponsored loans, and scholarships/grants available. Financial award application deadline: 2/15; financial award applicants required to submit FAFSA. *Faculty research:* Leadership in higher education, community colleges. *Unit head:* Dr. Trudy Day, Educational Policy and Practice Director, 415-955-2102, Fax: 415-955-2179, E-mail: admissions@alliant.edu. *Application contact:* Alliant International University Central Contact Center, 866-U-ALLIANT, Fax: 858-635-4555, E-mail: admissions@alliant.edu. Web site: http://www.alliant.edu/gsoe/.

Alverno College, School of Education, Milwaukee, WI 53234-3922. Offers adaptive education (MA); administrative leadership (MA); adult education and organizational development (MA); adult educational and instructional design (MA); adult educational and instructional technology (MA); global connections in the humanities (MA); instructional leadership (MA); instructional technology for K-12 settings (MA); professional development (MA); reading education (MA); reading education with adaptive education (MA); science education (MA); teaching in alternative schools (MA). *Accreditation:* NCATE. Part-time and evening/weekend programs available. *Faculty:* 22 full-time (18 women), 13 part-time/adjunct (all women). *Students:* 63 full-time (58 women), 91 part-time (81 women); includes 36 minority (29 Black or African American, non-Hispanic/Latino; 1 Asian, non-Hispanic/Latino; 4 Hispanic/Latino; 1 Native Hawaiian or other Pacific Islander, non-Hispanic/Latino; 1 Two or more races, non-Hispanic/Latino), 2 international. Average age 38. 151 applicants, 60% accepted, 62 enrolled. In 2011, 52 master's awarded. *Degree requirements:* For master's, presentation/defense of proposal, conference presentation of inquiry projects. *Entrance requirements:* For master's, bachelor's degree in related field, communication samples from work setting, 3 letters of recommendation. Additional exam requirements/recommendations for international students: Required—TOEFL. *Application deadline:* For fall admission, 7/15 priority date for domestic students, 7/15 for international students; for spring admission, 12/15 priority date for domestic students, 12/15 for international students. Applications are processed on a rolling basis. Application fee: $0. Electronic applications accepted. Application fee is waived when completed online. Tuition and fees vary according to program. *Financial support:* In 2011–12, 1 student received support. Federal Work-Study available. Support available to part-time students. Financial award application deadline: 4/15; financial award applicants required to submit FAFSA. *Faculty research:* Student self-assessment, self-reflection, integration of curriculum, identifying needs of students in strategic situations and designing appropriate classroom strategies. *Unit head:* Dr. Desiree Pointer-Mace, Associate Dean, Graduate Program, 414-382-6345, Fax: 414-382-6332, E-mail: desiree.pointer-mace@alverno.edu. *Application contact:* Mary Claire Jones, Graduate Recruiter, 414-382-6106, Fax: 414-382-6354, E-mail: maryclaire.jones@alverno.edu.

American College of Education, Graduate Programs, Chicago, IL 60606. Offers curriculum and instruction (M Ed), including bilingual, ESL; educational leadership (M Ed); educational technology (M Ed).

American InterContinental University Online, Program in Education, Hoffman Estates, IL 60192. Offers curriculum and instruction (M Ed); educational assessment and evaluation (M Ed); instructional technology (M Ed); leadership of educational organizations (M Ed). Evening/weekend programs available. Postbaccalaureate distance learning degree programs offered (no on-campus study). *Entrance requirements:* Additional exam requirements/recommendations for international students: Required—TOEFL (minimum score 550 paper-based; 213 computer-based). Electronic applications accepted.

American International College, School of Arts, Education and Sciences, Department of Education, Springfield, MA 01109-3189. Offers early childhood education (M Ed, CAGS); educational leadership and supervision (Ed D); elementary education (M Ed, CAGS); middle/secondary education (M Ed, CAGS); moderate disabilities (M Ed, CAGS); reading (M Ed, CAGS); school adjustment counseling (MA, CAGS); school administration (M Ed, CAGS); school guidance counseling (MA, CAGS); teaching (MA, MS); teaching and learning (Ed D). Part-time and evening/weekend programs available. Terminal master's awarded for partial completion of doctoral program. *Degree requirements:* For master's, comprehensive exam (for some programs), thesis (for some programs), practicum; for doctorate, comprehensive exam (for some programs), thesis/dissertation; for CAGS, practicum. *Entrance requirements:* For master's, minimum B-average in undergraduate course work; for doctorate, GRE General Test, interview. Additional exam requirements/recommendations for international students: Required—TOEFL. Electronic applications accepted.

American Public University System, AMU/APU Graduate Programs, Charles Town, WV 25414. Offers accounting (MBA, MS); administration and supervision (M Ed); criminal justice (MA); emergency and disaster management (MA); entrepreneurship (MBA); environmental policy and management (MS), including environmental planning, environmental sustainability, fish and wildlife management, general (MA, MS), global environmental management; finance (MBA); general (MBA); global business management (MBA); guidance and counseling (M Ed); history (MA), including American history, ancient and classical history, European history, global history, military and diplomatic history, public history; homeland security (MA); homeland security resource allocation (MBA); humanities (MA); information technology (MS), including digital forensics, enterprise software development, information assurance and security, IT project management; information technology management (MBA); intelligence studies (MA), including criminal intelligence, general (MA, MS), homeland security, intelligence analysis, intelligence collection, intelligence operations, terrorism studies; international relations and conflict resolution (MA), including comparative and security issues, conflict resolution, international and transnational security issues, peacekeeping; legal studies (MA); management (MA), including defense management, general (MA, MS), human resource management, organizational leadership, public administration, reverse logistics, strategic consulting; marketing (MBA); military history (MA), including American military history, American revolution, civil war, war since 1946, World War II; military studies (MA), including air warfare, asymmetrical warfare, joint warfare, land warfare, naval warfare, strategic leadership; national security studies (MA), including general (MA, MS), homeland security, regional security studies, security and intelligence analysis, terrorism studies; nonprofit management (MBA); political science (MA), including American politics and government, comparative government and development, public policy; psychology (MA); public administration (MA, MPA), including disaster management (MPA), environmental policy (MA), health policy (MPA), human resources (MPA), national security (MPA), organizational management (MPA), security management (MPA); public health (MA, MPH), including emergency management (MPH), environmental health (MPH), public administration (MA); reverse logistics management (MA); security management (MA); space studies (MS), including aerospace science, planetary science; sports and health sciences (MS); sports management (MS), including coaching theory and strategy, sports administration; teaching (M Ed), including curriculum and instruction for elementary teachers, elementary, elementary reading, English language learners, instructional leadership, online learning, secondary social sciences, special education; transportation and logistics management (MA), including maritime engineering management. Programs offered via distance learning only. Part-time and evening/weekend programs available. Postbaccalaureate distance learning degree programs offered (no on-campus study). *Faculty:* 445 full-time (241 women), 1,360 part-time/adjunct (617 women). *Students:* 688 full-time (338 women), 10,168 part-time (3,706 women); includes 3,130 minority (1,007 Black or African American, non-Hispanic/Latino; 103 American Indian or Alaska Native, non-Hispanic/Latino; 825 Asian, non-Hispanic/Latino; 810 Hispanic/Latino; 51 Native Hawaiian or other Pacific Islander, non-Hispanic/Latino; 334 Two or more races, non-Hispanic/Latino), 134 international. Average age 35. In 2011, 2,386 master's awarded. *Degree requirements:* For master's, comprehensive exam or practicum. *Entrance requirements:* For master's, official transcript showing earned bachelor's degree from institution accredited by recognized accrediting body. Additional exam requirements/recommendations for international students: Required—TOEFL (minimum score 550 paper-based; 213 computer-based), IELTS (minimum score 6.5). *Application deadline:* Applications are processed on a rolling basis. Application fee: $0. Electronic applications accepted. *Expenses: Tuition:* Part-time $325 per credit hour. *Financial support:* Applicants required to submit FAFSA. *Faculty research:* Military history, criminal justice, management performance, national security. *Unit head:* Dr. Karan Powell, Executive Vice President and Provost, 877-468-6268, Fax: 304-724-3780. *Application contact:* Terry Grant, Vice President of Enrollment Management, 877-468-6268, Fax: 304-724-3780, E-mail: info@apus.edu. Web site: http://www.apus.edu.

Andrews University, School of Graduate Studies, School of Education, Department of Leadership and Educational Administration, Program in Educational Administration and Leadership, Berrien Springs, MI 49104. Offers MA, Ed D, PhD, Ed S. *Faculty:* 4 full-time (0 women). *Students:* 2 full-time (1 woman), 21 part-time (8 women); includes 10 minority (7 Black or African American, non-Hispanic/Latino; 2 Hispanic/Latino; 1 Two or more races, non-Hispanic/Latino), 8 international. Average age 41. 25 applicants, 44% accepted, 2 enrolled. In 2011, 8 degrees awarded. *Degree requirements:* For master's, thesis or alternative; for doctorate, thesis/dissertation. *Entrance requirements:* For master's and doctorate, GRE Subject Test. Additional exam requirements/recommendations for international students: Required—TOEFL (minimum score 550 paper-based). *Application deadline:* Applications are processed on a rolling basis. Application fee: $40. *Financial support:* Research assistantships available. *Unit head:* Dr. Robson Marinho, Coordinator, 269-471-3487. *Application contact:* Carolyn Hurst, Supervisor of Graduate Admission, 800-253-2874, Fax: 269-471-6321, E-mail: graduate@andrews.edu.

Andrews University, School of Graduate Studies, School of Education, Department of Leadership and Educational Administration, Program in Leadership, Berrien Springs, MI 49104. Offers MA, Ed D, PhD, Ed S. *Students:* 97 part-time (37 women); includes 20 minority (11 Black or African American, non-Hispanic/Latino; 1 American Indian or Alaska Native, non-Hispanic/Latino; 3 Asian, non-Hispanic/Latino; 5 Hispanic/Latino), 15 international. Average age 49. 32 applicants, 44% accepted, 11 enrolled. In 2011, 9 degrees awarded. *Entrance requirements:* For master's, GRE. Additional exam requirements/recommendations for international students: Required—TOEFL (minimum score 550 paper-based). Application fee: $40. *Unit head:* Dr. Robson Marinhor, Chair, 269-471-6580. *Application contact:* Carolyn Hurst, Supervisor of Graduate Admission, 800-253-2874, Fax: 269-471-6321, E-mail: graduate@andrews.edu.

Angelo State University, College of Graduate Studies, College of Education, Department of Curriculum and Instruction, Program in School Administration, San Angelo, TX 76909. Offers principal (Certificate); school administration (M Ed); superintendent (Certificate). Part-time and evening/weekend programs available. *Faculty:* 17 full-time (12 women). *Students:* 9 full-time (8 women), 57 part-time (29 women); includes 17 minority (3 Black or African American, non-Hispanic/Latino; 1 American Indian or Alaska Native, non-Hispanic/Latino; 13 Hispanic/Latino). Average age 40. 38 applicants, 87% accepted, 28 enrolled. In 2011, 10 master's awarded. *Degree requirements:* For master's, comprehensive exam. *Entrance requirements:* Additional exam requirements/recommendations for international students: Required—TOEFL or IELTS. *Application deadline:* For fall admission, 7/15 priority date for domestic students, 6/10 for international students; for spring admission, 12/1 priority date for domestic students, 11/1 for international students. Applications are processed on a rolling basis. Application fee: $40 ($50 for international students). Electronic applications accepted. *Financial support:* In 2011–12, 19 students received support. Career-related internships or fieldwork, Federal Work-Study, scholarships/grants, and unspecified assistantships available. Support available to part-time students. Financial award application deadline: 3/1; financial award applicants required to submit FAFSA. *Unit head:* Dr. James Summerlin, 325-942-2052 Ext. 266, Fax: 325-942-2039, E-mail: jsummerlin@angelo.edu. *Application contact:* Aly Hunter, Graduate Admissions Assistant, 325-942-2169, Fax: 325-942-2194, E-mail: aly.hunter@angelo.edu. Web site: http://www.angelo.edu/dept/ci.

Antioch University New England, Graduate School, Department of Organization and Management, Program in Administration and Supervision, Keene, NH 03431-3552. Offers M Ed. *Degree requirements:* For master's, practicum. *Entrance requirements:* For master's, previous course work and work experience in organization and management. Additional exam requirements/recommendations for international students: Required—TOEFL (minimum score 600 paper-based; 250 computer-based). Electronic applications accepted. *Expenses:* Contact institution. *Faculty research:* Collaborative research programs in Waldorf schools and communities, shared decision making in schools, rational to creative problem solving, competency to shift paradigms of thinking.

Appalachian State University, Cratis D. Williams Graduate School, Department of Leadership and Educational Studies, Boone, NC 28608. Offers educational administration (Ed S); educational media (MA); higher education (MA, Ed S); library science (MLS); school administration (MSA). Part-time and evening/weekend programs available. Postbaccalaureate distance learning degree programs offered (no on-campus study). *Faculty:* 35 full-time (15 women), 1 (woman) part-time/adjunct. *Students:* 35 full-time (27 women), 369 part-time (293 women); includes 31 minority (26 Black or African American, non-Hispanic/Latino; 1 Asian, non-Hispanic/Latino; 4 Hispanic/Latino). 196 applicants, 83% accepted, 117 enrolled. In 2011, 195 master's, 32 other advanced degrees awarded. *Degree requirements:* For master's and Ed S, comprehensive exam, thesis optional. *Entrance requirements:* For master's and Ed S, GRE or MAT, 3 letters of recommendation. Additional exam requirements/recommendations for international students: Required—TOEFL (minimum score 570 paper-based; 230 computer-based; 79 iBT), IELTS (minimum score 6.5). *Application deadline:* For fall admission, 3/14 priority date for domestic students, 2/1 for international students; for spring admission, 11/1 for domestic students, 7/1 for international students. Applications are processed on a rolling basis. Application fee: $55. Electronic applications accepted. *Expenses:* Tuition, state resident: full-time $4040; part-time $180 per semester hour. Tuition, nonresident: full-time $15,900; part-time $760 per semester hour. *Required fees:* $2500; $20 per semester hour. Tuition and fees vary according to campus/location. *Financial support:* In 2011–12, 10 research assistantships (averaging $8,000 per year) were awarded; career-related internships or fieldwork, scholarships/grants, and unspecified assistantships also available. Financial award application deadline: 4/1; financial award applicants required to submit FAFSA. *Faculty research:* Brain, learning and meditation; leadership of teaching and learning. *Total annual research expenditures:* $515,000. *Unit head:* Dr. Robert Sanders, Interim Director, 828-262-3112, E-mail: sandersrl@appstate.edu. *Application contact:* Lori Dean, Graduate Student Coordinator, 828-262-6041, E-mail: deanlk@appstate.edu. Web site: http://www.les.appstate.edu.

Appalachian State University, Cratis D. Williams Graduate School, Program in Educational Leadership, Boone, NC 28608. Offers licensure (superintendent) (Ed D). *Accreditation:* NCATE. Part-time programs available. Postbaccalaureate distance learning degree programs offered (no on-campus study). *Students:* 10 full-time (9 women), 85 part-time (50 women); includes 14 minority (10 Black or African American, non-Hispanic/Latino; 1 American Indian or Alaska Native, non-Hispanic/Latino; 1 Asian, non-Hispanic/Latino; 2 Hispanic/Latino), 1 international. 45 applicants, 71% accepted, 26 enrolled. In 2011, 16 doctorates awarded. *Degree requirements:* For doctorate, comprehensive exam, thesis/dissertation. *Entrance requirements:* For doctorate, GRE General Test, 4 letters of recommendation. Additional exam requirements/recommendations for international students: Required—TOEFL (minimum score 570 paper-based; 230 computer-based; 79 iBT) or IELTS (minimum score 6.5). *Application deadline:* For fall admission, 3/1 for domestic students, 2/1 for international students; for spring admission, 7/1 for international students. Application fee: $55. Electronic applications accepted. *Expenses:* Tuition, state resident: full-time $4040; part-time $180 per semester hour. Tuition, nonresident: full-time $15,900; part-time $760 per semester hour. *Required fees:* $2500; $20 per semester hour. Tuition and fees vary according to campus/location. *Financial support:* In 2011–12, 8 research assistantships (averaging $16,000 per year) were awarded; Federal Work-Study, scholarships/grants, and unspecified assistantships also available. Financial award application deadline: 4/1; financial award applicants required to submit FAFSA. *Faculty research:* Sustainability of organizations, cultural pedagogy. *Unit head:* Dr. C. James Killacky, Director, 828-262-3168, E-mail: killackycj@appstate.edu. *Application contact:* Susan Musilli, Graduate Student Coordinator, 828-262-3168, E-mail: musillism@appstate.edu. Web site: http://www.edl.appstate.edu.

Arcadia University, Graduate Studies, Department of Education, Glenside, PA 19038-3295. Offers art education (M Ed); computer education (CAS); curriculum (CAS); curriculum studies (M Ed); early childhood education (M Ed, CAS), including individualized (M Ed), master teacher (M Ed), research in child development (M Ed); educational leadership (M Ed, Ed D, CAS); elementary education (M Ed, CAS); English education (MA Ed); environmental education (MA Ed, CAS); history education (MA Ed); instructional technology (M Ed); language arts (M Ed, CAS); library science (M Ed); mathematics education (M Ed, MA Ed, CAS); music education (MA Ed); psychology (MA Ed); reading (M Ed, CAS); science education (M Ed, CAS); secondary education (M Ed, CAS); special education (M Ed, Ed D, CAS); theater arts (MA Ed); written communication (MA Ed). *Accreditation:* NASAD. Part-time and evening/weekend programs available. Postbaccalaureate distance learning degree programs offered (minimal on-campus study). *Faculty:* 12 full-time (8 women), 38 part-time/adjunct (26 women). *Students:* 66 full-time (48 women), 590 part-time (477 women); includes 65 minority (53 Black or African American, non-Hispanic/Latino; 6 Asian, non-Hispanic/Latino; 3 Hispanic/Latino; 3 Two or more races, non-Hispanic/Latino), 4 international. Average age 36. In 2011, 229 master's, 5 doctorates awarded. *Application deadline:* Applications are processed on a rolling basis. Application fee: $50. Electronic applications accepted. *Expenses:* Contact institution. *Financial support:* Career-related internships or fieldwork, tuition waivers (partial), and unspecified assistantships available. *Unit head:* Dr. Steven P. Gulkus, Associate Professor, 215-572-2120, E-mail: gulkus@arcadia.edu. *Application contact:* 215-572-2925, Fax: 215-572-2126, E-mail: grad@arcadia.edu.

Argosy University, Atlanta, College of Education, Atlanta, GA 30328. Offers educational leadership (MAEd, Ed D, Ed S), including higher education administration (Ed D), K-12 education (Ed D); teaching and learning (MAEd, Ed D, Ed S), including education technology (Ed D), higher education (Ed D), K-12 education (Ed D).

See Close-Up on page 1017.

Argosy University, Chicago, College of Education, Chicago, IL 60601. Offers adult education and training (MA Ed); community college executive leadership (Ed D); educational leadership (MA Ed, Ed D, Ed S), including district leadership (Ed D), higher education administration (Ed D), K-12 education (Ed D); instructional leadership (Ed D, Ed S), including higher education (Ed D), K-12 education (Ed D). Postbaccalaureate distance learning degree programs offered (minimal on-campus study).

See Close-Up on page 769.

Argosy University, Dallas, College of Education, Farmers Branch, TX 75244. Offers educational administration (MA Ed); educational leadership (Ed D); higher and postsecondary education (MA Ed); instructional leadership (MA Ed); school psychology (MA).

See Close-Up on page 771.

Argosy University, Denver, College of Education, Denver, CO 80231. Offers community college executive leadership (Ed D); educational leadership (MA Ed, Ed D), including higher education (Ed D), K-12 education (Ed D); instructional leadership (MA Ed, Ed D), including higher education administration (Ed D), K-12 education (Ed D).

See Close-Up on page 773.

Argosy University, Hawai`i, College of Education, Honolulu, HI 96813. Offers adult education and training (MAEd); educational leadership (Ed D), including higher education administration, K-12 education; instructional leadership (Ed D), including higher education, K-12 education; school psychology (MA).

See Close-Up on page 775.

Argosy University, Inland Empire, College of Education, San Bernardino, CA 92408. Offers community college executive leadership (Ed D); educational leadership (MA Ed, Ed D), including higher education administration (Ed D), K-12 education (Ed D); instructional leadership (MA Ed, Ed D), including higher education (Ed D), K-12 education (Ed D), multiple subject teacher preparation (MA Ed), single subject teacher preparation (MA Ed).

See Close-Up on page 1019.

Argosy University, Los Angeles, College of Education, Santa Monica, CA 90045. Offers community college executive leadership (Ed D); educational leadership (MA Ed, Ed D), including higher education administration (Ed D), K-12 education (Ed D); instructional leadership (MA Ed, Ed D), including higher education (Ed D), K-12 education (Ed D), multiple subject teacher preparation (MA Ed), single subject teacher preparation (MA Ed).

See Close-Up on page 777.

Argosy University, Nashville, College of Education, Program in Educational Leadership, Nashville, TN 37214. Offers educational leadership (MA Ed, Ed S); higher education administration (Ed D); K-12 education (Ed D).

See Close-Up on page 1021.

Argosy University, Nashville, College of Education, Program in Instructional Leadership, Nashville, TN 37214. Offers education technology (Ed D); higher education administration (Ed D); instructional leadership (MA Ed, Ed S); K-12 education (Ed D).

See Close-Up on page 1021.

Argosy University, Orange County, College of Education, Orange, CA 92868. Offers community college executive leadership (Ed D); educational leadership (MA Ed, Ed D), including higher education administration (Ed D), K-12 education (Ed D); instructional leadership (MA Ed, Ed D), including education technology (Ed D), higher education (Ed D), K-12 education (Ed D), multiple subject teacher preparation (MA Ed), single subject teacher preparation (MA Ed).

See Close-Up on page 779.

Argosy University, Phoenix, College of Education, Phoenix, AZ 85021. Offers adult education and training (MA Ed); advanced educational administration (Ed D, Ed S); community college executive leadership (Ed D); educational administration (MA Ed); educational leadership (MA Ed, Ed D, Ed S), including education technology (Ed D), higher education administration (Ed D), K-12 education (Ed D); higher and postsecondary education (MA Ed); initial educational administration (Ed D, Ed S); school psychology (MA); teaching and learning (MA Ed, Ed D, Ed S), including education technology (Ed D), higher education (Ed D), K-12 education (Ed D).

See Close-Up on page 781.

Argosy University, Salt Lake City, College of Education, Draper, UT 84020. Offers educational leadership (MA Ed, Ed D).

See Close-Up on page 783.

Argosy University, San Diego, College of Education, San Diego, CA 92108. Offers community college executive leadership (Ed D); educational leadership (MA Ed, Ed D), including higher education administration (Ed D), K-12 education (Ed D); instructional leadership (MA Ed, Ed D), including higher education (Ed D), K-12 education (Ed D).

See Close-Up on page 785.

Argosy University, San Francisco Bay Area, College of Education, Alameda, CA 94501. Offers community college executive leadership (Ed D); educational leadership (MA Ed, Ed D), including education technology (Ed D), higher education administration (Ed D), K-12 education (Ed D); instructional leadership (MA Ed, Ed D), including education technology (Ed D), higher education (Ed D), K-12 education (Ed D), multiple subject teacher preparation (MA Ed), single subject teacher preparation (MA Ed).

See Close-Up on page 787.

Argosy University, Sarasota, College of Education, Sarasota, FL 34235. Offers community college executive leadership (Ed D); educational leadership (MA Ed, Ed D, Ed S), including higher education administration (Ed D), K-12 education (Ed D); school counseling (MA, Ed S); school psychology (MA); teaching and learning (MA Ed, Ed D, Ed S), including education technology (Ed D), higher education (Ed D), K-12 education (Ed D).

See Close-Up on page 789.

Argosy University, Schaumburg, College of Education, Schaumburg, IL 60173-5403. Offers community college executive leadership (Ed D); educational leadership (MA Ed, Ed D, Ed S), including district leadership (Ed D), higher education administration (Ed D), K-12 education (Ed D); instructional leadership (Ed D, Ed S), including higher education (Ed D), K-12 education (Ed D).

See Close-Up on page 791.

Argosy University, Seattle, College of Education, Seattle, WA 98121. Offers adult education and training (MA Ed); community college executive leadership (Ed D); educational leadership (MA Ed, Ed D), including higher education administration (Ed D), K-12 education (Ed D); higher and postsecondary education (MA Ed); instructional leadership (MA Ed, Ed D), including education technology (Ed D), higher education (Ed D), K-12 education (Ed D).

See Close-Up on page 793.

Argosy University, Tampa, College of Education, Tampa, FL 33607. Offers community college executive leadership (Ed D); educational leadership (MA Ed, Ed D, Ed S), including higher education administration (Ed D), K-12 education (Ed D); school counseling (MA); teaching and learning (MA Ed, Ed D, Ed S), including higher education (Ed D), K-12 education (Ed D).

See Close-Up on page 795.

Argosy University, Twin Cities, College of Education, Eagan, MN 55121. Offers advanced educational administration (Ed D, Ed S); educational leadership (MA Ed, Ed D, Ed S), including higher education administration (Ed D), K-12 education (Ed D); higher and postsecondary education (MA Ed); initial educational administration (Ed D, Ed S); instructional leadership (MA Ed, Ed D, Ed S), including education technology (Ed D), higher education (Ed D), K-12 education (Ed D).

See Close-Up on page 797.

Argosy University, Washington DC, College of Education, Arlington, VA 22209. Offers community college executive leadership (Ed D); educational leadership (MA Ed, Ed D, Ed S), including higher education administration (Ed D), K-12 education (Ed D); instructional leadership (MA Ed, Ed D, Ed S), including higher education (Ed D), K-12 education (Ed D).

See Close-Up on page 799.

Arizona State University, Mary Lou Fulton Teachers College, Program in Educational Administration and Supervision, Phoenix, AZ 85069. Offers educational administration and supervision (M Ed); leadership and innovation (Ed D). Part-time and evening/weekend programs available. Postbaccalaureate distance learning degree programs offered (minimal on-campus study). Terminal master's awarded for partial completion of doctoral program. *Degree requirements:* For master's, thesis or alternative, written portfolio, internship, interactive Program of Study (iPOS) submitted before completing 50 percent of required credit hours; for doctorate, thesis/dissertation, interactive Program of Study (iPOS) submitted before completing 50 percent of required credit hours. *Entrance requirements:* For master's, minimum GPA of 3.0 or equivalent in last 2 years of work leading to bachelor's degree, 1 year of teaching experience, 3 letters of recommendation, personal statement, writing sample, curriculum vitae or resume; for doctorate, master's degree in education or related field, resume, personal statement, writing samples based on short writing prompts, 3 letters of recommendation. Additional exam requirements/recommendations for international students: Required—TOEFL, IELTS, or Pearson Test of English. Electronic applications accepted.

Arizona State University, Mary Lou Fulton Teachers College, Program in Educational Leadership and Policy Studies, Phoenix, AZ 85069. Offers PhD. Fall admission only. *Degree requirements:* For doctorate, comprehensive exam, thesis/dissertation, interactive Program of Study (iPOS) submitted before completing 50 percent of required credit hours. *Entrance requirements:* For doctorate, GRE, minimum GPA of 3.0 or equivalent in last 2 years of work leading to bachelor's degree, 3 letters of recommendation, personal statement, writing sample, curriculum vitae or resume. Additional exam requirements/recommendations for international students: Required—TOEFL (minimum score 80 iBT), TOEFL, IELTS, or Pearson Test of English. Electronic applications accepted. *Expenses:* Contact institution. *Faculty research:* Education policy analysis, school finance and quantitative methods, school improvement in ethnically, linguistically and economically diverse communities, parent/teacher engagement, school choice, accountability polices, school finance litigation, school segregation.

Arkansas State University, Graduate School, College of Education, Department of Educational Leadership, Curriculum, and Special Education, Jonesboro, State University, AR 72467. Offers community college administration education (SCCT); curriculum and instruction (MSE); educational leadership (MSE, Ed D, PhD, Ed S), including curriculum and instruction (MSE, Ed S); special education (MSE), including gifted, talented, and creative, instructional specialist 4-12, instructional specialist P-4. *Accreditation:* NCATE. Part-time programs available. Postbaccalaureate distance learning degree programs offered (no on-campus study). *Faculty:* 12 full-time (5 women). *Students:* 11 full-time (6 women), 2,240 part-time (1,686 women); includes 374 minority (278 Black or African American, non-Hispanic/Latino; 14 American Indian or Alaska Native, non-Hispanic/Latino; 12 Asian, non-Hispanic/Latino; 46 Hispanic/Latino; 2 Native Hawaiian or other Pacific Islander, non-Hispanic/Latino; 22 Two or more races, non-Hispanic/Latino), 1 international. Average age 37. 1,519 applicants, 76% accepted, 790 enrolled. In 2011, 827 master's, 8 doctorates, 30 other advanced degrees awarded. *Degree requirements:* For master's, comprehensive exam, thesis or alternative; for doctorate, comprehensive exam, thesis/dissertation; for other advanced degree, comprehensive exam. *Entrance requirements:* For master's, GRE General Test or MAT, appropriate bachelor's degree, letters of reference, interview, official transcript, immunization records; for doctorate, GRE General Test or MAT, interview, master's degree, letters of reference, official transcript, personal statement, writing sample, immunization records; for other advanced degree, GRE General Test or MAT, interview, master's degree, letters of reference, official transcript, 3 years teaching experience, mentor, teaching license, immunization records. Additional exam requirements/recommendations for international students: Required—TOEFL (minimum score 550 paper-based; 213 computer-based; 79 iBT), IELTS (minimum score 6), Pearson Test of English Academic (minimum score 56). *Application deadline:* Applications are processed on a rolling basis. Application fee: $50. Electronic applications accepted. *Expenses:* Tuition, state resident: full-time $4044; part-time $225 per credit hour. Tuition, nonresident: full-time $8087; part-time $449 per credit hour. *Required fees:* $936; $52 per credit hour. $25 per term. One-time fee: $30. Tuition and fees vary according to course load and program. *Financial support:* In 2011–12, 6 students received support. Fellowships, teaching assistantships, career-related internships or fieldwork, scholarships/grants, and unspecified assistantships available. Financial award application deadline: 7/1; financial award applicants required to submit FAFSA. *Unit head:* Dr. Mitchell Holifield, Chair, 870-972-3062, Fax: 870-680-8130, E-mail: hfield@astate.edu. *Application contact:* Dr. Andrew Sustich, Dean of the Graduate School, 870-972-3029, Fax: 870-972-3857, E-mail: sustich@astate.edu. Web site: http://www.astate.edu/a/education/elcse/.

Arkansas Tech University, Center for Leadership and Learning, College of Education, Russellville, AR 72801. Offers college student personnel (MS); educational leadership (Ed S); elementary education (M Ed); instructional improvement (M Ed); instructional technology (M Ed); physical education (M Ed); school counseling and leadership (M Ed); teaching (MAT). *Accreditation:* NCATE. Part-time and evening/weekend programs available. Postbaccalaureate distance learning degree programs offered (no on-campus study). *Students:* 70 full-time (44 women), 247 part-time (189 women); includes 57 minority (38 Black or African American, non-Hispanic/Latino; 1 American Indian or Alaska Native, non-Hispanic/Latino; 8 Asian, non-Hispanic/Latino; 4 Hispanic/Latino; 6 Two or more races, non-Hispanic/Latino), 3 international. Average age 31. In 2011, 58 master's awarded. *Degree requirements:* For master's, comprehensive exam, thesis optional, action research project. *Entrance requirements:* Additional exam requirements/recommendations for international students: Required—TOEFL (minimum score 550 paper-based; 213 computer-based; 79 iBT), IELTS (minimum score 6.5). *Application deadline:* For fall admission, 3/1 priority date for domestic students, 5/1 for international students; for spring admission, 10/1 priority date for domestic students, 10/1 for international students. Applications are processed on a rolling basis. Application fee: $25 ($75 for international students). Electronic applications accepted. *Expenses:* Tuition, state resident: full-time $4968; part-time $207 per credit hour. Tuition, nonresident: full-time $9936; part-time $414 per credit hour. *Required fees:* $375 per semester. Tuition and fees vary according to course load. *Financial support:* In 2011–12, teaching assistantships with full tuition reimbursements (averaging $4,800 per year) were awarded; research assistantships with full tuition reimbursements, career-related internships or fieldwork, Federal Work-Study, scholarships/grants, health care benefits, and unspecified assistantships also available. Support available to part-time students. Financial award application deadline: 4/15; financial award applicants required to submit FAFSA. *Unit head:* Dr. Eldon G. Clary, Jr., Dean, 479-968-0350, Fax: 479-968-0350, E-mail: eclary@atu.edu. *Application contact:* Dr. Mary B. Gunter, Dean of Graduate College, 479-968-0398, Fax: 479-964-0542, E-mail: gradcollege@atu.edu. Web site: http://www.atu.edu/education/.

Asbury University, School of Graduate and Professional Studies, Wilmore, KY 40390-1198. Offers biology: alternative certificate (MA Ed); chemistry: alternative certificate (MA Ed); English (MA Ed); English as a second language (MA Ed); ESL (MA Ed); French (MA Ed); Latin: alternative certificate (MA Ed); mathematics: alternative certificate (MA Ed); reading/writing endorsement (MA Ed); social studies (MA Ed); social work (MSW), including child and family services; Spanish (MA Ed); special education (MA Ed); special education: alternative certificate (MA Ed); teacher as leader endorsement (MA Ed). *Accreditation:* NCATE. Part-time programs available. *Degree requirements:* For master's, action research project, portfolio. *Entrance requirements:* For master's, PRAXIS/NTE, minimum GPA of 2.75, letters of recommendation. Additional exam requirements/recommendations for international students: Required—TOEFL (minimum score 550 paper-based). Electronic applications accepted.

Ashland University, Dwight Schar College of Education, Department of Educational Administration, Ashland, OH 44805-3702. Offers curriculum specialist (M Ed); principalship (M Ed); pupil services (M Ed). Part-time programs available. *Faculty:* 7 full-time (3 women), 16 part-time/adjunct (4 women). *Students:* 108 full-time (72 women), 185 part-time (94 women); includes 34 minority (26 Black or African American, non-Hispanic/Latino; 2 American Indian or Alaska Native, non-Hispanic/Latino; 1 Asian, non-Hispanic/Latino; 2 Hispanic/Latino; 3 Two or more races, non-Hispanic/Latino), 2 international. Average age 33. 75 applicants, 100% accepted, 65 enrolled. In 2011, 143 master's awarded. *Degree requirements:* For master's, thesis or alternative, internship. *Entrance requirements:* For master's, teaching certificate or license, bachelor's degree, minimum cumulative GPA of 2.75. Additional exam requirements/recommendations for international students: Required—TOEFL. *Application deadline:* Applications are processed on a rolling basis. Application fee: $30. Electronic applications accepted. *Expenses: Tuition:* Full-time $5580; part-time $465 per credit hour. *Financial support:* Institutionally sponsored loans and scholarships/grants available. Financial award application deadline: 4/15. *Faculty research:* Gender and religious considerations in employment, ISLLC standards, adjunct faculty training, politics of school finance, ethnicity and employment. *Unit head:* Dr. Robert Thiede, Chair, 419-289-5258, Fax: 419-207-6702, E-mail: rthiede@ashland.edu. *Application contact:* Dr. Linda Billman, Director and Chair, Graduate Studies in Education/Associate Dean, 419-289-5369, Fax: 419-289-5331, E-mail: lbillman@ashland.edu.

Ashland University, Dwight Schar College of Education, Department of Educational Foundations, Ashland, OH 44805-3702. Offers teacher leader (M Ed). Part-time and evening/weekend programs available. *Faculty:* 12 full-time (9 women), 68 part-time/adjunct (33 women). *Students:* 3 full-time (2 women), 18 part-time (12 women); includes 1 minority (Two or more races, non-Hispanic/Latino), 2 international. Average age 28. 3 applicants, 100% accepted, 2 enrolled. In 2011, 15 master's awarded. *Degree requirements:* For master's, inquiry seminar, internship, or thesis. *Entrance requirements:* For master's, teaching certificate or license, bachelor's degree, minimum cumulative GPA of 2.75. Additional exam requirements/recommendations for international students: Required—TOEFL. *Application deadline:* Applications are processed on a rolling basis. Application fee: $30. Electronic applications accepted. *Expenses: Tuition:* Full-time $5580; part-time $465 per credit hour. *Financial support:* Application deadline: 4/15. *Faculty research:* Character education, teacher reflection, religion and education, professional education, environmental education. *Unit head:* Dr. Louise Fleming, Chair, 419-289-5347, E-mail: lfleming@ashland.edu. *Application contact:* Dr. Linda Billman, Associate Dean, 419-289-5369, Fax: 419-289-5331, E-mail: lbillman@ashland.edu. Web site: http://www.ashland.edu/academics/education/edfoundations/.

Ashland University, Dwight Schar College of Education, Doctoral Program in Educational Leadership Studies, Ashland, OH 44805-3702. Offers Ed D. Part-time and evening/weekend programs available. *Faculty:* 4 full-time (2 women), 1 (woman) part-time/adjunct. *Students:* 10 full-time (6 women), 44 part-time (17 women); includes 9 minority (all Black or African American, non-Hispanic/Latino), 2 international. Average age 40. In 2011, 5 doctorates awarded. *Degree requirements:* For doctorate, comprehensive exam, thesis/dissertation. *Entrance requirements:* For doctorate, GRE, master's degree, minimum GPA of 3.3, writing sample, letters of recommendation. Additional exam requirements/recommendations for international students: Required—TOEFL. *Application deadline:* For spring admission, 3/1 for domestic students. Applications are processed on a rolling basis. Application fee: $30. Electronic applications accepted. *Expenses:* Contact institution. *Financial support:* In 2011–12, 1 student received support. Teaching assistantships available. Financial award application deadline: 4/15. *Faculty research:* School funding, charter schools, administrative jobs, continuous improvement, marginalized groups, school finance, minority superintendent trends, teacher salaries, minority recruiting, women's issues. *Unit head:* Dr. Judy Alston, Director, 419-207-4983, Fax: 419-289-5097, E-mail: jalston@ashland.edu. *Application contact:* Administrative Assistant. Web site: http://www.ashland.edu/edd/.

Auburn University, Graduate School, College of Education, Department of Educational Foundations, Leadership, and Technology, Auburn University, AL 36849. Offers adult education (M Ed, MS, Ed D); curriculum and instruction (M Ed, MS, Ed D, Ed S); curriculum supervision (M Ed, MS, Ed D, Ed S); educational psychology (PhD); higher education administration (M Ed, MS, Ed D, Ed S); media instructional design (MS); media specialist (M Ed); school administration (M Ed, MS, Ed D, Ed S). *Accreditation:* NCATE. Part-time programs available. *Faculty:* 26 full-time (16 women), 3 part-time/adjunct (all women). *Students:* 58 full-time (28 women), 215 part-time (135 women); includes 89 minority (82 Black or African American, non-Hispanic/Latino; 1 American Indian or Alaska Native, non-Hispanic/Latino; 4 Asian, non-Hispanic/Latino; 2 Hispanic/Latino), 13 international. Average age 35. 140 applicants, 61% accepted, 56 enrolled. In 2011, 37 master's, 29 doctorates, 9 other advanced degrees awarded. *Degree requirements:* For master's, thesis (for some programs); for doctorate, thesis/dissertation; for Ed S, field project. *Entrance requirements:* For master's, doctorate, and Ed S, GRE General Test. *Application deadline:* For fall admission, 7/7 for domestic students; for spring admission, 11/24 for domestic students. Applications are processed on a rolling basis. Application fee: $50 ($60 for international students). Electronic applications accepted. *Expenses:* Tuition, state resident: full-time $7290; part-time $405 per credit hour. Tuition, nonresident: full-time $21,870; part-time $1215 per credit hour. *International tuition:* $22,000 full-time. *Required fees:* $1402. *Financial support:* Teaching assistantships and Federal Work-Study available. Support available to part-time students. Financial award application deadline: 3/15; financial award applicants required to submit FAFSA. *Unit head:* Dr. Sherida Downer, Head, 334-844-4460. *Application contact:* Dr. George Flowers, Dean of the Graduate School, 334-844-4700. Web site: http://www.education.auburn.edu/academic_departments/eflt/.

Auburn University Montgomery, School of Education, Department of Counselor, Leadership, and Special Education, Montgomery, AL 36124-4023. Offers counseling (M Ed, Ed S); education administration (M Ed, Ed S); special education (M Ed, Ed S). *Accreditation:* ACA; NCATE. Part-time and evening/weekend programs available. *Degree requirements:* For master's and Ed S, comprehensive exam. *Entrance requirements:* For master's, GRE General Test or MAT, certification, BS in teaching; for Ed S, GRE General Test or MAT, certification. Electronic applications accepted. *Expenses:* Tuition, state resident: full-time $5076. Tuition, nonresident: full-time $15,228.

Augusta State University, Graduate Studies, College of Education, Program in Educational Leadership, Augusta, GA 30904-2200. Offers M Ed, Ed S. *Accreditation:* NCATE. Part-time and evening/weekend programs available. *Faculty:* 10 full-time (3 women), 5 part-time/adjunct (3 women). *Students:* 46 full-time (33 women), 48 part-time (34 women); includes 44 minority (42 Black or African American, non-Hispanic/Latino; 2 Hispanic/Latino). Average age 37. 36 applicants, 42% accepted, 12 enrolled. In 2011, 21 master's, 47 Ed Ss awarded. *Degree requirements:* For master's, comprehensive exam; for Ed S, comprehensive exam, thesis. *Entrance requirements:* For master's, GRE, MAT, minimum GPA of 2.5; for Ed S, GRE, MAT. *Application deadline:* For fall admission, 8/1 priority date for domestic students. Applications are processed on a rolling basis. Application fee: $20. *Financial support:* In 2011–12, 2 students received support. Career-related internships or fieldwork, Federal Work-Study, institutionally sponsored loans, and unspecified assistantships available. Support available to part-time students. Financial award application deadline: 4/15; financial award applicants required to submit FAFSA. *Faculty research:* Restructuring schools, financing education, student transition. *Unit head:* Dr. Charles Jackson, Chair, 706-737-1497, Fax: 706-667-4706, E-mail: cjackson@aug.edu. *Application contact:* Andrea M. Scott, Secretary to the Dean, 706-737-1499, Fax: 706-667-4706, E-mail: ascott1@aug.edu.

Aurora University, College of Education, Aurora, IL 60506-4892. Offers curriculum and instruction (MA, Ed D); early childhood and special education (MA); education (MAT), including elementary certification; education and administration (Ed D); educational leadership (MEL); educational technology (MATL); reading instruction (MA); special education (MA). *Accreditation:* NCATE. Part-time and evening/weekend programs available. *Degree requirements:* For doctorate, comprehensive exam, thesis/dissertation. *Entrance requirements:* For master's, 2 years of teaching experience, valid teaching certificate. Additional exam requirements/recommendations for international students: Required—TOEFL (minimum score 550 paper-based; 213 computer-based). Electronic applications accepted. *Expenses:* Contact institution.

Austin Peay State University, College of Graduate Studies, College of Education, Department of Educational Specialties, Clarksville, TN 37044. Offers administration and supervision (Ed S); curriculum and instruction (MA Ed); education leadership (MA Ed); elementary education (Ed S); secondary education (Ed S); special education (MA Ed). Part-time and evening/weekend programs available. Postbaccalaureate distance learning degree programs offered. *Faculty:* 7 full-time (4 women), 4 part-time/adjunct (3 women). *Students:* 6 full-time (4 women), 86 part-time (66 women); includes 11 minority (6 Black or African American, non-Hispanic/Latino; 1 American Indian or Alaska Native, non-Hispanic/Latino; 4 Hispanic/Latino). Average age 37. 33 applicants, 100% accepted, 23 enrolled. In 2011, 32 master's, 7 Ed Ss awarded. *Degree requirements:* For master's, comprehensive exam, thesis optional. *Entrance requirements:* For master's, GRE General Test, 3 letters of recommendation, minimum undergraduate GPA of 2.75. Additional exam requirements/recommendations for international students: Required—TOEFL (minimum score 500 paper-based; 173 computer-based). *Application deadline:* For fall admission, 8/1 priority date for domestic students. Applications are processed on a rolling basis. Application fee: $25. Electronic applications accepted. *Expenses:* Tuition, state resident: part-time $350 per credit hour. Tuition, nonresident: full-time $20,644; part-time $971 per credit hour. *Required fees:* $1224; $61.20 per credit hour. *Financial support:* Career-related internships or fieldwork, Federal Work-Study, institutionally sponsored loans, scholarships/grants, and unspecified assistantships available. Support available to part-time students. Financial award application deadline: 3/1; financial award applicants required to submit FAFSA. *Unit head:* Dr. Moniqueka Gold, Chair, 931-221-7696, Fax: 931-221-1292, E-mail: goldm@apsu.edu. *Application contact:* Kendra Bryant, Graduate Admissions, 800-844-2778, Fax: 931-221-6188, E-mail: admissionsweb@apsu.edu.

Azusa Pacific University, School of Behavioral and Applied Sciences, Department of Doctoral Higher Education, Program in Higher Education Leadership, Azusa, CA 91702-7000. Offers Ed D.

Azusa Pacific University, School of Education, Program in School Administration, Azusa, CA 91702-7000. Offers MA. Part-time and evening/weekend programs available. *Degree requirements:* For master's, comprehensive exam or thesis, core exams, oral presentation. *Entrance requirements:* For master's, 12 units of course work in education, minimum GPA of 3.0. *Faculty research:* Instructional supervision, outcome-based education, technology and online searching, teacher preparation.

Baldwin Wallace University, Graduate Programs, Division of Education, Leadership in Higher Education Program, Berea, OH 44017-2088. Offers MA Ed. Part-time and evening/weekend programs available. *Faculty:* 9 full-time (4 women), 1 (woman) part-time/adjunct. *Students:* 23 full-time (14 women), 1 (woman) part-time; includes 1 minority (Black or African American, non-Hispanic/Latino). Average age 26. 57 applicants, 37% accepted, 15 enrolled. In 2011, 12 master's awarded. *Degree requirements:* For master's, comprehensive exam (for some programs). *Entrance requirements:* For master's, bachelor's degree in field, MAT or minimum GPA of 2.75. Additional exam requirements/recommendations for international students: Required—TOEFL (minimum score 523 paper-based; 193 computer-based; 70 iBT). *Application deadline:* For fall admission, 8/15 for domestic students; for spring admission, 12/15 for domestic students. Applications are processed on a rolling basis. Application fee: $25. Electronic applications accepted. Application fee is waived when completed online. *Expenses:* *Tuition:* Full-time $17,016; part-time $727 per credit hour. Tuition and fees vary according to program. *Faculty research:* Program development in higher education, leadership styles, the psychology of leadership and learning in higher education. *Unit head:* Dr. Debra Jamas, Director, 440-826-8177, Fax: 440-826-3779, E-mail: djamas@bw.edu. *Application contact:* Winifred W. Gerhardt, Director of Admission for the Evening and Weekend College, 440-826-2222, Fax: 440-826-3830, E-mail: admission@bw.edu. Web site: http://www.bw.edu/academics/mae/hedleader.

Baldwin Wallace University, Graduate Programs, Division of Education, Specialization in School Leadership, Berea, OH 44017-2088. Offers MA Ed. Part-time and evening/weekend programs available. Postbaccalaureate distance learning degree programs offered. *Faculty:* 2 full-time (0 women), 7 part-time/adjunct (2 women). *Students:* 14 full-time (12 women), 8 part-time (4 women); includes 7 minority (5 Black or African American, non-Hispanic/Latino; 2 Hispanic/Latino). Average age 36. 13 applicants, 54% accepted, 4 enrolled. In 2011, 18 master's awarded. *Degree requirements:* For master's, comprehensive exam. *Entrance requirements:* For master's, bachelor's degree in field, MAT or minimum GPA of 2.75. Additional exam requirements/recommendations for international students: Required—TOEFL (minimum score 523 paper-based; 193 computer-based; 70 iBT). *Application deadline:* For fall admission, 8/15 priority date for domestic students; for spring admission, 12/15 priority date for domestic students. Applications are processed on a rolling basis. Application fee: $25. Electronic applications accepted. Application fee is waived when completed online. *Expenses:* *Tuition:* Full-time $17,016; part-time $727 per credit hour. Tuition and fees vary according to program. *Financial support:* Career-related internships or fieldwork available. Support available to part-time students. Financial award application deadline: 5/1; financial award applicants required to submit FAFSA. *Faculty research:* Leadership styles, instructional strategies, formative assessment. *Unit head:* Dr. Karen Kaye, Chair, 440-826-2168, Fax: 440-826-3779, E-mail: kkaye@bw.edu. *Application contact:* Winifred W. Gerhardt, Director of Admission for the Evening and Weekend College, 440-826-2222, Fax: 440-826-3830, E-mail: admission@bw.edu. Web site: http://www.bw.edu/academics/mae/leader/.

Ball State University, Graduate School, Teachers College, Department of Educational Leadership, Program in Educational Administration, Muncie, IN 47306-1099. Offers MAE, Ed D. *Accreditation:* NCATE. *Faculty:* 7. *Students:* 109 full-time (50 women), 352 part-time (164 women); includes 38 minority (31 Black or African American, non-Hispanic/Latino; 1 American Indian or Alaska Native, non-Hispanic/Latino; 5 Hispanic/Latino; 1 Two or more races, non-Hispanic/Latino). Average age 29. 111 applicants, 90% accepted, 84 enrolled. In 2011, 101 master's, 6 doctorates awarded. *Degree requirements:* For doctorate, thesis/dissertation. *Entrance requirements:* For doctorate, GRE General Test, interview, minimum graduate GPA of 3.2. Application fee: $50. Tuition and fees vary according to program and reciprocity agreements. *Financial support:* In 2011–12, 14 students received support, including 2 teaching assistantships with full tuition reimbursements available (averaging $6,118 per year). Financial award application deadline: 3/1. *Unit head:* Dr. Joseph McKinney, Head, 765-285-2762. *Application contact:* Dr. Janet Sauer, Associate Provost for Research and Dean of the Graduate School. Web site: http://www.bsu.edu/teachers/departments/edld/.

Ball State University, Graduate School, Teachers College, Department of Educational Leadership, Program in School Superintendency, Muncie, IN 47306-1099. Offers Ed S. *Accreditation:* NCATE. *Faculty:* 7. *Students:* 13 full-time (5 women), 22 part-time (9 women); includes 4 minority (all Black or African American, non-Hispanic/Latino). Average age 38. 22 applicants, 73% accepted, 15 enrolled. In 2011, 15 Ed Ss awarded. *Degree requirements:* For Ed S, thesis. *Entrance requirements:* For degree, GRE General Test, interview. Application fee: $50. Tuition and fees vary according to program and reciprocity agreements. *Financial support:* In 2011–12, 2 students received support, including 1 teaching assistantship (averaging $1,658 per year). Financial award application deadline: 3/1. *Unit head:* Dr. Joseph McKinney, Director of Doctoral and Specialist Programs, 765-285-8488, Fax: 765-285-2166. *Application contact:* Dr. William Sharp, Associate Provost for Research and Dean of the Graduate School, 765-285-8488, E-mail: bsharp@bsu.edu.

Ball State University, Graduate School, Teachers College, Department of Educational Studies, Program in Executive Development, Muncie, IN 47306-1099. Offers MA. *Students:* 10 full-time (8 women), 37 part-time (25 women); includes 2 minority (both Black or African American, non-Hispanic/Latino), 1 international. Average age 31. 25 applicants, 60% accepted, 12 enrolled. In 2011, 36 master's awarded. Application fee: $50. Tuition and fees vary according to program and reciprocity agreements. *Financial support:* In 2011–12, 18 students received support, including 5 teaching assistantships (averaging $5,537 per year). Financial award application deadline: 3/1. *Unit head:* Jayne Beilke, Director, 765-285-5460, Fax: 765-285-5489. *Application contact:* Dr. Ruby Cain, Associate Provost for Research and Dean of the Graduate School. Web site: http://www.bsu.edu/teachers/departments/edstudies/.

Ball State University, Graduate School, Teachers College, Department of Educational Studies, Program in Student Affairs Administration in Higher Education, Muncie, IN 47306-1099. Offers MA. *Accreditation:* NCATE. *Students:* 36 full-time (25 women), 7 part-time (4 women); includes 15 minority (13 Black or African American, non-Hispanic/Latino; 1 Hispanic/Latino; 1 Two or more races, non-Hispanic/Latino), 1 international. Average age 22. 178 applicants, 22% accepted, 31 enrolled. In 2011, 23 master's awarded. *Entrance requirements:* For master's, GRE General Test, interview. Application fee: $50. Tuition and fees vary according to program and reciprocity agreements. *Financial support:* In 2011–12, 41 students received support, including 40 research assistantships with full tuition reimbursements available (averaging $15,978 per year). Financial award application deadline: 3/1. *Unit head:* Dr. Jayne Beilke, Director, 765-285-5486, Fax: 765-285-2464. *Application contact:* Dr. Roger Wessel,

Associate Provost for Research and Dean of the Graduate School, 765-285-8290, E-mail: rwessel@bsu.edu. Web site: http://www.bsu.edu/teachers/departments/edstudies/.

Bank Street College of Education, Graduate School, Programs in Educational Leadership, New York, NY 10025. Offers early childhood leadership (MS Ed); educational leadership (MS Ed); leadership for educational change (Ed M, MS Ed); leadership in community-based learning (MS Ed); leadership in mathematics education (MS Ed); leadership in museum education (MS Ed); leadership in the arts: creative writing (MS Ed); leadership in the arts: visual arts (MS Ed). *Students:* 77 full-time (66 women), 130 part-time (108 women); includes 68 minority (33 Black or African American, non-Hispanic/Latino; 8 Asian, non-Hispanic/Latino; 25 Hispanic/Latino; 2 Two or more races, non-Hispanic/Latino), 3 international. Average age 34. 148 applicants, 70% accepted, 92 enrolled. In 2011, 82 master's awarded. *Degree requirements:* For master's, thesis. *Entrance requirements:* For master's, interview, essays, minimum of 2 years experience as a classroom teacher. Additional exam requirements/recommendations for international students: Required—TOEFL (minimum score 600 paper-based; 250 computer-based; 100 iBT), IELTS (minimum score 7). *Application deadline:* For fall admission, 2/15 priority date for domestic students, 2/15 for international students; for spring admission, 11/1 priority date for domestic students, 11/1 for international students. Applications are processed on a rolling basis. Application fee: $65. Electronic applications accepted. *Expenses: Required fees:* $1240 per credit. $100 per term. One-time fee: $250 part-time. *Financial support:* Career-related internships or fieldwork, Federal Work-Study, scholarships/grants, traineeships, and unspecified assistantships available. Support available to part-time students. Financial award application deadline: 4/15; financial award applicants required to submit FAFSA. *Faculty research:* Leadership in small schools, mathematics in elementary schools, professional development in early childhood, leadership in arts education, leadership in special education. *Unit head:* Dr. Rima Shore, Chairperson, 212-875-4478, Fax: 212-875-8753, E-mail: rshore@bankstreet.edu. *Application contact:* Ann Morgan, Director of Graduate Admissions, 212-875-4403, Fax: 212-875-4678, E-mail: amorgan@bankstreet.edu. Web site: http://bankstreet.edu/graduate-school/academics/programs/leadership-programs-overview/.

Barry University, School of Education, Program in Educational Leadership, Miami Shores, FL 33161-6695. Offers MS, Ed D, Certificate, Ed S. Part-time and evening/weekend programs available. *Degree requirements:* For master's and other advanced degree, comprehensive exam. *Entrance requirements:* For master's, GRE General Test or MAT, minimum GPA of 3.0; for other advanced degree, GRE General Test, minimum GPA of 3.0. Electronic applications accepted.

Barry University, School of Education, Program in Higher Education Administration, Miami Shores, FL 33161-6695. Offers MS. Part-time and evening/weekend programs available. *Degree requirements:* For master's, comprehensive exam. *Entrance requirements:* For master's, GRE General Test or MAT, minimum GPA of 3.0. Electronic applications accepted.

Barry University, School of Education, Program in Leadership and Education, Miami Shores, FL 33161-6695. Offers educational technology (PhD); exceptional student education (PhD); higher education administration (PhD); human resource development (PhD); leadership (PhD). Part-time and evening/weekend programs available. *Degree requirements:* For doctorate, thesis/dissertation. *Entrance requirements:* For doctorate, GRE General Test, minimum GPA of 3.25. Electronic applications accepted.

Bayamón Central University, Graduate Programs, Program in Education, Bayamón, PR 00960-1725. Offers administration and supervision (MA Ed); commercial education (MA Ed); elementary education (K–3) (MA Ed); family counseling (Graduate Certificate); guidance and counseling (MA Ed); pre-elementary teacher (MA Ed); rehabilitation counseling (MA Ed); special education (MA Ed), including attention deficit disorder, education of the autistic, learning disabilities. Part-time and evening/weekend programs available. *Degree requirements:* For master's, comprehensive exam. *Entrance requirements:* For master's, EXADEP, bachelor's degree in education or related field.

Baylor University, Graduate School, School of Education, Department of Educational Administration, Waco, TX 76798. Offers MS Ed, Ed S. *Accreditation:* NCATE. *Students:* 27 full-time (18 women), 7 part-time (3 women); includes 4 minority (3 Black or African American, non-Hispanic/Latino; 1 Asian, non-Hispanic/Latino). 90 applicants, 44% accepted. In 2011, 17 master's awarded. *Entrance requirements:* For master's, GRE General Test. *Application deadline:* Applications are processed on a rolling basis. Application fee: $25. *Financial support:* In 2011–12, 20 students received support, including 2 research assistantships; teaching assistantships, Federal Work-Study, institutionally sponsored loans, and scholarships/grants also available. *Unit head:* Dr. Robert Cloud, Graduate Program Director, 254-710-6110, Fax: 254-710-3265, E-mail: robert_cloud@baylor.edu. *Application contact:* Julie Baker, Administrative Assistant, 254-710-3050, Fax: 254-710-3870, E-mail: julie_l_baker@baylor.edu. Web site: https://www.baylor.edu/soe/eda/.

Bay Path College, Program in Higher Education Administration, Longmeadow, MA 01106-2292. Offers enrollment management (MS); general administration (MS); institutional advancement (MS). Part-time programs available. Postbaccalaureate distance learning degree programs offered (no on-campus study). *Students:* 7 full-time (6 women), 39 part-time (32 women); includes 9 minority (6 Black or African American, non-Hispanic/Latino; 1 Asian, non-Hispanic/Latino; 2 Hispanic/Latino). Average age 35. 46 applicants, 74% accepted, 25 enrolled. In 2011, 10 master's awarded. *Application deadline:* Applications are processed on a rolling basis. Application fee: $45. Electronic applications accepted. Application fee is waived when completed online. *Expenses: Tuition:* Part-time $665 per credit. Tuition and fees vary according to program. *Financial support:* In 2011–12, 12 students received support. Scholarships/grants available. Financial award applicants required to submit FAFSA. *Application contact:* Lisa Adams, Director of Graduate Admissions, 413-565-1317, Fax: 413-565-1250, E-mail: ladams@baypath.edu.

Bellarmine University, Annsley Frazier Thornton School of Education, Louisville, KY 40205-0671. Offers early elementary education (MA Ed, MAT); education and social change (PhD); learning and behavior disorders (MA Ed, MAT); middle school education (MA Ed, MAT); principalship (Ed S); reading and writing endorsement (MA Ed); secondary school education (MAT); teacher leadership, grades P-12 (MA Ed). *Accreditation:* NCATE. Part-time and evening/weekend programs available. *Faculty:* 13 full-time (6 women), 12 part-time/adjunct (10 women). *Students:* 85 full-time (65 women), 186 part-time (144 women); includes 30 minority (22 Black or African American, non-Hispanic/Latino; 1 American Indian or Alaska Native, non-Hispanic/Latino; 6 Asian, non-Hispanic/Latino; 1 Hispanic/Latino). Average age 33. In 2011, 105 master's awarded. *Degree requirements:* For master's, comprehensive exam, thesis (for some programs); for doctorate, comprehensive exam, thesis/dissertation. *Entrance requirements:* For master's, GRE, baccalaureate degree from accredited institution; minimum overall GPA of 2.75, 3.0 in major; letters of recommendation; valid Kentucky provisional or professional certificate; for doctorate, GRE, minimum GPA of 3.5 in all graduate coursework completed at time of application; baccalaureate and master's degrees in education (MA, MS) or fields directly relevant to education; three letters of recommendation; two essays (no more than 1,000 words each); interview. Additional exam requirements/recommendations for international students: Required—TOEFL (minimum score 550 paper-based; 213 computer-based; 80 iBT). *Application deadline:* Applications are processed on a rolling basis. Application fee: $25. *Expenses:* Contact institution. *Financial support:* Scholarships/grants available. Financial award applicants required to submit FAFSA. *Faculty research:* Literacy, service-learning, dispositions, educational technology, special education. *Unit head:* Dr. Robert Cooter, Dean, 502-272-8191, Fax: 502-272-8189, E-mail: rcooter@bellarmine.edu. *Application contact:* Theresa Klapheke, Administrative Director of Graduate Programs, 502-272-8271, Fax: 502-272-8002, E-mail: tklapheke@bellarmine.edu. Web site: http://www.bellarmine.edu/education/graduate.

Benedictine College, Master of Arts Program in School Leadership, Atchison, KS 66002-1499. Offers MA. *Accreditation:* NCATE. Part-time and evening/weekend programs available. *Degree requirements:* For master's, comprehensive exam, practicum. *Entrance requirements:* For master's, MAT or GMAT, minimum GPA of 3.0. *Expenses:* Contact institution. *Faculty research:* Teacher leadership, special education issues, diversity in schools, Catholic school leadership, professional development.

Benedictine College, Master of Education Program in Teacher Leadership, Atchison, KS 66002-1499. Offers M Ed. *Entrance requirements:* For master's, minimum GPA of 3.0 in last two years (60 hours) of college course work from accredited institutions, official transcripts, bachelor's degree, teacher certification/licensure, resume, essay.

Benedictine University, Graduate Programs, Program in Education, Lisle, IL 60532-0900. Offers curriculum and instruction and collaborative teaching (M Ed); elementary education (MA Ed); leadership and administration (M Ed); reading and literacy (M Ed); secondary education (MA Ed); special education (MA Ed). Part-time and evening/weekend programs available. *Faculty:* 4 full-time (2 women), 52 part-time/adjunct (30 women). *Students:* 178 full-time (157 women), 239 part-time (211 women); includes 41 minority (29 Black or African American, non-Hispanic/Latino; 4 Asian, non-Hispanic/Latino; 8 Hispanic/Latino), 2 international. Average age 33. 177 applicants, 44% accepted, 68 enrolled. In 2011, 278 master's awarded. *Degree requirements:* For master's, comprehensive exam, thesis (for some programs). *Entrance requirements:* For master's, GRE or MAT. Additional exam requirements/recommendations for international students: Required—TOEFL (minimum score 550 paper-based; 213 computer-based). *Application deadline:* For fall admission, 9/1 for domestic students; for winter admission, 12/1 for domestic students; for spring admission, 2/15 for domestic students. Applications are processed on a rolling basis. Application fee: $40. Electronic applications accepted. *Expenses:* Contact institution. *Financial support:* Career-related internships or fieldwork and health care benefits available. Support available to part-time students. *Unit head:* MeShelda Jackson, Director, 630-829-6282, E-mail: mjackson@ben.edu. *Application contact:* Kari Gibbons, Associate Vice President, Enrollment Center, 630-829-6200, Fax: 630-829-6584, E-mail: kgibbons@ben.edu.

Benedictine University, Graduate Programs, Program in Higher Education and Organizational Change, Lisle, IL 60532-0900. Offers Ed D. *Faculty:* 2 full-time (1 woman). *Students:* 35 full-time (24 women), 65 part-time (38 women); includes 34 minority (24 Black or African American, non-Hispanic/Latino; 1 American Indian or Alaska Native, non-Hispanic/Latino; 2 Asian, non-Hispanic/Latino; 7 Hispanic/Latino), 2 international. 34 applicants, 71% accepted, 22 enrolled. In 2011, 7 degrees awarded. Application fee: $40. *Unit head:* Dr. Sunil Chand, Director, 630-829-1930, E-mail: schand@ben.edu. *Application contact:* Kari Gibbons, Associate Vice President, Enrollment Center, 630-829-6200, Fax: 630-829-6584, E-mail: kgibbons@ben.edu.

Bernard M. Baruch College of the City University of New York, School of Public Affairs, Program in Educational Leadership, New York, NY 10010-5585. Offers educational leadership (MS Ed); school building leadership (Advanced Certificate); school district leadership (Advanced Certificate). Part-time and evening/weekend programs available. *Faculty:* 45 full-time (17 women), 34 part-time/adjunct (12 women). *Students:* 57 full-time (44 women), 119 part-time (73 women); includes 64 minority (30 Black or African American, non-Hispanic/Latino; 6 Asian, non-Hispanic/Latino; 21 Hispanic/Latino; 7 Two or more races, non-Hispanic/Latino). *Degree requirements:* For master's, internship. *Entrance requirements:* For master's, GRE or master's degree. Additional exam requirements/recommendations for international students: Required—TOEFL. *Application deadline:* For fall admission, 4/1 priority date for domestic students, 4/1 for international students; for spring admission, 11/15 priority date for domestic students, 11/15 for international students. Applications are processed on a rolling basis. Application fee: $125. Electronic applications accepted. *Financial support:* Career-related internships or fieldwork, Federal Work-Study, and scholarships/grants available. Support available to part-time students. Financial award application deadline: 5/30; financial award applicants required to submit FAFSA. *Faculty research:* School administration, program development, school leadership, violence in schools, school leadership development, school reform, school discipline policy, program development. *Total annual research expenditures:* $429,000. *Unit head:* David S. Birdsell, Dean, 646-660-6700, Fax: 646-660-6721, E-mail: david.birdsell@baruch.cuny.edu. *Application contact:* Michael J. Lovaglio, Director of Student Affairs and Graduate Admissions, 646-660-6760, Fax: 646-660-6751, E-mail: michael.lovaglio@baruch.cuny.edu. Web site: http://www.baruch.cuny.edu/spa/academics/graduatedegrees/educationalleadership.php.

Bernard M. Baruch College of the City University of New York, School of Public Affairs, Program in Higher Education Administration, New York, NY 10010-5585. Offers MS Ed. Part-time and evening/weekend programs available. *Faculty:* 45 full-time (17 women), 34 part-time/adjunct (12 women). *Students:* 6 full-time (5 women), 115 part-time (83 women); includes 66 minority (31 Black or African American, non-Hispanic/Latino; 5 Asian, non-Hispanic/Latino; 27 Hispanic/Latino; 3 Two or more races, non-Hispanic/Latino). Average age 34. *Entrance requirements:* For master's, GRE General Test. Additional exam requirements/recommendations for international students: Required—TOEFL. *Application deadline:* For fall admission, 4/1 priority date for domestic students, 4/1 for international students; for spring admission, 11/15 priority date for domestic students, 11/15 for international students. Applications are processed on a rolling basis. Application fee: $125. Electronic applications accepted. *Expenses:* Contact institution. *Financial support:* In 2011–12, fellowships (averaging $3,000 per year) were awarded; research assistantships, teaching assistantships, career-related internships or fieldwork, Federal Work-Study, scholarships/grants, tuition waivers (partial), and unspecified assistantships also available. Support available to part-time students. Financial award application deadline: 5/15; financial award applicants required to submit FAFSA. *Unit head:* David S. Birdsell, Dean, 646-660-6700, Fax: 646-660-6721, E-mail: david.birdsell@baruch.cuny.edu. *Application contact:* Michael J. Lovaglio, Director of Student Affairs and Graduate Admissions, 646-660-6760, Fax: 646-660-6751, E-mail: michael.lovaglio@baruch.cuny.edu. Web site: http://www.baruch.cuny.edu/spa/academics/graduatedegrees/highereducationadmin.php.

Berry College, Graduate Programs, Graduate Programs in Education, Program in Leadership in Curriculum and Instruction, Mount Berry, GA 30149-0159. Offers curriculum and instruction (Ed S); educational leadership (Ed S). *Accreditation:* NCATE. *Faculty:* 6 part-time/adjunct (3 women). *Students:* 49 part-time (33 women); includes 7 minority (4 Black or African American, non-Hispanic/Latino; 1 Asian, non-Hispanic/Latino; 2 Hispanic/Latino). Average age 37. In 2011, 10 Ed Ss awarded. *Degree requirements:* For Ed S, thesis, portfolio, oral exams. *Entrance requirements:* For degree, M Ed from NCATE-accredited school, minimum GPA of 3.25. Additional exam requirements/recommendations for international students: Required—TOEFL (minimum score 550 paper-based; 213 computer-based). *Application deadline:* For fall admission, 5/1 for domestic and international students; for spring admission, 10/1 for domestic and international students. Applications are processed on a rolling basis. Application fee: $25 ($30 for international students). Electronic applications accepted. *Expenses:* Contact institution. *Financial support:* In 2011–12, 1 student received support. Scholarships/grants available. Support available to part-time students. Financial award application deadline: 3/1; financial award applicants required to submit FAFSA. *Faculty research:* Curriculum development, teacher training, pedagogy. *Unit head:* Dr. Jacqueline McDowell, 706-236-1717, Fax: 706-238-5827, E-mail: jmcdowell@berry.edu. *Application contact:* Brett Kennedy, Director of Admissions, 706-236-2215, Fax: 706-290-2178, E-mail: admissions@berry.edu. Web site: http://www.berry.edu/academics/education/graduate/.

Bethel University, Graduate Programs, McKenzie, TN 38201. Offers administration and supervision (MA Ed); business administration (MBA); conflict resolution (MA); physician assistant studies (MS). Part-time and evening/weekend programs available. *Degree requirements:* For master's, thesis (for some programs). *Entrance requirements:* For master's, GRE General Test or MAT, minimum undergraduate GPA of 2.5.

Bethel University, Graduate School, St. Paul, MN 55112-6999. Offers autism spectrum disorders (Certificate); business administration (MBA); communication (MA); counseling psychology (MA); education (M Ed); educational leadership (Ed D); gerontology (MA, Certificate); international baccalaureate education (Certificate); K-12 education (MA); literacy education (MA); nursing (MA); nursing education (Certificate); nursing leadership (Certificate); organizational leadership (MA); postsecondary teaching (Certificate); special education (MA); teaching (MA). Part-time and evening/weekend programs available. Postbaccalaureate distance learning degree programs offered (minimal on-campus study). *Faculty:* 8 full-time (3 women), 98 part-time/adjunct (46 women). *Students:* 651 full-time (419 women), 312 part-time (212 women); includes 79 minority (35 Black or African American, non-Hispanic/Latino; 2 American Indian or Alaska Native, non-Hispanic/Latino; 19 Asian, non-Hispanic/Latino; 17 Hispanic/Latino; 6 Two or more races, non-Hispanic/Latino), 6 international. Average age 36. In 2011, 245 master's, 4 doctorates, 32 other advanced degrees awarded. *Degree requirements:* For master's, comprehensive exam (for some programs), thesis (for some programs); for doctorate, comprehensive exam, thesis/dissertation. *Entrance requirements:* Additional exam requirements/recommendations for international students: Required—TOEFL (minimum score 550 paper-based; 213 computer-based; 80 iBT). *Application deadline:* Applications are processed on a rolling basis. Electronic applications accepted. Tuition and fees vary according to course load, degree level and program. *Financial support:* Applicants required to submit FAFSA. *Unit head:* Dick Crombie, Vice-President/Dean, 651-635-8000, Fax: 651-635-8004, E-mail: gs@bethel.edu. *Application contact:* Paul Ives, Director of Admissions, 651-635-8000, Fax: 651-635-8004, E-mail: gs@bethel.edu. Web site: http://gs.bethel.edu/.

Bob Jones University, Graduate Programs, Greenville, SC 29614. Offers accountancy (MS); Bible (MA); Bible translation (MA); Biblical studies (Certificate); broadcast management (MS); business administration (MBA); church history (MA, PhD); church ministries (MA); church music (MM); cinema and video production (MA); counseling (MS); curriculum and instruction (Ed D); divinity (M Div); dramatic production (MA); educational leadership (MS, Ed D, Ed S); elementary education (M Ed, MAT); English (M Ed, MA, MAT); fine arts (MA); graphic design (MA); history (M Ed, MA); illustration (MA); interpretative speech (MA); mathematics (M Ed, MAT); medical missions (Certificate); ministry (MM, D Min); multi-categorical special education (M Ed, MAT); music (M Ed); New Testament interpretation (PhD); Old Testament interpretation (PhD); orchestral instrument performance (MM); organ performance (MM); pastoral studies (MA); personnel services (MS, Ed S); piano pedagogy (MM); piano performance (MM); platform arts (MA); radio and television broadcasting (MS); rhetoric and public address (MA); secondary education (M Ed); studio art (MA); teaching Bible (MA); theology (MA, PhD); voice performance (MM); youth ministries (MA); M Div/MM.

Boise State University, Graduate College, College of Education, Department of Curriculum, Instruction and Foundational Studies, Boise, ID 83725-0399. Offers curriculum and instruction (Ed D); curriculum instruction (MA); educational leadership (M Ed). *Accreditation:* NCATE. Part-time programs available. *Degree requirements:* For master's, thesis optional. *Entrance requirements:* For master's, minimum GPA of 3.0. Electronic applications accepted.

Boston College, Lynch Graduate School of Education, Program in Educational Leadership, Chestnut Hill, MA 02467-3800. Offers M Ed, Ed D, CAES, JD/M Ed. Part-time and evening/weekend programs available. *Students:* 22 full-time (13 women), 67 part-time (36 women); includes 13 minority (5 Black or African American, non-Hispanic/Latino; 1 Asian, non-Hispanic/Latino; 5 Hispanic/Latino; 2 Two or more races, non-Hispanic/Latino), 7 international. 98 applicants, 45% accepted, 37 enrolled. In 2011, 16 master's, 4 doctorates, 4 CAESs awarded. *Degree requirements:* For master's and CAES, comprehensive exam. *Entrance requirements:* For master's and CAES, GRE General Test or MAT; for doctorate, GRE General Test. Additional exam requirements/recommendations for international students: Required—TOEFL (minimum score 550 paper-based; 213 computer-based; 79 iBT). Application fee: $65. Electronic applications accepted. *Financial support:* Fellowships with full and partial tuition reimbursements, research assistantships with full and partial tuition reimbursements, teaching assistantships with full and partial tuition reimbursements, career-related internships or fieldwork, Federal Work-Study, scholarships/grants, traineeships, health care benefits, tuition waivers (full and partial), and unspecified assistantships available. Support available to part-time students. Financial award applicants required to submit FAFSA. *Faculty research:* Politics of urban education, principalship, urban catholic schools, educational leadership, educational law and policy. *Unit head:* Dr. Ana M. Martinez-Aleman, Chairperson, 617-552-4214, Fax: 617-552-0398. *Application contact:* Adam Poluzzi, Director, Graduate Admission and Financial Aid, 617-552-4214, Fax: 617-552-0398, E-mail: poluzzi@bc.edu.

Boston College, Lynch Graduate School of Education, Program in Higher Education, Chestnut Hill, MA 02467-3800. Offers MA, PhD, JD/MA, MBA/MA. *Accreditation:* Teacher Education Accreditation Council. Part-time and evening/weekend programs available. *Students:* 73 full-time (51 women), 57 part-time (39 women); includes 27 minority (3 Black or African American, non-Hispanic/Latino; 9 Asian, non-Hispanic/Latino; 12 Hispanic/Latino; 3 Two or more races, non-Hispanic/Latino), 6 international. 248 applicants, 39% accepted, 57 enrolled. In 2011, 45 master's, 11 doctorates awarded. Terminal master's awarded for partial completion of doctoral program. *Degree requirements:* For master's, comprehensive exam; for doctorate, comprehensive exam, thesis/dissertation. *Entrance requirements:* For master's, GRE General Test or MAT; for doctorate, GRE General Test. Additional exam requirements/recommendations for international students: Required—TOEFL (minimum score 550 paper-based; 213 computer-based; 79 iBT). Application fee: $65. Electronic applications accepted. *Financial support:* Fellowships with full and partial tuition reimbursements, research assistantships with full and partial tuition reimbursements, teaching assistantships with full and partial tuition reimbursements, career-related internships or fieldwork, Federal Work-Study, scholarships/grants, traineeships, health care benefits, tuition waivers (full and partial), and unspecified assistantships available. Support available to part-time students. Financial award applicants required to submit FAFSA. *Faculty research:* Race, culture and gender in higher education; international education; college student development; Catholic higher education; organizational analysis. *Unit head:* Dr. Ana M. Martinez-Aleman, Chairperson, 617-552-4214, Fax: 617-552-0398. *Application contact:* Adam Poluzzi, Director, Graduate Admission and Financial Aid, 617-552-4214, Fax: 617-552-0398, E-mail: poluzzi@bc.edu.

Bowie State University, Graduate Programs, Program in Educational Leadership/Executive Fellows, Bowie, MD 20715-9465. Offers Ed D. Part-time and evening/weekend programs available. *Students:* 1 (woman) full-time, 37 part-time (26 women); includes 30 minority (all Black or African American, non-Hispanic/Latino). Average age 44. *Degree requirements:* For doctorate, comprehensive exam, thesis/dissertation. *Application deadline:* For fall admission, 4/1 priority date for domestic students, 4/1 for international students; for spring admission, 11/1 priority date for domestic students, 11/1 for international students. Applications are processed on a rolling basis. Electronic applications accepted. *Expenses:* Tuition, state resident: full-time $4140; part-time $3105 per semester. Tuition, nonresident: full-time $7836; part-time $5877 per semester. *Required fees:* $1715; $648 per semester. *Unit head:* Dr. Barbara Jackson, Chairperson, 301-860-3125, E-mail: bjackson@bowiestate.edu. *Application contact:* Angela Issac, Information Contact, 301-860-4000.

Bowie State University, Graduate Programs, Program in Elementary and Secondary School Administration, Bowie, MD 20715-9465. Offers M Ed. Part-time and evening/weekend programs available. *Students:* 5 full-time (1 woman), 27 part-time (19 women); includes 28 minority (27 Black or African American, non-Hispanic/Latino; 1 Two or more races, non-Hispanic/Latino). Average age 38. 14 applicants, 100% accepted, 14 enrolled. In 2011, 22 master's awarded. *Degree requirements:* For master's, comprehensive exam. *Entrance requirements:* For master's, copy of Advance Teaching Certificate, 3 years teaching experience, letter of recommendation from current supervisor. *Application deadline:* For fall admission, 4/11 priority date for domestic students, 4/1 for international students; for spring admission, 11/1 priority date for domestic students, 11/1 for international students. Applications are processed on a rolling basis. Application fee: $40. Electronic applications accepted. *Expenses:* Tuition, state resident: full-time $4140; part-time $3105 per semester. Tuition, nonresident: full-time $7836; part-time $5877 per semester. *Required fees:* $1715; $648 per semester. *Unit head:* Dr. Barbara Jackson, Program Coordinator, 301-860, E-mail: bjackson@bowiestate.edu. *Application contact:* Angela Issac, Information Contact, 301-860-4000.

Bowie State University, Graduate Programs, Program in School Administration and Supervision, Bowie, MD 20715-9465. Offers M Ed. Part-time and evening/weekend programs available. *Faculty:* 3 full-time (1 woman), 2 part-time/adjunct (1 woman). *Students:* 16 full-time (10 women), 23 part-time (15 women); includes 31 minority (29 Black or African American, non-Hispanic/Latino; 2 Hispanic/Latino). Average age 35. *Degree requirements:* For master's, comprehensive exam, thesis optional, research paper. *Entrance requirements:* For master's, minimum undergraduate GPA of 3.0, 3 years of teaching experience, teaching certificate. *Application deadline:* For fall admission, 8/16 priority date for domestic students. Applications are processed on a rolling basis. Application fee: $40. *Expenses:* Tuition, state resident: full-time $4140; part-time $3105 per semester. Tuition, nonresident: full-time $7836; part-time $5877 per semester. *Required fees:* $1715; $648 per semester. *Financial support:* Application deadline: 4/1. *Unit head:* Dr. Paul Hester, Coordinator, 301-860-3326. *Application contact:* Angela Issac, Information Contact, 301-860-4000.

Bowling Green State University, Graduate College, College of Education and Human Development, School of Leadership and Policy Studies, Program in Educational Administration and Supervision, Bowling Green, OH 43403. Offers educational administration and supervision (M Ed, Ed S); leadership studies (Ed D). *Accreditation:* NCATE. Part-time and evening/weekend programs available. *Degree requirements:* For master's, thesis or alternative; for doctorate, comprehensive exam, thesis/dissertation; for Ed S, thesis or alternative, field experience or internship. *Entrance requirements:* For master's, doctorate, and Ed S, GRE General Test. Additional exam requirements/recommendations for international students: Required—TOEFL. Electronic applications accepted. *Faculty research:* Professional development for school leaders, organizational development, school finance, legal challenges to school decision making, administering urban schools.

Bowling Green State University, Graduate College, College of Education and Human Development, School of Leadership and Policy Studies, Program in Higher Education Administration, Bowling Green, OH 43403. Offers PhD. *Accreditation:* NCATE. Part-time programs available. *Degree requirements:* For doctorate, comprehensive exam, thesis/dissertation. *Entrance requirements:* For doctorate, GRE General Test. Additional exam requirements/recommendations for international students: Required—TOEFL. Electronic applications accepted. *Faculty research:* Adult learners, legal issues, intellectual development.

Bradley University, Graduate School, College of Education and Health Sciences, Department of Educational Leadership and Human Development, Peoria, IL 61625-0002. Offers human development counseling (MA), including community and agency counseling, school counseling; leadership in educational administration (MA); leadership in human service administration (MA). *Accreditation:* ACA; NCATE. Part-time and evening/weekend programs available. *Degree requirements:* For master's, comprehensive exam, thesis optional. *Entrance requirements:* For master's, GRE General Test or MAT, interview, 3 letters of recommendation. Additional exam requirements/recommendations for international students: Required—TOEFL (minimum score 550 paper-based; 213 computer-based; 79 iBT).

Brandman University, School of Education, Irvine, CA 92618. Offers education (MA); educational leadership (MA); school counseling (MA); special education (MA); teaching (MA).

Brandon University, Faculty of Education, Brandon, MB R7A 6A9, Canada. Offers curriculum and instruction (M Ed, Diploma); educational administration (M Ed, Diploma); guidance and counseling (M Ed, Diploma); special education (M Ed, Diploma). *Degree requirements:* For master's, thesis. *Entrance requirements:* For master's, minimum GPA of 3.0, teaching certificate or equivalent. Additional exam requirements/recommendations for international students: Required—TOEFL. *Faculty research:* Comparative education, environmental studies, parent/school council.

Bridgewater State University, School of Graduate Studies, School of Education and Allied Studies, Department of Secondary Education and Professional Programs, Program in Educational Leadership, Bridgewater, MA 02325-0001. Offers M Ed, CAGS. *Accreditation:* NCATE. Part-time and evening/weekend programs available. *Degree requirements:* For master's and CAGS, comprehensive exam. *Entrance requirements:* For master's, GRE General Test or Massachusetts Test for Educator Licensure, work experience; for CAGS, master's degree.

Brigham Young University, Graduate Studies, David O. McKay School of Education, Department of Educational Leadership and Foundations, Provo, UT 84602. Offers M Ed, Ed D. Part-time and evening/weekend programs available. *Faculty:* 10 full-time (3 women), 2 part-time/adjunct (0 women). *Students:* 27 full-time (19 women), 64 part-time (24 women); includes 9 minority (1 American Indian or Alaska Native, non-Hispanic/

Latino; 1 Asian, non-Hispanic/Latino; 2 Hispanic/Latino; 5 Native Hawaiian or other Pacific Islander, non-Hispanic/Latino). Average age 39. 66 applicants, 61% accepted, 37 enrolled. In 2011, 33 master's, 4 doctorates awarded. *Degree requirements:* For master's, comprehensive exam, thesis or alternative; for doctorate, comprehensive exam, thesis/dissertation. *Entrance requirements:* For master's, GRE, MAT, LSAT, Utah Level II Teaching License (or equivalent); for doctorate, GRE, GMAT, LSAT. Additional exam requirements/recommendations for international students: Required—TOEFL (minimum score 580 paper-based; 237 computer-based; 85 iBT). *Application deadline:* For fall admission, 2/15 for domestic and international students; for spring admission, 3/1 for domestic and international students. Application fee: $50. Electronic applications accepted. *Expenses: Tuition:* Full-time $5760; part-time $320 per credit. Tuition and fees vary according to student's religious affiliation. *Financial support:* In 2011–12, 35 students received support, including research assistantships (averaging $914 per year); teaching assistantships and scholarships/grants also available. Financial award application deadline: 9/1. *Faculty research:* Mentoring, pre-service training of administrators, policy development, cross-cultural studies of educational leadership. *Unit head:* Dean Richard K. Young, Chair, 801-422-3695, Fax: 801-422-0200, E-mail: msesec@byu.edu. *Application contact:* Bonnie Bennett, Department Secretary, 801-422-3813, Fax: 801-422-0196, E-mail: bonnie_bennett@byu.edu. Web site: http://education.byu.edu/edlf/.

Brooklyn College of the City University of New York, Division of Graduate Studies, School of Education, Program in Educational Leadership, Brooklyn, NY 11210-2889. Offers MS Ed. Part-time and evening/weekend programs available. *Entrance requirements:* For master's, 2 supervisory letters of recommendation, essay, resume, teaching certificate, interview, supplemental application. Additional exam requirements/recommendations for international students: Required—TOEFL (minimum score 500 paper-based; 173 computer-based; 61 iBT). Electronic applications accepted.

Buffalo State College, State University of New York, The Graduate School, Faculty of Applied Science and Education, Department of Elementary Education and Reading, Program in Educational Leadership, Buffalo, NY 14222-1095. Offers CAS. *Accreditation:* NCATE. Part-time and evening/weekend programs available. *Degree requirements:* For CAS, internship. *Entrance requirements:* For degree, master's degree, New York teaching certificate, 3 years of teaching experience. Additional exam requirements/recommendations for international students: Required—TOEFL (minimum score 550 paper-based; 213 computer-based).

Butler University, College of Education, Indianapolis, IN 46208-3485. Offers administration (MS); elementary education (MS); reading (MS); school counseling (MS); secondary education (MS); special education (MS). *Accreditation:* ACA; NCATE. Part-time and evening/weekend programs available. *Faculty:* 7 full-time (4 women), 5 part-time/adjunct (all women). *Students:* 9 full-time (6 women), 136 part-time (105 women); includes 21 minority (14 Black or African American, non-Hispanic/Latino; 5 Asian, non-Hispanic/Latino; 1 Hispanic/Latino; 1 Two or more races, non-Hispanic/Latino), 1 international. Average age 31. 69 applicants, 94% accepted, 24 enrolled. In 2011, 66 master's awarded. *Entrance requirements:* For master's, GRE General Test, MAT, interview. *Application deadline:* For fall admission, 8/15 priority date for domestic students. Applications are processed on a rolling basis. Application fee: $35. Electronic applications accepted. *Expenses: Tuition:* Part-time $466 per credit. *Financial support:* Institutionally sponsored loans available. Support available to part-time students. Financial award application deadline: 7/15; financial award applicants required to submit FAFSA. *Faculty research:* Ethics in cybercounseling, history of sports for disabled, effect of fetal alcohol syndrome on perceptual learning, reading recovery's theoretical framework in teacher education. *Unit head:* Dr. Ena Shelley, Dean, 317-940-9752, Fax: 317-940-6481. *Application contact:* Karen Farrell, Department Secretary, 317-940-9220, E-mail: kfarrell@butler.edu.

Cairn University, School of Education, Langhorne, PA 19047-2990. Offers educational leadership and administration (MS El); teacher education (MS Ed). Part-time and evening/weekend programs available. *Faculty:* 3 full-time (2 women), 3 part-time/adjunct (all women). *Students:* 12 full-time (7 women), 41 part-time (30 women); includes 12 minority (7 Black or African American, non-Hispanic/Latino; 3 Asian, non-Hispanic/Latino; 1 Native Hawaiian or other Pacific Islander, non-Hispanic/Latino; 1 Two or more races, non-Hispanic/Latino), 3 international. Average age 35. 21 applicants, 71% accepted, 10 enrolled. In 2011, 22 master's awarded. *Entrance requirements:* Additional exam requirements/recommendations for international students: Required—TOEFL (minimum score 550 paper-based; 213 computer-based). *Application deadline:* Applications are processed on a rolling basis. Application fee: $25. Electronic applications accepted. *Expenses: Tuition:* Part-time $475 per credit hour. Tuition and fees vary according to program. *Financial support:* Scholarships/grants available. Support available to part-time students. Financial award applicants required to submit FAFSA. *Unit head:* Dr. Deborah MacCullough, Dean, 215-702-4360, E-mail: teacher.ed@pbu.edu. *Application contact:* Caitlin Lenker, Enrollment Counselor, Graduate Education, 800-572-2472, Fax: 215-702-4248, E-mail: clenker@pbu.edu.

Caldwell College, Graduate Studies, Division of Education, Caldwell, NJ 07006-6195. Offers curriculum and instruction (MA); educational administration (MA); learning disabilities teacher-consultant (Post-Master's Certificate); literacy instruction (MA); principal (Post-Master's Certificate); reading specialist (Post-Master's Certificate); special education (MA), including special education, teaching of students with disabilities, teaching of students with disabilities and learning disabilities teacher-consultant; superintendent (Post-Master's Certificate); supervisor (Post-Master's Certificate). Part-time and evening/weekend programs available. *Students:* 66 full-time (41 women), 230 part-time (188 women); includes 24 minority (14 Black or African American, non-Hispanic/Latino; 1 Asian, non-Hispanic/Latino; 9 Hispanic/Latino). *Entrance requirements:* Additional exam requirements/recommendations for international students: Required—TOEFL (minimum score 580 paper-based; 237 computer-based). *Application deadline:* Applications are processed on a rolling basis. Application fee: $40. Electronic applications accepted. *Expenses: Tuition:* Full-time $14,400; part-time $800 per credit. *Required fees:* $200; $100 per semester. *Financial support:* Applicants required to submit FAFSA. *Unit head:* Dr. Janice Stewart, Coordinator, 973-618-3626, E-mail: jstewart@caldwell.edu. *Application contact:* Vilma Mueller, Director of Graduate Studies, 973-618-3544, E-mail: graduate@caldwell.edu.

California Baptist University, Program in Education, Riverside, CA 92504-3206. Offers educational leadership for faith-based instruction (MS); educational leadership for public institutions (MS); educational technology (MS); instructional computer applications (MS); international education (MS); reading (MS); school counseling (MS); school psychology (MS); special education (MS); special education in mild/moderate disabilities (MS); special education in moderate/severe disabilities (MS); teaching (MS); teaching and learning with induction program (MS Ed). Part-time and evening/weekend programs available. *Faculty:* 16 full-time (10 women), 1 (woman) part-time/adjunct. *Students:* 380 full-time (323 women); includes 149 minority (28 Black or African American, non-Hispanic/Latino; 2 American Indian or Alaska Native, non-Hispanic/Latino; 13 Asian, non-Hispanic/Latino; 100 Hispanic/Latino; 2 Native Hawaiian or other Pacific Islander, non-Hispanic/Latino; 4 Two or more races, non-Hispanic/Latino). Average age 32. 181 applicants, 70% accepted, 111 enrolled. In 2011, 82 master's awarded. *Degree requirements:* For master's, comprehensive exam or thesis. *Entrance requirements:* For master's, minimum undergraduate GPA of 3.0; 18 semester units of prerequisite course work in education; three recommendations; essay; interview. Additional exam requirements/recommendations for international students: Required—TOEFL (minimum score 575 paper-based; 230 computer-based; 89 iBT). *Application deadline:* For fall admission, 8/1 priority date for domestic students, 7/1 for international students; for spring admission, 12/1 priority date for domestic students, 11/1 for international students. Applications are processed on a rolling basis. Application fee: $45. Electronic applications accepted. *Expenses:* Contact institution. *Financial support:* In 2011–12, 4 students received support. Federal Work-Study and institutionally sponsored loans available. Financial award applicants required to submit FAFSA. *Faculty research:* Special education, neurosciences and education, cultural influences on behavior, faith-based school leadership, social and philosophical contexts of education. *Unit head:* Dr. John Shoup, Dean, School of Education, 951-343-4205, Fax: 951-343-4516, E-mail: jshoup@calbaptist.edu. *Application contact:* Dr. James Heyman, Director, Master of Science Program in Education, 951-343-4243, Fax: 951-343-5095, E-mail: jheyman@calbaptist.edu. Web site: http://www.calbaptist.edu/mastersined/.

California Coast University, School of Education, Santa Ana, CA 92701. Offers administration (M Ed); curriculum and instruction (M Ed); educational administration (Ed D); educational psychology (Ed D); organizational leadership (Ed D). Postbaccalaureate distance learning degree programs offered (no on-campus study).

California Lutheran University, Graduate Studies, Graduate School of Education, Thousand Oaks, CA 91360-2787. Offers counseling and guidance (MS), including college student personnel, counseling and guidance; educational leadership (MA, Ed D), including educational leadership (K-12) (Ed D), higher education leadership (Ed D); special education (MS); teacher leadership (M Ed); teaching (M Ed). *Accreditation:* NCATE. Part-time and evening/weekend programs available. *Entrance requirements:* For master's, GRE General Test, interview, minimum GPA of 3.0.

California State University, Bakersfield, Division of Graduate Studies, School of Social Sciences and Education, Program in Educational Administration, Bakersfield, CA 93311. Offers MA. *Degree requirements:* For master's, thesis or alternative, project or culminating exam. *Application deadline:* Applications are processed on a rolling basis. Application fee: $55. *Expenses: Required fees:* $1302 per unit. Part-time tuition and fees vary according to course load and program. *Unit head:* Dr. Louis Wildman, Graduate Coordinator, 661-664-3047, Fax: 661-664-2278, E-mail: lwildman@csub.edu. Web site: http://www.csub.edu/sse/advanced_education/educational_administration/.

California State University Channel Islands, Extended Education, Program in Educational Leadership, Camarillo, CA 93012. Offers MAEd.

California State University, Chico, Office of Graduate Studies, College of Communication and Education, School of Education, Option in Educational Leadership Administration, Chico, CA 95929-0722. Offers MA. *Accreditation:* NCATE. *Faculty:* 12 full-time (9 women), 8 part-time/adjunct (5 women). *Students:* 38 full-time (30 women), 68 part-time (48 women); includes 16 minority (2 Black or African American, non-Hispanic/Latino; 2 American Indian or Alaska Native, non-Hispanic/Latino; 2 Asian, non-Hispanic/Latino; 10 Hispanic/Latino), 1 international. Average age 35. 63 applicants, 70% accepted, 32 enrolled. In 2011, 87 master's awarded. *Degree requirements:* For master's, comprehensive exam, thesis or project. *Entrance requirements:* Additional exam requirements/recommendations for international students: Required—TOEFL (minimum score 550 paper-based; 213 computer-based; 80 iBT), IELTS (minimum score 6.5). *Application deadline:* For fall admission, 3/1 priority date for domestic students, 3/1 for international students; for spring admission, 9/15 priority date for domestic students, 9/15 for international students. Application fee: $55. Electronic applications accepted. Tuition and fees vary according to class time, course load and degree level. *Financial support:* Fellowships, career-related internships or fieldwork, scholarships/grants, and stipends available. *Unit head:* Dr. Deborah Summers, Chair, 530-898-6421, Fax: 530-898-6177, E-mail: educ@csuchico.edu. *Application contact:* Judy I. Rice, Graduate Admissions Coordinator, 530-898-5416, Fax: 530-898-3342, E-mail: jlrice@csuchico.edu. Web site: http://www.csuchico.edu/soe/advanced/education/ed-leadership-admin.shtml.

California State University, Dominguez Hills, College of Professional Studies, School of Education, Division of Graduate Education, Program in Educational Administration, Carson, CA 90747-0001. Offers MA. Part-time and evening/weekend programs available. *Faculty:* 4 full-time (2 women), 8 part-time/adjunct (5 women). *Students:* 98 full-time (55 women), 30 part-time (17 women); includes 85 minority (20 Black or African American, non-Hispanic/Latino; 9 Asian, non-Hispanic/Latino; 53 Hispanic/Latino; 3 Two or more races, non-Hispanic/Latino), 1 international. Average age 39. 152 applicants, 88% accepted, 79 enrolled. In 2011, 91 master's awarded. *Degree requirements:* For master's, comprehensive exam. *Entrance requirements:* For master's, minimum GPA of 2.75. *Application deadline:* For fall admission, 6/1 for domestic students. Applications are processed on a rolling basis. Application fee: $55. *Faculty research:* Educational leadership, teacher retention, accountability, decision-making. *Unit head:* Dr. Ann Chlebicki, Chairperson, 310-243-2517, E-mail: achlebicki@csudh.edu. *Application contact:* Admissions Office, 310-243-3530. Web site: http://www.csudh.edu/cps/soe/programsdegrees/graduate-programs-ed-administration.shtml.

California State University, East Bay, Office of Academic Programs and Graduate Studies, College of Education and Allied Studies, Department of Educational Leadership, Hayward, CA 94542-3000. Offers educational leadership (MS, Ed D); urban teaching leadership (MS). *Accreditation:* NCATE. Part-time and evening/weekend programs available. Postbaccalaureate distance learning degree programs offered. *Faculty:* 7 full-time (3 women), 10 part-time/adjunct (7 women). *Students:* 77 full-time (42 women), 54 part-time (40 women); includes 61 minority (23 Black or African American, non-Hispanic/Latino; 13 Asian, non-Hispanic/Latino; 20 Hispanic/Latino; 5 Two or more races, non-Hispanic/Latino), 1 international. Average age 40. 87 applicants, 86% accepted, 33 enrolled. In 2011, 46 master's, 7 doctorates awarded. *Degree requirements:* For master's, comprehensive exam, project or thesis; for doctorate, thesis/dissertation. *Entrance requirements:* For master's, CBEST, teaching or services credential and experience; minimum GPA of 3.0; for doctorate, GRE, MA with minimum GPA of 3.0; PK-12 leadership position; portfolio of work samples; employer/district support agreement. Additional exam requirements/recommendations for international students: Required—TOEFL (minimum score 550 paper-based; 213 computer-based). *Application deadline:* For fall admission, 6/30 for domestic and international students. Application fee: $55. Electronic applications accepted. *Expenses:* Tuition, state resident: full-time $6738; part-time $1302 per quarter. Tuition, nonresident: full-time $12,690; part-time $2294 per quarter. *Required fees:* $449 per quarter. Tuition and fees vary according to degree level, program and reciprocity agreements. *Financial support:* Career-related internships or fieldwork, Federal Work-Study, and institutionally sponsored loans available. Support available to part-time students. Financial award application deadline: 3/2; financial award applicants required to submit FAFSA. *Unit head:* Prof. Ray Garcia, Chair, 510-885-4145, Fax: 510-885-4642, E-mail: ray.garcia@csueastbay.edu. *Application contact:* Prof. Gilberto Arriaza, Educational Leadership Graduate Advisor, 510-885-4145, Fax: 510-885-4642, E-mail: gilberto.arriaza@csueastbay.edu. Web site: http://www20.csueastbay.edu/ceas/departments/el/.

Educational Leadership and Administration

California State University, Fresno, Division of Graduate Studies, School of Education and Human Development, Department of Educational Research and Administration, Fresno, CA 93740-8027. Offers education (MA), including administration and supervision. *Accreditation:* NCATE. Part-time and evening/weekend programs available. *Degree requirements:* For master's, thesis or alternative. *Entrance requirements:* For master's, GRE General Test, MAT, minimum GPA of 2.75. Additional exam requirements/recommendations for international students: Required—TOEFL. Electronic applications accepted. *Faculty research:* Substance abuse on youth education.

California State University, Fresno, Division of Graduate Studies, School of Education and Human Development, Doctoral Program in Educational Leadership, Fresno, CA 93740-8027. Offers Ed D. Part-time programs available. *Degree requirements:* For doctorate, thesis/dissertation. *Entrance requirements:* For doctorate, GRE or MAT, minimum GPA of 3.2, master's degree. Additional exam requirements/recommendations for international students: Required—TOEFL. Electronic applications accepted. *Faculty research:* Minority special education leadership, literacy, ethics of leadership, organizational planning, language development.

California State University, Fullerton, Graduate Studies, College of Education, Department of Educational Leadership, Fullerton, CA 92834-9480. Offers MS, Ed D. *Accreditation:* NCATE. Part-time programs available. *Students:* 6 full-time (all women), 253 part-time (157 women); includes 139 minority (28 Black or African American, non-Hispanic/Latino; 1 American Indian or Alaska Native, non-Hispanic/Latino; 37 Asian, non-Hispanic/Latino; 66 Hispanic/Latino; 7 Two or more races, non-Hispanic/Latino), 10 international. Average age 36. 185 applicants, 57% accepted, 91 enrolled. In 2011, 84 master's, 11 doctorates awarded. *Degree requirements:* For master's, thesis or alternative, project. *Entrance requirements:* For master's, minimum GPA of 2.5. Application fee: $55. *Financial support:* Career-related internships or fieldwork, Federal Work-Study, institutionally sponsored loans, and scholarships/grants available. Support available to part-time students. Financial award application deadline: 3/1; financial award applicants required to submit FAFSA. *Faculty research:* Creation of a substance abuse prevention training and demonstration program. *Unit head:* Dr. Louise Adler, Head, 657-278-3911. *Application contact:* Admissions/Applications, 657-278-2371.

California State University, Long Beach, Graduate Studies, College of Education, Department of Advanced Studies in Education and Counseling, Program in Educational Administration, Long Beach, CA 90840. Offers MA, Ed D. *Students:* 16 full-time (9 women), 20 part-time (10 women); includes 17 minority (5 American Indian or Alaska Native, non-Hispanic/Latino; 3 Asian, non-Hispanic/Latino; 8 Hispanic/Latino; 1 Native Hawaiian or other Pacific Islander, non-Hispanic/Latino). Average age 35. 19 applicants, 68% accepted, 11 enrolled. In 2011, 21 master's awarded. *Degree requirements:* For master's, comprehensive exam, project or thesis. *Entrance requirements:* For master's, GRE General Test, minimum GPA of 2.75. *Application deadline:* For fall admission, 7/1 for domestic students; for spring admission, 12/1 for domestic students. Applications are processed on a rolling basis. Application fee: $55. Electronic applications accepted. *Financial support:* Federal Work-Study, institutionally sponsored loans, and scholarships/grants available. Financial award application deadline: 3/2. *Unit head:* Dr. Marilyn Korostoff, Coordinator, 562-985-5705, Fax: 562-985-4534, E-mail: marilynk@csulb.edu. *Application contact:* Nancy L. McGlothin, Coordinator for Graduate Studies and Research, 562-985-8476, Fax: 562-985-4951, E-mail: nmcgloth@csulb.edu.

California State University, Northridge, Graduate Studies, College of Education, Department of Educational Leadership and Policy Studies, Northridge, CA 91330. Offers education (MA); educational administration (MA); educational leadership (Ed D). *Accreditation:* NCATE. Part-time and evening/weekend programs available. *Entrance requirements:* For master's, 2 letters of recommendation. Additional exam requirements/recommendations for international students: Required—TOEFL. *Faculty research:* Bilingual educational training.

California State University, Sacramento, Office of Graduate Studies, College of Education, Department of Educational Leadership and Policy Studies, Sacramento, CA 95819-6079. Offers educational leadership (MA). Part-time programs available. *Faculty:* 7 full-time (4 women), 5 part-time/adjunct (4 women). *Students:* 106 full-time, 20 part-time; includes 50 minority (13 Black or African American, non-Hispanic/Latino; 2 Asian, non-Hispanic/Latino; 28 Hispanic/Latino; 3 Native Hawaiian or other Pacific Islander, non-Hispanic/Latino; 4 Two or more races, non-Hispanic/Latino). Average age 37. 90 applicants, 76% accepted, 52 enrolled. In 2011, 70 master's awarded. *Degree requirements:* For master's, thesis or project; writing proficiency exam. *Entrance requirements:* For master's, minimum GPA of 2.5. Additional exam requirements/recommendations for international students: Required—TOEFL. *Application deadline:* For fall admission, 3/1 for domestic and international students; for spring admission, 9/30 for international students. Applications are processed on a rolling basis. Application fee: $55. Electronic applications accepted. *Financial support:* Career-related internships or fieldwork and Federal Work-Study available. Support available to part-time students. Financial award application deadline: 3/1; financial award applicants required to submit FAFSA. *Unit head:* Dr. Francisco Reveles, Chair, 916-278-5388, Fax: 916-278-4608, E-mail: revelesf@csus.edu. *Application contact:* Jose Martinez, Outreach and Graduate Diversity Coordinator, 916-278-6470, Fax: 916-278-5669, E-mail: martinj@skymail.csus.edu. Web site: http://www.edweb.csus.edu/edlp.

California State University, San Bernardino, Graduate Studies, College of Education, Program in Educational Administration, San Bernardino, CA 92407-2397. Offers MA. Part-time and evening/weekend programs available. *Students:* 38 full-time (20 women), 38 part-time (21 women); includes 23 minority (5 Black or African American, non-Hispanic/Latino; 2 Asian, non-Hispanic/Latino; 15 Hispanic/Latino; 1 Native Hawaiian or other Pacific Islander, non-Hispanic/Latino). Average age 37. 90 applicants, 41% accepted, 22 enrolled. In 2011, 42 master's awarded. *Degree requirements:* For master's, thesis or alternative. *Entrance requirements:* For master's, minimum GPA of 3.0 in education. *Application deadline:* For fall admission, 8/31 priority date for domestic students. Application fee: $55. *Expenses:* Tuition, state resident: full-time $7356. Tuition, nonresident: full-time $7356. *Required fees:* $1077. Tuition and fees vary according to program. *Financial support:* Career-related internships or fieldwork available. Support available to part-time students. *Unit head:* Dr. Jay Fiene, Department Chair, 909-537-7621, Fax: 909-537-7510, E-mail: jfiene@csusb.edu. *Application contact:* Sandra Kamusikiri, Associate Vice-President/Dean of Graduate Studies, 909-537-6069, E-mail: skamusik@csusb.edu.

California State University, San Bernardino, Graduate Studies, College of Education, Program in Educational Leadership and Curriculum, San Bernardino, CA 92407-2397. Offers Ed D. *Students:* 43 full-time (29 women), 2 part-time (0 women); includes 10 minority (all Hispanic/Latino), 1 international. Average age 42. 23 applicants, 70% accepted, 14 enrolled. *Expenses:* Tuition, state resident: full-time $7356. Tuition, nonresident: full-time $7356. *Required fees:* $1077. Tuition and fees vary according to program. *Unit head:* Dr. Jay Feine, Interim Department Chair, 909-537-7621, E-mail: jfiene@csusb.edu. *Application contact:* Sandra Kamusikiri, Associate Vice-President/Dean of Graduate Studies, 909-537-5058, E-mail: skamusik@csusb.edu.

California State University, Stanislaus, College of Education, Program in Education (MA), Turlock, CA 95382. Offers curriculum and instruction (MA), including education technology, elementary education, multilingual education, physical education, reading, secondary education, special education; school administration (MA); school counseling (MA). Part-time and evening/weekend programs available. *Degree requirements:* For master's, comprehensive exam (for some programs), thesis (for some programs). *Entrance requirements:* For master's, MAT, GRE, or CBEST (varies by concentration), 3 letters of recommendation, personal statement. Additional exam requirements/recommendations for international students: Required—TOEFL (minimum score 550 paper-based; 213 computer-based). *Application deadline:* For fall admission, 5/1 for domestic students; for spring admission, 1/7 for domestic students. Application fee: $55. Electronic applications accepted. *Expenses: Required fees:* $4616 per year. *Financial support:* Federal Work-Study available. Financial award application deadline: 3/1; financial award applicants required to submit FAFSA. *Faculty research:* Children's perspectives on historical events, method elementary schools dual language education, K-12 reading and CYRM programs. *Unit head:* Dr. Kathy Norman, Dean, College of Education, 209-667-3652, Fax: 209-664-6613, E-mail: coe@csustan.edu. *Application contact:* Graduate School, 209-667-3129, Fax: 209-664-7025, E-mail: graduate_school@csustan.edu. Web site: http://www.csustan.edu/COE/.

California State University, Stanislaus, College of Education, Programs in Educational Leadership (Ed D), Turlock, CA 95382. Offers community college leadership (Ed D); P-12 leadership (Ed D). Part-time and evening/weekend programs available. *Degree requirements:* For doctorate, thesis/dissertation. *Entrance requirements:* For doctorate, GRE, minimum GPA of 3.0, 3 letters of reference, interview, personal statement. Additional exam requirements/recommendations for international students: Required—TOEFL (minimum score 550 paper-based; 213 computer-based). *Application deadline:* For spring admission, 2/1 priority date for domestic students. Application fee: $55. Electronic applications accepted. *Expenses: Required fees:* $4616 per year. *Financial support:* Career-related internships or fieldwork and Federal Work-Study available. Financial award application deadline: 3/1; financial award applicants required to submit FAFSA. *Unit head:* Dr. Kenneth White, Director, 209-664-6543, Fax: 209-667-3043, E-mail: edd@csustan.edu. *Application contact:* Graduate School, 209-667-3129, Fax: 209-664-7025, E-mail: graduate_school@csustan.edu. Web site: http://www.csustan.edu/EdD/.

California University of Pennsylvania, School of Graduate Studies and Research, College of Education and Human Services, Program in School Administration, California, PA 15419-1394. Offers M Ed. *Accreditation:* NCATE. Part-time and evening/weekend programs available. *Degree requirements:* For master's, comprehensive exam, thesis optional. *Entrance requirements:* For master's, MAT, interview, minimum GPA of 3.0, teaching certificate, 2 years of teaching experience. Additional exam requirements/recommendations for international students: Required—TOEFL (minimum score 550 paper-based; 213 computer-based; 80 iBT). Electronic applications accepted. *Faculty research:* Educational leadership, peer coaching, online education-effective teaching strategies, instruction strategies, school law.

Calumet College of Saint Joseph, Program in Leadership in Teaching, Whiting, IN 46394-2195. Offers MS Ed.

Calvin College, Graduate Programs in Education, Grand Rapids, MI 49546-4388. Offers curriculum and instruction (M Ed); educational leadership (M Ed); learning disabilities (M Ed); literacy (M Ed). Part-time programs available. *Degree requirements:* For master's, thesis or seminar. *Entrance requirements:* For master's, teaching certificate. Additional exam requirements/recommendations for international students: Required—TOEFL (minimum score 550 paper-based; 213 computer-based; 80 iBT). Electronic applications accepted. *Faculty research:* Literacy, racialized gender and gendered identity, teacher learning, learning disabilities identification.

Cambridge College, School of Education, Cambridge, MA 02138-5304. Offers autism specialist (M Ed); autism/behavior analyst (M Ed); behavior analyst (Post-Master's Certificate); behavioral management (M Ed); early childhood teacher (M Ed); education specialist in curriculum and instruction (CAGS); educational leadership (Ed D); elementary teacher (M Ed); English as a second language (M Ed, Certificate); general science (M Ed); health education (Post-Master's Certificate); health/family and consumer sciences (M Ed); history (M Ed); individualized (M Ed); information technology literacy (M Ed); instructional technology (M Ed); interdisciplinary studies (M Ed); library teacher (M Ed); literacy education (M Ed); mathematics (M Ed); mathematics specialist (Certificate); middle school mathematics and science (M Ed); school administration (M Ed, CAGS); school guidance counselor (M Ed); school nurse education (M Ed); school social worker/school adjustment counselor (M Ed); special education administrator (CAGS); special education/moderate disabilities (M Ed); teaching skills and methodologies (M Ed). Part-time and evening/weekend programs available. Postbaccalaureate distance learning degree programs offered (minimal on-campus study). *Degree requirements:* For master's, thesis, internship/practicum (licensure program only); for doctorate, thesis/dissertation; for other advanced degree, thesis. *Entrance requirements:* For master's, interview, resume, documentation of licensure, 2 professional references; for doctorate, official transcripts, interview, resume, documentation of licensure (if any), written personal statement/essay, portfolio of scholarly and professional work, qualifying assessment, 2 professional references, health insurance, immunizations form; for other advanced degree, official transcripts, interview, resume, documentation of licensure (if any), written personal statement/essay, 2 professional references, health insurance, immunizations form. Additional exam requirements/recommendations for international students: Required—TOEFL (minimum score 550 paper-based; 213 computer-based; 79 iBT); Recommended—IELTS (minimum score 6). Electronic applications accepted. *Expenses:* Contact institution. *Faculty research:* Adult education, accelerated learning, mathematics education, brain compatible learning, special education and law.

Cameron University, Office of Graduate Studies, Program in Educational Leadership, Lawton, OK 73505-6377. Offers MS. Part-time and evening/weekend programs available. *Degree requirements:* For master's, portfolio.

Campbell University, Graduate and Professional Programs, School of Education, Buies Creek, NC 27506. Offers administration (MSA); community counseling (MA); elementary education (M Ed); English education (M Ed); interdisciplinary studies (M Ed); mathematics education (M Ed); middle grades education (M Ed); physical education (M Ed); school counseling (M Ed); secondary education (M Ed); social science education (M Ed). *Accreditation:* NCATE. Part-time and evening/weekend programs available. *Degree requirements:* For master's, comprehensive exam. *Entrance requirements:* For master's, GRE General Test, minimum GPA of 2.7. *Faculty research:* Spiritual values and wellness issues in counseling, stress and professional burnout among counselors, thinking strategies, leadership, adaptive technology.

Canisius College, Graduate Division, School of Education and Human Services, Department of Graduate Education and Leadership, Buffalo, NY 14208-1098. Offers college student personnel (MS Ed); deaf education (MS Ed); deaf/adolescent education, grades 7-12 (MS Ed); deaf/childhood education, grades 1-6 (MS Ed); differential instruction (MS Ed); education administration (MS Ed); gifted education extention (Certificate); literacy (MS Ed); reading (Certificate); school building leadership (MS Ed, Certificate); school district leadership (Certificate). *Accreditation:* NCATE. Part-time and evening/weekend programs available. Postbaccalaureate distance learning degree programs offered (minimal on-campus study). *Faculty:* 7 full-time (6 women), 36 part-time/adjunct (22 women). *Students:* 149 full-time (114 women), 242 part-time (177 women); includes 42 minority (29 Black or African American, non-Hispanic/Latino; 2 American Indian or Alaska Native, non-Hispanic/Latino; 3 Asian, non-Hispanic/Latino; 6 Hispanic/Latino; 2 Two or more races, non-Hispanic/Latino), 3 international. Average age 30. 250 applicants, 84% accepted, 124 enrolled. In 2011, 135 degrees awarded. *Entrance requirements:* For master's, GRE if cumulative GPA less than 2.7, transcripts, two letters of recommendation. Additional exam requirements/recommendations for international students: Required—TOEFL. *Application deadline:* Applications are processed on a rolling basis. Application fee: $25. Electronic applications accepted. *Financial support:* Career-related internships or fieldwork, Federal Work-Study, scholarships/grants, tuition waivers (partial), and unspecified assistantships available. Support available to part-time students. Financial award application deadline: 4/30; financial award applicants required to submit FAFSA. *Faculty research:* Asperger's disease, autism, private higher education, reading strategies. *Unit head:* Dr. Rosemary K. Murray, Chair/Associate Professor of Graduate Education and Leadership, 716-888-3723, E-mail: murray1@canisius.edu. *Application contact:* Jim Bagwell, Director of Graduate Recruitment and Admissions, 716-888-2544, Fax: 716-888-3290, E-mail: bagwellj@canisius.edu. Web site: http://www.canisius.edu/education/graduate.asp.

Capella University, School of Education, Minneapolis, MN 55402. Offers college teaching (Certificate); curriculum and instruction (MS, PhD); education (MS); enrollment management (MS); instructional design for online learning (MS, PhD); k-12 studies in education (MS, PhD); leadership for higher education (MS, PhD); leadership in education administration (Certificate); leadership in educational administration (MS, PhD); postsecondary and adult education (MS, PhD); professional studies in education (MS, PhD); reading and literacy (MS); training and performance improvement (MS, PhD). Part-time and evening/weekend programs available. Postbaccalaureate distance learning degree programs offered (minimal on-campus study). Terminal master's awarded for partial completion of doctoral program. *Degree requirements:* For master's, thesis optional, integrative project; for doctorate, comprehensive exam, thesis/dissertation. *Entrance requirements:* Additional exam requirements/recommendations for international students: Required—TOEFL (minimum score 550 paper-based; 213 computer-based), TWE (minimum score 4). Electronic applications accepted. *Faculty research:* Higher education administration, distance learning, adult education, training and curriculum design.

Cardinal Stritch University, College of Education, Department of Education, Milwaukee, WI 53217-3985. Offers education (ME); educational leadership (MS); leadership for the advancement of learning and service (Ed D, PhD); teaching (MAT); urban education (MA). *Accreditation:* NCATE. Evening/weekend programs available. *Degree requirements:* For master's, comprehensive exam, thesis (for some programs), research project, faculty recommendation; for doctorate, thesis/dissertation, practica, field experience. *Entrance requirements:* For master's, letters of recommendation (3), minimum GPA of 3.0; for doctorate, minimum GPA of 3.5 in master's coursework, letters of recommendation (3).

Caribbean University, Graduate School, Bayamón, PR 00960-0493. Offers administration and supervision (MA Ed); criminal justice (MA); curriculum and instruction (MA Ed, PhD), including elementary education (MA Ed), English education (MA Ed), history education (MA Ed), mathematics education (MA Ed), primary education (MA Ed), science education (MA Ed), Spanish education (MA Ed); educational technology in instructional systems (MA Ed); gerontology (MSN); human resources (MBA); museology, archiving and art history (MA Ed); neonatal pediatrics (MSN); physical education (MA Ed); special education (MA Ed). *Entrance requirements:* For master's, interview, minimum GPA of 2.5.

Carson-Newman College, Graduate Program in Education, Jefferson City, TN 37760. Offers curriculum and instruction (M Ed); educational leadership (M Ed); elementary education (MAT); school counseling (MS); secondary education (MAT); teaching English as a second language (MATESL). *Accreditation:* NCATE. Part-time and evening/weekend programs available. *Faculty:* 5 full-time (2 women), 10 part-time/adjunct (3 women). *Students:* 85 full-time (55 women), 76 part-time (53 women); includes 8 minority (5 Black or African American, non-Hispanic/Latino; 2 Asian, non-Hispanic/Latino; 1 Two or more races, non-Hispanic/Latino), 23 international. Average age 32. 80 applicants, 96% accepted. In 2011, 90 master's awarded. *Degree requirements:* For master's, thesis or alternative. *Entrance requirements:* For master's, NTE, minimum GPA of 3.0 in major, 2.5 overall. *Application deadline:* For fall admission, 7/15 priority date for domestic students. Applications are processed on a rolling basis. Application fee: $25 ($50 for international students). *Expenses: Tuition:* Full-time $6750; part-time $375 per credit hour. *Required fees:* $200. *Financial support:* In 2011–12, 41 students received support. Federal Work-Study and unspecified assistantships available. Financial award application deadline: 4/1; financial award applicants required to submit FAFSA. *Unit head:* Dr. Sharon Teets, Chair, 865-471-3461. *Application contact:* Graduate Admissions and Services Adviser, 865-471-3460, Fax: 865-471-3875.

Carthage College, Division of Teacher Education, Kenosha, WI 53140. Offers classroom guidance and counseling (M Ed); creative arts (M Ed); gifted and talented children (M Ed); language arts (M Ed); modern language (M Ed); natural sciences (M Ed); reading (M Ed, Certificate); social sciences (M Ed); teacher leadership (M Ed). Part-time and evening/weekend programs available. *Degree requirements:* For master's, thesis optional. *Entrance requirements:* For master's, MAT, minimum B average, letters of reference.

Castleton State College, Division of Graduate Studies, Department of Education, Program in Educational Leadership, Castleton, VT 05735. Offers MA Ed, CAGS. Part-time and evening/weekend programs available. *Degree requirements:* For master's, thesis or alternative; for CAGS, publishable paper. *Entrance requirements:* For master's, GRE General Test, MAT, interview, minimum undergraduate GPA of 3.0; for CAGS, educational research, master's degree, minimum undergraduate GPA of 3.0.

The Catholic University of America, School of Arts and Sciences, Department of Education, Washington, DC 20064. Offers Catholic educational leadership and policy studies (PhD); Catholic school leadership (MA); education (Certificate); educational psychology (PhD); secondary education (MA); special education (MA). *Accreditation:* NCATE. Part-time programs available. *Faculty:* 10 full-time (8 women), 10 part-time/adjunct (8 women). *Students:* 4 full-time (all women), 44 part-time (34 women); includes 12 minority (6 Black or African American, non-Hispanic/Latino; 4 Hispanic/Latino; 2 Two or more races, non-Hispanic/Latino). Average age 39. 38 applicants, 24% accepted, 2 enrolled. In 2011, 5 master's, 4 doctorates, 3 other advanced degrees awarded. *Degree requirements:* For master's, comprehensive exam, thesis or alternative; for doctorate, comprehensive exam, thesis/dissertation; for Certificate, action research project. *Entrance requirements:* For master's and doctorate, GRE General Test or MAT, statement of purpose, official copies of academic transcripts, three letters of recommendation, interview; for Certificate, PRAXIS I, statement of purpose, official copies of academic transcripts, three letters of recommendation, interview. Additional exam requirements/recommendations for international students: Required—TOEFL (minimum score 580 paper-based; 237 computer-based). *Application deadline:* For fall admission, 8/1 priority date for domestic students, 7/15 for international students; for spring admission, 12/1 priority date for domestic students, 10/15 for international students. Applications are processed on a rolling basis. Application fee: $55. Electronic applications accepted. *Expenses: Tuition:* Full-time $35,260; part-time $1380 per credit. *Required fees:* $80; $40 per semester hour. One-time fee: $425. *Financial support:* Fellowships, research assistantships, teaching assistantships, Federal Work-Study, scholarships/grants, tuition waivers (full and partial), and unspecified assistantships available. Financial award application deadline: 2/1; financial award applicants required to submit FAFSA. *Faculty research:* Special education, early childhood education, educational psychology, Catholic school administration, leadership and policy studies, counseling, curriculum and instruction. *Total annual research expenditures:* $36,210. *Unit head:* Dr. Merylann J. Schuttloffel, Chair, 202-319-5805, Fax: 202-319-5815, E-mail: schuttloffel@cua.edu. *Application contact:* Andrew Woodall, Director of Graduate Admissions, 202-319-5057, Fax: 202-319-6533, E-mail: cua-admissions@cua.edu. Web site: http://education.cua.edu/.

Cedarville University, Graduate Programs, Cedarville, OH 45314-0601. Offers family nurse practitioner (MSN); global health nursing (MSN); nurse educator (MSN); teacher leader (M Ed). Part-time programs available. *Faculty:* 27 part-time/adjunct (14 women). *Students:* 13 full-time (11 women), 66 part-time (51 women), 2 international. Average age 33. 65 applicants, 83% accepted, 38 enrolled. In 2011, 2 master's awarded. *Degree requirements:* For master's, thesis. *Entrance requirements:* For master's, GRE, 2 professional recommendations. Additional exam requirements/recommendations for international students: Required—TOEFL (minimum score 550 paper-based; 80 iBT). *Application deadline:* For fall admission, 5/1 priority date for domestic students, 5/1 for international students; for spring admission, 11/1 priority date for domestic students, 11/1 for international students. Applications are processed on a rolling basis. Application fee: $30. Electronic applications accepted. *Financial support:* Scholarships/grants and unspecified assistantships available. Support available to part-time students. Financial award applicants required to submit FAFSA. *Unit head:* Dr. Andrew A. Runyan, Senior Associate Academic Vice-President/Dean of Graduate Studies, 937-766-3840, E-mail: arunyan@cedarville.edu. *Application contact:* Roscoe F. Smith, Associate Vice-President of Enrollment, 937-766-7700, Fax: 937-766-7575, E-mail: smithr@cedarville.edu. Web site: http://www.cedarville.edu/academics/graduate/.

Centenary College, Program in Education, Hackettstown, NJ 07840-2100. Offers educational leadership (MA); instructional leadership (MA); special education (MA). *Accreditation:* Teacher Education Accreditation Council. Part-time and evening/weekend programs available. Postbaccalaureate distance learning degree programs offered (minimal on-campus study). *Degree requirements:* For master's, thesis. *Entrance requirements:* For master's, interview, minimum undergraduate GPA of 2.8.

Centenary College of Louisiana, Graduate Programs, Department of Education, Shreveport, LA 71104. Offers administration (M Ed); elementary education (MAT); secondary education (MAT); supervision of instruction (M Ed). Part-time and evening/weekend programs available. *Degree requirements:* For master's, comprehensive exam. *Entrance requirements:* For master's, GRE General Test (M Ed), PRAXIS I and PRAXIS II (MAT), teacher certification (M Ed), minimum GPA of 2.5. *Expenses:* Contact institution. *Faculty research:* Teachers as advocates for teachers, portfolio assessment, disabled readers.

Central Connecticut State University, School of Graduate Studies, School of Education and Professional Studies, Department of Educational Leadership, Program in Educational Leadership, New Britain, CT 06050-4010. Offers MS, Ed D, Sixth Year Certificate. Part-time and evening/weekend programs available. *Students:* 8 full-time (7 women), 241 part-time (153 women); includes 40 minority (19 Black or African American, non-Hispanic/Latino; 4 Asian, non-Hispanic/Latino; 17 Hispanic/Latino), 1 international. Average age 41. 80 applicants, 71% accepted, 38 enrolled. In 2011, 85 master's, 6 doctorates, 52 other advanced degrees awarded. *Degree requirements:* For master's, thesis or alternative; for doctorate, thesis/dissertation or alternative; for Sixth Year Certificate, thesis or alternative, qualifying exam. *Entrance requirements:* For master's, minimum undergraduate GPA of 2.7; for doctorate, GRE, master's degree, essay, interview, resume; for Sixth Year Certificate, master's degree with minimum GPA of 3.0, essay, portfolio. Additional exam requirements/recommendations for international students: Required—TOEFL (minimum score 550 paper-based; 213 computer-based). *Application deadline:* For fall admission, 6/1 for domestic students, 5/1 for international students; for spring admission, 11/1 for domestic and international students. Applications are processed on a rolling basis. Application fee: $50. Electronic applications accepted. *Expenses: Tuition, area resident:* Full-time $5137; part-time $482 per credit. Tuition, state resident: full-time $7707; part-time $494 per credit. Tuition, nonresident: full-time $14,311; part-time $494 per credit. *Required fees:* $3865. One-time fee: $62 part-time. *Unit head:* Dr. Anthony Rigazio-Digilio, Chair, 860-832-2130, E-mail: digilio@ccsu.edu. *Application contact:* Patricia Gardner, Associate Director of Graduate Studies, 860-832-2350, Fax: 860-832-2352, E-mail: graduateadmissions@ccsu.edu.

Central Michigan University, Central Michigan University Global Campus, Program in Education, Mount Pleasant, MI 48859. Offers adult education (MA); college teaching (Graduate Certificate); community college (MA); educational leadership (MA), including charter school leadership; educational technology (MA); guidance and development (MA); instruction (MA); reading and literacy K-12 (MA); school principalship (MA); teacher leadership (MA). *Accreditation:* Teacher Education Accreditation Council. Part-time and evening/weekend programs available. *Entrance requirements:* For master's, minimum GPA of 2.7 in major. Additional exam requirements/recommendations for international students: Required—TOEFL. *Application deadline:* Applications are processed on a rolling basis. Application fee: $50. Electronic applications accepted. *Financial support:* Scholarships/grants available. Support available to part-time students. *Unit head:* Dr. Peter Ross, Director, 989-774-4456, E-mail: ross1pg@cmich.edu. *Application contact:* 877-268-4636, E-mail: cmuglobal@cmich.edu.

Central Michigan University, Central Michigan University Global Campus, Program in Educational Leadership, Mount Pleasant, MI 48859. Offers educational administration (Ed S); educational administration and community leadership (Ed D). Part-time and evening/weekend programs available. *Entrance requirements:* Additional exam requirements/recommendations for international students: Required—TOEFL. *Application deadline:* Applications are processed on a rolling basis. Application fee: $50. Electronic applications accepted. *Financial support:* Scholarships/grants available. Support available to part-time students. *Unit head:* Dr. Anne Hornak, Chair, 989-774-2215, E-mail: horna1am@cmich.edu. *Application contact:* 877-268-4636, E-mail: cmuglobal@cmich.edu.

Central Michigan University, College of Graduate Studies, College of Education and Human Services, Department of Educational Leadership, Mount Pleasant, MI 48859. Offers educational leadership (MA, Ed D), including charter school leadership (MA), educational technology (Ed D, Ed S), general educational leadership (MA), higher education administration (MA, Ed S), higher education leadership (Ed D), K-12 curriculum (Ed D), K-12 leadership (Ed D), student affairs administration (MA); general educational administration (Ed S), including administrative leadership K-12, educational technology (Ed D, Ed S), higher education administration (MA, Ed S), instructional leadership K-12; school principalship (MA); teacher leadership (MA). Part-time and evening/weekend programs available. *Degree requirements:* For master's and other advanced degree, thesis or alternative; for doctorate, thesis/dissertation. *Entrance* *requirements:* For doctorate, GRE or MAT, master's degree, minimum GPA of 3.5, 3 years of professional education experience. Electronic applications accepted. *Faculty research:* Elementary administration, secondary administration, student achievement, in-service training, internships in administration.

Central Washington University, Graduate Studies and Research, College of Education and Professional Studies, Department of Advanced Programs, Ellensburg, WA 98926. Offers school administration (M Ed); school instructional leadership (M Ed). *Faculty:* 4 full-time. *Students:* 1 full-time, 8 part-time (3 women). 6 applicants, 67% accepted, 4 enrolled. In 2011, 8 master's awarded. *Degree requirements:* For master's, comprehensive exam, thesis or alternative. *Entrance requirements:* Additional exam requirements/recommendations for international students: Required—TOEFL (minimum score 550 paper-based; 79 computer-based), IELTS (minimum score 6.5). *Application deadline:* For fall admission, 2/1 for domestic students; for winter admission, 10/1 for domestic students; for spring admission, 1/1 for domestic students. Applications are processed on a rolling basis. Application fee: $50. Electronic applications accepted. *Expenses:* Tuition, state resident: full-time $8112; part-time $270 per credit. Tuition, nonresident: full-time $18,069; part-time $602 per credit. *Required fees:* $924. *Financial support:* Career-related internships or fieldwork, Federal Work-Study, scholarships/grants, and unspecified assistantships available. Support available to part-time students. *Unit head:* Dr. Henry Williams, Chair, 509-963-1751. *Application contact:* Justine Eason, Admissions Program Coordinator, 509-963-3103, Fax: 509-963-1799, E-mail: masters@cwu.edu. Web site: http://www.cwu.edu/~ap/.

Chadron State College, School of Professional and Graduate Studies, Department of Education, Chadron, NE 69337. Offers business (MA Ed); community counseling (MA Ed); educational administration (MS Ed, Sp Ed); elementary education (MS Ed); history (MA Ed); language and literature (MA Ed); secondary administration (MS Ed); secondary education (MS Ed). *Accreditation:* NCATE. Part-time and evening/weekend programs available. Postbaccalaureate distance learning degree programs offered. *Degree requirements:* For master's, thesis optional. *Entrance requirements:* For master's, GRE General Test, GRE Writing Test, minimum GPA of 2.75 or 12 graduate hours at CSC with minimum GPA of 3.25. Additional exam requirements/recommendations for international students: Required—TOEFL. Electronic applications accepted. *Faculty research:* Rural education, technology, mental health.

Chaminade University of Honolulu, Graduate Services, Program in Education, Honolulu, HI 96816-1578. Offers child development (M Ed); educational leadership (M Ed); elementary education with licensure (MAT); instructional leadership (M Ed); Montessori credential (M Ed); Montessori emphasis (M Ed); secondary education with licensure (MAT), including English, math, science, social studies; special education with licensure (MAT). Part-time and evening/weekend programs available. Postbaccalaureate distance learning degree programs offered (minimal on-campus study). *Faculty:* 2 full-time (both women), 32 part-time/adjunct (25 women). *Students:* 53 full-time (38 women), 88 part-time (67 women); includes 77 minority (6 Black or African American, non-Hispanic/Latino; 1 American Indian or Alaska Native, non-Hispanic/Latino; 44 Asian, non-Hispanic/Latino; 5 Hispanic/Latino; 17 Native Hawaiian or other Pacific Islander, non-Hispanic/Latino; 4 Two or more races, non-Hispanic/Latino), 1 international. Average age 35. 40 applicants, 88% accepted, 30 enrolled. In 2011, 105 master's awarded. *Degree requirements:* For master's, thesis or alternative. *Entrance requirements:* For master's, PRAXIS (for MAT only), minimum GPA of 2.75, 3 letters of recommendation. Additional exam requirements/recommendations for international students: Required—TOEFL (minimum score 550 paper-based). *Application deadline:* For fall admission, 9/1 priority date for domestic students, 9/1 for international students; for winter admission, 12/1 priority date for domestic students, 12/1 for international students; for spring admission, 3/1 priority date for domestic students, 3/1 for international students. Applications are processed on a rolling basis. Application fee: $50. Electronic applications accepted. *Expenses: Required fees:* $600 per credit hour. One-time fee: $93 part-time. *Financial support:* In 2011–12, 172 students received support. Career-related internships or fieldwork, Federal Work-Study, institutionally sponsored loans, scholarships/grants, and tuition waivers (partial) available. Support available to part-time students. Financial award application deadline: 3/1; financial award applicants required to submit FAFSA. *Faculty research:* Peace and curriculum education. *Unit head:* Dr. Joseph Peters, Dean, 808-440-4251, Fax: 808-739-4607, E-mail: joseph.peters@chaminade.edu. *Application contact:* 808-739-4663, Fax: 808-739-8329, E-mail: gradserv@chaminade.edu. Web site: http://www.chaminade.edu/education/grad.php.

Charleston Southern University, School of Education, Charleston, SC 29423-8087. Offers administration and supervision (M Ed), including elementary, secondary; elementary education (M Ed); secondary education (M Ed). *Accreditation:* NCATE. Part-time and evening/weekend programs available. *Degree requirements:* For master's, thesis optional. *Entrance requirements:* For master's, GRE or MAT. Additional exam requirements/recommendations for international students: Required—TOEFL (minimum score 550 paper-based; 213 computer-based; 79 iBT). *Expenses:* Contact institution.

Chestnut Hill College, School of Graduate Studies, Department of Education, Program in Educational Leadership, Philadelphia, PA 19118-2693. Offers M Ed. Part-time and evening/weekend programs available. *Faculty:* 6 full-time (4 women), 50 part-time/adjunct (33 women). *Students:* 1 (woman) full-time, 8 part-time (7 women). Average age 31. 2 applicants, 100% accepted. In 2011, 1 master's awarded. *Degree requirements:* For master's, thesis optional. *Entrance requirements:* For master's, PRAXIS I or proof of teaching certification, letters of recommendation, writing sample, 6 graduate credits with minimum B grade if undergraduate GPA less than 3.0. Additional exam requirements/recommendations for international students: Required—TOEFL (minimum score 500 paper-based; 213 computer-based). *Application deadline:* For fall admission, 7/17 priority date for domestic students, 7/15 for international students; for spring admission, 12/15 priority date for domestic students, 12/15 for international students. Applications are processed on a rolling basis. Application fee: $55. *Expenses: Tuition:* Part-time $555 per credit hour. One-time fee: $55 part-time. Part-time tuition and fees vary according to degree level and program. *Financial support:* Unspecified assistantships available. *Faculty research:* Mentoring and induction programs. *Unit head:* Dr. Carol Pate, Chair, Education Department, 215-248-7127, Fax: 215-248-7155, E-mail: cmpate@chc.edu. *Application contact:* Amy Boorse, Administrative Assistant, School of Graduate Studies Office, 215-248-7170, Fax: 215-248-7161, E-mail: gradadmissions@chc.edu. Web site: http://www.chc.edu/Graduate/Programs/Masters/Education/.

Cheyney University of Pennsylvania, School of Education and Professional Studies, Program in Educational Administration and Supervision, Cheyney, PA 19319. Offers M Ed, Certificate. *Accreditation:* NCATE. Part-time and evening/weekend programs available. *Degree requirements:* For master's, thesis or alternative. *Entrance requirements:* For master's, GRE General Test, MAT, minimum GPA of 2.75. Electronic applications accepted. *Faculty research:* Teacher motivation, critical thinking.

Cheyney University of Pennsylvania, School of Education and Professional Studies, Program in Educational Administration of Adult and Continuing Education, Cheyney, PA 19319. Offers M Ed, MS. Part-time and evening/weekend programs available. *Degree requirements:* For master's, thesis or alternative. Electronic applications accepted.

Cheyney University of Pennsylvania, School of Education and Professional Studies, Program in Elementary and Secondary Principalship, Cheyney, PA 19319. Offers Certificate.

Chicago State University, School of Graduate and Professional Studies, College of Education, Department of Educational Leadership, Curriculum and Foundations, Program in Educational Leadership, Chicago, IL 60628. Offers educational leadership (Ed D); general administration (MA); higher education administration (MA). *Accreditation:* NCATE. *Degree requirements:* For master's, comprehensive exam, thesis optional. *Entrance requirements:* For master's, minimum GPA of 2.75.

Christian Brothers University, School of Arts, Memphis, TN 38104-5581. Offers Catholic studies (MACS); educational leadership (MSEL); teacher-leadership (M Ed); teaching (MAT). Part-time and evening/weekend programs available. *Entrance requirements:* For master's, GRE, GMAT, PRAXIS II. *Expenses:* Contact institution.

The Citadel, The Military College of South Carolina, Citadel Graduate College, School of Education, Program in Educational Administration, Charleston, SC 29409. Offers elementary/secondary school administration and supervision (M Ed); school superintendency (Ed S). *Accreditation:* NCATE. Part-time and evening/weekend programs available. *Faculty:* 12 full-time (8 women), 9 part-time/adjunct (4 women). *Students:* 70 part-time (48 women); includes 12 minority (8 Black or African American, non-Hispanic/Latino; 1 American Indian or Alaska Native, non-Hispanic/Latino; 2 Asian, non-Hispanic/Latino; 1 Hispanic/Latino). Average age 35. In 2011, 26 master's, 3 Ed Ss awarded. *Degree requirements:* For master's and Ed S, comprehensive exam, internship. *Entrance requirements:* For master's, GRE (minimum score 900) or MAT (minimum score 396), minimum undergraduate GPA of 2.5, valid South Carolina teaching certificate, one year of teaching experience; for Ed S, GRE (minimum score 900) or MAT (minimum score 396), minimum GPA of 3.5; South Carolina State Certificate in school administration or administrative position equivalent to assistant principal or higher in education; valid South Carolina teaching certificate; three years' teaching experience. Additional exam requirements/recommendations for international students: Required—TOEFL (minimum score 550 paper-based; 213 computer-based). *Application deadline:* Applications are processed on a rolling basis. Application fee: $30. Electronic applications accepted. *Expenses: Tuition, area resident:* Part-time $501 per credit hour. Tuition, state resident: part-time $501 per credit hour. Tuition, nonresident: part-time $824 per credit hour. *Required fees:* $40 per term. One-time fee: $30. *Financial support:* Career-related internships or fieldwork, health care benefits, and unspecified assistantships available. Support available to part-time students. Financial award application deadline: 7/1; financial award applicants required to submit FAFSA. *Unit head:* Dr. Mary Lou Yeatts, Coordinator, 843-953-5201, Fax: 843-953-7258, E-mail: marylou.yeatts@citadel.edu. *Application contact:* Dr. Steve A. Nida, Associate Provost, The Citadel Graduate College, 843-953-5089, Fax: 843-953-7630, E-mail: cgc@citadel.edu. Web site: http://www.citadel.edu/education/educational-leadership.html.

City College of the City University of New York, Graduate School, School of Education, Department of Leadership and Special Education, New York, NY 10031-9198. Offers bilingual special education (MS Ed); educational leadership (MS, AC); teacher of students with disabilities in childhood education (MS Ed); teacher of students with disabilities in middle childhood education (MS Ed). *Degree requirements:* For master's, thesis, research paper. *Entrance requirements:* For master's, Liberal Arts and Sciences Test (LAST), Content Specialty Test (CST), interview; minimum GPA of 3.0 in major, 2.5 overall. Additional exam requirements/recommendations for international students: Required—TOEFL. *Faculty research:* Dynamics of organizational change, impact of laws on educational policy, leadership development in schools.

City University of Seattle, Graduate Division, Albright School of Education, Bellevue, WA 98005. Offers administrator certification (Certificate); curriculum and instruction (M Ed); educational leadership (Ed D); elementary education (MIT); guidance and counseling (M Ed); higher education leadership (Ed D); leadership (M Ed); leadership and school counseling (M Ed); organizational leadership (Ed D); reading and literacy (M Ed); special education (MIT); superintendent certification (Certificate). Part-time and evening/weekend programs available. Postbaccalaureate distance learning degree programs offered (no on-campus study). *Faculty:* 23 full-time (15 women), 123 part-time/adjunct (82 women). *Students:* 353 full-time (263 women), 75 part-time (50 women); includes 40 minority (12 Black or African American, non-Hispanic/Latino; 5 American Indian or Alaska Native, non-Hispanic/Latino; 7 Asian, non-Hispanic/Latino; 8 Hispanic/Latino; 5 Native Hawaiian or other Pacific Islander, non-Hispanic/Latino; 3 Two or more races, non-Hispanic/Latino). Average age 36. 129 applicants, 98% accepted, 126 enrolled. In 2011, 351 master's, 30 Certificates awarded. *Degree requirements:* For master's, comprehensive exam (for some programs), thesis (for some programs); for doctorate, comprehensive exam, thesis/dissertation. *Entrance requirements:* Additional exam requirements/recommendations for international students: Required—TOEFL (minimum score 567 paper-based; 227 computer-based; 87 iBT); Recommended—IELTS. *Application deadline:* For fall admission, 9/1 for international students; for winter admission, 12/1 for international students; for spring admission, 3/1 for international students. Applications are processed on a rolling basis. Application fee: $50. Electronic applications accepted. *Expenses:* Contact institution. *Financial support:* In 2011–12, 40 students received support. Federal Work-Study and scholarships/grants available. Support available to part-time students. Financial award applicants required to submit FAFSA. *Unit head:* Craig Schieber, Dean, 425-637-101 Ext. 5460, Fax: 425-709-5363, E-mail: schieber@cityu.edu. *Application contact:* Alysa Borelli, 888-422-4898, Fax: 425-709-5363, E-mail: info@cityu.edu. Web site: http://www.cityu.edu/programs/soe/index.aspx.

Claremont Graduate University, Graduate Programs, School of Educational Studies, Claremont, CA 91711-6160. Offers Africana education (Certificate); education and policy (MA, PhD); higher education/student affairs (MA, PhD); human development (MA, PhD); public school administration (MA, PhD); quantitative evaluation (MA, PhD); special education (MA, PhD); teacher education (MA); teaching and learning (MA, PhD); urban leadership (PhD); MBA/PhD. PhD program offered jointly with San Diego State University. Part-time programs available. *Faculty:* 18 full-time (10 women), 2 part-time/adjunct (1 woman). *Students:* 307 full-time (220 women), 134 part-time (96 women); includes 228 minority (59 Black or African American, non-Hispanic/Latino; 3 American Indian or Alaska Native, non-Hispanic/Latino; 37 Asian, non-Hispanic/Latino; 110 Hispanic/Latino; 2 Native Hawaiian or other Pacific Islander, non-Hispanic/Latino; 17 Two or more races, non-Hispanic/Latino), 13 international. Average age 38. In 2011, 93 master's, 23 doctorates, 10 other advanced degrees awarded. Terminal master's awarded for partial completion of doctoral program. *Entrance requirements:* For master's and doctorate, GRE General Test. Additional exam requirements/recommendations for international students: Required—TOEFL (minimum score 550 paper-based; 213 computer-based; 80 iBT). *Application deadline:* For fall admission, 2/1 priority date for domestic students. Applications are processed on a rolling basis. Application fee: $60. Electronic applications accepted. *Expenses: Tuition:* Full-time $36,374; part-time $1581 per unit. *Required fees:* $165 per semester. *Financial support:* Fellowships, research assistantships, Federal Work-Study, institutionally sponsored loans, and scholarships/grants available. Support available to part-time students. Financial award application deadline: 2/15; financial award applicants required to submit FAFSA. *Faculty research:* Education administration, K-12 and higher education, multicultural education, education policy, diversity in higher education, faculty issues. *Unit head:* Margaret Grogan, Dean, 909-621-8075, Fax: 909-621-8734, E-mail: margaret.grogan@cgu.edu. *Application contact:* Julia Evans, Director of Central Recruitment, 909-607-3689, Fax: 909-607-7285, E-mail: admiss@cgu.edu. Web site: http://www.cgu.edu/pages/267.asp.

Clark Atlanta University, School of Education, Department of Educational Leadership, Atlanta, GA 30314. Offers MA, Ed D, Ed S. Part-time and evening/weekend programs available. *Faculty:* 5 full-time (2 women), 4 part-time/adjunct (2 women). *Students:* 24 full-time (15 women), 52 part-time (30 women); includes 72 minority (71 Black or African American, non-Hispanic/Latino; 1 Asian, non-Hispanic/Latino), 1 international. Average age 36. 37 applicants, 92% accepted, 14 enrolled. In 2011, 5 master's, 10 doctorates, 1 other advanced degree awarded. *Degree requirements:* For master's and Ed S, comprehensive exam; for doctorate, comprehensive exam, thesis/dissertation. *Entrance requirements:* For master's, GRE General Test, minimum undergraduate GPA of 2.6; for doctorate and Ed S, GRE General Test, minimum graduate GPA of 3.0. Additional exam requirements/recommendations for international students: Required—TOEFL (minimum score 500 paper-based; 173 computer-based; 61 iBT). *Application deadline:* For fall admission, 4/1 for domestic and international students; for spring admission, 11/1 for domestic and international students. Applications are processed on a rolling basis. Application fee: $40 ($55 for international students). Electronic applications accepted. *Expenses: Tuition:* Full-time $13,572; part-time $754 per credit hour. *Required fees:* $806; $403 per semester. *Financial support:* Career-related internships or fieldwork, Federal Work-Study, scholarships/grants, and unspecified assistantships available. Support available to part-time students. Financial award application deadline: 4/30; financial award applicants required to submit FAFSA. *Unit head:* Dr. Moses Norman, Chairperson, 404-880-8495, E-mail: mnorman@cau.edu. *Application contact:* Michelle Clark-Davis, Graduate Program Admissions, 404-880-6605, E-mail: cauadmissions@cau.edu.

Clarke University, Program in Education, Dubuque, IA 52001-3198. Offers early childhood/special education (MAE); educational administration: elementary and secondary (MAE); educational media: elementary and secondary (MAE); multi-categorical resource k-12 (MAE); multidisciplinary studies (MAE); reading: elementary (MAE); technology in education (MAE). Part-time and evening/weekend programs available. Postbaccalaureate distance learning degree programs offered (minimal on-campus study). *Faculty:* 4 full-time (3 women), 2 part-time/adjunct (1 woman). *Students:* 7 full-time (all women), 43 part-time (40 women). Average age 31. In 2011, 11 master's awarded. *Degree requirements:* For master's, comprehensive exam, thesis optional. *Entrance requirements:* For master's, GRE General Test or MAT, minimum GPA of 2.75. *Application deadline:* Applications are processed on a rolling basis. Application fee: $25. Electronic applications accepted. *Expenses: Tuition:* Part-time $690 per credit hour. *Required fees:* $35 per credit hour. Tuition and fees vary according to program and student level. *Financial support:* Career-related internships or fieldwork available. Financial award applicants required to submit FAFSA. *Unit head:* Dr. Larry Bice, Chair, 319-588-6397, Fax: 319-584-8604. *Application contact:* Joan Coates, Information Contact, 563-588-6354, Fax: 563-588-6789, E-mail: graduate@clarke.edu.

Clearwater Christian College, Program in Educational Leadership, Clearwater, FL 33759-4595. Offers M Ed. Part-time programs available. Postbaccalaureate distance learning degree programs offered (no on-campus study). *Faculty:* 9. *Students:* 3 full-time (2 women), 7 part-time (2 women). *Degree requirements:* For master's, thesis or practicum. *Entrance requirements:* For master's, GRE. Additional exam requirements/recommendations for international students: Required—TOEFL (minimum score 600 paper-based; 250 computer-based). *Application deadline:* For fall admission, 8/1 for domestic students; for spring admission, 1/3 for domestic students. Applications are processed on a rolling basis. Application fee: $50. Electronic applications accepted. *Expenses: Tuition:* Part-time $390 per credit hour. *Required fees:* $50 per course. *Financial support:* Applicants required to submit FAFSA. *Unit head:* Dr. Mary Draper, Chair of Graduate Education, 727-726-1153. *Application contact:* Debbie Edson, Secretary for Graduate Studies, 727-726-1153 Ext. 232, E-mail: graduatestudies@clearwater.edu. Web site: http://www.clearwater.edu/academics/graduate/program/.

Clemson University, Graduate School, College of Health, Education, and Human Development, Eugene T. Moore School of Education, Program in Administration and Supervision (K-12), Clemson, SC 29634. Offers M Ed, Ed S. Part-time and evening/weekend programs available. *Students:* 1 (woman) full-time, 65 part-time (40 women); includes 10 minority (9 Black or African American, non-Hispanic/Latino; 1 Hispanic/Latino). Average age 34. 50 applicants, 88% accepted, 21 enrolled. In 2011, 24 master's, 1 Ed S awarded. *Degree requirements:* For master's and Ed S, comprehensive exam. *Entrance requirements:* For master's, GRE General Test or MAT, 1 year of teaching experience; for Ed S, GRE General Test, 1 year of teaching experience. Additional exam requirements/recommendations for international students: Required—TOEFL; Recommended—IELTS. *Application deadline:* For fall admission, 3/1 for domestic and international students; for spring admission, 10/1 for domestic and international students. Applications are processed on a rolling basis. Application fee: $70 ($80 for international students). Electronic applications accepted. *Financial support:* Research assistantships with partial tuition reimbursements, institutionally sponsored loans, health care benefits, and unspecified assistantships available. Financial award application deadline: 6/1; financial award applicants required to submit FAFSA. *Faculty research:* School finance, educational assessment and accountability policies, politics of education, school improvement, complex organizations, school law. *Unit head:* Dr. Michael J. Padilla, Director/Associate Dean, 864-656-4444, Fax: 864-656-0311, E-mail: padilla@clemson.edu. *Application contact:* Dr. David Fleming, Graduate Coordinator, 864-656-1881, Fax: 864-656-0311, E-mail: dflemin@clemson.edu. Web site: http://www.clemson.edu/hehd/departments/education/academics/graduate/MEd-AS.html.

Clemson University, Graduate School, College of Health, Education, and Human Development, Eugene T. Moore School of Education, Program in Educational Leadership, Clemson, SC 29634. Offers higher education (PhD); K-12 (PhD). *Accreditation:* NCATE. Part-time and evening/weekend programs available. *Students:* 28 full-time (14 women), 66 part-time (38 women); includes 23 minority (19 Black or African American, non-Hispanic/Latino; 2 Hispanic/Latino; 2 Two or more races, non-Hispanic/Latino), 3 international. Average age 38. 37 applicants, 57% accepted, 13 enrolled. In 2011, 10 doctorates awarded. *Degree requirements:* For doctorate, comprehensive exam, thesis/dissertation, preliminary exam. *Entrance requirements:* For doctorate, GRE General Test, master's degree in related field. Additional exam requirements/recommendations for international students: Required—TOEFL; Recommended—IELTS. *Application deadline:* For fall admission, 3/1 for domestic and international students; for spring admission, 10/1 for domestic and international students. Application fee: $70 ($80 for international students). Electronic applications accepted. *Financial support:* In 2011–12, 19 students received support, including 1 fellowship with full and partial tuition reimbursement available (averaging $8,000 per year), 11 research assistantships with partial tuition reimbursements available (averaging $16,075 per year), 3 teaching assistantships with partial tuition reimbursements available (averaging $15,333 per year); institutionally sponsored loans, health care benefits, and unspecified assistantships also available. Financial award application deadline: 6/1; financial award applicants required to submit FAFSA. *Faculty research:* Higher education leadership, P-12 educational leadership. *Unit head:* Dr. Michael J. Padilla, Director/Associate Dean, 864-656-4444, Fax: 864-656-0311, E-mail: padilla@clemson.edu. *Application contact:* Dr. David Fleming, Graduate Coordinator, 864-656-1881, Fax: 864-656-0311, E-mail: dflemin@clemson.edu.

Cleveland State University, College of Graduate Studies, College of Education and Human Services, Department of Counseling, Administration, Supervision and Adult Learning (CASAL), Cleveland, OH 44115. Offers accelerated degree in adult learning and development (M Ed); adult learning and development (M Ed); chemical dependency counseling (Certificate); clinical mental health counseling (M Ed); early childhood mental health counseling (Certificate); educational administration and supervision (M Ed); organizational leadership (M Ed); school administration (Ed S); school counseling (M Ed). *Accreditation:* ACA (one or more programs are accredited). Part-time and evening/weekend programs available. *Faculty:* 15 full-time (8 women), 19 part-time/adjunct (10 women). *Students:* 58 full-time (49 women), 273 part-time (221 women); includes 121 minority (106 Black or African American, non-Hispanic/Latino; 2 Asian, non-Hispanic/Latino; 9 Hispanic/Latino; 4 Two or more races, non-Hispanic/Latino), 1 international. Average age 35. 192 applicants, 86% accepted, 105 enrolled. In 2011, 151 master's, 23 Certificates awarded. *Degree requirements:* For master's, comprehensive exam (for some programs), thesis optional, internship. *Entrance requirements:* For master's, GRE General Test or MAT, letter of recommendation and minimum GPA of 2.75 (for counseling); 2 letters of recommendation and interviews (for organizational leadership). Additional exam requirements/recommendations for international students: Required—TOEFL (minimum score 525 paper-based; 197 computer-based), IELTS (minimum score 6). *Application deadline:* For fall admission, 6/21 for domestic students, 5/15 for international students; for spring admission, 8/31 for domestic students, 11/1 for international students. Application fee: $30. Electronic applications accepted. *Expenses:* Tuition, state resident: full-time $6416; part-time $494 per credit hour. Tuition, nonresident: full-time $12,074; part-time $929 per credit hour. *Financial support:* In 2011–12, 19 students received support, including 10 research assistantships with full and partial tuition reimbursements available (averaging $11,882 per year), 5 teaching assistantships with full and partial tuition reimbursements available (averaging $11,882 per year); scholarships/grants and unspecified assistantships also available. Support available to part-time students. *Faculty research:* Education law, career development, bullying, psychopharmacology, counseling and spirituality. *Total annual research expenditures:* $225,821. *Unit head:* Dr. Ann L. Bauer, Chairperson, 216-687-4582, Fax: 216-687-5378, E-mail: a.l.bauer@csuohio.edu. *Application contact:* Deborah L. Brown, Interim Assistant Director, Graduate Admissions, 216-523-7572, Fax: 216-687-5400, E-mail: d.l.brown@csuohio.edu. Web site: http://www.csuohio.edu/cehs/departments/casal/.

Cleveland State University, College of Graduate Studies, College of Education and Human Services, Program in Urban Education, Cleveland, OH 44115. Offers counseling (PhD); counseling psychology (PhD); leadership and lifelong learning (PhD); learning and development (PhD); policy studies (PhD); school administration (PhD). Part-time programs available. *Faculty:* 16 full-time (8 women), 15 part-time/adjunct (12 women). *Students:* 33 full-time (27 women), 86 part-time (58 women); includes 39 minority (32 Black or African American, non-Hispanic/Latino; 4 Asian, non-Hispanic/Latino; 3 Hispanic/Latino), 8 international. Average age 40. 54 applicants, 44% accepted, 16 enrolled. In 2011, 17 doctorates awarded. *Degree requirements:* For doctorate, one foreign language, comprehensive exam, thesis/dissertation. *Entrance requirements:* For doctorate, GRE General Test, minimum graduate GPA of 3.25. Additional exam requirements/recommendations for international students: Required—TOEFL (minimum score 525 paper-based; 197 computer-based), IELTS (minimum score 6). *Application deadline:* For fall admission, 2/5 for domestic students. Application fee: $30. *Expenses:* Tuition, state resident: full-time $6416; part-time $494 per credit hour. Tuition, nonresident: full-time $12,074; part-time $929 per credit hour. *Financial support:* In 2011–12, 7 students received support, including 4 research assistantships with full and partial tuition reimbursements available (averaging $7,800 per year), 3 teaching assistantships with full and partial tuition reimbursements available (averaging $7,800 per year); tuition waivers (full) and unspecified assistantships also available. Financial award applicants required to submit FAFSA. *Faculty research:* Equity issues (race, ethnicity, and gender), education development consequences for special needs of urban populations, urban education programming, counseling the violent or aggressive adolescent. *Total annual research expenditures:* $5,662. *Unit head:* Dr. Joshua Bagakas, Director, 216-687-4591, Fax: 216-875-9697, E-mail: j.bagakas@csuohio.edu. *Application contact:* Wanda Butler, Administrative Assistant, 216-687-4697, Fax: 216-875-9697, E-mail: w.pruett-butler@csuohio.edu. Web site: http://www.csuohio.edu/coehs/departments/phd/.

Coastal Carolina University, William L. Spadoni College of Education, Conway, SC 29528-6054. Offers education (MAT); educational leadership (M Ed); learning and teaching (M Ed). *Accreditation:* NCATE. Part-time and evening/weekend programs available. *Faculty:* 15 full-time (7 women), 4 part-time/adjunct (1 woman). *Students:* 67 full-time (40 women), 190 part-time (143 women); includes 34 minority (27 Black or African American, non-Hispanic/Latino; 1 American Indian or Alaska Native, non-Hispanic/Latino; 2 Hispanic/Latino; 2 Native Hawaiian or other Pacific Islander, non-Hispanic/Latino; 2 Two or more races, non-Hispanic/Latino), 4 international. Average age 33. 171 applicants, 89% accepted, 119 enrolled. In 2011, 112 master's awarded. *Degree requirements:* For master's, comprehensive exam. *Entrance requirements:* For master's, GRE, MAT, 2 letters of recommendation, copy of teaching credential. Additional exam requirements/recommendations for international students: Required—TOEFL (minimum score 550 paper-based; 213 computer-based; 79 iBT). *Application deadline:* For fall admission, 7/1 priority date for domestic students, 7/1 for international students; for spring admission, 11/1 priority date for domestic students, 11/1 for international students. Applications are processed on a rolling basis. Application fee: $45. Electronic applications accepted. *Expenses:* Tuition, state resident: full-time $11,040; part-time $460 per credit hour. Tuition, nonresident: full-time $16,560; part-time $690 per credit hour. *Required fees:* $80; $40 per term. *Financial support:* Fellowships, research assistantships, and unspecified assistantships available. Support available to part-time students. Financial award application deadline: 3/1; financial award applicants required to submit FAFSA. *Unit head:* Dr. Edward Jadallah, Dean, 843-349-2773, Fax: 843-349-2106, E-mail: ejadalla@coastal.edu. *Application contact:* Dr. James O. Luken, Associate Provost/Director of Graduate Studies, 843-349-2235, Fax: 843-349-6444, E-mail: joluken@coastal.edu. Web site: http://www.coastal.edu/education/.

The College at Brockport, State University of New York, School of Education and Human Services, Department of Educational Administration, Brockport, NY 14420-2997. Offers school building leader/school district leader (CAS); school district business leader (CAS). Part-time programs available. *Students:* 7 full-time (6 women), 153 part-time (84 women); includes 12 minority (10 Black or African American, non-Hispanic/Latino; 1 American Indian or Alaska Native, non-Hispanic/Latino; 1 Hispanic/Latino). 63 applicants, 73% accepted, 38 enrolled. In 2011, 81 CASs awarded. *Degree requirements:* For CAS, thesis or alternative, internship. *Entrance requirements:* For degree, minimum GPA of 3.0. Additional exam requirements/recommendations for international students: Required—TOEFL (minimum score 550 paper-based; 213 computer-based; 79 iBT). *Application deadline:* For fall admission, 4/15 priority date for domestic students, 4/15 for international students; for spring admission, 11/15 priority date for domestic students, 11/15 for international students. Application fee: $80. Electronic applications accepted. *Financial support:* Federal Work-Study, scholarships/grants, and unspecified assistantships available. Support available to part-time students. Financial award application deadline: 3/15; financial award applicants required to submit FAFSA. *Faculty research:* Superintendency, budgeting, school business administration, leadership, special education administration. *Unit head:* Carol Godsave, Interim Chairperson, 585-395-5512, Fax: 585-395-2172, E-mail: cgodsave@brockport.edu. *Application contact:* Carol Godsave, 585-395-5512, Fax: 585-395-2172, E-mail: cgodsave@brockport.edu. Web site: http://www.brockport.edu/graduate/.

College of Mount St. Joseph, Graduate Education Program, Cincinnati, OH 45233-1670. Offers adolescent young adult education (MA); art (MA); inclusive early childhood education (MA); instructional leadership (MA); middle childhood education (MA); multi-age education (MA); multicultural special education (MA); music (MA); reading (MA). *Accreditation:* Teacher Education Accreditation Council. Part-time and evening/weekend programs available. *Faculty:* 22 full-time (12 women), 11 part-time/adjunct (8 women). *Students:* 51 full-time (40 women), 92 part-time (72 women); includes 17 minority (14 Black or African American, non-Hispanic/Latino; 1 American Indian or Alaska Native, non-Hispanic/Latino; 1 Asian, non-Hispanic/Latino; 1 Hispanic/Latino). Average age 34. 87 applicants, 44% accepted, 29 enrolled. In 2011, 61 master's awarded. *Degree requirements:* For master's, research project, student teaching, clinical and field-based experiences. *Entrance requirements:* For master's, GRE, PRAXIS II in teaching content area (math or science), 2 letters of recommendation, interview, resume. Additional exam requirements/recommendations for international students: Required—TOEFL (minimum score 560 paper-based; 220 computer-based; 83 iBT). *Application deadline:* Applications are processed on a rolling basis. Application fee: $50. Electronic applications accepted. *Expenses: Tuition:* Full-time $24,200; part-time $540 per credit hour. *Required fees:* $112.50 per semester. One-time fee: $200. *Financial support:* In 2011–12, 22 students received support. Scholarships/grants available. Financial award applicants required to submit FAFSA. *Faculty research:* Foreign and second language learning problems/reading disabilities/hyperlexia, multicultural/bilingual special education, alternative educator licensure, science education, pedagogical content knowledge. *Unit head:* Dr. Mary West, Chair, 513-244-3263, Fax: 513-244-4867, E-mail: mary_west@mail.msj.edu. *Application contact:* Marilyn Hoskins, Assistant Director of Graduate Recruitment, 513-244-4723, Fax: 513-244-4629, E-mail: marilyn_hoskins@mail.msj.edu. Web site: http://www.msj.edu/view/academics/graduate-programs/education.aspx.

The College of New Jersey, Graduate Studies, School of Education, Department of Educational Administration and Secondary Education, Program in Educational Leadership, Ewing, NJ 08628. Offers M Ed, Certificate. Part-time and evening/weekend programs available. *Degree requirements:* For master's, comprehensive exam. *Entrance requirements:* For master's, GRE, minimum GPA of 3.0 in field or 2.75 overall; for Certificate, previous master's degree or higher. Additional exam requirements/recommendations for international students: Required—TOEFL. Electronic applications accepted.

The College of New Rochelle, Graduate School, Division of Education, Program in School Administration and Supervision, New Rochelle, NY 10805-2308. Offers dual certification: school building leader/school district leader (MS); school building leader (MS, Advanced Certificate); school district leader (MS, Advanced Diploma). *Degree requirements:* For master's, internship. *Entrance requirements:* For master's, interview, minimum GPA of 3.0 in field, 2.7 overall, minimum 3 years teaching or education administration experience. *Faculty research:* Training administrators in Eastern Europe, leadership.

College of Saint Elizabeth, Department of Education, Morristown, NJ 07960-6989. Offers accelerated certification for teachers (Certificate); assistive technology (Certificate); education: human services leadership (MA); educational leadership (MA, Ed D); educational technology (MA). Part-time and evening/weekend programs available. *Faculty:* 10 full-time (3 women), 12 part-time/adjunct (6 women). *Students:* 69 full-time (50 women), 203 part-time (175 women); includes 43 minority (26 Black or African American, non-Hispanic/Latino; 1 Asian, non-Hispanic/Latino; 16 Hispanic/Latino). Average age 36. 114 applicants, 72% accepted, 70 enrolled. In 2011, 84 master's, 14 doctorates, 119 other advanced degrees awarded. *Degree requirements:* For master's, thesis or alternative, portfolio; for doctorate, thesis/dissertation. *Entrance requirements:* For master's, interview, minimum undergraduate GPA of 3.0; for doctorate, master's degree. *Application deadline:* For fall admission, 6/30 priority date for domestic students; for spring admission, 11/30 for domestic students. Applications are processed on a rolling basis. Application fee: $35. Electronic applications accepted. *Expenses: Tuition:* Part-time $899 per credit. *Required fees:* $73 per credit. *Financial support:* Career-related internships or fieldwork, tuition waivers (partial), and unspecified assistantships available. Support available to part-time students. Financial award application deadline: 3/15; financial award applicants required to submit FAFSA. *Faculty research:* Developmental stages for teaching and human services professionals, effectiveness of humanities core curriculum. *Unit head:* Dr. Alan H. Markowitz, Director of Graduate Education Programs, 973-290-4374, Fax: 973-290-4389, E-mail: amarkowitz@cse.edu. *Application contact:* Donna Tatarka, Dean of Admission, 973-290-4705, Fax: 973-290-4710, E-mail: dtatarka@cse.edu. Web site: http://www.cse.edu/academics/academic-areas/human-social-dev/education/?tabID-tabGraduate&divID-progGraduate.

College of Saint Mary, Program in Education, Omaha, NE 68106. Offers assessment leadership (MSE); English as a second language (MSE). Part-time programs available. *Entrance requirements:* For master's, technology competency test or equivalent, minimum cumulative GPA of 3.0, teaching certificate, 2 letters of reference, resume.

The College of Saint Rose, Graduate Studies, School of Education, Department of Counseling and Educational Administration, Program in Educational Administration and Supervision, Albany, NY 12203-1419. Offers college student services administration (MS Ed); educational administration and supervision (MS Ed, Certificate); school administrator and supervisor (Certificate). Part-time and evening/weekend programs available. *Degree requirements:* For master's, comprehensive exam or thesis. *Entrance requirements:* For master's, minimum undergraduate GPA of 3.0, timed writing sample, interview, permanent certification or 3 years teaching experience. Additional exam requirements/recommendations for international students: Required—TOEFL (minimum score 550 paper-based; 213 computer-based). Electronic applications accepted.

College of Staten Island of the City University of New York, Graduate Programs, Department of Education, Program in School Building and District Leadership, Staten Island, NY 10314-6600. Offers 6th Year Certificate. Part-time and evening/weekend programs available. *Faculty:* 1 (woman) full-time, 3 part-time/adjunct (all women). *Students:* 30 part-time (23 women). Average age 36. 28 applicants, 71% accepted, 15 enrolled. In 2011, 19 6th Year Certificates awarded. *Entrance requirements:* For degree, master's degree, minimum GPA of 3.0, 4 years of teaching experience, 3 professional recommendations, interview. Additional exam requirements/recommendations for international students: Required—TOEFL (minimum score 550 paper-based; 213 computer-based; 79 iBT), IELTS (minimum score 6.5). *Application deadline:* For fall admission, 5/1 for domestic and international students. Application fee: $125. Electronic applications accepted. *Expenses:* Tuition, state resident: full-time $8210; part-time $345 per credit. Tuition, nonresident: part-time $640 per credit. *Required fees:* $128 per semester. *Financial support:* Career-related internships or fieldwork, Federal Work-Study, and scholarships/grants available. Support available to part-time students. Financial award applicants required to submit FAFSA. *Unit head:* Dr. Ruth Silverberg, Coordinator, 718-982-3726, Fax: 718-982-3743, E-mail: ruth.silverberg@csi.cuny.edu. *Application contact:* Sasha Spence, Assistant Director for Graduate Admissions, 718-982-2699, Fax: 718-982-2500, E-mail: sasha.spence@csi.cuny.edu. Web site: http://www.csi.cuny.edu/catalog/graduate/graduate-programs-in-education.htm#o2614.

The College of William and Mary, School of Education, Program in Education Policy, Planning, and Leadership, Williamsburg, VA 23187-8795. Offers curriculum and educational technology (Ed D, PhD); curriculum leadership (Ed D, PhD); educational leadership (M Ed), including higher education administration (M Ed, Ed D, PhD), K-12 administration and supervision; educational policy, planning, and leadership (Ed D, PhD), including general education administration, gifted education administration, higher education administration (M Ed, Ed D, PhD), special education administration; gifted education administration (M Ed). *Accreditation:* NCATE. Part-time and evening/weekend programs available. *Faculty:* 11 full-time (5 women), 11 part-time/adjunct (9 women). *Students:* 50 full-time (38 women), 145 part-time (104 women); includes 45 minority (35 Black or African American, non-Hispanic/Latino; 2 Asian, non-Hispanic/Latino; 4 Hispanic/Latino; 4 Two or more races, non-Hispanic/Latino), 5 international. Average age 38. 173 applicants, 62% accepted, 75 enrolled. In 2011, 21 master's, 10 doctorates awarded. *Degree requirements:* For doctorate, comprehensive exam, thesis/dissertation. *Entrance requirements:* For master's, GRE or MAT, minimum GPA of 2.5; for doctorate, GRE or MAT, minimum GPA of 3.0. Additional exam requirements/recommendations for international students: Required—TOEFL. *Application deadline:* For fall admission, 1/15 for domestic and international students. Application fee: $50. Electronic applications accepted. *Expenses:* Tuition, state resident: full-time $6400; part-time $365 per credit hour. Tuition, nonresident: full-time $19,720; part-time $985 per credit hour. *Required fees:* $4562. *Financial support:* In 2011–12, 54 students received support, including 1 fellowship (averaging $20,000 per year), 38 research assistantships with full and partial tuition reimbursements available (averaging $15,000 per year); career-related internships or fieldwork, Federal Work-Study, institutionally sponsored loans, scholarships/grants, and unspecified assistantships also available. Support available to part-time students. Financial award application deadline: 1/15; financial award applicants required to submit FAFSA. *Faculty research:* Higher education policy, faculty incentives, history of adversity, resilience, leadership. *Unit head:* Dr. Pamela Eddy, Area Coordinator, 757-221-2349, E-mail: peddy@wm.edu. *Application contact:* Dorothy Smith Osborne, Assistant Dean for Admission, 757-221-2317, Fax: 757-221-2293, E-mail: dsosbo@wm.edu. Web site: http://education.wm.edu.

Colorado Mesa University, Center for Teacher Education, Grand Junction, CO 81501-3122. Offers educational leadership (MAEd); English for speakers of other languages (MAEd). *Accreditation:* NCATE. Part-time programs available. Postbaccalaureate distance learning degree programs offered (minimal on-campus study). *Degree requirements:* For master's, comprehensive exam, capstone presentation. *Entrance requirements:* For master's, GRE, 2 professional letters of recommendation. Additional exam requirements/recommendations for international students: Required—TOEFL (minimum score 550 paper-based; 207 computer-based). Electronic applications accepted.

Colorado State University, Graduate School, College of Applied Human Sciences, School of Education, Fort Collins, CO 80523-1588. Offers adult education and training (M Ed); community college leadership (PhD); counseling and career development (M Ed); education and human resource studies (M Ed, PhD); educational leadership (M Ed, PhD); interdisciplinary studies (PhD); organizational performance and change (M Ed, PhD); student affairs in higher education (MS). *Accreditation:* ACA; Teacher Education Accreditation Council. Part-time and evening/weekend programs available. *Faculty:* 18 full-time (11 women), 1 part-time/adjunct (0 women). *Students:* 161 full-time (106 women), 491 part-time (291 women); includes 130 minority (28 Black or African American, non-Hispanic/Latino; 5 American Indian or Alaska Native, non-Hispanic/Latino; 12 Asian, non-Hispanic/Latino; 68 Hispanic/Latino; 3 Native Hawaiian or other Pacific Islander, non-Hispanic/Latino; 14 Two or more races, non-Hispanic/Latino), 29 international. Average age 38. 468 applicants, 31% accepted, 112 enrolled. In 2011, 192 master's, 30 doctorates awarded. *Degree requirements:* For master's, comprehensive exam (for some programs), thesis optional; for doctorate, comprehensive exam, thesis/dissertation, minimum of 60 credits. *Entrance requirements:* For master's, GRE, minimum undergraduate GPA of 3.0, 3 letters of recommendation, curriculum vitae/resume; for doctorate, minimum GPA of 3.0, 3 letters of recommendation, curriculum vitae. Additional exam requirements/recommendations for international students: Required—TOEFL (minimum score 550 paper-based; 213 computer-based; 80 iBT). *Application deadline:* For fall admission, 2/15 priority date for domestic students, 2/15 for international students; for spring admission, 9/1 priority date for domestic students, 9/1 for international students. Applications are processed on a rolling basis. Application fee: $50. Electronic applications accepted. *Expenses:* Tuition, state resident: full-time $7992. Tuition, nonresident: full-time $19,592. *Required fees:* $1735; $58 per credit. *Financial support:* In 2011–12, 11 students received support, including 1 fellowship (averaging $37,500 per year), 3 research assistantships with full tuition reimbursements available (averaging $8,911 per year), 7 teaching assistantships with full tuition reimbursements available (averaging $12,691 per year); Federal Work-Study, scholarships/grants, and unspecified assistantships also available. Financial award application deadline: 2/15; financial award applicants required to submit FAFSA. *Faculty research:* Innovative instruction, diverse learners, transition, scientifically-based evaluation methods, leadership and organizational development, research methodology. *Total annual research expenditures:* $455,133. *Unit head:* Dr. Kevin Oltjenbruns, Interim Director, 970-491-6316, Fax: 970-491-1317, E-mail: kevin.oltjenbruns@colostate.edu. *Application contact:* Kathy Lucas, Graduate Contact, 970-491-1963, Fax: 970-491-1317, E-mail: kplucas@cahs.colostate.edu. Web site: http://www.soe.cahs.colostate.edu/.

Columbia International University, Columbia Graduate School, Columbia, SC 29230-3122. Offers Bible teaching (MABT); Christian higher education leadership (Ed D); Christian school educational leadership (Ed D); counseling (MACN); curriculum and instruction (M Ed), including Christian school guidance, English as a second language, learning disabilities, school technology; early childhood and elementary education (MAT); educational administration (M Ed); teaching English as a foreign language (Certificate); teaching English as a foreign language and intercultural studies (MATF). Part-time and evening/weekend programs available. *Degree requirements:* For master's, internships, professional project. *Entrance requirements:* For master's, Minnesota Multiphasic Personality Inventory, MAT, minimum GPA of 2.7. Additional exam requirements/recommendations for international students: Required—TOEFL. Electronic applications accepted.

Columbus State University, Graduate Studies, College of Education and Health Professions, Department of Counseling, Foundations, and Leadership, Columbus, GA 31907-5645. Offers community counseling (MS); curriculum and leadership (Ed D); educational leadership (M Ed, Ed S); higher education (M Ed); school counseling (M Ed,

Ed S). *Accreditation:* ACA; NCATE. Part-time and evening/weekend programs available. Postbaccalaureate distance learning degree programs offered (minimal on-campus study). *Degree requirements:* For master's, thesis, exit exam; for Ed S, thesis or alternative. *Entrance requirements:* For master's, GRE General Test, minimum GPA of 2.75; for doctorate, minimum graduate GPA of 3.5, four years of professional service; for Ed S, GRE General Test. Additional exam requirements/recommendations for international students: Required—TOEFL (minimum score 550 paper-based; 213 computer-based; 79 iBT). Electronic applications accepted.

Concordia University, College of Education, Portland, OR 97211-6099. Offers curriculum and instruction (elementary) (M Ed); educational administration (M Ed); elementary education (MAT); secondary education (MAT). Part-time programs available. Postbaccalaureate distance learning degree programs offered (no on-campus study). *Degree requirements:* For master's, comprehensive exam, work samples/ portfolio. *Entrance requirements:* For master's, California Basic Educational Skills Test or PRAXIS I, minimum undergraduate GPA of 2.8, graduate 3.0; 2 letters of recommendation. Additional exam requirements/recommendations for international students: Required—TOEFL (minimum score 525 paper-based; 195 computer-based). Electronic applications accepted. *Faculty research:* Learner centered classroom, brain-based learning future of on-line learning.

Concordia University, School of Education, Irvine, CA 92612-3299. Offers curriculum and instruction (MA); education and preliminary teaching credential (M Ed); educational administration and preliminary administrative services credential (MA); school counseling with pupil personnel services credential (MA). Part-time and evening/ weekend programs available. Postbaccalaureate distance learning degree programs offered (no on-campus study). *Faculty:* 16 full-time (11 women), 68 part-time/adjunct (32 women). *Students:* 556 full-time (434 women), 277 part-time (211 women); includes 278 minority (42 Black or African American, non-Hispanic/Latino; 1 American Indian or Alaska Native, non-Hispanic/Latino; 51 Asian, non-Hispanic/Latino; 172 Hispanic/Latino; 12 Two or more races, non-Hispanic/Latino), 1 international. Average age 39. 296 applicants, 96% accepted, 256 enrolled. In 2011, 378 master's awarded. *Degree requirements:* For master's, action research project. *Entrance requirements:* For master's, California Basic Educational Skills Test, California Subject Examinations for Teachers (M Ed and MA in educational administration and preliminary administrative services credential), official college transcript(s), signed statement of intent, two references, copy of credential. Additional exam requirements/recommendations for international students: Required—TOEFL. *Application deadline:* For fall admission, 7/15 priority date for domestic students, 6/1 for international students; for spring admission, 11/30 priority date for domestic students, 10/1 for international students. Applications are processed on a rolling basis. Application fee: $50 ($125 for international students). Electronic applications accepted. *Expenses:* Contact institution. *Financial support:* In 2011–12, 17 students received support. Scholarships/grants and unspecified assistantships available. Financial award applicants required to submit FAFSA. *Unit head:* Dr. Janice Nelson, Dean, 949-214-3334, E-mail: janice.nelson@cui.edu. *Application contact:* Scott Eskelson, 949-214-3362, Fax: 949-854-6894, E-mail: scott.eskelson@cui.edu.

Concordia University Ann Arbor, Graduate Programs, Ann Arbor, MI 48105-2797. Offers curriculum and instruction (MS); educational leadership (MS); organizational leadership and administration (MS). Part-time and evening/weekend programs available. *Faculty:* 3 full-time (2 women), 24 part-time/adjunct (10 women). *Students:* 123 full-time (79 women), 46 part-time (24 women); includes 26 minority (19 Black or African American, non-Hispanic/Latino; 2 American Indian or Alaska Native, non-Hispanic/Latino; 3 Asian, non-Hispanic/Latino; 1 Hispanic/Latino; 1 Two or more races, non-Hispanic/Latino), 1 international. Average age 37. 45 applicants, 84% accepted, 37 enrolled. In 2011, 74 degrees awarded. *Degree requirements:* For master's, thesis. *Entrance requirements:* Additional exam requirements/recommendations for international students: Required—TOEFL (minimum score 80 iBT); Recommended—IELTS (minimum score 6.5). *Application deadline:* For fall admission, 7/1 priority date for domestic students, 6/1 for international students; for spring admission, 8/26 priority date for domestic students, 7/26 for international students. Applications are processed on a rolling basis. Electronic applications accepted. *Financial support:* Applicants required to submit FAFSA. *Unit head:* Dr. Ross Stueber, Vice President of Academics, 734-995-7586, Fax: 734-995-7448, E-mail: stuebr@cuaa.edu. *Application contact:* Caroline Harris, Graduate Admission Coordinator, 734-995-7521, Fax: 734-995-7530, E-mail: harrica@cuaa.edu. Web site: http://www.cuaa.edu/graduate.

Concordia University Chicago, College of Education, Program in School Leadership, River Forest, IL 60305-1499. Offers MA, Ed D, CAS. MA offered jointly with the Chicago Consortium of Colleges and Universities. *Accreditation:* NCATE. Part-time and evening/ weekend programs available. *Degree requirements:* For master's, comprehensive exam, thesis optional; for CAS, thesis, final project. *Entrance requirements:* For master's, minimum GPA of 2.9; for CAS, master's degree. Additional exam requirements/recommendations for international students: Required—TOEFL (minimum score 550 paper-based; 195 computer-based). Electronic applications accepted. *Faculty research:* Effectiveness of urban Lutheran schools in impacting children's faith development, effectiveness of centers for urban ministries in supporting urban ministry and teaching science.

Concordia University, Nebraska, Graduate Programs in Education, Program in Educational Administration, Seward, NE 68434-1599. Offers elementary and secondary education (M Ed); elementary education (M Ed); secondary education (M Ed). *Accreditation:* NCATE. Part-time programs available. *Degree requirements:* For master's, thesis or alternative. *Entrance requirements:* For master's, GRE, MAT, or NTE, BS in education or equivalent, minimum GPA of 3.0.

Concordia University, St. Paul, College of Education, St. Paul, MN 55104-5494. Offers curriculum and instruction (MA Ed), including K-12 reading endorsement; differentiated instruction (MA Ed); early childhood education (MA Ed); educational leadership (MA Ed); educational technology (MA Ed); family life education (MA); K-12 reading endorsement (Certificate); special education (Certificate); sports management (MA). *Accreditation:* NCATE. Evening/weekend programs available. Postbaccalaureate distance learning degree programs offered (minimal on-campus study). *Faculty:* 7 full-time (3 women), 64 part-time/adjunct (42 women). *Students:* 617 full-time (495 women), 9 part-time (6 women); includes 57 minority (30 Black or African American, non-Hispanic/Latino; 2 American Indian or Alaska Native, non-Hispanic/Latino; 17 Asian, non-Hispanic/Latino; 5 Hispanic/Latino; 1 Native Hawaiian or other Pacific Islander, non-Hispanic/Latino; 2 Two or more races, non-Hispanic/Latino). Average age 36. 302 applicants, 83% accepted, 210 enrolled. In 2011, 320 master's, 68 other advanced degrees awarded. *Application deadline:* Applications are processed on a rolling basis. Application fee: $50. Electronic applications accepted. *Expenses: Tuition:* Full-time $8100; part-time $435 per credit. Tuition and fees vary according to program. *Financial support:* Applicants required to submit FAFSA. *Unit head:* Dr. Donald Helmstetter, Dean, 651-641-8227, Fax: 651-641-8807, E-mail: helmstetter@csp.edu. *Application contact:* Kimberly Craig, Director of Graduate and Cohort Admission, 651-603-6223, Fax: 651-603-6320, E-mail: craig@csp.edu.

Concordia University Wisconsin, Graduate Programs, Department of Education, Program in Educational Administration, Mequon, WI 53097-2402. Offers MS Ed. Part-time and evening/weekend programs available. Postbaccalaureate distance learning degree programs offered (minimal on-campus study). *Students:* 103 full-time (59 women), 148 part-time (66 women); includes 18 minority (8 Black or African American, non-Hispanic/Latino; 1 American Indian or Alaska Native, non-Hispanic/Latino; 2 Asian, non-Hispanic/Latino; 3 Hispanic/Latino; 4 Two or more races, non-Hispanic/Latino), 1 international. Average age 37. In 2011, 8 master's awarded. *Degree requirements:* For master's, comprehensive exam, thesis or alternative. *Entrance requirements:* For master's, minimum GPA of 3.0. Additional exam requirements/recommendations for international students: Required—TOEFL. Application fee: $35. *Financial support:* Application deadline: 8/1. *Unit head:* Dr. Ross Stueber, Head, 262-243-4285, Fax: 262-243-4428, E-mail: ross.stueber@cuw.edu. *Application contact:* Graduate Admissions, 262-243-4248, Fax: 262-243-4428.

Concord University, Graduate Studies, Athens, WV 24712-1000. Offers educational leadership and supervision (M Ed); geography (M Ed); health promotion (M Ed); reading specialist (M Ed). Part-time and evening/weekend programs available. Postbaccalaureate distance learning degree programs offered (no on-campus study). *Entrance requirements:* For master's, GRE or MAT, baccalaureate degree with minimum GPA of 2.5 from regionally-accredited institution; teaching license; 2 letters of recommendation; completed disposition assessment form. Electronic applications accepted.

Converse College, School of Education and Graduate Studies, Education Specialist Program, Spartanburg, SC 29302-0006. Offers administration and supervision (Ed S); curriculum and instruction (Ed S); marriage and family therapy (Ed S). *Accreditation:* AAMFT/COAMFTE. Part-time programs available. *Entrance requirements:* For degree, GRE or MAT (marriage and family therapy), minimum GPA of 3.0. Electronic applications accepted.

Converse College, School of Education and Graduate Studies, Program in Leadership, Spartanburg, SC 29302-0006. Offers M Ed. *Degree requirements:* For master's, capstone paper. *Entrance requirements:* For master's, NTE, minimum GPA of 2.75, nomination by school district, 3 recommendations. Electronic applications accepted.

Creighton University, Graduate School, College of Arts and Sciences, Department of Education, Program in Educational Leadership, Omaha, NE 68178-0001. Offers elementary school administration (MS); leadership (Ed D); secondary school administration (MS); teacher leadership (MS). Part-time and evening/weekend programs available. *Faculty:* 14 full-time (8 women). *Students:* 32 part-time (19 women); includes 1 minority (Hispanic/Latino). Average age 32. 2 applicants, 100% accepted, 2 enrolled. In 2011, 6 master's awarded. *Degree requirements:* For master's, portfolio. *Entrance requirements:* For master's, 2 writing samples, 3 letters of recommendation. Additional exam requirements/recommendations for international students: Required—TOEFL (minimum score 550 paper-based; 213 computer-based; 80 iBT). *Application deadline:* For fall admission, 7/1 for domestic students, 3/1 for international students; for winter admission, 10/1 for domestic students, 5/1 for international students; for spring admission, 3/1 for domestic students, 10/1 for international students. Applications are processed on a rolling basis. Application fee: $50. Electronic applications accepted. *Expenses: Tuition:* Full-time $12,672; part-time $704 per credit hour. *Required fees:* $1410; $136 per semester. Tuition and fees vary according to campus/location and reciprocity agreements. *Financial support:* Scholarships/grants and tuition waivers (partial) available. Support available to part-time students. Financial award application deadline: 5/1; financial award applicants required to submit FAFSA. *Unit head:* Dr. Barbara Brock, Professor of Education, 402-280-2551, E-mail: barbarabrock@creighton.edu. *Application contact:* Taunya Plater, Senior Program Coordinator, 402-280-2870, Fax: 402-280-2423, E-mail: taunyaplater@creighton.edu.

Creighton University, Graduate School, Interdisciplinary EdD Program in Leadership, Omaha, NE 68178-0001. Offers Ed D. *Entrance requirements:* For doctorate, master's or equivalent professional degree, current resume, official transcripts, three recommendations. Additional exam requirements/recommendations for international students: Required—TOEFL (minimum score 550 paper-based; 213 computer-based; 80 iBT). *Expenses: Tuition:* Full-time $12,672; part-time $704 per credit hour. *Required fees:* $1410; $136 per semester. Tuition and fees vary according to campus/location and reciprocity agreements.

Dakota Wesleyan University, Program in Education, Mitchell, SD 57301-4398. Offers curriculum and instruction (MA Ed); educational policy and administration (MA Ed); preK-12 principal certification (MA Ed); secondary certification (MA Ed). Part-time and evening/weekend programs available. *Degree requirements:* For master's, comprehensive exam, thesis optional, electronic portfolio. *Entrance requirements:* For master's, minimum GPA of 2.7, elementary statistics course, statement of purpose, official transcripts, resume, three letters of recommendation. Additional exam requirements/recommendations for international students: Required—TOEFL (minimum score 500 paper-based; 71 computer-based), IELTS (minimum score 6.5). Electronic applications accepted. *Faculty research:* Math, political policy, technology in the classroom.

Dallas Baptist University, Dorothy M. Bush College of Education, Program in Educational Leadership, Dallas, TX 75211-9299. Offers M Ed. Part-time and evening/ weekend programs available. *Entrance requirements:* For master's, GRE General Test, minimum GPA of 3.0. Additional exam requirements/recommendations for international students: Required—TOEFL, IELTS. *Application deadline:* Applications are processed on a rolling basis. Application fee: $25. Electronic applications accepted. *Expenses: Tuition:* Full-time $12,060; part-time $670 per credit hour. *Required fees:* $100; $50 per semester. *Financial support:* Federal Work-Study, institutionally sponsored loans, scholarships/grants, and tuition waivers (full and partial) available. Support available to part-time students. Financial award applicants required to submit FAFSA. *Faculty research:* Emerging literacy, self-directed schools. *Unit head:* Dr. Tam Jones, Director, 214-333-6841, Fax: 214-333-5551, E-mail: graduate@dbu.edu. *Application contact:* Kit P. Montgomery, Director of Graduate Programs, 214-333-5242, Fax: 214-333-5579, E-mail: graduate@dbu.edu. Web site: http://www3.dbu.edu/graduate/education.asp.

Dallas Theological Seminary, Graduate Programs, Dallas, TX 75204-6499. Offers adult education (Th M); apologetics (Th M); Bible backgrounds (Th M); Bible translation (Th M); Biblical and theological studies (Certificate); biblical counseling (MA); biblical exegesis and linguistics (MA); biblical exposition (PhD); biblical studies (MA); Biblical theology (Th M); children's education (Th M); Christian education (MA, D Min); Christian leadership (MA); cross-cultural ministries (MA); educational administration (Th M); educational leadership (Th M); evangelism and discipleship (Th M); exposition of Biblical books (Th M); family life education (Th M); general studies (Th M); Hebrew and cognate studies (Th M); hermeneutics (Th M); historical theology (Th M); homiletics (Th M); intercultural ministries (Th M); Jesus studies (Th M); leadership studies (Th M); media and communication (MA); media arts (Th M); ministry (D Min); ministry with women (Th M); New Testament studies (Th M, PhD); Old Testament studies (Th M, PhD); parachurch ministries (Th M); pastoral care and counseling (Th M); pastoral theology and practice (Th M); philosophy (Th M); sacred theology (STM); spiritual formation (Th M); systematic theology (Th M); teaching in Christian institutions (Th M); theological studies (PhD); urban ministries (Th M); worship studies (Th M); youth education (Th M). *Accreditation:* ATS (one or more programs are accredited). Part-time programs available. Postbaccalaureate distance learning degree programs offered (minimal on-campus study). *Faculty:* 68 full-time (3 women), 35 part-time/adjunct (8 women). *Students:* 809 full-time (181 women), 1,215 part-time (450 women); includes 487 minority (208 Black or African American, non-Hispanic/Latino; 6 American Indian or Alaska Native, non-Hispanic/Latino; 141 Asian, non-Hispanic/Latino; 96 Hispanic/Latino; 5 Native Hawaiian or other Pacific Islander, non-Hispanic/Latino; 31 Two or more races, non-Hispanic/Latino), 223 international. Average age 36. 891 applicants, 70% accepted, 372 enrolled. In 2011, 336 master's, 27 doctorates, 46 other advanced degrees awarded. *Degree requirements:* For master's, variable foreign language requirement, thesis (for some programs); for doctorate, 2 foreign languages, thesis/dissertation. *Entrance requirements:* For master's, GRE or MAT if minimum undergraduate cumulative GPA is below 2.5 or undergraduate degree is unaccredited. Additional exam requirements/recommendations for international students: Required—TOEFL (minimum score 575 paper-based; 233 computer-based; 85 iBT), TWE (minimum score 4.5). *Application deadline:* For fall admission, 7/1 for domestic students, 1/1 for international students; for winter admission, 11/1 for domestic students; for spring admission, 11/1 for domestic students. *Expenses: Tuition:* Full-time $12,450; part-time $440 per credit hour. *Required fees:* $380; $190 per semester. *Financial support:* In 2011–12, 1,030 students received support. Career-related internships or fieldwork, scholarships/grants, and tuition waivers (full and partial) available. Financial award application deadline: 2/28. *Unit head:* Dr. Mark L. Bailey, President, 214-841-3676, Fax: 214-841-3565. *Application contact:* Josh Bleeker, Director of Admissions and Student Advising, 214-841-3661, Fax: 214-841-3664, E-mail: admissions@dts.edu.

Delaware State University, Graduate Programs, College of Education, Health and Public Policy, Program in Educational Leadership, Dover, DE 19901-2277. Offers MA, Ed D. *Entrance requirements:* Additional exam requirements/recommendations for international students: Required—TOEFL (minimum score 550 paper-based).

Delaware Valley College, Program in Educational Leadership, Doylestown, PA 18901-2697. Offers instruction, curriculum and technology (MS); school administration and leadership (MS). Part-time and evening/weekend programs available. *Entrance requirements:* For master's, minimum undergraduate GPA of 3.0.

Delta State University, Graduate Programs, College of Education, Thad Cochran Center for Rural School Leadership and Research, Program in Professional Studies, Cleveland, MS 38733-0001. Offers counselor education (Ed D); educational leadership (Ed D); elementary education (Ed D); higher education (Ed D). Part-time and evening/weekend programs available. *Degree requirements:* For doctorate, thesis/dissertation. *Entrance requirements:* For doctorate, GRE General Test. *Expenses:* Tuition, state resident: full-time $4702; part-time $294 per credit hour. Tuition, nonresident: full-time $12,516; part-time $760 per credit hour. *Required fees:* $586.

Delta State University, Graduate Programs, College of Education, Thad Cochran Center for Rural School Leadership and Research, Programs in Educational Administration and Supervision, Cleveland, MS 38733-0001. Offers M Ed, Ed S. *Accreditation:* NCATE. Part-time and evening/weekend programs available. *Degree requirements:* For master's, thesis optional. *Entrance requirements:* For master's, GRE General Test or MAT; for Ed S, master's degree, teaching certificate. *Expenses:* Tuition, state resident: full-time $4702; part-time $294 per credit hour. Tuition, nonresident: full-time $12,516; part-time $760 per credit hour. *Required fees:* $586.

DePaul University, College of Education, Chicago, IL 60106. Offers bilingual bicultural education (M Ed, MA); counseling (M Ed, MA), including college student development, community counseling, school counseling; curriculum studies (M Ed, MA, Ed D); early childhood education (M Ed, MA); educational leadership (M Ed, MA, Ed D), including administration and supervision (M Ed, MA), physical education (M Ed, MA); middle school mathematics education (MS); reading specialist (M Ed, MA); social and cultural foundations in education (M Ed, MA), including curriculum studies/development (MA); special education (M Ed, MA); teaching and learning (M Ed, MA), including elementary education, secondary education; world languages education (M Ed, MA). Part-time and evening/weekend programs available. *Faculty:* 49 full-time (28 women), 94 part-time/adjunct (60 women). *Students:* 894 full-time (707 women), 473 part-time (361 women); includes 349 minority (159 Black or African American, non-Hispanic/Latino; 3 American Indian or Alaska Native, non-Hispanic/Latino; 45 Asian, non-Hispanic/Latino; 115 Hispanic/Latino; 2 Native Hawaiian or other Pacific Islander, non-Hispanic/Latino; 25 Two or more races, non-Hispanic/Latino), 21 international. Average age 30. 872 applicants, 64% accepted, 325 enrolled. In 2011, 499 master's, 10 doctorates awarded. *Median time to degree:* Of those who began their doctoral program in fall 2003, 32% received their degree in 8 years or less. *Degree requirements:* For master's, thesis/dissertation (for MA); capstone course or paper (for M Ed); for doctorate, thesis/dissertation. *Entrance requirements:* For master's, interview, minimum GPA of 2.75, 2 letters of recommendation, bachelor's degree conferred by accredited college or university; for doctorate, interview, master's degree, writing sample, 3 letters of recommendation. Additional exam requirements/recommendations for international students: Required—TOEFL (minimum score 550 paper-based; 213 computer-based; 80 iBT). *Application deadline:* For fall admission, 8/15 priority date for domestic students; for winter admission, 12/1 priority date for domestic students; for spring admission, 3/1 priority date for domestic students. Applications are processed on a rolling basis. Application fee: $40. Electronic applications accepted. *Financial support:* In 2011–12, 163 students received support, including 15 research assistantships with full tuition reimbursements available (averaging $6,375 per year); career-related internships or fieldwork, Federal Work-Study, scholarships/grants, and unspecified assistantships also available. Support available to part-time students. Financial award application deadline: 12/31; financial award applicants required to submit FAFSA. *Faculty research:* Reflective teaching, children at risk, loss, ethnicity, urban education. *Total annual research expenditures:* $916,310. *Unit head:* Dr. Paul Zionts, Dean, 773-325-7581, Fax: 773-325-7713, E-mail: pzionts@depaul.edu. *Application contact:* Brandon Washington, Enrollment Management Coordinator, 773-325-1152, Fax: 773-325-2270, E-mail: bwashin3@depaul.edu. Web site: http://education.depaul.edu.

Doane College, Program in Education, Crete, NE 68333-2430. Offers curriculum and instruction (M Ed); educational leadership (M Ed). *Accreditation:* NCATE. Part-time and evening/weekend programs available. *Students:* 126 full-time (103 women), 381 part-time (284 women); includes 20 minority (8 Black or African American, non-Hispanic/Latino; 2 American Indian or Alaska Native, non-Hispanic/Latino; 9 Hispanic/Latino; 1 Two or more races, non-Hispanic/Latino). Average age 33. In 2011, 312 master's awarded. *Degree requirements:* For master's, thesis. *Entrance requirements:* For master's, minimum GPA of 2.5. Additional exam requirements/recommendations for international students: Required—TOEFL. *Application deadline:* Applications are processed on a rolling basis. Electronic applications accepted. *Expenses:* Contact institution. *Financial support:* Applicants required to submit FAFSA. *Unit head:* Lyn C. Forester, Dean, 402-826-8604, Fax: 402-826-8278. *Application contact:* Wilma Daddario, Assistant Dean, 402-464-1223, Fax: 402-466-4228, E-mail: wdaddario@doane.edu. Web site: http://www.doane.edu/Admission/Graduate_Admission/Master_Of_Education/.

Dominican University, School of Education, River Forest, IL 60305-1099. Offers curriculum and instruction (MA Ed); early childhood education (MS); education (MAT); educational administration (MA); elementary (online) (MS); English as a second language (online) (MS); reading (online) (MS); special education (MS). Part-time and evening/weekend programs available. Postbaccalaureate distance learning degree programs offered (no on-campus study). *Faculty:* 19 full-time (13 women), 53 part-time/adjunct (41 women). *Students:* 24 full-time (19 women), 434 part-time (357 women); includes 95 minority (27 Black or African American, non-Hispanic/Latino; 1 American Indian or Alaska Native, non-Hispanic/Latino; 12 Asian, non-Hispanic/Latino; 48 Hispanic/Latino; 7 Two or more races, non-Hispanic/Latino), 1 international. Average age 33. 92 applicants, 99% accepted, 91 enrolled. In 2011, 267 master's awarded. *Entrance requirements:* For master's, Illinois certification test of basic skills. Additional exam requirements/recommendations for international students: Required—TOEFL (minimum score 550 paper-based; 213 computer-based; 79 iBT). *Application deadline:* Applications are processed on a rolling basis. Application fee: $25. *Expenses:* Contact institution. *Financial support:* Career-related internships or fieldwork, scholarships/grants, and tuition waivers (partial) available. Support available to part-time students. Financial award application deadline: 8/15; financial award applicants required to submit FAFSA. *Faculty research:* Governance of private education institutions, reading and language arts, inclusion, organizational planning, leadership and vision. *Unit head:* Dr. Colleen Reardon, Dean, 718-524-6643, Fax: 708-524-6665, E-mail: creardon@dom.edu. *Application contact:* Keven Hansen, Coordinator of Recruitment and Admissions, 708-524-6921, Fax: 708-524-6665, E-mail: educate@dom.edu. Web site: http://www.dom.edu/soe.

Dowling College, Graduate Programs in Education, Oakdale, NY 11769-1999. Offers adolescence education with middle childhood extension (MS); advanced certificate in gifted education (AC); childhood and early childhood education (MS); childhood and gifted education (MS); computers in education (AC); early childhood education (MS); educational administration (Ed D); educational technology leadership (MS); educational technology specialist (AC); literacy education (MS); literary education (AC); school building leader (AC); school district business leader (MBA, AC); school district leader (AC); special education (MS); sports management (MS). *Accreditation:* NCATE. Part-time and evening/weekend programs available. Postbaccalaureate distance learning degree programs offered (minimal on-campus study). *Faculty:* 23 full-time (12 women), 70 part-time/adjunct (44 women). *Students:* 336 full-time (245 women), 631 part-time (485 women); includes 83 minority (29 Black or African American, non-Hispanic/Latino; 2 American Indian or Alaska Native, non-Hispanic/Latino; 7 Asian, non-Hispanic/Latino; 45 Hispanic/Latino). Average age 32. 280 applicants, 85% accepted, 167 enrolled. In 2011, 425 master's, 27 doctorates, 40 other advanced degrees awarded. *Degree requirements:* For master's and AC, comprehensive exam; for doctorate, thesis/dissertation. *Entrance requirements:* For master's, minimum GPA of 3.0; for doctorate, GRE, master's degree; for AC, teaching certificate. Additional exam requirements/recommendations for international students: Required—TOEFL (minimum score 550 paper-based). *Application deadline:* For fall admission, 9/1 priority date for domestic students; for winter admission, 1/1 priority date for domestic students; for spring admission, 2/1 priority date for domestic students. Applications are processed on a rolling basis. Application fee: $50. Electronic applications accepted. *Expenses: Tuition:* Full-time $19,162; part-time $933 per credit. *Required fees:* $1330; $700 per year. Tuition and fees vary according to course load. *Financial support:* Career-related internships or fieldwork and Federal Work-Study available. Support available to part-time students. Financial award application deadline: 6/30; financial award applicants required to submit FAFSA. *Faculty research:* Natural readers, Korean styles and learning strategies, mothers of children with disabilities, computers in instruction, cultural background and organizational roadblocks to problem solving. *Unit head:* Carol Pulsonetti, Director of Operations, School of Education, 631-244-3243, E-mail: pulsonec@dowling.edu. *Application contact:* Ronnie S. Macdonald, Assistant Vice President for Enrollment Services/Dean of Admissions, 631-244-3357, Fax: 631-244-1059, E-mail: macdonar@dowling.edu.

Drexel University, Goodwin College of Professional Studies, School of Education, Program in Educational Administration: Collaborative Leadership, Philadelphia, PA 19104-2875. Offers MS.

Drexel University, Goodwin College of Professional Studies, School of Education, Program in Educational Leadership and Management, Philadelphia, PA 19104-2875. Offers Ed D.

Drexel University, Goodwin College of Professional Studies, School of Education, Program in Education Leadership Development and Learning Technologies, Philadelphia, PA 19104-2875. Offers PhD. *Degree requirements:* For doctorate, thesis/dissertation. Electronic applications accepted.

Duquesne University, School of Education, Department of Foundations and Leadership, Professional Doctorate in Educational Leadership Program (ProDEL), Pittsburgh, PA 15282-0001. Offers Ed D. Part-time and evening/weekend programs available. *Faculty:* 2 full-time (0 women). *Students:* 16 full-time (9 women); includes 7 minority (6 Black or African American, non-Hispanic/Latino; 1 Two or more races, non-Hispanic/Latino), 1 international. Average age 40. 74 applicants, 22% accepted, 16 enrolled. *Degree requirements:* For doctorate, thesis/dissertation. *Entrance requirements:* For doctorate, GRE, letters of recommendation, essay, interview, master's degree. Additional exam requirements/recommendations for international students: Required—TOEFL (minimum score 550 paper-based; 80 computer-based), IELTS (minimum score 7). *Application deadline:* For fall admission, 3/1 for domestic students. *Expenses: Tuition:* Full-time $16,596; part-time $922 per credit. *Required fees:* $1584; $88 per credit. Tuition and fees vary according to program. *Unit head:* Dr. Launcelot Brown, Chair, 412-396-1046, Fax: 412-396-6017, E-mail: brownli@duq.edu. *Application contact:* Michael Dolinger, Director of Student and Academic Services, 412-396-6647, Fax: 412-396-5585, E-mail: dolinger@duq.edu. Web site: http://www.duq.edu/prodel/index.cfm.

Duquesne University, School of Education, Department of Foundations and Leadership, Program in School Administration and Supervision, Pittsburgh, PA 15282-0001. Offers curriculum and instruction (Post-Master's Certificate); school administration K-12 (MS Ed, Post-Master's Certificate); school supervision (MS Ed). Part-time and evening/weekend programs available. Postbaccalaureate distance learning degree programs offered (minimal on-campus study). *Faculty:* 3 full-time (1 woman). *Students:* 30 full-time (16 women), 17 part-time (15 women); includes 4 minority (2 Black or African American, non-Hispanic/Latino; 2 Hispanic/Latino). Average age 35. 11 applicants, 64% accepted, 4 enrolled. In 2011, 35 degrees awarded. *Degree requirements:* For master's, thesis optional. *Entrance requirements:* For master's and Post-Master's Certificate, bachelor's degree. Additional exam requirements/recommendations for international students: Required—TOEFL (minimum score 550 paper-based; 80 computer-based), IELTS (minimum score 7). *Application deadline:* For fall admission, 9/1 for domestic students; for spring admission, 1/1 for domestic students. Applications are processed on a rolling basis. Application fee: $0. Electronic applications accepted. Application fee is waived when completed online. *Expenses: Tuition:* Full-time $16,596; part-time $922 per credit. *Required fees:* $1584; $88 per credit. Tuition and fees vary according to program. *Financial support:* Research assistantships available. Support available to part-time students. *Unit head:* Dr. Robert Furman, Director, 412-396-5274, Fax: 412-396-1274, E-mail: furman@duq.edu. *Application contact:* Michael Dolinger, Director of

Student and Academic Services, 412-396-6647, Fax: 412-396-5585, E-mail: dolingerm@duq.edu. Web site: http://www.duq.edu/education.

D'Youville College, Doctoral Programs, Buffalo, NY 14201-1084. Offers educational leadership (Ed D); health education (Ed D); health policy (Ed D). Part-time and evening/weekend programs available. *Faculty:* 6 full-time (2 women), 23 part-time/adjunct (13 women). *Students:* 28 full-time (14 women), 32 part-time (25 women); includes 3 minority (2 Black or African American, non-Hispanic/Latino; 1 Hispanic/Latino), 14 international. Average age 44. 38 applicants, 58% accepted, 18 enrolled. In 2011, 13 doctorates awarded. *Degree requirements:* For doctorate, comprehensive exam, thesis/dissertation, fieldwork. *Entrance requirements:* For doctorate, MS/MA; professional experience. *Expenses: Tuition:* Full-time $18,960; part-time $790 per credit hour. *Required fees:* $310. Tuition and fees vary according to degree level and program. *Financial support:* In 2011–12, research assistantships with tuition reimbursements (averaging $3,000 per year) were awarded; scholarships/grants also available. *Faculty research:* Educational assessment, assessment reform, culture and education, market-based reform, men's health, electronic records. *Unit head:* Dr. Mark Garrison, Director, 716-829-8125, E-mail: garrisonm@dyc.edu. *Application contact:* Linda Fisher, Graduate Admissions Director, 716-829-8400, Fax: 716-829-7900, E-mail: graduateadmissions@dyc.edu.

East Carolina University, Graduate School, College of Education, Department of Educational Leadership, Greenville, NC 27858-4353. Offers educational administration and supervision (Ed S); educational leadership (Ed D); school administration (MSA). *Accreditation:* NCATE. Part-time and evening/weekend programs available. Postbaccalaureate distance learning degree programs offered (minimal on-campus study). *Degree requirements:* For master's, comprehensive exam, thesis optional; for doctorate, thesis/dissertation. *Entrance requirements:* For master's, GRE General Test or MAT, interview, minimum GPA of 2.5, bachelor's degree in related field, teaching license (MA Ed); for doctorate, GRE or MAT, interview, minimum GPA of 3.5. Additional exam requirements/recommendations for international students: Required—TOEFL. *Application deadline:* For fall admission, 6/1 priority date for domestic students. Applications are processed on a rolling basis. Application fee: $50. *Expenses:* Tuition, state resident: full-time $3557; part-time $444.63 per semester hour. Tuition, nonresident: full-time $14,351; part-time $1793.88 per semester hour. *Required fees:* $2016; $252 per semester hour. Part-time tuition and fees vary according to course load, campus/location and program. *Financial support:* Research assistantships with partial tuition reimbursements, teaching assistantships with partial tuition reimbursements, and Federal Work-Study available. Support available to part-time students. Financial award application deadline: 6/1. *Unit head:* Wiliam A. Rouse, Interim Chair, 252-328-6763, E-mail: rousew@ecu.edu. *Application contact:* Dean of Graduate School, 252-328-6012, Fax: 252-328-6071, E-mail: gradschool@ecu.edu. Web site: http://www.ecu.edu/cs-educ/leed/index.cfm.

East Carolina University, Graduate School, College of Education, Department of Higher, Adult, and Counselor Education, Greenville, NC 27858-4353. Offers adult education (MA Ed); counselor education (MS); higher education administration (Ed D). *Accreditation:* NCATE. Part-time and evening/weekend programs available. *Degree requirements:* For master's, comprehensive exam, thesis optional. *Entrance requirements:* For master's, GRE General Test or MAT, interview, minimum GPA of 2.5, bachelor's degree in related field, teaching license (MA Ed). Additional exam requirements/recommendations for international students: Required—TOEFL. *Application deadline:* For fall admission, 5/15 priority date for domestic students. Applications are processed on a rolling basis. Application fee: $50. *Expenses:* Tuition, state resident: full-time $3557; part-time $444.63 per semester hour. Tuition, nonresident: full-time $14,351; part-time $1793.88 per semester hour. *Required fees:* $2016; $252 per semester hour. Part-time tuition and fees vary according to course load, campus/location and program. *Financial support:* Research assistantships with partial tuition reimbursements, teaching assistantships with partial tuition reimbursements, and Federal Work-Study available. Support available to part-time students. Financial award application deadline: 6/1. *Unit head:* Dr. Vivian W. Mott, Chair, 252-328-6177, Fax: 252-328-4368, E-mail: mottv@ecu.edu. *Application contact:* Dean of Graduate School, 252-328-6012, Fax: 252-328-6071, E-mail: gradschool@ecu.edu. Web site: http://www.ecu.edu/cs-educ/hace/index.cfm.

Eastern Illinois University, Graduate School, College of Education and Professional Studies, Department of Educational Leadership, Charleston, IL 61920-3099. Offers MS Ed, Ed S. *Accreditation:* NCATE. Part-time and evening/weekend programs available. *Degree requirements:* For master's, fieldwork; for Ed S, thesis. *Expenses:* Tuition, state resident: part-time $279 per credit hour. Tuition, nonresident: part-time $670 per credit hour. *Required fees:* $179.07 per credit hour. $1253 per semester.

Eastern Kentucky University, The Graduate School, College of Education, Department of Counseling and Educational Leadership, Richmond, KY 40475-3102. Offers human services (MA); instructional leadership (MA Ed); mental health counseling (MA); school counseling (MA Ed). *Accreditation:* ACA (one or more programs are accredited); NCATE. Part-time programs available. Postbaccalaureate distance learning degree programs offered. *Entrance requirements:* For master's, GRE General Test, minimum GPA of 2.5.

Eastern Michigan University, Graduate School, College of Education, Department of Leadership and Counseling, Programs in Leadership, Ypsilanti, MI 48197. Offers college student personnel (MA); community college leadership (Graduate Certificate); educational leadership (MA, Ed D, SPA); higher education general administration (MA); higher education student affairs (MA); K-12 administration (MA); K-12 basic administration (Post Master's Certificate). Part-time and evening/weekend programs available. Postbaccalaureate distance learning degree programs offered (no on-campus study). *Students:* 21 full-time (16 women), 418 part-time (258 women); includes 120 minority (104 Black or African American, non-Hispanic/Latino; 2 American Indian or Alaska Native, non-Hispanic/Latino; 4 Asian, non-Hispanic/Latino; 8 Hispanic/Latino; 2 Two or more races, non-Hispanic/Latino), 5 international. Average age 37. 215 applicants, 73% accepted, 93 enrolled. In 2011, 82 master's, 11 doctorates, 35 other advanced degrees awarded. *Degree requirements:* For master's, portfolio. *Entrance requirements:* For doctorate, GRE. Additional exam requirements/recommendations for international students: Required—TOEFL. *Application deadline:* For winter admission, 2/1 for domestic and international students. Applications are processed on a rolling basis. Application fee: $35. *Expenses:* Tuition, state resident: full-time $10,367; part-time $432 per credit hour. Tuition, nonresident: full-time $20,435; part-time $851 per credit hour. *Required fees:* $39 per credit hour. $46 per semester. One-time fee: $100. Tuition and fees vary according to course level, degree level and reciprocity agreements. *Financial support:* Fellowships, research assistantships with full tuition reimbursements, teaching assistantships with full tuition reimbursements, career-related internships or fieldwork, Federal Work-Study, institutionally sponsored loans, scholarships/grants, tuition waivers (partial), and unspecified assistantships available. Support available to part-time students. *Unit head:* Dr. Jaclynn Tracy, Department Head, 734-487-0255, Fax: 734-487-4608, E-mail: jtracy@emich.edu. *Application contact:* Dr. Elizabeth Broughton, Coordinator of Advising for Programs in Educational Leadership, 734-487-0255, Fax: 734-487-4608, E-mail: ebroughto@emich.edu.

Eastern Michigan University, Graduate School, College of Education, Department of Special Education, Programs in Special Education, Ypsilanti, MI 48197. Offers special education (MA); special education-administration and supervision (SPA); special education-curriculum development (SPA). *Accreditation:* NCATE. Part-time and evening/weekend programs available. Postbaccalaureate distance learning degree programs offered (minimal on-campus study). *Students:* 14 full-time (11 women), 49 part-time (40 women); includes 13 minority (7 Black or African American, non-Hispanic/Latino; 2 Asian, non-Hispanic/Latino; 4 Hispanic/Latino), 1 international. Average age 38. 23 applicants, 48% accepted, 8 enrolled. In 2011, 3 master's, 3 other advanced degrees awarded. *Entrance requirements:* For master's, GRE General Test. Additional exam requirements/recommendations for international students: Required—TOEFL. *Application deadline:* Applications are processed on a rolling basis. Application fee: $35. *Expenses:* Tuition, state resident: full-time $10,367; part-time $432 per credit hour. Tuition, nonresident: full-time $20,435; part-time $851 per credit hour. *Required fees:* $39 per credit hour. $46 per semester. One-time fee: $100. Tuition and fees vary according to course level, degree level and reciprocity agreements. *Financial support:* Fellowships, research assistantships with full tuition reimbursements, teaching assistantships with full tuition reimbursements, career-related internships or fieldwork, Federal Work-Study, institutionally sponsored loans, scholarships/grants, tuition waivers (partial), and unspecified assistantships available. Support available to part-time students. Financial award applicants required to submit FAFSA. *Unit head:* Dr. Philip Smith, Interim Department Head, 734-487-3300, Fax: 734-487-2473, E-mail: psmith16@emich.edu. *Application contact:* Graduate Admissions, 734-487-2400, Fax: 734-487-6559, E-mail: graduate.admissions@emich.edu.

Eastern Nazarene College, Adult and Graduate Studies, Division of Teacher Education, Quincy, MA 02170. Offers administration (M Ed); early childhood education (M Ed, Certificate); elementary education (M Ed, Certificate); English as a second language (Certificate); instructional enrichment and development (Certificate); middle school education (M Ed, Certificate); moderate special needs education (Certificate); principal (Certificate); program development and supervision (Certificate); secondary education (M Ed, Certificate); special education administrator (Certificate); special needs (M Ed); supervisor (Certificate); teacher of reading (M Ed, Certificate). M Ed also available through weekend program for administration, special needs, and teacher of reading only. Part-time and evening/weekend programs available. *Entrance requirements:* Additional exam requirements/recommendations for international students: Required—TOEFL (minimum score 550 paper-based).

Eastern New Mexico University, Graduate School, College of Education and Technology, Department of Educational Studies, Portales, NM 88130. Offers counseling (MA); education (M Ed), including educational adminstration, secondary education; school counseling (M Ed); special education (M Sp Ed), including early childhood special education, general. *Accreditation:* NCATE. Part-time and evening/weekend programs available. Postbaccalaureate distance learning degree programs offered (minimal on-campus study). *Degree requirements:* For master's, comprehensive exam, thesis optional. *Entrance requirements:* For master's, minimum GPA of 3.0, letter of recommendation, photocopy of teaching license, writing assessment, Level II teaching license (for M Ed in educational administration). Additional exam requirements/recommendations for international students: Required—TOEFL (minimum score 550 paper-based; 213 computer-based; 79 iBT), IELTS (minimum score 6). Electronic applications accepted.

Eastern Washington University, Graduate Studies, College of Arts, Letters and Education, Department of Education, Program in Educational Leadership, Cheney, WA 99004-2431. Offers M Ed. *Students:* 2 part-time (both women). Average age 38. 2 applicants, 0% accepted, 0 enrolled. In 2011, 4 master's awarded. *Degree requirements:* For master's, comprehensive exam, thesis or alternative. *Entrance requirements:* For master's, minimum GPA of 3.0. *Application deadline:* For fall admission, 4/1 priority date for domestic students; for spring admission, 1/15 for domestic students. Applications are processed on a rolling basis. Application fee: $50. *Financial support:* In 2011–12, teaching assistantships with partial tuition reimbursements (averaging $7,000 per year) were awarded; career-related internships or fieldwork, Federal Work-Study, institutionally sponsored loans, scholarships/grants, health care benefits, tuition waivers (partial), and unspecified assistantships also available. Support available to part-time students. Financial award application deadline: 2/1; financial award applicants required to submit FAFSA. *Unit head:* Dr. Les Portner, Director, 509-939-0846, Fax: 509-359-4822. *Application contact:* Dr. Kevin Pyatt, Graduate Program Coordinator, 509-359-6091.

East Tennessee State University, School of Graduate Studies, College of Education, Department of Educational Leadership and Policy Analysis, Johnson City, TN 37614. Offers administration endorsement (Ed S); administrative endorsement (Ed D); classroom leadership (Ed D); counselor leadership (Ed S); educational leadership (M Ed); post-secondary and private sector leadership (Ed D); school leadership (Ed D); school system leadership (Ed S); teacher leadership (Ed S). *Accreditation:* NCATE. Part-time programs available. Postbaccalaureate distance learning degree programs offered. *Faculty:* 8 full-time (5 women), 2 part-time/adjunct (0 women). *Students:* 24 full-time (16 women), 163 part-time (111 women); includes 28 minority (18 Black or African American, non-Hispanic/Latino; 1 American Indian or Alaska Native, non-Hispanic/Latino; 3 Asian, non-Hispanic/Latino; 4 Hispanic/Latino; 2 Two or more races, non-Hispanic/Latino), 1 international. Average age 41. 58 applicants, 41% accepted, 24 enrolled. In 2011, 5 master's, 38 doctorates, 6 other advanced degrees awarded. *Degree requirements:* For master's, comprehensive exam, portfolio development and presentation, performance assessment; for doctorate, comprehensive exam, thesis/dissertation, residency, internship; for Ed S, comprehensive exam, field experience; internship (for counselor leadership concentration). *Entrance requirements:* For master's, writing assessment, minimum GPA of 2.75, professional resume, teaching certificate and experience, interview; for doctorate, GRE General Test, writing assessment, professional resume, teaching certificate (except for post secondary and private sector leadership concentration), interview, four letters of recommendation; for Ed S, writing assessment, professional resume, teaching certificate (for counselor leadership concentration). Additional exam requirements/recommendations for international students: Required—TOEFL (minimum score 550 paper-based; 213 computer-based; 79 iBT). *Application deadline:* For fall admission, 5/1 for domestic students, 4/30 for international students; for spring admission, 10/1 for domestic students, 9/30 for international students. Application fee: $35 ($45 for international students). Electronic applications accepted. *Expenses:* Tuition, state resident: full-time $7312; part-time $350 per credit hour. Tuition, nonresident: full-time $18,490; part-time $621 per credit hour. *Required fees:* $63 per credit hour. Tuition and fees vary according to course load and program. *Financial support:* In 2011–12, 15 students received support, including 7 fellowships with full tuition reimbursements available (averaging $9,800 per year), 2 research assistantships with full tuition reimbursements available (averaging $6,000 per year), 1 teaching assistantship with full tuition reimbursement available (averaging $6,000 per year); career-related internships or fieldwork, institutionally sponsored loans, scholarships/grants, and unspecified assistantships also available. Financial award application deadline: 7/1; financial award applicants required to submit FAFSA. *Faculty research:* Needs of principals in the new century, funding accountability and policy formulation for U. S. community college systems, use of technology in principal preparation programs, multiple intelligence and the adult learner, leadership development in youth and young adults. *Unit head:* Dr. Pam Scott, Chair, 423-439-4430, Fax: 423-439-7636, E-mail: scottp@etsu.edu. *Application contact:* Cindy Hill, Graduate Specialist, 423-439-6590, Fax: 423-439-5624, E-mail: hillcc@etsu.edu.

Edgewood College, Program in Education, Madison, WI 53711-1997. Offers adult learning (MA Ed); bilingual teaching and learning (MA Ed); director of instruction (Certificate); director of special education and pupil services (Certificate); education (MA Ed); educational administration (MA Ed); educational leadership (Ed D); professional studies (MA Ed); program coordinator (Certificate); reading administration (MA Ed); school business administration (Certificate); school principalship K-12 (Certificate); special education (MA Ed); sustainability leadership (MA Ed); teaching and learning (MA Ed); teaching English to speakers of other languages (TESOL) (MA Ed). *Accreditation:* NCATE (one or more programs are accredited). Part-time and evening/weekend programs available. *Students:* 155 full-time (93 women), 152 part-time (116 women); includes 39 minority (13 Black or African American, non-Hispanic/Latino; 5 Asian, non-Hispanic/Latino; 17 Hispanic/Latino; 4 Two or more races, non-Hispanic/Latino), 9 international. Average age 36. In 2011, 39 master's, 32 doctorates awarded. *Degree requirements:* For master's, practicum, research project; for doctorate, comprehensive exam, thesis/dissertation. *Entrance requirements:* For master's, minimum GPA of 2.75, 2 letters of recommendation, personal statement; for doctorate, resume, letter of intent, 2 letters of recommendation, interview, writing sample. Additional exam requirements/recommendations for international students: Required—TOEFL (minimum score 525 paper-based; 197 computer-based; 72 iBT). *Application deadline:* For fall admission, 8/15 for domestic students, 5/1 for international students; for spring admission, 1/8 for domestic students, 11/1 for international students. Applications are processed on a rolling basis. Application fee: $25. Electronic applications accepted. *Expenses: Tuition:* Part-time $747 per credit. Part-time tuition and fees vary according to program. *Unit head:* Dr. Jane Belmore, Dean, 608-663-8336, Fax: 608-663-3291, E-mail: jbelmore@edgewood.edu. *Application contact:* Joann Eastman, Admissions Counselor, 608-663-3250, Fax: 608-663-2214, E-mail: gps@edgewood.edu. Web site: http://education.edgewood.edu/graduate.html.

Edinboro University of Pennsylvania, School of Education, Department of Professional Studies, Edinboro, PA 16444. Offers counseling (MA), including community counseling, elementary guidance, rehabilitation counseling, secondary guidance, student personnel services; educational leadership (M Ed), including elementary school administration, secondary school administration; educational psychology (M Ed); educational specialist school psychology (MS); elementary principal (Certificate); elementary school guidance counselor (Certificate); K-12 school administration (Certificate); letter of eligibility (Certificate); reading (M Ed); reading specialist (Certificate); school psychology (Certificate); school supervision (Certificate), including music, special education. Part-time and evening/weekend programs available. *Faculty:* 13 full-time (8 women). *Students:* 171 full-time (134 women), 563 part-time (441 women); includes 26 minority (20 Black or African American, non-Hispanic/Latino; 1 American Indian or Alaska Native, non-Hispanic/Latino; 1 Asian, non-Hispanic/Latino; 4 Hispanic/Latino). Average age 31. In 2011, 297 master's, 49 other advanced degrees awarded. *Degree requirements:* For master's, thesis or alternative, competency exam; for Certificate, thesis or alternative. *Entrance requirements:* For master's and Certificate, GRE or MAT, minimum QPA of 2.5. *Application deadline:* Applications are processed on a rolling basis. Application fee: $30. Electronic applications accepted. *Financial support:* In 2011–12, 60 research assistantships with full and partial tuition reimbursements (averaging $4,050 per year) were awarded; career-related internships or fieldwork, Federal Work-Study, scholarships/grants, and unspecified assistantships also available. Support available to part-time students. Financial award application deadline: 2/15; financial award applicants required to submit FAFSA. *Unit head:* Dr. Susan Norton, 814-732-2260, E-mail: scnorton@edinboro.edu. *Application contact:* Dr. Andrew Pushchack, Program Head, Educational Leadership, 814-732-1548, E-mail: apushchack@edinboro.edu.

Elizabeth City State University, School of Education and Psychology, Program in School Administration, Elizabeth City, NC 27909-7806. Offers MSA. Part-time and evening/weekend programs available. *Degree requirements:* For master's, thesis. *Entrance requirements:* For master's, MAT, GRE, minimum GPA of 3.0. Additional exam requirements/recommendations for international students: Required—TOEFL. Electronic applications accepted.

Ellis University, Program in Education, Chicago, IL 60606-7204. Offers early childhood education (MA Ed); education (MA Ed); teacher as a leader (MA Ed). *Degree requirements:* For master's, thesis or capstone.

Elmhurst College, Graduate Programs, Program in Teacher Leadership, Elmhurst, IL 60126-3296. Offers M Ed. Part-time and evening/weekend programs available. *Faculty:* 2 full-time (both women), 1 (woman) part-time/adjunct. *Students:* 25 part-time (21 women); includes 3 minority (1 Black or African American, non-Hispanic/Latino; 1 Asian, non-Hispanic/Latino; 1 Hispanic/Latino). Average age 33. 10 applicants, 40% accepted, 3 enrolled. In 2011, 3 master's awarded. *Entrance requirements:* For master's, 3 recommendations, resume, statement of purpose. Additional exam requirements/recommendations for international students: Required—TOEFL (minimum score 550 paper-based; 213 computer-based). *Application deadline:* Applications are processed on a rolling basis. Application fee: $0. Electronic applications accepted. *Expenses:* Contact institution. *Financial support:* In 2011–12, 2 students received support. Federal Work-Study and scholarships/grants available. Support available to part-time students. Financial award application deadline: 6/1; financial award applicants required to submit FAFSA. *Unit head:* Elizabeth D. Kuebler, Director of Adult and Graduate Admission, 630-617-3300, Fax: 630-617-5501, E-mail: oaga@elmhurst.edu. *Application contact:* Elizabeth D. Kuebler, Director of Adult and Graduate Admission, 630-617-3300, Fax: 630-617-5501, E-mail: oaga@elmhurst.edu.

Emmanuel College, Graduate and Professional Programs, Graduate Programs in Education, Boston, MA 02115. Offers educational leadership (CAGS); elementary education (MAT); school administration (M Ed); secondary education (MAT). Part-time and evening/weekend programs available. *Faculty:* 3 full-time (all women), 11 part-time/adjunct (3 women). *Students:* 12 full-time (11 women), 28 part-time (21 women); includes 9 minority (6 Black or African American, non-Hispanic/Latino; 1 American Indian or Alaska Native, non-Hispanic/Latino; 2 Hispanic/Latino). Average age 30. 9 applicants, 78% accepted, 6 enrolled. In 2011, 14 degrees awarded. *Degree requirements:* For master's, 36 credits, including 6-credit practicum. *Entrance requirements:* For master's and CAGS, transcripts from all regionally-accredited institutions attended (showing proof of bachelor's degree completion), 2 letters of recommendation, essay, resume, interview. Additional exam requirements/recommendations for international students: Required—TOEFL (minimum score 600 paper-based; 250 computer-based; 106 iBT) or IELTS (minimum score 6.5). *Application deadline:* For fall admission, 7/31 priority date for domestic students; for spring admission, 11/30 priority date for domestic students. Applications are processed on a rolling basis. Application fee: $0. Electronic applications accepted. *Expenses: Tuition:* Part-time $2139 per course. Tuition and fees vary according to program and reciprocity agreements. *Financial support:* Applicants required to submit FAFSA. *Faculty research:* Literature/reading, history of education, multicultural education, special education. *Unit head:* Dr. Joyce DeLeo, Vice President of Academic Affairs, 617-735-9700, Fax: 617-507-0434, E-mail: gpp@emmanuel.edu. *Application contact:* Enrollment Counselor, 617-735-9700, Fax: 617-507-0434, E-mail: gpp@emmanuel.edu. Web site: http://gpp.emmanuel.edu.

Emporia State University, Graduate School, Teachers College, Department of School Leadership and Middle/Secondary Education, Program in Curriculum and Instruction, Emporia, KS 66801-5087. Offers curriculum leadership (MS); effective practitioner (MS); national board certification (MS). *Accreditation:* NCATE. Part-time programs available. *Students:* 1 (woman) full-time, 126 part-time (105 women); includes 11 minority (5 Black or African American, non-Hispanic/Latino; 1 American Indian or Alaska Native, non-Hispanic/Latino; 5 Hispanic/Latino). 31 applicants, 94% accepted, 23 enrolled. In 2011, 57 master's awarded. *Degree requirements:* For master's, comprehensive exam or thesis, practicum. *Entrance requirements:* For master's, GRE or MAT, appropriate bachelor's degree, teacher certification, 1 year of teaching experience, letters of recommendation. *Application deadline:* For fall admission, 8/15 priority date for domestic students. Applications are processed on a rolling basis. Application fee: $30 ($75 for international students). Electronic applications accepted. *Expenses:* Tuition, state resident: full-time $2342; part-time $195 per credit hour. Tuition, nonresident: full-time $7254; part-time $605 per credit hour. *Required fees:* $66 per credit hour. Tuition and fees vary according to campus/location. *Financial support:* Career-related internships or fieldwork, Federal Work-Study, institutionally sponsored loans, health care benefits, and unspecified assistantships available. Financial award application deadline: 3/15; financial award applicants required to submit FAFSA. *Unit head:* Dr. Jerry Will, Chair, 620-341-5777, E-mail: jwill@emporia.edu. *Application contact:* Mary Sewell, Admissions Coordinator, 800-950-GRAD, Fax: 620-341-5909, E-mail: msewell@emporia.edu.

Emporia State University, Graduate School, Teachers College, Department of School Leadership and Middle/Secondary Education, Program in Educational Administration, Emporia, KS 66801-5087. Offers elementary administration (MS); elementary/secondary administration (MS); secondary administration (MS). *Accreditation:* NCATE. Part-time programs available. *Students:* 32 full-time (18 women), 93 part-time (43 women); includes 11 minority (3 Black or African American, non-Hispanic/Latino; 1 American Indian or Alaska Native, non-Hispanic/Latino; 1 Asian, non-Hispanic/Latino; 6 Hispanic/Latino). 30 applicants, 87% accepted, 13 enrolled. In 2011, 55 master's awarded. *Degree requirements:* For master's, comprehensive exam or thesis, practicum. *Entrance requirements:* For master's, GRE or MAT, appropriate bachelor's degree, letters of recommendation, teacher certification, 1 year teaching experience. *Application deadline:* For fall admission, 8/15 priority date for domestic students. Applications are processed on a rolling basis. Application fee: $30 ($75 for international students). Electronic applications accepted. *Expenses:* Tuition, state resident: full-time $2342; part-time $195 per credit hour. Tuition, nonresident: full-time $7254; part-time $605 per credit hour. *Required fees:* $66 per credit hour. Tuition and fees vary according to campus/location. *Financial support:* Career-related internships or fieldwork, Federal Work-Study, institutionally sponsored loans, health care benefits, and unspecified assistantships available. Financial award application deadline: 3/15; financial award applicants required to submit FAFSA. *Unit head:* Dr. Jerry Will, Chair, 620-341-5777, E-mail: jwill@emporia.edu. *Application contact:* Mary Sewell, Admissions Coordinator, 800-950-GRAD, Fax: 620-341-5909, E-mail: msewell@emporia.edu.

Emporia State University, Graduate School, Teachers College, Department of School Leadership and Middle/Secondary Education, Program in Instructional Leadership, Emporia, KS 66801-5087. Offers MS. Part-time and evening/weekend programs available. *Students:* 8 part-time (7 women). 4 applicants, 25% accepted, 0 enrolled. *Degree requirements:* For master's, comprehensive exam. *Entrance requirements:* For master's, GRE or MAT, minimum GPA of 2.5 on last 60 undergraduate hours; official transcripts; essay; two personal references; copy of teaching certificate. *Expenses:* Tuition, state resident: full-time $2342; part-time $195 per credit hour. Tuition, nonresident: full-time $7254; part-time $605 per credit hour. *Required fees:* $66 per credit hour. Tuition and fees vary according to campus/location. *Unit head:* Dr. Jerry Will, Chair, 620-341-5777, E-mail: jwill@emporia.edu. *Application contact:* Mary Sewell, Admissions Coordinator, 800-950-GRAD, Fax: 620-341-5909, E-mail: msewell@emporia.edu. Web site: http://www.emporia.edu/sleme/graduate-programs/instructional-leadership-masters-.html.

Evangel University, Department of Education, Springfield, MO 65802. Offers educational leadership (M Ed); reading education (M Ed); secondary teaching (M Ed); teaching (MA). *Accreditation:* NCATE. Part-time and evening/weekend programs available. *Faculty:* 4 full-time (1 woman), 2 part-time/adjunct (1 woman). *Students:* 10 full-time (5 women), 39 part-time (25 women). Average age 33. 14 applicants, 86% accepted, 11 enrolled. In 2011, 21 master's awarded. *Degree requirements:* For master's, comprehensive exam, thesis optional. *Entrance requirements:* For master's, PRAXIS II (preferred) or GRE. Additional exam requirements/recommendations for international students: Required—TOEFL (minimum score 550 paper-based; 213 computer-based). *Application deadline:* For fall admission, 7/15 priority date for domestic students; for spring admission, 11/15 priority date for domestic students. Applications are processed on a rolling basis. Application fee: $25. *Financial support:* In 2011–12, 3 students received support. Career-related internships or fieldwork, institutionally sponsored loans, and scholarships/grants available. Support available to part-time students. Financial award application deadline: 3/1; financial award applicants required to submit FAFSA. *Unit head:* Dr. Matt Stringer, Program Coordinator, 417-865-2815 Ext. 8563, E-mail: stringerm@evangel.edu. *Application contact:* Micah Hildreth, Admissions Representative, Graduate and Professional Studies, 417-865-2811 Ext. 7227, Fax: 417-865-9599, E-mail: hildrethm@evangel.edu. Web site: http://www.evangel.edu/departments/education/about-the-department/.

Fairleigh Dickinson University, College at Florham, University College: Arts, Sciences, and Professional Studies, Peter Sammartino School of Education, Program in Educational Leadership, Madison, NJ 07940-1099. Offers MA.

Fairleigh Dickinson University, Metropolitan Campus, University College: Arts, Sciences, and Professional Studies, Peter Sammartino School of Education, Program in Educational Leadership, Teaneck, NJ 07666-1914. Offers MA.

Fairmont State University, Programs in Education, Fairmont, WV 26554. Offers digital media, new literacies and learning (M Ed); education (MAT); exercise science, fitness and wellness (M Ed); leadership studies (M Ed); online learning (M Ed); professional studies (M Ed); reading (M Ed); special education (M Ed). *Accreditation:* NCATE. Part-time and evening/weekend programs available. Postbaccalaureate distance learning degree programs offered. *Faculty:* 16 part-time/adjunct (10 women). *Students:* 103 full-time (72 women), 142 part-time (103 women); includes 11 minority (2 Black or African American, non-Hispanic/Latino; 1 American Indian or Alaska Native, non-Hispanic/Latino; 6 Hispanic/Latino; 2 Two or more races, non-Hispanic/Latino), 2 international. Average age 33. 71 applicants, 85% accepted. In 2011, 58 master's awarded. *Entrance requirements:* For master's, GRE. *Application deadline:* For fall admission, 5/1 for domestic and international students. Applications are processed on a rolling basis. Application fee: $40. *Expenses:* Tuition, state resident: full-time $5900. Tuition, nonresident: full-time $12,596. *Unit head:* Dr. Van O. Dempsey, III, Dean, School of Education, 304-367-4241, Fax: 304-367-4599, E-mail: vdempsey@fairmontstate.edu. Web site: http://www.fairmontstate.edu/graduatestudies/default.asp.

Fayetteville State University, Graduate School, Programs in Educational Leadership and School Administration, Fayetteville, NC 28301-4298. Offers educational leadership (Ed D); school administration (MSA). *Accreditation:* NCATE (one or more programs are accredited). Part-time and evening/weekend programs available. *Faculty:* 7 full-time (4 women), 2 part-time/adjunct (1 woman). *Students:* 59 full-time (40 women), 28 part-time (22 women); includes 68 minority (61 Black or African American, non-Hispanic/Latino; 4 American Indian or Alaska Native, non-Hispanic/Latino; 2 Hispanic/Latino; 1 Two or more races, non-Hispanic/Latino). Average age 42. 51 applicants, 67% accepted, 34 enrolled. In 2011, 18 master's, 6 doctorates awarded. *Degree requirements:* For master's, internship, written and oral exams. *Entrance requirements:* For master's, GRE or MAT, minimum GPA of 2.5. *Application deadline:* For fall admission, 4/1 for domestic students. Applications are processed on a rolling basis. Application fee: $35. Electronic applications accepted. *Faculty research:* First-generation college students and academic successes, educational law and higher education, educational policy and K-12/higher education. *Total annual research expenditures:* $20,000. *Unit head:* 910-672-1731. *Application contact:* Katrina Hoffman, Graduate Admission Officer, 910-672-1374, Fax: 910-672-1470, E-mail: khoffma1@uncfsu.edu.

Felician College, Program in Education, Lodi, NJ 07644-2117. Offers education (MA); educational leadership (principal/supervision) (MA); educational supervision (PMC); principal (PMC); school nursing and health education (MA, Certificate). *Accreditation:* Teacher Education Accreditation Council. Part-time and evening/weekend programs available. *Students:* 12 full-time (9 women), 93 part-time (83 women); includes 15 minority (5 Black or African American, non-Hispanic/Latino; 1 Asian, non-Hispanic/Latino; 9 Hispanic/Latino), 3 international. Average age 37. 18 applicants, 50% accepted, 9 enrolled. *Degree requirements:* For master's, project. *Entrance requirements:* For master's, MAT, minimum GPA of 3.0, 3 letters of recommendation. Additional exam requirements/recommendations for international students: Recommended—TOEFL (minimum score 550 paper-based; 213 computer-based). *Application deadline:* Applications are processed on a rolling basis. Application fee: $40. *Expenses: Tuition:* Part-time $925 per credit. *Required fees:* $262.50 per semester. Part-time tuition and fees vary according to class time and student level. *Financial support:* Federal Work-Study available. *Unit head:* Dr. Rosemarie Liebmann, Associate Dean, 201-559-3537, E-mail: liebmannr@felician.edu. *Application contact:* Dr. Margaret Smolin, Associate Director, Graduate Admissions, 201-559-6077, Fax: 201-559-6138, E-mail: graduate@felician.edu.

See Display on page 702 and Close-Up on page 801.

Ferris State University, College of Education and Human Services, School of Education, Big Rapids, MI 49307. Offers administration (MSCTE); curriculum and instruction (M Ed), including administration, elementary education, experiential education, philanthropic education, reading, secondary education, special education, subject matter option; education technology (MSCTE); instructor (MSCTE); post-secondary administration (MSCTE); training and development (MSCTE). Part-time and evening/weekend programs available. Postbaccalaureate distance learning degree programs offered (minimal on-campus study). *Faculty:* 9 full-time (7 women), 9 part-time/adjunct (6 women). *Students:* 8 full-time (7 women), 132 part-time (75 women); includes 13 minority (11 Black or African American, non-Hispanic/Latino; 1 American Indian or Alaska Native, non-Hispanic/Latino; 1 Hispanic/Latino), 5 international. Average age 36. 20 applicants, 100% accepted, 8 enrolled. In 2011, 51 master's awarded. *Degree requirements:* For master's, thesis, research paper. *Entrance requirements:* For master's, 2 years of work experience for vocational setting, minimum GPA of 2.75. Additional exam requirements/recommendations for international students: Recommended—TOEFL (minimum score 500 paper-based; 173 computer-based; 61 iBT). *Application deadline:* For fall admission, 7/1 priority date for domestic students, 7/1 for international students; for spring admission, 11/1 priority date for domestic students, 11/1 for international students. Applications are processed on a rolling basis. Application fee: $30. Electronic applications accepted. Application fee is waived when completed online. *Financial support:* Career-related internships or fieldwork and scholarships/grants available. Support available to part-time students. Financial award applicants required to submit FAFSA. *Faculty research:* Suicide prevention, reading, women in education, special needs, administration. *Unit head:* Dr. James Powell, Director, 231-591-5362, Fax: 231-591-2043, E-mail: powelj20@ferris.edu. *Application contact:* Kimisue Worrall, Secretary, 231-591-5361, Fax: 231-591-2043. Web site: http://www.ferris.edu/education/education/.

Ferris State University, College of Professional and Technological Studies, Big Rapids, MI 49307. Offers community college leadership (Ed D). Evening/weekend programs available. Postbaccalaureate distance learning degree programs offered (minimal on-campus study). *Faculty:* 20 part-time/adjunct (11 women). *Students:* 41 part-time (27 women); includes 7 minority (6 Black or African American, non-Hispanic/Latino; 1 Hispanic/Latino). Average age 45. *Entrance requirements:* For doctorate, master's degree with minimum GPA of 3.25, fierce commitment to the mission of community colleges, essay, writing samples. *Application deadline:* For winter admission, 1/27 for domestic and international students; for spring admission, 4/15 for domestic and international students. Applications are processed on a rolling basis. Application fee: $30. Electronic applications accepted. Application fee is waived when completed online. *Financial support:* In 2011–12, 10 students received support. Applicants required to submit FAFSA. *Unit head:* Dr. Roberta Teahen, Director, 231-591-3805, E-mail: robertateahen@ferris.edu. *Application contact:* Andrea Wirgau, Coordinator, 231-591-2710, Fax: 231-591-3539, E-mail: andreawirgau@ferris.edu.

Fielding Graduate University, Graduate Programs, School of Educational Leadership and Change, Santa Barbara, CA 93105-3538. Offers collaborative educational leadership (MA); educational leadership and change (Ed D), including community college leadership and change, grounded theory/grounded action, leadership of higher education systems, media studies; teaching in the virtual classroom (Graduate Certificate). Postbaccalaureate distance learning degree programs offered (minimal on-campus study). *Faculty:* 15 full-time (8 women), 5 part-time/adjunct (3 women). *Students:* 201 full-time (141 women), 9 part-time (8 women); includes 108 minority (64 Black or African American, non-Hispanic/Latino; 6 American Indian or Alaska Native, non-Hispanic/Latino; 7 Asian, non-Hispanic/Latino; 21 Hispanic/Latino; 1 Native Hawaiian or other Pacific Islander, non-Hispanic/Latino; 9 Two or more races, non-Hispanic/Latino), 2 international. Average age 47. 27 applicants, 93% accepted, 19 enrolled. In 2011, 44 master's, 45 doctorates, 7 other advanced degrees awarded. *Degree requirements:* For master's, capstone research project; for doctorate, comprehensive exam, thesis/dissertation. *Entrance requirements:* For master's, minimum GPA of 2.5; for doctorate, resume, 2 letters of recommendation, writing sample. *Application deadline:* For fall admission, 6/10 for domestic and international students; for spring admission, 11/19 for domestic and international students. Application fee: $75. Electronic applications accepted. *Expenses:* Contact institution. *Financial support:* In 2011–12, 21 students received support. Scholarships/grants, health care benefits, and tuition waivers (partial) available. Support available to part-time students. Financial award applicants required to submit FAFSA. *Unit head:* Dr. Mario R. Borunda, Dean, 805-898-2940, E-mail: mborunda@fielding.edu. *Application contact:* Admission Counselor, 800-340-1099 Ext. 4098, Fax: 805-687-9793, E-mail: elcadmissions@fielding.edu. Web site: http://www.fielding.edu/programs/elc/default.aspx.

Fitchburg State University, Division of Graduate and Continuing Education, Program in Educational Leadership and Management, Fitchburg, MA 01420-2697. Offers educational technology (Certificate); higher education administration (CAGS); non-licensure (M Ed, CAGS); school principal (M Ed, CAGS); supervisor/director (M Ed, CAGS); technology leader (M Ed, CAGS). *Accreditation:* NCATE. Part-time and evening/weekend programs available. *Students:* 26 full-time (14 women), 49 part-time (22 women); includes 2 minority (1 Black or African American, non-Hispanic/Latino; 1 Hispanic/Latino). Average age 41. 10 applicants, 100% accepted, 9 enrolled. In 2011, 11 master's, 30 CAGSs awarded. *Entrance requirements:* Additional exam requirements/recommendations for international students: Required—TOEFL (minimum score 550 paper-based; 213 computer-based; 79 iBT). *Application deadline:* For fall admission, 7/15 for international students; for spring admission, 12/1 for international students. Applications are processed on a rolling basis. Application fee: $25 ($50 for international students). Electronic applications accepted. *Expenses:* Tuition, state resident: full-time $2700; part-time $150 per credit. Tuition, nonresident: full-time $2700; part-time $150 per credit. *Required fees:* $2286; $127 per credit. *Financial support:* In 2011–12, research assistantships with partial tuition reimbursements (averaging $5,500 per year) were awarded; Federal Work-Study, scholarships/grants, and unspecified assistantships also available. Support available to part-time students. Financial award application deadline: 3/1; financial award applicants required to submit FAFSA. *Unit head:* Dr. Randy Howe, Chair, 978-665-3544, Fax: 978-665-3658, E-mail: gce@fitchburgstate.edu. *Application contact:* Kay Reynolds, Director of Admissions, 978-665-3144, Fax: 978-665-4540, E-mail: admissions@fitchburgstate.edu. Web site: http://www.fitchburgstate.edu.

Florida Agricultural and Mechanical University, Division of Graduate Studies, Research, and Continuing Education, College of Education, Department of Educational Leadership and Human Services, Tallahassee, FL 32307-3200. Offers administration and supervision (M Ed, MS Ed, PhD); adult education (M Ed, MS Ed); educational leadership (PhD); guidance and counseling (M Ed, MS Ed). *Accreditation:* NCATE. *Degree requirements:* For master's, thesis (for some programs); for doctorate, thesis/dissertation. *Entrance requirements:* For master's, GRE General Test, minimum GPA of 3.0. Additional exam requirements/recommendations for international students: Required—TOEFL.

Florida Atlantic University, College of Education, Department of Educational Leadership and Research Methodology, Boca Raton, FL 33431-0991. Offers adult and community education (M Ed, PhD, Ed S); educational leadership (M Ed, PhD, Ed S); higher education (M Ed, PhD); K-12 school leadership (M Ed, PhD, Ed S). *Accreditation:* NCATE. Part-time and evening/weekend programs available. Postbaccalaureate distance learning degree programs offered (minimal on-campus study). *Faculty:* 20 full-time (11 women), 17 part-time/adjunct (7 women). *Students:* 100 full-time (75 women), 245 part-time (173 women); includes 126 minority (59 Black or African American, non-Hispanic/Latino; 15 Asian, non-Hispanic/Latino; 47 Hispanic/Latino; 5 Two or more races, non-Hispanic/Latino), 4 international. Average age 36. 253 applicants, 47% accepted, 66 enrolled. In 2011, 122 master's, 11 doctorates awarded. *Degree requirements:* For doctorate, comprehensive exam, thesis/dissertation, departmental qualifying exam; for Ed S, departmental qualifying exam. *Entrance requirements:* For master's, GRE General Test, minimum GPA of 3.0 during previous 2 years; for doctorate, GRE General Test, minimum GPA of 3.5; for Ed S, GRE General Test. *Application deadline:* For fall admission, 7/1 for domestic students, 2/15 for international students; for spring admission, 9/15 for domestic students, 7/15 for international students. Applications are processed on a rolling basis. Application fee: $30. Electronic applications accepted. *Expenses: Tuition, area resident:* Part-time $343.02 per credit hour. Tuition, state resident: full-time $8232. Tuition, nonresident: full-time $23,931; part-time $997.14 per credit hour. *Financial support:* Fellowships, research assistantships, teaching assistantships, career-related internships or fieldwork, and tuition waivers (partial) available. *Faculty research:* Self-directed learning, school reform issues, legal issues, mentoring, school leadership. *Unit head:* Dr. Robert Shockley, Chair, 561-297-3550, Fax: 561-297-3618, E-mail: shockley@fau.edu. *Application contact:* Catherine Politi, Senior Secretary, 561-297-3550, Fax: 561-297-3618, E-mail: edleadership@fau.edu. Web site: http://www.coe.fau.edu/academicdepartments/el/.

Florida Gulf Coast University, College of Education, Program in Educational Leadership, Fort Myers, FL 33965-6565. Offers M Ed, MA, Ed D, Ed S. Part-time and evening/weekend programs available. *Faculty:* 34 full-time (26 women), 57 part-time/adjunct (40 women). *Students:* 45 full-time (33 women), 17 part-time (15 women); includes 10 minority (3 Black or African American, non-Hispanic/Latino; 2 Asian, non-Hispanic/Latino; 4 Hispanic/Latino; 1 Two or more races, non-Hispanic/Latino). Average age 33. 29 applicants, 97% accepted, 24 enrolled. In 2011, 21 master's awarded. *Degree requirements:* For master's, thesis or alternative, learning and professional portfolios. *Entrance requirements:* For master's, GRE General Test, MAT, minimum GPA of 3.0. Additional exam requirements/recommendations for international students: Required—TOEFL (minimum score 550 paper-based; 213 computer-based). *Application deadline:* For fall admission, 7/1 priority date for domestic students; for spring admission, 10/15 for domestic students. Applications are processed on a rolling basis. Application fee: $30. Electronic applications accepted. *Expenses:* Tuition, state resident: full-time $8289. Tuition, nonresident: full-time $28,895. *Required fees:* $1831. One-time fee: $30 full-time. *Faculty research:* Inclusion, technology in teaching, curriculum development in educational leadership, education policy and law. *Unit head:* Dr. Robert Kenny, Department Chair, 239-590-1147, Fax: 239-590-7801, E-mail: rkenny@fgcu.edu. *Application contact:* Keiana Desmore, Adviser/Counselor, 239-590-7759, Fax: 239-590-7801, E-mail: kdesmore@fgcu.edu.

Florida International University, College of Education, Department of Educational Leadership and Policy Studies, Miami, FL 33199. Offers adult education (MS); adult education in human resource development (Ed D); clinical mental health counseling (MS); conflict resolution and consensus building (Certificate); counselor education (MS); educational administration and supervision (Ed D); educational leadership (MS, Certificate, Ed S); higher education (Ed D); higher education administration (MS); human resource development (MS); instruction in urban settings (MS); international/intercultural education (MS); learning technologies (MS); multicultural-bilingual (MS); multicultural-TESOL (MS); recreation and sport management (MS); recreation therapy (MS); rehabilitation counseling (MS); school counseling (MS); school psychology (Ed S); urban education (MS). Part-time and evening/weekend programs available. *Degree requirements:* For doctorate, thesis/dissertation. *Entrance requirements:* For master's, minimum GPA of 3.0; for doctorate and other advanced degree, GRE General Test. Additional exam requirements/recommendations for international students: Required—TOEFL (minimum score 550 paper-based; 213 computer-based; 80 iBT), IELTS (minimum score 6.3). Electronic applications accepted.

Florida State University, The Graduate School, College of Education, Department of Educational Leadership and Policy Studies, Program in Educational Leadership/Administration, Tallahassee, FL 32306. Offers MS, Ed D, PhD, Ed S. Part-time and evening/weekend programs available. *Faculty:* 10 full-time (9 women). *Students:* 28 full-time (18 women), 115 part-time (75 women); includes 42 minority (30 Black or African

American, non-Hispanic/Latino; 1 American Indian or Alaska Native, non-Hispanic/Latino; 11 Hispanic/Latino), 7 international. Average age 36. 77 applicants, 51% accepted, 24 enrolled. In 2011, 23 master's, 1 doctorate, 11 other advanced degrees awarded. Terminal master's awarded for partial completion of doctoral program. *Degree requirements:* For master's and Ed S, comprehensive exam, thesis optional; for doctorate, comprehensive exam, thesis/dissertation. *Entrance requirements:* For master's, GRE General Test, minimum GPA of 3.0; for doctorate and Ed S, GRE General Test, minimum graduate GPA of 3.0. Additional exam requirements/recommendations for international students: Required—TOEFL (minimum score 550 paper-based; 213 computer-based; 80 iBT). *Application deadline:* For fall admission, 7/1 for domestic and international students; for winter admission, 11/1 for domestic and international students; for spring admission, 3/1 for domestic and international students. Application fee: $30. Electronic applications accepted. *Expenses:* Tuition, state resident: full-time $9474; part-time $350.88 per credit hour. Tuition, nonresident: full-time $16,236; part-time $601.34 per credit hour. *Required fees:* $630 per semester. One-time fee: $20. Tuition and fees vary according to course load and campus/location. *Financial support:* Fellowships with full and partial tuition reimbursements, research assistantships with full and partial tuition reimbursements, teaching assistantships with full and partial tuition reimbursements, career-related internships or fieldwork, scholarships/grants, health care benefits, and unspecified assistantships available. Financial award application deadline: 1/15; financial award applicants required to submit FAFSA. *Faculty research:* Issues in higher education law; diversity, equity, and social justice; educational issues in Western and Non-Western countries. *Unit head:* Dr. Judith Irvin, Program Coordinator, 850-644-6777, Fax: 850-644-1258, E-mail: jirvin@fsu.edu. *Application contact:* Jimmy Pastrano, Program Assistant, 850-644-6777, Fax: 850-644-1258, E-mail: jpastrano@fsu.edu. Web site: http://www.coe.fsu.edu/Academic-Programs/Departments/Educational-Leadership-and-Policy-Studies-ELPS/Academic-Programs/Degree-Programs/Educational-Lead.

Fordham University, Graduate School of Education, Division of Educational Leadership, Administration and Policy, New York, NY 10023. Offers administration and supervision (MSE, Adv C); administration and supervision for church leaders (PhD); educational administration and supervision (Ed D, PhD); human resource program administration (MS). *Accreditation:* NCATE. *Degree requirements:* For doctorate, thesis/dissertation. *Entrance requirements:* For doctorate, MAT, GRE General Test. *Expenses: Tuition:* Full-time $30,480; part-time $1270 per credit. *Required fees:* $586; $293 per semester.

Fort Hays State University, Graduate School, College of Education and Technology, Department of Educational Administration and Counseling, Program in Educational Administration, Hays, KS 67601-4099. Offers MS, Ed S. *Accreditation:* NCATE. *Degree requirements:* For master's and Ed S, comprehensive exam, thesis or alternative. *Entrance requirements:* For master's, GRE General Test or MAT. Additional exam requirements/recommendations for international students: Required—TOEFL (minimum score 550 paper-based; 213 computer-based). Electronic applications accepted. *Faculty research:* Guide to negotiations, nutrition program for disadvantaged, accountability, student insurance practices, student liability.

Framingham State University, Division of Graduate and Continuing Education, Program in Educational Leadership, Framingham, MA 01701-9101. Offers MA. Part-time and evening/weekend programs available. *Entrance requirements:* For master's, MAT.

Franciscan University of Steubenville, Graduate Programs, Department of Education, Steubenville, OH 43952-1763. Offers administration (MS Ed); teaching (MS Ed). Part-time and evening/weekend programs available. *Degree requirements:* For master's, project. *Entrance requirements:* For master's, minimum undergraduate GPA of 2.5 or written exam. *Expenses:* Contact institution.

Freed-Hardeman University, Program in Education, Henderson, TN 38340-2399. Offers curriculum and instruction (M Ed); school counseling (M Ed), including administration and supervision, special education; school leadership (Ed S). *Accreditation:* NCATE. Part-time and evening/weekend programs available. *Degree requirements:* For master's, comprehensive exam, thesis optional; for Ed S, thesis. *Entrance requirements:* For master's, GRE General Test or NTE; for Ed S, 3 years of teaching experience. Additional exam requirements/recommendations for international students: Required—TOEFL (minimum score 500 paper-based; 173 computer-based).

Fresno Pacific University, Graduate Programs, School of Education, Division of Administration, Fresno, CA 93702-4709. Offers administrative services (MA Ed). Part-time and evening/weekend programs available. *Degree requirements:* For master's, thesis or alternative, 4 practica. *Entrance requirements:* Additional exam requirements/recommendations for international students: Required—TOEFL (minimum score 550 paper-based; 213 computer-based). Electronic applications accepted.

Frostburg State University, Graduate School, College of Education, Department of Educational Professions, Program in Educational Administration and Supervision, Frostburg, MD 21532-1099. Offers elementary (M Ed); secondary (M Ed). Part-time and evening/weekend programs available. *Degree requirements:* For master's, thesis or alternative. *Entrance requirements:* For master's, teaching certificate. Additional exam requirements/recommendations for international students: Required—TOEFL. Electronic applications accepted. *Faculty research:* Practicum experience in schools.

Furman University, Graduate Division, Department of Education, Greenville, SC 29613. Offers curriculum and instruction (MA); early childhood education (MA); educational leadership (Ed S); English as a second language (MA); literacy (MA); school leadership (MA); special education (MA). *Accreditation:* NCATE. Part-time programs available. Postbaccalaureate distance learning degree programs offered (minimal on-campus study). *Faculty:* 14 full-time (8 women), 6 part-time/adjunct (4 women). *Students:* 237 part-time (188 women); includes 27 minority (22 Black or African American, non-Hispanic/Latino; 1 Asian, non-Hispanic/Latino; 3 Hispanic/Latino; 1 Native Hawaiian or other Pacific Islander, non-Hispanic/Latino). Average age 29. 97 applicants, 100% accepted, 90 enrolled. In 2011, 34 master's awarded. *Degree requirements:* For master's, comprehensive exam (for some programs), thesis or alternative. *Entrance requirements:* For master's, PRAXIS II. *Application deadline:* For fall admission, 8/1 priority date for domestic students, 7/15 for international students; for spring admission, 12/1 priority date for domestic students, 12/1 for international students. Applications are processed on a rolling basis. Application fee: $50. *Financial support:* Scholarships/grants available. Financial award application deadline: 5/15; financial award applicants required to submit FAFSA. *Faculty research:* Literacy, pedagogy and practice, social justice, advanced leadership, achievement in high poverty schools. *Unit head:* Dr. Nelly Hecker, Head, 864-294-3385. *Application contact:* Helen Reynolds, Department Assistant, 864-294-2213, Fax: 864-294-3579, E-mail: helen.reynolds@furman.edu. Web site: http://www.furman.edu/gradstudies/.

Gannon University, School of Graduate Studies, College of Humanities, Education, and Social Sciences, School of Education, Program in Educational Leadership, Erie, PA 16541-0001. Offers M Ed. Part-time and evening/weekend programs available. *Students:* 2 applicants, 50% accepted, 0 enrolled. In 2011, 3 master's awarded. *Entrance requirements:* For master's, bachelor's degree, minimum GPA of 3.0, letters of recommendation. Additional exam requirements/recommendations for international students: Required—TOEFL (minimum score 79 iBT). *Application deadline:* Applications are processed on a rolling basis. Application fee: $25. Electronic applications accepted. *Expenses:* Contact institution. *Financial support:* Application deadline: 7/1; applicants required to submit FAFSA. *Faculty research:* English, natural sciences, environmental education. *Unit head:* Dr. Kathleen Kingston, Director, 814-871-5626, E-mail: kingston002@gannon.edu. *Application contact:* Kara Morgan, Director of Graduate Admissions, 814-871-5831, Fax: 814-871-5827, E-mail: graduate@gannon.edu.

Gannon University, School of Graduate Studies, College of Humanities, Education, and Social Sciences, School of Education, Program in Principal Certification, Erie, PA 16541-0001. Offers Certificate. Part-time and evening/weekend programs available. Postbaccalaureate distance learning degree programs offered (no on-campus study). *Students:* 24 part-time (16 women). Average age 33. 32 applicants, 97% accepted, 20 enrolled. *Entrance requirements:* For degree, master's degree, minimum GPA of 3.0, educational certification, 3 letters of recommendation. Additional exam requirements/recommendations for international students: Required—TOEFL (minimum score 79 iBT). *Application deadline:* Applications are processed on a rolling basis. Application fee: $25. Electronic applications accepted. *Expenses:* Contact institution. *Financial support:* Scholarships/grants available. Financial award application deadline: 7/1; financial award applicants required to submit FAFSA. *Faculty research:* Community engagement, teaching the skills and processes of reflection, re-conceptualizing the preparation of instructional leaders. *Unit head:* Dr. Kathleen Kingston, Director, 814-871-5626, E-mail: kingston002@gannon.edu. *Application contact:* Kara Morgan, Director of Graduate Admissions, 814-871-5831, Fax: 814-871-5827, E-mail: graduate@gannon.edu.

Gannon University, School of Graduate Studies, College of Humanities, Education, and Social Sciences, School of Education, Program in Superintendent Letter of Eligibility Certification, Erie, PA 16541-0001. Offers Certificate. Part-time and evening/weekend programs available. Postbaccalaureate distance learning degree programs offered (no on-campus study). *Students:* 18 part-time (5 women); includes 2 minority (1 Black or African American, non-Hispanic/Latino; 1 Native Hawaiian or other Pacific Islander, non-Hispanic/Latino). Average age 41. 21 applicants, 86% accepted, 14 enrolled. *Degree requirements:* For Certificate, thesis or alternative, superintendent internship, portfolio. *Entrance requirements:* For degree, master's degree; minimum GPA of 3.0; 6 years of educational experience, 3 under administrative or supervisory certificate, letters of recommendation. Additional exam requirements/recommendations for international students: Required—TOEFL (minimum score 79 iBT). *Application deadline:* Applications are processed on a rolling basis. Application fee: $25. Electronic applications accepted. *Expenses:* Contact institution. *Financial support:* Scholarships/grants available. Financial award application deadline: 7/1; financial award applicants required to submit FAFSA. *Faculty research:* Community engagement, teaching the skills and processes of reflection, re-conceptualizing the preparation of instructional leaders. *Unit head:* Dr. Kathleen Kingston, Director, 814-871-5626, E-mail: kingston002@gannon.edu. *Application contact:* Kara Morgan, Director of Graduate Admission, 814-871-5831, Fax: 814-871-5827, E-mail: graduate@gannon.edu.

Gannon University, School of Graduate Studies, College of Humanities, Education, and Social Sciences, School of Humanities, Program in Organizational Learning and Leadership, Erie, PA 16541-0001. Offers PhD. Part-time and evening/weekend programs available. *Students:* 2 full-time (1 woman), 59 part-time (33 women); includes 2 minority (both Black or African American, non-Hispanic/Latino). Average age 42. 41 applicants, 68% accepted, 20 enrolled. In 2011, 1 doctorate awarded. *Degree requirements:* For doctorate, thesis/dissertation. *Entrance requirements:* For doctorate, GRE (verbal, quantitative and written sections taken within the last 3 years), minimum graduate GPA of 3.5, 2 years post-baccalaureate work experience, letters of recommendation, statement of purpose. Additional exam requirements/recommendations for international students: Required—TOEFL (minimum score 79 iBT). *Application deadline:* For spring admission, 2/1 for domestic students. Application fee: $50. Electronic applications accepted. *Financial support:* Scholarships/grants and unspecified assistantships available. Financial award applicants required to submit FAFSA. *Unit head:* Dr. David B. Barker, Director, 814-871-7700, E-mail: barker002@gannon.edu. *Application contact:* Kara Morgan, Director of Graduate Admissions, 814-871-5831, Fax: 814-871-5827, E-mail: graduate@gannon.edu.

Gardner-Webb University, Graduate School, School of Education, Program in Educational Leadership, Boiling Springs, NC 28017. Offers Ed D. *Faculty:* 10 full-time (4 women), 20 part-time/adjunct (7 women). *Students:* 95 part-time (48 women); includes 34 minority (33 Black or African American, non-Hispanic/Latino; 1 Asian, non-Hispanic/Latino). Average age 40. In 2011, 7 doctorates awarded. *Expenses: Tuition:* Full-time $6300; part-time $350 per credit hour. *Unit head:* Dr. Alan D. Eury, Chair, 704-406-4402, Fax: 704-406-3921, E-mail: dsimmons@gardner-webb.edu. *Application contact:* Office of Graduate Admissions, 877-498-4723, Fax: 704-406-3895, E-mail: gradinfo@gardner-webb.edu.

Gardner-Webb University, Graduate School, School of Education, Program in School Administration, Boiling Springs, NC 28017. Offers MA. *Students:* 3 full-time (2 women), 124 part-time (90 women); includes 59 minority (58 Black or African American, non-Hispanic/Latino; 1 Asian, non-Hispanic/Latino). Average age 37. *Expenses: Tuition:* Full-time $6300; part-time $350 per credit hour. *Application contact:* Office of Graduate Admissions, 877-498-4723, Fax: 704-406-3895, E-mail: gradinfo@gardner-webb.edu.

Gardner-Webb University, Graduate School, School of Education, Program in School Administration, Boiling Springs, NC 28017. Offers MA. *Accreditation:* NCATE. Part-time and evening/weekend programs available. *Faculty:* 10 full-time (4 women), 20 part-time/adjunct (7 women). *Students:* 3 full-time (1 woman), 358 part-time (252 women); includes 95 minority (85 Black or African American, non-Hispanic/Latino; 3 American Indian or Alaska Native, non-Hispanic/Latino; 3 Asian, non-Hispanic/Latino; 4 Hispanic/Latino). Average age 37. In 2011, 80 master's awarded. *Degree requirements:* For master's, comprehensive exam. *Entrance requirements:* For master's, GRE General Test or NTE, PRAXIS, minimum GPA of 2.5. *Application deadline:* For fall admission, 8/1 priority date for domestic students. Applications are processed on a rolling basis. Application fee: $40. Electronic applications accepted. *Expenses: Tuition:* Full-time $6300; part-time $350 per credit hour. *Financial support:* Unspecified assistantships available. *Unit head:* Dr. Alan D. Eury, Dean of the School of Education, 704-406-4402. *Application contact:* Office of Graduate Admissions, 877-498-4723, Fax: 704-406-3895, E-mail: gradinfo@gardner-webb.edu.

Geneva College, Master of Arts in Higher Education Program, Beaver Falls, PA 15010-3599. Offers campus ministry (MA); college teaching (MA); educational leadership (MA); student affairs administration (MA). Part-time and evening/weekend programs available. Postbaccalaureate distance learning degree programs offered (minimal on-campus study). *Faculty:* 1 full-time (0 women), 4 part-time/adjunct (0 women). *Students:* 30 full-time (13 women), 34 part-time (21 women); includes 5 minority (3 Black or African American, non-Hispanic/Latino; 1 Native Hawaiian or other Pacific Islander, non-Hispanic/Latino; 1 Two or more races, non-Hispanic/Latino). Average age 25. 39 applicants, 90% accepted, 24 enrolled. In 2011, 23 master's awarded. *Degree requirements:* For master's, 36 hours (27 in core courses) including a capstone research project. *Entrance requirements:* For master's, minimum GPA of 3.0, writing sample, 3 letters of recommendation, essay on motivation for participation in the HED program. Additional exam requirements/recommendations for international students: Required—

TOEFL. *Application deadline:* For fall admission, 9/1 priority date for domestic students; for winter admission, 1/2 priority date for domestic students; for spring admission, 3/11 priority date for domestic students. Applications are processed on a rolling basis. Electronic applications accepted. *Expenses: Tuition:* Part-time $625 per credit hour. Tuition and fees vary according to program. *Financial support:* In 2011–12, 45 students received support. Unspecified assistantships available. Financial award application deadline: 8/1; financial award applicants required to submit FAFSA. *Faculty research:* Student development, learning theories, church-related higher education, assessment, organizational culture. *Unit head:* Dr. David Guthrie, Program Director, 724-847-5565, Fax: 724-847-6107, E-mail: hed@geneva.edu. *Application contact:* Jerryn S. Carson, Program Coordinator, 724-847-6510, Fax: 724-847-6696, E-mail: hed@geneva.edu. Web site: http://www.geneva.edu/.

George Fox University, School of Education, Educational Foundations and Leadership Program, Newberg, OR 97132-2697. Offers continuing administrator license (Certificate); curriculum and instruction (M Ed); educational leadership (M Ed, Ed D); ESOL (Certificate); higher education (M Ed); initial administrator license (Certificate); instructional leadership (Ed S); library media (M Ed, Certificate); literacy (M Ed); reading (M Ed); secondary education (M Ed). *Accreditation:* NCATE. Part-time and evening/weekend programs available. Postbaccalaureate distance learning degree programs offered (minimal on-campus study). *Faculty:* 10 full-time (3 women), 6 part-time/adjunct (3 women). *Students:* 2 full-time (both women), 111 part-time (83 women); includes 16 minority (2 American Indian or Alaska Native, non-Hispanic/Latino; 6 Asian, non-Hispanic/Latino; 7 Hispanic/Latino; 1 Native Hawaiian or other Pacific Islander, non-Hispanic/Latino), 3 international. Average age 39. 44 applicants, 98% accepted, 43 enrolled. In 2011, 34 master's, 7 doctorates, 76 Certificates awarded. *Degree requirements:* For master's, thesis (for some programs); for doctorate, comprehensive exam, thesis/dissertation, project. *Entrance requirements:* For master's, minimum undergraduate GPA of 3.0 during previous 2 years of course work, resume, 3 professional recommendations on university forms, official transcripts; for doctorate, GRE, master's degree with minimum GPA of 3.25, 3 years of relevant professional experience, interview, personal essay, scholarly work, 3 professional recommendations on university forms along with 3 written letters of recommendation, official transcripts. Additional exam requirements/recommendations for international students: Required—TOEFL (minimum score 577 paper-based; 233 computer-based; 90 iBT). *Application deadline:* For fall admission, 7/15 for domestic and international students; for winter admission, 11/1 for domestic and international students; for spring admission, 4/1 for domestic and international students. Applications are processed on a rolling basis. Application fee: $40. Electronic applications accepted. *Expenses:* Contact institution. *Financial support:* Career-related internships or fieldwork available. Financial award applicants required to submit FAFSA. *Unit head:* Dr. Scot Headley, Professor/Chair, 503-554-2836, E-mail: sheadley@georgefox.edu. *Application contact:* Alex Martin, Admissions Counselor, 800-631-0921, Fax: 503-554-3110, E-mail: amartin@georgefox.edu. Web site: http://www.georgefox.edu/education/index.html.

George Mason University, College of Education and Human Development, Program in Education Leadership, Fairfax, VA 22030. Offers M Ed. *Accreditation:* NCATE. *Faculty:* 7 full-time (3 women), 14 part-time/adjunct (8 women). *Students:* 6 full-time (4 women), 308 part-time (222 women); includes 60 minority (35 Black or African American, non-Hispanic/Latino; 1 American Indian or Alaska Native, non-Hispanic/Latino; 5 Asian, non-Hispanic/Latino; 16 Hispanic/Latino; 3 Two or more races, non-Hispanic/Latino), 2 international. Average age 36. 193 applicants, 82% accepted, 130 enrolled. In 2011, 141 degrees awarded. *Entrance requirements:* For master's, bachelor's degree from regionally-accredited institution with minimum GPA of 3.0 overall or in last 60 credit hours; 2 official transcripts; expanded goals statement; 3 letters of recommendation; 3 years of documented teaching experience. Additional exam requirements/recommendations for international students: Required—TOEFL (minimum score 570 paper-based; 230 computer-based; 88 iBT), IELTS, Pearson Test of English. *Application deadline:* For fall admission, 4/1 priority date for domestic students; for spring admission, 11/1 for domestic students. Applications are processed on a rolling basis. Application fee: $65 ($80 for international students). Electronic applications accepted. *Expenses:* Tuition, state resident: full-time $8750; part-time $364.58 per credit. Tuition, nonresident: full-time $24,092; part-time $1003.83 per credit. *Required fees:* $2514; $104.75 per credit. *Financial support:* Career-related internships or fieldwork, Federal Work-Study, scholarships/grants, unspecified assistantships, and health care benefits (full-time research or teaching assistantship recipients) available. Financial award application deadline: 3/1; financial award applicants required to submit FAFSA. *Faculty research:* Understanding of the complexities of change in schools, communities, and organizations; education law; foundations of education leadership, history and leadership. *Unit head:* Dr. David Brazer, Associate Professor, 703-993-3634, Fax: 703-993-2013, E-mail: sbrazer@gmu.edu. *Application contact:* Farnoosh Shahrokhi, Outreach and Administrative Coordinator, 703-993-2009, Fax: 703-993-3643, E-mail: fsharhrok@gmu.edu. Web site: http://gse.gmu.edu/programs/edleadership/.

The George Washington University, Graduate School of Education and Human Development, Department of Educational Leadership, Program in Educational Administration and Policy Studies, Washington, DC 20052. Offers education policy (Ed D); educational administration (Ed D). Educational administration program offered at Newport News and Alexandria, VA. *Accreditation:* NCATE. *Students:* 9 full-time (7 women), 155 part-time (108 women); includes 57 minority (44 Black or African American, non-Hispanic/Latino; 8 Asian, non-Hispanic/Latino; 5 Hispanic/Latino), 4 international. Average age 40. 46 applicants, 50% accepted. In 2011, 15 doctorates awarded. *Degree requirements:* For doctorate, comprehensive exam, thesis/dissertation. *Entrance requirements:* For doctorate, GRE General Test or MAT, interview, minimum GPA of 3.3. *Application deadline:* For fall admission, 1/15 priority date for domestic students; for spring admission, 10/1 for domestic students. Applications are processed on a rolling basis. Application fee: $75. *Financial support:* In 2011–12, 9 students received support. Fellowships, research assistantships, teaching assistantships, career-related internships or fieldwork, Federal Work-Study, and tuition waivers (partial) available. Financial award application deadline: 1/15; financial award applicants required to submit FAFSA. *Unit head:* Prof. Yas Nakib, Program Coordinator, 202-994-8816, E-mail: nakib@gwu.edu. *Application contact:* Sarah Lang, 202-994-1447, Fax: 202-994-7207, E-mail: slang@gwu.edu.

The George Washington University, Graduate School of Education and Human Development, Department of Educational Leadership, Program in Educational Leadership and Administration, Washington, DC 20052. Offers MA Ed, Certificate, Ed S. Programs offered at Newport News and Alexandria, VA. *Accreditation:* NCATE. Evening/weekend programs available. *Students:* 15 full-time (9 women), 148 part-time (102 women); includes 65 minority (50 Black or African American, non-Hispanic/Latino; 1 American Indian or Alaska Native, non-Hispanic/Latino; 3 Asian, non-Hispanic/Latino; 9 Hispanic/Latino; 1 Native Hawaiian or other Pacific Islander, non-Hispanic/Latino; 1 Two or more races, non-Hispanic/Latino). Average age 36. 128 applicants, 94% accepted. In 2011, 45 master's, 26 Certificates awarded. *Degree requirements:* For master's, comprehensive exam. *Entrance requirements:* For master's, GRE General Test or MAT, interview, minimum GPA of 2.75. *Application deadline:* For fall admission, 1/15 priority date for domestic students; for spring admission, 10/1 for domestic students. Applications are processed on a rolling basis. Application fee: $75. *Financial support:* Fellowships, teaching assistantships, career-related internships or fieldwork, and Federal Work-Study available. Financial award application deadline: 1/15; financial award applicants required to submit FAFSA. *Faculty research:* Organizational learning. *Unit head:* Dr. Linda K. Lemasters, Director, 757-269-2218, E-mail: lindal@gwu.edu. *Application contact:* Sarah Lang, Director of Graduate Admissions, 202-994-1447, Fax: 202-994-7207, E-mail: slang@gwu.edu.

The George Washington University, Graduate School of Education and Human Development, Department of Educational Leadership, Program in Higher Education Administration, Washington, DC 20052. Offers MA Ed, Ed D, Ed S. *Accreditation:* NCATE. *Students:* 19 full-time (11 women), 115 part-time (69 women); includes 48 minority (31 Black or African American, non-Hispanic/Latino; 5 Asian, non-Hispanic/Latino; 8 Hispanic/Latino; 4 Two or more races, non-Hispanic/Latino). Average age 34. 163 applicants, 78% accepted. In 2011, 22 master's, 9 doctorates, 2 other advanced degrees awarded. *Degree requirements:* For master's and Ed S, comprehensive exam; for doctorate, comprehensive exam, thesis/dissertation. *Entrance requirements:* For master's, GRE General Test or MAT, minimum GPA of 2.75; for doctorate, GRE General Test or MAT, interview, minimum GPA of 3.3; for Ed S, GRE General Test or MAT, minimum GPA of 3.3. *Application deadline:* For fall admission, 1/15 priority date for domestic students; for spring admission, 10/1 for domestic students. Applications are processed on a rolling basis. Application fee: $75. *Financial support:* In 2011–12, 17 students received support. Fellowships, research assistantships, career-related internships or fieldwork, Federal Work-Study, and tuition waivers (partial) available. Financial award application deadline: 1/15; financial award applicants required to submit FAFSA. *Faculty research:* Technology in higher education administration. *Unit head:* Virginia Roach, Chair, 202-994-3094, E-mail: vroach@gwu.edu. *Application contact:* Sarah Lang, Director of Graduate Admissions, 202-994-1447, Fax: 202-994-7207, E-mail: slang@gwu.edu.

The George Washington University, Graduate School of Education and Human Development, Department of Educational Leadership, Program in Leadership in Educational Technology, Washington, DC 20052. Offers Graduate Certificate.

Georgia College & State University, Graduate School, The John H. Lounsbury College of Education, Department of Special Education and Educational Leadership, Program in Educational Leadership, Milledgeville, GA 31061. Offers M Ed, Ed S. *Accreditation:* NCATE. Part-time and evening/weekend programs available. *Students:* 59 full-time (38 women), 3 part-time (all women); includes 26 minority (25 Black or African American, non-Hispanic/Latino; 1 Hispanic/Latino). Average age 37. 57 applicants, 63% accepted, 35 enrolled. In 2011, 15 master's, 21 Ed Ss awarded. *Entrance requirements:* For master's, on-site writing assessment, 2 recommendations, level 4 teaching certificate, transcripts. Additional exam requirements/recommendations for international students: Required—TOEFL (minimum score 550 paper-based; 213 computer-based; 79 iBT). *Application deadline:* For fall admission, 7/1 priority date for domestic students; for spring admission, 11/15 priority date for domestic students. Application fee: $40. Electronic applications accepted. *Expenses:* Tuition, state resident: full-time $4806; part-time $267 per credit hour. Tuition, nonresident: full-time $17,802; part-time $989 per credit hour. *Required fees:* $936 per semester. Tuition and fees vary according to course load and campus/location. *Financial support:* In 2011–12, 1 teaching assistantship with full tuition reimbursement was awarded. *Unit head:* Dr. Craig Smith, Chair, Special Education and Educational Leadership, 478-445-4577, E-mail: craig.smith@gcsu.edu. *Application contact:* Shanda Brand, Graduate Admission Coordinator, 478-445-1383.

Georgian Court University, School of Arts and Sciences, Lakewood, NJ 08701-2697. Offers biology (MA); Catholic school leadership (Certificate); clinical mental health counseling (MA); holistic health studies (MA); mathematics (MA); pastoral ministry (Certificate); religious education (Certificate); school psychology (Certificate); theology (MA, Certificate). Part-time and evening/weekend programs available. *Faculty:* 21 full-time (10 women), 6 part-time/adjunct (5 women). *Students:* 88 full-time (84 women), 126 part-time (107 women); includes 29 minority (11 Black or African American, non-Hispanic/Latino; 5 Asian, non-Hispanic/Latino; 12 Hispanic/Latino; 1 Two or more races, non-Hispanic/Latino), 1 international. Average age 39. 210 applicants, 54% accepted, 79 enrolled. In 2011, 5 master's awarded. *Degree requirements:* For master's, comprehensive exam (for some programs), thesis (for some programs). *Entrance requirements:* For master's, GRE, MAT, or NTE/PRAXIS, 3 letters of recommendation. Additional exam requirements/recommendations for international students: Required—TOEFL (minimum score 550 paper-based; 213 computer-based). *Application deadline:* For fall admission, 8/1 priority date for domestic students, 4/1 for international students; for spring admission, 1/1 priority date for domestic students, 7/1 for international students. Applications are processed on a rolling basis. Application fee: $40. Electronic applications accepted. *Expenses: Tuition:* Full-time $13,410; part-time $745 per credit. *Required fees:* $450 per year. Tuition and fees vary according to campus/location and program. *Financial support:* Scholarships/grants, health care benefits, and unspecified assistantships available. Financial award application deadline: 4/15; financial award applicants required to submit FAFSA. *Unit head:* Dr. Rita Kipp, Dean, 732-987-2493, Fax: 732-987-2007. *Application contact:* Patrick Givens, Assistant Director of Graduate Admissions, 732-987-2736, Fax: 732-987-2084, E-mail: graduateadmissions@georgian.edu. Web site: http://www.georgian.edu/arts_sciences/index.htm.

Georgian Court University, School of Education, Lakewood, NJ 08701-2697. Offers administration and leadership (MA); education (MA). *Accreditation:* Teacher Education Accreditation Council. Part-time and evening/weekend programs available. *Faculty:* 23 full-time (15 women), 25 part-time/adjunct (16 women). *Students:* 107 full-time (80 women), 365 part-time (321 women); includes 51 minority (8 Black or African American, non-Hispanic/Latino; 2 American Indian or Alaska Native, non-Hispanic/Latino; 2 Asian, non-Hispanic/Latino; 34 Hispanic/Latino; 1 Native Hawaiian or other Pacific Islander, non-Hispanic/Latino; 4 Two or more races, non-Hispanic/Latino). Average age 32. 537 applicants, 68% accepted, 197 enrolled. In 2011, 118 master's awarded. *Degree requirements:* For master's, comprehensive exam (for some programs), thesis (for some programs). *Entrance requirements:* For master's, GRE, MAT or NTE/PRAXIS, 3 letters of recommendation. Additional exam requirements/recommendations for international students: Required—TOEFL (minimum score 550 paper-based; 213 computer-based). *Application deadline:* For fall admission, 8/1 priority date for domestic students, 4/1 for international students; for spring admission, 1/1 priority date for domestic students, 7/1 for international students. Applications are processed on a rolling basis. Application fee: $40. Electronic applications accepted. *Expenses: Tuition:* Full-time $13,410; part-time $745 per credit. *Required fees:* $450 per year. Tuition and fees vary according to campus/location and program. *Financial support:* Scholarships/grants, health care benefits, and unspecified assistantships available. Financial award application deadline: 4/15; financial award applicants required to submit FAFSA. *Unit head:* Dr. Jacqueline Kress, Dean, 732-987-2729. *Application contact:* Patrick Givens, Assistant Director of Graduate Admissions, 732-987-2736, Fax: 732-987-2084, E-mail: graduateadmissions@georgian.edu. Web site: http://www.georgian.edu/education/index.htm.

Georgia Southern University, Jack N. Averitt College of Graduate Studies, College of Education, Department of Leadership, Technology, and Human Development, Program in Educational Administration, Statesboro, GA 30460. Offers Ed D. Part-time and evening/weekend programs available. *Students:* 6 full-time (4 women), 165 part-time (111 women); includes 85 minority (75 Black or African American, non-Hispanic/Latino; 1 American Indian or Alaska Native, non-Hispanic/Latino; 1 Asian, non-Hispanic/Latino; 4 Hispanic/Latino; 4 Two or more races, non-Hispanic/Latino). Average age 43. 21 applicants, 81% accepted, 4 enrolled. In 2011, 37 doctorates awarded. *Degree requirements:* For doctorate, thesis/dissertation, exams. *Entrance requirements:* For doctorate, GRE General Test or MAT, minimum GPA of 3.5, letters of reference, resume. Additional exam requirements/recommendations for international students: Required—TOEFL (minimum score 550 paper-based; 213 computer-based; 80 iBT). *Application deadline:* For fall admission, 3/1 for domestic and international students; for spring admission, 11/1 for domestic students, 10/1 for international students. Applications are processed on a rolling basis. Application fee: $50. Electronic applications accepted. *Expenses:* Tuition, state resident: full-time $6300; part-time $263 per semester hour. Tuition, nonresident: full-time $25,174; part-time $1049 per semester hour. *Required fees:* $1872. *Financial support:* In 2011–12, fellowships with partial tuition reimbursements (averaging $9,500 per year), teaching assistantships with partial tuition reimbursements (averaging $9,500 per year) were awarded; research assistantships with partial tuition reimbursements, Federal Work-Study, scholarships/grants, tuition waivers (partial), and unspecified assistantships also available. Support available to part-time students. Financial award application deadline: 4/15; financial award applicants required to submit FAFSA. *Faculty research:* National and local policies regarding school renewal, student achievement, and university leadership; roles and responsibilities of the Assistant Principal/Deputy Headteacher in the U. S., U. K. and China; development of an instrument to measure student dispositions; the impact of cultural context on leadership practices and behaviors; technology leadership preparation. *Unit head:* Dr. Russell Mays, Program Coordinator, 912-478-5605, Fax: 912-478-7140, E-mail: rmays@georgiasouthern.edu. *Application contact:* Amanda Gilliland, Coordinator for Graduate Student Recruitment, 912-478-5384, Fax: 912-478-0740, E-mail: gradadmissions@georgiasouthern.edu. Web site: http://coe.georgiasouthern.edu/ithd/leadership.html.

Georgia Southern University, Jack N. Averitt College of Graduate Studies, College of Education, Department of Leadership, Technology, and Human Development, Program in Educational Leadership, Statesboro, GA 30460. Offers M Ed, Ed S. *Accreditation:* NCATE. Part-time and evening/weekend programs available. *Students:* 26 full-time (16 women), 54 part-time (31 women); includes 27 minority (25 Black or African American, non-Hispanic/Latino; 1 Hispanic/Latino; 1 Two or more races, non-Hispanic/Latino). Average age 35. 29 applicants, 97% accepted, 10 enrolled. In 2011, 13 master's, 20 Ed Ss awarded. *Degree requirements:* For master's, comprehensive exam, transition point assessments; for Ed S, transition point assessments. *Entrance requirements:* For master's, GRE General Test or MAT, minimum GPA of 2.5, 3 years teaching experience; for Ed S, GRE General Test or MAT, minimum graduate GPA of 3.25. Additional exam requirements/recommendations for international students: Required—TOEFL (minimum score 550 paper-based; 213 computer-based; 80 iBT). *Application deadline:* For fall admission, 3/1 priority date for domestic students, 3/1 for international students; for spring admission, 10/1 priority date for domestic students, 10/1 for international students. Applications are processed on a rolling basis. Application fee: $50. Electronic applications accepted. *Expenses:* Tuition, state resident: full-time $6300; part-time $263 per semester hour. Tuition, nonresident: full-time $25,174; part-time $1049 per semester hour. *Required fees:* $1872. *Financial support:* In 2011–12, research assistantships with partial tuition reimbursements (averaging $7,200 per year), teaching assistantships with partial tuition reimbursements (averaging $7,200 per year) were awarded; career-related internships or fieldwork, Federal Work-Study, scholarships/grants, tuition waivers (partial), and unspecified assistantships also available. Support available to part-time students. Financial award application deadline: 4/15; financial award applicants required to submit FAFSA. *Faculty research:* Principalship, performance-based leadership preparation, instructional technology for school leaders, dispositions of educational leaders. *Unit head:* Dr. Linda Arthur, Assistant Professor, 912-478-0697, Fax: 912-478-7104, E-mail: larthur@georgiasouthern.edu. *Application contact:* Amanda Gilliland, Coordinator for Graduate Student Recruitment, 912-478-5384, Fax: 912-478-0740, E-mail: gradadmissions@georgiasouthern.edu. Web site: http://coe.georgiasouther.edu/ithd/leadership.html.

Georgia State University, College of Education, Department of Educational Policy Studies, Program in Educational Leadership, Atlanta, GA 30302-3083. Offers M Ed, PhD, Ed S. *Accreditation:* NCATE. Part-time and evening/weekend programs available. *Degree requirements:* For master's, comprehensive exam; for doctorate, comprehensive exam, thesis/dissertation. *Entrance requirements:* For master's, GRE General Test, minimum GPA of 2.5; for doctorate, GRE General Test or MAT, minimum GPA of 3.3; for Ed S, GRE General Test or MAT, minimum graduate GPA of 3.25. Electronic applications accepted. *Faculty research:* Principal effectiveness, teacher empowerment, restructuring of schools.

Golden Gate Baptist Theological Seminary, Graduate and Professional Programs, Mill Valley, CA 94941-3197. Offers divinity (M Div); early childhood education (Certificate); education leadership (MAEL, Diploma); ministry (D Min); theological studies (MTS); theology (Th M); youth ministry (Certificate). *Accreditation:* ACIPE; ATS (one or more programs are accredited). Part-time and evening/weekend programs available. *Degree requirements:* For master's, thesis (for some programs); for doctorate, 2 foreign languages, thesis/dissertation. *Entrance requirements:* For doctorate, MAT. Additional exam requirements/recommendations for international students: Required—TOEFL (minimum score 550 paper-based; 213 computer-based). Electronic applications accepted.

Gonzaga University, School of Education, Program in Administration and Curriculum, Spokane, WA 99258. Offers MAA. *Accreditation:* NCATE. *Degree requirements:* For master's, comprehensive exam. *Entrance requirements:* For master's, GRE General Test or MAT, minimum B average in undergraduate course work. Additional exam requirements/recommendations for international students: Required—TOEFL.

Gonzaga University, School of Education, Program in Educational Administration, Spokane, WA 99258. Offers MA Ed Ad.

Gonzaga University, School of Professional Studies, Program in Leadership Studies, Spokane, WA 99258. Offers PhD. *Entrance requirements:* For doctorate, MAT and/or GRE.

Governors State University, College of Education, Program in Educational Administration and Supervision, University Park, IL 60484. Offers MA. Part-time and evening/weekend programs available. *Students:* 11 full-time (7 women), 165 part-time (121 women); includes 48 minority (35 Black or African American, non-Hispanic/Latino; 1 American Indian or Alaska Native, non-Hispanic/Latino; 1 Asian, non-Hispanic/Latino; 10 Hispanic/Latino; 1 Two or more races, non-Hispanic/Latino). Average age 36. *Degree requirements:* For master's, comprehensive exam, practicum. *Entrance requirements:* For master's, minimum GPA of 2.75 in last 60 hours of undergraduate course work, 3.0 graduate. *Application deadline:* For fall admission, 7/15 priority date for domestic students; for spring admission, 11/10 for domestic students. Applications are processed on a rolling basis. Application fee: $25. *Financial support:* Career-related internships or fieldwork, Federal Work-Study, institutionally sponsored loans, and tuition waivers (full and partial) available. Support available to part-time students. Financial award application deadline: 5/1. *Unit head:* Dr. Deborah Bordelon, Dean, 708-534-4050.

Graceland University, Gleazer School of Education, Lamoni, IA 50140. Offers collaborative learning and teaching (M Ed); differentiated instruction (M Ed); management in the inclusive classroom (M Ed); mild/moderate special education (M Ed); technology integration (M Ed). *Accreditation:* NCATE. Part-time and evening/weekend programs available. Postbaccalaureate distance learning degree programs offered (no on-campus study). *Faculty:* 12 full-time (11 women), 18 part-time/adjunct (14 women). *Students:* 315 full-time (256 women), 69 part-time (51 women); includes 11 minority (4 Black or African American, non-Hispanic/Latino; 1 American Indian or Alaska Native, non-Hispanic/Latino; 2 Asian, non-Hispanic/Latino; 4 Hispanic/Latino), 8 international. *Degree requirements:* For master's, action research project. *Entrance requirements:* For master's, minimum GPA of 3.0, teaching certificate, current teaching contract. *Application deadline:* For fall admission, 7/15 for domestic students; for winter admission, 10/15 for domestic students; for spring admission, 1/15 priority date for domestic students. Application fee: $50. Electronic applications accepted. *Financial support:* Institutionally sponsored loans and scholarships/grants available. Financial award application deadline: 12/15; financial award applicants required to submit FAFSA. *Unit head:* Dr. Tammy Everett, Dean, 641-784-5000 Ext. 5226, E-mail: teverett@graceland.edu. *Application contact:* Cathy Porter, Program Consultant, 816-833-0524 Ext. 4516, E-mail: cgporter@graceland.edu. Web site: http://www.graceland.edu/education.

Grambling State University, School of Graduate Studies and Research, College of Education, Department of Educational Leadership, Grambling, LA 71245. Offers curriculum and instruction (Ed D); developmental education (MS, Ed D), including curriculum and instruction: reading (Ed D), English (MS), guidance and counseling (MS), higher education administration (Ed D), instructional systems and technology (Ed D), mathematics (MS), reading (MS), science (MS), student development and personnel services (Ed D); educational leadership (MS, Ed D). Part-time and evening/weekend programs available. *Degree requirements:* For master's, comprehensive exam, thesis (for some programs); for doctorate, comprehensive exam, thesis/dissertation. *Entrance requirements:* For master's, GRE, minimum GPA of 2.5 on last degree; for doctorate, GRE (minimum 1000, 500 on Verbal), master's degree, minimum GPA of 3.0 on last degree. Additional exam requirements/recommendations for international students: Required—TOEFL (minimum score 500 paper-based; 173 computer-based; 61 iBT). Electronic applications accepted. *Expenses:* Tuition, state resident: full-time $3546; part-time $192 per credit hour. Tuition, nonresident: full-time $3456; part-time $192 per credit hour. *Required fees:* $1829; $1829 per semester hour.

Grand Canyon University, College of Doctoral Studies, Phoenix, AZ 85017-1097. Offers business administration (DBA); general psychology (PhD), including cognition and instruction, industrial and organizational psychology; organizational leadership (Ed D, PhD), including behavioral health (PhD), education and effective schools (PhD), higher education (PhD), instructional leadership (PhD), organizational development (Ed D). *Degree requirements:* For doctorate, comprehensive exam, thesis/dissertation. *Entrance requirements:* For doctorate, minimum GPA of 3.4 on earned advanced degree from regionally-accredited institution; transcripts; goals statement.

Grand Canyon University, College of Education, Phoenix, AZ 85017-1097. Offers curriculum and instruction (M Ed); education administration (M Ed); elementary education (M Ed); secondary education (M Ed); special education (M Ed); teaching (MA). Part-time and evening/weekend programs available. Postbaccalaureate distance learning degree programs offered (no on-campus study). *Degree requirements:* For master's, publishable research paper (M Ed), e-portfolio. *Entrance requirements:* For master's, undergraduate degree from accredited, GCU-approved college, university, or program with minimum GPA 2.8. Additional exam requirements/recommendations for international students: Required—TOEFL (minimum score 550 paper-based; 213 computer-based; 79 iBT), IELTS (minimum score 6). Electronic applications accepted.

Grand Valley State University, College of Education, Program in Educational Leadership, Allendale, MI 49401-9403. Offers M Ed.

Grand Valley State University, College of Education, Program in Leadership, Allendale, MI 49401-9403. Offers Ed S. *Entrance requirements:* For degree, GRE, master's degree with minimum GPA of 3.0, resume, 3 recommendations. Electronic applications accepted.

Grand Valley State University, College of Education, Programs in General Education, Allendale, MI 49401-9403. Offers adult and higher education (M Ed); early childhood education (M Ed); educational differentiation (M Ed); educational leadership (M Ed); educational technology integration (M Ed); elementary education (M Ed); middle level education (M Ed); school library media services (M Ed); secondary level education (M Ed); teaching English to speakers of other languages (M Ed). Part-time and evening/weekend programs available. Postbaccalaureate distance learning degree programs offered (minimal on-campus study). *Degree requirements:* For master's, thesis. *Entrance requirements:* For master's, GRE General Test or minimum GPA of 3.0. Additional exam requirements/recommendations for international students: Required—TOEFL. Electronic applications accepted. *Faculty research:* Effectiveness of technology in education, parental involvement, effective teaching, effective schools research.

Gwynedd-Mercy College, School of Education, Gwynedd Valley, PA 19437-0901. Offers educational administration (MS); master teacher (MS); reading (MS); school counseling (MS); special education (MS). Part-time and evening/weekend programs available. *Faculty:* 8 full-time (5 women), 38 part-time/adjunct (24 women). *Students:* 33 full-time (22 women), 157 part-time (116 women); includes 33 minority (22 Black or African American, non-Hispanic/Latino; 6 Asian, non-Hispanic/Latino; 5 Hispanic/Latino), 1 international. Average age 33. In 2011, 186 master's awarded. *Degree requirements:* For master's, thesis, internship, practicum. *Entrance requirements:* For master's, GRE or MAT; PRAXIS I, minimum GPA of 3.0. *Application deadline:* Applications are processed on a rolling basis. Application fee: $25. *Expenses:* *Tuition:* Part-time $630 per credit hour. *Financial support:* In 2011–12, 2 research assistantships were awarded; career-related internships or fieldwork, Federal Work-Study, tuition waivers (full and partial), unspecified assistantships, and Federal Stafford loans, Federal work study, alternative loans, graduate assistantships also available. Financial award applicants required to submit FAFSA. *Faculty research:* Learning and the brain, reading literacy, ethics and moral judgment, leadership, teaching and multicultural education. *Unit head:* Dr. Sandra Mangano, Dean, 215-641-5549, Fax: 215-542-4695, E-mail: mangano.s@gmc.edu. *Application contact:* Graduate Program Coordinator. Web site: http://www.gmc.edu/academics/education/.

Hampton University, Graduate College, College of Education and Continuing Studies, Hampton, VA 23668. Offers counseling (MA), including college student development, community agency counseling, pastoral counseling, school counseling; educational leadership (MA); elementary education (MA); gifted education (MA); Montessori education (MA); teaching (MT), including early childhood education, middle school education, music education, secondary education, special education. *Accreditation:* NCATE. Part-time and evening/weekend programs available. *Entrance requirements:* For master's, GRE General Test.

Hampton University, Hampton U Online, Hampton, VA 23668. Offers business administration (PhD); educational management (PhD); health administration (MHA); nursing (MSN, PhD).

Harding University, College of Education, Searcy, AR 72149-0001. Offers advanced studies in teaching and learning (M Ed); art (MSE); behavioral science (MSE); counseling (MS, Ed S); early childhood special education (M Ed, MSE); education (MSE); educational leadership (M Ed, Ed S); elementary education (M Ed); English (MSE); French (MSE); history/social science (MSE); kinesiology (MSE); math (MSE); reading (M Ed); secondary education (M Ed); Spanish (MSE); teaching (MAT); teaching English as a second language (MSE). *Accreditation:* NCATE. Part-time and evening/weekend programs available. *Faculty:* 9 full-time (2 women), 48 part-time/adjunct (26 women). *Students:* 100 full-time (77 women), 333 part-time (239 women); includes 76 minority (59 Black or African American, non-Hispanic/Latino; 1 Asian, non-Hispanic/Latino; 10 Hispanic/Latino; 6 Two or more races, non-Hispanic/Latino), 2 international. Average age 36. 93 applicants, 91% accepted, 83 enrolled. In 2011, 159 master's, 10 other advanced degrees awarded. *Degree requirements:* For master's, comprehensive exam (for some programs), thesis optional, portfolio(s); for Ed S, comprehensive exam, portfolio, project. *Entrance requirements:* For master's, GRE, MAT, PRAXIS; for Ed S, MAT or GRE. Additional exam requirements/recommendations for international students: Required—TOEFL (minimum score 550 paper-based; 79 iBT). *Application deadline:* For fall admission, 8/1 for domestic and international students; for spring admission, 1/1 for domestic and international students. Applications are processed on a rolling basis. Application fee: $35. *Expenses: Tuition:* Full-time $10,512; part-time $584 per credit hour. *Required fees:* $500; $25 per credit hour. Tuition and fees vary according to course load, degree level and program. *Financial support:* In 2011–12, 37 students received support. Unspecified assistantships available. *Faculty research:* Reading, comprehension, school violence, educational technology, behavior, college choice, differentiated instruction, brain-based teaching. *Unit head:* Dr. Clara Carroll, Chair, 501-279-4501, Fax: 501-279-4083, E-mail: ccarroll@harding.edu. *Application contact:* Information Contact, 501-279-4315, E-mail: gradstudiesedu@harding.edu. Web site: http://www.harding.edu/education/grad.html.

Harvard University, Harvard Graduate School of Education, Doctoral Program in Education, Cambridge, MA 02138. Offers culture, communities and education (Ed D); education policy, leadership and instructional practice (Ed D); higher education (Ed D); human development and education (Ed D); quantitative policy analysis in education (Ed D). *Faculty:* 83 full-time (44 women), 67 part-time/adjunct (29 women). *Students:* 251 full-time (172 women), 16 part-time (7 women); includes 87 minority (32 Black or African American, non-Hispanic/Latino; 1 American Indian or Alaska Native, non-Hispanic/Latino; 26 Asian, non-Hispanic/Latino; 22 Hispanic/Latino; 1 Native Hawaiian or other Pacific Islander, non-Hispanic/Latino; 5 Two or more races, non-Hispanic/Latino), 30 international. Average age 34. 545 applicants, 7% accepted, 28 enrolled. In 2011, 47 doctorates awarded. Terminal master's awarded for partial completion of doctoral program. *Degree requirements:* For doctorate, thesis/dissertation. *Entrance requirements:* For doctorate, GRE General Test, statement of purpose, 3 letters of recommendation, resume, official transcripts. Additional exam requirements/recommendations for international students: Required—TOEFL (minimum score 613 paper-based; 104 computer-based; 100 iBT), TWE (minimum score 5). *Application deadline:* For fall admission, 12/14 for domestic and international students. Application fee: $85. Electronic applications accepted. *Expenses:* Contact institution. *Financial support:* In 2011–12, 203 students received support, including 62 fellowships with full and partial tuition reimbursements available (averaging $13,939 per year), 35 research assistantships (averaging $9,534 per year), 134 teaching assistantships (averaging $10,748 per year); career-related internships or fieldwork, Federal Work-Study, institutionally sponsored loans, scholarships/grants, health care benefits, tuition waivers (full and partial), and unspecified assistantships also available. Support available to part-time students. Financial award application deadline: 2/1; financial award applicants required to submit FAFSA. *Faculty research:* Learning and development, educational leadership and organizations, education policy analysis. *Total annual research expenditures:* $26 million. *Unit head:* Dr. Shu-Ling Chen, Assistant Dean, 617-496-4406. *Application contact:* Information Contact, 617-495-3414, Fax: 617-496-3577, E-mail: gseadmissions@harvard.edu. Web site: http://gse.harvard.edu/.

Harvard University, Harvard Graduate School of Education, Doctor of Education Leadership (Ed.L.D.) Program, Cambridge, MA 02138. Offers Ed L D. *Faculty:* 83 full-time (44 women), 67 part-time/adjunct (29 women). *Students:* 50 full-time (33 women); includes 29 minority (13 Black or African American, non-Hispanic/Latino; 5 Asian, non-Hispanic/Latino; 10 Hispanic/Latino; 1 Two or more races, non-Hispanic/Latino). Average age 34. 520 applicants, 5% accepted, 25 enrolled. *Degree requirements:* For doctorate, thesis/dissertation, capstone project. *Entrance requirements:* For doctorate, GRE or GMAT, statement of purpose, 3 letters of recommendation, resume, official transcripts, 2 short essay questions. Additional exam requirements/recommendations for international students: Required—TOEFL (minimum score 613 paper-based; 104 computer-based; 100 iBT), TWE. *Application deadline:* For fall admission, 12/14 for domestic and international students. Application fee: $85. Electronic applications accepted. *Expenses: Tuition:* Full-time $36,304. *Required fees:* $1186. Full-time tuition and fees vary according to program. *Financial support:* In 2011–12, 50 students received support, including 50 fellowships (averaging $21,373 per year), 17 teaching assistantships (averaging $5,773 per year); research assistantships, career-related internships or fieldwork, Federal Work-Study, institutionally sponsored loans, scholarships/grants, health care benefits, tuition waivers, and unspecified assistantships also available. Support available to part-time students. Financial award application deadline: 2/1; financial award applicants required to submit FAFSA. *Faculty research:* System level leadership in education. *Total annual research expenditures:* $26 million. *Unit head:* Dr. Elizabeth City, Executive Director, 617-495-1076. *Application contact:* Information Contact, 617-495-3414, Fax: 617-496-3577, E-mail: gseadmissions@harvard.edu. Web site: http://www.gse.harvard.edu/academics/doctorate/edld/index.html.

Harvard University, Harvard Graduate School of Education, Master's Programs in Education, Cambridge, MA 02138. Offers arts in education (Ed M); education policy and management (Ed M); higher education (Ed M); human development and psychology (Ed M); international education policy (Ed M); language and literacy (Ed M); learning and teaching (Ed M); mid-career mathematics and science (teaching certificate) (Ed M); mind brain and education (Ed M); prevention science and practice (Ed M); school leadership (Ed M); special studies (Ed M); teaching and curriculum (teaching certificate) (Ed M); technology innovation and education (Ed M). Part-time programs available. *Faculty:* 83 full-time (44 women), 67 part-time/adjunct (29 women). *Students:* 592 full-time (431 women), 75 part-time (54 women); includes 194 minority (41 Black or African American, non-Hispanic/Latino; 4 American Indian or Alaska Native, non-Hispanic/Latino; 75 Asian, non-Hispanic/Latino; 45 Hispanic/Latino; 2 Native Hawaiian or other Pacific Islander, non-Hispanic/Latino; 27 Two or more races, non-Hispanic/Latino), 95 international. Average age 28. 1,679 applicants, 52% accepted, 627 enrolled. In 2011, 653 master's awarded. *Entrance requirements:* For master's, GRE General Test, statement of purpose, 3 letters of recommendation, resume, official transcripts. Additional exam requirements/recommendations for international students: Required—TOEFL (minimum score 613 paper-based; 104 computer-based; 100 iBT), TWE (minimum score 5). *Application deadline:* For fall admission, 1/4 for domestic and international students. Application fee: $85. Electronic applications accepted. *Expenses:* Contact institution. *Financial support:* In 2011–12, 419 students received support, including 14 fellowships with full and partial tuition reimbursements available (averaging $12,831 per year); career-related internships or fieldwork, Federal Work-Study, institutionally sponsored loans, scholarships/grants, health care benefits, tuition waivers (full and partial), and unspecified assistantships also available. Support available to part-time students. Financial award application deadline: 2/1; financial award applicants required to submit FAFSA. *Faculty research:* Learning and development, educational leadership and organizations, educational policy analysis. *Total annual research expenditures:* $26 million. *Unit head:* Jennifer L. Petrallia, Assistant Dean, 617-495-8445. *Application contact:* Information Contact, 617-495-3414, Fax: 617-496-3577, E-mail: gseadmissions@harvard.edu. Web site: http://www.gse.harvard.edu/.

Henderson State University, Graduate Studies, Teachers College, Department of Educational Leadership, Arkadelphia, AR 71999-0001. Offers educational leadership (Ed S); school administration (MSE). Part-time programs available. *Entrance requirements:* For master's, GRE or MAT. Additional exam requirements/recommendations for international students: Required—TOEFL (minimum score 550 paper-based; 213 computer-based); Recommended—IELTS (minimum score 6). Electronic applications accepted.

Heritage University, Graduate Programs in Education, Program in Educational Administration, Toppenish, WA 98948-9599. Offers M Ed. Part-time and evening/weekend programs available. *Degree requirements:* For master's, comprehensive exam, thesis optional, special project. *Entrance requirements:* For master's, valid teaching certificate, 3 years of teaching experience, interview, letters of recommendation.

High Point University, Norcross Graduate School, High Point, NC 27262-3598. Offers business administration (MBA); educational leadership (M Ed); elementary education (M Ed); history (MA); nonprofit management (MA); secondary math (M Ed); special education (M Ed); strategic communication (MA); teaching elementary education k-6 (MAT); teaching secondary mathematics 9-12 (MAT). *Accreditation:* ACBSP; NCATE. Part-time and evening/weekend programs available. *Degree requirements:* For master's, comprehensive exam (for some programs), thesis (for some programs). *Entrance requirements:* For master's, GMAT (MBA), GRE, MAT, minimum GPA of 3.0. Additional exam requirements/recommendations for international students: Required—TOEFL (minimum score 550 paper-based). Electronic applications accepted.

Hofstra University, School of Education, Health, and Human Services, Department of Foundations, Leadership, and Policy Studies, Hempstead, NY 11549. Offers educational and policy leadership (MS Ed, Ed D), including higher education (MS Ed), K-12 (MS Ed); educational policy and leadership (Advanced Certificate), including school district business leader; foundations of education (MA, Advanced Certificate); Advanced Certificate/Advanced Certificate. Part-time and evening/weekend programs available. Postbaccalaureate distance learning degree programs offered (minimal on-campus study). *Students:* 22 full-time (16 women), 105 part-time (65 women); includes 45 minority (33 Black or African American, non-Hispanic/Latino; 1 Asian, non-Hispanic/Latino; 11 Hispanic/Latino), 2 international. Average age 37. 78 applicants, 94% accepted, 42 enrolled. In 2011, 12 master's, 6 doctorates, 12 other advanced degrees awarded. *Degree requirements:* For master's, one foreign language, comprehensive exam (for some programs), thesis or alternative, minimum GPA of 3.0; for doctorate, comprehensive exam (for some programs), thesis/dissertation (for some programs), minimum GPA of 3.0. *Entrance requirements:* For master's and Advanced Certificate, interview, writing sample, essay; for doctorate, GMAT, GRE, LSAT, or MAT, interview, 3 letters of recommendation, resume, essay. Additional exam requirements/recommendations for international students: Required—TOEFL (minimum score 550 paper-based; 213 computer-based; 80 iBT). *Application deadline:* Applications are processed on a rolling basis. Application fee: $70 ($75 for international students). Electronic applications accepted. *Expenses: Tuition:* Full-time $18,990; part-time $1055 per credit hour. *Required fees:* $970. Tuition and fees vary according to program. *Financial support:* In 2011–12, 66 students received support, including 44 fellowships with full and partial tuition reimbursements available (averaging $3,788 per year), 3 research assistantships with full and partial tuition reimbursements available (averaging $12,125 per year); Federal Work-Study, institutionally sponsored loans, scholarships/grants, tuition waivers (full and partial), and unspecified assistantships also available. Support available to part-time students. Financial award applicants required to submit FAFSA. *Faculty research:* School improvement, professional assessment - APPR, educational policy, professional development, race/gender in education. *Unit head:* Dr. Esther Fusco, Chairperson, 516-463-7704, Fax: 516-463-6196, E-mail: catezf@hofstra.edu. *Application contact:* Carol Drummer, Dean of Graduate Admissions, 516-463-4876, Fax: 516-463-4664, E-mail: gradstudent@hofstra.edu. Web site: http://www.hofstra.edu/education/.

Holy Family University, Graduate School, School of Education, Philadelphia, PA 19114. Offers education (M Ed); education leadership (M Ed); elementary education (M Ed); reading specialist (M Ed); secondary education (M Ed); special education (M Ed). Part-time and evening/weekend programs available. *Degree requirements:* For master's, thesis optional. *Entrance requirements:* For master's, GRE or MAT, interview. Electronic applications accepted. *Faculty research:* Cognition, developmental issues, sociological issues in education.

See Display on page 707 and Close-Up on page 803.

Hood College, Graduate School, Department of Education, Frederick, MD 21701-8575. Offers curriculum and instruction (MS), including early childhood education, elementary education, elementary school science and mathematics, secondary education, special education; educational leadership (MS, Certificate); reading specialization (MS). Part-time and evening/weekend programs available. *Degree requirements:* For master's, action research project, portfolio (reading). *Entrance requirements:* For master's, minimum GPA of 2.75, teaching certification. Additional exam requirements/recommendations for international students: Required—TOEFL (minimum score 575 paper-based; 231 computer-based; 89 iBT). Electronic applications accepted. *Faculty research:* Leadership, action research, brain research, learning styles.

Hope International University, School of Graduate and Professional Studies, Program in Education, Fullerton, CA 92831-3138. Offers education administration (MA); elementary education (ME); secondary education (ME). Part-time and evening/weekend programs available. *Degree requirements:* For master's, comprehensive exam (for some programs), thesis. *Entrance requirements:* For master's, minimum GPA of 3.0, 2 references. Additional exam requirements/recommendations for international students: Required—TOEFL (minimum score 550 paper-based; 213 computer-based; 86 iBT); Recommended—IELTS (minimum score 6.5). Electronic applications accepted. *Expenses:* Contact institution. *Faculty research:* Distance education.

Houston Baptist University, College of Education and Behavioral Sciences, Programs in Education, Houston, TX 77074-3298. Offers bilingual education (M Ed); counselor education (M Ed); curriculum and instruction (M Ed); educational administration (M Ed); educational diagnostician (M Ed); reading education (M Ed). Part-time programs available. *Entrance requirements:* For master's, GRE General Test or MAT. Additional exam requirements/recommendations for international students: Required—TOEFL (minimum score 550 paper-based; 213 computer-based).

Howard Payne University, Program in Instructional Leadership, Brownwood, TX 76801-2715. Offers M Ed. Postbaccalaureate distance learning degree programs offered (no on-campus study).

Howard University, School of Education, Department of Educational Administration and Policy, Program in Educational Administration and Policy, Washington, DC 20059-0002. Offers educational administration (M Ed, CAGS); educational administration and policy (Ed D). *Accreditation:* NCATE. Part-time programs available. *Faculty:* 5 full-time (2 women), 2 part-time/adjunct (1 woman). *Students:* 36 full-time (24 women), 46 part-time (29 women); includes 68 minority (67 Black or African American, non-Hispanic/Latino; 1 Hispanic/Latino), 9 international. Average age 39. 54 applicants, 54% accepted, 23 enrolled. In 2011, 12 master's, 4 doctorates awarded. *Degree requirements:* For master's, comprehensive exam, thesis (for some programs); for doctorate, comprehensive exam, thesis/dissertation, internship; for CAGS, thesis. *Entrance requirements:* For master's and doctorate, minimum GPA of 3.0. Additional exam requirements/recommendations for international students: Required—TOEFL (minimum score 550 paper-based). *Application deadline:* For fall admission, 4/15 priority date for domestic students, 4/1 for international students; for spring admission, 11/15 priority date for domestic students. Applications are processed on a rolling basis. Application fee: $45. Electronic applications accepted. *Financial support:* In 2011–12, 10 students received support, including 6 fellowships with full and partial tuition reimbursements available (averaging $16,000 per year), 2 research assistantships (averaging $4,000 per year); career-related internships or fieldwork, Federal Work-Study, institutionally sponsored loans, scholarships/grants, and unspecified assistantships also available. Financial award application deadline: 3/15; financial award applicants required to submit FAFSA. *Faculty research:* Educational policy, reform, achievement gap, disability reform policy, school governance delivery of social services to students. *Unit head:* Dr. Dawn G. Williams, Chair, Department of Educational Administration and Policy, 202-806-7342, Fax: 202-806-5310, E-mail: dgwilliams@howard.edu. *Application contact:* Naomi Black, Administrative Assistant, Department of Educational Administration and Policy, 202-806-7342, Fax: 202-806-5310, E-mail: nblack@howard.edu.

Hunter College of the City University of New York, Graduate School, School of Education, Department of Curriculum and Teaching, Program in Educational Supervision and Administration, New York, NY 10021-5085. Offers AC. *Faculty:* 9 part-time/adjunct (4 women). *Students:* 96 part-time (75 women); includes 20 minority (4 Black or African American, non-Hispanic/Latino; 6 Asian, non-Hispanic/Latino; 10 Hispanic/Latino). Average age 34. 40 applicants, 65% accepted, 22 enrolled. In 2011, 39 ACs awarded. *Degree requirements:* For AC, portfolio review. *Entrance requirements:* For degree, minimum B average in graduate course work, teaching certificate, minimum 3 years of full-time teaching experience, interview, 2 letters of support. Additional exam requirements/recommendations for international students: Required—TOEFL. *Application deadline:* For fall admission, 4/1 for domestic students, 2/1 for international students; for spring admission, 11/1 for domestic students, 9/1 for international students. Applications are processed on a rolling basis. Application fee: $125. *Expenses:* Tuition, state resident: full-time $8210; part-time $345 per credit. Tuition, nonresident: full-time $15,360; part-time $640 per credit. *Required fees:* $280 per semester. One-time fee: $125. Tuition and fees vary according to class time, campus/location and program. *Financial support:* Federal Work-Study and tuition waivers (partial) available. Support available to part-time students. *Faculty research:* Supervision of instruction, theory in action, human relations and leadership. *Unit head:* Dr. Marcia Knoll, Coordinator, 212-772-4761, E-mail: mknoll@hunter.cuny.edu. *Application contact:* William Zlata, Director for Graduate Admissions, 212-772-4482, Fax: 212-650-3336, E-mail: admissions@hunter.cuny.edu. Web site: http://www.hunter.cuny.edu/school-of-education/programs/graduate/administration-supervision.

Idaho State University, Office of Graduate Studies, College of Education, Department of Educational Foundations, Pocatello, ID 83209-8059. Offers child and family studies (M Ed); curriculum leadership (M Ed); education (M Ed); educational administration (M Ed); educational foundations (5th Year Certificate); elementary education (M Ed), including K-12 education, literacy, secondary education. Part-time programs available. *Degree requirements:* For master's, comprehensive exam, thesis optional, oral exam, written exam; for 5th Year Certificate, comprehensive exam, thesis (for some programs), oral exam, written exam. *Entrance requirements:* For master's, GRE General Test or MAT, minimum undergraduate GPA of 3.0; for 5th Year Certificate, GRE General Test, minimum undergraduate GPA of 3.0, master's degree. Additional exam requirements/recommendations for international students: Required—TOEFL (minimum score 550 paper-based; 213 computer-based; 80 iBT). Electronic applications accepted. *Faculty research:* Child and families studies; business education; special education; math, science, and technology education.

Idaho State University, Office of Graduate Studies, College of Education, Department of Educational Leadership and Instructional Design, Pocatello, ID 83209-8059. Offers educational administration (M Ed, 6th Year Certificate, Ed S); educational leadership (Ed D), including education training and development, educational administration, educational technology, higher education administration; educational leadership and instructional design (PhD); instructional technology (M Ed). Part-time programs available. *Degree requirements:* For master's, comprehensive exam, thesis optional, internship, oral exam or deferred thesis; for doctorate, comprehensive exam, thesis/dissertation, written exam; for other advanced degree, comprehensive exam, thesis (for some programs), written and oral exam. *Entrance requirements:* For master's, MAT, bachelor's degree, minimum GPA of 3.0, 1 year of training experience; for doctorate, GRE General Test or MAT, minimum GPA of 3.0 (undergraduate), 3.5 (graduate); departmental interview; for other advanced degree, GRE General Test, minimum GPA of 3.0, master's degree. Additional exam requirements/recommendations for international students: Required—TOEFL (minimum score 550 paper-based; 213 computer-based; 80 iBT). Electronic applications accepted. *Faculty research:* Educational leadership, gender issues in education and sport, staff development.

Illinois State University, Graduate School, College of Education, Department of Educational Administration and Foundations, Normal, IL 61790-2200. Offers college student personnel administration (MS); educational administration (MS, MS Ed, Ed D, PhD). *Accreditation:* NCATE. *Degree requirements:* For doctorate, variable foreign language requirement, thesis/dissertation, 2 terms of residency. *Entrance requirements:* For master's, GRE General Test, minimum GPA of 2.6 in last 60 hours of course work; for doctorate, GRE General Test, master's degree or equivalent, minimum GPA of 3.5. *Faculty research:* Illinois Association of School Administrators FY2007, Illinois Principals Association, special populations professional development and technical assistance project, Illinois state action for education leadership project.

Immaculata University, College of Graduate Studies, Program in Educational Leadership and Administration, Immaculata, PA 19345. Offers educational leadership and administration (MA, Ed D); elementary education (Certificate); school principal (Certificate); school superintendent (Certificate); secondary education (Certificate); special education (Certificate). Part-time and evening/weekend programs available. *Degree requirements:* For master's, comprehensive exam, thesis optional; for doctorate, comprehensive exam, thesis/dissertation. *Entrance requirements:* For master's, GRE or MAT, minimum GPA of 3.0; for doctorate, GRE General Test or MAT, minimum GPA of 3.5. Additional exam requirements/recommendations for international students: Required—TOEFL. Electronic applications accepted. *Faculty research:* Cooperative learning, school-based management, whole language, performance assessment.

Indiana State University, College of Graduate and Professional Studies, College of Education, Department of Educational Leadership, Administration, and Foundations, Terre Haute, IN 47809. Offers educational administration (PhD); leadership in higher education (PhD); school administration (Ed S); school administration and supervision (M Ed); student affairs in higher education (MS). *Accreditation:* NCATE. Part-time and evening/weekend programs available. Terminal master's awarded for partial completion of doctoral program. *Degree requirements:* For master's, thesis; for doctorate, thesis/dissertation. *Entrance requirements:* For master's, GRE General Test, minimum undergraduate GPA of 2.5; for doctorate, GRE General Test, minimum undergraduate GPA of 3.5; for Ed S, GRE General Test, minimum graduate GPA of 3.25. Electronic applications accepted.

Indiana University Bloomington, School of Education, Department of Educational Leadership and Policy Studies, Bloomington, IN 47405-7000. Offers education policy studies (PhD); educational leadership (MS, Ed D, Ed S); higher education (MS, Ed D, PhD); history and philosophy of education (MS); history of education (PhD); international and comparative education (MS, PhD); philosophy of education (PhD); student affairs administration (MS). *Accreditation:* NCATE. Part-time and evening/weekend programs available. *Degree requirements:* For master's, thesis optional; for doctorate, comprehensive exam, thesis/dissertation; for Ed S, comprehensive exam or project. *Entrance requirements:* For master's, doctorate, and Ed S, GRE General Test. Additional exam requirements/recommendations for international students: Required—TOEFL (minimum score 213 computer-based; 79 iBT). Electronic applications accepted. *Faculty research:* Student engagement at higher education institutions in the nation, Reading First professional development initiative, state finance policy on financial access to higher education, school reform, special needs studies.

Indiana University of Pennsylvania, School of Graduate Studies and Research, College of Education and Educational Technology, Department of Professional Studies in Education, Certification Program for Principal, Indiana, PA 15705-1087. Offers Certificate. Part-time and evening/weekend programs available. *Faculty:* 19 full-time (13 women), 1 (woman) part-time/adjunct. *Students:* 18 part-time (11 women). Average age 36. 22 applicants, 91% accepted, 12 enrolled. *Entrance requirements:* For degree, GRE General Test, GRE Subject Test, 2 letters of recommendation. Additional exam requirements/recommendations for international students: Required—TOEFL (minimum score 540 paper-based; 207 computer-based). *Application deadline:* For fall admission, 7/1 priority date for domestic students; for spring admission, 11/1 for domestic students. Applications are processed on a rolling basis. Application fee: $50. Electronic applications accepted. *Expenses:* Tuition, state resident: full-time $7488; part-time $416 per credit. Tuition, nonresident: full-time $11,232; part-time $624 per credit. *Required fees:* $2070; $192.20 per credit. $90 per semester. *Financial support:* Application deadline: 4/15; applicants required to submit FAFSA. *Unit head:* Dr. Cathy Kauffman, Graduate Coordinator, 724-357-3928, E-mail: ckaufman@iup.edu. *Application contact:* Dr. Edward Nardi, Associate Dean, 724-357-2480, Fax: 724-357-5595, E-mail: ewnardi@iup.edu. Web site: http://www.iup.edu/upper.aspx?id=49407.

Indiana University of Pennsylvania, School of Graduate Studies and Research, College of Education and Educational Technology, Department of Professional Studies in Education, Doctoral Program in Administration and Leadership Studies, Indiana, PA 15705-1087. Offers D Ed. Program offered jointly with East Stroudsburg University of Pennsylvania. Part-time and evening/weekend programs available. *Faculty:* 19 full-time (13 women), 1 (woman) part-time/adjunct. *Students:* 61 part-time (22 women); includes 4 minority (all Black or African American, non-Hispanic/Latino). Average age 42. 7 applicants, 0% accepted, 0 enrolled. In 2011, 14 doctorates awarded. *Degree requirements:* For doctorate, one foreign language, comprehensive exam, thesis/dissertation, written exam. *Entrance requirements:* For doctorate, 2 letters of recommendation, interview. Additional exam requirements/recommendations for international students: Required—TOEFL (minimum score 540 paper-based; 207 computer-based). *Application deadline:* Applications are processed on a rolling basis. Application fee: $50. Electronic applications accepted. *Expenses:* Tuition, state resident: full-time $7488; part-time $416 per credit. Tuition, nonresident: full-time $11,232; part-time $624 per credit. *Required fees:* $2070; $192.20 per credit. $90 per semester. *Financial support:* In 2011–12, 4 fellowships (averaging $1,000 per year), 1 teaching assistantship (averaging $1,000 per year) were awarded; research assistantships with full and partial tuition reimbursements also available. Financial award application deadline: 4/15; financial award applicants required to submit FAFSA. *Unit head:* Dr. Cathy Kaufmann, Graduate Coordinator, 724-357-5593, E-mail: cathy.kaufmann@iup.edu. *Application contact:* Dr. Edward Nardi, Associate Dean, 724-357-2480, Fax: 724-357-5595, E-mail: ewnardi@iup.edu. Web site: http://www.iup.edu/upper.aspx?id=92694.

Indiana University of Pennsylvania, School of Graduate Studies and Research, College of Humanities and Social Sciences, Department of Sociology, Program in Administration and Leadership Studies, Indiana, PA 15705-1087. Offers PhD. Part-time and evening/weekend programs available. *Faculty:* 12 full-time (7 women). *Students:* 4 full-time (0 women), 96 part-time (56 women); includes 14 minority (10 Black or African American, non-Hispanic/Latino; 1 Asian, non-Hispanic/Latino; 3 Hispanic/Latino). Average age 43. 46 applicants, 48% accepted, 20 enrolled. In 2011, 13 doctorates awarded. *Degree requirements:* For doctorate, comprehensive exam, thesis/dissertation. *Entrance requirements:* For doctorate, GRE, resume, writing sample, 3 letters of recommendation. Additional exam requirements/recommendations for international students: Required—TOEFL (minimum score 540 paper-based; 207 computer-based). *Application deadline:* For fall admission, 2/15 priority date for domestic students. Applications are processed on a rolling basis. Application fee: $50. Electronic applications accepted. *Expenses:* Tuition, state resident: full-time $7488; part-time $416 per credit. Tuition, nonresident: full-time $11,232; part-time $624 per credit. *Required fees:* $2070; $192.20 per credit. $90 per semester. *Financial support:* In 2011–12, 7 fellowships (averaging $857 per year), 5 research assistantships with full and partial tuition reimbursements (averaging $5,440 per year) were awarded. Financial award application deadline: 4/15; financial award applicants required to submit FAFSA. *Unit head:* Dr. John Anderson, Graduate Coordinator, 724-357-1291, E-mail: janderson@iup.edu. *Application contact:* Paula Stossel, Assistant Dean, 724-357-2222, Fax: 724-357-4862, E-mail: graduate-admissions@iup.edu. Web site: http://www.iup.edu/grad/ALS/default.aspx.

Indiana University–Purdue University Fort Wayne, College of Education and Public Policy, Department of Professional Studies, Fort Wayne, IN 46805-1499. Offers counselor education (MS Ed); educational leadership (MS Ed); marriage and family therapy (MS Ed); school counseling (MS Ed); special education (MS Ed, Certificate). Part-time programs available. *Faculty:* 6 full-time (5 women), 1 (woman) part-time/adjunct. *Students:* 2 full-time (1 woman), 158 part-time (124 women); includes 19 minority (11 Black or African American, non-Hispanic/Latino; 6 Hispanic/Latino; 2 Two or more races, non-Hispanic/Latino), 1 international. Average age 33. 59 applicants, 56% accepted, 32 enrolled. In 2011, 56 master's awarded. *Degree requirements:* For master's, comprehensive exam, practicum, internship, portfolio. *Entrance requirements:* For master's, minimum GPA of 2.5, three professional letters of recommendation. Additional exam requirements/recommendations for international students: Required—TOEFL (minimum score 550 paper-based; 213 computer-based; 77 iBT). *Application deadline:* For fall admission, 4/1 priority date for domestic students, 4/1 for international students. Applications are processed on a rolling basis. Application fee: $55. *Financial support:* Research assistantships, teaching assistantships, and scholarships/grants available. Support available to part-time students. Financial award application deadline: 3/1; financial award applicants required to submit FAFSA. *Faculty research:* Improving education with stronger collaborations. *Unit head:* Dr. James Burg, Interim Chair, 260-481-5406, Fax: 260-481-5408, E-mail: burgj@ipfw.edu. *Application contact:* Vicky L. Schmidt, Graduate Recorder, 260-481-6450, Fax: 260-481-5408, E-mail: schmidt@ipfw.edu. Web site: http://www.ipfw.edu/education.

Indiana University–Purdue University Indianapolis, School of Education, Indianapolis, IN 46202-2896. Offers computer education (Certificate); curriculum and instruction (MS); early childhood (MS); educational leadership (MS, Certificate); English as a second language (Certificate); higher education and student affairs (MS); kindergarten (Certificate); language education (MS); reading (Certificate); school counseling (MS); special education (MS, Certificate). Part-time and evening/weekend programs available. *Faculty:* 41 full-time, 80 part-time/adjunct. *Students:* 67 full-time (52 women), 467 part-time (360 women); includes 82 minority (44 Black or African American, non-Hispanic/Latino; 3 American Indian or Alaska Native, non-Hispanic/Latino; 8 Asian, non-Hispanic/Latino; 13 Hispanic/Latino; 14 Two or more races, non-Hispanic/Latino), 10 international. Average age 33. 63 applicants, 57% accepted, 29 enrolled. In 2011, 167 master's awarded. *Degree requirements:* For master's, thesis optional. *Entrance requirements:* For master's, GRE General Test, minimum GPA of 3.0. Additional exam requirements/recommendations for international students: Required—TOEFL. *Application deadline:* For fall admission, 5/1 priority date for domestic students; for spring admission, 11/1 for domestic students. Application fee: $55 ($65 for international students). *Financial support:* Fellowships, research assistantships with partial tuition reimbursements, teaching assistantships, Federal Work-Study, institutionally sponsored loans, scholarships/grants, and tuition waivers (partial) available. Support available to part-time students. *Faculty research:* Teachers in the process of change, learning cycles, children's concepts of science. *Total annual research expenditures:* $614,458. *Unit head:* Dr. Chris Leland, Interim Executive Associate Dean, 317-274-6801, Fax: 317-274-6864. *Application contact:* Sarah Brandenburg, Graduate Advisor, 317-274-6801, Fax: 317-274-6864, E-mail: edugrad@iupui.edu. Web site: http://education.iupui.edu/.

Indiana Wesleyan University, College of Adult and Professional Studies, School of Educational Leadership, Marion, IN 46953. Offers M Ed, Ed S. *Accreditation:* NCATE. Part-time and evening/weekend programs available. Postbaccalaureate distance learning degree programs offered (no on-campus study). *Degree requirements:* For master's, portfolio. *Entrance requirements:* For master's, minimum GPA of 2.75, teaching experience, teaching license. Additional exam requirements/recommendations for international students: Required—TOEFL (minimum score 550 paper-based; 213 computer-based). Electronic applications accepted. *Faculty research:* Mentoring, performance-based assessments, faith integration, integration of technology, program assessment.

Instituto Tecnologico de Santo Domingo, Graduate School, Area of Humanities and Social Sciences, Santo Domingo, Dominican Republic. Offers accounting (Certificate); adult education (Certificate); applied linguistics (MA); economics (MA); education (M Ed); educational psychology (MA, Certificate); gender and development (MA, Certificate); humanistic studies (MA); international marketing management (Certificate); international relations in the Caribbean basin (Certificate); intervention systems in family therapy (MA); linguistic and literary communication (Certificate); pedagogical support (MA); social science education (M Ed); sustainable human development (MA); terminal illness and death psychology (Certificate); youth and adult education (M Ed).

Instituto Tecnológico y de Estudios Superiores de Monterrey, Campus Central de Veracruz, Graduate Programs, Córdoba, Mexico. Offers administration (MA); administration of information technologies (MTI); computer sciences (MCC); education (MEE); educational institution administration (MAD); educational technology (MTE); electronic commerce (MCE); finance (MAF); humanistic studies (MEH); international business for Latin America (MNL); marketing (MMT); science (MCP). Part-time and evening/weekend programs available. Postbaccalaureate distance learning degree programs offered (minimal on-campus study). *Degree requirements:* For master's, thesis (for some programs). *Entrance requirements:* For master's, PAEP College Board. Electronic applications accepted.

Instituto Tecnológico y de Estudios Superiores de Monterrey, Campus Ciudad Juárez, Program in Educational Administration, Ciudad Juárez, Mexico. Offers MEA.

Instituto Tecnológico y de Estudios Superiores de Monterrey, Campus Estado de México, Professional and Graduate Division, Estado de Mexico, Mexico. Offers administration of information technologies (MITA); architecture (M Arch); business administration (GMBA, MBA); computer sciences (MCS, PhD); education (M Ed); educational institution administration (MAD); educational technology and innovation (PhD); electronic commerce (MEC); environmental systems (MS); finance (MAF); humanistic studies (MHS); information sciences and knowledge management (MISKM); information systems (MS); manufacturing systems (MS); marketing (MEM); quality systems and productivity (MS); science and materials engineering (PhD); telecommunications management (MTM). Part-time programs available. Postbaccalaureate distance learning degree programs offered (minimal on-campus study). *Degree requirements:* For master's, one foreign language, thesis (for some programs); for doctorate, one foreign language, thesis/dissertation. *Entrance requirements:* For master's, E-PAEP 500, interview; for doctorate, E-PAEP 500, research proposal. Additional exam requirements/recommendations for international students: Required—TOEFL (minimum score 550 paper-based). *Faculty research:* Surface treatments by plasmas, mechanical properties, robotics, graphical computing, mechatronics security protocols.

Instituto Tecnológico y de Estudios Superiores de Monterrey, Campus Irapuato, Graduate Programs, Irapuato, Mexico. Offers administration (MBA); administration of information technology (MAIT); administration of telecommunications (MAT); architecture (M Arch); computer science (MCS); education (M Ed); educational administration (MEA); educational innovation and technology (DEIT); educational technology (MET); electronic commerce (MBA); environmental administration and planning (MEAP); environmental systems (MES); finances (MBA); humanistic studies (MHS); international management for Latin American executives (MIMLAE); library and information science (MLIS); manufacturing quality management (MMQM); marketing research (MBA).

Inter American University of Puerto Rico, Aguadilla Campus, Graduate School, Aguadilla, PR 00605. Offers accounting (MBA); counseling psychology specializing in family (MS); criminal justice (MA); educative management and leadership (MA); elementary education (M Ed); finance (MBA); human resources (MBA); industrial management (MBA); management information systems (MBA); marketing (MBA). Part-time and evening/weekend programs available. *Degree requirements:* For master's, comprehensive exam. *Entrance requirements:* For master's, EXADEP, 2 letters of recommendation, minimum GPA of 2.5. Electronic applications accepted.

Inter American University of Puerto Rico, Arecibo Campus, Programs in Education, Arecibo, PR 00614-4050. Offers administration and educational supervision (MA Ed); counseling and guidance (MA Ed); curriculum and teaching (MA Ed), including biology education, English as a second language, history education, math education, Spanish; elementary education (MA Ed). *Degree requirements:* For master's, comprehensive exam, thesis optional. *Entrance requirements:* For master's, GRE, EXADEP, bachelor's degree in education or teaching license (administration and supervision) or courses in education and psychology (counseling and guidance), minimum GPA of 2.5 in last 60 credits.

Inter American University of Puerto Rico, Barranquitas Campus, Program in Education, Barranquitas, PR 00794. Offers curriculum and teaching (M Ed), including biology education, English as a second language, history education, mathematics education, Spanish; educational leadership and management (MA); elementary education (M Ed); information and library service technology (M Ed); special education (MA). *Degree requirements:* For master's, comprehensive exam, thesis optional. *Entrance requirements:* For master's, EXADEP, letter of recommendation. Electronic applications accepted.

Inter American University of Puerto Rico, Metropolitan Campus, Graduate Programs, Program in Education, San Juan, PR 00919-1293. Offers curriculum and instruction (Ed D); educational administration (Ed D); guidance and counseling (MA, Ed D); special education administration (Ed D). *Degree requirements:* For doctorate, comprehensive exam, thesis/dissertation. *Entrance requirements:* For doctorate, GRE, MAT, or EXADEP. Electronic applications accepted.

Iona College, School of Arts and Science, Program in Education, New Rochelle, NY 10801-1890. Offers adolescence education: biology (MS Ed, MST); adolescence education: English (MS Ed, MST); adolescence education: Italian (MS Ed, MST); adolescence education: mathematics (MS Ed, MST); adolescence education: social studies (MS Ed, MST); adolescence education: Spanish (MS Ed, MST); adolescence special education 5-12 (MST); adolescence special education/literacy 5-12 (MS Ed); childhood 1-6/special education 1-6 (MST); childhood education (MST); early childhood/childhood (MST); educational leadership (MS Ed); literacy birth-grade 6/special education 1-6 (MS Ed); literacy education: birth-grade 6 (MS Ed). *Accreditation:* NCATE. Part-time and evening/weekend programs available. *Faculty:* 21 full-time (13 women), 13 part-time/adjunct (8 women). *Students:* 59 full-time (45 women), 101 part-time (78 women); includes 11 minority (2 Black or African American, non-Hispanic/Latino; 2 Asian, non-Hispanic/Latino; 7 Hispanic/Latino). Average age 26. 74 applicants, 66% accepted, 35 enrolled. In 2011, 46 master's awarded. *Degree requirements:* For master's, thesis or alternative. *Entrance requirements:* For master's, minimum GPA of 2.5 (MST), New York teaching certificate (MS Ed). Additional exam requirements/recommendations for international students: Required—TOEFL (minimum score 550 paper-based; 213 computer-based). *Application deadline:* Applications are processed on a rolling basis. Application fee: $50. Electronic applications accepted. *Expenses: Tuition:* Part-time $872 per credit. *Required fees:* $225 per term. *Financial support:* Unspecified assistantships available. Support available to part-time students. Financial award application deadline: 4/15; financial award applicants required to submit FAFSA. *Faculty research:* Reading/writing, educational technology, administration, early literacy assessment, literacy development. *Unit head:* Dr. Catherine O'Callaghan, Chair, 914-633-2210, Fax: 914-633-2608, E-mail: cocallaghan@iona.edu. *Application contact:* Dr. Jeanne Zaino, Interim Dean, School of Arts and Science, 914-633-2112, Fax: 914-633-2023, E-mail: jzaino@iona.edu.

Iowa State University of Science and Technology, Department of Educational Leadership and Policy Studies, Ames, IA 50011. Offers counselor education (M Ed, MS); educational administration (M Ed, MS); educational leadership (PhD); higher education (M Ed, MS); organizational learning and human resource development (M Ed, MS); research and evaluation (MS); student affairs (MS). *Degree requirements:* For master's, thesis or alternative; for doctorate, thesis/dissertation. *Entrance requirements:* For master's and doctorate, GRE General Test. Additional exam requirements/recommendations for international students: Required—TOEFL (minimum score 560 paper-based; 83 iBT), IELTS (minimum score 6.5). *Application deadline:* For fall admission, 1/1 priority date for domestic students, 1/1 for international students. Application fee: $40 ($90 for international students). Electronic applications accepted. *Unit head:* Dr. Daniel Robinson, Director of Graduate Education, 515-294-1241, Fax: 515-294-4942, E-mail: edldrshp@iastate.edu. *Application contact:* Judy Weiland, Application Contact, 515-294-1241, Fax: 515-294-4942, E-mail: eldrshp@iastate.edu. Web site: http://www.elps.hs.iastate.edu/.

Jackson State University, Graduate School, College of Education and Human Development, Department of Educational Leadership, Jackson, MS 39217. Offers education administration (Ed S); educational administration (MS Ed, PhD); secondary education (MS Ed, Ed S), including educational technology (MS Ed). *Accreditation:* NCATE. Part-time and evening/weekend programs available. *Degree requirements:* For master's, comprehensive exam, thesis or alternative; for doctorate, comprehensive exam, thesis/dissertation; for Ed S, comprehensive exam, thesis. *Entrance requirements:* For master's, GRE General Test; for doctorate, MAT, GRE, teaching experience. Additional exam requirements/recommendations for international students: Required—TOEFL (minimum score 520 paper-based; 195 computer-based; 67 iBT).

Jacksonville State University, College of Graduate Studies and Continuing Education, College of Education and Professional Studies, Program in Educational Administration, Jacksonville, AL 36265-1602. Offers MS Ed, Ed S. *Accreditation:* NCATE. Part-time and evening/weekend programs available. *Degree requirements:* For master's, comprehensive exam, thesis (for some programs). *Entrance requirements:* For master's, GRE General Test or MAT. Electronic applications accepted. *Expenses:* Tuition, state resident: part-time $336 per hour. Tuition, nonresident: part-time $672 per hour. Part-time tuition and fees vary according to degree level.

Jacksonville University, School of Education, Jacksonville, FL 32211. Offers educational leadership (M Ed); instructional leadership and organizational development (M Ed); sport management and leadership (M Ed). Part-time and evening/weekend programs available. *Degree requirements:* For master's, comprehensive exam. *Entrance requirements:* For master's, GRE General Test, minimum GPA of 3.0. Additional exam requirements/recommendations for international students: Required—TOEFL (minimum score 550 paper-based), TWE. *Expenses:* Contact institution.

James Madison University, The Graduate School, College of Education, Adult Education Department, Program in Educational Leadership, Harrisonburg, VA 22807. Offers M Ed. *Accreditation:* NCATE. Part-time and evening/weekend programs available. *Students:* Average age 27. *Entrance requirements:* For master's, GRE General Test. Additional exam requirements/recommendations for international students: Required—TOEFL. *Application deadline:* For fall admission, 5/1 priority date for domestic students; for spring admission, 9/1 priority date for domestic students.

Applications are processed on a rolling basis. Application fee: $55. Electronic applications accepted. *Expenses:* Tuition, state resident: full-time $8016; part-time $334 per credit hour. Tuition, nonresident: full-time $22,656; part-time $944 per credit hour. *Financial support:* Federal Work-Study available. Financial award application deadline: 3/1; financial award applicants required to submit FAFSA. *Unit head:* Dr. Diane Foucar-Szocki, Academic Unit Head, 540-568-6794. *Application contact:* Lynette M. Bible, Director of Graduate Admissions, 540-568-6395, Fax: 540-568-7860, E-mail: biblelm@jmu.edu.

John Brown University, Graduate Business Programs, Siloam Springs, AR 72761-2121. Offers global continuous improvement (MBA); international community development leadership (MS); leadership and ethics (MBA, MS); leadership and higher education (MS). Part-time and evening/weekend programs available. Postbaccalaureate distance learning degree programs offered (minimal on-campus study). *Faculty:* 6 full-time (2 women), 31 part-time/adjunct (7 women). *Students:* 29 full-time (13 women), 185 part-time (90 women); includes 33 minority (12 Black or African American, non-Hispanic/Latino; 3 American Indian or Alaska Native, non-Hispanic/Latino; 4 Asian, non-Hispanic/Latino; 11 Hispanic/Latino; 3 Two or more races, non-Hispanic/Latino), 7 international. 75 applicants, 88% accepted. *Entrance requirements:* For master's, MAT, GMAT or GRE if undergraduate GPA is less than 3.0, recommendation forms from three people, 200-word essay describing professional plans and reason for seeking acceptance. Additional exam requirements/recommendations for international students: Required—TOEFL (minimum score 550 paper-based; 213 computer-based; 70 iBT). *Application deadline:* Applications are processed on a rolling basis. Application fee: $35 ($100 for international students). Electronic applications accepted. *Expenses: Tuition:* Part-time $470 per credit hour. *Financial support:* Fellowships, institutionally sponsored loans, and scholarships/grants available. *Unit head:* Dr. Joe Walenciak, Program Director, 479-524-7431, E-mail: jwalenci@jbu.edu. *Application contact:* Brent Young, Graduate Business Representative, 479-524-7450, E-mail: byoung@jbu.edu. Web site: http://www.jbu.edu/grad/business/.

John Carroll University, Graduate School, Department of Education and Allied Studies, Program in Administration, University Heights, OH 44118-4581. Offers M Ed, MA. *Accreditation:* NCATE. Part-time and evening/weekend programs available. *Degree requirements:* For master's, comprehensive exam, research essay or thesis (MA only). *Entrance requirements:* For master's, GRE General Test or MAT, minimum GPA of 2.75, interview, teachers license, 2 years experience. Electronic applications accepted.

The Johns Hopkins University, School of Education, Department of Interdisciplinary Studies in Education, Baltimore, MD 21218. Offers earth/space science (Certificate); education (MS), including educational studies; health care education (MEHP); mind, brain, and teaching (Certificate); teaching the adult learner (Certificate); urban education (Certificate). Part-time and evening/weekend programs available. Postbaccalaureate distance learning degree programs offered (minimal on-campus study). *Degree requirements:* For master's, capstone course. *Entrance requirements:* For master's and Certificate, minimum undergraduate GPA of 3.0. Additional exam requirements/recommendations for international students: Required—TOEFL (minimum score 600 paper-based; 250 computer-based; 100 iBT). Electronic applications accepted. *Faculty research:* Neuro-education, urban school reform, leadership development, teacher leadership, charter schools, techniques for teaching reading to adolescents with delayed reading skills, school culture.

The Johns Hopkins University, School of Education, Department of Teacher Development and Leadership, Baltimore, MD 21218-2699. Offers adolescent literacy education (Certificate); data-based decision making and organizational improvement (Certificate); education (MS), including reading, school administration and supervision, technology for educators; educational leadership for independent schools (Certificate); effective teaching of reading (Certificate); emergent literacy education (Certificate); English as a second language instruction (Certificate); gifted education (Certificate); leadership for school, family, and community collaboration (Certificate); leadership in technology integration (Certificate); school administration and supervision (Certificate); teacher development and leadership (Ed D); teacher leadership (Certificate). Part-time and evening/weekend programs available. Postbaccalaureate distance learning degree programs offered (minimal on-campus study). *Degree requirements:* For master's and Certificate, portfolio; for doctorate, comprehensive exam (for some programs), thesis/dissertation, portfolio or comprehensive exam. *Entrance requirements:* For master's and Certificate, bachelor's degree; minimum undergraduate GPA of 3.0; essay/statement of goals; for doctorate, GRE, essay/statement of goals; three letters of recommendation; curriculum vitae/resume; K-12 professional experience; interview; writing assessment. Additional exam requirements/recommendations for international students: Required—TOEFL (minimum score 600 paper-based; 250 computer-based; 100 iBT). Electronic applications accepted. *Faculty research:* Application of psychoanalytic concepts to teaching, schools, and education reform; adolescent literacies; use of emerging technologies for teaching, learning, and school leadership; quantitative analyses of the social contexts of education; school, family, and community collaboration; program evaluation methodologies.

Johnson & Wales University, The Alan Shawn Feinstein Graduate School, Ed D Program, Providence, RI 02903-3703. Offers higher education (Ed D); K-12 (Ed D). Part-time programs available. *Degree requirements:* For doctorate, thesis/dissertation. *Entrance requirements:* For doctorate, MAT, minimum GPA of 3.25; master's degree in appropriate field from accredited institution. Additional exam requirements/recommendations for international students: Required—TOEFL (minimum score 550 paper-based; 210 computer-based); Recommended—IELTS, TWE. *Faculty research:* Site-based management, collaborative learning, technology and education, K-16 education.

Jones International University, School of Education, Centennial, CO 80112. Offers adult education (M Ed); corporate training and knowledge management (M Ed); curriculum and instruction (M Ed), including elementary teacher licensure, secondary teacher licensure; e-learning technology and design (M Ed); educational leadership and administration (M Ed); educational leadership and administration: principal and administrator licensure (M Ed); elementary curriculum instruction and assessment (M Ed); higher education leadership and administration (M Ed); K-12 instructional technology (M Ed); K-12 instructional technology: teacher licensure (M Ed); secondary curriculum instruction and assessment (M Ed); technology and design (M Ed). Part-time and evening/weekend programs available. Postbaccalaureate distance learning degree programs offered (no on-campus study). *Entrance requirements:* For master's, minimum cumulative GPA of 2.5. Additional exam requirements/recommendations for international students: Recommended—TOEFL (minimum score 550 paper-based; 213 computer-based). Electronic applications accepted.

Kansas State University, Graduate School, College of Education, Department of Curriculum and Instruction, Manhattan, KS 66506. Offers career and technical education (Ed D, PhD); curriculum studies (Ed D, PhD); digital teaching and learning (MS); educational computing, design and online learning (MS); educational technology (Ed D, PhD); elementary/middle level (MS); English as a second language (MS); language/diversity education (Ed D, PhD); literacy education (Ed D, PhD); mathematics education (Ed D, PhD); middle level/secondary (MS); reading and language arts (MS); reading specialist endorsement (MS); science education (Ed D, PhD); social science education (Ed D, PhD); teacher education (Ed D, PhD); teacher leader/school improvement (MS, Ed D). *Accreditation:* NCATE. Part-time programs available. Postbaccalaureate distance learning degree programs offered (minimal on-campus study). *Faculty:* 15 full-time (12 women), 3 part-time/adjunct (2 women). *Students:* 37 full-time (30 women), 113 part-time (91 women); includes 14 minority (4 Black or African American, non-Hispanic/Latino; 1 American Indian or Alaska Native, non-Hispanic/Latino; 1 Asian, non-Hispanic/Latino; 7 Hispanic/Latino; 1 Two or more races, non-Hispanic/Latino), 15 international. Average age 37. 75 applicants, 51% accepted, 9 enrolled. In 2011, 48 master's, 14 doctorates awarded. *Degree requirements:* For master's, comprehensive exam, portfolio, project, report or thesis; for doctorate, comprehensive exam, thesis/dissertation, preliminary exam. *Entrance requirements:* For master's, minimum GPA of 3.0; for doctorate, GRE, minimum GPA of 3.0. Additional exam requirements/recommendations for international students: Required—TOEFL. *Application deadline:* For fall admission, 2/1 priority date for domestic students, 2/1 for international students; for spring admission, 8/1 priority date for domestic students, 8/1 for international students. Applications are processed on a rolling basis. Application fee: $40 ($55 for international students). Electronic applications accepted. *Financial support:* In 2011–12, 1 research assistantship (averaging $16,900 per year), 8 teaching assistantships (averaging $12,466 per year) were awarded; career-related internships or fieldwork, institutionally sponsored loans, and scholarships/grants also available. Support available to part-time students. Financial award application deadline: 3/1; financial award applicants required to submit FAFSA. *Faculty research:* Literacy and technology, critical race theory and diversity, achievement gaps, school improvement, teacher education. *Total annual research expenditures:* $510,907. *Unit head:* Dr. Gail Shroyer, Chair, 785-532-5550, Fax: 785-532-7304, E-mail: gshroyer@ksu.edu. *Application contact:* Dona Deam, Application Contact, 785-532-5595, Fax: 785-532-7304, E-mail: ddeam@ksu.edu. Web site: http://coe.k-state.edu/departments/currin/curringrad.htm.

Kansas State University, Graduate School, College of Education, Department of Educational Leadership, Manhattan, KS 66506. Offers adult, occupational and continuing education (MS, Ed D, PhD); educational leadership (MS, Ed D). *Accreditation:* NCATE. *Faculty:* 10 full-time (5 women), 1 part-time/adjunct (0 women). *Students:* 43 full-time (21 women), 185 part-time (91 women); includes 37 minority (14 Black or African American, non-Hispanic/Latino; 1 American Indian or Alaska Native, non-Hispanic/Latino; 4 Asian, non-Hispanic/Latino; 16 Hispanic/Latino; 2 Two or more races, non-Hispanic/Latino), 1 international. Average age 40. 96 applicants, 59% accepted, 37 enrolled. In 2011, 74 master's, 8 doctorates awarded. *Degree requirements:* For master's, comprehensive exam; for doctorate, comprehensive exam, thesis/dissertation. *Entrance requirements:* For master's, minimum undergraduate GPA of 3.0; for doctorate, GRE General Test, minimum GPA of 3.0 in last 60 hours. Additional exam requirements/recommendations for international students: Required—TOEFL. *Application deadline:* For fall admission, 2/1 priority date for domestic students, 2/1 for international students; for spring admission, 8/1 priority date for domestic students, 8/1 for international students. Applications are processed on a rolling basis. Application fee: $40 ($55 for international students). Electronic applications accepted. *Financial support:* Career-related internships or fieldwork, institutionally sponsored loans, and scholarships/grants available. Support available to part-time students. Financial award application deadline: 3/1; financial award applicants required to submit FAFSA. *Faculty research:* Educational law, school finance, school facilities, organizational leadership, adult learning, distance learning/education. *Total annual research expenditures:* $5,648. *Unit head:* David C. Thompson, Head, 785-532-5535, Fax: 785-532-7304, E-mail: thomsond@ksu.edu. *Application contact:* Dona Deam, Applications Contact, 785-532-5595, Fax: 785-532-7304, E-mail: ddeam@ksu.edu. Web site: http://coe.k-state.edu/departments/edlea/index.htm.

Kaplan University, Davenport Campus, School of Higher Education Studies, Davenport, IA 52807-2095. Offers college administration and leadership (MS); college teaching and learning (MS); student services (MS). Part-time and evening/weekend programs available. Postbaccalaureate distance learning degree programs offered (no on-campus study). *Entrance requirements:* Additional exam requirements/recommendations for international students: Required—TOEFL (minimum score 550 paper-based; 218 computer-based; 80 iBT).

Kean University, Nathan Weiss Graduate College, Program in Educational Administration, Union, NJ 07083. Offers school business administration (MA); supervisors and principals (MA). *Accreditation:* NCATE. *Faculty:* 6 full-time (3 women). *Students:* 8 full-time (6 women), 201 part-time (130 women); includes 67 minority (38 Black or African American, non-Hispanic/Latino; 5 Asian, non-Hispanic/Latino; 23 Hispanic/Latino; 1 Native Hawaiian or other Pacific Islander, non-Hispanic/Latino), 1 international. Average age 36. 72 applicants, 100% accepted, 58 enrolled. In 2011, 55 master's awarded. *Degree requirements:* For master's, comprehensive exam, portfolio, field experience, research component, internship, teaching experience. *Entrance requirements:* For master's, GRE General Test or MAT, minimum GPA of 3.0, interview, 2 letters of recommendation, transcripts, personal statement, transcript. Additional exam requirements/recommendations for international students: Required—TOEFL (minimum score 79 iBT). *Application deadline:* For fall admission, 6/1 for domestic and international students; for spring admission, 12/1 for domestic and international students. Applications are processed on a rolling basis. Application fee: $75 ($150 for international students). Electronic applications accepted. *Expenses:* Tuition, state resident: full-time $11,302; part-time $550 per credit. Tuition, nonresident: full-time $15,318; part-time $674 per credit. *Required fees:* $2849; $130 per credit. Tuition and fees vary according to degree level. *Financial support:* In 2011–12, research assistantships with full tuition reimbursements (averaging $3,263 per year) were awarded; unspecified assistantships also available. Financial award applicants required to submit FAFSA. *Unit head:* Dr. Efthimia Christie, Program Coordinator, 908-737-5974, E-mail: echristi@kean.edu. *Application contact:* Ann-Marie Kay, Assistant Director of Graduate Admissions, 908-737-5922, Fax: 908-737-5925, E-mail: akay@kean.edu. Web site: http://www.kean.edu/KU/School-Business-Administrator.

Kean University, Nathan Weiss Graduate College, Program in Urban Leadership, Union, NJ 07083. Offers Ed D. *Faculty:* 6 full-time (3 women). *Students:* 59 part-time (41 women); includes 43 minority (38 Black or African American, non-Hispanic/Latino; 5 Hispanic/Latino). Average age 44. 20 applicants, 65% accepted, 13 enrolled. *Degree requirements:* For doctorate, comprehensive exam, thesis/dissertation. *Entrance requirements:* For doctorate, GRE General Test, GRE Subject Test in psychology (taken within the last 5 years), master's degree from accredited college, minimum GPA of 3.0 in last degree attained, substantial experience working in education or family support agencies, 2 letters of recommendation, personal interview, transcripts, leadership portfolio, resume. Additional exam requirements/recommendations for international students: Required—TOEFL (minimum score 79 iBT). *Application deadline:* For fall admission, 6/1 for domestic and international students; for spring admission, 12/1 for domestic and international students. Applications are processed on a rolling basis. Application fee: $75 ($150 for international students). Electronic applications accepted. *Expenses:* Contact institution. *Financial support:* In 2011–12, research assistantships (averaging $3,263 per year) were awarded; unspecified assistantships also available. Financial award applicants required to submit FAFSA. *Unit head:* Dr. Effie Christie, Program Director, 908-737-5974, E-mail: echristi@kean.edu. *Application contact:* Reenat Hasan, Admissions Counselor, 908-737-5923, Fax: 908-737-5925, E-mail:

hasanr@kean.edu. Web site: http://www.kean.edu/KU/Doctor-of-Education-Ed-D-in-Urban-Leadership.

Keene State College, School of Professional and Graduate Studies, Keene, NH 03435. Offers curriculum and instruction (M Ed); education leadership (PMC); educational leadership (M Ed); safety and occupational health applied science (MS); school counselor (M Ed, PMC); special education (M Ed); teacher certification (Postbaccalaureate Certificate). *Accreditation:* NCATE. Part-time and evening/weekend programs available. *Faculty:* 11 full-time (7 women), 15 part-time/adjunct (8 women). *Students:* 36 full-time (32 women), 69 part-time (54 women); includes 1 minority (American Indian or Alaska Native, non-Hispanic/Latino), 1 international. Average age 33. 48 applicants, 83% accepted, 32 enrolled. In 2011, 39 master's, 12 other advanced degrees awarded. *Entrance requirements:* For master's, PRAXIS I, resume; minimum GPA of 2.5. Additional exam requirements/recommendations for international students: Required—TOEFL (minimum score 550 paper-based; 173 computer-based; 61 iBT). *Application deadline:* For fall admission, 4/1 for domestic students; for spring admission, 12/1 for domestic students. Applications are processed on a rolling basis. Application fee: $50. Electronic applications accepted. *Expenses:* Tuition, state resident: part-time $420 per credit. Tuition, nonresident: part-time $460 per credit. Tuition and fees vary according to course load. *Financial support:* Research assistantships, career-related internships or fieldwork, Federal Work-Study, institutionally sponsored loans, and unspecified assistantships available. Support available to part-time students. Financial award application deadline: 3/1; financial award applicants required to submit FAFSA. *Unit head:* Dr. Melinda Treadwell, Dean, 603-358-2220, E-mail: mtreadwe@keene.edu. *Application contact:* Peggy Richmond, Director of Admissions, 603-358-2276, Fax: 603-358-2767, E-mail: admissions@keene.edu. Web site: http://www.keene.edu/ps/.

Keiser University, Master of Science in Education Program, Fort Lauderdale, FL 33309. Offers college administration (MS Ed); leadership (MS Ed); teaching and learning (MS Ed). Part-time programs available. Postbaccalaureate distance learning degree programs offered (no on-campus study). *Entrance requirements:* For master's, minimum GPA of 2.7 from an accredited institution. Additional exam requirements/recommendations for international students: Required—TOEFL. Electronic applications accepted.

Keiser University, PhD in Educational Leadership Program, Fort Lauderdale, FL 33309. Offers PhD.

Kennesaw State University, Leland and Clarice C. Bagwell College of Education, Program in Graduate Education, Kennesaw, GA 30144-5591. Offers adolescent education (M Ed); educational leadership (M Ed); educational leadership technology (M Ed); elementary and early childhood education (M Ed); special education (M Ed); teaching English to speakers of other languages (M Ed). *Accreditation:* NCATE. Part-time programs available. *Students:* 42 full-time (39 women), 132 part-time (105 women); includes 31 minority (20 Black or African American, non-Hispanic/Latino; 4 Asian, non-Hispanic/Latino; 5 Hispanic/Latino; 2 Two or more races, non-Hispanic/Latino). Average age 34. 48 applicants, 79% accepted, 38 enrolled. In 2011, 117 master's awarded. *Degree requirements:* For master's, thesis or alternative. *Entrance requirements:* For master's, GRE General Test, T-4 state certification, minimum GPA of 2.75. Additional exam requirements/recommendations for international students: Required—TOEFL (minimum score 550 paper-based; 213 computer-based; 80 iBT), IELTS (minimum score 6). *Application deadline:* For fall admission, 7/1 for domestic and international students; for spring admission, 10/1 for domestic and international students. Application fee: $60. Electronic applications accepted. *Expenses:* Tuition, state resident: full-time $3000; part-time $250 per semester hour. Tuition, nonresident: full-time $10,836; part-time $903 per semester hour. *Required fees:* $774 per semester. *Financial support:* Federal Work-Study and unspecified assistantships available. Support available to part-time students. Financial award application deadline: 4/1; financial award applicants required to submit FAFSA. *Unit head:* Dr. Nita Paris, Associate Dean for Graduate Programs, 770-423-6636, E-mail: nparis@kennesaw.edu. *Application contact:* Alisha Bello, Administrative Coordinator, 770-423-6043, Fax: 770-420-4435, E-mail: abello1@kennesaw.edu. Web site: http://www.kennesaw.edu/education/grad/.

Kennesaw State University, Leland and Clarice C. Bagwell College of Education, Program in Leadership for Learning, Kennesaw, GA 30144-5591. Offers Ed D, Ed S. Part-time and evening/weekend programs available. *Students:* 19 full-time (14 women), 105 part-time (82 women); includes 30 minority (24 Black or African American, non-Hispanic/Latino; 2 Asian, non-Hispanic/Latino; 3 Hispanic/Latino; 1 Two or more races, non-Hispanic/Latino). Average age 41. 25 applicants, 92% accepted, 6 enrolled. In 2011, 16 doctorates, 31 other advanced degrees awarded. *Degree requirements:* For doctorate, thesis/dissertation. *Entrance requirements:* For doctorate, GRE General Test, minimum graduate GPA of 3.0, resume. Additional exam requirements/recommendations for international students: Required—TOEFL (minimum score 550 paper-based; 218 computer-based; 80 iBT), IELTS (minimum score 6). *Application deadline:* For fall admission, 6/1 for domestic and international students; for spring admission, 9/1 for domestic and international students. Application fee: $60. Electronic applications accepted. *Expenses:* Tuition, state resident: full-time $3000; part-time $250 per semester hour. Tuition, nonresident: full-time $10,836; part-time $903 per semester hour. *Required fees:* $774 per semester. *Financial support:* In 2011–12, 2 research assistantships with tuition reimbursements (averaging $4,000 per year) were awarded. Financial award application deadline: 4/1; financial award applicants required to submit FAFSA. *Unit head:* Dr. Nita Paris, Associate Dean for Graduate Programs, 770-423-6636, E-mail: nparis@kennesaw.edu. *Application contact:* Alisha Bello, Administrative Coordinator, 770-423-6043, Fax: 770-420-4435, E-mail: abello1@kennesaw.edu.

Kent State University, Graduate School of Education, Health, and Human Services, School of Foundations, Leadership and Administration, Program in K-12 Leadership, Kent, OH 44242-0001. Offers M Ed, PhD, Ed S. *Faculty:* 3 full-time (2 women), 7 part-time/adjunct (6 women). *Students:* 15 full-time (8 women), 49 part-time (33 women); includes 2 minority (1 Black or African American, non-Hispanic/Latino; 1 Asian, non-Hispanic/Latino). 39 applicants, 38% accepted. In 2011, 27 master's, 2 doctorates, 5 other advanced degrees awarded. *Degree requirements:* For master's, thesis optional; for doctorate, comprehensive exam, thesis/dissertation. *Entrance requirements:* For master's, GRE required if GPA is below 3.0, 2 letters of reference, goals statement; for doctorate, GRE, minimum master's-level GPA of 3.5, interview, resume, 2 letters of reference, goals statement; for Ed S, GRE. Additional exam requirements/recommendations for international students: Required—TOEFL (minimum score 550 paper-based; 213 computer-based; 80 iBT). *Application deadline:* Applications are processed on a rolling basis. Application fee: $30 ($60 for international students). Electronic applications accepted. *Expenses:* Tuition, state resident: full-time $8136; part-time $452 per credit hour. Tuition, nonresident: full-time $14,292; part-time $794 per credit hour. *Financial support:* In 2011–12, 1 research assistantship (averaging $12,000 per year) was awarded; fellowships, teaching assistantships, career-related internships or fieldwork, Federal Work-Study, institutionally sponsored loans, scholarships/grants, health care benefits, unspecified assistantships, and 1 administrative assistantship (averaging $8,500 per year) also available. Support available to part-time students. *Unit head:* Cathy Hackney, Coordinator, 330-672-0583, E-mail: chackne1@kent.edu. *Application contact:* Nancy Miller, Academic Program Coordinator, Office of Graduate Student Services, 330-672-2576, Fax: 330-672-9162, E-mail: ogs@kent.edu.

Kutztown University of Pennsylvania, College of Education, Program in Student Affairs in Higher Education, Kutztown, PA 19530-0730. Offers M Ed. *Accreditation:* NCATE. Part-time and evening/weekend programs available. *Faculty:* 2 full-time (both women). *Students:* 15 full-time (9 women), 12 part-time (8 women); includes 6 minority (3 Black or African American, non-Hispanic/Latino; 1 Asian, non-Hispanic/Latino; 2 Hispanic/Latino). Average age 27. 11 applicants, 100% accepted, 4 enrolled. In 2011, 9 master's awarded. *Degree requirements:* For master's, comprehensive exam. *Entrance requirements:* For master's, GRE General Test, interview. Additional exam requirements/recommendations for international students: Required—TOEFL (minimum score 550 paper-based; 79 iBT). *Application deadline:* For fall admission, 3/1 for domestic and international students; for spring admission, 10/1 for domestic and international students. Application fee: $35. Electronic applications accepted. *Expenses:* Tuition, state resident: full-time $7488; part-time $416 per credit. Tuition, nonresident: full-time $11,232; part-time $624 per credit. *Financial support:* Career-related internships or fieldwork, Federal Work-Study, scholarships/grants, and unspecified assistantships available. Financial award application deadline: 3/1; financial award applicants required to submit FAFSA. *Unit head:* Dr. Deborah Barlieb, Chairperson, 610-683-4204, Fax: 610-683-1585, E-mail: barlieb@kutztown.edu. *Application contact:* Kelly D. Burr, Associate Director, Graduate Admissions, 610-683-4200, Fax: 610-683-1393, E-mail: graduate@kutztown.edu.

Lake Erie College, School of Professional and Innovative Studies, Painesville, OH 44077-3389. Offers curriculum and instruction (MS Ed); education (MS Ed); educational leadership (MS Ed); reading (MS Ed). Part-time and evening/weekend programs available. *Faculty:* 3 full-time (all women), 1 part-time/adjunct (0 women). *Students:* 20 part-time (15 women); includes 14 minority (all American Indian or Alaska Native, non-Hispanic/Latino). Average age 35. 5 applicants, 100% accepted, 1 enrolled. In 2011, 7 master's awarded. *Degree requirements:* For master's, comprehensive exam (for some programs), thesis optional, applied research project. *Entrance requirements:* For master's, GRE General Test (minimum score of 440 verbal or 500 quantitative) or minimum GPA of 2.75; bachelor's degree from accredited 4-year institution; references; essay. Additional exam requirements/recommendations for international students: Required—TOEFL (minimum score 550 paper-based; 79 computer-based). *Application deadline:* For fall admission, 8/1 priority date for domestic students, 6/1 for international students; for spring admission, 12/15 for domestic students, 10/1 for international students. Applications are processed on a rolling basis. Application fee: $30. Electronic applications accepted. Application fee is waived when completed online. *Expenses:* Contact institution. *Financial support:* Teaching assistantships, tuition waivers, and unspecified assistantships available. Financial award applicants required to submit FAFSA. *Faculty research:* Cooperative learning, portfolio assessment, education systems abroad, Web-based instruction. *Unit head:* Prof. Dale Sheptak, Interim Dean of the School of Professional and Innovative Studies/Assistant Professor, 440-375-7131, E-mail: dsheptak@lec.edu. *Application contact:* Christopher Harris, Dean of Admissions and Financial Aid, 800-916-0904, Fax: 440-375-7000, E-mail: admissions@lec.edu. Web site: http://www.lec.edu/med.

Lamar University, College of Graduate Studies, College of Education and Human Development, Department of Educational Leadership, Beaumont, TX 77710. Offers counseling and development (M Ed, Certificate); education administration (M Ed); educational leadership (DE); principal (Certificate); school superintendent (Certificate); supervision (M Ed); technology application (Certificate). Part-time and evening/weekend programs available. *Faculty:* 19 full-time (8 women), 2 part-time/adjunct (1 woman). *Students:* 23 full-time (14 women), 1,716 part-time (1,106 women); includes 476 minority (246 Black or African American, non-Hispanic/Latino; 13 American Indian or Alaska Native, non-Hispanic/Latino; 18 Asian, non-Hispanic/Latino; 198 Hispanic/Latino; 1 Two or more races, non-Hispanic/Latino), 1 international. Average age 37. 956 applicants, 97% accepted, 547 enrolled. In 2011, 1,609 master's, 16 doctorates awarded. Terminal master's awarded for partial completion of doctoral program. *Degree requirements:* For master's, comprehensive exam, thesis optional; for doctorate, thesis/dissertation. *Entrance requirements:* For master's, GRE General Test, minimum GPA of 2.5; for doctorate, GRE. Additional exam requirements/recommendations for international students: Required—TOEFL. *Application deadline:* For fall admission, 8/1 priority date for domestic students; for spring admission, 12/1 priority date for domestic students. Applications are processed on a rolling basis. Application fee: $25 ($50 for international students). *Expenses:* Tuition, state resident: full-time $5430; part-time $272 per credit hour. Tuition, nonresident: full-time $11,540; part-time $577 per credit hour. *Required fees:* $1916. *Financial support:* In 2011–12, 3 fellowships (averaging $20,000 per year), 1 research assistantship with tuition reimbursement (averaging $6,500 per year) were awarded; teaching assistantships with tuition reimbursements, career-related internships or fieldwork, and scholarships/grants also available. Support available to part-time students. Financial award application deadline: 4/1. *Faculty research:* School dropouts, suicide prevention in public school students, school climate and gifted performance, teacher evaluation. *Unit head:* Dr. Carolyn Crawford, Chair, 409-880-8689, Fax: 409-880-8685. *Application contact:* Dr. Lula Henry, Director of Professional Service, 409-880-8218.

La Sierra University, School of Education, Department of Administration and Leadership, Riverside, CA 92515. Offers MA, Ed D, Ed S. Part-time and evening/weekend programs available. Terminal master's awarded for partial completion of doctoral program. *Degree requirements:* For master's, thesis optional; for doctorate, thesis/dissertation, fieldwork, qualifying exam; for Ed S, thesis optional, fieldwork. *Entrance requirements:* For master's, minimum GPA of 3.0; for doctorate, GRE General Test, GRE Subject Test, minimum GPA of 3.3, Ed S; for Ed S, master's degree, minimum GPA of 3.3.

Lee University, Program in Education, Cleveland, TN 37320-3450. Offers classroom teaching (M Ed, Ed S); educational leadership (M Ed, Ed S); elementary/secondary education (MAT); secondary education (MAT); special education (M Ed); special education (secondary) (MAT). Part-time programs available. *Faculty:* 14 full-time (6 women), 5 part-time/adjunct (3 women). *Students:* 43 full-time (27 women), 176 part-time (107 women); includes 19 minority (4 Black or African American, non-Hispanic/Latino; 3 American Indian or Alaska Native, non-Hispanic/Latino; 1 Asian, non-Hispanic/Latino; 8 Hispanic/Latino; 3 Two or more races, non-Hispanic/Latino), 4 international. Average age 33. 52 applicants, 100% accepted, 38 enrolled. In 2011, 90 master's, 14 other advanced degrees awarded. *Degree requirements:* For master's, variable foreign language requirement, comprehensive exam, thesis, internship. *Entrance requirements:* For master's, MAT or GRE General Test, minimum GPA of 2.75, 3 letters of recommendation, interview, writing sample. Additional exam requirements/recommendations for international students: Required—TOEFL (minimum score 450 paper-based; 45 computer-based). *Application deadline:* For fall admission, 4/1 priority date for domestic students; for spring admission, 10/1 priority date for domestic students. Applications are processed on a rolling basis. Application fee: $25. *Expenses:* *Tuition:* Full-time $12,120; part-time $506 per credit hour. *Required fees:* $560; $305 per term. Part-time tuition and fees vary according to course load. *Financial support:* In 2011–12, 18 teaching assistantships (averaging $1,966 per year) were awarded; career-related internships or fieldwork, Federal Work-Study, institutionally sponsored loans, scholarships/grants, and unspecified assistantships also available. Financial award application deadline: 3/1; financial award applicants required to submit FAFSA. *Unit head:* Dr. Gary Riggins, Director, 423-614-8193. *Application contact:* Vicki Glasscock, Graduate Admissions Director, 423-614-8059, E-mail: vglasscock@leeuniversity.edu. Web site: http://www.leeuniversity.edu/academics/graduate/education.

Lehigh University, College of Education, Program in Educational Leadership, Bethlehem, PA 18015. Offers educational leadership (M Ed, Ed D); principal certification K-12 (Certificate); pupil services (Certificate); special education (Certificate); superintendant certification (Certificate); supervisor of curriculum and instruction (Certificate); supervisor of pupil services (Certificate); MBA/M Ed. Part-time and evening/weekend programs available. Postbaccalaureate distance learning degree programs offered (minimal on-campus study). *Faculty:* 7 full-time (2 women), 8 part-time/adjunct (6 women). *Students:* 4 full-time (all women), 149 part-time (68 women); includes 6 minority (2 Black or African American, non-Hispanic/Latino; 2 Asian, non-Hispanic/Latino; 2 Hispanic/Latino), 19 international. Average age 38. 61 applicants, 52% accepted, 4 enrolled. In 2011, 36 master's, 5 doctorates awarded. *Degree requirements:* For doctorate, comprehensive exam, thesis/dissertation. *Entrance requirements:* For master's and Certificate, minimum undergraduate GPA of 3.0; for doctorate, GRE General Test or MAT, minimum graduate GPA of 3.6, 2 letters of recommendation, essay, transcript. Additional exam requirements/recommendations for international students: Required—TOEFL (minimum score 600 paper-based; 250 computer-based; 93 iBT). *Application deadline:* For fall admission, 1/15 for domestic and international students; for spring admission, 11/1 for domestic and international students. Applications are processed on a rolling basis. Application fee: $65. Electronic applications accepted. *Expenses:* Contact institution. *Financial support:* In 2011–12, 1 student received support, including 1 research assistantship with full and partial tuition reimbursement available (averaging $13,000 per year); fellowships with full and partial tuition reimbursements available, teaching assistantships with full and partial tuition reimbursements available, career-related internships or fieldwork, Federal Work-Study, institutionally sponsored loans, scholarships/grants, and tuition waivers (full and partial) also available. Financial award application deadline: 1/31. *Faculty research:* School finance and law, supervision of instruction, middle-level education, organizational change, leadership preparation and development, international school leadership, urban school leadership. *Unit head:* Dr. Floyd D. Beachum, Director, 610-758-5955, Fax: 610-758-3227, E-mail: fdb209@lehigh.edu. *Application contact:* Donna M. Johnson, Coordinator, 610-758-3231, Fax: 610-758-6223, E-mail: dmj4@lehigh.edu.

Le Moyne College, Department of Education, Syracuse, NY 13214. Offers adolescent education (MS Ed, MST); adolescent education/special education (MS Ed, MST); adolescent English (grades 7-12) (MST); adolescent history (grades 7-12) (MST); childhood education (MS Ed); childhood education/special education (MS Ed); elementary education (MS Ed); general professional education (MS Ed); inclusive childhood education (MST); literacy education (birth to grade 6) (MS Ed); literacy education (grades 5-12) (MS Ed); school building leadership (MS Ed, CAS); school district business leader (MS Ed, CAS); school district leadership (MS Ed, CAS); secondary education (MS Ed); special education (MS Ed); students with disabilities-generalist (grades 7-12) (MS Ed); TESOL (teaching English to speakers of other languages) (MS Ed); urban studies (MS Ed). *Accreditation:* Teacher Education Accreditation Council. Part-time and evening/weekend programs available. *Faculty:* 9 full-time (6 women), 51 part-time/adjunct (28 women). *Students:* 61 full-time (47 women), 311 part-time (222 women); includes 31 minority (19 Black or African American, non-Hispanic/Latino; 3 American Indian or Alaska Native, non-Hispanic/Latino; 4 Asian, non-Hispanic/Latino; 5 Hispanic/Latino), 2 international. Average age 30. 242 applicants, 90% accepted, 180 enrolled. In 2011, 168 master's, 23 CASs awarded. *Degree requirements:* For master's, thesis. *Entrance requirements:* For master's, GRE General Test, bachelor's degree, 2 letters of recommendation, written statement, transcripts. Additional exam requirements/recommendations for international students: Required—TOEFL (minimum score 550 paper-based; 213 computer-based; 79 iBT). *Application deadline:* For fall admission, 4/1 priority date for domestic students, 4/1 for international students; for spring admission, 10/1 priority date for domestic students, 10/1 for international students. Applications are processed on a rolling basis. Application fee: $50. *Expenses:* Contact institution. *Financial support:* In 2011–12, 32 students received support. Career-related internships or fieldwork and health care benefits available. Support available to part-time students. Financial award applicants required to submit FAFSA. *Faculty research:* Minority teachers, special education, multiculturalism, literacy, technology, video games learning, autism, school district organization, service-learning, higher level problem solving, teacher leadership. *Unit head:* Dr. Suzanne L. Gilmour, Chair, Department of Education and Director of Graduate Education Programs, 315-445-4376, Fax: 315-445-4744, E-mail: gilmous@lemoyne.edu. *Application contact:* Kristen P. Trapasso, Director of Graduate Admission, 315-445-4265, Fax: 315-445-6027, E-mail: trapaskp@lemoyne.edu. Web site: http://www.lemoyne.edu/education.

Lewis & Clark College, Graduate School of Education and Counseling, Department of Educational Leadership, Program in Educational Leadership, Portland, OR 97219-7899. Offers educational leadership (Ed D, Ed S). Part-time and evening/weekend programs available. *Faculty:* 4 full-time (all women), 19 part-time/adjunct (11 women). *Students:* 2 full-time (both women), 55 part-time (34 women); includes 8 minority (2 Black or African American, non-Hispanic/Latino; 1 American Indian or Alaska Native, non-Hispanic/Latino; 5 Hispanic/Latino). Average age 42. 32 applicants, 72% accepted, 19 enrolled. In 2011, 3 doctorates, 5 other advanced degrees awarded. *Degree requirements:* For doctorate, thesis/dissertation. *Entrance requirements:* For doctorate, master's degree plus minimum of 14 degree-applicable, post-master's semester credits; minimum undergraduate GPA of 2.75. Additional exam requirements/recommendations for international students: Required—TOEFL (minimum score 575 paper-based; 233 computer-based). *Application deadline:* For fall admission, 5/1 for domestic and international students. Applications are processed on a rolling basis. Application fee: $50. Electronic applications accepted. *Expenses: Tuition:* Part-time $738 per semester hour. Tuition and fees vary according to course level and campus/location. *Financial support:* In 2011–12, 4 students received support. Career-related internships or fieldwork, Federal Work-Study, institutionally sponsored loans, health care benefits, and tuition waivers (partial) available. Support available to part-time students. Financial award application deadline: 3/1; financial award applicants required to submit FAFSA. *Unit head:* Dr. Carolyn Carr, Department Chair, 503-768-6080, Fax: 503-768-6085, E-mail: eda@lclark.edu. *Application contact:* Becky Haas, Director of Admissions, 503-768-6200, Fax: 503-768-6205, E-mail: gseadmit@lclark.edu. Web site: http://www.lclark.edu/dept/eda/.

Lewis University, College of Education, Program in Advanced Study in Education, Romeoville, IL 60446. Offers general administrative (CAS); superintendent endorsement (CAS). Part-time and evening/weekend programs available. *Students:* 3 full-time (2 women), 11 part-time (8 women); includes 5 minority (all Black or African American, non-Hispanic/Latino). Average age 41. *Entrance requirements:* Additional exam requirements/recommendations for international students: Required—TOEFL (minimum score 550 paper-based; 213 computer-based; 80 iBT). *Application deadline:* For fall admission, 5/1 for international students; for spring admission, 11/15 for international students. Applications are processed on a rolling basis. Application fee: $40. Electronic applications accepted. *Financial support:* Institutionally sponsored loans and unspecified assistantships available. Support available to part-time students. Financial award application deadline: 5/1; financial award applicants required to submit FAFSA. *Unit head:* Dr. Barbara Mackey, Program Director, 815-838-0500 Ext. 5962, E-mail: mackeyba@lewisu.edu. *Application contact:* Kelly Lofgren, Graduate Admission Counselor, 815-836-5704, Fax: 815-836-5578, E-mail: lofgreke@lewisu.edu.

Lewis University, College of Education, Program in Educational Leadership, Romeoville, IL 60446. Offers M Ed, MA. Part-time and evening/weekend programs available. *Students:* 9 full-time (7 women), 68 part-time (49 women); includes 13 minority (10 Black or African American, non-Hispanic/Latino; 1 Asian, non-Hispanic/Latino; 2 Hispanic/Latino). Average age 34. In 2011, 53 master's awarded. *Entrance requirements:* For master's, departmental qualifying exams, writing exam, minimum GPA of 2.75, 2 letters of recommendation, interview. Additional exam requirements/recommendations for international students: Required—TOEFL (minimum score 550 paper-based; 213 computer-based; 80 iBT). *Application deadline:* For fall admission, 5/1 for international students; for spring admission, 11/15 for international students. Application fee: $40. *Financial support:* Federal Work-Study, scholarships/grants, and unspecified assistantships available. Financial award application deadline: 5/1; financial award applicants required to submit FAFSA. *Unit head:* Dr. Jane Petrek, Director, 815-838-0500 Ext. 5039, Fax: 815-836-5879, E-mail: petrekja@lewisu.edu. *Application contact:* Kelly Lofgren, Graduate Admission Counselor, 815-836-5704, Fax: 815-836-5578, E-mail: lofgreke@lewisu.edu.

Lewis University, College of Education, Program in Educational Leadership for Teaching and Learning, Romeoville, IL 60446. Offers Ed D. *Students:* 51 part-time (38 women); includes 20 minority (13 Black or African American, non-Hispanic/Latino; 1 Asian, non-Hispanic/Latino; 6 Hispanic/Latino), 1 international. Average age 41. In 2011, 7 doctorates awarded. *Degree requirements:* For doctorate, thesis/dissertation. *Entrance requirements:* For doctorate, GRE General Test, letters of recommendation, personal statement, academic and scholarly work. Application fee: $40. *Financial support:* Application deadline: 5/1; applicants required to submit FAFSA. *Unit head:* Dr. Lauren Hoffman, Program Director, 815-838-0500 Ext. 5501, E-mail: hoffmala@lewisu.edu. *Application contact:* Leslie Jacobson, Director, Graduate and Adult Enrollment Systems, 815-836-5821, E-mail: jacobsle@lewisu.edu.

Liberty University, School of Education, Lynchburg, VA 24502. Offers administration and supervision (M Ed); curriculum and instruction (M Ed); early childhood education (M Ed); educational leadership (Ed D, Ed S); educational technology and online instruction (M Ed); elementary education (M Ed, MAT); gifted education (M Ed); math specialist (M Ed); middle grades (M Ed); outdoor adventure sport (MS); reading specialist (M Ed); school counseling (M Ed); secondary education (M Ed, MAT); special education (M Ed, MAT); sports administration (MS); teaching and learning (Ed D, Ed S). *Accreditation:* NCATE. Part-time programs available. Postbaccalaureate distance learning degree programs offered (minimal on-campus study). *Students:* 2,245 full-time (1,572 women), 3,500 part-time (2,558 women); includes 1,141 minority (888 Black or African American, non-Hispanic/Latino; 19 American Indian or Alaska Native, non-Hispanic/Latino; 21 Asian, non-Hispanic/Latino; 123 Hispanic/Latino; 9 Native Hawaiian or other Pacific Islander, non-Hispanic/Latino; 81 Two or more races, non-Hispanic/Latino), 76 international. Average age 37. In 2011, 760 master's, 48 doctorates, 321 other advanced degrees awarded. *Degree requirements:* For doctorate, comprehensive exam, thesis/dissertation. *Entrance requirements:* For master's, GRE General Test or MAT (if taken in or before 1999), 2 letters of recommendation, minimum undergraduate GPA of 3.0, curriculum vitae; for doctorate, GRE General Test or MAT (if taken before 1999), minimum master's GPA of 3.0, 3 years of teacher experience; for Ed S, GRE General Test or MAT (if taken before 1999), minimum master's GPA of 3.0, 3 years of teaching experience. Additional exam requirements/recommendations for international students: Required—TOEFL (minimum score 600 paper-based; 250 computer-based). *Application deadline:* For fall admission, 6/1 priority date for domestic students; for spring admission, 11/1 for domestic students. Applications are processed on a rolling basis. Application fee: $50. Electronic applications accepted. *Expenses:* Contact institution. *Financial support:* Federal Work-Study and tuition waivers (partial) available. *Faculty research:* Self-determination, character education, bibliotherapy, learning styles, distance education. *Unit head:* Dr. Karen L. Parker, Dean, 434-582-2195, Fax: 434-582-2468, E-mail: kparker@liberty.edu. *Application contact:* Jay Bridge, Director of Graduate Admissions, 800-424-9595, Fax: 800-628-7977, E-mail: gradadmissions@liberty.edu. Web site: http://www.liberty.edu/academics/education/graduate/.

Lincoln Memorial University, Carter and Moyers School of Education, Harrogate, TN 37752-1901. Offers administration and supervision (M Ed, Ed S); counseling and guidance (M Ed); curriculum and instruction (M Ed, Ed D, Ed S); English (M Ed); executive leadership (Ed D); higher education administration (Ed D); human resource development (Ed D); leadership and administration (Ed D). Part-time and evening/weekend programs available. Postbaccalaureate distance learning degree programs offered. *Degree requirements:* For master's, comprehensive exam, thesis optional; for Ed S, comprehensive exam. *Entrance requirements:* For master's, PRAXIS, NTE, GRE, MAT, letters of recommendation; for Ed S, graduate transcripts. Additional exam requirements/recommendations for international students: Recommended—TOEFL. *Faculty research:* Brain compatible teaching and learning; poverty in Appalachia; leadership for change; ethics, moral responsibility and social justice; human and organizational learning.

Lincoln University, School of Graduate Studies and Continuing Education, Jefferson City, MO 65102. Offers business administration (MBA), including accounting, entrepreneurship, management, public administration and policy; educational leadership (Ed S), including elementary leadership, secondary leadership, superintendency; guidance and counseling (M Ed), including community/agency counseling, elementary school, secondary school; history (MA); school administration and supervision (M Ed), including elementary school administration, secondary school administration, special education administration; school teaching (M Ed), including elementary school teaching, secondary school teaching; social science (MA), including history, political science, sociology; sociology (MA); sociology/criminal justice (MA). Part-time and evening/weekend programs available. *Degree requirements:* For master's and Ed S, comprehensive exam, thesis optional. *Entrance requirements:* For master's and Ed S, GRE, MAT or GMAT, minimum GPA of 2.75 in major, 2.5 overall; 3 letters of recommendation; minimum C average in English composition; personal statement of purpose. Additional exam requirements/recommendations for international students: Required—TOEFL (minimum score 500 paper-based; 173 computer-based; 61 iBT). *Faculty research:* Suicide prevention.

Lindenwood University, Graduate Programs, School of Education, St. Charles, MO 63301-1695. Offers education (MA); educational administration (MA, Ed D, Ed S); human performance (MS); instructional leadership (Ed D, Ed S); library media (MA); professional and school counseling (MA); professional counseling (MA); school administration (Ed S); school counseling (MA); teaching (MA); teaching English to speakers of other languages (MA). Part-time and evening/weekend programs available. *Faculty:* 33 full-time (13 women), 176 part-time/adjunct (83 women). *Students:* 472 full-time (353 women), 1,772 part-time (1,373 women); includes 666 minority (605 Black or

African American, non-Hispanic/Latino; 15 American Indian or Alaska Native, non-Hispanic/Latino; 5 Asian, non-Hispanic/Latino; 2 Hispanic/Latino; 4 Native Hawaiian or other Pacific Islander, non-Hispanic/Latino; 35 Two or more races, non-Hispanic/Latino), 24 international. Average age 36. 472 applicants, 87% accepted, 366 enrolled. In 2011, 747 master's, 42 doctorates, 69 other advanced degrees awarded. *Degree requirements:* For master's, thesis (for some programs), minimum GPA of 3.0; for doctorate, thesis/dissertation, minimum GPA of 3.0; for Ed S, comprehensive exam, project, minimum GPA of 3.0. *Entrance requirements:* For master's, interview, minimum GPA of 3.0, writing sample, letter of recommendation; for doctorate, GRE, minimum graduate GPA of 3.4, resume, interview, writing sample, 4 letters of recommendation; for Ed S, master's degree in education, relevant work experience. Additional exam requirements/recommendations for international students: Required—TOEFL (minimum score 550 paper-based; 213 computer-based; 80 iBT). *Application deadline:* For fall admission, 8/26 priority date for domestic students, 8/26 for international students; for spring admission, 1/27 priority date for domestic students, 1/27 for international students. Applications are processed on a rolling basis. Application fee: $30 ($100 for international students). Electronic applications accepted. *Expenses: Tuition:* Full-time $13,650; part-time $395 per credit hour. *Required fees:* $150 per semester. Tuition and fees vary according to course level and course load. *Financial support:* In 2011–12, 153 students received support. Career-related internships or fieldwork, institutionally sponsored loans, tuition waivers (partial), and unspecified assistantships available. Financial award application deadline: 6/30; financial award applicants required to submit FAFSA. *Unit head:* Dr. Cynthia Bice, Dean, 636-949-4618, Fax: 636-949-4197, E-mail: cbice@lindenwood.edu. *Application contact:* Brett Barger, Dean of Evening Admissions and Extension Campuses, 636-949-4934, Fax: 636-949-4109, E-mail: adultadmissions@lindenwood.edu.

Lipscomb University, Program in Education, Nashville, TN 37204-3951. Offers educational leadership (M Ed); English language learning (M Ed); instructional practice (M Ed); instructional technology (M Ed); learning organizations and strategic change (Ed D); math specialty (M Ed); special education (M Ed); teaching, learning, and leading (M Ed). *Accreditation:* NCATE. Part-time and evening/weekend programs available. *Faculty:* 18 full-time (10 women), 23 part-time/adjunct (16 women). *Students:* 377 full-time (281 women), 117 part-time (85 women); includes 55 minority (39 Black or African American, non-Hispanic/Latino; 4 American Indian or Alaska Native, non-Hispanic/Latino; 5 Asian, non-Hispanic/Latino; 7 Hispanic/Latino). Average age 32. 300 applicants, 66% accepted, 142 enrolled. In 2011, 190 master's awarded. *Degree requirements:* For master's, comprehensive exam, portfolio, research project and presentation; for doctorate, practical capstone project in experiential setting. *Entrance requirements:* For master's, MAT or GRE General Test, 2 reference letters, goals statement, writing sample, interview; for doctorate, MAT or GRE General Test, 3 reference letters, artifact of demonstrated academic excellence, written personal statements, interview. Additional exam requirements/recommendations for international students: Required—TOEFL (minimum score 570 paper-based; 230 computer-based). *Application deadline:* For fall admission, 8/29 priority date for domestic students; for spring admission, 1/15 priority date for domestic students. Applications are processed on a rolling basis. Application fee: $50 ($75 for international students). *Expenses: Tuition:* Full-time $16,830; part-time $935 per credit hour. Tuition and fees vary according to degree level and program. *Financial support:* In 2011–12, 67 students received support. Scholarships/grants and tuition waivers (partial) available. Financial award applicants required to submit FAFSA. *Faculty research:* Facilitative learning styles, leadership, student assessment, interactive multimedia inclusion, learning organizations and strategic change. *Unit head:* Dr. Deborah Boyd, Director, 615-966-6263, E-mail: deborah.boyd@lipscomb.edu. *Application contact:* Kristin Baese, Assistant Director of Enrollment and Outreach, 615-966-7628 Ext. 6081, Fax: 615-966-5173, E-mail: kristin.baese@lipscomb.edu. Web site: http://graduateeducation.lipscomb.edu/.

Long Island University–Brooklyn Campus, School of Education, Department of Human Development and Leadership, Program in Leadership and Policy, Brooklyn, NY 11201-8423. Offers MS. *Degree requirements:* For master's, thesis optional. *Entrance requirements:* For master's, 2 letters of recommendation. Additional exam requirements/recommendations for international students: Required—TOEFL (minimum score 500 paper-based; 173 computer-based).

Long Island University–C. W. Post Campus, School of Education, Department of Educational Leadership and Administration, Brookville, NY 11548-1300. Offers school administration and supervision (MS Ed); school building leader (AC); school district business leader (AC); school district leader (AC). Part-time and evening/weekend programs available. *Degree requirements:* For master's, comprehensive exam or research project, internship; for AC, internship. *Entrance requirements:* For master's, minimum GPA of 3.0, 3 years of teaching experience. Electronic applications accepted. *Faculty research:* Leadership administration, computers in decision making, curricular innovation and school business administration.

Long Island University–C. W. Post Campus, School of Education, Program in Interdisciplinary Educational Studies, Brookville, NY 11548-1300. Offers educational leadership (Ed D); teaching and learning (Ed D). Part-time programs available. *Degree requirements:* For doctorate, comprehensive exam, thesis/dissertation, portfolio. *Entrance requirements:* For doctorate, master's degree in education or a related field, 3 letters of recommendation, writing sample, curriculum vitae/resume. Additional exam requirements/recommendations for international students: Required—TOEFL (minimum score 600 paper-based).

Long Island University–Hudson at Rockland, Graduate School, Program in Educational Leadership, Orangeburg, NY 10962. Offers MS Ed, Advanced Certificate. Part-time programs available. *Entrance requirements:* For master's, college transcripts, two letters of recommendation, resume.

Longwood University, Office of Graduate Studies, College of Education and Human Services, Farmville, VA 23909. Offers communication sciences and disorders (MS); community and college counseling (MS); curriculum and instruction specialist-elementary (MS), including mild disabilities, modern languages; curriculum and instruction specialist-secondary (MS), including English, mild disabilities, modern languages; educational leadership (MS); guidance and counseling (MS); literacy and culture (MS); school library media (MS). *Accreditation:* NCATE. Part-time and evening/weekend programs available. *Degree requirements:* For master's, comprehensive exam, thesis optional. *Entrance requirements:* For master's, GRE (communication sciences and disorders), minimum GPA of 2.75. Additional exam requirements/recommendations for international students: Required—TOEFL (minimum score 550 paper-based; 213 computer-based).

Loras College, Graduate Division, Program in Educational Leadership, Dubuque, IA 52004-0178. Offers MA. Part-time and evening/weekend programs available. *Degree requirements:* For master's, comprehensive exam, thesis optional. *Entrance requirements:* For master's, minimum cumulative undergraduate GPA of 3.0.

Louisiana State University and Agricultural and Mechanical College, Graduate School, College of Education, Department of Educational Theory, Policy and Practice, Baton Rouge, LA 70803. Offers counseling (M Ed, MA, Ed S); educational administration (M Ed, MA, PhD, Ed S); educational technology (MA); elementary education (M Ed, MAT); higher education (PhD); research methodology (PhD); secondary education (M Ed, MAT). PhD programs offered jointly with Louisiana State University in Shreveport. *Accreditation:* ACA (one or more programs are accredited); NCATE. Part-time and evening/weekend programs available. *Faculty:* 17 full-time (all women). *Students:* 188 full-time (145 women), 161 part-time (130 women); includes 104 minority (88 Black or African American, non-Hispanic/Latino; 1 American Indian or Alaska Native, non-Hispanic/Latino; 6 Asian, non-Hispanic/Latino; 5 Hispanic/Latino; 4 Two or more races, non-Hispanic/Latino), 9 international. Average age 31. 151 applicants, 61% accepted, 58 enrolled. In 2011, 129 master's, 17 doctorates, 11 other advanced degrees awarded. Terminal master's awarded for partial completion of doctoral program. *Degree requirements:* For doctorate, thesis/dissertation; for Ed S, thesis optional. *Entrance requirements:* For master's and doctorate, GRE General Test, minimum GPA of 3.0. Additional exam requirements/recommendations for international students: Required—TOEFL (minimum score 550 paper-based; 213 computer-based; 79 iBT) or IELTS (minimum score 6.5). *Application deadline:* For fall admission, 1/25 priority date for domestic students, 5/15 for international students; for spring admission, 10/15 for international students. Applications are processed on a rolling basis. Application fee: $50 ($70 for international students). Electronic applications accepted. *Financial support:* In 2011–12, 230 students received support, including 2 fellowships (averaging $19,353 per year), 24 research assistantships with full and partial tuition reimbursements available (averaging $10,052 per year), 53 teaching assistantships with full and partial tuition reimbursements available (averaging $12,218 per year); career-related internships or fieldwork, Federal Work-Study, institutionally sponsored loans, health care benefits, and unspecified assistantships also available. Support available to part-time students. Financial award applicants required to submit FAFSA. *Faculty research:* Literary, curriculum studies, science education, K-12 leadership, higher education. *Total annual research expenditures:* $774,887. *Unit head:* Dr. Earl Cheek, Jr., Chair, 225-578-6867, Fax: 225-578-9135, E-mail: echeek@lsu.edu. *Application contact:* Dr. Rita Culross, Graduate Coordinator, 225-578-6867, Fax: 225-578-9135, E-mail: acrita@lsu.edu.

Louisiana State University in Shreveport, College of Business, Education, and Human Development, Program in Education, Shreveport, LA 71115-2399. Offers education curriculum and instruction (M Ed); educational leadership (M Ed); school counseling (M Ed). Part-time programs available. *Students:* 6 full-time (all women), 55 part-time (40 women); includes 14 minority (12 Black or African American, non-Hispanic/Latino; 1 Asian, non-Hispanic/Latino; 1 Hispanic/Latino). Average age 35. 34 applicants, 97% accepted, 13 enrolled. In 2011, 14 master's awarded. *Degree requirements:* For master's, orally-presented project, 200-hour internship (educational leadership). *Entrance requirements:* For master's, GRE, minimum GPA of 2.5; teacher certification; recommendations and interview (for educational leadership). Additional exam requirements/recommendations for international students: Required—TOEFL (minimum score 550 paper-based; 213 computer-based; 80 iBT). *Application deadline:* For fall admission, 6/30 for domestic and international students; for spring admission, 11/30 for domestic and international students. Applications are processed on a rolling basis. Application fee: $10 ($20 for international students). *Financial support:* In 2011–12, 5 research assistantships (averaging $2,150 per year) were awarded. *Unit head:* Dr. Julie Bergeron, Coordinator, 318-797-5033, Fax: 318-798-4144, E-mail: julie.bergeron@lsus.edu. *Application contact:* Christianne Wojcik, Director of Academic Services, 318-797-5247, Fax: 318-798-4120, E-mail: christianne.wojcik@lsus.edu.

Louisiana Tech University, Graduate School, College of Education, Department of Curriculum, Instruction and Leadership, Ruston, LA 71272. Offers curriculum and instruction (MS, Ed D); educational leadership (Ed D); secondary education (M Ed), including business education, English education, foreign language education, health and physical education, mathematics education, science education, social studies education, speech education. *Accreditation:* NCATE. Part-time programs available. *Degree requirements:* For doctorate, thesis/dissertation. *Entrance requirements:* For master's and doctorate, GRE General Test.

Loyola Marymount University, School of Education, Department of Educational Leadership, Doctorate in Educational Leadership in Social Justice Program, Los Angeles, CA 90045. Offers Ed D. Part-time programs available. *Faculty:* 8 full-time (6 women), 8 part-time/adjunct (4 women). *Students:* 18 full-time (11 women), 48 part-time (29 women); includes 40 minority (9 Black or African American, non-Hispanic/Latino; 4 Asian, non-Hispanic/Latino; 26 Hispanic/Latino; 1 Two or more races, non-Hispanic/Latino), 1 international. Average age 37. 52 applicants, 44% accepted, 17 enrolled. In 2011, 11 doctorates awarded. *Degree requirements:* For doctorate, thesis/dissertation. *Entrance requirements:* For doctorate, GRE, interview, resume, 3 letters of recommendation. Additional exam requirements/recommendations for international students: Required—TOEFL (minimum score 600 paper-based; 250 computer-based; 100 iBT). *Application deadline:* For fall admission, 1/25 for domestic students. Application fee: $50. Electronic applications accepted. Application fee is waived when completed online. *Financial support:* In 2011–12, 53 students received support, including 1 research assistantship (averaging $1,200 per year); institutionally sponsored loans, scholarships/grants, and unspecified assistantships also available. Support available to part-time students. Financial award application deadline: 1/25; financial award applicants required to submit FAFSA. *Unit head:* Dr. Shane P. Martin, Dean, 310-338-7301, E-mail: smartin@lmu.edu. *Application contact:* Chake H. Kouyoumjian, Associate Dean of Graduate Studies, 310-338-2721, E-mail: ckouyoum@lmu.edu. Web site: http://soe.lmu.edu/centers/CEEL/programs/doctoral.htm.

Loyola Marymount University, School of Education, Department of Educational Leadership, Program in Catholic School Administration, Los Angeles, CA 90045. Offers MA. Part-time programs available. *Faculty:* 8 full-time (6 women), 8 part-time/adjunct (4 women). *Students:* 8 full-time (4 women), 21 part-time (15 women); includes 8 minority (4 Asian, non-Hispanic/Latino; 3 Hispanic/Latino; 1 Two or more races, non-Hispanic/Latino). Average age 38. 24 applicants, 96% accepted, 22 enrolled. In 2011, 5 master's awarded. *Degree requirements:* For master's, comprehensive exam. *Entrance requirements:* For master's, CBEST, CSET, 2 letters of recommendation, full-time employment in the Archdiocese of Los Angeles, mandatory information session. Additional exam requirements/recommendations for international students: Required—TOEFL (minimum score 600 paper-based; 250 computer-based; 100 iBT). *Application deadline:* For fall admission, 6/15 for domestic students; for spring admission, 11/15 for domestic students. Application fee: $50. Electronic applications accepted. *Financial support:* In 2011–12, 29 students received support. Institutionally sponsored loans, scholarships/grants, and unspecified assistantships available. Financial award application deadline: 6/15; financial award applicants required to submit FAFSA. *Unit head:* Dr. Franca Dell'Olio, Program Director, 310-258-8737, E-mail: fdellolio@lmu.edu. *Application contact:* Chake H. Kouyoumjian, Associate Dean of the Graduate Division, 310-338-2721, E-mail: ckouyoum@lmu.edu. Web site: http://soe.lmu.edu/admissions/programs/admin/catholicadmin.htm.

Loyola Marymount University, School of Education, Department of Educational Leadership, Program in School Administration, Los Angeles, CA 90045. Offers MA. Part-time and evening/weekend programs available. *Faculty:* 8 full-time (6 women), 8 part-time/adjunct (4 women). *Students:* 16 full-time (13 women), 1 (woman) part-time;

includes 12 minority (3 Black or African American, non-Hispanic/Latino; 1 Asian, non-Hispanic/Latino; 7 Hispanic/Latino; 1 Two or more races, non-Hispanic/Latino), 1 international. Average age 30. 15 applicants, 80% accepted, 9 enrolled. In 2011, 16 master's awarded. *Degree requirements:* For master's, comprehensive exam. *Entrance requirements:* For master's, CBEST, 2 letters of recommendation. Additional exam requirements/recommendations for international students: Required—TOEFL (minimum score 600 paper-based; 250 computer-based; 100 iBT). *Application deadline:* For fall admission, 5/1 for domestic students; for spring admission, 11/1 for domestic students. Application fee: $50. Electronic applications accepted. *Financial support:* In 2011–12, 15 students received support. Scholarships/grants and unspecified assistantships available. Support available to part-time students. Financial award application deadline: 5/1; financial award applicants required to submit FAFSA. *Unit head:* Dr. Franca Dell'Olio, Program Director, 310-258-8737, E-mail: fdellolio@lmu.edu. *Application contact:* Chake H. Kouyoumjian, Associate Dean of Graduate Studies, 310-338-2721, E-mail: ckouyoum@lmu.edu. Web site: http://soe.lmu.edu/admissions/programs/admin/schooladmin.htm.

Loyola University Chicago, School of Education, Program in Administration and Supervision, Chicago, IL 60660. Offers M Ed, Ed D, Certificate. Part-time and evening/weekend programs available. *Faculty:* 3 full-time (all women), 4 part-time/adjunct (2 women). *Students:* 88. Average age 35. 20 applicants, 60% accepted, 11 enrolled. In 2011, 25 master's, 9 doctorates awarded. *Degree requirements:* For master's, comprehensive exam; for doctorate, comprehensive exam, thesis/dissertation. *Entrance requirements:* For master's, minimum GPA of 3.0, letters of recommendation, resume, transcripts; for doctorate, GRE General Test, interview, minimum GPA of 3.0, letters of recommendation, resume. Additional exam requirements/recommendations for international students: Required—TOEFL (minimum score 550 paper-based; 213 computer-based; 79 iBT). *Application deadline:* For fall admission, 2/15 for domestic and international students; for spring admission, 11/1 for domestic and international students. Applications are processed on a rolling basis. Application fee: $50. Electronic applications accepted. Application fee is waived when completed online. *Expenses: Tuition:* Full-time $15,660; part-time $870 per credit hour. *Required fees:* $125 per semester. Tuition and fees vary according to course load and program. *Financial support:* Research assistantships with full tuition reimbursements, teaching assistantships, career-related internships or fieldwork, institutionally sponsored loans, scholarships/grants, tuition waivers, and unspecified assistantships available. Support available to part-time students. Financial award application deadline: 2/1; financial award applicants required to submit FAFSA. *Faculty research:* Leadership, school law, school administration, supervision, ethics. *Unit head:* Dr. Janis Fine, Director, 312-915-7022, Fax: 312-915-6980, E-mail: jfine@luc.edu. *Application contact:* Marie Rosin-Dittmar, Information Contact, 312-915-6800, E-mail: schleduc@luc.edu.

Loyola University Chicago, School of Education, Program in Instructional Leadership, Chicago, IL 60660. Offers M Ed. Part-time and evening/weekend programs available. *Faculty:* 7 full-time (6 women), 2 part-time/adjunct (1 woman). *Students:* 22. Average age 38. In 2011, 8 master's awarded. *Degree requirements:* For master's, comprehensive exam. *Entrance requirements:* For master's, minimum GPA of 3.0, letters of recommendation, resume. Additional exam requirements/recommendations for international students: Required—TOEFL (minimum score 550 paper-based; 213 computer-based; 79 iBT). *Application deadline:* For fall admission, 7/1 for domestic students; for spring admission, 11/1 for domestic students. Applications are processed on a rolling basis. Application fee: $50. Electronic applications accepted. Application fee is waived when completed online. *Expenses: Tuition:* Full-time $15,660; part-time $870 per credit hour. *Required fees:* $125 per semester. Tuition and fees vary according to course load and program. *Financial support:* Application deadline: 5/1. *Faculty research:* Staff development, school leadership, school change. *Unit head:* Dr. Janis Fine, Director, 312-915-7022, Fax: 312-915-6980, E-mail: jfine@luc.edu. *Application contact:* Marie Rosin-Dittmar, Information Contact, 312-915-6800, E-mail: schleduc@luc.edu.

Loyola University Maryland, Graduate Programs, Department of Education, Program in Educational Leadership, Baltimore, MD 21210-2699. Offers M Ed, MA, CAS, Certificate. Part-time programs available. *Faculty:* 57 full-time (32 women), 21 part-time/adjunct (10 women). *Students:* 2 full-time (1 woman), 55 part-time (40 women); includes 12 minority (9 Black or African American, non-Hispanic/Latino; 1 Asian, non-Hispanic/Latino; 2 Two or more races, non-Hispanic/Latino). Average age 32. In 2011, 27 master's, 1 other advanced degree awarded. *Degree requirements:* For master's, thesis. *Entrance requirements:* Additional exam requirements/recommendations for international students: Required—TOEFL (minimum score 550 paper-based; 213 computer-based). *Application deadline:* For fall admission, 6/15 priority date for domestic students; for spring admission, 11/1 priority date for domestic students. Application fee: $50. Electronic applications accepted. *Financial support:* Research assistantships, career-related internships or fieldwork, and unspecified assistantships available. Financial award application deadline: 4/15; financial award applicants required to submit FAFSA. *Unit head:* Peter R. Litchka, Director, 410-617-1656, E-mail: prlitchka@loyola.edu. *Application contact:* Maureen Faux, Executive Director, Graduate Admissions, 410-617-5020, Fax: 410-617-2002, E-mail: graduate@loyola.edu.

Lynchburg College, Graduate Studies, School of Education and Human Development, Leadership Studies (Ed.D.) Program, Lynchburg, VA 24501-3199. Offers Ed D. Evening/weekend programs available. *Faculty:* 9 full-time (2 women), 3 part-time/adjunct (0 women). *Students:* 2 full-time (both women), 25 part-time (15 women); includes 4 minority (3 Black or African American, non-Hispanic/Latino; 1 Asian, non-Hispanic/Latino), 1 international. Average age 40. *Degree requirements:* For doctorate, comprehensive exam, thesis/dissertation. *Entrance requirements:* For doctorate, GRE or GMAT, current resume of curriculum vitae, career goals statement, master's degree, official transcripts (bachelor's, master's, others of relevance), master's-level research course, three letters of recommendation, evidence of strong writing skills. Additional exam requirements/recommendations for international students: Required—TOEFL (minimum score 550 paper-based; 213 computer-based; 79 iBT), IELTS (minimum score 6.5). *Application deadline:* For fall admission, 7/31 for domestic students, 6/1 for international students; for spring admission, 11/30 for domestic students, 10/15 for international students. Applications are processed on a rolling basis. Application fee: $30. Electronic applications accepted. Application fee is waived when completed online. *Expenses: Tuition:* Full-time $7740; part-time $430 per credit hour. *Financial support:* Application deadline: 7/31; applicants required to submit FAFSA. *Unit head:* Dr. Roger Jones, Program Director, 434-544-8444, Fax: 434-544-8483, E-mail: jones@lynchburg.edu. *Application contact:* Anne Pingstock, Executive Assistant, 434-544-8383, Fax: 434-544-8483, E-mail: gradstudies@lynchburg.edu. Web site: http://www.lynchburg.edu/eddls.xml.

Lynchburg College, Graduate Studies, School of Education and Human Development, M Ed Program in Educational Leadership, Lynchburg, VA 24501-3199. Offers M Ed. Part-time and evening/weekend programs available. *Faculty:* 2 full-time (0 women), 1 part-time/adjunct (0 women). *Students:* 15 full-time (5 women), 34 part-time (22 women); includes 6 minority (5 Black or African American, non-Hispanic/Latino; 1 Hispanic/Latino). Average age 34. In 2011, 12 master's awarded. *Degree requirements:* For master's, internship; ISLLC exam or comprehensive exam. *Entrance requirements:* For master's, GRE, minimum GPA of 3.0 (preferred), official transcripts (bachelor's, others as relevant), three letters of recommendation, career goals statement. Additional exam requirements/recommendations for international students: Required—TOEFL (minimum score 550 paper-based; 213 computer-based; 79 iBT), IELTS (minimum score 6.5). *Application deadline:* For fall admission, 7/31 for domestic students, 6/1 for international students; for spring admission, 11/30 for domestic students, 10/5 for international students. Applications are processed on a rolling basis. Application fee: $30. Electronic applications accepted. Application fee is waived when completed online. *Expenses: Tuition:* Full-time $7740; part-time $430 per credit hour. *Financial support:* Fellowships, research assistantships, career-related internships or fieldwork, Federal Work-Study, scholarships/grants, health care benefits, and unspecified assistantships available. Support available to part-time students. Financial award application deadline: 7/31; financial award applicants required to submit FAFSA. *Unit head:* Dr. Roger Jones, Professor/Director, Leadership Studies, 434-544-8444, E-mail: jones@lynchburg.edu. *Application contact:* Anne Pingstock, Executive Assistant, Graduate Studies, 434-544-8383, Fax: 434-544-8483, E-mail: gradstudies@lynchburg.edu. Web site: http://www.lynchburg.edu/educationalleadership.xml.

Lynn University, Donald and Helen Ross College of Education, Boca Raton, FL 33431-5598. Offers educational leadership (M Ed, PhD); exceptional student education (M Ed); teacher preparation (PhD). Part-time and evening/weekend programs available. *Degree requirements:* For master's, thesis (for some programs); for doctorate, thesis/dissertation, qualifying paper. *Entrance requirements:* For master's, GRE, minimum undergraduate GPA of 3.0, resume, 2 letters of recommendation; for doctorate, GRE or GMAT, minimum GPA of 3.25, resume, 2 letters of recommendation. Additional exam requirements/recommendations for international students: Required—TOEFL (minimum score 550 paper-based; 213 computer-based). Electronic applications accepted. *Faculty research:* Non-traditional education, innovative curricula, multicultural education, simulation games.

Madonna University, Programs in Education, Livonia, MI 48150-1173. Offers Catholic school leadership (MSA); educational leadership (MSA); learning disabilities (MAT); literacy education (MAT); teaching and learning (MAT). *Accreditation:* NCATE. Part-time and evening/weekend programs available. *Degree requirements:* For master's, thesis or alternative. Electronic applications accepted.

Malone University, Graduate Program in Education, Canton, OH 44709. Offers curriculum and instruction (MA), including teacher leader endorsement; curriculum, instruction, and professional development (MA); educational leadership (MA), including principal license; intervention specialist (MA); reading (MA). Part-time and evening/weekend programs available. *Faculty:* 9 full-time (5 women), 8 part-time/adjunct (6 women). *Students:* 2 full-time (both women), 43 part-time (33 women); includes 2 minority (both Black or African American, non-Hispanic/Latino). Average age 36. 35 applicants, 91% accepted, 12 enrolled. In 2011, 11 master's awarded. *Degree requirements:* For master's, research project. *Entrance requirements:* For master's, minimum GPA of 3.0, teaching license. Additional exam requirements/recommendations for international students: Required—TOEFL (minimum score 550 paper-based; 213 computer-based; 79 iBT). *Application deadline:* Applications are processed on a rolling basis. *Expenses: Tuition:* Part-time $625 per semester hour. Part-time tuition and fees vary according to program. *Financial support:* Tuition waivers (partial) available. Support available to part-time students. Financial award application deadline: 6/30. *Faculty research:* Educational leadership styles: Jesus as master teacher, assessment accommodations for English language learners, preparing culturally proficient teachers, using naturally occurring text in the classroom to meet the syntactic needs of students with learning disabilities, using iPad instructional technology to meet the needs of students with disabilities. *Unit head:* Dr. Alice E. Christie, Director, 330-478-8541, Fax: 330-471-8563, E-mail: achristie@malone.edu. *Application contact:* Dan DePasquale, Senior Recruiter, 330-471-8381, Fax: 330-471-8343, E-mail: depasquale@malone.edu. Web site: http://www.malone.edu/admissions/graduate/education/.

Manhattan College, Graduate Division, School of Education, Program in School Building Leadership, Riverdale, NY 10471. Offers MS Ed, Professional Diploma. Part-time and evening/weekend programs available. *Faculty:* 1 (woman) full-time, 8 part-time/adjunct (6 women). *Students:* 2 full-time (1 woman), 47 part-time (37 women); includes 12 minority (5 Black or African American, non-Hispanic/Latino; 3 Hispanic/Latino; 4 Native Hawaiian or other Pacific Islander, non-Hispanic/Latino). Average age 39. 48 applicants, 75% accepted, 26 enrolled. In 2011, 7 master's awarded. *Degree requirements:* For master's, thesis, internship; for Professional Diploma, internship. *Entrance requirements:* For master's, minimum GPA of 3.0, 3 years teaching, professional recommendation; for Professional Diploma, minimum GPA of 3.0, Advanced Certificate. Additional exam requirements/recommendations for international students: Required—TOEFL. *Application deadline:* For fall admission, 8/1 priority date for domestic students, 5/1 for international students; for spring admission, 1/1 priority date for domestic students, 9/1 for international students. Applications are processed on a rolling basis. Application fee: $75. *Expenses: Tuition:* Full-time $14,850; part-time $825 per credit. *Required fees:* $390; $150. *Financial support:* Scholarships/grants, tuition waivers (full), and unspecified assistantships available. *Faculty research:* Distance learning and teacher efficacy, leadership and student achievement, professional development and student achievement, leadership development, professional development for teachers. *Unit head:* Sr. Remigia Kushner, Program Director, 718-862-7473, Fax: 718-862-7816, E-mail: sr.remigia.kushner@manhattan.edu. *Application contact:* William Bisset, Vice President for Enrollment, 718-862-7199, Fax: 718-862-8019, E-mail: william.bisset@manhattan.edu. Web site: http://home.manhattan.edu/~SBL/leadership/.

Manhattanville College, Graduate Studies, School of Education, Program in Educational Leadership, Purchase, NY 10577-2132. Offers MPS, Ed D. Part-time and evening/weekend programs available. *Entrance requirements:* For master's, minimum undergraduate GPA of 3.0, 2 letters of recommendation. Additional exam requirements/recommendations for international students: Required—TOEFL. Electronic applications accepted.

Marian University, School of Education, Fond du Lac, WI 54935-4699. Offers educational leadership (MAE, PhD); leadership studies (PhD); teacher development (MAE). PhD in leadership studies offered with Business Division. *Accreditation:* NCATE. Part-time programs available. *Faculty:* 20 full-time (11 women), 40 part-time/adjunct (23 women). *Students:* 29 full-time (23 women), 398 part-time (274 women); includes 18 minority (6 Black or African American, non-Hispanic/Latino; 3 American Indian or Alaska Native, non-Hispanic/Latino; 3 Asian, non-Hispanic/Latino; 6 Hispanic/Latino). Average age 36. 105 applicants, 80% accepted, 80 enrolled. In 2011, 227 master's, 7 doctorates awarded. *Degree requirements:* For master's, exam, field-based experience project, portfolio; for doctorate, comprehensive exam, thesis/dissertation, field-based experience. *Entrance requirements:* For master's, minimum GPA of 3.0, BA in education or related field, teaching license; for doctorate, GRE, MAT, resume, 2 writing samples, interview. Additional exam requirements/recommendations for international students: Required—TOEFL (minimum score 525 paper-based; 193 computer-based; 70 iBT). *Application deadline:* Applications are processed on a rolling basis. Application fee: $50. *Expenses: Tuition:* Part-time $428 per credit. Tuition and fees vary according to degree level and program. *Financial support:* Federal Work-Study and institutionally sponsored loans available. Support available to part-time students. Financial award application deadline: 3/1; financial award applicants required to submit FAFSA. *Faculty research:* At-risk youth, multicultural issues, values in education, teaching/learning strategies. *Unit head:* Sue Stoddart, Dean, 920-923-8099, Fax: 920-923-7663, E-mail: sstoddart@marianuniversity.edu. *Application contact:* Robert Bohnsack, Graduate Education Admissions, 920-923-8100, Fax: 920-923-7154, E-mail: bbohnsack@marianuniversity.edu. Web site: http://soe.marianuniversity.edu/.

Marquette University, Graduate School, College of Education, Department of Educational Policy and Leadership, Milwaukee, WI 53201-1881. Offers college student personnel administration (M Ed); curriculum and instruction (MA); education (MA); educational administration (M Ed); educational policy and foundations (MA); elementary education (Certificate); literacy (MA); principal (Certificate); reading specialist (Certificate); reading teacher (Certificate); secondary education (Certificate); superintendent (Certificate). Part-time and evening/weekend programs available. *Faculty:* 14 full-time (9 women). *Students:* 40 full-time (34 women), 137 part-time (80 women); includes 25 minority (14 Black or African American, non-Hispanic/Latino; 1 American Indian or Alaska Native, non-Hispanic/Latino; 2 Asian, non-Hispanic/Latino; 8 Hispanic/Latino), 2 international. Average age 32. 132 applicants, 73% accepted, 67 enrolled. In 2011, 46 master's, 3 doctorates, 5 other advanced degrees awarded. Terminal master's awarded for partial completion of doctoral program. *Degree requirements:* For master's, comprehensive exam, thesis (for some programs); for doctorate, thesis/dissertation, qualifying exam, supporting minor. *Entrance requirements:* For master's, GRE General Test or MAT, official transcripts from all current and previous colleges/universities except Marquette, three letters of recommendation, statement of purpose; for doctorate, GRE General Test, MAT, sample of written work, official transcripts from all current and previous colleges/universities except Marquette, three letters of recommendation, statement of purpose, resume/curriculum vitae; for Certificate, GRE General Test or MAT, master's degree. Additional exam requirements/recommendations for international students: Required—TOEFL (minimum score 530 paper-based; 78 computer-based). *Application deadline:* For fall admission, 1/15 for domestic and international students. Application fee: $50. *Expenses:* Contact institution. *Financial support:* In 2011–12, 130 students received support, including 1 fellowship with full tuition reimbursement available (averaging $18,780 per year), 5 research assistantships with full tuition reimbursements available (averaging $13,404 per year); health care benefits, tuition waivers (partial), and unspecified assistantships also available. Support available to part-time students. Financial award application deadline: 2/15. *Faculty research:* Leadership; social justice in education; development of lifelong learners; race, class, and schooling in historical perspective; urban teacher education. *Unit head:* Dr. Ellen Eckman, Chair, 414-288-1561, E-mail: ellen.eckman@marquette.edu. *Application contact:* Craig Pierce, Assistant Dean of the Graduate School, 414-288-5740, Fax: 414-288-1902, E-mail: craig.pierce@marquette.edu.

Marshall University, Academic Affairs Division, Graduate School of Education and Professional Development, Program in Leadership Studies, Huntington, WV 25755. Offers MA, MS, Ed D, Certificate, Ed S. Part-time and evening/weekend programs available. *Students:* 48 full-time (34 women), 284 part-time (192 women); includes 17 minority (9 Black or African American, non-Hispanic/Latino; 1 American Indian or Alaska Native, non-Hispanic/Latino; 3 Asian, non-Hispanic/Latino; 3 Hispanic/Latino; 1 Two or more races, non-Hispanic/Latino), 1 international. Average age 39. In 2011, 27 master's, 8 doctorates, 6 other advanced degrees awarded. *Degree requirements:* For master's, thesis optional, comprehensive or oral assessment. *Entrance requirements:* For master's, GRE General Test or MAT. Application fee: $40. *Financial support:* Career-related internships or fieldwork, Federal Work-Study, tuition waivers (full), and unspecified assistantships available. Support available to part-time students. Financial award applicants required to submit FAFSA. *Unit head:* Dr. Michael Cunningham, Program Director, 800-642-9842 Ext. 61912, E-mail: mcunningham@marshall.edu. *Application contact:* Information Contact, 304-746-1900, Fax: 304-746-1902, E-mail: services@marshall.edu.

Martin Luther College, Graduate Studies, New Ulm, MN 56073. Offers instruction (MS Ed); leadership (MS Ed); special education (MS Ed). Part-time programs available. Postbaccalaureate distance learning degree programs offered. *Degree requirements:* For master's, capstone project or comprehensive exam. *Entrance requirements:* For master's, undergraduate degree in education from an accredited college or university, minimum undergraduate GPA of 3.0. Electronic applications accepted.

Marygrove College, Graduate Division, Program in Educational Leadership, Detroit, MI 48221-2599. Offers MA. Part-time and evening/weekend programs available. *Degree requirements:* For master's, research project. *Entrance requirements:* For master's, MAT, interview, minimum undergraduate GPA of 3.0.

Marymount University, School of Education and Human Services, Program in Catholic School Leadership, Arlington, VA 22207-4299. Offers M Ed, Certificate. Part-time and evening/weekend programs available. Postbaccalaureate distance learning degree programs offered (minimal on-campus study). *Students:* 36 part-time (25 women); includes 6 minority (4 Black or African American, non-Hispanic/Latino; 2 Hispanic/Latino). Average age 43. In 2011, 9 master's awarded. *Degree requirements:* For master's, thesis or alternative. *Entrance requirements:* For master's, GRE General Test or MAT, 3 letters of recommendation, interview, resume; for Certificate, 3 letters of recommendation, interview, resume, essay. Additional exam requirements/recommendations for international students: Required—TOEFL (minimum score 600 paper-based; 250 computer-based; 96 iBT), IELTS (minimum score 6.5). *Application deadline:* For fall admission, 5/1 priority date for domestic students. Applications are processed on a rolling basis. Application fee: $40. Electronic applications accepted. *Expenses: Tuition:* Part-time $770 per credit hour. *Required fees:* $8 per credit hour. One-time fee: $180 full-time. *Financial support:* In 2011–12, 9 students received support. Research assistantships with full tuition reimbursements available, career-related internships or fieldwork, Federal Work-Study, scholarships/grants, and unspecified assistantships available. Support available to part-time students. Financial award applicants required to submit FAFSA. *Unit head:* Sr. Patricia Earl, Coordinator, 703-284-1517, Fax: 703-284-1631, E-mail: patricia.earl@marymount.edu. *Application contact:* Francesca Reed, Director, Graduate Admissions, 703-284-5901, Fax: 703-527-3815, E-mail: grad.admissions@marymount.edu. Web site: http://www.marymount.edu/academics/programs/edAdmin.

Maryville University of Saint Louis, School of Education, St. Louis, MO 63141-7299. Offers art education (MA Ed); early childhood education (MA Ed); educational leadership (Ed D); educational leadership: principal certification (MA Ed); elementary education (MA Ed); gifted education (MA Ed); higher education leadership (Ed D); literacy specialist (MA Ed); middle grades education (MA Ed); secondary teaching and inquiry (MA Ed); teacher as leader (MA Ed). *Accreditation:* NCATE. Part-time and evening/weekend programs available. *Faculty:* 10 full-time (6 women), 19 part-time/adjunct (15 women). *Students:* 33 full-time (25 women), 251 part-time (190 women); includes 42 minority (32 Black or African American, non-Hispanic/Latino; 1 American Indian or Alaska Native, non-Hispanic/Latino; 4 Asian, non-Hispanic/Latino; 2 Hispanic/Latino; 3 Two or more races, non-Hispanic/Latino). Average age 38. In 2011, 69 master's, 43 doctorates awarded. *Degree requirements:* For master's, thesis, project. *Entrance requirements:* For master's, minimum cumulative GPA of 3.0, 3 professional recommendations, essays, interview with program faculty; for doctorate, minimum GPA of 3.0, 3 professional recommendations, essay, interview, on-site writing sample. Additional exam requirements/recommendations for international students: Required—TOEFL (minimum score 550 paper-based). *Application deadline:* Applications are processed on a rolling basis. Application fee: $40 ($60 for international students). Electronic applications accepted. *Expenses: Tuition:* Full-time $21,922; part-time $675 per credit hour. *Required fees:* $233.75 per semester. *Financial support:* Career-related internships or fieldwork, Federal Work-Study, tuition waivers (partial), and professional educator discounts available. Financial award application deadline: 3/1; financial award applicants required to submit FAFSA. *Faculty research:* Collaboration with public schools, pre-service program development, mathematics, diversity, literacy. *Unit head:* Dr. Sam Hausfather, Dean, 314-529-9466, Fax: 314-529-9921, E-mail: shausfather@maryville.edu. *Application contact:* Holly Stanwich, Graduate Admissions Coordinator, 314-529-9542, Fax: 314-529-9921, E-mail: teachered@maryville.edu. Web site: http://www.maryville.edu/academics-ed-graduate.

Marywood University, Academic Affairs, Reap College of Education and Human Development, Department of Education, Program in Higher Education Administration, Scranton, PA 18509-1598. Offers MS. Part-time and evening/weekend programs available. *Entrance requirements:* Additional exam requirements/recommendations for international students: Required—TOEFL (minimum score 550 paper-based; 213 computer-based; 79 iBT). *Application deadline:* For fall admission, 4/1 priority date for domestic students, 3/31 for international students; for spring admission, 11/1 priority date for domestic students, 8/31 for international students. Applications are processed on a rolling basis. Application fee: $30. Electronic applications accepted. *Financial support:* Research assistantships with tuition reimbursements, career-related internships or fieldwork, scholarships/grants, and unspecified assistantships available. Support available to part-time students. Financial award application deadline: 6/30; financial award applicants required to submit FAFSA. *Faculty research:* Integrated thematic instruction. *Unit head:* Patricia S. Arter, Chairperson, 570-348-6211 Ext. 2511, E-mail: psarter@marywood.edu. *Application contact:* Tammy Manka, Assistant Director of Graduate Admissions, 570-348-6211 Ext. 2322, E-mail: tmanka@marywood.edu. Web site: http://www.marywood.edu/education/graduate-programs/ms_higher_education_administration.html.

Marywood University, Academic Affairs, Reap College of Education and Human Development, Department of Education, Program in Instructional Leadership, Scranton, PA 18509-1598. Offers M Ed. *Application deadline:* For fall admission, 4/1 for domestic students, 3/31 for international students; for spring admission, 11/1 for domestic students, 8/31 for international students. Applications are processed on a rolling basis. Electronic applications accepted. *Financial support:* Career-related internships or fieldwork, scholarships/grants, and unspecified assistantships available. Support available to part-time students. Financial award application deadline: 6/30. *Unit head:* Dr. Patricia S. Arter, Chairperson, 570-348-6211 Ext. 2511, E-mail: psarter@marywood.edu. *Application contact:* Tammy Manka, Assistant Director of Graduate Admissions, 570-348-6211 Ext. 2322, E-mail: tmanka@marywood.edu. Web site: http://www.marywood.edu/education/graduate-programs/med-instructional-leadership.html.

Marywood University, Academic Affairs, Reap College of Education and Human Development, Department of Education, Program in School Leadership with Principal Certification, Scranton, PA 18509-1598. Offers MS. *Accreditation:* NCATE. *Entrance requirements:* Additional exam requirements/recommendations for international students: Required—TOEFL (minimum score 550 paper-based; 213 computer-based; 79 iBT). *Application deadline:* For fall admission, 4/1 priority date for domestic students, 3/31 for international students; for spring admission, 11/1 priority date for domestic students, 8/31 for international students. Applications are processed on a rolling basis. Application fee: $35. Electronic applications accepted. *Financial support:* Career-related internships or fieldwork, scholarships/grants, and unspecified assistantships available. Support available to part-time students. Financial award application deadline: 6/30; financial award applicants required to submit FAFSA. *Faculty research:* School board leadership and development, site-based decision-making, educational administration. *Unit head:* Dr. Patricia S. Arter, Chairperson, 570-348-6211 Ext. 2511, E-mail: psarter@marywood.edu. *Application contact:* Tammy Manka, Assistant Director of Graduate Admissions, 570-348-6211 Ext. 2322, E-mail: tmanka@marywood.edu. Web site: http://www.marywood.edu/education/graduate-programs/ms-principal.html.

Marywood University, Academic Affairs, Reap College of Education and Human Development, Department of Human Development, Emphasis in Educational Administration, Scranton, PA 18509-1598. Offers PhD. *Entrance requirements:* Additional exam requirements/recommendations for international students: Required—TOEFL (minimum score 550 paper-based; 213 computer-based; 79 iBT). *Application deadline:* For fall admission, 1/30 priority date for domestic students, 1/30 for international students. Application fee: $35. Electronic applications accepted. *Expenses:* Contact institution. *Financial support:* Career-related internships or fieldwork, scholarships/grants, and unspecified assistantships available. Support available to part-time students. Financial award application deadline: 6/30; financial award applicants required to submit FAFSA. *Unit head:* Dr. Brook Cannon, Director, 570-348-6211 Ext. 2324, E-mail: cannonb@marywood.edu. *Application contact:* Tammy Manka, Assistant Director of Graduate Admissions, 570-348-6211 Ext. 2322, E-mail: tmanka@marywood.edu. Web site: http://www.marywood.edu/phd/specializations.html.

Marywood University, Academic Affairs, Reap College of Education and Human Development, Department of Human Development, Emphasis in Higher Education Administration, Scranton, PA 18509-1598. Offers PhD. *Entrance requirements:* Additional exam requirements/recommendations for international students: Required—TOEFL (minimum score 550 paper-based; 213 computer-based; 79 iBT). *Application deadline:* For fall admission, 1/30 for domestic and international students. Application fee: $35. Electronic applications accepted. *Expenses:* Contact institution. *Financial support:* Career-related internships or fieldwork, scholarships/grants, and unspecified assistantships available. Support available to part-time students. Financial award application deadline: 6/30; financial award applicants required to submit FAFSA. *Unit head:* Dr. Brook Cannon, Director, 570-348-6211 Ext. 2324, E-mail: cannonb@marywood.edu. *Application contact:* Tammy Manka, Assistant Director of Graduate Admissions, 570-348-6211 Ext. 2322, E-mail: tmanka@marywood.edu. Web site: http://www.marywood.edu/phd/specializations.html.

Marywood University, Academic Affairs, Reap College of Education and Human Development, Department of Human Development, Emphasis in Instructional Leadership, Scranton, PA 18509-1598. Offers PhD. *Entrance requirements:* Additional exam requirements/recommendations for international students: Required—TOEFL (minimum score 550 paper-based; 213 computer-based; 79 iBT). *Application deadline:* For fall admission, 1/30 priority date for domestic students, 1/30 for international students. Application fee: $35. Electronic applications accepted. *Expenses:* Contact institution. *Financial support:* Career-related internships or fieldwork, scholarships/grants, and unspecified assistantships available. Support available to part-time students. Financial award application deadline: 6/30; financial award applicants required to submit FAFSA. *Unit head:* Dr. Brook Cannon, Director, 570-348-6211 Ext. 2324, E-mail: cannonb@marywood.edu. *Application contact:* Tammy Manka, Assistant Director of

Graduate Admissions, 570-348-6211 Ext. 2322, E-mail: tmanka@marywood.edu. Web site: http://www.marywood.edu/phd/specializations.html.

Massachusetts College of Liberal Arts, Program in Education, North Adams, MA 01247-4100. Offers curriculum (M Ed); educational administration (M Ed); reading (M Ed); special education (M Ed). Part-time and evening/weekend programs available. *Degree requirements:* For master's, thesis. *Entrance requirements:* For master's, writing sample.

McDaniel College, Graduate and Professional Studies, Program in Educational Administration, Westminster, MD 21157-4390. Offers MS. Part-time and evening/weekend programs available. *Degree requirements:* For master's, comprehensive exam (for some programs), thesis optional, portfolio. *Entrance requirements:* For master's, GRE General Test, MAT, or NTE/PRAXIS I. Additional exam requirements/recommendations for international students: Required—TOEFL (minimum score 213 computer-based).

McGill University, Faculty of Graduate and Postdoctoral Studies, Faculty of Education, Department of Integrated Studies in Education, Montréal, QC H3A 2T5, Canada. Offers culture and values in education (MA, PhD); curriculum studies (MA); educational leadership (MA, Certificate); educational studies (PhD); integrated studies in education (M Ed); second language education (MA, PhD).

McKendree University, Graduate Programs, Master of Arts in Education Program, Lebanon, IL 62254-1299. Offers certification (MA Ed); educational administration and leadership (MA Ed); educational studies (MA Ed); higher education administrative services (MA Ed); music education (MA Ed); special education (MA Ed); teacher leadership (MA Ed); transition to teaching (MA Ed). *Accreditation:* NCATE. Part-time and evening/weekend programs available. Postbaccalaureate distance learning degree programs offered (no on-campus study). *Entrance requirements:* For master's, official transcripts from institutions attended, minimum GPA of 3.0, resume, references. Additional exam requirements/recommendations for international students: Required—TOEFL. Electronic applications accepted.

McNeese State University, Doré School of Graduate Studies, Burton College of Education, Department of Education Professions, Program in Educational Leadership, Lake Charles, LA 70609. Offers educational leadership (M Ed, Ed S); educational technology (Ed S). Evening/weekend programs available. *Faculty:* 4 full-time (0 women). *Students:* 2 full-time (1 woman), 68 part-time (27 women); includes 18 minority (all Black or African American, non-Hispanic/Latino). In 2011, 17 master's, 10 Ed Ss awarded. *Degree requirements:* For Ed S, comprehensive exam. *Entrance requirements:* For master's, GRE, teaching certificate, 3 years full-time teaching experience; for Ed S, teaching certificate, 3 years of teaching experience, 1 year of administration or supervision experience, master's degree with 12 semester hours in education. *Application deadline:* For fall admission, 5/15 priority date for domestic students, 5/15 for international students; for spring admission, 10/15 priority date for domestic students, 10/15 for international students. Applications are processed on a rolling basis. Application fee: $20 ($30 for international students). *Expenses:* Tuition, state resident: part-time $519 per credit hour. Tuition and fees vary according to course load. *Financial support:* Fellowships available. Financial award application deadline: 5/1. *Unit head:* Dr. Dustin M. Hebert, Director, 337-475-5424, Fax: 337-475-5272, E-mail: dhebert@mcneese.edu. *Application contact:* Dr. George F. Mead, Jr., Interim Dean of Dore' School of Graduate Studies, 337-475-5396, Fax: 337-475-5397, E-mail: admissions@mcneese.edu.

Memorial University of Newfoundland, School of Graduate Studies, Faculty of Education, St. John's, NL A1C 5S7, Canada. Offers counseling psychology (M Ed); curriculum, teaching, and learning studies (M Ed); education (PhD); educational leadership studies (M Ed); information technology (M Ed); post-secondary studies (M Ed, Diploma), including health professional education (Diploma). Part-time programs available. *Degree requirements:* For master's, thesis optional, internship, paper folio, project; for doctorate, comprehensive exam, thesis/dissertation, thesis seminar, oral defense of thesis. *Entrance requirements:* For master's, undergraduate degree with at least 2nd class standing, 1-2 years work experience; for doctorate, minimum A average in graduate course work, MA in education, 2 years professional experience; for Diploma, 2nd class degree, 2 years of work experience with adult learners, appropriate academic qualifications and work experience in a health-related field. Electronic applications accepted. *Faculty research:* Critical thinking, literacy, cognitive studies and counseling, educational change, technology in instruction.

Mercer University, Graduate Studies, Cecil B. Day Campus, Tift College of Education (Atlanta), Macon, GA 31207-0003. Offers curriculum and instruction (PhD); early childhood education (M Ed, MAT); educational leadership (PhD, Ed S); higher education leadership (M Ed); middle grades education (M Ed, MAT); reading education (M Ed); school counseling (Ed S); secondary education (M Ed, MAT); teacher leadership (Ed S). *Accreditation:* NCATE. Part-time and evening/weekend programs available. *Faculty:* 31 full-time (17 women), 6 part-time/adjunct (3 women). *Students:* 249 full-time (207 women), 413 part-time (326 women); includes 349 minority (322 Black or African American, non-Hispanic/Latino; 1 American Indian or Alaska Native, non-Hispanic/Latino; 18 Asian, non-Hispanic/Latino; 6 Hispanic/Latino; 2 Two or more races, non-Hispanic/Latino), 6 international. Average age 34. 204 applicants, 76% accepted, 125 enrolled. In 2011, 235 master's, 8 doctorates, 27 other advanced degrees awarded. *Degree requirements:* For master's and Ed S, research project; for doctorate, thesis/dissertation. *Entrance requirements:* For master's, GRE or MAT, minimum undergraduate GPA of 2.75; for doctorate, GRE; for Ed S, GRE or MAT, minimum GPA of 3.25, 3 years of teaching experience. Additional exam requirements/recommendations for international students: Required—TOEFL. *Application deadline:* For fall admission, 8/1 for domestic and international students; for spring admission, 12/1 for domestic and international students. Applications are processed on a rolling basis. Application fee: $25. *Expenses:* Contact institution. *Financial support:* Federal Work-Study available. Support available to part-time students. Financial award application deadline: 5/1. *Faculty research:* Educational technology, multicultural and minority issues in education, educational leadership (P-12 and higher education), school discipline and school bullying, standards-based mathematics education. *Unit head:* Dr. Carl R. Martray, Dean, 478-301-5397, Fax: 478-301-2280, E-mail: martray_cr@mercer.edu. *Application contact:* Dr. Allison Gilmore, Associate Dean for Graduate Teacher Education, 678-547-6333, Fax: 678-547-6055, E-mail: gilmore_a@mercer.edu. Web site: http://www.mercer.edu/education/.

Mercer University, Graduate Studies, Macon Campus, Tift College of Education (Macon), Macon, GA 31207-0003. Offers curriculum and instruction (PhD); early childhood education (M Ed); education leadership (PhD), including higher education, P-12; educational leadership (Ed S); higher education (M Ed); teacher leadership (Ed S). *Accreditation:* NCATE. Part-time and evening/weekend programs available. Postbaccalaureate distance learning degree programs offered (minimal on-campus study). *Faculty:* 26 full-time (17 women), 2 part-time/adjunct (0 women). *Students:* 87 full-time (78 women), 147 part-time (124 women); includes 92 minority (83 Black or African American, non-Hispanic/Latino; 3 American Indian or Alaska Native, non-Hispanic/Latino; 3 Asian, non-Hispanic/Latino; 3 Hispanic/Latino), 1 international. Average age 36. 122 applicants, 66% accepted, 72 enrolled. In 2011, 51 master's, 5 doctorates, 37 other advanced degrees awarded. *Degree requirements:* For master's, research project report; for doctorate, comprehensive exam, thesis/dissertation. *Entrance requirements:* For master's, GRE or MAT, minimum GPA of 2.75; for doctorate, GRE, minimum GPA of 3.5; interview; writing sample; 3 recommendations; for Ed S, GRE or MAT, minimum GPA of 3.5 (for Ed S in teacher leadership), 3.0 (for Ed S in educational leadership). Additional exam requirements/recommendations for international students: Required—TOEFL. *Application deadline:* For fall admission, 8/1 for domestic students; for spring admission, 12/1 for domestic students. Applications are processed on a rolling basis. Application fee: $35. *Expenses:* Contact institution. *Financial support:* Federal Work-Study and institutionally sponsored loans available. Support available to part-time students. Financial award application deadline: 5/1. *Faculty research:* Teacher effectiveness, specific learning disabilities, inclusion. *Unit head:* Dr. Carl R. Martray, Dean, 478-301-5397, Fax: 478-301-2280, E-mail: martray_cr@mercer.edu. *Application contact:* Tracey Wofford, Associate Director of Admissions, 678-547-6422, Fax: 678-547-6367, E-mail: wofford_tm@mercer.edu. Web site: http://education.mercer.edu.

Mercy College, School of Education, Advanced Certificate Program in School Building Leadership, Dobbs Ferry, NY 10522-1189. Offers Advanced Certificate. Part-time and evening/weekend programs available. *Degree requirements:* For Advanced Certificate, thesis or alternative, capstone. *Entrance requirements:* For degree, initial or professional teaching certification; interview with program director or faculty advisor; two years of teaching or specialty area experience; resume; master's degree from accredited institution. Additional exam requirements/recommendations for international students: Required—TOEFL (minimum score 600 paper-based; 250 computer-based; 100 iBT), IELTS (minimum score 8). Electronic applications accepted. *Faculty research:* School law, leadership, supervision.

Mercy College, School of Education, Master's Program in School Building Leadership, Dobbs Ferry, NY 10522-1189. Offers MS. Part-time and evening/weekend programs available. Postbaccalaureate distance learning degree programs offered (minimal on-campus study). *Degree requirements:* For master's, comprehensive exam. *Entrance requirements:* For master's, minimum undergraduate GPA of 3.0; resume; interview with program director; initial or professional teacher certification; two years of paid teaching or specialty area experience. Additional exam requirements/recommendations for international students: Required—TOEFL (minimum score 600 paper-based; 250 computer-based; 100 iBT), IELTS (minimum score 8). Electronic applications accepted. *Faculty research:* Proper school management, decisive and visionary leadership, school law.

Mercyhurst College, Graduate Studies, Program in Organizational Leadership, Erie, PA 16546. Offers accounting (MS); entrepreneurship (MS); higher education administration (MS); human resources (MS); nonprofit management (MS); organizational leadership (Certificate); sports leadership (MS). Part-time and evening/weekend programs available. *Faculty:* 1 full-time (0 women), 11 part-time/adjunct (4 women). *Students:* 42 full-time (16 women), 22 part-time (15 women); includes 5 minority (3 Black or African American, non-Hispanic/Latino; 1 American Indian or Alaska Native, non-Hispanic/Latino; 1 Hispanic/Latino), 9 international. Average age 30. 60 applicants, 62% accepted, 25 enrolled. In 2011, 27 master's, 2 other advanced degrees awarded. *Degree requirements:* For master's, thesis. *Entrance requirements:* For master's, GRE General Test or MAT, interview, resume, essay, three professional references, transcripts. Additional exam requirements/recommendations for international students: Required—TOEFL. *Application deadline:* For fall admission, 8/1 priority date for domestic students, 7/1 for international students; for winter admission, 11/1 for domestic students, 10/1 for international students; for spring admission, 2/1 for domestic students, 1/1 for international students. Applications are processed on a rolling basis. Application fee: $35. Electronic applications accepted. *Expenses: Tuition:* Part-time $570 per credit. *Required fees:* $90 per term. Tuition and fees vary according to program. *Financial support:* In 2011–12, 16 students received support, including 112 research assistantships with full and partial tuition reimbursements available (averaging $6,000 per year); career-related internships or fieldwork and unspecified assistantships also available. Support available to part-time students. Financial award application deadline: 5/1; financial award applicants required to submit FAFSA. *Faculty research:* Leadership training, organizational communication, leadership pedagogy. *Unit head:* Dr. Gilbert Jacobs, Director, 814-824-2390, E-mail: gjacobs@mercyhurst.edu. *Application contact:* Sarah Murphy, Academic Coordinator, 814-824-2297, Fax: 814-824-2055, E-mail: smurphy@mercyhurst.edu.

Mercyhurst College, Graduate Studies, Program in Special Education, Erie, PA 16546. Offers bilingual/bicultural special education (MS); educational leadership (Certificate); special education (MS). Part-time and evening/weekend programs available. *Faculty:* 1 full-time (0 women), 13 part-time/adjunct (8 women). *Students:* 60 full-time (51 women), 19 part-time (14 women); includes 8 minority (3 Black or African American, non-Hispanic/Latino; 1 American Indian or Alaska Native, non-Hispanic/Latino; 1 Asian, non-Hispanic/Latino; 3 Hispanic/Latino), 1 international. Average age 30. 32 applicants, 84% accepted, 18 enrolled. In 2011, 52 master's awarded. *Degree requirements:* For master's, thesis optional. *Entrance requirements:* For master's, GRE or PRAXIS I, interview, resume, essay, three professional references, transcripts. Additional exam requirements/recommendations for international students: Required—TOEFL. *Application deadline:* For fall admission, 8/1 priority date for domestic students, 8/1 for international students; for winter admission, 11/1 for domestic and international students; for spring admission, 2/1 for domestic and international students. Applications are processed on a rolling basis. Application fee: $35. Electronic applications accepted. *Expenses: Tuition:* Part-time $570 per credit. *Required fees:* $90 per term. Tuition and fees vary according to program. *Financial support:* In 2011–12, 25 students received support, including 15 research assistantships with full and partial tuition reimbursements available (averaging $8,000 per year); institutionally sponsored loans and unspecified assistantships also available. Support available to part-time students. Financial award application deadline: 5/15; financial award applicants required to submit FAFSA. *Faculty research:* College-age learning disabled program, teacher preparation/collaboration, applied behavior analysis, special education policy issues. *Total annual research expenditures:* $278,141. *Unit head:* Dr. Phillip J. Belfiore, Coordinator, 814-824-2267, Fax: 814-824-2438, E-mail: belfiore@mercyhurst.edu. *Application contact:* Sarah Murphy, Academic Coordinator, 814-824-2297, Fax: 814-824-2055, E-mail: smurphy@mercyhurst.edu. Web site: http://graduate.mercyhurst.edu/academics/graduate-degrees/special-education/.

Merrimack College, School of Education, North Andover, MA 01845-5800. Offers community engagement (M Ed); early childhood education (M Ed); elementary education (M Ed); elementary education plus moderate disabilities-dual license (M Ed); English as a second language (M Ed); general studies (M Ed); higher education (M Ed); middle (M Ed); moderate disabilities (preK-8) (M Ed); reading (M Ed); secondary (M Ed); teacher leadership (CAGS). Part-time and evening/weekend programs available. *Faculty:* 4 full-time (all women), 9 part-time/adjunct (7 women). *Students:* 70 full-time (60 women), 39 part-time (33 women); includes 2 minority (1 Asian, non-Hispanic/Latino; 1 Hispanic/Latino). Average age 27. In 2011, 26 master's awarded. *Degree requirements:* For master's, portfolio. *Entrance requirements:* Additional exam requirements/recommendations for international students: Required—TOEFL (minimum score 80 iBT). *Application deadline:* For fall admission, 8/1 priority date for domestic students, 7/15 for international students; for winter admission, 12/1 priority date for domestic students, 11/15 for international students; for spring admission, 3/1 priority date for domestic students, 2/15 for international students. Applications are processed on a rolling basis. Electronic applications accepted. *Expenses: Tuition:* Part-time $475 per credit. *Required fees:* $62.50 per semester. *Financial support:* In 2011–12, 50 fellowships were awarded; career-related internships or fieldwork and scholarships/grants also available. Financial award applicants required to submit FAFSA. *Faculty research:* Higher education, community engagement, literacy, leadership. *Unit head:* Dr. Theresa Kirk, Chair, 978-837-5436, E-mail: kirkt@merrimack.edu. *Application contact:* Jessica McCarthy, Program Coordinator, 978-837-5443, E-mail: mccarthyj@merrimack.edu. Web site: http://www.merrimack.edu/academics/education/med/.

Miami University, School of Education and Allied Professions, Department of Educational Leadership, Oxford, OH 45056. Offers curriculum and teacher leadership (M Ed); educational administration (Ed D, PhD); school leadership (MS); student affairs in higher education (MS, PhD). *Accreditation:* NCATE. Part-time programs available. *Students:* 102 full-time (63 women), 96 part-time (73 women); includes 45 minority (34 Black or African American, non-Hispanic/Latino; 1 American Indian or Alaska Native, non-Hispanic/Latino; 3 Asian, non-Hispanic/Latino; 2 Hispanic/Latino; 5 Two or more races, non-Hispanic/Latino), 7 international. Average age 32. In 2011, 52 master's, 7 doctorates awarded. *Entrance requirements:* For master's, MAT or GRE, minimum undergraduate GPA of 3.0 during previous 2 years or 2.75 overall; for doctorate, GRE, minimum GPA of 2.75 (undergraduate), 3.0 (graduate). Additional exam requirements/recommendations for international students: Required—TOEFL. Application fee: $50. *Expenses:* Tuition, state resident: full-time $12,023; part-time $501 per credit hour. Tuition, nonresident: full-time $26,554; part-time $1107 per credit hour. *Required fees:* $528. *Financial support:* Fellowships with full tuition reimbursements, research assistantships with full tuition reimbursements, teaching assistantships with full tuition reimbursements, career-related internships or fieldwork, Federal Work-Study, health care benefits, tuition waivers (full), and unspecified assistantships available. Financial award application deadline: 2/15; financial award applicants required to submit FAFSA. *Unit head:* Dr. Kate Rousmaniere, Chair, 513-529-6843, Fax: 513-529-1729, E-mail: rousmak@muohio.edu. Web site: http://www.units.muohio.edu/eap/edl/index.html.

Michigan State University, The Graduate School, College of Education, Department of Educational Administration, East Lansing, MI 48824. Offers higher, adult and lifelong education (MA, PhD); K–12 educational administration (MA, PhD, Ed S); student affairs administration (MA). Part-time programs available. *Entrance requirements:* Additional exam requirements/recommendations for international students: Required—TOEFL. Electronic applications accepted.

Middle Tennessee State University, College of Graduate Studies, College of Education, Department of Educational Leadership, Program in Administration and Supervision, Murfreesboro, TN 37132. Offers M Ed, Ed S. Part-time and evening/weekend programs available. Postbaccalaureate distance learning degree programs offered. *Faculty:* 22 full-time (11 women), 22 part-time/adjunct (12 women). *Students:* 2 full-time (both women), 318 part-time (256 women); includes 59 minority (46 Black or African American, non-Hispanic/Latino; 8 Asian, non-Hispanic/Latino; 3 Hispanic/Latino; 1 Native Hawaiian or other Pacific Islander, non-Hispanic/Latino; 1 Two or more races, non-Hispanic/Latino). 228 applicants, 97% accepted. In 2011, 60 master's, 58 Ed Ss awarded. *Degree requirements:* For master's, comprehensive exam; for Ed S, comprehensive exam, thesis or alternative. *Entrance requirements:* For master's and Ed S, GRE, MAT or current teaching license. Additional exam requirements/recommendations for international students: Required—TOEFL (minimum score 525 paper-based; 195 computer-based; 71 iBT) or IELTS (minimum score 6). *Application deadline:* For fall admission, 6/1 for domestic and international students. Applications are processed on a rolling basis. Application fee: $25 ($30 for international students). Electronic applications accepted. *Expenses:* Tuition, state resident: full-time $10,008. Tuition, nonresident: full-time $25,056. *Financial support:* Tuition waivers available. Support available to part-time students. Financial award application deadline: 5/1. *Unit head:* Dr. James Huffman, Chair, 615-898-2855, Fax: 615-898-2859. *Application contact:* Dr. Michael D. Allen, Dean and Vice Provost for Research, 615-898-2840, Fax: 615-904-8020, E-mail: michael.allen@mtsu.edu.

Midwestern State University, Graduate Studies, College of Education, Program in Educational Leadership and Technology, Wichita Falls, TX 76308. Offers ME. Part-time and evening/weekend programs available. *Degree requirements:* For master's, comprehensive exam. *Entrance requirements:* For master's, GRE General Test or MAT. Additional exam requirements/recommendations for international students: Required—TOEFL (minimum score 550 paper-based; 213 computer-based). Electronic applications accepted. *Faculty research:* Role of the principal in the twenty-first century, culturally proficient leadership, human diversity, immigration, teacher collaboration.

Mills College, Graduate Studies, MBA/MA Program in Educational Leadership, Oakland, CA 94613-1000. Offers MBA/MA. Program offered jointly between School of Education and Lorry I. Lokey Graduate School of Business. *Faculty:* 18 full-time (13 women), 17 part-time/adjunct (13 women). *Students:* 8 full-time (7 women); includes 6 minority (3 Black or African American, non-Hispanic/Latino; 1 American Indian or Alaska Native, non-Hispanic/Latino; 1 Asian, non-Hispanic/Latino; 1 Hispanic/Latino). Average age 29. 9 applicants, 89% accepted, 7 enrolled. *Entrance requirements:* Additional exam requirements/recommendations for international students: Required—TOEFL (minimum score 550 paper-based; 80 iBT) or IELTS (minimum score 6). *Application deadline:* For fall admission, 2/1 priority date for domestic students, 12/15 for international students. Applications are processed on a rolling basis. Application fee: $50. *Expenses: Tuition:* Full-time $28,280; part-time $15,640 per year. *Required fees:* $958. Tuition and fees vary according to program. *Financial support:* Application deadline: 2/1; applicants required to submit FAFSA. *Unit head:* Dr. Deborah Merrill-Sands, Dean of the Graduate School of Business, 510-430-3305, Fax: 510-430-2159, E-mail: grad-studies@mills.edu. *Application contact:* Tiana Kozoil, Graduate Admission Specialist, 510-430-3305, Fax: 510-430-2159, E-mail: grad-studies@mills.edu. Web site: http://www.mills.edu/MBAMAEdLdrshp.

Mills College, Graduate Studies, School of Education, Oakland, CA 94613-1000. Offers child life in hospitals (MA); early childhood education (MA); education (MA), including art education, curriculum and instruction, elementary education, English education, foreign language education, mathematics education, science education, secondary education, social studies education, teaching; educational leadership (MA, Ed D). Part-time and evening/weekend programs available. *Faculty:* 13 full-time (10 women), 14 part-time/adjunct (10 women). *Students:* 149 full-time (133 women), 69 part-time (61 women); includes 85 minority (32 Black or African American, non-Hispanic/Latino; 1 American Indian or Alaska Native, non-Hispanic/Latino; 16 Asian, non-Hispanic/Latino; 24 Hispanic/Latino; 1 Native Hawaiian or other Pacific Islander, non-Hispanic/Latino; 11 Two or more races, non-Hispanic/Latino), 3 international. Average age 28. 238 applicants, 84% accepted, 106 enrolled. In 2011, 41 master's, 2 doctorates awarded. Terminal master's awarded for partial completion of doctoral program. *Degree requirements:* For master's, comprehensive exam. *Entrance requirements:* For master's, statement of purpose, official transcript, 3 recommendations; for doctorate, GRE General Test. Additional exam requirements/recommendations for international students: Required—TOEFL (minimum score 550 paper-based; 80 iBT) or IELTS (minimum score 6). *Application deadline:* For fall admission, 12/31 priority date for domestic students, 12/15 for international students; for spring admission, 11/1 priority date for domestic students, 10/1 for international students. Applications are processed on a rolling basis. Application fee: $50. Electronic applications accepted. *Expenses: Tuition:* Full-time $28,280; part-time $15,640 per year. *Required fees:* $958. Tuition and fees vary according to program. *Financial support:* In 2011–12, 43 students received support, including 225 fellowships with full and partial tuition reimbursements available (averaging $6,020 per year), 43 teaching assistantships with full and partial tuition reimbursements available (averaging $6,782 per year); career-related internships or fieldwork and scholarships/grants also available. Support available to part-time students. Financial award application deadline: 2/1; financial award applicants required to submit FAFSA. *Faculty research:* Early childhood education, teacher preparation, educational leadership. *Total annual research expenditures:* $2.3 million. *Unit head:* Katherine Schultz, Chairperson, 510-430-3170, Fax: 510-430-3379, E-mail: grad-studies@mills.edu. *Application contact:* Tiana Kozoil, Graduate Admission Specialist, 510-430-3305, Fax: 510-430-2159, E-mail: grad-studies@mills.edu. Web site: http://www.mills.edu/education.

Minnesota State University Mankato, College of Graduate Studies, College of Education, Department of Educational Leadership, Program in Experiential Education, Mankato, MN 56001. Offers MS. *Accreditation:* NCATE. Part-time and evening/weekend programs available. *Students:* 24 full-time (12 women), 13 part-time (6 women). *Degree requirements:* For master's, thesis or alternative. *Entrance requirements:* For master's, minimum GPA of 3.0 during previous 2 years. Additional exam requirements/recommendations for international students: Required—TOEFL. *Application deadline:* For fall admission, 7/1 priority date for domestic students; for spring admission, 11/1 for domestic students. Applications are processed on a rolling basis. Application fee: $40. Electronic applications accepted. *Financial support:* Research assistantships with full tuition reimbursements, teaching assistantships with full tuition reimbursements, career-related internships or fieldwork, Federal Work-Study, and unspecified assistantships available. Support available to part-time students. Financial award application deadline: 3/15; financial award applicants required to submit FAFSA. *Unit head:* Dr. Jasper Hunt, Graduate Coordinator, 507-389-1116. *Application contact:* 507-389-2321, E-mail: grad@mnsu.edu.

Minnesota State University Moorhead, Graduate Studies, College of Education and Human Services, Program in Educational Leadership, Moorhead, MN 56563-0002. Offers MS, Ed S. MS, Ed S offered jointly with North Dakota State University. *Accreditation:* NCATE. Part-time programs available. *Degree requirements:* For master's, comprehensive exam, final oral exam, project or thesis. *Entrance requirements:* For master's, 2 letters of recommendation, minimum GPA of 3.0. Additional exam requirements/recommendations for international students: Required—TOEFL (minimum score 550 paper-based; 213 computer-based). Electronic applications accepted.

Mississippi College, Graduate School, School of Education, Department of Teacher Education and Leadership, Clinton, MS 39058. Offers art (M Ed); biological science (M Ed); business education (M Ed); computer science (M Ed); dyslexia therapy (M Ed); educational leadership (M Ed, Ed D, Ed S); elementary education (M Ed, Ed S); English (M Ed); higher education administration (MS); mathematics (M Ed); secondary education (M Ed); social studies (history) (M Ed); teaching arts (M Ed). Part-time programs available. Postbaccalaureate distance learning degree programs offered (no on-campus study). *Degree requirements:* For master's, comprehensive exam, thesis optional. *Entrance requirements:* For master's, NTE. Additional exam requirements/recommendations for international students: Recommended—TOEFL, IELTS. Electronic applications accepted.

Mississippi College, Graduate School, School of Education, Program in Higher Education Administration, Clinton, MS 39058. Offers MS. Part-time programs available. Postbaccalaureate distance learning degree programs offered (no on-campus study). *Degree requirements:* For master's, comprehensive exam, thesis optional. *Entrance requirements:* For master's, GRE or GMAT, minimum GPA of 3.0. Additional exam requirements/recommendations for international students: Recommended—TOEFL, IELTS.

Mississippi State University, College of Education, Department of Leadership and Foundations, Mississippi State, MS 39762. Offers MS, PhD, Ed S. MS in workforce educational leadership held jointly with Alcorn State University. *Faculty:* 9 full-time (3 women). *Students:* 58 full-time (30 women), 167 part-time (114 women); includes 122 minority (116 Black or African American, non-Hispanic/Latino; 1 American Indian or Alaska Native, non-Hispanic/Latino; 4 Hispanic/Latino; 1 Native Hawaiian or other Pacific Islander, non-Hispanic/Latino), 1 international. Average age 40. 95 applicants, 33% accepted, 27 enrolled. In 2011, 27 master's, 14 doctorates, 9 other advanced degrees awarded. *Degree requirements:* For master's and Ed S, comprehensive exam, thesis; for doctorate, comprehensive exam, thesis/dissertation. *Entrance requirements:* For master's, GRE, minimum GPA of 2.75 in junior and senior courses; for doctorate and Ed S, GRE. Additional exam requirements/recommendations for international students: Required—TOEFL (minimum score 550 paper-based; 213 computer-based; 79 iBT); Recommended—IELTS (minimum score 6.5). *Application deadline:* For fall admission, 7/1 for domestic students, 5/1 for international students; for spring admission, 11/1 for domestic students, 9/1 for international students. Application fee: $40. *Expenses:* Tuition, state resident: full-time $5805; part-time $322.50 per credit hour. Tuition, nonresident: full-time $14,670; part-time $815 per credit hour. *Financial support:* In 2011–12, 4 research assistantships (averaging $11,139 per year) were awarded; Federal Work-Study and institutionally sponsored loans also available. Financial award application deadline: 4/1; financial award applicants required to submit FAFSA. *Unit head:* Dr. Frankie K. Williams, Associate Professor and Department Head, 662-325-0974, Fax: 662-325-0975, E-mail: fwilliams@colled.msstate.edu. *Application contact:* Dr. Dwight Hare, Professor and Graduate Coordinator, 662-325-0969, Fax: 662-325-0975, E-mail: dhare@colled.msstate.edu. Web site: http://www.leadershipandfoundations.msstate.edu/.

Mississippi University for Women, Graduate School, College of Education and Human Sciences, Columbus, MS 39701-9998. Offers differentiated instruction (M Ed); educational leadership (M Ed); gifted studies (M Ed); reading/literacy (M Ed); teaching (MAT). *Accreditation:* ASHA; NCATE. Part-time programs available. *Degree requirements:* For master's, comprehensive exam, thesis optional. *Entrance requirements:* For master's, GRE General Test or NTE (M Ed in gifted education or MS in speech/language pathology), MAT (M Ed in instructional management), minimum QPA of 3.0.

Missouri Baptist University, Graduate Programs, St. Louis, MO 63141-8660. Offers business administration (MBA); Christian ministries (MACM); counseling (MAC); education (MSE); education administration (MEA); educational leadership (MSE, Ed S); teaching (MAT).

Missouri State University, Graduate College, College of Education, Department of Counseling, Leadership, and Special Education, Program in Educational Administration, Springfield, MO 65897. Offers educational administration (MS Ed, Ed S); elementary education (MS Ed); elementary principal (Ed S); secondary education (MS Ed); secondary principal (Ed S); superintendent (Ed S). Part-time and evening/weekend programs available. *Students:* 20 full-time (13 women), 109 part-time (73 women); includes 6 minority (1 Black or African American, non-Hispanic/Latino; 2 American Indian or Alaska Native, non-Hispanic/Latino; 1 Hispanic/Latino; 2 Two or more races, non-Hispanic/Latino), 5 international. Average age 35. 60 applicants, 98% accepted, 43 enrolled. In 2011, 51 master's, 16 Ed Ss awarded. *Degree requirements:* For master's and Ed S, comprehensive exam, thesis or alternative. *Entrance requirements:* For master's, minimum GPA of 2.75; for Ed S, GRE General Test, MAT, minimum GPA of 2.75. Additional exam requirements/recommendations for international students: Required—TOEFL (minimum score 550 paper-based; 213 computer-based; 79 iBT). *Application deadline:* For fall admission, 7/20 priority date for domestic students, 5/1 for international students; for spring admission, 12/20 priority date for domestic students, 9/1 for international students. Applications are processed on a rolling basis. Application fee: $35 ($50 for international students). Electronic applications accepted. *Expenses:* Tuition, state resident: full-time $4086; part-time $227 per credit hour. Tuition, nonresident: full-time $8172; part-time $454 per credit hour. *Required fees:* $275 per semester. Tuition and fees vary according to course load, campus/location and program. *Financial support:* Career-related internships or fieldwork, Federal Work-Study, institutionally sponsored loans, scholarships/grants, and unspecified assistantships available. Financial award application deadline: 3/31; financial award applicants required to submit FAFSA. *Unit head:* Dr. Kim Finch, Program Coordinator, 417-836-5192, Fax: 417-836-4918, E-mail: clse@missouristate.edu. *Application contact:* Misty Stewart, Coordinator of Admissions and Recruitment, 417-836-6079, Fax: 417-836-6200, E-mail: mistystewart@missouristate.edu. Web site: http://education.missouristate.edu/edadmin/.

Monmouth University, The Graduate School, School of Education, West Long Branch, NJ 07764-1898. Offers education (M Ed); initial certification (MAT), including elementary level, K-12, secondary level; learning disabilities-teacher consultant (Certificate); principal (MS Ed); principal/school administrator (MS Ed); reading specialist (MS Ed, Certificate); school counseling (MS Ed); special education (MS Ed), including autism, learning disabilities teacher consultant, teacher of students with disabilities, teaching in inclusive settings; supervisor (Certificate); teacher of the handicapped (Certificate); teaching English to speakers of other languages (TESOL) (Certificate). *Accreditation:* NCATE. Part-time and evening/weekend programs available. *Faculty:* 16 full-time (12 women), 24 part-time/adjunct (17 women). *Students:* 134 full-time (104 women), 293 part-time (246 women); includes 34 minority (11 Black or African American, non-Hispanic/Latino; 2 Asian, non-Hispanic/Latino; 18 Hispanic/Latino; 3 Two or more races, non-Hispanic/Latino), 2 international. Average age 29. 288 applicants, 92% accepted, 182 enrolled. In 2011, 173 master's awarded. *Entrance requirements:* For master's, minimum GPA of 3.0 in major, 2.75 overall; 2 letters of recommendation (for some programs). Additional exam requirements/recommendations for international students: Required—TOEFL (minimum score 550 paper-based; 213 computer-based; 79 iBT), IELTS (minimum score 5), Michigan English Language Assessment Battery (minimum score 77), Cambridge A, B, C. *Application deadline:* For fall admission, 7/15 priority date for domestic students, 7/1 for international students; for spring admission, 11/15 priority date for domestic students, 11/1 for international students. Applications are processed on a rolling basis. Application fee: $50. Electronic applications accepted. *Financial support:* In 2011–12, 274 students received support, including 291 fellowships (averaging $1,783 per year), 21 research assistantships (averaging $8,792 per year); career-related internships or fieldwork, scholarships/grants, and unspecified assistantships also available. Support available to part-time students. Financial award applicants required to submit FAFSA. *Faculty research:* Multicultural literacy, science and mathematics teaching strategies, teacher as reflective practitioner, children with disabilities. *Unit head:* Dr. Jason Barr, Program Director, 732-263-5238, Fax: 732-263-5277, E-mail: jbarr@monmouth.edu. *Application contact:* Kevin Roane, Director, Office of Graduate Admission, 732-571-3452, Fax: 732-263-5123, E-mail: gradadm@monmouth.edu. Web site: http://www.monmouth.edu/academics/schools/education/default.asp.

Montana State University, College of Graduate Studies, College of Education, Health, and Human Development, Department of Education, Bozeman, MT 59717. Offers adult and higher education (Ed D); curriculum and instruction (M Ed, Ed D), including professional educator (M Ed), technology education (M Ed); education (M Ed), including adult and higher education, educational leadership, school counseling; educational leadership (Ed D, Ed S). *Accreditation:* Teacher Education Accreditation Council. Part-time programs available. Postbaccalaureate distance learning degree programs offered (minimal on-campus study). *Degree requirements:* For master's, comprehensive exam; for doctorate, comprehensive exam, thesis/dissertation. *Entrance requirements:* For master's, GRE, 3 letters of reference, essays, BA transcripts; for doctorate, GRE, MAT, 3 letters of reference, essay, BA and M Ed transcripts; for Ed S, PRAXIS. Additional exam requirements/recommendations for international students: Required—TOEFL (minimum score 550 paper-based; 213 computer-based). Electronic applications accepted. *Faculty research:* Critical literacy; standards-based education; school Improvement, organizational change, leadership in rural education, leadership in Indian education; student Learning; multicultural/culturally responsive education for social justice Native American indigenous education, community-centered education teacher preparation.

Montclair State University, The Graduate School, College of Education and Human Services, Department of Counseling and Educational Leadership, Program in Educational Leadership, Montclair, NJ 07043-1624. Offers MA. Part-time and evening/weekend programs available. *Students:* 52 full-time (29 women), 94 part-time (48 women); includes 33 minority (17 Black or African American, non-Hispanic/Latino; 3 Asian, non-Hispanic/Latino; 12 Hispanic/Latino; 1 Two or more races, non-Hispanic/Latino), 1 international. Average age 31. 120 applicants, 78% accepted, 78 enrolled. In 2011, 90 degrees awarded. *Degree requirements:* For master's, comprehensive exam, thesis or alternative. *Entrance requirements:* For master's, GRE General Test, interview, 2 letters of recommendation. Additional exam requirements/recommendations for international students: Required—TOEFL (minimum score 83 iBT), IELTS (minimum score 6.5). *Application deadline:* For fall admission, 6/1 for international students; for spring admission, 10/1 for international students. Applications are processed on a rolling basis. Application fee: $60. Electronic applications accepted. *Financial support:* In 2011–12, 1 research assistantship with full tuition reimbursement (averaging $7,000 per year) was awarded; Federal Work-Study, scholarships/grants, and unspecified assistantships also available. Financial award application deadline: 3/1; financial award applicants required to submit FAFSA. *Unit head:* Dr. Larry Burlew, Chairperson, 973-655-7611. *Application contact:* Amy Aiello, Executive Director of The Graduate School, 973-655-5147, Fax: 973-655-7869, E-mail: graduate.school@montclair.edu. Web site: http://cehs.montclair.edu/academic/counseling/programs/masteradmin.shtml.

Montclair State University, The Graduate School, College of Education and Human Services, Doctoral Program in Teacher Education and Teacher Development, Montclair, NJ 07043-1624. Offers Ed D. Part-time and evening/weekend programs available. *Students:* 13 full-time (all women), 22 part-time (18 women); includes 6 minority (3 Black or African American, non-Hispanic/Latino; 1 Asian, non-Hispanic/Latino; 2 Hispanic/Latino). Average age 31. 51 applicants, 24% accepted, 11 enrolled. *Degree requirements:* For doctorate, comprehensive exam (for some programs), thesis/dissertation. *Entrance requirements:* For doctorate, GRE General Test, interview, 3 letters of recommendation, essay. Additional exam requirements/recommendations for international students: Required—TOEFL (minimum score 83 iBT), IELTS (minimum score 6.5). *Application deadline:* For fall admission, 2/1 for domestic and international students. Application fee: $60. Electronic applications accepted. *Financial support:* In 2011–12, 6 research assistantships with full tuition reimbursements (averaging $7,000 per year) were awarded; Federal Work-Study, scholarships/grants, and unspecified assistantships also available. Support available to part-time students. Financial award application deadline: 3/1; financial award applicants required to submit FAFSA. *Unit head:* Dr. Ada Beth Cutler, Dean, 973-655-5167, E-mail: cutler@mail.montclair.edu. *Application contact:* Amy Aiello, Executive Director of The Graduate School, 973-655-5147, Fax: 973-655-7869, E-mail: graduate.school@montclair.edu. Web site: http://www.montclair.edu/graduate/programs-of-study/doctoral-degrees/teacher-education-development-edd/.

Morehead State University, Graduate Programs, College of Education, Department of Foundational and Graduate Studies in Education, Morehead, KY 40351. Offers adult and higher education (MA, Ed S); certified professional counselor (Ed S); counseling P-12 (MA); curriculum and instruction (Ed S); educational technology (MA Ed); instructional leadership (Ed S); school administration (MA); school counseling (Ed S); teacher leader business and marketing content (MA Ed); teacher leader business and marketing technology (MA Ed); teacher leader educational technology (MA Ed); teacher leader English (MA Ed); teacher leader gifted education (MA Ed); teacher leader IECE certification (MA Ed); teacher leader interdisciplinary education P-5 (MA Ed); teacher leader middle grades (MA Ed); teacher leader non IECE certification (MA Ed); teacher leader reading/writing - non-certification (MA Ed); teacher leader reading/writing certification (MA Ed); teacher leader school communication - certification (MA Ed); teacher leader school communication - non-certification (MA Ed); teacher leader social studies (MA Ed); teacher leader special education (MA Ed). *Accreditation:* NCATE. Part-time and evening/weekend programs available. *Degree requirements:* For master's, thesis optional, oral and/or written comprehensive exams; for Ed S, thesis, oral exam. *Entrance requirements:* For master's, GRE General Test, minimum overall undergraduate GPA of 2.5; for Ed S, GRE General Test, interview, master's degree, minimum GPA of 3.5, work experience. Additional exam requirements/recommendations for international students: Required—TOEFL (minimum score 500 paper-based; 173 computer-based). Electronic applications accepted. *Faculty research:* Character education, school accountability, computer applications for school administrators.

Morgan State University, School of Graduate Studies, School of Education and Urban Studies, Department of Advanced Studies, Leadership and Policy, Program in Educational Administration and Supervision, Baltimore, MD 21251. Offers MS. *Accreditation:* NCATE. Part-time and evening/weekend programs available. *Degree requirements:* For master's, comprehensive exam, thesis optional. *Entrance requirements:* For master's, GRE General Test or MAT. *Faculty research:* Multicultural education, cooperative learning, psychology of cognition.

Morgan State University, School of Graduate Studies, School of Education and Urban Studies, Department of Advanced Studies, Leadership and Policy, Program in Higher Education Administration, Baltimore, MD 21251. Offers PhD. *Degree requirements:* For doctorate, comprehensive exam, thesis/dissertation. *Entrance requirements:* For doctorate, GRE General Test or MAT, minimum GPA of 3.0.

Morgan State University, School of Graduate Studies, School of Education and Urban Studies, Department of Advanced Studies, Leadership and Policy, Program in Higher Education-Community College Leadership, Baltimore, MD 21251. Offers Ed D. *Accreditation:* NCATE. Part-time and evening/weekend programs available. *Degree requirements:* For doctorate, comprehensive exam, thesis/dissertation. *Entrance requirements:* For doctorate, GRE General Test or MAT. Additional exam requirements/recommendations for international students: Required—TOEFL (minimum score 550 paper-based; 213 computer-based). *Faculty research:* Multicultural education, cooperative learning, psychology of cognition.

Mount St. Mary's College, Graduate Division, Department of Education, Specialization in Instructional Leadership, Los Angeles, CA 90049-1599. Offers MS, Certificate. Part-time and evening/weekend programs available. *Degree requirements:* For master's, thesis, research project. *Entrance requirements:* For master's, MAT, minimum GPA of 3.0. *Application deadline:* For fall admission, 7/15 priority date for domestic students; for spring admission, 11/15 priority date for domestic students. Application fee: $50 ($75 for international students). *Expenses: Tuition:* Part-time $752 per unit. Part-time tuition and fees vary according to degree level and program. *Financial support:* Institutionally sponsored loans, scholarships/grants, and tuition waivers (full and partial) available. Support available to part-time students. Financial award application deadline: 3/15; financial award applicants required to submit FAFSA. *Unit head:* Dr. Shelly Tochluk, Chair, Department of Education, 213-477-2623, E-mail: stochluk@msmc.la.edu.

Murray State University, College of Education, Department of Educational Studies, Leadership and Counseling, Program in School Administration, Murray, KY 42071. Offers MA Ed, Ed S. *Accreditation:* NCATE. Part-time programs available. *Degree requirements:* For master's and Ed S, comprehensive exam. *Entrance requirements:* For degree, GRE General Test. Additional exam requirements/recommendations for international students: Required—TOEFL.

National Louis University, National College of Education, Chicago, IL 60603. Offers administration and supervision (M Ed, Ed D, CAS, Ed S); curriculum and instruction (M Ed, MS Ed, CAS); early childhood administration (M Ed, CAS); early childhood education (M Ed, MAT, MS Ed, CAS); education (Ed D); educational psychology/human learning and development (M Ed, MS Ed, CAS, Ed S); elementary education (MAT); interdisciplinary curriculum and instruction (M Ed); mathematics education (M Ed, MS Ed, CAS); reading and language (M Ed, MS Ed, CAS); school psychology (M Ed, Ed S); science education (M Ed, MS Ed, CAS); secondary education (MAT); special education (M Ed, MAT, CAS); technology in education (M Ed, CAS). *Accreditation:* NCATE. Part-time and evening/weekend programs available. *Students:* 224 full-time (162 women), 2,336 part-time (1,767 women); includes 677 minority (366 Black or African American, non-Hispanic/Latino; 8 American Indian or Alaska Native, non-Hispanic/Latino; 68 Asian, non-Hispanic/Latino; 218 Hispanic/Latino; 2 Native Hawaiian or other Pacific Islander, non-Hispanic/Latino; 15 Two or more races, non-Hispanic/Latino), 2 international. Average age 34. In 2011, 1,711 master's, 76 doctorates, 86 other advanced degrees awarded. *Degree requirements:* For doctorate, comprehensive exam, thesis/dissertation. *Entrance requirements:* For master's, MAT or GRE, minimum GPA of 3.0; for doctorate, GRE General Test, minimum GPA of 3.25, interview, resume, writing sample, 4 recommendations. Additional exam requirements/recommendations for international students: Required—TOEFL (minimum score 550 paper-based; 213 computer-based; 79 iBT). *Application deadline:* Applications are processed on a rolling basis. Application fee: $40. *Financial support:* Fellowships, research assistantships, teaching assistantships, career-related internships or fieldwork, Federal Work-Study, institutionally sponsored loans, and scholarships/grants available. Support available to part-time students. Financial award applicants required to submit FAFSA. *Unit head:* Dr. Alison Hilsabeck, Dean, 312-361-3580, Fax: 312-261-2580, E-mail: ahilsabeck@nl.edu.

Application contact: Ken Kasprzak, Director of Admission, 888-658-8632, Fax: 847-947-5575, E-mail: kkasprzak@nl.edu.

National University, Academic Affairs, School of Education, Department of Educational Administration and School Counseling/Psychology, La Jolla, CA 92037-1011. Offers accomplished collaborative leadership (MA); applied behavior analysis (MS); applied school leadership (MS); educational administration (MS); educational counseling (MS); higher education administration (MS); innovative school leadership (MS); instructional leadership (MS); school psychology (MS). Part-time and evening/weekend programs available. Postbaccalaureate distance learning degree programs offered (no on-campus study). *Degree requirements:* For master's, thesis. *Entrance requirements:* For master's, interview, minimum GPA of 2.5. Additional exam requirements/recommendations for international students: Required—TOEFL (minimum score 550 paper-based; 213 computer-based; 79 iBT), IELTS (minimum score 6). *Application deadline:* Applications are processed on a rolling basis. Application fee: $60 ($65 for international students). Electronic applications accepted. *Financial support:* Career-related internships or fieldwork, institutionally sponsored loans, scholarships/grants, and tuition waivers (partial) available. Support available to part-time students. Financial award application deadline: 6/30; financial award applicants required to submit FAFSA. *Unit head:* Dr. Rollin Nordgren, Chair and Professor, 858-642-8144, Fax: 858-642-8724, E-mail: rnordgren@nu.edu. *Application contact:* Dominick Giovanniello, Associate Regional Dean, 800-NAT-UNIV, Fax: 858-541-7792, E-mail: dgiovann@nu.edu. Web site: http://www.nu.edu/OurPrograms/SchoolOfEducation/EducationalAdministration.html.

National University, Academic Affairs, School of Education, Department of Teacher Education, La Jolla, CA 92037-1011. Offers best practices (Certificate); early childhood education (Certificate); educational technology (Certificate); elementary education (M Ed); instructional technology (MS Ed); multiple or single subjects teaching (M Ed); national board certified teacher leadership (Certificate); secondary education (M Ed); teaching (MA). Part-time and evening/weekend programs available. Postbaccalaureate distance learning degree programs offered (no on-campus study). *Degree requirements:* For master's, thesis. *Entrance requirements:* For master's, interview, minimum GPA of 2.5. Additional exam requirements/recommendations for international students: Required—TOEFL (minimum score 550 paper-based; 213 computer-based; 79 iBT), IELTS (minimum score 6). *Application deadline:* Applications are processed on a rolling basis. Application fee: $60 ($65 for international students). Electronic applications accepted. *Financial support:* Career-related internships or fieldwork, institutionally sponsored loans, scholarships/grants, and tuition waivers (partial) available. Support available to part-time students. Financial award application deadline: 6/30; financial award applicants required to submit FAFSA. *Unit head:* Dr. Cynthia Schubert-Irastroza, Chair, 858-642-8339, Fax: 858-642-8724, E-mail: cshubert@nu.edu. *Application contact:* Dominick Giovanniello, Associate Regional Dean, 800-NAT-UNIV, Fax: 858-541-7792, E-mail: dgiovann@nu.edu. Web site: http://www.nu.edu/OurPrograms/SchoolOfEducation/TeacherEducation.html.

Neumann University, Program in Educational Leadership, Aston, PA 19014-1298. Offers Ed D. *Degree requirements:* For doctorate, comprehensive exam, thesis/dissertation. *Entrance requirements:* For doctorate, PRAXIS, GRE. *Expenses:* Contact institution.

New England College, Program in Education, Henniker, NH 03242-3293. Offers higher education administration (MS, Ed D); K-12 leadership (Ed D); literacy and language arts (M Ed); meeting the needs of all learners/special education (M Ed); teacher leadership/school reform (M Ed). Part-time and evening/weekend programs available.

New Jersey City University, Graduate Studies and Continuing Education, Debra Cannon Partridge Wolfe College of Education, Department of Educational Leadership, Jersey City, NJ 07305-1597. Offers basics and urban studies (MA); bilingual/bicultural education and English as a second language (MA); educational administration and supervision (MA). Part-time and evening/weekend programs available. *Students:* 16 full-time (12 women), 167 part-time (113 women); includes 72 minority (18 Black or African American, non-Hispanic/Latino; 3 Asian, non-Hispanic/Latino; 51 Hispanic/Latino), 6 international. Average age 34. In 2011, 126 master's awarded. *Entrance requirements:* Additional exam requirements/recommendations for international students: Required—TOEFL. *Application deadline:* For fall admission, 8/1 priority date for domestic students; for spring admission, 12/1 for domestic students. Applications are processed on a rolling basis. Application fee: $0. *Expenses:* Tuition, state resident: part-time $494 per credit. Tuition, nonresident: part-time $911.30 per credit. *Required fees:* $95.90 per year. *Financial support:* Fellowships, teaching assistantships, career-related internships or fieldwork, and unspecified assistantships available. *Unit head:* Dr. Catherine Rogers, Chairperson, 201-200-3012, E-mail: cshevey@njcu.edu. *Application contact:* Dr. William Bajor, Dean of Graduate Studies, 201-200-3409, Fax: 201-200-3411, E-mail: wbajor@njcu.edu.

Newman Theological College, Religious Education Programs, Edmonton, AB T6V 1H3, Canada. Offers catholic school administration (CCSA); religious education (MRE, GDRE). Part-time programs available. Postbaccalaureate distance learning degree programs offered (no on-campus study). *Faculty:* 15 part-time/adjunct (6 women). *Students:* 2 full-time (1 woman), 64 part-time (37 women). Average age 39. 30 applicants, 100% accepted, 30 enrolled. In 2011, 6 master's, 22 other advanced degrees awarded. *Degree requirements:* For master's, thesis or alternative. *Entrance requirements:* For master's, 2 years of successful teaching experience, graduate diploma in religious education; for other advanced degree, bachelor's degree in education, teaching certificate. Additional exam requirements/recommendations for international students: Required—TOEFL (minimum score 560 paper-based; 220 computer-based; 86 iBT). *Application deadline:* For fall admission, 8/6 priority date for domestic students; for winter admission, 1/3 priority date for domestic students; for spring admission, 5/7 priority date for domestic students. Applications are processed on a rolling basis. Application fee: $45 ($250 for international students). Tuition and fees charges are reported in Canadian dollars. *Expenses: Tuition:* Full-time $5880 Canadian dollars; part-time $588 Canadian dollars per course. *Required fees:* $230 Canadian dollars; $70 Canadian dollars per semester. *Financial support:* Tuition bursaries available. Support available to part-time students. Financial award application deadline: 5/31. *Unit head:* Sandra Talarico, Director, 780-392-2450 Ext. 5239, Fax: 780-462-4013, E-mail: sandra.talarico@newman.edu. *Application contact:* Maria Saulnier, Registrar, 780-392-2451, Fax: 780-462-4013, E-mail: registrar@newman.edu. Web site: http://www.newman.edu/.

Newman University, Master of Education Program, Wichita, KS 67213-2097. Offers building leadership (MS Ed); curriculum and instruction (MS Ed), including accountability, English as a second language, reading specialist. *Accreditation:* NCATE. Part-time and evening/weekend programs available. Postbaccalaureate distance learning degree programs offered (no on-campus study). *Faculty:* 4 full-time (2 women), 38 part-time/adjunct (all women). *Students:* 47 full-time (40 women), 414 part-time (318 women); includes 62 minority (20 Black or African American, non-Hispanic/Latino; 8 Asian, non-Hispanic/Latino; 30 Hispanic/Latino; 3 Native Hawaiian or other Pacific Islander, non-Hispanic/Latino; 1 Two or more races, non-Hispanic/Latino), 3 international. Average age 35. 42 applicants, 76% accepted, 27 enrolled. In 2011, 46 master's awarded. *Degree requirements:* For master's, thesis optional. *Entrance requirements:* For master's, interview, minimum GPA of 3.0, writing sample, 2 letters of recommendation, evidence of teaching certification. Additional exam requirements/recommendations for international students: Required—TOEFL (minimum score 600 paper-based; 250 computer-based; 100 iBT). *Application deadline:* For fall admission, 8/15 priority date for domestic students, 7/15 for international students; for spring admission, 1/10 priority date for domestic students, 11/15 for international students. Applications are processed on a rolling basis. Application fee: $25 ($40 for international students). Electronic applications accepted. *Expenses:* Contact institution. *Financial support:* In 2011–12, 18 students received support. Federal Work-Study available. Financial award application deadline: 8/15; financial award applicants required to submit FAFSA. *Unit head:* Dr. Guy Glidden, Director, Graduate Education, 316-942-4291 Ext. 2331, Fax: 316-942-4483, E-mail: gliddeng@newmanu.edu. *Application contact:* Linda Kay Sabala, Director of Graduate Admissions, 316-942-4291 Ext. 2230, Fax: 316-942-4483, E-mail: sabalal@newmanu.edu.

New Mexico Highlands University, Graduate Studies, School of Education, Las Vegas, NM 87701. Offers curriculum and instruction (MA); education (MA), including counseling, school counseling; educational leadership (MA); exercise and sport sciences (MA), including human performance and sport, sports administration, teacher education; guidance and counseling (MA), including professional counseling, rehabilitation counseling, school counseling; special education (MA), including). Part-time programs available. *Faculty:* 29 full-time (18 women). *Students:* 136 full-time (100 women), 275 part-time (219 women); includes 231 minority (8 Black or African American, non-Hispanic/Latino; 22 American Indian or Alaska Native, non-Hispanic/Latino; 2 Asian, non-Hispanic/Latino; 194 Hispanic/Latino; 1 Native Hawaiian or other Pacific Islander, non-Hispanic/Latino; 4 Two or more races, non-Hispanic/Latino), 14 international. Average age 39. 117 applicants, 82% accepted, 91 enrolled. In 2011, 105 master's awarded. *Degree requirements:* For master's, comprehensive exam, thesis or alternative. *Entrance requirements:* For master's, minimum undergraduate GPA of 3.0. Additional exam requirements/recommendations for international students: Required—TOEFL (minimum score 540 paper-based; 207 computer-based). *Application deadline:* For fall admission, 8/1 priority date for domestic students. Applications are processed on a rolling basis. Application fee: $15. *Expenses:* Tuition, state resident: full-time $2767; part-time $146 per credit hour. Tuition, nonresident: full-time $4879; part-time $234 per credit hour. *International tuition:* $5436 full-time. *Required fees:* $737. *Financial support:* In 2011–12, 12 students received support. Career-related internships or fieldwork, Federal Work-Study, institutionally sponsored loans, scholarships/grants, traineeships, tuition waivers (partial), and unspecified assistantships available. Support available to part-time students. Financial award application deadline: 3/1; financial award applicants required to submit FAFSA. *Faculty research:* Teaching the United States Constitution, middle school curriculum, integrated computer applications for pre-service classroom teachers, adolescent literacy, narrative cognitive modes in NM multicultural setting. *Unit head:* Dr. Michael Anderson, Interim Dean, 505-454-3213, E-mail: mfanderson@nmhu.edu. *Application contact:* Diane Trujillo, Administrative Assistant for Graduate Studies, 505-454-3266, Fax: 505-426-2117, E-mail: dtrujillo@nmhu.edu.

New Mexico State University, Graduate School, College of Education, Department of Educational Management and Development, Las Cruces, NM 88003-8001. Offers educational administration (MA, Ed D, PhD). *Accreditation:* NCATE. Part-time and evening/weekend programs available. Postbaccalaureate distance learning degree programs offered (minimal on-campus study). *Faculty:* 8 full-time (5 women). *Students:* 20 full-time (11 women), 117 part-time (85 women); includes 86 minority (1 Black or African American, non-Hispanic/Latino; 16 American Indian or Alaska Native, non-Hispanic/Latino; 1 Asian, non-Hispanic/Latino; 68 Hispanic/Latino), 2 international. Average age 42. 56 applicants, 50% accepted, 19 enrolled. In 2011, 23 master's, 11 doctorates awarded. *Degree requirements:* For master's, variable foreign language requirement, comprehensive exam, thesis optional, internship; for doctorate, variable foreign language requirement, comprehensive exam, thesis/dissertation, internship. *Entrance requirements:* For master's, minimum GPA of 3.0 in PK-12 educational administration, current teaching license, minimum 3 years of teaching in PK-12 sector; for doctorate, minimum GPA of 3.0, master's degree. Additional exam requirements/recommendations for international students: Required—TOEFL (minimum score 550 paper-based; 79 iBT), IELTS (minimum score 6.5). *Application deadline:* For fall admission, 7/15 for domestic and international students; for spring admission, 12/1 for domestic and international students. Applications are processed on a rolling basis. Application fee: $40 ($50 for international students). Electronic applications accepted. *Expenses:* Tuition, state resident: full-time $5004; part-time $208.50 per credit. Tuition, nonresident: full-time $17,446; part-time $726.90 per credit. *Financial support:* In 2011–12, 4 teaching assistantships (averaging $21,059 per year) were awarded; fellowships with tuition reimbursements, research assistantships, and health care benefits also available. *Faculty research:* Leadership in PK-12 and postsecondary education, community college administration, program evaluation, leadership for social justice, educational change. *Unit head:* Dr. Dana Christman, Academic Department Head, 575-646-3825, Fax: 575-646-4767, E-mail: danachri@nmsu.edu. *Application contact:* Dr. Marivel Oropeza, Programs Coordinator, 575-646-4050, Fax: 575-646-4767, E-mail: oropeza@nmsu.edu. Web site: http://education.nmsu.edu/emd/index.html.

New York Institute of Technology, Graduate Division, School of Education, Program in School Leadership and Technology, Old Westbury, NY 11568-8000. Offers Professional Diploma. Part-time and evening/weekend programs available. *Students:* 2 full-time (1 woman), 17 part-time (12 women); includes 3 minority (1 Black or African American, non-Hispanic/Latino; 2 Hispanic/Latino). Average age 36. 2 applicants, 50% accepted, 0 enrolled. In 2011, 8 Professional Diplomas awarded. *Degree requirements:* For Professional Diploma, internship. *Entrance requirements:* For degree, 3 years full-time teaching experience, permanent teacher certification in New York state. Additional exam requirements/recommendations for international students: Required—TOEFL (minimum score 550 paper-based; 213 computer-based). *Application deadline:* For fall admission, 7/1 for domestic students; for spring admission, 12/1 for domestic students. Application fee: $50. *Expenses: Tuition:* Part-time $930 per credit hour. *Financial support:* Career-related internships or fieldwork available. Financial award applicants required to submit FAFSA. *Unit head:* Dr. Michael Uttendorfer, Dean, 516-686-7706, Fax: 516-686-7655, E-mail: muttendo@nyit.edu. *Application contact:* Dr. Jacquelyn Nealon, Vice President for Enrollment Services, 516-686-7925, Fax: 516-686-7613, E-mail: jnealon@nyit.edu.

New York University, Steinhardt School of Culture, Education, and Human Development, Department of Administration, Leadership, and Technology, Program in Educational Leadership, New York, NY 10012-1019. Offers educational leadership (Ed D, PhD); educational leadership, politics and advocacy (MA); school building leader (MA); school district leader (Advanced Certificate). Part-time and evening/weekend programs available. *Faculty:* 4 full-time (3 women). *Students:* 33 full-time (21 women), 61 part-time (39 women); includes 46 minority (16 Black or African American, non-Hispanic/Latino; 10 Asian, non-Hispanic/Latino; 18 Hispanic/Latino; 2 Two or more races, non-Hispanic/Latino), 2 international. Average age 31. 167 applicants, 42% accepted, 37 enrolled. In 2011, 44 master's, 2 doctorates, 1 other advanced degree awarded. *Degree requirements:* For master's, thesis (for some programs); for doctorate, thesis/dissertation. *Entrance requirements:* For doctorate, GRE General Test, interview; for Advanced Certificate, master's degree. Additional exam requirements/recommendations for international students: Required—TOEFL. *Application deadline:*

Educational Leadership and Administration

For fall admission, 12/1 priority date for domestic students, 12/1 for international students; for spring admission, 11/1 for domestic and international students. Applications are processed on a rolling basis. Application fee: $75. Electronic applications accepted. *Financial support:* Fellowships with full and partial tuition reimbursements, teaching assistantships with partial tuition reimbursements, career-related internships or fieldwork, Federal Work-Study, institutionally sponsored loans, scholarships/grants, tuition waivers (partial), and unspecified assistantships available. Support available to part-time students. Financial award application deadline: 2/1; financial award applicants required to submit FAFSA. *Faculty research:* Schools and communities; critical theories of race, class and gender; school restructuring; educational reform; social organization of schools, educational advocacy. *Unit head:* Dr. Terry Astuto, Director, 212-998-5179, Fax: 212-995-4041, E-mail: terry.astuto@nyu.edu. *Application contact:* 212-998-5030, Fax: 212-995-4328, E-mail: steinhardt.gradadmissions@nyu.edu. Web site: http://steinhardt.nyu.edu/alt/edleadership.

New York University, Steinhardt School of Culture, Education, and Human Development, Department of Administration, Leadership, and Technology, Program in Higher Education, New York, NY 10012-1019. Offers higher and postsecondary education (PhD); higher education administration (Ed D); student personnel administration in higher education (MA). *Accreditation:* Teacher Education Accreditation Council. Part-time programs available. *Faculty:* 8 full-time (5 women). *Students:* 29 full-time (22 women), 104 part-time (73 women); includes 62 minority (27 Black or African American, non-Hispanic/Latino; 9 Asian, non-Hispanic/Latino; 19 Hispanic/Latino; 1 Native Hawaiian or other Pacific Islander, non-Hispanic/Latino; 6 Two or more races, non-Hispanic/Latino), 3 international. Average age 31. 235 applicants, 18% accepted, 38 enrolled. In 2011, 42 master's, 7 doctorates awarded. *Degree requirements:* For master's, thesis (for some programs); for doctorate, thesis/dissertation. *Entrance requirements:* For master's, interview, 2 letters of recommendation; for doctorate, GRE General Test, interview. Additional exam requirements/recommendations for international students: Required—TOEFL. *Application deadline:* For fall admission, 12/1 priority date for domestic students, 12/1 for international students; for spring admission, 11/1 for domestic and international students. Applications are processed on a rolling basis. Application fee: $75. Electronic applications accepted. *Financial support:* Fellowships with full and partial tuition reimbursements, career-related internships or fieldwork, Federal Work-Study, institutionally sponsored loans, scholarships/grants, tuition waivers (partial), and unspecified assistantships available. Support available to part-time students. Financial award application deadline: 2/1; financial award applicants required to submit FAFSA. *Faculty research:* Organizational theory and culture, systemic change, leadership development, access, equity and diversity. *Unit head:* Dr. Ann Marcus, Head, 212-998-4041, Fax: 212-995-4041. *Application contact:* 212-998-5030, Fax: 212-995-4328, E-mail: steinhardt.gradadmissions@nyu.edu. Web site: http://steinhardt.nyu.edu/alt/highered.

New York University, Steinhardt School of Culture, Education, and Human Development, Department of Teaching and Learning, Program in Early Childhood and Childhood Education, New York, NY 10012-1019. Offers childhood education (MA); childhood education/special education: childhood (MA); early childhood education (MA); positions of leadership: early childhood and elementary education (PhD). *Accreditation:* Teacher Education Accreditation Council. Part-time programs available. *Degree requirements:* For master's, thesis (for some programs); for doctorate, thesis/dissertation. *Entrance requirements:* For doctorate, GRE General Test, interview. Additional exam requirements/recommendations for international students: Required—TOEFL. Electronic applications accepted. *Faculty research:* Teacher evaluation and beliefs about teaching, early literacy development, language arts, child development and education, cultural differences.

Niagara University, Graduate Division of Education, Concentration in Educational Leadership, Niagara Falls, Niagara University, NY 14109. Offers administration/supervision (Certificate); educational administration/supervision (MS Ed); educational leadership school district building (MS Ed); school business administration (Certificate); school business leadership (MS Ed); school district administration (Certificate). Part-time and evening/weekend programs available. *Faculty:* 1 full-time (0 women), 7 part-time/adjunct (1 woman). *Students:* 5 full-time (3 women), 66 part-time (42 women); includes 3 minority (2 Black or African American, non-Hispanic/Latino; 1 Hispanic/Latino), 25 international. Average age 31. In 2011, 14 master's, 3 Certificates awarded. *Entrance requirements:* For master's, GRE General Test or MAT; for Certificate, GRE General Test and GRE Subject Test or MAT. Additional exam requirements/recommendations for international students: Required—TOEFL. *Application deadline:* For fall admission, 8/1 for domestic students. Applications are processed on a rolling basis. Application fee: $30. *Expenses:* Contact institution. *Financial support:* In 2011–12, 1 research assistantship was awarded; career-related internships or fieldwork, Federal Work-Study, and unspecified assistantships also available. Support available to part-time students. Financial award application deadline: 3/15. *Unit head:* Dr. Kristine Augustyniak, Chair, 716-286-8548, E-mail: kma@niagara.edu. *Application contact:* Dr. Debra A. Colley, Dean of Education, 716-286-8560, Fax: 716-286-8561, E-mail: dcolley@niagara.edu.

Nicholls State University, Graduate Studies, College of Education, Department of Teacher Education, Thibodaux, LA 70310. Offers administration and supervision (M Ed); counselor education (M Ed); curriculum and instruction (M Ed). *Accreditation:* NCATE. Part-time and evening/weekend programs available. *Degree requirements:* For master's, comprehensive exam, portfolio. *Entrance requirements:* For master's, GRE General Test, teaching license. Electronic applications accepted.

Norfolk State University, School of Graduate Studies, School of Education, Department of Secondary Education and School Leadership, Norfolk, VA 23504. Offers principal preparation (MA); secondary education (MAT); urban education/administration (MA), including teaching. *Accreditation:* NCATE. Part-time programs available. *Entrance requirements:* For master's, GRE General Test, PRAXIS I, minimum GPA of 3.0 in major, 2.5 overall. Additional exam requirements/recommendations for international students: Required—TOEFL (minimum score 500 paper-based).

North Carolina Agricultural and Technical State University, School of Graduate Studies, School of Education, Department of Human Development and Services, Greensboro, NC 27411. Offers adult education (MS); counseling (MS); school administration (MS). *Accreditation:* ACA. Part-time and evening/weekend programs available. *Degree requirements:* For master's, comprehensive exam, thesis, qualifying exam. *Entrance requirements:* For master's, GRE General Test, minimum GPA of 3.0.

North Carolina Central University, Division of Academic Affairs, School of Education, Program in School Administration, Durham, NC 27707-3129. Offers MSA.

North Carolina State University, Graduate School, College of Education, Department of Adult and Higher Education, Program in Higher Education Administration, Raleigh, NC 27695. Offers M Ed, MS, Ed D. *Degree requirements:* For master's, thesis (for some programs); for doctorate, thesis/dissertation. *Entrance requirements:* For master's and doctorate, GRE General Test or MAT, minimum GPA of 3.0 in major. Electronic applications accepted.

North Carolina State University, Graduate School, College of Education, Department of Educational Leadership and Policy Studies, Program in Educational Administration and Supervision, Raleigh, NC 27695. Offers Ed D. *Degree requirements:* For doctorate, thesis/dissertation. *Entrance requirements:* For doctorate, GRE General Test or MAT, minimum GPA of 3.0, interview, sample of work. Electronic applications accepted.

North Carolina State University, Graduate School, College of Education, Department of Educational Leadership and Policy Studies, Program in School Administration, Raleigh, NC 27695. Offers MSA. *Degree requirements:* For master's, comprehensive exam, thesis optional. *Entrance requirements:* For master's, GRE General Test or MAT, minimum GPA of 3.0 in major, 3 years of teaching experience. Electronic applications accepted. *Faculty research:* State and national policy, educational evaluation, cohort preparation programs.

North Central College, Graduate and Continuing Education Programs, Department of Education, Naperville, IL 60566-7063. Offers curriculum and instruction (MA Ed); leadership and administration (MA Ed). Part-time and evening/weekend programs available. *Faculty:* 10 full-time (6 women), 6 part-time/adjunct (3 women). *Students:* 7 full-time (all women), 23 part-time (16 women); includes 3 minority (all Hispanic/Latino). Average age 30. 25 applicants, 56% accepted, 12 enrolled. In 2011, 39 master's awarded. *Degree requirements:* For master's, thesis optional, clinical practicum, project. *Entrance requirements:* For master's, interview. Additional exam requirements/recommendations for international students: Required—TOEFL (minimum score 577 paper-based; 233 computer-based; 90 iBT). *Application deadline:* For fall admission, 8/15 for domestic students; for winter admission, 12/1 for domestic students; for spring admission, 2/1 for domestic students. Applications are processed on a rolling basis. Application fee: $25. *Expenses:* Contact institution. *Financial support:* In 2011–12, 4 students received support. Available to part-time students. *Unit head:* Dr. Kristine Servais, Graduate Program Coordinator, Education, 630-637-5739, Fax: 630-637-5844. *Application contact:* Wendy Kulpinski, Director of Graduate and Continuing Education Admission, 630-637-5808, Fax: 630-637-5844, E-mail: wekulpinski@noctrl.edu.

North Central College, Graduate and Continuing Education Programs, Program in Leadership Studies, Naperville, IL 60566-7063. Offers higher education leadership (MLS); professional leadership (MLS); social entrepreneurship (MLS); sports leadership (MLS). Part-time and evening/weekend programs available. *Faculty:* 9 full-time (1 woman), 11 part-time/adjunct (5 women). *Students:* 44 full-time (28 women), 32 part-time (20 women); includes 16 minority (9 Black or African American, non-Hispanic/Latino; 6 Hispanic/Latino; 1 Two or more races, non-Hispanic/Latino), 1 international. Average age 29. 69 applicants, 74% accepted, 32 enrolled. In 2011, 20 master's awarded. *Degree requirements:* For master's, thesis optional, project. *Entrance requirements:* For master's, interview. Additional exam requirements/recommendations for international students: Required—TOEFL (minimum score 570 paper-based; 233 computer-based; 90 iBT). *Application deadline:* For fall admission, 8/15 for domestic students; for winter admission, 12/1 for domestic students; for spring admission, 2/1 for domestic students. Applications are processed on a rolling basis. Application fee: $25. *Expenses:* Contact institution. *Financial support:* In 2011–12, 1 student received support. Scholarships/grants available. Support available to part-time students. *Unit head:* Dr. Thomas Cavenagh, Program Coordinator, Leadership Studies, 630-637-5285. *Application contact:* Wendy Kulpinski, Director of Graduate and Continuing Education Admission, 630-637-5808, Fax: 630-637-5844, E-mail: wekulpinski@noctrl.edu.

North Dakota State University, College of Graduate and Interdisciplinary Studies, College of Human Development and Education, School of Education, Program in Educational Leadership, Fargo, ND 58108. Offers M Ed, MS, Ed S. MS and Ed S offered jointly with Minnesota State University Moorhead. *Accreditation:* NCATE. Part-time and evening/weekend programs available. Postbaccalaureate distance learning degree programs offered (minimal on-campus study). *Students:* 26 full-time (14 women), 31 part-time (17 women); includes 3 minority (1 Black or African American, non-Hispanic/Latino; 1 American Indian or Alaska Native, non-Hispanic/Latino; 1 Two or more races, non-Hispanic/Latino), 2 international. Average age 32. 10 applicants, 90% accepted, 6 enrolled. In 2011, 17 master's awarded. *Entrance requirements:* For degree, GRE General Test, master's degree, minimum GPA of 3.25. Additional exam requirements/recommendations for international students: Required—TOEFL. *Application deadline:* Applications are processed on a rolling basis. Application fee: $35. *Financial support:* In 2011–12, 1 teaching assistantship with full tuition reimbursement (averaging $800 per year) was awarded; career-related internships or fieldwork, Federal Work-Study, institutionally sponsored loans, and tuition waivers (full) also available. Financial award application deadline: 4/15. *Faculty research:* Organizational change and development, goal setting and systematic planning, beginning teacher assistance. *Unit head:* Dr. Ann Clapper, Chair, 701-231-7202, Fax: 701-231-7205, E-mail: ann.clapper@ndsu.edu. *Application contact:* Vicki Ihry, Administrative Assistant, 701-231-9732, Fax: 701-231-7205, E-mail: vicki.ihry@ndsu.edu. Web site: http://www.ndsu.nodak.edu/ed_lead/.

Northeastern Illinois University, Graduate College, College of Education, Department of Educational Leadership and Development, Program in Educational Leadership, Chicago, IL 60625-4699. Offers educational administration and supervision (MA), including chief school business official, community college administration. Part-time and evening/weekend programs available. *Degree requirements:* For master's, comprehensive exam, practicum. *Entrance requirements:* For master's, 2 years of teaching experience, minimum GPA of 2.75. Additional exam requirements/recommendations for international students: Required—TOEFL (minimum score 550 paper-based; 213 computer-based; 79 iBT). Electronic applications accepted. *Faculty research:* Student motivation, leadership, teacher expectation, educational partnerships, community/school relations.

Northeastern Illinois University, Graduate College, College of Education, Department of Educational Leadership and Development, Program in Human Resource Development, Chicago, IL 60625-4699. Offers educational leadership (MA); human resource development (MA). Part-time and evening/weekend programs available. *Degree requirements:* For master's, comprehensive papers. *Entrance requirements:* For master's, minimum GPA of 2.75, BA in human resource development. Additional exam requirements/recommendations for international students: Required—TOEFL (minimum score 550 paper-based; 213 computer-based; 79 iBT). Electronic applications accepted. *Faculty research:* Analogics, development of expertise, case-based instruction, action science organizational development, theoretical model building.

Northeastern State University, Graduate College, College of Education, Department of Educational Foundations and Leadership, Higher Education Administration and Services Program, Tahlequah, OK 74464-2399. Offers MS. *Students:* 2 full-time (both women), 24 part-time (18 women); includes 7 minority (4 Black or African American, non-Hispanic/Latino; 2 American Indian or Alaska Native, non-Hispanic/Latino; 1 Hispanic/Latino). In 2011, 6 master's awarded. *Degree requirements:* For master's, thesis. *Entrance requirements:* For master's, MAT or GRE. Additional exam requirements/recommendations for international students: Required—TOEFL (minimum score 213 computer-based). *Application deadline:* For fall admission, 6/1 priority date for domestic students. Applications are processed on a rolling basis. Application fee: $25. Electronic applications accepted. *Financial support:* Application deadline: 3/1. *Unit head:* Dr. Susan Frusher, Head, 918-449-6000 Ext. 3714, E-mail: frusher@nsuok.edu.

Application contact: Margie Railey, Administrative Assistant, 918-456-5511 Ext. 2093, Fax: 918-458-2061, E-mail: railey@nsouk.edu.

Northeastern State University, Graduate College, College of Education, Department of Educational Foundations and Leadership, Program in School Administration, Tahlequah, OK 74464-2399. Offers M Ed. Part-time and evening/weekend programs available. *Students:* 13 full-time (7 women), 75 part-time (39 women); includes 24 minority (3 Black or African American, non-Hispanic/Latino; 19 American Indian or Alaska Native, non-Hispanic/Latino; 1 Asian, non-Hispanic/Latino; 1 Hispanic/Latino). In 2011, 34 master's awarded. *Degree requirements:* For master's, thesis. *Entrance requirements:* For master's, MAT or GRE, minimum GPA of 3.0. Additional exam requirements/recommendations for international students: Required—TOEFL (minimum score 213 computer-based). *Application deadline:* For fall admission, 6/1 priority date for domestic students. Applications are processed on a rolling basis. Application fee: $25. Electronic applications accepted. *Financial support:* Teaching assistantships and Federal Work-Study available. Financial award application deadline: 3/1. *Unit head:* Dr. Ken Hancock, Coordinator, 918-449-6000 Ext. 6563, Fax: 918-458-2351, E-mail: hancockl@nsuok.edu. *Application contact:* Margie Railey, Administrative Assistant, 918-456-5511 Ext. 2093, Fax: 918-458-2061, E-mail: railey@nsouk.edu.

Northern Arizona University, Graduate College, College of Education, Department of Educational Leadership, Flagstaff , AZ 86011. Offers community college/higher education (M Ed); educational foundations (M Ed); educational leadership (M Ed, Ed D); principal (Certificate); principal K-12 (M Ed); school leadership K-12 (M Ed); superintendent (Certificate). Part-time programs available. *Faculty:* 18 full-time (8 women). *Students:* 249 full-time (148 women), 737 part-time (460 women); includes 291 minority (51 Black or African American, non-Hispanic/Latino; 65 American Indian or Alaska Native, non-Hispanic/Latino; 14 Asian, non-Hispanic/Latino; 143 Hispanic/Latino; 2 Native Hawaiian or other Pacific Islander, non-Hispanic/Latino; 16 Two or more races, non-Hispanic/Latino), 1 international. Average age 32. 251 applicants, 94% accepted, 196 enrolled. In 2011, 356 master's, 12 doctorates, 74 Certificates awarded. *Degree requirements:* For master's, comprehensive exam, thesis (for some programs); for doctorate, comprehensive exam, thesis/dissertation. *Entrance requirements:* For master's, minimum GPA of 3.0; for doctorate, GRE or MAT, minimum GPA of 3.5. Additional exam requirements/recommendations for international students: Required—TOEFL (minimum score 550 paper-based; 213 computer-based; 80 iBT), IELTS (minimum score 7). *Application deadline:* For fall admission, 3/1 for international students; for spring admission, 9/15 for international students. Applications are processed on a rolling basis. Application fee: $65. Electronic applications accepted. *Expenses:* Tuition, state resident: full-time $7190; part-time $355 per credit hour. Tuition, nonresident: full-time $18,092; part-time $1005 per credit hour. *Required fees:* $818; $328 per semester. *Financial support:* In 2011–12, 1 research assistantship with partial tuition reimbursement (averaging $10,000 per year) was awarded. Financial award applicants required to submit FAFSA. *Unit head:* Dr. Michael Schwanenberger, Chair, 928-523-4212, Fax: 928-523-1929, E-mail: michael.schwanenberger@nau.edu. *Application contact:* Jennifer Offutt, Administrative Assistant, 928-523-5098, Fax: 928-523-1929, E-mail: jennifer.offutt@nau.edu. Web site: http://nau.edu/coe/ed-leadership/.

Northern Illinois University, Graduate School, College of Education, Department of Leadership, Educational Psychology and Foundations, De Kalb, IL 60115-2854. Offers educational administration (MS Ed, Ed D, Ed S); educational psychology (MS Ed, Ed D); foundations of education (MS Ed); school business management (MS Ed). Part-time and evening/weekend programs available. Postbaccalaureate distance learning degree programs offered (minimal on-campus study). *Faculty:* 23 full-time (12 women). *Students:* 8 full-time (6 women), 272 part-time (155 women); includes 46 minority (22 Black or African American, non-Hispanic/Latino; 1 American Indian or Alaska Native, non-Hispanic/Latino; 4 Asian, non-Hispanic/Latino; 17 Hispanic/Latino; 2 Two or more races, non-Hispanic/Latino), 6 international. Average age 39. 77 applicants, 74% accepted, 22 enrolled. In 2011, 81 master's, 8 doctorates, 39 other advanced degrees awarded. *Degree requirements:* For master's, comprehensive exam, thesis optional; for doctorate, thesis/dissertation, candidacy exam, dissertation defense. *Entrance requirements:* For master's, minimum undergraduate GPA of 2.75; for doctorate, GRE General Test, minimum undergraduate GPA of 2.75, 3.2 graduate; for Ed S, GRE General Test, minimum GPA of 2.75 (undergraduate), 3.2 (graduate). Additional exam requirements/recommendations for international students: Required—TOEFL (minimum score 550 paper-based; 213 computer-based). *Application deadline:* For fall admission, 6/1 for domestic students, 5/1 for international students; for spring admission, 11/1 for domestic students, 10/1 for international students. Applications are processed on a rolling basis. Application fee: $40. Electronic applications accepted. *Financial support:* In 2011–12, 4 research assistantships with full tuition reimbursements, 7 teaching assistantships with full tuition reimbursements were awarded; fellowships with full tuition reimbursements, career-related internships or fieldwork, Federal Work-Study, scholarships/grants, tuition waivers (full), and staff assistantships also available. Support available to part-time students. Financial award applicants required to submit FAFSA. *Faculty research:* Interpersonal forgiveness, learner-centered education, psychedelic studies, senior theory, professional growth. *Unit head:* Dr. Charles L. Howell, Chair, 815-753-4404, E-mail: chowell@niu.edu. *Application contact:* Graduate School Office, 815-753-0395, E-mail: gradsch@niu.edu. Web site: http://cedu.niu.edu/LEPF/.

Northern Illinois University, Graduate School, College of Education, Department of Special and Early Education, De Kalb, IL 60115-2854. Offers curriculum and instruction (MS Ed, Ed D), including curriculum leadership (Ed D), elementary education (Ed D), secondary education (Ed D); early childhood education (MS Ed); elementary education (MS Ed); special education (MS Ed). Part-time and evening/weekend programs available. *Faculty:* 22 full-time (14 women), 2 part-time/adjunct (both women). *Students:* 58 full-time (46 women), 241 part-time (189 women); includes 35 minority (17 Black or African American, non-Hispanic/Latino; 7 Asian, non-Hispanic/Latino; 9 Hispanic/Latino; 2 Two or more races, non-Hispanic/Latino), 3 international. Average age 35. 100 applicants, 65% accepted, 45 enrolled. In 2011, 186 master's, 7 doctorates awarded. *Degree requirements:* For master's, comprehensive exam, thesis optional; for doctorate, thesis/dissertation, candidacy exam, dissertation defense. *Entrance requirements:* For master's, GRE General Test or MAT, minimum undergraduate GPA of 2.75; for doctorate, GRE General Test or MAT, minimum undergraduate GPA of 2.75, graduate 3.2. Additional exam requirements/recommendations for international students: Required—TOEFL (minimum score 550 paper-based; 213 computer-based). *Application deadline:* For fall admission, 6/1 for domestic students, 5/1 for international students; for spring admission, 11/1 for domestic students, 10/1 for international students. Applications are processed on a rolling basis. Application fee: $40. Electronic applications accepted. *Financial support:* In 2011–12, 34 research assistantships with full tuition reimbursements were awarded; fellowships with full tuition reimbursements, teaching assistantships with full tuition reimbursements, career-related internships or fieldwork, Federal Work-Study, scholarships/grants, tuition waivers (full), and unspecified assistantships also available. Support available to part-time students. Financial award applicants required to submit FAFSA. *Faculty research:* Teacher certification, stress reduction during student teaching, teaching history, portfolios in student teaching. *Unit head:* Dr. Connie Fox, Interim Chair, 815-753-1619, E-mail: seed@niu.edu. *Application contact:* Gail Myers, 815-753-0381, E-mail: gmyers@niu.edu. Web site: http://www.cedu.niu.edu/seed/.

Northern Kentucky University, Office of Graduate Programs, College of Education and Human Services, Doctor of Education in Educational Leadership Program, Highland Heights, KY 41099. Offers Ed D. Part-time and evening/weekend programs available. *Students:* 27 full-time (17 women), 33 part-time (23 women); includes 10 minority (7 Black or African American, non-Hispanic/Latino; 1 Asian, non-Hispanic/Latino; 2 Hispanic/Latino). Average age 45. 35 applicants, 51% accepted, 13 enrolled. In 2011, 2 doctorates awarded. *Entrance requirements:* For doctorate, curriculum vitae, 500-word leadership situation account, 3 letters of recommendation, 5 professional references, interview. Additional exam requirements/recommendations for international students: Required—TOEFL (minimum score 550 paper-based; 213 computer-based; 79 iBT); Recommended—IELTS (minimum score 6.5). *Application deadline:* For fall admission, 7/1 priority date for domestic students, 6/1 for international students. Application fee: $50. Electronic applications accepted. *Expenses:* Tuition, state resident: full-time $7614; part-time $423 per credit hour. Tuition, nonresident: full-time $13,104; part-time $728 per credit hour. Tuition and fees vary according to degree level and reciprocity agreements. *Financial support:* Application deadline: 5/1; applicants required to submit FAFSA. *Faculty research:* Educator dispositions, civic engagement and service-learning in education, school leadership, technology in education, professional development. *Unit head:* Dr. Paul Wirtz, Director, 859-572-7899, E-mail: edd@nku.edu. *Application contact:* Dr. Peg Griffin, Director of Graduate Programs, 859-572-6934, Fax: 859-572-6670, E-mail: griffinp@nku.edu. Web site: http://coehs.nku.edu/gradprograms/edd/.

Northern Kentucky University, Office of Graduate Programs, College of Education and Human Services, Education Program: Teacher as a Leader, Highland Heights, KY 41099. Offers teacher as a leader (MA). Part-time and evening/weekend programs available. Postbaccalaureate distance learning degree programs offered (no on-campus study). *Faculty:* 16 full-time (9 women), 2 part-time/adjunct (0 women). *Students:* 4 full-time (3 women), 187 part-time (151 women); includes 5 minority (2 Black or African American, non-Hispanic/Latino; 3 Hispanic/Latino), 1 international. Average age 33. 50 applicants, 64% accepted, 25 enrolled. In 2011, 109 master's awarded. *Degree requirements:* For master's, thesis optional, portfolio. *Entrance requirements:* For master's, GRE, teacher certification, bachelor's degree in appropriate subject area, minimum GPA of 2.5, 3 letters of recommendation, 1 year of teaching experience. Additional exam requirements/recommendations for international students: Required—TOEFL (minimum score 550 paper-based; 213 computer-based; 79 iBT); Recommended—IELTS (minimum score 6.5). *Application deadline:* For fall admission, 7/1 for domestic students, 6/1 for international students; for spring admission, 11/1 priority date for domestic students, 10/1 for international students. Application fee: $40. Electronic applications accepted. *Expenses:* Tuition, state resident: full-time $7614; part-time $423 per credit hour. Tuition, nonresident: full-time $13,104; part-time $728 per credit hour. Tuition and fees vary according to degree level and reciprocity agreements. *Financial support:* Scholarships/grants and unspecified assistantships available. *Faculty research:* Teaching with technology, middle school education, children with disabilities, teaching in the content areas, diversifying faculty. *Unit head:* Dr. Shawn Faulkner, Chair for Teacher Education, 859-572-1910, Fax: 859-572-6096, E-mail: faulkners1@nku.edu. *Application contact:* Heidi Waters, Advising Coordinator, 859-572-5237, Fax: 859-572-1384, E-mail: watersh2@nku.edu. Web site: http://coehs.nku.edu/gradprograms/programs2/education.php.

Northern Kentucky University, Office of Graduate Programs, College of Education and Human Services, Education Specialist in Educational Leadership Program, Highland Heights, KY 41099. Offers Ed S. *Students:* 1 (woman) part-time. Average age 27. 9 applicants, 11% accepted, 1 enrolled. Application fee: $50. *Expenses:* Tuition, state resident: full-time $7614; part-time $423 per credit hour. Tuition, nonresident: full-time $13,104; part-time $728 per credit hour. Tuition and fees vary according to degree level and reciprocity agreements. *Unit head:* Dr. Mark Wasicsko, Dean, 859-572-5229, Fax: 859-572-6623, E-mail: wasicskom1@nku.edu. *Application contact:* Dr. Peg Griffin, Director of Graduate Programs, 859-572-6934, Fax: 859-572-6670, E-mail: griffinp@nku.edu.

Northern Kentucky University, Office of Graduate Programs, College of Education and Human Services, Program in Instructional Leadership, Highland Heights, KY 41099. Offers MA. Part-time and evening/weekend programs available. Postbaccalaureate distance learning degree programs offered (no on-campus study). *Students:* 3 full-time (all women), 42 part-time (20 women); includes 3 minority (2 Black or African American, non-Hispanic/Latino; 1 Hispanic/Latino). Average age 37. In 2011, 26 master's awarded. *Degree requirements:* For master's, comprehensive exam, portfolio. *Entrance requirements:* For master's, GRE, teaching certificate, 3 letters of recommendation, 3 years of teaching experience, letter of introduction and interest, 3 essays, interview. Additional exam requirements/recommendations for international students: Required—TOEFL (minimum score 550 paper-based; 213 computer-based; 79 iBT); Recommended—IELTS (minimum score 6.5). *Application deadline:* For fall admission, 7/1 for domestic students, 6/1 for international students; for spring admission, 12/1 priority date for domestic students, 10/1 for international students. Applications are processed on a rolling basis. Application fee: $40. Electronic applications accepted. *Expenses:* Tuition, state resident: full-time $7614; part-time $423 per credit hour. Tuition, nonresident: full-time $13,104; part-time $728 per credit hour. Tuition and fees vary according to degree level and reciprocity agreements. *Financial support:* Unspecified assistantships available. Financial award applicants required to submit FAFSA. *Faculty research:* Ethics, law, redesign of principal preparation, principal preparation for low-achieving poverty schools. *Unit head:* Dr. Rosa Weaver, Program Coordinator, 859-572-5536, Fax: 859-572-6592, E-mail: weaverro@nku.edu. *Application contact:* Dr. Peg Griffin, Director of Graduate Programs, 859-572-6934, Fax: 859-572-6670, E-mail: griffinp@nku.edu. Web site: http://coehs.nku.edu/gradprograms/instructionalleaders/index.php.

Northern Kentucky University, Office of Graduate Programs, College of Education and Human Services, Program in Teaching, Highland Heights, KY 41099. Offers rank 1 (Certificate); rank 1 supervisor of instruction (Certificate); school superintendent (Certificate); special education (MA, Certificate); teaching (MA). Part-time programs available. *Students:* 4 full-time (3 women), 50 part-time (28 women); includes 2 minority (both Black or African American, non-Hispanic/Latino). Average age 33. 57 applicants, 40% accepted, 21 enrolled. In 2011, 33 master's, 4 other advanced degrees awarded. *Degree requirements:* For master's, comprehensive exam, thesis optional, portfolio, student teaching or internship. *Entrance requirements:* For master's, GRE, PRAXIS II, minimum GPA of 2.5, criminal background check (state and federal), resume, letter to the reviewer, interview. Additional exam requirements/recommendations for international students: Required—TOEFL (minimum score 550 paper-based; 213 computer-based; 79 iBT); Recommended—IELTS (minimum score 6.5). *Application deadline:* For fall admission, 6/1 for domestic and international students; for spring admission, 10/1 for international students. Application fee: $40. Electronic applications accepted. *Expenses:* Tuition, state resident: full-time $7614; part-time $423 per credit hour. Tuition, nonresident: full-time $13,104; part-time $728 per credit hour. Tuition and fees vary according to degree level and reciprocity agreements. *Financial support:* Unspecified assistantships available. Financial award applicants required to submit FAFSA. *Faculty research:* Middle grades students, secondary students, rural classrooms, urban classrooms, teacher preparation. *Unit head:* Dr. Lenore Kinne, Director, Teacher Education Program, 859-572-1503, E-mail: kinnel1@nku.edu.

Application contact: Melissa Decker, Alternative Certification Coordinator, 859-572-6330, Fax: 859-572-1384, E-mail: deckerm@nku.edu.

Northern Michigan University, College of Graduate Studies, College of Professional Studies, School of Education, Program in Administration and Supervision, Marquette, MI 49855-5301. Offers MA Ed, Ed S. Part-time programs available. *Degree requirements:* For master's, thesis or alternative. *Entrance requirements:* For master's, GRE General Test, minimum GPA of 3.0. *Faculty research:* Supervision and improvement of instruction, the principal as educational leader, women in K–12 educational administration.

Northern State University, Division of Graduate Studies in Education, Program in Elementary and Secondary School Administration, Aberdeen, SD 57401-7198. Offers elementary school administration (MS Ed); secondary school administration (MS Ed). *Accreditation:* NCATE. Part-time and evening/weekend programs available. *Degree requirements:* For master's, thesis optional. *Entrance requirements:* For master's, minimum GPA of 2.75. Additional exam requirements/recommendations for international students: Required—TOEFL (minimum score 550 paper-based; 213 computer-based; 78 iBT), IELTS (minimum score 6). Electronic applications accepted.

North Georgia College & State University, School of Education, Dahlonega, GA 30597. Offers art education (MAT); early childhood education (M Ed); English education (MAT); history education (MAT); math education (MAT); middle grades education (M Ed, MAT); physical education (MS); school leadership (Ed S); secondary education (M Ed), including English education, history education, mathematics education, physical education; teacher education (MAT). *Accreditation:* NCATE. Part-time and evening/weekend programs available. Postbaccalaureate distance learning degree programs offered (no on-campus study). *Faculty:* 23 full-time (14 women), 16 part-time/adjunct (11 women). *Students:* 19 full-time (17 women), 199 part-time (147 women); includes 7 minority (3 Black or African American, non-Hispanic/Latino; 1 Asian, non-Hispanic/Latino; 3 Hispanic/Latino), 1 international. Average age 34. 259 applicants, 66% accepted, 112 enrolled. In 2011, 100 master's, 16 other advanced degrees awarded. *Degree requirements:* For master's, comprehensive exam, thesis optional. *Entrance requirements:* For master's, GRE or MAT, GACE, minimum GPA of 2.75; for Ed S, GRE General Test or MAT, 3 years of teaching experience, master's degree, minimum graduate GPA of 3.25, leadership position in the school. Additional exam requirements/recommendations for international students: Required—TOEFL (minimum score 550 paper-based; 213 computer-based; 79 iBT), IELTS (minimum score 6.5). *Application deadline:* For fall admission, 8/1 priority date for domestic students, 7/1 for international students; for spring admission, 12/1 priority date for domestic students, 11/1 for international students. Applications are processed on a rolling basis. Application fee: $40. Electronic applications accepted. *Expenses:* Tuition, state resident: full-time $3528; part-time $196 per credit hour. Tuition, nonresident: full-time $14,094; part-time $783 per credit hour. *Required fees:* $1718; $859 per semester. Tuition and fees vary according to course load, campus/location and program. *Financial support:* Teaching assistantships, career-related internships or fieldwork, scholarships/grants, and unspecified assistantships available. Financial award application deadline: 5/1; financial award applicants required to submit CSS PROFILE or FAFSA. *Faculty research:* Identification of professional development school structures supporting P-12 student achievement, impact of diverse field placement settings in teacher belief development among preservice teachers, use of inquiry methodology in social studies teaching with English language learners, use of instructional differentiation in the middle grades classroom, effects of international school placements on preservice teacher beliefs and attitudes. *Unit head:* Dr. Bob Michael, Dean, School of Education, 706-864-1998, Fax: 706-867-2850, E-mail: bmichael@northgeorgia.edu. *Application contact:* Susan L. Perry, Graduate Admissions Coordinator, 706-864-1543, Fax: 706-867-2795, E-mail: slperry@northgeorgia.edu. Web site: http://www.northgeorgia.edu/soe/.

Northwestern Oklahoma State University, School of Professional Studies, Program in Educational Leadership, Alva, OK 73717-2799. Offers M Ed. Part-time programs available. *Faculty:* 7 full-time (5 women). *Students:* 1 (woman) full-time, 12 part-time (7 women); includes 1 minority (American Indian or Alaska Native, non-Hispanic/Latino), 1 international. 4 applicants, 100% accepted, 4 enrolled. In 2011, 2 master's awarded. *Degree requirements:* For master's, thesis optional, portfolio. *Entrance requirements:* For master's, GRE General Test or MAT, minimum GPA of 2.75. Application fee: $15. *Financial support:* Federal Work-Study available. Support available to part-time students. Financial award application deadline: 5/1; financial award applicants required to submit FAFSA. *Unit head:* Dr. Beverly Warden, Education Division Chair, 580-327-8451, E-mail: bjwarden@nwosu.edu. *Application contact:* Sabrina Watson, Coordinator of Graduate Studies, 580-327-8410, E-mail: sdwatson@nwosu.edu.

Northwestern State University of Louisiana, Graduate Studies and Research, College of Education and Human Development, Programs in Educational Leadership and Instruction, Natchitoches, LA 71497. Offers counseling (Ed S); educational leadership (M Ed, Ed S); educational technology (Ed S); elementary teaching (Ed S); reading (Ed S); secondary teaching (Ed S); special education (Ed S). *Accreditation:* NASAD. *Students:* 7 full-time (6 women), 75 part-time (59 women); includes 22 minority (18 Black or African American, non-Hispanic/Latino; 2 American Indian or Alaska Native, non-Hispanic/Latino; 2 Hispanic/Latino). Average age 36. 30 applicants, 97% accepted, 15 enrolled. In 2011, 31 master's, 16 Ed Ss awarded. *Degree requirements:* For master's, comprehensive exam, thesis (for some programs). *Entrance requirements:* For master's and Ed S, GRE General Test. Additional exam requirements/recommendations for international students: Required—TOEFL. *Application deadline:* For fall admission, 3/15 priority date for domestic students; for spring admission, 10/15 priority date for domestic students. Applications are processed on a rolling basis. Application fee: $20 ($30 for international students). Electronic applications accepted. *Expenses:* Tuition, state resident: full-time $3440. Tuition, nonresident: full-time $12,010. *Unit head:* Dr. Vickie Gentry, Chair, 318-357-6288, Fax: 318-357-6275, E-mail: education@nsula.edu. *Application contact:* Dr. Steven G. Horton, Associate Provost/Dean, Graduate Studies, Research, and Information Systems, 318-357-5851, Fax: 318-357-5019, E-mail: grad_school@nsula.edu.

Northwest Missouri State University, Graduate School, College of Education and Human Services, Department of Educational Leadership, Program in Educational Leadership, Maryville, MO 64468-6001. Offers educational leadership: elementary (MS Ed); educational leadership: K-12 (MS Ed); educational leadership: secondary (MS Ed); elementary principalship (Ed S); secondary principalship (Ed S); superintendency (Ed S). *Accreditation:* NCATE. Part-time programs available. *Faculty:* 14 full-time (6 women). *Students:* 11 full-time (6 women), 86 part-time (58 women); includes 6 minority (all Black or African American, non-Hispanic/Latino). 20 applicants, 100% accepted, 7 enrolled. In 2011, 56 degrees awarded. *Degree requirements:* For master's, comprehensive exam; for Ed S, comprehensive exam, thesis. *Entrance requirements:* For master's, GRE General Test, minimum undergraduate GPA of 2.75, teaching certificate, writing sample; for Ed S, minimum graduate GPA of 3.25. Additional exam requirements/recommendations for international students: Required—TOEFL (minimum score 550 paper-based; 213 computer-based). *Application deadline:* For fall admission, 7/1 for domestic and international students; for spring admission, 11/15 for domestic and international students. Application fee: $0 ($50 for international students). *Financial support:* In 2011–12, research assistantships with full tuition reimbursements (averaging $6,000 per year), 5 teaching assistantships with full tuition reimbursements (averaging $6,000 per year) were awarded; unspecified assistantships also available. Financial award application deadline: 4/1; financial award applicants required to submit FAFSA. *Unit head:* Dr. Jan Glenn, Chairperson, 660-562-1064. *Application contact:* Dr. Gregory Haddock, Dean of Graduate School, 660-562-1145, Fax: 660-562-1096, E-mail: gradsch@nwmissouri.edu.

Northwest Nazarene University, Graduate Studies, Program in Teacher Education, Nampa, ID 83686-5897. Offers curriculum and instruction (M Ed); educational leadership (M Ed, Ed D, Ed S); exceptional child (M Ed); reading education (M Ed). *Accreditation:* ACA (one or more programs are accredited); NCATE. Part-time programs available. Postbaccalaureate distance learning degree programs offered (no on-campus study). *Faculty:* 15 full-time (9 women), 36 part-time/adjunct (21 women). *Students:* 80 full-time (54 women), 119 part-time (98 women); includes 13 minority (1 American Indian or Alaska Native, non-Hispanic/Latino; 10 Hispanic/Latino; 1 Native Hawaiian or other Pacific Islander, non-Hispanic/Latino; 1 Two or more races, non-Hispanic/Latino), 8 international. Average age 36. 60 applicants, 95% accepted, 39 enrolled. In 2011, 43 master's, 24 other advanced degrees awarded. *Degree requirements:* For master's, comprehensive exam (for some programs), action research project. *Entrance requirements:* For master's, minimum undergraduate GPA of 2.8 overall or 3.0 during final 30 semester credits. *Application deadline:* For fall admission, 9/1 for domestic students. Applications are processed on a rolling basis. Application fee: $25. *Faculty research:* Action research, cooperative learning, accountability, institutional accreditation. *Unit head:* Dr. Paula Kellerer, Chair, 208-467-8729, Fax: 208-467-8562. *Application contact:* Jackie Schober, 208-467-8341, Fax: 208-467-8786, E-mail: jsschober@nnu.edu. Web site: http://www.nnu.edu/graded/.

Notre Dame de Namur University, Division of Academic Affairs, School of Education and Leadership, Program in School Administration, Belmont, CA 94002-1908. Offers administrative services credential (Certificate); school administration (MA). Part-time and evening/weekend programs available. In 2011, 8 master's awarded. *Degree requirements:* For master's, thesis. *Entrance requirements:* Additional exam requirements/recommendations for international students: Required—TOEFL (minimum score 550 paper-based; 213 computer-based; 79 iBT). *Application deadline:* For fall admission, 8/1 priority date for domestic students; for spring admission, 12/1 priority date for domestic students. Applications are processed on a rolling basis. Application fee: $60. Electronic applications accepted. *Expenses: Tuition:* Full-time $14,220; part-time $790 per credit. *Required fees:* $35 per semester. Tuition and fees vary according to program. *Financial support:* Career-related internships or fieldwork available. Support available to part-time students. Financial award applicants required to submit FAFSA. *Unit head:* Prof. Samuel Johnson, Director, 650-508-3710, E-mail: sjohnson1@ndnu.edu. *Application contact:* Candace Hallmark, Associate Director of Admissions, 650-508-3600, Fax: 650-508-3426, E-mail: grad.admit@ndnu.edu.

Notre Dame of Maryland University, Graduate Studies, Leadership in Teaching Program, Baltimore, MD 21210-2476. Offers MA. *Entrance requirements:* For master's, interview, 1 year of teaching experience, minimum GPA of 3.0. Additional exam requirements/recommendations for international students: Required—TOEFL (minimum score 500 paper-based; 173 computer-based; 61 iBT). Electronic applications accepted.

Notre Dame of Maryland University, Graduate Studies, Program in Instructional Leadership for Changing Populations, Baltimore, MD 21210-2476. Offers PhD. *Entrance requirements:* Additional exam requirements/recommendations for international students: Required—TOEFL (minimum score 500 paper-based; 173 computer-based; 61 iBT).

Oakland City University, School of Education, Oakland City, IN 47660-1099. Offers educational leadership (Ed D); teaching (MA). *Accreditation:* NCATE. *Faculty:* 4 full-time (1 woman), 16 part-time/adjunct (8 women). *Students:* 39 full-time (23 women), 65 part-time (38 women); includes 9 minority (all Black or African American, non-Hispanic/Latino). Average age 32. 46 applicants, 91% accepted, 40 enrolled. In 2011, 64 master's, 8 doctorates awarded. Terminal master's awarded for partial completion of doctoral program. *Degree requirements:* For master's, thesis; for doctorate, comprehensive exam, thesis/dissertation. *Entrance requirements:* For master's, MAT, minimum GPA of 3.0, interview, resume, letters of recommendation; for doctorate, MAT, GRE, minimum GPA of 3.2, interview, resume, letters of recommendation. *Application deadline:* For spring admission, 5/1 for domestic students. Applications are processed on a rolling basis. Application fee: $35. *Expenses:* Contact institution. *Financial support:* Unspecified assistantships available. Financial award applicants required to submit FAFSA. *Faculty research:* Assessment, cultural diversity, teacher education, education leadership. *Unit head:* Dr. Mary Jo Beauchamp, Dean, 812-749-1399, Fax: 812-749-1511, E-mail: mbeauchamp@oak.edu. *Application contact:* Kim Heldt, Director of Admissions, 812-749-1218, E-mail: kheldt@oak.edu. Web site: http://www.oak.edu/.

Oakland University, Graduate Study and Lifelong Learning, School of Education and Human Services, Department of Educational Leadership, Rochester, MI 48309-4401. Offers educational leadership (M Ed, PhD); higher education (Certificate); higher education administration (Certificate); school administration (Ed S). *Entrance requirements:* Additional exam requirements/recommendations for international students: Required—TOEFL (minimum score 550 paper-based; 213 computer-based).

Oakland University, Graduate Study and Lifelong Learning, School of Education and Human Services, Department of Teacher Development and Educational Studies, Rochester, MI 48309-4401. Offers education studies (M Ed); secondary education (MAT). *Entrance requirements:* For master's, minimum GPA of 3.0 for unconditional admission. Electronic applications accepted. *Faculty research:* Earth science for middle and high school teachers through real world connections, learning communities, content enrichment.

Oglala Lakota College, Graduate Studies, Program in Educational Administration, Kyle, SD 57752-0490. Offers MA. Part-time and evening/weekend programs available. *Entrance requirements:* For master's, minimum GPA of 2.5.

The Ohio State University, Graduate School, College of Education and Human Ecology, School of Educational Policy and Leadership, Columbus, OH 43210. Offers M Ed, MA, PhD. *Accreditation:* NCATE. *Faculty:* 31. *Students:* 87 full-time (63 women), 168 part-time (103 women); includes 54 minority (27 Black or African American, non-Hispanic/Latino; 1 American Indian or Alaska Native, non-Hispanic/Latino; 11 Asian, non-Hispanic/Latino; 9 Hispanic/Latino; 6 Two or more races, non-Hispanic/Latino), 23 international. Average age 32. In 2011, 30 master's, 24 doctorates awarded. *Degree requirements:* For master's, thesis optional; for doctorate, thesis/dissertation. *Entrance requirements:* For doctorate, GRE General Test. Additional exam requirements/recommendations for international students: Required—TOEFL (minimum score 600 paper-based; 250 computer-based), Michigan English Language Assessment Battery (minimum score 82). *Application deadline:* For fall admission, 8/15 priority date for domestic students, 7/1 for international students; for winter admission, 12/1 priority date for domestic students, 11/1 for international students; for spring admission, 3/1 priority date for domestic students, 2/1 for international students. Applications are processed on a rolling basis. Application fee: $40 ($50 for international students). Electronic applications accepted. *Expenses:* Tuition, state resident: full-time $11,400. Tuition, nonresident: full-time $28,125. Tuition and fees vary according to course load, degree level, campus/location and program. *Financial support:* Fellowships, research assistantships, teaching assistantships, Federal Work-Study, institutionally sponsored loans, and unspecified assistantships available. Support available to part-time students. *Unit head:* Eric Anderman, Director, 614-688-3484, E-mail: anderman.1@osu.edu. *Application contact:* Deb Zabloudil, Director of Graduate Student Services, 614-688-4007, E-mail: zabloudil.1@osu.edu. Web site: http://ehe.osu.edu/epl/.

Ohio University, Graduate College, Gladys W. and David H. Patton College of Education and Human Services, Department of Educational Studies, Athens, OH 45701-2979. Offers computer education and technology (M Ed); cultural studies (M Ed); educational administration (M Ed, Ed D); educational research and evaluation (M Ed, PhD); instructional technology (PhD). Part-time and evening/weekend programs available. Postbaccalaureate distance learning degree programs offered (minimal on-campus study). *Students:* 121 full-time (76 women), 94 part-time (57 women); includes 21 minority (15 Black or African American, non-Hispanic/Latino; 1 American Indian or Alaska Native, non-Hispanic/Latino; 2 Hispanic/Latino; 3 Two or more races, non-Hispanic/Latino), 35 international. 73 applicants, 67% accepted, 32 enrolled. In 2011, 52 master's, 13 doctorates awarded. *Degree requirements:* For master's, thesis or alternative; for doctorate, comprehensive exam, thesis/dissertation. *Entrance requirements:* For master's, GRE General Test (if GPA less than 2.9); for doctorate, GRE General Test, GRE Subject Test, minimum GPA of 2.9, work experience, 3 letters of reference, autobiography. Additional exam requirements/recommendations for international students: Required—TOEFL (minimum score 550 paper-based; 80 iBT) or IELTS (minimum score 6.5). *Application deadline:* For fall admission, 3/1 priority date for domestic students, 3/1 for international students; for winter admission, 10/1 priority date for domestic students, 10/1 for international students; for spring admission, 1/30 priority date for domestic students, 1/1 for international students. Applications are processed on a rolling basis. Application fee: $50 ($55 for international students). Electronic applications accepted. *Financial support:* Research assistantships with full tuition reimbursements, teaching assistantships with full tuition reimbursements, Federal Work-Study, institutionally sponsored loans, tuition waivers (partial), and unspecified assistantships available. Financial award application deadline: 3/1. *Faculty research:* Race, class and gender; computer programs; development and organization theory; evaluation/development of instruments, leadership. *Total annual research expenditures:* $158,037. *Unit head:* Dr. David Richard Moore, Chair, 740-597-1322, Fax: 740-593-0477, E-mail: moored3@ohio.edu. *Application contact:* Floyd J. Doney, Director of Student Affairs, 740-593-4400, Fax: 740-593-9310, E-mail: doney@ohio.edu. Web site: http://www.cehs.ohio.edu/academics/es/.

Oklahoma State University, College of Education, School of Teaching and Curriculum Leadership, Stillwater, OK 74078. Offers MS, PhD. Part-time programs available. *Faculty:* 32 full-time (27 women), 21 part-time/adjunct (19 women). *Students:* 53 full-time (39 women), 219 part-time (165 women); includes 58 minority (22 Black or African American, non-Hispanic/Latino; 16 American Indian or Alaska Native, non-Hispanic/Latino; 1 Asian, non-Hispanic/Latino; 7 Hispanic/Latino; 12 Two or more races, non-Hispanic/Latino), 11 international. Average age 38. 134 applicants, 57% accepted, 54 enrolled. In 2011, 76 master's, 18 doctorates awarded. *Degree requirements:* For master's, thesis or alternative; for doctorate, comprehensive exam, thesis/dissertation. *Entrance requirements:* For master's and doctorate, GRE or GMAT. Additional exam requirements/recommendations for international students: Required—TOEFL (minimum score 550 paper-based; 79 iBT). *Application deadline:* For fall admission, 3/1 for international students; for spring admission, 8/1 for international students. Applications are processed on a rolling basis. Application fee: $40 ($75 for international students). Electronic applications accepted. *Expenses:* Tuition, state resident: full-time $4044; part-time $168.50 per credit hour. Tuition, nonresident: full-time $16,008; part-time $667 per credit hour. *Required fees:* $2122; $88.45 per credit hour. One-time fee: $50. Tuition and fees vary according to course load and campus/location. *Financial support:* In 2011–12, 15 research assistantships (averaging $9,475 per year), 8 teaching assistantships (averaging $14,925 per year) were awarded; career-related internships or fieldwork, Federal Work-Study, scholarships/grants, health care benefits, tuition waivers (partial), and unspecified assistantships also available. Support available to part-time students. Financial award application deadline: 3/1; financial award applicants required to submit FAFSA. *Unit head:* Dr. Pamela Brown, Interim Head, 405-744-7125, Fax: 405-744-6290. *Application contact:* Dr. Sheryl Tucker, Dean, 405-744-7099, Fax: 405-744-0355, E-mail: grad-i@okstate.edu. Web site: http://education.okstate.edu/index.php/academic-units/stcl.

Old Dominion University, Darden College of Education, Programs in Educational Leadership and Administration, Norfolk, VA 23529. Offers educational leadership (PhD, Ed S); educational training (MS Ed); principal preparation (MS Ed). *Accreditation:* NCATE. Part-time and evening/weekend programs available. Postbaccalaureate distance learning degree programs offered (minimal on-campus study). *Faculty:* 4 full-time (2 women), 5 part-time/adjunct (2 women). *Students:* 22 full-time (15 women), 95 part-time (57 women); includes 31 minority (24 Black or African American, non-Hispanic/Latino; 1 Asian, non-Hispanic/Latino; 2 Hispanic/Latino; 4 Two or more races, non-Hispanic/Latino), 1 international. Average age 38. 92 applicants, 73% accepted, 65 enrolled. In 2011, 15 master's, 1 doctorate, 16 other advanced degrees awarded. *Degree requirements:* For master's and Ed S, comprehensive exam, thesis optional, internship, portfolio, school leadership licensure assessment; for doctorate, comprehensive exam, thesis/dissertation. *Entrance requirements:* For master's, GRE General Test or MAT, minimum GPA of 3.0 in major, letter of recommendation; for doctorate, GRE, minimum graduate GPA of 3.5, 3 letters of recommendation; for Ed S, GRE General Test or MAT, minimum GPA of 3.0 in major, 2 letters of recommendation. Additional exam requirements/recommendations for international students: Required—TOEFL (minimum score 550 paper-based). *Application deadline:* For fall admission, 6/1 priority date for domestic students, 2/15 for international students; for winter admission, 10/1 for international students; for spring admission, 11/1 priority date for domestic students, 2/1 for international students. Applications are processed on a rolling basis. Application fee: $50. Electronic applications accepted. *Expenses:* Tuition, state resident: full-time $9096; part-time $379 per credit. Tuition, nonresident: full-time $23,064; part-time $961 per credit. *Required fees:* $127 per semester. One-time fee: $50. *Financial support:* In 2011–12, 48 students received support, including 1 fellowship with tuition reimbursement available (averaging $15,000 per year), 3 teaching assistantships with tuition reimbursements available (averaging $15,000 per year); career-related internships or fieldwork, scholarships/grants, and tuition waivers (partial) also available. Support available to part-time students. Financial award application deadline: 2/15; financial award applicants required to submit FAFSA. *Faculty research:* Principal and leadership preparation, supervision, policy studies, finance, teacher quality. *Total annual research expenditures:* $500,000. *Unit head:* Dr. William Owings, Graduate Program Director, 757-683-4954, Fax: 757-683-4413, E-mail: els@odu.edu. *Application contact:* William Heffelfinger, Director of Graduate Admissions, 757-683-5554, Fax: 757-683-3255, E-mail: gradadmit@odu.edu. Web site: http://education.odu.edu/efl/academics/educational/.

Old Dominion University, Darden College of Education, Programs in Higher Education, Norfolk, VA 23529. Offers educational leadership (MS Ed, Ed S), including higher education. Part-time programs available. *Faculty:* 3 full-time (1 woman), 10 part-time/adjunct (5 women). *Students:* 35 full-time (28 women), 20 part-time (13 women); includes 33 minority (28 Black or African American, non-Hispanic/Latino; 2 Asian, non-Hispanic/Latino; 2 Hispanic/Latino; 1 Two or more races, non-Hispanic/Latino). Average age 28. 43 applicants, 63% accepted, 20 enrolled. In 2011, 19 master's, 3 Ed Ss awarded. *Degree requirements:* For master's, comprehensive exam. *Entrance requirements:* For master's, GRE, minimum undergraduate GPA of 2.8; for Ed S, GRE, 2 letters of reference, minimum GPA of 3.5, master's degree. Additional exam requirements/recommendations for international students: Required—TOEFL. *Application deadline:* For fall admission, 3/1 priority date for domestic students, 3/1 for international students; for winter admission, 10/1 for domestic and international students; for spring admission, 3/1 for domestic and international students. Applications are processed on a rolling basis. Application fee: $50. Electronic applications accepted. *Expenses:* Tuition, state resident: full-time $9096; part-time $379 per credit. Tuition, nonresident: full-time $23,064; part-time $961 per credit. *Required fees:* $127 per semester. One-time fee: $50. *Financial support:* Research assistantships with partial tuition reimbursements, career-related internships or fieldwork, scholarships/grants, and unspecified assistantships available. *Faculty research:* Law leadership, student development, research administration, international higher education administration. *Unit head:* Dr. Dennis Gregory, Graduate Program Director, 757-683-5163, E-mail: hied@odu.edu. *Application contact:* William Heffelfinger, Director of Graduate Admissions, 757-683-5554, Fax: 757-683-3255, E-mail: gradadmit@odu.edu. Web site: http://education.odu.edu/efl/academics/highered/msed/msed_international_2.shtml.

Olivet Nazarene University, Graduate School, Division of Education, Program in School Leadership, Bourbonnais, IL 60914. Offers MAE.

Oral Roberts University, School of Education, Tulsa, OK 74171. Offers Christian school administration (K-12) (MA Ed, Ed D); Christian school curriculum development (MA Ed); college and higher education administration (Ed D); public school administration (K-12) (MA Ed, Ed D); public school teaching (MA Ed). *Accreditation:* NCATE. Part-time programs available. Postbaccalaureate distance learning degree programs offered (minimal on-campus study). *Degree requirements:* For master's, comprehensive exam, thesis optional; for doctorate, comprehensive exam, thesis/dissertation. *Entrance requirements:* For master's, GRE General Test or MAT, minimum GPA of 3.0; for doctorate, minimum GPA of 3.0. Additional exam requirements/recommendations for international students: Required—TOEFL (minimum score 500 paper-based; 173 computer-based). *Expenses:* Contact institution. *Faculty research:* Teacher effectiveness, college success in high achieving African-Americans, professional development practices.

Oregon State University, Graduate School, College of Education, Program in Adult Education and Higher Education Leadership, Corvallis, OR 97331. Offers Ed M, MAIS. *Accreditation:* NCATE. Part-time programs available. *Degree requirements:* For master's, thesis or alternative. *Entrance requirements:* For master's, minimum GPA of 3.0 in last 90 hours. Additional exam requirements/recommendations for international students: Required—TOEFL. *Faculty research:* Adult training and developmental psychology, cross-cultural communication, leadership development and human relations, adult literacy.

Ottawa University, Graduate Studies-Arizona, Program in Education, Ottawa, KS 66067-3399. Offers community college counseling (MA); curriculum and instruction (MA); early childhood (MA); education intervention (MA); education leadership (MA); education technology (MA); Montessori early childhood education (MA); Montessori elementary education (MA); professional development (MA); school guidance counseling (MA); special education - cross categorical (MA). Programs offered in Mesa, Phoenix, Tempe and West Valley, AZ. *Accreditation:* NCATE. Part-time programs available. *Degree requirements:* For master's, thesis or alternative. *Entrance requirements:* For master's, minimum undergraduate GPA of 3.0, copy of current state certification or teaching license. Additional exam requirements/recommendations for international students: Required—TOEFL (minimum score 550 paper-based; 213 computer-based). Electronic applications accepted. *Expenses:* Contact institution.

Our Lady of Holy Cross College, Program in Education and Counseling, New Orleans, LA 70131-7399. Offers administration and supervision (M Ed); curriculum and instruction (M Ed); marriage and family counseling (MA); school counseling (M Ed, MA). *Accreditation:* ACA; NCATE. Part-time and evening/weekend programs available. *Degree requirements:* For master's, thesis. *Entrance requirements:* For master's, GRE General Test, minimum GPA of 2.7.

Our Lady of the Lake University of San Antonio, School of Professional Studies, Program in Principal, San Antonio, TX 78207-4689. Offers M Ed. Part-time and evening/weekend programs available. *Degree requirements:* For master's, exam, internship. *Entrance requirements:* For master's, GRE General Test or MAT. Additional exam requirements/recommendations for international students: Required—TOEFL. Electronic applications accepted.

Pace University, School of Education, New York, NY 10038. Offers adolescent education (MST); childhood education (MST); educational leadership (MS Ed); educational technology studies (MS); literacy (MSE); school business management (Certificate); special education (MS Ed); teaching students with disabilities (MSE). *Accreditation:* NCATE. Part-time and evening/weekend programs available. *Students:* 164 full-time (131 women), 533 part-time (396 women); includes 157 minority (59 Black or African American, non-Hispanic/Latino; 2 American Indian or Alaska Native, non-Hispanic/Latino; 26 Asian, non-Hispanic/Latino; 54 Hispanic/Latino; 1 Native Hawaiian or other Pacific Islander, non-Hispanic/Latino; 15 Two or more races, non-Hispanic/Latino), 10 international. Average age 29. 256 applicants, 79% accepted, 114 enrolled. In 2011, 334 master's, 34 other advanced degrees awarded. *Degree requirements:* For master's, internship. *Entrance requirements:* For master's, interview, teaching certificate. Additional exam requirements/recommendations for international students: Required—TOEFL. *Application deadline:* For fall admission, 7/31 priority date for domestic students; for spring admission, 11/30 for domestic students. Applications are processed on a rolling basis. Application fee: $70. Electronic applications accepted. *Expenses:* Contact institution. *Financial support:* Research assistantships, career-related internships or fieldwork, and Federal Work-Study available. Support available to part-time students. Financial award applicants required to submit FAFSA. *Unit head:* Dr. Andrea M. Spencer, Dean, 212-346-1345, E-mail: aspencer@pace.edu. *Application contact:* Susan Ford-Goldschein, Director of Admissions, 212-346-1660, Fax: 212-346-1585, E-mail: gradnyc@pace.edu. Web site: http://www.pace.edu/.

Pacific Lutheran University, Division of Graduate Studies, School of Education, Program for Principal Certification, Tacoma, WA 98447. Offers MAE. *Expenses: Tuition:* Part-time $915 per semester hour. *Unit head:* Dr. John Lee, Dean, 253-535-7272. *Application contact:* Linda DuBay, Senior Office Assistant, 253-535-7151, Fax: 253-536-5136, E-mail: admissions@plu.edu.

Pacific Lutheran University, Division of Graduate Studies, School of Education, Program in Educational Leadership, Tacoma, WA 98447. Offers MAE. *Accreditation:* NCATE. Part-time and evening/weekend programs available. *Faculty:* 10 full-time (5 women), 1 (woman) part-time/adjunct. *Students:* 17 part-time (14 women); includes 2 minority (1 Black or African American, non-Hispanic/Latino; 1 Asian, non-Hispanic/Latino), 1 international. Average age 29. 22 applicants, 95% accepted, 15 enrolled. In 2011, 16 master's awarded. *Degree requirements:* For master's, comprehensive exam, thesis or alternative. *Entrance requirements:* For master's, GRE General Test or MAT, interview. Additional exam requirements/recommendations for international students: Required—TOEFL (minimum score 550 paper-based; 213 computer-based). *Application deadline:* For fall admission, 5/1 priority date for domestic students. Application fee: $40. *Expenses: Tuition:* Part-time $915 per semester hour. *Financial support:* In 2011–12, 13 students received support, including 8 fellowships (averaging $3,125 per year); research assistantships, Federal Work-Study, scholarships/grants, and unspecified assistantships also available. Financial award application deadline: 3/1. *Unit head:* Dr. Michael Hillis, Graduate Director, 253-535-7272, Fax: 253-535-7184, E-mail: hillis@plu.edu. *Application contact:* Linda DuBay, Senior Office Assistant, 253-535-7151, Fax: 253-536-5136, E-mail: admissions@plu.edu.

Park University, College of Graduate and Professional Studies, Kansas City, MO 54105. Offers adult education (M Ed); at-risk students (M Ed); disaster and emergency management (MPA); educational administration (M Ed); entrepreneurship (MBA); general business (MBA); general education (M Ed); government/business relations (MPA); healthcare/services management (MBA, MPA); international business (MBA); K-12 certification (MAT); management information systems (MBA); management of information systems (MPA); middle school certification (MAT); multi-cultural education (M Ed); nonprofit management (MPA); public management (MPA); school law (M Ed); secondary school certification (MAT); special education (M Ed). Part-time and evening/weekend programs available. Postbaccalaureate distance learning degree programs offered (no on-campus study). *Degree requirements:* For master's, comprehensive exam, thesis (for some programs). *Entrance requirements:* For master's, GRE, GMAT, teacher certification (M Ed). Additional exam requirements/recommendations for international students: Required—TOEFL (minimum score 550 paper-based). Electronic applications accepted. *Faculty research:* Literacy, leadership, brain based research, multicultural education, diversity.

Penn State University Park, Graduate School, College of Education, Department of Education Policy Studies, State College, University Park, PA 16802-1503. Offers college student affairs (M Ed); educational leadership (M Ed); educational theory and policy (MA, PhD); higher education (D Ed, PhD). *Accreditation:* NCATE. *Unit head:* Dr. David H. Monk, Dean, 814-865-2526, Fax: 814-865-0555, E-mail: dhm6@psu.edu. *Application contact:* Cynthia E. Nicosia, Director, Graduate Enrollment Services, 814-865-1834, E-mail: cey1@psu.edu. Web site: http://www.ed.psu.edu/educ/eps/.

Pepperdine University, Graduate School of Education and Psychology, Division of Education, Ed D Program in Educational Leadership, Administration, and Policy, Malibu, CA 90263. Offers Ed D. *Degree requirements:* For doctorate, thesis/dissertation. *Entrance requirements:* For doctorate, MAT, GRE (verbal and quantitative sections), or GMAT, 1,000- to 2,000-word statement of educational purpose, three recommendations, personal interviews, on-site writing sample. Additional exam requirements/recommendations for international students: Required—TOEFL. *Expenses:* Contact institution.

Pepperdine University, Graduate School of Education and Psychology, Division of Education, Ed D Program in Organizational Leadership, Malibu, CA 90263. Offers Ed D. Part-time and evening/weekend programs available. *Degree requirements:* For doctorate, thesis/dissertation. *Entrance requirements:* For doctorate, GMAT or GRE General Test, MAT, 1,000- to 2,000-word statement of educational purpose, three recommendations, personal interviews, on-site writing sample. Additional exam requirements/recommendations for international students: Required—TOEFL. *Expenses:* Contact institution.

Pepperdine University, Graduate School of Education and Psychology, Division of Education, Ed D Program in Organization Change, Malibu, CA 90263. Offers Ed D. Part-time and evening/weekend programs available. *Entrance requirements:* For doctorate, GMAT, GRE General Test, MAT, 1,000- to 2,000-word statement of educational purpose, three recommendations, personal interviews, on-site writing sample. Additional exam requirements/recommendations for international students: Required—TOEFL. *Expenses:* Contact institution.

Pepperdine University, Graduate School of Education and Psychology, Division of Education, MS Program in Administration and Preliminary Administrative Services Credential, Malibu, CA 90263. Offers MS. *Entrance requirements:* For master's, GRE General Test, CBEST, two recommendation forms; signed Principal's Consent form indicating support of principal or supervising administrator under whom the administrative field work will be accomplished; one- to two-page statement of educational purpose. Additional exam requirements/recommendations for international students: Required—TOEFL.

Piedmont College, School of Education, Demorest, GA 30535-0010. Offers early childhood education (MA, MAT); middle grades education (MA); secondary education (MA, MAT); special education (MA, MAT); teacher leadership (Ed S). Part-time and evening/weekend programs available. *Students:* 546 full-time (433 women), 809 part-time (698 women); includes 172 minority (139 Black or African American, non-Hispanic/Latino; 2 American Indian or Alaska Native, non-Hispanic/Latino; 6 Asian, non-Hispanic/Latino; 18 Hispanic/Latino; 7 Two or more races, non-Hispanic/Latino), 17 international. Average age 37. 342 applicants, 83% accepted, 234 enrolled. In 2011, 444 master's, 510 other advanced degrees awarded. *Degree requirements:* For master's, thesis, field experience in the classroom teaching ; for doctorate, thesis/dissertation. *Entrance requirements:* For master's, GRE General Test, MAT, minimum undergraduate GPA of 2.5; for Ed S, minimum graduate GPA of 3.5, valid teaching certificate. Additional exam requirements/recommendations for international students: Required—TOEFL (minimum score 550 paper-based; 213 computer-based). *Application deadline:* For fall admission, 7/15 for domestic students; for spring admission, 12/1 for domestic students. Applications are processed on a rolling basis. Application fee: $0. Electronic applications accepted. *Expenses: Tuition:* Part-time $407 per credit hour. Tuition and fees vary according to program. *Financial support:* Career-related internships or fieldwork, Federal Work-Study, and unspecified assistantships available. Support available to part-time students. Financial award applicants required to submit FAFSA. *Unit head:* Dr. Bob Cummings, Dean, 706-778-3000 Ext. 1201, Fax: 706-776-9608, E-mail: bcummings@piedmont.edu. *Application contact:* Penny Loggins, Director of Graduate Admissions, 706-778-8500 Ext. 1181, Fax: 706-778-0150, E-mail: ploggins@piedmont.edu.

Pittsburg State University, Graduate School, College of Education, Department of Special Services and Leadership Studies, Program in Educational Leadership, Pittsburg, KS 66762. Offers MS.

Pittsburg State University, Graduate School, College of Education, Department of Special Services and Leadership Studies, Program in General School Administration, Pittsburg, KS 66762. Offers Ed S.

Plymouth State University, College of Graduate Studies, Graduate Studies in Education, Program in Educational Leadership, Plymouth, NH 03264-1595. Offers M Ed. *Accreditation:* NCATE. Part-time and evening/weekend programs available. *Degree requirements:* For master's, PRAXIS. *Entrance requirements:* For master's, MAT, minimum GPA of 3.0.

Point Park University, School of Arts and Sciences, Department of Education, Pittsburgh, PA 15222-1984. Offers curriculum and instruction (MA); educational administration (MA); special education (M Ed); teaching and leadership (M Ed). Part-time and evening/weekend programs available. *Faculty:* 5 full-time, 9 part-time/adjunct. *Students:* 12 full-time (8 women), 40 part-time (31 women); includes 12 minority (11 Black or African American, non-Hispanic/Latino; 1 Asian, non-Hispanic/Latino), 2 international. Average age 33. 46 applicants, 61% accepted, 18 enrolled. In 2011, 15 master's awarded. *Degree requirements:* For master's, comprehensive exam (for some programs), thesis or alternative. *Entrance requirements:* For master's, minimum GPA of 3.0, resume, 2 letters of recommendation. Additional exam requirements/recommendations for international students: Required—TOEFL. *Application deadline:* Applications are processed on a rolling basis. Application fee: $30. Electronic applications accepted. *Expenses: Tuition:* Full-time $13,050; part-time $725 per credit. *Required fees:* $720; $40 per credit. *Financial support:* In 2011–12, 42 students received support, including 2 teaching assistantships with full tuition reimbursements available (averaging $6,400 per year); scholarships/grants also available. Financial award application deadline: 4/15; financial award applicants required to submit FAFSA. *Unit head:* Dr. Darlene Marnich, Chair, 412-392-3474, Fax: 412-392-3927, E-mail: dmarnich@pointpark.edu. *Application contact:* Lynn C. Ribar, Associate Director, Graduate and Adult Enrollment, 412-392-3908, Fax: 412-392-6164, E-mail: lribar@pointpark.edu.

Pontifical Catholic University of Puerto Rico, College of Education, Program in Educational Leadership and Administration, Ponce, PR 00717-0777. Offers PhD.

Portland State University, Graduate Studies, School of Education, Department of Educational Policy, Foundations, and Administrative Studies, Portland, OR 97207-0751. Offers educational leadership (MA, MS, Ed D); postsecondary, adult and continuing education (Ed D). *Accreditation:* NCATE. Part-time and evening/weekend programs available. *Degree requirements:* For master's, thesis or alternative, written exam or research project; for doctorate, comprehensive exam, thesis/dissertation. *Entrance requirements:* For master's, California Basic Educational Skills Test, minimum GPA of 3.0 in upper-division course work or 2.75 overall; for doctorate, GRE General Test or MAT. Additional exam requirements/recommendations for international students: Required—TOEFL (minimum score 550 paper-based; 213 computer-based). *Faculty research:* Leadership development and research, principals and urban schools, accelerated schools, cooperative learning, family involvement in schools.

Prairie View A&M University, College of Education, Department of Educational Leadership and Counseling, Prairie View, TX 77446-0519. Offers counseling (MA, MS Ed); educational administration (M Ed, MS Ed); educational leadership (PhD). *Accreditation:* NCATE. Part-time and evening/weekend programs available. *Degree requirements:* For master's, thesis optional; for doctorate, comprehensive exam, thesis/dissertation. *Entrance requirements:* For master's, GRE General Test, 3 letters of reference, minimum undergraduate GPA of 2.5; for doctorate, GRE General Test, 3 letters of reference. Additional exam requirements/recommendations for international students: Required—TOEFL (minimum score 550 paper-based). Electronic applications accepted. *Faculty research:* Mentoring, personality assessment, holistic/humanistic education.

Prescott College, Graduate Programs, Program in Education, Prescott, AZ 86301. Offers early childhood education (MA); early childhood special education (MA); education (MA); elementary education (MA); environmental education leadership and administration (MA); equine-assisted experiential learning (MA); school guidance counseling (MA); secondary education (MA); special education, learning disability (MA); special education, mental retardation (MA); special education, serious emotional disability (MA); student-directed independent study (MA); sustainability education (PhD). Part-time programs available. Postbaccalaureate distance learning degree programs offered (minimal on-campus study). *Faculty:* 2 full-time (both women), 47 part-time/adjunct (31 women). *Students:* 59 full-time (36 women), 48 part-time (30 women); includes 16 minority (3 Black or African American, non-Hispanic/Latino; 1 American Indian or Alaska Native, non-Hispanic/Latino; 1 Asian, non-Hispanic/Latino; 8 Hispanic/Latino; 3 Two or more races, non-Hispanic/Latino), 2 international. Average age 40. 75 applicants, 76% accepted, 36 enrolled. In 2011, 14 master's, 8 doctorates awarded. *Degree requirements:* For master's, thesis, fieldwork or internship, practicum; for doctorate, thesis/dissertation. *Entrance requirements:* For master's, 2 letters of recommendation, resume; for doctorate, 3 letters of recommendation, resume, official transcripts, personal statement, program proposal. Additional exam requirements/recommendations for international students: Required—TOEFL (minimum score 500 paper-based; 173 computer-based). *Application deadline:* For fall admission, 4/15 priority date for domestic students, 4/15 for international students; for spring admission, 9/15 priority date for domestic students, 9/15 for international students. Applications are processed on a rolling basis. Application fee: $40. Electronic applications accepted. *Expenses: Tuition:* Full-time $16,440; part-time $685 per credit. *Required fees:* $150 per semester. One-time fee: $350. *Financial support:* Career-related internships or fieldwork and Federal Work-Study available. Financial award applicants required to submit FAFSA. *Unit head:* Noel Caniglia, Chair, 928-358-3201, Fax: 928-776-5151, E-mail: ncaniglia@prescott.edu. *Application contact:* Kerstin Alicki, Admissions Counselor, 928-350-2100, Fax: 928-776-5242, E-mail: admissions@prescott.edu.

Providence College, Programs in Administration, Providence, RI 02918. Offers elementary administration (M Ed); secondary administration (M Ed). Part-time and evening/weekend programs available. *Faculty:* 11 part-time/adjunct (4 women). *Students:* 4 full-time (2 women), 81 part-time (45 women). Average age 36. 31 applicants, 94% accepted, 10 enrolled. In 2011, 18 master's awarded. *Degree requirements:* For master's, comprehensive exam. *Entrance requirements:* For master's, GRE General Test. Additional exam requirements/recommendations for international students: Required—TOEFL (minimum score 550 paper-based; 213 computer-based; 80 iBT). *Application deadline:* For fall admission, 8/1 priority date for domestic students, 8/1 for international students; for spring admission, 12/1 priority date for domestic students, 12/1 for international students. Applications are processed on a rolling basis. Application fee: $55. *Expenses: Tuition:* Part-time $404 per credit. *Required fees:* $404 per credit. *Financial support:* In 2011–12, research assistantships with full tuition reimbursements (averaging $8,400 per year) were awarded; career-related internships or fieldwork, institutionally sponsored loans, and unspecified assistantships also available. Support available to part-time students. Financial award application deadline: 8/1; financial award applicants required to submit FAFSA. *Unit head:* Francis J. Leary, Director, 401-865-2247, Fax: 401-865-1147, E-mail: fleary@providence.edu. *Application contact:* Carol A. Daniels, Coordinator of Graduate Faculty and Administrative Services, 401-865-2247, Fax: 401-865-1147, E-mail: daniels@providence.edu.

Purdue University, Graduate School, College of Education, Department of Educational Studies, West Lafayette, IN 47907. Offers administration (MS Ed, PhD, Ed S); counseling and development (MS Ed, PhD); education of the gifted (MS Ed); educational psychology (MS Ed, PhD); foundations of education (MS Ed, PhD); higher education administration (MS Ed, PhD); special education (MS Ed, PhD). *Accreditation:* ACA (one or more programs are accredited); NCATE (one or more programs are accredited). Part-time and evening/weekend programs available. *Faculty:* 23 full-time (17 women), 1 part-time/adjunct (0 women). *Students:* 111 full-time (79 women), 93 part-time (58 women); includes 34 minority (19 Black or African American, non-Hispanic/

Latino; 1 American Indian or Alaska Native, non-Hispanic/Latino; 4 Asian, non-Hispanic/Latino; 6 Hispanic/Latino; 4 Two or more races, non-Hispanic/Latino), 30 international. Average age 35. 249 applicants, 37% accepted, 46 enrolled. In 2011, 39 master's, 20 doctorates, 4 other advanced degrees awarded. *Degree requirements:* For master's, thesis optional; for doctorate, thesis/dissertation, oral and written exams; for Ed S, oral presentation, project. *Entrance requirements:* For master's, GRE General Test required for all Educational Studies program areas, except for Special Education if undergraduate GPA is higher than a 3.0, minimum undergraduate GPA of 3.0; for doctorate and Ed S, GRE general test is required, a combined score of 1000 (300 for revised GRE test) or more is expected., minimum undergraduate GPA of 3.0. Additional exam requirements/recommendations for international students: Required—TOEFL (minimum score 550 paper-based; 77 iBT), TWE (minimum score 5). *Application deadline:* Applications are processed on a rolling basis. Application fee: $60 ($75 for international students). Electronic applications accepted. *Financial support:* Fellowships with full tuition reimbursements, research assistantships with full tuition reimbursements, teaching assistantships with full tuition reimbursements, career-related internships or fieldwork, and tuition waivers (full) available. Support available to part-time students. Financial award application deadline: 3/1; financial award applicants required to submit FAFSA. *Faculty research:* Motivation, learning disabilities, school learning, group processes, cognitive development. *Unit head:* Dr. Ala Samrapungavan, Head, 765-494-9170, Fax: 765-496-1228, E-mail: ala@purdue.edu. *Application contact:* Sarah N. Prater, Graduate Contact, 765-494-2345, Fax: 765-494-5832, E-mail: prater0@purdue.edu. Web site: http://www.edst.purdue.edu/.

Purdue University Calumet, Graduate Studies Office, School of Education, Program in Educational Administration, Hammond, IN 46323-2094. Offers MS Ed. *Entrance requirements:* Additional exam requirements/recommendations for international students: Required—TOEFL.

Queens College of the City University of New York, Division of Graduate Studies, Division of Education, Department of Educational and Community Programs, Program in Educational Leadership, Flushing, NY 11367-1597. Offers AC. Part-time programs available. *Faculty:* 4 full-time (0 women). *Students:* 100 part-time (67 women); includes 19 minority (5 Black or African American, non-Hispanic/Latino; 4 Asian, non-Hispanic/Latino; 10 Hispanic/Latino), 1 international. 61 applicants, 48% accepted, 22 enrolled. In 2011, 44 ACs awarded. *Degree requirements:* For AC, thesis optional, internship. *Entrance requirements:* For degree, master's degree or equivalent. Additional exam requirements/recommendations for international students: Required—TOEFL. *Application deadline:* For fall admission, 4/1 for domestic students; for spring admission, 11/1 for domestic students. Applications are processed on a rolling basis. Application fee: $125. *Expenses:* Tuition, state resident: part-time $345 per credit. Tuition, nonresident: part-time $640 per credit. *Required fees:* $145.25 per semester. *Financial support:* Career-related internships or fieldwork, Federal Work-Study, institutionally sponsored loans, and tuition waivers (partial) available. Support available to part-time students. Financial award application deadline: 4/1; financial award applicants required to submit FAFSA. *Unit head:* Dr. Kenneth Dunn, Coordinator, 718-997-5240. *Application contact:* Mario Caruso, Director of Graduate Admissions, 718-997-5200, Fax: 718-997-5193, E-mail: graduate_admissions@qc.edu.

Queens University of Charlotte, Wayland H. Cato, Jr. School of Education, Charlotte, NC 28274-0002. Offers education in literacy (M Ed); elementary education (MAT); school administration (MSA). *Accreditation:* NCATE. Part-time and evening/weekend programs available. *Degree requirements:* For master's, comprehensive exam. *Entrance requirements:* For master's, GRE General Test. *Expenses:* Contact institution.

Quincy University, Program in Education, Quincy, IL 62301-2699. Offers alternative certification (MS Ed); curriculum and instruction (MS Ed); leadership (MS Ed); reading education (MS Ed); school administration (MS Ed); special education (MS Ed); teacher leader in reading (MS Ed); teaching certification (MS Ed). Part-time and evening/weekend programs available. Postbaccalaureate distance learning degree programs offered. *Students:* 221 full-time (168 women), 100 part-time (69 women); includes 104 minority (69 Black or African American, non-Hispanic/Latino; 1 American Indian or Alaska Native, non-Hispanic/Latino; 5 Asian, non-Hispanic/Latino; 27 Hispanic/Latino; 2 Two or more races, non-Hispanic/Latino). In 2011, 132 master's awarded. *Degree requirements:* For master's, comprehensive exam (for some programs), thesis or alternative. *Entrance requirements:* For master's, MAT or GRE. Additional exam requirements/recommendations for international students: Required—TOEFL (minimum score 550 paper-based; 79 iBT). *Application deadline:* Applications are processed on a rolling basis. Application fee: $25. Electronic applications accepted. *Expenses: Tuition:* Full-time $9120; part-time $380 per semester hour. *Required fees:* $360; $15 per semester hour. Tuition and fees vary according to course load, campus/location and program. *Financial support:* Applicants required to submit FAFSA. *Unit head:* Kristen Anguiano, Director, 217-228-5432 Ext. 3119, E-mail: anguikr@quincy.edu. *Application contact:* Office of Admissions, 217-228-5210, Fax: 217-228-5479, E-mail: admissions@quincy.edu. Web site: http://www.quincy.edu/academics/graduate-programs/education.

Quinnipiac University, School of Education, Program in Educational Leadership, Hamden, CT 06518-1940. Offers Diploma. Part-time and evening/weekend programs available. *Faculty:* 5 full-time (3 women), 7 part-time/adjunct (3 women). *Students:* 43 part-time (30 women); includes 3 minority (1 Black or African American, non-Hispanic/Latino; 2 Hispanic/Latino). 23 applicants, 91% accepted, 20 enrolled. In 2011, 25 Diplomas awarded. *Entrance requirements:* For degree, 3 years experience in pre K-12 setting, interview, 3 credits in special education course. *Application deadline:* For fall admission, 7/30 for domestic students; for spring admission, 12/15 for domestic students. Applications are processed on a rolling basis. Application fee: $45. Electronic applications accepted. *Expenses: Tuition:* Part-time $855 per credit. *Required fees:* $35 per credit. *Financial support:* In 2011–12, 5 students received support. Application deadline: 4/15; applicants required to submit FAFSA. *Faculty research:* Leadership and teacher quality, leadership and student achievement. *Unit head:* Gary Alger, Director, 203-582-3289, E-mail: gary.alger@quinnipiac.edu. *Application contact:* Jennifer Boutin, Associate Director of Graduate Admissions, 800-462-1944, Fax: 203-582-3443, E-mail: jennifer.boutin@quinnipiac.edu. Web site: http://www.quinnipiac.edu/sixthyear.

Quinnipiac University, School of Education, Program in Teacher Leadership, Hamden, CT 06518-1940. Offers MS. Part-time and evening/weekend programs available. Postbaccalaureate distance learning degree programs offered (no on-campus study). *Faculty:* 4 full-time (3 women), 4 part-time/adjunct (2 women). *Students:* 1 (woman) full-time, 42 part-time (37 women); includes 4 minority (1 Black or African American, non-Hispanic/Latino; 3 Hispanic/Latino). 26 applicants, 85% accepted, 22 enrolled. *Degree requirements:* For master's, capstone experience. *Application deadline:* For fall admission, 8/15 for domestic students; for spring admission, 1/15 for domestic students. Applications are processed on a rolling basis. Application fee: $45. Electronic applications accepted. *Expenses: Tuition:* Part-time $855 per credit. *Required fees:* $35 per credit. *Financial support:* In 2011–12, 7 students received support. Application deadline: 4/30; applicants required to submit FAFSA. *Unit head:* Gary Alger, Director, 203-582-3289, E-mail: gary.alger@quinnipiac.edu. *Application contact:* Quinnipiac University Online Admissions Office, 800-462-1944, E-mail: quonlineadmissions@quinnipiac.edu. Web site: http://www.quinnipiac.edu/qu-online/academics/degree-programs/ms-in-teacher-leadership.

Radford University, College of Graduate and Professional Studies, College of Education and Human Development, School of Teacher Education and Leadership, Program in Educational Leadership, Radford, VA 24142. Offers licensure option (MS). *Accreditation:* NCATE. Part-time and evening/weekend programs available. *Faculty:* 1 full-time (0 women), 2 part-time/adjunct (0 women). *Students:* 2 full-time (both women), 60 part-time (42 women); includes 4 minority (all Black or African American, non-Hispanic/Latino). Average age 36. 26 applicants, 100% accepted, 23 enrolled. In 2011, 33 master's awarded. *Degree requirements:* For master's, comprehensive exam. *Entrance requirements:* For master's, GRE or MAT, minimum GPA of 2.75, 3 years of K-12 classroom experience, writing sample, 3 letters of reference, resume, official transcripts. Additional exam requirements/recommendations for international students: Required—TOEFL (minimum score 550 paper-based; 213 computer-based; 79 iBT). *Application deadline:* For fall admission, 2/15 priority date for domestic students, 12/1 for international students; for spring admission, 7/1 for international students. Applications are processed on a rolling basis. Application fee: $50. Electronic applications accepted. *Expenses:* Tuition, state resident: full-time $6262; part-time $261 per credit hour. Tuition, nonresident: full-time $14,540; part-time $606 per credit hour. *Required fees:* $2812; $117 per credit hour. Tuition and fees vary according to program. *Financial support:* In 2011–12, 3 students received support. Career-related internships or fieldwork, Federal Work-Study, institutionally sponsored loans, scholarships/grants, and unspecified assistantships available. Financial award application deadline: 3/1; financial award applicants required to submit FAFSA. *Unit head:* Dr. Sandra Moore, Director, School of Teacher Education and Leadership, 540-831-5140, Fax: 540-831-5059. *Application contact:* Rebecca Conner, Graduate Admissions, 540-831-5431, Fax: 540-831-6061, E-mail: gradcollege@radford.edu. Web site: http://www.radford.edu/content/cehd/home/departments/teacher-ed/graduate-programs/educational-leadership.html.

Ramapo College of New Jersey, Master of Arts in Educational Leadership Program, Mahwah, NJ 07430-1680. Offers MA. Part-time and evening/weekend programs available. *Faculty:* 1 full-time (0 women), 3 part-time/adjunct (0 women). *Students:* 9 full-time (7 women), 5 part-time (2 women); includes 1 minority (Asian, non-Hispanic/Latino). Average age 34. 20 applicants, 85% accepted, 11 enrolled. *Degree requirements:* For master's, thesis. *Entrance requirements:* For master's, PRAXIS, interview; 2 professional references; immunizations; official transcript from accredited higher education institution with minimum cumulative GPA of 3.0; professional portfolio, including state-issued standard teaching certificate; minimum 2 years of successful teaching experience. Additional exam requirements/recommendations for international students: Required—TOEFL (minimum score 550 paper-based; 213 computer-based; 90 iBT). *Application deadline:* For fall admission, 9/1 priority date for domestic students, 9/1 for international students; for spring admission, 1/30 priority date for domestic students, 1/30 for international students. Applications are processed on a rolling basis. Application fee: $60. Electronic applications accepted. *Expenses: Tuition, area resident:* Part-time $551.05 per credit. Tuition, nonresident: part-time $708.30 per credit. *Required fees:* $122.50 per credit. *Unit head:* Dr. Brian P. Chinni, Assistant Professor, 201-684-7613, E-mail: bchinni@ramapo.edu. *Application contact:* Karen A. Viviani, Secretarial Assistant, 201-684-7638, E-mail: kdroubi@ramapo.edu. Web site: http://www.ramapo.edu/mael/.

Regent University, Graduate School, School of Education, Virginia Beach, VA 23464-9800. Offers adult education (Ed D); adult/staff development (Ed D, PhD); career switcher with licensure (M Ed), including alternative licensure; character education (Ed D, PhD); Christian education leadership (Ed D, PhD); Christian education specialist (Ed S); Christian school program (M Ed), including ACSI licensure; distance education (Ed D, PhD); education licensure (M Ed), including preK-6th grade; educational leadership (M Ed, PhD); educational leadership - special education (Ed S), including administration and supervision; educational psychology (Ed D, PhD), including learning and development, research and evaluation, special education; higher education (Ed D, PhD), including administration, research and institutional planning, teaching; higher education leadership (Ed D); individualized degree plan (M Ed), including behavior disorders, learning disabilities, mental retardation, reading specialist; K-12 school leadership (Ed D, PhD); leadership in character education (M Ed); master teacher (M Ed), including TESOL; mathematics education (M Ed); special education (PhD); student affairs (M Ed); TESOL (M Ed), including adult education, ESL: preK-12. *Accreditation:* Teacher Education Accreditation Council. Part-time and evening/weekend programs available. Postbaccalaureate distance learning degree programs offered (minimal on-campus study). *Faculty:* 26 full-time (13 women), 54 part-time/adjunct (34 women). *Students:* 140 full-time (109 women), 786 part-time (626 women); includes 218 minority (189 Black or African American, non-Hispanic/Latino; 2 American Indian or Alaska Native, non-Hispanic/Latino; 11 Asian, non-Hispanic/Latino; 16 Hispanic/Latino), 42 international. Average age 39. 673 applicants, 57% accepted, 298 enrolled. In 2011, 178 master's, 15 doctorates awarded. *Degree requirements:* For master's, thesis or alternative; for doctorate, comprehensive exam, thesis/dissertation. *Entrance requirements:* For master's, MAT, minimum undergraduate GPA of 2.75, writing sample, resume, recommendations, interview; for doctorate, GRE, writing sample, 3 years of relevant professional experience, master's-level paper, copies of published work, resume, transcripts, interview, recommendations. Additional exam requirements/recommendations for international students: Required—TOEFL (minimum score 577 paper-based; 233 computer-based). *Application deadline:* For fall admission, 4/1 priority date for domestic students; for spring admission, 10/15 priority date for domestic students. Applications are processed on a rolling basis. Application fee: $50. Electronic applications accepted. *Expenses:* Contact institution. *Financial support:* Fellowships, career-related internships or fieldwork, scholarships/grants, tuition waivers (full and partial), and unspecified assistantships available. Support available to part-time students. Financial award application deadline: 4/1; financial award applicants required to submit FAFSA. *Faculty research:* Character development and discipline for children, education leadership development, diversity in schools, classroom management, technology in education settings. *Unit head:* Dr. Alan A. Arroyo, Dean, 757-352-4261, Fax: 757-352-4318, E-mail: alanarr@regent.edu. *Application contact:* Matthew Chadwick, Director of Enrollment Support Services, 800-373-5504, Fax: 757-352-4381, E-mail: admissions@regent.edu. Web site: http://www.regent.edu/education/.

Regis University, College for Professional Studies, School of Education and Counseling, Department of Education, Denver, CO 80221-1099. Offers adult learning, training, and development (M Ed, Certificate); autism (Certificate); curriculum, instruction, and assessment (M Ed); educational leadership (Certificate); educational technology (Certificate); instructional technology (M Ed); literacy (Certificate); professional leadership (M Ed); reading (M Ed); self-designed (M Ed); space studies (M Ed). Program also offered in Henderson and Las Vegas (Summerlin), NV. *Accreditation:* Teacher Education Accreditation Council. Part-time and evening/weekend programs available. Postbaccalaureate distance learning degree programs offered (no on-campus study). *Degree requirements:* For master's, thesis. *Entrance requirements:* For master's, resume, minimum GPA of 2.75, criminal background check. Additional exam requirements/recommendations for international students: Required—TOEFL (minimum score 213 computer-based), TWE (minimum score 5). Electronic applications accepted. *Faculty research:* Issues of equity in the middle school classroom, professional learning communities, school reform, socialinguistic and discursive obstacles to student integration, inclusive language arts curriculum.

Educational Leadership and Administration

Rhode Island College, School of Graduate Studies, Feinstein School of Education and Human Development, Department of Counseling, Educational Leadership, and School Psychology, Providence, RI 02908-1991. Offers agency counseling (MA); co-occurring disorders (MA, CGS); educational leadership (M Ed); mental health counseling (CAGS); school counseling (MA); school psychology (CAGS). *Accreditation:* NCATE. Part-time and evening/weekend programs available. *Faculty:* 9 full-time (5 women), 13 part-time/adjunct (8 women). *Students:* 30 full-time (22 women), 147 part-time (111 women); includes 13 minority (4 Black or African American, non-Hispanic/Latino; 1 Asian, non-Hispanic/Latino; 8 Hispanic/Latino). Average age 33. In 2011, 48 master's, 15 other advanced degrees awarded. *Degree requirements:* For master's and other advanced degree, comprehensive exam (for some programs), thesis (for some programs). *Entrance requirements:* For master's, GRE General Test or MAT, undergraduate transcripts; minimum undergraduate GPA of 3.0; for other advanced degree, GRE or MAT (for most programs), undergraduate transcripts; minimum undergraduate GPA of 3.0; 3 letters of recommendation; current resume. Additional exam requirements/recommendations for international students: Recommended—TOEFL (minimum score 550 paper-based; 213 computer-based; 79 iBT). *Application deadline:* For fall admission, 3/1 for domestic students; for spring admission, 11/1 for domestic students. Applications are processed on a rolling basis. Application fee: $50. *Expenses:* Tuition, state resident: full-time $8592; part-time $358 per credit hour. Tuition, nonresident: full-time $16,800; part-time $700 per credit hour. *Required fees:* $602; $22 per credit. $72 per term. *Financial support:* Teaching assistantships with full tuition reimbursements, career-related internships or fieldwork, Federal Work-Study, scholarships/grants, health care benefits, and unspecified assistantships available. Support available to part-time students. Financial award application deadline: 5/15; financial award applicants required to submit FAFSA. *Unit head:* Dr. Monica Darcy, Chair, 401-456-8023. *Application contact:* Graduate Studies, 401-456-8700. Web site: http://www.ric.edu/counselingEducationalLeadershipSchoolPsychology/index.php.

The Richard Stockton College of New Jersey, School of Graduate and Continuing Studies, Program in Educational Leadership, Pomona, NJ 08240-0195. Offers MA. Part-time and evening/weekend programs available. *Faculty:* 1 full-time (0 women). *Students:* 18 part-time (13 women); includes 3 minority (2 Black or African American, non-Hispanic/Latino; 1 Hispanic/Latino). Average age 39. 8 applicants, 100% accepted, 8 enrolled. *Degree requirements:* For master's, thesis, final project, internship. *Entrance requirements:* For master's, MAT, GRE, teaching certificate. *Application deadline:* For fall admission, 7/1 for domestic students; for spring admission, 12/1 for domestic students. Applications are processed on a rolling basis. Application fee: $50. Electronic applications accepted. *Expenses:* Tuition, state resident: full-time $13,035; part-time $543 per credit. Tuition, nonresident: full-time $20,065; part-time $836 per credit. *Required fees:* $3920; $163 per credit. Tuition and fees vary according to degree level. *Financial support:* In 2011–12, 3 research assistantships with partial tuition reimbursements were awarded; fellowships, scholarships/grants, and unspecified assistantships also available. Support available to part-time students. Financial award application deadline: 3/1; financial award applicants required to submit FAFSA. *Unit head:* Dr. Ron Tinsley, Program Director, 609-626-3640, E-mail: gradschool@stockton.edu. *Application contact:* Tara Williams, Assistant Director of Graduate Enrollment Management, 609-626-3640, Fax: 609-626-6050, E-mail: gradschool@stockton.edu. Web site: http://www.stockton.edu/grad.

Rider University, Department of Graduate Education, Leadership and Counseling, Program in Curriculum, Instruction and Supervision, Lawrenceville, NJ 08648-3001. Offers curriculum, instruction and supervision (MA); supervisor (Certificate). *Accreditation:* NCATE. Part-time and evening/weekend programs available. *Degree requirements:* For master's, comprehensive exam, practicum project. *Entrance requirements:* For master's, interview, 2 letters of recommendation from current supervisors, resume. Additional exam requirements/recommendations for international students: Required—TOEFL (minimum score 550 paper-based; 213 computer-based). Electronic applications accepted. *Expenses: Tuition:* Full-time $32,820; part-time $710 per credit. *Required fees:* $350; $35 per course. Tuition and fees vary according to campus/location and program. *Faculty research:* Curriculum change, curriculum development, teacher evaluation.

Rider University, Department of Graduate Education, Leadership and Counseling, Program in Educational Administration, Lawrenceville, NJ 08648-3001. Offers educational administration (MA); principal (Certificate); school administrator (Certificate). *Accreditation:* NCATE. Part-time and evening/weekend programs available. *Degree requirements:* For master's, comprehensive exam, research project. *Entrance requirements:* For master's, interview, resume, 2 letters of recommendation. Additional exam requirements/recommendations for international students: Required—TOEFL (minimum score 550 paper-based; 213 computer-based). Electronic applications accepted. *Expenses: Tuition:* Full-time $32,820; part-time $710 per credit. *Required fees:* $350; $35 per course. Tuition and fees vary according to campus/location and program. *Faculty research:* National/state standards, urban education, administrative leadership, financing public education, community school linkages.

Rivier University, School of Graduate Studies, Department of Education, Nashua, NH 03060. Offers curriculum and instruction (M Ed); early childhood education (M Ed); educational administration (M Ed); educational studies (M Ed); elementary education (M Ed); elementary education and general special education (M Ed); emotional and behavioral disorders (M Ed); general social education (M Ed); leadership and learning (Ed D, CAGS); learning disabilities (M Ed); learning disabilities and reading (M Ed); mental health counseling (MA); reading (M Ed); school counseling (M Ed). Part-time and evening/weekend programs available. *Degree requirements:* For master's, comprehensive exam (for some programs), internships. *Entrance requirements:* For master's, GRE General Test or MAT.

Robert Morris University, Graduate Studies, School of Education and Social Sciences, Moon Township, PA 15108-1189. Offers business education (MS); education (Postbaccalaureate Certificate); instructional leadership (MS), including education, sport management; instructional management and leadership (PhD). *Accreditation:* Teacher Education Accreditation Council. Part-time and evening/weekend programs available. Postbaccalaureate distance learning degree programs offered (no on-campus study). *Faculty:* 14 full-time (3 women), 11 part-time/adjunct (6 women). *Students:* 326 part-time (217 women); includes 24 minority (21 Black or African American, non-Hispanic/Latino; 1 Asian, non-Hispanic/Latino; 2 Hispanic/Latino), 1 international. *Degree requirements:* For doctorate, thesis/dissertation. *Entrance requirements:* Additional exam requirements/recommendations for international students: Required—TOEFL (minimum score 550 paper-based; 213 computer-based; 79 iBT). *Application deadline:* For fall admission, 7/1 priority date for domestic students, 7/1 for international students; for spring admission, 11/1 priority date for domestic students, 11/1 for international students. Applications are processed on a rolling basis. Application fee: $35. Electronic applications accepted. *Expenses:* Contact institution. *Unit head:* Dr. John E. Graham, Dean, 412-397-6022, Fax: 412-397-2524, E-mail: graham@rmu.edu. *Application contact:* Debra Roach, Assistant Dean, Graduate Admissions, 412-397-5200, Fax: 412-397-2425, E-mail: graduateadmissions@rmu.edu. Web site: http://www.rmu.edu/web/cms/schools/sess/.

Robert Morris University Illinois, Morris Graduate School of Management, Chicago, IL 60605. Offers accounting (MBA); accounting/finance (MBA); design and media (MM); health care administration (MM); higher education administration (MM); human resource management (MBA); information systems (MIS); law enforcement administration (MM); management (MBA); management/finance (MIS); management/human resource management (MBA); sports administration (MM). Part-time and evening/weekend programs available. *Faculty:* 7 full-time (1 woman), 21 part-time/adjunct (5 women). *Students:* 296 full-time (172 women), 216 part-time (136 women); includes 273 minority (160 Black or African American, non-Hispanic/Latino; 1 American Indian or Alaska Native, non-Hispanic/Latino; 32 Asian, non-Hispanic/Latino; 78 Hispanic/Latino; 2 Two or more races, non-Hispanic/Latino), 28 international. Average age 32. 247 applicants, 69% accepted, 152 enrolled. In 2011, 244 master's awarded. *Entrance requirements:* Additional exam requirements/recommendations for international students: Required—TOEFL (minimum score 550 paper-based; 173 computer-based). *Application deadline:* Applications are processed on a rolling basis. Application fee: $20 ($100 for international students). Electronic applications accepted. *Expenses: Tuition:* Full-time $13,800; part-time $2300 per course. *Financial support:* In 2011–12, 643 students received support. Federal Work-Study, scholarships/grants, tuition waivers, and leadership and athletic scholarships available. Support available to part-time students. Financial award applicants required to submit FAFSA. *Unit head:* Kayed Akkawi, Dean, 312-935-6025, Fax: 312-935-6020, E-mail: kakkawi@robertmorris.edu. *Application contact:* Fernando Villeda, Dean of Morris Graduate School of Management, 312-935-6050, Fax: 312-935-6020, E-mail: fvilleda@robertmorris.edu.

Rocky Mountain College, Program in Educational Leadership, Billings, MT 59102-1796. Offers M Ed. *Faculty:* 2 full-time (both women), 2 part-time/adjunct (both women). *Students:* 18 full-time (10 women); includes 6 minority (4 American Indian or Alaska Native, non-Hispanic/Latino; 1 Asian, non-Hispanic/Latino; 1 Two or more races, non-Hispanic/Latino). Average age 36. In 2011, 2 master's awarded. *Application deadline:* Applications are processed on a rolling basis. Electronic applications accepted. *Expenses:* Contact institution. *Financial support:* Applicants required to submit FAFSA. *Unit head:* Dr. Stevie Schmitz, Director of Educational Leadership and Distance Elementary Education, 406-238-7366, E-mail: schmitzs@rocky.edu. *Application contact:* Kelly Edwards, Director of Admissions, 406-657-1026, Fax: 406-657-1189, E-mail: admissions@rocky.edu. Web site: http://rocky.edu/academics/academic-programs/graduate-programs/mel/index.php.

Roosevelt University, Graduate Division, College of Education, Program in Teacher Leadership (LEAD), Chicago, IL 60605. Offers MA.

Rowan University, Graduate School, College of Education, Department of Educational Leadership, Program in Educational Leadership, Glassboro, NJ 08028-1701. Offers Ed D. *Accreditation:* NCATE. Part-time and evening/weekend programs available. *Degree requirements:* For doctorate, thesis/dissertation. *Entrance requirements:* For doctorate, GRE General Test, master's degree. Additional exam requirements/recommendations for international students: Required—TOEFL. Electronic applications accepted.

Rowan University, Graduate School, College of Education, Department of Educational Leadership, Program in Higher Education Administration, Glassboro, NJ 08028-1701. Offers MA. *Accreditation:* NCATE. Part-time and evening/weekend programs available. *Degree requirements:* For master's, comprehensive exam, thesis. *Entrance requirements:* For master's, GRE General Test, minimum GPA of 2.8, 2 years of teaching experience. Additional exam requirements/recommendations for international students: Required—TOEFL. Electronic applications accepted.

Rowan University, Graduate School, College of Education, Department of Educational Leadership, Program in Principal Preparation, Glassboro, NJ 08028-1701. Offers CAGS. Part-time and evening/weekend programs available. *Degree requirements:* For CAGS, comprehensive exam, thesis, internship. *Entrance requirements:* For degree, GRE General Test, minimum GPA of 2.81, 1 year of teaching experience. Additional exam requirements/recommendations for international students: Required—TOEFL. Electronic applications accepted.

Rowan University, Graduate School, College of Education, Department of Educational Leadership, Program in School Administration, Glassboro, NJ 08028-1701. Offers business administration (MA); principal preparation (MA). *Accreditation:* NCATE. Part-time and evening/weekend programs available. *Degree requirements:* For master's, comprehensive exam, thesis, internship. *Entrance requirements:* For master's, GRE General Test, NTE, minimum GPA of 2.8, 2 years of teaching experience. Additional exam requirements/recommendations for international students: Required—TOEFL. Electronic applications accepted.

Rowan University, Graduate School, College of Education, Department of Educational Leadership, Program in School Business Administration, Glassboro, NJ 08028-1701. Offers MA. Part-time and evening/weekend programs available. *Degree requirements:* For master's, comprehensive exam, thesis. *Entrance requirements:* For master's, GRE General Test. Additional exam requirements/recommendations for international students: Required—TOEFL. Electronic applications accepted.

Rowan University, Graduate School, College of Education, Department of Teacher Education, Program in Standards-Based Practice, Glassboro, NJ 08028-1701. Offers M Ed. Part-time and evening/weekend programs available. *Degree requirements:* For master's, thesis. *Entrance requirements:* For master's, GRE General Test. Additional exam requirements/recommendations for international students: Required—TOEFL. Electronic applications accepted.

Rowan University, Graduate School, College of Education, Department of Teacher Education, Program in Teacher Leadership, Glassboro, NJ 08028-1701. Offers M Ed. Part-time and evening/weekend programs available. *Degree requirements:* For master's, thesis. *Entrance requirements:* For master's, GRE General Test, minimum GPA of 2.8, 1 year of teaching experience. Additional exam requirements/recommendations for international students: Required—TOEFL. Electronic applications accepted.

Rutgers, The State University of New Jersey, Camden, Graduate School of Arts and Sciences, Department of Public Policy and Administration, Camden, NJ 08102. Offers education policy and leadership (MPA); international public service and development (MPA); public management (MPA); JD/MPA; MPA/MA. *Accreditation:* NASPAA. Part-time and evening/weekend programs available. *Degree requirements:* For master's, directed study, research workshop, 42 credits. *Entrance requirements:* For master's, GRE General Test, GMAT or LSAT, 3 letters of recommendation; resume. Additional exam requirements/recommendations for international students: Required—TOEFL (minimum score 550 paper-based; 213 computer-based), IELTS. Electronic applications accepted. *Faculty research:* Nonprofit management, county and municipal administration, health and human services, government communication, administrative law, educational finance.

Rutgers, The State University of New Jersey, New Brunswick, Graduate School of Education, Department of Educational Theory, Policy and Administration, Programs in Educational Administration and Supervision, Piscataway, NJ 08854-8097. Offers Ed M, Ed D. Part-time and evening/weekend programs available. *Degree requirements:* For doctorate, thesis/dissertation, qualifying exam. *Entrance requirements:* For master's, GRE General Test, minimum GPA of 3.0; for doctorate, GRE General Test, minimum GPA of 3.0, master's degree in educational administration. Additional exam requirements/recommendations for international students: Required—TOEFL. Electronic applications accepted. *Faculty research:* Leadership of education, finance, law, schools as organizations.

Sacred Heart University, Graduate Programs, Isabelle Farrington College of Education, Fairfield, CT 06825-1000. Offers administration (CAS); educational technology (MAT); elementary education (MAT); reading (CAS); secondary education (MAT); teaching (CAS). Part-time and evening/weekend programs available. Postbaccalaureate distance learning degree programs offered (minimal on-campus study). *Degree requirements:* For master's, thesis or alternative. *Entrance requirements:* For master's, PRAXIS (teacher certification/MAT); for CAS, PRAXIS I. Additional exam requirements/recommendations for international students: Required—TOEFL (minimum score 550 paper-based; 213 computer-based). Electronic applications accepted. *Expenses:* Contact institution. *Faculty research:* Reading education, learning theory, teacher preparation, education of underachievers.

Sage Graduate School, Esteves School of Education, Program in Educational Leadership, Troy, NY 12180-4115. Offers Ed D. Part-time programs available. *Faculty:* 10 full-time (6 women), 3 part-time/adjunct (2 women). *Students:* 25 part-time (12 women); includes 5 minority (1 Black or African American, non-Hispanic/Latino; 2 American Indian or Alaska Native, non-Hispanic/Latino; 1 Asian, non-Hispanic/Latino; 1 Hispanic/Latino). Average age 47. 31 applicants, 42% accepted, 11 enrolled. In 2011, 11 doctorates awarded. *Degree requirements:* For doctorate, comprehensive exam. *Entrance requirements:* For doctorate, minimum GPA of 3.5, 60 graduate credits from an accredited institution, 3 references addressing leadership skill potential, writing sample, personal interview. Additional exam requirements/recommendations for international students: Required—TOEFL (minimum score 550 paper-based; 213 computer-based). *Application deadline:* Applications are processed on a rolling basis. Application fee: $40. *Expenses: Tuition:* Full-time $11,880; part-time $660 per credit hour. Tuition and fees vary according to program. *Financial support:* Fellowships, research assistantships, Federal Work-Study, scholarships/grants, and unspecified assistantships available. Support available to part-time students. *Unit head:* Dr. Lori Quigley, Dean, Esteves School of Education, 518-244-2326, Fax: 518-244-4571, E-mail: l.quigley@sage.edu. *Application contact:* Dr. Robert Bradley, Director, 518-292-8618, Fax: 518-292-1728, E-mail: bradlr2@sage.edu.

Saginaw Valley State University, College of Education, Program in Educational Leadership, University Center, MI 48710. Offers chief business officers (M Ed); education leadership (Ed S); educational administration and supervision (M Ed); principalship (M Ed); superintendency (M Ed). *Accreditation:* NCATE. Part-time and evening/weekend programs available. *Students:* 13 full-time (6 women), 211 part-time (117 women); includes 22 minority (8 Black or African American, non-Hispanic/Latino; 2 American Indian or Alaska Native, non-Hispanic/Latino; 3 Asian, non-Hispanic/Latino; 3 Hispanic/Latino; 6 Two or more races, non-Hispanic/Latino), 168 international. Average age 34. 9 applicants, 100% accepted, 6 enrolled. In 2011, 130 master's, 37 Ed Ss awarded. *Degree requirements:* For master's, practicum. *Entrance requirements:* For master's, minimum GPA of 3.0, teaching certificate. *Application deadline:* Applications are processed on a rolling basis. Application fee: $25. Electronic applications accepted. *Expenses:* Tuition, state resident: full-time $8300; part-time $5333 per year. Tuition, nonresident: full-time $15,613; part-time $10,209 per year. *International tuition:* $15,631 full-time. *Financial support:* Federal Work-Study and scholarships/grants available. Support available to part-time students. Financial award applicants required to submit FAFSA. *Unit head:* Dr. Steve P. Barbus, Jr., Dean, 989-964-6067, Fax: 989-790-4385, E-mail: barbus@svsu.edu. *Application contact:* Jeanne Chipman, Certification Officer, 989-964-4083, Fax: 989-964-4385, E-mail: jdc@svsu.edu.

St. Ambrose University, College of Education and Health Sciences, Program in Educational Administration, Davenport, IA 52803-2898. Offers MEA. Part-time and evening/weekend programs available. *Faculty:* 2 part-time/adjunct (0 women). *Students:* 18 part-time (11 women). Average age 35. 9 applicants, 78% accepted, 2 enrolled. In 2011, 6 master's awarded. *Entrance requirements:* Additional exam requirements/recommendations for international students: Required—TOEFL. *Application deadline:* Applications are processed on a rolling basis. Application fee: $25. Electronic applications accepted. *Expenses: Tuition:* Full-time $13,770; part-time $765 per credit hour. *Required fees:* $60 per semester. Tuition and fees vary according to degree level, program and reciprocity agreements. *Financial support:* In 2011–12, 15 students received support. Scholarships/grants available. *Unit head:* Dr. Charles Manges, Director, 563-388-7652, Fax: 563-388-7662, E-mail: mangescharles@sau.edu. *Application contact:* Susan M. Jameson, Administrative Assistant, 563-388-7660, Fax: 563-388-7662, E-mail: lovelesselizabethb@sau.edu. Web site: http://web.sau.edu/MEA/index.htm.

St. Bonaventure University, School of Graduate Studies, School of Education, Program in Educational Leadership, St. Bonaventure, NY 14778-2284. Offers educational leadership (MS Ed); school building leader (Adv C); school district leader (Adv C). Part-time and evening/weekend programs available. Postbaccalaureate distance learning degree programs offered (minimal on-campus study). *Faculty:* 2 full-time (1 woman), 1 (woman) part-time/adjunct. *Students:* 10 full-time (7 women), 31 part-time (18 women); includes 1 minority (Hispanic/Latino). Average age 36. 33 applicants, 94% accepted, 19 enrolled. In 2011, 5 master's awarded. *Degree requirements:* For master's, comprehensive exam, thesis optional, internship, portfolio. *Entrance requirements:* For master's, teaching or counseling certification, 3 years K-12 school experience, minimum GPA of 3.0, letters of recommendation, interview, writing sample. Additional exam requirements/recommendations for international students: Required—TOEFL (minimum score 550 paper-based; 213 computer-based; 79 iBT). *Application deadline:* For fall admission, 6/15 priority date for domestic students, 2/1 for international students; for spring admission, 11/1 for domestic students. Applications are processed on a rolling basis. Application fee: $30. Electronic applications accepted. *Expenses: Tuition:* Part-time $670 per credit. *Financial support:* Research assistantships, Federal Work-Study, scholarships/grants, health care benefits, tuition waivers (partial), and unspecified assistantships available. Support available to part-time students. Financial award application deadline: 4/15; financial award applicants required to submit FAFSA. *Unit head:* Dr. Greg Gibbs, Director, 716-375-2363, E-mail: ggibbs@sbu.edu. *Application contact:* Bruce Campbell, Director of Graduate Admissions, 716-375-2021, Fax: 716-375-4015, E-mail: gradsch@sbu.edu. Web site: http://www.sbu.edu/education.aspx?id-3016.

St. Cloud State University, School of Graduate Studies, College of Health and Human Services, Department of Counseling and Community Psychology, Program in Educational Administration and Leadership, St. Cloud, MN 56301-4498. Offers MS. Part-time programs available. *Degree requirements:* For master's, comprehensive exam (for some programs), thesis or alternative. *Entrance requirements:* For master's, GRE General Test, minimum GPA of 2.75. Additional exam requirements/recommendations for international students: Required—Michigan English Language Assessment Battery; Recommended—TOEFL (minimum score 550 paper-based; 213 computer-based), IELTS (minimum score 6.5). Electronic applications accepted.

St. Cloud State University, School of Graduate Studies, School of Education, Department of Educational Leadership and Higher Education, Program in Higher Education Administration, St. Cloud, MN 56301-4498. Offers MS, Ed D.

St. Edward's University, School of Education, Program in Teaching, Austin, TX 78704. Offers curriculum leadership (Certificate); instructional technology (Certificate); mediation (Certificate); mentoring and supervision (Certificate); special education (Certificate); sports management (Certificate); teaching (MA), including conflict resolution, initial teacher certification, liberal arts, special education, sports management, teacher leadership. Part-time and evening/weekend programs available. *Students:* 1 full-time (0 women), 32 part-time (22 women); includes 14 minority (2 Black or African American, non-Hispanic/Latino; 1 Asian, non-Hispanic/Latino; 10 Hispanic/Latino; 1 Two or more races, non-Hispanic/Latino), 1 international. Average age 32. 8 applicants, 75% accepted, 6 enrolled. In 2011, 13 master's awarded. *Degree requirements:* For master's, minimum of 24 resident hours. *Entrance requirements:* For master's, GRE General Test, minimum GPA of 3.0 in last 60 hours or 2.75 overall. Additional exam requirements/recommendations for international students: Required—TOEFL (minimum score 550 paper-based; 213 computer-based; 79 iBT) or IELTS (minimum score 6). *Application deadline:* For fall admission, 7/1 for domestic and international students; for spring admission, 11/1 for domestic and international students. Applications are processed on a rolling basis. Application fee: $45 ($50 for international students). Electronic applications accepted. *Expenses: Tuition:* Full-time $17,550; part-time $975 per credit hour. *Required fees:* $50 per trimester. Full-time tuition and fees vary according to course load and program. *Unit head:* Dr. David Hollier, Director, 512-448-8666, Fax: 512-428-1372, E-mail: davidrh@stedwards.edu. *Application contact:* Sarah Hennes, Graduate Admission Coordinator, 512-448-8600, Fax: 512-428-1032, E-mail: sarahhe@stedwards.edu. Web site: http://www.stedwards.edu.

Saint Francis University, Graduate Education Program, Loretto, PA 15940-0600. Offers education (M Ed); leadership (M Ed); reading (M Ed). Part-time and evening/weekend programs available. *Faculty:* 22 part-time/adjunct (9 women). *Students:* 130 part-time (95 women); includes 1 minority (Hispanic/Latino). Average age 30. 30 applicants, 100% accepted, 30 enrolled. In 2011, 53 master's awarded. *Degree requirements:* For master's, comprehensive exam, thesis optional. *Entrance requirements:* For master's, GRE or MAT (if undergraduate GPA less than 2.8), minimum undergraduate QPA of 2.5. *Application deadline:* Applications are processed on a rolling basis. Application fee: $30. *Expenses:* Contact institution. *Financial support:* Applicants required to submit FAFSA. *Unit head:* Dr. Janette D. Kelly, Director, 814-472-3068, Fax: 814-472-3864, E-mail: jkelly@francis.edu. *Application contact:* Sherri L. Toth, Coordinator, 814-472-3058, Fax: 814-472-3864, E-mail: stoth@francis.edu. Web site: http://www.francis.edu/medhome.htm.

St. Francis Xavier University, Graduate Studies, Graduate Studies in Education, Antigonish, NS B2G 2W5, Canada. Offers curriculum and instruction (M Ed); educational administration and leadership (M Ed). Part-time programs available. Postbaccalaureate distance learning degree programs offered (minimal on-campus study). *Degree requirements:* For master's, thesis. *Entrance requirements:* For master's, minimum undergraduate B average, 2 years of teaching experience. *Faculty research:* Inclusive education, qualitative research.

St. John Fisher College, Ralph C. Wilson Jr. School of Education, Educational Leadership Program, Rochester, NY 14618-3597. Offers MS Ed. Part-time and evening/weekend programs available. *Faculty:* 2 full-time (1 woman), 2 part-time/adjunct (both women). *Students:* 46 part-time (29 women); includes 12 minority (7 Black or African American, non-Hispanic/Latino; 1 Asian, non-Hispanic/Latino; 4 Hispanic/Latino). Average age 35. 24 applicants, 100% accepted, 18 enrolled. In 2011, 20 master's awarded. *Degree requirements:* For master's, capstone project, internship. *Entrance requirements:* For master's, teacher certification, minimum 2 years of teaching experience, 2 letters of recommendation, current resume. Additional exam requirements/recommendations for international students: Required—TOEFL (minimum score 575 paper-based; 233 computer-based; 80 iBT). *Application deadline:* Applications are processed on a rolling basis. Application fee: $30. Electronic applications accepted. *Expenses: Tuition:* Part-time $735 per credit. One-time fee: $50 part-time. Tuition and fees vary according to course load, degree level and program. *Financial support:* In 2011–12, 10 students received support. Scholarships/grants available. Financial award applicants required to submit FAFSA. *Faculty research:* Urban school leadership, assessment, effective school leadership. *Unit head:* Dr. William Stroud, Co-Director, 585-385-7258, E-mail: wstroud@sjfc.edu. *Application contact:* Jose Perales, Director of Graduate Admissions, 585-385-8067, E-mail: jperales@sjfc.edu.

St. John Fisher College, Ralph C. Wilson Jr. School of Education, Executive Leadership Program, Rochester, NY 14618-3597. Offers Ed D. Evening/weekend programs available. *Faculty:* 8 full-time (3 women), 4 part-time/adjunct (1 woman). *Students:* 97 full-time (64 women), 14 part-time (9 women); includes 59 minority (48 Black or African American, non-Hispanic/Latino; 1 Asian, non-Hispanic/Latino; 9 Hispanic/Latino; 1 Two or more races, non-Hispanic/Latino). Average age 45. 85 applicants, 73% accepted, 49 enrolled. In 2011, 22 doctorates awarded. *Degree requirements:* For doctorate, comprehensive exam, thesis/dissertation, field experiences. *Entrance requirements:* For doctorate, 3 professional writing samples, 2 letters of reference, interview, minimum 3 years management experience, master's degree. Additional exam requirements/recommendations for international students: Required—TOEFL (minimum score 575 paper-based; 233 computer-based; 80 iBT). *Application deadline:* For fall admission, 3/1 for domestic and international students. Applications are processed on a rolling basis. Electronic applications accepted. *Expenses: Tuition:* Part-time $735 per credit. One-time fee: $50 part-time. Tuition and fees vary according to course load, degree level and program. *Financial support:* In 2011–12, 19 students received support. Scholarships/grants available. Financial award applicants required to submit FAFSA. *Faculty research:* Leadership, organizational development. *Unit head:* Dr. Arthur Walton, Program Director, 585-385-8387, E-mail: awalton@sjfc.edu. *Application contact:* Jose Perales, Director of Graduate Admissions, 585-385-8067, E-mail: jperales@sjfc.edu. Web site: http://www.sjfc.edu/academics/education/departments/edd/index.dot.

St. John's University, The School of Education, Division of Administrative and Instructional Leadership, Instructional Leadership Program, Queens, NY 11439. Offers Ed D, Adv C. Part-time and evening/weekend programs available. *Students:* 7 full-time (6 women), 120 part-time (74 women); includes 41 minority (24 Black or African American, non-Hispanic/Latino; 8 Asian, non-Hispanic/Latino; 9 Hispanic/Latino), 2 international. Average age 42. 43 applicants, 77% accepted, 30 enrolled. In 2011, 9 doctorates, 3 Adv Cs awarded. *Degree requirements:* For doctorate, comprehensive exam, thesis/dissertation. *Entrance requirements:* For doctorate, GRE General Test, interview, minimum GPA of 3.2, 2 letters of recommendation, resume, writing samples; for Adv C, official transcript, minimum GPA of 3.0, 2 letters of recommendation. Additional exam requirements/recommendations for international students: Required—TOEFL (minimum score 600 paper-based; 250 computer-based; 100 iBT), IELTS (minimum score 5.5). *Application deadline:* For fall admission, 8/17 for domestic students, 5/1 for international students; for spring admission, 1/5 for domestic students,

11/1 for international students. Applications are processed on a rolling basis. Application fee: $70. Electronic applications accepted. *Expenses: Tuition:* Full-time $18,000; part-time $1000 per credit. *Required fees:* $170 per semester. Tuition and fees vary according to program. *Financial support:* Fellowships, research assistantships, career-related internships or fieldwork, and scholarships/grants available. Support available to part-time students. Financial award application deadline: 3/1; financial award applicants required to submit FAFSA. *Faculty research:* Mathematics learning disabilities and difficulties with students identified as learning disabled or students who are English Language Learners, identification of mathematical giftedness in students who are English Language Learner, effects of parental participation and parenting behaviors on the science and mathematics academic achievement of school-age students, analysis of major theoretical perspectives in curriculum design and implementation. *Unit head:* Dr. Rene Parmar, Chair, 718-990-5915, E-mail: parmarr@stjohns.edu. *Application contact:* Dr. Kelly K. Ronayne, Associate Dean of Graduate Admissions, 718-990-2304, Fax: 718-990-2343, E-mail: graded@stjohns.edu.

St. John's University, The School of Education, Division of Administrative and Instructional Leadership, Program in Educational Administration and Supervision, Queens, NY 11439. Offers administration and supervision (Ed D). Part-time and evening/weekend programs available. Postbaccalaureate distance learning degree programs offered. *Students:* 1 (woman) full-time, 95 part-time (59 women); includes 29 minority (18 Black or African American, non-Hispanic/Latino; 1 Asian, non-Hispanic/Latino; 8 Hispanic/Latino; 2 Two or more races, non-Hispanic/Latino), 6 international. Average age 41. 61 applicants, 57% accepted, 26 enrolled. In 2011, 20 doctorates, 1 Adv C awarded. *Degree requirements:* For doctorate, thesis/dissertation, clinical residency. *Entrance requirements:* For doctorate, GRE General Test, interview, minimum GPA of 3.2, 2 letters of recommendation, resume, writing samples. Additional exam requirements/recommendations for international students: Required—TOEFL (minimum score 600 paper-based; 250 computer-based; 100 iBT), IELTS (minimum score 5.5). *Application deadline:* For fall admission, 8/17 for domestic students, 5/1 for international students; for spring admission, 1/5 for domestic students, 11/1 for international students. Applications are processed on a rolling basis. Application fee: $70. Electronic applications accepted. *Expenses: Tuition:* Full-time $18,000; part-time $1000 per credit. *Required fees:* $170 per semester. Tuition and fees vary according to program. *Financial support:* Research assistantships and career-related internships or fieldwork available. Support available to part-time students. Financial award application deadline: 3/1; financial award applicants required to submit FAFSA. *Faculty research:* School administrators' accountability in response to New York State and federal regulations and reforms, including merit pay, decision-making in technology within the framework of instructional design; budgetary and expenditure decision-making among school district administrators in response to fiscal restraints, compliance, and changing demographics; twenty-first century technological tools in today's schools; teacher decision-making models based on decision theory. *Unit head:* Dr. Rene Parmar, Chair, 718-990-5915, E-mail: paramarr@stjohns.edu. *Application contact:* Dr. Kelly K. Ronayne, Associate Dean of Graduate Admissions, 718-990-2304, Fax: 718-990-2343, E-mail: graded@stjohns.edu.

St. John's University, The School of Education, Division of Administrative and Instructional Leadership, Program in School Building Leadership, Queens, NY 11439. Offers MS Ed, Adv C. Part-time and evening/weekend programs available. Postbaccalaureate distance learning degree programs offered. *Students:* 16 full-time (11 women), 156 part-time (113 women); includes 45 minority (23 Black or African American, non-Hispanic/Latino; 5 Asian, non-Hispanic/Latino; 16 Hispanic/Latino; 1 Two or more races, non-Hispanic/Latino), 5 international. Average age 37. 83 applicants, 98% accepted, 38 enrolled. In 2011, 60 master's, 17 Adv Cs awarded. *Degree requirements:* For master's and Adv C, comprehensive exam, internship. *Entrance requirements:* For master's, official transcript with minimum GPA of 3.0, minimum 3 years successful teaching experience, New York State Permanent Teaching Certification; for Adv C, minimum GPA of 3.5, minimum 3 years successful teaching experience, New York State Permanent Teaching Certification, essay, 2 letters of reference., transcripts. Additional exam requirements/recommendations for international students: Required—TOEFL (minimum score 600 paper-based; 250 computer-based; 100 iBT), IELTS (minimum score 5.5). *Application deadline:* For fall admission, 8/17 for domestic students, 5/1 for international students; for spring admission, 1/5 for domestic students, 11/1 for international students. Applications are processed on a rolling basis. Application fee: $70. Electronic applications accepted. *Expenses:* Contact institution. *Financial support:* Research assistantships, career-related internships or fieldwork, and scholarships/grants available. Support available to part-time students. Financial award application deadline: 3/1; financial award applicants required to submit FAFSA. *Faculty research:* Analysis of non-public school graduate student outcomes in programs and certification, Catholic school parents' perceptions of school and after school programs, issues in school business leadership from a financial management perspective. *Unit head:* Dr. Rene Parmar, Chair, 718-990-2915, E-mail: parmarr@stjohns.edu. *Application contact:* Dr. Kelly K. Ronayne, Associate Dean for Graduate Admissions, 718-990-2304, Fax: 718-990-2343, E-mail: graded@stjohns.edu.

St. John's University, The School of Education, Division of Administrative and Instructional Leadership, Program in School District Leadership, Queens, NY 11439. Offers Adv C. Part-time and evening/weekend programs available. Postbaccalaureate distance learning degree programs offered. *Students:* 8 part-time (5 women); includes 1 minority (Black or African American, non-Hispanic/Latino), 1 international. Average age 40. 1 applicant, 100% accepted, 1 enrolled. In 2011, 2 Adv Cs awarded. *Degree requirements:* For Adv C, comprehensive exam. *Entrance requirements:* For degree, minimum GPA of 3.5, minimum 3 years successful teaching experience, New York State Permanent Teaching Certification. Additional exam requirements/recommendations for international students: Required—TOEFL (minimum score 600 paper-based; 250 computer-based; 100 iBT), IELTS (minimum score 5.5). *Application deadline:* For fall admission, 8/17 for domestic students, 5/1 for international students; for spring admission, 1/5 for domestic students, 11/1 for international students. Applications are processed on a rolling basis. Application fee: $70. Electronic applications accepted. *Expenses: Tuition:* Full-time $18,000; part-time $1000 per credit. *Required fees:* $170 per semester. Tuition and fees vary according to program. *Financial support:* Research assistantships and career-related internships or fieldwork available. Support available to part-time students. Financial award application deadline: 3/1; financial award applicants required to submit FAFSA. *Faculty research:* Analysis of school district finances related to resource allocation and decision-making, responsiveness of districts to New York State proposition 13 (property tax caps), implementation of technology planning for the twenty-first century at the school district level. *Unit head:* Dr. Rene Parmar, Chair, 718-990-5915, E-mail: parmarr@stjohns.edu. *Application contact:* Dr. Kelly K. Ronayne, Associate Dean of Graduate Admissions, 718-990-2304, Fax: 718-990-2343, E-mail: graded@stjohns.edu.

Saint Joseph's College of Maine, Master of Science in Education Program, Standish, ME 04084. Offers adult education and training (MS Ed); Catholic school leadership (MS Ed); health care educator (MS Ed); school educator (MS Ed). Program available by correspondence. Part-time programs available. Postbaccalaureate distance learning degree programs offered (minimal on-campus study). *Faculty:* 20 part-time/adjunct (13 women). *Students:* 273 part-time (190 women); includes 21 minority (14 Black or African American, non-Hispanic/Latino; 1 American Indian or Alaska Native, non-Hispanic/Latino; 2 Asian, non-Hispanic/Latino; 4 Hispanic/Latino). Average age 43. In 2011, 25 master's awarded. *Application deadline:* Applications are processed on a rolling basis. Application fee: $50. Electronic applications accepted. One-time fee: $50. *Financial support:* Institutionally sponsored loans available. Support available to part-time students. Financial award applicants required to submit FAFSA. *Unit head:* Dr. Thomas Hancock, Director, 207-893-7841, Fax: 207-892-7987, E-mail: thancock@sjcme.edu. *Application contact:* Lynne Robinson, Director of Admissions, 800-752-4723, Fax: 207-892-7480, E-mail: info@sjcme.edu. Web site: http://online.sjcme.edu/master-science-education.php.

Saint Joseph's University, College of Arts and Sciences, Department of Education, Philadelphia, PA 19131-1395. Offers curriculum supervisor of instruction (Certificate); educational leadership (MS, Ed D); elementary education (MS, Certificate); elementary/middle years (Certificate); English second language specialist online (Certificate); hearing impaired: N-12th grade (Certificate); instructional technology (MS, Certificate); principal certification (Certificate); professional education (MS); reading specialist (MS, Certificate); reading supervisory (Certificate); secondary education (MS, Certificate); special education (MS, Certificate); superintendent's letter of eligibility (Certificate); supervisor of special education (Certificate); Wilson reading certificate online (Certificate). Part-time and evening/weekend programs available. Postbaccalaureate distance learning degree programs offered (no on-campus study). *Faculty:* 26 full-time (24 women), 83 part-time/adjunct (52 women). *Students:* 112 full-time (92 women), 923 part-time (709 women); includes 147 minority (92 Black or African American, non-Hispanic/Latino; 4 American Indian or Alaska Native, non-Hispanic/Latino; 19 Asian, non-Hispanic/Latino; 28 Hispanic/Latino; 4 Two or more races, non-Hispanic/Latino), 8 international. Average age 31. 285 applicants, 77% accepted, 176 enrolled. In 2011, 276 master's, 13 doctorates, 2 other advanced degrees awarded. *Entrance requirements:* For master's, 2 letters of recommendation, minimum GPA of 3.0, official transcripts, personal statement; for doctorate, GRE, master's degree from accredited institution, minimum graduate GPA of 3.5, computer competence, commitment to participate in cohort, interview with program director. Additional exam requirements/recommendations for international students: Required—TOEFL (minimum score 550 paper-based; 213 computer-based; 79 iBT). *Application deadline:* For fall admission, 7/15 priority date for domestic students, 4/15 for international students; for winter admission, 11/15 for domestic students, 1/15 for international students; for spring admission, 11/15 priority date for domestic students, 10/15 for international students. Applications are processed on a rolling basis. Application fee: $35. Electronic applications accepted. *Expenses:* Contact institution. *Financial support:* Unspecified assistantships available. Financial award applicants required to submit FAFSA. *Faculty research:* Public education professional development, factors predicting early mathematics skills for low income children. *Total annual research expenditures:* $92,975. *Unit head:* Dr. Jeanne Brady, Associate Dean, Education, 610-660-1580, E-mail: jebrady@sju.edu. *Application contact:* Kate McConnell, Director, Graduate College of Arts and Sciences Admissions and Retention, 610-660-3184, Fax: 610-660-3230, E-mail: kate.mcconnell@sju.edu.

St. Lawrence University, Department of Education, Program in Educational Leadership, Canton, NY 13617-1455. Offers combined school building leadership/school district leadership (CAS); educational leadership (M Ed); school building leadership (M Ed); school district leadership (CAS). Part-time and evening/weekend programs available. *Entrance requirements:* For master's, GRE General Test. *Faculty research:* Leadership.

Saint Leo University, Graduate Studies in Education, Saint Leo, FL 33574-6665. Offers educational leadership (M Ed); exceptional student education (M Ed); higher education leadership (Ed S); instructional design (MS); instructional leadership (M Ed); reading (M Ed); school leadership (Ed S). Part-time and evening/weekend programs available. Postbaccalaureate distance learning degree programs offered (minimal on-campus study). *Faculty:* 14 full-time (10 women), 21 part-time/adjunct (16 women). *Students:* 523 full-time (427 women), 20 part-time (17 women); includes 65 minority (43 Black or African American, non-Hispanic/Latino; 2 Asian, non-Hispanic/Latino; 16 Hispanic/Latino; 4 Two or more races, non-Hispanic/Latino), 3 international. Average age 37. In 2011, 153 master's, 18 other advanced degrees awarded. *Degree requirements:* For master's, comprehensive exam, appropriate State of Florida certification tests. *Entrance requirements:* For master's, GRE (minimum score of 1000) or MAT (minimum score of 410) if undergraduate GPA for last 60 hours of coursework was below 3.0 (for M Ed), bachelor's degree with minimum GPA of 3.0 for last 60 hours of coursework from regionally-accredited college or university, 2 recommendations, resume, statement of professional goals, copy of valid teaching certificate (for M Ed); for Ed S, GRE (minimum score 1000) or MAT (minimum score 410) if undergraduate GPA for last 60 hours of coursework less than 3.0, bachelor's degree with minimum GPA of 3.0 for last 60 hours of coursework from regionally-accredited college or university, 2 recommendations, resume, valid teaching certificate. Additional exam requirements/recommendations for international students: Required—TOEFL (minimum score 550 paper-based; 213 computer-based; 80 iBT). *Application deadline:* For fall admission, 7/1 priority date for domestic students, 7/1 for international students; for winter admission, 7/1 for international students; for spring admission, 11/1 priority date for domestic students. Applications are processed on a rolling basis. Application fee: $80. Electronic applications accepted. *Expenses:* Contact institution. *Financial support:* In 2011–12, 20 students received support. Career-related internships or fieldwork, Federal Work-Study, scholarships/grants, and health care benefits available. Financial award application deadline: 3/1; financial award applicants required to submit FAFSA. *Faculty research:* The role of the school leader in data analysis of student achievement, teacher recruitment, teacher effectiveness. *Unit head:* Dr. Sharyn Disabato, Director, 352-588-8309, Fax: 352-588-8861, E-mail: med@saintleo.edu. *Application contact:* Jared Welling, Director of Graduate Admission, 800-707-8846, Fax: 352-588-7873, E-mail: grad.admissions@saintleo.edu. Web site: http://www.saintleo.edu/Academics/School-of-Education-Social-Services/Graduate-Degree-Programs.

Saint Louis University, Graduate Education, College of Education and Public Service and Graduate Education, Department of Educational Leadership and Higher Education, St. Louis, MO 63103-2097. Offers Catholic school leadership (MA); educational administration (MA, Ed D, PhD, Ed S); higher education (MA, Ed D, PhD); student personnel administration (MA). *Accreditation:* NCATE. Part-time programs available. *Degree requirements:* For master's, comprehensive written and oral exam; for doctorate, comprehensive exam, thesis/dissertation, preliminary oral and written exams. *Entrance requirements:* For master's, GRE General Test, MAT, LSAT, GMAT or MCAT, letters of recommendation, resume; for doctorate and Ed S, GRE General Test, LSAT, GMAT or MCAT, letters of recommendation, resumé, goal statement, transcripts. Additional exam requirements/recommendations for international students: Required—TOEFL (minimum score 525 paper-based; 194 computer-based). Electronic applications accepted. *Faculty research:* Superintendent of schools, school finance, school facilities, student personal administration, building leadership.

Saint Martin's University, Graduate Programs, College of Education, Lacey, WA 98503. Offers administration (M Ed); English as a second language (M Ed); guidance and counseling (M Ed); reading (M Ed); special education (M Ed); teaching (MIT). *Accreditation:* Teacher Education Accreditation Council. Part-time and evening/weekend programs available. *Faculty:* 12 full-time (8 women), 9 part-time/adjunct (7 women). *Students:* 68 full-time (38 women), 28 part-time (20 women); includes 15 minority (2 Black or African American, non-Hispanic/Latino; 2 American Indian or Alaska Native, non-Hispanic/Latino; 7 Asian, non-Hispanic/Latino; 2 Hispanic/Latino; 2 Two or more races, non-Hispanic/Latino), 4 international. Average age 35. 17 applicants, 94% accepted, 15 enrolled. In 2011, 12 master's awarded. *Degree requirements:* For master's, comprehensive exam (for some programs), thesis or alternative, project or comprehensives. *Entrance requirements:* For master's, GRE General Test or MAT, resume. Additional exam requirements/recommendations for international students: Required—TOEFL (minimum score 560 paper-based; 220 computer-based; 83 iBT). *Application deadline:* For fall admission, 6/1 priority date for domestic students, 6/1 for international students; for spring admission, 10/1 priority date for domestic students, 10/1 for international students. Applications are processed on a rolling basis. Application fee: $35. *Expenses: Tuition:* Part-time $910 per credit hour. Tuition and fees vary according to course level, campus/location and program. *Financial support:* Career-related internships or fieldwork, Federal Work-Study, institutionally sponsored loans, and unspecified assistantships available. Support available to part-time students. Financial award application deadline: 3/1; financial award applicants required to submit FAFSA. *Faculty research:* Reader's theatre and reader/writer workshops, curriculum and assessment integration, gender and equity, classroom evaluations, organizational leadership. *Unit head:* Dr. Joyce Westgard, Dean, College of Education and Professional Psychology, 360-438-4509, Fax: 360-438-4486, E-mail: westgard@stmartin.edu. *Application contact:* Ryan M. Smith, Administrative Assistant, 360-438-4333, Fax: 360-438-4486, E-mail: ryan.smith@stmartin.edu. Web site: http://www.stmartin.edu/CEPP/.

Saint Mary's College of California, Kalmanovitz School of Education, Program in Early Childhood Education, Moraga, CA 94556. Offers curriculum and instruction (MA); supervision and leadership (MA). Part-time and evening/weekend programs available. *Students:* 9 part-time (all women); includes 1 minority (Black or African American, non-Hispanic/Latino). Average age 33. In 2011, 1 master's awarded. *Degree requirements:* For master's, thesis or alternative. *Entrance requirements:* For master's, interview, minimum GPA of 3.0. *Application deadline:* Applications are processed on a rolling basis. Application fee: $50. Tuition and fees vary according to course load, degree level and program. *Financial support:* Career-related internships or fieldwork available. Support available to part-time students. Financial award application deadline: 2/15. *Unit head:* Patricia Chambers, Coordinator, 925-631-4036, Fax: 925-376-8379, E-mail: pchambers@stmarys-ca.edu. *Application contact:* Jane Joyce, Coordinator, Recruitment and Admissions, 925-631-4700, Fax: 925-376-8379, E-mail: soereq@stmarys-ca.edu. Web site: http://www.stmarys-ca.edu/master-of-arts-degree-in-early-childhood-education.

Saint Mary's College of California, Kalmanovitz School of Education, Program in Educational Leadership, Moraga, CA 94556. Offers M Ed, MA, Ed D. Part-time and evening/weekend programs available. *Students:* 17 full-time (13 women), 78 part-time (54 women); includes 30 minority (15 Black or African American, non-Hispanic/Latino; 2 American Indian or Alaska Native, non-Hispanic/Latino; 5 Asian, non-Hispanic/Latino; 8 Hispanic/Latino), 1 international. Average age 39. 78 applicants, 67% accepted, 48 enrolled. In 2011, 18 master's, 7 doctorates awarded. *Degree requirements:* For master's, thesis or alternative; for doctorate, thesis/dissertation. *Entrance requirements:* For master's, interview, minimum GPA of 3.0, teaching credential; for doctorate, GRE or MAT, interview, MA, minimum GPA of 3.0. *Application deadline:* For fall admission, 12/15 priority date for domestic students; for spring admission, 4/15 priority date for domestic students. Applications are processed on a rolling basis. Application fee: $50. Tuition and fees vary according to course load, degree level and program. *Financial support:* Career-related internships or fieldwork available. Support available to part-time students. Financial award application deadline: 2/15. *Faculty research:* Building communities, programs in educational leadership, alignment of curriculum to standards. *Unit head:* Dr. Rebecca A. Proehl, Director, 925-631-4994, Fax: 925-376-8379, E-mail: rproehl@stmarys-ca.edu. *Application contact:* Jane Joyce, Coordinator, Recruitment and Admissions, 925-631-4700, Fax: 925-376-8379, E-mail: soereq@stmarys-ca.edu. Web site: http://www.stmarys-ca.edu/educational-leadership.

Saint Mary's College of California, Kalmanovitz School of Education, Teaching Leadership Program, Moraga, CA 94556. Offers MA. *Students:* 1 (woman) full-time, 41 part-time (37 women); includes 12 minority (4 Black or African American, non-Hispanic/Latino; 2 Asian, non-Hispanic/Latino; 6 Hispanic/Latino). Average age 38. In 2011, 3 master's awarded. Tuition and fees vary according to course load, degree level and program. *Unit head:* Katherine D. Perez, Unit Head, 925-631-4350, Fax: 925-376-8379, E-mail: kperez@stmarys-ca.edu. *Application contact:* Jane Joyce, Coordinator of Recruitment and Admissions, 925-631-4700, Fax: 925-376-8379, E-mail: soereq@stmarys-ca.edu. Web site: http://www.stmarys-ca.edu/master-of-arts-in-teaching-leadership.

St. Mary's University, Graduate School, Department of Teacher Education, Program in Catholic School Leadership, San Antonio, TX 78228-8507. Offers Catholic school administrators (Certificate); Catholic school leadership (MA); Catholic school teachers (Certificate). Part-time and evening/weekend programs available. Postbaccalaureate distance learning degree programs offered (minimal on-campus study). *Degree requirements:* For master's, comprehensive exam. *Entrance requirements:* For master's, GRE General Test. Additional exam requirements/recommendations for international students: Required—TOEFL (minimum score 550 paper-based; 213 computer-based; 80 iBT). Electronic applications accepted.

St. Mary's University, Graduate School, Department of Teacher Education, Program in Educational Leadership, San Antonio, TX 78228-8507. Offers educational leadership (MA); principalship (mid-management) (Certificate). Part-time programs available. *Degree requirements:* For master's, comprehensive exam. *Entrance requirements:* For master's, GRE. Additional exam requirements/recommendations for international students: Required—TOEFL (minimum score 550 paper-based; 213 computer-based; 80 iBT). Electronic applications accepted.

Saint Mary's University of Minnesota, Schools of Graduate and Professional Programs, Graduate School of Education, Educational Administration Program, Winona, MN 55987-1399. Offers educational administration (Certificate, Ed S), including director of special education, K-12 principal, superintendent. *Unit head:* Dr. William Bjorum, Director, 612-728-5126, Fax: 612-728-5121, E-mail: wbjorum@smumn.edu. *Application contact:* Yasin Alsaidi, Director of Admissions for Graduate and Professional Programs, 612-728-5207, Fax: 612-728-5121, E-mail: yalsaidi@smumn.edu. Web site: http://www.smumn.edu/graduate-home/areas-of-study/graduate-school-of-education/eds-in-educational-administration-director-of-special-education-k-12-pr.

Saint Mary's University of Minnesota, Schools of Graduate and Professional Programs, Graduate School of Education, Educational Leadership Program, Winona, MN 55987-1399. Offers MA, Ed D. *Unit head:* Dr. Nelson Updaw, Director, 612-728-5191, Fax: 612-728-5121, E-mail: nupdaw@smumn.edu. *Application contact:* Yasin Alsaidi, Director of Admissions for Graduate and Professional Programs, 612-728-5207, Fax: 612-728-5121, E-mail: yalsaidi@smumn.edu. Web site: http://www.smumn.edu/graduate-home/areas-of-study/graduate-school-of-education/edd-in-leadership.

Saint Mary's University of Minnesota, Schools of Graduate and Professional Programs, Graduate School of Education, Institute for LaSallian Studies, Winona, MN 55987-1399. Offers LaSallian leadership (MA); LaSallian studies (MA). *Unit head:* Dr. Roxanne Eubank, Director, 612-728-5217, E-mail: reubank@smumn.edu. *Application contact:* Yasin Alsaidi, Director of Admissions for Graduate and Professional Programs, 612-728-5207, Fax: 612-728-5121, E-mail: yalsaidi@smumn.edu. Web site: http://www.smumn.edu/graduate-home/areas-of-study/graduate-school-of-education/ma-in-lasallian-studies.

Saint Michael's College, Graduate Programs, Program in Education, Colchester, VT 05439. Offers administration (M Ed, CAGS); arts in education (CAGS); curriculum and instruction (M Ed, CAGS); information technology (CAGS); reading (M Ed); special education (M Ed, CAGS); technology (M Ed). Part-time and evening/weekend programs available. *Degree requirements:* For master's, thesis. *Entrance requirements:* For master's, minimum GPA of 3.0. Electronic applications accepted. *Faculty research:* Integrative curriculum, moral and spiritual dimensions of education, learning styles, multiple intelligences, integrating technology into the curriculum.

Saint Peter's University, Graduate Programs in Education, Program in Educational Leadership, Jersey City, NJ 07306-5997. Offers MA Ed, Ed D. Part-time and evening/weekend programs available. *Degree requirements:* For master's, comprehensive exam; for doctorate, comprehensive exam, thesis/dissertation. *Entrance requirements:* For master's and doctorate, GRE or MAT. Additional exam requirements/recommendations for international students: Required—TOEFL (minimum score 79 computer-based). Electronic applications accepted.

St. Thomas Aquinas College, Division of Teacher Education, Sparkill, NY 10976. Offers adolescence education (MST); childhood and special education (MST); childhood education (MST); educational leadership (MS Ed); reading (MS Ed, PMC); special education (MS Ed, PMC); teaching (MS Ed), including elementary education, middle school education, secondary education. *Accreditation:* NCATE. Part-time and evening/weekend programs available. *Degree requirements:* For master's, comprehensive exam, comprehensive professional portfolio; for PMC, action research project. *Entrance requirements:* For master's, New York State Qualifying Exam, GRE General Test or minimum GPA of 3.0, teaching certificate; for PMC, GRE General Test or minimum GPA of 3.0. Electronic applications accepted. *Faculty research:* Computer applications in education, adolescent special education students, literacy development, inclusive practices for special education students.

St. Thomas University, School of Leadership Studies, Institute for Education, Miami Gardens, FL 33054-6459. Offers earth/space science (Certificate); educational administration (MS, Certificate); educational leadership (Ed D); elementary education (MS); ESOL (Certificate); gifted education (Certificate); instructional technology (MS, Certificate); professional/studies (Certificate); reading (MS, Certificate); special education (MS). Part-time and evening/weekend programs available. *Degree requirements:* For master's, comprehensive exam; for doctorate, comprehensive exam, thesis/dissertation. *Entrance requirements:* For master's, interview, minimum GPA of 3.0 or GRE; for doctorate, GRE or MAT. Additional exam requirements/recommendations for international students: Required—TOEFL (minimum score 550 paper-based; 213 computer-based; 79 iBT). Electronic applications accepted.

Saint Vincent College, Program in Education, Latrobe, PA 15650-2690. Offers curriculum and instruction (MS); educational media and technology (MS); environmental education (MS); school administration and supervision (MS); special education (MS). Part-time and evening/weekend programs available. *Degree requirements:* For master's, comprehensive exam. *Entrance requirements:* For master's, GRE (if undergraduate GPA less than 3.0). Additional exam requirements/recommendations for international students: Required—TOEFL (minimum score 550 paper-based; 213 computer-based). *Faculty research:* Assessment and instructional technology.

Saint Xavier University, Graduate Studies, School of Education, Chicago, IL 60655-3105. Offers counseling (MA); curriculum and instruction (MA); early childhood education (MA); educational administration (MA); elementary education (MA); individualized studies (MA), including educational technology, English as a second language (ESL), ISTEM (integrative science, technology, engineering, and math), science education; music education (MA); reading (MA); secondary education (MA); Spanish education (MA); special education (MA); teaching and leadership (MA). *Accreditation:* NCATE. Part-time and evening/weekend programs available. *Degree requirements:* For master's, thesis or project. *Entrance requirements:* For master's, minimum GPA of 3.0. *Application deadline:* For fall admission, 8/15 priority date for domestic students. Applications are processed on a rolling basis. Application fee: $35. *Expenses:* Contact institution. *Financial support:* Career-related internships or fieldwork available. Support available to part-time students. Financial award applicants required to submit FAFSA. *Unit head:* Dr. Beverly Gulley, Dean, 773-298-3221, Fax: 773-779-9061, E-mail: gulley@sxu.edu. *Application contact:* Beth Gierach, Managing Director of Admission, 773-298-3053, Fax: 773-298-3076, E-mail: gierach@sxu.edu.

Salem International University, School of Education, Salem, WV 26426-0500. Offers curriculum and instruction (M Ed); educational leadership (M Ed). Part-time and evening/weekend programs available. Postbaccalaureate distance learning degree programs offered. *Degree requirements:* For master's, comprehensive exam (for some programs), thesis (for some programs). *Entrance requirements:* For master's, GRE, MAT, NTE, 3 letters of recommendation. Additional exam requirements/recommendations for international students: Required—TOEFL (minimum score 550 paper-based; 213 computer-based). Electronic applications accepted. *Expenses:* Contact institution. *Faculty research:* Improved classroom effectiveness.

Salem State University, School of Graduate Studies, Program in Educational Leadership, Salem, MA 01970-5353. Offers M Ed. *Entrance requirements:* For master's, GRE or MAT. Additional exam requirements/recommendations for international students: Required—TOEFL (minimum score 550 paper-based; 80 iBT) or IELTS (minimum score 5.5).

Salem State University, School of Graduate Studies, Program in Higher Education in Student Affairs, Salem, MA 01970-5353. Offers M Ed. Part-time and evening/weekend programs available. *Entrance requirements:* For master's, GRE or MAT. Additional exam requirements/recommendations for international students: Required—TOEFL (minimum score 550 paper-based; 80 iBT) or IELTS (minimum score 5.5).

Salisbury University, Graduate Division, Department of Education, Program in Education Administration, Salisbury, MD 21801-6837. Offers M Ed. Part-time and evening/weekend programs available. *Students:* 2 full-time (both women), 42 part-time (20 women); includes 2 minority (both Black or African American, non-Hispanic/Latino), 1 international. Average age 31. 4 applicants, 100% accepted, 4 enrolled. In 2011, 11 master's awarded. *Degree requirements:* For master's, comprehensive exam, internship. *Entrance requirements:* For master's, 2 recommendations, 2 years teaching performance, minimum undergraduate GPA of 3.0, interview. Additional exam requirements/recommendations for international students: Required—TOEFL (minimum score 550 paper-based; 79 iBT). *Application deadline:* Applications are processed on a rolling basis. Application fee: $45. Electronic applications accepted. *Expenses: Tuition, area resident:* Part-time $306 per credit hour. Tuition, state resident: part-time $306 per credit hour. Tuition, nonresident: part-time $595 per credit hour. *Required fees:* $68 per credit hour. *Financial support:* In 2011–12, 6 students received support. Career-related internships or fieldwork, institutionally sponsored loans, and unspecified assistantships available. Support available to part-time students. Financial award application deadline: 3/1; financial award applicants required to submit FAFSA. *Unit head:* Dr. Gwen Beegle, Director, 410-543-6280. *Application contact:* Tina Melczarek, Administrative Assistant I, 410-543-6281, Fax: 410-548-2593, E-mail: tmmelczarek@salisbury.edu. Web site: http://www.salisbury.edu/educationspecialties/med-edld.html.

Samford University, Orlean Bullard Beeson School of Education and Professional Studies, Birmingham, AL 35229. Offers early childhood education (Ed S); early childhood/elementary education (MS Ed); educational administration (Ed S); educational leadership (Ed D); elementary education (Ed S); gifted education (MS Ed); instructional leadership (MS Ed); secondary collaboration (MS Ed); M Div/MS Ed. *Accreditation:* NCATE. Part-time programs available. *Faculty:* 11 full-time (7 women), 9 part-time/adjunct (7 women). *Students:* 20 full-time (16 women), 169 part-time (122 women); includes 30 minority (26 Black or African American, non-Hispanic/Latino; 1 American Indian or Alaska Native, non-Hispanic/Latino; 1 Asian, non-Hispanic/Latino; 2 Hispanic/Latino), 1 international. Average age 39. 51 applicants, 92% accepted, 44 enrolled. In 2011, 57 master's, 9 doctorates, 35 other advanced degrees awarded. *Degree requirements:* For master's, comprehensive exam; for doctorate, comprehensive exam, thesis/dissertation. *Entrance requirements:* For master's, GRE or MAT, minimum GPA of 3.0; for doctorate, minimum GPA of 3.7; for Ed S, GRE, master's degree, teaching certificate, minimum GPA of 3.25. Additional exam requirements/recommendations for international students: Required—TOEFL (minimum score 550 paper-based; 213 computer-based). *Application deadline:* For fall admission, 7/15 for domestic students; for winter admission, 4/5 for domestic students; for spring admission, 12/4 for domestic students. Applications are processed on a rolling basis. Application fee: $25. *Expenses: Tuition:* Full-time $29,934; part-time $655 per credit. *Required fees:* $705. *Financial support:* Research assistantships, career-related internships or fieldwork, Federal Work-Study, scholarships/grants, and tuition waivers (partial) available. Support available to part-time students. Financial award applicants required to submit FAFSA. *Faculty research:* School law, the characteristics of beginning teachers, the nature of school reform, school culture, quality improvement in education, K-12 student achievement. *Unit head:* Dr. Jean Ann Box, Dean, 205-726-2565, E-mail: jabox@samford.edu. *Application contact:* Dr. Maurice Persall, Director, Graduate Office, 205-726-2019, E-mail: jmpersal@samford.edu. Web site: http://dlserver.samford.edu.

Sam Houston State University, College of Education, Department of Educational Leadership and Counseling, Huntsville, TX 77341. Offers administration (M Ed); counseling (M Ed, MA); counselor education (PhD); developmental education administration (Ed D); educational leadership (Ed D); higher education administration (MA); instructional leadership (M Ed, MA). Part-time programs available. *Faculty:* 27 full-time (17 women), 27 part-time/adjunct (14 women). *Students:* 98 full-time (78 women), 474 part-time (378 women); includes 182 minority (101 Black or African American, non-Hispanic/Latino; 10 American Indian or Alaska Native, non-Hispanic/Latino; 8 Asian, non-Hispanic/Latino; 63 Hispanic/Latino), 8 international. Average age 37. 407 applicants, 61% accepted, 194 enrolled. In 2011, 166 master's, 25 doctorates awarded. *Entrance requirements:* For master's, GRE General Test. Additional exam requirements/recommendations for international students: Required—TOEFL (minimum score 550 paper-based; 213 computer-based; 79 iBT). *Application deadline:* For fall admission, 8/1 for domestic students, 6/25 for international students; for spring admission, 12/1 for domestic students, 11/12 for international students. Applications are processed on a rolling basis. Application fee: $45 ($75 for international students). Electronic applications accepted. *Expenses:* Tuition, state resident: full-time $4420; part-time $221 per credit hour. Tuition, nonresident: full-time $10,680; part-time $534 per credit hour. *Required fees:* $329 per credit hour. *Financial support:* Career-related internships or fieldwork, Federal Work-Study, and institutionally sponsored loans available. Support available to part-time students. Financial award application deadline: 5/31; financial award applicants required to submit FAFSA. *Unit head:* Dr. Stacey Edmonson, Chair, 936-294-1752, Fax: 936-294-3886, E-mail: edu_sle01@shsu.edu. *Application contact:* Dr. Stacey Edmondson, Advisor, 936-294-1752, E-mail: sedmonson@shsu.edu. Web site: http://www.shsu.edu/~edu_elc/.

San Diego State University, Graduate and Research Affairs, College of Education, Department of Administration, Rehabilitation and Post-Secondary Education, San Diego, CA 92182. Offers educational leadership in post-secondary education (MA); rehabilitation counseling (MS), including deafness. Evening/weekend programs available. Postbaccalaureate distance learning degree programs offered. *Degree requirements:* For master's, comprehensive exam (for some programs), thesis (for some programs). *Entrance requirements:* For master's, GRE General Test, letters of reference. Additional exam requirements/recommendations for international students: Required—TOEFL. Electronic applications accepted. *Faculty research:* Rehabilitation in cultural diversity, distance learning technology.

San Diego State University, Graduate and Research Affairs, College of Education, Department of Educational Leadership, San Diego, CA 92182. Offers MA. *Accreditation:* NCATE. Evening/weekend programs available. *Entrance requirements:* For master's, GRE General Test, letters of reference. Additional exam requirements/recommendations for international students: Required—TOEFL. Electronic applications accepted.

San Francisco State University, Division of Graduate Studies, College of Education, Department of Administration and Interdisciplinary Studies, Program in Educational Administration, San Francisco, CA 94132-1722. Offers MA, AC. *Accreditation:* NCATE. *Application deadline:* Applications are processed on a rolling basis. *Unit head:* Dr. David Hemphill, Chair, 415-405-3681. *Application contact:* Dr. Andrew Dubin, Graduate Coordinator, 415-338-1300. Web site: http://coe.sfsu.edu/dais.

San Francisco State University, Division of Graduate Studies, College of Education, Program in Educational Leadership, San Francisco, CA 94132-1722. Offers Ed D. *Unit head:* Dr. Robert Gabriner, Director, 415-405-4103, E-mail: gabriner@sfsu.edu. *Application contact:* Dr. Norena Norton Badway, Graduate Coordinator, 415-405-4103, E-mail: nbadway@sfsu.edu. Web site: http://www.sfsu.edu/~edd/.

San Jose State University, Graduate Studies and Research, Connie L. Lurie College of Education, Department of Educational Leadership, San Jose, CA 95192-0001. Offers educational administration (K-12) (MA); higher education administration (MA). *Accreditation:* NCATE. *Degree requirements:* For master's, thesis or alternative. Electronic applications accepted.

Santa Clara University, School of Education and Counseling Psychology, Department of Education, Santa Clara, CA 95053. Offers educational administration (MA, Certificate); interdisciplinary education (MA); teacher education (Certificate), including multiple subject teaching, single subject teaching. Part-time and evening/weekend programs available. *Students:* 50 full-time (39 women), 187 part-time (148 women); includes 62 minority (4 Black or African American, non-Hispanic/Latino; 2 American Indian or Alaska Native, non-Hispanic/Latino; 19 Asian, non-Hispanic/Latino; 32 Hispanic/Latino; 3 Native Hawaiian or other Pacific Islander, non-Hispanic/Latino; 2 Two or more races, non-Hispanic/Latino), 5 international. Average age 33. 132 applicants, 64% accepted, 70 enrolled. In 2011, 86 master's, 124 other advanced degrees awarded. *Degree requirements:* For master's, comprehensive exam (for some programs), thesis (for some programs). *Entrance requirements:* For master's, statement of purpose, letters of recommendation, transcripts. Additional exam requirements/recommendations for international students: Required—TOEFL (minimum score 600 paper-based; 100 computer-based; 100 iBT). *Application deadline:* For fall admission, 6/15 for domestic and international students; for winter admission, 10/15 for domestic and international students; for spring admission, 1/31 for domestic and international students. Applications are processed on a rolling basis. Application fee: $50. Electronic applications accepted. *Expenses:* Contact institution. *Financial support:* In 2011–12, 66 students received support, including 66 fellowships (averaging $3,695 per year); Federal Work-Study, institutionally sponsored loans, and scholarships/grants also available. Support available to part-time students. Financial award application deadline: 5/15; financial award applicants required to submit FAFSA. *Faculty research:* Predispositions toward teaching science to diverse learners, environmental education, teacher practices and student motivation, critical thinking pedagogy and assessment, early childhood and elementary education, teacher technology integration. *Total annual research expenditures:* $396,365. *Unit head:* Dr. Atom Yee, Interim Dean, 408-554-4455, Fax: 408-554-5038, E-mail: ayee@scu.edu. *Application contact:* ECP Admissions, 408-554-4355, E-mail: ecpadmissions@scu.edu.

Seattle Pacific University, Educational Leadership Program, Seattle, WA 98119-1997. Offers educational leadership (M Ed, Ed D); principal (Certificate); program administrator (Certificate); superintendent (Certificate). *Accreditation:* NCATE. Part-time and evening/weekend programs available. *Degree requirements:* For master's, comprehensive exam; for doctorate, comprehensive exam, thesis/dissertation. *Entrance requirements:* For master's, GRE General Test or MAT, minimum GPA of 3.0; for doctorate, GRE General Test or MAT, minimum GPA of 3.0, formal interview. Electronic applications accepted.

Seattle University, College of Education, Program in Educational Administration, Seattle, WA 98122-1090. Offers M Ed, MA, Certificate, Ed S. *Accreditation:* NCATE. Part-time and evening/weekend programs available. *Students:* 1 (woman) full-time, 38 part-time (24 women); includes 9 minority (2 Black or African American, non-Hispanic/Latino; 1 American Indian or Alaska Native, non-Hispanic/Latino; 2 Asian, non-Hispanic/Latino; 1 Hispanic/Latino; 3 Two or more races, non-Hispanic/Latino), 1 international. Average age 36. 13 applicants, 85% accepted, 9 enrolled. In 2011, 5 master's, 1 other advanced degree awarded. *Degree requirements:* For master's and other advanced degree, comprehensive exam. *Entrance requirements:* For master's, GRE, MAT, or minimum GPA of 3.0; interview; 1 year of related experience. Additional exam requirements/recommendations for international students: Required—TOEFL. *Application deadline:* For fall admission, 8/20 priority date for domestic students; for winter admission, 11/20 for domestic students; for spring admission, 2/20 for domestic students. Applications are processed on a rolling basis. Application fee: $55. *Financial support:* Career-related internships or fieldwork and Federal Work-Study available. Support available to part-time students. Financial award applicants required to submit FAFSA. *Unit head:* Dr. Michael Silver, Director, 206-296-5798, E-mail: silverm@seattleu.edu. *Application contact:* Janet Shandley, Associate Dean of Graduate Admissions, 206-296-5900, Fax: 206-298-5656, E-mail: grad_admissions@seattleu.edu.

Seattle University, College of Education, Program in Educational Leadership, Seattle, WA 98122-1090. Offers Ed D. *Accreditation:* NCATE. Part-time and evening/weekend programs available. *Students:* 11 full-time (8 women), 51 part-time (29 women); includes 14 minority (8 Black or African American, non-Hispanic/Latino; 1 American Indian or Alaska Native, non-Hispanic/Latino; 2 Asian, non-Hispanic/Latino; 2 Hispanic/Latino; 1 Two or more races, non-Hispanic/Latino), 2 international. Average age 44. 2 applicants, 100% accepted, 2 enrolled. In 2011, 9 doctorates awarded. *Degree requirements:* For doctorate, comprehensive exam, thesis/dissertation. *Entrance requirements:* For doctorate, GRE General Test, MAT, interview, MA, minimum GPA of 3.5, 3 years of related experience. Additional exam requirements/recommendations for international students: Required—TOEFL. *Application deadline:* For fall admission, 4/1 for domestic students. Application fee: $55. *Expenses:* Contact institution. *Financial support:* Career-related internships or fieldwork and Federal Work-Study available. Support available to part-time students. Financial award applicants required to submit FAFSA. *Unit head:* Dr. Robert Pena, Chair, 206-296-6170, E-mail: penar@seattleu.edu. *Application contact:* Janet Shandley, Associate Dean of Graduate Admissions, 206-296-5900, Fax: 206-298-5656, E-mail: grad_admissions@seattleu.edu.

Seattle University, College of Education, Program in Student Development Administration, Seattle, WA 98122-1090. Offers M Ed, MA. Part-time and evening/weekend programs available. *Students:* 31 full-time (21 women), 44 part-time (37 women); includes 25 minority (6 Black or African American, non-Hispanic/Latino; 8 Asian, non-Hispanic/Latino; 8 Hispanic/Latino; 3 Two or more races, non-Hispanic/Latino), 1 international. Average age 26. 124 applicants, 51% accepted, 24 enrolled. In 2011, 14 master's awarded. *Degree requirements:* For master's, comprehensive exam. *Entrance requirements:* For master's, GRE, MAT, or minimum GPA of 3.0. Additional exam requirements/recommendations for international students: Required—TOEFL. *Application deadline:* For fall admission, 8/20 priority date for domestic students; for winter admission, 11/20 for domestic students; for spring admission, 2/20 for domestic students. Applications are processed on a rolling basis. Application fee: $55. *Financial support:* Career-related internships or fieldwork, Federal Work-Study, and unspecified assistantships available. Support available to part-time students. Financial award applicants required to submit FAFSA. *Unit head:* Dr. Jeremy Stringer, Coordinator, 206-296-6170, E-mail: stringer@seattleu.edu. *Application contact:* Janet Shandley, Associate Dean of Graduate Admissions, 206-296-5900, Fax: 206-298-5656, E-mail: grad_admissions@seattleu.edu.

Seton Hall University, College of Education and Human Services, Department of Education Leadership, Management and Policy, Program in Higher Education Administration, South Orange, NJ 07079-2697. Offers Ed D, PhD. *Accreditation:* NCATE. Part-time and evening/weekend programs available. *Faculty:* 12 full-time (4 women), 1 part-time/adjunct (0 women). *Students:* 14 full-time (8 women), 62 part-time (39 women); includes 19 minority (13 Black or African American, non-Hispanic/Latino; 6 Hispanic/Latino), 9 international. Average age 41. 26 applicants, 81% accepted, 16 enrolled. In 2011, 6 doctorates awarded. *Degree requirements:* For doctorate, comprehensive exam, thesis/dissertation, internship. *Entrance requirements:* For doctorate, GRE or MAT, interview, minimum GPA of 3.5. Additional exam requirements/recommendations for international students: Required—TOEFL. *Application deadline:* For fall admission, 2/1 priority date for domestic students; for spring admission, 10/1 for domestic students. Applications are processed on a rolling basis. Application fee: $50. *Expenses: Tuition:* Part-time $1033 per credit hour. *Required fees:* $85 per semester. *Financial support:* In 2011–12, 7 research assistantships with tuition reimbursements (averaging $5,000 per year) were awarded. Financial award application deadline: 2/1. *Unit head:* Dr. Michael Osnato, Chair, 973-275-2446, E-mail: osnatomi@shu.edu. *Application contact:* Dr. Manina Urgolo Huckvale, Associate Dean, 973-761-9668, Fax: 973-275-2187, E-mail: manina.urgolo-huckvale@shu.edu. Web site: http://www.shu.edu.

Seton Hall University, College of Education and Human Services, Department of Education Leadership, Management and Policy, Program in K–12 Leadership, Management and Policy, South Orange, NJ 07079-2697. Offers Ed D, Exec Ed D, Ed S. Part-time and evening/weekend programs available. *Faculty:* 12 full-time (4 women), 1 part-time/adjunct (0 women). *Students:* 73 full-time (41 women), 273 part-time (164 women); includes 66 minority (47 Black or African American, non-Hispanic/Latino; 4 Asian, non-Hispanic/Latino; 15 Hispanic/Latino), 2 international. Average age 43. 48 applicants, 81% accepted, 22 enrolled. In 2011, 38 doctorates, 13 other advanced degrees awarded. *Degree requirements:* For doctorate, comprehensive exam, thesis/dissertation. *Entrance requirements:* For doctorate, MAT or GRE, interview. *Application deadline:* For fall admission, 2/1 for domestic students; for spring admission, 12/1 for domestic students. Applications are processed on a rolling basis. Application fee: $50. *Expenses: Tuition:* Part-time $1033 per credit hour. *Required fees:* $85 per semester. *Financial support:* In 2011–12, 2 research assistantships with full tuition reimbursements (averaging $4,500 per year) were awarded; unspecified assistantships also available. Financial award application deadline: 2/1. *Unit head:* Dr. Michael Osnato, Chair, 973-275-2446, E-mail: osnatomi@shu.edu. *Application contact:* Dr. James Michael Caufield, Director, 973-761-9397.

Shasta Bible College, Program in School and Church Administration, Redding, CA 96002. Offers MS. Part-time and evening/weekend programs available. *Degree requirements:* For master's, comprehensive exam (for some programs), thesis or alternative. *Entrance requirements:* For master's, cumulative GPA of 3.0, 9 semester hours of education or psychology courses. Additional exam requirements/recommendations for international students: Required—TOEFL (minimum score 550 paper-based; 213 computer-based).

Shippensburg University of Pennsylvania, School of Graduate Studies, College of Education and Human Services, Department of Educational Leadership and Special Education, Shippensburg, PA 17257-2299. Offers school administration principal K-12 (M Ed); special education (M Ed), including comprehensive, emotional/behavior disorders, intellectual disabilities and autism, learning disabilities. *Accreditation:* NCATE. Part-time and evening/weekend programs available. *Faculty:* 9 full-time (3 women), 4 part-time/adjunct (2 women). *Students:* 29 full-time (24 women), 118 part-time (78 women); includes 4 minority (2 Black or African American, non-Hispanic/Latino; 1 Asian, non-Hispanic/Latino; 1 Hispanic/Latino), 2 international. Average age 31. 49 applicants, 73% accepted, 31 enrolled. In 2011, 66 master's awarded. *Degree requirements:* For master's, candidacy, thesis, or practicum. *Entrance requirements:* For master's, instructional or educational specialist certificate; 3 letters of reference; 2 years of successful teaching experience; interview and GRE or MAT (if GPA is less than 2.75); statement of purpose; writing sample; personal goals statement. Additional exam requirements/recommendations for international students: Required—TOEFL (minimum score 580 paper-based; 237 computer-based); Recommended—IELTS (minimum score 6). *Application deadline:* For fall admission, 1/6 for domestic students, 4/30 for international students; for spring admission, 1/9 for domestic students, 9/30 for international students. Applications are processed on a rolling basis. Application fee: $30. Electronic applications accepted. *Expenses: Tuition, area resident:* Part-time $416 per credit. Tuition, state resident: part-time $416 per credit. Tuition, nonresident: part-time $624 per credit. *Required fees:* $119 per credit. *Financial support:* In 2011–12, 6 research assistantships with full tuition reimbursements (averaging $5,000 per year) were awarded; career-related internships or fieldwork, scholarships/grants, unspecified assistantships, and resident hall director and student payroll positions also available. Support available to part-time students. Financial award application deadline: 3/1; financial award applicants required to submit FAFSA. *Unit head:* Dr. Christopher L. Schwilk, Chairperson, 717-477-1591, Fax: 717-477-4026, E-mail: clschwi@ship.edu. *Application contact:* Jeremy R. Goshorn, Assistant Dean of Graduate Admissions, 717-477-1231, Fax: 717-477-4016, E-mail: jrgoshorn@ship.edu. Web site: http://www.ship.edu/else/.

Siena Heights University, Graduate College, Program in Educational Leadership, Adrian, MI 49221-1796. Offers MA. *Expenses: Tuition:* Full-time $11,400; part-time $475 per credit hour. *Required fees:* $1000; $500 $125 per term. Tuition and fees vary according to degree level.

Sierra Nevada College, Teacher Education Program, Incline Village, NV 89451. Offers advanced teaching and leadership (M Ed); elementary education (MAT); secondary education (MAT). Part-time and evening/weekend programs available. Postbaccalaureate distance learning degree programs offered (minimal on-campus study). *Faculty:* 2 full-time (both women), 26 part-time/adjunct (16 women). *Students:* 247 full-time (192 women), 240 part-time (162 women); includes 234 minority (44 Black or African American, non-Hispanic/Latino; 8 American Indian or Alaska Native, non-Hispanic/Latino; 132 Asian, non-Hispanic/Latino; 38 Hispanic/Latino; 12 Native Hawaiian or other Pacific Islander, non-Hispanic/Latino). Average age 35. 147 applicants, 84% accepted, 124 enrolled. In 2011, 146 master's awarded. *Degree requirements:* For master's, comprehensive exam, thesis, PRAXIS I and II. *Entrance requirements:* For master's, 2 letters of recommendation, minimum GPA of 3.0. *Application deadline:* For fall admission, 8/6 priority date for domestic students; for winter admission, 1/7 priority date for domestic students; for spring admission, 5/6 priority date for domestic students. Applications are processed on a rolling basis. Application fee: $50. Electronic applications accepted. *Expenses: Tuition:* Full-time $7138; part-time $397 per credit. *Required fees:* $100 per semester. *Financial support:* In 2011–12, 334 students received support. Federal Work-Study available. Support available to part-time students. Financial award application deadline: 8/15; financial award applicants required to submit FAFSA. *Unit head:* Beth Bouchard, Chair of Education Department, 775-831-1314, Fax: 775-832-1686, E-mail: bbouchard@sierranevada.edu. *Application contact:* Katrina Midgley, Director of Graduate Admission, 775-831-1314 Ext. 7517, Fax: 775-832-1686, E-mail: kmidgley@sierranevada.edu. Web site: http://www.sierranevada.edu/.

Silver Lake College of the Holy Family, Division of Graduate Studies, Program in Education, Manitowoc, WI 54220-9319. Offers administrative leadership (MA Ed); teacher leadership (MA Ed). Part-time and evening/weekend programs available. Postbaccalaureate distance learning degree programs offered (no on-campus study). *Degree requirements:* For master's, comprehensive exam, thesis or alternative, public presentation of culminating project. *Entrance requirements:* For master's, minimum undergraduate GPA of 3.0, writing sample, 3 letters of recommendation. Additional exam requirements/recommendations for international students: Required—TOEFL. Electronic applications accepted.

Simmons College, College of Arts and Sciences Graduate Studies, Boston, MA 02115. Offers applied behavior analysis (PhD); behavior analysis (MS, Ed S); children's literature (MA); education (MS, CAGS, Ed S); educational leadership (PhD, CAGS); English (MA); gender and cultural studies (MA); health professions education (PhD); history (MA); Spanish (MA); special education moderate licensure (Certificate); special needs administration (Ed D); special needs education (Ed S); teaching (MAT); teaching English as a second language (MA, CAGS); urban education (CAGS); writing for children (MFA); MA/MA; MA/MS; MAT/MA. *Unit head:* Renee White, Dean. *Application contact:* Kristen Haack, Director, Graduate Studies Admission, 617-521-2917, Fax: 617-521-3058, E-mail: gsa@simmons.edu. Web site: http://www.simmons.edu/gradstudies/.

Simon Fraser University, Graduate Studies, Faculty of Education, Program in Educational Leadership, Burnaby, BC V5A 1S6, Canada. Offers M Ed, MA, Ed D. *Degree requirements:* For master's, project or thesis. *Entrance requirements:* For master's, minimum GPA of 3.0. Additional exam requirements/recommendations for international students: Required—TOEFL or IELTS.

Simpson University, School of Education, Redding, CA 96003-8606. Offers education (MA); education and preliminary administrative services (MA); education and preliminary teaching (MA); teaching (MA). Part-time and evening/weekend programs available. *Faculty:* 4 full-time (2 women), 16 part-time/adjunct (7 women). *Students:* 71 full-time (51 women), 84 part-time (57 women); includes 20 minority (1 Black or African American, non-Hispanic/Latino; 10 Asian, non-Hispanic/Latino; 9 Hispanic/Latino). Average age 33. 109 applicants, 83% accepted, 75 enrolled. In 2011, 42 master's awarded. *Degree requirements:* For master's, thesis optional. *Entrance requirements:* For master's, California Basic Educational Skills Test, CSET, 2 letters of reference. Additional exam requirements/recommendations for international students: Required—TOEFL (minimum score 550 paper-based; 180 computer-based). *Application deadline:* Applications are processed on a rolling basis. Application fee: $25. Electronic applications accepted. *Expenses: Tuition:* Full-time $5400; part-time $600 per unit. Tuition and fees vary according to program. *Financial support:* Scholarships/grants available. Financial award applicants required to submit FAFSA. *Unit head:* Dr. Glee Brooks, Dean, 530-226-4606, Fax: 530-226-4861, E-mail: edadmissions@simpsonu.edu. *Application contact:* Kendell Kluttz, Director of Enrollment Management, 530-226-4770, Fax: 530-226-4861, E-mail: edadmissions@simpsonu.edu.

Slippery Rock University of Pennsylvania, Graduate Studies (Recruitment), College of Education, Department of Secondary Education/Foundations of Education, Slippery Rock, PA 16057-1383. Offers educational leadership (M Ed); secondary education in English (M Ed); secondary education in math/science (M Ed); secondary education in social studies (M Ed). *Accreditation:* NCATE. Part-time and evening/weekend programs available. *Faculty:* 9 full-time (4 women), 3 part-time/adjunct (0 women). *Students:* 64 full-time (34 women), 16 part-time (8 women); includes 2 minority (1 Asian, non-Hispanic/Latino; 1 Two or more races, non-Hispanic/Latino). Average age 28. 68 applicants, 76% accepted, 27 enrolled. In 2011, 54 degrees awarded. *Degree requirements:* For master's, comprehensive exam, thesis (for some programs). *Entrance requirements:* For master's, GRE General Test, MAT, minimum GPA of 2.8 (depending on program). Additional exam requirements/recommendations for international students: Required—TOEFL (minimum score 550 paper-based; 213 computer-based; 80 iBT). *Application deadline:* For fall admission, 3/1 priority date for domestic students, 5/1 for international students; for spring admission, 10/1 priority date for domestic students, 9/1 for international students. Applications are processed on a rolling basis. Application fee: $25 ($30 for international students). Electronic applications accepted. *Expenses:* Tuition, state resident: full-time $7488; part-time $416 per credit. Tuition, nonresident: full-time $11,232; part-time $624 per credit. *International tuition:* $11,146 full-time. *Required fees:* $2722; $140 per credit. Tuition and fees vary according to degree level and program. *Financial support:* Career-related internships or fieldwork, Federal Work-Study, institutionally sponsored loans, scholarships/grants, tuition waivers (partial), and unspecified assistantships available. Support available to part-time students. Financial award application deadline: 5/1; financial award applicants required to submit FAFSA. *Unit head:* Dr. Jeffrey Lehman, Graduate Coordinator, 724-738-2311, Fax: 724-738-4987, E-mail: jeffrey.lehman@sru.edu. *Application contact:* Angela Barrett, Interim Director of Graduate Studies, 724-738-2051, Fax: 724-738-2146, E-mail: graduate.admissions@sru.edu.

Slippery Rock University of Pennsylvania, Graduate Studies (Recruitment), College of Education, Department of Special Education, Slippery Rock, PA 16057-1383. Offers autism (M Ed); birth to grade 8 (M Ed); grade 7 to grade 12 (M Ed); master teacher (M Ed); supervision (M Ed). *Accreditation:* NCATE. Part-time and evening/weekend programs available. Postbaccalaureate distance learning degree programs offered. *Faculty:* 7 full-time (3 women). *Students:* 15 full-time (12 women), 98 part-time (83 women); includes 3 minority (1 Black or African American, non-Hispanic/Latino; 2 Asian, non-Hispanic/Latino). Average age 31. 113 applicants, 70% accepted, 37 enrolled. In 2011, 62 degrees awarded. *Degree requirements:* For master's, thesis optional, portfolio presentation. *Entrance requirements:* For master's, GRE General Test, MAT, minimum GPA of 3.0, official transcripts, teaching certification. Additional exam requirements/recommendations for international students: Required—TOEFL (minimum score 550 paper-based; 213 computer-based; 80 iBT). *Application deadline:* For fall admission, 3/1 priority date for domestic students, 5/1 for international students; for spring admission, 10/1 priority date for domestic students, 9/1 for international students. Applications are processed on a rolling basis. Application fee: $25 ($30 for international students). Electronic applications accepted. *Expenses:* Contact institution. *Financial support:* Career-related internships or fieldwork, institutionally sponsored loans, scholarships/grants, and tuition waivers (partial) available. Support available to part-time students. Financial award application deadline: 5/1; financial award applicants required to submit FAFSA. *Unit head:* Dr. Robert Isherwood, Graduate Coordinator, 724-738-2614, Fax: 724-738-4395, E-mail: robert.isherwood@sru.edu. *Application contact:* Angela Barrett, Director of Graduate Admissions, 724-738-2051, Fax: 724-738-2146, E-mail: graduate.admissions@sru.edu.

South Carolina State University, School of Graduate Studies, Department of Education, Orangeburg, SC 29117-0001. Offers counseling education (M Ed); early childhood and special education (M Ed); early childhood education (MAT); educational leadership (Ed D, Ed S); elementary education (M Ed, MAT); engineering (MAT); general science (MAT); mathematics (MAT); secondary education (M Ed), including biology education, business education, counselor education, English education, home economics education, industrial education, mathematics education, science education, social studies education; special education (M Ed), including emotionally handicapped, learning disabilities, mentally handicapped. *Accreditation:* NCATE. Part-time and evening/weekend programs available. *Faculty:* 9 full-time (6 women), 6 part-time/adjunct (2 women). *Students:* 34 full-time (29 women), 50 part-time (40 women); includes 74 minority (72 Black or African American, non-Hispanic/Latino; 1 Asian, non-Hispanic/Latino; 1 Hispanic/Latino). Average age 34. 23 applicants, 91% accepted, 14 enrolled. In 2011, 11 master's awarded. *Degree requirements:* For master's, thesis optional, departmental qualifying exam. *Entrance requirements:* For master's, GRE General Test, NTE, interview, teaching certificate. *Application deadline:* For fall admission, 6/15 priority date for domestic students, 6/15 for international students; for spring admission, 11/1 for domestic and international students. Applications are processed on a rolling basis. Application fee: $25. Electronic applications accepted. *Expenses:* Tuition, state resident: full-time $8688; part-time $514 per credit hour. Tuition, nonresident: full-time $17,600; part-time $1009 per credit hour. *Required fees:* $570. *Financial support:* In 2011–12, 3 fellowships (averaging $5,020 per year) were awarded; career-related internships or fieldwork, Federal Work-Study, and institutionally sponsored loans also available. Financial award application deadline: 6/1. *Faculty research:* Critical thinking, child abuse, stress, test-taking skills, conflict resolution, mainstreaming. *Unit head:* Dr. Charlie Spell, Interim Chair, 803-536-7098, Fax: 803-516-4568, E-mail: cspell@scsu.edu. *Application contact:* Annette Hazzard-Jones, Program Coordinator II, 803-536-8809, Fax: 803-536-8812, E-mail: zs_ahazzard@scsu.edu.

South Dakota State University, Graduate School, College of Education and Human Sciences, Department of Educational Leadership, Brookings, SD 57007. Offers curriculum and instruction (M Ed); educational administration (M Ed). Part-time and evening/weekend programs available. Postbaccalaureate distance learning degree programs offered (minimal on-campus study). *Degree requirements:* For master's, portfolio, oral exam. *Entrance requirements:* For master's, minimum GPA of 2.75. Additional exam requirements/recommendations for international students: Required—TOEFL (minimum score 550 paper-based; 213 computer-based; 80 iBT). *Faculty research:* Inclusion school climate, K-12 reform and restructuring, rural development, ESL, leadership.

Southeastern Louisiana University, College of Education and Human Development, Department of Educational Leadership and Technology, Hammond, LA 70402. Offers educational leadership (M Ed, Ed D); educational technology leadership (M Ed). Part-time and evening/weekend programs available. *Faculty:* 16 full-time (6 women). *Students:* 16 full-time (12 women), 233 part-time (186 women); includes 77 minority (69 Black or African American, non-Hispanic/Latino; 1 Asian, non-Hispanic/Latino; 4 Hispanic/Latino; 3 Two or more races, non-Hispanic/Latino). Average age 38. 23 applicants, 100% accepted, 16 enrolled. In 2011, 105 master's, 19 doctorates awarded. *Degree requirements:* For master's, comprehensive exam; for doctorate, comprehensive exam, thesis/dissertation. *Entrance requirements:* For master's, GRE (verbal and quantitative); for doctorate, GRE, master's degree with minimum GPA of 3.25, 3.0 on the last 60 undergraduate hours. Additional exam requirements/recommendations for international students: Required—TOEFL (minimum score 500 paper-based; 173 computer-based; 61 iBT). *Application deadline:* For fall admission, 7/15 priority date for domestic students, 6/1 for international students; for spring admission, 12/1 priority date for domestic students, 10/1 for international students. Applications are processed on a rolling basis. Application fee: $20 ($30 for international students). Electronic applications accepted. *Expenses:* Tuition, state resident: full-time $3977; part-time $283 per semester hour. Tuition, nonresident: full-time $13,482; part-time $811 per semester hour. *Financial support:* Career-related internships or fieldwork, Federal Work-Study, institutionally sponsored loans, scholarships/grants, and unspecified assistantships available. Support available to part-time students. Financial award application deadline: 5/1; financial award applicants required to submit FAFSA. *Faculty research:* Technology leadership in schools, techno stress for educational leaders, dispositions of effective leaders. *Total annual research expenditures:* $176,799. *Unit head:* Dr. Michael D. Richardson, Department Head, 985-549-5713, Fax: 985-549-5712, E-mail: mrichardson@selu.edu. *Application contact:* Sandra Meyers, Graduate Admissions Analyst, 985-549-2066, Fax: 985-549-5632, E-mail: admissions@selu.edu. Web site: http://www.selu.edu/acad_research/depts/edlt.

Southeastern Oklahoma State University, School of Education, Durant, OK 74701-0609. Offers math specialist (M Ed); reading specialist (M Ed); school administration (M Ed); school counseling (M Ed); special education (M Ed). *Accreditation:* NCATE. Part-time and evening/weekend programs available. *Faculty:* 52 full-time (19 women), 1 (woman) part-time/adjunct. *Students:* 15 full-time (11 women), 54 part-time (40 women); includes 24 minority (2 Black or African American, non-Hispanic/Latino; 16 American Indian or Alaska Native, non-Hispanic/Latino; 6 Hispanic/Latino). Average age 34. 31 applicants, 94% accepted, 29 enrolled. *Degree requirements:* For master's, comprehensive exam, thesis optional, portfolio (M Ed). *Entrance requirements:* For master's, GRE General Test (MBS), minimum GPA of 3.0 in last 60 hours or 2.75 overall. Additional exam requirements/recommendations for international students: Required—TOEFL (minimum score 550 paper-based; 213 computer-based; 79 iBT). *Application deadline:* For fall admission, 8/1 for domestic students, 6/1 for international students; for spring admission, 1/5 for domestic students, 11/1 for international students. Application fee: $20 ($55 for international students). Electronic applications accepted. *Expenses:* Tuition, state resident: full-time $3537; part-time $173.95 per credit hour. Tuition, nonresident: full-time $8673; part-time $459.30 per credit hour. *Required fees:* $22.55 per credit hour. *Financial support:* In 2011–12, 1 teaching assistantship with full tuition reimbursement (averaging $5,000 per year) was awarded; Federal Work-Study, institutionally sponsored loans, and tuition waivers (partial) also available. Support available to part-time students. Financial award application deadline: 6/15; financial award applicants required to submit FAFSA. *Unit head:* Dr. John Love, M Ed Coordinator, 580-745-2226, Fax: 580-745-7508, E-mail: jlove@se.edu. *Application contact:* Carrie Williamson, Graduate Secretary, 580-745-2220, Fax: 580-745-7474, E-mail: cwilliamson@se.edu. Web site: http://www.se.edu/graduate-programs/master-of-education/.

Southeastern University, College of Education, Lakeland, FL 33801-6099. Offers educational leadership (M Ed); elementary education (M Ed); teaching and learning (M Ed).

Southeast Missouri State University, School of Graduate Studies, Department of Educational Leadership and Counseling, Program in Educational Administration, Cape Girardeau, MO 63701-4799. Offers educational administration (Ed S); educational leadership development (Ed S); elementary administration and supervision (MA); higher education administration (MA); secondary administration and supervision (MA); teacher leadership (MA). *Accreditation:* NCATE. Part-time and evening/weekend programs available. Postbaccalaureate distance learning degree programs offered (minimal on-campus study). *Faculty:* 12 full-time (7 women). *Students:* 32 full-time (23 women), 172 part-time (122 women); includes 10 minority (6 Black or African American, non-Hispanic/Latino; 3 Asian, non-Hispanic/Latino; 1 Hispanic/Latino), 1 international. Average age 34. 62 applicants, 95% accepted, 51 enrolled. In 2011, 34 master's, 13 other advanced degrees awarded. *Degree requirements:* For master's, comprehensive exam (for some programs), thesis (for some programs), minimum GPA of 3.25; paper, portfolio or oral exam (for some programs); for Ed S, comprehensive exam. *Entrance requirements:* For master's, minimum undergraduate GPA of 2.75, valid teacher certification; for Ed S, GRE General Test, PRAXIS or MAT, minimum graduate GPA of 3.5; master's degree; valid teaching certificate. Additional exam requirements/recommendations for international students: Required—TOEFL (minimum score 550 paper-based; 213 computer-based; 79 iBT); Recommended—IELTS (minimum score 6). *Application deadline:* For fall admission, 8/1 for domestic students, 7/1 for international students; for spring admission, 11/21 for domestic students, 11/1 for international students. Applications are processed on a rolling basis. Application fee: $30 ($40 for international students). Electronic applications accepted. *Expenses:* Tuition, state resident: full-time $4896; part-time $272 per credit hour. Tuition, nonresident: full-time $8649; part-time $480.50 per credit hour. *Financial support:* In 2011–12, 16 students received support. Career-related internships or fieldwork, Federal Work-Study, scholarships/grants, tuition waivers (full), and unspecified assistantships available. Financial award application deadline: 6/30; financial award applicants required to submit FAFSA. *Faculty research:* Teacher leadership, organizational leadership effectiveness, state assessment and accountability systems. *Unit head:* Dr. David Stader, 573-651-2417, E-mail: dstader@semo.edu. *Application contact:* Alisa Aleen McFerron, Assistant Director of Admissions for Operations, 573-651-5937, Fax: 573-651-5936, E-mail: amcferron@semo.edu. Web site: http://www4.semo.edu/edadmin/admin.

Southern Adventist University, School of Education and Psychology, Collegedale, TN 37315-0370. Offers clinical mental health counseling (MS); inclusive education (MS Ed); instructional leadership (MS Ed); literacy education (MS Ed); outdoor teacher education (MS Ed); school counseling (MS). *Accreditation:* NCATE. Part-time and evening/weekend programs available. *Degree requirements:* For master's, comprehensive exam (for some programs), thesis optional, position paper (MS), portfolio (MS Ed in outdoor teacher education). *Entrance requirements:* For master's, interview (MS); 9 semester hours of upper division course work in psychology or related field, including 1 course in psychology research or statistics; 9 semester hours of education (MS Ed). Additional exam requirements/recommendations for international students: Required—TOEFL (minimum score 600 paper-based; 250 computer-based; 100 iBT). Electronic applications accepted.

Southern Arkansas University–Magnolia, Graduate Programs, Magnolia, AR 71754. Offers agriculture (MS); business administration (MBA); computer and information sciences (MS); education (M Ed), including counseling and development, curriculum and instruction, educational administration and supervision, elementary education, middle level, reading, secondary education, TESOL; kinesiology (M Ed); library media and information specialist (M Ed); mental health and clinical counseling (MS); public administration (MPA); school counseling (M Ed); teaching (MAT). *Accreditation:* NCATE. Part-time and evening/weekend programs available. Postbaccalaureate distance learning degree programs offered. *Faculty:* 34 full-time (15 women), 8 part-time/adjunct (5 women). *Students:* 87 full-time (62 women), 320 part-time (224 women); includes 116 minority (111 Black or African American, non-Hispanic/Latino; 2 American Indian or Alaska Native, non-Hispanic/Latino; 2 Asian, non-Hispanic/Latino; 1 Hispanic/Latino), 25 international. Average age 33. 201 applicants, 98% accepted, 156 enrolled. In 2011, 162 master's awarded. *Degree requirements:* For master's, comprehensive exam (for some programs), thesis optional. *Entrance requirements:* For master's, GRE, MAT or GMAT, minimum GPA of 2.5. Additional exam requirements/recommendations for international students: Required—TOEFL (minimum score 173 computer-based). *Application deadline:* For fall admission, 7/15 for domestic and international students; for winter admission, 12/1 for domestic and international students; for spring admission, 12/1 for domestic and international students. Applications are processed on a rolling basis. Application fee: $25 ($35 for international students). Electronic applications accepted. *Expenses:* Tuition, state resident: part-time $232 per credit. Tuition, nonresident: part-time $339 per credit. *Required fees:* $44 per credit. Part-time tuition and fees vary according to course load. *Financial support:* Career-related internships or fieldwork, Federal Work-Study, scholarships/grants, tuition waivers (full), and unspecified assistantships available. Financial award applicants required to submit FAFSA. *Faculty research:* Alternative certification for teachers, supervision of instruction, instructional leadership, counseling. *Unit head:* Dr. Kim Bloss, Dean, School of Graduate Studies, 870-235-4150, Fax: 870-235-5227, E-mail: kkbloss@saumag.edu. *Application contact:* Gaye Calhoun, Admissions Specialist, 870-235-4150, Fax: 870-235-5227, E-mail: glcalhoun@saumag.edu. Web site: http://www.saumag.edu/graduate.

Southern Connecticut State University, School of Graduate Studies, School of Education, Department of Educational Leadership, New Haven, CT 06515-1355. Offers educational foundations (Diploma), including foundational studies; educational leadership (Ed D, Diploma); research, statistics, and measurement (MS). Part-time and evening/weekend programs available. *Faculty:* 13 full-time (7 women), 10 part-time/adjunct (4 women). *Students:* 13 full-time (6 women), 196 part-time (135 women); includes 34 minority (17 Black or African American, non-Hispanic/Latino; 3 Asian, non-Hispanic/Latino; 13 Hispanic/Latino; 1 Two or more races, non-Hispanic/Latino), 1 international. 203 applicants, 34% accepted, 59 enrolled. In 2011, 3 doctorates, 109 other advanced degrees awarded. *Entrance requirements:* For degree, master's degree, minimum GPA of 3.0, writing sample. *Application deadline:* For fall admission, 7/15 priority date for domestic students. Applications are processed on a rolling basis. Application fee: $50. Electronic applications accepted. *Expenses:* Tuition, state resident: full-time $5137; part-time $413 per credit. *Required fees:* $4008; $55 per term. *Financial support:* Application deadline: 4/15; applicants required to submit FAFSA. *Unit head:* Dr. Peter Madonia, Chairperson, 203-392-5441, E-mail: madoniap1@southernct.edu. *Application contact:* Dr. Cathryn Magno, Graduate Coordinator, 203-392-5170, Fax: 203-392-5347, E-mail: magnoc1@southernct.edu.

Southern Illinois University Carbondale, Graduate School, College of Education and Human Services, Department of Educational Administration and Higher Education, Program in Educational Administration, Carbondale, IL 62901-4701. Offers MS Ed, PhD. PhD offered jointly with Southeast Missouri State University. *Accreditation:* NCATE. Part-time programs available. *Faculty:* 9 full-time (3 women). *Students:* 21 full-time (6 women), 71 part-time (46 women); includes 23 minority (18 Black or African American, non-Hispanic/Latino; 1 Asian, non-Hispanic/Latino; 4 Hispanic/Latino), 3 international. 11 applicants, 45% accepted, 2 enrolled. In 2011, 10 master's, 3 doctorates awarded. *Degree requirements:* For master's, thesis or alternative; for doctorate, thesis/dissertation. *Entrance requirements:* For master's, GRE General Test, MAT, minimum GPA of 2.7; for doctorate, GRE General Test, MAT, minimum GPA of 3.5. Additional exam requirements/recommendations for international students: Required—TOEFL. *Application deadline:* For fall admission, 5/15 for domestic students; for spring admission, 9/15 for domestic students. Applications are processed on a rolling basis. Application fee: $20. *Financial support:* In 2011–12, 7 students received support, including 1 research assistantship with full tuition reimbursement available, 3 teaching assistantships with full tuition reimbursements available; fellowships with full tuition reimbursements available, career-related internships or fieldwork, Federal Work-Study, institutionally sponsored loans, and tuition waivers (full) also available. Support available to part-time students. Financial award application deadline: 4/1. *Faculty research:* School principalship, history and philosophy of education, supervision. *Unit head:* Dr. W. Bradley Colwell, Chair, 618-536-4434, Fax: 618-453-4338, E-mail: bcolwell@siu.edu. *Application contact:* Debra Mibb, Admissions Secretary, 618-536-4434, Fax: 618-453-4338, E-mail: dmibb@siu.edu.

Southern Illinois University Edwardsville, Graduate School, School of Education, Department of Educational Leadership, Program in Educational Administration, Edwardsville, IL 62026. Offers MS Ed, Ed S. *Accreditation:* NCATE. Part-time and evening/weekend programs available. *Students:* 3 full-time (1 woman), 166 part-time (110 women); includes 23 minority (17 Black or African American, non-Hispanic/Latino; 1 Asian, non-Hispanic/Latino; 2 Hispanic/Latino; 3 Two or more races, non-Hispanic/Latino), 1 international. 57 applicants, 42% accepted. In 2011, 37 master's, 25 Ed Ss awarded. *Degree requirements:* For master's, thesis or alternative, portfolio. *Entrance requirements:* Additional exam requirements/recommendations for international students: Required—TOEFL (minimum score 550 paper-based; 213 computer-based; 79 iBT), IELTS (minimum score 6.5). *Application deadline:* For fall admission, 7/22 for domestic students, 6/1 for international students; for spring admission, 12/9 for domestic students, 10/1 for international students. Applications are processed on a rolling basis. Application fee: $30. Electronic applications accepted. Tuition and fees vary according to course load and program. *Financial support:* Fellowships with tuition reimbursements, research assistantships with full tuition reimbursements, teaching assistantships with tuition reimbursements, institutionally sponsored loans, scholarships/grants, traineeships, and unspecified assistantships available. Financial award application deadline: 3/1; financial award applicants required to submit FAFSA. *Unit head:* Dr. Allison Reeves, Director, 618-650-3297, E-mail: alireev@siue.edu. *Application contact:* Michelle Robinson, Coordinator of Graduate Recruitment, 618-650-2811, Fax:

618-650-3523, E-mail: michero@siue.edu. Web site: http://www.siue.edu/education/edld/.

Southern Illinois University Edwardsville, Graduate School, School of Education, Department of Educational Leadership, Program in Educational Leadership, Edwardsville, IL 62026. Offers Ed D. Part-time and evening/weekend programs available. *Students:* 20 part-time (11 women); includes 5 minority (4 Black or African American, non-Hispanic/Latino; 1 Hispanic/Latino). *Degree requirements:* For doctorate, thesis/dissertation or alternative, project. *Entrance requirements:* For doctorate, GRE. Additional exam requirements/recommendations for international students: Required—TOEFL (minimum score 550 paper-based; 213 computer-based; 79 iBT), IELTS (minimum score 6.5). *Application deadline:* For fall admission, 7/20 for domestic students, 6/1 for international students; for spring admission, 12/7 for domestic students, 10/1 for international students. Applications are processed on a rolling basis. Application fee: $30. Electronic applications accepted. Tuition and fees vary according to course load and program. *Financial support:* Institutionally sponsored loans, scholarships/grants, and unspecified assistantships available. Financial award application deadline: 3/1; financial award applicants required to submit FAFSA. *Unit head:* Dr. Linda Morice, Chair, 618-650-3278, E-mail: lmorice@siue.edu. Web site: http://www.siue.edu/education/edld/.

Southern New Hampshire University, School of Education, Manchester, NH 03106-1045. Offers business education (MS); child development (M Ed); computer technology education (Certificate); curriculum and instruction (M Ed); education (M Ed, CAS); elementary education (M Ed); general special education (Certificate); school business administrator (Certificate); secondary education (M Ed); training and development (Certificate). Part-time and evening/weekend programs available. Postbaccalaureate distance learning degree programs offered (no on-campus study). *Degree requirements:* For master's, comprehensive exam (for some programs), thesis or alternative. *Entrance requirements:* For master's, PRAXIS I, minimum GPA of 2.75. Additional exam requirements/recommendations for international students: Required—TOEFL (minimum score 550 paper-based; 213 computer-based). Electronic applications accepted. *Expenses:* Contact institution.

Southern Oregon University, Graduate Studies, School of Education, Ashland, OR 97520. Offers elementary education (MA Ed, MS Ed), including classroom teacher, early childhood, handicapped learner, reading, supervision; secondary education (MA Ed, MS Ed), including classroom teacher, handicapped learner, reading, supervision; teaching (MAT). *Faculty:* 18 full-time (10 women), 10 part-time/adjunct (all women). *Students:* 128 full-time (88 women), 145 part-time (103 women); includes 32 minority (1 Black or African American, non-Hispanic/Latino; 3 American Indian or Alaska Native, non-Hispanic/Latino; 5 Asian, non-Hispanic/Latino; 13 Hispanic/Latino; 3 Native Hawaiian or other Pacific Islander, non-Hispanic/Latino; 7 Two or more races, non-Hispanic/Latino), 1 international. Average age 35. 48 applicants, 60% accepted, 23 enrolled. In 2011, 102 degrees awarded. *Degree requirements:* For master's, thesis optional. *Entrance requirements:* For master's, GRE General Test, minimum GPA of 3.0. *Application deadline:* For fall admission, 2/1 for domestic students. Application fee: $50. Electronic applications accepted. *Expenses:* Tuition, state resident: full-time $12,600; part-time $350 per credit. Tuition, nonresident: full-time $16,200; part-time $450 per credit. *Required fees:* $1590. *Financial support:* Research assistantships with partial tuition reimbursements available. *Unit head:* Dr. Geoff Mills, Dean, 541-552-6920, E-mail: mills@sou.edu. *Application contact:* Mark Bottorff, Director of Admissions, 541-552-6411, Fax: 541-552-8403, E-mail: admissions@sou.edu. Web site: http://www.sou.edu/education/.

Southern University and Agricultural and Mechanical College, Graduate School, College of Education, Department of Behavioral Studies and Educational Leadership, Program in Administration and Supervision, Baton Rouge, LA 70813. Offers M Ed.

Southern University and Agricultural and Mechanical College, Graduate School, College of Education, Department of Behavioral Studies and Educational Leadership, Program in Educational Leadership, Baton Rouge, LA 70813. Offers M Ed. *Entrance requirements:* For master's, GRE General Test.

Southwest Baptist University, Program in Education, Bolivar, MO 65613-2597. Offers education (MS); educational administration (MS, Ed S). Part-time programs available. *Degree requirements:* For master's, comprehensive exam, thesis optional, 6-hour residency; for Ed S, comprehensive exam, 5-hour residency. *Entrance requirements:* For master's, GRE or PRAXIS II, interviews, minimum GPA of 2.75; for Ed S, master's degree. Additional exam requirements/recommendations for international students: Required—TOEFL (minimum score 550 paper-based; 213 computer-based). *Faculty research:* At-risk programs, principal retention, mentoring beginning principals.

Southwestern Adventist University, Education Department, Keene, TX 76059. Offers curriculum and instruction with reading emphasis (M Ed); educational leadership (M Ed). Part-time and evening/weekend programs available. *Degree requirements:* For master's, thesis or alternative, professional paper. *Entrance requirements:* For master's, GRE General Test.

Southwestern Assemblies of God University, Thomas F. Harrison School of Graduate Studies, Program in Education, Waxahachie, TX 75165-5735. Offers Christian school administration (MS); curriculum development (MS); early education administration (M Ed); middle and secondary education (M Ed). *Degree requirements:* For master's, comprehensive written and oral exams. *Entrance requirements:* For master's, GRE General Test, minimum GPA of 2.5. Electronic applications accepted.

Southwestern Oklahoma State University, College of Professional and Graduate Studies, School of Behavioral Sciences and Education, Specialization in Educational Administration, Weatherford, OK 73096-3098. Offers M Ed. M Ed distance learning degree program offered to Oklahoma residents only. *Accreditation:* NCATE. Part-time and evening/weekend programs available. Postbaccalaureate distance learning degree programs offered (minimal on-campus study). *Degree requirements:* For master's, exam. *Entrance requirements:* For master's, GRE General Test or minimum undergraduate GPA of 3.0, portfolio. Additional exam requirements/recommendations for international students: Required—TOEFL.

Southwest Minnesota State University, Department of Education, Marshall, MN 56258. Offers ESL (MS); math (MS); reading (MS); special education (MS), including developmental disabilities, early childhood education, emotional behavioral disorders, learning disabilities; teaching, learning and leadership (MS). Part-time and evening/weekend programs available. Postbaccalaureate distance learning degree programs offered (no on-campus study). *Entrance requirements:* Additional exam requirements/recommendations for international students: Required—TOEFL or IELTS; Recommended—TOEFL (minimum score 550 paper-based; 213 computer-based; 80 iBT), IELTS.

Spalding University, Graduate Studies, College of Education, Program in Leadership Education, Louisville, KY 40203-2188. Offers M Ed, Ed D. *Accreditation:* NCATE. Part-time and evening/weekend programs available. *Faculty:* 6 part-time/adjunct (3 women). *Students:* 27 full-time (17 women), 43 part-time (32 women); includes 30 minority (28 Black or African American, non-Hispanic/Latino; 1 Asian, non-Hispanic/Latino; 1 Two or more races, non-Hispanic/Latino), 6 international. Average age 41. 28 applicants, 46% accepted, 11 enrolled. In 2011, 19 doctorates awarded. *Degree requirements:* For doctorate, comprehensive exam, thesis/dissertation. *Entrance requirements:* For doctorate, GRE General Test or MAT, interview, recommendations, resume. Additional exam requirements/recommendations for international students: Required—TOEFL (minimum score 535 paper-based; 203 computer-based). *Application deadline:* Applications are processed on a rolling basis. Electronic applications accepted. *Expenses: Tuition:* Full-time $12,438. Tuition and fees vary according to course load, degree level and program. *Financial support:* In 2011–12, 19 students received support. Scholarships/grants and unspecified assistantships available. Financial award application deadline: 3/15; financial award applicants required to submit FAFSA. *Faculty research:* Leadership of schools, achievement gap, women in leadership. *Unit head:* Dr. Beverly Keepers, Dean, 502-873-4268, E-mail: bkeepers@spalding.edu. *Application contact:* Dr. Rita Greer, Director, 502-873-4265, E-mail: rgreer@spalding.edu.

Spalding University, Graduate Studies, College of Education, Programs in Education, Louisville, KY 40203-2188. Offers elementary school education (MAT); general education (MA); high school education (MAT); middle school education (MAT); school administration (MA); special education (learning and behavioral disorders) (MAT); student guidance counselor (MA). MAT programs offered for first teaching certificate/license students. *Accreditation:* NCATE. Part-time and evening/weekend programs available. *Faculty:* 9 full-time (6 women), 32 part-time/adjunct (20 women). *Students:* 142 full-time (100 women), 71 part-time (53 women); includes 75 minority (65 Black or African American, non-Hispanic/Latino; 1 American Indian or Alaska Native, non-Hispanic/Latino; 6 Hispanic/Latino; 3 Two or more races, non-Hispanic/Latino). Average age 36. 96 applicants, 44% accepted, 41 enrolled. In 2011, 69 master's awarded. *Degree requirements:* For master's, portfolio, final project, clinical experience. *Entrance requirements:* For master's, GRE General Test or MAT, interview, recommendations, resume. Additional exam requirements/recommendations for international students: Required—TOEFL (minimum score 535 paper-based; 203 computer-based). *Application deadline:* Applications are processed on a rolling basis. Application fee: $30. Electronic applications accepted. *Expenses: Tuition:* Full-time $12,438. Tuition and fees vary according to course load, degree level and program. *Financial support:* In 2011–12, 72 students received support, including 3 research assistantships with partial tuition reimbursements available (averaging $4,490 per year); scholarships/grants, traineeships, and unspecified assistantships also available. Financial award application deadline: 3/15; financial award applicants required to submit FAFSA. *Faculty research:* Instructional technology, achievement gap, classroom management, assessment. *Unit head:* Dr. Beverly Keepers, Dean, 502-588-7121, Fax: 502-585-7123, E-mail: bkeepers@spalding.edu. *Application contact:* Bonnie Caughron, 502-873-4262, E-mail: bcaughron@spalding.edu.

Springfield College, Graduate Programs, Program in Education, Springfield, MA 01109-3797. Offers counseling and secondary education (M Ed, MS); early childhood education (M Ed, MS); education (M Ed, MS); educational administration (M Ed, MS); educational studies (M Ed, MS); elementary education (M Ed, MS); secondary education (M Ed, MS); special education (M Ed, MS). Part-time and evening/weekend programs available. *Entrance requirements:* Additional exam requirements/recommendations for international students: Required—TOEFL (minimum score 550 paper-based; 213 computer-based). Electronic applications accepted.

Stanford University, School of Education, Program in Social Sciences, Policy, and Educational Practice, Stanford, CA 94305-9991. Offers administration and policy analysis (Ed D, PhD); anthropology of education (PhD); economics of education (PhD); educational linguistics (PhD); evaluation (MA), including interdisciplinary studies; higher education (PhD); history of education (PhD); interdisciplinary studies (PhD); international comparative education (MA, PhD); international education administration and policy analysis (MA); philosophy of education (PhD); policy analysis (MA); prospective principal's program (MA); sociology of education (PhD). *Degree requirements:* For master's, thesis (for some programs); for doctorate, thesis/dissertation. *Entrance requirements:* For master's and doctorate, GRE General Test. Electronic applications accepted. *Expenses: Tuition:* Full-time $40,050; part-time $890 per credit.

State University of New York at Binghamton, Graduate School, College of Community and Public Affairs, Department of Student Affairs Administration, Binghamton, NY 13902-6000. Offers MS. *Faculty:* 3 full-time (2 women). *Students:* 23 full-time (12 women), 15 part-time (9 women); includes 9 minority (1 Black or African American, non-Hispanic/Latino; 1 Asian, non-Hispanic/Latino; 7 Hispanic/Latino), 3 international. Average age 28. 32 applicants, 66% accepted, 10 enrolled. In 2011, 17 master's awarded. *Financial support:* In 2011–12, 8 students received support, including fellowships with full tuition reimbursements available (averaging $9,000 per year), 3 teaching assistantships with full tuition reimbursements available (averaging $9,000 per year); career-related internships or fieldwork, Federal Work-Study, institutionally sponsored loans, scholarships/grants, health care benefits, and unspecified assistantships also available. Financial award application deadline: 2/15; financial award applicants required to submit FAFSA. *Unit head:* Dr. Mary Ann Swain, Chair, 607-777-9219, E-mail: mswain@binghamton.edu. *Application contact:* Catherine Smith, Recruiting and Admissions Coordinator, 607-777-2151, Fax: 607-777-2501, E-mail: cmsmith@binghamton.edu. Web site: http://www2.binghamton.edu/ccpa/student-affairs-administration/.

State University of New York at Fredonia, Graduate Studies, College of Education, Program in Educational Administration, Fredonia, NY 14063-1136. Offers CAS. Part-time and evening/weekend programs available. *Degree requirements:* For CAS, thesis or alternative. *Expenses:* Tuition, state resident: full-time $6666; part-time $370 per credit hour. Tuition, nonresident: full-time $11,376; part-time $632 per credit hour. *Required fees:* $1059.30; $58.85 per credit hour. Tuition and fees vary according to course load.

State University of New York at New Paltz, Graduate School, School of Education, Department of Educational Administration, New Paltz, NY 12561. Offers alternative certificate: school district leader (transition D) (CAS); school business leadership (CAS); school leadership (MS Ed, CAS). Part-time and evening/weekend programs available. *Faculty:* 2 full-time (1 woman), 6 part-time/adjunct (3 women). *Students:* 7 full-time (4 women), 83 part-time (55 women); includes 18 minority (9 Black or African American, non-Hispanic/Latino; 1 American Indian or Alaska Native, non-Hispanic/Latino; 3 Asian, non-Hispanic/Latino; 4 Hispanic/Latino; 1 Two or more races, non-Hispanic/Latino). Average age 39. 59 applicants, 75% accepted, 39 enrolled. In 2011, 4 master's, 66 CASs awarded. *Degree requirements:* For CAS, internship. *Entrance requirements:* For master's, GRE General Test or MAT, minimum GPA of 3.0, New York state teaching certificate; for CAS, minimum GPA of 3.0, proof of 3 years teaching experience, New York state teaching certificate. Additional exam requirements/recommendations for international students: Required—TOEFL (minimum score 550 paper-based; 213 computer-based; 80 iBT), IELTS (minimum score 6.5). *Application deadline:* For fall admission, 5/15 priority date for domestic students, 5/15 for international students; for spring admission, 11/15 priority date for domestic students, 11/15 for international students. Applications are processed on a rolling basis. Application fee: $50. Electronic applications accepted. *Expenses:* Tuition, state resident: full-time $8870; part-time $370 per credit. Tuition, nonresident: full-time $15,160; part-time $632 per credit. *Required* *fees:* $1188; $34 per credit. $184 per semester. *Financial support:* Career-related internships or fieldwork, Federal Work-Study, and institutionally sponsored loans available. Financial award application deadline: 8/1; financial award applicants required to submit FAFSA. *Faculty research:* Time management of administrators, social justice, women in educational leadership, diversity in educational leadership, superintendency. *Unit head:* Dr. Charles Khoury, Program Director, 845-257-2810, E-mail: khouryc@newpaltz.edu. *Application contact:* Caroline Murphy, Graduate Admissions Advisor, 845-257-3285, Fax: 845-257-3284, E-mail: gradschool@newpaltz.edu. Web site: http://www.newpaltz.edu/edadmin/.

State University of New York at Oswego, Graduate Studies, School of Education, Department of Educational Administration, Oswego, NY 13126. Offers educational administration and supervision (CAS); school building leadership (CAS). Part-time programs available. *Degree requirements:* For CAS, comprehensive exam, internship. *Entrance requirements:* For degree, interview, MA or MS, minimum GPA of 3.0, teaching certificate. Additional exam requirements/recommendations for international students: Required—TOEFL (minimum score 560 paper-based; 220 computer-based). *Faculty research:* Professional growth and development, leadership, governance, strategic planning, shared decision making.

State University of New York at Plattsburgh, Division of Education, Health, and Human Services, Program in Educational Leadership, Plattsburgh, NY 12901-2681. Offers CAS. Part-time and evening/weekend programs available. *Students:* 3 full-time (2 women), 55 part-time (30 women). Average age 39. *Entrance requirements:* Additional exam requirements/recommendations for international students: Required—TOEFL. *Application deadline:* For fall admission, 2/15 priority date for domestic students; for spring admission, 10/15 priority date for domestic students. Applications are processed on a rolling basis. Application fee: $75. *Financial support:* Federal Work-Study available. Support available to part-time students. Financial award application deadline: 4/15; financial award applicants required to submit FAFSA. *Unit head:* Michael Johnson, Coordinator, 518-792-5425 Ext. 105, E-mail: johnsomj@plattsburgh.edu. *Application contact:* Marguerite Adelman, Assistant Director, Graduate Admissions, 518-564-4723, Fax: 518-564-4722, E-mail: adelmaml@plattsburgh.edu.

State University of New York College at Cortland, Graduate Studies, School of Education, Program in Educational Leadership, Cortland, NY 13045. Offers CAS. Part-time and evening/weekend programs available. *Degree requirements:* For CAS, one foreign language. *Entrance requirements:* For degree, MS in education, permanent New York teaching certificate. Additional exam requirements/recommendations for international students: Required—TOEFL.

Stephen F. Austin State University, Graduate School, College of Education, Department of Secondary Education and Educational Leadership, Nacogdoches, TX 75962. Offers educational leadership (Ed D); secondary education (M Ed). *Accreditation:* NCATE. *Degree requirements:* For master's, comprehensive exam; for doctorate, thesis/dissertation. *Entrance requirements:* For master's, GRE General Test; for doctorate, GRE General Test, interview, writing sample. Additional exam requirements/recommendations for international students: Required—TOEFL. Electronic applications accepted.

Stetson University, College of Arts and Sciences, Division of Education, Department of Teacher Education, Program in Educational Leadership, DeLand, FL 32723. Offers M Ed, Ed S. *Accreditation:* NCATE. Evening/weekend programs available. *Students:* 37 full-time (27 women), 1 part-time (0 women); includes 8 minority (3 Black or African American, non-Hispanic/Latino; 2 Asian, non-Hispanic/Latino; 3 Hispanic/Latino), 1 international. Average age 34. In 2011, 47 master's awarded. *Degree requirements:* For master's, comprehensive exam. *Entrance requirements:* For master's and Ed S, GRE General Test or MAT. *Application deadline:* For fall admission, 3/1 priority date for domestic students; for spring admission, 11/1 for domestic students. Applications are processed on a rolling basis. Application fee: $25. *Financial support:* Career-related internships or fieldwork available. *Unit head:* Dr. Debra Touchton, Coordinator, 386-822-7075. *Application contact:* Diana Belian, Office of Graduate Studies, 386-822-7075, Fax: 386-822-7388, E-mail: dbelian@stetson.edu.

Stony Brook University, State University of New York, School of Professional Development, Stony Brook, NY 11794. Offers biology-grade 7-12 (MAT); chemistry-grade 7-12 (MAT); coaching (Graduate Certificate); coaching online (Graduate Certificate); computer integrated engineering (Graduate Certificate); earth science-grade 7-12 (MAT); educational computing (Graduate Certificate); educational leadership (Advanced Certificate); English-grade 7-12 (MAT); environmental management (Graduate Certificate); environmental/occupational health and safety (Graduate Certificate); French-grade 7-12 (MAT); German-grade 7-12 (MAT); human resource management (Graduate Certificate); human resource management online (Graduate Certificate); information systems management (Graduate Certificate); Italian-grade 7-12 (MAT); liberal studies (MA); liberal studies online (MAT); mathematics-grade 7-12 (MAT); operation research (Graduate Certificate); physics-grade 7-12 (MAT); professional studies online (MPS); school administration and supervision (Graduate Certificate); school building leadership (Graduate Certificate); school district administration (Graduate Certificate); school district business leadership (Advanced Certificate); school district leadership (Graduate Certificate); social science and the professions (MPS), including environmental waste management, human resource management; social studies-grade 7-12 (MAT); Spanish-grade 7-12 (MAT); waste management (Graduate Certificate). Part-time and evening/weekend programs available. Postbaccalaureate distance learning degree programs offered. *Degree requirements:* For master's, one foreign language, thesis or alternative.

Suffolk University, College of Arts and Sciences, Department of Education and Human Services, Boston, MA 02108-2770. Offers administration of higher education (M Ed, CAGS), including administration of higher education (M Ed), leadership (CAGS); human resource, learning and performance (MS, CAGS, Graduate Certificate), including global human resources (Graduate Certificate), human resources (MS, Graduate Certificate), organizational development (CAGS, Graduate Certificate), organizational learning and development (MS, Graduate Certificate); mental health counseling (MS, CAGS); school counseling (M Ed, CAGS); school teaching (M Ed, CAGS), including foundations of education (M Ed), middle school teaching (M Ed), secondary school teaching (M Ed); MPA/MSMHC; MS/Certificate. Part-time and evening/weekend programs available. *Faculty:* 10 full-time (6 women), 7 part-time/adjunct (3 women). *Students:* 53 full-time (39 women), 131 part-time (112 women); includes 21 minority (7 Black or African American, non-Hispanic/Latino; 2 American Indian or Alaska Native, non-Hispanic/Latino; 5 Asian, non-Hispanic/Latino; 5 Hispanic/Latino; 2 Two or more races, non-Hispanic/Latino), 9 international. Average age 28. 158 applicants, 73% accepted, 60 enrolled. In 2011, 72 master's, 8 other advanced degrees awarded. *Entrance requirements:* For master's, GRE General Test or MAT, 2 letters of recommendation, resume. Additional exam requirements/recommendations for international students: Required—TOEFL (minimum score 550 paper-based; 213 computer-based; 80 iBT). *Application deadline:* For fall admission, 6/15 priority date for domestic students, 6/15 for international students; for spring admission, 11/1 priority date for domestic students, 11/1 for international students. Applications are processed on a rolling basis. Application fee: $50. Electronic applications accepted. *Expenses:* Contact institution. *Financial support:* In 2011–12, 102 students received support, including 30 fellowships with full and partial tuition reimbursements available (averaging $10,664 per year); career-related internships or fieldwork, Federal Work-Study, and institutionally sponsored loans also available. Support available to part-time students. Financial award application deadline: 4/1; financial award applicants required to submit FAFSA. *Faculty research:* Predicting competent Head Start preschools, cultural differences. *Unit head:* Dr. Krisanne Bursik, Associate Dean and Acting Chair, 617-573-8261, Fax: 617-305-1743, E-mail: kbursik@suffolk.edu. *Application contact:* Ellen Driscoll, Director of Graduate Admissions, 617-573-8302, Fax: 617-305-1733, E-mail: grad.admission@suffolk.edu. Web site: http://www.suffolk.edu/college/9785.html.

Sul Ross State University, Rio Grande College of Sul Ross State University, Alpine, TX 79832. Offers business administration (MBA); teacher education (M Ed), including bilingual education, counseling, educational diagnostics, elementary education, general education, reading, school administration, secondary education. Part-time and evening/weekend programs available. Postbaccalaureate distance learning degree programs offered (no on-campus study). *Faculty:* 11 full-time (3 women), 4 part-time/adjunct (3 women). *Students:* 45 full-time (36 women), 255 part-time (168 women); includes 218 minority (2 Black or African American, non-Hispanic/Latino; 1 American Indian or Alaska Native, non-Hispanic/Latino; 215 Hispanic/Latino), 1 international. Average age 36. In 2011, 47 master's awarded. *Degree requirements:* For master's, comprehensive exam, thesis optional, minimum GPA of 3.0. *Entrance requirements:* For master's, GMAT or GRE General Test, minimum GPA of 2.5 in last 60 hours of undergraduate work. Additional exam requirements/recommendations for international students: Required—TOEFL. *Application deadline:* Applications are processed on a rolling basis. Application fee: $0 ($50 for international students). *Financial support:* Career-related internships or fieldwork, Federal Work-Study, and institutionally sponsored loans available. Support available to part-time students. Financial award application deadline: 5/1; financial award applicants required to submit FAFSA. *Unit head:* Dr. Paul Sorrels, Associate Provost/Dean, 512-278-3339, Fax: 512-278-3330. *Application contact:* Claudia R. Wright, Director of Admissions and Records, 915-837-8050, Fax: 915-837-8431, E-mail: rcullins@sulross.edu.

Sul Ross State University, School of Professional Studies, Department of Teacher Education, Program in School Administration, Alpine, TX 79832. Offers M Ed. Part-time and evening/weekend programs available. *Degree requirements:* For master's, thesis optional. *Entrance requirements:* For master's, GMAT or GRE General Test, minimum GPA of 2.5 in last 60 hours of undergraduate work.

Sul Ross State University, School of Professional Studies, Department of Teacher Education, Program in Supervision, Alpine, TX 79832. Offers M Ed. Part-time and evening/weekend programs available. *Degree requirements:* For master's, thesis optional. *Entrance requirements:* For master's, GMAT or GRE General Test, minimum GPA of 2.5 in last 60 hours of undergraduate work.

Syracuse University, School of Education, Program in Educational Leadership, Syracuse, NY 13244. Offers MS, Ed D, CAS. Part-time programs available. *Students:* 3 full-time (2 women), 67 part-time (46 women); includes 5 minority (2 Asian, non-Hispanic/Latino; 1 Hispanic/Latino; 2 Two or more races, non-Hispanic/Latino), 2 international. Average age 40. 17 applicants, 41% accepted, 5 enrolled. In 2011, 1 master's, 1 doctorate, 7 other advanced degrees awarded. *Degree requirements:* For master's, thesis or alternative; for doctorate, thesis/dissertation; for CAS, thesis. *Entrance requirements:* For doctorate, GRE, master's degree; for CAS, master's degree, minimum three years of teaching experience. Additional exam requirements/recommendations for international students: Required—TOEFL (minimum score 100 iBT). *Application deadline:* For fall admission, 2/1 priority date for domestic students, 2/1 for international students; for spring admission, 10/15 priority date for domestic students, 10/15 for international students. Applications are processed on a rolling basis. Application fee: $75. Electronic applications accepted. *Expenses: Tuition:* Part-time $1206 per credit. *Financial support:* Fellowships with full tuition reimbursements, research assistantships with full and partial tuition reimbursements, and teaching assistantships with full and partial tuition reimbursements available. Financial award application deadline: 1/1; financial award applicants required to submit FAFSA. *Unit head:* Dr. Joseph Shedd, Program Coordinator, 315-443-1468, E-mail: jbshedd@syr.edu. *Application contact:* Laurie Deyo, Graduate Recruiter, School of Education, 315-443-2505, E-mail: e-gradrcrt@syr.edu. Web site: http://soe.syr.edu/academic/teaching_and_leadership/graduate/CAS/educational_leadership/default.aspx.

Syracuse University, School of Education, Program in School District Business Leadership, Syracuse, NY 13244. Offers CAS. Part-time programs available. *Entrance requirements:* Additional exam requirements/recommendations for international students: Required—TOEFL (minimum score 100 iBT). *Application deadline:* For fall admission, 2/1 priority date for domestic students, 2/1 for international students. Applications are processed on a rolling basis. Electronic applications accepted. *Expenses: Tuition:* Part-time $1206 per credit. *Unit head:* Dr. Douglas Biklen, Dean, 315-443-4751. *Application contact:* Laurie Deyo, Graduate Recruiter, School of Education, 315-443-2505, E-mail: e-gradrcrt@syr.edu. Web site: http://soeweb.syr.edu/.

Tarleton State University, College of Graduate Studies, College of Education, Department of Educational Leadership and Policy Studies, Stephenville, TX 76402. Offers educational administration (M Ed); educational leadership (Ed D, Certificate). Part-time and evening/weekend programs available. Postbaccalaureate distance learning degree programs offered (minimal on-campus study). *Faculty:* 11 full-time (4 women), 6 part-time/adjunct (3 women). *Students:* 6 full-time (5 women), 129 part-time (89 women); includes 27 minority (12 Black or African American, non-Hispanic/Latino; 1 American Indian or Alaska Native, non-Hispanic/Latino; 12 Hispanic/Latino; 2 Two or more races, non-Hispanic/Latino). Average age 35. 37 applicants, 97% accepted, 30 enrolled. In 2011, 46 master's, 12 doctorates awarded. *Degree requirements:* For master's, comprehensive exam, thesis optional; for doctorate, thesis/dissertation. *Entrance requirements:* For master's, GRE General Test, minimum GPA of 3.0; for doctorate, GRE, 4 letters of reference, leadership portfolio. Additional exam requirements/recommendations for international students: Required—TOEFL (minimum score 550 paper-based; 213 computer-based; 80 iBT). *Application deadline:* For fall admission, 8/5 priority date for domestic students; for spring admission, 12/1 for domestic students. Applications are processed on a rolling basis. Application fee: $30 ($130 for international students). Electronic applications accepted. *Expenses:* Tuition, state resident: full-time $3131.46; part-time $174 per credit hour. Tuition, nonresident: full-time $8225; part-time $457 per credit hour. *Required fees:* $1446. Tuition and fees vary according to course load and campus/location. *Financial support:* Teaching assistantships, career-related internships or fieldwork, Federal Work-Study, and institutionally sponsored loans available. Support available to part-time students. Financial award application deadline: 5/1; financial award applicants required to submit FAFSA. *Unit head:* Dr. Mark Littleton, Interim Department Head, 254-968-9804, Fax: 254-968-9979, E-mail: mlittleton@tarleton.edu. *Application contact:* Information Contact, 254-968-9104, Fax: 254-968-9670, E-mail: gradoffice@tarleton.edu. Web site: http://www.tarleton.edu/~edd.

Tarleton State University, College of Graduate Studies, College of Education, Department of Psychology and Counseling, Stephenville, TX 76402. Offers counseling and psychology (M Ed), including counseling, counseling psychology, educational psychology; educational administration (M Ed); secondary education (Certificate); special education (Certificate). Part-time and evening/weekend programs available. Postbaccalaureate distance learning degree programs offered (minimal on-campus study). *Faculty:* 8 full-time (5 women), 13 part-time/adjunct (6 women). *Students:* 73 full-time (62 women), 219 part-time (186 women); includes 55 minority (25 Black or African American, non-Hispanic/Latino; 1 American Indian or Alaska Native, non-Hispanic/Latino; 1 Asian, non-Hispanic/Latino; 22 Hispanic/Latino; 1 Native Hawaiian or other Pacific Islander, non-Hispanic/Latino; 5 Two or more races, non-Hispanic/Latino), 1 international. Average age 35. 92 applicants, 91% accepted, 62 enrolled. In 2011, 65 master's awarded. *Degree requirements:* For master's, comprehensive exam, thesis optional. *Entrance requirements:* For master's, GRE General Test, minimum GPA of 3.0. Additional exam requirements/recommendations for international students: Required—TOEFL (minimum score 550 paper-based; 213 computer-based; 80 iBT). *Application deadline:* For fall admission, 8/5 priority date for domestic students; for spring admission, 12/1 for domestic students. Applications are processed on a rolling basis. Application fee: $30 ($130 for international students). Electronic applications accepted. *Expenses:* Tuition, state resident: full-time $3131.46; part-time $174 per credit hour. Tuition, nonresident: full-time $8225; part-time $457 per credit hour. *Required fees:* $1446. Tuition and fees vary according to course load and campus/location. *Financial support:* Research assistantships, teaching assistantships, career-related internships or fieldwork, Federal Work-Study, institutionally sponsored loans, and tuition waivers (partial) available. Support available to part-time students. Financial award application deadline: 5/1; financial award applicants required to submit FAFSA. *Unit head:* Dr. Bob Newby, Interim Department Head, 254-968-9813, Fax: 254-968-1991, E-mail: newby@tarleton.edu. *Application contact:* Information Contact, 254-968-9104, Fax: 254-968-9670, E-mail: gradoffice@tarleton.edu. Web site: http://www.tarleton.edu/~dpc.

Teacher Education University, Graduate Programs, Winter Park, FL 32789. Offers educational leadership (MA); educational technology (MA); elementary education K-6 (MA); instructional strategies (MA Ed); school guidance and counseling (MA).

Teachers College, Columbia University, Graduate Faculty of Education, Department of Education Policy and Social Analysis, Program in Leadership, Policy and Politics, New York, NY 10027-6696. Offers Ed M, MA, Ed D, PhD, MBA/Ed D. *Faculty:* 9 full-time (4 women), 3 part-time/adjunct (0 women). *Students:* 58 full-time (39 women), 174 part-time (97 women); includes 89 minority (37 Black or African American, non-Hispanic/Latino; 29 Asian, non-Hispanic/Latino; 20 Hispanic/Latino; 3 Two or more races, non-Hispanic/Latino), 8 international. Average age 32. 147 applicants, 61% accepted, 37 enrolled. *Degree requirements:* For doctorate, thesis/dissertation. *Entrance requirements:* For master's, GRE, at least 3 years of full-time teaching experience (private school leadership); at least 3 years of teaching and/or administrative experience (for Ed M in public school and school district leadership); for doctorate, GRE, at least three years of teaching and/or administrative experience (for Ed D in public school and school district leadership). *Application deadline:* For fall admission, 12/15 for domestic students. Application fee: $65. *Financial support:* Applicants required to submit FAFSA. *Faculty research:* Legal issues in education, educational equity, leadership for adult learning and development, decentralization in education, professional development of teachers and administrators. *Unit head:* Prof. Craig E. Richards, Coordinator/Program Director of Summer Principals Academy, 212-678-3420, E-mail: edleadership@tc.edu. *Application contact:* Debbie Lesperance, Assistant Director of Admission, 212-678-3710, Fax: 212-678-4171.

Teachers College, Columbia University, Graduate Faculty of Education, Department of Organization and Leadership, Program in Private School Leadership, New York,, NY 10027. Offers Ed M, MA. *Faculty:* 4 full-time (3 women), 3 part-time/adjunct (1 woman). *Entrance requirements:* For master's, minimum of three years full-time head teaching experience. *Application deadline:* For fall admission, 1/15 priority date for domestic students. *Faculty research:* Independent schools on issues of leadership, governance, professional development and the attraction and retention of teachers. *Unit head:* Prof. Pearl Rock Kane, Director of the Klingenstein Center, 212-678-3156. *Application contact:* Debbie Lesperance, Assistant Director of Admission, 212-678-3710, Fax: 212-678-4171. Web site: http://klingenstein.org/.

Teachers College, Columbia University, Graduate Faculty of Education, Department of Organization and Leadership, Urban Education Leaders Program, New York, NY 10027. Offers Ed D. *Faculty:* 6 full-time (2 women), 1 part-time/adjunct (0 women). *Entrance requirements:* For doctorate, GRE, master's degree in education leadership, curriculum and teaching, or another relevant field; at least 3 years of teaching experience. *Faculty research:* School leadership, qualitative research methods, and supporting adult development in K-12 schools; ABE/ESOL programs and higher education contexts; school choice reforms. *Unit head:* Dr. Brian Keith Perkins, Director, 212-678-3071, E-mail: bp58@tc.columbia.edu. *Application contact:* Gibran Majdalany, Associate Director, 212-678-3812, E-mail: gm84@tc.columbia.edu. Web site: http://uelp.tc.columbia.edu/.

Teachers College, Columbia University, Graduate Faculty of Education, Program in Administration and Supervision in Special Education, New York, NY 10027-6696. Offers Ed M, MA, Ed D, PhD. *Accreditation:* NCATE. *Faculty:* 7 full-time (4 women), 11 part-time/adjunct (10 women). *Students:* 1 part-time (0 women); minority (Asian, non-Hispanic/Latino). Average age 31. In 2011, 2 degrees awarded. *Degree requirements:* For doctorate, thesis/dissertation. *Application deadline:* For fall admission, 5/15 for domestic students. Application fee: $65. *Financial support:* Career-related internships or fieldwork, Federal Work-Study, institutionally sponsored loans, and tuition waivers (full and partial) available. Support available to part-time students. Financial award application deadline: 2/1. *Faculty research:* Cognition and comprehension, disability studies, self-determination, literacy development. *Unit head:* Stephen T. Peverly, Chair, 212-678-3964, Fax: 212-678-8259, E-mail: stp4@columbia.edu. *Application contact:* Thomas P. Rock, Director of Admissions, 212-678-3083, Fax: 212-678-4171, E-mail: rock@tc.edu. Web site: http://www.tc.columbia.edu/hbs/SpecialEd/.

Temple University, College of Education, Department of Educational Leadership and Policy Studies, Philadelphia, PA 19122-6096. Offers educational administration (Ed M, Ed D); urban education (Ed M, Ed D). Part-time and evening/weekend programs available. *Faculty:* 11 full-time (6 women). *Students:* 69 full-time (43 women), 97 part-time (58 women); includes 46 minority (36 Black or African American, non-Hispanic/Latino; 4 Asian, non-Hispanic/Latino; 2 Hispanic/Latino; 4 Two or more races, non-Hispanic/Latino), 1 international. Average age 34. 107 applicants, 56% accepted, 37 enrolled. In 2011, 29 master's, 11 doctorates awarded. Terminal master's awarded for partial completion of doctoral program. *Degree requirements:* For master's, comprehensive exam, thesis or alternative; for doctorate, thesis/dissertation, preliminary exam. *Entrance requirements:* For master's and doctorate, GRE General Test or MAT, minimum GPA of 3.0. Additional exam requirements/recommendations for international students: Required—TOEFL (minimum score 550 paper-based; 213 computer-based; 79 iBT). *Application deadline:* For fall admission, 12/15 for international students; for spring admission, 8/1 for international students. Application fee: $50. Electronic applications accepted. *Expenses:* Tuition, state resident: full-time $12,366; part-time $687 per credit hour. Tuition, nonresident: full-time $17,298; part-time $961 per credit hour. *Required fees:* $590; $213 per year. *Financial support:* Fellowships, research assistantships with full tuition reimbursements, teaching assistantships with full tuition reimbursements, career-related internships or fieldwork, and Federal Work-Study available. Financial award application deadline: 1/15; financial award applicants required to submit FAFSA. *Faculty research:* Women in education, school effectiveness, financial policy, school improvement in city schools, nongraded schools. *Unit head:* Dr. Corrinne Caldwell, Chair, 215-204-6174, Fax: 215-204-2743, E-mail: corrinne.caldwell@temple.edu. *Application contact:* Dr. Margo Greicar, Director for Graduate Academic and Student Affairs, 215-204-8011, Fax: 215-204-4383, E-mail: margo.greicar@temple.edu. Web site: http://www.temple.edu/education/elps.

Tennessee State University, The School of Graduate Studies and Research, College of Education, Department of Educational Administration, Nashville, TN 37209-1561. Offers administration and supervision (M Ed, Ed D, Ed S). *Accreditation:* NCATE. *Entrance requirements:* For master's, GRE General Test, GRE Subject Test, minimum GPA of 2.5; for doctorate, GRE General Test, MAT, interview, minimum GPA of 3.25, work experience.

Tennessee Technological University, Graduate School, College of Education, Department of Curriculum and Instruction, Program in Instructional Leadership, Cookeville, TN 38505. Offers MA, Ed S. *Accreditation:* NCATE. Part-time and evening/weekend programs available. *Faculty:* 9 full-time (3 women). *Students:* 89 part-time (65 women); includes 8 minority (5 Black or African American, non-Hispanic/Latino; 1 American Indian or Alaska Native, non-Hispanic/Latino; 1 Asian, non-Hispanic/Latino; 1 Hispanic/Latino). Average age 27. 42 applicants, 71% accepted, 20 enrolled. In 2011, 98 master's, 62 other advanced degrees awarded. *Degree requirements:* For master's and Ed S, comprehensive exam, thesis or alternative. *Entrance requirements:* For master's and Ed S, MAT or GRE. Additional exam requirements/recommendations for international students: Required—TOEFL (minimum score 550 paper-based; 71 iBT), IELTS (minimum score 5.5), Pearson Test of English Academic. *Application deadline:* For fall admission, 8/1 for domestic students, 5/1 for international students; for spring admission, 12/1 for domestic students, 10/1 for international students. Application fee: $25 ($30 for international students). Electronic applications accepted. *Expenses:* Tuition, state resident: full-time $8094; part-time $422 per credit hour. Tuition, nonresident: full-time $20,574; part-time $1046 per credit hour. *Financial support:* In 2011–12, 33 fellowships (averaging $8,000 per year), 11 research assistantships (averaging $4,000 per year), 7 teaching assistantships (averaging $4,000 per year) were awarded; career-related internships or fieldwork also available. Financial award application deadline: 4/1. *Faculty research:* School board member training, community school education. *Unit head:* Dr. Susan Gore, Interim Chairperson, 931-372-3181, Fax: 931-372-6270, E-mail: sgore@tntech.edu. *Application contact:* Shelia K. Kendrick, Coordinator of Graduate Admissions, 931-372-3808, Fax: 931-372-3497, E-mail: skendrick@tntech.edu.

Tennessee Temple University, Graduate Studies in Education, Program in Educational Leadership, Chattanooga, TN 37404-3587. Offers M Ed. *Degree requirements:* For master's, comprehensive exam, thesis or alternative. *Entrance requirements:* For master's, GRE, minimum cumulative undergraduate GPA of 3.0, 3 references.

Texas A&M International University, Office of Graduate Studies and Research, College of Education, Department of Professional Programs, Laredo, TX 78041-1900. Offers educational administration (MS Ed); generic special education (MS Ed); school counseling (MS). *Faculty:* 11 full-time (5 women), 1 part-time/adjunct (0 women). *Students:* 11 full-time (8 women), 115 part-time (90 women); includes 125 minority (2 Black or African American, non-Hispanic/Latino; 123 Hispanic/Latino). Average age 34. 33 applicants, 79% accepted, 18 enrolled. In 2011, 42 master's awarded. *Entrance requirements:* Additional exam requirements/recommendations for international students: Required—TOEFL (minimum score 550 paper-based; 213 computer-based; 79 iBT). *Application deadline:* For fall admission, 4/30 priority date for domestic students, 4/30 for international students; for spring admission, 11/30 priority date for domestic students, 10/1 for international students. Application fee: $35 ($50 for international students). *Expenses:* Tuition, state resident: full-time $5063. *Financial support:* In 2011–12, 5 students received support, including 3 fellowships, 2 research assistantships; Federal Work-Study, scholarships/grants, and unspecified assistantships also available. Financial award application deadline: 4/1. *Unit head:* Dr. Randel Brown, Chair, 956-326-2679, E-mail: brown@tamiu.edu. *Application contact:* Suzanne H. Alford, Director of Admissions, 956-326-3023, E-mail: graduateschool@tamiu.edu. Web site: http://www.tamiu.edu/coedu/DOPPPrograms.shtml.

Texas A&M University, College of Education and Human Development, Department of Educational Administration and Human Resource Development, College Station, TX 77843. Offers adult education (PhD); higher education administration (MS, PhD); human resource development (MS, PhD); public school administration (M Ed, Ed D, PhD). Part-time programs available. *Faculty:* 31. *Students:* 126 full-time (88 women), 270 part-time (156 women); includes 162 minority (65 Black or African American, non-Hispanic/Latino; 2 American Indian or Alaska Native, non-Hispanic/Latino; 15 Asian, non-Hispanic/Latino; 77 Hispanic/Latino; 3 Two or more races, non-Hispanic/Latino), 23 international. Average age 37. In 2011, 91 master's, 30 doctorates awarded. *Degree requirements:* For master's, thesis optional; for doctorate, thesis/dissertation. *Entrance requirements:* For master's, GRE General Test, writing exam, interview, professional experience; for doctorate, GRE General Test, writing exam, interview/presentation, professional experience. Additional exam requirements/recommendations for international students: Required—TOEFL. *Application deadline:* For fall admission, 12/1 for domestic and international students; for spring admission, 8/15 for domestic and international students. Application fee: $50 ($75 for international students). Electronic applications accepted. *Expenses:* Tuition, state resident: full-time $5437; part-time $226.55 per credit hour. Tuition, nonresident: full-time $12,949; part-time $539.55 per credit hour. *Required fees:* $2741. *Financial support:* In 2011–12, fellowships (averaging $20,000 per year), research assistantships (averaging $12,000 per year) were awarded; career-related internships or fieldwork and institutionally sponsored loans also available. Support available to part-time students. Financial award application deadline: 3/1; financial award applicants required to submit FAFSA. *Faculty research:* Higher education administration, public school administration, student affairs. *Unit head:* Dr. Fred M. Nafukho, Head, 979-862-3395, Fax: 979-862-4347, E-mail: fnafukho@tamu.edu. *Application contact:* Joyce Nelson, Director of Academic Advising, 979-847-9098, Fax: 979-862-4347, E-mail: jnelson@tamu.edu. Web site: http://eahr.tamu.edu.

Texas A&M University–Commerce, Graduate School, College of Education and Human Services, Department of Educational Leadership, Commerce, TX 75429-3011. Offers educational administration (M Ed, Ed D); educational technology (M Ed, MS); higher education (MS, Ed D); training and development (MS). Part-time programs available. Terminal master's awarded for partial completion of doctoral program. *Degree requirements:* For master's, comprehensive exam, thesis (for some programs); for doctorate, thesis/dissertation, departmental qualifying exam. *Entrance requirements:* For master's, GRE General Test; for doctorate, GRE General Test, writing skills exam, interview. Electronic applications accepted. *Faculty research:* Property tax reform, politics of education, administrative stress.

Texas A&M University–Corpus Christi, Graduate Studies and Research, College of Education, Program in Educational Administration, Corpus Christi, TX 78412-5503. Offers MS. Part-time and evening/weekend programs available. *Degree requirements:*

For master's, comprehensive exam, thesis (for some programs). *Entrance requirements:* For master's, GRE General Test. Additional exam requirements/recommendations for international students: Required—TOEFL. Electronic applications accepted.

Texas A&M University–Corpus Christi, Graduate Studies and Research, College of Education, Program in Educational Leadership, Corpus Christi, TX 78412-5503. Offers Ed D. Program offered jointly with Texas A&M University–Kingsville. Part-time and evening/weekend programs available. *Degree requirements:* For doctorate, comprehensive exam, thesis/dissertation. *Entrance requirements:* Additional exam requirements/recommendations for international students: Required—TOEFL. Electronic applications accepted.

Texas A&M University–Kingsville, College of Graduate Studies, College of Education, Department of Education, Program in Higher Education Administration Leadership, Kingsville, TX 78363. Offers PhD. Program offered jointly with Texas A&M University. *Degree requirements:* For doctorate, one foreign language, comprehensive exam, thesis/dissertation. *Entrance requirements:* For doctorate, GRE General Test, MAT, minimum GPA of 3.25.

Texas A&M University–Kingsville, College of Graduate Studies, College of Education, Department of Education, Program in School Administration, Kingsville, TX 78363. Offers MA, MS, Ed D. Ed D offered jointly with Texas A&M University–Corpus Christi. Part-time and evening/weekend programs available. *Degree requirements:* For master's, comprehensive exam, mini-thesis; for doctorate, one foreign language, comprehensive exam, thesis/dissertation. *Entrance requirements:* For master's, GRE General Test, MAT, minimum GPA of 3.0; for doctorate, GRE General Test, MAT, minimum GPA of 3.25. *Faculty research:* Funding sources in public education.

Texas A&M University–Kingsville, College of Graduate Studies, College of Education, Department of Education, Program in Supervision, Kingsville, TX 78363. Offers MA, MS. Part-time programs available. *Degree requirements:* For master's, comprehensive exam, mini-thesis. *Entrance requirements:* For master's, GRE General Test, MAT, minimum GPA of 3.0.

Texas A&M University–San Antonio, Department of Leadership and Counseling, San Antonio, TX 78224. Offers counseling and guidance (MA); educational leadership (MA). Part-time and evening/weekend programs available. *Faculty:* 12 full-time (7 women), 7 part-time/adjunct (5 women). *Students:* 108 full-time (83 women), 157 part-time (131 women). Average age 35. In 2011, 70 master's awarded. *Degree requirements:* For master's, comprehensive exam, thesis or alternative. *Entrance requirements:* For master's, MAT. Additional exam requirements/recommendations for international students: Required—TOEFL (minimum score 550 paper-based; 213 computer-based; 80 iBT), IELTS (minimum score 6). *Application deadline:* For fall admission, 8/15 priority date for domestic students, 6/1 for international students; for spring admission, 12/15 priority date for domestic students, 10/1 for international students. Applications are processed on a rolling basis. Application fee: $35 ($50 for international students). Electronic applications accepted. *Expenses:* Tuition, state resident: part-time $691.11 per course. Tuition, nonresident: part-time $1621.11 per course. *Financial support:* Application deadline: 3/31; applicants required to submit FAFSA. *Unit head:* Dr. Albert Valadez, Department Chair, 210-932-7843, E-mail: albert.valadez@tamusa.tamus.edu. *Application contact:* Jennifer M. Dovalina, Graduate Admissions Specialist, 210-784-1380, E-mail: graduateadmissions@tamusa.tamus.edu. Web site: http://www.tamusa.tamus.edu/leadership-counseling/.

Texas A&M University–Texarkana, Graduate Studies and Research, College of Education and Liberal Arts, Texarkana, TX 75505-5518. Offers adult education (MS); curriculum and instruction (M Ed); education (MS); educational administration (M Ed); English (MA); instructional technology (MS); interdisciplinary studies (MA, MS); special education (MS). Part-time and evening/weekend programs available. *Degree requirements:* For master's, comprehensive exam (for some programs), thesis optional. *Entrance requirements:* For master's, minimum GPA of 2.5 on last 60 hours of bachelor's degree. Additional exam requirements/recommendations for international students: Required—TOEFL. Electronic applications accepted.

Texas Christian University, College of Education, Ed D in Educational Leadership Program, Fort Worth, TX 76129-0002. Offers educational leadership (Ed D); higher education (Ed D). Part-time and evening/weekend programs available. *Faculty:* 27 full-time (21 women), 1 part-time/adjunct. *Students:* 8 full-time (7 women), 16 part-time (7 women); includes 8 minority (5 Black or African American, non-Hispanic/Latino; 1 American Indian or Alaska Native, non-Hispanic/Latino; 1 Asian, non-Hispanic/Latino; 1 Hispanic/Latino). Average age 37. 15 applicants, 40% accepted, 6 enrolled. In 2011, 7 doctorates awarded. *Degree requirements:* For doctorate, comprehensive exam, thesis/dissertation. *Entrance requirements:* For doctorate, GRE or MAT. Additional exam requirements/recommendations for international students: Required—TOEFL (minimum score 550 paper-based; 213 computer-based; 80 iBT). *Application deadline:* For winter admission, 2/1 for domestic and international students. Application fee: $60. Electronic applications accepted. *Expenses: Tuition:* Full-time $20,250; part-time $1125 per credit hour. Part-time tuition and fees vary according to course load and program. *Financial support:* Teaching assistantships with full tuition reimbursements, career-related internships or fieldwork, scholarships/grants, and unspecified assistantships available. Financial award application deadline: 2/1. *Unit head:* Dr. Jan Lacina, Associate Dean, 817-257-6786, E-mail: j.lacina@tcu.edu. *Application contact:* Patricia Garcia, Academic Program Specialist, 817-257-7661, E-mail: p.m.garcia@tcu.edu. Web site: http://www.coe.tcu.edu/187.asp.

Texas Christian University, College of Education, Program in Educational Leadership, Fort Worth, TX 76129-0002. Offers educational leadership (M Ed); principal (Certificate). Part-time and evening/weekend programs available. *Faculty:* 27 full-time (21 women), 1 part-time/adjunct. *Students:* 12 full-time (8 women), 31 part-time (15 women); includes 9 minority (5 Black or African American, non-Hispanic/Latino; 1 American Indian or Alaska Native, non-Hispanic/Latino; 1 Asian, non-Hispanic/Latino; 1 Hispanic/Latino; 1 Two or more races, non-Hispanic/Latino), 3 international. Average age 43. 28 applicants, 89% accepted, 18 enrolled. In 2011, 20 master's awarded. *Entrance requirements:* Additional exam requirements/recommendations for international students: Required—TOEFL (minimum score 550 paper-based; 213 computer-based; 80 iBT). *Application deadline:* For fall admission, 11/15 for domestic students, 11/16 for international students; for spring admission, 3/1 for domestic and international students. Application fee: $60. Electronic applications accepted. *Expenses: Tuition:* Full-time $20,250; part-time $1125 per credit hour. Part-time tuition and fees vary according to course load and program. *Financial support:* Teaching assistantships with full tuition reimbursements, career-related internships or fieldwork, scholarships/grants, and unspecified assistantships available. Financial award application deadline: 3/1. *Unit head:* Dr. Jan Lacina, Associate Dean, 817-257-6786, E-mail: j.lacina@tcu.edu. *Application contact:* Patricia Garcia, Academic Program Specialist, 817-257-7661, E-mail: p.m.garcia@tcu.edu. Web site: http://www.coe.tcu.edu/187.asp.

Texas Christian University, The Neeley School of Business at TCU, MBA/Ed D in Educational Leadership Joint Program, Fort Worth, TX 76129-0002. Offers MBA/Ed D. Part-time and evening/weekend programs available. *Faculty:* 44 full-time (23 women), 2 part-time/adjunct (1 woman). *Students:* 1 full-time. Average age 32. *Entrance requirements:* Additional exam requirements/recommendations for international students: Required—TOEFL (minimum score 550 paper-based; 213 computer-based; 80 iBT). *Application deadline:* For fall admission, 2/1 for domestic and international students. Application fee: $60. *Expenses: Tuition:* Full-time $20,250; part-time $1125 per credit hour. Part-time tuition and fees vary according to course load and program. *Financial support:* Teaching assistantships with full tuition reimbursements, career-related internships or fieldwork, scholarships/grants, and unspecified assistantships available. Support available to part-time students. Financial award application deadline: 3/1; financial award applicants required to submit FAFSA. *Unit head:* Dr. Jan Lacina, Associate Dean, 817-257-6786, E-mail: j.lacina@tcu.edu. *Application contact:* Patricia Garcia, Graduate Program Specialist, 817-257-7661, E-mail: p.m.garcia@tcu.edu. Web site: http://www.coe.tcu.edu/187.asp.

Texas Southern University, College of Education, Department of Educational Administration and Foundation, Houston, TX 77004-4584. Offers educational administration (M Ed, Ed D). Part-time and evening/weekend programs available. *Degree requirements:* For master's, comprehensive exam; for doctorate, comprehensive exam, thesis/dissertation. *Entrance requirements:* For master's, GRE General Test, minimum GPA of 2.5; for doctorate, GRE General Test or MAT, master's degree, minimum B+ average. Additional exam requirements/recommendations for international students: Required—TOEFL. Electronic applications accepted.

Texas State University–San Marcos, Graduate School, College of Education, Department of Counseling, Leadership, Adult Education, and School Psychology, Program in Educational Leadership, San Marcos, TX 78666. Offers M Ed, MA, PhD. Part-time and evening/weekend programs available. *Faculty:* 4 full-time (2 women), 10 part-time/adjunct (6 women). *Students:* 1 (woman) full-time, 81 part-time (65 women); includes 40 minority (8 Black or African American, non-Hispanic/Latino; 2 Asian, non-Hispanic/Latino; 29 Hispanic/Latino; 1 Two or more races, non-Hispanic/Latino). Average age 35. 77 applicants, 61% accepted, 38 enrolled. In 2011, 54 master's, 2 doctorates awarded. *Degree requirements:* For master's, comprehensive exam, thesis (for some programs). *Entrance requirements:* For master's, GRE General Test, minimum GPA of 2.75 in last 60 hours of course work. Additional exam requirements/recommendations for international students: Required—TOEFL (minimum score 550 paper-based; 213 computer-based; 78 iBT). *Application deadline:* For fall admission, 6/15 for domestic students, 6/1 for international students. Applications are processed on a rolling basis. Application fee: $40 ($90 for international students). Electronic applications accepted. *Expenses:* Tuition, state resident: full-time $6408; part-time $3204 per semester. Tuition, nonresident: full-time $14,832; part-time $7416 per semester. *Required fees:* $1824; $912 per semester. Tuition and fees vary according to course load. *Financial support:* In 2011–12, 47 students received support, including 2 research assistantships (averaging $23,157 per year), 2 teaching assistantships (averaging $18,528 per year); career-related internships or fieldwork, Federal Work-Study, and institutionally sponsored loans also available. Support available to part-time students. Financial award application deadline: 4/1; financial award applicants required to submit FAFSA. *Faculty research:* Superintendency, middle management, supervision, junior college. *Unit head:* Dr. Miguel Guajardo, Graduate Advisor, 512-245-2575, E-mail: mg50@txstate.edu. *Application contact:* Dr. J. Michael Willoughby, Dean of Graduate School, 512-245-2581, Fax: 512-245-8365, E-mail: gradcollege@txstate.edu. Web site: http://www.txstate.edu/clas/Educational-Leadership.html.

Texas State University–San Marcos, Graduate School, Interdisciplinary Studies Program in Educational Administration and Psychological Services, San Marcos, TX 78666. Offers MAIS. *Degree requirements:* For master's, comprehensive exam. *Entrance requirements:* Additional exam requirements/recommendations for international students: Required—TOEFL (minimum score 550 paper-based; 213 computer-based; 78 iBT). *Application deadline:* For fall admission, 6/15 priority date for domestic students; for spring admission, 10/15 priority date for domestic students. Applications are processed on a rolling basis. Application fee: $40 ($90 for international students). *Expenses:* Tuition, state resident: full-time $6408; part-time $3204 per semester. Tuition, nonresident: full-time $14,832; part-time $7416 per semester. *Required fees:* $1824; $912 per semester. Tuition and fees vary according to course load. *Financial support:* Application deadline: 4/1. *Unit head:* Dr. Stan Carpenter, Dean, 512-245-2575, Fax: 512-245-8345, E-mail: sc33@txstate.edu. *Application contact:* Dr. J. Michael Willoughby, Dean of Graduate School, 512-245-2581, Fax: 512-245-8365, E-mail: gradcollege@txstate.edu. Web site: http://www.txstate.edu/clas/Educational-Leadership/Program-Information.html.

Texas Tech University, Graduate School, College of Education, Department of Educational Psychology and Leadership, Lubbock, TX 79409. Offers counselor education (M Ed, PhD); educational leadership (M Ed, Ed D); educational psychology (M Ed, PhD); higher education (M Ed, Ed D); higher education: higher education research (PhD); instructional technology (M Ed, Ed D); instructional technology: distance education (M Ed); special education (M Ed, Ed D). *Accreditation:* ACA; NCATE. Part-time programs available. Postbaccalaureate distance learning degree programs offered (no on-campus study). *Students:* 180 full-time (133 women), 418 part-time (297 women); includes 127 minority (34 Black or African American, non-Hispanic/Latino; 3 American Indian or Alaska Native, non-Hispanic/Latino; 6 Asian, non-Hispanic/Latino; 76 Hispanic/Latino; 8 Two or more races, non-Hispanic/Latino), 41 international. Average age 36. 478 applicants, 42% accepted, 134 enrolled. In 2011, 139 master's, 30 doctorates awarded. *Degree requirements:* For master's, thesis optional; for doctorate, thesis/dissertation. *Entrance requirements:* For master's and doctorate, GRE General Test. Additional exam requirements/recommendations for international students: Required—TOEFL (minimum score 550 paper-based; 213 computer-based; 79 iBT). *Application deadline:* For fall admission, 6/1 priority date for domestic students, 1/15 for international students; for spring admission, 9/1 priority date for domestic students, 6/15 for international students. Applications are processed on a rolling basis. Application fee: $50 ($75 for international students). Electronic applications accepted. *Expenses:* Tuition, state resident: full-time $5899; part-time $245.80 per credit hour. Tuition, nonresident: full-time $13,411; part-time $558.80 per credit hour. *Required fees:* $2680.60; $86.50 per credit hour. $920.30 per semester. *Financial support:* In 2011–12, 142 students received support. Application deadline: 4/15; applicants required to submit FAFSA. *Faculty research:* Psychological processes of teaching and learning, teaching populations with special needs, instructional technology, educational administration in education, theories and practice in counseling and counselor education K-12 and higher. *Total annual research expenditures:* $1.4 million. *Unit head:* Dr. William Lan, Chair, 806-742-1998 Ext. 436, Fax: 806-742-2179, E-mail: william.lan@ttu.edu. *Application contact:* Dr. Hansel Burley, Associate Academic Dean, 806-742-1998 Ext. 447, Fax: 806-742-2179, E-mail: hansel.burley@ttu.edu.

Texas Woman's University, Graduate School, College of Professional Education, Department of Teacher Education, Denton, TX 76201. Offers administration (M Ed, MA); special education (M Ed, MA, PhD), including educational diagnostician (M Ed, MA); teaching, learning, and curriculum (M Ed). Part-time programs available. *Faculty:* 27 full-time (20 women), 2 part-time/adjunct (both women). *Students:* 14 full-time (12 women), 164 part-time (142 women); includes 68 minority (33 Black or African American, non-Hispanic/Latino; 1 American Indian or Alaska Native, non-Hispanic/Latino; 6 Asian, non-Hispanic/Latino; 28 Hispanic/Latino), 1 international. Average age 37. 38 applicants, 74% accepted, 24 enrolled. In 2011, 67 master's, 4 doctorates awarded. Terminal master's awarded for partial completion of doctoral program. *Degree requirements:* For master's, comprehensive exam, thesis, professional paper (M Ed); for doctorate, comprehensive exam, thesis/dissertation. *Entrance requirements:* For master's, minimum GPA of 3.0 on last 60 undergraduate hours, 2 letters of reference, resume, copy of certifications, teacher service record, statement of intent; for doctorate, GRE General Test, minimum GPA of 3.0, 3 letters of reference, resume, copy of certifications, teacher service record, statement of intent. Additional exam requirements/ recommendations for international students: Required—TOEFL (minimum score 550 paper-based; 213 computer-based; 79 iBT). *Application deadline:* For fall admission, 7/1 priority date for domestic students, 3/1 for international students; for spring admission, 11/1 priority date for domestic students, 7/1 for international students. Applications are processed on a rolling basis. Application fee: $50 ($75 for international students). Electronic applications accepted. *Expenses:* Tuition, state resident: full-time $3834; part-time $213 per credit hour. Tuition, nonresident: full-time $9468; part-time $526 per credit hour. *Required fees:* $213 per credit hour. Tuition and fees vary according to course load. *Financial support:* In 2011–12, 42 students received support, including 8 research assistantships (averaging $12,942 per year); career-related internships or fieldwork, Federal Work-Study, institutionally sponsored loans, scholarships/grants, traineeships, health care benefits, and unspecified assistantships also available. Support available to part-time students. Financial award application deadline: 3/1; financial award applicants required to submit FAFSA. *Faculty research:* Language and literacy, classroom management, learning disabilities, staff and professional development, leadership preparation practice. *Unit head:* Dr. Jane Pemberton, Chair, 940-898-2271, Fax: 940-898-2270, E-mail: mrule1@twu.edu. *Application contact:* Dr. Samuel Wheeler, Assistant Director of Admissions, 940-898-3188, Fax: 940-898-3081, E-mail: wheelersr@twu.edu. Web site: http://www.twu.edu/teacher-education/.

Thomas Edison State College, Heavin School of Arts and Sciences, Program in Educational Leadership, Trenton, NJ 08608-1176. Offers MAEL. Part-time programs available. Postbaccalaureate distance learning degree programs offered (no on-campus study). *Students:* 90 part-time (57 women); includes 22 minority (10 Black or African American, non-Hispanic/Latino; 1 Asian, non-Hispanic/Latino; 11 Hispanic/Latino). Average age 38. In 2011, 23 master's awarded. *Degree requirements:* For master's, field-based practicum, professional portfolio development. *Entrance requirements:* For master's, at least 3 years of teaching experience; valid teacher's certification; letter of recommendation from a building-level administrator; school setting and on-site mentor available to conduct site-based fieldwork and inquiry projects successfully for each course; statement of goals and objectives. Additional exam requirements/ recommendations for international students: Required—TOEFL (minimum score 550 paper-based; 213 computer-based; 79 iBT). *Application deadline:* For fall admission, 8/ 15 priority date for domestic students, 8/15 for international students; for winter admission, 11/15 priority date for domestic students, 11/15 for international students; for spring admission, 2/15 priority date for domestic students, 2/15 for international students. Applications are processed on a rolling basis. Application fee: $75. Electronic applications accepted. *Financial support:* Applicants required to submit FAFSA. *Unit head:* Dr. Susan Davenport, Dean, Heavin School of Arts and Sciences, 609-984-1130, Fax: 609-984-0740, E-mail: info@tesc.edu. *Application contact:* David Hoftiezer, Director of Admissions, 888-442-8372, Fax: 609-984-8447, E-mail: admissions@ tese.edu. Web site: http://www.tesc.edu/1844.php.

Touro College, Graduate School of Education, New York, NY 10010. Offers bilingual programs (Advanced Certificate); education and special education (MS); gifted and talented education (Advanced Certificate); instructional technology (MS); mathematics education (MS); school leadership (MS); teaching children with autism and other severe or multiple disabilities (Advanced Certificate); teaching English to speakers of other languages (MS, Advanced Certificate); teaching literacy (MS). Part-time and evening/ weekend programs available. Postbaccalaureate distance learning degree programs offered (no on-campus study). *Faculty:* 75 full-time, 131 part-time/adjunct. *Students:* 382 full-time (324 women), 3,790 part-time (3,196 women); includes 1,211 minority (537 Black or African American, non-Hispanic/Latino; 4 American Indian or Alaska Native, non-Hispanic/Latino; 187 Asian, non-Hispanic/Latino; 472 Hispanic/Latino; 3 Native Hawaiian or other Pacific Islander, non-Hispanic/Latino; 8 Two or more races, non-Hispanic/Latino), 1 international. 1,422 applicants, 50% accepted, 675 enrolled. In 2011, 6 master's, 4 other advanced degrees awarded. *Application deadline:* For fall admission, 8/26 for domestic students, 7/15 for international students; for spring admission, 12/31 for domestic students, 12/15 for international students. Applications are processed on a rolling basis. Application fee: $50. *Financial support:* Federal Work-Study available. Financial award applicants required to submit FAFSA. *Faculty research:* Equity assistance, language development, scholar communications, Latin American studies and cultural sensitivity, behavior management techniques and strategies in special education. *Unit head:* Dr. LaMar Miller, Dean, 212-463-0400 Ext. 5561, Fax: 212-462-4889, E-mail: lpmiller@touro.edu. *Application contact:* Natalie Arroyo, Admissions Assistant, 212-463-0400 Ext. 5119, E-mail: natalie.arroyo@touro.edu.

Trevecca Nazarene University, College of Lifelong Learning, School of Education, Major in Educational Leadership, Nashville, TN 37210-2877. Offers M Ed. Part-time and evening/weekend programs available. *Students:* 65 full-time (47 women), 4 part-time (3 women); includes 19 minority (all Black or African American, non-Hispanic/Latino). In 2011, 49 master's awarded. *Degree requirements:* For master's, exit assessment. *Entrance requirements:* For master's, GRE General Test, MAT, interview, minimum GPA of 2.7, 2 references. Additional exam requirements/recommendations for international students: Required—TOEFL (minimum score 550 paper-based; 213 computer-based). *Application deadline:* Applications are processed on a rolling basis. Application fee: $25. *Expenses:* Contact institution. *Financial support:* Applicants required to submit FAFSA. *Unit head:* Dr. Esther Swink, Dean, School of Education/ Director of Graduate Education Programs, 615-248-1201, Fax: 615-248-1597, E-mail: admissions.ged@trevecca.edu. *Application contact:* Melanie Eaton, Admissions, 615-248-1498, E-mail: admissions_ged@trevecca.edu. Web site: http://www.trevecca.edu/ soe/.

Trevecca Nazarene University, College of Lifelong Learning, School of Education, Major in Leadership and Professional Practice, Nashville, TN 37210-2877. Offers Ed D. *Students:* 63 full-time (39 women), 48 part-time (34 women); includes 23 minority (20 Black or African American, non-Hispanic/Latino; 1 Asian, non-Hispanic/Latino; 2 Two or more races, non-Hispanic/Latino), 1 international. Average age 40. In 2011, 23 doctorates awarded. *Degree requirements:* For doctorate, thesis/dissertation, proposal study, symposium presentation. *Entrance requirements:* For doctorate, GMAT, GRE, MAT, or NTE, minimum GPA of 3.4, resume, writing sample, interview. Additional exam requirements/recommendations for international students: Required—TOEFL (minimum score 550 paper-based; 213 computer-based). *Application deadline:* Applications are processed on a rolling basis. Application fee: $50. *Expenses:* Contact institution. *Financial support:* Applicants required to submit FAFSA. *Unit head:* Dr. Esther Swink, Dean, School of Education/Director of Graduate Education Program, 615-248-1201, Fax: 615-248-1597, E-mail: admissions_ged@trevecca.edu. *Application contact:* Melanie Eaton, Admissions, 615-248-1498, E-mail: admissions_ged@trevecca.edu. Web site: http://www.trevecca.edu/soe/edd.

Trident University International, College of Education, Program in Educational Leadership, Cypress, CA 90630. Offers e-learning leadership (MA Ed, PhD); educational leadership (MA Ed); higher education leadership (PhD); K-12 leadership (PhD). Part-time and evening/weekend programs available. Postbaccalaureate distance learning degree programs offered (no on-campus study). *Degree requirements:* For doctorate, comprehensive exam, thesis/dissertation, defense of dissertation. *Entrance requirements:* For master's, minimum GPA of 2.5 (students with GPA 3.0 or greater may transfer up to 30% of graduate level credits); for doctorate, minimum GPA of 3.4, course work in research methods or statistics. Additional exam requirements/recommendations for international students: Required—TOEFL. Electronic applications accepted.

Trinity Baptist College, Graduate Programs, Jacksonville, FL 32221. Offers educational leadership (M Ed); ministry (MA); special education (M Ed). Postbaccalaureate distance learning degree programs offered. *Entrance requirements:* For master's, GRE (M Ed), 2 letters of recommendation; minimum GPA of 2.5 (M Min) or 3.0 (M Ed); computer proficiency.

Trinity International University, Trinity Graduate School, Deerfield, IL 60015-1284. Offers bioethics (MA); communication and culture (MA); counseling psychology (MA); instructional leadership (M Ed); teaching (MA). Part-time and evening/weekend programs available. Postbaccalaureate distance learning degree programs offered (minimal on-campus study). *Degree requirements:* For master's, comprehensive exam. *Entrance requirements:* For master's, GRE General Test or MAT, minimum undergraduate GPA of 3.0. Additional exam requirements/recommendations for international students: Required—TOEFL (minimum score 580 paper-based; 237 computer-based), TWE (minimum score 4). Electronic applications accepted.

Trinity University, Department of Education, Program in School Administration, San Antonio, TX 78212-7200. Offers M Ed. *Accreditation:* NCATE. Part-time and evening/ weekend programs available. *Entrance requirements:* For master's, GRE General Test, interview, minimum GPA of 3.0.

Trinity Washington University, School of Education, Washington, DC 20017-1094. Offers counseling (MA); early childhood education (MAT); educating for change (M Ed); educational administration (MSA); elementary education (MAT); school counseling (MA); secondary education (MAT), including English, social studies; special education (MAT); teaching English as a second language (MAT); teaching English to speakers of other languages (M Ed); the teaching of reading (M Ed). *Accreditation:* NCATE. Part-time and evening/weekend programs available. *Degree requirements:* For master's, thesis (for some programs), capstone project(s). *Entrance requirements:* For master's, PRAXIS I, minimum GPA of 2.8. Additional exam requirements/recommendations for international students: Required—TOEFL (minimum score 550 paper-based; 213 computer-based). *Faculty research:* Technology, literacy, special education, organizations, inclusion models.

Trinity Western University, School of Graduate Studies, Program in Leadership, Langley, BC V2Y 1Y1, Canada. Offers business (MA, Certificate); Christian ministry (MA); education (MA, Certificate); healthcare (MA, Certificate); non-profit (MA, Certificate). Postbaccalaureate distance learning degree programs offered (minimal on-campus study). *Degree requirements:* For master's, major project. *Entrance requirements:* For master's, minimum GPA of 2.7. Additional exam requirements/ recommendations for international students: Required—TOEFL (minimum score 620 paper-based; 260 computer-based; 105 iBT). Electronic applications accepted. *Expenses:* Contact institution. *Faculty research:* Servant leadership.

Troy University, Graduate School, College of Education, Program in Educational Administration/Leadership, Troy, AL 36082. Offers MS, Ed S. *Accreditation:* NCATE. Part-time and evening/weekend programs available. *Faculty:* 9 full-time (3 women), 3 part-time/adjunct (1 woman). *Students:* 27 full-time (15 women), 46 part-time (25 women); includes 28 minority (24 Black or African American, non-Hispanic/Latino; 3 Hispanic/Latino; 1 Two or more races, non-Hispanic/Latino). Average age 38. 32 applicants, 88% accepted, 11 enrolled. In 2011, 26 master's, 16 other advanced degrees awarded. *Degree requirements:* For master's, comprehensive exam, thesis. *Entrance requirements:* For master's, minimum GPA of 2.5, bachelor's degree, 3 years of teaching experience; for Ed S, MS. Additional exam requirements/recommendations for international students: Required—TOEFL (minimum score 523 paper-based; 193 computer-based; 70 iBT), IELTS. *Application deadline:* Applications are processed on a rolling basis. Application fee: $50. Electronic applications accepted. *Expenses:* Tuition, state resident: full-time $6960; part-time $290 per credit hour. Tuition, nonresident: full-time $13,920; part-time $580 per credit hour. *Required fees:* $386 per term. *Financial support:* Available to part-time students. Applicants required to submit FAFSA. *Unit head:* Victoria Morin, Professor, 334-983-6556 Ext. 351, E-mail: vmorinr@troy.edu. *Application contact:* Jessida McConnell, Graduate Admissions, 334-448-5106, Fax: 334-448-5299, E-mail: jcmcconnell@troy.edu.

Troy University, Graduate School, College of Education, Program in Postsecondary Education, Troy, AL 36082. Offers adult education (M Ed); biology (M Ed); criminal justice (M Ed); English (M Ed); foundations of education (M Ed); general science (M Ed); higher education administration (M Ed); history (M Ed); instructional technology (M Ed); mathematics (M Ed); music industry (M Ed); physical fitness (M Ed); political science (M Ed); public administration (M Ed); social science (M Ed); teaching English (M Ed). *Accreditation:* NCATE. Part-time and evening/weekend programs available. *Faculty:* 53 full-time (21 women), 22 part-time/adjunct (8 women). *Students:* 74 full-time (51 women), 166 part-time (121 women); includes 148 minority (143 Black or African American, non-Hispanic/Latino; 1 American Indian or Alaska Native, non-Hispanic/ Latino; 2 Hispanic/Latino; 2 Two or more races, non-Hispanic/Latino). Average age 34. 174 applicants, 82% accepted, 88 enrolled. In 2011, 221 master's awarded. *Degree requirements:* For master's, comprehensive exam, thesis. *Entrance requirements:* For master's, MAT (minimum score 385), minimum GPA of 2.5. Additional exam requirements/recommendations for international students: Required—TOEFL (minimum score 523 paper-based; 193 computer-based; 70 iBT), IELTS (minimum score 6), or ACT COMPASS ESL (minimum listening, reading, and grammar score 270). *Application deadline:* Applications are processed on a rolling basis. Application fee: $50. Electronic applications accepted. *Expenses:* Tuition, state resident: full-time $6960; part-time $290 per credit hour. Tuition, nonresident: full-time $13,920; part-time $580 per credit hour. *Required fees:* $386 per term. *Financial support:* Available to part-time students. Applicants required to submit FAFSA. *Unit head:* Dr. Jan Oliver, Associate Professor, 334-670-3444, Fax: 334-670-3296, E-mail: oliver@troy.edu. *Application contact:* Brenda K. Campbell, Director of Graduate Admissions, 334-670-3178, Fax: 334-670-3733, E-mail: bcamp@troy.edu.

Union College, Graduate Programs, Department of Education, Barbourville, KY 40906-1499. Offers elementary education (MA); health and physical education (MA); middle grades (MA); music education (MA); principalship (MA); reading specialist (MA); secondary education (MA); special education (MA). *Degree requirements:* For master's, thesis optional. *Entrance requirements:* For master's, GRE General Test, NTE.

Union College, Graduate Programs, Educational Leadership Program, Barbourville, KY 40906-1499. Offers principalship (MA).

Union Graduate College, School of Education, Schenectady, NY 12308-3107. Offers biology (MAT, MS); chemistry (MAT); Chinese (MAT); earth science (MAT); English

(MAT); French (MAT); general science (MAT); German (MAT); Greek (MAT); languages (MAT); Latin (MAT); mathematics (MAT); mathematics and technology (MS); mentoring and teacher leadership (AC); middle childhood extension (AC); national board certificate and teacher leadership (AC); physical science (MS); physics (MAT); social studies (MAT); Spanish (MAT). *Accreditation:* Teacher Education Accreditation Council. *Faculty:* 3 full-time (1 woman), 51 part-time/adjunct (24 women). *Students:* 37 full-time (26 women), 25 part-time (16 women); includes 4 minority (3 Asian, non-Hispanic/Latino; 1 Hispanic/Latino). Average age 32. 66 applicants, 83% accepted, 41 enrolled. In 2011, 47 master's, 29 other advanced degrees awarded. *Degree requirements:* For master's, thesis or project. *Entrance requirements:* For master's, minimum GPA of 3.0, letters of recommendation. Additional exam requirements/recommendations for international students: Required—TOEFL (minimum score 550 paper-based; 213 computer-based). *Application deadline:* Applications are processed on a rolling basis. Application fee: $60. Electronic applications accepted. *Expenses:* Contact institution. *Financial support:* In 2011–12, 22 students received support. Career-related internships or fieldwork, Federal Work-Study, scholarships/grants, health care benefits, and tuition waivers (partial) available. Support available to part-time students. Financial award applicants required to submit FAFSA. *Faculty research:* Transformative learning, science education, National Board Certification, teacher leadership, teacher quality. *Unit head:* Dr. Patrick Allen, Dean, 518-631-9870, Fax: 518-631-9901. *Application contact:* Christine Angley, Assistant, 518-631-9871, Fax: 518-631-9903, E-mail: angleyc@uniongraduatecollege.edu.

Union Institute & University, Education Programs, Cincinnati, OH 45206-1925. Offers adult and higher education (M Ed); curriculum and instruction (M Ed); educational leadership (M Ed, Ed D); guidance and counseling (Ed S); higher education (Ed D); issues in education (M Ed); reading (Ed S). M Ed offered online and in Vermont and Florida, concentrations vary by location; Ed S offered in Florida; Ed D program is a hybrid (online with limited residency) offered in Ohio. Postbaccalaureate distance learning degree programs offered (minimal on-campus study). *Degree requirements:* For master's, comprehensive exam (for some programs), thesis (for some programs), electronic portfolio; for doctorate, comprehensive exam, thesis/dissertation, electronic portfolio.

Union University, School of Education, Jackson, TN 38305-3697. Offers education (M Ed, MA Ed); education administration generalist (Ed S); educational leadership (Ed D); educational supervision (Ed S); higher education (Ed D). M Ed also available at Germantown campus. *Accreditation:* NCATE. Part-time and evening/weekend programs available. *Degree requirements:* For master's, thesis (for some programs), capstone research course; for doctorate, comprehensive exam, thesis/dissertation; for Ed S, thesis or alternative. *Entrance requirements:* For master's, MAT, PRAXIS II or GRE, minimum GPA of 3.0, teaching license, writing sample; for doctorate, GRE, minimum graduate GPA of 3.2, writing sample; for Ed S, PRAXIS II, minimum graduate GPA of 3.2, writing sample. *Faculty research:* Mathematics education, direct instruction, language disorders and special education, brain compatible learning, empathy and school leadership.

United States University, School of Education, Cypress, CA 90630. Offers administration (MA Ed); early childhood education (MA Ed); general (MA Ed); higher education administration (MA Ed); Spanish language education (MA Ed); special education (MA Ed). *Degree requirements:* For master's, portfolio. *Entrance requirements:* For master's, minimum undergraduate GPA of 2.5. Additional exam requirements/recommendations for international students: Required—TOEFL (minimum score 500 paper-based; 173 computer-based; 61 iBT).

Universidad Adventista de las Antillas, EGECED Department, Mayagüez, PR 00681-0118. Offers curriculum and instruction (M Ed); health education (M Ed); medical surgical nursing (MN); pastoral theology (M Div); school administration and supervision (M Ed). *Degree requirements:* For master's, comprehensive exam (for some programs), thesis (for some programs). *Entrance requirements:* For master's, EXADEP or GRE General Test, recommendations. Electronic applications accepted.

Universidad del Turabo, Graduate Programs, Programs in Education, Program in Administration of School Libraries, Gurabo, PR 00778-3030. Offers M Ed, Certificate. *Students:* 2 full-time (1 woman), 1 (woman) part-time; all minorities (all Hispanic/Latino). Average age 34. 2 applicants, 100% accepted, 1 enrolled. *Unit head:* Angela Candelario, Dean, 787-743-7979 Ext. 4126. *Application contact:* Virginia Gonzalez, Admissions Officer, 787-746-3009.

Universidad del Turabo, Graduate Programs, Programs in Education, Program in Educational Administration, Gurabo, PR 00778-3030. Offers M Ed. *Students:* 36 full-time (29 women), 30 part-time (25 women); includes 59 minority (all Hispanic/Latino). Average age 38. 67 applicants, 87% accepted, 37 enrolled. In 2011, 13 master's awarded. *Unit head:* Angela Candelario, Dean, 787-743-7979 Ext. 4126. *Application contact:* Virginia Gonzalez, Admissions Officer, 787-746-3009.

Universidad del Turabo, Graduate Programs, Programs in Education, Program in Educational Leadership, Gurabo, PR 00778-3030. Offers D Ed. *Students:* 13 full-time (11 women), 44 part-time (30 women); includes 51 minority (all Hispanic/Latino). Average age 41. 23 applicants, 78% accepted, 15 enrolled. In 2011, 8 doctorates awarded. *Unit head:* Angela Candelario, Dean, 787-743-7979 Ext. 4126. *Application contact:* Virginia Gonzalez, Admissions Officer, 787-746-3009.

Universidad Iberoamericana, Graduate School, Santo Domingo D.N., Dominican Republic. Offers business administration (MBA, PMBA); constitutional law (LL M); dentistry (DMD); educational management (MA); integrated marketing communication (MA); psychopedagogical intervention (M Ed); real estate law (LL M); strategic management of human talent (MM).

Universidad Metropolitana, School of Education, Program in Educational Administration and Supervision, San Juan, PR 00928-1150. Offers M Ed. Part-time programs available. *Degree requirements:* For master's, thesis or alternative. *Entrance requirements:* For master's, EXADEP, interview. Electronic applications accepted.

Universidad Metropolitana, School of Education, Program in Pre-School Centers Administration, San Juan, PR 00928-1150. Offers M Ed. Part-time programs available. *Degree requirements:* For master's, thesis or alternative. *Entrance requirements:* For master's, EXADEP, interview. Electronic applications accepted.

Université de Moncton, Faculty of Education, Graduate Studies in Education, Moncton, NB E1A 3E9, Canada. Offers educational psychology (M Ed, MA Ed); guidance (M Ed, MA Ed); school administration (M Ed, MA Ed); teaching (M Ed, MA Ed). Part-time programs available. *Degree requirements:* For master's, proficiency in English and French. *Entrance requirements:* For master's, minimum GPA of 3.0. *Faculty research:* Guidance, ethnolinguistic vitality, children's rights, ecological education, entrepreneurship.

Université de Montréal, Faculty of Education, Department of Administration and Foundations of Education, Montréal, QC H3C 3J7, Canada. Offers M Ed, MA, PhD, DESS. Part-time programs available. *Degree requirements:* For master's, thesis; for doctorate, thesis/dissertation, general exam. *Entrance requirements:* For master's and DESS, bachelor's degree in related field with minimum B average; for doctorate, master's degree in related field with minimum B average. Electronic applications accepted. *Faculty research:* Pluriethnicity, formative education, comparative education, diagnostic evaluation.

Université de Sherbrooke, Faculty of Education, Program in School Administration, Sherbrooke, QC J1K 2R1, Canada. Offers M Ed. Part-time and evening/weekend programs available. *Degree requirements:* For master's, thesis.

Université du Québec à Trois-Rivières, Graduate Programs, Program in Educational Administration, Trois-Rivières, QC G9A 5H7, Canada. Offers DESS.

Université Laval, Faculty of Education, Department of Foundations and Interventions in Education, Programs in Educational Administration and Evaluation, Québec, QC G1K 7P4, Canada. Offers MA, PhD. Terminal master's awarded for partial completion of doctoral program. *Degree requirements:* For master's, thesis (for some programs); for doctorate, comprehensive exam, thesis/dissertation. *Entrance requirements:* For master's and doctorate, English exam (comprehension of written English), knowledge of French and English. Electronic applications accepted.

Université Laval, Faculty of Education, Department of Foundations and Interventions in Education, Programs in Educational Practice, Québec, QC G1K 7P4, Canada. Offers educational pedagogy (Diploma); pedagogy management and development (Diploma); school adaptation (Diploma). Part-time programs available. *Entrance requirements:* For degree, English exam (comprehension of written English), knowledge of French and English. Electronic applications accepted.

University at Albany, State University of New York, School of Education, Department of Educational Administration and Policy Studies, Albany, NY 12222-0001. Offers MS, PhD, CAS. Evening/weekend programs available. *Degree requirements:* For doctorate, one foreign language, thesis/dissertation. *Entrance requirements:* For doctorate, GRE General Test, GRE Subject Test. Additional exam requirements/recommendations for international students: Required—TOEFL (minimum score 550 paper-based; 213 computer-based). Electronic applications accepted.

University at Buffalo, the State University of New York, Graduate School, Graduate School of Education, Department of Educational Leadership and Policy, Buffalo, NY 14260. Offers educational administration (Ed M, PhD); educational culture, policy and society (PhD); general education (Ed M); higher education administration (Ed M, PhD); school building leadership (LIFTS) (Certificate); school business and human resource administration (Certificate); school district business leadership (LIFTS) (Certificate); school district leadership (LIFTS) (Certificate). Part-time and evening/weekend programs available. *Faculty:* 12 full-time (7 women), 9 part-time/adjunct (7 women). *Students:* 79 full-time (55 women), 136 part-time (76 women); includes 47 minority (24 Black or African American, non-Hispanic/Latino; 1 American Indian or Alaska Native, non-Hispanic/Latino; 9 Asian, non-Hispanic/Latino; 13 Hispanic/Latino), 17 international. Average age 35. 194 applicants, 40% accepted, 73 enrolled. In 2011, 44 master's, 18 doctorates, 25 other advanced degrees awarded. *Degree requirements:* For master's, comprehensive exam (for some programs), thesis optional; for doctorate, comprehensive exam, thesis/dissertation. *Entrance requirements:* For doctorate, GRE General Test or MAT, writing sample. Additional exam requirements/recommendations for international students: Required—TOEFL (minimum score 550 paper-based; 213 computer-based; 79 iBT). *Application deadline:* For fall admission, 3/1 priority date for domestic students, 3/1 for international students; for spring admission, 11/15 priority date for domestic students, 10/1 for international students. Applications are processed on a rolling basis. Application fee: $50. Electronic applications accepted. *Financial support:* In 2011–12, 21 fellowships (averaging $10,298 per year), 9 research assistantships (averaging $11,955 per year) were awarded; career-related internships or fieldwork, Federal Work-Study, institutionally sponsored loans, health care benefits, and unspecified assistantships also available. Financial award application deadline: 3/15; financial award applicants required to submit FAFSA. *Faculty research:* College access and choice, school leadership preparation and practice, public policy, curriculum and pedagogy, comparative and international education. *Unit head:* Dr. William C. Barba, Chairman, 716-645-2471, Fax: 716-645-2481, E-mail: barba@buffalo.edu. *Application contact:* Bonnie Reed, Admissions Assistant, 716-645-2110, Fax: 716-645-7937, E-mail: brfisher@buffalo.edu. Web site: http://gse.buffalo.edu/elp.

The University of Akron, Graduate School, College of Education, Department of Educational Foundations and Leadership, Program in Educational Leadership, Akron, OH 44325. Offers Ed D. *Accreditation:* NCATE. *Students:* 3 full-time (2 women), 16 part-time (11 women); includes 1 minority (Black or African American, non-Hispanic/Latino), 1 international. Average age 42. 9 applicants, 33% accepted, 1 enrolled. In 2011, 1 doctorate awarded. Terminal master's awarded for partial completion of doctoral program. *Degree requirements:* For doctorate, one foreign language, comprehensive exam, thesis/dissertation, written and oral exams. *Entrance requirements:* For doctorate, GRE, minimum GPA of 3.25 for master's degree, three letters of recommendation, statement of purpose indicating nature of interest in the program and future career goals, current curriculum vitae/resume. Additional exam requirements/recommendations for international students: Required—TOEFL (minimum score 550 paper-based; 213 computer-based; 79 iBT). *Application deadline:* For fall admission, 3/1 for domestic and international students; for spring admission, 10/15 for domestic and international students. Application fee: $30 ($40 for international students). Electronic applications accepted. *Expenses:* Tuition, state resident: full-time $7038; part-time $391 per credit hour. Tuition, nonresident: full-time $12,051; part-time $670 per credit hour. *Required fees:* $1274; $34 per credit hour. *Unit head:* Dr. Sharon Kruse, Coordinator, 330-972-7773, E-mail: skruse@uakron.edu. *Application contact:* Dr. Mark Tausig, Associate Dean, 330-972-6266, Fax: 330-972-6475, E-mail: mtausig@uakron.edu.

The University of Akron, Graduate School, College of Education, Department of Educational Foundations and Leadership, Program in Higher Education Administration, Akron, OH 44325. Offers MA, MS. *Accreditation:* NCATE. *Students:* 45 full-time (28 women), 40 part-time (26 women); includes 19 minority (15 Black or African American, non-Hispanic/Latino; 2 Hispanic/Latino; 2 Two or more races, non-Hispanic/Latino), 1 international. Average age 32. 43 applicants, 65% accepted, 15 enrolled. In 2011, 42 master's awarded. *Degree requirements:* For master's, comprehensive exam. *Entrance requirements:* For master's, GRE, minimum GPA of 2.75, declaration of intent that includes statement of professional goals and reasons for choosing the field of higher education administration and The University of Akron. Additional exam requirements/recommendations for international students: Required—TOEFL (minimum score 550 paper-based; 213 computer-based; 79 iBT). *Application deadline:* Applications are processed on a rolling basis. Application fee: $30 ($40 for international students). Electronic applications accepted. *Expenses:* Tuition, state resident: full-time $7038; part-time $391 per credit hour. Tuition, nonresident: full-time $12,051; part-time $670 per credit hour. *Required fees:* $1274; $34 per credit hour. *Financial support:* Fellowships, research assistantships, and teaching assistantships available. *Unit head:* Dr. Sharon Kruse, Coordinator, 330-972-8177, E-mail: skruse@uakron.edu. *Application contact:* Dr. Mark Tausig, Associate Dean, 330-972-6266, Fax: 330-972-6475, E-mail: mtausig@uakron.edu.

The University of Akron, Graduate School, College of Education, Department of Educational Foundations and Leadership, Program in Principalship, Akron, OH 44325. Offers MA, MS. *Students:* 3 full-time (all women), 78 part-time (50 women); includes 6 minority (3 Black or African American, non-Hispanic/Latino; 3 Two or more races, non-

Hispanic/Latino). Average age 33. 18 applicants, 89% accepted, 12 enrolled. In 2011, 54 master's awarded. *Degree requirements:* For master's, portfolio assessment. *Entrance requirements:* For master's, minimum GPA of 2.75, valid Ohio teacher license. Additional exam requirements/recommendations for international students: Required—TOEFL (minimum score 550 paper-based; 213 computer-based; 79 iBT). *Application deadline:* Applications are processed on a rolling basis. Application fee: $30 ($40 for international students). Electronic applications accepted. *Expenses:* Tuition, state resident: full-time $7038; part-time $391 per credit hour. Tuition, nonresident: full-time $12,051; part-time $670 per credit hour. *Required fees:* $1274; $34 per credit hour. *Unit head:* Dr. Sharon Kruse, Coordinator, 330-972-7773, E-mail: skruse@uakron.edu. *Application contact:* Dr. Mark Tausig, Associate Dean, 330-972-6266, Fax: 330-972-6475, E-mail: mtausig@uakron.edu.

The University of Alabama, Graduate School, College of Education, Department of Educational Leadership, Policy, and Technology Studies, Educational Administration Program, Tuscaloosa, AL 35487. Offers Ed D, PhD. Evening/weekend programs available. *Faculty:* 4 full-time (3 women). *Students:* 7 full-time (5 women), 68 part-time (40 women); includes 21 minority (18 Black or African American, non-Hispanic/Latino; 3 American Indian or Alaska Native, non-Hispanic/Latino), 1 international. Average age 43. 10 applicants, 70% accepted, 4 enrolled. In 2011, 15 degrees awarded. *Degree requirements:* For doctorate, comprehensive exam, thesis/dissertation. *Entrance requirements:* For doctorate, MAT, GRE, master's degree in field. *Application deadline:* For fall admission, 9/1 priority date for domestic students, 9/1 for international students; for winter admission, 2/1 priority date for domestic students, 2/1 for international students; for spring admission, 4/1 priority date for domestic students, 4/1 for international students. Applications are processed on a rolling basis. Application fee: $50 ($60 for international students). Electronic applications accepted. *Expenses:* Tuition, state resident: full-time $8600. Tuition, nonresident: full-time $21,900. *Financial support:* In 2011–12, 3 research assistantships with tuition reimbursements (averaging $14,000 per year), teaching assistantships with tuition reimbursements (averaging $14,000 per year) were awarded; unspecified assistantships also available. Financial award application deadline: 4/1. *Unit head:* Dr. David R. Dagley, Professor of Educational Leadership, 205-348-5159, Fax: 205-348-2161, E-mail: ddagley@bamaed.ua.edu. *Application contact:* Dr. Kathy S. Wetzel, Assistant Dean for Student Services, 205-348-1154, Fax: 205-348-0080, E-mail: kwetzel@bamaed.ua.edu. Web site: http://www.elpts.ua.edu.

The University of Alabama, Graduate School, College of Education, Department of Educational Leadership, Policy, and Technology Studies, Educational Leadership Program, Tuscaloosa, AL 35487. Offers MA, Ed S. Part-time and evening/weekend programs available. Postbaccalaureate distance learning degree programs offered (minimal on-campus study). *Faculty:* 7 full-time (3 women), 1 part-time/adjunct (0 women). *Students:* 4 full-time (3 women), 69 part-time (37 women); includes 7 minority (5 Black or African American, non-Hispanic/Latino; 1 Hispanic/Latino; 1 Two or more races, non-Hispanic/Latino). Average age 38. 39 applicants, 67% accepted, 23 enrolled. In 2011, 28 master's, 15 other advanced degrees awarded. *Degree requirements:* For master's, comprehensive exam, internship. *Entrance requirements:* For master's, MAT, GRE, 3 years of teaching experience, teaching certification. *Application deadline:* For fall admission, 9/1 priority date for domestic students, 9/1 for international students; for winter admission, 2/1 priority date for domestic students, 2/1 for international students; for spring admission, 4/1 priority date for domestic students, 4/1 for international students. Applications are processed on a rolling basis. Application fee: $50 ($60 for international students). Electronic applications accepted. *Expenses:* Tuition, state resident: full-time $8600. Tuition, nonresident: full-time $21,900. *Unit head:* Dr. David R. Dagley, Professor, 205-348-5159, Fax: 205-348-2161, E-mail: ddagley@bamaed.ua.edu. *Application contact:* Dr. Kathy S. Wetzel, Assistant Dean for Student Services, 205-348-1154, Fax: 205-348-0080, E-mail: kwetzel@bamaed.ua.edu.

The University of Alabama, Graduate School, College of Education, Department of Educational Leadership, Policy, and Technology Studies, Higher Education Administration Program, Tuscaloosa, AL 35487. Offers MA, Ed D, PhD. Evening/weekend programs available. *Faculty:* 8 full-time (3 women), 1 part-time/adjunct (0 women). *Students:* 54 full-time (25 women), 89 part-time (53 women); includes 28 minority (21 Black or African American, non-Hispanic/Latino; 2 American Indian or Alaska Native, non-Hispanic/Latino; 2 Asian, non-Hispanic/Latino; 1 Hispanic/Latino; 2 Two or more races, non-Hispanic/Latino), 1 international. Average age 37. 62 applicants, 61% accepted, 22 enrolled. In 2011, 13 master's, 11 doctorates awarded. Terminal master's awarded for partial completion of doctoral program. *Degree requirements:* For master's, comprehensive exam; for doctorate, comprehensive exam, thesis/dissertation. *Entrance requirements:* For master's, GRE, MAT or GMAT; for doctorate, GRE or MAT. Application fee: $50 ($60 for international students). Electronic applications accepted. *Expenses:* Tuition, state resident: full-time $8600. Tuition, nonresident: full-time $21,900. *Financial support:* In 2011–12, 5 students received support. Career-related internships or fieldwork, scholarships/grants, and unspecified assistantships available. *Unit head:* Dr. Claire H. Major, Coordinator and Associate Professor, 205-348-6871, Fax: 205-348-2161, E-mail: bea@bamaed.ua.edu. *Application contact:* Donna Smith, Administration Assistant, 205-348-6871, Fax: 205-348-2161, E-mail: dbsmith@bamaed.ua.edu.

The University of Alabama, Graduate School, College of Education, Department of Educational Leadership, Policy, and Technology Studies, Instructional Leadership Program, Tuscaloosa, AL 35487. Offers Ed D, PhD. Evening/weekend programs available. *Faculty:* 3 full-time (all women), 1 (woman) part-time/adjunct. *Students:* 73 full-time (64 women), 117 part-time (87 women); includes 43 minority (35 Black or African American, non-Hispanic/Latino; 3 American Indian or Alaska Native, non-Hispanic/Latino; 1 Asian, non-Hispanic/Latino; 1 Hispanic/Latino; 1 Native Hawaiian or other Pacific Islander, non-Hispanic/Latino; 2 Two or more races, non-Hispanic/Latino), 3 international. Average age 42. 43 applicants, 72% accepted, 22 enrolled. In 2011, 17 degrees awarded. *Degree requirements:* For doctorate, comprehensive exam, thesis/dissertation. *Entrance requirements:* For doctorate, GRE, MAT, master's degree. *Application deadline:* For fall admission, 9/1 priority date for domestic students, 9/1 for international students; for winter admission, 2/1 priority date for domestic students, 2/1 for international students; for spring admission, 4/1 priority date for domestic students, 4/1 for international students. Applications are processed on a rolling basis. Application fee: $50 ($60 for international students). Electronic applications accepted. *Expenses:* Tuition, state resident: full-time $8600. Tuition, nonresident: full-time $21,900. *Financial support:* In 2011–12, 2 research assistantships (averaging $14,000 per year), 2 teaching assistantships (averaging $14,000 per year) were awarded; health care benefits and unspecified assistantships also available. *Unit head:* Dr. John Petroric, Professor in Foundations of Education, 205-348-0465, Fax: 205-348-2161, E-mail: petroric@bamaed.ua.edu. *Application contact:* Dr. Kathy S. Wetzel, Assistant Dean for Student Services, 205-348-1154, Fax: 205-348-0080, E-mail: kwetzel@bamaed.ua.edu. Web site: http://www.elpts.ua.edu.

The University of Alabama at Birmingham, College of Arts and Sciences, School of Education, Program in Educational Leadership, Birmingham, AL 35294. Offers MA Ed, Ed D, PhD, Ed S. Ed D, PhD offered jointly with The University of Alabama (Tuscaloosa). *Accreditation:* NCATE. *Degree requirements:* For master's, thesis optional; for doctorate, thesis/dissertation; for Ed S, comprehensive exam, thesis optional. *Entrance requirements:* For master's, GRE General Test, MAT, or NTE, minimum GPA of 3.0; for doctorate, GRE General Test, MAT, minimum GPA of 3.25; for Ed S, GRE General Test, MAT, minimum GPA of 3.0, master's degree. *Application deadline:* Applications are processed on a rolling basis. Electronic applications accepted. *Expenses:* Tuition, state resident: full-time $5922; part-time $309 per hour. Tuition, nonresident: full-time $13,428; part-time $726 per hour. Tuition and fees vary according to program. *Unit head:* Dr. Kristi Menear, Chair, 205-975-7409, Fax: 205-975-8040, E-mail: kmenear@uab.edu. Web site: http://www.uab.edu/humanstudies/educationalleadership.

University of Alaska Anchorage, College of Education, Program in Educational Leadership, Anchorage, AK 99508. Offers educational leadership (M Ed); principal licensure (Certificate); superintendent (Certificate). Part-time programs available. *Entrance requirements:* For master's, GRE or MAT, interview, minimum GPA of 3.0. Additional exam requirements/recommendations for international students: Required—TOEFL (minimum score 550 paper-based; 213 computer-based).

University of Alberta, Faculty of Graduate Studies and Research, Department of Educational Policy Studies, Edmonton, AB T6G 2E1, Canada. Offers adult education (M Ed, Ed D, PhD); educational administration and leadership (M Ed, Ed D, PhD, Postgraduate Diploma); First Nations education (M Ed, Ed D, PhD); theoretical, cultural and international studies in education (M Ed, Ed D, PhD). *Degree requirements:* For master's, thesis (for some programs); for doctorate, thesis/dissertation. *Entrance requirements:* For master's, minimum GPA of 6.5 on a 9.0 scale; for doctorate, minimum GPA of 7.5 on a 9.0 scale. Additional exam requirements/recommendations for international students: Required—TOEFL (minimum score 580 paper-based; 237 computer-based). Electronic applications accepted.

The University of Arizona, College of Education, Department of Educational Policy Studies and Practice, Program of Educational Leadership, Tucson, AZ 85721. Offers M Ed, Ed D, Ed S. Part-time programs available. *Faculty:* 9 full-time (4 women). *Students:* 23 full-time (16 women), 52 part-time (35 women); includes 23 minority (4 Black or African American, non-Hispanic/Latino; 1 American Indian or Alaska Native, non-Hispanic/Latino; 16 Hispanic/Latino; 2 Two or more races, non-Hispanic/Latino), 2 international. Average age 38. 49 applicants, 53% accepted, 25 enrolled. In 2011, 15 master's, 2 doctorates awarded. *Degree requirements:* For master's and Ed S, capstone experience; for doctorate, comprehensive exam, thesis/dissertation. *Entrance requirements:* For master's, leadership experience; for doctorate, GRE General Test, minimum GPA of 3.5, 3 letters of recommendation, curriculum vitae, writing sample. Additional exam requirements/recommendations for international students: Required—TOEFL (minimum score 550 paper-based; 213 computer-based; 79 iBT). *Application deadline:* For fall admission, 3/1 for domestic students, 12/1 for international students. Applications are processed on a rolling basis. Application fee: $75. Electronic applications accepted. *Expenses:* Tuition, state resident: full-time $10,840. Tuition, nonresident: full-time $25,802. *Financial support:* Career-related internships or fieldwork, scholarships/grants, health care benefits, and unspecified assistantships available. *Faculty research:* School governance, higher order thinking, restructuring schools, bilingual education policy, authority in education. *Total annual research expenditures:* $292,015. *Unit head:* Dr. Kris Bosworth, Department Head, 520-621-6658, Fax: 520-626-6005, E-mail: edlprog@email.arizona.edu. *Application contact:* Kathy Bayham, Administrative Assistant, 520-621-6658, Fax: 520-626-6005, E-mail: edlprog@email.arizona.edu. Web site: http://grad.arizona.edu/live/programs/description/51.

University of Arkansas, Graduate School, College of Education and Health Professions, Department of Curriculum and Instruction, Program in Educational Leadership, Fayetteville, AR 72701-1201. Offers M Ed, Ed D, Ed S. *Accreditation:* NCATE. Part-time and evening/weekend programs available. *Students:* 2 full-time (both women), 46 part-time (27 women); includes 7 minority (3 Black or African American, non-Hispanic/Latino; 1 American Indian or Alaska Native, non-Hispanic/Latino; 1 Asian, non-Hispanic/Latino; 2 Two or more races, non-Hispanic/Latino). In 2011, 12 master's, 4 doctorates, 2 other advanced degrees awarded. *Degree requirements:* For doctorate, thesis/dissertation. *Entrance requirements:* For master's, GRE General Test, MAT or minimum GPA of 3.0; for doctorate, GRE General Test or MAT. *Application deadline:* For fall admission, 4/1 for international students; for spring admission, 10/1 for international students. Applications are processed on a rolling basis. Application fee: $40 ($50 for international students). Electronic applications accepted. *Financial support:* Fellowships with tuition reimbursements, research assistantships, teaching assistantships, career-related internships or fieldwork, and Federal Work-Study available. Support available to part-time students. Financial award application deadline: 4/1; financial award applicants required to submit FAFSA. *Unit head:* Dr. Michael Daugherty, Departmental Chairperson, 479-575-4209, Fax: 479-575-5119, E-mail: mkd03@uark.edu. *Application contact:* Dr. Barbara Gartin, Graduate Coordinator, 479-575-7525, Fax: 479-575-6676, E-mail: bgartin@uark.edu. Web site: http://cied.uark.edu.

University of Arkansas at Little Rock, Graduate School, College of Education, Department of Educational Leadership, Program in Educational Administration, Little Rock, AR 72204-1099. Offers educational administration (M Ed, Ed S); educational administration and supervision (Ed D). Part-time and evening/weekend programs available. *Degree requirements:* For master's, comprehensive exam; for doctorate, comprehensive exam, oral defense of dissertation, residency; for Ed S, comprehensive exam, professional project. *Entrance requirements:* For master's, GRE General Test or MAT, 4 years of work experience (minimum 3 in teaching), interview, minimum GPA of 2.75, teaching certificate; for doctorate, GRE General Test or MAT, 4 years of work experience, minimum graduate GPA of 3.0, teaching certificate; for Ed S, GRE General Test or MAT, 4 years of work experience, minimum GPA of 2.75, teaching certificate.

University of Arkansas at Little Rock, Graduate School, College of Education, Department of Educational Leadership, Program in Higher Education Administration, Little Rock, AR 72204-1099. Offers Ed D. *Degree requirements:* For doctorate, comprehensive exam, oral defense of dissertation, residency. *Entrance requirements:* For doctorate, GRE General Test or MAT, interview, minimum graduate GPA of 3.0, teaching certificate, work experience.

University of Arkansas at Monticello, School of Education, Monticello, AR 71656. Offers education (M Ed, MAT); educational leadership (M Ed). *Accreditation:* NCATE. Part-time and evening/weekend programs available. Postbaccalaureate distance learning degree programs offered (minimal on-campus study). *Degree requirements:* For master's, comprehensive exam. *Entrance requirements:* For master's, minimum GPA of 3.0. Additional exam requirements/recommendations for international students: Required—TOEFL (minimum score 550 paper-based; 213 computer-based). Electronic applications accepted.

University of Atlanta, Graduate Programs, Atlanta, GA 30360. Offers business (MS); business administration (Exec MBA, MBA); computer science (MS); educational leadership (MS, Ed D); healthcare administration (MS, D Sc, Graduate Certificate); information technology for management (Graduate Certificate); international project management (Graduate Certificate); law (JD); managerial science (DBA); project management (Graduate Certificate); social science (MS). Postbaccalaureate distance learning degree programs offered. *Entrance requirements:* For master's, minimum cumulative GPA of 2.5.

University of Bridgeport, School of Education, Department of Education, Bridgeport, CT 06604. Offers education (MS); educational management (Ed D, Diploma), including intermediate administrator or supervisor (Diploma), leadership (Ed D); elementary education (MS, Diploma), including early childhood education, elementary education; middle school education (MS); music education (MS); remedial reading and language arts (Diploma); secondary education (MS, Diploma), including computer specialist (Diploma), international education (Diploma), reading specialist, secondary education. Part-time and evening/weekend programs available. *Faculty:* 12 full-time (5 women), 108 part-time/adjunct (60 women). *Students:* 232 full-time (161 women), 216 part-time (160 women); includes 61 minority (21 Black or African American, non-Hispanic/Latino; 8 Asian, non-Hispanic/Latino; 22 Hispanic/Latino; 10 Two or more races, non-Hispanic/Latino), 34 international. Average age 30. 412 applicants, 63% accepted, 147 enrolled. In 2011, 216 master's, 7 other advanced degrees awarded. *Degree requirements:* For master's, final exam, final project, or thesis; for doctorate, comprehensive exam, thesis/dissertation; for Diploma, thesis or alternative, final project. *Entrance requirements:* For master's, minimum undergraduate QPA of 2.67; for doctorate, GRE, MAT; for Diploma, GRE General Test or MAT, minimum graduate QPA of 3.0. Additional exam requirements/recommendations for international students: Recommended—TOEFL (minimum score 550 paper-based; 213 computer-based; 80 iBT), IELTS (minimum score 6.5). *Application deadline:* For fall admission, 8/1 priority date for domestic students, 8/1 for international students; for spring admission, 12/1 priority date for domestic students, 12/1 for international students. Applications are processed on a rolling basis. Application fee: $50. Electronic applications accepted. *Expenses: Tuition:* Full-time $22,880; part-time $700 per credit. *Required fees:* $1870; $95 per semester. Tuition and fees vary according to course load and program. *Financial support:* In 2011–12, 120 students received support. Fellowships, research assistantships, teaching assistantships, career-related internships or fieldwork, Federal Work-Study, and institutionally sponsored loans available. Support available to part-time students. Financial award application deadline: 6/1; financial award applicants required to submit FAFSA. *Faculty research:* Self-concept, internship assessment, stress and situational development, follow-up of graduation, trend analysis. *Unit head:* Dr. Allen P. Cook, Dean, 203-576-4192, Fax: 203-576-4200, E-mail: acook@bridgeport.edu. *Application contact:* Karissa Peckham, Dean of Admissions, 203-576-4552, Fax: 203-576-4941, E-mail: admit@bridgeport.edu.

University of Bridgeport, School of Education, Department of Educational Leadership, Bridgeport, CT 06604. Offers intermediate administrator or supervisor (Diploma); leadership (Ed D). *Faculty:* 2 full-time (0 women), 4 part-time/adjunct (2 women). *Students:* 14 full-time (8 women), 90 part-time (57 women); includes 12 minority (6 Black or African American, non-Hispanic/Latino; 1 Asian, non-Hispanic/Latino; 5 Hispanic/Latino), 3 international. Average age 38. 65 applicants, 63% accepted, 13 enrolled. In 2011, 10 doctorates, 21 Diplomas awarded. *Degree requirements:* For doctorate, comprehensive exam, thesis/dissertation; for Diploma, thesis or alternative, final project. *Entrance requirements:* For doctorate, GRE, MAT; for Diploma, GRE General Test or MAT, minimum graduate QPA of 3.0. Additional exam requirements/recommendations for international students: Recommended—TOEFL (minimum score 550 paper-based; 213 computer-based; 80 iBT), IELTS (minimum score 6.5). *Application deadline:* For fall admission, 8/1 priority date for domestic students, 8/1 for international students; for spring admission, 12/1 priority date for domestic students, 12/1 for international students. Applications are processed on a rolling basis. Application fee: $50. Electronic applications accepted. *Expenses:* Contact institution. *Financial support:* In 2011–12, 20 students received support. Fellowships, research assistantships, teaching assistantships, career-related internships or fieldwork, Federal Work-Study, and institutionally sponsored loans available. Support available to part-time students. Financial award application deadline: 6/1; financial award applicants required to submit FAFSA. *Unit head:* Dr. Thomas W. Christ, Chairman, 203-576-4028, Fax: 203-576-4102, E-mail: tchrist@bridgeport.edu. *Application contact:* Karissa Peckham, Dean of Admissions, 203-576-4552, Fax: 203-576-4941, E-mail: admit@bridgeport.edu.

The University of British Columbia, Faculty of Education, Department of Educational Studies, Vancouver, BC V6T 1Z1, Canada. Offers adult education (M Ed, MA); adult learning and global change (M Ed); educational administration (M Ed, MA); educational leadership and policy (Ed D); educational studies (PhD); higher education (M Ed, MA); society, culture and politics in education (M Ed, MA). Part-time and evening/weekend programs available. Terminal master's awarded for partial completion of doctoral program. *Degree requirements:* For master's, thesis; for doctorate, comprehensive exam, thesis/dissertation, master's thesis. *Entrance requirements:* For master's, minimum B+ average, 4-year undergraduate degree, field-related experience; for doctorate, minimum B+ average, 4-year undergraduate degree, master's degree, field-related experience. Additional exam requirements/recommendations for international students: Required—TOEFL (minimum score 600 paper-based; 250 computer-based; 100 iBT) or IELTS (minimum score 6.5). Electronic applications accepted. *Faculty research:* Educational leadership educational administration adult education politics in education, global change and adult learning.

University of Calgary, Faculty of Graduate Studies, Faculty of Education, Graduate Division of Educational Research, Calgary, AB T2N 1N4, Canada. Offers community rehabilitation and disability studies (M Ed, M Sc, Ed D, PhD, Graduate Certificate, Graduate Diploma); curriculum, teaching and learning (M Ed, M Sc, MA, Ed D, PhD, Graduate Certificate, Graduate Diploma); educational contexts (M Ed, MA, Ed D, PhD, Graduate Certificate, Graduate Diploma); educational leadership (M Ed, MA, Ed D, PhD, Graduate Certificate, Graduate Diploma); educational technology (M Ed, M Sc, MA, Ed D, PhD, Graduate Certificate, Graduate Diploma); gifted education (M Sc, MA, Ed D, PhD, Graduate Certificate, Graduate Diploma); higher education administration (Ed D); interpretive studies in education (M Ed, M Sc, MA, Ed D, PhD, Graduate Certificate, Graduate Diploma); second language teaching (M Ed, Ed D, PhD, Graduate Certificate, Graduate Diploma); teaching English as a second language (M Ed, M Sc, MA, Ed D, PhD, Graduate Certificate, Graduate Diploma); workplace and adult learning (M Ed, MA, Ed D, PhD, Graduate Certificate, Graduate Diploma). Ed D in both higher education administration and educational leadership offered via distance delivery. Part-time and evening/weekend programs available. Postbaccalaureate distance learning degree programs offered (minimal on-campus study). *Degree requirements:* For master's, thesis (for some programs); for doctorate, thesis/dissertation, candidacy exam. *Entrance requirements:* For master's, minimum GPA of 3.0, 3 letters of reference; for doctorate, minimum GPA of 3.5, 3 letters of reference; for other advanced degree, minimum GPA of 3.0. Additional exam requirements/recommendations for international students: Required—TOEFL, IELTS. Electronic applications accepted. *Faculty research:* Curriculum, leadership, technology, contexts, gifted, second language teaching, work place and adult learning.

University of California, Irvine, Department of Education, Irvine, CA 92697. Offers educational administration (Ed D); educational administration and leadership (Ed D); elementary and secondary education (MAT). Part-time and evening/weekend programs available. *Students:* 246 full-time (185 women), 8 part-time (5 women); includes 121 minority (4 Black or African American, non-Hispanic/Latino; 1 American Indian or Alaska Native, non-Hispanic/Latino; 65 Asian, non-Hispanic/Latino; 37 Hispanic/Latino; 2 Native Hawaiian or other Pacific Islander, non-Hispanic/Latino; 12 Two or more races, non-Hispanic/Latino), 7 international. Average age 28. 455 applicants, 75% accepted, 185 enrolled. In 2011, 146 master's, 12 doctorates awarded. *Degree requirements:* For doctorate, thesis/dissertation. *Entrance requirements:* For master's, GRE, minimum GPA of 3.0; for doctorate, GRE General Test, minimum GPA of 3.0. Additional exam requirements/recommendations for international students: Required—TOEFL (minimum score 550 paper-based; 213 computer-based). *Application deadline:* For fall admission, 1/2 priority date for domestic students, 1/2 for international students. Application fee: $80 ($100 for international students). Electronic applications accepted. *Financial support:* Fellowships, research assistantships with full tuition reimbursements, institutionally sponsored loans, traineeships, health care benefits, and unspecified assistantships available. Financial award application deadline: 3/1; financial award applicants required to submit FAFSA. *Faculty research:* Education technology, learning theory, social theory, cultural diversity, postmodernism. *Unit head:* Deborah L. Vandell, Chair, 949-824-8026, Fax: 949-824-3968, E-mail: dvandell@uci.edu. *Application contact:* Sarah K. Singh, Credential Program Counselor, 949-824-6673, Fax: 949-824-9103, E-mail: sksingh@uci.edu. Web site: http://www.gse.uci.edu/.

University of California, Los Angeles, Graduate Division, Graduate School of Education and Information Studies, Program in Educational Leadership, Los Angeles, CA 90095. Offers Ed D. Evening/weekend programs available. *Degree requirements:* For doctorate, thesis/dissertation, oral and written qualifying exams. *Entrance requirements:* For doctorate, GRE General Test, minimum undergraduate GPA of 3.0, resume. Electronic applications accepted.

University of California, Riverside, Graduate Division, Graduate School of Education, Riverside, CA 92521-0102. Offers autism (M Ed); diversity and equity (M Ed); education, society and culture (MA, PhD); educational psychology (MA, PhD); general education (M Ed); higher education administration and policy (M Ed, PhD); reading (M Ed); school psychology (PhD); special education (M Ed, MA, PhD). *Faculty:* 19 full-time (9 women), 9 part-time/adjunct (6 women). *Students:* 181 full-time (128 women); includes 79 minority (8 Black or African American, non-Hispanic/Latino; 1 American Indian or Alaska Native, non-Hispanic/Latino; 26 Asian, non-Hispanic/Latino; 34 Hispanic/Latino; 10 Two or more races, non-Hispanic/Latino), 5 international. Average age 31. 200 applicants, 48% accepted, 76 enrolled. In 2011, 67 master's, 12 doctorates awarded. Terminal master's awarded for partial completion of doctoral program. *Degree requirements:* For master's, thesis optional, comprehensive exams or thesis (MA), case study or analytical report (M Ed); for doctorate, thesis/dissertation, written and oral qualifying exams, college teaching practicum. *Entrance requirements:* For master's, GRE General Test, CBEST, CSET, minimum GPA of 3.2; for doctorate, GRE General Test, master's degree (desirable), minimum GPA of 3.2. Additional exam requirements/recommendations for international students: Required—TOEFL (minimum score 550 paper-based; 213 computer-based; 80 iBT), IELTS (minimum score 7). *Application deadline:* For fall admission, 9/1 for domestic students, 4/1 for international students; for winter admission, 12/1 for domestic students, 7/1 for international students; for spring admission, 3/1 for domestic students, 10/1 for international students. Applications are processed on a rolling basis. Application fee: $80 ($100 for international students). Electronic applications accepted. *Financial support:* In 2011–12, 59 students received support, including 9 fellowships with full and partial tuition reimbursements available (averaging $26,587 per year), 21 research assistantships with full and partial tuition reimbursements available (averaging $14,517 per year), 1 teaching assistantship with full and partial tuition reimbursement available (averaging $17,307 per year); career-related internships or fieldwork, Federal Work-Study, institutionally sponsored loans, scholarships/grants, and unspecified assistantships also available. Financial award application deadline: 1/5. *Faculty research:* Responsiveness to intervention, faculty core, response to intervention of English language learners, advanced modeling techniques, study on social capital, trust, and motivation. *Total annual research expenditures:* $2.8 million. *Unit head:* Prof. Douglas Mitchell, Interim Dean, 951-827-5802, Fax: 951-827-3942, E-mail: douglas.mitchell@ucr.edu. *Application contact:* Prof. Robert Ream, Graduate Advisor for Admission, 951-827-6362, Fax: 951-827-3291, E-mail: edgrad@ucr.edu. Web site: http://www.education.ucr.edu/.

University of California, Santa Barbara, Graduate Division, Gevirtz Graduate School of Education, Santa Barbara, CA 93106-9490. Offers counseling, clinical and school psychology (M Ed, MA, PhD, Credential), including clinical psychology (PhD), counseling psychology (MA, PhD), school psychology (M Ed, PhD), school psychology: pupil personnel services (Credential); education (M Ed, MA, PhD, Credential), including child and adolescent development (MA, PhD), cultural perspectives and comparative education (MA, PhD), educational leadership and organizations (MA, PhD), multiple subject teaching (Credential), research methodology (MA, PhD), single subject teaching (Credential), special education (Credential), special education disabilities and risk studies (MA), special education, disabilities and risk studies (PhD), teaching (M Ed), teaching and learning (MA, PhD); MA/PhD. *Accreditation:* APA (one or more programs are accredited). *Faculty:* 40 full-time (21 women), 2 part-time/adjunct (both women). *Students:* 389 full-time (301 women); includes 131 minority (14 Black or African American, non-Hispanic/Latino; 2 American Indian or Alaska Native, non-Hispanic/Latino; 41 Asian, non-Hispanic/Latino; 69 Hispanic/Latino; 1 Native Hawaiian or other Pacific Islander, non-Hispanic/Latino; 4 Two or more races, non-Hispanic/Latino), 25 international. Average age 28. 691 applicants, 35% accepted, 154 enrolled. In 2011, 145 master's, 45 doctorates, 118 other advanced degrees awarded. Terminal master's awarded for partial completion of doctoral program. *Degree requirements:* For master's, comprehensive exam (for some programs), thesis (for some programs); for doctorate, comprehensive exam (for some programs), thesis/dissertation; for Credential, CA state requirements (varies by credential). *Entrance requirements:* For master's and doctorate, GRE; for Credential, GRE or MAT, CSET and CBEST. Additional exam requirements/recommendations for international students: Required—TOEFL (minimum score 550 paper-based; 80 iBT), IELTS (minimum score 7). Application fee: $80 ($100 for international students). Electronic applications accepted. *Expenses:* Tuition, state resident: full-time $12,192. Tuition, nonresident: full-time $27,294. *Required fees:* $764.13. *Financial support:* In 2011–12, 301 students received support, including 429 fellowships with partial tuition reimbursements available (averaging $5,017 per year), 83 research assistantships with full and partial tuition reimbursements available (averaging $6,262 per year), 55 teaching assistantships with partial tuition reimbursements available (averaging $8,655 per year); career-related internships or fieldwork also available. Financial award applicants required to submit FAFSA. *Faculty research:* Needs of diverse students, school accountability and leadership, school violence, language learning and literacy, science/math education. *Total annual research expenditures:* $3 million. *Unit head:* Arlis Markel, Assistant Dean, 805-893-5492, Fax: 805-893-2588, E-mail: arlis@education.ucsb.edu. *Application contact:* Kathryn Marie Tucciarone, Student Affairs Officer, 805-893-2137, Fax: 805-893-2588, E-mail: katiet@education.ucsb.edu. Web site: http://www.education.ucsb.edu/.

University of Central Arkansas, Graduate School, College of Education, Department of Leadership Studies, Conway, AR 72035-0001. Offers college student personnel (MS); educational leadership - district level (Ed S); instructional technology (MS); library media and information technology (MS); school counseling (MS); school leadership (MS).

Accreditation: NCATE. Part-time programs available. *Students:* 48 full-time (31 women), 170 part-time (142 women); includes 40 minority (27 Black or African American, non-Hispanic/Latino; 5 American Indian or Alaska Native, non-Hispanic/Latino; 2 Asian, non-Hispanic/Latino; 4 Hispanic/Latino; 2 Two or more races, non-Hispanic/Latino), 3 international. Average age 33. 73 applicants, 100% accepted, 62 enrolled. In 2011, 93 master's, 2 other advanced degrees awarded. *Degree requirements:* For master's and Ed S, comprehensive exam. *Entrance requirements:* For master's, GRE. Additional exam requirements/recommendations for international students: Required—TOEFL. *Application deadline:* For fall admission, 3/1 priority date for domestic students; for spring admission, 10/1 priority date for domestic students. Applications are processed on a rolling basis. Application fee: $25 ($40 for international students). *Expenses:* Contact institution. *Financial support:* Federal Work-Study, scholarships/grants, and tuition waivers (partial) available. Financial award application deadline: 2/15; financial award applicants required to submit FAFSA. *Unit head:* Dr. Terry James, Interim Chair, 501-450-5209, Fax: 501-450-5302. *Application contact:* Sandy Burks, Administrative Specialist, 501-450-3124, Fax: 501-450-5678, E-mail: slburks@uca.edu.

University of Central Florida, College of Education, Department of Educational and Human Sciences, Program in Educational Leadership, Orlando, FL 32816. Offers educational leadership (MA, Ed D), including community college education (MA), higher education (Ed D), student personnel (MA). Part-time and evening/weekend programs available. *Students:* 82 full-time (55 women), 179 part-time (126 women); includes 53 minority (27 Black or African American, non-Hispanic/Latino; 3 Asian, non-Hispanic/Latino; 19 Hispanic/Latino; 4 Two or more races, non-Hispanic/Latino), 1 international. Average age 35. 142 applicants, 69% accepted, 62 enrolled. In 2011, 60 master's, 26 doctorates awarded. *Degree requirements:* For master's, thesis or alternative; for doctorate, thesis/dissertation, candidacy exam. *Entrance requirements:* For master's, GRE General Test; for doctorate, GRE General Test, GRE Subject Test, minimum GPA of 3.0, resume. Additional exam requirements/recommendations for international students: Required—TOEFL. *Application deadline:* For fall admission, 2/20 priority date for domestic students; for spring admission, 9/20 priority date for domestic students. Application fee: $30. Electronic applications accepted. *Expenses:* Tuition, state resident: part-time $277.08 per credit hour. Tuition, nonresident: part-time $277.08 per credit hour. Part-time tuition and fees vary according to degree level and program. *Financial support:* In 2011–12, 17 students received support, including 4 fellowships with partial tuition reimbursements available (averaging $8,300 per year), 14 research assistantships with partial tuition reimbursements available (averaging $7,000 per year), 2 teaching assistantships with partial tuition reimbursements available (averaging $1,000 per year); career-related internships or fieldwork, Federal Work-Study, institutionally sponsored loans, tuition waivers (partial), and unspecified assistantships also available. Financial award application deadline: 3/1; financial award applicants required to submit FAFSA. *Unit head:* Dr. Rosa Cintron, Program Coordinator, 407-832-1248, E-mail: rosa.cintrondelgado@ucf.edu. *Application contact:* Barbara Rodriguez, Director, Admissions and Registration, 407-823-2766, Fax: 407-823-6442, E-mail: gradadmissions@ucf.edu. Web site: http://education.ucf.edu/departments.cfm.

University of Central Florida, College of Education, School of Teaching, Learning, and Leadership, Program in Art Education, Orlando, FL 32816. Offers teacher education (MAT); teacher leadership (M Ed). *Accreditation:* NCATE. Part-time and evening/weekend programs available. *Students:* 4 full-time (3 women), 16 part-time (14 women); includes 2 minority (1 Black or African American, non-Hispanic/Latino; 1 Hispanic/Latino). Average age 32. 4 applicants, 75% accepted, 1 enrolled. In 2011, 6 master's awarded. *Degree requirements:* For master's, thesis or alternative, research report, internship (MA). *Entrance requirements:* Additional exam requirements/recommendations for international students: Required—TOEFL. *Application deadline:* For fall admission, 7/15 for domestic students; for spring admission, 12/1 for domestic students. Application fee: $30. Electronic applications accepted. *Expenses:* Tuition, state resident: part-time $277.08 per credit hour. Tuition, nonresident: part-time $277.08 per credit hour. Part-time tuition and fees vary according to degree level and program. *Financial support:* Fellowships with partial tuition reimbursements, research assistantships with tuition reimbursements, teaching assistantships with partial tuition reimbursements, career-related internships or fieldwork, Federal Work-Study, institutionally sponsored loans, tuition waivers (partial), and unspecified assistantships available. Financial award application deadline: 3/1; financial award applicants required to submit FAFSA. *Unit head:* Dr. Janet B. Andreasen, Program Coordinator, 407-823-5430, E-mail: janet.andreasen@ucf.edu. *Application contact:* Barbara Rodriguez, Director, Admissions and Registration, 407-823-2766, Fax: 407-823-6442, E-mail: gradadmissions@ucf.edu. Web site: http://education.ucf.edu/departments.cfm.

University of Central Florida, College of Education, School of Teaching, Learning, and Leadership, Program in English Language Arts Education, Orlando, FL 32816. Offers teacher education (MAT), including ESOL endorsement; teacher leadership (M Ed). *Accreditation:* NCATE. Part-time and evening/weekend programs available. *Students:* 18 full-time (15 women), 30 part-time (25 women); includes 14 minority (5 Black or African American, non-Hispanic/Latino; 2 Asian, non-Hispanic/Latino; 6 Hispanic/Latino; 1 Two or more races, non-Hispanic/Latino). Average age 29. 14 applicants, 71% accepted, 9 enrolled. In 2011, 14 master's awarded. *Degree requirements:* For master's, thesis or alternative, research project. *Entrance requirements:* For master's, GRE General Test. Additional exam requirements/recommendations for international students: Required—TOEFL. *Application deadline:* For fall admission, 7/15 for domestic students; for spring admission, 12/1 for domestic students. Application fee: $30. Electronic applications accepted. *Expenses:* Tuition, state resident: part-time $277.08 per credit hour. Tuition, nonresident: part-time $277.08 per credit hour. Part-time tuition and fees vary according to degree level and program. *Financial support:* In 2011–12, 1 student received support. Fellowships with partial tuition reimbursements available, research assistantships with partial tuition reimbursements available, teaching assistantships with partial tuition reimbursements available, career-related internships or fieldwork, Federal Work-Study, institutionally sponsored loans, tuition waivers (partial), and unspecified assistantships available. Financial award application deadline: 3/1; financial award applicants required to submit FAFSA. *Unit head:* Dr. Janet B. Andreasen, Program Coordinator, 407-823-5430, E-mail: janet.andreasen@ucf.edu. *Application contact:* Barbara Rodriguez, Director, Admissions and Registration, 407-823-2766, Fax: 407-823-6442, E-mail: gradadmissions@ucf.edu.

University of Central Florida, College of Education, School of Teaching, Learning, and Leadership, Program in Mathematics Education, Orlando, FL 32816. Offers teacher education (MAT), including mathematics education, middle school mathematics; teacher leadership (M Ed). *Accreditation:* NCATE. Part-time and evening/weekend programs available. *Students:* 10 full-time (9 women), 32 part-time (23 women); includes 11 minority (4 Black or African American, non-Hispanic/Latino; 3 Asian, non-Hispanic/Latino; 4 Hispanic/Latino). Average age 35. 16 applicants, 63% accepted, 7 enrolled. In 2011, 16 master's awarded. *Entrance requirements:* For master's, GRE General Test. Additional exam requirements/recommendations for international students: Required—TOEFL. *Application deadline:* For fall admission, 7/15 for domestic students; for spring admission, 12/1 for domestic students. Application fee: $30. Electronic applications accepted. *Expenses:* Tuition, state resident: part-time $277.08 per credit hour. Tuition, nonresident: part-time $277.08 per credit hour. Part-time tuition and fees vary according to degree level and program. *Financial support:* In 2011–12, 1 student received support, including 1 research assistantship with partial tuition reimbursement available (averaging $6,900 per year); fellowships with partial tuition reimbursements available, teaching assistantships with partial tuition reimbursements available, career-related internships or fieldwork, Federal Work-Study, institutionally sponsored loans, tuition waivers (partial), and unspecified assistantships also available. Financial award application deadline: 3/1; financial award applicants required to submit FAFSA. *Unit head:* Dr. Janet B. Andreasen, Program Coordinator, 407-823-5430, E-mail: janet.andreasen@ucf.edu. *Application contact:* Barbara Rodriguez, Director, Admissions and Registration, 407-823-2766, Fax: 407-823-6442, E-mail: gradadmissions@ucf.edu.

University of Central Florida, College of Education, School of Teaching, Learning, and Leadership, Program in Science Education, Orlando, FL 32816. Offers teacher education (MAT), including biology, middle school science, physics; teacher leadership (M Ed), including science education. *Accreditation:* NCATE. Part-time and evening/weekend programs available. *Students:* 9 full-time (6 women), 19 part-time (12 women); includes 5 minority (1 Asian, non-Hispanic/Latino; 3 Hispanic/Latino; 1 Two or more races, non-Hispanic/Latino). Average age 33. 19 applicants, 58% accepted, 7 enrolled. In 2011, 21 master's awarded. *Entrance requirements:* For master's, GRE General Test. Additional exam requirements/recommendations for international students: Required—TOEFL. *Application deadline:* For fall admission, 7/15 for domestic students; for spring admission, 12/1 for domestic students. Application fee: $30. Electronic applications accepted. *Expenses:* Tuition, state resident: part-time $277.08 per credit hour. Tuition, nonresident: part-time $277.08 per credit hour. Part-time tuition and fees vary according to degree level and program. *Financial support:* Career-related internships or fieldwork, Federal Work-Study, institutionally sponsored loans, tuition waivers (partial), and unspecified assistantships available. Financial award application deadline: 3/1; financial award applicants required to submit FAFSA. *Unit head:* Dr. Janet B. Andreasen, Program Coordinator, 407-823-5430, E-mail: janet.andreasen@ucf.edu. *Application contact:* Barbara Rodriguez, Director, Admissions and Registration, 407-823-2766, Fax: 407-823-6442, E-mail: gradadmissions@ucf.edu.

University of Central Florida, College of Education, School of Teaching, Learning, and Leadership, Program in Social Science Education, Orlando, FL 32816. Offers teacher education (MAT); teacher leadership (M Ed). *Accreditation:* NCATE. Part-time and evening/weekend programs available. *Students:* 14 full-time (6 women), 47 part-time (27 women); includes 5 minority (3 Black or African American, non-Hispanic/Latino; 2 Hispanic/Latino). Average age 31. 22 applicants, 68% accepted, 14 enrolled. In 2011, 28 master's awarded. *Entrance requirements:* For master's, GRE General Test. Additional exam requirements/recommendations for international students: Required—TOEFL. *Application deadline:* For fall admission, 7/15 for domestic students; for spring admission, 12/1 for domestic students. Application fee: $12. Electronic applications accepted. *Expenses:* Tuition, state resident: part-time $277.08 per credit hour. Tuition, nonresident: part-time $277.08 per credit hour. Part-time tuition and fees vary according to degree level and program. *Financial support:* In 2011–12, 2 students received support, including 2 research assistantships (averaging $4,100 per year), 1 teaching assistantship (averaging $4,900 per year); career-related internships or fieldwork, Federal Work-Study, institutionally sponsored loans, tuition waivers (partial), and unspecified assistantships also available. Financial award application deadline: 3/1; financial award applicants required to submit FAFSA. *Unit head:* Dr. Janet B. Andreasen, Program Coordinator, 407-823-5430, E-mail: janet.andreasen@ucf.edu. *Application contact:* Barbara Rodriguez, Director, Admissions and Registration, 407-823-2766, Fax: 407-823-6442, E-mail: gradadmissions@ucf.edu.

University of Central Florida, College of Education, School of Teaching, Learning, and Leadership, Teacher Leadership and Educational Leadership Program, Orlando, FL 32816. Offers educational leadership (Ed S); teacher leadership (M Ed). *Students:* 9 full-time (6 women), 64 part-time (51 women); includes 14 minority (6 Black or African American, non-Hispanic/Latino; 2 Asian, non-Hispanic/Latino; 5 Hispanic/Latino; 1 Two or more races, non-Hispanic/Latino), 1 international. Average age 32. 58 applicants, 90% accepted, 37 enrolled. In 2011, 13 master's, 16 Ed Ss awarded. Application fee: $30. Electronic applications accepted. *Expenses:* Tuition, state resident: part-time $277.08 per credit hour. Tuition, nonresident: part-time $277.08 per credit hour. Part-time tuition and fees vary according to degree level and program. *Financial support:* In 2011–12, 1 student received support, including 1 fellowship (averaging $10,000 per year). *Unit head:* Dr. Carolyn Hopp, Program Coordinator, 407-823-0392, E-mail: carolyn.hopp@ucf.edu. *Application contact:* Barbara Rodriguez, Director, Admissions and Registration, 407-823-2766, Fax: 407-823-6442, E-mail: gradadmissions@ucf.edu. Web site: http://education.ucf.edu/departments.cfm.

University of Central Missouri, The Graduate School, College of Education, Warrensburg, MO 64093. Offers career and technical education administration (MS); career and technical education industry training (MS); career and technical education leadership/teaching (MS); college student personnel administration (MS); counseling (MS); curriculum and instruction (Ed S); educational leadership (Ed D); educational technology (MS); elementary education/educational foundations and literacy (MSE); elementary school administration (MSE); elementary school principalship (Ed S); human services/learning resources (Ed S); human services/professional counseling (Ed S); human services/special education (Ed S); human services/technology and occupational education (Ed S); K-12 education/educational foundations and literacy (MSE); K-12 special education (MSE); library science and information services (MS); literacy education (MSE); secondary education/educational foundations & literacy (MSE); secondary school administration (MSE); secondary school principalship (Ed S); superintendency (Ed S); teaching (MAT). Ed D offered jointly with University of Missouri. Part-time programs available. Postbaccalaureate distance learning degree programs offered. *Entrance requirements:* Additional exam requirements/recommendations for international students: Required—TOEFL (minimum score 550 paper-based; 79 computer-based). Electronic applications accepted.

University of Central Oklahoma, College of Graduate Studies and Research, College of Education and Professional Studies, Department of Advanced Professional and Special Services, Program in Educational Leadership, Edmond, OK 73034-5209. Offers M Ed. *Accreditation:* NCATE. Part-time programs available. *Entrance requirements:* For master's, GRE General Test. Additional exam requirements/recommendations for international students: Required—TOEFL (minimum score 550 paper-based; 213 computer-based). *Application deadline:* For fall admission, 7/1 for international students; for spring admission, 11/1 for international students. Applications are processed on a rolling basis. Application fee: $50. Electronic applications accepted. *Expenses:* Tuition, state resident: full-time $3901; part-time $218.30 per credit hour. Tuition, nonresident: full-time $9198; part-time $511.20 per credit hour. Tuition and fees vary according to program. *Financial support:* Unspecified assistantships available. Financial award application deadline: 3/31; financial award applicants required to submit FAFSA. *Unit head:* Dr. J. Kirk Webster, Coordinator, 405-974-5448, Fax: 405-974-3822. *Application contact:* Dr. Richard Bernard, Dean, Jackson College of Graduate Studies, 405-974-3493, Fax: 405-974-3852, E-mail: gradcoll@uco.edu. Web site: http://www.uco.edu/ceps/dept/apss/educational-leadership/index.asp.

University of Cincinnati, Graduate School, College of Education, Criminal Justice, and Human Services, Division of Educational Studies, Program in Educational Leadership,

Cincinnati, OH 45221. Offers M Ed, Ed S. *Accreditation:* NCATE. Part-time programs available. Postbaccalaureate distance learning degree programs offered. *Degree requirements:* For master's, thesis or alternative. *Entrance requirements:* For master's, GRE General Test, 3 letters of reference, resume, minimum GPA of 2.8; for Ed S, references, interview. Additional exam requirements/recommendations for international students: Required—TOEFL (minimum score 550 paper-based). Electronic applications accepted.

University of Cincinnati, Graduate School, College of Education, Criminal Justice, and Human Services, Division of Educational Studies, Program in Urban Educational Leadership, Cincinnati, OH 45221. Offers Ed D. *Degree requirements:* For doctorate, thesis/dissertation. *Entrance requirements:* For doctorate, GRE General Test, GRE Subject Test. Additional exam requirements/recommendations for international students: Required—TOEFL (minimum score 550 paper-based), OEPT.

University of Colorado at Colorado Springs, College of Education, Colorado Springs, CO 80933-7150. Offers counseling and human services (MA); curriculum and instruction (MA); educational administration (MA); educational leadership (MA, PhD); special education (MA). *Accreditation:* ACA; NCATE. Part-time and evening/weekend programs available. Postbaccalaureate distance learning degree programs offered (minimal on-campus study). *Faculty:* 26 full-time (16 women), 9 part-time/adjunct (5 women). *Students:* 307 full-time (203 women), 115 part-time (92 women); includes 82 minority (24 Black or African American, non-Hispanic/Latino; 3 American Indian or Alaska Native, non-Hispanic/Latino; 12 Asian, non-Hispanic/Latino; 36 Hispanic/Latino; 1 Native Hawaiian or other Pacific Islander, non-Hispanic/Latino; 6 Two or more races, non-Hispanic/Latino), 1 international. Average age 36. 99 applicants, 86% accepted, 61 enrolled. In 2011, 165 master's, 6 doctorates awarded. *Degree requirements:* For master's, comprehensive exam, thesis or alternative, microcomputer proficiency; for doctorate, comprehensive exam, thesis/dissertation, research lab. *Entrance requirements:* For master's, GRE General Test. Additional exam requirements/recommendations for international students: Recommended—TOEFL. *Application deadline:* For fall admission, 2/28 priority date for domestic students, 2/28 for international students; for spring admission, 10/15 for domestic and international students. Applications are processed on a rolling basis. Application fee: $60 ($75 for international students). *Expenses:* Tuition, state resident: part-time $660 per credit hour. Tuition, nonresident: part-time $1133 per credit hour. Tuition and fees vary according to degree level, program and student level. *Financial support:* In 2011–12, 57 students received support. Career-related internships or fieldwork, Federal Work-Study, and scholarships/grants available. Support available to part-time students. Financial award application deadline: 3/1; financial award applicants required to submit FAFSA. *Faculty research:* Job training for special populations, materials development for classroom. *Total annual research expenditures:* $1.6 million. *Unit head:* Dr. Mary Snyder, Dean, 719-255-3701, Fax: 719-262-4133, E-mail: msnyder3@uccs.edu. *Application contact:* Juliane Field, Director, 719-255-4526, Fax: 719-255-4110, E-mail: jfield@uccs.edu. Web site: http://www.uccs.edu/coe.

University of Colorado Denver, School of Education and Human Development, Administrative Leadership and Policy Studies Program, Denver, CO 80217. Offers MA, Ed S. *Accreditation:* NCATE. Part-time and evening/weekend programs available. *Students:* 95 full-time (65 women), 9 part-time (6 women); includes 14 minority (3 Black or African American, non-Hispanic/Latino; 1 Asian, non-Hispanic/Latino; 10 Hispanic/Latino). Average age 36. 16 applicants, 94% accepted, 14 enrolled. In 2011, 21 master's, 22 other advanced degrees awarded. *Degree requirements:* For master's, comprehensive exam, 9 credit hours beyond the 32 required for principal-administrator licensure; for Ed S, comprehensive exam, 9 credit hours beyond the 32 required for principal-administrator licensure (for those already holding MA). *Entrance requirements:* For master's and Ed S, GRE or MAT (if GPA is below 2.75), minimum GPA of 2.75, interview, 3 letters of recommendation, resume. Additional exam requirements/recommendations for international students: Required—TOEFL (minimum score 525 paper-based). *Application deadline:* For fall admission, 6/15 for domestic students, 6/1 for international students; for spring admission, 10/1 for domestic students, 9/15 for international students. Application fee: $50 ($75 for international students). Electronic applications accepted. *Expenses:* Contact institution. *Financial support:* Research assistantships, teaching assistantships, and Federal Work-Study available. Financial award application deadline: 4/1; financial award applicants required to submit FAFSA. *Faculty research:* Learning cultures, teaching and learning in educational administration. *Unit head:* Connie Fulmer, Professor, 303-315-4962, E-mail: connie.fulmer@ucdenver.edu. *Application contact:* Rebecca Schell, Academic Advisor, 303-315-4978, E-mail: rebecca.schell@ucdenver.edu. Web site: http://www.ucdenver.edu/academics/colleges/SchoolOfEducation/Apply/Pages/AdministrativeLeadershipPolicyStudies.aspx.

University of Colorado Denver, School of Education and Human Development, Program in Educational Leadership and Innovation, Denver, CO 80217-3364. Offers educational studies and research (PhD), including administrative leadership and policy, early childhood special education, math education, research, assessment and evaluation, science education, urban ecologies. Part-time and evening/weekend programs available. *Students:* 21 full-time (15 women), 25 part-time (17 women); includes 10 minority (5 Black or African American, non-Hispanic/Latino; 1 American Indian or Alaska Native, non-Hispanic/Latino; 3 Asian, non-Hispanic/Latino; 1 Hispanic/Latino), 1 international. Average age 43. 11 applicants, 45% accepted, 3 enrolled. In 2011, 11 doctorates awarded. *Degree requirements:* For doctorate, comprehensive exam, thesis/dissertation, 75 credit hours (for PhD). *Entrance requirements:* For doctorate, GRE or equivalent, resume or curriculum vitae, written statement, letters of recommendation, master's degree or equivalent, completion of basic or advanced statistics course with minimum B grade. Additional exam requirements/recommendations for international students: Required—TOEFL (minimum score 525 paper-based; 197 computer-based). *Application deadline:* Applications are processed on a rolling basis. Application fee: $50 ($75 for international students). Electronic applications accepted. *Expenses:* Contact institution. *Financial support:* Fellowships, research assistantships, teaching assistantships, scholarships/grants, and unspecified assistantships available. Financial award application deadline: 4/1; financial award applicants required to submit FAFSA. *Faculty research:* Administrative leadership and policy studies, early childhood education, research in diversity, paraprofessionals in education, urban schools lab. *Unit head:* Dr. Deanna Sands, Associate Dean, Research and Professional Development, 303-315-4931, E-mail: deanna.sands@ucdenver.edu. *Application contact:* Student Services Center, 303-315-6300, Fax: 303-315-6311, E-mail: education@ucdenver.edu. Web site: http://www.ucdenver.edu/ACADEMICS/COLLEGES/SCHOOLOFEDUCATION/ACADEMICS/Pages/AcademicPrograms.aspx.

University of Colorado Denver, School of Education and Human Development, Program in Leadership for Educational Equity, Denver, CO 80217. Offers executive leadership (Ed D); instructional leadership (Ed D). *Students:* 31 full-time (23 women), 2 part-time (both women); includes 3 minority (all Hispanic/Latino). Average age 40. 1 applicant, 100% accepted, 1 enrolled. *Degree requirements:* For doctorate, thesis/dissertation, 69 credit hours, including 24 credits in dissertation and independent study. *Entrance requirements:* For doctorate, GRE General Test (minimum score of 1000), resume with minimum of 5 years experience in an educational background, 2-3 professional artifacts illuminating leadership experiences, three professional letters of recommendation, master's degree with recommended minimum GPA of 3.2. Additional exam requirements/recommendations for international students: Required—TOEFL (minimum score 550 paper-based; 213 computer-based; 80 iBT). *Application deadline:* For spring admission, 10/1 for international students. Applications are processed on a rolling basis. Application fee: $50 ($75 for international students). *Financial support:* Application deadline: 4/1; applicants required to submit FAFSA. *Unit head:* Dr. Shelley Zion, Executive Director of the Center for Continuing Professional Education, 303-315-4920, E-mail: shelley.zion@ucdenver.edu. *Application contact:* Student Services Center, 303-315-6300, Fax: 303-315-6311, E-mail: education@ucdenver.edu. Web site: http://www.ucdenver.edu/academics/colleges/SchoolOfEducation/Academics/Doctorate/Pages/EdD.aspx.

University of Connecticut, Graduate School, Neag School of Education, Department of Educational Leadership, Field of Educational Administration, Storrs, CT 06269. Offers Ed D, PhD, Post-Master's Certificate. *Accreditation:* NCATE. *Degree requirements:* For doctorate, thesis/dissertation. *Entrance requirements:* For doctorate, GRE General Test. Additional exam requirements/recommendations for international students: Required—TOEFL (minimum score 550 paper-based; 213 computer-based). Electronic applications accepted.

University of Dayton, Department of Counselor Education and Human Services, Dayton, OH 45469-1300. Offers college student personnel (MS Ed); community counseling (MS Ed); higher education administration (MS Ed); human services (MS Ed); school counseling (MS Ed); school psychology (MS Ed, Ed S). *Accreditation:* ACA; NCATE. Part-time and evening/weekend programs available. *Faculty:* 12 full-time (9 women), 30 part-time/adjunct (20 women). *Students:* 223 full-time (184 women), 189 part-time (147 women); includes 91 minority (83 Black or African American, non-Hispanic/Latino; 1 American Indian or Alaska Native, non-Hispanic/Latino; 2 Asian, non-Hispanic/Latino; 3 Hispanic/Latino; 2 Two or more races, non-Hispanic/Latino), 5 international. Average age 34. 336 applicants, 40% accepted, 96 enrolled. In 2011, 170 master's, 10 Ed Ss awarded. *Degree requirements:* For master's, comprehensive exam (for some programs), thesis (for some programs), exit exam. *Entrance requirements:* For master's, MAT or GRE (if GPA less than 2.75), interview, writing sample. Additional exam requirements/recommendations for international students: Required—TOEFL (minimum score 550 paper-based; 213 computer-based; 80 iBT). *Application deadline:* For fall admission, 4/10 for domestic students, 3/1 for international students; for winter admission, 9/10 for domestic students, 7/1 for international students; for spring admission, 1/10 for domestic students, 1/1 for international students. Application fee: $0 ($50 for international students). Electronic applications accepted. *Expenses: Tuition:* Full-time $8400; part-time $700 per credit hour. *Required fees:* $25 per semester. Tuition and fees vary according to degree level. *Financial support:* In 2011–12, 7 research assistantships with full and partial tuition reimbursements (averaging $8,550 per year) were awarded; career-related internships or fieldwork, institutionally sponsored loans, health care benefits, and unspecified assistantships also available. Financial award applicants required to submit FAFSA. *Faculty research:* Mindfulness, forgiveness in relationships, positive psychology in couples counseling, traumatic brain injury responses. *Unit head:* Dr. Moly Schaller, Chairperson, 937-229-3644, Fax: 937-229-1055, E-mail: mschaller1@udayton.edu. *Application contact:* Kathleen Brown, 937-229-3644, Fax: 937-229-1055, E-mail: kbrown1@udayton.edu. Web site: http://soeap.udayton.edu/edc.

University of Dayton, Department of Teacher Education, Dayton, OH 45469-1300. Offers adolescent/young adult (MS Ed); art education (MS Ed); early childhood education (MS Ed); early childhood leadership advocacy (MS Ed); inclusive early childhood (MS Ed); interdisciplinary education (MS Ed); intervention specialist education, mild/moderate (MS Ed); literacy (MS Ed); middle childhood (MS Ed); multi-age education (MS Ed); music education (MS Ed); teacher as leader (MS Ed); technology in education (MS Ed). Part-time and evening/weekend programs available. Postbaccalaureate distance learning degree programs offered (no on-campus study). *Faculty:* 15 full-time (11 women), 22 part-time/adjunct (20 women). *Students:* 41 full-time (29 women), 95 part-time (87 women); includes 13 minority (9 Black or African American, non-Hispanic/Latino; 1 Asian, non-Hispanic/Latino; 3 Hispanic/Latino), 9 international. Average age 32. 111 applicants, 55% accepted, 38 enrolled. In 2011, 97 degrees awarded. *Degree requirements:* For master's, thesis, capstone research project. *Entrance requirements:* For master's, GRE General Test, minimum GPA of 2.75. Additional exam requirements/recommendations for international students: Required—TOEFL (minimum score 550 paper-based; 213 computer-based; 80 iBT). *Application deadline:* For fall admission, 3/1 priority date for domestic students, 3/1 for international students; for winter admission, 7/1 for international students; for spring admission, 1/1 for international students. Applications are processed on a rolling basis. Application fee: $0 ($50 for international students). Electronic applications accepted. *Expenses:* Contact institution. *Financial support:* In 2011–12, 5 research assistantships with full and partial tuition reimbursements (averaging $8,470 per year) were awarded; career-related internships or fieldwork, institutionally sponsored loans, health care benefits, and unspecified assistantships also available. Financial award applicants required to submit FAFSA. *Faculty research:* Diversity, literacy, art representation by young children, preservice teacher preparation. *Unit head:* Dr. Katie A. Kinnucan-Welsch, Chair, 937-229-3346. *Application contact:* Alexsandar Popovski, Enrollment Management Administrator, 937-229-2357, Fax: 937-229-4729, E-mail: alex.popovski@notes.udayton.edu.

University of Dayton, Doctoral Program in Educational Leadership, Dayton, OH 45469-1300. Offers PhD. Evening/weekend programs available. *Faculty:* 12 full-time (4 women). *Students:* 55 full-time (36 women); includes 4 minority (all Black or African American, non-Hispanic/Latino). Average age 42. 26 applicants, 35% accepted, 7 enrolled. In 2011, 4 doctorates awarded. *Degree requirements:* For doctorate, comprehensive exam, thesis/dissertation. *Entrance requirements:* For doctorate, GRE, administration experience, minimum GPA of 3.25. Additional exam requirements/recommendations for international students: Required—TOEFL (minimum score 550 paper-based; 213 computer-based; 80 iBT). *Application deadline:* For fall admission, 3/1 for international students; for winter admission, 7/1 for international students; for spring admission, 1/1 for international students. Applications are processed on a rolling basis. Application fee: $0 ($50 for international students). Electronic applications accepted. *Expenses: Tuition:* Full-time $8400; part-time $700 per credit hour. *Required fees:* $25 per semester. Tuition and fees vary according to degree level. *Financial support:* In 2011–12, 1 fellowship (averaging $12,800 per year), 6 research assistantships with full tuition reimbursements (averaging $12,350 per year) were awarded; institutionally sponsored loans, health care benefits, and unspecified assistantships also available. Financial award applicants required to submit FAFSA. *Unit head:* Dr. A. William Place, Director, 937-229-4003, Fax: 937-229-4003, E-mail: aplace1@udayton.edu. *Application contact:* Nancy Crouchley, Administrative Assistant, 937-229-4003, Fax: 937-229-4729, E-mail: ncrouchley1@udayton.edu. Web site: http://www.udayton.edu/education/phd/.

University of Dayton, Educational Leadership Program, Dayton, OH 45469-1300. Offers education administration (Ed S); educational leadership (MS Ed). Part-time and evening/weekend programs available. Postbaccalaureate distance learning degree programs offered (no on-campus study). *Faculty:* 11 full-time (3 women), 20 part-time/adjunct (5 women). *Students:* 90 full-time (55 women), 159 part-time (103 women);

includes 18 minority (16 Black or African American, non-Hispanic/Latino; 2 Hispanic/Latino), 19 international. Average age 34. 91 applicants, 58% accepted, 34 enrolled. In 2011, 224 master's, 3 Ed Ss awarded. *Degree requirements:* For master's, comprehensive exam (for some programs), thesis or alternative. *Entrance requirements:* For master's, MAT or GRE (if GPA less than 2.75), minimum GPA of 2.75. Additional exam requirements/recommendations for international students: Required—TOEFL (minimum score 550 paper-based; 213 computer-based; 80 iBT). *Application deadline:* For fall admission, 1/20 priority date for domestic students, 6/1 for international students; for winter admission, 10/10 for domestic students, 10/1 for international students; for spring admission, 1/14 for domestic students, 1/1 for international students. Applications are processed on a rolling basis. Application fee: $0 ($50 for international students). Electronic applications accepted. *Expenses: Tuition:* Full-time $8400; part-time $700 per credit hour. *Required fees:* $25 per semester. Tuition and fees vary according to degree level. *Financial support:* In 2011–12, 5 research assistantships with full tuition reimbursements (averaging $9,200 per year) were awarded; career-related internships or fieldwork, institutionally sponsored loans, health care benefits, and unspecified assistantships also available. Financial award applicants required to submit FAFSA. *Faculty research:* Preparation for school superintendents, issues in diversity, legal issues in special education, online education, Catholic school leadership. *Unit head:* Dr. David D. Dolph, Chair, 937-229-3737, E-mail: ddolph1@udayton.edu. *Application contact:* Janice Keivel, Administrative Associate, 937-229-3755, Fax: 937-229-3392, E-mail: jkeivel1@udayton.edu. Web site: http://www.udayton.edu/education/edl.

University of Delaware, College of Education and Human Development, School of Education, Newark, DE 19716. Offers education (PhD); educational leadership (Ed D); higher education (M Ed); instruction (MI); reading (M Ed); school leadership (M Ed); school psychology (MA, Ed S); teaching English as a second language (TESL) (MA). *Accreditation:* NCATE. Part-time and evening/weekend programs available. Terminal master's awarded for partial completion of doctoral program. *Degree requirements:* For master's, comprehensive exam (for some programs), thesis (for some programs); for doctorate, comprehensive exam (for some programs), thesis/dissertation. *Entrance requirements:* For master's and doctorate, GRE, 3 letters of recommendation. Additional exam requirements/recommendations for international students: Required—TOEFL (minimum score 600 paper-based; 250 computer-based). Electronic applications accepted. *Faculty research:* Teacher education; curriculum theory and development; community based education models, educational leadership.

University of Denver, Morgridge College of Education, Denver, CO 80208. Offers advanced study in law librarianship (Certificate); child and family studies (MA, PhD); counseling psychology (MA, PhD); curriculum and instruction (MA, PhD, Certificate); educational leadership (Ed D, PhD); educational leadership and policy studies (MA, Certificate); higher education (MA, PhD); library and information science (MLIS); research methods and statistics (MA, PhD); school administration (PhD); school psychology (Ed S). *Accreditation:* ALA; APA (one or more programs are accredited). Part-time and evening/weekend programs available. Postbaccalaureate distance learning degree programs offered (no on-campus study). *Faculty:* 34 full-time (25 women), 70 part-time/adjunct (54 women). *Students:* 385 full-time (289 women), 386 part-time (303 women); includes 168 minority (49 Black or African American, non-Hispanic/Latino; 8 American Indian or Alaska Native, non-Hispanic/Latino; 25 Asian, non-Hispanic/Latino; 71 Hispanic/Latino; 1 Native Hawaiian or other Pacific Islander, non-Hispanic/Latino; 14 Two or more races, non-Hispanic/Latino), 17 international. Average age 33. 668 applicants, 72% accepted, 256 enrolled. In 2011, 308 master's, 43 doctorates, 55 other advanced degrees awarded. Terminal master's awarded for partial completion of doctoral program. *Degree requirements:* For master's, comprehensive exam; for doctorate, 2 foreign languages, comprehensive exam, thesis/dissertation. *Entrance requirements:* For master's and doctorate, GRE General Test or GMAT. Additional exam requirements/recommendations for international students: Required—TOEFL (minimum score 550 paper-based; 80 iBT). *Application deadline:* Applications are processed on a rolling basis. Application fee: $60. Electronic applications accepted. *Financial support:* In 2011–12, 72 teaching assistantships with full and partial tuition reimbursements (averaging $9,049 per year) were awarded; career-related internships or fieldwork, Federal Work-Study, institutionally sponsored loans, scholarships/grants, and unspecified assistantships also available. Support available to part-time students. Financial award application deadline: 2/15; financial award applicants required to submit FAFSA. *Faculty research:* Parkinson's disease, personnel training, development and assessments, gifted education, service-learning, transportation, public schools. *Unit head:* Dr. Gregory M. Anderson, Dean, 303-871-3665, E-mail: gregory.m.anderson@du.edu. *Application contact:* Chris Dowen, Director, MCE Admission Office, 303-871-2783, E-mail: chris.dowen@du.edu. Web site: http://www.du.edu/education/.

University of Detroit Mercy, College of Liberal Arts and Education, Department of Education, Program in Educational Administration, Detroit, MI 48221. Offers MA. *Degree requirements:* For master's, thesis or alternative. *Entrance requirements:* For master's, minimum GPA of 2.75.

The University of Findlay, Graduate and Professional Studies, College of Education, Findlay, OH 45840-3653. Offers administration (MA Ed); children's literature (MA Ed); early childhood (MA Ed); human resource development (MA Ed); reading endorsement (MA Ed); science (MA Ed); special education (MA Ed); technology (MA Ed). *Accreditation:* NCATE. Part-time and evening/weekend programs available. Postbaccalaureate distance learning degree programs offered (no on-campus study). *Faculty:* 16 full-time (12 women), 5 part-time/adjunct (2 women). *Students:* 72 full-time (49 women), 198 part-time (119 women); includes 10 minority (7 Black or African American, non-Hispanic/Latino; 1 Asian, non-Hispanic/Latino; 2 Hispanic/Latino), 16 international. Average age 30. 75 applicants, 88% accepted, 36 enrolled. In 2011, 76 master's awarded. *Degree requirements:* For master's, thesis, cumulative project. *Entrance requirements:* For master's, bachelor's degree from accredited institution, minimum undergraduate GPA of 2.75 in last 62 hours of course work. Additional exam requirements/recommendations for international students: Required—TOEFL (minimum score 550 paper-based; 213 computer-based; 80 iBT). *Application deadline:* Applications are processed on a rolling basis. Application fee: $25. Electronic applications accepted. *Expenses:* Contact institution. *Financial support:* In 2011–12, 5 research assistantships with full and partial tuition reimbursements (averaging $4,200 per year) were awarded; Federal Work-Study, health care benefits, and unspecified assistantships also available. Financial award application deadline: 4/1; financial award applicants required to submit FAFSA. *Faculty research:* Children's literature, books and artwork, educational technology, professional development. *Unit head:* Dr. Julie McIntosh, Dean, 419-434-4862, Fax: 419-434-4822. *Application contact:* Heather Riffle, Assistant Director, Graduate and Professional Studies, 419-434-4640, Fax: 419-434-5517, E-mail: riffle@findlay.edu. Web site: http://www.findlay.edu.

University of Florida, Graduate School, College of Education, Department of Educational Administration and Policy, Gainesville, FL 32611. Offers curriculum and instruction (Ed D, PhD); educational leadership (M Ed, MAE, Ed D, PhD, Ed S); higher education administration (Ed D, PhD, Ed S); student personnel in higher education (M Ed, MAE); PhD/JD. *Accreditation:* NCATE. Part-time and evening/weekend programs available. Postbaccalaureate distance learning degree programs offered. Terminal master's awarded for partial completion of doctoral program. *Degree requirements:* For master's, thesis (for some programs); for doctorate, comprehensive exam (for some programs), thesis/dissertation (for some programs). *Entrance requirements:* For master's, GRE General Test, minimum GPA of 3.0, teaching experience; for doctorate and Ed S, GRE General Test, minimum GPA of 3.0. Additional exam requirements/recommendations for international students: Required—TOEFL (minimum score 550 paper-based; 213 computer-based; 80 iBT), IELTS (minimum score 6). *Application deadline:* For fall admission, 2/15 for domestic students, 12/1 for international students; for spring admission, 9/15 for domestic students, 3/1 for international students. Applications are processed on a rolling basis. Application fee: $30. Electronic applications accepted. *Financial support:* Career-related internships or fieldwork and unspecified assistantships available. Financial award applicants required to submit FAFSA.

University of Georgia, College of Education, Department of Lifelong Education, Administration and Policy, Athens, GA 30602. Offers adult education (M Ed, Ed D, PhD, Ed S); educational administration and policy (M Ed, PhD, Ed S); educational leadership (Ed D); human resource and organizational design (M Ed). *Accreditation:* NCATE. *Faculty:* 25 full-time (18 women), 1 part-time/adjunct (0 women). *Students:* 74 full-time (56 women), 216 part-time (136 women); includes 73 minority (62 Black or African American, non-Hispanic/Latino; 4 Asian, non-Hispanic/Latino; 3 Hispanic/Latino; 4 Two or more races, non-Hispanic/Latino), 23 international. Average age 37. 123 applicants, 64% accepted, 45 enrolled. In 2011, 54 master's, 19 doctorates, 14 other advanced degrees awarded. *Entrance requirements:* For master's and Ed S, GRE General Test or MAT; for doctorate, GRE General Test. *Application deadline:* For fall admission, 7/1 priority date for domestic students; for spring admission, 11/15 for domestic students. Application fee: $50. Electronic applications accepted. *Unit head:* Dr. Janette Hill, Head, 706-542-4035, Fax: 706-542-5873, E-mail: janette@.uga.edu. *Application contact:* Dr. Robert B. Hill, Graduate Coordinator, 706-542-4016, Fax: 706-542-5873, E-mail: bobhill@uga.edu. Web site: http://www.coe.uga.edu/leap/.

University of Georgia, College of Education, Department of Workforce Education, Leadership and Social Foundations, Athens, GA 30602. Offers educational leadership (Ed D); human resources and organization design (M Ed); occupational studies (MAT, Ed D, PhD, Ed S); social foundations of education (PhD). *Accreditation:* NCATE. *Faculty:* 14 full-time (7 women). *Students:* 27 full-time (15 women), 70 part-time (46 women); includes 24 minority (23 Black or African American, non-Hispanic/Latino; 1 Native Hawaiian or other Pacific Islander, non-Hispanic/Latino), 5 international. Average age 37. 40 applicants, 63% accepted, 8 enrolled. In 2011, 16 master's, 23 doctorates, 5 other advanced degrees awarded. *Entrance requirements:* For master's, GRE General Test, MAT; for doctorate, GRE General Test; for Ed S, GRE General Test or MAT. *Application deadline:* For fall admission, 7/1 priority date for domestic students; for spring admission, 11/15 for domestic students. Application fee: $50. Electronic applications accepted. *Financial support:* Fellowships, research assistantships, teaching assistantships, and unspecified assistantships available. *Unit head:* Dr. Roger B. Hill, Interim Head, 706-542-4100, Fax: 706-542-4054, E-mail: rbhill@uga.edu. *Application contact:* Dr. Robert C. Wicklein, Graduate Coordinator, 706-542-4503, Fax: 706-542-4054, E-mail: wickone@uga.edu. Web site: http://www.coe.uga.edu/welsf/.

University of Guam, Office of Graduate Studies, School of Education, Program in Administration and Supervision, Mangilao, GU 96923. Offers M Ed. *Degree requirements:* For master's, comprehensive oral and written exams, special project or thesis. *Entrance requirements:* For master's, GRE General Test. Additional exam requirements/recommendations for international students: Required—TOEFL.

University of Hartford, College of Education, Nursing, and Health Professions, Doctoral Program in Educational Leadership, West Hartford, CT 06117-1599. Offers Ed D. *Accreditation:* NCATE. Part-time and evening/weekend programs available. *Degree requirements:* For doctorate, thesis/dissertation. *Entrance requirements:* For doctorate, MAT, 3 letters of recommendation, writing samples, interview, resume, letter of support from employer. *Expenses:* Contact institution.

University of Hartford, College of Education, Nursing, and Health Professions, Program in Educational Leadership, West Hartford, CT 06117-1599. Offers administration and supervision (CAGS). *Accreditation:* NCATE. Part-time and evening/weekend programs available. *Degree requirements:* For CAGS, comprehensive exam or research project. *Entrance requirements:* For degree, GRE General Test or MAT, interview. Additional exam requirements/recommendations for international students: Required—TOEFL (minimum score 550 paper-based; 213 computer-based). Electronic applications accepted.

University of Hawaii at Manoa, Graduate Division, College of Education, Department of Educational Administration, Honolulu, HI 96822. Offers M Ed. Part-time programs available. *Degree requirements:* For master's, thesis optional. *Entrance requirements:* Additional exam requirements/recommendations for international students: Required—TOEFL (minimum score 600 paper-based; 250 computer-based; 100 iBT), IELTS (minimum score 7). *Faculty research:* Leadership, educational policy, organizational processes, finance.

University of Hawaii at Manoa, Graduate Division, College of Education, Ed D in Professional Practice Program, Honolulu, HI 96822. Offers Ed D. *Entrance requirements:* Additional exam requirements/recommendations for international students: Required—TOEFL (minimum score 600 paper-based; 100 iBT).

University of Hawaii at Manoa, Graduate Division, College of Education, PhD in Education Program, Honolulu, HI 96822. Offers curriculum and instruction (PhD); educational administration (PhD); educational foundations (PhD); educational policy studies (PhD); educational technology (PhD); exceptionalities (PhD); kinesiology (PhD). Part-time and evening/weekend programs available. *Degree requirements:* For doctorate, thesis/dissertation. *Entrance requirements:* For doctorate, GRE General Test, sample of written work. Additional exam requirements/recommendations for international students: Required—TOEFL (minimum score 600 paper-based; 250 computer-based; 100 iBT), IELTS (minimum score 7).

University of Houston, College of Education, Department of Curriculum and Instruction, Houston, TX 77204. Offers administration and supervision (M Ed); curriculum and instruction (M Ed, Ed D); professional leadership (Ed D). *Accreditation:* NCATE. Part-time and evening/weekend programs available. *Degree requirements:* For master's, comprehensive exam, thesis optional; for doctorate, comprehensive exam, thesis/dissertation. *Entrance requirements:* For master's and doctorate, GRE, minimum cumulative undergraduate GPA of 2.6, 3 letters of recommendation, resume/vita, goal statement. Additional exam requirements/recommendations for international students: Required—TOEFL (minimum score 550 paper-based; 79 iBT). Electronic applications accepted. *Faculty research:* Teaching-learning process, instructional technology in schools, teacher education, classroom management, at-risk students.

University of Houston, College of Education, Department of Educational Leadership and Cultural Studies, Houston, TX 77204. Offers administration and supervision (M Ed, Ed D); higher education (M Ed); historical, social, and cultural foundations of education (M Ed). *Accreditation:* NCATE. Part-time and evening/weekend programs available. *Degree requirements:* For master's, comprehensive exam or thesis; for doctorate, comprehensive exam, thesis/dissertation. *Entrance requirements:* For master's, GRE General Test, minimum cumulative GPA of 2.6, 3 letters of recommendation, resume/

vitae, goal statement; for doctorate, GRE General Test, minimum cumulative GPA of 2.6, 3 letters of recommendation, resume/vitae, goal statement, writing sample, interview. Additional exam requirements/recommendations for international students: Required—TOEFL (minimum score 550 paper-based; 79 iBT). Electronic applications accepted. *Faculty research:* Change, supervision, multiculturalism, evaluation, policy.

University of Houston, College of Education, Department of Educational Psychology, Houston, TX 77204. Offers administration and supervision - higher education (M Ed); counseling (M Ed); counseling psychology (PhD); educational psychology (M Ed); school psychology (PhD); school psychology and individual differences (PhD); special education (M Ed). *Accreditation:* NCATE. Part-time and evening/weekend programs available. Postbaccalaureate distance learning degree programs offered. *Degree requirements:* For master's, comprehensive exam or thesis; for doctorate, comprehensive exam, thesis/dissertation. *Entrance requirements:* For master's, GRE, transcripts, 3 letters of recommendation, curriculum vita, goal statement; for doctorate, GRE, transcripts, 3 letters of recommendation, curriculum vita, goal statement, writing sample, interview. Additional exam requirements/recommendations for international students: Required—TOEFL (minimum score 550 paper-based; 79 iBT), IELTS (minimum score 6.5). Electronic applications accepted. *Faculty research:* Evidence-based assessment and intervention, multicultural issues in psychology, social and cultural context of learning, systemic barriers to college, motivational aspects of self-regulated learning.

University of Houston–Clear Lake, School of Education, Program in Educational Leadership, Houston, TX 77058-1098. Offers educational leadership (Ed D); educational management (MS). *Degree requirements:* For master's, thesis optional; for doctorate, comprehensive exam, thesis/dissertation.

University of Houston–Victoria, School of Education and Human Development, Victoria, TX 77901-4450. Offers administration and supervision (M Ed); counseling (M Ed); curriculum and instruction (M Ed); special education (M Ed). Part-time and evening/weekend programs available. Postbaccalaureate distance learning degree programs offered (minimal on-campus study). *Degree requirements:* For master's, comprehensive exam, project or thesis. *Entrance requirements:* For master's, GRE General Test. Additional exam requirements/recommendations for international students: Required—TOEFL. Electronic applications accepted. *Faculty research:* Reading and language arts education, evaluation and diagnosis of special children's abilities.

University of Idaho, College of Graduate Studies, College of Education, Department of Leadership and Counseling, Program in Educational Leadership, Boise, ID 83702. Offers M Ed, Ed S. *Accreditation:* NCATE. *Students:* 15 full-time, 133 part-time. Average age 37. In 2011, 84 master's, 26 Ed Ss awarded. *Entrance requirements:* For master's, minimum GPA of 2.8. *Application deadline:* For fall admission, 8/1 for domestic students; for spring admission, 12/15 for domestic students. Applications are processed on a rolling basis. Application fee: $60. Electronic applications accepted. *Expenses:* Tuition, state resident: full-time $3874; part-time $334 per credit hour. Tuition, nonresident: full-time $16,394; part-time $861 per credit hour. *Required fees:* $2808; $99 per credit hour. Tuition and fees vary according to program. *Financial support:* Applicants required to submit FAFSA. *Unit head:* Dr. Russell A. Joki, Chair, 208-364-4099, E-mail: rjoki@uidaho.edu. *Application contact:* Erick Larson, Director of Graduate Admissions, 208-885-4723, E-mail: gadms@uidaho.edu. Web site: http://www.uidaho.edu/ed/leadershipcounseling.

University of Illinois at Chicago, Graduate College, College of Education, Department of Educational Policy Studies, Chicago, IL 60607-7128. Offers policy studies (M Ed); policy studies in urban education (PhD); urban education leadership (Ed D).

University of Illinois at Springfield, Graduate Programs, College of Education and Human Services, Department of Educational Leadership, Springfield, IL 62703-5407. Offers educational leadership (MA); teacher leadership (MA). Part-time and evening/weekend programs available. Postbaccalaureate distance learning degree programs offered (no on-campus study). *Faculty:* 8 full-time (1 woman), 11 part-time/adjunct (4 women). *Students:* 3 full-time (1 woman), 165 part-time (123 women); includes 14 minority (10 Black or African American, non-Hispanic/Latino; 2 Asian, non-Hispanic/Latino; 2 Hispanic/Latino). Average age 33. 54 applicants, 72% accepted, 34 enrolled. In 2011, 81 master's awarded. *Degree requirements:* For master's, project or thesis, capstone course (for teacher leadership option). *Entrance requirements:* For master's, minimum undergraduate GPA of 3.0. Additional exam requirements/recommendations for international students: Required—TOEFL (minimum score 500 paper-based; 176 computer-based; 61 iBT). *Application deadline:* Applications are processed on a rolling basis. Application fee: $50 ($60 for international students). Electronic applications accepted. *Expenses:* Tuition, state resident: full-time $6978; part-time $290.75 per credit hour. Tuition, nonresident: full-time $15,282; part-time $636.75 per credit hour. *Required fees:* $2106; $87.75 per credit hour. *Financial support:* In 2011–12, fellowships with full tuition reimbursements (averaging $8,550 per year), research assistantships with full tuition reimbursements (averaging $8,550 per year), teaching assistantships with full tuition reimbursements (averaging $8,550 per year) were awarded; career-related internships or fieldwork, Federal Work-Study, scholarships/grants, health care benefits, and unspecified assistantships also available. Support available to part-time students. Financial award application deadline: 11/15; financial award applicants required to submit FAFSA. *Unit head:* Dr. Scott Day, Program Administrator, 217-206-7520, Fax: 217-206-6775, E-mail: day.scott@uis.edu. *Application contact:* Dr. Lynn Pardie, Office of Graduate Studies, 800-252-8533, Fax: 217-206-7623, E-mail: lpard1@uis.edu. Web site: http://www.uis.edu/educationalleadership.

University of Illinois at Urbana–Champaign, Graduate College, College of Education, Department of Education Policy, Organization, and Leadership, Champaign, IL 61820. Offers educational organization and leadership (Ed M, MS, Ed D, PhD, CAS); educational policy studies (Ed M, MA, PhD); human resource education (Ed M, MS, Ed D, PhD, CAS). Part-time programs available. Postbaccalaureate distance learning degree programs offered (minimal on-campus study). *Faculty:* 30 full-time (13 women), 3 part-time/adjunct (2 women). *Students:* 185 full-time (117 women), 391 part-time (249 women); includes 199 minority (107 Black or African American, non-Hispanic/Latino; 3 American Indian or Alaska Native, non-Hispanic/Latino; 28 Asian, non-Hispanic/Latino; 49 Hispanic/Latino; 12 Two or more races, non-Hispanic/Latino), 52 international. 327 applicants, 60% accepted, 100 enrolled. In 2011, 201 master's, 34 doctorates, 3 other advanced degrees awarded. *Entrance requirements:* For master's, minimum GPA of 3.0; for doctorate, GRE General Test, minimum GPA of 3.0, writing samples, interview. Additional exam requirements/recommendations for international students: Required—TOEFL (minimum score 620 paper-based; 260 computer-based; 105 iBT). *Application deadline:* Applications are processed on a rolling basis. Application fee: $75 ($90 for international students). Electronic applications accepted. *Financial support:* In 2011–12, 29 fellowships, 60 research assistantships, 60 teaching assistantships were awarded; tuition waivers (full and partial) also available. *Unit head:* James Anderson, Head, 217-333-2446, Fax: 217-244-5632, E-mail: janders@illinois.edu. *Application contact:* Rebecca Grady, 217-265-5404, Fax: 217-244-5632, E-mail: rgrady@illinois.edu. Web site: http://education.illinois.edu/epol.

University of Indianapolis, Graduate Programs, School of Education, Indianapolis, IN 46227-3697. Offers art education (MAT); biology (MAT); chemistry (MAT); curriculum and instruction (MA); earth sciences (MAT); education (MA, MAT); educational leadership (MA); elementary education (MA); English (MAT); French (MAT); math (MAT); physical education (MAT); physics (MAT); secondary education (MA), including art education, education, English education, social studies education; social studies (MAT); Spanish (MAT). *Accreditation:* NCATE. Part-time and evening/weekend programs available. *Faculty:* 3 full-time (2 women), 3 part-time/adjunct (2 women). *Students:* 32 full-time (18 women), 97 part-time (56 women); includes 22 minority (20 Black or African American, non-Hispanic/Latino; 1 Asian, non-Hispanic/Latino; 1 Hispanic/Latino), 3 international. Average age 33. In 2011, 78 master's awarded. *Entrance requirements:* For master's, GRE Subject Test, PRAXIS I, minimum GPA of 2.5, 3 letters of recommendation, interview, writing exercise. Additional exam requirements/recommendations for international students: Required—TOEFL (minimum score 550 paper-based; 213 computer-based). *Application deadline:* Applications are processed on a rolling basis. Application fee: $50. Tuition and fees vary according to degree level and program. *Financial support:* Federal Work-Study available. Financial award application deadline: 5/1; financial award applicants required to submit FAFSA. *Faculty research:* Assessment of teacher education, perceptions of prospective teachers by parents. *Unit head:* Dr. Kathy Moran, Dean, 317-788-3285, Fax: 317-788-3300, E-mail: kmoran@uindy.edu. *Application contact:* Jeni Kirby, 317-788-2113, E-mail: kirbyj@uindy.edu. Web site: http://education.uindy.edu/.

The University of Iowa, Graduate College, College of Education, Department of Counseling, Rehabilitation, and Student Development, Iowa City, IA 52242-1316. Offers administration and research (PhD); community/rehabilitation counseling (MA); counselor education and supervision (PhD); rehabilitation counselor education (PhD); school counseling (MA); student development (MA, PhD). *Accreditation:* ACA (one or more programs are accredited); CORE (one or more programs are accredited). *Degree requirements:* For master's, thesis optional, exam; for doctorate, comprehensive exam, thesis/dissertation. *Entrance requirements:* For master's and doctorate, GRE General Test, minimum GPA of 3.0. Additional exam requirements/recommendations for international students: Required—TOEFL (minimum score 550 paper-based; 213 computer-based; 81 iBT). Electronic applications accepted.

The University of Iowa, Graduate College, College of Education, Department of Educational Policy and Leadership Studies, Program in Educational Administration, Iowa City, IA 52242-1316. Offers MA, PhD, Ed S. *Degree requirements:* For master's and Ed S, exam; for doctorate, comprehensive exam, thesis/dissertation. *Entrance requirements:* For master's, doctorate, and Ed S, GRE General Test, minimum GPA of 3.0. Additional exam requirements/recommendations for international students: Required—TOEFL (minimum score 550 paper-based; 213 computer-based; 81 iBT). Electronic applications accepted.

The University of Kansas, Graduate Studies, School of Education, Department of Educational Leadership and Policy Studies, Education Leadership and Policy Program, Lawrence, KS 66045-3101. Offers educational administration (Ed D, PhD); foundations (PhD); higher education (Ed D, PhD); policy studies (PhD). Part-time and evening/weekend programs available. *Faculty:* 16. *Students:* 99 full-time (65 women), 52 part-time (28 women); includes 31 minority (10 Black or African American, non-Hispanic/Latino; 5 American Indian or Alaska Native, non-Hispanic/Latino; 5 Asian, non-Hispanic/Latino; 7 Hispanic/Latino; 4 Two or more races, non-Hispanic/Latino), 10 international. Average age 38. 44 applicants, 73% accepted, 22 enrolled. In 2011, 26 degrees awarded. *Degree requirements:* For doctorate, comprehensive exam, thesis/dissertation. *Entrance requirements:* For doctorate, GRE General Test, minimum graduate GPA of 3.5. Additional exam requirements/recommendations for international students: Required—TOEFL (minimum score 570 paper-based; 230 computer-based; 80 iBT). *Application deadline:* For fall admission, 7/1 for domestic and international students; for spring admission, 11/1 for domestic and international students. Applications are processed on a rolling basis. Application fee: $55 ($65 for international students). Electronic applications accepted. Tuition and fees vary according to course load, campus/location, program and reciprocity agreements. *Financial support:* Fellowships, research assistantships with full and partial tuition reimbursements, teaching assistantships with full and partial tuition reimbursements, scholarships/grants, and unspecified assistantships available. Financial award application deadline: 3/15. *Faculty research:* Historical and philosophical issues in education, education policy and leadership, higher education faculty, research on college students, education technology. *Unit head:* Dr. Susan Twombly, Chair, 785-864-9721, Fax: 785-864-4697, E-mail: stwombly@ku.edu. *Application contact:* Denise Brubaker, Admissions Coordinator, 785-864-4458, Fax: 785-864-4697, E-mail: elps@ku.edu. Web site: http://soe.ku.edu/elps/.

The University of Kansas, Graduate Studies, School of Education, Department of Educational Leadership and Policy Studies, Program in Educational Administration, Lawrence, KS 66045-3101. Offers MS Ed, Ed D, PhD. Program begins in summer semester only. Part-time and evening/weekend programs available. *Faculty:* 6. *Students:* 3 full-time (2 women), 18 part-time (11 women); includes 4 minority (1 Black or African American, non-Hispanic/Latino; 1 Asian, non-Hispanic/Latino; 2 Hispanic/Latino), 3 international. Average age 28. 11 applicants, 73% accepted, 7 enrolled. *Degree requirements:* For master's, comprehensive exam; for doctorate, comprehensive exam, thesis/dissertation. *Entrance requirements:* For master's, minimum GPA of 3.0; for doctorate, GRE General Test, minimum graduate GPA of 3.5. Additional exam requirements/recommendations for international students: Required—TOEFL (minimum score 570 paper-based; 230 computer-based; 80 iBT). *Application deadline:* For fall admission, 3/1 for domestic and international students. Application fee: $55 ($65 for international students). Electronic applications accepted. Tuition and fees vary according to course load, campus/location, program and reciprocity agreements. *Financial support:* Application deadline: 3/1. *Faculty research:* Policy studies, law, personnel, leadership, organizational studies. *Unit head:* Dr. Susan Twombly, Chair, 785-864-9721, Fax: 785-864-4697, E-mail: stwombly@ku.edu. *Application contact:* Denise Brubaker, Admissions Coordinator, 785-864-4458, Fax: 785-864-4697, E-mail: elps@ku.edu. Web site: http://soe.ku.edu/elps/academics/edadmin/mse/.

University of Kentucky, Graduate School, College of Education, Program in Educational Leadership Studies, Lexington, KY 40506-0032. Offers administration and supervision (Ed S); instruction and administration (Ed D); school administration (M Ed). *Degree requirements:* For master's and Ed S, comprehensive exam; for doctorate, comprehensive exam, thesis/dissertation. *Entrance requirements:* For master's, GRE General Test, minimum undergraduate GPA of 2.75; for doctorate, GRE General Test, minimum graduate GPA of 3.0. Additional exam requirements/recommendations for international students: Required—TOEFL (minimum score 550 paper-based; 213 computer-based). Electronic applications accepted. *Faculty research:* School governance, teacher empowerment, planned change, systemic reform, issues of equity and fairness.

University of La Verne, College of Education and Organizational Leadership, Doctoral Program in Organizational Leadership, La Verne, CA 91750-4443. Offers Ed D. Part-time programs available. *Faculty:* 19 full-time (12 women), 28 part-time/adjunct (22 women). *Students:* 130 full-time (79 women), 97 part-time (74 women); includes 104 minority (41 Black or African American, non-Hispanic/Latino; 2 American Indian or Alaska Native, non-Hispanic/Latino; 12 Asian, non-Hispanic/Latino; 48 Hispanic/Latino; 1 Native Hawaiian or other Pacific Islander, non-Hispanic/Latino), 2 international. Average age 45. In 2011, 42 doctorates awarded. *Degree requirements:* For doctorate, thesis/dissertation. *Entrance requirements:* For doctorate, GRE or MAT, minimum graduate GPA of 3.0, resume, 2 endorsement forms. Additional exam requirements/recommendations for international students: Required—TOEFL (minimum score 550 paper-based; 213 computer-based). *Application deadline:* Applications are processed on a rolling basis. Application fee: $75. *Expenses:* Contact institution. *Financial support:* Institutionally sponsored loans available. Financial award application deadline: 3/2; financial award applicants required to submit FAFSA. *Unit head:* Dr. Hyatt Laura, Chairperson, 909-593-3511 Ext. 4583, Fax: 909-392-2700, E-mail: lhyatt@laverne.edu. *Application contact:* Christy Ranells, Program and Admission Specialist, 909-593-3511 Ext. 4644, Fax: 909-392-2761, E-mail: cranells@laverne.edu. Web site: http://laverne.edu/education/.

University of La Verne, College of Education and Organizational Leadership, Program in Educational Management, La Verne, CA 91750-4443. Offers educational management (M Ed); preliminary administrative services (Credential); professional administrative services (Credential). *Faculty:* 19 full-time (12 women), 28 part-time/adjunct (22 women). *Students:* 2 full-time (0 women), 13 part-time (7 women); includes 4 minority (1 Asian, non-Hispanic/Latino; 3 Hispanic/Latino). Average age 35. In 2011, 18 master's awarded. *Entrance requirements:* For master's, California Basic Educational Skills Test, 2 years experience in teaching, pupil personnel services, health, or librarian services; California teaching credential. Additional exam requirements/recommendations for international students: Required—TOEFL (minimum score 550 paper-based; 213 computer-based). *Application deadline:* Applications are processed on a rolling basis. Application fee: $50. *Expenses:* Contact institution. *Financial support:* Institutionally sponsored loans available. Financial award application deadline: 3/2; financial award applicants required to submit FAFSA. *Unit head:* Patricia Ensey, Chair, 909-593-3511 Ext. 4385, E-mail: pensey@laverne.edu. *Application contact:* Christy Ranells, Program and Admission Specialist, 909-593-3511 Ext. 4644, Fax: 909-392-2761, E-mail: cranells@laverne.edu. Web site: http://laverne.edu/education/.

University of La Verne, Regional Campus Administration, Master's Programs in Education, California Statewide Campus, La Verne, CA 91750-4443. Offers educational management (M Ed), including preliminary administrative services credential; multiple or single subject teaching credential (M Ed); school counseling (MS), including public personnel services credential. *Entrance requirements:* For master's, California Basic Educational Skills Test, 3 letters of recommendation, teaching credential. *Expenses:* Contact institution.

University of Lethbridge, School of Graduate Studies, Lethbridge, AB T1K 3M4, Canada. Offers accounting (MScM); addictions counseling (M Sc); agricultural biotechnology (M Sc); agricultural studies (M Sc, MA); anthropology (MA); archaeology (MA); art (MA, MFA); biochemistry (M Sc); biological sciences (M Sc); biomolecular science (PhD); biosystems and biodiversity (PhD); Canadian studies (MA); chemistry (M Sc); computer science (M Sc); computer science and geographical information science (M Sc); counseling psychology (M Ed); dramatic arts (MA); earth, space, and physical science (PhD); economics (MA); educational leadership (M Ed); English (MA); environmental science (M Sc); evolution and behavior (PhD); exercise science (M Sc); finance (MScM); French (MA); French/German (MA); French/Spanish (MA); general education (M Ed); general management (MScM); geography (M Sc, MA); German (MA); health science (M Sc); history (MA); human resource management and labour relations (MScM); individualized multidisciplinary (M Sc, MA); information systems (MScM); international management (MScM); kinesiology (M Sc, MA); management (M Sc, MA); marketing (MScM); mathematics (M Sc); music (M Mus, MA); Native American studies (MA); neuroscience (M Sc, PhD); new media (MA); nursing (M Sc); philosophy (MA); physics (M Sc); policy and strategy (MScM); political science (MA); psychology (M Sc, MA); religious studies (MA); social sciences (MA); sociology (MA); theatre and dramatic arts (MFA); theoretical and computational science (PhD); urban and regional studies (MA); women's studies (MA). Part-time and evening/weekend programs available. *Degree requirements:* For doctorate, comprehensive exam, thesis/dissertation. *Entrance requirements:* For master's, GMAT (M Sc in management), bachelor's degree in related field, minimum GPA of 3.0 during previous 20 graded semester courses, 2 years teaching or related experience (M Ed); for doctorate, master's degree, minimum graduate GPA of 3.5. Additional exam requirements/recommendations for international students: Required—TOEFL. *Faculty research:* Movement and brain plasticity, gibberellin physiology, photosynthesis, carbon cycling, molecular properties of main-group ring components.

University of Louisiana at Lafayette, College of Education, Graduate Studies and Research in Education, Program in Administration and Supervision, Lafayette, LA 70504. Offers M Ed. *Degree requirements:* For master's, thesis or alternative. *Entrance requirements:* For master's, GRE General Test, teaching certificate. Additional exam requirements/recommendations for international students: Required—TOEFL (minimum score 550 paper-based; 213 computer-based). Electronic applications accepted.

University of Louisiana at Lafayette, College of Education, Graduate Studies and Research in Education, Program in Educational Leadership, Lafayette, LA 70504. Offers M Ed, Ed D. *Entrance requirements:* Additional exam requirements/recommendations for international students: Required—TOEFL (minimum score 550 paper-based; 213 computer-based).

University of Louisiana at Monroe, Graduate School, College of Education and Human Development, Department of Educational Leadership and Counseling, Program in Educational Leadership, Monroe, LA 71209-0001. Offers Ed D. *Accreditation:* NCATE. *Faculty:* 4 full-time (2 women). *Students:* 31 full-time (19 women), 72 part-time (44 women); includes 37 minority (34 Black or African American, non-Hispanic/Latino; 2 Asian, non-Hispanic/Latino; 1 Hispanic/Latino). Average age 34. 23 applicants, 65% accepted, 14 enrolled. In 2011, 1 doctorate awarded. *Degree requirements:* For doctorate, comprehensive exam, thesis/dissertation, internship. *Entrance requirements:* For doctorate, GRE General Test, minimum GPA of 2.75, 3 letters of recommendation. Additional exam requirements/recommendations for international students: Required—TOEFL (minimum score 500 paper-based; 173 computer-based; 61 iBT). *Application deadline:* For fall admission, 8/24 priority date for domestic students, 7/1 for international students; for winter admission, 12/14 for domestic students; for spring admission, 1/19 for domestic students, 11/1 for international students. Applications are processed on a rolling basis. Application fee: $20 ($30 for international students). Electronic applications accepted. *Expenses:* Tuition, state resident: full-time $3436; part-time $240 per credit hour. Tuition, nonresident: full-time $3436; part-time $240 per credit hour. *International tuition:* $10,733 full-time. *Required fees:* $1460.90. *Financial support:* In 2011–12, 17 research assistantships with full tuition reimbursements (averaging $3,750 per year) were awarded; career-related internships or fieldwork, Federal Work-Study, and unspecified assistantships also available. Financial award application deadline: 4/1; financial award applicants required to submit FAFSA. *Unit head:* Dr. Bob Cage, Director, 318-342-1288, Fax: 318-342-3131, E-mail: cage@ulm.edu. *Application contact:* Dr. Jack Palmer, Director of Graduate Studies, 318-342-1250, Fax: 318-342-1240, E-mail: palmer@ulm.edu. Web site: http://www.ulm.edu/elc/index.html.

University of Louisville, Graduate School, College of Education and Human Development, Department of Leadership, Foundations and Human Resource Education, Louisville, KY 40292-0001. Offers educational leadership and organizational development (Ed D, PhD); higher education (MA); human resource education (MS); P-12 educational administration (M Ed, Ed S). *Accreditation:* NCATE. Part-time and evening/weekend programs available. Postbaccalaureate distance learning degree programs offered. *Degree requirements:* For doctorate, comprehensive exam, thesis/dissertation. *Entrance requirements:* For master's, doctorate, and Ed S, GRE General Test. Additional exam requirements/recommendations for international students: Required—TOEFL (minimum score 560 paper-based; 210 computer-based; 83 iBT). Electronic applications accepted. *Expenses:* Tuition, state resident: full-time $9692; part-time $539 per credit hour. Tuition, nonresident: full-time $20,168; part-time $1121 per credit hour. Tuition and fees vary according to program and reciprocity agreements. *Faculty research:* Evaluation of methods and programs to improve elementary and secondary education; research on organizational and human resource development; student access, retention and success in post-secondary education; educational policy analysis; multivariate quantitative research methods.

University of Louisville, Graduate School, College of Education and Human Development, Department of Teaching and Learning, Louisville, KY 40292-0001. Offers art education (MAT); curriculum and instruction (PhD); early elementary education (MAT); instructional technology (M Ed); interdisciplinary early childhood education (MAT); middle school education (MAT); music education (MAT); reading education (M Ed); secondary education (MAT); special education (M Ed, MAT); teacher leadership (M Ed). Part-time and evening/weekend programs available. *Degree requirements:* For doctorate, comprehensive exam, thesis/dissertation. *Entrance requirements:* For master's, GRE General Test, PRAXIS II (for some programs); for doctorate, GRE General Test. Additional exam requirements/recommendations for international students: Required—TOEFL (minimum score 560 paper-based; 210 computer-based; 83 iBT). Electronic applications accepted. *Expenses:* Tuition, state resident: full-time $9692; part-time $539 per credit hour. Tuition, nonresident: full-time $20,168; part-time $1121 per credit hour. Tuition and fees vary according to program and reciprocity agreements. *Faculty research:* Mathematics teacher education and ongoing professional development in pedagogy and content knowledge; development of literacy, including early literacy in science and mathematics and literacy development for English language learners; immersive visualizations for promoting STEM education from nanoscience to cosmic scales; evidence-based practices for students with disabilities; urban education, including teacher response to intervention systems in schools and cross-cultural competence.

University of Maine, Graduate School, College of Education and Human Development, Program in Educational Leadership, Orono, ME 04469. Offers M Ed, Ed D, CAS. *Accreditation:* NCATE. Part-time and evening/weekend programs available. *Students:* 9 full-time (2 women), 90 part-time (50 women); includes 3 minority (1 Black or African American, non-Hispanic/Latino; 2 Hispanic/Latino). Average age 40. 29 applicants, 86% accepted, 25 enrolled. In 2011, 32 master's, 4 doctorates, 10 CASs awarded. *Degree requirements:* For master's, thesis or alternative; for doctorate, thesis/dissertation. *Entrance requirements:* For master's, MAT; for doctorate, GRE General Test, MA, M Ed, or MS; for CAS, MA, M Ed, or MS. Additional exam requirements/recommendations for international students: Required—TOEFL. *Application deadline:* For fall admission, 2/1 priority date for domestic students. Applications are processed on a rolling basis. Application fee: $65. Electronic applications accepted. *Expenses:* Tuition, state resident: full-time $5016. Tuition, nonresident: full-time $14,424. *Financial support:* Career-related internships or fieldwork, Federal Work-Study, institutionally sponsored loans, tuition waivers (full and partial), and unspecified assistantships available. Support available to part-time students. Financial award application deadline: 3/1. *Unit head:* Dr. Janet Spector, Coordinator, 207-581-2444, Fax: 207-581-2423. *Application contact:* Scott G. Delcourt, Associate Dean of the Graduate School, 207-581-3291, Fax: 207-581-3232, E-mail: graduate@maine.edu. Web site: http://www2.umaine.edu/graduate/.

University of Maine at Farmington, Program in Education, Farmington, ME 04938-1990. Offers early childhood education (MS Ed); educational leadership (MS Ed). *Accreditation:* NCATE. Part-time and evening/weekend programs available. Postbaccalaureate distance learning degree programs offered (minimal on-campus study). *Degree requirements:* For master's, capstone project (for educational leadership). *Entrance requirements:* For master's, baccalaureate degree from accredited institution, valid teaching certificate or professional experience in education, professional employment by school district or other educational institution (exceptions may be made by the Assistant Dean), minimum of two years experience in professional education. *Faculty research:* School improvement strategies, technology integration.

University of Manitoba, Faculty of Graduate Studies, Faculty of Education, Department of Educational Administration, Foundations and Psychology, Winnipeg, MB R3T 2N2, Canada. Offers adult and post-secondary education (M Ed); educational administration (M Ed); guidance and counseling (M Ed); inclusive special education (M Ed); social foundations of education (M Ed). *Degree requirements:* For master's, thesis or alternative.

University of Mary, School of Education and Behavioral Sciences, Department of Education, Bismarck, ND 58504-9652. Offers college teaching (M Ed); curriculum, instruction and assessment (M Ed); early childhood education (M Ed); early childhood special education (M Ed); elementary administration (M Ed); emotional disorders (M Ed); learning disabilities (M Ed); reading (M Ed); secondary administration (M Ed); special education strategist (M Ed). Part-time programs available. *Faculty:* 6 full-time (5 women), 12 part-time/adjunct (8 women). *Students:* 5 full-time (4 women), 77 part-time (56 women); includes 9 minority (1 Black or African American, non-Hispanic/Latino; 4 American Indian or Alaska Native, non-Hispanic/Latino; 1 Asian, non-Hispanic/Latino; 3 Hispanic/Latino), 1 international. Average age 30. 58 applicants, 55% accepted, 29 enrolled. In 2011, 16 master's awarded. *Degree requirements:* For master's, portfolio or thesis. *Entrance requirements:* For master's, interview, letters of reference, minimum GPA of 2.5. Additional exam requirements/recommendations for international students: Required—TOEFL (minimum score 500 paper-based; 197 computer-based; 71 iBT). *Application deadline:* Applications are processed on a rolling basis. Application fee: $40. Electronic applications accepted. *Financial support:* In 2011–12, 1 teaching assistantship with full tuition reimbursement was awarded; career-related internships or fieldwork also available. Financial award application deadline: 8/1; financial award applicants required to submit FAFSA. *Faculty research:* Innovative pedagogy in higher education, technology in education, content standards, children of poverty, children with diverse learning needs. *Unit head:* Dr. Rebecca Yunker Salveson, Director, 701-355-8186, E-mail: rysalves@umary.edu. *Application contact:* Leona Friedig, Administrative Secretary, 701-355-8058, E-mail: lfriedig@umary.edu.

University of Mary Hardin-Baylor, Graduate Studies in Education, Belton, TX 76513. Offers administration of intervention programs (M Ed); curriculum and instruction (M Ed); educational administration (M Ed, Ed D). Part-time and evening/weekend programs available. *Faculty:* 17 full-time (9 women), 3 part-time/adjunct (2 women). *Students:* 39 full-time (21 women), 88 part-time (51 women); includes 43 minority (24 Black or African American, non-Hispanic/Latino; 2 Asian, non-Hispanic/Latino; 17 Hispanic/Latino), 3 international. Average age 37. 32 applicants, 66% accepted, 12 enrolled. In 2011, 20 master's, 14 doctorates awarded. *Degree requirements:* For master's, comprehensive exam; for doctorate, thesis/dissertation. *Entrance requirements:* For master's, GRE General Test, minimum GPA of 2.75, Texas teaching certificate; for doctorate, GRE, minimum GPA of 3.5, interview, essay. *Application deadline:* For fall admission, 6/1 priority date for domestic students; for spring admission, 11/1 for domestic students. Applications are processed on a rolling basis. Application fee: $35 ($135 for international students). Electronic applications accepted. *Expenses: Tuition:* Full-time $12,780. *Required fees:* $2350. *Financial support:* Federal Work-Study and scholarships (for some active duty military personnel only) available. Support available to part-time students. Financial award application deadline: 6/1; financial award applicants required to submit FAFSA. *Unit head:* Dr. Austin Vasek, Program Director, 254-295-4185, Fax: 254-295-4480, E-mail: austin.vasek@umhb.edu. *Application contact:* Melissa Ford, Director of Graduate Admissions, 254-295-4020, Fax: 254-295-5301, E-mail: mford@umhb.edu.

University of Maryland, College Park, Academic Affairs, College of Education, Department of Counseling and Personnel Services, College Park, MD 20742. Offers college student personnel (M Ed, MA); college student personnel administration (PhD); community counseling (CAGS); community/career counseling (M Ed, MA); counseling and personnel services (M Ed, MA, PhD), including art therapy (M Ed), college student personnel (M Ed), counseling and personnel services (PhD), counseling psychology (M Ed), mental health counseling (M Ed), school counseling (M Ed); counseling psychology (PhD); counselor education (PhD); rehabilitation counseling (M Ed, MA, AGSC); school counseling (M Ed, MA); school psychology (M Ed, MA, PhD). *Accreditation:* ACA (one or more programs are accredited); APA (one or more programs are accredited); CORE (one or more programs are accredited); NCATE. Part-time and evening/weekend programs available. Postbaccalaureate distance learning degree programs offered (no on-campus study). *Faculty:* 29 full-time (15 women), 6 part-time/adjunct (5 women). *Students:* 114 full-time (88 women), 12 part-time (9 women); includes 45 minority (17 Black or African American, non-Hispanic/Latino; 16 Asian, non-Hispanic/Latino; 10 Hispanic/Latino; 2 Two or more races, non-Hispanic/Latino), 15 international. 266 applicants, 12% accepted, 16 enrolled. In 2011, 30 master's, 15 doctorates awarded. *Median time to degree:* Of those who began their doctoral program in fall 2003, 60% received their degree in 8 years or less. *Degree requirements:* For master's, thesis (for some programs); for doctorate, thesis/dissertation. *Entrance requirements:* For master's, GRE General Test or MAT, minimum GPA of 3.0, 3 letters of recommendation; for doctorate, GRE General Test or MAT, minimum GPA of 3.5, 3 letters of recommendation. Additional exam requirements/recommendations for international students: Required—TOEFL. *Application deadline:* For fall admission, 12/15 for domestic and international students; for spring admission, 6/1 for international students. Applications are processed on a rolling basis. Application fee: $75. Electronic applications accepted. *Expenses: Tuition, area resident:* Part-time $525 per credit hour. Tuition, state resident: part-time $525 per credit hour. Tuition, nonresident: part-time $1131 per credit hour. *Required fees:* $386.31 per term. Tuition and fees vary according to program. *Financial support:* In 2011–12, 8 fellowships with full and partial tuition reimbursements (averaging $11,286 per year), 1 research assistantship (averaging $20,861 per year), 71 teaching assistantships with tuition reimbursements (averaging $16,237 per year) were awarded; career-related internships or fieldwork, Federal Work-Study, and scholarships/grants also available. Support available to part-time students. Financial award applicants required to submit FAFSA. *Faculty research:* Educational psychology, counseling, health. *Total annual research expenditures:* $589,600. *Unit head:* Dr. Dennis Kivlighan, Chair, 301-405-2858, E-mail: dennisk@umd.edu. *Application contact:* Dr. Charles A. Caramello, Dean of Graduate School, 301-405-0358, Fax: 301-314-9305.

University of Maryland, College Park, Academic Affairs, College of Education, Department of Education Policy and Leadership, College Park, MD 20742. Offers curriculum and educational communications (M Ed, MA, Ed D, PhD); social foundations of education (M Ed, MA, Ed D, PhD, CAGS). *Accreditation:* NCATE. Part-time and evening/weekend programs available. Postbaccalaureate distance learning degree programs offered (minimal on-campus study). *Students:* 93 full-time (67 women), 9 part-time (5 women); includes 46 minority (29 Black or African American, non-Hispanic/Latino; 8 Asian, non-Hispanic/Latino; 8 Hispanic/Latino; 1 Two or more races, non-Hispanic/Latino), 3 international. In 2011, 5 master's, 15 doctorates awarded. *Degree requirements:* For master's, thesis or alternative, internship and/or field experience; for doctorate, comprehensive exam, thesis/dissertation, practicum or internship. *Entrance requirements:* For master's, GRE General Test or MAT, minimum GPA of 3.0, scholarly writing sample, 3 letters of recommendation; for doctorate, GRE General Test or MAT, scholarly writing sample; minimum undergraduate GPA of 3.0, graduate 3.5. *Expenses: Tuition, area resident:* Part-time $525 per credit hour. Tuition, state resident: part-time $525 per credit hour. Tuition, nonresident: part-time $1131 per credit hour. *Required fees:* $386.31 per term. Tuition and fees vary according to program. *Financial support:* In 2011–12, 2 fellowships with full and partial tuition reimbursements (averaging $13,060 per year), 2 research assistantships (averaging $16,176 per year), 8 teaching assistantships (averaging $16,791 per year) were awarded; career-related internships or fieldwork, Federal Work-Study, and scholarships/grants also available. Support available to part-time students. Financial award applicants required to submit FAFSA. *Faculty research:* Educational technology, adult and higher education. *Total annual research expenditures:* $848. *Unit head:* Dennis Kivlighan, Chair, 301-405-2858, E-mail: dennisk@umd.edu. *Application contact:* Dr. Charles A. Caramello, Dean of Graduate School, 301-405-0358, Fax: 301-314-9305.

University of Maryland Eastern Shore, Graduate Programs, Department of Education, Program in Education Leadership, Princess Anne, MD 21853-1299. Offers Ed D. Evening/weekend programs available. *Degree requirements:* For doctorate, comprehensive exam, thesis/dissertation, internship. *Entrance requirements:* For doctorate, interview, writing sample, state certification in a standard area, 3 years recent teaching or successful professional experience in a k-12 school setting. Additional exam requirements/recommendations for international students: Required—TOEFL (minimum score 213 computer-based; 80 iBT). Electronic applications accepted.

University of Massachusetts Amherst, Graduate School, School of Education, Program in Education, Amherst, MA 01003. Offers bilingual, English as a second language, and multicultural education (M Ed, CAGS); child study and early education (M Ed); children, families and schools (Ed D, CAGS); early childhood and elementary teacher education (M Ed); educational leadership (M Ed, CAGS); educational policy and leadership (Ed D); higher education (M Ed, CAGS); international education (M Ed); language, literacy and culture (Ed D); learning, media and technology (M Ed, CAGS); mathematics, science, and learning technologies (Ed D); policy studies in education (CAGS); psychometric methods, educational statistics and research methods (Ed D); reading and writing (M Ed); school counselor education (M Ed, CAGS); science education (CAGS); secondary teacher education (M Ed); social justice education (M Ed, Ed D, CAGS); special education (M Ed, Ed D, CAGS). *Accreditation:* NCATE. Part-time programs available. Postbaccalaureate distance learning degree programs offered (minimal on-campus study). *Faculty:* 81 full-time (46 women). *Students:* 341 full-time (240 women), 333 part-time (226 women); includes 113 minority (36 Black or African American, non-Hispanic/Latino; 1 American Indian or Alaska Native, non-Hispanic/Latino; 14 Asian, non-Hispanic/Latino; 51 Hispanic/Latino; 1 Native Hawaiian or other Pacific Islander, non-Hispanic/Latino; 10 Two or more races, non-Hispanic/Latino), 98 international. Average age 36. 721 applicants, 57% accepted, 202 enrolled. In 2011, 166 master's, 33 doctorates, 25 CAGSs awarded. Terminal master's awarded for partial completion of doctoral program. *Degree requirements:* For doctorate, comprehensive exam, thesis/dissertation. *Entrance requirements:* Additional exam requirements/recommendations for international students: Required—TOEFL (minimum score 550 paper-based; 213 computer-based; 80 iBT), IELTS (minimum score 6.5). *Application deadline:* For fall admission, 1/15 for domestic and international students. Applications are processed on a rolling basis. Application fee: $50 ($65 for international students). Electronic applications accepted. Tuition and fees vary according to course load, campus/location and program. *Financial support:* Fellowships with full and partial tuition reimbursements, research assistantships with full and partial tuition reimbursements, teaching assistantships with full and partial tuition reimbursements, career-related internships or fieldwork, Federal Work-Study, scholarships/grants, traineeships, health care benefits, tuition waivers (full and partial), and unspecified assistantships available. Support available to part-time students. Financial award application deadline: 1/15. *Unit head:* Dr. Linda L. Griffin, Graduate Program Director, 413-545-6984, Fax: 413-545-1523. *Application contact:* Lindsay DeSantis, Interim Supervisor of Admissions, 413-545-0722, Fax: 413-577-0010, E-mail: gradadm@grad.umass.edu. Web site: http://www.umass.edu/education/.

University of Massachusetts Boston, Office of Graduate Studies, Graduate College of Education, School Organization, Curriculum and Instruction Department, Program in Educational Administration, Boston, MA 02125-3393. Offers M Ed, CAGS. Part-time and evening/weekend programs available. *Degree requirements:* For master's, comprehensive exam, practicum; for CAGS, comprehensive exam. *Entrance requirements:* For master's, GRE General Test or MAT, 2 years of teaching experience, minimum GPA of 2.75; for CAGS, minimum GPA of 2.75. *Faculty research:* Power in the classroom, teacher leadership, professional development schools.

University of Massachusetts Boston, Office of Graduate Studies, Graduate College of Education, School Organization, Curriculum and Instruction Department, Program in Education, Track in Higher Education Administration, Boston, MA 02125-3393. Offers Ed D. Part-time and evening/weekend programs available. *Degree requirements:* For doctorate, comprehensive exam, thesis/dissertation. *Entrance requirements:* For doctorate, GRE General Test or MAT, minimum GPA of 2.75. *Faculty research:* Women, higher education and professionalization, school reform, urban classroom, higher education policy.

University of Massachusetts Boston, Office of Graduate Studies, Graduate College of Education, School Organization, Curriculum and Instruction Department, Program in Education, Track in Urban School Leadership, Boston, MA 02125-3393. Offers Ed D. Part-time and evening/weekend programs available. *Degree requirements:* For doctorate, comprehensive exam, thesis/dissertation. *Entrance requirements:* For doctorate, GRE General Test or MAT, minimum GPA of 2.75. *Faculty research:* School reform, race and culture in schools, race and higher education, language, literacy and writing.

University of Massachusetts Lowell, Graduate School of Education, Lowell, MA 01854-2881. Offers administration, planning, and policy (CAGS); curriculum and instruction (M Ed, CAGS); educational administration (M Ed); language arts and literacy (Ed D); leadership in schooling (Ed D); math and science education (Ed D); reading and language (M Ed, CAGS). *Accreditation:* NCATE. Part-time and evening/weekend programs available. Postbaccalaureate distance learning degree programs offered (no on-campus study). Terminal master's awarded for partial completion of doctoral program. *Degree requirements:* For doctorate, thesis/dissertation. *Entrance requirements:* For master's, doctorate, and CAGS, GRE General Test. Additional exam requirements/recommendations for international students: Required—TOEFL. Electronic applications accepted.

University of Memphis, Graduate School, College of Education, Department of Leadership, Memphis, TN 38152. Offers adult education (Ed D); educational leadership (Ed D); higher education (Ed D); leadership (MS); policy studies (Ed D); school administration and supervision (MS). *Accreditation:* NCATE. Part-time and evening/weekend programs available. Postbaccalaureate distance learning degree programs offered (minimal on-campus study). *Degree requirements:* For master's, comprehensive exam, thesis optional; for doctorate, comprehensive exam, thesis/dissertation. *Entrance requirements:* For master's and doctorate, GRE. Electronic applications accepted. *Faculty research:* School improvement, social justice, online learning, adult learning, diversity.

University of Michigan–Dearborn, School of Education, Doctoral Program in Education, Dearborn, MI 48126. Offers curriculum and practice (Ed D); educational leadership (Ed D); educational psychology/special education (Ed D); metropolitan education (Ed D). Part-time and evening/weekend programs available. *Faculty:* 8 full-time (6 women), 2 part-time/adjunct (0 women). *Students:* 47 part-time (34 women); includes 12 minority (6 Black or African American, non-Hispanic/Latino; 3 Asian, non-Hispanic/Latino; 1 Hispanic/Latino; 2 Two or more races, non-Hispanic/Latino). Average age 40. 55 applicants, 35% accepted, 17 enrolled. *Degree requirements:* For doctorate, comprehensive exam, thesis/dissertation. *Entrance requirements:* For doctorate, GRE (taken within the last 5 years), master's degree with minimum GPA of 3.3, 3 letters of recommendation (1 from faculty), 3 years' professional and/or teaching experience. Additional exam requirements/recommendations for international students: Required—TOEFL (minimum score 550 paper-based). *Application deadline:* For fall admission, 3/1 for domestic and international students. Application fee: $60 ($75 for international students). *Financial support:* Scholarships/grants available. *Faculty research:* Educational leadership, metropolitan education, curriculum and practice, educational psychology, special education, assessment. *Unit head:* Bonnie Beyer, Coordinator, 313-593-5583, E-mail: beyer@umd.umich.edu. *Application contact:* Catherine Parkins, Customer Service Assistant, 313-583-6349, Fax: 313-593-4748, E-mail: cparkins@umd.umich.edu. Web site: http://www.soe.umd.umich.edu/soe_edd/.

University of Michigan–Dearborn, School of Education, Program in Educational Leadership, Dearborn, MI 48126. Offers MA. Part-time and evening/weekend programs available. Postbaccalaureate distance learning degree programs offered (minimal on-campus study). *Faculty:* 2 full-time (both women), 5 part-time/adjunct (4 women). *Students:* 2 full-time (1 woman), 33 part-time (22 women); includes 9 minority (6 Black or African American, non-Hispanic/Latino; 2 Asian, non-Hispanic/Latino; 1 Hispanic/Latino). Average age 32. 8 applicants, 100% accepted, 8 enrolled. In 2011, 10 master's awarded. *Entrance requirements:* For master's, minimum GPA of 3.0; interview; official transcripts of all undergraduate/graduate work completed; 3 recommendation forms and letters on letterhead; statement of purpose/personal statement; teaching certificate. Additional exam requirements/recommendations for international students: Required—TOEFL (minimum score 560 paper-based; 220 computer-based; 84 iBT). *Application deadline:* For fall admission, 9/5 for domestic students; for winter admission, 12/22 for domestic students; for spring admission, 5/5 for domestic students. Applications are processed on a rolling basis. Application fee: $60 ($75 for international students). Electronic applications accepted. *Financial support:* Applicants required to submit FAFSA. *Unit head:* Dr. Bonnie Beyer, Professor/Program Coordinator, 313-593-5583, Fax: 313-593-4748, E-mail: beyere@umd.umich.edu. *Application contact:* Elizabeth

Morden, Customer Service Assistant, 313-583-6333, Fax: 313-593-4748, E-mail: emorden@umd.umich.edu. Web site: http://www.soe.umd.umich.edu/soe_mael/.

University of Minnesota, Twin Cities Campus, Graduate School, College of Education and Human Development, Department of Organizational Leadership, Policy and Development, Program in Educational Administration, Minneapolis, MN 55455-0213. Offers MA, Ed D, PhD. *Students:* 45 full-time (26 women), 109 part-time (70 women); includes 22 minority (14 Black or African American, non-Hispanic/Latino; 1 American Indian or Alaska Native, non-Hispanic/Latino; 4 Asian, non-Hispanic/Latino; 3 Hispanic/Latino), 9 international. Average age 41. 127 applicants, 76% accepted, 79 enrolled. In 2011, 43 master's, 13 doctorates awarded. Application fee: $55. *Unit head:* Dr. Rebecca Ropers-Huilman, Chair, 612-624-1006, Fax: 612-624-3377, E-mail: ropers@umn.edu. *Application contact:* Dr. Jennifer Engler, Assistant Dean, 612-626-2887, Fax: 612-626-7496, E-mail: engle009@umn.edu. Web site: http://www.cehd.umn.edu/EdPA/EdAd/.

University of Mississippi, Graduate School, School of Education, Department of Educational Leadership and Counselor Education, Oxford, University, MS 38677. Offers counselor education (M Ed, PhD, Specialist); educational leadership (PhD); educational leadership and counselor education (M Ed, MA, Ed D, Ed S); higher education/student personnel (MA). *Accreditation:* ACA; NCATE. *Students:* 155 full-time (106 women), 177 part-time (110 women); includes 100 minority (91 Black or African American, non-Hispanic/Latino; 1 Asian, non-Hispanic/Latino; 5 Hispanic/Latino; 3 Two or more races, non-Hispanic/Latino), 7 international. In 2011, 82 master's, 13 doctorates, 36 other advanced degrees awarded. *Degree requirements:* For doctorate, thesis/dissertation. *Entrance requirements:* For master's, GRE General Test, minimum GPA of 3.0; for doctorate, GRE General Test. Additional exam requirements/recommendations for international students: Required—TOEFL. *Application deadline:* For fall admission, 4/1 for domestic students; for spring admission, 10/1 for domestic students. Applications are processed on a rolling basis. Application fee: $25. Electronic applications accepted. *Financial support:* Scholarships/grants available. Financial award application deadline: 3/1; financial award applicants required to submit FAFSA. *Unit head:* Dr. Timothy Letzring, Acting Chair, 662-915-7063, Fax: 662-915-7249. *Application contact:* Dr. Christy M. Wyandt, Associate Dean, 662-915-7474, Fax: 662-915-7577, E-mail: cwyandt@olemiss.edu.

University of Missouri, Graduate School, College of Education, Department of Educational Leadership and Policy Analysis, Columbia, MO 65211. Offers education administration (M Ed, MA, Ed D, PhD, Ed S); higher and adult education (M Ed, MA, Ed D, PhD, Ed S). Part-time programs available. *Faculty:* 15 full-time (8 women), 5 part-time/adjunct (4 women). *Students:* 139 full-time (85 women), 273 part-time (158 women); includes 55 minority (38 Black or African American, non-Hispanic/Latino; 1 American Indian or Alaska Native, non-Hispanic/Latino; 6 Asian, non-Hispanic/Latino; 6 Hispanic/Latino; 4 Two or more races, non-Hispanic/Latino), 13 international. Average age 38. 186 applicants, 74% accepted, 91 enrolled. In 2011, 19 master's, 56 doctorates, 16 other advanced degrees awarded. *Degree requirements:* For doctorate, variable foreign language requirement, comprehensive exam (for some programs), thesis/dissertation. *Entrance requirements:* For master's, doctorate, and Ed S, minimum GPA of 3.0. Additional exam requirements/recommendations for international students: Required—TOEFL (minimum score 500 paper-based; 173 computer-based; 61 iBT), IELTS (minimum score 5.5). *Application deadline:* For fall admission, 2/15 priority date for domestic students; for spring admission, 10/15 for domestic students. Applications are processed on a rolling basis. Application fee: $55 ($75 for international students). Electronic applications accepted. *Expenses:* Tuition, state resident: full-time $5881. Tuition, nonresident: full-time $15,183. *Required fees:* $952. Tuition and fees vary according to campus/location and program. *Financial support:* In 2011–12, 2 fellowships with full tuition reimbursements, 32 research assistantships with full tuition reimbursements, 4 teaching assistantships with full tuition reimbursements were awarded; institutionally sponsored loans, scholarships/grants, health care benefits, and unspecified assistantships also available. *Faculty research:* Administrative communication and behavior, middle schools leadership, administration of special education. *Unit head:* Dr. Jay Scribner, Department Chair, E-mail: scribnerj@missouri.edu. *Application contact:* Betty Kissane, 573-882-8231, E-mail: kissaneb@missouri.edu. Web site: http://education.missouri.edu/ELPA/index.php.

University of Missouri–Kansas City, School of Education, Kansas City, MO 64110-2499. Offers administration (Ed D); counseling and guidance (MA, Ed S); counseling psychology (PhD); curriculum and instruction (MA, Ed S); education (PhD); educational administration (MA, Ed S); reading education (MA, Ed S); special education (MA). PhD in education offered through the School of Graduate Studies. *Accreditation:* NCATE. Part-time and evening/weekend programs available. *Faculty:* 59 full-time (47 women), 57 part-time/adjunct (42 women). *Students:* 221 full-time (155 women), 379 part-time (271 women); includes 140 minority (95 Black or African American, non-Hispanic/Latino; 1 American Indian or Alaska Native, non-Hispanic/Latino; 15 Asian, non-Hispanic/Latino; 27 Hispanic/Latino; 2 Two or more races, non-Hispanic/Latino), 16 international. Average age 33. 332 applicants, 51% accepted, 136 enrolled. In 2011, 131 master's, 4 doctorates, 25 other advanced degrees awarded. *Degree requirements:* For doctorate, thesis/dissertation, internship, practicum. *Entrance requirements:* For master's, GRE, minimum GPA of 2.75, 2 letters of reference, written statement of purpose; for doctorate, GRE, minimum GPA of 3.0; for Ed S, minimum GPA of 3.0. Additional exam requirements/recommendations for international students: Required—TOEFL (minimum score 550 paper-based; 213 computer-based; 80 iBT). *Application deadline:* For fall admission, 4/1 priority date for domestic students, 4/1 for international students; for spring admission, 11/1 priority date for domestic students, 11/1 for international students. Applications are processed on a rolling basis. Application fee: $45 ($50 for international students). *Expenses:* Tuition, state resident: full-time $5798; part-time $322.10 per credit hour. Tuition, nonresident: full-time $14,969; part-time $831.60 per credit hour. *Required fees:* $93.51 per credit hour. *Financial support:* In 2011–12, 15 research assistantships with partial tuition reimbursements (averaging $10,720 per year) were awarded; career-related internships or fieldwork, Federal Work-Study, institutionally sponsored loans, and tuition waivers (full and partial) also available. Support available to part-time students. Financial award application deadline: 3/1; financial award applicants required to submit FAFSA. *Faculty research:* Urban education, inquiry-based field study, theories of counseling and psychotherapy, school literacy, educational technology. *Unit head:* Dr. Wanda Blanchett, Dean, 816-235-2234, Fax: 816-235-5270, E-mail: education@umkc.edu. *Application contact:* Erica Hernandez-Scott, Student Recruiter, 816-235-1295, Fax: 816-235-5270, E-mail: hernandeze@umkc.edu. Web site: http://education.umkc.edu.

University of Missouri–St. Louis, College of Education, Division of Educational Leadership and Policy Studies, St. Louis, MO 63121. Offers adult and higher education (M Ed), including adult education, higher education; educational administration (M Ed, Ed S), including community education (M Ed), elementary education (M Ed), secondary education (M Ed); institutional research (Certificate). *Accreditation:* NCATE. Part-time and evening/weekend programs available. *Faculty:* 17 full-time (8 women), 7 part-time/adjunct (5 women). *Students:* 23 full-time (15 women), 187 part-time (137 women); includes 103 minority (96 Black or African American, non-Hispanic/Latino; 2 Asian, non-Hispanic/Latino; 4 Hispanic/Latino; 1 Two or more races, non-Hispanic/Latino), 4 international. Average age 35. 95 applicants, 86% accepted, 68 enrolled. In 2011, 57 master's, 19 Certificates awarded. *Degree requirements:* For master's, comprehensive exam (for some programs). *Entrance requirements:* Additional exam requirements/recommendations for international students: Required—TOEFL (minimum score 550 paper-based; 213 computer-based). *Application deadline:* For fall admission, 7/1 priority date for domestic students, 7/1 for international students; for spring admission, 12/1 priority date for domestic students, 12/1 for international students. Applications are processed on a rolling basis. Application fee: $35 ($40 for international students). Electronic applications accepted. *Expenses:* Tuition, state resident: full-time $6273; part-time $3866 per year. Tuition, nonresident: full-time $14,969; part-time $9980 per year. *Required fees:* $315 per year. *Financial support:* In 2011–12, 12 research assistantships (averaging $12,000 per year), 1 teaching assistantship (averaging $10,500 per year) were awarded. Financial award application deadline: 4/1; financial award applicants required to submit FAFSA. *Faculty research:* Educational policy research; philosophy of education; higher, adult, and vocational education; school initiatives, change, and reform. *Unit head:* Dr. E. Paulette Savage, Chair, 514-516-5944. *Application contact:* 314-516-5458, Fax: 314-516-6996, E-mail: gradadm@umsl.edu. Web site: http://coe.umsl.edu/web/divisions/elaps/index.html.

University of Missouri–St. Louis, College of Education, Interdisciplinary Doctoral Programs, St. Louis, MO 63121. Offers adult and higher education (Ed D); counseling (PhD); counselor education (Ed D); educational administration (Ed D); educational leadership and policy studies (PhD); educational psychology (PhD); teaching-learning processes (Ed D, PhD). *Faculty:* 72 full-time (33 women). *Students:* 44 full-time (29 women), 199 part-time (138 women); includes 65 minority (52 Black or African American, non-Hispanic/Latino; 3 American Indian or Alaska Native, non-Hispanic/Latino; 5 Asian, non-Hispanic/Latino; 5 Hispanic/Latino), 6 international. Average age 43. 47 applicants, 34% accepted, 11 enrolled. In 2011, 27 doctorates awarded. *Degree requirements:* For doctorate, thesis/dissertation. *Entrance requirements:* For doctorate, GRE General Test, 3 letters of recommendation; personal interview. Additional exam requirements/recommendations for international students: Recommended—TOEFL (minimum score 550 paper-based; 230 computer-based). *Application deadline:* For fall admission, 3/1 for domestic and international students; for spring admission, 10/1 for domestic and international students. Application fee: $35 ($40 for international students). Electronic applications accepted. *Expenses:* Tuition, state resident: full-time $6273; part-time $3866 per year. Tuition, nonresident: full-time $14,969; part-time $9980 per year. *Required fees:* $315 per year. *Financial support:* In 2011–12, 15 research assistantships (averaging $12,240 per year), 8 teaching assistantships (averaging $12,240 per year) were awarded. Financial award application deadline: 4/1; financial award applicants required to submit FAFSA. *Faculty research:* Higher education law and policy, gender and higher education, student retention, lifelong learning orientation, school counselor's role in violence prevention. *Unit head:* Dr. Kathleen Haywood, Director of Graduate Studies, 314-516-5483, Fax: 314-516-5227, E-mail: kathleen_haywood@umsl.edu. *Application contact:* 314-516-5458, Fax: 314-516-6996, E-mail: gradadm@umsl.edu.

The University of Montana, Graduate School, Phyllis J. Washington College of Education and Human Sciences, Department of Educational Leadership and Counseling, Program in Educational Leadership, Missoula, MT 59812-0002. Offers M Ed, Ed D, Ed S. *Degree requirements:* For doctorate, thesis/dissertation; for Ed S, thesis. *Entrance requirements:* For master's and Ed S, GRE General Test. Additional exam requirements/recommendations for international students: Required—TOEFL.

University of Montevallo, College of Education, Program in Instructional Leadership, Montevallo, AL 35115. Offers M Ed, Ed S. *Accreditation:* NCATE. Part-time and evening/weekend programs available. *Students:* 11 full-time (10 women), 75 part-time (55 women); includes 31 minority (all Black or African American, non-Hispanic/Latino). In 2011, 10 master's, 32 Ed Ss awarded. *Degree requirements:* For master's and Ed S, comprehensive exam. *Entrance requirements:* For master's, GRE General Test or MAT. Additional exam requirements/recommendations for international students: Required—TOEFL (minimum score 550 paper-based). *Application deadline:* For fall admission, 7/15 for domestic students; for spring admission, 11/15 for domestic students. Application fee: $25. *Financial support:* Federal Work-Study, scholarships/grants, and unspecified assistantships available. *Unit head:* Dr. Leland Doebler, Chair, 205-665-6380. *Application contact:* Rebecca Hartley, Coordinator for Graduate Studies, 205-665-6350, Fax: 205-665-6353, E-mail: hartleyrs@montevallo.edu.

University of Nebraska at Kearney, Graduate Studies, College of Education, Department of Educational Administration, Kearney, NE 68849-0001. Offers educational administration (MA Ed, Ed S); supervisor (MA Ed). *Accreditation:* NCATE. Part-time and evening/weekend programs available. *Degree requirements:* For master's, thesis optional; for Ed S, thesis. *Entrance requirements:* For master's, letters of recommendation. Additional exam requirements/recommendations for international students: Required—TOEFL (minimum score 550 paper-based; 213 computer-based). Electronic applications accepted. *Faculty research:* Leadership and organizational behavior.

University of Nebraska at Omaha, Graduate Studies, College of Education, Department of Counseling, Omaha, NE 68182. Offers community counseling (MA, MS); counseling gerontology (MA, MS); school counseling (MA, MS); student affairs practice in higher education (MA, MS). *Accreditation:* ACA (one or more programs are accredited); NCATE. Part-time and evening/weekend programs available. *Faculty:* 3 full-time (0 women). *Students:* 44 full-time (38 women), 138 part-time (113 women); includes 10 minority (7 Black or African American, non-Hispanic/Latino; 1 American Indian or Alaska Native, non-Hispanic/Latino; 1 Hispanic/Latino; 1 Two or more races, non-Hispanic/Latino). Average age 31. 47 applicants, 55% accepted, 23 enrolled. In 2011, 40 master's awarded. *Degree requirements:* For master's, comprehensive exam, thesis (for some programs). *Entrance requirements:* For master's, GRE General Test, MAT, department test, interview, minimum GPA of 3.0, 3 letters of recommendation. Additional exam requirements/recommendations for international students: Required—TOEFL (minimum score 550 paper-based; 213 computer-based; 80 iBT). *Application deadline:* For fall admission, 3/1 for domestic students; for spring admission, 10/1 for domestic students. Applications are processed on a rolling basis. Application fee: $45. Electronic applications accepted. *Financial support:* In 2011–12, 24 students received support, including 10 research assistantships with tuition reimbursements available, 3 teaching assistantships with tuition reimbursements available; fellowships, Federal Work-Study, institutionally sponsored loans, scholarships/grants, tuition waivers (partial), and unspecified assistantships also available. Support available to part-time students. Financial award application deadline: 3/1; financial award applicants required to submit FAFSA. *Unit head:* Dr. Paul Barnes, Chairperson, 402-554-2727. *Application contact:* Dr. Paul Barnes, 402-554-2341, Fax: 402-554-3143, E-mail: graduate@unomaha.edu.

University of Nebraska at Omaha, Graduate Studies, College of Education, Department of Educational Administration and Supervision, Omaha, NE 68182. Offers MS, Ed D, Ed S. *Accreditation:* NCATE. Part-time and evening/weekend programs available. *Faculty:* 7 full-time (3 women). *Students:* 9 full-time (5 women), 103 part-time (58 women); includes 7 minority (5 Black or African American, non-Hispanic/Latino; 1 American Indian or Alaska Native, non-Hispanic/Latino; 1 Hispanic/Latino), 1 international. Average age 37. 43 applicants, 56% accepted, 21 enrolled. In 2011, 39 master's, 15 doctorates awarded. *Degree requirements:* For master's, comprehensive exam, thesis (for some programs); for doctorate, comprehensive exam, thesis/dissertation; for Ed S, comprehensive exam, thesis. *Entrance requirements:* For master's, minimum GPA of 3.0, 2 letters of recommendations, statement of purpose; for doctorate, GRE General Test, resume, 3 samples of research/written work, letters of recommendation, statement of purpose. Additional exam requirements/recommendations for international students: Required—TOEFL (minimum score 500 paper-based; 173 computer-based; 61 iBT). *Application deadline:* For fall admission, 2/1 priority date for domestic students; for spring admission, 10/15 priority date for domestic students. Applications are processed on a rolling basis. Application fee: $45. Electronic applications accepted. *Financial support:* In 2011–12, 7 students received support, including 1 research assistantship with tuition reimbursement available; Federal Work-Study, institutionally sponsored loans, scholarships/grants, tuition waivers (partial), and unspecified assistantships also available. Support available to part-time students. Financial award application deadline: 3/1. *Unit head:* Dr. John Hill, Chairperson, 402-554-2721. *Application contact:* Dr. Kay Keiser, 402-554-2341, Fax: 402-554-3143, E-mail: graduate@unomaha.edu.

University of Nebraska–Lincoln, Graduate College, College of Education and Human Sciences, Department of Educational Administration, Lincoln, NE 68588. Offers M Ed, MA, Ed D, Certificate. Ed D offered jointly with University of Nebraska at Omaha. *Accreditation:* NCATE. *Degree requirements:* For master's, thesis optional; for doctorate, comprehensive exam, thesis/dissertation. *Entrance requirements:* For master's, GRE or MAT; for doctorate, GRE General Test, administrative certification. Additional exam requirements/recommendations for international students: Required—TOEFL (minimum score 550 paper-based; 213 computer-based). Electronic applications accepted. *Faculty research:* Educational policy, school finance, school law, school restructuring, leadership behavior.

University of Nebraska–Lincoln, Graduate College, College of Education and Human Sciences, Interdepartmental Area of Administration, Curriculum and Instruction, Lincoln, NE 68588. Offers Ed D, PhD, JD/PhD. *Accreditation:* NCATE. Postbaccalaureate distance learning degree programs offered. *Degree requirements:* For doctorate, comprehensive exam, thesis/dissertation. *Entrance requirements:* For doctorate, GRE, curriculum vitae. Additional exam requirements/recommendations for international students: Required—TOEFL (minimum score 550 paper-based; 213 computer-based). Electronic applications accepted.

University of Nevada, Las Vegas, Graduate College, College of Education, Department of Educational Research, Cognition, and Development, Las Vegas, NV 89154-3002. Offers educational leadership (M Ed, MS, Ed D, PhD); educational leadership-executive (Ed D); educational psychology (MS, PhD, Ed S); higher education leadership (PhD); learning and technology (PhD); school psychology (PhD); PhD/JD. *Accreditation:* NCATE. Part-time and evening/weekend programs available. *Faculty:* 28 full-time (14 women), 13 part-time/adjunct (9 women). *Students:* 54 full-time (40 women), 184 part-time (124 women); includes 68 minority (26 Black or African American, non-Hispanic/Latino; 1 American Indian or Alaska Native, non-Hispanic/Latino; 9 Asian, non-Hispanic/Latino; 21 Hispanic/Latino; 2 Native Hawaiian or other Pacific Islander, non-Hispanic/Latino; 9 Two or more races, non-Hispanic/Latino), 4 international. Average age 37. 70 applicants, 69% accepted, 41 enrolled. In 2011, 94 master's, 34 doctorates, 12 other advanced degrees awarded. *Degree requirements:* For master's, comprehensive exam (for some programs), thesis (for some programs); for doctorate, comprehensive exam (for some programs), thesis/dissertation; for Ed S, comprehensive exam, thesis. *Entrance requirements:* For master's, GMAT or GRE General Test; for doctorate, GRE General Test, writing exam; for Ed S, GRE General Test. Additional exam requirements/recommendations for international students: Required—TOEFL (minimum score 550 paper-based; 213 computer-based; 80 iBT), IELTS (minimum score 7). *Application deadline:* For fall admission, 2/1 for domestic students, 5/1 for international students; for spring admission, 10/1 for international students. Application fee: $60 ($95 for international students). Electronic applications accepted. *Financial support:* In 2011–12, 44 students received support, including 16 research assistantships with partial tuition reimbursements available (averaging $9,428 per year), 28 teaching assistantships with partial tuition reimbursements available (averaging $10,783 per year); institutionally sponsored loans, scholarships/grants, health care benefits, and unspecified assistantships also available. Financial award application deadline: 3/1. *Faculty research:* Innovation and change in educational settings; educational policy, finance, and marketing; psycho-educational assessment; student retention, persistence, development, language, and culture; statistical modeling, program evaluation, qualitative and quantitative research methods. *Total annual research expenditures:* $269,710. *Unit head:* Dr. LeAnn Putney, Chair/Professor, 702-895-4879, Fax: 702-895-3492, E-mail: leann.putney@unlv.edu. *Application contact:* Graduate College Admissions Evaluator, 702-895-3320, Fax: 702-895-4180, E-mail: gradcollege@unlv.edu. Web site: http://education.unlv.edu/ercd/.

University of Nevada, Reno, Graduate School, College of Education, Department of Educational Leadership, Reno, NV 89557. Offers M Ed, MA, MS, Ed D, PhD, Ed S. *Accreditation:* NCATE. Terminal master's awarded for partial completion of doctoral program. *Degree requirements:* For master's, comprehensive exam, thesis optional; for doctorate, comprehensive exam, thesis/dissertation. *Entrance requirements:* For master's, minimum GPA of 2.75; for doctorate, GRE General Test, minimum GPA of 3.0. Additional exam requirements/recommendations for international students: Required—TOEFL (minimum score 500 paper-based; 173 computer-based; 61 iBT), IELTS (minimum score 6). Electronic applications accepted. *Faculty research:* Law, finance, supervision, organizational theory, principalship.

University of New England, College of Arts and Sciences, Program in Education, Biddeford, ME 04005-9526. Offers advanced educational leadership (CAGS); curriculum and instruction strategies (CAGS); curriculum and instruction strategy (MS Ed); educational leadership (MS Ed, CAGS); general studies (MS Ed); inclusion education (MS Ed); leadership, ethics and change (CAGS); literacy K-12 (MS Ed, CAGS); teaching methodologies (MS Ed). Part-time programs available. Postbaccalaureate distance learning degree programs offered (minimal on-campus study). *Faculty:* 20 part-time/adjunct. *Students:* 514 full-time (417 women), 218 part-time (165 women). In 2011, 307 master's, 86 CAGSs awarded. *Degree requirements:* For master's, collaborative action research project, integrative seminar portfolio. *Entrance requirements:* For master's, teaching certificate, 2 years of teaching experience. Additional exam requirements/recommendations for international students: Required—TOEFL. *Application deadline:* For fall admission, 9/15 for domestic students; for spring admission, 1/15 for domestic students. Applications are processed on a rolling basis. Application fee: $40. Electronic applications accepted. *Expenses:* Contact institution. *Financial support:* Application deadline: 5/1; applicants required to submit FAFSA. *Faculty research:* Distance learning, effective teaching, transition planning, adult learning. *Unit head:* Dr. Doug Lynch, Chair of Education Department, 207-283-0171 Ext. 2888, E-mail: dlynch@une.edu. *Application contact:* Stacy Gato, Assistant Director of Graduate Admissions, 207-221-4225, Fax: 207-221-4898, E-mail: gradadmissions@une.edu.

University of New England, College of Arts and Sciences, Program in Educational Leadership, Biddeford, ME 04005-9526. Offers CAGS. Part-time programs available. Postbaccalaureate distance learning degree programs offered (minimal on-campus study). *Entrance requirements:* For degree, 3 years of teaching experience in an accredited school, master's degree. *Application deadline:* For fall admission, 8/15 priority date for domestic students; for winter admission, 11/15 priority date for domestic students; for spring admission, 4/15 priority date for domestic students. Applications are processed on a rolling basis. Application fee: $40. Electronic applications accepted. *Expenses:* Contact institution. *Financial support:* Application deadline: 5/1; applicants required to submit FAFSA. *Unit head:* Dr. Doug Lynch, Chair of Education Department, 207-283-0171 Ext. 2888, E-mail: dlynch@une.edu. *Application contact:* Stacy Gato, Assistant Director of Graduate Admissions, 207-221-4225, Fax: 207-221-4898, E-mail: gradadmissions@une.edu. Web site: http://uneonline.org/.

University of New Hampshire, Graduate School, College of Liberal Arts, Department of Education, Program in Educational Administration, Durham, NH 03824. Offers M Ed, Ed S. Part-time programs available. *Faculty:* 32 full-time. *Students:* 2 full-time (1 woman), 26 part-time (14 women). Average age 39. 7 applicants, 57% accepted, 2 enrolled. In 2011, 2 master's awarded. *Degree requirements:* For master's, thesis or alternative. *Entrance requirements:* For master's and Ed S, GRE General Test. Additional exam requirements/recommendations for international students: Required—TOEFL (minimum score 550 paper-based; 213 computer-based; 80 iBT). *Application deadline:* For fall admission, 2/1 priority date for domestic students, 2/1 for international students; for spring admission, 12/1 for domestic students. Applications are processed on a rolling basis. Application fee: $65. *Expenses:* Tuition, state resident: full-time $12,360; part-time $687 per credit hour. Tuition, nonresident: full-time $25,680; part-time $1058 per credit hour. *International tuition:* $29,550 full-time. *Required fees:* $1666; $833 per course. $416.50 per semester. Tuition and fees vary according to course load and degree level. *Financial support:* In 2011–12, 4 students received support. Fellowships, research assistantships, teaching assistantships, career-related internships or fieldwork, Federal Work-Study, scholarships/grants, and tuition waivers (full and partial) available. Support available to part-time students. Financial award application deadline: 2/15. *Faculty research:* School principalship, supervision, superintendency. *Unit head:* Dr. Todd Demitchell, Chair, 603-862-5043, E-mail: education.department@unh.edu. *Application contact:* Lisa Wilder, Graduate Coordinator, 603-862-2310, E-mail: education.department@unh.edu. Web site: http://www.unh.edu/education.

University of New Hampshire, Graduate School, College of Liberal Arts, Department of Education, Program in Teacher Leadership, Durham, NH 03824. Offers M Ed, Postbaccalaureate Certificate. Part-time programs available. *Faculty:* 32 full-time. *Students:* 1 (woman) full-time, 12 part-time (10 women); includes 1 minority (Asian, non-Hispanic/Latino). Average age 38. 7 applicants, 43% accepted, 1 enrolled. In 2011, 7 master's awarded. *Degree requirements:* For master's, oral exam or thesis. *Entrance requirements:* For master's, GRE. Additional exam requirements/recommendations for international students: Required—TOEFL (minimum score 550 paper-based; 213 computer-based; 80 iBT). *Application deadline:* For fall admission, 3/1 for domestic and international students; for spring admission, 4/1 for domestic students. Applications are processed on a rolling basis. Application fee: $65. Electronic applications accepted. *Expenses:* Tuition, state resident: full-time $12,360; part-time $687 per credit hour. Tuition, nonresident: full-time $25,680; part-time $1058 per credit hour. *International tuition:* $29,550 full-time. *Required fees:* $1666; $833 per course. $416.50 per semester. Tuition and fees vary according to course load and degree level. *Financial support:* Fellowships, research assistantships, teaching assistantships, Federal Work-Study, and scholarships/grants available. Support available to part-time students. Financial award application deadline: 2/15. *Unit head:* Dr. Michael Middleton, Coordinator, 603-862-7054, E-mail: education.department@unh.edu. *Application contact:* Lisa Wilder, Graduate Coordinator, 603-862-2310, E-mail: education.department@unh.edu. Web site: http://www.unh.edu/education.

University of New Hampshire, Graduate School Manchester Campus, Manchester, NH 03101. Offers business administration (MBA); counseling (M Ed); education (M Ed, MAT); educational administration and supervision (M Ed, Ed S); information technology (MS); management of technology (MS); public administration (MPA); public health (MPH, Certificate); social work (MSW); software systems engineering (Certificate). Part-time and evening/weekend programs available. *Students:* 78 full-time (50 women), 130 part-time (65 women); includes 62 minority (2 Black or African American, non-Hispanic/Latino; 56 Asian, non-Hispanic/Latino; 4 Hispanic/Latino), 4 international. Average age 34. 132 applicants, 55% accepted, 57 enrolled. In 2011, 66 master's, 9 other advanced degrees awarded. *Degree requirements:* For master's, thesis or alternative. *Entrance requirements:* Additional exam requirements/recommendations for international students: Required—TOEFL (minimum score 550 paper-based; 213 computer-based; 80 iBT). *Application deadline:* For fall admission, 6/1 for domestic students, 4/1 for international students; for spring admission, 12/1 for domestic students. Applications are processed on a rolling basis. Application fee: $65. Electronic applications accepted. *Expenses:* Tuition, state resident: full-time $12,360; part-time $687 per credit hour. Tuition, nonresident: full-time $25,680; part-time $1058 per credit hour. *International tuition:* $29,550 full-time. *Required fees:* $1666; $833 per course. $416.50 per semester. Tuition and fees vary according to course load and degree level. *Financial support:* In 2011–12, 11 students received support, including 2 teaching assistantships; fellowships, research assistantships, Federal Work-Study, scholarships/grants, health care benefits, and unspecified assistantships also available. Support available to part-time students. Financial award application deadline: 3/1; financial award applicants required to submit FAFSA. *Unit head:* Candice Brown, Director, 603-641-4313, E-mail: unhm.gradcenter@unh.edu. *Application contact:* Graduate Admissions Office, 603-862-3000, Fax: 603-862-0275, E-mail: grad.school@unh.edu. Web site: http://www.gradschool.unh.edu/manchester/.

University of New Mexico, Graduate School, College of Education, Department of Educational Leadership and Organizational Learning, Program in Educational Leadership, Albuquerque, NM 87131-2039. Offers MA, Ed D, PhD, Ed S. *Accreditation:* NCATE. Part-time and evening/weekend programs available. Postbaccalaureate distance learning degree programs offered. *Students:* 24 full-time (21 women), 84 part-time (53 women); includes 61 minority (3 Black or African American, non-Hispanic/Latino; 7 American Indian or Alaska Native, non-Hispanic/Latino; 2 Asian, non-Hispanic/Latino; 47 Hispanic/Latino; 2 Two or more races, non-Hispanic/Latino), 1 international. Average age 42. 42 applicants, 45% accepted, 13 enrolled. In 2011, 10 master's, 1 doctorate, 13 other advanced degrees awarded. *Degree requirements:* For master's, comprehensive exam; for doctorate, comprehensive exam, thesis/dissertation. *Entrance requirements:* For master's, bachelor's degree; for doctorate, GRE, master's degree. *Application deadline:* For fall admission, 6/1 for domestic students; for spring admission, 10/1 for domestic students. Applications are processed on a rolling basis. Application fee: $50. Electronic applications accepted. *Financial support:* In 2011–12, 25 students received support, including 1 research assistantship (averaging $14,000 per year); career-related internships or fieldwork and scholarships/grants also available. Financial award application deadline: 3/1; financial award applicants required to submit FAFSA. *Faculty research:* K-20 educational and organizational leadership, individual and organizational learning, policy, legal and political contexts. *Unit head:* Dr. Patricia

Boverie, Head, 505-277-2408, Fax: 505-277-5553, E-mail: pboverie@unm.edu. *Application contact:* Linda Wood, Information Contact, 505-277-0441, Fax: 505-277-5553, E-mail: woodl@unm.edu. Web site: http://coe.unm.edu/departments/elol/educational-leadership-program.html.

University of New Orleans, Graduate School, College of Education and Human Development, Department of Educational Leadership, Counseling, and Foundations, Program in Educational Leadership, New Orleans, LA 70148. Offers M Ed, PhD, GCE. *Accreditation:* NCATE. Evening/weekend programs available. Terminal master's awarded for partial completion of doctoral program. *Degree requirements:* For doctorate, variable foreign language requirement, thesis/dissertation. *Entrance requirements:* For master's and doctorate, GRE General Test. Additional exam requirements/recommendations for international students: Required—TOEFL (minimum score 550 paper-based; 213 computer-based; 79 iBT). Electronic applications accepted.

University of North Alabama, College of Education, Department of Secondary Education, Program in Education Leadership, Florence, AL 35632-0001. Offers Ed S. *Accreditation:* NCATE. Part-time and evening/weekend programs available. *Faculty:* 2 part-time/adjunct (1 woman). *Students:* 2 full-time (1 woman), 11 part-time (5 women); includes 1 minority (American Indian or Alaska Native, non-Hispanic/Latino). Average age 41. In 2011, 6 Ed Ss awarded. *Application deadline:* For fall admission, 7/1 priority date for domestic students; for spring admission, 12/1 for domestic students. Applications are processed on a rolling basis. Application fee: $25. Electronic applications accepted. *Financial support:* Application deadline: 4/1. *Unit head:* Dr. Peggy Campbell, Coordinator, 256-765-4575, Fax: 256-765-4159, E-mail: pccampbell@una.edu. *Application contact:* Kim Mauldin, Director of Admissions, 256-765-4608, Fax: 256-765-4960, E-mail: komauldin@una.edu. Web site: http://www.una.edu/education.

The University of North Carolina at Chapel Hill, Graduate School, School of Education, Programs in Educational Leadership and School Administration, Chapel Hill, NC 27599. Offers educational leadership (Ed D); school administration (MSA). *Accreditation:* NCATE. Part-time programs available. *Degree requirements:* For master's, comprehensive exam; for doctorate, comprehensive exam, thesis/dissertation. *Entrance requirements:* For master's, GRE General Test or MAT, minimum GPA of 3.2 during last 2 years of undergraduate course work, 3 years of school-based professional experience; for doctorate, GRE General Test, minimum GPA of 3.2 during last 2 years of undergraduate course work, 3 years of school-based professional experience. Additional exam requirements/recommendations for international students: Required—TOEFL (minimum score 550 paper-based; 213 computer-based). *Faculty research:* Gender, race, and class issues; school leadership; school finance and reform.

The University of North Carolina at Charlotte, Graduate School, College of Education, Department of Educational Leadership, Charlotte, NC 28223-0001. Offers curriculum and supervision (M Ed); educational leadership (Ed D); instructional systems technology (M Ed); school administration (MSA). Part-time and evening/weekend programs available. *Faculty:* 24 full-time (12 women), 2 part-time/adjunct (0 women). *Students:* 32 full-time (22 women), 180 part-time (120 women); includes 74 minority (68 Black or African American, non-Hispanic/Latino; 1 American Indian or Alaska Native, non-Hispanic/Latino; 2 Asian, non-Hispanic/Latino; 2 Hispanic/Latino; 1 Two or more races, non-Hispanic/Latino), 1 international. Average age 38. 26 applicants, 92% accepted, 21 enrolled. In 2011, 46 master's, 27 doctorates awarded. *Degree requirements:* For master's, thesis. *Entrance requirements:* For master's and doctorate, GRE or MAT. Additional exam requirements/recommendations for international students: Required—TOEFL (minimum score 550 paper-based; 220 computer-based; 83 iBT). *Application deadline:* For fall admission, 7/1 for domestic students, 5/1 for international students; for spring admission, 11/1 for domestic students, 10/1 for international students. Applications are processed on a rolling basis. Application fee: $65 ($75 for international students). Electronic applications accepted. *Expenses:* Tuition, state resident: full-time $3689. Tuition, nonresident: full-time $15,226. *Required fees:* $2198. Tuition and fees vary according to course load and program. *Financial support:* In 2011–12, 4 students received support, including 4 research assistantships (averaging $6,031 per year); career-related internships or fieldwork, institutionally sponsored loans, scholarships/grants, and unspecified assistantships also available. Support available to part-time students. Financial award application deadline: 4/1; financial award applicants required to submit FAFSA. *Faculty research:* Educational leadership theory and practice, instructional systems technology, educational research methodology, curriculum and supervision in the schools, school law and finance. *Total annual research expenditures:* $638,519. *Unit head:* Dr. Dawson R. Hancock, Chair, 704-687-8863, Fax: 704-687-3493, E-mail: dhancock@uncc.edu. *Application contact:* Kathy B. Giddings, Director of Graduate Admissions, 704-687-5503, Fax: 704-687-3279, E-mail: gradadm@uncc.edu. Web site: http://education.uncc.edu/eart/programs.htm.

The University of North Carolina at Greensboro, Graduate School, School of Education, Department of Curriculum and Instruction, Greensboro, NC 27412-5001. Offers college teaching and adult learning (Certificate); curriculum and instruction (M Ed), including chemistry education, elementary education, English as a second language, French education, instructional technology, mathematics education, middle grades education, reading education, science education, social studies education, Spanish education; curriculum and teaching (PhD), including higher education, teacher education and development; English as a second language (Certificate); higher education (M Ed); supervision (M Ed). *Accreditation:* NCATE. Part-time programs available. *Degree requirements:* For doctorate, thesis/dissertation. *Entrance requirements:* For master's and doctorate, GRE General Test. Additional exam requirements/recommendations for international students: Required—TOEFL. Electronic applications accepted. *Faculty research:* Community college literacy program, middle school mathematics/computer mathematics.

The University of North Carolina at Greensboro, Graduate School, School of Education, Department of Educational Leadership and Cultural Foundations, Greensboro, NC 27412-5001. Offers curriculum and teaching (PhD), including cultural studies; educational leadership (Ed D, Ed S); school administration (MSA). *Accreditation:* NCATE. *Degree requirements:* For doctorate, thesis/dissertation. *Entrance requirements:* For master's, doctorate, and Ed S, GRE General Test. Additional exam requirements/recommendations for international students: Required—TOEFL. Electronic applications accepted.

The University of North Carolina at Pembroke, Graduate Studies, School of Education, Program in School Administration, Pembroke, NC 28372-1510. Offers MSA. Part-time and evening/weekend programs available. *Degree requirements:* For master's, internship. *Entrance requirements:* For master's, GRE General Test or MAT, minimum GPA of 3.0 in major, 2.5 overall; 3 years teaching experience. Additional exam requirements/recommendations for international students: Required—TOEFL.

The University of North Carolina Wilmington, Watson School of Education, Department of Educational Leadership, Programs in Educational Leadership, Wilmington, NC 28403-3297. Offers educational leadership and administration (Ed D); school administration (MSA). *Degree requirements:* For master's, comprehensive exam.

University of North Dakota, Graduate School, College of Education and Human Development, Program in Educational Leadership, Grand Forks, ND 58202. Offers M Ed, MS, Ed D, PhD, Specialist. *Accreditation:* NCATE. Part-time and evening/weekend programs available. Postbaccalaureate distance learning degree programs offered (minimal on-campus study). *Degree requirements:* For master's and Specialist, comprehensive exam, thesis or alternative; for doctorate, comprehensive exam, thesis/dissertation, final exam. *Entrance requirements:* For master's, minimum GPA of 3.0; for doctorate, minimum GPA of 3.5. Additional exam requirements/recommendations for international students: Required—TOEFL (minimum score 550 paper-based; 213 computer-based; 79 iBT), IELTS (minimum score 6.5). Electronic applications accepted.

University of Northern Colorado, Graduate School, College of Education and Behavioral Sciences, Department of Leadership, Policy and Development: Higher Education and P-12 Education, Educational Leadership and Policy Studies Program, Greeley, CO 80639. Offers educational leadership (MA, Ed D, Ed S). *Accreditation:* NCATE. Part-time and evening/weekend programs available. Postbaccalaureate distance learning degree programs offered. *Degree requirements:* For master's, comprehensive exam, thesis or alternative; for doctorate, comprehensive exam, thesis/dissertation; for Ed S, comprehensive exam, thesis. *Entrance requirements:* For master's, resume, interview; for doctorate, GRE General Test, resume, interview; for Ed S, resume. Electronic applications accepted.

University of Northern Colorado, Graduate School, College of Education and Behavioral Sciences, School of Teacher Education, Program in Educational Studies, Greeley, CO 80639. Offers MAT, Ed D. Part-time and evening/weekend programs available. Electronic applications accepted.

University of Northern Iowa, Graduate College, College of Education, Department of Educational Leadership, Counseling, and Postsecondary Education, Program in Educational Leadership, Cedar Falls, IA 50614. Offers educational leadership (Ed D); principalship (MAE). Part-time and evening/weekend programs available. *Students:* 98 part-time (46 women); includes 12 minority (7 Black or African American, non-Hispanic/Latino; 1 Asian, non-Hispanic/Latino; 3 Hispanic/Latino; 1 Two or more races, non-Hispanic/Latino). 39 applicants, 64% accepted, 24 enrolled. In 2011, 23 master's, 2 doctorates awarded. *Degree requirements:* For master's, comprehensive exam (for some programs), thesis or alternative, minimum of 1 year successful teaching appropriate to the major; for doctorate, thesis/dissertation. *Entrance requirements:* For master's, minimum GPA of 3.0; for doctorate, GRE, master's degree, minimum GPA of 3.5. Additional exam requirements/recommendations for international students: Required—TOEFL (minimum score 500 paper-based; 180 computer-based; 61 iBT). *Application deadline:* For fall admission, 8/1 priority date for domestic students. Applications are processed on a rolling basis. Application fee: $50 ($70 for international students). Electronic applications accepted. *Expenses:* Tuition, state resident: full-time $7476. Tuition, nonresident: full-time $16,410. *Required fees:* $942. *Financial support:* Career-related internships or fieldwork, Federal Work-Study, and tuition waivers (full and partial) available. Support available to part-time students. Financial award application deadline: 2/1. *Unit head:* Dr. Robert Decker, Coordinator, 319-273-2443, Fax: 319-273-5175, E-mail: robert.decker@uni.edu. *Application contact:* Laurie S. Russell, Record Analyst, 319-273-2623, Fax: 319-273-2885, E-mail: laurie.russell@uni.edu. Web site: http://www.uni.edu/coe/elpe/.

University of North Florida, College of Education and Human Services, Department of Leadership, School Counseling and Sport Management, Jacksonville, FL 32224. Offers counselor education (M Ed), including school counseling; educational leadership (M Ed, Ed D), including athletic administration (M Ed), educational leadership (Ed D), educational leadership (certification) (M Ed), educational technology (M Ed), instructional leadership (M Ed). Part-time and evening/weekend programs available. *Faculty:* 15 full-time (9 women). *Students:* 48 full-time (35 women), 200 part-time (135 women); includes 67 minority (47 Black or African American, non-Hispanic/Latino; 2 American Indian or Alaska Native, non-Hispanic/Latino; 6 Asian, non-Hispanic/Latino; 10 Hispanic/Latino; 2 Two or more races, non-Hispanic/Latino), 2 international. Average age 36. 97 applicants, 48% accepted, 41 enrolled. In 2011, 84 master's, 6 doctorates awarded. *Degree requirements:* For doctorate, thesis/dissertation. *Entrance requirements:* For master's, GRE General Test, minimum GPA of 3.0 in last 60 hours, interview, 3 letters of recommendation; for doctorate, GRE General Test, master's degree, interview, 3 letters of recommendation, writing sample. Additional exam requirements/recommendations for international students: Required—TOEFL (minimum score 500 paper-based; 173 computer-based). *Application deadline:* For fall admission, 7/1 priority date for domestic students, 5/1 for international students; for spring admission, 11/1 priority date for domestic students, 10/1 for international students. Applications are processed on a rolling basis. Application fee: $30. Electronic applications accepted. *Expenses:* Tuition, state resident: full-time $8793; part-time $366.38 per credit hour. Tuition, nonresident: full-time $23,502; part-time $979.24 per credit hour. *Required fees:* $1384; $57.66 per credit hour. Tuition and fees vary according to course load and program. *Financial support:* In 2011–12, 68 students received support, including 2 research assistantships (averaging $6,200 per year), 2 teaching assistantships (averaging $6,250 per year); career-related internships or fieldwork, Federal Work-Study, scholarships/grants, tuition waivers (partial), and unspecified assistantships also available. Support available to part-time students. Financial award application deadline: 4/1; financial award applicants required to submit FAFSA. *Faculty research:* Counseling: ethics; lesbian, bisexual and transgender issues; educational leadership: school culture and climate; educational assessment and accountability; school safety and student discipline. *Total annual research expenditures:* $137,500. *Unit head:* Dr. Edgar N. Jackson, Jr., Chair, 904-620-1829, E-mail: newton.jackson@unf.edu. *Application contact:* Lillith Richardson, Assistant Director, The Graduate School, 904-620-1360, Fax: 904-620-1362, E-mail: graduateschool@unf.edu. Web site: http://www.unf.edu/coehs/lscsm/.

University of North Texas, Toulouse Graduate School, College of Education, Department of Teacher Education and Administration, Program in Educational Administration, Denton, TX 76203. Offers M Ed, Ed D, PhD. *Accreditation:* NCATE. *Degree requirements:* For master's, internship/practicum; for doctorate, comprehensive exam, thesis/dissertation. *Entrance requirements:* For master's, GRE General Test, letter of recommendation, resume; for doctorate, GRE General Test, admission exam, 3 letters of recommendation, resume, teaching experience, essay, academic writing sample. Additional exam requirements/recommendations for international students: Recommended—TOEFL (minimum score 550 paper-based; 213 computer-based). Electronic applications accepted. *Expenses:* Tuition, state resident: part-time $100 per credit hour. Tuition, nonresident: part-time $413 per credit hour. *Faculty research:* Professional learning communities, early college high schools, growth model analysis of student achievement.

University of Oklahoma, Jeannine Rainbolt College of Education, Department of Educational Leadership and Policy Studies, Program in Educational Administration, Curriculum and Supervision, Norman, OK 73019. Offers curriculum and supervision (M Ed); education administration (M Ed, Ed D, PhD); law and policy (M Ed); technology leadership (M Ed). *Accreditation:* NCATE. Part-time and evening/weekend programs available. *Students:* 35 full-time (19 women), 136 part-time (95 women); includes 42 minority (20 Black or African American, non-Hispanic/Latino; 14 American Indian or Alaska Native, non-Hispanic/Latino; 2 Asian, non-Hispanic/Latino; 3 Hispanic/Latino; 1 Native Hawaiian or other Pacific Islander, non-Hispanic/Latino; 2 Two or more races, non-Hispanic/Latino). Average age 39. 47 applicants, 79% accepted, 28 enrolled. In 2011, 38 master's, 9 doctorates awarded. Terminal master's awarded for partial completion of doctoral program. *Degree requirements:* For master's, thesis optional; for doctorate, variable foreign language requirement, thesis/dissertation, general exam. *Entrance requirements:* For master's, 12 hours of course work in education; for doctorate, GRE General Test, master's degree, 3 letters of reference, writing sample. Additional exam requirements/recommendations for international students: Required—TOEFL (minimum score 550 paper-based; 79 iBT). *Application deadline:* For fall admission, 6/1 priority date for domestic students, 3/1 for international students; for spring admission, 10/1 for domestic students, 9/1 for international students. Application fee: $40 ($90 for international students). Electronic applications accepted. *Expenses:* Tuition, state resident: full-time $4087; part-time $170.30 per credit hour. Tuition, nonresident: full-time $14,875; part-time $619.80 per credit hour. *Required fees:* $2659; $100.25 per credit hour. Tuition and fees vary according to course load and degree level. *Financial support:* In 2011–12, 76 students received support. Unspecified assistantships available. Financial award applicants required to submit FAFSA. *Faculty research:* Collective and student trust, urban school district renewal and community revitalization, single gender education, female secondary school leaders, school-university social order. *Unit head:* David Tan, Chair, 405-325-4202, Fax: 405-325-2403, E-mail: dtan@ou.edu. *Application contact:* Geri Evans, Graduate Programs Representative, 405-325-5978, Fax: 405-325-2403, E-mail: gevans@ou.edu. Web site: http://education.ou.edu/departments_1/eacs_1/.

University of Oklahoma, Jeannine Rainbolt College of Education, Department of Instructional Leadership and Academic Curriculum, Norman, OK 73072. Offers communication, culture and pedagogy for Hispanic populations in educational settings (Graduate Certificate); instructional leadership and academic curriculum (M Ed, PhD), including bilingual education, early childhood education, elementary education, English education, instructional leadership, mathematics education, reading education, science education, science, technology, engineering and mathematics education (M Ed), secondary education, social studies education, teacher education (M Ed). *Accreditation:* NCATE. Part-time and evening/weekend programs available. *Faculty:* 19 full-time (13 women), 1 (woman) part-time/adjunct. *Students:* 73 full-time (63 women), 114 part-time (87 women); includes 29 minority (5 Black or African American, non-Hispanic/Latino; 12 American Indian or Alaska Native, non-Hispanic/Latino; 5 Asian, non-Hispanic/Latino; 3 Hispanic/Latino; 1 Native Hawaiian or other Pacific Islander, non-Hispanic/Latino; 3 Two or more races, non-Hispanic/Latino), 7 international. Average age 33. 87 applicants, 86% accepted, 68 enrolled. In 2011, 36 master's, 6 doctorates awarded. Terminal master's awarded for partial completion of doctoral program. *Degree requirements:* For doctorate, thesis/dissertation. *Entrance requirements:* For master's, 12 hours of course work in education; for doctorate, GRE General Test, master's degree, minimum graduate GPA of 3.0. Additional exam requirements/recommendations for international students: Required—TOEFL (minimum score 550 paper-based; 79 iBT). *Application deadline:* For fall admission, 6/1 priority date for domestic students, 3/1 for international students; for spring admission, 11/1 for domestic students, 9/1 for international students. Applications are processed on a rolling basis. Application fee: $40 ($90 for international students). Electronic applications accepted. *Expenses:* Tuition, state resident: full-time $4087; part-time $170.30 per credit hour. Tuition, nonresident: full-time $14,875; part-time $619.80 per credit hour. *Required fees:* $2659; $100.25 per credit hour. Tuition and fees vary according to course load and degree level. *Financial support:* In 2011–12, 128 students received support, including 2 research assistantships with partial tuition reimbursements available (averaging $12,431 per year), 12 teaching assistantships with partial tuition reimbursements available (averaging $10,161 per year); institutionally sponsored loans, scholarships/grants, and unspecified assistantships also available. Financial award applicants required to submit FAFSA. *Faculty research:* Engineering in practice for sustainable future, no child left behind (reading), early childhood learning games impact study, Educare randomized control startup, Oklahoma mentoring professional development. *Total annual research expenditures:* $1.1 million. *Unit head:* Lawrence Baines, Chair, 405-325-1498, Fax: 405-325-4061, E-mail: lbaines@ou.edu. *Application contact:* Lynn Crussel, Graduate Programs Officer, 405-325-4843, Fax: 405-325-4061, E-mail: lcrussel@ou.edu. Web site: http://education.ou.edu/departments/ilac.

University of Pennsylvania, Graduate School of Education, Division of Teaching, Learning, and Leadership, Program in Educational Leadership, Philadelphia, PA 19104. Offers MS Ed, Ed D, PhD. Part-time programs available. *Students:* 27 full-time (11 women), 3 part-time (0 women); includes 7 minority (3 Black or African American, non-Hispanic/Latino; 1 Asian, non-Hispanic/Latino; 3 Two or more races, non-Hispanic/Latino), 1 international. 30 applicants, 17% accepted, 4 enrolled. In 2011, 2 master's, 3 doctorates awarded. *Degree requirements:* For master's, comprehensive exam, thesis; for doctorate, comprehensive exam, thesis/dissertation, oral exams. *Entrance requirements:* For master's, GRE or MAT; for doctorate, GRE. *Application deadline:* For fall admission, 12/15 priority date for domestic students; for spring admission, 12/1 for domestic students. Applications are processed on a rolling basis. Application fee: $70. Electronic applications accepted. *Expenses:* Contact institution. *Financial support:* Institutionally sponsored loans, scholarships/grants, traineeships, health care benefits, and unspecified assistantships available. *Faculty research:* Public policy, curriculum and instruction, organization theory/leadership, school reform. *Unit head:* Dr. Andrew Porter, Dean, 215-898-7014.

University of Pennsylvania, Graduate School of Education, Division of Teaching, Learning, and Leadership, Program in School Leadership, Philadelphia, PA 19104. Offers MS Ed. *Students:* 31 full-time (16 women), 5 part-time (3 women); includes 8 minority (6 Black or African American, non-Hispanic/Latino; 2 Hispanic/Latino). 61 applicants, 70% accepted, 36 enrolled. In 2011, 17 degrees awarded. *Degree requirements:* For master's, 360-hour internship, research project, paper. *Expenses: Tuition:* Full-time $26,660; part-time $4944 per course. *Required fees:* $2318; $291 per course. Tuition and fees vary according to course load, degree level and program. *Unit head:* Dr. Andrew Porter, Dean, 215-898-7014. *Application contact:* Liz Ulivella, Coordinator, 215-746-2718, E-mail: ulivella@gse.upenn.edu.

University of Pennsylvania, Graduate School of Education, Mid-Career Doctoral Program in Educational Leadership, Philadelphia, PA 19104. Offers Ed D. *Students:* 83 full-time (53 women), 1 (woman) part-time; includes 32 minority (26 Black or African American, non-Hispanic/Latino; 1 Asian, non-Hispanic/Latino; 4 Hispanic/Latino; 1 Two or more races, non-Hispanic/Latino). 108 applicants, 28% accepted, 25 enrolled. In 2011, 17 degrees awarded. *Application deadline:* For fall admission, 2/1 for domestic students. *Expenses: Tuition:* Full-time $26,660; part-time $4944 per course. *Required fees:* $2318; $291 per course. Tuition and fees vary according to course load, degree level and program. *Unit head:* Dr. Michael Johanek, Director, 215-746-6573, E-mail: midcareer@gse.upenn.edu. *Application contact:* Alyssa D'Alconzo, Associate Director, Admissions, 215-898-6415, Fax: 215-746-6884, E-mail: admissions@gse.upenn.edu. Web site: http://www.gse.upenn.edu/degrees_programs/midcareer.

University of Pennsylvania, Graduate School of Education, Penn Chief Learning Officer (CLO) Executive Doctoral Program, Philadelphia, PA 19104. Offers MS Ed, Ed D. *Students:* 34 full-time (12 women), 2 part-time (0 women); includes 2 minority (1 Hispanic/Latino; 1 Two or more races, non-Hispanic/Latino). 25 applicants, 56% accepted, 12 enrolled. In 2011, 9 degrees awarded. *Application deadline:* For fall admission, 7/15 for domestic students. *Expenses: Tuition:* Full-time $26,660; part-time $4944 per course. *Required fees:* $2318; $291 per course. Tuition and fees vary according to course load, degree level and program. *Unit head:* Rona Rosenberg, Interim Director, 215-573-2872, E-mail: ronar@exchange.upenn.edu. *Application contact:* Alyssa D'Alconzo, Associate Director, Admissions, 215-898-6415, Fax: 215-746-6884, E-mail: admissions@gse.upenn.edu. Web site: http://pennclo.com/.

University of Phoenix–Bay Area Campus, College of Education, San Jose, CA 95134-1805. Offers administration and supervision (MA Ed); adult education and training (MA Ed); early childhood education (MA Ed); education (Ed S); educational leadership (Ed D); elementary teacher education (MA Ed); higher education administration (PhD); secondary teacher education (MA Ed); special education (MA Ed); teacher leadership (MA Ed). Evening/weekend programs available. Postbaccalaureate distance learning degree programs offered (no on-campus study). *Degree requirements:* For master's, thesis (for some programs). *Entrance requirements:* For master's, minimum undergraduate GPA of 2.5, 3 years of work experience. Additional exam requirements/recommendations for international students: Required—TOEFL (minimum score 550 paper-based; 213 computer-based; 79 iBT). Electronic applications accepted.

University of Phoenix–Central Florida Campus, College of Education, Maitland, FL 32751-7057. Offers administration and supervision (MA Ed); curriculum and instruction (MA Ed); curriculum and instruction-computer education (MA Ed); curriculum and instruction-mathematics education (MA Ed); early childhood education (MA Ed); elementary teacher education (MA Ed); secondary teacher education (MA Ed). Evening/weekend programs available. *Degree requirements:* For master's, thesis (for some programs). *Entrance requirements:* For master's, 3 years of work experience, minimum undergraduate GPA of 2.5. Additional exam requirements/recommendations for international students: Required—TOEFL (minimum score 550 paper-based; 213 computer-based; 79 iBT). Electronic applications accepted.

University of Phoenix–Chattanooga Campus, College of Education, Chattanooga, TN 37421-3707. Offers administration and supervision (MA Ed); curriculum and instruction (MA Ed); elementary teacher education (MA Ed); secondary teacher education (MA Ed).

University of Phoenix–Denver Campus, College of Education, Lone Tree, CO 80124-5453. Offers administration and supervision (MAEd); curriculum instruction (MAEd); elementary teacher education (MAEd); school counseling (MSC); secondary teacher education (MAEd). Evening/weekend programs available. *Degree requirements:* For master's, thesis (for some programs). *Entrance requirements:* For master's, minimum undergraduate GPA of 2.5, 3 years work experience. Additional exam requirements/recommendations for international students: Required—TOEFL (minimum score 550 paper-based; 213 computer-based; 79 iBT). Electronic applications accepted.

University of Phoenix–Hawaii Campus, College of Education, Honolulu, HI 96813-4317. Offers administration and supervision (MA Ed); curriculum and instruction (MA Ed); elementary education (MA Ed); secondary education (MA Ed); special education (MA Ed); teacher education for elementary licensure (MA Ed). Evening/weekend programs available. *Degree requirements:* For master's, thesis (for some programs). *Entrance requirements:* For master's, minimum undergraduate GPA of 2.5, 3 years of work experience. Additional exam requirements/recommendations for international students: Required—TOEFL (minimum score 550 paper-based; 213 computer-based; 79 iBT). Electronic applications accepted.

University of Phoenix–Idaho Campus, College of Education, Meridian, ID 83642-5114. Offers administration and supervision (MA Ed); curriculum and instruction (MA Ed); elementary teacher education (MA Ed); secondary teacher education (MA Ed). Evening/weekend programs available. *Degree requirements:* For master's, thesis (for some programs). *Entrance requirements:* For master's, minimum undergraduate GPA of 2.5, 3 years of work experience. Additional exam requirements/recommendations for international students: Required—TOEFL (minimum score 550 paper-based; 213 computer-based). Electronic applications accepted.

University of Phoenix–Kansas City Campus, College of Education, Kansas City, MO 64131-4517. Offers administration and supervision (MA Ed). Postbaccalaureate distance learning degree programs offered.

University of Phoenix–Las Vegas Campus, College of Education, Las Vegas, NV 89128. Offers administration and supervision (MA Ed); curriculum and instruction (MA Ed); school counseling (MSC); teacher education-elementary licensure (MA Ed). Evening/weekend programs available. *Degree requirements:* For master's, thesis (for some programs). *Entrance requirements:* For master's, minimum undergraduate GPA of 2.5, 3 years of work experience. Additional exam requirements/recommendations for international students: Required—TOEFL (minimum score 550 paper-based; 213 computer-based; 79 iBT). Electronic applications accepted.

University of Phoenix–Madison Campus, College of Education, Madison, WI 53718-2416. Offers education (Ed S); educational leadership (Ed D); educational leadership: curriculum and instruction (Ed D); higher education administration (PhD).

University of Phoenix–Memphis Campus, College of Education, Cordova, TN 38018. Offers administration and supervision (MA Ed); curriculum and instruction (MA Ed); elementary teacher education (MA Ed); secondary teacher education (MA Ed).

University of Phoenix–Metro Detroit Campus, College of Education, Troy, MI 48098-2623. Offers administration and supervision (MA Ed); elementary teacher education (MA Ed); secondary teacher education (MA Ed); special education (MA Ed). Evening/weekend programs available. *Degree requirements:* For master's, thesis (for some programs). *Entrance requirements:* For master's, 3 years of work experience, minimum undergraduate GPA of 2.5. Additional exam requirements/recommendations for international students: Required—TOEFL (minimum score 550 paper-based; 213 computer-based; 79 iBT). Electronic applications accepted.

University of Phoenix–Milwaukee Campus, College of Education, Milwaukee, WI 53045. Offers curriculum and instruction (MA Ed, Ed D); education (Ed S); educational leadership (Ed D); English as a second language (MA Ed); higher education administration (PhD).

University of Phoenix–Nashville Campus, College of Education, Nashville, TN 37214-5048. Offers administration and supervision (MA Ed); curriculum and instruction (MA Ed); elementary teacher education (MA Ed); secondary teacher education (MA Ed). Evening/weekend programs available. *Degree requirements:* For master's, thesis (for some programs). *Entrance requirements:* For master's, minimum undergraduate GPA of 2.5, 3 years work experience. Additional exam requirements/recommendations for international students: Required—TOEFL (minimum score 500 paper-based; 213 computer-based; 79 iBT). Electronic applications accepted.

University of Phoenix–New Mexico Campus, College of Education, Albuquerque, NM 87113-1570. Offers administration and supervision (MAEd); curriculum and instruction (MAEd); elementary teacher education (MAEd); school counseling (MSC); secondary teacher education (MAEd). Evening/weekend programs available. *Degree requirements:* For master's, thesis (for some programs). *Entrance requirements:* For master's, minimum undergraduate GPA of 2.5, 3 years of work experience. Additional exam requirements/recommendations for international students: Required—TOEFL (minimum score 550 paper-based; 213 computer-based; 79 iBT). Electronic applications accepted.

University of Phoenix–Northern Nevada Campus, College of Education, Reno, NV 89521-5862. Offers administration and supervision (MA Ed); curriculum and instruction (MA Ed); elementary teacher education (MA Ed); secondary teacher education (MA Ed).

University of Phoenix–Northern Virginia Campus, College of Education, Reston, VA 20190. Offers administration and supervision (MA Ed).

University of Phoenix–North Florida Campus, College of Education, Jacksonville, FL 32216-0959. Offers administration and supervision (MA Ed); curriculum and instruction (MA Ed), including computer education, mathematics education; early childhood education (MA Ed); elementary teacher education (MA Ed); secondary teacher education (MA Ed). Evening/weekend programs available. *Degree requirements:* For master's, thesis (for some programs). *Entrance requirements:* For master's, 3 years of work experience, minimum undergraduate GPA of 2.5. Additional exam requirements/recommendations for international students: Required—TOEFL (minimum score 550 paper-based; 213 computer-based; 49 iBT). Electronic applications accepted.

University of Phoenix–Omaha Campus, College of Education, Omaha, NE 68154-5240. Offers administration and supervision (MA Ed); curriculum and instruction (MA Ed), including adult education, computer education, curriculum and instruction, English and language arts education, English as a second language, mathematics education; elementary teacher education (MA Ed); secondary teacher education (MA Ed); special education (MA Ed).

University of Phoenix–Online Campus, College of Education, Phoenix, AZ 85034-7209. Offers administration and supervision (MAEd, Graduate Certificate); adult education and training (MAEd); curriculum and instruction (MAEd); curriculum and instruction reading (MAEd); curriculum and instruction-computer education (MAEd); curriculum and instruction-language arts (MAEd); curriculum and instruction-mathematics (MAEd); early childhood education (MAEd); educational studies (MAEd); elementary teacher education (MAEd); elementary teacher education-early childhood (MAEd); secondary teacher education (MAEd); special education (MAEd); teacher education - elementary/middle level (MAEd); teacher education middle level generalist (MAEd); teacher education middle level mathematics (MAEd); teacher education middle level science (MAEd); teacher education secondary mathematics (MAEd); teacher education secondary science (MAEd); teacher leadership (MAEd). *Accreditation:* Teacher Education Accreditation Council. Evening/weekend programs available. Postbaccalaureate distance learning degree programs offered. *Students:* 9,180 full-time (7,178 women); includes 2,913 minority (2,069 Black or African American, non-Hispanic/Latino; 50 American Indian or Alaska Native, non-Hispanic/Latino; 100 Asian, non-Hispanic/Latino; 542 Hispanic/Latino; 48 Native Hawaiian or other Pacific Islander, non-Hispanic/Latino; 104 Two or more races, non-Hispanic/Latino), 147 international. Average age 36. *Entrance requirements:* Additional exam requirements/recommendations for international students: Required—TOEFL, TOEIC (Test of English as an International Communication), Berlitz Online English Proficiency Exam, Pearson Test of English, or IELTS. *Application deadline:* Applications are processed on a rolling basis. Application fee: $45. Electronic applications accepted. *Expenses:* Contact institution. *Financial support:* Scholarships/grants available. Financial award applicants required to submit FAFSA. *Application contact:* 866-766-0766. Web site: http://www.phoenix.edu/colleges_divisions/education.html.

University of Phoenix–Online Campus, School of Advanced Studies, Phoenix, AZ 85034-7209. Offers business administration (DBA); education (Ed S); educational leadership (Ed D), including curriculum and instruction, education technology, educational leadership; health administration (DHA); higher education administration (PhD); industrial/organizational psychology (PhD); nursing (PhD); organizational leadership (DM), including information systems and technology, organizational leadership. Evening/weekend programs available. Postbaccalaureate distance learning degree programs offered. *Students:* 7,581 full-time (5,042 women); includes 3,199 minority (2,505 Black or African American, non-Hispanic/Latino; 68 American Indian or Alaska Native, non-Hispanic/Latino; 158 Asian, non-Hispanic/Latino; 395 Hispanic/Latino; 46 Native Hawaiian or other Pacific Islander, non-Hispanic/Latino; 27 Two or more races, non-Hispanic/Latino), 397 international. Average age 44. *Degree requirements:* For doctorate, thesis/dissertation. *Entrance requirements:* Additional exam requirements/recommendations for international students: Required—TOEFL, TOEIC (Test of English as an International Communication), Berlitz Online English Proficiency Exam, Pearson Test of English, or IELTS. *Application deadline:* Applications are processed on a rolling basis. Application fee: $45. Electronic applications accepted. *Expenses:* Contact institution. *Financial support:* Scholarships/grants available. Financial award applicants required to submit FAFSA. *Unit head:* Dr. Jeremy Moreland, Executive Dean. *Application contact:* 866-766-0766. Web site: http://www.phoenix.edu/colleges_divisions/doctoral.html.

University of Phoenix–Phoenix Main Campus, College of Education, Tempe, AZ 85282-2371. Offers administration and supervision (MA Ed); adult education and training (MA Ed); curriculum and instruction reading (MA Ed); curriculum instruction (MA Ed); early childhood education (MA Ed); education studies (MA Ed); elementary teacher education (MA Ed); secondary teacher education (MA Ed); special education (MA Ed); teacher leadership (MA Ed). Evening/weekend programs available. Postbaccalaureate distance learning degree programs offered. *Students:* 297 full-time (203 women); includes 53 minority (19 Black or African American, non-Hispanic/Latino; 1 American Indian or Alaska Native, non-Hispanic/Latino; 6 Asian, non-Hispanic/Latino; 21 Hispanic/Latino; 2 Native Hawaiian or other Pacific Islander, non-Hispanic/Latino; 4 Two or more races, non-Hispanic/Latino), 3 international. Average age 35. *Entrance requirements:* Additional exam requirements/recommendations for international students: Required—TOEFL, TOEIC (Test of English as an International Communication), Berlitz Online English Proficiency Exam, Pearson Test of English, or IELTS. *Application deadline:* Applications are processed on a rolling basis. Application fee: $45. Electronic applications accepted. *Expenses:* Contact institution. *Financial support:* Scholarships/grants available. Financial award applicants required to submit FAFSA. *Application contact:* 866-766-0766. Web site: http://www.phoenix.edu/colleges_divisions/education.html.

University of Phoenix–Puerto Rico Campus, College of Education, Guaynabo, PR 00968. Offers administration and supervision (MA Ed); early childhood education (MA Ed); school counselor (MSC). Evening/weekend programs available. *Degree requirements:* For master's, thesis (for some programs). *Entrance requirements:* For master's, minimum undergraduate GPA of 2.5, 3 years work experience. Additional exam requirements/recommendations for international students: Required—TOEFL (minimum score 550 paper-based; 213 computer-based; 79 iBT). Electronic applications accepted.

University of Phoenix–Richmond Campus, College of Education, Richmond, VA 23230. Offers administration and supervision (MA Ed); curriculum and instruction (MA Ed).

University of Phoenix–Southern Arizona Campus, College of Education, Tucson, AZ 85711. Offers administration and supervision (MA Ed); adult education and training (MA Ed); curriculum instruction (MA Ed); educational counseling (MA Ed); elementary teacher education (MA Ed); school counseling (MSC); secondary teacher education (MA Ed); special education (MA Ed, Certificate). Evening/weekend programs available. *Degree requirements:* For master's, thesis (for some programs). *Entrance requirements:* For master's, minimum undergraduate GPA of 2.5, 3 years of work experience. Additional exam requirements/recommendations for international students: Required—TOEFL (minimum score 550 paper-based; 213 computer-based; 79 iBT). Electronic applications accepted.

University of Phoenix–Southern California Campus, College of Education, Costa Mesa, CA 92626. Offers administration and supervision (MA Ed); adult education and training (MA Ed); educational studies (MA Ed); teacher leadership (MA Ed). Evening/weekend programs available. Postbaccalaureate distance learning degree programs offered. *Students:* 190 full-time (132 women); includes 82 minority (25 Black or African American, non-Hispanic/Latino; 5 Asian, non-Hispanic/Latino; 46 Hispanic/Latino; 4 Native Hawaiian or other Pacific Islander, non-Hispanic/Latino; 2 Two or more races, non-Hispanic/Latino), 3 international. Average age 35. *Entrance requirements:* Additional exam requirements/recommendations for international students: Required—TOEFL, TOEIC (Test of English as an International Communication), Berlitz Online English Proficiency Exam, Pearson Test of English, or IELTS. *Application deadline:* Applications are processed on a rolling basis. Application fee: $45. Electronic applications accepted. *Expenses:* Contact institution. *Financial support:* Scholarships/grants available. Financial award applicants required to submit FAFSA. *Application contact:* 866-766-0766. Web site: http://www.phoenix.edu/colleges_divisions/education.html.

University of Phoenix–Southern Colorado Campus, College of Education, Colorado Springs, CO 80919-2335. Offers administration and supervision (MA Ed); curriculum and instruction (MA Ed); elementary teacher education (MA Ed); principal licensure certification (Certificate); school counseling (MSC); secondary teacher education (MA Ed). Evening/weekend programs available. *Degree requirements:* For master's, thesis (for some programs). *Entrance requirements:* For master's, minimum undergraduate GPA of 2.5, 3 years of work experience. Additional exam requirements/recommendations for international students: Required—TOEFL (minimum score 550 paper-based; 213 computer-based; 79 iBT). Electronic applications accepted.

University of Phoenix–South Florida Campus, College of Education, Fort Lauderdale, FL 33309. Offers administration and supervision (MA Ed); curriculum and instruction (MA Ed), including computer education, curriculum and instruction, mathematics education; early childhood education (MA Ed); elementary teacher education (MA Ed); secondary teacher education (MA Ed). Evening/weekend programs available. *Degree requirements:* For master's, thesis (for some programs). *Entrance requirements:* For master's, 3 years of work experience, minimum undergraduate GPA of 2.5. Additional exam requirements/recommendations for international students: Required—TOEFL (minimum score 550 paper-based; 213 computer-based; 79 iBT). Electronic applications accepted.

University of Phoenix–Springfield Campus, College of Education, Springfield, MO 65804-7211. Offers administration and supervision (MA Ed); curriculum and instruction (MA Ed), including computer education, curriculum and instruction, English and language arts education, English as a second language, mathematics education; English and language arts education (MA Ed).

University of Phoenix–Utah Campus, College of Education, Salt Lake City, UT 84123-4617. Offers administration and supervision (MA Ed); curriculum and instruction (MA Ed); elementary teacher education (MA Ed); school counseling (MSC); secondary teacher education (MA Ed); special education (MA Ed). Evening/weekend programs available. *Degree requirements:* For master's, thesis (for some programs). *Entrance requirements:* For master's, minimum undergraduate GPA of 2.5, 3 years work experience. Additional exam requirements/recommendations for international students: Required—TOEFL (minimum score 550 paper-based; 213 computer-based; 79 iBT). Electronic applications accepted.

University of Phoenix–Vancouver Campus, The Artemis School, College of Education, Burnaby, BC V5C 6G9, Canada. Offers administration and supervision (MA Ed); curriculum and instruction (MA Ed), including computer education, curriculum and instruction. Evening/weekend programs available. *Degree requirements:* For master's, thesis (for some programs). *Entrance requirements:* For master's, minimum undergraduate GPA of 2.5, 3 years work experience. Additional exam requirements/recommendations for international students: Required—TOEFL (minimum score 550 paper-based; 213 computer-based; 79 iBT). Electronic applications accepted.

University of Phoenix–Washington D.C. Campus, College of Education, Washington, DC 20001. Offers administration and supervision (MA Ed); adult education and training (MA Ed); computer education (MA Ed); curriculum and instruction (MA Ed, Ed D); early childhood education (MA Ed); education (Ed S); educational leadership (Ed D); educational technology (Ed D); elementary teacher education (MA Ed); English and language arts education (MA Ed); English as a second language (MA Ed); higher education administration (PhD); mathematics education (MA Ed); secondary teacher education (MA Ed); special education (MA Ed); teacher leadership (MA Ed).

University of Phoenix–West Florida Campus, College of Education, Temple Terrace, FL 33637. Offers administration and supervision (MA Ed); curriculum and instruction (MA Ed), including computer education, curriculum and instruction, mathematics education; curriculum and technology (MA Ed); early childhood education (MA Ed); elementary teacher education (MA Ed); secondary teacher education (MA Ed). Evening/weekend programs available. *Degree requirements:* For master's, thesis (for some programs). *Entrance requirements:* For master's, 3 years of work experience, minimum undergraduate GPA of 2.5. Additional exam requirements/recommendations for international students: Required—TOEFL (minimum score 550 paper-based; 213 computer-based; 79 iBT).

University of Pittsburgh, School of Education, Department of Administrative and Policy Studies, Program in School Leadership, Pittsburgh, PA 15260. Offers M Ed, Ed D, PhD. Part-time and evening/weekend programs available. *Students:* 10 full-time (7 women), 107 part-time (57 women); includes 7 minority (all Black or African American, non-Hispanic/Latino), 2 international. Average age 39. 19 applicants, 68% accepted, 13 enrolled. In 2011, 27 master's, 8 doctorates awarded. *Degree requirements:* For master's, thesis; for doctorate, thesis/dissertation. *Entrance requirements:* For doctorate, GRE General Test. Additional exam requirements/recommendations for international students: Required—TOEFL (minimum score 213 computer-based; 80 iBT). *Application deadline:* For fall admission, 2/15 priority date for domestic students, 2/15 for international students; for spring admission, 11/1 priority date for domestic students, 11/1 for international students. Applications are processed on a rolling basis. Application fee: $50. Electronic applications accepted. *Expenses:* Tuition, state resident: full-time $18,774; part-time $760 per credit. Tuition, nonresident: full-time $30,736; part-time $1258 per credit. *Required fees:* $740; $200 per term. Tuition and fees vary according to program. *Financial support:* Fellowships, research assistantships, teaching assistantships, Federal Work-Study, institutionally sponsored loans, scholarships/grants, health care benefits, tuition waivers (partial), and unspecified assistantships available. Support available to part-time students. Financial award application deadline: 3/15; financial award applicants required to submit FAFSA. *Unit* *head:* Dr. Mary Margaret Kerr, Chair, 412-648-7205, Fax: 412-648-1784, E-mail: mmkerr@pitt.edu. *Application contact:* Lauren Pasquini, Enrollment Manager, 412-648-2230, Fax: 412-648-1899, E-mail: soeinfo@pitt.edu. Web site: http://www.education.pitt.edu/.

University of Prince Edward Island, Faculty of Education, Charlottetown, PE C1A 4P3, Canada. Offers leadership and learning (M Ed). Part-time programs available. *Degree requirements:* For master's, thesis. *Entrance requirements:* For master's, 2 years of professional experience, bachelor of education, professional certificate. Additional exam requirements/recommendations for international students: Required—TOEFL (minimum score 550 paper-based; 213 computer-based; 80 iBT), Canadian Academic English Language Assessment, Michigan English Language Assessment Battery, Canadian Test of English for Scholars and Trainees. *Faculty research:* Distance learning, aboriginal communities and education leadership development, international development, immersion language learning.

University of Puerto Rico, Río Piedras, College of Education, Program in School Administration and Supervision, San Juan, PR 00931-3300. Offers M Ed, Ed D. Part-time programs available. *Degree requirements:* For master's, thesis; for doctorate, thesis/dissertation, internship. *Entrance requirements:* For master's, PAEG or GRE, minimum GPA of 3.0, letter of recommendation; for doctorate, GRE or PAEG, interview, master's degree, minimum GPA of 3.0, letter of recommendation.

University of Regina, Faculty of Graduate Studies and Research, Faculty of Education, Department of Educational Administration, Regina, SK S4S 0A2, Canada. Offers M Ed. *Faculty:* 2 full-time (0 women). *Students:* 4 full-time (3 women), 53 part-time (24 women). 43 applicants, 84% accepted. In 2011, 6 master's awarded. *Degree requirements:* For master's, thesis optional, practicum, project, or thesis. *Entrance requirements:* For master's, bachelor's degree in education, two years teaching experience. Additional exam requirements/recommendations for international students: Required—TOEFL (minimum score 580 paper-based; 80 iBT), IELTS (minimum score 6.5). *Application deadline:* 2/15 for domestic and international students. Application fee: $100. Electronic applications accepted. *Financial support:* Fellowships, research assistantships, and teaching assistantships available. Financial award application deadline: 6/15. *Faculty research:* Legal aspects of school administration, economics of education, education planning, politics of education, administrative behavior in education. *Unit head:* Dr. Rod Dolmage, Head/Executive Director, 306-585-4816, Fax: 306-585-5387, E-mail: rod.dolmage@uregina.ca. *Application contact:* Tania Gates, Graduate Program Coordinator, 306-585-4506, Fax: 306-585-5387, E-mail: edgrad@uregina.ca.

University of Rochester, Margaret Warner Graduate School of Education and Human Development, Doctoral Programs in Education, Rochester, NY 14627. Offers counseling (Ed D); educational administration (Ed D); educational policy and theory (PhD); higher education (PhD); human development in educational context (PhD); teaching, curriculum, and change (PhD). *Expenses: Tuition:* Full-time $41,040.

University of Rochester, Margaret Warner Graduate School of Education and Human Development, Master's Program in School Leadership, Rochester, NY 14627. Offers MS. *Expenses: Tuition:* Full-time $41,040.

University of St. Francis, College of Education, Joliet, IL 60435-6169. Offers educational leadership (MS, Ed D); elementary education certification (M Ed); reading (MS); secondary education certification (M Ed), including English education, math education, science education, social studies education, visual arts education; special education (M Ed); teaching and learning (MS). *Accreditation:* NCATE. Part-time and evening/weekend programs available. Postbaccalaureate distance learning degree programs offered (no on-campus study). *Faculty:* 7 full-time (5 women), 21 part-time/adjunct (14 women). *Students:* 32 full-time (21 women), 230 part-time (175 women); includes 23 minority (7 Black or African American, non-Hispanic/Latino; 2 Asian, non-Hispanic/Latino; 13 Hispanic/Latino; 1 Two or more races, non-Hispanic/Latino), 1 international. Average age 32. 147 applicants, 60% accepted, 57 enrolled. In 2011, 156 master's awarded. *Entrance requirements:* For doctorate, master's degree, IL Type 75 or Principal's endorsement, interview. Additional exam requirements/recommendations for international students: Required—TOEFL (minimum score 550 paper-based; 213 computer-based). *Application deadline:* Applications are processed on a rolling basis. Application fee: $30. Electronic applications accepted. *Expenses:* Contact institution. *Financial support:* In 2011–12, 23 students received support. Federal Work-Study, scholarships/grants, tuition waivers (partial), and unspecified assistantships available. Support available to part-time students. Financial award applicants required to submit FAFSA. *Unit head:* Dr. John Gambro, Dean, 815-740-3829, Fax: 815-740-2264, E-mail: jgambro@stfrancis.edu. *Application contact:* Sandra Sloka, Director of Admissions for Graduate and Degree Completion Programs, 800-735-7500, Fax: 815-740-5032, E-mail: ssloka@stfrancis.edu. Web site: http://www.stfrancis.edu/academics/college-of-education/.

University of St. Thomas, Graduate Studies, School of Education, Department of Leadership, Policy and Administration, St. Paul, MN 55105-1096. Offers community education administration (MA); educational leadership (Ed S); educational leadership and administration (MA); international leadership (MA, Certificate); leadership (Ed D); leadership in student affairs (MA, Certificate); police leadership (MA); public policy and leadership (MA, Certificate). Part-time and evening/weekend programs available. *Faculty:* 8 full-time (3 women), 17 part-time/adjunct (7 women). *Students:* 47 full-time (34 women), 325 part-time (172 women); includes 54 minority (26 Black or African American, non-Hispanic/Latino; 3 American Indian or Alaska Native, non-Hispanic/Latino; 14 Asian, non-Hispanic/Latino; 7 Hispanic/Latino; 4 Two or more races, non-Hispanic/Latino), 11 international. Average age 37. 170 applicants, 80% accepted, 93 enrolled. In 2011, 72 master's, 17 doctorates, 39 other advanced degrees awarded. Terminal master's awarded for partial completion of doctoral program. *Degree requirements:* For master's, thesis (for some programs); for doctorate, thesis/dissertation; for other advanced degree, thesis or alternative. *Entrance requirements:* For master's, minimum GPA of 3.0 or MAT; for doctorate, MAT, minimum graduate GPA of 3.5; for other advanced degree, minimum graduate GPA of 3.25 or MAT. Additional exam requirements/recommendations for international students: Required—TOEFL (minimum score 550 paper-based; 213 computer-based; 20 iBT). *Application deadline:* For fall admission, 6/1 priority date for domestic students; for spring admission, 11/1 priority date for domestic students. Applications are processed on a rolling basis. Application fee: $50. *Expenses:* Contact institution. *Financial support:* Fellowships, research assistantships, institutionally sponsored loans, and scholarships/grants available. Support available to part-time students. Financial award applicants required to submit FAFSA. *Unit head:* Dr. Donald R. LaMagdeleine, Chair, 651-962-4893, Fax: 651-962-4169, E-mail: drlamagdelei@stthomas.edu. *Application contact:* Jackie Grossklaus, Department Assistant, 651-962-4885, Fax: 651-962-4169, E-mail: jmgrossklaus@stthomas.edu. Web site: http://www.stthomas.edu/education.

University of St. Thomas, School of Education, Houston, TX 77006-4696. Offers all level teaching (M Ed); bilingual/dual language (M Ed); Catholic school teaching (M Ed); Catholic/private school leadership (M Ed); counselor education (M Ed); curriculum and instruction (M Ed); educational leadership (M Ed); elementary teaching (M Ed); English as a second language (M Ed); exceptionality/ educational diagnostician (M Ed); exceptionality/special education (M Ed); generalist (M Ed); reading (M Ed); secondary teaching (M Ed). Part-time and evening/weekend programs available. Postbaccalaureate distance learning degree programs offered (no on-campus study). *Faculty:* 30 full-time (17 women), 54 part-time/adjunct (37 women). *Students:* 66 full-time (43 women), 1,178 part-time (1,044 women); includes 777 minority (313 Black or African American, non-Hispanic/Latino; 5 American Indian or Alaska Native, non-Hispanic/Latino; 29 Asian, non-Hispanic/Latino; 395 Hispanic/Latino; 2 Native Hawaiian or other Pacific Islander, non-Hispanic/Latino; 33 Two or more races, non-Hispanic/Latino), 26 international. Average age 36. 551 applicants, 94% accepted, 416 enrolled. In 2011, 72 master's awarded. *Degree requirements:* For master's, thesis, field experience. *Entrance requirements:* For master's, GRE or MAT if GPA is below 3.0, bachelor's degree; minimum GPA of 2.75 in bachelor's degree or last 60 credit hours; official transcripts from all institutions; goal statement of 250-300 words; 1 reference. Additional exam requirements/recommendations for international students: Required—TOEFL. *Application deadline:* Applications are processed on a rolling basis. Application fee: $35. Electronic applications accepted. *Expenses:* Contact institution. *Financial support:* In 2011–12, 9 students received support. Federal Work-Study, scholarships/grants, and state work-study, institutional employment available. Support available to part-time students. Financial award application deadline: 4/15; financial award applicants required to submit FAFSA. *Faculty research:* Leadership, diversity, personality traits, second language acquisition. *Unit head:* Dr. Nora Hutto, Dean, 713-525-3540, Fax: 713-525-3871, E-mail: education@stthom.edu. *Application contact:* Paula C. Hollis, Administrative Assistant, 713-525-3540, Fax: 713-525-3871, E-mail: education@stthom.edu. Web site: http://www.stthom.edu/Schools_Centers_of_Excellence/Schools_of_Study/School_of_Education/Index.aqf.

University of San Diego, School of Leadership and Education Sciences, Department of Leadership Studies, San Diego, CA 92110-2492. Offers higher education leadership (MA); leadership studies (MA, PhD); nonprofit leadership and management (MA, Certificate). Part-time and evening/weekend programs available. *Faculty:* 11 full-time (6 women), 16 part-time/adjunct (8 women). *Students:* 14 full-time (9 women), 202 part-time (139 women); includes 65 minority (16 Black or African American, non-Hispanic/Latino; 11 Asian, non-Hispanic/Latino; 30 Hispanic/Latino; 3 Native Hawaiian or other Pacific Islander, non-Hispanic/Latino; 5 Two or more races, non-Hispanic/Latino), 8 international. Average age 35. 236 applicants, 51% accepted, 75 enrolled. In 2011, 53 master's, 11 doctorates awarded. *Degree requirements:* For master's, thesis (for some programs), portfolio; for doctorate, comprehensive exam, thesis/dissertation. *Entrance requirements:* For master's, minimum GPA of 3.0, interview; for doctorate, GRE, master's degree, minimum GPA of 3.5 (recommended), interview, writing sample, resume. Additional exam requirements/recommendations for international students: Required—TOEFL (minimum score 580 paper-based; 237 computer-based; 83 iBT), TWE. *Application deadline:* For fall admission, 1/15 for domestic and international students. Application fee: $45. Electronic applications accepted. *Expenses: Tuition:* Full-time $22,482; part-time $1249 per unit. *Required fees:* $224. Full-time tuition and fees vary according to course load and degree level. *Financial support:* In 2011–12, 161 students received support. Career-related internships or fieldwork, Federal Work-Study, institutionally sponsored loans, unspecified assistantships, and stipends available. Support available to part-time students. Financial award application deadline: 4/1; financial award applicants required to submit FAFSA. *Faculty research:* Higher education administration policy and relations, organizational leadership, nonprofits and philanthropy, student affairs leadership. *Unit head:* Dr. Cheryl Getz, Graduate Program Director, 619-260-4289, Fax: 619-260-6835, E-mail: cgetz@sandiego.edu. *Application contact:* Monica Mahon, Associate Director of Graduate Admissions, 619-260-4524, Fax: 619-260-4158, E-mail: grads@sandiego.edu. Web site: http://www.sandiego.edu/soles/programs/leadership_studies/.

University of San Francisco, School of Education, Catholic Educational Leadership Program, San Francisco, CA 94117-1080. Offers Catholic school leadership (MA, Ed D); Catholic school teaching (MA). *Faculty:* 2 full-time (1 woman), 2 part-time/adjunct (both women). *Students:* 9 full-time (4 women), 25 part-time (11 women); includes 6 minority (1 Black or African American, non-Hispanic/Latino; 2 Asian, non-Hispanic/Latino; 3 Hispanic/Latino), 3 international. Average age 41. 24 applicants, 71% accepted, 8 enrolled. In 2011, 2 master's, 6 doctorates awarded. *Degree requirements:* For doctorate, thesis/dissertation. Application fee: $55 ($65 for international students). *Expenses: Tuition:* Full-time $20,070; part-time $1115 per unit. Tuition and fees vary according to course load, campus/location and program. *Financial support:* In 2011–12, 1 student received support. Fellowships, research assistantships, and teaching assistantships available. Financial award application deadline: 3/2; financial award applicants required to submit FAFSA. *Unit head:* Dr. Christopher Thomas, Chair, 415-422-2204. *Application contact:* Beth Teague, Associate Director of Graduate Outreach, 415-422-5467, E-mail: schoolofeducation@usfca.edu. Web site: http://www.soe.usfca.edu/departments/leadership/cel_index.html.

University of San Francisco, School of Education, Organization and Leadership Program, San Francisco, CA 94117-1080. Offers MA, Ed D. *Faculty:* 3 full-time (all women), 6 part-time/adjunct (4 women). *Students:* 75 full-time (53 women), 36 part-time (29 women); includes 59 minority (12 Black or African American, non-Hispanic/Latino; 2 American Indian or Alaska Native, non-Hispanic/Latino; 15 Asian, non-Hispanic/Latino; 23 Hispanic/Latino; 1 Native Hawaiian or other Pacific Islander, non-Hispanic/Latino; 6 Two or more races, non-Hispanic/Latino), 6 international. Average age 36. 91 applicants, 78% accepted, 35 enrolled. In 2011, 23 master's, 26 doctorates awarded. *Degree requirements:* For doctorate, thesis/dissertation. Application fee: $55 ($65 for international students). *Expenses: Tuition:* Full-time $20,070; part-time $1115 per unit. Tuition and fees vary according to course load, campus/location and program. *Financial support:* In 2011–12, 16 students received support. Fellowships, research assistantships, and teaching assistantships available. Financial award application deadline: 3/2; financial award applicants required to submit FAFSA. *Unit head:* Dr. Christopher Thomas, Chair, 415-422-2204. *Application contact:* Beth Teague, Associate Director of Graduate Outreach, 415-422-5467, E-mail: schoolofeducation@usfca.edu. Web site: http://www.soe.usfca.edu/departments/leadership/ol_index.html.

University of Saskatchewan, College of Graduate Studies and Research, College of Education, Department of Educational Administration, Saskatoon, SK S7N 5A2, Canada. Offers M Ed, PhD, Diploma. Part-time programs available. *Degree requirements:* For master's, thesis (for some programs); for doctorate, comprehensive exam (for some programs), thesis/dissertation. *Entrance requirements:* Additional exam requirements/recommendations for international students: Required—TOEFL (minimum score 80 iBT); Recommended—IELTS (minimum score 6.5). Electronic applications accepted.

The University of Scranton, College of Graduate and Continuing Education, Department of Education, Program in Educational Administration, Scranton, PA 18510. Offers MS. *Accreditation:* NCATE. Part-time and evening/weekend programs available. Postbaccalaureate distance learning degree programs offered (no on-campus study). *Students:* 104 full-time (53 women), 217 part-time (114 women); includes 19 minority (13 Black or African American, non-Hispanic/Latino; 1 American Indian or Alaska Native, non-Hispanic/Latino; 1 Asian, non-Hispanic/Latino; 4 Hispanic/Latino). Average age 34. 59 applicants, 95% accepted. In 2011, 169 master's awarded. *Degree requirements:* For master's, comprehensive exam, capstone experience. *Entrance requirements:* For master's, minimum GPA of 2.75. Additional exam requirements/recommendations for international students: Required—TOEFL (minimum score 500 paper-based; 173 computer-based), IELTS (minimum score 5.5). *Application deadline:* Applications are processed on a rolling basis. Application fee: $50. *Financial support:* Teaching assistantships, career-related internships or fieldwork, Federal Work-Study, and unspecified assistantships available. Support available to part-time students. Financial award application deadline: 3/1. *Unit head:* Dr. Art Chambers, Director, 570-941-4668, Fax: 570-941-5515, E-mail: chambersa2@scranton.edu. *Application contact:* Joseph M. Roback, Director of Admissions, 570-941-4385, Fax: 570-941-5928, E-mail: robackj2@scranton.edu.

University of Sioux Falls, Fredrikson School of Education, Sioux Falls, SD 57105-1699. Offers educational administration (Ed S), including principal leadership, superintendent and district leadership; leadership in reading (M Ed); leadership in schools (M Ed); leadership in technology (M Ed); teaching (M Ed). Admission in summer only. *Accreditation:* NCATE. Part-time and evening/weekend programs available. *Faculty:* 9 full-time (8 women), 10 part-time/adjunct (7 women). *Students:* 196 part-time (144 women); includes 2 minority (1 Black or African American, non-Hispanic/Latino; 1 American Indian or Alaska Native, non-Hispanic/Latino). 55 applicants, 100% accepted, 47 enrolled. *Degree requirements:* For master's, comprehensive exam (for some programs), research application project; for Ed S, comprehensive exam, portfolio. *Entrance requirements:* For master's, minimum GPA of 3.0, 1 year of teaching experience; for Ed S, minimum 3 years of teaching experience, minimum cumulative GPA of 3.5, 1 year of administrative experience. Additional exam requirements/recommendations for international students: Required—TOEFL. *Application deadline:* Applications are processed on a rolling basis. Application fee: $25. *Expenses: Tuition:* Part-time $345 per semester hour. *Required fees:* $35 per term. Part-time tuition and fees vary according to degree level and program. *Financial support:* Available to part-time students. Applicants required to submit FAFSA. *Faculty research:* Reading, literacy, leadership. *Unit head:* Dawn Olson, Director of Graduate Programs in Education, 605-575-2083, Fax: 605-575-2079, E-mail: dawn.olson@usiouxfalls.edu. *Application contact:* Student Contact, 605-331-5000.

University of South Africa, College of Human Sciences, Pretoria, South Africa. Offers adult education (M Ed); African languages (MA, PhD); African politics (MA, PhD); Afrikaans (MA, PhD); ancient history (MA, PhD); ancient Near Eastern studies (MA, PhD); anthropology (MA, PhD); applied linguistics (MA); Arabic (MA, PhD); archaeology (MA); art history (MA); Biblical archaeology (MA); Biblical studies (M Th, D Th, PhD); Christian spirituality (M Th, D Th); church history (M Th, D Th); classical studies (MA, PhD); clinical psychology (MA); communication (MA, PhD); comparative education (M Ed, Ed D); consulting psychology (D Admin, D Com, PhD); curriculum studies (M Ed, Ed D); development studies (M Admin, MA, D Admin, PhD); didactics (M Ed, Ed D); education (M Tech); education management (M Ed, Ed D); educational psychology (M Ed); English (MA); environmental education (M Ed); French (MA, PhD); German (MA, PhD); Greek (MA); guidance and counseling (M Ed); health studies (MA, PhD), including health sciences education (MA), health services management (MA), medical and surgical nursing science (critical care general) (MA), midwifery and neonatal nursing science (MA), trauma and emergency care (MA); history (MA, PhD); history of education (Ed D); inclusive education (M Ed, Ed D); information and communications technology policy and regulation (MA); information science (MA, MIS, PhD); international politics (MA, PhD); Islamic studies (MA, PhD); Italian (MA, PhD); Judaica (MA, PhD); linguistics (MA, PhD); mathematical education (M Ed); mathematics education (MA); missiology (M Th, D Th); modern Hebrew (MA, PhD); musicology (MA, MMus, D Mus, PhD); natural science education (M Ed); New Testament (M Th, D Th); Old Testament (D Th); pastoral therapy (M Th, D Th); philosophy (MA); philosophy of education (M Ed, Ed D); politics (MA, PhD); Portuguese (MA, PhD); practical theology (M Th, D Th); psychology (MA, MS, PhD); psychology of education (M Ed, Ed D); public health (MA); religious studies (MA, D Th, PhD); Romance languages (MA); Russian (MA, PhD); Semitic languages (MA, PhD); social behavior studies in HIV/AIDS (MA); social science (mental health) (MA); social science in development studies (MA); social science in psychology (MA); social science in social work (MA); social science in sociology (MA); social work (MSW, DSW, PhD); socio-education (M Ed, Ed D); sociolinguistics (MA); sociology (MA, PhD); Spanish (MA, PhD); systematic theology (M Th, D Th); TESOL (teaching English to speakers of other languages) (MA); theological ethics (M Th, D Th); theory of literature (MA, PhD); urban ministries (D Th); urban ministry (M Th).

University of South Alabama, Graduate School, College of Education, Department of Leadership and Teacher Education, Mobile, AL 36688-0002. Offers early childhood education (M Ed); educational administration (Ed S); educational leadership (M Ed); elementary education (M Ed); reading education (M Ed); science education (M Ed); secondary education (M Ed); special education (M Ed, Ed S). *Accreditation:* NCATE. Part-time programs available. *Faculty:* 20 full-time (14 women). *Students:* 135 full-time (106 women), 75 part-time (62 women); includes 50 minority (40 Black or African American, non-Hispanic/Latino; 3 American Indian or Alaska Native, non-Hispanic/Latino; 3 Asian, non-Hispanic/Latino; 3 Hispanic/Latino; 1 Two or more races, non-Hispanic/Latino), 1 international. 89 applicants, 49% accepted, 36 enrolled. In 2011, 88 master's, 13 Ed Ss awarded. *Degree requirements:* For master's, comprehensive exam. *Entrance requirements:* For master's, GRE General Test or MAT, minimum GPA of 3.0. *Application deadline:* For fall admission, 7/15 priority date for domestic students, 6/15 for international students; for spring admission, 12/1 priority date for domestic students, 11/1 for international students. Applications are processed on a rolling basis. Application fee: $35. *Expenses:* Tuition, state resident: full-time $7968; part-time $332 per credit hour. Tuition, nonresident: full-time $15,936; part-time $664 per credit hour. *Financial support:* Research assistantships and career-related internships or fieldwork available. Support available to part-time students. Financial award application deadline: 4/1. *Unit head:* Dr. Harold Dodge, Jr., Chair, 251-380-2894. *Application contact:* Dr. Abigail Baxter, Director of Graduate Studies, 251-460-6310, Fax: 251-461-1513, E-mail: kharriso@usouthal.edu. Web site: http://www.southalabama.edu/coe/lted.

University of South Carolina, The Graduate School, College of Education, Department of Educational Leadership and Policies, Program in Educational Administration, Columbia, SC 29208. Offers M Ed, PhD, Ed S. *Accreditation:* NCATE. Part-time and evening/weekend programs available. Postbaccalaureate distance learning degree programs offered (no on-campus study). *Degree requirements:* For master's, comprehensive exam, thesis (for some programs), foreign language (MA); for doctorate, comprehensive exam, thesis/dissertation. *Entrance requirements:* For master's, GRE General Test or MAT, letter of reference, resume; for doctorate and Ed S, GRE General Test or MAT, interview, letter of intent, letter of reference, transcripts, resum&e. Electronic applications accepted.

The University of South Dakota, Graduate School, School of Education, Division of Educational Administration, Vermillion, SD 57069-2390. Offers MA, Ed D, Ed S. *Accreditation:* NCATE. Part-time and evening/weekend programs available. Postbaccalaureate distance learning degree programs offered (no on-campus study). *Degree requirements:* For master's and Ed S, comprehensive exam, thesis or alternative; for doctorate, comprehensive exam, thesis/dissertation. *Entrance requirements:* For master's and doctorate, GRE General Test, MAT, minimum GPA of 2.7. Additional exam requirements/recommendations for international students: Required—TOEFL (minimum score 550 paper-based; 213 computer-based; 79 iBT). Electronic applications accepted. *Expenses:* Tuition, state resident: full-time $3118.50; part-time $173.25 per credit hour. Tuition, nonresident: full-time $6601; part-time $366.70 per credit hour. *Required fees:* $2268; $126 per credit hour. Tuition and fees vary according to program.

University of Southern California, Graduate School, Rossier School of Education, Doctor of Education Programs, Los Angeles, CA 90089. Offers educational psychology (Ed D); higher education administration (Ed D); K-12 leadership in urban school settings (Ed D); teacher education in multicultural societies (Ed D). Part-time and evening/weekend programs available. *Degree requirements:* For doctorate, thesis/dissertation. *Entrance requirements:* For doctorate, GRE. Additional exam requirements/recommendations for international students: Required—TOEFL (minimum score 250 computer-based; 100 iBT). Electronic applications accepted. *Faculty research:* Data-driven decision-making in K-12 schools and districts; examination of college and university leadership and management in U. S. and Asia; studies in facilitating student learning; organizational change and the role of leaders; leadership, diversity, learning and accountability.

University of Southern California, Graduate School, Rossier School of Education, Doctor of Philosophy in Education Programs, Los Angeles, CA 90089. Offers educational psychology (PhD); higher education administration and policy (PhD); K-12 policy and practice (PhD). *Degree requirements:* For doctorate, thesis/dissertation, 63 units; qualifying exam; dissertation proposal and defense. *Entrance requirements:* For doctorate, GRE. Additional exam requirements/recommendations for international students: Required—TOEFL (minimum score 250 computer-based; 100 iBT). Electronic applications accepted. *Faculty research:* Diversity in higher education, organizational change, educational psychology, policy and politics of educational reform, economics of education and education policy.

University of Southern Maine, School of Education and Human Development, Educational Leadership Program, Portland, ME 04104-9300. Offers assistant principal (Certificate); athletic administration (Certificate); educational leadership (MS Ed, CAS); middle-level education (Certificate). Part-time and evening/weekend programs available. Postbaccalaureate distance learning degree programs offered (minimal on-campus study). *Degree requirements:* For master's, thesis or alternative, practicum, internship; for other advanced degree, thesis or alternative. *Entrance requirements:* For master's, three years of documented teaching; for other advanced degree, master's degree. Additional exam requirements/recommendations for international students: Required—TOEFL (minimum score 550 paper-based; 213 computer-based; 79 iBT). Electronic applications accepted.

University of Southern Mississippi, Graduate School, College of Education and Psychology, Department of Educational Leadership and School Counseling, Hattiesburg, MS 39401. Offers education (Ed D, PhD, Ed S), including educational leadership and school counseling (Ed D, PhD); educational administration (M Ed). Part-time programs available. *Faculty:* 9 full-time (5 women), 3 part-time/adjunct (1 woman). *Students:* 35 full-time (26 women), 266 part-time (184 women); includes 103 minority (93 Black or African American, non-Hispanic/Latino; 5 Hispanic/Latino; 5 Two or more races, non-Hispanic/Latino). Average age 39. 27 applicants, 74% accepted, 18 enrolled. In 2011, 85 master's, 25 doctorates, 18 other advanced degrees awarded. *Degree requirements:* For master's, comprehensive exam, thesis optional, internship; for doctorate, comprehensive exam, thesis/dissertation; for Ed S, comprehensive exam, thesis optional. *Entrance requirements:* For master's, GRE General Test, minimum GPA of 2.75; for doctorate, GRE General Test, minimum GPA of 3.5; for Ed S, GRE General Test, minimum GPA of 3.25. Additional exam requirements/recommendations for international students: Required—TOEFL, IELTS. *Application deadline:* For fall admission, 3/1 priority date for domestic students, 3/1 for international students; for spring admission, 1/10 for domestic and international students. Application fee: $50. *Financial support:* In 2011–12, research assistantships (averaging $9,000 per year), teaching assistantships (averaging $9,000 per year) were awarded; career-related internships or fieldwork, Federal Work-Study, institutionally sponsored loans, scholarships/grants, health care benefits, and unspecified assistantships also available. Financial award application deadline: 3/15; financial award applicants required to submit FAFSA. *Unit head:* Dr. Thelma Roberson, Interim Chair, 601-266-4556, Fax: 601-266-4233, E-mail: thelma.roberson@usm.edu. *Application contact:* Dr. Thelma Roberson, Interim Chair, 601-266-4556, Fax: 601-266-4233, E-mail: thelma.roberson@usm.edu. Web site: http://www.usm.edu/graduateschool/table.php.

University of Southern Mississippi, Graduate School, College of Education and Psychology, Department of Educational Studies and Research, Hattiesburg, MS 39406-0001. Offers adult education (Graduate Certificate); community college leadership (Graduate Certificate); counseling and personnel services (college) (M Ed); education (PhD, Ed S), including adult education, research, evaluation and statistics (PhD); education (Ed D), including educational administration, educational research; education: educational leadership and research (Ed S), including higher education administration; educational administration and supervision (M Ed); higher education administration (Ed D, PhD); institutional research (Graduate Certificate). *Faculty:* 7 full-time (1 woman), 5 part-time/adjunct (1 woman). *Students:* 33 full-time (25 women), 104 part-time (25 women); includes 46 minority (40 Black or African American, non-Hispanic/Latino; 1 Asian, non-Hispanic/Latino; 3 Hispanic/Latino; 2 Two or more races, non-Hispanic/Latino), 1 international. Average age 36. 27 applicants, 48% accepted, 1 enrolled. In 2011, 27 master's, 13 doctorates, 1 other advanced degree awarded. *Degree requirements:* For master's and other advanced degree, comprehensive exam, thesis (for some programs); for doctorate, comprehensive exam, thesis/dissertation. *Entrance requirements:* For master's, doctorate, and other advanced degree, GRE General Test, minimum GPA of 2.75. Additional exam requirements/recommendations for international students: Required—TOEFL. *Application deadline:* For fall admission, 2/1 for domestic students, 3/1 for international students. Applications are processed on a rolling basis. Application fee: $35. *Financial support:* Career-related internships or fieldwork, Federal Work-Study, and institutionally sponsored loans available. Financial award application deadline: 3/15; financial award applicants required to submit FAFSA. *Total annual research expenditures:* $88,500. *Unit head:* Dr. Thomas V. O'Brien, Chair, 601-266-6093, E-mail: thomas.obrien@usm.edu. *Application contact:* Shonna Breland, Manager of Graduate Admissions, 601-266-6563, Fax: 601-266-5138. Web site: http://www.usm.edu/cep/esr/.

University of South Florida, Graduate School, College of Education, Department of Educational Leadership and Policy Studies, Tampa, FL 33620-9951. Offers educational leadership (M Ed, Ed D, Ed S). Part-time programs available. *Faculty:* 10 full-time (5 women), 9 part-time/adjunct (4 women). *Students:* 6 full-time (5 women), 126 part-time (95 women); includes 42 minority (23 Black or African American, non-Hispanic/Latino; 2 Asian, non-Hispanic/Latino; 14 Hispanic/Latino; 3 Two or more races, non-Hispanic/Latino). Average age 39. 98 applicants, 42% accepted, 31 enrolled. In 2011, 52 master's, 13 doctorates, 5 other advanced degrees awarded. *Degree requirements:* For master's, comprehensive exam, portfolio; for doctorate, comprehensive exam, thesis/dissertation, philosophies of inquiry; multiple research methods; for Ed S, comprehensive exam, thesis. *Entrance requirements:* For master's, minimum GPA of

3.0 in last 60 hours of coursework; Florida Professional Teaching Certificate; 2 years' post bachelor's teaching experience; for doctorate, GRE General Test, master's degree in educational leadership or educational leadership certification; for Ed S, GRE General Test, educational leadership certification. Additional exam requirements/recommendations for international students: Required—TOEFL (minimum score 550 paper-based; 213 computer-based; 79 iBT). *Application deadline:* For fall admission, 2/15 for domestic students, 1/2 for international students; for spring admission, 10/15 for domestic students, 6/1 for international students. Application fee: $30. Electronic applications accepted. *Financial support:* In 2011–12, 8 students received support, including 2 teaching assistantships with full tuition reimbursements available (averaging $10,500 per year); scholarships/grants, health care benefits, and unspecified assistantships also available. Financial award application deadline: 3/22; financial award applicants required to submit FAFSA. *Faculty research:* Multicultural education and social justice, educational accountability policy, school reform, community development and school success, school governance, teacher and principal preparation. *Total annual research expenditures:* $76,508. *Unit head:* Dr. Anthony Rolle, Chairperson, 813-974-6036, Fax: 813-974-5423. *Application contact:* Lisa Mullen, Academic Advisor, 813-974-1344, Fax: 813-974-5423, E-mail: lmullen@usf.edu. Web site: http://www.coedu.usf.edu/main/departments/edlead/edlead.html.

University of South Florida–Polytechnic, College of Human and Social Sciences, Lakeland, FL 33803. Offers counselor education (MA), including clinical mental health, professional school counseling; educational leadership (M Ed); reading education (MA).

University of South Florida–St. Petersburg Campus, College of Education, St. Petersburg, FL 33701. Offers educational leadership development (M Ed); elementary education (MA), including math/science; English education (MA); middle grades STEM education (MS); reading education (MA). Part-time programs available. *Students:* 30 full-time (27 women), 130 part-time (109 women); includes 28 minority (14 Black or African American, non-Hispanic/Latino; 4 Asian, non-Hispanic/Latino; 9 Hispanic/Latino; 1 Two or more races, non-Hispanic/Latino). Average age 34. 63 applicants, 70% accepted, 36 enrolled. In 2011, 74 master's awarded. *Degree requirements:* For master's, comprehensive exam, practicum, internship, comprehensive portfolio. *Entrance requirements:* For master's, State of Florida General Knowledge Test (GKT), Florida Teaching Certificate (for non-initial certification programs), letters of recommendation. Additional exam requirements/recommendations for international students: Required—TOEFL (minimum score 550 paper-based; 79 iBT); Recommended—IELTS. *Application deadline:* For fall admission, 6/1 priority date for domestic students, 6/1 for international students; for spring admission, 10/15 priority date for domestic students, 10/15 for international students. Applications are processed on a rolling basis. Application fee: $30. Electronic applications accepted. *Expenses:* Tuition, state resident: full-time $8847. Tuition, nonresident: full-time $18,423. One-time fee: $35 full-time. Full-time tuition and fees vary according to course load and program. *Financial support:* Applicants required to submit FAFSA. *Unit head:* Dr. Harold W. Heller, Dean, 727-873-4155, Fax: 727-873-4191, E-mail: hheller@usfsp.edu. *Application contact:* Eric Douthirt, Enrollment Management Specialist, 727-873-4450, E-mail: douthirt@usfsp.edu. Web site: http://www1.usfsp.edu/coe/index.asp.

University of South Florida Sarasota-Manatee, College of Education, Sarasota, FL 34243. Offers educational leadership (M Ed), including curriculum leadership, K-12, non-public/charter school leadership; elementary education K-6 (MA); K-6 with ESOL endorsement (MAT); reading education K-12 (MA); MAT/MA. Part-time and evening/weekend programs available. *Faculty:* 12 full-time (8 women), 4 part-time/adjunct (3 women). *Students:* 19 full-time (17 women), 64 part-time (50 women); includes 7 minority (1 Black or African American, non-Hispanic/Latino; 1 Asian, non-Hispanic/Latino; 4 Hispanic/Latino; 1 Two or more races, non-Hispanic/Latino). Average age 33. 50 applicants, 62% accepted, 21 enrolled. In 2011, 41 master's awarded. *Degree requirements:* For master's, comprehensive exam (for some programs). *Entrance requirements:* For master's, GRE. Additional exam requirements/recommendations for international students: Required—TOEFL (minimum score 213 computer-based; 79 iBT) or IELTS. *Application deadline:* For fall admission, 2/15 for domestic students, 1/2 for international students; for spring admission, 10/15 for domestic students, 6/1 for international students. Applications are processed on a rolling basis. Application fee: $30. Electronic applications accepted. *Expenses:* Tuition, state resident: full-time $9301; part-time $387.55 per credit hour. Tuition, nonresident: full-time $19,412; part-time $808.85 per credit hour. *Required fees:* $15; $5 per semester. One-time fee: $30. *Financial support:* Federal Work-Study, scholarships/grants, health care benefits, and unspecified assistantships available. Support available to part-time students. Financial award application deadline: 3/1; financial award applicants required to submit FAFSA. *Faculty research:* Child development, student achievement, intergenerational studies. *Unit head:* Dr. Terry A. Osborn, Dean, 941-359-4531, E-mail: terryosborn@sar.usf.edu. *Application contact:* Jo Lynn Raudebaugh, Graduate Admissions Advisor, 941-359-4587, E-mail: jraudeba@sar.usf.edu. Web site: http://www.sarasota.usf.edu/Academics/COE/.

The University of Tampa, Program in Teaching, Tampa, FL 33606-1490. Offers curricula and instructional leadership (M Ed); teaching (M Ed). Part-time and evening/weekend programs available. *Faculty:* 5 full-time (2 women), 7 part-time/adjunct (6 women). *Students:* 25 full-time (12 women), 2 part-time (both women); includes 6 minority (5 Hispanic/Latino; 1 Two or more races, non-Hispanic/Latino). Average age 30. 102 applicants, 38% accepted, 27 enrolled. In 2011, 43 master's awarded. *Entrance requirements:* For master's, Florida Teacher Certification Exam, PRAXIS, GRE, or GMAT, bachelor's degree in education or professional teaching certificate. Additional exam requirements/recommendations for international students: Required—TOEFL (minimum score 577 paper-based; 230 computer-based; 90 iBT), IELTS (minimum score 7). *Application deadline:* For fall admission, 5/1 for domestic students. Applications are processed on a rolling basis. Application fee: $40. Electronic applications accepted. *Expenses: Tuition:* Full-time $8320; part-time $520 per credit hour. *Required fees:* $40 per semester. Tuition and fees vary according to program. *Financial support:* In 2011–12, 8 students received support. Grants available. Financial award applicants required to submit FAFSA. *Faculty research:* Diversity in the classroom, technology integration, assessment methodologies, complex and ill-structured problem solving, and communities of practice.. *Unit head:* Dr. Anne Gormly, Dean, College of Social Sciences, Mathematics and Education, 813-253-3333 Ext. 6262, E-mail: agormly@ut.edu. *Application contact:* Charlene Tobie, Associate Director, Graduate and Continuing Studies, 813-258-7409, Fax: 813-258-7451, E-mail: ctobie@ut.edu. Web site: http://www.ut.edu/graduate.

The University of Tennessee, Graduate School, College of Education, Health and Human Sciences, Program in Education, Knoxville, TN 37996. Offers art education (MS); counseling education (PhD); cultural studies in education (PhD); curriculum (MS, Ed S); curriculum, educational research and evaluation (Ed D, PhD); early childhood education (PhD); early childhood special education (MS); education of deaf and hard of hearing (MS); educational administration and policy studies (Ed D, PhD); educational administration and supervision (Ed S); educational psychology (Ed D, PhD); elementary education (MS, Ed S); elementary teaching (MS); English education (MS, Ed S); exercise science (PhD); foreign language/ESL education (MS, Ed S); instructional technology (MS, Ed D, PhD, Ed S); literacy, language and ESL education (PhD); literacy, language education, and ESL education (Ed D); mathematics education (MS, Ed S); modified and comprehensive special education (MS); reading education (MS, Ed S); school counseling (Ed S); school psychology (PhD, Ed S); science education (MS, Ed S); secondary teaching (MS); social foundations (MS); social science education (MS, Ed S); socio-cultural foundations of sports and education (PhD); special education (Ed S); teacher education (Ed D, PhD). *Accreditation:* NCATE. Part-time and evening/weekend programs available. *Degree requirements:* For master's and Ed S, thesis optional; for doctorate, variable foreign language requirement, thesis/dissertation. *Entrance requirements:* For master's, minimum GPA of 2.7; for doctorate and Ed S, GRE General Test, minimum GPA of 2.7. Additional exam requirements/recommendations for international students: Required—TOEFL. Electronic applications accepted. *Expenses:* Tuition, state resident: full-time $8332; part-time $464 per credit hour. Tuition, nonresident: full-time $25,174; part-time $1400 per credit hour. *Required fees:* $1162; $56 per credit hour. Tuition and fees vary according to program.

The University of Tennessee, Graduate School, College of Education, Health and Human Sciences, Program in Educational Administration and Policy Studies, Knoxville, TN 37996. Offers educational administration and policy studies (Ed D); educational administration and supervision (MS). *Accreditation:* NCATE. Part-time and evening/weekend programs available. Postbaccalaureate distance learning degree programs offered (no on-campus study). *Degree requirements:* For master's, thesis optional. *Entrance requirements:* For master's, minimum GPA of 2.7. Additional exam requirements/recommendations for international students: Required—TOEFL. Electronic applications accepted. *Expenses:* Tuition, state resident: full-time $8332; part-time $464 per credit hour. Tuition, nonresident: full-time $25,174; part-time $1400 per credit hour. *Required fees:* $1162; $56 per credit hour. Tuition and fees vary according to program.

The University of Tennessee at Chattanooga, Graduate School, College of Health, Education and Professional Studies, School of Education, Chattanooga, TN 37403-2598. Offers counseling (M Ed), including community counseling, school counseling; education (M Ed, Post-Master's Certificate), including elementary education (M Ed), school leadership, secondary education (M Ed), special education (M Ed); educational specialist (Ed S), including educational technology, school psychology; learning and leadership (Ed D), including educational leadership. *Accreditation:* ACA; NCATE. Part-time and evening/weekend programs available. Postbaccalaureate distance learning degree programs offered (no on-campus study). *Faculty:* 25 full-time (17 women), 10 part-time/adjunct (3 women). *Students:* 145 full-time (104 women), 319 part-time (236 women); includes 63 minority (43 Black or African American, non-Hispanic/Latino; 4 American Indian or Alaska Native, non-Hispanic/Latino; 2 Asian, non-Hispanic/Latino; 6 Hispanic/Latino; 8 Two or more races, non-Hispanic/Latino), 2 international. Average age 34. 226 applicants, 79% accepted, 111 enrolled. In 2011, 120 master's, 9 doctorates, 17 other advanced degrees awarded. *Degree requirements:* For master's, comprehensive exam, thesis optional, culminating experience; for doctorate, comprehensive exam, thesis/dissertation; for other advanced degree, internship. *Entrance requirements:* For master's, GRE General Test, PPST 1, teaching certificate; for doctorate, GRE General Test, master's degree, two years of practical work experience in organizational environment; for other advanced degree, GRE General Test, letters of reference. Additional exam requirements/recommendations for international students: Required—TOEFL (minimum score 550 paper-based; 213 computer-based; 79 iBT), IELTS (minimum score 6). *Application deadline:* For fall admission, 8/1 for domestic students, 6/1 for international students; for spring admission, 12/1 for domestic students, 10/1 for international students. Applications are processed on a rolling basis. Application fee: $35. Electronic applications accepted. *Expenses:* Tuition, state resident: full-time $6472; part-time $359 per credit hour. Tuition, nonresident: full-time $20,006; part-time $1111 per credit hour. *Required fees:* $1320; $160 per credit hour. *Financial support:* Career-related internships or fieldwork, institutionally sponsored loans, scholarships/grants, and unspecified assistantships available. Support available to part-time students. Financial award applicants required to submit FAFSA. *Faculty research:* School counseling, community counseling, elementary and secondary education, school leadership and administration. *Total annual research expenditures:* $675,479. *Unit head:* Dr. John Freeman, Head, 423-425-4133, Fax: 423-425-5380, E-mail: john-freeman@utc.edu. *Application contact:* Dr. Jerald Ainsworth, Dean of Graduate Studies, 423-425-4478, Fax: 423-425-5223, E-mail: jerald-ainsworth@utc.edu. Web site: http://www.utc.edu/Administration/HealthEducationAndProfessionalStudies/Graduate_Studies/graduate_studies.html.

The University of Tennessee at Martin, Graduate Programs, College of Education, Health, and Behavioral Sciences, Program in Educational Leadership, Martin, TN 38238-1000. Offers MS Ed. Part-time programs available. Postbaccalaureate distance learning degree programs offered. *Students:* 26 (15 women); includes 4 minority (all Black or African American, non-Hispanic/Latino). 19 applicants, 68% accepted, 11 enrolled. In 2011, 19 master's awarded. *Degree requirements:* For master's, comprehensive exam. *Entrance requirements:* For master's, GRE General Test, minimum GPA of 2.5, letters of reference, teaching license, resume, teaching experience. Additional exam requirements/recommendations for international students: Required—TOEFL (minimum score 525 paper-based; 197 computer-based; 71 iBT). *Application deadline:* For fall admission, 8/1 priority date for domestic students, 6/15 for international students; for spring admission, 12/15 priority date for domestic students, 12/1 for international students. Applications are processed on a rolling basis. Application fee: $30 ($130 for international students). Electronic applications accepted. *Expenses:* Tuition, state resident: full-time $6726; part-time $374 per credit hour. Tuition, nonresident: full-time $19,136; part-time $1064 per credit hour. *Required fees:* $61 per credit hour. *Financial support:* Research assistantships with full tuition reimbursements, teaching assistantships with full tuition reimbursements, scholarships/grants, and unspecified assistantships available. Support available to part-time students. Financial award application deadline: 2/15; financial award applicants required to submit FAFSA. *Application contact:* Linda S. Arant, Student Services Specialist, 731-881-7012, Fax: 731-881-7499, E-mail: larant@utm.edu.

The University of Texas at Arlington, Graduate School, College of Education and Health Professions, Department of Educational Leadership and Policy Studies, Arlington, TX 76019. Offers dual language (M Ed); education leadership and policy studies (PhD); higher education (M Ed); principal certification (M Ed). Part-time and evening/weekend programs available. Postbaccalaureate distance learning degree programs offered (no on-campus study). *Faculty:* 12 full-time (9 women). *Students:* 31 full-time (25 women), 749 part-time (523 women); includes 334 minority (165 Black or African American, non-Hispanic/Latino; 5 American Indian or Alaska Native, non-Hispanic/Latino; 11 Asian, non-Hispanic/Latino; 140 Hispanic/Latino; 13 Two or more races, non-Hispanic/Latino), 9 international. 342 applicants, 84% accepted, 247 enrolled. In 2011, 183 master's, 1 doctorate awarded. *Degree requirements:* For master's, 2 field-based practica; for doctorate, comprehensive exam, thesis/dissertation, 2 research-based practica. *Entrance requirements:* For master's, GRE, 3 references forms, minimum undergraduate GPA of 3.0 in the last 60 hours of course work; for doctorate, GRE, resume, statement of intent, 3 reference forms, applicable master's degree. Application fee: $50. *Financial support:* In 2011–12, 6 students received support, including 4 fellowships (averaging $6,700 per year), 2 research assistantships (averaging $8,000 per year). Financial award applicants required to submit FAFSA.

Faculty research: Lived realities of students of color in K-16 contexts, K-16 faculty, K-16 policy and law, K-16 student access, K-16 student success. *Unit head:* Dr. Adrienne E. Hyle, Chair, 817-272-2841, Fax: 817-272-2127, E-mail: ahyle@uta.edu. *Application contact:* Paige Cordor, Graduate Advisor, 817-272-5051, Fax: 817-272-2127, E-mail: paigec@uta.edu. Web site: http://www.uta.edu/coehp/educleadership/.

The University of Texas at Austin, Graduate School, College of Education, Department of Educational Administration, Austin, TX 78712-1111. Offers M Ed, Ed D, PhD. *Degree requirements:* For doctorate, thesis/dissertation. *Entrance requirements:* For master's and doctorate, GRE General Test. *Application deadline:* For fall admission, 3/1 priority date for domestic students. Application fee: $50 ($75 for international students). Electronic applications accepted. *Financial support:* Fellowships available. Financial award application deadline: 2/1. *Unit head:* Norma Cantu, Chair, 512-471-7551, Fax: 512-471-5975, E-mail: metrocan2@aol.com. *Application contact:* Dr. Martha N. Ovando, Graduate Advisor, 512-475-8575, Fax: 512-471-5975, E-mail: movando@mail.utexas.edu. Web site: http://www.edb.utexas.edu/coe/depts/edadmin/eda/index.html.

The University of Texas at Austin, Graduate School, College of Education, Department of Special Education, Austin, TX 78712-1111. Offers autism and developmental disabilities (Ed D, PhD); autism and developmental disability (M Ed, MA); early childhood special education (M Ed, MA, Ed D, PhD); learning disabilities (Ed D, PhD); learning disabilities/behavior disorders (M Ed, MA); multicultural special education (M Ed, MA, Ed D, PhD); rehabilitation counselor (M Ed); rehabilitation counselor education (Ed D, PhD); special education administration (Ed D, PhD). *Accreditation:* CORE. Part-time and evening/weekend programs available. Postbaccalaureate distance learning degree programs offered (no on-campus study). *Degree requirements:* For master's, thesis or alternative; for doctorate, thesis/dissertation. *Entrance requirements:* For master's and doctorate, GRE General Test. *Application deadline:* For fall admission, 2/1 priority date for domestic students; for spring admission, 10/1 priority date for domestic students. Applications are processed on a rolling basis. Application fee: $50 ($75 for international students). *Financial support:* Fellowships with tuition reimbursements, research assistantships with partial tuition reimbursements, teaching assistantships with partial tuition reimbursements, career-related internships or fieldwork, Federal Work-Study, institutionally sponsored loans, scholarships/grants, tuition waivers (full and partial), and unspecified assistantships available. Financial award application deadline: 2/1. *Faculty research:* Anchored instruction, reading disabilities, multicultural/bilingual. *Unit head:* Herbert J. Rieth, Jr., Chairman, 512-475-6552, Fax: 512-471-2471, E-mail: rieth.herb@mail.utexas.edu. *Application contact:* James Schaller, Graduate Adviser, 512-475-6543, E-mail: jschaller@mail.utexas.edu. Web site: http://www.edb.utexas.edu/coe/depts/sped.html.

The University of Texas at Brownsville, Graduate Studies, School of Education, Brownsville, TX 78520-4991. Offers bilingual education (M Ed); counseling and guidance (M Ed); curriculum and instruction (M Ed); early childhood education (M Ed); educational administration (M Ed); educational technology (M Ed); English as a second language (M Ed); reading specialist (M Ed); special education/educational diagnostician (M Ed). Part-time and evening/weekend programs available. Postbaccalaureate distance learning degree programs offered (minimal on-campus study). *Degree requirements:* For master's, thesis optional. *Entrance requirements:* For master's, GRE General Test. Additional exam requirements/recommendations for international students: Required—TOEFL.

The University of Texas at El Paso, Graduate School, College of Education, Department of Educational Leadership and Foundations, El Paso, TX 79968-0001. Offers educational administration (M Ed); educational leadership and administration (Ed D). Part-time and evening/weekend programs available. *Students:* 204 (135 women); includes 164 minority (5 Black or African American, non-Hispanic/Latino; 2 Asian, non-Hispanic/Latino; 157 Hispanic/Latino), 9 international. Average age 34. 43 applicants, 79% accepted, 27 enrolled. In 2011, 22 master's, 2 doctorates awarded. *Degree requirements:* For master's, thesis optional; for doctorate, thesis/dissertation. *Entrance requirements:* For doctorate, GRE General Test, minimum graduate GPA of 3.0. Additional exam requirements/recommendations for international students: Required—TOEFL. *Application deadline:* For fall admission, 2/1 for domestic students. Applications are processed on a rolling basis. Application fee: $15 ($65 for international students). Electronic applications accepted. *Financial support:* In 2011–12, research assistantships with partial tuition reimbursements (averaging $16,642 per year), teaching assistantships with partial tuition reimbursements (averaging $13,314 per year) were awarded; fellowships with partial tuition reimbursements, Federal Work-Study, institutionally sponsored loans, scholarships/grants, and tuition waivers (partial) also available. Financial award application deadline: 3/15; financial award applicants required to submit FAFSA. *Unit head:* Dr. Gary D. Brooks, Chairperson, 915-747-7593, Fax: 915-747-5838, E-mail: gdbrooks@utep.edu. *Application contact:* Dr. Benjamin Flores, Interim Dean of the Graduate School, 915-747-5491, Fax: 915-747-5788, E-mail: bflores@utep.edu.

The University of Texas at San Antonio, College of Education and Human Development, Department of Educational Leadership and Policy Studies, San Antonio, TX 78249-0617. Offers educational leadership (Ed D); educational leadership and policy studies (M Ed), including educational leadership, higher education administration; higher education administration (M Ed). Part-time programs available. *Faculty:* 17 full-time (8 women), 26 part-time/adjunct (13 women). *Students:* 71 full-time (52 women), 269 part-time (185 women); includes 213 minority (33 Black or African American, non-Hispanic/Latino; 3 Asian, non-Hispanic/Latino; 171 Hispanic/Latino; 6 Two or more races, non-Hispanic/Latino), 4 international. Average age 36. 155 applicants, 77% accepted, 95 enrolled. In 2011, 102 master's, 8 doctorates awarded. *Degree requirements:* For master's, comprehensive exam, thesis or alternative; for doctorate, comprehensive exam, thesis/dissertation. *Entrance requirements:* For master's, bachelor's degree with 18 credit hours in field of study or in another appropriate field of study, resume, letter of recommendation; for doctorate, GRE General Test, minimum GPA of 3.5 in a master's program, resume, three letters of recommendation, statement of purpose. Additional exam requirements/recommendations for international students: Required—TOEFL (minimum score 550 paper-based; 61 iBT), IELTS (minimum score 5). *Application deadline:* For fall admission, 7/1 for domestic students, 4/1 for international students; for spring admission, 11/1 for domestic students, 9/1 for international students. Application fee: $45 ($85 for international students). *Expenses:* Tuition, state resident: full-time $3148; part-time $2176 per semester. Tuition, nonresident: full-time $8782; part-time $5932 per semester. *Required fees:* $719 per semester. *Financial support:* In 2011–12, 6 students received support, including 6 fellowships with full and partial tuition reimbursements available (averaging $40,000 per year). Financial award application deadline: 2/1. *Faculty research:* Urban and international school leadership, student success, college access, higher education policy, multiculturalism, minority student achievement. *Unit head:* Dr. David P. Thompson, Department Chair, 210-458-5404, Fax: 210-458-5848, E-mail: david.thompson@utsa.edu. *Application contact:* Elisha Reynolds, Student Development Specialist, 210-458-6620, Fax: 210-458-5848, E-mail: grelisha.reynolds@utsa.edu.

The University of Texas at Tyler, College of Education and Psychology, Department of Educational Leadership, Tyler, TX 75799-0001. Offers M Ed. Part-time and evening/weekend programs available. Postbaccalaureate distance learning degree programs offered (no on-campus study). *Degree requirements:* For master's, comprehensive exam, 2 years of teaching experience. *Entrance requirements:* For master's, GRE General Test. Additional exam requirements/recommendations for international students: Required—TOEFL (minimum score 79 computer-based). *Faculty research:* Effective schools, restructuring of schools, leadership.

The University of Texas of the Permian Basin, Office of Graduate Studies, School of Education, Program in Educational Leadership, Odessa, TX 79762-0001. Offers MA. *Degree requirements:* For master's, comprehensive exam (for some programs), thesis (for some programs). *Entrance requirements:* For master's, GRE General Test. Additional exam requirements/recommendations for international students: Required—TOEFL (minimum score 550 paper-based; 213 computer-based).

The University of Texas–Pan American, College of Education, Department of Educational Leadership, Edinburg, TX 78539. Offers M Ed, Ed D. Part-time and evening/weekend programs available. *Degree requirements:* For master's, comprehensive exam, thesis optional; for doctorate, comprehensive exam, thesis/dissertation. *Entrance requirements:* For master's, GRE; for doctorate, master's degree. Additional exam requirements/recommendations for international students: Required—TOEFL. *Application deadline:* For fall admission, 8/15 priority date for domestic students; for spring admission, 11/15 priority date for domestic students. Application fee: $0. Electronic applications accepted. Tuition and fees vary according to course load, program and student level. *Financial support:* In 2011–12, fellowships (averaging $30,000 per year), research assistantships (averaging $30,000 per year), teaching assistantships (averaging $30,000 per year) were awarded; career-related internships or fieldwork and institutionally sponsored loans also available. Support available to part-time students. Financial award application deadline: 4/15. *Faculty research:* Community perceptions of education, leadership and gender studies, continuous improvement processes, leadership. *Unit head:* Dr. Velma Menchaca, Chair, 956-665-2943, E-mail: menchaca@utpa.edu. Web site: http://portal.utpa.edu/utpa_main/daa_home/coed_home/lead_home.

University of the Cumberlands, Graduate Programs in Education, Williamsburg, KY 40769-1372. Offers all grades (P-12) (M Ed); business and marketing (MA Ed, MAT); director of pupil personnel (Certificate); director of special education (Certificate); educational administration and supervision (Ed S); educational leadership (Ed D); elementary education (MA Ed, MAT); instructional leadership - principalship (MA Ed); instructional leadership - school principal (Certificate); middle school education (MA Ed, MAT); reading and writing (MA Ed); school counseling (MA Ed); school superintendent (Certificate); secondary education (MA Ed, MAT); special education (MAT); supervisor of instruction (Certificate); teacher leader (MA Ed). Part-time and evening/weekend programs available. Postbaccalaureate distance learning degree programs offered. *Degree requirements:* For master's, comprehensive exam. Electronic applications accepted.

University of the Incarnate Word, Extended Academic Programs, Program in Teacher Leadership, San Antonio, TX 78209-6397. Offers M Ed. *Faculty:* 1 (woman) full-time, 4 part-time/adjunct (1 woman). *Students:* 7 part-time (5 women); includes 4 minority (all Hispanic/Latino). Average age 39. 2 applicants, 100% accepted, 1 enrolled. In 2011, 4 master's awarded. *Expenses: Tuition:* Part-time $725 per credit hour. Tuition and fees vary according to degree level. *Unit head:* Dr. Cyndi Porter, Vice President, 877-603-1130, E-mail: porter@uiwtx.edu. *Application contact:* Julie Weber, Director of Marketing and Recruitment, 210-832-2100, Fax: 210-829-2756, E-mail: eapadmission@uiwtx.edu. Web site: http://online.uiw.edu/master_of_education_in_teacher_leadership.

University of the Incarnate Word, School of Graduate Studies and Research, Dreeben School of Education, Programs in Education, San Antonio, TX 78209-6397. Offers adult education (M Ed, MA); cross-cultural education (M Ed, MA); early childhood literacy (M Ed, MA); general education (M Ed, MA); higher education (PhD); instructional technology (M Ed, MA); international education and entrepreneurship (PhD); kinesiology (M Ed, MA); literacy (M Ed, MA); organizational leadership (PhD); organizational learning and learning (M Ed, MA); reading (M Ed, MA); special education (M Ed, MA); teacher leadership (M Ed, MA). Part-time and evening/weekend programs available. *Faculty:* 14 full-time (8 women), 10 part-time/adjunct (9 women). *Students:* 13 full-time (7 women), 197 part-time (129 women); includes 111 minority (23 Black or African American, non-Hispanic/Latino; 2 American Indian or Alaska Native, non-Hispanic/Latino; 1 Asian, non-Hispanic/Latino; 85 Hispanic/Latino), 26 international. Average age 41. 78 applicants, 79% accepted, 34 enrolled. In 2011, 21 master's, 12 doctorates awarded. *Degree requirements:* For master's, capstone; for doctorate, thesis/dissertation, qualifying exam. *Entrance requirements:* For master's, baccalaureate degree; minimum foundation GPA of 2.5; interview; for doctorate, master's degree; interview; supervised writing sample. Additional exam requirements/recommendations for international students: Required—TOEFL (minimum score 560 paper-based; 220 computer-based; 83 iBT). *Application deadline:* Applications are processed on a rolling basis. Application fee: $20. Electronic applications accepted. *Expenses: Tuition:* Part-time $725 per credit hour. Tuition and fees vary according to degree level. *Financial support:* In 2011–12, 5 research assistantships were awarded; Federal Work-Study and scholarships/grants also available. Financial award applicants required to submit FAFSA. *Unit head:* Dr. Denise Staudt, Dean, Dreeben School of Education, 210-829-2762, E-mail: staudt@uiwtx.edu. *Application contact:* Andrea Cyterski-Acosta, Dean of Enrollment, 210-829-6005, Fax: 210-829-3921, E-mail: admis@uiwtx.edu. Web site: http://www.uiw.edu/education/index.htm.

University of the Pacific, School of Education, Department of Educational Administration and Leadership, Stockton, CA 95211-0197. Offers educational administration (MA, Ed D). *Accreditation:* NCATE. *Faculty:* 4 full-time (2 women). *Students:* 26 full-time (14 women), 90 part-time (61 women); includes 44 minority (12 Black or African American, non-Hispanic/Latino; 20 Asian, non-Hispanic/Latino; 12 Hispanic/Latino), 8 international. Average age 32. 51 applicants, 63% accepted, 22 enrolled. In 2011, 34 master's, 25 doctorates awarded. *Degree requirements:* For master's, thesis (for some programs); for doctorate, thesis/dissertation. *Entrance requirements:* For master's and doctorate, GRE General Test, GRE Subject Test. Additional exam requirements/recommendations for international students: Required—TOEFL (minimum score 475 paper-based; 150 computer-based). *Application deadline:* For fall admission, 3/1 priority date for domestic students; for spring admission, 10/1 priority date for domestic students. Applications are processed on a rolling basis. Application fee: $75. *Expenses: Tuition:* Full-time $18,900; part-time $1181 per unit. *Required fees:* $949. *Financial support:* Application deadline: 3/1; applicants required to submit FAFSA. *Unit head:* Dr. Dennis Brennan, Chairperson, 209-946-2580, E-mail: dbrennan@pacific.edu. *Application contact:* Office of Graduate Admissions, 209-946-2344.

University of the Southwest, Graduate Programs, Hobbs, NM 88240-9129. Offers business administration (MBA); curriculum and instruction (MSE); curriculum and instruction: bilingual (MSE); curriculum and instruction: TESOL (MSE); early childhood education (MSE); educational administration (MSE); mental health counseling (MSE); school counseling (MSE); special education (MSE); sports management (MBA). Part-time and evening/weekend programs available. Postbaccalaureate distance learning degree programs offered (no on-campus study). *Faculty:* 13 full-time (6 women), 28 part-time/adjunct (17 women). *Students:* 76 full-time (63 women), 229 part-time (194 women); includes 104 minority (50 Black or African American, non-Hispanic/Latino; 2 American Indian or Alaska Native, non-Hispanic/Latino; 8 Asian, non-Hispanic/Latino; 44 Hispanic/Latino). Average age 38. 173 applicants, 71% accepted, 101 enrolled. In 2011, 75 master's awarded. *Degree requirements:* For master's, comprehensive exam, thesis (for some programs). *Entrance requirements:* Additional exam requirements/recommendations for international students: Recommended—TOEFL. *Application deadline:* Applications are processed on a rolling basis. Application fee: $50. Electronic applications accepted. *Expenses: Tuition:* Full-time $12,288; part-time $512 per credit hour. One-time fee: $50. Tuition and fees vary according to course load. *Financial support:* In 2011–12, 47 students received support. Federal Work-Study available. Financial award application deadline: 4/1; financial award applicants required to submit FAFSA. *Unit head:* Dr. Mary Harris, Dean of Education, 575-492-2162, Fax: 575-392-6006, E-mail: mharris@usw.edu. *Application contact:* Melissa Mitchell, Senior Online Program Advisor, 575-492-2142, Fax: 575-392-6006, E-mail: mmitchell@usw.edu. Web site: http://www.usw.edu/admissions/graduate_admission/graduate_admissions.

The University of Toledo, College of Graduate Studies, Judith Herb College of Education, Health Science and Human Service, Department of Educational Foundations and Leadership, Toledo, OH 43606-3390. Offers educational administration and supervision (ME, DE, Ed S); educational psychology (ME, DE, PhD); educational research and measurement (ME, PhD); educational sociology (DE, PhD); educational theory and social foundations (ME); foundations of education (DE, PhD); higher education (ME, PhD); history of education (PhD); philosophy of education (PhD). *Accreditation:* NCATE. Part-time and evening/weekend programs available. *Faculty:* 32. *Students:* 26 full-time (14 women), 222 part-time (134 women); includes 78 minority (57 Black or African American, non-Hispanic/Latino; 5 Asian, non-Hispanic/Latino; 15 Hispanic/Latino; 1 Two or more races, non-Hispanic/Latino), 5 international. Average age 40. 85 applicants, 61% accepted, 34 enrolled. In 2011, 37 master's, 7 doctorates, 18 other advanced degrees awarded. *Degree requirements:* For master's, comprehensive exam, thesis or alternative; for doctorate, comprehensive exam, thesis/dissertation; for Ed S, thesis optional. *Entrance requirements:* For master's, doctorate, and Ed S, minimum cumulative GPA of 2.7 for all previous academic work, letters of recommendation. Additional exam requirements/recommendations for international students: Required—TOEFL (minimum score 550 paper-based; 213 computer-based; 80 iBT), IELTS (minimum score 6.5). *Application deadline:* For fall admission, 1/15 priority date for domestic students, 1/15 for international students. Applications are processed on a rolling basis. Application fee: $45 ($75 for international students). Electronic applications accepted. *Financial support:* In 2011–12, 10 research assistantships with full and partial tuition reimbursements (averaging $6,734 per year), 8 teaching assistantships with full and partial tuition reimbursements (averaging $9,000 per year) were awarded; career-related internships or fieldwork, Federal Work-Study, institutionally sponsored loans, scholarships/grants, tuition waivers (full and partial), unspecified assistantships, and administrative assistantships also available. Support available to part-time students. *Unit head:* Dr. William Gray, Interim Chair, 419-530-2565, Fax: 419-530-8447, E-mail: william.gray@utoledo.edu. *Application contact:* Graduate School Office, 419-530-4723, Fax: 419-530-4724, E-mail: grdsch@utnet.utoledo.edu. Web site: http://www.utoledo.edu/eduhshs/.

University of Utah, Graduate School, College of Education, Department of Educational Leadership and Policy, Salt Lake City, UT 84112. Offers M Ed, PhD, MPA/PhD. Part-time and evening/weekend programs available. *Faculty:* 14 full-time (9 women), 2 part-time/adjunct (both women). *Students:* 50 full-time (33 women), 80 part-time (49 women); includes 27 minority (2 Black or African American, non-Hispanic/Latino; 1 American Indian or Alaska Native, non-Hispanic/Latino; 2 Asian, non-Hispanic/Latino; 15 Hispanic/Latino; 2 Native Hawaiian or other Pacific Islander, non-Hispanic/Latino; 5 Two or more races, non-Hispanic/Latino), 5 international. Average age 37. 80 applicants, 33% accepted, 22 enrolled. In 2011, 43 master's, 7 doctorates awarded. *Median time to degree:* Of those who began their doctoral program in fall 2003, 80% received their degree in 8 years or less. *Degree requirements:* For master's, comprehensive exam, internship; for doctorate, thesis/dissertation, qualifying exam. *Entrance requirements:* For master's, minimum undergraduate GPA of 3.0, 3 years' teaching or leadership experience, Level 2 UT educator's license, valid bachelor's degree (for K-12 programs only); for doctorate, GRE General Test, minimum undergraduate GPA of 3.0, valid master's degree. Additional exam requirements/recommendations for international students: Required—TOEFL (minimum score 500 paper-based; 173 computer-based). *Application deadline:* For fall admission, 12/15 for domestic and international students; for winter admission, 2/1 for domestic and international students. Application fee: $55 ($65 for international students). Electronic applications accepted. *Financial support:* In 2011–12, 30 students received support, including 1 fellowship with full tuition reimbursement available (averaging $12,000 per year), 1 research assistantship with full tuition reimbursement available (averaging $12,000 per year), 7 teaching assistantships with full tuition reimbursements available (averaging $12,000 per year); career-related internships or fieldwork, scholarships/grants, and unspecified assistantships also available. Financial award application deadline: 2/1; financial award applicants required to submit CSS PROFILE. *Faculty research:* Education accountability, college student diversity, social leadership, student affairs, higher education. *Total annual research expenditures:* $50,949. *Unit head:* Dr. Paula Smith, Chair, 801-581-6017, Fax: 801-585-6756, E-mail: paula.smith@utah.edu. *Application contact:* Dr. Amy A. Bergerson, Director of Graduate Studies, 801-581-6714, Fax: 801-585-6756, E-mail: amy.bergerson@utah.edu. Web site: http://www.ed.utah.edu/ELP/.

University of Vermont, Graduate College, College of Education and Social Services, Department of Leadership and Developmental Sciences, Program in Educational Leadership, Burlington, VT 05405. Offers M Ed. *Accreditation:* NCATE. *Students:* 20 (13 women), 1 international. 17 applicants, 88% accepted, 5 enrolled. In 2011, 12 master's awarded. *Degree requirements:* For master's, thesis or alternative. *Entrance requirements:* Additional exam requirements/recommendations for international students: Required—TOEFL (minimum score 550 paper-based; 213 computer-based; 80 iBT). *Application deadline:* For fall admission, 4/30 priority date for domestic students, 4/30 for international students; for spring admission, 11/1 priority date for domestic students. Application fee: $40. Electronic applications accepted. *Financial support:* Research assistantships, teaching assistantships, and career-related internships or fieldwork available. Financial award application deadline: 3/1. *Application contact:* Dr. Jill Tarule, Coordinator, 802-656-2936.

University of Vermont, Graduate College, College of Education and Social Services, Department of Leadership and Developmental Sciences, Program in Educational Leadership and Policy Studies, Burlington, VT 05405. Offers Ed D, PhD. *Accreditation:* NCATE. *Students:* 51 (36 women); includes 10 minority (4 Black or African American, non-Hispanic/Latino; 1 Asian, non-Hispanic/Latino; 5 Hispanic/Latino), 1 international. 47 applicants, 36% accepted, 10 enrolled. In 2011, 18 doctorates awarded. *Degree requirements:* For doctorate, thesis/dissertation. *Entrance requirements:* For doctorate, GRE, resume (for Ed D), writing sample. Additional exam requirements/recommendations for international students: Required—TOEFL (minimum score 550 paper-based; 213 computer-based; 80 iBT). *Application deadline:* For fall admission, 1/15 priority date for domestic students, 1/15 for international students. Application fee: $40. Electronic applications accepted. *Financial support:* Research assistantships and teaching assistantships available. *Unit head:* Prof. Cynthia Gerstl-Pepin, PhD Director and Coordinator, 802-656-0259. *Application contact:* Prof. Kieran Killeen, Ed D Coordinator, 802-656-1442, Fax: 802-656-0519, E-mail: graduate.admissions@uvm.edu.

University of Vermont, Graduate College, College of Education and Social Services, Department of Leadership and Developmental Sciences, Program in Higher Education and Student Affairs Administration, Burlington, VT 05405. Offers M Ed. *Accreditation:* NCATE. *Students:* 30 (22 women); includes 12 minority (7 Black or African American, non-Hispanic/Latino; 3 Asian, non-Hispanic/Latino; 2 Hispanic/Latino), 2 international. 179 applicants, 17% accepted, 16 enrolled. In 2011, 16 master's awarded. *Degree requirements:* For master's, thesis or alternative. *Entrance requirements:* For master's, resume. Additional exam requirements/recommendations for international students: Required—TOEFL (minimum score 550 paper-based; 213 computer-based; 80 iBT). *Application deadline:* For fall admission, 12/15 for domestic and international students. Applications are processed on a rolling basis. Application fee: $40. Electronic applications accepted. *Financial support:* Application deadline: 1/1. *Unit head:* Prof. Kathleen Manning, Director, 802-656-2030. *Application contact:* Prof. Kathleen Manning, Coordinator, 802-656-2030.

University of Victoria, Faculty of Graduate Studies, Faculty of Education, Department of Educational Psychology and Leadership Studies, Victoria, BC V8W 2Y2, Canada. Offers aboriginal communities counseling (M Ed); counseling (M Ed, MA); educational psychology (M Ed, MA, PhD), including counseling psychology (M Ed, MA), leadership studies (PhD), learning and development (MA, PhD), measurement and evaluation, special education (M Ed, MA); leadership studies (M Ed, MA). Part-time programs available. *Degree requirements:* For master's, thesis (for some programs), comprehensive exam (M Ed); for doctorate, comprehensive exam, thesis/dissertation, candidacy exam. *Entrance requirements:* For master's, 2 years of work experience in a relevant field; for doctorate, GRE, 2 years of work experience in a relevant field, minimum B average. Additional exam requirements/recommendations for international students: Required—TOEFL (minimum score 575 paper-based; 233 computer-based), IELTS (minimum score 7). *Faculty research:* Learning and development (child, adolescent and adult), special education and exceptional children.

University of Virginia, Curry School of Education, Department of Leadership, Foundations and Policy, Program in Administration and Supervision, Charlottesville, VA 22903. Offers M Ed, Ed D, Ed S. *Students:* 3 full-time (2 women), 44 part-time (24 women); includes 2 minority (both Hispanic/Latino). Average age 38. 45 applicants, 89% accepted, 39 enrolled. In 2011, 31 master's, 19 doctorates, 20 other advanced degrees awarded. *Entrance requirements:* For master's, doctorate, and Ed S, GRE General Test, letters of recommendation. *Application deadline:* Applications are processed on a rolling basis. Application fee: $60. Electronic applications accepted. *Financial support:* Fellowships, research assistantships, and teaching assistantships available. Financial award applicants required to submit FAFSA. *Unit head:* Pam Tucker, Program Coordinator. *Application contact:* Lisa Miller, Assistant to the Chair, 434-982-2849, E-mail: lam3v@virgnina.edu. Web site: http://curry.virginia.edu/academics/areas-of-study/administration-supervision.

University of Virginia, Curry School of Education, Program in Education, Charlottesville, VA 22903. Offers administration and supervision (PhD); applied developmental science (PhD); counselor education (PhD); curriculum and instruction (PhD); early childhood-developmental risk (MT); education evaluation (PhD); educational psychology (PhD); educational research (PhD); elementary (MT, PhD); English education (MT, PhD); foreign language education (MT); higher education (PhD); instructional technology (PhD); kinesiology (MT, PhD); math education (PhD); reading education (PhD); research statistics and evaluation (PhD); school psychology (PhD); science education (PhD); social studies education (MT, PhD); special education (PhD); world languages education (MT). *Students:* 299 full-time (216 women), 60 part-time (33 women); includes 46 minority (18 Black or African American, non-Hispanic/Latino; 17 Asian, non-Hispanic/Latino; 7 Hispanic/Latino; 4 Two or more races, non-Hispanic/Latino), 23 international. Average age 30. 307 applicants, 42% accepted, 80 enrolled. In 2011, 113 master's, 62 doctorates awarded. *Degree requirements:* For master's, comprehensive exam (for some programs), field project; for doctorate, comprehensive exam, thesis/dissertation. *Entrance requirements:* For doctorate, GRE General Test. Additional exam requirements/recommendations for international students: Required—TOEFL (minimum score 600 paper-based; 250 computer-based; 90 iBT), IELTS (minimum score 7). *Application deadline:* Applications are processed on a rolling basis. Application fee: $60. Electronic applications accepted. *Financial support:* Fellowships, research assistantships, and teaching assistantships available. Financial award application deadline: 1/5; financial award applicants required to submit FAFSA. *Unit head:* Robert C. Pianta, Dean, 434-924-3334. *Application contact:* Joanne McNergney, Assistant Dean for Admissions and Student Services, 434-924-3334, E-mail: curry-admissions@virginia.edu.

University of Washington, Graduate School, College of Education, Seattle, WA 98195. Offers curriculum and instruction (M Ed, Ed D, PhD), including educational technology, general curriculum (Ed D, PhD), language, literacy, and culture, mathematics education, multicultural education, reading and language arts education (Ed D), science education, social studies education, teaching and curriculum (M Ed); educational leadership and policy studies (M Ed, Ed D, PhD), including administration (Ed D), educational policy, organization, and leadership (M Ed, PhD), higher education, leadership for learning (Ed D), social and cultural foundations of education (M Ed, PhD); educational psychology (M Ed, PhD), including educational psychology (PhD), human development and cognition (M Ed), learning sciences, measurement, statistics and research design (M Ed), school psychology (M Ed); instructional leadership (M Ed); intercollegiate athletic leadership (M Ed); special education (M Ed, Ed D, PhD), including early childhood special education (M Ed), emotional and behavioral disabilities (M Ed), learning disabilities (M Ed), low-incidence disabilities (M Ed), severe disabilities (M Ed), special education (Ed D, PhD); teacher education (MIT). *Accreditation:* APA. Part-time and evening/weekend programs available. *Degree requirements:* For master's, thesis optional; for doctorate, thesis/dissertation. *Entrance requirements:* For master's and doctorate, GRE General Test, minimum GPA of 3.0. Additional exam requirements/recommendations for international students: Required—TOEFL. Electronic applications accepted. *Faculty research:* School restructuring/effective schools, special education interventions, literacy and writing, technology, school partnerships, teacher preparation.

University of Washington, Bothell, Program in Education, Bothell, WA 98011-8246. Offers education (M Ed); leadership development for educators (M Ed); secondary/middle level endorsement (M Ed). Part-time and evening/weekend programs available. *Faculty:* 14 full-time (10 women), 1 (woman) part-time/adjunct. *Students:* 52 full-time (40 women), 115 part-time (94 women); includes 19 minority (3 Black or African American, non-Hispanic/Latino; 9 Asian, non-Hispanic/Latino; 4 Hispanic/Latino; 3 Two or more races, non-Hispanic/Latino). Average age 35. 76 applicants, 80% accepted, 57 enrolled. In 2011, 74 master's awarded. *Degree requirements:* For master's, thesis. *Entrance requirements:* Additional exam requirements/recommendations for international students: Required—TOEFL. *Application deadline:* For fall admission, 8/14 priority date for domestic students, 8/14 for international students; for spring admission, 4/7 priority date for domestic students, 11/1 for international students. Applications are processed on a rolling basis. Application fee: $75. Electronic applications accepted. *Financial support:* In 2011–12, 2 students received support. Federal Work-Study and unspecified assistantships available. Financial award application deadline: 5/2. *Faculty research:* Multicultural education in citizenship education, intercultural education, knowledge and practice in the principalship, educational public policy, national board certification for teachers, teacher learning in literacy, technology and its impact on teaching and learning of mathematics, reading assessments, professional development in literacy education and mobility, digital media, education and class. *Unit head:* Dr. Bradley S. Portin, Director/Professor, 425-352-3482, Fax: 425-352-5234, E-mail: bportin@uwb.edu. *Application contact:* Nick Brownlee, Advisor, 425-352-5369, Fax: 425-352-5369, E-mail: nbrownlee@uwb.edu.

University of Washington, Tacoma, Graduate Programs, Program in Education, Tacoma, WA 98402-3100. Offers education (M Ed); educational administration (principal or program administrator certification) (M Ed); elementary education teacher certification (M Ed); elementary education/special education teacher certification (M Ed); secondary science or math teacher certification (M Ed). Part-time and evening/weekend programs available. *Degree requirements:* For master's, culminating project. *Entrance requirements:* For master's, WEST-B, WEST-E (teacher certification programs only), official sealed transcript from every college/university attended, personal goal statement, letters of recommendation, copy of valid teaching certificate. Additional exam requirements/recommendations for international students: Required—TOEFL (minimum score 580 paper-based; 237 computer-based; 92 iBT). Electronic applications accepted. *Faculty research:* Global learning communities for English/Chinese languages, evaluation of mathematics and reading intervention programs, response to intervention, school-wide behavioral and emotional support, mathematics education and culturally responsive mathematics education.

The University of West Alabama, School of Graduate Studies, College of Education, Departments of Instructional Leadership and Support/Curriculum and Instruction, Program in Instructional Leadership, Livingston, AL 35470. Offers M Ed. *Accreditation:* NCATE. Part-time programs available. *Faculty:* 8 full-time (6 women). *Students:* 84 (43 women); includes 56 minority (all Black or African American, non-Hispanic/Latino). *Degree requirements:* For master's, comprehensive exam. *Entrance requirements:* For master's, GRE General Test, MAT, minimum GPA of 2.75. Additional exam requirements/recommendations for international students: Required—TOEFL (minimum score 61 computer-based). *Application deadline:* For fall admission, 9/10 priority date for domestic students; for spring admission, 3/24 for domestic students. Applications are processed on a rolling basis. Application fee: $25 ($50 for international students). *Expenses:* Tuition, state resident: full-time $5112; part-time $284 per credit hour. Tuition, nonresident: full-time $10,224; part-time $568 per credit hour. *Required fees:* $180; $40 per semester. One-time fee: $65. Tuition and fees vary according to class time, course load, campus/location and program. *Financial support:* Teaching assistantships, career-related internships or fieldwork, Federal Work-Study, scholarships/grants, and unspecified assistantships available. Support available to part-time students. Financial award application deadline: 3/1. *Unit head:* Dr. Jan Miller, Chair of Instructional Leadership and Support, 205-652-3445, Fax: 205-652-3706, E-mail: jmiller@uwa.edu. *Application contact:* Dr. Kathy Chandler, Dean of Graduate Studies, 205-652-3421, Fax: 205-652-3706, E-mail: kchandler@uwa.edu. Web site: http://www.uwa.edu/medinstructionalleadership.aspx.

University of West Florida, College of Professional Studies, Department of Applied Science, Technology and Administration, Program in Administration, Pensacola, FL 32514-5750. Offers acquisition and contract administration (MSA); biomedical/pharmaceutical (MSA); criminal justice administration (MSA); database administration (MSA); education leadership (MSA); healthcare administration (MSA); human performance technology (MSA); leadership (MSA); nursing administration (MSA); public administration (MSA); software engineering administration (MSA). Part-time and evening/weekend programs available. Postbaccalaureate distance learning degree programs offered (no on-campus study). *Students:* 36 full-time (28 women), 158 part-time (95 women); includes 61 minority (31 Black or African American, non-Hispanic/Latino; 4 American Indian or Alaska Native, non-Hispanic/Latino; 4 Asian, non-Hispanic/Latino; 17 Hispanic/Latino; 2 Native Hawaiian or other Pacific Islander, non-Hispanic/Latino; 3 Two or more races, non-Hispanic/Latino), 1 international. Average age 34. 102 applicants, 59% accepted, 40 enrolled. In 2011, 62 master's awarded. *Entrance requirements:* For master's, GRE General Test, letter of intent, names of references. Additional exam requirements/recommendations for international students: Required—TOEFL (minimum score 550 paper-based; 213 computer-based). *Application deadline:* For fall admission, 6/1 for domestic and international students; for spring admission, 10/1 for domestic and international students. Applications are processed on a rolling basis. Application fee: $30. *Expenses:* Tuition, state resident: full-time $5729; part-time $302 per credit hour. Tuition, nonresident: full-time $20,059; part-time $961 per credit hour. *Required fees:* $1509; $63 per credit hour. *Financial support:* Unspecified assistantships available. Financial award application deadline: 4/15; financial award applicants required to submit FAFSA. *Unit head:* Dr. Karen Rasmussen, Chairperson, 850-474-2301, Fax: 850-474-2804, E-mail: krasmuss@uwf.edu. *Application contact:* Terry McCray, Assistant Director of Graduate Admissions, 850-473-7718, Fax: 850-473-7714, E-mail: gradadmissions@uwf.edu. Web site: http://uwf.edu/msaprogram/.

University of West Florida, College of Professional Studies, Department of Applied Science, Technology and Administration, Program in Educational Leadership - ETMS, Pensacola, FL 32514-5750. Offers education and training management (M Ed). Part-time and evening/weekend programs available. Postbaccalaureate distance learning degree programs offered (no on-campus study). *Students:* 5 full-time (1 woman), 14 part-time (7 women); includes 4 minority (3 Black or African American, non-Hispanic/Latino; 1 Hispanic/Latino). Average age 38. 14 applicants, 57% accepted, 6 enrolled. In 2011, 2 master's awarded. *Entrance requirements:* For master's, GRE, minimum undergraduate GPA of 3.0. *Application deadline:* For fall admission, 6/1 for domestic and international students; for spring admission, 10/1 for domestic students. Applications are processed on a rolling basis. *Expenses:* Tuition, state resident: full-time $5729; part-time $302 per credit hour. Tuition, nonresident: full-time $20,059; part-time $961 per credit hour. *Required fees:* $1509; $63 per credit hour. *Unit head:* Dr. Karen Rasmussen, Chairperson, 850-474-2300, E-mail: krasmuss@uwf.edu. *Application contact:* Terry McCray, Assistant Director of Graduate Admissions, 850-473-7718, Fax: 850-473-7714, E-mail: gradadmissions@uwf.edu.

University of West Florida, College of Professional Studies, Department of Applied Science, Technology and Administration, Program in Instructional Technology, Pensacola, FL 32514-5750. Offers educational leadership (M Ed); instructional technology (M Ed). *Students:* 3 full-time (1 woman), 16 part-time (11 women); includes 7 minority (4 Black or African American, non-Hispanic/Latino; 1 Hispanic/Latino; 2 Two or more races, non-Hispanic/Latino), 1 international. Average age 42. 10 applicants, 50% accepted, 3 enrolled. In 2011, 17 master's awarded. *Entrance requirements:* For master's, MAT, GRE or GMAT, letter of intent, names of references. Additional exam requirements/recommendations for international students: Required—TOEFL (minimum score 550 paper-based; 213 computer-based). *Application deadline:* For fall admission, 6/1 for domestic and international students; for spring admission, 10/1 for domestic and international students. Applications are processed on a rolling basis. Application fee: $30. Electronic applications accepted. *Expenses:* Tuition, state resident: full-time $5729; part-time $302 per credit hour. Tuition, nonresident: full-time $20,059; part-time $961 per credit hour. *Required fees:* $1509; $63 per credit hour. *Financial support:* Application deadline: 4/15; applicants required to submit FAFSA. *Unit head:* Dr. Karen Rasmussen, Chairperson, 850-474-2301, Fax: 850-474-2804, E-mail: krasmuss@uwf.edu. *Application contact:* Terry McCray, Assistant Director of Graduate Admissions, 850-473-7718, Fax: 850-473-7714, E-mail: gradadmissions@uwf.edu.

University of West Florida, College of Professional Studies, Department of Research and Applied Studies, Pensacola, FL 32514-5750. Offers administration (MSA), including acquisition and contract administration, biomedical/pharmaceutical, criminal justice administration, database administration, education leadership, healthcare administration, human performance technology, leadership, nursing administration, public administration, software engineering and administration; college student personnel administration (M Ed), including college personnel administration, guidance and counseling; curriculum and instruction (M Ed, Ed S); educational leadership (M Ed); middle and secondary level education and ESOL (M Ed). Part-time and evening/weekend programs available. *Faculty:* 2 full-time (both women), 3 part-time/adjunct (2 women). *Students:* 26 full-time (15 women), 13 part-time (9 women); includes 8 minority (4 Black or African American, non-Hispanic/Latino; 2 American Indian or Alaska Native, non-Hispanic/Latino; 1 Hispanic/Latino; 1 Two or more races, non-Hispanic/Latino), 1 international. Average age 26. 51 applicants, 51% accepted, 16 enrolled. In 2011, 17 master's, 49 Ed Ss awarded. *Entrance requirements:* For master's, GRE or MAT, official transcripts; minimum undergraduate GPA of 3.0; letter of intent; three letters of recommendation; resume. Additional exam requirements/recommendations for international students: Required—TOEFL (minimum score 550 paper-based; 213 computer-based). *Application deadline:* For fall admission, 6/1 for domestic and international students; for spring admission, 10/1 for domestic and international students. Applications are processed on a rolling basis. Application fee: $30. *Expenses:* Tuition, state resident: full-time $5729; part-time $302 per credit hour. Tuition, nonresident: full-time $20,059; part-time $961 per credit hour. *Required fees:* $1509; $63 per credit hour. *Financial support:* In 2011–12, 33 fellowships (averaging $860 per year), 10 research assistantships (averaging $3,280 per year), 2 teaching assistantships (averaging $3,760 per year) were awarded; unspecified assistantships also available. Financial award application deadline: 4/15; financial award applicants required to submit FAFSA. *Unit head:* Dr. Joyce Nichols, Chairperson, 850-857-6042, E-mail: jcoleman0@uwf.edu. *Application contact:* Terry McCray, Assistant Director of Graduate Admissions, 850-473-7718, Fax: 850-473-7714, E-mail: gradadmissions@uwf.edu. Web site: http://uwf.edu/pcl/.

University of West Florida, College of Professional Studies, Ed D Programs, Specialization in Curriculum and Instruction: Administrative Studies, Pensacola, FL 32514-5750. Offers Ed D. *Students:* 2 full-time (1 woman), 24 part-time (18 women); includes 8 minority (6 Black or African American, non-Hispanic/Latino; 2 Two or more races, non-Hispanic/Latino). Average age 47. In 2011, 5 doctorates awarded. *Degree requirements:* For doctorate, comprehensive exam, thesis/dissertation. *Entrance requirements:* For doctorate, GRE, MAT, or GMAT, letter of intent; writing sample; three letters of recommendation; two completed disposition assessment forms; written statement of goals; interview with admissions committee. Additional exam requirements/recommendations for international students: Required—TOEFL (minimum score 550 paper-based; 213 computer-based). *Application deadline:* For fall admission, 6/1 for domestic and international students; for spring admission, 10/1 for domestic students. *Expenses:* Tuition, state resident: full-time $5729; part-time $302 per credit hour. Tuition, nonresident: full-time $20,059; part-time $961 per credit hour. *Required fees:* $1509; $63 per credit hour. *Unit head:* Dr. Pam Northrup, Interim Dean, 850-474-2769, Fax: 850-474-3205. *Application contact:* Terry McCray, Assistant Director of Graduate Admissions, 850-473-7718, Fax: 850-473-7714, E-mail: gradadmissions@uwf.edu. Web site: http://uwf.edu/edd/administration.cfm.

University of West Florida, College of Professional Studies, School of Education, Program in Educational Leadership, Pensacola, FL 32514-5750. Offers M Ed. *Accreditation:* NCATE. Part-time and evening/weekend programs available. Postbaccalaureate distance learning degree programs offered (no on-campus study). *Students:* 53 full-time (33 women), 138 part-time (95 women); includes 45 minority (27 Black or African American, non-Hispanic/Latino; 1 Asian, non-Hispanic/Latino; 13 Hispanic/Latino; 1 Native Hawaiian or other Pacific Islander, non-Hispanic/Latino; 3 Two or more races, non-Hispanic/Latino). Average age 35. 74 applicants, 73% accepted, 45 enrolled. In 2011, 19 master's awarded. *Degree requirements:* For master's, thesis optional. *Entrance requirements:* For master's, GRE General Test or minimum GPA of 3.0. Additional exam requirements/recommendations for international students: Required—TOEFL (minimum score 550 paper-based; 213 computer-based). *Application deadline:* For fall admission, 6/1 for domestic students, 5/15 for international students; for spring admission, 10/1 for domestic and international students. Applications are processed on a rolling basis. Application fee: $30. *Expenses:* Tuition, state resident: full-time $5729; part-time $302 per credit hour. Tuition, nonresident: full-time $20,059; part-time $961 per credit hour. *Required fees:* $1509; $63 per credit hour. *Financial support:* Career-related internships or fieldwork, Federal Work-Study, scholarships/grants, and tuition waivers (partial) available. Support available to part-time students. Financial award application deadline: 4/15; financial award applicants required to submit FAFSA. *Unit head:* Dr. Karen L. Rasmussen, Interim Chairperson, 850-474-2300, Fax: 850-857-6288, E-mail: krasmuss@uwf.edu. *Application contact:* Terry McCray, Assistant Director of Graduate Admissions, 850-473-7718, Fax: 850-473-7714, E-mail: gradadmissions@uwf.edu. Web site: http://uwf.edu/education/educationalleadership_med.cfm.

University of West Georgia, College of Education, Department of Leadership and Applied Instruction, Carrollton, GA 30118. Offers art education (M Ed); art teacher education (Ed S); biology - secondary education (M Ed); biology/secondary education (Ed S); business education (M Ed, Ed S); chemistry/secondary education (Ed S); earth science/secondary education (Ed S); economics/secondary education (Ed S); educational leadership (M Ed, Ed S); English teacher education (M Ed, Ed S); French teacher education (M Ed, Ed S); history teacher education (Ed S); mathematics teacher education (M Ed, Ed S); middle grades education (M Ed, Ed S); physical education and recreation (Ed S); physical education teaching and coaching (M Ed); physics/secondary education (Ed S); science teacher education (M Ed, Ed S); secondary education (M Ed); social science - secondary education (M Ed); social science teacher education (M Ed); Spanish (M Ed); Spanish teacher education (M Ed, Ed S); sports management (M Ed). *Accreditation:* NCATE. Part-time and evening/weekend programs available. *Faculty:* 18 full-time (9 women). *Students:* 75 full-time (49 women), 169 part-time (109 women); includes 90 minority (85 Black or African American, non-Hispanic/Latino; 3 Hispanic/Latino; 2 Two or more races, non-Hispanic/Latino), 1 international. Average age 36. 115 applicants, 67% accepted, 19 enrolled. In 2011, 73 master's, 53 Ed Ss awarded. *Degree requirements:* For master's, internship; for Ed S, research project. *Entrance requirements:* For master's, GRE General Test, minimum GPA of 2.7; for Ed S, GRE General Test, master's degree, minimum graduate GPA of 3.0, district appointment. Additional exam requirements/recommendations for international students: Required—TOEFL (minimum score 523 paper-based; 193 computer-based; 69 iBT); Recommended—IELTS (minimum score 6). *Application deadline:* For fall admission, 7/

21 for domestic students, 6/1 for international students; for spring admission, 11/30 for domestic students, 10/15 for international students. Applications are processed on a rolling basis. Application fee: $30. Electronic applications accepted. *Expenses:* Tuition, state resident: full-time $4336; part-time $181 per credit hour. Tuition, nonresident: full-time $17,362; part-time $724 per credit hour. Tuition and fees vary according to course load, degree level, campus/location and program. *Financial support:* In 2011–12, 1 research assistantship with full tuition reimbursement (averaging $7,444 per year) was awarded; career-related internships or fieldwork, scholarships/grants, and unspecified assistantships also available. Support available to part-time students. Financial award application deadline: 7/1; financial award applicants required to submit FAFSA. *Total annual research expenditures:* $5,000. *Unit head:* Dr. Frank Butts, Chair, 678-839-6530, Fax: 678-839-6195, E-mail: fbutts@westga.edu. *Application contact:* Deanna Richards, Coordinator, Graduate Studies, 678-839-5946, E-mail: drichard@westga.edu. Web site: http://www.westga.edu/coelai.

University of Wisconsin–Madison, Graduate School, School of Education, Department of Educational Leadership and Policy Analysis, Madison, WI 53706-1380. Offers administration (Certificate); educational policy (MS, PhD). *Degree requirements:* For doctorate, thesis/dissertation. *Entrance requirements:* For master's and doctorate, GRE General Test. *Application deadline:* For fall admission, 1/15 for domestic and international students. Application fee: $56. Electronic applications accepted. *Expenses:* Tuition, state resident: full-time $10,296; part-time $643.51 per credit. Tuition, nonresident: full-time $24,054; part-time $1503.40 per credit. *Required fees:* $70.06 per credit. Tuition and fees vary according to course load, campus/location, program and reciprocity agreements. *Financial support:* Fellowships with full tuition reimbursements, research assistantships with full tuition reimbursements, teaching assistantships with full tuition reimbursements, and project assistantships available. *Unit head:* Dr. Julie Mead, Chair, 608-262-3106, E-mail: jmead@education.wisc.edu. *Application contact:* 608-262-2433, Fax: 608-262-5134, E-mail: gradadmiss@mail.bascom.wisc.edu. Web site: http://www.education.wisc.edu/elpa.

University of Wisconsin–Milwaukee, Graduate School, School of Education, Department of Administrative Leadership, Milwaukee, WI 53201-0413. Offers administrative leadership and supervision in education (MS); specialist in administrative leadership (Certificate); teaching and learning in higher education (Certificate). Part-time programs available. *Faculty:* 9 full-time (6 women), 1 part-time/adjunct (0 women). *Students:* 29 full-time (21 women), 122 part-time (87 women); includes 37 minority (22 Black or African American, non-Hispanic/Latino; 5 Asian, non-Hispanic/Latino; 2 Hispanic/Latino; 8 Two or more races, non-Hispanic/Latino), 3 international. Average age 34. 79 applicants, 68% accepted, 30 enrolled. In 2011, 44 degrees awarded. *Degree requirements:* For master's, comprehensive exam, thesis or alternative. *Entrance requirements:* For master's, GRE General Test. Additional exam requirements/recommendations for international students: Required—TOEFL (minimum score 550 paper-based; 79 iBT), IELTS (minimum score 6.5). *Application deadline:* For fall admission, 1/1 priority date for domestic students; for spring admission, 9/1 for domestic students. Applications are processed on a rolling basis. Application fee: $56 ($96 for international students). Electronic applications accepted. One-time fee: $506.10 full-time. Tuition and fees vary according to course load and reciprocity agreements. *Financial support:* In 2011–12, 2 fellowships were awarded; research assistantships, teaching assistantships, career-related internships or fieldwork, health care benefits, unspecified assistantships, and project assistantships also available. Support available to part-time students. Financial award application deadline: 4/15; financial award applicants required to submit FAFSA. *Total annual research expenditures:* $31,569. *Unit head:* Larry Martin, Department Chair, 414-229-5754, Fax: 414-229-5300, E-mail: lmartin@uwm.edu. *Application contact:* General Information Contact, 414-229-4982, Fax: 414-229-6967, E-mail: gradschool@uwm.edu. Web site: http://www.uwm.edu/Dept/Ad_Ldsp/.

University of Wisconsin–Milwaukee, Graduate School, School of Education, Program in Urban Education, Milwaukee, WI 53201-0413. Offers adult and continuing education (PhD); curriculum and instruction (PhD); educational administration (PhD); educational and media technology (PhD); educational psychology (PhD); multicultural studies (PhD); social foundations of education (PhD). *Students:* 65 full-time (45 women), 37 part-time (25 women); includes 39 minority (18 Black or African American, non-Hispanic/Latino; 1 American Indian or Alaska Native, non-Hispanic/Latino; 6 Asian, non-Hispanic/Latino; 6 Hispanic/Latino; 8 Two or more races, non-Hispanic/Latino), 5 international. Average age 41. 26 applicants, 62% accepted, 2 enrolled. In 2011, 13 degrees awarded. *Degree requirements:* For doctorate, comprehensive exam, thesis/dissertation. *Entrance requirements:* For doctorate, GRE General Test, minimum undergraduate GPA of 2.85, graduate 3.5. Additional exam requirements/recommendations for international students: Required—TOEFL (minimum score 550 paper-based; 79 iBT), IELTS (minimum score 6.5). *Application deadline:* For fall admission, 1/1 priority date for domestic students; for spring admission, 9/1 for domestic students. Applications are processed on a rolling basis. Application fee: $56 ($96 for international students). Electronic applications accepted. One-time fee: $506.10 full-time. Tuition and fees vary according to course load and reciprocity agreements. *Financial support:* In 2011–12, 11 fellowships, 1 teaching assistantship were awarded; research assistantships, career-related internships or fieldwork, health care benefits, unspecified assistantships, and project assistantships also available. Support available to part-time students. Financial award application deadline: 4/15; financial award applicants required to submit FAFSA. *Unit head:* Larry Martin, Representative, 414-229-4729, Fax: 414-229-2920, E-mail: lmartin@uwm.edu. *Application contact:* General Information Contact, 414-229-4982, Fax: 414-229-6967, E-mail: gradschool@uwm.edu. Web site: http://www.uwm.edu/Dept/UrbanEd/.

University of Wisconsin–Oshkosh, Graduate Studies, College of Education and Human Services, Department of Educational Leadership and Human Services, Oshkosh, WI 54901. Offers educational leadership (MS). Part-time and evening/weekend programs available. *Degree requirements:* For master's, comprehensive exam, thesis optional. *Entrance requirements:* For master's, bachelor's degree in education or related field. Additional exam requirements/recommendations for international students: Required—TOEFL (minimum score 550 paper-based; 213 computer-based; 79 iBT). Electronic applications accepted. *Faculty research:* Supervision models, learning styles, total quality management, cooperative learning, school choice.

University of Wisconsin–Stevens Point, College of Professional Studies, School of Education, Program in Educational Administration, Stevens Point, WI 54481-3897. Offers MSE. Program offered jointly with University of Wisconsin–Superior. *Degree requirements:* For master's, comprehensive exam, thesis or alternative.

University of Wisconsin–Superior, Graduate Division, Department of Educational Administration, Superior, WI 54880-4500. Offers MSE, Ed S. MSE, Ed S offered jointly with University of Wisconsin–Eau Claire, University of Wisconsin–Stevens Point. Part-time and evening/weekend programs available. Postbaccalaureate distance learning degree programs offered (minimal on-campus study). *Degree requirements:* For master's, thesis or alternative, research project or position paper, written exam; for Ed S, thesis, internship, oral and written exams. *Entrance requirements:* For master's, GRE General Test or MAT, minimum GPA of 2.75, teaching license, 3 years teaching experience; for Ed S, MAT, GRE, master's degree, 3 years of teaching experience, teaching license. *Faculty research:* Postsecondary disabilities, educational partnerships, K-12.

University of Wisconsin–Whitewater, School of Graduate Studies, College of Business and Economics, Program in School Business Management, Whitewater, WI 53190-1790. Offers MSE. Part-time and evening/weekend programs available. Postbaccalaureate distance learning degree programs offered (no on-campus study). *Students:* 7 full-time (2 women), 41 part-time (15 women); includes 4 minority (2 Black or African American, non-Hispanic/Latino; 2 Hispanic/Latino). Average age 36. 15 applicants, 93% accepted, 11 enrolled. In 2011, 14 master's awarded. *Entrance requirements:* For master's, minimum GPA of 2.75. Additional exam requirements/recommendations for international students: Required—TOEFL (minimum score 550 paper-based; 213 computer-based; 80 iBT), IELTS (minimum score 6). *Application deadline:* For fall admission, 7/15 priority date for domestic students; for spring admission, 12/1 priority date for domestic students. Applications are processed on a rolling basis. Application fee: $56. Electronic applications accepted. *Expenses:* Tuition, state resident: full-time $4088. Tuition, nonresident: full-time $8817. Tuition and fees vary according to program. *Financial support:* Federal Work-Study, unspecified assistantships, and out-of-state fee waivers available. Support available to part-time students. Financial award application deadline: 3/15; financial award applicants required to submit FAFSA. *Unit head:* Dr. Debra Towns, Coordinator, 262-472-6947, E-mail: townsd@uww.edu. *Application contact:* Sally A. Lange, School of Graduate Studies, 262-472-1006, Fax: 262-472-5027, E-mail: gradschl@uww.edu.

University of Wisconsin–Whitewater, School of Graduate Studies, College of Education and Professional Studies, Department of Curriculum and Instruction, Whitewater, WI 53190-1790. Offers professional development (MS), including bilingual education, challenging advanced learners, curriculum and instruction, educational leadership, health, human performance and recreation, health, physical education and coaching, information technologies and libraries, reading. *Accreditation:* NCATE. Part-time and evening/weekend programs available. Postbaccalaureate distance learning degree programs offered. *Students:* 25 full-time (12 women), 68 part-time (51 women); includes 26 minority (15 Black or African American, non-Hispanic/Latino; 3 Asian, non-Hispanic/Latino; 8 Hispanic/Latino). Average age 33. 29 applicants, 86% accepted, 16 enrolled. In 2011, 44 master's awarded. *Degree requirements:* For master's, thesis or integrated project. *Entrance requirements:* Additional exam requirements/recommendations for international students: Required—TOEFL (minimum score 550 paper-based; 213 computer-based; 80 iBT), IELTS (minimum score 6). *Application deadline:* For fall admission, 7/15 priority date for domestic students, 7/15 for international students; for spring admission, 12/1 priority date for domestic students, 12/1 for international students. Applications are processed on a rolling basis. Application fee: $56. Electronic applications accepted. *Expenses:* Tuition, state resident: full-time $4088. Tuition, nonresident: full-time $8817. Tuition and fees vary according to program. *Financial support:* Research assistantships, Federal Work-Study, unspecified assistantships, and out-of-state fee waivers available. Support available to part-time students. Financial award application deadline: 3/15; financial award applicants required to submit FAFSA. *Faculty research:* Hybrid of exercise physiology and psychology; gender equity; education, pedagogy, and technology; comprehensive school health education. *Unit head:* Dr. John Zbikowski, Coordinator, 262-472-4860, Fax: 262-472-1988, E-mail: zbikowskij@uww.edu. *Application contact:* Sally A. Lange, School of Graduate Studies, 262-472-1006, Fax: 262-472-5027, E-mail: gradschl@uww.edu.

University of Wyoming, College of Education, Programs in Educational Leadership, Laramie, WY 82070. Offers MA, Ed D, Certificate. Part-time programs available. Postbaccalaureate distance learning degree programs offered (minimal on-campus study). *Degree requirements:* For master's, thesis; for doctorate, comprehensive exam, thesis/dissertation; for Certificate, comprehensive exam, thesis, residency. *Entrance requirements:* For master's and Certificate, GRE; for doctorate, MA, 3 years' teaching experience. Additional exam requirements/recommendations for international students: Required—TOEFL (minimum score 520 paper-based). *Faculty research:* School leadership, leadership preparation, leadership skills.

Upper Iowa University, Online Master's Programs, Fayette, IA 52142-1857. Offers accounting (MBA); corporate financial management (MBA); global business (MBA); health and human services (MPA); higher education administration (MHEA); homeland security (MPA); human resources management (MBA); justice administration (MPA); organizational development (MBA); public personnel management (MPA); quality management (MBA). MBA also available at Madison, WI campus. Part-time programs available. Postbaccalaureate distance learning degree programs offered (no on-campus study). *Degree requirements:* For master's, research project. *Entrance requirements:* For master's, GMAT, GRE, or minimum GPA of 2.7 during last 60 hours. Additional exam requirements/recommendations for international students: Required—TOEFL (minimum score 570 paper-based; 230 computer-based). Electronic applications accepted. *Faculty research:* Total quality management, CQI, teams, organization culture and climate, management.

Ursuline College, School of Graduate Studies, Program in Educational Administration, Pepper Pike, OH 44124-4398. Offers MA. Part-time programs available. *Faculty:* 1 full-time (0 women), 3 part-time/adjunct (0 women). *Students:* 3 full-time (all women), 59 part-time (37 women); includes 11 minority (10 Black or African American, non-Hispanic/Latino; 1 Two or more races, non-Hispanic/Latino). Average age 37. 13 applicants, 92% accepted, 8 enrolled. In 2011, 17 master's awarded. *Degree requirements:* For master's, thesis or alternative. *Entrance requirements:* For master's, minimum undergraduate GPA of 3.0, teaching certificate, professional experience. Additional exam requirements/recommendations for international students: Required—TOEFL (minimum score 500 paper-based; 173 computer-based). *Application deadline:* For fall admission, 8/1 priority date for domestic students. Applications are processed on a rolling basis. Application fee: $25. *Expenses:* Contact institution. *Financial support:* Federal Work-Study available. Financial award application deadline: 3/1; financial award applicants required to submit FAFSA. *Unit head:* Martin Kane, Director, 440-646-8148, Fax: 440-646-8328, E-mail: mkane@ursuline.edu. *Application contact:* Melanie Steele, Graduate Admission Assistant, 440-464-8199, Fax: 440-684-6138, E-mail: graduateadmissions@ursuline.edu.

Valdosta State University, Program in Educational Leadership, Valdosta, GA 31698. Offers M Ed, Ed D, Ed S. *Accreditation:* NCATE. *Faculty:* 17 full-time (8 women). *Students:* 69 full-time (41 women), 210 part-time (143 women); includes 88 minority (80 Black or African American, non-Hispanic/Latino; 2 American Indian or Alaska Native, non-Hispanic/Latino; 3 Asian, non-Hispanic/Latino; 1 Hispanic/Latino; 2 Two or more races, non-Hispanic/Latino). Average age 25. 123 applicants, 78% accepted, 65 enrolled. In 2011, 41 master's, 5 doctorates awarded. *Degree requirements:* For master's, thesis (for some programs), comprehensive written and/or oral exams; for doctorate, thesis/dissertation, comprehensive written and/or oral exams; for Ed S, thesis. *Entrance requirements:* For master's and Ed S, GRE General Test or MAT; for doctorate, GRE General Test, minimum GPA of 3.5, 3 years experience. Additional exam requirements/recommendations for international students: Required—TOEFL (minimum score 523 paper-based; 193 computer-based). *Application deadline:* For fall admission, 7/1 for domestic and international students; for spring admission, 11/15 for domestic and international students. Applications are processed on a rolling basis. Application fee: $35. Electronic applications accepted. *Expenses:* Tuition, state resident: full-time $7098; part-time $217 per hour. Tuition, nonresident: full-time $20,630; part-time $780 per hour. *Financial support:* In 2011–12, 4 students received support, including 4 research assistantships with full tuition reimbursements available (averaging $3,652 per year); institutionally sponsored loans, scholarships/grants, and unspecified assistantships also available. Support available to part-time students. Financial award application deadline: 7/1; financial award applicants required to submit FAFSA. *Faculty research:* Student transition, mentoring in higher education, contemporary issues in higher education. *Unit head:* Dr. Don Leech, 229-333-5633, E-mail: dwleech@valdosta.edu. *Application contact:* Rebecca Waters, Coordinator of Graduate Programs, 229-333-5694, Fax: 229-245-3853, E-mail: rlwaters@valdosta.edu.

Valparaiso University, Graduate School, Department of Education, Program in Instructional Leadership, Valparaiso, IN 46383. Offers M Ed. Part-time and evening/weekend programs available. Postbaccalaureate distance learning degree programs offered (minimal on-campus study). *Degree requirements:* For master's, research project. *Entrance requirements:* For master's, valid teaching license, minimum undergraduate GPA of 3.0, two letters of recommendation. Additional exam requirements/recommendations for international students: Required—TOEFL (minimum score 550 paper-based; 213 computer-based; 80 iBT). *Application deadline:* Applications are processed on a rolling basis. Application fee: $30 ($50 for international students). Electronic applications accepted. *Expenses: Tuition:* Part-time $560 per credit hour. Tuition and fees vary according to course load and program. *Financial support:* Available to part-time students. Applicants required to submit FAFSA. *Unit head:* Dr. David L. Rowland, Dean, Graduate School and Continuing Education/Associate Provost, 219-464-5313, Fax: 219-464-5381, E-mail: david.rowland@valpo.edu. *Application contact:* Dustin Jesch, Coordinator, U.S. Student Engagement, 219-464-5313, Fax: 219-464-5381, E-mail: dustin.jesch@valpo.edu. Web site: http://valpo.edu/grad/ed/instldrshp.php.

Vanderbilt University, Graduate School, Program in Leadership and Policy Studies, Nashville, TN 37240-1001. Offers PhD. *Faculty:* 18 full-time (6 women), 5 part-time/adjunct (1 woman). *Students:* 42 full-time (22 women), 1 (woman) part-time; includes 6 minority (2 Black or African American, non-Hispanic/Latino; 2 Hispanic/Latino; 2 Two or more races, non-Hispanic/Latino), 9 international. Average age 33. 164 applicants, 7% accepted, 5 enrolled. In 2011, 5 doctorates awarded. *Degree requirements:* For doctorate, comprehensive exam, thesis/dissertation. *Entrance requirements:* For doctorate, GRE General Test. Additional exam requirements/recommendations for international students: Required—TOEFL (minimum score 570 paper-based; 230 computer-based; 88 iBT). *Application deadline:* For fall admission, 12/31 for domestic and international students. Application fee: $0. Electronic applications accepted. *Financial support:* Fellowships with full and partial tuition reimbursements, research assistantships with full tuition reimbursements, teaching assistantships with full tuition reimbursements, Federal Work-Study, institutionally sponsored loans, scholarships/grants, traineeships, and health care benefits available. Financial award application deadline: 1/15; financial award applicants required to submit CSS PROFILE or FAFSA. *Unit head:* Dr. Ellen Goldring, Chair, 615-322-8037, Fax: 615-343-7094, E-mail: ellen.b.goldring@vanderbilt.edu. *Application contact:* Dr. Thomas M. Smith, Director of Graduate Studies, 615-322-5519, Fax: 615-343-7094, E-mail: thomas.smith@vanderbilt.edu. Web site: http://peabody.vanderbilt.edu/admissions_and_programs/phd_programs/phd_program_choices.xml.

Vanderbilt University, Peabody College, Department of Leadership, Policy, and Organizations, Nashville, TN 37240-1001. Offers education policy (MPP); educational leadership and policy (Ed D); higher education (M Ed); higher education, leadership and policy (Ed D); international education policy and management (M Ed); leadership and organizational performance (M Ed). Part-time and evening/weekend programs available. *Faculty:* 27 full-time (12 women), 10 part-time/adjunct (3 women). *Students:* 165 full-time (117 women), 98 part-time (46 women); includes 35 minority (15 Black or African American, non-Hispanic/Latino; 4 Asian, non-Hispanic/Latino; 10 Hispanic/Latino; 6 Two or more races, non-Hispanic/Latino), 30 international. Average age 28. 465 applicants, 54% accepted, 87 enrolled. In 2011, 102 master's, 25 doctorates awarded. *Degree requirements:* For master's, comprehensive exam, thesis optional; for doctorate, thesis/dissertation, qualifying exams, residency. *Entrance requirements:* For master's and doctorate, GRE General Test. Additional exam requirements/recommendations for international students: Required—TOEFL (minimum score 550 paper-based; 213 computer-based). *Application deadline:* For fall admission, 12/31 priority date for domestic students, 12/31 for international students; for spring admission, 11/1 priority date for domestic students, 11/1 for international students. Applications are processed on a rolling basis. Application fee: $0. Electronic applications accepted. *Financial support:* Fellowships with full and partial tuition reimbursements, research assistantships with full and partial tuition reimbursements, teaching assistantships with full and partial tuition reimbursements, Federal Work-Study, institutionally sponsored loans, scholarships/grants, tuition waivers (partial), and unspecified assistantships available. Support available to part-time students. Financial award application deadline: 2/1; financial award applicants required to submit FAFSA. *Faculty research:* Education policy, education reform, school choice, equity and diversity, higher education. *Unit head:* Dr. Ellen B. Goldring, Chair, 615-322-8000, Fax: 615-343-7094, E-mail: ellen.b.goldring@vanderbilt.edu. *Application contact:* Rosie Moody, Educational Coordinator, 615-322-8019, Fax: 615-343-7094, E-mail: rosie.moody@vanderbilt.edu.

Villanova University, Graduate School of Liberal Arts and Sciences, Department of Education and Counseling, Program in Teacher Leadership, Villanova, PA 19085-1699. Offers MA. Part-time and evening/weekend programs available. *Students:* 9 full-time (8 women), 9 part-time (6 women); includes 2 minority (1 Asian, non-Hispanic/Latino; 1 Hispanic/Latino), 1 international. Average age 28. In 2011, 8 master's awarded. *Degree requirements:* For master's, comprehensive exam. *Entrance requirements:* For master's, GRE or MAT, minimum GPA of 3.0. Additional exam requirements/recommendations for international students: Required—TOEFL. *Application deadline:* Applications are processed on a rolling basis. Application fee: $50. Electronic applications accepted. *Expenses: Tuition:* Part-time $675 per credit. Part-time tuition and fees vary according to degree level and program. *Financial support:* Career-related internships or fieldwork and Federal Work-Study available. Financial award applicants required to submit FAFSA. *Unit head:* Dr. Edward Fierros, Chairperson, 610-519-4625. *Application contact:* Dean, Graduate School of Liberal Arts and Sciences.

Virginia Commonwealth University, Graduate School, School of Education, Doctoral Program in Education, Educational Leadership Track, Richmond, VA 23284-9005. Offers PhD. *Entrance requirements:* For doctorate, GRE. Additional exam requirements/recommendations for international students: Required—TOEFL (minimum score 600 paper-based; 250 computer-based; 100 iBT). Electronic applications accepted. *Expenses:* Tuition, state resident: full-time $9133; part-time $507 per credit. Tuition, nonresident: full-time $18,777; part-time $1043 per credit. *Required fees:* $77 per credit. Tuition and fees vary according to degree level, campus/location, program and student level.

Virginia Commonwealth University, Graduate School, School of Education, Doctoral Program in Education, Instructional Leadership Track, Richmond, VA 23284-9005. Offers PhD. *Entrance requirements:* For doctorate, GRE. Additional exam requirements/recommendations for international students: Required—TOEFL (minimum score 600 paper-based; 250 computer-based; 100 iBT). Electronic applications accepted. *Expenses:* Tuition, state resident: full-time $9133; part-time $507 per credit. Tuition, nonresident: full-time $18,777; part-time $1043 per credit. *Required fees:* $77 per credit. Tuition and fees vary according to degree level, campus/location, program and student level.

Virginia Polytechnic Institute and State University, Graduate School, College of Liberal Arts and Human Sciences, School of Education, Department of Educational Leadership and Policy Studies, Blacksburg, VA 24061. Offers administration and supervision of special education (Ed D, PhD); counselor education (MA, PhD); educational leadership and policy studies (MA, Ed D, PhD, Ed S); educational research and evaluation (PhD); higher education (MA, PhD). *Accreditation:* ACA; NCATE. *Degree requirements:* For master's, comprehensive exam (for some programs), thesis (for some programs); for doctorate, comprehensive exam (for some programs), thesis/dissertation (for some programs). *Entrance requirements:* For master's and doctorate, GRE. Additional exam requirements/recommendations for international students: Required—TOEFL (minimum score 550 paper-based; 213 computer-based). *Application deadline:* For fall admission, 7/1 for domestic and international students; for spring admission, 12/1 for domestic and international students. Applications are processed on a rolling basis. Application fee: $65. Electronic applications accepted. *Expenses:* Tuition, state resident: full-time $10,048; part-time $558.25 per credit hour. Tuition, nonresident: full-time $19,497; part-time $1083.25 per credit hour. *Required fees:* $405 per semester. Tuition and fees vary according to course load, campus/location and program. *Financial support:* Career-related internships or fieldwork, Federal Work-Study, scholarships/grants, health care benefits, and unspecified assistantships available. Financial award application deadline: 1/15. *Unit head:* Dr. M. David Alexander, Unit Head, 540-231-9723, Fax: 540-231-7845, E-mail: mdavid@vt.edu. *Application contact:* Daisy Stewart, Information Contact, 540-231-8180, Fax: 540-231-7845, E-mail: daisys@vt.edu. Web site: http://www.soe.vt.edu/elps/index.html.

Virginia Polytechnic Institute and State University, Graduate School, College of Liberal Arts and Human Sciences, School of Education, Department of Teaching and Learning, Blacksburg, VA 24061. Offers career and technical education (MS Ed, Ed D, PhD, Ed S); cognition and education (Certificate); counselor education (MA, PhD); curriculum and instruction (MA Ed, Ed D, PhD, Ed S); educational research, evaluation (PhD); higher education administration (Certificate); integrative STEM education (Certificate). *Accreditation:* NCATE. Postbaccalaureate distance learning degree programs offered (no on-campus study). Terminal master's awarded for partial completion of doctoral program. *Degree requirements:* For master's, comprehensive exam (for some programs), thesis (for some programs); for doctorate, comprehensive exam (for some programs), thesis/dissertation (for some programs). *Entrance requirements:* For master's and doctorate, GRE. Additional exam requirements/recommendations for international students: Required—TOEFL (minimum score 550 paper-based; 213 computer-based). *Application deadline:* For fall admission, 7/1 for domestic and international students; for spring admission, 12/1 for domestic and international students. Applications are processed on a rolling basis. Application fee: $65. Electronic applications accepted. *Expenses:* Tuition, state resident: full-time $10,048; part-time $558.25 per credit hour. Tuition, nonresident: full-time $19,497; part-time $1083.25 per credit hour. *Required fees:* $405 per semester. Tuition and fees vary according to course load, campus/location and program. *Financial support:* Career-related internships or fieldwork, Federal Work-Study, scholarships/grants, health care benefits, and unspecified assistantships available. Financial award application deadline: 1/15. *Faculty research:* Instructional technology, teacher evaluation, school change, literacy, teaching strategies. *Unit head:* Dr. Daisy L. Stewart, Unit Head, 540-231-8180, Fax: 540-231-3717, E-mail: daisys@vt.edu. *Application contact:* Daisy Stewart, Contact, 540-231-8180, Fax: 540-231-3717, E-mail: daisys@vt.edu. Web site: http://www.soe.vt.edu/.

Virginia State University, School of Graduate Studies, Research, and Outreach, School of Liberal Arts and Education, Department of Graduate Professional Education Programs, Program in Educational Administration and Supervision, Petersburg, VA 23806-0001. Offers M Ed, MS. *Accreditation:* NCATE. *Degree requirements:* For master's, thesis optional.

Wagner College, Division of Graduate Studies, Department of Education, Program in Educational Leadership, Staten Island, NY 10301-4495. Offers school building leader (MS Ed). Evening/weekend programs available. *Faculty:* 1 full-time (0 women), 5 part-time/adjunct (2 women). *Students:* 3 full-time (all women). Average age 29. 4 applicants, 100% accepted, 2 enrolled. In 2011, 3 master's awarded. *Entrance requirements:* Additional exam requirements/recommendations for international students: Required—TOEFL (minimum score 550 paper-based; 217 computer-based; 79 iBT). *Application deadline:* For fall admission, 5/1 priority date for domestic students, 3/1 for international students; for spring admission, 11/1 priority date for domestic students, 10/1 for international students. *Expenses: Tuition:* Full-time $16,200; part-time $890 per credit. *Financial support:* Applicants required to submit FAFSA. *Unit head:* Dr. Stephen Preskill, Graduate Coordinator, 718-420-4070, Fax: 718-390-3456, E-mail: stephen.preskill@wagner.edu. *Application contact:* Patricia Clancy, Administrative Assistant, Admissions, 718-420-4464, Fax: 718-390-3105, E-mail: patricia.clancy@wagner.edu.

Walden University, Graduate Programs, Richard W. Riley College of Education and Leadership, Minneapolis, MN 55401. Offers administrator leadership for teaching and learning (Ed D, Ed S); adult education (Ed D, Ed S); adult learning (MS, Postbaccalaureate Certificate), including developmental education (MS), online teaching (MS), teaching adults English as a second language (MS), training and performance management (MS); college teaching and learning (Ed D, Ed S, Postbaccalaureate Certificate); curriculum, instruction and assessment (Ed D, Postbaccalaureate Certificate); curriculum, instruction, and professional development (Ed S); developmental education (Postbaccalaureate Certificate); early childhood administration, management, and leadership (Postbaccalaureate Certificate); early childhood education (birth-grade 3) (MAT); early childhood public policy and advocacy (Postbaccalaureate Certificate); early childhood studies (MS), including administration, management and leadership, early childhood public policy and advocacy, teaching adults in the early childhood field, teaching and diversity; education (MS, PhD), including adolescent literacy and technology (grades 6-12) (MS), adult education leadership (PhD), assessment, evaluation, and accountability (PhD), community college leadership (PhD), curriculum, instruction, and assessment, early childhood education (PhD), educational technology (PhD), elementary reading and literacy (MS), elementary reading and mathematics (MS), general program, global and comparative education (PhD), higher education (PhD), integrating technology in the classroom (MS), K-12 educational leadership (PhD), leadership, policy and change (PhD), learning, instruction and innovation (PhD), literacy and learning in the content areas (MS), mathematics (grades 6-8) (MS), mathematics (grades K-5) (MS), middle level education (grades 5-8) (MS), professional development (MS), science (grades K-8) (MS), self-designed (PhD), special education (PhD), special education (non-licensure) (MS), teacher leadership (grades K-12) (MS), teaching English language learners (grades K-12) (MS);

educational leadership and administration (principal preparation) (Ed S); educational technology (Ed S); elementary reading and literacy (Postbaccalaureate Certificate); engaging culturally diverse learners (Postbaccalaureate Certificate); enrollment management and institutional marketing (Postbaccalaureate Certificate); higher education (MS), including college teaching and learning, enrollment management and institutional planning, global higher education, leadership for student success, online and distance learning; higher education leadership (Ed D); instructional design (Postbaccalaureate Certificate); instructional design and technology (MS), including general program (MS, PhD), online learning, training and performance improvement; integrating technology in the classroom (Postbaccalaureate Certificate); online teaching for adult learners (Postbaccalaureate Certificate); professional development (Postbaccalaureate Certificate); reading and literacy leadership (Ed D); science K-8 (Postbaccalaureate Certificate); special education (Ed D, Ed S); special education: emotional/behavioral disorders (K-12) (MAT); special education: learning disabilities (K-12) (MAT); teacher leadership (Ed D, Ed S, Postbaccalaureate Certificate); training and performance management (Postbaccalaureate Certificate). Part-time and evening/weekend programs available. Postbaccalaureate distance learning degree programs offered (minimal on-campus study). *Faculty:* 71 full-time (48 women), 853 part-time/adjunct (585 women). *Students:* 11,326 full-time (9,212 women), 2,148 part-time (1,795 women); includes 5,346 minority (4,403 Black or African American, non-Hispanic/Latino; 76 American Indian or Alaska Native, non-Hispanic/Latino; 140 Asian, non-Hispanic/Latino; 561 Hispanic/Latino; 21 Native Hawaiian or other Pacific Islander, non-Hispanic/Latino; 145 Two or more races, non-Hispanic/Latino), 322 international. Average age 39. In 2011, 3,477 master's, 318 doctorates, 471 other advanced degrees awarded. *Degree requirements:* For doctorate, thesis/dissertation (for some programs), residency; for other advanced degree, residency (for some programs). *Entrance requirements:* For master's, bachelor's degree or equivalent in related field; minimum GPA of 2.5; official transcripts; goal statement; access to computer and Internet; for doctorate, master's degree or equivalent in related field; minimum GPA of 3.0; official transcripts; three years' related professional/academic experience (preferred); access to computer and Internet; for other advanced degree, master's degree or equivalent in related field; minimum GPA of 3.0; 3 years related professional/academic experience (preferred); access to computer and Internet (Ed S). Additional exam requirements/recommendations for international students: Required—TOEFL (minimum score 550 paper-based; 213 computer-based), IELTS (minimum score 6.5), or Michigan English Language Assessment Battery (minimum score 82). *Application deadline:* Applications are processed on a rolling basis. Application fee: $50. Electronic applications accepted. *Financial support:* Federal Work-Study, scholarships/grants, unspecified assistantships, and family tuition reduction, active duty/veteran tuition reduction, group tuition reduction, interest-free payment plans, employee tuition reduction available. Support available to part-time students. Financial award applicants required to submit FAFSA. *Unit head:* Dr. Kate Steffens, Dean, 800-925-3368. *Application contact:* Jennifer Hall, Vice President of Enrollment Management, 866-4-WALDEN, E-mail: info@waldenu.edu. Web site: http://www.waldenu.edu/Colleges-and-Schools/College-of-Education-and-Leadership.htm.

Walla Walla University, Graduate School, School of Education and Psychology, College Place, WA 99324-1198. Offers counseling psychology (MA); curriculum and instruction (M Ed, MA, MAT); educational leadership (M Ed, MA, MAT); literacy instruction (M Ed, MA, MAT); students at risk (M Ed, MA, MAT); teaching (MAT). Part-time programs available. *Entrance requirements:* For master's, GRE General Test, minimum GPA of 2.75. Additional exam requirements/recommendations for international students: Required—TOEFL (minimum score 550 paper-based; 213 computer-based; 79 iBT). Electronic applications accepted. *Faculty research:* Admissions/retention, instructional psychology, moral development, teaching of reading.

Washburn University, College of Arts and Sciences, Department of Education, Topeka, KS 66621. Offers curriculum and instruction (M Ed); educational leadership (M Ed); reading (M Ed); special education (M Ed). *Accreditation:* NCATE. Part-time programs available. *Faculty:* 6 full-time (3 women), 1 (woman) part-time/adjunct. *Students:* 2 full-time (both women), 26 part-time (16 women). Average age 36. In 2011, 17 master's awarded. *Degree requirements:* For master's, comprehensive exam, thesis or alternative, portfolio, comprehensive paper, or action research project. *Entrance requirements:* For master's, department graduate admissions test, GRE General Test, or MAT, minimum GPA of 3.0 in graduate coursework or last 60 hours of undergraduate coursework. Additional exam requirements/recommendations for international students: Required—TOEFL (minimum score 550 paper-based; 80 iBT). *Application deadline:* For fall admission, 8/1 for domestic and international students; for spring admission, 11/1 for domestic and international students. Applications are processed on a rolling basis. *Expenses:* Tuition, state resident: full-time $5346; part-time $297 per credit hour. Tuition, nonresident: full-time $10,908; part-time $606 per credit hour. *Required fees:* $86; $43 per semester. *Financial support:* Federal Work-Study, institutionally sponsored loans, and scholarships/grants available. Support available to part-time students. Financial award applicants required to submit FAFSA. *Faculty research:* Reading/literature/literacy, foundations, educational administration/leadership, special education, diversity. *Unit head:* Dr. Judith McConnell-Farmer, Interim Chairperson, 785-670-1472, Fax: 785-670-1046, E-mail: judy.mcconnell-farmer@washburn.edu. *Application contact:* Tara Porter, Licensure Officer, 785-670-1434, Fax: 785-670-1046, E-mail: tara.porter@washburn.edu. Web site: http://www.washburn.edu/academics/college-schools/arts-sciences/departments/education/index.html.

Washington State University, Graduate School, College of Education, Department of Educational Leadership and Counseling Psychology, Program in Educational Leadership, Pullman, WA 99164. Offers M Ed, MA, Ed D, PhD. *Accreditation:* NCATE. *Degree requirements:* For master's, comprehensive exam (for some programs), thesis (for some programs), oral or written exam; for doctorate, comprehensive exam, thesis/dissertation, oral exam, written exam. *Entrance requirements:* For master's, minimum GPA of 3.0, 3 letters of recommendation; for doctorate, GRE General Test, minimum GPA of 3.0, 3 letters of recommendation. Additional exam requirements/recommendations for international students: Recommended—TOEFL (minimum score 550 paper-based; 213 computer-based). *Application deadline:* For fall admission, 3/15 for domestic students, 3/1 for international students; for spring admission, 10/1 for domestic students, 7/1 for international students. Electronic applications accepted. *Financial support:* Research assistantships with partial tuition reimbursements, teaching assistantships with partial tuition reimbursements, career-related internships or fieldwork, Federal Work-Study, institutionally sponsored loans, scholarships/grants, and unspecified assistantships available. Financial award application deadline: 4/1. *Faculty research:* Cross-cultural personality study, language, learning school as community. *Unit head:* Dennis Ray, Director, 509-358-7941, E-mail: dray@wsu.edu. *Application contact:* Graduate School Admissions, 800-GRADWSU, Fax: 509-335-1949, E-mail: gradsch@wsu.edu. Web site: http://www.educ.wsu.edu/elcp/.

Washington State University Spokane, Graduate Programs, Program in Education, Spokane, WA 99210. Offers educational leadership (Ed M, MA); principal (Certificate); professional certification for teachers (Certificate); program administrator (Certificate); school psychologist (Certificate); superintendent (Certificate); teaching (MIT). *Faculty:* 24. *Students:* 11 full-time (10 women), 25 part-time (17 women); includes 1 minority (Hispanic/Latino). Average age 37. 27 applicants, 67% accepted, 18 enrolled. In 2011, 8 degrees awarded. *Degree requirements:* For master's, comprehensive exam (for some programs), thesis (for some programs). *Entrance requirements:* For master's, GRE or GMAT, minimum GPA of 3.0, 3 letters of recommendation, resume. Additional exam requirements/recommendations for international students: Required—TOEFL (minimum score 550 paper-based; 213 computer-based). *Application deadline:* For fall admission, 1/10 priority date for domestic students, 1/10 for international students; for spring admission, 7/1 priority date for domestic students, 7/1 for international students. Application fee: $50. *Financial support:* In 2011–12, 33 students received support, including research assistantships (averaging $14,634 per year), teaching assistantships (averaging $13,383 per year). *Total annual research expenditures:* $16,557. *Unit head:* Dr. Joan Kingrey, Director, 509-358-7939, Fax: 509-358-7900, E-mail: kingrey@wsu.edu. *Application contact:* Graduate School Admissions, 800-GRADWSU, Fax: 509-335-1949, E-mail: gradsch@wsu.edu.

Washington State University Tri-Cities, Graduate Programs, Program in Education, Richland, WA 99352-1671. Offers counseling (Ed M); educational leadership (Ed M, Ed D); literacy (Ed M); secondary certification (Ed M); teaching (MIT). Part-time programs available. *Faculty:* 24. *Students:* 19 full-time (14 women), 73 part-time (46 women); includes 18 minority (1 Black or African American, non-Hispanic/Latino; 3 Asian, non-Hispanic/Latino; 14 Hispanic/Latino). Average age 34. 26 applicants, 69% accepted, 18 enrolled. In 2011, 31 master's awarded. *Degree requirements:* For master's, comprehensive exam, thesis or alternative; for doctorate, comprehensive exam, thesis/dissertation. *Entrance requirements:* For master's, GRE, minimum GPA of 3.0, Working with Youth form, Character and Fitness form, 3 letters of recommendation. Additional exam requirements/recommendations for international students: Required—TOEFL. *Application deadline:* For fall admission, 1/10 priority date for domestic students, 1/10 for international students; for spring admission, 7/1 priority date for domestic students, 7/1 for international students. Applications are processed on a rolling basis. Application fee: $75. Electronic applications accepted. *Financial support:* In 2011–12, 59 students received support, including research assistantships (averaging $14,634 per year), teaching assistantships (averaging $13,383 per year); Federal Work-Study, scholarships/grants, and unspecified assistantships also available. Financial award application deadline: 2/15. *Faculty research:* Multicultural counseling, socio-cultural influences in schools, diverse learners, teacher education, K-12 educational leadership. *Unit head:* Dr. Elizabeth Nagel, Director, 509-372-7398, E-mail: elizabeth_nagel@tricity.wsu.edu. *Application contact:* Helen Berry, Academic Coordinator, 800-GRADWSU, Fax: 509-372-3796, E-mail: hberry@tricity.wsu.edu. Web site: http://www.tricity.wsu.edu/education/graduate.html.

Wayland Baptist University, Graduate Programs, Program in Education, Plainview, TX 79072-6998. Offers education administration (M Ed); higher education administration (M Ed); instructional leadership (M Ed); instructional technology (M Ed); special education (M Ed). Part-time and evening/weekend programs available. Postbaccalaureate distance learning degree programs offered (no on-campus study). *Degree requirements:* For master's, comprehensive exam, capstone course. *Entrance requirements:* For master's, GRE, GMAT or MAT. Additional exam requirements/recommendations for international students: Required—TOEFL (minimum score 500 paper-based; 173 computer-based; 61 iBT). Electronic applications accepted.

Wayne State College, School of Education and Counseling, Department of Educational Foundations and Leadership, Program in Educational Administration, Wayne, NE 68787. Offers educational administration (Ed S); elementary administration (MSE); elementary and secondary administration (MSE); secondary administration (MSE). *Accreditation:* NCATE. Part-time and evening/weekend programs available. *Degree requirements:* For master's, comprehensive exam, thesis optional, research paper. *Entrance requirements:* For master's, GRE General Test, minimum GPA of 2.5; for Ed S, GRE General Test, minimum GPA of 3.2. Additional exam requirements/recommendations for international students: Required—TOEFL (minimum score 550 paper-based; 213 computer-based). Electronic applications accepted.

Wayne State University, College of Education, Division of Administrative and Organizational Studies, Detroit, MI 48202. Offers college and university teaching (Certificate); educational leadership (M Ed); educational leadership and policy studies (Ed D, PhD); general administration and supervision (Ed S); instructional technology (M Ed, Ed D, PhD, Ed S); online teaching (Certificate); secondary curriculum and instruction (Ed S). *Students:* 86 full-time (62 women), 261 part-time (172 women); includes 171 minority (145 Black or African American, non-Hispanic/Latino; 1 American Indian or Alaska Native, non-Hispanic/Latino; 8 Asian, non-Hispanic/Latino; 16 Hispanic/Latino; 1 Two or more races, non-Hispanic/Latino), 8 international. Average age 39. 122 applicants, 40% accepted, 28 enrolled. In 2011, 73 master's, 9 doctorates, 50 other advanced degrees awarded. *Degree requirements:* For doctorate, thesis/dissertation. *Entrance requirements:* For doctorate, GRE or MAT, interview; autobiography or curriculum vitae; references; master's degree; minimum undergraduate GPA of 3.0, graduate 3.75; 3 years relevant experience; foundational course work; for other advanced degree, minimum GPA of 3.4. Additional exam requirements/recommendations for international students: Required—TOEFL (minimum score 550 paper-based; 213 computer-based), TWE (minimum score 5.5). *Application deadline:* For fall admission, 6/1 priority date for domestic students, 5/1 for international students; for winter admission, 10/1 priority date for domestic students, 9/1 for international students; for spring admission, 2/1 priority date for domestic students, 1/1 for international students. Applications are processed on a rolling basis. Application fee: $50. Electronic applications accepted. *Expenses:* Tuition, state resident: part-time $512.85 per credit. Tuition, nonresident: part-time $1132.65 per credit. *Required fees:* $26.60 per credit. $199.65 per semester. Tuition and fees vary according to course load and program. *Financial support:* In 2011–12, 59 students received support, including 1 fellowship with tuition reimbursement available (averaging $17,347 per year), 4 research assistantships with tuition reimbursements available (averaging $15,713 per year); career-related internships or fieldwork, Federal Work-Study, institutionally sponsored loans, scholarships/grants, health care benefits, and unspecified assistantships also available. Support available to part-time students. *Faculty research:* Total quality management, participatory management, administering educational technology, school improvement, principalship. *Total annual research expenditures:* $22,232. *Unit head:* Dr. Alan Hoffman, Interim Assistant Dean, 313-577-5235, E-mail: alanhoffman@wayne.edu. *Application contact:* Janice Green, Assistant Dean, 313-577-1605, E-mail: jwgreen@wayne.edu. Web site: http://coe.wayne.edu/aos/index.php.

Webster University, School of Education, Department of Multidisciplinary Studies, St. Louis, MO 63119-3194. Offers administrative leadership (Ed S); education leadership (Ed S); educational technology (MAT); mathematics (MAT); multidisciplinary studies (MAT); school systems, superintendency and leadership (Ed S); social science (MAT); special education (MAT). Part-time programs available. *Entrance requirements:* For master's, minimum GPA of 2.5. Additional exam requirements/recommendations for international students: Required—TOEFL. *Expenses: Tuition:* Full-time $10,890; part-time $605 per credit hour. Tuition and fees vary according to campus/location and program.

Western Carolina University, Graduate School, College of Education and Allied Professions, School of Teaching and Learning, Cullowhee, NC 28723. Offers community college and higher education (MA Ed), including community college administration, community college teaching; comprehensive education (MA Ed, MAT);

educational leadership (MA Ed, MSA, Ed D, Ed S), including educational leadership (MSA, Ed D, Ed S), educational supervision (MA Ed); teaching (MA Ed, MAT), including comprehensive education (MA Ed), physical education (MA Ed), teaching (MAT). *Accreditation:* NCATE. Part-time and evening/weekend programs available. Postbaccalaureate distance learning degree programs offered. *Students:* 40 full-time (24 women), 150 part-time (133 women); includes 13 minority (6 Black or African American, non-Hispanic/Latino; 2 American Indian or Alaska Native, non-Hispanic/Latino; 4 Hispanic/Latino; 1 Two or more races, non-Hispanic/Latino), 9 international. Average age 32. 96 applicants, 90% accepted, 71 enrolled. In 2011, 86 master's, 13 doctorates, 5 other advanced degrees awarded. *Degree requirements:* For master's, comprehensive exam; for doctorate, comprehensive exam, thesis/dissertation. *Entrance requirements:* For master's, GRE, appropriate undergraduate degree, 3 letters of recommendation; for doctorate, GRE General Test, minimum graduate GPA of 3.5, appropriate master's degree; for other advanced degree, GRE General Test, minimum graduate GPA of 3.5, work experience, appropriate master's degree. Additional exam requirements/recommendations for international students: Required—TOEFL (minimum score 550 paper-based; 270 computer-based; 79 iBT). *Application deadline:* For fall admission, 2/1 for domestic students; for spring admission, 9/1 priority date for domestic students. Applications are processed on a rolling basis. Application fee: $50. *Expenses:* Tuition, state resident: full-time $3348. Tuition, nonresident: full-time $12,933. *Required fees:* $3155. *Financial support:* In 2011–12, 2 fellowships were awarded; research assistantships with full and partial tuition reimbursements, teaching assistantships with full and partial tuition reimbursements, career-related internships or fieldwork, institutionally sponsored loans, scholarships/grants, and unspecified assistantships also available. Financial award application deadline: 3/31; financial award applicants required to submit FAFSA. *Faculty research:* Educational leadership, special education, rural education, organizational theory and practice, interinstitutional partnership, program evaluation. *Unit head:* Dr. William Dee Nichols, Department Head, 828-227-7108, Fax: 828-227-7607, E-mail: wdnichols@wcu.edu. *Application contact:* Admissions Specialist for Educational Leadership and Foundations, 828-227-7398, Fax: 828-227-7480, E-mail: gradsch@email.wcu.edu. Web site: http://www.wcu.edu/3067.asp.

Western Connecticut State University, Division of Graduate Studies, School of Professional Studies, Department of Education and Educational Psychology, Program in Instructional Leadership, Danbury, CT 06810-6885. Offers Ed D. Part-time programs available. *Faculty:* 7 full-time (5 women), 4 part-time/adjunct (all women). *Students:* 6 full-time (4 women), 51 part-time (34 women); includes 6 minority (2 Black or African American, non-Hispanic/Latino; 2 American Indian or Alaska Native, non-Hispanic/Latino; 2 Hispanic/Latino). Average age 44. 18 applicants, 72% accepted, 12 enrolled. In 2011, 2 degrees awarded. *Degree requirements:* For doctorate, comprehensive exam, thesis/dissertation, completion of program in 6 years. *Entrance requirements:* For doctorate, GRE or MAT, resume, three recommendations (one in a supervisory capacity in an educational setting), satisfactory interview with WCSU representatives from the EdD Admissions Committee. Additional exam requirements/recommendations for international students: Recommended—TOEFL (minimum score 550 paper-based; 213 computer-based; 79 iBT), IELTS (minimum score 6). *Application deadline:* For fall admission, 3/30 priority date for domestic students. Application fee: $100. *Expenses:* Contact institution. *Faculty research:* Differentiated instruction, the transition of teacher learning, teacher retention, relationship building through the evaluation process, leadership development. *Unit head:* Dr. Marcia A. Delcourt, Coordinator, 203-837-9121, Fax: 203-837-8413, E-mail: delcourtm@wcsu.edu. *Application contact:* Chris Shankle, Associate Director of Graduate Studies, 203-837-9005, Fax: 203-837-8326, E-mail: shanklec@wcsu.edu.

Western Governors University, Teachers College, Salt Lake City, UT 84107. Offers curriculum and instruction (MS); educational leadership (MS); educational studies (MA); educational studies (5-12) (MA), including mathematics; elementary education (k-8) (Postbaccalaureate Certificate); English language learning (K-12) (MA); instructional design (MAT); learning and technology (M Ed, MA); management and innovation (M Ed); mathematics (5-12) (Postbaccalaureate Certificate); mathematics (5-9) (Postbaccalaureate Certificate); mathematics education (5-12) (MA); mathematics education (5-9) (MA); mathematics education (K-6) (MA); measurement and evaluation (M Ed); science (5-12) (Postbaccalaureate Certificate); science (5-9) (Postbaccalaureate Certificate); science education (5-12) (MA), including biology, chemistry, geology, physics; science education (5-9) (MA); social science (5-12) (MAT); special education (MAT). *Accreditation:* NCATE. Evening/weekend programs available. Postbaccalaureate distance learning degree programs offered (no on-campus study). *Students:* 3,746 full-time (2,811 women); includes 652 minority (332 Black or African American, non-Hispanic/Latino; 37 American Indian or Alaska Native, non-Hispanic/Latino; 74 Asian, non-Hispanic/Latino; 139 Hispanic/Latino; 70 Two or more races, non-Hispanic/Latino), 12 international. Average age 37. In 2011, 1,080 master's, 242 other advanced degrees awarded. *Degree requirements:* For master's, capstone project. *Entrance requirements:* For master's and Postbaccalaureate Certificate, Readiness Assessment, commitment counseling discussion, transcript submissions, completion of orientation. Additional exam requirements/recommendations for international students: Required—TOEFL (minimum score 450 paper-based; 80 iBT). *Application deadline:* Applications are processed on a rolling basis. Application fee: $65. Electronic applications accepted. *Expenses:* Contact institution. *Financial support:* Scholarships/grants and tuition waivers (partial) available. Financial award applicants required to submit FAFSA. *Unit head:* Dr. Philip Schmidt, Dean of the Teachers College, 845-255-4656. *Application contact:* Enrollment Department, 866-225-5948, Fax: 801-274-3306, E-mail: info@wgu.edu.

Western Illinois University, School of Graduate Studies, College of Education and Human Services, Department of Educational Leadership, Macomb, IL 61455-1390. Offers MS Ed, Ed D, Ed S. *Accreditation:* NCATE. Part-time and evening/weekend programs available. *Students:* 8 full-time (6 women), 224 part-time (117 women); includes 13 minority (7 Black or African American, non-Hispanic/Latino; 1 American Indian or Alaska Native, non-Hispanic/Latino; 4 Hispanic/Latino; 1 Two or more races, non-Hispanic/Latino), 3 international. Average age 38. 30 applicants, 73% accepted. In 2011, 33 master's, 9 doctorates, 21 other advanced degrees awarded. *Degree requirements:* For master's, thesis or alternative; for doctorate, comprehensive exam, thesis/dissertation, electronic portfolio. *Entrance requirements:* For master's and Ed S, interview; for doctorate, GRE General Test. Additional exam requirements/recommendations for international students: Required—TOEFL (minimum score 575 paper-based; 230 computer-based; 88 iBT). *Application deadline:* Applications are processed on a rolling basis. Application fee: $30. Electronic applications accepted. *Expenses:* Tuition, state resident: part-time $281.16 per credit hour. Tuition, nonresident: part-time $562.32 per credit hour. Part-time tuition and fees vary according to campus/location and reciprocity agreements. *Financial support:* In 2011–12, research assistantships with full tuition reimbursements (averaging $7,360 per year) were awarded. Financial award applicants required to submit FAFSA. *Unit head:* Dr. Jess House, Interim Chairperson, 309-298-1070. *Application contact:* Dr. Nancy Parsons, Interim Associate Provost and Director of Graduate Studies, 309-298-1806, Fax: 309-298-2345, E-mail: grad-office@wiu.edu. Web site: http://wiu.edu/educationalleadership.

Western Kentucky University, Graduate Studies, College of Education and Behavioral Sciences, Department of Educational Administration, Leadership, and Research, Bowling Green, KY 42101. Offers adult education (MAE); educational leadership (Ed D); school administration (Ed S); school principal (MAE). *Accreditation:* NCATE. Part-time and evening/weekend programs available. *Degree requirements:* For master's, comprehensive exam, thesis or applied project and oral defense; for Ed S, thesis. *Entrance requirements:* For master's, GRE General Test, minimum GPA of 2.75. Additional exam requirements/recommendations for international students: Required—TOEFL (minimum score 555 paper-based; 213 computer-based; 79 iBT). *Faculty research:* Principal internship, superintendent assessment, administrative leadership, group training for residential workers.

Western Michigan University, Graduate College, College of Education and Human Development, Department of Educational Leadership, Research and Technology, Kalamazoo, MI 49008. Offers educational leadership (MA, PhD, Ed S); educational technology (MA, Graduate Certificate); evaluation, measurement and research (MA, PhD).

Western New Mexico University, Graduate Division, School of Education, Silver City, NM 88062-0680. Offers bilingual education (MAT); counseling (MA); educational leadership (MA); elementary education (MAT); reading (MAT); school psychology (MA); secondary education (MAT); special education (MAT); TESOL (teaching English to speakers of other languages) (MAT). *Accreditation:* NCATE. *Degree requirements:* For master's, comprehensive exam. *Entrance requirements:* For master's, GRE General Test, GRE Subject Test, minimum GPA of 3.2 in last 64 hours of undergraduate study. Additional exam requirements/recommendations for international students: Required—TOEFL (minimum score 550 paper-based; 213 computer-based). Electronic applications accepted.

Western State College of Colorado, Graduate Programs in Education, Gunnison, CO 81231. Offers education administrator leadership (MA); reading leadership (MA); teacher leadership (MA). Postbaccalaureate distance learning degree programs offered (minimal on-campus study). *Degree requirements:* For master's, capstone.

Western Washington University, Graduate School, Woodring College of Education, Department of Educational Leadership, Educational Administration Program, Bellingham, WA 98225-5996. Offers M Ed. *Accreditation:* NCATE. Part-time programs available. *Degree requirements:* For master's, comprehensive exam, thesis optional. *Entrance requirements:* For master's, GRE General Test or MAT, minimum GPA of 3.0 in last 60 semester hours or last 90 quarter hours, certification. Additional exam requirements/recommendations for international students: Required—TOEFL (minimum score 567 paper-based; 227 computer-based). Electronic applications accepted. *Faculty research:* Principal efficacy, collaborative school leadership, school/university partnerships, case study methodology, ethical leadership.

Western Washington University, Graduate School, Woodring College of Education, Department of Educational Leadership, Program in Student Affairs Administration, Bellingham, WA 98225-5996. Offers M Ed. *Accreditation:* NCATE. Part-time programs available. *Degree requirements:* For master's, comprehensive exam, thesis optional, research project. *Entrance requirements:* For master's, GRE General Test or MAT, minimum GPA of 3.0 in last 60 semester hours or last 90 quarter hours. Additional exam requirements/recommendations for international students: Required—TOEFL (minimum score 567 paper-based; 227 computer-based). Electronic applications accepted. *Faculty research:* Outcomes assessment, adult learning, best practices/student affairs, college health promotion, cultural pluralism.

Westfield State University, Division of Graduate and Continuing Education, Department of Education, Program in School Administration, Westfield, MA 01086. Offers M Ed, CAGS. Part-time and evening/weekend programs available. *Degree requirements:* For master's, comprehensive exam, practicum; for CAGS, research-based field internship. *Entrance requirements:* For master's, GRE General Test or MAT, minimum undergraduate GPA of 2.7; for CAGS, master's degree. *Faculty research:* Collaborative teacher education, developmental early childhood education.

Westminster College, Programs in Education, Program in Administration, New Wilmington, PA 16172-0001. Offers M Ed, Certificate. Part-time and evening/weekend programs available. *Degree requirements:* For master's, comprehensive exam. *Entrance requirements:* For master's, GRE or MAT, minimum GPA of 3.0.

West Texas A&M University, College of Education and Social Sciences, Division of Education, Program in Administration, Canyon, TX 79016-0001. Offers M Ed. Part-time and evening/weekend programs available. Postbaccalaureate distance learning degree programs offered (minimal on-campus study). *Degree requirements:* For master's, comprehensive exam, thesis optional. *Entrance requirements:* For master's, GRE General Test. Additional exam requirements/recommendations for international students: Required—TOEFL (minimum score 550 paper-based). Electronic applications accepted. *Faculty research:* Teacher quality, leadership, recruitment, retention.

West Virginia University, College of Human Resources and Education, Department of Educational Leadership Studies, Morgantown, WV 26506. Offers educational leadership (Ed D); higher education administration (MA); public school administration (MA). *Accreditation:* NCATE. Part-time programs available. *Degree requirements:* For master's, content exams; for doctorate, comprehensive exam, thesis/dissertation. *Entrance requirements:* For master's, minimum GPA of 2.75 or MA Degree or MAT of 4107; for doctorate, GRE General Test or MAT, minimum GPA of 3.25. Additional exam requirements/recommendations for international students: Required—TOEFL. Electronic applications accepted. *Faculty research:* Evaluation, collective bargaining, educational law, international higher education, superintendency.

Wheeling Jesuit University, Department of Education, Wheeling, WV 26003-6295. Offers MEL. Part-time and evening/weekend programs available. Postbaccalaureate distance learning degree programs offered (no on-campus study). *Faculty:* 3 full-time (all women), 3 part-time/adjunct (1 woman). *Students:* 24 full-time (13 women), 23 part-time (20 women); includes 1 minority (Hispanic/Latino). Average age 36. 47 applicants, 89% accepted, 42 enrolled. In 2011, 2 master's awarded. *Degree requirements:* For master's, thesis. *Entrance requirements:* For master's, GRE or MAT, minimum GPA of 2.5, professional teaching certificate. Additional exam requirements/recommendations for international students: Required—TOEFL (minimum score 600 paper-based; 250 computer-based; 100 iBT). *Application deadline:* For fall admission, 8/1 priority date for domestic students, 8/1 for international students; for spring admission, 12/15 priority date for domestic students, 12/1 for international students. Applications are processed on a rolling basis. Application fee: $25. Electronic applications accepted. Application fee is waived when completed online. *Expenses: Tuition:* Full-time $9720; part-time $540 per credit hour. *Required fees:* $250. *Financial support:* Application deadline: 8/1; applicants required to submit FAFSA. *Faculty research:* Education leadership, school improvement, student achievement. *Unit head:* Dr. Bonnie Ritz, Assistant Professor in Professional Education and Program Director, 304-243-2175, Fax: 304-243-8167, E-mail: britz@wju.edu. *Application contact:* Dan Angalich, Associate Director of Admissions for School of Education, 304-243-2642, Fax: 304-243-2397, E-mail: dangalich@wju.edu. Web site: http://www.wju.edu/adulted/mel/default.asp.

Educational Leadership and Administration

Wheelock College, Graduate Programs, Division of Education, Boston, MA 02215-4176. Offers early childhood education (MS); education leadership (MS); elementary education (MS); language, literacy, and reading (MS); teaching students with moderate disabilities (MS). *Accreditation:* NCATE. Postbaccalaureate distance learning degree programs offered (minimal on-campus study). *Degree requirements:* For master's, comprehensive exam. *Entrance requirements:* Additional exam requirements/recommendations for international students: Required—TOEFL. Electronic applications accepted. *Faculty research:* Symbolic learning, emergent literacy, diversity inclusion, beginning reading language and culture, math education.

Whittier College, Graduate Programs, Department of Education and Child Development, Program in Educational Administration, Whittier, CA 90608-0634. Offers MA Ed. Part-time and evening/weekend programs available. *Degree requirements:* For master's, thesis. *Entrance requirements:* For master's, GRE General Test, MAT. *Faculty research:* Candidate leadership development.

Whitworth University, School of Education, Graduate Studies in Education, Program in Administration, Spokane, WA 99251-0001. Offers M Ed. *Accreditation:* NCATE. Part-time and evening/weekend programs available. *Degree requirements:* For master's, comprehensive exam, internship, practicum, research project, or thesis. *Entrance requirements:* For master's, GRE General Test, MAT. Tuition and fees vary according to program. *Faculty research:* Rural staff development.

Wichita State University, Graduate School, College of Education, Department of Counseling, Educational Leadership, Educational and School Psychology, Wichita, KS 67260. Offers counseling (M Ed); educational leadership (M Ed, Ed D); educational psychology (M Ed); school psychology (Ed S). *Accreditation:* NCATE. Part-time and evening/weekend programs available. *Expenses:* Tuition, state resident: full-time $4746; part-time $263.65 per credit. Tuition, nonresident: full-time $11,669; part-time $648.30 per credit. *Unit head:* Dr. Jean Patterson, Chairperson, 316-978-3325, Fax: 316-978-3102, E-mail: jean.patterson@wichita.edu. *Application contact:* Carrie C. Henderson, Admissions Coordinator, 316-978-3095, Fax: 316-978-3253, E-mail: carrie.henderson@wichita.edu. Web site: http://www.wichita.edu/.

Widener University, School of Human Service Professions, Center for Education, Chester, PA 19013-5792. Offers adult education (M Ed); counseling in higher education (M Ed); counselor education (M Ed); early childhood education (M Ed); educational foundations (M Ed); educational leadership (M Ed); educational psychology (M Ed); elementary education (M Ed); English and language arts (M Ed); health education (M Ed); higher education leadership (Ed D); home and school visitor (M Ed); human sexuality (M Ed, PhD); mathematics education (M Ed); middle school education (M Ed); principalship (M Ed); reading and language arts (Ed D); reading education (M Ed); school administration (Ed D); science education (M Ed); social studies education (M Ed); special education (M Ed); technology education (M Ed). *Accreditation:* NCATE. Part-time and evening/weekend programs available. Terminal master's awarded for partial completion of doctoral program. *Degree requirements:* For doctorate, thesis/dissertation. *Entrance requirements:* For master's, minimum GPA of 2.5; for doctorate, GRE or MAT, minimum GPA of 2.0 (undergraduate), 3.5 (graduate). Electronic applications accepted. *Expenses:* Contact institution. *Faculty research:* Reading and cognition, adult education, technology education, educational leadership, special education.

Wilkes University, College of Graduate and Professional Studies, School of Education, Wilkes-Barre, PA 18766-0002. Offers art and science of teaching (MS Ed); classroom technology (MS Ed); early childhood literacy (MS Ed); educational computing (MS Ed); educational development and strategies (MS Ed); educational leadership (MS Ed); educational technology (Ed D); higher education administration (Ed D); instructional media (MS Ed); instructional technology (MS Ed); K-12 administration (Ed D); online teaching (MS Ed); reading (MS Ed); school business leadership (MS Ed); secondary education (MS Ed), including biology, chemistry, English, history, mathematics; special education (MS Ed); teaching English as a second language (MS Ed); twenty-first century teaching and learning (MS Ed). Part-time and evening/weekend programs available. Postbaccalaureate distance learning degree programs offered (minimal on-campus study). *Students:* 92 full-time (63 women), 2,005 part-time (1,459 women); includes 89 minority (23 Black or African American, non-Hispanic/Latino; 1 American Indian or Alaska Native, non-Hispanic/Latino; 14 Asian, non-Hispanic/Latino; 33 Hispanic/Latino; 1 Native Hawaiian or other Pacific Islander, non-Hispanic/Latino; 17 Two or more races, non-Hispanic/Latino), 6 international. Average age 33. In 2011, 1,150 master's, 3 doctorates awarded. *Entrance requirements:* Additional exam requirements/recommendations for international students: Required—TOEFL (minimum score 550 paper-based; 213 computer-based; 79 iBT). *Application deadline:* Applications are processed on a rolling basis. Application fee: $45. Electronic applications accepted. *Expenses:* Contact institution. *Financial support:* Federal Work-Study and unspecified assistantships available. Financial award application deadline: 3/1; financial award applicants required to submit FAFSA. *Unit head:* Dr. Michael Speziale, Dean, 570-408-4679, Fax: 570-408-4905, E-mail: michael.speziale@wilkes.edu. *Application contact:* Erin Sutzko, Director of Extended Learning, 570-408-4253, Fax: 570-408-7846, E-mail: erin.sutzko@wilkes.edu. Web site: http://www.wilkes.edu/pages/383.asp.

William Paterson University of New Jersey, College of Education, Wayne, NJ 07470-8420. Offers curriculum and learning (M Ed); educational leadership (M Ed); reading (M Ed); special education and counseling services (M Ed), including counseling services, special education; teaching (MAT). *Accreditation:* NCATE. Part-time and evening/weekend programs available. *Degree requirements:* For master's, comprehensive exam. *Entrance requirements:* For master's, GRE General Test, MAT, minimum GPA of 2.75, teaching certificate. Electronic applications accepted. *Faculty research:* Urban community service.

William Woods University, Graduate and Adult Studies, Fulton, MO 65251-1098. Offers administration (Ed S); agriculture (MBA); athletic/activities administration (M Ed); curriculum and instruction (M Ed); curriculum leadership (Ed S); elementary administration (M Ed); health management (MBA); human resources (MBA); principalship (Ed S); secondary administration (M Ed); special education director (M Ed). Evening/weekend programs available. *Degree requirements:* For master's, capstone course (MBA), action research (M Ed); for Ed S, field experience. *Entrance requirements:* For master's, 2 recommendations, resumé, BA/BS; teaching certification (M Ed); course work in economics and accounting (MBA); for Ed S, M Ed, 2 letters of recommendation, resume, teaching certification. Additional exam requirements/recommendations for international students: Required—TOEFL (minimum score 550 paper-based). Electronic applications accepted.

Wilmington University, College of Education, New Castle, DE 19720-6491. Offers applied technology in education (M Ed); career and technical education (M Ed); educational leadership (Ed D); elementary and secondary school counseling (M Ed); elementary studies (M Ed); ESOL literacy (M Ed); higher education leadership (Ed D); instruction: gifted and talented (M Ed); instruction: teacher of reading (M Ed); instruction: teaching and learning (M Ed); organizational leadership (Ed D); school leadership (M Ed); secondary education (MAT); special education (M Ed). *Accreditation:* NCATE. Part-time and evening/weekend programs available. *Faculty:* 7 full-time (4 women). *Students:* 638 full-time (425 women), 2,014 part-time (1,635 women). Average age 33. *Entrance requirements:* For master's, 2 letters of recommendation, interview. Additional exam requirements/recommendations for international students: Required—TOEFL (minimum score 500 paper-based; 173 computer-based). *Application deadline:* For fall admission, 4/30 for domestic students. Applications are processed on a rolling basis. Application fee: $35. Electronic applications accepted. *Expenses: Tuition:* Part-time $534 per credit hour. *Required fees:* $25 per term. *Financial support:* Applicants required to submit FAFSA. *Unit head:* Dr. John C. Gray, Dean, 302-295-1139. *Application contact:* Chris Ferguson, Director of Admissions, 302-356-4636 Ext. 256, Fax: 302-328-5164, E-mail: inquire@wilmcoll.edu. Web site: http://www.wilmu.edu/education/.

Wingate University, Thayer School of Education, Wingate, NC 28174-0159. Offers community college leadership (Ed D); educational leadership (MA Ed, Ed D); elementary education (MA Ed, MAT); health and physical education (MA Ed); sport administration (MA Ed). *Accreditation:* NCATE. Part-time and evening/weekend programs available. *Faculty:* 5 full-time (3 women), 10 part-time/adjunct (3 women). *Students:* 7 full-time (4 women), 251 part-time (152 women); includes 68 minority (63 Black or African American, non-Hispanic/Latino; 1 American Indian or Alaska Native, non-Hispanic/Latino; 1 Asian, non-Hispanic/Latino; 3 Hispanic/Latino), 2 international. Average age 35. In 2011, 29 master's awarded. *Degree requirements:* For master's, portfolio. *Entrance requirements:* For master's, GRE General Test or MAT, teaching certificate (MA Ed). *Application deadline:* For fall admission, 8/15 priority date for domestic students; for spring admission, 12/15 for domestic students. Applications are processed on a rolling basis. Application fee: $0. *Expenses: Tuition:* Part-time $455 per credit hour. Part-time tuition and fees vary according to degree level and program. *Financial support:* In 2011–12, 20 students received support. Scholarships/grants available. Support available to part-time students. Financial award applicants required to submit FAFSA. *Unit head:* Dr. Sarah Harrison-Burns, Dean, 704-233-8128, E-mail: shburns@wingate.edu. *Application contact:* Theresa Hopkins, Secretary, 704-321-1470, Fax: 704-233-8273, E-mail: t.hopkins@wingate.edu.

Winona State University, College of Education, Department of Education Leadership, Winona, MN 55987. Offers educational leadership (Ed S), including general superintendency, K-12 principalship; general school leadership (MS); K-12 principalship (MS); outdoor education/adventure-based leadership (MS); sports management (MS); teacher leadership (MS). *Accreditation:* NCATE. Part-time and evening/weekend programs available. *Students:* 52 full-time (24 women), 57 part-time (18 women); includes 8 minority (5 Black or African American, non-Hispanic/Latino; 1 Asian, non-Hispanic/Latino; 1 Hispanic/Latino; 1 Two or more races, non-Hispanic/Latino), 3 international. Average age 34. In 2011, 17 master's, 10 other advanced degrees awarded. *Degree requirements:* For master's, comprehensive exam, thesis optional; for Ed S, thesis optional. *Application deadline:* For fall admission, 8/8 for domestic students; for spring admission, 12/10 for domestic students. Applications are processed on a rolling basis. Application fee: $20. *Financial support:* Federal Work-Study available. Support available to part-time students. Financial award applicants required to submit FAFSA. *Unit head:* Dr. George P. Morrow, Chair, 507-457-5346, Fax: 507-457-5882, E-mail: gmorrow@winona.edu. *Application contact:* Dr. George P. Morrow, 507-457-5346, Fax: 507-457-5882, E-mail: gmorrow@winona.edu. Web site: http://www.winona.edu/educationleadership/.

Winthrop University, College of Education, Program in Educational Leadership, Rock Hill, SC 29733. Offers M Ed. *Entrance requirements:* For master's, GRE General Test or MAT, 3 years of experience, South Carolina Class III Teaching Certificate, recommendations from current principal and district-level administrator, pre-entrance assessment. Electronic applications accepted.

Worcester State University, Graduate Studies, Department of Education, Program in Leadership and Administration, Worcester, MA 01602-2597. Offers M Ed, CAGS. Part-time programs available. *Faculty:* 12 full-time (9 women), 22 part-time/adjunct (10 women). *Students:* 65 part-time (42 women); includes 7 minority (2 Black or African American, non-Hispanic/Latino; 1 Asian, non-Hispanic/Latino; 3 Hispanic/Latino; 1 Two or more races, non-Hispanic/Latino). Average age 40. 80 applicants, 75% accepted, 29 enrolled. In 2011, 20 master's, 28 CAGSs awarded. *Degree requirements:* For master's, comprehensive exam (for some programs), thesis optional. *Entrance requirements:* For master's, GRE General Test or MAT, teaching certificate; for CAGS, Massachusetts Tests for Educator Licensure (communications and literacy skills), M Ed or master's degree in related field. Additional exam requirements/recommendations for international students: Required—TOEFL (minimum score 500 paper-based; 61 iBT). *Application deadline:* For fall admission, 6/15 for domestic and international students; for spring admission, 4/1 for domestic and international students. Applications are processed on a rolling basis. Application fee: $40. Electronic applications accepted. *Expenses:* Tuition, state resident: full-time $2700; part-time $150 per credit. Tuition, nonresident: full-time $2700; part-time $150 per credit. *Required fees:* $2016; $112 per credit. *Financial support:* Career-related internships or fieldwork, scholarships/grants, and unspecified assistantships available. Financial award application deadline: 3/1; financial award applicants required to submit FAFSA. *Unit head:* Dr. Audrey Wright, Coordinator, 508-929-8594, Fax: 508-929-8164, E-mail: awright1@worcester.edu. *Application contact:* Sara Grady, Assistant Dean of Graduate and Continuing Education, 508-929-8787, Fax: 508-929-8100, E-mail: sara.grady@worcester.edu.

Wright State University, School of Graduate Studies, College of Education and Human Services, Department of Educational Leadership, Program in Advanced Educational Leadership, Dayton, OH 45435. Offers advanced curriculum and instruction (Ed S); higher education-adult education (Ed S); superintendent (Ed S). *Accreditation:* NCATE. *Degree requirements:* For Ed S, thesis. *Entrance requirements:* For degree, GRE General Test, MAT. Additional exam requirements/recommendations for international students: Required—TOEFL.

Wright State University, School of Graduate Studies, College of Education and Human Services, Department of Educational Leadership, Programs in Educational Leadership, Dayton, OH 45435. Offers curriculum and instruction: teacher leader (MA); educational administrative specialist: teacher leader (M Ed); educational administrative specialist: vocational education administration (M Ed, MA); student affairs in higher education-administration (M Ed, MA). *Accreditation:* NCATE. *Degree requirements:* For master's, thesis (for some programs). *Entrance requirements:* For master's, GRE General Test, MAT. Additional exam requirements/recommendations for international students: Required—TOEFL.

Xavier University, College of Social Sciences, Health and Education, School of Education, Department of Educational Leadership and Human Resource Development, Program in Educational Administration, Cincinnati, OH 45207. Offers M Ed. Part-time and evening/weekend programs available. *Faculty:* 7 full-time (0 women), 18 part-time/adjunct (4 women). *Students:* 5 full-time (1 woman), 63 part-time (30 women); includes 8 minority (all Black or African American, non-Hispanic/Latino), 1 international. Average age 35. 12 applicants, 100% accepted, 10 enrolled. In 2011, 61 master's awarded. *Degree requirements:* For master's, comprehensive exam, thesis. *Entrance requirements:* For master's, MAT or GRE. *Application deadline:* Applications are processed on a rolling basis. Application fee: $35. Electronic applications accepted. *Expenses: Tuition:* Part-time $576 per credit hour. *Financial support:* In 2011–12, 34 students received support. Tuition waivers (partial) and unspecified assistantships available. Financial award applicants required to submit FAFSA. *Faculty research:* Educational leadership, hidden curriculum, internship effectiveness, neuroleadership, school leadership. *Unit head:* Dr. Leo Bradley, Chair, 513-745-3701, Fax: 513-745-3504, E-mail: bradley@xavier.edu. *Application contact:* Roger Bosse, Graduate Services Director, 513-745-3357, Fax: 513-745-1048, E-mail: bosse@xavier.edu. Web site: http://www.xavier.edu/administration-grad/.

Xavier University of Louisiana, Graduate School, Programs in Education, New Orleans, LA 70125-1098. Offers curriculum and instruction (MA); education administration and supervision (MA); guidance and counseling (MA). *Accreditation:* NCATE. Part-time and evening/weekend programs available. *Degree requirements:* For master's, comprehensive exam, thesis or alternative. *Entrance requirements:* For master's, GRE General Test, MAT, minimum GPA of 2.5. Additional exam requirements/recommendations for international students: Required—TOEFL.

Yeshiva University, Azrieli Graduate School of Jewish Education and Administration, New York, NY 10033-4391. Offers MS, Ed D, Specialist. Part-time and evening/weekend programs available. Terminal master's awarded for partial completion of doctoral program. *Degree requirements:* For master's, one foreign language, student teaching experience, comprehensive exam or thesis; for doctorate, one foreign language, comprehensive exam, thesis/dissertation, certifying exams, internship; for Specialist, one foreign language, comprehensive exam, certifying exams, internship. *Entrance requirements:* For master's, GRE General Test, BA in Jewish studies or equivalent; for doctorate and Specialist, GRE General Test, master's degree in Jewish education, 2 years of teaching experience. *Expenses:* Contact institution. *Faculty research:* Social patterns of American and Israeli Jewish population, special education, adult education, technology in education, return to religious values.

York College of Pennsylvania, Department of Education, York, PA 17405-7199. Offers educational leadership (M Ed); reading specialist (M Ed). Part-time and evening/weekend programs available. *Faculty:* 3 full-time (2 women), 4 part-time/adjunct (2 women). *Students:* 82 part-time (65 women). 10 applicants, 60% accepted, 5 enrolled. In 2011, 17 master's awarded. *Degree requirements:* For master's, comprehensive exam, thesis optional, portfolio. *Entrance requirements:* For master's, GRE, MAT or PRAXIS, letters of recommendation, portfolio. *Application deadline:* For fall admission, 7/15 priority date for domestic students; for spring admission, 11/15 priority date for domestic students. Applications are processed on a rolling basis. Application fee: $50. Electronic applications accepted. *Expenses: Tuition:* Full-time $12,060; part-time $670 per credit hour. *Required fees:* $340 per semester. Tuition and fees vary according to degree level. *Faculty research:* Mentoring, principal development, principal retention. *Unit head:* Dr. Philip Monteith, Director, 717-815-6406, E-mail: med@ycp.edu. *Application contact:* Irene Z. Altland, Administrative Assistant, 717-815-6406, Fax: 717-849-1629, E-mail: med@ycp.edu. Web site: http://www.ycp.edu/academics/academic-departments/education/.

Youngstown State University, Graduate School, Beeghly College of Education, Department of Educational Foundations, Research, Technology, and Leadership, Youngstown, OH 44555-0001. Offers educational administration (MS Ed); educational leadership (Ed D). *Accreditation:* NCATE. Part-time and evening/weekend programs available. *Degree requirements:* For master's, comprehensive exam; for doctorate, comprehensive exam, thesis/dissertation. *Entrance requirements:* For master's, GRE, MAT, or teaching certificate; minimum GPA of 2.7; for doctorate, GRE General Test, GRE Subject Test, interview, minimum GPA of 3.5. Additional exam requirements/recommendations for international students: Required—TOEFL. *Faculty research:* Administrative theory, computer applications, education law, school and community relations, finance principalship.

Educational Measurement and Evaluation

American InterContinental University Online, Program in Education, Hoffman Estates, IL 60192. Offers curriculum and instruction (M Ed); educational assessment and evaluation (M Ed); instructional technology (M Ed); leadership of educational organizations (M Ed). Evening/weekend programs available. Postbaccalaureate distance learning degree programs offered (no on-campus study). *Entrance requirements:* Additional exam requirements/recommendations for international students: Required—TOEFL (minimum score 550 paper-based; 213 computer-based). Electronic applications accepted.

Boston College, Lynch Graduate School of Education, Program in Educational Research, Measurement, and Evaluation, Chestnut Hill, MA 02467-3800. Offers M Ed, PhD. Part-time and evening/weekend programs available. *Students:* 37 full-time (29 women), 7 part-time (6 women); includes 8 minority (2 Black or African American, non-Hispanic/Latino; 2 Asian, non-Hispanic/Latino; 3 Hispanic/Latino; 1 Two or more races, non-Hispanic/Latino), 10 international. 68 applicants, 34% accepted, 13 enrolled. In 2011, 5 master's, 6 doctorates awarded. Terminal master's awarded for partial completion of doctoral program. *Degree requirements:* For master's, comprehensive exam; for doctorate, comprehensive exam, thesis/dissertation. *Entrance requirements:* For master's, GRE General Test or MAT; for doctorate, GRE General Test. Additional exam requirements/recommendations for international students: Required—TOEFL (minimum score 550 paper-based; 213 computer-based; 79 iBT). Application fee: $65. Electronic applications accepted. *Financial support:* Fellowships with full and partial tuition reimbursements, research assistantships with full and partial tuition reimbursements, teaching assistantships with full and partial tuition reimbursements, career-related internships or fieldwork, Federal Work-Study, institutionally sponsored loans, scholarships/grants, traineeships, health care benefits, tuition waivers (full and partial), and unspecified assistantships available. Support available to part-time students. Financial award applicants required to submit FAFSA. *Faculty research:* Testing and educational public policy, statistical modeling, classroom use of technology, international comparisons of student achievement, psychometrics. *Unit head:* Dr. Larry Ludlow, Chairperson, 617-552-4214, Fax: 617-552-0398. *Application contact:* Adam Poluzzi, Director, Graduate Admission and Financial Aid, 617-552-4214, Fax: 617-552-0398, E-mail: poluzzi@bc.edu.

Cambridge College, School of Education, Cambridge, MA 02138-5304. Offers autism specialist (M Ed); autism/behavior analyst (M Ed); behavior analyst (Post-Master's Certificate); behavioral management (M Ed); early childhood teacher (M Ed); education specialist in curriculum and instruction (CAGS); educational leadership (Ed D); elementary teacher (M Ed); English as a second language (M Ed, Certificate); general science (M Ed); health education (Post-Master's Certificate); health/family and consumer sciences (M Ed); history (M Ed); individualized (M Ed); information technology literacy (M Ed); instructional technology (M Ed); interdisciplinary studies (M Ed); library teacher (M Ed); literacy education (M Ed); mathematics (M Ed); mathematics specialist (Certificate); middle school mathematics and science (M Ed); school administration (M Ed, CAGS); school guidance counselor (M Ed); school nurse education (M Ed); school social worker/school adjustment counselor (M Ed); special education administrator (CAGS); special education/moderate disabilities (M Ed); teaching skills and methodologies (M Ed). Part-time and evening/weekend programs available. Postbaccalaureate distance learning degree programs offered (minimal on-campus study). *Degree requirements:* For master's, thesis, internship/practicum (licensure program only); for doctorate, thesis/dissertation; for other advanced degree, thesis. *Entrance requirements:* For master's, interview, resume, documentation of licensure, 2 professional references; for doctorate, official transcripts, interview, resume, documentation of licensure (if any), written personal statement/essay, portfolio of scholarly and professional work, qualifying assessment, 2 professional references, health insurance, immunizations form; for other advanced degree, official transcripts, interview, resume, documentation of licensure (if any), written personal statement/essay, 2 professional references, health insurance, immunizations form. Additional exam requirements/recommendations for international students: Required—TOEFL (minimum score 550 paper-based; 213 computer-based; 79 iBT); Recommended—IELTS (minimum score 6). Electronic applications accepted. *Expenses:* Contact institution. *Faculty research:* Adult education, accelerated learning, mathematics education, brain compatible learning, special education and law.

Claremont Graduate University, Graduate Programs, School of Educational Studies, Claremont, CA 91711-6160. Offers Africana education (Certificate); education and policy (MA, PhD); higher education/student affairs (MA, PhD); human development (MA, PhD); public school administration (MA, PhD); quantitative evaluation (MA, PhD); special education (MA, PhD); teacher education (MA); teaching and learning (MA, PhD); urban leadership (PhD); MBA/PhD. PhD program offered jointly with San Diego State University. Part-time programs available. *Faculty:* 18 full-time (10 women), 2 part-time/adjunct (1 woman). *Students:* 307 full-time (220 women), 134 part-time (96 women); includes 228 minority (59 Black or African American, non-Hispanic/Latino; 3 American Indian or Alaska Native, non-Hispanic/Latino; 37 Asian, non-Hispanic/Latino; 110 Hispanic/Latino; 2 Native Hawaiian or other Pacific Islander, non-Hispanic/Latino; 17 Two or more races, non-Hispanic/Latino), 13 international. Average age 38. In 2011, 93 master's, 23 doctorates, 10 other advanced degrees awarded. Terminal master's awarded for partial completion of doctoral program. *Entrance requirements:* For master's and doctorate, GRE General Test. Additional exam requirements/recommendations for international students: Required—TOEFL (minimum score 550 paper-based; 213 computer-based; 80 iBT). *Application deadline:* For fall admission, 2/1 priority date for domestic students. Applications are processed on a rolling basis. Application fee: $60. Electronic applications accepted. *Expenses: Tuition:* Full-time $36,374; part-time $1581 per unit. *Required fees:* $165 per semester. *Financial support:* Fellowships, research assistantships, Federal Work-Study, institutionally sponsored loans, and scholarships/grants available. Support available to part-time students. Financial award application deadline: 2/15; financial award applicants required to submit FAFSA. *Faculty research:* Education administration, K-12 and higher education, multicultural education, education policy, diversity in higher education, faculty issues. *Unit head:* Margaret Grogan, Dean, 909-621-8075, Fax: 909-621-8734, E-mail: margaret.grogan@cgu.edu. *Application contact:* Julia Evans, Director of Central Recruitment, 909-607-3689, Fax: 909-607-7285, E-mail: admiss@cgu.edu. Web site: http://www.cgu.edu/pages/267.asp.

College of Saint Mary, Program in Education, Omaha, NE 68106. Offers assessment leadership (MSE); English as a second language (MSE). Part-time programs available. *Entrance requirements:* For master's, technology competency test or equivalent, minimum cumulative GPA of 3.0, teaching certificate, 2 letters of reference, resume.

Duquesne University, School of Education, Department of Foundations and Leadership, Pittsburgh, PA 15282-0001. Offers counselor education and supervision (PhD); educational leadership (Ed D); educational studies (MS Ed); program evaluation (MS Ed); school administration and supervision (MS Ed, Post-Master's Certificate), including curriculum and instruction (Post-Master's Certificate), school administration K-12, school supervision (MS Ed). Part-time and evening/weekend programs available. Postbaccalaureate distance learning degree programs offered (no on-campus study). *Faculty:* 16 full-time (7 women). *Students:* 78 full-time (45 women), 40 part-time (35 women); includes 17 minority (14 Black or African American, non-Hispanic/Latino; 2 Hispanic/Latino; 1 Two or more races, non-Hispanic/Latino), 17 international. Average age 38. 131 applicants, 37% accepted, 41 enrolled. In 2011, 45 master's, 3 doctorates awarded. *Degree requirements:* For master's, thesis optional; for doctorate, thesis/dissertation optional. *Entrance requirements:* For master's, letters of recommendation, letter of intent, essay, interview, bachelor's degree; for doctorate, GRE, letters of recommendation, letter of intent, essay, interview, master's degree; for Post-Master's Certificate, letters of recommendation, letter of intent, essay, interview, bachelor's/master's degree. Additional exam requirements/recommendations for international students: Required—TOEFL (minimum score 550 paper-based; 80 computer-based), IELTS (minimum score 7). *Application deadline:* For fall admission, 9/1 for domestic students; for spring admission, 3/1 for domestic students. Applications are processed on a rolling basis. Application fee: $0. Electronic applications accepted. Application fee is waived when completed online. *Expenses: Tuition:* Full-time $16,596; part-time $922 per credit. *Required fees:* $1584; $88 per credit. Tuition and fees vary according to program. *Financial support:* Research assistantships available. Support available to part-time students. *Unit head:* Dr. Launcelot Brown, Chair, 412-396-1046, Fax: 412-396-6017, E-mail: brownli@duq.edu. *Application contact:* Michael Dolinger, Director of Student and Academic Services, 412-396-6647, Fax: 412-396-5585, E-mail: dolingerm@duq.edu.

Eastern Michigan University, Graduate School, College of Education, Department of Teacher Education, Programs in Educational Psychology and Assessment, Ypsilanti, MI 48197. Offers educational assessment (Graduate Certificate); educational psychology (MA), including development/personality, research and assessment, research and evaluation, the developing learner. *Accreditation:* NCATE. Part-time and evening/weekend programs available. Postbaccalaureate distance learning degree programs offered (minimal on-campus study). *Students:* 2 full-time (both women), 58 part-time (55 women); includes 8 minority (all Black or African American, non-Hispanic/Latino), 3 international. Average age 33. 27 applicants, 74% accepted, 13 enrolled. In 2011, 8 degrees awarded. *Degree requirements:* For master's, thesis or alternative. *Entrance* *requirements:* For master's, GRE. Additional exam requirements/recommendations for international students: Required—TOEFL. *Application deadline:* Applications are processed on a rolling basis. Application fee: $35. *Expenses:* Tuition, state resident: full-time $10,367; part-time $432 per credit hour. Tuition, nonresident: full-time $20,435; part-time $851 per credit hour. *Required fees:* $39 per credit hour. $46 per semester. One-time fee: $100. Tuition and fees vary according to course level, degree level and reciprocity agreements. *Financial support:* Fellowships, research assistantships with full tuition reimbursements, teaching assistantships with full tuition reimbursements, career-related internships or fieldwork, Federal Work-Study, institutionally sponsored loans, scholarships/grants, tuition waivers (partial), and unspecified assistantships available. Support available to part-time students. Financial award applicants required to submit FAFSA. *Unit head:* Dr. Pat Pokay, Coordinator, 734-487-3260, Fax: 734-487-2101, E-mail: ppokay@emich.edu. *Application contact:* Dr. Anne Bednar, Advisor, 734-487-3260, Fax: 734-487-2101, E-mail: anne.bednar@emich.edu.

Florida State University, The Graduate School, College of Education, Department of Educational Leadership and Policy Studies, Program in Program Evaluation, Tallahassee, FL 32306. Offers MS, PhD, Ed S. *Faculty:* 1 (woman) full-time. *Students:* 4 part-time (all women); includes 2 minority (both Black or African American, non-Hispanic/Latino). Average age 45. 1 applicant, 0% accepted. In 2011, 2 degrees awarded. *Median time to degree:* Of those who began their doctoral program in fall 2003, 100% received their degree in 8 years or less. *Degree requirements:* For master's and doctorate, comprehensive exam. *Entrance requirements:* Additional exam requirements/recommendations for international students: Required—TOEFL (minimum score 550 paper-based; 213 computer-based; 80 iBT). *Application deadline:* For fall admission, 7/1 for domestic and international students; for winter admission, 11/1 for domestic and international students; for spring admission, 3/1 for domestic and international students. Application fee: $30. Electronic applications accepted. *Expenses:* Tuition, state resident: full-time $9474; part-time $350.88 per credit hour. Tuition, nonresident: full-time $16,236; part-time $601.34 per credit hour. *Required fees:* $630 per semester. One-time fee: $20. Tuition and fees vary according to course load and campus/location. *Financial support:* Fellowships with full and partial tuition reimbursements, research assistantships with full and partial tuition reimbursements, teaching assistantships with full and partial tuition reimbursements, career-related internships or fieldwork, scholarships/grants, health care benefits, and unspecified assistantships available. *Faculty research:* Evaluation services for state, federal and human resource organizations; career counseling. *Unit head:* Dr. Linda Schrader, Head, 850-644-6777, Fax: 850-644-1258, E-mail: lschrader@fsu.edu. *Application contact:* Jimmy Pastrano, Program Assistant, 850-644-6777, Fax: 850-644-1258, E-mail: jpastrano@fsu.edu. Web site: http://www.coe.fsu.edu/Academic-Programs/Departments/Educational-Leadership-and-Policy-Studies-ELPS/Academic-Programs/Degree-Programs/Educational-Lead.

Florida State University, The Graduate School, College of Education, Department of Educational Psychology and Learning Systems, Program in Measurement and Statistics, Tallahassee, FL 32306. Offers MS, PhD, Ed S. *Faculty:* 4 full-time (2 women). *Students:* 28 full-time (17 women), 6 part-time (0 women); includes 3 minority (2 Black or African American, non-Hispanic/Latino; 1 Asian, non-Hispanic/Latino), 23 international. Average age 33. 15 applicants, 67% accepted, 2 enrolled. In 2011, 2 master's, 4 doctorates awarded. *Median time to degree:* Of those who began their doctoral program in fall 2003, 67% received their degree in 8 years or less. *Degree requirements:* For master's, comprehensive exam; for doctorate, comprehensive exam, thesis/dissertation, preliminary exam, prospectus. *Entrance requirements:* Additional exam requirements/recommendations for international students: Required—TOEFL (minimum score 550 paper-based; 213 computer-based; 80 iBT). *Application deadline:* For fall admission, 7/1 for domestic and international students; for winter admission, 11/1 for domestic and international students; for spring admission, 3/1 for domestic and international students. Application fee: $30. Electronic applications accepted. *Expenses:* Tuition, state resident: full-time $9474; part-time $350.88 per credit hour. Tuition, nonresident: full-time $16,236; part-time $601.34 per credit hour. *Required fees:* $630 per semester. One-time fee: $20. Tuition and fees vary according to course load and campus/location. *Financial support:* Fellowships with full and partial tuition reimbursements, research assistantships with full and partial tuition reimbursements, teaching assistantships with full and partial tuition reimbursements, Federal Work-Study, scholarships/grants, health care benefits, and unspecified assistantships available. *Faculty research:* Methods for meta analysis; IRT/mixIRT; CBT; modeling, especially of large data sets. *Unit head:* Dr. Betsy Becker, Program Leader, 850-645-2371, Fax: 850-644-8776, E-mail: bbecker@fsu.edu. *Application contact:* Peggy Lollie, Program Assistant, 850-644-8786, Fax: 850-644-8776, E-mail: plollie@fsu.edu.

George Mason University, College of Education and Human Development, Program in New Professional Studies, Fairfax, VA 22030. Offers MA. *Expenses:* Tuition, state resident: full-time $8750; part-time $364.58 per credit. Tuition, nonresident: full-time $24,092; part-time $1003.83 per credit. *Required fees:* $2514; $104.75 per credit. *Financial support:* Career-related internships or fieldwork, Federal Work-Study, scholarships/grants, unspecified assistantships, and health care benefits (full-time research or teaching assistantship recipients) available. Financial award applicants required to submit FAFSA. Web site: http://gse.gmu.edu/iet/academics/.

Georgia State University, College of Education, Department of Educational Policy Studies, Program in Educational Research, Atlanta, GA 30302-3083. Offers educational research (MS); research, measurements and statistics (PhD). *Accreditation:* NCATE. *Degree requirements:* For master's, thesis or project; for doctorate, comprehensive exam, thesis/dissertation. *Entrance requirements:* For master's, GRE General Test, minimum GPA of 2.5, 2 letters of recommendation, resume; for doctorate, GRE General Test or MAT, minimum GPA of 3.3, goals statement, 2 letters of recommendation, resum/curriculum vitae. Electronic applications accepted. *Faculty research:* Educational statistics, item response theory, instructional computing, measurement.

Harvard University, Harvard Graduate School of Education, Doctoral Program in Education, Cambridge, MA 02138. Offers culture, communities and education (Ed D); education policy, leadership and instructional practice (Ed D); higher education (Ed D); human development and education (Ed D); quantitative policy analysis in education (Ed D). *Faculty:* 83 full-time (44 women), 67 part-time/adjunct (29 women). *Students:* 251 full-time (172 women), 16 part-time (7 women); includes 87 minority (32 Black or African American, non-Hispanic/Latino; 1 American Indian or Alaska Native, non-Hispanic/Latino; 26 Asian, non-Hispanic/Latino; 22 Hispanic/Latino; 1 Native Hawaiian or other Pacific Islander, non-Hispanic/Latino; 5 Two or more races, non-Hispanic/Latino), 30 international. Average age 34. 545 applicants, 7% accepted, 28 enrolled. In 2011, 47 doctorates awarded. Terminal master's awarded for partial completion of doctoral program. *Degree requirements:* For doctorate, thesis/dissertation. *Entrance requirements:* For doctorate, GRE General Test, statement of purpose, 3 letters of recommendation, resume, official transcripts. Additional exam requirements/recommendations for international students: Required—TOEFL (minimum score 613 paper-based; 104 computer-based; 100 iBT), TWE (minimum score 5). *Application deadline:* For fall admission, 12/14 for domestic and international students. Application fee: $85. Electronic applications accepted. *Expenses:* Contact institution. *Financial support:* In 2011–12, 203 students received support, including 62 fellowships with full and partial tuition reimbursements available (averaging $13,939 per year), 35 research assistantships (averaging $9,534 per year), 134 teaching assistantships (averaging $10,748 per year); career-related internships or fieldwork, Federal Work-Study, institutionally sponsored loans, scholarships/grants, health care benefits, tuition waivers (full and partial), and unspecified assistantships also available. Support available to part-time students. Financial award application deadline: 2/1; financial award applicants required to submit FAFSA. *Faculty research:* Learning and development, educational leadership and organizations, education policy analysis. *Total annual research expenditures:* $26 million. *Unit head:* Dr. Shu-Ling Chen, Assistant Dean, 617-496-4406. *Application contact:* Information Contact, 617-495-3414, Fax: 617-496-3577, E-mail: gseadmissions@harvard.edu. Web site: http://gse.harvard.edu/.

Houston Baptist University, College of Education and Behavioral Sciences, Programs in Education, Houston, TX 77074-3298. Offers bilingual education (M Ed); counselor education (M Ed); curriculum and instruction (M Ed); educational administration (M Ed); educational diagnostician (M Ed); reading education (M Ed). Part-time programs available. *Entrance requirements:* For master's, GRE General Test or MAT. Additional exam requirements/recommendations for international students: Required—TOEFL (minimum score 550 paper-based; 213 computer-based).

Indiana University Bloomington, School of Education, Department of Counseling and Educational Psychology, Bloomington, IN 47405-1006. Offers counseling (MS, PhD, Ed S); counselor education (MS, Ed S); educational psychology (MS, PhD); inquiry methodology (PhD); learning and developmental sciences (MS, PhD); school psychology (PhD, Ed S). *Accreditation:* ACA (one or more programs are accredited); APA (one or more programs are accredited); NCATE. Terminal master's awarded for partial completion of doctoral program. *Degree requirements:* For master's, thesis optional; for doctorate, thesis/dissertation; for Ed S, comprehensive exam or project. *Entrance requirements:* For master's, doctorate, and Ed S, GRE General Test. Additional exam requirements/recommendations for international students: Required—TOEFL. Electronic applications accepted. *Faculty research:* Counseling psychology, inquiry methodology, school psychology, learning sciences, human development, educational psychology.

Indiana University Bloomington, School of Education, Program in Inquiry Methodology, Bloomington, IN 47405-7000. Offers PhD.

Iowa State University of Science and Technology, Department of Educational Leadership and Policy Studies, Ames, IA 50011. Offers counselor education (M Ed, MS); educational administration (M Ed, MS); educational leadership (PhD); higher education (M Ed, MS); organizational learning and human resource development (M Ed, MS); research and evaluation (MS); student affairs (MS). *Degree requirements:* For master's, thesis or alternative; for doctorate, thesis/dissertation. *Entrance requirements:* For master's and doctorate, GRE General Test. Additional exam requirements/recommendations for international students: Required—TOEFL (minimum score 560 paper-based; 83 iBT), IELTS (minimum score 6.5). *Application deadline:* For fall admission, 1/1 priority date for domestic students, 1/1 for international students. Application fee: $40 ($90 for international students). Electronic applications accepted. *Unit head:* Dr. Daniel Robinson, Director of Graduate Education, 515-294-1241, Fax: 515-294-4942, E-mail: edldrshp@iastate.edu. *Application contact:* Judy Weiland, Application Contact, 515-294-1241, Fax: 515-294-4942, E-mail: eldrshp@iastate.edu. Web site: http://www.elps.hs.iastate.edu/.

Kent State University, Graduate School of Education, Health, and Human Services, School of Foundations, Leadership and Administration, Program in Evaluation and Measurement, Kent, OH 44242-0001. Offers M Ed, PhD. *Faculty:* 4 full-time (2 women), 3 part-time/adjunct (1 woman). *Students:* 14 full-time (8 women), 26 part-time (19 women); includes 3 minority (2 Black or African American, non-Hispanic/Latino; 1 Asian, non-Hispanic/Latino). 24 applicants, 38% accepted. In 2011, 29 master's, 2 doctorates awarded. *Degree requirements:* For doctorate, comprehensive exam, thesis/dissertation. *Entrance requirements:* For master's, minimum GPA of 2.75, 2 letters of reference, goals statement; for doctorate, GRE, minimum GPA of 3.5 from master's degree, resume, 2 letters of reference, goal statement. Additional exam requirements/recommendations for international students: Required—TOEFL (minimum score 550 paper-based; 213 computer-based; 80 iBT). Application fee: $30 ($60 for international students). *Expenses:* Tuition, state resident: full-time $8136; part-time $452 per credit hour. Tuition, nonresident: full-time $14,292; part-time $794 per credit hour. *Financial support:* In 2011–12, 1 fellowship (averaging $12,000 per year), 4 research assistantships (averaging $12,000 per year), teaching assistantships (averaging $12,000 per year) were awarded; career-related internships or fieldwork, Federal Work-Study, institutionally sponsored loans, scholarships/grants, health care benefits, unspecified assistantships, and 2 administrative assistantships (averaging $10,250 per year) also available. Support available to part-time students. *Unit head:* Dr. Tricia Niesz, Coordinator, 330-672-0591, E-mail: tniesz@kent.edu. *Application contact:* Nancy Miller, Academic Program Coordinator, Office of Graduate Student Services, 330-672-2576, Fax: 330-672-9162, E-mail: ogs@kent.edu. Web site: http://www.kent.edu/ehhs/eval/.

Louisiana State University and Agricultural and Mechanical College, Graduate School, College of Education, Department of Educational Theory, Policy and Practice, Baton Rouge, LA 70803. Offers counseling (M Ed, MA, Ed S); educational administration (M Ed, MA, PhD, Ed S); educational technology (MA); elementary education (M Ed, MAT); higher education (PhD); research methodology (PhD); secondary education (M Ed, MAT). PhD programs offered jointly with Louisiana State University in Shreveport. *Accreditation:* ACA (one or more programs are accredited); NCATE. Part-time and evening/weekend programs available. *Faculty:* 17 full-time (all women). *Students:* 188 full-time (145 women), 161 part-time (130 women); includes 104 minority (88 Black or African American, non-Hispanic/Latino; 1 American Indian or Alaska Native, non-Hispanic/Latino; 6 Asian, non-Hispanic/Latino; 5 Hispanic/Latino; 4 Two or more races, non-Hispanic/Latino), 9 international. Average age 31. 151 applicants, 61% accepted, 58 enrolled. In 2011, 129 master's, 17 doctorates, 11 other advanced degrees awarded. Terminal master's awarded for partial completion of doctoral program. *Degree requirements:* For doctorate, thesis/dissertation; for Ed S, thesis optional. *Entrance requirements:* For master's and doctorate, GRE General Test, minimum GPA of 3.0. Additional exam requirements/recommendations for international students: Required—TOEFL (minimum score 550 paper-based; 213 computer-based; 79 iBT) or IELTS (minimum score 6.5). *Application deadline:* For fall admission, 1/25 priority date for domestic students, 5/15 for international students; for spring admission, 10/15 for international students. Applications are processed on a rolling basis. Application fee: $50 ($70 for international students). Electronic applications accepted. *Financial support:* In 2011–12, 230 students received support, including 2 fellowships (averaging $19,353 per year), 24 research assistantships with full and partial tuition reimbursements available (averaging $10,052 per year), 53 teaching assistantships with full and partial tuition reimbursements available (averaging $12,218 per year); career-related internships or fieldwork, Federal Work-Study, institutionally sponsored loans, health care benefits, and unspecified assistantships also available. Support available to part-time students. Financial award applicants required to submit FAFSA. *Faculty research:* Literary, curriculum studies, science education, K-12 leadership, higher education. *Total annual research expenditures:* $774,887. *Unit head:* Dr. Earl Cheek, Jr., Chair, 225-578-6867, Fax: 225-578-9135, E-mail: echeek@lsu.edu. *Application* *contact:* Dr. Rita Culross, Graduate Coordinator, 225-578-6867, Fax: 225-578-9135, E-mail: acrita@lsu.edu.

Loyola University Chicago, School of Education, Program in Research Methods, Chicago, IL 60660. Offers M Ed, MA, PhD. MA and PhD offered through the Graduate School. Part-time and evening/weekend programs available. *Faculty:* 3 full-time (all women), 2 part-time/adjunct (both women). *Students:* 23. Average age 25. 9 applicants, 89% accepted, 8 enrolled. In 2011, 1 master's, 2 doctorates awarded. *Degree requirements:* For master's, comprehensive exam (M Ed), thesis (MA); for doctorate, comprehensive exam, thesis/dissertation. *Entrance requirements:* For master's, GRE General Test, letters of recommendation, resume, minimum GPA of 3.0; for doctorate, GRE General Test, interview. Additional exam requirements/recommendations for international students: Required—TOEFL (minimum score 550 paper-based; 213 computer-based; 79 iBT). *Application deadline:* For fall admission, 12/1 for domestic and international students. Applications are processed on a rolling basis. Application fee: $50. Electronic applications accepted. Application fee is waived when completed online. *Expenses: Tuition:* Full-time $15,660; part-time $870 per credit hour. *Required fees:* $125 per semester. Tuition and fees vary according to course load and program. *Financial support:* In 2011–12, 3 research assistantships with full tuition reimbursements (averaging $12,000 per year) were awarded; institutionally sponsored loans, scholarships/grants, health care benefits, and unspecified assistantships also available. Support available to part-time students. Financial award application deadline: 2/1; financial award applicants required to submit FAFSA. *Faculty research:* Circular statistics, program evaluation, psychological measurement, infant attachment, adolescent development. *Unit head:* Dr. Pamela Fenning, Director, 312-915-6803, E-mail: pfennin@luc.edu. *Application contact:* Marie Rosin-Dittmar, Information Contact, 312-915-6800, E-mail: schleduc@luc.edu.

McNeese State University, Doré School of Graduate Studies, Burton College of Education, Department of Education Professions, Program in Special Education, Lake Charles, LA 70609. Offers autism (M Ed); educational diagnostician (M Ed); mild moderate (M Ed). *Faculty:* 10 full-time (5 women). *Students:* 10 part-time (8 women); includes 2 minority (both Black or African American, non-Hispanic/Latino). In 2011, 1 master's awarded. *Entrance requirements:* For master's, GRE, teaching certificate. *Application deadline:* For fall admission, 5/15 priority date for domestic students, 5/15 for international students; for spring admission, 10/15 priority date for domestic students, 10/15 for international students. Applications are processed on a rolling basis. Application fee: $20 ($30 for international students). *Expenses:* Tuition, state resident: part-time $519 per credit hour. Tuition and fees vary according to course load. *Financial support:* Application deadline: 5/1. *Unit head:* Dr. Dustin M. Hebert, Director, 337-475-5424, Fax: 337-475-5272, E-mail: dhebert@mcneese.edu. *Application contact:* Dr. George F. Mead, Jr., Interim Dean of Dore' School of Graduate Studies, 337-475-5396, Fax: 337-475-5397, E-mail: admissions@mcneese.edu.

Michigan State University, The Graduate School, College of Education, Department of Counseling, Educational Psychology and Special Education, East Lansing, MI 48824. Offers counseling (MA); educational psychology and educational technology (PhD); educational technology (MA); measurement and quantitative methods (PhD); rehabilitation counseling (MA); rehabilitation counselor education (PhD); school psychology (MA, PhD, Ed S); special education (MA, PhD). *Accreditation:* APA (one or more programs are accredited); CORE (one or more programs are accredited). Part-time programs available. *Entrance requirements:* Additional exam requirements/ recommendations for international students: Required—TOEFL. Electronic applications accepted.

Missouri Western State University, Program in Assessment, St. Joseph, MO 64507-2294. Offers autism spectrum disorders (MAS); learning improvement (MAS); TESOL (MAS); writing (MAS). Part-time programs available. In 2011, 10 degrees awarded. *Application deadline:* Applications are processed on a rolling basis. Application fee: $45 ($50 for international students). Electronic applications accepted. *Expenses:* Tuition, state resident: full-time $4697; part-time $261 per credit hour. Tuition, nonresident: full-time $9355; part-time $520 per credit hour. *Required fees:* $343; $19.10 per credit hour. $30 per semester. Tuition and fees vary according to course load. *Application contact:* Dr. Brian C. Cronk, Dean of the Graduate School, 816-271-4394, E-mail: graduate@missouriwestern.edu.

North Carolina State University, Graduate School, College of Education, Department of Educational Leadership and Policy Studies, Program in Educational Research and Policy Analysis, Raleigh, NC 27695. Offers PhD. *Degree requirements:* For doctorate, thesis/dissertation. *Entrance requirements:* For doctorate, GRE General Test, minimum GPA of 3.0, interview, sample of work. Electronic applications accepted.

Ohio University, Graduate College, Gladys W. and David H. Patton College of Education and Human Services, Department of Educational Studies, Athens, OH 45701-2979. Offers computer education and technology (M Ed); cultural studies (M Ed); educational administration (M Ed, Ed D); educational research and evaluation (M Ed, PhD); instructional technology (PhD). Part-time and evening/weekend programs available. Postbaccalaureate distance learning degree programs offered (minimal on-campus study). *Students:* 121 full-time (76 women), 94 part-time (57 women); includes 21 minority (15 Black or African American, non-Hispanic/Latino; 1 American Indian or Alaska Native, non-Hispanic/Latino; 2 Hispanic/Latino; 3 Two or more races, non-Hispanic/Latino), 35 international. 73 applicants, 67% accepted, 32 enrolled. In 2011, 52 master's, 13 doctorates awarded. *Degree requirements:* For master's, thesis or alternative; for doctorate, comprehensive exam, thesis/dissertation. *Entrance requirements:* For master's, GRE General Test (if GPA less than 2.9); for doctorate, GRE General Test, GRE Subject Test, minimum GPA of 2.9, work experience, 3 letters of reference, autobiography. Additional exam requirements/recommendations for international students: Required—TOEFL (minimum score 550 paper-based; 80 iBT) or IELTS (minimum score 6.5). *Application deadline:* For fall admission, 3/1 priority date for domestic students, 3/1 for international students; for winter admission, 10/1 priority date for domestic students, 10/1 for international students; for spring admission, 1/30 priority date for domestic students, 1/1 for international students. Applications are processed on a rolling basis. Application fee: $50 ($55 for international students). Electronic applications accepted. *Financial support:* Research assistantships with full tuition reimbursements, teaching assistantships with full tuition reimbursements, Federal Work-Study, institutionally sponsored loans, tuition waivers (partial), and unspecified assistantships available. Financial award application deadline: 3/1. *Faculty research:* Race, class and gender; computer programs; development and organization theory; evaluation/development of instruments, leadership. *Total annual research expenditures:* $158,037. *Unit head:* Dr. David Richard Moore, Chair, 740-597-1322, Fax: 740-593-0477, E-mail: moored3@ohio.edu. *Application contact:* Floyd J. Doney, Director of Student Affairs, 740-593-4400, Fax: 740-593-9310, E-mail: doney@ohio.edu. Web site: http://www.cehs.ohio.edu/academics/es/.

Regent University, Graduate School, School of Education, Virginia Beach, VA 23464-9800. Offers adult education (Ed D); adult/staff development (Ed D, PhD); career switcher with licensure (M Ed), including alternative licensure; character education (Ed D, PhD); Christian education leadership (Ed D, PhD); Christian education specialist (Ed S); Christian school program (M Ed), including ACSI licensure; distance education (Ed D, PhD); education licensure (M Ed), including preK-6th grade; educational leadership (M Ed, PhD); educational leadership - special education (Ed S), including administration and supervision; educational psychology (Ed D, PhD), including learning and development, research and evaluation, special education; higher education (Ed D, PhD), including administration, research and institutional planning, teaching; higher education leadership (Ed D); individualized degree plan (M Ed), including behavior disorders, learning disabilities, mental retardation, reading specialist; K-12 school leadership (Ed D, PhD); leadership in character education (M Ed); master teacher (M Ed), including TESOL; mathematics education (M Ed); special education (PhD); student affairs (M Ed); TESOL (M Ed), including adult education, ESL: preK-12. *Accreditation:* Teacher Education Accreditation Council. Part-time and evening/weekend programs available. Postbaccalaureate distance learning degree programs offered (minimal on-campus study). *Faculty:* 26 full-time (13 women), 54 part-time/adjunct (34 women). *Students:* 140 full-time (109 women), 786 part-time (626 women); includes 218 minority (189 Black or African American, non-Hispanic/Latino; 2 American Indian or Alaska Native, non-Hispanic/Latino; 11 Asian, non-Hispanic/Latino; 16 Hispanic/Latino), 42 international. Average age 39. 673 applicants, 57% accepted, 298 enrolled. In 2011, 178 master's, 15 doctorates awarded. *Degree requirements:* For master's, thesis or alternative; for doctorate, comprehensive exam, thesis/dissertation. *Entrance requirements:* For master's, MAT, minimum undergraduate GPA of 2.75, writing sample, resume, recommendations, interview; for doctorate, GRE, writing sample, 3 years of relevant professional experience, master's-level paper, copies of published work, resume, transcripts, interview, recommendations. Additional exam requirements/ recommendations for international students: Required—TOEFL (minimum score 577 paper-based; 233 computer-based). *Application deadline:* For fall admission, 4/1 priority date for domestic students; for spring admission, 10/15 priority date for domestic students. Applications are processed on a rolling basis. Application fee: $50. Electronic applications accepted. *Expenses:* Contact institution. *Financial support:* Fellowships, career-related internships or fieldwork, scholarships/grants, tuition waivers (full and partial), and unspecified assistantships available. Support available to part-time students. Financial award application deadline: 4/1; financial award applicants required to submit FAFSA. *Faculty research:* Character development and discipline for children, education leadership development, diversity in schools, classroom management, technology in education settings. *Unit head:* Dr. Alan A. Arroyo, Dean, 757-352-4261, Fax: 757-352-4318, E-mail: alanarr@regent.edu. *Application contact:* Matthew Chadwick, Director of Enrollment Support Services, 800-373-5504, Fax: 757-352-4381, E-mail: admissions@regent.edu. Web site: http://www.regent.edu/education/.

Rutgers, The State University of New Jersey, New Brunswick, Graduate School of Education, Department of Educational Psychology, Program in Educational Statistics, Measurement and Evaluation, Piscataway, NJ 08854-8097. Offers Ed M. Part-time and evening/weekend programs available. *Entrance requirements:* For master's, GRE General Test, 3 letters of recommendation. Additional exam requirements/ recommendations for international students: Required—TOEFL (minimum score 550 paper-based; 233 computer-based; 83 iBT). Electronic applications accepted. *Faculty research:* Program evaluation of student assessment, Type I error and power comparisons, test performance factors, theory building in participatory program evaluation, test validity in higher education admissions.

Seton Hall University, College of Education and Human Services, Department of Education Leadership, Management and Policy, South Orange, NJ 07079-2697. Offers college student personnel administration (MA); education research, assessment and program evaluation (PhD); higher education administration (Ed D, PhD); human resource training and development (MA); K–12 administration and supervision (Ed D, Exec Ed D, Ed S); K–12 leadership, management and policy (Ed D, Exec Ed D, Ed S). Part-time and evening/weekend programs available. Postbaccalaureate distance learning degree programs offered (no on-campus study). *Faculty:* 15 full-time (7 women), 21 part-time/adjunct (4 women). *Students:* 73 full-time (34 women), 402 part-time (176 women); includes 186 minority (119 Black or African American, non-Hispanic/ Latino; 1 American Indian or Alaska Native, non-Hispanic/Latino; 10 Asian, non-Hispanic/Latino; 55 Hispanic/Latino; 1 Native Hawaiian or other Pacific Islander, non-Hispanic/Latino), 17 international. Average age 39. 135 applicants, 87% accepted, 90 enrolled. In 2011, 143 master's, 35 doctorates, 47 other advanced degrees awarded. *Degree requirements:* For master's, comprehensive exam, thesis or alternative; for doctorate, thesis/dissertation, oral exam, written exam; for Ed S, internship, research project. *Entrance requirements:* For master's, GRE or MAT, minimum GPA of 3.0; for doctorate, GRE or MAT, interview, minimum GPA of 3.5; for Ed S, GRE or MAT, minimum GPA of 3.5. *Application deadline:* Applications are processed on a rolling basis. Application fee: $50. *Expenses: Tuition:* Part-time $1033 per credit hour. *Required fees:* $85 per semester. *Financial support:* In 2011–12, 2 research assistantships with full tuition reimbursements (averaging $4,500 per year) were awarded; unspecified assistantships also available. Financial award application deadline: 2/1; financial award applicants required to submit FAFSA. *Unit head:* Dr. Michael Osnato, Chair, 973-275-2446, E-mail: osnatomi@shu.edu. *Application contact:* Dr. Manina Urgolo Huckvale, Associate Dean, 973-761-9668, Fax: 973-275-2187, E-mail: manina.urgolo-huckvale@shu.edu.

Southern Connecticut State University, School of Graduate Studies, School of Education, Department of Educational Leadership, New Haven, CT 06515-1355. Offers educational foundations (Diploma), including foundational studies; educational leadership (Ed D, Diploma); research, statistics, and measurement (MS). Part-time and evening/weekend programs available. *Faculty:* 13 full-time (7 women), 10 part-time/ adjunct (4 women). *Students:* 13 full-time (6 women), 196 part-time (135 women); includes 34 minority (17 Black or African American, non-Hispanic/Latino; 3 Asian, non-Hispanic/Latino; 13 Hispanic/Latino; 1 Two or more races, non-Hispanic/Latino), 1 international. 203 applicants, 34% accepted, 59 enrolled. In 2011, 3 doctorates, 109 other advanced degrees awarded. *Entrance requirements:* For degree, master's degree, minimum GPA of 3.0, writing sample. *Application deadline:* For fall admission, 7/15 priority date for domestic students. Applications are processed on a rolling basis. Application fee: $50. Electronic applications accepted. *Expenses:* Tuition, state resident: full-time $5137; part-time $413 per credit. *Required fees:* $4008; $55 per term. *Financial support:* Application deadline: 4/15; applicants required to submit FAFSA. *Unit head:* Dr. Peter Madonia, Chairperson, 203-392-5441, E-mail: madoniap1@southernct.edu. *Application contact:* Dr. Cathryn Magno, Graduate Coordinator, 203-392-5170, Fax: 203-392-5347, E-mail: magnoc1@southernct.edu.

Southern Illinois University Carbondale, Graduate School, College of Education and Human Services, Department of Educational Psychology and Special Education, Program in Educational Psychology, Carbondale, IL 62901-4701. Offers counselor education (MS Ed, PhD); educational psychology (PhD); human learning and development (MS Ed); measurement and statistics (PhD). *Accreditation:* NCATE. *Faculty:* 19 full-time (9 women), 7 part-time/adjunct (2 women). *Students:* 47 full-time (33 women), 20 part-time (12 women); includes 12 minority (10 Black or African American, non-Hispanic/Latino; 1 Asian, non-Hispanic/Latino; 1 Hispanic/Latino), 11 international. Average age 36. 29 applicants, 62% accepted, 8 enrolled. In 2011, 21 master's, 3 doctorates awarded. *Degree requirements:* For master's, thesis; for doctorate, thesis/dissertation. *Entrance requirements:* For master's, GRE General Test, minimum GPA of 2.7; for doctorate, minimum GPA of 3.25. Additional exam requirements/recommendations for international students: Required—TOEFL.

Application deadline: For fall admission, 6/15 priority date for domestic students. Applications are processed on a rolling basis. Application fee: $20. *Financial support:* In 2011–12, 36 students received support, including 2 fellowships with full tuition reimbursements available, 4 research assistantships with full tuition reimbursements available; teaching assistantships with full tuition reimbursements available, career-related internships or fieldwork, Federal Work-Study, institutionally sponsored loans, and tuition waivers (full) also available. Support available to part-time students. Financial award application deadline: 5/1. *Faculty research:* Career development, problem solving, learning and instruction, cognitive development, family assessment. *Total annual research expenditures:* $10,000. *Unit head:* Dr. Lyle White, Chairperson, 618-536-7763, E-mail: lwhite@siu.edu. *Application contact:* Cathy Earnhart, Administrative Clerk, 618-453-6932, E-mail: pern@siu.edu.

Southwestern Oklahoma State University, College of Professional and Graduate Studies, School of Behavioral Sciences and Education, Specialization in School Psychometry, Weatherford, OK 73096-3098. Offers M Ed. M Ed distance learning degree program offered to Oklahoma residents only. *Accreditation:* NCATE. Part-time and evening/weekend programs available. *Degree requirements:* For master's, exam. *Entrance requirements:* For master's, GRE General Test or minimum undergraduate GPA of 3.0, portfolio. Additional exam requirements/recommendations for international students: Required—TOEFL.

Stanford University, School of Education, Program in Social Sciences, Policy, and Educational Practice, Stanford, CA 94305-9991. Offers administration and policy analysis (Ed D, PhD); anthropology of education (PhD); economics of education (PhD); educational linguistics (PhD); evaluation (MA), including interdisciplinary studies; higher education (PhD); history of education (PhD); interdisciplinary studies (PhD); international comparative education (MA, PhD); international education administration and policy analysis (MA); philosophy of education (PhD); policy analysis (MA); prospective principal's program (MA); sociology of education (PhD). *Degree requirements:* For master's, thesis (for some programs); for doctorate, thesis/dissertation. *Entrance requirements:* For master's and doctorate, GRE General Test. Electronic applications accepted. *Expenses: Tuition:* Full-time $40,050; part-time $890 per credit.

Sul Ross State University, Rio Grande College of Sul Ross State University, Alpine, TX 79832. Offers business administration (MBA); teacher education (M Ed), including bilingual education, counseling, educational diagnostics, elementary education, general education, reading, school administration, secondary education. Part-time and evening/weekend programs available. Postbaccalaureate distance learning degree programs offered (no on-campus study). *Faculty:* 11 full-time (3 women), 4 part-time/adjunct (3 women). *Students:* 45 full-time (36 women), 255 part-time (168 women); includes 218 minority (2 Black or African American, non-Hispanic/Latino; 1 American Indian or Alaska Native, non-Hispanic/Latino; 215 Hispanic/Latino), 1 international. Average age 36. In 2011, 47 master's awarded. *Degree requirements:* For master's, comprehensive exam, thesis optional, minimum GPA of 3.0. *Entrance requirements:* For master's, GMAT or GRE General Test, minimum GPA of 2.5 in last 60 hours of undergraduate work. Additional exam requirements/recommendations for international students: Required—TOEFL. *Application deadline:* Applications are processed on a rolling basis. Application fee: $0 ($50 for international students). *Financial support:* Career-related internships or fieldwork, Federal Work-Study, and institutionally sponsored loans available. Support available to part-time students. Financial award application deadline: 5/1; financial award applicants required to submit FAFSA. *Unit head:* Dr. Paul Sorrels, Associate Provost/Dean, 512-278-3339, Fax: 512-278-3330. *Application contact:* Claudia R. Wright, Director of Admissions and Records, 915-837-8050, Fax: 915-837-8431, E-mail: rcullins@sulross.edu.

Sul Ross State University, School of Professional Studies, Department of Teacher Education, Program in Educational Diagnostics, Alpine, TX 79832. Offers M Ed. Part-time and evening/weekend programs available. *Degree requirements:* For master's, thesis optional. *Entrance requirements:* For master's, GMAT or GRE General Test, minimum GPA of 2.5 in last 60 hours of undergraduate work.

Syracuse University, School of Education, Program in Instructional Design, Development, and Evaluation, Syracuse, NY 13244. Offers MS, PhD, CAS. Part-time programs available. *Students:* 32 full-time (23 women), 21 part-time (11 women); includes 13 minority (6 Black or African American, non-Hispanic/Latino; 3 Asian, non-Hispanic/Latino; 4 Hispanic/Latino), 16 international. Average age 38. 28 applicants, 61% accepted, 8 enrolled. In 2011, 14 master's, 1 doctorate, 1 other advanced degree awarded. *Degree requirements:* For master's, thesis or alternative; for doctorate, thesis/dissertation. *Entrance requirements:* For doctorate, GRE, interview, master's degree; for CAS, GRE (recommended), interview. Additional exam requirements/recommendations for international students: Required—TOEFL (minimum score 100 iBT). *Application deadline:* For fall admission, 2/1 priority date for domestic students, 2/1 for international students; for spring admission, 10/15 priority date for domestic students, 10/15 for international students. Applications are processed on a rolling basis. Application fee: $75. Electronic applications accepted. *Expenses: Tuition:* Part-time $1206 per credit. *Financial support:* Fellowships with full tuition reimbursements, research assistantships with full and partial tuition reimbursements, and teaching assistantships with full and partial tuition reimbursements available. Financial award application deadline: 1/1; financial award applicants required to submit FAFSA. *Faculty research:* Cultural pluralism and instructional design, corrections training, aging and learning, the University and social change, investigative evaluation. *Unit head:* Dr. Nick Smith, Chair, 315-443-2685, E-mail: nlsmith@syr.edu. *Application contact:* Laurie Deyo, Graduate Recruiter, School of Education, 315-443-2505, E-mail: e-gradrcrt@syr.edu. Web site: http://soeweb.syr.edu/idde/instrucdesign.html.

Teachers College, Columbia University, Graduate Faculty of Education, Department of Human Development, Program in Measurement, Evaluation, and Statistics, New York, NY 10027. Offers MA, MS, Ed D, PhD. *Faculty:* 4 full-time (1 woman), 1 (woman) part-time/adjunct. *Students:* 14 full-time (8 women), 30 part-time (18 women); includes 11 minority (3 Black or African American, non-Hispanic/Latino; 8 Asian, non-Hispanic/Latino), 20 international. Average age 30. 37 applicants, 81% accepted, 10 enrolled. In 2011, 12 master's, 7 doctorates awarded. *Degree requirements:* For master's, project; for doctorate, comprehensive exam, thesis/dissertation, empirical, research paper. *Entrance requirements:* For master's and doctorate, GRE. *Application deadline:* For fall admission, 12/15 for domestic students; for spring admission, 11/1 for domestic students. Applications are processed on a rolling basis. Application fee: $65. Electronic applications accepted. *Financial support:* Career-related internships or fieldwork, Federal Work-Study, institutionally sponsored loans, and tuition waivers (full and partial) available. Support available to part-time students. Financial award application deadline: 2/1; financial award applicants required to submit FAFSA. *Faculty research:* Probability and inference, potentially biased test items, research design, clustering and scaling methods for multivariate data. *Unit head:* Prof. Lawrence T. DeCarlo, Program Coordinator, 212-678-4150, E-mail: decarlo@tc.edu. *Application contact:* Melba Remice, Assistant Director of Admission, 212-678-4035, Fax: 212-678-4171, E-mail: ms2545@columbia.edu. Web site: http://www.tc.columbia.edu/hud/measurement/.

Tennessee Technological University, Graduate School, College of Education, Department of Curriculum and Instruction, Program in Exceptional Learning, Cookeville, TN 38505. Offers applied behavior and learning (PhD); literacy (PhD); program planning and evaluation (PhD); STEM education (PhD). Part-time and evening/weekend programs available. *Students:* 11 full-time (7 women), 12 part-time (9 women); includes 2 minority (both Black or African American, non-Hispanic/Latino), 1 international. 18 applicants, 50% accepted, 8 enrolled. In 2011, 7 doctorates awarded. *Degree requirements:* For doctorate, comprehensive exam, thesis/dissertation. *Entrance requirements:* For doctorate, GRE, minimum GPA of 3.0. Additional exam requirements/recommendations for international students: Required—TOEFL (minimum score 550 paper-based; 71 iBT), IELTS (minimum score 5.5), Pearson Test of English Academic. *Application deadline:* For fall admission, 8/1 for domestic students, 5/1 for international students; for spring admission, 12/1 for domestic students, 10/1 for international students. Application fee: $25 ($30 for international students). Electronic applications accepted. *Expenses:* Tuition, state resident: full-time $8094; part-time $422 per credit hour. Tuition, nonresident: full-time $20,574; part-time $1046 per credit hour. *Financial support:* In 2011–12, 4 fellowships (averaging $8,000 per year), 10 research assistantships (averaging $12,000 per year), 1 teaching assistantship (averaging $12,000 per year) were awarded. Financial award application deadline: 4/1. *Unit head:* Dr. Lisa Zagumny, Director, 931-372-3078, Fax: 931-372-3517, E-mail: lzagumny@tntech.edu. *Application contact:* Shelia K. Kendrick, Coordinator of Graduate Admissions, 931-372-3808, Fax: 931-372-3497, E-mail: skendrick@tntech.edu.

Texas A&M University, College of Education and Human Development, Department of Educational Psychology, College Station, TX 77843. Offers bilingual education (M Ed, PhD); cognition, creativity, instruction and development (MS, PhD); counseling psychology (PhD); educational psychology (PhD); educational technology (PhD); research, measurement and statistics (MS); research, measurement, and statistics (PhD); school psychology (PhD); special education (M Ed, PhD). *Accreditation:* APA (one or more programs are accredited). Part-time and evening/weekend programs available. Postbaccalaureate distance learning degree programs offered (no on-campus study). *Faculty:* 46. *Students:* 151 full-time (124 women), 123 part-time (101 women); includes 97 minority (20 Black or African American, non-Hispanic/Latino; 11 Asian, non-Hispanic/Latino; 59 Hispanic/Latino; 7 Two or more races, non-Hispanic/Latino), 50 international. In 2011, 58 master's, 33 doctorates awarded. *Degree requirements:* For master's, thesis optional; for doctorate, thesis/dissertation. *Entrance requirements:* For master's and doctorate, GRE General Test. Additional exam requirements/recommendations for international students: Required—TOEFL. Application fee: $50 ($75 for international students). Electronic applications accepted. *Expenses:* Tuition, state resident: full-time $5437; part-time $226.55 per credit hour. Tuition, nonresident: full-time $12,949; part-time $539.55 per credit hour. *Required fees:* $2741. *Financial support:* In 2011–12, fellowships (averaging $12,000 per year), research assistantships (averaging $9,000 per year), teaching assistantships (averaging $9,000 per year) were awarded; career-related internships or fieldwork, institutionally sponsored loans, scholarships/grants, and unspecified assistantships also available. Financial award applicants required to submit FAFSA. *Unit head:* Dr. Victor Willson, Head, 979-845-1800. *Application contact:* Carol A. Wagner, Director of Advising, 979-845-1833, Fax: 979-862-1256, E-mail: epsyadvisor@tamu.edu. Web site: http://epsy.tamu.edu.

Texas A&M University–San Antonio, Department of Curriculum and Kinesiology, San Antonio, TX 78224. Offers bilingual education (MA); early childhood education (M Ed); kinesiology (MS); reading (MS); special education (M Ed), including educational diagnostician, instructional specialist. Part-time and evening/weekend programs available. *Students:* 76 full-time (51 women), 240 part-time (180 women). Average age 37. *Degree requirements:* For master's, comprehensive exam, thesis or alternative. *Entrance requirements:* For master's, MAT. Additional exam requirements/recommendations for international students: Required—TOEFL (minimum score 550 paper-based; 213 computer-based; 80 iBT), IELTS (minimum score 6). *Application deadline:* For fall admission, 8/15 priority date for domestic students, 6/1 for international students; for spring admission, 12/15 priority date for domestic students, 10/1 for international students. Applications are processed on a rolling basis. Application fee: $35 ($50 for international students). Electronic applications accepted. *Expenses:* Tuition, state resident: part-time $691.11 per course. Tuition, nonresident: part-time $1621.11 per course. *Financial support:* Application deadline: 3/31; applicants required to submit FAFSA. *Unit head:* Dr. Samuel Garcia, Department Chair, 210-784-2505, E-mail: samuel.garcia@tamusa.tamus.edu. *Application contact:* Jennifer M. Dovalina, Graduate Admissions Specialist, 210-784-1380, E-mail: graduateadmissions@tamusa.tamus.edu. Web site: http://www.tamusa.tamus.edu/education/index.html.

Université Laval, Faculty of Education, Department of Foundations and Interventions in Education, Québec, QC G1K 7P4, Canada. Offers educational administration and evaluation (MA, PhD); educational practice (Diploma), including educational pedagogy, pedagogy management and development, school adaptation; orientation sciences (MA, PhD). *Degree requirements:* For doctorate, comprehensive exam, thesis/dissertation. Electronic applications accepted.

University at Albany, State University of New York, School of Education, Department of Educational and Counseling Psychology, Albany, NY 12222-0001. Offers counseling psychology (MS, PhD, CAS); educational psychology (Ed D); educational psychology and statistics (MS); measurements and evaluation (Ed D); rehabilitation counseling (MS), including counseling psychology; school counselor (CAS); school psychology (Psy D, CAS); special education (MS); statistics and research design (Ed D). *Accreditation:* APA (one or more programs are accredited). Evening/weekend programs available. *Degree requirements:* For doctorate, thesis/dissertation. *Entrance requirements:* For doctorate, GRE General Test. Additional exam requirements/recommendations for international students: Required—TOEFL (minimum score 550 paper-based; 213 computer-based). Electronic applications accepted.

University of Arkansas, Graduate School, College of Education and Health Professions, Department of Curriculum and Instruction, Program in Educational Statistics and Research Methods, Fayetteville, AR 72701-1201. Offers MS, PhD. *Students:* 5 full-time (3 women), 7 part-time (5 women), 1 international. In 2011, 1 master's, 1 doctorate awarded. *Application deadline:* For fall admission, 4/1 for international students; for spring admission, 10/1 for international students. Applications are processed on a rolling basis. Application fee: $40 ($50 for international students). Electronic applications accepted. *Financial support:* In 2011–12, 14 research assistantships were awarded; fellowships and teaching assistantships also available. *Unit head:* Dr. Michael Daugherty, Departmental Chairperson, 479-575-4209, Fax: 479-575-5119, E-mail: mkd03@uark.edu. *Application contact:* Dr. Barbara Gartin, Graduate Coordinator, 479-575-7525, Fax: 479-575-6676, E-mail: bgartin@uark.edu. Web site: http://cied.uark.edu/.

The University of British Columbia, Faculty of Education, Department of Educational and Counseling Psychology, and Special Education, Vancouver, BC V6T 1Z1, Canada. Offers counseling psychology (M Ed, MA, PhD); development, learning and culture (PhD); guidance studies (Diploma); human development, learning and culture (M Ed, MA); measurement and evaluation and research methodology (M Ed); measurement, evaluation and research methodology (MA); measurement, evaluation, and research methodology (PhD); school psychology (M Ed, MA, PhD); special education (M Ed, MA, PhD, Diploma). Part-time programs available. *Degree requirements:* For master's, thesis (for some programs); for doctorate, comprehensive exam, thesis/dissertation. *Entrance* *requirements:* For master's, GRE General Test (counseling psychology MA); for doctorate, GRE General Test. Additional exam requirements/recommendations for international students: Required—TOEFL. Electronic applications accepted. *Faculty research:* Women, family, social problems, career transition, stress and coping problems.

University of Calgary, Faculty of Graduate Studies, Faculty of Education, Graduate Division of Educational Research, Calgary, AB T2N 1N4, Canada. Offers community rehabilitation and disability studies (M Ed, M Sc, Ed D, PhD, Graduate Certificate, Graduate Diploma); curriculum, teaching and learning (M Ed, M Sc, MA, Ed D, PhD, Graduate Certificate, Graduate Diploma); educational contexts (M Ed, MA, Ed D, PhD, Graduate Certificate, Graduate Diploma); educational leadership (M Ed, MA, Ed D, PhD, Graduate Certificate, Graduate Diploma); educational technology (M Ed, M Sc, MA, Ed D, PhD, Graduate Certificate, Graduate Diploma); gifted education (M Sc, MA, Ed D, PhD, Graduate Certificate, Graduate Diploma); higher education administration (Ed D); interpretive studies in education (M Ed, M Sc, MA, Ed D, PhD, Graduate Certificate, Graduate Diploma); second language teaching (M Ed, Ed D, PhD, Graduate Certificate, Graduate Diploma); teaching English as a second language (M Ed, M Sc, MA, Ed D, PhD, Graduate Certificate, Graduate Diploma); workplace and adult learning (M Ed, MA, Ed D, PhD, Graduate Certificate, Graduate Diploma). Ed D in both higher education administration and educational leadership offered via distance delivery. Part-time and evening/weekend programs available. Postbaccalaureate distance learning degree programs offered (minimal on-campus study). *Degree requirements:* For master's, thesis (for some programs); for doctorate, thesis/dissertation, candidacy exam. *Entrance requirements:* For master's, minimum GPA of 3.0, 3 letters of reference; for doctorate, minimum GPA of 3.5, 3 letters of reference; for other advanced degree, minimum GPA of 3.0. Additional exam requirements/recommendations for international students: Required—TOEFL, IELTS. Electronic applications accepted. *Faculty research:* Curriculum, leadership, technology, contexts, gifted, second language teaching, work place and adult learning.

University of California, Santa Barbara, Graduate Division, Gevirtz Graduate School of Education, Santa Barbara, CA 93106-9490. Offers counseling, clinical and school psychology (M Ed, MA, PhD, Credential), including clinical psychology (PhD), counseling psychology (MA, PhD), school psychology (M Ed, PhD), school psychology: pupil personnel services (Credential); education (M Ed, MA, PhD, Credential), including child and adolescent development (MA, PhD), cultural perspectives and comparative education (MA, PhD), educational leadership and organizations (MA, PhD), multiple subject teaching (Credential), research methodology (MA, PhD), single subject teaching (Credential), special education (Credential), special education disabilities and risk studies (MA), special education, disabilities and risk studies (PhD), teaching (M Ed), teaching and learning (MA, PhD); MA/PhD. *Accreditation:* APA (one or more programs are accredited). *Faculty:* 40 full-time (21 women), 2 part-time/adjunct (both women). *Students:* 389 full-time (301 women); includes 131 minority (14 Black or African American, non-Hispanic/Latino; 2 American Indian or Alaska Native, non-Hispanic/Latino; 41 Asian, non-Hispanic/Latino; 69 Hispanic/Latino; 1 Native Hawaiian or other Pacific Islander, non-Hispanic/Latino; 4 Two or more races, non-Hispanic/Latino), 25 international. Average age 28. 691 applicants, 35% accepted, 154 enrolled. In 2011, 145 master's, 45 doctorates, 118 other advanced degrees awarded. Terminal master's awarded for partial completion of doctoral program. *Degree requirements:* For master's, comprehensive exam (for some programs), thesis (for some programs); for doctorate, comprehensive exam (for some programs), thesis/dissertation; for Credential, CA state requirements (varies by credential). *Entrance requirements:* For master's and doctorate, GRE; for Credential, GRE or MAT, CSET and CBEST. Additional exam requirements/recommendations for international students: Required—TOEFL (minimum score 550 paper-based; 80 iBT), IELTS (minimum score 7). Application fee: $80 ($100 for international students). Electronic applications accepted. *Expenses:* Tuition, state resident: full-time $12,192. Tuition, nonresident: full-time $27,294. *Required fees:* $764.13. *Financial support:* In 2011–12, 301 students received support, including 429 fellowships with partial tuition reimbursements available (averaging $5,017 per year), 83 research assistantships with full and partial tuition reimbursements available (averaging $6,262 per year), 55 teaching assistantships with partial tuition reimbursements available (averaging $8,655 per year); career-related internships or fieldwork also available. Financial award applicants required to submit FAFSA. *Faculty research:* Needs of diverse students, school accountability and leadership, school violence, language learning and literacy, science/math education. *Total annual research expenditures:* $3 million. *Unit head:* Arlis Markel, Assistant Dean, 805-893-5492, Fax: 805-893-2588, E-mail: arlis@education.ucsb.edu. *Application contact:* Kathryn Marie Tucciarone, Student Affairs Officer, 805-893-2137, Fax: 805-893-2588, E-mail: katiet@education.ucsb.edu. Web site: http://www.education.ucsb.edu/.

University of Colorado Boulder, Graduate School, School of Education, Division of Research and Evaluation Methodologies, Boulder, CO 80309. Offers PhD. *Accreditation:* NCATE. *Students:* 7 full-time (5 women), 2 part-time (1 woman); includes 2 minority (1 Asian, non-Hispanic/Latino; 1 Hispanic/Latino), 1 international. Average age 30. 15 applicants, 13% accepted, 1 enrolled. In 2011, 4 doctorates awarded. *Degree requirements:* For doctorate, one foreign language, comprehensive exam, thesis/dissertation. *Entrance requirements:* For doctorate, GRE General Test, minimum undergraduate GPA of 2.75. *Application deadline:* For fall admission, 2/1 priority date for domestic students, 12/1 for international students; for spring admission, 9/1 for domestic students, 12/1 for international students. Application fee: $40 ($60 for international students). Electronic applications accepted. *Financial support:* In 2011–12, 17 students received support, including 6 fellowships (averaging $5,166 per year), 6 research assistantships with full and partial tuition reimbursements available (averaging $19,639 per year), 2 teaching assistantships with full and partial tuition reimbursements available (averaging $14,291 per year); institutionally sponsored loans, scholarships/grants, health care benefits, and unspecified assistantships also available. Financial award applicants required to submit FAFSA. *Application contact:* E-mail: edadvise@colorado.edu. Web site: http://www.colorado.edu/education/.

University of Colorado Denver, School of Education and Human Development, Program in Educational Leadership and Innovation, Denver, CO 80217-3364. Offers educational studies and research (PhD), including administrative leadership and policy, early childhood special education, math education, research, assessment and evaluation, science education, urban ecologies. Part-time and evening/weekend programs available. *Students:* 21 full-time (15 women), 25 part-time (17 women); includes 10 minority (5 Black or African American, non-Hispanic/Latino; 1 American Indian or Alaska Native, non-Hispanic/Latino; 3 Asian, non-Hispanic/Latino; 1 Hispanic/Latino), 1 international. Average age 43. 11 applicants, 45% accepted, 3 enrolled. In 2011, 11 doctorates awarded. *Degree requirements:* For doctorate, comprehensive exam, thesis/dissertation, 75 credit hours (for PhD). *Entrance requirements:* For doctorate, GRE or equivalent, resume or curriculum vitae, written statement, letters of recommendation, master's degree or equivalent, completion of basic or advanced statistics course with minimum B grade. Additional exam requirements/recommendations for international students: Required—TOEFL (minimum score 525 paper-based; 197 computer-based). *Application deadline:* Applications are processed on a rolling basis. Application fee: $50 ($75 for international students). Electronic applications accepted. *Expenses:* Contact institution. *Financial support:* Fellowships, research assistantships, teaching assistantships, scholarships/grants, and unspecified assistantships available. Financial award application deadline: 4/1; financial award applicants required to submit FAFSA. *Faculty research:* Administrative leadership and policy studies, early childhood education, research in diversity, paraprofessionals in education, urban schools lab. *Unit head:* Dr. Deanna Sands, Associate Dean, Research and Professional Development, 303-315-4931, E-mail: deanna.sands@ucdenver.edu. *Application contact:* Student Services Center, 303-315-6300, Fax: 303-315-6311, E-mail: education@ucdenver.edu. Web site: http://www.ucdenver.edu/ACADEMICS/COLLEGES/SCHOOLOFEDUCATION/ACADEMICS/Pages/AcademicPrograms.aspx.

University of Colorado Denver, School of Education and Human Development, Programs in Educational and School Psychology, Denver, CO 80217. Offers educational psychology (MA), including educational assessment, educational psychology, human development, human learning, partner schools, research and evaluation; school psychology (Ed S). Part-time and evening/weekend programs available. *Students:* 105 full-time (86 women), 46 part-time (40 women); includes 12 minority (1 Black or African American, non-Hispanic/Latino; 5 Asian, non-Hispanic/Latino; 5 Hispanic/Latino; 1 Two or more races, non-Hispanic/Latino), 2 international. Average age 30. 77 applicants, 79% accepted, 40 enrolled. In 2011, 58 master's, 23 other advanced degrees awarded. *Degree requirements:* For master's, comprehensive exam, 9 hours of core courses, embedded within a minimum of 36 to 38 hours of relevant coursework, including an educational psychology practicum, independent study project or thesis (recommended); for Ed S, comprehensive exam, minimum of 75 semester hours (61 hours of coursework, 6 of 500-hour practicum in field, and 8 of 1200-hour internship); PRAXIS II. *Entrance requirements:* For master's, GRE if undergraduate GPA below 2.75, resume, written statement, three letters of recommendation, transcripts; for Ed S, GRE, resume, written statement, letters of recommendation, transcripts. Additional exam requirements/recommendations for international students: Required—TOEFL. *Application deadline:* For fall admission, 4/15 for domestic students, 4/1 for international students; for spring admission, 9/15 for domestic students, 9/1 for international students. Application fee: $50 ($75 for international students). Electronic applications accepted. *Expenses:* Contact institution. *Financial support:* Application deadline: 4/1; applicants required to submit FAFSA. *Faculty research:* Crisis response and Intervention, school violence prevention, immigrant experience, educational environments for English language learners, culturally competent assessment and intervention, child and youth suicide. *Unit head:* Dr. Jung-In Kim, Assistant Professor of Educational Psychology, 303-315-4965, E-mail: jung-in.kim@ucdenver.edu. *Application contact:* Student Services Center, 303-315-6300, Fax: 303-315-6311, E-mail: education@ucdenver.edu. Web site: http://www.ucdenver.edu/academics/colleges/SchoolOfEducation/Academics/EdS/Pages/EdSinSchoolPsychology.aspx.

University of Connecticut, Graduate School, Neag School of Education, Department of Educational Psychology, Program in Measurement, Evaluation, and Assessment, Storrs, CT 06269. Offers MA, PhD, Post-Master's Certificate. Terminal master's awarded for partial completion of doctoral program. *Degree requirements:* For master's, comprehensive exam, thesis or alternative; for doctorate, thesis/dissertation. *Entrance requirements:* For doctorate, GRE General Test. Additional exam requirements/recommendations for international students: Required—TOEFL (minimum score 550 paper-based; 213 computer-based). Electronic applications accepted.

University of Florida, Graduate School, College of Education, Department of Educational Psychology, Gainesville, FL 32611. Offers educational psychology (M Ed, MAE, Ed D, PhD, Ed S); research and evaluation methodology (M Ed, MAE, Ed D, PhD, Ed S). *Accreditation:* NCATE. Terminal master's awarded for partial completion of doctoral program. *Degree requirements:* For master's, thesis (MAE); for doctorate, variable foreign language requirement, thesis/dissertation. *Entrance requirements:* For master's and doctorate, GRE General Test, minimum GPA of 3.0; for Ed S, GRE General Test. Additional exam requirements/recommendations for international students: Required—TOEFL (minimum score 550 paper-based; 213 computer-based; 80 iBT), IELTS (minimum score 6). *Application deadline:* For fall admission, 6/1 priority date for domestic students. Applications are processed on a rolling basis. Application fee: $30. Electronic applications accepted. *Financial support:* Fellowships, research assistantships, teaching assistantships, career-related internships or fieldwork, and unspecified assistantships available. Financial award application deadline: 4/30; financial award applicants required to submit FAFSA. *Faculty research:* School improvement, teaching and learning, item response theory.

The University of Iowa, Graduate College, College of Education, Department of Psychological and Quantitative Foundations, Iowa City, IA 52242-1316. Offers counseling psychology (PhD); educational measurement and statistics (MA, PhD); educational psychology (MA, PhD); school psychology (PhD, Ed S); JD/PhD. *Accreditation:* APA. *Degree requirements:* For master's, thesis optional, exam; for doctorate, comprehensive exam, thesis/dissertation; for Ed S, exam. *Entrance requirements:* For master's, doctorate, and Ed S, GRE General Test, minimum GPA of 3.0. Additional exam requirements/recommendations for international students: Required—TOEFL (minimum score 550 paper-based; 213 computer-based; 81 iBT). Electronic applications accepted.

The University of Kansas, Graduate Studies, School of Education, Department of Psychology and Research in Education, Program in Educational Psychology and Research, Lawrence, KS 66045. Offers MS Ed, PhD. *Faculty:* 4 full-time (1 woman). *Students:* 37 full-time (29 women), 8 part-time (5 women); includes 3 minority (all Black or African American, non-Hispanic/Latino), 20 international. Average age 32. 18 applicants, 61% accepted, 5 enrolled. In 2011, 1 master's, 2 doctorates awarded. *Degree requirements:* For master's, thesis; for doctorate, comprehensive exam, thesis/dissertation. *Entrance requirements:* For master's, GRE General Test, minimum GPA of 3.0; for doctorate, GRE General Test. Additional exam requirements/recommendations for international students: Required—TOEFL. *Application deadline:* For fall admission, 4/15 for domestic students; for spring admission, 11/15 for domestic students. Applications are processed on a rolling basis. Application fee: $55 ($65 for international students). Electronic applications accepted. Tuition and fees vary according to course load, campus/location, program and reciprocity agreements. *Financial support:* Fellowships, research assistantships with full and partial tuition reimbursements, teaching assistantships with full and partial tuition reimbursements, career-related internships or fieldwork, institutionally sponsored loans, scholarships/grants, traineeships, health care benefits, tuition waivers (full and partial), and unspecified assistantships available. Support available to part-time students. Financial award application deadline: 2/1. *Faculty research:* Educational measurement, applied statistics, research design, program evaluation, learning and development. *Unit head:* William Skorupski, Director of Training, 785-864-3931, E-mail: bfrey@ku.edu. *Application contact:* Loretta Warren, Admissions Coordinator, 785-864-9645, Fax: 785-864-3820, E-mail: preadmit@ku.edu. Web site: http://www.soe.ku.edu/PRE/.

University of Kentucky, Graduate School, College of Education, Program in Educational Policy Studies and Evaluation, Lexington, KY 40506-0032. Offers educational policy studies and evaluation (Ed D); higher education (MS Ed, PhD). *Accreditation:* NCATE. Terminal master's awarded for partial completion of doctoral program. *Degree requirements:* For master's, comprehensive exam, thesis optional; for doctorate, comprehensive exam, thesis/dissertation. *Entrance requirements:* For master's, GRE General Test, minimum undergraduate GPA of 2.75; for doctorate, GRE General Test, minimum graduate GPA of 3.0. Additional exam requirements/ recommendations for international students: Required—TOEFL (minimum score 550 paper-based; 213 computer-based). Electronic applications accepted. *Faculty research:* Studies in higher education; comparative and international education; evaluation of educational programs, policies, and reform; student, teacher, and faculty cultures; gender and education.

University of Louisiana at Monroe, Graduate School, College of Education and Human Development, Department of Curriculum and Instruction, Program in Curriculum and Instruction, Monroe, LA 71209-0001. Offers curriculum and instruction (Ed D); elementary education (1-5) (M Ed); reading education (K-12) (M Ed); SPED-academically gifted education (K-12) (M Ed); SPED-early intervention education (birth-3) (M Ed); SPED-educational diagnostics education (PreK-12) (M Ed). *Accreditation:* NCATE. *Students:* 42 full-time (37 women), 54 part-time (47 women); includes 20 minority (18 Black or African American, non-Hispanic/Latino; 1 Asian, non-Hispanic/ Latino; 1 Hispanic/Latino), 12 international. Average age 36. 55 applicants, 95% accepted, 38 enrolled. In 2011, 27 master's, 1 doctorate awarded. *Degree requirements:* For master's, comprehensive exam (for some programs), thesis; for doctorate, thesis/ dissertation, internships. *Entrance requirements:* For master's, GRE General Test; for doctorate, GRE General Test, minimum undergraduate GPA of 2.75, graduate 3.25. Additional exam requirements/recommendations for international students: Required—TOEFL (minimum score 500 paper-based; 173 computer-based; 61 iBT). *Application deadline:* For fall admission, 8/24 priority date for domestic students, 7/1 for international students; for winter admission, 12/14 priority date for domestic students; for spring admission, 1/19 for domestic students, 11/1 for international students. Applications are processed on a rolling basis. Application fee: $20 ($30 for international students). Electronic applications accepted. *Expenses:* Tuition, state resident: full-time $3436; part-time $240 per credit hour. Tuition, nonresident: full-time $3436; part-time $240 per credit hour. *International tuition:* $10,733 full-time. *Required fees:* $1460.90. *Financial support:* In 2011–12, 12 research assistantships with full tuition reimbursements (averaging $2,500 per year) were awarded; career-related internships or fieldwork, Federal Work-Study, and unspecified assistantships also available. Financial award application deadline: 4/1; financial award applicants required to submit FAFSA. *Unit head:* Dr. Dorothy Schween, Coordinator, 318-342-1269, Fax: 318-342-3131, E-mail: schween@ulm.edu. *Application contact:* Whitney Sutherland, Administrative Assistant to the Department Head, 318-342-1266, Fax: 318-342-3131, E-mail: sutherland@ulm.edu. Web site: http://www.ulm.edu/ci/.

University of Maryland, College Park, Academic Affairs, College of Education, Department of Measurement, Statistics, and Evaluation, College Park, MD 20742. Offers measurement (MA, PhD); program evaluation (MA, PhD); statistics (MA, PhD). *Accreditation:* NCATE. Part-time and evening/weekend programs available. Postbaccalaureate distance learning degree programs offered (minimal on-campus study). *Faculty:* 9 full-time (3 women), 4 part-time/adjunct (1 woman). *Students:* 30 full-time (21 women), 10 part-time (8 women); includes 4 minority (1 Black or African American, non-Hispanic/Latino; 2 Hispanic/Latino; 1 Two or more races, non-Hispanic/ Latino), 23 international. 48 applicants, 29% accepted, 7 enrolled. In 2011, 6 master's, 6 doctorates awarded. *Degree requirements:* For master's, comprehensive exam, thesis optional; for doctorate, thesis/dissertation, preliminary and comprehensive written exams. *Entrance requirements:* For master's and doctorate, GRE General Test or MAT, minimum GPA of 3.0, 3 letters of recommendation. Additional exam requirements/ recommendations for international students: Required—TOEFL. *Application deadline:* For fall admission, 3/15 for domestic students, 2/1 for international students; for spring admission, 10/1 for domestic students, 6/1 for international students. Applications are processed on a rolling basis. Application fee: $75. Electronic applications accepted. *Expenses: Tuition, area resident:* Part-time $525 per credit hour. Tuition, state resident: part-time $525 per credit hour. Tuition, nonresident: part-time $1131 per credit hour. *Required fees:* $386.31 per term. Tuition and fees vary according to program. *Financial support:* In 2011–12, 2 fellowships with partial tuition reimbursements (averaging $14,141 per year), 19 teaching assistantships (averaging $15,892 per year) were awarded; research assistantships, Federal Work-Study, and scholarships/grants also available. Support available to part-time students. Financial award applicants required to submit FAFSA. *Total annual research expenditures:* $817,012. *Unit head:* Francine Hultgren, Chair, 301-405-3117, E-mail: fh@umd.edu. *Application contact:* Dr. Charles A. Caramello, Dean of Graduate School, 301-405-0358, Fax: 301-314-9305.

University of Massachusetts Amherst, Graduate School, School of Education, Program in Education, Amherst, MA 01003. Offers bilingual, English as a second language, and multicultural education (M Ed, CAGS); child study and early education (M Ed); children, families and schools (Ed D, CAGS); early childhood and elementary teacher education (M Ed); educational leadership (M Ed, CAGS); educational policy and leadership (Ed D); higher education (M Ed, CAGS); international education (M Ed); language, literacy and culture (Ed D); learning, media and technology (M Ed, CAGS); mathematics, science, and learning technologies (Ed D); policy studies in education (CAGS); psychometric methods, educational statistics and research methods (Ed D); reading and writing (M Ed); school counselor education (M Ed, CAGS); science education (CAGS); secondary teacher education (M Ed); social justice education (M Ed, Ed D, CAGS); special education (M Ed, Ed D, CAGS). *Accreditation:* NCATE. Part-time programs available. Postbaccalaureate distance learning degree programs offered (minimal on-campus study). *Faculty:* 81 full-time (46 women). *Students:* 341 full-time (240 women), 333 part-time (226 women); includes 113 minority (36 Black or African American, non-Hispanic/Latino; 1 American Indian or Alaska Native, non-Hispanic/ Latino; 14 Asian, non-Hispanic/Latino; 51 Hispanic/Latino; 1 Native Hawaiian or other Pacific Islander, non-Hispanic/Latino; 10 Two or more races, non-Hispanic/Latino), 98 international. Average age 36. 721 applicants, 57% accepted, 202 enrolled. In 2011, 166 master's, 33 doctorates, 25 CAGSs awarded. Terminal master's awarded for partial completion of doctoral program. *Degree requirements:* For doctorate, comprehensive exam, thesis/dissertation. *Entrance requirements:* Additional exam requirements/ recommendations for international students: Required—TOEFL (minimum score 550 paper-based; 213 computer-based; 80 iBT), IELTS (minimum score 6.5). *Application deadline:* For fall admission, 1/15 for domestic and international students. Applications are processed on a rolling basis. Application fee: $50 ($65 for international students). Electronic applications accepted. Tuition and fees vary according to course load, campus/location and program. *Financial support:* Fellowships with full and partial tuition reimbursements, research assistantships with full and partial tuition reimbursements, teaching assistantships with full and partial tuition reimbursements, career-related internships or fieldwork, Federal Work-Study, scholarships/grants, traineeships, health care benefits, tuition waivers (full and partial), and unspecified assistantships available. Support available to part-time students. Financial award application deadline: 1/15. *Unit head:* Dr. Linda L. Griffin, Graduate Program Director, 413-545-6984, Fax: 413-545-1523. *Application contact:* Lindsay DeSantis, Interim Supervisor of Admissions, 413-545-0722, Fax: 413-577-0010, E-mail: gradadm@grad.umass.edu. Web site: http:// www.umass.edu/education/.

University of Memphis, Graduate School, College of Education, Department of Counseling, Educational Psychology and Research, Memphis, TN 38152. Offers counseling (MS, Ed D), including community counseling (MS), rehabilitation counseling (MS), school counseling (MS); counseling psychology (PhD); educational psychology and research (MS, PhD), including educational psychology, educational research. *Accreditation:* ACA (one or more programs are accredited); APA (one or more programs are accredited); CORE (one or more programs are accredited); NCATE. *Degree requirements:* For master's, comprehensive exam, thesis or alternative; for doctorate, comprehensive exam, thesis/dissertation. *Entrance requirements:* For master's, GRE General Test or MAT, minimum GPA of 2.5; for doctorate, GRE General Test. *Faculty research:* Anger management, aging and disability, supervision, multicultural counseling.

University of Miami, Graduate School, School of Education and Human Development, Department of Educational and Psychological Studies, Program in Research, Measurement, and Evaluation, Coral Gables, FL 33124. Offers MS Ed, PhD. Part-time and evening/weekend programs available. *Faculty:* 3 full-time (1 woman). *Students:* 6 full-time (4 women), 4 part-time (all women); includes 3 minority (all Hispanic/Latino), 3 international. Average age 28. 10 applicants, 10% accepted, 0 enrolled. Terminal master's awarded for partial completion of doctoral program. *Degree requirements:* For master's, comprehensive exam, thesis optional; for doctorate, thesis/dissertation, qualifying exam. *Entrance requirements:* For master's and doctorate, GRE General Test. Additional exam requirements/recommendations for international students: Required—TOEFL (minimum score 550 paper-based; 80 iBT); Recommended—IELTS (minimum score 6.5). *Application deadline:* For fall admission, 10/15 for international students. Applications are processed on a rolling basis. Application fee: $65. Electronic applications accepted. *Financial support:* In 2011–12, 9 students received support. Health care benefits and unspecified assistantships available. Support available to part-time students. Financial award application deadline: 3/1; financial award applicants required to submit FAFSA. *Faculty research:* Psychometric theory, computer-based testing, quantitative research methods. *Unit head:* Dr. Nicholas Myers, Associate Professor and Program Director, 305-284-9803, Fax: 305-284-3003, E-mail: nmyers@ miami.edu. *Application contact:* Lois Heffernan, Graduate Admissions Coordinator, 305-284-2167, Fax: 305-284-9395, E-mail: lheffernan@miami.edu.

University of Minnesota, Twin Cities Campus, Graduate School, College of Education and Human Development, Department of Organizational Leadership, Policy and Development, Program in Evaluation Studies, Minneapolis, MN 55455-0213. Offers MA, PhD. *Students:* 18 full-time (15 women), 12 part-time (11 women); includes 4 minority (1 Black or African American, non-Hispanic/Latino; 3 Asian, non-Hispanic/ Latino), 3 international. Average age 37. 10 applicants, 80% accepted, 5 enrolled. In 2011, 3 master's, 2 doctorates awarded. Application fee: $55. *Unit head:* Dr. Rebecca Ropers-Huilman, Chair, 612-624-1006, Fax: 612-624-3377, E-mail: ropers@umn.edu. *Application contact:* Dr. Jennifer Engler, Assistant Dean, 612-626-2887, Fax: 612-626-7496, E-mail: engle009@umn.edu. Web site: http://www.cehd.umn.edu/EdPA/ Evaluation.

University of Missouri–St. Louis, College of Education, Division of Educational Leadership and Policy Studies, St. Louis, MO 63121. Offers adult and higher education (M Ed), including adult education, higher education; educational administration (M Ed, Ed S), including community education (M Ed), elementary education (M Ed), secondary education (M Ed); institutional research (Certificate). *Accreditation:* NCATE. Part-time and evening/weekend programs available. *Faculty:* 17 full-time (8 women), 7 part-time/ adjunct (5 women). *Students:* 23 full-time (15 women), 187 part-time (137 women); includes 103 minority (96 Black or African American, non-Hispanic/Latino; 2 Asian, non-Hispanic/Latino; 4 Hispanic/Latino; 1 Two or more races, non-Hispanic/Latino), 4 international. Average age 35. 95 applicants, 86% accepted, 68 enrolled. In 2011, 57 master's, 19 Certificates awarded. *Degree requirements:* For master's, comprehensive exam (for some programs). *Entrance requirements:* Additional exam requirements/ recommendations for international students: Required—TOEFL (minimum score 550 paper-based; 213 computer-based). *Application deadline:* For fall admission, 7/1 priority date for domestic students, 7/1 for international students; for spring admission, 12/1 priority date for domestic students, 12/1 for international students. Applications are processed on a rolling basis. Application fee: $35 ($40 for international students). Electronic applications accepted. *Expenses:* Tuition, state resident: full-time $6273; part-time $3866 per year. Tuition, nonresident: full-time $14,969; part-time $9980 per year. *Required fees:* $315 per year. *Financial support:* In 2011–12, 12 research assistantships (averaging $12,000 per year), 1 teaching assistantship (averaging $10,500 per year) were awarded. Financial award application deadline: 4/1; financial award applicants required to submit FAFSA. *Faculty research:* Educational policy research; philosophy of education; higher, adult, and vocational education; school initiatives, change, and reform. *Unit head:* Dr. E. Paulette Savage, Chair, 514-516-5944. *Application contact:* 314-516-5458, Fax: 314-516-6996, E-mail: gradadm@umsl.edu. Web site: http://coe.umsl.edu/web/divisions/elaps/index.html.

University of Missouri–St. Louis, College of Education, Division of Educational Psychology, Research, and Evaluation, St. Louis, MO 63121. Offers program evaluation and assessment (Certificate); school psychology (Ed S). *Faculty:* 11 full-time (4 women), 9 part-time/adjunct (3 women). *Students:* 26 full-time (23 women), 2 part-time (1 woman); includes 3 minority (2 Black or African American, non-Hispanic/Latino; 1 Asian, non-Hispanic/Latino), 4 international. Average age 27. 32 applicants, 38% accepted, 7 enrolled. In 2011, 7 degrees awarded. *Degree requirements:* For other advanced degree, internship. *Entrance requirements:* For degree, GRE General Test, 2-4 letters of recommendation, personal interview. Additional exam requirements/recommendations for international students: Recommended—TOEFL (minimum score 550 paper-based; 213 computer-based). *Application deadline:* For fall admission, 2/15 for domestic and international students. Application fee: $35 ($40 for international students). Electronic applications accepted. *Expenses:* Tuition, state resident: full-time $6273; part-time $3866 per year. Tuition, nonresident: full-time $14,969; part-time $9980 per year. *Required fees:* $315 per year. *Financial support:* In 2011–12, 2 research assistantships with full and partial tuition reimbursements (averaging $13,089 per year) were awarded. Financial award application deadline: 4/1; financial award applicants required to submit FAFSA. *Faculty research:* Child/adolescent psychology, quantitative and qualitative methodology, evaluation processes, measurement and assessment. *Unit head:* Dr. Matthew Keefer, Chairperson, 314-516-5783, Fax: 314-516-5784, E-mail: keefer@ umsl.edu. *Application contact:* 314-516-5458, Fax: 314-516-6996, E-mail: gradadm@ umsl.edu. Web site: http://coe.umsl.edu/web/divisions/edpsych/index.html.

University of Nebraska–Lincoln, Graduate College, College of Education and Human Sciences, Department of Educational Psychology, Lincoln, NE 68588. Offers cognition, learning and development (MA); counseling psychology (MA); educational psychology (MA, Ed S); psychological studies in education (PhD), including cognition, learning and development, counseling psychology, quantitative, qualitative, and psychometric methods, school psychology; quantitative, qualitative, and psychometric methods (MA); school psychology (MA, Ed S). *Accreditation:* APA (one or more programs are accredited); NCATE. *Degree requirements:* For master's, thesis optional. *Entrance requirements:* For master's, GRE General Test. Additional exam requirements/ recommendations for international students: Required—TOEFL (minimum score 500 paper-based; 173 computer-based). Electronic applications accepted. *Faculty research:* Measurement and assessment, metacognition, academic skills, child development, multicultural education and counseling.

University of New England, College of Arts and Sciences, Program in Education, Biddeford, ME 04005-9526. Offers advanced educational leadership (CAGS); curriculum and instruction strategies (CAGS); curriculum and instruction strategy (MS Ed); educational leadership (MS Ed, CAGS); general studies (MS Ed); inclusion education (MS Ed); leadership, ethics and change (CAGS); literacy K-12 (MS Ed, CAGS); teaching methodologies (MS Ed). Part-time programs available. Postbaccalaureate distance learning degree programs offered (minimal on-campus study). *Faculty:* 20 part-time/adjunct. *Students:* 514 full-time (417 women), 218 part-time (165 women). In 2011, 307 master's, 86 CAGSs awarded. *Degree requirements:* For master's, collaborative action research project, integrative seminar portfolio. *Entrance requirements:* For master's, teaching certificate, 2 years of teaching experience. Additional exam requirements/recommendations for international students: Required—TOEFL. *Application deadline:* For fall admission, 9/15 for domestic students; for spring admission, 1/15 for domestic students. Applications are processed on a rolling basis. Application fee: $40. Electronic applications accepted. *Expenses:* Contact institution. *Financial support:* Application deadline: 5/1; applicants required to submit FAFSA. *Faculty research:* Distance learning, effective teaching, transition planning, adult learning. *Unit head:* Dr. Doug Lynch, Chair of Education Department, 207-283-0171 Ext. 2888, E-mail: dlynch@une.edu. *Application contact:* Stacy Gato, Assistant Director of Graduate Admissions, 207-221-4225, Fax: 207-221-4898, E-mail: gradadmissions@une.edu.

The University of North Carolina at Chapel Hill, Graduate School, School of Education, Program in Education, Chapel Hill, NC 27599. Offers culture, curriculum and change (MA, PhD); early childhood, intervention and literacy (MA, PhD); educational psychology, measurement and evaluation (MA, PhD). *Accreditation:* NCATE. *Degree requirements:* For master's, thesis; for doctorate, comprehensive exam, thesis/dissertation. *Entrance requirements:* For master's, GRE General Test, minimum GPA of 3.0 during last 2 years of undergraduates course work; for doctorate, GRE General Test, minimum GPA of 3.0 during last 2 years of undergraduate course work. Additional exam requirements/recommendations for international students: Required—TOEFL (minimum score 550 paper-based; 213 computer-based). Electronic applications accepted.

The University of North Carolina at Greensboro, Graduate School, School of Education, Department of Educational Research Methodology, Greensboro, NC 27412-5001. Offers educational research, measurement and evaluation (PhD); MS/PhD. *Accreditation:* NCATE. *Degree requirements:* For doctorate, thesis/dissertation. *Entrance requirements:* For doctorate, GRE General Test. Additional exam requirements/recommendations for international students: Required—TOEFL. Electronic applications accepted.

University of North Dakota, Graduate School, College of Education and Human Development, Teaching and Learning Program, Grand Forks, ND 58202. Offers elementary education (Ed D, PhD); measurement and statistics (Ed D, PhD); secondary education (Ed D, PhD); special education (Ed D, PhD). *Accreditation:* NCATE. Postbaccalaureate distance learning degree programs offered (minimal on-campus study). *Degree requirements:* For doctorate, comprehensive exam, thesis/dissertation, final exam. *Entrance requirements:* For doctorate, minimum GPA of 3.5. Additional exam requirements/recommendations for international students: Required—TOEFL (minimum score 550 paper-based; 213 computer-based; 79 iBT), IELTS (minimum score 6.5). Electronic applications accepted.

University of Northern Colorado, Graduate School, College of Education and Behavioral Sciences, Program in Applied Statistics and Research Methods, Greeley, CO 80639. Offers MS, PhD. Part-time programs available. *Degree requirements:* For master's, comprehensive exam; for doctorate, comprehensive exam, thesis/dissertation. *Entrance requirements:* For master's, 3 letters of reference; for doctorate, GRE General Test, 3 letters of reference. Electronic applications accepted.

University of North Texas, Toulouse Graduate School, College of Education, Department of Educational Psychology, Program in Educational Research, Denton, TX 76203. Offers PhD. *Accreditation:* NCATE. *Degree requirements:* For doctorate, one foreign language, thesis/dissertation, internship. *Entrance requirements:* For doctorate, GRE General Test, admissions exam. Additional exam requirements/recommendations for international students: Recommended—TOEFL (minimum score 550 paper-based; 213 computer-based; 79 iBT). Electronic applications accepted. *Expenses:* Tuition, state resident: part-time $100 per credit hour. Tuition, nonresident: part-time $413 per credit hour. *Faculty research:* Applied general linear modeling, reliability, factor analysis, structural equation modeling, learning environments and social/historical factors.

University of Oklahoma, Jeannine Rainbolt College of Education, Department of Educational Psychology, Program in Instructional Psychology and Technology, Norman, OK 73019. Offers instructional psychology and technology (M Ed, PhD), including educational psychology (M Ed), general (M Ed), instructional design (M Ed), integrating technology in teaching (M Ed), interactive learning technologies (M Ed), teaching and assessment (M Ed), teaching with technology (M Ed). Part-time and evening/weekend programs available. *Students:* 23 full-time (16 women), 27 part-time (20 women); includes 14 minority (8 Black or African American, non-Hispanic/Latino; 1 American Indian or Alaska Native, non-Hispanic/Latino; 3 Hispanic/Latino; 2 Two or more races, non-Hispanic/Latino), 9 international. Average age 33. 22 applicants, 77% accepted, 17 enrolled. In 2011, 12 master's, 2 doctorates awarded. *Degree requirements:* For master's, comprehensive exam (for some programs), thesis optional; for doctorate, thesis/dissertation, general exam. *Entrance requirements:* For master's, minimum GPA of 3.0; for doctorate, GRE General Test, master's degree, minimum graduate GPA of 3.25. Additional exam requirements/recommendations for international students: Required—TOEFL (minimum score 550 paper-based; 79 iBT). *Application deadline:* For fall admission, 3/15 for domestic students, 3/1 for international students; for spring admission, 10/15 for domestic and international students. Applications are processed on a rolling basis. Application fee: $40 ($90 for international students). Electronic applications accepted. *Expenses:* Tuition, state resident: full-time $4087; part-time $170.30 per credit hour. Tuition, nonresident: full-time $14,875; part-time $619.80 per credit hour. *Required fees:* $2659; $100.25 per credit hour. Tuition and fees vary according to course load and degree level. *Financial support:* In 2011–12, 39 students received support. Career-related internships or fieldwork, Federal Work-Study, scholarships/grants, health care benefits, and unspecified assistantships available. Support available to part-time students. Financial award applicants required to submit FAFSA. *Faculty research:* Cognition and instruction, motivation and instruction, instructional design, technology integration in education, interactive learning technologies, measurement and assessment. *Unit head:* Dr. Terri K. Debacker, Chair, 405-325-1068, Fax: 405-325-6655, E-mail: debacker@ou.edu. *Application contact:* Shannon Vazquez, Graduate Programs Officer, 405-325-4525, Fax: 405-325-6655, E-mail: shannonv@ou.edu. Web site: http://education.ou.edu/ipt.

University of Pennsylvania, Graduate School of Education, Division of Quantitative Methods, Program in Policy Research, Evaluation, and Measurement, Philadelphia, PA 19104. Offers M Phil, MS, PhD. Part-time programs available. *Students:* 8 full-time (3 women), 1 (woman) part-time; includes 1 minority (Asian, non-Hispanic/Latino), 3 international. 32 applicants, 16% accepted, 2 enrolled. In 2011, 2 degrees awarded. *Degree requirements:* For master's, exam; for doctorate, thesis/dissertation, exam. *Entrance requirements:* For master's, GRE General Test; for doctorate, GRE General Test, GRE Subject Test. *Application deadline:* For fall admission, 12/15 for domestic students. Applications are processed on a rolling basis. Application fee: $70. Electronic applications accepted. *Expenses:* Contact institution. *Financial support:* Fellowships and scholarships/grants available. Support available to part-time students. Financial award applicants required to submit FAFSA. *Faculty research:* Multivariate analysis of behavioral data, behavioral research design. *Unit head:* Dr. Andrew Porter, Dean, 215-898-7014. *Application contact:* Christine Lee, 215-898-0505, E-mail: cplee@gse.upenn.edu. Web site: http://www.gse.upenn.edu/degrees_programs/prem.

University of Pennsylvania, Graduate School of Education, Division of Quantitative Methods, Program in Statistics, Measurement, Assessment, and Research Technology (SMART), Philadelphia, PA 19104. Offers MS. *Students:* 16 full-time (12 women), 10 part-time (5 women); includes 4 minority (3 Black or African American, non-Hispanic/Latino; 1 Asian, non-Hispanic/Latino), 10 international. 29 applicants, 62% accepted, 11 enrolled. In 2011, 7 degrees awarded. *Expenses: Tuition:* Full-time $26,660; part-time $4944 per course. *Required fees:* $2318; $291 per course. Tuition and fees vary according to course load, degree level and program. *Unit head:* Dr. Andrew Porter, Dean, 215-898-7014. *Application contact:* 215-898-2444, E-mail: pme@gse.upenn.edu.

University of Pittsburgh, School of Education, Department of Psychology in Education, Program in Research Methodology, Pittsburgh, PA 15260. Offers M Ed, MA, PhD. Part-time and evening/weekend programs available. *Students:* 13 full-time (9 women), 15 part-time (9 women); includes 2 minority (both Asian, non-Hispanic/Latino), 8 international. Average age 34. 15 applicants, 67% accepted, 4 enrolled. Terminal master's awarded for partial completion of doctoral program. *Degree requirements:* For master's, thesis; for doctorate, thesis/dissertation. *Entrance requirements:* For doctorate, GRE General Test. Additional exam requirements/recommendations for international students: Required—TOEFL. *Application deadline:* For fall admission, 2/1 for domestic students. Application fee: $50. Electronic applications accepted. *Expenses:* Tuition, state resident: full-time $18,774; part-time $760 per credit. Tuition, nonresident: full-time $30,736; part-time $1258 per credit. *Required fees:* $740; $200 per term. Tuition and fees vary according to program. *Financial support:* Fellowships, research assistantships with partial tuition reimbursements, Federal Work-Study, tuition waivers (partial), and unspecified assistantships available. Support available to part-time students. Financial award application deadline: 3/15; financial award applicants required to submit FAFSA. *Unit head:* Dr. Carl N. Johnson, Chairman, 412-624-6942, Fax: 412-624-7231, E-mail: johnson@pitt.edu. *Application contact:* Maggie Sikora, Graduate Enrollment Manager, 412-648-2230, Fax: 412-648-1899, E-mail: soeinfo@pitt.edu. Web site: http://www.education.pitt.edu/AcademicDepartments/PsychologyinEducation/Programs/ResearchMethodology.aspx.

University of Puerto Rico, Río Piedras, College of Education, Program in Educational Research and Evaluation, San Juan, PR 00931-3300. Offers M Ed. Part-time programs available. *Degree requirements:* For master's, thesis. *Entrance requirements:* For master's, PAEG or GRE, interview, minimum GPA of 3.0, letter of recommendation.

University of St. Thomas, School of Education, Houston, TX 77006-4696. Offers all level teaching (M Ed); bilingual/dual language (M Ed); Catholic school teaching (M Ed); Catholic/private school leadership (M Ed); counselor education (M Ed); curriculum and instruction (M Ed); educational leadership (M Ed); elementary teaching (M Ed); English as a second language (M Ed); exceptionality/ educational diagnostician (M Ed); exceptionality/special education (M Ed); generalist (M Ed); reading (M Ed); secondary teaching (M Ed). Part-time and evening/weekend programs available. Postbaccalaureate distance learning degree programs offered (no on-campus study). *Faculty:* 30 full-time (17 women), 54 part-time/adjunct (37 women). *Students:* 66 full-time (43 women), 1,178 part-time (1,044 women); includes 777 minority (313 Black or African American, non-Hispanic/Latino; 5 American Indian or Alaska Native, non-Hispanic/Latino; 29 Asian, non-Hispanic/Latino; 395 Hispanic/Latino; 2 Native Hawaiian or other Pacific Islander, non-Hispanic/Latino; 33 Two or more races, non-Hispanic/Latino), 26 international. Average age 36. 551 applicants, 94% accepted, 416 enrolled. In 2011, 72 master's awarded. *Degree requirements:* For master's, thesis, field experience. *Entrance requirements:* For master's, GRE or MAT if GPA is below 3.0, bachelor's degree; minimum GPA of 2.75 in bachelor's degree or last 60 credit hours; official transcripts from all institutions; goal statement of 250-300 words; 1 reference. Additional exam requirements/recommendations for international students: Required—TOEFL. *Application deadline:* Applications are processed on a rolling basis. Application fee: $35. Electronic applications accepted. *Expenses:* Contact institution. *Financial support:* In 2011–12, 9 students received support. Federal Work-Study, scholarships/grants, and state work-study, institutional employment available. Support available to part-time students. Financial award application deadline: 4/15; financial award applicants required to submit FAFSA. *Faculty research:* Leadership, diversity, personality traits, second language acquisition. *Unit head:* Dr. Nora Hutto, Dean, 713-525-3540, Fax: 713-525-3871, E-mail: education@stthom.edu. *Application contact:* Paula C. Hollis, Administrative Assistant, 713-525-3540, Fax: 713-525-3871, E-mail: education@stthom.edu. Web site: http://www.stthom.edu/Schools_Centers_of_Excellence/Schools_of_Study/School_of_Education/Index.aqf.

University of South Carolina, The Graduate School, College of Education, Department of Educational Studies, Program in Educational Psychology, Research, Columbia, SC 29208. Offers M Ed, PhD. *Accreditation:* NCATE. Part-time programs available. *Degree requirements:* For master's, comprehensive exam, thesis (for some programs); for doctorate, comprehensive exam, thesis/dissertation. *Entrance requirements:* For master's, GRE General Test; for doctorate, GRE General Test, interview. Electronic applications accepted. *Faculty research:* Problem solving, higher order thinking skills, psychometric research, methodology.

University of Southern Mississippi, Graduate School, College of Education and Psychology, Department of Educational Studies and Research, Hattiesburg, MS 39406-0001. Offers adult education (Graduate Certificate); community college leadership (Graduate Certificate); counseling and personnel services (college) (M Ed); education (PhD, Ed S), including adult education, research, evaluation and statistics (PhD); education (Ed D), including educational administration, educational research; education: educational leadership and research (Ed S), including higher education administration; educational administration and supervision (M Ed); higher education administration (Ed D, PhD); institutional research (Graduate Certificate). *Faculty:* 7 full-time (1 woman), 5 part-time/adjunct (1 woman). *Students:* 33 full-time (25 women), 104 part-time (25 women); includes 46 minority (40 Black or African American, non-Hispanic/Latino; 1 Asian, non-Hispanic/Latino; 3 Hispanic/Latino; 2 Two or more races, non-Hispanic/Latino), 1 international. Average age 36. 27 applicants, 48% accepted, 1 enrolled. In 2011, 27 master's, 13 doctorates, 1 other advanced degree awarded. *Degree requirements:* For master's and other advanced degree, comprehensive exam, thesis (for some programs); for doctorate, comprehensive exam, thesis/dissertation. *Entrance requirements:* For master's, doctorate, and other advanced degree, GRE General Test, minimum GPA of 2.75. Additional exam requirements/recommendations for international students: Required—TOEFL. *Application deadline:* For fall admission, 2/1 for domestic students, 3/1 for international students. Applications are processed on a rolling basis. Application fee: $35. *Financial support:* Career-related internships or fieldwork, Federal Work-Study, and institutionally sponsored loans available. Financial award application deadline: 3/15; financial award applicants required to submit FAFSA.

Total annual research expenditures: $88,500. *Unit head:* Dr. Thomas V. O'Brien, Chair, 601-266-6093, E-mail: thomas.obrien@usm.edu. *Application contact:* Shonna Breland, Manager of Graduate Admissions, 601-266-6563, Fax: 601-266-5138. Web site: http://www.usm.edu/cep/esr/.

University of South Florida, Graduate School, College of Education, Department of Educational Measurement and Research, Tampa, FL 33620-9951. Offers measurement and evaluation (M Ed, PhD, Ed S). *Accreditation:* NCATE. Part-time programs available. *Faculty:* 7 full-time (2 women), 3 part-time/adjunct (2 women). *Students:* 21 full-time (17 women), 27 part-time (14 women); includes 14 minority (5 Black or African American, non-Hispanic/Latino; 3 Asian, non-Hispanic/Latino; 6 Hispanic/Latino), 8 international. Average age 40. 6 applicants, 100% accepted, 6 enrolled. In 2011, 4 master's, 2 doctorates awarded. *Median time to degree:* Of those who began their doctoral program in fall 2003, 100% received their degree in 8 years or less. *Degree requirements:* For master's, comprehensive exam; for doctorate, comprehensive exam, thesis/dissertation, philosophies of inquiry; multiple research methods. *Entrance requirements:* For master's, GRE General Test, minimum GPA of 3.0 in last 60 hours of course work; for doctorate, GRE General Test, minimum undergraduate GPA of 3.0 on upper-division coursework, master's degree or Ed S from regionally-accredited institution; for Ed S, GRE General Test, minimum undergraduate GPA of 3.0 on upper-division coursework, master's degree from regionally-accredited institution. Additional exam requirements/recommendations for international students: Required—TOEFL (minimum score 550 paper-based; 213 computer-based; 79 iBT). *Application deadline:* For fall admission, 2/15 for domestic students, 1/2 for international students; for spring admission, 10/15 for domestic students, 6/1 for international students. Applications are processed on a rolling basis. Application fee: $30. Electronic applications accepted. *Financial support:* In 2011–12, 1 student received support, including 1 fellowship with full tuition reimbursement available (averaging $10,000 per year), 8 research assistantships with full tuition reimbursements available (averaging $10,553 per year), 4 teaching assistantships with full tuition reimbursements available (averaging $10,553 per year); career-related internships or fieldwork, scholarships/grants, health care benefits, and unspecified assistantships also available. Financial award application deadline: 6/15; financial award applicants required to submit FAFSA. *Faculty research:* Multilevel modeling, methods for analyzing single case data, collaborative evaluation, validity of statistical inferences, secondary data analysis, effect sizes, meta-analyses. *Total annual research expenditures:* $252,886. *Unit head:* Dr. John Ferron, Chairperson, 813-974-5361, Fax: 813-974-4495, E-mail: ferron@tempest.coedu.usf.edu. *Application contact:* Dr. Diane Briscoe, Coordinator of Graduate Studies, 813-974-1804, Fax: 813-974-3391, E-mail: briscoe@usf.edu. Web site: http://www.coedu.usf.edu/main/departments/me/me.html.

The University of Tennessee, Graduate School, College of Education, Health and Human Sciences, Program in Education, Knoxville, TN 37996. Offers art education (MS); counseling education (PhD); cultural studies in education (PhD); curriculum (MS, Ed S); curriculum, educational research and evaluation (Ed D, PhD); early childhood education (PhD); early childhood special education (MS); education of deaf and hard of hearing (MS); educational administration and policy studies (Ed D, PhD); educational administration and supervision (Ed S); educational psychology (Ed D, PhD); elementary education (MS, Ed S); elementary teaching (MS); English education (MS, Ed S); exercise science (PhD); foreign language/ESL education (MS, Ed S); instructional technology (MS, Ed D, PhD, Ed S); literacy, language and ESL education (PhD); literacy, language education, and ESL education (Ed D); mathematics education (MS, Ed S); modified and comprehensive special education (MS); reading education (MS, Ed S); school counseling (Ed S); school psychology (PhD, Ed S); science education (MS, Ed S); secondary teaching (MS); social foundations (MS); social science education (MS, Ed S); socio-cultural foundations of sports and education (PhD); special education (Ed S); teacher education (Ed D, PhD). *Accreditation:* NCATE. Part-time and evening/weekend programs available. *Degree requirements:* For master's and Ed S, thesis optional; for doctorate, variable foreign language requirement, thesis/dissertation. *Entrance requirements:* For master's, minimum GPA of 2.7; for doctorate and Ed S, GRE General Test, minimum GPA of 2.7. Additional exam requirements/recommendations for international students: Required—TOEFL. Electronic applications accepted. *Expenses:* Tuition, state resident: full-time $8332; part-time $464 per credit hour. Tuition, nonresident: full-time $25,174; part-time $1400 per credit hour. *Required fees:* $1162; $56 per credit hour. Tuition and fees vary according to program.

The University of Texas at El Paso, Graduate School, College of Education, Department of Educational Psychology and Special Services, El Paso, TX 79968-0001. Offers educational diagnostics (M Ed); guidance and counseling (M Ed); special education (M Ed). Part-time and evening/weekend programs available. *Students:* 289 (250 women); includes 252 minority (9 Black or African American, non-Hispanic/Latino; 1 American Indian or Alaska Native, non-Hispanic/Latino; 2 Asian, non-Hispanic/Latino; 240 Hispanic/Latino), 11 international. Average age 34. 85 applicants, 71% accepted, 53 enrolled. In 2011, 53 master's awarded. *Degree requirements:* For master's, thesis optional. *Entrance requirements:* For master's, minimum GPA of 3.0. Additional exam requirements/recommendations for international students: Required—TOEFL. *Application deadline:* For fall admission, 7/1 priority date for domestic students, 3/1 for international students; for spring admission, 11/1 priority date for domestic students, 9/1 for international students. Applications are processed on a rolling basis. Application fee: $15 ($65 for international students). Electronic applications accepted. *Financial support:* In 2011–12, research assistantships with partial tuition reimbursements (averaging $16,642 per year), teaching assistantships with partial tuition reimbursements (averaging $13,314 per year) were awarded; Federal Work-Study, institutionally sponsored loans, and tuition waivers (partial) also available. Financial award application deadline: 3/15; financial award applicants required to submit FAFSA. *Unit head:* Dr. Don C. Combs, Interim Chair, 915-747-7585, E-mail: dcombs@utep.edu. *Application contact:* Dr. Benjamin Flores, Interim Dean of the Graduate School, 915-747-5491, Fax: 915-747-5788, E-mail: bflores@utep.edu.

The University of Texas–Pan American, College of Education, Department of Educational Psychology, Edinburg, TX 78539. Offers educational diagnostician (M Ed); gifted education (M Ed); guidance and counseling (M Ed); school psychology (MA); special education (M Ed). Part-time and evening/weekend programs available. *Degree requirements:* For master's, comprehensive exam (for some programs), thesis (for some programs). *Entrance requirements:* For master's, GRE General Test, interview. *Application deadline:* For fall admission, 7/17 for domestic students; for spring admission, 11/16 for domestic students. Application fee: $0. Tuition and fees vary according to course load, program and student level. *Financial support:* Research assistantships, career-related internships or fieldwork, Federal Work-Study, and institutionally sponsored loans available. Support available to part-time students. Financial award application deadline: 4/15. *Faculty research:* Reading instruction, assessment practice, behavior interventions consultation, mental retardation. *Unit head:* Dr. Paul Sale, Chair, 956-665-2433, E-mail: psale@utpa.edu. *Application contact:* Dr. Sylvia Ramirez, Associate Dean of Graduate Studies, 956-665-3488, E-mail: ramirezs@utpa.edu. Web site: http://portal.utpa.edu/utpa_main/daa_home/coed_home/edpsy_home.

The University of Toledo, College of Graduate Studies, Judith Herb College of Education, Health Science and Human Service, Department of Educational Foundations and Leadership, Toledo, OH 43606-3390. Offers educational administration and supervision (ME, DE, Ed S); educational psychology (ME, DE, PhD); educational research and measurement (ME, PhD); educational sociology (DE, PhD); educational theory and social foundations (ME); foundations of education (DE, PhD); higher education (ME, PhD); history of education (PhD); philosophy of education (PhD). *Accreditation:* NCATE. Part-time and evening/weekend programs available. *Faculty:* 32. *Students:* 26 full-time (14 women), 222 part-time (134 women); includes 78 minority (57 Black or African American, non-Hispanic/Latino; 5 Asian, non-Hispanic/Latino; 15 Hispanic/Latino; 1 Two or more races, non-Hispanic/Latino), 5 international. Average age 40. 85 applicants, 61% accepted, 34 enrolled. In 2011, 37 master's, 7 doctorates, 18 other advanced degrees awarded. *Degree requirements:* For master's, comprehensive exam, thesis or alternative; for doctorate, comprehensive exam, thesis/dissertation; for Ed S, thesis optional. *Entrance requirements:* For master's, doctorate, and Ed S, minimum cumulative GPA of 2.7 for all previous academic work, letters of recommendation. Additional exam requirements/recommendations for international students: Required—TOEFL (minimum score 550 paper-based; 213 computer-based; 80 iBT), IELTS (minimum score 6.5). *Application deadline:* For fall admission, 1/15 priority date for domestic students, 1/15 for international students. Applications are processed on a rolling basis. Application fee: $45 ($75 for international students). Electronic applications accepted. *Financial support:* In 2011–12, 10 research assistantships with full and partial tuition reimbursements (averaging $6,734 per year), 8 teaching assistantships with full and partial tuition reimbursements (averaging $9,000 per year) were awarded; career-related internships or fieldwork, Federal Work-Study, institutionally sponsored loans, scholarships/grants, tuition waivers (full and partial), unspecified assistantships, and administrative assistantships also available. Support available to part-time students. *Unit head:* Dr. William Gray, Interim Chair, 419-530-2565, Fax: 419-530-8447, E-mail: william.gray@utoledo.edu. *Application contact:* Graduate School Office, 419-530-4723, Fax: 419-530-4724, E-mail: grdsch@utnet.utoledo.edu. Web site: http://www.utoledo.edu/eduhshs/.

University of Victoria, Faculty of Graduate Studies, Faculty of Education, Department of Educational Psychology and Leadership Studies, Victoria, BC V8W 2Y2, Canada. Offers aboriginal communities counseling (M Ed); counseling (M Ed, MA); educational psychology (M Ed, MA, PhD), including counseling psychology (M Ed, MA), leadership studies (PhD), learning and development (MA, PhD), measurement and evaluation, special education (M Ed, MA); leadership studies (M Ed, MA). Part-time programs available. *Degree requirements:* For master's, thesis (for some programs), comprehensive exam (M Ed); for doctorate, comprehensive exam, thesis/dissertation, candidacy exam. *Entrance requirements:* For master's, 2 years of work experience in a relevant field; for doctorate, GRE, 2 years of work experience in a relevant field, minimum B average. Additional exam requirements/recommendations for international students: Required—TOEFL (minimum score 575 paper-based; 233 computer-based), IELTS (minimum score 7). *Faculty research:* Learning and development (child, adolescent and adult), special education and exceptional children.

University of Virginia, Curry School of Education, Department of Leadership, Foundations and Policy, Educational Policy Studies Program, Charlottesville, VA 22903. Offers M Ed, Ed D. *Students:* 1 full-time (0 women). Average age 56. *Entrance requirements:* For master's and doctorate, GRE General Test, 2 letters of recommendation. Additional exam requirements/recommendations for international students: Required—TOEFL (minimum score 600 paper-based; 250 computer-based; 90 iBT), IELTS (minimum score 7). *Application deadline:* Applications are processed on a rolling basis. Application fee: $60. Electronic applications accepted. *Financial support:* Fellowships, research assistantships, and teaching assistantships available. Financial award application deadline: 1/5; financial award applicants required to submit FAFSA. *Unit head:* James H. Wyckoff, Director, Educational Policy PhD Program, 434-924-0842, E-mail: jhw4n@virginia.edu. *Application contact:* Lisa Miller, Assistant to the Chair, 434-982-2849, E-mail: lam3v@virgnina.edu. Web site: http://curry.virginia.edu/academics/areas-of-study/education-policy.

University of Virginia, Curry School of Education, Department of Leadership, Foundations and Policy, Program in Educational Psychology, Charlottesville, VA 22903. Offers applied developmental science (M Ed); educational evaluation (M Ed); educational psychology (M Ed, Ed D, Ed S); educational research (Ed D); gifted education (M Ed); instructional technology (M Ed, Ed S); research statistics and evaluation (Ed D); school psychology (Ed D). *Students:* 17 full-time (12 women), 10 part-time (7 women); includes 2 minority (1 Black or African American, non-Hispanic/Latino; 1 Hispanic/Latino), 1 international. Average age 29. 56 applicants, 77% accepted, 23 enrolled. In 2011, 40 master's, 1 doctorate awarded. *Degree requirements:* For master's, comprehensive exam. *Entrance requirements:* For master's and doctorate, GRE General Test, 2 letters of recommendation. Additional exam requirements/recommendations for international students: Required—TOEFL (minimum score 600 paper-based; 250 computer-based; 90 iBT), IELTS (minimum score 7). *Application deadline:* Applications are processed on a rolling basis. Application fee: $60. Electronic applications accepted. *Financial support:* Fellowships, research assistantships, and teaching assistantships available. Financial award application deadline: 1/5; financial award applicants required to submit FAFSA. *Unit head:* Christopher De La Cerda, Program Coordinator, 434-243-2021, E-mail: cjd8kn@virginia.edu. *Application contact:* Lisa Miller, Assistant to the Chair, 434-982-2849, E-mail: lam3v@virgnina.edu.

University of Virginia, Curry School of Education, Program in Education, Charlottesville, VA 22903. Offers administration and supervision (PhD); applied developmental science (PhD); counselor education (PhD); curriculum and instruction (PhD); early childhood-developmental risk (MT); education evaluation (PhD); educational psychology (PhD); educational research (PhD); elementary (MT, PhD); English education (MT, PhD); foreign language education (MT); higher education (PhD); instructional technology (PhD); kinesiology (MT, PhD); math education (PhD); reading education (PhD); research statistics and evaluation (PhD); school psychology (PhD); science education (PhD); social studies education (MT, PhD); special education (PhD); world languages education (MT). *Students:* 299 full-time (216 women), 60 part-time (33 women); includes 46 minority (18 Black or African American, non-Hispanic/Latino; 17 Asian, non-Hispanic/Latino; 7 Hispanic/Latino; 4 Two or more races, non-Hispanic/Latino), 23 international. Average age 30. 307 applicants, 42% accepted, 80 enrolled. In 2011, 113 master's, 62 doctorates awarded. *Degree requirements:* For master's, comprehensive exam (for some programs), field project; for doctorate, comprehensive exam, thesis/dissertation. *Entrance requirements:* For doctorate, GRE General Test. Additional exam requirements/recommendations for international students: Required—TOEFL (minimum score 600 paper-based; 250 computer-based; 90 iBT), IELTS (minimum score 7). *Application deadline:* Applications are processed on a rolling basis. Application fee: $60. Electronic applications accepted. *Financial support:* Fellowships, research assistantships, and teaching assistantships available. Financial award application deadline: 1/5; financial award applicants required to submit FAFSA. *Unit head:* Robert C. Pianta, Dean, 434-924-3334. *Application contact:* Joanne McNergney, Assistant Dean for Admissions and Student Services, 434-924-3334, E-mail: curry-admissions@virginia.edu.

University of Washington, Graduate School, College of Education, Program in Educational Psychology, Seattle, WA 98195. Offers educational psychology (PhD); human development and cognition (M Ed); learning sciences (M Ed, PhD); measurement, statistics and research design (M Ed); school psychology (M Ed). *Accreditation:* APA. *Degree requirements:* For master's, thesis optional; for doctorate, thesis/dissertation. *Entrance requirements:* For master's and doctorate, GRE General Test, minimum GPA of 3.0. Additional exam requirements/recommendations for international students: Required—TOEFL.

University of Wisconsin–Milwaukee, Graduate School, School of Education, Department of Educational Psychology, Milwaukee, WI 53201-0413. Offers counseling (school, community) (MS); counseling psychology (PhD); learning and development (MS); research methodology (MS, PhD); school psychology (PhD). *Accreditation:* APA. Part-time programs available. *Faculty:* 15 full-time (9 women), 1 (woman) part-time/adjunct. *Students:* 146 full-time (110 women), 60 part-time (46 women); includes 42 minority (14 Black or African American, non-Hispanic/Latino; 10 Asian, non-Hispanic/Latino; 4 Hispanic/Latino; 14 Two or more races, non-Hispanic/Latino), 11 international. Average age 30. 240 applicants, 52% accepted, 52 enrolled. In 2011, 78 master's, 15 doctorates awarded. *Degree requirements:* For master's, comprehensive exam, thesis; for doctorate, thesis/dissertation. *Entrance requirements:* For master's, minimum GPA of 3.0; for doctorate, GRE General Test, minimum GPA of 3.0. Additional exam requirements/recommendations for international students: Required—TOEFL (minimum score 550 paper-based; 79 iBT), IELTS (minimum score 6.5). *Application deadline:* For fall admission, 1/1 priority date for domestic students; for spring admission, 9/1 for domestic students. Applications are processed on a rolling basis. Application fee: $56 ($96 for international students). Electronic applications accepted. One-time fee: $506.10 full-time. Tuition and fees vary according to course load and reciprocity agreements. *Financial support:* In 2011–12, 14 fellowships, 1 research assistantship, 8 teaching assistantships were awarded; career-related internships or fieldwork, health care benefits, unspecified assistantships, and project assistantships also available. Support available to part-time students. Financial award application deadline: 4/15; financial award applicants required to submit FAFSA. *Total annual research expenditures:* $287,260. *Unit head:* Nadya Fouad, Department Chair, 414-229-6830, Fax: 414-229-4939, E-mail: nadya@uwm.edu. *Application contact:* General Information Contact, 414-229-4982, Fax: 414-229-6967, E-mail: gradschool@uwm.edu. Web site: http://www.uwm.edu/Dept/EdPsych/.

Utah State University, School of Graduate Studies, Emma Eccles Jones College of Education and Human Services, Department of Psychology, Logan, UT 84322. Offers clinical/counseling/school psychology (PhD); research and evaluation methodology (PhD); school counseling (MS); school psychology (MS). *Accreditation:* APA (one or more programs are accredited). Part-time and evening/weekend programs available. Postbaccalaureate distance learning degree programs offered (no on-campus study). Terminal master's awarded for partial completion of doctoral program. *Degree requirements:* For master's, thesis (for some programs); for doctorate, thesis/dissertation. *Entrance requirements:* For master's, GRE General Test (school psychology), MAT (school counseling), minimum GPA of 3.5; for doctorate, GRE General Test, minimum GPA of 3.5. Additional exam requirements/recommendations for international students: Required—TOEFL. *Faculty research:* Hearing loss detection in infancy, ADHD, eating disorders, domestic violence, neuropsychology, bilingual/Spanish speaking students/parents.

Utah State University, School of Graduate Studies, Emma Eccles Jones College of Education and Human Services, Doctoral Program in Education, Logan, UT 84322. Offers business information systems (Ed D, PhD); curriculum and instruction (Ed D, PhD); research and evaluation (PhD). *Degree requirements:* For doctorate, comprehensive exam, thesis/dissertation. *Entrance requirements:* For doctorate, GRE General Test, minimum GPA of 3.0, master's degree. Additional exam requirements/recommendations for international students: Required—TOEFL. Electronic applications accepted. *Faculty research:* Language and literacy development, math and science education, instructional technology, hearing problems/deafness, domestic violence and animal abuse.

Vanderbilt University, Graduate School, Department of Physics and Astronomy, Nashville, TN 37240-1001. Offers astronomy (MS); physics (MA, MAT, MS, PhD). *Faculty:* 34 full-time (4 women), 2 part-time/adjunct (0 women). *Students:* 78 full-time (20 women), 3 part-time (0 women); includes 13 minority (6 Black or African American, non-Hispanic/Latino; 1 Asian, non-Hispanic/Latino; 4 Hispanic/Latino; 2 Two or more races, non-Hispanic/Latino), 22 international. Average age 28. 171 applicants, 25% accepted, 15 enrolled. In 2011, 8 master's, 4 doctorates awarded. *Degree requirements:* For master's, thesis; for doctorate, comprehensive exam, thesis/dissertation, final and qualifying exams. *Entrance requirements:* For master's, GRE General Test; for doctorate, GRE General Test, GRE Subject Test. Additional exam requirements/recommendations for international students: Required—TOEFL (minimum score 570 paper-based; 230 computer-based; 88 iBT). *Application deadline:* For fall admission, 1/15 for domestic and international students. Application fee: $0. Electronic applications accepted. *Financial support:* Fellowships with full and partial tuition reimbursements, research assistantships with full tuition reimbursements, teaching assistantships with full tuition reimbursements, career-related internships or fieldwork, Federal Work-Study, and institutionally sponsored loans available. Financial award application deadline: 1/15; financial award applicants required to submit CSS PROFILE or FAFSA. *Faculty research:* Experimental and theoretical physics, free electron laser, living-state physics, heavy-ion physics, nuclear structure. *Unit head:* Dr. Robert J. Scherrer, Chair, 615-322-2828, Fax: 615-343-7263, E-mail: robert.scherrer@vanderbilt.edu. *Application contact:* Dr. Julia Velkovska, Director of Graduate Studies, 615-322-0656, Fax: 615-343-7263, E-mail: julia.velkovska@vanderbilt.edu. Web site: http://www.vanderbilt.edu/physics/.

Virginia Commonwealth University, Graduate School, School of Education, Doctoral Program in Education, Research and Evaluation Track, Richmond, VA 23284-9005. Offers PhD. *Entrance requirements:* For doctorate, GRE. Additional exam requirements/recommendations for international students: Required—TOEFL (minimum score 600 paper-based; 250 computer-based; 100 iBT). Electronic applications accepted. *Expenses:* Tuition, state resident: full-time $9133; part-time $507 per credit. Tuition, nonresident: full-time $18,777; part-time $1043 per credit. *Required fees:* $77 per credit. Tuition and fees vary according to degree level, campus/location, program and student level.

Virginia Polytechnic Institute and State University, Graduate School, College of Liberal Arts and Human Sciences, School of Education, Department of Educational Leadership and Policy Studies, Blacksburg, VA 24061. Offers administration and supervision of special education (Ed D, PhD); counselor education (MA, PhD); educational leadership and policy studies (MA, Ed D, PhD, Ed S); educational research and evaluation (PhD); higher education (MA, PhD). *Accreditation:* ACA; NCATE. *Degree requirements:* For master's, comprehensive exam (for some programs), thesis (for some programs); for doctorate, comprehensive exam (for some programs), thesis/dissertation (for some programs). *Entrance requirements:* For master's and doctorate, GRE. Additional exam requirements/recommendations for international students: Required—TOEFL (minimum score 550 paper-based; 213 computer-based). *Application deadline:* For fall admission, 7/1 for domestic and international students; for spring admission, 12/1 for domestic and international students. Applications are processed on a rolling basis. Application fee: $65. Electronic applications accepted. *Expenses:* Tuition, state resident: full-time $10,048; part-time $558.25 per credit hour. Tuition, nonresident: full-time $19,497; part-time $1083.25 per credit hour. *Required fees:* $405 per semester. Tuition and fees vary according to course load, campus/location and program. *Financial support:* Career-related internships or fieldwork, Federal Work-Study, scholarships/grants, health care benefits, and unspecified assistantships available. Financial award application deadline: 1/15. *Unit head:* Dr. M. David Alexander, Unit Head, 540-231-9723, Fax: 540-231-7845, E-mail: mdavid@vt.edu. *Application contact:* Daisy Stewart, Information Contact, 540-231-8180, Fax: 540-231-7845, E-mail: daisys@vt.edu. Web site: http://www.soe.vt.edu/elps/index.html.

Virginia Polytechnic Institute and State University, Graduate School, College of Liberal Arts and Human Sciences, School of Education, Department of Teaching and Learning, Blacksburg, VA 24061. Offers career and technical education (MS Ed, Ed D, PhD, Ed S); cognition and education (Certificate); counselor education (MA, PhD); curriculum and instruction (MA Ed, Ed D, PhD, Ed S); educational research, evaluation (PhD); higher education administration (Certificate); integrative STEM education (Certificate). *Accreditation:* NCATE. Postbaccalaureate distance learning degree programs offered (no on-campus study). Terminal master's awarded for partial completion of doctoral program. *Degree requirements:* For master's, comprehensive exam (for some programs), thesis (for some programs); for doctorate, comprehensive exam (for some programs), thesis/dissertation (for some programs). *Entrance requirements:* For master's and doctorate, GRE. Additional exam requirements/recommendations for international students: Required—TOEFL (minimum score 550 paper-based; 213 computer-based). *Application deadline:* For fall admission, 7/1 for domestic and international students; for spring admission, 12/1 for domestic and international students. Applications are processed on a rolling basis. Application fee: $65. Electronic applications accepted. *Expenses:* Tuition, state resident: full-time $10,048; part-time $558.25 per credit hour. Tuition, nonresident: full-time $19,497; part-time $1083.25 per credit hour. *Required fees:* $405 per semester. Tuition and fees vary according to course load, campus/location and program. *Financial support:* Career-related internships or fieldwork, Federal Work-Study, scholarships/grants, health care benefits, and unspecified assistantships available. Financial award application deadline: 1/15. *Faculty research:* Instructional technology, teacher evaluation, school change, literacy, teaching strategies. *Unit head:* Dr. Daisy L. Stewart, Unit Head, 540-231-8180, Fax: 540-231-3717, E-mail: daisys@vt.edu. *Application contact:* Daisy Stewart, Contact, 540-231-8180, Fax: 540-231-3717, E-mail: daisys@vt.edu. Web site: http://www.soe.vt.edu/.

Walden University, Graduate Programs, Richard W. Riley College of Education and Leadership, Minneapolis, MN 55401. Offers administrator leadership for teaching and learning (Ed D, Ed S); adult education (Ed D, Ed S); adult learning (MS, Postbaccalaureate Certificate), including developmental education (MS), online teaching (MS), teaching adults English as a second language (MS), training and performance management (MS); college teaching and learning (Ed D, Ed S, Postbaccalaureate Certificate); curriculum, instruction and assessment (Ed D, Postbaccalaureate Certificate); curriculum, instruction, and professional development (Ed S); developmental education (Postbaccalaureate Certificate); early childhood administration, management, and leadership (Postbaccalaureate Certificate); early childhood education (birth-grade 3) (MAT); early childhood public policy and advocacy (Postbaccalaureate Certificate); early childhood studies (MS), including administration, management and leadership, early childhood public policy and advocacy, teaching adults in the early childhood field, teaching and diversity; education (MS, PhD), including adolescent literacy and technology (grades 6-12) (MS), adult education leadership (PhD), assessment, evaluation, and accountability (PhD), community college leadership (PhD), curriculum, instruction, and assessment, early childhood education (PhD), educational technology (PhD), elementary reading and literacy (MS), elementary reading and mathematics (MS), general program, global and comparative education (PhD), higher education (PhD), integrating technology in the classroom (MS), K-12 educational leadership (PhD), leadership, policy and change (PhD), learning, instruction and innovation (PhD), literacy and learning in the content areas (MS), mathematics (grades 6-8) (MS), mathematics (grades K-5) (MS), middle level education (grades 5-8) (MS), professional development (MS), science (grades K-8) (MS), self-designed (PhD), special education (PhD), special education (non-licensure) (MS), teacher leadership (grades K-12) (MS), teaching English language learners (grades K-12) (MS); educational leadership and administration (principal preparation) (Ed S); educational technology (Ed S); elementary reading and literacy (Postbaccalaureate Certificate); engaging culturally diverse learners (Postbaccalaureate Certificate); enrollment management and institutional marketing (Postbaccalaureate Certificate); higher education (MS), including college teaching and learning, enrollment management and institutional planning, global higher education, leadership for student success, online and distance learning; higher education leadership (Ed D); instructional design (Postbaccalaureate Certificate); instructional design and technology (MS), including general program (MS, PhD), online learning, training and performance improvement; integrating technology in the classroom (Postbaccalaureate Certificate); online teaching for adult learners (Postbaccalaureate Certificate); professional development (Postbaccalaureate Certificate); reading and literacy leadership (Ed D); science K-8 (Postbaccalaureate Certificate); special education (Ed D, Ed S); special education: emotional/behavioral disorders (K-12) (MAT); special education: learning disabilities (K-12) (MAT); teacher leadership (Ed D, Ed S, Postbaccalaureate Certificate); training and performance management (Postbaccalaureate Certificate). Part-time and evening/weekend programs available. Postbaccalaureate distance learning degree programs offered (minimal on-campus study). *Faculty:* 71 full-time (48 women), 853 part-time/adjunct (585 women). *Students:* 11,326 full-time (9,212 women), 2,148 part-time (1,795 women); includes 5,346 minority (4,403 Black or African American, non-Hispanic/Latino; 76 American Indian or Alaska Native, non-Hispanic/Latino; 140 Asian, non-Hispanic/Latino; 561 Hispanic/Latino; 21 Native Hawaiian or other Pacific Islander, non-Hispanic/Latino; 145 Two or more races, non-Hispanic/Latino), 322 international. Average age 39. In 2011, 3,477 master's, 318 doctorates, 471 other advanced degrees awarded. *Degree requirements:* For doctorate, thesis/dissertation (for some programs), residency; for other advanced degree, residency (for some programs). *Entrance requirements:* For master's, bachelor's degree or equivalent in related field; minimum GPA of 2.5; official transcripts; goal statement; access to computer and Internet; for doctorate, master's degree or equivalent in related field; minimum GPA of 3.0; official transcripts; three years' related professional/academic experience (preferred); access to computer and Internet; for other advanced degree, master's degree or equivalent in related field; minimum GPA of 3.0; 3 years related professional/academic experience (preferred); access to computer and Internet (Ed S). Additional exam requirements/recommendations for international students: Required—TOEFL (minimum score 550 paper-based; 213 computer-based), IELTS (minimum score 6.5), or Michigan English Language Assessment Battery (minimum score 82). *Application deadline:* Applications are processed on a rolling basis. Application fee: $50. Electronic applications accepted. *Financial support:* Federal Work-Study, scholarships/grants, unspecified assistantships, and family tuition reduction, active duty/veteran tuition reduction, group tuition reduction, interest-free payment plans, employee tuition reduction available. Support available to part-time students. Financial award applicants required to submit FAFSA. *Unit head:* Dr. Kate Steffens, Dean, 800-925-3368. *Application contact:* Jennifer Hall, Vice President of Enrollment Management, 866-4-WALDEN, E-mail: info@waldenu.edu. Web site: http://www.waldenu.edu/Colleges-and-Schools/College-of-Education-and-Leadership.htm.

Washington University in St. Louis, Graduate School of Arts and Sciences, Department of Education, Program in Educational Research, St. Louis, MO 63130-4899. Offers PhD. *Entrance requirements:* For doctorate, GRE General Test. Electronic applications accepted.

Wayne State University, College of Education, Division of Theoretical and Behavioral Foundations, Detroit, MI 48202. Offers counseling (M Ed, MA, Ed D, PhD, Ed S); education evaluation and research (M Ed, Ed D, PhD); educational psychology (M Ed, Ed D, PhD, Ed S); educational sociology (M Ed, Ed D, PhD, Ed S); history and philosophy of education (M Ed, Ed D, PhD); rehabilitation counseling and community inclusion (MA, Ed S); school and community psychology (MA, Ed S); school clinical psychology (Ed S). *Accreditation:* ACA (one or more programs are accredited); CORE (one or more programs are accredited). Evening/weekend programs available. *Students:* 199 full-time (156 women), 215 part-time (187 women); includes 162 minority (145 Black or African American, non-Hispanic/Latino; 1 American Indian or Alaska Native, non-Hispanic/Latino; 5 Asian, non-Hispanic/Latino; 5 Hispanic/Latino; 1 Native Hawaiian or other Pacific Islander, non-Hispanic/Latino; 5 Two or more races, non-Hispanic/Latino), 21 international. Average age 35. 278 applicants, 30% accepted, 56 enrolled. In 2011, 94 master's, 15 doctorates, 1 other advanced degree awarded. *Degree requirements:* For master's, thesis (for some programs); for doctorate, thesis/dissertation. *Entrance requirements:* For master's, GRE; for doctorate, GRE, interview, minimum GPA of 3.0, curriculum vitae, references. Additional exam requirements/recommendations for international students: Required—TOEFL (minimum score 550 paper-based; 213 computer-based), TWE (minimum score 5.5). *Application deadline:* For fall admission, 6/1 priority date for domestic students, 5/1 for international students; for winter admission, 10/1 priority date for domestic students, 9/1 for international students; for spring admission, 2/1 priority date for domestic students, 1/1 for international students. Applications are processed on a rolling basis. Application fee: $50. Electronic applications accepted. *Expenses:* Tuition, state resident: part-time $512.85 per credit. Tuition, nonresident: part-time $1132.65 per credit. *Required fees:* $26.60 per credit. $199.65 per semester. Tuition and fees vary according to course load and program. *Financial support:* In 2011–12, 64 students received support, including 3 fellowships with tuition reimbursements available (averaging $16,371 per year), 2 research assistantships with tuition reimbursements available (averaging $15,713 per year), 1 teaching assistantship (averaging $18,000 per year); career-related internships or fieldwork, Federal Work-Study, institutionally sponsored loans, scholarships/grants, health care benefits, and unspecified assistantships also available. *Faculty research:* Adolescents at risk, supervision of counseling. *Total annual research expenditures:* $5,019. *Unit head:* Dr. Alan Hoffman, Assistant Dean, 313-577-5235, E-mail: alanhoffman@wayne.edu. *Application contact:* Janice Green, Assistant Dean, 313-577-1605, E-mail: jwgreen@wayne.edu. Web site: http://coe.wayne.edu/tbf/index.php.

Western Governors University, Teachers College, Salt Lake City, UT 84107. Offers curriculum and instruction (MS); educational leadership (MS); educational studies (MA); educational studies (5-12) (MA), including mathematics; elementary education (k-8) (Postbaccalaureate Certificate); English language learning (K-12) (MA); instructional design (MAT); learning and technology (M Ed, MA); management and innovation (M Ed); mathematics (5-12) (Postbaccalaureate Certificate); mathematics (5-9) (Postbaccalaureate Certificate); mathematics education (5-12) (MA); mathematics education (5-9) (MA); mathematics education (K-6) (MA); measurement and evaluation (M Ed); science (5-12) (Postbaccalaureate Certificate); science (5-9) (Postbaccalaureate Certificate); science education (5-12) (MA), including biology, chemistry, geology, physics; science education (5-9) (MA); social science (5-12) (MAT); special education (MAT). *Accreditation:* NCATE. Evening/weekend programs available. Postbaccalaureate distance learning degree programs offered (no on-campus study). *Students:* 3,746 full-time (2,811 women); includes 652 minority (332 Black or African American, non-Hispanic/Latino; 37 American Indian or Alaska Native, non-Hispanic/Latino; 74 Asian, non-Hispanic/Latino; 139 Hispanic/Latino; 70 Two or more races, non-Hispanic/Latino), 12 international. Average age 37. In 2011, 1,080 master's, 242 other advanced degrees awarded. *Degree requirements:* For master's, capstone project. *Entrance requirements:* For master's and Postbaccalaureate Certificate, Readiness Assessment, commitment counseling discussion, transcript submissions, completion of orientation. Additional exam requirements/recommendations for international students: Required—TOEFL (minimum score 450 paper-based; 80 iBT). *Application deadline:* Applications are processed on a rolling basis. Application fee: $65. Electronic applications accepted. *Expenses:* Contact institution. *Financial support:* Scholarships/grants and tuition waivers (partial) available. Financial award applicants required to submit FAFSA. *Unit head:* Dr. Philip Schmidt, Dean of the Teachers College, 845-255-4656. *Application contact:* Enrollment Department, 866-225-5948, Fax: 801-274-3306, E-mail: info@wgu.edu.

Western Michigan University, Graduate College, College of Education and Human Development, Department of Educational Leadership, Research and Technology, Kalamazoo, MI 49008. Offers educational leadership (MA, PhD, Ed S); educational technology (MA, Graduate Certificate); evaluation, measurement and research (MA, PhD).

Western Michigan University, Graduate College, The Evaluation Center, Kalamazoo, MI 49008. Offers PhD.

West Texas A&M University, College of Education and Social Sciences, Division of Education, Program in Educational Diagnostician, Canyon, TX 79016-0001. Offers M Ed. Part-time programs available. Postbaccalaureate distance learning degree programs offered (minimal on-campus study). *Degree requirements:* For master's, comprehensive exam, thesis optional. *Entrance requirements:* For master's, GRE General Test, 3 years teaching experience, competency in diagnosis and prescription. Additional exam requirements/recommendations for international students: Required—TOEFL (minimum score 550 paper-based). Electronic applications accepted. *Faculty research:* Teacher preparation through web-based instruction, developmental disabilities.

Wilkes University, College of Graduate and Professional Studies, School of Education, Wilkes-Barre, PA 18766-0002. Offers art and science of teaching (MS Ed); classroom technology (MS Ed); early childhood literacy (MS Ed); educational computing (MS Ed); educational development and strategies (MS Ed); educational leadership (MS Ed); educational technology (Ed D); higher education administration (Ed D); instructional media (MS Ed); instructional technology (MS Ed); K-12 administration (Ed D); online teaching (MS Ed); reading (MS Ed); school business leadership (MS Ed); secondary education (MS Ed), including biology, chemistry, English, history, mathematics; special education (MS Ed); teaching English as a second language (MS Ed); twenty-first century teaching and learning (MS Ed). Part-time and evening/weekend programs available. Postbaccalaureate distance learning degree programs offered (minimal on-campus study). *Students:* 92 full-time (63 women), 2,005 part-time (1,459 women); includes 89 minority (23 Black or African American, non-Hispanic/Latino; 1 American Indian or Alaska Native, non-Hispanic/Latino; 14 Asian, non-Hispanic/Latino; 33 Hispanic/Latino; 1 Native Hawaiian or other Pacific Islander, non-Hispanic/Latino; 17 Two or more races, non-Hispanic/Latino), 6 international. Average age 33. In 2011, 1,150 master's, 3 doctorates awarded. *Entrance requirements:* Additional exam requirements/recommendations for international students: Required—TOEFL (minimum score 550 paper-based; 213 computer-based; 79 iBT). *Application deadline:* Applications are processed on a rolling basis. Application fee: $45. Electronic applications accepted. *Expenses:* Contact institution. *Financial support:* Federal Work-Study and unspecified assistantships available. Financial award application deadline: 3/1; financial award applicants required to submit FAFSA. *Unit head:* Dr. Michael Speziale, Dean, 570-408-4679, Fax: 570-408-4905, E-mail: michael.speziale@wilkes.edu. *Application contact:* Erin Sutzko, Director of Extended Learning, 570-408-4253, Fax: 570-408-7846, E-mail: erin.sutzko@wilkes.edu. Web site: http://www.wilkes.edu/pages/383.asp.

Educational Media/Instructional Technology

Abilene Christian University, Graduate School, College of Education and Human Services, Graduate Studies in Education, Leadership of Learning Program, Abilene, TX 79699-9100. Offers leadership of digital learning (Certificate); leadership of learning (M Ed). Part-time programs available. Postbaccalaureate distance learning degree programs offered (no on-campus study). *Faculty:* 4 full-time (1 woman). *Students:* 3 full-time (1 woman), 69 part-time (51 women); includes 15 minority (8 Black or African American, non-Hispanic/Latino; 1 Asian, non-Hispanic/Latino; 5 Hispanic/Latino; 1 Two or more races, non-Hispanic/Latino), 2 international. 41 applicants, 39% accepted, 12 enrolled. In 2011, 32 master's, 5 Certificates awarded. *Degree requirements:* For master's, comprehensive exam, practicum. *Entrance requirements:* Additional exam requirements/recommendations for international students: Required—TOEFL (minimum score 550 paper-based; 213 computer-based; 80 iBT), IELTS (minimum score 6). *Application deadline:* For fall admission, 8/15 priority date for domestic students; for winter admission, 10/1 priority date for domestic students; for spring admission, 12/15 priority date for domestic students. Applications are processed on a rolling basis. Application fee: $50. Electronic applications accepted. *Expenses: Tuition:* Full-time $14,168; part-time $787 per hour. *Required fees:* $82 per hour. $10 per term. *Financial support:* In 2011–12, 1 student received support. Application deadline: 4/1; applicants required to submit FAFSA. *Unit head:* Dr. Lloyd Goldsmith, Graduate Director, 325-674-2946, Fax: 325-674-2123, E-mail: lloyd.goldsmith@acu.edu. *Application contact:* David Pittman, Graduate Admissions Counselor, 325-674-2656, Fax: 325-674-6717, E-mail: gradinfo@acu.edu.

Acadia University, Faculty of Professional Studies, School of Education, Program in Curriculum Studies, Wolfville, NS B4P 2R6, Canada. Offers cultural and media studies (M Ed); learning and technology (M Ed); science, math and technology (M Ed). Part-time programs available. *Degree requirements:* For master's, thesis optional. *Entrance requirements:* For master's, B Ed or the equivalent, minimum B average in undergraduate course work, 2 years of teaching experience. Additional exam requirements/recommendations for international students: Required—TOEFL (minimum score 580 paper-based; 237 computer-based; 93 iBT), IELTS (minimum score 6.5). *Faculty research:* Literacy development, postmodern philosophy and curriculum theory, historiography, philosophy of education, learning and technology.

Adelphi University, Ruth S. Ammon School of Education, Program in Educational Leadership and Technology, Garden City, NY 11530-0701. Offers MA, Certificate. *Students:* 1 (woman) full-time, 34 part-time (23 women); includes 17 minority (10 Black or African American, non-Hispanic/Latino; 5 Hispanic/Latino; 2 Two or more races, non-Hispanic/Latino). Average age 35. In 2011, 13 master's, 13 other advanced degrees awarded. *Entrance requirements:* For master's, 2 letters of recommendation, resume, letter attesting to teaching experience (3 years full-time K-12). Additional exam requirements/recommendations for international students: Required—TOEFL (minimum score 550 paper-based; 213 computer-based; 80 iBT). *Application deadline:* For fall admission, 8/15 priority date for domestic students, 4/1 for international students; for spring admission, 1/15 priority date for domestic students, 11/1 for international students. Applications are processed on a rolling basis. Application fee: $50. Electronic applications accepted. *Expenses: Tuition:* Full-time $29,600; part-time $930 per credit. *Required fees:* $1100. *Financial support:* Research assistantships with partial tuition reimbursements and institutionally sponsored loans available. Financial award application deadline: 2/15; financial award applicants required to submit FAFSA. *Faculty research:* Technology methodology focusing on in-service and pre-service curriculum. *Unit head:* Dr. Devin Thornburg, Director, 516-877-4026, E-mail: thornburg@adelphi.edu. *Application contact:* Christine Murphy, Director of Admissions, 516-877-3050, Fax: 516-877-3039, E-mail: graduateadmissions@adelphi.edu.

Alabama State University, Department of Instructional Support, Library Education Media Program, Montgomery, AL 36101-0271. Offers M Ed, Ed S. Part-time programs available. *Students:* 1 (woman) full-time, 14 part-time (12 women); includes 13 minority (all Black or African American, non-Hispanic/Latino). Average age 35. 6 applicants, 100% accepted, 0 enrolled. In 2011, 5 degrees awarded. *Degree requirements:* For master's, comprehensive exam; for Ed S, comprehensive exam, thesis. *Entrance requirements:* For master's, GRE General Test or MAT, writing competency test, 2 letters of recommendation; for Ed S, writing competency test, GRE or MAT, 2 letters of recommendation. Additional exam requirements/recommendations for international students: Required—TOEFL (minimum score 500 paper-based; 173 computer-based). *Application deadline:* For fall admission, 7/15 for domestic students; for spring admission, 12/15 for domestic students. Applications are processed on a rolling basis. Application fee: $10. *Financial support:* In 2011–12, research assistantships (averaging $9,450 per year) were awarded. *Faculty research:* Developing research capabilities through media, computer and media usage for teaching young children, use of media for in-service. *Unit head:* Dr. Agnes Helen Bellel, Coordinator, 334-229-8801, E-mail:

abellel@alasu.edu. *Application contact:* Dr. Doris Screws, Dean of Graduate Studies, 334-229-4274, Fax: 334-229-4928, E-mail: dscrews@alasu.edu. Web site: http://www.alasu.edu/academics/colleges—departments/college-of-education/instructional-support-programs/library-education-media/index.aspx.

Alliant International University–Irvine, Shirley M. Hufstedler School of Education, Teacher Education Programs, Irvine, CA 92612. Offers auditory oral education (Certificate); CLAD (Certificate); preliminary multiple subject (Credential); preliminary multiple subject with BCLAD (Credential); preliminary single subject (Credential); professional clear multiple subject (Credential); professional clear single subject (Credential); teaching (MA, Credential); technology and learning (MA). Part-time and evening/weekend programs available. *Students:* 4. In 2011, 6 master's awarded. *Entrance requirements:* For degree, California Basic Educational Skills Test, minimum GPA of 2.5. Additional exam requirements/recommendations for international students: Required—TOEFL (minimum score 550 paper-based; 213 computer-based), TWE. *Application deadline:* For fall admission, 7/1 priority date for domestic students, 7/1 for international students; for spring admission, 12/1 priority date for domestic students, 12/1 for international students. Applications are processed on a rolling basis. Application fee: $55. Electronic applications accepted. *Financial support:* Career-related internships or fieldwork, Federal Work-Study, institutionally sponsored loans, and scholarships/grants available. Financial award applicants required to submit FAFSA. *Unit head:* Dr. Trudy Day, Assistant Dean, 866-825-5426, Fax: 949-833-3507, E-mail: admissions@alliant.edu. *Application contact:* Alliant International University Central Contact Center, 866-U-ALLIANT, Fax: 858-635-4555, E-mail: admissions@alliant.edu. Web site: http://www.alliant.edu/gsoe.

Alverno College, School of Education, Milwaukee, WI 53234-3922. Offers adaptive education (MA); administrative leadership (MA); adult education and organizational development (MA); adult educational and instructional design (MA); adult educational and instructional technology (MA); global connections in the humanities (MA); instructional leadership (MA); instructional technology for K-12 settings (MA); professional development (MA); reading education (MA); reading education with adaptive education (MA); science education (MA); teaching in alternative schools (MA). *Accreditation:* NCATE. Part-time and evening/weekend programs available. *Faculty:* 22 full-time (18 women), 13 part-time/adjunct (all women). *Students:* 63 full-time (58 women), 91 part-time (81 women); includes 36 minority (29 Black or African American, non-Hispanic/Latino; 1 Asian, non-Hispanic/Latino; 4 Hispanic/Latino; 1 Native Hawaiian or other Pacific Islander, non-Hispanic/Latino; 1 Two or more races, non-Hispanic/Latino), 2 international. Average age 38. 151 applicants, 60% accepted, 62 enrolled. In 2011, 52 master's awarded. *Degree requirements:* For master's, presentation/defense of proposal, conference presentation of inquiry projects. *Entrance requirements:* For master's, bachelor's degree in related field, communication samples from work setting, 3 letters of recommendation. Additional exam requirements/recommendations for international students: Required—TOEFL. *Application deadline:* For fall admission, 7/15 priority date for domestic students, 7/15 for international students; for spring admission, 12/15 priority date for domestic students, 12/15 for international students. Applications are processed on a rolling basis. Application fee: $0. Electronic applications accepted. Application fee is waived when completed online. Tuition and fees vary according to program. *Financial support:* In 2011–12, 1 student received support. Federal Work-Study available. Support available to part-time students. Financial award application deadline: 4/15; financial award applicants required to submit FAFSA. *Faculty research:* Student self-assessment, self-reflection, integration of curriculum, identifying needs of students in strategic situations and designing appropriate classroom strategies. *Unit head:* Dr. Desiree Pointer-Mace, Associate Dean, Graduate Program, 414-382-6345, Fax: 414-382-6332, E-mail: desiree.pointer-mace@alverno.edu. *Application contact:* Mary Claire Jones, Graduate Recruiter, 414-382-6106, Fax: 414-382-6354, E-mail: maryclaire.jones@alverno.edu.

American College of Education, Graduate Programs, Chicago, IL 60606. Offers curriculum and instruction (M Ed), including bilingual, ESL; educational leadership (M Ed); educational technology (M Ed).

American InterContinental University Online, Program in Education, Hoffman Estates, IL 60192. Offers curriculum and instruction (M Ed); educational assessment and evaluation (M Ed); instructional technology (M Ed); leadership of educational organizations (M Ed). Evening/weekend programs available. Postbaccalaureate distance learning degree programs offered (no on-campus study). *Entrance requirements:* Additional exam requirements/recommendations for international students: Required—TOEFL (minimum score 550 paper-based; 213 computer-based). Electronic applications accepted.

American InterContinental University South Florida, Program in Instructional Technology, Weston, FL 33326. Offers M Ed. Part-time and evening/weekend programs available. *Entrance requirements:* Additional exam requirements/recommendations for international students: Required—TOEFL (minimum score 670 paper-based). Electronic applications accepted.

Appalachian State University, Cratis D. Williams Graduate School, Department of Curriculum and Instruction, Boone, NC 28608. Offers curriculum specialist (MA); educational media (MA); elementary education (MA); middle grades education (MA), including language arts, mathematics, science, social studies. *Accreditation:* NCATE. Part-time and evening/weekend programs available. Postbaccalaureate distance learning degree programs offered (no on-campus study). *Faculty:* 33 full-time (23 women), 5 part-time/adjunct (2 women). *Students:* 23 full-time (18 women), 110 part-time (90 women); includes 7 minority (4 Black or African American, non-Hispanic/Latino; 1 Asian, non-Hispanic/Latino; 2 Hispanic/Latino). 79 applicants, 94% accepted, 64 enrolled. In 2011, 87 master's awarded. *Degree requirements:* For master's, comprehensive exam, thesis or alternative. *Entrance requirements:* For master's, GRE General Test or MAT, 3 letters of recommendation. Additional exam requirements/recommendations for international students: Required—TOEFL (minimum score 570 paper-based; 230 computer-based; 79 iBT), IELTS (minimum score 6.5). *Application deadline:* For fall admission, 3/14 for domestic students, 2/1 for international students; for spring admission, 11/1 for domestic students, 7/1 for international students. Applications are processed on a rolling basis. Application fee: $55. Electronic applications accepted. *Expenses:* Tuition, state resident: full-time $4040; part-time $180 per semester hour. Tuition, nonresident: full-time $15,900; part-time $760 per semester hour. *Required fees:* $2500; $20 per semester hour. Tuition and fees vary according to campus/location. *Financial support:* In 2011–12, 6 teaching assistantships (averaging $8,000 per year) were awarded; fellowships, research assistantships, career-related internships or fieldwork, Federal Work-Study, scholarships/grants, and unspecified assistantships also available. Financial award application deadline: 4/1; financial award applicants required to submit FAFSA. *Faculty research:* Media literacy, elementary teaching, curriculum development, online learning environments. *Total annual research expenditures:* $480,000. *Unit head:* Dr. Michael Jacobson, Chairperson, 828-262-2224. *Application contact:* Sandy Krause, Director of Admissions and Recruiting, 828-262-2130, Fax: 828-262-2709, E-mail: krausesl@appstate.edu. Web site: http://www.ced.appstate.edu/departments/ci.

Appalachian State University, Cratis D. Williams Graduate School, Department of Leadership and Educational Studies, Boone, NC 28608. Offers educational administration (Ed S); educational media (MA); higher education (MA, Ed S); library science (MLS); school administration (MSA). Part-time and evening/weekend programs available. Postbaccalaureate distance learning degree programs offered (no on-campus study). *Faculty:* 35 full-time (15 women), 1 (woman) part-time/adjunct. *Students:* 35 full-time (27 women), 369 part-time (293 women); includes 31 minority (26 Black or African American, non-Hispanic/Latino; 1 Asian, non-Hispanic/Latino; 4 Hispanic/Latino). 196 applicants, 83% accepted, 117 enrolled. In 2011, 195 master's, 32 other advanced degrees awarded. *Degree requirements:* For master's and Ed S, comprehensive exam, thesis optional. *Entrance requirements:* For master's and Ed S, GRE or MAT, 3 letters of recommendation. Additional exam requirements/recommendations for international students: Required—TOEFL (minimum score 570 paper-based; 230 computer-based; 79 iBT), IELTS (minimum score 6.5). *Application deadline:* For fall admission, 3/14 priority date for domestic students, 2/1 for international students; for spring admission, 11/1 for domestic students, 7/1 for international students. Applications are processed on a rolling basis. Application fee: $55. Electronic applications accepted. *Expenses:* Tuition, state resident: full-time $4040; part-time $180 per semester hour. Tuition, nonresident: full-time $15,900; part-time $760 per semester hour. *Required fees:* $2500; $20 per semester hour. Tuition and fees vary according to campus/location. *Financial support:* In 2011–12, 10 research assistantships (averaging $8,000 per year) were awarded; career-related internships or fieldwork, scholarships/grants, and unspecified assistantships also available. Financial award application deadline: 4/1; financial award applicants required to submit FAFSA. *Faculty research:* Brain, learning and meditation; leadership of teaching and learning. *Total annual research expenditures:* $515,000. *Unit head:* Dr. Robert Sanders, Interim Director, 828-262-3112, E-mail: sandersrl@appstate.edu. *Application contact:* Lori Dean, Graduate Student Coordinator, 828-262-6041, E-mail: deanlk@appstate.edu. Web site: http://www.les.appstate.edu.

Arcadia University, Graduate Studies, Department of Education, Glenside, PA 19038-3295. Offers art education (M Ed); computer education (CAS); curriculum (CAS); curriculum studies (M Ed); early childhood education (M Ed, CAS), including individualized (M Ed), master teacher (M Ed), research in child development (M Ed); educational leadership (M Ed, Ed D, CAS); elementary education (M Ed, CAS); English education (MA Ed); environmental education (MA Ed, CAS); history education (MA Ed); instructional technology (M Ed); language arts (M Ed, CAS); library science (M Ed); mathematics education (M Ed, MA Ed, CAS); music education (MA Ed); psychology (MA Ed); reading (M Ed, CAS); science education (M Ed, CAS); secondary education (M Ed, CAS); special education (M Ed, Ed D, CAS); theater arts (MA Ed); written communication (MA Ed). *Accreditation:* NASAD. Part-time and evening/weekend programs available. Postbaccalaureate distance learning degree programs offered (minimal on-campus study). *Faculty:* 12 full-time (8 women), 38 part-time/adjunct (26 women). *Students:* 66 full-time (48 women), 590 part-time (477 women); includes 65 minority (53 Black or African American, non-Hispanic/Latino; 6 Asian, non-Hispanic/Latino; 3 Hispanic/Latino; 3 Two or more races, non-Hispanic/Latino), 4 international. Average age 36. In 2011, 229 master's, 5 doctorates awarded. *Application deadline:* Applications are processed on a rolling basis. Application fee: $50. Electronic applications accepted. *Expenses:* Contact institution. *Financial support:* Career-related internships or fieldwork, tuition waivers (partial), and unspecified assistantships available. *Unit head:* Dr. Steven P. Gulkus, Associate Professor, 215-572-2120, E-mail: gulkus@arcadia.edu. *Application contact:* 215-572-2925, Fax: 215-572-2126, E-mail: grad@arcadia.edu.

Argosy University, Atlanta, College of Education, Atlanta, GA 30328. Offers educational leadership (MAEd, Ed D, Ed S), including higher education administration (Ed D), K-12 education (Ed D); teaching and learning (MAEd, Ed D, Ed S), including education technology (Ed D), higher education (Ed D), K-12 education (Ed D).

See Close-Up on page 1017.

Argosy University, Denver, College of Education, Denver, CO 80231. Offers community college executive leadership (Ed D); educational leadership (MA Ed, Ed D), including higher education (Ed D), K-12 education (Ed D); instructional leadership (MA Ed, Ed D), including higher education administration (Ed D), K-12 education (Ed D).

See Close-Up on page 773.

Argosy University, Nashville, College of Education, Program in Instructional Leadership, Nashville, TN 37214. Offers education technology (Ed D); higher education administration (Ed D); instructional leadership (MA Ed, Ed S); K-12 education (Ed D).

See Close-Up on page 1021.

Argosy University, Orange County, College of Education, Orange, CA 92868. Offers community college executive leadership (Ed D); educational leadership (MA Ed, Ed D), including higher education administration (Ed D), K-12 education (Ed D); instructional leadership (MA Ed, Ed D), including education technology (Ed D), higher education (Ed D), K-12 education (Ed D), multiple subject teacher preparation (MA Ed), single subject teacher preparation (MA Ed).

See Close-Up on page 779.

Argosy University, Phoenix, College of Education, Phoenix, AZ 85021. Offers adult education and training (MA Ed); advanced educational administration (Ed D, Ed S); community college executive leadership (Ed D); educational administration (MA Ed); educational leadership (MA Ed, Ed D, Ed S), including education technology (Ed D), higher education administration (Ed D), K-12 education (Ed D); higher and postsecondary education (MA Ed); initial educational administration (Ed D, Ed S); school psychology (MA); teaching and learning (MA Ed, Ed D, Ed S), including education technology (Ed D), higher education (Ed D), K-12 education (Ed D).

See Close-Up on page 781.

Argosy University, San Francisco Bay Area, College of Education, Alameda, CA 94501. Offers community college executive leadership (Ed D); educational leadership (MA Ed, Ed D), including education technology (Ed D), higher education administration (Ed D), K-12 education (Ed D); instructional leadership (MA Ed, Ed D), including education technology (Ed D), higher education (Ed D), K-12 education (Ed D), multiple subject teacher preparation (MA Ed), single subject teacher preparation (MA Ed).

See Close-Up on page 787.

Argosy University, Sarasota, College of Education, Sarasota, FL 34235. Offers community college executive leadership (Ed D); educational leadership (MA Ed, Ed D, Ed S), including higher education administration (Ed D), K-12 education (Ed D); school counseling (MA, Ed S); school psychology (MA); teaching and learning (MA Ed, Ed D, Ed S), including education technology (Ed D), higher education (Ed D), K-12 education (Ed D).

See Close-Up on page 789.

Argosy University, Seattle, College of Education, Seattle, WA 98121. Offers adult education and training (MA Ed); community college executive leadership (Ed D); educational leadership (MA Ed, Ed D), including higher education administration (Ed D), K-12 education (Ed D); higher and postsecondary education (MA Ed); instructional leadership (MA Ed, Ed D), including education technology (Ed D), higher education (Ed D), K-12 education (Ed D).

See Close-Up on page 793.

Argosy University, Twin Cities, College of Education, Eagan, MN 55121. Offers advanced educational administration (Ed D, Ed S); educational leadership (MA Ed, Ed D, Ed S), including higher education administration (Ed D), K-12 education (Ed D); higher and postsecondary education (MA Ed); initial educational administration (Ed D, Ed S); instructional leadership (MA Ed, Ed D, Ed S), including education technology (Ed D), higher education (Ed D), K-12 education (Ed D).

See Close-Up on page 797.

Arizona State University, Mary Lou Fulton Teachers College, Program in Educational Technology, Phoenix, AZ 85069. Offers educational technology (M Ed, PhD); instructional design and performance improvement (Graduate Certificate); online teaching for grades K-12 (Graduate Certificate). Part-time and evening/weekend programs available. Postbaccalaureate distance learning degree programs offered (minimal on-campus study). Terminal master's awarded for partial completion of doctoral program. *Degree requirements:* For master's, thesis or alternative, applied project, interactive Program of Study (iPOS) submitted before completing 50 percent of required credit hours; for doctorate, comprehensive exam, thesis/dissertation, interactive Program of Study (iPOS) submitted before completing 50 percent of required credit hours. *Entrance requirements:* For master's, GRE (Verbal section) or MAT (for students with less than 3 years of professional experience as teacher, trainer or instructional designer), minimum GPA of 3.0 or equivalent in last 2 years of work leading to bachelor's degree, 3 letters of recommendation, personal statement, curriculum vitae or resume; for doctorate, GRE (minimum scores of 500 on each of the verbal and quantitative sections and 4 on the analytical writing section), minimum GPA of 3.2 or equivalent in last 2 years of work leading to bachelor's degree, 3 letters of recommendation, personal statement of professional goals, writing sample, curriculum vitae or resume. Additional exam requirements/recommendations for international students: Required—TOEFL (minimum score 600 paper-based; 250 computer-based; 100 iBT). Electronic applications accepted. *Faculty research:* Virtual environments; innovative technologies; theory, design, and implementation of computer-based learning environments; impact of technology into curricula on student achievement/attitude; electronic portfolios for learning and assessment.

Arkansas Tech University, Center for Leadership and Learning, College of Education, Russellville, AR 72801. Offers college student personnel (MS); educational leadership (Ed S); elementary education (M Ed); instructional improvement (M Ed); instructional technology (M Ed); physical education (M Ed); school counseling and leadership (M Ed); teaching (MAT). *Accreditation:* NCATE. Part-time and evening/weekend programs available. Postbaccalaureate distance learning degree programs offered (no on-campus study). *Students:* 70 full-time (44 women), 247 part-time (189 women); includes 57 minority (38 Black or African American, non-Hispanic/Latino; 1 American Indian or Alaska Native, non-Hispanic/Latino; 8 Asian, non-Hispanic/Latino; 4 Hispanic/Latino; 6 Two or more races, non-Hispanic/Latino), 3 international. Average age 31. In 2011, 58 master's awarded. *Degree requirements:* For master's, comprehensive exam, thesis optional, action research project. *Entrance requirements:* Additional exam requirements/recommendations for international students: Required—TOEFL (minimum score 550 paper-based; 213 computer-based; 79 iBT), IELTS (minimum score 6.5). *Application deadline:* For fall admission, 3/1 priority date for domestic students, 5/1 for international students; for spring admission, 10/1 priority date for domestic students, 10/1 for international students. Applications are processed on a rolling basis. Application fee: $25 ($75 for international students). Electronic applications accepted. *Expenses:* Tuition, state resident: full-time $4968; part-time $207 per credit hour. Tuition, nonresident: full-time $9936; part-time $414 per credit hour. *Required fees:* $375 per semester. Tuition and fees vary according to course load. *Financial support:* In 2011–12, teaching assistantships with full tuition reimbursements (averaging $4,800 per year) were awarded; research assistantships with full tuition reimbursements, career-related internships or fieldwork, Federal Work-Study, scholarships/grants, health care benefits, and unspecified assistantships also available. Support available to part-time students. Financial award application deadline: 4/15; financial award applicants required to submit FAFSA. *Unit head:* Dr. Eldon G. Clary, Jr., Dean, 479-968-0350, Fax: 479-968-0350, E-mail: eclary@atu.edu. *Application contact:* Dr. Mary B. Gunter, Dean of Graduate College, 479-968-0398, Fax: 479-964-0542, E-mail: gradcollege@atu.edu. Web site: http://www.atu.edu/education/.

Ashland University, Dwight Schar College of Education, Department of Curriculum and Instruction, Ashland, OH 44805-3702. Offers classroom instruction (M Ed); literacy (M Ed); technology facilitator (M Ed). *Accreditation:* NCATE. Part-time and evening/weekend programs available. *Faculty:* 10 full-time (6 women), 39 part-time/adjunct (23 women). *Students:* 75 full-time (62 women), 218 part-time (183 women); includes 17 minority (14 Black or African American, non-Hispanic/Latino; 1 Asian, non-Hispanic/Latino; 2 Hispanic/Latino), 8 international. Average age 36. 72 applicants, 100% accepted, 63 enrolled. In 2011, 256 master's awarded. *Degree requirements:* For master's, thesis or alternative, internship, practicum, inquiry seminar. *Entrance requirements:* For master's, teaching certificate or license, bachelor's degree, minimum cumulative GPA of 2.75. Additional exam requirements/recommendations for international students: Required—TOEFL. *Application deadline:* For fall admission, 8/27 for domestic students; for spring admission, 1/15 for domestic students. Applications are processed on a rolling basis. Application fee: $30. Electronic applications accepted. *Expenses: Tuition:* Full-time $5580; part-time $465 per credit hour. *Financial support:* Institutionally sponsored loans and scholarships/grants available. Financial award application deadline: 4/15. *Faculty research:* Gender equity, postmodern children's and young adult literature, outdoor/experimental education, re-examining literature study in middle grades, morality and giftedness. *Unit head:* Dr. David J. Kommer, Chair, 419-289-5203, Fax: 419-207-4949, E-mail: dkommer@ashland.edu. *Application contact:* Dr. Linda Billman, Associate Dean, 419-289-5369, Fax: 419-289-5331, E-mail: lbillman@ashland.edu.

Auburn University, Graduate School, College of Education, Department of Educational Foundations, Leadership, and Technology, Auburn University, AL 36849. Offers adult education (M Ed, MS, Ed D); curriculum and instruction (M Ed, MS, Ed D, Ed S); curriculum supervision (M Ed, MS, Ed D, Ed S); educational psychology (PhD); higher education administration (M Ed, MS, Ed D, Ed S); media instructional design (MS); media specialist (M Ed); school administration (M Ed, MS, Ed D, Ed S). *Accreditation:* NCATE. Part-time programs available. *Faculty:* 26 full-time (16 women), 3 part-time/adjunct (all women). *Students:* 58 full-time (28 women), 215 part-time (135 women); includes 89 minority (82 Black or African American, non-Hispanic/Latino; 1 American Indian or Alaska Native, non-Hispanic/Latino; 4 Asian, non-Hispanic/Latino; 2 Hispanic/Latino), 13 international. Average age 35. 140 applicants, 61% accepted, 56 enrolled. In 2011, 37 master's, 29 doctorates, 9 other advanced degrees awarded. *Degree requirements:* For master's, thesis (for some programs); for doctorate, thesis/dissertation; for Ed S, field project. *Entrance requirements:* For master's, doctorate, and Ed S, GRE General Test. *Application deadline:* For fall admission, 7/7 for domestic students; for spring admission, 11/24 for domestic students. Applications are processed on a rolling basis. Application fee: $50 ($60 for international students). Electronic applications accepted. *Expenses:* Tuition, state resident: full-time $7290; part-time $405 per credit hour. Tuition, nonresident: full-time $21,870; part-time $1215 per credit hour. *International tuition:* $22,000 full-time. *Required fees:* $1402. *Financial support:* Teaching assistantships and Federal Work-Study available. Support available to part-time students. Financial award application deadline: 3/15; financial award applicants required to submit FAFSA. *Unit head:* Dr. Sherida Downer, Head, 334-844-4460. *Application contact:* Dr. George Flowers, Dean of the Graduate School, 334-844-4700. Web site: http://www.education.auburn.edu/academic_departments/eflt/.

Aurora University, College of Education, Aurora, IL 60506-4892. Offers curriculum and instruction (MA, Ed D); early childhood and special education (MA); education (MAT), including elementary certification; education and administration (Ed D); educational leadership (MEL); educational technology (MATL); reading instruction (MA); special education (MA). *Accreditation:* NCATE. Part-time and evening/weekend programs available. *Degree requirements:* For doctorate, comprehensive exam, thesis/dissertation. *Entrance requirements:* For master's, 2 years of teaching experience, valid teaching certificate. Additional exam requirements/recommendations for international students: Required—TOEFL (minimum score 550 paper-based; 213 computer-based). Electronic applications accepted. *Expenses:* Contact institution.

Azusa Pacific University, School of Education, Department of Advanced Studies, Program in Digital Teaching and Learning, Azusa, CA 91702-7000. Offers MA Ed.

Azusa Pacific University, School of Education, Department of Advanced Studies, Program in Educational Technology, Azusa, CA 91702-7000. Offers M Ed. Part-time and evening/weekend programs available. *Degree requirements:* For master's, comprehensive exam, core exam, oral presentation. *Entrance requirements:* For master's, 12 units of course work in education, minimum GPA of 3.0.

Azusa Pacific University, School of Education, Department of Advanced Studies, Program in Educational Technology and Learning, Azusa, CA 91702-7000. Offers MA. Postbaccalaureate distance learning degree programs offered.

Azusa Pacific University, School of Education, Department of Special Education, Program in Special Education and Educational Technology, Azusa, CA 91702-7000. Offers M Ed.

Baldwin Wallace University, Graduate Programs, Division of Education, Specialization in Educational Technology, Berea, OH 44017-2088. Offers MA Ed. Part-time and evening/weekend programs available. *Faculty:* 1 full-time, 4 part-time/adjunct (1 woman). *Students:* 14 full-time (7 women), 17 part-time (10 women); includes 2 minority (1 Black or African American, non-Hispanic/Latino; 1 Hispanic/Latino). Average age 31. 13 applicants, 77% accepted, 5 enrolled. In 2011, 35 master's awarded. *Degree requirements:* For master's, comprehensive exam. *Entrance requirements:* For master's, bachelor's degree in field, MAT or minimum GPA of 2.75. Additional exam requirements/recommendations for international students: Required—TOEFL (minimum score 523 paper-based; 193 computer-based; 70 iBT). *Application deadline:* For fall admission, 8/15 priority date for domestic students; for spring admission, 12/15 priority date for domestic students. Applications are processed on a rolling basis. Application fee: $25. Electronic applications accepted. Application fee is waived when completed online. *Expenses: Tuition:* Full-time $17,016; part-time $727 per credit hour. Tuition and fees vary according to program. *Financial support:* Career-related internships or fieldwork available. Support available to part-time students. Financial award application deadline: 5/1. *Faculty research:* No cost software, online resources for building a classroom learning management system. *Unit head:* Dr. Karen Kaye, Chair, 440-826-2168, Fax: 440-826-3779, E-mail: kkaye@bw.edu. *Application contact:* Winifred W. Gerhardt, Director of Admission for the Evening and Weekend College, 440-826-2222, Fax: 440-826-3830, E-mail: admission@bw.edu. Web site: http://www.bw.edu/academics/mae/tech/.

Barry University, School of Education, Graduate Certificate Programs, Miami Shores, FL 33161-6695. Offers advanced teaching and learning with technology (Certificate); distance education (Certificate); higher education technology integration (Certificate); human resources: not for profit and religious organizations (Certificate); K-12 technology integration (Certificate).

Barry University, School of Education, Program in Educational Technology Applications, Miami Shores, FL 33161-6695. Offers educational computing and technology (MS, Ed S). Part-time and evening/weekend programs available. Postbaccalaureate distance learning degree programs offered (minimal on-campus study). *Degree requirements:* For master's and Ed S, comprehensive exam. *Entrance requirements:* For master's, GRE General Test or MAT, minimum GPA of 3.0; for Ed S, GRE General Test, minimum GPA of 3.0.

Barry University, School of Education, Program in Leadership and Education, Miami Shores, FL 33161-6695. Offers educational technology (PhD); exceptional student education (PhD); higher education administration (PhD); human resource development (PhD); leadership (PhD). Part-time and evening/weekend programs available. *Degree requirements:* For doctorate, thesis/dissertation. *Entrance requirements:* For doctorate, GRE General Test, minimum GPA of 3.25. Electronic applications accepted.

Barry University, School of Education, Program in Technology and TESOL, Miami Shores, FL 33161-6695. Offers MS, Ed S.

Bellevue University, Graduate School, College of Professional Studies, Bellevue, NE 68005-3098. Offers instructional design and development (MS); justice administration and criminal management (MS); leadership (MA); organizational performance (MS); public administration (MPA); security management (MS).

Bloomsburg University of Pennsylvania, School of Graduate Studies, College of Science and Technology, Department of Instructional Technology, Bloomsburg, PA 17815-1301. Offers instructional technology (MS), including corporate track, education track, eLearning certificate. Postbaccalaureate distance learning degree programs offered (no on-campus study). *Degree requirements:* For master's, thesis or alternative. *Entrance requirements:* For master's, minimum QPA of 3.0, 3 letters of recommendation. Additional exam requirements/recommendations for international students: Required—TOEFL (minimum score 550 paper-based; 213 computer-based; 79 iBT). Electronic applications accepted. *Faculty research:* Instructional design and computing, interactive graphics, authoring tools.

Boise State University, Graduate College, College of Education, Programs in Teacher Education, Department of Educational Technology, Boise, ID 83725-0399. Offers MET, MS, MS Ed. *Accreditation:* NCATE. Part-time programs available. Postbaccalaureate distance learning degree programs offered (no on-campus study). *Degree requirements:* For master's, thesis optional. *Entrance requirements:* For master's, minimum GPA of 3.0. Electronic applications accepted.

Boise State University, Graduate College, College of Engineering, Department of Instructional and Performance Technology, Boise, ID 83725-0399. Offers MS. Part-time programs available. Postbaccalaureate distance learning degree programs offered (no on-campus study). *Degree requirements:* For master's, thesis optional. *Entrance requirements:* For master's, minimum GPA of 3.0. Electronic applications accepted.

Bowling Green State University, Graduate College, College of Education and Human Development, School of Education and Intervention Services, Intervention Services Division, Program in Special Education, Bowling Green, OH 43403. Offers assistive technology (M Ed); early childhood intervention (M Ed); gifted education (M Ed); hearing impaired intervention (M Ed); mild/moderate intervention (M Ed); moderate/intensive intervention (M Ed). *Accreditation:* NCATE. Part-time programs available. *Degree requirements:* For master's, thesis or alternative. *Entrance requirements:* For master's, GRE General Test. Additional exam requirements/recommendations for international students: Required—TOEFL. Electronic applications accepted. *Faculty research:* Reading and special populations, deafness, early childhood, gifted and talented, behavior disorders.

Bowling Green State University, Graduate College, College of Education and Human Development, School of Education and Intervention Services, Teaching and Learning Division, Program in Classroom Technology, Bowling Green, OH 43403. Offers M Ed. *Accreditation:* NCATE. Part-time and evening/weekend programs available. *Degree requirements:* For master's, thesis or alternative. *Entrance requirements:* For master's, GRE General Test. Additional exam requirements/recommendations for international students: Required—TOEFL. Electronic applications accepted.

Bridgewater State University, School of Graduate Studies, School of Education and Allied Studies, Department of Secondary Education and Professional Programs, Program in Instructional Technology, Bridgewater, MA 02325-0001. Offers M Ed. Part-time and evening/weekend programs available. *Entrance requirements:* For master's, GRE General Test or Massachusetts Test for Educator Licensure.

Brigham Young University, Graduate Studies, David O. McKay School of Education, Department of Instructional Psychology and Technology, Provo, UT 84602. Offers MS, PhD. *Faculty:* 9 full-time (0 women), 3 part-time/adjunct (0 women). *Students:* 56 full-time (24 women), 20 part-time (9 women); includes 7 minority (3 Asian, non-Hispanic/Latino; 3 Hispanic/Latino; 1 Native Hawaiian or other Pacific Islander, non-Hispanic/Latino), 6 international. Average age 35. 27 applicants, 70% accepted, 19 enrolled. In 2011, 9 master's, 9 doctorates awarded. *Degree requirements:* For master's, thesis; for doctorate, comprehensive exam, thesis/dissertation. *Entrance requirements:* For master's and doctorate, GRE General Test. Additional exam requirements/recommendations for international students: Required—TOEFL. *Application deadline:* For fall and winter admission, 2/1 for domestic and international students. Application fee: $50. Electronic applications accepted. *Expenses: Tuition:* Full-time $5760; part-time $320 per credit. Tuition and fees vary according to student's religious affiliation. *Financial support:* In 2011–12, 34 students received support, including 14 research assistantships with full and partial tuition reimbursements available (averaging $10,000 per year), 12 teaching assistantships with full and partial tuition reimbursements available (averaging $6,500 per year); career-related internships or fieldwork, scholarships/grants, tuition waivers (full and partial), and unspecified assistantships also available. Support available to part-time students. *Faculty research:* Interactive learning, learning theory, instructional designed development, research and evaluation, measurement. *Unit head:* Dr. Andrew S. Gibbons, Chair, 801-422-5097, Fax: 801-422-0314, E-mail: andy_gibbons@byu.edu. *Application contact:* Michele Bray, Department Secretary, 801-422-2746, Fax: 801-422-0314, E-mail: michele_bray@byu.edu. Web site: http://education.byu.edu/ipt/.

Brigham Young University, Graduate Studies, Ira A. Fulton College of Engineering and Technology, School of Technology, Provo, UT 84602-1001. Offers construction management (MS); information technology (MS); manufacturing systems (MS); technology and engineering education (MS). *Faculty:* 26 full-time (0 women). *Students:* 25 full-time (2 women), 9 part-time (3 women); includes 3 minority (1 Asian, non-Hispanic/Latino; 2 Hispanic/Latino), 5 international. Average age 25. 27 applicants, 59% accepted, 14 enrolled. In 2011, 12 master's awarded. *Degree requirements:* For master's, thesis. *Entrance requirements:* For master's, GRE General Test; GMAT or GRE (for construction management emphasis), minimum GPA of 3.0 in last 60 hours of course work. Additional exam requirements/recommendations for international students: Required—TOEFL (minimum score 580 paper-based; 237 computer-based; 85 iBT). *Application deadline:* For fall admission, 2/15 for domestic and international students; for winter admission, 9/15 for domestic and international students; for spring admission, 2/15 for domestic and international students. Application fee: $50. Electronic applications accepted. *Expenses: Tuition:* Full-time $5760; part-time $320 per credit. Tuition and fees vary according to student's religious affiliation. *Financial support:* In 2011–12, 34 students received support, including 11 research assistantships (averaging $3,506 per year), 7 teaching assistantships (averaging $3,254 per year); scholarships/grants also available. *Faculty research:* Information assurance and security, computerized systems in CM, pedagogy in technology and engineering, manufacturing planning. *Total annual research expenditures:* $220,300. *Unit head:* Val D. Hawks, Director, 801-422-6300, Fax: 801-422-0490, E-mail: hawksv@byu.edu. *Application contact:* Barry M. Lunt, Graduate Coordinator, 801-422-2264, Fax: 801-422-0490, E-mail: ralowe@byu.edu. Web site: http://www.et.byu.edu/sot/.

Buffalo State College, State University of New York, The Graduate School, Faculty of Applied Science and Education, Department of Computer Information Systems, Program in Educational Computing, Buffalo, NY 14222-1095. Offers MS Ed. *Accreditation:* NCATE. Part-time and evening/weekend programs available. *Degree requirements:* For master's, thesis, project. *Entrance requirements:* Additional exam requirements/recommendations for international students: Required—TOEFL (minimum score 550 paper-based; 213 computer-based).

California Baptist University, Program in Education, Riverside, CA 92504-3206. Offers educational leadership for faith-based instruction (MS); educational leadership for public institutions (MS); educational technology (MS); instructional computer applications (MS); international education (MS); reading (MS); school counseling (MS); school psychology (MS); special education (MS); special education in mild/moderate disabilities (MS); special education in moderate/severe disabilities (MS); teaching (MS); teaching and learning with induction program (MS Ed). Part-time and evening/weekend programs available. *Faculty:* 16 full-time (10 women), 1 (woman) part-time/adjunct. *Students:* 380 full-time (323 women); includes 149 minority (28 Black or African American, non-Hispanic/Latino; 2 American Indian or Alaska Native, non-Hispanic/Latino; 13 Asian, non-Hispanic/Latino; 100 Hispanic/Latino; 2 Native Hawaiian or other Pacific Islander, non-Hispanic/Latino; 4 Two or more races, non-Hispanic/Latino). Average age 32. 181 applicants, 70% accepted, 111 enrolled. In 2011, 82 master's awarded. *Degree requirements:* For master's, comprehensive exam or thesis. *Entrance requirements:* For master's, minimum undergraduate GPA of 3.0; 18 semester units of prerequisite course work in education; three recommendations; essay; interview. Additional exam requirements/recommendations for international students: Required—TOEFL (minimum score 575 paper-based; 230 computer-based; 89 iBT). *Application deadline:* For fall admission, 8/1 priority date for domestic students, 7/1 for international students; for spring admission, 12/1 priority date for domestic students, 11/1 for international students. Applications are processed on a rolling basis. Application fee: $45. Electronic applications accepted. *Expenses:* Contact institution. *Financial support:* In 2011–12, 4 students received support. Federal Work-Study and institutionally sponsored loans available. Financial award applicants required to submit FAFSA. *Faculty research:* Special education, neurosciences and education, cultural influences on behavior, faith-based school leadership, social and philosophical contexts of education. *Unit head:* Dr. John Shoup, Dean, School of Education, 951-343-4205, Fax: 951-343-4516, E-mail: jshoup@calbaptist.edu. *Application contact:* Dr. James Heyman, Director, Master of Science Program in Education, 951-343-4243, Fax: 951-343-5095, E-mail: jheyman@calbaptist.edu. Web site: http://www.calbaptist.edu/mastersined/.

California State University, Dominguez Hills, College of Professional Studies, School of Education, Division of Graduate Education, Program in Technology-Based Education, Carson, CA 90747-0001. Offers MA, Certificate. Part-time and evening/weekend programs available. *Faculty:* 1 (woman) full-time. *Students:* 7 full-time (4 women), 35 part-time (19 women); includes 30 minority (10 Black or African American, non-Hispanic/Latino; 4 Asian, non-Hispanic/Latino; 14 Hispanic/Latino; 1 Native Hawaiian or other Pacific Islander, non-Hispanic/Latino; 1 Two or more races, non-Hispanic/Latino), 1 international. Average age 38. 23 applicants, 91% accepted, 16 enrolled. In 2011, 27 master's awarded. *Degree requirements:* For master's, comprehensive exam, thesis or alternative. *Entrance requirements:* For master's, minimum GPA of 2.75. *Application deadline:* For fall admission, 6/1 for domestic students. Application fee: $55. *Faculty research:* Media literacy, assistive technology. *Unit head:* Dr. Peter Desberg, Unit Head, 310-243-3908, E-mail: pdesberg@csudh.edu. *Application contact:* Admissions Office, 310-243-3530. Web site: http://www.csudh.edu/cps/soe/programsdegrees/graduate-programs-technology.shtml.

California State University, East Bay, Office of Academic Programs and Graduate Studies, College of Education and Allied Studies, Department of Teacher Education, Hayward, CA 94542-3000. Offers education (MS), including curriculum, early childhood education, educational technology leadership, online teaching and learning, reading instruction. Postbaccalaureate distance learning degree programs offered. *Faculty:* 5 full-time (4 women), 2 part-time/adjunct (both women). *Students:* 64 full-time (53 women), 55 part-time (39 women); includes 50 minority (14 Black or African American, non-Hispanic/Latino; 17 Asian, non-Hispanic/Latino; 15 Hispanic/Latino; 4 Two or more races, non-Hispanic/Latino), 3 international. Average age 35. 98 applicants, 69% accepted, 30 enrolled. In 2011, 149 master's awarded. *Degree requirements:* For master's, project or thesis. *Entrance requirements:* For master's, minimum GPA of 3.0 in field, 2.5 overall; teaching experience; baccalaureate degree; 3 letters of recommendation. Additional exam requirements/recommendations for international students: Required—TOEFL (minimum score 550 paper-based; 213 computer-based), IELTS. *Application deadline:* For fall admission, 6/30 for domestic and international students. Application fee: $55. Electronic applications accepted. *Expenses:* Tuition, state resident: full-time $6738; part-time $1302 per quarter. Tuition, nonresident: full-time $12,690; part-time $2294 per quarter. *Required fees:* $449 per quarter. Tuition and fees vary according to degree level, program and reciprocity agreements. *Financial support:* Career-related internships or fieldwork, Federal Work-Study, and institutionally sponsored loans available. Support available to part-time students. Financial award application deadline: 3/2; financial award applicants required to submit FAFSA. *Faculty research:* Online, pedagogy, writing, learning, teaching. *Unit head:* Dr. Jeanette Bicais, Chair, 510-885-3027, Fax: 510-885-4632, E-mail: jeanette.bicais@csueastbay.edu. *Application contact:* Prof. Valerie Helgren-Lempesis, Education Graduate Advisor, 510-885-3006, Fax: 510-885-4632, E-mail: valerie.lempesis@csueastbay.edu. Web site: http://www20.csueastbay.edu/ceas/departments/ted/index.html.

California State University, Fullerton, Graduate Studies, College of Education, Program of Instructional Design and Technology, Fullerton, CA 92834-9480. Offers MS. Part-time programs available. Postbaccalaureate distance learning degree programs offered. *Students:* 55 part-time (32 women); includes 19 minority (3 Black or African American, non-Hispanic/Latino; 3 Asian, non-Hispanic/Latino; 11 Hispanic/Latino; 2 Two or more races, non-Hispanic/Latino). Average age 41. 54 applicants, 78% accepted, 33 enrolled. In 2011, 19 master's awarded. Application fee: $55. *Financial support:* Career-related internships or fieldwork, Federal Work-Study, institutionally sponsored loans, and scholarships/grants available. Support available to part-time students. Financial award application deadline: 3/1; financial award applicants required to submit FAFSA. *Unit head:* Dr. Jo Ann Carter-Wells, Chair, 657-278-3357. *Application contact:* Admissions/Applications, 657-278-2371.

California State University, Monterey Bay, College of Science, Media Arts and Technology, School of Information Technology and Communication Design, Seaside, CA 93955-8001. Offers interdisciplinary studies (MA), including instructional science and technology; management and information technology (MA). *Degree requirements:* For master's, capstone or thesis. *Entrance requirements:* For master's, GRE, 2 letters of recommendation, minimum GPA of 3.0, technology screening assessment. Additional exam requirements/recommendations for international students: Required—TOEFL (minimum score 550 paper-based; 213 computer-based; 71 iBT). Electronic applications accepted. *Faculty research:* Electronic commerce, e-learning, knowledge management, international business, business and public policy.

California State University, Northridge, Graduate Studies, College of Education, Department of Secondary Education, Northridge, CA 91330. Offers educational technology (MA); English education (MA); mathematics education (MA); secondary science education (MA); teaching and learning (MA). *Accreditation:* NCATE. Part-time programs available. *Degree requirements:* For master's, thesis optional. *Entrance requirements:* For master's, GRE General Test or minimum GPA of 3.0. Additional exam requirements/recommendations for international students: Required—TOEFL.

California State University, San Bernardino, Graduate Studies, College of Education, Program in Instructional Technology, San Bernardino, CA 92407-2397. Offers MA. *Students:* 39 full-time (26 women), 24 part-time (18 women); includes 23 minority (8 Black or African American, non-Hispanic/Latino; 2 Asian, non-Hispanic/Latino; 12 Hispanic/Latino; 1 Two or more races, non-Hispanic/Latino), 2 international. Average age 31. In 2011, 9 master's awarded. *Degree requirements:* For master's, comprehensive exam (for some programs), thesis optional, advancement to candidacy. *Entrance requirements:* For master's, minimum GPA of 2.5. *Application deadline:* For fall admission, 8/31 priority date for domestic students. Application fee: $55. *Expenses:* Tuition, state resident: full-time $7356. Tuition, nonresident: full-time $7356. *Required fees:* $1077. Tuition and fees vary according to program. *Unit head:* Dr. Herbert Brunkhorst, Chair, 909-537-5613, Fax: 909-537-7522, E-mail: hkbrunkh@csusb.edu. *Application contact:* Sandra Kamusikiri, Associate Vice-President/Dean of Graduate Studies, 909-5375058, E-mail: skamusik@csusb.edu.

California State University, Stanislaus, College of Education, Program in Education (MA), Turlock, CA 95382. Offers curriculum and instruction (MA), including education technology, elementary education, multilingual education, physical education, reading, secondary education, special education; school administration (MA); school counseling (MA). Part-time and evening/weekend programs available. *Degree requirements:* For master's, comprehensive exam (for some programs), thesis (for some programs). *Entrance requirements:* For master's, MAT, GRE, or CBEST (varies by concentration), 3 letters of recommendation, personal statement. Additional exam requirements/recommendations for international students: Required—TOEFL (minimum score 550 paper-based; 213 computer-based). *Application deadline:* For fall admission, 5/1 for domestic students; for spring admission, 1/7 for domestic students. Application fee: $55. Electronic applications accepted. *Expenses: Required fees:* $4616 per year. *Financial support:* Federal Work-Study available. Financial award application deadline: 3/1;

financial award applicants required to submit FAFSA. *Faculty research:* Children's perspectives on historical events, method elementary schools dual language education, K-12 reading and CYRM programs. *Unit head:* Dr. Kathy Norman, Dean, College of Education, 209-667-3652, Fax: 209-664-6613, E-mail: coe@csustan.edu. *Application contact:* Graduate School, 209-667-3129, Fax: 209-664-7025, E-mail: graduate_school@csustan.edu. Web site: http://www.csustan.edu/COE/.

Cambridge College, School of Education, Cambridge, MA 02138-5304. Offers autism specialist (M Ed); autism/behavior analyst (M Ed); behavior analyst (Post-Master's Certificate); behavioral management (M Ed); early childhood teacher (M Ed); education specialist in curriculum and instruction (CAGS); educational leadership (Ed D); elementary teacher (M Ed); English as a second language (M Ed, Certificate); general science (M Ed); health education (Post-Master's Certificate); health/family and consumer sciences (M Ed); history (M Ed); individualized (M Ed); information technology literacy (M Ed); instructional technology (M Ed); interdisciplinary studies (M Ed); library teacher (M Ed); literacy education (M Ed); mathematics (M Ed); mathematics specialist (Certificate); middle school mathematics and science (M Ed); school administration (M Ed, CAGS); school guidance counselor (M Ed); school nurse education (M Ed); school social worker/school adjustment counselor (M Ed); special education administrator (CAGS); special education/moderate disabilities (M Ed); teaching skills and methodologies (M Ed). Part-time and evening/weekend programs available. Postbaccalaureate distance learning degree programs offered (minimal on-campus study). *Degree requirements:* For master's, thesis, internship/practicum (licensure program only); for doctorate, thesis/dissertation; for other advanced degree, thesis. *Entrance requirements:* For master's, interview, resume, documentation of licensure, 2 professional references; for doctorate, official transcripts, interview, resume, documentation of licensure (if any), written personal statement/essay, portfolio of scholarly and professional work, qualifying assessment, 2 professional references, health insurance, immunizations form; for other advanced degree, official transcripts, interview, resume, documentation of licensure (if any), written personal statement/essay, 2 professional references, health insurance, immunizations form. Additional exam requirements/recommendations for international students: Required—TOEFL (minimum score 550 paper-based; 213 computer-based; 79 iBT); Recommended—IELTS (minimum score 6). Electronic applications accepted. *Expenses:* Contact institution. *Faculty research:* Adult education, accelerated learning, mathematics education, brain compatible learning, special education and law.

Capella University, School of Education, Minneapolis, MN 55402. Offers college teaching (Certificate); curriculum and instruction (MS, PhD); education (MS); enrollment management (MS); instructional design for online learning (MS, PhD); k-12 studies in education (MS, PhD); leadership for higher education (MS, PhD); leadership in education administration (Certificate); leadership in educational administration (MS, PhD); postsecondary and adult education (MS, PhD); professional studies in education (MS, PhD); reading and literacy (MS); training and performance improvement (MS, PhD). Part-time and evening/weekend programs available. Postbaccalaureate distance learning degree programs offered (minimal on-campus study). Terminal master's awarded for partial completion of doctoral program. *Degree requirements:* For master's, thesis optional, integrative project; for doctorate, comprehensive exam, thesis/dissertation. *Entrance requirements:* Additional exam requirements/recommendations for international students: Required—TOEFL (minimum score 550 paper-based; 213 computer-based), TWE (minimum score 4). Electronic applications accepted. *Faculty research:* Higher education administration, distance learning, adult education, training and curriculum design.

Cardinal Stritch University, College of Education, Department of Educational Computing, Milwaukee, WI 53217-3985. Offers instructional technology (ME, MS). Part-time and evening/weekend programs available. *Degree requirements:* For master's, comprehensive exam, thesis, faculty recommendation. *Entrance requirements:* For master's, letters of recommendation (2), minimum GPA of 2.75.

Caribbean University, Graduate School, Bayamón, PR 00960-0493. Offers administration and supervision (MA Ed); criminal justice (MA); curriculum and instruction (MA Ed, PhD), including elementary education (MA Ed), English education (MA Ed), history education (MA Ed), mathematics education (MA Ed), primary education (MA Ed), science education (MA Ed), Spanish education (MA Ed); educational technology in instructional systems (MA Ed); gerontology (MSN); human resources (MBA); museology, archiving and art history (MA Ed); neonatal pediatrics (MSN); physical education (MA Ed); special education (MA Ed). *Entrance requirements:* For master's, interview, minimum GPA of 2.5.

Carlow University, School of Education, Program in Education, Pittsburgh, PA 15213-3165. Offers art education (M Ed); early childhood education (M Ed); instructional technology specialist (M Ed); middle level education (M Ed); secondary education (M Ed); special education (M Ed). Part-time and evening/weekend programs available. *Students:* 72 full-time (58 women), 16 part-time (13 women); includes 16 minority (15 Black or African American, non-Hispanic/Latino; 1 Hispanic/Latino). Average age 32. 68 applicants, 28% accepted, 11 enrolled. In 2011, 41 master's awarded. *Entrance requirements:* For master's, resume, 3 letters of recommendation, minimum GPA of 3.0, interview. Additional exam requirements/recommendations for international students: Required—TOEFL. *Application deadline:* For fall admission, 6/15 priority date for domestic students, 6/15 for international students; for spring admission, 11/15 priority date for domestic students, 11/15 for international students. Applications are processed on a rolling basis. Application fee: $20. Electronic applications accepted. *Expenses: Tuition:* Full-time $10,290; part-time $686 per credit. Tuition and fees vary according to course load, degree level and program. *Financial support:* Applicants required to submit FAFSA. *Unit head:* Dr. Marilyn J. Llewellyn, Director, 412-578-6011, Fax: 412-578-0816, E-mail: llewellynmj@carlow.edu. *Application contact:* Jo Danhires, Administrative Assistant, Admissions, 412-578-6089, Fax: 412-578-6321, E-mail: gradstudies@carlow.edu. Web site: http://www.carlow.edu.

Central Connecticut State University, School of Graduate Studies, School of Education and Professional Studies, Department of Educational Leadership, Program in Educational Technology and Media, New Britain, CT 06050-4010. Offers MS. Part-time and evening/weekend programs available. *Students:* 41 part-time (23 women); includes 5 minority (1 Black or African American, non-Hispanic/Latino; 1 Asian, non-Hispanic/Latino; 1 Native Hawaiian or other Pacific Islander, non-Hispanic/Latino; 2 Two or more races, non-Hispanic/Latino). Average age 33. 13 applicants, 100% accepted, 10 enrolled. In 2011, 22 master's awarded. *Degree requirements:* For master's, thesis or alternative. *Entrance requirements:* For master's, minimum undergraduate GPA of 2.7. Additional exam requirements/recommendations for international students: Required—TOEFL (minimum score 550 paper-based; 213 computer-based). *Application deadline:* For fall admission, 6/1 for domestic students, 5/1 for international students; for spring admission, 11/1 for domestic and international students. Applications are processed on a rolling basis. Application fee: $50. Electronic applications accepted. *Expenses: Tuition, area resident:* Full-time $5137; part-time $482 per credit. Tuition, state resident: full-time $7707; part-time $494 per credit. Tuition, nonresident: full-time $14,311; part-time $494 per credit. *Required fees:* $3865. One-time fee: $62 part-time. *Faculty research:* Design and development of multimedia packages, semiotics, perceptual theories, integrated media presentations, distance teaching. *Unit head:* Dr. Anthony Rigazio-Digilio, Chair, 860-832-2130, E-mail: digilio@ccsu.edu. *Application contact:* Patricia Gardner, Associate Director of Graduate Studies, 860-832-2350, Fax: 860-832-2352, E-mail: graduateadmissions@ccsu.edu.

Central Michigan University, Central Michigan University Global Campus, Program in Education, Mount Pleasant, MI 48859. Offers adult education (MA); college teaching (Graduate Certificate); community college (MA); educational leadership (MA), including charter school leadership; educational technology (MA); guidance and development (MA); instruction (MA); reading and literacy K-12 (MA); school principalship (MA); teacher leadership (MA). *Accreditation:* Teacher Education Accreditation Council. Part-time and evening/weekend programs available. *Entrance requirements:* For master's, minimum GPA of 2.7 in major. Additional exam requirements/recommendations for international students: Required—TOEFL. *Application deadline:* Applications are processed on a rolling basis. Application fee: $50. Electronic applications accepted. *Financial support:* Scholarships/grants available. Support available to part-time students. *Unit head:* Dr. Peter Ross, Director, 989-774-4456, E-mail: ross1pg@cmich.edu. *Application contact:* 877-268-4636, E-mail: cmuglobal@cmich.edu.

Central Michigan University, College of Graduate Studies, College of Education and Human Services, Department of Educational Leadership, Mount Pleasant, MI 48859. Offers educational leadership (MA, Ed D), including charter school leadership (MA), educational technology (Ed D, Ed S), general educational leadership (MA), higher education administration (MA, Ed S), higher education leadership (Ed D), K-12 curriculum (Ed D), K-12 leadership (Ed D), student affairs administration (MA); general educational administration (Ed S), including administrative leadership K-12, educational technology (Ed D, Ed S), higher education administration (MA, Ed S), instructional leadership K-12; school principalship (MA); teacher leadership (MA). Part-time and evening/weekend programs available. *Degree requirements:* For master's and other advanced degree, thesis or alternative; for doctorate, thesis/dissertation. *Entrance requirements:* For doctorate, GRE or MAT, master's degree, minimum GPA of 3.5, 3 years of professional education experience. Electronic applications accepted. *Faculty research:* Elementary administration, secondary administration, student achievement, in-service training, internships in administration.

Central Michigan University, College of Graduate Studies, College of Education and Human Services, Department of Teacher Education and Professional Development, Mount Pleasant, MI 48859. Offers educational technology (MA, Graduate Certificate); elementary education (MA), including classroom teaching, early childhood; middle level education (MA); reading and literacy K-12 (MA); secondary education (MA). Part-time and evening/weekend programs available. *Degree requirements:* For master's, thesis or alternative. Electronic applications accepted. *Faculty research:* Integrating literacy across the curriculum, science teaching and aesthetic learning in science, diversity education, educational technology, educational psychology and child development.

Chestnut Hill College, School of Graduate Studies, Program in Instructional Technology, Philadelphia, PA 19118-2693. Offers MS, CAS. Part-time and evening/weekend programs available. *Faculty:* 1 full-time (0 women), 5 part-time/adjunct (2 women). *Students:* 3 full-time (1 woman), 19 part-time (8 women); includes 2 minority (both Black or African American, non-Hispanic/Latino). Average age 34. 4 applicants, 100% accepted, 4 enrolled. In 2011, 4 master's awarded. *Degree requirements:* For master's, special project/internship. *Entrance requirements:* For master's, GRE General Test or MAT, letters of recommendation, writing sample. Additional exam requirements/recommendations for international students: Required—TOEFL (minimum score 500 paper-based; 213 computer-based). *Application deadline:* For fall admission, 7/17 priority date for domestic students, 7/15 for international students; for spring admission, 12/15 priority date for domestic students, 12/15 for international students. Applications are processed on a rolling basis. Application fee: $55. *Expenses: Tuition:* Part-time $555 per credit hour. One-time fee: $55 part-time. Part-time tuition and fees vary according to degree level and program. *Financial support:* Unspecified assistantships available. *Faculty research:* Instructional design, learning management systems and related technologies, video as a teaching and learning tool, Web 2.0 technologies and virtual worlds as a learning tool, utilization of laptops and iPads in the classroom. *Unit head:* Dr. Yefim kats, Coordinator, 215-248-7008, Fax: 215-248-7155, E-mail: katsy@chc.edu. *Application contact:* Amy Boorse, Administrative Assistant, School of Graduate Studies Office, 215-248-7170, Fax: 215-248-7161, E-mail: gradadmissions@chc.edu. Web site: http://www.chc.edu/Graduate/Programs/Masters/Instructional_Technology/.

Chicago State University, School of Graduate and Professional Studies, College of Education, Department of Reading, Elementary Education, Library Information and Media Studies, Program in Library Information and Media Studies, Chicago, IL 60628. Offers MS Ed. *Entrance requirements:* For master's, minimum GPA of 2.75.

Chicago State University, School of Graduate and Professional Studies, College of Education, Department of Technology and Education, Chicago, IL 60628. Offers secondary education (MAT); technology and education (MS Ed). Postbaccalaureate distance learning degree programs offered. *Degree requirements:* For master's, thesis optional. *Entrance requirements:* For master's, minimum GPA of 2.75.

Clarion University of Pennsylvania, Office of Graduate Programs, Master of Education Program, Clarion, PA 16214. Offers curriculum and instruction (M Ed); early childhood (M Ed, Certificate); English (M Ed); instructional technology specialist (K-12) (Certificate); literacy (M Ed); mathematics education (M Ed); reading specialist (M Ed, Certificate); science education (M Ed); special education (M Ed); technology (M Ed); world language (M Ed). *Accreditation:* NCATE. Part-time programs available. *Students:* 14 full-time (11 women), 207 part-time (163 women); includes 3 minority (1 Black or African American, non-Hispanic/Latino; 2 Hispanic/Latino). Average age 31. In 2011, 96 master's awarded. *Degree requirements:* For master's, thesis or alternative. *Entrance requirements:* For master's, minimum QPA of 3.0. *Application deadline:* Applications are processed on a rolling basis. *Expenses:* Tuition, state resident: part-time $429 per credit. Tuition, nonresident: part-time $644 per credit. *Financial support:* Research assistantships with full and partial tuition reimbursements and career-related internships or fieldwork available. Support available to part-time students. Financial award application deadline: 3/1. *Unit head:* Dr. John Groves, Dean, 814-393-2146, Fax: 514-393-2446. *Application contact:* Dr. Brenda Sanders Dede, Assistant Vice President for Academic Affairs, 814-393-2337, Fax: 814-393-2030, E-mail: bdede@clarion.edu. Web site: http://www.clarion.edu/25887/.

Clarke University, Program in Education, Dubuque, IA 52001-3198. Offers early childhood/special education (MAE); educational administration: elementary and secondary (MAE); educational media: elementary and secondary (MAE); multi-categorical resource k-12 (MAE); multidisciplinary studies (MAE); reading: elementary (MAE); technology in education (MAE). Part-time and evening/weekend programs available. Postbaccalaureate distance learning degree programs offered (minimal on-campus study). *Faculty:* 4 full-time (3 women), 2 part-time/adjunct (1 woman). *Students:* 7 full-time (all women), 43 part-time (40 women). Average age 31. In 2011, 11 master's awarded. *Degree requirements:* For master's, comprehensive exam, thesis optional. *Entrance requirements:* For master's, GRE General Test or MAT, minimum GPA of 2.75. *Application deadline:* Applications are processed on a rolling basis. Application fee: $25. Electronic applications accepted. *Expenses: Tuition:* Part-time $690 per credit hour. *Required fees:* $35 per credit hour. Tuition and fees vary according to program and student level. *Financial support:* Career-related internships or fieldwork available. Financial award applicants required to submit FAFSA. *Unit head:* Dr. Larry Bice, Chair, 319-588-6397, Fax: 319-584-8604. *Application contact:* Joan Coates, Information Contact, 563-588-6354, Fax: 563-588-6789, E-mail: graduate@clarke.edu.

College of Mount Saint Vincent, School of Professional and Continuing Studies, Department of Teacher Education, Riverdale, NY 10471-1093. Offers instructional technology and global perspectives (Certificate); middle level education (Certificate); multicultural studies (Certificate); urban and multicultural education (MS Ed). *Accreditation:* Teacher Education Accreditation Council. Part-time programs available. *Degree requirements:* For master's, comprehensive exam. *Entrance requirements:* For master's, interview, New York teaching certificate. Additional exam requirements/recommendations for international students: Required—TOEFL.

College of Saint Elizabeth, Department of Education, Morristown, NJ 07960-6989. Offers accelerated certification for teachers (Certificate); assistive technology (Certificate); education: human services leadership (MA); educational leadership (MA, Ed D); educational technology (MA). Part-time and evening/weekend programs available. *Faculty:* 10 full-time (3 women), 12 part-time/adjunct (6 women). *Students:* 69 full-time (50 women), 203 part-time (175 women); includes 43 minority (26 Black or African American, non-Hispanic/Latino; 1 Asian, non-Hispanic/Latino; 16 Hispanic/Latino). Average age 36. 114 applicants, 72% accepted, 70 enrolled. In 2011, 84 master's, 14 doctorates, 119 other advanced degrees awarded. *Degree requirements:* For master's, thesis or alternative, portfolio; for doctorate, thesis/dissertation. *Entrance requirements:* For master's, interview, minimum undergraduate GPA of 3.0; for doctorate, master's degree. *Application deadline:* For fall admission, 6/30 priority date for domestic students; for spring admission, 11/30 for domestic students. Applications are processed on a rolling basis. Application fee: $35. Electronic applications accepted. *Expenses: Tuition:* Part-time $899 per credit. *Required fees:* $73 per credit. *Financial support:* Career-related internships or fieldwork, tuition waivers (partial), and unspecified assistantships available. Support available to part-time students. Financial award application deadline: 3/15; financial award applicants required to submit FAFSA. *Faculty research:* Developmental stages for teaching and human services professionals, effectiveness of humanities core curriculum. *Unit head:* Dr. Alan H. Markowitz, Director of Graduate Education Programs, 973-290-4374, Fax: 973-290-4389, E-mail: amarkowitz@cse.edu. *Application contact:* Donna Tatarka, Dean of Admission, 973-290-4705, Fax: 973-290-4710, E-mail: dtatarka@cse.edu. Web site: http://www.cse.edu/academics/academic-areas/human-social-dev/education/?tabID-tabGraduate&divID-progGraduate.

The College of Saint Rose, Graduate Studies, School of Education, Educational and School Psychology Department, Albany, NY 12203-1419. Offers applied technology education (MS Ed); educational psychology (MS Ed); school psychology (MS, Certificate). Part-time and evening/weekend programs available. *Entrance requirements:* For master's, minimum undergraduate GPA of 3.0. Additional exam requirements/recommendations for international students: Required—TOEFL (minimum score 550 paper-based; 213 computer-based). Electronic applications accepted.

The College of William and Mary, School of Education, Program in Education Policy, Planning, and Leadership, Williamsburg, VA 23187-8795. Offers curriculum and educational technology (Ed D, PhD); curriculum leadership (Ed D, PhD); educational leadership (M Ed), including higher education administration (M Ed, Ed D, PhD), K-12 administration and supervision; educational policy, planning, and leadership (Ed D, PhD), including general education administration, gifted education administration, higher education administration (M Ed, Ed D, PhD), special education administration; gifted education administration (M Ed). *Accreditation:* NCATE. Part-time and evening/weekend programs available. *Faculty:* 11 full-time (5 women), 11 part-time/adjunct (9 women). *Students:* 50 full-time (38 women), 145 part-time (104 women); includes 45 minority (35 Black or African American, non-Hispanic/Latino; 2 Asian, non-Hispanic/Latino; 4 Hispanic/Latino; 4 Two or more races, non-Hispanic/Latino), 5 international. Average age 38. 173 applicants, 62% accepted, 75 enrolled. In 2011, 21 master's, 10 doctorates awarded. *Degree requirements:* For doctorate, comprehensive exam, thesis/dissertation. *Entrance requirements:* For master's, GRE or MAT, minimum GPA of 2.5; for doctorate, GRE or MAT, minimum GPA of 3.0. Additional exam requirements/recommendations for international students: Required—TOEFL. *Application deadline:* For fall admission, 1/15 for domestic and international students. Application fee: $50. Electronic applications accepted. *Expenses:* Tuition, state resident: full-time $6400; part-time $365 per credit hour. Tuition, nonresident: full-time $19,720; part-time $985 per credit hour. *Required fees:* $4562. *Financial support:* In 2011–12, 54 students received support, including 1 fellowship (averaging $20,000 per year), 38 research assistantships with full and partial tuition reimbursements available (averaging $15,000 per year); career-related internships or fieldwork, Federal Work-Study, institutionally sponsored loans, scholarships/grants, and unspecified assistantships also available. Support available to part-time students. Financial award application deadline: 1/15; financial award applicants required to submit FAFSA. *Faculty research:* Higher education policy, faculty incentives, history of adversity, resilience, leadership. *Unit head:* Dr. Pamela Eddy, Area Coordinator, 757-221-2349, E-mail: peddy@wm.edu. *Application contact:* Dorothy Smith Osborne, Assistant Dean for Admission, 757-221-2317, Fax: 757-221-2293, E-mail: dsosbo@wm.edu. Web site: http://education.wm.edu.

Colorado Christian University, Program in Curriculum and Instruction, Lakewood, CO 80226. Offers corporate education (MACI); early childhood educator (MACI); elementary educator (MACI); instructional technology (MACI); master educator (MACI); online course developer (MACI); online teaching and learning (MACI); special education generalist (MACI). Part-time and evening/weekend programs available. *Degree requirements:* For master's, thesis optional, practicum. *Entrance requirements:* For master's, interviews, letters of recommendation. Additional exam requirements/recommendations for international students: Required—TOEFL. Electronic applications accepted. *Expenses:* Contact institution.

Colorado State University–Pueblo, College of Education, Engineering and Professional Studies, Education Program, Pueblo, CO 81001-4901. Offers art education (M Ed); foreign language education (M Ed); health and physical education (M Ed); instructional technology (M Ed); linguistically diverse education (M Ed); music education (M Ed); special education (M Ed). *Accreditation:* Teacher Education Accreditation Council. Part-time programs available. *Degree requirements:* For master's, portfolio. *Entrance requirements:* For master's, 3 recommendations, teaching license. Additional exam requirements/recommendations for international students: Required—TOEFL (minimum score 500 paper-based; 173 computer-based). Electronic applications accepted. *Faculty research:* Portfolio assessment, math education, science education.

Columbia International University, Columbia Graduate School, Columbia, SC 29230-3122. Offers Bible teaching (MABT); Christian higher education leadership (Ed D); Christian school educational leadership (Ed D); counseling (MACN); curriculum and instruction (M Ed), including Christian school guidance, English as a second language, learning disabilities, school technology; early childhood and elementary education (MAT); educational administration (M Ed); teaching English as a foreign language (Certificate); teaching English as a foreign language and intercultural studies (MATF). Part-time and evening/weekend programs available. *Degree requirements:* For master's, internships, professional project. *Entrance requirements:* For master's, Minnesota Multiphasic Personality Inventory, MAT, minimum GPA of 2.7. Additional exam requirements/recommendations for international students: Required—TOEFL. Electronic applications accepted.

Columbus State University, Graduate Studies, College of Education and Health Professions, Department of Teacher Education, Columbus, GA 31907-5645. Offers accomplished teaching (M Ed); early childhood education (M Ed, MAT, Ed S); health and physical education (M Ed, MAT); middle grades education (M Ed, MAT, Ed S); school library media (M Ed, MAT); secondary education (M Ed, MAT, Ed S), including English/language arts (M Ed, Ed S), general science (M Ed), mathematics (M Ed), social science (M Ed); special education (M Ed, Ed S), including general curriculum (M Ed). *Accreditation:* NCATE. Part-time and evening/weekend programs available. Postbaccalaureate distance learning degree programs offered (minimal on-campus study). *Degree requirements:* For master's, thesis, exit exam; for Ed S, thesis or alternative. *Entrance requirements:* For master's, GRE General Test, minimum GPA of 2.75; for Ed S, GRE General Test. Additional exam requirements/recommendations for international students: Required—TOEFL (minimum score 550 paper-based; 213 computer-based; 79 iBT). Electronic applications accepted.

Concordia University, School of Graduate Studies, Faculty of Arts and Science, Department of Education, Program in Educational Technology, Montréal, QC H3G 1M8, Canada. Offers MA, PhD. *Degree requirements:* For master's, one foreign language, thesis optional, internship; for doctorate, comprehensive exam, thesis/dissertation. *Entrance requirements:* For doctorate, MA in educational technology or equivalent. *Faculty research:* Instructional design and tele-education, educational cybernetics and systems analysis, media research and theory development, distance education.

Concordia University, School of Graduate Studies, Faculty of Arts and Science, Department of Education, Program in Instructional Technology, Montréal, QC H3G 1M8, Canada. Offers Diploma. *Entrance requirements:* For degree, BA in related field.

Concordia University Chicago, College of Graduate and Innovative Programs, Program in Educational Technology, River Forest, IL 60305-1499. Offers MA.

Concordia University, St. Paul, College of Education, St. Paul, MN 55104-5494. Offers curriculum and instruction (MA Ed), including K-12 reading endorsement; differentiated instruction (MA Ed); early childhood education (MA Ed); educational leadership (MA Ed); educational technology (MA Ed); family life education (MA); K-12 reading endorsement (Certificate); special education (Certificate); sports management (MA). *Accreditation:* NCATE. Evening/weekend programs available. Postbaccalaureate distance learning degree programs offered (minimal on-campus study). *Faculty:* 7 full-time (3 women), 64 part-time/adjunct (42 women). *Students:* 617 full-time (495 women), 9 part-time (6 women); includes 57 minority (30 Black or African American, non-Hispanic/Latino; 2 American Indian or Alaska Native, non-Hispanic/Latino; 17 Asian, non-Hispanic/Latino; 5 Hispanic/Latino; 1 Native Hawaiian or other Pacific Islander, non-Hispanic/Latino; 2 Two or more races, non-Hispanic/Latino). Average age 36. 302 applicants, 83% accepted, 210 enrolled. In 2011, 320 master's, 68 other advanced degrees awarded. *Application deadline:* Applications are processed on a rolling basis. Application fee: $50. Electronic applications accepted. *Expenses: Tuition:* Full-time $8100; part-time $435 per credit. Tuition and fees vary according to program. *Financial support:* Applicants required to submit FAFSA. *Unit head:* Dr. Donald Helmstetter, Dean, 651-641-8227, Fax: 651-641-8807, E-mail: helmstetter@csp.edu. *Application contact:* Kimberly Craig, Director of Graduate and Cohort Admission, 651-603-6223, Fax: 651-603-6320, E-mail: craig@csp.edu.

Dakota State University, College of Education, Madison, SD 57042-1799. Offers instructional technology (MSET). *Accreditation:* NCATE. Part-time and evening/weekend programs available. Postbaccalaureate distance learning degree programs offered (minimal on-campus study). *Faculty:* 6 full-time (3 women), 2 part-time/adjunct (0 women). *Students:* 1 full-time (0 women), 24 part-time (15 women); includes 3 minority (all Hispanic/Latino), 1 international. Average age 33. 5 applicants, 100% accepted, 5 enrolled. In 2011, 9 master's awarded. *Degree requirements:* For master's, thesis, portfolio. *Entrance requirements:* For master's, GRE General Test, demonstration of technology skills, minimum GPA of 2.7. Additional exam requirements/recommendations for international students: Required—TOEFL (minimum score 550 paper-based; 213 computer-based; 78 iBT). *Application deadline:* For fall admission, 6/15 for domestic and international students; for spring admission, 11/15 for domestic and international students. Applications are processed on a rolling basis. Application fee: $35 ($85 for international students). *Financial support:* In 2011–12, 14 students received support, including 3 research assistantships with partial tuition reimbursements available (averaging $11,116 per year); teaching assistantships, Federal Work-Study, scholarships/grants, tuition waivers (partial), unspecified assistantships, and administrative assistantships also available. Support available to part-time students. Financial award applicants required to submit FAFSA. *Faculty research:* Educational technology evaluation, computer-supported collaborative learning, cognitive theory and visual representation of the effects of ambiguitous wireless computing on student learning and productivity. *Unit head:* Dr. Judy Dittman, Dean, 605-256-5177, Fax: 605-256-7300, E-mail: judy.dittman@dsu.edu. *Application contact:* Erin Blankespoor, Secretary, Office of Graduate Studies and Research, 605-256-5799, Fax: 605-256-5093, E-mail: erin.blankespoor@dsu.edu. Web site: http://www.dsu.edu/educate/index.aspx.

Delaware Valley College, Program in Educational Leadership, Doylestown, PA 18901-2697. Offers instruction, curriculum and technology (MS); school administration and leadership (MS). Part-time and evening/weekend programs available. *Entrance requirements:* For master's, minimum undergraduate GPA of 3.0.

DeSales University, Graduate Division, Program in Education, Center Valley, PA 18034-9568. Offers academic standards and reform (M Ed); academic standards for K-6 (M Ed); English as a second language (M Ed); instructional technology for K-12 (M Ed); special education (M Ed); teaching English to speakers of other languages (M Ed). Part-time and evening/weekend programs available. Postbaccalaureate distance learning degree programs offered (no on-campus study). *Degree requirements:* For master's, thesis project. *Entrance requirements:* Additional exam requirements/recommendations for international students: Required—TOEFL. *Application deadline:* Applications are processed on a rolling basis. Electronic applications accepted. Tuition and fees vary according to degree level. *Financial support:* Application deadline: 5/1. *Unit head:* Dr. Judith Rance-Roney, Interim Director, 610-282-1100 Ext. 1323, E-mail: judith.rance-roney@desales.edu. *Application contact:* Caryn Stopper, Director of Graduate Admissions, 610-282-1100 Ext. 1768, Fax: 610-282-0525, E-mail: caryn.stopper@desales.edu.

Dowling College, Graduate Programs in Education, Oakdale, NY 11769-1999. Offers adolescence education with middle childhood extension (MS); advanced certificate in gifted education (AC); childhood and early childhood education (MS); childhood and gifted education (MS); computers in education (AC); early childhood education (MS); educational administration (Ed D); educational technology leadership (MS); educational technology specialist (AC); literacy education (MS); literary education (AC); school building leader (AC); school district business leader (MBA, AC); school district leader (AC); special education (MS); sports management (MS). *Accreditation:* NCATE. Part-time and evening/weekend programs available. Postbaccalaureate distance learning degree programs offered (minimal on-campus study). *Faculty:* 23 full-time (12 women), 70 part-time/adjunct (44 women). *Students:* 336 full-time (245 women), 631 part-time (485 women); includes 83 minority (29 Black or African American, non-Hispanic/Latino; 2 American Indian or Alaska Native, non-Hispanic/Latino; 7 Asian, non-Hispanic/Latino; 45 Hispanic/Latino). Average age 32. 280 applicants, 85% accepted, 167 enrolled. In 2011, 425 master's, 27 doctorates, 40 other advanced degrees awarded. *Degree requirements:* For master's and AC, comprehensive exam; for doctorate, thesis/dissertation. *Entrance requirements:* For master's, minimum GPA of 3.0; for doctorate, GRE, master's degree; for AC, teaching certificate. Additional exam requirements/recommendations for international students: Required—TOEFL (minimum score 550 paper-based). *Application deadline:* For fall admission, 9/1 priority date for domestic students; for winter admission, 1/1 priority date for domestic students; for spring admission, 2/1 priority date for domestic students. Applications are processed on a rolling basis. Application fee: $50. Electronic applications accepted. *Expenses: Tuition:* Full-time $19,162; part-time $933 per credit. *Required fees:* $1330; $700 per year. Tuition and fees vary according to course load. *Financial support:* Career-related internships or fieldwork and Federal Work-Study available. Support available to part-time students. Financial award application deadline: 6/30; financial award applicants required to submit FAFSA. *Faculty research:* Natural readers, Korean styles and learning strategies, mothers of children with disabilities, computers in instruction, cultural background and organizational roadblocks to problem solving. *Unit head:* Carol Pulsonetti, Director of Operations, School of Education, 631-244-3243, E-mail: pulsonec@dowling.edu. *Application contact:* Ronnie S. Macdonald, Assistant Vice President for Enrollment Services/Dean of Admissions, 631-244-3357, Fax: 631-244-1059, E-mail: macdonar@dowling.edu.

Drexel University, Goodwin College of Professional Studies, School of Education, Program in Education Leadership Development and Learning Technologies, Philadelphia, PA 19104-2875. Offers PhD. *Degree requirements:* For doctorate, thesis/dissertation. Electronic applications accepted.

Drexel University, Goodwin College of Professional Studies, School of Education, Program in Learning Technologies, Philadelphia, PA 19104-2875. Offers MS.

Drexel University, Goodwin College of Professional Studies, School of Technology and Professional Studies, Philadelphia, PA 19104-2875. Offers construction management (MS); engineering technology (MS); food science (MS); hospitality management (MS); professional studies: creativity studies (MS); professional studies: e-learning leadership (MS); professional studies: homeland security management (MS); project management (MS); property management (MS); sport management (MS). Postbaccalaureate distance learning degree programs offered.

Drexel University, The iSchool at Drexel, College of Information Science and Technology, Master of Science in Library and Information Science Program, Philadelphia, PA 19104-2875. Offers archival studies (MS); competitive intelligence and knowledge management (MS); digital libraries (MS); library and information services (MS); school library media (MS); youth services (MS). Part-time and evening/weekend programs available. Postbaccalaureate distance learning degree programs offered (no on-campus study). *Faculty:* 30 full-time (20 women), 29 part-time/adjunct (15 women). *Students:* 198 full-time (155 women), 437 part-time (353 women); includes 79 minority (30 Black or African American, non-Hispanic/Latino; 6 American Indian or Alaska Native, non-Hispanic/Latino; 20 Asian, non-Hispanic/Latino; 23 Hispanic/Latino), 15 international. Average age 33. 464 applicants, 72% accepted, 202 enrolled. In 2011, 261 master's awarded. *Entrance requirements:* For master's, GRE General Test. Additional exam requirements/recommendations for international students: Required—TOEFL (minimum score 600 paper-based; 250 computer-based; 100 iBT). *Application deadline:* For fall admission, 8/1 for domestic and international students; for spring admission, 2/1 for domestic and international students. Applications are processed on a rolling basis. Electronic applications accepted. *Expenses:* Contact institution. *Financial support:* In 2011–12, 217 students received support, including 252 fellowships with partial tuition reimbursements available (averaging $22,500 per year); institutionally sponsored loans and scholarships/grants also available. Support available to part-time students. Financial award application deadline: 3/1; financial award applicants required to submit FAFSA. *Faculty research:* Library and information resources and services, knowledge organization and representation, information retrieval/information visualization/bibliometrics, information needs and behaviors, digital libraries. *Total annual research expenditures:* $2 million. *Unit head:* Dr. David E. Fenske, Dean/Professor of Information Science, 215-895-2475, Fax: 215-895-6378, E-mail: fenske@drexel.edu. *Application contact:* Matthew Lechtenberg, Graduate Admissions Manager, 215-895-1951, Fax: 215-895-2303, E-mail: ml333@drexel.edu.

Drury University, Graduate Programs in Education, Springfield, MO 65802. Offers elementary education (M Ed); gifted education (M Ed); human services (M Ed); instructional mathematics K-8 (M Ed); instructional technology (M Ed); middle school teaching (M Ed); secondary education (M Ed); special education (M Ed); special reading (M Ed). *Accreditation:* NCATE. Part-time and evening/weekend programs available. *Degree requirements:* For master's, thesis. *Entrance requirements:* For master's, GRE or MAT, minimum GPA of 2.75. Additional exam requirements/recommendations for international students: Required—TOEFL. Electronic applications accepted. *Faculty research:* Cultural enrichment, research skills, parental involvement relating to reading skills, reading strategies for mainstreaming children.

Duquesne University, School of Education, Department of Instruction and Leadership, Program in Instructional Technology, Pittsburgh, PA 15282-0001. Offers business, computer, and information technology (MS Ed); instructional technology (MS Ed, Ed D, Post-Master's Certificate). Part-time and evening/weekend programs available. Postbaccalaureate distance learning degree programs offered (minimal on-campus study). *Faculty:* 3 full-time (1 woman), 13 part-time/adjunct (10 women). *Students:* 82 full-time (50 women), 14 part-time (9 women); includes 4 minority (2 Black or African American, non-Hispanic/Latino; 2 Hispanic/Latino), 4 international. Average age 32. 23 applicants, 65% accepted, 11 enrolled. In 2011, 30 master's, 1 doctorate awarded. *Degree requirements:* For master's, thesis optional; for doctorate, thesis/dissertation. *Entrance requirements:* For master's, bachelor's degree; for doctorate, GRE, master's degree; for Post-Master's Certificate, bachelor's/master's degree. Additional exam requirements/recommendations for international students: Required—TOEFL (minimum score 550 paper-based; 80 computer-based), IELTS (minimum score 7). *Application deadline:* For fall admission, 9/1 for domestic students; for spring admission, 1/1 for domestic students. Applications are processed on a rolling basis. Application fee: $0. Electronic applications accepted. Application fee is waived when completed online. *Expenses: Tuition:* Full-time $16,596; part-time $922 per credit. *Required fees:* $1584; $88 per credit. Tuition and fees vary according to program. *Financial support:* Available to part-time students. *Unit head:* Dr. David Carbonara, Director, 412-396-4039, Fax: 412-396-1997, E-mail: carbonara@duq.edu. *Application contact:* Michael Dolinger, Director of Student and Academic Services, 412-396-6647, Fax: 412-396-5585, E-mail: dolingerm@duq.edu. Web site: http://www.duq.edu/education.

East Carolina University, Graduate School, College of Education, Department of Curriculum and Instruction, Greenville, NC 27858-4353. Offers assistive technology (Certificate); autism (Certificate); deaf/blindness (Certificate); elementary education (MA Ed); English education (MA Ed); history (MA Ed); middle grade education (MA Ed); reading education (MA Ed); special education (MA Ed); teaching (MAT). Part-time programs available. Postbaccalaureate distance learning degree programs offered. *Degree requirements:* For master's, comprehensive exam, thesis optional. *Entrance requirements:* For master's, GRE General Test or MAT, interview, bachelor's degree in related field, minimum GPA of 2.5, teaching license. Additional exam requirements/recommendations for international students: Required—TOEFL. *Application deadline:* For fall admission, 6/1 priority date for domestic students. Applications are processed on a rolling basis. Application fee: $50. *Expenses:* Tuition, state resident: full-time $3557; part-time $444.63 per semester hour. Tuition, nonresident: full-time $14,351; part-time $1793.88 per semester hour. *Required fees:* $2016; $252 per semester hour. Part-time tuition and fees vary according to course load, campus/location and program. *Financial support:* Research assistantships, teaching assistantships, and Federal Work-Study available. Support available to part-time students. Financial award application deadline: 6/1; financial award applicants required to submit FAFSA. *Unit head:* Carolyn C. Ledford, Interim Chair, 252-328-1100, E-mail: ledfordc@ecu.edu. *Application contact:* Dean of Graduate School, 252-328-6012, Fax: 252-328-6071, E-mail: gradschool@ecu.edu. Web site: http://www.ecu.edu/cs-educ/ci/Graduate.cfm.

East Carolina University, Graduate School, College of Education, Department of Mathematics, Science, and Instructional Technology Education, Greenville, NC 27858-4353. Offers computer-based instruction (Certificate); distance learning and administration (Certificate); instructional technology (MA Ed, MS); mathematics (MA Ed); performance improvement (Certificate); science education (MA, MA Ed); special endorsement in computer education (Certificate). Part-time and evening/weekend programs available. *Degree requirements:* For master's, comprehensive exam, thesis optional. *Entrance requirements:* For master's, GRE General Test or MAT, interview, minimum GPA of 2.5, bachelor's degree in related field, teaching license (MA Ed). Additional exam requirements/recommendations for international students: Required—TOEFL. *Application deadline:* For fall admission, 6/1 priority date for domestic students. Applications are processed on a rolling basis. Application fee: $50. *Expenses:* Tuition, state resident: full-time $3557; part-time $444.63 per semester hour. Tuition, nonresident: full-time $14,351; part-time $1793.88 per semester hour. *Required fees:* $2016; $252 per semester hour. Part-time tuition and fees vary according to course load, campus/location and program. *Financial support:* Research assistantships, teaching assistantships, and Federal Work-Study available. Support available to part-time students. Financial award application deadline: 6/1. *Unit head:* Susan Ganter, Chair, 252-328-9353, E-mail: ganters@ecu.edu. *Application contact:* Dean of Graduate School, 252-328-6012, Fax: 252-328-6071, E-mail: gradschool@ecu.edu.

Eastern Connecticut State University, School of Education and Professional Studies/Graduate Division, Program in Educational Technology, Willimantic, CT 06226-2295. Offers MS. Part-time and evening/weekend programs available. *Degree requirements:* For master's, comprehensive exam or thesis. *Entrance requirements:* For master's, minimum GPA of 2.7. Additional exam requirements/recommendations for international students: Required—TOEFL (minimum score 550 paper-based; 213 computer-based). Electronic applications accepted.

Eastern Michigan University, Graduate School, College of Education, Department of Teacher Education, Program in Educational Media and Technology, Ypsilanti, MI 48197. Offers MA, Graduate Certificate. Part-time and evening/weekend programs available. Postbaccalaureate distance learning degree programs offered (minimal on-campus study). *Students:* 61 part-time (44 women); includes 5 minority (2 Black or African American, non-Hispanic/Latino; 2 Asian, non-Hispanic/Latino; 1 Native Hawaiian or other Pacific Islander, non-Hispanic/Latino). Average age 33. 32 applicants, 69% accepted, 10 enrolled. In 2011, 24 master's, 1 other advanced degree awarded. *Entrance requirements:* Additional exam requirements/recommendations for international students: Required—TOEFL. *Application deadline:* Applications are processed on a rolling basis. Application fee: $35. *Expenses:* Tuition, state resident: full-time $10,367; part-time $432 per credit hour. Tuition, nonresident: full-time $20,435; part-time $851 per credit hour. *Required fees:* $39 per credit hour. $46 per semester. One-time fee: $100. Tuition and fees vary according to course level, degree level and reciprocity agreements. *Financial support:* Fellowships, research assistantships with full tuition reimbursements, teaching assistantships with full tuition reimbursements, career-related internships or fieldwork, Federal Work-Study, institutionally sponsored loans, scholarships/grants, tuition waivers (partial), and unspecified assistantships available. Support available to part-time students. Financial award applicants required to submit FAFSA. *Unit head:* Dr. Nancy Copeland, Coordinator, 734-487-3260, Fax: 734-487-2101, E-mail: ncopeland@emich.edu. *Application contact:* Dr. Anne Bednar, Advisor, 734-487-3260, Fax: 734-487-2101, E-mail: anne.bednar@emich.edu.

Eastern New Mexico University, Graduate School, College of Education and Technology, Department of Curriculum and Instruction, Portales, NM 88130. Offers bilingual education (M Ed); educational technology (M Ed); elementary education (M Ed); English as a second language (M Ed); pedagogy and learning (M Ed); professional technical education (M Ed); reading/literacy (M Ed). Part-time programs available. Postbaccalaureate distance learning degree programs offered (minimal on-campus study). *Degree requirements:* For master's, comprehensive exam, thesis optional. *Entrance requirements:* For master's, minimum GPA of 3.0, photocopy of teaching license, writing assessment, letter of recommendation. Additional exam requirements/recommendations for international students: Required—TOEFL (minimum score 550 paper-based; 213 computer-based; 79 iBT), IELTS (minimum score 6). Electronic applications accepted.

Eastern Washington University, Graduate Studies, College of Arts, Letters and Education, Department of Education, Program in Instructional Media and Technology, Cheney, WA 99004-2431. Offers M Ed. *Students:* 2 full-time (both women), 4 part-time (2 women), 3 international. Average age 38. 17 applicants. *Unit head:* Robin Showalter, Program Coordinator, 509-359-6492, E-mail: rshowalter@mail.ewu.edu. *Application contact:* Dr. Kevin Pyatt, Assistant Professor, Science and Technology, 509-359-6091, E-mail: kpyatt@ewu.edu.

East Stroudsburg University of Pennsylvania, Graduate School, College of Education, Department of Media Communications and Technology, East Stroudsburg, PA 18301-2999. Offers instructional technology (M Ed). Part-time and evening/weekend programs available. *Degree requirements:* For master's, comprehensive exam, comprehensive portfolio, internship. *Entrance requirements:* For master's, two letters of recommendation, portfolio or interview, minimum overall undergraduate QPA of 2.5, internship. Additional exam requirements/recommendations for international students: Required—TOEFL (minimum score 560 paper-based; 220 computer-based; 83 iBT).

East Tennessee State University, School of Graduate Studies, College of Education, Department of Curriculum and Instruction, Johnson City, TN 37614. Offers educational media/educational technology (M Ed), including educational communications and technology, school library media; elementary education (M Ed); reading (MA), including reading education, storytelling; school library professional (Post-Master's Certificate); secondary education (M Ed), including classroom technology, secondary education (M Ed, MAT); storytelling (Postbaccalaureate Certificate); teacher education with multiple levels (initial licensure) (MAT), including elementary education, middle grades education, secondary education (M Ed, MAT). *Accreditation:* NCATE. Part-time and evening/weekend programs available. Postbaccalaureate distance learning degree programs offered (no on-campus study). *Faculty:* 20 full-time (13 women), 3 part-time/adjunct (all women). *Students:* 108 full-time (76 women), 107 part-time (97 women); includes 9 minority (4 Black or African American, non-Hispanic/Latino; 1 Asian, non-Hispanic/Latino; 2 Hispanic/Latino; 2 Two or more races, non-Hispanic/Latino), 2 international. Average age 33. 141 applicants, 57% accepted, 79 enrolled. In 2011, 129 master's awarded. *Degree requirements:* For master's, comprehensive exam, thesis optional, student teaching, practicum; for other advanced degree, field work (school library); culminating experience (storytelling). *Entrance requirements:* For master's, GRE, SAT, ACT, PRAXIS, minimum GPA of 3.0; for other advanced degree, master's degree, TN teaching license (school library professional post-master's certificate); three letters of recommendation (storytelling certificate). Additional exam requirements/recommendations for international students: Required—TOEFL (minimum score 550 paper-based; 213 computer-based; 79 iBT). *Application deadline:* For fall admission, 6/1 for domestic students, 4/30 for international students; for spring admission, 11/1 for domestic students, 4/30 for international students. Application fee: $35 ($45 for international students). Electronic applications accepted. *Expenses:* Tuition, state resident: full-time $7312; part-time $350 per credit hour. Tuition, nonresident: full-time $18,490; part-time $621 per credit hour. *Required fees:* $63 per credit hour. Tuition and fees vary according to course load and program. *Financial support:* In 2011–12, 60 students received support, including 7 research assistantships with full tuition reimbursements available (averaging $6,000 per year), 11 teaching assistantships with full tuition reimbursements available (averaging $6,000 per year); career-related internships or fieldwork, institutionally sponsored loans, scholarships/grants, and unspecified assistantships also available. Financial award application deadline: 7/1; financial award applicants required to submit FAFSA. *Faculty research:* Critical thinking; curriculum development in reading, math, and science education; cultural diversity; cognitive processes; effective teaching strategies. *Unit head:* Dr. Rhona Hurwitz, Chair, 423-439-7598, Fax: 423-439-8362, E-mail: hurwitz@etsu.edu. *Application contact:* Fiona Goodyear, Graduate Specialist, 423-439-6148, Fax: 423-439-5624, E-mail: goodyear@etsu.edu.

Ellis University, Program in Instructional Technology, Chicago, IL 60606-7204. Offers MS. *Degree requirements:* For master's, research and field project.

Emporia State University, Graduate School, Teachers College, Department of Instructional Design and Technology, Emporia, KS 66801-5087. Offers MS. *Accreditation:* NCATE. Part-time programs available. Postbaccalaureate distance learning degree programs offered (minimal on-campus study). *Faculty:* 6 full-time (3 women). *Students:* 20 full-time (9 women), 90 part-time (62 women); includes 16 minority (6 Black or African American, non-Hispanic/Latino; 2 Asian, non-Hispanic/Latino; 5 Hispanic/Latino; 1 Native Hawaiian or other Pacific Islander, non-Hispanic/Latino; 2 Two or more races, non-Hispanic/Latino), 17 international. 23 applicants, 87% accepted, 13 enrolled. In 2011, 41 master's awarded. *Degree requirements:* For master's, comprehensive exam (for some programs), thesis (for some programs), project. *Entrance requirements:* For master's, appropriate bachelor's degree, letters of recommendation. Additional exam requirements/recommendations for international students: Required—TOEFL (minimum score 520 paper-based; 133 computer-based; 68 iBT). *Application deadline:* For fall admission, 8/15 priority date for domestic students. Applications are processed on a rolling basis. Application fee: $30 ($75 for international students). Electronic applications accepted. *Expenses:* Tuition, state resident: full-time $2342; part-time $195 per credit hour. Tuition, nonresident: full-time $7254; part-time $605 per credit hour. *Required fees:* $66 per credit hour. Tuition and fees vary according to campus/location. *Financial support:* In 2011–12, 6 teaching assistantships with full tuition reimbursements (averaging $6,471 per year) were awarded; Federal Work-Study, institutionally sponsored loans, health care benefits, and unspecified assistantships also available. Financial award application deadline: 3/15; financial award applicants required to submit FAFSA. *Unit head:* Dr. Marcus Childress, Chair, 620-341-5627, E-mail: mchildre@emporia.edu. *Application contact:* Mary Sewell, Admissions Coordinator, 800-950-GRAD, Fax: 620-341-5909, E-mail: msewell@emporia.edu. Web site: http://www.emporia.edu/idt/.

Fairfield University, Graduate School of Education and Allied Professions, Fairfield, CT 06824-5195. Offers applied psychology (MA); bilingual education (CAS); clinical mental health counseling (MA, CAS); educational technology (MA); elementary education (MA); family studies (MA); marriage and family therapy (MA); school counseling (MA, CAS); school psychology (MA, CAS); special education (MA); teaching (Certificate); teaching and foundations (MA, CAS); TESOL foreign language and bilingual/multicultural education (MA, CAS). *Accreditation:* NCATE. Part-time and evening/weekend programs available. *Faculty:* 24 full-time (19 women). *Students:* 147 full-time (120 women), 391 part-time (321 women); includes 60 minority (13 Black or African American, non-Hispanic/Latino; 8 Asian, non-Hispanic/Latino; 35 Hispanic/Latino; 4 Two or more races, non-Hispanic/Latino), 1 international. Average age 34. 319 applicants, 48% accepted, 80 enrolled. In 2011, 185 master's, 20 other advanced degrees awarded. *Degree requirements:* For master's, comprehensive exam. *Entrance requirements:* For master's, PRAXIS I (for certification programs), minimum QPA of 3.0, 2 recommendations, resume. Additional exam requirements/recommendations for international students: Required—TOEFL (minimum score 550 paper-based; 213 computer-based; 84 iBT) or IELTS (minimum score 7.5). *Application deadline:* For fall admission, 2/15 for international students; for spring admission, 10/1 for international students. Application fee: $60. Electronic applications accepted. *Expenses: Tuition:* Part-time $600 per credit hour. *Required fees:* $25 per term. *Financial support:* In 2011–12, 45 students received support. Career-related internships or fieldwork and unspecified assistantships available. Financial award applicants required to submit FAFSA. *Faculty research:* Literacy, adolescent psychology, special education, early childhood education, teaching development. *Unit head:* Dr. Susan D. Franzosa, Dean, 203-254-4000 Ext. 4250, Fax: 203-254-4241, E-mail: sfranzosa@fairfield.edu. *Application contact:* Marianne Gumpper, Director of Graduate and Continuing Studies Admission, 203-254-4184, Fax: 203-254-4073, E-mail: gradadmis@fairfield.edu. Web site: http://www.fairfield.edu/gseap/gseap_grad_1.html.

Fairleigh Dickinson University, College at Florham, University College: Arts, Sciences, and Professional Studies, Peter Sammartino School of Education, Madison, NJ 07940-1099. Offers education for certified teachers (MA, Certificate); educational leadership (MA); instructional technology (Certificate); literacy/reading (Certificate); teaching (MAT).

Fairleigh Dickinson University, Metropolitan Campus, University College: Arts, Sciences, and Professional Studies, Peter Sammartino School of Education, Teaneck, NJ 07666-1914. Offers dyslexia specialist (Certificate); education for certified teachers (MA); educational leadership (MA); instructional technology (Certificate); learning disabilities (MA); literacy/reading (Certificate); multilingual education (MA); teacher of the handicapped (Certificate); teaching (MAT). *Accreditation:* Teacher Education Accreditation Council. Part-time programs available. *Degree requirements:* For master's, research project (MAT).

Fairmont State University, Programs in Education, Fairmont, WV 26554. Offers digital media, new literacies and learning (M Ed); education (MAT); exercise science, fitness and wellness (M Ed); leadership studies (M Ed); online learning (M Ed); professional studies (M Ed); reading (M Ed); special education (M Ed). *Accreditation:* NCATE. Part-time and evening/weekend programs available. Postbaccalaureate distance learning degree programs offered. *Faculty:* 16 part-time/adjunct (10 women). *Students:* 103 full-time (72 women), 142 part-time (103 women); includes 11 minority (2 Black or African American, non-Hispanic/Latino; 1 American Indian or Alaska Native, non-Hispanic/Latino; 6 Hispanic/Latino; 2 Two or more races, non-Hispanic/Latino), 2 international. Average age 33. 71 applicants, 85% accepted. In 2011, 58 master's awarded. *Entrance requirements:* For master's, GRE. *Application deadline:* For fall admission, 5/1 for domestic and international students. Applications are processed on a rolling basis. Application fee: $40. *Expenses:* Tuition, state resident: full-time $5900. Tuition, nonresident: full-time $12,596. *Unit head:* Dr. Van O. Dempsey, III, Dean, School of Education, 304-367-4241, Fax: 304-367-4599, E-mail: vdempsey@fairmontstate.edu. Web site: http://www.fairmontstate.edu/graduatestudies/default.asp.

Ferris State University, College of Education and Human Services, School of Education, Big Rapids, MI 49307. Offers administration (MSCTE); curriculum and instruction (M Ed), including administration, elementary education, experiential education, philanthropic education, reading, secondary education, special education, subject matter option; education technology (MSCTE); instructor (MSCTE); post-secondary administration (MSCTE); training and development (MSCTE). Part-time and evening/weekend programs available. Postbaccalaureate distance learning degree programs offered (minimal on-campus study). *Faculty:* 9 full-time (7 women), 9 part-time/adjunct (6 women). *Students:* 8 full-time (7 women), 132 part-time (75 women); includes 13 minority (11 Black or African American, non-Hispanic/Latino; 1 American Indian or Alaska Native, non-Hispanic/Latino; 1 Hispanic/Latino), 5 international. Average age 36. 20 applicants, 100% accepted, 8 enrolled. In 2011, 51 master's awarded. *Degree requirements:* For master's, thesis, research paper. *Entrance requirements:* For master's, 2 years of work experience for vocational setting, minimum GPA of 2.75. Additional exam requirements/recommendations for international students: Recommended—TOEFL (minimum score 500 paper-based; 173 computer-based; 61 iBT). *Application deadline:* For fall admission, 7/1 priority date for domestic students, 7/1 for international students; for spring admission, 11/1 priority date for domestic students, 11/1 for international students. Applications are processed on a rolling basis. Application fee: $30. Electronic applications accepted. Application fee is waived when completed online. *Financial support:* Career-related internships or fieldwork and scholarships/grants available. Support available to part-time students. Financial award applicants required to submit FAFSA. *Faculty research:* Suicide prevention, reading, women in education, special needs, administration. *Unit head:* Dr. James Powell, Director, 231-591-5362, Fax: 231-591-2043, E-mail: powelj20@ferris.edu. *Application contact:* Kimisue Worrall, Secretary, 231-591-5361, Fax: 231-591-2043. Web site: http://www.ferris.edu/education/education/.

Fielding Graduate University, Graduate Programs, School of Educational Leadership and Change, Santa Barbara, CA 93105-3538. Offers collaborative educational leadership (MA); educational leadership and change (Ed D), including community college leadership and change, grounded theory/grounded action, leadership of higher education systems, media studies; teaching in the virtual classroom (Graduate Certificate). Postbaccalaureate distance learning degree programs offered (minimal on-campus study). *Faculty:* 15 full-time (8 women), 5 part-time/adjunct (3 women). *Students:* 201 full-time (141 women), 9 part-time (8 women); includes 108 minority (64 Black or African American, non-Hispanic/Latino; 6 American Indian or Alaska Native, non-Hispanic/Latino; 7 Asian, non-Hispanic/Latino; 21 Hispanic/Latino; 1 Native Hawaiian or other Pacific Islander, non-Hispanic/Latino; 9 Two or more races, non-Hispanic/Latino), 2 international. Average age 47. 27 applicants, 93% accepted, 19 enrolled. In 2011, 44 master's, 45 doctorates, 7 other advanced degrees awarded. *Degree requirements:* For master's, capstone research project; for doctorate, comprehensive exam, thesis/dissertation. *Entrance requirements:* For master's, minimum GPA of 2.5; for doctorate, resume, 2 letters of recommendation, writing sample. *Application deadline:* For fall admission, 6/10 for domestic and international students; for spring admission, 11/19 for domestic and international students. Application fee: $75. Electronic applications accepted. *Expenses:* Contact institution. *Financial support:* In 2011–12, 21 students received support. Scholarships/grants, health care benefits, and tuition waivers (partial) available. Support available to part-time students. Financial award applicants required to submit FAFSA. *Unit head:* Dr. Mario R. Borunda, Dean, 805-898-2940, E-mail: mborunda@fielding.edu. *Application contact:* Admission Counselor, 800-340-1099 Ext. 4098, Fax: 805-687-9793, E-mail: elcadmissions@fielding.edu. Web site: http://www.fielding.edu/programs/elc/default.aspx.

Fitchburg State University, Division of Graduate and Continuing Education, Program in Applied Communications, Fitchburg, MA 01420-2697. Offers applied communications (MS, Certificate); health communication (MS); library media (MS); technical and professional writing (MS). Part-time and evening/weekend programs available. *Students:* 3 full-time (1 woman), 7 part-time (5 women); includes 1 minority (Hispanic/Latino), 1 international. Average age 33. 9 applicants, 100% accepted, 6 enrolled. In 2011, 3 master's awarded. *Entrance requirements:* Additional exam requirements/recommendations for international students: Required—TOEFL (minimum score 550 paper-based; 213 computer-based; 79 iBT). *Application deadline:* For fall admission, 7/15 for international students; for spring admission, 12/1 for international students. Applications are processed on a rolling basis. Application fee: $25 ($50 for international students). Electronic applications accepted. *Expenses:* Tuition, state resident: full-time $2700; part-time $150 per credit. Tuition, nonresident: full-time $2700; part-time $150 per credit. *Required fees:* $2286; $127 per credit. *Financial support:* In 2011–12, research assistantships with partial tuition reimbursements (averaging $5,500 per year) were awarded; Federal Work-Study, scholarships/grants, and unspecified assistantships also available. Support available to part-time students. Financial award application deadline: 3/1; financial award applicants required to submit FAFSA. *Unit head:* Dr. John Chetro-Szivos, Chair, 978-665-3261, Fax: 978-665-3658, E-mail: gce@fitchburgstate.edu. *Application contact:* Kay Reynolds, Director of Admissions, 978-665-3144, Fax: 978-665-4540, E-mail: admissions@fsc.edu. Web site: http://www.fitchburgstate.edu/.

Florida Gulf Coast University, College of Education, Program in Curriculum and Instruction, Fort Myers, FL 33965-6565. Offers curriculum and instruction (Ed D, Ed S); educational technology (M Ed, MA); English education (M Ed). Part-time and evening/weekend programs available. Postbaccalaureate distance learning degree programs offered (minimal on-campus study). *Faculty:* 34 full-time (26 women), 57 part-time/adjunct (40 women). *Students:* 19 full-time (18 women), 8 part-time (all women); includes 2 minority (both Hispanic/Latino). Average age 34. 13 applicants, 85% accepted, 10 enrolled. In 2011, 9 master's awarded. *Degree requirements:* For master's, final project or portfolio. *Entrance requirements:* For master's, GRE General Test, MAT, minimum undergraduate GPA of 3.0 in last 2 years. Additional exam requirements/recommendations for international students: Required—TOEFL (minimum score 550 paper-based; 213 computer-based). *Application deadline:* For fall admission, 7/1 priority date for domestic students; for spring admission, 10/15 for domestic students. Applications are processed on a rolling basis. Application fee: $30. Electronic applications accepted. *Expenses:* Tuition, state resident: full-time $8289. Tuition, nonresident: full-time $28,895. *Required fees:* $1831. One-time fee: $30 full-time.

Faculty research: Internet in schools, technology in pre-service and in-service teacher training. *Unit head:* Dr. Diane Schmidt, Department Chair, 239-590-7741, Fax: 239-590-7801, E-mail: dschmidt@fgcu.edu. *Application contact:* Keiana Desmore, Adviser/Counselor, 239-590-7759, Fax: 239-590-7801, E-mail: kdesmore@fgcu.edu. Web site: http://edtech.fgcu.edu/.

Florida International University, College of Education, Department of Curriculum and Instruction, Miami, FL 33199. Offers art education (MAT, MS, Ed D); curriculum and instruction (Ed S); curriculum development (MS); curriculum studies (PhD); early childhood education (MS, Ed D); elementary education (MS, Ed D); English education (MAT, MS, Ed D); foreign language education - teaching English to speakers of other languages (TESOL) (MS, Certificate), including foreign language education (Certificate), teaching English (MS); French education - initial teacher preparation (MAT); international and intercultural development education (Ed D); international and intercultural developmental education (MS); language, literacy and culture (PhD); learning technologies (MS, Ed D, PhD); mathematics education (MAT, MS, Ed D, PhD); modern language education/bilingual education (MS, Ed D); physical education (MS); reading education (MS, Ed D); science education (MAT, MS, Ed D, PhD); social studies education (MAT, MS, Ed D); Spanish education - initial teacher preparation (MAT); special education (MS). Part-time and evening/weekend programs available. *Degree requirements:* For doctorate, comprehensive exam, thesis/dissertation. *Entrance requirements:* For master's, GRE General Test, Florida General Knowledge Test or Florida College Level Academic Skills Test; for doctorate and other advanced degree, GRE General Test. Additional exam requirements/recommendations for international students: Required—TOEFL (minimum score 550 paper-based; 213 computer-based; 80 iBT), IELTS (minimum score 6.3). Electronic applications accepted.

Florida International University, College of Education, Department of Educational Leadership and Policy Studies, Miami, FL 33199. Offers adult education (MS); adult education in human resource development (Ed D); clinical mental health counseling (MS); conflict resolution and consensus building (Certificate); counselor education (MS); educational administration and supervision (Ed D); educational leadership (MS, Certificate, Ed S); higher education (Ed D); higher education administration (MS); human resource development (MS); instruction in urban settings (MS); international/intercultural education (MS); learning technologies (MS); multicultural-bilingual (MS); multicultural-TESOL (MS); recreation and sport management (MS); recreation therapy (MS); rehabilitation counseling (MS); school counseling (MS); school psychology (Ed S); urban education (MS). Part-time and evening/weekend programs available. *Degree requirements:* For doctorate, thesis/dissertation. *Entrance requirements:* For master's, minimum GPA of 3.0; for doctorate and other advanced degree, GRE General Test. Additional exam requirements/recommendations for international students: Required—TOEFL (minimum score 550 paper-based; 213 computer-based; 80 iBT), IELTS (minimum score 6.3). Electronic applications accepted.

Florida State University, The Graduate School, College of Education, Department of Educational Psychology and Learning Systems, Program in Instructional Systems, Tallahassee, FL 32306. Offers instructional systems (MS, PhD, Ed S); open and distance learning (MS); performance improvement and human resources (MS). *Faculty:* 6 full-time (4 women), 1 (woman) part-time/adjunct. *Students:* 68 full-time (47 women), 78 part-time (48 women); includes 19 minority (8 Black or African American, non-Hispanic/Latino; 1 American Indian or Alaska Native, non-Hispanic/Latino; 6 Asian, non-Hispanic/Latino; 4 Hispanic/Latino), 48 international. Average age 36. 60 applicants, 27% accepted, 7 enrolled. In 2011, 31 master's, 3 doctorates awarded. *Median time to degree:* Of those who began their doctoral program in fall 2003, 50% received their degree in 8 years or less. *Degree requirements:* For master's and Ed S, comprehensive exam, thesis optional; for doctorate, comprehensive exam, thesis/dissertation. *Entrance requirements:* For master's, doctorate, and Ed S, GRE General Test, minimum GPA of 3.0. Additional exam requirements/recommendations for international students: Required—TOEFL (minimum score 550 paper-based; 213 computer-based; 80 iBT). *Application deadline:* For fall admission, 7/1 for domestic and international students; for winter admission, 11/1 for domestic and international students; for spring admission, 3/1 for domestic and international students. Applications are processed on a rolling basis. Application fee: $30. Electronic applications accepted. *Expenses:* Tuition, state resident: full-time $9474; part-time $350.88 per credit hour. Tuition, nonresident: full-time $16,236; part-time $601.34 per credit hour. *Required fees:* $630 per semester. One-time fee: $20. Tuition and fees vary according to course load and campus/location. *Financial support:* Fellowships with full and partial tuition reimbursements, research assistantships with full and partial tuition reimbursements, teaching assistantships with full and partial tuition reimbursements, career-related internships or fieldwork, scholarships/grants, health care benefits, and unspecified assistantships available. Financial award applicants required to submit FAFSA. *Faculty research:* Human performance improvement, educational semiotics, development of software tools to measure online interaction among learners. *Unit head:* Dr. Vanessa Dennen, Program Leader, 850-644-8783, Fax: 850-644-8776, E-mail: vdennen@fsu.edu. *Application contact:* Mary Kate McKee, Program Coordinator, 850-644-8792, Fax: 850-644-8776, E-mail: mmckee@campus.fsu.edu.

Fort Hays State University, Graduate School, College of Education and Technology, Department of Technology Studies, Hays, KS 67601-4099. Offers instructional technology (MS). *Degree requirements:* For master's, comprehensive exam, thesis or alternative. *Entrance requirements:* Additional exam requirements/recommendations for international students: Required—TOEFL (minimum score 550 paper-based; 213 computer-based). Electronic applications accepted.

Framingham State University, Division of Graduate and Continuing Education, Program in Curriculum and Instructional Technology, Framingham, MA 01701-9101. Offers M Ed. Postbaccalaureate distance learning degree programs offered.

Franklin University, Instructional Design and Performance Technology Program, Columbus, OH 43215-5399. Offers MS.

Fresno Pacific University, Graduate Programs, School of Education, Fresno, CA 93702-4709. Offers administration (MA Ed), including administrative services; foundations, curriculum and teaching (MA Ed), including curriculum and teaching, school library and information technology; language, literacy, and culture (MA Ed), including bilingual/cross-cultural education, language development, multilingual contexts, reading; mathematics/science/computer education (MA Ed), including educational technology, integrated mathematics/science education, mathematics education; pupil personnel services (MA Ed), including school counseling, school psychology; special education (MA Ed), including mild/moderate, moderate/severe, physical and health impairments. Part-time and evening/weekend programs available. *Degree requirements:* For master's, thesis (for some programs). *Entrance requirements:* For master's, interview; GMAT, GRE, MAT, or 6 units of course work with a faculty recommendation. Additional exam requirements/recommendations for international students: Required—TOEFL (minimum score 550 paper-based; 213 computer-based). Electronic applications accepted.

Fresno Pacific University, Graduate Programs, School of Education, Division of Foundations, Curriculum and Teaching, Program in School Library and Information Technology, Fresno, CA 93702-4709. Offers MA Ed. Part-time and evening/weekend programs available. *Degree requirements:* For master's, thesis or alternative. *Entrance requirements:* Additional exam requirements/recommendations for international students: Required—TOEFL (minimum score 550 paper-based; 213 computer-based). Electronic applications accepted.

Fresno Pacific University, Graduate Programs, School of Education, Division of Mathematics/Science/Computer Education, Program in Educational Technology, Fresno, CA 93702-4709. Offers MA Ed. Part-time and evening/weekend programs available. *Degree requirements:* For master's, thesis or alternative. *Entrance requirements:* Additional exam requirements/recommendations for international students: Required—TOEFL (minimum score 550 paper-based; 213 computer-based).

Frostburg State University, Graduate School, College of Education, Department of Educational Professions, Program in Curriculum and Instruction, Frostburg, MD 21532-1099. Offers educational technology (M Ed); elementary education (M Ed); secondary education (M Ed). Part-time and evening/weekend programs available. *Degree requirements:* For master's, thesis or alternative. *Entrance requirements:* For master's, teaching certificate. Additional exam requirements/recommendations for international students: Required—TOEFL. Electronic applications accepted.

Full Sail University, Education Media Design and Technology Master of Science Program - Online, Winter Park, FL 32792-7437. Offers MS. Postbaccalaureate distance learning degree programs offered (no on-campus study). *Entrance requirements:* Additional exam requirements/recommendations for international students: Required—TOEFL (minimum score 550 paper-based; 213 computer-based; 79 iBT).

Gannon University, School of Graduate Studies, College of Humanities, Education, and Social Sciences, School of Education, Program in Educational Computing Technology, Erie, PA 16541-0001. Offers M Ed. Part-time and evening/weekend programs available. *Degree requirements:* For master's, comprehensive exam, thesis. *Entrance requirements:* For master's, GRE or MAT, interview, teaching certificate. Additional exam requirements/recommendations for international students: Required—TOEFL (minimum score 79 iBT). *Application deadline:* Applications are processed on a rolling basis. Application fee: $25. Electronic applications accepted. *Expenses:* Contact institution. *Financial support:* Application deadline: 7/1; applicants required to submit FAFSA. *Unit head:* Dr. Kathleen Kingston, Director, 814-871-5626, E-mail: kingston002@gannon.edu. *Application contact:* Kara Morgan, Director of Graduate Admissions, 814-871-5831, Fax: 814-871-5827, E-mail: graduate@gannon.edu.

George Fox University, School of Education, Educational Foundations and Leadership Program, Newberg, OR 97132-2697. Offers continuing administrator license (Certificate); curriculum and instruction (M Ed); educational leadership (M Ed, Ed D); ESOL (Certificate); higher education (M Ed); initial administrator license (Certificate); instructional leadership (Ed S); library media (M Ed, Certificate); literacy (M Ed); reading (M Ed); secondary education (M Ed). *Accreditation:* NCATE. Part-time and evening/weekend programs available. Postbaccalaureate distance learning degree programs offered (minimal on-campus study). *Faculty:* 10 full-time (3 women), 6 part-time/adjunct (3 women). *Students:* 2 full-time (both women), 111 part-time (83 women); includes 16 minority (2 American Indian or Alaska Native, non-Hispanic/Latino; 6 Asian, non-Hispanic/Latino; 7 Hispanic/Latino; 1 Native Hawaiian or other Pacific Islander, non-Hispanic/Latino), 3 international. Average age 39. 44 applicants, 98% accepted, 43 enrolled. In 2011, 34 master's, 7 doctorates, 76 Certificates awarded. *Degree requirements:* For master's, thesis (for some programs); for doctorate, comprehensive exam, thesis/dissertation, project. *Entrance requirements:* For master's, minimum undergraduate GPA of 3.0 during previous 2 years of course work, resume, 3 professional recommendations on university forms, official transcripts; for doctorate, GRE, master's degree with minimum GPA of 3.25, 3 years of relevant professional experience, interview, personal essay, scholarly work, 3 professional recommendations on university forms along with 3 written letters of recommendation, official transcripts. Additional exam requirements/recommendations for international students: Required—TOEFL (minimum score 577 paper-based; 233 computer-based; 90 iBT). *Application deadline:* For fall admission, 7/15 for domestic and international students; for winter admission, 11/1 for domestic and international students; for spring admission, 4/1 for domestic and international students. Applications are processed on a rolling basis. Application fee: $40. Electronic applications accepted. *Expenses:* Contact institution. *Financial support:* Career-related internships or fieldwork available. Financial award applicants required to submit FAFSA. *Unit head:* Dr. Scot Headley, Professor/Chair, 503-554-2836, E-mail: sheadley@georgefox.edu. *Application contact:* Alex Martin, Admissions Counselor, 800-631-0921, Fax: 503-554-3110, E-mail: amartin@georgefox.edu. Web site: http://www.georgefox.edu/education/index.html.

The George Washington University, Graduate School of Education and Human Development, Department of Educational Leadership, Program in Educational Technology Leadership, Washington, DC 20052. Offers MA Ed. *Accreditation:* NCATE. Part-time and evening/weekend programs available. *Students:* 3 full-time (all women), 53 part-time (33 women); includes 14 minority (7 Black or African American, non-Hispanic/Latino; 2 Asian, non-Hispanic/Latino; 5 Hispanic/Latino), 1 international. Average age 39. 20 applicants, 100% accepted. In 2011, 16 master's awarded. *Degree requirements:* For master's, comprehensive exam, thesis or alternative. *Entrance requirements:* For master's, GRE General Test or MAT, minimum GPA of 2.75. *Application deadline:* For fall admission, 1/15 priority date for domestic students; for spring admission, 10/1 for domestic students. Applications are processed on a rolling basis. Application fee: $75. *Expenses:* Contact institution. *Financial support:* Fellowships, research assistantships, teaching assistantships, and career-related internships or fieldwork available. Financial award application deadline: 1/15. *Faculty research:* Interactive multimedia, distance education, federal technology policy. *Unit head:* Dr. Michael Corry, Director, 202-994-9295, E-mail: mcorry@gwu.edu. *Application contact:* Sarah Lang, Director of Graduate Admissions, 202-994-1447, Fax: 202-994-7207, E-mail: slang@gwu.edu.

The George Washington University, Graduate School of Education and Human Development, Department of Educational Leadership, Program in Instructional Design, Washington, DC 20052. Offers Graduate Certificate.

The George Washington University, Graduate School of Education and Human Development, Department of Educational Leadership, Program in Integrating Technology into Education, Washington, DC 20052. Offers Graduate Certificate.

The George Washington University, Graduate School of Education and Human Development, Department of Educational Leadership, Program in Leadership in Educational Technology, Washington, DC 20052. Offers Graduate Certificate.

The George Washington University, Graduate School of Education and Human Development, Department of Educational Leadership, Program in Multimedia Development, Washington, DC 20052. Offers Graduate Certificate.

The George Washington University, Graduate School of Education and Human Development, Department of Educational Leadership, Program in Training and Educational Technology, Washington, DC 20052. Offers Graduate Certificate.

Georgia College & State University, Graduate School, The John H. Lounsbury College of Education, Department of Foundations and Secondary Education, Milledgeville, GA 31061. Offers curriculum and instruction (Ed S), including secondary education; educational technology (M Ed), including library media; educational technology (M Ed), including instructional technology; secondary education (M Ed, MAT). *Accreditation:* NCATE. Part-time and evening/weekend programs available. *Students:* 84 full-time (47 women), 120 part-time (98 women); includes 51 minority (43 Black or African American, non-Hispanic/Latino; 2 Asian, non-Hispanic/Latino; 4 Hispanic/Latino; 2 Two or more races, non-Hispanic/Latino), 1 international. Average age 31. 69 applicants, 51% accepted, 28 enrolled. In 2011, 105 master's, 33 other advanced degrees awarded. *Degree requirements:* For master's, comprehensive exam; for Ed S, comprehensive exam, electronic portfolio presentation. *Entrance requirements:* For master's, on-site writing assessment, 2 letters of recommendation, level 4 teaching certificate; for Ed S, on-site writing assessment, master's degree, 2 letters of recommendation, 2 years of teaching experience, level 5 teacher certification. Additional exam requirements/recommendations for international students: Recommended—TOEFL (minimum score 550 paper-based; 213 computer-based; 79 iBT). *Application deadline:* For fall admission, 7/1 priority date for domestic students, 4/1 for international students; for spring admission, 11/15 priority date for domestic students, 9/1 for international students. Applications are processed on a rolling basis. Application fee: $40. Electronic applications accepted. *Expenses:* Tuition, state resident: full-time $4806; part-time $267 per credit hour. Tuition, nonresident: full-time $17,802; part-time $989 per credit hour. *Required fees:* $936 per semester. Tuition and fees vary according to course load and campus/location. *Financial support:* In 2011–12, 12 research assistantships with full tuition reimbursements were awarded; career-related internships or fieldwork and Federal Work-Study also available. Support available to part-time students. Financial award applicants required to submit FAFSA. *Unit head:* Dr. Brian Mumma, Interim Chair, 478-445-2517, E-mail: brian.mumma@gcsu.edu. *Application contact:* Shanda Brand, Graduate Advisor, 478-445-1383, E-mail: shanda.brand@gcsu.edu.

Georgia Southern University, Jack N. Averitt College of Graduate Studies, College of Education, Department of Leadership, Technology, and Human Development, Program in Instructional Technology, Statesboro, GA 30460. Offers M Ed. Part-time and evening/weekend programs available. Postbaccalaureate distance learning degree programs offered (no on-campus study). *Students:* 33 full-time (28 women), 208 part-time (172 women); includes 57 minority (52 Black or African American, non-Hispanic/Latino; 1 American Indian or Alaska Native, non-Hispanic/Latino; 1 Hispanic/Latino; 3 Two or more races, non-Hispanic/Latino), 1 international. Average age 35. 67 applicants, 100% accepted, 33 enrolled. In 2011, 86 master's awarded. *Degree requirements:* For master's, portfolio, transition point assessments. *Entrance requirements:* For master's, GRE General Test or MAT, minimum GPA of 2.5. Additional exam requirements/recommendations for international students: Required—TOEFL (minimum score 550 paper-based; 213 computer-based; 80 iBT). *Application deadline:* For fall admission, 3/1 priority date for domestic students, 3/1 for international students; for spring admission, 10/1 priority date for domestic students, 10/1 for international students. Applications are processed on a rolling basis. Application fee: $50. Electronic applications accepted. *Expenses:* Tuition, state resident: full-time $6300; part-time $263 per semester hour. Tuition, nonresident: full-time $25,174; part-time $1049 per semester hour. *Required fees:* $1872. *Financial support:* Research assistantships, teaching assistantships, career-related internships or fieldwork, and scholarships/grants available. Support available to part-time students. Financial award application deadline: 4/15; financial award applicants required to submit FAFSA. *Faculty research:* Online learning in higher education and K-12, instructional technology leadership, school library media programs, twenty-first century skills, instructional technology in the content areas. *Unit head:* Dr. Judith Repman, Coordinator, 912-478-5394, Fax: 912-478-7104, E-mail: edowns@georgiasouthern.edu. *Application contact:* Amanda Gilliland, Coordinator for Graduate Student Recruitment, 912-478-5384, Fax: 912-478-0740, E-mail: gradadmissions@georgiasouthern.edu. Web site: http://coe.georgiasouthern.edu/ithd/itech.html.

Georgia State University, College of Education, Department of Middle-Secondary Education and Instructional Technology, Library Science/Media Unit, Atlanta, GA 30302-3083. Offers instructional technology (MS, PhD, Ed S); library media technology (MLM, PhD, Ed S). Part-time and evening/weekend programs available. *Degree requirements:* For master's, comprehensive exam; for doctorate, comprehensive exam, thesis/dissertation; for Ed S, project/exam. *Entrance requirements:* For master's, GRE General Test, minimum GPA of 2.5; for doctorate, GRE General Test or MAT, minimum GPA of 3.3; for Ed S, GRE General Test or MAT, minimum graduate GPA of 3.25. *Faculty research:* Automation, children's literature, cataloging, electronic resources.

Governors State University, College of Arts and Sciences, Program in Communication and Training, University Park, IL 60484. Offers communication studies (MA); instructional and training technology (MA); media communication (MA). Part-time and evening/weekend programs available. *Students:* 24 full-time (20 women), 120 part-time (104 women); includes 108 minority (100 Black or African American, non-Hispanic/Latino; 1 American Indian or Alaska Native, non-Hispanic/Latino; 6 Hispanic/Latino; 1 Two or more races, non-Hispanic/Latino), 1 international. Average age 35. *Degree requirements:* For master's, thesis or alternative. *Application deadline:* For fall admission, 7/15 priority date for domestic students; for spring admission, 11/10 for domestic students. Applications are processed on a rolling basis. Application fee: $25. *Financial support:* Research assistantships, Federal Work-Study, institutionally sponsored loans, and scholarships/grants available. Support available to part-time students. Financial award application deadline: 5/1. *Unit head:* Dr. James Howley, Chair, Division of Liberal Arts, 708-534-7893. *Application contact:* Yakeea Daniels, Interim Director of Admission, 708-534-4510, E-mail: ydaniels@govst.edu.

Graceland University, Gleazer School of Education, Lamoni, IA 50140. Offers collaborative learning and teaching (M Ed); differentiated instruction (M Ed); management in the inclusive classroom (M Ed); mild/moderate special education (M Ed); technology integration (M Ed). *Accreditation:* NCATE. Part-time and evening/weekend programs available. Postbaccalaureate distance learning degree programs offered (no on-campus study). *Faculty:* 12 full-time (11 women), 18 part-time/adjunct (14 women). *Students:* 315 full-time (256 women), 69 part-time (51 women); includes 11 minority (4 Black or African American, non-Hispanic/Latino; 1 American Indian or Alaska Native, non-Hispanic/Latino; 2 Asian, non-Hispanic/Latino; 4 Hispanic/Latino), 8 international. *Degree requirements:* For master's, action research project. *Entrance requirements:* For master's, minimum GPA of 3.0, teaching certificate, current teaching contract. *Application deadline:* For fall admission, 7/15 for domestic students; for winter admission, 10/15 for domestic students; for spring admission, 1/15 priority date for domestic students. Application fee: $50. Electronic applications accepted. *Financial support:* Institutionally sponsored loans and scholarships/grants available. Financial award application deadline: 12/15; financial award applicants required to submit FAFSA. *Unit head:* Dr. Tammy Everett, Dean, 641-784-5000 Ext. 5226, E-mail: teverett@graceland.edu. *Application contact:* Cathy Porter, Program Consultant, 816-833-0524 Ext. 4516, E-mail: cgporter@graceland.edu. Web site: http://www.graceland.edu/education.

Grambling State University, School of Graduate Studies and Research, College of Education, Department of Educational Leadership, Grambling, LA 71245. Offers curriculum and instruction (Ed D); developmental education (MS, Ed D), including curriculum and instruction: reading (Ed D), English (MS), guidance and counseling (MS), higher education administration (Ed D), instructional systems and technology (Ed D), mathematics (MS), reading (MS), science (MS), student development and personnel services (Ed D); educational leadership (MS, Ed D). Part-time and evening/weekend programs available. *Degree requirements:* For master's, comprehensive exam, thesis (for some programs); for doctorate, comprehensive exam, thesis/dissertation. *Entrance requirements:* For master's, GRE, minimum GPA of 2.5 on last degree; for doctorate, GRE (minimum 1000, 500 on Verbal), master's degree, minimum GPA of 3.0 on last degree. Additional exam requirements/recommendations for international students: Required—TOEFL (minimum score 500 paper-based; 173 computer-based; 61 iBT). Electronic applications accepted. *Expenses:* Tuition, state resident: full-time $3546; part-time $192 per credit hour. Tuition, nonresident: full-time $3456; part-time $192 per credit hour. *Required fees:* $1829; $1829 per semester hour.

Grand Valley State University, College of Education, Programs in General Education, Allendale, MI 49401-9403. Offers adult and higher education (M Ed); early childhood education (M Ed); educational differentiation (M Ed); educational leadership (M Ed); educational technology integration (M Ed); elementary education (M Ed); middle level education (M Ed); school library media services (M Ed); secondary level education (M Ed); teaching English to speakers of other languages (M Ed). Part-time and evening/weekend programs available. Postbaccalaureate distance learning degree programs offered (minimal on-campus study). *Degree requirements:* For master's, thesis. *Entrance requirements:* For master's, GRE General Test or minimum GPA of 3.0. Additional exam requirements/recommendations for international students: Required—TOEFL. Electronic applications accepted. *Faculty research:* Effectiveness of technology in education, parental involvement, effective teaching, effective schools research.

Gratz College, Graduate Programs, Program in Educational Technology, Melrose Park, PA 19027. Offers Graduate Certificate. Postbaccalaureate distance learning degree programs offered. *Degree requirements:* For Graduate Certificate, final paper and project. *Unit head:* Deborah Nagler, Program Director, 215-635-7300 Ext. 182, E-mail: dnagler@gratz.edu. *Application contact:* Joanna Boeing Bratton, Director of Admissions, 215-635-7300 Ext. 140, Fax: 215-635-7399, E-mail: admissions@gratz.edu.

Harrisburg University of Science and Technology, Program in Learning Technologies, Harrisburg, PA 17101. Offers learning technologies (MS). Part-time and evening/weekend programs available. *Entrance requirements:* Additional exam requirements/recommendations for international students: Required—TOEFL (minimum score 520 paper-based; 200 computer-based; 80 iBT). Electronic applications accepted.

Harvard University, Extension School, Cambridge, MA 02138-3722. Offers applied sciences (CAS); biotechnology (ALM); educational technologies (ALM); educational technology (CET); English for graduate and professional studies (DGP); environmental management (ALM, CEM); information technology (ALM); journalism (ALM); liberal arts (ALM); management (ALM, CM); mathematics for teaching (ALM); museum studies (ALM); premedical studies (Diploma); publication and communication (CPC). Part-time and evening/weekend programs available. *Degree requirements:* For master's, thesis. *Entrance requirements:* For master's, 3 completed graduate courses with grade of B or higher. Additional exam requirements/recommendations for international students: Required—TOEFL (minimum score 600 paper-based; 250 computer-based), TWE (minimum score 5). *Expenses:* Contact institution.

Harvard University, Harvard Graduate School of Education, Master's Programs in Education, Cambridge, MA 02138. Offers arts in education (Ed M); education policy and management (Ed M); higher education (Ed M); human development and psychology (Ed M); international education policy (Ed M); language and literacy (Ed M); learning and teaching (Ed M); mid-career mathematics and science (teaching certificate) (Ed M); mind brain and education (Ed M); prevention science and practice (Ed M); school leadership (Ed M); special studies (Ed M); teaching and curriculum (teaching certificate) (Ed M); technology innovation and education (Ed M). Part-time programs available. *Faculty:* 83 full-time (44 women), 67 part-time/adjunct (29 women). *Students:* 592 full-time (431 women), 75 part-time (54 women); includes 194 minority (41 Black or African American, non-Hispanic/Latino; 4 American Indian or Alaska Native, non-Hispanic/Latino; 75 Asian, non-Hispanic/Latino; 45 Hispanic/Latino; 2 Native Hawaiian or other Pacific Islander, non-Hispanic/Latino; 27 Two or more races, non-Hispanic/Latino), 95 international. Average age 28. 1,679 applicants, 52% accepted, 627 enrolled. In 2011, 653 master's awarded. *Entrance requirements:* For master's, GRE General Test, statement of purpose, 3 letters of recommendation, resume, official transcripts. Additional exam requirements/recommendations for international students: Required—TOEFL (minimum score 613 paper-based; 104 computer-based; 100 iBT), TWE (minimum score 5). *Application deadline:* For fall admission, 1/4 for domestic and international students. Application fee: $85. Electronic applications accepted. *Expenses:* Contact institution. *Financial support:* In 2011–12, 419 students received support, including 14 fellowships with full and partial tuition reimbursements available (averaging $12,831 per year); career-related internships or fieldwork, Federal Work-Study, institutionally sponsored loans, scholarships/grants, health care benefits, tuition waivers (full and partial), and unspecified assistantships also available. Support available to part-time students. Financial award application deadline: 2/1; financial award applicants required to submit FAFSA. *Faculty research:* Learning and development, educational leadership and organizations, educational policy analysis. *Total annual research expenditures:* $26 million. *Unit head:* Jennifer L. Petrallia, Assistant Dean, 617-495-8445. *Application contact:* Information Contact, 617-495-3414, Fax: 617-496-3577, E-mail: gseadmissions@harvard.edu. Web site: http://www.gse.harvard.edu/.

Hofstra University, School of Education, Health, and Human Services, Program in Elementary Education, Hempstead, NY 11549. Offers early childhood and childhood education (MS Ed); early childhood education (MA, MS Ed); educational technology (MA); elementary education (MS Ed); literacy (MA); math specialist (Advanced Certificate); math, science, technology (MA); multiculturalism (MA). Part-time and evening/weekend programs available. Postbaccalaureate distance learning degree programs offered (minimal on-campus study). *Students:* 54 full-time (48 women), 43 part-time (37 women); includes 17 minority (10 Black or African American, non-Hispanic/Latino; 2 Asian, non-Hispanic/Latino; 5 Hispanic/Latino), 2 international. Average age 29. 65 applicants, 88% accepted, 18 enrolled. In 2011, 58 master's awarded. *Degree requirements:* For master's, comprehensive exam, thesis (for some programs), 35 semester hours (for MA); 38-41 semester hours (for MS Ed), minimum GPA of 3.0. *Entrance requirements:* For master's, 2 letters of recommendation, teacher certification (MA), interview, essay. Additional exam requirements/recommendations for international students: Required—TOEFL (minimum score 550 paper-based; 213 computer-based; 80 iBT). *Application deadline:* Applications are processed on a rolling basis. Application fee: $70 ($75 for international students). Electronic applications accepted. *Expenses: Tuition:* Full-time $18,990; part-time $1055 per credit hour. *Required fees:* $970. Tuition and fees vary according to program. *Financial support:* In 2011–12, 45 students received support, including 22 fellowships with full and partial tuition reimbursements available (averaging $2,560 per year), 2 research assistantships with full and partial tuition reimbursements available (averaging $21,993 per year); career-related internships or fieldwork, Federal Work-Study, institutionally sponsored loans, scholarships/grants, tuition waivers (full and partial), and unspecified assistantships also available. Support available to part-time students. Financial award applicants required to submit FAFSA. *Faculty research:* Dynamic-themes curriculum/complexity theory, joyful learning, teacher education, multicultural education, multiple authentic assessments. *Unit head:* Dr. Esther Fusco, Chairperson, 516-463-7704, Fax: 516-463-6196, E-mail: catezf@hofstra.edu. *Application contact:* Carol Drummer, Dean of Graduate Admissions, 516-463-4876, Fax: 516-463-4664, E-mail: gradstudent@hofstra.edu. Web site: http://www.hofstra.edu/education/.

Hofstra University, School of Education, Health, and Human Services, Programs in Teaching - Secondary Education, Hempstead, NY 11549. Offers business education (MS Ed); education technology (Advanced Certificate); English education (MA, MS Ed); foreign language and TESOL (MS Ed); foreign language education (MA, MS Ed), including French, German, Russian, Spanish; mathematics education (MA, MS Ed); science education (MA, MS Ed), including biology, chemistry, earth science, geology, physics; secondary education (Advanced Certificate); social studies education (MA, MS Ed). Part-time and evening/weekend programs available. Postbaccalaureate distance learning degree programs offered (minimal on-campus study). *Students:* 72 full-time (47 women), 51 part-time (30 women); includes 21 minority (9 Black or African American, non-Hispanic/Latino; 7 Asian, non-Hispanic/Latino; 5 Hispanic/Latino). Average age 28. 103 applicants, 91% accepted, 41 enrolled. In 2011, 86 master's, 6 other advanced degrees awarded. *Degree requirements:* For master's, one foreign language, comprehensive exam (for some programs), thesis (for some programs), exit project, electronic portfolio, student teaching, fieldwork, curriculum project, minimum GPA of 3.0; for Advanced Certificate, 3 foreign languages, comprehensive exam (for some programs), thesis project, minimum GPA of 3.0. *Entrance requirements:* For master's, 2 letters of recommendation, teacher certification (MA), essay; for Advanced Certificate, 2 letters of recommendation, essay. Additional exam requirements/recommendations for international students: Required—TOEFL (minimum score 550 paper-based; 213 computer-based; 80 iBT). *Application deadline:* Applications are processed on a rolling basis. Application fee: $70 ($75 for international students). Electronic applications accepted. *Expenses: Tuition:* Full-time $18,990; part-time $1055 per credit hour. *Required fees:* $970. Tuition and fees vary according to program. *Financial support:* In 2011–12, 90 students received support, including 13 fellowships with full and partial tuition reimbursements available (averaging $3,202 per year), 1 research assistantship with full and partial tuition reimbursement available (averaging $11,645 per year); career-related internships or fieldwork, Federal Work-Study, institutionally sponsored loans, scholarships/grants, tuition waivers (full and partial), and unspecified assistantships also available. Support available to part-time students. Financial award applicants required to submit FAFSA. *Faculty research:* Appropriate content and pedagogy in secondary school disciplines, appropriate pedagogy in secondary school disciplines, adolescent development, secondary school organization, alternative secondary school programs. *Unit head:* Dr. Esther Fusco, Chairperson, 516-463-7704, Fax: 516-463-6196, E-mail: catezf@hofstra.edu. *Application contact:* Carol Drummer, Dean of Graduate Admissions, 516-463-4876, Fax: 516-463-4664, E-mail: gradstudent@hofstra.edu. Web site: http://www.hofstra.edu/education/.

Idaho State University, Office of Graduate Studies, College of Education, Department of Educational Leadership and Instructional Design, Pocatello, ID 83209-8059. Offers educational administration (M Ed, 6th Year Certificate, Ed S); educational leadership (Ed D), including education training and development, educational administration, educational technology, higher education administration; educational leadership and instructional design (PhD); instructional technology (M Ed). Part-time programs available. *Degree requirements:* For master's, comprehensive exam, thesis optional, internship, oral exam or deferred thesis; for doctorate, comprehensive exam, thesis/dissertation, written exam; for other advanced degree, comprehensive exam, thesis (for some programs), written and oral exam. *Entrance requirements:* For master's, MAT, bachelor's degree, minimum GPA of 3.0, 1 year of training experience; for doctorate, GRE General Test or MAT, minimum GPA of 3.0 (undergraduate), 3.5 (graduate); departmental interview; for other advanced degree, GRE General Test, minimum GPA of 3.0, master's degree. Additional exam requirements/recommendations for international students: Required—TOEFL (minimum score 550 paper-based; 213 computer-based; 80 iBT). Electronic applications accepted. *Faculty research:* Educational leadership, gender issues in education and sport, staff development.

Idaho State University, Office of Graduate Studies, College of Education, Program in Instructional Methods and Technology, Pocatello, ID 83209. Offers instructional design (PhD); instructional technology (M Ed). Part-time programs available. *Degree requirements:* For master's, comprehensive exam, thesis optional, minimum 36 credits; for doctorate, comprehensive exam, thesis/dissertation (for some programs). *Entrance requirements:* For master's, GRE or MAT, bachelor's degree; for doctorate, GRE or MAT, master's degree. Additional exam requirements/recommendations for international students: Required—TOEFL (minimum score 550 paper-based; 213 computer-based; 80 iBT). Electronic applications accepted.

Indiana State University, College of Graduate and Professional Studies, College of Education, Department of Curriculum, Instruction, and Media Technology, Terre Haute, IN 47809. Offers curriculum and instruction (M Ed, PhD); educational technology (MS). *Accreditation:* NCATE. *Degree requirements:* For doctorate, thesis/dissertation. *Entrance requirements:* For doctorate, GRE General Test. Electronic applications accepted. *Faculty research:* Discipline FERPA reading, teacher strengths and needs.

Indiana University Bloomington, School of Education, Department of Instructional Systems Technology, Bloomington, IN 47405-1006. Offers MS, PhD. Postbaccalaureate distance learning degree programs offered (no on-campus study). Terminal master's awarded for partial completion of doctoral program. *Degree requirements:* For master's, thesis optional, portfolio; for doctorate, comprehensive exam, thesis/dissertation, dossier review. *Entrance requirements:* For master's and doctorate, GRE General Test, minimum GPA of 2.75. Additional exam requirements/recommendations for international students: Required—TOEFL. Electronic applications accepted. *Faculty research:* Instructional design and theory development, e-learning and distance education, systemic change, serious simulations and games, human performance improvement, technology integration in education.

Indiana University of Pennsylvania, School of Graduate Studies and Research, College of Education and Educational Technology, Department of Adult and Community Education, Program in Adult Education and Communications Technology, Indiana, PA 15705-1087. Offers MA. Part-time and evening/weekend programs available. *Faculty:* 2 full-time (0 women). *Students:* 21 full-time (6 women), 7 part-time (2 women); includes 2 minority (1 Black or African American, non-Hispanic/Latino; 1 Two or more races, non-Hispanic/Latino), 1 international. Average age 28. 29 applicants, 69% accepted, 14 enrolled. In 2011, 23 master's awarded. *Degree requirements:* For master's, thesis optional. *Entrance requirements:* For master's, 2 letters of recommendation, writing sample. Additional exam requirements/recommendations for international students: Required—TOEFL (minimum score 540 paper-based; 207 computer-based). *Application deadline:* Applications are processed on a rolling basis. Application fee: $50. Electronic applications accepted. *Expenses:* Tuition, state resident: full-time $7488; part-time $416 per credit. Tuition, nonresident: full-time $11,232; part-time $624 per credit. *Required fees:* $2070; $192.20 per credit. $90 per semester. *Financial support:* In 2011–12, 7 research assistantships with full and partial tuition reimbursements (averaging $5,440 per year) were awarded; fellowships, teaching assistantships with partial tuition reimbursements, career-related internships or fieldwork, and Federal Work-Study also available. Support available to part-time students. Financial award application deadline: 4/15; financial award applicants required to submit FAFSA. *Unit head:* Dr. Gary Dean, Chairperson, 724-357-2470, E-mail: gjdean@iup.edu. *Application contact:* Dr. Edward Nardi, Associate Dean, 724-357-2480, Fax: 724-357-5595, E-mail: ewnardi@iup.edu. Web site: http://www.iup.edu/upper.aspx?id=93738.

Indiana University of Pennsylvania, School of Graduate Studies and Research, College of Education and Educational Technology, Department of Communications Media, Indiana, PA 15705-1087. Offers adult education and communications technology (MA); communications media and instructional technology (PhD). Part-time and evening/weekend programs available. *Faculty:* 10 full-time (3 women), 1 part-time/adjunct (0 women). *Students:* 20 full-time (9 women), 40 part-time (20 women); includes 5 minority (3 Black or African American, non-Hispanic/Latino; 1 Asian, non-Hispanic/Latino; 1 Two or more races, non-Hispanic/Latino), 2 international. Average age 38. 46 applicants, 46% accepted, 17 enrolled. *Degree requirements:* For doctorate, thesis/dissertation. *Entrance requirements:* For master's, 2 letters of recommendation. Additional exam requirements/recommendations for international students: Required—TOEFL (minimum score 540 paper-based; 207 computer-based). *Application deadline:* Applications are processed on a rolling basis. Application fee: $50. Electronic applications accepted. *Expenses:* Tuition, state resident: full-time $7488; part-time $416 per credit. Tuition, nonresident: full-time $11,232; part-time $624 per credit. *Required fees:* $2070; $192.20 per credit. $90 per semester. *Financial support:* In 2011–12, 4 fellowships with full tuition reimbursements (averaging $1,879 per year), 8 research assistantships with full and partial tuition reimbursements (averaging $5,222 per year), 3 teaching assistantships with partial tuition reimbursements (averaging $22,398 per year) were awarded; career-related internships or fieldwork, Federal Work-Study, scholarships/grants, and tuition waivers (full) also available. Support available to part-time students. Financial award application deadline: 4/15; financial award applicants required to submit FAFSA. *Unit head:* Dr. Mark Piwinsky, Chairperson, 724-357-3954, Fax: 724-357-5503, E-mail: mark.piwinsky@iup.edu. *Application contact:* Dr. Edward Nardi, Associate Dean, 724-357-2480, Fax: 724-357-5595, E-mail: ewnardi@iup.edu. Web site: http://www.iup.edu/commmedia/.

Instituto Tecnológico y de Estudios Superiores de Monterrey, Campus Central de Veracruz, Graduate Programs, Córdoba, Mexico. Offers administration (MA); administration of information technologies (MTI); computer sciences (MCC); education (MEE); educational institution administration (MAD); educational technology (MTE); electronic commerce (MCE); finance (MAF); humanistic studies (MEH); international business for Latin America (MNL); marketing (MMT); science (MCP). Part-time and evening/weekend programs available. Postbaccalaureate distance learning degree programs offered (minimal on-campus study). *Degree requirements:* For master's, thesis (for some programs). *Entrance requirements:* For master's, PAEP College Board. Electronic applications accepted.

Instituto Tecnológico y de Estudios Superiores de Monterrey, Campus Ciudad de México, Virtual University Division, Ciudad de Mexico, Mexico. Offers administration of information technologies (MA); computer sciences (MA); education (MA, PhD); educational technology (MA); environmental engineering (MA); environmental systems (MA); humanistic studies (MA); industrial engineering (MA); international business for Latin America (MA); quality systems (MA); quality systems and productivity (MA). Part-time and evening/weekend programs available. Postbaccalaureate distance learning degree programs offered (minimal on-campus study). *Entrance requirements:* For master's and doctorate, Instituto entrance exam. Additional exam requirements/recommendations for international students: Required—TOEFL.

Instituto Tecnológico y de Estudios Superiores de Monterrey, Campus Ciudad Juárez, Program in Educational Innovation, Ciudad Juárez, Mexico. Offers DE.

Instituto Tecnológico y de Estudios Superiores de Monterrey, Campus Ciudad Juárez, Program in Educational Technology, Ciudad Juárez, Mexico. Offers MTE.

Instituto Tecnológico y de Estudios Superiores de Monterrey, Campus Estado de México, Professional and Graduate Division, Estado de Mexico, Mexico. Offers administration of information technologies (MITA); architecture (M Arch); business administration (GMBA, MBA); computer sciences (MCS, PhD); education (M Ed); educational institution administration (MAD); educational technology and innovation (PhD); electronic commerce (MEC); environmental systems (MS); finance (MAF); humanistic studies (MHS); information sciences and knowledge management (MISKM); information systems (MS); manufacturing systems (MS); marketing (MEM); quality systems and productivity (MS); science and materials engineering (PhD); telecommunications management (MTM). Part-time programs available. Postbaccalaureate distance learning degree programs offered (minimal on-campus study). *Degree requirements:* For master's, one foreign language, thesis (for some programs); for doctorate, one foreign language, thesis/dissertation. *Entrance requirements:* For master's, E-PAEP 500, interview; for doctorate, E-PAEP 500, research proposal. Additional exam requirements/recommendations for international students: Required—TOEFL (minimum score 550 paper-based). *Faculty research:* Surface treatments by plasmas, mechanical properties, robotics, graphical computing, mechatronics security protocols.

Instituto Tecnológico y de Estudios Superiores de Monterrey, Campus Irapuato, Graduate Programs, Irapuato, Mexico. Offers administration (MBA); administration of information technology (MAIT); administration of telecommunications (MAT); architecture (M Arch); computer science (MCS); education (M Ed); educational administration (MEA); educational innovation and technology (DEIT); educational technology (MET); electronic commerce (MBA); environmental administration and planning (MEAP); environmental systems (MES); finances (MBA); humanistic studies (MHS); international management for Latin American executives (MIMLAE); library and information science (MLIS); manufacturing quality management (MMQM); marketing research (MBA).

Inter American University of Puerto Rico, Metropolitan Campus, Graduate Programs, Program in Educational Computing, San Juan, PR 00919-1293. Offers MA. *Degree requirements:* For master's, comprehensive exam, portfolio. *Entrance requirements:* For master's, GRE or EXADEP, minimum GPA of 2.5. Electronic applications accepted. *Faculty research:* Effectiveness of multimedia, World Wide Web for distance learning.

Iowa State University of Science and Technology, Department of Curriculum and Instruction, Ames, IA 50011. Offers curriculum and instructional technology (M Ed, MS, PhD); elementary education (M Ed, MS); historical, philosophical, and comparative studies in education (M Ed, MS); special education (M Ed, MS, PhD). *Degree requirements:* For master's, thesis or alternative; for doctorate, thesis/dissertation. *Entrance requirements:* For master's and doctorate, GRE General Test. Additional exam requirements/recommendations for international students: Required—TOEFL (minimum score 560 paper-based; 83 iBT), IELTS (minimum score 6.5). *Application deadline:* For fall admission, 1/1 priority date for domestic students, 1/1 for international students; for spring admission, 9/1 for domestic and international students. Application fee: $40 ($90 for international students). Electronic applications accepted. *Unit head:* Dr. Anne Foegen, Director of Graduate Education, 515-294-7021, Fax: 515-294-6206, E-mail: cigrad@iastate.edu. *Application contact:* Phyllis Kendall, Director of Graduate

Education, 515-294-7021, Fax: 515-294-6206, E-mail: cigrad@iastate.edu. Web site: http://www.ci.hs.iastate.edu.

Jackson State University, Graduate School, College of Education and Human Development, Department of Educational Leadership, Jackson, MS 39217. Offers education administration (Ed S); educational administration (MS Ed, PhD); secondary education (MS Ed, Ed S), including educational technology (MS Ed). *Accreditation:* NCATE. Part-time and evening/weekend programs available. *Degree requirements:* For master's, comprehensive exam, thesis or alternative; for doctorate, comprehensive exam, thesis/dissertation; for Ed S, comprehensive exam, thesis. *Entrance requirements:* For master's, GRE General Test; for doctorate, MAT, GRE, teaching experience. Additional exam requirements/recommendations for international students: Required—TOEFL (minimum score 520 paper-based; 195 computer-based; 67 iBT).

Jacksonville State University, College of Graduate Studies and Continuing Education, College of Education and Professional Studies, Program in Instructional Media, Jacksonville, AL 36265-1602. Offers MS Ed. Part-time and evening/weekend programs available. *Degree requirements:* For master's, comprehensive exam, thesis (for some programs). *Entrance requirements:* For master's, GRE General Test or MAT. Electronic applications accepted. *Expenses:* Tuition, state resident: part-time $336 per hour. Tuition, nonresident: part-time $672 per hour. Part-time tuition and fees vary according to degree level.

The Johns Hopkins University, School of Education, Department of Special Education, Baltimore, MD 21218. Offers advanced methods for differentiated instruction and inclusive education (Certificate); assistive technology (Certificate); early intervention/preschool special education specialist (Certificate); education of students with autism and other pervasive developmental disorders (Certificate); education of students with severe disabilities (Certificate); special education (MS, Ed D, CAGS), including early childhood special education (MS), general special education studies (MS), mild to moderate disabilities (MS), severe disabilities (MS), technology in special education (MS). *Accreditation:* NCATE. Part-time and evening/weekend programs available. Postbaccalaureate distance learning degree programs offered (minimal on-campus study). *Degree requirements:* For master's, internships, professional portfolio, and PRAXIS II (for licensure); for doctorate, comprehensive exam, thesis/dissertation. *Entrance requirements:* For master's, PRAXIS I, SAT, ACT, or GRE, minimum undergraduate GPA of 3.0, 2 letters of recommendation (for cohort programs); for doctorate, GRE, degree in special education (or related field); minimum GPA of 3.0 in all prior academic work; 3 letters of recommendation; curriculum vitae/resume; professional experience; for other advanced degree, minimum undergraduate GPA of 3.0, master's degree (for CAGS). Additional exam requirements/recommendations for international students: Required—TOEFL (minimum score 600 paper-based; 250 computer-based; 100 iBT). Electronic applications accepted. *Faculty research:* Alternative licensure programs for special educators, collaborative programming, data-based decision-making and knowledge management as keys to school reform, parent training, natural environment teaching (NET).

The Johns Hopkins University, School of Education, Department of Teacher Development and Leadership, Baltimore, MD 21218-2699. Offers adolescent literacy education (Certificate); data-based decision making and organizational improvement (Certificate); education (MS), including reading, school administration and supervision, technology for educators; educational leadership for independent schools (Certificate); effective teaching of reading (Certificate); emergent literacy education (Certificate); English as a second language instruction (Certificate); gifted education (Certificate); leadership for school, family, and community collaboration (Certificate); leadership in technology integration (Certificate); school administration and supervision (Certificate); teacher development and leadership (Ed D); teacher leadership (Certificate). Part-time and evening/weekend programs available. Postbaccalaureate distance learning degree programs offered (minimal on-campus study). *Degree requirements:* For master's and Certificate, portfolio; for doctorate, comprehensive exam (for some programs), thesis/dissertation, portfolio or comprehensive exam. *Entrance requirements:* For master's and Certificate, bachelor's degree; minimum undergraduate GPA of 3.0; essay/statement of goals; for doctorate, GRE, essay/statement of goals; three letters of recommendation; curriculum vitae/resume; K-12 professional experience; interview; writing assessment. Additional exam requirements/recommendations for international students: Required—TOEFL (minimum score 600 paper-based; 250 computer-based; 100 iBT). Electronic applications accepted. *Faculty research:* Application of psychoanalytic concepts to teaching, schools, and education reform; adolescent literacies; use of emerging technologies for teaching, learning, and school leadership; quantitative analyses of the social contexts of education; school, family, and community collaboration; program evaluation methodologies.

Johnson University, Teacher Education Program, Knoxville, TN 37998-1001. Offers Bible and educational technology (MA); holistic education (MA). Part-time programs available. *Degree requirements:* For master's, multimedia action research presentation. *Entrance requirements:* For master's, interview, minimum GPA of 3.0, portfolio, teaching license. Additional exam requirements/recommendations for international students: Required—TOEFL. *Faculty research:* Instructional technology.

Jones International University, School of Education, Centennial, CO 80112. Offers adult education (M Ed); corporate training and knowledge management (M Ed); curriculum and instruction (M Ed), including elementary teacher licensure, secondary teacher licensure; e-learning technology and design (M Ed); educational leadership and administration (M Ed); educational leadership and administration: principal and administrator licensure (M Ed); elementary curriculum instruction and assessment (M Ed); higher education leadership and administration (M Ed); K-12 instructional technology (M Ed); K-12 instructional technology: teacher licensure (M Ed); secondary curriculum instruction and assessment (M Ed); technology and design (M Ed). Part-time and evening/weekend programs available. Postbaccalaureate distance learning degree programs offered (no on-campus study). *Entrance requirements:* For master's, minimum cumulative GPA of 2.5. Additional exam requirements/recommendations for international students: Recommended—TOEFL (minimum score 550 paper-based; 213 computer-based). Electronic applications accepted.

Kansas State University, Graduate School, College of Education, Department of Curriculum and Instruction, Manhattan, KS 66506. Offers career and technical education (Ed D, PhD); curriculum studies (Ed D, PhD); digital teaching and learning (MS); educational computing, design and online learning (MS); educational technology (Ed D, PhD); elementary/middle level (MS); English as a second language (MS); language/diversity education (Ed D, PhD); literacy education (Ed D, PhD); mathematics education (Ed D, PhD); middle level/secondary (MS); reading and language arts (MS); reading specialist endorsement (MS); science education (Ed D, PhD); social science education (Ed D, PhD); teacher education (Ed D, PhD); teacher leader/school improvement (MS, Ed D). *Accreditation:* NCATE. Part-time programs available. Postbaccalaureate distance learning degree programs offered (minimal on-campus study). *Faculty:* 15 full-time (12 women), 3 part-time/adjunct (2 women). *Students:* 37 full-time (30 women), 113 part-time (91 women); includes 14 minority (4 Black or African American, non-Hispanic/Latino; 1 American Indian or Alaska Native, non-Hispanic/Latino; 1 Asian, non-Hispanic/Latino; 7 Hispanic/Latino; 1 Two or more races, non-Hispanic/Latino), 15 international. Average age 37. 75 applicants, 51% accepted, 9 enrolled. In 2011, 48 master's, 14 doctorates awarded. *Degree requirements:* For master's, comprehensive exam, portfolio, project, report or thesis; for doctorate, comprehensive exam, thesis/dissertation, preliminary exam. *Entrance requirements:* For master's, minimum GPA of 3.0; for doctorate, GRE, minimum GPA of 3.0. Additional exam requirements/recommendations for international students: Required—TOEFL. *Application deadline:* For fall admission, 2/1 priority date for domestic students, 2/1 for international students; for spring admission, 8/1 priority date for domestic students, 8/1 for international students. Applications are processed on a rolling basis. Application fee: $40 ($55 for international students). Electronic applications accepted. *Financial support:* In 2011–12, 1 research assistantship (averaging $16,900 per year), 8 teaching assistantships (averaging $12,466 per year) were awarded; career-related internships or fieldwork, institutionally sponsored loans, and scholarships/grants also available. Support available to part-time students. Financial award application deadline: 3/1; financial award applicants required to submit FAFSA. *Faculty research:* Literacy and technology, critical race theory and diversity, achievement gaps, school improvement, teacher education. *Total annual research expenditures:* $510,907. *Unit head:* Dr. Gail Shroyer, Chair, 785-532-5550, Fax: 785-532-7304, E-mail: gshroyer@ksu.edu. *Application contact:* Dona Deam, Application Contact, 785-532-5595, Fax: 785-532-7304, E-mail: ddeam@ksu.edu. Web site: http://coe.k-state.edu/departments/currin/curringrad.htm.

Kaplan University, Davenport Campus, School of Teacher Education, Davenport, IA 52807-2095. Offers education (M Ed); secondary education (M Ed); teaching and learning (MA); teaching literacy and language: grades 6-12 (MA); teaching literacy and language: grades K-6 (MA); teaching mathematics: grades 6-8 (MA); teaching mathematics: grades 9-12 (MA); teaching mathematics: grades K-5 (MA); teaching science: grades 6-12 (MA); teaching science: grades K-6 (MA); teaching students with special needs (MA); teaching with technology (MA). Part-time and evening/weekend programs available. Postbaccalaureate distance learning degree programs offered (no on-campus study). *Entrance requirements:* Additional exam requirements/recommendations for international students: Required—TOEFL (minimum score 550 paper-based; 218 computer-based; 80 iBT).

Keiser University, PhD in Instructional Design and Technology Program, Fort Lauderdale, FL 33309. Offers PhD.

Kennesaw State University, Leland and Clarice C. Bagwell College of Education, Program in Graduate Education, Kennesaw, GA 30144-5591. Offers adolescent education (M Ed); educational leadership (M Ed); educational leadership technology (M Ed); elementary and early childhood education (M Ed); special education (M Ed); teaching English to speakers of other languages (M Ed). *Accreditation:* NCATE. Part-time programs available. *Students:* 42 full-time (39 women), 132 part-time (105 women); includes 31 minority (20 Black or African American, non-Hispanic/Latino; 4 Asian, non-Hispanic/Latino; 5 Hispanic/Latino; 2 Two or more races, non-Hispanic/Latino). Average age 34. 48 applicants, 79% accepted, 38 enrolled. In 2011, 117 master's awarded. *Degree requirements:* For master's, thesis or alternative. *Entrance requirements:* For master's, GRE General Test, T-4 state certification, minimum GPA of 2.75. Additional exam requirements/recommendations for international students: Required—TOEFL (minimum score 550 paper-based; 213 computer-based; 80 iBT), IELTS (minimum score 6). *Application deadline:* For fall admission, 7/1 for domestic and international students; for spring admission, 10/1 for domestic and international students. Application fee: $60. Electronic applications accepted. *Expenses:* Tuition, state resident: full-time $3000; part-time $250 per semester hour. Tuition, nonresident: full-time $10,836; part-time $903 per semester hour. *Required fees:* $774 per semester. *Financial support:* Federal Work-Study and unspecified assistantships available. Support available to part-time students. Financial award application deadline: 4/1; financial award applicants required to submit FAFSA. *Unit head:* Dr. Nita Paris, Associate Dean for Graduate Programs, 770-423-6636, E-mail: nparis@kennesaw.edu. *Application contact:* Alisha Bello, Administrative Coordinator, 770-423-6043, Fax: 770-420-4435, E-mail: abello1@kennesaw.edu. Web site: http://www.kennesaw.edu/education/grad/.

Kent State University, Graduate School of Education, Health, and Human Services, School of Lifespan Development and Educational Sciences, Program in Instructional Technology, Kent, OH 44242-0001. Offers computer technology (M Ed); general instructional technology (M Ed). *Accreditation:* NCATE. *Faculty:* 12 full-time (4 women), 3 part-time/adjunct (2 women). *Students:* 11 full-time (9 women), 53 part-time (38 women); includes 5 minority (4 Black or African American, non-Hispanic/Latino; 1 Hispanic/Latino). 21 applicants, 71% accepted. In 2011, 29 master's awarded. *Degree requirements:* For master's, thesis (for some programs). *Entrance requirements:* For master's, 2 letters of reference, goals statement, minimum GPA of 2.75. Additional exam requirements/recommendations for international students: Required—TOEFL (minimum score 550 paper-based; 213 computer-based; 80 iBT). *Application deadline:* Applications are processed on a rolling basis. Application fee: $30 ($60 for international students). *Expenses:* Tuition, state resident: full-time $8136; part-time $452 per credit hour. Tuition, nonresident: full-time $14,292; part-time $794 per credit hour. *Financial support:* Fellowships with full tuition reimbursements, research assistantships with full tuition reimbursements, teaching assistantships with full tuition reimbursements, Federal Work-Study, scholarships/grants, unspecified assistantships, and 1 administrative assistantship (averaging $8,500 per year) available. Financial award application deadline: 4/1; financial award applicants required to submit FAFSA. *Faculty research:* Cooperative learning, aesthetics, computers in schools. *Unit head:* Dr. Drew Tiene, Coordinator, 330-672-0607, E-mail: dtiene@kent.edu. *Application contact:* Nancy Miller, Academic Program Coordinator, Office of Graduate Student Services, 330-672-2576, Fax: 330-672-9162, E-mail: ogs@kent.edu. Web site: http://www.kent.edu/ehhs/itec/.

Kutztown University of Pennsylvania, College of Education, Program in Instructional Technology, Kutztown, PA 19530-0730. Offers M Ed. Part-time and evening/weekend programs available. *Students:* 1 full-time (0 women), 18 part-time (10 women); includes 1 minority (Asian, non-Hispanic/Latino). Average age 32. 2 applicants, 100% accepted, 2 enrolled. In 2011, 13 master's awarded. *Degree requirements:* For master's, comprehensive exam. *Entrance requirements:* Additional exam requirements/recommendations for international students: Required—TOEFL (minimum score 550 paper-based; 79 iBT). *Application deadline:* For fall admission, 8/1 priority date for domestic students, 8/1 for international students; for spring admission, 12/1 priority date for domestic students, 12/1 for international students. Applications are processed on a rolling basis. Application fee: $35. Electronic applications accepted. *Expenses:* Tuition, state resident: full-time $7488; part-time $416 per credit. Tuition, nonresident: full-time $11,232; part-time $624 per credit. *Financial support:* Career-related internships or fieldwork, Federal Work-Study, scholarships/grants, and unspecified assistantships available. Financial award application deadline: 3/1; financial award applicants required to submit FAFSA. *Unit head:* Dr. Eloise Long, Chairperson, 610-683-4302, Fax: 610-683-1326, E-mail: long@kutztown.edu. *Application contact:* Kelly D. Burr, Associate Director, Graduate Admissions, 610-683-4200, Fax: 610-683-1393, E-mail: graduate@kutztown.edu.

Lamar University, College of Graduate Studies, College of Education and Human Development, Department of Educational Leadership, Beaumont, TX 77710. Offers counseling and development (M Ed, Certificate); education administration (M Ed); educational leadership (DE); principal (Certificate); school superintendent (Certificate); supervision (M Ed); technology application (Certificate). Part-time and evening/weekend programs available. *Faculty:* 19 full-time (8 women), 2 part-time/adjunct (1 woman). *Students:* 23 full-time (14 women), 1,716 part-time (1,106 women); includes 476 minority (246 Black or African American, non-Hispanic/Latino; 13 American Indian or Alaska Native, non-Hispanic/Latino; 18 Asian, non-Hispanic/Latino; 198 Hispanic/Latino; 1 Two or more races, non-Hispanic/Latino), 1 international. Average age 37. 956 applicants, 97% accepted, 547 enrolled. In 2011, 1,609 master's, 16 doctorates awarded. Terminal master's awarded for partial completion of doctoral program. *Degree requirements:* For master's, comprehensive exam, thesis optional; for doctorate, thesis/dissertation. *Entrance requirements:* For master's, GRE General Test, minimum GPA of 2.5; for doctorate, GRE. Additional exam requirements/recommendations for international students: Required—TOEFL. *Application deadline:* For fall admission, 8/1 priority date for domestic students; for spring admission, 12/1 priority date for domestic students. Applications are processed on a rolling basis. Application fee: $25 ($50 for international students). *Expenses:* Tuition, state resident: full-time $5430; part-time $272 per credit hour. Tuition, nonresident: full-time $11,540; part-time $577 per credit hour. *Required fees:* $1916. *Financial support:* In 2011–12, 3 fellowships (averaging $20,000 per year), 1 research assistantship with tuition reimbursement (averaging $6,500 per year) were awarded; teaching assistantships with tuition reimbursements, career-related internships or fieldwork, and scholarships/grants also available. Support available to part-time students. Financial award application deadline: 4/1. *Faculty research:* School dropouts, suicide prevention in public school students, school climate and gifted performance, teacher evaluation. *Unit head:* Dr. Carolyn Crawford, Chair, 409-880-8689, Fax: 409-880-8685. *Application contact:* Dr. Lula Henry, Director of Professional Service, 409-880-8218.

La Salle University, Program in Instructional Technology Management, Philadelphia, PA 19141-1199. Offers MS. *Degree requirements:* For master's, capstone project. *Entrance requirements:* For master's, GRE, MAT, or GMAT, 3 to 5 years professional experience in corporate training, human resources, information technology or business; resume; 2 letters of recommendation. Additional exam requirements/recommendations for international students: Required—TOEFL. Electronic applications accepted.

Lawrence Technological University, College of Arts and Sciences, Southfield, MI 48075-1058. Offers computer science (MS); educational technology (MS); educational technology - training and performance (MA); integrated science (MSE); science education (MSE); technical and professional communication (MS). Part-time and evening/weekend programs available. *Faculty:* 9 full-time (5 women), 16 part-time/adjunct (8 women). *Students:* 5 full-time (1 woman), 79 part-time (48 women); includes 30 minority (18 Black or African American, non-Hispanic/Latino; 8 Asian, non-Hispanic/Latino; 1 Hispanic/Latino; 3 Two or more races, non-Hispanic/Latino), 6 international. Average age 37. 382 applicants, 66% accepted, 17 enrolled. In 2011, 32 master's awarded. *Degree requirements:* For master's, thesis (for some programs). *Entrance requirements:* For master's, GRE. Additional exam requirements/recommendations for international students: Required—TOEFL (minimum score 550 paper-based; 213 computer-based; 79 iBT). *Application deadline:* For fall admission, 6/27 priority date for domestic students, 5/23 for international students; for spring admission, 11/15 priority date for domestic students, 11/15 for international students. Applications are processed on a rolling basis. Application fee: $50. Electronic applications accepted. *Financial support:* In 2011–12, 25 students received support, including 3 research assistantships (averaging $18,480 per year); Federal Work-Study also available. Financial award application deadline: 4/1; financial award applicants required to submit FAFSA. *Unit head:* Dr. Hsiao-Ping Moore, Dean, 248-204-3500, Fax: 248-204-3518, E-mail: scidean@itu.edu. *Application contact:* Jane Rohrback, Director of Admissions, 248-204-3160, Fax: 248-204-2228, E-mail: admissions@ltu.edu. Web site: http://www.ltu.edu/arts_sciences/graduate.asp.

Lehigh University, College of Education, Program in Comparative and International Education, Bethlehem, PA 18015. Offers comparative and international education (MA); globalization and educational change (M Ed); international counseling (Certificate); international development in education (Certificate); special education (Certificate); technology use in schools (Certificate); TESOL (Certificate). Part-time programs available. Postbaccalaureate distance learning degree programs offered (no on-campus study). *Faculty:* 4 full-time (2 women). *Students:* 25 full-time (10 women), 45 part-time (31 women); includes 5 minority (all Asian, non-Hispanic/Latino), 16 international. Average age 34. 45 applicants, 71% accepted, 12 enrolled. In 2011, 21 master's awarded. *Degree requirements:* For master's, thesis (MA). *Entrance requirements:* For master's, 2 letters of recommendation. Additional exam requirements/recommendations for international students: Required—TOEFL (minimum score 600 paper-based; 250 computer-based; 93 iBT). *Application deadline:* For fall and spring admission, 2/1 for domestic and international students. Application fee: $65. Electronic applications accepted. *Financial support:* In 2011–12, 8 students received support, including 3 research assistantships with full and partial tuition reimbursements available (averaging $13,000 per year). Financial award application deadline: 3/15. *Faculty research:* Comparative education, rural education, gender equity in education, post-socialist education transformation, educational borrowing, comparing education systems, education policy an globalization, family-school relationships, China, international testing, social inequities. *Unit head:* Dr. Iveta Silova, Program Director and Associate Professor, 610-758-5750, Fax: 610-758-6223, E-mail: ism207@lehigh.edu. *Application contact:* Donna M. Johnson, Coordinator, 610-758-3231, Fax: 610-758-6223, E-mail: dmj4@lehigh.edu. Web site: http://www.lehigh.edu/education/cie.

Lehigh University, College of Education, Program in Teaching, Learning and Technology, Bethlehem, PA 18015. Offers elementary education with certification (M Ed); instructional technology (MS); learning sciences and technology (PhD); teaching and learning (M Ed, MA); technology use in the schools (Graduate Certificate); M Ed/MA. Part-time programs available. *Faculty:* 5 full-time (2 women), 9 part-time/adjunct (5 women). *Students:* 49 full-time (37 women), 48 part-time (38 women); includes 12 minority (2 Black or African American, non-Hispanic/Latino; 6 Asian, non-Hispanic/Latino; 3 Hispanic/Latino; 1 Native Hawaiian or other Pacific Islander, non-Hispanic/Latino), 4 international. Average age 31. 72 applicants, 76% accepted, 18 enrolled. In 2011, 46 master's, 2 doctorates awarded. Terminal master's awarded for partial completion of doctoral program. *Degree requirements:* For master's, comprehensive exam and thesis/dissertation (for M Ed); for doctorate, comprehensive exam, thesis/dissertation. *Entrance requirements:* For master's, minimum GPA of 3.0, 2 letters of recommendation, essay, transcript; for doctorate, GRE General Test, minimum graduate GPA of 3.0, writing sample, 2 letters of recommendation, essay, transcript. Additional exam requirements/recommendations for international students: Required—TOEFL (minimum score 600 paper-based; 250 computer-based; 93 iBT). *Application deadline:* For fall admission, 2/1 for domestic and international students; for spring admission, 11/1 for domestic and international students. Applications are processed on a rolling basis. Application fee: $65. Electronic applications accepted. *Financial support:* In 2011–12, 18 students received support, including 1 fellowship with full and partial tuition reimbursement available (averaging $16,000 per year), 2 research assistantships with full and partial tuition reimbursements available (averaging $18,000 per year); career-related internships or fieldwork, institutionally sponsored loans, scholarships/grants, and tuition waivers (full and partial) also available. Financial award application deadline: 1/31. *Faculty research:* Instructional media and delivery systems, technologies to enhance education, technical and informal education, Web-based learning. *Unit head:* Dr. M. J. Bishop, Director, 610-758-3235, Fax: 610-758-3243, E-mail: mjba@lehigh.edu. *Application contact:* Donna M. Johnson, Coordinator, 610-758-3231, Fax: 610-758-6223, E-mail: dmj4@lehigh.edu.

Lewis University, College of Education, Program in Curriculum and Instruction: Instructional Technology, Romeoville, IL 60446. Offers M Ed. Part-time and evening/weekend programs available. *Students:* 16 part-time (13 women); includes 1 minority (Black or African American, non-Hispanic/Latino). Average age 31. In 2011, 7 master's awarded. *Entrance requirements:* For master's, departmental qualifying exam, writing exam, minimum GPA of 2.75, 2 letters of recommendation, interview. Additional exam requirements/recommendations for international students: Required—TOEFL (minimum score 550 paper-based; 213 computer-based; 80 iBT). *Application deadline:* For fall admission, 5/1 for international students; for spring admission, 11/15 for international students. Applications are processed on a rolling basis. Application fee: $40. Electronic applications accepted. *Financial support:* Institutionally sponsored loans and unspecified assistantships available. Support available to part-time students. Financial award application deadline: 5/1; financial award applicants required to submit FAFSA. *Unit head:* Dr. Seung Kim, Program Director, 815-838-0500, E-mail: kimse@lewisu.edu. *Application contact:* Kelly Lofgren, Graduate Admission Counselor, 815-836-5704, Fax: 815-836-5578, E-mail: lofgreke@lewisu.edu.

Liberty University, School of Education, Lynchburg, VA 24502. Offers administration and supervision (M Ed); curriculum and instruction (M Ed); early childhood education (M Ed); educational leadership (Ed D, Ed S); educational technology and online instruction (M Ed); elementary education (M Ed, MAT); gifted education (M Ed); math specialist (M Ed); middle grades (M Ed); outdoor adventure sport (MS); reading specialist (M Ed); school counseling (M Ed); secondary education (M Ed, MAT); special education (M Ed, MAT); sports administration (MS); teaching and learning (Ed D, Ed S). *Accreditation:* NCATE. Part-time programs available. Postbaccalaureate distance learning degree programs offered (minimal on-campus study). *Students:* 2,245 full-time (1,572 women), 3,500 part-time (2,558 women); includes 1,141 minority (888 Black or African American, non-Hispanic/Latino; 19 American Indian or Alaska Native, non-Hispanic/Latino; 21 Asian, non-Hispanic/Latino; 123 Hispanic/Latino; 9 Native Hawaiian or other Pacific Islander, non-Hispanic/Latino; 81 Two or more races, non-Hispanic/Latino), 76 international. Average age 37. In 2011, 760 master's, 48 doctorates, 321 other advanced degrees awarded. *Degree requirements:* For doctorate, comprehensive exam, thesis/dissertation. *Entrance requirements:* For master's, GRE General Test or MAT (if taken in or before 1999), 2 letters of recommendation, minimum undergraduate GPA of 3.0, curriculum vitae; for doctorate, GRE General Test or MAT (if taken before 1999), minimum master's GPA of 3.0, 3 years of teacher experience; for Ed S, GRE General Test or MAT (if taken before 1999), minimum master's GPA of 3.0, 3 years of teaching experience. Additional exam requirements/recommendations for international students: Required—TOEFL (minimum score 600 paper-based; 250 computer-based). *Application deadline:* For fall admission, 6/1 priority date for domestic students; for spring admission, 11/1 for domestic students. Applications are processed on a rolling basis. Application fee: $50. Electronic applications accepted. *Expenses:* Contact institution. *Financial support:* Federal Work-Study and tuition waivers (partial) available. *Faculty research:* Self-determination, character education, bibliotherapy, learning styles, distance education. *Unit head:* Dr. Karen L. Parker, Dean, 434-582-2195, Fax: 434-582-2468, E-mail: kparker@liberty.edu. *Application contact:* Jay Bridge, Director of Graduate Admissions, 800-424-9595, Fax: 800-628-7977, E-mail: gradadmissions@liberty.edu. Web site: http://www.liberty.edu/academics/education/graduate/.

Lindenwood University, Graduate Programs, School of Education, St. Charles, MO 63301-1695. Offers education (MA); educational administration (MA, Ed D, Ed S); human performance (MS); instructional leadership (Ed D, Ed S); library media (MA); professional and school counseling (MA); professional counseling (MA); school administration (Ed S); school counseling (MA); teaching (MA); teaching English to speakers of other languages (MA). Part-time and evening/weekend programs available. *Faculty:* 33 full-time (13 women), 176 part-time/adjunct (83 women). *Students:* 472 full-time (353 women), 1,772 part-time (1,373 women); includes 666 minority (605 Black or African American, non-Hispanic/Latino; 15 American Indian or Alaska Native, non-Hispanic/Latino; 5 Asian, non-Hispanic/Latino; 2 Hispanic/Latino; 4 Native Hawaiian or other Pacific Islander, non-Hispanic/Latino; 35 Two or more races, non-Hispanic/Latino), 24 international. Average age 36. 472 applicants, 87% accepted, 366 enrolled. In 2011, 747 master's, 42 doctorates, 69 other advanced degrees awarded. *Degree requirements:* For master's, thesis (for some programs), minimum GPA of 3.0; for doctorate, thesis/dissertation, minimum GPA of 3.0; for Ed S, comprehensive exam, project, minimum GPA of 3.0. *Entrance requirements:* For master's, interview, minimum GPA of 3.0, writing sample, letter of recommendation; for doctorate, GRE, minimum graduate GPA of 3.4, resume, interview, writing sample, 4 letters of recommendation; for Ed S, master's degree in education, relevant work experience. Additional exam requirements/recommendations for international students: Required—TOEFL (minimum score 550 paper-based; 213 computer-based; 80 iBT). *Application deadline:* For fall admission, 8/26 priority date for domestic students, 8/26 for international students; for spring admission, 1/27 priority date for domestic students, 1/27 for international students. Applications are processed on a rolling basis. Application fee: $30 ($100 for international students). Electronic applications accepted. *Expenses: Tuition:* Full-time $13,650; part-time $395 per credit hour. *Required fees:* $150 per semester. Tuition and fees vary according to course level and course load. *Financial support:* In 2011–12, 153 students received support. Career-related internships or fieldwork, institutionally sponsored loans, tuition waivers (partial), and unspecified assistantships available. Financial award application deadline: 6/30; financial award applicants required to submit FAFSA. *Unit head:* Dr. Cynthia Bice, Dean, 636-949-4618, Fax: 636-949-4197, E-mail: cbice@lindenwood.edu. *Application contact:* Brett Barger, Dean of Evening Admissions and Extension Campuses, 636-949-4934, Fax: 636-949-4109, E-mail: adultadmissions@lindenwood.edu.

Lipscomb University, Program in Education, Nashville, TN 37204-3951. Offers educational leadership (M Ed); English language learning (M Ed); instructional practice (M Ed); instructional technology (M Ed); learning organizations and strategic change (Ed D); math specialty (M Ed); special education (M Ed); teaching, learning, and leading (M Ed). *Accreditation:* NCATE. Part-time and evening/weekend programs available. *Faculty:* 18 full-time (10 women), 23 part-time/adjunct (16 women). *Students:* 377 full-time (281 women), 117 part-time (85 women); includes 55 minority (39 Black or African American, non-Hispanic/Latino; 4 American Indian or Alaska Native, non-Hispanic/Latino; 5 Asian, non-Hispanic/Latino; 7 Hispanic/Latino). Average age 32. 300 applicants, 66% accepted, 142 enrolled. In 2011, 190 master's awarded. *Degree requirements:* For master's, comprehensive exam, portfolio, research project and presentation; for doctorate, practical capstone project in experiential setting. *Entrance requirements:* For master's, MAT or GRE General Test, 2 reference letters, goals statement, writing sample, interview; for doctorate, MAT or GRE General Test, 3 reference letters, artifact of demonstrated academic excellence, written personal statements, interview. Additional exam requirements/recommendations for international students: Required—TOEFL (minimum score 570 paper-based; 230 computer-based). *Application deadline:* For fall admission, 8/29 priority date for domestic students; for spring admission, 1/15 priority date for domestic students. Applications are processed on a rolling basis. Application fee: $50 ($75 for international students). *Expenses:*

Tuition: Full-time $16,830; part-time $935 per credit hour. Tuition and fees vary according to degree level and program. *Financial support:* In 2011–12, 67 students received support. Scholarships/grants and tuition waivers (partial) available. Financial award applicants required to submit FAFSA. *Faculty research:* Facilitative learning styles, leadership, student assessment, interactive multimedia inclusion, learning organizations and strategic change. *Unit head:* Dr. Deborah Boyd, Director, 615-966-6263, E-mail: deborah.boyd@lipscomb.edu. *Application contact:* Kristin Baese, Assistant Director of Enrollment and Outreach, 615-966-7628 Ext. 6081, Fax: 615-966-5173, E-mail: kristin.baese@lipscomb.edu. Web site: http://graduateeducation.lipscomb.edu/.

Long Island University–Brooklyn Campus, School of Education, Department of Teaching and Learning, Program in Computers in Education, Brooklyn, NY 11201-8423. Offers MS. *Degree requirements:* For master's, thesis optional. *Entrance requirements:* For master's, 2 letters of recommendation. Additional exam requirements/recommendations for international students: Required—TOEFL (minimum score 500 paper-based; 173 computer-based).

Long Island University–C. W. Post Campus, School of Education, Department of Educational Technology, Brookville, NY 11548-1300. Offers computers in education (MS). Part-time and evening/weekend programs available. *Degree requirements:* For master's, research project. *Entrance requirements:* For master's, interview; minimum GPA of 2.75 in major, 2.5 overall. Electronic applications accepted. *Faculty research:* Desktop publishing, higher-order thinking skills, interactive learning environments.

Longwood University, Office of Graduate Studies, College of Education and Human Services, Farmville, VA 23909. Offers communication sciences and disorders (MS); community and college counseling (MS); curriculum and instruction specialist-elementary (MS), including mild disabilities, modern languages; curriculum and instruction specialist-secondary (MS), including English, mild disabilities, modern languages; educational leadership (MS); guidance and counseling (MS); literacy and culture (MS); school library media (MS). *Accreditation:* NCATE. Part-time and evening/weekend programs available. *Degree requirements:* For master's, comprehensive exam, thesis optional. *Entrance requirements:* For master's, GRE (communication sciences and disorders), minimum GPA of 2.75. Additional exam requirements/recommendations for international students: Required—TOEFL (minimum score 550 paper-based; 213 computer-based).

Louisiana State University and Agricultural and Mechanical College, Graduate School, College of Education, Department of Educational Theory, Policy and Practice, Baton Rouge, LA 70803. Offers counseling (M Ed, MA, Ed S); educational administration (M Ed, MA, PhD, Ed S); educational technology (MA); elementary education (M Ed, MAT); higher education (PhD); research methodology (PhD); secondary education (M Ed, MAT). PhD programs offered jointly with Louisiana State University in Shreveport. *Accreditation:* ACA (one or more programs are accredited); NCATE. Part-time and evening/weekend programs available. *Faculty:* 17 full-time (all women). *Students:* 188 full-time (145 women), 161 part-time (130 women); includes 104 minority (88 Black or African American, non-Hispanic/Latino; 1 American Indian or Alaska Native, non-Hispanic/Latino; 6 Asian, non-Hispanic/Latino; 5 Hispanic/Latino; 4 Two or more races, non-Hispanic/Latino), 9 international. Average age 31. 151 applicants, 61% accepted, 58 enrolled. In 2011, 129 master's, 17 doctorates, 11 other advanced degrees awarded. Terminal master's awarded for partial completion of doctoral program. *Degree requirements:* For doctorate, thesis/dissertation; for Ed S, thesis optional. *Entrance requirements:* For master's and doctorate, GRE General Test, minimum GPA of 3.0. Additional exam requirements/recommendations for international students: Required—TOEFL (minimum score 550 paper-based; 213 computer-based; 79 iBT) or IELTS (minimum score 6.5). *Application deadline:* For fall admission, 1/25 priority date for domestic students, 5/15 for international students; for spring admission, 10/15 for international students. Applications are processed on a rolling basis. Application fee: $50 ($70 for international students). Electronic applications accepted. *Financial support:* In 2011–12, 230 students received support, including 2 fellowships (averaging $19,353 per year), 24 research assistantships with full and partial tuition reimbursements available (averaging $10,052 per year), 53 teaching assistantships with full and partial tuition reimbursements available (averaging $12,218 per year); career-related internships or fieldwork, Federal Work-Study, institutionally sponsored loans, health care benefits, and unspecified assistantships also available. Support available to part-time students. Financial award applicants required to submit FAFSA. *Faculty research:* Literary, curriculum studies, science education, K-12 leadership, higher education. *Total annual research expenditures:* $774,887. *Unit head:* Dr. Earl Cheek, Jr., Chair, 225-578-6867, Fax: 225-578-9135, E-mail: echeek@lsu.edu. *Application contact:* Dr. Rita Culross, Graduate Coordinator, 225-578-6867, Fax: 225-578-9135, E-mail: acrita@lsu.edu.

Lourdes University, Graduate School, Program in Education, Sylvania, OH 43560-2898. Offers endorsement in computer technology (M Ed). *Accreditation:* Teacher Education Accreditation Council. Evening/weekend programs available. *Entrance requirements:* Additional exam requirements/recommendations for international students: Required—TOEFL.

Loyola University Chicago, School of Education, Program in Teaching and Learning, Chicago, IL 60660. Offers elementary education (M Ed); English as a second language (Certificate); math education (M Ed); reading specialist (M Ed); reading teacher endorsement (Certificate); school technology (M Ed); science education (M Ed); secondary education (M Ed); special education (M Ed). *Accreditation:* NCATE. *Faculty:* 12 full-time (9 women), 12 part-time/adjunct (6 women). *Students:* 131. Average age 28. 115 applicants, 65% accepted, 30 enrolled. In 2011, 80 master's awarded. *Degree requirements:* For master's, comprehensive exam. *Entrance requirements:* For master's, Illinois Basic Skills Test, 3 letters of recommendation, minimum GPA of 3.0, resume. Additional exam requirements/recommendations for international students: Required—TOEFL (minimum score 550 paper-based; 213 computer-based; 79 iBT). *Application deadline:* For fall admission, 7/1 priority date for domestic students, 7/1 for international students; for spring admission, 11/1 priority date for domestic students, 11/1 for international students. Applications are processed on a rolling basis. Application fee: $50. Electronic applications accepted. Application fee is waived when completed online. *Expenses: Tuition:* Full-time $15,660; part-time $870 per credit hour. *Required fees:* $125 per semester. Tuition and fees vary according to course load and program. *Financial support:* Institutionally sponsored loans, scholarships/grants, and unspecified assistantships available. Support available to part-time students. Financial award application deadline: 2/1; financial award applicants required to submit FAFSA. *Faculty research:* Positive behavior support, school reform, school improvement. *Unit head:* Dr. Dorothy Giroux, Director, 312-915-7027, E-mail: dgiroux@luc.edu. *Application contact:* Marie Rosin-Dittmar, Information Contact, 312-915-6800, E-mail: schleduc@luc.edu.

Loyola University Maryland, Graduate Programs, Department of Education, Program in Educational Technology, Baltimore, MD 21210-2699. Offers M Ed, MA. Part-time programs available. *Faculty:* 57 full-time (32 women), 21 part-time/adjunct (10 women). *Students:* 1 (woman) full-time, 55 part-time (45 women); includes 7 minority (1 Black or African American, non-Hispanic/Latino; 1 Asian, non-Hispanic/Latino; 3 Hispanic/Latino; 2 Two or more races, non-Hispanic/Latino). Average age 30. In 2011, 5 master's awarded. *Degree requirements:* For master's, thesis. *Entrance requirements:* Additional exam requirements/recommendations for international students: Required—TOEFL (minimum score 550 paper-based; 213 computer-based). *Application deadline:* For fall admission, 6/15 for domestic students. Application fee: $50. Electronic applications accepted. *Financial support:* Research assistantships and unspecified assistantships available. Financial award application deadline: 4/15; financial award applicants required to submit FAFSA. *Unit head:* Dr. David M. Marcovitz, Director, 410-617-2250, E-mail: marco@loyola.edu. *Application contact:* Maureen Faux, Executive Director, Graduate Admissions, 410-617-5020, Fax: 410-617-2002, E-mail: graduate@loyola.edu.

Marlboro College, Graduate School, Program in Teaching with Technology, Marlboro, VT 05344. Offers MAT. Part-time and evening/weekend programs available. Postbaccalaureate distance learning degree programs offered (minimal on-campus study). *Degree requirements:* For master's, 30 credits including capstone project. *Entrance requirements:* For master's, letter of intent, 2 letters of recommendation, transcripts. Electronic applications accepted.

McDaniel College, Graduate and Professional Studies, Program in Media/Library Science, Westminster, MD 21157-4390. Offers MS. Part-time and evening/weekend programs available. *Degree requirements:* For master's, comprehensive exam, thesis optional. *Entrance requirements:* For master's, GRE General Test, MAT, or NTE/PRAXIS I, letters of reference (3). Additional exam requirements/recommendations for international students: Required—TOEFL (minimum score 213 computer-based).

McNeese State University, Doré School of Graduate Studies, Burton College of Education, Department of Education Professions, Program in Educational Leadership, Lake Charles, LA 70609. Offers educational leadership (M Ed, Ed S); educational technology (Ed S). Evening/weekend programs available. *Faculty:* 4 full-time (0 women). *Students:* 2 full-time (1 woman), 68 part-time (27 women); includes 18 minority (all Black or African American, non-Hispanic/Latino). In 2011, 17 master's, 10 Ed Ss awarded. *Degree requirements:* For Ed S, comprehensive exam. *Entrance requirements:* For master's, GRE, teaching certificate, 3 years full-time teaching experience; for Ed S, teaching certificate, 3 years of teaching experience, 1 year of administration or supervision experience, master's degree with 12 semester hours in education. *Application deadline:* For fall admission, 5/15 priority date for domestic students, 5/15 for international students; for spring admission, 10/15 priority date for domestic students, 10/15 for international students. Applications are processed on a rolling basis. Application fee: $20 ($30 for international students). *Expenses:* Tuition, state resident: part-time $519 per credit hour. Tuition and fees vary according to course load. *Financial support:* Fellowships available. Financial award application deadline: 5/1. *Unit head:* Dr. Dustin M. Hebert, Director, 337-475-5424, Fax: 337-475-5272, E-mail: dhebert@mcneese.edu. *Application contact:* Dr. George F. Mead, Jr., Interim Dean of Dore' School of Graduate Studies, 337-475-5396, Fax: 337-475-5397, E-mail: admissions@mcneese.edu.

McNeese State University, Doré School of Graduate Studies, Burton College of Education, Department of Education Professions, Program in Educational Technology Leadership, Lake Charles, LA 70609. Offers M Ed. Evening/weekend programs available. *Faculty:* 3 full-time (2 women). *Students:* 6 full-time (5 women), 11 part-time (10 women); includes 5 minority (all Black or African American, non-Hispanic/Latino). In 2011, 12 master's awarded. *Entrance requirements:* For master's, GRE, teaching certificate. *Application deadline:* For fall admission, 5/15 priority date for domestic students, 5/15 for international students; for spring admission, 10/15 priority date for domestic students, 10/15 for international students. Applications are processed on a rolling basis. Application fee: $20 ($30 for international students). *Expenses:* Tuition, state resident: part-time $519 per credit hour. Tuition and fees vary according to course load. *Financial support:* Fellowships available. Financial award application deadline: 5/1. *Unit head:* Dr. Dustin M. Hebert, Director, 337-475-5424, Fax: 337-475-5272, E-mail: dhebert@mcneese.edu. *Application contact:* Dr. George F. Mead, Jr., Interim Dean of Dore' School of Graduate Studies, 337-475-5396, Fax: 337-475-5397, E-mail: admissions@mcneese.edu.

McNeese State University, Doré School of Graduate Studies, Burton College of Education, Department of Education Professions, Program in Instructional Technology, Lake Charles, LA 70609. Offers MS. Evening/weekend programs available. *Faculty:* 3 full-time (2 women). *Students:* 13 full-time (10 women), 18 part-time (13 women); includes 11 minority (all Black or African American, non-Hispanic/Latino), 5 international. In 2011, 5 master's awarded. *Entrance requirements:* For master's, GRE. *Application deadline:* For fall admission, 5/15 priority date for domestic students, 5/15 for international students; for spring admission, 10/15 priority date for domestic students, 10/15 for international students. Applications are processed on a rolling basis. Application fee: $20 ($30 for international students). *Expenses:* Tuition, state resident: part-time $519 per credit hour. Tuition and fees vary according to course load. *Financial support:* Application deadline: 5/1. *Unit head:* Dr. Dustin M. Hebert, Director, 337-475-5424, Fax: 337-475-5272, E-mail: dhebert@mcneese.edu. *Application contact:* Dr. George F. Mead, Jr., Interim Dean of Dore' School of Graduate Studies, 337-475-5396, Fax: 337-475-5397, E-mail: admissions@mcneese.edu.

Memorial University of Newfoundland, School of Graduate Studies, Faculty of Education, St. John's, NL A1C 5S7, Canada. Offers counseling psychology (M Ed); curriculum, teaching, and learning studies (M Ed); education (PhD); educational leadership studies (M Ed); information technology (M Ed); post-secondary studies (M Ed, Diploma), including health professional education (Diploma). Part-time programs available. *Degree requirements:* For master's, thesis optional, internship, paper folio, project; for doctorate, comprehensive exam, thesis/dissertation, thesis seminar, oral defense of thesis. *Entrance requirements:* For master's, undergraduate degree with at least 2nd class standing, 1-2 years work experience; for doctorate, minimum A average in graduate course work, MA in education, 2 years professional experience; for Diploma, 2nd class degree, 2 years of work experience with adult learners, appropriate academic qualifications and work experience in a health-related field. Electronic applications accepted. *Faculty research:* Critical thinking, literacy, cognitive studies and counseling, educational change, technology in instruction.

Miami University, School of Education and Allied Professions, Department of Educational Psychology, Oxford, OH 45056. Offers educational psychology (M Ed); instructional design and technology (M Ed, MA); school psychology (MS, Ed S); special education (M Ed). *Accreditation:* NCATE. *Students:* 49 full-time (40 women), 39 part-time (31 women); includes 8 minority (1 Black or African American, non-Hispanic/Latino; 5 Asian, non-Hispanic/Latino; 2 Two or more races, non-Hispanic/Latino), 28 international. Average age 29. In 2011, 50 master's awarded. *Entrance requirements:* For master's, GRE General Test or MAT, minimum undergraduate GPA of 3.0 during previous 2 years or 2.75 overall; for Ed S, GRE General Test or MAT. Additional exam requirements/recommendations for international students: Required—TOEFL. Application fee: $50. *Expenses:* Tuition, state resident: full-time $12,023; part-time $501 per credit hour. Tuition, nonresident: full-time $26,554; part-time $1107 per credit hour. *Required fees:* $528. *Financial support:* Fellowships with full tuition reimbursements, research assistantships with full tuition reimbursements, teaching assistantships with full tuition reimbursements, career-related internships or fieldwork, Federal Work-Study, health care benefits, tuition waivers (full), and unspecified assistantships available. Financial award application deadline: 2/15; financial award applicants required to submit FAFSA. *Unit head:* Dr. Nelda Cambron-McCabe, Chair, 513-529-6836, Fax: 513-529-

6621, E-mail: cambron@muohio.edu. *Application contact:* Jennifer Turner, Administrative Assistant, 513-529-6621, Fax: 513-529-3646, E-mail: hillje@muohio.edu. Web site: http://www.units.muohio.edu/eap/departments/edp/edp.htm.

Michigan State University, The Graduate School, College of Education, Department of Counseling, Educational Psychology and Special Education, East Lansing, MI 48824. Offers counseling (MA); educational psychology and educational technology (PhD); educational technology (MA); measurement and quantitative methods (PhD); rehabilitation counseling (MA); rehabilitation counselor education (PhD); school psychology (MA, PhD, Ed S); special education (MA, PhD). *Accreditation:* APA (one or more programs are accredited); CORE (one or more programs are accredited). Part-time programs available. *Entrance requirements:* Additional exam requirements/recommendations for international students: Required—TOEFL. Electronic applications accepted.

MidAmerica Nazarene University, Graduate Studies in Education, Olathe, KS 66062-1899. Offers ESOL (M Ed); professional teaching (M Ed); special education (MA); technology enhanced teaching (M Ed). *Accreditation:* NCATE. Part-time and evening/weekend programs available. Postbaccalaureate distance learning degree programs offered (no on-campus study). *Degree requirements:* For master's, thesis or alternative, creative project, technology leadership practicum. *Entrance requirements:* For master's, minimum undergraduate GPA of 2.8, 2 years of teaching experience. *Expenses:* Contact institution.

Middle Tennessee State University, College of Graduate Studies, College of Education, Department of Educational Leadership, Program in Curriculum and Instruction, Murfreesboro, TN 37132. Offers curriculum and instruction (M Ed, Ed S); English as a second language (M Ed, Ed S); secondary education (M Ed); technology and curriculum design (Ed S). *Accreditation:* NCATE. Part-time and evening/weekend programs available. Postbaccalaureate distance learning degree programs offered. *Faculty:* 22 full-time (11 women), 22 part-time/adjunct (12 women). *Students:* 13 full-time (7 women), 208 part-time (167 women); includes 38 minority (29 Black or African American, non-Hispanic/Latino; 2 Asian, non-Hispanic/Latino; 2 Hispanic/Latino; 5 Two or more races, non-Hispanic/Latino). 154 applicants, 97% accepted. In 2011, 144 master's, 40 Ed Ss awarded. *Degree requirements:* For master's, comprehensive exam; for Ed S, comprehensive exam, thesis or alternative. *Entrance requirements:* For master's and Ed S, GRE, MAT or PRAXIS. Additional exam requirements/recommendations for international students: Required—TOEFL (minimum score 525 paper-based; 195 computer-based; 71 iBT) or IELTS (minimum score 6). *Application deadline:* For fall admission, 6/1 for domestic and international students. Applications are processed on a rolling basis. Application fee: $25 ($30 for international students). Electronic applications accepted. *Expenses:* Tuition, state resident: full-time $10,008. Tuition, nonresident: full-time $25,056. *Financial support:* Tuition waivers available. Support available to part-time students. Financial award application deadline: 5/1. *Unit head:* Dr. James Huffman, Chair, 615-898-2855, Fax: 615-898-2859. *Application contact:* Dr. Michael D. Allen, Dean and Vice Provost for Research, 615-898-2840, Fax: 615-904-8020, E-mail: michael.allen@mtsu.edu.

Midwestern State University, Graduate Studies, College of Education, Program in Educational Leadership and Technology, Wichita Falls, TX 76308. Offers ME. Part-time and evening/weekend programs available. *Degree requirements:* For master's, comprehensive exam. *Entrance requirements:* For master's, GRE General Test or MAT. Additional exam requirements/recommendations for international students: Required—TOEFL (minimum score 550 paper-based; 213 computer-based). Electronic applications accepted. *Faculty research:* Role of the principal in the twenty-first century, culturally proficient leadership, human diversity, immigration, teacher collaboration.

Minnesota State University Mankato, College of Graduate Studies, College of Education, Department of Educational Studies: K–12 and Secondary Programs, Program in Library Media Education, Mankato, MN 56001. Offers MS, Certificate. *Accreditation:* NCATE. Part-time programs available. *Students:* 1 full-time (0 women), 21 part-time (19 women). *Degree requirements:* For master's, comprehensive exam, thesis or alternative; for Certificate, comprehensive exam, thesis. *Entrance requirements:* For master's, GRE General Test (if GPA less than 3.0), minimum GPA of 3.0 during previous 2 years; for Certificate, minimum GPA of 3.0. Additional exam requirements/recommendations for international students: Required—TOEFL. *Application deadline:* For fall admission, 7/1 priority date for domestic students; for spring admission, 11/1 for domestic students. Applications are processed on a rolling basis. Application fee: $40. Electronic applications accepted. *Financial support:* Research assistantships with full tuition reimbursements, teaching assistantships with full tuition reimbursements, career-related internships or fieldwork, Federal Work-Study, and institutionally sponsored loans available. Support available to part-time students. Financial award application deadline: 3/15; financial award applicants required to submit FAFSA. *Unit head:* Dr. Deborah Jesseman, Graduate Coordinator, 507-389-1965. *Application contact:* 507-389-2321, E-mail: grad@mnsu.edu. Web site: http://ed.mnsu.edu/ksp/.

Mississippi State University, College of Education, Department of Instructional Systems and Workforce Development, Mississippi State, MS 39762. Offers MS, MSIT, Ed D, PhD, Ed S. *Faculty:* 9 full-time (6 women), 1 (woman) part-time/adjunct. *Students:* 24 full-time (15 women), 84 part-time (66 women); includes 61 minority (59 Black or African American, non-Hispanic/Latino; 2 Asian, non-Hispanic/Latino), 2 international. Average age 37. 36 applicants, 56% accepted, 17 enrolled. In 2011, 18 master's, 4 doctorates, 4 other advanced degrees awarded. *Degree requirements:* For master's, thesis optional, comprehensive oral or written exam; for doctorate, thesis/dissertation, comprehensive oral and written exam; for Ed S, thesis, comprehensive written exam. *Entrance requirements:* For master's, GRE, minimum GPA of 2.75 in junior and senior courses; for doctorate and Ed S, GRE. Additional exam requirements/recommendations for international students: Required—TOEFL (minimum score 550 paper-based; 213 computer-based; 79 iBT); Recommended—IELTS (minimum score 6.5). *Application deadline:* For fall admission, 7/1 for domestic students, 5/1 for international students; for spring admission, 11/1 for domestic students, 9/1 for international students. Applications are processed on a rolling basis. Application fee: $40. Electronic applications accepted. *Expenses:* Tuition, state resident: full-time $5805; part-time $322.50 per credit hour. Tuition, nonresident: full-time $14,670; part-time $815 per credit hour. *Financial support:* In 2011–12, 1 teaching assistantship with full tuition reimbursement (averaging $10,800 per year) was awarded; Federal Work-Study, institutionally sponsored loans, and unspecified assistantships also available. Financial award application deadline: 4/1; financial award applicants required to submit FAFSA. *Faculty research:* Computer technology, nontraditional students, interactive video, instructional technology, educational leadership. *Unit head:* Dr. Connie Forde, Professor and Department Head, 662-325-7258, Fax: 662-325-7599, E-mail: cforde@colled.msstate.edu. *Application contact:* Dr. James Adams, Associate Professor and Graduate Coordinator, 662-325-7563, Fax: 662-325-7258, E-mail: jadams@colled.msstate.edu. Web site: http://www.msstate.edu/dept/teched/.

Missouri Southern State University, Program in Instructional Technology, Joplin, MO 64801-1595. Offers MS Ed. Program offered jointly with Northwest Missouri State University. *Degree requirements:* For master's, comprehensive exam, research paper. *Entrance requirements:* For master's, GRE (minimum combined score of 700), writing assessment, minimum overall undergraduate GPA of 3.0.

Missouri State University, Graduate College, College of Education, Department of Reading, Foundations, and Technology, Program in Educational Technology, Springfield, MO 65897. Offers MS Ed. Part-time programs available. *Students:* 2 full-time (both women), 18 part-time (10 women); includes 2 minority (1 Asian, non-Hispanic/Latino; 1 Two or more races, non-Hispanic/Latino), 1 international. Average age 34. 7 applicants, 100% accepted, 6 enrolled. In 2011, 5 master's awarded. *Degree requirements:* For master's, comprehensive exam, thesis or alternative. *Entrance requirements:* Additional exam requirements/recommendations for international students: Required—TOEFL (minimum score 550 paper-based; 213 computer-based; 79 iBT). *Application deadline:* For fall admission, 7/20 for domestic students, 5/1 for international students; for spring admission, 12/20 for domestic students, 9/1 for international students. Applications are processed on a rolling basis. Application fee: $35 ($50 for international students). Electronic applications accepted. *Expenses:* Tuition, state resident: full-time $4086; part-time $227 per credit hour. Tuition, nonresident: full-time $8172; part-time $454 per credit hour. *Required fees:* $275 per semester. Tuition and fees vary according to course load, campus/location and program. *Financial support:* Federal Work-Study, institutionally sponsored loans, scholarships/grants, and unspecified assistantships available. Financial award application deadline: 3/31; financial award applicants required to submit FAFSA. *Unit head:* Dr. Fred Groves, Graduate Program Coordinator, 417-836-6769, E-mail: fredgroves@missouristate.edu. *Application contact:* Misty Stewart, Coordinator of Graduate Recruitment, 417-836-6079, Fax: 417-836-6200, E-mail: mistystewart@missouristate.edu. Web site: http://education.missouristate.edu/rft/.

Montana State University Billings, College of Education, Department of Educational Theory and Practice, Option in Educational Technology, Billings, MT 59101-0298. Offers M Ed. *Accreditation:* NCATE. Part-time programs available. *Degree requirements:* For master's, professional paper or thesis. *Entrance requirements:* For master's, GRE General Test or MAT, minimum GPA of 3.0 (undergraduate), 3.25 (graduate).

Montclair State University, The Graduate School, College of Education and Human Services, Department of Early Childhood, Elementary and Literacy Education, New Literacies, Digital Technologies and Learning Certificate Program, Montclair, NJ 07043-1624. Offers Certificate. Part-time and evening/weekend programs available. *Students:* 3 part-time (all women). Average age 31. 3 applicants, 33% accepted, 0 enrolled. In 2011, 4 Certificates awarded. *Degree requirements:* For Certificate, comprehensive exam. *Entrance requirements:* Additional exam requirements/recommendations for international students: Required—TOEFL (minimum score 83 iBT), IELTS (minimum score 6.5). *Application deadline:* Applications are processed on a rolling basis. Application fee: $60. Electronic applications accepted. *Financial support:* Federal Work-Study, scholarships/grants, and unspecified assistantships available. Support available to part-time students. Financial award application deadline: 3/1; financial award applicants required to submit FAFSA. *Unit head:* Dr. Tina Jacobowitz, Chairperson, 973-655-7191. *Application contact:* Amy Aiello, Executive Director of The Graduate School, 973-655-5147, Fax: 973-655-7869, E-mail: graduate.school@montclair.edu. Web site: http://cehs.montclair.edu/academic/ecele/programs/newliteracies.shtml.

Morehead State University, Graduate Programs, College of Education, Department of Foundational and Graduate Studies in Education, Morehead, KY 40351. Offers adult and higher education (MA, Ed S); certified professional counselor (Ed S); counseling P-12 (MA); curriculum and instruction (Ed S); educational technology (MA Ed); instructional leadership (Ed S); school administration (MA); school counseling (Ed S); teacher leader business and marketing content (MA Ed); teacher leader business and marketing technology (MA Ed); teacher leader educational technology (MA Ed); teacher leader English (MA Ed); teacher leader gifted education (MA Ed); teacher leader IECE certification (MA Ed); teacher leader interdisciplinary education P-5 (MA Ed); teacher leader middle grades (MA Ed); teacher leader non IECE certification (MA Ed); teacher leader reading/writing - non-certification (MA Ed); teacher leader reading/writing certification (MA Ed); teacher leader school communication - certification (MA Ed); teacher leader school communication - non-certification (MA Ed); teacher leader social studies (MA Ed); teacher leader special education (MA Ed). *Accreditation:* NCATE. Part-time and evening/weekend programs available. *Degree requirements:* For master's, thesis optional, oral and/or written comprehensive exams; for Ed S, thesis, oral exam. *Entrance requirements:* For master's, GRE General Test, minimum overall undergraduate GPA of 2.5; for Ed S, GRE General Test, interview, master's degree, minimum GPA of 3.5, work experience. Additional exam requirements/recommendations for international students: Required—TOEFL (minimum score 500 paper-based; 173 computer-based). Electronic applications accepted. *Faculty research:* Character education, school accountability, computer applications for school administrators.

National Louis University, National College of Education, Chicago, IL 60603. Offers administration and supervision (M Ed, Ed D, CAS, Ed S); curriculum and instruction (M Ed, MS Ed, CAS); early childhood administration (M Ed, CAS); early childhood education (M Ed, MAT, MS Ed, CAS); education (Ed D); educational psychology/human learning and development (M Ed, MS Ed, CAS, Ed S); elementary education (MAT); interdisciplinary curriculum and instruction (M Ed); mathematics education (M Ed, MS Ed, CAS); reading and language (M Ed, MS Ed, CAS); school psychology (M Ed, Ed S); science education (M Ed, MS Ed, CAS); secondary education (MAT); special education (M Ed, MAT, CAS); technology in education (M Ed, CAS). *Accreditation:* NCATE. Part-time and evening/weekend programs available. *Students:* 224 full-time (162 women), 2,336 part-time (1,767 women); includes 677 minority (366 Black or African American, non-Hispanic/Latino; 8 American Indian or Alaska Native, non-Hispanic/Latino; 68 Asian, non-Hispanic/Latino; 218 Hispanic/Latino; 2 Native Hawaiian or other Pacific Islander, non-Hispanic/Latino; 15 Two or more races, non-Hispanic/Latino), 2 international. Average age 34. In 2011, 1,711 master's, 76 doctorates, 86 other advanced degrees awarded. *Degree requirements:* For doctorate, comprehensive exam, thesis/dissertation. *Entrance requirements:* For master's, MAT or GRE, minimum GPA of 3.0; for doctorate, GRE General Test, minimum GPA of 3.25, interview, resume, writing sample, 4 recommendations. Additional exam requirements/recommendations for international students: Required—TOEFL (minimum score 550 paper-based; 213 computer-based; 79 iBT). *Application deadline:* Applications are processed on a rolling basis. Application fee: $40. *Financial support:* Fellowships, research assistantships, teaching assistantships, career-related internships or fieldwork, Federal Work-Study, institutionally sponsored loans, and scholarships/grants available. Support available to part-time students. Financial award applicants required to submit FAFSA. *Unit head:* Dr. Alison Hilsabeck, Dean, 312-361-3580, Fax: 312-261-2580, E-mail: ahilsabeck@nl.edu. *Application contact:* Ken Kasprzak, Director of Admission, 888-658-8632, Fax: 847-947-5575, E-mail: kkasprzak@nl.edu.

National University, Academic Affairs, School of Education, Department of Teacher Education, La Jolla, CA 92037-1011. Offers best practices (Certificate); early childhood education (Certificate); educational technology (Certificate); elementary education (M Ed); instructional technology (MS Ed); multiple or single subjects teaching (M Ed); national board certified teacher leadership (Certificate); secondary education (M Ed); teaching (MA). Part-time and evening/weekend programs available. Postbaccalaureate distance learning degree programs offered (no on-campus study). *Degree requirements:* For master's, thesis. *Entrance requirements:* For master's, interview, minimum GPA of 2.5. Additional exam requirements/recommendations for international students: Required—TOEFL (minimum score 550 paper-based; 213 computer-based; 79 iBT), IELTS (minimum score 6). *Application deadline:* Applications are processed on a rolling basis. Application fee: $60 ($65 for international students). Electronic applications accepted. *Financial support:* Career-related internships or fieldwork, institutionally sponsored loans, scholarships/grants, and tuition waivers (partial) available. Support available to part-time students. Financial award application deadline: 6/30; financial award applicants required to submit FAFSA. *Unit head:* Dr. Cynthia Schubert-Irastroza, Chair, 858-642-8339, Fax: 858-642-8724, E-mail: cshubert@nu.edu. *Application contact:* Dominick Giovanniello, Associate Regional Dean, 800-NAT-UNIV, Fax: 858-541-7792, E-mail: dgiovann@nu.edu. Web site: http://www.nu.edu/OurPrograms/SchoolOfEducation/TeacherEducation.html.

Nazareth College of Rochester, Graduate Studies, Department of Education, Program in Educational Technology/Computer Education, Rochester, NY 14618-3790. Offers MS Ed. Part-time and evening/weekend programs available. *Entrance requirements:* For master's, minimum GPA of 3.0.

New Jersey City University, Graduate Studies and Continuing Education, Debra Cannon Partridge Wolfe College of Education, Concentration in Educational Technology, Jersey City, NJ 07305-1597. Offers MA. *Accreditation:* NCATE. Part-time and evening/weekend programs available. Postbaccalaureate distance learning degree programs offered (minimal on-campus study). *Students:* 3 full-time (2 women), 86 part-time (66 women); includes 11 minority (4 Black or African American, non-Hispanic/Latino; 4 Asian, non-Hispanic/Latino; 3 Hispanic/Latino), 1 international. Average age 37. In 2011, 53 master's awarded. *Degree requirements:* For master's, internship. *Entrance requirements:* Additional exam requirements/recommendations for international students: Required—TOEFL. *Application deadline:* For fall admission, 8/1 priority date for domestic students; for spring admission, 12/1 for domestic students. Applications are processed on a rolling basis. Application fee: $0. *Expenses:* Tuition, state resident: part-time $494 per credit. Tuition, nonresident: part-time $911.30 per credit. *Required fees:* $95.90 per year. *Financial support:* Unspecified assistantships available. *Unit head:* Dr. Cordelia Twomey, Chairperson, 201-200-3421, E-mail: ctwomey@njcu.edu. *Application contact:* Dr. William Bajor, Dean of Graduate Studies, 201-200-3409, Fax: 201-200-3411, E-mail: wbajor@njcu.edu.

New York Institute of Technology, Graduate Division, School of Education, Program in Instructional Technology, Old Westbury, NY 11568-8000. Offers distance learning (Advanced Certificate); instructional technology (MS); multimedia (Advanced Certificate). Part-time and evening/weekend programs available. Postbaccalaureate distance learning degree programs offered. *Students:* 24 full-time (15 women), 251 part-time (166 women); includes 61 minority (28 Black or African American, non-Hispanic/Latino; 2 American Indian or Alaska Native, non-Hispanic/Latino; 11 Asian, non-Hispanic/Latino; 20 Hispanic/Latino), 3 international. Average age 33. In 2011, 93 master's, 4 other advanced degrees awarded. *Degree requirements:* For master's, thesis. *Entrance requirements:* For master's, minimum QPA of 3.0; for Advanced Certificate, master's degree, minimum GPA of 3.0, 3 years of teaching experience, New York teaching certificate, 2 letters of recommendation. Additional exam requirements/recommendations for international students: Required—TOEFL (minimum score 550 paper-based; 213 computer-based). *Application deadline:* For fall admission, 7/1 priority date for domestic students; for spring admission, 12/1 priority date for domestic students. Applications are processed on a rolling basis. Application fee: $50. Electronic applications accepted. *Expenses: Tuition:* Part-time $930 per credit hour. *Financial support:* Research assistantships with partial tuition reimbursements, career-related internships or fieldwork, institutionally sponsored loans, and tuition waivers (full and partial) available. Support available to part-time students. Financial award applicants required to submit FAFSA. *Faculty research:* Distance learning, teacher training resources and strategies. *Unit head:* Dr. Sarah McPherson, Department Chair, 516-686-1053, Fax: 516-686-7655, E-mail: smcphers@nyit.edu. *Application contact:* Dr. Jacquelyn Nealon, Vice President for Enrollment Services, 516-686-7925, Fax: 516-686-7597, E-mail: jnealon@nyit.edu.

New York Institute of Technology, Graduate Division, School of Education, Program in School Leadership and Technology, Old Westbury, NY 11568-8000. Offers Professional Diploma. Part-time and evening/weekend programs available. *Students:* 2 full-time (1 woman), 17 part-time (12 women); includes 3 minority (1 Black or African American, non-Hispanic/Latino; 2 Hispanic/Latino). Average age 36. 2 applicants, 50% accepted, 0 enrolled. In 2011, 8 Professional Diplomas awarded. *Degree requirements:* For Professional Diploma, internship. *Entrance requirements:* For degree, 3 years full-time teaching experience, permanent teacher certification in New York state. Additional exam requirements/recommendations for international students: Required—TOEFL (minimum score 550 paper-based; 213 computer-based). *Application deadline:* For fall admission, 7/1 for domestic students; for spring admission, 12/1 for domestic students. Application fee: $50. *Expenses: Tuition:* Part-time $930 per credit hour. *Financial support:* Career-related internships or fieldwork available. Financial award applicants required to submit FAFSA. *Unit head:* Dr. Michael Uttendorfer, Dean, 516-686-7706, Fax: 516-686-7655, E-mail: muttendo@nyit.edu. *Application contact:* Dr. Jacquelyn Nealon, Vice President for Enrollment Services, 516-686-7925, Fax: 516-686-7613, E-mail: jnealon@nyit.edu.

New York University, Steinhardt School of Culture, Education, and Human Development, Department of Administration, Leadership, and Technology, Program in Educational Communication and Technology, New York, NY 10012-1019. Offers MA, PhD, Advanced Certificate. Part-time programs available. *Faculty:* 4 full-time (2 women). *Students:* 19 full-time (14 women), 27 part-time (16 women); includes 17 minority (4 Black or African American, non-Hispanic/Latino; 3 Asian, non-Hispanic/Latino; 9 Hispanic/Latino; 1 Two or more races, non-Hispanic/Latino), 11 international. Average age 34. 62 applicants, 53% accepted, 12 enrolled. In 2011, 20 master's, 3 doctorates awarded. *Degree requirements:* For master's, thesis (for some programs); for doctorate, thesis/dissertation. *Entrance requirements:* For doctorate, GRE General Test, interview; for Advanced Certificate, master's degree. Additional exam requirements/recommendations for international students: Required—TOEFL. *Application deadline:* For fall admission, 12/1 priority date for domestic students, 12/1 for international students; for spring admission, 11/1 for domestic and international students. Applications are processed on a rolling basis. Application fee: $75. Electronic applications accepted. *Financial support:* Fellowships with full and partial tuition reimbursements, research assistantships with full and partial tuition reimbursements, teaching assistantships with partial tuition reimbursements, career-related internships or fieldwork, Federal Work-Study, institutionally sponsored loans, scholarships/grants, tuition waivers (partial), and unspecified assistantships available. Support available to part-time students. Financial award application deadline: 2/1; financial award applicants required to submit FAFSA. *Faculty research:* Digital design for learning, critical evaluation of games, multimedia, cognitive science, individual differences in multimedia learning, serious games. *Unit head:* Dr. Ricki Goldman, Director, 212-998-5520, Fax: 212-995-4047. *Application contact:* 212-998-5030, Fax: 212-995-4328, E-mail: steinhardt.gradadmissions@nyu.edu. Web site: http://steinhardt.nyu.edu/alt/ect.

North Carolina Agricultural and Technical State University, School of Graduate Studies, School of Education, Department of Curriculum and Instruction, Greensboro, NC 27411. Offers elementary education (MA Ed); instructional technology (MS); reading education (MA Ed); teaching (MAT). *Accreditation:* NCATE. Part-time and evening/weekend programs available. *Degree requirements:* For master's, comprehensive exam, qualifying exam. *Entrance requirements:* For master's, GRE General Test, minimum GPA of 3.0.

North Carolina Central University, Division of Academic Affairs, School of Education, Program in Educational Technology, Durham, NC 27707-3129. Offers MA. *Accreditation:* NCATE. Part-time and evening/weekend programs available. *Degree requirements:* For master's, comprehensive exam, thesis or alternative. *Entrance requirements:* For master's, GRE, minimum GPA of 3.0 in major, 2.5 overall. Additional exam requirements/recommendations for international students: Required—TOEFL. *Faculty research:* Role of media in school libraries, media and implications for educational gerontology.

North Carolina Central University, Division of Academic Affairs, School of Education, Program in Instructional Technology, Durham, NC 27707-3129. Offers M Ed.

North Carolina State University, Graduate School, College of Education, Department of Curriculum and Instruction, Program in Instructional Technology, Raleigh, NC 27695. Offers M Ed, MS. *Entrance requirements:* For master's, MAT or GRE, minimum GPA of 3.0, 3 letters of reference.

North Carolina State University, Graduate School, College of Education, Department of Mathematics, Science, and Technology Education, Program in Technology Education, Raleigh, NC 27695. Offers M Ed, MS, Ed D. *Degree requirements:* For master's, thesis (for some programs); for doctorate, thesis/dissertation. *Entrance requirements:* For master's, GRE or MAT; for doctorate, GRE General Test or MAT, minimum GPA of 3.0, interview. Electronic applications accepted.

Northeastern State University, Graduate College, College of Education, Program in Library Media and Information Technology, Tahlequah, OK 74464-2399. Offers MS Ed. *Students:* 2 full-time (both women), 58 part-time (54 women); includes 13 minority (12 American Indian or Alaska Native, non-Hispanic/Latino; 1 Hispanic/Latino). In 2011, 19 master's awarded. *Entrance requirements:* Additional exam requirements/recommendations for international students: Required—TOEFL (minimum score 213 computer-based). *Application deadline:* For fall admission, 6/1 for domestic students. Application fee: $25. *Unit head:* Dr. Barbara Ray, Head, 918-449-6000 Ext. 6451. *Application contact:* Margie Railey, Administrative Assistant, 918-456-5511 Ext. 2093, Fax: 918-458-2061, E-mail: railey@nsouk.edu.

Northern Arizona University, Graduate College, College of Education, Department of Educational Specialties, Flagstaff , AZ 86011. Offers autism spectrum disorders (Certificate); bilingual/multicultural education (M Ed), including bilingual education, ESL education; career and technical education (M Ed, Certificate); curriculum and instruction (Ed D); early childhood special education (M Ed); early intervention (Certificate); educational technology (M Ed, Certificate); special education (M Ed). *Faculty:* 28 full-time (19 women). *Students:* 113 full-time (91 women), 206 part-time (158 women); includes 104 minority (8 Black or African American, non-Hispanic/Latino; 17 American Indian or Alaska Native, non-Hispanic/Latino; 6 Asian, non-Hispanic/Latino; 65 Hispanic/Latino; 2 Native Hawaiian or other Pacific Islander, non-Hispanic/Latino; 6 Two or more races, non-Hispanic/Latino), 3 international. Average age 30. 141 applicants, 75% accepted, 76 enrolled. In 2011, 167 master's, 7 Certificates awarded. *Degree requirements:* For master's, comprehensive exam (for some programs), thesis (for some programs). *Entrance requirements:* For master's, minimum GPA of 3.0. Additional exam requirements/recommendations for international students: Required—TOEFL (minimum score 550 paper-based; 213 computer-based; 80 iBT), IELTS (minimum score 7). *Application deadline:* For fall admission, 3/1 for international students; for spring admission, 9/15 for international students. Applications are processed on a rolling basis. Application fee: $65. Electronic applications accepted. *Expenses:* Tuition, state resident: full-time $7190; part-time $355 per credit hour. Tuition, nonresident: full-time $18,092; part-time $1005 per credit hour. *Required fees:* $818; $328 per semester. *Financial support:* Applicants required to submit FAFSA. *Unit head:* Dr. Jennifer Prior, Chair, 928-523-5064, Fax: 928-523-1929, E-mail: jennifer.prior@nau.edu. *Application contact:* Shirley Robinson, Coordinator, 928-523-4348, Fax: 928-523-8950, E-mail: shirley.robinson@nau.edu. Web site: http://nau.edu/coe/ed-specialties/.

Northern Illinois University, Graduate School, College of Education, Department of Educational Technology, Research and Assessment, De Kalb, IL 60115-2854. Offers educational research and evaluation (MS); instructional technology (MS Ed, Ed D). Part-time and evening/weekend programs available. *Faculty:* 13 full-time (7 women). *Students:* 43 full-time (31 women), 114 part-time (72 women); includes 31 minority (17 Black or African American, non-Hispanic/Latino; 8 Asian, non-Hispanic/Latino; 4 Hispanic/Latino; 2 Two or more races, non-Hispanic/Latino), 13 international. Average age 39. 46 applicants, 78% accepted, 23 enrolled. In 2011, 34 master's, 10 doctorates awarded. Terminal master's awarded for partial completion of doctoral program. *Degree requirements:* For master's, comprehensive exam, thesis optional; for doctorate, thesis/dissertation, candidacy exam, dissertation defense. *Entrance requirements:* For master's, GRE General Test or MAT, minimum GPA of 2.75; for doctorate, GRE General Test or MAT, minimum undergraduate GPA of 2.75, 3.2 graduate. Additional exam requirements/recommendations for international students: Required—TOEFL (minimum score 550 paper-based; 213 computer-based). *Application deadline:* For fall admission, 6/1 for domestic students, 5/1 for international students; for spring admission, 11/1 for domestic students, 10/1 for international students. Applications are processed on a rolling basis. Application fee: $40. Electronic applications accepted. *Financial support:* In 2011–12, 5 research assistantships with full tuition reimbursements, 3 teaching assistantships with full tuition reimbursements were awarded; fellowships with full tuition reimbursements, career-related internships or fieldwork, Federal Work-Study, scholarships/grants, tuition waivers (full), and unspecified assistantships also available. Support available to part-time students. Financial award applicants required to submit FAFSA. *Faculty research:* Distance education, Web-based training, copyright assessment during student teaching, instructional software. *Unit head:* Dr. Lara Leutkehans, Chair, 815-753-9339, E-mail: etra@niu.edu. *Application contact:* Graduate School Office, 815-753-0395, E-mail: gradsch@niu.edu. Web site: http://www.cedu.niu.edu/etra/index.html.

Northern State University, Division of Graduate Studies in Education, Center for Statewide E-Learning, Aberdeen, SD 57401-7198. Offers e-learning design and instruction (MS Ed); e-learning technology and administration (MS). Part-time and evening/weekend programs available. *Degree requirements:* For master's, thesis optional. *Entrance requirements:* For master's, minimum GPA of 2.75. Additional exam requirements/recommendations for international students: Required—TOEFL (minimum score 550 paper-based; 213 computer-based; 78 iBT), IELTS (minimum score 6). Electronic applications accepted.

Northwestern State University of Louisiana, Graduate Studies and Research, College of Education and Human Development, Program in Educational Technology Leadership, Natchitoches, LA 71497. Offers M Ed. *Students:* 6 full-time (4 women), 48 part-time (40 women); includes 5 minority (4 Black or African American, non-Hispanic/

Latino; 1 Asian, non-Hispanic/Latino), 1 international. Average age 37. 11 applicants, 100% accepted, 10 enrolled. In 2011, 24 master's awarded. *Degree requirements:* For master's, comprehensive exam, thesis (for some programs). *Entrance requirements:* For master's, GRE General Test. Additional exam requirements/recommendations for international students: Required—TOEFL. *Application deadline:* For fall admission, 3/15 priority date for domestic students; for spring admission, 10/15 priority date for domestic students. Applications are processed on a rolling basis. Application fee: $20 ($30 for international students). Electronic applications accepted. *Expenses:* Tuition, state resident: full-time $3440. Tuition, nonresident: full-time $12,010. *Financial support:* Application deadline: 5/1; applicants required to submit FAFSA. *Unit head:* Dr. Vickie Gentry, Chair, 318-357-6288, Fax: 318-357-6275, E-mail: education@nsula.edu. *Application contact:* Dr. Steven G. Horton, Associate Provost/Dean, Graduate Studies, Research, and Information Systems, 318-357-5851, Fax: 318-357-5019, E-mail: grad_school@nsula.edu.

Northwestern State University of Louisiana, Graduate Studies and Research, College of Education and Human Development, Programs in Educational Leadership and Instruction, Natchitoches, LA 71497. Offers counseling (Ed S); educational leadership (M Ed, Ed S); educational technology (Ed S); elementary teaching (Ed S); reading (Ed S); secondary teaching (Ed S); special education (Ed S). *Accreditation:* NASAD. *Students:* 7 full-time (6 women), 75 part-time (59 women); includes 22 minority (18 Black or African American, non-Hispanic/Latino; 2 American Indian or Alaska Native, non-Hispanic/Latino; 2 Hispanic/Latino). Average age 36. 30 applicants, 97% accepted, 15 enrolled. In 2011, 31 master's, 16 Ed Ss awarded. *Degree requirements:* For master's, comprehensive exam, thesis (for some programs). *Entrance requirements:* For master's and Ed S, GRE General Test. Additional exam requirements/recommendations for international students: Required—TOEFL. *Application deadline:* For fall admission, 3/15 priority date for domestic students; for spring admission, 10/15 priority date for domestic students. Applications are processed on a rolling basis. Application fee: $20 ($30 for international students). Electronic applications accepted. *Expenses:* Tuition, state resident: full-time $3440. Tuition, nonresident: full-time $12,010. *Unit head:* Dr. Vickie Gentry, Chair, 318-357-6288, Fax: 318-357-6275, E-mail: education@nsula.edu. *Application contact:* Dr. Steven G. Horton, Associate Provost/Dean, Graduate Studies, Research, and Information Systems, 318-357-5851, Fax: 318-357-5019, E-mail: grad_school@nsula.edu.

Northwestern University, The Graduate School, School of Education and Social Policy, Program in Learning Sciences, Evanston, IL 60208. Offers MA, PhD. Admissions and degrees offered through The Graduate School. Terminal master's awarded for partial completion of doctoral program. *Degree requirements:* For master's, thesis or alternative, portfolio; for doctorate, thesis/dissertation, qualifying exam. *Entrance requirements:* For doctorate, GRE General Test. Additional exam requirements/recommendations for international students: Required—TOEFL (minimum score 600 paper-based; 250 computer-based; 100 iBT). Electronic applications accepted. *Expenses:* Contact institution. *Faculty research:* Technologically supported learning environments; inquiry-based learning in mathematics, science, and literacy; learning social contexts; cognitive models of learning and problem solving; changing roles for teachers involved in innovative design and practice.

Northwest Missouri State University, Graduate School, Melvin and Valorie Booth College of Business and Professional Studies, Department of Computer Science and Information Systems, Program in Teaching Instructional Technology, Maryville, MO 64468-6001. Offers MS Ed. Part-time programs available. *Faculty:* 10 full-time (6 women). *Students:* 27 part-time (21 women). 7 applicants, 100% accepted, 3 enrolled. In 2011, 9 master's awarded. *Degree requirements:* For master's, comprehensive exam. *Entrance requirements:* For master's, GRE General Test, minimum GPA of 2.5, teaching certificate, writing sample. Additional exam requirements/recommendations for international students: Required—TOEFL (minimum score 550 paper-based; 213 computer-based). *Application deadline:* For fall admission, 7/1 for domestic and international students; for spring admission, 12/1 for domestic students, 11/15 for international students. Applications are processed on a rolling basis. Application fee: $0 ($50 for international students). *Financial support:* Application deadline: 4/1; applicants required to submit FAFSA. *Unit head:* Dr. Jan Glenn, Program Director, 660-562-1721. *Application contact:* Dr. Gregory Haddock, Dean of Graduate School, 660-562-1145, Fax: 660-562-1096, E-mail: gradsch@nwmissouri.edu.

Notre Dame de Namur University, Division of Academic Affairs, School of Education and Leadership, Program in Teacher Education, Belmont, CA 94002-1908. Offers curriculum and instruction (MA); disciplinary studies (MA); educational technology (MA); multiple subject teaching credential (Certificate); single subject teaching credential (Certificate). Part-time and evening/weekend programs available. *Students:* 93 full-time (71 women), 128 part-time (89 women); includes 40 minority (3 Black or African American, non-Hispanic/Latino; 2 American Indian or Alaska Native, non-Hispanic/Latino; 14 Asian, non-Hispanic/Latino; 19 Hispanic/Latino; 1 Native Hawaiian or other Pacific Islander, non-Hispanic/Latino; 1 Two or more races, non-Hispanic/Latino), 2 international. In 2011, 18 master's awarded. *Entrance requirements:* Additional exam requirements/recommendations for international students: Required—TOEFL (minimum score 550 paper-based; 213 computer-based; 79 iBT). Application fee: $60. *Expenses: Tuition:* Full-time $14,220; part-time $790 per credit. *Required fees:* $35 per semester. Tuition and fees vary according to program. *Financial support:* Career-related internships or fieldwork available. Support available to part-time students. Financial award applicants required to submit FAFSA. *Unit head:* Dr. Kim Tolley, Director, 650-508-3464, E-mail: ktolley@ndnu.edu. *Application contact:* Candace Hallmark, Associate Director of Admissions, 650-508-3592, Fax: 650-508-3426, E-mail: grad.admit@ndnu.edu.

Nova Southeastern University, Abraham S. Fischler School of Education, Fort Lauderdale, FL 33314-7796. Offers education (MS, Ed D, Ed S); instructional design and diversity education (MS); instructional technology and distance education (MS); speech language pathology (MS, SLPD); teaching and learning (MA). Part-time and evening/weekend programs available. *Students:* 3,832 full-time (3,039 women), 4,222 part-time (3,452 women); includes 4,795 minority (3,209 Black or African American, non-Hispanic/Latino; 27 American Indian or Alaska Native, non-Hispanic/Latino; 97 Asian, non-Hispanic/Latino; 1,394 Hispanic/Latino; 16 Native Hawaiian or other Pacific Islander, non-Hispanic/Latino; 52 Two or more races, non-Hispanic/Latino), 54 international. Average age 40. In 2011, 1,669 master's, 383 doctorates, 402 other advanced degrees awarded. *Degree requirements:* For master's, practicum, internship; for doctorate, thesis/dissertation; for Ed S, thesis, practicum, internship. *Entrance requirements:* For master's, MAT or GRE (for some programs), CLAST, PRAXIS I, CBEST, General Knowledge Test, teaching certification, minimum GPA of 2.5, verification of teaching, BS; for doctorate, MAT or GRE, master's degree, minimum cumulative GPA of 3.0; for Ed S, MAT or GRE, master's degree, teaching certificate; minimum GPA of 3.0. Additional exam requirements/recommendations for international students: Recommended—TOEFL (minimum score 550 paper-based; 213 computer-based; 80 iBT), IELTS (minimum score 6). *Application deadline:* Applications are processed on a rolling basis. Application fee: $50. Electronic applications accepted. *Financial support:* In 2011–12, 2 fellowships with full tuition reimbursements (averaging $30,000 per year) were awarded; career-related internships or fieldwork, Federal Work-Study, and tuition waivers (full) also available. Support available to part-time students. Financial award application deadline: 4/15; financial award applicants required to submit FAFSA. *Unit head:* Dr. H. Wells Singleton, Provost/Dean, 954-262-8730, Fax: 954-262-3894, E-mail: singlew@nova.edu. *Application contact:* Dr. Jennifer Quinones Nottingham, Dean of Student Affairs, 800-986-3223 Ext. 8500, E-mail: jlquinon@nova.edu. Web site: http://www.fischlerschool.nova.edu/.

Nova Southeastern University, Graduate School of Computer and Information Sciences, Fort Lauderdale, FL 33314-7796. Offers computer information systems (MS, PhD); computer science (MS, PhD); computing technology in education (PhD); information security (MS); information systems (PhD); information technology (MS); information technology in education (MS); management information systems (MS). Part-time and evening/weekend programs available. Postbaccalaureate distance learning degree programs offered (no on-campus study). *Faculty:* 20 full-time (5 women), 21 part-time/adjunct (3 women). *Students:* 130 full-time (37 women), 960 part-time (291 women); includes 496 minority (221 Black or African American, non-Hispanic/Latino; 4 American Indian or Alaska Native, non-Hispanic/Latino; 78 Asian, non-Hispanic/Latino; 178 Hispanic/Latino; 15 Two or more races, non-Hispanic/Latino), 49 international. Average age 41. 486 applicants, 45% accepted. In 2011, 131 master's, 39 doctorates awarded. Terminal master's awarded for partial completion of doctoral program. *Degree requirements:* For master's, thesis optional; for doctorate, thesis/dissertation. *Entrance requirements:* For master's, minimum undergraduate GPA of 2.5; 3.0 in major; for doctorate, master's degree, minimum graduate GPA of 3.25. Additional exam requirements/recommendations for international students: Required—TOEFL (minimum score 213 computer-based; 79 iBT), IELTS (minimum score 6). *Application deadline:* Applications are processed on a rolling basis. Application fee: $50. Electronic applications accepted. *Expenses:* Contact institution. *Financial support:* Federal Work-Study, scholarships/grants, and unspecified assistantships available. Support available to part-time students. Financial award application deadline: 5/1. *Faculty research:* Artificial intelligence, database management, human-computer interaction, distance education, information security. *Unit head:* Dr. Eric S. Ackerman, Interim Dean, 954-262-7300. *Application contact:* 954-262-2000, Fax: 954-262-2752, E-mail: scisinfo@nova.edu. Web site: http://www.scis.nova.edu/.

Oakland University, Graduate Study and Lifelong Learning, School of Education and Human Services, Program in Microcomputer Applications in Education, Rochester, MI 48309-4401. Offers advanced microcomputer applications (Certificate); microcomputer applications (Certificate). *Entrance requirements:* Additional exam requirements/recommendations for international students: Required—TOEFL (minimum score 550 paper-based; 213 computer-based). Electronic applications accepted.

Ohio University, Graduate College, Gladys W. and David H. Patton College of Education and Human Services, Department of Educational Studies, Athens, OH 45701-2979. Offers computer education and technology (M Ed); cultural studies (M Ed); educational administration (M Ed, Ed D); educational research and evaluation (M Ed, PhD); instructional technology (PhD). Part-time and evening/weekend programs available. Postbaccalaureate distance learning degree programs offered (minimal on-campus study). *Students:* 121 full-time (76 women), 94 part-time (57 women); includes 21 minority (15 Black or African American, non-Hispanic/Latino; 1 American Indian or Alaska Native, non-Hispanic/Latino; 2 Hispanic/Latino; 3 Two or more races, non-Hispanic/Latino), 35 international. 73 applicants, 67% accepted, 32 enrolled. In 2011, 52 master's, 13 doctorates awarded. *Degree requirements:* For master's, thesis or alternative; for doctorate, comprehensive exam, thesis/dissertation. *Entrance requirements:* For master's, GRE General Test (if GPA less than 2.9); for doctorate, GRE General Test, GRE Subject Test, minimum GPA of 2.9, work experience, 3 letters of reference, autobiography. Additional exam requirements/recommendations for international students: Required—TOEFL (minimum score 550 paper-based; 80 iBT) or IELTS (minimum score 6.5). *Application deadline:* For fall admission, 3/1 priority date for domestic students, 3/1 for international students; for winter admission, 10/1 priority date for domestic students, 10/1 for international students; for spring admission, 1/30 priority date for domestic students, 1/1 for international students. Applications are processed on a rolling basis. Application fee: $50 ($55 for international students). Electronic applications accepted. *Financial support:* Research assistantships with full tuition reimbursements, teaching assistantships with full tuition reimbursements, Federal Work-Study, institutionally sponsored loans, tuition waivers (partial), and unspecified assistantships available. Financial award application deadline: 3/1. *Faculty research:* Race, class and gender; computer programs; development and organization theory; evaluation/development of instruments, leadership. *Total annual research expenditures:* $158,037. *Unit head:* Dr. David Richard Moore, Chair, 740-597-1322, Fax: 740-593-0477, E-mail: moored3@ohio.edu. *Application contact:* Floyd J. Doney, Director of Student Affairs, 740-593-4400, Fax: 740-593-9310, E-mail: doney@ohio.edu. Web site: http://www.cehs.ohio.edu/academics/es/.

Old Dominion University, Darden College of Education, Program in Elementary/Middle Education, Norfolk, VA 23529. Offers elementary education (MS Ed); instructional technology (MS Ed); library science (MS Ed); middle school education (MS Ed). *Accreditation:* NCATE. Part-time and evening/weekend programs available. Postbaccalaureate distance learning degree programs offered (no on-campus study). *Faculty:* 18 full-time (16 women), 34 part-time/adjunct (27 women). *Students:* 151 full-time (140 women), 118 part-time (96 women); includes 53 minority (27 Black or African American, non-Hispanic/Latino; 3 Asian, non-Hispanic/Latino; 10 Hispanic/Latino; 2 Native Hawaiian or other Pacific Islander, non-Hispanic/Latino; 11 Two or more races, non-Hispanic/Latino). Average age 31. 291 applicants, 50% accepted, 123 enrolled. In 2011, 167 master's awarded. *Degree requirements:* For master's, comprehensive exam. *Entrance requirements:* For master's, GRE General Test or MAT; PRAXIS I, SAT or ACT, minimum GPA of 2.8. Additional exam requirements/recommendations for international students: Required—TOEFL (minimum score 600 paper-based; 250 computer-based). *Application deadline:* For fall admission, 6/1 priority date for domestic students; for winter admission, 11/1 priority date for domestic students; for spring admission, 3/1 priority date for domestic students. Applications are processed on a rolling basis. Application fee: $50. Electronic applications accepted. *Expenses:* Tuition, state resident: full-time $9096; part-time $379 per credit. Tuition, nonresident: full-time $23,064; part-time $961 per credit. *Required fees:* $127 per semester. One-time fee: $50. *Financial support:* In 2011–12, 180 students received support, including teaching assistantships (averaging $9,000 per year); career-related internships or fieldwork, Federal Work-Study, institutionally sponsored loans, and scholarships/grants also available. Support available to part-time students. Financial award application deadline: 2/15; financial award applicants required to submit FAFSA. *Faculty research:* Education pre-K to 6, school librarianship. *Unit head:* Dr. Lea Lee, Graduate Program Director, 757-683-4801, Fax: 757-683-5862, E-mail: lxlee@odu.edu. *Application contact:* William Heffelfinger, Director of Graduate Admissions, 757-683-5554, Fax: 757-683-3255, E-mail: gradadmit@odu.edu. Web site: http://education.odu.edu/eci/.

Old Dominion University, Darden College of Education, Program in Instructional Design and Technology, Norfolk, VA 23529. Offers PhD. Part-time and evening/weekend programs available. Postbaccalaureate distance learning degree programs offered (no on-campus study). *Faculty:* 6 full-time (3 women). *Students:* 8 full-time (2 women), 60 part-time (36 women); includes 9 minority (8 Black or African American, non-Hispanic/Latino; 1 Hispanic/Latino), 4 international. Average age 42. 30 applicants, 43% accepted, 13 enrolled. In 2011, 2 doctorates awarded. *Degree requirements:* For doctorate, comprehensive exam, thesis/dissertation. *Entrance requirements:* For doctorate, GRE, references, interview, essay of 500 words. Additional exam requirements/recommendations for international students: Required—TOEFL (minimum score 550 paper-based; 213 computer-based). *Application deadline:* For fall admission, 6/1 priority date for domestic students, 2/1 for international students; for winter admission, 11/1 priority date for domestic students, 11/1 for international students. Applications are processed on a rolling basis. Application fee: $50. Electronic applications accepted. *Expenses:* Tuition, state resident: full-time $9096; part-time $379 per credit. Tuition, nonresident: full-time $23,064; part-time $961 per credit. *Required fees:* $127 per semester. One-time fee: $50. *Financial support:* In 2011–12, 4 students received support, including 3 research assistantships with full tuition reimbursements available (averaging $15,000 per year); career-related internships or fieldwork and unspecified assistantships also available. Financial award application deadline: 2/15; financial award applicants required to submit FAFSA. *Faculty research:* Instructional design, cognitive load, distance education, pedagogical agents, human performance technology, gaming, simulation design, distance education. *Total annual research expenditures:* $2 million. *Unit head:* Dr. Gary R. Morrison, Graduate Program Director, 757-683-4305, Fax: 757-683-5227, E-mail: gmorriso@odu.edu. *Application contact:* Alice McAdory, Director of Admissions, 757-683-3685, Fax: 757-683-3255, E-mail: gradadmit@odu.edu. Web site: http://education.odu.edu/eci/idt.

Old Dominion University, Darden College of Education, Programs in Secondary Education, Norfolk, VA 23529. Offers biology (MS Ed); chemistry (MS Ed); English (MS Ed); instructional technology (MS Ed); library science (MS Ed); secondary education (MS Ed). *Accreditation:* NCATE. Part-time and evening/weekend programs available. Postbaccalaureate distance learning degree programs offered (minimal on-campus study). *Faculty:* 20 full-time (16 women). *Students:* 82 full-time (49 women), 95 part-time (63 women); includes 37 minority (21 Black or African American, non-Hispanic/Latino; 3 Asian, non-Hispanic/Latino; 8 Hispanic/Latino; 5 Two or more races, non-Hispanic/Latino), 1 international. Average age 32. 67 applicants, 79% accepted, 53 enrolled. In 2011, 84 degrees awarded. *Degree requirements:* For master's, comprehensive exam, thesis. *Entrance requirements:* For master's, GRE General Test or MAT, PRAXIS I (for licensure), minimum GPA of 2.8, teaching certificate. Additional exam requirements/recommendations for international students: Required—TOEFL. *Application deadline:* For fall admission, 6/1 for domestic and international students; for winter admission, 11/1 for domestic and international students; for spring admission, 3/1 for domestic and international students. Applications are processed on a rolling basis. Application fee: $50. Electronic applications accepted. *Expenses:* Tuition, state resident: full-time $9096; part-time $379 per credit. Tuition, nonresident: full-time $23,064; part-time $961 per credit. *Required fees:* $127 per semester. One-time fee: $50. *Financial support:* In 2011–12, 56 students received support, including fellowships (averaging $15,000 per year), 2 research assistantships with tuition reimbursements available (averaging $9,000 per year), 3 teaching assistantships with tuition reimbursements available (averaging $12,500 per year); career-related internships or fieldwork, Federal Work-Study, institutionally sponsored loans, scholarships/grants, and tuition waivers (partial) also available. Support available to part-time students. Financial award application deadline: 2/15; financial award applicants required to submit FAFSA. *Faculty research:* Use of technology, writing project for teachers, geography teaching, reading. *Unit head:* Dr. Robert Lucking, Graduate Program Director, 757-683-5545, Fax: 757-683-5862, E-mail: rlucking@odu.edu. *Application contact:* William Heffelfinger, Director of Graduate Admissions, 757-683-5554, Fax: 757-683-3255, E-mail: gradadmit@odu.edu. Web site: http://education.odu.edu/eci/secondary/.

Ottawa University, Graduate Studies-Arizona, Program in Education, Ottawa, KS 66067-3399. Offers community college counseling (MA); curriculum and instruction (MA); early childhood (MA); education intervention (MA); education leadership (MA); education technology (MA); Montessori early childhood education (MA); Montessori elementary education (MA); professional development (MA); school guidance counseling (MA); special education - cross categorical (MA). Programs offered in Mesa, Phoenix, Tempe and West Valley, AZ. *Accreditation:* NCATE. Part-time programs available. *Degree requirements:* For master's, thesis or alternative. *Entrance requirements:* For master's, minimum undergraduate GPA of 3.0, copy of current state certification or teaching license. Additional exam requirements/recommendations for international students: Required—TOEFL (minimum score 550 paper-based; 213 computer-based). Electronic applications accepted. *Expenses:* Contact institution.

Our Lady of the Lake University of San Antonio, School of Professional Studies, Program in Learning Resources Specialist, San Antonio, TX 78207-4689. Offers M Ed. Part-time and evening/weekend programs available. *Degree requirements:* For master's, comprehensive exam. *Entrance requirements:* For master's, GRE General Test or MAT. Additional exam requirements/recommendations for international students: Required—TOEFL. Electronic applications accepted. *Faculty research:* Automation and libraries, electronic books.

Pace University, School of Education, New York, NY 10038. Offers adolescent education (MST); childhood education (MST); educational leadership (MS Ed); educational technology studies (MS); literacy (MSE); school business management (Certificate); special education (MS Ed); teaching students with disabilities (MSE). *Accreditation:* NCATE. Part-time and evening/weekend programs available. *Students:* 164 full-time (131 women), 533 part-time (396 women); includes 157 minority (59 Black or African American, non-Hispanic/Latino; 2 American Indian or Alaska Native, non-Hispanic/Latino; 26 Asian, non-Hispanic/Latino; 54 Hispanic/Latino; 1 Native Hawaiian or other Pacific Islander, non-Hispanic/Latino; 15 Two or more races, non-Hispanic/Latino), 10 international. Average age 29. 256 applicants, 79% accepted, 114 enrolled. In 2011, 334 master's, 34 other advanced degrees awarded. *Degree requirements:* For master's, internship. *Entrance requirements:* For master's, interview, teaching certificate. Additional exam requirements/recommendations for international students: Required—TOEFL. *Application deadline:* For fall admission, 7/31 priority date for domestic students; for spring admission, 11/30 for domestic students. Applications are processed on a rolling basis. Application fee: $70. Electronic applications accepted. *Expenses:* Contact institution. *Financial support:* Research assistantships, career-related internships or fieldwork, and Federal Work-Study available. Support available to part-time students. Financial award applicants required to submit FAFSA. *Unit head:* Dr. Andrea M. Spencer, Dean, 212-346-1345, E-mail: aspencer@pace.edu. *Application contact:* Susan Ford-Goldschein, Director of Admissions, 212-346-1660, Fax: 212-346-1585, E-mail: gradnyc@pace.edu. Web site: http://www.pace.edu/.

Penn State University Park, Graduate School, College of Education, Department of Learning and Performance Systems, State College, University Park, PA 16802-1503. Offers adult education (M Ed, D Ed, PhD, Certificate); instructional systems (M Ed, MS, D Ed, PhD); workforce education and development (M Ed, MS, PhD). *Unit head:* Dr. David H. Monk, Dean, 814-865-2526, Fax: 814-865-0555, E-mail: dhm6@psu.edu. *Application contact:* Cynthia E. Nicosia, Director, Graduate Enrollment Services, 814-865-1834, E-mail: cey1@psu.edu. Web site: http://www.ed.psu.edu/educ/lps/dept-lps.

Pepperdine University, Graduate School of Education and Psychology, Division of Education, Ed D Program in Learning Technologies, Malibu, CA 90263. Offers Ed D. Part-time and evening/weekend programs available. Postbaccalaureate distance learning degree programs offered (minimal on-campus study). *Entrance requirements:* For doctorate, MAT or GRE verbal and quantitative sections (all taken within last five years), two recommendations; three-part statement describing vision for technology, experience/background in technology, and personal goals related to pursuit of degree (minimum of 2,000 words); personal interview. Additional exam requirements/recommendations for international students: Required—TOEFL.

Pepperdine University, Graduate School of Education and Psychology, Division of Education, MA Program in Learning Technologies, Malibu, CA 90263. Offers MA. Part-time and evening/weekend programs available. Postbaccalaureate distance learning degree programs offered (minimal on-campus study). *Entrance requirements:* For master's, personal interviews; two letters of recommendation; three-part statement describing vision for technology in educational settings, experience/background in technology, and personal goals related to pursuit of degree (minimum of 2000 words). Additional exam requirements/recommendations for international students: Required—TOEFL. *Expenses:* Contact institution.

Pittsburg State University, Graduate School, College of Education, Department of Special Services and Leadership Studies, Program in Educational Technology, Pittsburg, KS 66762. Offers MS. *Accreditation:* NCATE. *Degree requirements:* For master's, thesis or alternative. *Entrance requirements:* For master's, GRE General Test or MAT.

Portland State University, Graduate Studies, School of Education, Department of Curriculum and Instruction, Portland, OR 97207-0751. Offers early childhood education (MA, MS); education (M Ed, MA, MS); educational leadership: curriculum and instruction (Ed D); educational media/school librarianship (MA, MS); elementary education (M Ed, MAT, MST); reading (MA, MS); secondary education (M Ed, MAT, MST). *Accreditation:* NCATE. Part-time programs available. *Degree requirements:* For master's, comprehensive exam, thesis or alternative; for doctorate, thesis/dissertation. *Entrance requirements:* For master's, California Basic Educational Skills Test, minimum GPA of 3.0 in upper-division course work or 2.75 overall. Additional exam requirements/recommendations for international students: Required—TOEFL (minimum score 550 paper-based; 213 computer-based). *Faculty research:* Early literacy, characteristics of successful teachers of at-risk students, participation of women/minorities in technology courses, selection of cooperating teachers.

Post University, Program in Education, Waterbury, CT 06723-2540. Offers education (M Ed); instructional design and technology (M Ed); teaching and learning (M Ed). Postbaccalaureate distance learning degree programs offered.

Purdue University, Graduate School, College of Education, Department of Curriculum and Instruction, West Lafayette, IN 47907. Offers agricultural and extension education (PhD, Ed S); agriculture and extension education (MS, MS Ed); art education (PhD); consumer and family sciences and extension education (MS Ed, PhD, Ed S); curriculum studies (MS Ed, PhD, Ed S); educational technology (MS Ed, PhD, Ed S); elementary education (MS Ed); foreign language education (MS Ed, PhD, Ed S); industrial technology (PhD, Ed S); language arts (MS Ed, PhD, Ed S); literacy (MS Ed, PhD, Ed S); mathematics/science education (MS, MS Ed, PhD, Ed S); social studies (MS Ed, PhD); social studies education (Ed S); vocational/industrial education (MS Ed, PhD, Ed S); vocational/technical education (MS Ed, PhD, Ed S). *Accreditation:* NCATE. Part-time and evening/weekend programs available. *Faculty:* 30 full-time (21 women), 1 (woman) part-time/adjunct. *Students:* 89 full-time (64 women), 134 part-time (84 women); includes 31 minority (12 Black or African American, non-Hispanic/Latino; 3 American Indian or Alaska Native, non-Hispanic/Latino; 7 Asian, non-Hispanic/Latino; 9 Hispanic/Latino), 49 international. Average age 36. 136 applicants, 83% accepted, 72 enrolled. In 2011, 26 master's, 13 doctorates awarded. *Degree requirements:* For master's, thesis optional; for doctorate, thesis/dissertation, oral and written exams; for Ed S, oral presentation, project. *Entrance requirements:* For master's, GRE general test is required if undergraduate GPA is below 3.0, minimum undergraduate GPA of 3.0 or equivalent; for doctorate, GRE General Test, a combined GRE verbal and quantitative score of 1000 (300 for revised GRE Test) or more is expected, minimum undergraduate GPA of 3.0 or equivalent; master's degree with minimum GPA of 3.0 or equivalent; for Ed S, GRE general test, a combined GRE verbal and quantitative score of 1000 (300 for revised GRE Test) or more is expected, minimum undergraduate GPA of 3.0 or equivalent; master's degree. Additional exam requirements/recommendations for international students: Required—TOEFL (minimum score 550 paper-based; 77 iBT). *Application deadline:* For fall admission, 12/15 priority date for domestic students, 3/1 for international students; for spring admission, 9/15 for domestic students, 8/1 for international students. Application fee: $60 ($75 for international students). Electronic applications accepted. *Financial support:* Fellowships with full tuition reimbursements, research assistantships with full tuition reimbursements, teaching assistantships with full tuition reimbursements, career-related internships or fieldwork, and tuition waivers (full) available. Support available to part-time students. Financial award application deadline: 3/1; financial award applicants required to submit FAFSA. *Faculty research:* Literacy acquisition and development, teacher beliefs and knowledge, recruitment and retention of underrepresented students, economic education, literacy discourse. *Unit head:* Dr. Philip J. VanFossen, Head, 765-494-7935, Fax: 765-496-1622, E-mail: vanfoss@purdue.edu. *Application contact:* Sarah N. Prater, Graduate Contact, 765-494-2345, Fax: 765-494-5832, E-mail: prater0@purdue.edu. Web site: http://www.edci.purdue.edu/.

Purdue University, Graduate School, College of Technology, West Lafayette, IN 47907. Offers MS, PhD. Postbaccalaureate distance learning degree programs offered. *Faculty:* 141 full-time (26 women), 3 part-time/adjunct (0 women). *Students:* 213 full-time (71 women), 246 part-time (66 women); includes 61 minority (28 Black or African American, non-Hispanic/Latino; 2 American Indian or Alaska Native, non-Hispanic/Latino; 10 Asian, non-Hispanic/Latino; 17 Hispanic/Latino; 4 Two or more races, non-Hispanic/Latino), 104 international. Average age 32. 441 applicants, 55% accepted, 155 enrolled. In 2011, 96 master's, 10 doctorates awarded. *Degree requirements:* For master's, oral exam. *Entrance requirements:* For master's, GRE, minimum GPA of 3.0; for doctorate, GRE. Additional exam requirements/recommendations for international students: Required—TOEFL. *Application deadline:* Applications are processed on a rolling basis. Application fee: $60 ($75 for international students). Electronic applications accepted. *Financial support:* In 2011–12, 37 teaching assistantships were awarded; fellowships also available. Support available to part-time students. Financial award applicants required to submit FAFSA. *Unit head:* Dr. Gary R. Bertoline, Dean, 765-496-6071, E-mail: bertoline@purdue.edu.

Purdue University Calumet, Graduate Studies Office, School of Education, Program in Instructional Technology, Hammond, IN 46323-2094. Offers MS Ed. *Entrance requirements:* Additional exam requirements/recommendations for international students: Required—TOEFL.

Ramapo College of New Jersey, Master of Science in Educational Technology Program, Mahwah, NJ 07430. Offers MS. Part-time programs available. *Faculty:* 10 part-time/adjunct (6 women). *Students:* 2 full-time (1 woman), 73 part-time (48 women); includes 9 minority (2 Black or African American, non-Hispanic/Latino; 1 American Indian or Alaska Native, non-Hispanic/Latino; 2 Asian, non-Hispanic/Latino; 4 Hispanic/

Latino). Average age 34. 42 applicants, 86% accepted, 28 enrolled. In 2011, 73 master's awarded. *Degree requirements:* For master's, 34 semester credits with 18 in required courses. *Entrance requirements:* For master's, interview; 2 letters of reference; immunizations; official transcript from accredited higher education institution with minimum cumulative GPA of 3.0; essay describing interest in MSET program and personal intellectual goals. Additional exam requirements/recommendations for international students: Required—TOEFL (minimum score 550 paper-based; 213 computer-based; 90 iBT). *Application deadline:* For fall admission, 9/1 priority date for domestic students, 9/1 for international students; for spring admission, 1/29 priority date for domestic students, 1/30 for international students. Applications are processed on a rolling basis. Application fee: $60. Electronic applications accepted. *Expenses: Tuition, area resident:* Part-time $551.05 per credit. Tuition, nonresident: part-time $708.30 per credit. *Required fees:* $122.50 per credit. *Financial support:* Scholarships/grants available. Financial award application deadline: 3/1; financial award applicants required to submit FAFSA. *Faculty research:* Integrity technology in the curriculum of K-12 learning environment. *Unit head:* Dr. Angela Cristini, Dean/Executive Director of Special Programs, Office Of The Provost, 201-684-7721, Fax: 201-684-6699, E-mail: acristin@ramapo.edu. *Application contact:* Joyce Wilson, Administrative Assistant, 201-684-7721, Fax: 201-684-6699, E-mail: mlafayet@ramapo.edu. Web site: http://www.ramapo.edu/catalog_09_10/mset.html.

Regis University, College for Professional Studies, School of Education and Counseling, Department of Education, Denver, CO 80221-1099. Offers adult learning, training, and development (M Ed, Certificate); autism (Certificate); curriculum, instruction, and assessment (M Ed); educational leadership (Certificate); educational technology (Certificate); instructional technology (M Ed); literacy (Certificate); professional leadership (M Ed); reading (M Ed); self-designed (M Ed); space studies (M Ed). Program also offered in Henderson and Las Vegas (Summerlin), NV. *Accreditation:* Teacher Education Accreditation Council. Part-time and evening/weekend programs available. Postbaccalaureate distance learning degree programs offered (no on-campus study). *Degree requirements:* For master's, thesis. *Entrance requirements:* For master's, resume, minimum GPA of 2.75, criminal background check. Additional exam requirements/recommendations for international students: Required—TOEFL (minimum score 213 computer-based), TWE (minimum score 5). Electronic applications accepted. *Faculty research:* Issues of equity in the middle school classroom, professional learning communities, school reform, socialinguistic and discursive obstacles to student integration, inclusive language arts curriculum.

The Richard Stockton College of New Jersey, School of Graduate and Continuing Studies, Program in Instructional Technology, Pomona, NJ 08240-0195. Offers MA. Part-time and evening/weekend programs available. *Faculty:* 3 full-time (2 women), 3 part-time/adjunct (2 women). *Students:* 76 part-time (48 women); includes 5 minority (1 Black or African American, non-Hispanic/Latino; 1 Asian, non-Hispanic/Latino; 2 Hispanic/Latino; 1 Two or more races, non-Hispanic/Latino), 1 international. Average age 39. 20 applicants, 85% accepted, 14 enrolled. In 2011, 20 master's awarded. *Degree requirements:* For master's, final project. *Entrance requirements:* For master's, GRE or MAT, minimum GPA of 3.0. Additional exam requirements/recommendations for international students: Required—TOEFL. *Application deadline:* For fall admission, 7/1 priority date for domestic students, 7/1 for international students; for spring admission, 12/1 for domestic students, 12/5 for international students. Applications are processed on a rolling basis. Application fee: $50. Electronic applications accepted. *Expenses:* Tuition, state resident: full-time $13,035; part-time $543 per credit. Tuition, nonresident: full-time $20,065; part-time $836 per credit. *Required fees:* $3920; $163 per credit. Tuition and fees vary according to degree level. *Financial support:* In 2011–12, 7 students received support, including 1 fellowship, 11 research assistantships with partial tuition reimbursements available; career-related internships or fieldwork, Federal Work-Study, scholarships/grants, and unspecified assistantships also available. Support available to part-time students. Financial award application deadline: 3/1; financial award applicants required to submit FAFSA. *Faculty research:* Ethics, digital imaging, virtual reality in the classroom, 3-D art in multimedia, technology projects for job-skills training, community computing networks. *Unit head:* Dr. Amy Ackerman, Director, 609-626-3640, E-mail: mait@stockton.edu. *Application contact:* Tara Williams, Assistant Director of Graduate Enrollment, 609-626-3640, Fax: 609-626-6050, E-mail: gradschool@stockton.edu. Web site: http://www.stockton.edu/grad.

Sacred Heart University, Graduate Programs, Isabelle Farrington College of Education, Fairfield, CT 06825-1000. Offers administration (CAS); educational technology (MAT); elementary education (MAT); reading (CAS); secondary education (MAT); teaching (CAS). Part-time and evening/weekend programs available. Postbaccalaureate distance learning degree programs offered (minimal on-campus study). *Degree requirements:* For master's, thesis or alternative. *Entrance requirements:* For master's, PRAXIS (teacher certification/MAT); for CAS, PRAXIS I. Additional exam requirements/recommendations for international students: Required—TOEFL (minimum score 550 paper-based; 213 computer-based). Electronic applications accepted. *Expenses:* Contact institution. *Faculty research:* Reading education, learning theory, teacher preparation, education of underachievers.

Saginaw Valley State University, College of Education, Program in Instructional Technology, University Center, MI 48710. Offers MAT. Part-time and evening/weekend programs available. *Students:* 11 full-time (6 women), 63 part-time (42 women); includes 6 minority (3 Black or African American, non-Hispanic/Latino; 1 American Indian or Alaska Native, non-Hispanic/Latino; 1 Asian, non-Hispanic/Latino; 1 Hispanic/Latino), 6 international. Average age 34. 14 applicants, 100% accepted, 10 enrolled. In 2011, 4 master's awarded. *Entrance requirements:* Additional exam requirements/recommendations for international students: Required—TOEFL (minimum score 525 paper-based; 197 computer-based; 71 iBT). Application fee: $25. *Expenses:* Tuition, state resident: full-time $8300; part-time $5333 per year. Tuition, nonresident: full-time $15,613; part-time $10,209 per year. *International tuition:* $15,631 full-time. *Financial support:* Federal Work-Study and scholarships/grants available. Support available to part-time students. Financial award applicants required to submit FAFSA. *Unit head:* Dr. Steve P. Barbus, Jr., Dean, 989-964-6067, Fax: 989-790-4385, E-mail: barbus@svsu.edu. *Application contact:* Kathy Lopez, Certification Officer, 989-964-4661, Fax: 989-964-4385, E-mail: klopez@svsu.edu.

St. Cloud State University, School of Graduate Studies, School of Education, Center for Information Media, St. Cloud, MN 56301-4498. Offers MS. Postbaccalaureate distance learning degree programs offered (no on-campus study). *Faculty:* 11 full-time (5 women), 6 part-time/adjunct (3 women). *Students:* 6 full-time (5 women), 26 part-time (16 women), 10 international. 8 applicants, 100% accepted. In 2011, 8 master's awarded. *Degree requirements:* For master's, comprehensive exam, thesis or alternative. *Entrance requirements:* For master's, minimum GPA of 2.75. Additional exam requirements/recommendations for international students: Required—Michigan English Language Assessment Battery; Recommended—TOEFL (minimum score 550 paper-based; 213 computer-based), IELTS (minimum score 6.5). *Application deadline:* For fall admission, 6/1 priority date for domestic students, 4/1 for international students; for spring admission, 10/1 priority date for domestic students, 8/1 for international students. Applications are processed on a rolling basis. Application fee: $35. Electronic applications accepted. *Financial support:* Federal Work-Study, scholarships/grants, and unspecified assistantships available. Financial award application deadline: 3/1. *Unit head:* Dr. Marcia Thompson, Graduate Coordinator, 320-308-2120, E-mail: mthompson@stcloudstate.edu. *Application contact:* Linda Lou Krueger, School of Graduate Studies, 320-308-2113, Fax: 320-308-5371, E-mail: lekrueger@stcloudstate.edu.

St. Edward's University, School of Education, Program in Teaching, Austin, TX 78704. Offers curriculum leadership (Certificate); instructional technology (Certificate); mediation (Certificate); mentoring and supervision (Certificate); special education (Certificate); sports management (Certificate); teaching (MA), including conflict resolution, initial teacher certification, liberal arts, special education, sports management, teacher leadership. Part-time and evening/weekend programs available. *Students:* 1 full-time (0 women), 32 part-time (22 women); includes 14 minority (2 Black or African American, non-Hispanic/Latino; 1 Asian, non-Hispanic/Latino; 10 Hispanic/Latino; 1 Two or more races, non-Hispanic/Latino), 1 international. Average age 32. 8 applicants, 75% accepted, 6 enrolled. In 2011, 13 master's awarded. *Degree requirements:* For master's, minimum of 24 resident hours. *Entrance requirements:* For master's, GRE General Test, minimum GPA of 3.0 in last 60 hours or 2.75 overall. Additional exam requirements/recommendations for international students: Required—TOEFL (minimum score 550 paper-based; 213 computer-based; 79 iBT) or IELTS (minimum score 6). *Application deadline:* For fall admission, 7/1 for domestic and international students; for spring admission, 11/1 for domestic and international students. Applications are processed on a rolling basis. Application fee: $45 ($50 for international students). Electronic applications accepted. *Expenses: Tuition:* Full-time $17,550; part-time $975 per credit hour. *Required fees:* $50 per trimester. Full-time tuition and fees vary according to course load and program. *Unit head:* Dr. David Hollier, Director, 512-448-8666, Fax: 512-428-1372, E-mail: davidrh@stedwards.edu. *Application contact:* Sarah Hennes, Graduate Admission Coordinator, 512-448-8600, Fax: 512-428-1032, E-mail: sarahhe@stedwards.edu. Web site: http://www.stedwards.edu.

Saint Joseph's University, College of Arts and Sciences, Department of Education, Philadelphia, PA 19131-1395. Offers curriculum supervisor of instruction (Certificate); educational leadership (MS, Ed D); elementary education (MS, Certificate); elementary/middle years (Certificate); English second language specialist online (Certificate); hearing impaired: N-12th grade (Certificate); instructional technology (MS, Certificate); principal certification (Certificate); professional education (MS); reading specialist (MS, Certificate); reading supervisory (Certificate); secondary education (MS, Certificate); special education (MS, Certificate); superintendent's letter of eligibility (Certificate); supervisor of special education (Certificate); Wilson reading certificate online (Certificate). Part-time and evening/weekend programs available. Postbaccalaureate distance learning degree programs offered (no on-campus study). *Faculty:* 26 full-time (24 women), 83 part-time/adjunct (52 women). *Students:* 112 full-time (92 women), 923 part-time (709 women); includes 147 minority (92 Black or African American, non-Hispanic/Latino; 4 American Indian or Alaska Native, non-Hispanic/Latino; 19 Asian, non-Hispanic/Latino; 28 Hispanic/Latino; 4 Two or more races, non-Hispanic/Latino), 8 international. Average age 31. 285 applicants, 77% accepted, 176 enrolled. In 2011, 276 master's, 13 doctorates, 2 other advanced degrees awarded. *Entrance requirements:* For master's, 2 letters of recommendation, minimum GPA of 3.0, official transcripts, personal statement; for doctorate, GRE, master's degree from accredited institution, minimum graduate GPA of 3.5, computer competence, commitment to participate in cohort, interview with program director. Additional exam requirements/recommendations for international students: Required—TOEFL (minimum score 550 paper-based; 213 computer-based; 79 iBT). *Application deadline:* For fall admission, 7/15 priority date for domestic students, 4/15 for international students; for winter admission, 11/15 for domestic students, 1/15 for international students; for spring admission, 11/15 priority date for domestic students, 10/15 for international students. Applications are processed on a rolling basis. Application fee: $35. Electronic applications accepted. *Expenses:* Contact institution. *Financial support:* Unspecified assistantships available. Financial award applicants required to submit FAFSA. *Faculty research:* Public education professional development, factors predicting early mathematics skills for low income children. *Total annual research expenditures:* $92,975. *Unit head:* Dr. Jeanne Brady, Associate Dean, Education, 610-660-1580, E-mail: jebrady@sju.edu. *Application contact:* Kate McConnell, Director, Graduate College of Arts and Sciences Admissions and Retention, 610-660-3184, Fax: 610-660-3230, E-mail: kate.mcconnell@sju.edu.

Saint Leo University, Graduate Studies in Education, Saint Leo, FL 33574-6665. Offers educational leadership (M Ed); exceptional student education (M Ed); higher education leadership (Ed S); instructional design (MS); instructional leadership (M Ed); reading (M Ed); school leadership (Ed S). Part-time and evening/weekend programs available. Postbaccalaureate distance learning degree programs offered (minimal on-campus study). *Faculty:* 14 full-time (10 women), 21 part-time/adjunct (16 women). *Students:* 523 full-time (427 women), 20 part-time (17 women); includes 65 minority (43 Black or African American, non-Hispanic/Latino; 2 Asian, non-Hispanic/Latino; 16 Hispanic/Latino; 4 Two or more races, non-Hispanic/Latino), 3 international. Average age 37. In 2011, 153 master's, 18 other advanced degrees awarded. *Degree requirements:* For master's, comprehensive exam, appropriate State of Florida certification tests. *Entrance requirements:* For master's, GRE (minimum score of 1000) or MAT (minimum score of 410) if undergraduate GPA for last 60 hours of coursework was below 3.0 (for M Ed), bachelor's degree with minimum GPA of 3.0 for last 60 hours of coursework from regionally-accredited college or university, 2 recommendations, resume, statement of professional goals, copy of valid teaching certificate (for M Ed); for Ed S, GRE (minimum score 1000) or MAT (minimum score 410) if undergraduate GPA for last 60 hours of coursework less than 3.0, bachelor's degree with minimum GPA of 3.0 for last 60 hours of coursework from regionally-accredited college or university, 2 recommendations, resume, valid teaching certificate. Additional exam requirements/recommendations for international students: Required—TOEFL (minimum score 550 paper-based; 213 computer-based; 80 iBT). *Application deadline:* For fall admission, 7/1 priority date for domestic students, 7/1 for international students; for winter admission, 7/1 for international students; for spring admission, 11/1 priority date for domestic students. Applications are processed on a rolling basis. Application fee: $80. Electronic applications accepted. *Expenses:* Contact institution. *Financial support:* In 2011–12, 20 students received support. Career-related internships or fieldwork, Federal Work-Study, scholarships/grants, and health care benefits available. Financial award application deadline: 3/1; financial award applicants required to submit FAFSA. *Faculty research:* The role of the school leader in data analysis of student achievement, teacher recruitment, teacher effectiveness. *Unit head:* Dr. Sharyn Disabato, Director, 352-588-8309, Fax: 352-588-8861, E-mail: med@saintleo.edu. *Application contact:* Jared Welling, Director of Graduate Admission, 800-707-8846, Fax: 352-588-7873, E-mail: grad.admissions@saintleo.edu. Web site: http://www.saintleo.edu/Academics/School-of-Education-Social-Services/Graduate-Degree-Programs.

Saint Michael's College, Graduate Programs, Program in Education, Colchester, VT 05439. Offers administration (M Ed, CAGS); arts in education (CAGS); curriculum and instruction (M Ed, CAGS); information technology (CAGS); reading (M Ed); special education (M Ed, CAGS); technology (M Ed). Part-time and evening/weekend programs available. *Degree requirements:* For master's, thesis. *Entrance requirements:* For master's, minimum GPA of 3.0. Electronic applications accepted. *Faculty research:*

Integrative curriculum, moral and spiritual dimensions of education, learning styles, multiple intelligences, integrating technology into the curriculum.

St. Thomas University, School of Leadership Studies, Institute for Education, Miami Gardens, FL 33054-6459. Offers earth/space science (Certificate); educational administration (MS, Certificate); educational leadership (Ed D); elementary education (MS); ESOL (Certificate); gifted education (Certificate); instructional technology (MS, Certificate); professional/studies (Certificate); reading (MS, Certificate); special education (MS). Part-time and evening/weekend programs available. *Degree requirements:* For master's, comprehensive exam; for doctorate, comprehensive exam, thesis/dissertation. *Entrance requirements:* For master's, interview, minimum GPA of 3.0 or GRE; for doctorate, GRE or MAT. Additional exam requirements/recommendations for international students: Required—TOEFL (minimum score 550 paper-based; 213 computer-based; 79 iBT). Electronic applications accepted.

Saint Vincent College, Program in Education, Latrobe, PA 15650-2690. Offers curriculum and instruction (MS); educational media and technology (MS); environmental education (MS); school administration and supervision (MS); special education (MS). Part-time and evening/weekend programs available. *Degree requirements:* For master's, comprehensive exam. *Entrance requirements:* For master's, GRE (if undergraduate GPA less than 3.0). Additional exam requirements/recommendations for international students: Required—TOEFL (minimum score 550 paper-based; 213 computer-based). *Faculty research:* Assessment and instructional technology.

Saint Xavier University, Graduate Studies, School of Education, Chicago, IL 60655-3105. Offers counseling (MA); curriculum and instruction (MA); early childhood education (MA); educational administration (MA); elementary education (MA); individualized studies (MA), including educational technology, English as a second language (ESL), ISTEM (integrative science, technology, engineering, and math), science education; music education (MA); reading (MA); secondary education (MA); Spanish education (MA); special education (MA); teaching and leadership (MA). *Accreditation:* NCATE. Part-time and evening/weekend programs available. *Degree requirements:* For master's, thesis or project. *Entrance requirements:* For master's, minimum GPA of 3.0. *Application deadline:* For fall admission, 8/15 priority date for domestic students. Applications are processed on a rolling basis. Application fee: $35. *Expenses:* Contact institution. *Financial support:* Career-related internships or fieldwork available. Support available to part-time students. Financial award applicants required to submit FAFSA. *Unit head:* Dr. Beverly Gulley, Dean, 773-298-3221, Fax: 773-779-9061, E-mail: gulley@sxu.edu. *Application contact:* Beth Gierach, Managing Director of Admission, 773-298-3053, Fax: 773-298-3076, E-mail: gierach@sxu.edu.

Salem State University, School of Graduate Studies, Program in Library Media Studies, Salem, MA 01970-5353. Offers M Ed. *Accreditation:* NCATE. Part-time and evening/weekend programs available. *Entrance requirements:* For master's, GRE or MAT. Additional exam requirements/recommendations for international students: Required—TOEFL (minimum score 550 paper-based; 80 iBT) or IELTS (minimum score 5.5).

Salem State University, School of Graduate Studies, Program in Technology in Education, Salem, MA 01970-5353. Offers M Ed. Part-time and evening/weekend programs available. *Entrance requirements:* For master's, GRE or MAT. Additional exam requirements/recommendations for international students: Required—TOEFL (minimum score 550 paper-based; 80 iBT) or IELTS (minimum score 5.5).

Sam Houston State University, College of Education, Department of Curriculum and Instruction, Huntsville, TX 77341. Offers curriculum and instruction (M Ed, MA); instructional technology (M Ed). *Accreditation:* NCATE. Part-time and evening/weekend programs available. *Faculty:* 13 full-time (8 women), 1 part-time/adjunct (0 women). *Students:* 25 full-time (17 women), 192 part-time (156 women); includes 72 minority (37 Black or African American, non-Hispanic/Latino; 3 American Indian or Alaska Native, non-Hispanic/Latino; 4 Asian, non-Hispanic/Latino; 27 Hispanic/Latino; 1 Native Hawaiian or other Pacific Islander, non-Hispanic/Latino). Average age 33. 285 applicants, 51% accepted, 86 enrolled. In 2011, 53 master's awarded. *Entrance requirements:* For master's, GRE General Test. Additional exam requirements/recommendations for international students: Required—TOEFL (minimum score 550 paper-based; 213 computer-based; 79 iBT). *Application deadline:* For fall admission, 8/1 for domestic students, 6/25 for international students; for spring admission, 12/1 for domestic students, 11/12 for international students. Application fee: $45 ($75 for international students). *Expenses:* Tuition, state resident: full-time $4420; part-time $221 per credit hour. Tuition, nonresident: full-time $10,680; part-time $534 per credit hour. *Required fees:* $329 per credit hour. *Financial support:* Teaching assistantships and institutionally sponsored loans available. Financial award application deadline: 5/31; financial award applicants required to submit FAFSA. *Unit head:* Dr. Daphne Johnson, Chair, 936-294-3875, Fax: 936-294-1056, E-mail: edu_dxe@shsu.edu. *Application contact:* Dr. Eren Johnson, Advisor, 936-294-1140, E-mail: edu_mej@shsu.edu. Web site: http://www.shsu.edu/~cai_www/.

San Diego State University, Graduate and Research Affairs, College of Education, Department of Educational Technology, San Diego, CA 92182. Offers educational technology (MA); educational technology and teaching and learning (Ed D). *Accreditation:* NCATE. Evening/weekend programs available. *Entrance requirements:* For master's, GRE General Test, letters of reference. Additional exam requirements/recommendations for international students: Required—TOEFL. Electronic applications accepted.

San Francisco State University, Division of Graduate Studies, College of Education, Department of Instructional Technologies, San Francisco, CA 94132-1722. Offers instructional technologies (MA); training systems development (AC). *Unit head:* Dr. Brian Beatty, Chair, 415-338-6833, E-mail: bjbeatty@sfsu.edu. *Application contact:* Anna Kozubek, Academic Office Coordinator, 415-338-1509, E-mail: annak@sfsu.edu. Web site: http://www.sfsu.edu/~itec.

Seton Hall University, College of Education and Human Services, Department of Educational Studies, Program in Instructional Design, South Orange, NJ 07079-2697. Offers MA. Part-time and evening/weekend programs available. *Faculty:* 22 full-time (14 women). *Students:* 10 full-time (4 women), 16 part-time (7 women); includes 5 minority (1 Black or African American, non-Hispanic/Latino; 2 Asian, non-Hispanic/Latino; 2 Hispanic/Latino), 2 international. Average age 38. 6 applicants, 100% accepted, 6 enrolled. In 2011, 15 master's awarded. *Degree requirements:* For master's, comprehensive exam. *Entrance requirements:* For master's, GRE General Test or MAT, minimum GPA of 2.75. *Application deadline:* For fall admission, 5/1 for domestic students; for spring admission, 10/1 for domestic students. Applications are processed on a rolling basis. Application fee: $50. *Expenses: Tuition:* Part-time $1033 per credit hour. *Required fees:* $85 per semester. *Financial support:* Application deadline: 2/1. *Unit head:* Dr. Joseph Martinelli, Chair, 973-275-2733, E-mail: joseph.martinelli@shu.edu.

Simmons College, Graduate School of Library and Information Science, Boston, MA 02115. Offers archives management (MS, Certificate); instructional technology licensure (Certificate); library and information science (MS, PhD); managerial leadership in the informational professions (PhD); school library teacher (MS, Certificate); MS/MA. *Accreditation:* ALA (one or more programs are accredited). *Unit head:* Dr. Michele V. Cloonan, Dean, 617-521-2806, Fax: 617-521-3192, E-mail: michele.cloonan@simmons.edu. *Application contact:* Sarah Petrakos, Assistant Dean, Admission and Recruitment, 617-521-2868, Fax: 617-521-3192, E-mail: gslisadm@simmons.edu. Web site: http://www.simmons.edu/gslis/.

Simon Fraser University, Graduate Studies, Faculty of Education, Program in Educational Technology and Learning Design, Burnaby, BC V5A 1S6, Canada. Offers M Ed, MA, PhD. *Degree requirements:* For master's, thesis or comprehensive exam.

Southeastern Louisiana University, College of Education and Human Development, Department of Educational Leadership and Technology, Hammond, LA 70402. Offers educational leadership (M Ed, Ed D); educational technology leadership (M Ed). Part-time and evening/weekend programs available. *Faculty:* 16 full-time (6 women). *Students:* 16 full-time (12 women), 233 part-time (186 women); includes 77 minority (69 Black or African American, non-Hispanic/Latino; 1 Asian, non-Hispanic/Latino; 4 Hispanic/Latino; 3 Two or more races, non-Hispanic/Latino). Average age 38. 23 applicants, 100% accepted, 16 enrolled. In 2011, 105 master's, 19 doctorates awarded. *Degree requirements:* For master's, comprehensive exam; for doctorate, comprehensive exam, thesis/dissertation. *Entrance requirements:* For master's, GRE (verbal and quantitative); for doctorate, GRE, master's degree with minimum GPA of 3.25, 3.0 on the last 60 undergraduate hours. Additional exam requirements/recommendations for international students: Required—TOEFL (minimum score 500 paper-based; 173 computer-based; 61 iBT). *Application deadline:* For fall admission, 7/15 priority date for domestic students, 6/1 for international students; for spring admission, 12/1 priority date for domestic students, 10/1 for international students. Applications are processed on a rolling basis. Application fee: $20 ($30 for international students). Electronic applications accepted. *Expenses:* Tuition, state resident: full-time $3977; part-time $283 per semester hour. Tuition, nonresident: full-time $13,482; part-time $811 per semester hour. *Financial support:* Career-related internships or fieldwork, Federal Work-Study, institutionally sponsored loans, scholarships/grants, and unspecified assistantships available. Support available to part-time students. Financial award application deadline: 5/1; financial award applicants required to submit FAFSA. *Faculty research:* Technology leadership in schools, techno stress for educational leaders, dispositions of effective leaders. *Total annual research expenditures:* $176,799. *Unit head:* Dr. Michael D. Richardson, Department Head, 985-549-5713, Fax: 985-549-5712, E-mail: mrichardson@selu.edu. *Application contact:* Sandra Meyers, Graduate Admissions Analyst, 985-549-2066, Fax: 985-549-5632, E-mail: admissions@selu.edu. Web site: http://www.selu.edu/acad_research/depts/edlt.

Southeast Missouri State University, School of Graduate Studies, Department of Middle and Secondary Education, Cape Girardeau, MO 63701-4799. Offers secondary education (MA), including education studies, education technology. *Accreditation:* NCATE. Part-time and evening/weekend programs available. *Faculty:* 4 full-time (3 women). *Students:* 3 full-time (2 women), 18 part-time (14 women); includes 2 minority (both Black or African American, non-Hispanic/Latino), 1 international. Average age 30. 7 applicants, 86% accepted, 6 enrolled. In 2011, 12 master's awarded. *Degree requirements:* For master's, comprehensive exam, research paper. *Entrance requirements:* For master's, minimum undergraduate GPA of 2.75. Additional exam requirements/recommendations for international students: Required—TOEFL (minimum score 550 paper-based; 213 computer-based; 79 iBT); Recommended—IELTS (minimum score 6). *Application deadline:* For fall admission, 8/1 for domestic students, 7/1 for international students; for spring admission, 11/21 for domestic students, 11/1 for international students. Applications are processed on a rolling basis. Application fee: $30 ($40 for international students). Electronic applications accepted. *Expenses:* Tuition, state resident: full-time $4896; part-time $272 per credit hour. Tuition, nonresident: full-time $8649; part-time $480.50 per credit hour. *Financial support:* In 2011–12, 4 students received support. Career-related internships or fieldwork, Federal Work-Study, scholarships/grants, tuition waivers (full), and unspecified assistantships available. Financial award application deadline: 6/30; financial award applicants required to submit FAFSA. *Faculty research:* Pedagogy of teaching, multicultural education, reading and writing strategies, use of technology in the classroom. *Unit head:* Dr. Simin L. Cwick, Chairperson and Graduate Coordinator, 573-651-5965, Fax: 573-986-6141, E-mail: scwick@semo.edu. *Application contact:* Alisa Aleen McFerron, Assistant Director of Admissions for Operations, 573-651-5937, Fax: 573-651-5936, E-mail: amcferron@semo.edu. Web site: http://www5.semo.edu/middleandsec/.

Southern Illinois University Edwardsville, Graduate School, School of Education, Department of Educational Leadership, Program in Instructional Technology, Edwardsville, IL 62026. Offers MS Ed. *Accreditation:* NCATE. Part-time and evening/weekend programs available. *Students:* 33 part-time (21 women); includes 4 minority (3 Black or African American, non-Hispanic/Latino; 1 Hispanic/Latino). 16 applicants, 50% accepted. In 2011, 7 master's awarded. *Degree requirements:* For master's, thesis or alternative, portfolio. *Entrance requirements:* Additional exam requirements/recommendations for international students: Required—TOEFL (minimum score 550 paper-based; 213 computer-based; 79 iBT), IELTS (minimum score 6.5). *Application deadline:* For fall admission, 7/22 for domestic students, 6/1 for international students; for spring admission, 12/9 for domestic students, 10/1 for international students. Applications are processed on a rolling basis. Application fee: $30. Electronic applications accepted. Tuition and fees vary according to course load and program. *Financial support:* Fellowships, research assistantships, teaching assistantships, institutionally sponsored loans, scholarships/grants, and unspecified assistantships available. Financial award application deadline: 3/1; financial award applicants required to submit FAFSA. *Unit head:* Dr. Melissa Thomeczek, Program Director, 618-650-3290, E-mail: mthomec@siue.edu. *Application contact:* Michelle Robinson, Coordinator of Graduate Recruitment, 618-650-2811, Fax: 618-650-3523, E-mail: michero@siue.edu. Web site: http://www.siue.edu/education/edld/.

Southern Illinois University Edwardsville, Graduate School, School of Education, Department of Educational Leadership, Program in Web-Based Learning, Edwardsville, IL 62026. Offers Postbaccalaureate Certificate. Part-time programs available. *Students:* 1 part-time (0 women), all international. 4 applicants, 50% accepted. In 2011, 1 Postbaccalaureate Certificate awarded. *Entrance requirements:* Additional exam requirements/recommendations for international students: Required—TOEFL (minimum score 550 paper-based; 213 computer-based; 79 iBT), IELTS (minimum score 6.5). *Application deadline:* For fall admission, 7/22 for domestic students, 6/1 for international students; for spring admission, 12/9 for domestic students, 10/1 for international students. Applications are processed on a rolling basis. Application fee: $30. Electronic applications accepted. Tuition and fees vary according to course load and program. *Financial support:* Institutionally sponsored loans, scholarships/grants, and unspecified assistantships available. Financial award application deadline: 3/1; financial award applicants required to submit FAFSA. *Unit head:* Dr. Melissa Thomeczek, Director, 618-650-3290, E-mail: mthomec@siue.edu. *Application contact:* Michelle Robinson, Coordinator of Graduate Recruitment, 618-650-2811, Fax: 618-650-3523, E-mail: michero@siue.edu. Web site: http://www.siue.edu/education/edld/.

Southern Polytechnic State University, School of Arts and Sciences, Department of English, Technical Communication, and Media Arts, Marietta, GA 30060-2896. Offers communications management (AGC); content development (AGC); information and instructional design (MSIID); information design and communication (MS); instructional design (AGC); technical communication (Graduate Certificate); visual communication and graphics (AGC). Part-time and evening/weekend programs available. Postbaccalaureate distance learning degree programs offered (no on-campus study). *Faculty:* 5 full-time (3 women), 2 part-time/adjunct (both women). *Students:* 1 full-time (0 women), 44 part-time (34 women); includes 13 minority (all Black or African American, non-Hispanic/Latino), 1 international. Average age 36. 24 applicants, 88% accepted, 16 enrolled. In 2011, 7 master's, 5 other advanced degrees awarded. *Degree requirements:* For master's, thesis optional; for other advanced degree, thesis optional, 18 hours completed through thesis option (6 hours), internship option (6 hours) or advanced coursework option (6 hours). *Entrance requirements:* For master's, GRE, statement of purpose, writing sample, timed essay; for other advanced degree, writing sample, professional recommendations. Additional exam requirements/recommendations for international students: Required—TOEFL (minimum score 550 paper-based; 213 computer-based; 79 iBT), IELTS (minimum score 6.5). *Application deadline:* For fall admission, 7/1 priority date for domestic students, 5/1 for international students; for spring admission, 11/1 priority date for domestic students, 9/1 for international students. Applications are processed on a rolling basis. Application fee: $50. Electronic applications accepted. *Expenses:* Tuition, state resident: full-time $2592; part-time $216 per semester hour. Tuition, nonresident: full-time $9408; part-time $784 per semester hour. *Required fees:* $698 per term. *Financial support:* Research assistantships with tuition reimbursements, teaching assistantships with tuition reimbursements, career-related internships or fieldwork, Federal Work-Study, scholarships/grants, and unspecified assistantships available. Support available to part-time students. Financial award application deadline: 5/1; financial award applicants required to submit FAFSA. *Faculty research:* Usability, user-centered design, instructional design, information architecture, information design, content strategy. *Unit head:* Dr. Mark Nunes, Chair, 678-915-7202, Fax: 678-915-7425, E-mail: mnunes@spsu.edu. *Application contact:* Donna McPherson, Program Assistant, 678-915-7202, Fax: 678-915-7425, E-mail: donna@@spsu.edu. Web site: http://www.spsu.edu/arts/departments.htm.

Southern University and Agricultural and Mechanical College, Graduate School, College of Education, Department of Curriculum and Instruction, Baton Rouge, LA 70813. Offers elementary education (M Ed); media (M Ed); secondary education (M Ed). *Degree requirements:* For master's, comprehensive exam, thesis optional. *Entrance requirements:* For master's, GMAT or GRE General Test. Additional exam requirements/recommendations for international students: Required—TOEFL (minimum score 525 paper-based; 193 computer-based).

State University of New York College at Oneonta, Graduate Education, Division of Education, Oneonta, NY 13820-4015. Offers educational psychology and counseling (MS Ed, CAS), including school counselor K-12; educational technology specialist (MS Ed); elementary education and reading (MS Ed), including childhood education, literacy education; secondary education (MS Ed), including adolescence education, family and consumer science education; special education (MS Ed), including adolescence, childhood. *Accreditation:* NCATE. Part-time and evening/weekend programs available. *Entrance requirements:* For master's, GRE General Test.

State University of New York College at Potsdam, School of Education and Professional Studies, Program in Information and Communication Technology, Potsdam, NY 13676. Offers educational technology specialist (MS Ed); organizational performance, leadership and technology (MS Ed). Part-time and evening/weekend programs available. *Faculty:* 3 full-time (0 women), 2 part-time/adjunct (1 woman). *Students:* 22 full-time (12 women), 41 part-time (24 women); includes 3 minority (all Black or African American, non-Hispanic/Latino), 7 international. 31 applicants, 100% accepted, 25 enrolled. In 2011, 31 master's awarded. *Degree requirements:* For master's, culminating experience. *Entrance requirements:* For master's, minimum GPA of 3.0 in last 60 hours of course work. Additional exam requirements/recommendations for international students: Required—TOEFL (minimum score 550 paper-based; 213 computer-based; 80 iBT), IELTS (minimum score 6). *Application deadline:* For fall admission, 4/1 for domestic and international students; for winter admission, 10/15 for domestic and international students; for spring admission, 3/1 for domestic and international students. Applications are processed on a rolling basis. Application fee: $50. *Expenses:* Tuition, state resident: full-time $8870; part-time $370 per credit hour. Tuition, nonresident: full-time $15,160; part-time $632 per credit hour. *Required fees:* $1066; $44.10 per credit hour. One-time fee: $3. *Financial support:* Fellowships, teaching assistantships, career-related internships or fieldwork, Federal Work-Study, scholarships/grants, and unspecified assistantships available. Support available to part-time students. Financial award application deadline: 3/1; financial award applicants required to submit FAFSA. *Unit head:* Dr. Timothy V. Fossum, Chairperson, 315-267-2056, Fax: 315-267-3207, E-mail: fossumtv@potsdam.edu. *Application contact:* Peter Cutler, Graduate Admissions Counselor, 315-267-2165, Fax: 315-267-4802, E-mail: graduate@potsdam.edu.

Stony Brook University, State University of New York, Graduate School, College of Engineering and Applied Sciences, Department of Technology and Society, Program in Educational Technology, Stony Brook, NY 11794. Offers MS. *Accreditation:* NCATE. Electronic applications accepted.

Stony Brook University, State University of New York, School of Professional Development, Stony Brook, NY 11794. Offers biology-grade 7-12 (MAT); chemistry-grade 7-12 (MAT); coaching (Graduate Certificate); coaching online (Graduate Certificate); computer integrated engineering (Graduate Certificate); earth science-grade 7-12 (MAT); educational computing (Graduate Certificate); educational leadership (Advanced Certificate); English-grade 7-12 (MAT); environmental management (Graduate Certificate); environmental/occupational health and safety (Graduate Certificate); French-grade 7-12 (MAT); German-grade 7-12 (MAT); human resource management (Graduate Certificate); human resource management online (Graduate Certificate); information systems management (Graduate Certificate); Italian-grade 7-12 (MAT); liberal studies (MA); liberal studies online (MAT); mathematics-grade 7-12 (MAT); operation research (Graduate Certificate); physics-grade 7-12 (MAT); professional studies online (MPS); school administration and supervision (Graduate Certificate); school building leadership (Graduate Certificate); school district administration (Graduate Certificate); school district business leadership (Advanced Certificate); school district leadership (Graduate Certificate); social science and the professions (MPS), including environmental waste management, human resource management; social studies-grade 7-12 (MAT); Spanish-grade 7-12 (MAT); waste management (Graduate Certificate). Part-time and evening/weekend programs available. Postbaccalaureate distance learning degree programs offered. *Degree requirements:* For master's, one foreign language, thesis or alternative.

Strayer University, Graduate Studies, Washington, DC 20005-2603. Offers accounting (MS); acquisition (MBA); business administration (MBA); communications technology (MS); educational management (M Ed); finance (MBA); health services administration (MHSA); hospitality and tourism management (MBA); human resource management (MBA); information systems (MS), including computer security management, decision support system management, enterprise resource management, network management, software engineering management, systems development management; management (MBA); management information systems (MS); marketing (MBA); professional accounting (MS), including accounting information systems, controllership, taxation; public administration (MPA); supply chain management (MBA); technology in education (M Ed). Programs also offered at campus locations in Birmingham, AL; Chamblee, GA; Cobb County, GA; Morrow, GA; White Marsh, MD; Charleston, SC; Columbia, SC; Greensboro, NC; Greenville, SC; Lexington, KY; Louisville, KY; Nashville, TN; North Raleigh, NC; Washington, DC. Part-time and evening/weekend programs available. Postbaccalaureate distance learning degree programs offered (minimal on-campus study). *Degree requirements:* For master's, thesis. *Entrance requirements:* For master's, GMAT, GRE General Test, bachelor's degree from an accredited college or university, minimum undergraduate GPA of 2.75. Electronic applications accepted.

Syracuse University, School of Education, Program in Educational Technology, Syracuse, NY 13244. Offers CAS. *Accreditation:* ACA. Part-time programs available. In 2011, 14 degrees awarded. *Degree requirements:* For CAS, thesis or alternative. *Entrance requirements:* Additional exam requirements/recommendations for international students: Required—TOEFL (minimum score 100 iBT). *Application deadline:* For fall admission, 2/1 priority date for domestic students, 2/1 for international students; for spring admission, 10/15 priority date for domestic students, 10/15 for international students. Applications are processed on a rolling basis. Application fee: $75. Electronic applications accepted. *Expenses: Tuition:* Part-time $1206 per credit. *Financial support:* Application deadline: 1/1. *Faculty research:* Academics and athletics, drug free schools, group counseling, prejudice prevention, culture-centered counseling. *Unit head:* Nick Smith, Chair, 315-443-3703, E-mail: nlsmith@syr.edu. *Application contact:* Laurie Deyo, Graduate Recruiter, School of Education, 315-443-2505, E-mail: e-gradrcrt@syr.edu. Web site: http://soeweb.syr.edu/chs/.

Syracuse University, School of Education, Program in Instructional Technology, Syracuse, NY 13244. Offers MS. *Students:* 6 full-time (all women), 1 part-time (0 women); includes 1 minority (Black or African American, non-Hispanic/Latino). Average age 24. 2 applicants, 100% accepted, 2 enrolled. *Entrance requirements:* For master's, New York state teacher certification or eligibility for certification, resume. Additional exam requirements/recommendations for international students: Required—TOEFL (minimum score 100 iBT). *Application deadline:* For fall admission, 2/1 for domestic and international students. Application fee: $75. Electronic applications accepted. *Expenses: Tuition:* Part-time $1206 per credit. *Financial support:* Fellowships with full tuition reimbursements and research assistantships with full and partial tuition reimbursements available. Financial award application deadline: 1/1. *Unit head:* Dr. Nick Smith, Department Chair, 315-443-5293, E-mail: nlsmith@syr.edu. *Application contact:* Laurie Deyo, Graduate Recruiter, School of Education, 315-443-2505, E-mail: e-gradrcrt@syr.edu. Web site: http://soeweb.syr.edu/academic/Instructional_Design_Development_and_Evaluation/graduate/masters/instructional_technology/default.aspx.

Syracuse University, School of Education, Program in Professional Practice in Educational Technology, Syracuse, NY 13244. Offers Certificate. Part-time programs available. Application fee: $75. *Expenses: Tuition:* Part-time $1206 per credit. *Unit head:* Dr. Douglas Biklen, Dean, 315-443-4751. *Application contact:* Laurie Deyo, Graduate Recruiter, School of Education, 315-443-2505, E-mail: e-gradrcrt@syr.edu. Web site: http://soeweb.syr.edu/.

Syracuse University, School of Information Studies, Program in Library and Information Science: School Media, Syracuse, NY 13244. Offers MS. Part-time and evening/weekend programs available. Postbaccalaureate distance learning degree programs offered (minimal on-campus study). *Students:* 19 full-time (17 women), 42 part-time (41 women); includes 4 minority (2 Black or African American, non-Hispanic/Latino; 1 Asian, non-Hispanic/Latino; 1 Two or more races, non-Hispanic/Latino). Average age 35. 33 applicants, 94% accepted, 22 enrolled. In 2011, 32 degrees awarded. *Entrance requirements:* For master's, GRE. Additional exam requirements/recommendations for international students: Required—TOEFL (minimum score 100 iBT). *Application deadline:* For fall admission, 2/1 priority date for domestic students, 2/1 for international students; for spring admission, 10/15 priority date for domestic students, 10/15 for international students. Applications are processed on a rolling basis. Application fee: $75. Electronic applications accepted. *Expenses: Tuition:* Part-time $1206 per credit. *Financial support:* Application deadline: 1/1. *Unit head:* Blythe Bennett, Program Director, 315-443-2911, E-mail: babennet@syr.edu. *Application contact:* Susan Corieri, Director of Enrollment Management, 315-443-2575, E-mail: ischool@syr.edu. Web site: http://ischool.syr.edu/academics/graduate/mls/mediaprogram/index.aspx.

See Display on page 1637 and Close-Up on page 1653.

Syracuse University, School of Information Studies, Program in School Media, Syracuse, NY 13244. Offers CAS. Part-time and evening/weekend programs available. Postbaccalaureate distance learning degree programs offered. *Students:* 6 part-time (all women); includes 1 minority (American Indian or Alaska Native, non-Hispanic/Latino). Average age 36. 3 applicants, 100% accepted, 2 enrolled. In 2011, 3 degrees awarded. *Entrance requirements:* For degree, MS in library and information science. Additional exam requirements/recommendations for international students: Required—TOEFL (minimum score 100 iBT). *Application deadline:* For fall admission, 2/1 priority date for domestic students, 2/1 for international students; for spring admission, 10/15 priority date for domestic students, 10/15 for international students. Applications are processed on a rolling basis. Application fee: $75. Electronic applications accepted. *Expenses: Tuition:* Part-time $1206 per credit. *Financial support:* Application deadline: 1/1. *Unit head:* R. David Lankes, Director, 315-443-1707, E-mail: rdlankes@iis.syr.edu. *Application contact:* Susan Corieri, Director of Enrollment Management, 315-443-2575, E-mail: ist@syr.edu.

See Display on page 1637 and Close-Up on page 1653.

Teacher Education University, Graduate Programs, Winter Park, FL 32789. Offers educational leadership (MA); educational technology (MA); elementary education K-6 (MA); instructional strategies (MA Ed); school guidance and counseling (MA).

Teachers College, Columbia University, Graduate Faculty of Education, Department of Math, Science and Technology, Program in Educational Media/Instructional Technology, New York, NY 10027. Offers Ed M, MA, Ed D. *Faculty:* 12 full-time (5 women), 13 part-time/adjunct (7 women). *Students:* 23 full-time (15 women), 80 part-time (47 women); includes 33 minority (10 Black or African American, non-Hispanic/Latino; 1 American Indian or Alaska Native, non-Hispanic/Latino; 10 Asian, non-Hispanic/Latino; 8 Hispanic/Latino; 4 Two or more races, non-Hispanic/Latino), 33 international. Average age 34. 40 applicants, 88% accepted, 14 enrolled. *Degree requirements:* For master's, integrative project; for doctorate, comprehensive exam, thesis/dissertation. *Entrance requirements:* For doctorate, GRE General Test or MAT. *Application deadline:* For fall admission, 1/15 for domestic students; for spring admission, 11/1 for domestic students. Applications are processed on a rolling basis. Application fee: $65. Electronic applications accepted. *Financial support:* Career-related internships or fieldwork, Federal Work-Study, institutionally sponsored loans, and tuition waivers (full and partial) available. Support available to part-time students. Financial award applicants required to submit FAFSA. *Faculty research:* Video and interactive learning. *Unit head:* Prof. Charles Kinzer, Chair, 212-678-3344, Fax: 212-678-8227, E-mail: tcccte@tc.edu. *Application contact:* Deanna Ghozati, Assistant Director of

Admission, 212-678-4018, Fax: 212-678-4171, E-mail: ghozati@tc.edu. Web site: http://www.tc.edu/mst/ccte/.

Texas A&M University, College of Education and Human Development, Department of Educational Psychology, College Station, TX 77843. Offers bilingual education (M Ed, PhD); cognition, creativity, instruction and development (MS, PhD); counseling psychology (PhD); educational psychology (PhD); educational technology (PhD); research, measurement and statistics (MS); research, measurement, and statistics (PhD); school psychology (PhD); special education (M Ed, PhD). *Accreditation:* APA (one or more programs are accredited). Part-time and evening/weekend programs available. Postbaccalaureate distance learning degree programs offered (no on-campus study). *Faculty:* 46. *Students:* 151 full-time (124 women), 123 part-time (101 women); includes 97 minority (20 Black or African American, non-Hispanic/Latino; 11 Asian, non-Hispanic/Latino; 59 Hispanic/Latino; 7 Two or more races, non-Hispanic/Latino), 50 international. In 2011, 58 master's, 33 doctorates awarded. *Degree requirements:* For master's, thesis optional; for doctorate, thesis/dissertation. *Entrance requirements:* For master's and doctorate, GRE General Test. Additional exam requirements/recommendations for international students: Required—TOEFL. Application fee: $50 ($75 for international students). Electronic applications accepted. *Expenses:* Tuition, state resident: full-time $5437; part-time $226.55 per credit hour. Tuition, nonresident: full-time $12,949; part-time $539.55 per credit hour. *Required fees:* $2741. *Financial support:* In 2011–12, fellowships (averaging $12,000 per year), research assistantships (averaging $9,000 per year), teaching assistantships (averaging $9,000 per year) were awarded; career-related internships or fieldwork, institutionally sponsored loans, scholarships/grants, and unspecified assistantships also available. Financial award applicants required to submit FAFSA. *Unit head:* Dr. Victor Willson, Head, 979-845-1800. *Application contact:* Carol A. Wagner, Director of Advising, 979-845-1833, Fax: 979-862-1256, E-mail: epsyadvisor@tamu.edu. Web site: http://epsy.tamu.edu.

Texas A&M University–Commerce, Graduate School, College of Education and Human Services, Department of Educational Leadership, Commerce, TX 75429-3011. Offers educational administration (M Ed, Ed D); educational technology (M Ed, MS); higher education (MS, Ed D); training and development (MS). Part-time programs available. Terminal master's awarded for partial completion of doctoral program. *Degree requirements:* For master's, comprehensive exam, thesis (for some programs); for doctorate, thesis/dissertation, departmental qualifying exam. *Entrance requirements:* For master's, GRE General Test; for doctorate, GRE General Test, writing skills exam, interview. Electronic applications accepted. *Faculty research:* Property tax reform, politics of education, administrative stress.

Texas A&M University–Corpus Christi, Graduate Studies and Research, College of Education, Corpus Christi, TX 78412-5503. Offers counseling (MS, PhD), including counseling (MS), counselor education (PhD); curriculum and instruction (MS, Ed D); early childhood education (MS); educational administration (MS); educational leadership (Ed D); educational technology (MS); elementary education (MS); kinesiology (MS); reading (MS); secondary education (MS); special education (MS). Part-time and evening/weekend programs available. *Degree requirements:* For master's, comprehensive exam, thesis (for some programs); for doctorate, comprehensive exam, thesis/dissertation. *Entrance requirements:* For master's, GRE General Test. Additional exam requirements/recommendations for international students: Required—TOEFL. Electronic applications accepted.

Texas A&M University–Texarkana, Graduate Studies and Research, College of Education and Liberal Arts, Texarkana, TX 75505-5518. Offers adult education (MS); curriculum and instruction (M Ed); education (MS); educational administration (M Ed); English (MA); instructional technology (MS); interdisciplinary studies (MA, MS); special education (MS). Part-time and evening/weekend programs available. *Degree requirements:* For master's, comprehensive exam (for some programs), thesis optional. *Entrance requirements:* For master's, minimum GPA of 2.5 on last 60 hours of bachelor's degree. Additional exam requirements/recommendations for international students: Required—TOEFL. Electronic applications accepted.

Texas State University–San Marcos, Graduate School, College of Education, Department of Curriculum and Instruction, Education Technology, San Marcos, TX 78666. Offers M Ed, MA. Part-time and evening/weekend programs available. *Faculty:* 2 full-time (0 women). *Students:* 14 full-time (10 women), 22 part-time (17 women); includes 15 minority (3 Black or African American, non-Hispanic/Latino; 1 American Indian or Alaska Native, non-Hispanic/Latino; 9 Hispanic/Latino; 2 Two or more races, non-Hispanic/Latino). Average age 36. 22 applicants, 73% accepted, 7 enrolled. In 2011, 9 master's awarded. *Degree requirements:* For master's, comprehensive exam, thesis optional. *Entrance requirements:* For master's, minimum GPA of 2.75 in undergraduate work. Additional exam requirements/recommendations for international students: Required—TOEFL (minimum score 550 paper-based; 213 computer-based; 78 iBT). *Application deadline:* For fall admission, 6/15 priority date for domestic students, 6/1 for international students; for spring admission, 10/15 priority date for domestic students, 10/1 for international students. Applications are processed on a rolling basis. Application fee: $40 ($90 for international students). Electronic applications accepted. *Expenses:* Tuition, state resident: full-time $6408; part-time $3204 per semester. Tuition, nonresident: full-time $14,832; part-time $7416 per semester. *Required fees:* $1824; $912 per semester. Tuition and fees vary according to course load. *Financial support:* In 2011–12, 23 students received support. Application deadline: 4/1. *Unit head:* Dr. David Bynum, Graduate Advisor, 512-245-2041, Fax: 512-245-7911, E-mail: db15@txstate.edu. *Application contact:* Dr. J. Michael Willoughby, Dean of Graduate School, 512-245-2581, Fax: 512-245-8365, E-mail: gradcollege@txstate.edu. Web site: http://www.education.txstate.edu/ci/degrees-programs/graduate/elementary-education.html.

Texas Tech University, Graduate School, College of Education, Department of Educational Psychology and Leadership, Lubbock, TX 79409. Offers counselor education (M Ed, PhD); educational leadership (M Ed, Ed D); educational psychology (M Ed, PhD); higher education (M Ed, Ed D); higher education: higher education research (PhD); instructional technology (M Ed, Ed D); instructional technology: distance education (M Ed); special education (M Ed, Ed D). *Accreditation:* ACA; NCATE. Part-time programs available. Postbaccalaureate distance learning degree programs offered (no on-campus study). *Students:* 180 full-time (133 women), 418 part-time (297 women); includes 127 minority (34 Black or African American, non-Hispanic/Latino; 3 American Indian or Alaska Native, non-Hispanic/Latino; 6 Asian, non-Hispanic/Latino; 76 Hispanic/Latino; 8 Two or more races, non-Hispanic/Latino), 41 international. Average age 36. 478 applicants, 42% accepted, 134 enrolled. In 2011, 139 master's, 30 doctorates awarded. *Degree requirements:* For master's, thesis optional; for doctorate, thesis/dissertation. *Entrance requirements:* For master's and doctorate, GRE General Test. Additional exam requirements/recommendations for international students: Required—TOEFL (minimum score 550 paper-based; 213 computer-based; 79 iBT). *Application deadline:* For fall admission, 6/1 priority date for domestic students, 1/15 for international students; for spring admission, 9/1 priority date for domestic students, 6/15 for international students. Applications are processed on a rolling basis. Application fee: $50 ($75 for international students). Electronic applications accepted. *Expenses:* Tuition, state resident: full-time $5899; part-time $245.80 per credit hour. Tuition, nonresident: full-time $13,411; part-time $558.80 per credit hour. *Required fees:* $2680.60; $86.50 per credit hour. $920.30 per semester. *Financial support:* In 2011–12, 142 students received support. Application deadline: 4/15; applicants required to submit FAFSA. *Faculty research:* Psychological processes of teaching and learning, teaching populations with special needs, instructional technology, educational administration in education, theories and practice in counseling and counselor education K-12 and higher. *Total annual research expenditures:* $1.4 million. *Unit head:* Dr. William Lan, Chair, 806-742-1998 Ext. 436, Fax: 806-742-2179, E-mail: william.lan@ttu.edu. *Application contact:* Dr. Hansel Burley, Associate Academic Dean, 806-742-1998 Ext. 447, Fax: 806-742-2179, E-mail: hansel.burley@ttu.edu.

Thomas Edison State College, Heavin School of Arts and Sciences, Program in Online Learning and Teaching, Trenton, NJ 08608-1176. Offers Graduate Certificate. Part-time programs available. Postbaccalaureate distance learning degree programs offered (no on-campus study). *Students:* 23 part-time (14 women); includes 10 minority (6 Black or African American, non-Hispanic/Latino; 4 Hispanic/Latino). Average age 48. In 2011, 10 Graduate Certificates awarded. *Entrance requirements:* Additional exam requirements/recommendations for international students: Required—TOEFL (minimum score 550 paper-based; 213 computer-based; 79 iBT). *Application deadline:* For fall admission, 8/15 priority date for domestic students, 8/15 for international students; for winter admission, 11/15 priority date for domestic students, 11/15 for international students; for spring admission, 2/15 priority date for domestic students, 2/15 for international students. Applications are processed on a rolling basis. Application fee: $75. Electronic applications accepted. *Financial support:* Applicants required to submit FAFSA. *Unit head:* Dr. Susan Davenport, Dean, Heavin School of Arts and Sciences, 609-984-1130, Fax: 609-984-0740, E-mail: info@tesc.edu. *Application contact:* David Hoftiezer, Director of Admissions, 888-442-8372, Fax: 609-984-8447, E-mail: admissions@tesc.edu. Web site: http://www.tesc.edu/1880.php.

Touro College, Graduate School of Education, New York, NY 10010. Offers bilingual programs (Advanced Certificate); education and special education (MS); gifted and talented education (Advanced Certificate); instructional technology (MS); mathematics education (MS); school leadership (MS); teaching children with autism and other severe or multiple disabilities (Advanced Certificate); teaching English to speakers of other languages (MS, Advanced Certificate); teaching literacy (MS). Part-time and evening/weekend programs available. Postbaccalaureate distance learning degree programs offered (no on-campus study). *Faculty:* 75 full-time, 131 part-time/adjunct. *Students:* 382 full-time (324 women), 3,790 part-time (3,196 women); includes 1,211 minority (537 Black or African American, non-Hispanic/Latino; 4 American Indian or Alaska Native, non-Hispanic/Latino; 187 Asian, non-Hispanic/Latino; 472 Hispanic/Latino; 3 Native Hawaiian or other Pacific Islander, non-Hispanic/Latino; 8 Two or more races, non-Hispanic/Latino), 1 international. 1,422 applicants, 50% accepted, 675 enrolled. In 2011, 6 master's, 4 other advanced degrees awarded. *Application deadline:* For fall admission, 8/26 for domestic students, 7/15 for international students; for spring admission, 12/31 for domestic students, 12/15 for international students. Applications are processed on a rolling basis. Application fee: $50. *Financial support:* Federal Work-Study available. Financial award applicants required to submit FAFSA. *Faculty research:* Equity assistance, language development, scholar communications, Latin American studies and cultural sensitivity, behavior management techniques and strategies in special education. *Unit head:* Dr. LaMar Miller, Dean, 212-463-0400 Ext. 5561, Fax: 212-462-4889, E-mail: lpmiller@touro.edu. *Application contact:* Natalie Arroyo, Admissions Assistant, 212-463-0400 Ext. 5119, E-mail: natalie.arroyo@touro.edu.

Touro College, Graduate School of Technology, New York, NY 10010. Offers information systems (MS); instructional technology (MS); Web and multimedia design (MA). *Students:* 87 full-time (17 women), 19 part-time (17 women); includes 46 minority (15 Black or African American, non-Hispanic/Latino; 15 Asian, non-Hispanic/Latino; 9 Hispanic/Latino; 7 Native Hawaiian or other Pacific Islander, non-Hispanic/Latino), 2 international. *Unit head:* Dr. Isaac Herskowitz, Dean of the Graduate School of Technology, 202-463-0400 Ext. 5231, E-mail: ssac.herskowitz@touro.edu. Web site: http://www.touro.edu/gst/.

Towson University, Program in Instructional Technology, Towson, MD 21252-0001. Offers instructional design and training (MS); instructional technology (Ed D). Part-time and evening/weekend programs available. *Students:* 7 full-time (3 women), 217 part-time (184 women); includes 25 minority (16 Black or African American, non-Hispanic/Latino; 2 American Indian or Alaska Native, non-Hispanic/Latino; 3 Asian, non-Hispanic/Latino; 1 Hispanic/Latino; 3 Two or more races, non-Hispanic/Latino), 5 international. *Degree requirements:* For master's, thesis optional; for doctorate, comprehensive exam, thesis/dissertation. *Entrance requirements:* For master's, minimum GPA of 3.0, technological literacy; for doctorate, GRE, writing sample, letters of recommendation. Additional exam requirements/recommendations for international students: Required—TOEFL (minimum score 600 paper-based). *Application deadline:* For fall admission, 8/1 priority date for domestic students, 7/15 for international students. Applications are processed on a rolling basis. Application fee: $50. Electronic applications accepted. *Expenses:* Tuition, state resident: part-time $337 per credit. Tuition, nonresident: part-time $709 per credit. *Required fees:* $99 per credit. *Financial support:* Application deadline: 4/1; applicants required to submit FAFSA. *Unit head:* Bill Sadera, Ed D Program Director, 410-704-2731, E-mail: bsadera@towson.edu.

Trident University International, College of Education, Program in Educational Leadership, Cypress, CA 90630. Offers e-learning leadership (MA Ed, PhD); educational leadership (MA Ed); higher education leadership (PhD); K-12 leadership (PhD). Part-time and evening/weekend programs available. Postbaccalaureate distance learning degree programs offered (no on-campus study). *Degree requirements:* For doctorate, comprehensive exam, thesis/dissertation, defense of dissertation. *Entrance requirements:* For master's, minimum GPA of 2.5 (students with GPA 3.0 or greater may transfer up to 30% of graduate level credits); for doctorate, minimum GPA of 3.4, course work in research methods or statistics. Additional exam requirements/recommendations for international students: Required—TOEFL. Electronic applications accepted.

Troy University, Graduate School, College of Education, Program in Postsecondary Education, Troy, AL 36082. Offers adult education (M Ed); biology (M Ed); criminal justice (M Ed); English (M Ed); foundations of education (M Ed); general science (M Ed); higher education administration (M Ed); history (M Ed); instructional technology (M Ed); mathematics (M Ed); music industry (M Ed); physical fitness (M Ed); political science (M Ed); public administration (M Ed); social science (M Ed); teaching English (M Ed). *Accreditation:* NCATE. Part-time and evening/weekend programs available. *Faculty:* 53 full-time (21 women), 22 part-time/adjunct (8 women). *Students:* 74 full-time (51 women), 166 part-time (121 women); includes 148 minority (143 Black or African American, non-Hispanic/Latino; 1 American Indian or Alaska Native, non-Hispanic/Latino; 2 Hispanic/Latino; 2 Two or more races, non-Hispanic/Latino). Average age 34. 174 applicants, 82% accepted, 88 enrolled. In 2011, 221 master's awarded. *Degree requirements:* For master's, comprehensive exam, thesis. *Entrance requirements:* For master's, MAT (minimum score 385), minimum GPA of 2.5. Additional exam requirements/recommendations for international students: Required—TOEFL (minimum score 523 paper-based; 193 computer-based; 70 iBT), IELTS (minimum score 6), or ACT COMPASS ESL (minimum listening, reading, and grammar score 270). *Application deadline:* Applications are processed on a rolling basis. Application fee: $50. Electronic applications accepted. *Expenses:* Tuition, state resident: full-time $6960;

part-time $290 per credit hour. Tuition, nonresident: full-time $13,920; part-time $580 per credit hour. *Required fees:* $386 per term. *Financial support:* Available to part-time students. Applicants required to submit FAFSA. *Unit head:* Dr. Jan Oliver, Associate Professor, 334-670-3444, Fax: 334-670-3296, E-mail: oliver@troy.edu. *Application contact:* Brenda K. Campbell, Director of Graduate Admissions, 334-670-3178, Fax: 334-670-3733, E-mail: bcamp@troy.edu.

Université Laval, Faculty of Education, Department of Teaching and Learning Studies, Programs in Teaching Technology, Québec, QC G1K 7P4, Canada. Offers MA, PhD. Terminal master's awarded for partial completion of doctoral program. *Degree requirements:* For master's, thesis (for some programs); for doctorate, comprehensive exam, thesis/dissertation. *Entrance requirements:* For master's and doctorate, English exam (comprehension of written English), knowledge of French. Electronic applications accepted.

University at Albany, State University of New York, School of Education, Department of Educational Theory and Practice, Albany, NY 12222-0001. Offers curriculum and instruction (MS, Ed D, CAS); curriculum planning and development (MA); educational communications (MS, CAS). Evening/weekend programs available. *Degree requirements:* For doctorate, one foreign language, thesis/dissertation. *Entrance requirements:* For doctorate, GRE General Test. Additional exam requirements/recommendations for international students: Required—TOEFL (minimum score 550 paper-based; 213 computer-based). Electronic applications accepted.

University at Buffalo, the State University of New York, Graduate School, Graduate School of Education, Department of Learning and Instruction, Buffalo, NY 14260. Offers biology education (Ed M, Certificate); chemistry education (Ed M, Certificate); childhood education (Ed M); childhood education with bilingual extension (Ed M); early childhood education (Ed M); early childhood education with bilingual extension (birth-grade 2) (Ed M); earth science education (Ed M, Certificate); educational technology and new literacies (Certificate); educational technology and new literacies (online) (Certificate); elementary education (Ed D, PhD); English education (Ed M, PhD, Certificate); English for speakers of other languages (Ed M); foreign and second language education (PhD); French education (Ed M, Certificate); general education (Ed M); German education (Ed M, Certificate); gifted education (online) (Certificate); Latin education (Ed M, Certificate); literacy teaching and learning (Certificate); literary specialist (Ed M); mathematics education (Ed M, PhD, Certificate); music education (Ed M, Certificate); physics education (Ed M, Certificate); reading education (PhD); science and the public (online) (Ed M); science education (PhD); social studies education (Ed M, Certificate); Spanish education (Ed M, Certificate); special education (PhD); teaching and leading for diversity (Certificate); teaching English to speakers of other languages (Ed M). Part-time and evening/weekend programs available. Postbaccalaureate distance learning degree programs offered (no on-campus study). *Faculty:* 32 full-time (23 women), 54 part-time/adjunct (43 women). *Students:* 294 full-time (222 women), 350 part-time (261 women); includes 75 minority (19 Black or African American, non-Hispanic/Latino; 6 American Indian or Alaska Native, non-Hispanic/Latino; 40 Asian, non-Hispanic/Latino; 10 Hispanic/Latino), 76 international. Average age 29. 548 applicants, 52% accepted, 253 enrolled. In 2011, 225 master's, 17 doctorates, 37 other advanced degrees awarded. *Degree requirements:* For master's, comprehensive exam; for doctorate, thesis/dissertation, research analysis exam, research experience component. *Entrance requirements:* For doctorate, GRE General Test or MAT, interview, writing sample, letters of recommendation. Additional exam requirements/recommendations for international students: Required—TOEFL (minimum score 600 paper-based; 96 iBT). *Application deadline:* For fall admission, 2/1 priority date for domestic students, 2/1 for international students; for spring admission, 11/15 priority date for domestic students, 10/1 for international students. Applications are processed on a rolling basis. Application fee: $50. Electronic applications accepted. *Financial support:* In 2011–12, 40 fellowships (averaging $12,991 per year), 46 research assistantships (averaging $10,986 per year) were awarded; teaching assistantships with full tuition reimbursements, career-related internships or fieldwork, Federal Work-Study, institutionally sponsored loans, scholarships/grants, and unspecified assistantships also available. Financial award application deadline: 2/28; financial award applicants required to submit FAFSA. *Faculty research:* Science assessment, foreign language teaching and learning, early learning, new literacies, gender and education. *Unit head:* Dr. Julie Sarama, Chair, 716-645-2455, Fax: 716-645-3161, E-mail: jcollins@buffalo.edu. *Application contact:* Cathy Dimino, Admissions Assistant, 716-645-2110, Fax: 716-645-7937, E-mail: cadimino@buffalo.edu.

University at Buffalo, the State University of New York, Graduate School, Graduate School of Education, Department of Library and Information Studies, Buffalo, NY 14260. Offers library and information studies (MLS, Certificate); library and information studies (online) (MLS); library media specialist (online) (MLS). *Accreditation:* ALA (one or more programs are accredited). Part-time programs available. Postbaccalaureate distance learning degree programs offered (no on-campus study). *Faculty:* 11 full-time (8 women), 26 part-time/adjunct (14 women). *Students:* 115 full-time (84 women), 218 part-time (167 women); includes 31 minority (15 Black or African American, non-Hispanic/Latino; 1 American Indian or Alaska Native, non-Hispanic/Latino; 8 Asian, non-Hispanic/Latino; 7 Hispanic/Latino), 5 international. Average age 34. 250 applicants, 57% accepted, 137 enrolled. In 2011, 112 master's, 4 other advanced degrees awarded. *Degree requirements:* For master's, thesis optional; for Certificate, thesis. *Entrance requirements:* For master's, minimum GPA of 3.0. Additional exam requirements/recommendations for international students: Required—TOEFL (minimum score 550 paper-based; 79 iBT). *Application deadline:* For fall admission, 4/1 priority date for domestic students, 4/1 for international students; for spring admission, 10/15 priority date for domestic students, 10/15 for international students. Applications are processed on a rolling basis. Application fee: $50. Electronic applications accepted. *Financial support:* In 2011–12, 14 fellowships (averaging $5,115 per year), 6 research assistantships (averaging $9,000 per year) were awarded; teaching assistantships, career-related internships or fieldwork, Federal Work-Study, institutionally sponsored loans, and unspecified assistantships also available. Support available to part-time students. Financial award application deadline: 3/1; financial award applicants required to submit FAFSA. *Faculty research:* Information-seeking behavior, thesauri, impact of technology, questioning behaviors, educational informatics. *Unit head:* Dr. Dagobert Soergel, Chair, 716-645-2412, Fax: 716-645-3775, E-mail: dsoergel@buffalo.edu. *Application contact:* Dr. Radhika Suresh, Director of Graduate Admissions and Student Services, 716-645-2110, Fax: 716-645-7937, E-mail: gse-info@buffalo.edu. Web site: http://www.gse.buffalo.edu/lis/.

University of Alaska Southeast, Graduate Programs, Program in Education, Juneau, AK 99801. Offers early childhood education (M Ed, MAT); educational technology (M Ed); elementary education (MAT); reading (M Ed); secondary education (MAT). *Accreditation:* NCATE. Part-time and evening/weekend programs available. Postbaccalaureate distance learning degree programs offered (minimal on-campus study). *Degree requirements:* For master's, comprehensive exam or project, portfolio. *Entrance requirements:* For master's, PRAXIS, minimum GPA of 3.0, writing sample, letters of recommendation. Electronic applications accepted. *Faculty research:* Applied classroom research, culturally responsive practices, action research, teaching effectiveness.

University of Alberta, Faculty of Graduate Studies and Research, Department of Educational Psychology, Edmonton, AB T6G 2E1, Canada. Offers counseling psychology (M Ed, PhD); educational psychology (M Ed, PhD); instructional technology (M Ed); school counseling (M Ed); school psychology (M Ed, PhD); special education (M Ed, PhD); special education-deafness studies (M Ed); teaching English as a second language (M Ed). Part-time programs available. *Degree requirements:* For master's, thesis optional; for doctorate, comprehensive exam, thesis/dissertation. *Entrance requirements:* For master's and doctorate, minimum GPA of 3.0. Additional exam requirements/recommendations for international students: Required—TOEFL. *Faculty research:* Human learning, development and assessment.

University of Arkansas, Graduate School, College of Education and Health Professions, Department of Curriculum and Instruction, Program in Educational Technology, Fayetteville, AR 72701-1201. Offers M Ed. *Accreditation:* NCATE. Part-time and evening/weekend programs available. *Students:* 3 full-time (all women), 36 part-time (26 women); includes 5 minority (3 Black or African American, non-Hispanic/Latino; 2 Two or more races, non-Hispanic/Latino). In 2011, 5 master's awarded. *Entrance requirements:* For master's, GRE General Test, MAT or minimum GPA of 3.0. *Application deadline:* For fall admission, 4/1 for international students; for spring admission, 10/1 for international students. Applications are processed on a rolling basis. Application fee: $40 ($50 for international students). Electronic applications accepted. *Financial support:* Fellowships with tuition reimbursements, research assistantships, teaching assistantships, career-related internships or fieldwork, and Federal Work-Study available. Support available to part-time students. Financial award application deadline: 4/1; financial award applicants required to submit FAFSA. *Unit head:* Dr. Michael Daugherty, Departmental Chairperson, 479-575-4209, E-mail: mkd03@uark.edu. *Application contact:* Dr. Barbara Gartin, Graduate Coordinator, 479-575-7525, Fax: 479-575-6676, E-mail: bgartin@uark.edu. Web site: http://etec.uark.edu/.

University of Arkansas at Little Rock, Graduate School, College of Education, Department of Educational Leadership, Program in Learning Systems Technology, Little Rock, AR 72204-1099. Offers M Ed. *Degree requirements:* For master's, comprehensive exam or defense of portfolio. *Entrance requirements:* For master's, GRE General Test, interview, minimum GPA of 2.75. *Faculty research:* Instructional program development, educational technology product development, educational technology management.

University of Calgary, Faculty of Graduate Studies, Faculty of Education, Graduate Division of Educational Research, Calgary, AB T2N 1N4, Canada. Offers community rehabilitation and disability studies (M Ed, M Sc, Ed D, PhD, Graduate Certificate, Graduate Diploma); curriculum, teaching and learning (M Ed, M Sc, MA, Ed D, PhD, Graduate Certificate, Graduate Diploma); educational contexts (M Ed, MA, Ed D, PhD, Graduate Certificate, Graduate Diploma); educational leadership (M Ed, MA, Ed D, PhD, Graduate Certificate, Graduate Diploma); educational technology (M Ed, M Sc, MA, Ed D, PhD, Graduate Certificate, Graduate Diploma); gifted education (M Sc, MA, Ed D, PhD, Graduate Certificate, Graduate Diploma); higher education administration (Ed D); interpretive studies in education (M Ed, M Sc, MA, Ed D, PhD, Graduate Certificate, Graduate Diploma); second language teaching (M Ed, Ed D, PhD, Graduate Certificate, Graduate Diploma); teaching English as a second language (M Ed, M Sc, MA, Ed D, PhD, Graduate Certificate, Graduate Diploma); workplace and adult learning (M Ed, MA, Ed D, PhD, Graduate Certificate, Graduate Diploma). Ed D in both higher education administration and educational leadership offered via distance delivery. Part-time and evening/weekend programs available. Postbaccalaureate distance learning degree programs offered (minimal on-campus study). *Degree requirements:* For master's, thesis (for some programs); for doctorate, thesis/dissertation, candidacy exam. *Entrance requirements:* For master's, minimum GPA of 3.0, 3 letters of reference; for doctorate, minimum GPA of 3.5, 3 letters of reference; for other advanced degree, minimum GPA of 3.0. Additional exam requirements/recommendations for international students: Required—TOEFL, IELTS. Electronic applications accepted. *Faculty research:* Curriculum, leadership, technology, contexts, gifted, second language teaching, work place and adult learning.

University of Central Arkansas, Graduate School, College of Education, Department of Leadership Studies, Program in Library Media and Information Technology, Conway, AR 72035-0001. Offers MS. Part-time programs available. *Students:* 5 full-time (4 women), 87 part-time (all women); includes 8 minority (2 Black or African American, non-Hispanic/Latino; 5 American Indian or Alaska Native, non-Hispanic/Latino; 1 Hispanic/Latino). Average age 36. 29 applicants, 100% accepted, 26 enrolled. In 2011, 49 master's awarded. *Degree requirements:* For master's, comprehensive exam. *Entrance requirements:* For master's, GRE General Test, minimum GPA of 2.7. Additional exam requirements/recommendations for international students: Required—TOEFL (minimum score 550 paper-based; 213 computer-based). *Application deadline:* For fall admission, 3/1 priority date for domestic students, 3/1 for international students; for spring admission, 10/1 priority date for domestic students, 10/1 for international students. Applications are processed on a rolling basis. Application fee: $25 ($50 for international students). *Expenses:* Tuition, state resident: full-time $4834; part-time $398.35 per credit hour. Tuition, nonresident: full-time $8686. *Financial support:* Federal Work-Study, scholarships/grants, and tuition waivers (partial) available. Financial award application deadline: 2/15; financial award applicants required to submit FAFSA. *Unit head:* Stephanie Huffman, Head, 501-450-5430, Fax: 501-450-5680, E-mail: steph@uca.edu. *Application contact:* Susan Wood, Administrative Specialist, 501-450-3124, Fax: 501-450-5678, E-mail: swood@uca.edu.

University of Central Florida, College of Education, Department of Educational and Human Sciences, Program in Instructional Systems, Orlando, FL 32816. Offers instructional design for simulations (Certificate); instructional systems (MA). *Students:* 17 full-time (9 women), 43 part-time (29 women); includes 15 minority (5 Black or African American, non-Hispanic/Latino; 3 Asian, non-Hispanic/Latino; 6 Hispanic/Latino; 1 Two or more races, non-Hispanic/Latino), 3 international. Average age 35. 25 applicants, 88% accepted, 17 enrolled. In 2011, 6 master's, 6 other advanced degrees awarded. Application fee: $30. Electronic applications accepted. *Expenses:* Tuition, state resident: part-time $277.08 per credit hour. Tuition, nonresident: part-time $277.08 per credit hour. Part-time tuition and fees vary according to degree level and program. *Financial support:* Fellowships with partial tuition reimbursements, research assistantships with partial tuition reimbursements, and teaching assistantships with partial tuition reimbursements available. *Unit head:* Dr. Atsusi Hirumi, Program Coordinator, 407-823-1760, E-mail: atsusi.hirumi@ucf.edu. *Application contact:* Barbara Rodriguez, Director, Admissions and Registration, 407-823-2766, Fax: 407-823-6442, E-mail: gradadmissions@ucf.edu.

University of Central Florida, College of Education, Education Doctoral Programs, Orlando, FL 32816. Offers communication sciences and disorders (PhD); counselor education (PhD); education (Ed D); elementary education (PhD); exceptional education (PhD); exercise physiology (PhD); higher education (PhD); hospitality education (PhD); instructional technology (PhD); mathematics education (PhD); reading education (PhD); science education (PhD); social science education (PhD); TESOL (PhD). *Students:* 135 full-time (87 women), 73 part-time (51 women); includes 49 minority (21 Black or African American, non-Hispanic/Latino; 4 Asian, non-Hispanic/Latino; 20 Hispanic/Latino; 4 Two or more races, non-Hispanic/Latino), 18 international. Average age 39. 125 applicants,

46% accepted, 46 enrolled. In 2011, 43 doctorates awarded. Application fee: $30. Electronic applications accepted. *Expenses:* Tuition, state resident: part-time $277.08 per credit hour. Tuition, nonresident: part-time $277.08 per credit hour. Part-time tuition and fees vary according to degree level and program. *Financial support:* In 2011–12, 85 students received support, including 48 fellowships with partial tuition reimbursements available (averaging $5,900 per year), 36 research assistantships with partial tuition reimbursements available (averaging $6,900 per year), 59 teaching assistantships with partial tuition reimbursements available (averaging $6,900 per year). *Unit head:* Dr. Rex Culp, Associate Dean, 407-823-5391, E-mail: rex.culp@ucf.edu. *Application contact:* Barbara Rodriguez, Associate Director, Admissions and Registration, 407-823-2766, Fax: 407-823-6442, E-mail: gradadmissions@ucf.edu. Web site: http://education.ucf.edu/departments.cfm.

University of Central Florida, College of Education, School of Teaching, Learning, and Leadership, Program in Educational Technology, Orlando, FL 32816. Offers educational technology (Certificate); instructional technology/media (MA), including e-learning, educational technology. *Students:* 19 full-time (17 women), 77 part-time (49 women); includes 23 minority (11 Black or African American, non-Hispanic/Latino; 2 Asian, non-Hispanic/Latino; 10 Hispanic/Latino), 6 international. Average age 36. 42 applicants, 90% accepted, 32 enrolled. In 2011, 11 master's, 3 other advanced degrees awarded. *Degree requirements:* For master's, thesis or alternative. *Application deadline:* For fall admission, 7/15 for domestic students; for spring admission, 12/1 for domestic students. Application fee: $30. Electronic applications accepted. *Expenses:* Tuition, state resident: part-time $277.08 per credit hour. Tuition, nonresident: part-time $277.08 per credit hour. Part-time tuition and fees vary according to degree level and program. *Financial support:* In 2011–12, 2 students received support, including 2 teaching assistantships (averaging $7,300 per year); career-related internships or fieldwork, Federal Work-Study, institutionally sponsored loans, tuition waivers (partial), and unspecified assistantships also available. *Unit head:* Dr. Glenda A. Gunter, Program Coordinator, 407-823-3502, E-mail: glenda.gunter@ucf.edu. *Application contact:* Barbara Rodriguez, Director, Admissions and Registration, 407-823-2766, Fax: 407-823-6442, E-mail: gradadmissions@ucf.edu.

University of Central Missouri, The Graduate School, College of Education, Warrensburg, MO 64093. Offers career and technical education administration (MS); career and technical education industry training (MS); career and technical education leadership/teaching (MS); college student personnel administration (MS); counseling (MS); curriculum and instruction (Ed S); educational leadership (Ed D); educational technology (MS); elementary education/educational foundations and literacy (MSE); elementary school administration (MSE); elementary school principalship (Ed S); human services/learning resources (Ed S); human services/professional counseling (Ed S); human services/special education (Ed S); human services/technology and occupational education (Ed S); K-12 education/educational foundations and literacy (MSE); K-12 special education (MSE); library science and information services (MS); literacy education (MSE); secondary education/educational foundations & literacy (MSE); secondary school administration (MSE); secondary school principalship (Ed S); superintendency (Ed S); teaching (MAT). Ed D offered jointly with University of Missouri. Part-time programs available. Postbaccalaureate distance learning degree programs offered. *Entrance requirements:* Additional exam requirements/recommendations for international students: Required—TOEFL (minimum score 550 paper-based; 79 computer-based). Electronic applications accepted.

University of Central Oklahoma, College of Graduate Studies and Research, College of Education and Professional Studies, Department of Advanced Professional and Special Services, Program in Library Media Education, Edmond, OK 73034-5209. Offers M Ed. *Accreditation:* NCATE. Part-time programs available. *Entrance requirements:* For master's, GRE General Test. Additional exam requirements/recommendations for international students: Required—TOEFL (minimum score 550 paper-based; 213 computer-based). *Application deadline:* For fall admission, 7/1 for international students; for spring admission, 11/1 for international students. Applications are processed on a rolling basis. Application fee: $25. Electronic applications accepted. *Expenses:* Tuition, state resident: full-time $3901; part-time $218.30 per credit hour. Tuition, nonresident: full-time $9198; part-time $511.20 per credit hour. Tuition and fees vary according to program. *Financial support:* Unspecified assistantships available. Financial award application deadline: 3/31; financial award applicants required to submit FAFSA. *Unit head:* Dr. Pat Couts, Adviser, 405-974-5888, Fax: 405-974-3822. *Application contact:* Dr. Richard Bernard, Dean, Jackson College of Graduate Studies, 405-974-3493, Fax: 405-974-3852, E-mail: gradcoll@uco.edu. Web site: http://www.uco.edu/ceps/dept/apss/instructional-media/index.asp.

University of Colorado Denver, School of Education and Human Development, Information and Learning Technologies Program, Denver, CO 80217-3364. Offers e-learning design and implementation (MA); instructional design and adult learning (MA); K-12 teaching (MA). Part-time and evening/weekend programs available. Postbaccalaureate distance learning degree programs offered (no on-campus study). *Students:* 82 full-time (65 women), 46 part-time (38 women); includes 13 minority (2 Black or African American, non-Hispanic/Latino; 3 Asian, non-Hispanic/Latino; 8 Hispanic/Latino), 3 international. Average age 38. 35 applicants, 89% accepted, 27 enrolled. In 2011, 79 master's awarded. *Degree requirements:* For master's, comprehensive exam (for some programs), comprehensive exam or online portfolio; 30 credit hours. *Entrance requirements:* For master's, GRE or MAT (if GPA is below 2.75), resume, statement of intent, three letters of recommendation. Additional exam requirements/recommendations for international students: Required—TOEFL (minimum score 525 paper-based; 197 computer-based). *Application deadline:* For fall admission, 5/15 for domestic students; for spring admission, 11/15 for domestic students. Application fee: $50 ($75 for international students). *Expenses:* Contact institution. *Financial support:* Scholarships/grants available. Financial award application deadline: 4/1; financial award applicants required to submit FAFSA. *Faculty research:* Technology for educational management, instructional design foundations, e-Learning, educational design. *Unit head:* Brent Wilson, Professor, 303-315-4963, E-mail: brent.wilson@ucdenver.edu. *Application contact:* Hans Broers, Academic Advisor, 303-315-6351, Fax: 303-315-6311, E-mail: hans.broers@ucdenver.edu. Web site: http://www.ucdenver.edu/ACADEMICS/COLLEGES/SCHOOLOFEDUCATION/ACADEMICS/Pages/AcademicPrograms.aspx.

University of Connecticut, Graduate School, Neag School of Education, Department of Educational Psychology, Program in Learning Technology, Storrs, CT 06269. Offers MA, PhD, Post-Master's Certificate. *Accreditation:* NCATE. Terminal master's awarded for partial completion of doctoral program. *Degree requirements:* For master's, comprehensive exam, thesis or alternative; for doctorate, thesis/dissertation. *Entrance requirements:* For master's and doctorate, GRE General Test. Additional exam requirements/recommendations for international students: Required—TOEFL (minimum score 550 paper-based; 213 computer-based). Electronic applications accepted.

University of Dayton, Department of Teacher Education, Dayton, OH 45469-1300. Offers adolescent/young adult (MS Ed); art education (MS Ed); early childhood education (MS Ed); early childhood leadership advocacy (MS Ed); inclusive early childhood (MS Ed); interdisciplinary education (MS Ed); intervention specialist education, mild/moderate (MS Ed); literacy (MS Ed); middle childhood (MS Ed); multi-age education (MS Ed); music education (MS Ed); teacher as leader (MS Ed); technology in education (MS Ed). Part-time and evening/weekend programs available. Postbaccalaureate distance learning degree programs offered (no on-campus study). *Faculty:* 15 full-time (11 women), 22 part-time/adjunct (20 women). *Students:* 41 full-time (29 women), 95 part-time (87 women); includes 13 minority (9 Black or African American, non-Hispanic/Latino; 1 Asian, non-Hispanic/Latino; 3 Hispanic/Latino), 9 international. Average age 32. 111 applicants, 55% accepted, 38 enrolled. In 2011, 97 degrees awarded. *Degree requirements:* For master's, thesis, capstone research project. *Entrance requirements:* For master's, GRE General Test, minimum GPA of 2.75. Additional exam requirements/recommendations for international students: Required—TOEFL (minimum score 550 paper-based; 213 computer-based; 80 iBT). *Application deadline:* For fall admission, 3/1 priority date for domestic students, 3/1 for international students; for winter admission, 7/1 for international students; for spring admission, 1/1 for international students. Applications are processed on a rolling basis. Application fee: $0 ($50 for international students). Electronic applications accepted. *Expenses:* Contact institution. *Financial support:* In 2011–12, 5 research assistantships with full and partial tuition reimbursements (averaging $8,470 per year) were awarded; career-related internships or fieldwork, institutionally sponsored loans, health care benefits, and unspecified assistantships also available. Financial award applicants required to submit FAFSA. *Faculty research:* Diversity, literacy, art representation by young children, preservice teacher preparation. *Unit head:* Dr. Katie A. Kinnucan-Welsch, Chair, 937-229-3346. *Application contact:* Alexsandar Popovski, Enrollment Management Administrator, 937-229-2357, Fax: 937-229-4729, E-mail: alex.popovski@notes.udayton.edu.

The University of Findlay, Graduate and Professional Studies, College of Education, Findlay, OH 45840-3653. Offers administration (MA Ed); children's literature (MA Ed); early childhood (MA Ed); human resource development (MA Ed); reading endorsement (MA Ed); science (MA Ed); special education (MA Ed); technology (MA Ed). *Accreditation:* NCATE. Part-time and evening/weekend programs available. Postbaccalaureate distance learning degree programs offered (no on-campus study). *Faculty:* 16 full-time (12 women), 5 part-time/adjunct (2 women). *Students:* 72 full-time (49 women), 198 part-time (119 women); includes 10 minority (7 Black or African American, non-Hispanic/Latino; 1 Asian, non-Hispanic/Latino; 2 Hispanic/Latino), 16 international. Average age 30. 75 applicants, 88% accepted, 36 enrolled. In 2011, 76 master's awarded. *Degree requirements:* For master's, thesis, cumulative project. *Entrance requirements:* For master's, bachelor's degree from accredited institution, minimum undergraduate GPA of 2.75 in last 62 hours of course work. Additional exam requirements/recommendations for international students: Required—TOEFL (minimum score 550 paper-based; 213 computer-based; 80 iBT). *Application deadline:* Applications are processed on a rolling basis. Application fee: $25. Electronic applications accepted. *Expenses:* Contact institution. *Financial support:* In 2011–12, 5 research assistantships with full and partial tuition reimbursements (averaging $4,200 per year) were awarded; Federal Work-Study, health care benefits, and unspecified assistantships also available. Financial award application deadline: 4/1; financial award applicants required to submit FAFSA. *Faculty research:* Children's literature, books and artwork, educational technology, professional development. *Unit head:* Dr. Julie McIntosh, Dean, 419-434-4862, Fax: 419-434-4822. *Application contact:* Heather Riffle, Assistant Director, Graduate and Professional Studies, 419-434-4640, Fax: 419-434-5517, E-mail: riffle@findlay.edu. Web site: http://www.findlay.edu.

University of Georgia, College of Education, Department of Educational Psychology and Instructional Technology, Athens, GA 30602. Offers education of the gifted (Ed D); educational psychology (M Ed, MA, Ed D, PhD, Ed S); instructional technology (M Ed, PhD, Ed S). *Accreditation:* NCATE. *Faculty:* 27 full-time (11 women). *Students:* 109 full-time (82 women), 130 part-time (99 women); includes 38 minority (25 Black or African American, non-Hispanic/Latino; 1 American Indian or Alaska Native, non-Hispanic/Latino; 6 Asian, non-Hispanic/Latino; 5 Hispanic/Latino; 1 Two or more races, non-Hispanic/Latino), 47 international. Average age 33. 151 applicants, 36% accepted, 25 enrolled. In 2011, 51 master's, 23 doctorates, 32 other advanced degrees awarded. *Entrance requirements:* For master's and Ed S, GRE General Test or MAT; for doctorate, GRE General Test. *Application deadline:* For fall admission, 7/1 priority date for domestic students; for spring admission, 11/15 for domestic students. Application fee: $50. Electronic applications accepted. *Financial support:* Fellowships, research assistantships, teaching assistantships, and unspecified assistantships available. *Unit head:* Dr. Roy P. Martin, Acting Head, 706-542-4261, Fax: 706-542-4240, E-mail: rpmartin@uga.edu. *Application contact:* Dr. Bonnie Crammond, Graduate Coordinator, 706-542-4248, E-mail: bcrammond@uga.edu. Web site: http://www.coe.uga.edu/epit.

University of Hartford, College of Education, Nursing, and Health Professions, Program in Educational Technology, West Hartford, CT 06117-1599. Offers M Ed. *Accreditation:* NCATE. Part-time and evening/weekend programs available. *Degree requirements:* For master's, comprehensive exam. *Entrance requirements:* For master's, interview, 2 letters of recommendation. Additional exam requirements/recommendations for international students: Required—TOEFL (minimum score 550 paper-based; 213 computer-based). Electronic applications accepted.

University of Hawaii at Manoa, Graduate Division, College of Education, Department of Educational Technology, Honolulu, HI 96822. Offers M Ed. Part-time programs available. *Degree requirements:* For master's, thesis optional. *Entrance requirements:* Additional exam requirements/recommendations for international students: Required—TOEFL (minimum score 650 paper-based; 280 computer-based; 114 iBT), IELTS (minimum score 7). *Faculty research:* Distance education-interaction via electronic means.

University of Hawaii at Manoa, Graduate Division, College of Education, PhD in Education Program, Honolulu, HI 96822. Offers curriculum and instruction (PhD); educational administration (PhD); educational foundations (PhD); educational policy studies (PhD); educational technology (PhD); exceptionalities (PhD); kinesiology (PhD). Part-time and evening/weekend programs available. *Degree requirements:* For doctorate, thesis/dissertation. *Entrance requirements:* For doctorate, GRE General Test, sample of written work. Additional exam requirements/recommendations for international students: Required—TOEFL (minimum score 600 paper-based; 250 computer-based; 100 iBT), IELTS (minimum score 7).

University of Houston–Clear Lake, School of Education, Program in Curriculum and Instruction, Houston, TX 77058-1098. Offers curriculum and instruction (MS); early childhood education (MS); reading (MS); school library and information science (MS). Part-time and evening/weekend programs available. *Degree requirements:* For master's, thesis (for some programs). *Entrance requirements:* For master's, GRE or minimum GPA of 3.0 in last 60 hours. Additional exam requirements/recommendations for international students: Required—TOEFL (minimum score 550 paper-based; 213 computer-based). Electronic applications accepted.

University of Houston–Clear Lake, School of Education, Program in Foundations and Professional Studies, Houston, TX 77058-1098. Offers counseling (MS); instructional technology (MS); multicultural studies (MS). Part-time and evening/weekend programs available. *Degree requirements:* For master's, thesis optional. *Entrance requirements:* For master's, GRE or minimum GPA of 3.0 in last 60 hours. Additional exam

requirements/recommendations for international students: Required—TOEFL (minimum score 550 paper-based; 213 computer-based). Electronic applications accepted.

University of Kentucky, Graduate School, College of Education, Program in Curriculum and Instruction, Lexington, KY 40506-0032. Offers curriculum and instruction (MA Ed, Ed D); instruction and administration (Ed D); instruction system design (MS Ed); middle school education (MS Ed). *Accreditation:* NCATE. *Degree requirements:* For master's, comprehensive exam, thesis optional; for doctorate, comprehensive exam, thesis/dissertation. *Entrance requirements:* For master's, GRE General Test, minimum undergraduate GPA of 2.75; for doctorate, GRE General Test, minimum graduate GPA of 3.0. Additional exam requirements/recommendations for international students: Required—TOEFL (minimum score 550 paper-based; 213 computer-based). Electronic applications accepted. *Faculty research:* Educational reform, multicultural education, classroom instructional practices, performance based assessment, primary school programs.

University of Maine, Graduate School, College of Education and Human Development, Program in Instructional Technology, Orono, ME 04469. Offers M Ed. Part-time and evening/weekend programs available. *Students:* 7 full-time (2 women), 13 part-time (8 women). Average age 35. 4 applicants, 100% accepted, 4 enrolled. In 2011, 5 degrees awarded. *Degree requirements:* For master's, thesis or alternative. *Entrance requirements:* For master's, MAT. Additional exam requirements/recommendations for international students: Required—TOEFL. *Application deadline:* Applications are processed on a rolling basis. Application fee: $65. Electronic applications accepted. *Expenses:* Tuition, state resident: full-time $5016. Tuition, nonresident: full-time $14,424. *Financial support:* Application deadline: 3/1. *Unit head:* Dr. Janet Spector, Coordinator, 207-581-2444, Fax: 207-581-2423. *Application contact:* Scott G. Delcourt, Associate Dean of the Graduate School, 207-581-3291, Fax: 207-581-3232, E-mail: graduate@maine.edu. Web site: http://www2.umaine.edu/graduate/.

University of Maryland, Baltimore County, Graduate School, College of Arts, Humanities and Social Sciences, Department of Education, Program in Instructional Systems Development, Baltimore, MD 21250. Offers distance education (Graduate Certificate); instructional design for e-learning (Graduate Certificate); instructional systems development (MA, Graduate Certificate); instructional technology (Graduate Certificate). Part-time and evening/weekend programs available. Postbaccalaureate distance learning degree programs offered (no on-campus study). *Faculty:* 2 full-time (0 women), 13 part-time/adjunct (4 women). *Students:* 5 full-time (3 women), 68 part-time (53 women); includes 51 minority (35 Black or African American, non-Hispanic/Latino; 1 American Indian or Alaska Native, non-Hispanic/Latino; 6 Asian, non-Hispanic/Latino; 7 Hispanic/Latino; 2 Two or more races, non-Hispanic/Latino), 4 international. Average age 44. 97 applicants, 85% accepted, 45 enrolled. In 2011, 38 master's, 47 other advanced degrees awarded. *Entrance requirements:* Additional exam requirements/recommendations for international students: Required—TOEFL (minimum score 550 paper-based; 213 computer-based; 80 iBT). *Application deadline:* For fall admission, 6/1 priority date for domestic students, 1/1 for international students; for spring admission, 11/1 priority date for domestic students, 6/1 for international students. Applications are processed on a rolling basis. Application fee: $50. Electronic applications accepted. *Financial support:* Applicants required to submit FAFSA. *Faculty research:* E-learning, distance education, instructional design. *Unit head:* Dr. Greg Williams, Director, 410-455-6773, Fax: 410-455-1344, E-mail: gregw@umbc.edu. *Application contact:* Sharese Essien, Program Coordinator, 410-455-8670, Fax: 410-455-1344, E-mail: sharese@umbc.edu. Web site: http://www.umbc.edu/isd.

University of Maryland, College Park, Academic Affairs, College of Education, Department of Education Policy and Leadership, College Park, MD 20742. Offers curriculum and educational communications (M Ed, MA, Ed D, PhD); social foundations of education (M Ed, MA, Ed D, PhD, CAGS). *Accreditation:* NCATE. Part-time and evening/weekend programs available. Postbaccalaureate distance learning degree programs offered (minimal on-campus study). *Students:* 93 full-time (67 women), 9 part-time (5 women); includes 46 minority (29 Black or African American, non-Hispanic/Latino; 8 Asian, non-Hispanic/Latino; 8 Hispanic/Latino; 1 Two or more races, non-Hispanic/Latino), 3 international. In 2011, 5 master's, 15 doctorates awarded. *Degree requirements:* For master's, thesis or alternative, internship and/or field experience; for doctorate, comprehensive exam, thesis/dissertation, practicum or internship. *Entrance requirements:* For master's, GRE General Test or MAT, minimum GPA of 3.0, scholarly writing sample, 3 letters of recommendation; for doctorate, GRE General Test or MAT, scholarly writing sample; minimum undergraduate GPA of 3.0, graduate 3.5. *Expenses: Tuition, area resident:* Part-time $525 per credit hour. Tuition, state resident: part-time $525 per credit hour. Tuition, nonresident: part-time $1131 per credit hour. *Required fees:* $386.31 per term. Tuition and fees vary according to program. *Financial support:* In 2011–12, 2 fellowships with full and partial tuition reimbursements (averaging $13,060 per year), 2 research assistantships (averaging $16,176 per year), 8 teaching assistantships (averaging $16,791 per year) were awarded; career-related internships or fieldwork, Federal Work-Study, and scholarships/grants also available. Support available to part-time students. Financial award applicants required to submit FAFSA. *Faculty research:* Educational technology, adult and higher education. *Total annual research expenditures:* $848. *Unit head:* Dennis Kivlighan, Chair, 301-405-2858, E-mail: dennisk@umd.edu. *Application contact:* Dr. Charles A. Caramello, Dean of Graduate School, 301-405-0358, Fax: 301-314-9305.

University of Massachusetts Amherst, Graduate School, School of Education, Program in Education, Amherst, MA 01003. Offers bilingual, English as a second language, and multicultural education (M Ed, CAGS); child study and early education (M Ed); children, families and schools (Ed D, CAGS); early childhood and elementary teacher education (M Ed); educational leadership (M Ed, CAGS); educational policy and leadership (Ed D); higher education (M Ed, CAGS); international education (M Ed); language, literacy and culture (Ed D); learning, media and technology (M Ed, CAGS); mathematics, science, and learning technologies (Ed D); policy studies in education (CAGS); psychometric methods, educational statistics and research methods (Ed D); reading and writing (M Ed); school counselor education (M Ed, CAGS); science education (CAGS); secondary teacher education (M Ed); social justice education (M Ed, Ed D, CAGS); special education (M Ed, Ed D, CAGS). *Accreditation:* NCATE. Part-time programs available. Postbaccalaureate distance learning degree programs offered (minimal on-campus study). *Faculty:* 81 full-time (46 women). *Students:* 341 full-time (240 women), 333 part-time (226 women); includes 113 minority (36 Black or African American, non-Hispanic/Latino; 1 American Indian or Alaska Native, non-Hispanic/Latino; 14 Asian, non-Hispanic/Latino; 51 Hispanic/Latino; 1 Native Hawaiian or other Pacific Islander, non-Hispanic/Latino; 10 Two or more races, non-Hispanic/Latino), 98 international. Average age 36. 721 applicants, 57% accepted, 202 enrolled. In 2011, 166 master's, 33 doctorates, 25 CAGSs awarded. Terminal master's awarded for partial completion of doctoral program. *Degree requirements:* For doctorate, comprehensive exam, thesis/dissertation. *Entrance requirements:* Additional exam requirements/recommendations for international students: Required—TOEFL (minimum score 550 paper-based; 213 computer-based; 80 iBT), IELTS (minimum score 6.5). *Application deadline:* For fall admission, 1/15 for domestic and international students. Applications are processed on a rolling basis. Application fee: $50 ($65 for international students). Electronic applications accepted. Tuition and fees vary according to course load, campus/location and program. *Financial support:* Fellowships with full and partial tuition reimbursements, research assistantships with full and partial tuition reimbursements, teaching assistantships with full and partial tuition reimbursements, career-related internships or fieldwork, Federal Work-Study, scholarships/grants, traineeships, health care benefits, tuition waivers (full and partial), and unspecified assistantships available. Support available to part-time students. Financial award application deadline: 1/15. *Unit head:* Dr. Linda L. Griffin, Graduate Program Director, 413-545-6984, Fax: 413-545-1523. *Application contact:* Lindsay DeSantis, Interim Supervisor of Admissions, 413-545-0722, Fax: 413-577-0010, E-mail: gradadm@grad.umass.edu. Web site: http://www.umass.edu/education/.

University of Memphis, Graduate School, College of Education, Department of Instruction and Curriculum Leadership, Memphis, TN 38152. Offers early childhood education (MAT, MS, Ed D); elementary education (MAT); instruction and curriculum (MS, Ed D); instruction design and technology (MS, Ed D); middle grades education (MAT); reading (MS, Ed D); secondary education (MAT); special education (MAT, MS, Ed D). *Accreditation:* NCATE (one or more programs are accredited). Part-time programs available. Terminal master's awarded for partial completion of doctoral program. *Degree requirements:* For master's, comprehensive exam, thesis or alternative; for doctorate, comprehensive exam, thesis/dissertation. *Entrance requirements:* For master's, GRE General Test, minimum GPA of 2.5; for doctorate, GRE General Test, GRE Subject Test, 2 years of teaching experience. Electronic applications accepted. *Faculty research:* Effective urban teachers, preparation and retention of urban teachers, technology utilization in schools, field-based teacher preparation programs, effective use of online instruction.

University of Michigan, Horace H. Rackham School of Graduate Studies, School of Information, Ann Arbor, MI 48109-1285. Offers archives and records management (MSI); community informatics (MSI); health informatics (MS); human computer interaction (MSI); information (PhD); information analysis and retrieval (MSI); information economics for management (MSI); information policy (MSI); library and information science (MSI); preservation of information (MSI); school library media (MSI); social computing (MSI). *Accreditation:* ALA (one or more programs are accredited). *Entrance requirements:* For master's and doctorate, GRE General Test. Additional exam requirements/recommendations for international students: Required—TOEFL (minimum score 600 paper-based; 100 iBT). Electronic applications accepted.

University of Michigan–Flint, School of Education and Human Services, Department of Education, Flint, MI 48502-1950. Offers education (MA); elementary education with teaching certification (MA); literacy (K-12) (MA); special education (MA); technology in education (MA). Part-time programs available. *Entrance requirements:* For master's, BS with minimum GPA of 3.0. Additional exam requirements/recommendations for international students: Required—TOEFL (minimum score 560 paper-based; 220 computer-based; 84 iBT), IELTS (minimum score 6.5). *Expenses:* Contact institution.

University of Minnesota, Twin Cities Campus, Graduate School, College of Education and Human Development, Department of Curriculum and Instruction, Minneapolis, MN 55455-0213. Offers art education (M Ed, MA, PhD); children's literature (M Ed, MA, PhD); curriculum and instruction (MA, PhD); early childhood education (M Ed, PhD); elementary education (M Ed, MA, PhD); English education (MA, PhD); environmental education (M Ed); family education (M Ed, MA, Ed D, PhD); instructional systems and technology (M Ed, MA, PhD); language arts (MA, PhD); language immersion education (Certificate); literacy education (MA); mathematics education (MA, PhD); reading education (MA, PhD); science education (MA, PhD); second languages and cultures education (MA, PhD); social studies education (MA, PhD); teaching (M Ed), including Chinese, earth science, elementary special education, English, English as a second language, French, German, Hebrew, Japanese, life sciences, mathematics, middle school science, science, second languages and cultures, social studies, Spanish; technology enhanced learning (Certificate); writing education (M Ed, MA, PhD). *Faculty:* 34 full-time (22 women). *Students:* 433 full-time (319 women), 310 part-time (239 women); includes 97 minority (34 Black or African American, non-Hispanic/Latino; 6 American Indian or Alaska Native, non-Hispanic/Latino; 35 Asian, non-Hispanic/Latino; 22 Hispanic/Latino), 47 international. Average age 33. 660 applicants, 68% accepted, 395 enrolled. In 2011, 518 master's, 19 doctorates, 14 other advanced degrees awarded. Application fee: $55. *Financial support:* In 2011–12, 6 fellowships (averaging $9,308 per year), 39 research assistantships with full tuition reimbursements (averaging $8,301 per year), 61 teaching assistantships with full tuition reimbursements (averaging $9,206 per year) were awarded. *Faculty research:* Teaching and learning; quality of education; influence of cultural, linguistic, social, political, technological and economic factors on teaching, learning and educational research; relationship between educational practice and a democratic and just society. *Total annual research expenditures:* $943,365. *Unit head:* Dr. Nina Asher, Chair, 612-624-4772, Fax: 612-624-1357, E-mail: nasher@umn.edu. *Application contact:* Dr. Jennifer Engler, Assistant Dean, 612-626-2887, Fax: 612-626-7496, E-mail: engle009@umn.edu. Web site: http://www.cehd.umn.edu/ci.

University of Missouri, Graduate School, College of Education, School of Information Science and Learning Technologies, Columbia, MO 65211. Offers educational technology (M Ed, Ed S); information science and learning technology (PhD); library science (MA). *Accreditation:* ALA (one or more programs are accredited). Part-time and evening/weekend programs available. *Faculty:* 16 full-time (11 women), 1 (woman) part-time/adjunct. *Students:* 125 full-time (89 women), 296 part-time (214 women); includes 19 minority (6 Black or African American, non-Hispanic/Latino; 1 American Indian or Alaska Native, non-Hispanic/Latino; 3 Asian, non-Hispanic/Latino; 8 Hispanic/Latino; 1 Two or more races, non-Hispanic/Latino), 22 international. Average age 34. 159 applicants, 66% accepted, 78 enrolled. In 2011, 154 master's, 3 doctorates, 20 other advanced degrees awarded. *Entrance requirements:* For master's, GRE General Test or MAT, minimum GPA of 3.0. Additional exam requirements/recommendations for international students: Required—TOEFL (minimum score 540 paper-based; 207 computer-based; 76 iBT). *Application deadline:* For fall admission, 3/1 priority date for domestic students; for winter admission, 10/1 priority date for domestic students; for spring admission, 3/1 priority date for domestic students. Applications are processed on a rolling basis. Application fee: $55 ($75 for international students). *Expenses:* Tuition, state resident: full-time $5881. Tuition, nonresident: full-time $15,183. *Required fees:* $952. Tuition and fees vary according to campus/location and program. *Financial support:* Fellowships and teaching assistantships available. *Faculty research:* Problem-based learning, technology usability in classrooms, computer-based performance support tools for children and youth with learning disabilities and/or emotional/behavioral disorders, engineering education collaboration environment , effectiveness of activities designed to recruit and retain women in engineering and science. *Unit head:* Dr. John Wedman, Director, E-mail: wedmanj@missouri.edu. *Application contact:* Amy Adam, 573-884-1391, E-mail: adamae@missouri.edu. Web site: http://education.missouri.edu/SISLT/.

University of Nebraska at Kearney, Graduate Studies, College of Education, Department of Teacher Education, Kearney, NE 68849-0001. Offers curriculum and instruction (MS Ed); instructional technology (MS Ed); reading education (MA Ed); special education (MA Ed). Part-time and evening/weekend programs available. *Degree requirements:* For master's, comprehensive exam, thesis optional. *Entrance* *requirements:* For master's, portfolio or GRE. Additional exam requirements/recommendations for international students: Required—TOEFL (minimum score 550 paper-based; 213 computer-based). Electronic applications accepted.

University of Nebraska at Omaha, Graduate Studies, College of Education, Department of Teacher Education, Omaha, NE 68182. Offers elementary education (MA, MS); instruction in urban schools (Certificate); instructional technology (Certificate); reading education (MS); secondary education (MA, MS). Part-time and evening/weekend programs available. *Faculty:* 20 full-time (14 women). *Students:* 20 full-time (17 women), 253 part-time (217 women); includes 11 minority (3 Black or African American, non-Hispanic/Latino; 1 American Indian or Alaska Native, non-Hispanic/Latino; 2 Asian, non-Hispanic/Latino; 5 Hispanic/Latino), 1 international. Average age 33. 62 applicants, 77% accepted, 34 enrolled. In 2011, 99 master's, 3 other advanced degrees awarded. *Degree requirements:* For master's, comprehensive exam (for some programs), thesis (for some programs). *Entrance requirements:* For master's, minimum GPA of 3.0. Additional exam requirements/recommendations for international students: Required—TOEFL (minimum score 550 paper-based; 213 computer-based; 80 iBT). *Application deadline:* For fall admission, 8/1 priority date for domestic students; for spring admission, 12/1 priority date for domestic students. Applications are processed on a rolling basis. Application fee: $45. Electronic applications accepted. *Financial support:* In 2011–12, 23 students received support, including 5 research assistantships with tuition reimbursements available; fellowships, teaching assistantships with tuition reimbursements available, Federal Work-Study, institutionally sponsored loans, scholarships/grants, tuition waivers (partial), and unspecified assistantships also available. Support available to part-time students. Financial award application deadline: 3/1; financial award applicants required to submit FAFSA. *Unit head:* Dr. Lana Danielson, Advisor, 402-554-2212. *Application contact:* Dr. Wilma Kuhlman, Student Contact, 402-554-2212.

University of Nevada, Las Vegas, Graduate College, College of Education, Department of Educational Research, Cognition, and Development, Las Vegas, NV 89154-3002. Offers educational leadership (M Ed, MS, Ed D, PhD); educational leadership-executive (Ed D); educational psychology (MS, PhD, Ed S); higher education leadership (PhD); learning and technology (PhD); school psychology (PhD); PhD/JD. *Accreditation:* NCATE. Part-time and evening/weekend programs available. *Faculty:* 28 full-time (14 women), 13 part-time/adjunct (9 women). *Students:* 54 full-time (40 women), 184 part-time (124 women); includes 68 minority (26 Black or African American, non-Hispanic/Latino; 1 American Indian or Alaska Native, non-Hispanic/Latino; 9 Asian, non-Hispanic/Latino; 21 Hispanic/Latino; 2 Native Hawaiian or other Pacific Islander, non-Hispanic/Latino; 9 Two or more races, non-Hispanic/Latino), 4 international. Average age 37. 70 applicants, 69% accepted, 41 enrolled. In 2011, 94 master's, 34 doctorates, 12 other advanced degrees awarded. *Degree requirements:* For master's, comprehensive exam (for some programs), thesis (for some programs); for doctorate, comprehensive exam (for some programs), thesis/dissertation; for Ed S, comprehensive exam, thesis. *Entrance requirements:* For master's, GMAT or GRE General Test; for doctorate, GRE General Test, writing exam; for Ed S, GRE General Test. Additional exam requirements/recommendations for international students: Required—TOEFL (minimum score 550 paper-based; 213 computer-based; 80 iBT), IELTS (minimum score 7). *Application deadline:* For fall admission, 2/1 for domestic students, 5/1 for international students; for spring admission, 10/1 for international students. Application fee: $60 ($95 for international students). Electronic applications accepted. *Financial support:* In 2011–12, 44 students received support, including 16 research assistantships with partial tuition reimbursements available (averaging $9,428 per year), 28 teaching assistantships with partial tuition reimbursements available (averaging $10,783 per year); institutionally sponsored loans, scholarships/grants, health care benefits, and unspecified assistantships also available. Financial award application deadline: 3/1. *Faculty research:* Innovation and change in educational settings; educational policy, finance, and marketing; psycho-educational assessment; student retention, persistence, development, language, and culture; statistical modeling, program evaluation, qualitative and quantitative research methods. *Total annual research expenditures:* $269,710. *Unit head:* Dr. LeAnn Putney, Chair/Professor, 702-895-4879, Fax: 702-895-3492, E-mail: leann.putney@unlv.edu. *Application contact:* Graduate College Admissions Evaluator, 702-895-3320, Fax: 702-895-4180, E-mail: gradcollege@unlv.edu. Web site: http://education.unlv.edu/ercd/.

University of New Mexico, Graduate School, College of Education, Department of Educational Leadership and Organizational Learning, Program in Organizational Learning and Instructional Technologies, Albuquerque, NM 87131-2039. Offers MA, PhD, Ed S. *Accreditation:* NCATE. Part-time and evening/weekend programs available. Postbaccalaureate distance learning degree programs offered (no on-campus study). *Students:* 26 full-time (18 women), 95 part-time (67 women); includes 52 minority (5 Black or African American, non-Hispanic/Latino; 2 American Indian or Alaska Native, non-Hispanic/Latino; 3 Asian, non-Hispanic/Latino; 41 Hispanic/Latino; 1 Two or more races, non-Hispanic/Latino), 4 international. Average age 45. 54 applicants, 50% accepted, 18 enrolled. In 2011, 18 master's, 8 doctorates awarded. *Degree requirements:* For master's, comprehensive exam, thesis or alternative; for doctorate, comprehensive exam, thesis/dissertation. *Entrance requirements:* For master's, minimum GPA of 3.0 in last 60 hours of course work, bachelor's degree; for doctorate, GRE General Test, MAT, master's degree, minimum GPA of 3.5. Additional exam requirements/recommendations for international students: Required—TOEFL. *Application deadline:* For fall admission, 3/15 for domestic and international students; for spring admission, 10/15 for domestic and international students. Application fee: $50. Electronic applications accepted. *Financial support:* In 2011–12, 47 students received support, including 3 fellowships (averaging $2,290 per year), 3 research assistantships (averaging $8,333 per year), 2 teaching assistantships with tuition reimbursements available (averaging $8,396 per year); career-related internships or fieldwork also available. Financial award application deadline: 3/1; financial award applicants required to submit FAFSA. *Faculty research:* Adult learning, distance education, instructional multimedia, organizational learning and development, transformational learning, workplace and learning environment factors that enhance learning and productivity, program and organization evaluation and reform, effects of technology on learning and problem solving. *Total annual research expenditures:* $40,000. *Unit head:* Dr. Mark Salisbury, Program Director, 505-277-9678, Fax: 505-277-5553, E-mail: salisbu@unm.edu. *Application contact:* Linda Wood, Program Coordinator, 505-277-4131, Fax: 505-277-5553, E-mail: woodl@unm.edu. Web site: http://www.unm.edu/~olit/.

The University of North Carolina at Charlotte, Graduate School, College of Education, Department of Educational Leadership, Charlotte, NC 28223-0001. Offers curriculum and supervision (M Ed); educational leadership (Ed D); instructional systems technology (M Ed); school administration (MSA). Part-time and evening/weekend programs available. *Faculty:* 24 full-time (12 women), 2 part-time/adjunct (0 women). *Students:* 32 full-time (22 women), 180 part-time (120 women); includes 74 minority (68 Black or African American, non-Hispanic/Latino; 1 American Indian or Alaska Native, non-Hispanic/Latino; 2 Asian, non-Hispanic/Latino; 2 Hispanic/Latino; 1 Two or more races, non-Hispanic/Latino), 1 international. Average age 38. 26 applicants, 92% accepted, 21 enrolled. In 2011, 46 master's, 27 doctorates awarded. *Degree requirements:* For master's, thesis. *Entrance requirements:* For master's and doctorate, GRE or MAT. Additional exam requirements/recommendations for international students: Required—TOEFL (minimum score 550 paper-based; 220 computer-based; 83 iBT). *Application deadline:* For fall admission, 7/1 for domestic students, 5/1 for international students; for spring admission, 11/1 for domestic students, 10/1 for international students. Applications are processed on a rolling basis. Application fee: $65 ($75 for international students). Electronic applications accepted. *Expenses:* Tuition, state resident: full-time $3689. Tuition, nonresident: full-time $15,226. *Required fees:* $2198. Tuition and fees vary according to course load and program. *Financial support:* In 2011–12, 4 students received support, including 4 research assistantships (averaging $6,031 per year); career-related internships or fieldwork, institutionally sponsored loans, scholarships/grants, and unspecified assistantships also available. Support available to part-time students. Financial award application deadline: 4/1; financial award applicants required to submit FAFSA. *Faculty research:* Educational leadership theory and practice, instructional systems technology, educational research methodology, curriculum and supervision in the schools, school law and finance. *Total annual research expenditures:* $638,519. *Unit head:* Dr. Dawson R. Hancock, Chair, 704-687-8863, Fax: 704-687-3493, E-mail: dhancock@uncc.edu. *Application contact:* Kathy B. Giddings, Director of Graduate Admissions, 704-687-5503, Fax: 704-687-3279, E-mail: gradadm@uncc.edu. Web site: http://education.uncc.uncc.edu/eart/programs.htm.

The University of North Carolina at Greensboro, Graduate School, School of Education, Department of Curriculum and Instruction, Greensboro, NC 27412-5001. Offers college teaching and adult learning (Certificate); curriculum and instruction (M Ed), including chemistry education, elementary education, English as a second language, French education, instructional technology, mathematics education, middle grades education, reading education, science education, social studies education, Spanish education; curriculum and teaching (PhD), including higher education, teacher education and development; English as a second language (Certificate); higher education (M Ed); supervision (M Ed). *Accreditation:* NCATE. Part-time programs available. *Degree requirements:* For doctorate, thesis/dissertation. *Entrance requirements:* For master's and doctorate, GRE General Test. Additional exam requirements/recommendations for international students: Required—TOEFL. Electronic applications accepted. *Faculty research:* Community college literacy program, middle school mathematics/computer mathematics.

The University of North Carolina Wilmington, Watson School of Education, Department of Elementary, Middle Level and Literacy Education, Program in Middle Grades Education, Wilmington, NC 28403-3297. Offers instructional technology (MS); secondary education (M Ed). *Degree requirements:* For master's, comprehensive exam.

The University of North Carolina Wilmington, Watson School of Education, Department of Instructional Technology, Foundations and Secondary Education, Wilmington, NC 28403-3297. Offers instructional technology (MS); secondary education (M Ed); teaching (MAT). *Degree requirements:* For master's, comprehensive exam, thesis or alternative. *Entrance requirements:* Additional exam requirements/recommendations for international students: Required—TOEFL (minimum score 550 paper-based; 217 computer-based; 79 iBT), IELTS (minimum score 6.5).

University of North Dakota, Graduate School, College of Education and Human Development, Department of Instructional Design and Technology, Grand Forks, ND 58202. Offers M Ed, MS. *Degree requirements:* For master's, comprehensive exam, thesis or alternative. *Entrance requirements:* For master's, minimum GPA of 3.0. Additional exam requirements/recommendations for international students: Required—TOEFL (minimum score 550 paper-based; 213 computer-based; 79 iBT), IELTS (minimum score 6.5). Electronic applications accepted.

University of Northern Colorado, Graduate School, College of Education and Behavioral Sciences, Department of Educational Technology, Greeley, CO 80639. Offers educational technology (MA, PhD); school library education (MA). *Accreditation:* NCATE. Part-time programs available. Postbaccalaureate distance learning degree programs offered (minimal on-campus study). *Degree requirements:* For master's, comprehensive exam, thesis or alternative; for doctorate, comprehensive exam, thesis/dissertation. *Entrance requirements:* For master's and doctorate, GRE General Test, 3 letters of reference. Electronic applications accepted.

University of Northern Iowa, Graduate College, College of Education, Department of Curriculum and Instruction, Program in Instructional Technology, Cedar Falls, IA 50614. Offers curriculum and instruction (MA); curriculum and instruction: instructional technology school library endorsement (MA); performance and training technology (MA). *Students:* 9 full-time (3 women), 26 part-time (23 women); includes 6 minority (4 Black or African American, non-Hispanic/Latino; 2 Hispanic/Latino), 4 international. 14 applicants, 79% accepted, 9 enrolled. In 2011, 8 master's awarded. *Degree requirements:* For master's, comprehensive exam, thesis or alternative. *Entrance requirements:* For master's, minimum GPA of 3.0. Additional exam requirements/recommendations for international students: Required—TOEFL (minimum score 500 paper-based; 180 computer-based; 61 iBT). *Application deadline:* For fall admission, 8/1 priority date for domestic students. Applications are processed on a rolling basis. Application fee: $50 ($70 for international students). Electronic applications accepted. *Expenses:* Tuition, state resident: full-time $7476. Tuition, nonresident: full-time $16,410. *Required fees:* $942. *Financial support:* Application deadline: 2/1. *Unit head:* Dr. Leigh Zeitz, Coordinator, 319-273-3249, Fax: 319-273-5886, E-mail: zeitz@uni.edu. *Application contact:* Laurie S. Russell, Record Analyst, 319-273-2623, Fax: 319-273-2885, E-mail: laurie.russell@uni.edu. Web site: http://www.uni.edu/coe/ci/.

University of Northern Iowa, Graduate College, College of Education, Department of Curriculum and Instruction, Program in School Library Media Studies, Cedar Falls, IA 50614. Offers MA. Part-time and evening/weekend programs available. *Students:* 1 (woman) full-time, 48 part-time (44 women); includes 2 minority (both Hispanic/Latino). 26 applicants, 69% accepted, 17 enrolled. In 2011, 25 master's awarded. *Degree requirements:* For master's, comprehensive exam (for some programs), thesis or alternative, comprehensive portfolio. *Entrance requirements:* For master's, minimum GPA of 3.0. Additional exam requirements/recommendations for international students: Required—TOEFL (minimum score 500 paper-based; 180 computer-based; 61 iBT). *Application deadline:* For fall admission, 8/1 priority date for domestic students. Applications are processed on a rolling basis. Application fee: $50 ($70 for international students). Electronic applications accepted. *Expenses:* Tuition, state resident: full-time $7476. Tuition, nonresident: full-time $16,410. *Required fees:* $942. *Financial support:* Career-related internships or fieldwork, Federal Work-Study, scholarships/grants, and tuition waivers (full and partial) available. Support available to part-time students. Financial award application deadline: 2/1. *Unit head:* Dr. Karla Krueger, Coordinator, 319-273-2050, Fax: 319-273-5886, E-mail: karla.krueger@uni.edu. *Application contact:* Laurie S. Russell, Record Analyst, 319-273-2623, Fax: 319-273-2885, E-mail: laurie.russell@uni.edu. Web site: http://www.uni.edu/coe/ci/slm/index.shtml.

University of North Florida, College of Education and Human Services, Department of Leadership, School Counseling and Sport Management, Jacksonville, FL 32224. Offers counselor education (M Ed), including school counseling; educational leadership (M Ed, Ed D), including athletic administration (M Ed), educational leadership (Ed D), educational leadership (certification) (M Ed), educational technology (M Ed), instructional leadership (M Ed). Part-time and evening/weekend programs available.

Faculty: 15 full-time (9 women). *Students:* 48 full-time (35 women), 200 part-time (135 women); includes 67 minority (47 Black or African American, non-Hispanic/Latino; 2 American Indian or Alaska Native, non-Hispanic/Latino; 6 Asian, non-Hispanic/Latino; 10 Hispanic/Latino; 2 Two or more races, non-Hispanic/Latino), 2 international. Average age 36. 97 applicants, 48% accepted, 41 enrolled. In 2011, 84 master's, 6 doctorates awarded. *Degree requirements:* For doctorate, thesis/dissertation. *Entrance requirements:* For master's, GRE General Test, minimum GPA of 3.0 in last 60 hours, interview, 3 letters of recommendation; for doctorate, GRE General Test, master's degree, interview, 3 letters of recommendation, writing sample. Additional exam requirements/recommendations for international students: Required—TOEFL (minimum score 500 paper-based; 173 computer-based). *Application deadline:* For fall admission, 7/1 priority date for domestic students, 5/1 for international students; for spring admission, 11/1 priority date for domestic students, 10/1 for international students. Applications are processed on a rolling basis. Application fee: $30. Electronic applications accepted. *Expenses:* Tuition, state resident: full-time $8793; part-time $366.38 per credit hour. Tuition, nonresident: full-time $23,502; part-time $979.24 per credit hour. *Required fees:* $1384; $57.66 per credit hour. Tuition and fees vary according to course load and program. *Financial support:* In 2011–12, 68 students received support, including 2 research assistantships (averaging $6,200 per year), 2 teaching assistantships (averaging $6,250 per year); career-related internships or fieldwork, Federal Work-Study, scholarships/grants, tuition waivers (partial), and unspecified assistantships also available. Support available to part-time students. Financial award application deadline: 4/1; financial award applicants required to submit FAFSA. *Faculty research:* Counseling: ethics; lesbian, bisexual and transgender issues; educational leadership: school culture and climate; educational assessment and accountability; school safety and student discipline. *Total annual research expenditures:* $137,500. *Unit head:* Dr. Edgar N. Jackson, Jr., Chair, 904-620-1829, E-mail: newton.jackson@unf.edu. *Application contact:* Lillith Richardson, Assistant Director, The Graduate School, 904-620-1360, Fax: 904-620-1362, E-mail: graduateschool@unf.edu. Web site: http://www.unf.edu/coehs/lscsm/.

University of North Texas, Toulouse Graduate School, College of Information, Department of Learning Technologies, Program in Educational Computing, Denton, TX 76203. Offers PhD. *Entrance requirements:* Additional exam requirements/recommendations for international students: Recommended—TOEFL (minimum score 550 paper-based; 213 computer-based; 79 iBT). Electronic applications accepted. *Expenses:* Tuition, state resident: part-time $100 per credit hour. Tuition, nonresident: part-time $413 per credit hour.

University of North Texas, Toulouse Graduate School, College of Information, Department of Library and Information Sciences, Denton, TX 76203. Offers information science (MS, PhD); learning technologies (M Ed, Ed D), including applied technology, training and development (M Ed), computer education and cognitive systems, educational computing; library science (MS). *Accreditation:* ALA (one or more programs are accredited). Part-time and evening/weekend programs available. *Degree requirements:* For master's, comprehensive exam; for doctorate, comprehensive exam, thesis/dissertation. *Entrance requirements:* For master's, GRE General Test, MAT; for doctorate, GRE General Test. Additional exam requirements/recommendations for international students: Recommended—TOEFL (minimum score 550 paper-based; 213 computer-based; 79 iBT). Electronic applications accepted. *Expenses:* Tuition, state resident: part-time $100 per credit hour. Tuition, nonresident: part-time $413 per credit hour. *Faculty research:* Information resources and services, information management and retrieval, computer-based information systems, human information behavior.

University of Oklahoma, Jeannine Rainbolt College of Education, Department of Educational Psychology, Program in Instructional Psychology and Technology, Norman, OK 73019. Offers instructional psychology and technology (M Ed, PhD), including educational psychology (M Ed), general (M Ed), instructional design (M Ed), integrating technology in teaching (M Ed), interactive learning technologies (M Ed), teaching and assessment (M Ed), teaching with technology (M Ed). Part-time and evening/weekend programs available. *Students:* 23 full-time (16 women), 27 part-time (20 women); includes 14 minority (8 Black or African American, non-Hispanic/Latino; 1 American Indian or Alaska Native, non-Hispanic/Latino; 3 Hispanic/Latino; 2 Two or more races, non-Hispanic/Latino), 9 international. Average age 33. 22 applicants, 77% accepted, 17 enrolled. In 2011, 12 master's, 2 doctorates awarded. *Degree requirements:* For master's, comprehensive exam (for some programs), thesis optional; for doctorate, thesis/dissertation, general exam. *Entrance requirements:* For master's, minimum GPA of 3.0; for doctorate, GRE General Test, master's degree, minimum graduate GPA of 3.25. Additional exam requirements/recommendations for international students: Required—TOEFL (minimum score 550 paper-based; 79 iBT). *Application deadline:* For fall admission, 3/15 for domestic students, 3/1 for international students; for spring admission, 10/15 for domestic and international students. Applications are processed on a rolling basis. Application fee: $40 ($90 for international students). Electronic applications accepted. *Expenses:* Tuition, state resident: full-time $4087; part-time $170.30 per credit hour. Tuition, nonresident: full-time $14,875; part-time $619.80 per credit hour. *Required fees:* $2659; $100.25 per credit hour. Tuition and fees vary according to course load and degree level. *Financial support:* In 2011–12, 39 students received support. Career-related internships or fieldwork, Federal Work-Study, scholarships/grants, health care benefits, and unspecified assistantships available. Support available to part-time students. Financial award applicants required to submit FAFSA. *Faculty research:* Cognition and instruction, motivation and instruction, instructional design, technology integration in education, interactive learning technologies, measurement and assessment. *Unit head:* Dr. Terri K. Debacker, Chair, 405-325-1068, Fax: 405-325-6655, E-mail: debacker@ou.edu. *Application contact:* Shannon Vazquez, Graduate Programs Officer, 405-325-4525, Fax: 405-325-6655, E-mail: shannonv@ou.edu. Web site: http://education.ou.edu/ipt.

University of Pennsylvania, Graduate School of Education, Division of Teaching, Learning, and Leadership, Programs in Learning Science and Technologies, Philadelphia, PA 19104. Offers MS Ed. *Students:* 3 full-time (2 women), 2 part-time (1 woman); includes 1 minority (Black or African American, non-Hispanic/Latino), 3 international. 18 applicants, 61% accepted, 2 enrolled. In 2011, 1 master's awarded. *Degree requirements:* For master's, comprehensive exam or portfolio. *Entrance requirements:* For master's, GRE, MAT. *Application deadline:* For fall admission, 12/15 priority date for domestic students. Applications are processed on a rolling basis. Application fee: $70. Electronic applications accepted. *Expenses:* Contact institution. *Financial support:* Applicants required to submit FAFSA. *Unit head:* Dr. Andrew Porter, Dean, 215-898-7014. *Application contact:* Vernell Edwards, 215-746-2566, E-mail: edwardsv@gse.upenn.edu.

University of Phoenix–Online Campus, School of Advanced Studies, Phoenix, AZ 85034-7209. Offers business administration (DBA); education (Ed S); educational leadership (Ed D), including curriculum and instruction, education technology, educational leadership; health administration (DHA); higher education administration (PhD); industrial/organizational psychology (PhD); nursing (PhD); organizational leadership (DM), including information systems and technology, organizational leadership. Evening/weekend programs available. Postbaccalaureate distance learning degree programs offered. *Students:* 7,581 full-time (5,042 women); includes 3,199 minority (2,505 Black or African American, non-Hispanic/Latino; 68 American Indian or Alaska Native, non-Hispanic/Latino; 158 Asian, non-Hispanic/Latino; 395 Hispanic/Latino; 46 Native Hawaiian or other Pacific Islander, non-Hispanic/Latino; 27 Two or more races, non-Hispanic/Latino), 397 international. Average age 44. *Degree requirements:* For doctorate, thesis/dissertation. *Entrance requirements:* Additional exam requirements/recommendations for international students: Required—TOEFL, TOEIC (Test of English as an International Communication), Berlitz Online English Proficiency Exam, Pearson Test of English, or IELTS. *Application deadline:* Applications are processed on a rolling basis. Application fee: $45. Electronic applications accepted. *Expenses:* Contact institution. *Financial support:* Scholarships/grants available. Financial award applicants required to submit FAFSA. *Unit head:* Dr. Jeremy Moreland, Executive Dean. *Application contact:* 866-766-0766. Web site: http://www.phoenix.edu/colleges_divisions/doctoral.html.

University of Phoenix–Washington D.C. Campus, College of Education, Washington, DC 20001. Offers administration and supervision (MA Ed); adult education and training (MA Ed); computer education (MA Ed); curriculum and instruction (MA Ed, Ed D); early childhood education (MA Ed); education (Ed S); educational leadership (Ed D); educational technology (Ed D); elementary teacher education (MA Ed); English and language arts education (MA Ed); English as a second language (MA Ed); higher education administration (PhD); mathematics education (MA Ed); secondary teacher education (MA Ed); special education (MA Ed); teacher leadership (MA Ed).

University of Phoenix–West Florida Campus, College of Education, Temple Terrace, FL 33637. Offers administration and supervision (MA Ed); curriculum and instruction (MA Ed), including computer education, curriculum and instruction, mathematics education; curriculum and technology (MA Ed); early childhood education (MA Ed); elementary teacher education (MA Ed); secondary teacher education (MA Ed). Evening/weekend programs available. *Degree requirements:* For master's, thesis (for some programs). *Entrance requirements:* For master's, 3 years of work experience, minimum undergraduate GPA of 2.5. Additional exam requirements/recommendations for international students: Required—TOEFL (minimum score 550 paper-based; 213 computer-based; 79 iBT).

University of St. Thomas, Graduate Studies, School of Education, Program in Organization Learning and Development, St. Paul, MN 55105-1096. Offers e-learning (Certificate); human resource management (Certificate); learning technology (MA); organization development (Ed D, Certificate); strategic resources and change leadership (MA). Part-time and evening/weekend programs available. Postbaccalaureate distance learning degree programs offered (minimal on-campus study). *Faculty:* 6 full-time (4 women), 15 part-time/adjunct (8 women). *Students:* 6 full-time (all women), 125 part-time (96 women); includes 26 minority (13 Black or African American, non-Hispanic/Latino; 5 Asian, non-Hispanic/Latino; 4 Hispanic/Latino; 1 Native Hawaiian or other Pacific Islander, non-Hispanic/Latino; 3 Two or more races, non-Hispanic/Latino), 9 international. Average age 38. 40 applicants, 85% accepted, 28 enrolled. In 2011, 31 master's, 9 doctorates awarded. *Degree requirements:* For master's, practicum; for doctorate, comprehensive exam, thesis/dissertation. *Entrance requirements:* For master's, minimum GPA of 3.0, 2 letters of reference, personal statement, 2-5 years of organization experience; for doctorate, minimum GPA of 3.5, interview, 5-7 years of OD or leadership experience; for Certificate, minimum graduate GPA of 3.25. Additional exam requirements/recommendations for international students: Required—TOEFL (minimum score 550 paper-based; 213 computer-based). *Application deadline:* For fall admission, 8/1 priority date for domestic students, 8/1 for international students; for winter admission, 12/1 priority date for domestic students, 12/1 for international students; for spring admission, 12/1 priority date for domestic students, 12/1 for international students. Applications are processed on a rolling basis. Application fee: $50. Electronic applications accepted. *Expenses:* Contact institution. *Financial support:* In 2011–12, 1 student received support. Fellowships, research assistantships, institutionally sponsored loans, and scholarships/grants available. Support available to part-time students. Financial award applicants required to submit FAFSA. *Faculty research:* Workplace conflict, physician leaders, virtual teams, technology use in schools/workplace, developing masterful practitioners. *Unit head:* Dr. David W. Jamieson, Department Chair, 651-962-4387, Fax: 651-962-4169, E-mail: djamieson@stthomas.edu. *Application contact:* Liz G. Knight, Program Manager, 651-962-4459, Fax: 651-962-4169, E-mail: egknight@stthomas.edu. Web site: http://www.stthomas.edu/education.

University of San Francisco, School of Education, Department of Learning and Instruction, San Francisco, CA 94117-1080. Offers digital media and learning (MA); learning and instruction (MA, Ed D); teaching (MA); teaching reading (MA). *Faculty:* 10 full-time (6 women), 1 part-time/adjunct (0 women). *Students:* 275 full-time (201 women), 67 part-time (42 women); includes 97 minority (7 Black or African American, non-Hispanic/Latino; 3 American Indian or Alaska Native, non-Hispanic/Latino; 32 Asian, non-Hispanic/Latino; 34 Hispanic/Latino; 1 Native Hawaiian or other Pacific Islander, non-Hispanic/Latino; 20 Two or more races, non-Hispanic/Latino), 4 international. Average age 32. 310 applicants, 72% accepted, 135 enrolled. In 2011, 118 master's, 10 doctorates awarded. *Degree requirements:* For doctorate, thesis/dissertation. Application fee: $55 ($65 for international students). *Expenses: Tuition:* Full-time $20,070; part-time $1115 per unit. Tuition and fees vary according to course load, campus/location and program. *Financial support:* In 2011–12, 54 students received support. Fellowships, research assistantships, and teaching assistantships available. Financial award application deadline: 3/2; financial award applicants required to submit FAFSA. *Unit head:* Dr. Robert Burns, Chair, 415-422-6289. *Application contact:* Beth Teague, Associate Director of Graduate Outreach, 415-422-5467, E-mail: schoolofeducation@usfca.edu.

University of Sioux Falls, Fredrikson School of Education, Sioux Falls, SD 57105-1699. Offers educational administration (Ed S), including principal leadership, superintendent and district leadership; leadership in reading (M Ed); leadership in schools (M Ed); leadership in technology (M Ed); teaching (M Ed). Admission in summer only. *Accreditation:* NCATE. Part-time and evening/weekend programs available. *Faculty:* 9 full-time (8 women), 10 part-time/adjunct (7 women). *Students:* 196 part-time (144 women); includes 2 minority (1 Black or African American, non-Hispanic/Latino; 1 American Indian or Alaska Native, non-Hispanic/Latino). 55 applicants, 100% accepted, 47 enrolled. *Degree requirements:* For master's, comprehensive exam (for some programs), research application project; for Ed S, comprehensive exam, portfolio. *Entrance requirements:* For master's, minimum GPA of 3.0, 1 year of teaching experience; for Ed S, minimum 3 years of teaching experience, minimum cumulative GPA of 3.5, 1 year of administrative experience. Additional exam requirements/recommendations for international students: Required—TOEFL. *Application deadline:* Applications are processed on a rolling basis. Application fee: $25. *Expenses: Tuition:* Part-time $345 per semester hour. *Required fees:* $35 per term. Part-time tuition and fees vary according to degree level and program. *Financial support:* Available to part-time students. Applicants required to submit FAFSA. *Faculty research:* Reading, literacy, leadership. *Unit head:* Dawn Olson, Director of Graduate Programs in Education, 605-575-2083, Fax: 605-575-2079, E-mail: dawn.olson@usiouxfalls.edu. *Application contact:* Student Contact, 605-331-5000.

University of South Africa, College of Human Sciences, Pretoria, South Africa. Offers adult education (M Ed); African languages (MA, PhD); African politics (MA, PhD); Afrikaans (MA, PhD); ancient history (MA, PhD); ancient Near Eastern studies (MA, PhD); anthropology (MA, PhD); applied linguistics (MA); Arabic (MA, PhD); archaeology (MA); art history (MA); Biblical archaeology (MA); Biblical studies (M Th, D Th, PhD); Christian spirituality (M Th, D Th); church history (M Th, D Th); classical studies (MA, PhD); clinical psychology (MA); communication (MA, PhD); comparative education (M Ed, Ed D); consulting psychology (D Admin, D Com, PhD); curriculum studies (M Ed, Ed D); development studies (M Admin, MA, D Admin, PhD); didactics (M Ed, Ed D); education (M Tech); education management (M Ed, Ed D); educational psychology (M Ed); English (MA); environmental education (M Ed); French (MA, PhD); German (MA, PhD); Greek (MA); guidance and counseling (M Ed); health studies (MA, PhD), including health sciences education (MA), health services management (MA), medical and surgical nursing science (critical care general) (MA), midwifery and neonatal nursing science (MA), trauma and emergency care (MA); history (MA, PhD); history of education (Ed D); inclusive education (M Ed, Ed D); information and communications technology policy and regulation (MA); information science (MA, MIS, PhD); international politics (MA, PhD); Islamic studies (MA, PhD); Italian (MA, PhD); Judaica (MA, PhD); linguistics (MA, PhD); mathematical education (M Ed); mathematics education (MA); missiology (M Th, D Th); modern Hebrew (MA, PhD); musicology (MA, MMus, D Mus, PhD); natural science education (M Ed); New Testament (M Th, D Th); Old Testament (D Th); pastoral therapy (M Th, D Th); philosophy (MA); philosophy of education (M Ed, Ed D); politics (MA, PhD); Portuguese (MA, PhD); practical theology (M Th, D Th); psychology (MA, MS, PhD); psychology of education (M Ed, Ed D); public health (MA); religious studies (MA, D Th, PhD); Romance languages (MA); Russian (MA, PhD); Semitic languages (MA, PhD); social behavior studies in HIV/AIDS (MA); social science (mental health) (MA); social science in development studies (MA); social science in psychology (MA); social science in social work (MA); social science in sociology (MA); social work (MSW, DSW, PhD); socio-education (M Ed, Ed D); sociolinguistics (MA); sociology (MA, PhD); Spanish (MA, PhD); systematic theology (M Th, D Th); TESOL (teaching English to speakers of other languages) (MA); theological ethics (M Th, D Th); theory of literature (MA, PhD); urban ministries (D Th); urban ministry (M Th).

University of South Alabama, Graduate School, College of Education, Department of Professional Studies, Mobile, AL 36688-0002. Offers community counseling (MS); educational media (M Ed, MS); instructional design and development (MS, PhD); rehabilitation counseling (MS); school counseling (M Ed); school psychometry (M Ed). *Accreditation:* NCATE. Part-time programs available. *Faculty:* 14 full-time (7 women). *Students:* 89 full-time (70 women), 116 part-time (96 women); includes 46 minority (41 Black or African American, non-Hispanic/Latino; 1 American Indian or Alaska Native, non-Hispanic/Latino; 1 Asian, non-Hispanic/Latino; 2 Hispanic/Latino; 1 Two or more races, non-Hispanic/Latino), 5 international. 53 applicants, 49% accepted, 25 enrolled. In 2011, 32 master's, 4 doctorates awarded. *Degree requirements:* For master's, comprehensive exam. *Entrance requirements:* For master's, GRE General Test or MAT, minimum GPA of 3.0. *Application deadline:* For fall admission, 6/15 priority date for domestic students; for spring admission, 11/1 priority date for domestic students. Applications are processed on a rolling basis. Application fee: $35. *Expenses:* Tuition, state resident: full-time $7968; part-time $332 per credit hour. Tuition, nonresident: full-time $15,936; part-time $664 per credit hour. *Financial support:* In 2011–12, 5 research assistantships were awarded; career-related internships or fieldwork also available. Support available to part-time students. Financial award application deadline: 4/1. *Faculty research:* Agency counseling, rehabilitation counseling, school psychometry. *Unit head:* Dr. Charles Guest, Chair, 251-380-2861. *Application contact:* Dr. Abigail Baxter, Director of Graduate Studies, 251-380-6310. Web site: http://www.southalabama.edu/coe/profstudies/.

University of South Carolina, The Graduate School, College of Education, Department of Educational Studies, Program in Educational Technology, Columbia, SC 29208. Offers M Ed. *Accreditation:* NCATE. Part-time programs available. Postbaccalaureate distance learning degree programs offered. *Degree requirements:* For master's, comprehensive exam. *Entrance requirements:* For master's, GRE or MAT, interview, letters of intent and reference.

University of South Carolina Aiken, Program in Educational Technology, Aiken, SC 29801-6309. Offers M Ed. Part-time and evening/weekend programs available. Postbaccalaureate distance learning degree programs offered (no on-campus study). *Faculty:* 3 full-time (1 woman). *Students:* 2 full-time (1 woman), 18 part-time (16 women); includes 5 minority (1 Black or African American, non-Hispanic/Latino; 1 American Indian or Alaska Native, non-Hispanic/Latino; 2 Hispanic/Latino; 1 Two or more races, non-Hispanic/Latino). Average age 36. 10 applicants, 90% accepted, 7 enrolled. In 2011, 5 master's awarded. *Degree requirements:* For master's, comprehensive exam. *Entrance requirements:* For master's, GRE or MAT. Additional exam requirements/recommendations for international students: Required—TOEFL (minimum score 550 paper-based; 213 computer-based). *Application deadline:* Applications are processed on a rolling basis. Application fee: $45. Electronic applications accepted. *Expenses:* Tuition, state resident: full-time $10,916; part-time $455 per credit hour. Tuition, nonresident: full-time $23,444; part-time $977 per credit hour. *Required fees:* $9 per credit hour. $25 per semester. *Financial support:* In 2011–12, 5 students received support. Career-related internships or fieldwork, Federal Work-Study, scholarships/grants, tuition waivers (partial), and unspecified assistantships available. Support available to part-time students. Financial award application deadline: 3/15; financial award applicants required to submit FAFSA. *Faculty research:* Hybrid courses, integrating technology into the curriculum, Web-based courses, assistive technology, assessment technology. *Total annual research expenditures:* $685,500. *Unit head:* Dr. Tom Smyth, Coordinator, 803-641-3527. *Application contact:* Karen Morris, Graduate Studies Coordinator, 803-641-3489, E-mail: karenm@usca.edu. Web site: http://edtech.usca.edu/.

The University of South Dakota, Graduate School, School of Education, Division of Curriculum and Instruction, Program in Technology for Education and Training, Vermillion, SD 57069-2390. Offers MS, Ed S. Part-time and evening/weekend programs available. Postbaccalaureate distance learning degree programs offered (no on-campus study). *Degree requirements:* For master's and Ed S, comprehensive exam, thesis or alternative. *Entrance requirements:* For master's and Ed S, GRE, minimum GPA of 2.7. Additional exam requirements/recommendations for international students: Required—TOEFL (minimum score 550 paper-based; 213 computer-based; 79 iBT). Electronic applications accepted. *Expenses:* Tuition, state resident: full-time $3118.50; part-time $173.25 per credit hour. Tuition, nonresident: full-time $6601; part-time $366.70 per credit hour. *Required fees:* $2268; $126 per credit hour. Tuition and fees vary according to program.

University of South Florida, Graduate School, College of Education, Department of Secondary Education, Tampa, FL 33620-9951. Offers English education (M Ed, MA, MAT, PhD); foreign language education/ESOL (M Ed, MA, MAT); instructional technology (M Ed, PhD, Ed S); mathematics education (M Ed, MA, MAT, PhD, Ed S); science education (M Ed, MA, MAT, PhD); second language acquisition/instructional technology (PhD); secondary education (M Ed, PhD); secondary education/TESOL (M Ed); social science education (M Ed, MA, MAT); teaching and learning in the content area (PhD). *Accreditation:* NCATE. Part-time and evening/weekend programs available. *Faculty:* 28 full-time (17 women), 3 part-time/adjunct (1 woman). *Students:* 174 full-time (116 women), 268 part-time (184 women); includes 103 minority (26 Black or African American, non-Hispanic/Latino; 10 Asian, non-Hispanic/Latino; 58 Hispanic/Latino; 9 Two or more races, non-Hispanic/Latino), 32 international. Average age 37. 229 applicants, 73% accepted, 141 enrolled. In 2011, 115 master's, 16 doctorates, 5 other advanced degrees awarded. *Degree requirements:* For master's, variable foreign language requirement, comprehensive exam, project (for some programs); for doctorate, variable foreign language requirement, comprehensive exam, thesis/dissertation, philosophies of inquiry; multiple research methods. *Entrance requirements:* For master's, GRE General Test or General Knowledge Test, minimum GPA of 3.0; for doctorate, GRE General Test, minimum GPA of 3.5; for Ed S, GRE General Test. Additional exam requirements/recommendations for international students: Required—TOEFL (minimum score 550 paper-based; 213 computer-based; 79 iBT). *Application deadline:* For fall admission, 2/15 for domestic students, 1/2 for international students; for spring admission, 10/15 for domestic students, 6/1 for international students. Application fee: $30. Electronic applications accepted. *Financial support:* In 2011–12, 7 students received support, including 1 research assistantship with full tuition reimbursement available (averaging $10,000 per year), 55 teaching assistantships with full and partial tuition reimbursements available (averaging $7,900 per year); scholarships/grants and unspecified assistantships also available. Financial award application deadline: 4/15; financial award applicants required to submit FAFSA. *Faculty research:* English language learners/multicultural, social science education, mathematics education, science education, instructional technology. *Total annual research expenditures:* $336,023. *Unit head:* Dr. Stephen Thornton, Chairperson, 813-974-3533, Fax: 813-974-3837, E-mail: thornton@usf.edu. *Application contact:* Dr. Diane Briscoe, Coordinator of Graduate Studies, 813-974-1804, Fax: 813-974-3391, E-mail: briscoe@usf.edu. Web site: http://www.coedu.usf.edu/main/departments/seced/seced.html.

The University of Tennessee, Graduate School, College of Education, Health and Human Sciences, Program in Education, Knoxville, TN 37996. Offers art education (MS); counseling education (PhD); cultural studies in education (PhD); curriculum (MS, Ed S); curriculum, educational research and evaluation (Ed D, PhD); early childhood education (PhD); early childhood special education (MS); education of deaf and hard of hearing (MS); educational administration and policy studies (Ed D, PhD); educational administration and supervision (Ed S); educational psychology (Ed D, PhD); elementary education (MS, Ed S); elementary teaching (MS); English education (MS, Ed S); exercise science (PhD); foreign language/ESL education (MS, Ed S); instructional technology (MS, Ed D, PhD, Ed S); literacy, language and ESL education (PhD); literacy, language education, and ESL education (Ed D); mathematics education (MS, Ed S); modified and comprehensive special education (MS); reading education (MS, Ed S); school counseling (Ed S); school psychology (PhD, Ed S); science education (MS, Ed S); secondary teaching (MS); social foundations (MS); social science education (MS, Ed S); socio-cultural foundations of sports and education (PhD); special education (Ed S); teacher education (Ed D, PhD). *Accreditation:* NCATE. Part-time and evening/weekend programs available. *Degree requirements:* For master's and Ed S, thesis optional; for doctorate, variable foreign language requirement, thesis/dissertation. *Entrance requirements:* For master's, minimum GPA of 2.7; for doctorate and Ed S, GRE General Test, minimum GPA of 2.7. Additional exam requirements/recommendations for international students: Required—TOEFL. Electronic applications accepted. *Expenses:* Tuition, state resident: full-time $8332; part-time $464 per credit hour. Tuition, nonresident: full-time $25,174; part-time $1400 per credit hour. *Required fees:* $1162; $56 per credit hour. Tuition and fees vary according to program.

The University of Tennessee at Chattanooga, Graduate School, College of Health, Education and Professional Studies, School of Education, Chattanooga, TN 37403-2598. Offers counseling (M Ed), including community counseling, school counseling; education (M Ed, Post-Master's Certificate), including elementary education (M Ed), school leadership, secondary education (M Ed), special education (M Ed); educational specialist (Ed S), including educational technology, school psychology; learning and leadership (Ed D), including educational leadership. *Accreditation:* ACA; NCATE. Part-time and evening/weekend programs available. Postbaccalaureate distance learning degree programs offered (no on-campus study). *Faculty:* 25 full-time (17 women), 10 part-time/adjunct (3 women). *Students:* 145 full-time (104 women), 319 part-time (236 women); includes 63 minority (43 Black or African American, non-Hispanic/Latino; 4 American Indian or Alaska Native, non-Hispanic/Latino; 2 Asian, non-Hispanic/Latino; 6 Hispanic/Latino; 8 Two or more races, non-Hispanic/Latino), 2 international. Average age 34. 226 applicants, 79% accepted, 111 enrolled. In 2011, 120 master's, 9 doctorates, 17 other advanced degrees awarded. *Degree requirements:* For master's, comprehensive exam, thesis optional, culminating experience; for doctorate, comprehensive exam, thesis/dissertation; for other advanced degree, internship. *Entrance requirements:* For master's, GRE General Test, PPST 1, teaching certificate; for doctorate, GRE General Test, master's degree, two years of practical work experience in organizational environment; for other advanced degree, GRE General Test, letters of reference. Additional exam requirements/recommendations for international students: Required—TOEFL (minimum score 550 paper-based; 213 computer-based; 79 iBT), IELTS (minimum score 6). *Application deadline:* For fall admission, 8/1 for domestic students, 6/1 for international students; for spring admission, 12/1 for domestic students, 10/1 for international students. Applications are processed on a rolling basis. Application fee: $35. Electronic applications accepted. *Expenses:* Tuition, state resident: full-time $6472; part-time $359 per credit hour. Tuition, nonresident: full-time $20,006; part-time $1111 per credit hour. *Required fees:* $1320; $160 per credit hour. *Financial support:* Career-related internships or fieldwork, institutionally sponsored loans, scholarships/grants, and unspecified assistantships available. Support available to part-time students. Financial award applicants required to submit FAFSA. *Faculty research:* School counseling, community counseling, elementary and secondary education, school leadership and administration. *Total annual research expenditures:* $675,479. *Unit head:* Dr. John Freeman, Head, 423-425-4133, Fax: 423-425-5380, E-mail: john-freeman@utc.edu. *Application contact:* Dr. Jerald Ainsworth, Dean of Graduate Studies, 423-425-4478, Fax: 423-425-5223, E-mail: jerald-ainsworth@utc.edu. Web site: http://www.utc.edu/Administration/HealthEducationAndProfessionalStudies/Graduate_Studies/graduate_studies.html.

The University of Texas at Austin, Graduate School, College of Education, Department of Curriculum and Instruction, Austin, TX 78712-1111. Offers bilingual/bicultural education (M Ed, MA, PhD); cultural studies in education (M Ed, MA, PhD); early childhood education (M Ed, MA, PhD); language and literacy studies (M Ed, PhD); learning technologies (M Ed, MA, PhD); physical education (M Ed, MA, PhD). Terminal master's awarded for partial completion of doctoral program. *Degree requirements:* For doctorate, thesis/dissertation. *Entrance requirements:* For master's and doctorate, GRE General Test. *Application deadline:* For fall admission, 3/1 for domestic students; for spring admission, 10/1 for domestic students. Applications are processed on a rolling basis. Application fee: $50 ($75 for international students). Electronic applications accepted. *Financial support:* Fellowships and teaching assistantships with partial tuition reimbursements available. Financial award application deadline: 2/1. *Unit head:* Betty Maloch, Chair, 512-232-4262, E-mail: bmaloch@austin.utexas.edu. *Application contact:*

Educational Media/Instructional Technology

Stephen Flynn, Graduate Coordinator, 512-471-3747, E-mail: sflynn@austin.utexas.edu. Web site: http://www.edb.utexas.edu/coe/depts/ci/cti.html.

The University of Texas at Brownsville, Graduate Studies, School of Education, Brownsville, TX 78520-4991. Offers bilingual education (M Ed); counseling and guidance (M Ed); curriculum and instruction (M Ed); early childhood education (M Ed); educational administration (M Ed); educational technology (M Ed); English as a second language (M Ed); reading specialist (M Ed); special education/educational diagnostician (M Ed). Part-time and evening/weekend programs available. Postbaccalaureate distance learning degree programs offered (minimal on-campus study). *Degree requirements:* For master's, thesis optional. *Entrance requirements:* For master's, GRE General Test. Additional exam requirements/recommendations for international students: Required—TOEFL.

The University of Texas at San Antonio, College of Education and Human Development, Department of Interdisciplinary Learning and Teaching, San Antonio, TX 78249-0617. Offers adult learning and teaching (MA); education (MA), including curriculum and instruction, early childhood and elementary education, educational psychology/special education, instructional technology, reading and literacy education; interdisciplinary learning and teaching (PhD). Part-time and evening/weekend programs available. *Faculty:* 26 full-time (21 women), 1 (woman) part-time/adjunct. *Students:* 131 full-time (100 women), 357 part-time (283 women); includes 275 minority (31 Black or African American, non-Hispanic/Latino; 9 Asian, non-Hispanic/Latino; 227 Hispanic/Latino; 8 Two or more races, non-Hispanic/Latino), 31 international. Average age 33. 239 applicants, 75% accepted, 120 enrolled. In 2011, 119 master's awarded. *Degree requirements:* For master's, comprehensive exam, thesis optional, 36 hours of course work without thesis (33 with thesis); for doctorate, comprehensive exam, thesis/dissertation, minimum of 60 semester credit hours. *Entrance requirements:* For master's, GRE General Test, bachelor's degree with minimum GPA of 3.0 in last 60 hours of coursework; resume; two letters of recommendation; statement of purpose; for doctorate, GRE, transcripts from all colleges and universities attended, professional vitae demonstrating experience in work environment where education was primary professional emphasis, 3 letters of recommendation, statement of purpose, master's degree transcript documenting minimum GPA of 3.5. Additional exam requirements/recommendations for international students: Required—TOEFL (minimum score 500 paper-based; 61 iBT), IELTS (minimum score 5). *Application deadline:* For fall admission, 7/1 for domestic students, 4/1 for international students; for spring admission, 11/1 for domestic students, 9/1 for international students. Application fee: $45 ($85 for international students). *Expenses:* Tuition, state resident: full-time $3148; part-time $2176 per semester. Tuition, nonresident: full-time $8782; part-time $5932 per semester. *Required fees:* $719 per semester. *Financial support:* In 2011–12, 9 fellowships with partial tuition reimbursements (averaging $27,000 per year) were awarded; career-related internships or fieldwork, Federal Work-Study, and scholarships/grants also available. Support available to part-time students. *Faculty research:* Explorations of science, learning and teaching, family Involvement in early childhood, culturally-responsive literacy instruction in diverse settings, STEM education, autism spectrum disorders. *Total annual research expenditures:* $5.9 million. *Unit head:* Dr. Maria R. Cortez, Department Chair, 210-458-5969, Fax: 210-458-7281, E-mail: mari.cortez@utsa.edu. *Application contact:* Erin Doran, Student Development Specialist, 210-458-7443, Fax: 210-458-7281, E-mail: erin.doran@utsa.edu.

University of the Incarnate Word, School of Graduate Studies and Research, Dreeben School of Education, Programs in Education, San Antonio, TX 78209-6397. Offers adult education (M Ed, MA); cross-cultural education (M Ed, MA); early childhood literacy (M Ed, MA); general education (M Ed, MA); higher education (PhD); instructional technology (M Ed, MA); international education and entrepreneurship (PhD); kinesiology (M Ed, MA); literacy (M Ed, MA); organizational leadership (PhD); organizational learning and learning (M Ed, MA); reading (M Ed, MA); special education (M Ed, MA); teacher leadership (M Ed, MA). Part-time and evening/weekend programs available. *Faculty:* 14 full-time (8 women), 10 part-time/adjunct (9 women). *Students:* 13 full-time (7 women), 197 part-time (129 women); includes 111 minority (23 Black or African American, non-Hispanic/Latino; 2 American Indian or Alaska Native, non-Hispanic/Latino; 1 Asian, non-Hispanic/Latino; 85 Hispanic/Latino), 26 international. Average age 41. 78 applicants, 79% accepted, 34 enrolled. In 2011, 21 master's, 12 doctorates awarded. *Degree requirements:* For master's, capstone; for doctorate, thesis/dissertation, qualifying exam. *Entrance requirements:* For master's, baccalaureate degree; minimum foundation GPA of 2.5; interview; for doctorate, master's degree; interview; supervised writing sample. Additional exam requirements/recommendations for international students: Required—TOEFL (minimum score 560 paper-based; 220 computer-based; 83 iBT). *Application deadline:* Applications are processed on a rolling basis. Application fee: $20. Electronic applications accepted. *Expenses: Tuition:* Part-time $725 per credit hour. Tuition and fees vary according to degree level. *Financial support:* In 2011–12, 5 research assistantships were awarded; Federal Work-Study and scholarships/grants also available. Financial award applicants required to submit FAFSA. *Unit head:* Dr. Denise Staudt, Dean, Dreeben School of Education, 210-829-2762, E-mail: staudt@uiwtx.edu. *Application contact:* Andrea Cyterski-Acosta, Dean of Enrollment, 210-829-6005, Fax: 210-829-3921, E-mail: admis@uiwtx.edu. Web site: http://www.uiw.edu/education/index.htm.

University of the Incarnate Word, School of Graduate Studies and Research, H-E-B School of Business and Administration, Programs in Administration, San Antonio, TX 78209-6397. Offers adult education (MAA); applied administration (MAA); communication arts (MAA); healthcare administration (MAA); instructional technology (MAA); international business (Certificate); nutrition (MAA); organizational development (MAA, Certificate); project management (Certificate); sports management (MAA). Part-time and evening/weekend programs available. Postbaccalaureate distance learning degree programs offered (no on-campus study). *Faculty:* 23 full-time (10 women), 26 part-time/adjunct (12 women). *Students:* 25 full-time (18 women), 54 part-time (33 women); includes 50 minority (10 Black or African American, non-Hispanic/Latino; 40 Hispanic/Latino), 5 international. Average age 34. 35 applicants, 94% accepted, 19 enrolled. In 2011, 38 master's awarded. *Degree requirements:* For master's, capstone. *Entrance requirements:* For master's, GRE, GMAT, undergraduate degree, minimum GPA of 2.5. Additional exam requirements/recommendations for international students: Required—TOEFL (minimum score 560 paper-based; 220 computer-based; 83 iBT). *Application deadline:* Applications are processed on a rolling basis. Application fee: $20. Electronic applications accepted. *Expenses: Tuition:* Part-time $725 per credit hour. Tuition and fees vary according to degree level. *Financial support:* Federal Work-Study and scholarships/grants available. Financial award applicants required to submit FAFSA. *Unit head:* Dr. Mark Teachout, MAA Programs Director, 210-829-3177, Fax: 210-805-3564, E-mail: teachout@uiwtx.edu. *Application contact:* Andrea Cyterski-Acosta, Dean of Enrollment, 210-829-6005, Fax: 210-829-3921, E-mail: admis@uiwtx.edu. Web site: http://www.uiw.edu/maa/index.htm and http://www.uiw.edu/maa/admissions.html.

University of the Sacred Heart, Graduate Programs, Department of Education, Program in Instruction Systems and Education Technology, San Juan, PR 00914-0383. Offers M Ed. Part-time and evening/weekend programs available. *Degree requirements:* For master's, thesis. *Entrance requirements:* For master's, EXADEP, interview, minimum undergraduate GPA of 2.75.

The University of Toledo, College of Graduate Studies, Judith Herb College of Education, Health Science and Human Service, Department of Curriculum and Instruction, Toledo, OH 43606-3390. Offers art education (ME); career and technical education (ME); curriculum and instruction (ME, PhD, Ed S); education and anthropology (MAE); education and biology (MES); education and chemistry (MES); education and classics (MAE); education and economics (MAE); education and English (MAE); education and French (MAE); education and geography (MAE); education and geology (MES); education and German (MAE); education and history (MAE); education and mathematics (MAE, MES); education and physics (MES); education and political science (MAE); education and sociology (MAE); education and Spanish (MAE); educational media (PhD); educational technology (ME); English as a second language (MAE); gifted and talented (PhD); middle childhood education licensure (ME); music education (MME); secondary education (PhD); secondary education licensure (ME). *Accreditation:* NCATE. Part-time and evening/weekend programs available. *Faculty:* 24. *Students:* 60 full-time (31 women), 211 part-time (161 women); includes 23 minority (21 Black or African American, non-Hispanic/Latino; 2 Hispanic/Latino), 20 international. Average age 35. 115 applicants, 73% accepted, 74 enrolled. In 2011, 105 master's, 3 doctorates, 4 other advanced degrees awarded. *Degree requirements:* For master's, comprehensive exam, thesis or alternative; for doctorate, comprehensive exam, thesis/dissertation; for Ed S, thesis optional. *Entrance requirements:* For master's, doctorate, and Ed S, minimum cumulative GPA of 2.7 for all previous academic work, letters of recommendation. Additional exam requirements/recommendations for international students: Required—TOEFL (minimum score 550 paper-based; 213 computer-based; 80 iBT), IELTS (minimum score 6.5). *Application deadline:* For fall admission, 1/15 priority date for domestic students, 1/15 for international students. Applications are processed on a rolling basis. Application fee: $45 ($75 for international students). Electronic applications accepted. *Financial support:* In 2011–12, 9 research assistantships with full and partial tuition reimbursements (averaging $7,184 per year), 12 teaching assistantships with full and partial tuition reimbursements (averaging $8,425 per year) were awarded; career-related internships or fieldwork, Federal Work-Study, institutionally sponsored loans, scholarships/grants, tuition waivers (full and partial), unspecified assistantships, and administrative assistantships also available. Support available to part-time students. *Unit head:* Dr. Leigh Chiarelott, Chair, 419-530-5371, E-mail: eigh.chiarelott@utoledo.edu. *Application contact:* Graduate School Office, 419-530-4723, Fax: 419-530-4724, E-mail: grdsch@utnet.utoledo.edu. Web site: http://www.utoledo.edu/eduhshs/.

University of Utah, Graduate School, College of Education, Department of Educational Psychology, Salt Lake City, UT 84112. Offers counseling psychology (PhD); educational psychology (MA); elementary education (M Ed); instructional design and educational technology (M Ed); instructional design and technology (M Ed, MS); learning and cognition (MS, PhD); learning sciences (MA); professional counseling (MS); professional psychology (M Ed); reading and literacy (M Ed, PhD); school counseling (M Ed, MS); school psychology (M Ed, MS, PhD); statistics (M Stat). *Accreditation:* APA (one or more programs are accredited). Evening/weekend programs available. Postbaccalaureate distance learning degree programs offered (minimal on-campus study). *Faculty:* 23 full-time (12 women), 9 part-time/adjunct (7 women). *Students:* 104 full-time (85 women), 107 part-time (78 women); includes 26 minority (1 American Indian or Alaska Native, non-Hispanic/Latino; 4 Asian, non-Hispanic/Latino; 17 Hispanic/Latino; 1 Native Hawaiian or other Pacific Islander, non-Hispanic/Latino; 3 Two or more races, non-Hispanic/Latino), 4 international. Average age 32. 213 applicants, 27% accepted, 48 enrolled. In 2011, 39 master's, 9 doctorates awarded. *Median time to degree:* Of those who began their doctoral program in fall 2003, 50% received their degree in 8 years or less. *Degree requirements:* For master's, variable foreign language requirement, comprehensive exam, thesis (for some programs); for doctorate, variable foreign language requirement, thesis/dissertation, oral exam. *Entrance requirements:* For master's and doctorate, GRE General Test, minimum GPA of 3.0. Additional exam requirements/recommendations for international students: Required—TOEFL (minimum score 500 paper-based; 173 computer-based). *Application deadline:* For fall admission, 4/1 for domestic and international students; for spring admission, 11/1 for domestic and international students. Application fee: $55 ($65 for international students). *Expenses:* Contact institution. *Financial support:* In 2011–12, 59 students received support, including 25 fellowships with full and partial tuition reimbursements available (averaging $12,000 per year), 7 research assistantships with full and partial tuition reimbursements available (averaging $12,000 per year), 27 teaching assistantships with full and partial tuition reimbursements available (averaging $12,000 per year); career-related internships or fieldwork, Federal Work-Study, institutionally sponsored loans, scholarships/grants, and unspecified assistantships also available. Financial award application deadline: 2/1; financial award applicants required to submit FAFSA. *Faculty research:* Autism, computer technology and instruction, cognitive behavior, aging, group counseling. *Total annual research expenditures:* $371,256. *Unit head:* Dr. Elaine Clark, Chair, 801-581-7148, Fax: 801-581-5566, E-mail: clark@ed.utah.edu. *Application contact:* Kendra Lee Wiebke, Academic Program Specialist, 801-581-7148, Fax: 801-581-5566, E-mail: kendra.wiebke@utah.edu. Web site: http://www.ed.utah.edu/edps/.

University of Virginia, Curry School of Education, Department of Leadership, Foundations and Policy, Program in Educational Psychology, Charlottesville, VA 22903. Offers applied developmental science (M Ed); educational evaluation (M Ed); educational psychology (M Ed, Ed D, Ed S); educational research (Ed D); gifted education (M Ed); instructional technology (M Ed, Ed S); research statistics and evaluation (Ed D); school psychology (Ed D). *Students:* 17 full-time (12 women), 10 part-time (7 women); includes 2 minority (1 Black or African American, non-Hispanic/Latino; 1 Hispanic/Latino), 1 international. Average age 29. 56 applicants, 77% accepted, 23 enrolled. In 2011, 40 master's, 1 doctorate awarded. *Degree requirements:* For master's, comprehensive exam. *Entrance requirements:* For master's and doctorate, GRE General Test, 2 letters of recommendation. Additional exam requirements/recommendations for international students: Required—TOEFL (minimum score 600 paper-based; 250 computer-based; 90 iBT), IELTS (minimum score 7). *Application deadline:* Applications are processed on a rolling basis. Application fee: $60. Electronic applications accepted. *Financial support:* Fellowships, research assistantships, and teaching assistantships available. Financial award application deadline: 1/5; financial award applicants required to submit FAFSA. *Unit head:* Christopher De La Cerda, Program Coordinator, 434-243-2021, E-mail: cjd8kn@virginia.edu. *Application contact:* Lisa Miller, Assistant to the Chair, 434-982-2849, E-mail: lam3v@virgnina.edu.

University of Virginia, Curry School of Education, Program in Education, Charlottesville, VA 22903. Offers administration and supervision (PhD); applied developmental science (PhD); counselor education (PhD); curriculum and instruction (PhD); early childhood-developmental risk (MT); education evaluation (PhD); educational psychology (PhD); educational research (PhD); elementary (MT, PhD); English education (MT, PhD); foreign language education (MT); higher education (PhD); instructional technology (PhD); kinesiology (MT, PhD); math education (PhD); reading education (PhD); research statistics and evaluation (PhD); school psychology (PhD); science education (PhD); social studies education (MT, PhD); special education (PhD); world languages education (MT). *Students:* 299 full-time (216 women), 60 part-time (33 women); includes 46 minority (18 Black or African American, non-Hispanic/Latino; 17 Asian, non-Hispanic/Latino; 7 Hispanic/Latino; 4 Two or more races, non-Hispanic/Latino), 23 international. Average age 30. 307 applicants, 42% accepted, 80 enrolled. In 2011, 113 master's, 62 doctorates awarded. *Degree requirements:* For master's, comprehensive exam (for some programs), field project; for doctorate, comprehensive exam, thesis/dissertation. *Entrance requirements:* For doctorate, GRE General Test. Additional exam requirements/recommendations for international students: Required—TOEFL (minimum score 600 paper-based; 250 computer-based; 90 iBT), IELTS (minimum score 7). *Application deadline:* Applications are processed on a rolling basis. Application fee: $60. Electronic applications accepted. *Financial support:* Fellowships, research assistantships, and teaching assistantships available. Financial award application deadline: 1/5; financial award applicants required to submit FAFSA. *Unit head:* Robert C. Pianta, Dean, 434-924-3334. *Application contact:* Joanne McNergney, Assistant Dean for Admissions and Student Services, 434-924-3334, E-mail: curry-admissions@virginia.edu.

University of Washington, Graduate School, College of Education, Seattle, WA 98195. Offers curriculum and instruction (M Ed, Ed D, PhD), including educational technology, general curriculum (Ed D, PhD), language, literacy, and culture, mathematics education, multicultural education, reading and language arts education (Ed D), science education, social studies education, teaching and curriculum (M Ed); educational leadership and policy studies (M Ed, Ed D, PhD), including administration (Ed D), educational policy, organization, and leadership (M Ed, PhD), higher education, leadership for learning (Ed D), social and cultural foundations of education (M Ed, PhD); educational psychology (M Ed, PhD), including educational psychology (PhD), human development and cognition (M Ed), learning sciences, measurement, statistics and research design (M Ed), school psychology (M Ed); instructional leadership (M Ed); intercollegiate athletic leadership (M Ed); special education (M Ed, Ed D, PhD), including early childhood special education (M Ed), emotional and behavioral disabilities (M Ed), learning disabilities (M Ed), low-incidence disabilities (M Ed), severe disabilities (M Ed), special education (Ed D, PhD); teacher education (MIT). *Accreditation:* APA. Part-time and evening/weekend programs available. *Degree requirements:* For master's, thesis optional; for doctorate, thesis/dissertation. *Entrance requirements:* For master's and doctorate, GRE General Test, minimum GPA of 3.0. Additional exam requirements/recommendations for international students: Required—TOEFL. Electronic applications accepted. *Faculty research:* School restructuring/effective schools, special education interventions, literacy and writing, technology, school partnerships, teacher preparation.

The University of West Alabama, School of Graduate Studies, College of Education, Departments of Instructional Leadership and Support/Curriculum and Instruction, Program in Library Media, Livingston, AL 35470. Offers M Ed. Part-time programs available. *Faculty:* 8 full-time (6 women). *Students:* 213 (199 women); includes 74 minority (71 Black or African American, non-Hispanic/Latino; 2 American Indian or Alaska Native, non-Hispanic/Latino; 1 Hispanic/Latino). In 2011, 33 master's awarded. *Degree requirements:* For master's, comprehensive exam. *Entrance requirements:* For master's, GRE General Test, MAT, minimum GPA of 2.75. Additional exam requirements/recommendations for international students: Required—TOEFL (minimum score 61 computer-based). *Application deadline:* For fall admission, 9/10 priority date for domestic students; for spring admission, 3/24 for domestic students. Applications are processed on a rolling basis. Application fee: $25 ($50 for international students). *Expenses:* Tuition, state resident: full-time $5112; part-time $284 per credit hour. Tuition, nonresident: full-time $10,224; part-time $568 per credit hour. *Required fees:* $180; $40 per semester. One-time fee: $65. Tuition and fees vary according to class time, course load, campus/location and program. *Financial support:* Teaching assistantships, career-related internships or fieldwork, Federal Work-Study, scholarships/grants, and unspecified assistantships available. Support available to part-time students. Financial award application deadline: 3/1. *Unit head:* Dr. Jan Miller, Chair of Instructional Leadership and Support, 205-652-3445, Fax: 205-652-3706, E-mail: jmiller@uwa.edu. *Application contact:* Dr. Kathy Chandler, Dean of Graduate Studies, 205-652-3421, Fax: 205-652-3706, E-mail: kchandler@uwa.edu. Web site: http://www.uwa.edu/medlibrarymedia.aspx.

University of West Florida, College of Professional Studies, Department of Applied Science, Technology and Administration, Program in Instructional Technology, Pensacola, FL 32514-5750. Offers educational leadership (M Ed); instructional technology (M Ed). *Students:* 3 full-time (1 woman), 16 part-time (11 women); includes 7 minority (4 Black or African American, non-Hispanic/Latino; 1 Hispanic/Latino; 2 Two or more races, non-Hispanic/Latino), 1 international. Average age 42. 10 applicants, 50% accepted, 3 enrolled. In 2011, 17 master's awarded. *Entrance requirements:* For master's, MAT, GRE or GMAT, letter of intent, names of references. Additional exam requirements/recommendations for international students: Required—TOEFL (minimum score 550 paper-based; 213 computer-based). *Application deadline:* For fall admission, 6/1 for domestic and international students; for spring admission, 10/1 for domestic and international students. Applications are processed on a rolling basis. Application fee: $30. Electronic applications accepted. *Expenses:* Tuition, state resident: full-time $5729; part-time $302 per credit hour. Tuition, nonresident: full-time $20,059; part-time $961 per credit hour. *Required fees:* $1509; $63 per credit hour. *Financial support:* Application deadline: 4/15; applicants required to submit FAFSA. *Unit head:* Dr. Karen Rasmussen, Chairperson, 850-474-2301, Fax: 850-474-2804, E-mail: krasmuss@uwf.edu. *Application contact:* Terry McCray, Assistant Director of Graduate Admissions, 850-473-7718, Fax: 850-473-7714, E-mail: gradadmissions@uwf.edu.

University of West Florida, College of Professional Studies, Ed D Programs, Specialization in Curriculum and Instruction: Instructional Technology, Pensacola, FL 32514-5750. Offers Ed D. *Students:* 6 full-time (3 women), 64 part-time (40 women); includes 12 minority (8 Black or African American, non-Hispanic/Latino; 2 Asian, non-Hispanic/Latino; 1 Hispanic/Latino; 1 Native Hawaiian or other Pacific Islander, non-Hispanic/Latino). Average age 46. 7 applicants, 71% accepted, 4 enrolled. In 2011, 6 doctorates awarded. *Degree requirements:* For doctorate, comprehensive exam, thesis/dissertation. *Entrance requirements:* For doctorate, GRE, MAT, or GMAT, letter of intent; writing sample; three letters of recommendation; two completed disposition assessment forms; written statement of goals; interview with admissions committee. Additional exam requirements/recommendations for international students: Required—TOEFL (minimum score 550 paper-based; 213 computer-based). *Application deadline:* For fall admission, 6/1 for domestic and international students; for spring admission, 10/1 for domestic students. Applications are processed on a rolling basis. Application fee: $30. *Expenses:* Tuition, state resident: full-time $5729; part-time $302 per credit hour. Tuition, nonresident: full-time $20,059; part-time $961 per credit hour. *Required fees:* $1509; $63 per credit hour. *Unit head:* Dr. Karen Rasmussen, Chairperson, 850-474-2300, E-mail: krasmuss@uwf.edu. *Application contact:* Terry McCray, Assistant Director of Graduate Admissions, 850-473-7718, Fax: 850-473-7714, E-mail: gradadmissions@uwf.edu.

University of West Georgia, College of Education, Department of Educational Innovation, Carrollton, GA 30118. Offers media (M Ed, Ed S). Part-time and evening/weekend programs available. Postbaccalaureate distance learning degree programs offered (no on-campus study). *Faculty:* 17 full-time (10 women), 1 (woman) part-time/adjunct. *Students:* 6 full-time (5 women), 254 part-time (215 women); includes 39 minority (32 Black or African American, non-Hispanic/Latino; 3 Hispanic/Latino; 4 Two or more races, non-Hispanic/Latino). Average age 38. 82 applicants, 82% accepted, 32 enrolled. In 2011, 47 master's, 52 Ed Ss awarded. *Degree requirements:* For master's, comprehensive exam, electronic portfolio; for Ed S, comprehensive exam, research project. *Entrance requirements:* For master's, minimum GPA of 2.7, teaching certificate; for Ed S, GRE General Test, MAT, master's degree, minimum graduate GPA of 3.0. Additional exam requirements/recommendations for international students: Required—TOEFL (minimum score 523 paper-based; 193 computer-based; 69 iBT); Recommended—IELTS (minimum score 6). *Application deadline:* For fall admission, 7/21 for domestic students, 6/1 for international students; for spring admission, 11/30 for domestic students, 10/15 for international students. Applications are processed on a rolling basis. Application fee: $30. Electronic applications accepted. *Expenses:* Tuition, state resident: full-time $4336; part-time $181 per credit hour. Tuition, nonresident: full-time $17,362; part-time $724 per credit hour. Tuition and fees vary according to course load, degree level, campus/location and program. *Financial support:* In 2011–12, 2 students received support, including 2 research assistantships with full tuition reimbursements available (averaging $6,000 per year); career-related internships or fieldwork, scholarships/grants, and unspecified assistantships also available. Support available to part-time students. Financial award application deadline: 7/1; financial award applicants required to submit FAFSA. *Faculty research:* Distance education, technology integration, collaboration, e-books for children, instructional design. *Unit head:* Dr. Barbera Kawulich, Interim Chair, 678-839-6558, Fax: 678-839-6151, E-mail: bkawulic@westga.edu. *Application contact:* Deanna Richards, Coordinator, Graduate Studies, 678-839-5946, E-mail: drichard@westga.edu. Web site: http://www.westga.edu/coeei.

University of Wisconsin–Milwaukee, Graduate School, School of Education, Program in Urban Education, Milwaukee, WI 53201-0413. Offers adult and continuing education (PhD); curriculum and instruction (PhD); educational administration (PhD); educational and media technology (PhD); educational psychology (PhD); multicultural studies (PhD); social foundations of education (PhD). *Students:* 65 full-time (45 women), 37 part-time (25 women); includes 39 minority (18 Black or African American, non-Hispanic/Latino; 1 American Indian or Alaska Native, non-Hispanic/Latino; 6 Asian, non-Hispanic/Latino; 6 Hispanic/Latino; 8 Two or more races, non-Hispanic/Latino), 5 international. Average age 41. 26 applicants, 62% accepted, 2 enrolled. In 2011, 13 degrees awarded. *Degree requirements:* For doctorate, comprehensive exam, thesis/dissertation. *Entrance requirements:* For doctorate, GRE General Test, minimum undergraduate GPA of 2.85, graduate 3.5. Additional exam requirements/recommendations for international students: Required—TOEFL (minimum score 550 paper-based; 79 iBT), IELTS (minimum score 6.5). *Application deadline:* For fall admission, 1/1 priority date for domestic students; for spring admission, 9/1 for domestic students. Applications are processed on a rolling basis. Application fee: $56 ($96 for international students). Electronic applications accepted. One-time fee: $506.10 full-time. Tuition and fees vary according to course load and reciprocity agreements. *Financial support:* In 2011–12, 11 fellowships, 1 teaching assistantship were awarded; research assistantships, career-related internships or fieldwork, health care benefits, unspecified assistantships, and project assistantships also available. Support available to part-time students. Financial award application deadline: 4/15; financial award applicants required to submit FAFSA. *Unit head:* Larry Martin, Representative, 414-229-4729, Fax: 414-229-2920, E-mail: lmartin@uwm.edu. *Application contact:* General Information Contact, 414-229-4982, Fax: 414-229-6967, E-mail: gradschool@uwm.edu. Web site: http://www.uwm.edu/Dept/UrbanEd/.

University of Wyoming, College of Education, Program in Instructional Technology, Laramie, WY 82070. Offers MS, Ed D, PhD. Part-time programs available. Postbaccalaureate distance learning degree programs offered (no on-campus study). *Degree requirements:* For master's, thesis or alternative; for doctorate, comprehensive exam, thesis/dissertation. *Entrance requirements:* For master's, GRE, minimum GPA of 3.0; for doctorate, MS or MA, minimum GPA of 3.0. Additional exam requirements/recommendations for international students: Required—TOEFL. Electronic applications accepted. *Faculty research:* Web based instruction, instructional decision, adult education history, literacy in adults, international distance education.

Utah State University, School of Graduate Studies, Emma Eccles Jones College of Education and Human Services, Department of Instructional Technology and Learning Sciences, Logan, UT 84322. Offers M Ed, MS, PhD, Ed S. Part-time and evening/weekend programs available. Postbaccalaureate distance learning degree programs offered (minimal on-campus study). Terminal master's awarded for partial completion of doctoral program. *Degree requirements:* For master's, thesis (for some programs); for doctorate, comprehensive exam, thesis/dissertation. *Entrance requirements:* For master's, GRE General Test or MAT, minimum GPA of 3.0, 3 recommendation letters; for doctorate, GRE General Test, minimum GPA of 3.0, 3 recommendation letters, transcripts, letter of intent; for Ed S, GRE General Test, GRE Subject Test, minimum GPA of 3.0. Additional exam requirements/recommendations for international students: Required—TOEFL (minimum score 550 paper-based; 213 computer-based). Electronic applications accepted. *Faculty research:* Interactive learning environments, computer-assisted instruction, learning, distance education, corporate training.

Valley City State University, Online Master of Education Program, Valley City, ND 58072. Offers library and information technologies (M Ed); teaching and technology (M Ed); teaching English language learners (ELL) (M Ed); technology education (M Ed). *Accreditation:* NCATE. Part-time and evening/weekend programs available. Postbaccalaureate distance learning degree programs offered (no on-campus study). *Faculty:* 25 full-time (18 women), 2 part-time/adjunct (both women). *Students:* 4 full-time (3 women), 147 part-time (99 women); includes 6 minority (1 Black or African American, non-Hispanic/Latino; 1 American Indian or Alaska Native, non-Hispanic/Latino; 2 Asian, non-Hispanic/Latino; 2 Hispanic/Latino). Average age 34. 40 applicants, 83% accepted, 30 enrolled. In 2011, 30 master's awarded. *Degree requirements:* For master's, action research report, comprehensive portfolio. *Entrance requirements:* For master's, GRE, MAT, PRAXIS II or National Teaching Board for Professional Standards (if GPA less than 3.0). Additional exam requirements/recommendations for international students: Required—TOEFL (minimum score 525 paper-based; 70 iBT). *Application deadline:* For fall admission, 5/23 priority date for domestic students, 5/28 for international students; for spring admission, 4/20 priority date for domestic students, 4/23 for international students. Applications are processed on a rolling basis. Application fee: $35. Electronic applications accepted. *Expenses:* Tuition, state resident: full-time $4533.30; part-time $251.85 per credit hour. Tuition, nonresident: full-time $4533; part-time $251.85 per credit hour. *Required fees:* $1239.48; $68.86 per credit hour. *Financial support:* In 2011–12, 27 students received support. Tuition waivers (full and partial) available. Financial award application deadline: 5/15; financial award applicants required to submit FAFSA. *Faculty research:* Academically at-risk students in higher education, communication pedagogy and technology, gender communication, computer-mediated communication, creativity in music. *Total annual research expenditures:* $26,000. *Unit head:* Dr. Gary Thompson, Dean, 701-845-7197, E-mail: gary.thompson@vcsu.edu. *Application contact:* Misty Lindgren, 701-845-7303, Fax: 701-845-7305, E-mail: misty.lindgren@vcsu.edu. Web site: http://www.vcsu.edu/graduate.

Educational Media/Instructional Technology

Virginia Commonwealth University, Graduate School, School of Education, Program in Adult Learning, Richmond, VA 23284-9005. Offers adult literacy (M Ed); human resource development (M Ed); teaching and learning with technology (M Ed). *Accreditation:* NCATE. Part-time programs available. *Entrance requirements:* For master's, GRE General Test or MAT. Additional exam requirements/recommendations for international students: Required—TOEFL (minimum score 600 paper-based; 250 computer-based; 100 iBT). Electronic applications accepted. *Expenses:* Tuition, state resident: full-time $9133; part-time $507 per credit. Tuition, nonresident: full-time $18,777; part-time $1043 per credit. *Required fees:* $77 per credit. Tuition and fees vary according to degree level, campus/location, program and student level. *Faculty research:* Adult development and learning, program planning and evaluation.

Virginia Polytechnic Institute and State University, VT Online, Blacksburg, VA 24061. Offers advanced transportation systems (Certificate); aerospace engineering (MS); agricultural and life sciences (MSLFS); business information systems (Graduate Certificate); career and technical education (MS); civil engineering (MS); computer engineering (M Eng, MS); decision support systems (Graduate Certificate); eLearning leadership (MA); electrical engineering (M Eng, MS); engineering administration (MEA); environmental engineering (Certificate); environmental politics and policy (Graduate Certificate); environmental sciences and engineering (MS); foundations of political analysis (Graduate Certificate); health product risk management (Graduate Certificate); industrial and systems engineering (MS); information policy and society (Graduate Certificate); information security (Graduate Certificate); information technology (MIT); instructional technology (MA); integrative STEM education (MA Ed); liberal arts (Graduate Certificate); life sciences: health product risk management (MS); natural resources (MNR, Graduate Certificate); networking (Graduate Certificate); nonprofit and nongovernmental organization management (Graduate Certificate); ocean engineering (MS); political science (MA); security studies (Graduate Certificate); software development (Graduate Certificate). *Expenses:* Tuition, state resident: full-time $10,048; part-time $558.25 per credit hour. Tuition, nonresident: full-time $19,497; part-time $1083.25 per credit hour. *Required fees:* $405 per semester. Tuition and fees vary according to course load, campus/location and program. *Application contact:* Graduate School Applications General Assistance, 540-231-8636, Fax: 540-231-2039, E-mail: gradappl@vt.edu. Web site: http://www.vto.vt.edu/.

Walden University, Graduate Programs, Richard W. Riley College of Education and Leadership, Minneapolis, MN 55401. Offers administrator leadership for teaching and learning (Ed D, Ed S); adult education (Ed D, Ed S); adult learning (MS, Postbaccalaureate Certificate), including developmental education (MS), online teaching (MS), teaching adults English as a second language (MS), training and performance management (MS); college teaching and learning (Ed D, Ed S, Postbaccalaureate Certificate); curriculum, instruction and assessment (Ed D, Postbaccalaureate Certificate); curriculum, instruction, and professional development (Ed S); developmental education (Postbaccalaureate Certificate); early childhood administration, management, and leadership (Postbaccalaureate Certificate); early childhood education (birth-grade 3) (MAT); early childhood public policy and advocacy (Postbaccalaureate Certificate); early childhood studies (MS), including administration, management and leadership, early childhood public policy and advocacy, teaching adults in the early childhood field, teaching and diversity; education (MS, PhD), including adolescent literacy and technology (grades 6-12) (MS), adult education leadership (PhD), assessment, evaluation, and accountability (PhD), community college leadership (PhD), curriculum, instruction, and assessment, early childhood education (PhD), educational technology (PhD), elementary reading and literacy (MS), elementary reading and mathematics (MS), general program, global and comparative education (PhD), higher education (PhD), integrating technology in the classroom (MS), K-12 educational leadership (PhD), leadership, policy and change (PhD), learning, instruction and innovation (PhD), literacy and learning in the content areas (MS), mathematics (grades 6-8) (MS), mathematics (grades K-5) (MS), middle level education (grades 5-8) (MS), professional development (MS), science (grades K-8) (MS), self-designed (PhD), special education (PhD), special education (non-licensure) (MS), teacher leadership (grades K-12) (MS), teaching English language learners (grades K-12) (MS); educational leadership and administration (principal preparation) (Ed S); educational technology (Ed S); elementary reading and literacy (Postbaccalaureate Certificate); engaging culturally diverse learners (Postbaccalaureate Certificate); enrollment management and institutional marketing (Postbaccalaureate Certificate); higher education (MS), including college teaching and learning, enrollment management and institutional planning, global higher education, leadership for student success, online and distance learning; higher education leadership (Ed D); instructional design (Postbaccalaureate Certificate); instructional design and technology (MS), including general program (MS, PhD), online learning, training and performance improvement; integrating technology in the classroom (Postbaccalaureate Certificate); online teaching for adult learners (Postbaccalaureate Certificate); professional development (Postbaccalaureate Certificate); reading and literacy leadership (Ed D); science K-8 (Postbaccalaureate Certificate); special education (Ed D, Ed S); special education: emotional/behavioral disorders (K-12) (MAT); special education: learning disabilities (K-12) (MAT); teacher leadership (Ed D, Ed S, Postbaccalaureate Certificate); training and performance management (Postbaccalaureate Certificate). Part-time and evening/weekend programs available. Postbaccalaureate distance learning degree programs offered (minimal on-campus study). *Faculty:* 71 full-time (48 women), 853 part-time/adjunct (585 women). *Students:* 11,326 full-time (9,212 women), 2,148 part-time (1,795 women); includes 5,346 minority (4,403 Black or African American, non-Hispanic/Latino; 76 American Indian or Alaska Native, non-Hispanic/Latino; 140 Asian, non-Hispanic/Latino; 561 Hispanic/Latino; 21 Native Hawaiian or other Pacific Islander, non-Hispanic/Latino; 145 Two or more races, non-Hispanic/Latino), 322 international. Average age 39. In 2011, 3,477 master's, 318 doctorates, 471 other advanced degrees awarded. *Degree requirements:* For doctorate, thesis/dissertation (for some programs), residency; for other advanced degree, residency (for some programs). *Entrance requirements:* For master's, bachelor's degree or equivalent in related field; minimum GPA of 2.5; official transcripts; goal statement; access to computer and Internet; for doctorate, master's degree or equivalent in related field; minimum GPA of 3.0; official transcripts; three years' related professional/academic experience (preferred); access to computer and Internet; for other advanced degree, master's degree or equivalent in related field; minimum GPA of 3.0; 3 years related professional/academic experience (preferred); access to computer and Internet (Ed S). Additional exam requirements/recommendations for international students: Required—TOEFL (minimum score 550 paper-based; 213 computer-based), IELTS (minimum score 6.5), or Michigan English Language Assessment Battery (minimum score 82). *Application deadline:* Applications are processed on a rolling basis. Application fee: $50. Electronic applications accepted. *Financial support:* Federal Work-Study, scholarships/grants, unspecified assistantships, and family tuition reduction, active duty/veteran tuition reduction, group tuition reduction, interest-free payment plans, employee tuition reduction available. Support available to part-time students. Financial award applicants required to submit FAFSA. *Unit head:* Dr. Kate Steffens, Dean, 800-925-3368. *Application contact:* Jennifer Hall, Vice President of Enrollment Management, 866-4-WALDEN, E-mail: info@waldenu.edu. Web site: http://www.waldenu.edu/Colleges-and-Schools/College-of-Education-and-Leadership.htm.

Walden University, Graduate Programs, School of Psychology, Minneapolis, MN 55401. Offers clinical psychology (MS), including counseling; forensic psychology (MS), including forensic psychology in the community, general program, mental health applications, program planning and evaluation in forensic settings, psychology and legal systems; organizational psychology and development (Postbaccalaureate Certificate); psychology (MS, PhD), including applied psychology (MS), clinical psychology (PhD), counseling psychology (PhD), crisis management and response (MS), educational psychology, general psychology, health psychology, leadership development and coaching (MS), media psychology (MS), organizational psychology, organizational psychology and nonprofit management (MS), program evaluation and research (MS), psychology of culture (MS), psychology, public administration, and social change (MS), social psychology, terrorism and security (MS); teaching online (Post-Master's Certificate). Part-time and evening/weekend programs available. Postbaccalaureate distance learning degree programs offered (minimal on-campus study). *Faculty:* 35 full-time (23 women), 237 part-time/adjunct (124 women). *Students:* 3,206 full-time (2,508 women), 1,510 part-time (1,240 women); includes 2,028 minority (1,483 Black or African American, non-Hispanic/Latino; 43 American Indian or Alaska Native, non-Hispanic/Latino; 99 Asian, non-Hispanic/Latino; 308 Hispanic/Latino; 4 Native Hawaiian or other Pacific Islander, non-Hispanic/Latino; 91 Two or more races, non-Hispanic/Latino), 158 international. Average age 40. In 2011, 645 master's, 113 doctorates, 30 other advanced degrees awarded. Terminal master's awarded for partial completion of doctoral program. *Degree requirements:* For master's, thesis optional; for doctorate, thesis/dissertation, residency. *Entrance requirements:* For master's, bachelor's degree or equivalent in related field; minimum GPA of 2.5; official transcripts; goal statement; access to computer and Internet; for doctorate, master's degree or equivalent in related field; minimum GPA of 3.0; 3 years of related professional/academic experience (preferred). Additional exam requirements/recommendations for international students: Required—TOEFL (minimum score 550 paper-based; 213 computer-based), IELTS (minimum score 6.5), or Michigan English Language Assessment Battery (minimum score 82). *Application deadline:* Applications are processed on a rolling basis. Application fee: $50. Electronic applications accepted. *Financial support:* Federal Work-Study, scholarships/grants, unspecified assistantships, and family tuition reduction, active duty/veteran tuition reduction, group tuition reduction, interest-free payment plans, employee tuition reduction available. Support available to part-time students. Financial award applicants required to submit FAFSA. *Unit head:* Dr. Melanie Storms, Vice President, 800-925-3368. *Application contact:* Jennifer Hall, Vice President of Enrollment Management, 866-4-WALDEN, E-mail: info@waldenu.edu. Web site: http://www.waldenu.edu/Colleges-and-Schools/College-of-Social-and-Behavioral-Sciences/School-of%20-Psychology.htm.

Wayland Baptist University, Graduate Programs, Program in Education, Plainview, TX 79072-6998. Offers education administration (M Ed); higher education administration (M Ed); instructional leadership (M Ed); instructional technology (M Ed); special education (M Ed). Part-time and evening/weekend programs available. Postbaccalaureate distance learning degree programs offered (no on-campus study). *Degree requirements:* For master's, comprehensive exam, capstone course. *Entrance requirements:* For master's, GRE, GMAT or MAT. Additional exam requirements/recommendations for international students: Required—TOEFL (minimum score 500 paper-based; 173 computer-based; 61 iBT). Electronic applications accepted.

Waynesburg University, Graduate and Professional Studies, Waynesburg, PA 15370-1222. Offers business (MBA), including finance, health systems, human resources, leadership, market development; counseling (MA), including addictions counseling, clinical mental health; education (MAT); nursing (MSN), including administration, education, informatics, palliative care; nursing practice (DNP); special education (M Ed); technology (M Ed); MSN/MBA. *Accreditation:* AACN. Part-time and evening/weekend programs available. *Degree requirements:* For doctorate, thesis/dissertation. *Entrance requirements:* Additional exam requirements/recommendations for international students: Required—TOEFL. Electronic applications accepted.

Wayne State University, College of Education, Division of Administrative and Organizational Studies, Detroit, MI 48202. Offers college and university teaching (Certificate); educational leadership (M Ed); educational leadership and policy studies (Ed D, PhD); general administration and supervision (Ed S); instructional technology (M Ed, Ed D, PhD, Ed S); online teaching (Certificate); secondary curriculum and instruction (Ed S). *Students:* 86 full-time (62 women), 261 part-time (172 women); includes 171 minority (145 Black or African American, non-Hispanic/Latino; 1 American Indian or Alaska Native, non-Hispanic/Latino; 8 Asian, non-Hispanic/Latino; 16 Hispanic/Latino; 1 Two or more races, non-Hispanic/Latino), 8 international. Average age 39. 122 applicants, 40% accepted, 28 enrolled. In 2011, 73 master's, 9 doctorates, 50 other advanced degrees awarded. *Degree requirements:* For doctorate, thesis/dissertation. *Entrance requirements:* For doctorate, GRE or MAT, interview; autobiography or curriculum vitae; references; master's degree; minimum undergraduate GPA of 3.0, graduate 3.75; 3 years relevant experience; foundational course work; for other advanced degree, minimum GPA of 3.4. Additional exam requirements/recommendations for international students: Required—TOEFL (minimum score 550 paper-based; 213 computer-based), TWE (minimum score 5.5). *Application deadline:* For fall admission, 6/1 priority date for domestic students, 5/1 for international students; for winter admission, 10/1 priority date for domestic students, 9/1 for international students; for spring admission, 2/1 priority date for domestic students, 1/1 for international students. Applications are processed on a rolling basis. Application fee: $50. Electronic applications accepted. *Expenses:* Tuition, state resident: part-time $512.85 per credit. Tuition, nonresident: part-time $1132.65 per credit. *Required fees:* $26.60 per credit. $199.65 per semester. Tuition and fees vary according to course load and program. *Financial support:* In 2011–12, 59 students received support, including 1 fellowship with tuition reimbursement available (averaging $17,347 per year), 4 research assistantships with tuition reimbursements available (averaging $15,713 per year); career-related internships or fieldwork, Federal Work-Study, institutionally sponsored loans, scholarships/grants, health care benefits, and unspecified assistantships also available. Support available to part-time students. *Faculty research:* Total quality management, participatory management, administering educational technology, school improvement, principalship. *Total annual research expenditures:* $22,232. *Unit head:* Dr. Alan Hoffman, Interim Assistant Dean, 313-577-5235, E-mail: alanhoffman@wayne.edu. *Application contact:* Janice Green, Assistant Dean, 313-577-1605, E-mail: jwgreen@wayne.edu. Web site: http://coe.wayne.edu/aos/index.php.

Wayne State University, School of Library and Information Science, Detroit, MI 48202. Offers archival administration (MLIS, Certificate); arts and museum librarianship (Certificate); general librarianship (MLIS); health sciences librarianship (MLIS); information management for librarians (Certificate); information science (MLIS); law librarianship (MLIS); library and information science (MLIS, Spec), including academic libraries (MLIS); organization of information (MLIS); public libraries (MLIS); public library services to children and young adults (MLIS, Certificate); records and information management (Certificate); records management (MLIS); references services (MLIS); school library media (Spec); school library media specialist endorsement (MLIS); special libraries (MLIS); urban librarianship (Certificate); urban libraries (MLIS); MLIS/MA. *Accreditation:* ALA (one or more programs are accredited). Part-time and evening/weekend programs available. Postbaccalaureate distance learning degree programs offered (no on-campus study). *Faculty:* 13 full-time (8 women), 25 part-time/adjunct (19 women). *Students:* 121 full-time (93 women), 447 part-time (346 women); includes 57 minority (37 Black or African American, non-Hispanic/Latino; 1 American Indian or Alaska Native, non-Hispanic/Latino; 4 Asian, non-Hispanic/Latino; 7 Hispanic/Latino; 8 Two or more races, non-Hispanic/Latino), 4 international. Average age 33. 336 applicants, 62% accepted, 135 enrolled. In 2011, 212 master's, 38 other advanced degrees awarded. *Entrance requirements:* For master's and other advanced degree, GRE or MAT (if undergraduate GPA is between 2.5 and 2.99), minimum undergraduate GPA of 3.0 or graduate degree, personal statement, new student orientation. Additional exam requirements/recommendations for international students: Required—TOEFL (minimum score 550 paper-based; 213 computer-based); Recommended—TWE (minimum score 5.5). *Application deadline:* For fall admission, 7/1 for domestic students, 5/1 for international students; for winter admission, 10/1 for domestic students, 9/1 for international students; for spring admission, 3/15 for domestic students, 1/1 for international students. Applications are processed on a rolling basis. Application fee: $50. Electronic applications accepted. *Expenses:* Tuition, state resident: part-time $512.85 per credit. Tuition, nonresident: part-time $1132.65 per credit. *Required fees:* $26.60 per credit. $199.65 per semester. Tuition and fees vary according to course load and program. *Financial support:* In 2011–12, 1 research assistantship with tuition reimbursement (averaging $12,250 per year) was awarded; fellowships with tuition reimbursements, career-related internships or fieldwork, Federal Work-Study, institutionally sponsored loans, scholarships/grants, and unspecified assistantships also available. Support available to part-time students. Financial award application deadline: 5/15. *Faculty research:* Convergence of academic libraries and other academic services, competitive intelligence and data mining, impact of digitization on libraries, international librarianship, consumer health information, urban library issues, human-computer interaction, universal access to libraries and instructional support services. *Unit head:* Dr. Sandra Yee, Dean, 313-577-4059, Fax: 313-577-7563, E-mail: aj0533@wayne.edu. *Application contact:* Dr. Stephen Fredericks, Associate Dean and Director, 313-577-7563, E-mail: bajjaly@wayne.edu. Web site: http://www.lisp.wayne.edu/.

Webster University, School of Education, Department of Multidisciplinary Studies, St. Louis, MO 63119-3194. Offers administrative leadership (Ed S); education leadership (Ed S); educational technology (MAT); mathematics (MAT); multidisciplinary studies (MAT); school systems, superintendency and leadership (Ed S); social science (MAT); special education (MAT). Part-time programs available. *Entrance requirements:* For master's, minimum GPA of 2.5. Additional exam requirements/recommendations for international students: Required—TOEFL. *Expenses: Tuition:* Full-time $10,890; part-time $605 per credit hour. Tuition and fees vary according to campus/location and program.

West Chester University of Pennsylvania, College of Education, Department of Professional and Secondary Education, West Chester, PA 19383. Offers education for sustainability (Certificate); entrepreneurial education (Certificate); secondary education (M Ed, Teaching Certificate); teaching and learning with technology (Certificate). Part-time programs available. *Faculty:* 1 (woman) full-time, 9 part-time/adjunct (7 women). *Students:* 5 full-time (all women), 26 part-time (11 women); includes 4 minority (2 Black or African American, non-Hispanic/Latino; 1 Asian, non-Hispanic/Latino; 1 Two or more races, non-Hispanic/Latino). Average age 33. 34 applicants, 56% accepted, 10 enrolled. In 2011, 6 master's, 4 Certificates awarded. *Degree requirements:* For master's, comprehensive exam, thesis (for some programs). *Entrance requirements:* For master's, teaching certification (strongly recommended). Additional exam requirements/recommendations for international students: Required—TOEFL (minimum score 550 paper-based; 213 computer-based; 80 iBT). *Application deadline:* For fall admission, 4/15 priority date for domestic students, 3/15 for international students; for spring admission, 10/15 priority date for domestic students, 9/1 for international students. Applications are processed on a rolling basis. Application fee: $45. Electronic applications accepted. *Expenses:* Tuition, state resident: full-time $7488; part-time $416 per credit. Tuition, nonresident: full-time $11,232; part-time $624 per credit. *Required fees:* $1784.64; $67.59 per credit. Tuition and fees vary according to program. *Financial support:* Unspecified assistantships available. Support available to part-time students. Financial award application deadline: 2/15; financial award applicants required to submit FAFSA. *Faculty research:* Technology integration: preparing our teachers for the twenty-first century, critical pedagogy. *Unit head:* Dr. John Elmore, Chair, 610-436-6934, Fax: 610-436-3102, E-mail: jelmore@wcupa.edu. *Application contact:* Dr. David Bolton, Graduate Coordinator, 610-436-6914, Fax: 610-436-3102, E-mail: dbolton@wcupa.edu. Web site: http://www.wcupa.edu/_academics/sch_sed.prof&seced/.

West Chester University of Pennsylvania, College of Education, Department of Special Education, West Chester, PA 19383. Offers autism (Certificate); special education (M Ed, Certificate, Teaching Certificate); special education: distance education (M Ed); universal design for learning and assistive technology (Certificate); universal design for learning and assistive technology: distance education (Certificate). *Accreditation:* NCATE. Part-time and evening/weekend programs available. Postbaccalaureate distance learning degree programs offered (no on-campus study). *Faculty:* 1 full-time (0 women), 5 part-time/adjunct (all women). *Students:* 11 full-time (10 women), 87 part-time (74 women); includes 9 minority (1 Black or African American, non-Hispanic/Latino; 4 Asian, non-Hispanic/Latino; 4 Hispanic/Latino). Average age 29. 56 applicants, 73% accepted, 22 enrolled. In 2011, 12 degrees awarded. *Degree requirements:* For master's, thesis optional, minimum GPA of 3.0. *Entrance requirements:* For master's, GMAT, GRE General Test, or MAT, interview, minimum GPA of 2.8, two letters of recommendation. Additional exam requirements/recommendations for international students: Required—TOEFL (minimum score 550 paper-based; 213 computer-based; 80 iBT). *Application deadline:* For fall admission, 4/15 priority date for domestic students, 3/15 for international students; for spring admission, 10/15 priority date for domestic students, 9/1 for international students. Applications are processed on a rolling basis. Application fee: $45. Electronic applications accepted. *Expenses:* Tuition, state resident: full-time $7488; part-time $416 per credit. Tuition, nonresident: full-time $11,232; part-time $624 per credit. *Required fees:* $1784.64; $67.59 per credit. Tuition and fees vary according to program. *Financial support:* Unspecified assistantships available. Support available to part-time students. Financial award application deadline: 2/15; financial award applicants required to submit FAFSA. *Faculty research:* Developing online instruction for children with disabilities. *Unit head:* Dr. Donna Wandry, Chair, 610-436-3431, Fax: 610-436-3102, E-mail: dwandry@wcupa.edu. *Application contact:* Dr. Vicki McGinley, Graduate Coordinator, 610-436-2867, E-mail: vmcginley@wcupa.edu. Web site: http://www.wcupa.edu/_academics/sch_sed.earlyspecialed/.

Western Connecticut State University, Division of Graduate Studies, School of Professional Studies, Department of Education and Educational Psychology, Instructional Technology Option, Danbury, CT 06810-6885. Offers MS. Part-time programs available. *Faculty:* 2 full-time (0 women). *Students:* 19 part-time (13 women); includes 1 minority (Hispanic/Latino). Average age 33. 2 applicants, 100% accepted, 2 enrolled. In 2011, 11 degrees awarded. *Degree requirements:* For master's, thesis or research project, completion of program in 6 years. *Entrance requirements:* For master's, minimum GPA of 2.8, teaching certificate. Additional exam requirements/recommendations for international students: Recommended—TOEFL (minimum score 550 paper-based; 213 computer-based; 79 iBT), IELTS (minimum score 6). *Application deadline:* For fall admission, 8/5 priority date for domestic students; for spring admission, 1/5 priority date for domestic students. Applications are processed on a rolling basis. Application fee: $50. Tuition and fees vary according to course level, course load, degree level and program. *Financial support:* Application deadline: 5/1; applicants required to submit FAFSA. *Faculty research:* Connectivism in education. *Unit head:* Dr. Adeline Merrill, Chairperson, Department of Education and Educational Psychology, 203-837-3267, Fax: 203-837-8413, E-mail: merrilla@wcsu.edu. *Application contact:* Chris Shankle, Associate Director of Graduate Studies, 203-837-9005, Fax: 203-837-8326, E-mail: shanklec@wcsu.edu.

Western Governors University, Teachers College, Salt Lake City, UT 84107. Offers curriculum and instruction (MS); educational leadership (MS); educational studies (MA); educational studies (5-12) (MA), including mathematics; elementary education (k-8) (Postbaccalaureate Certificate); English language learning (K-12) (MA); instructional design (MAT); learning and technology (M Ed, MA); management and innovation (M Ed); mathematics (5-12) (Postbaccalaureate Certificate); mathematics (5-9) (Postbaccalaureate Certificate); mathematics education (5-12) (MA); mathematics education (5-9) (MA); mathematics education (K-6) (MA); measurement and evaluation (M Ed); science (5-12) (Postbaccalaureate Certificate); science (5-9) (Postbaccalaureate Certificate); science education (5-12) (MA), including biology, chemistry, geology, physics; science education (5-9) (MA); social science (5-12) (MAT); special education (MAT). *Accreditation:* NCATE. Evening/weekend programs available. Postbaccalaureate distance learning degree programs offered (no on-campus study). *Students:* 3,746 full-time (2,811 women); includes 652 minority (332 Black or African American, non-Hispanic/Latino; 37 American Indian or Alaska Native, non-Hispanic/Latino; 74 Asian, non-Hispanic/Latino; 139 Hispanic/Latino; 70 Two or more races, non-Hispanic/Latino), 12 international. Average age 37. In 2011, 1,080 master's, 242 other advanced degrees awarded. *Degree requirements:* For master's, capstone project. *Entrance requirements:* For master's and Postbaccalaureate Certificate, Readiness Assessment, commitment counseling discussion, transcript submissions, completion of orientation. Additional exam requirements/recommendations for international students: Required—TOEFL (minimum score 450 paper-based; 80 iBT). *Application deadline:* Applications are processed on a rolling basis. Application fee: $65. Electronic applications accepted. *Expenses:* Contact institution. *Financial support:* Scholarships/grants and tuition waivers (partial) available. Financial award applicants required to submit FAFSA. *Unit head:* Dr. Philip Schmidt, Dean of the Teachers College, 845-255-4656. *Application contact:* Enrollment Department, 866-225-5948, Fax: 801-274-3306, E-mail: info@wgu.edu.

Western Illinois University, School of Graduate Studies, College of Education and Human Services, Department of Instructional Design and Technology, Macomb, IL 61455-1390. Offers distance learning (Certificate); educational technology specialist (Certificate); graphic applications (Certificate); instructional design and technology (MS); multimedia (Certificate); technology integration in education (Certificate); training development (Certificate). Part-time programs available. Postbaccalaureate distance learning degree programs offered (no on-campus study). *Students:* 23 full-time (16 women), 58 part-time (35 women); includes 15 minority (8 Black or African American, non-Hispanic/Latino; 1 American Indian or Alaska Native, non-Hispanic/Latino; 2 Asian, non-Hispanic/Latino; 4 Hispanic/Latino), 7 international. Average age 35. 25 applicants, 80% accepted. In 2011, 20 master's, 8 other advanced degrees awarded. *Degree requirements:* For master's, thesis or alternative. *Entrance requirements:* Additional exam requirements/recommendations for international students: Required—TOEFL (minimum score 550 paper-based; 213 computer-based; 80 iBT). *Application deadline:* Applications are processed on a rolling basis. Application fee: $30. Electronic applications accepted. *Expenses:* Tuition, state resident: part-time $281.16 per credit hour. Tuition, nonresident: part-time $562.32 per credit hour. Part-time tuition and fees vary according to campus/location and reciprocity agreements. *Financial support:* In 2011–12, 13 students received support, including 10 research assistantships with full tuition reimbursements available (averaging $7,360 per year), 3 teaching assistantships with full tuition reimbursements available (averaging $8,480 per year). Financial award applicants required to submit FAFSA. *Unit head:* Dr. Hoyet Hemphill, Chairperson, 309-298-1952. *Application contact:* Dr. Nancy Parsons, Interim Associate Provost and Director of Graduate Studies, 309-298-1806, Fax: 309-298-2345, E-mail: grad-office@wiu.edu. Web site: http://wiu.edu/idt.

Western Kentucky University, Graduate Studies, College of Education and Behavioral Sciences, School of Teacher Education, Bowling Green, KY 42101. Offers elementary education (MAE, Ed S); exceptional education: learning and behavioral disorders (MAE); exceptional education: moderate and severe disabilities (MAE); instructional design (MS); interdisciplinary early childhood education (MAE); library media education (MS); literacy education (MAE); middle grades education (MAE); secondary education (MAE, Ed S). Part-time and evening/weekend programs available. Postbaccalaureate distance learning degree programs offered (minimal on-campus study). *Degree requirements:* For master's, comprehensive exam. *Entrance requirements:* For master's, GRE General Test. Additional exam requirements/recommendations for international students: Required—TOEFL (minimum score 555 paper-based; 213 computer-based; 79 iBT). *Faculty research:* Teacher preparation in moderate/severe disabilities.

Western Michigan University, Graduate College, College of Education and Human Development, Department of Educational Leadership, Research and Technology, Kalamazoo, MI 49008. Offers educational leadership (MA, PhD, Ed S); educational technology (MA, Graduate Certificate); evaluation, measurement and research (MA, PhD).

Western Oregon University, Graduate Programs, College of Education, Division of Teacher Education, Program in Information Technology, Monmouth, OR 97361-1394. Offers MS Ed. *Accreditation:* NCATE. Part-time and evening/weekend programs available. Postbaccalaureate distance learning degree programs offered (minimal on-campus study). *Degree requirements:* For master's, written exams. *Entrance requirements:* For master's, interview, minimum GPA of 3.0, teaching license. Additional exam requirements/recommendations for international students: Required—TOEFL (minimum score 550 paper-based; 213 computer-based; 79 iBT), IELTS (minimum score 6.5). *Faculty research:* Impact of technology on teaching and learning.

Westfield State University, Division of Graduate and Continuing Education, Department of Education, Program in Technology for Educators, Westfield, MA 01086. Offers M Ed. Part-time and evening/weekend programs available. *Degree requirements:* For master's, comprehensive exam or project. *Entrance requirements:* For master's, GRE General Test or MAT, minimum undergraduate GPA of 2.7.

West Texas A&M University, College of Education and Social Sciences, Division of Education, Program in Educational Technology, Canyon, TX 79016-0001. Offers M Ed. Part-time and evening/weekend programs available. Postbaccalaureate distance learning degree programs offered (minimal on-campus study). *Degree requirements:* For master's, comprehensive exam, thesis optional. *Entrance requirements:* For master's, GRE General Test, approval from the instructional technology admissions committee. Additional exam requirements/recommendations for international students: Required—TOEFL (minimum score 550 paper-based). Electronic applications accepted.

Faculty research: Mathematics and science instruction, technology, developing online courses for freshmen, integrity of online courses.

West Virginia University, College of Human Resources and Education, Department of Technology, Learning and Culture, Program in Instructional Design and Technology, Morgantown, WV 26506. Offers MA, Ed D. *Accreditation:* NCATE. *Degree requirements:* For master's, thesis; for doctorate, thesis/dissertation. *Entrance requirements:* For master's, GRE General Test, minimum GPA of 2.75; for doctorate, GRE, minimum GPA of 2.75. Additional exam requirements/recommendations for international students: Required—TOEFL. *Faculty research:* Appropriate technology, alternative energy, computer applications for education and training, telecommunication, professional development.

Widener University, School of Human Service Professions, Center for Education, Chester, PA 19013-5792. Offers adult education (M Ed); counseling in higher education (M Ed); counselor education (M Ed); early childhood education (M Ed); educational foundations (M Ed); educational leadership (M Ed); educational psychology (M Ed); elementary education (M Ed); English and language arts (M Ed); health education (M Ed); higher education leadership (Ed D); home and school visitor (M Ed); human sexuality (M Ed, PhD); mathematics education (M Ed); middle school education (M Ed); principalship (M Ed); reading and language arts (Ed D); reading education (M Ed); school administration (Ed D); science education (M Ed); social studies education (M Ed); special education (M Ed); technology education (M Ed). *Accreditation:* NCATE. Part-time and evening/weekend programs available. Terminal master's awarded for partial completion of doctoral program. *Degree requirements:* For doctorate, thesis/dissertation. *Entrance requirements:* For master's, minimum GPA of 2.5; for doctorate, GRE or MAT, minimum GPA of 2.0 (undergraduate), 3.5 (graduate). Electronic applications accepted. *Expenses:* Contact institution. *Faculty research:* Reading and cognition, adult education, technology education, educational leadership, special education.

Wilkes University, College of Graduate and Professional Studies, School of Education, Wilkes-Barre, PA 18766-0002. Offers art and science of teaching (MS Ed); classroom technology (MS Ed); early childhood literacy (MS Ed); educational computing (MS Ed); educational development and strategies (MS Ed); educational leadership (MS Ed); educational technology (Ed D); higher education administration (Ed D); instructional media (MS Ed); instructional technology (MS Ed); K-12 administration (Ed D); online teaching (MS Ed); reading (MS Ed); school business leadership (MS Ed); secondary education (MS Ed), including biology, chemistry, English, history, mathematics; special education (MS Ed); teaching English as a second language (MS Ed); twenty-first century teaching and learning (MS Ed). Part-time and evening/weekend programs available. Postbaccalaureate distance learning degree programs offered (minimal on-campus study). *Students:* 92 full-time (63 women), 2,005 part-time (1,459 women); includes 89 minority (23 Black or African American, non-Hispanic/Latino; 1 American Indian or Alaska Native, non-Hispanic/Latino; 14 Asian, non-Hispanic/Latino; 33 Hispanic/Latino; 1 Native Hawaiian or other Pacific Islander, non-Hispanic/Latino; 17 Two or more races, non-Hispanic/Latino), 6 international. Average age 33. In 2011, 1,150 master's, 3 doctorates awarded. *Entrance requirements:* Additional exam requirements/recommendations for international students: Required—TOEFL (minimum score 550 paper-based; 213 computer-based; 79 iBT). *Application deadline:* Applications are processed on a rolling basis. Application fee: $45. Electronic applications accepted. *Expenses:* Contact institution. *Financial support:* Federal Work-Study and unspecified assistantships available. Financial award application deadline: 3/1; financial award applicants required to submit FAFSA. *Unit head:* Dr. Michael Speziale, Dean, 570-408-4679, Fax: 570-408-4905, E-mail: michael.speziale@wilkes.edu. *Application contact:* Erin Sutzko, Director of Extended Learning, 570-408-4253, Fax: 570-408-7846, E-mail: erin.sutzko@wilkes.edu. Web site: http://www.wilkes.edu/pages/383.asp.

Wilmington University, College of Education, New Castle, DE 19720-6491. Offers applied technology in education (M Ed); career and technical education (M Ed); educational leadership (Ed D); elementary and secondary school counseling (M Ed); elementary studies (M Ed); ESOL literacy (M Ed); higher education leadership (Ed D); instruction: gifted and talented (M Ed); instruction: teacher of reading (M Ed); instruction: teaching and learning (M Ed); organizational leadership (Ed D); school leadership (M Ed); secondary education (MAT); special education (M Ed). *Accreditation:* NCATE. Part-time and evening/weekend programs available. *Faculty:* 7 full-time (4 women). *Students:* 638 full-time (425 women), 2,014 part-time (1,635 women). Average age 33. *Entrance requirements:* For master's, 2 letters of recommendation, interview. Additional exam requirements/recommendations for international students: Required—TOEFL (minimum score 500 paper-based; 173 computer-based). *Application deadline:* For fall admission, 4/30 for domestic students. Applications are processed on a rolling basis. Application fee: $35. Electronic applications accepted. *Expenses: Tuition:* Part-time $534 per credit hour. *Required fees:* $25 per term. *Financial support:* Applicants required to submit FAFSA. *Unit head:* Dr. John C. Gray, Dean, 302-295-1139. *Application contact:* Chris Ferguson, Director of Admissions, 302-356-4636 Ext. 256, Fax: 302-328-5164, E-mail: inquire@wilmcoll.edu. Web site: http://www.wilmu.edu/education/.

Worcester Polytechnic Institute, Graduate Studies and Research, Program in Learning Sciences and Technologies, Worcester, MA 01609-2280. Offers MS, PhD. Program offered jointly between Department of Social Science and Policy Studies and Department of Computer Science. Part-time and evening/weekend programs available. *Students:* 6 full-time (2 women); includes 1 minority (Asian, non-Hispanic/Latino), 1 international. 8 applicants, 63% accepted, 2 enrolled. *Entrance requirements:* For master's and doctorate, GRE (strongly recommended). Additional exam requirements/recommendations for international students: Required—TOEFL (minimum score 563 paper-based; 223 computer-based; 84 iBT), IELTS (minimum score 7). *Application deadline:* For fall admission, 1/1 for domestic and international students; for spring admission, 10/1 for domestic and international students. Applications are processed on a rolling basis. Application fee: $70. Electronic applications accepted. *Financial support:* Research assistantships and teaching assistantships available. *Unit head:* Janice Gobert, Co-Director, 508-831-5296, E-mail: jgobert@wpi.edu. *Application contact:* Lynne Dougherty, Administrative Assistant, 508-831-5301, Fax: 508-831-5717, E-mail: grad@wpi.edu. Web site: http://www.wpi.edu/academics/Majors/LST/progra586.html.

Youngstown State University, Graduate School, Beeghly College of Education, Department of Teacher Education, Youngstown, OH 44555-0001. Offers adolescent/young adult education (MS Ed); content area concentration (MS Ed); early childhood education (MS Ed); educational technology (MS Ed); literacy (MS Ed); middle childhood education (MS Ed); special education (MS Ed), including gifted and talented education, special education. *Accreditation:* NCATE. Part-time and evening/weekend programs available. *Degree requirements:* For master's, comprehensive exam. *Entrance requirements:* For master's, GRE, MAT, or teaching certificate; minimum GPA of 2.7. Additional exam requirements/recommendations for international students: Required—TOEFL. *Faculty research:* Multicultural literacy, hands-on mathematics teaching, integrated instruction, reading comprehension, emergent curriculum.

Educational Policy

Alabama State University, Department of Instructional Support, Program in Educational Administration, Montgomery, AL 36101-0271. Offers educational administration (M Ed, Ed S); educational leadership, policy and law (Ed D). Part-time programs available. *Students:* 30 full-time (17 women), 91 part-time (56 women); includes 91 minority (86 Black or African American, non-Hispanic/Latino; 3 Asian, non-Hispanic/Latino; 2 Hispanic/Latino). Average age 43. 48 applicants, 50% accepted, 8 enrolled. In 2011, 5 master's awarded. *Degree requirements:* For master's, comprehensive exam, thesis optional; for Ed S, thesis. *Entrance requirements:* For master's, GRE General Test, MAT, graduate writing competency test; for Ed S, graduate writing competency test, GRE, MAT. Additional exam requirements/recommendations for international students: Required—TOEFL (minimum score 500 paper-based; 173 computer-based). *Application deadline:* For fall admission, 7/15 for domestic students; for spring admission, 12/15 for domestic students. Applications are processed on a rolling basis. Application fee: $10. *Financial support:* In 2011–12, research assistantships (averaging $9,450 per year) were awarded. *Faculty research:* Nontraditional roles, computer applications for principals, women in educational administration. *Unit head:* Dr. Hyacinth Findlay, Coordinator, 334-229-4417, E-mail: hfindlay@alasu.edu. *Application contact:* Dr. Doris Screws, Dean of Graduate Studies, 334-229-4274, Fax: 334-229-4928, E-mail: dscrews@alasu.edu. Web site: http://www.alasu.edu/academics/colleges—departments/college-of-education/instructional-support-programs/instructional-leadership/eds-in-educational-a.

Arizona State University, Mary Lou Fulton Teachers College, Program in Educational Leadership and Policy Studies, Phoenix, AZ 85069. Offers PhD. Fall admission only. *Degree requirements:* For doctorate, comprehensive exam, thesis/dissertation, interactive Program of Study (iPOS) submitted before completing 50 percent of required credit hours. *Entrance requirements:* For doctorate, GRE, minimum GPA of 3.0 or equivalent in last 2 years of work leading to bachelor's degree, 3 letters of recommendation, personal statement, writing sample, curriculum vitae or resume. Additional exam requirements/recommendations for international students: Required—TOEFL (minimum score 80 iBT), TOEFL, IELTS, or Pearson Test of English. Electronic applications accepted. *Expenses:* Contact institution. *Faculty research:* Education policy analysis, school finance and quantitative methods, school improvement in ethnically, linguistically and economically diverse communities, parent/teacher engagement, school choice, accountability polices, school finance litigation, school segregation.

The Catholic University of America, School of Arts and Sciences, Department of Education, Washington, DC 20064. Offers Catholic educational leadership and policy studies (PhD); Catholic school leadership (MA); education (Certificate); educational psychology (PhD); secondary education (MA); special education (MA). *Accreditation:* NCATE. Part-time programs available. *Faculty:* 10 full-time (8 women), 10 part-time/adjunct (8 women). *Students:* 4 full-time (all women), 44 part-time (34 women); includes 12 minority (6 Black or African American, non-Hispanic/Latino; 4 Hispanic/Latino; 2 Two or more races, non-Hispanic/Latino). Average age 39. 38 applicants, 24% accepted, 2 enrolled. In 2011, 5 master's, 4 doctorates, 3 other advanced degrees awarded. *Degree requirements:* For master's, comprehensive exam, thesis or alternative; for doctorate, comprehensive exam, thesis/dissertation; for Certificate, action research project. *Entrance requirements:* For master's and doctorate, GRE General Test or MAT, statement of purpose, official copies of academic transcripts, three letters of recommendation, interview; for Certificate, PRAXIS I, statement of purpose, official copies of academic transcripts, three letters of recommendation, interview. Additional exam requirements/recommendations for international students: Required—TOEFL (minimum score 580 paper-based; 237 computer-based). *Application deadline:* For fall admission, 8/1 priority date for domestic students, 7/15 for international students; for spring admission, 12/1 priority date for domestic students, 10/15 for international students. Applications are processed on a rolling basis. Application fee: $55. Electronic applications accepted. *Expenses: Tuition:* Full-time $35,260; part-time $1380 per credit. *Required fees:* $80; $40 per semester hour. One-time fee: $425. *Financial support:* Fellowships, research assistantships, teaching assistantships, Federal Work-Study, scholarships/grants, tuition waivers (full and partial), and unspecified assistantships available. Financial award application deadline: 2/1; financial award applicants required to submit FAFSA. *Faculty research:* Special education, early childhood education, educational psychology, Catholic school administration, leadership and policy studies, counseling, curriculum and instruction. *Total annual research expenditures:* $36,210. *Unit head:* Dr. Merylann J. Schuttloffel, Chair, 202-319-5805, Fax: 202-319-5815, E-mail: schuttloffel@cua.edu. *Application contact:* Andrew Woodall, Director of Graduate Admissions, 202-319-5057, Fax: 202-319-6533, E-mail: cua-admissions@cua.edu. Web site: http://education.cua.edu/.

The College of William and Mary, School of Education, Program in Education Policy, Planning, and Leadership, Williamsburg, VA 23187-8795. Offers curriculum and educational technology (Ed D, PhD); curriculum leadership (Ed D, PhD); educational leadership (M Ed), including higher education administration (M Ed, Ed D, PhD), K-12 administration and supervision; educational policy, planning, and leadership (Ed D, PhD), including general education administration, gifted education administration, higher education administration (M Ed, Ed D, PhD), special education administration; gifted education administration (M Ed). *Accreditation:* NCATE. Part-time and evening/weekend programs available. *Faculty:* 11 full-time (5 women), 11 part-time/adjunct (9 women). *Students:* 50 full-time (38 women), 145 part-time (104 women); includes 45 minority (35 Black or African American, non-Hispanic/Latino; 2 Asian, non-Hispanic/Latino; 4 Hispanic/Latino; 4 Two or more races, non-Hispanic/Latino), 5 international. Average age 38. 173 applicants, 62% accepted, 75 enrolled. In 2011, 21 master's, 10 doctorates awarded. *Degree requirements:* For doctorate, comprehensive exam, thesis/dissertation. *Entrance requirements:* For master's, GRE or MAT, minimum GPA of 2.5; for doctorate, GRE or MAT, minimum GPA of 3.0. Additional exam requirements/recommendations for international students: Required—TOEFL. *Application deadline:* For fall admission, 1/15 for domestic and international students. Application fee: $50.

Electronic applications accepted. *Expenses:* Tuition, state resident: full-time $6400; part-time $365 per credit hour. Tuition, nonresident: full-time $19,720; part-time $985 per credit hour. *Required fees:* $4562. *Financial support:* In 2011–12, 54 students received support, including 1 fellowship (averaging $20,000 per year), 38 research assistantships with full and partial tuition reimbursements available (averaging $15,000 per year); career-related internships or fieldwork, Federal Work-Study, institutionally sponsored loans, scholarships/grants, and unspecified assistantships also available. Support available to part-time students. Financial award application deadline: 1/15; financial award applicants required to submit FAFSA. *Faculty research:* Higher education policy, faculty incentives, history of adversity, resilience, leadership. *Unit head:* Dr. Pamela Eddy, Area Coordinator, 757-221-2349, E-mail: peddy@wm.edu. *Application contact:* Dorothy Smith Osborne, Assistant Dean for Admission, 757-221-2317, Fax: 757-221-2293, E-mail: dsosbo@wm.edu. Web site: http://education.wm.edu.

Florida State University, The Graduate School, College of Education, Department of Educational Leadership and Policy Studies, Tallahassee, FL 32306-4452. Offers educational leadership/administration (MS, Ed D, PhD, Ed S), including educational administration/leadership; educational policy and planning analysis (PhD, Ed S); higher education (MS, Ed D, PhD, Ed S), including higher education; program evaluation (MS, PhD, Ed S); social, history and philosophy of education (MS, PhD, Ed S), including history and philosophy of education, international and intercultural education (PhD); sociocultural and international developmental education (MS, PhD, Ed S). Part-time and evening/weekend programs available. *Faculty:* 19 full-time (10 women), 17 part-time/adjunct (10 women). *Students:* 145 full-time (95 women), 163 part-time (104 women); includes 85 minority (61 Black or African American, non-Hispanic/Latino; 3 American Indian or Alaska Native, non-Hispanic/Latino; 4 Asian, non-Hispanic/Latino; 17 Hispanic/Latino), 27 international. Average age 33. 283 applicants, 57% accepted, 75 enrolled. In 2011, 65 master's, 19 doctorates, 13 other advanced degrees awarded. Terminal master's awarded for partial completion of doctoral program. *Degree requirements:* For master's and Ed S, comprehensive exam, thesis optional; for doctorate, comprehensive exam, thesis/dissertation. *Entrance requirements:* For master's, doctorate, and Ed S, GRE General Test, minimum GPA of 3.0. Additional exam requirements/recommendations for international students: Required—TOEFL (minimum score 550 paper-based; 213 computer-based; 80 iBT). *Application deadline:* For fall admission, 7/1 for domestic and international students; for winter admission, 11/1 for domestic and international students; for spring admission, 3/1 for domestic and international students. Application fee: $30. Electronic applications accepted. *Expenses:* Tuition, state resident: full-time $9474; part-time $350.88 per credit hour. Tuition, nonresident: full-time $16,236; part-time $601.34 per credit hour. *Required fees:* $630 per semester. One-time fee: $20. Tuition and fees vary according to course load and campus/location. *Financial support:* In 2011–12, 8 students received support, including 4 fellowships with full and partial tuition reimbursements available, 23 research assistantships with full and partial tuition reimbursements available, 18 teaching assistantships with full and partial tuition reimbursements available; career-related internships or fieldwork, scholarships/grants, health care benefits, and unspecified assistantships also available. Financial award application deadline: 1/15; financial award applicants required to submit FAFSA. *Faculty research:* Study and implementation of educational policy on all applicable levels, from neighborhood schools to international agencies. *Total annual research expenditures:* $509,546. *Unit head:* Dr. Patrice Iatarola, Chair, 850-644-6777, Fax: 850-644-1258, E-mail: piatarola@fsu.edu. *Application contact:* Jimmy Pastrano, Program Assistant, 850-644-6777, Fax: 850-644-1258, E-mail: jpastrano@fsu.edu. Web site: http://www.fsu.edu/~elps/.

The George Washington University, Graduate School of Education and Human Development, Department of Educational Leadership, Program in Educational Administration and Policy Studies, Washington, DC 20052. Offers education policy (Ed D); educational administration (Ed D). Educational administration program offered at Newport News and Alexandria, VA. *Accreditation:* NCATE. *Students:* 9 full-time (7 women), 155 part-time (108 women); includes 57 minority (44 Black or African American, non-Hispanic/Latino; 8 Asian, non-Hispanic/Latino; 5 Hispanic/Latino), 4 international. Average age 40. 46 applicants, 50% accepted. In 2011, 15 doctorates awarded. *Degree requirements:* For doctorate, comprehensive exam, thesis/dissertation. *Entrance requirements:* For doctorate, GRE General Test or MAT, interview, minimum GPA of 3.3. *Application deadline:* For fall admission, 1/15 priority date for domestic students; for spring admission, 10/1 for domestic students. Applications are processed on a rolling basis. Application fee: $75. *Financial support:* In 2011–12, 9 students received support. Fellowships, research assistantships, teaching assistantships, career-related internships or fieldwork, Federal Work-Study, and tuition waivers (partial) available. Financial award application deadline: 1/15; financial award applicants required to submit FAFSA. *Unit head:* Prof. Yas Nakib, Program Coordinator, 202-994-8816, E-mail: nakib@gwu.edu. *Application contact:* Sarah Lang, 202-994-1447, Fax: 202-994-7207, E-mail: slang@gwu.edu.

The George Washington University, Graduate School of Education and Human Development, Department of Educational Leadership, Program in Education Policy Studies, Washington, DC 20052. Offers MA Ed. *Accreditation:* NCATE. *Students:* 13 full-time (11 women), 10 part-time (9 women); includes 5 minority (2 Black or African American, non-Hispanic/Latino; 1 Asian, non-Hispanic/Latino; 2 Hispanic/Latino). Average age 29. 79 applicants, 65% accepted. In 2011, 9 master's awarded. *Degree requirements:* For master's, comprehensive exam. *Entrance requirements:* For master's, GRE General Test or MAT, interview, minimum GPA of 2.75. *Application deadline:* For fall admission, 1/15 priority date for domestic students; for spring admission, 10/1 for domestic students. Applications are processed on a rolling basis. Application fee: $75. *Financial support:* In 2011–12, 10 students received support. Fellowships, career-related internships or fieldwork, Federal Work-Study, and tuition waivers (partial) available. Financial award application deadline: 1/15. *Unit head:* Prof. Yas Nakib, Coordinator, 202-994-8816, E-mail: nakib@gwu.edu. *Application contact:* Sarah Lang, Director of Graduate Admissions, 202-994-1447, Fax: 202-994-7207, E-mail: slang@gwu.edu.

Georgia State University, College of Education, Department of Educational Policy Studies, Atlanta, GA 30302-3083. Offers educational leadership (M Ed, PhD, Ed S); educational research (MS, PhD), including educational research (MS), research, measurements and statistics (PhD); social foundations of education (MS, PhD). Part-time and evening/weekend programs available. *Degree requirements:* For master's, thesis or project; for doctorate, thesis/dissertation. *Entrance requirements:* For master's, GRE General Test, minimum GPA of 2.5, 2 letters of recommendation, resume; for doctorate, GRE General Test or MAT, minimum GPA of 3.3, goal statement, 2 letters of recommendation, resum; for Ed S, GRE General Test or MAT, minimum GPA of 3.25, goal statement, 1 letter of recommendation. Electronic applications accepted. *Faculty research:* Policy studies, organizational studies, education and culture.

Harvard University, Harvard Graduate School of Education, Master's Programs in Education, Cambridge, MA 02138. Offers arts in education (Ed M); education policy and management (Ed M); higher education (Ed M); human development and psychology (Ed M); international education policy (Ed M); language and literacy (Ed M); learning and teaching (Ed M); mid-career mathematics and science (teaching certificate) (Ed M); mind brain and education (Ed M); prevention science and practice (Ed M); school leadership (Ed M); special studies (Ed M); teaching and curriculum (teaching certificate) (Ed M); technology innovation and education (Ed M). Part-time programs available. *Faculty:* 83 full-time (44 women), 67 part-time/adjunct (29 women). *Students:* 592 full-time (431 women), 75 part-time (54 women); includes 194 minority (41 Black or African American, non-Hispanic/Latino; 4 American Indian or Alaska Native, non-Hispanic/Latino; 75 Asian, non-Hispanic/Latino; 45 Hispanic/Latino; 2 Native Hawaiian or other Pacific Islander, non-Hispanic/Latino; 27 Two or more races, non-Hispanic/Latino), 95 international. Average age 28. 1,679 applicants, 52% accepted, 627 enrolled. In 2011, 653 master's awarded. *Entrance requirements:* For master's, GRE General Test, statement of purpose, 3 letters of recommendation, resume, official transcripts. Additional exam requirements/recommendations for international students: Required—TOEFL (minimum score 613 paper-based; 104 computer-based; 100 iBT), TWE (minimum score 5). *Application deadline:* For fall admission, 1/4 for domestic and international students. Application fee: $85. Electronic applications accepted. *Expenses:* Contact institution. *Financial support:* In 2011–12, 419 students received support, including 14 fellowships with full and partial tuition reimbursements available (averaging $12,831 per year); career-related internships or fieldwork, Federal Work-Study, institutionally sponsored loans, scholarships/grants, health care benefits, tuition waivers (full and partial), and unspecified assistantships also available. Support available to part-time students. Financial award application deadline: 2/1; financial award applicants required to submit FAFSA. *Faculty research:* Learning and development, educational leadership and organizations, educational policy analysis. *Total annual research expenditures:* $26 million. *Unit head:* Jennifer L. Petrallia, Assistant Dean, 617-495-8445. *Application contact:* Information Contact, 617-495-3414, Fax: 617-496-3577, E-mail: gseadmissions@harvard.edu. Web site: http://www.gse.harvard.edu/.

Hofstra University, School of Education, Health, and Human Services, Department of Foundations, Leadership, and Policy Studies, Hempstead, NY 11549. Offers educational and policy leadership (MS Ed, Ed D), including higher education (MS Ed), K-12 (MS Ed); educational policy and leadership (Advanced Certificate), including school district business leader; foundations of education (MA, Advanced Certificate); Advanced Certificate/Advanced Certificate. Part-time and evening/weekend programs available. Postbaccalaureate distance learning degree programs offered (minimal on-campus study). *Students:* 22 full-time (16 women), 105 part-time (65 women); includes 45 minority (33 Black or African American, non-Hispanic/Latino; 1 Asian, non-Hispanic/Latino; 11 Hispanic/Latino), 2 international. Average age 37. 78 applicants, 94% accepted, 42 enrolled. In 2011, 12 master's, 6 doctorates, 12 other advanced degrees awarded. *Degree requirements:* For master's, one foreign language, comprehensive exam (for some programs), thesis or alternative, minimum GPA of 3.0; for doctorate, comprehensive exam (for some programs), thesis/dissertation (for some programs), minimum GPA of 3.0. *Entrance requirements:* For master's and Advanced Certificate, interview, writing sample, essay; for doctorate, GMAT, GRE, LSAT, or MAT, interview, 3 letters of recommendation, resume, essay. Additional exam requirements/recommendations for international students: Required—TOEFL (minimum score 550 paper-based; 213 computer-based; 80 iBT). *Application deadline:* Applications are processed on a rolling basis. Application fee: $70 ($75 for international students). Electronic applications accepted. *Expenses: Tuition:* Full-time $18,990; part-time $1055 per credit hour. *Required fees:* $970. Tuition and fees vary according to program. *Financial support:* In 2011–12, 66 students received support, including 44 fellowships with full and partial tuition reimbursements available (averaging $3,788 per year), 3 research assistantships with full and partial tuition reimbursements available (averaging $12,125 per year); Federal Work-Study, institutionally sponsored loans, scholarships/grants, tuition waivers (full and partial), and unspecified assistantships also available. Support available to part-time students. Financial award applicants required to submit FAFSA. *Faculty research:* School improvement, professional assessment - APPR, educational policy, professional development, race/gender in education. *Unit head:* Dr. Esther Fusco, Chairperson, 516-463-7704, Fax: 516-463-6196, E-mail: catezf@hofstra.edu. *Application contact:* Carol Drummer, Dean of Graduate Admissions, 516-463-4876, Fax: 516-463-4664, E-mail: gradstudent@hofstra.edu. Web site: http://www.hofstra.edu/education/.

Illinois State University, Graduate School, College of Education, Department of Curriculum and Instruction, Normal, IL 61790-2200. Offers curriculum and instruction (MS, MS Ed, Ed D); educational policies (Ed D); postsecondary education (Ed D); reading (MS Ed); supervision (Ed D). *Accreditation:* NCATE. *Degree requirements:* For master's, variable foreign language requirement, thesis or alternative; for doctorate, variable foreign language requirement, thesis/dissertation, 2 terms of residency, internship. *Entrance requirements:* For master's, GRE General Test, minimum GPA of 3.0 in last 60 hours of course work; for doctorate, GRE General Test. *Faculty research:* In-service and pre-service teacher education for teachers of English language learners; teachers for all children: developing a model for alternative, bilingual elementary certification for paraprofessionals in Illinois; Illinois Geographic Alliance, Connections Project.

Indiana University Bloomington, School of Education, Department of Educational Leadership and Policy Studies, Bloomington, IN 47405-7000. Offers education policy studies (PhD); educational leadership (MS, Ed D, Ed S); higher education (MS, Ed D, PhD); history and philosophy of education (MS); history of education (PhD); international and comparative education (MS, PhD); philosophy of education (PhD); student affairs administration (MS). *Accreditation:* NCATE. Part-time and evening/weekend programs available. *Degree requirements:* For master's, thesis optional; for doctorate, comprehensive exam, thesis/dissertation; for Ed S, comprehensive exam or project. *Entrance requirements:* For master's, doctorate, and Ed S, GRE General Test. Additional exam requirements/recommendations for international students: Required—TOEFL (minimum score 213 computer-based; 79 iBT). Electronic applications accepted. *Faculty research:* Student engagement at higher education institutions in the nation, Reading First professional development initiative, state finance policy on financial access to higher education, school reform, special needs studies.

Loyola University Chicago, School of Education, Program in Cultural and Educational Policy Studies, Chicago, IL 60660. Offers M Ed, MA, Ed D, PhD. Part-time programs available. *Faculty:* 4 full-time (1 woman), 4 part-time/adjunct (2 women). *Students:* 68. Average age 30. 79 applicants, 67% accepted, 19 enrolled. In 2011, 20 master's, 12 doctorates awarded. *Degree requirements:* For master's, comprehensive exam (M Ed), thesis (MA); for doctorate, comprehensive exam, thesis/dissertation, oral candidacy exam. *Entrance requirements:* For master's, letters of recommendation, minimum GPA of 3.0; for doctorate, GRE General Test, interview, letter of recommendation, resume, minimum GPA of 3.0. Additional exam requirements/recommendations for international students: Required—TOEFL (minimum score 550 paper-based; 218 computer-based; 79 iBT). *Application deadline:* For fall admission, 7/1 for domestic and international students; for spring admission, 11/1 for domestic and international students. Applications are processed on a rolling basis. Application fee: $50. Application fee is waived when completed online. *Expenses: Tuition:* Full-time $15,660; part-time $870 per credit hour. *Required fees:* $125 per semester. Tuition and fees vary according to course load and program. *Financial support:* In 2011–12, 4 fellowships with full tuition reimbursements (averaging $13,000 per year), 5 research assistantships with full tuition reimbursements (averaging $12,000 per year) were awarded; career-related internships or fieldwork, institutionally sponsored loans, scholarships/grants, health care benefits, tuition waivers (partial), and unspecified assistantships also available. Support available to part-time students. Financial award application deadline: 2/1; financial award applicants required to submit FAFSA. *Faculty research:* Politics of education, cultural foundations, policy studies, qualitative research methods, multicultural diversity. *Unit head:* Dr. Noah Sobe, Director, 312-915-6954, E-mail: nsobe@luc.edu. *Application contact:* Marie Rosin-Dittmar, Information Contact, 312-915-6800, E-mail: schleduc@luc.edu.

Marquette University, Graduate School, College of Education, Department of Educational Policy and Leadership, Milwaukee, WI 53201-1881. Offers college student personnel administration (M Ed); curriculum and instruction (MA); education (MA); educational administration (M Ed); educational policy and foundations (MA); elementary education (Certificate); literacy (MA); principal (Certificate); reading specialist (Certificate); reading teacher (Certificate); secondary education (Certificate); superintendent (Certificate). Part-time and evening/weekend programs available. *Faculty:* 14 full-time (9 women). *Students:* 40 full-time (34 women), 137 part-time (80 women); includes 25 minority (14 Black or African American, non-Hispanic/Latino; 1 American Indian or Alaska Native, non-Hispanic/Latino; 2 Asian, non-Hispanic/Latino; 8 Hispanic/Latino), 2 international. Average age 32. 132 applicants, 73% accepted, 67 enrolled. In 2011, 46 master's, 3 doctorates, 5 other advanced degrees awarded. Terminal master's awarded for partial completion of doctoral program. *Degree requirements:* For master's, comprehensive exam, thesis (for some programs); for doctorate, thesis/dissertation, qualifying exam, supporting minor. *Entrance requirements:* For master's, GRE General Test or MAT, official transcripts from all current and previous colleges/universities except Marquette, three letters of recommendation, statement of purpose; for doctorate, GRE General Test, MAT, sample of written work, official transcripts from all current and previous colleges/universities except Marquette, three letters of recommendation, statement of purpose, resume/curriculum vitae; for Certificate, GRE General Test or MAT, master's degree. Additional exam requirements/recommendations for international students: Required—TOEFL (minimum score 530 paper-based; 78 computer-based). *Application deadline:* For fall admission, 1/15 for domestic and international students. Application fee: $50. *Expenses:* Contact institution. *Financial support:* In 2011–12, 130 students received support, including 1 fellowship with full tuition reimbursement available (averaging $18,780 per year), 5 research assistantships with full tuition reimbursements available (averaging $13,404 per year); health care benefits, tuition waivers (partial), and unspecified assistantships also available. Support available to part-time students. Financial award application deadline: 2/15. *Faculty research:* Leadership; social justice in education; development of lifelong learners; race, class, and schooling in historical perspective; urban teacher education. *Unit head:* Dr. Ellen Eckman, Chair, 414-288-1561, E-mail: ellen.eckman@marquette.edu. *Application contact:* Craig Pierce, Assistant Dean of the Graduate School, 414-288-5740, Fax: 414-288-1902, E-mail: craig.pierce@marquette.edu.

Michigan State University, The Graduate School, College of Education, Program in Educational Policy, East Lansing, MI 48824. Offers PhD. *Entrance requirements:* Additional exam requirements/recommendations for international students: Required—TOEFL. Electronic applications accepted.

New York University, Steinhardt School of Culture, Education, and Human Development, Department of Humanities and Social Sciences in the Professions, Program in Sociology of Education, New York, NY 10012-1019. Offers education and social policy (MA); sociology of education (MA, PhD), including education policy (MA), social and cultural studies of education (MA). Part-time programs available. *Faculty:* 14 full-time (7 women). *Students:* 43 full-time (35 women), 22 part-time (16 women); includes 19 minority (10 Black or African American, non-Hispanic/Latino; 3 Asian, non-Hispanic/Latino; 5 Hispanic/Latino; 1 Two or more races, non-Hispanic/Latino), 13 international. Average age 29. 127 applicants, 86% accepted, 33 enrolled. In 2011, 7 master's, 1 doctorate awarded. *Degree requirements:* For master's, thesis (for some programs); for doctorate, thesis/dissertation. *Entrance requirements:* For master's, letters of recommendation; for doctorate, GRE General Test, interview. Additional exam requirements/recommendations for international students: Required—TOEFL. *Application deadline:* For fall admission, 12/1 priority date for domestic students, 12/1 for international students; for spring admission, 11/1 for domestic and international students. Applications are processed on a rolling basis. Application fee: $75. Electronic applications accepted. *Financial support:* Fellowships with full and partial tuition reimbursements, Federal Work-Study, institutionally sponsored loans, scholarships/grants, and tuition waivers (partial) available. Support available to part-time students. Financial award application deadline: 2/1; financial award applicants required to submit FAFSA. *Faculty research:* Legal and institutional environments of schools; social inequality; high school reform and achievement; urban schooling, economics and education, educational policy. *Unit head:* Dr. Floyd M. Hammack, Program Director, 212-998-5542, Fax: 212-995-4832, E-mail: fmhl@nyu.edu. *Application contact:* 212-998-5030, Fax: 212-995-4328, E-mail: steinhardt.gradadmissions@nyu.edu. Web site: http://steinhardt.nyu.edu/humsocsci/sociology.

The Ohio State University, Graduate School, College of Education and Human Ecology, School of Educational Policy and Leadership, Columbus, OH 43210. Offers M Ed, MA, PhD. *Accreditation:* NCATE. *Faculty:* 31. *Students:* 87 full-time (63 women), 168 part-time (103 women); includes 54 minority (27 Black or African American, non-Hispanic/Latino; 1 American Indian or Alaska Native, non-Hispanic/Latino; 11 Asian, non-Hispanic/Latino; 9 Hispanic/Latino; 6 Two or more races, non-Hispanic/Latino), 23 international. Average age 32. In 2011, 30 master's, 24 doctorates awarded. *Degree requirements:* For master's, thesis optional; for doctorate, thesis/dissertation. *Entrance requirements:* For doctorate, GRE General Test. Additional exam requirements/recommendations for international students: Required—TOEFL (minimum score 600 paper-based; 250 computer-based), Michigan English Language Assessment Battery (minimum score 82). *Application deadline:* For fall admission, 8/15 priority date for domestic students, 7/1 for international students; for winter admission, 12/1 priority date for domestic students, 11/1 for international students; for spring admission, 3/1 priority date for domestic students, 2/1 for international students. Applications are processed on a rolling basis. Application fee: $40 ($50 for international students). Electronic applications accepted. *Expenses:* Tuition, state resident: full-time $11,400. Tuition, nonresident: full-time $28,125. Tuition and fees vary according to course load, degree level, campus/location and program. *Financial support:* Fellowships, research assistantships, teaching assistantships, Federal Work-Study, institutionally sponsored loans, and unspecified assistantships available. Support available to part-time students. *Unit head:* Eric Anderman, Director, 614-688-3484, E-mail: anderman.1@osu.edu. *Application contact:* Deb Zabloudil, Director of Graduate Student Services, 614-688-4007, E-mail: zabloudil.1@osu.edu. Web site: http://ehe.osu.edu/epl/.

Penn State University Park, Graduate School, College of Education, Department of Education Policy Studies, State College, University Park, PA 16802-1503. Offers college student affairs (M Ed); educational leadership (M Ed); educational theory and policy (MA, PhD); higher education (D Ed, PhD). *Accreditation:* NCATE. *Unit head:* Dr. David H. Monk, Dean, 814-865-2526, Fax: 814-865-0555, E-mail: dhm6@psu.edu. *Application contact:* Cynthia E. Nicosia, Director, Graduate Enrollment Services, 814-865-1834, E-mail: cey1@psu.edu. Web site: http://www.ed.psu.edu/educ/eps/.

Rutgers, The State University of New Jersey, Camden, Graduate School of Arts and Sciences, Department of Public Policy and Administration, Camden, NJ 08102. Offers education policy and leadership (MPA); international public service and development (MPA); public management (MPA); JD/MPA; MPA/MA. *Accreditation:* NASPAA. Part-time and evening/weekend programs available. *Degree requirements:* For master's, directed study, research workshop, 42 credits. *Entrance requirements:* For master's, GRE General Test, GMAT or LSAT, 3 letters of recommendation; resume. Additional exam requirements/recommendations for international students: Required—TOEFL (minimum score 550 paper-based; 213 computer-based), IELTS. Electronic applications accepted. *Faculty research:* Nonprofit management, county and municipal administration, health and human services, government communication, administrative law, educational finance.

Rutgers, The State University of New Jersey, New Brunswick, Graduate School of Education, Doctoral Program in Education, New Brunswick, NJ 08901. Offers educational policy (PhD); educational psychology (PhD); literacy education (PhD); mathematics education (PhD). Part-time programs available. *Degree requirements:* For doctorate, thesis/dissertation, qualifying exam. *Entrance requirements:* For doctorate, GRE General Test, GRE Subject Test (mathematics education). Additional exam requirements/recommendations for international students: Required—TOEFL (minimum score 575 paper-based; 233 computer-based; 83 iBT). Electronic applications accepted. *Faculty research:* Literacy education, math education, educational psychology, educational policy, learning sciences.

University of Alberta, Faculty of Graduate Studies and Research, Department of Educational Policy Studies, Edmonton, AB T6G 2E1, Canada. Offers adult education (M Ed, Ed D, PhD); educational administration and leadership (M Ed, Ed D, PhD, Postgraduate Diploma); First Nations education (M Ed, Ed D, PhD); theoretical, cultural and international studies in education (M Ed, Ed D, PhD). *Degree requirements:* For master's, thesis (for some programs); for doctorate, thesis/dissertation. *Entrance requirements:* For master's, minimum GPA of 6.5 on a 9.0 scale; for doctorate, minimum GPA of 7.5 on a 9.0 scale. Additional exam requirements/recommendations for international students: Required—TOEFL (minimum score 580 paper-based; 237 computer-based). Electronic applications accepted.

University of Arkansas, Graduate School, College of Education and Health Professions, Department of Curriculum and Instruction, Program in Education Policy, Fayetteville, AR 72701-1201. Offers PhD. *Students:* 9 full-time (4 women), 6 part-time (0 women); includes 2 minority (1 Black or African American, non-Hispanic/Latino; 1 Hispanic/Latino), 1 international. *Application deadline:* For fall admission, 4/1 for international students; for spring admission, 10/1 for international students. Applications are processed on a rolling basis. Electronic applications accepted. *Financial support:* In 2011–12, 14 research assistantships were awarded; fellowships and teaching assistantships also available. *Unit head:* Dr. Michael Daugherty, Department Head, 479-575-4209, E-mail: mkd03@uark.edu. *Application contact:* Dr. Barbara Gartin, Graduate Admissions, 479-575-7525, Fax: 479-575-6676, E-mail: bgartin@uark.edu.

The University of British Columbia, Faculty of Education, Department of Educational Studies, Vancouver, BC V6T 1Z1, Canada. Offers adult education (M Ed, MA); adult learning and global change (M Ed); educational administration (M Ed, MA); educational leadership and policy (Ed D); educational studies (PhD); higher education (M Ed, MA); society, culture and politics in education (M Ed, MA). Part-time and evening/weekend programs available. Terminal master's awarded for partial completion of doctoral program. *Degree requirements:* For master's, thesis; for doctorate, comprehensive exam, thesis/dissertation, master's thesis. *Entrance requirements:* For master's, minimum B+ average, 4-year undergraduate degree, field-related experience; for doctorate, minimum B+ average, 4-year undergraduate degree, master's degree, field-related experience. Additional exam requirements/recommendations for international students: Required—TOEFL (minimum score 600 paper-based; 250 computer-based; 100 iBT) or IELTS (minimum score 6.5). Electronic applications accepted. *Faculty research:* Educational leadership educational administration adult education politics in education, global change and adult learning.

University of Colorado Boulder, Graduate School, School of Education, Division of Educational Foundations, Policy, and Practice, Boulder, CO 80309. Offers MA, PhD. *Students:* 43 full-time (27 women), 12 part-time (9 women); includes 20 minority (5 Black or African American, non-Hispanic/Latino; 5 Asian, non-Hispanic/Latino; 9 Hispanic/Latino; 1 Two or more races, non-Hispanic/Latino). Average age 34. 67 applicants, 45% accepted, 14 enrolled. In 2011, 11 master's, 3 doctorates awarded. *Entrance requirements:* For master's, minimum undergraduate GPA of 2.75. *Application deadline:* For fall admission, 2/1 for domestic students, 12/1 for international students; for spring admission, 9/1 for domestic students, 12/1 for international students. Electronic applications accepted. *Financial support:* In 2011–12, 68 students received support, including 24 fellowships (averaging $5,502 per year), 13 research assistantships with full and partial tuition reimbursements available (averaging $14,062 per year), 20 teaching assistantships with full and partial tuition reimbursements available (averaging $14,814 per year); institutionally sponsored loans, scholarships/grants, health care benefits, and unspecified assistantships also available. Financial award applicants required to submit FAFSA. *Application contact:* E-mail: edadvise@colorado.edu.

University of Colorado Denver, School of Education and Human Development, Program in Educational Leadership and Innovation, Denver, CO 80217-3364. Offers educational studies and research (PhD), including administrative leadership and policy, early childhood special education, math education, research, assessment and evaluation, science education, urban ecologies. Part-time and evening/weekend programs available. *Students:* 21 full-time (15 women), 25 part-time (17 women); includes 10 minority (5 Black or African American, non-Hispanic/Latino; 1 American Indian or Alaska Native, non-Hispanic/Latino; 3 Asian, non-Hispanic/Latino; 1 Hispanic/Latino), 1 international. Average age 43. 11 applicants, 45% accepted, 3 enrolled. In 2011, 11 doctorates awarded. *Degree requirements:* For doctorate, comprehensive exam, thesis/dissertation, 75 credit hours (for PhD). *Entrance requirements:* For doctorate, GRE or equivalent, resume or curriculum vitae, written statement, letters of recommendation, master's degree or equivalent, completion of basic or advanced statistics course with minimum B grade. Additional exam requirements/recommendations for international students: Required—TOEFL (minimum score 525 paper-based; 197 computer-based). *Application deadline:* Applications are processed on a rolling basis. Application fee: $50 ($75 for international students). Electronic applications accepted. *Expenses:* Contact institution. *Financial support:* Fellowships, research assistantships, teaching assistantships, scholarships/grants, and unspecified assistantships available. Financial award application deadline: 4/1; financial award applicants required to submit FAFSA. *Faculty research:* Administrative leadership and policy studies, early childhood education, research in diversity, paraprofessionals in education, urban schools lab. *Unit head:* Dr. Deanna Sands, Associate Dean, Research and Professional Development, 303-315-4931, E-mail: deanna.sands@ucdenver.edu. *Application contact:* Student Services Center, 303-315-6300, Fax: 303-315-6311, E-mail: education@ucdenver.edu. Web site: http://www.ucdenver.edu/ACADEMICS/COLLEGES/SCHOOLOFEDUCATION/ACADEMICS/Pages/AcademicPrograms.aspx.

University of Denver, Morgridge College of Education, Denver, CO 80208. Offers advanced study in law librarianship (Certificate); child and family studies (MA, PhD); counseling psychology (MA, PhD); curriculum and instruction (MA, PhD, Certificate); educational leadership (Ed D, PhD); educational leadership and policy studies (MA, Certificate); higher education (MA, PhD); library and information science (MLIS); research methods and statistics (MA, PhD); school administration (PhD); school psychology (Ed S). *Accreditation:* ALA; APA (one or more programs are accredited). Part-time and evening/weekend programs available. Postbaccalaureate distance learning degree programs offered (no on-campus study). *Faculty:* 34 full-time (25 women), 70 part-time/adjunct (54 women). *Students:* 385 full-time (289 women), 386 part-time (303 women); includes 168 minority (49 Black or African American, non-Hispanic/Latino; 8 American Indian or Alaska Native, non-Hispanic/Latino; 25 Asian, non-Hispanic/Latino; 71 Hispanic/Latino; 1 Native Hawaiian or other Pacific Islander, non-Hispanic/Latino; 14 Two or more races, non-Hispanic/Latino), 17 international. Average age 33. 668 applicants, 72% accepted, 256 enrolled. In 2011, 308 master's, 43 doctorates, 55 other advanced degrees awarded. Terminal master's awarded for partial completion of doctoral program. *Degree requirements:* For master's, comprehensive exam; for doctorate, 2 foreign languages, comprehensive exam, thesis/dissertation. *Entrance requirements:* For master's and doctorate, GRE General Test or GMAT. Additional exam requirements/recommendations for international students: Required—TOEFL (minimum score 550 paper-based; 80 iBT). *Application deadline:* Applications are processed on a rolling basis. Application fee: $60. Electronic applications accepted. *Financial support:* In 2011–12, 72 teaching assistantships with full and partial tuition reimbursements (averaging $9,049 per year) were awarded; career-related internships or fieldwork, Federal Work-Study, institutionally sponsored loans, scholarships/grants, and unspecified assistantships also available. Support available to part-time students. Financial award application deadline: 2/15; financial award applicants required to submit FAFSA. *Faculty research:* Parkinson's disease, personnel training, development and assessments, gifted education, service-learning, transportation, public schools. *Unit head:* Dr. Gregory M. Anderson, Dean, 303-871-3665, E-mail: gregory.m.anderson@du.edu. *Application contact:* Chris Dowen, Director, MCE Admission Office, 303-871-2783, E-mail: chris.dowen@du.edu. Web site: http://www.du.edu/education/.

University of Georgia, College of Education, Department of Lifelong Education, Administration and Policy, Athens, GA 30602. Offers adult education (M Ed, Ed D, PhD, Ed S); educational administration and policy (M Ed, PhD, Ed S); educational leadership (Ed D); human resource and organizational design (M Ed). *Accreditation:* NCATE. *Faculty:* 25 full-time (18 women), 1 part-time/adjunct (0 women). *Students:* 74 full-time (56 women), 216 part-time (136 women); includes 73 minority (62 Black or African American, non-Hispanic/Latino; 4 Asian, non-Hispanic/Latino; 3 Hispanic/Latino; 4 Two or more races, non-Hispanic/Latino), 23 international. Average age 37. 123 applicants, 64% accepted, 45 enrolled. In 2011, 54 master's, 19 doctorates, 14 other advanced degrees awarded. *Entrance requirements:* For master's and Ed S, GRE General Test or MAT; for doctorate, GRE General Test. *Application deadline:* For fall admission, 7/1 priority date for domestic students; for spring admission, 11/15 for domestic students. Application fee: $50. Electronic applications accepted. *Unit head:* Dr. Janette Hill, Head, 706-542-4035, Fax: 706-542-5873, E-mail: janette@.uga.edu. *Application contact:* Dr. Robert B. Hill, Graduate Coordinator, 706-542-4016, Fax: 706-542-5873, E-mail: bobhill@uga.edu. Web site: http://www.coe.uga.edu/leap/.

University of Hawaii at Manoa, Graduate Division, College of Education, PhD in Education Program, Honolulu, HI 96822. Offers curriculum and instruction (PhD); educational administration (PhD); educational foundations (PhD); educational policy studies (PhD); educational technology (PhD); exceptionalities (PhD); kinesiology (PhD). Part-time and evening/weekend programs available. *Degree requirements:* For doctorate, thesis/dissertation. *Entrance requirements:* For doctorate, GRE General Test, sample of written work. Additional exam requirements/recommendations for international students: Required—TOEFL (minimum score 600 paper-based; 250 computer-based; 100 iBT), IELTS (minimum score 7).

University of Illinois at Chicago, Graduate College, College of Education, Department of Educational Policy Studies, Chicago, IL 60607-7128. Offers policy studies (M Ed); policy studies in urban education (PhD); urban education leadership (Ed D).

University of Illinois at Urbana–Champaign, Graduate College, College of Education, Department of Education Policy, Organization, and Leadership, Champaign, IL 61820. Offers educational organization and leadership (Ed M, MS, Ed D, PhD, CAS); educational policy studies (Ed M, MA, PhD); human resource education (Ed M, MS, Ed D, PhD, CAS). Part-time programs available. Postbaccalaureate distance learning degree programs offered (minimal on-campus study). *Faculty:* 30 full-time (13 women), 3 part-time/adjunct (2 women). *Students:* 185 full-time (117 women), 391 part-time (249 women); includes 199 minority (107 Black or African American, non-Hispanic/Latino; 3 American Indian or Alaska Native, non-Hispanic/Latino; 28 Asian, non-Hispanic/Latino; 49 Hispanic/Latino; 12 Two or more races, non-Hispanic/Latino), 52 international. 327 applicants, 60% accepted, 100 enrolled. In 2011, 201 master's, 34 doctorates, 3 other advanced degrees awarded. *Entrance requirements:* For master's, minimum GPA of 3.0; for doctorate, GRE General Test, minimum GPA of 3.0, writing samples, interview. Additional exam requirements/recommendations for international students: Required—TOEFL (minimum score 620 paper-based; 260 computer-based; 105 iBT). *Application deadline:* Applications are processed on a rolling basis. Application fee: $75 ($90 for international students). Electronic applications accepted. *Financial support:* In 2011–12, 29 fellowships, 60 research assistantships, 60 teaching assistantships were awarded; tuition waivers (full and partial) also available. *Unit head:* James Anderson, Head, 217-333-2446, Fax: 217-244-5632, E-mail: janders@illinois.edu. *Application contact:* Rebecca Grady, 217-265-5404, Fax: 217-244-5632, E-mail: rgrady@illinois.edu. Web site: http://education.illinois.edu/epol.

The University of Iowa, Graduate College, College of Education, Department of Educational Policy and Leadership Studies, Iowa City, IA 52242-1316. Offers educational administration (MA, PhD, Ed S); higher education (MA, PhD, Ed S); social foundations (MA, PhD); JD/PhD. *Degree requirements:* For master's and Ed S, exam; for doctorate, comprehensive exam, thesis/dissertation. *Entrance requirements:* For master's, doctorate, and Ed S, GRE General Test, minimum GPA of 3.0. Additional exam requirements/recommendations for international students: Required—TOEFL (minimum score 550 paper-based; 213 computer-based; 81 iBT). Electronic applications accepted.

The University of Kansas, Graduate Studies, School of Education, Department of Educational Leadership and Policy Studies, Education Leadership and Policy Program, Lawrence, KS 66045-3101. Offers educational administration (Ed D, PhD); foundations (PhD); higher education (Ed D, PhD); policy studies (PhD). Part-time and evening/weekend programs available. *Faculty:* 16. *Students:* 99 full-time (65 women), 52 part-time (28 women); includes 31 minority (10 Black or African American, non-Hispanic/Latino; 5 American Indian or Alaska Native, non-Hispanic/Latino; 5 Asian, non-Hispanic/Latino; 7 Hispanic/Latino; 4 Two or more races, non-Hispanic/Latino), 10 international. Average age 38. 44 applicants, 73% accepted, 22 enrolled. In 2011, 26 degrees awarded. *Degree requirements:* For doctorate, comprehensive exam, thesis/dissertation. *Entrance requirements:* For doctorate, GRE General Test, minimum graduate GPA of 3.5. Additional exam requirements/recommendations for international students: Required—TOEFL (minimum score 570 paper-based; 230 computer-based; 80 iBT). *Application deadline:* For fall admission, 7/1 for domestic and international students; for spring admission, 11/1 for domestic and international students. Applications are processed on a rolling basis. Application fee: $55 ($65 for international students). Electronic applications accepted. Tuition and fees vary according to course load, campus/location, program and reciprocity agreements. *Financial support:* Fellowships, research assistantships with full and partial tuition reimbursements, teaching assistantships with full and partial tuition reimbursements, scholarships/grants, and unspecified assistantships available. Financial award application deadline: 3/15. *Faculty research:* Historical and philosophical issues in education, education policy and leadership, higher education faculty, research on college students, education technology . *Unit head:* Dr. Susan Twombly, Chair, 785-864-9721, Fax: 785-864-4697, E-mail: stwombly@ku.edu. *Application contact:* Denise Brubaker, Admissions Coordinator, 785-864-4458, Fax: 785-864-4697, E-mail: elps@ku.edu. Web site: http://soe.ku.edu/elps/.

University of Kentucky, Graduate School, College of Education, Program in Educational Policy Studies and Evaluation, Lexington, KY 40506-0032. Offers educational policy studies and evaluation (Ed D); higher education (MS Ed, PhD). *Accreditation:* NCATE. Terminal master's awarded for partial completion of doctoral program. *Degree requirements:* For master's, comprehensive exam, thesis optional; for doctorate, comprehensive exam, thesis/dissertation. *Entrance requirements:* For master's, GRE General Test, minimum undergraduate GPA of 2.75; for doctorate, GRE General Test, minimum graduate GPA of 3.0. Additional exam requirements/recommendations for international students: Required—TOEFL (minimum score 550 paper-based; 213 computer-based). Electronic applications accepted. *Faculty research:* Studies in higher education; comparative and international education; evaluation of educational programs, policies, and reform; student, teacher, and faculty cultures; gender and education.

University of Maryland, Baltimore County, Graduate School, College of Arts, Humanities and Social Sciences, Department of Public Policy, Program in Public Policy, Baltimore, MD 21250. Offers economics (PhD); educational policy (MPP, PhD); evaluation and analytical methods (MPP, PhD); health policy (MPP, PhD); policy history (PhD); public management (MPP, PhD); urban policy (MPP, PhD). Part-time and evening/weekend programs available. *Faculty:* 10 full-time (2 women), 2 part-time/adjunct (0 women). *Students:* 61 full-time (30 women), 88 part-time (45 women); includes 26 minority (14 Black or African American, non-Hispanic/Latino; 5 Asian, non-Hispanic/Latino; 3 Hispanic/Latino; 1 Native Hawaiian or other Pacific Islander, non-Hispanic/Latino; 3 Two or more races, non-Hispanic/Latino), 14 international. Average age 36. 101 applicants, 60% accepted, 22 enrolled. In 2011, 10 master's, 8 doctorates awarded. Terminal master's awarded for partial completion of doctoral program. *Degree requirements:* For master's, thesis optional, public analysis paper, internship for pre-service; for doctorate, thesis/dissertation, comprehensive and field qualifying exams. *Entrance requirements:* For master's, GRE General Test, 3 academic letters of reference, transcripts, resume; for doctorate, GRE General Test, 3 academic letters of reference, transcripts, resume, research paper. Additional exam requirements/recommendations for international students: Required—TOEFL (minimum score 550 paper-based; 213 computer-based; 80 iBT). *Application deadline:* For fall admission, 1/15 priority date for domestic students, 1/1 for international students; for spring admission, 11/1 priority date for domestic students, 5/1 for international students. Applications are processed on a rolling basis. Application fee: $50. Electronic applications accepted. *Financial support:* In 2011–12, 26 students received support, including 6 fellowships with full tuition reimbursements available (averaging $17,400 per year), 23 research assistantships with full tuition reimbursements available (averaging $17,400 per year), 1 teaching assistantship with full tuition reimbursement available (averaging $17,400 per year); career-related internships or fieldwork, Federal Work-Study, scholarships/grants, health care benefits, and unspecified assistantships also available. Support available to part-time students. Financial award application deadline: 1/15; financial award applicants required to submit FAFSA. *Faculty research:* Health policy, education policy, urban policy, public management, evaluation and analytical methods. *Unit head:* Dr. Donald Norris, Chair, 410-455-1455, E-mail: norris@umbc.edu. *Application contact:* Sally F. Helms, Administrator of Academic Affairs, 410-455-3202, Fax: 410-455-1172, E-mail: gradposi@umbc.edu. Web site: http://www.umbc.edu/pubpol.

University of Maryland, College Park, Academic Affairs, College of Education, Department of Education Policy Studies, College Park, MD 20742. Offers M Ed, MA, PhD. *Faculty:* 7 full-time (3 women), 3 part-time/adjunct (2 women). *Students:* 14 full-time (13 women), 35 part-time (26 women); includes 12 minority (4 Black or African American, non-Hispanic/Latino; 1 American Indian or Alaska Native, non-Hispanic/Latino; 4 Asian, non-Hispanic/Latino; 1 Hispanic/Latino; 1 Native Hawaiian or other Pacific Islander, non-Hispanic/Latino; 1 Two or more races, non-Hispanic/Latino), 2 international. 90 applicants, 51% accepted, 29 enrolled. In 2011, 3 master's awarded. *Application deadline:* For fall admission, 11/15 for domestic and international students; for spring admission, 6/1 for domestic and international students. Application fee: $75. *Expenses: Tuition, area resident:* Part-time $525 per credit hour. Tuition, state resident: part-time $525 per credit hour. Tuition, nonresident: part-time $1131 per credit hour. *Required fees:* $386.31 per term. Tuition and fees vary according to program. *Financial support:* In 2011–12, 2 fellowships with full tuition reimbursements (averaging $15,321 per year), 11 teaching assistantships (averaging $15,828 per year) were awarded. *Total annual research expenditures:* $82,677. *Unit head:* Dr. Francine Hultgren, Chair, 301-405-4562, E-mail: fh@umd.edu. *Application contact:* Dr. Charles A. Caramello, Dean of Graduate School, 301-405-0358, Fax: 301-314-9305. Web site: http://www.education.umd.edu/EDPS/.

University of Massachusetts Amherst, Graduate School, School of Education, Program in Education, Amherst, MA 01003. Offers bilingual, English as a second language, and multicultural education (M Ed, CAGS); child study and early education (M Ed); children, families and schools (Ed D, CAGS); early childhood and elementary teacher education (M Ed); educational leadership (M Ed, CAGS); educational policy and leadership (Ed D); higher education (M Ed, CAGS); international education (M Ed); language, literacy and culture (Ed D); learning, media and technology (M Ed, CAGS); mathematics, science, and learning technologies (Ed D); policy studies in education (CAGS); psychometric methods, educational statistics and research methods (Ed D); reading and writing (M Ed); school counselor education (M Ed, CAGS); science education (CAGS); secondary teacher education (M Ed); social justice education (M Ed, Ed D, CAGS); special education (M Ed, Ed D, CAGS). *Accreditation:* NCATE. Part-time programs available. Postbaccalaureate distance learning degree programs offered (minimal on-campus study). *Faculty:* 81 full-time (46 women). *Students:* 341 full-time (240 women), 333 part-time (226 women); includes 113 minority (36 Black or African American, non-Hispanic/Latino; 1 American Indian or Alaska Native, non-Hispanic/Latino; 14 Asian, non-Hispanic/Latino; 51 Hispanic/Latino; 1 Native Hawaiian or other Pacific Islander, non-Hispanic/Latino; 10 Two or more races, non-Hispanic/Latino), 98 international. Average age 36. 721 applicants, 57% accepted, 202 enrolled. In 2011, 166 master's, 33 doctorates, 25 CAGSs awarded. Terminal master's awarded for partial completion of doctoral program. *Degree requirements:* For doctorate, comprehensive exam, thesis/dissertation. *Entrance requirements:* Additional exam requirements/recommendations for international students: Required—TOEFL (minimum score 550 paper-based; 213 computer-based; 80 iBT), IELTS (minimum score 6.5). *Application deadline:* For fall admission, 1/15 for domestic and international students. Applications are processed on a rolling basis. Application fee: $50 ($65 for international students). Electronic applications accepted. Tuition and fees vary according to course load, campus/location and program. *Financial support:* Fellowships with full and partial tuition reimbursements, research assistantships with full and partial tuition reimbursements, teaching assistantships with full and partial tuition reimbursements, career-related internships or fieldwork, Federal Work-Study, scholarships/grants, traineeships, health care benefits, tuition waivers (full and partial), and unspecified assistantships available. Support available to part-time students. Financial award application deadline: 1/15. *Unit head:* Dr. Linda L. Griffin, Graduate Program Director, 413-545-6984, Fax: 413-545-1523. *Application contact:* Lindsay DeSantis, Interim Supervisor of Admissions, 413-545-0722, Fax: 413-577-0010, E-mail: gradadm@grad.umass.edu. Web site: http://www.umass.edu/education/.

University of Massachusetts Dartmouth, Graduate School, School of Education, Public Policy, and Civic Engagement, Department of Public Policy, North Dartmouth, MA 02747-2300. Offers educational policy (Postbaccalaureate Certificate); environmental policy (Postbaccalaureate Certificate); public policy (MPP). Part-time programs available. Postbaccalaureate distance learning degree programs offered (minimal on-campus study). *Faculty:* 8 full-time (2 women). *Students:* 12 full-time (10 women), 44 part-time (23 women); includes 12 minority (5 Black or African American, non-Hispanic/Latino; 1 American Indian or Alaska Native, non-Hispanic/Latino; 2 Asian, non-Hispanic/Latino; 3 Hispanic/Latino; 1 Two or more races, non-Hispanic/Latino), 1 international. Average age 34. 52 applicants, 98% accepted, 32 enrolled. In 2011, 6 master's, 11 other advanced degrees awarded. *Entrance requirements:* For master's and Postbaccalaureate Certificate, GRE or GMAT, 2 letters of recommendation, resume, statement of intent. Additional exam requirements/recommendations for international students: Required—TOEFL (minimum score 600 paper-based; 250 computer-based). *Application deadline:* For fall admission, 3/1 for domestic students, 2/1 for international students; for spring admission, 11/15 for domestic students, 10/15 for international students. Applications are processed on a rolling basis. Application fee: $40 ($60 for international students). Electronic applications accepted. *Expenses:* Tuition, state resident: full-time $2071; part-time $86.29 per credit. Tuition, nonresident: full-time $8099; part-time $337.46 per credit. *Required fees:* $438.58 per credit. Part-time tuition and fees vary according to class time, course load, degree level and reciprocity agreements. *Financial support:* In 2011–12, 3 research assistantships with full tuition reimbursements (averaging $6,916 per year), 1 teaching assistantship with full tuition reimbursement (averaging $6,000 per year) were awarded; Federal Work-Study and unspecified assistantships also available. Support available to part-time students. Financial award application deadline: 3/1. *Faculty research:* Demographic analysis, legal and regulatory framework. *Total annual research expenditures:* $123,168. *Unit head:* Dr. Michael Goodman, Graduate Program Director, 508-990-9660, Fax: 508-999-8374, E-mail: mgoodman@umassd.edu. *Application contact:* Elan Turcotte-Shamski, Graduate Admissions Officer, 508-999-8604, Fax: 508-999-8183, E-mail: graduate@umassd.edu. Web site: http://www.umassd.edu/seppce/publicpolicy/index.html.

University of Minnesota, Twin Cities Campus, Graduate School, College of Education and Human Development, Department of Organizational Leadership, Policy and Development, Minneapolis, MN 55455-0213. Offers adult education (M Ed, MA, Ed D, PhD, Certificate); agricultural, food and environmental education (M Ed, MA, Ed D, PhD); business and industry education (M Ed, MA, Ed D, PhD); business education (M Ed); comparative and international development education (MA, PhD); disability policy and services (Certificate); educational administration (MA, Ed D, PhD); evaluation studies (MA, PhD); higher education (MA, PhD); human resource development (M Ed, MA, Ed D, PhD, Certificate); marketing education (M Ed); postsecondary administration (Ed D); program evaluation (Certificate); school-to-work (Certificate); staff development (Certificate); teacher leadership (M Ed); technical education (Certificate); technology education (M Ed, MA); work and human resource education (M Ed, MA, Ed D, PhD); youth development leadership (M Ed). *Faculty:* 28 full-time (12 women). *Students:* 265 full-time (183 women), 196 part-time (43 women); includes 97 minority (48 Black or African American, non-Hispanic/Latino; 5 American Indian or Alaska Native, non-Hispanic/Latino; 30 Asian, non-Hispanic/Latino; 14 Hispanic/Latino), 75 international. Average age 38. 419 applicants, 68% accepted, 202 enrolled. In 2011, 140 master's, 48 doctorates, 149 other advanced degrees awarded. Application fee: $55. *Financial support:* In 2011–12, 2 fellowships (averaging $14,581 per year), 46 research assistantships with full tuition reimbursements (averaging $8,130 per year), 14 teaching assistantships with full tuition reimbursements (averaging $8,800 per year) were awarded. *Faculty research:* Organizational change in schools, universities, and other organizations; international education and development; program evaluation to facilitate organizational reform; international human resource development and change; interactions of gender and race/ethnicity on learning and leadership; development of initiatives to develop intercultural sensitivity and global awareness; leadership theory and development in educational, work-based, and other organizations. *Total annual research expenditures:* $787,672. *Unit head:* Dr. Rebecca Ropers-Huilman, Chair, 612-624-1006, Fax: 612-624-3377, E-mail: ropers@umn.edu. *Application contact:* Dr. Jennifer Engler, Assistant Dean, 612-626-2887, Fax: 612-626-7496, E-mail: engle009@umn.edu. Web site: http://www.education.umn.edu/edpa/.

University of Pennsylvania, Graduate School of Education, Division of Education Policy, Philadelphia, PA 19104. Offers MS Ed, PhD. *Students:* 33 full-time (25 women), 3 part-time (2 women); includes 12 minority (7 Black or African American, non-Hispanic/Latino; 3 Asian, non-Hispanic/Latino; 2 Hispanic/Latino), 6 international. 186 applicants, 39% accepted, 19 enrolled. In 2011, 19 degrees awarded. *Expenses: Tuition:* Full-time $26,660; part-time $4944 per course. *Required fees:* $2318; $291 per course. Tuition and fees vary according to course load, degree level and program. *Unit head:* Dr. Andrew Porter, Dean, 215-898-7014. *Application contact:* Janet White, 215-898-0597, E-mail: jawhite@gse.upenn.edu.

University of Pittsburgh, School of Education, Learning Sciences and Policy Program, Pittsburgh, PA 15260. Offers PhD. Part-time and evening/weekend programs available. *Students:* 13 full-time (8 women), 2 part-time (1 woman); includes 1 minority (Black or African American, non-Hispanic/Latino), 3 international. Average age 32. 18 applicants, 28% accepted, 3 enrolled. *Degree requirements:* For doctorate, comprehensive exam, thesis/dissertation. *Entrance requirements:* Additional exam requirements/recommendations for international students: Required—TOEFL (minimum score 550 paper-based; 213 computer-based; 80 iBT). *Application deadline:* For fall admission, 2/1 priority date for domestic students, 2/1 for international students; for spring admission, 11/15 for domestic students, 7/1 for international students. Application fee: $50. *Expenses:* Tuition, state resident: full-time $18,774; part-time $760 per credit. Tuition, nonresident: full-time $30,736; part-time $1258 per credit. *Required fees:* $740; $200 per term. Tuition and fees vary according to program. *Financial support:* Fellowships with full and partial tuition reimbursements, research assistantships with full and partial tuition reimbursements, and teaching assistantships with full and partial tuition reimbursements available. Financial award applicants required to submit FAFSA. *Unit head:* Dr. Mary Kay Stein, Head, 412-648-7116, E-mail: mkstein@pitt.edu. *Application contact:* Maggie Sikora, Graduate Enrollment Manager, 412-648-2230, Fax: 412-648-1899, E-mail: soeinfo@pitt.edu. Web site: http://www.education.pitt.edu/lsap/.

University of Rochester, Margaret Warner Graduate School of Education and Human Development, Doctoral Programs in Education, Rochester, NY 14627. Offers counseling (Ed D); educational administration (Ed D); educational policy and theory (PhD); higher education (PhD); human development in educational context (PhD); teaching, curriculum, and change (PhD). *Expenses: Tuition:* Full-time $41,040.

University of Rochester, Margaret Warner Graduate School of Education and Human Development, Master's Program in Educational Policy, Rochester, NY 14627. Offers MS. *Expenses: Tuition:* Full-time $41,040.

University of St. Thomas, Graduate Studies, School of Education, Department of Leadership, Policy and Administration, St. Paul, MN 55105-1096. Offers community education administration (MA); educational leadership (Ed S); educational leadership and administration (MA); international leadership (MA, Certificate); leadership (Ed D); leadership in student affairs (MA, Certificate); police leadership (MA); public policy and leadership (MA, Certificate). Part-time and evening/weekend programs available. *Faculty:* 8 full-time (3 women), 17 part-time/adjunct (7 women). *Students:* 47 full-time (34 women), 325 part-time (172 women); includes 54 minority (26 Black or African American, non-Hispanic/Latino; 3 American Indian or Alaska Native, non-Hispanic/Latino; 14 Asian, non-Hispanic/Latino; 7 Hispanic/Latino; 4 Two or more races, non-Hispanic/Latino), 11 international. Average age 37. 170 applicants, 80% accepted, 93 enrolled. In 2011, 72 master's, 17 doctorates, 39 other advanced degrees awarded. Terminal master's awarded for partial completion of doctoral program. *Degree requirements:* For master's, thesis (for some programs); for doctorate, thesis/dissertation; for other advanced degree, thesis or alternative. *Entrance requirements:* For master's, minimum GPA of 3.0 or MAT; for doctorate, MAT, minimum graduate GPA of 3.5; for other advanced degree, minimum graduate GPA of 3.25 or MAT. Additional exam requirements/recommendations for international students: Required—TOEFL (minimum score 550 paper-based; 213 computer-based; 20 iBT). *Application deadline:* For fall admission, 6/1 priority date for domestic students; for spring admission, 11/1 priority date for domestic students. Applications are processed on a rolling basis. Application fee: $50. *Expenses:* Contact institution. *Financial support:* Fellowships, research assistantships, institutionally sponsored loans, and scholarships/grants available. Support available to part-time students. Financial award applicants required to submit FAFSA. *Unit head:* Dr. Donald R. LaMagdeleine, Chair, 651-962-4893, Fax: 651-962-4169, E-mail: drlamagdelei@stthomas.edu. *Application contact:* Jackie Grossklaus, Department Assistant, 651-962-4885, Fax: 651-962-4169, E-mail: jmgrossklaus@stthomas.edu. Web site: http://www.stthomas.edu/education.

University of Southern California, Graduate School, Rossier School of Education, Doctor of Philosophy in Education Programs, Los Angeles, CA 90089. Offers educational psychology (PhD); higher education administration and policy (PhD); K-12 policy and practice (PhD). *Degree requirements:* For doctorate, thesis/dissertation, 63 units; qualifying exam; dissertation proposal and defense. *Entrance requirements:* For doctorate, GRE. Additional exam requirements/recommendations for international students: Required—TOEFL (minimum score 250 computer-based; 100 iBT). Electronic applications accepted. *Faculty research:* Diversity in higher education, organizational change, educational psychology, policy and politics of educational reform, economics of education and education policy.

The University of Texas at Arlington, Graduate School, College of Education and Health Professions, Department of Educational Leadership and Policy Studies, Arlington, TX 76019. Offers dual language (M Ed); education leadership and policy studies (PhD); higher education (M Ed); principal certification (M Ed). Part-time and evening/weekend programs available. Postbaccalaureate distance learning degree programs offered (no on-campus study). *Faculty:* 12 full-time (9 women). *Students:* 31 full-time (25 women), 749 part-time (523 women); includes 334 minority (165 Black or African American, non-Hispanic/Latino; 5 American Indian or Alaska Native, non-Hispanic/Latino; 11 Asian, non-Hispanic/Latino; 140 Hispanic/Latino; 13 Two or more races, non-Hispanic/Latino), 9 international. 342 applicants, 84% accepted, 247 enrolled. In 2011, 183 master's, 1 doctorate awarded. *Degree requirements:* For master's, 2 field-based practica; for doctorate, comprehensive exam, thesis/dissertation, 2 research-based practica. *Entrance requirements:* For master's, GRE, 3 references forms, minimum undergraduate GPA of 3.0 in the last 60 hours of course work; for doctorate, GRE, resume, statement of intent, 3 reference forms, applicable master's degree. Application fee: $50. *Financial support:* In 2011–12, 6 students received support, including 4 fellowships (averaging $6,700 per year), 2 research assistantships (averaging $8,000 per year). Financial award applicants required to submit FAFSA. *Faculty research:* Lived realities of students of color in K-16 contexts, K-16 faculty, K-16 policy and law, K-16 student access, K-16 student success. *Unit head:* Dr. Adrienne E. Hyle, Chair, 817-272-2841, Fax: 817-272-2127, E-mail: ahyle@uta.edu. *Application contact:* Paige Cordor, Graduate Advisor, 817-272-5051, Fax: 817-272-2127, E-mail: paigec@uta.edu. Web site: http://www.uta.edu/coehp/educleadership/.

University of Washington, Graduate School, College of Education, Seattle, WA 98195. Offers curriculum and instruction (M Ed, Ed D, PhD), including educational technology, general curriculum (Ed D, PhD), language, literacy, and culture, mathematics education, multicultural education, reading and language arts education (Ed D), science education, social studies education, teaching and curriculum (M Ed); educational leadership and policy studies (M Ed, Ed D, PhD), including administration (Ed D), educational policy, organization, and leadership (M Ed, PhD), higher education, leadership for learning (Ed D), social and cultural foundations of education (M Ed, PhD); educational psychology (M Ed, PhD), including educational psychology (PhD), human development and cognition (M Ed), learning sciences, measurement, statistics and research design (M Ed), school psychology (M Ed); instructional leadership (M Ed); intercollegiate athletic leadership (M Ed); special education (M Ed, Ed D, PhD), including early childhood special education (M Ed), emotional and behavioral disabilities (M Ed), learning disabilities (M Ed), low-incidence disabilities (M Ed), severe disabilities (M Ed), special education (Ed D, PhD); teacher education (MIT). *Accreditation:* APA. Part-time and evening/weekend programs available. *Degree requirements:* For master's, thesis optional; for doctorate, thesis/dissertation. *Entrance requirements:* For master's and doctorate, GRE General Test, minimum GPA of 3.0. Additional exam requirements/recommendations for international students: Required—TOEFL. Electronic applications accepted. *Faculty research:* School restructuring/effective schools, special education interventions, literacy and writing, technology, school partnerships, teacher preparation.

The University of Western Ontario, Faculty of Graduate Studies, Social Sciences Division, Faculty of Education, Program in Educational Studies, London, ON N6A 5B8, Canada. Offers curriculum studies (M Ed); educational policy studies (M Ed); educational psychology/special education (M Ed). Part-time programs available. *Faculty research:* Reflective practice, gender and schooling, feminist pedagogy, narrative inquiry, second language, multiculturalism in Canada, education and law.

University of Wisconsin–Madison, Graduate School, School of Education, Department of Educational Leadership and Policy Analysis, Madison, WI 53706-1380. Offers administration (Certificate); educational policy (MS, PhD). *Degree requirements:* For doctorate, thesis/dissertation. *Entrance requirements:* For master's and doctorate, GRE General Test. *Application deadline:* For fall admission, 1/15 for domestic and international students. Application fee: $56. Electronic applications accepted. *Expenses:* Tuition, state resident: full-time $10,296; part-time $643.51 per credit. Tuition, nonresident: full-time $24,054; part-time $1503.40 per credit. *Required fees:* $70.06 per credit. Tuition and fees vary according to course load, campus/location, program and reciprocity agreements. *Financial support:* Fellowships with full tuition reimbursements, research assistantships with full tuition reimbursements, teaching assistantships with full tuition reimbursements, and project assistantships available. *Unit head:* Dr. Julie Mead, Chair, 608-262-3106, E-mail: jmead@education.wisc.edu. *Application contact:* 608-262-2433, Fax: 608-262-5134, E-mail: gradadmiss@mail.bascom.wisc.edu. Web site: http://www.education.wisc.edu/elpa.

University of Wisconsin–Madison, Graduate School, School of Education, Department of Educational Policy Studies, Madison, WI 53706-1380. Offers MA, PhD. *Degree requirements:* For doctorate, thesis/dissertation. *Entrance requirements:* For master's and doctorate, GRE General Test. *Application deadline:* For fall admission, 1/1 for domestic and international students; for spring admission, 10/15 for domestic and international students. Application fee: $56. Electronic applications accepted. *Expenses:* Tuition, state resident: full-time $10,296; part-time $643.51 per credit. Tuition, nonresident: full-time $24,054; part-time $1503.40 per credit. *Required fees:* $70.06 per credit. Tuition and fees vary according to course load, campus/location, program and reciprocity agreements. *Financial support:* Project assistantships available. *Unit head:* Dr. Stacey Lee, Chair, 608-262-1760, E-mail: slee@education.wisc.edu. *Application contact:* 608-262-2433, Fax: 608-262-5134, E-mail: gradadmiss@mail.bascom.wisc.edu. Web site: http://www.education.wisc.edu/eps.

Vanderbilt University, Peabody College, Department of Leadership, Policy, and Organizations, Nashville, TN 37240-1001. Offers education policy (MPP); educational leadership and policy (Ed D); higher education (M Ed); higher education, leadership and policy (Ed D); international education policy and management (M Ed); leadership and organizational performance (M Ed). Part-time and evening/weekend programs available. *Faculty:* 27 full-time (12 women), 10 part-time/adjunct (3 women). *Students:* 165 full-time (117 women), 98 part-time (46 women); includes 35 minority (15 Black or African American, non-Hispanic/Latino; 4 Asian, non-Hispanic/Latino; 10 Hispanic/Latino; 6 Two or more races, non-Hispanic/Latino), 30 international. Average age 28. 465 applicants, 54% accepted, 87 enrolled. In 2011, 102 master's, 25 doctorates awarded. *Degree requirements:* For master's, comprehensive exam, thesis optional; for doctorate, thesis/dissertation, qualifying exams, residency. *Entrance requirements:* For master's and doctorate, GRE General Test. Additional exam requirements/recommendations for international students: Required—TOEFL (minimum score 550 paper-based; 213 computer-based). *Application deadline:* For fall admission, 12/31 priority date for domestic students, 12/31 for international students; for spring admission, 11/1 priority date for domestic students, 11/1 for international students. Applications are processed on a rolling basis. Application fee: $0. Electronic applications accepted. *Financial support:* Fellowships with full and partial tuition reimbursements, research assistantships with full and partial tuition reimbursements, teaching assistantships with full and partial tuition reimbursements, Federal Work-Study, institutionally sponsored loans, scholarships/grants, tuition waivers (partial), and unspecified assistantships available. Support available to part-time students. Financial award application deadline: 2/1; financial award applicants required to submit FAFSA. *Faculty research:* Education policy, education reform, school choice, equity and diversity, higher education. *Unit head:* Dr. Ellen B. Goldring, Chair, 615-322-8000, Fax: 615-343-7094, E-mail: ellen.b.goldring@vanderbilt.edu. *Application contact:* Rosie Moody, Educational Coordinator, 615-322-8019, Fax: 615-343-7094, E-mail: rosie.moody@vanderbilt.edu.

Virginia Commonwealth University, Graduate School, School of Education, Doctoral Program in Education, Richmond, VA 23284-9005. Offers educational leadership (PhD); educational psychology (PhD); instructional leadership (PhD); leadership (Ed D); research and evaluation (PhD); special education and disability leadership (PhD); urban services leadership (PhD). *Accreditation:* NCATE. Part-time programs available. *Degree requirements:* For doctorate, thesis/dissertation. *Entrance requirements:* For doctorate, GRE (for PhD), MAT (for Ed D), interview, master's degree, writing sample. Additional exam requirements/recommendations for international students: Required—TOEFL (minimum score 600 paper-based; 250 computer-based; 100 iBT). Electronic applications accepted. *Expenses:* Tuition, state resident: full-time $9133; part-time $507 per credit. Tuition, nonresident: full-time $18,777; part-time $1043 per credit. *Required fees:* $77 per credit. Tuition and fees vary according to degree level, campus/location, program and student level.

Virginia Polytechnic Institute and State University, Graduate School, College of Liberal Arts and Human Sciences, School of Education, Department of Educational Leadership and Policy Studies, Blacksburg, VA 24061. Offers administration and supervision of special education (Ed D, PhD); counselor education (MA, PhD); educational leadership and policy studies (MA, Ed D, PhD, Ed S); educational research and evaluation (PhD); higher education (MA, PhD). *Accreditation:* ACA; NCATE. *Degree requirements:* For master's, comprehensive exam (for some programs), thesis (for some programs); for doctorate, comprehensive exam (for some programs), thesis/dissertation (for some programs). *Entrance requirements:* For master's and doctorate, GRE. Additional exam requirements/recommendations for international students: Required—TOEFL (minimum score 550 paper-based; 213 computer-based). *Application deadline:* For fall admission, 7/1 for domestic and international students; for spring admission, 12/1 for domestic and international students. Applications are processed on a rolling basis. Application fee: $65. Electronic applications accepted. *Expenses:* Tuition, state resident: full-time $10,048; part-time $558.25 per credit hour. Tuition, nonresident: full-time $19,497; part-time $1083.25 per credit hour. *Required fees:* $405 per semester. Tuition and fees vary according to course load, campus/location and program. *Financial support:* Career-related internships or fieldwork, Federal Work-Study, scholarships/grants, health care benefits, and unspecified assistantships available. Financial award application deadline: 1/15. *Unit head:* Dr. M. David Alexander, Unit Head, 540-231-9723, Fax: 540-231-7845, E-mail: mdavid@vt.edu. *Application contact:* Daisy Stewart, Information Contact, 540-231-8180, Fax: 540-231-7845, E-mail: daisys@vt.edu. Web site: http://www.soe.vt.edu/elps/index.html.

Walden University, Graduate Programs, Richard W. Riley College of Education and Leadership, Minneapolis, MN 55401. Offers administrator leadership for teaching and learning (Ed D, Ed S); adult education (Ed D, Ed S); adult learning (MS, Postbaccalaureate Certificate), including developmental education (MS), online teaching (MS), teaching adults English as a second language (MS), training and performance management (MS); college teaching and learning (Ed D, Ed S, Postbaccalaureate Certificate); curriculum, instruction and assessment (Ed D, Postbaccalaureate Certificate); curriculum, instruction, and professional development (Ed S); developmental education (Postbaccalaureate Certificate); early childhood administration, management, and leadership (Postbaccalaureate Certificate); early childhood education (birth-grade 3) (MAT); early childhood public policy and advocacy (Postbaccalaureate Certificate); early childhood studies (MS), including administration, management and leadership, early childhood public policy and advocacy, teaching adults in the early childhood field, teaching and diversity; education (MS, PhD), including adolescent literacy and technology (grades 6-12) (MS), adult education leadership (PhD), assessment, evaluation, and accountability (PhD), community college leadership (PhD), curriculum, instruction, and assessment, early childhood education (PhD), educational technology (PhD), elementary reading and literacy (MS), elementary reading and mathematics (MS), general program, global and comparative education (PhD), higher education (PhD), integrating technology in the classroom (MS), K-12 educational leadership (PhD), leadership, policy and change (PhD), learning, instruction and innovation (PhD), literacy and learning in the content areas (MS), mathematics (grades 6-8) (MS), mathematics (grades K-5) (MS), middle level education (grades 5-8) (MS), professional development (MS), science (grades K-8) (MS), self-designed (PhD), special education (PhD), special education (non-licensure) (MS), teacher leadership (grades K-12) (MS), teaching English language learners (grades K-12) (MS); educational leadership and administration (principal preparation) (Ed S); educational technology (Ed S); elementary reading and literacy (Postbaccalaureate Certificate); engaging culturally diverse learners (Postbaccalaureate Certificate); enrollment management and institutional marketing (Postbaccalaureate Certificate); higher education (MS), including college teaching and learning, enrollment management and institutional planning, global higher education, leadership for student success, online and distance learning; higher education leadership (Ed D); instructional design (Postbaccalaureate Certificate); instructional design and technology (MS), including general program (MS, PhD), online learning, training and performance improvement; integrating technology in the classroom (Postbaccalaureate Certificate); online teaching for adult learners (Postbaccalaureate Certificate); professional development (Postbaccalaureate Certificate); reading and literacy leadership (Ed D); science K-8 (Postbaccalaureate Certificate); special education (Ed D, Ed S); special education: emotional/behavioral disorders (K-12) (MAT); special education: learning disabilities (K-12) (MAT); teacher leadership (Ed D, Ed S, Postbaccalaureate Certificate); training and performance management (Postbaccalaureate Certificate). Part-time and evening/weekend programs available. Postbaccalaureate distance learning degree programs offered (minimal on-campus study). *Faculty:* 71 full-time (48 women), 853 part-time/adjunct (585 women). *Students:* 11,326 full-time (9,212 women), 2,148 part-time (1,795 women); includes 5,346 minority (4,403 Black or African American, non-Hispanic/Latino; 76 American Indian or Alaska Native, non-Hispanic/Latino; 140 Asian, non-Hispanic/Latino; 561 Hispanic/Latino; 21 Native Hawaiian or other Pacific Islander, non-Hispanic/Latino; 145 Two or more races, non-Hispanic/Latino), 322 international. Average age 39. In 2011, 3,477 master's, 318 doctorates, 471 other advanced degrees awarded. *Degree requirements:* For doctorate, thesis/dissertation (for some programs), residency; for other advanced degree, residency (for some programs). *Entrance requirements:* For master's, bachelor's degree or equivalent in related field; minimum GPA of 2.5; official transcripts; goal statement; access to computer and Internet; for doctorate, master's degree or equivalent in related field; minimum GPA of 3.0; official transcripts; three years' related professional/academic experience (preferred); access to computer and Internet; for other advanced degree, master's degree or equivalent in related field; minimum GPA of 3.0; 3 years related professional/academic experience (preferred); access to computer and Internet (Ed S). Additional exam requirements/recommendations for international students: Required—TOEFL (minimum score 550 paper-based; 213 computer-based), IELTS (minimum score 6.5), or Michigan English Language Assessment Battery (minimum score 82). *Application deadline:* Applications are processed on a rolling basis. Application fee: $50. Electronic applications accepted. *Financial support:* Federal Work-Study, scholarships/grants, unspecified assistantships, and family tuition reduction, active duty/veteran tuition reduction, group tuition reduction, interest-free payment plans, employee tuition reduction available. Support available to part-time students. Financial award applicants required to submit FAFSA. *Unit head:* Dr. Kate Steffens, Dean, 800-925-3368. *Application contact:* Jennifer Hall, Vice President of Enrollment Management, 866-4-WALDEN, E-mail: info@waldenu.edu. Web site: http://www.waldenu.edu/Colleges-and-Schools/College-of-Education-and-Leadership.htm.

Wayne State University, College of Education, Division of Administrative and Organizational Studies, Detroit, MI 48202. Offers college and university teaching (Certificate); educational leadership (M Ed); educational leadership and policy studies (Ed D, PhD); general administration and supervision (Ed S); instructional technology (M Ed, Ed D, PhD, Ed S); online teaching (Certificate); secondary curriculum and instruction (Ed S). *Students:* 86 full-time (62 women), 261 part-time (172 women); includes 171 minority (145 Black or African American, non-Hispanic/Latino; 1 American Indian or Alaska Native, non-Hispanic/Latino; 8 Asian, non-Hispanic/Latino; 16 Hispanic/Latino; 1 Two or more races, non-Hispanic/Latino), 8 international. Average age 39. 122 applicants, 40% accepted, 28 enrolled. In 2011, 73 master's, 9 doctorates, 50 other advanced degrees awarded. *Degree requirements:* For doctorate, thesis/dissertation. *Entrance requirements:* For doctorate, GRE or MAT, interview, autobiography or curriculum vitae; references; master's degree; minimum undergraduate GPA of 3.0, graduate 3.75; 3 years relevant experience; foundational course work; for other advanced degree, minimum GPA of 3.4. Additional exam requirements/recommendations for international students: Required—TOEFL (minimum score 550 paper-based; 213 computer-based), TWE (minimum score 5.5). *Application deadline:* For fall admission, 6/1 priority date for domestic students, 5/1 for international students; for winter admission, 10/1 priority date for domestic students, 9/1 for international students; for spring admission, 2/1 priority date for domestic students, 1/1 for international students. Applications are processed on a rolling basis. Application fee: $50. Electronic applications accepted. *Expenses:* Tuition, state resident: part-time $512.85 per credit. Tuition, nonresident: part-time $1132.65 per credit. *Required fees:* $26.60 per credit. $199.65 per semester. Tuition and fees vary according to course load and program. *Financial support:* In 2011–12, 59 students received support, including 1 fellowship with tuition reimbursement available (averaging $17,347 per year), 4 research assistantships with tuition reimbursements available (averaging $15,713 per year); career-related internships or fieldwork, Federal Work-Study, institutionally sponsored loans, scholarships/grants, health care benefits, and unspecified assistantships also available. Support available to part-time students. *Faculty research:* Total quality management, participatory management, administering educational technology, school improvement, principalship. *Total annual research expenditures:* $22,232. *Unit head:* Dr. Alan Hoffman, Interim Assistant Dean, 313-577-5235, E-mail: alanhoffman@wayne.edu. *Application contact:* Janice Green, Assistant Dean, 313-577-1605, E-mail: jwgreen@wayne.edu. Web site: http://coe.wayne.edu/aos/index.php.

Educational Psychology

Alliant International University–Irvine, Shirley M. Hufstedler School of Education, Educational Psychology Programs, Irvine, CA 92612. Offers educational psychology (Psy D); pupil personnel services (Credential); school psychology (MA). Part-time programs available. *Faculty:* 1 full-time, 15 part-time/adjunct (10 women). *Students:* 19 full-time (16 women), 17 part-time (16 women); includes 12 minority (7 Asian, non-Hispanic/Latino; 5 Hispanic/Latino). Average age 32. In 2011, 6 master's, 4 doctorates awarded. *Degree requirements:* For doctorate, thesis/dissertation. *Entrance requirements:* For master's, minimum GPA of 2.5, letters of recommendation; for doctorate, interview, minimum GPA of 3.0, letters of recommendation. Additional exam requirements/recommendations for international students: Required—TOEFL (minimum score 550 paper-based; 213 computer-based; 80 iBT), TWE (minimum score 5). *Application deadline:* For fall admission, 7/1 priority date for domestic students, 7/1 for international students; for spring admission, 12/1 priority date for domestic students, 12/1 for international students. Application fee: $55. *Financial support:* Career-related internships or fieldwork, Federal Work-Study, institutionally sponsored loans, and scholarships/grants available. Financial award application deadline: 2/15; financial award applicants required to submit FAFSA. *Faculty research:* School-based mental health. *Unit head:* Dr. Don Wofford, Program Director, 949-833-2651, Fax: 949-833-3507, E-mail: admissions@alliant.edu. *Application contact:* Alliant International University Central Contact Center, 866-U-ALLIANT, Fax: 858-635-4555, E-mail: admissions@alliant.edu.

Alliant International University–Los Angeles, Shirley M. Hufstedler School of Education, Educational Psychology Programs, Alhambra, CA 91803-1360. Offers educational psychology (Psy D); pupil personnel services (Credential); school psychology (MA). Part-time programs available. *Students:* 11 full-time (10 women), 28 part-time (24 women); includes 24 minority (7 Black or African American, non-Hispanic/Latino; 12 Hispanic/Latino; 5 Two or more races, non-Hispanic/Latino). Average age 35. 21 applicants, 67% accepted, 9 enrolled. In 2011, 1 master's, 5 doctorates awarded. *Degree requirements:* For doctorate, thesis/dissertation. *Entrance requirements:* For master's, minimum GPA of 2.5, letters of recommendation; for doctorate, interview, minimum GPA of 3.0, letters of recommendation. Additional exam requirements/recommendations for international students: Required—TOEFL (minimum score 550 paper-based; 213 computer-based), TWE (minimum score 5). *Application deadline:* For fall admission, 7/1 priority date for domestic students, 7/1 for international students; for spring admission, 12/1 priority date for domestic students, 12/1 for international students. Applications are processed on a rolling basis. Application fee: $55. Electronic applications accepted. *Financial support:* Career-related internships or fieldwork, Federal Work-Study, institutionally sponsored loans, and scholarships/grants available. Financial award application deadline: 2/15; financial award applicants required to submit FAFSA. *Faculty research:* Early identification and intervention with high-risk preschoolers, pediatric neuropsychology, interpersonal violence, ADHD, learning theories. *Unit head:* Dr. Carlton Parks, Program Director, 626-270-3379, Fax: 626-284-0550, E-mail: admissions@alliant.edu. *Application contact:* Alliant International University Central Contact Center, 866-U-ALLIANT, Fax: 858-635-4555, E-mail: admissions@alliant.edu. Web site: http://www.alliant.edu/hsoe/.

Alliant International University–San Diego, Shirley M. Hufstedler School of Education, Educational Psychology Programs, San Diego, CA 92131-1799. Offers educational psychology (Psy D); pupil personnel services (Credential); school neuropsychology (Certificate); school psychology (MA); school-based mental health (Certificate). Part-time programs available. *Faculty:* 1 full-time (0 women), 14 part-time/adjunct (9 women). *Students:* 28 full-time (26 women), 31 part-time (25 women); includes 14 minority (5 Black or African American, non-Hispanic/Latino; 9 Hispanic/Latino). Average age 32. In 2011, 10 master's, 2 doctorates awarded. *Degree requirements:* For doctorate, thesis/dissertation, internship. *Entrance requirements:* For master's, minimum GPA of 2.5, letters of recommendation; for doctorate, minimum GPA of 3.0, letters of recommendation. Additional exam requirements/recommendations for international students: Required—TOEFL (minimum score 550 paper-based; 213 computer-based), TWE (minimum score 5). *Application deadline:* For fall admission, 7/1 priority date for domestic students, 7/1 for international students; for spring admission, 12/1 priority date for domestic students, 12/1 for international students. Applications are processed on a rolling basis. Application fee: $55. Electronic applications accepted. Tuition and fees vary according to degree level and program. *Financial support:* Career-related internships or fieldwork, Federal Work-Study, institutionally sponsored loans, and scholarships/grants available. Financial award application deadline: 2/15; financial award applicants required to submit FAFSA. *Faculty research:* School-based mental health, pupil personnel services, childhood mood, school-based assessment. *Unit head:* Dr. Steve Fisher, Program Director, 828-635-4825, Fax: 858-635-4739, E-mail: admissions@alliant.edu. *Application contact:* Alliant International University Central Contact Center, 866-U-ALLIANT, Fax: 858-635-4555, E-mail: admissions@alliant.edu. Web site: http://www.alliant.edu/gsoe.

Alliant International University–San Francisco, Shirley M. Hufstedler School of Education, Educational Psychology Programs, San Francisco, CA 94133-1221. Offers educational psychology (Psy D); pupil personnel services (Credential); school psychology (MA). Part-time programs available. *Faculty:* 1 full-time, 9 part-time/adjunct (7 women). *Students:* 20 full-time (17 women), 11 part-time (10 women). Average age 34. In 2011, 4 master's, 4 doctorates awarded. Terminal master's awarded for partial completion of doctoral program. *Degree requirements:* For doctorate, thesis/dissertation. *Entrance requirements:* For master's, minimum GPA of 3.0, letters of recommendation; for doctorate, interview, minimum GPA of 3.0, letters of recommendation. Additional exam requirements/recommendations for international students: Required—TOEFL (minimum score 550 paper-based; 213 computer-based), TWE (minimum score 5). *Application deadline:* For fall admission, 7/1 priority date for domestic students, 7/1 for international students; for spring admission, 12/1 priority date for domestic students, 12/1 for international students. Applications are processed on a rolling basis. Application fee: $55. Electronic applications accepted. *Financial support:* Career-related internships or fieldwork, Federal Work-Study, institutionally sponsored loans, and scholarships/grants available. Financial award application deadline: 2/15; financial award applicants required to submit FAFSA. *Faculty research:* Social skills, ADHD, cognitive functioning and learning, innovative teaching methods. *Unit head:* Dr. James Hiromto, Systemwide Program Director, 415-955-2087, Fax: 415-955-2179, E-mail: admissions@alliant.edu. *Application contact:* Alliant International University Central Contact Center, 866-U-ALLIANT, Fax: 858-635-4555, E-mail: admissions@alliant.edu.

American International College, School of Arts, Education and Sciences, Department of Psychology, Springfield, MA 01109-3189. Offers clinical psychology (MA); educational psychology (MA, Ed D); forensic psychology (MS). Part-time and evening/weekend programs available. *Degree requirements:* For master's, comprehensive exam (for some programs), thesis (for some programs), practicum. *Entrance requirements:* For master's, minimum GPA of 3.0; for doctorate, GRE General Test, interview. Additional exam requirements/recommendations for international students: Required—TOEFL. Electronic applications accepted.

Andrews University, School of Graduate Studies, School of Education, Department of Educational and Counseling Psychology, Program in Educational and Developmental Psychology, Berrien Springs, MI 49104. Offers educational and developmental psychology (MA); educational psychology (Ed D, PhD). *Students:* 6 full-time (3 women), 12 part-time (9 women); includes 6 minority (3 Black or African American, non-Hispanic/Latino; 2 Asian, non-Hispanic/Latino; 1 Hispanic/Latino), 3 international. Average age 34. 24 applicants, 50% accepted, 5 enrolled. In 2011, 8 master's awarded. *Degree requirements:* For master's, thesis optional. *Entrance requirements:* For master's, GRE. Additional exam requirements/recommendations for international students: Required—TOEFL (minimum score 550 paper-based). *Application deadline:* Applications are processed on a rolling basis. Application fee: $40. *Unit head:* Dr. Jimmy Kijai, Coordinator, 269-471-6240. *Application contact:* Carolyn Hurst, Supervisor of Graduate Admission, 800-253-2874, Fax: 269-471-6321, E-mail: graduate@andrews.edu.

Auburn University, Graduate School, College of Education, Department of Educational Foundations, Leadership, and Technology, Auburn University, AL 36849. Offers adult education (M Ed, MS, Ed D); curriculum and instruction (M Ed, MS, Ed D, Ed S); curriculum supervision (M Ed, MS, Ed D, Ed S); educational psychology (PhD); higher education administration (M Ed, MS, Ed D, Ed S); media instructional design (MS); media specialist (M Ed); school administration (M Ed, MS, Ed D, Ed S). *Accreditation:* NCATE. Part-time programs available. *Faculty:* 26 full-time (16 women), 3 part-time/adjunct (all women). *Students:* 58 full-time (28 women), 215 part-time (135 women); includes 89 minority (82 Black or African American, non-Hispanic/Latino; 1 American Indian or Alaska Native, non-Hispanic/Latino; 4 Asian, non-Hispanic/Latino; 2 Hispanic/Latino), 13 international. Average age 35. 140 applicants, 61% accepted, 56 enrolled. In 2011, 37 master's, 29 doctorates, 9 other advanced degrees awarded. *Degree requirements:* For master's, thesis (for some programs); for doctorate, thesis/dissertation; for Ed S, field project. *Entrance requirements:* For master's, doctorate, and Ed S, GRE General Test. *Application deadline:* For fall admission, 7/7 for domestic students; for spring admission, 11/24 for domestic students. Applications are processed on a rolling basis. Application fee: $50 ($60 for international students). Electronic applications accepted. *Expenses:* Tuition, state resident: full-time $7290; part-time $405 per credit hour. Tuition, nonresident: full-time $21,870; part-time $1215 per credit hour. *International tuition:* $22,000 full-time. *Required fees:* $1402. *Financial support:* Teaching assistantships and Federal Work-Study available. Support available to part-time students. Financial award application deadline: 3/15; financial award applicants required to submit FAFSA. *Unit head:* Dr. Sherida Downer, Head, 334-844-4460. *Application contact:* Dr. George Flowers, Dean of the Graduate School, 334-844-4700. Web site: http://www.education.auburn.edu/academic_departments/eflt/.

Ball State University, Graduate School, Teachers College, Department of Educational Psychology, Program in Educational Psychology, Muncie, IN 47306-1099. Offers MA, PhD, Ed S. *Accreditation:* NCATE. *Students:* 6 full-time (all women), 34 part-time (31 women); includes 2 minority (1 Black or African American, non-Hispanic/Latino; 1 American Indian or Alaska Native, non-Hispanic/Latino). Average age 27. 61 applicants, 62% accepted, 23 enrolled. In 2011, 14 master's, 1 other advanced degree awarded. *Degree requirements:* For doctorate, thesis/dissertation; for Ed S, thesis. *Entrance requirements:* For master's and Ed S, GRE General Test; for doctorate, GRE General Test, minimum graduate GPA of 3.2. Application fee: $50. Tuition and fees vary according to program and reciprocity agreements. *Financial support:* In 2011–12, 23 students received support, including 23 teaching assistantships with tuition reimbursements available (averaging $13,287 per year); research assistantships with tuition reimbursements available also available. Financial award application deadline: 3/1. *Unit head:* Dr. Felicia Dixon, Head, 785-285-8500, Fax: 785-285-3653. *Application contact:* Dr. Robert Morris, Associate Provost for Research and Dean of the Graduate School, 765-285-1300, E-mail: rmorris@bsu.edu. Web site: http://www.bsu.edu/teachers/departments/edpsy/.

Baylor University, Graduate School, School of Education, Department of Educational Psychology, Waco, TX 76798-7301. Offers applied behavior analysis (MS Ed); educational psychology (MA); exceptionalities (PhD); gifted (PhD); quantitative (PhD); school psychology (PhD, Ed S). *Accreditation:* NCATE. Part-time programs available. *Faculty:* 7 full-time (4 women), 2 part-time/adjunct (1 woman). *Students:* 42 full-time (34 women), 11 part-time (9 women); includes 15 minority (5 Black or African American, non-Hispanic/Latino; 5 Asian, non-Hispanic/Latino; 3 Hispanic/Latino; 2 Two or more races, non-Hispanic/Latino), 2 international. Average age 28. 31 applicants, 48% accepted, 13 enrolled. In 2011, 3 master's, 5 doctorates, 7 other advanced degrees awarded. *Degree requirements:* For master's, thesis optional; for doctorate, comprehensive exam, thesis/dissertation; for Ed S, comprehensive exam, thesis or alternative. *Entrance requirements:* For master's and Ed S, GRE General Test; for doctorate, GRE General Test, master's degree. Additional exam requirements/recommendations for international students: Required—TOEFL. *Application deadline:* For fall admission, 2/1 priority date for domestic students, 2/1 for international students. Application fee: $50. Electronic applications accepted. *Financial support:* In 2011–12, 20 students received support, including 20 research assistantships with full and partial tuition reimbursements available; career-related internships or fieldwork, Federal Work-Study, institutionally sponsored loans, scholarships/grants, health care benefits, tuition waivers (full and partial), unspecified assistantships, and stipends also available. Financial award application deadline: 2/1. *Faculty research:* Individual differences, quantitative methods, gifted and talented, special education, school psychology, autism, applied behavior analysis. *Unit head:* Dr. Marley W. Watkins, Professor and Chairman, 254-710-4234, Fax: 254-710-3987, E-mail: marley_watkins@baylor.edu. *Application contact:* Lisa Rowe, Administrative Assistant, 254-710-3112, Fax: 254-710-3112, E-mail: lisa_rowe@baylor.edu. Web site: http://www.baylor.edu/soe/EDP/.

Boston College, Lynch Graduate School of Education, Program in Applied Developmental and Educational Psychology, Chestnut Hill, MA 02467-3800. Offers MA, PhD. Part-time and evening/weekend programs available. *Students:* 51 full-time (45 women), 5 part-time (3 women); includes 13 minority (6 Black or African American, non-Hispanic/Latino; 1 Asian, non-Hispanic/Latino; 3 Hispanic/Latino; 3 Two or more races, non-Hispanic/Latino), 10 international. 153 applicants, 37% accepted, 21 enrolled. In 2011, 21 master's, 3 doctorates awarded. Terminal master's awarded for partial completion of doctoral program. *Degree requirements:* For master's, comprehensive exam; for doctorate, comprehensive exam, thesis/dissertation. *Entrance requirements:* For master's and doctorate, GRE General Test. Additional exam requirements/recommendations for international students: Required—TOEFL (minimum score 550 paper-based; 213 computer-based; 79 iBT). Application fee: $65. Electronic applications accepted. *Financial support:* Fellowships with full and partial tuition reimbursements, research assistantships with full and partial tuition reimbursements, teaching assistantships with full and partial tuition reimbursements, career-related internships or fieldwork, Federal Work-Study, scholarships/grants, traineeships, health care benefits, tuition waivers (full and partial), and unspecified assistantships available. Support available to part-time students. Financial award applicants required to submit FAFSA. *Faculty research:* Cognitive learning and culture, effects of social policy reform on children and families, psychosocial trauma, human rights and international justice, positive youth development, children and adolescents living in poverty. *Unit head:* Dr. M. Brinton Lykes, Chairperson, 617-552-4214, Fax: 617-552-0812. *Application contact:* Adam Poluzzi, Director, Graduate Admission and Financial Aid, 617-552-4214, Fax: 617-552-0398, E-mail: poluzzi@bc.edu.

Brigham Young University, Graduate Studies, David O. McKay School of Education, Department of Instructional Psychology and Technology, Provo, UT 84602. Offers MS, PhD. *Faculty:* 9 full-time (0 women), 3 part-time/adjunct (0 women). *Students:* 56 full-time (24 women), 20 part-time (9 women); includes 7 minority (3 Asian, non-Hispanic/Latino; 3 Hispanic/Latino; 1 Native Hawaiian or other Pacific Islander, non-Hispanic/Latino), 6 international. Average age 35. 27 applicants, 70% accepted, 19 enrolled. In 2011, 9 master's, 9 doctorates awarded. *Degree requirements:* For master's, thesis; for doctorate, comprehensive exam, thesis/dissertation. *Entrance requirements:* For master's and doctorate, GRE General Test. Additional exam requirements/recommendations for international students: Required—TOEFL. *Application deadline:* For fall and winter admission, 2/1 for domestic and international students. Application fee: $50. Electronic applications accepted. *Expenses: Tuition:* Full-time $5760; part-time $320 per credit. Tuition and fees vary according to student's religious affiliation. *Financial support:* In 2011–12, 34 students received support, including 14 research assistantships with full and partial tuition reimbursements available (averaging $10,000 per year), 12 teaching assistantships with full and partial tuition reimbursements available (averaging $6,500 per year); career-related internships or fieldwork, scholarships/grants, tuition waivers (full and partial), and unspecified assistantships also available. Support available to part-time students. *Faculty research:* Interactive learning, learning theory, instructional designed development, research and evaluation, measurement. *Unit head:* Dr. Andrew S. Gibbons, Chair, 801-422-5097, Fax: 801-422-0314, E-mail: andy_gibbons@byu.edu. *Application contact:* Michele Bray, Department Secretary, 801-422-2746, Fax: 801-422-0314, E-mail: michele_bray@byu.edu. Web site: http://education.byu.edu/ipt/.

California Coast University, School of Education, Santa Ana, CA 92701. Offers administration (M Ed); curriculum and instruction (M Ed); educational administration (Ed D); educational psychology (Ed D); organizational leadership (Ed D). Postbaccalaureate distance learning degree programs offered (no on-campus study).

California State University, Long Beach, Graduate Studies, College of Education, Department of Advanced Studies in Education and Counseling, Program in Educational Psychology, Long Beach, CA 90840. Offers MA. *Students:* 33 full-time (27 women), 7 part-time (6 women); includes 17 minority (1 Black or African American, non-Hispanic/Latino; 4 Asian, non-Hispanic/Latino; 12 Hispanic/Latino), 2 international. Average age 26. 86 applicants, 16% accepted, 13 enrolled. In 2011, 20 master's awarded. *Degree requirements:* For master's, thesis. *Entrance requirements:* For master's, GRE General Test, minimum GPA of 2.75. *Application deadline:* For fall admission, 7/1 for domestic students; for spring admission, 12/1 for domestic students. Applications are processed on a rolling basis. Application fee: $55. Electronic applications accepted. *Financial support:* Federal Work-Study, institutionally sponsored loans, and scholarships/grants available. Financial award application deadline: 3/2. *Unit head:* Dr. Hiromi Masunaga, Coordinator, 562-985-5613, E-mail: hmasunag@csulb.edu. *Application contact:* Nancy L. McGlothin, Coordinator for Graduate Studies and Research, 562-985-8476, Fax: 562-985-4951, E-mail: nmcgloth@csulb.edu.

California State University, Northridge, Graduate Studies, College of Education, Department of Educational Psychology and Counseling, Northridge, CA 91330. Offers counseling (MS), including career counseling, college counseling and student services, marriage and family therapy, school counseling, school psychology; educational psychology (MA Ed), including development, learning, and instruction, early childhood education. *Accreditation:* ACA (one or more programs are accredited); NCATE. Part-time and evening/weekend programs available. *Entrance requirements:* For master's, GRE General Test or minimum GPA of 3.0. Additional exam requirements/recommendations for international students: Required—TOEFL.

Capella University, Harold Abel School of Psychology, Minneapolis, MN 55402. Offers child and adolescent development (MS); clinical psychology (MS, Psy D); counseling psychology (MS); educational psychology (MS, PhD); evaluation, research, and measurement (MS); general psychology (MS, PhD); industrial/organizational psychology (MS, PhD); leadership coaching psychology (MS); organizational leader development (MS); school psychology (MS); sport psychology (MS). Part-time and evening/weekend programs available. Postbaccalaureate distance learning degree programs offered (minimal on-campus study). Terminal master's awarded for partial completion of doctoral program. *Degree requirements:* For master's, thesis optional, project; for doctorate, thesis/dissertation. *Entrance requirements:* For degree, master's degree in school psychology. Additional exam requirements/recommendations for international students: Required—TOEFL (minimum score 550 paper-based; 213 computer-based), TWE (minimum score 4); Recommended—IELTS. Electronic applications accepted.

The Catholic University of America, School of Arts and Sciences, Department of Education, Washington, DC 20064. Offers Catholic educational leadership and policy studies (PhD); Catholic school leadership (MA); education (Certificate); educational psychology (PhD); secondary education (MA); special education (MA). *Accreditation:* NCATE. Part-time programs available. *Faculty:* 10 full-time (8 women), 10 part-time/adjunct (8 women). *Students:* 4 full-time (all women), 44 part-time (34 women); includes 12 minority (6 Black or African American, non-Hispanic/Latino; 4 Hispanic/Latino; 2 Two or more races, non-Hispanic/Latino). Average age 39. 38 applicants, 24% accepted, 2 enrolled. In 2011, 5 master's, 4 doctorates, 3 other advanced degrees awarded. *Degree requirements:* For master's, comprehensive exam, thesis or alternative; for doctorate, comprehensive exam, thesis/dissertation; for Certificate, action research project. *Entrance requirements:* For master's and doctorate, GRE General Test or MAT, statement of purpose, official copies of academic transcripts, three letters of recommendation, interview; for Certificate, PRAXIS I, statement of purpose, official copies of academic transcripts, three letters of recommendation, interview. Additional exam requirements/recommendations for international students: Required—TOEFL (minimum score 580 paper-based; 237 computer-based). *Application deadline:* For fall admission, 8/1 priority date for domestic students, 7/15 for international students; for spring admission, 12/1 priority date for domestic students, 10/15 for international students. Applications are processed on a rolling basis. Application fee: $55. Electronic applications accepted. *Expenses: Tuition:* Full-time $35,260; part-time $1380 per credit. *Required fees:* $80; $40 per semester hour. One-time fee: $425. *Financial support:* Fellowships, research assistantships, teaching assistantships, Federal Work-Study, scholarships/grants, tuition waivers (full and partial), and unspecified assistantships available. Financial award application deadline: 2/1; financial award applicants required to submit FAFSA. *Faculty research:* Special education, early childhood education, educational psychology, Catholic school administration, leadership and policy studies, counseling, curriculum and instruction. *Total annual research expenditures:* $36,210. *Unit head:* Dr. Merylann J. Schuttloffel, Chair, 202-319-5805, Fax: 202-319-5815, E-mail: schuttloffel@cua.edu. *Application contact:* Andrew Woodall, Director of Graduate Admissions, 202-319-5057, Fax: 202-319-6533, E-mail: cua-admissions@cua.edu. Web site: http://education.cua.edu/.

Chapman University, College of Educational Studies, Orange, CA 92866. Offers communication sciences and disorders (MS); counseling (MA), including school counseling (MA, Credential); education (MA, PhD), including cultural and curricular studies (PhD), disability studies (PhD), school psychology (PhD, Credential); educational psychology (MA); professional clear (Credential); pupil personnel services (Credential), including school counseling (MA, Credential), school psychology (PhD, Credential); school psychology (Ed S); single subject (Credential); special education (MA); special education (level ii) (Credential), including mild/moderate, moderate/severe; special education (preliminary) (Credential), including mild/moderate, moderate/severe; speech language pathology (Credential); teaching (MA), including elementary education, secondary education. *Accreditation:* Teacher Education Accreditation Council. Part-time and evening/weekend programs available. *Faculty:* 27 full-time (18 women), 35 part-time/adjunct (24 women). *Students:* 220 full-time (188 women), 164 part-time (128 women); includes 140 minority (12 Black or African American, non-Hispanic/Latino; 1 American Indian or Alaska Native, non-Hispanic/Latino; 44 Asian, non-Hispanic/Latino; 73 Hispanic/Latino; 4 Native Hawaiian or other Pacific Islander, non-Hispanic/Latino; 6 Two or more races, non-Hispanic/Latino), 1 international. Average age 29. 436 applicants, 38% accepted, 126 enrolled. In 2011, 130 master's, 5 doctorates awarded. *Entrance requirements:* Additional exam requirements/recommendations for international students: Required—TOEFL (minimum score 550 paper-based; 213 computer-based; 80 iBT). *Application deadline:* Applications are processed on a rolling basis. Application fee: $60. Electronic applications accepted. Tuition and fees vary according to degree level and program. *Financial support:* Fellowships and scholarships/grants available. Financial award application deadline: 6/30; financial award applicants required to submit FAFSA. *Unit head:* Dr. Don Cardinal, Dean, 714-997-6781, E-mail: cardinal@chapman.edu. *Application contact:* Admissions Coordinator, 714-997-6714. Web site: http://www.chapman.edu/CES/.

Clark Atlanta University, School of Education, Department of Counseling and Psychological Studies, Atlanta, GA 30314. Offers MA. Part-time programs available. *Faculty:* 1 (woman) full-time, 5 part-time/adjunct (4 women). *Students:* 19 full-time (15 women), 13 part-time (7 women); includes 30 minority (all Black or African American, non-Hispanic/Latino). Average age 26. 21 applicants, 86% accepted, 8 enrolled. In 2011, 14 master's awarded. *Degree requirements:* For master's, comprehensive exam. *Entrance requirements:* For master's, GRE General Test, minimum undergraduate GPA of 2.6. Additional exam requirements/recommendations for international students: Required—TOEFL (minimum score 500 paper-based; 173 computer-based; 61 iBT). *Application deadline:* For fall admission, 4/1 for domestic and international students; for spring admission, 11/1 for domestic and international students. Applications are processed on a rolling basis. Application fee: $40 ($55 for international students). Electronic applications accepted. *Expenses: Tuition:* Full-time $13,572; part-time $754 per credit hour. *Required fees:* $806; $403 per semester. *Financial support:* Career-related internships or fieldwork, Federal Work-Study, scholarships/grants, and unspecified assistantships available. Support available to part-time students. Financial award application deadline: 4/30; financial award applicants required to submit FAFSA. *Unit head:* Dr. Noran Moffett, Interim Chairperson, 404-880-6330, E-mail: nmoffett@cau.edu. *Application contact:* Michelle Clark-Davis, Graduate Program Admissions, 404-880-6605, E-mail: cauadmissions@cau.edu.

The College of Saint Rose, Graduate Studies, School of Education, Educational and School Psychology Department, Albany, NY 12203-1419. Offers applied technology education (MS Ed); educational psychology (MS Ed); school psychology (MS, Certificate). Part-time and evening/weekend programs available. *Entrance requirements:* For master's, minimum undergraduate GPA of 3.0. Additional exam requirements/recommendations for international students: Required—TOEFL (minimum score 550 paper-based; 213 computer-based). Electronic applications accepted.

Dowling College, Graduate Programs in Education, Oakdale, NY 11769-1999. Offers adolescence education with middle childhood extension (MS); advanced certificate in gifted education (AC); childhood and early childhood education (MS); childhood and gifted education (MS); computers in education (AC); early childhood education (MS); educational administration (Ed D); educational technology leadership (MS); educational technology specialist (AC); literacy education (MS); literary education (AC); school building leader (AC); school district business leader (MBA, AC); school district leader (AC); special education (MS); sports management (MS). *Accreditation:* NCATE. Part-time and evening/weekend programs available. Postbaccalaureate distance learning degree programs offered (minimal on-campus study). *Faculty:* 23 full-time (12 women), 70 part-time/adjunct (44 women). *Students:* 336 full-time (245 women), 631 part-time (485 women); includes 83 minority (29 Black or African American, non-Hispanic/Latino; 2 American Indian or Alaska Native, non-Hispanic/Latino; 7 Asian, non-Hispanic/Latino; 45 Hispanic/Latino). Average age 32. 280 applicants, 85% accepted, 167 enrolled. In 2011, 425 master's, 27 doctorates, 40 other advanced degrees awarded. *Degree requirements:* For master's and AC, comprehensive exam; for doctorate, thesis/dissertation. *Entrance requirements:* For master's, minimum GPA of 3.0; for doctorate, GRE, master's degree; for AC, teaching certificate. Additional exam requirements/recommendations for international students: Required—TOEFL (minimum score 550 paper-based). *Application deadline:* For fall admission, 9/1 priority date for domestic students; for winter admission, 1/1 priority date for domestic students; for spring admission, 2/1 priority date for domestic students. Applications are processed on a rolling basis. Application fee: $50. Electronic applications accepted. *Expenses: Tuition:* Full-time $19,162; part-time $933 per credit. *Required fees:* $1330; $700 per year. Tuition and fees vary according to course load. *Financial support:* Career-related internships or fieldwork and Federal Work-Study available. Support available to part-time students. Financial award application deadline: 6/30; financial award applicants required to submit FAFSA. *Faculty research:* Natural readers, Korean styles and learning strategies, mothers of children with disabilities, computers in instruction, cultural background and organizational roadblocks to problem solving. *Unit head:* Carol Pulsonetti, Director of Operations, School of Education, 631-244-3243, E-mail: pulsonec@dowling.edu. *Application contact:* Ronnie S. Macdonald, Assistant Vice President for Enrollment Services/Dean of Admissions, 631-244-3357, Fax: 631-244-1059, E-mail: macdonar@dowling.edu.

Eastern Michigan University, Graduate School, College of Education, Department of Teacher Education, Programs in Educational Psychology and Assessment, Ypsilanti, MI 48197. Offers educational assessment (Graduate Certificate); educational psychology (MA), including development/personality, research and assessment, research and evaluation, the developing learner. *Accreditation:* NCATE. Part-time and evening/weekend programs available. Postbaccalaureate distance learning degree programs offered (minimal on-campus study). *Students:* 2 full-time (both women), 58 part-time (55 women); includes 8 minority (all Black or African American, non-Hispanic/Latino), 3 international. Average age 33. 27 applicants, 74% accepted, 13 enrolled. In 2011, 8 degrees awarded. *Degree requirements:* For master's, thesis or alternative. *Entrance requirements:* For master's, GRE. Additional exam requirements/recommendations for international students: Required—TOEFL. *Application deadline:* Applications are processed on a rolling basis. Application fee: $35. *Expenses:* Tuition, state resident: full-time $10,367; part-time $432 per credit hour. Tuition, nonresident: full-time $20,435; part-time $851 per credit hour. *Required fees:* $39 per credit hour. $46 per semester. One-time fee: $100. Tuition and fees vary according to course level, degree level and reciprocity agreements. *Financial support:* Fellowships, research assistantships with full tuition reimbursements, teaching assistantships with full tuition reimbursements, career-related internships or fieldwork, Federal Work-Study, institutionally sponsored loans, scholarships/grants, tuition waivers (partial), and unspecified assistantships available. Support available to part-time students. Financial award applicants required to submit FAFSA. *Unit head:* Dr. Pat Pokay, Coordinator, 734-487-3260, Fax: 734-487-2101, E-mail: ppokay@emich.edu. *Application contact:* Dr. Anne Bednar, Advisor, 734-487-3260, Fax: 734-487-2101, E-mail: anne.bednar@emich.edu.

Edinboro University of Pennsylvania, School of Education, Department of Professional Studies, Edinboro, PA 16444. Offers counseling (MA), including community counseling, elementary guidance, rehabilitation counseling, secondary guidance, student personnel services; educational leadership (M Ed), including elementary school administration, secondary school administration; educational psychology (M Ed); educational specialist school psychology (MS); elementary principal (Certificate); elementary school guidance counselor (Certificate); K-12 school administration (Certificate); letter of eligibility (Certificate); reading (M Ed); reading specialist (Certificate); school psychology (Certificate); school supervision (Certificate), including music, special education. Part-time and evening/weekend programs available. *Faculty:* 13 full-time (8 women). *Students:* 171 full-time (134 women), 563 part-time (441 women); includes 26 minority (20 Black or African American, non-Hispanic/Latino; 1 American Indian or Alaska Native, non-Hispanic/Latino; 1 Asian, non-Hispanic/Latino; 4 Hispanic/Latino). Average age 31. In 2011, 297 master's, 49 other advanced degrees awarded. *Degree requirements:* For master's, thesis or alternative, competency exam; for Certificate, thesis or alternative. *Entrance requirements:* For master's and Certificate, GRE or MAT, minimum QPA of 2.5. *Application deadline:* Applications are processed on a rolling basis. Application fee: $30. Electronic applications accepted. *Financial support:* In 2011–12, 60 research assistantships with full and partial tuition reimbursements (averaging $4,050 per year) were awarded; career-related internships or fieldwork, Federal Work-Study, scholarships/grants, and unspecified assistantships also available. Support available to part-time students. Financial award application deadline: 2/15; financial award applicants required to submit FAFSA. *Unit head:* Dr. Susan Norton, 814-732-2260, E-mail: scnorton@edinboro.edu. *Application contact:* Dr. Andrew Pushchack, Program Head, Educational Leadership, 814-732-1548, E-mail: apushchack@edinboro.edu.

Florida State University, The Graduate School, College of Education, Department of Educational Psychology and Learning Systems, Program in Educational Psychology, Tallahassee, FL 32306. Offers learning and cognition (MS, PhD, Ed S); sports psychology (MS, PhD). *Faculty:* 6 full-time (4 women). *Students:* 55 full-time (38 women), 19 part-time (10 women); includes 13 minority (7 Black or African American, non-Hispanic/Latino; 1 Asian, non-Hispanic/Latino; 5 Hispanic/Latino), 20 international. Average age 30. 102 applicants, 58% accepted, 17 enrolled. In 2011, 7 master's, 3 doctorates, 1 other advanced degree awarded. *Degree requirements:* For master's, comprehensive exam, thesis optional; for doctorate, comprehensive exam, thesis/dissertation. *Entrance requirements:* For master's and doctorate, GRE General Test, minimum GPA of 3.0. Additional exam requirements/recommendations for international students: Required—TOEFL (minimum score 550 paper-based; 213 computer-based; 80 iBT). *Application deadline:* For fall admission, 7/1 for domestic and international students; for winter admission, 11/1 for domestic and international students; for spring admission, 3/1 for domestic and international students. Applications are processed on a rolling basis. Application fee: $30. Electronic applications accepted. *Expenses:* Tuition, state resident: full-time $9474; part-time $350.88 per credit hour. Tuition, nonresident: full-time $16,236; part-time $601.34 per credit hour. *Required fees:* $630 per semester. One-time fee: $20. Tuition and fees vary according to course load and campus/location. *Financial support:* In 2011–12, 5 fellowships with full and partial tuition reimbursements, 30 research assistantships with full and partial tuition reimbursements, 43 teaching assistantships with full and partial tuition reimbursements were awarded; career-related internships or fieldwork, scholarships/grants, health care benefits, and unspecified assistantships also available. Financial award application deadline: 1/15; financial award applicants required to submit FAFSA. *Faculty research:* Learning and cognition, skill acquisition, self-perception, processes of motivation. *Unit head:* Dr. Susan Losh, Program Leader, 850-644-8776, Fax: 850-644-8776, E-mail: slosh@fsu.edu. *Application contact:* Peggy Lollie, Program Assistant, 850-644-8786, Fax: 850-644-8776, E-mail: plollie@fsu.edu.

Fordham University, Graduate School of Education, Division of Psychological and Educational Services, New York, NY 10023. Offers counseling and personnel services (MSE, Adv C); counseling psychology (PhD); educational psychology (MSE, PhD); school psychology (PhD); urban and urban bilingual school psychology (Adv C). *Accreditation:* APA (one or more programs are accredited); NCATE. *Degree requirements:* For doctorate, thesis/dissertation. *Entrance requirements:* For doctorate, GRE General Test. *Expenses: Tuition:* Full-time $30,480; part-time $1270 per credit. *Required fees:* $586; $293 per semester.

George Mason University, College of Education and Human Development, Program in Educational Psychology, Fairfax, VA 22030. Offers MS, Certificate. *Faculty:* 8 full-time (5 women). *Students:* 11 full-time (8 women), 33 part-time (30 women); includes 10 minority (2 Black or African American, non-Hispanic/Latino; 5 Asian, non-Hispanic/Latino; 3 Hispanic/Latino), 2 international. Average age 31. 27 applicants, 78% accepted, 17 enrolled. In 2011, 14 degrees awarded. *Entrance requirements:* For master's, GRE, official transcripts; 3 letters of recommendation; expanded goals statement. Additional exam requirements/recommendations for international students: Required—TOEFL (minimum score 570 paper-based; 230 computer-based; 88 iBT), IELTS, Pearson Test of English. *Application deadline:* For fall admission, 4/1 for domestic students; for spring admission, 11/1 for domestic students. Application fee: $65 ($80 for international students). *Expenses:* Tuition, state resident: full-time $8750; part-time $364.58 per credit. Tuition, nonresident: full-time $24,092; part-time $1003.83 per credit. *Required fees:* $2514; $104.75 per credit. *Financial support:* In 2011–12, 8 students received support, including 8 research assistantships with full and partial tuition reimbursements available (averaging $8,453 per year); career-related internships or fieldwork, Federal Work-Study, scholarships/grants, unspecified assistantships, and health care benefits (full-time research or teaching assistantship recipients) also available. Support available to part-time students. Financial award application deadline: 3/1; financial award applicants required to submit FAFSA. *Unit head:* Anastasia Kitsantas, Professor, 703-993-2688, Fax: 703-993-3678, E-mail: akitsant@gmu.edu. *Application contact:* Kim Howe, Enrollment and Course Coordinator, 703-993-3679, Fax: 703-993-3678, E-mail: khowe1@gmu.edu. Web site: http://gse.gmu.edu/programs/edpsych/.

Georgia State University, College of Education, Department of Educational Psychology and Special Education, Program in Educational Psychology, Atlanta, GA 30302-3083. Offers MS, PhD. *Accreditation:* NCATE. Part-time and evening/weekend programs available. *Degree requirements:* For master's, thesis or project; for doctorate, comprehensive exam, thesis/dissertation. *Entrance requirements:* For master's, GRE General Test, minimum GPA of 2.5; for doctorate, GRE General Test, minimum GPA of 3.3. *Faculty research:* Cognitive and language development, language development of deaf children, reading in adult populations.

Graduate School and University Center of the City University of New York, Graduate Studies, Program in Educational Psychology, New York, NY 10016-4039. Offers PhD. *Accreditation:* APA. *Degree requirements:* For doctorate, 2 foreign languages, thesis/dissertation. *Entrance requirements:* For doctorate, GRE General Test, interview, minimum GPA of 3.0. Additional exam requirements/recommendations for international students: Required—TOEFL. Electronic applications accepted.

Harvard University, Harvard Graduate School of Education, Master's Programs in Education, Cambridge, MA 02138. Offers arts in education (Ed M); education policy and management (Ed M); higher education (Ed M); human development and psychology (Ed M); international education policy (Ed M); language and literacy (Ed M); learning and teaching (Ed M); mid-career mathematics and science (teaching certificate) (Ed M); mind brain and education (Ed M); prevention science and practice (Ed M); school leadership (Ed M); special studies (Ed M); teaching and curriculum (teaching certificate) (Ed M); technology innovation and education (Ed M). Part-time programs available. *Faculty:* 83 full-time (44 women), 67 part-time/adjunct (29 women). *Students:* 592 full-time (431 women), 75 part-time (54 women); includes 194 minority (41 Black or African American, non-Hispanic/Latino; 4 American Indian or Alaska Native, non-Hispanic/Latino; 75 Asian, non-Hispanic/Latino; 45 Hispanic/Latino; 2 Native Hawaiian or other Pacific Islander, non-Hispanic/Latino; 27 Two or more races, non-Hispanic/Latino), 95 international. Average age 28. 1,679 applicants, 52% accepted, 627 enrolled. In 2011, 653 master's awarded. *Entrance requirements:* For master's, GRE General Test, statement of purpose, 3 letters of recommendation, resume, official transcripts. Additional exam requirements/recommendations for international students: Required—TOEFL (minimum score 613 paper-based; 104 computer-based; 100 iBT), TWE (minimum score 5). *Application deadline:* For fall admission, 1/4 for domestic and international students. Application fee: $85. Electronic applications accepted. *Expenses:* Contact institution. *Financial support:* In 2011–12, 419 students received support, including 14 fellowships with full and partial tuition reimbursements available (averaging $12,831 per year); career-related internships or fieldwork, Federal Work-Study, institutionally sponsored loans, scholarships/grants, health care benefits, tuition waivers (full and partial), and unspecified assistantships also available. Support available to part-time students. Financial award application deadline: 2/1; financial award applicants required to submit FAFSA. *Faculty research:* Learning and development, educational leadership and organizations, educational policy analysis. *Total annual research expenditures:* $26 million. *Unit head:* Jennifer L. Petrallia, Assistant Dean, 617-495-8445. *Application contact:* Information Contact, 617-495-3414, Fax: 617-496-3577, E-mail: gseadmissions@harvard.edu. Web site: http://www.gse.harvard.edu/.

Holy Names University, Graduate Division, Department of Education, Oakland, CA 94619-1699. Offers educational therapy (Certificate); level 1 education specialist mild/moderate disabilities (Credential); level 2 education specialist mild/moderate disabilities (Credential); multiple subject teaching credential (Credential); single subject teaching credential (Credential); teaching English as a second language (TESL) (M Ed); urban education: educational therapy (M Ed); urban education: K-12 education (M Ed); urban education: special education (M Ed). Part-time programs available. *Degree requirements:* For master's, comprehensive exam, research paper, thesis or project. *Entrance requirements:* For master's, minimum undergraduate GPA of 2.6 overall, 3.0 in major. Additional exam requirements/recommendations for international students: Required—TOEFL (minimum score 550 paper-based; 213 computer-based; 80 iBT). *Faculty research:* Cognitive development, language development, learning handicaps.

Howard University, School of Education, Department of Human Development and Psychoeducational Studies, Program in Educational Psychology, Washington, DC 20059-0002. Offers PhD. Part-time programs available. *Faculty:* 4 full-time (3 women). *Students:* 14 full-time (9 women), 12 part-time (8 women); includes 25 minority (all Black or African American, non-Hispanic/Latino), 1 international. Average age 29. 8 applicants, 38% accepted, 3 enrolled. In 2011, 1 degree awarded. *Degree requirements:* For doctorate, one foreign language, comprehensive exam, thesis/dissertation, expository writing exam, internship. *Entrance requirements:* For doctorate, GRE General Test, minimum GPA of 3.4. Additional exam requirements/recommendations for international students: Required—TOEFL (minimum score 550 paper-based). *Application deadline:* For fall admission, 2/15 priority date for domestic students; for spring admission, 11/1 for domestic students. Applications are processed on a rolling basis. Application fee: $45. Electronic applications accepted. *Financial support:* In 2011–12, 2 students received support, including 2 fellowships with full and partial tuition reimbursements available (averaging $16,000 per year); research assistantships, teaching assistantships, career-related internships or fieldwork, Federal Work-Study, institutionally sponsored loans, and scholarships/grants also available. Financial award application deadline: 3/15; financial award applicants required to submit FAFSA. *Unit head:* Dr. Kimberly E. Freeman, Assistant Professor/Coordinator, 202-806-6514, Fax: 202-806-5205, E-mail: kefreeman@howard.edu. *Application contact:* Menbere Endale, Administration Assistant, Department of Human Development and Psychoeducational Studies, 202-806-7351, Fax: 202-806-5205, E-mail: mendale@howard.edu.

Illinois State University, Graduate School, College of Arts and Sciences, Department of Psychology, Normal, IL 61790-2200. Offers psychology (MA, MS), including clinical psychology, counseling psychology, developmental psychology, educational psychology, experimental psychology, measurement-evaluation, organizational-industrial psychology; school psychology (PhD, SSP). *Accreditation:* APA. *Degree requirements:* For master's, thesis or alternative; for doctorate, variable foreign language requirement, thesis/dissertation, 2 terms of residency, internship, practicum. *Entrance requirements:* For master's, GRE General Test, GRE Subject Test, minimum GPA of 3.0 in last 60 hours of course work; for doctorate, GRE General Test. *Faculty research:* Comprehensive evaluation system for the central region professional development grant, Illinois school psychology internship consortium, for children's sake.

Indiana University Bloomington, School of Education, Department of Counseling and Educational Psychology, Bloomington, IN 47405-1006. Offers counseling (MS, PhD, Ed S); counselor education (MS, Ed S); educational psychology (MS, PhD); inquiry methodology (PhD); learning and developmental sciences (MS, PhD); school psychology (PhD, Ed S). *Accreditation:* ACA (one or more programs are accredited); APA (one or more programs are accredited); NCATE. Terminal master's awarded for partial completion of doctoral program. *Degree requirements:* For master's, thesis optional; for doctorate, thesis/dissertation; for Ed S, comprehensive exam or project. *Entrance requirements:* For master's, doctorate, and Ed S, GRE General Test. Additional exam requirements/recommendations for international students: Required—TOEFL. Electronic applications accepted. *Faculty research:* Counseling psychology, inquiry methodology, school psychology, learning sciences, human development, educational psychology.

Indiana University of Pennsylvania, School of Graduate Studies and Research, College of Education and Educational Technology, Department of Educational and School Psychology, Program in Educational Psychology, Indiana, PA 15705-1087. Offers M Ed, Certificate. *Accreditation:* NCATE. Part-time and evening/weekend programs available. *Faculty:* 7 full-time (2 women), 1 (woman) part-time/adjunct. *Students:* 17 full-time (12 women), 3 part-time (2 women). Average age 26. 37 applicants, 59% accepted, 20 enrolled. In 2011, 15 master's awarded. *Degree requirements:* For master's, thesis optional. *Entrance requirements:* For master's, GRE General Test, GRE Subject Test, 2 letters of recommendation. Additional exam requirements/recommendations for international students: Required—TOEFL (minimum score 540 paper-based; 207 computer-based). *Application deadline:* For fall admission, 2/1 priority date for domestic students. Application fee: $50. Electronic applications accepted. *Expenses:* Tuition, state resident: full-time $7488; part-time $416 per credit. Tuition, nonresident: full-time $11,232; part-time $624 per credit. *Required fees:* $2070; $192.20 per credit. $90 per semester. *Financial support:* In 2011–12, 1 fellowship with full tuition reimbursement (averaging $5,944 per year), 15 research assistantships with full and partial tuition reimbursements (averaging $4,896 per year) were awarded; teaching assistantships with partial tuition reimbursements, career-related internships or fieldwork, and Federal Work-Study also available. Support available to part-time students. Financial award application deadline: 4/15; financial award applicants required to submit FAFSA. *Unit head:* Dr. Mark R. McGowan, Graduate Coordinator, 724-357-2174, E-mail: mmcgowan@iup.edu. *Application contact:* Dr. Edward Nardi, Associate Dean, 724-357-2480, Fax: 724-357-5595, E-mail: ewnardi@iup.edu. Web site: http://www.iup.edu/upper.aspx?id=93725.

Instituto Tecnologico de Santo Domingo, Graduate School, Area of Humanities and Social Sciences, Santo Domingo, Dominican Republic. Offers accounting (Certificate); adult education (Certificate); applied linguistics (MA); economics (MA); education (M Ed); educational psychology (MA, Certificate); gender and development (MA, Certificate); humanistic studies (MA); international marketing management (Certificate); international relations in the Caribbean basin (Certificate); intervention systems in family therapy (MA); linguistic and literary communication (Certificate); pedagogical support (MA); social science education (M Ed); sustainable human development (MA); terminal illness and death psychology (Certificate); youth and adult education (M Ed).

John Carroll University, Graduate School, Department of Education and Allied Studies, Program in Educational and School Psychology, University Heights, OH 44118-4581. Offers M Ed, MA. *Accreditation:* NCATE. Part-time and evening/weekend programs available. *Degree requirements:* For master's, comprehensive exam, research essay or thesis (MA only). *Entrance requirements:* For master's, GRE General Test or MAT, minimum GPA of 2.75, Educ. or Psych. degree, questionnaire, interview. Electronic applications accepted.

The Johns Hopkins University, School of Education, Department of Interdisciplinary Studies in Education, Baltimore, MD 21218. Offers earth/space science (Certificate); education (MS), including educational studies; health care education (MEHP); mind, brain, and teaching (Certificate); teaching the adult learner (Certificate); urban education (Certificate). Part-time and evening/weekend programs available. Postbaccalaureate distance learning degree programs offered (minimal on-campus study). *Degree requirements:* For master's, capstone course. *Entrance requirements:* For master's and Certificate, minimum undergraduate GPA of 3.0. Additional exam requirements/recommendations for international students: Required—TOEFL (minimum score 600 paper-based; 250 computer-based; 100 iBT). Electronic applications accepted. *Faculty research:* Neuro-education, urban school reform, leadership development, teacher leadership, charter schools, techniques for teaching reading to adolescents with delayed reading skills, school culture.

Kent State University, Graduate School of Education, Health, and Human Services, School of Lifespan Development and Educational Sciences, Program in Educational Psychology, Kent, OH 44242-0001. Offers M Ed, MA, PhD. *Faculty:* 4 full-time (2 women), 1 (woman) part-time/adjunct. *Students:* 30 full-time (16 women), 24 part-time (17 women); includes 1 minority (Hispanic/Latino). 25 applicants, 32% accepted. In 2011, 5 master's, 2 doctorates awarded. *Degree requirements:* For master's, thesis optional; for doctorate, comprehensive exam, thesis/dissertation. *Entrance requirements:* For master's, 2 letters of reference, minimum master's GPA of 3.5, goals statement; for doctorate, GRE, 2 letters of reference, minimum undergraduate GPA of 3.0, goals statement, resume, interview. Additional exam requirements/recommendations for international students: Required—TOEFL (minimum score 550 paper-based; 213 computer-based; 80 iBT). *Application deadline:* Applications are processed on a rolling basis. Application fee: $30 ($60 for international students). Electronic applications accepted. *Expenses:* Tuition, state resident: full-time $8136; part-time $452 per credit hour. Tuition, nonresident: full-time $14,292; part-time $794 per credit hour. *Financial support:* In 2011–12, 2 fellowships (averaging $12,000 per year), 3 research assistantships (averaging $12,000 per year) were awarded; career-related internships or fieldwork, Federal Work-Study, institutionally sponsored loans, scholarships/grants, health care benefits, and unspecified assistantships also available. Support available to part-time students. *Unit head:* Dr. Drew Tiene, Coordinator, 330-672-0607, E-mail: dtiene@kent.edu. *Application contact:* Nancy Miller, Academic Program Coordinator, Office of Graduate Student Services, 330-672-2576, Fax: 330-672-9162, E-mail: ogs@kent.edu. Web site: http://www.kent.edu/ehhs/edpf/.

La Sierra University, School of Education, Department of School Psychology and Counseling, Riverside, CA 92515. Offers counseling (MA); educational psychology (Ed S); school psychology (Ed S). Part-time and evening/weekend programs available. *Degree requirements:* For master's, thesis optional; for Ed S, practicum (educational psychology). *Entrance requirements:* For master's, California Basic Educational Skills Test, NTE, minimum GPA of 3.0; for Ed S, minimum GPA of 3.3. *Faculty research:* Equivalent score scales, self perception.

Long Island University–Hudson at Westchester, Programs in Education-School Counselor and School Psychology, Purchase, NY 10577. Offers school counselor (MS Ed); school psychologist (MS Ed). Part-time and evening/weekend programs available.

Loyola University Chicago, School of Education, Program in Educational Psychology, Chicago, IL 60660. Offers M Ed. Part-time and evening/weekend programs available. *Faculty:* 7 full-time (5 women), 4 part-time/adjunct (2 women). *Students:* 27. Average age 28. 94 applicants, 52% accepted, 20 enrolled. In 2011, 28 master's awarded. Terminal master's awarded for partial completion of doctoral program. *Degree requirements:* For master's, comprehensive exam, thesis (for some programs). *Entrance requirements:* For master's, GRE General Test, letters of recommendation, minimum GPA of 3.0. Additional exam requirements/recommendations for international students: Required—TOEFL (minimum score 550 paper-based; 213 computer-based; 79 iBT). *Application deadline:* For fall admission, 12/1 for domestic and international students. Application fee: $50. Electronic applications accepted. Application fee is waived when completed online. *Expenses: Tuition:* Full-time $15,660; part-time $870 per credit hour. *Required fees:* $125 per semester. Tuition and fees vary according to course load and program. *Financial support:* Institutionally sponsored loans and scholarships/grants available. Support available to part-time students. Financial award application deadline: 2/1; financial award applicants required to submit FAFSA. *Faculty research:* Learning theory and teaching; cognitive, social, and cultural constructivism; school reform; workplace training and adult education. *Unit head:* Dr. Lynne Golomb, Director, 312-915-6218, E-mail: lgolomb@luc.edu. *Application contact:* Marie Rosin-Dittmar, Information Contact, 312-915-6800, E-mail: schleduc@luc.edu.

McGill University, Faculty of Graduate and Postdoctoral Studies, Faculty of Education, Department of Educational and Counseling Psychology, Montréal, QC H3A 2T5, Canada. Offers counseling psychology (MA, PhD); educational psychology (M Ed, MA, PhD); school/applied child psychology and applied developmental psychology (M Ed, MA, PhD, Diploma), including school psychology. *Accreditation:* APA.

Memorial University of Newfoundland, School of Graduate Studies, Faculty of Education, St. John's, NL A1C 5S7, Canada. Offers counseling psychology (M Ed); curriculum, teaching, and learning studies (M Ed); education (PhD); educational leadership studies (M Ed); information technology (M Ed); post-secondary studies (M Ed, Diploma), including health professional education (Diploma). Part-time programs available. *Degree requirements:* For master's, thesis optional, internship, paper folio, project; for doctorate, comprehensive exam, thesis/dissertation, thesis seminar, oral defense of thesis. *Entrance requirements:* For master's, undergraduate degree with at least 2nd class standing, 1-2 years work experience; for doctorate, minimum A average in graduate course work, MA in education, 2 years professional experience; for Diploma, 2nd class degree, 2 years of work experience with adult learners, appropriate academic qualifications and work experience in a health-related field. Electronic applications accepted. *Faculty research:* Critical thinking, literacy, cognitive studies and counseling, educational change, technology in instruction.

Miami University, School of Education and Allied Professions, Department of Educational Psychology, Oxford, OH 45056. Offers educational psychology (M Ed); instructional design and technology (M Ed, MA); school psychology (MS, Ed S); special education (M Ed). *Accreditation:* NCATE. *Students:* 49 full-time (40 women), 39 part-time (31 women); includes 8 minority (1 Black or African American, non-Hispanic/Latino; 5 Asian, non-Hispanic/Latino; 2 Two or more races, non-Hispanic/Latino), 28 international. Average age 29. In 2011, 50 master's awarded. *Entrance requirements:* For master's, GRE General Test or MAT, minimum undergraduate GPA of 3.0 during previous 2 years or 2.75 overall; for Ed S, GRE General Test or MAT. Additional exam requirements/recommendations for international students: Required—TOEFL. Application fee: $50. *Expenses:* Tuition, state resident: full-time $12,023; part-time $501 per credit hour. Tuition, nonresident: full-time $26,554; part-time $1107 per credit hour. *Required fees:* $528. *Financial support:* Fellowships with full tuition reimbursements, research assistantships with full tuition reimbursements, teaching assistantships with full tuition reimbursements, career-related internships or fieldwork, Federal Work-Study, health care benefits, tuition waivers (full), and unspecified assistantships available. Financial award application deadline: 2/15; financial award applicants required to submit FAFSA. *Unit head:* Dr. Nelda Cambron-McCabe, Chair, 513-529-6836, Fax: 513-529-6621, E-mail: cambron@muohio.edu. *Application contact:* Jennifer Turner, Administrative Assistant, 513-529-6621, Fax: 513-529-3646, E-mail: hillje@muohio.edu. Web site: http://www.units.muohio.edu/eap/departments/edp/edp.htm.

Michigan School of Professional Psychology, MA and Psy D Program in Clinical Psychology, Farmington Hills, MI 48334. Offers MA, Psy D. Part-time and evening/weekend programs available. *Faculty:* 8 full-time (3 women), 24 part-time/adjunct (16 women). *Students:* 112 full-time (90 women), 37 part-time (27 women); includes 34 minority (22 Black or African American, non-Hispanic/Latino; 6 Asian, non-Hispanic/Latino; 3 Hispanic/Latino; 3 Two or more races, non-Hispanic/Latino). 117 applicants, 72% accepted, 68 enrolled. In 2011, 32 master's, 15 doctorates awarded. *Median time to degree:* Of those who began their doctoral program in fall 2003, 100% received their degree in 8 years or less. *Degree requirements:* For master's, practicum; for doctorate, comprehensive exam, thesis/dissertation, internship, practicum. *Entrance requirements:* For master's, undergraduate degree from accredited institution with minimum GPA of 2.5; major in psychology, social work, or counseling; for doctorate, undergraduate degree from accredited institution with minimum GPA of 2.5; graduate degree in psychology, social work, or counseling from accredited institution with minimum GPA of 3.25; 500 graduate-level practicum hours or equivalent field experience. Additional exam requirements/recommendations for international students: Required—TOEFL (minimum score 550 paper-based; 213 computer-based; 79 iBT). *Application deadline:* Applications are processed on a rolling basis. Application fee: $75. Tuition and fees vary according to course level, course load, degree level and program. *Financial support:* In 2011–12, 6 students received support, including 3 research assistantships (averaging $12,000 per year), 1 teaching assistantship (averaging $12,000 per year); career-related internships or fieldwork, institutionally sponsored loans, and scholarships/grants also available. Financial award application deadline: 6/30; financial award applicants required to submit FAFSA. *Faculty research:* Qualitative research, existential, phenomenological psychology, clinical practice, humanistic. *Unit head:* Dr. Kerry Moustakas, President, 248-476-1122, Fax: 248-476-1125. *Application contact:* Amanda Ming, Admissions and Recruitment Coordinator, 248-476-1122 Ext. 117, Fax: 248-476-1125, E-mail: aming@mispp.edu. Web site: http://www.mispp.edu.

Michigan State University, The Graduate School, College of Education, Department of Counseling, Educational Psychology and Special Education, East Lansing, MI 48824. Offers counseling (MA); educational psychology and educational technology (PhD); educational technology (MA); measurement and quantitative methods (PhD); rehabilitation counseling (MA); rehabilitation counselor education (PhD); school psychology (MA, PhD, Ed S); special education (MA, PhD). *Accreditation:* APA (one or more programs are accredited); CORE (one or more programs are accredited). Part-time programs available. *Entrance requirements:* Additional exam requirements/recommendations for international students: Required—TOEFL. Electronic applications accepted.

Mississippi State University, College of Education, Department of Counseling and Educational Psychology, Mississippi State, MS 39762. Offers college/postsecondary student counseling and personnel services (PhD); counselor education (MS); education (Ed S), including counselor education, school psychology; educational psychology (MS, PhD). *Accreditation:* ACA (one or more programs are accredited); APA; CORE (one or more programs are accredited); NCATE. Part-time programs available. Postbaccalaureate distance learning degree programs offered (minimal on-campus study). *Faculty:* 18 full-time (13 women), 2 part-time/adjunct (1 woman). *Students:* 167 full-time (133 women), 87 part-time (78 women); includes 81 minority (70 Black or African American, non-Hispanic/Latino; 4 American Indian or Alaska Native, non-Hispanic/Latino; 4 Asian, non-Hispanic/Latino; 1 Native Hawaiian or other Pacific Islander, non-Hispanic/Latino; 2 Two or more races, non-Hispanic/Latino), 7 international. Average age 31. 197 applicants, 55% accepted, 79 enrolled. In 2011, 52 master's, 2 doctorates, 7 other advanced degrees awarded. Terminal master's awarded for partial completion of doctoral program. *Degree requirements:* For master's, comprehensive exam, thesis optional; for doctorate, thesis/dissertation, comprehensive oral and written exam. *Entrance requirements:* For master's, GRE, minimum QPA of 3.0; for doctorate, GRE, interview, minimum GPA of 3.4; for Ed S, GRE, MS in counseling or related field. Additional exam requirements/recommendations for international students: Required—TOEFL (minimum score 475 paper-based; 153 computer-based; 53 iBT); Recommended—IELTS (minimum score 4.5). *Application deadline:* For fall admission,

2/1 priority date for domestic students, 2/1 for international students. Applications are processed on a rolling basis. Application fee: $40. Electronic applications accepted. *Expenses:* Tuition, state resident: full-time $5805; part-time $322.50 per credit hour. Tuition, nonresident: full-time $14,670; part-time $815 per credit hour. *Financial support:* In 2011–12, 7 research assistantships (averaging $10,750 per year), 6 teaching assistantships with full tuition reimbursements (averaging $10,151 per year) were awarded; career-related internships or fieldwork, Federal Work-Study, institutionally sponsored loans, and unspecified assistantships also available. Financial award application deadline: 2/1; financial award applicants required to submit FAFSA. *Faculty research:* HIV-AIDS in college population, substance abuse in youth and college students, ADHD and conduct disorders in youth, assessment and identification of early childhood disabilities, assessment and vocational transition of the disabled. *Unit head:* Dr. Daniel Wong, Professor/Head, 662-325-7928, Fax: 662-325-3263, E-mail: dwong@colled.msstate.edu. *Application contact:* Dr. Tony Doggett, Associate Professor and Graduate Coordinator, 662-325-3312, Fax: 662-325-3263, E-mail: tdoggett@colled.msstate.edu. Web site: http://www.cep.msstate.edu/.

Mount Saint Vincent University, Graduate Programs, Faculty of Education, Program in Educational Psychology, Halifax, NS B3M 2J6, Canada. Offers education of the blind or visually impaired (M Ed, MA Ed); education of the deaf or hard of hearing (M Ed, MA Ed); educational psychology (MA-R); human relations (M Ed, MA Ed). Part-time and evening/weekend programs available. Postbaccalaureate distance learning degree programs offered (minimal on-campus study). *Degree requirements:* For master's, thesis (for some programs). *Entrance requirements:* For master's, bachelor's degree in related field, 1 year of teaching experience. Electronic applications accepted. *Faculty research:* Personality measurement, values reasoning, aggression and sexuality, power and control, quantitative and qualitative research methodologies.

National Louis University, National College of Education, Chicago, IL 60603. Offers administration and supervision (M Ed, Ed D, CAS, Ed S); curriculum and instruction (M Ed, MS Ed, CAS); early childhood administration (M Ed, CAS); early childhood education (M Ed, MAT, MS Ed, CAS); education (Ed D); educational psychology/human learning and development (M Ed, MS Ed, CAS, Ed S); elementary education (MAT); interdisciplinary curriculum and instruction (M Ed); mathematics education (M Ed, MS Ed, CAS); reading and language (M Ed, MS Ed, CAS); school psychology (M Ed, Ed S); science education (M Ed, MS Ed, CAS); secondary education (MAT); special education (M Ed, MAT, CAS); technology in education (M Ed, CAS). *Accreditation:* NCATE. Part-time and evening/weekend programs available. *Students:* 224 full-time (162 women), 2,336 part-time (1,767 women); includes 677 minority (366 Black or African American, non-Hispanic/Latino; 8 American Indian or Alaska Native, non-Hispanic/Latino; 68 Asian, non-Hispanic/Latino; 218 Hispanic/Latino; 2 Native Hawaiian or other Pacific Islander, non-Hispanic/Latino; 15 Two or more races, non-Hispanic/Latino), 2 international. Average age 34. In 2011, 1,711 master's, 76 doctorates, 86 other advanced degrees awarded. *Degree requirements:* For doctorate, comprehensive exam, thesis/dissertation. *Entrance requirements:* For master's, MAT or GRE, minimum GPA of 3.0; for doctorate, GRE General Test, minimum GPA of 3.25, interview, resume, writing sample, 4 recommendations. Additional exam requirements/recommendations for international students: Required—TOEFL (minimum score 550 paper-based; 213 computer-based; 79 iBT). *Application deadline:* Applications are processed on a rolling basis. Application fee: $40. *Financial support:* Fellowships, research assistantships, teaching assistantships, career-related internships or fieldwork, Federal Work-Study, institutionally sponsored loans, and scholarships/grants available. Support available to part-time students. Financial award applicants required to submit FAFSA. *Unit head:* Dr. Alison Hilsabeck, Dean, 312-361-3580, Fax: 312-261-2580, E-mail: ahilsabeck@nl.edu. *Application contact:* Ken Kasprzak, Director of Admission, 888-658-8632, Fax: 847-947-5575, E-mail: kkasprzak@nl.edu.

New Jersey City University, Graduate Studies and Continuing Education, William J. Maxwell College of Arts and Sciences, Program in Educational Psychology, Jersey City, NJ 07305-1597. Offers educational psychology (MA); school psychology (PD). Part-time and evening/weekend programs available. *Students:* 21 full-time (15 women), 8 part-time (6 women); includes 17 minority (5 Black or African American, non-Hispanic/Latino; 12 Hispanic/Latino). Average age 30. In 2011, 19 master's, 5 other advanced degrees awarded. *Degree requirements:* For PD, summer internship or externship. *Entrance requirements:* For degree, GRE General Test. Additional exam requirements/recommendations for international students: Required—TOEFL. *Application deadline:* For fall admission, 8/1 priority date for domestic students; for spring admission, 12/1 for domestic students. Applications are processed on a rolling basis. Application fee: $0. *Expenses:* Tuition, state resident: part-time $494 per credit. Tuition, nonresident: part-time $911.30 per credit. *Required fees:* $95.90 per year. *Financial support:* Unspecified assistantships available. *Unit head:* Dr. James Lennon, Director, 201-200-3309, E-mail: jlennon@njcu.edu. *Application contact:* Dr. William Bajor, Dean of Graduate Studies, 201-200-3409, Fax: 201-200-3411, E-mail: wbajor@njcu.edu.

New York University, Steinhardt School of Culture, Education, and Human Development, Department of Applied Psychology, Programs in Educational and Developmental Psychology, New York, NY 10012-1019. Offers educational psychology (MA); human development and social intervention (MA); psychological development (PhD); psychology and social intervention (PhD). *Accreditation:* APA (one or more programs are accredited). Part-time programs available. *Faculty:* 26 full-time (18 women). *Students:* 60 full-time (57 women), 20 part-time (19 women); includes 25 minority (12 Black or African American, non-Hispanic/Latino; 9 Asian, non-Hispanic/Latino; 4 Hispanic/Latino), 17 international. Average age 33. 223 applicants, 37% accepted, 16 enrolled. In 2011, 16 master's, 3 doctorates awarded. *Degree requirements:* For master's, thesis (for some programs); for doctorate, thesis/dissertation. *Entrance requirements:* For doctorate, GRE General Test, interview. Additional exam requirements/recommendations for international students: Required—TOEFL. *Application deadline:* For fall admission, 12/1 priority date for domestic students, 12/1 for international students. Applications are processed on a rolling basis. Application fee: $75. Electronic applications accepted. *Financial support:* Teaching assistantships with partial tuition reimbursements, career-related internships or fieldwork, Federal Work-Study, institutionally sponsored loans, and tuition waivers (partial) available. Support available to part-time students. Financial award application deadline: 2/1; financial award applicants required to submit FAFSA. *Faculty research:* High risk children and youth; child and adolescent developments; families and schooling; infant cognition; exploration, language, and symbolic play in toddlerhood. *Unit head:* Dr. LaRue Allen, Director, 212-998-5555, Fax: 212-995-4358. *Application contact:* 212-998-5030, Fax: 212-995-4328, E-mail: steinhardt.gradadmissions@nyu.edu. Web site: http://steinhardt.nyu.edu/appsych.

Northern Arizona University, Graduate College, College of Education, Department of Educational Psychology, Flagstaff, AZ 86011. Offers counseling (MA); educational psychology (PhD), including counseling psychology, learning and instruction, school psychology; human relations (M Ed); school counseling (M Ed); school psychology (Certificate, Ed S); student affairs (M Ed). Part-time programs available. Postbaccalaureate distance learning degree programs offered. *Faculty:* 18 full-time (8 women). *Students:* 280 full-time (220 women), 241 part-time (198 women); includes 194 minority (29 Black or African American, non-Hispanic/Latino; 37 American Indian or Alaska Native, non-Hispanic/Latino; 8 Asian, non-Hispanic/Latino; 105 Hispanic/Latino; 1 Native Hawaiian or other Pacific Islander, non-Hispanic/Latino; 14 Two or more races, non-Hispanic/Latino), 2 international. 274 applicants, 76% accepted, 141 enrolled. In 2011, 172 master's, 4 doctorates awarded. Terminal master's awarded for partial completion of doctoral program. *Median time to degree:* Of those who began their doctoral program in fall 2003, 75% received their degree in 8 years or less. *Degree requirements:* For master's, internship (for some programs); for doctorate, comprehensive exam, thesis/dissertation, internship. *Entrance requirements:* Additional exam requirements/recommendations for international students: Required—TOEFL (minimum score 550 paper-based; 213 computer-based; 80 iBT), IELTS (minimum score 7). *Application deadline:* For fall admission, 9/15 for domestic students; for spring admission, 1/15 for domestic students. Applications are processed on a rolling basis. Application fee: $65. Electronic applications accepted. *Expenses:* Tuition, state resident: full-time $7190; part-time $355 per credit hour. Tuition, nonresident: full-time $18,092; part-time $1005 per credit hour. *Required fees:* $818; $328 per semester. *Financial support:* In 2011–12, 20 students received support, including 1 research assistantship with partial tuition reimbursement available (averaging $10,222 per year), 14 teaching assistantships with partial tuition reimbursements available (averaging $9,660 per year); career-related internships or fieldwork, Federal Work-Study, scholarships/grants, health care benefits, tuition waivers (full and partial), and unspecified assistantships also available. Financial award applicants required to submit FAFSA. *Unit head:* Dr. Kathy Bohan, Chair, 928-523-0362, Fax: 928-523-9284, E-mail: kathy.bohan@nau.edu. *Application contact:* Hope DeMello, Administrative Assistant, 928-523-7103, Fax: 928-523-9284, E-mail: eps@nau.edu. Web site: http://nau.edu/coe/ed-psych/.

Northern Illinois University, Graduate School, College of Education, Department of Leadership, Educational Psychology and Foundations, De Kalb, IL 60115-2854. Offers educational administration (MS Ed, Ed D, Ed S); educational psychology (MS Ed, Ed D); foundations of education (MS Ed); school business management (MS Ed). Part-time and evening/weekend programs available. Postbaccalaureate distance learning degree programs offered (minimal on-campus study). *Faculty:* 23 full-time (12 women). *Students:* 8 full-time (6 women), 272 part-time (155 women); includes 46 minority (22 Black or African American, non-Hispanic/Latino; 1 American Indian or Alaska Native, non-Hispanic/Latino; 4 Asian, non-Hispanic/Latino; 17 Hispanic/Latino; 2 Two or more races, non-Hispanic/Latino), 6 international. Average age 39. 77 applicants, 74% accepted, 22 enrolled. In 2011, 81 master's, 8 doctorates, 39 other advanced degrees awarded. *Degree requirements:* For master's, comprehensive exam, thesis optional; for doctorate, thesis/dissertation, candidacy exam, dissertation defense. *Entrance requirements:* For master's, minimum undergraduate GPA of 2.75; for doctorate, GRE General Test, minimum undergraduate GPA of 2.75, 3.2 graduate; for Ed S, GRE General Test, minimum GPA of 2.75 (undergraduate), 3.2 (graduate). Additional exam requirements/recommendations for international students: Required—TOEFL (minimum score 550 paper-based; 213 computer-based). *Application deadline:* For fall admission, 6/1 for domestic students, 5/1 for international students; for spring admission, 11/1 for domestic students, 10/1 for international students. Applications are processed on a rolling basis. Application fee: $40. Electronic applications accepted. *Financial support:* In 2011–12, 4 research assistantships with full tuition reimbursements, 7 teaching assistantships with full tuition reimbursements were awarded; fellowships with full tuition reimbursements, career-related internships or fieldwork, Federal Work-Study, scholarships/grants, tuition waivers (full), and staff assistantships also available. Support available to part-time students. Financial award applicants required to submit FAFSA. *Faculty research:* Interpersonal forgiveness, learner-centered education, psychedelic studies, senior theory, professional growth. *Unit head:* Dr. Charles L. Howell, Chair, 815-753-4404, E-mail: chowell@niu.edu. *Application contact:* Graduate School Office, 815-753-0395, E-mail: gradsch@niu.edu. Web site: http://cedu.niu.edu/LEPF/.

Oklahoma State University, College of Education, School of Applied Health and Educational Psychology, Stillwater, OK 74078. Offers applied behavioral studies (Ed D); applied health and educational psychology (MS, PhD, Ed S). *Accreditation:* APA (one or more programs are accredited). Part-time programs available. *Faculty:* 40 full-time (19 women), 17 part-time/adjunct (9 women). *Students:* 192 full-time (137 women), 150 part-time (102 women); includes 85 minority (22 Black or African American, non-Hispanic/Latino; 18 American Indian or Alaska Native, non-Hispanic/Latino; 8 Asian, non-Hispanic/Latino; 17 Hispanic/Latino; 20 Two or more races, non-Hispanic/Latino), 11 international. Average age 31. 234 applicants, 30% accepted, 55 enrolled. In 2011, 72 master's, 26 doctorates awarded. *Degree requirements:* For master's, thesis (for some programs); for doctorate, comprehensive exam, thesis/dissertation. *Entrance requirements:* For master's and doctorate, GRE or GMAT. Additional exam requirements/recommendations for international students: Required—TOEFL (minimum score 550 paper-based; 79 iBT). *Application deadline:* For fall admission, 3/1 for international students; for spring admission, 8/1 for international students. Applications are processed on a rolling basis. Application fee: $40 ($75 for international students). Electronic applications accepted. *Expenses:* Tuition, state resident: full-time $4044; part-time $168.50 per credit hour. Tuition, nonresident: full-time $16,008; part-time $667 per credit hour. *Required fees:* $2122; $88.45 per credit hour. One-time fee: $50. Tuition and fees vary according to course load and campus/location. *Financial support:* In 2011–12, 17 research assistantships (averaging $9,302 per year), 70 teaching assistantships (averaging $8,447 per year) were awarded; career-related internships or fieldwork, Federal Work-Study, scholarships/grants, health care benefits, tuition waivers (partial), and unspecified assistantships also available. Support available to part-time students. Financial award application deadline: 3/1; financial award applicants required to submit FAFSA. *Unit head:* Dr. John Romans, Head, 405-744-6040, Fax: 405-744-6779. *Application contact:* Dr. Sheryl Tucker, Dean, 405-744-7099, Fax: 405-744-0355, E-mail: grad-i@okstate.edu. Web site: http://education.okstate.edu/index.php/academic-units/school-of-applied-health-a-educational-psychology.

Penn State University Park, Graduate School, College of Education, Department of Educational Psychology and Special Education, State College, University Park, PA 16802-1503. Offers counselor education (M Ed, MS, PhD); educational psychology (MS, PhD, Certificate); school psychology (M Ed, MS, PhD, Certificate); special education (M Ed, MS, PhD, Certificate). *Unit head:* Dr. David H. Monk, Dean, 814-865-2526, Fax: 814-865-0555, E-mail: dhm6@psu.edu. *Application contact:* Cynthia E. Nicosia, Director, Graduate Enrollment Services, 814-865-1834, E-mail: cey1@psu.edu. Web site: http://www.ed.psu.edu/educ/epcse.

Pontifical Catholic University of Puerto Rico, College of Education, Program in Educational Psychology, Ponce, PR 00717-0777. Offers M Ed. *Degree requirements:* For master's, comprehensive exam, thesis (for some programs). *Entrance requirements:* For master's, GRE, 2 letters of recommendation, interview, minimum GPA of 2.75.

Purdue University, Graduate School, College of Education, Department of Educational Studies, West Lafayette, IN 47907. Offers administration (MS Ed, PhD, Ed S); counseling and development (MS Ed, PhD); education of the gifted (MS Ed); educational psychology (MS Ed, PhD); foundations of education (MS Ed, PhD); higher education administration (MS Ed, PhD); special education (MS Ed, PhD). *Accreditation:* ACA (one or more programs are accredited); NCATE (one or more programs are accredited). Part-time and evening/weekend programs available. *Faculty:* 23 full-time

(17 women), 1 part-time/adjunct (0 women). *Students:* 111 full-time (79 women), 93 part-time (58 women); includes 34 minority (19 Black or African American, non-Hispanic/ Latino; 1 American Indian or Alaska Native, non-Hispanic/Latino; 4 Asian, non-Hispanic/ Latino; 6 Hispanic/Latino; 4 Two or more races, non-Hispanic/Latino), 30 international. Average age 35. 249 applicants, 37% accepted, 46 enrolled. In 2011, 39 master's, 20 doctorates, 4 other advanced degrees awarded. *Degree requirements:* For master's, thesis optional; for doctorate, thesis/dissertation, oral and written exams; for Ed S, oral presentation, project. *Entrance requirements:* For master's, GRE General Test required for all Educational Studies program areas, except for Special Education if undergraduate GPA is higher than a 3.0, minimum undergraduate GPA of 3.0; for doctorate and Ed S, GRE general test is required, a combined score of 1000 (300 for revised GRE test) or more is expected., minimum undergraduate GPA of 3.0. Additional exam requirements/ recommendations for international students: Required—TOEFL (minimum score 550 paper-based; 77 iBT), TWE (minimum score 5). *Application deadline:* Applications are processed on a rolling basis. Application fee: $60 ($75 for international students). Electronic applications accepted. *Financial support:* Fellowships with full tuition reimbursements, research assistantships with full tuition reimbursements, teaching assistantships with full tuition reimbursements, career-related internships or fieldwork, and tuition waivers (full) available. Support available to part-time students. Financial award application deadline: 3/1; financial award applicants required to submit FAFSA. *Faculty research:* Motivation, learning disabilities, school learning, group processes, cognitive development. *Unit head:* Dr. Ala Samrapungavan, Head, 765-494-9170, Fax: 765-496-1228, E-mail: ala@purdue.edu. *Application contact:* Sarah N. Prater, Graduate Contact, 765-494-2345, Fax: 765-494-5832, E-mail: prater0@purdue.edu. Web site: http://www.edst.purdue.edu/.

Regent University, Graduate School, School of Education, Virginia Beach, VA 23464-9800. Offers adult education (Ed D); adult/staff development (Ed D, PhD); career switcher with licensure (M Ed), including alternative licensure; character education (Ed D, PhD); Christian education leadership (Ed D, PhD); Christian education specialist (Ed S); Christian school program (M Ed), including ACSI licensure; distance education (Ed D, PhD); education licensure (M Ed), including preK-6th grade; educational leadership (M Ed, PhD); educational leadership - special education (Ed S), including administration and supervision; educational psychology (Ed D, PhD), including learning and development, research and evaluation, special education; higher education (Ed D, PhD), including administration, research and institutional planning, teaching; higher education leadership (Ed D); individualized degree plan (M Ed), including behavior disorders, learning disabilities, mental retardation, reading specialist; K-12 school leadership (Ed D, PhD); leadership in character education (M Ed); master teacher (M Ed), including TESOL; mathematics education (M Ed); special education (PhD); student affairs (M Ed); TESOL (M Ed), including adult education, ESL: preK-12. *Accreditation:* Teacher Education Accreditation Council. Part-time and evening/weekend programs available. Postbaccalaureate distance learning degree programs offered (minimal on-campus study). *Faculty:* 26 full-time (13 women), 54 part-time/adjunct (34 women). *Students:* 140 full-time (109 women), 786 part-time (626 women); includes 218 minority (189 Black or African American, non-Hispanic/Latino; 2 American Indian or Alaska Native, non-Hispanic/Latino; 11 Asian, non-Hispanic/Latino; 16 Hispanic/Latino), 42 international. Average age 39. 673 applicants, 57% accepted, 298 enrolled. In 2011, 178 master's, 15 doctorates awarded. *Degree requirements:* For master's, thesis or alternative; for doctorate, comprehensive exam, thesis/dissertation. *Entrance requirements:* For master's, MAT, minimum undergraduate GPA of 2.75, writing sample, resume, recommendations, interview; for doctorate, GRE, writing sample, 3 years of relevant professional experience, master's-level paper, copies of published work, resume, transcripts, interview, recommendations. Additional exam requirements/ recommendations for international students: Required—TOEFL (minimum score 577 paper-based; 233 computer-based). *Application deadline:* For fall admission, 4/1 priority date for domestic students; for spring admission, 10/15 priority date for domestic students. Applications are processed on a rolling basis. Application fee: $50. Electronic applications accepted. *Expenses:* Contact institution. *Financial support:* Fellowships, career-related internships or fieldwork, scholarships/grants, tuition waivers (full and partial), and unspecified assistantships available. Support available to part-time students. Financial award application deadline: 4/1; financial award applicants required to submit FAFSA. *Faculty research:* Character development and discipline for children, education leadership development, diversity in schools, classroom management, technology in education settings. *Unit head:* Dr. Alan A. Arroyo, Dean, 757-352-4261, Fax: 757-352-4318, E-mail: alanarr@regent.edu. *Application contact:* Matthew Chadwick, Director of Enrollment Support Services, 800-373-5504, Fax: 757-352-4381, E-mail: admissions@regent.edu. Web site: http://www.regent.edu/education/.

Rutgers, The State University of New Jersey, New Brunswick, Graduate School of Education, Department of Educational Psychology, Program in Learning, Cognition and Development, Piscataway, NJ 08854-8097. Offers Ed M. Part-time and evening/ weekend programs available. *Entrance requirements:* For master's, GRE General Test, 3 letters of recommendation. Additional exam requirements/recommendations for international students: Required—TOEFL (minimum score 550 paper-based; 233 computer-based; 83 iBT). Electronic applications accepted. *Faculty research:* Cognitive development, gender roles, cognition and instruction, peer learning, infancy and early childhood.

Rutgers, The State University of New Jersey, New Brunswick, Graduate School of Education, Doctoral Program in Education, New Brunswick, NJ 08901. Offers educational policy (PhD); educational psychology (PhD); literacy education (PhD); mathematics education (PhD). Part-time programs available. *Degree requirements:* For doctorate, thesis/dissertation, qualifying exam. *Entrance requirements:* For doctorate, GRE General Test, GRE Subject Test (mathematics education). Additional exam requirements/recommendations for international students: Required—TOEFL (minimum score 575 paper-based; 233 computer-based; 83 iBT). Electronic applications accepted. *Faculty research:* Literacy education, math education, educational psychology, educational policy, learning sciences.

Simon Fraser University, Graduate Studies, Faculty of Education, Program in Educational Psychology, Burnaby, BC V5A 1S6, Canada. Offers M Ed, MA, PhD. *Degree requirements:* For master's, project or thesis; for doctorate, thesis/dissertation. *Entrance requirements:* For master's, minimum GPA of 3.0; for doctorate, GRE, master's degree or exceptional record in a bachelor's degree, minimum GPA of 3.5. Additional exam requirements/recommendations for international students: Required—TOEFL or IELTS.

Southern Illinois University Carbondale, Graduate School, College of Education and Human Services, Department of Educational Psychology and Special Education, Program in Educational Psychology, Carbondale, IL 62901-4701. Offers counselor education (MS Ed, PhD); educational psychology (PhD); human learning and development (MS Ed); measurement and statistics (PhD). *Accreditation:* NCATE. *Faculty:* 19 full-time (9 women), 7 part-time/adjunct (2 women). *Students:* 47 full-time (33 women), 20 part-time (12 women); includes 12 minority (10 Black or African American, non-Hispanic/Latino; 1 Asian, non-Hispanic/Latino; 1 Hispanic/Latino), 11 international. Average age 36. 29 applicants, 62% accepted, 8 enrolled. In 2011, 21 master's, 3 doctorates awarded. *Degree requirements:* For master's, thesis; for doctorate, thesis/dissertation. *Entrance requirements:* For master's, GRE General Test, minimum GPA of 2.7; for doctorate, minimum GPA of 3.25. Additional exam requirements/recommendations for international students: Required—TOEFL. *Application deadline:* For fall admission, 6/15 priority date for domestic students. Applications are processed on a rolling basis. Application fee: $20. *Financial support:* In 2011–12, 36 students received support, including 2 fellowships with full tuition reimbursements available, 4 research assistantships with full tuition reimbursements available; teaching assistantships with full tuition reimbursements available, career-related internships or fieldwork, Federal Work-Study, institutionally sponsored loans, and tuition waivers (full) also available. Support available to part-time students. Financial award application deadline: 5/1. *Faculty research:* Career development, problem solving, learning and instruction, cognitive development, family assessment. *Total annual research expenditures:* $10,000. *Unit head:* Dr. Lyle White, Chairperson, 618-536-7763, E-mail: lwhite@siu.edu. *Application contact:* Cathy Earnhart, Administrative Clerk, 618-453-6932, E-mail: pern@siu.edu.

Stanford University, School of Education, Program in Psychological Studies in Education, Stanford, CA 94305-9991. Offers child and adolescent development (PhD); counseling psychology (PhD); educational psychology (PhD). *Degree requirements:* For doctorate, thesis/dissertation. *Entrance requirements:* For doctorate, GRE General Test. Electronic applications accepted. *Expenses: Tuition:* Full-time $40,050; part-time $890 per credit.

State University of New York College at Oneonta, Graduate Education, Division of Education, Department of Educational Psychology and Counseling, Oneonta, NY 13820-4015. Offers school counselor K-12 (MS Ed, CAS). *Accreditation:* NCATE. Part-time and evening/weekend programs available. *Degree requirements:* For master's, comprehensive exam. *Entrance requirements:* For master's, GRE General Test.

Teachers College, Columbia University, Graduate Faculty of Education, Department of Health and Behavioral Studies, Program in Applied Educational Psychology–School Psychology, New York, NY 10027. Offers Ed M, MA, Ed D, PhD. *Accreditation:* APA (one or more programs are accredited). *Faculty:* 4 full-time (2 women), 12 part-time/ adjunct (10 women). *Students:* 41 full-time (39 women), 63 part-time (55 women); includes 21 minority (4 Black or African American, non-Hispanic/Latino; 5 Asian, non-Hispanic/Latino; 8 Hispanic/Latino; 3 Native Hawaiian or other Pacific Islander, non-Hispanic/Latino; 1 Two or more races, non-Hispanic/Latino), 7 international. Average age 26. 151 applicants, 30% accepted, 25 enrolled. In 2011, 25 master's, 8 doctorates awarded. *Degree requirements:* For master's, project; for doctorate, comprehensive exam, thesis/dissertation. *Entrance requirements:* For master's, GRE General Test (for Ed M); for doctorate, GRE General Test. *Application deadline:* For fall admission, 12/15 for domestic students. Application fee: $65. *Financial support:* Fellowships, research assistantships, career-related internships or fieldwork, Federal Work-Study, institutionally sponsored loans, and tuition waivers (full and partial) available. Support available to part-time students. Financial award application deadline: 2/1; financial award applicants required to submit FAFSA. *Faculty research:* Psychoeducational assessment, observation and concept acquisition in young children, reading, mathematical thinking, memory. *Unit head:* Prof. Marla Brassard, Chair, 212-678-3942, E-mail: brassard@tc.edu. *Application contact:* Peter Shon, Assistant Director of Admission, 212-678-3305, Fax: 212-678-4171, E-mail: shon@ exchange.tc.columbia.edu. Web site: http://www.tc.edu/hbs/SchoolPsych/.

Teachers College, Columbia University, Graduate Faculty of Education, Department of Human Development, Program in Educational Psychology-Human Cognition and Learning, New York, NY 10027-6696. Offers Ed M, MA, Ed D, PhD. *Accreditation:* APA (one or more programs are accredited). Part-time programs available. *Faculty:* 4 full-time (2 women). *Students:* 19 full-time (15 women), 73 part-time (49 women); includes 23 minority (9 Black or African American, non-Hispanic/Latino; 13 Asian, non-Hispanic/ Latino; 1 Hispanic/Latino), 18 international. Average age 33. 56 applicants, 80% accepted, 15 enrolled. Terminal master's awarded for partial completion of doctoral program. *Degree requirements:* For master's, integrative paper; for doctorate, thesis/ dissertation, integrative project. *Entrance requirements:* For doctorate, GRE General Test. *Application deadline:* For fall admission, 5/15 for domestic students; for spring admission, 12/1 for domestic students. Application fee: $65. *Financial support:* Fellowships, research assistantships, career-related internships or fieldwork, Federal Work-Study, institutionally sponsored loans, and tuition waivers (full and partial) available. Support available to part-time students. Financial award application deadline: 2/1. *Faculty research:* Early reading, text comprehension, learning disabilities, mathematical thinking, reasoning. *Unit head:* Prof. John B. Black, Program Coordinator, 212-678-4150. *Application contact:* David Estrella, Associate Director of Admission, 212-678-3710, Fax: 212-678-4171, E-mail: tcinfo@tc.edu.

Temple University, College of Education, Department of Psychological Studies in Education, Program in Educational Psychology, Philadelphia, PA 19122-6096. Offers Ed M, PhD. Part-time and evening/weekend programs available. *Students:* 36 full-time (28 women), 29 part-time (18 women); includes 12 minority (9 Black or African American, non-Hispanic/Latino; 1 Asian, non-Hispanic/Latino; 2 Hispanic/Latino), 3 international. Average age 36. 33 applicants, 70% accepted, 16 enrolled. In 2011, 8 master's, 11 doctorates awarded. Terminal master's awarded for partial completion of doctoral program. *Degree requirements:* For master's, thesis or alternative; for doctorate, thesis/dissertation. *Entrance requirements:* For master's and doctorate, GRE General Test or MAT, minimum GPA of 3.0. Additional exam requirements/ recommendations for international students: Required—TOEFL (minimum score 550 paper-based; 213 computer-based; 79 iBT). *Application deadline:* For fall admission, 5/1 for domestic students, 12/15 for international students; for spring admission, 11/1 for domestic students, 8/1 for international students. Applications are processed on a rolling basis. Application fee: $50. Electronic applications accepted. *Expenses:* Tuition, state resident: full-time $12,366; part-time $687 per credit hour. Tuition, nonresident: full-time $17,298; part-time $961 per credit hour. *Required fees:* $590; $213 per year. *Financial support:* Fellowships, research assistantships with full tuition reimbursements, and teaching assistantships with full tuition reimbursements available. Financial award application deadline: 1/15; financial award applicants required to submit FAFSA. *Faculty research:* Computers in education, student motivation, school improvement in city schools, individual differences in learning, teaching strategies. *Unit head:* Dr. Joseph Ducette, Head, 215-204-4998, E-mail: joseph.ducette@temple.edu. *Application contact:* Dr. Margo Greicar, Director for Graduate Academic and Student Affairs, 215-204-8011, Fax: 215-204-4383, E-mail: margo.greicar@temple.edu. Web site: http:// www.temple.edu/education/edpsych/index.html.

Tennessee Technological University, Graduate School, College of Education, Department of Counseling and Psychology, Cookeville, TN 38505. Offers agency counselor (MA, Ed S); case management and supervision (MA); educational psychology (MA, Ed S); mental health counseling (MA); school counselor (MA, Ed S); school psychology (MA, Ed S). *Accreditation:* NCATE (one or more programs are accredited). Part-time and evening/weekend programs available. *Faculty:* 24 full-time (6 women). *Students:* 72 full-time (56 women), 49 part-time (39 women); includes 8 minority (6 Black or African American, non-Hispanic/Latino; 1 American Indian or Alaska Native, non-Hispanic/Latino; 1 Native Hawaiian or other Pacific Islander, non-Hispanic/Latino), 1 international. Average age 27. 62 applicants, 77% accepted, 33 enrolled. In 2011, 38 master's, 8 other advanced degrees awarded. *Degree requirements:* For master's and Ed S, comprehensive exam, thesis or alternative. *Entrance requirements:* For master's and Ed S, MAT or GRE. Additional exam requirements/recommendations for international students: Required—TOEFL (minimum score 527 paper-based; 71 iBT), IELTS (minimum score 5.5), Pearson Test of English Academic. *Application deadline:* For fall admission, 8/1 for domestic students, 5/1 for international students; for spring admission, 12/1 for domestic students, 10/1 for international students. Application fee: $25 ($30 for international students). Electronic applications accepted. *Expenses:* Tuition, state resident: full-time $8094; part-time $422 per credit hour. Tuition, nonresident: full-time $20,574; part-time $1046 per credit hour. *Financial support:* In 2011–12, 1 fellowship (averaging $8,000 per year), 8 research assistantships (averaging $4,000 per year), 3 teaching assistantships (averaging $4,000 per year) were awarded; career-related internships or fieldwork also available. Financial award application deadline: 4/1. *Unit head:* Dr. Barry Stein, Interim Chairperson, 931-372-3457, Fax: 931-372-6319, E-mail: bstein@tntech.edu. *Application contact:* Shelia K. Kendrick, Coordinator of Graduate Admissions, 931-372-3808, Fax: 931-372-3497, E-mail: skendrick@tntech.edu.

Texas A&M University, College of Education and Human Development, Department of Educational Psychology, College Station, TX 77843. Offers bilingual education (M Ed, PhD); cognition, creativity, instruction and development (MS, PhD); counseling psychology (PhD); educational psychology (PhD); educational technology (PhD); research, measurement and statistics (MS); research, measurement, and statistics (PhD); school psychology (PhD); special education (M Ed, PhD). *Accreditation:* APA (one or more programs are accredited). Part-time and evening/weekend programs available. Postbaccalaureate distance learning degree programs offered (no on-campus study). *Faculty:* 46. *Students:* 151 full-time (124 women), 123 part-time (101 women); includes 97 minority (20 Black or African American, non-Hispanic/Latino; 11 Asian, non-Hispanic/Latino; 59 Hispanic/Latino; 7 Two or more races, non-Hispanic/Latino), 50 international. In 2011, 58 master's, 33 doctorates awarded. *Degree requirements:* For master's, thesis optional; for doctorate, thesis/dissertation. *Entrance requirements:* For master's and doctorate, GRE General Test. Additional exam requirements/recommendations for international students: Required—TOEFL. Application fee: $50 ($75 for international students). Electronic applications accepted. *Expenses:* Tuition, state resident: full-time $5437; part-time $226.55 per credit hour. Tuition, nonresident: full-time $12,949; part-time $539.55 per credit hour. *Required fees:* $2741. *Financial support:* In 2011–12, fellowships (averaging $12,000 per year), research assistantships (averaging $9,000 per year), teaching assistantships (averaging $9,000 per year) were awarded; career-related internships or fieldwork, institutionally sponsored loans, scholarships/grants, and unspecified assistantships also available. Financial award applicants required to submit FAFSA. *Unit head:* Dr. Victor Willson, Head, 979-845-1800. *Application contact:* Carol A. Wagner, Director of Advising, 979-845-1833, Fax: 979-862-1256, E-mail: epsyadvisor@tamu.edu. Web site: http://epsy.tamu.edu.

Texas Christian University, College of Education, Program in Counseling, Fort Worth, TX 76129-0002. Offers counseling (M Ed, PhD); LPC (Certificate); school counseling (Certificate). Part-time and evening/weekend programs available. *Faculty:* 27 full-time (21 women), 1 part-time/adjunct. *Students:* 18 full-time (14 women), 29 part-time (25 women); includes 13 minority (4 Black or African American, non-Hispanic/Latino; 9 Hispanic/Latino). Average age 29. 28 applicants, 82% accepted, 21 enrolled. In 2011, 16 master's awarded. *Degree requirements:* For master's, oral exam. *Entrance requirements:* Additional exam requirements/recommendations for international students: Required—TOEFL (minimum score 550 paper-based; 213 computer-based; 80 iBT). *Application deadline:* For fall admission, 11/1 for domestic students, 11/16 for international students; for winter admission, 2/1 for domestic and international students; for spring admission, 3/1 for domestic and international students. Application fee: $50. Electronic applications accepted. *Expenses: Tuition:* Full-time $20,250; part-time $1125 per credit hour. Part-time tuition and fees vary according to course load and program. *Financial support:* Teaching assistantships with full tuition reimbursements, career-related internships or fieldwork, scholarships/grants, and unspecified assistantships available. Financial award application deadline: 3/1. *Unit head:* Dr. Jan Lacina, Associate Dean, 817-257-6786, E-mail: j.lacina@tcu.edu. *Application contact:* Patricia Garcia, Academic Program Specialist, 817-257-7661, E-mail: p.m.garcia@tcu.edu. Web site: http://www.coe.tcu.edu/283.asp.

Texas Christian University, College of Science and Engineering, Department of Psychology, Fort Worth, TX 76129-0002. Offers experimental psychology (PhD), including cognitive psychology, learning, neuropsychology, social psychology; psychology (MA, MS). *Faculty:* 13 full-time (3 women), 4 part-time/adjunct. *Students:* 14 full-time (8 women), 15 part-time (11 women); includes 1 minority (Two or more races, non-Hispanic/Latino), 5 international. Average age 29. 38 applicants, 42% accepted, 11 enrolled. In 2011, 10 master's, 5 doctorates awarded. Terminal master's awarded for partial completion of doctoral program. *Degree requirements:* For master's, thesis; for doctorate, thesis/dissertation. *Entrance requirements:* For master's and doctorate, GRE General Test. Additional exam requirements/recommendations for international students: Required—TOEFL. *Application deadline:* For fall admission, 3/1 for domestic and international students; for spring admission, 12/1 for domestic students. Applications are processed on a rolling basis. Application fee: $60. Electronic applications accepted. *Expenses: Tuition:* Full-time $20,250; part-time $1125 per credit hour. Part-time tuition and fees vary according to course load and program. *Financial support:* In 2011–12, 20 students received support. Teaching assistantships with full tuition reimbursements available and unspecified assistantships available. Financial award application deadline: 3/1. *Unit head:* Dr. Gary W. Boehm, Coordinator of Graduate Studies, 817-257-7410, Fax: 817-257-7681, E-mail: g.boehm@tcu.edu. *Application contact:* Tami Joyce, Department Manager, 817-257-6437, Fax: 817-257-7681, E-mail: t.joyce@tcu.edu. Web site: http://www.psy.tcu.edu/gradpro.html.

Texas Tech University, Graduate School, College of Education, Department of Educational Psychology and Leadership, Lubbock, TX 79409. Offers counselor education (M Ed, PhD); educational leadership (M Ed, Ed D); educational psychology (M Ed, PhD); higher education (M Ed, Ed D); higher education: higher education research (PhD); instructional technology (M Ed, Ed D); instructional technology: distance education (M Ed); special education (M Ed, Ed D). *Accreditation:* ACA; NCATE. Part-time programs available. Postbaccalaureate distance learning degree programs offered (no on-campus study). *Students:* 180 full-time (133 women), 418 part-time (297 women); includes 127 minority (34 Black or African American, non-Hispanic/Latino; 3 American Indian or Alaska Native, non-Hispanic/Latino; 6 Asian, non-Hispanic/Latino; 76 Hispanic/Latino; 8 Two or more races, non-Hispanic/Latino), 41 international. Average age 36. 478 applicants, 42% accepted, 134 enrolled. In 2011, 139 master's, 30 doctorates awarded. *Degree requirements:* For master's, thesis optional; for doctorate, thesis/dissertation. *Entrance requirements:* For master's and doctorate, GRE General Test. Additional exam requirements/recommendations for international students: Required—TOEFL (minimum score 550 paper-based; 213 computer-based; 79 iBT). *Application deadline:* For fall admission, 6/1 priority date for domestic students, 1/15 for international students; for spring admission, 9/1 priority date for domestic students, 6/15 for international students. Applications are processed on a rolling basis. Application fee: $50 ($75 for international students). Electronic applications accepted. *Expenses:* Tuition, state resident: full-time $5899; part-time $245.80 per credit hour. Tuition, nonresident: full-time $13,411; part-time $558.80 per credit hour. *Required fees:* $2680.60; $86.50 per credit hour. $920.30 per semester. *Financial support:* In 2011–12, 142 students received support. Application deadline: 4/15; applicants required to submit FAFSA. *Faculty research:* Psychological processes of teaching and learning, teaching populations with special needs, instructional technology, educational administration in education, theories and practice in counseling and counselor education K-12 and higher. *Total annual research expenditures:* $1.4 million. *Unit head:* Dr. William Lan, Chair, 806-742-1998 Ext. 436, Fax: 806-742-2179, E-mail: william.lan@ttu.edu. *Application contact:* Dr. Hansel Burley, Associate Academic Dean, 806-742-1998 Ext. 447, Fax: 806-742-2179, E-mail: hansel.burley@ttu.edu.

Union Institute & University, Programs in Psychology and Counseling, Brattleboro, VT 05301. Offers clinical mental health counseling (MA); clinical psychology (Psy D); counseling psychology (MA); counselor education and supervision (CAGS); developmental psychology (MA); educational psychology (MA); human development and wellness (CAGS); organizational psychology (MA); psychology education (CAGS). Psy D offered in Ohio and Vermont. Postbaccalaureate distance learning degree programs offered (minimal on-campus study). *Degree requirements:* For master's, thesis, internship (depending on concentration); for doctorate, thesis/dissertation, internship, practicum. Electronic applications accepted.

Universidad de Iberoamerica, Graduate School, San Jose, Costa Rica. Offers clinical neuropsychology (PhD); clinical psychology (M Psych); educational psychology (M Psych); forensic psychology (M Psych); hospital management (MHA); intensive care nursing (MN); medicine (MD).

Université de Moncton, Faculty of Education, Graduate Studies in Education, Moncton, NB E1A 3E9, Canada. Offers educational psychology (M Ed, MA Ed); guidance (M Ed, MA Ed); school administration (M Ed, MA Ed); teaching (M Ed, MA Ed). Part-time programs available. *Degree requirements:* For master's, proficiency in English and French. *Entrance requirements:* For master's, minimum GPA of 3.0. *Faculty research:* Guidance, ethnolinguistic vitality, children's rights, ecological education, entrepreneurship.

Université de Montréal, Faculty of Education, Department of Psychopedagogy and Andragogy, Montréal, QC H3C 3J7, Canada. Offers M Ed, MA, PhD, DESS. Part-time and evening/weekend programs available. Terminal master's awarded for partial completion of doctoral program. *Degree requirements:* For master's, thesis (for some programs); for doctorate, thesis/dissertation, general exam. *Entrance requirements:* For doctorate, MA or M Ed. Electronic applications accepted.

Université du Québec à Trois-Rivières, Graduate Programs, Program in Psychoeducation, Trois-Rivières, QC G9A 5H7, Canada. Offers M Ed, PhD. M Ed offered jointly with Université du Québec en Outaouais. *Entrance requirements:* For master's, appropriate bachelor's degree, proficiency in French. *Faculty research:* Troubled youth intervention.

Université du Québec en Outaouais, Graduate Programs, Program in Psychoéducation, Gatineau, QC J8X 3X7, Canada. Offers M Ed, MA. Part-time programs available. *Students:* 69 full-time, 47 part-time, 1 international. *Degree requirements:* For master's, thesis (for some programs). *Entrance requirements:* For master's, appropriate bachelor's degree, proficiency in French. *Application deadline:* For fall admission, 6/1 priority date for domestic students, 3/1 for international students; for winter admission, 11/1 priority date for domestic students, 10/1 for international students. Application fee: $30 Canadian dollars. *Financial support:* Fellowships, research assistantships, and teaching assistantships available. *Unit head:* Line Leblanc, Director, 819-595-3900 Ext. 2289, Fax: 819-595-2250, E-mail: line.leblanc@uqo.ca. *Application contact:* Registrar's Office, 819-773-1850, Fax: 819-773-1835, E-mail: registraire@uqo.ca.

Université Laval, Faculty of Education, Department of Teaching and Learning Studies, Programs in Educational Psychology, Québec, QC G1K 7P4, Canada. Offers MA, PhD. Terminal master's awarded for partial completion of doctoral program. *Degree requirements:* For master's, thesis (for some programs); for doctorate, comprehensive exam, thesis/dissertation. *Entrance requirements:* For master's and doctorate, English exam (comprehension of written English), knowledge of French. Electronic applications accepted. *Faculty research:* Emotional, social, and cognitive development; learning and motivation in school; language development; reading acquisition; computer and learning strategies.

University at Albany, State University of New York, School of Education, Department of Educational and Counseling Psychology, Albany, NY 12222-0001. Offers counseling psychology (MS, PhD, CAS); educational psychology (Ed D); educational psychology and statistics (MS); measurements and evaluation (Ed D); rehabilitation counseling (MS), including counseling psychology; school counselor (CAS); school psychology (Psy D, CAS); special education (MS); statistics and research design (Ed D). *Accreditation:* APA (one or more programs are accredited). Evening/weekend programs available. *Degree requirements:* For doctorate, thesis/dissertation. *Entrance requirements:* For doctorate, GRE General Test. Additional exam requirements/recommendations for international students: Required—TOEFL (minimum score 550 paper-based; 213 computer-based). Electronic applications accepted.

University at Buffalo, the State University of New York, Graduate School, Graduate School of Education, Department of Counseling, School, and Educational Psychology, Buffalo, NY 14260. Offers counseling/school psychology (PhD); counselor education (PhD); educational psychology (MA, PhD); general education (Ed M); mental health counseling (MS); mental health counseling (online) (Certificate); rehabilitation counseling (MS); school counseling (Ed M, Certificate). *Accreditation:* CORE (one or more programs are accredited). Part-time programs available. Postbaccalaureate distance learning degree programs offered (no on-campus study). *Faculty:* 22 full-time (14 women), 30 part-time/adjunct (26 women). *Students:* 154 full-time (123 women), 116 part-time (92 women); includes 45 minority (24 Black or African American, non-Hispanic/Latino; 3 American Indian or Alaska Native, non-Hispanic/Latino; 9 Asian, non-Hispanic/Latino; 9 Hispanic/Latino), 24 international. Average age 30. 344 applicants, 30% accepted, 98 enrolled. In 2011, 57 master's, 13 doctorates, 19 other advanced degrees awarded. *Degree requirements:* For master's, comprehensive exam (for some programs), thesis (for some programs); for doctorate, comprehensive exam, thesis/dissertation. *Entrance requirements:* For master's and doctorate, GRE General Test, interview, letters of reference. Additional exam requirements/recommendations for international students: Required—TOEFL (minimum score 79 iBT). *Application deadline:* For fall admission, 2/1 priority date for domestic students, 2/1 for international students. Application fee: $50. Electronic applications accepted. *Financial support:* In 2011–12, 25 fellowships (averaging $9,000 per year), 47 research assistantships (averaging $10,074 per year) were awarded; teaching assistantships with tuition reimbursements, career-related internships or fieldwork, Federal Work-Study, institutionally sponsored loans, and unspecified assistantships also available. Financial award application deadline: 2/1; financial award applicants required to submit FAFSA. *Faculty research:* Multicultural counseling, class size effects, good work in counseling, eating disorders, outcome assessment, change agents and therapeutic factors in group counseling. *Unit head:* Dr. Timothy Janikowski, Chair, 716-645-2484, Fax: 716-645-6616, E-mail:

tjanikow@buffalo.edu. *Application contact:* Rochelle Cohen, Admissions Assistant, 716-645-2110, Fax: 716-645-7937, E-mail: recohen@buffalo.edu.

University of Alberta, Faculty of Graduate Studies and Research, Department of Educational Psychology, Edmonton, AB T6G 2E1, Canada. Offers counseling psychology (M Ed, PhD); educational psychology (M Ed, PhD); instructional technology (M Ed); school counseling (M Ed); school psychology (M Ed, PhD); special education (M Ed, PhD); special education-deafness studies (M Ed); teaching English as a second language (M Ed). Part-time programs available. *Degree requirements:* For master's, thesis optional; for doctorate, comprehensive exam, thesis/dissertation. *Entrance requirements:* For master's and doctorate, minimum GPA of 3.0. Additional exam requirements/recommendations for international students: Required—TOEFL. *Faculty research:* Human learning, development and assessment.

The University of Arizona, College of Education, Department of Educational Psychology, Tucson, AZ 85721. Offers educational psychology (MA, PhD, Ed S); school counseling and guidance (M Ed). *Accreditation:* APA (one or more programs are accredited). Part-time programs available. *Faculty:* 1 (woman) full-time. *Students:* 39 full-time (25 women), 7 part-time (5 women); includes 14 minority (2 Black or African American, non-Hispanic/Latino; 1 American Indian or Alaska Native, non-Hispanic/Latino; 1 Asian, non-Hispanic/Latino; 5 Hispanic/Latino; 1 Native Hawaiian or other Pacific Islander, non-Hispanic/Latino; 4 Two or more races, non-Hispanic/Latino), 4 international. Average age 30. 36 applicants, 36% accepted, 9 enrolled. In 2011, 4 master's, 6 doctorates awarded. Terminal master's awarded for partial completion of doctoral program. *Degree requirements:* For master's, comprehensive exam (for some programs), thesis optional; for doctorate, comprehensive exam, thesis/dissertation. *Entrance requirements:* For master's, minimum GPA of 3.0, 3 letters of recommendation, 500-word professional writing sample; for doctorate, GRE General Test, minimum GPA of 3.0, 3 letters of recommendation, statement of purpose, 500-word professional writing sample. Additional exam requirements/recommendations for international students: Required—TOEFL (minimum score 600 paper-based; 250 computer-based). *Application deadline:* For fall admission, 3/1 for domestic students; for spring admission, 10/1 for domestic students. Applications are processed on a rolling basis. Application fee: $65. Electronic applications accepted. *Expenses:* Tuition, state resident: full-time $10,840. Tuition, nonresident: full-time $25,802. *Financial support:* In 2011–12, 1 research assistantship with full tuition reimbursement (averaging $26,438 per year), 10 teaching assistantships with full tuition reimbursements (averaging $21,191 per year) were awarded; career-related internships or fieldwork, scholarships/grants, health care benefits, tuition waivers (partial), and unspecified assistantships also available. *Faculty research:* School reform, motivational learning in classroom settings, measurement and evaluation of learning outcomes, student resilience, preadolescent and adolescent development. *Total annual research expenditures:* $344,778. *Unit head:* Dr. Thomas Good, Department Head, 520-621-7828, Fax: 520-621-2909, E-mail: goodt@u.arizona.edu. *Application contact:* Toni Sollars, Administrative Associate, 520-621-7828, Fax: 520-621-2909, E-mail: tsollars@u.arizona.edu. Web site: http://www.coe.arizona.edu/ep.

University of California, Davis, Graduate Studies, Graduate Group in Education, Davis, CA 95616. Offers education (MA, Ed D); instructional studies (PhD); psychological studies (PhD); sociocultural studies (PhD). Ed D offered jointly with California State University, Fresno. Terminal master's awarded for partial completion of doctoral program. *Degree requirements:* For master's, comprehensive exam (for some programs), thesis (for some programs); for doctorate, thesis/dissertation. *Entrance requirements:* For master's and doctorate, GRE. Additional exam requirements/recommendations for international students: Required—TOEFL (minimum score 550 paper-based; 213 computer-based). Electronic applications accepted. *Faculty research:* Language and literacy, mathematics education, science education, teacher development, school psychology.

University of California, Riverside, Graduate Division, Graduate School of Education, Riverside, CA 92521-0102. Offers autism (M Ed); diversity and equity (M Ed); education, society and culture (MA, PhD); educational psychology (MA, PhD); general education (M Ed); higher education administration and policy (M Ed, PhD); reading (M Ed); school psychology (PhD); special education (M Ed, MA, PhD). *Faculty:* 19 full-time (9 women), 9 part-time/adjunct (6 women). *Students:* 181 full-time (128 women); includes 79 minority (8 Black or African American, non-Hispanic/Latino; 1 American Indian or Alaska Native, non-Hispanic/Latino; 26 Asian, non-Hispanic/Latino; 34 Hispanic/Latino; 10 Two or more races, non-Hispanic/Latino), 5 international. Average age 31. 200 applicants, 48% accepted, 76 enrolled. In 2011, 67 master's, 12 doctorates awarded. Terminal master's awarded for partial completion of doctoral program. *Degree requirements:* For master's, thesis optional, comprehensive exams or thesis (MA), case study or analytical report (M Ed); for doctorate, thesis/dissertation, written and oral qualifying exams, college teaching practicum. *Entrance requirements:* For master's, GRE General Test, CBEST, CSET, minimum GPA of 3.2; for doctorate, GRE General Test, master's degree (desirable), minimum GPA of 3.2. Additional exam requirements/recommendations for international students: Required—TOEFL (minimum score 550 paper-based; 213 computer-based; 80 iBT), IELTS (minimum score 7). *Application deadline:* For fall admission, 9/1 for domestic students, 4/1 for international students; for winter admission, 12/1 for domestic students, 7/1 for international students; for spring admission, 3/1 for domestic students, 10/1 for international students. Applications are processed on a rolling basis. Application fee: $80 ($100 for international students). Electronic applications accepted. *Financial support:* In 2011–12, 59 students received support, including 9 fellowships with full and partial tuition reimbursements available (averaging $26,587 per year), 21 research assistantships with full and partial tuition reimbursements available (averaging $14,517 per year), 1 teaching assistantship with full and partial tuition reimbursement available (averaging $17,307 per year); career-related internships or fieldwork, Federal Work-Study, institutionally sponsored loans, scholarships/grants, and unspecified assistantships also available. Financial award application deadline: 1/5. *Faculty research:* Responsiveness to intervention, faculty core, response to intervention of English language learners, advanced modeling techniques, study on social capital, trust, and motivation. *Total annual research expenditures:* $2.8 million. *Unit head:* Prof. Douglas Mitchell, Interim Dean, 951-827-5802, Fax: 951-827-3942, E-mail: douglas.mitchell@ucr.edu. *Application contact:* Prof. Robert Ream, Graduate Advisor for Admission, 951-827-6362, Fax: 951-827-3291, E-mail: edgrad@ucr.edu. Web site: http://www.education.ucr.edu/.

University of Colorado Boulder, Graduate School, School of Education, Division of Educational and Psychological Studies, Boulder, CO 80309. Offers MA, PhD. *Accreditation:* NCATE. *Students:* 13 full-time (9 women), 1 (woman) part-time; includes 6 minority (1 Black or African American, non-Hispanic/Latino; 1 American Indian or Alaska Native, non-Hispanic/Latino; 1 Asian, non-Hispanic/Latino; 2 Hispanic/Latino; 1 Two or more races, non-Hispanic/Latino). Average age 33. 17 applicants, 35% accepted, 2 enrolled. In 2011, 3 master's, 4 doctorates awarded. Terminal master's awarded for partial completion of doctoral program. *Degree requirements:* For master's, comprehensive exam, thesis or alternative; for doctorate, one foreign language, comprehensive exam, thesis/dissertation. *Entrance requirements:* For master's, GRE General Test or MAT, minimum undergraduate GPA of 2.75; for doctorate, GRE General Test. *Application deadline:* For fall admission, 2/1 priority date for domestic students, 12/1 for international students; for spring admission, 9/1 for domestic students, 12/1 for international students. Application fee: $50 ($60 for international students). Electronic applications accepted. *Financial support:* In 2011–12, 23 students received support, including 9 fellowships (averaging $5,678 per year), 5 research assistantships with full and partial tuition reimbursements available (averaging $16,784 per year), 6 teaching assistantships with full and partial tuition reimbursements available (averaging $14,973 per year); institutionally sponsored loans, scholarships/grants, health care benefits, and unspecified assistantships also available. Financial award applicants required to submit FAFSA. *Application contact:* E-mail: edadvise@colorado.edu. Web site: http://www.colorado.edu/education/.

University of Colorado Denver, School of Education and Human Development, Programs in Educational and School Psychology, Denver, CO 80217. Offers educational psychology (MA), including educational assessment, educational psychology, human development, human learning, partner schools, research and evaluation; school psychology (Ed S). Part-time and evening/weekend programs available. *Students:* 105 full-time (86 women), 46 part-time (40 women); includes 12 minority (1 Black or African American, non-Hispanic/Latino; 5 Asian, non-Hispanic/Latino; 5 Hispanic/Latino; 1 Two or more races, non-Hispanic/Latino), 2 international. Average age 30. 77 applicants, 79% accepted, 40 enrolled. In 2011, 58 master's, 23 other advanced degrees awarded. *Degree requirements:* For master's, comprehensive exam, 9 hours of core courses, embedded within a minimum of 36 to 38 hours of relevant coursework, including an educational psychology practicum, independent study project or thesis (recommended); for Ed S, comprehensive exam, minimum of 75 semester hours (61 hours of coursework, 6 of 500-hour practicum in field, and 8 of 1200-hour internship); PRAXIS II. *Entrance requirements:* For master's, GRE if undergraduate GPA below 2.75, resume, written statement, three letters of recommendation, transcripts; for Ed S, GRE, resume, written statement, letters of recommendation, transcripts. Additional exam requirements/recommendations for international students: Required—TOEFL. *Application deadline:* For fall admission, 4/15 for domestic students, 4/1 for international students; for spring admission, 9/15 for domestic students, 9/1 for international students. Application fee: $50 ($75 for international students). Electronic applications accepted. *Expenses:* Contact institution. *Financial support:* Application deadline: 4/1; applicants required to submit FAFSA. *Faculty research:* Crisis response and Intervention, school violence prevention, immigrant experience, educational environments for English language learners, culturally competent assessment and intervention, child and youth suicide. *Unit head:* Dr. Jung-In Kim, Assistant Professor of Educational Psychology, 303-315-4965, E-mail: jung-in.kim@ucdenver.edu. *Application contact:* Student Services Center, 303-315-6300, Fax: 303-315-6311, E-mail: education@ucdenver.edu. Web site: http://www.ucdenver.edu/academics/colleges/SchoolOfEducation/Academics/EdS/Pages/EdSinSchoolPsychology.aspx.

University of Connecticut, Graduate School, Neag School of Education, Department of Educational Psychology, Storrs, CT 06269. Offers cognition and instruction (MA, PhD, Post-Master's Certificate); counseling psychology (MA, PhD, Post-Master's Certificate), including counseling psychology (PhD), school counseling (MA, Post-Master's Certificate); gifted and talented education (MA, PhD, Post-Master's Certificate); learning technology (MA, PhD, Post-Master's Certificate); measurement, evaluation, and assessment (MA, PhD, Post-Master's Certificate); school psychology (MA, PhD, Post-Master's Certificate); special education (MA, PhD, Post-Master's Certificate). *Degree requirements:* For master's, comprehensive exam; for doctorate, thesis/dissertation. *Entrance requirements:* For doctorate, GRE General Test. Additional exam requirements/recommendations for international students: Required—TOEFL (minimum score 550 paper-based; 213 computer-based). Electronic applications accepted.

University of Florida, Graduate School, College of Education, Department of Educational Psychology, Gainesville, FL 32611. Offers educational psychology (M Ed, MAE, Ed D, PhD, Ed S); research and evaluation methodology (M Ed, MAE, Ed D, PhD, Ed S). *Accreditation:* NCATE. Terminal master's awarded for partial completion of doctoral program. *Degree requirements:* For master's, thesis (MAE); for doctorate, variable foreign language requirement, thesis/dissertation. *Entrance requirements:* For master's and doctorate, GRE General Test, minimum GPA of 3.0; for Ed S, GRE General Test. Additional exam requirements/recommendations for international students: Required—TOEFL (minimum score 550 paper-based; 213 computer-based; 80 iBT), IELTS (minimum score 6). *Application deadline:* For fall admission, 6/1 priority date for domestic students. Applications are processed on a rolling basis. Application fee: $30. Electronic applications accepted. *Financial support:* Fellowships, research assistantships, teaching assistantships, career-related internships or fieldwork, and unspecified assistantships available. Financial award application deadline: 4/30; financial award applicants required to submit FAFSA. *Faculty research:* School improvement, teaching and learning, item response theory.

University of Georgia, College of Education, Department of Educational Psychology and Instructional Technology, Athens, GA 30602. Offers education of the gifted (Ed D); educational psychology (M Ed, MA, Ed D, PhD, Ed S); instructional technology (M Ed, PhD, Ed S). *Accreditation:* NCATE. *Faculty:* 27 full-time (11 women). *Students:* 109 full-time (82 women), 130 part-time (99 women); includes 38 minority (25 Black or African American, non-Hispanic/Latino; 1 American Indian or Alaska Native, non-Hispanic/Latino; 6 Asian, non-Hispanic/Latino; 5 Hispanic/Latino; 1 Two or more races, non-Hispanic/Latino), 47 international. Average age 33. 151 applicants, 36% accepted, 25 enrolled. In 2011, 51 master's, 23 doctorates, 32 other advanced degrees awarded. *Entrance requirements:* For master's and Ed S, GRE General Test or MAT; for doctorate, GRE General Test. *Application deadline:* For fall admission, 7/1 priority date for domestic students; for spring admission, 11/15 for domestic students. Application fee: $50. Electronic applications accepted. *Financial support:* Fellowships, research assistantships, teaching assistantships, and unspecified assistantships available. *Unit head:* Dr. Roy P. Martin, Acting Head, 706-542-4261, Fax: 706-542-4240, E-mail: rpmartin@uga.edu. *Application contact:* Dr. Bonnie Crammond, Graduate Coordinator, 706-542-4248, E-mail: bcrammond@uga.edu. Web site: http://www.coe.uga.edu/epit.

University of Hawaii at Manoa, Graduate Division, College of Education, Department of Educational Psychology, Honolulu, HI 96822. Offers M Ed, PhD. Part-time programs available. *Degree requirements:* For master's, thesis optional; for doctorate, comprehensive exam, thesis/dissertation. *Entrance requirements:* Additional exam requirements/recommendations for international students: Required—TOEFL (minimum score 600 paper-based; 250 computer-based; 100 iBT), IELTS (minimum score 7). *Faculty research:* Human learning and development, measurement, research methods, statistics.

University of Houston, College of Education, Department of Educational Psychology, Houston, TX 77204. Offers administration and supervision - higher education (M Ed); counseling (M Ed); counseling psychology (PhD); educational psychology (M Ed); school psychology (PhD); school psychology and individual differences (PhD); special education (M Ed). *Accreditation:* NCATE. Part-time and evening/weekend programs available. Postbaccalaureate distance learning degree programs offered. *Degree requirements:* For master's, comprehensive exam or thesis; for doctorate, comprehensive exam, thesis/dissertation. *Entrance requirements:* For master's, GRE, transcripts, 3 letters of recommendation, curriculum vita, goal statement; for doctorate, GRE, transcripts, 3 letters of recommendation, curriculum vita, goal statement, writing sample, interview. Additional exam requirements/recommendations for international students: Required—TOEFL (minimum score 550 paper-based; 79 iBT), IELTS (minimum score 6.5). Electronic applications accepted. *Faculty research:* Evidence-based assessment and intervention, multicultural issues in psychology, social and cultural context of learning, systemic barriers to college, motivational aspects of self-regulated learning.

University of Illinois at Chicago, Graduate College, College of Education, Department of Educational Psychology, Chicago, IL 60607-7128. Offers PhD.

University of Illinois at Urbana–Champaign, Graduate College, College of Education, Department of Educational Psychology, Champaign, IL 61820. Offers Ed M, MA, MS, PhD, CAS. *Accreditation:* APA (one or more programs are accredited). Part-time programs available. Postbaccalaureate distance learning degree programs offered. *Faculty:* 16 full-time (8 women). *Students:* 60 full-time (46 women), 35 part-time (30 women); includes 26 minority (9 Black or African American, non-Hispanic/Latino; 2 Asian, non-Hispanic/Latino; 12 Hispanic/Latino; 3 Two or more races, non-Hispanic/Latino), 32 international. 50 applicants, 46% accepted, 13 enrolled. In 2011, 23 master's, 18 doctorates awarded. *Entrance requirements:* For master's, minimum GPA of 3.5; for doctorate, GRE General Test, minimum GPA of 3.5. Additional exam requirements/recommendations for international students: Required—TOEFL (minimum score 610 paper-based; 253 computer-based; 102 iBT). *Application deadline:* Applications are processed on a rolling basis. Application fee: $75 ($90 for international students). Electronic applications accepted. *Financial support:* In 2011–12, 13 fellowships, 37 research assistantships, 39 teaching assistantships were awarded; tuition waivers (full and partial) also available. *Unit head:* Jose Mestre, Chair, 217-333-0098, Fax: 217-244-7620, E-mail: mestre@illinois.edu. *Application contact:* Myranda Lyons, Office Support Specialist, 217-244-3391, Fax: 217-244-7620, E-mail: mjlyons@illinois.edu. Web site: http://education.illinois.edu/EDPSY/.

The University of Iowa, Graduate College, College of Education, Department of Psychological and Quantitative Foundations, Iowa City, IA 52242-1316. Offers counseling psychology (PhD); educational measurement and statistics (MA, PhD); educational psychology (MA, PhD); school psychology (PhD, Ed S); JD/PhD. *Accreditation:* APA. *Degree requirements:* For master's, thesis optional, exam; for doctorate, comprehensive exam, thesis/dissertation; for Ed S, exam. *Entrance requirements:* For master's, doctorate, and Ed S, GRE General Test, minimum GPA of 3.0. Additional exam requirements/recommendations for international students: Required—TOEFL (minimum score 550 paper-based; 213 computer-based; 81 iBT). Electronic applications accepted.

The University of Kansas, Graduate Studies, School of Education, Department of Psychology and Research in Education, Program in Educational Psychology and Research, Lawrence, KS 66045. Offers MS Ed, PhD. *Faculty:* 4 full-time (1 woman). *Students:* 37 full-time (29 women), 8 part-time (5 women); includes 3 minority (all Black or African American, non-Hispanic/Latino), 20 international. Average age 32. 18 applicants, 61% accepted, 5 enrolled. In 2011, 1 master's, 2 doctorates awarded. *Degree requirements:* For master's, thesis; for doctorate, comprehensive exam, thesis/dissertation. *Entrance requirements:* For master's, GRE General Test, minimum GPA of 3.0; for doctorate, GRE General Test. Additional exam requirements/recommendations for international students: Required—TOEFL. *Application deadline:* For fall admission, 4/15 for domestic students; for spring admission, 11/15 for domestic students. Applications are processed on a rolling basis. Application fee: $55 ($65 for international students). Electronic applications accepted. Tuition and fees vary according to course load, campus/location, program and reciprocity agreements. *Financial support:* Fellowships, research assistantships with full and partial tuition reimbursements, teaching assistantships with full and partial tuition reimbursements, career-related internships or fieldwork, institutionally sponsored loans, scholarships/grants, traineeships, health care benefits, tuition waivers (full and partial), and unspecified assistantships available. Support available to part-time students. Financial award application deadline: 2/1. *Faculty research:* Educational measurement, applied statistics, research design, program evaluation, learning and development. *Unit head:* William Skorupski, Director of Training, 785-864-3931, E-mail: bfrey@ku.edu. *Application contact:* Loretta Warren, Admissions Coordinator, 785-864-9645, Fax: 785-864-3820, E-mail: preadmit@ku.edu. Web site: http://www.soe.ku.edu/PRE/.

University of Kentucky, Graduate School, College of Education, Program in Educational and Counseling Psychology, Lexington, KY 40506-0032. Offers counseling psychology (MS Ed, PhD, Ed S); educational and counseling psychology (MS Ed); educational psychology (Ed D, PhD, Ed S); school psychometrist and school psychology (MA Ed). *Accreditation:* APA (one or more programs are accredited); NCATE. *Degree requirements:* For master's, comprehensive exam, thesis optional; for doctorate, comprehensive exam, thesis/dissertation; for Ed S, comprehensive exam. *Entrance requirements:* For master's, GRE General Test, minimum undergraduate GPA of 2.75; for doctorate, GRE General Test, minimum graduate GPA of 3.0; for Ed S, GRE General Test. Additional exam requirements/recommendations for international students: Required—TOEFL (minimum score 550 paper-based; 213 computer-based). Electronic applications accepted.

University of Louisville, Graduate School, College of Education and Human Development, Department of Educational and Counseling Psychology, Louisville, KY 40292-0001. Offers counseling and personnel services (M Ed, PhD). *Accreditation:* APA; NCATE. Part-time and evening/weekend programs available. *Degree requirements:* For doctorate, comprehensive exam, thesis/dissertation. *Entrance requirements:* For master's and doctorate, GRE General Test. Additional exam requirements/recommendations for international students: Required—TOEFL (minimum score 560 paper-based; 210 computer-based; 83 iBT). Electronic applications accepted. *Expenses:* Tuition, state resident: full-time $9692; part-time $539 per credit hour. Tuition, nonresident: full-time $20,168; part-time $1121 per credit hour. Tuition and fees vary according to program and reciprocity agreements. *Faculty research:* Classroom processes, school outcomes, adolescent and adult development issues/prevention and treatment, multicultural counseling, spirituality, therapeutic outcomes, college student success, college student affairs administration, career development.

The University of Manchester, School of Education, Manchester, United Kingdom. Offers counseling (D Couns); counseling psychology (D Couns); education (M Phil, Ed D, PhD); educational and child psychology (Ed D); educational psychology (Ed D).

University of Manitoba, Faculty of Graduate Studies, Faculty of Education, Department of Educational Administration, Foundations and Psychology, Winnipeg, MB R3T 2N2, Canada. Offers adult and post-secondary education (M Ed); educational administration (M Ed); guidance and counseling (M Ed); inclusive special education (M Ed); social foundations of education (M Ed). *Degree requirements:* For master's, thesis or alternative.

University of Maryland, College Park, Academic Affairs, College of Education, Department of Human Development, College Park, MD 20742. Offers early childhood/elementary education (M Ed, MA, Ed D, PhD); human development (M Ed, MA, Ed D, PhD). *Accreditation:* NCATE. Part-time and evening/weekend programs available. Postbaccalaureate distance learning degree programs offered. *Faculty:* 50 full-time (43 women), 18 part-time/adjunct (16 women). *Students:* 58 full-time (52 women), 23 part-time (20 women); includes 23 minority (7 Black or African American, non-Hispanic/Latino; 7 Asian, non-Hispanic/Latino; 7 Hispanic/Latino; 1 Native Hawaiian or other Pacific Islander, non-Hispanic/Latino; 1 Two or more races, non-Hispanic/Latino), 7 international. 108 applicants, 22% accepted, 21 enrolled. In 2011, 21 master's, 6 doctorates awarded. *Degree requirements:* For master's, comprehensive exam, thesis optional; for doctorate, comprehensive exam, thesis/dissertation, essay, exam, research paper. *Entrance requirements:* For master's, GRE General Test, minimum GPA of 3.0, 3 letters of recommendation; for doctorate, GRE General Test or MAT, minimum undergraduate GPA of 3.0, graduate 3.5; 3 letters of recommendation. Additional exam requirements/recommendations for international students: Required—TOEFL. *Application deadline:* For fall admission, 3/15 for domestic students, 12/15 for international students; for spring admission, 10/1 priority date for domestic students, 6/1 for international students. Applications are processed on a rolling basis. Application fee: $75. Electronic applications accepted. *Expenses: Tuition, area resident:* Part-time $525 per credit hour. Tuition, state resident: part-time $525 per credit hour. Tuition, nonresident: part-time $1131 per credit hour. *Required fees:* $386.31 per term. Tuition and fees vary according to program. *Financial support:* In 2011–12, 5 fellowships with full and partial tuition reimbursements (averaging $16,476 per year), 38 teaching assistantships (averaging $17,258 per year) were awarded; Federal Work-Study and scholarships/grants also available. Support available to part-time students. Financial award applicants required to submit FAFSA. *Faculty research:* Developmental science, educational psychology, cognitive development, language development. *Total annual research expenditures:* $3.4 million. *Unit head:* Dr. Kathryn Wentzel, Interim Chair, 301-405-1659, Fax: 301-405-2891, E-mail: wentzel@umd.edu. *Application contact:* Dr. Charles A. Caramello, Dean of Graduate School, 301-405-0358, Fax: 301-314-9305.

University of Memphis, Graduate School, College of Education, Department of Counseling, Educational Psychology and Research, Memphis, TN 38152. Offers counseling (MS, Ed D), including community counseling (MS), rehabilitation counseling (MS), school counseling (MS); counseling psychology (PhD); educational psychology and research (MS, PhD), including educational psychology, educational research. *Accreditation:* ACA (one or more programs are accredited); APA (one or more programs are accredited); CORE (one or more programs are accredited); NCATE. *Degree requirements:* For master's, comprehensive exam, thesis or alternative; for doctorate, comprehensive exam, thesis/dissertation. *Entrance requirements:* For master's, GRE General Test or MAT, minimum GPA of 2.5; for doctorate, GRE General Test. *Faculty research:* Anger management, aging and disability, supervision, multicultural counseling.

University of Michigan–Dearborn, School of Education, Doctoral Program in Education, Dearborn, MI 48126. Offers curriculum and practice (Ed D); educational leadership (Ed D); educational psychology/special education (Ed D); metropolitan education (Ed D). Part-time and evening/weekend programs available. *Faculty:* 8 full-time (6 women), 2 part-time/adjunct (0 women). *Students:* 47 part-time (34 women); includes 12 minority (6 Black or African American, non-Hispanic/Latino; 3 Asian, non-Hispanic/Latino; 1 Hispanic/Latino; 2 Two or more races, non-Hispanic/Latino). Average age 40. 55 applicants, 35% accepted, 17 enrolled. *Degree requirements:* For doctorate, comprehensive exam, thesis/dissertation. *Entrance requirements:* For doctorate, GRE (taken within the last 5 years), master's degree with minimum GPA of 3.3, 3 letters of recommendation (1 from faculty), 3 years' professional and/or teaching experience. Additional exam requirements/recommendations for international students: Required—TOEFL (minimum score 550 paper-based). *Application deadline:* For fall admission, 3/1 for domestic and international students. Application fee: $60 ($75 for international students). *Financial support:* Scholarships/grants available. *Faculty research:* Educational leadership, metropolitan education, curriculum and practice, educational psychology, special education, assessment. *Unit head:* Bonnie Beyer, Coordinator, 313-593-5583, E-mail: beyer@umd.umich.edu. *Application contact:* Catherine Parkins, Customer Service Assistant, 313-583-6349, Fax: 313-593-4748, E-mail: cparkins@umd.umich.edu. Web site: http://www.soe.umd.umich.edu/soe_edd/.

University of Minnesota, Twin Cities Campus, Graduate School, College of Education and Human Development, Department of Educational Psychology, Minneapolis, MN 55455-0213. Offers counseling and student personnel psychology (MA, PhD, Ed S); early childhood education (M Ed, MA, PhD); educational psychology (PhD); psychological foundations of education (MA, PhD, Ed S); school psychology (MA, PhD, Ed S); special education (M Ed, MA, PhD, Ed S); talent development and gifted education (Certificate). *Accreditation:* APA (one or more programs are accredited). *Faculty:* 31 full-time (13 women). *Students:* 312 full-time (231 women), 88 part-time (67 women); includes 54 minority (20 Black or African American, non-Hispanic/Latino; 5 American Indian or Alaska Native, non-Hispanic/Latino; 18 Asian, non-Hispanic/Latino; 11 Hispanic/Latino), 5,149 international. Average age 30. 440 applicants, 48% accepted, 127 enrolled. In 2011, 98 master's, 21 doctorates, 22 other advanced degrees awarded. *Financial support:* In 2011–12, 4 fellowships (averaging $20,729 per year), 62 research assistantships (averaging $10,014 per year), 36 teaching assistantships (averaging $10,014 per year) were awarded. *Faculty research:* Learning, cognitive and social processes; multicultural education and counseling; measurement and statistical processes; performance assessment; instructional design/strategies for students with special needs. *Total annual research expenditures:* $4 million. *Unit head:* Dr. Susan Hupp, Chair, 612-624-1003, Fax: 612-624-8241, E-mail: shupp@umn.edu. *Application contact:* Dr. Jennifer Engler, Assistant Dean, 612-626-2887, Fax: 612-626-7496, E-mail: engle009@umn.edu. Web site: http://www.cehd.umn.edu/EdPsych.

University of Missouri, Graduate School, College of Education, Department of Educational, School, and Counseling Psychology, Columbia, MO 65211. Offers counseling psychology (M Ed, MA, PhD, Ed S); educational psychology (M Ed, MA, PhD, Ed S); learning and instruction (M Ed); school psychology (M Ed, MA, PhD, Ed S). *Accreditation:* APA (one or more programs are accredited). Part-time programs available. *Faculty:* 25 full-time (13 women), 4 part-time/adjunct (2 women). *Students:* 161 full-time (124 women), 54 part-time (40 women); includes 29 minority (15 Black or African American, non-Hispanic/Latino; 1 American Indian or Alaska Native, non-Hispanic/Latino; 2 Asian, non-Hispanic/Latino; 9 Hispanic/Latino; 2 Two or more races, non-Hispanic/Latino), 41 international. Average age 28. 262 applicants, 53% accepted, 118 enrolled. In 2011, 59 master's, 14 doctorates, 17 other advanced degrees awarded. *Degree requirements:* For doctorate, thesis/dissertation. *Entrance requirements:* For master's, doctorate, and Ed S, GRE General Test, minimum GPA of 3.0. Additional exam requirements/recommendations for international students: Required—TOEFL (minimum score 580 paper-based; 237 computer-based; 92 iBT). *Application deadline:* For fall admission, 1/8 priority date for domestic students. Applications are processed on a rolling basis. Application fee: $55 ($75 for international students). *Expenses:* Tuition, state resident: full-time $5881. Tuition, nonresident: full-time $15,183. *Required fees:* $952. Tuition and fees vary according to campus/location and program. *Financial support:* Fellowships, research assistantships, teaching assistantships, and institutionally sponsored loans available. *Faculty research:* Out-of-school learning, social cognitive career theory, black psychology and the intersectionality of social identities, test session behavior. *Unit head:* Dr. Deborah Carr, Department Chair, 573-882-5081, E-mail: carrd@missouri.edu. *Application contact:* Latoya Owens, 573-882-7732, E-mail: owensla@missouri.edu. Web site: http://education.missouri.edu/ESCP/.

University of Missouri–St. Louis, College of Education, Interdisciplinary Doctoral Programs, St. Louis, MO 63121. Offers adult and higher education (Ed D); counseling (PhD); counselor education (Ed D); educational administration (Ed D); educational leadership and policy studies (PhD); educational psychology (PhD); teaching-learning processes (Ed D, PhD). *Faculty:* 72 full-time (33 women). *Students:* 44 full-time (29 women), 199 part-time (138 women); includes 65 minority (52 Black or African American, non-Hispanic/Latino; 3 American Indian or Alaska Native, non-Hispanic/Latino; 5 Asian, non-Hispanic/Latino; 5 Hispanic/Latino), 6 international. Average age 43. 47 applicants, 34% accepted, 11 enrolled. In 2011, 27 doctorates awarded. *Degree requirements:* For doctorate, thesis/dissertation. *Entrance requirements:* For doctorate, GRE General Test, 3 letters of recommendation; personal interview. Additional exam requirements/recommendations for international students: Recommended—TOEFL (minimum score 550 paper-based; 230 computer-based). *Application deadline:* For fall admission, 3/1 for domestic and international students; for spring admission, 10/1 for domestic and international students. Application fee: $35 ($40 for international students). Electronic applications accepted. *Expenses:* Tuition, state resident: full-time $6273; part-time $3866 per year. Tuition, nonresident: full-time $14,969; part-time $9980 per year. *Required fees:* $315 per year. *Financial support:* In 2011–12, 15 research assistantships (averaging $12,240 per year), 8 teaching assistantships (averaging $12,240 per year) were awarded. Financial award application deadline: 4/1; financial award applicants required to submit FAFSA. *Faculty research:* Higher education law and policy, gender and higher education, student retention, lifelong learning orientation, school counselor's role in violence prevention. *Unit head:* Dr. Kathleen Haywood, Director of Graduate Studies, 314-516-5483, Fax: 314-516-5227, E-mail: kathleen_haywood@umsl.edu. *Application contact:* 314-516-5458, Fax: 314-516-6996, E-mail: gradadm@umsl.edu.

University of Nebraska at Omaha, Graduate Studies, College of Arts and Sciences, Department of Psychology, Omaha, NE 68182. Offers developmental psychology (PhD); industrial/organizational psychology (MS, PhD); psychobiology (PhD); psychology (MA); school psychology (MS, Ed S). Part-time programs available. *Faculty:* 18 full-time (8 women). *Students:* 53 full-time (38 women), 43 part-time (33 women); includes 8 minority (1 Black or African American, non-Hispanic/Latino; 6 Hispanic/Latino; 1 Two or more races, non-Hispanic/Latino), 3 international. Average age 27. 118 applicants, 31% accepted, 35 enrolled. In 2011, 16 master's, 2 doctorates, 6 other advanced degrees awarded. *Degree requirements:* For master's, comprehensive exam, thesis (for some programs); for doctorate, comprehensive exam, thesis/dissertation. *Entrance requirements:* For master's, GRE General Test, GRE Subject Test, previous course work in psychology, including statistics and a laboratory course; minimum GPA of 3.0, 3 letters of recommendation, resume, statement of purpose, writing sample; for doctorate, GRE General Test. Additional exam requirements/recommendations for international students: Required—TOEFL (minimum score 500 paper-based; 173 computer-based; 61 iBT). *Application deadline:* For fall admission, 1/5 for domestic students. Application fee: $45. Electronic applications accepted. *Financial support:* In 2011–12, 53 students received support, including 2 fellowships with tuition reimbursements available, 22 research assistantships with tuition reimbursements available, 24 teaching assistantships with tuition reimbursements available; career-related internships or fieldwork, Federal Work-Study, institutionally sponsored loans, scholarships/grants, tuition waivers (partial), and unspecified assistantships also available. Support available to part-time students. Financial award application deadline: 3/1; financial award applicants required to submit FAFSA. *Unit head:* Dr. Brigette Ryalls, Chairperson, 402-554-2592. *Application contact:* Dr. Joseph Brown, Student Contact, 402-554-2592.

University of Nebraska–Lincoln, Graduate College, College of Education and Human Sciences, Department of Educational Psychology, Lincoln, NE 68588. Offers cognition, learning and development (MA); counseling psychology (MA); educational psychology (MA, Ed S); psychological studies in education (PhD), including cognition, learning and development, counseling psychology, quantitative, qualitative, and psychometric methods, school psychology; quantitative, qualitative, and psychometric methods (MA); school psychology (MA, Ed S). *Accreditation:* APA (one or more programs are accredited); NCATE. *Degree requirements:* For master's, thesis optional. *Entrance requirements:* For master's, GRE General Test. Additional exam requirements/recommendations for international students: Required—TOEFL (minimum score 500 paper-based; 173 computer-based). Electronic applications accepted. *Faculty research:* Measurement and assessment, metacognition, academic skills, child development, multicultural education and counseling.

University of Nevada, Las Vegas, Graduate College, College of Education, Department of Educational Research, Cognition, and Development, Las Vegas, NV 89154-3002. Offers educational leadership (M Ed, MS, Ed D, PhD); educational leadership-executive (Ed D); educational psychology (MS, PhD, Ed S); higher education leadership (PhD); learning and technology (PhD); school psychology (PhD); PhD/JD. *Accreditation:* NCATE. Part-time and evening/weekend programs available. *Faculty:* 28 full-time (14 women), 13 part-time/adjunct (9 women). *Students:* 54 full-time (40 women), 184 part-time (124 women); includes 68 minority (26 Black or African American, non-Hispanic/Latino; 1 American Indian or Alaska Native, non-Hispanic/Latino; 9 Asian, non-Hispanic/Latino; 21 Hispanic/Latino; 2 Native Hawaiian or other Pacific Islander, non-Hispanic/Latino; 9 Two or more races, non-Hispanic/Latino), 4 international. Average age 37. 70 applicants, 69% accepted, 41 enrolled. In 2011, 94 master's, 34 doctorates, 12 other advanced degrees awarded. *Degree requirements:* For master's, comprehensive exam (for some programs), thesis (for some programs); for doctorate, comprehensive exam (for some programs), thesis/dissertation; for Ed S, comprehensive exam, thesis. *Entrance requirements:* For master's, GMAT or GRE General Test; for doctorate, GRE General Test, writing exam; for Ed S, GRE General Test. Additional exam requirements/recommendations for international students: Required—TOEFL (minimum score 550 paper-based; 213 computer-based; 80 iBT), IELTS (minimum score 7). *Application deadline:* For fall admission, 2/1 for domestic students, 5/1 for international students; for spring admission, 10/1 for international students. Application fee: $60 ($95 for international students). Electronic applications accepted. *Financial support:* In 2011–12, 44 students received support, including 16 research assistantships with partial tuition reimbursements available (averaging $9,428 per year), 28 teaching assistantships with partial tuition reimbursements available (averaging $10,783 per year); institutionally sponsored loans, scholarships/grants, health care benefits, and unspecified assistantships also available. Financial award application deadline: 3/1. *Faculty research:* Innovation and change in educational settings; educational policy, finance, and marketing; psycho-educational assessment; student retention, persistence, development, language, and culture; statistical modeling, program evaluation, qualitative and quantitative research methods. *Total annual research expenditures:* $269,710. *Unit head:* Dr. LeAnn Putney, Chair/Professor, 702-895-4879, Fax: 702-895-3492, E-mail: leann.putney@unlv.edu. *Application contact:* Graduate College Admissions Evaluator, 702-895-3320, Fax: 702-895-4180, E-mail: gradcollege@unlv.edu. Web site: http://education.unlv.edu/ercd/.

University of Nevada, Reno, Graduate School, College of Education, Department of Counseling and Educational Psychology, Reno, NV 89557. Offers M Ed, MA, MS, Ed D, PhD, Ed S. *Accreditation:* ACA (one or more programs are accredited); NCATE. Terminal master's awarded for partial completion of doctoral program. *Degree requirements:* For master's, comprehensive exam, thesis optional; for doctorate, comprehensive exam, thesis/dissertation, qualifying exam. *Entrance requirements:* For master's, GRE, minimum GPA of 2.75; for doctorate, GRE, minimum GPA of 3.0. Additional exam requirements/recommendations for international students: Required—TOEFL (minimum score 500 paper-based; 173 computer-based; 61 iBT), IELTS (minimum score 6). Electronic applications accepted. *Faculty research:* Marriage and family counseling, substance abuse attitudes of teachers, current supply of counseling educators, HIV-positive services for patients, family counseling for youth at risk.

University of New Mexico, Graduate School, College of Education, Department of Individual, Family and Community Education, Program in Educational Psychology, Albuquerque, NM 87131-2039. Offers MA, PhD. *Accreditation:* NCATE. Part-time and evening/weekend programs available. *Students:* 8 full-time (6 women), 27 part-time (21 women); includes 7 minority (2 Black or African American, non-Hispanic/Latino; 5 Hispanic/Latino), 1 international. Average age 43. 11 applicants, 55% accepted, 4 enrolled. In 2011, 5 degrees awarded. Terminal master's awarded for partial completion of doctoral program. *Degree requirements:* For master's, comprehensive exam (for some programs), thesis (for some programs); for doctorate, comprehensive exam, thesis/dissertation. *Entrance requirements:* For master's, GRE General Test or MAT, minimum GPA of 3.0 in last 2 years of undergraduate study, 3 letters of reference, interview with 3 faculty; for doctorate, GRE General Test or MAT, minimum GPA of 3.0 in last 2 years of undergraduate study, 3 letters of reference, interview with 3 faculty, writing sample. *Application deadline:* For fall admission, 3/1 for domestic students; for spring admission, 10/1 for domestic students. Application fee: $50. Electronic applications accepted. *Financial support:* In 2011–12, 14 students received support, including 2 research assistantships with partial tuition reimbursements available (averaging $9,000 per year), 8 teaching assistantships with full and partial tuition reimbursements available (averaging $9,070 per year). Financial award application deadline: 3/1; financial award applicants required to submit FAFSA. *Faculty research:* Measurement and assessment, cognitive strategies, accountability, motivation, instructional technology, educational research, human lifespan development, beliefs. *Unit head:* Dr. Jay Parkes, Department Chair, 505-277-3320, Fax: 505-277-8361, E-mail: edpsy@unm.edu. *Application contact:* Cynthia Salas, Department Administrator, 505-277-4535, Fax: 505-277-8361, E-mail: divbse@unm.edu. Web site: http://coe.unm.edu/departments/ifce/educational-psychology.html.

The University of North Carolina at Chapel Hill, Graduate School, School of Education, Program in Education, Chapel Hill, NC 27599. Offers culture, curriculum and change (MA, PhD); early childhood, intervention and literacy (MA, PhD); educational psychology, measurement and evaluation (MA, PhD). *Accreditation:* NCATE. *Degree requirements:* For master's, thesis; for doctorate, comprehensive exam, thesis/dissertation. *Entrance requirements:* For master's, GRE General Test, minimum GPA of 3.0 during last 2 years of undergraduates course work; for doctorate, GRE General Test, minimum GPA of 3.0 during last 2 years of undergraduate course work. Additional exam requirements/recommendations for international students: Required—TOEFL (minimum score 550 paper-based; 213 computer-based). Electronic applications accepted.

University of Northern Colorado, Graduate School, College of Education and Behavioral Sciences, School of Psychological Sciences, Program in Educational Psychology, Greeley, CO 80639. Offers early childhood education (MA); educational psychology (MA, PhD). *Accreditation:* NCATE. Part-time programs available. *Degree requirements:* For master's, comprehensive exam, thesis or alternative; for doctorate, comprehensive exam, thesis/dissertation. *Entrance requirements:* For master's, GRE General Test, letters of recommendation; for doctorate, GRE General Test, letters of recommendation, resume. Electronic applications accepted.

University of Northern Iowa, Graduate College, College of Education, Department of Educational Psychology and Foundations, Cedar Falls, IA 50614. Offers educational psychology (MAE); professional development for teachers (MAE); school psychology (Ed S). Part-time and evening/weekend programs available. *Students:* 22 full-time (16 women), 24 part-time (20 women), 7 international. 49 applicants, 61% accepted, 26 enrolled. In 2011, 18 master's, 5 other advanced degrees awarded. *Degree requirements:* For master's, comprehensive exam (for some programs), thesis or alternative; for Ed S, thesis or alternative. *Entrance requirements:* For master's, GRE General Test, minimum GPA of 3.0; for Ed S, GRE General Test. Additional exam requirements/recommendations for international students: Required—TOEFL (minimum score 500 paper-based; 180 computer-based; 61 iBT). *Application deadline:* For fall admission, 8/1 priority date for domestic students. Applications are processed on a rolling basis. Application fee: $50 ($70 for international students). Electronic applications accepted. *Expenses:* Tuition, state resident: full-time $7476. Tuition, nonresident: full-time $16,410. *Required fees:* $942. *Financial support:* Career-related internships or fieldwork, Federal Work-Study, scholarships/grants, and tuition waivers (full and partial) available. Support available to part-time students. Financial award application deadline: 2/1. *Unit head:* Dr. Radhi Al-Mabuk, Interim Head, 319-273-2609, Fax: 319-273-7732, E-mail: radhi.al-mabuk@uni.edu. *Application contact:* Laurie S. Russell, Record Analyst, 319-273-2623, Fax: 319-273-2885, E-mail: laurie.russell@uni.edu. Web site: http://www.uni.edu/coe/epf/.

University of North Texas, Toulouse Graduate School, College of Education, Department of Educational Psychology, Program in Educational Psychology, Denton, TX 76203. Offers MS. *Degree requirements:* For master's, thesis optional. *Entrance requirements:* For master's, GRE General Test. Additional exam requirements/recommendations for international students: Recommended—TOEFL (minimum score 550 paper-based; 213 computer-based; 79 iBT). *Expenses:* Tuition, state resident: part-time $100 per credit hour. Tuition, nonresident: part-time $413 per credit hour. *Faculty research:* Structural equation modeling, applied general linear modeling, reliability, factor analysis, learning environments, social historical factors.

University of Oklahoma, Jeannine Rainbolt College of Education, Department of Educational Psychology, Program in Instructional Psychology and Technology, Norman, OK 73019. Offers instructional psychology and technology (M Ed, PhD), including educational psychology (M Ed), general (M Ed), instructional design (M Ed), integrating technology in teaching (M Ed), interactive learning technologies (M Ed), teaching and assessment (M Ed), teaching with technology (M Ed). Part-time and evening/weekend programs available. *Students:* 23 full-time (16 women), 27 part-time (20 women); includes 14 minority (8 Black or African American, non-Hispanic/Latino; 1 American Indian or Alaska Native, non-Hispanic/Latino; 3 Hispanic/Latino; 2 Two or more races, non-Hispanic/Latino), 9 international. Average age 33. 22 applicants, 77% accepted, 17 enrolled. In 2011, 12 master's, 2 doctorates awarded. *Degree requirements:* For master's, comprehensive exam (for some programs), thesis optional; for doctorate, thesis/dissertation, general exam. *Entrance requirements:* For master's, minimum GPA of 3.0; for doctorate, GRE General Test, master's degree, minimum graduate GPA of 3.25. Additional exam requirements/recommendations for international students: Required—TOEFL (minimum score 550 paper-based; 79 iBT). *Application deadline:* For fall admission, 3/15 for domestic students, 3/1 for international students; for spring admission, 10/15 for domestic and international students. Applications are processed on a rolling basis. Application fee: $40 ($90 for international students). Electronic applications accepted. *Expenses:* Tuition, state resident: full-time $4087; part-time $170.30 per credit hour. Tuition, nonresident: full-time $14,875; part-time $619.80 per credit hour. *Required fees:* $2659; $100.25 per credit hour. Tuition and fees vary according to course load and degree level. *Financial support:* In 2011–12, 39 students received support. Career-related internships or fieldwork, Federal Work-Study, scholarships/grants, health care benefits, and unspecified assistantships available. Support available to part-time students. Financial award applicants required to submit FAFSA. *Faculty research:* Cognition and instruction, motivation and instruction, instructional design, technology integration in education, interactive learning technologies, measurement and assessment. *Unit head:* Dr. Terri K. Debacker, Chair, 405-325-1068, Fax: 405-325-6655, E-mail: debacker@ou.edu. *Application contact:* Shannon Vazquez, Graduate Programs Officer, 405-325-4525, Fax: 405-325-6655, E-mail: shannonv@ou.edu. Web site: http://education.ou.edu/ipt.

University of Phoenix–Southern Arizona Campus, College of Education, Tucson, AZ 85711. Offers administration and supervision (MA Ed); adult education and training (MA Ed); curriculum instruction (MA Ed); educational counseling (MA Ed); elementary teacher education (MA Ed); school counseling (MSC); secondary teacher education (MA Ed); special education (MA Ed, Certificate). Evening/weekend programs available. *Degree requirements:* For master's, thesis (for some programs). *Entrance requirements:* For master's, minimum undergraduate GPA of 2.5, 3 years of work experience. Additional exam requirements/recommendations for international students: Required—TOEFL (minimum score 550 paper-based; 213 computer-based; 79 iBT). Electronic applications accepted.

University of Regina, Faculty of Graduate Studies and Research, Faculty of Education, Department of Educational Psychology, Regina, SK S4S 0A2, Canada. Offers M Ed. Part-time programs available. *Faculty:* 7 full-time (4 women). *Students:* 23 full-time (18 women), 42 part-time (36 women). 33 applicants, 33% accepted. In 2011, 17 master's awarded. *Degree requirements:* For master's, thesis (for some programs), practicum, project, or thesis. *Entrance requirements:* For master's, bachelor's degree in education. Additional exam requirements/recommendations for international students: Required—TOEFL (minimum score 580 paper-based; 80 iBT), IELTS (minimum score 6.5). *Application deadline:* 2/15 for domestic and international students. Application fee: $100. Electronic applications accepted. *Financial support:* In 2011–12, 2 fellowships (averaging $6,000 per year), 5 teaching assistantships (averaging $2,298 per year) were awarded; research assistantships, career-related internships or fieldwork, and scholarships/grants also available. Financial award application deadline: 6/15. *Faculty research:* Theories of counseling, psychology of learning, aptitude and achievement analysis, education and vocational guidance, resilience: re-conceptualizing PRAXIS. *Unit head:* Dr. Rod Dolmage, Associate Dean, Research and Graduate Programs, 306-585-4816, Fax: 306-585-5387, E-mail: rod.dolmage@uregina.ca. *Application contact:* Tania Gates, Graduate Program Coordinator, 306-585-4506, Fax: 306-585-5387, E-mail: edgrad@uregina.ca.

University of Saskatchewan, College of Graduate Studies and Research, College of Education, Department of Educational Psychology and Special Education, Saskatoon, SK S7N 5A2, Canada. Offers M Ed, PhD, Diploma. *Degree requirements:* For master's, thesis (for some programs); for doctorate, comprehensive exam (for some programs), thesis/dissertation. *Entrance requirements:* Additional exam requirements/recommendations for international students: Required—TOEFL (minimum score 80 iBT); Recommended—IELTS (minimum score 6.5). Electronic applications accepted.

University of South Africa, College of Human Sciences, Pretoria, South Africa. Offers adult education (M Ed); African languages (MA, PhD); African politics (MA, PhD); Afrikaans (MA, PhD); ancient history (MA, PhD); ancient Near Eastern studies (MA, PhD); anthropology (MA, PhD); applied linguistics (MA); Arabic (MA, PhD); archaeology (MA); art history (MA); Biblical archaeology (MA); Biblical studies (M Th, D Th, PhD); Christian spirituality (M Th, D Th); church history (M Th, D Th); classical studies (MA, PhD); clinical psychology (MA); communication (MA, PhD); comparative education (M Ed, Ed D); consulting psychology (D Admin, D Com, PhD); curriculum studies (M Ed, Ed D); development studies (M Admin, MA, D Admin, PhD); didactics (M Ed, Ed D); education (M Tech); education management (M Ed, Ed D); educational psychology (M Ed); English (MA); environmental education (M Ed); French (MA, PhD); German (MA, PhD); Greek (MA); guidance and counseling (M Ed); health studies (MA, PhD), including health sciences education (MA), health services management (MA), medical and surgical nursing science (critical care general) (MA), midwifery and neonatal nursing science (MA), trauma and emergency care (MA); history (MA, PhD); history of education (Ed D); inclusive education (M Ed, Ed D); information and communications technology policy and regulation (MA); information science (MA, MIS, PhD); international politics (MA, PhD); Islamic studies (MA, PhD); Italian (MA, PhD); Judaica (MA, PhD); linguistics (MA, PhD); mathematical education (M Ed); mathematics education (MA); missiology (M Th, D Th); modern Hebrew (MA, PhD); musicology (MA, MMus, D Mus, PhD); natural science education (M Ed); New Testament (M Th, D Th); Old Testament (D Th); pastoral therapy (M Th, D Th); philosophy (MA); philosophy of education (M Ed, Ed D); politics (MA, PhD); Portuguese (MA, PhD); practical theology (M Th, D Th); psychology (MA, MS, PhD); psychology of education (M Ed, Ed D); public health (MA); religious studies (MA, D Th, PhD); Romance languages (MA); Russian (MA, PhD); Semitic languages (MA, PhD); social behavior studies in HIV/AIDS (MA); social science (mental health) (MA); social science in development studies (MA); social science in psychology (MA); social science in social work (MA); social science in sociology (MA); social work (MSW, DSW, PhD); socio-education (M Ed, Ed D); sociolinguistics (MA); sociology (MA, PhD); Spanish (MA, PhD); systematic theology (M Th, D Th); TESOL (teaching English to speakers of other languages) (MA); theological ethics (M Th, D Th); theory of literature (MA, PhD); urban ministry (D Th); urban ministry (M Th).

University of South Carolina, The Graduate School, College of Education, Department of Educational Studies, Program in Educational Psychology, Research, Columbia, SC 29208. Offers M Ed, PhD. *Accreditation:* NCATE. Part-time programs available. *Degree requirements:* For master's, comprehensive exam, thesis (for some programs); for doctorate, comprehensive exam, thesis/dissertation. *Entrance requirements:* For master's, GRE General Test; for doctorate, GRE General Test, interview. Electronic applications accepted. *Faculty research:* Problem solving, higher order thinking skills, psychometric research, methodology.

The University of South Dakota, Graduate School, School of Education, Division of Counseling and Psychology in Education, Vermillion, SD 57069-2390. Offers MA, PhD, Ed S. *Accreditation:* ACA (one or more programs are accredited); NCATE. Part-time programs available. *Degree requirements:* For master's and Ed S, comprehensive exam, thesis or alternative; for doctorate, comprehensive exam, thesis/dissertation. *Entrance requirements:* For master's and doctorate, GRE General Test, minimum GPA of 3.0. Additional exam requirements/recommendations for international students: Required—TOEFL (minimum score 550 paper-based; 213 computer-based; 79 iBT). Electronic applications accepted. *Expenses:* Tuition, state resident: full-time $3118.50; part-time $173.25 per credit hour. Tuition, nonresident: full-time $6601; part-time $366.70 per credit hour. *Required fees:* $2268; $126 per credit hour. Tuition and fees vary according to program.

University of Southern California, Graduate School, Rossier School of Education, Doctor of Education Programs, Los Angeles, CA 90089. Offers educational psychology (Ed D); higher education administration (Ed D); K-12 leadership in urban school settings (Ed D); teacher education in multicultural societies (Ed D). Part-time and evening/weekend programs available. *Degree requirements:* For doctorate, thesis/dissertation. *Entrance requirements:* For doctorate, GRE. Additional exam requirements/recommendations for international students: Required—TOEFL (minimum score 250 computer-based; 100 iBT). Electronic applications accepted. *Faculty research:* Data-driven decision-making in K-12 schools and districts; examination of college and university leadership and management in U. S. and Asia; studies in facilitating student learning; organizational change and the role of leaders; leadership, diversity, learning and accountability.

University of Southern California, Graduate School, Rossier School of Education, Doctor of Philosophy in Education Programs, Los Angeles, CA 90089. Offers educational psychology (PhD); higher education administration and policy (PhD); K-12 policy and practice (PhD). *Degree requirements:* For doctorate, thesis/dissertation, 63 units; qualifying exam; dissertation proposal and defense. *Entrance requirements:* For doctorate, GRE. Additional exam requirements/recommendations for international students: Required—TOEFL (minimum score 250 computer-based; 100 iBT). Electronic applications accepted. *Faculty research:* Diversity in higher education, organizational change, educational psychology, policy and politics of educational reform, economics of education and education policy.

University of Southern Maine, School of Education and Human Development, Program in Educational Psychology, Portland, ME 04104-9300. Offers applied behavior analysis (MS, Certificate). Part-time and evening/weekend programs available. *Entrance requirements:* For master's, GRE or MAT. Additional exam requirements/recommendations for international students: Required—TOEFL (minimum score 550 paper-based; 213 computer-based; 79 iBT). Electronic applications accepted.

The University of Tennessee, Graduate School, College of Education, Health and Human Sciences, Department of Educational Psychology and Counseling, Knoxville, TN 37996. Offers adult education (MS); applied educational psychology (MS); collaborative learning (Ed D); college student personnel (MS); mental health counseling (MS); rehabilitation counseling (MS); school counseling (MS). *Accreditation:* ACA (one or more programs are accredited); CORE (one or more programs are accredited); NCATE. Part-time and evening/weekend programs available. *Degree requirements:* For master's, thesis optional. *Entrance requirements:* For master's, GRE General Test, minimum GPA of 2.7. Additional exam requirements/recommendations for international students: Required—TOEFL. Electronic applications accepted. *Expenses:* Tuition, state resident: full-time $8332; part-time $464 per credit hour. Tuition, nonresident: full-time $25,174; part-time $1400 per credit hour. *Required fees:* $1162; $56 per credit hour. Tuition and fees vary according to program.

The University of Tennessee, Graduate School, College of Education, Health and Human Sciences, Program in Education, Knoxville, TN 37996. Offers art education (MS); counseling education (PhD); cultural studies in education (PhD); curriculum (MS, Ed S); curriculum, educational research and evaluation (Ed D, PhD); early childhood education (PhD); early childhood special education (MS); education of deaf and hard of hearing (MS); educational administration and policy studies (Ed D, PhD); educational administration and supervision (Ed S); educational psychology (Ed D, PhD); elementary education (MS, Ed S); elementary teaching (MS); English education (MS, Ed S); exercise science (PhD); foreign language/ESL education (MS, Ed S); instructional technology (MS, Ed D, PhD, Ed S); literacy, language and ESL education (PhD); literacy, language education, and ESL education (Ed D); mathematics education (MS, Ed S); modified and comprehensive special education (MS); reading education (MS, Ed S); school counseling (Ed S); school psychology (PhD, Ed S); science education (MS, Ed S); secondary teaching (MS); social foundations (MS); social science education (MS, Ed S); socio-cultural foundations of sports and education (PhD); special education (Ed S); teacher education (Ed D, PhD). *Accreditation:* NCATE. Part-time and evening/weekend programs available. *Degree requirements:* For master's and Ed S, thesis optional; for doctorate, variable foreign language requirement, thesis/dissertation. *Entrance requirements:* For master's, minimum GPA of 2.7; for doctorate and Ed S, GRE General Test, minimum GPA of 2.7. Additional exam requirements/recommendations for international students: Required—TOEFL. Electronic applications accepted. *Expenses:* Tuition, state resident: full-time $8332; part-time $464 per credit hour. Tuition, nonresident: full-time $25,174; part-time $1400 per credit hour. *Required fees:* $1162; $56 per credit hour. Tuition and fees vary according to program.

The University of Texas at Austin, Graduate School, College of Education, Department of Educational Psychology, Austin, TX 78712-1111. Offers academic educational psychology (M Ed, MA); counseling psychology (PhD); counselor education (M Ed); human development, culture and learning sciences (PhD); program evaluation (MA); quantitative methods (M Ed, MA, PhD); school psychology (MA, PhD). *Accreditation:* APA (one or more programs are accredited). *Degree requirements:* For master's, thesis optional; for doctorate, thesis/dissertation. *Entrance requirements:* For master's and doctorate, GRE General Test, 3 letters of recommendation. Additional exam requirements/recommendations for international students: Required—TOEFL. *Application deadline:* For fall admission, 1/15 priority date for domestic students, 1/15 for international students; for spring admission, 10/1 priority date for domestic students, 10/1 for international students. Applications are processed on a rolling basis. Application fee: $50 ($75 for international students). *Financial support:* Fellowships with full and partial tuition reimbursements, research assistantships with partial tuition reimbursements, teaching assistantships with partial tuition reimbursements, career-related internships or fieldwork, Federal Work-Study, institutionally sponsored loans, scholarships/grants, tuition waivers (full and partial), and unspecified assistantships available. Financial award application deadline: 1/15. *Unit head:* Dr. Cindy Carlson, Chair, 512-471-0276, Fax: 512-471-1288, E-mail: ccarlson@austin.utexas.edu. *Application contact:* Diane Schallert, Graduate Adviser, 512-232-4835, E-mail: dschallert@mail.utexas.edu. Web site: http://www.edb.utexas.edu/coe/depts/edp/edp.html.

The University of Texas at El Paso, Graduate School, College of Education, Department of Educational Psychology and Special Services, El Paso, TX 79968-0001. Offers educational diagnostics (M Ed); guidance and counseling (M Ed); special education (M Ed). Part-time and evening/weekend programs available. *Students:* 289 (250 women); includes 252 minority (9 Black or African American, non-Hispanic/Latino; 1 American Indian or Alaska Native, non-Hispanic/Latino; 2 Asian, non-Hispanic/Latino; 240 Hispanic/Latino), 11 international. Average age 34. 85 applicants, 71% accepted, 53 enrolled. In 2011, 53 master's awarded. *Degree requirements:* For master's, thesis optional. *Entrance requirements:* For master's, minimum GPA of 3.0. Additional exam requirements/recommendations for international students: Required—TOEFL. *Application deadline:* For fall admission, 7/1 priority date for domestic students, 3/1 for international students; for spring admission, 11/1 priority date for domestic students, 9/1 for international students. Applications are processed on a rolling basis. Application fee: $15 ($65 for international students). Electronic applications accepted. *Financial support:* In 2011–12, research assistantships with partial tuition reimbursements (averaging $16,642 per year), teaching assistantships with partial tuition reimbursements (averaging $13,314 per year) were awarded; Federal Work-Study, institutionally sponsored loans, and tuition waivers (partial) also available. Financial award application deadline: 3/15; financial award applicants required to submit FAFSA. *Unit head:* Dr. Don C. Combs, Interim Chair, 915-747-7585, E-mail: dcombs@utep.edu. *Application* *contact:* Dr. Benjamin Flores, Interim Dean of the Graduate School, 915-747-5491, Fax: 915-747-5788, E-mail: bflores@utep.edu.

The University of Texas at San Antonio, College of Education and Human Development, Department of Interdisciplinary Learning and Teaching, San Antonio, TX 78249-0617. Offers adult learning and teaching (MA); education (MA), including curriculum and instruction, early childhood and elementary education, educational psychology/special education, instructional technology, reading and literacy education; interdisciplinary learning and teaching (PhD). Part-time and evening/weekend programs available. *Faculty:* 26 full-time (21 women), 1 (woman) part-time/adjunct. *Students:* 131 full-time (100 women), 357 part-time (283 women); includes 275 minority (31 Black or African American, non-Hispanic/Latino; 9 Asian, non-Hispanic/Latino; 227 Hispanic/Latino; 8 Two or more races, non-Hispanic/Latino), 31 international. Average age 33. 239 applicants, 75% accepted, 120 enrolled. In 2011, 119 master's awarded. *Degree requirements:* For master's, comprehensive exam, thesis optional, 36 hours of course work without thesis (33 with thesis); for doctorate, comprehensive exam, thesis/dissertation, minimum of 60 semester credit hours. *Entrance requirements:* For master's, GRE General Test, bachelor's degree with minimum GPA of 3.0 in last 60 hours of coursework; resume; two letters of recommendation; statement of purpose; for doctorate, GRE, transcripts from all colleges and universities attended, professional vitae demonstrating experience in work environment where education was primary professional emphasis, 3 letters of recommendation, statement of purpose, master's degree transcript documenting minimum GPA of 3.5. Additional exam requirements/recommendations for international students: Required—TOEFL (minimum score 500 paper-based; 61 iBT), IELTS (minimum score 5). *Application deadline:* For fall admission, 7/1 for domestic students, 4/1 for international students; for spring admission, 11/1 for domestic students, 9/1 for international students. Application fee: $45 ($85 for international students). *Expenses:* Tuition, state resident: full-time $3148; part-time $2176 per semester. Tuition, nonresident: full-time $8782; part-time $5932 per semester. *Required fees:* $719 per semester. *Financial support:* In 2011–12, 9 fellowships with partial tuition reimbursements (averaging $27,000 per year) were awarded; career-related internships or fieldwork, Federal Work-Study, and scholarships/grants also available. Support available to part-time students. *Faculty research:* Explorations of science, learning and teaching, family Involvement in early childhood, culturally-responsive literacy instruction in diverse settings, STEM education, autism spectrum disorders. *Total annual research expenditures:* $5.9 million. *Unit head:* Dr. Maria R. Cortez, Department Chair, 210-458-5969, Fax: 210-458-7281, E-mail: mari.cortez@utsa.edu. *Application contact:* Erin Doran, Student Development Specialist, 210-458-7443, Fax: 210-458-7281, E-mail: erin.doran@utsa.edu.

The University of Texas–Pan American, College of Education, Department of Educational Psychology, Edinburg, TX 78539. Offers educational diagnostician (M Ed); gifted education (M Ed); guidance and counseling (M Ed); school psychology (MA); special education (M Ed). Part-time and evening/weekend programs available. *Degree requirements:* For master's, comprehensive exam (for some programs), thesis (for some programs). *Entrance requirements:* For master's, GRE General Test, interview. *Application deadline:* For fall admission, 7/17 for domestic students; for spring admission, 11/16 for domestic students. Application fee: $0. Tuition and fees vary according to course load, program and student level. *Financial support:* Research assistantships, career-related internships or fieldwork, Federal Work-Study, and institutionally sponsored loans available. Support available to part-time students. Financial award application deadline: 4/15. *Faculty research:* Reading instruction, assessment practice, behavior interventions consultation, mental retardation. *Unit head:* Dr. Paul Sale, Chair, 956-665-2433, E-mail: psale@utpa.edu. *Application contact:* Dr. Sylvia Ramirez, Associate Dean of Graduate Studies, 956-665-3488, E-mail: ramirezs@utpa.edu. Web site: http://portal.utpa.edu/utpa_main/daa_home/coed_home/edpsy_home.

University of the Pacific, School of Education, Department of Educational and School Psychology, Stockton, CA 95211-0197. Offers educational psychology (MA, Ed D); school psychology (Ed S). *Accreditation:* NCATE. *Faculty:* 6 full-time (3 women). *Students:* 17 full-time (16 women), 9 part-time (5 women); includes 11 minority (1 Black or African American, non-Hispanic/Latino; 1 American Indian or Alaska Native, non-Hispanic/Latino; 4 Asian, non-Hispanic/Latino; 5 Hispanic/Latino). Average age 27. 12 applicants, 58% accepted, 5 enrolled. In 2011, 7 master's, 1 doctorate awarded. *Degree requirements:* For master's, thesis; for doctorate, thesis/dissertation. *Entrance requirements:* For master's and doctorate, GRE General Test, GRE Subject Test. Additional exam requirements/recommendations for international students: Required—TOEFL (minimum score 475 paper-based; 150 computer-based). *Application deadline:* For fall admission, 3/1 priority date for domestic students; for spring admission, 10/1 priority date for domestic students. Applications are processed on a rolling basis. Application fee: $75. *Expenses: Tuition:* Full-time $18,900; part-time $1181 per unit. *Required fees:* $949. *Financial support:* In 2011–12, 6 teaching assistantships were awarded. Financial award application deadline: 3/1; financial award applicants required to submit FAFSA. *Unit head:* Dr. Linda Webster, Chairperson, 209-946-2559, E-mail: lwebster@pacific.edu. *Application contact:* Office of Graduate Admissions, 209-946-2344.

The University of Toledo, College of Graduate Studies, Judith Herb College of Education, Health Science and Human Service, Department of Educational Foundations and Leadership, Toledo, OH 43606-3390. Offers educational administration and supervision (ME, DE, Ed S); educational psychology (ME, DE, PhD); educational research and measurement (ME, PhD); educational sociology (DE, PhD); educational theory and social foundations (ME); foundations of education (DE, PhD); higher education (ME, PhD); history of education (PhD); philosophy of education (PhD). *Accreditation:* NCATE. Part-time and evening/weekend programs available. *Faculty:* 32. *Students:* 26 full-time (14 women), 222 part-time (134 women); includes 78 minority (57 Black or African American, non-Hispanic/Latino; 5 Asian, non-Hispanic/Latino; 15 Hispanic/Latino; 1 Two or more races, non-Hispanic/Latino), 5 international. Average age 40. 85 applicants, 61% accepted, 34 enrolled. In 2011, 37 master's, 7 doctorates, 18 other advanced degrees awarded. *Degree requirements:* For master's, comprehensive exam, thesis or alternative; for doctorate, comprehensive exam, thesis/dissertation; for Ed S, thesis optional. *Entrance requirements:* For master's, doctorate, and Ed S, minimum cumulative GPA of 2.7 for all previous academic work, letters of recommendation. Additional exam requirements/recommendations for international students: Required—TOEFL (minimum score 550 paper-based; 213 computer-based; 80 iBT), IELTS (minimum score 6.5). *Application deadline:* For fall admission, 1/15 priority date for domestic students, 1/15 for international students. Applications are processed on a rolling basis. Application fee: $45 ($75 for international students). Electronic applications accepted. *Financial support:* In 2011–12, 10 research assistantships with full and partial tuition reimbursements (averaging $6,734 per year), 8 teaching assistantships with full and partial tuition reimbursements (averaging $9,000 per year) were awarded; career-related internships or fieldwork, Federal Work-Study, institutionally sponsored loans, scholarships/grants, tuition waivers (full and partial), unspecified assistantships, and administrative assistantships also available. Support available to part-time students. *Unit head:* Dr. William Gray, Interim Chair, 419-530-2565, Fax: 419-530-8447, E-mail: william.gray@utoledo.edu. *Application contact:* Graduate School Office, 419-530-4723, Fax: 419-530-4724, E-mail: grdsch@utnet.utoledo.edu. Web site: http://www.utoledo.edu/eduhshs/.

University of Utah, Graduate School, College of Education, Department of Educational Psychology, Salt Lake City, UT 84112. Offers counseling psychology (PhD); educational psychology (MA); elementary education (M Ed); instructional design and educational technology (M Ed); instructional design and technology (M Ed, MS); learning and cognition (MS, PhD); learning sciences (MA); professional counseling (MS); professional psychology (M Ed); reading and literacy (M Ed, PhD); school counseling (M Ed, MS); school psychology (M Ed, MS, PhD); statistics (M Stat). *Accreditation:* APA (one or more programs are accredited). Evening/weekend programs available. Postbaccalaureate distance learning degree programs offered (minimal on-campus study). *Faculty:* 23 full-time (12 women), 9 part-time/adjunct (7 women). *Students:* 104 full-time (85 women), 107 part-time (78 women); includes 26 minority (1 American Indian or Alaska Native, non-Hispanic/Latino; 4 Asian, non-Hispanic/Latino; 17 Hispanic/Latino; 1 Native Hawaiian or other Pacific Islander, non-Hispanic/Latino; 3 Two or more races, non-Hispanic/Latino), 4 international. Average age 32. 213 applicants, 27% accepted, 48 enrolled. In 2011, 39 master's, 9 doctorates awarded. *Median time to degree:* Of those who began their doctoral program in fall 2003, 50% received their degree in 8 years or less. *Degree requirements:* For master's, variable foreign language requirement, comprehensive exam, thesis (for some programs); for doctorate, variable foreign language requirement, thesis/dissertation, oral exam. *Entrance requirements:* For master's and doctorate, GRE General Test, minimum GPA of 3.0. Additional exam requirements/recommendations for international students: Required—TOEFL (minimum score 500 paper-based; 173 computer-based). *Application deadline:* For fall admission, 4/1 for domestic and international students; for spring admission, 11/1 for domestic and international students. Application fee: $55 ($65 for international students). *Expenses:* Contact institution. *Financial support:* In 2011–12, 59 students received support, including 25 fellowships with full and partial tuition reimbursements available (averaging $12,000 per year), 7 research assistantships with full and partial tuition reimbursements available (averaging $12,000 per year), 27 teaching assistantships with full and partial tuition reimbursements available (averaging $12,000 per year); career-related internships or fieldwork, Federal Work-Study, institutionally sponsored loans, scholarships/grants, and unspecified assistantships also available. Financial award application deadline: 2/1; financial award applicants required to submit FAFSA. *Faculty research:* Autism, computer technology and instruction, cognitive behavior, aging, group counseling. *Total annual research expenditures:* $371,256. *Unit head:* Dr. Elaine Clark, Chair, 801-581-7148, Fax: 801-581-5566, E-mail: clark@ed.utah.edu. *Application contact:* Kendra Lee Wiebke, Academic Program Specialist, 801-581-7148, Fax: 801-581-5566, E-mail: kendra.wiebke@utah.edu. Web site: http://www.ed.utah.edu/edps/.

University of Utah, Graduate School, Interdepartmental Program in Statistics, Salt Lake City, UT 84112-1107. Offers biostatistics (M Stat); econometrics (M Stat); educational psychology (M Stat); mathematics (M Stat); sociology (M Stat); statistics (M Stat). Part-time programs available. *Students:* 25 full-time (10 women), 28 part-time (8 women); includes 8 minority (2 Black or African American, non-Hispanic/Latino; 3 Asian, non-Hispanic/Latino; 3 Hispanic/Latino), 15 international. Average age 33. 59 applicants, 44% accepted, 12 enrolled. In 2011, 18 master's awarded. *Degree requirements:* For master's, comprehensive exam, projects. *Entrance requirements:* For master's, GRE General Test (sociology and educational psychology), minimum GPA of 3.0; course work in calculus, matrix theory, statistics. Additional exam requirements/recommendations for international students: Required—TOEFL (minimum score 500 paper-based; 173 computer-based; 61 iBT). *Application deadline:* For fall admission, 7/1 for domestic students, 4/1 for international students. Applications are processed on a rolling basis. Application fee: $55 ($65 for international students). *Financial support:* Career-related internships or fieldwork available. *Faculty research:* Biostatistics, management, economics, educational psychology, mathematics. *Unit head:* Richard Fowles, Chair, University Statistics Committee, 801-581-4577, E-mail: fowles@economics.utah.edu. *Application contact:* Laura Egbert, Coordinator, 801-585-6853, E-mail: laura.egbert@utah.edu. Web site: http://www.math.utah.edu/mstat/.

University of Victoria, Faculty of Graduate Studies, Faculty of Education, Department of Educational Psychology and Leadership Studies, Victoria, BC V8W 2Y2, Canada. Offers aboriginal communities counseling (M Ed); counseling (M Ed, MA); educational psychology (M Ed, MA, PhD), including counseling psychology (M Ed, MA), leadership studies (PhD), learning and development (MA, PhD), measurement and evaluation, special education (M Ed, MA); leadership studies (M Ed, MA). Part-time programs available. *Degree requirements:* For master's, thesis (for some programs), comprehensive exam (M Ed); for doctorate, comprehensive exam, thesis/dissertation, candidacy exam. *Entrance requirements:* For master's, 2 years of work experience in a relevant field; for doctorate, GRE, 2 years of work experience in a relevant field, minimum B average. Additional exam requirements/recommendations for international students: Required—TOEFL (minimum score 575 paper-based; 233 computer-based), IELTS (minimum score 7). *Faculty research:* Learning and development (child, adolescent and adult), special education and exceptional children.

University of Virginia, Curry School of Education, Department of Leadership, Foundations and Policy, Program in Educational Psychology, Charlottesville, VA 22903. Offers applied developmental science (M Ed); educational evaluation (M Ed); educational psychology (M Ed, Ed D, Ed S); educational research (Ed D); gifted education (M Ed); instructional technology (M Ed, Ed S); research statistics and evaluation (Ed D); school psychology (Ed D). *Students:* 17 full-time (12 women), 10 part-time (7 women); includes 2 minority (1 Black or African American, non-Hispanic/Latino; 1 Hispanic/Latino), 1 international. Average age 29. 56 applicants, 77% accepted, 23 enrolled. In 2011, 40 master's, 1 doctorate awarded. *Degree requirements:* For master's, comprehensive exam. *Entrance requirements:* For master's and doctorate, GRE General Test, 2 letters of recommendation. Additional exam requirements/recommendations for international students: Required—TOEFL (minimum score 600 paper-based; 250 computer-based; 90 iBT), IELTS (minimum score 7). *Application deadline:* Applications are processed on a rolling basis. Application fee: $60. Electronic applications accepted. *Financial support:* Fellowships, research assistantships, and teaching assistantships available. Financial award application deadline: 1/5; financial award applicants required to submit FAFSA. *Unit head:* Christopher De La Cerda, Program Coordinator, 434-243-2021, E-mail: cjd8kn@virginia.edu. *Application contact:* Lisa Miller, Assistant to the Chair, 434-982-2849, E-mail: lam3v@virgnina.edu.

University of Virginia, Curry School of Education, Program in Education, Charlottesville, VA 22903. Offers administration and supervision (PhD); applied developmental science (PhD); counselor education (PhD); curriculum and instruction (PhD); early childhood-developmental risk (MT); education evaluation (PhD); educational psychology (PhD); educational research (PhD); elementary (MT, PhD); English education (MT, PhD); foreign language education (MT); higher education (PhD); instructional technology (PhD); kinesiology (MT, PhD); math education (PhD); reading education (PhD); research statistics and evaluation (PhD); school psychology (PhD); science education (PhD); social studies education (MT, PhD); special education (PhD); world languages education (MT). *Students:* 299 full-time (216 women), 60 part-time (33 women); includes 46 minority (18 Black or African American, non-Hispanic/Latino; 17 Asian, non-Hispanic/Latino; 7 Hispanic/Latino; 4 Two or more races, non-Hispanic/

Latino), 23 international. Average age 30. 307 applicants, 42% accepted, 80 enrolled. In 2011, 113 master's, 62 doctorates awarded. *Degree requirements:* For master's, comprehensive exam (for some programs), field project; for doctorate, comprehensive exam, thesis/dissertation. *Entrance requirements:* For doctorate, GRE General Test. Additional exam requirements/recommendations for international students: Required—TOEFL (minimum score 600 paper-based; 250 computer-based; 90 iBT), IELTS (minimum score 7). *Application deadline:* Applications are processed on a rolling basis. Application fee: $60. Electronic applications accepted. *Financial support:* Fellowships, research assistantships, and teaching assistantships available. Financial award application deadline: 1/5; financial award applicants required to submit FAFSA. *Unit head:* Robert C. Pianta, Dean, 434-924-3334. *Application contact:* Joanne McNergney, Assistant Dean for Admissions and Student Services, 434-924-3334, E-mail: curry-admissions@virginia.edu.

University of Washington, Graduate School, College of Education, Program in Educational Psychology, Seattle, WA 98195. Offers educational psychology (PhD); human development and cognition (M Ed); learning sciences (M Ed, PhD); measurement, statistics and research design (M Ed); school psychology (M Ed). *Accreditation:* APA. *Degree requirements:* For master's, thesis optional; for doctorate, thesis/dissertation. *Entrance requirements:* For master's and doctorate, GRE General Test, minimum GPA of 3.0. Additional exam requirements/recommendations for international students: Required—TOEFL.

The University of Western Ontario, Faculty of Graduate Studies, Social Sciences Division, Faculty of Education, Program in Educational Studies, London, ON N6A 5B8, Canada. Offers curriculum studies (M Ed); educational policy studies (M Ed); educational psychology/special education (M Ed). Part-time programs available. *Faculty research:* Reflective practice, gender and schooling, feminist pedagogy, narrative inquiry, second language, multiculturalism in Canada, education and law.

University of Wisconsin–Madison, Graduate School, School of Education, Department of Educational Psychology, Madison, WI 53706-1380. Offers MS, PhD. *Accreditation:* APA (one or more programs are accredited). *Degree requirements:* For doctorate, thesis/dissertation. *Entrance requirements:* For master's and doctorate, GRE General Test. *Application deadline:* For fall admission, 12/1 for domestic and international students; for spring admission, 10/1 for domestic and international students. Application fee: $56. Electronic applications accepted. *Expenses:* Tuition, state resident: full-time $10,296; part-time $643.51 per credit. Tuition, nonresident: full-time $24,054; part-time $1503.40 per credit. *Required fees:* $70.06 per credit. Tuition and fees vary according to course load, campus/location, program and reciprocity agreements. *Financial support:* Fellowships with full tuition reimbursements, research assistantships with full tuition reimbursements, teaching assistantships with full tuition reimbursements, and project assistantships available. *Unit head:* Dr. Charles Kalish, Chair, 608-262-3432, E-mail: cwkalish@wisc.edu. *Application contact:* 608-262-2433, Fax: 608-262-5134, E-mail: gradadmiss@mail.bascom.wisc.edu. Web site: http://www.education.wisc.edu/edpsych/.

University of Wisconsin–Milwaukee, Graduate School, School of Education, Department of Educational Psychology, Milwaukee, WI 53201-0413. Offers counseling (school, community) (MS); counseling psychology (PhD); learning and development (MS); research methodology (MS, PhD); school psychology (PhD). *Accreditation:* APA. Part-time programs available. *Faculty:* 15 full-time (9 women), 1 (woman) part-time/adjunct. *Students:* 146 full-time (110 women), 60 part-time (46 women); includes 42 minority (14 Black or African American, non-Hispanic/Latino; 10 Asian, non-Hispanic/Latino; 4 Hispanic/Latino; 14 Two or more races, non-Hispanic/Latino), 11 international. Average age 30. 240 applicants, 52% accepted, 52 enrolled. In 2011, 78 master's, 15 doctorates awarded. *Degree requirements:* For master's, comprehensive exam, thesis; for doctorate, thesis/dissertation. *Entrance requirements:* For master's, minimum GPA of 3.0; for doctorate, GRE General Test, minimum GPA of 3.0. Additional exam requirements/recommendations for international students: Required—TOEFL (minimum score 550 paper-based; 79 iBT), IELTS (minimum score 6.5). *Application deadline:* For fall admission, 1/1 priority date for domestic students; for spring admission, 9/1 for domestic students. Applications are processed on a rolling basis. Application fee: $56 ($96 for international students). Electronic applications accepted. One-time fee: $506.10 full-time. Tuition and fees vary according to course load and reciprocity agreements. *Financial support:* In 2011–12, 14 fellowships, 1 research assistantship, 8 teaching assistantships were awarded; career-related internships or fieldwork, health care benefits, unspecified assistantships, and project assistantships also available. Support available to part-time students. Financial award application deadline: 4/15; financial award applicants required to submit FAFSA. *Total annual research expenditures:* $287,260. *Unit head:* Nadya Fouad, Department Chair, 414-229-6830, Fax: 414-229-4939, E-mail: nadya@uwm.edu. *Application contact:* General Information Contact, 414-229-4982, Fax: 414-229-6967, E-mail: gradschool@uwm.edu. Web site: http://www.uwm.edu/Dept/EdPsych/.

University of Wisconsin–Milwaukee, Graduate School, School of Education, Program in Urban Education, Milwaukee, WI 53201-0413. Offers adult and continuing education (PhD); curriculum and instruction (PhD); educational administration (PhD); educational and media technology (PhD); educational psychology (PhD); multicultural studies (PhD); social foundations of education (PhD). *Students:* 65 full-time (45 women), 37 part-time (25 women); includes 39 minority (18 Black or African American, non-Hispanic/Latino; 1 American Indian or Alaska Native, non-Hispanic/Latino; 6 Asian, non-Hispanic/Latino; 6 Hispanic/Latino; 8 Two or more races, non-Hispanic/Latino), 5 international. Average age 41. 26 applicants, 62% accepted, 2 enrolled. In 2011, 13 degrees awarded. *Degree requirements:* For doctorate, comprehensive exam, thesis/dissertation. *Entrance requirements:* For doctorate, GRE General Test, minimum undergraduate GPA of 2.85, graduate 3.5. Additional exam requirements/recommendations for international students: Required—TOEFL (minimum score 550 paper-based; 79 iBT), IELTS (minimum score 6.5). *Application deadline:* For fall admission, 1/1 priority date for domestic students; for spring admission, 9/1 for domestic students. Applications are processed on a rolling basis. Application fee: $56 ($96 for international students). Electronic applications accepted. One-time fee: $506.10 full-time. Tuition and fees vary according to course load and reciprocity agreements. *Financial support:* In 2011–12, 11 fellowships, 1 teaching assistantship were awarded; research assistantships, career-related internships or fieldwork, health care benefits, unspecified assistantships, and project assistantships also available. Support available to part-time students. Financial award application deadline: 4/15; financial award applicants required to submit FAFSA. *Unit head:* Larry Martin, Representative, 414-229-4729, Fax: 414-229-2920, E-mail: lmartin@uwm.edu. *Application contact:* General Information Contact, 414-229-4982, Fax: 414-229-6967, E-mail: gradschool@uwm.edu. Web site: http://www.uwm.edu/Dept/UrbanEd/.

Virginia Commonwealth University, Graduate School, School of Education, Doctoral Program in Education, Educational Psychology Track, Richmond, VA 23284-9005. Offers PhD. *Entrance requirements:* For doctorate, GRE. Additional exam requirements/recommendations for international students: Required—TOEFL (minimum score 600 paper-based; 250 computer-based; 100 iBT). Electronic applications accepted. *Expenses:* Tuition, state resident: full-time $9133; part-time $507 per credit. Tuition, nonresident: full-time $18,777; part-time $1043 per credit. *Required fees:* $77 per credit. Tuition and fees vary according to degree level, campus/location, program and student level.

Walden University, Graduate Programs, School of Psychology, Minneapolis, MN 55401. Offers clinical psychology (MS), including counseling; forensic psychology (MS), including forensic psychology in the community, general program, mental health applications, program planning and evaluation in forensic settings, psychology and legal systems; organizational psychology and development (Postbaccalaureate Certificate); psychology (MS, PhD), including applied psychology (MS), clinical psychology (PhD), counseling psychology (PhD), crisis management and response (MS), educational psychology, general psychology, health psychology, leadership development and coaching (MS), media psychology (MS), organizational psychology, organizational psychology and nonprofit management (MS), program evaluation and research (MS), psychology of culture (MS), psychology, public administration, and social change (MS), social psychology, terrorism and security (MS); teaching online (Post-Master's Certificate). Part-time and evening/weekend programs available. Postbaccalaureate distance learning degree programs offered (minimal on-campus study). *Faculty:* 35 full-time (23 women), 237 part-time/adjunct (124 women). *Students:* 3,206 full-time (2,508 women), 1,510 part-time (1,240 women); includes 2,028 minority (1,483 Black or African American, non-Hispanic/Latino; 43 American Indian or Alaska Native, non-Hispanic/Latino; 99 Asian, non-Hispanic/Latino; 308 Hispanic/Latino; 4 Native Hawaiian or other Pacific Islander, non-Hispanic/Latino; 91 Two or more races, non-Hispanic/Latino), 158 international. Average age 40. In 2011, 645 master's, 113 doctorates, 30 other advanced degrees awarded. Terminal master's awarded for partial completion of doctoral program. *Degree requirements:* For master's, thesis optional; for doctorate, thesis/dissertation, residency. *Entrance requirements:* For master's, bachelor's degree or equivalent in related field; minimum GPA of 2.5; official transcripts; goal statement; access to computer and Internet; for doctorate, master's degree or equivalent in related field; minimum GPA of 3.0; 3 years of related professional/academic experience (preferred). Additional exam requirements/recommendations for international students: Required—TOEFL (minimum score 550 paper-based; 213 computer-based), IELTS (minimum score 6.5), or Michigan English Language Assessment Battery (minimum score 82). *Application deadline:* Applications are processed on a rolling basis. Application fee: $50. Electronic applications accepted. *Financial support:* Federal Work-Study, scholarships/grants, unspecified assistantships, and family tuition reduction, active duty/veteran tuition reduction, group tuition reduction, interest-free payment plans, employee tuition reduction available. Support available to part-time students. Financial award applicants required to submit FAFSA. *Unit head:* Dr. Melanie Storms, Vice President, 800-925-3368. *Application contact:* Jennifer Hall, Vice President of Enrollment Management, 866-4-WALDEN, E-mail: info@waldenu.edu. Web site: http://www.waldenu.edu/Colleges-and-Schools/College-of-Social-and-Behavioral-Sciences/School-of%20-Psychology.htm.

Washington State University, Graduate School, College of Education, Department of Educational Leadership and Counseling Psychology, Pullman, WA 99164. Offers counseling psychology (Ed M, MA, PhD, Certificate), including counseling psychology (Ed M, MA, PhD), school psychologist (Certificate); educational leadership (M Ed, MA, Ed D, PhD); educational psychology (Ed M, MA, PhD); higher education (Ed M, MA, Ed D, PhD), including higher education administration (PhD), sport management (PhD), student affairs (PhD); higher education with sport management (Ed M). *Accreditation:* NCATE. *Faculty:* 12. *Students:* 103 full-time (68 women), 59 part-time (29 women); includes 36 minority (6 Black or African American, non-Hispanic/Latino; 10 Asian, non-Hispanic/Latino; 16 Hispanic/Latino; 4 Two or more races, non-Hispanic/Latino), 18 international. Average age 30. 244 applicants, 29% accepted, 45 enrolled. In 2011, 44 master's, 11 doctorates awarded. Terminal master's awarded for partial completion of doctoral program. *Degree requirements:* For master's, comprehensive exam (for some programs), thesis (for some programs), oral or written exam; for doctorate, comprehensive exam, thesis/dissertation, oral and written exams. *Entrance requirements:* For master's and doctorate, GRE General Test, minimum GPA of 3.0, 3 letters of recommendation. Additional exam requirements/recommendations for international students: Required—TOEFL (minimum score 550 paper-based; 213 computer-based). *Application deadline:* For fall admission, 3/1 for domestic and international students; for spring admission, 10/1 for domestic students, 7/1 for international students. Application fee: $75. *Financial support:* In 2011–12, 1 research assistantship (averaging $18,204 per year), 4 teaching assistantships (averaging $18,204 per year) were awarded; career-related internships or fieldwork, Federal Work-Study, institutionally sponsored loans, scholarships/grants, tuition waivers (partial), and unspecified assistantships also available. Financial award application deadline: 4/1; financial award applicants required to submit FAFSA. *Faculty research:* Attentional processes, cross-cultural psychology, faculty development in higher education. *Total annual research expenditures:* $554,000. *Unit head:* Dr. Phyllis Erdman, Associate Dean, 509-335-9117, E-mail: perdman@wsu.edu. *Application contact:* Graduate School Admissions, 800-GRADWSU, Fax: 509-335-1949, E-mail: gradsch@wsu.edu. Web site: http://www.educ.wsu.edu/elcp/.

Wayne State University, College of Education, Division of Theoretical and Behavioral Foundations, Detroit, MI 48202. Offers counseling (M Ed, MA, Ed D, PhD, Ed S); education evaluation and research (M Ed, Ed D, PhD); educational psychology (M Ed, Ed D, PhD, Ed S); educational sociology (M Ed, Ed D, PhD, Ed S); history and philosophy of education (M Ed, Ed D, PhD); rehabilitation counseling and community inclusion (MA, Ed S); school and community psychology (MA, Ed S); school clinical psychology (Ed S). *Accreditation:* ACA (one or more programs are accredited); CORE (one or more programs are accredited). Evening/weekend programs available. *Students:* 199 full-time (156 women), 215 part-time (187 women); includes 162 minority (145 Black or African American, non-Hispanic/Latino; 1 American Indian or Alaska Native, non-Hispanic/Latino; 5 Asian, non-Hispanic/Latino; 5 Hispanic/Latino; 1 Native Hawaiian or other Pacific Islander, non-Hispanic/Latino; 5 Two or more races, non-Hispanic/Latino), 21 international. Average age 35. 278 applicants, 30% accepted, 56 enrolled. In 2011, 94 master's, 15 doctorates, 1 other advanced degree awarded. *Degree requirements:* For master's, thesis (for some programs); for doctorate, thesis/dissertation. *Entrance requirements:* For master's, GRE; for doctorate, GRE, interview, minimum GPA of 3.0, curriculum vitae, references. Additional exam requirements/recommendations for international students: Required—TOEFL (minimum score 550 paper-based; 213 computer-based), TWE (minimum score 5.5). *Application deadline:* For fall admission, 6/1 priority date for domestic students, 5/1 for international students; for winter admission, 10/1 priority date for domestic students, 9/1 for international students; for spring admission, 2/1 priority date for domestic students, 1/1 for international students. Applications are processed on a rolling basis. Application fee: $50. Electronic applications accepted. *Expenses:* Tuition, state resident: part-time $512.85 per credit. Tuition, nonresident: part-time $1132.65 per credit. *Required fees:* $26.60 per credit. $199.65 per semester. Tuition and fees vary according to course load and program. *Financial support:* In 2011–12, 64 students received support, including 3 fellowships with tuition reimbursements available (averaging $16,371 per year), 2 research assistantships with tuition reimbursements available (averaging $15,713 per year), 1 teaching assistantship (averaging $18,000 per year); career-related internships or fieldwork, Federal Work-Study, institutionally sponsored loans, scholarships/grants, health care benefits, and unspecified assistantships also available. *Faculty research:*

Adolescents at risk, supervision of counseling. *Total annual research expenditures:* $5,019. *Unit head:* Dr. Alan Hoffman, Assistant Dean, 313-577-5235, E-mail: alanhoffman@wayne.edu. *Application contact:* Janice Green, Assistant Dean, 313-577-1605, E-mail: jwgreen@wayne.edu. Web site: http://coe.wayne.edu/tbf/index.php.

West Virginia University, College of Human Resources and Education, Department of Technology, Learning and Culture, Program in Educational Psychology, Morgantown, WV 26506. Offers MA. *Accreditation:* NCATE. Evening/weekend programs available. *Degree requirements:* For master's, thesis, content exams. *Entrance requirements:* For master's, GRE General Test (minimum score 1100 verbal and quantitative) or MAT (minimum score 55), minimum GPA of 3.0, interview. Additional exam requirements/recommendations for international students: Required—TOEFL (minimum score 550 paper-based). *Faculty research:* Learning, development, instructional design, stimulus control, rehabilitation.

Wichita State University, Graduate School, College of Education, Department of Counseling, Educational Leadership, Educational and School Psychology, Wichita, KS 67260. Offers counseling (M Ed); educational leadership (M Ed, Ed D); educational psychology (M Ed); school psychology (Ed S). *Accreditation:* NCATE. Part-time and evening/weekend programs available. *Expenses:* Tuition, state resident: full-time $4746; part-time $263.65 per credit. Tuition, nonresident: full-time $11,669; part-time $648.30 per credit. *Unit head:* Dr. Jean Patterson, Chairperson, 316-978-3325, Fax: 316-978-3102, E-mail: jean.patterson@wichita.edu. *Application contact:* Carrie C. Henderson, Admissions Coordinator, 316-978-3095, Fax: 316-978-3253, E-mail: carrie.henderson@wichita.edu. Web site: http://www.wichita.edu/.

Widener University, School of Human Service Professions, Center for Education, Chester, PA 19013-5792. Offers adult education (M Ed); counseling in higher education (M Ed); counselor education (M Ed); early childhood education (M Ed); educational foundations (M Ed); educational leadership (M Ed); educational psychology (M Ed); elementary education (M Ed); English and language arts (M Ed); health education (M Ed); higher education leadership (Ed D); home and school visitor (M Ed); human sexuality (M Ed, PhD); mathematics education (M Ed); middle school education (M Ed); principalship (M Ed); reading and language arts (Ed D); reading education (M Ed); school administration (Ed D); science education (M Ed); social studies education (M Ed); special education (M Ed); technology education (M Ed). *Accreditation:* NCATE. Part-time and evening/weekend programs available. Terminal master's awarded for partial completion of doctoral program. *Degree requirements:* For doctorate, thesis/dissertation. *Entrance requirements:* For master's, minimum GPA of 2.5; for doctorate, GRE or MAT, minimum GPA of 2.0 (undergraduate), 3.5 (graduate). Electronic applications accepted. *Expenses:* Contact institution. *Faculty research:* Reading and cognition, adult education, technology education, educational leadership, special education.

Foundations and Philosophy of Education

Antioch University New England, Graduate School, Department of Education, Experienced Educators Program, Keene, NH 03431-3552. Offers M Ed. *Degree requirements:* For master's, thesis, practicum. *Entrance requirements:* For master's, previous course work and work experience in education. Additional exam requirements/recommendations for international students: Required—TOEFL (minimum score 600 paper-based; 250 computer-based). Electronic applications accepted. *Expenses:* Contact institution. *Faculty research:* Classroom action research, school restructuring, problem-based learning, brain-based learning.

Arizona State University, Mary Lou Fulton Teachers College, Program in Social and Philosophical Foundations of Education, Phoenix, AZ 85069. Offers MA. Part-time and evening/weekend programs available. *Degree requirements:* For master's, thesis optional, interactive Program of Study (iPOS) submitted before completing 50 percent of required credit hours. *Entrance requirements:* For master's, minimum GPA of 3.0 or equivalent in last 2 years of work leading to bachelor's degree, 3 letters of recommendation, professional statement, curriculum vitae or resume. Additional exam requirements/recommendations for international students: Required—TOEFL (minimum score 80 iBT), TOEFL, IELTS, or Pearson Test of English. Electronic applications accepted.

Ashland University, Dwight Schar College of Education, Department of Educational Foundations, Ashland, OH 44805-3702. Offers teacher leader (M Ed). Part-time and evening/weekend programs available. *Faculty:* 12 full-time (9 women), 68 part-time/adjunct (33 women). *Students:* 3 full-time (2 women), 18 part-time (12 women); includes 1 minority (Two or more races, non-Hispanic/Latino), 2 international. Average age 28. 3 applicants, 100% accepted, 2 enrolled. In 2011, 15 master's awarded. *Degree requirements:* For master's, inquiry seminar, internship, or thesis. *Entrance requirements:* For master's, teaching certificate or license, bachelor's degree, minimum cumulative GPA of 2.75. Additional exam requirements/recommendations for international students: Required—TOEFL. *Application deadline:* Applications are processed on a rolling basis. Application fee: $30. Electronic applications accepted. *Expenses: Tuition:* Full-time $5580; part-time $465 per credit hour. *Financial support:* Application deadline: 4/15. *Faculty research:* Character education, teacher reflection, religion and education, professional education, environmental education. *Unit head:* Dr. Louise Fleming, Chair, 419-289-5347, E-mail: lfleming@ashland.edu. *Application contact:* Dr. Linda Billman, Associate Dean, 419-289-5369, Fax: 419-289-5331, E-mail: lbillman@ashland.edu. Web site: http://www.ashland.edu/academics/education/edfoundations/.

Azusa Pacific University, School of Education, Department of Foundations and Transdisciplinary Studies, Azusa, CA 91702-7000. Offers curriculum and instruction in multicultural contexts (MA Ed); teaching (MA Ed).

Ball State University, Graduate School, Teachers College, Department of Educational Studies, Program in Educational Studies, Muncie, IN 47306-1099. Offers PhD. *Students:* 3 full-time (2 women), 8 part-time (4 women), 1 international. 25 applicants, 40% accepted, 6 enrolled. In 2011, 2 doctorates awarded. Tuition and fees vary according to program and reciprocity agreements. *Financial support:* In 2011–12, 6 students received support, including 6 teaching assistantships (averaging $6,979 per year). *Unit head:* Dr. Jayne Beilke, Chairman, 765-285-5400, Fax: 765-285-5489. *Application contact:* Dr. Thalia Mulvihill, Associate Provost for Research and Dean of the Graduate School.

Bank Street College of Education, Graduate School, Studies in Education, New York, NY 10025. Offers Ed M, MS Ed. *Students:* 4 full-time (all women), 4 part-time (3 women); includes 4 minority (3 Black or African American, non-Hispanic/Latino; 1 Hispanic/Latino), 1 international. Average age 31. 5 applicants, 80% accepted, 2 enrolled. In 2011, 6 master's awarded. *Degree requirements:* For master's, thesis. *Entrance requirements:* For master's, interview, essays. Additional exam requirements/recommendations for international students: Required—TOEFL (minimum score 600 paper-based; 250 computer-based; 100 iBT), IELTS (minimum score 7). *Application deadline:* For fall admission, 2/15 priority date for domestic students, 2/15 for international students; for spring admission, 11/1 priority date for domestic students, 11/1 for international students. Applications are processed on a rolling basis. Application fee: $65. Electronic applications accepted. *Expenses: Required fees:* $1240 per credit. $100 per term. One-time fee: $250 part-time. *Financial support:* Career-related internships or fieldwork, Federal Work-Study, scholarships/grants, and unspecified assistantships available. Support available to part-time students. Financial award application deadline: 4/15; financial award applicants required to submit FAFSA. *Unit head:* Nancy Gropper, Director, 212-875-4477, Fax: 212-875-4753, E-mail: ngropper@bankstreet.edu. *Application contact:* Ann Morgan, Director of Graduate Admissions, 212-875-4403, Fax: 212-875-4678, E-mail: amorgan@bankstreet.edu. Web site: http://bankstreet.edu/graduate-school/academics/programs/individualized-programs/studies-education/.

Brigham Young University, Graduate Studies, David O. McKay School of Education, Department of Educational Leadership and Foundations, Provo, UT 84602. Offers M Ed, Ed D. Part-time and evening/weekend programs available. *Faculty:* 10 full-time (3 women), 2 part-time/adjunct (0 women). *Students:* 27 full-time (19 women), 64 part-time (24 women); includes 9 minority (1 American Indian or Alaska Native, non-Hispanic/Latino; 1 Asian, non-Hispanic/Latino; 2 Hispanic/Latino; 5 Native Hawaiian or other Pacific Islander, non-Hispanic/Latino). Average age 39. 66 applicants, 61% accepted, 37 enrolled. In 2011, 33 master's, 4 doctorates awarded. *Degree requirements:* For master's, comprehensive exam, thesis or alternative; for doctorate, comprehensive exam, thesis/dissertation. *Entrance requirements:* For master's, GRE, MAT, LSAT, Utah Level II Teaching License (or equivalent); for doctorate, GRE, GMAT, LSAT. Additional exam requirements/recommendations for international students: Required—TOEFL (minimum score 580 paper-based; 237 computer-based; 85 iBT). *Application deadline:* For fall admission, 2/15 for domestic and international students; for spring admission, 3/1 for domestic and international students. Application fee: $50. Electronic applications accepted. *Expenses: Tuition:* Full-time $5760; part-time $320 per credit. Tuition and fees vary according to student's religious affiliation. *Financial support:* In 2011–12, 35 students received support, including research assistantships (averaging $914 per year); teaching assistantships and scholarships/grants also available. Financial award application deadline: 9/1. *Faculty research:* Mentoring, pre-service training of administrators, policy development, cross-cultural studies of educational leadership. *Unit head:* Dean Richard K. Young, Chair, 801-422-3695, Fax: 801-422-0200, E-mail: msesec@byu.edu. *Application contact:* Bonnie Bennett, Department Secretary, 801-422-3813, Fax: 801-422-0196, E-mail: bonnie_bennett@byu.edu. Web site: http://education.byu.edu/edlf/.

Central Connecticut State University, School of Graduate Studies, School of Education and Professional Studies, Department of Teacher Education, Program in Educational Foundations Policy/Secondary Education, New Britain, CT 06050-4010. Offers MS. Part-time and evening/weekend programs available. *Students:* 11 part-time (7 women). Average age 37. In 2011, 8 master's awarded. *Degree requirements:* For master's, comprehensive exam, thesis or alternative. *Entrance requirements:* For master's, minimum undergraduate GPA of 2.7. Additional exam requirements/recommendations for international students: Required—TOEFL (minimum score 550 paper-based; 213 computer-based). *Application deadline:* For fall admission, 6/1 for domestic students, 5/1 for international students; for spring admission, 11/1 for domestic and international students. Applications are processed on a rolling basis. Application fee: $50. Electronic applications accepted. *Expenses: Tuition, area resident:* Full-time $5137; part-time $482 per credit. Tuition, state resident: full-time $7707; part-time $494 per credit. Tuition, nonresident: full-time $14,311; part-time $494 per credit. *Required fees:* $3865. One-time fee: $62 part-time. *Unit head:* Dr. Ronnie Casella, Chair, 860-832-2415, E-mail: casellar@ccsu.edu. *Application contact:* Patricia Gardner, Associate Director of Graduate Studies, 860-832-2350, Fax: 860-832-2352, E-mail: graduateadmissions@ccsu.edu.

Central Washington University, Graduate Studies and Research, College of Education and Professional Studies, Department of Educational Foundations and Curriculum, Ellensburg, WA 98926. Offers master teacher (M Ed). Part-time programs available. *Faculty:* 19 full-time (9 women). *Students:* 22 part-time (21 women). 14 applicants, 64% accepted, 9 enrolled. In 2011, 12 master's awarded. *Degree requirements:* For master's, comprehensive exam (for some programs), thesis or alternative. *Entrance requirements:* For master's, 1 year contracted teaching experience. Additional exam requirements/recommendations for international students: Required—TOEFL (minimum score 550 paper-based; 213 computer-based; 79 iBT), IELTS (minimum score 6.5). *Application deadline:* For fall admission, 2/1 for domestic students; for winter admission, 10/1 for domestic students; for spring admission, 1/1 for domestic students. Applications are processed on a rolling basis. Application fee: $50. Electronic applications accepted. *Expenses:* Tuition, state resident: full-time $8112; part-time $270 per credit. Tuition, nonresident: full-time $18,069; part-time $602 per credit. *Required fees:* $924. *Financial support:* In 2011–12, 1 teaching assistantship (averaging $9,234 per year) was awarded; Federal Work-Study, scholarships/grants, health care benefits, and unspecified assistantships also available. Support available to part-time students. Financial award application deadline: 3/1; financial award applicants required to submit FAFSA. *Unit head:* Dr. Barry Donahue, Chair, 509-963-1448. *Application contact:* Justine Eason, Admissions Program Coordinator, 509-963-3103, Fax: 509-963-1799, E-mail: masters@cwu.edu. Web site: http://www.cwu.edu/~edfoundations/.

Chicago State University, School of Graduate and Professional Studies, College of Education, Department of Educational Leadership, Curriculum and Foundations, Program in Curriculum and Instruction, Chicago, IL 60628. Offers instructional foundations (MS Ed). *Degree requirements:* For master's, comprehensive exam, thesis optional. *Entrance requirements:* For master's, minimum GPA of 2.75.

Curry College, Graduate Studies, Program in Education, Milton, MA 02186-9984. Offers elementary education (M Ed); foundations (non-license) (M Ed); reading (M Ed, Certificate); special education (M Ed). Part-time and evening/weekend programs available. *Degree requirements:* For master's, project or thesis. *Entrance requirements:* For master's, interview, recommendations, resume, written statement. Additional exam requirements/recommendations for international students: Required—TOEFL (minimum score 550 paper-based; 213 computer-based; 80 iBT). *Expenses:* Contact institution. *Faculty research:* Classroom trauma, therapeutic writing, inclusionary practices.

DePaul University, College of Education, Chicago, IL 60106. Offers bilingual bicultural education (M Ed, MA); counseling (M Ed, MA), including college student development, community counseling, school counseling; curriculum studies (M Ed, MA, Ed D); early childhood education (M Ed, MA); educational leadership (M Ed, MA, Ed D), including administration and supervision (M Ed, MA), physical education (M Ed, MA); middle school mathematics education (MS); reading specialist (M Ed, MA); social and cultural foundations in education (M Ed, MA), including curriculum studies/development (MA); special education (M Ed, MA); teaching and learning (M Ed, MA), including elementary education, secondary education; world languages education (M Ed, MA). Part-time and evening/weekend programs available. *Faculty:* 49 full-time (28 women), 94 part-time/adjunct (60 women). *Students:* 894 full-time (707 women), 473 part-time (361 women); includes 349 minority (159 Black or African American, non-Hispanic/Latino; 3 American Indian or Alaska Native, non-Hispanic/Latino; 45 Asian, non-Hispanic/Latino; 115 Hispanic/Latino; 2 Native Hawaiian or other Pacific Islander, non-Hispanic/Latino; 25 Two or more races, non-Hispanic/Latino), 21 international. Average age 30. 872 applicants, 64% accepted, 325 enrolled. In 2011, 499 master's, 10 doctorates awarded. *Median time to degree:* Of those who began their doctoral program in fall 2003, 32% received their degree in 8 years or less. *Degree requirements:* For master's, thesis/dissertation (for MA); capstone course or paper (for M Ed); for doctorate, thesis/dissertation. *Entrance requirements:* For master's, interview, minimum GPA of 2.75, 2 letters of recommendation, bachelor's degree conferred by accredited college or university; for doctorate, interview, master's degree, writing sample, 3 letters of recommendation. Additional exam requirements/recommendations for international students: Required—TOEFL (minimum score 550 paper-based; 213 computer-based; 80 iBT). *Application deadline:* For fall admission, 8/15 priority date for domestic students; for winter admission, 12/1 priority date for domestic students; for spring admission, 3/1 priority date for domestic students. Applications are processed on a rolling basis. Application fee: $40. Electronic applications accepted. *Financial support:* In 2011–12, 163 students received support, including 15 research assistantships with full tuition reimbursements available (averaging $6,375 per year); career-related internships or fieldwork, Federal Work-Study, scholarships/grants, and unspecified assistantships also available. Support available to part-time students. Financial award application deadline: 12/31; financial award applicants required to submit FAFSA. *Faculty research:* Reflective teaching, children at risk, loss, ethnicity, urban education. *Total annual research expenditures:* $916,310. *Unit head:* Dr. Paul Zionts, Dean, 773-325-7581, Fax: 773-325-7713, E-mail: pzionts@depaul.edu. *Application contact:* Brandon Washington, Enrollment Management Coordinator, 773-325-1152, Fax: 773-325-2270, E-mail: bwashin3@depaul.edu. Web site: http://education.depaul.edu.

Duquesne University, School of Education, Department of Foundations and Leadership, Program in Educational Studies, Pittsburgh, PA 15282-0001. Offers MS Ed. Part-time and evening/weekend programs available. Postbaccalaureate distance learning degree programs offered (no on-campus study). *Faculty:* 1 (woman) full-time. *Students:* 12 full-time (7 women), 18 part-time (16 women); includes 3 minority (all Black or African American, non-Hispanic/Latino), 15 international. Average age 36. 39 applicants, 56% accepted, 19 enrolled. In 2011, 10 degrees awarded. *Degree requirements:* For master's, thesis optional. *Entrance requirements:* For master's, bachelor's degree. Additional exam requirements/recommendations for international students: Required—TOEFL (minimum score 550 paper-based; 80 computer-based), IELTS (minimum score 7). *Application deadline:* For fall admission, 9/1 for domestic students; for spring admission, 1/1 for domestic students. Applications are processed on a rolling basis. Application fee: $0. Electronic applications accepted. *Expenses: Tuition:* Full-time $16,596; part-time $922 per credit. *Required fees:* $1584; $88 per credit. Tuition and fees vary according to program. *Financial support:* Research assistantships available. Support available to part-time students. *Unit head:* Dr. Connie Marie Moss, Director, 412-396-4778, Fax: 412-396-5454, E-mail: moss@duq.edu. *Application contact:* Michael Dolinger, Director of Student and Academic Services, 412-396-6647, Fax: 412-396-5585, E-mail: dolingerm@duq.edu. Web site: http://www.duq.edu/education.

Eastern Michigan University, Graduate School, College of Education, Department of Teacher Education, Program in Social Foundations, Ypsilanti, MI 48197. Offers MA. *Accreditation:* NCATE. Part-time and evening/weekend programs available. Postbaccalaureate distance learning degree programs offered (minimal on-campus study). *Students:* 3 full-time (all women), 11 part-time (10 women); includes 5 minority (3 Black or African American, non-Hispanic/Latino; 1 Hispanic/Latino; 1 Two or more races, non-Hispanic/Latino), 2 international. Average age 32. 9 applicants, 100% accepted, 4 enrolled. In 2011, 4 degrees awarded. *Entrance requirements:* For master's, GRE. Additional exam requirements/recommendations for international students: Required—TOEFL. *Application deadline:* Applications are processed on a rolling basis. Application fee: $35. *Expenses:* Tuition, state resident: full-time $10,367; part-time $432 per credit hour. Tuition, nonresident: full-time $20,435; part-time $851 per credit hour. *Required fees:* $39 per credit hour. $46 per semester. One-time fee: $100. Tuition and fees vary according to course level, degree level and reciprocity agreements. *Financial support:* Fellowships, research assistantships with full tuition reimbursements, teaching assistantships with full tuition reimbursements, career-related internships or fieldwork, Federal Work-Study, institutionally sponsored loans, scholarships/grants, tuition waivers (partial), and unspecified assistantships available. Support available to part-time students. Financial award applicants required to submit FAFSA. *Unit head:* Dr. Joe Ramsey, Coordinator, 734-487-3260, Fax: 734-487-2101, E-mail: pramsey1@emich.edu. *Application contact:* Dr. Anne Bednar, Advisor, 734-487-3260, Fax: 734-487-2101, E-mail: anne.bednar@emich.edu.

Eastern Washington University, Graduate Studies, College of Arts, Letters and Education, Department of Education, Program in Foundations of Education, Cheney, WA 99004-2431. Offers M Ed. *Students:* 2 part-time (1 woman); includes 1 minority (Asian, non-Hispanic/Latino), 1 international. Average age 40. 2 applicants, 0% accepted, 0 enrolled. In 2011, 3 master's awarded. *Degree requirements:* For master's, comprehensive exam. *Entrance requirements:* For master's, minimum GPA of 3.0. *Application deadline:* For fall admission, 4/1 priority date for domestic students; for spring admission, 1/15 for domestic students. Applications are processed on a rolling basis. Application fee: $50. *Financial support:* In 2011–12, teaching assistantships with partial tuition reimbursements (averaging $7,000 per year) were awarded; career-related internships or fieldwork, Federal Work-Study, institutionally sponsored loans, scholarships/grants, health care benefits, tuition waivers (partial), and unspecified assistantships also available. Support available to part-time students. Financial award application deadline: 2/1; financial award applicants required to submit FAFSA. *Unit head:* Robin Showalter, Program Coordinator, 509-359-6492, E-mail: rshowalter@mail.ewu.edu. *Application contact:* Dr. Kevin Pyatt, Graduate Program Coordinator, 509-359-6091.

Fairfield University, Graduate School of Education and Allied Professions, Fairfield, CT 06824-5195. Offers applied psychology (MA); bilingual education (CAS); clinical mental health counseling (MA, CAS); educational technology (MA); elementary education (MA); family studies (MA); marriage and family therapy (MA); school counseling (MA, CAS); school psychology (MA, CAS); special education (MA); teaching (Certificate); teaching and foundations (MA, CAS); TESOL foreign language and bilingual/multicultural education (MA, CAS). *Accreditation:* NCATE. Part-time and evening/weekend programs available. *Faculty:* 24 full-time (19 women). *Students:* 147 full-time (120 women), 391 part-time (321 women); includes 60 minority (13 Black or African American, non-Hispanic/Latino; 8 Asian, non-Hispanic/Latino; 35 Hispanic/Latino; 4 Two or more races, non-Hispanic/Latino), 1 international. Average age 34. 319 applicants, 48% accepted, 80 enrolled. In 2011, 185 master's, 20 other advanced degrees awarded. *Degree requirements:* For master's, comprehensive exam. *Entrance requirements:* For master's, PRAXIS I (for certification programs), minimum QPA of 3.0, 2 recommendations, resume. Additional exam requirements/recommendations for international students: Required—TOEFL (minimum score 550 paper-based; 213 computer-based; 84 iBT) or IELTS (minimum score 7.5). *Application deadline:* For fall admission, 2/15 for international students; for spring admission, 10/1 for international students. Application fee: $60. Electronic applications accepted. *Expenses: Tuition:* Part-time $600 per credit hour. *Required fees:* $25 per term. *Financial support:* In 2011–12, 45 students received support. Career-related internships or fieldwork and unspecified assistantships available. Financial award applicants required to submit FAFSA. *Faculty research:* Literacy, adolescent psychology, special education, early childhood education, teaching development. *Unit head:* Dr. Susan D. Franzosa, Dean, 203-254-4000 Ext. 4250, Fax: 203-254-4241, E-mail: sfranzosa@fairfield.edu. *Application contact:* Marianne Gumpper, Director of Graduate and Continuing Studies Admission, 203-254-4184, Fax: 203-254-4073, E-mail: gradadmis@fairfield.edu. Web site: http://www.fairfield.edu/gseap/gseap_grad_1.html.

Fairleigh Dickinson University, Metropolitan Campus, University College: Arts, Sciences, and Professional Studies, School of Computer Sciences and Engineering, Program in Mathematical Foundation, Teaneck, NJ 07666-1914. Offers MS.

Florida Atlantic University, College of Education, Department of Teaching and Learning, Boca Raton, FL 33431-0991. Offers curriculum and instruction (M Ed); elementary education (M Ed); environmental education (M Ed); reading education (M Ed); social foundations of education (M Ed). *Accreditation:* NCATE. Part-time and evening/weekend programs available. *Faculty:* 32 full-time (25 women), 90 part-time/adjunct (68 women). *Students:* 34 full-time (30 women), 103 part-time (96 women); includes 29 minority (8 Black or African American, non-Hispanic/Latino; 7 Asian, non-Hispanic/Latino; 11 Hispanic/Latino; 3 Two or more races, non-Hispanic/Latino), 1 international. Average age 32. 96 applicants, 66% accepted, 24 enrolled. In 2011, 71 master's awarded. *Entrance requirements:* For master's, GRE General Test, minimum GPA of 3.0 in last 2 years of undergraduate course work. Additional exam requirements/recommendations for international students: Required—TOEFL. *Application deadline:* For fall admission, 7/1 for domestic students, 2/15 for international students; for spring admission, 11/1 for domestic students, 7/15 for international students. Applications are processed on a rolling basis. Application fee: $30. *Expenses: Tuition, area resident:* Part-time $343.02 per credit hour. Tuition, state resident: full-time $8232. Tuition, nonresident: full-time $23,931; part-time $997.14 per credit hour. *Financial support:* Fellowships with partial tuition reimbursements, research assistantships with partial tuition reimbursements, teaching assistantships with partial tuition reimbursements, career-related internships or fieldwork, scholarships/grants, and unspecified assistantships available. *Faculty research:* Technology, teaching English to speakers of other languages, math teaching, electronic portfolio assessment, global perspectives through social studies. *Unit head:* Dr. Barbara Ridener, Chairperson, 561-297-3588. *Application contact:* Dr. Eliah Watlington, Associate Dean, 561-296-8520, Fax: 261-297-2991, E-mail: ewatling@fau.edu. Web site: http://www.coe.fau.edu/academicdepartments/tl/.

Florida State University, The Graduate School, College of Education, Department of Educational Leadership and Policy Studies, Program in Social, History and Philosophy of Education, Tallahassee, FL 32306. Offers history and philosophy of education (MS, PhD, Ed S); international and intercultural education (PhD). *Faculty:* 2 full-time (0 women). *Students:* 29 full-time (19 women), 17 part-time (8 women); includes 8 minority (5 Black or African American, non-Hispanic/Latino; 1 Asian, non-Hispanic/Latino; 2 Hispanic/Latino), 14 international. Average age 36. 42 applicants, 76% accepted, 10 enrolled. In 2011, 11 master's, 5 doctorates, 2 other advanced degrees awarded. *Degree requirements:* For master's and Ed S, comprehensive exam, thesis optional; for doctorate, comprehensive exam, thesis/dissertation. *Entrance requirements:* For master's, doctorate, and Ed S, GRE General Test, minimum GPA of 3.0. Additional exam requirements/recommendations for international students: Required—TOEFL (minimum score 550 paper-based; 213 computer-based; 80 iBT). *Application deadline:* For fall admission, 7/1 for domestic and international students; for winter admission, 11/1 for domestic and international students; for spring admission, 3/1 for domestic and international students. Application fee: $30. Electronic applications accepted. *Expenses:* Tuition, state resident: full-time $9474; part-time $350.88 per credit hour. Tuition, nonresident: full-time $16,236; part-time $601.34 per credit hour. *Required fees:* $630 per semester. One-time fee: $20. Tuition and fees vary according to course load and campus/location. *Financial support:* Fellowships with full and partial tuition reimbursements, research assistantships with full and partial tuition reimbursements, teaching assistantships with full and partial tuition reimbursements, career-related internships or fieldwork, scholarships/grants, health care benefits, and unspecified assistantships available. Financial award applicants required to submit FAFSA. *Faculty research:* Social, historical, philosophical content of educational policies; religion, gender, diversity, and social justice in educational policy; interdisciplinary. *Unit head:* Dr. Jeffrey A. Milligan, Assistant Professor/Program Coordinator, 850-644-8171, Fax: 850-644-1258, E-mail: jmilligan@fsu.edu. *Application contact:* Jimmy Pastrano, Program Assistant, 850-644-6777, Fax: 850-644-1258, E-mail: jpastrano@fsu.edu. Web site: http://www.coe.fsu.edu/SHPFE.

The George Washington University, Graduate School of Education and Human Development, Department of Curriculum and Pedagogy, Program in Professional Teaching Standards, Washington, DC 20052. Offers Graduate Certificate.

Georgia State University, College of Education, Department of Educational Policy Studies, Program in Social Foundations of Education, Atlanta, GA 30302-3083. Offers MS, PhD. *Accreditation:* NCATE. Part-time and evening/weekend programs available. *Degree requirements:* For master's, thesis or project; for doctorate, comprehensive exam, thesis/dissertation. *Entrance requirements:* For master's, GRE General Test, minimum GPA of 2.5, 2 letters of recommendation, resume; for doctorate, GRE General Test or MAT, minimum GPA of 3.3, 3 letters of recommendation, resum/curriculum vitae, statement of goals. *Faculty research:* Teacher unionism, African and African-American history and culture, multicultural and workplace education, teacher autonomy and epistemology.

Harvard University, Extension School, Cambridge, MA 02138-3722. Offers applied sciences (CAS); biotechnology (ALM); educational technologies (ALM); educational technology (CET); English for graduate and professional studies (DGP); environmental management (ALM, CEM); information technology (ALM); journalism (ALM); liberal arts (ALM); management (ALM, CM); mathematics for teaching (ALM); museum studies (ALM); premedical studies (Diploma); publication and communication (CPC). Part-time and evening/weekend programs available. *Degree requirements:* For master's, thesis.

Entrance requirements: For master's, 3 completed graduate courses with grade of B or higher. Additional exam requirements/recommendations for international students: Required—TOEFL (minimum score 600 paper-based; 250 computer-based), TWE (minimum score 5). *Expenses:* Contact institution.

Hofstra University, School of Education, Health, and Human Services, Department of Foundations, Leadership, and Policy Studies, Hempstead, NY 11549. Offers educational and policy leadership (MS Ed, Ed D), including higher education (MS Ed), K-12 (MS Ed); educational policy and leadership (Advanced Certificate), including school district business leader; foundations of education (MA, Advanced Certificate); Advanced Certificate/Advanced Certificate. Part-time and evening/weekend programs available. Postbaccalaureate distance learning degree programs offered (minimal on-campus study). *Students:* 22 full-time (16 women), 105 part-time (65 women); includes 45 minority (33 Black or African American, non-Hispanic/Latino; 1 Asian, non-Hispanic/Latino; 11 Hispanic/Latino), 2 international. Average age 37. 78 applicants, 94% accepted, 42 enrolled. In 2011, 12 master's, 6 doctorates, 12 other advanced degrees awarded. *Degree requirements:* For master's, one foreign language, comprehensive exam (for some programs), thesis or alternative, minimum GPA of 3.0; for doctorate, comprehensive exam (for some programs), thesis/dissertation (for some programs), minimum GPA of 3.0. *Entrance requirements:* For master's and Advanced Certificate, interview, writing sample, essay; for doctorate, GMAT, GRE, LSAT, or MAT, interview, 3 letters of recommendation, resume, essay. Additional exam requirements/recommendations for international students: Required—TOEFL (minimum score 550 paper-based; 213 computer-based; 80 iBT). *Application deadline:* Applications are processed on a rolling basis. Application fee: $70 ($75 for international students). Electronic applications accepted. *Expenses: Tuition:* Full-time $18,990; part-time $1055 per credit hour. *Required fees:* $970. Tuition and fees vary according to program. *Financial support:* In 2011–12, 66 students received support, including 44 fellowships with full and partial tuition reimbursements available (averaging $3,788 per year), 3 research assistantships with full and partial tuition reimbursements available (averaging $12,125 per year); Federal Work-Study, institutionally sponsored loans, scholarships/grants, tuition waivers (full and partial), and unspecified assistantships also available. Support available to part-time students. Financial award applicants required to submit FAFSA. *Faculty research:* School improvement, professional assessment - APPR, educational policy, professional development, race/gender in education. *Unit head:* Dr. Esther Fusco, Chairperson, 516-463-7704, Fax: 516-463-6196, E-mail: catezf@hofstra.edu. *Application contact:* Carol Drummer, Dean of Graduate Admissions, 516-463-4876, Fax: 516-463-4664, E-mail: gradstudent@hofstra.edu. Web site: http://www.hofstra.edu/education/.

Indiana University Bloomington, School of Education, Department of Educational Leadership and Policy Studies, Bloomington, IN 47405-7000. Offers education policy studies (PhD); educational leadership (MS, Ed D, Ed S); higher education (MS, Ed D, PhD); history and philosophy of education (MS); history of education (PhD); international and comparative education (MS, PhD); philosophy of education (PhD); student affairs administration (MS). *Accreditation:* NCATE. Part-time and evening/weekend programs available. *Degree requirements:* For master's, thesis optional; for doctorate, comprehensive exam, thesis/dissertation; for Ed S, comprehensive exam or project. *Entrance requirements:* For master's, doctorate, and Ed S, GRE General Test. Additional exam requirements/recommendations for international students: Required—TOEFL (minimum score 213 computer-based; 79 iBT). Electronic applications accepted. *Faculty research:* Student engagement at higher education institutions in the nation, Reading First professional development initiative, state finance policy on financial access to higher education, school reform, special needs studies.

Indiana University Bloomington, University Graduate School, College of Arts and Sciences, Department of East Asian Languages and Cultures, Bloomington, IN 47408. Offers Chinese (MA, PhD); Chinese - flagship track (MA); Chinese language pedagogy (MA); East Asian studies (MA); Japanese (MA, PhD); Japanese language pedagogy (MA). Part-time programs available. *Faculty:* 18 full-time (9 women), 12 part-time/adjunct (6 women). *Students:* 29 full-time (14 women), 8 part-time (5 women); includes 2 minority (both Black or African American, non-Hispanic/Latino), 7 international. Average age 29. 98 applicants, 31% accepted, 7 enrolled. In 2011, 8 master's, 1 doctorate awarded. *Degree requirements:* For master's, one foreign language, thesis; for doctorate, 2 foreign languages, comprehensive exam, thesis/dissertation. *Entrance requirements:* Additional exam requirements/recommendations for international students: Required—TOEFL (minimum score 93 iBT). *Application deadline:* For fall admission, 1/15 for domestic students, 12/1 for international students. Application fee: $55 ($65 for international students). Electronic applications accepted. *Financial support:* In 2011–12, 21 students received support, including 5 fellowships with full tuition reimbursements available (averaging $15,000 per year), 18 teaching assistantships with full tuition reimbursements available (averaging $13,400 per year). Financial award application deadline: 3/1. *Faculty research:* Postwar/postmodern Japanese fiction, modern Chinese film and literature, classical Chinese literature and philosophy, Chinese and Japanese linguistics and pedagogy, East Asian politics and economics, Chinese and Japanese history, Korean language. *Unit head:* Natsuko Tsujimura, Chair, 812-855-0856, Fax: 812-855-6402, E-mail: tsujimur@indiana.edu. *Application contact:* Scott O'Bryan, Director of Graduate Studies, 812-855-2454, Fax: 812-855-6402, E-mail: spobryan@indiana.edu. Web site: http://www.indiana.edu/~ealc/index.shtml.

Iowa State University of Science and Technology, Department of Curriculum and Instruction, Ames, IA 50011. Offers curriculum and instructional technology (M Ed, MS, PhD); elementary education (M Ed, MS); historical, philosophical, and comparative studies in education (M Ed, MS); special education (M Ed, MS, PhD). *Degree requirements:* For master's, thesis or alternative; for doctorate, thesis/dissertation. *Entrance requirements:* For master's and doctorate, GRE General Test. Additional exam requirements/recommendations for international students: Required—TOEFL (minimum score 560 paper-based; 83 iBT), IELTS (minimum score 6.5). *Application deadline:* For fall admission, 1/1 priority date for domestic students, 1/1 for international students; for spring admission, 9/1 for domestic and international students. Application fee: $40 ($90 for international students). Electronic applications accepted. *Unit head:* Dr. Anne Foegen, Director of Graduate Education, 515-294-7021, Fax: 515-294-6206, E-mail: cigrad@iastate.edu. *Application contact:* Phyllis Kendall, Director of Graduate Education, 515-294-7021, Fax: 515-294-6206, E-mail: cigrad@iastate.edu. Web site: http://www.ci.hs.iastate.edu.

Kent State University, Graduate School of Education, Health, and Human Services, School of Foundations, Leadership and Administration, Program in Cultural Foundations, Kent, OH 44242-0001. Offers M Ed, MA, PhD. *Accreditation:* NCATE. *Faculty:* 6 full-time (5 women), 1 (woman) part-time/adjunct. *Students:* 29 full-time (21 women), 20 part-time (15 women); includes 17 minority (10 Black or African American, non-Hispanic/Latino; 1 American Indian or Alaska Native, non-Hispanic/Latino; 4 Asian, non-Hispanic/Latino; 2 Hispanic/Latino). 22 applicants, 41% accepted. In 2011, 6 master's, 6 doctorates awarded. *Degree requirements:* For master's, thesis optional; for doctorate, comprehensive exam, thesis/dissertation. *Entrance requirements:* For master's, minimum GPA of 2.75, 2 letters of reference, goal statement; for doctorate, GRE General Test, minimum GPA of 3.5, master's degree, resume, interview, goal statement, 2 letters of reference. Additional exam requirements/recommendations for international students: Required—TOEFL (minimum score 550 paper-based; 213 computer-based; 80 iBT). *Application deadline:* Applications are processed on a rolling basis. Application fee: $30 ($60 for international students). Electronic applications accepted. *Expenses:* Tuition, state resident: full-time $8136; part-time $452 per credit hour. Tuition, nonresident: full-time $14,292; part-time $794 per credit hour. *Financial support:* In 2011–12, 5 research assistantships with full tuition reimbursements (averaging $12,000 per year) were awarded; fellowships with full tuition reimbursements, teaching assistantships with full tuition reimbursements, career-related internships or fieldwork, Federal Work-Study, institutionally sponsored loans, scholarships/grants, health care benefits, and unspecified assistantships also available. Support available to part-time students. Financial award application deadline: 4/1; financial award applicants required to submit FAFSA. *Faculty research:* Public politics, intercultural communication and training, research paradigms, comparative and international education. *Unit head:* Dr. Averil McClelland, Coordinator, 330-672-0594, E-mail: amcclell@kent.edu. *Application contact:* Nancy Miller, Academic Program Coordinator, Office of Graduate Student Services, 330-672-2576, Fax: 330-672-9162, E-mail: ogs@kent.edu. Web site: http://www.kent.edu/ehhs/cult/.

Marquette University, Graduate School, College of Education, Department of Educational Policy and Leadership, Milwaukee, WI 53201-1881. Offers college student personnel administration (M Ed); curriculum and instruction (MA); education (MA); educational administration (M Ed); educational policy and foundations (MA); elementary education (Certificate); literacy (MA); principal (Certificate); reading specialist (Certificate); reading teacher (Certificate); secondary education (Certificate); superintendent (Certificate). Part-time and evening/weekend programs available. *Faculty:* 14 full-time (9 women). *Students:* 40 full-time (34 women), 137 part-time (80 women); includes 25 minority (14 Black or African American, non-Hispanic/Latino; 1 American Indian or Alaska Native, non-Hispanic/Latino; 2 Asian, non-Hispanic/Latino; 8 Hispanic/Latino), 2 international. Average age 32. 132 applicants, 73% accepted, 67 enrolled. In 2011, 46 master's, 3 doctorates, 5 other advanced degrees awarded. Terminal master's awarded for partial completion of doctoral program. *Degree requirements:* For master's, comprehensive exam, thesis (for some programs); for doctorate, thesis/dissertation, qualifying exam, supporting minor. *Entrance requirements:* For master's, GRE General Test or MAT, official transcripts from all current and previous colleges/universities except Marquette, three letters of recommendation, statement of purpose; for doctorate, GRE General Test, MAT, sample of written work, official transcripts from all current and previous colleges/universities except Marquette, three letters of recommendation, statement of purpose, resume/curriculum vitae; for Certificate, GRE General Test or MAT, master's degree. Additional exam requirements/recommendations for international students: Required—TOEFL (minimum score 530 paper-based; 78 computer-based). *Application deadline:* For fall admission, 1/15 for domestic and international students. Application fee: $50. *Expenses:* Contact institution. *Financial support:* In 2011–12, 130 students received support, including 1 fellowship with full tuition reimbursement available (averaging $18,780 per year), 5 research assistantships with full tuition reimbursements available (averaging $13,404 per year); health care benefits, tuition waivers (partial), and unspecified assistantships also available. Support available to part-time students. Financial award application deadline: 2/15. *Faculty research:* Leadership; social justice in education; development of lifelong learners; race, class, and schooling in historical perspective; urban teacher education. *Unit head:* Dr. Ellen Eckman, Chair, 414-288-1561, E-mail: ellen.eckman@marquette.edu. *Application contact:* Craig Pierce, Assistant Dean of the Graduate School, 414-288-5740, Fax: 414-288-1902, E-mail: craig.pierce@marquette.edu.

McGill University, Faculty of Graduate and Postdoctoral Studies, Faculty of Education, Department of Integrated Studies in Education, Montréal, QC H3A 2T5, Canada. Offers culture and values in education (MA, PhD); curriculum studies (MA); educational leadership (MA, Certificate); educational studies (PhD); integrated studies in education (M Ed); second language education (MA, PhD).

Millersville University of Pennsylvania, College of Graduate and Professional Studies, School of Education, Department of Educational Foundations, Millersville, PA 17551-0302. Offers leadership for teaching and learning (M Ed). Part-time and evening/weekend programs available. *Faculty:* 12 full-time (6 women), 11 part-time/adjunct (5 women). *Students:* 25 part-time (15 women). Average age 31. 3 applicants, 100% accepted, 2 enrolled. In 2011, 9 master's awarded. *Degree requirements:* For master's, graded portfolio. *Entrance requirements:* For master's, GRE or MAT, 3 letters of recommendation; interview (in-person). Additional exam requirements/recommendations for international students: Required—TOEFL (minimum score 500 paper-based; 183 computer-based; 65 iBT). *Application deadline:* For fall admission, 1/15 priority date for domestic students, 1/15 for international students; for winter admission, 10/1 priority date for domestic students, 10/1 for international students; for spring admission, 10/1 priority date for domestic students, 10/1 for international students. Applications are processed on a rolling basis. Application fee: $40 ($50 for international students). Electronic applications accepted. *Expenses:* Tuition, state resident: full-time $3744; part-time $416 per credit. Tuition, nonresident: full-time $5616; part-time $624 per credit. *Required fees:* $1130; $125.50 per credit. Tuition and fees vary according to course load. *Financial support:* In 2011–12, 1 research assistantship (averaging $1,563 per year) was awarded; institutionally sponsored loans and unspecified assistantships also available. Support available to part-time students. Financial award application deadline: 3/15; financial award applicants required to submit FAFSA. *Faculty research:* Teacher reflection, math learning disabilities, motivation for learning, teacher development, urban education. *Total annual research expenditures:* $20,000. *Unit head:* Dr. John R. Ward, Chair, 717-871-3835, Fax: 717-872-3856, E-mail: john.ward@millersville.edu. *Application contact:* Dr. Victor S. DeSantis, Dean, College of Graduate and Professional Studies, 717-872-3099, Fax: 717-872-3453, E-mail: victor.desantis@millersville.edu. Web site: http://www.millersville.edu/edfoundations/.

Montclair State University, The Graduate School, College of Education and Human Services, Department of Educational Foundations, Montclair, NJ 07043-1624. Offers educational foundations (Certificate); pedagogy and philosophy (Ed D). Part-time and evening/weekend programs available. *Faculty:* 13 full-time (5 women), 10 part-time/adjunct (7 women). *Students:* 1 part-time (0 women); minority (Hispanic/Latino). Average age 31. *Entrance requirements:* For doctorate, GRE General Test, 3 years of classroom teaching experience, interview, writing sample. Additional exam requirements/recommendations for international students: Required—TOEFL (minimum score 83 iBT) or IELTS. *Application deadline:* For fall admission, 2/1 for domestic students, 2/15 for international students; for spring admission, 10/15 for domestic and international students. Applications are processed on a rolling basis. Application fee: $60. Electronic applications accepted. *Financial support:* In 2011–12, 3 research assistantships with full tuition reimbursements (averaging $7,000 per year) were awarded; Federal Work-Study and scholarships/grants also available. Support available to part-time students. Financial award application deadline: 3/1; financial award applicants required to submit FAFSA. *Faculty research:* Pragmatism and education: theoretical and practical, history of education, children and philosophy, academic development, developing theory and practice - transforming K-12 school pedagogy. *Unit head:* Dr. Jeremy Price, Chairperson, 973-655-7039. *Application contact:* Amy Aiello, Executive Director of The Graduate School, 973-655-5147, Fax: 973-655-7869, E-mail:

graduate.school@montclair.edu. Web site: http://www.montclair.edu/cehs/academics/departments/educational-foundations/.

Mount Saint Vincent University, Graduate Programs, Faculty of Education, Program in Educational Foundations, Halifax, NS B3M 2J6, Canada. Offers M Ed, MA Ed, MA-R. Part-time and evening/weekend programs available. *Degree requirements:* For master's, thesis (for some programs). *Entrance requirements:* For master's, bachelor's degree in related field, minimum B average. Electronic applications accepted. *Faculty research:* Research paradigms, moral aspects of education and teaching, private/independent schools, theory of critical thinking, teachers as workers and as agents of social change.

New York University, Steinhardt School of Culture, Education, and Human Development, Department of Humanities and Social Sciences in the Professions, Program in History of Education, New York, NY 10012-1019. Offers MA, PhD. Part-time programs available. *Faculty:* 2 full-time (0 women). *Students:* 2 full-time (1 woman), 1 (woman) part-time. Average age 27. 12 applicants, 42% accepted, 2 enrolled. In 2011, 3 doctorates awarded. *Degree requirements:* For master's, thesis (for some programs); for doctorate, thesis/dissertation. *Entrance requirements:* For doctorate, GRE General Test, interview. Additional exam requirements/recommendations for international students: Required—TOEFL. *Application deadline:* For fall admission, 12/1 priority date for domestic students, 12/1 for international students; for spring admission, 11/1 for domestic and international students. Applications are processed on a rolling basis. Application fee: $75. Electronic applications accepted. *Financial support:* Fellowships with full and partial tuition reimbursements, Federal Work-Study, institutionally sponsored loans, scholarships/grants, and tuition waivers (partial) available. Support available to part-time students. Financial award application deadline: 2/1; financial award applicants required to submit FAFSA. *Faculty research:* American educational thought, democratic community and education, twentieth century history of education, Jewish history. *Unit head:* Dr. Jonathan L. Zimmerman, Director, 212-992-9475, Fax: 212-995-4832, E-mail: jlzimm@aol.com. *Application contact:* 212-998-5030, Fax: 212-995-4328, E-mail: steinhardt.gradadmissions@nyu.edu. Web site: http://steinhardt.nyu.edu/humsocsci/history.

Niagara University, Graduate Division of Education, Concentration in Foundations of Teaching, Niagara Falls, Niagara University, NY 14109. Offers MA, MS Ed. *Accreditation:* NCATE. Part-time and evening/weekend programs available. *Degree requirements:* For master's, thesis. *Entrance requirements:* For master's, GRE General Test or MAT. *Application deadline:* For fall admission, 8/1 for domestic students. Applications are processed on a rolling basis. Application fee: $30. *Expenses:* Contact institution. *Financial support:* Application deadline: 3/15. *Unit head:* Dr. Chandra Foote, Chair, 716-286-8549. *Application contact:* Dr. Debra A. Colley, Dean of Education, 716-286-8560, Fax: 716-286-8560, E-mail: dcolley@niagara.edu.

Northeastern State University, Graduate College, College of Education, Department of Educational Foundations and Leadership, Tahlequah, OK 74464-2399. Offers collegiate scholarship and services (MS); higher education administration and services (MS); school administration (M Ed); teaching (M Ed). Part-time and evening/weekend programs available. *Students:* 24 full-time (17 women), 123 part-time (77 women); includes 42 minority (9 Black or African American, non-Hispanic/Latino; 28 American Indian or Alaska Native, non-Hispanic/Latino; 1 Asian, non-Hispanic/Latino; 4 Hispanic/Latino). In 2011, 58 master's awarded. *Degree requirements:* For master's, thesis. *Entrance requirements:* For master's, MAT or GRE. Additional exam requirements/recommendations for international students: Required—TOEFL (minimum score 213 computer-based). *Application deadline:* For fall admission, 6/1 priority date for domestic students. Applications are processed on a rolling basis. Application fee: $25. Electronic applications accepted. *Financial support:* Teaching assistantships and Federal Work-Study available. Financial award application deadline: 3/1. *Unit head:* Dr. Marion Morgan, Head, 918-449-6000 Ext. 6589, E-mail: morgan@nsuok.edu. *Application contact:* Margie Railey, Administrative Assistant, 918-456-5511 Ext. 2093, Fax: 918-458-2061, E-mail: railey@nsouk.edu.

Northern Arizona University, Graduate College, College of Education, Department of Educational Leadership, Flagstaff , AZ 86011. Offers community college/higher education (M Ed); educational foundations (M Ed); educational leadership (M Ed, Ed D); principal (Certificate); principal K-12 (M Ed); school leadership K-12 (M Ed); superintendent (Certificate). Part-time programs available. *Faculty:* 18 full-time (8 women). *Students:* 249 full-time (148 women), 737 part-time (460 women); includes 291 minority (51 Black or African American, non-Hispanic/Latino; 65 American Indian or Alaska Native, non-Hispanic/Latino; 14 Asian, non-Hispanic/Latino; 143 Hispanic/Latino; 2 Native Hawaiian or other Pacific Islander, non-Hispanic/Latino; 16 Two or more races, non-Hispanic/Latino), 1 international. Average age 32. 251 applicants, 94% accepted, 196 enrolled. In 2011, 356 master's, 12 doctorates, 74 Certificates awarded. *Degree requirements:* For master's, comprehensive exam, thesis (for some programs); for doctorate, comprehensive exam, thesis/dissertation. *Entrance requirements:* For master's, minimum GPA of 3.0; for doctorate, GRE or MAT, minimum GPA of 3.5. Additional exam requirements/recommendations for international students: Required—TOEFL (minimum score 550 paper-based; 213 computer-based; 80 iBT), IELTS (minimum score 7). *Application deadline:* For fall admission, 3/1 for international students; for spring admission, 9/15 for international students. Applications are processed on a rolling basis. Application fee: $65. Electronic applications accepted. *Expenses:* Tuition, state resident: full-time $7190; part-time $355 per credit hour. Tuition, nonresident: full-time $18,092; part-time $1005 per credit hour. *Required fees:* $818; $328 per semester. *Financial support:* In 2011–12, 1 research assistantship with partial tuition reimbursement (averaging $10,000 per year) was awarded. Financial award applicants required to submit FAFSA. *Unit head:* Dr. Michael Schwanenberger, Chair, 928-523-4212, Fax: 928-523-1929, E-mail: michael.schwanenberger@nau.edu. *Application contact:* Jennifer Offutt, Administrative Assistant, 928-523-5098, Fax: 928-523-1929, E-mail: jennifer.offutt@nau.edu. Web site: http://nau.edu/coe/ed-leadership/.

Northern Illinois University, Graduate School, College of Education, Department of Leadership, Educational Psychology and Foundations, De Kalb, IL 60115-2854. Offers educational administration (MS Ed, Ed D, Ed S); educational psychology (MS Ed, Ed D); foundations of education (MS Ed); school business management (MS Ed). Part-time and evening/weekend programs available. Postbaccalaureate distance learning degree programs offered (minimal on-campus study). *Faculty:* 23 full-time (12 women). *Students:* 8 full-time (6 women), 272 part-time (155 women); includes 46 minority (22 Black or African American, non-Hispanic/Latino; 1 American Indian or Alaska Native, non-Hispanic/Latino; 4 Asian, non-Hispanic/Latino; 17 Hispanic/Latino; 2 Two or more races, non-Hispanic/Latino), 6 international. Average age 39. 77 applicants, 74% accepted, 22 enrolled. In 2011, 81 master's, 8 doctorates, 39 other advanced degrees awarded. *Degree requirements:* For master's, comprehensive exam, thesis optional; for doctorate, thesis/dissertation, candidacy exam, dissertation defense. *Entrance requirements:* For master's, minimum undergraduate GPA of 2.75; for doctorate, GRE General Test, minimum undergraduate GPA of 2.75, 3.2 graduate; for Ed S, GRE General Test, minimum GPA of 2.75 (undergraduate), 3.2 (graduate). Additional exam requirements/recommendations for international students: Required—TOEFL (minimum score 550 paper-based; 213 computer-based). *Application deadline:* For fall admission, 6/1 for domestic students, 5/1 for international students; for spring admission, 11/1 for domestic students, 10/1 for international students. Applications are processed on a rolling basis. Application fee: $40. Electronic applications accepted. *Financial support:* In 2011–12, 4 research assistantships with full tuition reimbursements, 7 teaching assistantships with full tuition reimbursements were awarded; fellowships with full tuition reimbursements, career-related internships or fieldwork, Federal Work-Study, scholarships/grants, tuition waivers (full), and staff assistantships also available. Support available to part-time students. Financial award applicants required to submit FAFSA. *Faculty research:* Interpersonal forgiveness, learner-centered education, psychedelic studies, senior theory, professional growth. *Unit head:* Dr. Charles L. Howell, Chair, 815-753-4404, E-mail: chowell@niu.edu. *Application contact:* Graduate School Office, 815-753-0395, E-mail: gradsch@niu.edu. Web site: http://cedu.niu.edu/LEPF/.

Oakland University, Graduate Study and Lifelong Learning, School of Education and Human Services, Department of Teacher Development and Educational Studies, Rochester, MI 48309-4401. Offers education studies (M Ed); secondary education (MAT). *Entrance requirements:* For master's, minimum GPA of 3.0 for unconditional admission. Electronic applications accepted. *Faculty research:* Earth science for middle and high school teachers through real world connections, learning communities, content enrichment.

Purdue University, Graduate School, College of Education, Department of Educational Studies, West Lafayette, IN 47907. Offers administration (MS Ed, PhD, Ed S); counseling and development (MS Ed, PhD); education of the gifted (MS Ed); educational psychology (MS Ed, PhD); foundations of education (MS Ed, PhD); higher education administration (MS Ed, PhD); special education (MS Ed, PhD). *Accreditation:* ACA (one or more programs are accredited); NCATE (one or more programs are accredited). Part-time and evening/weekend programs available. *Faculty:* 23 full-time (17 women), 1 part-time/adjunct (0 women). *Students:* 111 full-time (79 women), 93 part-time (58 women); includes 34 minority (19 Black or African American, non-Hispanic/Latino; 1 American Indian or Alaska Native, non-Hispanic/Latino; 4 Asian, non-Hispanic/Latino; 6 Hispanic/Latino; 4 Two or more races, non-Hispanic/Latino), 30 international. Average age 35. 249 applicants, 37% accepted, 46 enrolled. In 2011, 39 master's, 20 doctorates, 4 other advanced degrees awarded. *Degree requirements:* For master's, thesis optional; for doctorate, thesis/dissertation, oral and written exams; for Ed S, oral presentation, project. *Entrance requirements:* For master's, GRE General Test required for all Educational Studies program areas, except for Special Education if undergraduate GPA is higher than a 3.0, minimum undergraduate GPA of 3.0; for doctorate and Ed S, GRE general test is required, a combined score of 1000 (300 for revised GRE test) or more is expected., minimum undergraduate GPA of 3.0. Additional exam requirements/recommendations for international students: Required—TOEFL (minimum score 550 paper-based; 77 iBT), TWE (minimum score 5). *Application deadline:* Applications are processed on a rolling basis. Application fee: $60 ($75 for international students). Electronic applications accepted. *Financial support:* Fellowships with full tuition reimbursements, research assistantships with full tuition reimbursements, teaching assistantships with full tuition reimbursements, career-related internships or fieldwork, and tuition waivers (full) available. Support available to part-time students. Financial award application deadline: 3/1; financial award applicants required to submit FAFSA. *Faculty research:* Motivation, learning disabilities, school learning, group processes, cognitive development. *Unit head:* Dr. Ala Samrapungavan, Head, 765-494-9170, Fax: 765-496-1228, E-mail: ala@purdue.edu. *Application contact:* Sarah N. Prater, Graduate Contact, 765-494-2345, Fax: 765-494-5832, E-mail: prater0@purdue.edu. Web site: http://www.edst.purdue.edu/.

Regis University, College for Professional Studies, School of Education and Counseling, Department of Education, Denver, CO 80221-1099. Offers adult learning, training, and development (M Ed, Certificate); autism (Certificate); curriculum, instruction, and assessment (M Ed); educational leadership (Certificate); educational technology (Certificate); instructional technology (M Ed); literacy (Certificate); professional leadership (M Ed); reading (M Ed); self-designed (M Ed); space studies (M Ed). Program also offered in Henderson and Las Vegas (Summerlin), NV. *Accreditation:* Teacher Education Accreditation Council. Part-time and evening/weekend programs available. Postbaccalaureate distance learning degree programs offered (no on-campus study). *Degree requirements:* For master's, thesis. *Entrance requirements:* For master's, resume, minimum GPA of 2.75, criminal background check. Additional exam requirements/recommendations for international students: Required—TOEFL (minimum score 213 computer-based), TWE (minimum score 5). Electronic applications accepted. *Faculty research:* Issues of equity in the middle school classroom, professional learning communities, school reform, socialinguistic and discursive obstacles to student integration, inclusive language arts curriculum.

Rutgers, The State University of New Jersey, New Brunswick, Graduate School of Education, Department of Educational Theory, Policy and Administration, Program in Social and Philosophical Foundations of Education, Piscataway, NJ 08854-8097. Offers Ed M, Ed D. Part-time and evening/weekend programs available. *Degree requirements:* For doctorate, thesis/dissertation, qualifying exam. *Entrance requirements:* For master's, GRE General Test; for doctorate, GRE General Test, writing sample. Additional exam requirements/recommendations for international students: Required—TOEFL. Electronic applications accepted. *Faculty research:* Anthropology, history, sociology, philosophy, comparative education.

Saint Louis University, Graduate Education, College of Education and Public Service, Department of Educational Studies, St. Louis, MO 63103-2097. Offers curriculum and instruction (MA, Ed D, PhD); educational foundations (MA, Ed D, PhD); special education (MA); teaching (MAT). *Accreditation:* NCATE. Part-time programs available. *Degree requirements:* For master's, comprehensive exam; for doctorate, comprehensive exam, thesis/dissertation, preliminary oral and written exams. *Entrance requirements:* For master's, GRE General Test or MAT, letters of recommendation, resume; for doctorate, GRE General Test, letters of recommendation, resumé, goal statement, transcripts. Additional exam requirements/recommendations for international students: Required—TOEFL (minimum score 525 paper-based; 194 computer-based). Electronic applications accepted. *Faculty research:* Teacher preparation, multicultural issues, children with special needs, qualitative research in education, inclusion.

Simon Fraser University, Graduate Studies, Faculty of Education, Programs in Curriculum and Instruction, Burnaby, BC V5A 1S6, Canada. Offers curriculum theory and implementation (PhD); foundations (M Ed, MA); philosophy of education (PhD). *Degree requirements:* For master's, project or thesis; for doctorate, thesis/dissertation. *Entrance requirements:* For master's, minimum GPA of 3.0; for doctorate, GRE, master's degree or exceptional record in a bachelor's degree, minimum GPA of 3.5. Additional exam requirements/recommendations for international students: Required—TOEFL or IELTS.

Southeast Missouri State University, School of Graduate Studies, Department of Middle and Secondary Education, Cape Girardeau, MO 63701-4799. Offers secondary education (MA), including education studies, education technology. *Accreditation:* NCATE. Part-time and evening/weekend programs available. *Faculty:* 4 full-time (3 women). *Students:* 3 full-time (2 women), 18 part-time (14 women); includes 2 minority (both Black or African American, non-Hispanic/Latino), 1 international. Average age 30. 7 applicants, 86% accepted, 6 enrolled. In 2011, 12 master's awarded. *Degree requirements:* For master's, comprehensive exam, research paper. *Entrance* *requirements:* For master's, minimum undergraduate GPA of 2.75. Additional exam requirements/recommendations for international students: Required—TOEFL (minimum score 550 paper-based; 213 computer-based; 79 iBT); Recommended—IELTS (minimum score 6). *Application deadline:* For fall admission, 8/1 for domestic students, 7/1 for international students; for spring admission, 11/21 for domestic students, 11/1 for international students. Applications are processed on a rolling basis. Application fee: $30 ($40 for international students). Electronic applications accepted. *Expenses:* Tuition, state resident: full-time $4896; part-time $272 per credit hour. Tuition, nonresident: full-time $8649; part-time $480.50 per credit hour. *Financial support:* In 2011–12, 4 students received support. Career-related internships or fieldwork, Federal Work-Study, scholarships/grants, tuition waivers (full), and unspecified assistantships available. Financial award application deadline: 6/30; financial award applicants required to submit FAFSA. *Faculty research:* Pedagogy of teaching, multicultural education, reading and writing strategies, use of technology in the classroom. *Unit head:* Dr. Simin L. Cwick, Chairperson and Graduate Coordinator, 573-651-5965, Fax: 573-986-6141, E-mail: scwick@semo.edu. *Application contact:* Alisa Aleen McFerron, Assistant Director of Admissions for Operations, 573-651-5937, Fax: 573-651-5936, E-mail: amcferron@semo.edu. Web site: http://www5.semo.edu/middleandsec/.

Southern Connecticut State University, School of Graduate Studies, School of Education, Department of Educational Leadership, New Haven, CT 06515-1355. Offers educational foundations (Diploma), including foundational studies; educational leadership (Ed D, Diploma); research, statistics, and measurement (MS). Part-time and evening/weekend programs available. *Faculty:* 13 full-time (7 women), 10 part-time/adjunct (4 women). *Students:* 13 full-time (6 women), 196 part-time (135 women); includes 34 minority (17 Black or African American, non-Hispanic/Latino; 3 Asian, non-Hispanic/Latino; 13 Hispanic/Latino; 1 Two or more races, non-Hispanic/Latino), 1 international. 203 applicants, 34% accepted, 59 enrolled. In 2011, 3 doctorates, 109 other advanced degrees awarded. *Entrance requirements:* For degree, master's degree, minimum GPA of 3.0, writing sample. *Application deadline:* For fall admission, 7/15 priority date for domestic students. Applications are processed on a rolling basis. Application fee: $50. Electronic applications accepted. *Expenses:* Tuition, state resident: full-time $5137; part-time $413 per credit. *Required fees:* $4008; $55 per term. *Financial support:* Application deadline: 4/15; applicants required to submit FAFSA. *Unit head:* Dr. Peter Madonia, Chairperson, 203-392-5441, E-mail: madoniap1@southernct.edu. *Application contact:* Dr. Cathryn Magno, Graduate Coordinator, 203-392-5170, Fax: 203-392-5347, E-mail: magnoc1@southernct.edu.

Southern Illinois University Edwardsville, Graduate School, School of Education, Department of Educational Leadership, Program in Learning, Culture, and Society, Edwardsville, IL 62026. Offers MS Ed. Part-time programs available. *Students:* 1 full-time (0 women), 9 part-time (all women); includes 3 minority (1 Black or African American, non-Hispanic/Latino; 1 Hispanic/Latino; 1 Two or more races, non-Hispanic/Latino), 2 international. 7 applicants, 57% accepted. In 2011, 4 master's awarded. *Degree requirements:* For master's, thesis or alternative, project, oral defense. *Entrance requirements:* Additional exam requirements/recommendations for international students: Required—TOEFL (minimum score 550 paper-based; 213 computer-based; 79 iBT), IELTS (minimum score 6.5). *Application deadline:* For fall admission, 7/22 for domestic students, 6/1 for international students; for spring admission, 12/9 for domestic students, 10/1 for international students. Applications are processed on a rolling basis. Application fee: $30. Electronic applications accepted. Tuition and fees vary according to course load and program. *Financial support:* In 2011–12, 2 research assistantships with full tuition reimbursements (averaging $9,927 per year) were awarded; fellowships, teaching assistantships, institutionally sponsored loans, scholarships/grants, and unspecified assistantships also available. Financial award application deadline: 3/1; financial award applicants required to submit FAFSA. *Unit head:* Dr. Laurel Puchner, Director, 618-650-3286, E-mail: lpuchne@siue.edu. *Application contact:* Michelle Robinson, Coordinator of Graduate Recruitment, 618-650-2811, Fax: 618-650-3523, E-mail: michero@siue.edu. Web site: http://www.siue.edu/education/edld/.

Spring Hill College, Graduate Programs, Program in Education, Mobile, AL 36608-1791. Offers early childhood education (MAT, MS Ed); educational theory (MS Ed); elementary education (MAT, MS Ed); secondary education (MAT, MS Ed). Part-time programs available. *Faculty:* 3 full-time (2 women), 3 part-time/adjunct (all women). *Students:* 7 full-time (6 women), 21 part-time (18 women); includes 7 minority (6 Black or African American, non-Hispanic/Latino; 1 Asian, non-Hispanic/Latino). Average age 31. In 2011, 13 master's awarded. *Degree requirements:* For master's, comprehensive exam, completion of program within 6 calendar years of entrance into graduate studies at Spring Hill; documentation of course field assignments (MS) or completion of internship (MAT). *Entrance requirements:* For master's, GRE, MAT, or PRAXIS (varies by program), bachelor's degree with minimum undergraduate GPA of 3.0; class B certificate (MS) or minimum number of hours in specific fields (MAT). Additional exam requirements/recommendations for international students: Required—TOEFL (minimum score 550 paper-based; 213 computer-based; 80 iBT), IELTS (minimum score 6.5), CPE or CAE (minimum score C),Michigan English Language Assessment Battery (minimum score 90). *Application deadline:* For fall admission, 8/1 priority date for domestic students, 8/1 for international students; for spring admission, 12/1 priority date for domestic students, 12/1 for international students. Applications are processed on a rolling basis. Application fee: $25 ($35 for international students). Electronic applications accepted. *Expenses:* Contact institution. *Financial support:* Applicants required to submit FAFSA. *Unit head:* Dr. Ann A. Adams, Chair of Teacher Education, 251-380-3479, Fax: 251-460-2184, E-mail: aadams@shc.edu. *Application contact:* Donna B. Tarasavage, Director of Admissions, Graduate and Continuing Studies, 251-380-3067, Fax: 251-460-2190, E-mail: dtarasavage@shc.edu. Web site: http://www.shc.edu/grad/academics/teaching.

Stanford University, School of Education, Program in Social Sciences, Policy, and Educational Practice, Stanford, CA 94305-9991. Offers administration and policy analysis (Ed D, PhD); anthropology of education (PhD); economics of education (PhD); educational linguistics (PhD); evaluation (MA), including interdisciplinary studies; higher education (PhD); history of education (PhD); interdisciplinary studies (PhD); international comparative education (MA, PhD); international education administration and policy analysis (MA); philosophy of education (PhD); policy analysis (MA); prospective principal's program (MA); sociology of education (PhD). *Degree requirements:* For master's, thesis (for some programs); for doctorate, thesis/dissertation. *Entrance requirements:* For master's and doctorate, GRE General Test. Electronic applications accepted. *Expenses: Tuition:* Full-time $40,050; part-time $890 per credit.

State University of New York at Binghamton, Graduate School, School of Education, Program in Educational Theory and Practice, Binghamton, NY 13902-6000. Offers Ed D. *Students:* 14 full-time (13 women), 73 part-time (55 women); includes 8 minority (6 Black or African American, non-Hispanic/Latino; 1 American Indian or Alaska Native, non-Hispanic/Latino; 1 Native Hawaiian or other Pacific Islander, non-Hispanic/Latino), 6 international. Average age 41. 39 applicants, 74% accepted, 23 enrolled. In 2011, 3 doctorates awarded. *Degree requirements:* For doctorate, thesis/dissertation. *Entrance requirements:* For doctorate, GRE General Test, writing sample. Additional exam requirements/recommendations for international students: Required—TOEFL (minimum score 550 paper-based; 213 computer-based; 80 iBT). *Application deadline:* For fall admission, 2/1 priority date for domestic students, 2/1 for international students. Applications are processed on a rolling basis. Application fee: $60. Electronic applications accepted. *Financial support:* In 2011–12, 17 students received support, including 3 fellowships with full tuition reimbursements available (averaging $12,000 per year), 2 research assistantships with full tuition reimbursements available (averaging $12,000 per year), 3 teaching assistantships with full tuition reimbursements available (averaging $12,000 per year); career-related internships or fieldwork, Federal Work-Study, institutionally sponsored loans, scholarships/grants, health care benefits, tuition waivers (full), and unspecified assistantships also available. Financial award application deadline: 2/15; financial award applicants required to submit FAFSA. *Unit head:* Dr. James Carpenter, Coordinator, 607-777-4678, E-mail: jcarpent@binghamton.edu. *Application contact:* Catherine Smith, Recruiting and Admissions Coordinator, 607-777-2151, Fax: 607-777-2501, E-mail: cmsmith@binghamton.edu. Web site: http://www2.binghamton.edu/gse/doctoral-program/index.html.

Suffolk University, College of Arts and Sciences, Department of Education and Human Services, Boston, MA 02108-2770. Offers administration of higher education (M Ed, CAGS), including administration of higher education (M Ed), leadership (CAGS); human resource, learning and performance (MS, CAGS, Graduate Certificate), including global human resources (Graduate Certificate), human resources (MS, Graduate Certificate), organizational development (CAGS, Graduate Certificate), organizational learning and development (MS, Graduate Certificate); mental health counseling (MS, CAGS); school counseling (M Ed, CAGS); school teaching (M Ed, CAGS), including foundations of education (M Ed), middle school teaching (M Ed), secondary school teaching (M Ed); MPA/MSMHC; MS/Certificate. Part-time and evening/weekend programs available. *Faculty:* 10 full-time (6 women), 7 part-time/adjunct (3 women). *Students:* 53 full-time (39 women), 131 part-time (112 women); includes 21 minority (7 Black or African American, non-Hispanic/Latino; 2 American Indian or Alaska Native, non-Hispanic/Latino; 5 Asian, non-Hispanic/Latino; 5 Hispanic/Latino; 2 Two or more races, non-Hispanic/Latino), 9 international. Average age 28. 158 applicants, 73% accepted, 60 enrolled. In 2011, 72 master's, 8 other advanced degrees awarded. *Entrance requirements:* For master's, GRE General Test or MAT, 2 letters of recommendation, resume. Additional exam requirements/recommendations for international students: Required—TOEFL (minimum score 550 paper-based; 213 computer-based; 80 iBT). *Application deadline:* For fall admission, 6/15 priority date for domestic students, 6/15 for international students; for spring admission, 11/1 priority date for domestic students, 11/1 for international students. Applications are processed on a rolling basis. Application fee: $50. Electronic applications accepted. *Expenses:* Contact institution. *Financial support:* In 2011–12, 102 students received support, including 30 fellowships with full and partial tuition reimbursements available (averaging $10,664 per year); career-related internships or fieldwork, Federal Work-Study, and institutionally sponsored loans also available. Support available to part-time students. Financial award application deadline: 4/1; financial award applicants required to submit FAFSA. *Faculty research:* Predicting competent Head Start preschools, cultural differences. *Unit head:* Dr. Krisanne Bursik, Associate Dean and Acting Chair, 617-573-8261, Fax: 617-305-1743, E-mail: kbursik@suffolk.edu. *Application contact:* Ellen Driscoll, Director of Graduate Admissions, 617-573-8302, Fax: 617-305-1733, E-mail: grad.admission@suffolk.edu. Web site: http://www.suffolk.edu/college/9785.html.

Syracuse University, School of Education, Program in Cultural Foundations of Education, Syracuse, NY 13244. Offers MS, PhD. Part-time programs available. *Students:* 41 full-time (30 women), 22 part-time (15 women); includes 18 minority (8 Black or African American, non-Hispanic/Latino; 1 American Indian or Alaska Native, non-Hispanic/Latino; 3 Asian, non-Hispanic/Latino; 4 Hispanic/Latino; 2 Two or more races, non-Hispanic/Latino), 9 international. Average age 35. 52 applicants, 48% accepted, 9 enrolled. In 2011, 14 master's, 3 doctorates awarded. *Degree requirements:* For master's, thesis or alternative; for doctorate, thesis/dissertation. *Entrance requirements:* For doctorate, GRE, master's degree. Additional exam requirements/recommendations for international students: Required—TOEFL (minimum score 100 iBT). *Application deadline:* For fall admission, 2/1 priority date for domestic students, 2/1 for international students; for spring admission, 10/15 priority date for domestic students, 10/15 for international students. Applications are processed on a rolling basis. Application fee: $75. Electronic applications accepted. *Expenses: Tuition:* Part-time $1206 per credit. *Financial support:* Fellowships with full tuition reimbursements, research assistantships with full and partial tuition reimbursements, and teaching assistantships with full and partial tuition reimbursements available. Financial award application deadline: 1/1; financial award applicants required to submit FAFSA. *Faculty research:* Gender and education, history of women's education, the role of science in liberal education, student attrition. *Unit head:* Dr. Sari Knopp Biklen, Chair, 315-443-9075. *Application contact:* Laurie Deyo, Graduate Recruiter, School of Education, 315-443-2505, E-mail: e-gradrcrt@syr.edu. Web site: http://soeweb.syr.edu/cfe/culturalfound.html.

Teachers College, Columbia University, Graduate Faculty of Education, Department of Arts and Humanities, Program in Philosophy and Education, New York, NY 10027. Offers Ed M, MA, Ed D, PhD. *Faculty:* 2 full-time (1 woman). *Students:* 16 full-time (11 women), 41 part-time (15 women); includes 10 minority (3 Black or African American, non-Hispanic/Latino; 3 Asian, non-Hispanic/Latino; 4 Hispanic/Latino), 12 international. Average age 31. 37 applicants, 62% accepted, 16 enrolled. In 2011, 12 master's, 2 doctorates awarded. *Degree requirements:* For master's, project; for doctorate, one foreign language, thesis/dissertation. *Entrance requirements:* For master's, previous course work in philosophy; for doctorate, GRE, previous course work in philosophy (Ed D), undergraduate degree in philosophy (PhD). *Application deadline:* For fall admission, 12/15 for domestic students; for spring admission, 11/1 for domestic students. Applications are processed on a rolling basis. Application fee: $65. *Financial support:* Career-related internships or fieldwork, Federal Work-Study, institutionally sponsored loans, and tuition waivers (full and partial) available. Support available to part-time students. Financial award application deadline: 2/1. *Faculty research:* Philosophy and its relationship to educational thought, ethics and education, social theory and ideology. *Unit head:* Prof. David T. Hansen, Program Coordinator, 212-678-4138, E-mail: dth2006@tc.columbia.edu. *Application contact:* Thomas P. Rock, Director of Admissions, 212-678-3083, Fax: 212-678-4171, E-mail: rock@tc.edu. Web site: http://www.tc.edu/philosophy/.

Troy University, Graduate School, College of Education, Program in Postsecondary Education, Troy, AL 36082. Offers adult education (M Ed); biology (M Ed); criminal justice (M Ed); English (M Ed); foundations of education (M Ed); general science (M Ed); higher education administration (M Ed); history (M Ed); instructional technology (M Ed); mathematics (M Ed); music industry (M Ed); physical fitness (M Ed); political science (M Ed); public administration (M Ed); social science (M Ed); teaching English (M Ed). *Accreditation:* NCATE. Part-time and evening/weekend programs available. *Faculty:* 53 full-time (21 women), 22 part-time/adjunct (8 women). *Students:* 74 full-time (51 women), 166 part-time (121 women); includes 148 minority (143 Black or African American, non-Hispanic/Latino; 1 American Indian or Alaska Native, non-Hispanic/Latino; 2 Hispanic/Latino; 2 Two or more races, non-Hispanic/Latino). Average age 34. 174 applicants, 82% accepted, 88 enrolled. In 2011, 221 master's awarded. *Degree requirements:* For master's, comprehensive exam, thesis. *Entrance requirements:* For master's, MAT (minimum score 385), minimum GPA of 2.5. Additional exam requirements/recommendations for international students: Required—TOEFL (minimum score 523 paper-based; 193 computer-based; 70 iBT), IELTS (minimum score 6), or ACT COMPASS ESL (minimum listening, reading, and grammar score 270). *Application deadline:* Applications are processed on a rolling basis. Application fee: $50. Electronic applications accepted. *Expenses:* Tuition, state resident: full-time $6960; part-time $290 per credit hour. Tuition, nonresident: full-time $13,920; part-time $580 per credit hour. *Required fees:* $386 per term. *Financial support:* Available to part-time students. Applicants required to submit FAFSA. *Unit head:* Dr. Jan Oliver, Associate Professor, 334-670-3444, Fax: 334-670-3296, E-mail: oliver@troy.edu. *Application contact:* Brenda K. Campbell, Director of Graduate Admissions, 334-670-3178, Fax: 334-670-3733, E-mail: bcamp@troy.edu.

University at Buffalo, the State University of New York, Graduate School, Graduate School of Education, Department of Educational Leadership and Policy, Buffalo, NY 14260. Offers educational administration (Ed M, PhD); educational culture, policy and society (PhD); general education (Ed M); higher education administration (Ed M, PhD); school building leadership (LIFTS) (Certificate); school business and human resource administration (Certificate); school district business leadership (LIFTS) (Certificate); school district leadership (LIFTS) (Certificate). Part-time and evening/weekend programs available. *Faculty:* 12 full-time (7 women), 9 part-time/adjunct (7 women). *Students:* 79 full-time (55 women), 136 part-time (76 women); includes 47 minority (24 Black or African American, non-Hispanic/Latino; 1 American Indian or Alaska Native, non-Hispanic/Latino; 9 Asian, non-Hispanic/Latino; 13 Hispanic/Latino), 17 international. Average age 35. 194 applicants, 40% accepted, 73 enrolled. In 2011, 44 master's, 18 doctorates, 25 other advanced degrees awarded. *Degree requirements:* For master's, comprehensive exam (for some programs), thesis optional; for doctorate, comprehensive exam, thesis/dissertation. *Entrance requirements:* For doctorate, GRE General Test or MAT, writing sample. Additional exam requirements/recommendations for international students: Required—TOEFL (minimum score 550 paper-based; 213 computer-based; 79 iBT). *Application deadline:* For fall admission, 3/1 priority date for domestic students, 3/1 for international students; for spring admission, 11/15 priority date for domestic students, 10/1 for international students. Applications are processed on a rolling basis. Application fee: $50. Electronic applications accepted. *Financial support:* In 2011–12, 21 fellowships (averaging $10,298 per year), 9 research assistantships (averaging $11,955 per year) were awarded; career-related internships or fieldwork, Federal Work-Study, institutionally sponsored loans, health care benefits, and unspecified assistantships also available. Financial award application deadline: 3/15; financial award applicants required to submit FAFSA. *Faculty research:* College access and choice, school leadership preparation and practice, public policy, curriculum and pedagogy, comparative and international education. *Unit head:* Dr. William C. Barba, Chairman, 716-645-2471, Fax: 716-645-2481, E-mail: barba@buffalo.edu. *Application contact:* Bonnie Reed, Admissions Assistant, 716-645-2110, Fax: 716-645-7937, E-mail: brfisher@buffalo.edu. Web site: http://gse.buffalo.edu/elp.

The University of British Columbia, Faculty of Education, Department of Educational Studies, Vancouver, BC V6T 1Z1, Canada. Offers adult education (M Ed, MA); adult learning and global change (M Ed); educational administration (M Ed, MA); educational leadership and policy (Ed D); educational studies (PhD); higher education (M Ed, MA); society, culture and politics in education (M Ed, MA). Part-time and evening/weekend programs available. Terminal master's awarded for partial completion of doctoral program. *Degree requirements:* For master's, thesis; for doctorate, comprehensive exam, thesis/dissertation, master's thesis. *Entrance requirements:* For master's, minimum B+ average, 4-year undergraduate degree, field-related experience; for doctorate, minimum B+ average, 4-year undergraduate degree, master's degree, field-related experience. Additional exam requirements/recommendations for international students: Required—TOEFL (minimum score 600 paper-based; 250 computer-based; 100 iBT) or IELTS (minimum score 6.5). Electronic applications accepted. *Faculty research:* Educational leadership educational administration adult education politics in education, global change and adult learning.

University of Calgary, Faculty of Graduate Studies, Faculty of Education, Graduate Division of Educational Research, Calgary, AB T2N 1N4, Canada. Offers community rehabilitation and disability studies (M Ed, M Sc, Ed D, PhD, Graduate Certificate, Graduate Diploma); curriculum, teaching and learning (M Ed, M Sc, MA, Ed D, PhD, Graduate Certificate, Graduate Diploma); educational contexts (M Ed, MA, Ed D, PhD, Graduate Certificate, Graduate Diploma); educational leadership (M Ed, MA, Ed D, PhD, Graduate Certificate, Graduate Diploma); educational technology (M Ed, M Sc, MA, Ed D, PhD, Graduate Certificate, Graduate Diploma); gifted education (M Sc, MA, Ed D, PhD, Graduate Certificate, Graduate Diploma); higher education administration (Ed D); interpretive studies in education (M Ed, M Sc, MA, Ed D, PhD, Graduate Certificate, Graduate Diploma); second language teaching (M Ed, Ed D, PhD, Graduate Certificate, Graduate Diploma); teaching English as a second language (M Ed, M Sc, MA, Ed D, PhD, Graduate Certificate, Graduate Diploma); workplace and adult learning (M Ed, MA, Ed D, PhD, Graduate Certificate, Graduate Diploma). Ed D in both higher education administration and educational leadership offered via distance delivery. Part-time and evening/weekend programs available. Postbaccalaureate distance learning degree programs offered (minimal on-campus study). *Degree requirements:* For master's, thesis (for some programs); for doctorate, thesis/dissertation, candidacy exam. *Entrance requirements:* For master's, minimum GPA of 3.0, 3 letters of reference; for doctorate, minimum GPA of 3.5, 3 letters of reference; for other advanced degree, minimum GPA of 3.0. Additional exam requirements/recommendations for international students: Required—TOEFL, IELTS. Electronic applications accepted. *Faculty research:* Curriculum, leadership, technology, contexts, gifted, second language teaching, work place and adult learning.

University of California, Riverside, Graduate Division, Graduate School of Education, Riverside, CA 92521-0102. Offers autism (M Ed); diversity and equity (M Ed); education, society and culture (MA, PhD); educational psychology (MA, PhD); general education (M Ed); higher education administration and policy (M Ed, PhD); reading (M Ed); school psychology (PhD); special education (M Ed, MA, PhD). *Faculty:* 19 full-time (9 women), 9 part-time/adjunct (6 women). *Students:* 181 full-time (128 women); includes 79 minority (8 Black or African American, non-Hispanic/Latino; 1 American Indian or Alaska Native, non-Hispanic/Latino; 26 Asian, non-Hispanic/Latino; 34 Hispanic/Latino; 10 Two or more races, non-Hispanic/Latino), 5 international. Average age 31. 200 applicants, 48% accepted, 76 enrolled. In 2011, 67 master's, 12 doctorates awarded. Terminal master's awarded for partial completion of doctoral program. *Degree requirements:* For master's, thesis optional, comprehensive exams or thesis (MA), case study or analytical report (M Ed); for doctorate, thesis/dissertation, written and oral qualifying exams, college teaching practicum. *Entrance requirements:* For master's, GRE General Test, CBEST, CSET, minimum GPA of 3.2; for doctorate, GRE General Test, master's degree (desirable), minimum GPA of 3.2. Additional exam requirements/recommendations for international students: Required—TOEFL (minimum score 550 paper-based; 213 computer-based; 80 iBT), IELTS (minimum score 7). *Application deadline:* For fall admission, 9/1 for domestic students, 4/1 for international students; for winter admission, 12/1 for domestic students, 7/1 for international students; for spring admission, 3/1 for domestic students, 10/1 for international students. Applications are processed on a rolling basis. Application fee: $80 ($100 for international students). Electronic applications accepted. *Financial support:* In 2011–12, 59 students received support, including 9 fellowships with full and partial tuition reimbursements available (averaging $26,587 per year), 21 research assistantships with full and partial tuition reimbursements available (averaging $14,517 per year), 1 teaching assistantship with full and partial tuition reimbursement available (averaging $17,307 per year); career-related internships or fieldwork, Federal Work-Study, institutionally sponsored loans, scholarships/grants, and unspecified assistantships also available. Financial award application deadline: 1/5. *Faculty research:* Responsiveness to intervention, faculty core, response to intervention of English language learners, advanced modeling techniques, study on social capital, trust, and motivation. *Total annual research expenditures:* $2.8 million. *Unit head:* Prof. Douglas Mitchell, Interim Dean, 951-827-5802, Fax: 951-827-3942, E-mail: douglas.mitchell@ucr.edu. *Application contact:* Prof. Robert Ream, Graduate Advisor for Admission, 951-827-6362, Fax: 951-827-3291, E-mail: edgrad@ucr.edu. Web site: http://www.education.ucr.edu/.

University of Central Missouri, The Graduate School, College of Education, Warrensburg, MO 64093. Offers career and technical education administration (MS); career and technical education industry training (MS); career and technical education leadership/teaching (MS); college student personnel administration (MS); counseling (MS); curriculum and instruction (Ed S); educational leadership (Ed D); educational technology (MS); elementary education/educational foundations and literacy (MSE); elementary school administration (MSE); elementary school principalship (Ed S); human services/learning resources (Ed S); human services/professional counseling (Ed S); human services/special education (Ed S); human services/technology and occupational education (Ed S); K-12 education/educational foundations and literacy (MSE); K-12 special education (MSE); library science and information services (MS); literacy education (MSE); secondary education/educational foundations & literacy (MSE); secondary school administration (MSE); secondary school principalship (Ed S); superintendency (Ed S); teaching (MAT). Ed D offered jointly with University of Missouri. Part-time programs available. Postbaccalaureate distance learning degree programs offered. *Entrance requirements:* Additional exam requirements/recommendations for international students: Required—TOEFL (minimum score 550 paper-based; 79 computer-based). Electronic applications accepted.

University of Cincinnati, Graduate School, College of Education, Criminal Justice, and Human Services, Division of Educational Studies, Program in Educational Studies, Cincinnati, OH 45221. Offers M Ed, PhD. *Accreditation:* NCATE. Part-time programs available. *Degree requirements:* For master's, thesis optional; for doctorate, comprehensive exam, thesis/dissertation. *Entrance requirements:* For master's, GRE General Test; for doctorate, GRE General Test, GRE Subject Test. Additional exam requirements/recommendations for international students: Required—TOEFL (minimum score 520 paper-based; 190 computer-based), OEPT 3. Electronic applications accepted.

University of Connecticut, Graduate School, Neag School of Education, Department of Educational Leadership, Center for Education Policy Analysis, Storrs, CT 06269. Offers PhD. *Accreditation:* NCATE. *Degree requirements:* For doctorate, thesis/dissertation. *Entrance requirements:* For doctorate, GRE General Test. Additional exam requirements/recommendations for international students: Required—TOEFL (minimum score 550 paper-based; 213 computer-based). Electronic applications accepted.

University of Florida, Graduate School, College of Education, School of Teaching and Learning, Gainesville, FL 32611. Offers bilingual/ESOL education (M Ed, MAE, Ed D, PhD, Ed S); curriculum and instruction (M Ed, MAE, Ed D, PhD, Ed S); elementary education (M Ed, MAE); English education (M Ed, MAE); mathematics education (M Ed, MAE); reading education (M Ed, MAE); science education (M Ed, MAE); social foundations of education (M Ed, MAE, Ed D, PhD); social studies education (M Ed, MAE). *Accreditation:* NCATE. Part-time and evening/weekend programs available. Postbaccalaureate distance learning degree programs offered (no on-campus study). *Faculty:* 26 full-time (19 women). *Students:* 247 full-time (201 women), 236 part-time (196 women); includes 100 minority (32 Black or African American, non-Hispanic/Latino; 2 American Indian or Alaska Native, non-Hispanic/Latino; 15 Asian, non-Hispanic/Latino; 51 Hispanic/Latino), 32 international. Average age 33. 290 applicants, 60% accepted, 122 enrolled. In 2011, 284 master's, 19 doctorates, 29 other advanced degrees awarded. Terminal master's awarded for partial completion of doctoral program. *Degree requirements:* For master's, comprehensive exam (for some programs), thesis (for some programs); for doctorate, comprehensive exam (for some programs), thesis/dissertation (for some programs). *Entrance requirements:* For master's and doctorate, GRE General Test, minimum GPA of 3.0; for Ed S, GRE General Test. Additional exam requirements/recommendations for international students: Required—TOEFL (minimum score 550 paper-based; 213 computer-based; 80 iBT), IELTS (minimum score 6). *Application deadline:* For fall admission, 2/15 for domestic students, 12/1 for international students; for spring admission, 9/15 for domestic students, 3/1 for international students. Applications are processed on a rolling basis. Application fee: $30. Electronic applications accepted. *Financial support:* Fellowships, research assistantships, teaching assistantships, career-related internships or fieldwork, and unspecified assistantships available. Financial award applicants required to submit FAFSA. *Faculty research:* Early childhood, child and adolescents, diverse learners, race/ethnicity issues, teacher education, professional development, language and literacy development, policy development. *Unit head:* Dr. Elizabeth Bondy, Chair, 352-273-4242, Fax: 352-392-9193, E-mail: bondy@coe.ufl.edu. *Application contact:* Wevan Terzian, Graduate Coordinator, 352-273-4216, Fax: 352-392-9193, E-mail: sterzian@coe.ufl.edu. Web site: http://education.ufl.edu/school-teaching-learning/.

University of Georgia, College of Education, Department of Workforce Education, Leadership and Social Foundations, Athens, GA 30602. Offers educational leadership (Ed D); human resources and organization design (M Ed); occupational studies (MAT, Ed D, PhD, Ed S); social foundations of education (PhD). *Accreditation:* NCATE. *Faculty:* 14 full-time (7 women). *Students:* 27 full-time (15 women), 70 part-time (46 women); includes 24 minority (23 Black or African American, non-Hispanic/Latino; 1 Native Hawaiian or other Pacific Islander, non-Hispanic/Latino), 5 international. Average age 37. 40 applicants, 63% accepted, 8 enrolled. In 2011, 16 master's, 23 doctorates, 5 other advanced degrees awarded. *Entrance requirements:* For master's, GRE General Test, MAT; for doctorate, GRE General Test; for Ed S, GRE General Test or MAT. *Application deadline:* For fall admission, 7/1 priority date for domestic students; for spring admission, 11/15 for domestic students. Application fee: $50. Electronic applications accepted. *Financial support:* Fellowships, research assistantships, teaching assistantships, and unspecified assistantships available. *Unit head:* Dr. Roger B. Hill, Interim Head, 706-542-4100, Fax: 706-542-4054, E-mail: rbhill@uga.edu. *Application contact:* Dr. Robert C. Wicklein, Graduate Coordinator, 706-542-4503, Fax: 706-542-4054, E-mail: wickone@uga.edu. Web site: http://www.coe.uga.edu/welsf/.

University of Hawaii at Manoa, Graduate Division, College of Education, Department of Educational Foundations, Honolulu, HI 96822. Offers M Ed. Part-time and evening/weekend programs available. *Degree requirements:* For master's, thesis optional. *Entrance requirements:* Additional exam requirements/recommendations for international students: Required—TOEFL (minimum score 580 paper-based; 237 computer-based; 92 iBT), IELTS (minimum score 5). *Faculty research:* Multiculturalethnic education, comparative education, educational policy, interdisciplinary inquiry, moral/political education.

University of Hawaii at Manoa, Graduate Division, College of Education, PhD in Education Program, Honolulu, HI 96822. Offers curriculum and instruction (PhD); educational administration (PhD); educational foundations (PhD); educational policy studies (PhD); educational technology (PhD); exceptionalities (PhD); kinesiology (PhD). Part-time and evening/weekend programs available. *Degree requirements:* For doctorate, thesis/dissertation. *Entrance requirements:* For doctorate, GRE General Test, sample of written work. Additional exam requirements/recommendations for international students: Required—TOEFL (minimum score 600 paper-based; 250 computer-based; 100 iBT), IELTS (minimum score 7).

University of Houston, College of Education, Department of Educational Leadership and Cultural Studies, Houston, TX 77204. Offers administration and supervision (M Ed, Ed D); higher education (M Ed); historical, social, and cultural foundations of education (M Ed). *Accreditation:* NCATE. Part-time and evening/weekend programs available. *Degree requirements:* For master's, comprehensive exam or thesis; for doctorate, comprehensive exam, thesis/dissertation. *Entrance requirements:* For master's, GRE General Test, minimum cumulative GPA of 2.6, 3 letters of recommendation, resume/vitae, goal statement; for doctorate, GRE General Test, minimum cumulative GPA of 2.6, 3 letters of recommendation, resume/vitae, goal statement, writing sample, interview. Additional exam requirements/recommendations for international students: Required—TOEFL (minimum score 550 paper-based; 79 iBT). Electronic applications accepted. *Faculty research:* Change, supervision, multiculturalism, evaluation, policy.

University of Houston–Clear Lake, School of Education, Program in Foundations and Professional Studies, Houston, TX 77058-1098. Offers counseling (MS); instructional technology (MS); multicultural studies (MS). Part-time and evening/weekend programs available. *Degree requirements:* For master's, thesis optional. *Entrance requirements:* For master's, GRE or minimum GPA of 3.0 in last 60 hours. Additional exam requirements/recommendations for international students: Required—TOEFL (minimum score 550 paper-based; 213 computer-based). Electronic applications accepted.

The University of Iowa, Graduate College, College of Education, Department of Educational Policy and Leadership Studies, Program in Social Foundations, Iowa City, IA 52242-1316. Offers MA, PhD. *Degree requirements:* For master's, thesis optional, exam; for doctorate, comprehensive exam, thesis/dissertation. *Entrance requirements:* For master's and doctorate, GRE General Test, minimum GPA of 3.0. Additional exam requirements/recommendations for international students: Required—TOEFL (minimum score 550 paper-based; 213 computer-based; 81 iBT). Electronic applications accepted.

The University of Iowa, Graduate College, College of Education, Department of Psychological and Quantitative Foundations, Iowa City, IA 52242-1316. Offers counseling psychology (PhD); educational measurement and statistics (MA, PhD); educational psychology (MA, PhD); school psychology (PhD, Ed S); JD/PhD. *Accreditation:* APA. *Degree requirements:* For master's, thesis optional, exam; for doctorate, comprehensive exam, thesis/dissertation; for Ed S, exam. *Entrance requirements:* For master's, doctorate, and Ed S, GRE General Test, minimum GPA of 3.0. Additional exam requirements/recommendations for international students: Required—TOEFL (minimum score 550 paper-based; 213 computer-based; 81 iBT). Electronic applications accepted.

The University of Kansas, Graduate Studies, School of Education, Department of Educational Leadership and Policy Studies, Education Leadership and Policy Program, Lawrence, KS 66045-3101. Offers educational administration (Ed D, PhD); foundations (PhD); higher education (Ed D, PhD); policy studies (PhD). Part-time and evening/weekend programs available. *Faculty:* 16. *Students:* 99 full-time (65 women), 52 part-time (28 women); includes 31 minority (10 Black or African American, non-Hispanic/Latino; 5 American Indian or Alaska Native, non-Hispanic/Latino; 5 Asian, non-Hispanic/Latino; 7 Hispanic/Latino; 4 Two or more races, non-Hispanic/Latino), 10 international. Average age 38. 44 applicants, 73% accepted, 22 enrolled. In 2011, 26 degrees awarded. *Degree requirements:* For doctorate, comprehensive exam, thesis/dissertation. *Entrance requirements:* For doctorate, GRE General Test, minimum graduate GPA of 3.5. Additional exam requirements/recommendations for international students: Required—TOEFL (minimum score 570 paper-based; 230 computer-based; 80 iBT). *Application deadline:* For fall admission, 7/1 for domestic and international students; for spring admission, 11/1 for domestic and international students. Applications are processed on a rolling basis. Application fee: $55 ($65 for international students). Electronic applications accepted. Tuition and fees vary according to course load, campus/location, program and reciprocity agreements. *Financial support:* Fellowships, research assistantships with full and partial tuition reimbursements, teaching assistantships with full and partial tuition reimbursements, scholarships/grants, and unspecified assistantships available. Financial award application deadline: 3/15. *Faculty research:* Historical and philosophical issues in education, education policy and leadership, higher education faculty, research on college students, education technology . *Unit head:* Dr. Susan Twombly, Chair, 785-864-9721, Fax: 785-864-4697, E-mail: stwombly@ku.edu. *Application contact:* Denise Brubaker, Admissions Coordinator, 785-864-4458, Fax: 785-864-4697, E-mail: elps@ku.edu. Web site: http://soe.ku.edu/elps/.

University of Manitoba, Faculty of Graduate Studies, Faculty of Education, Department of Educational Administration, Foundations and Psychology, Winnipeg, MB R3T 2N2, Canada. Offers adult and post-secondary education (M Ed); educational administration (M Ed); guidance and counseling (M Ed); inclusive special education (M Ed); social foundations of education (M Ed). *Degree requirements:* For master's, thesis or alternative.

University of Maryland, College Park, Academic Affairs, College of Education, Department of Education Policy and Leadership, College Park, MD 20742. Offers curriculum and educational communications (M Ed, MA, Ed D, PhD); social foundations of education (M Ed, MA, Ed D, PhD, CAGS). *Accreditation:* NCATE. Part-time and evening/weekend programs available. Postbaccalaureate distance learning degree programs offered (minimal on-campus study). *Students:* 93 full-time (67 women), 9 part-time (5 women); includes 46 minority (29 Black or African American, non-Hispanic/Latino; 8 Asian, non-Hispanic/Latino; 8 Hispanic/Latino; 1 Two or more races, non-Hispanic/Latino), 3 international. In 2011, 5 master's, 15 doctorates awarded. *Degree requirements:* For master's, thesis or alternative, internship and/or field experience; for doctorate, comprehensive exam, thesis/dissertation, practicum or internship. *Entrance requirements:* For master's, GRE General Test or MAT, minimum GPA of 3.0, scholarly writing sample, 3 letters of recommendation; for doctorate, GRE General Test or MAT, scholarly writing sample; minimum undergraduate GPA of 3.0, graduate 3.5. *Expenses: Tuition, area resident:* Part-time $525 per credit hour. Tuition, state resident: part-time $525 per credit hour. Tuition, nonresident: part-time $1131 per credit hour. *Required fees:* $386.31 per term. Tuition and fees vary according to program. *Financial support:* In 2011–12, 2 fellowships with full and partial tuition reimbursements (averaging $13,060 per year), 2 research assistantships (averaging $16,176 per year), 8 teaching assistantships (averaging $16,791 per year) were awarded; career-related internships or fieldwork, Federal Work-Study, and scholarships/grants also available. Support available to part-time students. Financial award applicants required to submit FAFSA. *Faculty research:* Educational technology, adult and higher education. *Total annual research expenditures:* $848. *Unit head:* Dennis Kivlighan, Chair, 301-405-2858, E-mail: dennisk@umd.edu. *Application contact:* Dr. Charles A. Caramello, Dean of Graduate School, 301-405-0358, Fax: 301-314-9305.

University of Minnesota, Twin Cities Campus, Graduate School, College of Education and Human Development, Department of Educational Psychology, Program in Psychological Foundations of Education, Minneapolis, MN 55455-0213. Offers MA, PhD, Ed S. *Students:* 53 full-time (31 women), 24 part-time (16 women); includes 12 minority (5 Black or African American, non-Hispanic/Latino; 4 Asian, non-Hispanic/Latino; 3 Hispanic/Latino), 18 international. Average age 34. 45 applicants, 60% accepted, 15 enrolled. In 2011, 8 master's, 4 doctorates awarded. Application fee: $55. *Unit head:* Dr. Susan Hupp, Chair, 612-624-1003, Fax: 612-624-8241, E-mail: shupp@umn.edu. *Application contact:* Dr. Jennifer Engler, Assistant Dean, 612-626-2887, Fax: 612-626-7496, E-mail: engle009@.umn.edu. Web site: http://www.cehd.umn.edu/EdPsych/Foundations.

University of New Mexico, Graduate School, College of Education, Department of Language, Literacy and Sociocultural Studies, Program in Language, Literacy and Sociocultural Studies, Albuquerque, NM 87131. Offers American Indian education (MA); bilingual education (MA, PhD); educational linguistics (PhD); educational thought and sociocultural studies (MA, PhD); literacy/language arts (MA, PhD); social studies (MA); TESOL (MA, PhD). *Faculty:* 19 full-time (12 women), 12 part-time/adjunct (10 women). *Students:* 40 full-time (30 women), 47 part-time (17 women); includes 85 minority (4 Black or African American, non-Hispanic/Latino; 14 American Indian or Alaska Native, non-Hispanic/Latino; 4 Asian, non-Hispanic/Latino; 59 Hispanic/Latino; 4 Two or more races, non-Hispanic/Latino), 14 international. Average age 41. 63 applicants, 57% accepted, 22 enrolled. In 2011, 44 master's, 8 doctorates awarded. *Degree requirements:* For master's, comprehensive exam, thesis optional; for doctorate, comprehensive exam, thesis/dissertation, research skills. *Entrance requirements:* For master's, letter of intent, 3 letters of recommendation, resume, BA/BS, department demographic form, transcripts; for doctorate, writing sample, letter of intent, 3 letters of recommendation, resume, BA/BS, department demographic form, transcripts. Additional exam requirements/recommendations for international students: Required—TOEFL. *Application deadline:* For fall admission, 12/1 for domestic and international students; for spring admission, 9/15 for domestic and international students. Application fee: $50. Electronic applications accepted. *Financial support:* In 2011–12, 7 students received support, including 7 fellowships (averaging $3,170 per year), 1,318 teaching assistantships with tuition reimbursements available (averaging $3,789 per year); research assistantships, career-related internships or fieldwork, institutionally sponsored loans, scholarships/grants, and unspecified assistantships also available. Support available to part-time students. Financial award application deadline: 3/1; financial award applicants required to submit FAFSA. *Faculty research:* School reform, professional development, history of education, Native American education, politics of education, feminism and issues of sexual identity, critical race theory, bilingualism, literacy reading, adolescent literature, second language acquisition, critical theory and schooling, indigenous languages. *Unit head:* Dr. Lois M. Meyer, Chair, 505-277-7244, Fax: 505-277-8362, E-mail: lsmeyer@unm.edu. *Application contact:* Debra Schaffer, Administrative Assistant, 505-277-0437, Fax: 505-277-8362, E-mail: schaffer@unm.edu. Web site: http://coe.unm.edu/departments/department-of-language-literacy-and-sociocultural-studies/llss-program.html.

University of Pennsylvania, Graduate School of Education, Division of Education, Culture and Society, Program in Education, Culture and Society, Philadelphia, PA 19104. Offers MS Ed, PhD. *Students:* 41 full-time (27 women), 6 part-time (3 women); includes 12 minority (8 Black or African American, non-Hispanic/Latino; 1 Asian, non-Hispanic/Latino; 3 Hispanic/Latino), 9 international. 180 applicants, 29% accepted, 23 enrolled. In 2011, 16 master's, 1 doctorate awarded. *Expenses: Tuition:* Full-time $26,660; part-time $4944 per course. *Required fees:* $2318; $291 per course. Tuition and fees vary according to course load, degree level and program. *Unit head:* Dr. Andrew Porter, Dean, 215-898-7014. *Application contact:* Vernell Edwards, 215-746-2566, E-mail: edwardsv@gse.upenn.edu.

University of Pittsburgh, School of Education, Department of Administrative and Policy Studies, Program in Social and Comparative Analysis in Education, Pittsburgh, PA 15260. Offers M Ed, MA, Ed D, PhD. Evening/weekend programs available. *Students:* 64 full-time (46 women), 39 part-time (26 women); includes 11 minority (6 Black or African American, non-Hispanic/Latino; 4 Asian, non-Hispanic/Latino; 1 Hispanic/Latino), 26 international. Average age 36. 79 applicants, 80% accepted, 37 enrolled. In 2011, 6 master's, 20 doctorates awarded. *Degree requirements:* For master's, thesis; for doctorate, thesis/dissertation. *Entrance requirements:* For doctorate, GRE General Test. Additional exam requirements/recommendations for international students: Required—TOEFL (minimum score 213 computer-based; 80 iBT). *Application deadline:* For fall admission, 2/1 priority date for domestic students, 2/1 for international students; for spring admission, 11/15 priority date for domestic students, 7/1 for international students. Applications are processed on a rolling basis. Application fee: $50. Electronic applications accepted. *Expenses:* Tuition, state resident: full-time $18,774; part-time $760 per credit. Tuition, nonresident: full-time $30,736; part-time $1258 per credit. *Required fees:* $740; $200 per term. Tuition and fees vary according to program. *Financial support:* Research assistantships, teaching assistantships, Federal Work-Study, institutionally sponsored loans, scholarships/grants, health care benefits, tuition waivers (partial), and unspecified assistantships available. Support available to part-time students. Financial award application deadline: 3/15; financial award applicants required to submit FAFSA. *Unit head:* Dr. Mary Margaret Kerr, Chair, 412-648-7205, Fax: 412-648-1784, E-mail: mmkerr@pitt.edu. *Application contact:* Lauren Spadafora, Enrollment Manager, 412-648-2230, Fax: 412-648-1899, E-mail: soeinfo@pitt.edu. Web site: http://www.education.pitt.edu/AcademicDepartments/AdministrativePolicyStudies/Programs/SocialComparativeAnalysisinEducation.aspx.

University of Rochester, Margaret Warner Graduate School of Education and Human Development, Doctoral Programs in Education, Rochester, NY 14627. Offers counseling (Ed D); educational administration (Ed D); educational policy and theory (PhD); higher education (PhD); human development in educational context (PhD); teaching, curriculum, and change (PhD). *Expenses: Tuition:* Full-time $41,040.

University of Saskatchewan, College of Graduate Studies and Research, College of Education, Department of Educational Foundations, Saskatoon, SK S7N 5A2, Canada. Offers M Ed, MC Ed, PhD, Diploma. Part-time programs available. *Degree requirements:* For master's, thesis (for some programs); for doctorate, comprehensive exam (for some programs), thesis/dissertation. *Entrance requirements:* Additional exam requirements/recommendations for international students: Required—TOEFL (minimum score 80 iBT); Recommended—IELTS (minimum score 6.5). Electronic applications accepted. *Faculty research:* Indian and northern education, adult and continuing education, international education.

University of South Africa, College of Human Sciences, Pretoria, South Africa. Offers adult education (M Ed); African languages (MA, PhD); African politics (MA, PhD); Afrikaans (MA, PhD); ancient history (MA, PhD); ancient Near Eastern studies (MA, PhD); anthropology (MA, PhD); applied linguistics (MA); Arabic (MA, PhD); archaeology (MA); art history (MA); Biblical archaeology (MA); Biblical studies (M Th, D Th, PhD); Christian spirituality (M Th, D Th); church history (M Th, D Th); classical studies (MA,

PhD); clinical psychology (MA); communication (MA, PhD); comparative education (M Ed, Ed D); consulting psychology (D Admin, D Com, PhD); curriculum studies (M Ed, Ed D); development studies (M Admin, MA, D Admin, PhD); didactics (M Ed, Ed D); education (M Tech); education management (M Ed, Ed D); educational psychology (M Ed); English (MA); environmental education (M Ed); French (MA, PhD); German (MA, PhD); Greek (MA); guidance and counseling (M Ed); health studies (MA, PhD), including health sciences education (MA), health services management (MA), medical and surgical nursing science (critical care general) (MA), midwifery and neonatal nursing science (MA), trauma and emergency care (MA); history (MA, PhD); history of education (Ed D); inclusive education (M Ed, Ed D); information and communications technology policy and regulation (MA); information science (MA, MIS, PhD); international politics (MA, PhD); Islamic studies (MA, PhD); Italian (MA, PhD); Judaica (MA, PhD); linguistics (MA, PhD); mathematical education (M Ed); mathematics education (MA); missiology (M Th, D Th); modern Hebrew (MA, PhD); musicology (MA, MMus, D Mus, PhD); natural science education (M Ed); New Testament (M Th, D Th); Old Testament (D Th); pastoral therapy (M Th, D Th); philosophy (MA); philosophy of education (M Ed, Ed D); politics (MA, PhD); Portuguese (MA, PhD); practical theology (M Th, D Th); psychology (MA, MS, PhD); psychology of education (M Ed, Ed D); public health (MA); religious studies (MA, D Th, PhD); Romance languages (MA); Russian (MA, PhD); Semitic languages (MA, PhD); social behavior studies in HIV/AIDS (MA); social science (mental health) (MA); social science in development studies (MA); social science in psychology (MA); social science in social work (MA); social science in sociology (MA); social work (MSW, DSW, PhD); socio-education (M Ed, Ed D); sociolinguistics (MA); sociology (MA, PhD); Spanish (MA, PhD); systematic theology (M Th, D Th); TESOL (teaching English to speakers of other languages) (MA); theological ethics (M Th, D Th); theory of literature (MA, PhD); urban ministries (D Th); urban ministry (M Th).

University of South Carolina, The Graduate School, College of Education, Department of Educational Studies, Program in Foundations in Education, Columbia, SC 29208. Offers PhD. *Accreditation:* NCATE. Part-time programs available. *Degree requirements:* For doctorate, comprehensive exam, thesis/dissertation. *Entrance requirements:* For doctorate, GRE General Test or MAT, interview. Electronic applications accepted. *Faculty research:* Oral history, educational biography, home schooling, international education.

The University of Tennessee, Graduate School, College of Education, Health and Human Sciences, Program in Education, Knoxville, TN 37996. Offers art education (MS); counseling education (PhD); cultural studies in education (PhD); curriculum (MS, Ed S); curriculum, educational research and evaluation (Ed D, PhD); early childhood education (PhD); early childhood special education (MS); education of deaf and hard of hearing (MS); educational administration and policy studies (Ed D, PhD); educational administration and supervision (Ed S); educational psychology (Ed D, PhD); elementary education (MS, Ed S); elementary teaching (MS); English education (MS, Ed S); exercise science (PhD); foreign language/ESL education (MS, Ed S); instructional technology (MS, Ed D, PhD, Ed S); literacy, language and ESL education (PhD); literacy, language education, and ESL education (Ed D); mathematics education (MS, Ed S); modified and comprehensive special education (MS); reading education (MS, Ed S); school counseling (Ed S); school psychology (PhD, Ed S); science education (MS, Ed S); secondary teaching (MS); social foundations (MS); social science education (MS, Ed S); socio-cultural foundations of sports and education (PhD); special education (Ed S); teacher education (Ed D, PhD). *Accreditation:* NCATE. Part-time and evening/weekend programs available. *Degree requirements:* For master's and Ed S, thesis optional; for doctorate, variable foreign language requirement, thesis/dissertation. *Entrance requirements:* For master's, minimum GPA of 2.7; for doctorate and Ed S, GRE General Test, minimum GPA of 2.7. Additional exam requirements/recommendations for international students: Required—TOEFL. Electronic applications accepted. *Expenses:* Tuition, state resident: full-time $8332; part-time $464 per credit hour. Tuition, nonresident: full-time $25,174; part-time $1400 per credit hour. *Required fees:* $1162; $56 per credit hour. Tuition and fees vary according to program.

The University of Texas of the Permian Basin, Office of Graduate Studies, School of Education, Program in Professional Education, Odessa, TX 79762-0001. Offers MA. *Degree requirements:* For master's, comprehensive exam (for some programs), thesis (for some programs). *Entrance requirements:* For master's, GRE General Test. Additional exam requirements/recommendations for international students: Required—TOEFL (minimum score 550 paper-based; 213 computer-based).

The University of Toledo, College of Graduate Studies, Judith Herb College of Education, Health Science and Human Service, Department of Educational Foundations and Leadership, Toledo, OH 43606-3390. Offers educational administration and supervision (ME, DE, Ed S); educational psychology (ME, DE, PhD); educational research and measurement (ME, PhD); educational sociology (DE, PhD); educational theory and social foundations (ME); foundations of education (DE, PhD); higher education (ME, PhD); history of education (PhD); philosophy of education (PhD). *Accreditation:* NCATE. Part-time and evening/weekend programs available. *Faculty:* 32. *Students:* 26 full-time (14 women), 222 part-time (134 women); includes 78 minority (57 Black or African American, non-Hispanic/Latino; 5 Asian, non-Hispanic/Latino; 15 Hispanic/Latino; 1 Two or more races, non-Hispanic/Latino), 5 international. Average age 40. 85 applicants, 61% accepted, 34 enrolled. In 2011, 37 master's, 7 doctorates, 18 other advanced degrees awarded. *Degree requirements:* For master's, comprehensive exam, thesis or alternative; for doctorate, comprehensive exam, thesis/dissertation; for Ed S, thesis optional. *Entrance requirements:* For master's, doctorate, and Ed S, minimum cumulative GPA of 2.7 for all previous academic work, letters of recommendation. Additional exam requirements/recommendations for international students: Required—TOEFL (minimum score 550 paper-based; 213 computer-based; 80 iBT), IELTS (minimum score 6.5). *Application deadline:* For fall admission, 1/15 priority date for domestic students, 1/15 for international students. Applications are processed on a rolling basis. Application fee: $45 ($75 for international students). Electronic applications accepted. *Financial support:* In 2011–12, 10 research assistantships with full and partial tuition reimbursements (averaging $6,734 per year), 8 teaching assistantships with full and partial tuition reimbursements (averaging $9,000 per year) were awarded; career-related internships or fieldwork, Federal Work-Study, institutionally sponsored loans, scholarships/grants, tuition waivers (full and partial), unspecified assistantships, and administrative assistantships also available. Support available to part-time students. *Unit head:* Dr. William Gray, Interim Chair, 419-530-2565, Fax: 419-530-8447, E-mail: william.gray@utoledo.edu. *Application contact:* Graduate School Office, 419-530-4723, Fax: 419-530-4724, E-mail: grdsch@utnet.utoledo.edu. Web site: http://www.utoledo.edu/eduhshs/.

University of Utah, Graduate School, College of Education, Department of Education, Culture, and Society, Salt Lake City, UT 84112-1107. Offers M Ed, MA, MS, PhD. Evening/weekend programs available. *Faculty:* 13 full-time (8 women). *Students:* 62 full-time (42 women), 47 part-time (36 women); includes 35 minority (3 Black or African American, non-Hispanic/Latino; 5 American Indian or Alaska Native, non-Hispanic/Latino; 5 Asian, non-Hispanic/Latino; 20 Hispanic/Latino; 2 Native Hawaiian or other Pacific Islander, non-Hispanic/Latino), 5 international. Average age 31. 101 applicants, 47% accepted, 29 enrolled. In 2011, 13 master's, 6 doctorates awarded. *Median time to degree:* Of those who began their doctoral program in fall 2003, 40% received their degree in 8 years or less. *Degree requirements:* For master's, comprehensive exam, thesis (for some programs); for doctorate, thesis/dissertation. *Entrance requirements:* For master's and doctorate, minimum GPA of 3.0. Additional exam requirements/recommendations for international students: Required—TOEFL (minimum score 650 paper-based; 278 computer-based; 114 iBT). *Application deadline:* For fall admission, 2/1 priority date for domestic students, 2/1 for international students. Application fee: $55 ($65 for international students). Electronic applications accepted. *Financial support:* In 2011–12, 4 students received support, including 9 teaching assistantships with full tuition reimbursements available (averaging $15,000 per year); tuition waivers (full) and unspecified assistantships also available. Financial award application deadline: 3/1; financial award applicants required to submit FAFSA. *Faculty research:* History, philosophy and sociology of education, language, culture and curriculum. *Total annual research expenditures:* $6,404. *Unit head:* Dr. Harvey Kantor, Chair, 801-581-7805, Fax: 801-587-7801, E-mail: harvey.kantor@.utah.edu. Web site: http://www.ed.utah.edu/ecs/.

University of Victoria, Faculty of Graduate Studies, Faculty of Education, Department of Curriculum and Instruction, Victoria, BC V8W 2Y2, Canada. Offers art education (M Ed, PhD); curriculum studies (M Ed, MA, PhD); early childhood education (M Ed, PhD); educational studies (PhD); language and literacy (M Ed, MA, PhD); mathematics (M Ed, MA, PhD); music education (M Ed, MA, PhD); science (M Ed, MA, PhD); social studies (M Ed, MA); social, cultural and foundational studies (MA, PhD); technology and environmental education (PhD). Part-time programs available. *Degree requirements:* For master's, thesis, project (M Ed); for doctorate, comprehensive exam, thesis/dissertation. *Entrance requirements:* For master's, minimum B average. Additional exam requirements/recommendations for international students: Required—TOEFL (minimum score 575 paper-based; 233 computer-based), IELTS (minimum score 7). Electronic applications accepted. *Faculty research:* Elementary and secondary English, language arts, curriculum theory and practice, educational media and technology, educational administration and leadership, history and philosophy of education.

University of Washington, Graduate School, College of Education, Seattle, WA 98195. Offers curriculum and instruction (M Ed, Ed D, PhD), including educational technology, general curriculum (Ed D, PhD), language, literacy, and culture, mathematics education, multicultural education, reading and language arts education (Ed D), science education, social studies education, teaching and curriculum (M Ed); educational leadership and policy studies (M Ed, Ed D, PhD), including administration (Ed D), educational policy, organization, and leadership (M Ed, PhD), higher education, leadership for learning (Ed D), social and cultural foundations of education (M Ed, PhD); educational psychology (M Ed, PhD), including educational psychology (PhD), human development and cognition (M Ed), learning sciences, measurement, statistics and research design (M Ed), school psychology (M Ed); instructional leadership (M Ed); intercollegiate athletic leadership (M Ed); special education (M Ed, Ed D, PhD), including early childhood special education (M Ed), emotional and behavioral disabilities (M Ed), learning disabilities (M Ed), low-incidence disabilities (M Ed), severe disabilities (M Ed), special education (Ed D, PhD); teacher education (MIT). *Accreditation:* APA. Part-time and evening/weekend programs available. *Degree requirements:* For master's, thesis optional; for doctorate, thesis/dissertation. *Entrance requirements:* For master's and doctorate, GRE General Test, minimum GPA of 3.0. Additional exam requirements/recommendations for international students: Required—TOEFL. Electronic applications accepted. *Faculty research:* School restructuring/effective schools, special education interventions, literacy and writing, technology, school partnerships, teacher preparation.

University of Wisconsin–Milwaukee, Graduate School, School of Education, MS Program in Cultural Foundations of Education, Milwaukee, WI 53201-0413. Offers MS. Part-time programs available. *Students:* 20 full-time (13 women), 31 part-time (23 women); includes 29 minority (20 Black or African American, non-Hispanic/Latino; 1 Asian, non-Hispanic/Latino; 3 Hispanic/Latino; 5 Two or more races, non-Hispanic/Latino), 1 international. Average age 33. 39 applicants, 62% accepted, 13 enrolled. In 2011, 8 degrees awarded. *Degree requirements:* For master's, thesis or alternative. *Entrance requirements:* Additional exam requirements/recommendations for international students: Required—TOEFL (minimum score 550 paper-based; 79 iBT), IELTS (minimum score 6.5). *Application deadline:* For fall admission, 1/1 priority date for domestic students; for spring admission, 9/1 for domestic students. Applications are processed on a rolling basis. Application fee: $56 ($96 for international students). Electronic applications accepted. One-time fee: $506.10 full-time. Tuition and fees vary according to course load and reciprocity agreements. *Financial support:* In 2011–12, 3 fellowships with full tuition reimbursements were awarded; research assistantships, teaching assistantships, career-related internships or fieldwork, health care benefits, and unspecified assistantships also available. Support available to part-time students. Financial award application deadline: 4/15; financial award applicants required to submit FAFSA. *Faculty research:* Human relations in education, international and multicultural education. *Unit head:* Michael Bonds, Representative, 414-229-2256, Fax: 414-229-3700, E-mail: mbonds@uwm.edu. *Application contact:* General Information Contact, 414-229-4982, Fax: 414-229-6967, E-mail: gradschool@uwm.edu. Web site: http://www4.uwm.edu/soe/departments/ed_policy/degrees_pgm_study/mstr_prgm_cult_found.cfm.

University of Wisconsin–Milwaukee, Graduate School, School of Education, Program in Urban Education, Milwaukee, WI 53201-0413. Offers adult and continuing education (PhD); curriculum and instruction (PhD); educational administration (PhD); educational and media technology (PhD); educational psychology (PhD); multicultural studies (PhD); social foundations of education (PhD). *Students:* 65 full-time (45 women), 37 part-time (25 women); includes 39 minority (18 Black or African American, non-Hispanic/Latino; 1 American Indian or Alaska Native, non-Hispanic/Latino; 6 Asian, non-Hispanic/Latino; 6 Hispanic/Latino; 8 Two or more races, non-Hispanic/Latino), 5 international. Average age 41. 26 applicants, 62% accepted, 2 enrolled. In 2011, 13 degrees awarded. *Degree requirements:* For doctorate, comprehensive exam, thesis/dissertation. *Entrance requirements:* For doctorate, GRE General Test, minimum undergraduate GPA of 2.85, graduate 3.5. Additional exam requirements/recommendations for international students: Required—TOEFL (minimum score 550 paper-based; 79 iBT), IELTS (minimum score 6.5). *Application deadline:* For fall admission, 1/1 priority date for domestic students; for spring admission, 9/1 for domestic students. Applications are processed on a rolling basis. Application fee: $56 ($96 for international students). Electronic applications accepted. One-time fee: $506.10 full-time. Tuition and fees vary according to course load and reciprocity agreements. *Financial support:* In 2011–12, 11 fellowships, 1 teaching assistantship were awarded; research assistantships, career-related internships or fieldwork, health care benefits, unspecified assistantships, and project assistantships also available. Support available to part-time students. Financial award application deadline: 4/15; financial award applicants required to submit FAFSA. *Unit head:* Larry Martin, Representative, 414-229-4729, Fax: 414-229-2920, E-mail: lmartin@uwm.edu. *Application contact:* General Information Contact, 414-229-4982, Fax: 414-229-6967, E-mail: gradschool@uwm.edu. Web site: http://www.uwm.edu/Dept/UrbanEd/.

Wayne State University, College of Education, Division of Theoretical and Behavioral Foundations, Detroit, MI 48202. Offers counseling (M Ed, MA, Ed D, PhD, Ed S); education evaluation and research (M Ed, Ed D, PhD); educational psychology (M Ed,

Ed D, PhD, Ed S); educational sociology (M Ed, Ed D, PhD, Ed S); history and philosophy of education (M Ed, Ed D, PhD); rehabilitation counseling and community inclusion (MA, Ed S); school and community psychology (MA, Ed S); school clinical psychology (Ed S). *Accreditation:* ACA (one or more programs are accredited); CORE (one or more programs are accredited). Evening/weekend programs available. *Students:* 199 full-time (156 women), 215 part-time (187 women); includes 162 minority (145 Black or African American, non-Hispanic/Latino; 1 American Indian or Alaska Native, non-Hispanic/Latino; 5 Asian, non-Hispanic/Latino; 5 Hispanic/Latino; 1 Native Hawaiian or other Pacific Islander, non-Hispanic/Latino; 5 Two or more races, non-Hispanic/Latino), 21 international. Average age 35. 278 applicants, 30% accepted, 56 enrolled. In 2011, 94 master's, 15 doctorates, 1 other advanced degree awarded. *Degree requirements:* For master's, thesis (for some programs); for doctorate, thesis/dissertation. *Entrance requirements:* For master's, GRE; for doctorate, GRE, interview, minimum GPA of 3.0, curriculum vitae, references. Additional exam requirements/recommendations for international students: Required—TOEFL (minimum score 550 paper-based; 213 computer-based), TWE (minimum score 5.5). *Application deadline:* For fall admission, 6/1 priority date for domestic students, 5/1 for international students; for winter admission, 10/1 priority date for domestic students, 9/1 for international students; for spring admission, 2/1 priority date for domestic students, 1/1 for international students. Applications are processed on a rolling basis. Application fee: $50. Electronic applications accepted. *Expenses:* Tuition, state resident: part-time $512.85 per credit. Tuition, nonresident: part-time $1132.65 per credit. *Required fees:* $26.60 per credit. $199.65 per semester. Tuition and fees vary according to course load and program. *Financial support:* In 2011–12, 64 students received support, including 3 fellowships with tuition reimbursements available (averaging $16,371 per year), 2 research assistantships with tuition reimbursements available (averaging $15,713 per year), 1 teaching assistantship (averaging $18,000 per year); career-related internships or fieldwork, Federal Work-Study, institutionally sponsored loans, scholarships/grants, health care benefits, and unspecified assistantships also available. *Faculty research:* Adolescents at risk, supervision of counseling. *Total annual research expenditures:* $5,019. *Unit head:* Dr. Alan Hoffman, Assistant Dean, 313-577-5235, E-mail: alanhoffman@wayne.edu. *Application contact:* Janice Green, Assistant Dean, 313-577-1605, E-mail: jwgreen@wayne.edu. Web site: http://coe.wayne.edu/tbf/index.php.

Western Illinois University, School of Graduate Studies, College of Education and Human Services, Department of Educational and Interdisciplinary Studies, Program in Educational and Interdisciplinary Studies, Macomb, IL 61455-1390. Offers educational and interdisciplinary studies (MS Ed); teaching English to speakers of other languages (Certificate). *Accreditation:* NCATE. Part-time programs available. *Students:* 13 full-time (10 women), 47 part-time (32 women); includes 9 minority (4 Black or African American, non-Hispanic/Latino; 1 Asian, non-Hispanic/Latino; 4 Hispanic/Latino). Average age 37. 12 applicants, 83% accepted. In 2011, 46 master's, 4 Certificates awarded. *Degree requirements:* For master's, thesis or alternative. *Entrance requirements:* For master's, minimum GPA of 2.75, interview. Additional exam requirements/recommendations for international students: Required—TOEFL (minimum score 550 paper-based; 213 computer-based; 80 iBT). *Application deadline:* Applications are processed on a rolling basis. Application fee: $30. Electronic applications accepted. *Expenses:* Tuition, state resident: part-time $281.16 per credit hour. Tuition, nonresident: part-time $562.32 per credit hour. Part-time tuition and fees vary according to campus/location and reciprocity agreements. *Financial support:* In 2011–12, 5 students received support, including 5 research assistantships with full tuition reimbursements available (averaging $7,360 per year). Financial award applicants required to submit FAFSA. *Unit head:* Dr. Tom Cody, Graduate Committee Chairperson, 309-298-1183. *Application contact:* Dr. Nancy Parsons, Interim Associate Provost and Director of Graduate Studies, 309-298-1806, Fax: 309-298-2345, E-mail: grad-office@wiu.edu. Web site: http://wiu.edu/eis.

Widener University, School of Human Service Professions, Center for Education, Chester, PA 19013-5792. Offers adult education (M Ed); counseling in higher education (M Ed); counselor education (M Ed); early childhood education (M Ed); educational foundations (M Ed); educational leadership (M Ed); educational psychology (M Ed); elementary education (M Ed); English and language arts (M Ed); health education (M Ed); higher education leadership (Ed D); home and school visitor (M Ed); human sexuality (M Ed, PhD); mathematics education (M Ed); middle school education (M Ed); principalship (M Ed); reading and language arts (Ed D); reading education (M Ed); school administration (Ed D); science education (M Ed); social studies education (M Ed); special education (M Ed); technology education (M Ed). *Accreditation:* NCATE. Part-time and evening/weekend programs available. Terminal master's awarded for partial completion of doctoral program. *Degree requirements:* For doctorate, thesis/dissertation. *Entrance requirements:* For master's, minimum GPA of 2.5; for doctorate, GRE or MAT, minimum GPA of 2.0 (undergraduate), 3.5 (graduate). Electronic applications accepted. *Expenses:* Contact institution. *Faculty research:* Reading and cognition, adult education, technology education, educational leadership, special education.

International and Comparative Education

American University, College of Arts and Sciences, School of Education, Teaching, and Health, Program in International Training and Education, Washington, DC 20016-8001. Offers MA, MAT. *Students:* 20 full-time (all women), 17 part-time (16 women); includes 5 minority (2 Black or African American, non-Hispanic/Latino; 1 Asian, non-Hispanic/Latino; 1 Hispanic/Latino; 1 Two or more races, non-Hispanic/Latino), 1 international. Average age 28. 58 applicants, 79% accepted, 9 enrolled. In 2011, 18 master's awarded. *Degree requirements:* For master's, one foreign language, comprehensive exam, volunteer experience. *Entrance requirements:* For master's, GRE General Test, minimum GPA of 3.0, six months international/cultural experience (preferred). *Application deadline:* For fall admission, 2/1 priority date for domestic students; for spring admission, 10/1 priority date for domestic students. Applications are processed on a rolling basis. Application fee: $80. *Expenses: Tuition:* Full-time $24,264; part-time $1348 per credit hour. *Required fees:* $430. Tuition and fees vary according to course load and program. *Financial support:* Application deadline: 2/1. *Unit head:* Sarah Irvine-Belson, Dean, 202-885-3714, Fax: 202-885-1187, E-mail: educate@american.edu. *Application contact:* Kathleen Clowery, Director, Graduate Admissions, 202-885-3621, Fax: 202-885-1505, E-mail: clowery@american.edu. Web site: http://www.american.edu/cas/seth/.

The American University in Cairo, Graduate School of Education, New Cairo 11835, Egypt. Offers international and comparative education (MA). Part-time programs available. *Faculty:* 7 full-time (6 women), 4 part-time/adjunct (0 women). *Students:* 17 full-time (13 women), 23 part-time (18 women). 59 applicants, 81% accepted, 19 enrolled. *Degree requirements:* For master's, thesis. *Entrance requirements:* Additional exam requirements/recommendations for international students: Required—TOEFL (minimum score 450 paper-based; 133 computer-based; 45 iBT). *Application deadline:* For fall admission, 2/1 priority date for domestic students, 2/1 for international students; for spring admission, 11/1 priority date for domestic students, 11/1 for international students. Applications are processed on a rolling basis. Application fee: $50. Electronic applications accepted. *Expenses: Tuition:* Part-time $932 per credit hour. Tuition and fees vary according to course load, degree level and program. *Financial support:* Fellowships with partial tuition reimbursements and scholarships/grants available. Financial award application deadline: 5/12. *Unit head:* Dr. Samiha Peterson, 20-2-2615-1490, E-mail: peterss@aucegypt.edu. *Application contact:* Wesley Clark, Coordinator of Student Affairs, 212-646-810-9433 Ext. 4547, E-mail: wclark@aucnyo.edu. Web site: http://www.aucegypt.edu/GSE/Pages/Home.aspx.

Bowling Green State University, Graduate College, College of Education and Human Development, School of Leadership and Policy Studies, Program in Cross-Cultural and International Education, Bowling Green, OH 43403. Offers MA. Part-time programs available. *Degree requirements:* For master's, thesis or alternative. *Entrance requirements:* For master's, GRE General Test. Additional exam requirements/recommendations for international students: Required—TOEFL.

California Baptist University, Program in Education, Riverside, CA 92504-3206. Offers educational leadership for faith-based instruction (MS); educational leadership for public institutions (MS); educational technology (MS); instructional computer applications (MS); international education (MS); reading (MS); school counseling (MS); school psychology (MS); special education (MS); special education in mild/moderate disabilities (MS); special education in moderate/severe disabilities (MS); teaching (MS); teaching and learning with induction program (MS Ed). Part-time and evening/weekend programs available. *Faculty:* 16 full-time (10 women), 1 (woman) part-time/adjunct. *Students:* 380 full-time (323 women); includes 149 minority (28 Black or African American, non-Hispanic/Latino; 2 American Indian or Alaska Native, non-Hispanic/Latino; 13 Asian, non-Hispanic/Latino; 100 Hispanic/Latino; 2 Native Hawaiian or other Pacific Islander, non-Hispanic/Latino; 4 Two or more races, non-Hispanic/Latino). Average age 32. 181 applicants, 70% accepted, 111 enrolled. In 2011, 82 master's awarded. *Degree requirements:* For master's, comprehensive exam or thesis. *Entrance requirements:* For master's, minimum undergraduate GPA of 3.0; 18 semester units of prerequisite course work in education; three recommendations; essay; interview. Additional exam requirements/recommendations for international students: Required—TOEFL (minimum score 575 paper-based; 230 computer-based; 89 iBT). *Application deadline:* For fall admission, 8/1 priority date for domestic students, 7/1 for international students; for spring admission, 12/1 priority date for domestic students, 11/1 for international students. Applications are processed on a rolling basis. Application fee: $45. Electronic applications accepted. *Expenses:* Contact institution. *Financial support:* In 2011–12, 4 students received support. Federal Work-Study and institutionally sponsored loans available. Financial award applicants required to submit FAFSA. *Faculty research:* Special education, neurosciences and education, cultural influences on behavior, faith-based school leadership, social and philosophical contexts of education. *Unit head:* Dr. John Shoup, Dean, School of Education, 951-343-4205, Fax: 951-343-4516, E-mail: jshoup@calbaptist.edu. *Application contact:* Dr. James Heyman, Director, Master of Science Program in Education, 951-343-4243, Fax: 951-343-5095, E-mail: jheyman@calbaptist.edu. Web site: http://www.calbaptist.edu/mastersined/.

California State University, Dominguez Hills, College of Extended and International Education, Carson, CA 90747-0001. Offers MA, MS. Part-time and evening/weekend programs available. Postbaccalaureate distance learning degree programs offered. *Faculty:* 9 full-time (4 women), 47 part-time/adjunct (16 women). *Students:* 12 full-time (2 women), 564 part-time (312 women); includes 170 minority (39 Black or African American, non-Hispanic/Latino; 3 American Indian or Alaska Native, non-Hispanic/Latino; 50 Asian, non-Hispanic/Latino; 31 Hispanic/Latino; 2 Native Hawaiian or other Pacific Islander, non-Hispanic/Latino; 45 Two or more races, non-Hispanic/Latino), 30 international. Average age 42. 425 applicants, 91% accepted, 120 enrolled. In 2011, 100 master's awarded. *Degree requirements:* For master's, thesis. *Entrance requirements:* Additional exam requirements/recommendations for international students: Required—TOEFL. Application fee: $55. Electronic applications accepted. *Expenses:* Contact institution. *Unit head:* Dr. Margaret Gordon, Dean, 310-243-3737, Fax: 310-516-4423, E-mail: mgordon@csudh.edu. *Application contact:* Dr. Timothy Mozia, Director of Operations, 310-243-3741, E-mail: tmozia@csudh.edu. Web site: http://www.csudh.edu/ee/.

The College of New Jersey, Graduate Studies, Office of Global Programs, Program in Overseas Education, Ewing, NJ 08628. Offers M Ed, Certificate. Part-time programs available. *Degree requirements:* For master's, comprehensive exam. *Entrance requirements:* For master's, GRE, minimum GPA of 3.0 in field or 2.75 overall; for Certificate, previous master's degree or higher. Additional exam requirements/recommendations for international students: Required—TOEFL. Electronic applications accepted.

Drexel University, Goodwin College of Professional Studies, School of Education, Program in Global and International Education, Philadelphia, PA 19104-2875. Offers MS.

Florida International University, College of Education, Department of Curriculum and Instruction, Miami, FL 33199. Offers art education (MAT, MS, Ed D); curriculum and instruction (Ed S); curriculum development (MS); curriculum studies (PhD); early childhood education (MS, Ed D); elementary education (MS, Ed D); English education (MAT, MS, Ed D); foreign language education - teaching English to speakers of other languages (TESOL) (MS, Certificate), including foreign language education (Certificate), teaching English (MS); French education - initial teacher preparation (MAT); international and intercultural development education (Ed D); international and intercultural developmental education (MS); language, literacy and culture (PhD); learning technologies (MS, Ed D, PhD); mathematics education (MAT, MS, Ed D, PhD); modern language education/bilingual education (MS, Ed D); physical education (MS); reading education (MS, Ed D); science education (MAT, MS, Ed D, PhD); social studies education (MAT, MS, Ed D); Spanish education - initial teacher preparation (MAT); special education (MS). Part-time and evening/weekend programs available. *Degree requirements:* For doctorate, comprehensive exam, thesis/dissertation. *Entrance requirements:* For master's, GRE General Test, Florida General Knowledge Test or Florida College Level Academic Skills Test; for doctorate and other advanced degree,

International and Comparative Education

GRE General Test. Additional exam requirements/recommendations for international students: Required—TOEFL (minimum score 550 paper-based; 213 computer-based; 80 iBT), IELTS (minimum score 6.3). Electronic applications accepted.

Florida International University, College of Education, Department of Educational Leadership and Policy Studies, Miami, FL 33199. Offers adult education (MS); adult education in human resource development (Ed D); clinical mental health counseling (MS); conflict resolution and consensus building (Certificate); counselor education (MS); educational administration and supervision (Ed D); educational leadership (MS, Certificate, Ed S); higher education (Ed D); higher education administration (MS); human resource development (MS); instruction in urban settings (MS); international/intercultural education (MS); learning technologies (MS); multicultural-bilingual (MS); multicultural-TESOL (MS); recreation and sport management (MS); recreation therapy (MS); rehabilitation counseling (MS); school counseling (MS); school psychology (Ed S); urban education (MS). Part-time and evening/weekend programs available. *Degree requirements:* For doctorate, thesis/dissertation. *Entrance requirements:* For master's, minimum GPA of 3.0; for doctorate and other advanced degree, GRE General Test. Additional exam requirements/recommendations for international students: Required—TOEFL (minimum score 550 paper-based; 213 computer-based; 80 iBT), IELTS (minimum score 6.3). Electronic applications accepted.

Florida State University, The Graduate School, College of Education, Department of Educational Leadership and Policy Studies, Program in Social, History and Philosophy of Education, Tallahassee, FL 32306. Offers history and philosophy of education (MS, PhD, Ed S); international and intercultural education (PhD). *Faculty:* 2 full-time (0 women). *Students:* 29 full-time (19 women), 17 part-time (8 women); includes 8 minority (5 Black or African American, non-Hispanic/Latino; 1 Asian, non-Hispanic/Latino; 2 Hispanic/Latino), 14 international. Average age 36. 42 applicants, 76% accepted, 10 enrolled. In 2011, 11 master's, 5 doctorates, 2 other advanced degrees awarded. *Degree requirements:* For master's and Ed S, comprehensive exam, thesis optional; for doctorate, comprehensive exam, thesis/dissertation. *Entrance requirements:* For master's, doctorate, and Ed S, GRE General Test, minimum GPA of 3.0. Additional exam requirements/recommendations for international students: Required—TOEFL (minimum score 550 paper-based; 213 computer-based; 80 iBT). *Application deadline:* For fall admission, 7/1 for domestic and international students; for winter admission, 11/1 for domestic and international students; for spring admission, 3/1 for domestic and international students. Application fee: $30. Electronic applications accepted. *Expenses:* Tuition, state resident: full-time $9474; part-time $350.88 per credit hour. Tuition, nonresident: full-time $16,236; part-time $601.34 per credit hour. *Required fees:* $630 per semester. One-time fee: $20. Tuition and fees vary according to course load and campus/location. *Financial support:* Fellowships with full and partial tuition reimbursements, research assistantships with full and partial tuition reimbursements, teaching assistantships with full and partial tuition reimbursements, career-related internships or fieldwork, scholarships/grants, health care benefits, and unspecified assistantships available. Financial award applicants required to submit FAFSA. *Faculty research:* Social, historical, philosophical content of educational policies; religion, gender, diversity, and social justice in educational policy; interdisciplinary. *Unit head:* Dr. Jeffrey A. Milligan, Assistant Professor/Program Coordinator, 850-644-8171, Fax: 850-644-1258, E-mail: jmilligan@fsu.edu. *Application contact:* Jimmy Pastrano, Program Assistant, 850-644-6777, Fax: 850-644-1258, E-mail: jpastrano@fsu.edu. Web site: http://www.coe.fsu.edu/SHPFE.

Gallaudet University, The Graduate School, Washington, DC 20002-3625. Offers audiology (Au D); clinical psychology (PhD); critical studies in the education of deaf learners (PhD); deaf and hard of hearing infants, toddlers, and their families (Certificate); deaf education (Ed S); deaf education: advanced studies (MA); deaf education: special programs in deaf education (MA); deaf history (Certificate); deaf studies (MA, Certificate); education deaf students with disabilities (Certificate); education: teacher preparation (MA), including deaf education, early childhood education and deaf education, elementary education and deaf education, secondary education and deaf education; hearing, speech and language sciences (MS, PhD); international development (MA); interpretation (MA, PhD); linguistics (MA, PhD); mental health counseling (MA); public administration (MA); school counseling (MA); school psychology (Psy S); sign language teaching (MA); social work (MSW); speech-language pathology (MS). Part-time programs available. *Faculty:* 62 full-time (44 women). *Students:* 300 full-time (246 women), 110 part-time (82 women); includes 80 minority (27 Black or African American, non-Hispanic/Latino; 1 American Indian or Alaska Native, non-Hispanic/Latino; 11 Asian, non-Hispanic/Latino; 25 Hispanic/Latino; 1 Native Hawaiian or other Pacific Islander, non-Hispanic/Latino; 15 Two or more races, non-Hispanic/Latino), 24 international. Average age 30. 498 applicants, 45% accepted, 168 enrolled. In 2011, 129 master's, 24 doctorates, 19 other advanced degrees awarded. Terminal master's awarded for partial completion of doctoral program. *Degree requirements:* For master's, comprehensive exam (for some programs), thesis optional; for doctorate, comprehensive exam, thesis/dissertation. *Entrance requirements:* For master's and doctorate, GRE General Test or MAT, letters of recommendation, interviews, goals statement, ASL proficiency interview, written English competency. Additional exam requirements/recommendations for international students: Required—TOEFL. *Application deadline:* For fall admission, 2/15 for domestic students. Applications are processed on a rolling basis. Application fee: $50. Electronic applications accepted. *Expenses: Tuition:* Full-time $12,770; part-time $710 per credit. *Required fees:* $376. *Financial support:* In 2011–12, 287 students received support. Fellowships, research assistantships, teaching assistantships, career-related internships or fieldwork, Federal Work-Study, scholarships/grants, tuition waivers (partial), and unspecified assistantships available. Support available to part-time students. Financial award applicants required to submit FAFSA. *Faculty research:* Bimodal bilingualism development, audiology, telecommunications access, early childhood education, linguistics, visual language and visual learning, rehabilitation and hearing enhancement. *Unit head:* Dr. Carol J. Erting, Dean, 202-651-5520, Fax: 202-651-5027, E-mail: carol.erting@gallaudet.edu. *Application contact:* Wednesday Luria, Coordinator of Prospective Graduate Student Services, 202-651-5400, Fax: 202-651-5295, E-mail: graduate.school@gallaudet.edu. Web site: http://www.gallaudet.edu/x26696.xml.

George Mason University, College of Humanities and Social Sciences, Program in Global Affairs, Fairfax, VA 22030. Offers MA. *Expenses:* Tuition, state resident: full-time $8750; part-time $364.58 per credit. Tuition, nonresident: full-time $24,092; part-time $1003.83 per credit. *Required fees:* $2514; $104.75 per credit. *Application contact:* Laura Layland, Graduate Admissions Assistant, 703-993-2409, E-mail: llayland@gmu.edu.

The George Washington University, Graduate School of Education and Human Development, Department of Educational Leadership, Program in International Education, Washington, DC 20052. Offers MA Ed. *Accreditation:* NCATE. *Students:* 34 full-time (25 women), 54 part-time (50 women); includes 16 minority (4 Black or African American, non-Hispanic/Latino; 6 Asian, non-Hispanic/Latino; 5 Hispanic/Latino; 1 Two or more races, non-Hispanic/Latino), 6 international. Average age 27. 139 applicants, 96% accepted. In 2011, 32 master's awarded. *Degree requirements:* For master's, comprehensive exam. *Entrance requirements:* For master's, GRE General Test or MAT, minimum GPA of 2.75. *Application deadline:* For fall admission, 1/15 priority date for domestic students; for spring admission, 10/1 for domestic students. Applications are processed on a rolling basis. Application fee: $75. *Financial support:* In 2011–12, 13 students received support. Fellowships, research assistantships, career-related internships or fieldwork, Federal Work-Study, and tuition waivers available. Financial award application deadline: 1/15; financial award applicants required to submit FAFSA. *Faculty research:* Education and development. *Unit head:* Dr. William K. Cummings, Coordinator, 202-994-4698, E-mail: wkcum@gwu.edu. *Application contact:* Sarah Lang, Director of Graduate Admissions, 202-994-1447, Fax: 202-994-7207, E-mail: slang@gwu.edu.

Harvard University, Harvard Graduate School of Education, Master's Programs in Education, Cambridge, MA 02138. Offers arts in education (Ed M); education policy and management (Ed M); higher education (Ed M); human development and psychology (Ed M); international education policy (Ed M); language and literacy (Ed M); learning and teaching (Ed M); mid-career mathematics and science (teaching certificate) (Ed M); mind brain and education (Ed M); prevention science and practice (Ed M); school leadership (Ed M); special studies (Ed M); teaching and curriculum (teaching certificate) (Ed M); technology innovation and education (Ed M). Part-time programs available. *Faculty:* 83 full-time (44 women), 67 part-time/adjunct (29 women). *Students:* 592 full-time (431 women), 75 part-time (54 women); includes 194 minority (41 Black or African American, non-Hispanic/Latino; 4 American Indian or Alaska Native, non-Hispanic/Latino; 75 Asian, non-Hispanic/Latino; 45 Hispanic/Latino; 2 Native Hawaiian or other Pacific Islander, non-Hispanic/Latino; 27 Two or more races, non-Hispanic/Latino), 95 international. Average age 28. 1,679 applicants, 52% accepted, 627 enrolled. In 2011, 653 master's awarded. *Entrance requirements:* For master's, GRE General Test, statement of purpose, 3 letters of recommendation, resume, official transcripts. Additional exam requirements/recommendations for international students: Required—TOEFL (minimum score 613 paper-based; 104 computer-based; 100 iBT), TWE (minimum score 5). *Application deadline:* For fall admission, 1/4 for domestic and international students. Application fee: $85. Electronic applications accepted. *Expenses:* Contact institution. *Financial support:* In 2011–12, 419 students received support, including 14 fellowships with full and partial tuition reimbursements available (averaging $12,831 per year); career-related internships or fieldwork, Federal Work-Study, institutionally sponsored loans, scholarships/grants, health care benefits, tuition waivers (full and partial), and unspecified assistantships also available. Support available to part-time students. Financial award application deadline: 2/1; financial award applicants required to submit FAFSA. *Faculty research:* Learning and development, educational leadership and organizations, educational policy analysis. *Total annual research expenditures:* $26 million. *Unit head:* Jennifer L. Petrallia, Assistant Dean, 617-495-8445. *Application contact:* Information Contact, 617-495-3414, Fax: 617-496-3577, E-mail: gseadmissions@harvard.edu. Web site: http://www.gse.harvard.edu/.

Indiana University Bloomington, School of Education, Department of Educational Leadership and Policy Studies, Bloomington, IN 47405-7000. Offers education policy studies (PhD); educational leadership (MS, Ed D, Ed S); higher education (MS, Ed D, PhD); history and philosophy of education (MS); history of education (PhD); international and comparative education (MS, PhD); philosophy of education (PhD); student affairs administration (MS). *Accreditation:* NCATE. Part-time and evening/weekend programs available. *Degree requirements:* For master's, thesis optional; for doctorate, comprehensive exam, thesis/dissertation; for Ed S, comprehensive exam or project. *Entrance requirements:* For master's, doctorate, and Ed S, GRE General Test. Additional exam requirements/recommendations for international students: Required—TOEFL (minimum score 213 computer-based; 79 iBT). Electronic applications accepted. *Faculty research:* Student engagement at higher education institutions in the nation, Reading First professional development initiative, state finance policy on financial access to higher education, school reform, special needs studies.

Lehigh University, College of Education, Program in Comparative and International Education, Bethlehem, PA 18015. Offers comparative and international education (MA); globalization and educational change (M Ed); international counseling (Certificate); international development in education (Certificate); special education (Certificate); technology use in schools (Certificate); TESOL (Certificate). Part-time programs available. Postbaccalaureate distance learning degree programs offered (no on-campus study). *Faculty:* 4 full-time (2 women). *Students:* 25 full-time (10 women), 45 part-time (31 women); includes 5 minority (all Asian, non-Hispanic/Latino), 16 international. Average age 34. 45 applicants, 71% accepted, 12 enrolled. In 2011, 21 master's awarded. *Degree requirements:* For master's, thesis (MA). *Entrance requirements:* For master's, 2 letters of recommendation. Additional exam requirements/recommendations for international students: Required—TOEFL (minimum score 600 paper-based; 250 computer-based; 93 iBT). *Application deadline:* For fall and spring admission, 2/1 for domestic and international students. Application fee: $65. Electronic applications accepted. *Financial support:* In 2011–12, 8 students received support, including 3 research assistantships with full and partial tuition reimbursements available (averaging $13,000 per year). Financial award application deadline: 3/15. *Faculty research:* Comparative education, rural education, gender equity in education, post-socialist education transformation, educational borrowing, comparing education systems, education policy an globalization, family-school relationships, China, international testing, social inequities. *Unit head:* Dr. Iveta Silova, Program Director and Associate Professor, 610-758-5750, Fax: 610-758-6223, E-mail: ism207@lehigh.edu. *Application contact:* Donna M. Johnson, Coordinator, 610-758-3231, Fax: 610-758-6223, E-mail: dmj4@lehigh.edu. Web site: http://www.lehigh.edu/education/cie.

Louisiana State University and Agricultural and Mechanical College, Graduate School, College of Agriculture, School of Human Resource Education and Workforce Development, Baton Rouge, LA 70803. Offers agriculture and extension education and youth development (MS, PhD); career and technical education (MS, PhD); comprehensive vocational education (MS, PhD); extension and international education (MS, PhD); human resource and leadership development (MS, PhD); industrial education (MS); vocational agriculture education (MS, PhD); vocational business education (MS); vocational home economics education (MS). *Accreditation:* NCATE. Part-time programs available. *Faculty:* 9 full-time (5 women), 3 part-time/adjunct (0 women). *Students:* 51 full-time (36 women), 85 part-time (59 women); includes 28 minority (23 Black or African American, non-Hispanic/Latino; 1 Asian, non-Hispanic/Latino; 4 Hispanic/Latino), 3 international. Average age 36. 29 applicants, 83% accepted, 20 enrolled. In 2011, 15 master's, 17 doctorates awarded. Terminal master's awarded for partial completion of doctoral program. *Degree requirements:* For master's, thesis (for some programs); for doctorate, thesis/dissertation. *Entrance requirements:* For master's and doctorate, GRE General Test, minimum GPA of 3.0. Additional exam requirements/recommendations for international students: Required—TOEFL (minimum score 550 paper-based; 213 computer-based; 79 iBT) or IELTS (minimum score 6.5). *Application deadline:* For fall admission, 1/25 priority date for domestic students, 5/15 for international students; for spring admission, 10/15 for international students. Applications are processed on a rolling basis. Application fee: $50 ($70 for international students). Electronic applications accepted. *Financial support:* In 2011–12, 84 students received support, including 3 fellowships with full and partial tuition reimbursements available (averaging $14,986 per year), 4 research assistantships with full and partial tuition reimbursements available (averaging $12,000 per year), 11 teaching assistantships with partial tuition reimbursements available (averaging $13,300 per year); career-related internships or fieldwork, Federal Work-Study, institutionally sponsored loans, health care benefits, tuition waivers (full and partial), and unspecified assistantships also available. Financial award application deadline: 3/1; financial award applicants required to submit FAFSA. *Faculty research:* Adult education, history and philosophy of vocational education, curriculum and instruction, career decision-making. *Unit head:* Dr. Michael F. Burnett, Director, 225-578-5748, Fax: 225-578-2526, E-mail: vocbur@lsu.edu. Web site: http://www.lsu.edu/hrleader/.

Morehead State University, Graduate Programs, College of Education, Department of Curriculum and Instruction, Morehead, KY 40351. Offers curriculum and instruction (Ed S); elementary education (MA Ed), including elementary education, international education, middle school education, reading; secondary education (MA Ed); special education (MA Ed); teaching (MAT). Part-time and evening/weekend programs available. *Degree requirements:* For master's, comprehensive exam, thesis optional; for Ed S, thesis, oral exam. *Entrance requirements:* For master's, GRE General Test, minimum GPA of 2.75, teaching certificate; for Ed S, GRE General Test, interview, master's degree, minimum GPA of 3.5, work experience. Additional exam requirements/recommendations for international students: Required—TOEFL (minimum score 500 paper-based; 173 computer-based). Electronic applications accepted. *Faculty research:* Communicative competence of learning-disabled students, teaching social studies in elementary schools, ungraded primary school organization, study skills.

New York University, Steinhardt School of Culture, Education, and Human Development, Department of Humanities and Social Sciences in the Professions, Program in International Education, New York, NY 10012-1019. Offers human development and social intervention (MA); international education (MA, PhD, Advanced Certificate), including cross cultural exchange and training (PhD), global education (PhD), international development education (PhD). Part-time programs available. *Faculty:* 3 full-time (2 women). *Students:* 83 full-time (63 women), 53 part-time (47 women); includes 40 minority (7 Black or African American, non-Hispanic/Latino; 17 Asian, non-Hispanic/Latino; 14 Hispanic/Latino; 2 Two or more races, non-Hispanic/Latino), 22 international. Average age 31. 290 applicants, 58% accepted, 50 enrolled. In 2011, 55 master's, 3 doctorates awarded. *Degree requirements:* For master's, thesis (for some programs); for doctorate, thesis/dissertation. *Entrance requirements:* For doctorate, GRE General Test, interview; for Advanced Certificate, master's degree. Additional exam requirements/recommendations for international students: Required—TOEFL. *Application deadline:* For fall admission, 12/1 priority date for domestic students, 12/1 for international students; for spring admission, 11/1 for domestic and international students. Applications are processed on a rolling basis. Application fee: $75. Electronic applications accepted. *Financial support:* Fellowships with full and partial tuition reimbursements, career-related internships or fieldwork, Federal Work-Study, institutionally sponsored loans, and scholarships/grants available. Support available to part-time students. Financial award application deadline: 2/1; financial award applicants required to submit FAFSA. *Faculty research:* Civic education, ethnic identity among students and teachers, comparative education, education during emergencies, cross-cultural exchange. *Unit head:* Dr. Philip Hosay, Director, 212-998-5496, Fax: 212-995-4832, E-mail: pmh2@nyu.edu. *Application contact:* 212-998-5030, Fax: 212-995-4328, E-mail: steinhardt.gradadmissions@nyu.edu. Web site: http://steinhardt.nyu.edu/humsocsci/international.

New York University, Steinhardt School of Culture, Education, and Human Development, Department of Teaching and Learning, Program in English Education, New York, NY 10012-1019. Offers secondary and college (PhD), including applied linguistics, comparative education, curriculum, literature and reading, media education; teachers of English 7-12 (MA); teachers of English language and literature in college (Advanced Certificate). *Accreditation:* Teacher Education Accreditation Council. Part-time programs available. *Degree requirements:* For master's, thesis (for some programs); for doctorate, thesis/dissertation. *Entrance requirements:* For doctorate, GRE General Test, interview; for Advanced Certificate, master's degree. Additional exam requirements/recommendations for international students: Required—TOEFL. Electronic applications accepted. *Faculty research:* Making meaning of literature, teaching of literature, urban adolescent literacy and equity, literacy development and globalization, digital media and literacy.

SIT Graduate Institute, Graduate Programs, Master's Programs in Intercultural Service, Leadership, and Management, Brattleboro, VT 05302-0676. Offers conflict transformation (MA); intercultural service, leadership, and management (MA); international education (MA); sustainable development (MA). Postbaccalaureate distance learning degree programs offered (minimal on-campus study). *Degree requirements:* For master's, one foreign language, thesis. *Entrance requirements:* For master's, 3 letters of reference. Additional exam requirements/recommendations for international students: Required—TOEFL. *Faculty research:* Intercultural communication, conflict resolution, advising and training, world issues, international business.

Stanford University, School of Education, Program in Social Sciences, Policy, and Educational Practice, Stanford, CA 94305-9991. Offers administration and policy analysis (Ed D, PhD); anthropology of education (PhD); economics of education (PhD); educational linguistics (PhD); evaluation (MA), including interdisciplinary studies; higher education (PhD); history of education (PhD); interdisciplinary studies (PhD); international comparative education (MA, PhD); international education administration and policy analysis (MA); philosophy of education (PhD); policy analysis (MA); prospective principal's program (MA); sociology of education (PhD). *Degree requirements:* For master's, thesis (for some programs); for doctorate, thesis/dissertation. *Entrance requirements:* For master's and doctorate, GRE General Test. Electronic applications accepted. *Expenses: Tuition:* Full-time $40,050; part-time $890 per credit.

Teachers College, Columbia University, Graduate Faculty of Education, Department of International and Transcultural Studies, Program in Comparative and International Education, New York, NY 10027. Offers Ed M, MA, Ed D, PhD. *Faculty:* 9 full-time (8 women), 3 part-time/adjunct (all women). *Students:* 13 full-time (9 women), 37 part-time (29 women); includes 11 minority (3 Black or African American, non-Hispanic/Latino; 8 Asian, non-Hispanic/Latino), 21 international. Average age 31. 75 applicants, 27% accepted, 4 enrolled. In 2011, 5 master's, 1 doctorate awarded. *Degree requirements:* For master's, integrative project; for doctorate, variable foreign language requirement, comprehensive exam, thesis/dissertation. *Entrance requirements:* For doctorate, academic writing sample. *Application deadline:* For fall admission, 12/15 for domestic students. Application fee: $65. Electronic applications accepted. *Financial support:* Career-related internships or fieldwork, Federal Work-Study, institutionally sponsored loans, and tuition waivers (full and partial) available. Support available to part-time students. Financial award application deadline: 2/1; financial award applicants required to submit FAFSA. *Faculty research:* Comparative analysis of national educational systems, identity and community in local and transcultural settings. *Unit head:* Prof. Hope Jensen Leichter, Program Coordinator, 212-678-3184, E-mail: iedcieinfo@tc.columbia.edu. *Application contact:* Deanna Ghozati, Assistant Director of Admission, 212-678-4018, Fax: 212-678-4171, E-mail: ghozati@tc.edu. Web site: http://www.tc.columbia.edu/its/cie%26ied/.

Teachers College, Columbia University, Graduate Faculty of Education, Department of International and Transcultural Studies, Program in International Educational Development, New York, NY 10027. Offers Ed M, MA, Ed D, PhD. *Faculty:* 9 full-time (8 women), 3 part-time/adjunct (all women). *Students:* 54 full-time (49 women), 164 part-time (141 women); includes 73 minority (15 Black or African American, non-Hispanic/Latino; 2 American Indian or Alaska Native, non-Hispanic/Latino; 27 Asian, non-Hispanic/Latino; 19 Hispanic/Latino; 10 Two or more races, non-Hispanic/Latino), 51 international. Average age 30. 283 applicants, 55% accepted, 63 enrolled. In 2011, 81 master's, 12 doctorates awarded. *Degree requirements:* For master's, integrative project; for doctorate, comprehensive exam, thesis/dissertation. *Entrance requirements:* For master's, master's degree (for Ed M applicants); for doctorate, master's degree. Additional exam requirements/recommendations for international students: Required—TOEFL (minimum score 600 paper-based). *Application deadline:* For fall admission, 5/15 for domestic students; for spring admission, 12/1 for domestic students. Application fee: $65. Electronic applications accepted. *Financial support:* Career-related internships or fieldwork, Federal Work-Study, institutionally sponsored loans, and tuition waivers (full and partial) available. Support available to part-time students. Financial award application deadline: 2/1; financial award applicants required to submit FAFSA. *Faculty research:* Application of formal and nonformal education to programs of social and economic development in Third World countries. *Unit head:* Prof. Hope Jensen Leichter, Program Coordinator, 212-678-3184, E-mail: iedcieinfo@tc.columbia.edu. *Application contact:* Deanna Ghozati, Assistant Director of Admission, 212-678-4018, Fax: 212-678-4171, E-mail: ghozati@tc.edu. Web site: http://www.tc.columbia.edu/its/cie&ied/.

University of Bridgeport, School of Education, Department of Education, Bridgeport, CT 06604. Offers education (MS); educational management (Ed D, Diploma), including intermediate administrator or supervisor (Diploma), leadership (Ed D); elementary education (MS, Diploma), including early childhood education, elementary education; middle school education (MS); music education (MS); remedial reading and language arts (Diploma); secondary education (MS, Diploma), including computer specialist (Diploma), international education (Diploma), reading specialist, secondary education. Part-time and evening/weekend programs available. *Faculty:* 12 full-time (5 women), 108 part-time/adjunct (60 women). *Students:* 232 full-time (161 women), 216 part-time (160 women); includes 61 minority (21 Black or African American, non-Hispanic/Latino; 8 Asian, non-Hispanic/Latino; 22 Hispanic/Latino; 10 Two or more races, non-Hispanic/Latino), 34 international. Average age 30. 412 applicants, 63% accepted, 147 enrolled. In 2011, 216 master's, 7 other advanced degrees awarded. *Degree requirements:* For master's, final exam, final project, or thesis; for doctorate, comprehensive exam, thesis/dissertation; for Diploma, thesis or alternative, final project. *Entrance requirements:* For master's, minimum undergraduate QPA of 2.67; for doctorate, GRE, MAT; for Diploma, GRE General Test or MAT, minimum graduate QPA of 3.0. Additional exam requirements/recommendations for international students: Recommended—TOEFL (minimum score 550 paper-based; 213 computer-based; 80 iBT), IELTS (minimum score 6.5). *Application deadline:* For fall admission, 8/1 priority date for domestic students, 8/1 for international students; for spring admission, 12/1 priority date for domestic students, 12/1 for international students. Applications are processed on a rolling basis. Application fee: $50. Electronic applications accepted. *Expenses: Tuition:* Full-time $22,880; part-time $700 per credit. *Required fees:* $1870; $95 per semester. Tuition and fees vary according to course load and program. *Financial support:* In 2011–12, 120 students received support. Fellowships, research assistantships, teaching assistantships, career-related internships or fieldwork, Federal Work-Study, and institutionally sponsored loans available. Support available to part-time students. Financial award application deadline: 6/1; financial award applicants required to submit FAFSA. *Faculty research:* Self-concept, internship assessment, stress and situational development, follow-up of graduation, trend analysis. *Unit head:* Dr. Allen P. Cook, Dean, 203-576-4192, Fax: 203-576-4200, E-mail: acook@bridgeport.edu. *Application contact:* Karissa Peckham, Dean of Admissions, 203-576-4552, Fax: 203-576-4941, E-mail: admit@bridgeport.edu.

University of California, Santa Barbara, Graduate Division, Gevirtz Graduate School of Education, Santa Barbara, CA 93106-9490. Offers counseling, clinical and school psychology (M Ed, MA, PhD, Credential), including clinical psychology (PhD), counseling psychology (MA, PhD), school psychology (M Ed, PhD), school psychology: pupil personnel services (Credential); education (M Ed, MA, PhD, Credential), including child and adolescent development (MA, PhD), cultural perspectives and comparative education (MA, PhD), educational leadership and organizations (MA, PhD), multiple subject teaching (Credential), research methodology (MA, PhD), single subject teaching (Credential), special education (Credential), special education disabilities and risk studies (MA), special education, disabilities and risk studies (PhD), teaching (M Ed), teaching and learning (MA, PhD); MA/PhD. *Accreditation:* APA (one or more programs are accredited). *Faculty:* 40 full-time (21 women), 2 part-time/adjunct (both women). *Students:* 389 full-time (301 women); includes 131 minority (14 Black or African American, non-Hispanic/Latino; 2 American Indian or Alaska Native, non-Hispanic/Latino; 41 Asian, non-Hispanic/Latino; 69 Hispanic/Latino; 1 Native Hawaiian or other Pacific Islander, non-Hispanic/Latino; 4 Two or more races, non-Hispanic/Latino), 25 international. Average age 28. 691 applicants, 35% accepted, 154 enrolled. In 2011, 145 master's, 45 doctorates, 118 other advanced degrees awarded. Terminal master's awarded for partial completion of doctoral program. *Degree requirements:* For master's, comprehensive exam (for some programs), thesis (for some programs); for doctorate, comprehensive exam (for some programs), thesis/dissertation; for Credential, CA state requirements (varies by credential). *Entrance requirements:* For master's and doctorate, GRE; for Credential, GRE or MAT, CSET and CBEST. Additional exam requirements/recommendations for international students: Required—TOEFL (minimum score 550 paper-based; 80 iBT), IELTS (minimum score 7). Application fee: $80 ($100 for international students). Electronic applications accepted. *Expenses:* Tuition, state resident: full-time $12,192. Tuition, nonresident: full-time $27,294. *Required fees:* $764.13. *Financial support:* In 2011–12, 301 students received support, including 429 fellowships with partial tuition reimbursements available (averaging $5,017 per year), 83 research assistantships with full and partial tuition reimbursements available (averaging $6,262 per year), 55 teaching assistantships with partial tuition reimbursements available (averaging $8,655 per year); career-related internships or fieldwork also available. Financial award applicants required to submit FAFSA. *Faculty research:* Needs of diverse students, school accountability and leadership, school violence, language learning and literacy, science/math education. *Total annual research expenditures:* $3 million. *Unit head:* Arlis Markel, Assistant Dean, 805-893-5492, Fax: 805-893-2588, E-mail: arlis@education.ucsb.edu. *Application contact:* Kathryn Marie Tucciarone, Student Affairs Officer, 805-893-2137, Fax: 805-893-2588, E-mail: katiet@education.ucsb.edu. Web site: http://www.education.ucsb.edu/.

University of Central Florida, College of Education, School of Teaching, Learning, and Leadership, Applied Learning and Instruction Program, Orlando, FL 32816. Offers applied learning and instruction (MA); community college education (Certificate); gifted education (Certificate); global and comparative education (Certificate); initial teacher professional preparation (Certificate); urban education (Certificate). *Accreditation:* NCATE. Part-time and evening/weekend programs available. *Students:* 12 full-time (10 women), 79 part-time (65 women); includes 23 minority (6 Black or African American, non-Hispanic/Latino; 1 American Indian or Alaska Native, non-Hispanic/Latino; 3 Asian, non-Hispanic/Latino; 12 Hispanic/Latino; 1 Two or more races, non-Hispanic/Latino), 1 international. Average age 31. 53 applicants, 72% accepted, 24 enrolled. In 2011, 11 master's, 24 other advanced degrees awarded. *Degree requirements:* For Certificate, thesis or alternative, final exam. *Entrance requirements:* For degree, GRE General Test, minimum GPA of 3.0, resume. Additional exam requirements/recommendations for international students: Required—TOEFL. *Application deadline:* For fall admission, 2/20 for domestic students; for spring admission, 9/20 for domestic students. Application fee: $30. Electronic applications accepted. *Expenses:* Tuition, state resident: part-time $277.08 per credit hour. Tuition, nonresident: part-time $277.08 per credit hour. Part-time tuition and fees vary according to degree level and program. *Financial support:* In 2011–12, 3 students received support, including 2 research assistantships with partial tuition reimbursements available (averaging $7,100 per year), 1 teaching assistantship with partial tuition reimbursement available (averaging $6,900 per year); fellowships with partial tuition reimbursements available, career-related internships or fieldwork, Federal Work-Study, institutionally sponsored loans, and unspecified assistantships also available. Financial award application deadline: 3/1; financial award applicants required to submit FAFSA. *Unit head:* Dr. Bobby Hoffman, Program Coordinator, 407-823-1770, E-mail: bobby.hoffman@ucf.edu. *Application contact:* Barbara Rodriguez, Director, Admissions and Registration, 407-823-2766, Fax: 407-823-6442, E-mail: gradadmissions@ucf.edu. Web site: http://education.ucf.edu/departments.cfm.

University of Maryland, College Park, Academic Affairs, College of Education, Department of Education Leadership, Higher Education and International Education, College Park, MD 20742. Offers MA, Ed D, PhD. *Faculty:* 13 full-time (8 women), 3 part-time/adjunct (2 women). *Students:* 56 full-time (43 women), 21 part-time (12 women); includes 25 minority (13 Black or African American, non-Hispanic/Latino; 2 Asian, non-Hispanic/Latino; 8 Hispanic/Latino; 2 Two or more races, non-Hispanic/Latino), 8 international. 235 applicants, 11% accepted, 15 enrolled. In 2011, 25 master's, 1 doctorate awarded. *Entrance requirements:* Additional exam requirements/recommendations for international students: Required—TOEFL. *Application deadline:* For fall admission, 12/15 for domestic and international students. Application fee: $75. *Expenses: Tuition, area resident:* Part-time $525 per credit hour. Tuition, state resident: part-time $525 per credit hour. Tuition, nonresident: part-time $1131 per credit hour. *Required fees:* $386.31 per term. Tuition and fees vary according to program. *Financial support:* In 2011–12, 6 fellowships with full and partial tuition reimbursements (averaging $11,552 per year), 46 teaching assistantships (averaging $16,671 per year) were awarded. *Total annual research expenditures:* $250,238. *Unit head:* Dennis Kivlighan, Chair, 301-405-2858, E-mail: dennisk@umd.edu. *Application contact:* Dr. Charles A. Caramello, Dean of Graduate School, 301-405-0358, Fax: 301-314-9305. Web site: http://www.education.umd.edu/EDHI/.

University of Massachusetts Amherst, Graduate School, School of Education, Program in Education, Amherst, MA 01003. Offers bilingual, English as a second language, and multicultural education (M Ed, CAGS); child study and early education (M Ed); children, families and schools (Ed D, CAGS); early childhood and elementary teacher education (M Ed); educational leadership (M Ed, CAGS); educational policy and leadership (Ed D); higher education (M Ed, CAGS); international education (M Ed); language, literacy and culture (Ed D); learning, media and technology (M Ed, CAGS); mathematics, science, and learning technologies (Ed D); policy studies in education (CAGS); psychometric methods, educational statistics and research methods (Ed D); reading and writing (M Ed); school counselor education (M Ed, CAGS); science education (CAGS); secondary teacher education (M Ed); social justice education (M Ed, Ed D, CAGS); special education (M Ed, Ed D, CAGS). *Accreditation:* NCATE. Part-time programs available. Postbaccalaureate distance learning degree programs offered (minimal on-campus study). *Faculty:* 81 full-time (46 women). *Students:* 341 full-time (240 women), 333 part-time (226 women); includes 113 minority (36 Black or African American, non-Hispanic/Latino; 1 American Indian or Alaska Native, non-Hispanic/Latino; 14 Asian, non-Hispanic/Latino; 51 Hispanic/Latino; 1 Native Hawaiian or other Pacific Islander, non-Hispanic/Latino; 10 Two or more races, non-Hispanic/Latino), 98 international. Average age 36. 721 applicants, 57% accepted, 202 enrolled. In 2011, 166 master's, 33 doctorates, 25 CAGSs awarded. Terminal master's awarded for partial completion of doctoral program. *Degree requirements:* For doctorate, comprehensive exam, thesis/dissertation. *Entrance requirements:* Additional exam requirements/recommendations for international students: Required—TOEFL (minimum score 550 paper-based; 213 computer-based; 80 iBT), IELTS (minimum score 6.5). *Application deadline:* For fall admission, 1/15 for domestic and international students. Applications are processed on a rolling basis. Application fee: $50 ($65 for international students). Electronic applications accepted. Tuition and fees vary according to course load, campus/location and program. *Financial support:* Fellowships with full and partial tuition reimbursements, research assistantships with full and partial tuition reimbursements, teaching assistantships with full and partial tuition reimbursements, career-related internships or fieldwork, Federal Work-Study, scholarships/grants, traineeships, health care benefits, tuition waivers (full and partial), and unspecified assistantships available. Support available to part-time students. Financial award application deadline: 1/15. *Unit head:* Dr. Linda L. Griffin, Graduate Program Director, 413-545-6984, Fax: 413-545-1523. *Application contact:* Lindsay DeSantis, Interim Supervisor of Admissions, 413-545-0722, Fax: 413-577-0010, E-mail: gradadm@grad.umass.edu. Web site: http://www.umass.edu/education/.

University of Minnesota, Twin Cities Campus, Graduate School, College of Education and Human Development, Department of Organizational Leadership, Policy and Development, Program in Comparative and International Development Education, Minneapolis, MN 55455-0213. Offers MA, PhD. *Students:* 68 full-time (50 women), 44 part-time (27 women); includes 15 minority (6 Black or African American, non-Hispanic/Latino; 6 Asian, non-Hispanic/Latino; 3 Hispanic/Latino), 23 international. Average age 33. 104 applicants, 58% accepted, 24 enrolled. In 2011, 26 master's, 8 doctorates awarded. Application fee: $55. *Unit head:* Dr. Rebecca Ropers-Huilman, Chair, 612-624-1006, Fax: 612-624-3377, E-mail: ropers@umn.edu. *Application contact:* Dr. Jennifer Engler, Assistant Dean, 612-626-2887, Fax: 612-626-7496, E-mail: engle009@umn.edu. Web site: http://www.cehd.umn.edu/EdPA/CIDE.

University of North Texas, Toulouse Graduate School, College of Public Affairs and Community Service, Department of Sociology, Denton, TX 76203. Offers global and comparative (PhD); health and illness (PhD); social stratification and inequality (PhD); sociology (MA, MS). Terminal master's awarded for partial completion of doctoral program. *Degree requirements:* For master's, variable foreign language requirement, comprehensive exam, thesis (for some programs); for doctorate, variable foreign language requirement, comprehensive exam, thesis/dissertation. *Entrance requirements:* For master's, GRE General Test, 4 letters of recommendation; for doctorate, GRE General Test, master's degree, 4 letters of recommendation. Additional exam requirements/recommendations for international students: Required—TOEFL (minimum score 550 paper-based; 213 computer-based; 79 iBT). Electronic applications accepted. *Expenses:* Tuition, state resident: part-time $100 per credit hour. Tuition, nonresident: part-time $413 per credit hour. *Faculty research:* Health and illness, social inequality, globalization and development, family.

University of Pennsylvania, Graduate School of Education, Division of Education, Culture and Society, Program in International Educational Development, Philadelphia, PA 19104. Offers MS Ed. *Students:* 25 full-time (22 women), 4 part-time (all women); includes 8 minority (1 Black or African American, non-Hispanic/Latino; 3 Asian, non-Hispanic/Latino; 2 Hispanic/Latino; 2 Two or more races, non-Hispanic/Latino), 10 international. 115 applicants, 65% accepted, 22 enrolled. In 2011, 14 degrees awarded. *Expenses: Tuition:* Full-time $26,660; part-time $4944 per course. *Required fees:* $2318; $291 per course. Tuition and fees vary according to course load, degree level and program. *Unit head:* Dr. Dan Wagner, Director, 215-898-5199. *Application contact:* Vernell Edwards, 215-746-2566, E-mail: edwardsv@gse.upenn.edu. Web site: http://www.gse.upenn.edu/iedp.

University of Pittsburgh, School of Education, Department of Administrative and Policy Studies, Program in Social and Comparative Analysis in Education, Pittsburgh, PA 15260. Offers M Ed, MA, Ed D, PhD. Evening/weekend programs available. *Students:* 64 full-time (46 women), 39 part-time (26 women); includes 11 minority (6 Black or African American, non-Hispanic/Latino; 4 Asian, non-Hispanic/Latino; 1 Hispanic/Latino), 26 international. Average age 36. 79 applicants, 80% accepted, 37 enrolled. In 2011, 6 master's, 20 doctorates awarded. *Degree requirements:* For master's, thesis; for doctorate, thesis/dissertation. *Entrance requirements:* For doctorate, GRE General Test. Additional exam requirements/recommendations for international students: Required—TOEFL (minimum score 213 computer-based; 80 iBT). *Application deadline:* For fall admission, 2/1 priority date for domestic students, 2/1 for international students; for spring admission, 11/15 priority date for domestic students, 7/1 for international students. Applications are processed on a rolling basis. Application fee: $50. Electronic applications accepted. *Expenses:* Tuition, state resident: full-time $18,774; part-time $760 per credit. Tuition, nonresident: full-time $30,736; part-time $1258 per credit. *Required fees:* $740; $200 per term. Tuition and fees vary according to program. *Financial support:* Research assistantships, teaching assistantships, Federal Work-Study, institutionally sponsored loans, scholarships/grants, health care benefits, tuition waivers (partial), and unspecified assistantships available. Support available to part-time students. Financial award application deadline: 3/15; financial award applicants required to submit FAFSA. *Unit head:* Dr. Mary Margaret Kerr, Chair, 412-648-7205, Fax: 412-648-1784, E-mail: mmkerr@pitt.edu. *Application contact:* Lauren Spadafora, Enrollment Manager, 412-648-2230, Fax: 412-648-1899, E-mail: soeinfo@pitt.edu. Web site: http://www.education.pitt.edu/AcademicDepartments/AdministrativePolicyStudies/Programs/SocialComparativeAnalysisinEducation.aspx.

University of San Francisco, School of Education, Department of International and Multicultural Education, San Francisco, CA 94117-1080. Offers international and multicultural education (MA, Ed D); multicultural literature for children and young adults (MA); teaching English as a second language (MA). *Faculty:* 3 full-time (all women), 6 part-time/adjunct (3 women). *Students:* 128 full-time (105 women), 52 part-time (43 women); includes 84 minority (15 Black or African American, non-Hispanic/Latino; 21 Asian, non-Hispanic/Latino; 39 Hispanic/Latino; 9 Two or more races, non-Hispanic/Latino), 26 international. Average age 36. 203 applicants, 58% accepted, 50 enrolled. In 2011, 35 master's, 5 doctorates awarded. *Degree requirements:* For doctorate, thesis/dissertation. Application fee: $55 ($65 for international students). *Expenses: Tuition:* Full-time $20,070; part-time $1115 per unit. Tuition and fees vary according to course load, campus/location and program. *Financial support:* In 2011–12, 11 students received support. Fellowships, research assistantships, and teaching assistantships available. Financial award application deadline: 3/2; financial award applicants required to submit FAFSA. *Unit head:* Dr. Katz Susan, Chair, 415-422-6878. *Application contact:* Beth Teague, Associate Director of Graduate Outreach, 415-422-5467, E-mail: schoolofeducation@usfca.edu.

University of South Africa, College of Human Sciences, Pretoria, South Africa. Offers adult education (M Ed); African languages (MA, PhD); African politics (MA, PhD); Afrikaans (MA, PhD); ancient history (MA, PhD); ancient Near Eastern studies (MA, PhD); anthropology (MA, PhD); applied linguistics (MA); Arabic (MA, PhD); archaeology (MA); art history (MA); Biblical archaeology (MA); Biblical studies (M Th, D Th, PhD); Christian spirituality (M Th, D Th); church history (M Th, D Th); classical studies (MA, PhD); clinical psychology (MA); communication (MA, PhD); comparative education (M Ed, Ed D); consulting psychology (D Admin, D Com, PhD); curriculum studies (M Ed, Ed D); development studies (M Admin, MA, D Admin, PhD); didactics (M Ed, Ed D); education (M Tech); education management (M Ed, Ed D); educational psychology (M Ed); English (MA); environmental education (M Ed); French (MA, PhD); German (MA, PhD); Greek (MA); guidance and counseling (M Ed); health studies (MA, PhD), including health sciences education (MA), health services management (MA), medical and surgical nursing science (critical care general) (MA), midwifery and neonatal nursing science (MA), trauma and emergency care (MA); history (MA, PhD); history of education (Ed D); inclusive education (M Ed, Ed D); information and communications technology policy and regulation (MA); information science (MA, MIS, PhD); international politics (MA, PhD); Islamic studies (MA, PhD); Italian (MA, PhD); Judaica (MA, PhD); linguistics (MA, PhD); mathematical education (M Ed); mathematics education (MA); missiology (M Th, D Th); modern Hebrew (MA, PhD); musicology (MA, MMus, D Mus, PhD); natural science education (M Ed); New Testament (M Th, D Th); Old Testament (D Th); pastoral therapy (M Th, D Th); philosophy (MA); philosophy of education (M Ed, Ed D); politics (MA, PhD); Portuguese (MA, PhD); practical theology (M Th, D Th); psychology (MA, MS, PhD); psychology of education (M Ed, Ed D); public health (MA); religious studies (MA, D Th, PhD); Romance languages (MA); Russian (MA, PhD); Semitic languages (MA, PhD); social behavior studies in HIV/AIDS (MA); social science (mental health) (MA); social science in development studies (MA); social science in psychology (MA); social science in social work (MA); social science in sociology (MA); social work (MSW, DSW, PhD); socio-education (M Ed, Ed D); sociolinguistics (MA); sociology (MA, PhD); Spanish (MA, PhD); systematic theology (M Th, D Th); TESOL (teaching English to speakers of other languages) (MA); theological ethics (M Th, D Th); theory of literature (MA, PhD); urban ministries (D Th); urban ministry (M Th).

Vanderbilt University, Peabody College, Department of Leadership, Policy, and Organizations, Nashville, TN 37240-1001. Offers education policy (MPP); educational leadership and policy (Ed D); higher education (M Ed); higher education, leadership and policy (Ed D); international education policy and management (M Ed); leadership and organizational performance (M Ed). Part-time and evening/weekend programs available. *Faculty:* 27 full-time (12 women), 10 part-time/adjunct (3 women). *Students:* 165 full-time (117 women), 98 part-time (46 women); includes 35 minority (15 Black or African American, non-Hispanic/Latino; 4 Asian, non-Hispanic/Latino; 10 Hispanic/Latino; 6 Two or more races, non-Hispanic/Latino), 30 international. Average age 28. 465 applicants, 54% accepted, 87 enrolled. In 2011, 102 master's, 25 doctorates awarded. *Degree requirements:* For master's, comprehensive exam, thesis optional; for doctorate, thesis/dissertation, qualifying exams, residency. *Entrance requirements:* For master's and doctorate, GRE General Test. Additional exam requirements/recommendations for international students: Required—TOEFL (minimum score 550 paper-based; 213 computer-based). *Application deadline:* For fall admission, 12/31 priority date for domestic students, 12/31 for international students; for spring admission, 11/1 priority date for domestic students, 11/1 for international students. Applications are processed on a rolling basis. Application fee: $0. Electronic applications accepted. *Financial support:* Fellowships with full and partial tuition reimbursements, research assistantships with full and partial tuition reimbursements, teaching assistantships with full and partial tuition reimbursements, Federal Work-Study, institutionally sponsored loans, scholarships/grants, tuition waivers (partial), and unspecified assistantships available. Support available to part-time students. Financial award application deadline: 2/1; financial award applicants required to submit FAFSA. *Faculty research:* Education policy, education reform, school choice, equity and diversity, higher education. *Unit head:* Dr. Ellen B. Goldring, Chair, 615-322-8000, Fax: 615-343-7094, E-mail: ellen.b.goldring@vanderbilt.edu. *Application contact:* Rosie Moody, Educational Coordinator, 615-322-8019, Fax: 615-343-7094, E-mail: rosie.moody@vanderbilt.edu.

Walden University, Graduate Programs, Richard W. Riley College of Education and Leadership, Minneapolis, MN 55401. Offers administrator leadership for teaching and learning (Ed D, Ed S); adult education (Ed D, Ed S); adult learning (MS, Postbaccalaureate Certificate), including developmental education (MS), online teaching (MS), teaching adults English as a second language (MS), training and performance management (MS); college teaching and learning (Ed D, Ed S, Postbaccalaureate Certificate); curriculum, instruction and assessment (Ed D, Postbaccalaureate Certificate); curriculum, instruction, and professional development (Ed S); developmental education (Postbaccalaureate Certificate); early childhood administration, management, and leadership (Postbaccalaureate Certificate); early childhood education (birth-grade 3) (MAT); early childhood public policy and advocacy (Postbaccalaureate Certificate); early childhood studies (MS), including administration, management and leadership, early childhood public policy and advocacy, teaching adults in the early childhood field, teaching and diversity; education (MS, PhD), including adolescent literacy and technology (grades 6-12) (MS), adult education leadership (PhD), assessment, evaluation, and accountability (PhD), community college leadership (PhD), curriculum, instruction, and assessment, early childhood education (PhD), educational technology (PhD), elementary reading and literacy (MS), elementary reading and mathematics (MS), general program, global and comparative education (PhD), higher education (PhD), integrating technology in the classroom (MS), K-12 educational leadership (PhD), leadership, policy and change (PhD), learning, instruction and innovation (PhD), literacy and learning in the content areas (MS), mathematics (grades 6-8) (MS), mathematics (grades K-5) (MS), middle level education (grades 5-8) (MS), professional development (MS), science (grades K-8) (MS), self-designed (PhD), special education (PhD), special education (non-licensure) (MS), teacher leadership (grades K-12) (MS), teaching English language learners (grades K-12) (MS); educational leadership and administration (principal preparation) (Ed S); educational technology (Ed S); elementary reading and literacy (Postbaccalaureate Certificate); engaging culturally diverse learners (Postbaccalaureate Certificate); enrollment management and institutional marketing (Postbaccalaureate Certificate); higher education (MS), including college teaching and learning, enrollment management and institutional planning, global higher education, leadership for student success, online and distance learning; higher education leadership (Ed D); instructional design (Postbaccalaureate Certificate); instructional design and technology (MS), including general program (MS, PhD), online learning, training and performance improvement; integrating technology in the classroom (Postbaccalaureate Certificate); online teaching for adult learners (Postbaccalaureate Certificate); professional development (Postbaccalaureate Certificate); reading and literacy leadership (Ed D); science K-8 (Postbaccalaureate Certificate); special education (Ed D, Ed S); special education: emotional/behavioral disorders (K-12) (MAT); special education: learning disabilities (K-12) (MAT); teacher leadership (Ed D, Ed S, Postbaccalaureate Certificate); training and performance management (Postbaccalaureate Certificate). Part-time and evening/weekend programs available. Postbaccalaureate distance learning degree programs offered (minimal on-campus study). *Faculty:* 71 full-time (48 women), 853 part-time/adjunct (585 women). *Students:* 11,326 full-time (9,212 women), 2,148 part-time (1,795 women); includes 5,346 minority (4,403 Black or African American, non-Hispanic/Latino; 76 American Indian or Alaska Native, non-Hispanic/Latino; 140 Asian, non-Hispanic/Latino; 561 Hispanic/Latino; 21 Native Hawaiian or other Pacific Islander, non-Hispanic/Latino; 145 Two or more races, non-Hispanic/Latino), 322 international. Average age 39. In 2011, 3,477 master's, 318 doctorates, 471 other advanced degrees awarded. *Degree requirements:* For doctorate, thesis/dissertation (for some programs), residency; for other advanced degree, residency (for some programs). *Entrance requirements:* For master's, bachelor's degree or equivalent in related field; minimum GPA of 2.5; official transcripts; goal statement; access to computer and Internet; for doctorate, master's degree or equivalent in related field; minimum GPA of 3.0; official transcripts; three years' related professional/academic experience (preferred); access to computer and Internet; for other advanced degree, master's degree or equivalent in related field; minimum GPA of 3.0; 3 years related professional/academic experience (preferred); access to computer and Internet (Ed S). Additional exam requirements/recommendations for international students: Required—TOEFL (minimum score 550 paper-based; 213 computer-based), IELTS (minimum score 6.5), or Michigan English Language Assessment Battery (minimum score 82). *Application deadline:* Applications are processed on a rolling basis. Application fee: $50. Electronic applications accepted. *Financial support:* Federal Work-Study, scholarships/grants, unspecified assistantships, and family tuition reduction, active duty/veteran tuition reduction, group tuition reduction, interest-free payment plans, employee tuition reduction available. Support available to part-time students. Financial award applicants required to submit FAFSA. *Unit head:* Dr. Kate Steffens, Dean, 800-925-3368. *Application contact:* Jennifer Hall, Vice President of Enrollment Management, 866-4-WALDEN, E-mail: info@waldenu.edu. Web site: http://www.waldenu.edu/Colleges-and-Schools/College-of-Education-and-Leadership.htm.

Wright State University, School of Graduate Studies, College of Liberal Arts, Program in Applied Behavioral Science, Dayton, OH 45435. Offers criminal justice and social problems (MA); international and comparative politics (MA). *Degree requirements:* For master's, thesis optional. *Entrance requirements:* Additional exam requirements/recommendations for international students: Required—TOEFL. *Faculty research:* Training and development, criminal justice and social problems, community systems, human factors, industrial/organizational psychology.

Student Affairs

Alliant International University–Los Angeles, Shirley M. Hufstedler School of Education, Educational Psychology Programs, Alhambra, CA 91803-1360. Offers educational psychology (Psy D); pupil personnel services (Credential); school psychology (MA). Part-time programs available. *Students:* 11 full-time (10 women), 28 part-time (24 women); includes 24 minority (7 Black or African American, non-Hispanic/Latino; 12 Hispanic/Latino; 5 Two or more races, non-Hispanic/Latino). Average age 35. 21 applicants, 67% accepted, 9 enrolled. In 2011, 1 master's, 5 doctorates awarded. *Degree requirements:* For doctorate, thesis/dissertation. *Entrance requirements:* For master's, minimum GPA of 2.5, letters of recommendation; for doctorate, interview, minimum GPA of 3.0, letters of recommendation. Additional exam requirements/recommendations for international students: Required—TOEFL (minimum score 550 paper-based; 213 computer-based), TWE (minimum score 5). *Application deadline:* For fall admission, 7/1 priority date for domestic students, 7/1 for international students; for spring admission, 12/1 priority date for domestic students, 12/1 for international students. Applications are processed on a rolling basis. Application fee: $55. Electronic applications accepted. *Financial support:* Career-related internships or fieldwork, Federal Work-Study, institutionally sponsored loans, and scholarships/grants available. Financial award application deadline: 2/15; financial award applicants required to submit FAFSA. *Faculty research:* Early identification and intervention with high-risk preschoolers, pediatric neuropsychology, interpersonal violence, ADHD, learning theories. *Unit head:* Dr. Carlton Parks, Program Director, 626-270-3379, Fax: 626-284-0550, E-mail: admissions@alliant.edu. *Application contact:* Alliant International University Central Contact Center, 866-U-ALLIANT, Fax: 858-635-4555, E-mail: admissions@alliant.edu. Web site: http://www.alliant.edu/hsoe/.

Alliant International University–San Diego, Shirley M. Hufstedler School of Education, Educational Psychology Programs, San Diego, CA 92131-1799. Offers educational psychology (Psy D); pupil personnel services (Credential); school neuropsychology (Certificate); school psychology (MA); school-based mental health (Certificate). Part-time programs available. *Faculty:* 1 full-time (0 women), 14 part-time/adjunct (9 women). *Students:* 28 full-time (26 women), 31 part-time (25 women); includes 14 minority (5 Black or African American, non-Hispanic/Latino; 9 Hispanic/Latino). Average age 32. In 2011, 10 master's, 2 doctorates awarded. *Degree requirements:* For doctorate, thesis/dissertation, internship. *Entrance requirements:* For master's, minimum GPA of 2.5, letters of recommendation; for doctorate, minimum GPA of 3.0, letters of recommendation. Additional exam requirements/recommendations for international students: Required—TOEFL (minimum score 550 paper-based; 213 computer-based), TWE (minimum score 5). *Application deadline:* For fall admission, 7/1 priority date for domestic students, 7/1 for international students; for spring admission, 12/1 priority date for domestic students, 12/1 for international students. Applications are processed on a rolling basis. Application fee: $55. Electronic applications accepted. Tuition and fees vary according to degree level and program. *Financial support:* Career-related internships or fieldwork, Federal Work-Study, institutionally sponsored loans, and scholarships/grants available. Financial award application deadline: 2/15; financial award applicants required to submit FAFSA. *Faculty research:* School-based mental health, pupil personnel services, childhood mood, school-based assessment. *Unit head:* Dr. Steve Fisher, Program Director, 828-635-4825, Fax: 858-635-4739, E-mail: admissions@alliant.edu. *Application contact:* Alliant International University Central Contact Center, 866-U-ALLIANT, Fax: 858-635-4555, E-mail: admissions@alliant.edu. Web site: http://www.alliant.edu/gsoe.

Appalachian State University, Cratis D. Williams Graduate School, Department of Human Development and Psychological Counseling, Boone, NC 28608. Offers clinical mental health counseling (MA); college student development (MA); marriage and family therapy (MA); school counseling (MA). *Accreditation:* AAMFT/COAMFTE; ACA; NCATE. Part-time programs available. *Faculty:* 13 full-time (8 women), 8 part-time/adjunct (6 women). *Students:* 165 full-time (128 women), 20 part-time (15 women); includes 14 minority (10 Black or African American, non-Hispanic/Latino; 3 Asian, non-Hispanic/Latino; 1 Hispanic/Latino), 1 international. 337 applicants, 33% accepted, 80 enrolled. In 2011, 68 master's awarded. *Degree requirements:* For master's, comprehensive exam (for some programs), thesis optional, internships. *Entrance requirements:* For master's, GRE General Test, 3 letters of recommendation. Additional exam requirements/recommendations for international students: Required—TOEFL (minimum score 570 paper-based; 230 computer-based; 79 iBT), IELTS (minimum score 6.5). *Application deadline:* For fall admission, 2/1 priority date for domestic students, 2/1 for international students; for spring admission, 2/1 for international students. Applications are processed on a rolling basis. Application fee: $55. Electronic applications accepted. *Expenses:* Tuition, state resident: full-time $4040; part-time $180 per semester hour. Tuition, nonresident: full-time $15,900; part-time $760 per semester hour. *Required fees:* $2500; $20 per semester hour. Tuition and fees vary according to campus/location. *Financial support:* In 2011–12, 20 research assistantships (averaging $8,000 per year), 7 teaching assistantships (averaging $8,000 per year) were awarded; fellowships, career-related internships or fieldwork, Federal Work-Study, scholarships/grants, and unspecified assistantships also available. Financial award application deadline: 4/1; financial award applicants required to submit FAFSA. *Faculty research:* Multicultural counseling, addictions counseling, play therapy, expressive arts, child and adolescent therapy, sexual abuse counseling. *Unit head:* Dr. Lee Baruth, Chairman, 828-262-2055, E-mail: baruthlg@appstate.edu. *Application contact:* Sandy Krause, Director of Admissions and Recruiting, 828-262-2130, Fax: 828-262-2709, E-mail: krausesl@appstate.edu. Web site: http://www.ced.appstate.edu/departments/hpc.

Arkansas State University, Graduate School, College of Education, Department of Psychology and Counseling, Jonesboro, State University, AR 72467. Offers college student personnel services (MS); mental health counseling (Certificate); psychology and counseling (Ed S); rehabilitation counseling (MRC); school counseling (MSE); student affairs (Certificate). *Accreditation:* ACA (one or more programs are accredited); CORE (one or more programs are accredited); NCATE. Part-time programs available. *Faculty:* 15 full-time (9 women). *Students:* 45 full-time (32 women), 91 part-time (73 women); includes 38 minority (all Black or African American, non-Hispanic/Latino), 1 international. Average age 33. 75 applicants, 68% accepted, 40 enrolled. In 2011, 14 master's, 20 other advanced degrees awarded. *Degree requirements:* For master's and other advanced degree, comprehensive exam, thesis or alternative. *Entrance requirements:* For master's, GRE General Test or MAT (MSE), appropriate bachelor's degree, interview, letters of reference, official transcripts, immunization records, written statement, 2-3 page autobiography; for other advanced degree, GRE General Test, interview, master's degree, letters of reference, official transcript, personal statement, immunization records. Additional exam requirements/recommendations for international students: Required—TOEFL (minimum score 550 paper-based; 213 computer-based; 79 iBT), IELTS (minimum score 6), Pearson Test of English Academic (minimum score 56). *Application deadline:* Applications are processed on a rolling basis. Application fee: $30 ($40 for international students). Electronic applications accepted. *Expenses:* Tuition, state resident: full-time $4044; part-time $225 per credit hour. Tuition, nonresident: full-time $8087; part-time $449 per credit hour. *Required fees:* $936; $52 per credit hour. $25 per term. One-time fee: $30. Tuition and fees vary according to course load and program. *Financial support:* In 2011–12, 27 students received support. Teaching assistantships, career-related internships or fieldwork, scholarships/grants, and unspecified assistantships available. Financial award application deadline: 7/1;

financial award applicants required to submit FAFSA. *Unit head:* Dr. Loretta McGregor, Chair, 870-972-3064, Fax: 870-972-3962, E-mail: lmcgregor@astate.edu. *Application contact:* Dr. Andrew Sustich, Dean of the Graduate School, 870-972-3029, Fax: 870-972-3857, E-mail: sustich@astate.edu. Web site: http://www.astate.edu/a/education/psychologycounseling/index.dot.

Arkansas Tech University, Center for Leadership and Learning, College of Education, Russellville, AR 72801. Offers college student personnel (MS); educational leadership (Ed S); elementary education (M Ed); instructional improvement (M Ed); instructional technology (M Ed); physical education (M Ed); school counseling and leadership (M Ed); teaching (MAT). *Accreditation:* NCATE. Part-time and evening/weekend programs available. Postbaccalaureate distance learning degree programs offered (no on-campus study). *Students:* 70 full-time (44 women), 247 part-time (189 women); includes 57 minority (38 Black or African American, non-Hispanic/Latino; 1 American Indian or Alaska Native, non-Hispanic/Latino; 8 Asian, non-Hispanic/Latino; 4 Hispanic/Latino; 6 Two or more races, non-Hispanic/Latino), 3 international. Average age 31. In 2011, 58 master's awarded. *Degree requirements:* For master's, comprehensive exam, thesis optional, action research project. *Entrance requirements:* Additional exam requirements/recommendations for international students: Required—TOEFL (minimum score 550 paper-based; 213 computer-based; 79 iBT), IELTS (minimum score 6.5). *Application deadline:* For fall admission, 3/1 priority date for domestic students, 5/1 for international students; for spring admission, 10/1 priority date for domestic students, 10/1 for international students. Applications are processed on a rolling basis. Application fee: $25 ($75 for international students). Electronic applications accepted. *Expenses:* Tuition, state resident: full-time $4968; part-time $207 per credit hour. Tuition, nonresident: full-time $9936; part-time $414 per credit hour. *Required fees:* $375 per semester. Tuition and fees vary according to course load. *Financial support:* In 2011–12, teaching assistantships with full tuition reimbursements (averaging $4,800 per year) were awarded; research assistantships with full tuition reimbursements, career-related internships or fieldwork, Federal Work-Study, scholarships/grants, health care benefits, and unspecified assistantships also available. Support available to part-time students. Financial award application deadline: 4/15; financial award applicants required to submit FAFSA. *Unit head:* Dr. Eldon G. Clary, Jr., Dean, 479-968-0350, Fax: 479-968-0350, E-mail: eclary@atu.edu. *Application contact:* Dr. Mary B. Gunter, Dean of Graduate College, 479-968-0398, Fax: 479-964-0542, E-mail: gradcollege@atu.edu. Web site: http://www.atu.edu/education/.

Ashland University, Dwight Schar College of Education, Department of Educational Administration, Ashland, OH 44805-3702. Offers curriculum specialist (M Ed); principalship (M Ed); pupil services (M Ed). Part-time programs available. *Faculty:* 7 full-time (3 women), 16 part-time/adjunct (4 women). *Students:* 108 full-time (72 women), 185 part-time (94 women); includes 34 minority (26 Black or African American, non-Hispanic/Latino; 2 American Indian or Alaska Native, non-Hispanic/Latino; 1 Asian, non-Hispanic/Latino; 2 Hispanic/Latino; 3 Two or more races, non-Hispanic/Latino), 2 international. Average age 33. 75 applicants, 100% accepted, 65 enrolled. In 2011, 143 master's awarded. *Degree requirements:* For master's, thesis or alternative, internship. *Entrance requirements:* For master's, teaching certificate or license, bachelor's degree, minimum cumulative GPA of 2.75. Additional exam requirements/recommendations for international students: Required—TOEFL. *Application deadline:* Applications are processed on a rolling basis. Application fee: $30. Electronic applications accepted. *Expenses: Tuition:* Full-time $5580; part-time $465 per credit hour. *Financial support:* Institutionally sponsored loans and scholarships/grants available. Financial award application deadline: 4/15. *Faculty research:* Gender and religious considerations in employment, ISLLC standards, adjunct faculty training, politics of school finance, ethnicity and employment. *Unit head:* Dr. Robert Thiede, Chair, 419-289-5258, Fax: 419-207-6702, E-mail: rthiede@ashland.edu. *Application contact:* Dr. Linda Billman, Director and Chair, Graduate Studies in Education/Associate Dean, 419-289-5369, Fax: 419-289-5331, E-mail: lbillman@ashland.edu.

Azusa Pacific University, School of Behavioral and Applied Sciences, Department of Higher Education and Organizational Leadership, Program in College Student Affairs, Azusa, CA 91702-7000. Offers M Ed. Part-time and evening/weekend programs available. *Degree requirements:* For master's, exam. *Entrance requirements:* For master's, 12 units of course work in social science, minimum GPA of 3.0.

Bloomsburg University of Pennsylvania, School of Graduate Studies, College of Education, Department of Educational Studies and Secondary Education, Program in Guidance Counseling and Student Affairs, Bloomsburg, PA 17815-1301. Offers M Ed. *Entrance requirements:* For master's, GRE, 3 letters of recommendation, resume.

Bob Jones University, Graduate Programs, Greenville, SC 29614. Offers accountancy (MS); Bible (MA); Bible translation (MA); Biblical studies (Certificate); broadcast management (MS); business administration (MBA); church history (MA, PhD); church ministries (MA); church music (MM); cinema and video production (MA); counseling (MS); curriculum and instruction (Ed D); divinity (M Div); dramatic production (MA); educational leadership (MS, Ed D, Ed S); elementary education (M Ed, MAT); English (M Ed, MA, MAT); fine arts (MA); graphic design (MA); history (M Ed, MA); illustration (MA); interpretative speech (MA); mathematics (M Ed, MAT); medical missions (Certificate); ministry (MM, D Min); multi-categorical special education (M Ed, MAT); music (M Ed); New Testament interpretation (PhD); Old Testament interpretation (PhD); orchestral instrument performance (MM); organ performance (MM); pastoral studies (MA); personnel services (MS, Ed S); piano pedagogy (MM); piano performance (MM); platform arts (MA); radio and television broadcasting (MS); rhetoric and public address (MA); secondary education (M Ed); studio art (MA); teaching Bible (MA); theology (MA, PhD); voice performance (MM); youth ministries (MA); M Div/MM.

Bowling Green State University, Graduate College, College of Education and Human Development, School of Leadership and Policy Studies, Program in College Student Personnel, Bowling Green, OH 43403. Offers MA. Part-time programs available. *Degree requirements:* For master's, thesis or alternative. *Entrance requirements:* For master's, GRE General Test, interview. Additional exam requirements/recommendations for international students: Required—TOEFL. Electronic applications accepted. *Faculty research:* Adult learning, legal issues, moral and ethical development.

Bucknell University, Graduate Studies, College of Arts and Sciences, Department of Education, Lewisburg, PA 17837. Offers college student personnel (MS Ed). Part-time programs available. *Faculty:* 12 full-time (9 women), 4 part-time/adjunct (2 women). *Students:* 10 full-time (6 women), 7 part-time (6 women). 5 applicants, 60% accepted, 3 enrolled. In 2011, 18 master's awarded. *Degree requirements:* For master's, comprehensive exam (for some programs), thesis or alternative. *Entrance requirements:* For master's, GRE General Test, minimum GPA of 3.0. Additional exam requirements/recommendations for international students: Required—TOEFL (minimum score 600 paper-based). *Application deadline:* For fall admission, 2/1 priority date for domestic students, 1/1 for international students. Application fee: $25. *Financial support:* In 2011–12, 10 students received support, including 2 fellowships with full and partial tuition reimbursements available (averaging $20,000 per year); scholarships/grants and tuition waivers (full and partial) also available. Financial award application deadline: 2/1. *Unit head:* Dr. Joe Murray, Head, 717-577-1324. *Application contact:* Gretchen H. Fegley, Coordinator, 570-577-3655, Fax: 570-577-3760, E-mail: gfegley@bucknell.edu. Web site: http://www.bucknell.edu/education.

Buffalo State College, State University of New York, The Graduate School, Faculty of Applied Science and Education, Department of Educational Foundations, Program in Student Personnel Administration, Buffalo, NY 14222-1095. Offers MS. *Degree requirements:* For master's, comprehensive exam. *Entrance requirements:* For master's, minimum GPA of 2.75 in last 60 hours of undergraduate course work. Additional exam requirements/recommendations for international students: Required—TOEFL (minimum score 550 paper-based; 213 computer-based).

California State University, Bakersfield, Division of Graduate Studies, School of Social Sciences and Education, Program in Counseling, Bakersfield, CA 93311. Offers school counseling (MS); student affairs (MS). *Accreditation:* NCATE. *Degree requirements:* For master's, thesis or alternative, culminating projects. *Entrance requirements:* For master's, CBEST (school counseling). *Application deadline:* Applications are processed on a rolling basis. Application fee: $55. *Expenses: Required fees:* $1302 per unit. Part-time tuition and fees vary according to course load and program. *Unit head:* Julia Bavier, Evaluator, Advanced Educational Studies, 661-654-3193, Fax: 661-665-6916, E-mail: jbavier@csub.edu. Web site: http://www.csub.edu/sse/advanced_education/counseling_and_personnel_services/.

California State University, Long Beach, Graduate Studies, College of Education, Department of Advanced Studies in Education and Counseling, Master of Science in Counseling Program, Long Beach, CA 90840. Offers marriage and family therapy (MS); school counseling (MS); student development in higher education (MS). *Accreditation:* NCATE. *Students:* 150 full-time (114 women), 65 part-time (48 women); includes 153 minority (23 Black or African American, non-Hispanic/Latino; 3 American Indian or Alaska Native, non-Hispanic/Latino; 32 Asian, non-Hispanic/Latino; 86 Hispanic/Latino; 1 Native Hawaiian or other Pacific Islander, non-Hispanic/Latino; 8 Two or more races, non-Hispanic/Latino), 3 international. Average age 28. 488 applicants, 18% accepted, 68 enrolled. In 2011, 59 master's awarded. *Degree requirements:* For master's, comprehensive exam or thesis. *Application deadline:* For fall admission, 3/1 for domestic students. Applications are processed on a rolling basis. Application fee: $55. Electronic applications accepted. *Financial support:* Federal Work-Study, institutionally sponsored loans, and scholarships/grants available. Financial award application deadline: 3/2. *Unit head:* Dr. Jennifer Coots, Chair, 562-985-4517, Fax: 562-985-4534, E-mail: jcoots@csulb.edu. *Application contact:* Dr. Bita Ghafoori, Assistant Chair, 562-985-7864, Fax: 562-985-4534, E-mail: bghafoor@csulb.edu.

Canisius College, Graduate Division, School of Education and Human Services, Department of Graduate Education and Leadership, Buffalo, NY 14208-1098. Offers college student personnel (MS Ed); deaf education (MS Ed); deaf/adolescent education, grades 7-12 (MS Ed); deaf/childhood education, grades 1-6 (MS Ed); differential instruction (MS Ed); education administration (MS Ed); gifted education extention (Certificate); literacy (MS Ed); reading (Certificate); school building leadership (MS Ed, Certificate); school district leadership (Certificate). *Accreditation:* NCATE. Part-time and evening/weekend programs available. Postbaccalaureate distance learning degree programs offered (minimal on-campus study). *Faculty:* 7 full-time (6 women), 36 part-time/adjunct (22 women). *Students:* 149 full-time (114 women), 242 part-time (177 women); includes 42 minority (29 Black or African American, non-Hispanic/Latino; 2 American Indian or Alaska Native, non-Hispanic/Latino; 3 Asian, non-Hispanic/Latino; 6 Hispanic/Latino; 2 Two or more races, non-Hispanic/Latino), 3 international. Average age 30. 250 applicants, 84% accepted, 124 enrolled. In 2011, 135 degrees awarded. *Entrance requirements:* For master's, GRE if cumulative GPA less than 2.7, transcripts, two letters of recommendation. Additional exam requirements/recommendations for international students: Required—TOEFL. *Application deadline:* Applications are processed on a rolling basis. Application fee: $25. Electronic applications accepted. *Financial support:* Career-related internships or fieldwork, Federal Work-Study, scholarships/grants, tuition waivers (partial), and unspecified assistantships available. Support available to part-time students. Financial award application deadline: 4/30; financial award applicants required to submit FAFSA. *Faculty research:* Asperger's disease, autism, private higher education, reading strategies. *Unit head:* Dr. Rosemary K. Murray, Chair/Associate Professor of Graduate Education and Leadership, 716-888-3723, E-mail: murray1@canisius.edu. *Application contact:* Jim Bagwell, Director of Graduate Recruitment and Admissions, 716-888-2544, Fax: 716-888-3290, E-mail: bagwellj@canisius.edu. Web site: http://www.canisius.edu/education/graduate.asp.

Central Michigan University, College of Graduate Studies, College of Education and Human Services, Department of Educational Leadership, Mount Pleasant, MI 48859. Offers educational leadership (MA, Ed D), including charter school leadership (MA), educational technology (Ed D, Ed S), general educational leadership (MA), higher education administration (MA, Ed S), higher education leadership (Ed D), K-12 curriculum (Ed D), K-12 leadership (Ed D), student affairs administration (MA); general educational administration (Ed S), including administrative leadership K-12, educational technology (Ed D, Ed S), higher education administration (MA, Ed S), instructional leadership K-12; school principalship (MA); teacher leadership (MA). Part-time and evening/weekend programs available. *Degree requirements:* For master's and other advanced degree, thesis or alternative; for doctorate, thesis/dissertation. *Entrance requirements:* For doctorate, GRE or MAT, master's degree, minimum GPA of 3.5, 3 years of professional education experience. Electronic applications accepted. *Faculty research:* Elementary administration, secondary administration, student achievement, in-service training, internships in administration.

The Citadel, The Military College of South Carolina, Citadel Graduate College, School of Education, Program in Guidance and Counseling, Charleston, SC 29409. Offers elementary/secondary school counseling (M Ed); student affairs and college counseling (M Ed). *Accreditation:* ACA; NCATE. Part-time and evening/weekend programs available. *Faculty:* 12 full-time (8 women), 9 part-time/adjunct (4 women). *Students:* 24 full-time (22 women), 36 part-time (31 women); includes 9 minority (8 Black or African American, non-Hispanic/Latino; 1 Hispanic/Latino). Average age 31. In 2011, 22 master's awarded. *Degree requirements:* For master's, comprehensive exam, practicum or internship. *Entrance requirements:* For master's, GRE (minimum score 900) or MAT (minimum score 396), minimum undergraduate GPA of 3.0, 3 letters of reference, group interview. Additional exam requirements/recommendations for international students: Required—TOEFL (minimum score 550 paper-based; 213 computer-based; 79 iBT). *Application deadline:* For fall admission, 6/1 for domestic students; for spring admission, 10/1 for domestic students. Application fee: $30. Electronic applications accepted. *Expenses: Tuition, area resident:* Part-time $501 per credit hour. Tuition, state resident: part-time $501 per credit hour. Tuition, nonresident: part-time $824 per credit hour. *Required fees:* $40 per term. One-time fee: $30. *Financial support:* Career-related internships or fieldwork, health care benefits, and unspecified assistantships available. Support available to part-time students. Financial award application deadline: 7/1; financial award applicants required to submit FAFSA. *Unit head:* Dr. George T. Williams, Director, 843-953-2205, Fax: 843-953-7258, E-mail: williamsg@citadel.edu. *Application contact:* Dr. Steve A. Nida, Associate Provost, The Citadel Graduate College, 843-953-5089, Fax: 843-953-7630, E-mail: cgc@citadel.edu. Web site: http://www.citadel.edu/education/counselor.html.

Claremont Graduate University, Graduate Programs, School of Educational Studies, Claremont, CA 91711-6160. Offers Africana education (Certificate); education and policy (MA, PhD); higher education/student affairs (MA, PhD); human development (MA,

PhD); public school administration (MA, PhD); quantitative evaluation (MA, PhD); special education (MA, PhD); teacher education (MA); teaching and learning (MA, PhD); urban leadership (PhD); MBA/PhD. PhD program offered jointly with San Diego State University. Part-time programs available. *Faculty:* 18 full-time (10 women), 2 part-time/adjunct (1 woman). *Students:* 307 full-time (220 women), 134 part-time (96 women); includes 228 minority (59 Black or African American, non-Hispanic/Latino; 3 American Indian or Alaska Native, non-Hispanic/Latino; 37 Asian, non-Hispanic/Latino; 110 Hispanic/Latino; 2 Native Hawaiian or other Pacific Islander, non-Hispanic/Latino; 17 Two or more races, non-Hispanic/Latino), 13 international. Average age 38. In 2011, 93 master's, 23 doctorates, 10 other advanced degrees awarded. Terminal master's awarded for partial completion of doctoral program. *Entrance requirements:* For master's and doctorate, GRE General Test. Additional exam requirements/recommendations for international students: Required—TOEFL (minimum score 550 paper-based; 213 computer-based; 80 iBT). *Application deadline:* For fall admission, 2/1 priority date for domestic students. Applications are processed on a rolling basis. Application fee: $60. Electronic applications accepted. *Expenses: Tuition:* Full-time $36,374; part-time $1581 per unit. *Required fees:* $165 per semester. *Financial support:* Fellowships, research assistantships, Federal Work-Study, institutionally sponsored loans, and scholarships/grants available. Support available to part-time students. Financial award application deadline: 2/15; financial award applicants required to submit FAFSA. *Faculty research:* Education administration, K-12 and higher education, multicultural education, education policy, diversity in higher education, faculty issues. *Unit head:* Margaret Grogan, Dean, 909-621-8075, Fax: 909-621-8734, E-mail: margaret.grogan@cgu.edu. *Application contact:* Julia Evans, Director of Central Recruitment, 909-607-3689, Fax: 909-607-7285, E-mail: admiss@cgu.edu. Web site: http://www.cgu.edu/pages/267.asp.

Clemson University, Graduate School, College of Health, Education, and Human Development, Eugene T. Moore School of Education, Program in Counselor Education, Clemson, SC 29634. Offers clinical mental health counseling (M Ed); community mental health (M Ed); school counseling (K-12) (M Ed); student affairs (higher education) (M Ed). *Accreditation:* ACA; NCATE. Part-time and evening/weekend programs available. *Students:* 127 full-time (101 women), 28 part-time (19 women); includes 23 minority (14 Black or African American, non-Hispanic/Latino; 3 Asian, non-Hispanic/Latino; 2 Hispanic/Latino; 1 Native Hawaiian or other Pacific Islander, non-Hispanic/Latino; 3 Two or more races, non-Hispanic/Latino), 1 international. Average age 28. 186 applicants, 58% accepted, 45 enrolled. In 2011, 66 master's awarded. *Degree requirements:* For master's, comprehensive exam. *Entrance requirements:* For master's, GRE General Test. Additional exam requirements/recommendations for international students: Required—TOEFL; Recommended—IELTS. *Application deadline:* For fall admission, 2/1 priority date for domestic students; for spring admission, 10/1 for domestic students. Applications are processed on a rolling basis. Application fee: $70 ($80 for international students). Electronic applications accepted. *Expenses:* Contact institution. *Financial support:* In 2011–12, 74 students received support, including 10 research assistantships with partial tuition reimbursements available (averaging $8,402 per year), 1 teaching assistantship with partial tuition reimbursement available (averaging $12,528 per year); institutionally sponsored loans, health care benefits, and unspecified assistantships also available. Financial award application deadline: 6/1; financial award applicants required to submit FAFSA. *Faculty research:* At-risk youth, ethnic identity development across the life span, postsecondary transitions and college readiness, distance and distributed learning environments, the student veteran experience in college, student development theory. *Unit head:* Dr. Michael J. Padilla, Director/Associate Dean, 864-656-4444, Fax: 864-656-0311, E-mail: padilla@clemson.edu. *Application contact:* Dr. David Fleming, Graduate Coordinator, 864-656-1881, Fax: 864-656-0311, E-mail: dflemin@clemson.edu.

College of Saint Elizabeth, Department of Psychology, Morristown, NJ 07960-6989. Offers counseling psychology (MA); forensic psychology (MA); mental health counseling (Certificate); student affairs in higher education (Certificate). Part-time and evening/weekend programs available. *Faculty:* 5 full-time (3 women), 5 part-time/adjunct (4 women). *Students:* 28 full-time (23 women), 72 part-time (67 women); includes 28 minority (18 Black or African American, non-Hispanic/Latino; 2 Asian, non-Hispanic/Latino; 8 Hispanic/Latino), 2 international. Average age 29. 85 applicants, 47% accepted, 29 enrolled. In 2011, 26 master's, 1 other advanced degree awarded. *Degree requirements:* For master's, thesis or alternative, portfolio. *Entrance requirements:* For master's, minimum GPA of 3.0, BA in psychology (preferred), 12 credits of course work in psychology. Additional exam requirements/recommendations for international students: Required—TOEFL (minimum score 550 paper-based). *Application deadline:* For fall admission, 4/1 priority date for domestic students; for spring admission, 11/15 for domestic students. Applications are processed on a rolling basis. Application fee: $35. Electronic applications accepted. *Expenses: Tuition:* Part-time $899 per credit. *Required fees:* $73 per credit. *Financial support:* Career-related internships or fieldwork, tuition waivers (partial), and unspecified assistantships available. Support available to part-time students. Financial award application deadline: 3/15; financial award applicants required to submit FAFSA. *Faculty research:* Family systems, dissociative identity disorder, multicultural counseling, outcomes assessment. *Unit head:* Dr. Valerie Scott, Director of the Graduate Program in Counseling Psychology, 973-290-4102, Fax: 973-290-4676, E-mail: vscott@cse.edu. *Application contact:* Donna Tatarka, Dean of Admission, 973-290-4705, Fax: 973-290-4710, E-mail: dtatarka@cse.edu. Web site: http://www.cse.edu/academics/academic-areas/human-social-dev/psychology/?tabID-tabGraduate&divID-progGraduate.

The College of Saint Rose, Graduate Studies, School of Education, Department of Counseling and Educational Administration, Program in Counseling, Albany, NY 12203-1419. Offers college student personnel (MS Ed); community counseling (MS Ed); school counseling (MS Ed). *Accreditation:* NCATE. Part-time and evening/weekend programs available. *Degree requirements:* For master's, comprehensive exam or thesis. *Entrance requirements:* For master's, interview, minimum undergraduate GPA of 3.0, 9 hours of psychology coursework. Additional exam requirements/recommendations for international students: Required—TOEFL (minimum score 550 paper-based; 213 computer-based). Electronic applications accepted.

The College of Saint Rose, Graduate Studies, School of Education, Department of Counseling and Educational Administration, Program in Educational Administration and Supervision, Albany, NY 12203-1419. Offers college student services administration (MS Ed); educational administration and supervision (MS Ed, Certificate); school administrator and supervisor (Certificate). Part-time and evening/weekend programs available. *Degree requirements:* For master's, comprehensive exam or thesis. *Entrance requirements:* For master's, minimum undergraduate GPA of 3.0, timed writing sample, interview, permanent certification or 3 years teaching experience. Additional exam requirements/recommendations for international students: Required—TOEFL (minimum score 550 paper-based; 213 computer-based). Electronic applications accepted.

Colorado State University, Graduate School, College of Applied Human Sciences, School of Education, Fort Collins, CO 80523-1588. Offers adult education and training (M Ed); community college leadership (PhD); counseling and career development (M Ed); education and human resource studies (M Ed, PhD); educational leadership (M Ed, PhD); interdisciplinary studies (PhD); organizational performance and change (M Ed, PhD); student affairs in higher education (MS). *Accreditation:* ACA; Teacher Education Accreditation Council. Part-time and evening/weekend programs available. *Faculty:* 18 full-time (11 women), 1 part-time/adjunct (0 women). *Students:* 161 full-time (106 women), 491 part-time (291 women); includes 130 minority (28 Black or African American, non-Hispanic/Latino; 5 American Indian or Alaska Native, non-Hispanic/Latino; 12 Asian, non-Hispanic/Latino; 68 Hispanic/Latino; 3 Native Hawaiian or other Pacific Islander, non-Hispanic/Latino; 14 Two or more races, non-Hispanic/Latino), 29 international. Average age 38. 468 applicants, 31% accepted, 112 enrolled. In 2011, 192 master's, 30 doctorates awarded. *Degree requirements:* For master's, comprehensive exam (for some programs), thesis optional; for doctorate, comprehensive exam, thesis/dissertation, minimum of 60 credits. *Entrance requirements:* For master's, GRE, minimum undergraduate GPA of 3.0, 3 letters of recommendation, curriculum vitae/resume; for doctorate, minimum GPA of 3.0, 3 letters of recommendation, curriculum vitae. Additional exam requirements/recommendations for international students: Required—TOEFL (minimum score 550 paper-based; 213 computer-based; 80 iBT). *Application deadline:* For fall admission, 2/15 priority date for domestic students, 2/15 for international students; for spring admission, 9/1 priority date for domestic students, 9/1 for international students. Applications are processed on a rolling basis. Application fee: $50. Electronic applications accepted. *Expenses:* Tuition, state resident: full-time $7992. Tuition, nonresident: full-time $19,592. *Required fees:* $1735; $58 per credit. *Financial support:* In 2011–12, 11 students received support, including 1 fellowship (averaging $37,500 per year), 3 research assistantships with full tuition reimbursements available (averaging $8,911 per year), 7 teaching assistantships with full tuition reimbursements available (averaging $12,691 per year); Federal Work-Study, scholarships/grants, and unspecified assistantships also available. Financial award application deadline: 2/15; financial award applicants required to submit FAFSA. *Faculty research:* Innovative instruction, diverse learners, transition, scientifically-based evaluation methods, leadership and organizational development, research methodology. *Total annual research expenditures:* $455,133. *Unit head:* Dr. Kevin Oltjenbruns, Interim Director, 970-491-6316, Fax: 970-491-1317, E-mail: kevin.oltjenbruns@colostate.edu. *Application contact:* Kathy Lucas, Graduate Contact, 970-491-1963, Fax: 970-491-1317, E-mail: kplucas@cahs.colostate.edu. Web site: http://www.soe.cahs.colostate.edu/.

Concordia University Wisconsin, Graduate Programs, School of Business and Legal Studies, Program in Student Personnel Administration, Mequon, WI 53097-2402. Offers MSSPA. *Students:* 11 full-time (8 women), 57 part-time (33 women); includes 18 minority (12 Black or African American, non-Hispanic/Latino; 2 Asian, non-Hispanic/Latino; 2 Hispanic/Latino; 2 Two or more races, non-Hispanic/Latino), 2 international. Average age 31. In 2011, 4 master's awarded. *Degree requirements:* For master's, comprehensive exam, thesis or alternative. *Entrance requirements:* Additional exam requirements/recommendations for international students: Required—TOEFL. Application fee: $35 ($125 for international students). *Financial support:* Application deadline: 8/1. *Unit head:* Dr. Andrew Luptak, Director, 262-243-4331, E-mail: andy.luptak@cuw.edu. *Application contact:* Mary Eberhardt, Graduate Admissions, 262-243-4551, Fax: 262-243-4428, E-mail: mary.eberhardt@cuw.edu.

Creighton University, Graduate School, College of Arts and Sciences, Department of Education, Program in Counselor Education, Omaha, NE 68178-0001. Offers college student affairs (MS); community counseling (MS); elementary school guidance (MS); secondary school guidance (MS). Part-time and evening/weekend programs available. *Faculty:* 13 full-time (8 women). *Students:* 2 full-time (1 woman), 28 part-time (22 women); includes 3 minority (1 Black or African American, non-Hispanic/Latino; 1 American Indian or Alaska Native, non-Hispanic/Latino; 1 Hispanic/Latino), 2 international. Average age 33. 12 applicants, 75% accepted, 9 enrolled. In 2011, 8 master's awarded. *Degree requirements:* For master's, comprehensive exam. *Entrance requirements:* For master's, GRE General Test, resume, 3 letters of recommendation, personal statement. Additional exam requirements/recommendations for international students: Required—TOEFL (minimum score 550 paper-based; 213 computer-based; 80 iBT). *Application deadline:* For fall admission, 7/1 for domestic students, 3/1 for international students; for winter admission, 10/1 for domestic students, 7/1 for international students; for spring admission, 3/1 for domestic students, 9/1 for international students. Applications are processed on a rolling basis. Application fee: $50. Electronic applications accepted. *Expenses: Tuition:* Full-time $12,672; part-time $704 per credit hour. *Required fees:* $1410; $136 per semester. Tuition and fees vary according to campus/location and reciprocity agreements. *Financial support:* Scholarships/grants available. Support available to part-time students. Financial award applicants required to submit FAFSA. *Unit head:* Dr. Jeffrey Smith, Associate Professor of Education, 402-280-2413, E-mail: jefsmith@creighton.edu. *Application contact:* Taunya Plater, Senior Program Coordinator, 402-280-2870, Fax: 402-280-2423, E-mail: taunyaplater@creighton.edu.

DePaul University, College of Education, Chicago, IL 60106. Offers bilingual bicultural education (M Ed, MA); counseling (M Ed, MA), including college student development, community counseling, school counseling; curriculum studies (M Ed, MA, Ed D); early childhood education (M Ed, MA); educational leadership (M Ed, MA, Ed D), including administration and supervision (M Ed, MA), physical education (M Ed, MA); middle school mathematics education (MS); reading specialist (M Ed, MA); social and cultural foundations in education (M Ed, MA), including curriculum studies/development (MA); special education (M Ed, MA); teaching and learning (M Ed, MA), including elementary education, secondary education; world languages education (M Ed, MA). Part-time and evening/weekend programs available. *Faculty:* 49 full-time (28 women), 94 part-time/adjunct (60 women). *Students:* 894 full-time (707 women), 473 part-time (361 women); includes 349 minority (159 Black or African American, non-Hispanic/Latino; 3 American Indian or Alaska Native, non-Hispanic/Latino; 45 Asian, non-Hispanic/Latino; 115 Hispanic/Latino; 2 Native Hawaiian or other Pacific Islander, non-Hispanic/Latino; 25 Two or more races, non-Hispanic/Latino), 21 international. Average age 30. 872 applicants, 64% accepted, 325 enrolled. In 2011, 499 master's, 10 doctorates awarded. *Median time to degree:* Of those who began their doctoral program in fall 2003, 32% received their degree in 8 years or less. *Degree requirements:* For master's, thesis/dissertation (for MA); capstone course or paper (for M Ed); for doctorate, thesis/dissertation. *Entrance requirements:* For master's, interview, minimum GPA of 2.75, 2 letters of recommendation, bachelor's degree conferred by accredited college or university; for doctorate, interview, master's degree, writing sample, 3 letters of recommendation. Additional exam requirements/recommendations for international students: Required—TOEFL (minimum score 550 paper-based; 213 computer-based; 80 iBT). *Application deadline:* For fall admission, 8/15 priority date for domestic students; for winter admission, 12/1 priority date for domestic students; for spring admission, 3/1 priority date for domestic students. Applications are processed on a rolling basis. Application fee: $40. Electronic applications accepted. *Financial support:* In 2011–12, 163 students received support, including 15 research assistantships with full tuition reimbursements available (averaging $6,375 per year); career-related internships or fieldwork, Federal Work-Study, scholarships/grants, and unspecified assistantships also available. Support available to part-time students. Financial award application deadline: 12/31; financial award applicants required to submit FAFSA. *Faculty research:* Reflective teaching, children at risk, loss, ethnicity, urban education. *Total annual research expenditures:* $916,310. *Unit head:* Dr. Paul Zionts, Dean, 773-325-7581, Fax: 773-325-7713, E-mail: pzionts@depaul.edu. *Application contact:*

Brandon Washington, Enrollment Management Coordinator, 773-325-1152, Fax: 773-325-2270, E-mail: bwashin3@depaul.edu. Web site: http://education.depaul.edu.

Eastern Illinois University, Graduate School, College of Education and Professional Studies, Department of Counseling and Student Development, Charleston, IL 61920-3099. Offers clinical counseling (MS); college student affairs (MS); school counseling (MS). *Accreditation:* ACA; NCATE. Part-time and evening/weekend programs available. *Degree requirements:* For master's, comprehensive exam. *Entrance requirements:* For master's, GRE General Test or MAT. *Expenses:* Tuition, state resident: part-time $279 per credit hour. Tuition, nonresident: part-time $670 per credit hour. *Required fees:* $179.07 per credit hour. $1253 per semester.

Fresno Pacific University, Graduate Programs, School of Education, Division of Pupil Personnel Services, Fresno, CA 93702-4709. Offers school counseling (MA Ed); school psychology (MA Ed). Part-time programs available. *Degree requirements:* For master's, thesis or alternative. *Entrance requirements:* Additional exam requirements/recommendations for international students: Required—TOEFL (minimum score 550 paper-based; 213 computer-based).

Grambling State University, School of Graduate Studies and Research, College of Education, Department of Educational Leadership, Grambling, LA 71245. Offers curriculum and instruction (Ed D); developmental education (MS, Ed D), including curriculum and instruction: reading (Ed D), English (MS), guidance and counseling (MS), higher education administration (Ed D), instructional systems and technology (Ed D), mathematics (MS), reading (MS), science (MS), student development and personnel services (Ed D); educational leadership (MS, Ed D). Part-time and evening/weekend programs available. *Degree requirements:* For master's, comprehensive exam, thesis (for some programs); for doctorate, comprehensive exam, thesis/dissertation. *Entrance requirements:* For master's, GRE, minimum GPA of 2.5 on last degree; for doctorate, GRE (minimum 1000, 500 on Verbal), master's degree, minimum GPA of 3.0 on last degree. Additional exam requirements/recommendations for international students: Required—TOEFL (minimum score 500 paper-based; 173 computer-based; 61 iBT). Electronic applications accepted. *Expenses:* Tuition, state resident: full-time $3546; part-time $192 per credit hour. Tuition, nonresident: full-time $3456; part-time $192 per credit hour. *Required fees:* $1829; $1829 per semester hour.

Hampton University, Graduate College, College of Education and Continuing Studies, Program in Counseling, Hampton, VA 23668. Offers college student development (MA); community agency counseling (MA); pastoral counseling (MA); school counseling (MA). *Accreditation:* NCATE. Part-time and evening/weekend programs available. *Entrance requirements:* For master's, GRE General Test.

Illinois State University, Graduate School, College of Education, Department of Educational Administration and Foundations, Program in College Student Personnel Administration, Normal, IL 61790-2200. Offers MS.

Indiana State University, College of Graduate and Professional Studies, College of Education, Department of Educational Leadership, Administration, and Foundations, Terre Haute, IN 47809. Offers educational administration (PhD); leadership in higher education (PhD); school administration (Ed S); school administration and supervision (M Ed); student affairs in higher education (MS). *Accreditation:* NCATE. Part-time and evening/weekend programs available. Terminal master's awarded for partial completion of doctoral program. *Degree requirements:* For master's, thesis; for doctorate, thesis/dissertation. *Entrance requirements:* For master's, GRE General Test, minimum undergraduate GPA of 2.5; for doctorate, GRE General Test, minimum undergraduate GPA of 3.5; for Ed S, GRE General Test, minimum graduate GPA of 3.25. Electronic applications accepted.

Indiana University of Pennsylvania, School of Graduate Studies and Research, College of Education and Educational Technology, Department of Student Affairs in Higher Education, Indiana, PA 15705-1087. Offers MA. *Accreditation:* NCATE. Part-time programs available. *Faculty:* 4 full-time (2 women). *Students:* 57 full-time (40 women), 6 part-time (4 women); includes 5 minority (4 Black or African American, non-Hispanic/Latino; 1 Two or more races, non-Hispanic/Latino). Average age 24. 136 applicants, 52% accepted, 35 enrolled. In 2011, 26 master's awarded. *Degree requirements:* For master's, comprehensive exam, thesis optional. *Entrance requirements:* For master's, resume, interview, 2 letters of recommendation, writing sample. Additional exam requirements/recommendations for international students: Required—TOEFL (minimum score 540 paper-based; 207 computer-based). *Application deadline:* For fall admission, 1/15 priority date for domestic students. Application fee: $50. Electronic applications accepted. *Expenses:* Tuition, state resident: full-time $7488; part-time $416 per credit. Tuition, nonresident: full-time $11,232; part-time $624 per credit. *Required fees:* $2070; $192.20 per credit. $90 per semester. *Financial support:* In 2011–12, 1 fellowship (averaging $500 per year), 17 research assistantships with full and partial tuition reimbursements (averaging $5,284 per year) were awarded; career-related internships or fieldwork and Federal Work-Study also available. Support available to part-time students. Financial award application deadline: 4/15; financial award applicants required to submit FAFSA. *Unit head:* Dr. Linda W. Hall, Chairperson and Graduate Coordinator, 724-357-4535, E-mail: linda.hall@iup.edu. *Application contact:* Dr. Edward Nardi, Interim Associate Dean, 724-357-2480, Fax: 724-357-5595, E-mail: ewnardi@iup.edu. Web site: http://www.iup.edu/upper.aspx?id=216.

Indiana University–Purdue University Indianapolis, School of Education, Indianapolis, IN 46202-2896. Offers computer education (Certificate); curriculum and instruction (MS); early childhood (MS); educational leadership (MS, Certificate); English as a second language (Certificate); higher education and student affairs (MS); kindergarten (Certificate); language education (MS); reading (Certificate); school counseling (MS); special education (MS, Certificate). Part-time and evening/weekend programs available. *Faculty:* 41 full-time, 80 part-time/adjunct. *Students:* 67 full-time (52 women), 467 part-time (360 women); includes 82 minority (44 Black or African American, non-Hispanic/Latino; 3 American Indian or Alaska Native, non-Hispanic/Latino; 8 Asian, non-Hispanic/Latino; 13 Hispanic/Latino; 14 Two or more races, non-Hispanic/Latino), 10 international. Average age 33. 63 applicants, 57% accepted, 29 enrolled. In 2011, 167 master's awarded. *Degree requirements:* For master's, thesis optional. *Entrance requirements:* For master's, GRE General Test, minimum GPA of 3.0. Additional exam requirements/recommendations for international students: Required—TOEFL. *Application deadline:* For fall admission, 5/1 priority date for domestic students; for spring admission, 11/1 for domestic students. Application fee: $55 ($65 for international students). *Financial support:* Fellowships, research assistantships with partial tuition reimbursements, teaching assistantships, Federal Work-Study, institutionally sponsored loans, scholarships/grants, and tuition waivers (partial) available. Support available to part-time students. *Faculty research:* Teachers in the process of change, learning cycles, children's concepts of science. *Total annual research expenditures:* $614,458. *Unit head:* Dr. Chris Leland, Interim Executive Associate Dean, 317-274-6801, Fax: 317-274-6864. *Application contact:* Sarah Brandenburg, Graduate Advisor, 317-274-6801, Fax: 317-274-6864, E-mail: edugrad@iupui.edu. Web site: http://education.iupui.edu/.

Iowa State University of Science and Technology, Department of Educational Leadership and Policy Studies, Ames, IA 50011. Offers counselor education (M Ed, MS); educational administration (M Ed, MS); educational leadership (PhD); higher education (M Ed, MS); organizational learning and human resource development (M Ed, MS); research and evaluation (MS); student affairs (MS). *Degree requirements:* For master's, thesis or alternative; for doctorate, thesis/dissertation. *Entrance requirements:* For master's and doctorate, GRE General Test. Additional exam requirements/recommendations for international students: Required—TOEFL (minimum score 560 paper-based; 83 iBT), IELTS (minimum score 6.5). *Application deadline:* For fall admission, 1/1 priority date for domestic students, 1/1 for international students. Application fee: $40 ($90 for international students). Electronic applications accepted. *Unit head:* Dr. Daniel Robinson, Director of Graduate Education, 515-294-1241, Fax: 515-294-4942, E-mail: edldrshp@iastate.edu. *Application contact:* Judy Weiland, Application Contact, 515-294-1241, Fax: 515-294-4942, E-mail: eldrshp@iastate.edu. Web site: http://www.elps.hs.iastate.edu/.

Kansas State University, Graduate School, College of Education, Department of Special Education, Counseling and Student Affairs, Manhattan, KS 66506. Offers academic advising (MS); counseling and student development (MS, Ed D, PhD), including college student development (MS), counselor education and supervision (PhD), school counseling (MS), student affairs in higher education (PhD); special education (MS, Ed D). *Accreditation:* ACA; NCATE. Part-time programs available. *Faculty:* 8 full-time (4 women), 4 part-time/adjunct (1 woman). *Students:* 87 full-time (64 women), 323 part-time (251 women); includes 62 minority (27 Black or African American, non-Hispanic/Latino; 4 American Indian or Alaska Native, non-Hispanic/Latino; 5 Asian, non-Hispanic/Latino; 19 Hispanic/Latino; 2 Native Hawaiian or other Pacific Islander, non-Hispanic/Latino; 5 Two or more races, non-Hispanic/Latino), 4 international. Average age 34. 236 applicants, 70% accepted, 83 enrolled. In 2011, 111 master's, 2 doctorates awarded. *Degree requirements:* For master's, comprehensive exam; for doctorate, comprehensive exam, thesis/dissertation. *Entrance requirements:* For master's, minimum undergraduate GPA of 3.0; for doctorate, GRE General Test, minimum GPA of 3.0 in last 60 hours. Additional exam requirements/recommendations for international students: Required—TOEFL. *Application deadline:* For fall admission, 2/1 priority date for domestic students, 2/1 for international students; for spring admission, 8/1 priority date for domestic students, 8/1 for international students. Applications are processed on a rolling basis. Application fee: $40 ($55 for international students). Electronic applications accepted. *Financial support:* In 2011–12, 3 teaching assistantships (averaging $18,090 per year) were awarded; career-related internships or fieldwork, institutionally sponsored loans, and scholarships/grants also available. Financial award application deadline: 3/1; financial award applicants required to submit FAFSA. *Faculty research:* Counseling supervision, academic advising, career development, student development, universal design for learning, autism, learning disabilities. *Total annual research expenditures:* $2,678. *Unit head:* Kenneth Hughey, Head, 785-532-6445, Fax: 785-532-7304, E-mail: khughey@ksu.edu. *Application contact:* Dona Deam, Application Contact, 785-532-5595, Fax: 785-532-7304, E-mail: ddeam@ksu.edu. Web site: http://coe.ksu.edu/departments/secsa/index.htm.

Kaplan University, Davenport Campus, School of Higher Education Studies, Davenport, IA 52807-2095. Offers college administration and leadership (MS); college teaching and learning (MS); student services (MS). Part-time and evening/weekend programs available. Postbaccalaureate distance learning degree programs offered (no on-campus study). *Entrance requirements:* Additional exam requirements/recommendations for international students: Required—TOEFL (minimum score 550 paper-based; 218 computer-based; 80 iBT).

Kent State University, Graduate School of Education, Health, and Human Services, School of Foundations, Leadership and Administration, Program in Higher Education and Student Personnel, Kent, OH 44242-0001. Offers M Ed. *Accreditation:* NCATE. Part-time and evening/weekend programs available. *Faculty:* 5 full-time (3 women), 6 part-time/adjunct (4 women). *Students:* 75 full-time (58 women), 31 part-time (23 women); includes 10 minority (4 Black or African American, non-Hispanic/Latino; 2 Asian, non-Hispanic/Latino; 4 Hispanic/Latino). 112 applicants, 39% accepted. In 2011, 35 master's awarded. *Entrance requirements:* For master's, GRE required if undergraduate GPA is below 3.0, resume, interview, 2 letters of recommendation, goals statement. Additional exam requirements/recommendations for international students: Required—TOEFL (minimum score 550 paper-based; 213 computer-based; 80 iBT). *Application deadline:* Applications are processed on a rolling basis. Application fee: $30 ($60 for international students). Electronic applications accepted. *Expenses:* Tuition, state resident: full-time $8136; part-time $452 per credit hour. Tuition, nonresident: full-time $14,292; part-time $794 per credit hour. *Financial support:* In 2011–12, 2 research assistantships with full tuition reimbursements (averaging $8,500 per year) were awarded; teaching assistantships with full tuition reimbursements, Federal Work-Study, scholarships/grants, unspecified assistantships, and 5 administrative assistantships (averaging $8,500 per year) also available. Financial award application deadline: 4/1; financial award applicants required to submit FAFSA. *Faculty research:* History/sociology of higher education, organization and administration in higher education. *Unit head:* Dr. Mark Kretovics, Coordinator, 330-672-0642, E-mail: mkretov1@kent.edu. *Application contact:* Nancy Miller, Academic Program Coordinator, Office of Graduate Student Services, 330-672-2576, Fax: 330-672-9162, E-mail: ogs@kent.edu.

Lamar University, College of Graduate Studies, College of Education and Human Development, Department of Counseling and Special Populations, Beaumont, TX 77710. Offers counseling and development (M Ed); school counseling (M Ed); special education (M Ed); student affairs (Certificate). *Faculty:* 7 full-time (5 women). *Students:* 9 full-time (5 women), 654 part-time (619 women); includes 239 minority (140 Black or African American, non-Hispanic/Latino; 8 American Indian or Alaska Native, non-Hispanic/Latino; 8 Asian, non-Hispanic/Latino; 83 Hispanic/Latino). Average age 36. 525 applicants, 96% accepted, 201 enrolled. In 2011, 15 master's awarded. *Application deadline:* For fall admission, 8/1 for domestic students; for spring admission, 12/1 for domestic students. Applications are processed on a rolling basis. Application fee: $25 ($50 for international students). *Expenses:* Tuition, state resident: full-time $5430; part-time $272 per credit hour. Tuition, nonresident: full-time $11,540; part-time $577 per credit hour. *Required fees:* $1916. *Unit head:* Dr. Carl J. Sheperis, Chair, 409-880-8978, Fax: 409-880-2263. *Application contact:* Dr. Lula Henry, Director of Professional Service, 409-880-8218. Web site: http://dept.lamar.edu/counseling/.

Lee University, Graduate Studies in Counseling, Cleveland, TN 37320-3450. Offers college student development (MS); holistic child development (MS); marriage and family therapy (MS); school counseling (MS). Part-time programs available. *Faculty:* 6 full-time (0 women), 7 part-time/adjunct (2 women). *Students:* 66 full-time (53 women), 34 part-time (29 women); includes 6 minority (1 American Indian or Alaska Native, non-Hispanic/Latino; 1 Asian, non-Hispanic/Latino; 3 Hispanic/Latino; 1 Two or more races, non-Hispanic/Latino), 6 international. Average age 27. 57 applicants, 56% accepted, 30 enrolled. In 2011, 44 master's awarded. *Degree requirements:* For master's, variable foreign language requirement, comprehensive exam, thesis, internship. *Entrance requirements:* For master's, GRE General Test or MAT, minimum undergraduate GPA of 3.0, 3 letters of recommendation, interview. Additional exam requirements/recommendations for international students: Required—TOEFL (minimum score 450 paper-based; 45 computer-based). *Application deadline:* For fall admission, 4/1 priority date for domestic students, 4/1 for international students; for spring admission, 10/1 priority date for domestic students, 10/1 for international students. Applications are processed on a rolling basis. Application fee: $25. *Expenses: Tuition:* Full-time $12,120; part-time $506 per credit hour. *Required fees:* $560; $305 per term. Part-time tuition and fees vary according to course load. *Financial support:* In 2011–12, 21 teaching assistantships (averaging $569 per year) were awarded; career-related internships or fieldwork, Federal Work-Study, institutionally sponsored loans, scholarships/grants, and unspecified assistantships also available. Financial award application deadline: 3/1; financial award applicants required to submit FAFSA. *Unit head:* Dr. Trevor Milliron, Director, 423-614-8126, Fax: 423-614-8129, E-mail: tmilliron@leeuniversity.edu. *Application contact:* Vicki Glasscock, Graduate Admissions Director, 423-614-8059, E-mail: vglasscock@leeuniversity.edu. Web site: http://www.leeuniversity.edu/academics/graduate/arts.

Lehigh University, College of Education, Program in Educational Leadership, Bethlehem, PA 18015. Offers educational leadership (M Ed, Ed D); principal certification K-12 (Certificate); pupil services (Certificate); special education (Certificate); superintendant certification (Certificate); supervisor of curriculum and instruction (Certificate); supervisor of pupil services (Certificate); MBA/M Ed. Part-time and evening/weekend programs available. Postbaccalaureate distance learning degree programs offered (minimal on-campus study). *Faculty:* 7 full-time (2 women), 8 part-time/adjunct (6 women). *Students:* 4 full-time (all women), 149 part-time (68 women); includes 6 minority (2 Black or African American, non-Hispanic/Latino; 2 Asian, non-Hispanic/Latino; 2 Hispanic/Latino), 19 international. Average age 38. 61 applicants, 52% accepted, 4 enrolled. In 2011, 36 master's, 5 doctorates awarded. *Degree requirements:* For doctorate, comprehensive exam, thesis/dissertation. *Entrance requirements:* For master's and Certificate, minimum undergraduate GPA of 3.0; for doctorate, GRE General Test or MAT, minimum graduate GPA of 3.6, 2 letters of recommendation, essay, transcript. Additional exam requirements/recommendations for international students: Required—TOEFL (minimum score 600 paper-based; 250 computer-based; 93 iBT). *Application deadline:* For fall admission, 1/15 for domestic and international students; for spring admission, 11/1 for domestic and international students. Applications are processed on a rolling basis. Application fee: $65. Electronic applications accepted. *Expenses:* Contact institution. *Financial support:* In 2011–12, 1 student received support, including 1 research assistantship with full and partial tuition reimbursement available (averaging $13,000 per year); fellowships with full and partial tuition reimbursements available, teaching assistantships with full and partial tuition reimbursements available, career-related internships or fieldwork, Federal Work-Study, institutionally sponsored loans, scholarships/grants, and tuition waivers (full and partial) also available. Financial award application deadline: 1/31. *Faculty research:* School finance and law, supervision of instruction, middle-level education, organizational change, leadership preparation and development, international school leadership, urban school leadership. *Unit head:* Dr. Floyd D. Beachum, Director, 610-758-5955, Fax: 610-758-3227, E-mail: fdb209@lehigh.edu. *Application contact:* Donna M. Johnson, Coordinator, 610-758-3231, Fax: 610-758-6223, E-mail: dmj4@lehigh.edu.

Lewis University, College of Arts and Sciences, Program in Organizational Leadership, Romeoville, IL 60446. Offers higher education/student services (MA); non-for-profit management (MA); organizational management (MA); public administration (MA); training and development (MA). Part-time and evening/weekend programs available. Postbaccalaureate distance learning degree programs offered (no on-campus study). *Faculty:* 2 full-time (0 women), 9 part-time/adjunct (2 women). *Students:* 15 full-time (14 women), 193 part-time (143 women); includes 61 minority (50 Black or African American, non-Hispanic/Latino; 2 Asian, non-Hispanic/Latino; 9 Hispanic/Latino). Average age 36. In 2011, 46 master's awarded. *Entrance requirements:* For master's, bachelor's degree, at least 25 years of age, minimum of 3 years of work experience, minimum GPA of 3.0, letter of recommendation, interview. Additional exam requirements/recommendations for international students: Required—TOEFL (minimum score 550 paper-based; 213 computer-based). *Application deadline:* For fall admission, 5/1 for international students; for spring admission, 11/15 for international students. Applications are processed on a rolling basis. Application fee: $40. Electronic applications accepted. *Financial support:* Federal Work-Study, scholarships/grants, tuition waivers, and unspecified assistantships available. Financial award application deadline: 5/1; financial award applicants required to submit FAFSA. *Unit head:* Dr. Rich Walsh, Director, 815-838-0500, E-mail: walshri@lewisu.edu. *Application contact:* Julie Branchaw, Assistant Director, Graduate and Adult Admission, 815-836-5574, Fax: 815-836-5578, E-mail: branchju@lewisu.edu.

Manhattan College, Graduate Division, School of Education, Program in Counseling, Riverdale, NY 10471. Offers bilingual pupil personnel services (Advanced Certificate); mental health counseling (MS, Advanced Certificate); school counseling (MA, Diploma). Part-time and evening/weekend programs available. *Faculty:* 4 full-time (2 women), 17 part-time/adjunct (10 women). *Students:* 66 full-time (55 women), 66 part-time (55 women); includes 65 minority (26 Black or African American, non-Hispanic/Latino; 5 Asian, non-Hispanic/Latino; 32 Hispanic/Latino; 2 Two or more races, non-Hispanic/Latino), 4 international. 174 applicants, 95% accepted, 48 enrolled. In 2011, 32 master's, 17 other advanced degrees awarded. *Degree requirements:* For master's, thesis, internship. *Entrance requirements:* For master's, minimum GPA of 3.0. Additional exam requirements/recommendations for international students: Recommended—TOEFL. *Application deadline:* For fall admission, 7/1 priority date for domestic students; for spring admission, 12/20 priority date for domestic students. Applications are processed on a rolling basis. Application fee: $60. *Expenses: Tuition:* Full-time $14,850; part-time $825 per credit. *Required fees:* $390; $150. *Financial support:* In 2011–12, 1 research assistantship with partial tuition reimbursement (averaging $18,000 per year) was awarded; Federal Work-Study, scholarships/grants, health care benefits, and unspecified assistantships also available. Financial award application deadline: 2/1; financial award applicants required to submit FAFSA. *Faculty research:* College advising, cognition, family counseling, group dynamics, cultural attitudes, bullying. *Unit head:* Dr. Corine Fitzpatrick, Director, 718-862-7497, Fax: 718-862-7472, E-mail: corine.fitzpatrick@manhattan.edu. *Application contact:* Dr. Corine Fitzpatrick, Director, 718-862-7497, Fax: 718-862-7472, E-mail: corine.fitzpatrick@manhattan.edu.

Marquette University, Graduate School, College of Education, Department of Educational Policy and Leadership, Milwaukee, WI 53201-1881. Offers college student personnel administration (M Ed); curriculum and instruction (MA); education (MA); educational administration (M Ed); educational policy and foundations (MA); elementary education (Certificate); literacy (MA); principal (Certificate); reading specialist (Certificate); reading teacher (Certificate); secondary education (Certificate); superintendent (Certificate). Part-time and evening/weekend programs available. *Faculty:* 14 full-time (9 women). *Students:* 40 full-time (34 women), 137 part-time (80 women); includes 25 minority (14 Black or African American, non-Hispanic/Latino; 1 American Indian or Alaska Native, non-Hispanic/Latino; 2 Asian, non-Hispanic/Latino; 8 Hispanic/Latino), 2 international. Average age 32. 132 applicants, 73% accepted, 67 enrolled. In 2011, 46 master's, 3 doctorates, 5 other advanced degrees awarded. Terminal master's awarded for partial completion of doctoral program. *Degree requirements:* For master's, comprehensive exam, thesis (for some programs); for doctorate, thesis/dissertation, qualifying exam, supporting minor. *Entrance requirements:* For master's, GRE General Test or MAT, official transcripts from all current and previous colleges/universities except Marquette, three letters of recommendation, statement of purpose; for doctorate, GRE General Test, MAT, sample of written work, official transcripts from all current and previous colleges/universities except Marquette, three letters of recommendation, statement of purpose, resume/curriculum vitae; for Certificate, GRE General Test or MAT, master's degree. Additional exam requirements/recommendations for international students: Required—TOEFL (minimum score 530 paper-based; 78 computer-based). *Application deadline:* For fall admission, 1/15 for domestic and international students. Application fee: $50. *Expenses:* Contact institution. *Financial support:* In 2011–12, 130 students received support, including 1 fellowship with full tuition reimbursement available (averaging $18,780 per year), 5 research assistantships with full tuition reimbursements available (averaging $13,404 per year); health care benefits, tuition waivers (partial), and unspecified assistantships also available. Support available to part-time students. Financial award application deadline: 2/15. *Faculty research:* Leadership; social justice in education; development of lifelong learners; race, class, and schooling in historical perspective; urban teacher education. *Unit head:* Dr. Ellen Eckman, Chair, 414-288-1561, E-mail: ellen.eckman@marquette.edu. *Application contact:* Craig Pierce, Assistant Dean of the Graduate School, 414-288-5740, Fax: 414-288-1902, E-mail: craig.pierce@marquette.edu.

Massachusetts School of Professional Psychology, Graduate Programs, Boston, MA 02132. Offers applied psychology in higher education student personnel administration (MA); clinical psychology (Psy D); counseling psychology (MA); counseling psychology and community mental health (MA); counseling psychology and global mental health (MA); executive coaching (Graduate Certificate); forensic and counseling psychology (MA); leadership psychology (Psy D); organizational psychology (MA); primary care psychology (MA); respecialization in clinical psychology (Certificate); school psychology (Psy D); MA/CAGS. *Accreditation:* APA. *Degree requirements:* For master's, comprehensive exam (for some programs); for doctorate, thesis/dissertation (for some programs). Electronic applications accepted.

Messiah College, Program in Higher Education, Mechanicsburg, PA 17055. Offers college athletics management (MA); self-designed concentration (MA); student affairs (MA). Part-time programs available. *Faculty:* 2 full-time (1 woman), 3 part-time/adjunct (2 women). *Students:* 2 full-time (1 woman), 2 part-time (both women). Average age 25. *Application deadline:* For fall admission, 6/1 priority date for domestic students; for winter admission, 11/1 priority date for domestic students; for spring admission, 11/1 priority date for domestic students. Applications are processed on a rolling basis. Application fee: $30. Electronic applications accepted. *Expenses: Tuition:* Full-time $9648; part-time $536 per credit hour. *Required fees:* $150; $25 per course. *Financial support:* Federal Work-Study and unspecified assistantships available. Financial award applicants required to submit FAFSA. *Faculty research:* College athletics management, assessment and student learning outcomes, the life and legacy of Ernest L. Boyer, common learning, student affairs practice. *Unit head:* Dr. Cynthia Wells, Assistant Professor of Higher Education/Program Coordinator, 717-766-2511 Ext. 7378, E-mail: cwells@messiah.edu. *Application contact:* Jackie Gehman, Graduate Enrollment Coordinator, 717-796-5061, Fax: 717-691-2386, E-mail: jgehman@messiah.edu. Web site: http://www.messiah.edu/academics/graduate_studies/Higher-Ed/.

Miami University, School of Education and Allied Professions, Department of Educational Leadership, Oxford, OH 45056. Offers curriculum and teacher leadership (M Ed); educational administration (Ed D, PhD); school leadership (MS); student affairs in higher education (MS, PhD). *Accreditation:* NCATE. Part-time programs available. *Students:* 102 full-time (63 women), 96 part-time (73 women); includes 45 minority (34 Black or African American, non-Hispanic/Latino; 1 American Indian or Alaska Native, non-Hispanic/Latino; 3 Asian, non-Hispanic/Latino; 2 Hispanic/Latino; 5 Two or more races, non-Hispanic/Latino), 7 international. Average age 32. In 2011, 52 master's, 7 doctorates awarded. *Entrance requirements:* For master's, MAT or GRE, minimum undergraduate GPA of 3.0 during previous 2 years or 2.75 overall; for doctorate, GRE, minimum GPA of 2.75 (undergraduate), 3.0 (graduate). Additional exam requirements/recommendations for international students: Required—TOEFL. Application fee: $50. *Expenses:* Tuition, state resident: full-time $12,023; part-time $501 per credit hour. Tuition, nonresident: full-time $26,554; part-time $1107 per credit hour. *Required fees:* $528. *Financial support:* Fellowships with full tuition reimbursements, research assistantships with full tuition reimbursements, teaching assistantships with full tuition reimbursements, career-related internships or fieldwork, Federal Work-Study, health care benefits, tuition waivers (full), and unspecified assistantships available. Financial award application deadline: 2/15; financial award applicants required to submit FAFSA. *Unit head:* Dr. Kate Rousmaniere, Chair, 513-529-6843, Fax: 513-529-1729, E-mail: rousmak@muohio.edu. Web site: http://www.units.muohio.edu/eap/edl/index.html.

Minnesota State University Mankato, College of Graduate Studies, College of Education, Department of Counseling and Student Personnel, Mankato, MN 56001. Offers college student affairs (MS); counselor education and supervision (Ed D); marriage and family counseling (Certificate); mental health counseling (MS); professional school counseling (MS). *Accreditation:* ACA (one or more programs are accredited); NCATE. *Students:* 174 full-time (61 women), 42 part-time (30 women). *Degree requirements:* For master's, comprehensive exam, thesis or alternative. *Entrance requirements:* For master's, GRE General Test or MAT (if GPA less than 3.0 for last 2 years), minimum GPA of 3.0 during previous 2 years, 3 letters of reference. Additional exam requirements/recommendations for international students: Required—TOEFL. *Application deadline:* For fall admission, 1/15 priority date for domestic students. Applications are processed on a rolling basis. Application fee: $40. Electronic applications accepted. *Financial support:* Research assistantships with full tuition reimbursements, teaching assistantships with full tuition reimbursements, career-related internships or fieldwork, Federal Work-Study, institutionally sponsored loans, and unspecified assistantships available. Support available to part-time students. Financial award application deadline: 3/15; financial award applicants required to submit FAFSA. *Unit head:* Dr. Jacqueline Lewis, Chairperson, 507-389-5658. *Application contact:* 507-389-2321, E-mail: grad@mnsu.edu.

Mississippi State University, College of Education, Department of Counseling and Educational Psychology, Mississippi State, MS 39762. Offers college/postsecondary student counseling and personnel services (PhD); counselor education (MS); education (Ed S), including counselor education, school psychology; educational psychology (MS, PhD). *Accreditation:* ACA (one or more programs are accredited); APA; CORE (one or more programs are accredited); NCATE. Part-time programs available. Postbaccalaureate distance learning degree programs offered (minimal on-campus study). *Faculty:* 18 full-time (13 women), 2 part-time/adjunct (1 woman). *Students:* 167 full-time (133 women), 87 part-time (78 women); includes 81 minority (70 Black or African American, non-Hispanic/Latino; 4 American Indian or Alaska Native, non-Hispanic/Latino; 4 Asian, non-Hispanic/Latino; 1 Native Hawaiian or other Pacific Islander, non-Hispanic/Latino; 2 Two or more races, non-Hispanic/Latino), 7 international. Average age 31. 197 applicants, 55% accepted, 79 enrolled. In 2011, 52 master's, 2 doctorates, 7 other advanced degrees awarded. Terminal master's awarded for partial completion of doctoral program. *Degree requirements:* For master's, comprehensive exam, thesis optional; for doctorate, thesis/dissertation, comprehensive oral and written exam. *Entrance requirements:* For master's, GRE, minimum QPA of 3.0; for doctorate, GRE, interview, minimum GPA of 3.4; for Ed S, GRE, MS in counseling or related field. Additional exam requirements/recommendations for international students:

Required—TOEFL (minimum score 475 paper-based; 153 computer-based; 53 iBT); Recommended—IELTS (minimum score 4.5). *Application deadline:* For fall admission, 2/1 priority date for domestic students, 2/1 for international students. Applications are processed on a rolling basis. Application fee: $40. Electronic applications accepted. *Expenses:* Tuition, state resident: full-time $5805; part-time $322.50 per credit hour. Tuition, nonresident: full-time $14,670; part-time $815 per credit hour. *Financial support:* In 2011–12, 7 research assistantships (averaging $10,750 per year), 6 teaching assistantships with full tuition reimbursements (averaging $10,151 per year) were awarded; career-related internships or fieldwork, Federal Work-Study, institutionally sponsored loans, and unspecified assistantships also available. Financial award application deadline: 2/1; financial award applicants required to submit FAFSA. *Faculty research:* HIV-AIDS in college population, substance abuse in youth and college students, ADHD and conduct disorders in youth, assessment and identification of early childhood disabilities, assessment and vocational transition of the disabled. *Unit head:* Dr. Daniel Wong, Professor/Head, 662-325-7928, Fax: 662-325-3263, E-mail: dwong@colled.msstate.edu. *Application contact:* Dr. Tony Doggett, Associate Professor and Graduate Coordinator, 662-325-3312, Fax: 662-325-3263, E-mail: tdoggett@colled.msstate.edu. Web site: http://www.cep.msstate.edu/.

Missouri State University, Graduate College, College of Education, Department of Counseling, Leadership, and Special Education, Program in Student Affairs in Higher Education, Springfield, MO 65897. Offers MS. Part-time programs available. *Students:* 29 full-time (17 women), 13 part-time (12 women); includes 10 minority (4 Black or African American, non-Hispanic/Latino; 3 Asian, non-Hispanic/Latino; 2 Hispanic/Latino; 1 Two or more races, non-Hispanic/Latino). Average age 27. 36 applicants, 83% accepted, 21 enrolled. In 2011, 18 master's awarded. *Degree requirements:* For master's, comprehensive exam, thesis or alternative. *Entrance requirements:* For master's, statement of purpose; three references. Additional exam requirements/recommendations for international students: Required—TOEFL (minimum score 550 paper-based; 213 computer-based; 79 iBT). *Application deadline:* For fall admission, 7/20 priority date for domestic students, 5/1 for international students; for spring admission, 12/20 priority date for domestic students, 9/1 for international students. Applications are processed on a rolling basis. Application fee: $35 ($50 for international students). Electronic applications accepted. *Expenses:* Tuition, state resident: full-time $4086; part-time $227 per credit hour. Tuition, nonresident: full-time $8172; part-time $454 per credit hour. *Required fees:* $275 per semester. Tuition and fees vary according to course load, campus/location and program. *Financial support:* Federal Work-Study, institutionally sponsored loans, scholarships/grants, and unspecified assistantships available. Financial award application deadline: 3/31; financial award applicants required to submit FAFSA. *Unit head:* Dr. Gilbert Brown, Program Director, 417-836-4428, E-mail: gilbertbrown@missouristate.edu. *Application contact:* Misty Stewart, Coordinator of Graduate Recruitment, 417-836-6079, Fax: 417-836-6200, E-mail: mistystewart@missouristate.edu. Web site: http://education.missouristate.edu/edadmin/MSEDSA.htm.

New York University, Steinhardt School of Culture, Education, and Human Development, Department of Administration, Leadership, and Technology, Program in Higher Education, New York, NY 10012-1019. Offers higher and postsecondary education (PhD); higher education administration (Ed D); student personnel administration in higher education (MA). *Accreditation:* Teacher Education Accreditation Council. Part-time programs available. *Faculty:* 8 full-time (5 women). *Students:* 29 full-time (22 women), 104 part-time (73 women); includes 62 minority (27 Black or African American, non-Hispanic/Latino; 9 Asian, non-Hispanic/Latino; 19 Hispanic/Latino; 1 Native Hawaiian or other Pacific Islander, non-Hispanic/Latino; 6 Two or more races, non-Hispanic/Latino), 3 international. Average age 31. 235 applicants, 18% accepted, 38 enrolled. In 2011, 42 master's, 7 doctorates awarded. *Degree requirements:* For master's, thesis (for some programs); for doctorate, thesis/dissertation. *Entrance requirements:* For master's, interview, 2 letters of recommendation; for doctorate, GRE General Test, interview. Additional exam requirements/recommendations for international students: Required—TOEFL. *Application deadline:* For fall admission, 12/1 priority date for domestic students, 12/1 for international students; for spring admission, 11/1 for domestic and international students. Applications are processed on a rolling basis. Application fee: $75. Electronic applications accepted. *Financial support:* Fellowships with full and partial tuition reimbursements, career-related internships or fieldwork, Federal Work-Study, institutionally sponsored loans, scholarships/grants, tuition waivers (partial), and unspecified assistantships available. Support available to part-time students. Financial award application deadline: 2/1; financial award applicants required to submit FAFSA. *Faculty research:* Organizational theory and culture, systemic change, leadership development, access, equity and diversity. *Unit head:* Dr. Ann Marcus, Head, 212-998-4041, Fax: 212-995-4041. *Application contact:* 212-998-5030, Fax: 212-995-4328, E-mail: steinhardt.gradadmissions@nyu.edu. Web site: http://steinhardt.nyu.edu/alt/highered.

Northeastern University, Bouvé College of Health Sciences, Department of Counseling and Applied Educational Psychology, Program in College Student Development and Counseling, Boston, MA 02115-5096. Offers MS, CAGS. Part-time and evening/weekend programs available. *Faculty:* 5. *Students:* 45 full-time (35 women), 6 part-time (all women). 53 applicants, 77% accepted, 22 enrolled. In 2011, 25 master's awarded. *Entrance requirements:* For master's, GRE General Test or MAT. Additional exam requirements/recommendations for international students: Required—TOEFL (minimum score 100 iBT). *Application deadline:* For fall admission, 8/1 for domestic students; for spring admission, 12/1 for domestic students. Applications are processed on a rolling basis. Application fee: $50. Electronic applications accepted. *Financial support:* Career-related internships or fieldwork, Federal Work-Study, scholarships/grants, tuition waivers (partial), and unspecified assistantships available. Support available to part-time students. Financial award application deadline: 3/1; financial award applicants required to submit FAFSA. *Unit head:* Prof. Vanessa Johnson, Director, 617-373-4634, E-mail: v.johnson@neu.edu. *Application contact:* Margaret Schnabel, Director of Graduate Admissions, 617-373-2708, E-mail: bouvegrad@neu.edu. Web site: http://www.northeastern.edu/bouve/programs/mstudentdev.html.

Northern Arizona University, Graduate College, College of Education, Department of Educational Psychology, Flagstaff, AZ 86011. Offers counseling (MA); educational psychology (PhD), including counseling psychology, learning and instruction, school psychology; human relations (M Ed); school counseling (M Ed); school psychology (Certificate, Ed S); student affairs (M Ed). Part-time programs available. Postbaccalaureate distance learning degree programs offered. *Faculty:* 18 full-time (8 women). *Students:* 280 full-time (220 women), 241 part-time (198 women); includes 194 minority (29 Black or African American, non-Hispanic/Latino; 37 American Indian or Alaska Native, non-Hispanic/Latino; 8 Asian, non-Hispanic/Latino; 105 Hispanic/Latino; 1 Native Hawaiian or other Pacific Islander, non-Hispanic/Latino; 14 Two or more races, non-Hispanic/Latino), 2 international. 274 applicants, 76% accepted, 141 enrolled. In 2011, 172 master's, 4 doctorates awarded. Terminal master's awarded for partial completion of doctoral program. *Median time to degree:* Of those who began their doctoral program in fall 2003, 75% received their degree in 8 years or less. *Degree requirements:* For master's, internship (for some programs); for doctorate, comprehensive exam, thesis/dissertation, internship. *Entrance requirements:* Additional exam requirements/recommendations for international students: Required—TOEFL (minimum score 550 paper-based; 213 computer-based; 80 iBT), IELTS (minimum score 7). *Application deadline:* For fall admission, 9/15 for domestic students; for spring admission, 1/15 for domestic students. Applications are processed on a rolling basis. Application fee: $65. Electronic applications accepted. *Expenses:* Tuition, state resident: full-time $7190; part-time $355 per credit hour. Tuition, nonresident: full-time $18,092; part-time $1005 per credit hour. *Required fees:* $818; $328 per semester. *Financial support:* In 2011–12, 20 students received support, including 1 research assistantship with partial tuition reimbursement available (averaging $10,222 per year), 14 teaching assistantships with partial tuition reimbursements available (averaging $9,660 per year); career-related internships or fieldwork, Federal Work-Study, scholarships/grants, health care benefits, tuition waivers (full and partial), and unspecified assistantships also available. Financial award applicants required to submit FAFSA. *Unit head:* Dr. Kathy Bohan, Chair, 928-523-0362, Fax: 928-523-9284, E-mail: kathy.bohan@nau.edu. *Application contact:* Hope DeMello, Administrative Assistant, 928-523-7103, Fax: 928-523-9284, E-mail: eps@nau.edu. Web site: http://nau.edu/coe/ed-psych/.

Northern Kentucky University, Office of Graduate Programs, College of Education and Human Services, Clinical Mental Health Counseling Program, Highland Heights, KY 41099. Offers clinical mental health counseling (MS); college student development (Certificate). Part-time and evening/weekend programs available. *Faculty:* 12 full-time (7 women), 1 part-time/adjunct (0 women). *Students:* 37 full-time (33 women), 25 part-time (20 women); includes 2 minority (1 Black or African American, non-Hispanic/Latino; 1 Native Hawaiian or other Pacific Islander, non-Hispanic/Latino). Average age 32. 40 applicants, 60% accepted, 24 enrolled. In 2011, 13 master's, 7 other advanced degrees awarded. *Degree requirements:* For master's, comprehensive exam, internship. *Entrance requirements:* For master's, GRE, minimum GPA of 2.75, 3 letters of reference, criminal background check (state and federal), resume. Additional exam requirements/recommendations for international students: Required—TOEFL (minimum score 550 paper-based; 213 computer-based; 79 iBT); Recommended—IELTS (minimum score 6.5). *Application deadline:* For fall admission, 7/1 priority date for domestic students, 6/1 for international students; for spring admission, 11/1 priority date for domestic students, 10/1 for international students. Application fee: $40. Electronic applications accepted. *Expenses:* Tuition, state resident: full-time $7614; part-time $423 per credit hour. Tuition, nonresident: full-time $13,104; part-time $728 per credit hour. Tuition and fees vary according to degree level and reciprocity agreements. *Financial support:* Applicants required to submit FAFSA. *Faculty research:* Best practices and evidence-based treatment in counseling, assessment in counseling, counseling children and adolescents, clinical mental health and school counselors working together in best interests of children adolescents and families, professional gatekeeping in counselor education programs. *Unit head:* Dr. Kerry Sebera, Program Director, 859-572-7841, Fax: 859-572-6592, E-mail: seberak1@nku.edu. *Application contact:* Dr. Peg Griffin, Director, Graduate Programs, 859-572-6934, Fax: 859-572-6670, E-mail: griffinp@nku.edu. Web site: http://coehs.nku.edu/gradprograms/counseling/clinicalmentalhealthcounseling.html.

Northwestern State University of Louisiana, Graduate Studies and Research, College of Education and Human Development, Program in Student Affairs in Higher Education, Natchitoches, LA 71497. Offers MA. *Accreditation:* NCATE. *Faculty:* 3 full-time (2 women). *Students:* 14 full-time (10 women), 5 part-time (1 woman); includes 7 minority (all Black or African American, non-Hispanic/Latino). Average age 29. 14 applicants, 93% accepted, 6 enrolled. In 2011, 10 master's awarded. *Degree requirements:* For master's, comprehensive exam, thesis or alternative. *Entrance requirements:* For master's, GRE General Test, GRE Subject Test, minimum undergraduate GPA of 2.5. Additional exam requirements/recommendations for international students: Required—TOEFL. *Application deadline:* For fall admission, 3/15 priority date for domestic students; for spring admission, 10/15 priority date for domestic students. Applications are processed on a rolling basis. Application fee: $20 ($30 for international students). Electronic applications accepted. *Expenses:* Tuition, state resident: full-time $3440. Tuition, nonresident: full-time $12,010. *Financial support:* Application deadline: 7/15. *Unit head:* Dr. Vickie Gentry, Chair, 318-357-6288, Fax: 318-357-6275, E-mail: education@nsula.edu. *Application contact:* Dr. Steven G. Horton, Associate Provost/Dean, Graduate Studies, Research, and Information Systems, 318-357-5851, Fax: 318-357-5019, E-mail: grad_school@nsula.edu. Web site: http://www.education.nsula.edu/programs.asp/.

Nova Southeastern University, Graduate School of Humanities and Social Sciences, Fort Lauderdale, FL 33314-7796. Offers advanced conflict resolution practice (Certificate); college student affairs (MS); college student personnel administration (Certificate); conflict analysis and resolution (MS, PhD); cross-disciplinary studies (MA); family systems healthcare (Certificate); family therapy (MS, PhD); marriage and family therapy (DMFT); national security affairs (MS); peace studies (Certificate); qualitative research (Certificate); JD/MS; PhD/JD. *Accreditation:* AAMFT/COAMFTE (one or more programs are accredited). Part-time and evening/weekend programs available. Postbaccalaureate distance learning degree programs offered (minimal on-campus study). *Faculty:* 24 full-time (13 women), 33 part-time/adjunct (22 women). *Students:* 442 full-time (320 women), 413 part-time (303 women); includes 438 minority (265 Black or African American, non-Hispanic/Latino; 1 American Indian or Alaska Native, non-Hispanic/Latino; 21 Asian, non-Hispanic/Latino; 134 Hispanic/Latino; 1 Native Hawaiian or other Pacific Islander, non-Hispanic/Latino; 16 Two or more races, non-Hispanic/Latino), 60 international. Average age 37. 420 applicants, 53% accepted, 171 enrolled. In 2011, 114 master's, 25 doctorates awarded. *Degree requirements:* For master's, comprehensive exam, thesis optional, portfolios (for some programs); for doctorate, comprehensive exam, thesis/dissertation, qualifying exams, portfolios (for some programs). *Entrance requirements:* For master's, interview, minimum GPA of 3.0, writing sample; for doctorate, interview, minimum GPA of 3.5, master's degree in related field, writing sample. Additional exam requirements/recommendations for international students: Required—TOEFL. *Application deadline:* For fall admission, 6/1 priority date for domestic students, 6/1 for international students; for winter admission, 10/1 priority date for domestic students, 10/1 for international students; for spring admission, 3/1 priority date for domestic students, 3/1 for international students. Applications are processed on a rolling basis. Application fee: $50. Electronic applications accepted. *Financial support:* In 2011–12, 21 students received support, including 30 research assistantships (averaging $15,600 per year); career-related internships or fieldwork, Federal Work-Study, scholarships/grants, and unspecified assistantships also available. Financial award application deadline: 4/1; financial award applicants required to submit CSS PROFILE. *Faculty research:* Conflict resolution, family therapy, peace research, international conflict, multi-disciplinary studies, college student affairs, national security affairs, health care conflict resolution, family systems health care. *Unit head:* Dr. Honggang Yang, Dean, 954-262-3016, Fax: 954-262-3968, E-mail: yangh@nova.edu. *Application contact:* Marcia Arango, Student Recruitment Coordinator, 954-262-3006, Fax: 954-262-3968, E-mail: marango@nsu.nova.edu. Web site: http://shss.nova.edu/.

Ohio University, Graduate College, Gladys W. and David H. Patton College of Education and Human Services, Department of Counseling and Higher Education, Athens, OH 45701-2979. Offers college student personnel (M Ed); community/agency counseling (M Ed); counselor education (PhD); higher education (PhD); rehabilitation counseling (M Ed); school counseling (M Ed). *Accreditation:* ACA; CORE. Part-time and evening/weekend programs available. *Students:* 174 full-time (133 women), 40 part-time (25 women); includes 38 minority (21 Black or African American, non-Hispanic/Latino; 2 American Indian or Alaska Native, non-Hispanic/Latino; 2 Asian, non-Hispanic/Latino; 7 Hispanic/Latino; 6 Two or more races, non-Hispanic/Latino), 9 international. 130 applicants, 59% accepted, 62 enrolled. In 2011, 45 master's, 7 doctorates awarded. *Degree requirements:* For master's, comprehensive exam (for some programs), thesis or alternative; for doctorate, comprehensive exam, thesis/dissertation. *Entrance requirements:* For master's, GRE General Test or MAT (if GPA less than 2.9), 3 letters of reference; for doctorate, GRE General Test, work experience, minimum GPA of 3.4. Additional exam requirements/recommendations for international students: Required—TOEFL (minimum score 550 paper-based; 80 iBT) or IELTS (minimum score 6.5). *Application deadline:* For fall admission, 1/15 for domestic and international students. Application fee: $50 ($55 for international students). Electronic applications accepted. *Financial support:* Research assistantships with full tuition reimbursements, teaching assistantships with full tuition reimbursements, Federal Work-Study, institutionally sponsored loans, tuition waivers (partial), and unspecified assistantships available. Financial award application deadline: 1/15. *Faculty research:* Youth violence, gender studies, student affairs, chemical dependency, disabilities issues. *Total annual research expenditures:* $527,983. *Unit head:* Dr. Tracy Leinbaugh, Chair, 740-593-0846, Fax: 740-593-0477, E-mail: leinbaug@ohio.edu. *Application contact:* Floyd J. Doney, Director of Student Affairs, 740-593-4400, Fax: 740-593-9310, E-mail: doney@ohio.edu. Web site: http://www.cehs.ohio.edu/academics/che/.

Oregon State University, Graduate School, College of Education, Program in College Student Services Administration, Corvallis, OR 97331. Offers Ed M, MS. *Degree requirements:* For master's, thesis or alternative. *Entrance requirements:* For master's, minimum GPA of 3.0 in last 90 hours of course work. Additional exam requirements/recommendations for international students: Required—TOEFL. *Faculty research:* Improvement of student activities, administering recreational sports programs.

Penn State University Park, Graduate School, College of Education, Department of Education Policy Studies, State College, University Park, PA 16802-1503. Offers college student affairs (M Ed); educational leadership (M Ed); educational theory and policy (MA, PhD); higher education (D Ed, PhD). *Accreditation:* NCATE. *Unit head:* Dr. David H. Monk, Dean, 814-865-2526, Fax: 814-865-0555, E-mail: dhm6@psu.edu. *Application contact:* Cynthia E. Nicosia, Director, Graduate Enrollment Services, 814-865-1834, E-mail: cey1@psu.edu. Web site: http://www.ed.psu.edu/educ/eps/.

Providence College and Theological Seminary, Theological Seminary, Otterburne, MB R0A 1G0, Canada. Offers children's ministry (Certificate); Christian studies (MA, Certificate); counseling (MA); cross-cultural discipleship (Certificate); divinity (M Div); educational studies (MA), including counseling psychology, educational ministries, student development, teaching English to speakers of other languages, training teachers of English to speakers of other languages; global studies (MA); lay counseling (Diploma); ministry (D Min); teaching English to speakers of other languages (Certificate); theological studies (MA); training teacher of English to speakers of other languages (Certificate); youth ministry (Certificate). *Accreditation:* ATS. Part-time programs available. *Degree requirements:* For master's, variable foreign language requirement, thesis (for some programs); for doctorate, thesis/dissertation. *Entrance requirements:* Additional exam requirements/recommendations for international students: Recommended—TOEFL (minimum score 550 paper-based; 213 computer-based). *Faculty research:* Studies in Isaiah, theology of sin.

Regent University, Graduate School, School of Education, Virginia Beach, VA 23464-9800. Offers adult education (Ed D); adult/staff development (Ed D, PhD); career switcher with licensure (M Ed), including alternative licensure; character education (Ed D, PhD); Christian education leadership (Ed D, PhD); Christian education specialist (Ed S); Christian school program (M Ed), including ACSI licensure; distance education (Ed D, PhD); education licensure (M Ed), including preK-6th grade; educational leadership (M Ed, PhD); educational leadership - special education (Ed S), including administration and supervision; educational psychology (Ed D, PhD), including learning and development, research and evaluation, special education; higher education (Ed D, PhD), including administration, research and institutional planning, teaching; higher education leadership (Ed D); individualized degree plan (M Ed), including behavior disorders, learning disabilities, mental retardation, reading specialist; K-12 school leadership (Ed D, PhD); leadership in character education (M Ed); master teacher (M Ed), including TESOL; mathematics education (M Ed); special education (PhD); student affairs (M Ed); TESOL (M Ed), including adult education, ESL: preK-12. *Accreditation:* Teacher Education Accreditation Council. Part-time and evening/weekend programs available. Postbaccalaureate distance learning degree programs offered (minimal on-campus study). *Faculty:* 26 full-time (13 women), 54 part-time/adjunct (34 women). *Students:* 140 full-time (109 women), 786 part-time (626 women); includes 218 minority (189 Black or African American, non-Hispanic/Latino; 2 American Indian or Alaska Native, non-Hispanic/Latino; 11 Asian, non-Hispanic/Latino; 16 Hispanic/Latino), 42 international. Average age 39. 673 applicants, 57% accepted, 298 enrolled. In 2011, 178 master's, 15 doctorates awarded. *Degree requirements:* For master's, thesis or alternative; for doctorate, comprehensive exam, thesis/dissertation. *Entrance requirements:* For master's, MAT, minimum undergraduate GPA of 2.75, writing sample, resume, recommendations, interview; for doctorate, GRE, writing sample, 3 years of relevant professional experience, master's-level paper, copies of published work, resume, transcripts, interview, recommendations. Additional exam requirements/recommendations for international students: Required—TOEFL (minimum score 577 paper-based; 233 computer-based). *Application deadline:* For fall admission, 4/1 priority date for domestic students; for spring admission, 10/15 priority date for domestic students. Applications are processed on a rolling basis. Application fee: $50. Electronic applications accepted. *Expenses:* Contact institution. *Financial support:* Fellowships, career-related internships or fieldwork, scholarships/grants, tuition waivers (full and partial), and unspecified assistantships available. Support available to part-time students. Financial award application deadline: 4/1; financial award applicants required to submit FAFSA. *Faculty research:* Character development and discipline for children, education leadership development, diversity in schools, classroom management, technology in education settings. *Unit head:* Dr. Alan A. Arroyo, Dean, 757-352-4261, Fax: 757-352-4318, E-mail: alanarr@regent.edu. *Application contact:* Matthew Chadwick, Director of Enrollment Support Services, 800-373-5504, Fax: 757-352-4381, E-mail: admissions@regent.edu. Web site: http://www.regent.edu/education/.

Rutgers, The State University of New Jersey, New Brunswick, Graduate School of Education, Department of Educational Psychology, Program in College Student Affairs, Piscataway, NJ 08854-8097. Offers Ed M. *Accreditation:* ACA. *Degree requirements:* For master's, comprehensive exam. *Entrance requirements:* For master's, GRE General Test, 3 letters of recommendation, resume. Additional exam requirements/recommendations for international students: Required—TOEFL (minimum score 550 paper-based; 233 computer-based; 83 iBT). Electronic applications accepted. *Faculty research:* Higher education equality, Latino college student experience.

St. Cloud State University, School of Graduate Studies, School of Education, Department of Educational Leadership and Higher Education, Program in College Counseling and Student Development, St. Cloud, MN 56301-4498. Offers MS. *Degree requirements:* For master's, comprehensive exam, thesis or alternative. *Entrance requirements:* For master's, GRE General Test, minimum GPA of 2.75. Additional exam requirements/recommendations for international students: Required—Michigan English Language Assessment Battery; Recommended—TOEFL (minimum score 550 paper-based; 213 computer-based), IELTS (minimum score 6.5). Electronic applications accepted.

St. Edward's University, New College, Program in College Student Development, Austin, TX 78704. Offers MA. Part-time and evening/weekend programs available. *Students:* 2 full-time (both women), 26 part-time (22 women); includes 11 minority (3 Black or African American, non-Hispanic/Latino; 8 Hispanic/Latino). Average age 36. 17 applicants, 88% accepted, 8 enrolled. In 2011, 8 master's awarded. *Entrance requirements:* For master's, GRE, minimum GPA of 3.0 in last 60 hours or 2.75 overall. Additional exam requirements/recommendations for international students: Required—TOEFL (minimum score 550 paper-based; 213 computer-based; 79 iBT) or IELTS (minimum score 6). *Application deadline:* For fall admission, 7/1 for domestic and international students; for spring admission, 11/1 for domestic and international students. Applications are processed on a rolling basis. Application fee: $45 ($50 for international students). Electronic applications accepted. *Expenses: Tuition:* Full-time $17,550; part-time $975 per credit hour. *Required fees:* $50 per trimester. Full-time tuition and fees vary according to course load and program. *Unit head:* Dr. Richard A. Parsells, Director, 512-637-1978, Fax: 512-448-8492, E-mail: richp@stedwards.edu. *Application contact:* Carrie Martin, Graduate Admissions Coordinator, 512-448-8600, Fax: 512-428-1032, E-mail: carriem@stedwards.edu. Web site: http://www.stedwards.edu.

Saint Louis University, Graduate Education, College of Education and Public Service and Graduate Education, Department of Educational Leadership and Higher Education, St. Louis, MO 63103-2097. Offers Catholic school leadership (MA); educational administration (MA, Ed D, PhD, Ed S); higher education (MA, Ed D, PhD); student personnel administration (MA). *Accreditation:* NCATE. Part-time programs available. *Degree requirements:* For master's, comprehensive written and oral exam; for doctorate, comprehensive exam, thesis/dissertation, preliminary oral and written exams. *Entrance requirements:* For master's, GRE General Test, MAT, LSAT, GMAT or MCAT, letters of recommendation, resume; for doctorate and Ed S, GRE General Test, LSAT, GMAT or MCAT, letters of recommendation, resumé, goal statement, transcripts. Additional exam requirements/recommendations for international students: Required—TOEFL (minimum score 525 paper-based; 194 computer-based). Electronic applications accepted. *Faculty research:* Superintendent of schools, school finance, school facilities, student personal administration, building leadership.

San Jose State University, Graduate Studies and Research, Connie L. Lurie College of Education, Department of Counselor Education, San Jose, CA 95192-0001. Offers MA. *Accreditation:* NCATE. Evening/weekend programs available. *Degree requirements:* For master's, thesis or alternative. Electronic applications accepted.

Seton Hall University, College of Education and Human Services, Department of Education Leadership, Management and Policy, Program in College Student Personnel Administration, South Orange, NJ 07079-2697. Offers MA. Part-time and evening/weekend programs available. *Faculty:* 12 full-time (4 women), 1 part-time/adjunct (0 women). *Students:* 5 full-time (3 women), 5 part-time (2 women); includes 2 minority (both Black or African American, non-Hispanic/Latino). Average age 33. 12 applicants, 100% accepted, 4 enrolled. In 2011, 3 master's awarded. *Entrance requirements:* For master's, GRE or MAT (within past 5 years), minimum GPA of 3.0. Additional exam requirements/recommendations for international students: Required—TOEFL. *Application deadline:* Applications are processed on a rolling basis. Application fee: $50. *Expenses: Tuition:* Part-time $1033 per credit hour. *Required fees:* $85 per semester. *Unit head:* Dr. Michael Osnato, Chair, 973-275-2446, E-mail: osnatomi@shu.edu. *Application contact:* Information Contact, 973-761-9668. Web site: http://www.shu.edu.

Springfield College, Graduate Programs, Programs in Psychology and Counseling, Springfield, MA 01109-3797. Offers athletic counseling (M Ed, MS, CAGS); industrial/organizational psychology (M Ed, MS, CAGS); marriage and family therapy (M Ed, MS, CAGS); mental health counseling (M Ed, MS, CAGS); school guidance and counseling (M Ed, MS, CAGS); student personnel in higher education (M Ed, MS, CAGS). Part-time programs available. *Degree requirements:* For master's, research project, portfolio. *Entrance requirements:* Additional exam requirements/recommendations for international students: Required—TOEFL (minimum score 550 paper-based; 213 computer-based). Electronic applications accepted.

State University of New York at Binghamton, Graduate School, College of Community and Public Affairs, Department of Student Affairs Administration, Binghamton, NY 13902-6000. Offers MS. *Faculty:* 3 full-time (2 women). *Students:* 23 full-time (12 women), 15 part-time (9 women); includes 9 minority (1 Black or African American, non-Hispanic/Latino; 1 Asian, non-Hispanic/Latino; 7 Hispanic/Latino), 3 international. Average age 28. 32 applicants, 66% accepted, 10 enrolled. In 2011, 17 master's awarded. *Financial support:* In 2011–12, 8 students received support, including fellowships with full tuition reimbursements available (averaging $9,000 per year), 3 teaching assistantships with full tuition reimbursements available (averaging $9,000 per year); career-related internships or fieldwork, Federal Work-Study, institutionally sponsored loans, scholarships/grants, health care benefits, and unspecified assistantships also available. Financial award application deadline: 2/15; financial award applicants required to submit FAFSA. *Unit head:* Dr. Mary Ann Swain, Chair, 607-777-9219, E-mail: mswain@binghamton.edu. *Application contact:* Catherine Smith, Recruiting and Admissions Coordinator, 607-777-2151, Fax: 607-777-2501, E-mail: cmsmith@binghamton.edu. Web site: http://www2.binghamton.edu/ccpa/student-affairs-administration/.

State University of New York at Plattsburgh, Division of Education, Health, and Human Services, Department of Counselor Education, Plattsburgh, NY 12901-2681. Offers school counselor (MS Ed, CAS); student affairs counseling (MS), including clinical mental health counseling. *Accreditation:* ACA (one or more programs are accredited); Teacher Education Accreditation Council. Part-time programs available. *Students:* 54 full-time (45 women), 11 part-time (9 women); includes 4 minority (2 Black or African American, non-Hispanic/Latino; 2 Hispanic/Latino), 1 international. Average age 29. *Entrance requirements:* For master's, GRE General Test or MAT, minimum GPA of 2.8. Additional exam requirements/recommendations for international students: Required—TOEFL. *Application deadline:* For fall admission, 2/15 priority date for domestic students; for spring admission, 10/15 priority date for domestic students. Applications are processed on a rolling basis. Application fee: $75. *Financial support:* Research assistantships, teaching assistantships, career-related internships or fieldwork, Federal Work-Study, and administrative assistantships, editorial assistantships available. Support available to part-time students. Financial award application deadline: 4/15; financial award applicants required to submit FAFSA. *Faculty research:* Campus violence, program accreditation, substance abuse, vocational assessment, group counseling, divorce. *Unit head:* Dr. David Stone, Coordinator, 518-564-4170, E-mail: stoneda@plattsburgh.edu. *Application contact:* Marguerite Adelman, Assistant Director, Graduate Admissions, 518-564-4723, Fax: 518-564-4722, E-mail: adelmaml@plattsburgh.edu.

Student Affairs

Syracuse University, School of Education, Program in Student Affairs Counseling, Syracuse, NY 13244. Offers MS. Part-time programs available. *Students:* 3 full-time (1 woman), 2 part-time (both women); includes 1 minority (Two or more races, non-Hispanic/Latino). Average age 29. 11 applicants, 45% accepted, 2 enrolled. In 2011, 3 master's awarded. *Entrance requirements:* For master's, GRE General Test or MAT, interview. Additional exam requirements/recommendations for international students: Required—TOEFL (minimum score 100 iBT). *Application deadline:* For fall admission, 2/1 for domestic and international students; for spring admission, 10/15 for domestic and international students. Applications are processed on a rolling basis. Application fee: $75. Electronic applications accepted. *Expenses: Tuition:* Part-time $1206 per credit. *Financial support:* Fellowships with full tuition reimbursements and teaching assistantships with full and partial tuition reimbursements available. Financial award application deadline: 1/1; financial award applicants required to submit FAFSA. *Unit head:* Dr. Dennis Gilbride, Chair, 315-443-2266, E-mail: ddgilbr@syr.edu. *Application contact:* Laurie Deyo, Graduate Recruiter, School of Education, 315-443-2505, E-mail: e-gradrcrt@syr.edu. Web site: http://soeweb.syr.edu/.

Teachers College, Columbia University, Graduate Faculty of Education, Department of Organization and Leadership, New York, NY 10027-6696. Offers adult education guided intensive study (Ed D); adult learning and leadership (Ed M, MA, Ed D); educational administration (Ed M, MA, Ed D, PhD); higher education (Ed M, MA, Ed D); inquiry in education leadership (Ed D); nurse executive (MA, Ed D), including administration studies (MA), nurse executive (Ed D), professorial studies (MA); private school leadership (Ed M, MA); social and organizational psychology (MA), including change leadership, social-organizational psychology; student personnel administration (Ed M, MA, Ed D); urban education leadership (Ed D). Part-time and evening/weekend programs available. *Students:* 294 full-time (196 women), 319 part-time (231 women); includes 208 minority (85 Black or African American, non-Hispanic/Latino; 57 Asian, non-Hispanic/Latino; 66 Hispanic/Latino), 70 international. Average age 34. 456 applicants, 66% accepted, 144 enrolled. In 2011, 193 master's, 31 doctorates awarded. *Degree requirements:* For doctorate, thesis/dissertation. Application fee: $65. *Financial support:* Fellowships, research assistantships, career-related internships or fieldwork, Federal Work-Study, institutionally sponsored loans, and tuition waivers (full and partial) available. Support available to part-time students. Financial award application deadline: 2/1. *Unit head:* Warner Burke, Chair, 212-678-3258. *Application contact:* Debbie Lesperance, Assistant Director of Admission, 212-678-3710, Fax: 212-678-4171.

Texas State University–San Marcos, Graduate School, College of Education, Department of Counseling, Leadership, Adult Education, and School Psychology, Program of Student Affairs in Higher Education, San Marcos, TX 78666. Offers M Ed. *Accreditation:* ACA. Part-time and evening/weekend programs available. *Faculty:* 2 full-time (1 woman), 3 part-time/adjunct (1 woman). *Students:* 29 full-time (22 women), 13 part-time (all women); includes 12 minority (3 Black or African American, non-Hispanic/Latino; 2 Asian, non-Hispanic/Latino; 5 Hispanic/Latino; 2 Two or more races, non-Hispanic/Latino), 1 international. Average age 29. 39 applicants, 49% accepted, 11 enrolled. In 2011, 41 master's awarded. *Degree requirements:* For master's, comprehensive exam, thesis (for some programs). *Entrance requirements:* For master's, GRE General Test, minimum GPA of 3.0 in last 60 hours of course work. Additional exam requirements/recommendations for international students: Required—TOEFL (minimum score 550 paper-based; 213 computer-based; 78 iBT). *Application deadline:* For fall admission, 4/15 for domestic students, 3/15 for international students; for spring admission, 10/1 for domestic and international students. Applications are processed on a rolling basis. Application fee: $40 ($90 for international students). Electronic applications accepted. *Expenses:* Tuition, state resident: full-time $6408; part-time $3204 per semester. Tuition, nonresident: full-time $14,832; part-time $7416 per semester. *Required fees:* $1824; $912 per semester. Tuition and fees vary according to course load. *Financial support:* In 2011–12, 26 students received support, including 22 research assistantships (averaging $9,720 per year), 1 teaching assistantship (averaging $5,076 per year); career-related internships or fieldwork, Federal Work-Study, and institutionally sponsored loans also available. Support available to part-time students. Financial award application deadline: 4/1; financial award applicants required to submit FAFSA. *Unit head:* Dr. Paige Haber, Graduate Advisor, 512-245-7628, Fax: 512-245-8872, E-mail: ph31@txstate.edu. *Application contact:* Dr. J. Michael Willoughby, Dean of Graduate School, 512-245-2581, Fax: 512-245-8365, E-mail: gradcollege@txstate.edu. Web site: http://www.txstate.edu/clas/Student-Affairs/student-affairs-in-higher-ed2.html.

University of Bridgeport, School of Arts and Sciences, Department of Counseling, Bridgeport, CT 06604. Offers clinical mental health counseling (MS); college student personnel (MS); community counseling (MS); human resource development (MS); human service (MS). Part-time and evening/weekend programs available. *Faculty:* 7 full-time (4 women), 13 part-time/adjunct (7 women). *Students:* 26 full-time (22 women), 98 part-time (73 women); includes 76 minority (52 Black or African American, non-Hispanic/Latino; 1 Asian, non-Hispanic/Latino; 18 Hispanic/Latino; 5 Two or more races, non-Hispanic/Latino), 2 international. Average age 36. 99 applicants, 47% accepted, 34 enrolled. In 2011, 23 master's awarded. *Degree requirements:* For master's, thesis, project. *Entrance requirements:* Additional exam requirements/recommendations for international students: Recommended—TOEFL (minimum score 550 paper-based; 213 computer-based; 80 iBT), IELTS (minimum score 6.5). *Application deadline:* For fall admission, 8/1 priority date for domestic students, 8/1 for international students; for spring admission, 12/1 priority date for domestic students, 12/1 for international students. Applications are processed on a rolling basis. Application fee: $50. Electronic applications accepted. *Expenses: Tuition:* Full-time $22,880; part-time $700 per credit. *Required fees:* $1870; $95 per semester. Tuition and fees vary according to course load and program. *Financial support:* In 2011–12, 27 students received support. Fellowships, research assistantships, teaching assistantships, career-related internships or fieldwork, Federal Work-Study, and institutionally sponsored loans available. Support available to part-time students. Financial award application deadline: 6/1; financial award applicants required to submit FAFSA. *Faculty research:* Corporate elder care programs. *Unit head:* Dr. Sara L. Connolly, Director, Division of Counseling and Human Resources, 203-576-4183, Fax: 203-576-4219, E-mail: sconnoll@bridgeport.edu. *Application contact:* Karissa Peckham, Dean of Admissions, 203-576-4552, Fax: 203-576-4941, E-mail: admit@bridgeport.edu.

University of Central Arkansas, Graduate School, College of Education, Department of Leadership Studies, Program in College Student Personnel, Conway, AR 72035-0001. Offers MS. *Students:* 33 full-time (18 women), 5 part-time (2 women); includes 11 minority (9 Black or African American, non-Hispanic/Latino; 2 Asian, non-Hispanic/Latino), 3 international. Average age 25. 19 applicants, 100% accepted, 15 enrolled. In 2011, 17 master's awarded. *Degree requirements:* For master's, comprehensive exam, thesis. *Entrance requirements:* For master's, GRE General Test, minimum GPA of 2.7. Additional exam requirements/recommendations for international students: Required—TOEFL (minimum score 550 paper-based; 213 computer-based). *Application deadline:* For fall admission, 3/1 priority date for domestic students; for spring admission, 10/1 priority date for domestic students. Applications are processed on a rolling basis. Application fee: $25 ($40 for international students). *Expenses:* Contact institution. *Financial support:* Applicants required to submit FAFSA. *Unit head:* Dr. Charlotte Cone, Coordinator, 501-450-5303, Fax: 501-450-5469, E-mail: johns@uca.edu. *Application contact:* Susan Wood, Admissions Assistant, 501-450-3124, Fax: 501-450-5678, E-mail: swood@uca.edu.

University of Central Florida, College of Education, Department of Educational and Human Sciences, Program in Educational Leadership, Orlando, FL 32816. Offers educational leadership (MA, Ed D), including community college education (MA), higher education (Ed D), student personnel (MA). Part-time and evening/weekend programs available. *Students:* 82 full-time (55 women), 179 part-time (126 women); includes 53 minority (27 Black or African American, non-Hispanic/Latino; 3 Asian, non-Hispanic/Latino; 19 Hispanic/Latino; 4 Two or more races, non-Hispanic/Latino), 1 international. Average age 35. 142 applicants, 69% accepted, 62 enrolled. In 2011, 60 master's, 26 doctorates awarded. *Degree requirements:* For master's, thesis or alternative; for doctorate, thesis/dissertation, candidacy exam. *Entrance requirements:* For master's, GRE General Test; for doctorate, GRE General Test, GRE Subject Test, minimum GPA of 3.0, resume. Additional exam requirements/recommendations for international students: Required—TOEFL. *Application deadline:* For fall admission, 2/20 priority date for domestic students; for spring admission, 9/20 priority date for domestic students. Application fee: $30. Electronic applications accepted. *Expenses:* Tuition, state resident: part-time $277.08 per credit hour. Tuition, nonresident: part-time $277.08 per credit hour. Part-time tuition and fees vary according to degree level and program. *Financial support:* In 2011–12, 17 students received support, including 4 fellowships with partial tuition reimbursements available (averaging $8,300 per year), 14 research assistantships with partial tuition reimbursements available (averaging $7,000 per year), 2 teaching assistantships with partial tuition reimbursements available (averaging $1,000 per year); career-related internships or fieldwork, Federal Work-Study, institutionally sponsored loans, tuition waivers (partial), and unspecified assistantships also available. Financial award application deadline: 3/1; financial award applicants required to submit FAFSA. *Unit head:* Dr. Rosa Cintron, Program Coordinator, 407-832-1248, E-mail: rosa.cintrondelgado@ucf.edu. *Application contact:* Barbara Rodriguez, Director, Admissions and Registration, 407-823-2766, Fax: 407-823-6442, E-mail: gradadmissions@ucf.edu. Web site: http://education.ucf.edu/departments.cfm.

University of Central Missouri, The Graduate School, College of Education, Warrensburg, MO 64093. Offers career and technical education administration (MS); career and technical education industry training (MS); career and technical education leadership/teaching (MS); college student personnel administration (MS); counseling (MS); curriculum and instruction (Ed S); educational leadership (Ed D); educational technology (MS); elementary education/educational foundations and literacy (MSE); elementary school administration (MSE); elementary school principalship (Ed S); human services/learning resources (Ed S); human services/professional counseling (Ed S); human services/special education (Ed S); human services/technology and occupational education (Ed S); K-12 education/educational foundations and literacy (MSE); K-12 special education (MSE); library science and information services (MS); literacy education (MSE); secondary education/educational foundations & literacy (MSE); secondary school administration (MSE); secondary school principalship (Ed S); superintendency (Ed S); teaching (MAT). Ed D offered jointly with University of Missouri. Part-time programs available. Postbaccalaureate distance learning degree programs offered. *Entrance requirements:* Additional exam requirements/recommendations for international students: Required—TOEFL (minimum score 550 paper-based; 79 computer-based). Electronic applications accepted.

University of Dayton, Department of Counselor Education and Human Services, Dayton, OH 45469-1300. Offers college student personnel (MS Ed); community counseling (MS Ed); higher education administration (MS Ed); human services (MS Ed); school counseling (MS Ed); school psychology (MS Ed, Ed S). *Accreditation:* ACA; NCATE. Part-time and evening/weekend programs available. *Faculty:* 12 full-time (9 women), 30 part-time/adjunct (20 women). *Students:* 223 full-time (184 women), 189 part-time (147 women); includes 91 minority (83 Black or African American, non-Hispanic/Latino; 1 American Indian or Alaska Native, non-Hispanic/Latino; 2 Asian, non-Hispanic/Latino; 3 Hispanic/Latino; 2 Two or more races, non-Hispanic/Latino), 5 international. Average age 34. 336 applicants, 40% accepted, 96 enrolled. In 2011, 170 master's, 10 Ed Ss awarded. *Degree requirements:* For master's, comprehensive exam (for some programs), thesis (for some programs), exit exam. *Entrance requirements:* For master's, MAT or GRE (if GPA less than 2.75), interview, writing sample. Additional exam requirements/recommendations for international students: Required—TOEFL (minimum score 550 paper-based; 213 computer-based; 80 iBT). *Application deadline:* For fall admission, 4/10 for domestic students, 3/1 for international students; for winter admission, 9/10 for domestic students, 7/1 for international students; for spring admission, 1/10 for domestic students, 1/1 for international students. Application fee: $0 ($50 for international students). Electronic applications accepted. *Expenses: Tuition:* Full-time $8400; part-time $700 per credit hour. *Required fees:* $25 per semester. Tuition and fees vary according to degree level. *Financial support:* In 2011–12, 7 research assistantships with full and partial tuition reimbursements (averaging $8,550 per year) were awarded; career-related internships or fieldwork, institutionally sponsored loans, health care benefits, and unspecified assistantships also available. Financial award applicants required to submit FAFSA. *Faculty research:* Mindfulness, forgiveness in relationships, positive psychology in couples counseling, traumatic brain injury responses. *Unit head:* Dr. Moly Schaller, Chairperson, 937-229-3644, Fax: 937-229-1055, E-mail: mschaller1@udayton.edu. *Application contact:* Kathleen Brown, 937-229-3644, Fax: 937-229-1055, E-mail: kbrown1@udayton.edu. Web site: http://soeap.udayton.edu/edc.

University of Florida, Graduate School, College of Education, Department of Educational Administration and Policy, Gainesville, FL 32611. Offers curriculum and instruction (Ed D, PhD); educational leadership (M Ed, MAE, Ed D, PhD, Ed S); higher education administration (Ed D, PhD, Ed S); student personnel in higher education (M Ed, MAE); PhD/JD. *Accreditation:* NCATE. Part-time and evening/weekend programs available. Postbaccalaureate distance learning degree programs offered. Terminal master's awarded for partial completion of doctoral program. *Degree requirements:* For master's, thesis (for some programs); for doctorate, comprehensive exam (for some programs), thesis/dissertation (for some programs). *Entrance requirements:* For master's, GRE General Test, minimum GPA of 3.0, teaching experience; for doctorate and Ed S, GRE General Test, minimum GPA of 3.0. Additional exam requirements/recommendations for international students: Required—TOEFL (minimum score 550 paper-based; 213 computer-based; 80 iBT), IELTS (minimum score 6). *Application deadline:* For fall admission, 2/15 for domestic students, 12/1 for international students; for spring admission, 9/15 for domestic students, 3/1 for international students. Applications are processed on a rolling basis. Application fee: $30. Electronic applications accepted. *Financial support:* Career-related internships or fieldwork and unspecified assistantships available. Financial award applicants required to submit FAFSA.

University of Georgia, College of Education, Department of Counseling and Human Development Services, Athens, GA 30602. Offers college student affairs administration (M Ed, PhD); counseling and student personnel (PhD); counseling psychology (PhD); professional counseling (M Ed); professional school counseling (Ed S); recreation and leisure studies (M Ed, MA, PhD). *Accreditation:* ACA (one or more programs are accredited); APA (one or more programs are accredited); NCATE. *Faculty:* 23 full-time

(14 women). *Students:* 173 full-time (126 women), 78 part-time (46 women); includes 82 minority (70 Black or African American, non-Hispanic/Latino; 3 Asian, non-Hispanic/Latino; 7 Hispanic/Latino; 1 Native Hawaiian or other Pacific Islander, non-Hispanic/Latino; 1 Two or more races, non-Hispanic/Latino), 1 international. Average age 30. 375 applicants, 26% accepted, 53 enrolled. In 2011, 48 master's, 27 doctorates, 14 other advanced degrees awarded. *Degree requirements:* For master's, thesis (MA); for doctorate, variable foreign language requirement, thesis/dissertation. *Entrance requirements:* For master's, GRE General Test or MAT; for doctorate, GRE General Test. *Application deadline:* For fall admission, 7/1 priority date for domestic students; for spring admission, 11/15 for domestic students. Application fee: $50. Electronic applications accepted. *Financial support:* Fellowships, research assistantships, teaching assistantships, and unspecified assistantships available. *Unit head:* Dr. Rosemary E. Phelps, Head, 706-542-4221, Fax: 706-542-4130, E-mail: rephelps@uga.edu. *Application contact:* Dr. Corey W. Johnson, Graduate Coordinator, 706-542-4335, Fax: 706-542-4130, E-mail: cwjohns@uga.edu. Web site: http://www.coe.uga.edu/chds/.

The University of Iowa, Graduate College, College of Education, Department of Counseling, Rehabilitation, and Student Development, Iowa City, IA 52242-1316. Offers administration and research (PhD); community/rehabilitation counseling (MA); counselor education and supervision (PhD); rehabilitation counselor education (PhD); school counseling (MA); student development (MA, PhD). *Accreditation:* ACA (one or more programs are accredited); CORE (one or more programs are accredited). *Degree requirements:* For master's, thesis optional, exam; for doctorate, comprehensive exam, thesis/dissertation. *Entrance requirements:* For master's and doctorate, GRE General Test, minimum GPA of 3.0. Additional exam requirements/recommendations for international students: Required—TOEFL (minimum score 550 paper-based; 213 computer-based; 81 iBT). Electronic applications accepted.

University of La Verne, College of Arts and Sciences, Department of Psychology, Programs in Counseling, La Verne, CA 91750-4443. Offers counseling (MS), including student services; marriage and family therapy (MS). Part-time programs available. *Faculty:* 7 full-time (3 women), 13 part-time/adjunct (9 women). *Students:* 34 full-time (31 women), 43 part-time (38 women); includes 49 minority (12 Black or African American, non-Hispanic/Latino; 2 Asian, non-Hispanic/Latino; 34 Hispanic/Latino; 1 Two or more races, non-Hispanic/Latino). Average age 29. In 2011, 48 master's awarded. *Degree requirements:* For master's, thesis, competency exam, personal psychotherapy. *Entrance requirements:* For master's, minimum undergraduate GPA of 3.0; 3 letters of recommendations; interview. Additional exam requirements/recommendations for international students: Required—TOEFL (minimum score 600 paper-based; 250 computer-based). *Application deadline:* Applications are processed on a rolling basis. Application fee: $50. *Expenses:* Contact institution. *Financial support:* Career-related internships or fieldwork, institutionally sponsored loans, and scholarships/grants available. Financial award application deadline: 3/2; financial award applicants required to submit FAFSA. *Unit head:* Patricia Long, 909-593-3511 Ext. 4091, E-mail: plong@laverne.edu. *Application contact:* Barbara Cox, Program and Admission Specialist, 909-593-3511 Ext. 4004, Fax: 909-392-2761, E-mail: gradadmission@laverne.edu. Web site: http://www.laverne.edu/academics/arts-sciences/psychology/index.php.

University of Louisville, Graduate School, College of Education and Human Development, Department of Educational and Counseling Psychology, Louisville, KY 40292-0001. Offers counseling and personnel services (M Ed, PhD). *Accreditation:* APA; NCATE. Part-time and evening/weekend programs available. *Degree requirements:* For doctorate, comprehensive exam, thesis/dissertation. *Entrance requirements:* For master's and doctorate, GRE General Test. Additional exam requirements/recommendations for international students: Required—TOEFL (minimum score 560 paper-based; 210 computer-based; 83 iBT). Electronic applications accepted. *Expenses:* Tuition, state resident: full-time $9692; part-time $539 per credit hour. Tuition, nonresident: full-time $20,168; part-time $1121 per credit hour. Tuition and fees vary according to program and reciprocity agreements. *Faculty research:* Classroom processes, school outcomes, adolescent and adult development issues/prevention and treatment, multicultural counseling, spirituality, therapeutic outcomes, college student success, college student affairs administration, career development.

University of Mary, School of Education and Behavioral Sciences, Department of Behavioral Sciences, Bismarck, ND 58504-9652. Offers addiction counseling (MSC); community counseling (MSC); school counseling (MSC); student affairs counseling (MSC). Part-time programs available. Postbaccalaureate distance learning degree programs offered (minimal on-campus study). *Faculty:* 5 full-time (3 women), 9 part-time/adjunct (5 women). *Students:* 44 full-time (35 women), 12 part-time (7 women); includes 2 minority (both Black or African American, non-Hispanic/Latino). Average age 32. 43 applicants, 70% accepted, 25 enrolled. In 2011, 14 master's awarded. *Degree requirements:* For master's, thesis, internship. *Entrance requirements:* For master's, coursework/experience in psychology, statistics, minimum GPA of 3.0. Additional exam requirements/recommendations for international students: Required—TOEFL (minimum score 500 paper-based; 197 computer-based; 71 iBT). *Application deadline:* For fall admission, 8/1 priority date for domestic students. Application fee: $40. *Financial support:* Application deadline: 8/1; applicants required to submit FAFSA. *Unit head:* James Renner, Program Director for Counseling Graduate Studies, 701-355-8177, Fax: 701-255-7687, E-mail: jrenner@umary.edu. *Application contact:* Jeanette Shaeffer, Accelerated and Distance Education Administrative Assistant, 701-355-8128, Fax: 701-255-7687, E-mail: jgschae@umary.edu.

University of Maryland, College Park, Academic Affairs, College of Education, Department of Counseling and Personnel Services, College Park, MD 20742. Offers college student personnel (M Ed, MA); college student personnel administration (PhD); community counseling (CAGS); community/career counseling (M Ed, MA); counseling and personnel services (M Ed, MA, PhD), including art therapy (M Ed), college student personnel (M Ed), counseling and personnel services (PhD), counseling psychology (M Ed), mental health counseling (M Ed), school counseling (M Ed); counseling psychology (PhD); counselor education (PhD); rehabilitation counseling (M Ed, MA, AGSC); school counseling (M Ed, MA); school psychology (M Ed, MA, PhD). *Accreditation:* ACA (one or more programs are accredited); APA (one or more programs are accredited); CORE (one or more programs are accredited); NCATE. Part-time and evening/weekend programs available. Postbaccalaureate distance learning degree programs offered (no on-campus study). *Faculty:* 29 full-time (15 women), 6 part-time/adjunct (5 women). *Students:* 114 full-time (88 women), 12 part-time (9 women); includes 45 minority (17 Black or African American, non-Hispanic/Latino; 16 Asian, non-Hispanic/Latino; 10 Hispanic/Latino; 2 Two or more races, non-Hispanic/Latino), 15 international. 266 applicants, 12% accepted, 16 enrolled. In 2011, 30 master's, 15 doctorates awarded. *Median time to degree:* Of those who began their doctoral program in fall 2003, 60% received their degree in 8 years or less. *Degree requirements:* For master's, thesis (for some programs); for doctorate, thesis/dissertation. *Entrance requirements:* For master's, GRE General Test or MAT, minimum GPA of 3.0, 3 letters of recommendation; for doctorate, GRE General Test or MAT, minimum GPA of 3.5, 3 letters of recommendation. Additional exam requirements/recommendations for international students: Required—TOEFL. *Application deadline:* For fall admission, 12/15 for domestic and international students; for spring admission, 6/1 for international students. Applications are processed on a rolling basis. Application fee: $75. Electronic applications accepted. *Expenses: Tuition, area resident:* Part-time $525 per credit hour. Tuition, state resident: part-time $525 per credit hour. Tuition, nonresident: part-time $1131 per credit hour. *Required fees:* $386.31 per term. Tuition and fees vary according to program. *Financial support:* In 2011–12, 8 fellowships with full and partial tuition reimbursements (averaging $11,286 per year), 1 research assistantship (averaging $20,861 per year), 71 teaching assistantships with tuition reimbursements (averaging $16,237 per year) were awarded; career-related internships or fieldwork, Federal Work-Study, and scholarships/grants also available. Support available to part-time students. Financial award applicants required to submit FAFSA. *Faculty research:* Educational psychology, counseling, health. *Total annual research expenditures:* $589,600. *Unit head:* Dr. Dennis Kivlighan, Chair, 301-405-2858, E-mail: dennisk@umd.edu. *Application contact:* Dr. Charles A. Caramello, Dean of Graduate School, 301-405-0358, Fax: 301-314-9305.

University of Minnesota, Twin Cities Campus, Graduate School, College of Education and Human Development, Department of Educational Psychology, Program in Counseling and Student Personnel Psychology, Minneapolis, MN 55455-0213. Offers MA, PhD, Ed S. *Students:* 97 full-time (60 women), 15 part-time (13 women); includes 18 minority (8 Black or African American, non-Hispanic/Latino; 3 American Indian or Alaska Native, non-Hispanic/Latino; 5 Asian, non-Hispanic/Latino; 2 Hispanic/Latino), 21 international. Average age 28. 197 applicants, 42% accepted, 38 enrolled. In 2011, 38 master's, 7 doctorates, 1 other advanced degree awarded. Application fee: $55. *Unit head:* Dr. Susan Hupp, Chair, 612-624-1003, Fax: 612-624-8241, E-mail: shupp@umn.edu. *Application contact:* Dr. Jennifer Engler, Assistant Dean, 612-626-2887, Fax: 612-626-7496, E-mail: engle009@umn.edu. Web site: http://www.cehd.umn.edu/EdPsych/CSPP.

University of Mississippi, Graduate School, School of Education, Department of Educational Leadership and Counselor Education, Oxford, University, MS 38677. Offers counselor education (M Ed, PhD, Specialist); educational leadership (PhD); educational leadership and counselor education (M Ed, MA, Ed D, Ed S); higher education/student personnel (MA). *Accreditation:* ACA; NCATE. *Students:* 155 full-time (106 women), 177 part-time (110 women); includes 100 minority (91 Black or African American, non-Hispanic/Latino; 1 Asian, non-Hispanic/Latino; 5 Hispanic/Latino; 3 Two or more races, non-Hispanic/Latino), 7 international. In 2011, 82 master's, 13 doctorates, 36 other advanced degrees awarded. *Degree requirements:* For doctorate, thesis/dissertation. *Entrance requirements:* For master's, GRE General Test, minimum GPA of 3.0; for doctorate, GRE General Test. Additional exam requirements/recommendations for international students: Required—TOEFL. *Application deadline:* For fall admission, 4/1 for domestic students; for spring admission, 10/1 for domestic students. Applications are processed on a rolling basis. Application fee: $25. Electronic applications accepted. *Financial support:* Scholarships/grants available. Financial award application deadline: 3/1; financial award applicants required to submit FAFSA. *Unit head:* Dr. Timothy Letzring, Acting Chair, 662-915-7063, Fax: 662-915-7249. *Application contact:* Dr. Christy M. Wyandt, Associate Dean, 662-915-7474, Fax: 662-915-7577, E-mail: cwyandt@olemiss.edu.

University of Northern Colorado, Graduate School, College of Education and Behavioral Sciences, Department of Leadership, Policy and Development: Higher Education and P-12 Education, Program in Higher Education and Student Affairs Leadership, Greeley, CO 80639. Offers PhD. Part-time programs available. *Entrance requirements:* For doctorate, GRE General Test, transcripts, 3 letters of recommendation. Electronic applications accepted.

University of Northern Iowa, Graduate College, College of Education, Department of Educational Leadership, Counseling, and Postsecondary Education, Program in Postsecondary Education, Cedar Falls, IA 50614. Offers student affairs (MAE). *Students:* 26 full-time (19 women), 13 part-time (11 women); includes 10 minority (5 Black or African American, non-Hispanic/Latino; 1 Asian, non-Hispanic/Latino; 4 Hispanic/Latino). 48 applicants, 50% accepted, 17 enrolled. In 2011, 6 master's awarded. *Degree requirements:* For master's, comprehensive exam, thesis or alternative. *Entrance requirements:* For master's, minimum GPA of 3.0. Additional exam requirements/recommendations for international students: Required—TOEFL (minimum score 500 paper-based; 180 computer-based; 61 iBT). *Application deadline:* For fall admission, 8/1 priority date for domestic students. Applications are processed on a rolling basis. Application fee: $50 ($70 for international students). Electronic applications accepted. *Expenses:* Tuition, state resident: full-time $7476. Tuition, nonresident: full-time $16,410. *Required fees:* $942. *Financial support:* Career-related internships or fieldwork, Federal Work-Study, scholarships/grants, and tuition waivers (full) available. Financial award application deadline: 2/1. *Unit head:* Dr. Michael Waggoner, Professor, 319-273-2605, Fax: 319-273-5175, E-mail: mike.waggoner@uni.edu. *Application contact:* Laurie S. Russell, Record Analyst, 319-273-2623, Fax: 319-273-2885, E-mail: laurie.russell@uni.edu. Web site: http://www.uni.edu/coe/elpe/.

University of Rhode Island, Graduate School, College of Human Science and Services, Department of Human Development and Family Studies, Kingston, RI 02881. Offers college student personnel (MS); human development and family studies (MS); marriage and family therapy (MS). *Accreditation:* AAMFT/COAMFTE. Part-time programs available. *Faculty:* 13 full-time (10 women), 2 part-time/adjunct (both women). *Students:* 48 full-time (37 women), 13 part-time (10 women); includes 8 minority (3 Black or African American, non-Hispanic/Latino; 1 Asian, non-Hispanic/Latino; 3 Hispanic/Latino; 1 Native Hawaiian or other Pacific Islander, non-Hispanic/Latino), 2 international. In 2011, 22 master's awarded. *Degree requirements:* For master's, comprehensive exam (for some programs), thesis optional. *Entrance requirements:* For master's, GRE or MAT, 2 letters of recommendation. Additional exam requirements/recommendations for international students: Required—TOEFL (minimum score 550 paper-based; 213 computer-based). Application fee: $65. Electronic applications accepted. *Expenses:* Tuition, state resident: full-time $10,432; part-time $580 per credit hour. Tuition, nonresident: full-time $23,130; part-time $1285 per credit hour. *Required fees:* $1362; $36 per credit hour. $35 per semester. One-time fee: $130. *Financial support:* In 2011–12, 2 research assistantships with full and partial tuition reimbursements (averaging $8,043 per year), 4 teaching assistantships with full and partial tuition reimbursements (averaging $7,939 per year) were awarded. Financial award applicants required to submit FAFSA. *Unit head:* Dr. Jerome Adams, Chair, 401-874-5962, Fax: 401-874-4020, E-mail: jadams@uri.edu. *Application contact:* Nasser H. Zawia, Dean of the Graduate School, 401-874-5909, Fax: 401-874-5787, E-mail: nzawia@uri.edu. Web site: http://www.uri.edu/hss/hdf/.

University of Rochester, Margaret Warner Graduate School of Education and Human Development, Master's Program in Higher Education, Rochester, NY 14627. Offers higher education (MS); higher education student affairs (MS). *Expenses: Tuition:* Full-time $41,040.

University of St. Thomas, Graduate Studies, School of Education, Department of Leadership, Policy and Administration, St. Paul, MN 55105-1096. Offers community education administration (MA); educational leadership (Ed S); educational leadership and administration (MA); international leadership (MA, Certificate); leadership (Ed D); leadership in student affairs (MA, Certificate); police leadership (MA); public policy and leadership (MA, Certificate). Part-time and evening/weekend programs available.

Faculty: 8 full-time (3 women), 17 part-time/adjunct (7 women). *Students:* 47 full-time (34 women), 325 part-time (172 women); includes 54 minority (26 Black or African American, non-Hispanic/Latino; 3 American Indian or Alaska Native, non-Hispanic/ Latino; 14 Asian, non-Hispanic/Latino; 7 Hispanic/Latino; 4 Two or more races, non-Hispanic/Latino), 11 international. Average age 37. 170 applicants, 80% accepted, 93 enrolled. In 2011, 72 master's, 17 doctorates, 39 other advanced degrees awarded. Terminal master's awarded for partial completion of doctoral program. *Degree requirements:* For master's, thesis (for some programs); for doctorate, thesis/ dissertation; for other advanced degree, thesis or alternative. *Entrance requirements:* For master's, minimum GPA of 3.0 or MAT; for doctorate, MAT, minimum graduate GPA of 3.5; for other advanced degree, minimum graduate GPA of 3.25 or MAT. Additional exam requirements/recommendations for international students: Required—TOEFL (minimum score 550 paper-based; 213 computer-based; 20 iBT). *Application deadline:* For fall admission, 6/1 priority date for domestic students; for spring admission, 11/1 priority date for domestic students. Applications are processed on a rolling basis. Application fee: $50. *Expenses:* Contact institution. *Financial support:* Fellowships, research assistantships, institutionally sponsored loans, and scholarships/grants available. Support available to part-time students. Financial award applicants required to submit FAFSA. *Unit head:* Dr. Donald R. LaMagdeleine, Chair, 651-962-4893, Fax: 651-962-4169, E-mail: drlamagdelei@stthomas.edu. *Application contact:* Jackie Grossklaus, Department Assistant, 651-962-4885, Fax: 651-962-4169, E-mail: jmgrossklaus@stthomas.edu. Web site: http://www.stthomas.edu/education.

University of South Carolina, The Graduate School, College of Education, Department of Educational Leadership and Policies, Program in Higher Education and Student Affairs, Columbia, SC 29208. Offers M Ed. *Accreditation:* NCATE. Part-time programs available. *Degree requirements:* For master's, comprehensive exam, thesis (for some programs). *Entrance requirements:* For master's, GRE General Test or MAT, letters of reference. Electronic applications accepted. *Faculty research:* Minorities in higher education, community college transfer problem, federal role in educational research.

University of Southern California, Graduate School, Rossier School of Education, Master's Programs in Education, Los Angeles, CA 90089-4038. Offers educational counseling (ME); marriage, family and child counseling (MMFT); postsecondary administration and student affairs [PASA] (ME); school counseling (ME); teaching (online) (MAT); teaching and teaching credential (MAT); teaching English to speakers of other languages (MAT). Part-time and evening/weekend programs available. Postbaccalaureate distance learning degree programs offered (no on-campus study). *Degree requirements:* For master's, thesis optional. *Entrance requirements:* For master's, GRE (for all programs except MAT). Additional exam requirements/ recommendations for international students: Required—TOEFL (minimum score 250 computer-based; 100 iBT). Electronic applications accepted. *Faculty research:* College access and equity, preparing teachers for culturally diverse populations, sociocultural basis of learning as mediated by instruction with focus on reading and literacy in English learners, social and political aspects of teaching and learning English, school counselor development and training.

University of Southern Mississippi, Graduate School, College of Education and Psychology, Department of Educational Studies and Research, Hattiesburg, MS 39406-0001. Offers adult education (Graduate Certificate); community college leadership (Graduate Certificate); counseling and personnel services (college) (M Ed); education (PhD, Ed S), including adult education, research, evaluation and statistics (PhD); education (Ed D), including educational administration, educational research; education: educational leadership and research (Ed S), including higher education administration; educational administration and supervision (M Ed); higher education administration (Ed D, PhD); institutional research (Graduate Certificate). *Faculty:* 7 full-time (1 woman), 5 part-time/adjunct (1 woman). *Students:* 33 full-time (25 women), 104 part-time (25 women); includes 46 minority (40 Black or African American, non-Hispanic/ Latino; 1 Asian, non-Hispanic/Latino; 3 Hispanic/Latino; 2 Two or more races, non-Hispanic/Latino), 1 international. Average age 36. 27 applicants, 48% accepted, 1 enrolled. In 2011, 27 master's, 13 doctorates, 1 other advanced degree awarded. *Degree requirements:* For master's and other advanced degree, comprehensive exam, thesis (for some programs); for doctorate, comprehensive exam, thesis/dissertation. *Entrance requirements:* For master's, doctorate, and other advanced degree, GRE General Test, minimum GPA of 2.75. Additional exam requirements/recommendations for international students: Required—TOEFL. *Application deadline:* For fall admission, 2/ 1 for domestic students, 3/1 for international students. Applications are processed on a rolling basis. Application fee: $35. *Financial support:* Career-related internships or fieldwork, Federal Work-Study, and institutionally sponsored loans available. Financial award application deadline: 3/15; financial award applicants required to submit FAFSA. *Total annual research expenditures:* $88,500. *Unit head:* Dr. Thomas V. O'Brien, Chair, 601-266-6093, E-mail: thomas.obrien@usm.edu. *Application contact:* Shonna Breland, Manager of Graduate Admissions, 601-266-6563, Fax: 601-266-5138. Web site: http://www.usm.edu/cep/esr/.

University of South Florida, Graduate School, College of Education, Department of Psychological and Social Foundations, Tampa, FL 33620-9951. Offers college student affairs (M Ed); counselor education (MA, PhD, Ed S); interdisciplinary (PhD, Ed S); school psychology (PhD, Ed S). Part-time and evening/weekend programs available. *Faculty:* 22 full-time (13 women), 6 part-time/adjunct (4 women). *Students:* 172 full-time (135 women), 81 part-time (61 women); includes 59 minority (28 Black or African American, non-Hispanic/Latino; 4 Asian, non-Hispanic/Latino; 22 Hispanic/Latino; 5 Two or more races, non-Hispanic/Latino), 7 international. Average age 30. 243 applicants, 57% accepted, 110 enrolled. In 2011, 70 master's, 15 doctorates, 5 other advanced degrees awarded. *Degree requirements:* For master's, comprehensive exam, thesis (for some programs); for doctorate, comprehensive exam, thesis/dissertation, multiple research methods; philosophies of inquiry (for some programs). *Entrance requirements:* For master's, GRE General Test, minimum GPA of 3.5 in last 60 hours of course work; for doctorate, GRE General Test, MAT, minimum GPA of 3.5 in last 60 hours of course work; for Ed S, GRE General Test. Additional exam requirements/recommendations for international students: Required—TOEFL (minimum score 550 paper-based; 213 computer-based; 79 iBT). *Application deadline:* For fall admission, 1/1 for domestic students, 1/2 for international students. Application fee: $30. Electronic applications accepted. *Financial support:* In 2011–12, 47 students received support, including 6 fellowships with full tuition reimbursements available (averaging $10,000 per year), 6 research assistantships with full tuition reimbursements available (averaging $15,000 per year), 21 teaching assistantships with full tuition reimbursements available (averaging $10,200 per year); career-related internships or fieldwork, scholarships/ grants, and unspecified assistantships also available. Financial award application deadline: 1/1; financial award applicants required to submit CSS PROFILE. *Faculty research:* College student affairs, counselor education, educational psychology, school psychology, social foundations. *Total annual research expenditures:* $4.2 million. *Unit head:* Dr. Herbert Exum, Chairperson, 813-974-8395, Fax: 813-974-5814, E-mail: exum@tempest.coedu.usf.edu. *Application contact:* Dr. Kathy Bradley, Program Director, School Psychology, 813-974-9486, Fax: 813-974-5814, E-mail: kbradley@usf.edu. Web site: http://www.coedu.usf.edu/main/departments/psf/psf.html.

The University of Tennessee, Graduate School, College of Education, Health and Human Sciences, Department of Educational Psychology and Counseling, Program in College Student Personnel, Knoxville, TN 37996. Offers MS. *Accreditation:* NCATE. Part-time programs available. *Degree requirements:* For master's, thesis optional. *Entrance requirements:* For master's, GRE General Test, minimum GPA of 2.7. Additional exam requirements/recommendations for international students: Required—TOEFL. Electronic applications accepted. *Expenses:* Tuition, state resident: full-time $8332; part-time $464 per credit hour. Tuition, nonresident: full-time $25,174; part-time $1400 per credit hour. *Required fees:* $1162; $56 per credit hour. Tuition and fees vary according to program.

University of the Cumberlands, Graduate Programs in Education, Williamsburg, KY 40769-1372. Offers all grades (P-12) (M Ed); business and marketing (MA Ed, MAT); director of pupil personnel (Certificate); director of special education (Certificate); educational administration and supervision (Ed S); educational leadership (Ed D); elementary education (MA Ed, MAT); instructional leadership - principalship (MA Ed); instructional leadership - school principal (Certificate); middle school education (MA Ed, MAT); reading and writing (MA Ed); school counseling (MA Ed); school superintendent (Certificate); secondary education (MA Ed, MAT); special education (MAT); supervisor of instruction (Certificate); teacher leader (MA Ed). Part-time and evening/weekend programs available. Postbaccalaureate distance learning degree programs offered. *Degree requirements:* For master's, comprehensive exam. Electronic applications accepted.

University of Virginia, Curry School of Education, Department of Leadership, Foundations and Policy, Program in Higher Education, Charlottesville, VA 22903. Offers higher education (Ed S); student affairs practice (M Ed). *Students:* 23 full-time (12 women), 18 part-time (9 women); includes 6 minority (5 Black or African American, non-Hispanic/Latino; 1 Asian, non-Hispanic/Latino). Average age 31. 15 applicants, 60% accepted, 8 enrolled. In 2011, 16 master's awarded. *Entrance requirements:* For master's, doctorate, and Ed S, GRE General Test, 2 letters of recommendation. Additional exam requirements/recommendations for international students: Required—TOEFL (minimum score 600 paper-based; 250 computer-based; 90 iBT), IELTS (minimum score 7). *Application deadline:* Applications are processed on a rolling basis. Application fee: $60. Electronic applications accepted. *Financial support:* Fellowships, research assistantships, and teaching assistantships available. Financial award applicants required to submit FAFSA. *Unit head:* Brian Pusser, Associate Professor and Director, 434-924-7782, E-mail: highered@virginia.edu. *Application contact:* Lisa Miller, Assistant to the Chair, 434-982-2849, E-mail: lam3v@virgnina.edu. Web site: http://curry.virginia.edu/academics/areas-of-study/higher-education.

The University of West Alabama, School of Graduate Studies, College of Education, Departments of Instructional Leadership and Support/Curriculum and Instruction, Livinston, AL 35470. Offers college student development (MSCE); continuing education (MSCE); early childhood education (M Ed); elementary education (M Ed); guidance and counseling (M Ed, MSCE), including continuing education (MSCE), guidance and counseling (M Ed); instructional leadership (M Ed); library media (M Ed); secondary education (MAT); special education (M Ed). *Accreditation:* NCATE. Part-time and evening/weekend programs available. *Faculty:* 37 full-time (19 women), 80 part-time/ adjunct (53 women). *Students:* 2,849 full-time (2,450 women), 333 part-time (267 women); includes 1,988 minority (1,947 Black or African American, non-Hispanic/Latino; 17 American Indian or Alaska Native, non-Hispanic/Latino; 3 Asian, non-Hispanic/ Latino; 18 Hispanic/Latino; 3 Two or more races, non-Hispanic/Latino), 3 international. In 2011, 944 master's awarded. *Degree requirements:* For master's, comprehensive exam. *Entrance requirements:* For master's, GRE General Test, MAT, minimum GPA of 2.75. Additional exam requirements/recommendations for international students: Required—TOEFL (minimum score 61 computer-based). *Application deadline:* For fall admission, 9/10 priority date for domestic students; for spring admission, 3/24 for domestic students. Applications are processed on a rolling basis. Application fee: $25 ($50 for international students). *Expenses:* Tuition, state resident: full-time $5112; part-time $284 per credit hour. Tuition, nonresident: full-time $10,224; part-time $568 per credit hour. *Required fees:* $180; $40 per semester. One-time fee: $65. Tuition and fees vary according to class time, course load, campus/location and program. *Financial support:* In 2011–12, 35 students received support, including 35 teaching assistantships (averaging $9,600 per year); career-related internships or fieldwork, Federal Work-Study, scholarships/grants, and unspecified assistantships also available. Support available to part-time students. Financial award application deadline: 3/1. *Unit head:* Dr. Jan Miller, Chair of Instructional Leadership and Support, 205-652-3445, Fax: 205-652-3706, E-mail: jmiller@uwa.edu. *Application contact:* Dr. Kathy Chandler, Dean of Graduate Studies, 205-652-3421, Fax: 205-652-3670, E-mail: kchandler@uwa.edu. Web site: http://www.uwa.edu/ils/.

University of West Florida, College of Professional Studies, Department of Research and Applied Studies, Pensacola, FL 32514-5750. Offers administration (MSA), including acquisition and contract administration, biomedical/pharmaceutical, criminal justice administration, database administration, education leadership, healthcare administration, human performance technology, leadership, nursing administration, public administration, software engineering and administration; college student personnel administration (M Ed), including college personnel administration, guidance and counseling; curriculum and instruction (M Ed, Ed S); educational leadership (M Ed); middle and secondary level education and ESOL (M Ed). Part-time and evening/ weekend programs available. *Faculty:* 2 full-time (both women), 3 part-time/adjunct (2 women). *Students:* 26 full-time (15 women), 13 part-time (9 women); includes 8 minority (4 Black or African American, non-Hispanic/Latino; 2 American Indian or Alaska Native, non-Hispanic/Latino; 1 Hispanic/Latino; 1 Two or more races, non-Hispanic/Latino), 1 international. Average age 26. 51 applicants, 51% accepted, 16 enrolled. In 2011, 17 master's, 49 Ed Ss awarded. *Entrance requirements:* For master's, GRE or MAT, official transcripts; minimum undergraduate GPA of 3.0; letter of intent; three letters of recommendation; resume. Additional exam requirements/recommendations for international students: Required—TOEFL (minimum score 550 paper-based; 213 computer-based). *Application deadline:* For fall admission, 6/1 for domestic and international students; for spring admission, 10/1 for domestic and international students. Applications are processed on a rolling basis. Application fee: $30. *Expenses:* Tuition, state resident: full-time $5729; part-time $302 per credit hour. Tuition, nonresident: full-time $20,059; part-time $961 per credit hour. *Required fees:* $1509; $63 per credit hour. *Financial support:* In 2011–12, 33 fellowships (averaging $860 per year), 10 research assistantships (averaging $3,280 per year), 2 teaching assistantships (averaging $3,760 per year) were awarded; unspecified assistantships also available. Financial award application deadline: 4/15; financial award applicants required to submit FAFSA. *Unit head:* Dr. Joyce Nichols, Chairperson, 850-857-6042, E-mail: jcoleman0@uwf.edu. *Application contact:* Terry McCray, Assistant Director of Graduate Admissions, 850-473-7718, Fax: 850-473-7714, E-mail: gradadmissions@uwf.edu. Web site: http://uwf.edu/pcl/.

University of Wisconsin–La Crosse, Office of University Graduate Studies, College of Liberal Studies, Department of Student Affairs Administration in Higher Education, La Crosse, WI 54601-3742. Offers MS Ed. Part-time programs available. Postbaccalaureate distance learning degree programs offered (no on-campus study).

Faculty: 1 full-time (0 women), 11 part-time/adjunct (5 women). *Students:* 34 full-time (25 women), 42 part-time (30 women); includes 8 minority (2 Black or African American, non-Hispanic/Latino; 1 American Indian or Alaska Native, non-Hispanic/Latino; 2 Asian, non-Hispanic/Latino; 2 Hispanic/Latino; 1 Two or more races, non-Hispanic/Latino). Average age 29. 71 applicants, 55% accepted, 16 enrolled. In 2011, 36 master's awarded. *Degree requirements:* For master's, comprehensive exam (for some programs), thesis optional, electronic portfolio, applied research project. *Entrance requirements:* For master's, interview, writing sample, references, experience in the field. Additional exam requirements/recommendations for international students: Required—TOEFL (minimum score 550 paper-based; 213 computer-based; 79 iBT). *Application deadline:* For fall admission, 2/1 priority date for domestic students, 2/1 for international students. Application fee: $56. Electronic applications accepted. *Expenses:* Tuition, state resident: full-time $8391; part-time $481.17 per credit. Tuition, nonresident: full-time $17,850; part-time $1006.68 per credit. *Required fees:* $2 per credit. $18.25 per semester. Tuition and fees vary according to course load, program, reciprocity agreements and student level. *Financial support:* In 2011–12, 32 research assistantships with partial tuition reimbursements (averaging $10,016 per year) were awarded; Federal Work-Study, scholarships/grants, and health care benefits also available. Support available to part-time students. Financial award application deadline: 3/15; financial award applicants required to submit FAFSA. *Unit head:* Dr. Jodie Rindt, Director, 608-785-6450, E-mail: rindt.jodi@uwlax.edu. *Application contact:* Kathryn Kiefer, Director of Admissions, 608-785-8939, E-mail: admissions@uwlax.edu. Web site: http://www.uwlax.edu/saa/.

University of Wyoming, College of Education, Programs in Counselor Education, Laramie, WY 82070. Offers community mental health (MS); counselor education and supervision (PhD); school counseling (MS); student affairs (MS). *Accreditation:* ACA (one or more programs are accredited). *Degree requirements:* For master's, comprehensive exam (for some programs), thesis optional; for doctorate, thesis/dissertation, video demonstration. *Entrance requirements:* For master's, interview, background check; for doctorate, video tape session, interview, writing sample, master's degree, background check. Additional exam requirements/recommendations for international students: Required—TOEFL. *Faculty research:* Wyoming SAGE photovoice project; accountable school counseling programs; GLBT issues; addictions; play therapy-early childhood mental health.

Virginia Commonwealth University, Graduate School, School of Education, Program in Counselor Education, Richmond, VA 23284-9005. Offers college student development and counseling (M Ed); school counseling (M Ed). *Accreditation:* ACA; NCATE. *Entrance requirements:* For master's, GRE General Test or MAT. Additional exam requirements/recommendations for international students: Required—TOEFL (minimum score 600 paper-based; 250 computer-based; 100 iBT). Electronic applications accepted. *Expenses:* Tuition, state resident: full-time $9133; part-time $507 per credit. Tuition, nonresident: full-time $18,777; part-time $1043 per credit. *Required fees:* $77 per credit. Tuition and fees vary according to degree level, campus/location, program and student level.

Washington State University, Graduate School, College of Education, Department of Educational Leadership and Counseling Psychology, Pullman, WA 99164. Offers counseling psychology (Ed M, MA, PhD, Certificate), including counseling psychology (Ed M, MA, PhD), school psychologist (Certificate); educational leadership (M Ed, MA, Ed D, PhD); educational psychology (Ed M, MA, PhD); higher education (Ed M, MA, Ed D, PhD), including higher education administration (PhD), sport management (PhD), student affairs (PhD); higher education with sport management (Ed M). *Accreditation:* NCATE. *Faculty:* 12. *Students:* 103 full-time (68 women), 59 part-time (29 women); includes 36 minority (6 Black or African American, non-Hispanic/Latino; 10 Asian, non-Hispanic/Latino; 16 Hispanic/Latino; 4 Two or more races, non-Hispanic/Latino), 18 international. Average age 30. 244 applicants, 29% accepted, 45 enrolled. In 2011, 44 master's, 11 doctorates awarded. Terminal master's awarded for partial completion of doctoral program. *Degree requirements:* For master's, comprehensive exam (for some programs), thesis (for some programs), oral or written exam; for doctorate, comprehensive exam, thesis/dissertation, oral and written exams. *Entrance requirements:* For master's and doctorate, GRE General Test, minimum GPA of 3.0, 3 letters of recommendation. Additional exam requirements/recommendations for international students: Required—TOEFL (minimum score 550 paper-based; 213 computer-based). *Application deadline:* For fall admission, 3/1 for domestic and international students; for spring admission, 10/1 for domestic students, 7/1 for international students. Application fee: $75. *Financial support:* In 2011–12, 1 research assistantship (averaging $18,204 per year), 4 teaching assistantships (averaging $18,204 per year) were awarded; career-related internships or fieldwork, Federal Work-Study, institutionally sponsored loans, scholarships/grants, tuition waivers (partial), and unspecified assistantships also available. Financial award application deadline: 4/1; financial award applicants required to submit FAFSA. *Faculty research:* Attentional processes, cross-cultural psychology, faculty development in higher education. *Total annual research expenditures:* $554,000. *Unit head:* Dr. Phyllis Erdman, Associate Dean, 509-335-9117, E-mail: perdman@wsu.edu. *Application contact:* Graduate School Admissions, 800-GRADWSU, Fax: 509-335-1949, E-mail: gradsch@wsu.edu. Web site: http://www.educ.wsu.edu/elcp/.

Western Illinois University, School of Graduate Studies, College of Education and Human Services, Department of Educational and Interdisciplinary Studies, Program in College Student Personnel, Macomb, IL 61455-1390. Offers MS. *Accreditation:* NCATE. Part-time programs available. *Students:* 42 full-time (27 women); includes 8 minority (5 Black or African American, non-Hispanic/Latino; 1 Asian, non-Hispanic/Latino; 1 Hispanic/Latino; 1 Two or more races, non-Hispanic/Latino), 2 international. Average age 24. 98 applicants, 22% accepted. In 2011, 21 master's awarded. *Degree requirements:* For master's, thesis or alternative. *Entrance requirements:* For master's, interview. Additional exam requirements/recommendations for international students: Required—TOEFL (minimum score 550 paper-based; 213 computer-based; 80 iBT). *Application deadline:* For fall admission, 1/15 priority date for domestic students. Applications are processed on a rolling basis. Application fee: $30. Electronic applications accepted. *Expenses:* Tuition, state resident: part-time $281.16 per credit hour. Tuition, nonresident: part-time $562.32 per credit hour. Part-time tuition and fees vary according to campus/location and reciprocity agreements. *Financial support:* In 2011–12, 42 students received support, including 42 research assistantships with full tuition reimbursements available (averaging $7,360 per year). Financial award applicants required to submit FAFSA. *Unit head:* Dr. Tracy Davis, Coordinator, 309-298-1183. *Application contact:* Dr. Nancy Parsons, Interim Associate Provost and Director of Graduate Studies, 309-298-1806, Fax: 309-298-2345, E-mail: grad-office@wiu.edu. Web site: http://wiu.edu/csp/.

Western Kentucky University, Graduate Studies, College of Education and Behavioral Sciences, Department of Counseling and Student Affairs, Bowling Green, KY 42101. Offers counseling (MA Ed), including marriage and family therapy, mental health counseling; school counseling (P-12) (MA Ed); student affairs in higher education (MA Ed). *Accreditation:* ACA; NCATE. Part-time and evening/weekend programs available. *Degree requirements:* For master's, comprehensive exam, thesis optional. *Entrance requirements:* For master's, GRE General Test. Additional exam requirements/recommendations for international students: Required—TOEFL (minimum score 555 paper-based; 213 computer-based; 79 iBT). *Faculty research:* Counselor education, research for residential workers.

ARGOSY UNIVERSITY, ATLANTA

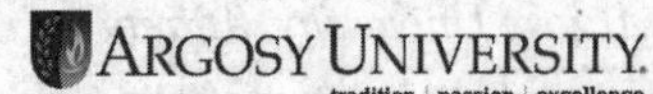

College of Education

Programs of Study

Argosy University, Atlanta, offers Master of Arts in Education (M.A.Ed.) degrees in Curriculum and Instruction, Curriculum and Instruction: ELL/ESL, Curriculum and Instruction: Reading, Curriculum and Instruction: Special Education, Educational Leadership, Higher and Postsecondary Education, and Teaching and Learning; Doctor of Education (Ed.D.) degrees in Curriculum and Instruction, Higher and Postsecondary Education, Teacher Leadership, and Teaching and Learning; and Education Specialist (Ed.S.) degrees in Curriculum and Instruction, Higher and Postsecondary Education and Teaching and Learning.

The Master of Arts in Education (M.A.Ed.) in Curriculum and Instruction degree program is intended to prepare educators who work in the P–12 setting as change agents who engage actively in their communities, using appropriate pedagogy and technology to foster the development of global citizens. In addition to the core course requirements, students enrolled in this degree program will complete a four-course sequence designed to strengthen educators' knowledge and skills in order to work more effectively in the current classroom environment. This degree program does not lead to certification or credential endorsement.

The Master of Arts in Education (M.A.Ed.) in Curriculum and Instruction: ELL/ESL degree program is a 30-credit-hour degree program intended to prepare educators who work in the P–12 setting as change agents who engage actively in their communities, using appropriate pedagogy and technology to foster the development of global citizens. In addition to the core course requirements, students enrolled in this degree program will complete a four course sequence designed to strengthen educators' knowledge and skills when working with students who are classified as English Language Learners (ELL) or English as a Second Language (ESL). This degree program does not lead to certification or credential endorsement.

The Master of Arts in Education (M.A.Ed.) in Curriculum and Instruction: Reading degree program is a 30-credit-hour program intended to prepare educators who work in the P–12 setting as change agents who engage actively in their communities, using appropriate pedagogy and technology to foster the development of global citizens. Students enrolled in this program will complete a four course sequence in reading designed to strengthen educators' knowledge and skills in this specific area of focus. This program does not lead to certification or credential endorsement.

The Master of Arts in Education (M.A.Ed.) in Curriculum and Instruction: Special Education degree program is a 30-credit-hour program intended to prepare educators who work in the P-12 setting as change agents who engage actively in their communities, using appropriate pedagogy and technology to foster the development of global citizens. Students enrolled in this program will complete a four course sequence designed to strengthen educators' knowledge and skills when working with students with special learning needs. This program does not lead to certification or credential endorsement.

The Master of Arts in Education (M.A.Ed.) in Educational Leadership noncertification program is designed to prepare graduates for roles as effective leaders in education. Students have the opportunity to develop core practical and academic skills in analysis, oral and written communication, problem solving, critical thinking, team-building, and computer technology, through courses that examine the practical, historical, philosophical, psychological, social, technical, and theoretical aspects of education.

The Master of Arts in Education (M.A.Ed.) in Higher and Postsecondary Education program is designed for individuals who seek administrative and other positions in noninstructional units at higher education and postsecondary institutions. Graduates of this program will have enhanced practical skills, knowledge, and experiences as professionals and leaders in universities, colleges, and postsecondary educational institutions. A bachelor's degree is required for admission to this program.

The Master of Arts in Education (M.A.Ed.) in Teaching and Learning noncertification program is for students who wish to develop or enhance classroom skills, become curriculum supervisors, or become educational leaders with instruction as their main focus.

The Doctor of Education (Ed.D.) in Curriculum and Instruction degree program is designed to prepare educators as change agents and leaders in the P-12 setting who engage actively in their communities, using appropriate pedagogy and technology to foster the development of global citizens. This program does not lead to certification or credential endorsement.

The Doctor of Education (Ed.D.) in Higher and Postsecondary Education program is designed for students to enhance their professional competence as educational leaders, instructors, or consultants in academic affairs, student affairs, or student services divisions within community colleges, technical schools and institutes, and four-year colleges and universities, as well as in government, military, religious, and profit or nonprofit postsecondary educational organizations and divisions. The program offers three concentrations: student affairs and services, teaching and learning, and interdisciplinary studies.

The Doctor of Education (Ed.D.) in Teacher Leadership degree program is a 60-credit-hour program designed for classroom teachers who are looking to expand their content knowledge, develop leadership skills, teach more effectively, and support the professional development of their peers. Candidates in this degree program will have the opportunity to become skillful in building collaborative relationships and learning communities that focus on student learning and support a strong positive climate in the school. Peer mentoring and coaching are modeled and practiced throughout the program in field experiences and the culminating research project. The program culminates in a dissertation related to teacher leadership and is designed to add knowledge to the field of teacher leadership. The Ed.D. in Teacher Leadership degree program does not prepare for or lead to teacher or school administrative certification/ licensure.

The Doctor of Education (Ed.D.) in Teaching and Learning noncertification program is designed for students who wish to master teaching methodologies, become curriculum supervisors, or become educational leaders with curriculum and instruction as their main focus. Students must choose a concentration in education technology, higher education, or K–12 education.

The Education Specialist (Ed.S.) in Curriculum and Instruction degree program is designed to prepare educators as change agents and leaders in the P-12 setting who engage actively in their communities, using appropriate pedagogy and technology to foster the development of global citizens. This program does not lead to certification or any credential endorsement.

The Education Specialist (Ed.S.) in Higher and Postsecondary Education program is designed for students to enhance their professional competence as educational leaders, instructors, or consultants in academic affairs, student affairs, or student services divisions within community colleges, technical schools and institutes, four-year colleges and universities, as well as in government, military, religious, profit or nonprofit postsecondary educational organizations and divisions. The program offers three concentrations: student affairs and services, teaching and learning, and interdisciplinary studies.

The Education Specialist (Ed.S.) in Teaching and Learning noncertification program prepares educators to serve in the P–12 setting as change agents and leaders who engage actively in their communities, using appropriate pedagogy and technology to foster the development of global citizens.

Research Facilities

Argosy University libraries provide curriculum support and educational resources, including current text materials, diagnostic training documents, reference materials and databases, journals and dissertations, and major and current titles in program areas. There is an online public-access catalog of library resources available throughout the Argosy University system. Students have remote access to the campus library database, enabling them to study and conduct research at home. Academic databases offer dissertation abstracts, academic journals, and professional periodicals. All library computers are Internet accessible. Software applications include Word, Excel, PowerPoint, SPSS, and various test-scoring programs.

Financial Aid

Financial aid is available to those who qualify. Argosy University, Atlanta, offers access to federal and state aid programs, merit-based awards, grants, loans, and a work-study program. As a first step, students should complete the Free Application for Federal Student Aid (FAFSA). Prospective students can apply electronically at http://www.fafsa.ed.gov or at the campus.

Cost of Study

Tuition varies by program. Students should contact Argosy University, Atlanta, for tuition information.

Living and Housing Costs

Students typically live in apartments in the metropolitan Atlanta area. Living expenses vary according to each student's preferred standard of living, housing, and transportation. The University does not offer or operate student housing. Most of the students are full-time working professionals who live within driving distance of the campus. Several nearby hotels offer special rates for those who commute from long distances. The Admissions Department also maintains a list of housing options, including contact information for University students who wish to share housing. For more information, students should contact the Admissions Department.

Student Group

Admission to Argosy University, Atlanta, is selective to ensure a dynamic and engaged student body. It encourages diversity in academic and employment backgrounds and promotes integration of the student body into professional life through established connections with local and national professional associations. Argosy University offers a professionally oriented education with rich opportunities to gain practical experience in class, field placements, and internships. Full-time students and working professionals gain the extensive knowledge and range of skills necessary for effective performance in their chosen fields.

Student Outcomes

Students can register with the University's online career-services system and use select services from a distance, such as degree-specific career e-mail lists, national job posts, and virtual job fairs. Students should contact the University for more information.

Location

Argosy University, Atlanta, is housed in a modern building in Sandy Springs, a northern suburb of Atlanta. The campus features a cafe and outdoor lakeside terrace. Beyond the University, students find a wide selection of affordable housing options. This major metropolitan area offers many social and recreational opportunities, from clubs and concerts to galleries and museums, from a growing restaurant scene to Braves baseball games and rollerblading in Piedmont Park.

Many educational institutions and agencies in the area provide varied opportunities for student training. Atlanta's business environment includes technology companies such as EarthLink and Macquarium, as well as corporate giants such as the Coca-Cola Company, CNN, Delta Air Lines, AT&T, and Georgia Pacific.

The University

Argosy University is a private institution with nineteen locations across the nation. Argosy University, Atlanta, provides students with a career resources office, an academic resources center, and extensive information access for research. It offers the resources of a large university, plus the friendliness and personal attention of a small campus. Argosy University, Atlanta, is closely associated with the Franklin, Tennessee campus, an approved degree site near Nashville.

The innovative programs feature dynamic, relevant, and practical curricula delivered in flexible class formats. Students enjoy scheduling options that make it easier to fit school into their busy lives, choosing from day and evening courses, on campus or online. Many students find a combination of class formats to be an ideal way of continuing their education while meeting family and professional demands.

Argosy University is accredited by the Accrediting Commission for Senior Colleges and Universities of the Western Association of Schools and Colleges (985 Atlantic Avenue, Suite 100, Alameda, California, 94501, http://www.wascsenior.org).

Applying

Argosy University, Atlanta, accepts students year-round on a rolling admissions basis, depending on availability of required courses. Applications for admission are available online or by contacting the campus.

Correspondence and Information

Argosy University, Atlanta
980 Hammond Drive, Suite 100
Atlanta, Georgia 30328
United States
Phone: 770-671-1200
888-671-4777 (toll-free)
Fax: 770-671-9055
E-mail: auadmissions@argosy.edu
Web site: http://www.argosy.edu/atlanta

THE FACULTY

The Argosy University faculty comprises working professionals who are eager to help students succeed. Members bring real-world experience and the latest practice innovations to the academic setting. The diverse faculty members of the College of Education are widely recognized for contributions to the field. Many are published scholars, and most hold doctoral degrees. They provide a substantive education that combines comprehensive knowledge with critical skills and practical workplace relevance. Above all, faculty members are committed to their students' personal and professional development.

ARGOSY UNIVERSITY, INLAND EMPIRE

College of Education

Programs of Study

Argosy University, Inland Empire, offers Master of Arts in Education (M.A.Ed.) degrees in Educational Administration, Higher and Postsecondary Education, Teaching and Learning: ELL/ESL, Teaching and Learning: Reading, and Teaching and Learning: Special Education; Doctor of Education (Ed.D.) degrees in Higher and Postsecondary Education, Initial Educational Administration, and Teaching and Learning; and Educational Specialist (Ed.S.) degrees in Higher and Postsecondary Education and Initial Educational Administration.

The Master of Arts in Education (M.A.Ed.) in Educational Administration program prepares individuals to serve as school administrators. The program is designed for practicing educators who have already completed a bachelor's degree program from a regionally accredited institution and are seeking administrative credentialing. Based on state requirements, students may be required to complete additional experiences or course work.

The Master of Arts in Education (M.A.Ed.) in Higher and Postsecondary Education program is designed for individuals who seek administrative and other positions in noninstructional units at higher education and postsecondary institutions. Graduates of this program will have enhanced practical skills, knowledge, and experiences as professionals and leaders in universities, colleges, and postsecondary educational institutions. A bachelor's degree is required for admission to this program.

The Master of Arts in Education (M.A.Ed.) in Teaching and Learning: ELL/ESL is a 30-credit-hour degree program intended to prepare educators who work in the P–12 setting as change agents who engage actively in their communities, using appropriate pedagogy and technology to foster the development of global citizens. In addition to the core course requirements, students will complete a four-course sequence to strengthen knowledge and skills when working with students who are classified as English Language Learners (ELL) or English as a Second Language (ESL). This program does not lead to certification or credential endorsement.

The Master of Arts in Education (M.A.Ed.) in Teaching and Learning: Reading is a 30-credit program intended to prepare educators who work in the P–12 setting as change agents who engage actively in their communities, using appropriate pedagogy and technology to foster the development of global citizens. Students enrolled in this program will complete a four-course sequence in reading to strengthen knowledge and skills in this specific area. This program does not lead to certification or credential endorsement.

The Master of Arts in Education (M.A.Ed.) in Teaching and Learning: Special Education is a 30-credit program intended to prepare educators who work in the P–12 setting as change agents who engage actively in their communities, using appropriate pedagogy and technology to foster the development of global citizens. Students enrolled in this program will complete a four-course sequence designed to strengthen knowledge and skills when working with students with special learning needs. This program does not lead to certification or credential endorsement.

The Doctor of Education (Ed.D.) in Higher and Postsecondary Education program is designed for students to enhance their professional competence as educational leaders, instructors, or consultants in academic affairs, student affairs, or student services divisions within community colleges, technical schools and institutes, and four-year colleges and universities, as well as in government, military, religious, and profit or nonprofit postsecondary educational organizations and divisions. The program offers three concentrations: student affairs and services, teaching and learning, and interdisciplinary studies.

The Doctor of Education (Ed.D.) in Initial Educational Administration program prepares individuals to serve as school principals and/or building-level administrators. The program is designed for practicing educators who have already completed a graduate-level program from a regionally accredited institution or an appropriately certified foreign institution, and are seeking administrative licensure at the initial or K–12 level. Completion of the program results in a terminal degree which includes a specific writing, research, and dissertation sequence.

The Doctor of Education (Ed.D.) in Teaching and Learning is designed to prepare educators in P–12 settings to serve as change agents and leaders who engage actively in their communities, using appropriate pedagogy and technology to foster the development of global citizens. This program does not lead to certification or credential endorsement.

The Education Specialist (Ed.S.) in Higher and Postsecondary Education program is designed for students to enhance their professional competence as educational leaders, instructors, or consultants in academic affairs, student affairs, or student services divisions within community colleges, technical schools and institutes, four-year colleges and universities, as well as in government, military, religious, profit or nonprofit postsecondary educational organizations and divisions. The program offers three concentrations: student affairs and services, teaching and learning, and interdisciplinary studies.

The Education Specialist (Ed.S.) in Initial Educational Administration program prepares individuals to serve as school administrators. The program is designed for practicing educators who have already completed a master's degree program from a regionally accredited institution and are seeking administrative credentialing. Based on state requirements, students may be required to complete additional experiences or course work.

Research Facilities

Argosy University libraries provide curriculum support and educational resources, including current text materials, diagnostic training documents, reference materials and databases, journals and dissertations, and major and current titles in program areas. There is an online public-access catalog of library resources available throughout the Argosy University system. Students have remote access to the campus library database, enabling them to study and conduct research at home. Academic databases offer dissertation abstracts, academic journals, and professional periodicals. All library computers are Internet accessible. Software applications include Word, Excel, PowerPoint, SPSS, and various test-scoring programs.

Financial Aid

Financial aid is available to those who qualify. Argosy University, Inland Empire, offers access to federal and state aid programs, merit-based awards, grants, loans, and a work-study program. As a first step, students should complete the Free Application for Federal Student Aid (FAFSA). Prospective students can apply electronically at http://www.fafsa.ed.gov or at the campus.

Cost of Study

Tuition varies by program. Students should contact Argosy University, Inland Empire, for tuition information.

Living and Housing Costs

Students typically live in apartments in the metropolitan area. Living expenses vary according to each student's preferred standard of living, housing, and transportation. The University does not offer or operate student housing. Most of the students are full-time working professionals who live within driving distance of the campus. Several nearby hotels offer special rates for those who commute from long distances. The Admissions Department also maintains a list of housing options, including contact information for University students who wish to share housing. For more information, students should contact the Admissions Department.

Student Group

Admission to Argosy University, Inland Empire, is selective to ensure a dynamic and engaged student body. It encourages diversity in academic and employment backgrounds and promotes integration of the student body into professional life through established connections with local and national professional associations. Argosy University offers a professionally oriented education with rich opportunities to gain practical experience in class, field placements, and internships. Full-time students and working professionals gain the extensive knowledge and range of skills necessary for effective performance in their chosen fields.

Student Outcomes

Students can register with the University's online career-services system and use select services from a distance, such as degree-specific career e-mail lists, national job posts, and virtual job fairs. Students should contact the University for more information.

Location

Argosy University's Inland Empire facility features classrooms, computer labs, a resource center with Internet access, a student lounge, staff and faculty offices, and proximity to the region's many cultural and recreational attractions. Argosy University provides a supportive educational environment with convenient class options that enable students to earn a degree while fulfilling other life responsibilities. All of the programs are thoroughly oriented to the real working world. The University focuses on developing technical proficiency in each student's field, as well as an overall professional career approach. Many educational institutions and agencies in the area provide varied opportunities for student training.

The University

Argosy University is a private institution with nineteen locations across the nation. Argosy University, Inland Empire, provides students with a career resources office, an academic resources center, and extensive information access for research. It offers the resources of a large university, plus the friendliness and personal attention of a small campus.

The innovative programs feature dynamic, relevant, and practical curricula delivered in flexible class formats. Students enjoy scheduling options that make it easier to fit school into their busy lives, choosing from day and evening courses, on campus or online. Many students find a combination of class formats to be an ideal way of continuing their education while meeting family and professional demands.

Argosy University is accredited by the Accrediting Commission for Senior Colleges and Universities of the Western Association for Schools and Colleges (985 Atlantic Avenue, Suite 100, Alameda, California, 94501, http://www.wascsenior.org).

Applying

Argosy University, Inland Empire, accepts students year-round on a rolling admissions basis, depending on availability of required courses. Applications for admission are available online or by contacting the campus.

Correspondence and Information

Argosy University, Inland Empire
3401 Centre Lake Drive, Suite 200
Ontario, California 91761
United States
Phone: 909-472-0800
866-217-9075 (toll-free)
Fax: 909-472-0801
E-mail: auadmissions@argosy.edu
Web site: http://www.argosy.edu/inlandempire

THE FACULTY

The Argosy University faculty comprises working professionals who are eager to help students succeed. Members bring real-world experience and the latest practice innovations to the academic setting. The diverse faculty members of the College of Education are widely recognized for contributions to the field. Most hold doctoral degrees. They provide a substantive education that combines comprehensive knowledge with critical skills and practical workplace relevance. Above all, faculty members are committed to their students' personal and professional development.

ARGOSY UNIVERSITY, NASHVILLE

College of Education

Programs of Study

Argosy University, Nashville, offers Master of Arts in Education (M.A.Ed.) degrees in Higher and Postsecondary Education, Instructional Leadership, Teaching and Learning: ELL/ESL, Teaching and Learning: Reading and Teaching and Learning: Special Education; Education Specialist (Ed.S.) degrees in Higher and Postsecondary Education, Instructional Leadership, and Teaching and Learning; and Doctor of Education (Ed.D.) degrees in Higher and Postsecondary Education, Instructional Leadership , and Teaching and Learning.

The Master of Arts in Education (M.A.Ed.) in Higher and Postsecondary Education program is designed for individuals who seek administrative and other positions in noninstructional units at higher education and postsecondary institutions. Graduates of this program will have enhanced practical skills, knowledge, and experiences as professionals and leaders in universities, colleges, and postsecondary educational institutions. A bachelor's degree is required for admission to this program.

The Master of Arts in Education (M.A.Ed.) in Instructional Leadership noncertification program is designed for students who wish to develop or enhance classroom skills, become curriculum supervisors, or become educational leaders with instruction as their main focus. This program is designed to prepare graduates for responsible roles as leaders in the field of instructional leadership. The foundation courses include an array of subjects oriented toward the challenges and problems encountered in a modern educational environment. Students have opportunities to develop core practical and academic skills in analysis, oral and written communication, problem solving, critical thinking, team-building, and computer technology, through courses that examine the practical, historical, philosophical, psychological, social, technical, and theoretical aspects of education.

The Master of Arts in Education (M.A.Ed.) in Teaching and Learning: ELL/ESL is a 30-credit-hour degree program intended to prepare educators who work in the P–12 setting as change agents who engage actively in their communities, using appropriate pedagogy and technology to foster the development of global citizens. In addition to the core course requirements, students will complete a four-course sequence to strengthen knowledge and skills when working with students who are classified as English Language Learners (ELL) or English as a Second Language (ESL). This program does not lead to certification or credential endorsement.

The Master of Arts in Education (M.A.Ed.) in Teaching and Learning: Reading is a 30-credit program intended to prepare educators who work in the P–12 setting as change agents who engage actively in their communities, using appropriate pedagogy and technology to foster the development of global citizens. Students enrolled in this program will complete a four-course sequence in reading to strengthen knowledge and skills in this specific area. This program does not lead to certification or credential endorsement.

The Master of Arts in Education (M.A.Ed.) in Teaching and Learning: Special Education is a 30-credit program intended to prepare educators who work in the P–12 setting as change agents who engage actively in their communities, using appropriate pedagogy and technology to foster the development of global citizens. Students enrolled in this program will complete a four-course sequence designed to strengthen knowledge and skills when working with students with special learning needs. This program does not lead to certification or credential endorsement.

The Education Specialist (Ed.S.) in Higher and Postsecondary Education program is designed for students to enhance their professional competence as educational leaders, instructors, or consultants in academic affairs, student affairs, or student services divisions within community colleges, technical schools and institutes, four-year colleges and universities, as well as in government, military, religious, profit or nonprofit postsecondary educational organizations and divisions. The program offers three concentrations: student affairs and services, teaching and learning, and interdisciplinary studies.

The Education Specialist (Ed.S.) in Instructional Leadership program enables experienced teachers to become more effective practitioners and leaders with a focus on instruction. Course work is designed to satisfy the requirements of students seeking career advancement and those who are working toward a doctoral degree.

The Doctor of Education (Ed.D.) in Higher and Postsecondary Education program is designed for students to enhance their professional competence as educational leaders, instructors, or consultants in academic affairs, student affairs, or student services divisions within community colleges, technical schools and institutes, and four-year colleges and universities, as well as in government, military, religious, and profit or nonprofit postsecondary educational organizations and divisions. The program offers three concentrations: student affairs and services, teaching and learning, and interdisciplinary studies.

The Doctor of Education (Ed.D.) in Instructional Leadership noncertification program is designed for students who wish to master teaching methodologies, become curriculum supervisors, or become educational leaders with curriculum and instruction as their main focus. Students must choose either education technology, higher education, or K–12 education as an area of concentration. Not all concentrations are available at all campuses. Students should check with the campus dean or program chair at their campus of record to determine the available concentrations.

The Doctor of Education (Ed.D.) in Teaching and Learning program is designed to prepare educators in P–12 settings to serve as change agents and leaders who engage actively in their communities, using appropriate pedagogy and technology to foster the development of global citizens. This program does not lead to certification or credential endorsement.

Research Facilities

Argosy University libraries provide curriculum support and educational resources, including current text materials, diagnostic training documents, reference materials and databases, journals and dissertations, and major and current titles in program areas. There is an online public-access catalog of library resources available throughout the Argosy University system. Students have remote access to the campus library database, enabling them to study and conduct research at home. Academic databases offer dissertation abstracts, academic journals, and professional periodicals. All library computers are Internet accessible. Software applications include Word, Excel, PowerPoint, SPSS, and various test-scoring programs.

Financial Aid

Financial aid is available to those who qualify. Argosy University, Nashville, offers access to federal and state aid programs, merit-based awards, grants, loans, and a work-study program. As a first step, students should complete the Free Application for Federal Student Aid (FAFSA). Prospective students can apply electronically at http://www.fafsa.ed.gov or at the campus.

Cost of Study

Tuition varies by program. Students should contact Argosy University, Nashville, for tuition information.

Living and Housing Costs

Students typically live in apartments in the metropolitan Nashville area. Living expenses vary according to each student's preferred standard of living, housing, and transportation. The University does not offer or operate student housing. Most of the students are full-time working professionals who live within driving distance of the campus. Several nearby hotels offer special rates for those who commute from long distances. The Admissions Department also maintains a list of housing options, including contact information, for University students who wish to share housing. For more information, students should contact the Admissions Department.

Student Group

Admission to Argosy University, Nashville, is selective to ensure a dynamic and engaged student body. It encourages diversity in academic and employment backgrounds and promotes integration of the student body into professional life through established connections with local and national professional associations. Argosy University offers a professionally oriented education with rich opportunities to gain practical experience in class, field placements, and internships. Full-time students and working professionals gain the extensive knowledge and range of skills necessary for effective performance in their chosen fields.

Student Outcomes

Students can register with the University's online career-services system and use select services from a distance, such as degree-specific career e-mail lists, national job posts, and virtual job fairs. Students should contact the University for more information.

Location

Argosy University, Nashville, is located at 100 Centerview Drive in Nashville, Tennessee. This growing city offers a variety of recreational activities, including the ballet and symphony, the newly established Frist Museum of Art, and professional sports. Nashville is known as Music City, USA, and is home to the Country Music Hall of Fame. Many educational institutions and agencies in the area provide varied opportunities for student training. The business environment includes companies such as Moses Cone Health Systems, Inc., and Novant Health, Inc.

The University

Argosy University is a private institution with nineteen locations across the nation. Argosy University, Nashville, provides students with a career resources office, an academic resources center, and extensive information access for research. It offers the resources of a large university, plus the friendliness and personal attention of a small campus. The innovative programs feature dynamic, relevant, and practical curricula delivered in flexible class formats. Students enjoy scheduling options that make it easier to fit school into their busy lives, choosing from day and evening courses, on campus or online. Many students find a combination of class formats to be an ideal way of continuing their education while meeting family and professional demands.

Argosy University is accredited by the Accrediting Commission for Senior Colleges and Universities of the Western Association for Schools and Colleges (985 Atlantic Avenue, Suite 100, Alameda, California, 94501, http://www.wascsenior.org).

Applying

Argosy University, Nashville, accepts students year-round on a rolling admissions basis, depending on availability of required courses. Applications for admission are available online or by contacting the campus.

Correspondence and Information

Argosy University, Nashville
100 Centerview Drive, Suite 225
Nashville, Tennessee 37214
United States
Phone: 615-525-2800
866-833-6598 (toll-free)
Fax: 615-525-2900
E-mail: auadmissions@argosy.edu
Web site: http://www.argosy.edu/nashville

THE FACULTY

The Argosy University faculty comprises working professionals who are eager to help students succeed. Members bring real-world experience and the latest practice innovations to the academic setting. The diverse faculty members of the College of Education are widely recognized for contributions to the field. Most hold doctoral degrees. They provide a substantive education that combines comprehensive knowledge with critical skills and practical workplace relevance. Above all, faculty members are committed to their students' personal and professional development.

Section 24
Instructional Levels

This section contains a directory of institutions offering graduate work in instructional levels, followed by an in-depth entry submitted by an institution that chose to prepare a detailed program description. Additional information about programs listed in the directory but not augmented by an in-depth entry may be obtained by writing directly to the dean of a graduate school or chair of a department at the address given in the directory.

For programs offering related work, see also in this book *Administration, Instruction, and Theory; Education; Leisure Studies and Recreation; Physical Education and Kinesiology; Special Focus;* and *Subject Areas.* In other guides in this series:

Graduate Programs in the Humanities, Arts & Social Sciences
See *Psychology and Counseling (School Psychology)*

Graduate Programs in the Biological/Biomedical Sciences & Health-Related Medical Professions
See *Health-Related Professions*

CONTENTS

Program Directories

Displays and Close-Ups

Adult Education

Alverno College, School of Education, Milwaukee, WI 53234-3922. Offers adaptive education (MA); administrative leadership (MA); adult education and organizational development (MA); adult educational and instructional design (MA); adult educational and instructional technology (MA); global connections in the humanities (MA); instructional leadership (MA); instructional technology for K-12 settings (MA); professional development (MA); reading education (MA); reading education with adaptive education (MA); science education (MA); teaching in alternative schools (MA). *Accreditation:* NCATE. Part-time and evening/weekend programs available. *Faculty:* 22 full-time (18 women), 13 part-time/adjunct (all women). *Students:* 63 full-time (58 women), 91 part-time (81 women); includes 36 minority (29 Black or African American, non-Hispanic/Latino; 1 Asian, non-Hispanic/Latino; 4 Hispanic/Latino; 1 Native Hawaiian or other Pacific Islander, non-Hispanic/Latino; 1 Two or more races, non-Hispanic/Latino), 2 international. Average age 38. 151 applicants, 60% accepted, 62 enrolled. In 2011, 52 master's awarded. *Degree requirements:* For master's, presentation/defense of proposal, conference presentation of inquiry projects. *Entrance requirements:* For master's, bachelor's degree in related field, communication samples from work setting, 3 letters of recommendation. Additional exam requirements/recommendations for international students: Required—TOEFL. *Application deadline:* For fall admission, 7/15 priority date for domestic students, 7/15 for international students; for spring admission, 12/15 priority date for domestic students, 12/15 for international students. Applications are processed on a rolling basis. Application fee: $0. Electronic applications accepted. Application fee is waived when completed online. Tuition and fees vary according to program. *Financial support:* In 2011–12, 1 student received support. Federal Work-Study available. Support available to part-time students. Financial award application deadline: 4/15; financial award applicants required to submit FAFSA. *Faculty research:* Student self-assessment, self-reflection, integration of curriculum, identifying needs of students in strategic situations and designing appropriate classroom strategies. *Unit head:* Dr. Desiree Pointer-Mace, Associate Dean, Graduate Program, 414-382-6345, Fax: 414-382-6332, E-mail: desiree.pointer-mace@alverno.edu. *Application contact:* Mary Claire Jones, Graduate Recruiter, 414-382-6106, Fax: 414-382-6354, E-mail: maryclaire.jones@alverno.edu.

Argosy University, Chicago, College of Education, Chicago, IL 60601. Offers adult education and training (MA Ed); community college executive leadership (Ed D); educational leadership (MA Ed, Ed D, Ed S), including district leadership (Ed D), higher education administration (Ed D), K-12 education (Ed D); instructional leadership (Ed D, Ed S), including higher education (Ed D), K-12 education (Ed D). Postbaccalaureate distance learning degree programs offered (minimal on-campus study).

See Close-Up on page 769.

Argosy University, Hawai`i, College of Education, Honolulu, HI 96813. Offers adult education and training (MAEd); educational leadership (Ed D), including higher education administration, K-12 education; instructional leadership (Ed D), including higher education, K-12 education; school psychology (MA).

See Close-Up on page 775.

Argosy University, Phoenix, College of Education, Phoenix, AZ 85021. Offers adult education and training (MA Ed); advanced educational administration (Ed D, Ed S); community college executive leadership (Ed D); educational administration (MA Ed); educational leadership (MA Ed, Ed D, Ed S), including education technology (Ed D), higher education administration (Ed D), K-12 education (Ed D); higher and postsecondary education (MA Ed); initial educational administration (Ed D, Ed S); school psychology (MA); teaching and learning (MA Ed, Ed D, Ed S), including education technology (Ed D), higher education (Ed D), K-12 education (Ed D).

See Close-Up on page 781.

Argosy University, Seattle, College of Education, Seattle, WA 98121. Offers adult education and training (MA Ed); community college executive leadership (Ed D); educational leadership (MA Ed, Ed D), including higher education administration (Ed D), K-12 education (Ed D); higher and postsecondary education (MA Ed); instructional leadership (MA Ed, Ed D), including education technology (Ed D), higher education (Ed D), K-12 education (Ed D).

See Close-Up on page 793.

Armstrong Atlantic State University, School of Graduate Studies, Program in Education, Savannah, GA 31419-1997. Offers adult education (M Ed); curriculum and instruction (M Ed); early childhood education (M Ed); education (M Ed); elementary education (M Ed); middle grades education (M Ed); secondary education (M Ed), including business education, English education, mathematics education, science education, social science education; special education (M Ed), including behavioral disorders, learning disabilities, speech-language pathology. *Accreditation:* NCATE. Part-time and evening/weekend programs available. Postbaccalaureate distance learning degree programs offered (minimal on-campus study). *Faculty:* 33 full-time (23 women), 3 part-time/adjunct (2 women). *Students:* 97 full-time (91 women), 262 part-time (227 women); includes 83 minority (70 Black or African American, non-Hispanic/Latino; 3 Asian, non-Hispanic/Latino; 8 Hispanic/Latino; 2 Two or more races, non-Hispanic/Latino), 5 international. Average age 34. 169 applicants, 69% accepted, 102 enrolled. In 2011, 227 master's awarded. *Degree requirements:* For master's, comprehensive exam, portfolio. *Entrance requirements:* For master's, GRE General Test or MAT, minimum GPA of 2.5, letters of recommendation. Additional exam requirements/recommendations for international students: Required—TOEFL (minimum score 523 paper-based; 193 computer-based). *Application deadline:* For fall admission, 7/1 priority date for domestic students, 5/1 for international students; for spring admission, 11/15 priority date for domestic students, 9/15 for international students. Applications are processed on a rolling basis. Application fee: $30. Electronic applications accepted. *Expenses:* Tuition, state resident: full-time $3402. Tuition, nonresident: full-time $12,636. *Financial support:* In 2011–12, research assistantships with full tuition reimbursements (averaging $5,000 per year) were awarded; career-related internships or fieldwork, Federal Work-Study, scholarships/grants, and unspecified assistantships also available. Support available to part-time students. Financial award applicants required to submit FAFSA. *Unit head:* Dr. Patricia Wachholz, Dean, College of Education, 912-344-2797, E-mail: patricia.wachholz@armstrong.edu. *Application contact:* Jill Bell, Director, Graduate Enrollment Services, 912-344-2798, Fax: 912-344-3488, E-mail: graduate@armstrong.edu. Web site: http://www.armstrong.edu/Education/coe_deans_office/coe_education_welcome.

Athabasca University, Centre for Integrated Studies, Athabasca, AB T9S 3A3, Canada. Offers adult education (MA); community studies (MA); cultural studies (MA); educational studies (MA); global change (MA); work, organization, and leadership (MA). Part-time and evening/weekend programs available. Postbaccalaureate distance learning degree programs offered (no on-campus study). *Degree requirements:* For master's, project. *Entrance requirements:* Additional exam requirements/recommendations for international students: Required—TOEFL (minimum score 560 paper-based; 220 computer-based). Electronic applications accepted. *Faculty research:* Women's history, literature and culture studies, sustainable development, labor and education.

Auburn University, Graduate School, College of Education, Department of Educational Foundations, Leadership, and Technology, Auburn University, AL 36849. Offers adult education (M Ed, MS, Ed D); curriculum and instruction (M Ed, MS, Ed D, Ed S); curriculum supervision (M Ed, MS, Ed D, Ed S); educational psychology (PhD); higher education administration (M Ed, MS, Ed D, Ed S); media instructional design (MS); media specialist (M Ed); school administration (M Ed, MS, Ed D, Ed S). *Accreditation:* NCATE. Part-time programs available. *Faculty:* 26 full-time (16 women), 3 part-time/adjunct (all women). *Students:* 58 full-time (28 women), 215 part-time (135 women); includes 89 minority (82 Black or African American, non-Hispanic/Latino; 1 American Indian or Alaska Native, non-Hispanic/Latino; 4 Asian, non-Hispanic/Latino; 2 Hispanic/Latino), 13 international. Average age 35. 140 applicants, 61% accepted, 56 enrolled. In 2011, 37 master's, 29 doctorates, 9 other advanced degrees awarded. *Degree requirements:* For master's, thesis (for some programs); for doctorate, thesis/dissertation; for Ed S, field project. *Entrance requirements:* For master's, doctorate, and Ed S, GRE General Test. *Application deadline:* For fall admission, 7/7 for domestic students; for spring admission, 11/24 for domestic students. Applications are processed on a rolling basis. Application fee: $50 ($60 for international students). Electronic applications accepted. *Expenses:* Tuition, state resident: full-time $7290; part-time $405 per credit hour. Tuition, nonresident: full-time $21,870; part-time $1215 per credit hour. *International tuition:* $22,000 full-time. *Required fees:* $1402. *Financial support:* Teaching assistantships and Federal Work-Study available. Support available to part-time students. Financial award application deadline: 3/15; financial award applicants required to submit FAFSA. *Unit head:* Dr. Sherida Downer, Head, 334-844-4460. *Application contact:* Dr. George Flowers, Dean of the Graduate School, 334-844-4700. Web site: http://www.education.auburn.edu/academic_departments/eflt/.

Ball State University, Graduate School, Teachers College, Department of Educational Studies, Program in Adult Education, Muncie, IN 47306-1099. Offers adult and community education (MA); adult, community, and higher education (Ed D). *Accreditation:* NCATE. *Students:* 31 full-time (21 women), 82 part-time (57 women); includes 19 minority (13 Black or African American, non-Hispanic/Latino; 1 Asian, non-Hispanic/Latino; 2 Hispanic/Latino; 3 Two or more races, non-Hispanic/Latino), 2 international. Average age 34. 39 applicants, 67% accepted, 21 enrolled. In 2011, 19 master's, 7 doctorates awarded. *Degree requirements:* For doctorate, thesis/dissertation. *Entrance requirements:* For doctorate, GRE General Test, minimum graduate GPA of 3.2. Application fee: $50. Tuition and fees vary according to program and reciprocity agreements. *Financial support:* In 2011–12, 37 students received support, including 22 teaching assistantships with full tuition reimbursements available (averaging $6,202 per year); career-related internships or fieldwork also available. Financial award application deadline: 3/1. *Faculty research:* Community education, executive development for public services, applied gerontology. *Unit head:* Jayne Beilke, Director of Doctoral Program, 765-285-5348, Fax: 765-285-5489. *Application contact:* Dr. Thalia Mulvihill, Associate Provost for Research and Dean of the Graduate School. Web site: http://www.bsu.edu/teachers/departments/edstudies/.

Buffalo State College, State University of New York, The Graduate School, Faculty of Applied Science and Education, Department of Educational Foundations, Program in Adult Education, Buffalo, NY 14222-1095. Offers adult education (MS, Certificate); human resources development (Certificate). Part-time and evening/weekend programs available. Postbaccalaureate distance learning degree programs offered (no on-campus study). *Degree requirements:* For master's, comprehensive exam. *Entrance requirements:* Additional exam requirements/recommendations for international students: Required—TOEFL (minimum score 550 paper-based; 213 computer-based).

Capella University, School of Education, Minneapolis, MN 55402. Offers college teaching (Certificate); curriculum and instruction (MS, PhD); education (MS); enrollment management (MS); instructional design for online learning (MS, PhD); k-12 studies in education (MS, PhD); leadership for higher education (MS, PhD); leadership in education administration (Certificate); leadership in educational administration (MS, PhD); postsecondary and adult education (MS, PhD); professional studies in education (MS, PhD); reading and literacy (MS); training and performance improvement (MS, PhD). Part-time and evening/weekend programs available. Postbaccalaureate distance learning degree programs offered (minimal on-campus study). Terminal master's awarded for partial completion of doctoral program. *Degree requirements:* For master's, thesis optional, integrative project; for doctorate, comprehensive exam, thesis/dissertation. *Entrance requirements:* Additional exam requirements/recommendations for international students: Required—TOEFL (minimum score 550 paper-based; 213 computer-based), TWE (minimum score 4). Electronic applications accepted. *Faculty research:* Higher education administration, distance learning, adult education, training and curriculum design.

Central Michigan University, Central Michigan University Global Campus, Program in Education, Mount Pleasant, MI 48859. Offers adult education (MA); college teaching (Graduate Certificate); community college (MA); educational leadership (MA), including charter school leadership; educational technology (MA); guidance and development (MA); instruction (MA); reading and literacy K-12 (MA); school principalship (MA); teacher leadership (MA). *Accreditation:* Teacher Education Accreditation Council. Part-time and evening/weekend programs available. *Entrance requirements:* For master's, minimum GPA of 2.7 in major. Additional exam requirements/recommendations for international students: Required—TOEFL. *Application deadline:* Applications are processed on a rolling basis. Application fee: $50. Electronic applications accepted. *Financial support:* Scholarships/grants available. Support available to part-time students. *Unit head:* Dr. Peter Ross, Director, 989-774-4456, E-mail: ross1pg@cmich.edu. *Application contact:* 877-268-4636, E-mail: cmuglobal@cmich.edu.

Cheyney University of Pennsylvania, School of Education and Professional Studies, Program in Adult and Continuing Education, Cheyney, PA 19319. Offers MS. Part-time and evening/weekend programs available. *Degree requirements:* For master's, thesis or alternative. *Entrance requirements:* For master's, GRE General Test, MAT, minimum GPA of 2.75. Electronic applications accepted.

Cheyney University of Pennsylvania, School of Education and Professional Studies, Program in Educational Administration of Adult and Continuing Education, Cheyney, PA 19319. Offers M Ed, MS. Part-time and evening/weekend programs available. *Degree requirements:* For master's, thesis or alternative. Electronic applications accepted.

Cleveland State University, College of Graduate Studies, College of Education and Human Services, Department of Counseling, Administration, Supervision and Adult Learning (CASAL), Cleveland, OH 44115. Offers accelerated degree in adult learning and development (M Ed); adult learning and development (M Ed); chemical dependency counseling (Certificate); clinical mental health counseling (M Ed); early childhood mental health counseling (Certificate); educational administration and supervision (M Ed); organizational leadership (M Ed); school administration (Ed S); school counseling (M Ed). *Accreditation:* ACA (one or more programs are accredited). Part-time and evening/weekend programs available. *Faculty:* 15 full-time (8 women), 19 part-time/adjunct (10 women). *Students:* 58 full-time (49 women), 273 part-time (221 women); includes 121 minority (106 Black or African American, non-Hispanic/Latino; 2 Asian, non-Hispanic/Latino; 9 Hispanic/Latino; 4 Two or more races, non-Hispanic/Latino), 1 international. Average age 35. 192 applicants, 86% accepted, 105 enrolled. In 2011, 151 master's, 23 Certificates awarded. *Degree requirements:* For master's, comprehensive exam (for some programs), thesis optional, internship. *Entrance requirements:* For master's, GRE General Test or MAT, letter of recommendation and minimum GPA of 2.75 (for counseling); 2 letters of recommendation and interviews (for organizational leadership). Additional exam requirements/recommendations for international students: Required—TOEFL (minimum score 525 paper-based; 197 computer-based), IELTS (minimum score 6). *Application deadline:* For fall admission, 6/21 for domestic students, 5/15 for international students; for spring admission, 8/31 for domestic students, 11/1 for international students. Application fee: $30. Electronic applications accepted. *Expenses:* Tuition, state resident: full-time $6416; part-time $494 per credit hour. Tuition, nonresident: full-time $12,074; part-time $929 per credit hour. *Financial support:* In 2011–12, 19 students received support, including 10 research assistantships with full and partial tuition reimbursements available (averaging $11,882 per year), 5 teaching assistantships with full and partial tuition reimbursements available (averaging $11,882 per year); scholarships/grants and unspecified assistantships also available. Support available to part-time students. *Faculty research:* Education law, career development, bullying, psychopharmacology, counseling and spirituality. *Total annual research expenditures:* $225,821. *Unit head:* Dr. Ann L. Bauer, Chairperson, 216-687-4582, Fax: 216-687-5378, E-mail: a.l.bauer@csuohio.edu. *Application contact:* Deborah L. Brown, Interim Assistant Director, Graduate Admissions, 216-523-7572, Fax: 216-687-5400, E-mail: d.l.brown@csuohio.edu. Web site: http://www.csuohio.edu/cehs/departments/casal/.

Colorado State University, Graduate School, College of Applied Human Sciences, School of Education, Fort Collins, CO 80523-1588. Offers adult education and training (M Ed); community college leadership (PhD); counseling and career development (M Ed); education and human resource studies (M Ed, PhD); educational leadership (M Ed, PhD); interdisciplinary studies (PhD); organizational performance and change (M Ed, PhD); student affairs in higher education (MS). *Accreditation:* ACA; Teacher Education Accreditation Council. Part-time and evening/weekend programs available. *Faculty:* 18 full-time (11 women), 1 part-time/adjunct (0 women). *Students:* 161 full-time (106 women), 491 part-time (291 women); includes 130 minority (28 Black or African American, non-Hispanic/Latino; 5 American Indian or Alaska Native, non-Hispanic/Latino; 12 Asian, non-Hispanic/Latino; 68 Hispanic/Latino; 3 Native Hawaiian or other Pacific Islander, non-Hispanic/Latino; 14 Two or more races, non-Hispanic/Latino), 29 international. Average age 38. 468 applicants, 31% accepted, 112 enrolled. In 2011, 192 master's, 30 doctorates awarded. *Degree requirements:* For master's, comprehensive exam (for some programs), thesis optional; for doctorate, comprehensive exam, thesis/dissertation, minimum of 60 credits. *Entrance requirements:* For master's, GRE, minimum undergraduate GPA of 3.0, 3 letters of recommendation, curriculum vitae/resume; for doctorate, minimum GPA of 3.0, 3 letters of recommendation, curriculum vitae. Additional exam requirements/recommendations for international students: Required—TOEFL (minimum score 550 paper-based; 213 computer-based; 80 iBT). *Application deadline:* For fall admission, 2/15 priority date for domestic students, 2/15 for international students; for spring admission, 9/1 priority date for domestic students, 9/1 for international students. Applications are processed on a rolling basis. Application fee: $50. Electronic applications accepted. *Expenses:* Tuition, state resident: full-time $7992. Tuition, nonresident: full-time $19,592. *Required fees:* $1735; $58 per credit. *Financial support:* In 2011–12, 11 students received support, including 1 fellowship (averaging $37,500 per year), 3 research assistantships with full tuition reimbursements available (averaging $8,911 per year), 7 teaching assistantships with full tuition reimbursements available (averaging $12,691 per year); Federal Work-Study, scholarships/grants, and unspecified assistantships also available. Financial award application deadline: 2/15; financial award applicants required to submit FAFSA. *Faculty research:* Innovative instruction, diverse learners, transition, scientifically-based evaluation methods, leadership and organizational development, research methodology. *Total annual research expenditures:* $455,133. *Unit head:* Dr. Kevin Oltjenbruns, Interim Director, 970-491-6316, Fax: 970-491-1317, E-mail: kevin.oltjenbruns@colostate.edu. *Application contact:* Kathy Lucas, Graduate Contact, 970-491-1963, Fax: 970-491-1317, E-mail: kplucas@cahs.colostate.edu. Web site: http://www.soe.cahs.colostate.edu/.

Concordia University, School of Graduate Studies, Faculty of Arts and Science, Department of Education, Program in Adult Education, Montréal, QC H3G 1M8, Canada. Offers Diploma. *Degree requirements:* For Diploma, internship. *Entrance requirements:* For degree, interview. *Faculty research:* Staff development, human relations training, adult learning, professional development, learning in the workplace.

Concordia University, School of Graduate Studies, Faculty of Arts and Science, Department of Education, Program in Educational Studies, Montréal, QC H3G 1M8, Canada. Offers MA. *Degree requirements:* For master's, one foreign language, thesis optional. *Faculty research:* Social aspects of microtechnology, gender and education, minorities and immigrants in Canadian education, professional development, political education.

Coppin State University, Division of Graduate Studies, Division of Education, Department of Adult and General Education, Baltimore, MD 21216-3698. Offers MS. Part-time and evening/weekend programs available. *Degree requirements:* For master's, thesis optional, research paper, internship. *Entrance requirements:* For master's, GRE or PRAXIS, minimum GPA of 2.5, interview, resume, references.

Cornell University, Graduate School, Graduate Fields of Agriculture and Life Sciences, Field of Education, Ithaca, NY 14853-0001. Offers agricultural education (MAT); biology (7-12) (MAT); chemistry (7-12) (MAT); curriculum and instruction (MPS, MS, PhD); earth science (7-12) (MAT); extension, and adult education (MPS, MS, PhD); mathematics (7-12) (MAT); physics (7-12) (MAT). *Faculty:* 23 full-time (10 women). *Students:* 32 full-time (18 women); includes 6 minority (4 Asian, non-Hispanic/Latino; 2 Hispanic/Latino), 1 international. Average age 30. 60 applicants, 33% accepted, 12 enrolled. In 2011, 22 master's, 7 doctorates awarded. Terminal master's awarded for partial completion of doctoral program. *Degree requirements:* For master's, thesis (MS); for doctorate, comprehensive exam, thesis/dissertation. *Entrance requirements:* For master's and doctorate, GRE General Test, sample of written work (recommended), 2 letters of recommendation. Additional exam requirements/recommendations for international students: Required—TOEFL (minimum score 550 paper-based; 213 computer-based; 77 iBT). *Application deadline:* For fall admission, 2/15 for domestic students. Application fee: $95. Electronic applications accepted. *Financial support:* In 2011–12, 2 fellowships with full tuition reimbursements, 4 research assistantships with full tuition reimbursements, 12 teaching assistantships with full tuition reimbursements were awarded; institutionally sponsored loans, scholarships/grants, health care benefits, tuition waivers (full and partial), and unspecified assistantships also available. Financial award applicants required to submit FAFSA. *Faculty research:* Moral development and professional ethics, public issues education and community development, socio/political issues in public education, teacher education and curriculum in agricultural science and mathematics, extension research. *Unit head:* Director of Graduate Studies, 607-255-4278, Fax: 607-255-7905. *Application contact:* Graduate Field Assistant, 607-255-4278, Fax: 607-255-7905, E-mail: rh22@cornell.edu. Web site: http://www.gradschool.cornell.edu/fields.php?id-80&a-2.

Dallas Theological Seminary, Graduate Programs, Dallas, TX 75204-6499. Offers adult education (Th M); apologetics (Th M); Bible backgrounds (Th M); Bible translation (Th M); Biblical and theological studies (Certificate); biblical counseling (MA); biblical exegesis and linguistics (MA); biblical exposition (PhD); biblical studies (MA); Biblical theology (Th M); children's education (Th M); Christian education (MA, D Min); Christian leadership (MA); cross-cultural ministries (MA); educational administration (Th M); educational leadership (Th M); evangelism and discipleship (Th M); exposition of Biblical books (Th M); family life education (Th M); general studies (Th M); Hebrew and cognate studies (Th M); hermeneutics (Th M); historical theology (Th M); homiletics (Th M); intercultural ministries (Th M); Jesus studies (Th M); leadership studies (Th M); media and communication (MA); media arts (Th M); ministry (D Min); ministry with women (Th M); New Testament studies (Th M, PhD); Old Testament studies (Th M, PhD); parachurch ministries (Th M); pastoral care and counseling (Th M); pastoral theology and practice (Th M); philosophy (Th M); sacred theology (STM); spiritual formation (Th M); systematic theology (Th M); teaching in Christian institutions (Th M); theological studies (PhD); urban ministries (Th M); worship studies (Th M); youth education (Th M). *Accreditation:* ATS (one or more programs are accredited). Part-time programs available. Postbaccalaureate distance learning degree programs offered (minimal on-campus study). *Faculty:* 68 full-time (3 women), 35 part-time/adjunct (8 women). *Students:* 809 full-time (181 women), 1,215 part-time (450 women); includes 487 minority (208 Black or African American, non-Hispanic/Latino; 6 American Indian or Alaska Native, non-Hispanic/Latino; 141 Asian, non-Hispanic/Latino; 96 Hispanic/Latino; 5 Native Hawaiian or other Pacific Islander, non-Hispanic/Latino; 31 Two or more races, non-Hispanic/Latino), 223 international. Average age 36. 891 applicants, 70% accepted, 372 enrolled. In 2011, 336 master's, 27 doctorates, 46 other advanced degrees awarded. *Degree requirements:* For master's, variable foreign language requirement, thesis (for some programs); for doctorate, 2 foreign languages, thesis/dissertation. *Entrance requirements:* For master's, GRE or MAT if minimum undergraduate cumulative GPA is below 2.5 or undergraduate degree is unaccredited. Additional exam requirements/recommendations for international students: Required—TOEFL (minimum score 575 paper-based; 233 computer-based; 85 iBT), TWE (minimum score 4.5). *Application deadline:* For fall admission, 7/1 for domestic students, 1/1 for international students; for winter admission, 11/1 for domestic students; for spring admission, 11/1 for domestic students. *Expenses: Tuition:* Full-time $12,450; part-time $440 per credit hour. *Required fees:* $380; $190 per semester. *Financial support:* In 2011–12, 1,030 students received support. Career-related internships or fieldwork, scholarships/grants, and tuition waivers (full and partial) available. Financial award application deadline: 2/28. *Unit head:* Dr. Mark L. Bailey, President, 214-841-3676, Fax: 214-841-3565. *Application contact:* Josh Bleeker, Director of Admissions and Student Advising, 214-841-3661, Fax: 214-841-3664, E-mail: admissions@dts.edu.

Defiance College, Program in Education, Defiance, OH 43512-1610. Offers adolescent and young adult licensure (MA); mild and moderate intervention specialist (MA). Part-time programs available. *Faculty:* 7 full-time (4 women), 1 part-time/adjunct (0 women). *Students:* 34 part-time (25 women). *Degree requirements:* For master's, thesis (for some programs). *Entrance requirements:* For master's, teaching certificate. *Application deadline:* For fall admission, 8/1 for domestic students. Applications are processed on a rolling basis. Application fee: $25. *Expenses: Tuition:* Full-time $10,800; part-time $450 per credit hour. *Required fees:* $95; $35 per semester. *Unit head:* Dr. Suzanne McFarland, Coordinator, 419-783-2315, Fax: 419-784-0426, E-mail: smcfarland@defiance.edu. *Application contact:* Sally Bissell, Director of Continuing Education, 419-783-2350, Fax: 419-784-0426, E-mail: sbissell@defiance.edu.

Delaware State University, Graduate Programs, College of Education, Health and Public Policy, Program in Adult Literacy and Basic Education, Dover, DE 19901-2277. Offers MA. *Entrance requirements:* Additional exam requirements/recommendations for international students: Required—TOEFL (minimum score 550 paper-based). Electronic applications accepted.

DePaul University, School for New Learning, Chicago, IL 60604. Offers applied professional studies (MA); applied technology (MS); educating adults (MA). Part-time and evening/weekend programs available. *Faculty:* 11 full-time (6 women), 12 part-time/adjunct (8 women). *Students:* 8 full-time (2 women), 160 part-time (119 women); includes 87 minority (64 Black or African American, non-Hispanic/Latino; 4 Asian, non-Hispanic/Latino; 15 Hispanic/Latino; 4 Two or more races, non-Hispanic/Latino). Average age 44. 53 applicants, 60% accepted, 29 enrolled. In 2011, 20 master's awarded. *Degree requirements:* For master's, thesis or alternative. *Entrance requirements:* For master's, 3 years of work experience, current related employment. *Application deadline:* For fall admission, 9/1 priority date for domestic students; for spring admission, 3/1 priority date for domestic students. Applications are processed on a rolling basis. Application fee: $25. Electronic applications accepted. *Financial support:* In 2011–12, 7 students received support. Scholarships/grants and tuition waivers (partial) available. Financial award applicants required to submit FAFSA. *Faculty research:* Interactive problem-based learning, liberal learning and professional competence, effective instructional practice. *Unit head:* Dr. Russ Rogers, Program Director, 312-362-8512, Fax: 312-362-8809, E-mail: rrogers@depaul.edu. *Application contact:* Sarah Hellstrom, Assistant Director, 312-362-5744, Fax: 312-362-8809, E-mail: shellstr@depaul.edu. Web site: http://snl.depaul.edu/.

East Carolina University, Graduate School, College of Education, Department of Higher, Adult, and Counselor Education, Greenville, NC 27858-4353. Offers adult education (MA Ed); counselor education (MS); higher education administration (Ed D). *Accreditation:* NCATE. Part-time and evening/weekend programs available. *Degree requirements:* For master's, comprehensive exam, thesis optional. *Entrance requirements:* For master's, GRE General Test or MAT, interview, minimum GPA of 2.5, bachelor's degree in related field, teaching license (MA Ed). Additional exam requirements/recommendations for international students: Required—TOEFL. *Application deadline:* For fall admission, 5/15 priority date for domestic students. Applications are processed on a rolling basis. Application fee: $50. *Expenses:* Tuition, state resident: full-time $3557; part-time $444.63 per semester hour. Tuition, nonresident: full-time $14,351; part-time $1793.88 per semester hour. *Required fees:* $2016; $252 per semester hour. Part-time tuition and fees vary according to course load, campus/location and program. *Financial support:* Research assistantships with partial tuition reimbursements, teaching assistantships with partial tuition reimbursements, and Federal Work-Study available. Support available to part-time students. Financial award application deadline: 6/1. *Unit head:* Dr. Vivian W. Mott, Chair, 252-328-6177, Fax: 252-328-4368, E-mail: mottv@ecu.edu. *Application contact:* Dean of Graduate School, 252-328-6012, Fax: 252-328-6071, E-mail: gradschool@ecu.edu. Web site: http://www.ecu.edu/cs-educ/hace/index.cfm.

Adult Education

Eastern Washington University, Graduate Studies, College of Arts, Letters and Education, Department of Education, Program in Adult Education, Cheney, WA 99004-2431. Offers M Ed. *Students:* 3 full-time (2 women). Average age 41. 9 applicants, 56% accepted, 3 enrolled. In 2011, 4 master's awarded. *Degree requirements:* For master's, comprehensive exam, thesis or alternative. *Entrance requirements:* For master's, minimum GPA of 3.0. *Application deadline:* For fall admission, 4/1 priority date for domestic students; for spring admission, 1/15 for domestic students. Applications are processed on a rolling basis. Application fee: $35. *Financial support:* In 2011–12, teaching assistantships with partial tuition reimbursements (averaging $7,000 per year) were awarded; career-related internships or fieldwork, Federal Work-Study, institutionally sponsored loans, scholarships/grants, health care benefits, tuition waivers (partial), and unspecified assistantships also available. Support available to part-time students. Financial award application deadline: 2/1; financial award applicants required to submit FAFSA. *Unit head:* Robin Showalter, Program Coordinator, 509-359-6492, E-mail: rshowalter@mail.ewu.edu. *Application contact:* Dr. Kevin Pyatt, Graduate Program Coordinator, 509-359-6091, Fax: 509-359-4822.

Edgewood College, Program in Education, Madison, WI 53711-1997. Offers adult learning (MA Ed); bilingual teaching and learning (MA Ed); director of instruction (Certificate); director of special education and pupil services (Certificate); education (MA Ed); educational administration (MA Ed); educational leadership (Ed D); professional studies (MA Ed); program coordinator (Certificate); reading administration (MA Ed); school business administration (Certificate); school principalship K-12 (Certificate); special education (MA Ed); sustainability leadership (MA Ed); teaching and learning (MA Ed); teaching English to speakers of other languages (TESOL) (MA Ed). *Accreditation:* NCATE (one or more programs are accredited). Part-time and evening/weekend programs available. *Students:* 155 full-time (93 women), 152 part-time (116 women); includes 39 minority (13 Black or African American, non-Hispanic/Latino; 5 Asian, non-Hispanic/Latino; 17 Hispanic/Latino; 4 Two or more races, non-Hispanic/Latino), 9 international. Average age 36. In 2011, 39 master's, 32 doctorates awarded. *Degree requirements:* For master's, practicum, research project; for doctorate, comprehensive exam, thesis/dissertation. *Entrance requirements:* For master's, minimum GPA of 2.75, 2 letters of recommendation, personal statement; for doctorate, resume, letter of intent, 2 letters of recommendation, interview, writing sample. Additional exam requirements/recommendations for international students: Required—TOEFL (minimum score 525 paper-based; 197 computer-based; 72 iBT). *Application deadline:* For fall admission, 8/15 for domestic students, 5/1 for international students; for spring admission, 1/8 for domestic students, 11/1 for international students. Applications are processed on a rolling basis. Application fee: $25. Electronic applications accepted. *Expenses: Tuition:* Part-time $747 per credit. Part-time tuition and fees vary according to program. *Unit head:* Dr. Jane Belmore, Dean, 608-663-8336, Fax: 608-663-3291, E-mail: jbelmore@edgewood.edu. *Application contact:* Joann Eastman, Admissions Counselor, 608-663-3250, Fax: 608-663-2214, E-mail: gps@edgewood.edu. Web site: http://education.edgewood.edu/graduate.html.

Florida Agricultural and Mechanical University, Division of Graduate Studies, Research, and Continuing Education, College of Education, Department of Educational Leadership and Human Services, Tallahassee, FL 32307-3200. Offers administration and supervision (M Ed, MS Ed, PhD); adult education (M Ed, MS Ed); educational leadership (PhD); guidance and counseling (M Ed, MS Ed). *Accreditation:* NCATE. *Degree requirements:* For master's, thesis (for some programs); for doctorate, thesis/dissertation. *Entrance requirements:* For master's, GRE General Test, minimum GPA of 3.0. Additional exam requirements/recommendations for international students: Required—TOEFL.

Florida Atlantic University, College of Education, Department of Educational Leadership and Research Methodology, Boca Raton, FL 33431-0991. Offers adult and community education (M Ed, PhD, Ed S); educational leadership (M Ed, PhD, Ed S); higher education (M Ed, PhD); K-12 school leadership (M Ed, PhD, Ed S). *Accreditation:* NCATE. Part-time and evening/weekend programs available. Postbaccalaureate distance learning degree programs offered (minimal on-campus study). *Faculty:* 20 full-time (11 women), 17 part-time/adjunct (7 women). *Students:* 100 full-time (75 women), 245 part-time (173 women); includes 126 minority (59 Black or African American, non-Hispanic/Latino; 15 Asian, non-Hispanic/Latino; 47 Hispanic/Latino; 5 Two or more races, non-Hispanic/Latino), 4 international. Average age 36. 253 applicants, 47% accepted, 66 enrolled. In 2011, 122 master's, 11 doctorates awarded. *Degree requirements:* For doctorate, comprehensive exam, thesis/dissertation, departmental qualifying exam; for Ed S, departmental qualifying exam. *Entrance requirements:* For master's, GRE General Test, minimum GPA of 3.0 during previous 2 years; for doctorate, GRE General Test, minimum GPA of 3.5; for Ed S, GRE General Test. *Application deadline:* For fall admission, 7/1 for domestic students, 2/15 for international students; for spring admission, 9/15 for domestic students, 7/15 for international students. Applications are processed on a rolling basis. Application fee: $30. Electronic applications accepted. *Expenses: Tuition, area resident:* Part-time $343.02 per credit hour. Tuition, state resident: full-time $8232. Tuition, nonresident: full-time $23,931; part-time $997.14 per credit hour. *Financial support:* Fellowships, research assistantships, teaching assistantships, career-related internships or fieldwork, and tuition waivers (partial) available. *Faculty research:* Self-directed learning, school reform issues, legal issues, mentoring, school leadership. *Unit head:* Dr. Robert Shockley, Chair, 561-297-3550, Fax: 561-297-3618, E-mail: shockley@fau.edu. *Application contact:* Catherine Politi, Senior Secretary, 561-297-3550, Fax: 561-297-3618, E-mail: edleadership@fau.edu. Web site: http://www.coe.fau.edu/academicdepartments/el/.

Florida International University, College of Education, Department of Educational Leadership and Policy Studies, Miami, FL 33199. Offers adult education (MS); adult education in human resource development (Ed D); clinical mental health counseling (MS); conflict resolution and consensus building (Certificate); counselor education (MS); educational administration and supervision (Ed D); educational leadership (MS, Certificate, Ed S); higher education (Ed D); higher education administration (MS); human resource development (MS); instruction in urban settings (MS); international/intercultural education (MS); learning technologies (MS); multicultural-bilingual (MS); multicultural-TESOL (MS); recreation and sport management (MS); recreation therapy (MS); rehabilitation counseling (MS); school counseling (MS); school psychology (Ed S); urban education (MS). Part-time and evening/weekend programs available. *Degree requirements:* For doctorate, thesis/dissertation. *Entrance requirements:* For master's, minimum GPA of 3.0; for doctorate and other advanced degree, GRE General Test. Additional exam requirements/recommendations for international students: Required—TOEFL (minimum score 550 paper-based; 213 computer-based; 80 iBT), IELTS (minimum score 6.3). Electronic applications accepted.

Fordham University, Graduate School of Education, Division of Curriculum and Teaching, New York, NY 10023. Offers adult education (MS, MSE); bilingual teacher education (MSE); curriculum and teaching (MSE); early childhood education (MSE); elementary education (MST); language, literacy, and learning (PhD); reading education (MSE, Adv C); secondary education (MAT, MSE); special education (MSE, Adv C); teaching English as a second language (MSE). *Accreditation:* NCATE. *Degree requirements:* For doctorate, thesis/dissertation; for Adv C, thesis. *Entrance requirements:* For doctorate, MAT, GRE General Test. *Expenses: Tuition:* Full-time $30,480; part-time $1270 per credit. *Required fees:* $586; $293 per semester.

The George Washington University, Graduate School of Education and Human Development, Department of Human and Organizational Learning, Program in Design and Assessment of Adult Learning, Washington, DC 20052. Offers Graduate Certificate. *Entrance requirements:* For degree, two letters of recommendation, resume, statement of purpose. Electronic applications accepted.

Grand Valley State University, College of Education, Programs in General Education, Allendale, MI 49401-9403. Offers adult and higher education (M Ed); early childhood education (M Ed); educational differentiation (M Ed); educational leadership (M Ed); educational technology integration (M Ed); elementary education (M Ed); middle level education (M Ed); school library media services (M Ed); secondary level education (M Ed); teaching English to speakers of other languages (M Ed). Part-time and evening/weekend programs available. Postbaccalaureate distance learning degree programs offered (minimal on-campus study). *Degree requirements:* For master's, thesis. *Entrance requirements:* For master's, GRE General Test or minimum GPA of 3.0. Additional exam requirements/recommendations for international students: Required—TOEFL. Electronic applications accepted. *Faculty research:* Effectiveness of technology in education, parental involvement, effective teaching, effective schools research.

Indiana University of Pennsylvania, School of Graduate Studies and Research, College of Education and Educational Technology, Department of Adult and Community Education, Program in Adult and Community Education, Indiana, PA 15705-1087. Offers MA. Part-time programs available. Postbaccalaureate distance learning degree programs offered (no on-campus study). *Faculty:* 2 full-time (0 women). *Students:* 2 full-time (both women), 21 part-time (16 women); includes 4 minority (3 Black or African American, non-Hispanic/Latino; 1 Hispanic/Latino), 2 international. Average age 37. 19 applicants, 74% accepted, 11 enrolled. In 2011, 7 master's awarded. *Degree requirements:* For master's, thesis optional. *Entrance requirements:* Additional exam requirements/recommendations for international students: Required—TOEFL (minimum score 540 paper-based; 207 computer-based). *Application deadline:* Applications are processed on a rolling basis. Application fee: $50. Electronic applications accepted. *Expenses:* Tuition, state resident: full-time $7488; part-time $416 per credit. Tuition, nonresident: full-time $11,232; part-time $624 per credit. *Required fees:* $2070; $192.20 per credit. $90 per semester. *Financial support:* Application deadline: 4/15; applicants required to submit FAFSA. *Unit head:* Dr. Gary Dean, Chairperson, 724-357-2470, E-mail: gjdean@iup.edu. *Application contact:* Dr. Edward Nardi, Associate Dean, 724-357-2480, Fax: 724-357-5595, E-mail: ewnardi@iup.edu. Web site: http://www.iup.edu/upper.aspx?id=49407.

Indiana University of Pennsylvania, School of Graduate Studies and Research, College of Education and Educational Technology, Department of Adult and Community Education, Program in Adult Education and Communications Technology, Indiana, PA 15705-1087. Offers MA. Part-time and evening/weekend programs available. *Faculty:* 2 full-time (0 women). *Students:* 21 full-time (6 women), 7 part-time (2 women); includes 2 minority (1 Black or African American, non-Hispanic/Latino; 1 Two or more races, non-Hispanic/Latino), 1 international. Average age 28. 29 applicants, 69% accepted, 14 enrolled. In 2011, 23 master's awarded. *Degree requirements:* For master's, thesis optional. *Entrance requirements:* For master's, 2 letters of recommendation, writing sample. Additional exam requirements/recommendations for international students: Required—TOEFL (minimum score 540 paper-based; 207 computer-based). *Application deadline:* Applications are processed on a rolling basis. Application fee: $50. Electronic applications accepted. *Expenses:* Tuition, state resident: full-time $7488; part-time $416 per credit. Tuition, nonresident: full-time $11,232; part-time $624 per credit. *Required fees:* $2070; $192.20 per credit. $90 per semester. *Financial support:* In 2011–12, 7 research assistantships with full and partial tuition reimbursements (averaging $5,440 per year) were awarded; fellowships, teaching assistantships with partial tuition reimbursements, career-related internships or fieldwork, and Federal Work-Study also available. Support available to part-time students. Financial award application deadline: 4/15; financial award applicants required to submit FAFSA. *Unit head:* Dr. Gary Dean, Chairperson, 724-357-2470, E-mail: gjdean@iup.edu. *Application contact:* Dr. Edward Nardi, Associate Dean, 724-357-2480, Fax: 724-357-5595, E-mail: ewnardi@iup.edu. Web site: http://www.iup.edu/upper.aspx?id=93738.

Indiana University of Pennsylvania, School of Graduate Studies and Research, College of Education and Educational Technology, Department of Communications Media, Indiana, PA 15705-1087. Offers adult education and communications technology (MA); communications media and instructional technology (PhD). Part-time and evening/weekend programs available. *Faculty:* 10 full-time (3 women), 1 part-time/adjunct (0 women). *Students:* 20 full-time (9 women), 40 part-time (20 women); includes 5 minority (3 Black or African American, non-Hispanic/Latino; 1 Asian, non-Hispanic/Latino; 1 Two or more races, non-Hispanic/Latino), 2 international. Average age 38. 46 applicants, 46% accepted, 17 enrolled. *Degree requirements:* For doctorate, thesis/dissertation. *Entrance requirements:* For master's, 2 letters of recommendation. Additional exam requirements/recommendations for international students: Required—TOEFL (minimum score 540 paper-based; 207 computer-based). *Application deadline:* Applications are processed on a rolling basis. Application fee: $50. Electronic applications accepted. *Expenses:* Tuition, state resident: full-time $7488; part-time $416 per credit. Tuition, nonresident: full-time $11,232; part-time $624 per credit. *Required fees:* $2070; $192.20 per credit. $90 per semester. *Financial support:* In 2011–12, 4 fellowships with full tuition reimbursements (averaging $1,879 per year), 8 research assistantships with full and partial tuition reimbursements (averaging $5,222 per year), 3 teaching assistantships with partial tuition reimbursements (averaging $22,398 per year) were awarded; career-related internships or fieldwork, Federal Work-Study, scholarships/grants, and tuition waivers (full) also available. Support available to part-time students. Financial award application deadline: 4/15; financial award applicants required to submit FAFSA. *Unit head:* Dr. Mark Piwinsky, Chairperson, 724-357-3954, Fax: 724-357-5503, E-mail: mark.piwinsky@iup.edu. *Application contact:* Dr. Edward Nardi, Associate Dean, 724-357-2480, Fax: 724-357-5595, E-mail: ewnardi@iup.edu. Web site: http://www.iup.edu/commmedia/.

Indiana University–Purdue University Indianapolis, School of Continuing Studies, Indianapolis, IN 46202-2896. Offers MS. *Students:* 2 full-time (both women), 81 part-time (64 women); includes 8 minority (3 Black or African American, non-Hispanic/Latino; 2 American Indian or Alaska Native, non-Hispanic/Latino; 2 Asian, non-Hispanic/Latino; 1 Hispanic/Latino). Average age 41. 42 applicants, 86% accepted, 33 enrolled. In 2011, 21 master's awarded. *Application contact:* Dr. Sherry Queener, Director, Graduate Studies and Associate Dean, 317-274-1577, Fax: 317-278-2380. Web site: http://www.scs.indiana.edu/graduate/welcome.shtml.

Instituto Tecnologico de Santo Domingo, Graduate School, Area of Humanities and Social Sciences, Santo Domingo, Dominican Republic. Offers accounting (Certificate); adult education (Certificate); applied linguistics (MA); economics (MA); education (M Ed); educational psychology (MA, Certificate); gender and development (MA, Certificate); humanistic studies (MA); international marketing management (Certificate); international relations in the Caribbean basin (Certificate); intervention systems in family therapy (MA); linguistic and literary communication (Certificate); pedagogical support

(MA); social science education (M Ed); sustainable human development (MA); terminal illness and death psychology (Certificate); youth and adult education (M Ed).

The Johns Hopkins University, School of Education, Department of Interdisciplinary Studies in Education, Baltimore, MD 21218. Offers earth/space science (Certificate); education (MS), including educational studies; health care education (MEHP); mind, brain, and teaching (Certificate); teaching the adult learner (Certificate); urban education (Certificate). Part-time and evening/weekend programs available. Postbaccalaureate distance learning degree programs offered (minimal on-campus study). *Degree requirements:* For master's, capstone course. *Entrance requirements:* For master's and Certificate, minimum undergraduate GPA of 3.0. Additional exam requirements/recommendations for international students: Required—TOEFL (minimum score 600 paper-based; 250 computer-based; 100 iBT). Electronic applications accepted. *Faculty research:* Neuro-education, urban school reform, leadership development, teacher leadership, charter schools, techniques for teaching reading to adolescents with delayed reading skills, school culture.

Jones International University, School of Education, Centennial, CO 80112. Offers adult education (M Ed); corporate training and knowledge management (M Ed); curriculum and instruction (M Ed), including elementary teacher licensure, secondary teacher licensure; e-learning technology and design (M Ed); educational leadership and administration (M Ed); educational leadership and administration: principal and administrator licensure (M Ed); elementary curriculum instruction and assessment (M Ed); higher education leadership and administration (M Ed); K-12 instructional technology (M Ed); K-12 instructional technology: teacher licensure (M Ed); secondary curriculum instruction and assessment (M Ed); technology and design (M Ed). Part-time and evening/weekend programs available. Postbaccalaureate distance learning degree programs offered (no on-campus study). *Entrance requirements:* For master's, minimum cumulative GPA of 2.5. Additional exam requirements/recommendations for international students: Recommended—TOEFL (minimum score 550 paper-based; 213 computer-based). Electronic applications accepted.

Kansas State University, Graduate School, College of Education, Department of Educational Leadership, Manhattan, KS 66506. Offers adult, occupational and continuing education (MS, Ed D, PhD); educational leadership (MS, Ed D). *Accreditation:* NCATE. *Faculty:* 10 full-time (5 women), 1 part-time/adjunct (0 women). *Students:* 43 full-time (21 women), 185 part-time (91 women); includes 37 minority (14 Black or African American, non-Hispanic/Latino; 1 American Indian or Alaska Native, non-Hispanic/Latino; 4 Asian, non-Hispanic/Latino; 16 Hispanic/Latino; 2 Two or more races, non-Hispanic/Latino), 1 international. Average age 40. 96 applicants, 59% accepted, 37 enrolled. In 2011, 74 master's, 8 doctorates awarded. *Degree requirements:* For master's, comprehensive exam; for doctorate, comprehensive exam, thesis/dissertation. *Entrance requirements:* For master's, minimum undergraduate GPA of 3.0; for doctorate, GRE General Test, minimum GPA of 3.0 in last 60 hours. Additional exam requirements/recommendations for international students: Required—TOEFL. *Application deadline:* For fall admission, 2/1 priority date for domestic students, 2/1 for international students; for spring admission, 8/1 priority date for domestic students, 8/1 for international students. Applications are processed on a rolling basis. Application fee: $40 ($55 for international students). Electronic applications accepted. *Financial support:* Career-related internships or fieldwork, institutionally sponsored loans, and scholarships/grants available. Support available to part-time students. Financial award application deadline: 3/1; financial award applicants required to submit FAFSA. *Faculty research:* Educational law, school finance, school facilities, organizational leadership, adult learning, distance learning/education. *Total annual research expenditures:* $5,648. *Unit head:* David C. Thompson, Head, 785-532-5535, Fax: 785-532-7304, E-mail: thomsond@ksu.edu. *Application contact:* Dona Deam, Applications Contact, 785-532-5595, Fax: 785-532-7304, E-mail: ddeam@ksu.edu. Web site: http://coe.k-state.edu/departments/edlea/index.htm.

Kean University, College of Education, Program in Reading Specialization, Union, NJ 07083. Offers adult literacy (MA); basic skills (MA); reading specialization (MA). *Faculty:* 11 full-time (all women). *Students:* 1 (woman) full-time, 36 part-time (35 women); includes 1 minority (Black or African American, non-Hispanic/Latino). Average age 29. 4 applicants, 100% accepted, 1 enrolled. In 2011, 20 master's awarded. *Degree requirements:* For master's, thesis, practicum, clinical, research seminar, 2 years of teaching experience by end of program (for certification). *Entrance requirements:* For master's, GRE General Test or MAT, minimum GPA of 3.0, 2 letters of recommendation, interview, teaching certification, transcripts, personal statement. Additional exam requirements/recommendations for international students: Required—TOEFL (minimum score 79 iBT). *Application deadline:* For fall admission, 6/1 for domestic and international students; for spring admission, 12/1 for domestic and international students. Applications are processed on a rolling basis. Application fee: $75 ($150 for international students). Electronic applications accepted. *Expenses:* Tuition, state resident: full-time $11,302; part-time $550 per credit. Tuition, nonresident: full-time $15,318; part-time $674 per credit. *Required fees:* $2849; $130 per credit. Tuition and fees vary according to degree level. *Financial support:* In 2011–12, 1 research assistantship with full tuition reimbursement (averaging $3,263 per year) was awarded; unspecified assistantships also available. Financial award applicants required to submit FAFSA. *Unit head:* Dr. Joan M. Kastner, Program Coordinator, 908-737-3942, E-mail: jkastner@kean.edu. *Application contact:* Reenat Hasan, Admission Counselor, 908-737-5923, Fax: 908-737-5925, E-mail: rhasan@exchange.kean.edu. Web site: http://www.kean.edu/KU/Adult-Literacy.

Marshall University, Academic Affairs Division, Graduate School of Education and Professional Development, Division of Adult and Technical Education, Huntington, WV 25755. Offers MS. *Accreditation:* NCATE. Evening/weekend programs available. *Students:* 40 full-time (19 women), 67 part-time (49 women); includes 11 minority (9 Black or African American, non-Hispanic/Latino; 2 Asian, non-Hispanic/Latino), 6 international. Average age 38. In 2011, 65 master's awarded. *Degree requirements:* For master's, thesis optional, comprehensive assessment. Application fee: $40. *Unit head:* Dr. Lee Olson, Program Coordinator, 304-696-6757, E-mail: olsonl@marshall.edu. *Application contact:* Graduate Admission.

Memorial University of Newfoundland, School of Graduate Studies, Faculty of Education, St. John's, NL A1C 5S7, Canada. Offers counseling psychology (M Ed); curriculum, teaching, and learning studies (M Ed); education (PhD); educational leadership studies (M Ed); information technology (M Ed); post-secondary studies (M Ed, Diploma), including health professional education (Diploma). Part-time programs available. *Degree requirements:* For master's, thesis optional, internship, paper folio, project; for doctorate, comprehensive exam, thesis/dissertation, thesis seminar, oral defense of thesis. *Entrance requirements:* For master's, undergraduate degree with at least 2nd class standing, 1-2 years work experience; for doctorate, minimum A average in graduate course work, MA in education, 2 years professional experience; for Diploma, 2nd class degree, 2 years of work experience with adult learners, appropriate academic qualifications and work experience in a health-related field. Electronic applications accepted. *Faculty research:* Critical thinking, literacy, cognitive studies and counseling, educational change, technology in instruction.

Michigan State University, The Graduate School, College of Education, Department of Educational Administration, East Lansing, MI 48824. Offers higher, adult and lifelong education (MA, PhD); K–12 educational administration (MA, PhD, Ed S); student affairs administration (MA). Part-time programs available. *Entrance requirements:* Additional exam requirements/recommendations for international students: Required—TOEFL. Electronic applications accepted.

Montana State University, College of Graduate Studies, College of Education, Health, and Human Development, Department of Education, Bozeman, MT 59717. Offers adult and higher education (Ed D); curriculum and instruction (M Ed, Ed D), including professional educator (M Ed), technology education (M Ed); education (M Ed), including adult and higher education, educational leadership, school counseling; educational leadership (Ed D, Ed S). *Accreditation:* Teacher Education Accreditation Council. Part-time programs available. Postbaccalaureate distance learning degree programs offered (minimal on-campus study). *Degree requirements:* For master's, comprehensive exam; for doctorate, comprehensive exam, thesis/dissertation. *Entrance requirements:* For master's, GRE, 3 letters of reference, essays, BA transcripts; for doctorate, GRE, MAT, 3 letters of reference, essay, BA and M Ed transcripts; for Ed S, PRAXIS. Additional exam requirements/recommendations for international students: Required—TOEFL (minimum score 550 paper-based; 213 computer-based). Electronic applications accepted. *Faculty research:* Critical literacy; standards-based education; school Improvement, organizational change, leadership in rural education, leadership in Indian education; student Learning; multicultural/culturally responsive education for social justice Native American indigenous education, community-centered education teacher preparation.

Morehead State University, Graduate Programs, College of Education, Department of Foundational and Graduate Studies in Education, Morehead, KY 40351. Offers adult and higher education (MA, Ed S); certified professional counselor (Ed S); counseling P-12 (MA); curriculum and instruction (Ed S); educational technology (MA Ed); instructional leadership (Ed S); school administration (MA); school counseling (Ed S); teacher leader business and marketing content (MA Ed); teacher leader business and marketing technology (MA Ed); teacher leader educational technology (MA Ed); teacher leader English (MA Ed); teacher leader gifted education (MA Ed); teacher leader IECE certification (MA Ed); teacher leader interdisciplinary education P-5 (MA Ed); teacher leader middle grades (MA Ed); teacher leader non IECE certification (MA Ed); teacher leader reading/writing - non-certification (MA Ed); teacher leader reading/writing certification (MA Ed); teacher leader school communication - certification (MA Ed); teacher leader school communication - non-certification (MA Ed); teacher leader social studies (MA Ed); teacher leader special education (MA Ed). *Accreditation:* NCATE. Part-time and evening/weekend programs available. *Degree requirements:* For master's, thesis optional, oral and/or written comprehensive exams; for Ed S, thesis, oral exam. *Entrance requirements:* For master's, GRE General Test, minimum overall undergraduate GPA of 2.5; for Ed S, GRE General Test, interview, master's degree, minimum GPA of 3.5, work experience. Additional exam requirements/recommendations for international students: Required—TOEFL (minimum score 500 paper-based; 173 computer-based). Electronic applications accepted. *Faculty research:* Character education, school accountability, computer applications for school administrators.

Mount Saint Vincent University, Graduate Programs, Faculty of Education, Program in Adult Education, Halifax, NS B3M 2J6, Canada. Offers M Ed, MA Ed, MA-R. Part-time and evening/weekend programs available. Postbaccalaureate distance learning degree programs offered (minimal on-campus study). *Degree requirements:* For master's, thesis (for some programs), practicum. *Entrance requirements:* For master's, bachelor's degree in related field, minimum B average. Electronic applications accepted.

National Louis University, College of Arts and Sciences, Chicago, IL 60603. Offers adult education (Ed D); counseling and human services (MS); language and academic development (M Ed, Certificate); psychology (MA, PhD, Certificate); public policy (MA); written communication (MS, Certificate). Part-time and evening/weekend programs available. Postbaccalaureate distance learning degree programs offered (minimal on-campus study). *Students:* 33 full-time (25 women), 466 part-time (388 women); includes 233 minority (176 Black or African American, non-Hispanic/Latino; 1 American Indian or Alaska Native, non-Hispanic/Latino; 12 Asian, non-Hispanic/Latino; 41 Hispanic/Latino; 3 Two or more races, non-Hispanic/Latino). Average age 38. In 2011, 196 master's, 7 doctorates, 48 other advanced degrees awarded. *Degree requirements:* For master's and Certificate, comprehensive exam (for some programs), thesis (for some programs); for doctorate, thesis/dissertation. *Entrance requirements:* For master's, MAT or GRE, 3 professional or academic references, interview, minimum GPA of 3.0; for doctorate, GRE General Test, MAT, or Watson-Glaser Critical Thinking Appraisal, three professional or academic references, statement of academic and professional goals, 3 years of experience in field, interview, master's degree, resume, writing sample; for Certificate, GRE, MAT, or Watson-Glaser Critical Thinking Appraisal, three professional or academic references, statement of academic and professional goals, interview, minimum GPA of 3.0. Additional exam requirements/recommendations for international students: Required—Department of Language Studies Assessment or TOEFL (minimum score 550 paper-based; 213 computer-based; 79 iBT). *Application deadline:* Applications are processed on a rolling basis. Application fee: $40. Electronic applications accepted. *Financial support:* Career-related internships or fieldwork, Federal Work-Study, institutionally sponsored loans, scholarships/grants, and tuition waivers available. Support available to part-time students. Financial award applicants required to submit FAFSA. *Unit head:* Dr. Walter Roettger, Interim Dean, 312-261-3073, Fax: 312-261-3073, E-mail: walter.roettger@nl.edu. *Application contact:* Dr. Ken Kasprzak, Director of Admissions, 888-658-8632, Fax: 847-947-5575, E-mail: kkasprzak@nl.edu.

North Carolina Agricultural and Technical State University, School of Graduate Studies, School of Education, Department of Human Development and Services, Greensboro, NC 27411. Offers adult education (MS); counseling (MS); school administration (MS). *Accreditation:* ACA. Part-time and evening/weekend programs available. *Degree requirements:* For master's, comprehensive exam, thesis, qualifying exam. *Entrance requirements:* For master's, GRE General Test, minimum GPA of 3.0.

North Carolina State University, Graduate School, College of Education, Department of Adult and Higher Education, Program in Adult and Community College Education, Raleigh, NC 27695. Offers M Ed, MS, Ed D. *Degree requirements:* For master's, thesis (for some programs); for doctorate, thesis/dissertation. *Entrance requirements:* For master's and doctorate, GRE or MAT. Electronic applications accepted.

North Dakota State University, College of Graduate and Interdisciplinary Studies, College of Human Development and Education, School of Education, Fargo, ND 58108. Offers agricultural education (M Ed, MS), including agricultural education, agricultural extension education (MS); counseling (M Ed, MS, PhD); curriculum and instruction (M Ed, MS), including pedagogy, physical education and athletic administration; education (PhD); educational leadership (M Ed, MS, Ed S); family and consumer sciences education (M Ed, MS); history education (M Ed, MS); institutional analysis (Ed D); mathematics education (M Ed, MS); music education (M Ed, MS); occupational and adult education (Ed D); science education (M Ed, MS). *Accreditation:* NCATE. Part-time and evening/weekend programs available. Postbaccalaureate distance learning degree programs offered (minimal on-campus study). *Faculty:* 24 full-time (10 women), 2 part-time/adjunct (1 woman). *Students:* 91 full-time (64 women), 114 part-time (78 women); includes 13 minority (4 Black or African American, non-Hispanic/Latino; 5 American Indian or Alaska Native, non-Hispanic/Latino; 1 Hispanic/Latino; 3 Two or more races, non-Hispanic/Latino), 8 international. 88 applicants, 67% accepted, 56 enrolled. In 2011, 43 master's, 12 doctorates awarded. *Degree requirements:* For master's, comprehensive exam; for doctorate, thesis/dissertation; for Ed S, thesis. *Entrance requirements:* For degree, GRE General Test, master's degree, minimum GPA of 3.25. Additional exam requirements/recommendations for international students: Required—TOEFL. *Application deadline:* Applications are processed on a rolling basis. Application fee: $45 ($60 for international students). *Financial support:* Research assistantships, teaching assistantships, career-related internships or fieldwork, Federal Work-Study, institutionally sponsored loans, and tuition waivers (full) available. Financial award application deadline: 4/15. *Unit head:* Dr. William Martin, Chair, 701-231-7202, Fax: 701-231-7416, E-mail: william.martin@ndsu.edu. *Application contact:* Sonya Goergen, Marketing, Recruitment, and Public Relations Coordinator, 701-231-7033, Fax: 701-231-6524. Web site: http://www.ndsu.nodak.edu/school_of_education/.

Northern Illinois University, Graduate School, College of Education, Department of Counseling, Adult and Higher Education, De Kalb, IL 60115-2854. Offers adult and higher education (MS Ed, Ed D); counseling (MS Ed, Ed D). *Accreditation:* ACA. Part-time and evening/weekend programs available. *Faculty:* 19 full-time (11 women), 2 part-time/adjunct (1 woman). *Students:* 122 full-time (84 women), 292 part-time (215 women); includes 149 minority (109 Black or African American, non-Hispanic/Latino; 1 American Indian or Alaska Native, non-Hispanic/Latino; 14 Asian, non-Hispanic/Latino; 20 Hispanic/Latino; 5 Two or more races, non-Hispanic/Latino), 14 international. Average age 36. 115 applicants, 55% accepted, 42 enrolled. In 2011, 58 master's, 21 doctorates awarded. Terminal master's awarded for partial completion of doctoral program. *Degree requirements:* For master's, comprehensive exam, thesis optional; for doctorate, thesis/dissertation, candidacy exam, dissertation defense. *Entrance requirements:* For master's, GRE General Test or MAT, minimum undergraduate GPA of 2.75, interview (counseling); for doctorate, GRE General Test, minimum undergraduate GPA of 2.75, 3.2 graduate, interview (counseling). Additional exam requirements/recommendations for international students: Required—TOEFL (minimum score 550 paper-based; 213 computer-based). *Application deadline:* For fall admission, 6/1 for domestic students, 5/1 for international students; for spring admission, 11/1 for domestic students, 10/1 for international students. Applications are processed on a rolling basis. Application fee: $40. Electronic applications accepted. *Financial support:* In 2011–12, 5 research assistantships with full tuition reimbursements, 1 teaching assistantship with full tuition reimbursement were awarded; fellowships with full tuition reimbursements, career-related internships or fieldwork, Federal Work-Study, scholarships/grants, tuition waivers (full), and staff assistantships also available. Support available to part-time students. Financial award applicants required to submit FAFSA. *Unit head:* Dr. Barbara Johnson, Interim Chair, 815-753-1448, E-mail: cahe@niu.edu. *Application contact:* Graduate School Office, 815-753-0395, E-mail: gradsch@niu.edu. Web site: http://www.cedu.niu.edu/cahe/index.html.

Northwestern Oklahoma State University, School of Professional Studies, Program in Adult Education Management and Administration, Alva, OK 73717-2799. Offers M Ed. Part-time programs available. *Faculty:* 5 full-time (2 women). *Students:* 1 (woman) full-time, 14 part-time (6 women); includes 2 minority (1 American Indian or Alaska Native, non-Hispanic/Latino; 1 Hispanic/Latino). 7 applicants, 86% accepted, 6 enrolled. In 2011, 5 master's awarded. *Degree requirements:* For master's, thesis optional, portfolio. *Entrance requirements:* For master's, GRE or MAT, minimum GPA of 2.75. *Application deadline:* Applications are processed on a rolling basis. Application fee: $15. *Financial support:* Application deadline: 5/1; applicants required to submit FAFSA. *Unit head:* Dr. Beverly Warden. *Application contact:* Sabrina Watson, Coordinator of Graduate Studies, 580-327-8410, E-mail: sdwatson@nwosu.edu.

Northwestern State University of Louisiana, Graduate Studies and Research, College of Education and Human Development, Program in Adult and Continuing Education, Natchitoches, LA 71497. Offers MA. *Students:* 16 full-time (11 women), 58 part-time (34 women); includes 27 minority (25 Black or African American, non-Hispanic/Latino; 1 Hispanic/Latino; 1 Two or more races, non-Hispanic/Latino). Average age 39. 37 applicants, 97% accepted, 29 enrolled. In 2011, 18 master's awarded. *Degree requirements:* For master's, comprehensive exam, thesis or alternative. *Entrance requirements:* For master's, GRE General Test, minimum undergraduate GPA of 2.5. Additional exam requirements/recommendations for international students: Required—TOEFL. *Application deadline:* For fall admission, 3/15 priority date for domestic students; for spring admission, 10/15 priority date for domestic students. Applications are processed on a rolling basis. Application fee: $20 ($30 for international students). Electronic applications accepted. *Expenses:* Tuition, state resident: full-time $3440. Tuition, nonresident: full-time $12,010. *Financial support:* Application deadline: 5/1; applicants required to submit FAFSA. *Unit head:* Dr. Vickie Gentry, Chair, 318-357-6288, Fax: 318-357-6275, E-mail: education@nsula.edu. *Application contact:* Dr. Steven G. Horton, Associate Provost/Dean, Graduate Studies, Research, and Information Systems, 318-357-5851, Fax: 318-357-5019, E-mail: grad_school@nsula.edu.

Oregon State University, Graduate School, College of Education, Program in Adult Education and Higher Education Leadership, Corvallis, OR 97331. Offers Ed M, MAIS. *Accreditation:* NCATE. Part-time programs available. *Degree requirements:* For master's, thesis or alternative. *Entrance requirements:* For master's, minimum GPA of 3.0 in last 90 hours. Additional exam requirements/recommendations for international students: Required—TOEFL. *Faculty research:* Adult training and developmental psychology, cross-cultural communication, leadership development and human relations, adult literacy.

Penn State University Park, Graduate School, College of Education, Department of Learning and Performance Systems, State College, University Park, PA 16802-1503. Offers adult education (M Ed, D Ed, PhD, Certificate); instructional systems (M Ed, MS, D Ed, PhD); workforce education and development (M Ed, MS, PhD). *Unit head:* Dr. David H. Monk, Dean, 814-865-2526, Fax: 814-865-0555, E-mail: dhm6@psu.edu. *Application contact:* Cynthia E. Nicosia, Director, Graduate Enrollment Services, 814-865-1834, E-mail: cey1@psu.edu. Web site: http://www.ed.psu.edu/educ/lps/dept-lps.

Plymouth State University, College of Graduate Studies, Graduate Studies in Education, Program in Learning, Leadership and Community, Plymouth, NH 03264-1595. Offers Ed D.

Portland State University, Graduate Studies, School of Education, Department of Educational Policy, Foundations, and Administrative Studies, Portland, OR 97207-0751. Offers educational leadership (MA, MS, Ed D); postsecondary, adult and continuing education (Ed D). *Accreditation:* NCATE. Part-time and evening/weekend programs available. *Degree requirements:* For master's, thesis or alternative, written exam or research project; for doctorate, comprehensive exam, thesis/dissertation. *Entrance requirements:* For master's, California Basic Educational Skills Test, minimum GPA of 3.0 in upper-division course work or 2.75 overall; for doctorate, GRE General Test or MAT. Additional exam requirements/recommendations for international students: Required—TOEFL (minimum score 550 paper-based; 213 computer-based). *Faculty research:* Leadership development and research, principals and urban schools, accelerated schools, cooperative learning, family involvement in schools.

Regent University, Graduate School, School of Education, Virginia Beach, VA 23464-9800. Offers adult education (Ed D); adult/staff development (Ed D, PhD); career switcher with licensure (M Ed), including alternative licensure; character education (Ed D, PhD); Christian education leadership (Ed D, PhD); Christian education specialist (Ed S); Christian school program (M Ed), including ACSI licensure; distance education (Ed D, PhD); education licensure (M Ed), including preK-6th grade; educational leadership (M Ed, PhD); educational leadership - special education (Ed S), including administration and supervision; educational psychology (Ed D, PhD), including learning and development, research and evaluation, special education; higher education (Ed D, PhD), including administration, research and institutional planning, teaching; higher education leadership (Ed D); individualized degree plan (M Ed), including behavior disorders, learning disabilities, mental retardation, reading specialist; K-12 school leadership (Ed D, PhD); leadership in character education (M Ed); master teacher (M Ed), including TESOL; mathematics education (M Ed); special education (PhD); student affairs (M Ed); TESOL (M Ed), including adult education, ESL: preK-12. *Accreditation:* Teacher Education Accreditation Council. Part-time and evening/weekend programs available. Postbaccalaureate distance learning degree programs offered (minimal on-campus study). *Faculty:* 26 full-time (13 women), 54 part-time/adjunct (34 women). *Students:* 140 full-time (109 women), 786 part-time (626 women); includes 218 minority (189 Black or African American, non-Hispanic/Latino; 2 American Indian or Alaska Native, non-Hispanic/Latino; 11 Asian, non-Hispanic/Latino; 16 Hispanic/Latino), 42 international. Average age 39. 673 applicants, 57% accepted, 298 enrolled. In 2011, 178 master's, 15 doctorates awarded. *Degree requirements:* For master's, thesis or alternative; for doctorate, comprehensive exam, thesis/dissertation. *Entrance requirements:* For master's, MAT, minimum undergraduate GPA of 2.75, writing sample, resume, recommendations, interview; for doctorate, GRE, writing sample, 3 years of relevant professional experience, master's-level paper, copies of published work, resume, transcripts, interview, recommendations. Additional exam requirements/recommendations for international students: Required—TOEFL (minimum score 577 paper-based; 233 computer-based). *Application deadline:* For fall admission, 4/1 priority date for domestic students; for spring admission, 10/15 priority date for domestic students. Applications are processed on a rolling basis. Application fee: $50. Electronic applications accepted. *Expenses:* Contact institution. *Financial support:* Fellowships, career-related internships or fieldwork, scholarships/grants, tuition waivers (full and partial), and unspecified assistantships available. Support available to part-time students. Financial award application deadline: 4/1; financial award applicants required to submit FAFSA. *Faculty research:* Character development and discipline for children, education leadership development, diversity in schools, classroom management, technology in education settings. *Unit head:* Dr. Alan A. Arroyo, Dean, 757-352-4261, Fax: 757-352-4318, E-mail: alanarr@regent.edu. *Application contact:* Matthew Chadwick, Director of Enrollment Support Services, 800-373-5504, Fax: 757-352-4381, E-mail: admissions@regent.edu. Web site: http://www.regent.edu/education/.

Regis University, College for Professional Studies, School of Education and Counseling, Department of Education, Denver, CO 80221-1099. Offers adult learning, training, and development (M Ed, Certificate); autism (Certificate); curriculum, instruction, and assessment (M Ed); educational leadership (Certificate); educational technology (Certificate); instructional technology (M Ed); literacy (Certificate); professional leadership (M Ed); reading (M Ed); self-designed (M Ed); space studies (M Ed). Program also offered in Henderson and Las Vegas (Summerlin), NV. *Accreditation:* Teacher Education Accreditation Council. Part-time and evening/weekend programs available. Postbaccalaureate distance learning degree programs offered (no on-campus study). *Degree requirements:* For master's, thesis. *Entrance requirements:* For master's, resume, minimum GPA of 2.75, criminal background check. Additional exam requirements/recommendations for international students: Required—TOEFL (minimum score 213 computer-based), TWE (minimum score 5). Electronic applications accepted. *Faculty research:* Issues of equity in the middle school classroom, professional learning communities, school reform, socialinguistic and discursive obstacles to student integration, inclusive language arts curriculum.

St. Francis Xavier University, Graduate Studies, Department of Adult Education, Antigonish, NS B2G 2W5, Canada. Offers M Ad Ed. Part-time programs available. Postbaccalaureate distance learning degree programs offered (minimal on-campus study). *Degree requirements:* For master's, thesis. *Entrance requirements:* For master's, minimum undergraduate B average, 2 years of work experience in field. Additional exam requirements/recommendations for international students: Required—TOEFL (minimum score 580 paper-based; 236 computer-based). *Faculty research:* Adult learning and development, religious education, women's issues, literacy, action research.

Saint Joseph's College of Maine, Master of Science in Education Program, Standish, ME 04084. Offers adult education and training (MS Ed); Catholic school leadership (MS Ed); health care educator (MS Ed); school educator (MS Ed). Program available by correspondence. Part-time programs available. Postbaccalaureate distance learning degree programs offered (minimal on-campus study). *Faculty:* 20 part-time/adjunct (13 women). *Students:* 273 part-time (190 women); includes 21 minority (14 Black or African American, non-Hispanic/Latino; 1 American Indian or Alaska Native, non-Hispanic/Latino; 2 Asian, non-Hispanic/Latino; 4 Hispanic/Latino). Average age 43. In 2011, 25 master's awarded. *Application deadline:* Applications are processed on a rolling basis. Application fee: $50. Electronic applications accepted. One-time fee: $50. *Financial support:* Institutionally sponsored loans available. Support available to part-time students. Financial award applicants required to submit FAFSA. *Unit head:* Dr. Thomas Hancock, Director, 207-893-7841, Fax: 207-892-7987, E-mail: thancock@sjcme.edu. *Application contact:* Lynne Robinson, Director of Admissions, 800-752-4723, Fax: 207-892-7480, E-mail: info@sjcme.edu. Web site: http://online.sjcme.edu/master-science-education.php.

Saint Joseph's University, College of Arts and Sciences, Organization Development and Leadership Programs, Philadelphia, PA 19131-1395. Offers adult learning and training (MS, Certificate); organization dynamics and leadership (MS, Certificate); organizational psychology and development (MS, Certificate). Part-time and evening/weekend programs available. Postbaccalaureate distance learning degree programs offered (no on-campus study). *Faculty:* 2 full-time (both women), 3 part-time/adjunct (1 woman). *Students:* 8 full-time (all women), 159 part-time (111 women); includes 50 minority (35 Black or African American, non-Hispanic/Latino; 1 American Indian or Alaska Native, non-Hispanic/Latino; 5 Asian, non-Hispanic/Latino; 7 Hispanic/Latino; 1 Native Hawaiian or other Pacific Islander, non-Hispanic/Latino; 1 Two or more races, non-Hispanic/Latino), 5 international. Average age 37. 57 applicants, 84% accepted, 42 enrolled. In 2011, 41 master's awarded. *Entrance requirements:* For master's, GRE (if GPA less than 2.7), minimum GPA of 2.7, 2 letters of recommendation, resume. Additional exam requirements/recommendations for international students: Required—TOEFL (minimum score 550 paper-based; 213 computer-based; 79 iBT). *Application deadline:* For fall admission, 7/15 priority date for domestic students, 4/15 for international students; for winter admission, 1/15 for international students; for spring admission, 11/15 priority date for domestic students, 10/15 for international students. Applications are processed on a rolling basis. Application fee: $35. Electronic applications accepted. *Expenses: Tuition:* Part-time $735 per credit hour. Tuition and fees vary according to degree level and program. *Financial support:* Applicants required to submit FAFSA. *Unit head:* Dr. Felice Tilin, Director, 610-660-1575, E-mail: ftilin@

sju.edu. *Application contact:* Kate McConnell, Director, Graduate College of Arts and Sciences Admissions and Retention, 610-660-3184, Fax: 610-660-3230, E-mail: kate.mcconnell@sju.edu. Web site: http://www.sju.edu/academics/cas/grad/odl/index.html.

San Francisco State University, Division of Graduate Studies, College of Education, Department of Administration and Interdisciplinary Studies, Program in Adult Education, San Francisco, CA 94132-1722. Offers MA, AC. *Accreditation:* NCATE. *Unit head:* Dr. David Hemphill, Chair, 415-338-1653, E-mail: mstepney@sfsu.edu. *Application contact:* Dr. Ming Yeh Lee, Graduate Coordinator, 415-338-1081, E-mail: mylee@sfsu.edu. Web site: http://coe.sfsu.edu/dais.

Seattle University, College of Education, Program in Adult Education and Training, Seattle, WA 98122-1090. Offers M Ed, MA, Certificate. *Accreditation:* NCATE. Part-time and evening/weekend programs available. *Students:* 1 (woman) full-time, 26 part-time (21 women); includes 5 minority (2 Black or African American, non-Hispanic/Latino; 3 Asian, non-Hispanic/Latino), 1 international. Average age 34. 13 applicants, 85% accepted, 9 enrolled. In 2011, 16 master's awarded. *Degree requirements:* For master's, comprehensive exam. *Entrance requirements:* For master's, GRE, MAT, or minimum GPA of 3.0; 1 year of related experience. Additional exam requirements/recommendations for international students: Required—TOEFL. *Application deadline:* For fall admission, 8/20 priority date for domestic students; for winter admission, 11/20 for domestic students; for spring admission, 2/20 for domestic students. Applications are processed on a rolling basis. Application fee: $55. *Financial support:* Career-related internships or fieldwork and Federal Work-Study available. Support available to part-time students. Financial award applicants required to submit FAFSA. *Unit head:* Dr. Carol Weaver, Director, 206-296-5908, E-mail: cweaver@seattleu.edu. *Application contact:* Janet Shandley, Associate Dean of Graduate Admissions, 206-296-5900, Fax: 206-298-5656, E-mail: grad_admissions@seattleu.edu.

Suffolk University, College of Arts and Sciences, Department of Education and Human Services, Boston, MA 02108-2770. Offers administration of higher education (M Ed, CAGS), including administration of higher education (M Ed), leadership (CAGS); human resource, learning and performance (MS, CAGS, Graduate Certificate), including global human resources (Graduate Certificate), human resources (MS, Graduate Certificate), organizational development (CAGS, Graduate Certificate), organizational learning and development (MS, Graduate Certificate); mental health counseling (MS, CAGS); school counseling (M Ed, CAGS); school teaching (M Ed, CAGS), including foundations of education (M Ed), middle school teaching (M Ed), secondary school teaching (M Ed); MPA/MSMHC; MS/Certificate. Part-time and evening/weekend programs available. *Faculty:* 10 full-time (6 women), 7 part-time/adjunct (3 women). *Students:* 53 full-time (39 women), 131 part-time (112 women); includes 21 minority (7 Black or African American, non-Hispanic/Latino; 2 American Indian or Alaska Native, non-Hispanic/Latino; 5 Asian, non-Hispanic/Latino; 5 Hispanic/Latino; 2 Two or more races, non-Hispanic/Latino), 9 international. Average age 28. 158 applicants, 73% accepted, 60 enrolled. In 2011, 72 master's, 8 other advanced degrees awarded. *Entrance requirements:* For master's, GRE General Test or MAT, 2 letters of recommendation, resume. Additional exam requirements/recommendations for international students: Required—TOEFL (minimum score 550 paper-based; 213 computer-based; 80 iBT). *Application deadline:* For fall admission, 6/15 priority date for domestic students, 6/15 for international students; for spring admission, 11/1 priority date for domestic students, 11/1 for international students. Applications are processed on a rolling basis. Application fee: $50. Electronic applications accepted. *Expenses:* Contact institution. *Financial support:* In 2011–12, 102 students received support, including 30 fellowships with full and partial tuition reimbursements available (averaging $10,664 per year); career-related internships or fieldwork, Federal Work-Study, and institutionally sponsored loans also available. Support available to part-time students. Financial award application deadline: 4/1; financial award applicants required to submit FAFSA. *Faculty research:* Predicting competent Head Start preschools, cultural differences. *Unit head:* Dr. Krisanne Bursik, Associate Dean and Acting Chair, 617-573-8261, Fax: 617-305-1743, E-mail: kbursik@suffolk.edu. *Application contact:* Ellen Driscoll, Director of Graduate Admissions, 617-573-8302, Fax: 617-305-1733, E-mail: grad.admission@suffolk.edu. Web site: http://www.suffolk.edu/college/9785.html.

Syracuse University, School of Education, Program in Lifelong Learning and Continuing Education, Syracuse, NY 13244. Offers Certificate. Part-time programs available. *Entrance requirements:* Additional exam requirements/recommendations for international students: Required—TOEFL. Application fee: $75. *Expenses: Tuition:* Part-time $1206 per credit. *Unit head:* Dr. Douglas Biklen, Dean, 315-443-4751. *Application contact:* Laurie Deyo, Graduate Recruiter, School of Education, 315-443-2505, E-mail: e-gradrcrt@syr.edu. Web site: http://soeweb.syr.edu/.

Teachers College, Columbia University, Graduate Faculty of Education, Department of Organization and Leadership, Adult Education Guided Intensive Study (AEGIS) Program, New York, NY 10027. Offers Ed D. *Accreditation:* NCATE. *Faculty:* 1 full-time (0 women), 16 part-time/adjunct (9 women). *Students:* 45 full-time (28 women), 76 part-time (50 women); includes 44 minority (23 Black or African American, non-Hispanic/Latino; 9 Asian, non-Hispanic/Latino; 12 Hispanic/Latino), 16 international. Average age 42. 33 applicants, 55% accepted, 11 enrolled. In 2011, 13 doctorates awarded. *Degree requirements:* For doctorate, comprehensive exam, thesis/dissertation, qualifying paper. *Entrance requirements:* For doctorate, 3-5 years of professional experience. *Application deadline:* For fall admission, 10/1 priority date for domestic students. Application fee: $65. Electronic applications accepted. *Financial support:* Career-related internships or fieldwork, Federal Work-Study, institutionally sponsored loans, and tuition waivers (full and partial) available. Support available to part-time students. Financial award applicants required to submit FAFSA. *Faculty research:* Adult learning, perspective transformation, training and evaluation, workplace learning, theory to practice. *Unit head:* Lyle Yorks, Program Coordinator, 212-678-3760, E-mail: ly84@columbia.edu. *Application contact:* Debbie Lesperance, Assistant Director of Admission, 212-678-3710, Fax: 212-678-4171. Web site: http://www.tc.columbia.edu/o&l/adulted/index.asp?Id=Program+Information&Info=AEGIS.

Teachers College, Columbia University, Graduate Faculty of Education, Department of Organization and Leadership, Program in Adult Learning and Leadership, New York, NY 10027. Offers Ed M, MA, Ed D. *Faculty:* 3 full-time (2 women), 16 part-time/adjunct (9 women). *Degree requirements:* For master's, culminating integrative project; for doctorate, comprehensive exam, thesis/dissertation. *Entrance requirements:* For master's, academic writing sample (for Ed M applicants); for doctorate, academic writing sample. *Application deadline:* For fall admission, 1/2 for domestic students. Electronic applications accepted. *Faculty research:* Informal workplace learning, team learning, action learning, strategic organizational learning and knowledge management, cultivation of learning communities. *Unit head:* Prof. Victoria Marsick, Program Coordinator, 212-678-3760, E-mail: al&l@tc.edu. *Application contact:* Debbie Lesperance, Assistant Director of Admission, 212-678-3710, Fax: 212-678-4171. Web site: http://www.tc.edu/o%26l/AdultEd/.

Texas A&M University, College of Education and Human Development, Department of Educational Administration and Human Resource Development, College Station, TX 77843. Offers adult education (PhD); higher education administration (MS, PhD); human resource development (MS, PhD); public school administration (M Ed, Ed D, PhD). Part-time programs available. *Faculty:* 31. *Students:* 126 full-time (88 women), 270 part-time (156 women); includes 162 minority (65 Black or African American, non-Hispanic/Latino; 2 American Indian or Alaska Native, non-Hispanic/Latino; 15 Asian, non-Hispanic/Latino; 77 Hispanic/Latino; 3 Two or more races, non-Hispanic/Latino), 23 international. Average age 37. In 2011, 91 master's, 30 doctorates awarded. *Degree requirements:* For master's, thesis optional; for doctorate, thesis/dissertation. *Entrance requirements:* For master's, GRE General Test, writing exam, interview, professional experience; for doctorate, GRE General Test, writing exam, interview/presentation, professional experience. Additional exam requirements/recommendations for international students: Required—TOEFL. *Application deadline:* For fall admission, 12/1 for domestic and international students; for spring admission, 8/15 for domestic and international students. Application fee: $50 ($75 for international students). Electronic applications accepted. *Expenses:* Tuition, state resident: full-time $5437; part-time $226.55 per credit hour. Tuition, nonresident: full-time $12,949; part-time $539.55 per credit hour. *Required fees:* $2741. *Financial support:* In 2011–12, fellowships (averaging $20,000 per year), research assistantships (averaging $12,000 per year) were awarded; career-related internships or fieldwork and institutionally sponsored loans also available. Support available to part-time students. Financial award application deadline: 3/1; financial award applicants required to submit FAFSA. *Faculty research:* Higher education administration, public school administration, student affairs. *Unit head:* Dr. Fred M. Nafukho, Head, 979-862-3395, Fax: 979-862-4347, E-mail: fnafukho@tamu.edu. *Application contact:* Joyce Nelson, Director of Academic Advising, 979-847-9098, Fax: 979-862-4347, E-mail: jnelson@tamu.edu. Web site: http://eahr.tamu.edu.

Texas A&M University–Kingsville, College of Graduate Studies, College of Education, Department of Education, Program in Adult Education, Kingsville, TX 78363. Offers M Ed. Program offered jointly with Texas A&M University. Part-time and evening/weekend programs available. *Degree requirements:* For master's, comprehensive exam, mini-thesis. *Entrance requirements:* For master's, GRE General Test, MAT, minimum GPA of 3.0. *Faculty research:* Continuing education efforts in south Texas, adult education methodologies.

Texas A&M University–Texarkana, Graduate Studies and Research, College of Education and Liberal Arts, Texarkana, TX 75505-5518. Offers adult education (MS); curriculum and instruction (M Ed); education (MS); educational administration (M Ed); English (MA); instructional technology (MS); interdisciplinary studies (MA, MS); special education (MS). Part-time and evening/weekend programs available. *Degree requirements:* For master's, comprehensive exam (for some programs), thesis optional. *Entrance requirements:* For master's, minimum GPA of 2.5 on last 60 hours of bachelor's degree. Additional exam requirements/recommendations for international students: Required—TOEFL. Electronic applications accepted.

Texas State University–San Marcos, Graduate School, College of Education, Department of Counseling, Leadership, Adult Education, and School Psychology, Program in Adult, Professional and Community Education, San Marcos, TX 78666. Offers adult, professional, and community education (PhD); developmental and adult education (MA). Part-time programs available. *Faculty:* 19 full-time (7 women), 1 part-time/adjunct (0 women). *Students:* 16 full-time (11 women), 46 part-time (21 women); includes 26 minority (11 Black or African American, non-Hispanic/Latino; 1 American Indian or Alaska Native, non-Hispanic/Latino; 1 Asian, non-Hispanic/Latino; 13 Hispanic/Latino), 3 international. Average age 45. 15 applicants, 73% accepted, 9 enrolled. In 2011, 7 master's, 7 doctorates awarded. *Degree requirements:* For master's, comprehensive exam, thesis, internship. *Entrance requirements:* For master's, minimum GPA of 2.75 in last 60 hours of course work. Additional exam requirements/recommendations for international students: Required—TOEFL (minimum score 550 paper-based; 213 computer-based; 78 iBT). *Application deadline:* For fall admission, 6/15 for domestic students, 6/1 for international students; for spring admission, 10/1 for domestic and international students. Applications are processed on a rolling basis. Application fee: $40 ($90 for international students). Electronic applications accepted. *Expenses:* Tuition, state resident: full-time $6408; part-time $3204 per semester. Tuition, nonresident: full-time $14,832; part-time $7416 per semester. *Required fees:* $1824; $912 per semester. Tuition and fees vary according to course load. *Financial support:* In 2011–12, 12 students received support, including 4 research assistantships (averaging $17,280 per year), 7 teaching assistantships (averaging $18,522 per year); career-related internships or fieldwork, Federal Work-Study, and institutionally sponsored loans also available. Support available to part-time students. Financial award application deadline: 4/1; financial award applicants required to submit FAFSA. *Unit head:* Dr. Jovita Ross-Gordan, Graduate Advisor, 512-245-3083, Fax: 512-245-8872, E-mail: jr24@txstate.edu. *Application contact:* Dr. J. Michael Willoughby, Dean of Graduate School, 512-245-2531, Fax: 512-245-8365, E-mail: gradcollege@txstate.edu. Web site: http://www.gradcollege.txstate.edu/Prospect_Students/Pgms_Apps/Doctoral/Ed_Ad_Pro_Comm_Ed.html.

Trident University International, College of Education, Program in Education, Cypress, CA 90630. Offers adult education (MA Ed); aviation education (MA Ed); children's literacy development (MA Ed); e-learning (MA Ed); early childhood education (MA Ed); enrollment management (MA Ed); higher education (MA Ed); teaching and instruction (MA Ed); training and development (MA Ed). Part-time and evening/weekend programs available. Postbaccalaureate distance learning degree programs offered (no on-campus study). *Degree requirements:* For master's, capstone project with integrative paper. *Entrance requirements:* For master's, minimum GPA of 2.5 (students with GPA 3.0 or greater may transfer up to 30% of graduate level credits). Additional exam requirements/recommendations for international students: Required—TOEFL (minimum score 525 paper-based). Electronic applications accepted.

Troy University, Graduate School, College of Education, Program in Adult Education, Troy, AL 36082. Offers MS. Part-time and evening/weekend programs available. *Faculty:* 5 full-time (2 women), 6 part-time/adjunct (2 women). *Students:* 4 full-time (3 women), 44 part-time (36 women); includes 33 minority (32 Black or African American, non-Hispanic/Latino; 1 Asian, non-Hispanic/Latino). Average age 42. 23 applicants, 91% accepted, 12 enrolled. In 2011, 19 master's awarded. *Degree requirements:* For master's, comprehensive exam, thesis or alternative. *Entrance requirements:* For master's, MAT (minimum score 385), bachelor's degree. Additional exam requirements/recommendations for international students: Required—TOEFL (minimum score 523 paper-based; 193 computer-based; 70 iBT), IELTS (minimum score 6), or ACT COMPASS ESL (minimum listening, reading, and grammar score 270). *Application deadline:* Applications are processed on a rolling basis. Application fee: $50. Electronic applications accepted. *Expenses:* Tuition, state resident: full-time $6960; part-time $290 per credit hour. Tuition, nonresident: full-time $13,920; part-time $580 per credit hour. *Required fees:* $386 per term. *Unit head:* Dr. Joe H. Reynolds, Coordinator, 334-241-8577, Fax: 334-240-7320, E-mail: jreynolds45@troy.edu. *Application contact:* Beth Potts, Graduate Actions Coordinator, 334-241-9707, Fax: 334-241-9586, E-mail: lizrichmond@troy.edu.

Troy University, Graduate School, College of Education, Program in Postsecondary Education, Troy, AL 36082. Offers adult education (M Ed); biology (M Ed); criminal justice (M Ed); English (M Ed); foundations of education (M Ed); general science (M Ed); higher education administration (M Ed); history (M Ed); instructional technology (M Ed); mathematics (M Ed); music industry (M Ed); physical fitness (M Ed); political science

(M Ed); public administration (M Ed); social science (M Ed); teaching English (M Ed). *Accreditation:* NCATE. Part-time and evening/weekend programs available. *Faculty:* 53 full-time (21 women), 22 part-time/adjunct (8 women). *Students:* 74 full-time (51 women), 166 part-time (121 women); includes 148 minority (143 Black or African American, non-Hispanic/Latino; 1 American Indian or Alaska Native, non-Hispanic/Latino; 2 Hispanic/Latino; 2 Two or more races, non-Hispanic/Latino). Average age 34. 174 applicants, 82% accepted, 88 enrolled. In 2011, 221 master's awarded. *Degree requirements:* For master's, comprehensive exam, thesis. *Entrance requirements:* For master's, MAT (minimum score 385), minimum GPA of 2.5. Additional exam requirements/recommendations for international students: Required—TOEFL (minimum score 523 paper-based; 193 computer-based; 70 iBT), IELTS (minimum score 6), or ACT COMPASS ESL (minimum listening, reading, and grammar score 270). *Application deadline:* Applications are processed on a rolling basis. Application fee: $50. Electronic applications accepted. *Expenses:* Tuition, state resident: full-time $6960; part-time $290 per credit hour. Tuition, nonresident: full-time $13,920; part-time $580 per credit hour. *Required fees:* $386 per term. *Financial support:* Available to part-time students. Applicants required to submit FAFSA. *Unit head:* Dr. Jan Oliver, Associate Professor, 334-670-3444, Fax: 334-670-3296, E-mail: oliver@troy.edu. *Application contact:* Brenda K. Campbell, Director of Graduate Admissions, 334-670-3178, Fax: 334-670-3733, E-mail: bcamp@troy.edu.

Tusculum College, Graduate School, Program in Education, Greeneville, TN 37743-9997. Offers adult education (MA Ed); K–12 (MA Ed). Evening/weekend programs available. *Degree requirements:* For master's, thesis or alternative. *Entrance requirements:* For master's, 3 years of work experience, minimum GPA of 2.75.

Union Institute & University, Education Programs, Cincinnati, OH 45206-1925. Offers adult and higher education (M Ed); curriculum and instruction (M Ed); educational leadership (M Ed, Ed D); guidance and counseling (Ed S); higher education (Ed D); issues in education (M Ed); reading (Ed S). M Ed offered online and in Vermont and Florida, concentrations vary by location; Ed S offered in Florida; Ed D program is a hybrid (online with limited residency) offered in Ohio. Postbaccalaureate distance learning degree programs offered (minimal on-campus study). *Degree requirements:* For master's, comprehensive exam (for some programs), thesis (for some programs), electronic portfolio; for doctorate, comprehensive exam, thesis/dissertation, electronic portfolio.

Universidad del Este, Graduate School, Carolina, PR 00984. Offers accounting (MBA); adult education (M Ed); agribusiness (MBA); criminal justice and criminology (MA); curriculum and instruction - early education (M Ed); curriculum and instruction - elementary (M Ed); curriculum and instruction - English (M Ed); curriculum and instruction - Spanish (M Ed); human resources (MBA); information security management (MBA); information technology and Web business development (MBA); management (MBA); public policy (MPA); social work (MA), including clinical social work; special education (M Ed); strategic leadership (MBA).

Universidad Metropolitana, School of Education, Program in Teaching of Physical Education, San Juan, PR 00928-1150. Offers teaching of adult physical education (M Ed); teaching of elementary physical education (M Ed); teaching of secondary physical education (M Ed). *Degree requirements:* For master's, thesis or alternative. *Entrance requirements:* For master's, EXADEP, interview. Electronic applications accepted.

Université du Québec en Outaouais, Graduate Programs, Program in Adult Education, Gatineau, QC J8X 3X7, Canada. Offers andragogy (DESS). Part-time programs available. *Students:* 42 full-time, 104 part-time. *Entrance requirements:* For degree, appropriate bachelor's degree, proficiency in French. *Application deadline:* For fall admission, 6/1 for domestic students, 3/1 for international students; for winter admission, 11/1 for domestic students, 10/1 for international students. Application fee: $30 Canadian dollars. *Financial support:* Fellowships, research assistantships, and teaching assistantships available. *Unit head:* Francine D'Ortun, Director, 819-595-3900 Ext. 4439, Fax: 819-773-1788, E-mail: francine.dortun@uqo.ca. *Application contact:* Registrar's Office, 819-773-1850, Fax: 819-773-1835, E-mail: registraire@ugo.ca.

University of Alaska Anchorage, College of Education, Program in Adult Education, Anchorage, AK 99508. Offers M Ed. Part-time programs available. *Degree requirements:* For master's, thesis or alternative. *Entrance requirements:* For master's, interview, minimum GPA of 3.0, writing exercise. Additional exam requirements/recommendations for international students: Required—TOEFL (minimum score 550 paper-based; 213 computer-based).

University of Alberta, Faculty of Graduate Studies and Research, Department of Educational Policy Studies, Edmonton, AB T6G 2E1, Canada. Offers adult education (M Ed, Ed D, PhD); educational administration and leadership (M Ed, Ed D, PhD, Postgraduate Diploma); First Nations education (M Ed, Ed D, PhD); theoretical, cultural and international studies in education (M Ed, Ed D, PhD). *Degree requirements:* For master's, thesis (for some programs); for doctorate, thesis/dissertation. *Entrance requirements:* For master's, minimum GPA of 6.5 on a 9.0 scale; for doctorate, minimum GPA of 7.5 on a 9.0 scale. Additional exam requirements/recommendations for international students: Required—TOEFL (minimum score 580 paper-based; 237 computer-based). Electronic applications accepted.

University of Arkansas at Little Rock, Graduate School, College of Education, Department of Counseling, Adult and Rehabilitation Education, Program in Adult Education, Little Rock, AR 72204-1099. Offers M Ed. *Accreditation:* NCATE. Part-time programs available. *Degree requirements:* For master's, comprehensive exam. *Entrance requirements:* For master's, interview, minimum GPA of 2.75, GRE General Test or teaching certificate. *Faculty research:* Adult literacy, volunteer training, in-services education.

The University of British Columbia, Faculty of Education, Department of Educational Studies, Vancouver, BC V6T 1Z1, Canada. Offers adult education (M Ed, MA); adult learning and global change (M Ed); educational administration (M Ed, MA); educational leadership and policy (Ed D); educational studies (PhD); higher education (M Ed, MA); society, culture and politics in education (M Ed, MA). Part-time and evening/weekend programs available. Terminal master's awarded for partial completion of doctoral program. *Degree requirements:* For master's, thesis; for doctorate, comprehensive exam, thesis/dissertation, master's thesis. *Entrance requirements:* For master's, minimum B+ average, 4-year undergraduate degree, field-related experience; for doctorate, minimum B+ average, 4-year undergraduate degree, master's degree, field-related experience. Additional exam requirements/recommendations for international students: Required—TOEFL (minimum score 600 paper-based; 250 computer-based; 100 iBT) or IELTS (minimum score 6.5). Electronic applications accepted. *Faculty research:* Educational leadership educational administration adult education politics in education, global change and adult learning.

University of Central Oklahoma, College of Graduate Studies and Research, College of Education and Professional Studies, Department of Occupational and Technical Education, Edmond, OK 73034-5209. Offers adult education (M Ed), including community services, gerontology; general education (M Ed); professional health occupations (M Ed). Part-time programs available. *Faculty:* 11 full-time (5 women), 11 part-time/adjunct (6 women). *Students:* 23 full-time (17 women), 76 part-time (59 women); includes 28 minority (15 Black or African American, non-Hispanic/Latino; 4 American Indian or Alaska Native, non-Hispanic/Latino; 6 Hispanic/Latino; 3 Two or more races, non-Hispanic/Latino), 3 international. Average age 40. In 2011, 64 master's awarded. *Entrance requirements:* For master's, GRE General Test. Additional exam requirements/recommendations for international students: Required—TOEFL (minimum score 550 paper-based; 213 computer-based). *Application deadline:* Applications are processed on a rolling basis. Application fee: $50. Electronic applications accepted. *Expenses:* Tuition, state resident: full-time $3901; part-time $218.30 per credit hour. Tuition, nonresident: full-time $9198; part-time $511.20 per credit hour. Tuition and fees vary according to program. *Financial support:* Unspecified assistantships available. Financial award application deadline: 3/31; financial award applicants required to submit FAFSA. *Faculty research:* Violence in the workplace/schools, aging issues, trade and industrial education. *Unit head:* Dr. Candy Sebert, Chairman, 405-974-5780, Fax: 405-974-3822. *Application contact:* Dr. Richard Bernard, Dean, Graduate College, 405-974-3493, Fax: 405-974-3852, E-mail: gradcoll@uco.edu.

University of Cincinnati, Graduate School, College of Education, Criminal Justice, and Human Services, Division of Teacher Education, Cincinnati, OH 45221. Offers curriculum and instruction (M Ed, Ed D); deaf studies (Certificate); early childhood education (M Ed); middle childhood education (M Ed); postsecondary literacy instruction (Certificate); reading/literacy (M Ed, Ed D); secondary education (M Ed); special education (M Ed, Ed D); teaching English as a second language (M Ed, Ed D, Certificate); teaching science (MS). Part-time programs available. *Degree requirements:* For doctorate, thesis/dissertation. *Entrance requirements:* For master's, GRE General Test. Additional exam requirements/recommendations for international students: Required—TOEFL (minimum score 550 paper-based). Electronic applications accepted.

University of Colorado Denver, School of Education and Human Development, Information and Learning Technologies Program, Denver, CO 80217-3364. Offers e-learning design and implementation (MA); instructional design and adult learning (MA); K-12 teaching (MA). Part-time and evening/weekend programs available. Postbaccalaureate distance learning degree programs offered (no on-campus study). *Students:* 82 full-time (65 women), 46 part-time (38 women); includes 13 minority (2 Black or African American, non-Hispanic/Latino; 3 Asian, non-Hispanic/Latino; 8 Hispanic/Latino), 3 international. Average age 38. 35 applicants, 89% accepted, 27 enrolled. In 2011, 79 master's awarded. *Degree requirements:* For master's, comprehensive exam (for some programs), comprehensive exam or online portfolio; 30 credit hours. *Entrance requirements:* For master's, GRE or MAT (if GPA is below 2.75), resume, statement of intent, three letters of recommendation. Additional exam requirements/recommendations for international students: Required—TOEFL (minimum score 525 paper-based; 197 computer-based). *Application deadline:* For fall admission, 5/15 for domestic students; for spring admission, 11/15 for domestic students. Application fee: $50 ($75 for international students). *Expenses:* Contact institution. *Financial support:* Scholarships/grants available. Financial award application deadline: 4/1; financial award applicants required to submit FAFSA. *Faculty research:* Technology for educational management, instructional design foundations, e-Learning, educational design. *Unit head:* Brent Wilson, Professor, 303-315-4963, E-mail: brent.wilson@ucdenver.edu. *Application contact:* Hans Broers, Academic Advisor, 303-315-6351, Fax: 303-315-6311, E-mail: hans.broers@ucdenver.edu. Web site: http://www.ucdenver.edu/ACADEMICS/COLLEGES/SCHOOLOFEDUCATION/ACADEMICS/Pages/AcademicPrograms.aspx.

University of Connecticut, Graduate School, Neag School of Education, Department of Educational Leadership, Field of Adult Learning, Storrs, CT 06269. Offers MA, PhD. *Accreditation:* NCATE. Terminal master's awarded for partial completion of doctoral program. *Degree requirements:* For master's, comprehensive exam, thesis or alternative; for doctorate, thesis/dissertation. *Entrance requirements:* For master's and doctorate, GRE General Test. Additional exam requirements/recommendations for international students: Required—TOEFL (minimum score 550 paper-based; 213 computer-based). Electronic applications accepted.

University of Georgia, College of Education, Department of Lifelong Education, Administration and Policy, Athens, GA 30602. Offers adult education (M Ed, Ed D, PhD, Ed S); educational administration and policy (M Ed, PhD, Ed S); educational leadership (Ed D); human resource and organizational design (M Ed). *Accreditation:* NCATE. *Faculty:* 25 full-time (18 women), 1 part-time/adjunct (0 women). *Students:* 74 full-time (56 women), 216 part-time (136 women); includes 73 minority (62 Black or African American, non-Hispanic/Latino; 4 Asian, non-Hispanic/Latino; 3 Hispanic/Latino; 4 Two or more races, non-Hispanic/Latino), 23 international. Average age 37. 123 applicants, 64% accepted, 45 enrolled. In 2011, 54 master's, 19 doctorates, 14 other advanced degrees awarded. *Entrance requirements:* For master's and Ed S, GRE General Test or MAT; for doctorate, GRE General Test. *Application deadline:* For fall admission, 7/1 priority date for domestic students; for spring admission, 11/15 for domestic students. Application fee: $50. Electronic applications accepted. *Unit head:* Dr. Janette Hill, Head, 706-542-4035, Fax: 706-542-5873, E-mail: janette@.uga.edu. *Application contact:* Dr. Robert B. Hill, Graduate Coordinator, 706-542-4016, Fax: 706-542-5873, E-mail: bobhill@uga.edu. Web site: http://www.coe.uga.edu/leap/.

University of Manitoba, Faculty of Graduate Studies, Faculty of Education, Department of Educational Administration, Foundations and Psychology, Winnipeg, MB R3T 2N2, Canada. Offers adult and post-secondary education (M Ed); educational administration (M Ed); guidance and counseling (M Ed); inclusive special education (M Ed); social foundations of education (M Ed). *Degree requirements:* For master's, thesis or alternative.

University of Memphis, Graduate School, College of Education, Department of Leadership, Memphis, TN 38152. Offers adult education (Ed D); educational leadership (Ed D); higher education (Ed D); leadership (MS); policy studies (Ed D); school administration and supervision (MS). *Accreditation:* NCATE. Part-time and evening/weekend programs available. Postbaccalaureate distance learning degree programs offered (minimal on-campus study). *Degree requirements:* For master's, comprehensive exam, thesis optional; for doctorate, comprehensive exam, thesis/dissertation. *Entrance requirements:* For master's and doctorate, GRE. Electronic applications accepted. *Faculty research:* School improvement, social justice, online learning, adult learning, diversity.

University of Minnesota, Twin Cities Campus, Graduate School, College of Education and Human Development, Department of Organizational Leadership, Policy and Development, Program in Adult Education, Minneapolis, MN 55455-0213. Offers M Ed, MA, Ed D, PhD, Certificate. *Students:* 12 full-time (all women), 21 part-time (16 women); includes 2 minority (both Asian, non-Hispanic/Latino), 1 international. Average age 36. 18 applicants, 78% accepted, 14 enrolled. In 2011, 16 master's, 30 other advanced degrees awarded. Application fee: $55. *Unit head:* Rebecca Ropers-Huilman, Chair, 612-626-9809, Fax: 612-624-2231, E-mail: ropers@umn.edu. *Application contact:* Dr. Jennifer Engler, Assistant Dean, 612-626-2887, Fax: 612-626-7496, E-mail: engle009@umn.edu. Web site: http://www.education.umn.edu/edpa/.

University of Missouri, Graduate School, College of Education, Department of Educational Leadership and Policy Analysis, Columbia, MO 65211. Offers education administration (M Ed, MA, Ed D, PhD, Ed S); higher and adult education (M Ed, MA,

Ed D, PhD, Ed S). Part-time programs available. *Faculty:* 15 full-time (8 women), 5 part-time/adjunct (4 women). *Students:* 139 full-time (85 women), 273 part-time (158 women); includes 55 minority (38 Black or African American, non-Hispanic/Latino; 1 American Indian or Alaska Native, non-Hispanic/Latino; 6 Asian, non-Hispanic/Latino; 6 Hispanic/Latino; 4 Two or more races, non-Hispanic/Latino), 13 international. Average age 38. 186 applicants, 74% accepted, 91 enrolled. In 2011, 19 master's, 56 doctorates, 16 other advanced degrees awarded. *Degree requirements:* For doctorate, variable foreign language requirement, comprehensive exam (for some programs), thesis/dissertation. *Entrance requirements:* For master's, doctorate, and Ed S, minimum GPA of 3.0. Additional exam requirements/recommendations for international students: Required—TOEFL (minimum score 500 paper-based; 173 computer-based; 61 iBT), IELTS (minimum score 5.5). *Application deadline:* For fall admission, 2/15 priority date for domestic students; for spring admission, 10/15 for domestic students. Applications are processed on a rolling basis. Application fee: $55 ($75 for international students). Electronic applications accepted. *Expenses:* Tuition, state resident: full-time $5881. Tuition, nonresident: full-time $15,183. *Required fees:* $952. Tuition and fees vary according to campus/location and program. *Financial support:* In 2011–12, 2 fellowships with full tuition reimbursements, 32 research assistantships with full tuition reimbursements, 4 teaching assistantships with full tuition reimbursements were awarded; institutionally sponsored loans, scholarships/grants, health care benefits, and unspecified assistantships also available. *Faculty research:* Administrative communication and behavior, middle schools leadership, administration of special education. *Unit head:* Dr. Jay Scribner, Department Chair, E-mail: scribnerj@missouri.edu. *Application contact:* Betty Kissane, 573-882-8231, E-mail: kissaneb@missouri.edu. Web site: http://education.missouri.edu/ELPA/index.php.

University of Missouri–St. Louis, College of Education, Division of Educational Leadership and Policy Studies, St. Louis, MO 63121. Offers adult and higher education (M Ed), including adult education, higher education; educational administration (M Ed, Ed S), including community education (M Ed), elementary education (M Ed), secondary education (M Ed); institutional research (Certificate). *Accreditation:* NCATE. Part-time and evening/weekend programs available. *Faculty:* 17 full-time (8 women), 7 part-time/adjunct (5 women). *Students:* 23 full-time (15 women), 187 part-time (137 women); includes 103 minority (96 Black or African American, non-Hispanic/Latino; 2 Asian, non-Hispanic/Latino; 4 Hispanic/Latino; 1 Two or more races, non-Hispanic/Latino), 4 international. Average age 35. 95 applicants, 86% accepted, 68 enrolled. In 2011, 57 master's, 19 Certificates awarded. *Degree requirements:* For master's, comprehensive exam (for some programs). *Entrance requirements:* Additional exam requirements/recommendations for international students: Required—TOEFL (minimum score 550 paper-based; 213 computer-based). *Application deadline:* For fall admission, 7/1 priority date for domestic students, 7/1 for international students; for spring admission, 12/1 priority date for domestic students, 12/1 for international students. Applications are processed on a rolling basis. Application fee: $35 ($40 for international students). Electronic applications accepted. *Expenses:* Tuition, state resident: full-time $6273; part-time $3866 per year. Tuition, nonresident: full-time $14,969; part-time $9980 per year. *Required fees:* $315 per year. *Financial support:* In 2011–12, 12 research assistantships (averaging $12,000 per year), 1 teaching assistantship (averaging $10,500 per year) were awarded. Financial award application deadline: 4/1; financial award applicants required to submit FAFSA. *Faculty research:* Educational policy research; philosophy of education; higher, adult, and vocational education; school initiatives, change, and reform. *Unit head:* Dr. E. Paulette Savage, Chair, 514-516-5944. *Application contact:* 314-516-5458, Fax: 314-516-6996, E-mail: gradadm@umsl.edu. Web site: http://coe.umsl.edu/web/divisions/elaps/index.html.

University of Missouri–St. Louis, College of Education, Interdisciplinary Doctoral Programs, St. Louis, MO 63121. Offers adult and higher education (Ed D); counseling (PhD); counselor education (Ed D); educational administration (Ed D); educational leadership and policy studies (PhD); educational psychology (PhD); teaching-learning processes (Ed D, PhD). *Faculty:* 72 full-time (33 women). *Students:* 44 full-time (29 women), 199 part-time (138 women); includes 65 minority (52 Black or African American, non-Hispanic/Latino; 3 American Indian or Alaska Native, non-Hispanic/Latino; 5 Asian, non-Hispanic/Latino; 5 Hispanic/Latino), 6 international. Average age 43. 47 applicants, 34% accepted, 11 enrolled. In 2011, 27 doctorates awarded. *Degree requirements:* For doctorate, thesis/dissertation. *Entrance requirements:* For doctorate, GRE General Test, 3 letters of recommendation; personal interview. Additional exam requirements/recommendations for international students: Recommended—TOEFL (minimum score 550 paper-based; 230 computer-based). *Application deadline:* For fall admission, 3/1 for domestic and international students; for spring admission, 10/1 for domestic and international students. Application fee: $35 ($40 for international students). Electronic applications accepted. *Expenses:* Tuition, state resident: full-time $6273; part-time $3866 per year. Tuition, nonresident: full-time $14,969; part-time $9980 per year. *Required fees:* $315 per year. *Financial support:* In 2011–12, 15 research assistantships (averaging $12,240 per year), 8 teaching assistantships (averaging $12,240 per year) were awarded. Financial award application deadline: 4/1; financial award applicants required to submit FAFSA. *Faculty research:* Higher education law and policy, gender and higher education, student retention, lifelong learning orientation, school counselor's role in violence prevention. *Unit head:* Dr. Kathleen Haywood, Director of Graduate Studies, 314-516-5483, Fax: 314-516-5227, E-mail: kathleen_haywood@umsl.edu. *Application contact:* 314-516-5458, Fax: 314-516-6996, E-mail: gradadm@umsl.edu.

University of Nebraska–Lincoln, Graduate College, College of Education and Human Sciences, Department of Teaching, Learning and Teacher Education, Lincoln, NE 68588. Offers adult and continuing education (MA); educational studies (Ed D, PhD), including special education (Ed D); teaching, learning and teacher education (M Ed, MA, MST, Ed D, PhD); vocational and adult education (M Ed, MA). *Accreditation:* NCATE. *Degree requirements:* For master's, thesis optional. *Entrance requirements:* Additional exam requirements/recommendations for international students: Required—TOEFL (minimum score 550 paper-based; 213 computer-based). Electronic applications accepted. *Faculty research:* Teacher education, instructional leadership, literacy education, technology, improvement of school curriculum.

The University of North Carolina at Greensboro, Graduate School, School of Education, Department of Curriculum and Instruction, Greensboro, NC 27412-5001. Offers college teaching and adult learning (Certificate); curriculum and instruction (M Ed), including chemistry education, elementary education, English as a second language, French education, instructional technology, mathematics education, middle grades education, reading education, science education, social studies education, Spanish education; curriculum and teaching (PhD), including higher education, teacher education and development; English as a second language (Certificate); higher education (M Ed); supervision (M Ed). *Accreditation:* NCATE. Part-time programs available. *Degree requirements:* For doctorate, thesis/dissertation. *Entrance requirements:* For master's and doctorate, GRE General Test. Additional exam requirements/recommendations for international students: Required—TOEFL. Electronic applications accepted. *Faculty research:* Community college literacy program, middle school mathematics/computer mathematics.

University of North Florida, College of Education and Human Services, Department of Foundations and Secondary Education, Jacksonville, FL 32224. Offers adult learning (M Ed); professional education (M Ed). *Accreditation:* NCATE. Part-time and evening/weekend programs available. *Faculty:* 11 full-time (4 women). *Students:* 9 full-time (8 women), 19 part-time (12 women); includes 2 minority (1 Black or African American, non-Hispanic/Latino; 1 Asian, non-Hispanic/Latino), 5 international. Average age 33. 13 applicants, 38% accepted, 5 enrolled. In 2011, 12 master's awarded. *Entrance requirements:* For master's, GRE General Test, minimum GPA of 3.0 in last 60 hours, interview, 3 letters of recommendation. Additional exam requirements/recommendations for international students: Required—TOEFL (minimum score 500 paper-based; 173 computer-based; 61 iBT). *Application deadline:* For fall admission, 7/1 priority date for domestic students, 5/1 for international students; for spring admission, 11/1 priority date for domestic students, 10/1 for international students. Applications are processed on a rolling basis. Application fee: $30. Electronic applications accepted. *Expenses:* Tuition, state resident: full-time $8793; part-time $366.38 per credit hour. Tuition, nonresident: full-time $23,502; part-time $979.24 per credit hour. *Required fees:* $1384; $57.66 per credit hour. Tuition and fees vary according to course load and program. *Financial support:* In 2011–12, 6 students received support. Teaching assistantships, career-related internships or fieldwork, Federal Work-Study, and tuition waivers (partial) available. Support available to part-time students. Financial award application deadline: 4/1; financial award applicants required to submit FAFSA. *Faculty research:* Using children's literature to enhance metalinguistic awareness, education, oral language diagnosis of middle-schoolers, science inquiry teaching and learning. *Total annual research expenditures:* $429. *Unit head:* Dr. Jeffery Cornett, Chair, 904-620-2610, Fax: 904-620-1821, E-mail: jcornett@unf.edu. *Application contact:* Lillith Richardson, Assistant Director, The Graduate School, 904-620-1360, Fax: 904-620-1362, E-mail: graduateschool@unf.edu. Web site: http://www.unf.edu/coehs/fse/.

University of Oklahoma, Jeannine Rainbolt College of Education, Department of Educational Leadership and Policy Studies, Program in Adult and Higher Education, Norman, OK 73019. Offers M Ed, PhD. *Accreditation:* NCATE. Part-time and evening/weekend programs available. *Students:* 131 full-time (71 women), 88 part-time (47 women); includes 64 minority (32 Black or African American, non-Hispanic/Latino; 12 American Indian or Alaska Native, non-Hispanic/Latino; 4 Asian, non-Hispanic/Latino; 7 Hispanic/Latino; 9 Two or more races, non-Hispanic/Latino), 6 international. Average age 29. 134 applicants, 67% accepted, 59 enrolled. In 2011, 65 master's, 3 doctorates awarded. Terminal master's awarded for partial completion of doctoral program. *Degree requirements:* For master's, comprehensive exam; for doctorate, variable foreign language requirement, thesis/dissertation, general exam. *Entrance requirements:* For master's, minimum GPA of 3.0 in last 60 hours of undergraduate course work; for doctorate, GRE General Test, resume, 3 letters of reference, scholarly writing sample. Additional exam requirements/recommendations for international students: Required—TOEFL (minimum score 550 paper-based; 79 iBT). *Application deadline:* For fall admission, 6/1 for domestic students, 3/1 for international students; for spring admission, 10/1 for domestic students, 9/1 for international students. Application fee: $40 ($90 for international students). Electronic applications accepted. *Expenses:* Tuition, state resident: full-time $4087; part-time $170.30 per credit hour. Tuition, nonresident: full-time $14,875; part-time $619.80 per credit hour. *Required fees:* $2659; $100.25 per credit hour. Tuition and fees vary according to course load and degree level. *Financial support:* In 2011–12, 201 students received support. Unspecified assistantships available. Financial award applicants required to submit FAFSA. *Faculty research:* Spirituality and identity; academic performance, persistence and graduation of college athletes; autobiography as a movement toward possibility; virtual learning; leadership, policy, and public good. *Unit head:* David Tan, Chair, 405-325-4202, Fax: 405-325-2403, E-mail: dtan@ou.edu. *Application contact:* Geri Evans, Graduate Programs Representative, 405-325-5978, Fax: 405-325-2403, E-mail: gevans@ou.edu. Web site: http://education.ou.edu/departments_1/edah_1.

University of Phoenix–Bay Area Campus, College of Education, San Jose, CA 95134-1805. Offers administration and supervision (MA Ed); adult education and training (MA Ed); early childhood education (MA Ed); education (Ed S); educational leadership (Ed D); elementary teacher education (MA Ed); higher education administration (PhD); secondary teacher education (MA Ed); special education (MA Ed); teacher leadership (MA Ed). Evening/weekend programs available. Postbaccalaureate distance learning degree programs offered (no on-campus study). *Degree requirements:* For master's, thesis (for some programs). *Entrance requirements:* For master's, minimum undergraduate GPA of 2.5, 3 years of work experience. Additional exam requirements/recommendations for international students: Required—TOEFL (minimum score 550 paper-based; 213 computer-based; 79 iBT). Electronic applications accepted.

University of Phoenix–Omaha Campus, College of Education, Omaha, NE 68154-5240. Offers administration and supervision (MA Ed); curriculum and instruction (MA Ed), including adult education, computer education, curriculum and instruction, English and language arts education, English as a second language, mathematics education; elementary teacher education (MA Ed); secondary teacher education (MA Ed); special education (MA Ed).

University of Phoenix–Online Campus, College of Education, Phoenix, AZ 85034-7209. Offers administration and supervision (MAEd, Graduate Certificate); adult education and training (MAEd); curriculum and instruction (MAEd); curriculum and instruction reading (MAEd); curriculum and instruction-computer education (MAEd); curriculum and instruction-language arts (MAEd); curriculum and instruction-mathematics (MAEd); early childhood education (MAEd); educational studies (MAEd); elementary teacher education (MAEd); elementary teacher education-early childhood (MAEd); secondary teacher education (MAEd); special education (MAEd); teacher education - elementary/middle level (MAEd); teacher education middle level generalist (MAEd); teacher education middle level mathematics (MAEd); teacher education middle level science (MAEd); teacher education secondary mathematics (MAEd); teacher education secondary science (MAEd); teacher leadership (MAEd). *Accreditation:* Teacher Education Accreditation Council. Evening/weekend programs available. Postbaccalaureate distance learning degree programs offered. *Students:* 9,180 full-time (7,178 women); includes 2,913 minority (2,069 Black or African American, non-Hispanic/Latino; 50 American Indian or Alaska Native, non-Hispanic/Latino; 100 Asian, non-Hispanic/Latino; 542 Hispanic/Latino; 48 Native Hawaiian or other Pacific Islander, non-Hispanic/Latino; 104 Two or more races, non-Hispanic/Latino), 147 international. Average age 36. *Entrance requirements:* Additional exam requirements/recommendations for international students: Required—TOEFL, TOEIC (Test of English as an International Communication), Berlitz Online English Proficiency Exam, Pearson Test of English, or IELTS. *Application deadline:* Applications are processed on a rolling basis. Application fee: $45. Electronic applications accepted. *Expenses:* Contact institution. *Financial support:* Scholarships/grants available. Financial award applicants required to submit FAFSA. *Application contact:* 866-766-0766. Web site: http://www.phoenix.edu/colleges_divisions/education.html.

University of Phoenix–Phoenix Main Campus, College of Education, Tempe, AZ 85282-2371. Offers administration and supervision (MA Ed); adult education and training (MA Ed); curriculum and instruction reading (MA Ed); curriculum instruction (MA Ed); early childhood education (MA Ed); education studies (MA Ed); elementary teacher education (MA Ed); secondary teacher education (MA Ed); special education (MA Ed); teacher leadership (MA Ed). Evening/weekend programs available. Postbaccalaureate distance learning degree programs offered. *Students:* 297 full-time (203 women); includes 53 minority (19 Black or African American, non-Hispanic/Latino; 1 American Indian or Alaska Native, non-Hispanic/Latino; 6 Asian, non-Hispanic/Latino; 21 Hispanic/Latino; 2 Native Hawaiian or other Pacific Islander, non-Hispanic/Latino; 4 Two or more races, non-Hispanic/Latino), 3 international. Average age 35. *Entrance requirements:* Additional exam requirements/recommendations for international students: Required—TOEFL, TOEIC (Test of English as an International Communication), Berlitz Online English Proficiency Exam, Pearson Test of English, or IELTS. *Application deadline:* Applications are processed on a rolling basis. Application fee: $45. Electronic applications accepted. *Expenses:* Contact institution. *Financial support:* Scholarships/grants available. Financial award applicants required to submit FAFSA. *Application contact:* 866-766-0766. Web site: http://www.phoenix.edu/colleges_divisions/education.html.

University of Phoenix–Sacramento Valley Campus, College of Education, Sacramento, CA 95833-3632. Offers adult education (MA Ed); curriculum instruction (MA Ed); elementary teacher education (MA Ed); secondary teacher education (MA Ed); teacher education (Certificate). Evening/weekend programs available. *Degree requirements:* For master's, thesis (for some programs). *Entrance requirements:* For master's, 3 years of work experience, minimum undergraduate GPA of 2.5. Additional exam requirements/recommendations for international students: Required—TOEFL (minimum score 550 paper-based; 213 computer-based; 79 iBT). Electronic applications accepted.

University of Phoenix–Southern Arizona Campus, College of Education, Tucson, AZ 85711. Offers administration and supervision (MA Ed); adult education and training (MA Ed); curriculum instruction (MA Ed); educational counseling (MA Ed); elementary teacher education (MA Ed); school counseling (MSC); secondary teacher education (MA Ed); special education (MA Ed, Certificate). Evening/weekend programs available. *Degree requirements:* For master's, thesis (for some programs). *Entrance requirements:* For master's, minimum undergraduate GPA of 2.5, 3 years of work experience. Additional exam requirements/recommendations for international students: Required—TOEFL (minimum score 550 paper-based; 213 computer-based; 79 iBT). Electronic applications accepted.

University of Phoenix–Southern California Campus, College of Education, Costa Mesa, CA 92626. Offers administration and supervision (MA Ed); adult education and training (MA Ed); educational studies (MA Ed); teacher leadership (MA Ed). Evening/weekend programs available. Postbaccalaureate distance learning degree programs offered. *Students:* 190 full-time (132 women); includes 82 minority (25 Black or African American, non-Hispanic/Latino; 5 Asian, non-Hispanic/Latino; 46 Hispanic/Latino; 4 Native Hawaiian or other Pacific Islander, non-Hispanic/Latino; 2 Two or more races, non-Hispanic/Latino), 3 international. Average age 35. *Entrance requirements:* Additional exam requirements/recommendations for international students: Required—TOEFL, TOEIC (Test of English as an International Communication), Berlitz Online English Proficiency Exam, Pearson Test of English, or IELTS. *Application deadline:* Applications are processed on a rolling basis. Application fee: $45. Electronic applications accepted. *Expenses:* Contact institution. *Financial support:* Scholarships/grants available. Financial award applicants required to submit FAFSA. *Application contact:* 866-766-0766. Web site: http://www.phoenix.edu/colleges_divisions/education.html.

University of Phoenix–Washington D.C. Campus, College of Education, Washington, DC 20001. Offers administration and supervision (MA Ed); adult education and training (MA Ed); computer education (MA Ed); curriculum and instruction (MA Ed, Ed D); early childhood education (MA Ed); education (Ed S); educational leadership (Ed D); educational technology (Ed D); elementary teacher education (MA Ed); English and language arts education (MA Ed); English as a second language (MA Ed); higher education administration (PhD); mathematics education (MA Ed); secondary teacher education (MA Ed); special education (MA Ed); teacher leadership (MA Ed).

University of Regina, Faculty of Graduate Studies and Research, Faculty of Education, Department of Adult Education, Regina, SK S4S 0A2, Canada. Offers MA Ed. Part-time programs available. *Faculty:* 3 full-time (2 women). *Students:* 5 full-time (4 women), 13 part-time (11 women). 16 applicants, 88% accepted. In 2011, 7 degrees awarded. *Degree requirements:* For master's, thesis (for some programs), practicum, project, or thesis. *Entrance requirements:* For master's, bachelor's degree in education, 2 years of teaching experience. Additional exam requirements/recommendations for international students: Required—TOEFL (minimum score 580 paper-based; 80 iBT), IELTS (minimum score 6.5). *Application deadline:* For fall admission, 2/15 for domestic students; for winter admission, 2/15 for domestic students; for spring admission, 2/15 for domestic students. Application fee: $100. Electronic applications accepted. *Financial support:* In 2011–12, 1 fellowship (averaging $6,000 per year) was awarded; research assistantships, teaching assistantships, and scholarships/grants also available. Financial award application deadline: 6/15. *Faculty research:* Program and instruction. *Unit head:* Dr. Abu Bockarie, Director, 306-585-5601, Fax: 306-585-5387, E-mail: abu.bockarie@uregina.ca. *Application contact:* Tania Gates, Graduate Program Coordinator, 306-585-4506, Fax: 306-585-5387, E-mail: edgrad@uregina.ca.

University of Rhode Island, Graduate School, College of Human Science and Services, School of Education, Kingston, RI 02881. Offers adult education (MA); education (PhD); elementary education (MA); music education (MM); reading education (MA); secondary education (MA); special education (MA); MS/PhD. *Accreditation:* NCATE. Part-time and evening/weekend programs available. *Faculty:* 21 full-time (13 women), 3 part-time/adjunct (1 woman). *Students:* 54 full-time (48 women), 108 part-time (86 women); includes 14 minority (3 Black or African American, non-Hispanic/Latino; 4 Asian, non-Hispanic/Latino; 7 Hispanic/Latino), 4 international. In 2011, 56 master's, 8 doctorates awarded. *Degree requirements:* For master's, comprehensive exam (for some programs), thesis optional; for doctorate, comprehensive exam, thesis/dissertation. *Entrance requirements:* For master's, 2 letters of recommendation; interview (for special education applicants); for doctorate, GRE, 3 letters of recommendation, resume. Additional exam requirements/recommendations for international students: Required—TOEFL (minimum score 600 paper-based; 250 computer-based; 100 iBT). *Application deadline:* For fall admission, 1/31 for international students. Application fee: $65. Electronic applications accepted. *Expenses:* Tuition, state resident: full-time $10,432; part-time $580 per credit hour. Tuition, nonresident: full-time $23,130; part-time $1285 per credit hour. *Required fees:* $1362; $36 per credit hour. $35 per semester. One-time fee: $130. *Financial support:* In 2011–12, 4 teaching assistantships with full and partial tuition reimbursements (averaging $12,157 per year) were awarded; career-related internships or fieldwork also available. Financial award applicants required to submit FAFSA. *Unit head:* Dr. David Byrd, Director, 401-874-5484, Fax: 401-874-5471, E-mail: dbyrd@uri.edu. *Application contact:* Dr. John Boulmetis, Coordinator of Graduate Studies, 401-874-4159, Fax: 401-874-7610, E-mail: johnb@uri.edu. Web site: http://www.uri.edu/hss/education/.

University of South Africa, College of Human Sciences, Pretoria, South Africa. Offers adult education (M Ed); African languages (MA, PhD); African politics (MA, PhD); Afrikaans (MA, PhD); ancient history (MA, PhD); ancient Near Eastern studies (MA, PhD); anthropology (MA, PhD); applied linguistics (MA); Arabic (MA, PhD); archaeology (MA); art history (MA); Biblical archaeology (MA); Biblical studies (M Th, D Th, PhD); Christian spirituality (M Th, D Th); church history (M Th, D Th); classical studies (MA, PhD); clinical psychology (MA); communication (MA, PhD); comparative education (M Ed, Ed D); consulting psychology (D Admin, D Com, PhD); curriculum studies (M Ed, Ed D); development studies (M Admin, MA, D Admin, PhD); didactics (M Ed, Ed D); education (M Tech); education management (M Ed, Ed D); educational psychology (M Ed); English (MA); environmental education (M Ed); French (MA, PhD); German (MA, PhD); Greek (MA); guidance and counseling (M Ed); health studies (MA, PhD), including health sciences education (MA), health services management (MA), medical and surgical nursing science (critical care general) (MA), midwifery and neonatal nursing science (MA), trauma and emergency care (MA); history (MA, PhD); history of education (Ed D); inclusive education (M Ed, Ed D); information and communications technology policy and regulation (MA); information science (MA, MIS, PhD); international politics (MA, PhD); Islamic studies (MA, PhD); Italian (MA, PhD); Judaica (MA, PhD); linguistics (MA, PhD); mathematical education (M Ed); mathematics education (MA); missiology (M Th, D Th); modern Hebrew (MA, PhD); musicology (MA, MMus, D Mus, PhD); natural science education (M Ed); New Testament (M Th, D Th); Old Testament (D Th); pastoral therapy (M Th, D Th); philosophy (MA); philosophy of education (M Ed, Ed D); politics (MA, PhD); Portuguese (MA, PhD); practical theology (M Th, D Th); psychology (MA, MS, PhD); psychology of education (M Ed, Ed D); public health (MA); religious studies (MA, D Th, PhD); Romance languages (MA); Russian (MA, PhD); Semitic languages (MA, PhD); social behavior studies in HIV/AIDS (MA); social science (mental health) (MA); social science in development studies (MA); social science in psychology (MA); social science in social work (MA); social science in sociology (MA); social work (MSW, DSW, PhD); socio-education (M Ed, Ed D); sociolinguistics (MA); sociology (MA, PhD); Spanish (MA, PhD); systematic theology (M Th, D Th); TESOL (teaching English to speakers of other languages) (MA); theological ethics (M Th, D Th); theory of literature (MA, PhD); urban ministries (D Th); urban ministry (M Th).

University of Southern Maine, School of Education and Human Development, Program in Adult Education, Portland, ME 04104-9300. Offers adult and higher education (MS); adult learning (CAS). *Accreditation:* Teacher Education Accreditation Council. Part-time and evening/weekend programs available. Postbaccalaureate distance learning degree programs offered (minimal on-campus study). *Degree requirements:* For master's and CAS, thesis or alternative. *Entrance requirements:* For master's, interview; for CAS, master's degree. Additional exam requirements/recommendations for international students: Required—TOEFL (minimum score 550 paper-based; 213 computer-based; 79 iBT). Electronic applications accepted. *Faculty research:* Workplace education, gerontology.

University of Southern Mississippi, Graduate School, College of Education and Psychology, Department of Educational Studies and Research, Hattiesburg, MS 39406-0001. Offers adult education (Graduate Certificate); community college leadership (Graduate Certificate); counseling and personnel services (college) (M Ed); education (PhD, Ed S), including adult education, research, evaluation and statistics (PhD); education (Ed D), including educational administration, educational research; education: educational leadership and research (Ed S), including higher education administration; educational administration and supervision (M Ed); higher education administration (Ed D, PhD); institutional research (Graduate Certificate). *Faculty:* 7 full-time (1 woman), 5 part-time/adjunct (1 woman). *Students:* 33 full-time (25 women), 104 part-time (25 women); includes 46 minority (40 Black or African American, non-Hispanic/Latino; 1 Asian, non-Hispanic/Latino; 3 Hispanic/Latino; 2 Two or more races, non-Hispanic/Latino), 1 international. Average age 36. 27 applicants, 48% accepted, 1 enrolled. In 2011, 27 master's, 13 doctorates, 1 other advanced degree awarded. *Degree requirements:* For master's and other advanced degree, comprehensive exam, thesis (for some programs); for doctorate, comprehensive exam, thesis/dissertation. *Entrance requirements:* For master's, doctorate, and other advanced degree, GRE General Test, minimum GPA of 2.75. Additional exam requirements/recommendations for international students: Required—TOEFL. *Application deadline:* For fall admission, 2/1 for domestic students, 3/1 for international students. Applications are processed on a rolling basis. Application fee: $35. *Financial support:* Career-related internships or fieldwork, Federal Work-Study, and institutionally sponsored loans available. Financial award application deadline: 3/15; financial award applicants required to submit FAFSA. *Total annual research expenditures:* $88,500. *Unit head:* Dr. Thomas V. O'Brien, Chair, 601-266-6093, E-mail: thomas.obrien@usm.edu. *Application contact:* Shonna Breland, Manager of Graduate Admissions, 601-266-6563, Fax: 601-266-5138. Web site: http://www.usm.edu/cep/esr/.

University of South Florida, Graduate School, College of Education, Department of Adult, Career and Higher Education, Tampa, FL 33620-9951. Offers adult education (MA, Ed D, PhD, Ed S); career and technical education (MA); career and workforce education (PhD); higher education/community college teaching (MA, Ed D, PhD); vocational education (Ed S). Part-time programs available. Postbaccalaureate distance learning degree programs offered (minimal on-campus study). *Faculty:* 9 full-time (3 women), 4 part-time/adjunct (3 women). *Students:* 38 full-time (21 women), 169 part-time (115 women); includes 59 minority (37 Black or African American, non-Hispanic/Latino; 5 Asian, non-Hispanic/Latino; 14 Hispanic/Latino; 3 Two or more races, non-Hispanic/Latino), 6 international. Average age 44. 98 applicants, 70% accepted, 42 enrolled. In 2011, 33 master's, 13 doctorates awarded. *Median time to degree:* Of those who began their doctoral program in fall 2003, 50% received their degree in 8 years or less. *Degree requirements:* For master's, comprehensive exam; for doctorate, comprehensive exam, thesis/dissertation, philosophies of inquiry; multiple research methods; for Ed S, comprehensive exam, thesis. *Entrance requirements:* For master's, minimum GPA of 3.0 in last 60 hours of course work; for doctorate and Ed S, GRE General Test, GRE Writing Test. Additional exam requirements/recommendations for international students: Required—TOEFL (minimum score 500 paper-based; 213 computer-based; 91 iBT). *Application deadline:* For fall admission, 2/15 for domestic students, 1/2 for international students; for spring admission, 10/15 for domestic students, 6/1 for international students. Applications are processed on a rolling basis. Application fee: $30. Electronic applications accepted. *Financial support:* In 2011–12, 5 students received support, including 5 teaching assistantships with full tuition reimbursements available (averaging $15,000 per year); career-related internships or fieldwork, scholarships/grants, and unspecified assistantships also available. Financial award applicants required to submit FAFSA. *Faculty research:* Community college leadership; integration of academic, career and technical education; competency-based education; continuing education administration; adult learning and development. *Total annual research expenditures:* $9,807. *Unit head:* Dr. Ann Cranston-Gingras, Chairperson, 813-974-6036, Fax: 813-974-3366, E-mail: cranston@usf.edu. *Application contact:* Dr. William Young, Program Director, 813-974-1861, Fax: 813-974-3366, E-mail: williamyoung@usf.edu.

The University of Tennessee, Graduate School, College of Education, Health and Human Sciences, Department of Educational Psychology and Counseling, Knoxville, TN 37996. Offers adult education (MS); applied educational psychology (MS); collaborative learning (Ed D); college student personnel (MS); mental health counseling (MS); rehabilitation counseling (MS); school counseling (MS). *Accreditation:* ACA (one or more programs are accredited); CORE (one or more programs are accredited); NCATE. Part-time and evening/weekend programs available. *Degree requirements:* For master's, thesis optional. *Entrance requirements:* For master's, GRE General Test, minimum GPA of 2.7. Additional exam requirements/recommendations for international students: Required—TOEFL. Electronic applications accepted. *Expenses:* Tuition, state resident: full-time $8332; part-time $464 per credit hour. Tuition, nonresident: full-time $25,174; part-time $1400 per credit hour. *Required fees:* $1162; $56 per credit hour. Tuition and fees vary according to program.

The University of Texas at San Antonio, College of Education and Human Development, Department of Interdisciplinary Learning and Teaching, San Antonio, TX 78249-0617. Offers adult learning and teaching (MA); education (MA), including curriculum and instruction, early childhood and elementary education, educational psychology/special education, instructional technology, reading and literacy education; interdisciplinary learning and teaching (PhD). Part-time and evening/weekend programs available. *Faculty:* 26 full-time (21 women), 1 (woman) part-time/adjunct. *Students:* 131 full-time (100 women), 357 part-time (283 women); includes 275 minority (31 Black or African American, non-Hispanic/Latino; 9 Asian, non-Hispanic/Latino; 227 Hispanic/Latino; 8 Two or more races, non-Hispanic/Latino), 31 international. Average age 33. 239 applicants, 75% accepted, 120 enrolled. In 2011, 119 master's awarded. *Degree requirements:* For master's, comprehensive exam, thesis optional, 36 hours of course work without thesis (33 with thesis); for doctorate, comprehensive exam, thesis/dissertation, minimum of 60 semester credit hours. *Entrance requirements:* For master's, GRE General Test, bachelor's degree with minimum GPA of 3.0 in last 60 hours of coursework; resume; two letters of recommendation; statement of purpose; for doctorate, GRE, transcripts from all colleges and universities attended, professional vitae demonstrating experience in work environment where education was primary professional emphasis, 3 letters of recommendation, statement of purpose, master's degree transcript documenting minimum GPA of 3.5. Additional exam requirements/recommendations for international students: Required—TOEFL (minimum score 500 paper-based; 61 iBT), IELTS (minimum score 5). *Application deadline:* For fall admission, 7/1 for domestic students, 4/1 for international students; for spring admission, 11/1 for domestic students, 9/1 for international students. Application fee: $45 ($85 for international students). *Expenses:* Tuition, state resident: full-time $3148; part-time $2176 per semester. Tuition, nonresident: full-time $8782; part-time $5932 per semester. *Required fees:* $719 per semester. *Financial support:* In 2011–12, 9 fellowships with partial tuition reimbursements (averaging $27,000 per year) were awarded; career-related internships or fieldwork, Federal Work-Study, and scholarships/grants also available. Support available to part-time students. *Faculty research:* Explorations of science, learning and teaching, family Involvement in early childhood, culturally-responsive literacy instruction in diverse settings, STEM education, autism spectrum disorders. *Total annual research expenditures:* $5.9 million. *Unit head:* Dr. Maria R. Cortez, Department Chair, 210-458-5969, Fax: 210-458-7281, E-mail: mari.cortez@utsa.edu. *Application contact:* Erin Doran, Student Development Specialist, 210-458-7443, Fax: 210-458-7281, E-mail: erin.doran@utsa.edu.

University of the Incarnate Word, School of Graduate Studies and Research, Dreeben School of Education, Programs in Education, San Antonio, TX 78209-6397. Offers adult education (M Ed, MA); cross-cultural education (M Ed, MA); early childhood literacy (M Ed, MA); general education (M Ed, MA); higher education (PhD); instructional technology (M Ed, MA); international education and entrepreneurship (PhD); kinesiology (M Ed, MA); literacy (M Ed, MA); organizational leadership (PhD); organizational learning and learning (M Ed, MA); reading (M Ed, MA); special education (M Ed, MA); teacher leadership (M Ed, MA). Part-time and evening/weekend programs available. *Faculty:* 14 full-time (8 women), 10 part-time/adjunct (9 women). *Students:* 13 full-time (7 women), 197 part-time (129 women); includes 111 minority (23 Black or African American, non-Hispanic/Latino; 2 American Indian or Alaska Native, non-Hispanic/Latino; 1 Asian, non-Hispanic/Latino; 85 Hispanic/Latino), 26 international. Average age 41. 78 applicants, 79% accepted, 34 enrolled. In 2011, 21 master's, 12 doctorates awarded. *Degree requirements:* For master's, capstone; for doctorate, thesis/dissertation, qualifying exam. *Entrance requirements:* For master's, baccalaureate degree; minimum foundation GPA of 2.5; interview; for doctorate, master's degree; interview; supervised writing sample. Additional exam requirements/recommendations for international students: Required—TOEFL (minimum score 560 paper-based; 220 computer-based; 83 iBT). *Application deadline:* Applications are processed on a rolling basis. Application fee: $20. Electronic applications accepted. *Expenses: Tuition:* Part-time $725 per credit hour. Tuition and fees vary according to degree level. *Financial support:* In 2011–12, 5 research assistantships were awarded; Federal Work-Study and scholarships/grants also available. Financial award applicants required to submit FAFSA. *Unit head:* Dr. Denise Staudt, Dean, Dreeben School of Education, 210-829-2762, E-mail: staudt@uiwtx.edu. *Application contact:* Andrea Cyterski-Acosta, Dean of Enrollment, 210-829-6005, Fax: 210-829-3921, E-mail: admis@uiwtx.edu. Web site: http://www.uiw.edu/education/index.htm.

University of the Incarnate Word, School of Graduate Studies and Research, H-E-B School of Business and Administration, Programs in Administration, San Antonio, TX 78209-6397. Offers adult education (MAA); applied administration (MAA); communication arts (MAA); healthcare administration (MAA); instructional technology (MAA); international business (Certificate); nutrition (MAA); organizational development (MAA, Certificate); project management (Certificate); sports management (MAA). Part-time and evening/weekend programs available. Postbaccalaureate distance learning degree programs offered (no on-campus study). *Faculty:* 23 full-time (10 women), 26 part-time/adjunct (12 women). *Students:* 25 full-time (18 women), 54 part-time (33 women); includes 50 minority (10 Black or African American, non-Hispanic/Latino; 40 Hispanic/Latino), 5 international. Average age 34. 35 applicants, 94% accepted, 19 enrolled. In 2011, 38 master's awarded. *Degree requirements:* For master's, capstone. *Entrance requirements:* For master's, GRE, GMAT, undergraduate degree, minimum GPA of 2.5. Additional exam requirements/recommendations for international students: Required—TOEFL (minimum score 560 paper-based; 220 computer-based; 83 iBT). *Application deadline:* Applications are processed on a rolling basis. Application fee: $20. Electronic applications accepted. *Expenses: Tuition:* Part-time $725 per credit hour. Tuition and fees vary according to degree level. *Financial support:* Federal Work-Study and scholarships/grants available. Financial award applicants required to submit FAFSA. *Unit head:* Dr. Mark Teachout, MAA Programs Director, 210-829-3177, Fax: 210-805-3564, E-mail: teachout@uiwtx.edu. *Application contact:* Andrea Cyterski-Acosta, Dean of Enrollment, 210-829-6005, Fax: 210-829-3921, E-mail: admis@uiwtx.edu. Web site: http://www.uiw.edu/maa/index.htm and http://www.uiw.edu/maa/admissions.html.

The University of West Alabama, School of Graduate Studies, College of Education, Departments of Instructional Leadership and Support/Curriculum and Instruction, Program in Continuing Education, Livingston, AL 35470. Offers MSCE. *Accreditation:* NCATE. Part-time programs available. *Faculty:* 21 full-time (6 women). *Students:* 103 (85 women); includes 86 minority (all Black or African American, non-Hispanic/Latino). In 2011, 11 master's awarded. *Degree requirements:* For master's, comprehensive exam. *Entrance requirements:* For master's, GRE General Test, MAT, minimum GPA of 2.75. Additional exam requirements/recommendations for international students: Required—TOEFL (minimum score 61 computer-based). *Application deadline:* For fall admission, 9/10 priority date for domestic students; for spring admission, 3/24 for domestic students. Applications are processed on a rolling basis. Application fee: $25 ($50 for international students). *Expenses:* Tuition, state resident: full-time $5112; part-time $284 per credit hour. Tuition, nonresident: full-time $10,224; part-time $568 per credit hour. *Required fees:* $180; $40 per semester. One-time fee: $65. Tuition and fees vary according to class time, course load, campus/location and program. *Financial support:* Teaching assistantships, career-related internships or fieldwork, Federal Work-Study, scholarships/grants, and unspecified assistantships available. Support available to part-time students. *Unit head:* Dr. Jan Miller, Chair of Instructional Leadership and Support, 205-652-3445, Fax: 205-652-3706, E-mail: jmiller@uwa.edu. *Application contact:* Dr. Kathy Chandler, Dean of Graduate Studies, 205-652-3421, Fax: 205-652-3670, E-mail: kchandler@uwa.edu.

The University of West Alabama, School of Graduate Studies, College of Education, Departments of Instructional Leadership and Support/Curriculum and Instruction, Program in Guidance and Counseling, Livingston, AL 35470. Offers continuing education (MSCE); guidance and counseling (M Ed). *Accreditation:* NCATE. Part-time and evening/weekend programs available. *Faculty:* 8 full-time (6 women). *Students:* 183 (155 women); includes 136 minority (130 Black or African American, non-Hispanic/Latino; 1 American Indian or Alaska Native, non-Hispanic/Latino; 2 Asian, non-Hispanic/Latino; 3 Hispanic/Latino). In 2011, 116 master's awarded. *Degree requirements:* For master's, comprehensive exam. *Entrance requirements:* For master's, GRE General Test, MAT, minimum GPA of 2.75. Additional exam requirements/recommendations for international students: Required—TOEFL (minimum score 61 computer-based). *Application deadline:* For fall admission, 9/10 priority date for domestic students; for spring admission, 3/21 for domestic students. Applications are processed on a rolling basis. Application fee: $25 ($50 for international students). *Expenses:* Tuition, state resident: full-time $5112; part-time $284 per credit hour. Tuition, nonresident: full-time $10,224; part-time $568 per credit hour. *Required fees:* $180; $40 per semester. One-time fee: $65. Tuition and fees vary according to class time, course load, campus/location and program. *Financial support:* Teaching assistantships, career-related internships or fieldwork, Federal Work-Study, scholarships/grants, and unspecified assistantships available. Support available to part-time students. Financial award application deadline: 3/1. *Unit head:* Dr. Jan Miller, Chair of Instructional Leadership and Support, 205-652-3421, Fax: 205-652-3706, E-mail: jmiller@uwa.edu. *Application contact:* Dr. Kathy Chandler, Dean of Graduate Studies, 205-652-3421, Fax: 205-652-3706, E-mail: kchandler@uwa.edu. Web site: http://www.uwa.edu/msceguidancecounseling.aspx.

University of Wisconsin–Milwaukee, Graduate School, School of Education, Program in Urban Education, Milwaukee, WI 53201-0413. Offers adult and continuing education (PhD); curriculum and instruction (PhD); educational administration (PhD); educational and media technology (PhD); educational psychology (PhD); multicultural studies (PhD); social foundations of education (PhD). *Students:* 65 full-time (45 women), 37 part-time (25 women); includes 39 minority (18 Black or African American, non-Hispanic/Latino; 1 American Indian or Alaska Native, non-Hispanic/Latino; 6 Asian, non-Hispanic/Latino; 6 Hispanic/Latino; 8 Two or more races, non-Hispanic/Latino), 5 international. Average age 41. 26 applicants, 62% accepted, 2 enrolled. In 2011, 13 degrees awarded. *Degree requirements:* For doctorate, comprehensive exam, thesis/dissertation. *Entrance requirements:* For doctorate, GRE General Test, minimum undergraduate GPA of 2.85, graduate 3.5. Additional exam requirements/recommendations for international students: Required—TOEFL (minimum score 550 paper-based; 79 iBT), IELTS (minimum score 6.5). *Application deadline:* For fall admission, 1/1 priority date for domestic students; for spring admission, 9/1 for domestic students. Applications are processed on a rolling basis. Application fee: $56 ($96 for international students). Electronic applications accepted. One-time fee: $506.10 full-time. Tuition and fees vary according to course load and reciprocity agreements. *Financial support:* In 2011–12, 11 fellowships, 1 teaching assistantship were awarded; research assistantships, career-related internships or fieldwork, health care benefits, unspecified assistantships, and project assistantships also available. Support available to part-time students. Financial award application deadline: 4/15; financial award applicants required to submit FAFSA. *Unit head:* Larry Martin, Representative, 414-229-4729, Fax: 414-229-2920, E-mail: lmartin@uwm.edu. *Application contact:* General Information Contact, 414-229-4982, Fax: 414-229-6967, E-mail: gradschool@uwm.edu. Web site: http://www.uwm.edu/Dept/UrbanEd/.

University of Wisconsin–Platteville, School of Graduate Studies, College of Liberal Arts and Education, School of Education, Platteville, WI 53818-3099. Offers adult education (MSE); elementary education (MSE); English education (MSE); middle school education (MSE); secondary education (MSE). *Accreditation:* NCATE. Part-time programs available. *Faculty:* 8 part-time/adjunct (3 women). *Students:* 62 full-time (47 women), 86 part-time (69 women); includes 22 minority (20 Black or African American, non-Hispanic/Latino; 2 Hispanic/Latino), 55 international. 17 applicants, 76% accepted. In 2011, 82 master's awarded. *Degree requirements:* For master's, comprehensive exam, thesis or alternative. *Entrance requirements:* Additional exam requirements/recommendations for international students: Required—TOEFL (minimum score 500 paper-based; 61 iBT), IELTS (minimum score 6). *Application deadline:* For fall admission, 7/1 priority date for domestic students; for spring admission, 11/1 for domestic students. Applications are processed on a rolling basis. Application fee: $56. Electronic applications accepted. *Financial support:* Research assistantships with partial tuition reimbursements, career-related internships or fieldwork, Federal Work-Study, institutionally sponsored loans, scholarships/grants, and unspecified assistantships available. Support available to part-time students. Financial award applicants required to submit FAFSA. *Unit head:* Dr. Karen Stinson, Director, 608-342-1131, Fax: 608-342-1133, E-mail: stinsonk@uwplatt.edu. *Application contact:* Lisa Popp, School of Graduate Studies, 608-342-1322, Fax: 608-342-1389, E-mail: poppl@uwplatt.edu. Web site: http://www.uwplatt.edu/.

Virginia Commonwealth University, Graduate School, School of Education, Program in Adult Learning, Richmond, VA 23284-9005. Offers adult literacy (M Ed); human resource development (M Ed); teaching and learning with technology (M Ed). *Accreditation:* NCATE. Part-time programs available. *Entrance requirements:* For master's, GRE General Test or MAT. Additional exam requirements/recommendations for international students: Required—TOEFL (minimum score 600 paper-based; 250 computer-based; 100 iBT). Electronic applications accepted. *Expenses:* Tuition, state resident: full-time $9133; part-time $507 per credit. Tuition, nonresident: full-time $18,777; part-time $1043 per credit. *Required fees:* $77 per credit. Tuition and fees vary according to degree level, campus/location, program and student level. *Faculty research:* Adult development and learning, program planning and evaluation.

Walden University, Graduate Programs, Richard W. Riley College of Education and Leadership, Minneapolis, MN 55401. Offers administrator leadership for teaching and learning (Ed D, Ed S); adult education (Ed D, Ed S); adult learning (MS, Postbaccalaureate Certificate), including developmental education (MS), online teaching (MS), teaching adults English as a second language (MS), training and performance management (MS); college teaching and learning (Ed D, Ed S, Postbaccalaureate Certificate); curriculum, instruction and assessment (Ed D, Postbaccalaureate Certificate); curriculum, instruction, and professional development (Ed S); developmental education (Postbaccalaureate Certificate); early childhood administration, management, and leadership (Postbaccalaureate Certificate); early childhood education (birth-grade 3) (MAT); early childhood public policy and advocacy (Postbaccalaureate Certificate); early childhood studies (MS), including administration, management and leadership, early childhood public policy and advocacy, teaching adults in the early childhood field, teaching and diversity; education (MS, PhD), including adolescent literacy and technology (grades 6-12) (MS), adult education leadership (PhD), assessment, evaluation, and accountability (PhD), community college leadership (PhD), curriculum, instruction, and assessment, early childhood education (PhD), educational technology (PhD), elementary reading and literacy (MS), elementary reading and mathematics (MS), general program, global and comparative education (PhD), higher education (PhD), integrating technology in the classroom (MS), K-12 educational leadership (PhD), leadership, policy and change (PhD), learning, instruction and innovation (PhD), literacy and learning in the content areas (MS), mathematics (grades 6-8) (MS), mathematics (grades K-5) (MS), middle level education (grades 5-8) (MS), professional development (MS), science (grades K-8) (MS), self-designed (PhD), special education (PhD), special education (non-licensure) (MS), teacher leadership (grades K-12) (MS), teaching English language learners (grades K-12) (MS); educational leadership and administration (principal preparation) (Ed S); educational technology (Ed S); elementary reading and literacy (Postbaccalaureate Certificate); engaging culturally diverse learners (Postbaccalaureate Certificate); enrollment management and institutional marketing (Postbaccalaureate Certificate); higher education (MS), including college teaching and learning, enrollment management and institutional planning, global higher education, leadership for student success, online and distance learning; higher education leadership (Ed D); instructional design (Postbaccalaureate Certificate); instructional design and technology (MS), including general program (MS, PhD), online learning, training and performance improvement; integrating technology in the classroom (Postbaccalaureate Certificate); online teaching for adult learners (Postbaccalaureate Certificate); professional development (Postbaccalaureate Certificate); reading and literacy leadership (Ed D); science K-8 (Postbaccalaureate Certificate); special education (Ed D, Ed S); special education: emotional/behavioral disorders (K-12) (MAT); special education: learning disabilities (K-12) (MAT); teacher leadership (Ed D, Ed S, Postbaccalaureate Certificate); training and performance management (Postbaccalaureate Certificate). Part-time and evening/weekend programs available. Postbaccalaureate distance learning degree programs offered (minimal on-campus study). *Faculty:* 71 full-time (48 women), 853 part-time/adjunct (585 women). *Students:* 11,326 full-time (9,212 women), 2,148 part-time (1,795 women); includes 5,346 minority (4,403 Black or African American, non-Hispanic/Latino; 76 American Indian or Alaska Native, non-Hispanic/Latino; 140 Asian, non-Hispanic/Latino; 561 Hispanic/Latino; 21 Native Hawaiian or other Pacific Islander, non-Hispanic/Latino; 145 Two or more races, non-Hispanic/Latino), 322 international. Average age 39. In 2011, 3,477 master's, 318 doctorates, 471 other advanced degrees awarded. *Degree requirements:* For doctorate, thesis/dissertation (for some programs), residency; for other advanced degree, residency (for some programs). *Entrance requirements:* For master's, bachelor's degree or equivalent in related field; minimum GPA of 2.5; official transcripts; goal statement; access to computer and Internet; for doctorate, master's degree or equivalent in related field; minimum GPA of 3.0; official transcripts; three years' related professional/academic experience (preferred); access to computer and Internet; for other advanced degree, master's degree or equivalent in related field; minimum GPA of 3.0; 3 years related professional/academic experience (preferred); access to computer and Internet (Ed S). Additional exam requirements/recommendations for international students: Required—TOEFL (minimum score 550 paper-based; 213 computer-based), IELTS (minimum score 6.5), or Michigan English Language Assessment Battery (minimum score 82). *Application deadline:* Applications are processed on a rolling basis. Application fee: $50. Electronic applications accepted. *Financial support:* Federal Work-Study, scholarships/grants, unspecified assistantships, and family tuition reduction, active duty/veteran tuition reduction, group tuition reduction, interest-free payment plans, employee tuition reduction available. Support available to part-time students. Financial award applicants required to submit FAFSA. *Unit head:* Dr. Kate Steffens, Dean, 800-925-3368. *Application contact:* Jennifer Hall, Vice President of Enrollment Management, 866-4-WALDEN, E-mail: info@waldenu.edu. Web site: http://www.waldenu.edu/Colleges-and-Schools/College-of-Education-and-Leadership.htm.

Western Kentucky University, Graduate Studies, College of Education and Behavioral Sciences, Department of Educational Administration, Leadership, and Research, Bowling Green, KY 42101. Offers adult education (MAE); educational leadership (Ed D); school administration (Ed S); school principal (MAE). *Accreditation:* NCATE. Part-time and evening/weekend programs available. *Degree requirements:* For master's, comprehensive exam, thesis or applied project and oral defense; for Ed S, thesis. *Entrance requirements:* For master's, GRE General Test, minimum GPA of 2.75. Additional exam requirements/recommendations for international students: Required—TOEFL (minimum score 555 paper-based; 213 computer-based; 79 iBT). *Faculty research:* Principal internship, superintendent assessment, administrative leadership, group training for residential workers.

Western Washington University, Graduate School, Woodring College of Education, Department of Educational Leadership, Program in Continuing and College Education, Bellingham, WA 98225-5996. Offers M Ed. Part-time and evening/weekend programs available. Postbaccalaureate distance learning degree programs offered (minimal on-campus study). *Degree requirements:* For master's, comprehensive exam, thesis optional. *Entrance requirements:* For master's, GRE General Test or MAT, minimum GPA of 3.0 in last 60 semester hours or last 90 quarter hours. Additional exam requirements/recommendations for international students: Required—TOEFL (minimum score 567 paper-based; 227 computer-based). Electronic applications accepted. *Faculty research:* Transfer of learning, postsecondary faculty development, action research as professional development, literacy education in community colleges, adult education in the Middle East, distance learning tools for graduate students.

Widener University, School of Human Service Professions, Center for Education, Chester, PA 19013-5792. Offers adult education (M Ed); counseling in higher education (M Ed); counselor education (M Ed); early childhood education (M Ed); educational foundations (M Ed); educational leadership (M Ed); educational psychology (M Ed); elementary education (M Ed); English and language arts (M Ed); health education (M Ed); higher education leadership (Ed D); home and school visitor (M Ed); human sexuality (M Ed, PhD); mathematics education (M Ed); middle school education (M Ed); principalship (M Ed); reading and language arts (Ed D); reading education (M Ed); school administration (Ed D); science education (M Ed); social studies education (M Ed); special education (M Ed); technology education (M Ed). *Accreditation:* NCATE. Part-time and evening/weekend programs available. Terminal master's awarded for partial completion of doctoral program. *Degree requirements:* For doctorate, thesis/dissertation. *Entrance requirements:* For master's, minimum GPA of 2.5; for doctorate, GRE or MAT, minimum GPA of 2.0 (undergraduate), 3.5 (graduate). Electronic applications accepted. *Expenses:* Contact institution. *Faculty research:* Reading and cognition, adult education, technology education, educational leadership, special education.

Wright State University, School of Graduate Studies, College of Education and Human Services, Department of Educational Leadership, Program in Advanced Educational Leadership, Dayton, OH 45435. Offers advanced curriculum and instruction (Ed S); higher education-adult education (Ed S); superintendent (Ed S). *Accreditation:* NCATE. *Degree requirements:* For Ed S, thesis. *Entrance requirements:* For degree, GRE General Test, MAT. Additional exam requirements/recommendations for international students: Required—TOEFL.

Community College Education

Argosy University, Chicago, College of Education, Chicago, IL 60601. Offers adult education and training (MA Ed); community college executive leadership (Ed D); educational leadership (MA Ed, Ed D, Ed S), including district leadership (Ed D), higher education administration (Ed D), K-12 education (Ed D); instructional leadership (Ed D, Ed S), including higher education (Ed D), K-12 education (Ed D). Postbaccalaureate distance learning degree programs offered (minimal on-campus study).

See Close-Up on page 769.

Argosy University, Denver, College of Education, Denver, CO 80231. Offers community college executive leadership (Ed D); educational leadership (MA Ed, Ed D), including higher education (Ed D), K-12 education (Ed D); instructional leadership (MA Ed, Ed D), including higher education administration (Ed D), K-12 education (Ed D).

See Close-Up on page 773.

Argosy University, Inland Empire, College of Education, San Bernardino, CA 92408. Offers community college executive leadership (Ed D); educational leadership (MA Ed, Ed D), including higher education administration (Ed D), K-12 education (Ed D); instructional leadership (MA Ed, Ed D), including higher education (Ed D), K-12 education (Ed D), multiple subject teacher preparation (MA Ed), single subject teacher preparation (MA Ed).

See Close-Up on page 1019.

Argosy University, Los Angeles, College of Education, Santa Monica, CA 90045. Offers community college executive leadership (Ed D); educational leadership (MA Ed, Ed D), including higher education administration (Ed D), K-12 education (Ed D); instructional leadership (MA Ed, Ed D), including higher education (Ed D), K-12 education (Ed D), multiple subject teacher preparation (MA Ed), single subject teacher preparation (MA Ed).

See Close-Up on page 777.

Argosy University, Orange County, College of Education, Orange, CA 92868. Offers community college executive leadership (Ed D); educational leadership (MA Ed, Ed D), including higher education administration (Ed D), K-12 education (Ed D); instructional leadership (MA Ed, Ed D), including education technology (Ed D), higher education (Ed D), K-12 education (Ed D), multiple subject teacher preparation (MA Ed), single subject teacher preparation (MA Ed).

See Close-Up on page 779.

Argosy University, Phoenix, College of Education, Phoenix, AZ 85021. Offers adult education and training (MA Ed); advanced educational administration (Ed D, Ed S); community college executive leadership (Ed D); educational administration (MA Ed); educational leadership (MA Ed, Ed D, Ed S), including education technology (Ed D), higher education administration (Ed D), K-12 education (Ed D); higher and postsecondary education (MA Ed); initial educational administration (Ed D, Ed S); school psychology (MA); teaching and learning (MA Ed, Ed D, Ed S), including education technology (Ed D), higher education (Ed D), K-12 education (Ed D).

See Close-Up on page 781.

Argosy University, San Diego, College of Education, San Diego, CA 92108. Offers community college executive leadership (Ed D); educational leadership (MA Ed, Ed D), including higher education administration (Ed D), K-12 education (Ed D); instructional leadership (MA Ed, Ed D), including higher education (Ed D), K-12 education (Ed D).

See Close-Up on page 785.

Argosy University, San Francisco Bay Area, College of Education, Alameda, CA 94501. Offers community college executive leadership (Ed D); educational leadership (MA Ed, Ed D), including education technology (Ed D), higher education administration (Ed D), K-12 education (Ed D); instructional leadership (MA Ed, Ed D), including education technology (Ed D), higher education (Ed D), K-12 education (Ed D), multiple subject teacher preparation (MA Ed), single subject teacher preparation (MA Ed).

See Close-Up on page 787.

Argosy University, Schaumburg, College of Education, Schaumburg, IL 60173-5403. Offers community college executive leadership (Ed D); educational leadership (MA Ed, Ed D, Ed S), including district leadership (Ed D), higher education administration (Ed D), K-12 education (Ed D); instructional leadership (Ed D, Ed S), including higher education (Ed D), K-12 education (Ed D).

See Close-Up on page 791.

Argosy University, Seattle, College of Education, Seattle, WA 98121. Offers adult education and training (MA Ed); community college executive leadership (Ed D); educational leadership (MA Ed, Ed D), including higher education administration (Ed D), K-12 education (Ed D); higher and postsecondary education (MA Ed); instructional leadership (MA Ed, Ed D), including education technology (Ed D), higher education (Ed D), K-12 education (Ed D).

See Close-Up on page 793.

Argosy University, Tampa, College of Education, Tampa, FL 33607. Offers community college executive leadership (Ed D); educational leadership (MA Ed, Ed D, Ed S), including higher education administration (Ed D), K-12 education (Ed D); school counseling (MA); teaching and learning (MA Ed, Ed D, Ed S), including higher education (Ed D), K-12 education (Ed D).

See Close-Up on page 795.

Argosy University, Washington DC, College of Education, Arlington, VA 22209. Offers community college executive leadership (Ed D); educational leadership (MA Ed, Ed D, Ed S), including higher education administration (Ed D), K-12 education (Ed D); instructional leadership (MA Ed, Ed D, Ed S), including higher education (Ed D), K-12 education (Ed D).

See Close-Up on page 799.

Arkansas State University, Graduate School, College of Education, Department of Educational Leadership, Curriculum, and Special Education, Jonesboro, State University, AR 72467. Offers community college administration education (SCCT); curriculum and instruction (MSE); educational leadership (MSE, Ed D, PhD, Ed S), including curriculum and instruction (MSE, Ed S); special education (MSE), including gifted, talented, and creative, instructional specialist 4-12, instructional specialist P-4. *Accreditation:* NCATE. Part-time programs available. Postbaccalaureate distance learning degree programs offered (no on-campus study). *Faculty:* 12 full-time (5 women). *Students:* 11 full-time (6 women), 2,240 part-time (1,686 women); includes 374 minority (278 Black or African American, non-Hispanic/Latino; 14 American Indian or Alaska Native, non-Hispanic/Latino; 12 Asian, non-Hispanic/Latino; 46 Hispanic/Latino; 2 Native Hawaiian or other Pacific Islander, non-Hispanic/Latino; 22 Two or more races, non-Hispanic/Latino), 1 international. Average age 37. 1,519 applicants, 76% accepted, 790 enrolled. In 2011, 827 master's, 8 doctorates, 30 other advanced degrees awarded. *Degree requirements:* For master's, comprehensive exam, thesis or alternative; for doctorate, comprehensive exam, thesis/dissertation; for other advanced degree, comprehensive exam. *Entrance requirements:* For master's, GRE General Test or MAT, appropriate bachelor's degree, letters of reference, interview, official transcript, immunization records; for doctorate, GRE General Test or MAT, interview, master's degree, letters of reference, official transcript, personal statement, writing sample, immunization records; for other advanced degree, GRE General Test or MAT, interview, master's degree, letters of reference, official transcript, 3 years teaching experience, mentor, teaching license, immunization records. Additional exam requirements/recommendations for international students: Required—TOEFL (minimum score 550 paper-based; 213 computer-based; 79 iBT), IELTS (minimum score 6), Pearson Test of English Academic (minimum score 56). *Application deadline:* Applications are processed on a rolling basis. Application fee: $50. Electronic applications accepted. *Expenses:* Tuition, state resident: full-time $4044; part-time $225 per credit hour. Tuition, nonresident: full-time $8087; part-time $449 per credit hour. *Required fees:* $936; $52 per credit hour. $25 per term. One-time fee: $30. Tuition and fees vary according to course load and program. *Financial support:* In 2011–12, 6 students received support. Fellowships, teaching assistantships, career-related internships or fieldwork, scholarships/grants, and unspecified assistantships available. Financial award application deadline: 7/1; financial award applicants required to submit FAFSA. *Unit head:* Dr. Mitchell Holifield, Chair, 870-972-3062, Fax: 870-680-8130, E-mail: hfield@astate.edu. *Application contact:* Dr. Andrew Sustich, Dean of the Graduate School, 870-972-3029, Fax: 870-972-3857, E-mail: sustich@astate.edu. Web site: http://www.astate.edu/a/education/elcse/.

California State University, Stanislaus, College of Education, Programs in Educational Leadership (Ed D), Turlock, CA 95382. Offers community college leadership (Ed D); P-12 leadership (Ed D). Part-time and evening/weekend programs available. *Degree requirements:* For doctorate, thesis/dissertation. *Entrance requirements:* For doctorate, GRE, minimum GPA of 3.0, 3 letters of reference, interview, personal statement. Additional exam requirements/recommendations for international students: Required—TOEFL (minimum score 550 paper-based; 213 computer-based). *Application deadline:* For spring admission, 2/1 priority date for domestic students. Application fee: $55. Electronic applications accepted. *Expenses: Required fees:* $4616 per year. *Financial support:* Career-related internships or fieldwork and Federal Work-Study available. Financial award application deadline: 3/1; financial award applicants required to submit FAFSA. *Unit head:* Dr. Kenneth White, Director, 209-664-6543, Fax: 209-667-3043, E-mail: edd@csustan.edu. *Application contact:* Graduate School, 209-667-3129, Fax: 209-664-7025, E-mail: graduate_school@csustan.edu. Web site: http://www.csustan.edu/EdD/.

Central Michigan University, Central Michigan University Global Campus, Program in Education, Mount Pleasant, MI 48859. Offers adult education (MA); college teaching (Graduate Certificate); community college (MA); educational leadership (MA), including charter school leadership; educational technology (MA); guidance and development (MA); instruction (MA); reading and literacy K-12 (MA); school principalship (MA); teacher leadership (MA). *Accreditation:* Teacher Education Accreditation Council. Part-time and evening/weekend programs available. *Entrance requirements:* For master's, minimum GPA of 2.7 in major. Additional exam requirements/recommendations for international students: Required—TOEFL. *Application deadline:* Applications are processed on a rolling basis. Application fee: $50. Electronic applications accepted. *Financial support:* Scholarships/grants available. Support available to part-time students. *Unit head:* Dr. Peter Ross, Director, 989-774-4456, E-mail: ross1pg@cmich.edu. *Application contact:* 877-268-4636, E-mail: cmuglobal@cmich.edu.

Colorado State University, Graduate School, College of Applied Human Sciences, School of Education, Fort Collins, CO 80523-1588. Offers adult education and training (M Ed); community college leadership (PhD); counseling and career development (M Ed); education and human resource studies (M Ed, PhD); educational leadership (M Ed, PhD); interdisciplinary studies (PhD); organizational performance and change (M Ed, PhD); student affairs in higher education (MS). *Accreditation:* ACA; Teacher Education Accreditation Council. Part-time and evening/weekend programs available. *Faculty:* 18 full-time (11 women), 1 part-time/adjunct (0 women). *Students:* 161 full-time (106 women), 491 part-time (291 women); includes 130 minority (28 Black or African American, non-Hispanic/Latino; 5 American Indian or Alaska Native, non-Hispanic/Latino; 12 Asian, non-Hispanic/Latino; 68 Hispanic/Latino; 3 Native Hawaiian or other Pacific Islander, non-Hispanic/Latino; 14 Two or more races, non-Hispanic/Latino), 29 international. Average age 38. 468 applicants, 31% accepted, 112 enrolled. In 2011, 192 master's, 30 doctorates awarded. *Degree requirements:* For master's, comprehensive exam (for some programs), thesis optional; for doctorate, comprehensive exam, thesis/dissertation, minimum of 60 credits. *Entrance requirements:* For master's, GRE, minimum undergraduate GPA of 3.0, 3 letters of recommendation, curriculum vitae/resume; for doctorate, minimum GPA of 3.0, 3 letters of recommendation, curriculum vitae. Additional exam requirements/recommendations for international students: Required—TOEFL (minimum score 550 paper-based; 213 computer-based; 80 iBT). *Application deadline:* For fall admission, 2/15 priority date for domestic students, 2/15 for international students; for spring admission, 9/1 priority date for domestic students, 9/1 for international students. Applications are processed on a rolling basis. Application fee: $50. Electronic applications accepted. *Expenses:* Tuition, state resident: full-time $7992. Tuition, nonresident: full-time $19,592. *Required fees:* $1735; $58 per credit. *Financial support:* In 2011–12, 11 students received support, including 1 fellowship (averaging $37,500 per year), 3 research assistantships with full tuition reimbursements available (averaging $8,911 per year), 7 teaching assistantships with full tuition reimbursements available (averaging $12,691 per year); Federal Work-Study, scholarships/grants, and unspecified assistantships also available. Financial award application deadline: 2/15; financial award applicants required to submit FAFSA. *Faculty research:* Innovative instruction, diverse learners, transition, scientifically-based evaluation methods, leadership and organizational development, research methodology. *Total annual research expenditures:* $455,133. *Unit head:* Dr. Kevin Oltjenbruns, Interim Director, 970-491-6316, Fax: 970-491-1317, E-mail: kevin.oltjenbruns@colostate.edu. *Application contact:* Kathy Lucas, Graduate Contact, 970-491-1963, Fax: 970-491-1317, E-mail: kplucas@cahs.colostate.edu. Web site: http://www.soe.cahs.colostate.edu/.

East Carolina University, Graduate School, Thomas Harriot College of Arts and Sciences, Department of Mathematics, Greenville, NC 27858-4353. Offers mathematics (MA); mathematics in the community college (MA); statistics (MA, Certificate). Part-time and evening/weekend programs available. *Degree requirements:* For master's, comprehensive exam. *Entrance requirements:* For master's, GRE General Test, MAT. Additional exam requirements/recommendations for international students: Required—TOEFL. *Application deadline:* For fall admission, 6/1 for domestic students; for spring admission, 10/15 for domestic students. Applications are processed on a rolling basis. Application fee: $50. *Expenses:* Tuition, state resident: full-time $3557; part-time $444.63 per semester hour. Tuition, nonresident: full-time $14,351; part-time $1793.88 per semester hour. *Required fees:* $2016; $252 per semester hour. Part-time tuition and fees vary according to course load, campus/location and program. *Financial support:* Research assistantships with partial tuition reimbursements and teaching assistantships with partial tuition reimbursements available. Financial award application deadline: 6/1. *Unit head:* Dr. Johannes H. Hattingh, Chair, 252-328-6461, E-mail: hattinghj@ecu.edu. *Application contact:* Dean of Graduate School, 252-328-6012, Fax: 252-328-6071, E-mail: gradschool@ecu.edu. Web site: http://www.ecu.edu/cs-cas/math/graduateprogram.cfm.

Eastern Illinois University, Graduate School, College of Arts and Humanities, Department of Communication Studies, Charleston, IL 61920-3099. Offers community college pedagogy (MA). Part-time programs available. *Faculty:* 11 full-time (2 women). *Students:* 28 full-time (18 women). In 2011, 6 master's awarded. *Degree requirements:* For master's, major paper. *Application deadline:* For fall admission, 3/31 priority date for domestic students. Applications are processed on a rolling basis. Application fee: $30. *Expenses:* Tuition, state resident: part-time $279 per credit hour. Tuition, nonresident: part-time $670 per credit hour. *Required fees:* $179.07 per credit hour. $1253 per semester. *Financial support:* In 2011–12, 1 research assistantship with full tuition reimbursement (averaging $8,100 per year), 6 teaching assistantships with full tuition reimbursements (averaging $8,100 per year) were awarded. *Unit head:* Dr. Mark Borzi, Chairperson, 217-581-2016, E-mail: cfmgb@eiu.edu. *Application contact:* Dr. Matt Gill, Coordinator, 217-581-6306, E-mail: mjgill@eiu.edu.

Ferris State University, College of Professional and Technological Studies, Big Rapids, MI 49307. Offers community college leadership (Ed D). Evening/weekend programs available. Postbaccalaureate distance learning degree programs offered (minimal on-campus study). *Faculty:* 20 part-time/adjunct (11 women). *Students:* 41 part-time (27 women); includes 7 minority (6 Black or African American, non-Hispanic/Latino; 1 Hispanic/Latino). Average age 45. *Entrance requirements:* For doctorate, master's degree with minimum GPA of 3.25, fierce commitment to the mission of community colleges, essay, writing samples. *Application deadline:* For winter admission, 1/27 for domestic and international students; for spring admission, 4/15 for domestic and international students. Applications are processed on a rolling basis. Application fee: $30. Electronic applications accepted. Application fee is waived when completed online. *Financial support:* In 2011–12, 10 students received support. Applicants required to submit FAFSA. *Unit head:* Dr. Roberta Teahen, Director, 231-591-3805, E-mail: robertateahen@ferris.edu. *Application contact:* Andrea Wirgau, Coordinator, 231-591-2710, Fax: 231-591-3539, E-mail: andreawirgau@ferris.edu.

Fielding Graduate University, Graduate Programs, School of Educational Leadership and Change, Santa Barbara, CA 93105-3538. Offers collaborative educational leadership (MA); educational leadership and change (Ed D), including community college leadership and change, grounded theory/grounded action, leadership of higher education systems, media studies; teaching in the virtual classroom (Graduate Certificate). Postbaccalaureate distance learning degree programs offered (minimal on-campus study). *Faculty:* 15 full-time (8 women), 5 part-time/adjunct (3 women). *Students:* 201 full-time (141 women), 9 part-time (8 women); includes 108 minority (64 Black or African American, non-Hispanic/Latino; 6 American Indian or Alaska Native, non-Hispanic/Latino; 7 Asian, non-Hispanic/Latino; 21 Hispanic/Latino; 1 Native Hawaiian or other Pacific Islander, non-Hispanic/Latino; 9 Two or more races, non-Hispanic/Latino), 2 international. Average age 47. 27 applicants, 93% accepted, 19 enrolled. In 2011, 44 master's, 45 doctorates, 7 other advanced degrees awarded. *Degree requirements:* For master's, capstone research project; for doctorate, comprehensive exam, thesis/dissertation. *Entrance requirements:* For master's, minimum GPA of 2.5; for doctorate, resume, 2 letters of recommendation, writing sample. *Application deadline:* For fall admission, 6/10 for domestic and international students; for spring admission, 11/19 for domestic and international students. Application fee: $75. Electronic applications accepted. *Expenses:* Contact institution. *Financial support:* In 2011–12, 21 students received support. Scholarships/grants, health care benefits, and tuition waivers (partial) available. Support available to part-time students. Financial award applicants required to submit FAFSA. *Unit head:* Dr. Mario R. Borunda, Dean, 805-898-2940, E-mail: mborunda@fielding.edu. *Application contact:* Admission Counselor, 800-340-1099 Ext. 4098, Fax: 805-687-9793, E-mail: elcadmissions@fielding.edu. Web site: http://www.fielding.edu/programs/elc/default.aspx.

George Mason University, College of Humanities and Social Sciences, Higher Education Program, Fairfax, VA 22030. Offers college teaching (Certificate); community college education (DA Ed); higher education administration (Certificate). *Faculty:* 4 full-time (3 women), 2 part-time/adjunct (0 women). *Students:* 5 full-time (4 women), 47 part-time (28 women); includes 15 minority (9 Black or African American, non-Hispanic/Latino; 2 Asian, non-Hispanic/Latino; 4 Hispanic/Latino). Average age 47. 23 applicants, 48% accepted, 6 enrolled. In 2011, 5 doctorates, 7 Certificates awarded. *Degree requirements:* For doctorate, thesis/dissertation, internship. *Entrance requirements:* For doctorate, GRE, 3 letters of recommendation; writing sample; resume; master's degree; expanded goals statement; official transcripts; for Certificate, official transcripts; expanded goals statement; 3 letters of recommendation; resume. Additional exam requirements/recommendations for international students: Required—TOEFL (minimum score 570 paper-based; 230 computer-based; 88 iBT), IELTS, Pearson Test of English. *Application deadline:* For fall admission, 4/15 priority date for domestic students; for spring admission, 11/1 priority date for domestic students. Application fee: $65 ($80 for international students). Electronic applications accepted. *Expenses:* Tuition, state resident: full-time $8750; part-time $364.58 per credit. Tuition, nonresident: full-time $24,092; part-time $1003.83 per credit. *Required fees:* $2514; $104.75 per credit. *Financial support:* In 2011–12, 3 students received support, including 1 research assistantship with full and partial tuition reimbursement available (averaging $14,500 per year), 2 teaching assistantships with full and partial tuition reimbursements available (averaging $6,504 per year); career-related internships or fieldwork, Federal Work-Study, scholarships/grants, unspecified assistantships, and health care benefits (full-time research or teaching assistantship recipients) also available. Support available to part-time students. Financial award application deadline: 3/1; financial award applicants required to submit FAFSA. *Faculty research:* Leadership, the scholarship of teaching, learning, and assessment; ethical leadership; assessment; information technology; diversity. *Unit head:* John S. O'Connor, Director, 703-993-1455, Fax: 703-993-2307, E-mail: joconnor@gmu.edu. *Application contact:* Nina Joshi, Administrative Coordinator, 703-993-2310, Fax: 703-993-2307, E-mail: njoshi@gmu.edu. Web site: http://highered.gmu.edu/.

George Mason University, College of Humanities and Social Sciences, Interdisciplinary Studies Program, Fairfax, VA 22030. Offers community college teaching (MAIS). *Faculty:* 6 full-time (3 women), 4 part-time/adjunct (2 women). *Students:* 13 full-time (10 women), 94 part-time (65 women); includes 21 minority (7 Black or African American, non-Hispanic/Latino; 3 Asian, non-Hispanic/Latino; 10 Hispanic/Latino; 1 Two or more races, non-Hispanic/Latino), 4 international. Average age 34. 87 applicants, 47% accepted, 26 enrolled. In 2011, 27 degrees awarded. *Degree requirements:* For master's, project or thesis. *Entrance requirements:* For master's, 3 letters of recommendation; writing sample; official transcript; resume. Additional exam requirements/recommendations for international students: Required—TOEFL (minimum score 570 paper-based; 230 computer-based; 88 iBT), IELTS, Pearson Test of English. *Application deadline:* For fall admission, 3/1 priority date for domestic students; for spring admission, 10/15 for domestic students. Application fee: $65 ($80 for international students). Electronic applications accepted. *Expenses:* Tuition, state resident: full-time $8750; part-time $364.58 per credit. Tuition, nonresident: full-time $24,092; part-time $1003.83 per credit. *Required fees:* $2514; $104.75 per credit. *Financial support:* In 2011–12, 5 students received support, including 1 research assistantship with full and partial tuition reimbursement available (averaging $1,000 per year), 5 teaching assistantships with full and partial tuition reimbursements available (averaging $10,350 per year); career-related internships or fieldwork, Federal Work-Study, scholarships/grants, unspecified assistantships, and health care benefits (full-time research or teaching assistantship recipients) also available. Support available to part-time students. Financial award application deadline: 3/1; financial award applicants required to submit FAFSA. *Faculty research:* Combined English and folklore, religious and cultural studies (Christianity and Muslim society). *Unit head:* Matt Zingraff, Director, 703-993-4769, E-mail: zingraff@gmu.edu. *Application contact:* Allison Millward, Administrative Coordinator, 703-993-8762, E-mail: amillwar@gmu.edu. Web site: http://mais.gmu.edu.

Morgan State University, School of Graduate Studies, School of Education and Urban Studies, Department of Advanced Studies, Leadership and Policy, Program in Higher Education-Community College Leadership, Baltimore, MD 21251. Offers Ed D. *Accreditation:* NCATE. Part-time and evening/weekend programs available. *Degree requirements:* For doctorate, comprehensive exam, thesis/dissertation. *Entrance requirements:* For doctorate, GRE General Test or MAT. Additional exam requirements/recommendations for international students: Required—TOEFL (minimum score 550 paper-based; 213 computer-based). *Faculty research:* Multicultural education, cooperative learning, psychology of cognition.

North Carolina State University, Graduate School, College of Education, Department of Adult and Higher Education, Program in Adult and Community College Education, Raleigh, NC 27695. Offers M Ed, MS, Ed D. *Degree requirements:* For master's, thesis (for some programs); for doctorate, thesis/dissertation. *Entrance requirements:* For master's and doctorate, GRE or MAT. Electronic applications accepted.

Northern Arizona University, Graduate College, College of Education, Department of Educational Leadership, Flagstaff , AZ 86011. Offers community college/higher education (M Ed); educational foundations (M Ed); educational leadership (M Ed, Ed D); principal (Certificate); principal K-12 (M Ed); school leadership K-12 (M Ed); superintendent (Certificate). Part-time programs available. *Faculty:* 18 full-time (8 women). *Students:* 249 full-time (148 women), 737 part-time (460 women); includes 291 minority (51 Black or African American, non-Hispanic/Latino; 65 American Indian or Alaska Native, non-Hispanic/Latino; 14 Asian, non-Hispanic/Latino; 143 Hispanic/Latino; 2 Native Hawaiian or other Pacific Islander, non-Hispanic/Latino; 16 Two or more races, non-Hispanic/Latino), 1 international. Average age 32. 251 applicants, 94% accepted, 196 enrolled. In 2011, 356 master's, 12 doctorates, 74 Certificates awarded. *Degree requirements:* For master's, comprehensive exam, thesis (for some programs); for doctorate, comprehensive exam, thesis/dissertation. *Entrance requirements:* For master's, minimum GPA of 3.0; for doctorate, GRE or MAT, minimum GPA of 3.5. Additional exam requirements/recommendations for international students: Required—TOEFL (minimum score 550 paper-based; 213 computer-based; 80 iBT), IELTS (minimum score 7). *Application deadline:* For fall admission, 3/1 for international students; for spring admission, 9/15 for international students. Applications are processed on a rolling basis. Application fee: $65. Electronic applications accepted. *Expenses:* Tuition, state resident: full-time $7190; part-time $355 per credit hour. Tuition, nonresident: full-time $18,092; part-time $1005 per credit hour. *Required fees:* $818; $328 per semester. *Financial support:* In 2011–12, 1 research assistantship with partial tuition reimbursement (averaging $10,000 per year) was awarded. Financial award applicants required to submit FAFSA. *Unit head:* Dr. Michael Schwanenberger, Chair, 928-523-4212, Fax: 928-523-1929, E-mail: michael.schwanenberger@nau.edu. *Application contact:* Jennifer Offutt, Administrative Assistant, 928-523-5098, Fax: 928-523-1929, E-mail: jennifer.offutt@nau.edu. Web site: http://nau.edu/coe/ed-leadership/.

Old Dominion University, Darden College of Education, Doctoral Program in Community College Leadership, Norfolk, VA 23529. Offers PhD. Part-time programs available. Postbaccalaureate distance learning degree programs offered (minimal on-campus study). *Faculty:* 2 full-time (1 woman), 10 part-time/adjunct (5 women). *Students:* 1 full-time (0 women), 50 part-time (32 women); includes 12 minority (7 Black or African American, non-Hispanic/Latino; 1 American Indian or Alaska Native, non-Hispanic/Latino; 2 Asian, non-Hispanic/Latino; 1 Hispanic/Latino; 1 Two or more races, non-Hispanic/Latino). Average age 46. 29 applicants, 41% accepted, 12 enrolled. In 2011, 9 doctorates awarded. *Degree requirements:* For doctorate, comprehensive exam, thesis/dissertation, internship. *Entrance requirements:* For doctorate, GRE, master's degree, minimum GPA of 3.5, 3 letters of reference, essay, interview with faculty. Additional exam requirements/recommendations for international students: Required—TOEFL (minimum score 600 paper-based). *Application deadline:* For spring admission, 2/1 for domestic and international students. Application fee: $50. Electronic applications accepted. *Expenses:* Tuition, state resident: full-time $9096; part-time $379 per credit. Tuition, nonresident: full-time $23,064; part-time $961 per credit. *Required fees:* $127 per semester. One-time fee: $50. *Financial support:* In 2011–12, 12 fellowships with partial tuition reimbursements (averaging $1,500 per year), 1 research assistantship with full tuition reimbursement (averaging $15,000 per year) were awarded; career-related internships or fieldwork and unspecified assistantships also available. Financial award application deadline: 4/15. *Faculty research:* Rural community colleges, inter-institutional collaboration in higher education. *Unit head:* Dr. Mitchell Williams, Interim Graduate Program Director, 757-683-4375, Fax: 757-683-5756, E-mail: mrwillia@odu.edu. *Application contact:* Vanessa Malo-Kurzinski, Office Manager, 757-683-4344, Fax: 757-683-5756, E-mail: vmaloku@odu.edu. Web site: http://education.odu.edu/efl/academics/commcollege/.

Old Dominion University, Darden College of Education, Programs in Occupational and Technical Studies, Norfolk, VA 23529. Offers business and industry training (MS); career and technical education (MS, PhD); community college teaching (MS); human resources training (PhD); STEM education (MS); technology education (PhD). *Accreditation:* NCATE (one or more programs are accredited). Part-time and evening/weekend programs available. Postbaccalaureate distance learning degree programs offered (minimal on-campus study). *Faculty:* 7 full-time (1 woman), 8 part-time/adjunct (3 women). *Students:* 14 full-time (10 women), 59 part-time (33 women); includes 28 minority (18 Black or African American, non-Hispanic/Latino; 1 American Indian or Alaska Native, non-Hispanic/Latino; 2 Asian, non-Hispanic/Latino; 6 Hispanic/Latino; 1 Two or more races, non-Hispanic/Latino), 1 international. Average age 42. 44 applicants, 95% accepted, 37 enrolled. In 2011, 27 master's, 5 doctorates awarded. *Degree requirements:* For master's, comprehensive exam, thesis optional, writing exam, candidacy exam; for doctorate, comprehensive exam, thesis/dissertation, writing exam, candidacy exam. *Entrance requirements:* For master's, GRE General Test or MAT, minimum GPA of 2.8, 2 letters of reference; for doctorate, GRE, minimum GPA of 3.0, 3 letters of reference. Additional exam requirements/recommendations for international students: Required—TOEFL. *Application deadline:* For fall admission, 6/1 priority date for domestic students, 6/1 for international students; for winter admission, 11/1 priority date for domestic students, 11/1 for international students; for spring admission, 3/1 priority date for domestic students, 3/1 for international students. Applications are processed on a rolling basis. Application fee: $50. Electronic applications accepted. *Expenses:* Tuition, state resident: full-time $9096; part-time $379 per credit. Tuition, nonresident: full-time $23,064; part-time $961 per credit. *Required fees:* $127 per semester. One-time fee: $50. *Financial support:* In 2011–12, 19 students received support, including 1 fellowship with full tuition reimbursement available (averaging $15,000 per year), 2 research assistantships with partial tuition reimbursements available (averaging $9,000 per year), 4 teaching assistantships with partial tuition reimbursements available (averaging $15,000 per year); career-related internships or fieldwork, scholarships/grants, tuition waivers (partial), and unspecified assistantships also available. Support available to part-time students. Financial award application deadline: 2/15; financial award applicants required to submit FAFSA. *Faculty research:* Training and development, marketing, technology, special populations, STEM education. *Total annual research expenditures:* $799,773. *Unit head:* Dr. John M. Ritz, Graduate Program Director, 757-683-5226, Fax: 757-683-5227, E-mail: jritz@odu.edu. *Application contact:* William Heffelfinger, Director of Graduate Admissions, 757-683-5554, Fax: 757-683-3255, E-mail: gradadmit@odu.edu. Web site: http://education.odu.edu/ots/.

Pittsburg State University, Graduate School, College of Education, Department of Special Services and Leadership Studies, Program in Community College and Higher Education, Pittsburg, KS 66762. Offers Ed S. *Accreditation:* NCATE.

University of Central Florida, College of Education, Department of Educational and Human Sciences, Program in Educational Leadership, Orlando, FL 32816. Offers educational leadership (MA, Ed D), including community college education (MA), higher education (Ed D), student personnel (MA). Part-time and evening/weekend programs available. *Students:* 82 full-time (55 women), 179 part-time (126 women); includes 53 minority (27 Black or African American, non-Hispanic/Latino; 3 Asian, non-Hispanic/Latino; 19 Hispanic/Latino; 4 Two or more races, non-Hispanic/Latino), 1 international. Average age 35. 142 applicants, 69% accepted, 62 enrolled. In 2011, 60 master's, 26 doctorates awarded. *Degree requirements:* For master's, thesis or alternative; for doctorate, thesis/dissertation, candidacy exam. *Entrance requirements:* For master's, GRE General Test; for doctorate, GRE General Test, GRE Subject Test, minimum GPA of 3.0, resume. Additional exam requirements/recommendations for international students: Required—TOEFL. *Application deadline:* For fall admission, 2/20 priority date for domestic students; for spring admission, 9/20 priority date for domestic students. Application fee: $30. Electronic applications accepted. *Expenses:* Tuition, state resident: part-time $277.08 per credit hour. Tuition, nonresident: part-time $277.08 per credit hour. Part-time tuition and fees vary according to degree level and program. *Financial support:* In 2011–12, 17 students received support, including 4 fellowships with partial tuition reimbursements available (averaging $8,300 per year), 14 research assistantships with partial tuition reimbursements available (averaging $7,000 per year), 2 teaching assistantships with partial tuition reimbursements available (averaging $1,000 per year); career-related internships or fieldwork, Federal Work-Study, institutionally sponsored loans, tuition waivers (partial), and unspecified assistantships also available. Financial award application deadline: 3/1; financial award applicants required to submit FAFSA. *Unit head:* Dr. Rosa Cintron, Program Coordinator, 407-832-1248, E-mail: rosa.cintrondelgado@ucf.edu. *Application contact:* Barbara Rodriguez, Director, Admissions and Registration, 407-823-2766, Fax: 407-823-6442, E-mail: gradadmissions@ucf.edu. Web site: http://education.ucf.edu/departments.cfm.

University of Central Florida, College of Education, School of Teaching, Learning, and Leadership, Applied Learning and Instruction Program, Orlando, FL 32816. Offers applied learning and instruction (MA); community college education (Certificate); gifted education (Certificate); global and comparative education (Certificate); initial teacher professional preparation (Certificate); urban education (Certificate). *Accreditation:* NCATE. Part-time and evening/weekend programs available. *Students:* 12 full-time (10 women), 79 part-time (65 women); includes 23 minority (6 Black or African American, non-Hispanic/Latino; 1 American Indian or Alaska Native, non-Hispanic/Latino; 3 Asian, non-Hispanic/Latino; 12 Hispanic/Latino; 1 Two or more races, non-Hispanic/Latino), 1 international. Average age 31. 53 applicants, 72% accepted, 24 enrolled. In 2011, 11 master's, 24 other advanced degrees awarded. *Degree requirements:* For Certificate, thesis or alternative, final exam. *Entrance requirements:* For degree, GRE General Test, minimum GPA of 3.0, resume. Additional exam requirements/recommendations for international students: Required—TOEFL. *Application deadline:* For fall admission, 2/20 for domestic students; for spring admission, 9/20 for domestic students. Application fee: $30. Electronic applications accepted. *Expenses:* Tuition, state resident: part-time $277.08 per credit hour. Tuition, nonresident: part-time $277.08 per credit hour. Part-time tuition and fees vary according to degree level and program. *Financial support:* In 2011–12, 3 students received support, including 2 research assistantships with partial tuition reimbursements available (averaging $7,100 per year), 1 teaching assistantship with partial tuition reimbursement available (averaging $6,900 per year); fellowships with partial tuition reimbursements available, career-related internships or fieldwork, Federal Work-Study, institutionally sponsored loans, and unspecified assistantships also available. Financial award application deadline: 3/1; financial award applicants required to submit FAFSA. *Unit head:* Dr. Bobby Hoffman, Program Coordinator, 407-823-1770, E-mail: bobby.hoffman@ucf.edu. *Application contact:* Barbara Rodriguez, Director, Admissions and Registration, 407-823-2766, Fax: 407-823-6442, E-mail: gradadmissions@ucf.edu. Web site: http://education.ucf.edu/departments.cfm.

University of Southern Mississippi, Graduate School, College of Education and Psychology, Department of Educational Studies and Research, Hattiesburg, MS 39406-0001. Offers adult education (Graduate Certificate); community college leadership (Graduate Certificate); counseling and personnel services (college) (M Ed); education

(PhD, Ed S), including adult education, research, evaluation and statistics (PhD); education (Ed D), including educational administration, educational research; education: educational leadership and research (Ed S), including higher education administration; educational administration and supervision (M Ed); higher education administration (Ed D, PhD); institutional research (Graduate Certificate). *Faculty:* 7 full-time (1 woman), 5 part-time/adjunct (1 woman). *Students:* 33 full-time (25 women), 104 part-time (25 women); includes 46 minority (40 Black or African American, non-Hispanic/Latino; 1 Asian, non-Hispanic/Latino; 3 Hispanic/Latino; 2 Two or more races, non-Hispanic/Latino), 1 international. Average age 36. 27 applicants, 48% accepted, 1 enrolled. In 2011, 27 master's, 13 doctorates, 1 other advanced degree awarded. *Degree requirements:* For master's and other advanced degree, comprehensive exam, thesis (for some programs); for doctorate, comprehensive exam, thesis/dissertation. *Entrance requirements:* For master's, doctorate, and other advanced degree, GRE General Test, minimum GPA of 2.75. Additional exam requirements/recommendations for international students: Required—TOEFL. *Application deadline:* For fall admission, 2/1 for domestic students, 3/1 for international students. Applications are processed on a rolling basis. Application fee: $35. *Financial support:* Career-related internships or fieldwork, Federal Work-Study, and institutionally sponsored loans available. Financial award application deadline: 3/15; financial award applicants required to submit FAFSA. *Total annual research expenditures:* $88,500. *Unit head:* Dr. Thomas V. O'Brien, Chair, 601-266-6093, E-mail: thomas.obrien@usm.edu. *Application contact:* Shonna Breland, Manager of Graduate Admissions, 601-266-6563, Fax: 601-266-5138. Web site: http://www.usm.edu/cep/esr/.

University of South Florida, Graduate School, College of Education, Department of Adult, Career and Higher Education, Tampa, FL 33620-9951. Offers adult education (MA, Ed D, PhD, Ed S); career and technical education (MA); career and workforce education (PhD); higher education/community college teaching (MA, Ed D, PhD); vocational education (Ed S). Part-time programs available. Postbaccalaureate distance learning degree programs offered (minimal on-campus study). *Faculty:* 9 full-time (3 women), 4 part-time/adjunct (3 women). *Students:* 38 full-time (21 women), 169 part-time (115 women); includes 59 minority (37 Black or African American, non-Hispanic/Latino; 5 Asian, non-Hispanic/Latino; 14 Hispanic/Latino; 3 Two or more races, non-Hispanic/Latino), 6 international. Average age 44. 98 applicants, 70% accepted, 42 enrolled. In 2011, 33 master's, 13 doctorates awarded. *Median time to degree:* Of those who began their doctoral program in fall 2003, 50% received their degree in 8 years or less. *Degree requirements:* For master's, comprehensive exam; for doctorate, comprehensive exam, thesis/dissertation, philosophies of inquiry; multiple research methods; for Ed S, comprehensive exam, thesis. *Entrance requirements:* For master's, minimum GPA of 3.0 in last 60 hours of course work; for doctorate and Ed S, GRE General Test, GRE Writing Test. Additional exam requirements/recommendations for international students: Required—TOEFL (minimum score 500 paper-based; 213 computer-based; 91 iBT). *Application deadline:* For fall admission, 2/15 for domestic students, 1/2 for international students; for spring admission, 10/15 for domestic students, 6/1 for international students. Applications are processed on a rolling basis. Application fee: $30. Electronic applications accepted. *Financial support:* In 2011–12, 5 students received support, including 5 teaching assistantships with full tuition reimbursements available (averaging $15,000 per year); career-related internships or fieldwork, scholarships/grants, and unspecified assistantships also available. Financial award applicants required to submit FAFSA. *Faculty research:* Community college leadership; integration of academic, career and technical education; competency-based education; continuing education administration; adult learning and development. *Total annual research expenditures:* $9,807. *Unit head:* Dr. Ann Cranston-Gingras, Chairperson, 813-974-6036, Fax: 813-974-3366, E-mail: cranston@usf.edu. *Application contact:* Dr. William Young, Program Director, 813-974-1861, Fax: 813-974-3366, E-mail: williamyoung@usf.edu.

Walden University, Graduate Programs, Richard W. Riley College of Education and Leadership, Minneapolis, MN 55401. Offers administrator leadership for teaching and learning (Ed D, Ed S); adult education (Ed D, Ed S); adult learning (MS, Postbaccalaureate Certificate), including developmental education (MS), online teaching (MS), teaching adults English as a second language (MS), training and performance management (MS); college teaching and learning (Ed D, Ed S, Postbaccalaureate Certificate); curriculum, instruction and assessment (Ed D, Postbaccalaureate Certificate); curriculum, instruction, and professional development (Ed S); developmental education (Postbaccalaureate Certificate); early childhood administration, management, and leadership (Postbaccalaureate Certificate); early childhood education (birth-grade 3) (MAT); early childhood public policy and advocacy (Postbaccalaureate Certificate); early childhood studies (MS), including administration, management and leadership, early childhood public policy and advocacy, teaching adults in the early childhood field, teaching and diversity; education (MS, PhD), including adolescent literacy and technology (grades 6-12) (MS), adult education leadership (PhD), assessment, evaluation, and accountability (PhD), community college leadership (PhD), curriculum, instruction, and assessment, early childhood education (PhD), educational technology (PhD), elementary reading and literacy (MS), elementary reading and mathematics (MS), general program, global and comparative education (PhD), higher education (PhD), integrating technology in the classroom (MS), K-12 educational leadership (PhD), leadership, policy and change (PhD), learning, instruction and innovation (PhD), literacy and learning in the content areas (MS), mathematics (grades 6-8) (MS), mathematics (grades K-5) (MS), middle level education (grades 5-8) (MS), professional development (MS), science (grades K-8) (MS), self-designed (PhD), special education (PhD), special education (non-licensure) (MS), teacher leadership (grades K-12) (MS), teaching English language learners (grades K-12) (MS); educational leadership and administration (principal preparation) (Ed S); educational technology (Ed S); elementary reading and literacy (Postbaccalaureate Certificate); engaging culturally diverse learners (Postbaccalaureate Certificate); enrollment management and institutional marketing (Postbaccalaureate Certificate); higher education (MS), including college teaching and learning, enrollment management and institutional planning, global higher education, leadership for student success, online and distance learning; higher education leadership (Ed D); instructional design (Postbaccalaureate Certificate); instructional design and technology (MS), including general program (MS, PhD), online learning, training and performance improvement; integrating technology in the classroom (Postbaccalaureate Certificate); online teaching for adult learners (Postbaccalaureate Certificate); professional development (Postbaccalaureate Certificate); reading and literacy leadership (Ed D); science K-8 (Postbaccalaureate Certificate); special education (Ed D, Ed S); special education: emotional/behavioral disorders (K-12) (MAT); special education: learning disabilities (K-12) (MAT); teacher leadership (Ed D, Ed S, Postbaccalaureate Certificate); training and performance management (Postbaccalaureate Certificate). Part-time and evening/weekend programs available. Postbaccalaureate distance learning degree programs offered (minimal on-campus study). *Faculty:* 71 full-time (48 women), 853 part-time/adjunct (585 women). *Students:* 11,326 full-time (9,212 women), 2,148 part-time (1,795 women); includes 5,346 minority (4,403 Black or African American, non-Hispanic/Latino; 76 American Indian or Alaska Native, non-Hispanic/Latino; 140 Asian, non-Hispanic/Latino; 561 Hispanic/Latino; 21 Native Hawaiian or other Pacific Islander, non-Hispanic/Latino; 145 Two or more races, non-Hispanic/Latino), 322 international. Average age 39. In 2011, 3,477 master's, 318 doctorates, 471 other advanced degrees awarded. *Degree requirements:* For doctorate, thesis/dissertation (for some programs), residency; for other advanced degree, residency (for some programs). *Entrance requirements:* For master's, bachelor's degree or equivalent in related field; minimum GPA of 2.5; official transcripts; goal statement; access to computer and Internet; for doctorate, master's degree or equivalent in related field; minimum GPA of 3.0; official transcripts; three years' related professional/academic experience (preferred); access to computer and Internet; for other advanced degree, master's degree or equivalent in related field; minimum GPA of 3.0; 3 years related professional/academic experience (preferred); access to computer and Internet (Ed S). Additional exam requirements/recommendations for international students: Required—TOEFL (minimum score 550 paper-based; 213 computer-based), IELTS (minimum score 6.5), or Michigan English Language Assessment Battery (minimum score 82). *Application deadline:* Applications are processed on a rolling basis. Application fee: $50. Electronic applications accepted. *Financial support:* Federal Work-Study, scholarships/grants, unspecified assistantships, and family tuition reduction, active duty/veteran tuition reduction, group tuition reduction, interest-free payment plans, employee tuition reduction available. Support available to part-time students. Financial award applicants required to submit FAFSA. *Unit head:* Dr. Kate Steffens, Dean, 800-925-3368. *Application contact:* Jennifer Hall, Vice President of Enrollment Management, 866-4-WALDEN, E-mail: info@waldenu.edu. Web site: http://www.waldenu.edu/Colleges-and-Schools/College-of-Education-and-Leadership.htm.

Western Carolina University, Graduate School, College of Education and Allied Professions, School of Teaching and Learning, Cullowhee, NC 28723. Offers community college and higher education (MA Ed), including community college administration, community college teaching; comprehensive education (MA Ed, MAT); educational leadership (MA Ed, MSA, Ed D, Ed S), including educational leadership (MSA, Ed D, Ed S), educational supervision (MA Ed); teaching (MA Ed, MAT), including comprehensive education (MA Ed), physical education (MA Ed), teaching (MAT). *Accreditation:* NCATE. Part-time and evening/weekend programs available. Postbaccalaureate distance learning degree programs offered. *Students:* 40 full-time (24 women), 150 part-time (133 women); includes 13 minority (6 Black or African American, non-Hispanic/Latino; 2 American Indian or Alaska Native, non-Hispanic/Latino; 4 Hispanic/Latino; 1 Two or more races, non-Hispanic/Latino), 9 international. Average age 32. 96 applicants, 90% accepted, 71 enrolled. In 2011, 86 master's, 13 doctorates, 5 other advanced degrees awarded. *Degree requirements:* For master's, comprehensive exam; for doctorate, comprehensive exam, thesis/dissertation. *Entrance requirements:* For master's, GRE, appropriate undergraduate degree, 3 letters of recommendation; for doctorate, GRE General Test, minimum graduate GPA of 3.5, appropriate master's degree; for other advanced degree, GRE General Test, minimum graduate GPA of 3.5, work experience, appropriate master's degree. Additional exam requirements/recommendations for international students: Required—TOEFL (minimum score 550 paper-based; 270 computer-based; 79 iBT). *Application deadline:* For fall admission, 2/1 for domestic students; for spring admission, 9/1 priority date for domestic students. Applications are processed on a rolling basis. Application fee: $50. *Expenses:* Tuition, state resident: full-time $3348. Tuition, nonresident: full-time $12,933. *Required fees:* $3155. *Financial support:* In 2011–12, 2 fellowships were awarded; research assistantships with full and partial tuition reimbursements, teaching assistantships with full and partial tuition reimbursements, career-related internships or fieldwork, institutionally sponsored loans, scholarships/grants, and unspecified assistantships also available. Financial award application deadline: 3/31; financial award applicants required to submit FAFSA. *Faculty research:* Educational leadership, special education, rural education, organizational theory and practice, interinstitutional partnership, program evaluation. *Unit head:* Dr. William Dee Nichols, Department Head, 828-227-7108, Fax: 828-227-7607, E-mail: wdnichols@wcu.edu. *Application contact:* Admissions Specialist for Educational Leadership and Foundations, 828-227-7398, Fax: 828-227-7480, E-mail: gradsch@email.wcu.edu. Web site: http://www.wcu.edu/3067.asp.

Wingate University, Thayer School of Education, Wingate, NC 28174-0159. Offers community college leadership (Ed D); educational leadership (MA Ed, Ed D); elementary education (MA Ed, MAT); health and physical education (MA Ed); sport administration (MA Ed). *Accreditation:* NCATE. Part-time and evening/weekend programs available. *Faculty:* 5 full-time (3 women), 10 part-time/adjunct (3 women). *Students:* 7 full-time (4 women), 251 part-time (152 women); includes 68 minority (63 Black or African American, non-Hispanic/Latino; 1 American Indian or Alaska Native, non-Hispanic/Latino; 1 Asian, non-Hispanic/Latino; 3 Hispanic/Latino), 2 international. Average age 35. In 2011, 29 master's awarded. *Degree requirements:* For master's, portfolio. *Entrance requirements:* For master's, GRE General Test or MAT, teaching certificate (MA Ed). *Application deadline:* For fall admission, 8/15 priority date for domestic students; for spring admission, 12/15 for domestic students. Applications are processed on a rolling basis. Application fee: $0. *Expenses: Tuition:* Part-time $455 per credit hour. Part-time tuition and fees vary according to degree level and program. *Financial support:* In 2011–12, 20 students received support. Scholarships/grants available. Support available to part-time students. Financial award applicants required to submit FAFSA. *Unit head:* Dr. Sarah Harrison-Burns, Dean, 704-233-8128, E-mail: shburns@wingate.edu. *Application contact:* Theresa Hopkins, Secretary, 704-321-1470, Fax: 704-233-8273, E-mail: t.hopkins@wingate.edu.

Early Childhood Education

Adelphi University, Ruth S. Ammon School of Education, Program in Early Childhood Education, Garden City, NY 11530-0701. Offers early childhood education (Certificate); in-service (MA); pre-certification (MA). *Students:* 8 part-time (all women). Average age 29. In 2011, 12 master's awarded. *Entrance requirements:* For master's, 2 letters of recommendation, resume; for Certificate, 2 letters of recommendation, resume, 6 credits in literacy. Additional exam requirements/recommendations for international students: Required—TOEFL (minimum score 550 paper-based; 213 computer-based; 80 iBT). *Application deadline:* For fall admission, 4/1 for domestic and international students; for spring admission, 11/1 for domestic and international students. Application fee: $50. Electronic applications accepted. *Expenses: Tuition:* Full-time $29,600; part-time $930 per credit. *Required fees:* $1100. *Faculty research:* Gifted education; impact of family, culture and school in child development; teacher training; assessment of young children; classrooms as respectful communities. *Unit head:* Dr. Dorothy Phalen, Director, 516-877-4025, E-mail: phalen2@adelphi.edu. *Application contact:* Christine Murphy, Director of Admissions, 516-877-3050, Fax: 516-877-3039, E-mail: graduateadmissions@adelphi.edu.

Alabama Agricultural and Mechanical University, School of Graduate Studies, School of Education, Area in Elementary and Early Childhood Education, Huntsville, AL 35811. Offers early childhood education (MS Ed, Ed S); elementary education (MS Ed, Ed S). *Accreditation:* NCATE. Evening/weekend programs available. *Degree requirements:* For master's, comprehensive exam; for Ed S, thesis. *Entrance requirements:* For master's, GRE General Test. Additional exam requirements/recommendations for international students: Required—TOEFL (minimum score 500 paper-based; 173 computer-based; 61 iBT). Electronic applications accepted. *Faculty research:* Multicultural education, learning styles, diagnostic-prescriptive instruction.

Alabama State University, Department of Curriculum and Instruction, Program in Early Childhood Education, Montgomery, AL 36101-0271. Offers M Ed, Ed S. Part-time programs available. *Faculty:* 3 full-time (2 women). *Students:* 6 full-time (all women), 25 part-time (24 women); includes 30 minority (all Black or African American, non-Hispanic/Latino). Average age 37. 6 applicants, 50% accepted, 0 enrolled. In 2011, 2 degrees awarded. *Degree requirements:* For master's, comprehensive exam; for Ed S, comprehensive exam, thesis. *Entrance requirements:* For master's, GRE General Test, MAT or NTE, graduate writing competency test; for Ed S, graduate writing competency test, GRE, MAT. Additional exam requirements/recommendations for international students: Required—TOEFL (minimum score 500 paper-based; 173 computer-based). *Application deadline:* For fall admission, 7/15 for domestic students; for spring admission, 12/15 for domestic students. Applications are processed on a rolling basis. Application fee: $10. *Unit head:* Dr. Kathleen Tyler, Coordinator, 334-229-4268. *Application contact:* Dr. Doris Screws, Dean of Graduate Studies, 334-229-4274, Fax: 334-229-4928, E-mail: dscrews@alasu.edu. Web site: http://www.alasu.edu/academics/graduate-school/degree-programs/med-in-early-childhood-education/index.aspx.

Albany State University, College of Education, Albany, GA 31705-2717. Offers early childhood education (M Ed); education specialist (Ed S); educational leadership and administration (M Ed); health, physical education and recreation (M Ed); middle grades education (M Ed); school counseling (M Ed); special education (M Ed). *Accreditation:* NCATE. Part-time and evening/weekend programs available. Postbaccalaureate distance learning degree programs offered (minimal on-campus study). *Faculty:* 19 full-time (13 women), 7 part-time/adjunct (5 women). *Students:* 90 full-time (69 women), 118 part-time (92 women); includes 152 minority (151 Black or African American, non-Hispanic/Latino; 1 American Indian or Alaska Native, non-Hispanic/Latino), 1 international. Average age 35. 93 applicants, 78% accepted, 38 enrolled. In 2011, 43 master's, 8 Ed Ss awarded. *Degree requirements:* For master's, comprehensive exam, internship, GACE Content Exam. *Entrance requirements:* For master's, GRE or MAT. *Application deadline:* For fall admission, 6/1 for domestic students, 5/1 for international students; for spring admission, 11/1 for domestic students, 10/1 for international students. Applications are processed on a rolling basis. Application fee: $20. Electronic applications accepted. *Expenses:* Tuition, state resident: full-time $3204; part-time $178 per credit hour. Tuition, nonresident: full-time $12,816; part-time $712 per credit hour. *Required fees:* $379 per semester. *Financial support:* Scholarships/grants available. Financial award application deadline: 4/15; financial award applicants required to submit FAFSA. *Faculty research:* GACE preparation, STEM (science, technology, engineering, and mathematics), technology education, special education, professional teacher development, health implications liberation philosophy, NET-Q, learning community, disabled or at-risk students. *Total annual research expenditures:* $252,502. *Unit head:* Dr. Kimberly King-Jupiter, Dean, 229-430-1718, Fax: 229-430-4993, E-mail: kimberly.king-jupiter@asurams.edu. *Application contact:* Jeffrey Pierce, II, Graduate Admissions Counselor, 229-430-4646, Fax: 229-430-4105, E-mail: jeffrey.pierce@asurams.edu. Web site: http://asu-sacs.asurams.edu/ASUCatalog/Graduate/index.html.

Albright College, Graduate Division, Reading, PA 19612-5234. Offers early childhood education (MS); elementary education (MS); English as a second language (MA); general education (MA); special education (MS). Part-time and evening/weekend programs available. *Degree requirements:* For master's, thesis. *Entrance requirements:* For master's, GRE General Test or MAT, minimum undergraduate GPA of 3.0, 2 letters of recommendation, interview. Additional exam requirements/recommendations for international students: Recommended—TOEFL (minimum score 525 paper-based; 197 computer-based). Electronic applications accepted.

American International College, School of Arts, Education and Sciences, Department of Education, Springfield, MA 01109-3189. Offers early childhood education (M Ed, CAGS); educational leadership and supervision (Ed D); elementary education (M Ed, CAGS); middle/secondary education (M Ed, CAGS); moderate disabilities (M Ed, CAGS); reading (M Ed, CAGS); school adjustment counseling (MA, CAGS); school administration (M Ed, CAGS); school guidance counseling (MA, CAGS); teaching (MA, MS); teaching and learning (Ed D). Part-time and evening/weekend programs available. Terminal master's awarded for partial completion of doctoral program. *Degree requirements:* For master's, comprehensive exam (for some programs), thesis (for some programs), practicum; for doctorate, comprehensive exam (for some programs), thesis/dissertation; for CAGS, practicum. *Entrance requirements:* For master's, minimum B-average in undergraduate course work; for doctorate, GRE General Test, interview. Additional exam requirements/recommendations for international students: Required—TOEFL. Electronic applications accepted.

American University, College of Arts and Sciences, School of Education, Teaching, and Health, Washington, DC 20016-8030. Offers curriculum and instruction (M Ed, Certificate); early childhood education (MAT, Certificate); elementary education (MAT); English for speakers of other languages (MAT, Certificate); health promotion management (MS, Certificate); international training and education (MA, MAT); nutrition education (Certificate); secondary teaching (MAT, Certificate); special education (MA), including special education: learning disabilities; MAT/MA. *Accreditation:* NCATE. Part-time and evening/weekend programs available. *Faculty:* 14 full-time (10 women), 58 part-time/adjunct (41 women). *Students:* 69 full-time (61 women), 257 part-time (188 women); includes 55 minority (35 Black or African American, non-Hispanic/Latino; 2 American Indian or Alaska Native, non-Hispanic/Latino; 5 Asian, non-Hispanic/Latino; 10 Hispanic/Latino; 3 Two or more races, non-Hispanic/Latino), 4 international. Average age 28. 221 applicants, 81% accepted, 96 enrolled. In 2011, 226 master's, 5 other advanced degrees awarded. *Degree requirements:* For master's, comprehensive exam, thesis or alternative, PRAXIS II. *Entrance requirements:* For master's, GRE General Test, two letters of recommendation; for Certificate, bachelor's degree. Additional exam requirements/recommendations for international students: Required—TOEFL. *Application deadline:* For fall admission, 2/1 priority date for domestic students; for spring admission, 10/1 priority date for domestic students. Applications are processed on a rolling basis. Application fee: $80. *Expenses: Tuition:* Full-time $24,264; part-time $1348 per credit hour. *Required fees:* $430. Tuition and fees vary according to course load and program. *Financial support:* Fellowships, research assistantships with full and partial tuition reimbursements, teaching assistantships with full and partial tuition reimbursements, career-related internships or fieldwork, Federal Work-Study, and institutionally sponsored loans available. Support available to part-time students. Financial award application deadline: 2/1; financial award applicants required to submit FAFSA. *Faculty research:* Gender equity, socioeconomic technology, learning disabilities, gifted and talented education. *Unit head:* Dr. Sarah Irvine-Belson, Dean, 202-885-3714, Fax: 202-885-1187, E-mail: educate@american.edu. *Application contact:* Kathleen Clowery, Director, Graduate Admissions, 202-885-3621, Fax: 202-885-1505, E-mail: clowery@american.edu. Web site: http://www.american.edu/cas/seth/.

Anna Maria College, Graduate Division, Program in Education, Paxton, MA 01612. Offers early childhood education (M Ed); education (CAGS); elementary education (M Ed); English language arts (M Ed); visual arts (M Ed). Part-time and evening/weekend programs available. *Entrance requirements:* For master's, bachelor's degree in liberal arts or sciences, minimum GPA of 3.0. Additional exam requirements/recommendations for international students: Required—TOEFL (minimum score 500 paper-based). Electronic applications accepted.

Antioch University New England, Graduate School, Department of Education, Keene, NH 03431-3552. Offers experienced educators (M Ed); integrated learning (M Ed), including early childhood education, elementary education; Waldorf teacher training (M Ed). *Degree requirements:* For master's, thesis (for some programs), internship. *Entrance requirements:* Additional exam requirements/recommendations for international students: Required—TOEFL (minimum score 600 paper-based; 250 computer-based). *Expenses:* Contact institution. *Faculty research:* Classroom and school restructuring, problem-based learning, Waldorf collaborative leadership, ecological literacy.

Antioch University New England, Graduate School, Department of Education, Integrated Learning Program, Concentration in Early Childhood Education, Keene, NH 03431-3552. Offers M Ed.

Arcadia University, Graduate Studies, Department of Education, Glenside, PA 19038-3295. Offers art education (M Ed); computer education (CAS); curriculum (CAS); curriculum studies (M Ed); early childhood education (M Ed, CAS), including individualized (M Ed), master teacher (M Ed), research in child development (M Ed); educational leadership (M Ed, Ed D, CAS); elementary education (M Ed, CAS); English education (MA Ed); environmental education (MA Ed, CAS); history education (MA Ed); instructional technology (M Ed); language arts (M Ed, CAS); library science (M Ed); mathematics education (M Ed, MA Ed, CAS); music education (MA Ed); psychology (MA Ed); reading (M Ed, CAS); science education (M Ed, CAS); secondary education (M Ed, CAS); special education (M Ed, Ed D, CAS); theater arts (MA Ed); written communication (MA Ed). *Accreditation:* NASAD. Part-time and evening/weekend programs available. Postbaccalaureate distance learning degree programs offered (minimal on-campus study). *Faculty:* 12 full-time (8 women), 38 part-time/adjunct (26 women). *Students:* 66 full-time (48 women), 590 part-time (477 women); includes 65 minority (53 Black or African American, non-Hispanic/Latino; 6 Asian, non-Hispanic/Latino; 3 Hispanic/Latino; 3 Two or more races, non-Hispanic/Latino), 4 international. Average age 36. In 2011, 229 master's, 5 doctorates awarded. *Application deadline:* Applications are processed on a rolling basis. Application fee: $50. Electronic applications accepted. *Expenses:* Contact institution. *Financial support:* Career-related internships or fieldwork, tuition waivers (partial), and unspecified assistantships available. *Unit head:* Dr. Steven P. Gulkus, Associate Professor, 215-572-2120, E-mail: gulkus@arcadia.edu. *Application contact:* 215-572-2925, Fax: 215-572-2126, E-mail: grad@arcadia.edu.

Arkansas State University, Graduate School, College of Education, Department of Teacher Education, Jonesboro, State University, AR 72467. Offers early childhood education (MAT, MSE); early childhood services (MS); middle level education (MAT, MSE); reading (MSE, Ed S). *Accreditation:* NCATE. Part-time programs available. *Faculty:* 16 full-time (11 women). *Students:* 47 full-time (44 women), 81 part-time (76 women); includes 52 minority (49 Black or African American, non-Hispanic/Latino; 1 Hispanic/Latino; 2 Two or more races, non-Hispanic/Latino), 2 international. Average age 33. 114 applicants, 58% accepted, 57 enrolled. In 2011, 35 master's awarded. *Degree requirements:* For master's, comprehensive exam, thesis or alternative; for Ed S, comprehensive exam. *Entrance requirements:* For master's, GRE General Test or MAT, appropriate bachelor's degree, official transcripts, immunization records; for Ed S, GRE General Test or MAT, interview, master's degree, official transcript, immunization records. Additional exam requirements/recommendations for international students: Required—TOEFL (minimum score 550 paper-based; 213 computer-based; 79 iBT), IELTS (minimum score 6), Pearson Test of English Academic (minimum score 56). *Application deadline:* For fall admission, 7/1 for domestic and international students; for spring admission, 11/15 for domestic students, 11/14 for international students. Applications are processed on a rolling basis. Application fee: $30 ($40 for international students). Electronic applications accepted. *Expenses:* Tuition, state resident: full-time $4044; part-time $225 per credit hour. Tuition, nonresident: full-time $8087; part-time $449 per credit hour. *Required fees:* $936; $52 per credit hour. $25 per term. One-time fee: $30. Tuition and fees vary according to course load and program. *Financial support:* In 2011–12, 5 students received support. Teaching assistantships, career-related internships or fieldwork, scholarships/grants, and unspecified assistantships available. Financial award application deadline: 7/1; financial award applicants required to submit FAFSA. *Unit head:* Dr. Lina Owens, Chair, 870-972-3059, Fax: 870-972-3344, E-mail: llowens@astate.edu. *Application contact:* Dr. Andrew Sustich, Dean of the Graduate School, 870-972-3029, Fax: 870-972-3857, E-mail: sustich@astate.edu. Web site: http://www.astate.edu/a/education/teachered/.

Armstrong Atlantic State University, School of Graduate Studies, Program in Education, Savannah, GA 31419-1997. Offers adult education (M Ed); curriculum and instruction (M Ed); early childhood education (M Ed); education (M Ed); elementary education (M Ed); middle grades education (M Ed); secondary education (M Ed), including business education, English education, mathematics education, science education, social science education; special education (M Ed), including behavioral disorders, learning disabilities, speech-language pathology. *Accreditation:* NCATE. Part-time and evening/weekend programs available. Postbaccalaureate distance learning degree programs offered (minimal on-campus study). *Faculty:* 33 full-time (23 women), 3 part-time/adjunct (2 women). *Students:* 97 full-time (91 women), 262 part-time (227 women); includes 83 minority (70 Black or African American, non-Hispanic/Latino; 3 Asian, non-Hispanic/Latino; 8 Hispanic/Latino; 2 Two or more races, non-Hispanic/Latino), 5 international. Average age 34. 169 applicants, 69% accepted, 102 enrolled. In 2011, 227 master's awarded. *Degree requirements:* For master's, comprehensive exam, portfolio. *Entrance requirements:* For master's, GRE General Test or MAT, minimum GPA of 2.5, letters of recommendation. Additional exam requirements/recommendations for international students: Required—TOEFL (minimum score 523 paper-based; 193 computer-based). *Application deadline:* For fall admission, 7/1 priority date for domestic students, 5/1 for international students; for spring admission, 11/15 priority date for domestic students, 9/15 for international students. Applications are processed on a rolling basis. Application fee: $30. Electronic applications accepted. *Expenses:* Tuition, state resident: full-time $3402. Tuition, nonresident: full-time $12,636. *Financial support:* In 2011–12, research assistantships with full tuition reimbursements (averaging $5,000 per year) were awarded; career-related internships or fieldwork, Federal Work-Study, scholarships/grants, and unspecified assistantships also available. Support available to part-time students. Financial award applicants required to submit FAFSA. *Unit head:* Dr. Patricia Wachholz, Dean, College of Education, 912-344-2797, E-mail: patricia.wachholz@armstrong.edu. *Application contact:* Jill Bell, Director, Graduate Enrollment Services, 912-344-2798, Fax: 912-344-3488, E-mail: graduate@armstrong.edu. Web site: http://www.armstrong.edu/Education/coe_deans_office/coe_education_welcome.

Auburn University, Graduate School, College of Education, Department of Curriculum and Teaching, Auburn University, AL 36849. Offers business education (M Ed, MS, PhD); early childhood education (M Ed, MS, PhD, Ed S); elementary education (M Ed, MS, PhD, Ed S); foreign languages (M Ed, MS); music education (M Ed, MS, PhD, Ed S); postsecondary education (PhD); reading education (PhD, Ed S); secondary education (M Ed, MS, PhD, Ed S), including English language arts, mathematics, science, social studies. *Accreditation:* NASM (one or more programs are accredited); NCATE. Part-time programs available. *Faculty:* 22 full-time (17 women), 3 part-time/adjunct (all women). *Students:* 80 full-time (58 women), 181 part-time (126 women); includes 42 minority (28 Black or African American, non-Hispanic/Latino; 7 Asian, non-Hispanic/Latino; 7 Hispanic/Latino). Average age 34. 184 applicants, 53% accepted, 60 enrolled. In 2011, 77 master's, 10 doctorates, 35 other advanced degrees awarded. *Degree requirements:* For master's, thesis (for some programs); for doctorate, thesis/dissertation; for Ed S, field project. *Entrance requirements:* For master's, doctorate, and Ed S, GRE General Test. *Application deadline:* For fall admission, 7/7 for domestic students; for spring admission, 11/24 for domestic students. Applications are processed on a rolling basis. Application fee: $50 ($60 for international students). Electronic applications accepted. *Expenses:* Tuition, state resident: full-time $7290; part-time $405 per credit hour. Tuition, nonresident: full-time $21,870; part-time $1215 per credit hour. *International tuition:* $22,000 full-time. *Required fees:* $1402. *Financial support:* Fellowships, teaching assistantships, career-related internships or fieldwork, and Federal Work-Study available. Support available to part-time students. Financial award application deadline: 3/15; financial award applicants required to submit FAFSA. *Faculty research:* Emerging literacy, reading attitudes, music for at-risk youth, portfolio assessment. *Unit head:* Dr. Kimberly Walls, Head, 334-844-4434. *Application contact:* Dr. George Flowers, Dean of the Graduate School, 334-844-2125. Web site: http://education.auburn.edu/academic_departments/curr/.

Auburn University, Graduate School, College of Education, Department of Special Education, Rehabilitation, Counseling and School Psychology, Auburn University, AL 36849. Offers collaborative teacher special education (M Ed, MS); early childhood special education (M Ed, MS); rehabilitation counseling (M Ed, MS, PhD). *Accreditation:* CORE; NCATE. Part-time programs available. *Faculty:* 21 full-time (14 women), 5 part-time/adjunct (3 women). *Students:* 153 full-time (126 women), 101 part-time (78 women); includes 67 minority (60 Black or African American, non-Hispanic/Latino; 2 American Indian or Alaska Native, non-Hispanic/Latino; 2 Asian, non-Hispanic/Latino; 3 Hispanic/Latino), 4 international. Average age 30. 221 applicants, 50% accepted, 89 enrolled. In 2011, 75 master's, 12 doctorates awarded. *Degree requirements:* For master's, thesis (for some programs); for doctorate, thesis/dissertation. *Entrance requirements:* For master's, GRE General Test; for doctorate, GRE General Test, interview. *Application deadline:* For fall admission, 7/7 for domestic students; for spring admission, 11/24 for domestic students. Applications are processed on a rolling basis. Application fee: $50 ($60 for international students). Electronic applications accepted. *Expenses:* Tuition, state resident: full-time $7290; part-time $405 per credit hour. Tuition, nonresident: full-time $21,870; part-time $1215 per credit hour. *International tuition:* $22,000 full-time. *Required fees:* $1402. *Financial support:* Research assistantships, teaching assistantships, and Federal Work-Study available. Support available to part-time students. Financial award application deadline: 3/15; financial award applicants required to submit FAFSA. *Faculty research:* Emotional conflict/behavior disorders, gifted and talented, learning disabilities, mental retardation, multi-handicapped. *Unit head:* Dr. E. Davis Martin, Jr., Head, 334-844-7676. *Application contact:* Dr. George Flowers, Dean of the Graduate School, 334-844-2125.

Auburn University Montgomery, School of Education, Department of Early Childhood, Elementary, and Reading Education, Montgomery, AL 36124-4023. Offers early childhood education (M Ed, Ed S); elementary education (M Ed, Ed S); reading education (M Ed, Ed S). *Accreditation:* NCATE. Part-time and evening/weekend programs available. *Degree requirements:* For master's and Ed S, comprehensive exam. *Entrance requirements:* For master's, GRE General Test or MAT, certification, BS in teaching; for Ed S, GRE General Test or MAT, certification. Electronic applications accepted. *Expenses:* Tuition, state resident: full-time $5076. Tuition, nonresident: full-time $15,228.

Aurora University, College of Education, Aurora, IL 60506-4892. Offers curriculum and instruction (MA, Ed D); early childhood and special education (MA); education (MAT), including elementary certification; education and administration (Ed D); educational leadership (MEL); educational technology (MATL); reading instruction (MA); special education (MA). *Accreditation:* NCATE. Part-time and evening/weekend programs available. *Degree requirements:* For doctorate, comprehensive exam, thesis/dissertation. *Entrance requirements:* For master's, 2 years of teaching experience, valid teaching certificate. Additional exam requirements/recommendations for international students: Required—TOEFL (minimum score 550 paper-based; 213 computer-based). Electronic applications accepted. *Expenses:* Contact institution.

Bank Street College of Education, Graduate School, Program in Early Childhood Education, New York, NY 10025. Offers MS Ed. *Students:* 14 full-time (13 women), 36 part-time (35 women); includes 8 minority (3 Black or African American, non-Hispanic/Latino; 2 Asian, non-Hispanic/Latino; 2 Hispanic/Latino; 1 Two or more races, non-Hispanic/Latino), 1 international. Average age 29. 32 applicants, 69% accepted, 16 enrolled. In 2011, 23 master's awarded. *Degree requirements:* For master's, thesis. *Entrance requirements:* For master's, interview, essays. Additional exam requirements/recommendations for international students: Required—TOEFL (minimum score 600 paper-based; 250 computer-based; 100 iBT), IELTS (minimum score 7). *Application deadline:* For fall admission, 2/15 priority date for domestic students, 2/15 for international students; for spring admission, 11/1 priority date for domestic students, 11/1 for international students. Applications are processed on a rolling basis. Application fee: $65. Electronic applications accepted. *Expenses: Required fees:* $1240 per credit. $100 per term. One-time fee: $250 part-time. *Financial support:* Career-related internships or fieldwork, Federal Work-Study, scholarships/grants, and unspecified assistantships available. Support available to part-time students. Financial award application deadline: 4/15; financial award applicants required to submit FAFSA. *Faculty research:* Play in early childhood settings, early childhood learning environments, family-teacher interaction, child-centered education, developmental interaction. *Unit head:* Dr. Peggy McNamara, Chairperson, 212-875-4586, Fax: 212-875-4753, E-mail: mam@bankstreet.edu. *Application contact:* Seena Berg, Associate Director of Graduate Admissions, 212-875-4402, Fax: 212-875-4678, E-mail: sberg@bankstreet.edu. Web site: http://bankstreet.edu/graduate-school/academics/programs/general-teacher-education-programs-overview/.

Bank Street College of Education, Graduate School, Program in Infant and Family Development and Early Intervention, New York, NY 10025. Offers infant and family development (MS Ed); infant and family early childhood special and general education (MS Ed); infant and family/early childhood special education (Ed M). *Students:* 15 full-time (14 women), 19 part-time (18 women); includes 13 minority (6 Black or African American, non-Hispanic/Latino; 1 Asian, non-Hispanic/Latino; 3 Hispanic/Latino; 3 Two or more races, non-Hispanic/Latino), 1 international. Average age 28. 31 applicants, 74% accepted, 15 enrolled. In 2011, 15 master's awarded. *Degree requirements:* For master's, thesis. *Entrance requirements:* For master's, interview, essays. Additional exam requirements/recommendations for international students: Required—TOEFL (minimum score 600 paper-based; 250 computer-based; 100 iBT), IELTS (minimum score 7). *Application deadline:* For fall admission, 2/15 priority date for domestic students, 2/15 for international students; for spring admission, 11/1 priority date for domestic students, 11/1 for international students. Applications are processed on a rolling basis. Application fee: $65. Electronic applications accepted. *Expenses: Required fees:* $1240 per credit. $100 per term. One-time fee: $250 part-time. *Financial support:* Career-related internships or fieldwork, Federal Work-Study, scholarships/grants, and unspecified assistantships available. Support available to part-time students. Financial award application deadline: 4/15; financial award applicants required to submit FAFSA. *Faculty research:* Early intervention, early attachment practice in infant and toddler childcare, parenting skills in adolescents. *Unit head:* Dr. Virginia Casper, Director, 212-875-4703, Fax: 212-875-4753, E-mail: vcasper@bankstreet.edu. *Application contact:* Ann Morgan, Director of Graduate Admissions, 212-875-4403, Fax: 212-875-4678, E-mail: amorgan@bankstreet.edu. Web site: http://bankstreet.edu/graduate-school/academics/programs/infant-and-family-development-programs-overview/.

Bank Street College of Education, Graduate School, Program in Reading and Literacy, New York, NY 10025. Offers advanced literacy specialization (Ed M); reading and literacy (MS Ed); teaching literacy (MS Ed); teaching literacy and childhood general education (MS Ed). *Students:* 38 full-time (34 women), 56 part-time (52 women); includes 25 minority (10 Black or African American, non-Hispanic/Latino; 4 Asian, non-Hispanic/Latino; 8 Hispanic/Latino; 3 Two or more races, non-Hispanic/Latino), 2 international. Average age 30. 56 applicants, 82% accepted, 32 enrolled. In 2011, 27 master's awarded. *Degree requirements:* For master's, thesis. *Entrance requirements:* For master's, interview, essays. Additional exam requirements/recommendations for international students: Required—TOEFL (minimum score 600 paper-based; 250 computer-based; 100 iBT), IELTS (minimum score 7). *Application deadline:* For fall admission, 2/15 priority date for domestic students, 2/15 for international students; for spring admission, 11/1 priority date for domestic students, 11/1 for international students. Applications are processed on a rolling basis. Application fee: $65. Electronic applications accepted. *Expenses: Required fees:* $1240 per credit. $100 per term. One-time fee: $250 part-time. *Financial support:* Career-related internships or fieldwork, Federal Work-Study, scholarships/grants, and unspecified assistantships available. Support available to part-time students. Financial award application deadline: 4/15; financial award applicants required to submit FAFSA. *Faculty research:* Language development, children's literature, whole language, the reading and writing processes, reading difficulties in multicultural classrooms. *Unit head:* Dr. Susan Goetz-Haver, Director, 212-875-4692, Fax: 212-875-4753, E-mail: sgoetz-haver@bankstreet.edu. *Application contact:* Ann Morgan, Director of Graduate Admissions, 212-875-4403, Fax: 212-875-4678, E-mail: amorgan@bankstreet.edu. Web site: http://bankstreet.edu/graduate-school/academics/programs/reading-and-literacy-program-overview/.

Bank Street College of Education, Graduate School, Programs in Educational Leadership, New York, NY 10025. Offers early childhood leadership (MS Ed); educational leadership (MS Ed); leadership for educational change (Ed M, MS Ed); leadership in community-based learning (MS Ed); leadership in mathematics education (MS Ed); leadership in museum education (MS Ed); leadership in the arts: creative writing (MS Ed); leadership in the arts: visual arts (MS Ed). *Students:* 77 full-time (66 women), 130 part-time (108 women); includes 68 minority (33 Black or African American, non-Hispanic/Latino; 8 Asian, non-Hispanic/Latino; 25 Hispanic/Latino; 2 Two or more races, non-Hispanic/Latino), 3 international. Average age 34. 148 applicants, 70% accepted, 92 enrolled. In 2011, 82 master's awarded. *Degree requirements:* For master's, thesis. *Entrance requirements:* For master's, interview, essays, minimum of 2 years experience as a classroom teacher. Additional exam requirements/recommendations for international students: Required—TOEFL (minimum score 600 paper-based; 250 computer-based; 100 iBT), IELTS (minimum score 7). *Application deadline:* For fall admission, 2/15 priority date for domestic students, 2/15 for international students; for spring admission, 11/1 priority date for domestic students, 11/1 for international students. Applications are processed on a rolling basis. Application fee: $65. Electronic applications accepted. *Expenses: Required fees:* $1240 per credit. $100 per term. One-time fee: $250 part-time. *Financial support:* Career-related internships or fieldwork, Federal Work-Study, scholarships/grants, traineeships, and unspecified assistantships available. Support available to part-time students. Financial award application deadline: 4/15; financial award applicants required to submit FAFSA. *Faculty research:* Leadership in small schools, mathematics in elementary schools, professional development in early childhood, leadership in arts education, leadership in special education. *Unit head:* Dr. Rima Shore, Chairperson, 212-875-4478, Fax: 212-875-8753, E-mail: rshore@bankstreet.edu. *Application contact:* Ann Morgan, Director of Graduate Admissions, 212-875-4403, Fax: 212-875-4678, E-mail: amorgan@bankstreet.edu. Web site: http://bankstreet.edu/graduate-school/academics/programs/leadership-programs-overview/.

Barry University, School of Education, Program in Curriculum and Instruction, Miami Shores, FL 33161-6695. Offers accomplished teacher (Ed S); culture, language and literacy (TESOL) (PhD); curriculum evaluation and research (PhD); early childhood (Ed S); early childhood education (PhD); elementary (Ed S); elementary education (PhD); ESOL (Ed S); gifted (Ed S); Montessori (Ed S); PKP/elementary (Ed S); reading (Ed S); reading, language and cognition (PhD). *Entrance requirements:* For doctorate, GRE, minimum GPA of 3.25.

Barry University, School of Education, Program in Montessori Education, Miami Shores, FL 33161-6695. Offers MS, Ed S. Part-time and evening/weekend programs available. *Degree requirements:* For master's, comprehensive exam, practicum; for Ed S, practicum. *Entrance requirements:* For master's, GRE General Test or MAT, minimum GPA of 3.0; for Ed S, GRE General Test, minimum GPA of 3.0. Electronic applications accepted.

Barry University, School of Education, Program in Pre-Kindergarten and Primary Education, Miami Shores, FL 33161-6695. Offers pre-k/primary (MS); pre-k/primary/ESOL (MS). Part-time and evening/weekend programs available. *Degree requirements:* For master's, comprehensive exam, practicum. *Entrance requirements:* For master's, GRE General Test or MAT, minimum GPA of 3.0. Electronic applications accepted.

Bayamón Central University, Graduate Programs, Program in Education, Bayamón, PR 00960-1725. Offers administration and supervision (MA Ed); commercial education (MA Ed); elementary education (K–3) (MA Ed); family counseling (Graduate Certificate);

guidance and counseling (MA Ed); pre-elementary teacher (MA Ed); rehabilitation counseling (MA Ed); special education (MA Ed), including attention deficit disorder, education of the autistic, learning disabilities. Part-time and evening/weekend programs available. *Degree requirements:* For master's, comprehensive exam. *Entrance requirements:* For master's, EXADEP, bachelor's degree in education or related field.

Bellarmine University, Annsley Frazier Thornton School of Education, Louisville, KY 40205-0671. Offers early elementary education (MA Ed, MAT); education and social change (PhD); learning and behavior disorders (MA Ed, MAT); middle school education (MA Ed, MAT); principalship (Ed S); reading and writing endorsement (MA Ed); secondary school education (MAT); teacher leadership, grades P-12 (MA Ed). *Accreditation:* NCATE. Part-time and evening/weekend programs available. *Faculty:* 13 full-time (6 women), 12 part-time/adjunct (10 women). *Students:* 85 full-time (65 women), 186 part-time (144 women); includes 30 minority (22 Black or African American, non-Hispanic/Latino; 1 American Indian or Alaska Native, non-Hispanic/Latino; 6 Asian, non-Hispanic/Latino; 1 Hispanic/Latino). Average age 33. In 2011, 105 master's awarded. *Degree requirements:* For master's, comprehensive exam, thesis (for some programs); for doctorate, comprehensive exam, thesis/dissertation. *Entrance requirements:* For master's, GRE, baccalaureate degree from accredited institution; minimum overall GPA of 2.75, 3.0 in major; letters of recommendation; valid Kentucky provisional or professional certificate; for doctorate, GRE, minimum GPA of 3.5 in all graduate coursework completed at time of application; baccalaureate and master's degrees in education (MA, MS) or fields directly relevant to education; three letters of recommendation; two essays (no more than 1,000 words each); interview. Additional exam requirements/recommendations for international students: Required—TOEFL (minimum score 550 paper-based; 213 computer-based; 80 iBT). *Application deadline:* Applications are processed on a rolling basis. Application fee: $25. *Expenses:* Contact institution. *Financial support:* Scholarships/grants available. Financial award applicants required to submit FAFSA. *Faculty research:* Literacy, service-learning, dispositions, educational technology, special education. *Unit head:* Dr. Robert Cooter, Dean, 502-272-8191, Fax: 502-272-8189, E-mail: rcooter@bellarmine.edu. *Application contact:* Theresa Klapheke, Administrative Director of Graduate Programs, 502-272-8271, Fax: 502-272-8002, E-mail: tklapheke@bellarmine.edu. Web site: http://www.bellarmine.edu/education/graduate.

Belmont University, College of Arts and Sciences, Department of Education, Nashville, TN 37212-3757. Offers education (M Ed); elementary education (MAT), including early childhood education, elementary education, language arts education; English (MAT); history (MAT); mathematics (MAT); middle grade education (MAT); science (MAT); secondary education (MAT); special education (MAT); sports administration (MSA). *Accreditation:* NCATE. Part-time and evening/weekend programs available. *Faculty:* 11 full-time (8 women), 23 part-time/adjunct (12 women). *Students:* 83 full-time (77 women), 205 part-time (162 women); includes 50 minority (36 Black or African American, non-Hispanic/Latino; 1 American Indian or Alaska Native, non-Hispanic/Latino; 1 Asian, non-Hispanic/Latino; 7 Hispanic/Latino; 5 Two or more races, non-Hispanic/Latino), 2 international. Average age 30. 83 applicants, 67% accepted, 35 enrolled. In 2011, 169 master's awarded. *Degree requirements:* For master's, thesis (for some programs). *Entrance requirements:* For master's, MAT or GRE and/or GMAT, minimum GPA of 2.75. Additional exam requirements/recommendations for international students: Required—TOEFL. *Application deadline:* For fall admission, 8/1 priority date for domestic students, 6/1 for international students; for spring admission, 12/1 priority date for domestic students, 10/1 for international students. Applications are processed on a rolling basis. Application fee: $50. *Expenses:* Contact institution. *Financial support:* In 2011–12, 30 students received support. Fellowships with partial tuition reimbursements available, teaching assistantships with partial tuition reimbursements available, institutionally sponsored loans, tuition waivers (partial), and unspecified assistantships available. Financial award application deadline: 4/15; financial award applicants required to submit FAFSA. *Faculty research:* Improving secondary literacy, Montessori, classroom management strategies, teacher residency programs, online professional development, mentoring, leadership, faculty development. *Total annual research expenditures:* $2,500. *Unit head:* Dr. Cynthia R. Watkins, Associate Dean, 615-460-6053, Fax: 615-460-5556, E-mail: cynthia.watkins@belmont.edu. *Application contact:* Andrea McClain, Admission/Licensure Officer, 615-460-5483, Fax: 615-460-5556, E-mail: andrea.mcclain@belmont.edu.

Berry College, Graduate Programs, Graduate Programs in Education, Program in Early Childhood Education, Mount Berry, GA 30149-0159. Offers M Ed, MAT. *Accreditation:* NCATE. Part-time programs available. *Faculty:* 15 part-time/adjunct (10 women). *Students:* 7 full-time (all women), 21 part-time (15 women); includes 1 minority (Black or African American, non-Hispanic/Latino). Average age 32. In 2011, 14 master's awarded. *Degree requirements:* For master's, thesis optional, oral exams. *Entrance requirements:* For master's, GRE General Test, MAT, or NTE, minimum GPA of 2.5. Additional exam requirements/recommendations for international students: Required—TOEFL (minimum score 550 paper-based; 213 computer-based). *Application deadline:* For fall admission, 5/1 for domestic and international students; for spring admission, 10/1 for domestic and international students. Applications are processed on a rolling basis. Application fee: $25 ($30 for international students). *Expenses:* Contact institution. *Financial support:* In 2011–12, 4 students received support, including 3 research assistantships with full tuition reimbursements available (averaging $5,405 per year); scholarships/grants and unspecified assistantships also available. Support available to part-time students. Financial award application deadline: 3/1; financial award applicants required to submit FAFSA. *Faculty research:* Curriculum development, teacher training, pedagogy, ESOL, reading. *Unit head:* Dr. Jacqueline McDowell, 706-236-1717, Fax: 706-238-5827, E-mail: jmcdowell@berry.edu. *Application contact:* Brett Kennedy, Director of Admissions, 706-236-2215, Fax: 706-290-2178, E-mail: admissions@berry.edu. Web site: http://www.berry.edu/academics/education/graduate/.

Bloomsburg University of Pennsylvania, School of Graduate Studies, College of Education, Department of Early Childhood and Adolescent Education, Program in Early Childhood Education, Bloomsburg, PA 17815-1301. Offers MS. *Accreditation:* NCATE. *Degree requirements:* For master's, thesis optional. *Entrance requirements:* For master's, MAT, minimum QPA of 3.0. Additional exam requirements/recommendations for international students: Required—TOEFL. Electronic applications accepted. *Faculty research:* Child development, children's literature, theory, administration.

Boise State University, Graduate College, College of Education, Programs in Teacher Education, Program in Early Childhood Education, Boise, ID 83725-0399. Offers M Ed, MA. *Accreditation:* NCATE. Part-time programs available. *Degree requirements:* For master's, thesis optional. *Entrance requirements:* For master's, minimum GPA of 3.0. Electronic applications accepted.

Boston College, Lynch Graduate School of Education, Program in Early Childhood Education, Chestnut Hill, MA 02467-3800. Offers M Ed. *Accreditation:* Teacher Education Accreditation Council. Part-time and evening/weekend programs available. *Students:* 5 full-time (all women), 2 part-time (both women). 27 applicants, 48% accepted, 4 enrolled. In 2011, 4 degrees awarded. *Degree requirements:* For master's, comprehensive exam. *Entrance requirements:* For master's, GRE General Test or MAT. Additional exam requirements/recommendations for international students: Required—TOEFL (minimum score 550 paper-based; 213 computer-based; 79 iBT). *Application deadline:* For fall admission, 1/1 priority date for domestic students. Application fee: $65. Electronic applications accepted. *Financial support:* Fellowships with full and partial tuition reimbursements, research assistantships with full and partial tuition reimbursements, teaching assistantships with full and partial tuition reimbursements, career-related internships or fieldwork, Federal Work-Study, scholarships/grants, traineeships, health care benefits, tuition waivers (full and partial), and unspecified assistantships available. Support available to part-time students. Financial award applicants required to submit FAFSA. *Faculty research:* Early childhood testing and assessment, selective attention abilities in children, problem-solving, dual language learning and literacy. *Unit head:* Dr. Maria E. Brisk, Chairperson, 617-552-4214, Fax: 617-552-0398. *Application contact:* Adam Poluzzi, Director, Graduate Admission and Financial Aid, 617-552-4214, Fax: 617-552-0398, E-mail: poluzzi@bc.edu.

Bowling Green State University, Graduate College, College of Education and Human Development, School of Education and Intervention Services, Intervention Services Division, Program in Special Education, Bowling Green, OH 43403. Offers assistive technology (M Ed); early childhood intervention (M Ed); gifted education (M Ed); hearing impaired intervention (M Ed); mild/moderate intervention (M Ed); moderate/intensive intervention (M Ed). *Accreditation:* NCATE. Part-time programs available. *Degree requirements:* For master's, thesis or alternative. *Entrance requirements:* For master's, GRE General Test. Additional exam requirements/recommendations for international students: Required—TOEFL. Electronic applications accepted. *Faculty research:* Reading and special populations, deafness, early childhood, gifted and talented, behavior disorders.

Brenau University, Sydney O. Smith Graduate School, School of Education, Gainesville, GA 30501. Offers early childhood (Ed S); early childhood education (M Ed, MAT); middle grades (Ed S); middle grades education (M Ed, MAT); secondary education (MAT); special education (M Ed, MAT). *Accreditation:* NCATE. Part-time and evening/weekend programs available. Postbaccalaureate distance learning degree programs offered (no on-campus study). *Degree requirements:* For master's, thesis optional, comprehensive exam or applied research project, effective portfolio; for Ed S, thesis, applied research project. *Entrance requirements:* For master's, GRE, MAT, interview, minimum GPA of 3.0, 3 references, writing samples; for Ed S, GRE, MAT, master's degree, minimum GPA of 3.0, writing sample, letters of reference. Additional exam requirements/recommendations for international students: Required—TOEFL (minimum score 500 paper-based; 173 computer-based; 61 iBT); Recommended—IELTS (minimum score 5). Electronic applications accepted. *Expenses:* Contact institution.

Bridgewater State University, School of Graduate Studies, School of Education and Allied Studies, Department of Elementary and Early Childhood Education, Program in Early Childhood Education, Bridgewater, MA 02325-0001. Offers M Ed. *Accreditation:* NCATE. Part-time and evening/weekend programs available. *Entrance requirements:* For master's, GRE General Test or Massachusetts Test for Educator Licensure.

Brooklyn College of the City University of New York, Division of Graduate Studies, School of Education, Program in Early Childhood Education, Brooklyn, NY 11210-2889. Offers birth-grade 2 (MS Ed). Part-time and evening/weekend programs available. *Entrance requirements:* For master's, LAST, bachelor's degree in early childhood education, resume, 2 letters of recommendation, essay. Additional exam requirements/recommendations for international students: Required—TOEFL (minimum score 500 paper-based; 173 computer-based; 61 iBT). Electronic applications accepted. *Faculty research:* Children's narrations, language acquisition, culture and education.

Buffalo State College, State University of New York, The Graduate School, Faculty of Applied Science and Education, Department of Elementary Education and Reading, Program in Elementary Education, Buffalo, NY 14222-1095. Offers childhood education (grades 1-6) (MS Ed); early childhood and childhood curriculum and instruction (MS Ed); early childhood education (birth-grade 2) (MS Ed). *Accreditation:* NCATE. Part-time programs available. *Degree requirements:* For master's, thesis or project. *Entrance requirements:* For master's, minimum GPA of 2.5 in last 60 hours, New York teaching certificate. Additional exam requirements/recommendations for international students: Required—TOEFL (minimum score 550 paper-based; 213 computer-based).

California State University, East Bay, Office of Academic Programs and Graduate Studies, College of Education and Allied Studies, Department of Teacher Education, Hayward, CA 94542-3000. Offers education (MS), including curriculum, early childhood education, educational technology leadership, online teaching and learning, reading instruction. Postbaccalaureate distance learning degree programs offered. *Faculty:* 5 full-time (4 women), 2 part-time/adjunct (both women). *Students:* 64 full-time (53 women), 55 part-time (39 women); includes 50 minority (14 Black or African American, non-Hispanic/Latino; 17 Asian, non-Hispanic/Latino; 15 Hispanic/Latino; 4 Two or more races, non-Hispanic/Latino), 3 international. Average age 35. 98 applicants, 69% accepted, 30 enrolled. In 2011, 149 master's awarded. *Degree requirements:* For master's, project or thesis. *Entrance requirements:* For master's, minimum GPA of 3.0 in field, 2.5 overall; teaching experience; baccalaureate degree; 3 letters of recommendation. Additional exam requirements/recommendations for international students: Required—TOEFL (minimum score 550 paper-based; 213 computer-based), IELTS. *Application deadline:* For fall admission, 6/30 for domestic and international students. Application fee: $55. Electronic applications accepted. *Expenses:* Tuition, state resident: full-time $6738; part-time $1302 per quarter. Tuition, nonresident: full-time $12,690; part-time $2294 per quarter. *Required fees:* $449 per quarter. Tuition and fees vary according to degree level, program and reciprocity agreements. *Financial support:* Career-related internships or fieldwork, Federal Work-Study, and institutionally sponsored loans available. Support available to part-time students. Financial award application deadline: 3/2; financial award applicants required to submit FAFSA. *Faculty research:* Online, pedagogy, writing, learning, teaching. *Unit head:* Dr. Jeanette Bicais, Chair, 510-885-3027, Fax: 510-885-4632, E-mail: jeanette.bicais@csueastbay.edu. *Application contact:* Prof. Valerie Helgren-Lempesis, Education Graduate Advisor, 510-885-3006, Fax: 510-885-4632, E-mail: valerie.lempesis@csueastbay.edu. Web site: http://www20.csueastbay.edu/ceas/departments/ted/index.html.

California State University, Fresno, Division of Graduate Studies, School of Education and Human Development, Department of Literacy and Early Education, Fresno, CA 93740-8027. Offers education (MA), including early childhood education, reading/language arts. *Accreditation:* NCATE. Part-time and evening/weekend programs available. *Degree requirements:* For master's, thesis or alternative. *Entrance requirements:* For master's, GRE General Test, MAT, minimum GPA of 2.75. Additional exam requirements/recommendations for international students: Required—TOEFL. Electronic applications accepted. *Faculty research:* Reading recovery, monitoring/tutoring programs, character and academics, professional ethics, low-performing partnership schools.

California State University, Northridge, Graduate Studies, College of Education, Department of Educational Psychology and Counseling, Northridge, CA 91330. Offers counseling (MS), including career counseling, college counseling and student services, marriage and family therapy, school counseling, school psychology; educational psychology (MA Ed), including development, learning, and instruction, early childhood education. *Accreditation:* ACA (one or more programs are accredited); NCATE. Part-time and evening/weekend programs available. *Entrance requirements:* For master's, GRE General Test or minimum GPA of 3.0. Additional exam requirements/recommendations for international students: Required—TOEFL.

California State University, Sacramento, Office of Graduate Studies, College of Education, Department of Teacher Education, Sacramento, CA 95819-6079. Offers curriculum and instruction (MA); early childhood education (MA); reading education (MA). Part-time programs available. *Faculty:* 30 full-time (19 women), 23 part-time/adjunct (21 women). *Students:* 116 full-time, 313 part-time; includes 116 minority (7 Black or African American, non-Hispanic/Latino; 4 American Indian or Alaska Native, non-Hispanic/Latino; 28 Asian, non-Hispanic/Latino; 51 Hispanic/Latino; 10 Native Hawaiian or other Pacific Islander, non-Hispanic/Latino; 16 Two or more races, non-Hispanic/Latino). Average age 37. 284 applicants, 96% accepted, 225 enrolled. In 2011, 49 master's awarded. *Entrance requirements:* Additional exam requirements/recommendations for international students: Required—TOEFL. *Application deadline:* For fall admission, 3/1 for domestic and international students; for spring admission, 9/15 for domestic students, 9/30 for international students. Applications are processed on a rolling basis. Application fee: $55. Electronic applications accepted. *Financial support:* Teaching assistantships, career-related internships or fieldwork, and Federal Work-Study available. Support available to part-time students. Financial award application deadline: 3/1; financial award applicants required to submit FAFSA. *Faculty research:* Technology integration and psychological implications for teaching and learning; inquiry-based research and learning in science and technology; uncovering the process of everyday creativity in teachers and other leaders; universal design as a foundation for inclusion; bullying, cyber-bullying and impact on school success; diversity, social justice in adult/vocational education. *Unit head:* Dr. Rita Johnson, Chair, 916-278-6155, Fax: 916-278-6643, E-mail: rjohnson@csus.edu. *Application contact:* Jose Martinez, Outreach and Graduate Diversity Coordinator, 916-278-6470, Fax: 916-278-5669, E-mail: martinj@skymail.csus.edu. Web site: http://www.edweb.csus.edu/edte.

Cambridge College, School of Education, Cambridge, MA 02138-5304. Offers autism specialist (M Ed); autism/behavior analyst (M Ed); behavior analyst (Post-Master's Certificate); behavioral management (M Ed); early childhood teacher (M Ed); education specialist in curriculum and instruction (CAGS); educational leadership (Ed D); elementary teacher (M Ed); English as a second language (M Ed, Certificate); general science (M Ed); health education (Post-Master's Certificate); health/family and consumer sciences (M Ed); history (M Ed); individualized (M Ed); information technology literacy (M Ed); instructional technology (M Ed); interdisciplinary studies (M Ed); library teacher (M Ed); literacy education (M Ed); mathematics (M Ed); mathematics specialist (Certificate); middle school mathematics and science (M Ed); school administration (M Ed, CAGS); school guidance counselor (M Ed); school nurse education (M Ed); school social worker/school adjustment counselor (M Ed); special education administrator (CAGS); special education/moderate disabilities (M Ed); teaching skills and methodologies (M Ed). Part-time and evening/weekend programs available. Postbaccalaureate distance learning degree programs offered (minimal on-campus study). *Degree requirements:* For master's, thesis, internship/practicum (licensure program only); for doctorate, thesis/dissertation; for other advanced degree, thesis. *Entrance requirements:* For master's, interview, resume, documentation of licensure, 2 professional references; for doctorate, official transcripts, interview, resume, documentation of licensure (if any), written personal statement/essay, portfolio of scholarly and professional work, qualifying assessment, 2 professional references, health insurance, immunizations form; for other advanced degree, official transcripts, interview, resume, documentation of licensure (if any), written personal statement/essay, 2 professional references, health insurance, immunizations form. Additional exam requirements/recommendations for international students: Required—TOEFL (minimum score 550 paper-based; 213 computer-based; 79 iBT); Recommended—IELTS (minimum score 6). Electronic applications accepted. *Expenses:* Contact institution. *Faculty research:* Adult education, accelerated learning, mathematics education, brain compatible learning, special education and law.

Canisius College, Graduate Division, School of Education and Human Services, Education Department, Buffalo, NY 14208-1098. Offers general education non-matriculated (MS Ed); middle childhood (MS Ed); special education/adolescent (MS Ed); special education/advanced (MS Ed); special education/childhood (MS Ed); special education/childhood education grades 1-6 (MS Ed). Part-time and evening/weekend programs available. Postbaccalaureate distance learning degree programs offered (minimal on-campus study). *Faculty:* 17 full-time (13 women), 23 part-time/adjunct (11 women). *Students:* 139 full-time (103 women), 62 part-time (47 women); includes 10 minority (9 Black or African American, non-Hispanic/Latino; 1 Hispanic/Latino), 67 international. Average age 30. 135 applicants, 70% accepted, 53 enrolled. In 2011, 125 master's awarded. *Degree requirements:* For master's, research project or thesis. *Entrance requirements:* For master's, GRE if cumulative GPA less than 2.7, transcripts, two letters of recommendation. Additional exam requirements/recommendations for international students: Required—TOEFL. *Application deadline:* Applications are processed on a rolling basis. Application fee: $25. Electronic applications accepted. *Financial support:* Career-related internships or fieldwork, Federal Work-Study, scholarships/grants, tuition waivers (partial), and unspecified assistantships available. Support available to part-time students. Financial award application deadline: 4/30; financial award applicants required to submit FAFSA. *Faculty research:* Family as faculty, tutorial experiences in modern math, integrating digital technologies in the classroom. *Unit head:* Dr. Julie Henry, Chair/Professor, 716-888-3729, E-mail: henry1@canisius.edu. *Application contact:* Jim Bagwell, Director of Graduate Recruitment and Admissions, 716-888-2544, Fax: 716-888-3290, E-mail: bagwellj@canisius.edu. Web site: http://www.canisius.edu/education/facultystaff.asp.

Caribbean University, Graduate School, Bayamón, PR 00960-0493. Offers administration and supervision (MA Ed); criminal justice (MA); curriculum and instruction (MA Ed, PhD), including elementary education (MA Ed), English education (MA Ed), history education (MA Ed), mathematics education (MA Ed), primary education (MA Ed), science education (MA Ed), Spanish education (MA Ed); educational technology in instructional systems (MA Ed); gerontology (MSN); human resources (MBA); museology, archiving and art history (MA Ed); neonatal pediatrics (MSN); physical education (MA Ed); special education (MA Ed). *Entrance requirements:* For master's, interview, minimum GPA of 2.5.

Carlow University, School of Education, Program in Early Childhood Education, Pittsburgh, PA 15213-3165. Offers M Ed. Part-time and evening/weekend programs available. *Students:* 37 full-time (35 women), 26 part-time (25 women); includes 12 minority (all Black or African American, non-Hispanic/Latino). Average age 33. 59 applicants, 31% accepted, 16 enrolled. In 2011, 17 master's awarded. *Degree requirements:* For master's, thesis or alternative. *Entrance requirements:* Additional exam requirements/recommendations for international students: Required—TOEFL. *Application deadline:* For fall admission, 6/15 priority date for domestic students, 6/15 for international students; for spring admission, 11/15 priority date for domestic students, 11/15 for international students. Applications are processed on a rolling basis. Application fee: $20. Electronic applications accepted. *Expenses: Tuition:* Full-time $10,290; part-time $686 per credit. Tuition and fees vary according to course load, degree level and program. *Financial support:* Application deadline: 4/1; applicants required to submit FAFSA. *Faculty research:* Understanding children's play, infant and toddler development, effects of violence on children, supervision and staff development. *Unit head:* Roberta Schomburg, Associate Dean and Director, 412-578-6312, E-mail: schomburgrl@carlow.edu. *Application contact:* Jo Danhires, Administrative Assistant, Admissions, 412-578-6092, Fax: 412-578-6321, E-mail: gradstudies@carlow.edu. Web site: http://www.carlow.edu/.

Carlow University, School of Education, Program in Early Childhood Supervision, Pittsburgh, PA 15213-3165. Offers M Ed. Part-time and evening/weekend programs available. *Students:* 1 (woman) part-time. Average age 40. 7 applicants, 14% accepted, 0 enrolled. In 2011, 1 master's awarded. *Degree requirements:* For master's, thesis or alternative. *Entrance requirements:* Additional exam requirements/recommendations for international students: Required—TOEFL. *Application deadline:* For fall admission, 6/15 priority date for domestic students, 6/15 for international students; for spring admission, 11/15 priority date for domestic students, 11/15 for international students. Applications are processed on a rolling basis. Application fee: $20. Electronic applications accepted. *Expenses: Tuition:* Full-time $10,290; part-time $686 per credit. Tuition and fees vary according to course load, degree level and program. *Financial support:* Federal Work-Study and scholarships/grants available. Support available to part-time students. Financial award application deadline: 4/1; financial award applicants required to submit FAFSA. *Faculty research:* Leadership styles, learning styles, feminist pedagogy. *Unit head:* Dr. Roberta L. Schomburg, Associate Dean and Director, 412-578-6312, E-mail: schomburgrl@carlow.edu. *Application contact:* Jo Danhires, Administrative Assistant, Admissions, 412-578-6059, Fax: 412-578-6321, E-mail: gradstudies@carlow.edu.

Carlow University, School of Education, Program in Education, Pittsburgh, PA 15213-3165. Offers art education (M Ed); early childhood education (M Ed); instructional technology specialist (M Ed); middle level education (M Ed); secondary education (M Ed); special education (M Ed). Part-time and evening/weekend programs available. *Students:* 72 full-time (58 women), 16 part-time (13 women); includes 16 minority (15 Black or African American, non-Hispanic/Latino; 1 Hispanic/Latino). Average age 32. 68 applicants, 28% accepted, 11 enrolled. In 2011, 41 master's awarded. *Entrance requirements:* For master's, resume, 3 letters of recommendation, minimum GPA of 3.0, interview. Additional exam requirements/recommendations for international students: Required—TOEFL. *Application deadline:* For fall admission, 6/15 priority date for domestic students, 6/15 for international students; for spring admission, 11/15 priority date for domestic students, 11/15 for international students. Applications are processed on a rolling basis. Application fee: $20. Electronic applications accepted. *Expenses: Tuition:* Full-time $10,290; part-time $686 per credit. Tuition and fees vary according to course load, degree level and program. *Financial support:* Applicants required to submit FAFSA. *Unit head:* Dr. Marilyn J. Llewellyn, Director, 412-578-6011, Fax: 412-578-0816, E-mail: llewellynmj@carlow.edu. *Application contact:* Jo Danhires, Administrative Assistant, Admissions, 412-578-6089, Fax: 412-578-6321, E-mail: gradstudies@carlow.edu. Web site: http://www.carlow.edu.

Central Connecticut State University, School of Graduate Studies, School of Education and Professional Studies, Department of Teacher Education, Program in Early Childhood Education, New Britain, CT 06050-4010. Offers MS. Part-time and evening/weekend programs available. *Students:* 1 (woman) full-time, 12 part-time (all women). Average age 34. 9 applicants, 56% accepted, 3 enrolled. In 2011, 8 master's awarded. *Degree requirements:* For master's, comprehensive exam, thesis or alternative. *Entrance requirements:* For master's, minimum undergraduate GPA of 2.7. Additional exam requirements/recommendations for international students: Required—TOEFL (minimum score 550 paper-based; 213 computer-based). *Application deadline:* For fall admission, 6/1 for domestic students, 5/1 for international students; for spring admission, 11/1 for domestic and international students. Applications are processed on a rolling basis. Application fee: $50. Electronic applications accepted. *Expenses: Tuition, area resident:* Full-time $5137; part-time $482 per credit. Tuition, state resident: full-time $7707; part-time $494 per credit. Tuition, nonresident: full-time $14,311; part-time $494 per credit. *Required fees:* $3865. One-time fee: $62 part-time. *Faculty research:* Pre-kindergarten and early learning research, early learning environments. *Unit head:* Dr. Ronnie Casella, Chair, 860-832-2415, E-mail: casellar@ccsu.edu. *Application contact:* Patricia Gardner, Associate Director of Graduate Studies, 860-832-2350, Fax: 860-832-2352, E-mail: graduateadmissions@ccsu.edu.

Central Michigan University, College of Graduate Studies, College of Education and Human Services, Department of Teacher Education and Professional Development, Mount Pleasant, MI 48859. Offers educational technology (MA, Graduate Certificate); elementary education (MA), including classroom teaching, early childhood; middle level education (MA); reading and literacy K-12 (MA); secondary education (MA). Part-time and evening/weekend programs available. *Degree requirements:* For master's, thesis or alternative. Electronic applications accepted. *Faculty research:* Integrating literacy across the curriculum, science teaching and aesthetic learning in science, diversity education, educational technology, educational psychology and child development.

Chatham University, Program in Education, Pittsburgh, PA 15232-2826. Offers early childhood education (MAT); elementary education (MAT); environmental education (K-12) (MAT); secondary art (MAT); secondary biology education (MAT); secondary chemistry education (MAT); secondary English education (MAT); secondary math education (MAT); secondary physics education (MAT); secondary social studies education (MAT); special education (MAT). *Students:* 52 full-time (42 women), 17 part-time (16 women); includes 2 minority (1 Black or African American, non-Hispanic/Latino; 1 Hispanic/Latino). Average age 29. 39 applicants, 82% accepted, 23 enrolled. In 2011, 37 master's awarded. *Degree requirements:* For master's, thesis, teaching experience. *Entrance requirements:* For master's, minimum GPA of 3.0, sample of written work, recommendation letters. Additional exam requirements/recommendations for international students: Required—TOEFL (minimum score 600 paper-based; 250 computer-based; 100 iBT), IELTS (minimum score 7), TWE. *Application deadline:* For fall admission, 4/1 priority date for domestic students, 4/1 for international students; for spring admission, 11/1 priority date for domestic students, 10/1 for international students. Applications are processed on a rolling basis. Application fee: $45. Electronic applications accepted. Application fee is waived when completed online. *Expenses: Tuition:* Full-time $13,896. Tuition and fees vary according to program. *Financial support:* Career-related internships or fieldwork available. Financial award applicants required to submit FAFSA. *Faculty research:* Gifted education, environmental education, technology in education, writing as learning, class size and achievement. *Unit head:* Dr. Elvira Sanatullova-Allison, Director of Education Programs, 412-365-2773, E-mail: esanatullovaallison@chatham.edu. *Application contact:* Dory Perry, Associate Director of Graduate Admission, 412-365-2758, Fax: 412-365-1609, E-mail: gradadmissions@chatham.edu. Web site: http://www.chatham.edu/mat.

Chestnut Hill College, School of Graduate Studies, Department of Education, Program in Early Education, Philadelphia, PA 19118-2693. Offers M Ed. Part-time and evening/weekend programs available. *Faculty:* 6 full-time (4 women), 50 part-time/adjunct (33 women). *Students:* 4 full-time (3 women), 49 part-time (47 women); includes 11 minority (6 Black or African American, non-Hispanic/Latino; 1 Asian, non-Hispanic/Latino; 4 Hispanic/Latino). Average age 33. 16 applicants, 100% accepted. In 2011, 12 master's awarded. *Degree requirements:* For master's, thesis optional. *Entrance requirements:* For master's, PRAXIS I or proof of teaching certification, writing sample, letters of recommendation, 6 graduate credits with minimum B grade if undergraduate GPA is below 3.0. Additional exam requirements/recommendations for international students: Required—TOEFL (minimum score 500 paper-based). *Application deadline:* For fall admission, 7/15 priority date for domestic students, 7/15 for international students; for spring admission, 12/15 priority date for domestic students, 12/15 for international students. Applications are processed on a rolling basis. Application fee: $55. *Expenses: Tuition:* Part-time $555 per credit hour. One-time fee: $55 part-time. Part-time tuition and fees vary according to degree level and program. *Financial support:* Unspecified assistantships available. *Faculty research:* Gender issues, ECE standardized testing. *Unit head:* Dr. Carol Pate, Chair, Education Department, 215-248-7127, Fax: 215-148-7155, E-mail: cmpate@chc.edu. *Application contact:* Amy Boorse, Administrative Assistant, School of Graduate Studies Office, 215-248-7170, Fax: 215-248-7161, E-mail: gradadmissions@chc.edu. Web site: http://www.chc.edu/Graduate/Programs/Masters/Education/.

Cheyney University of Pennsylvania, School of Education and Professional Studies, Program in Early Childhood Education, Cheyney, PA 19319. Offers Certificate. Part-time and evening/weekend programs available. *Degree requirements:* For Certificate, thesis or alternative. *Entrance requirements:* For degree, GRE General Test, MAT, minimum GPA of 2.75. Electronic applications accepted.

Chicago State University, School of Graduate and Professional Studies, College of Education, Department of Special Education, Early Childhood Education and Bilingual Education, Program in Early Childhood Education, Chicago, IL 60628. Offers MAT, MS Ed. *Accreditation:* NCATE. *Degree requirements:* For master's, thesis optional. *Entrance requirements:* For master's, minimum GPA of 2.75.

City College of the City University of New York, Graduate School, School of Education, Department of Childhood Education, New York, NY 10031-9198. Offers MS. *Accreditation:* NCATE. *Degree requirements:* For master's, thesis. *Entrance requirements:* For master's, Liberal Arts and Sciences Test (LAST), Content Specialty Test (CST). Additional exam requirements/recommendations for international students: Required—TOEFL.

Clarion University of Pennsylvania, Office of Graduate Programs, Master of Education Program, Clarion, PA 16214. Offers curriculum and instruction (M Ed); early childhood (M Ed, Certificate); English (M Ed); instructional technology specialist (K-12) (Certificate); literacy (M Ed); mathematics education (M Ed); reading specialist (M Ed, Certificate); science education (M Ed); special education (M Ed); technology (M Ed); world language (M Ed). *Accreditation:* NCATE. Part-time programs available. *Students:* 14 full-time (11 women), 207 part-time (163 women); includes 3 minority (1 Black or African American, non-Hispanic/Latino; 2 Hispanic/Latino). Average age 31. In 2011, 96 master's awarded. *Degree requirements:* For master's, thesis or alternative. *Entrance requirements:* For master's, minimum QPA of 3.0. *Application deadline:* Applications are processed on a rolling basis. *Expenses:* Tuition, state resident: part-time $429 per credit. Tuition, nonresident: part-time $644 per credit. *Financial support:* Research assistantships with full and partial tuition reimbursements and career-related internships or fieldwork available. Support available to part-time students. Financial award application deadline: 3/1. *Unit head:* Dr. John Groves, Dean, 814-393-2146, Fax: 514-393-2446. *Application contact:* Dr. Brenda Sanders Dede, Assistant Vice President for Academic Affairs, 814-393-2337, Fax: 814-393-2030, E-mail: bdede@clarion.edu. Web site: http://www.clarion.edu/25887/.

Clarke University, Program in Education, Dubuque, IA 52001-3198. Offers early childhood/special education (MAE); educational administration: elementary and secondary (MAE); educational media: elementary and secondary (MAE); multi-categorical resource k-12 (MAE); multidisciplinary studies (MAE); reading: elementary (MAE); technology in education (MAE). Part-time and evening/weekend programs available. Postbaccalaureate distance learning degree programs offered (minimal on-campus study). *Faculty:* 4 full-time (3 women), 2 part-time/adjunct (1 woman). *Students:* 7 full-time (all women), 43 part-time (40 women). Average age 31. In 2011, 11 master's awarded. *Degree requirements:* For master's, comprehensive exam, thesis optional. *Entrance requirements:* For master's, GRE General Test or MAT, minimum GPA of 2.75. *Application deadline:* Applications are processed on a rolling basis. Application fee: $25. Electronic applications accepted. *Expenses: Tuition:* Part-time $690 per credit hour. *Required fees:* $35 per credit hour. Tuition and fees vary according to program and student level. *Financial support:* Career-related internships or fieldwork available. Financial award applicants required to submit FAFSA. *Unit head:* Dr. Larry Bice, Chair, 319-588-6397, Fax: 319-584-8604. *Application contact:* Joan Coates, Information Contact, 563-588-6354, Fax: 563-588-6789, E-mail: graduate@clarke.edu.

Clemson University, Graduate School, College of Health, Education, and Human Development, Eugene T. Moore School of Education, Program in Early Childhood Education, Clemson, SC 29634. Offers early childhood education (M Ed); elementary education (M Ed); secondary English (M Ed); secondary math (M Ed); secondary science (M Ed); secondary social studies (M Ed). Part-time and evening/weekend programs available. *Students:* 5 applicants, 0% accepted, 0 enrolled. In 2011, 3 master's awarded. *Degree requirements:* For master's, comprehensive exam. *Entrance requirements:* For master's, GRE, valid teaching certificate. Additional exam requirements/recommendations for international students: Required—TOEFL; Recommended—IELTS. *Application deadline:* Applications are processed on a rolling basis. Application fee: $70 ($80 for international students). Electronic applications accepted. *Expenses:* Contact institution. *Financial support:* Institutionally sponsored loans, health care benefits, and unspecified assistantships available. Financial award application deadline: 3/1; financial award applicants required to submit FAFSA. *Faculty research:* Elementary education, mathematics education, social studies education, English education, science education. *Unit head:* Dr. Michael J. Padilla, Director/Associate Dean, 864-656-4444, Fax: 864-656-0311, E-mail: padilla@clemson.edu. *Application contact:* Dr. David Fleming, Graduate Programs Coordinator, 864-656-1881, Fax: 864-656-0311, E-mail: dflemin@clemson.edu.

Cleveland State University, College of Graduate Studies, College of Education and Human Services, Department of Teacher Education, Cleveland, OH 44115. Offers art education (M Ed); early childhood education (M Ed); foreign language education (M Ed); mathematics and science education (M Ed); middle childhood education (M Ed); special education (M Ed), including mild/moderate disabilities, moderate/intensive disabilities; teaching English to speakers of other languages (M Ed). Part-time and evening/weekend programs available. *Faculty:* 20 full-time (12 women), 26 part-time/adjunct (20 women). *Students:* 108 full-time (77 women), 388 part-time (306 women); includes 126 minority (100 Black or African American, non-Hispanic/Latino; 8 Asian, non-Hispanic/Latino; 15 Hispanic/Latino; 1 Native Hawaiian or other Pacific Islander, non-Hispanic/Latino; 2 Two or more races, non-Hispanic/Latino), 25 international. Average age 33. 249 applicants, 73% accepted, 118 enrolled. In 2011, 286 master's awarded. *Degree requirements:* For master's, comprehensive exam (for some programs), thesis or alternative. *Entrance requirements:* For master's, GRE General Test or MAT, minimum GPA of 2.75. Additional exam requirements/recommendations for international students: Required—TOEFL (minimum score 525 paper-based; 197 computer-based), IELTS (minimum score 6). *Application deadline:* For fall admission, 7/15 priority date for domestic students. Applications are processed on a rolling basis. Application fee: $30. *Expenses:* Tuition, state resident: full-time $6416; part-time $494 per credit hour. Tuition, nonresident: full-time $12,074; part-time $929 per credit hour. *Financial support:* In 2011–12, 12 research assistantships with full tuition reimbursements (averaging $3,480 per year) were awarded; tuition waivers (partial) and unspecified assistantships also available. *Faculty research:* Early literacy, professional development in reading, reading recovery, dual language, induction programs. *Total annual research expenditures:* $6.2 million. *Unit head:* Dr. Clifford T. Bennett, Chairperson, 216-523-7105, Fax: 216-687-5379, E-mail: c.t.bennett@csuohio.edu. *Application contact:* Deborah L. Brown, Interim Assistant Director, Graduate Admissions, 216-523-7572, E-mail: d.l.brown@csuohio.edu. Web site: http://www.csuohio.edu/coehs/departments/te.

College of Charleston, Graduate School, School of Education, Health, and Human Performance, Department of Elementary and Early Childhood Education, Program in Early Childhood Education, Charleston, SC 29424-0001. Offers MAT. *Accreditation:* NCATE. Part-time and evening/weekend programs available. *Faculty:* 34 full-time (25 women), 9 part-time/adjunct (all women). *Students:* 36 full-time (32 women), 5 part-time (4 women); includes 6 minority (5 Black or African American, non-Hispanic/Latino; 1 Two or more races, non-Hispanic/Latino). Average age 28. 22 applicants, 55% accepted, 8 enrolled. In 2011, 26 degrees awarded. *Degree requirements:* For master's, thesis or alternative, written qualifying exam, student teaching experience (MAT). *Entrance requirements:* For master's, GRE, minimum GPA of 2.5, 2 letters of recommendation. Additional exam requirements/recommendations for international students: Required—TOEFL (minimum score 81 iBT). *Application deadline:* For fall admission, 4/1 for domestic students; for spring admission, 11/1 for domestic students. Applications are processed on a rolling basis. Application fee: $45. Electronic applications accepted. *Expenses:* Tuition, state resident: full-time $5455; part-time $455 per credit. Tuition, nonresident: full-time $13,917; part-time $1160 per credit. *Financial support:* In 2011–12, teaching assistantships (averaging $13,300 per year) were awarded; research assistantships, Federal Work-Study, and unspecified assistantships also available. Support available to part-time students. Financial award application deadline: 4/1; financial award applicants required to submit FAFSA. *Faculty research:* Teacher education and creative arts, integrated curriculum, multicultural awareness, teaching models, cooperative learning. *Unit head:* Dr. Angela Cozart, Director, 843-953-6353, E-mail: cozarta@cofc.edu. *Application contact:* Susan Hallatt, Director of Graduate Admissions, 843-953-5614, Fax: 843-953-1434, E-mail: hallatts@cofc.edu. Web site: http://teachered.cofc.edu/grad-progs/edec.php.

College of Mount St. Joseph, Graduate Education Program, Cincinnati, OH 45233-1670. Offers adolescent young adult education (MA); art (MA); inclusive early childhood education (MA); instructional leadership (MA); middle childhood education (MA); multi-age education (MA); multicultural special education (MA); music (MA); reading (MA). *Accreditation:* Teacher Education Accreditation Council. Part-time and evening/weekend programs available. *Faculty:* 22 full-time (12 women), 11 part-time/adjunct (8 women). *Students:* 51 full-time (40 women), 92 part-time (72 women); includes 17 minority (14 Black or African American, non-Hispanic/Latino; 1 American Indian or Alaska Native, non-Hispanic/Latino; 1 Asian, non-Hispanic/Latino; 1 Hispanic/Latino). Average age 34. 87 applicants, 44% accepted, 29 enrolled. In 2011, 61 master's awarded. *Degree requirements:* For master's, research project, student teaching, clinical and field-based experiences. *Entrance requirements:* For master's, GRE, PRAXIS II in teaching content area (math or science), 2 letters of recommendation, interview, resume. Additional exam requirements/recommendations for international students: Required—TOEFL (minimum score 560 paper-based; 220 computer-based; 83 iBT). *Application deadline:* Applications are processed on a rolling basis. Application fee: $50. Electronic applications accepted. *Expenses: Tuition:* Full-time $24,200; part-time $540 per credit hour. *Required fees:* $112.50 per semester. One-time fee: $200. *Financial support:* In 2011–12, 22 students received support. Scholarships/grants available. Financial award applicants required to submit FAFSA. *Faculty research:* Foreign and second language learning problems/reading disabilities/hyperlexia, multicultural/bilingual special education, alternative educator licensure, science education, pedagogical content knowledge. *Unit head:* Dr. Mary West, Chair, 513-244-3263, Fax: 513-244-4867, E-mail: mary_west@mail.msj.edu. *Application contact:* Marilyn Hoskins, Assistant Director of Graduate Recruitment, 513-244-4723, Fax: 513-244-4629, E-mail: marilyn_hoskins@mail.msj.edu. Web site: http://www.msj.edu/view/academics/graduate-programs/education.aspx.

The College of New Jersey, Graduate Studies, School of Education, Department of Elementary and Early Childhood Education, Program in School Personnel Licensure: Preschool-Grade 3, Ewing, NJ 08628. Offers M Ed, MAT. Part-time programs available. *Entrance requirements:* For master's, GRE, minimum GPA of 3.0 in field or 2.75 overall. Additional exam requirements/recommendations for international students: Required—TOEFL. Electronic applications accepted.

The College of New Rochelle, Graduate School, Division of Education, Program in Elementary Education/Early Childhood Education, New Rochelle, NY 10805-2308. Offers MS Ed. Part-time programs available. *Degree requirements:* For master's, comprehensive exam (for some programs), thesis (for some programs), practicum. *Entrance requirements:* For master's, interview, minimum GPA of 3.0 in field, 2.7 overall.

The College of Saint Rose, Graduate Studies, School of Education, Teacher Education Department, Albany, NY 12203-1419. Offers business and marketing (MS Ed); childhood education (MS Ed); curriculum and instruction (MS Ed); early childhood education (MS Ed); elementary education (K-6) (MS Ed); secondary education (MS Ed, Certificate); teacher education (MS Ed, Certificate), including bilingual pupil personnel services (Certificate), teacher education (MS Ed). Part-time and evening/weekend programs available. *Entrance requirements:* For master's, minimum undergraduate GPA of 3.0. Additional exam requirements/recommendations for international students: Required—TOEFL (minimum score 550 paper-based; 213 computer-based). Electronic applications accepted.

Colorado Christian University, Program in Curriculum and Instruction, Lakewood, CO 80226. Offers corporate education (MACI); early childhood educator (MACI); elementary educator (MACI); instructional technology (MACI); master educator (MACI); online course developer (MACI); online teaching and learning (MACI); special education generalist (MACI). Part-time and evening/weekend programs available. *Degree requirements:* For master's, thesis optional, practicum. *Entrance requirements:* For master's, interviews, letters of recommendation. Additional exam requirements/recommendations for international students: Required—TOEFL. Electronic applications accepted. *Expenses:* Contact institution.

Columbia International University, Columbia Graduate School, Columbia, SC 29230-3122. Offers Bible teaching (MABT); Christian higher education leadership (Ed D); Christian school educational leadership (Ed D); counseling (MACN); curriculum and instruction (M Ed), including Christian school guidance, English as a second language, learning disabilities, school technology; early childhood and elementary education (MAT); educational administration (M Ed); teaching English as a foreign language (Certificate); teaching English as a foreign language and intercultural studies (MATF). Part-time and evening/weekend programs available. *Degree requirements:* For master's, internships, professional project. *Entrance requirements:* For master's, Minnesota Multiphasic Personality Inventory, MAT, minimum GPA of 2.7. Additional exam requirements/recommendations for international students: Required—TOEFL. Electronic applications accepted.

Columbus State University, Graduate Studies, College of Education and Health Professions, Department of Teacher Education, Columbus, GA 31907-5645. Offers accomplished teaching (M Ed); early childhood education (M Ed, MAT, Ed S); health and physical education (M Ed, MAT); middle grades education (M Ed, MAT, Ed S); school library media (M Ed, MAT); secondary education (M Ed, MAT, Ed S), including English/language arts (M Ed, Ed S), general science (M Ed), mathematics (M Ed), social science (M Ed); special education (M Ed, Ed S), including general curriculum (M Ed). *Accreditation:* NCATE. Part-time and evening/weekend programs available. Postbaccalaureate distance learning degree programs offered (minimal on-campus study). *Degree requirements:* For master's, thesis, exit exam; for Ed S, thesis or alternative. *Entrance requirements:* For master's, GRE General Test, minimum GPA of 2.75; for Ed S, GRE General Test. Additional exam requirements/recommendations for international students: Required—TOEFL (minimum score 550 paper-based; 213 computer-based; 79 iBT). Electronic applications accepted.

Concordia University Chicago, College of Education, Program in Early Childhood Education, River Forest, IL 60305-1499. Offers MA, Ed D. Part-time and evening/weekend programs available. *Degree requirements:* For master's, comprehensive exam, thesis. *Entrance requirements:* For master's, minimum GPA of 2.9; for doctorate, MAT or GRE, minimum graduate GPA of 3.5. Additional exam requirements/recommendations for international students: Required—TOEFL (minimum score 550 paper-based; 195 computer-based). Electronic applications accepted. *Faculty research:* Child care training project, "Children in Worship" project, ethical development of children.

Concordia University Chicago, College of Education, Program in Teaching, River Forest, IL 60305-1499. Offers early childhood education (MAT); elementary education (MAT); secondary education (MAT). *Degree requirements:* For master's, thesis or alternative. *Entrance requirements:* For master's, minimum GPA of 2.9. Additional exam requirements/recommendations for international students: Required—TOEFL (minimum score 550 paper-based; 195 computer-based). Electronic applications accepted.

Concordia University, Nebraska, Graduate Programs in Education, Program in Early Childhood Education, Seward, NE 68434-1599. Offers M Ed. *Accreditation:* NCATE. Part-time programs available. *Degree requirements:* For master's, comprehensive exam, thesis or alternative. *Entrance requirements:* For master's, GRE, MAT, or NTE, minimum GPA of 3.0, BS in education or equivalent. Additional exam requirements/recommendations for international students: Required—TOEFL.

Concordia University, St. Paul, College of Education, St. Paul, MN 55104-5494. Offers curriculum and instruction (MA Ed), including K-12 reading endorsement; differentiated instruction (MA Ed); early childhood education (MA Ed); educational leadership (MA Ed); educational technology (MA Ed); family life education (MA); K-12 reading endorsement (Certificate); special education (Certificate); sports management (MA). *Accreditation:* NCATE. Evening/weekend programs available. Postbaccalaureate distance learning degree programs offered (minimal on-campus study). *Faculty:* 7 full-time (3 women), 64 part-time/adjunct (42 women). *Students:* 617 full-time (495 women), 9 part-time (6 women); includes 57 minority (30 Black or African American, non-Hispanic/Latino; 2 American Indian or Alaska Native, non-Hispanic/Latino; 17 Asian, non-Hispanic/Latino; 5 Hispanic/Latino; 1 Native Hawaiian or other Pacific Islander, non-Hispanic/Latino; 2 Two or more races, non-Hispanic/Latino). Average age 36. 302 applicants, 83% accepted, 210 enrolled. In 2011, 320 master's, 68 other advanced degrees awarded. *Application deadline:* Applications are processed on a rolling basis. Application fee: $50. Electronic applications accepted. *Expenses: Tuition:* Full-time $8100; part-time $435 per credit. Tuition and fees vary according to program. *Financial support:* Applicants required to submit FAFSA. *Unit head:* Dr. Donald Helmstetter, Dean, 651-641-8227, Fax: 651-641-8807, E-mail: helmstetter@csp.edu. *Application contact:* Kimberly Craig, Director of Graduate and Cohort Admission, 651-603-6223, Fax: 651-603-6320, E-mail: craig@csp.edu.

Concordia University Wisconsin, Graduate Programs, Department of Education, Program in Early Childhood, Mequon, WI 53097-2402. Offers MS Ed. *Students:* 4 full-time (all women), 27 part-time (25 women); includes 5 minority (3 Black or African American, non-Hispanic/Latino; 1 Asian, non-Hispanic/Latino; 1 Two or more races, non-Hispanic/Latino), 3 international. Average age 37. In 2011, 2 master's awarded. *Degree requirements:* For master's, comprehensive exam, thesis or alternative. *Entrance requirements:* For master's, minimum GPA of 3.0, teaching license. Additional exam requirements/recommendations for international students: Required—TOEFL. Application fee: $35. *Financial support:* Application deadline: 8/1. *Unit head:* Dr. Candyce Seider, Head, 262-243-4221, E-mail: candyce.seider@cuw.edu. *Application contact:* Graduate Admissions, 262-243-4248, Fax: 262-243-4428, E-mail: candyce.seider@cuw.edu.

Converse College, School of Education and Graduate Studies, Spartanburg, SC 29302-0006. Offers art education (M Ed); early childhood education (MAT); education (Ed S), including administration and supervision, curriculum and instruction, marriage and family therapy; elementary education (M Ed, MAT); gifted education (M Ed); leadership (M Ed); liberal arts (MLA), including English (M Ed, MAT, MLA), history, political science; secondary education (M Ed, MAT), including biology (MAT), chemistry (MAT), English (M Ed, MAT, MLA), mathematics, natural sciences (M Ed), social sciences; special education (M Ed, MAT), including learning disabilities (MAT), mental disabilities (MAT), special education (M Ed). *Accreditation:* NASAD; NCATE. Part-time and evening/weekend programs available. *Entrance requirements:* For master's, PRAXIS II (M Ed), minimum GPA of 2.75; for Ed S, GRE or MAT, minimum GPA of 3.0. Electronic applications accepted. *Faculty research:* Motivation, classroom management, predictors of success in classroom teaching, sex equity in public education, gifted research.

Daemen College, Education Department, Amherst, NY 14226-3592. Offers adolescence education (MS); childhood education (MS); childhood special education (MS); childhood special-alternative certification (MS); early childhood special-alternative certification (MS). Part-time programs available. *Degree requirements:* For master's, thesis optional, research thesis in lieu of comprehensive exam; completion of degree within 5 years. *Entrance requirements:* For master's, 2 letters of recommendation (professional and character), proof of initial certificate of license for professional programs, resume. Additional exam requirements/recommendations for international students: Required—TOEFL (minimum score 500 paper-based; 173 computer-based; 63 iBT), IELTS (minimum score 5.5). Electronic applications accepted. *Faculty research:* Transition for students with disabilities, early childhood special education, traumatic brain injury (TBI), reading assessment.

Dallas Baptist University, Dorothy M. Bush College of Education, Teaching Program, Dallas, TX 75211-9299. Offers all-level (MAT); distance learning (MAT); elementary (MAT); English as a second language (MAT); Montessori (MAT); multisensory (MAT); secondary (MAT). Part-time and evening/weekend programs available. *Entrance requirements:* For master's, GRE General Test, minimum GPA of 3.0. Additional exam requirements/recommendations for international students: Required—TOEFL, IELTS. *Application deadline:* Applications are processed on a rolling basis. Application fee: $25. Electronic applications accepted. *Expenses: Tuition:* Full-time $12,060; part-time $670 per credit hour. *Required fees:* $100; $50 per semester. *Financial support:* Federal Work-Study, institutionally sponsored loans, scholarships/grants, and tuition waivers (full and partial) available. Support available to part-time students. Financial award applicants required to submit FAFSA. *Unit head:* Dara Owen, Acting Director, 214-333-5413, Fax: 214-333-5551, E-mail: graduate@dbu.edu. *Application contact:* Kit P. Montgomery, Director of Graduate Programs, 214-333-5242, Fax: 214-333-5579, E-mail: graduate@dbu.edu. Web site: http://www3.dbu.edu/graduate/mat.asp.

DePaul University, College of Education, Chicago, IL 60106. Offers bilingual bicultural education (M Ed, MA); counseling (M Ed, MA), including college student development, community counseling, school counseling; curriculum studies (M Ed, MA, Ed D); early childhood education (M Ed, MA); educational leadership (M Ed, MA, Ed D), including administration and supervision (M Ed, MA), physical education (M Ed, MA); middle school mathematics education (MS); reading specialist (M Ed, MA); social and cultural foundations in education (M Ed, MA), including curriculum studies/development (MA); special education (M Ed, MA); teaching and learning (M Ed, MA), including elementary education, secondary education; world languages education (M Ed, MA). Part-time and evening/weekend programs available. *Faculty:* 49 full-time (28 women), 94 part-time/adjunct (60 women). *Students:* 894 full-time (707 women), 473 part-time (361 women); includes 349 minority (159 Black or African American, non-Hispanic/Latino; 3 American Indian or Alaska Native, non-Hispanic/Latino; 45 Asian, non-Hispanic/Latino; 115 Hispanic/Latino; 2 Native Hawaiian or other Pacific Islander, non-Hispanic/Latino; 25 Two or more races, non-Hispanic/Latino), 21 international. Average age 30. 872 applicants, 64% accepted, 325 enrolled. In 2011, 499 master's, 10 doctorates awarded. *Median time to degree:* Of those who began their doctoral program in fall 2003, 32% received their degree in 8 years or less. *Degree requirements:* For master's, thesis/dissertation (for MA); capstone course or paper (for M Ed); for doctorate, thesis/dissertation. *Entrance requirements:* For master's, interview, minimum GPA of 2.75, 2 letters of recommendation, bachelor's degree conferred by accredited college or university; for doctorate, interview, master's degree, writing sample, 3 letters of recommendation. Additional exam requirements/recommendations for international students: Required—TOEFL (minimum score 550 paper-based; 213 computer-based; 80 iBT). *Application deadline:* For fall admission, 8/15 priority date for domestic students; for winter admission, 12/1 priority date for domestic students; for spring admission, 3/1 priority date for domestic students. Applications are processed on a rolling basis. Application fee: $40. Electronic applications accepted. *Financial support:* In 2011–12, 163 students received support, including 15 research assistantships with full tuition reimbursements available (averaging $6,375 per year); career-related internships or fieldwork, Federal Work-Study, scholarships/grants, and unspecified assistantships also available. Support available to part-time students. Financial award application deadline: 12/31; financial award applicants required to submit FAFSA. *Faculty research:* Reflective teaching, children at risk, loss, ethnicity, urban education. *Total annual research expenditures:* $916,310. *Unit head:* Dr. Paul Zionts, Dean, 773-325-7581, Fax: 773-325-7713, E-mail: pzionts@depaul.edu. *Application contact:* Brandon Washington, Enrollment Management Coordinator, 773-325-1152, Fax: 773-325-2270, E-mail: bwashin3@depaul.edu. Web site: http://education.depaul.edu.

Dominican University, School of Education, River Forest, IL 60305-1099. Offers curriculum and instruction (MA Ed); early childhood education (MS); education (MAT); educational administration (MA); elementary (online) (MS); English as a second language (online) (MS); reading (online) (MS); special education (MS). Part-time and evening/weekend programs available. Postbaccalaureate distance learning degree programs offered (no on-campus study). *Faculty:* 19 full-time (13 women), 53 part-time/adjunct (41 women). *Students:* 24 full-time (19 women), 434 part-time (357 women); includes 95 minority (27 Black or African American, non-Hispanic/Latino; 1 American Indian or Alaska Native, non-Hispanic/Latino; 12 Asian, non-Hispanic/Latino; 48 Hispanic/Latino; 7 Two or more races, non-Hispanic/Latino), 1 international. Average age 33. 92 applicants, 99% accepted, 91 enrolled. In 2011, 267 master's awarded. *Entrance requirements:* For master's, Illinois certification test of basic skills. Additional exam requirements/recommendations for international students: Required—TOEFL (minimum score 550 paper-based; 213 computer-based; 79 iBT). *Application deadline:* Applications are processed on a rolling basis. Application fee: $25. *Expenses:* Contact institution. *Financial support:* Career-related internships or fieldwork, scholarships/grants, and tuition waivers (partial) available. Support available to part-time students. Financial award application deadline: 8/15; financial award applicants required to submit FAFSA. *Faculty research:* Governance of private education institutions, reading and language arts, inclusion, organizational planning, leadership and vision. *Unit head:* Dr. Colleen Reardon, Dean, 718-524-6643, Fax: 708-524-6665, E-mail: creardon@dom.edu. *Application contact:* Keven Hansen, Coordinator of Recruitment and Admissions, 708-524-6921, Fax: 708-524-6665, E-mail: educate@dom.edu. Web site: http://www.dom.edu/soe.

Dowling College, Graduate Programs in Education, Oakdale, NY 11769-1999. Offers adolescence education with middle childhood extension (MS); advanced certificate in gifted education (AC); childhood and early childhood education (MS); childhood and gifted education (MS); computers in education (AC); early childhood education (MS); educational administration (Ed D); educational technology leadership (MS); educational technology specialist (AC); literacy education (MS); literary education (AC); school building leader (AC); school district business leader (MBA, AC); school district leader (AC); special education (MS); sports management (MS). *Accreditation:* NCATE. Part-time and evening/weekend programs available. Postbaccalaureate distance learning degree programs offered (minimal on-campus study). *Faculty:* 23 full-time (12 women), 70 part-time/adjunct (44 women). *Students:* 336 full-time (245 women), 631 part-time (485 women); includes 83 minority (29 Black or African American, non-Hispanic/Latino; 2 American Indian or Alaska Native, non-Hispanic/Latino; 7 Asian, non-Hispanic/Latino; 45 Hispanic/Latino). Average age 32. 280 applicants, 85% accepted, 167 enrolled. In 2011, 425 master's, 27 doctorates, 40 other advanced degrees awarded. *Degree requirements:* For master's and AC, comprehensive exam; for doctorate, thesis/dissertation. *Entrance requirements:* For master's, minimum GPA of 3.0; for doctorate, GRE, master's degree; for AC, teaching certificate. Additional exam requirements/recommendations for international students: Required—TOEFL (minimum score 550 paper-based). *Application deadline:* For fall admission, 9/1 priority date for domestic students; for winter admission, 1/1 priority date for domestic students; for spring admission, 2/1 priority date for domestic students. Applications are processed on a rolling basis. Application fee: $50. Electronic applications accepted. *Expenses: Tuition:* Full-time $19,162; part-time $933 per credit. *Required fees:* $1330; $700 per year. Tuition and fees vary according to course load. *Financial support:* Career-related internships or fieldwork and Federal Work-Study available. Support available to part-time students. Financial award application deadline: 6/30; financial award applicants required to submit FAFSA. *Faculty research:* Natural readers, Korean styles and learning strategies, mothers of children with disabilities, computers in instruction, cultural background and organizational roadblocks to problem solving. *Unit head:* Carol Pulsonetti, Director of Operations, School of Education, 631-244-3243, E-mail: pulsonec@dowling.edu. *Application contact:* Ronnie S. Macdonald, Assistant Vice President for Enrollment Services/Dean of Admissions, 631-244-3357, Fax: 631-244-1059, E-mail: macdonar@dowling.edu.

Early Childhood Education

Duquesne University, School of Education, Department of Instruction and Leadership, Program in Early Level (PreK-4) Education, Pittsburgh, PA 15282-0001. Offers MS Ed. Part-time and evening/weekend programs available. *Faculty:* 2 full-time (both women), 6 part-time/adjunct (2 women). *Students:* 4 full-time (all women); includes 1 minority (Black or African American, non-Hispanic/Latino). Average age 24. 13 applicants, 38% accepted, 4 enrolled. *Degree requirements:* For master's, thesis optional. *Entrance requirements:* For master's, bachelor's degree. Additional exam requirements/recommendations for international students: Required—TOEFL (minimum score 550 paper-based; 80 computer-based), IELTS (minimum score 7). *Application deadline:* For fall admission, 9/1 for domestic students; for spring admission, 1/1 for domestic students. Applications are processed on a rolling basis. Electronic applications accepted. Application fee is waived when completed online. *Expenses: Tuition:* Full-time $16,596; part-time $922 per credit. *Required fees:* $1584; $88 per credit. Tuition and fees vary according to program. *Unit head:* Dr. Julia Williams, Assistant Professor, 412-396-6098, Fax: 412-396-5388, E-mail: williamsj@duq.edu. *Application contact:* Michael Dolinger, Director of Student and Academic Services, 412-396-6647, Fax: 412-396-5585, E-mail: dolingerm@duq.edu. Web site: http://www.duq.edu/education/prek-4/index.cfm.

East Carolina University, Graduate School, College of Human Ecology, Department of Child Development and Family Relations, Greenville, NC 27858-4353. Offers birth through kindergarten education (MA Ed); child development and family relations (MS); family and consumer sciences (MA Ed); marriage and family therapy (MS). *Accreditation:* AAMFT/COAMFTE. Part-time programs available. *Degree requirements:* For master's, comprehensive exam, thesis optional. *Application deadline:* For fall admission, 1/15 for domestic students; for spring admission, 10/15 for domestic students. Applications are processed on a rolling basis. Application fee: $50. *Expenses:* Tuition, state resident: full-time $3557; part-time $444.63 per semester hour. Tuition, nonresident: full-time $14,351; part-time $1793.88 per semester hour. *Required fees:* $2016; $252 per semester hour. Part-time tuition and fees vary according to course load, campus/location and program. *Financial support:* Research assistantships, teaching assistantships, career-related internships or fieldwork, Federal Work-Study, institutionally sponsored loans, and scholarships/grants available. Support available to part-time students. Financial award application deadline: 6/1. *Faculty research:* Child care quality, mental health delivery systems for children, family violence. *Unit head:* Dr. Cynthia Johnson, Chairperson, 252-328-4273, E-mail: johnsoncy@ecu.edu. *Application contact:* Dean of Graduate School, 252-328-6012, Fax: 252-328-6071, E-mail: gradschool@ecu.edu.

Eastern Connecticut State University, School of Education and Professional Studies/Graduate Division, Program in Early Childhood Education, Willimantic, CT 06226-2295. Offers MS. *Accreditation:* NCATE. Part-time and evening/weekend programs available. *Degree requirements:* For master's, comprehensive exam or thesis. *Entrance requirements:* For master's, PRAXIS I, minimum GPA of 2.7. Additional exam requirements/recommendations for international students: Required—TOEFL (minimum score 550 paper-based; 213 computer-based).

Eastern Illinois University, Graduate School, College of Education and Professional Studies, Department of Early Childhood, Elementary and Middle Level Education, Charleston, IL 61920-3099. Offers elementary education (MS Ed). *Accreditation:* NCATE. Part-time programs available. *Degree requirements:* For master's, comprehensive exam. *Expenses:* Tuition, state resident: part-time $279 per credit hour. Tuition, nonresident: part-time $670 per credit hour. *Required fees:* $179.07 per credit hour. $1253 per semester.

Eastern Michigan University, Graduate School, College of Education, Department of Teacher Education, Program in Early Childhood Education, Ypsilanti, MI 48197. Offers MA. *Accreditation:* NCATE. Part-time and evening/weekend programs available. *Students:* 67 part-time (66 women); includes 5 minority (2 Black or African American, non-Hispanic/Latino; 1 Asian, non-Hispanic/Latino; 1 Hispanic/Latino; 1 Two or more races, non-Hispanic/Latino). Average age 34. 16 applicants, 63% accepted, 6 enrolled. In 2011, 24 degrees awarded. *Degree requirements:* For master's, thesis optional. *Entrance requirements:* For master's, GRE. Additional exam requirements/recommendations for international students: Required—TOEFL. *Application deadline:* Applications are processed on a rolling basis. Application fee: $35. *Expenses:* Tuition, state resident: full-time $10,367; part-time $432 per credit hour. Tuition, nonresident: full-time $20,435; part-time $851 per credit hour. *Required fees:* $39 per credit hour. $46 per semester. One-time fee: $100. Tuition and fees vary according to course level, degree level and reciprocity agreements. *Financial support:* Fellowships and teaching assistantships available. Support available to part-time students. Financial award applicants required to submit FAFSA. *Unit head:* Dr. Brigid Beaubien, Coordinator, 734-487-3260, Fax: 734-487-2101, E-mail: bbeaubi1@emich.edu. *Application contact:* Dr. Anne Bednar, Advisor, 734-487-3260, Fax: 734-487-2101, E-mail: anne.bednar@emich.edu.

Eastern Nazarene College, Adult and Graduate Studies, Division of Teacher Education, Quincy, MA 02170. Offers administration (M Ed); early childhood education (M Ed, Certificate); elementary education (M Ed, Certificate); English as a second language (Certificate); instructional enrichment and development (Certificate); middle school education (M Ed, Certificate); moderate special needs education (Certificate); principal (Certificate); program development and supervision (Certificate); secondary education (M Ed, Certificate); special education administrator (Certificate); special needs (M Ed); supervisor (Certificate); teacher of reading (M Ed, Certificate). M Ed also available through weekend program for administration, special needs, and teacher of reading only. Part-time and evening/weekend programs available. *Entrance requirements:* Additional exam requirements/recommendations for international students: Required—TOEFL (minimum score 550 paper-based).

Eastern New Mexico University, Graduate School, College of Education and Technology, Department of Educational Studies, Program in Special Education, Portales, NM 88130. Offers early childhood special education (M Sp Ed); general (M Sp Ed). Part-time programs available. *Degree requirements:* For master's, comprehensive exam, thesis optional. *Entrance requirements:* For master's, minimum GPA of 3.0, letter of recommendation, photocopy of teaching license or confirmation of entrance into alternative licensure program, writing assessment, 2 letters of application, special education license or minimum 30 hours of undergraduate course work. Additional exam requirements/recommendations for international students: Required—TOEFL (minimum score 550 paper-based; 213 computer-based; 79 iBT), IELTS (minimum score 6). Electronic applications accepted.

Eastern Washington University, Graduate Studies, College of Arts, Letters and Education, Department of Education, Program in Early Childhood Education, Cheney, WA 99004-2431. Offers M Ed. *Students:* 11 full-time (8 women), 1 part-time; includes 1 minority (Hispanic/Latino). In 2011, 1 master's awarded. *Unit head:* Robin Showalter, Program Coordinator, 509-359-6492, E-mail: rshowalter@mail.ewu.edu. *Application contact:* Dr. Kevin Pyatt, Graduate Program Coordinator, 509-359-6091, E-mail: kpyatt@ewu.edu.

East Tennessee State University, School of Graduate Studies, College of Education, Department of Human Development and Learning, Johnson City, TN 37614. Offers counseling (MA), including community agency counseling, elementary and secondary (school counseling), higher education counseling, marriage and family therapy; early childhood education (MA, PhD), including initial licensure in PreK-3 (MA), master teacher (MA), researcher (MA); special education (MA), including advanced practitioner, early childhood special education, special education. *Accreditation:* ACA; NCATE. Part-time programs available. *Faculty:* 31 full-time (22 women), 5 part-time/adjunct (all women). *Students:* 112 full-time (90 women), 41 part-time (36 women); includes 8 minority (5 Black or African American, non-Hispanic/Latino; 3 Two or more races, non-Hispanic/Latino), 4 international. Average age 32. 145 applicants, 34% accepted, 46 enrolled. In 2011, 34 master's awarded. Terminal master's awarded for partial completion of doctoral program. *Degree requirements:* For master's, comprehensive exam, thesis optional, internship, student teaching, culminating experience; for doctorate, comprehensive exam, thesis/dissertation, research apprenticeship. *Entrance requirements:* For master's, GRE General Test, minimum GPA of 3.0; for doctorate, GRE General Test, professional resume, master's degree in early childhood or related field, interview. Additional exam requirements/recommendations for international students: Required—TOEFL (minimum score 550 paper-based; 213 computer-based; 79 iBT). *Application deadline:* For fall admission, 2/1 for domestic and international students. Application fee: $35 ($45 for international students). Electronic applications accepted. *Expenses:* Tuition, state resident: full-time $7312; part-time $350 per credit hour. Tuition, nonresident: full-time $18,490; part-time $621 per credit hour. *Required fees:* $63 per credit hour. Tuition and fees vary according to course load and program. *Financial support:* In 2011–12, 86 students received support, including 6 fellowships with full tuition reimbursements available (averaging $18,000 per year), 28 research assistantships with full tuition reimbursements available (averaging $6,000 per year), 10 teaching assistantships with full tuition reimbursements available (averaging $6,000 per year); career-related internships or fieldwork, institutionally sponsored loans, scholarships/grants, traineeships, and unspecified assistantships also available. Financial award application deadline: 7/1; financial award applicants required to submit FAFSA. *Faculty research:* Drug and alcohol abuse, marriage and family counseling, severe mental retardation, parenting of children with disabilities. *Total annual research expenditures:* $2,600. *Unit head:* Dr. Pamela Evanshen, Chair, 423-439-7694, Fax: 423-439-7790, E-mail: evanshep@etsu.edu. *Application contact:* Fiona Goodyear, Graduate Specialist, 423-439-6148, Fax: 423-439-5624, E-mail: goodyear@etsu.edu.

Edinboro University of Pennsylvania, School of Education, Department of Early Childhood and Special Education, Edinboro, PA 16444. Offers behavior management (Certificate); character education (Certificate); online special education (M Ed); special education (M Ed). Part-time and evening/weekend programs available. *Faculty:* 5 full-time (all women). *Students:* 22 full-time (19 women), 154 part-time (129 women); includes 4 minority (3 Black or African American, non-Hispanic/Latino; 1 Two or more races, non-Hispanic/Latino). Average age 31. In 2011, 26 master's, 5 Certificates awarded. *Degree requirements:* For master's, thesis or alternative, competency exam; for Certificate, thesis or alternative. *Entrance requirements:* For master's and Certificate, GRE or MAT, minimum QPA of 2.5. *Application deadline:* Applications are processed on a rolling basis. Application fee: $30. Electronic applications accepted. *Financial support:* In 2011–12, 4 research assistantships with full and partial tuition reimbursements (averaging $4,050 per year) were awarded; career-related internships or fieldwork, Federal Work-Study, scholarships/grants, and unspecified assistantships also available. Support available to part-time students. Financial award application deadline: 2/15; financial award applicants required to submit FAFSA. *Unit head:* Dr. Maureen Walcavich, Program Head, Early Childhood, 814-732-2303, E-mail: mwalcavich@edinboro.edu. *Application contact:* Dr. Mary Jo Melvin, Program Head, Special Education, 814-732-2154, E-mail: mmelvin@edinboro.edu.

Ellis University, Program in Education, Chicago, IL 60606-7204. Offers early childhood education (MA Ed); education (MA Ed); teacher as a leader (MA Ed). *Degree requirements:* For master's, thesis or capstone.

Elms College, Division of Education, Chicopee, MA 01013-2839. Offers early childhood education (MAT); education (M Ed, CAGS); elementary education (MAT); English as a second language (MAT); reading (MAT); secondary education (MAT), including biology education, English education, Spanish education; special education (MAT). Part-time and evening/weekend programs available. *Degree requirements:* For master's, thesis (for some programs). *Entrance requirements:* For master's, Massachusetts Educators Certification Test, minimum GPA of 3.0; for CAGS, master's degree in education. Additional exam requirements/recommendations for international students: Required—TOEFL.

Emporia State University, Graduate School, Teachers College, Department of Elementary Education, Early Childhood, and Special Education, Program in Early Childhood Education, Emporia, KS 66801-5087. Offers early childhood curriculum (MS); early childhood special education (MS). *Accreditation:* NCATE. Part-time programs available. Postbaccalaureate distance learning degree programs offered. *Students:* 3 full-time (all women), 61 part-time (59 women); includes 9 minority (2 Asian, non-Hispanic/Latino; 6 Hispanic/Latino; 1 Native Hawaiian or other Pacific Islander, non-Hispanic/Latino). 17 applicants, 100% accepted, 15 enrolled. In 2011, 13 master's awarded. *Degree requirements:* For master's, comprehensive exam or thesis, practicum. *Entrance requirements:* For master's, GRE General Test or MAT, graduate essay exam, appropriate bachelor's degree, letters of recommendation. Additional exam requirements/recommendations for international students: Required—TOEFL (minimum score 520 paper-based; 133 computer-based; 68 iBT). *Application deadline:* For fall admission, 8/15 priority date for domestic students. Applications are processed on a rolling basis. Application fee: $30 ($75 for international students). Electronic applications accepted. *Expenses:* Tuition, state resident: full-time $2342; part-time $195 per credit hour. Tuition, nonresident: full-time $7254; part-time $605 per credit hour. *Required fees:* $66 per credit hour. Tuition and fees vary according to campus/location. *Financial support:* Federal Work-Study, institutionally sponsored loans, health care benefits, and unspecified assistantships available. Financial award application deadline: 3/15; financial award applicants required to submit FAFSA. *Unit head:* Dr. Jean Morrow, Chair, 620-341-5766, E-mail: jmorrow@emporia.edu. *Application contact:* Mary Sewell, Admissions Coordinator, 800-950-GRAD, Fax: 620-341-5909, E-mail: msewell@emporia.edu.

Endicott College, Van Loan School of Graduate and Professional Studies, Program in Montessori Integrative Learning, Beverly, MA 01915-2096. Offers M Ed. *Faculty:* 2 full-time (1 woman). *Students:* 12 full-time (10 women), 13 part-time (all women); includes 2 minority (both Hispanic/Latino). Average age 36. 19 applicants, 95% accepted, 15 enrolled. In 2011, 14 master's awarded. *Entrance requirements:* Additional exam requirements/recommendations for international students: Required—TOEFL. *Application deadline:* Applications are processed on a rolling basis. Tuition and fees vary according to degree level and program. *Financial support:* Applicants required to submit FAFSA. *Unit head:* Enid E. Larsen.

Erikson Institute, Erikson Institute, Chicago, IL 60654. Offers child development (MS); early childhood education (M Ed, MS, PhD). PhD offered through the Graduate School. *Accreditation:* NCA . *Degree requirements:* For master's, comprehensive exam, internship; for doctorate, one foreign language, comprehensive exam, thesis/dissertation. *Entrance requirements:* For master's, experience working with young children, interview; for doctorate, GRE General Test, interview. *Faculty research:* Early childhood development, cognitive development, sociocultural contexts, early childhood education, family and culture, early literacy.

Erikson Institute, Academic Programs, Program in Early Childhood Education, Chicago, IL 60654. Offers MS. *Degree requirements:* For master's, comprehensive exam. *Entrance requirements:* For master's, 3 letters of recommendation, minimum GPA of 2.75. Additional exam requirements/recommendations for international students: Required—TOEFL.

Fitchburg State University, Division of Graduate and Continuing Education, Program in Early Childhood Education, Fitchburg, MA 01420-2697. Offers M Ed. *Accreditation:* NCATE. Part-time and evening/weekend programs available. *Students:* 3 full-time (all women), 23 part-time (all women); includes 1 minority (Two or more races, non-Hispanic/Latino). Average age 33. 5 applicants, 100% accepted, 4 enrolled. In 2011, 8 master's awarded. *Entrance requirements:* Additional exam requirements/recommendations for international students: Recommended—TOEFL (minimum score 550 paper-based; 213 computer-based; 79 iBT). *Application deadline:* For fall admission, 7/15 for international students; for spring admission, 12/1 for international students. Applications are processed on a rolling basis. Application fee: $25 ($50 for international students). Electronic applications accepted. *Expenses:* Tuition, state resident: full-time $2700; part-time $150 per credit. Tuition, nonresident: full-time $2700; part-time $150 per credit. *Required fees:* $2286; $127 per credit. *Financial support:* In 2011–12, research assistantships with partial tuition reimbursements (averaging $5,500 per year) were awarded; Federal Work-Study, scholarships/grants, and unspecified assistantships also available. Support available to part-time students. Financial award application deadline: 3/1; financial award applicants required to submit FAFSA. *Unit head:* Richard Beardmore, Chair, 978-665-3193, Fax: 978-665-3658, E-mail: gce@fitchburgstate.edu. *Application contact:* Kay Reynolds, Director of Admissions, 978-665-3144, Fax: 978-665-4540, E-mail: admissions@fitchburgstate.edu. Web site: http://www.fitchburgstate.edu.

Florida Agricultural and Mechanical University, Division of Graduate Studies, Research, and Continuing Education, College of Education, Department of Elementary Education, Tallahassee, FL 32307-3200. Offers early childhood and elementary education (M Ed, MS Ed). *Accreditation:* NCATE. *Degree requirements:* For master's, thesis (for some programs). *Entrance requirements:* For master's, GRE General Test, minimum GPA of 3.0. Additional exam requirements/recommendations for international students: Required—TOEFL.

Florida Atlantic University, College of Education, Department of Curriculum, Culture, and Educational Inquiry, Boca Raton, FL 33431-0991. Offers curriculum and instruction (Ed D, Ed S); early childhood education (M Ed); multicultural education (M Ed); teaching English to speakers of other languages (TESOL) (M Ed). *Faculty:* 14 full-time (11 women), 16 part-time/adjunct (13 women). *Students:* 28 full-time (21 women), 138 part-time (106 women); includes 46 minority (18 Black or African American, non-Hispanic/Latino; 1 American Indian or Alaska Native, non-Hispanic/Latino; 3 Asian, non-Hispanic/Latino; 23 Hispanic/Latino; 1 Two or more races, non-Hispanic/Latino), 7 international. Average age 36. 120 applicants, 53% accepted, 32 enrolled. In 2011, 33 master's, 2 doctorates awarded. *Application deadline:* For fall admission, 7/1 for domestic students, 2/15 for international students; for spring admission, 11/1 for domestic students, 7/15 for international students. *Expenses: Tuition, area resident:* Part-time $343.02 per credit hour. Tuition, state resident: full-time $8232. Tuition, nonresident: full-time $23,931; part-time $997.14 per credit hour. *Faculty research:* Multicultural education, early intervention strategies, family literacy, religious diversity in schools, early childhood curriculum. *Unit head:* Dr. James McLaughlin, Interim Chair, 561-297-3965, E-mail: jmclau17@fau.edu. *Application contact:* Dr. Eliah Watlington, Associate Dean, 561-296-8520, Fax: 261-297-2991, E-mail: ewatling@fau.edu. Web site: http://www.coe.fau.edu/academicdepartments/ccei/.

Florida International University, College of Education, Department of Curriculum and Instruction, Miami, FL 33199. Offers art education (MAT, MS, Ed D); curriculum and instruction (Ed S); curriculum development (MS); curriculum studies (PhD); early childhood education (MS, Ed D); elementary education (MS, Ed D); English education (MAT, MS, Ed D); foreign language education - teaching English to speakers of other languages (TESOL) (MS, Certificate), including foreign language education (Certificate), teaching English (MS); French education - initial teacher preparation (MAT); international and intercultural development education (Ed D); international and intercultural developmental education (MS); language, literacy and culture (PhD); learning technologies (MS, Ed D, PhD); mathematics education (MAT, MS, Ed D, PhD); modern language education/bilingual education (MS, Ed D); physical education (MS); reading education (MS, Ed D); science education (MAT, MS, Ed D, PhD); social studies education (MAT, MS, Ed D); Spanish education - initial teacher preparation (MAT); special education (MS). Part-time and evening/weekend programs available. *Degree requirements:* For doctorate, comprehensive exam, thesis/dissertation. *Entrance requirements:* For master's, GRE General Test, Florida General Knowledge Test or Florida College Level Academic Skills Test; for doctorate and other advanced degree, GRE General Test. Additional exam requirements/recommendations for international students: Required—TOEFL (minimum score 550 paper-based; 213 computer-based; 80 iBT), IELTS (minimum score 6.3). Electronic applications accepted.

Florida State University, The Graduate School, College of Education, School of Teacher Education, Tallahassee, FL 32306. Offers early childhood education (MS, Ed D, PhD, Ed S); elementary education (MS, Ed D, PhD, Ed S); English education (MS, PhD, Ed S); mathematics education (MS, PhD, Ed S); reading education/language arts (MS, Ed D, PhD, Ed S); science education (MS, PhD, Ed S); social science education (MS, PhD, Ed S); special education (MS, PhD, Ed S), including emotional disturbance/learning disabilities (MS), mental retardation (MS), rehabilitation counseling, special education (PhD, Ed S), visual disabilities (MS). Part-time programs available. *Faculty:* 34 full-time (25 women), 20 part-time/adjunct (17 women). *Students:* 160 full-time (130 women), 116 part-time (98 women); includes 64 minority (36 Black or African American, non-Hispanic/Latino; 4 American Indian or Alaska Native, non-Hispanic/Latino; 6 Asian, non-Hispanic/Latino; 18 Hispanic/Latino), 28 international. Average age 31. 180 applicants, 62% accepted, 53 enrolled. In 2011, 142 master's, 17 doctorates, 8 other advanced degrees awarded. *Degree requirements:* For master's and Ed S, comprehensive exam, thesis optional; for doctorate, comprehensive exam, thesis/dissertation, preliminary exam, prospectus defense. *Entrance requirements:* For master's, doctorate, and Ed S, GRE General Test, minimum GPA of 3.0. Additional exam requirements/recommendations for international students: Required—TOEFL (minimum score 550 paper-based; 213 computer-based; 80 iBT). *Application deadline:* For fall admission, 7/1 for domestic and international students; for winter admission, 10/1 for domestic students, 11/1 for international students; for spring admission, 3/1 for domestic and international students. Applications are processed on a rolling basis. Application fee: $30. Electronic applications accepted. *Expenses:* Tuition, state resident: full-time $9474; part-time $350.88 per credit hour. Tuition, nonresident: full-time $16,236; part-time $601.34 per credit hour. *Required fees:* $630 per semester. One-time fee: $20. Tuition and fees vary according to course load and campus/location. *Financial support:* In 2011–12, 32 research assistantships with full and partial tuition reimbursements, 15 teaching assistantships with full and partial tuition reimbursements were awarded; fellowships with full and partial tuition reimbursements, career-related internships or fieldwork, scholarships/grants, health care benefits, and unspecified assistantships also available. Financial award application deadline: 1/15; financial award applicants required to submit FAFSA. *Faculty research:* Teaching and learning practices and policies, twenty-first century literacies, impact of teacher education programs on student gains. *Total annual research expenditures:* $723,234. *Unit head:* Dr. Lawrence Scharmann, Chair, 850-644-4880, Fax: 850-644-1880, E-mail: lscharmann@fsu.edu. *Application contact:* Harriet Kasper, Program Assistant, 850-644-2122, Fax: 850-644-7736, E-mail: hkasper@fsu.edu. Web site: http://www.coe.fsu.edu/Academic-Programs/Departments/School-of-Teacher-Education-STE.

Fordham University, Graduate School of Education, Division of Curriculum and Teaching, New York, NY 10023. Offers adult education (MS, MSE); bilingual teacher education (MSE); curriculum and teaching (MSE); early childhood education (MSE); elementary education (MST); language, literacy, and learning (PhD); reading education (MSE, Adv C); secondary education (MAT, MSE); special education (MSE, Adv C); teaching English as a second language (MSE). *Accreditation:* NCATE. *Degree requirements:* For doctorate, thesis/dissertation; for Adv C, thesis. *Entrance requirements:* For doctorate, MAT, GRE General Test. *Expenses: Tuition:* Full-time $30,480; part-time $1270 per credit. *Required fees:* $586; $293 per semester.

Framingham State University, Division of Graduate and Continuing Education, Program in Early Childhood Education, Framingham, MA 01701-9101. Offers M Ed.

Francis Marion University, Graduate Programs, School of Education, Florence, SC 29502-0547. Offers early childhood education (M Ed); elementary education (M Ed); learning disabilities (M Ed, MAT); remedial education (M Ed); secondary education (M Ed). *Accreditation:* NCATE. Part-time programs available. *Faculty:* 20 full-time (16 women), 1 (woman) part-time/adjunct. *Students:* 10 full-time (8 women), 115 part-time (88 women); includes 30 minority (26 Black or African American, non-Hispanic/Latino; 3 Asian, non-Hispanic/Latino; 1 Hispanic/Latino), 1 international. Average age 32. 249 applicants, 33% accepted, 77 enrolled. In 2011, 41 master's awarded. *Degree requirements:* For master's, comprehensive exam. *Entrance requirements:* For master's, GRE General Test, MAT, NTE, or PRAXIS II. *Application deadline:* For fall admission, 3/15 priority date for domestic students; for spring admission, 10/15 priority date for domestic students. Applications are processed on a rolling basis. Application fee: $31. *Expenses:* Tuition, state resident: full-time $8467; part-time $443.35 per credit hour. Tuition, nonresident: full-time $16,934; part-time $866.70 per credit hour. *Required fees:* $335; $12.25 per credit hour. $30 per semester. *Financial support:* In 2011–12, 3 research assistantships (averaging $6,000 per year) were awarded; scholarships/grants and unspecified assistantships also available. Support available to part-time students. Financial award application deadline: 3/1; financial award applicants required to submit FAFSA. *Faculty research:* Identification and alternate assessment of at-risk students. *Unit head:* Dr. James R. Faulkenberry, Dean, 843-661-1460, Fax: 843-661-4647. *Application contact:* Rannie Gamble, Administrative Manager, 843-661-1286, Fax: 843-661-4688, E-mail: rgamble@fmarion.edu.

Furman University, Graduate Division, Department of Education, Greenville, SC 29613. Offers curriculum and instruction (MA); early childhood education (MA); educational leadership (Ed S); English as a second language (MA); literacy (MA); school leadership (MA); special education (MA). *Accreditation:* NCATE. Part-time programs available. Postbaccalaureate distance learning degree programs offered (minimal on-campus study). *Faculty:* 14 full-time (8 women), 6 part-time/adjunct (4 women). *Students:* 237 part-time (188 women); includes 27 minority (22 Black or African American, non-Hispanic/Latino; 1 Asian, non-Hispanic/Latino; 3 Hispanic/Latino; 1 Native Hawaiian or other Pacific Islander, non-Hispanic/Latino). Average age 29. 97 applicants, 100% accepted, 90 enrolled. In 2011, 34 master's awarded. *Degree requirements:* For master's, comprehensive exam (for some programs), thesis or alternative. *Entrance requirements:* For master's, PRAXIS II. *Application deadline:* For fall admission, 8/1 priority date for domestic students, 7/15 for international students; for spring admission, 12/1 priority date for domestic students, 12/1 for international students. Applications are processed on a rolling basis. Application fee: $50. *Financial support:* Scholarships/grants available. Financial award application deadline: 5/15; financial award applicants required to submit FAFSA. *Faculty research:* Literacy, pedagogy and practice, social justice, advanced leadership, achievement in high poverty schools. *Unit head:* Dr. Nelly Hecker, Head, 864-294-3385. *Application contact:* Helen Reynolds, Department Assistant, 864-294-2213, Fax: 864-294-3579, E-mail: helen.reynolds@furman.edu. Web site: http://www.furman.edu/gradstudies/.

Gallaudet University, The Graduate School, Washington, DC 20002-3625. Offers audiology (Au D); clinical psychology (PhD); critical studies in the education of deaf learners (PhD); deaf and hard of hearing infants, toddlers, and their families (Certificate); deaf education (Ed S); deaf education: advanced studies (MA); deaf education: special programs in deaf education (MA); deaf history (Certificate); deaf studies (MA, Certificate); education deaf students with disabilities (Certificate); education: teacher preparation (MA), including deaf education, early childhood education and deaf education, elementary education and deaf education, secondary education and deaf education; hearing, speech and language sciences (MS, PhD); international development (MA); interpretation (MA, PhD); linguistics (MA, PhD); mental health counseling (MA); public administration (MA); school counseling (MA); school psychology (Psy S); sign language teaching (MA); social work (MSW); speech-language pathology (MS). Part-time programs available. *Faculty:* 62 full-time (44 women). *Students:* 300 full-time (246 women), 110 part-time (82 women); includes 80 minority (27 Black or African American, non-Hispanic/Latino; 1 American Indian or Alaska Native, non-Hispanic/Latino; 11 Asian, non-Hispanic/Latino; 25 Hispanic/Latino; 1 Native Hawaiian or other Pacific Islander, non-Hispanic/Latino; 15 Two or more races, non-Hispanic/Latino), 24 international. Average age 30. 498 applicants, 45% accepted, 168 enrolled. In 2011, 129 master's, 24 doctorates, 19 other advanced degrees awarded. Terminal master's awarded for partial completion of doctoral program. *Degree requirements:* For master's, comprehensive exam (for some programs), thesis optional; for doctorate, comprehensive exam, thesis/dissertation. *Entrance requirements:* For master's and doctorate, GRE General Test or MAT, letters of recommendation, interviews, goals statement, ASL proficiency interview, written English competency. Additional exam requirements/recommendations for international students: Required—TOEFL. *Application deadline:* For fall admission, 2/15 for domestic students. Applications are processed on a rolling basis. Application fee: $50. Electronic applications accepted. *Expenses: Tuition:* Full-time $12,770; part-time $710 per credit. *Required fees:* $376. *Financial support:* In 2011–12, 287 students received support. Fellowships, research assistantships, teaching assistantships, career-related internships or fieldwork, Federal Work-Study, scholarships/grants, tuition waivers (partial), and unspecified assistantships available. Support available to part-time students. Financial award applicants required to submit FAFSA. *Faculty research:* Bimodal bilingualism development, audiology, telecommunications access, early childhood education, linguistics, visual language and visual learning, rehabilitation and hearing enhancement. *Unit head:* Dr. Carol J. Erting, Dean, 202-651-5520, Fax: 202-651-5027, E-mail: carol.erting@gallaudet.edu. *Application contact:* Wednesday Luria, Coordinator of Prospective Graduate Student Services, 202-651-5400, Fax: 202-651-5295, E-mail: graduate.school@gallaudet.edu. Web site: http://www.gallaudet.edu/x26696.xml.

Early Childhood Education

Gannon University, School of Graduate Studies, College of Humanities, Education, and Social Sciences, School of Education, Program in Early Intervention, Erie, PA 16541-0001. Offers MS. Part-time and evening/weekend programs available. *Degree requirements:* For master's, comprehensive exam, research project. *Entrance requirements:* For master's, interview, teaching certificate. Additional exam requirements/recommendations for international students: Required—TOEFL (minimum score 79 iBT). *Application deadline:* Applications are processed on a rolling basis. Application fee: $25. Electronic applications accepted. *Expenses:* Contact institution. *Financial support:* Career-related internships or fieldwork available. Financial award application deadline: 7/1; financial award applicants required to submit FAFSA. *Unit head:* Dr. Kathleen Kingston, Director, 814-871-5626, E-mail: kingston002@gannon.edu. *Application contact:* Kara Morgan, Assistant Director of Graduate Admissions, 814-871-5831, Fax: 814-871-5827, E-mail: graduate@gannon.edu.

The George Washington University, Graduate School of Education and Human Development, Department of Special Education and Disability Studies, Program in Early Childhood Special Education, Washington, DC 20052. Offers MA Ed. *Accreditation:* NCATE. *Degree requirements:* For master's, comprehensive exam. *Entrance requirements:* For master's, GRE General Test or MAT, minimum GPA of 2.75. *Faculty research:* Computer-assisted instruction and learning, disabled learner assessment of preschool, handicapped children.

Georgia College & State University, Graduate School, The John H. Lounsbury College of Education, Department of Early Childhood and Middle Grades Education, Milledgeville, GA 31061. Offers early childhood education (M Ed, Ed S); middle grades education (M Ed, Ed S). *Accreditation:* NCATE. Part-time and evening/weekend programs available. *Students:* 6 full-time (5 women), 38 part-time (33 women); includes 10 minority (7 Black or African American, non-Hispanic/Latino; 2 Hispanic/Latino; 1 Two or more races, non-Hispanic/Latino). Average age 34. 23 applicants, 52% accepted, 8 enrolled. In 2011, 26 master's awarded. *Degree requirements:* For master's, comprehensive exam, exit portfolio; for Ed S, comprehensive exam, electronic portfolio presentation. *Entrance requirements:* For master's, on-site writing assessment, level 4 teaching certificate, 2 recommendations; for Ed S, on-site writing assessment, master's degree, 2 years of teaching experience, 2 professional recommendations, level 5 teacher certification. Additional exam requirements/recommendations for international students: Recommended—TOEFL (minimum score 550 paper-based; 213 computer-based; 79 iBT). *Application deadline:* For fall admission, 7/1 priority date for domestic students; for spring admission, 11/15 priority date for domestic students. Applications are processed on a rolling basis. Application fee: $40. Electronic applications accepted. *Expenses:* Tuition, state resident: full-time $4806; part-time $267 per credit hour. Tuition, nonresident: full-time $17,802; part-time $989 per credit hour. *Required fees:* $936 per semester. Tuition and fees vary according to course load and campus/location. *Financial support:* In 2011–12, 2 research assistantships were awarded; career-related internships or fieldwork, Federal Work-Study, and unspecified assistantships also available. Support available to part-time students. Financial award applicants required to submit FAFSA. *Unit head:* Dr. Nancy Mizelle, Chair, 478-445-5479, Fax: 478-445-6695, E-mail: nancy.mizelle@gcsu.edu. *Application contact:* Shanda Brand, Graduate Coordinator, 478-445-1383, E-mail: shanda.brand@gcsu.edu.

Georgia Southern University, Jack N. Averitt College of Graduate Studies, College of Education, Department of Teaching and Learning, Statesboro, GA 30460. Offers accomplished teaching (M Ed); art education (M Ed, MAT); business education (M Ed, MAT); curriculum and instruction - accomplished teaching (M Ed); early childhood education (MAT); English education (M Ed, MAT); French education (M Ed); mathematics education (M Ed, MAT); middle grades education (M Ed, MAT); science education (M Ed, MAT); secondary education/family and consumer sciences (MAT); social science education (M Ed, MAT); Spanish education (MAT); special education (M Ed, MAT); teaching and learning (M Ed, Ed S). Part-time and evening/weekend programs available. Postbaccalaureate distance learning degree programs offered (no on-campus study). *Students:* 124 full-time (97 women), 328 part-time (268 women); includes 113 minority (96 Black or African American, non-Hispanic/Latino; 2 Asian, non-Hispanic/Latino; 10 Hispanic/Latino; 1 Native Hawaiian or other Pacific Islander, non-Hispanic/Latino; 4 Two or more races, non-Hispanic/Latino), 2 international. Average age 31. 153 applicants, 93% accepted, 90 enrolled. In 2011, 114 master's, 60 other advanced degrees awarded. *Degree requirements:* For master's, exit assessment, portfolio, transition point assessments; for Ed S, exit assessment, transition point assessments. *Entrance requirements:* For master's, GRE General Test or MAT, minimum GPA of 2.5; for Ed S, GRE General Test or MAT, minimum graduate GPA of 3.25. Additional exam requirements/recommendations for international students: Required—TOEFL (minimum score 550 paper-based; 213 computer-based; 80 iBT). *Application deadline:* For fall admission, 3/1 priority date for domestic students, 3/1 for international students; for spring admission, 10/1 priority date for domestic students, 10/1 for international students. Applications are processed on a rolling basis. Application fee: $50. Electronic applications accepted. *Expenses:* Tuition, state resident: full-time $6300; part-time $263 per semester hour. Tuition, nonresident: full-time $25,174; part-time $1049 per semester hour. *Required fees:* $1872. *Financial support:* In 2011–12, 291 students received support, including research assistantships with partial tuition reimbursements available (averaging $7,200 per year), teaching assistantships with partial tuition reimbursements available (averaging $7,200 per year); career-related internships or fieldwork, Federal Work-Study, scholarships/grants, tuition waivers (partial), and unspecified assistantships also available. Support available to part-time students. Financial award application deadline: 4/15; financial award applicants required to submit FAFSA. *Total annual research expenditures:* $203,081. *Unit head:* Dr. Ronnie Sheppard, Chair, 912-478-0198, Fax: 912-478-0026, E-mail: sheppard@georgiasouthern.edu. *Application contact:* Amanda Gilliland, Coordinator for Graduate Student Recruitment, 912-478-5384, Fax: 912-478-0740, E-mail: gradschool@georgiasouthern.edu. Web site: http://coe.georgiasouthern.edu/tandl/.

Georgia Southwestern State University, Graduate Studies, School of Education, Americus, GA 31709-4693. Offers early childhood education (M Ed, Ed S); health and physical education (M Ed); middle grades education (M Ed, Ed S); reading (M Ed); secondary education (M Ed); special education (M Ed). *Accreditation:* NCATE. *Degree requirements:* For master's, comprehensive exam. *Entrance requirements:* For master's, GRE General Test or MAT, minimum GPA of 2.5; for Ed S, GRE General Test or MAT, minimum graduate GPA of 3.25, M Ed from accredited college or university, 3 years teaching experience. Electronic applications accepted.

Georgia State University, College of Education, Department of Early Childhood Education, Atlanta, GA 30302-3083. Offers M Ed, MAT, PhD, Ed S. *Accreditation:* NCATE. Part-time and evening/weekend programs available. *Degree requirements:* For master's, comprehensive exam; for doctorate, comprehensive exam, thesis/dissertation. *Entrance requirements:* For master's, GRE General Test, minimum GPA of 2.75; for doctorate, GRE General Test, minimum GPA of 3.3; for Ed S, GRE General Test or MAT, minimum graduate GPA of 3.25. Electronic applications accepted. *Faculty research:* Teacher training program evaluation, pre-kindergarten program evaluation, literacy development, children's literature, alternative assessment strategies, children in poverty.

Golden Gate Baptist Theological Seminary, Graduate and Professional Programs, Mill Valley, CA 94941-3197. Offers divinity (M Div); early childhood education (Certificate); education leadership (MAEL, Diploma); ministry (D Min); theological studies (MTS); theology (Th M); youth ministry (Certificate). *Accreditation:* ACIPE; ATS (one or more programs are accredited). Part-time and evening/weekend programs available. *Degree requirements:* For master's, thesis (for some programs); for doctorate, 2 foreign languages, thesis/dissertation. *Entrance requirements:* For doctorate, MAT. Additional exam requirements/recommendations for international students: Required—TOEFL (minimum score 550 paper-based; 213 computer-based). Electronic applications accepted.

Governors State University, College of Education, Program in Early Childhood Education, University Park, IL 60484. Offers MA. *Accreditation:* NCATE. *Students:* 2 full-time (both women), 20 part-time (all women); includes 9 minority (all Black or African American, non-Hispanic/Latino). Average age 37. *Degree requirements:* For master's, comprehensive exam, practicum. *Entrance requirements:* For master's, minimum GPA of 2.75 in last 60 hours of undergraduate course work, 3.0 graduate. *Application deadline:* For fall admission, 7/15 priority date for domestic students; for spring admission, 11/10 for domestic students. Applications are processed on a rolling basis. Application fee: $25. *Financial support:* Application deadline: 5/1. *Unit head:* Dr. Deborah Bordelon, Dean, 708-534-4050.

Grand Valley State University, College of Education, Program in Special Education, Allendale, MI 49401-9403. Offers cognitive impairment (M Ed); early childhood developmental delay (M Ed); emotional impairment (M Ed); learning disabilities (M Ed); special education endorsements (M Ed). *Accreditation:* NCATE. Part-time and evening/weekend programs available. *Degree requirements:* For master's, thesis. *Entrance requirements:* For master's, GRE General Test or minimum GPA of 3.0. Additional exam requirements/recommendations for international students: Required—TOEFL. Electronic applications accepted. *Faculty research:* Evaluation of special education program effects, adaptive behavior assessment, language development, writing disorders, comparative effects of presentation methods.

Grand Valley State University, College of Education, Programs in General Education, Allendale, MI 49401-9403. Offers adult and higher education (M Ed); early childhood education (M Ed); educational differentiation (M Ed); educational leadership (M Ed); educational technology integration (M Ed); elementary education (M Ed); middle level education (M Ed); school library media services (M Ed); secondary level education (M Ed); teaching English to speakers of other languages (M Ed). Part-time and evening/weekend programs available. Postbaccalaureate distance learning degree programs offered (minimal on-campus study). *Degree requirements:* For master's, thesis. *Entrance requirements:* For master's, GRE General Test or minimum GPA of 3.0. Additional exam requirements/recommendations for international students: Required—TOEFL. Electronic applications accepted. *Faculty research:* Effectiveness of technology in education, parental involvement, effective teaching, effective schools research.

Hampton University, Graduate College, College of Education and Continuing Studies, Program in Teaching, Hampton, VA 23668. Offers early childhood education (MT); middle school education (MT); music education (MT); secondary education (MT); special education (MT). *Entrance requirements:* For master's, GRE General Test.

Harding University, College of Education, Searcy, AR 72149-0001. Offers advanced studies in teaching and learning (M Ed); art (MSE); behavioral science (MSE); counseling (MS, Ed S); early childhood special education (M Ed, MSE); education (MSE); educational leadership (M Ed, Ed S); elementary education (M Ed); English (MSE); French (MSE); history/social science (MSE); kinesiology (MSE); math (MSE); reading (M Ed); secondary education (M Ed); Spanish (MSE); teaching (MAT); teaching English as a second language (MSE). *Accreditation:* NCATE. Part-time and evening/weekend programs available. *Faculty:* 9 full-time (2 women), 48 part-time/adjunct (26 women). *Students:* 100 full-time (77 women), 333 part-time (239 women); includes 76 minority (59 Black or African American, non-Hispanic/Latino; 1 Asian, non-Hispanic/Latino; 10 Hispanic/Latino; 6 Two or more races, non-Hispanic/Latino), 2 international. Average age 36. 93 applicants, 91% accepted, 83 enrolled. In 2011, 159 master's, 10 other advanced degrees awarded. *Degree requirements:* For master's, comprehensive exam (for some programs), thesis optional, portfolio(s); for Ed S, comprehensive exam, portfolio, project. *Entrance requirements:* For master's, GRE, MAT, PRAXIS; for Ed S, MAT or GRE. Additional exam requirements/recommendations for international students: Required—TOEFL (minimum score 550 paper-based; 79 iBT). *Application deadline:* For fall admission, 8/1 for domestic and international students; for spring admission, 1/1 for domestic and international students. Applications are processed on a rolling basis. Application fee: $35. *Expenses: Tuition:* Full-time $10,512; part-time $584 per credit hour. *Required fees:* $500; $25 per credit hour. Tuition and fees vary according to course load, degree level and program. *Financial support:* In 2011–12, 37 students received support. Unspecified assistantships available. *Faculty research:* Reading, comprehension, school violence, educational technology, behavior, college choice, differentiated instruction, brain-based teaching. *Unit head:* Dr. Clara Carroll, Chair, 501-279-4501, Fax: 501-279-4083, E-mail: ccarroll@harding.edu. *Application contact:* Information Contact, 501-279-4315, E-mail: gradstudiesedu@harding.edu. Web site: http://www.harding.edu/education/grad.html.

Hebrew College, Shoolman Graduate School of Jewish Education, Newton Centre, MA 02459. Offers early childhood Jewish education (Certificate); Jewish day school education (Certificate); Jewish education (MJ Ed); Jewish family education (Certificate); Jewish special education (Certificate); Jewish youth education, informal education and camping (Certificate). Part-time and evening/weekend programs available. Postbaccalaureate distance learning degree programs offered. *Degree requirements:* For master's, one foreign language. *Entrance requirements:* For master's, GRE, interview. Additional exam requirements/recommendations for international students: Required—TOEFL.

Henderson State University, Graduate Studies, Teachers College, Department of Advanced Instructional Studies, Arkadelphia, AR 71999-0001. Offers early childhood (P-4) (MSE); education (MAT); middle school (MSE); reading (MSE); special education (MSE). *Accreditation:* NCATE. Part-time programs available. *Entrance requirements:* For master's, GRE General Test or MAT, minimum GPA of 2.7, teacher certification. Additional exam requirements/recommendations for international students: Required—TOEFL (minimum score 550 paper-based; 213 computer-based); Recommended—IELTS (minimum score 6). Electronic applications accepted.

Hofstra University, School of Education, Health, and Human Services, Department of Literacy Studies, Hempstead, NY 11549. Offers advanced literacy studies (PD), including birth-grade 6 (MA, MS Ed, PD); advanced literary studies (PD), including grades 5-12 (MA, PD); birth-grade 6 (MS Ed, Advanced Certificate); grades 5-12 (Advanced Certificate); literacy studies (Ed D, PhD); special education (MS Ed), including birth-grade 2, birth-grade 6 (MA, MS Ed, PD); special education (MS Ed), including birth-grade 2; teaching of writing (MA), including birth-grade 6 (MA, MS Ed, PD), grades 5-12 (MA, PD). Part-time and evening/weekend programs available. *Students:* 43 full-time (42 women), 70 part-time (63 women); includes 15 minority (7 Black or African American, non-Hispanic/Latino; 1 Asian, non-Hispanic/Latino; 7 Hispanic/Latino). Average age 33. 67 applicants, 81% accepted, 32 enrolled. In 2011,

47 master's, 1 doctorate, 10 other advanced degrees awarded. *Degree requirements:* For master's, comprehensive exam, portfolio, minimum GPA of 3.0; for doctorate, one foreign language, comprehensive exam, thesis/dissertation, qualifying hearing, minimum GPA of 3.0. *Entrance requirements:* For master's, interview, teaching certificate, 2 letters of recommendation; for doctorate, GRE or MAT, interview, resume, essay, master's degree, 3 letters of recommendation, writing sample; for other advanced degree, 2 letters of recommendation, interview, teaching certificate, essay, master's degree. Additional exam requirements/recommendations for international students: Required—TOEFL (minimum score 550 paper-based; 213 computer-based; 80 iBT). *Application deadline:* Applications are processed on a rolling basis. Application fee: $70 ($75 for international students). Electronic applications accepted. *Expenses: Tuition:* Full-time $18,990; part-time $1055 per credit hour. *Required fees:* $970. Tuition and fees vary according to program. *Financial support:* In 2011–12, 78 students received support, including 36 fellowships with full and partial tuition reimbursements available (averaging $3,622 per year); research assistantships with full and partial tuition reimbursements available, career-related internships or fieldwork, Federal Work-Study, institutionally sponsored loans, scholarships/grants, tuition waivers (full and partial), and unspecified assistantships also available. Support available to part-time students. Financial award applicants required to submit FAFSA. *Faculty research:* Research literacy practices of immigrant and urban youth, literature for children and adolescents, eye movement/miscue analysis, literacy strategies for effective instruction, transnational literacies. *Unit head:* Dr. Esther Fusco, Chairperson, 516-463-7704, Fax: 516-463-6196, E-mail: catezf@hofstra.edu. *Application contact:* Carol Drummer, Dean of Graduate Admissions, 516-463-4876, Fax: 516-463-4664, E-mail: gradstudent@hofstra.edu. Web site: http://www.hofstra.edu/education/.

Hofstra University, School of Education, Health, and Human Services, Program in Elementary Education, Hempstead, NY 11549. Offers early childhood and childhood education (MS Ed); early childhood education (MA, MS Ed); educational technology (MA); elementary education (MS Ed); literacy (MA); math specialist (Advanced Certificate); math, science, technology (MA); multiculturalism (MA). Part-time and evening/weekend programs available. Postbaccalaureate distance learning degree programs offered (minimal on-campus study). *Students:* 54 full-time (48 women), 43 part-time (37 women); includes 17 minority (10 Black or African American, non-Hispanic/Latino; 2 Asian, non-Hispanic/Latino; 5 Hispanic/Latino), 2 international. Average age 29. 65 applicants, 88% accepted, 18 enrolled. In 2011, 58 master's awarded. *Degree requirements:* For master's, comprehensive exam, thesis (for some programs), 35 semester hours (for MA); 38-41 semester hours (for MS Ed), minimum GPA of 3.0. *Entrance requirements:* For master's, 2 letters of recommendation, teacher certification (MA), interview, essay. Additional exam requirements/recommendations for international students: Required—TOEFL (minimum score 550 paper-based; 213 computer-based; 80 iBT). *Application deadline:* Applications are processed on a rolling basis. Application fee: $70 ($75 for international students). Electronic applications accepted. *Expenses: Tuition:* Full-time $18,990; part-time $1055 per credit hour. *Required fees:* $970. Tuition and fees vary according to program. *Financial support:* In 2011–12, 45 students received support, including 22 fellowships with full and partial tuition reimbursements available (averaging $2,560 per year), 2 research assistantships with full and partial tuition reimbursements available (averaging $21,993 per year); career-related internships or fieldwork, Federal Work-Study, institutionally sponsored loans, scholarships/grants, tuition waivers (full and partial), and unspecified assistantships also available. Support available to part-time students. Financial award applicants required to submit FAFSA. *Faculty research:* Dynamic-themes curriculum/complexity theory, joyful learning, teacher education, multicultural education, multiple authentic assessments. *Unit head:* Dr. Esther Fusco, Chairperson, 516-463-7704, Fax: 516-463-6196, E-mail: catezf@hofstra.edu. *Application contact:* Carol Drummer, Dean of Graduate Admissions, 516-463-4876, Fax: 516-463-4664, E-mail: gradstudent@hofstra.edu. Web site: http://www.hofstra.edu/education/.

Hood College, Graduate School, Department of Education, Frederick, MD 21701-8575. Offers curriculum and instruction (MS), including early childhood education, elementary education, elementary school science and mathematics, secondary education, special education; educational leadership (MS, Certificate); reading specialization (MS). Part-time and evening/weekend programs available. *Degree requirements:* For master's, action research project, portfolio (reading). *Entrance requirements:* For master's, minimum GPA of 2.75, teaching certification. Additional exam requirements/recommendations for international students: Required—TOEFL (minimum score 575 paper-based; 231 computer-based; 89 iBT). Electronic applications accepted. *Faculty research:* Leadership, action research, brain research, learning styles.

Howard University, School of Education, Department of Curriculum and Instruction, Program in Early Childhood Education, Washington, DC 20059-0002. Offers M Ed. *Accreditation:* NCATE. Part-time programs available. *Faculty:* 2 full-time (both women). *Students:* 10 full-time (all women); all minorities (all Black or African American, non-Hispanic/Latino). Average age 22. 12 applicants, 92% accepted, 8 enrolled. In 2011, 5 master's awarded. *Degree requirements:* For master's, comprehensive exam, thesis (for some programs), expository writing exam, internships, practicum. *Entrance requirements:* For master's, minimum GPA of 2.7. Additional exam requirements/recommendations for international students: Required—TOEFL (minimum score 550 paper-based). *Application deadline:* For fall admission, 2/15 priority date for domestic students; for spring admission, 11/1 for domestic students. Applications are processed on a rolling basis. Application fee: $45. Electronic applications accepted. *Financial support:* In 2011–12, 5 students received support, including 3 fellowships with full and partial tuition reimbursements available (averaging $16,000 per year), 1 research assistantship (averaging $2,000 per year); career-related internships or fieldwork, Federal Work-Study, institutionally sponsored loans, scholarships/grants, and unspecified assistantships also available. Financial award application deadline: 3/15; financial award applicants required to submit FAFSA. *Faculty research:* Parental factors on child development, early attachment, cross-culture. *Unit head:* Dr. James T. Jackson, Chair, Department of Curriculum and Instruction, 202-806-5300, Fax: 202-806-5297, E-mail: jt_jackson@howard.edu. *Application contact:* June L. Harris, Administrative Assistant, Department of Curriculum and Instruction, 202-806-7343, Fax: 202-806-5297, E-mail: jlharris@howard.edu.

Hunter College of the City University of New York, Graduate School, School of Education, Department of Curriculum and Teaching, New York, NY 10021-5085. Offers bilingual education (MS); corrective reading (K-12) (MS Ed); early childhood education (MS); educational supervision and administration (AC); elementary education (MS); literacy education (MS); teaching English as a second language (MA). *Faculty:* 31 full-time (20 women), 103 part-time/adjunct (66 women). *Students:* 96 full-time (77 women), 650 part-time (542 women); includes 316 minority (49 Black or African American, non-Hispanic/Latino; 7 American Indian or Alaska Native, non-Hispanic/Latino; 66 Asian, non-Hispanic/Latino; 194 Hispanic/Latino), 11 international. Average age 31. 506 applicants, 62% accepted, 211 enrolled. In 2011, 311 master's, 39 other advanced degrees awarded. *Degree requirements:* For master's, thesis; for AC, portfolio review. *Entrance requirements:* For degree, minimum B average in graduate course work, teaching certificate, minimum 3 years of full-time teaching experience, interview, 2 letters of support. Additional exam requirements/recommendations for international students: Required—TOEFL, TWE. *Application deadline:* For fall admission, 4/1 for domestic students; for spring admission, 11/1 for domestic students. Applications are processed on a rolling basis. Application fee: $125. *Expenses:* Tuition, state resident: full-time $8210; part-time $345 per credit. Tuition, nonresident: full-time $15,360; part-time $640 per credit. *Required fees:* $280 per semester. One-time fee: $125. Tuition and fees vary according to class time, campus/location and program. *Financial support:* Federal Work-Study, scholarships/grants, and tuition waivers (partial) available. Support available to part-time students. *Faculty research:* Teacher opportunity corps-mentor program for first-year teachers, adult literacy, student literacy corporation. *Unit head:* Dr. Anne M. Ediger, Head, 212-777-4686, E-mail: anne.ediger@hunter.cuny.edu. *Application contact:* Milena Solo, Director for Graduate Admissions, 212-772-4482, Fax: 212-650-3336, E-mail: milena.solo@hunter.cuny.edu. Web site: http://www.hunter.cuny.edu/school-of-education/faculty/curriculum-teaching.

Indiana State University, College of Graduate and Professional Studies, College of Education, Department of Elementary, Early and Special Education, Terre Haute, IN 47809. Offers early childhood education (M Ed); elementary education (M Ed); MA/MS. *Accreditation:* NCATE. Electronic applications accepted.

Indiana University–Purdue University Indianapolis, School of Education, Indianapolis, IN 46202-2896. Offers computer education (Certificate); curriculum and instruction (MS); early childhood (MS); educational leadership (MS, Certificate); English as a second language (Certificate); higher education and student affairs (MS); kindergarten (Certificate); language education (MS); reading (Certificate); school counseling (MS); special education (MS, Certificate). Part-time and evening/weekend programs available. *Faculty:* 41 full-time, 80 part-time/adjunct. *Students:* 67 full-time (52 women), 467 part-time (360 women); includes 82 minority (44 Black or African American, non-Hispanic/Latino; 3 American Indian or Alaska Native, non-Hispanic/Latino; 8 Asian, non-Hispanic/Latino; 13 Hispanic/Latino; 14 Two or more races, non-Hispanic/Latino), 10 international. Average age 33. 63 applicants, 57% accepted, 29 enrolled. In 2011, 167 master's awarded. *Degree requirements:* For master's, thesis optional. *Entrance requirements:* For master's, GRE General Test, minimum GPA of 3.0. Additional exam requirements/recommendations for international students: Required—TOEFL. *Application deadline:* For fall admission, 5/1 priority date for domestic students; for spring admission, 11/1 for domestic students. Application fee: $55 ($65 for international students). *Financial support:* Fellowships, research assistantships with partial tuition reimbursements, teaching assistantships, Federal Work-Study, institutionally sponsored loans, scholarships/grants, and tuition waivers (partial) available. Support available to part-time students. *Faculty research:* Teachers in the process of change, learning cycles, children's concepts of science. *Total annual research expenditures:* $614,458. *Unit head:* Dr. Chris Leland, Interim Executive Associate Dean, 317-274-6801, Fax: 317-274-6864. *Application contact:* Sarah Brandenburg, Graduate Advisor, 317-274-6801, Fax: 317-274-6864, E-mail: edugrad@iupui.edu. Web site: http://education.iupui.edu/.

Inter American University of Puerto Rico, Guayama Campus, Department of Education and Social Sciences, Guayama, PR 00785. Offers early childhood education (0-4 years) (M Ed); elementary education (M Ed). Part-time programs available. *Entrance requirements:* For master's, GRE, MAT, EXADEP, letters of recommendation, minimum GPA of 2.5. Electronic applications accepted.

Iona College, School of Arts and Science, Program in Education, New Rochelle, NY 10801-1890. Offers adolescence education: biology (MS Ed, MST); adolescence education: English (MS Ed, MST); adolescence education: Italian (MS Ed, MST); adolescence education: mathematics (MS Ed, MST); adolescence education: social studies (MS Ed, MST); adolescence education: Spanish (MS Ed, MST); adolescence special education 5-12 (MST); adolescence special education/literacy 5-12 (MS Ed); childhood 1-6/special education 1-6 (MST); childhood education (MST); early childhood/childhood (MST); educational leadership (MS Ed); literacy birth-grade 6/special education 1-6 (MS Ed); literacy education: birth-grade 6 (MS Ed). *Accreditation:* NCATE. Part-time and evening/weekend programs available. *Faculty:* 21 full-time (13 women), 13 part-time/adjunct (8 women). *Students:* 59 full-time (45 women), 101 part-time (78 women); includes 11 minority (2 Black or African American, non-Hispanic/Latino; 2 Asian, non-Hispanic/Latino; 7 Hispanic/Latino). Average age 26. 74 applicants, 66% accepted, 35 enrolled. In 2011, 46 master's awarded. *Degree requirements:* For master's, thesis or alternative. *Entrance requirements:* For master's, minimum GPA of 2.5 (MST), New York teaching certificate (MS Ed). Additional exam requirements/recommendations for international students: Required—TOEFL (minimum score 550 paper-based; 213 computer-based). *Application deadline:* Applications are processed on a rolling basis. Application fee: $50. Electronic applications accepted. *Expenses: Tuition:* Part-time $872 per credit. *Required fees:* $225 per term. *Financial support:* Unspecified assistantships available. Support available to part-time students. Financial award application deadline: 4/15; financial award applicants required to submit FAFSA. *Faculty research:* Reading/writing, educational technology, administration, early literacy assessment, literacy development. *Unit head:* Dr. Catherine O'Callaghan, Chair, 914-633-2210, Fax: 914-633-2608, E-mail: cocallaghan@iona.edu. *Application contact:* Dr. Jeanne Zaino, Interim Dean, School of Arts and Science, 914-633-2112, Fax: 914-633-2023, E-mail: jzaino@iona.edu.

Jackson State University, Graduate School, College of Education and Human Development, Department of Elementary and Early Childhood Education, Jackson, MS 39217. Offers early childhood education (MS Ed, Ed D); elementary education (MS Ed, Ed S). *Accreditation:* NCATE. Evening/weekend programs available. Terminal master's awarded for partial completion of doctoral program. *Degree requirements:* For master's, comprehensive exam, thesis or alternative; for doctorate, comprehensive exam, thesis/dissertation. *Entrance requirements:* For master's, GRE General Test; for doctorate, MAT, teaching experience. Additional exam requirements/recommendations for international students: Required—TOEFL (minimum score 520 paper-based; 195 computer-based; 67 iBT).

Jacksonville State University, College of Graduate Studies and Continuing Education, College of Education and Professional Studies, Program in Early Childhood Education, Jacksonville, AL 36265-1602. Offers MS Ed. *Accreditation:* NCATE. Part-time and evening/weekend programs available. *Faculty:* 10 full-time (8 women). *Students:* 4 full-time (all women), 10 part-time (all women); includes 2 minority (both Black or African American, non-Hispanic/Latino). Average age 33. 16 applicants, 19% accepted, 3 enrolled. In 2011, 6 degrees awarded. *Degree requirements:* For master's, comprehensive exam, thesis (for some programs). *Entrance requirements:* For master's, GRE General Test or MAT. *Application deadline:* Applications are processed on a rolling basis. Application fee: $30. Electronic applications accepted. *Expenses:* Tuition, state resident: part-time $336 per hour. Tuition, nonresident: part-time $672 per hour. Part-time tuition and fees vary according to degree level. *Financial support:* In 2011–12, 11 students received support. Available to part-time students. Application deadline: 4/1; applicants required to submit FAFSA. *Unit head:* Dr. Elizabeth Engley, Head, 256-782-5844. *Application contact:* Dr. Jean Pugliese, Associate Dean, 256-782-8279, Fax: 256-782-5321, E-mail: pugliese@jsu.edu.

James Madison University, The Graduate School, College of Education, Early, Elementary, and Reading Education Department, Program in Early Childhood Education, Harrisonburg, VA 22807. Offers M Ed. *Accreditation:* NCATE. Part-time programs available. *Students:* Average age 27. *Entrance requirements:* For master's,

GRE General Test or MAT, PRAXIS I and II, 2-3 page written statement, faculty interview, minimum undergraduate GPA of 2.75. Additional exam requirements/recommendations for international students: Required—TOEFL. *Application deadline:* For fall admission, 5/1 priority date for domestic students; for spring admission, 9/1 priority date for domestic students. Applications are processed on a rolling basis. Application fee: $55. Electronic applications accepted. *Expenses:* Tuition, state resident: full-time $8016; part-time $334 per credit hour. Tuition, nonresident: full-time $22,656; part-time $944 per credit hour. *Financial support:* Career-related internships or fieldwork and unspecified assistantships available. Financial award application deadline: 3/1; financial award applicants required to submit FAFSA. *Unit head:* Dr. Martha Ross, Academic Unit Head, 540-568-6255. *Application contact:* Lynette M. Bible, Director of Graduate Admissions, 540-568-6395, Fax: 540-568-7860, E-mail: biblelm@jmu.edu.

John Carroll University, Graduate School, Department of Education and Allied Studies, Program in School Based Early Childhood Education, University Heights, OH 44118-4581. Offers M Ed. *Accreditation:* NCATE. *Degree requirements:* For master's, comprehensive exam. *Entrance requirements:* For master's, GRE General Test or MAT, minimum GPA of 2.75, interview. Additional exam requirements/recommendations for international students: Required—TOEFL. Electronic applications accepted.

The Johns Hopkins University, School of Education, Department of Special Education, Baltimore, MD 21218. Offers advanced methods for differentiated instruction and inclusive education (Certificate); assistive technology (Certificate); early intervention/preschool special education specialist (Certificate); education of students with autism and other pervasive developmental disorders (Certificate); education of students with severe disabilities (Certificate); special education (MS, Ed D, CAGS), including early childhood special education (MS), general special education studies (MS), mild to moderate disabilities (MS), severe disabilities (MS), technology in special education (MS). *Accreditation:* NCATE. Part-time and evening/weekend programs available. Postbaccalaureate distance learning degree programs offered (minimal on-campus study). *Degree requirements:* For master's, internships, professional portfolio, and PRAXIS II (for licensure); for doctorate, comprehensive exam, thesis/dissertation. *Entrance requirements:* For master's, PRAXIS I, SAT, ACT, or GRE, minimum undergraduate GPA of 3.0, 2 letters of recommendation (for cohort programs); for doctorate, GRE, degree in special education (or related field); minimum GPA of 3.0 in all prior academic work; 3 letters of recommendation; curriculum vitae/resume; professional experience; for other advanced degree, minimum undergraduate GPA of 3.0, master's degree (for CAGS). Additional exam requirements/recommendations for international students: Required—TOEFL (minimum score 600 paper-based; 250 computer-based; 100 iBT). Electronic applications accepted. *Faculty research:* Alternative licensure programs for special educators, collaborative programming, data-based decision-making and knowledge management as keys to school reform, parent training, natural environment teaching (NET).

The Johns Hopkins University, School of Education, Department of Teacher Preparation, Baltimore, MD 21218. Offers early childhood education (MAT); education (MS), including educational studies; elementary education (MAT); English for speakers of other languages (MAT); K-8 mathematics lead-teacher (Certificate); K-8 science lead-teacher (Certificate); secondary education (MAT), including biology, chemistry, earth/space/environmental science, English, French, mathematics, physics, social studies, Spanish. Part-time and evening/weekend programs available. *Degree requirements:* For master's, portfolio, PRAXIS II, internship. *Entrance requirements:* For master's, PRAXIS I, SAT, ACT, or GRE (MAT), minimum undergraduate GPA of 3.0, interview, 1 letter of recommendation, curriculum vitae/resume; for Certificate, bachelor's degree, minimum undergraduate GPA of 3.0, essay/statement of goals, interview. Additional exam requirements/recommendations for international students: Required—TOEFL (minimum score 600 paper-based; 250 computer-based; 100 iBT). Electronic applications accepted. *Faculty research:* Teacher retention, STEM education reform, alternative certification programs, school-university partnerships, urban education, action research/data-informed instruction, family engagement.

Kansas State University, Graduate School, College of Human Ecology, School of Family Studies and Human Services, Manhattan, KS 66506. Offers communication sciences and disorders (MS); early childhood education (MS); family studies (MS); life span human development (MS); marriage and family therapy (MS). *Accreditation:* AAMFT/COAMFTE; ASHA. Part-time programs available. *Faculty:* 28 full-time (18 women), 4 part-time/adjunct (3 women). *Students:* 56 full-time (47 women), 158 part-time (100 women); includes 34 minority (19 Black or African American, non-Hispanic/Latino; 3 American Indian or Alaska Native, non-Hispanic/Latino; 4 Asian, non-Hispanic/Latino; 7 Hispanic/Latino; 1 Two or more races, non-Hispanic/Latino), 2 international. Average age 32. 195 applicants, 41% accepted, 46 enrolled. In 2011, 56 master's awarded. *Degree requirements:* For master's, thesis or alternative, oral exam, residency. *Entrance requirements:* For master's, GRE, minimum GPA of 3.0 in last 2 years of undergraduate study. Additional exam requirements/recommendations for international students: Required—TOEFL (minimum score 600 paper-based; 250 computer-based). *Application deadline:* For fall admission, 2/1 priority date for domestic students, 2/1 for international students; for spring admission, 8/1 priority date for domestic students, 8/1 for international students. Applications are processed on a rolling basis. Application fee: $40 ($55 for international students). Electronic applications accepted. *Financial support:* In 2011–12, 27 research assistantships (averaging $12,839 per year), 17 teaching assistantships with full and partial tuition reimbursements (averaging $12,771 per year) were awarded; Federal Work-Study, institutionally sponsored loans, scholarships/grants, and unspecified assistantships also available. Support available to part-time students. Financial award application deadline: 3/1; financial award applicants required to submit FAFSA. *Faculty research:* Health and security of military families, personal and family risk assessment and evaluation, disorders of communication and swallowing, families and health. *Total annual research expenditures:* $13.5 million. *Unit head:* Dr. Maurice McDonald, Head, 785-532-5510, Fax: 785-532-5505, E-mail: morey@ksu.edu. *Application contact:* Connie Fechter, Administrative Specialist, 785-532-5510, Fax: 785-532-5505, E-mail: fechter@ksu.edu. Web site: http://www.he.k-state.edu/fshs/.

Kean University, College of Education, Program in Early Childhood Education, Union, NJ 07083. Offers administration in early childhood and family studies (MA); advanced curriculum and teaching (MA); classroom instruction (MA), including preschool-third grade; education for family living (MA). *Accreditation:* NCATE. *Faculty:* 22 full-time (12 women). *Students:* 9 full-time (all women), 40 part-time (38 women); includes 15 minority (7 Black or African American, non-Hispanic/Latino; 1 American Indian or Alaska Native, non-Hispanic/Latino; 2 Asian, non-Hispanic/Latino; 5 Hispanic/Latino), 2 international. Average age 33. 26 applicants, 100% accepted, 19 enrolled. In 2011, 12 master's awarded. *Degree requirements:* For master's, portfolio. *Entrance requirements:* For master's, GRE General Test, minimum GPA of 3.0, 2 letters of recommendation, interview, teacher certification (for some programs), writing sample, official transcripts, resume. Additional exam requirements/recommendations for international students: Required—TOEFL (minimum score 79 iBT). *Application deadline:* For fall admission, 6/1 for domestic and international students; for spring admission, 12/1 for domestic and international students. Applications are processed on a rolling basis. Application fee: $75 ($150 for international students). Electronic applications accepted. *Expenses:* Tuition, state resident: full-time $11,302; part-time $550 per credit. Tuition, nonresident: full-time $15,318; part-time $674 per credit. *Required fees:* $2849; $130 per credit. Tuition and fees vary according to degree level. *Financial support:* In 2011–12, 1 research assistantship with full tuition reimbursement (averaging $3,263 per year) was awarded; unspecified assistantships also available. Financial award applicants required to submit FAFSA. *Unit head:* Dr. Jennifer Chen, Program Coordinator, 908-737-3809, E-mail: jchen@kean.edu. *Application contact:* Ann-Marie Kay, Assistant Director of Graduate Admissions, 908-737-5922, Fax: 908-737-5925, E-mail: akay@kean.edu. Web site: http://www.kean.edu/KU/Administration-in-Early-Childhood-Family-Studies.

Kennesaw State University, Leland and Clarice C. Bagwell College of Education, Program in Graduate Education, Kennesaw, GA 30144-5591. Offers adolescent education (M Ed); educational leadership (M Ed); educational leadership technology (M Ed); elementary and early childhood education (M Ed); special education (M Ed); teaching English to speakers of other languages (M Ed). *Accreditation:* NCATE. Part-time programs available. *Students:* 42 full-time (39 women), 132 part-time (105 women); includes 31 minority (20 Black or African American, non-Hispanic/Latino; 4 Asian, non-Hispanic/Latino; 5 Hispanic/Latino; 2 Two or more races, non-Hispanic/Latino). Average age 34. 48 applicants, 79% accepted, 38 enrolled. In 2011, 117 master's awarded. *Degree requirements:* For master's, thesis or alternative. *Entrance requirements:* For master's, GRE General Test, T-4 state certification, minimum GPA of 2.75. Additional exam requirements/recommendations for international students: Required—TOEFL (minimum score 550 paper-based; 213 computer-based; 80 iBT), IELTS (minimum score 6). *Application deadline:* For fall admission, 7/1 for domestic and international students; for spring admission, 10/1 for domestic and international students. Application fee: $60. Electronic applications accepted. *Expenses:* Tuition, state resident: full-time $3000; part-time $250 per semester hour. Tuition, nonresident: full-time $10,836; part-time $903 per semester hour. *Required fees:* $774 per semester. *Financial support:* Federal Work-Study and unspecified assistantships available. Support available to part-time students. Financial award application deadline: 4/1; financial award applicants required to submit FAFSA. *Unit head:* Dr. Nita Paris, Associate Dean for Graduate Programs, 770-423-6636, E-mail: nparis@kennesaw.edu. *Application contact:* Alisha Bello, Administrative Coordinator, 770-423-6043, Fax: 770-420-4435, E-mail: abello1@kennesaw.edu. Web site: http://www.kennesaw.edu/education/grad/.

Kent State University, Graduate School of Education, Health, and Human Services, School of Lifespan Development and Educational Sciences, Kent, OH 44242-0001. Offers clinical mental health counseling (M Ed); counseling (Ed S); counseling and human development services (PhD); educational interpreter K-12 (M Ed); educational psychology (M Ed, MA, PhD); human development and family studies (MA); instructional technology (M Ed), including computer technology, general instructional technology; rehabilitation counseling (M Ed); school counseling (M Ed); school psychology (M Ed, PhD, Ed S); special education (M Ed, PhD, Ed S), including deaf education (M Ed), early childhood intervention specialist (M Ed), general special education (M Ed), gifted education (M Ed), mild/moderate intervention (M Ed), moderate/intensive intervention (M Ed), special education (PhD, Ed S), transition to work (M Ed). Part-time and evening/weekend programs available. *Faculty:* 142 full-time (72 women), 155 part-time/adjunct (117 women). *Students:* 409 full-time (334 women), 327 part-time (264 women); includes 65 minority (48 Black or African American, non-Hispanic/Latino; 5 Asian, non-Hispanic/Latino; 11 Hispanic/Latino; 1 Native Hawaiian or other Pacific Islander, non-Hispanic/Latino). 374 applicants, 52% accepted. In 2011, 198 master's, 10 doctorates, 15 other advanced degrees awarded. *Degree requirements:* For master's, thesis optional; for doctorate, comprehensive exam, thesis/dissertation. *Entrance requirements:* For master's, doctorate, and Ed S, GRE General Test. Additional exam requirements/recommendations for international students: Required—TOEFL (minimum score 550 paper-based; 213 computer-based; 80 iBT). *Application deadline:* Applications are processed on a rolling basis. Application fee: $30 ($60 for international students). Electronic applications accepted. *Expenses:* Tuition, state resident: full-time $8136; part-time $452 per credit hour. Tuition, nonresident: full-time $14,292; part-time $794 per credit hour. *Financial support:* In 2011–12, 6 fellowships with full tuition reimbursements (averaging $12,000 per year), 27 research assistantships with full tuition reimbursements (averaging $9,426 per year) were awarded; teaching assistantships with full tuition reimbursements, Federal Work-Study, scholarships/grants, unspecified assistantships, and 14 administrative assistantships (averaging $9,250 per year) also available. Financial award application deadline: 4/1. *Unit head:* Dr. Mary Dellmann-Jenkins, Director, 330-672-6958, E-mail: mdellman@kent.edu. *Application contact:* Nancy Miller, Academic Program Coordinator, Office of Graduate Student Services, 330-672-2576, Fax: 330-672-9162, E-mail: ogs@kent.edu. Web site: http://www.kent.edu/ehhs/ldes/.

Kent State University, Graduate School of Education, Health, and Human Services, School of Teaching, Learning and Curriculum Studies, Program in Early Childhood Education, Kent, OH 44242-0001. Offers M Ed, MA, MAT. *Accreditation:* NCATE. *Faculty:* 5 full-time (all women), 1 (woman) part-time/adjunct. *Students:* 21 full-time (19 women), 7 part-time (all women). 30 applicants, 40% accepted. In 2011, 13 master's awarded. *Degree requirements:* For master's, thesis (for some programs). *Entrance requirements:* For master's, GRE General Test (for licensure), 2 letters of reference, goals statement. Additional exam requirements/recommendations for international students: Required—TOEFL (minimum score 550 paper-based; 213 computer-based; 80 iBT). *Application deadline:* For spring admission, 3/1 for domestic students. Applications are processed on a rolling basis. Application fee: $30 ($60 for international students). Electronic applications accepted. *Expenses:* Tuition, state resident: full-time $8136; part-time $452 per credit hour. Tuition, nonresident: full-time $14,292; part-time $794 per credit hour. *Financial support:* Research assistantships with full tuition reimbursements, Federal Work-Study, scholarships/grants, and unspecified assistantships available. Financial award application deadline: 4/1; financial award applicants required to submit FAFSA. *Faculty research:* Parent-child relationships, professional preparation, curriculum and assessment. *Unit head:* Martha Lash, Coordinator, 330-672-0628, E-mail: mlash@kent.edu. *Application contact:* Nancy Miller, Academic Program Coordinator, Office of Graduate Student Services, 330-672-2576, Fax: 330-672-9162, E-mail: ogs@kent.edu.

Keuka College, Program in Childhood Education/Literacy, Keuka Park, NY 14478-0098. Offers MS. Part-time and evening/weekend programs available. *Degree requirements:* For master's, thesis, research project, portfolio. *Entrance requirements:* For master's, minimum undergraduate GPA of 3.0, 2 letters of recommendation, provisional New York state certification. Additional exam requirements/recommendations for international students: Required—TOEFL (minimum score 550 paper-based; 213 computer-based). *Expenses:* Contact institution. *Faculty research:* Reading and writing across the curriculum, science education, elementary mathematics education, special education, critical thinking.

Lehman College of the City University of New York, Division of Education, Department of Early Childhood and Elementary Education, Program in Early Childhood Education, Bronx, NY 10468-1589. Offers MS Ed. *Accreditation:* NCATE. Part-time and evening/weekend programs available. *Entrance requirements:* For master's, minimum GPA of 2.7. *Faculty research:* TV programming, literacy, children's trauma conceptualization.

Le Moyne College, Department of Education, Syracuse, NY 13214. Offers adolescent education (MS Ed, MST); adolescent education/special education (MS Ed, MST); adolescent English (grades 7-12) (MST); adolescent history (grades 7-12) (MST); childhood education (MS Ed); childhood education/special education (MS Ed); elementary education (MS Ed); general professional education (MS Ed); inclusive childhood education (MST); literacy education (birth to grade 6) (MS Ed); literacy education (grades 5-12) (MS Ed); school building leadership (MS Ed, CAS); school district business leader (MS Ed, CAS); school district leadership (MS Ed, CAS); secondary education (MS Ed); special education (MS Ed); students with disabilities-generalist (grades 7-12) (MS Ed); TESOL (teaching English to speakers of other languages) (MS Ed); urban studies (MS Ed). *Accreditation:* Teacher Education Accreditation Council. Part-time and evening/weekend programs available. *Faculty:* 9 full-time (6 women), 51 part-time/adjunct (28 women). *Students:* 61 full-time (47 women), 311 part-time (222 women); includes 31 minority (19 Black or African American, non-Hispanic/Latino; 3 American Indian or Alaska Native, non-Hispanic/Latino; 4 Asian, non-Hispanic/Latino; 5 Hispanic/Latino), 2 international. Average age 30. 242 applicants, 90% accepted, 180 enrolled. In 2011, 168 master's, 23 CASs awarded. *Degree requirements:* For master's, thesis. *Entrance requirements:* For master's, GRE General Test, bachelor's degree, 2 letters of recommendation, written statement, transcripts. Additional exam requirements/recommendations for international students: Required—TOEFL (minimum score 550 paper-based; 213 computer-based; 79 iBT). *Application deadline:* For fall admission, 4/1 priority date for domestic students, 4/1 for international students; for spring admission, 10/1 priority date for domestic students, 10/1 for international students. Applications are processed on a rolling basis. Application fee: $50. *Expenses:* Contact institution. *Financial support:* In 2011–12, 32 students received support. Career-related internships or fieldwork and health care benefits available. Support available to part-time students. Financial award applicants required to submit FAFSA. *Faculty research:* Minority teachers, special education, multiculturalism, literacy, technology, video games learning, autism, school district organization, service-learning, higher level problem solving, teacher leadership. *Unit head:* Dr. Suzanne L. Gilmour, Chair, Department of Education and Director of Graduate Education Programs, 315-445-4376, Fax: 315-445-4744, E-mail: gilmous@lemoyne.edu. *Application contact:* Kristen P. Trapasso, Director of Graduate Admission, 315-445-4265, Fax: 315-445-6027, E-mail: trapaskp@lemoyne.edu. Web site: http://www.lemoyne.edu/education.

Lenoir-Rhyne University, Graduate Programs, School of Education, Program in Birth through Kindergarten Education, Hickory, NC 28601. Offers MA. Part-time and evening/weekend programs available. *Degree requirements:* For master's, comprehensive exam, thesis optional. *Entrance requirements:* For master's, GRE General Test or MAT, minimum undergraduate GPA of 2.7, graduate 3.0. Additional exam requirements/recommendations for international students: Required—TOEFL (minimum score 600 paper-based). Electronic applications accepted.

Lesley University, School of Education, Cambridge, MA 02138-2790. Offers curriculum and instruction (M Ed, CAGS); early childhood education (M Ed); educational studies (PhD); elementary education (M Ed); individually designed (M Ed); middle school education (M Ed); moderate special needs (M Ed); reading (M Ed, CAGS); science in education (M Ed); severe special needs (M Ed); special needs (CAGS); technology in education (M Ed, CAGS). *Accreditation:* Teacher Education Accreditation Council. Part-time and evening/weekend programs available. Postbaccalaureate distance learning degree programs offered (no on-campus study). *Faculty:* 36 full-time (27 women), 170 part-time/adjunct (129 women). *Students:* 552 full-time (437 women), 1,971 part-time (1,697 women); includes 364 minority (189 Black or African American, non-Hispanic/Latino; 19 American Indian or Alaska Native, non-Hispanic/Latino; 45 Asian, non-Hispanic/Latino; 83 Hispanic/Latino; 2 Native Hawaiian or other Pacific Islander, non-Hispanic/Latino; 26 Two or more races, non-Hispanic/Latino), 28 international. Average age 37. In 2011, 1,390 master's, 8 doctorates, 42 other advanced degrees awarded. *Degree requirements:* For master's, practicum; for doctorate, thesis/dissertation. *Entrance requirements:* For doctorate, GRE General Test or MAT, interview, master's degree, resume; for CAGS, interview, master's degree. Additional exam requirements/recommendations for international students: Required—TOEFL (minimum score 550 paper-based; 213 computer-based; 80 iBT). *Application deadline:* Applications are processed on a rolling basis. Application fee: $50. Electronic applications accepted. *Financial support:* In 2011–12, research assistantships (averaging $3,400 per year), teaching assistantships (averaging $3,400 per year) were awarded; career-related internships or fieldwork, Federal Work-Study, scholarships/grants, and unspecified assistantships also available. Support available to part-time students. Financial award application deadline: 4/15; financial award applicants required to submit FAFSA. *Faculty research:* Assessment in literacy, mathematics and science; autism spectrum disorders; instructional technology and online learning; multicultural education and ELL. *Unit head:* Dr. Mario Borunda, Dean, 617-349-8375, Fax: 617-349-8607, E-mail: mborunda@lesley.edu. *Application contact:* Rosie Davis, Senior Assistant Director of Admissions, 617-349-8851, Fax: 617-349-8313, E-mail: rdavis4@lesley.edu. Web site: http://www.lesley.edu/soe.html.

Lewis & Clark College, Graduate School of Education and Counseling, Department of Teacher Education, Program in Early Childhood/Elementary Education, Portland, OR 97219-7899. Offers MAT. *Accreditation:* NCATE. *Faculty:* 5 full-time (4 women), 2 part-time/adjunct (1 woman). *Students:* 54 full-time (47 women), 4 part-time (1 woman); includes 12 minority (1 Black or African American, non-Hispanic/Latino; 3 American Indian or Alaska Native, non-Hispanic/Latino; 4 Asian, non-Hispanic/Latino; 2 Hispanic/Latino; 2 Two or more races, non-Hispanic/Latino), 1 international. Average age 29. 98 applicants, 85% accepted, 55 enrolled. In 2011, 69 master's awarded. *Entrance requirements:* For master's, minimum undergraduate GPA of 2.75; history of work, either volunteer or paid, with children in grades K-6. Additional exam requirements/recommendations for international students: Required—TOEFL (minimum score 575 paper-based; 233 computer-based). *Application deadline:* For fall admission, 12/1 priority date for domestic students, 12/1 for international students. Application fee: $50. Electronic applications accepted. *Expenses: Tuition:* Part-time $738 per semester hour. Tuition and fees vary according to course level and campus/location. *Financial support:* In 2011–12, 11 students received support. Career-related internships or fieldwork, Federal Work-Study, institutionally sponsored loans, scholarships/grants, health care benefits, and tuition waivers (partial) available. Support available to part-time students. Financial award application deadline: 3/1; financial award applicants required to submit FAFSA. *Faculty research:* Classroom ethnography, assessing student learning, reading, moral development, language arts. *Unit head:* Dr. Linda Griffin, Program Director, 503-768-6100, Fax: 503-768-6115, E-mail: lcteach@lclark.edu. *Application contact:* Becky Haas, Director of Admissions, 503-768-6200, Fax: 503-768-6205, E-mail: gseadmit@lclark.edu. Web site: http://graduate.lclark.edu/departments/teacher_education/prospective_teachers/early_childhood_elementary/.

Lewis University, College of Education, Romeoville, IL 60446. Offers advanced study in education (CAS), including general administrative, superintendent endorsement; curriculum and instruction: instructional technology (M Ed); early childhood education (MA); educational leadership (M Ed, MA); educational leadership for teaching and learning (Ed D); elementary education (MA); English as a second language (M Ed); instructional technology (M Ed); reading and literacy (M Ed, MA); secondary education (MA), including biology, chemistry, English, history, math, physics, psychology and social science; special education (MA). *Accreditation:* NCATE. Part-time and evening/weekend programs available. *Faculty:* 23 full-time (16 women), 40 part-time/adjunct (25 women). *Students:* 76 full-time (55 women), 388 part-time (312 women); includes 101 minority (56 Black or African American, non-Hispanic/Latino; 7 Asian, non-Hispanic/Latino; 36 Hispanic/Latino; 1 Native Hawaiian or other Pacific Islander, non-Hispanic/Latino; 1 Two or more races, non-Hispanic/Latino), 1 international. Average age 34. In 2011, 111 master's, 7 doctorates awarded. *Degree requirements:* For master's, thesis optional; for doctorate, thesis/dissertation. *Entrance requirements:* For master's, departmental qualifying exam, writing exam, minimum GPA of 2.75, 3 letters of recommendation, interview. Additional exam requirements/recommendations for international students: Required—TOEFL (minimum score 550 paper-based; 213 computer-based; 80 iBT). *Application deadline:* For fall admission, 5/1 for international students; for spring admission, 11/15 for international students. Applications are processed on a rolling basis. Application fee: $40. Electronic applications accepted. *Financial support:* Federal Work-Study, scholarships/grants, tuition waivers (partial), and unspecified assistantships available. Financial award application deadline: 5/1; financial award applicants required to submit FAFSA. *Unit head:* Dr. Jeanette Mines, Dean, 815-838-0500 Ext. 5316, Fax: 815-836-5879, E-mail: minesje@lewisu.edu. *Application contact:* Kelly Lofgren, Graduate Admission Counselor, 815-836-5704, Fax: 815-836-5578, E-mail: lofgreke@lewisu.edu.

Liberty University, School of Education, Lynchburg, VA 24502. Offers administration and supervision (M Ed); curriculum and instruction (M Ed); early childhood education (M Ed); educational leadership (Ed D, Ed S); educational technology and online instruction (M Ed); elementary education (M Ed, MAT); gifted education (M Ed); math specialist (M Ed); middle grades (M Ed); outdoor adventure sport (MS); reading specialist (M Ed); school counseling (M Ed); secondary education (M Ed, MAT); special education (M Ed, MAT); sports administration (MS); teaching and learning (Ed D, Ed S). *Accreditation:* NCATE. Part-time programs available. Postbaccalaureate distance learning degree programs offered (minimal on-campus study). *Students:* 2,245 full-time (1,572 women), 3,500 part-time (2,558 women); includes 1,141 minority (888 Black or African American, non-Hispanic/Latino; 19 American Indian or Alaska Native, non-Hispanic/Latino; 21 Asian, non-Hispanic/Latino; 123 Hispanic/Latino; 9 Native Hawaiian or other Pacific Islander, non-Hispanic/Latino; 81 Two or more races, non-Hispanic/Latino), 76 international. Average age 37. In 2011, 760 master's, 48 doctorates, 321 other advanced degrees awarded. *Degree requirements:* For doctorate, comprehensive exam, thesis/dissertation. *Entrance requirements:* For master's, GRE General Test or MAT (if taken in or before 1999), 2 letters of recommendation, minimum undergraduate GPA of 3.0, curriculum vitae; for doctorate, GRE General Test or MAT (if taken before 1999), minimum master's GPA of 3.0, 3 years of teacher experience; for Ed S, GRE General Test or MAT (if taken before 1999), minimum master's GPA of 3.0, 3 years of teaching experience. Additional exam requirements/recommendations for international students: Required—TOEFL (minimum score 600 paper-based; 250 computer-based). *Application deadline:* For fall admission, 6/1 priority date for domestic students; for spring admission, 11/1 for domestic students. Applications are processed on a rolling basis. Application fee: $50. Electronic applications accepted. *Expenses:* Contact institution. *Financial support:* Federal Work-Study and tuition waivers (partial) available. *Faculty research:* Self-determination, character education, bibliotherapy, learning styles, distance education. *Unit head:* Dr. Karen L. Parker, Dean, 434-582-2195, Fax: 434-582-2468, E-mail: kparker@liberty.edu. *Application contact:* Jay Bridge, Director of Graduate Admissions, 800-424-9595, Fax: 800-628-7977, E-mail: gradadmissions@liberty.edu. Web site: http://www.liberty.edu/academics/education/graduate/.

Lincoln University, Graduate Center, Lincoln University, PA 19352. Offers administration (MSA), including finance, human resources management; early childhood education (M Ed); elementary education (M Ed); human services (M Hum Svcs); reading (MSR). Evening/weekend programs available. *Degree requirements:* For master's, thesis. *Entrance requirements:* For master's, 5 years of work experience in human services. *Faculty research:* Gerontology/minority aging, computers in composition instruction.

Long Island University–Brentwood Campus, School of Education, Brentwood, NY 11717. Offers childhood education (MS); early childhood education (MS); literacy (MS); mental health counseling (MS); school counseling (MS); special education (MS). Part-time and evening/weekend programs available.

Long Island University–C. W. Post Campus, School of Education, Department of Curriculum and Instruction, Brookville, NY 11548-1300. Offers adolescence education (MS); adolescence education: biology (MS); adolescence education: earth science (MS); adolescence education: English (MS); adolescence education: mathematics (MS); adolescence education: social studies (MS); adolescence education: Spanish (MS); art education (MS); bilingual education (MS); childhood education (MS); early childhood education (MS); middle childhood education (MS); music education (MS); teaching English to speakers of other languages (MS). Part-time and evening/weekend programs available. *Degree requirements:* For master's, comprehensive exam or thesis, student teaching. *Entrance requirements:* For master's, minimum GPA of 2.75 in major, 2.5 overall. Electronic applications accepted. *Faculty research:* Ethics and education, teaching strategies.

Long Island University–Hudson at Rockland, Graduate School, Program in Curriculum and Instruction, Orangeburg, NY 10962. Offers adolescence education (MS Ed); childhood education (MS Ed). Part-time and evening/weekend programs available. *Degree requirements:* For master's, LAST and CST exams. *Entrance requirements:* For master's, college transcripts, letters of recommendation, personal statement.

Long Island University–Hudson at Westchester, Programs in Education-Teaching, Program in Early Childhood Education, Purchase, NY 10577. Offers MS Ed, Advanced Certificate.

Long Island University–Riverhead, Education Division, Program in Childhood Education, Riverhead, NY 11901. Offers childhood education (MS Ed); elementary education (MS Ed). *Accreditation:* Teacher Education Accreditation Council. *Faculty:* 1 full-time (0 women), 11 part-time/adjunct (7 women). *Students:* 19 full-time (17 women), 17 part-time (16 women); includes 4 minority (2 Black or African American, non-Hispanic/Latino; 2 Hispanic/Latino). Average age 30. In 2011, 22 master's awarded. *Degree requirements:* For master's, thesis. *Entrance requirements:* For master's, minimum undergraduate GPA of 2.75, on-campus writing sample. Additional exam requirements/recommendations for international students: Required—TOEFL (minimum score 550 paper-based; 250 computer-based). *Application deadline:* Applications are processed on a rolling basis. Application fee: $30. Electronic applications accepted. *Expenses: Tuition:* Part-time $1028 per credit. *Financial support:* In 2011–12, 1 research assistantship with full tuition reimbursement was awarded; scholarships/grants and unspecified assistantships also available. Support available to part-time students. Financial award applicants required to submit FAFSA. *Unit head:* Prof. David S. Schultz, Head, 631-287-8010, Fax: 631-287-8253. *Application contact:* Andrea Borra, Admissions Counselor, 631-287-8010, Fax: 631-287-8253, E-mail: andrea.borra@liu.edu.

Early Childhood Education

Loyola Marymount University, School of Education, Department of Elementary and Secondary Education, Program in Early Childhood Education, Los Angeles, CA 90045. Offers MA. Part-time and evening/weekend programs available. *Faculty:* 7 full-time (6 women), 17 part-time/adjunct (10 women). *Students:* 39 full-time (37 women), 1 (woman) part-time; includes 25 minority (5 Black or African American, non-Hispanic/Latino; 1 American Indian or Alaska Native, non-Hispanic/Latino; 8 Asian, non-Hispanic/Latino; 8 Hispanic/Latino; 3 Two or more races, non-Hispanic/Latino), 1 international. Average age 26. 27 applicants, 89% accepted, 21 enrolled. In 2011, 15 master's awarded. *Degree requirements:* For master's, comprehensive exam. *Entrance requirements:* For master's, 3 letters of recommendation. Additional exam requirements/recommendations for international students: Required—TOEFL (minimum score 600 paper-based; 250 computer-based; 100 iBT). *Application deadline:* For fall admission, 6/15 for domestic students. Application fee: $50. Electronic applications accepted. *Financial support:* In 2011–12, 19 students received support, including 1 research assistantship (averaging $983 per year); scholarships/grants and unspecified assistantships also available. Support available to part-time students. Financial award application deadline: 6/15; financial award applicants required to submit FAFSA. *Unit head:* Dr. Leslie Ponciano, Program Director, 310-338-6595, E-mail: lponcian@lmu.edu. *Application contact:* Chake H. Kouyoumjian, Director, Graduate Admissions, 310-338-2721, E-mail: ckouyoum@lmu.edu. Web site: http://soe.lmu.edu/admissions/programs/ece.htm.

Loyola University Maryland, Graduate Programs, Department of Education, Program in Montessori Education, Baltimore, MD 21210-2699. Offers elementary education (M Ed); infant education (M Ed); Montessori education (CAS); primary education (M Ed). *Accreditation:* NCATE. *Faculty:* 11 full-time (all women). *Students:* 35 full-time (31 women), 1 (woman) part-time; includes 4 minority (1 Asian, non-Hispanic/Latino; 2 Hispanic/Latino; 1 Two or more races, non-Hispanic/Latino), 6 international. Average age 29. In 2011, 98 master's awarded. *Entrance requirements:* Additional exam requirements/recommendations for international students: Required—TOEFL (minimum score 550 paper-based; 213 computer-based). *Application deadline:* For fall admission, 10/1 priority date for domestic students. Application fee: $50. Electronic applications accepted. *Financial support:* Research assistantships and unspecified assistantships available. Financial award application deadline: 4/15; financial award applicants required to submit FAFSA. *Unit head:* Dr. Sharon Dubble, Director, 410-617-7772, E-mail: sdubble@loyola.edu. *Application contact:* Maureen Faux, Executive Director, Graduate Admissions, 410-617-5020, Fax: 410-617-2002, E-mail: graduate@loyola.edu.

Loyola University Maryland, Graduate Programs, Department of Education, Program in Special Education, Baltimore, MD 21210-2699. Offers early childhood education (M Ed, CAS); elementary/middle education (M Ed, CAS); secondary education (M Ed, CAS). *Accreditation:* NCATE. Part-time programs available. *Faculty:* 57 full-time (32 women), 21 part-time/adjunct (10 women). *Students:* 6 full-time (5 women), 33 part-time (31 women); includes 3 minority (all Black or African American, non-Hispanic/Latino). Average age 29. In 2011, 11 master's awarded. *Entrance requirements:* For master's and CAS, PRAXIS, SAT, ACT, or GRE. Additional exam requirements/recommendations for international students: Required—TOEFL (minimum score 550 paper-based; 213 computer-based). *Application deadline:* For fall admission, 6/15 priority date for domestic students; for spring admission, 11/1 priority date for domestic students. Application fee: $50. Electronic applications accepted. *Financial support:* Research assistantships and unspecified assistantships available. Financial award application deadline: 4/15; financial award applicants required to submit FAFSA. *Unit head:* Monica J. Phelps, Director, 410-617-2671, E-mail: mphelps@loyola.edu. *Application contact:* Maureen Faux, Executive Director, Graduate Admissions, 410-617-5020, Fax: 410-617-2002, E-mail: graduate@loyola.edu.

Manhattan College, Graduate Division, School of Education, Program in Special Education, Riverdale, NY 10471. Offers autism spectrum disorder (Professional Diploma); bilingual special education (Certificate); dual childhood/special education (MS Ed); special education (MS Ed). Part-time and evening/weekend programs available. *Faculty:* 7 full-time (5 women), 22 part-time/adjunct (19 women). *Students:* 29 full-time (27 women), 59 part-time (50 women). Average age 24. 62 applicants, 92% accepted, 57 enrolled. In 2011, 30 master's awarded. *Degree requirements:* For master's, thesis, internship (if not certified). *Entrance requirements:* For master's, LAST, minimum GPA of 3.0. Additional exam requirements/recommendations for international students: Required—TOEFL (minimum score 550 paper-based). *Application deadline:* For fall admission, 8/10 priority date for domestic students; for spring admission, 1/7 priority date for domestic students. Applications are processed on a rolling basis. Application fee: $75. *Expenses:* Contact institution. *Financial support:* Federal Work-Study, scholarships/grants, and unspecified assistantships available. Financial award application deadline: 2/1. *Unit head:* Dr. Elizabeth Mary Kosky, Director of Childhood Special Education Programs, 718-862-7969, Fax: 718-862-7816, E-mail: elizabeth.kosky@manhattan.edu. *Application contact:* William Bisset, Information Contact, 718-862-8000.

Manhattanville College, Graduate Studies, School of Education, Program in Childhood Education, Purchase, NY 10577-2132. Offers childhood and special education (MPS); childhood education (MAT); special education childhood (MPS). Part-time and evening/weekend programs available. *Degree requirements:* For master's, comprehensive exam or research project, field experience. *Entrance requirements:* For master's, minimum undergraduate GPA of 3.0, 2 letters of recommendation. Additional exam requirements/recommendations for international students: Required—TOEFL.

Manhattanville College, Graduate Studies, School of Education, Program in Early Childhood Education, Purchase, NY 10577-2132. Offers childhood and early childhood education (MAT); early childhood education (birth-grade 2) (MAT); literacy (birth-grade 6) (MPS), including reading, writing; literacy (birth-grade 6) and special education (grades 1-6) (MPS); special education (birth-grade 2) (MPS); special education (birth-grade 6) (MPS). Part-time and evening/weekend programs available. *Degree requirements:* For master's, comprehensive exam or research project, field experience. *Entrance requirements:* For master's, minimum undergraduate GPA of 3.0, 2 letters of recommendation. Additional exam requirements/recommendations for international students: Required—TOEFL. Electronic applications accepted.

Marshall University, Academic Affairs Division, Graduate School of Education and Professional Development, Program in Early Childhood Education, Huntington, WV 25755. Offers MA. *Accreditation:* NCATE. Evening/weekend programs available. *Students:* 4 full-time (all women), 10 part-time (all women). Average age 34. In 2011, 2 master's awarded. *Degree requirements:* For master's, thesis optional, comprehensive or oral assessment. *Entrance requirements:* For master's, GRE General Test or MAT. Application fee: $40. *Unit head:* Dr. Lisa Heaton, Director, 304-746-2026, E-mail: heaton@marshall.edu. *Application contact:* Information Contact, Graduate Admissions, 304-746-1900, Fax: 304-746-1902, E-mail: services@marshall.edu.

Maryville University of Saint Louis, School of Education, St. Louis, MO 63141-7299. Offers art education (MA Ed); early childhood education (MA Ed); educational leadership (Ed D); educational leadership: principal certification (MA Ed); elementary education (MA Ed); gifted education (MA Ed); higher education leadership (Ed D); literacy specialist (MA Ed); middle grades education (MA Ed); secondary teaching and inquiry (MA Ed); teacher as leader (MA Ed). *Accreditation:* NCATE. Part-time and evening/weekend programs available. *Faculty:* 10 full-time (6 women), 19 part-time/adjunct (15 women). *Students:* 33 full-time (25 women), 251 part-time (190 women); includes 42 minority (32 Black or African American, non-Hispanic/Latino; 1 American Indian or Alaska Native, non-Hispanic/Latino; 4 Asian, non-Hispanic/Latino; 2 Hispanic/Latino; 3 Two or more races, non-Hispanic/Latino). Average age 38. In 2011, 69 master's, 43 doctorates awarded. *Degree requirements:* For master's, thesis, project. *Entrance requirements:* For master's, minimum cumulative GPA of 3.0, 3 professional recommendations, essays, interview with program faculty; for doctorate, minimum GPA of 3.0, 3 professional recommendations, essay, interview, on-site writing sample. Additional exam requirements/recommendations for international students: Required—TOEFL (minimum score 550 paper-based). *Application deadline:* Applications are processed on a rolling basis. Application fee: $40 ($60 for international students). Electronic applications accepted. *Expenses: Tuition:* Full-time $21,922; part-time $675 per credit hour. *Required fees:* $233.75 per semester. *Financial support:* Career-related internships or fieldwork, Federal Work-Study, tuition waivers (partial), and professional educator discounts available. Financial award application deadline: 3/1; financial award applicants required to submit FAFSA. *Faculty research:* Collaboration with public schools, pre-service program development, mathematics, diversity, literacy. *Unit head:* Dr. Sam Hausfather, Dean, 314-529-9466, Fax: 314-529-9921, E-mail: shausfather@maryville.edu. *Application contact:* Holly Stanwich, Graduate Admissions Coordinator, 314-529-9542, Fax: 314-529-9921, E-mail: teachered@maryville.edu. Web site: http://www.maryville.edu/academics-ed-graduate.

Marywood University, Academic Affairs, Reap College of Education and Human Development, Department of Education, Program in Early Childhood Intervention, Scranton, PA 18509-1598. Offers MS. *Accreditation:* NCATE. *Entrance requirements:* Additional exam requirements/recommendations for international students: Required—TOEFL (minimum score 550 paper-based; 213 computer-based; 79 iBT). *Application deadline:* For fall admission, 4/1 priority date for domestic students, 3/31 for international students; for spring admission, 11/1 priority date for domestic students, 8/31 for international students. Applications are processed on a rolling basis. Application fee: $35. Electronic applications accepted. *Financial support:* Career-related internships or fieldwork, scholarships/grants, and unspecified assistantships available. Support available to part-time students. Financial award application deadline: 6/30; financial award applicants required to submit FAFSA. *Faculty research:* Montessori education, developmentally appropriate practice, child care environment. *Unit head:* Dr. Patricia S. Arter, Chairperson, 570-348-6211 Ext. 2511, E-mail: psarter@marywood.edu. *Application contact:* Tammy Manka, Assistant Director of Graduate Admissions, 570-348-6211 Ext. 2322, E-mail: tmanka@marywood.edu. Web site: http://www.marywood.edu/education/graduate-programs/ms-early-childhood-intervention.html.

McNeese State University, Doré School of Graduate Studies, Burton College of Education, Department of Education Professions, Program in Curriculum and Instruction, Lake Charles, LA 70609. Offers early childhood education (M Ed); elementary education (M Ed); reading (M Ed); secondary education (M Ed). Evening/weekend programs available. *Faculty:* 10 full-time (5 women). *Students:* 8 full-time (7 women), 11 part-time (all women); includes 6 minority (all Black or African American, non-Hispanic/Latino), 1 international. In 2011, 6 master's awarded. *Entrance requirements:* For master's, GRE, teaching certificate. *Application deadline:* For fall admission, 5/15 priority date for domestic students, 5/15 for international students; for spring admission, 10/15 priority date for domestic students, 10/15 for international students. Applications are processed on a rolling basis. Application fee: $20 ($30 for international students). *Expenses:* Tuition, state resident: part-time $519 per credit hour. Tuition and fees vary according to course load. *Financial support:* Application deadline: 5/1. *Unit head:* Dr. Dustin M. Hebert, Director, 337-475-5424, Fax: 337-475-5272, E-mail: dhebert@mcneese.edu. *Application contact:* Dr. George F. Mead, Jr., Interim Dean of Dore' School of Graduate Studies, 337-475-5396, Fax: 337-475-5397, E-mail: admissions@mcneese.edu.

Mercer University, Graduate Studies, Cecil B. Day Campus, Tift College of Education (Atlanta), Macon, GA 31207-0003. Offers curriculum and instruction (PhD); early childhood education (M Ed, MAT); educational leadership (PhD, Ed S); higher education leadership (M Ed); middle grades education (M Ed, MAT); reading education (M Ed); school counseling (Ed S); secondary education (M Ed, MAT); teacher leadership (Ed S). *Accreditation:* NCATE. Part-time and evening/weekend programs available. *Faculty:* 31 full-time (17 women), 6 part-time/adjunct (3 women). *Students:* 249 full-time (207 women), 413 part-time (326 women); includes 349 minority (322 Black or African American, non-Hispanic/Latino; 1 American Indian or Alaska Native, non-Hispanic/Latino; 18 Asian, non-Hispanic/Latino; 6 Hispanic/Latino; 2 Two or more races, non-Hispanic/Latino), 6 international. Average age 34. 204 applicants, 76% accepted, 125 enrolled. In 2011, 235 master's, 8 doctorates, 27 other advanced degrees awarded. *Degree requirements:* For master's and Ed S, research project; for doctorate, thesis/dissertation. *Entrance requirements:* For master's, GRE or MAT, minimum undergraduate GPA of 2.75; for doctorate, GRE; for Ed S, GRE or MAT, minimum GPA of 3.25, 3 years of teaching experience. Additional exam requirements/recommendations for international students: Required—TOEFL. *Application deadline:* For fall admission, 8/1 for domestic and international students; for spring admission, 12/1 for domestic and international students. Applications are processed on a rolling basis. Application fee: $25. *Expenses:* Contact institution. *Financial support:* Federal Work-Study available. Support available to part-time students. Financial award application deadline: 5/1. *Faculty research:* Educational technology, multicultural and minority issues in education, educational leadership (P-12 and higher education), school discipline and school bullying, standards-based mathematics education. *Unit head:* Dr. Carl R. Martray, Dean, 478-301-5397, Fax: 478-301-2280, E-mail: martray_cr@mercer.edu. *Application contact:* Dr. Allison Gilmore, Associate Dean for Graduate Teacher Education, 678-547-6333, Fax: 678-547-6055, E-mail: gilmore_a@mercer.edu. Web site: http://www.mercer.edu/education/.

Mercer University, Graduate Studies, Macon Campus, Tift College of Education (Macon), Macon, GA 31207-0003. Offers curriculum and instruction (PhD); early childhood education (M Ed); education leadership (PhD), including higher education, P-12; educational leadership (Ed S); higher education (M Ed); teacher leadership (Ed S). *Accreditation:* NCATE. Part-time and evening/weekend programs available. Postbaccalaureate distance learning degree programs offered (minimal on-campus study). *Faculty:* 26 full-time (17 women), 2 part-time/adjunct (0 women). *Students:* 87 full-time (78 women), 147 part-time (124 women); includes 92 minority (83 Black or African American, non-Hispanic/Latino; 3 American Indian or Alaska Native, non-Hispanic/Latino; 3 Asian, non-Hispanic/Latino; 3 Hispanic/Latino), 1 international. Average age 36. 122 applicants, 66% accepted, 72 enrolled. In 2011, 51 master's, 5 doctorates, 37 other advanced degrees awarded. *Degree requirements:* For master's, research project report; for doctorate, comprehensive exam, thesis/dissertation. *Entrance requirements:* For master's, GRE or MAT, minimum GPA of 2.75; for doctorate, GRE, minimum GPA of 3.5; interview; writing sample; 3 recommendations; for Ed S, GRE or MAT, minimum GPA of 3.5 (for Ed S in teacher leadership), 3.0 (for Ed S in educational leadership). Additional exam requirements/recommendations for international students: Required—TOEFL. *Application deadline:* For fall admission, 8/1 for domestic students; for spring admission, 12/1 for domestic students. Applications are processed on a rolling basis. Application fee: $35. *Expenses:* Contact institution. *Financial support:* Federal Work-Study and institutionally sponsored loans available. Support available to part-time students. Financial award application deadline: 5/1. *Faculty research:* Teacher effectiveness, specific learning disabilities, inclusion. *Unit head:* Dr. Carl R. Martray, Dean, 478-301-5397, Fax: 478-301-2280, E-mail: martray_cr@mercer.edu. *Application contact:* Tracey Wofford, Associate Director of Admissions, 678-547-6422, Fax: 678-547-6367, E-mail: wofford_tm@mercer.edu. Web site: http://education.mercer.edu.

Mercy College, School of Education, Program in Early Childhood Education, Birth-Grade 2, Dobbs Ferry, NY 10522-1189. Offers MS. Part-time and evening/weekend programs available. Postbaccalaureate distance learning degree programs offered (no on-campus study). *Degree requirements:* For master's, comprehensive exam. *Entrance requirements:* Additional exam requirements/recommendations for international students: Required—TOEFL (minimum score 600 paper-based; 250 computer-based; 100 iBT), IELTS (minimum score 8). Electronic applications accepted. *Faculty research:* Correcting literacy problems, teaching-learning process, behavior management application for children.

Merrimack College, School of Education, North Andover, MA 01845-5800. Offers community engagement (M Ed); early childhood education (M Ed); elementary education (M Ed); elementary education plus moderate disabilities-dual license (M Ed); English as a second language (M Ed); general studies (M Ed); higher education (M Ed); middle (M Ed); moderate disabilities (preK-8) (M Ed); reading (M Ed); secondary (M Ed); teacher leadership (CAGS). Part-time and evening/weekend programs available. *Faculty:* 4 full-time (all women), 9 part-time/adjunct (7 women). *Students:* 70 full-time (60 women), 39 part-time (33 women); includes 2 minority (1 Asian, non-Hispanic/Latino; 1 Hispanic/Latino). Average age 27. In 2011, 26 master's awarded. *Degree requirements:* For master's, portfolio. *Entrance requirements:* Additional exam requirements/recommendations for international students: Required—TOEFL (minimum score 80 iBT). *Application deadline:* For fall admission, 8/1 priority date for domestic students, 7/15 for international students; for winter admission, 12/1 priority date for domestic students, 11/15 for international students; for spring admission, 3/1 priority date for domestic students, 2/15 for international students. Applications are processed on a rolling basis. Electronic applications accepted. *Expenses: Tuition:* Part-time $475 per credit. *Required fees:* $62.50 per semester. *Financial support:* In 2011–12, 50 fellowships were awarded; career-related internships or fieldwork and scholarships/grants also available. Financial award applicants required to submit FAFSA. *Faculty research:* Higher education, community engagement, literacy, leadership. *Unit head:* Dr. Theresa Kirk, Chair, 978-837-5436, E-mail: kirkt@merrimack.edu. *Application contact:* Jessica McCarthy, Program Coordinator, 978-837-5443, E-mail: mccarthyj@merrimack.edu. Web site: http://www.merrimack.edu/academics/education/med/.

Miami University, School of Education and Allied Professions, Department of Teacher Education, Oxford, OH 45056. Offers elementary education (M Ed, MAT); reading education (M Ed); secondary education (M Ed, MAT), including adolescent education (MAT), elementary mathematics education (M Ed), secondary education. Part-time programs available. *Students:* 32 full-time (19 women), 40 part-time (37 women); includes 6 minority (3 Black or African American, non-Hispanic/Latino; 2 Hispanic/Latino; 1 Two or more races, non-Hispanic/Latino), 3 international. Average age 28. In 2011, 42 master's awarded. *Entrance requirements:* For master's, GRE (for MAT), minimum undergraduate GPA of 3.0 during previous 2 years or 2.75 overall. *Application deadline:* Applications are processed on a rolling basis. Application fee: $50. Electronic applications accepted. *Expenses:* Tuition, state resident: full-time $12,023; part-time $501 per credit hour. Tuition, nonresident: full-time $26,554; part-time $1107 per credit hour. *Required fees:* $528. *Financial support:* Fellowships with full tuition reimbursements, research assistantships, teaching assistantships, career-related internships or fieldwork, Federal Work-Study, scholarships/grants, health care benefits, tuition waivers (full), and unspecified assistantships available. Financial award application deadline: 2/15. *Unit head:* Dr. James Shiveley, Chair, 513-529-6443, Fax: 513-529-4931, E-mail: shiveljm@muohio.edu. *Application contact:* Linda Dennett, Program Associate, 513-529-5708, E-mail: dennetlg@muohio.edu. Web site: http://www.units.muohio.edu/eap/departments/edt/.

Middle Tennessee State University, College of Graduate Studies, College of Education, Department of Elementary and Special Education, Major in Curriculum and Instruction, Murfreesboro, TN 37132. Offers early childhood education (M Ed); elementary education (M Ed, Ed S); middle school education (M Ed). *Accreditation:* NCATE. Part-time and evening/weekend programs available. Postbaccalaureate distance learning degree programs offered. *Faculty:* 14 full-time (9 women), 7 part-time/adjunct (all women). *Students:* 16 full-time (13 women), 144 part-time (129 women); includes 18 minority (16 Black or African American, non-Hispanic/Latino; 1 Asian, non-Hispanic/Latino; 1 Hispanic/Latino). 110 applicants, 73% accepted. In 2011, 55 master's awarded. *Degree requirements:* For master's, comprehensive exam; for Ed S, comprehensive exam, thesis or alternative. *Entrance requirements:* For master's and Ed S, GRE, MAT or PRAXIS. Additional exam requirements/recommendations for international students: Required—TOEFL (minimum score 525 paper-based; 195 computer-based; 71 iBT) or IELTS (minimum score 6). *Application deadline:* For fall admission, 8/1 priority date for domestic students. Applications are processed on a rolling basis. Application fee: $25. Electronic applications accepted. *Expenses:* Tuition, state resident: full-time $10,008. Tuition, nonresident: full-time $25,056. *Financial support:* Tuition waivers available. Support available to part-time students. Financial award application deadline: 5/1. *Unit head:* Dr. Kathleen Burriss, Interim Chair, 615-898-2323, Fax: 615-898-5309, E-mail: kathleen.burris@mtsu.edu. *Application contact:* Dr. Michael D. Allen, Dean and Vice Provost for Research, 615-898-2840, Fax: 615-904-8020, E-mail: michael.allen@mtsu.edu.

Millersville University of Pennsylvania, College of Graduate and Professional Studies, School of Education, Department of Elementary and Early Childhood Education, Program in Early Childhood Education, Millersville, PA 17551-0302. Offers M Ed. Part-time and evening/weekend programs available. *Faculty:* 16 full-time (12 women), 8 part-time/adjunct (5 women). *Students:* 23 part-time (all women); includes 2 minority (1 Black or African American, non-Hispanic/Latino; 1 Asian, non-Hispanic/Latino). Average age 30. 7 applicants, 100% accepted, 5 enrolled. In 2011, 7 master's awarded. *Degree requirements:* For master's, thesis optional. *Entrance requirements:* For master's, 3 letters of recommendation; copy of teaching certificate. Additional exam requirements/recommendations for international students: Required—TOEFL (minimum score 500 paper-based; 183 computer-based; 65 iBT). *Application deadline:* For fall admission, 1/15 priority date for domestic students, 1/15 for international students; for winter admission, 10/1 priority date for domestic students, 10/1 for international students; for spring admission, 10/1 priority date for domestic students, 10/1 for international students. Applications are processed on a rolling basis. Application fee: $40 ($50 for international students). Electronic applications accepted. *Expenses:* Tuition, state resident: full-time $3744; part-time $416 per credit. Tuition, nonresident: full-time $5616; part-time $624 per credit. *Required fees:* $1130; $125.50 per credit. Tuition and fees vary according to course load. *Financial support:* In 2011–12, 1 research assistantship (averaging $1,563 per year) was awarded; institutionally sponsored loans and unspecified assistantships also available. Support available to part-time students. Financial award application deadline: 3/15; financial award applicants required to submit FAFSA. *Faculty research:* Play, creative expression, alternative method of education, parent involvement in education. *Unit head:* Dr. Marcia L. Nell, Coordinator, 717-872-2170, Fax: 717-871-5462, E-mail: marcia.nell@millersville.edu. *Application contact:* Dr. Victor S. DeSantis, Dean, College of Graduate and Professional Studies, 717-872-3099, Fax: 717-872-3453, E-mail: victor.desantis@millersville.edu. Web site: http://www.millersville.edu/academics/educ/eled/graduate.php.

Mills College, Graduate Studies, Program in Infant Mental Health, Oakland, CA 94613-1000. Offers MA. Part-time programs available. *Faculty:* 2 full-time (both women). *Students:* 9 full-time (all women); includes 2 minority (1 Black or African American, non-Hispanic/Latino; 1 Hispanic/Latino). Average age 29. 12 applicants, 83% accepted, 6 enrolled. In 2011, 4 master's awarded. *Entrance requirements:* For master's, bachelor's degree, preferably in psychology, and the following prerequisite courses: fundamentals of psychology, developmental psychology, psychopathology, analytical methods/statistics, research methods; three letters of recommendation; statement of purpose essay. Additional exam requirements/recommendations for international students: Required—TOEFL (minimum score 550 paper-based; 80 iBT) or IELTS (minimum score 6). *Application deadline:* For fall admission, 12/31 priority date for domestic students, 12/15 for international students. Applications are processed on a rolling basis. *Expenses: Tuition:* Full-time $28,280; part-time $15,640 per year. *Required fees:* $958. Tuition and fees vary according to program. *Financial support:* Fellowships with full and partial tuition reimbursements, teaching assistantships with full and partial tuition reimbursements, and scholarships/grants available. Financial award application deadline: 2/1; financial award applicants required to submit FAFSA. *Faculty research:* Development and sequelae of attachment in children and adults in normative and clinical/risk populations, identifying the mental health needs of young children who have experienced extraordinary traumatic situations during critical points in their early development, examining the effects of early childhood trauma, work on helping professionals' psychological well-being. *Unit head:* Linda Perez, Professor of Education, 510-430-3170, Fax: 510-430-3379, E-mail: imh@mills.edu. *Application contact:* Tiana Kozoil, Graduate Admission Specialist, 510-430-3305, Fax: 510-430-2159, E-mail: grad-studies@mills.edu. Web site: http://www.mills.edu/imh/.

Mills College, Graduate Studies, School of Education, Oakland, CA 94613-1000. Offers child life in hospitals (MA); early childhood education (MA); education (MA), including art education, curriculum and instruction, elementary education, English education, foreign language education, mathematics education, science education, secondary education, social studies education, teaching; educational leadership (MA, Ed D). Part-time and evening/weekend programs available. *Faculty:* 13 full-time (10 women), 14 part-time/adjunct (10 women). *Students:* 149 full-time (133 women), 69 part-time (61 women); includes 85 minority (32 Black or African American, non-Hispanic/Latino; 1 American Indian or Alaska Native, non-Hispanic/Latino; 16 Asian, non-Hispanic/Latino; 24 Hispanic/Latino; 1 Native Hawaiian or other Pacific Islander, non-Hispanic/Latino; 11 Two or more races, non-Hispanic/Latino), 3 international. Average age 28. 238 applicants, 84% accepted, 106 enrolled. In 2011, 41 master's, 2 doctorates awarded. Terminal master's awarded for partial completion of doctoral program. *Degree requirements:* For master's, comprehensive exam. *Entrance requirements:* For master's, statement of purpose, official transcript, 3 recommendations; for doctorate, GRE General Test. Additional exam requirements/recommendations for international students: Required—TOEFL (minimum score 550 paper-based; 80 iBT) or IELTS (minimum score 6). *Application deadline:* For fall admission, 12/31 priority date for domestic students, 12/15 for international students; for spring admission, 11/1 priority date for domestic students, 10/1 for international students. Applications are processed on a rolling basis. Application fee: $50. Electronic applications accepted. *Expenses: Tuition:* Full-time $28,280; part-time $15,640 per year. *Required fees:* $958. Tuition and fees vary according to program. *Financial support:* In 2011–12, 43 students received support, including 225 fellowships with full and partial tuition reimbursements available (averaging $6,020 per year), 43 teaching assistantships with full and partial tuition reimbursements available (averaging $6,782 per year); career-related internships or fieldwork and scholarships/grants also available. Support available to part-time students. Financial award application deadline: 2/1; financial award applicants required to submit FAFSA. *Faculty research:* Early childhood education, teacher preparation, educational leadership. *Total annual research expenditures:* $2.3 million. *Unit head:* Katherine Schultz, Chairperson, 510-430-3170, Fax: 510-430-3379, E-mail: grad-studies@mills.edu. *Application contact:* Tiana Kozoil, Graduate Admission Specialist, 510-430-3305, Fax: 510-430-2159, E-mail: grad-studies@mills.edu. Web site: http://www.mills.edu/education.

Minnesota State University Mankato, College of Graduate Studies, College of Education, Department of Elementary and Early Childhood Education, Mankato, MN 56001. Offers MS, Certificate. *Accreditation:* NCATE. Part-time programs available. *Students:* 12 full-time (all women), 77 part-time (73 women). *Degree requirements:* For master's, comprehensive exam, thesis or alternative. *Entrance requirements:* For master's, GRE General Test or MAT, minimum GPA of 3.0 during previous 2 years. Additional exam requirements/recommendations for international students: Required—TOEFL. *Application deadline:* For fall admission, 7/1 priority date for domestic students; for spring admission, 11/1 for domestic students. Applications are processed on a rolling basis. Application fee: $40. Electronic applications accepted. *Financial support:* Application deadline: 3/15; applicants required to submit FAFSA. *Unit head:* Dr. Peggy Ballard, Graduate Coordinator, 507-389-1516. *Application contact:* 507-389-2321, E-mail: grad@mnsu.edu. Web site: http://ed.mnsu.edu/eec/.

Minot State University, Graduate School, Program in Special Education, Minot, ND 58707-0002. Offers education of the deaf (MS); learning disabilities (MS); special education strategist (MS), including early childhood special education, severe multiple handicaps. *Accreditation:* NCATE. *Degree requirements:* For master's, comprehensive exam (for some programs), thesis (for some programs). *Entrance requirements:* For master's, GRE General Test or minimum GPA of 3.0. Additional exam requirements/recommendations for international students: Required—TOEFL. *Faculty research:* Special education team diagnostic unit; individual diagnostic assessments of mentally retarded, learning-disabled, hearing-impaired, and speech-impaired youth; educational programming for the hearing impaired.

Missouri Southern State University, Program in Early Childhood Education, Joplin, MO 64801-1595. Offers MS Ed. Program offered jointly with Northwest Missouri State University. *Accreditation:* NCATE. *Entrance requirements:* For master's, GRE, minimum cumulative undergraduate GPA of 2.5.

Missouri State University, Graduate College, College of Education, Department of Childhood Education and Family Studies, Springfield, MO 65897. Offers early childhood and family development (MS); elementary education (MS Ed). Part-time programs available. *Faculty:* 11 full-time (8 women), 1 (woman) part-time/adjunct. *Students:* 15 full-time (14 women), 50 part-time (45 women); includes 3 minority (1 Asian, non-Hispanic/Latino; 2 Hispanic/Latino), 4 international. Average age 30. 20 applicants, 100% accepted, 16 enrolled. In 2011, 29 master's awarded. *Degree requirements:* For master's, comprehensive exam. *Entrance requirements:* For master's, GRE, minimum GPA of 3.0. Additional exam requirements/recommendations for international students:

Required—TOEFL (minimum score 550 paper-based; 213 computer-based; 79 iBT). *Application deadline:* For fall admission, 7/20 priority date for domestic students, 5/1 for international students; for spring admission, 12/20 priority date for domestic students, 9/1 for international students. Applications are processed on a rolling basis. Application fee: $35 ($50 for international students). Electronic applications accepted. *Expenses:* Tuition, state resident: full-time $4086; part-time $227 per credit hour. Tuition, nonresident: full-time $8172; part-time $454 per credit hour. *Required fees:* $275 per semester. Tuition and fees vary according to course load, campus/location and program. *Financial support:* Federal Work-Study, institutionally sponsored loans, scholarships/grants, and unspecified assistantships available. Financial award applicants required to submit FAFSA. *Unit head:* Dr. Josephine Agnew-Talley, Acting Head, 417-836-8915, Fax: 417-836-8900, E-mail: cefs@missouristate.edu. *Application contact:* Misty Stewart, Coordinator of Graduate Recruitment, 417-836-6079, Fax: 417-836-6200, E-mail: mistystewart@missouristate.edu. Web site: http://education.missouristate.edu/cefs/.

Montana State University Billings, College of Education, Department of Special Education, Counseling, Reading and Early Childhood, Option in Early Childhood Education, Billings, MT 59101-0298. Offers M Ed. *Accreditation:* NCATE. Part-time programs available. *Degree requirements:* For master's, thesis or professional paper and/or field experience. *Entrance requirements:* For master's, GRE General Test or MAT, minimum GPA of 3.0 (undergraduate), 3.25 (graduate). *Faculty research:* Bilingual education.

Montclair State University, The Graduate School, College of Education and Human Services, Department of Early Childhood, Elementary and Literacy Education, Program in Early Childhood and Elementary Education, Montclair, NJ 07043-1624. Offers M Ed. Part-time and evening/weekend programs available. *Students:* 14 part-time (all women); includes 2 minority (both Black or African American, non-Hispanic/Latino). 8 applicants, 13% accepted, 0 enrolled. In 2011, 7 master's awarded. *Degree requirements:* For master's, comprehensive exam, thesis or alternative. *Entrance requirements:* For master's, GRE General Test, interview, 2 letters of recommendation. Additional exam requirements/recommendations for international students: Required—TOEFL (minimum score 83 iBT), IELTS (minimum score 6.5). *Application deadline:* Applications are processed on a rolling basis. Application fee: $60. Electronic applications accepted. *Financial support:* Federal Work-Study, scholarships/grants, and unspecified assistantships available. Support available to part-time students. Financial award application deadline: 3/1; financial award applicants required to submit FAFSA. *Unit head:* Dr. Tina Jacobowitz, Chairperson, 973-655-7191. *Application contact:* Amy Aiello, Director of Graduate Admissions and Operations, 973-655-5147, Fax: 973-655-7869, E-mail: graduate.school@montclair.edu. Web site: http://cehs.montclair.edu/academic/ecele/programs/masterspecial1.shtml.

Montclair State University, The Graduate School, College of Education and Human Services, Department of Early Childhood, Elementary and Literacy Education, Program in Teaching Early Childhood, Montclair, NJ 07043-1624. Offers MAT. *Students:* 34 full-time (31 women), 82 part-time (70 women); includes 38 minority (11 Black or African American, non-Hispanic/Latino; 7 Asian, non-Hispanic/Latino; 19 Hispanic/Latino; 1 Native Hawaiian or other Pacific Islander, non-Hispanic/Latino), 1 international. Average age 31. 45 applicants, 56% accepted, 17 enrolled. *Degree requirements:* For master's, comprehensive exam, thesis or alternative. *Entrance requirements:* For master's, GRE General Test, interview, essay, 2 letters of recommendation. Additional exam requirements/recommendations for international students: Required—TOEFL (minimum score 83 iBT), IELTS (minimum score 6.5). *Application deadline:* Applications are processed on a rolling basis. Application fee: $60. Electronic applications accepted. *Financial support:* Federal Work-Study, scholarships/grants, and unspecified assistantships available. Support available to part-time students. Financial award application deadline: 3/1; financial award applicants required to submit FAFSA. *Unit head:* Dr. Tina Jacobowitz, Chairperson, 973-655-7191. *Application contact:* Amy Aiello, Director of Graduate Admissions and Operations, 973-655-5147, Fax: 973-655-7869, E-mail: graduate.school@montclair.edu. Web site: http://cehs.montclair.edu/academic/ecele/programs/masterearly.shtml.

Mount Saint Mary College, Division of Education, Newburgh, NY 12550-3494. Offers adolescence and special education (MS Ed); adolescence education (MS Ed); childhood and special education (MS Ed); childhood education (MS Ed); literacy (5-12) (Advanced Certificate); literacy (birth-6) (Advanced Certificate); literacy and special education (MS Ed); literacy/childhood (MS Ed); middle school (5-6) (MS Ed); middle school (7-9) (MS Ed); special education (1-6) (MS Ed); special education (7-12) (MS Ed). *Accreditation:* NCATE. Part-time and evening/weekend programs available. *Faculty:* 14 full-time (12 women), 14 part-time/adjunct (8 women). *Students:* 55 full-time (42 women), 158 part-time (125 women); includes 23 minority (4 Black or African American, non-Hispanic/Latino; 1 Asian, non-Hispanic/Latino; 18 Hispanic/Latino). Average age 29. 119 applicants, 45% accepted, 24 enrolled. In 2011, 107 master's awarded. *Application deadline:* Applications are processed on a rolling basis. Application fee: $45. Application fee is waived when completed online. *Expenses: Tuition:* Full-time $13,356; part-time $742 per credit. *Required fees:* $70 per semester. *Financial support:* In 2011–12, 99 students received support. Unspecified assistantships available. Financial award application deadline: 4/15; financial award applicants required to submit FAFSA. *Faculty research:* Learning and teaching styles, computers in special education, language development. *Unit head:* Dr. Theresa Lewis, Coordinator, 845-569-3149, Fax: 845-569-3535, E-mail: tlewis@msmc.edu. *Application contact:* Courtney McDermott, Graduate Recruiter, 845-569-3402, Fax: 845-569-3450, E-mail: courtney.mcdermott@msmc.edu. Web site: http://www.msmc.edu/Academics/Graduate_Programs/Master_of_Science_in_Education.

Murray State University, College of Education, Department of Early Childhood and Elementary Education, Program in Interdisciplinary Early Childhood Education, Murray, KY 42071. Offers MA Ed. Part-time programs available. *Degree requirements:* For master's, portfolio. *Entrance requirements:* For master's, minimum GPA of 2.5 for conditional admittance, 3.0 for unconditional.

National Louis University, National College of Education, Chicago, IL 60603. Offers administration and supervision (M Ed, Ed D, CAS, Ed S); curriculum and instruction (M Ed, MS Ed, CAS); early childhood administration (M Ed, CAS); early childhood education (M Ed, MAT, MS Ed, CAS); education (Ed D); educational psychology/human learning and development (M Ed, MS Ed, CAS, Ed S); elementary education (MAT); interdisciplinary curriculum and instruction (M Ed); mathematics education (M Ed, MS Ed, CAS); reading and language (M Ed, MS Ed, CAS); school psychology (M Ed, Ed S); science education (M Ed, MS Ed, CAS); secondary education (MAT); special education (M Ed, MAT, CAS); technology in education (M Ed, CAS). *Accreditation:* NCATE. Part-time and evening/weekend programs available. *Students:* 224 full-time (162 women), 2,336 part-time (1,767 women); includes 677 minority (366 Black or African American, non-Hispanic/Latino; 8 American Indian or Alaska Native, non-Hispanic/Latino; 68 Asian, non-Hispanic/Latino; 218 Hispanic/Latino; 2 Native Hawaiian or other Pacific Islander, non-Hispanic/Latino; 15 Two or more races, non-Hispanic/Latino), 2 international. Average age 34. In 2011, 1,711 master's, 76 doctorates, 86 other advanced degrees awarded. *Degree requirements:* For doctorate, comprehensive exam, thesis/dissertation. *Entrance requirements:* For master's, MAT or GRE, minimum GPA of 3.0; for doctorate, GRE General Test, minimum GPA of 3.25, interview, resume, writing sample, 4 recommendations. Additional exam requirements/recommendations for international students: Required—TOEFL (minimum score 550 paper-based; 213 computer-based; 79 iBT). *Application deadline:* Applications are processed on a rolling basis. Application fee: $40. *Financial support:* Fellowships, research assistantships, teaching assistantships, career-related internships or fieldwork, Federal Work-Study, institutionally sponsored loans, and scholarships/grants available. Support available to part-time students. Financial award applicants required to submit FAFSA. *Unit head:* Dr. Alison Hilsabeck, Dean, 312-361-3580, Fax: 312-261-2580, E-mail: ahilsabeck@nl.edu. *Application contact:* Ken Kasprzak, Director of Admission, 888-658-8632, Fax: 847-947-5575, E-mail: kkasprzak@nl.edu.

National University, Academic Affairs, School of Education, Department of Teacher Education, La Jolla, CA 92037-1011. Offers best practices (Certificate); early childhood education (Certificate); educational technology (Certificate); elementary education (M Ed); instructional technology (MS Ed); multiple or single subjects teaching (M Ed); national board certified teacher leadership (Certificate); secondary education (M Ed); teaching (MA). Part-time and evening/weekend programs available. Postbaccalaureate distance learning degree programs offered (no on-campus study). *Degree requirements:* For master's, thesis. *Entrance requirements:* For master's, interview, minimum GPA of 2.5. Additional exam requirements/recommendations for international students: Required—TOEFL (minimum score 550 paper-based; 213 computer-based; 79 iBT), IELTS (minimum score 6). *Application deadline:* Applications are processed on a rolling basis. Application fee: $60 ($65 for international students). Electronic applications accepted. *Financial support:* Career-related internships or fieldwork, institutionally sponsored loans, scholarships/grants, and tuition waivers (partial) available. Support available to part-time students. Financial award application deadline: 6/30; financial award applicants required to submit FAFSA. *Unit head:* Dr. Cynthia Schubert-Irastroza, Chair, 858-642-8339, Fax: 858-642-8724, E-mail: cshubert@nu.edu. *Application contact:* Dominick Giovanniello, Associate Regional Dean, 800-NAT-UNIV, Fax: 858-541-7792, E-mail: dgiovann@nu.edu. Web site: http://www.nu.edu/OurPrograms/SchoolOfEducation/TeacherEducation.html.

Nazareth College of Rochester, Graduate Studies, Department of Education, Program in Inclusive Education-Early Childhood Level, Rochester, NY 14618-3790. Offers MS Ed. *Accreditation:* Teacher Education Accreditation Council. Part-time and evening/weekend programs available. *Entrance requirements:* For master's, minimum GPA of 3.0.

New Jersey City University, Graduate Studies and Continuing Education, Debra Cannon Partridge Wolfe College of Education, Department of Early Childhood Education, Jersey City, NJ 07305-1597. Offers MA. Part-time and evening/weekend programs available. *Students:* 12 full-time (all women), 66 part-time (64 women); includes 39 minority (13 Black or African American, non-Hispanic/Latino; 6 Asian, non-Hispanic/Latino; 20 Hispanic/Latino). Average age 34. In 2011, 103 master's awarded. *Entrance requirements:* Additional exam requirements/recommendations for international students: Required—TOEFL. *Application deadline:* For fall admission, 8/1 priority date for domestic students; for spring admission, 12/1 for domestic students. Applications are processed on a rolling basis. Application fee: $0. *Expenses:* Tuition, state resident: part-time $494 per credit. Tuition, nonresident: part-time $911.30 per credit. *Required fees:* $95.90 per year. *Financial support:* Career-related internships or fieldwork and unspecified assistantships available. *Unit head:* Dr. Regina Adesanya, Coordinator, 201-200-2114, E-mail: radesanya@njcu.edu. *Application contact:* Dr. William Bajor, Dean of Graduate Studies, 201-200-3409, Fax: 201-200-3411, E-mail: wbajor@njcu.edu.

New York University, Steinhardt School of Culture, Education, and Human Development, Department of Teaching and Learning, Program in Early Childhood and Childhood Education, New York, NY 10012-1019. Offers childhood education (MA); childhood education/special education: childhood (MA); early childhood education (MA); positions of leadership: early childhood and elementary education (PhD). *Accreditation:* Teacher Education Accreditation Council. Part-time programs available. *Degree requirements:* For master's, thesis (for some programs); for doctorate, thesis/dissertation. *Entrance requirements:* For doctorate, GRE General Test, interview. Additional exam requirements/recommendations for international students: Required—TOEFL. Electronic applications accepted. *Faculty research:* Teacher evaluation and beliefs about teaching, early literacy development, language arts, child development and education, cultural differences.

New York University, Steinhardt School of Culture, Education, and Human Development, Department of Teaching and Learning, Program in Special Education, New York, NY 10012-1019. Offers childhood (MA); dual certification: childhood education/childhood special education (MA); dual certification: early childhood education/early childhood special education (MA); early childhood (MA). *Accreditation:* Teacher Education Accreditation Council. Part-time programs available. *Degree requirements:* For master's, thesis (for some programs). *Entrance requirements:* Additional exam requirements/recommendations for international students: Required—TOEFL. Electronic applications accepted. *Faculty research:* Special education referrals, attention deficit disorders in children, mainstreaming, curriculum-based assessment and program implementation, special education policy.

Niagara University, Graduate Division of Education, Concentration in Teacher Education, Niagara Falls, Niagara University, NY 14109. Offers early childhood and childhood education (MS Ed); middle and adolescence education (MS Ed); special education (grades 1-12) (MS Ed). *Accreditation:* NCATE. *Faculty:* 4 full-time (1 woman), 6 part-time/adjunct (4 women). *Students:* 249 full-time (162 women), 56 part-time (39 women); includes 11 minority (5 Black or African American, non-Hispanic/Latino; 1 American Indian or Alaska Native, non-Hispanic/Latino; 1 Asian, non-Hispanic/Latino; 2 Hispanic/Latino; 2 Two or more races, non-Hispanic/Latino), 176 international. Average age 24. In 2011, 233 master's, 1 Certificate awarded. *Entrance requirements:* For master's, GRE General Test or MAT. *Application deadline:* For fall admission, 8/1 for domestic students. Applications are processed on a rolling basis. Application fee: $30. *Expenses:* Contact institution. *Financial support:* Career-related internships or fieldwork, Federal Work-Study, and scholarships/grants available. Financial award application deadline: 3/15. *Unit head:* Dr. Chandra Foote, Chair, 716-286-8549. *Application contact:* Dr. Debra A. Colley, Dean of Education, 716-286-8560, Fax: 716-286-8561, E-mail: dcolley@niagara.edu.

Norfolk State University, School of Graduate Studies, School of Education, Department of Early Childhood and Elementary Education, Norfolk, VA 23504. Offers early childhood education (MAT); pre-elementary education (MA). *Accreditation:* NCATE. Part-time programs available. *Degree requirements:* For master's, comprehensive exam, thesis or alternative. *Entrance requirements:* For master's, PRAXIS I and II, minimum GPA of 2.5, letters of recommendation, interview. *Faculty research:* Parent involvement in education.

North Carolina Agricultural and Technical State University, School of Graduate Studies, School of Agriculture and Environmental Sciences, Department of Family and Consumer Sciences, Greensboro, NC 27411. Offers child development early education and family studies (MAT); family and consumer sciences (MAT); food and nutrition (MS). Part-time and evening/weekend programs available. *Degree requirements:* For master's, comprehensive exam, thesis or alternative, qualifying exam. *Entrance requirements:* For master's, GRE General Test, minimum GPA of 2.6.

Northeastern State University, Graduate College, College of Education, Department of Curriculum and Instruction, Program in Early Childhood Education, Tahlequah, OK 74464-2399. Offers M Ed. Part-time and evening/weekend programs available. *Students:* 3 full-time (all women), 16 part-time (all women); includes 3 minority (2 American Indian or Alaska Native, non-Hispanic/Latino; 1 Hispanic/Latino). In 2011, 6 master's awarded. *Degree requirements:* For master's, thesis. *Entrance requirements:* For master's, GRE or MAT, minimum GPA of 2.5. Additional exam requirements/recommendations for international students: Required—TOEFL (minimum score 213 computer-based). *Application deadline:* For fall admission, 6/1 priority date for domestic students. Applications are processed on a rolling basis. Application fee: $25. Electronic applications accepted. *Financial support:* Teaching assistantships and Federal Work-Study available. Financial award application deadline: 3/1. *Unit head:* Dr. Deborah Landry, Chair, 918-456-5511 Ext. 3710, Fax: 918-458-2351, E-mail: landryd@nsuok.edu. *Application contact:* Margie Railey, Administrative Assistant, 918-456-5511 Ext. 2093, Fax: 918-458-2061, E-mail: railey@nsouk.edu.

Northern Arizona University, Graduate College, College of Education, Department of Teaching and Learning, Flagstaff , AZ 86011. Offers early childhood education (M Ed); elementary education - certification (M Ed); elementary education - continuing professional (M Ed); secondary education - certification (M Ed); secondary education - continuing professional (M Ed). Part-time programs available. *Faculty:* 32 full-time (23 women). *Students:* 297 full-time (238 women), 368 part-time (333 women); includes 193 minority (16 Black or African American, non-Hispanic/Latino; 43 American Indian or Alaska Native, non-Hispanic/Latino; 11 Asian, non-Hispanic/Latino; 113 Hispanic/Latino; 10 Two or more races, non-Hispanic/Latino), 8 international. Average age 29. 182 applicants, 91% accepted, 118 enrolled. In 2011, 415 master's awarded. *Degree requirements:* For master's, comprehensive exam (for some programs), thesis (for some programs). *Entrance requirements:* For master's, minimum GPA of 3.0. Additional exam requirements/recommendations for international students: Required—TOEFL (minimum score 550 paper-based; 213 computer-based; 80 iBT), IELTS (minimum score 7). *Application deadline:* For fall admission, 3/1 for international students; for spring admission, 9/15 for international students. Applications are processed on a rolling basis. Application fee: $65. Electronic applications accepted. *Expenses:* Tuition, state resident: full-time $7190; part-time $355 per credit hour. Tuition, nonresident: full-time $18,092; part-time $1005 per credit hour. *Required fees:* $818; $328 per semester. *Financial support:* In 2011–12, 7 teaching assistantships with partial tuition reimbursements (averaging $10,000 per year) were awarded; Federal Work-Study, scholarships/grants, health care benefits, tuition waivers (full and partial), and unspecified assistantships also available. Financial award applicants required to submit FAFSA. *Unit head:* Dr. Sandra J. Stone, Chair, 928-523-4280, Fax: 928-523-1929, E-mail: sandra.stone@nau.edu. *Application contact:* Kay Quillen, Administrative Assistant, 928-523-9316, Fax: 928-523-1929, E-mail: kay.quillen@nau.edu. Web site: http://nau.edu/coe/teaching-and-learning/.

Northern Illinois University, Graduate School, College of Education, Department of Special and Early Education, De Kalb, IL 60115-2854. Offers curriculum and instruction (MS Ed, Ed D), including curriculum leadership (Ed D), elementary education (Ed D), secondary education (Ed D); early childhood education (MS Ed); elementary education (MS Ed); special education (MS Ed). Part-time and evening/weekend programs available. *Faculty:* 22 full-time (14 women), 2 part-time/adjunct (both women). *Students:* 58 full-time (46 women), 241 part-time (189 women); includes 35 minority (17 Black or African American, non-Hispanic/Latino; 7 Asian, non-Hispanic/Latino; 9 Hispanic/Latino; 2 Two or more races, non-Hispanic/Latino), 3 international. Average age 35. 100 applicants, 65% accepted, 45 enrolled. In 2011, 186 master's, 7 doctorates awarded. *Degree requirements:* For master's, comprehensive exam, thesis optional; for doctorate, thesis/dissertation, candidacy exam, dissertation defense. *Entrance requirements:* For master's, GRE General Test or MAT, minimum undergraduate GPA of 2.75; for doctorate, GRE General Test or MAT, minimum undergraduate GPA of 2.75, graduate 3.2. Additional exam requirements/recommendations for international students: Required—TOEFL (minimum score 550 paper-based; 213 computer-based). *Application deadline:* For fall admission, 6/1 for domestic students, 5/1 for international students; for spring admission, 11/1 for domestic students, 10/1 for international students. Applications are processed on a rolling basis. Application fee: $40. Electronic applications accepted. *Financial support:* In 2011–12, 34 research assistantships with full tuition reimbursements were awarded; fellowships with full tuition reimbursements, teaching assistantships with full tuition reimbursements, career-related internships or fieldwork, Federal Work-Study, scholarships/grants, tuition waivers (full), and unspecified assistantships also available. Support available to part-time students. Financial award applicants required to submit FAFSA. *Faculty research:* Teacher certification, stress reduction during student teaching, teaching history, portfolios in student teaching. *Unit head:* Dr. Connie Fox, Interim Chair, 815-753-1619, E-mail: seed@niu.edu. *Application contact:* Gail Myers, 815-753-0381, E-mail: gmyers@niu.edu. Web site: http://www.cedu.niu.edu/seed/.

North Georgia College & State University, School of Education, Dahlonega, GA 30597. Offers art education (MAT); early childhood education (M Ed); English education (MAT); history education (MAT); math education (MAT); middle grades education (M Ed, MAT); physical education (MS); school leadership (Ed S); secondary education (M Ed), including English education, history education, mathematics education, physical education; teacher education (MAT). *Accreditation:* NCATE. Part-time and evening/weekend programs available. Postbaccalaureate distance learning degree programs offered (no on-campus study). *Faculty:* 23 full-time (14 women), 16 part-time/adjunct (11 women). *Students:* 19 full-time (17 women), 199 part-time (147 women); includes 7 minority (3 Black or African American, non-Hispanic/Latino; 1 Asian, non-Hispanic/Latino; 3 Hispanic/Latino), 1 international. Average age 34. 259 applicants, 66% accepted, 112 enrolled. In 2011, 100 master's, 16 other advanced degrees awarded. *Degree requirements:* For master's, comprehensive exam, thesis optional. *Entrance requirements:* For master's, GRE or MAT, GACE, minimum GPA of 2.75; for Ed S, GRE General Test or MAT, 3 years of teaching experience, master's degree, minimum graduate GPA of 3.25, leadership position in the school. Additional exam requirements/recommendations for international students: Required—TOEFL (minimum score 550 paper-based; 213 computer-based; 79 iBT), IELTS (minimum score 6.5). *Application deadline:* For fall admission, 8/1 priority date for domestic students, 7/1 for international students; for spring admission, 12/1 priority date for domestic students, 11/1 for international students. Applications are processed on a rolling basis. Application fee: $40. Electronic applications accepted. *Expenses:* Tuition, state resident: full-time $3528; part-time $196 per credit hour. Tuition, nonresident: full-time $14,094; part-time $783 per credit hour. *Required fees:* $1718; $859 per semester. Tuition and fees vary according to course load, campus/location and program. *Financial support:* Teaching assistantships, career-related internships or fieldwork, scholarships/grants, and unspecified assistantships available. Financial award application deadline: 5/1; financial award applicants required to submit CSS PROFILE or FAFSA. *Faculty research:* Identification of professional development school structures supporting P-12 student achievement, impact of diverse field placement settings in teacher belief development among preservice teachers, use of inquiry methodology in social studies teaching with English language learners, use of instructional differentiation in the middle grades classroom, effects of international school placements on preservice teacher beliefs and attitudes. *Unit head:* Dr. Bob Michael, Dean, School of Education, 706-864-1998, Fax: 706-867-2850, E-mail: bmichael@northgeorgia.edu. *Application contact:* Susan L. Perry, Graduate Admissions Coordinator, 706-864-1543, Fax: 706-867-2795, E-mail: slperry@northgeorgia.edu. Web site: http://www.northgeorgia.edu/soe/.

Northwestern State University of Louisiana, Graduate Studies and Research, College of Education and Human Development, Program in Early Childhood Education, Natchitoches, LA 71497. Offers early childhood education and teaching (M Ed, MAT). *Students:* 2 full-time (both women), 42 part-time (41 women); includes 1 minority (Black or African American, non-Hispanic/Latino). Average age 31. 7 applicants, 100% accepted, 7 enrolled. In 2011, 6 master's awarded. *Degree requirements:* For master's, comprehensive exam, thesis or alternative. *Entrance requirements:* For master's, GRE General Test. Additional exam requirements/recommendations for international students: Required—TOEFL. *Application deadline:* For fall admission, 3/15 priority date for domestic students; for spring admission, 3/15 for domestic students. Applications are processed on a rolling basis. Application fee: $20 ($30 for international students). Electronic applications accepted. *Expenses:* Tuition, state resident: full-time $3440. Tuition, nonresident: full-time $12,010. *Unit head:* Dr. Vickie Gentry, Chair, 318-357-6288, Fax: 318-357-6275, E-mail: education@nsula.edu. *Application contact:* Dr. Steven G. Horton, Associate Provost/Dean, Graduate Studies, Research, and Information Systems, 318-357-5851, Fax: 318-357-5019, E-mail: grad_school@nsula.edu.

Northwest Missouri State University, Graduate School, College of Education and Human Services, Department of Curriculum and Instruction, Program in Teaching: Early Childhood, Maryville, MO 64468-6001. Offers MS Ed. *Accreditation:* NCATE. Part-time programs available. *Faculty:* 11 full-time (all women). *Students:* 7 part-time (all women); includes 1 minority (Two or more races, non-Hispanic/Latino). 3 applicants, 100% accepted, 1 enrolled. In 2011, 3 master's awarded. *Degree requirements:* For master's, comprehensive exam. *Entrance requirements:* For master's, GRE General Test, teaching certificate, minimum undergraduate GPA of 2.75, writing sample. Additional exam requirements/recommendations for international students: Required—TOEFL (minimum score 550 paper-based; 213 computer-based). *Application deadline:* For fall admission, 7/1 for domestic and international students; for spring admission, 11/15 for domestic and international students. Applications are processed on a rolling basis. Application fee: $0 ($50 for international students). *Financial support:* Application deadline: 4/1; applicants required to submit FAFSA. *Unit head:* Dr. Barbara Martin, Director, 660-562-1779. *Application contact:* Dr. Gregory Haddock, Dean of Graduate School, 660-562-1145, Fax: 660-562-1096, E-mail: gradsch@nwmissouri.edu.

Oakland University, Graduate Study and Lifelong Learning, School of Education and Human Services, Department of Human Development and Child Studies, Program in Early Childhood Education, Rochester, MI 48309-4401. Offers early childhood education (M Ed, PhD, Certificate); early mathematics education (Certificate). *Accreditation:* Teacher Education Accreditation Council. *Degree requirements:* For doctorate, thesis/dissertation. *Entrance requirements:* For master's, minimum GPA of 3.0 for unconditional admission; for doctorate, GRE General Test, minimum GPA of 3.0 for unconditional admission. Additional exam requirements/recommendations for international students: Required—TOEFL (minimum score 550 paper-based; 213 computer-based).

Oglethorpe University, Division of Education, Atlanta, GA 30319-2797. Offers early childhood education (MAT). Part-time programs available. *Degree requirements:* For master's, comprehensive exam. *Entrance requirements:* For master's, GRE General Test, PRAXIS, minimum GPA of 2.8, 3 recommendations.

The Ohio State University at Lima, Graduate Programs, Lima, OH 45804. Offers early childhood education (M Ed); education (MA); middle childhood education (M Ed); social work (MSW). Part-time programs available. *Faculty:* 41. *Students:* 27 full-time (13 women), 39 part-time (33 women); includes 3 minority (1 Black or African American, non-Hispanic/Latino; 2 Two or more races, non-Hispanic/Latino). Average age 34. Terminal master's awarded for partial completion of doctoral program. *Degree requirements:* For master's, comprehensive exam (for some programs), thesis (for some programs). *Entrance requirements:* For master's, GRE, minimum GPA of 3.0. Additional exam requirements/recommendations for international students: Required—TOEFL (minimum score 550 paper-based; 79 iBT), Michigan English Language Assessment Battery (minimum score 82); Recommended—IELTS (minimum score 7), TWE. *Application deadline:* For fall admission, 6/1 priority date for domestic students, 6/1 for international students; for spring admission, 10/15 priority date for domestic students, 10/15 for international students. Applications are processed on a rolling basis. Application fee: $40 ($50 for international students). Electronic applications accepted. *Expenses:* Tuition, state resident: full-time $11,130. Tuition, nonresident: full-time $27,855. *Financial support:* Application deadline: 2/1. *Unit head:* Dr. John Snyder, Dean/Director, 419-995-8481, E-mail: snyder.4@osu.edu. *Application contact:* Graduate Admissions, 614-292-9444, Fax: 614-292-3895, E-mail: domestic.grad@osu.edu.

The Ohio State University at Marion, Graduate Programs, Marion, OH 43302-5695. Offers early childhood education (pre-K to grade 3) (M Ed); education - teaching and learning (MA); middle childhood education (grades 4-9) (M Ed). Part-time programs available. *Faculty:* 38. *Students:* 67 full-time (49 women), 13 part-time (9 women); includes 2 minority (1 American Indian or Alaska Native, non-Hispanic/Latino; 1 Hispanic/Latino). Average age 32. *Degree requirements:* For master's, comprehensive exam (for some programs), thesis (for some programs). *Entrance requirements:* For master's, GRE, minimum undergraduate GPA of 3.0. Additional exam requirements/recommendations for international students: Required—Michigan English Language Assessment Battery (minimum score 82); Recommended—TOEFL (minimum score 650 paper-based; 79 iBT), IELTS (minimum score 7). *Application deadline:* For fall admission, 6/1 priority date for domestic students, 6/1 for international students; for spring admission, 10/15 priority date for domestic students, 10/15 for international students. Applications are processed on a rolling basis. Application fee: $40 ($50 for international students). Electronic applications accepted. *Expenses:* Tuition, state resident: full-time $11,130. Tuition, nonresident: full-time $27,855. Tuition and fees vary according to course load. *Financial support:* Application deadline: 1/15; applicants required to submit FAFSA. *Unit head:* Dr. Gregory S. Rose, Dean/Director, 740-389-6786 Ext. 6218, E-mail: rose.9@osu.edu. *Application contact:* Graduate Admissions, 614-292-9444, Fax: 614-292-3895, E-mail: domestic.grad@osu.edu.

The Ohio State University–Mansfield Campus, Graduate Programs, Mansfield, OH 44906-1599. Offers early childhood education (M Ed); education (MA); middle childhood education (M Ed); social work (MSW). Part-time programs available. *Faculty:* 41. *Students:* 21 full-time (15 women), 57 part-time (48 women); includes 5 minority (2 Black or African American, non-Hispanic/Latino; 1 Asian, non-Hispanic/Latino; 1 Hispanic/Latino; 1 Two or more races, non-Hispanic/Latino), 1 international. Average age 33. *Degree requirements:* For master's, comprehensive exam (for some programs), thesis (for some programs). *Entrance requirements:* For master's, GRE, minimum GPA of 3.0. Additional exam requirements/recommendations for international students: Required—TOEFL (minimum score 550 paper-based; 79 iBT), Michigan English Language Assessment Battery (minimum score 82); Recommended—IELTS (minimum score 7).

Application deadline: For fall admission, 6/1 priority date for domestic students, 6/1 for international students; for spring admission, 10/15 priority date for domestic students, 10/15 for international students. Applications are processed on a rolling basis. Application fee: $40 ($50 for international students). Electronic applications accepted. *Expenses:* Tuition, state resident: full-time $11,130. Tuition, nonresident: full-time $27,855. Tuition and fees vary according to course load. *Financial support:* Teaching assistantships with full tuition reimbursements, Federal Work-Study, and scholarships/grants available. Support available to part-time students. Financial award application deadline: 2/1. *Unit head:* Dr. Stephen M. Gavazzi, Dean and Director, 419-755-4221, Fax: 419-755-4241, E-mail: gavazzi.1@osu.edu. *Application contact:* Graduate Admissions, 614-292-9444, Fax: 614-292-3895, E-mail: domestic.grad@osu.edu.

The Ohio State University–Newark Campus, Graduate Programs, Newark, OH 43055-1797. Offers early/middle childhood education (M Ed); education - teaching and learning (MA); social work (MSW). Part-time programs available. *Faculty:* 56. *Students:* 63 full-time (55 women), 46 part-time (39 women); includes 6 minority (1 Black or African American, non-Hispanic/Latino; 1 Asian, non-Hispanic/Latino; 3 Hispanic/Latino; 1 Two or more races, non-Hispanic/Latino). Average age 31. Terminal master's awarded for partial completion of doctoral program. *Degree requirements:* For master's, comprehensive exam (for some programs), thesis (for some programs). *Entrance requirements:* For master's, GRE, minimum GPA of 3.0. Additional exam requirements/recommendations for international students: Required—Michigan English Language Assessment Battery (minimum score 82); Recommended—TOEFL (minimum score 550 paper-based; 79 iBT), IELTS (minimum score 7). *Application deadline:* For fall admission, 6/1 priority date for domestic students, 6/1 for international students; for spring admission, 10/15 priority date for domestic students, 2/1 for international students. Applications are processed on a rolling basis. Application fee: $40 ($50 for international students). Electronic applications accepted. *Unit head:* Dr. William L. MacDonald, Dean/Director, 740-366-9333 Ext. 330, E-mail: macdonald.24@osu.edu. *Application contact:* Graduate Admissions, 614-292-9444, Fax: 614-292-3985, E-mail: domestic.grad@osu.edu.

Oklahoma City University, Petree College of Arts and Sciences, Programs in Education, Oklahoma City, OK 73106-1402. Offers applied behavioral studies (M Ed); early childhood education (M Ed); elementary education (M Ed). Part-time and evening/weekend programs available. *Faculty:* 4 full-time (2 women), 2 part-time/adjunct (1 woman). *Students:* 34 full-time (31 women), 14 part-time (11 women); includes 14 minority (11 Black or African American, non-Hispanic/Latino; 2 Hispanic/Latino; 1 Two or more races, non-Hispanic/Latino), 6 international. Average age 30. 34 applicants, 79% accepted, 18 enrolled. In 2011, 21 master's awarded. *Entrance requirements:* For master's, minimum GPA of 3.0. Additional exam requirements/recommendations for international students: Required—TOEFL (minimum score 550 paper-based). *Application deadline:* Applications are processed on a rolling basis. Application fee: $50 ($70 for international students). Electronic applications accepted. *Expenses: Tuition:* Full-time $16,848; part-time $936 per credit hour. *Required fees:* $2070; $115 per credit hour. One-time fee: $300. *Financial support:* Career-related internships or fieldwork, Federal Work-Study, and tuition waivers available. Support available to part-time students. Financial award application deadline: 6/1; financial award applicants required to submit FAFSA. *Faculty research:* Adult literacy, cognition, reading strategies. *Unit head:* Dr. Lois Lawler-Brown, Chair, 405-208-5374, Fax: 405-208-6012, E-mail: llbrown@okcu.edu. *Application contact:* Michelle Cook, Director, Admissions, 800-633-7242, Fax: 405-208-5916, E-mail: gadmissions@okcu.edu. Web site: http://www.okcu.edu/petree/education/graduate.aspx.

Old Dominion University, Darden College of Education, Program in Early Childhood Education, Norfolk, VA 23529. Offers MS Ed, PhD. *Accreditation:* NCATE. Part-time and evening/weekend programs available. *Faculty:* 15 full-time (14 women), 34 part-time/adjunct (27 women). *Students:* 25 full-time (all women), 19 part-time (17 women); includes 15 minority (7 Black or African American, non-Hispanic/Latino; 1 American Indian or Alaska Native, non-Hispanic/Latino; 4 Asian, non-Hispanic/Latino; 1 Hispanic/Latino; 2 Two or more races, non-Hispanic/Latino). Average age 30. 43 applicants, 42% accepted, 18 enrolled. In 2011, 32 degrees awarded. *Degree requirements:* For master's, comprehensive exam, written exams; for doctorate, comprehensive exam, thesis/dissertation. *Entrance requirements:* For master's, GRE General Test, PRAXIS I, minimum undergraduate GPA of 2.5; for doctorate, GRE General Test. Additional exam requirements/recommendations for international students: Required—TOEFL. *Application deadline:* For fall admission, 7/1 for domestic students; for winter admission, 7/1 for domestic students; for spring admission, 11/1 for domestic students. Applications are processed on a rolling basis. Application fee: $50. *Expenses:* Tuition, state resident: full-time $9096; part-time $379 per credit. Tuition, nonresident: full-time $23,064; part-time $961 per credit. *Required fees:* $127 per semester. One-time fee: $50. *Financial support:* In 2011–12, 40 students received support, including fellowships with full tuition reimbursements available (averaging $15,000 per year), research assistantships with tuition reimbursements available (averaging $9,000 per year), 2 teaching assistantships with full tuition reimbursements available (averaging $9,000 per year); career-related internships or fieldwork, scholarships/grants, and tuition waivers (partial) also available. Financial award application deadline: 2/15; financial award applicants required to submit FAFSA. *Faculty research:* Child abuse, day care, parenting, discipline (positive), bullying. *Unit head:* Dr. Andrea Debruin-Parecki, Graduate Program Director, 757-683-6759, Fax: 757-683-5593, E-mail: adebruin@odu.edu. *Application contact:* William Heffelfinger, Director of Graduate Admissions, 757-683-5554, Fax: 757-683-3255, E-mail: gradadmit@odu.edu. Web site: http://education.odu.edu/esse/academics/degrees/ecedeg.shtml.

Ottawa University, Graduate Studies-Arizona, Program in Education, Ottawa, KS 66067-3399. Offers community college counseling (MA); curriculum and instruction (MA); early childhood (MA); education intervention (MA); education leadership (MA); education technology (MA); Montessori early childhood education (MA); Montessori elementary education (MA); professional development (MA); school guidance counseling (MA); special education - cross categorical (MA). Programs offered in Mesa, Phoenix, Tempe and West Valley, AZ. *Accreditation:* NCATE. Part-time programs available. *Degree requirements:* For master's, thesis or alternative. *Entrance requirements:* For master's, minimum undergraduate GPA of 3.0, copy of current state certification or teaching license. Additional exam requirements/recommendations for international students: Required—TOEFL (minimum score 550 paper-based; 213 computer-based). Electronic applications accepted. *Expenses:* Contact institution.

Our Lady of the Lake University of San Antonio, School of Professional Studies, Program in Curriculum and Instruction, San Antonio, TX 78207-4689. Offers bilingual (M Ed); early childhood education (M Ed); English as a second language (M Ed); integrated math teaching (M Ed); integrated science teaching (M Ed); master reading teacher (M Ed); master technology teacher (M Ed); reading specialist (M Ed).

Pace University, School of Education, New York, NY 10038. Offers adolescent education (MST); childhood education (MST); educational leadership (MS Ed); educational technology studies (MS); literacy (MSE); school business management (Certificate); special education (MS Ed); teaching students with disabilities (MSE). *Accreditation:* NCATE. Part-time and evening/weekend programs available. *Students:* 164 full-time (131 women), 533 part-time (396 women); includes 157 minority (59 Black or African American, non-Hispanic/Latino; 2 American Indian or Alaska Native, non-Hispanic/Latino; 26 Asian, non-Hispanic/Latino; 54 Hispanic/Latino; 1 Native Hawaiian or other Pacific Islander, non-Hispanic/Latino; 15 Two or more races, non-Hispanic/Latino), 10 international. Average age 29. 256 applicants, 79% accepted, 114 enrolled. In 2011, 334 master's, 34 other advanced degrees awarded. *Degree requirements:* For master's, internship. *Entrance requirements:* For master's, interview, teaching certificate. Additional exam requirements/recommendations for international students: Required—TOEFL. *Application deadline:* For fall admission, 7/31 priority date for domestic students; for spring admission, 11/30 for domestic students. Applications are processed on a rolling basis. Application fee: $70. Electronic applications accepted. *Expenses:* Contact institution. *Financial support:* Research assistantships, career-related internships or fieldwork, and Federal Work-Study available. Support available to part-time students. Financial award applicants required to submit FAFSA. *Unit head:* Dr. Andrea M. Spencer, Dean, 212-346-1345, E-mail: aspencer@pace.edu. *Application contact:* Susan Ford-Goldschein, Director of Admissions, 212-346-1660, Fax: 212-346-1585, E-mail: gradnyc@pace.edu. Web site: http://www.pace.edu/.

Pacific University, College of Education, Forest Grove, OR 97116-1797. Offers early childhood education (MAT); education (MAE); elementary education (MAT); high school education (MAT); middle school education (MAT); special education (MAT); visual function in learning (M Ed). *Accreditation:* NCATE. Part-time and evening/weekend programs available. *Degree requirements:* For master's, research project. *Entrance requirements:* For master's, California Basic Educational Skills Test, PRAXIS II, minimum undergraduate GPA of 2.75, 3.0 graduate. Additional exam requirements/recommendations for international students: Required—TOEFL. Electronic applications accepted. *Expenses:* Contact institution. *Faculty research:* Defining a culturally competent classroom, technology in the k-12 classroom, Socratic seminars, social studies education.

Piedmont College, School of Education, Demorest, GA 30535-0010. Offers early childhood education (MA, MAT); middle grades education (MA); secondary education (MA, MAT); special education (MA, MAT); teacher leadership (Ed S). Part-time and evening/weekend programs available. *Students:* 546 full-time (433 women), 809 part-time (698 women); includes 172 minority (139 Black or African American, non-Hispanic/Latino; 2 American Indian or Alaska Native, non-Hispanic/Latino; 6 Asian, non-Hispanic/Latino; 18 Hispanic/Latino; 7 Two or more races, non-Hispanic/Latino), 17 international. Average age 37. 342 applicants, 83% accepted, 234 enrolled. In 2011, 444 master's, 510 other advanced degrees awarded. *Degree requirements:* For master's, thesis, field experience in the classroom teaching ; for doctorate, thesis/dissertation. *Entrance requirements:* For master's, GRE General Test, MAT, minimum undergraduate GPA of 2.5; for Ed S, minimum graduate GPA of 3.5, valid teaching certificate. Additional exam requirements/recommendations for international students: Required—TOEFL (minimum score 550 paper-based; 213 computer-based). *Application deadline:* For fall admission, 7/15 for domestic students; for spring admission, 12/1 for domestic students. Applications are processed on a rolling basis. Application fee: $0. Electronic applications accepted. *Expenses: Tuition:* Part-time $407 per credit hour. Tuition and fees vary according to program. *Financial support:* Career-related internships or fieldwork, Federal Work-Study, and unspecified assistantships available. Support available to part-time students. Financial award applicants required to submit FAFSA. *Unit head:* Dr. Bob Cummings, Dean, 706-778-3000 Ext. 1201, Fax: 706-776-9608, E-mail: bcummings@piedmont.edu. *Application contact:* Penny Loggins, Director of Graduate Admissions, 706-778-8500 Ext. 1181, Fax: 706-778-0150, E-mail: ploggins@piedmont.edu.

Pittsburg State University, Graduate School, College of Education, Department of Curriculum and Instruction, Pittsburg, KS 66762. Offers classroom reading teacher (MS); early childhood education (MS); elementary education (MS); reading (MS); reading specialist (MS); secondary education (MS); teaching (MAT). *Accreditation:* NCATE. *Degree requirements:* For master's, thesis or alternative. *Entrance requirements:* For master's, GRE or MAT.

Pontificia Universidad Catolica Madre y Maestra, Graduate School, Faculty of Sciences and Humanities, Santiago, Dominican Republic. Offers architecture (M Arch), including architecture of interiors, architecture of tourist lodgings, landscaping; early childhood education (M Ed).

Portland State University, Graduate Studies, School of Education, Department of Curriculum and Instruction, Portland, OR 97207-0751. Offers early childhood education (MA, MS); education (M Ed, MA, MS); educational leadership: curriculum and instruction (Ed D); educational media/school librarianship (MA, MS); elementary education (M Ed, MAT, MST); reading (MA, MS); secondary education (M Ed, MAT, MST). *Accreditation:* NCATE. Part-time programs available. *Degree requirements:* For master's, comprehensive exam, thesis or alternative; for doctorate, thesis/dissertation. *Entrance requirements:* For master's, California Basic Educational Skills Test, minimum GPA of 3.0 in upper-division course work or 2.75 overall. Additional exam requirements/recommendations for international students: Required—TOEFL (minimum score 550 paper-based; 213 computer-based). *Faculty research:* Early literacy, characteristics of successful teachers of at-risk students, participation of women/minorities in technology courses, selection of cooperating teachers.

Prescott College, Graduate Programs, Program in Education, Prescott, AZ 86301. Offers early childhood education (MA); early childhood special education (MA); education (MA); elementary education (MA); environmental education leadership and administration (MA); equine-assisted experiential learning (MA); school guidance counseling (MA); secondary education (MA); special education, learning disability (MA); special education, mental retardation (MA); special education, serious emotional disability (MA); student-directed independent study (MA); sustainability education (PhD). Part-time programs available. Postbaccalaureate distance learning degree programs offered (minimal on-campus study). *Faculty:* 2 full-time (both women), 47 part-time/adjunct (31 women). *Students:* 59 full-time (36 women), 48 part-time (30 women); includes 16 minority (3 Black or African American, non-Hispanic/Latino; 1 American Indian or Alaska Native, non-Hispanic/Latino; 1 Asian, non-Hispanic/Latino; 8 Hispanic/Latino; 3 Two or more races, non-Hispanic/Latino), 2 international. Average age 40. 75 applicants, 76% accepted, 36 enrolled. In 2011, 14 master's, 8 doctorates awarded. *Degree requirements:* For master's, thesis, fieldwork or internship, practicum; for doctorate, thesis/dissertation. *Entrance requirements:* For master's, 2 letters of recommendation, resume; for doctorate, 3 letters of recommendation, resume, official transcripts, personal statement, program proposal. Additional exam requirements/recommendations for international students: Required—TOEFL (minimum score 500 paper-based; 173 computer-based). *Application deadline:* For fall admission, 4/15 priority date for domestic students, 4/15 for international students; for spring admission, 9/15 priority date for domestic students, 9/15 for international students. Applications are processed on a rolling basis. Application fee: $40. Electronic applications accepted. *Expenses: Tuition:* Full-time $16,440; part-time $685 per credit. *Required fees:* $150 per semester. One-time fee: $350. *Financial support:* Career-related internships or fieldwork and Federal Work-Study available. Financial award applicants required to submit FAFSA. *Unit head:* Noel Caniglia, Chair, 928-358-3201, Fax: 928-776-5151, E-mail: ncaniglia@prescott.edu. *Application contact:* Kerstin Alicki, Admissions Counselor, 928-350-2100, Fax: 928-776-5242, E-mail: admissions@prescott.edu.

Queens College of the City University of New York, Division of Graduate Studies, Division of Education, Department of Elementary and Early Childhood Education, Flushing, NY 11367-1597. Offers bilingual education (MS Ed); childhood education (MA); early childhood education (MA); elementary education (MS Ed, AC); literacy (MS Ed). Part-time and evening/weekend programs available. *Faculty:* 31 full-time (25 women). *Students:* 87 full-time (74 women), 561 part-time (522 women); includes 226 minority (49 Black or African American, non-Hispanic/Latino; 68 Asian, non-Hispanic/ Latino; 109 Hispanic/Latino), 5 international. 436 applicants, 64% accepted, 212 enrolled. In 2011, 229 master's, 1 other advanced degree awarded. *Degree requirements:* For master's, research project; for AC, thesis optional. *Entrance requirements:* For master's, minimum GPA of 3.0. Additional exam requirements/ recommendations for international students: Required—TOEFL. *Application deadline:* For fall admission, 4/1 for domestic students; for spring admission, 11/1 for domestic students. Applications are processed on a rolling basis. Application fee: $125. *Expenses:* Tuition, state resident: part-time $345 per credit. Tuition, nonresident: part-time $640 per credit. *Required fees:* $145.25 per semester. *Financial support:* Career-related internships or fieldwork, Federal Work-Study, institutionally sponsored loans, and tuition waivers (partial) available. Support available to part-time students. Financial award application deadline: 4/1; financial award applicants required to submit FAFSA. *Unit head:* Dr. Myra Zarnowski, Chairperson, 718-997-5328. *Application contact:* Mario Caruso, Director of Graduate Admissions, 718-997-5200, Fax: 718-997-5193, E-mail: graduate_admissions@qc.edu.

Radford University, College of Graduate and Professional Studies, College of Education and Human Development, School of Teacher Education and Leadership, Program in Special Education, Radford, VA 24142. Offers adapted curriculum (MS); early childhood special education (MS); general curriculum (MS); hearing impairments (MS); visual impairment (MS). *Accreditation:* NCATE. Part-time and evening/weekend programs available. *Faculty:* 9 full-time (8 women), 12 part-time/adjunct (11 women). *Students:* 19 full-time (all women), 39 part-time (31 women); includes 2 minority (both Black or African American, non-Hispanic/Latino). Average age 32. 24 applicants, 92% accepted, 19 enrolled. In 2011, 34 master's awarded. *Degree requirements:* For master's, comprehensive exam. *Entrance requirements:* For master's, GRE, minimum GPA of 2.75, 3 letters of reference, resume, personal essay, official transcripts. Additional exam requirements/recommendations for international students: Required—TOEFL (minimum score 550 paper-based; 213 computer-based; 79 iBT). *Application deadline:* For fall admission, 2/15 for domestic students, 12/1 for international students; for spring admission, 7/1 for international students. Applications are processed on a rolling basis. Application fee: $50. Electronic applications accepted. *Expenses:* Tuition, state resident: full-time $6262; part-time $261 per credit hour. Tuition, nonresident: full-time $14,540; part-time $606 per credit hour. *Required fees:* $2812; $117 per credit hour. Tuition and fees vary according to program. *Financial support:* In 2011–12, 19 students received support, including 5 research assistantships (averaging $7,875 per year); career-related internships or fieldwork, Federal Work-Study, institutionally sponsored loans, scholarships/grants, and unspecified assistantships also available. Financial award application deadline: 3/1; financial award applicants required to submit FAFSA. *Unit head:* Dr. Elizabeth Altieri, Coordinator, 540-831-5590, Fax: 540-831-5059, E-mail: ealtieri@radford.edu. *Application contact:* Rebecca Conner, Graduate Admissions, 540-831-5431, Fax: 540-831-6061, E-mail: gradcollege@radford.edu. Web site: http://www.radford.edu/content/cehd/home/departments/teacher-ed/graduate-programs/special-education.html.

Reinhardt University, Program in Early Childhood Education, Waleska, GA 30183-2981. Offers M Ed, MAT. Part-time and evening/weekend programs available. Postbaccalaureate distance learning degree programs offered. *Faculty:* 12 full-time (8 women), 6 part-time/adjunct (5 women). *Degree requirements:* For master's, comprehensive exam. *Entrance requirements:* For master's, GACE, background check. Additional exam requirements/recommendations for international students: Required—TOEFL. *Application deadline:* For fall admission, 5/7 for domestic and international students. Applications are processed on a rolling basis. Application fee: $25. Electronic applications accepted. *Expenses: Tuition:* Full-time $7020; part-time $390 per credit hour. *Required fees:* $70 per semester hour. *Financial support:* Application deadline: 5/ 1; applicants required to submit FAFSA. *Unit head:* Nancy Carter, Director of Graduate Studies, 770-720-5948, Fax: 770-720-9173, E-mail: ntc@reinhardt.edu. *Application contact:* Ray Schumacher, Admissions Counselor, 770-993-6971, Fax: 770-475-0263, E-mail: res@reinhardt.edu.

Rhode Island College, School of Graduate Studies, Feinstein School of Education and Human Development, Department of Elementary Education, Providence, RI 02908-1991. Offers early childhood education (M Ed); elementary education (M Ed, MAT); reading (M Ed). *Accreditation:* NCATE. Part-time and evening/weekend programs available. *Faculty:* 11 full-time (7 women), 2 part-time/adjunct (both women). *Students:* 23 full-time (20 women), 37 part-time (36 women); includes 3 minority (1 Black or African American, non-Hispanic/Latino; 1 Asian, non-Hispanic/Latino; 1 Hispanic/Latino). Average age 31. In 2011, 30 master's awarded. *Degree requirements:* For master's, comprehensive exam (for some programs), comprehensive assessment. *Entrance requirements:* For master's, GRE General Test or MAT, PRAXIS II (elementary content knowledge), undergraduate transcripts; minimum undergraduate GPA of 3.0; 3 letters of recommendation. Additional exam requirements/recommendations for international students: Recommended—TOEFL (minimum score 550 paper-based; 213 computer-based; 79 iBT). *Application deadline:* For fall admission, 3/1 for domestic students; for spring admission, 11/1 for domestic students. Applications are processed on a rolling basis. Application fee: $50. *Expenses:* Tuition, state resident: full-time $8592; part-time $358 per credit hour. Tuition, nonresident: full-time $16,800; part-time $700 per credit hour. *Required fees:* $602; $22 per credit. $72 per term. *Financial support:* Teaching assistantships with full tuition reimbursements, Federal Work-Study, scholarships/ grants, and health care benefits available. Support available to part-time students. Financial award application deadline: 5/15; financial award applicants required to submit FAFSA. *Unit head:* Dr. Patricia Cordeiro, Chair, 401-456-8016. *Application contact:* Graduate Studies, 401-456-8700. Web site: http://www.ric.edu/elementaryEducation/.

Rivier University, School of Graduate Studies, Department of Education, Nashua, NH 03060. Offers curriculum and instruction (M Ed); early childhood education (M Ed); educational administration (M Ed); educational studies (M Ed); elementary education (M Ed); elementary education and general special education (M Ed); emotional and behavioral disorders (M Ed); general social education (M Ed); leadership and learning (Ed D, CAGS); learning disabilities (M Ed); learning disabilities and reading (M Ed); mental health counseling (MA); reading (M Ed); school counseling (M Ed). Part-time and evening/weekend programs available. *Degree requirements:* For master's, comprehensive exam (for some programs), internships. *Entrance requirements:* For master's, GRE General Test or MAT.

Roberts Wesleyan College, Division of Teacher Education, Rochester, NY 14624-1997. Offers adolescence education (M Ed); childhood and special education (M Ed); literacy education (M Ed); urban education (M Ed). Part-time and evening/weekend programs available. *Degree requirements:* For master's, thesis.

Rockford College, Graduate Studies, Department of Education, Program in Early Childhood Education, Rockford, IL 61108-2393. Offers MAT. Part-time and evening/ weekend programs available. *Degree requirements:* For master's, thesis optional. *Entrance requirements:* For master's, GRE General Test, basic skills test (for students seeking certification), 3 letters of recommendation. Additional exam requirements/ recommendations for international students: Required—TOEFL. *Application deadline:* Applications are processed on a rolling basis. Application fee: $50. Electronic applications accepted. *Expenses: Tuition:* Full-time $16,200; part-time $675 per credit. *Required fees:* $80; $40 per semester. Tuition and fees vary according to class time, course level, course load, degree level, campus/location and program. *Unit head:* Dr. Michelle M. McReynolds, Director, 815-226-3390, Fax: 815-394-3706, E-mail: mmcreynolds@rockford.edu. *Application contact:* Michele Mehren, Office Manager for Graduate Studies, 815-226-4041, Fax: 815-394-3706, E-mail: mmehren@rockford.edu. Web site: http://www.rockford.edu/?page=MAT.

Roosevelt University, Graduate Division, College of Education, Department of Teaching and Learning, Chicago, IL 60605. Offers early childhood education (MA); elementary education (MA); special education (MA).

Rutgers, The State University of New Jersey, New Brunswick, Graduate School of Education, Department of Learning and Teaching, Program in Early Childhood/ Elementary Education, Piscataway, NJ 08854-8097. Offers Ed M, Ed D. Part-time programs available. Terminal master's awarded for partial completion of doctoral program. *Degree requirements:* For master's, comprehensive exam (for some programs); for doctorate, thesis/dissertation, qualifying exam. *Entrance requirements:* For master's, GRE General Test, minimum GPA of 3.0; for doctorate, GRE General Test, minimum GPA of 3.5. Additional exam requirements/recommendations for international students: Required—TOEFL. Electronic applications accepted.

Saginaw Valley State University, College of Education, Program in Early Childhood Education, University Center, MI 48710. Offers MAT. *Accreditation:* NCATE. Part-time and evening/weekend programs available. *Students:* 5 full-time (all women), 111 part-time (110 women); includes 2 minority (1 Black or African American, non-Hispanic/ Latino; 1 Hispanic/Latino). Average age 31. 21 applicants, 95% accepted, 15 enrolled. In 2011, 35 master's awarded. *Degree requirements:* For master's, practicum. *Entrance requirements:* For master's, minimum GPA of 3.0, teaching certificate. Additional exam requirements/recommendations for international students: Required—TOEFL (minimum score 525 paper-based; 197 computer-based; 71 iBT). *Application deadline:* Applications are processed on a rolling basis. Application fee: $25. Electronic applications accepted. *Expenses:* Tuition, state resident: full-time $8300; part-time $5333 per year. Tuition, nonresident: full-time $15,613; part-time $10,209 per year. *International tuition:* $15,631 full-time. *Financial support:* Federal Work-Study and scholarships/grants available. Support available to part-time students. Financial award applicants required to submit FAFSA. *Unit head:* Dr. Steve P. Barbus, Jr., Dean, 989-964-6067, Fax: 989-790-4385, E-mail: barbus@svsu.edu. *Application contact:* Kathy Lopez, Certification Officer, 989-964-4661, Fax: 989-964-4385, E-mail: klopez@ svsu.edu.

St. Bonaventure University, School of Graduate Studies, School of Education, Literacy Programs, St. Bonaventure, NY 14778-2284. Offers adolescent literacy 5-12 (MS Ed); childhood literacy B-6 (MS Ed). *Accreditation:* NCATE. Part-time and evening/weekend programs available. *Faculty:* 2 full-time (both women). *Students:* 18 full-time (16 women), 33 part-time (32 women). Average age 24. 33 applicants, 67% accepted, 15 enrolled. In 2011, 50 master's awarded. *Degree requirements:* For master's, comprehensive exam, thesis optional, literacy coaching internship, portfolio. *Entrance requirements:* For master's, interview, writing sample, minimum undergraduate GPA of 3.0, references, teaching certificate in matching area. Additional exam requirements/ recommendations for international students: Required—TOEFL (minimum score 550 paper-based; 213 computer-based; 80 iBT). *Application deadline:* For fall admission, 6/ 15 priority date for domestic students, 2/1 for international students; for spring admission, 11/15 priority date for domestic students, 7/1 for international students. Applications are processed on a rolling basis. Application fee: $30. Electronic applications accepted. *Expenses: Tuition:* Part-time $670 per credit. *Financial support:* In 2011–12, 4 research assistantships with full and partial tuition reimbursements were awarded; Federal Work-Study, scholarships/grants, health care benefits, and unspecified assistantships also available. Support available to part-time students. Financial award application deadline: 4/15; financial award applicants required to submit FAFSA. *Unit head:* Dr. Pamela Sharp Crawford, Director, 716-375-2387, E-mail: pcrawfor@sbu.edu. *Application contact:* Bruce Campbell, 716-375-2429, Fax: 716-375-4015, E-mail: gradsch@sbu.edu. Web site: http://www.sbu.edu/education.aspx?id-2994.

St. John's University, The School of Education, Department of Curriculum and Instruction, Program in Early Childhood Education, Queens, NY 11439. Offers early childhood (MS Ed). *Students:* 27 full-time (all women), 28 part-time (27 women); includes 26 minority (9 Black or African American, non-Hispanic/Latino; 5 Asian, non-Hispanic/Latino; 11 Hispanic/Latino; 1 Two or more races, non-Hispanic/Latino), 2 international. Average age 29. 44 applicants, 77% accepted, 18 enrolled. In 2011, 14 master's awarded. *Degree requirements:* For master's, comprehensive exam. *Entrance requirements:* For master's, minimum GPA of 3.0, 2 letters of recommendation, qualification for the New York State provisional (initial) teaching certificate. Additional exam requirements/recommendations for international students: Required—TOEFL (minimum score 600 paper-based; 250 computer-based; 100 iBT), IELTS (minimum score 5.5). *Application deadline:* For fall admission, 8/17 for domestic students, 5/1 for international students; for spring admission, 1/5 for domestic students, 11/1 for international students. Applications are processed on a rolling basis. Application fee: $70. Electronic applications accepted. *Expenses: Tuition:* Full-time $18,000; part-time $1000 per credit. *Required fees:* $170 per semester. Tuition and fees vary according to program. *Financial support:* Research assistantships available. *Faculty research:* Improving children's learning in math, science and technology; health and nutrition education to prevent obesity; oral language and literacy development in diverse populations; home-school collaborations in literacy among young ELLS; multicultural and international education; bilingual education; at-risk children; arts education; parent, home and community partnership; special needs and inclusive education. *Unit head:* Dr. Judith McVarish, Chair, 718-990-2334, E-mail: mcvarisj@stjohns.edu. *Application contact:* Dr. Kelly K. Ronayne, Associate Dean of Graduate Admissions, 718-990-2304, Fax: 718-990-2343, E-mail: graded@stjohns.edu.

St. Joseph's College, Long Island Campus, Program in Infant/Toddler Early Childhood Special Education, Patchogue, NY 11772-2399. Offers MA. Part-time and evening/weekend programs available. *Degree requirements:* For master's, thesis, full-time practicum experience. *Entrance requirements:* For master's, 1 course in child development, 2 courses in special education, minimum undergraduate GPA of 3.0, New York state teaching certificate, interview. Additional exam requirements/ recommendations for international students: Required—TOEFL (minimum score 550 paper-based; 213 computer-based).

St. Joseph's College, New York, Graduate Programs, Program in Education, Field of Infant/Toddler Early Childhood Special Education, Brooklyn, NY 11205-3688. Offers MA.

Early Childhood Education

Saint Mary's College of California, Kalmanovitz School of Education, Program in Early Childhood Education, Moraga, CA 94556. Offers curriculum and instruction (MA); supervision and leadership (MA). Part-time and evening/weekend programs available. *Students:* 9 part-time (all women); includes 1 minority (Black or African American, non-Hispanic/Latino). Average age 33. In 2011, 1 master's awarded. *Degree requirements:* For master's, thesis or alternative. *Entrance requirements:* For master's, interview, minimum GPA of 3.0. *Application deadline:* Applications are processed on a rolling basis. Application fee: $50. Tuition and fees vary according to course load, degree level and program. *Financial support:* Career-related internships or fieldwork available. Support available to part-time students. Financial award application deadline: 2/15. *Unit head:* Patricia Chambers, Coordinator, 925-631-4036, Fax: 925-376-8379, E-mail: pchambers@stmarys-ca.edu. *Application contact:* Jane Joyce, Coordinator, Recruitment and Admissions, 925-631-4700, Fax: 925-376-8379, E-mail: soereq@stmarys-ca.edu. Web site: http://www.stmarys-ca.edu/master-of-arts-degree-in-early-childhood-education.

Saint Mary's College of California, Kalmanovitz School of Education, Program in Montessori Education, Moraga, CA 94556. Offers reading and language arts (M Ed, MA). *Students:* 56 part-time (51 women); includes 23 minority (2 Black or African American, non-Hispanic/Latino; 1 American Indian or Alaska Native, non-Hispanic/Latino; 11 Asian, non-Hispanic/Latino; 9 Hispanic/Latino), 1 international. Average age 34. Tuition and fees vary according to course load, degree level and program. *Unit head:* Dr. Phyllis Metcalf-Turner, Dean, 925-631-4309, Fax: 925-376-8379. *Application contact:* Jane Joyce, Coordinator, Recruitment and Admissions, 925-631-4700, Fax: 925-376-8379, E-mail: soereq@stmarys-ca.edu. Web site: http://www.stmarys-ca.edu/montessori-education.

Saint Xavier University, Graduate Studies, School of Education, Chicago, IL 60655-3105. Offers counseling (MA); curriculum and instruction (MA); early childhood education (MA); educational administration (MA); elementary education (MA); individualized studies (MA), including educational technology, English as a second language (ESL), ISTEM (integrative science, technology, engineering, and math), science education; music education (MA); reading (MA); secondary education (MA); Spanish education (MA); special education (MA); teaching and leadership (MA). *Accreditation:* NCATE. Part-time and evening/weekend programs available. *Degree requirements:* For master's, thesis or project. *Entrance requirements:* For master's, minimum GPA of 3.0. *Application deadline:* For fall admission, 8/15 priority date for domestic students. Applications are processed on a rolling basis. Application fee: $35. *Expenses:* Contact institution. *Financial support:* Career-related internships or fieldwork available. Support available to part-time students. Financial award applicants required to submit FAFSA. *Unit head:* Dr. Beverly Gulley, Dean, 773-298-3221, Fax: 773-779-9061, E-mail: gulley@sxu.edu. *Application contact:* Beth Gierach, Managing Director of Admission, 773-298-3053, Fax: 773-298-3076, E-mail: gierach@sxu.edu.

Salem State University, School of Graduate Studies, Program in Early Childhood Education, Salem, MA 01970-5353. Offers M Ed. *Accreditation:* NCATE. Part-time and evening/weekend programs available. *Entrance requirements:* For master's, GRE or MAT. Additional exam requirements/recommendations for international students: Required—TOEFL (minimum score 550 paper-based; 80 iBT) or IELTS (minimum score 5.5).

Samford University, Orlean Bullard Beeson School of Education and Professional Studies, Birmingham, AL 35229. Offers early childhood education (Ed S); early childhood/elementary education (MS Ed); educational administration (Ed S); educational leadership (Ed D); elementary education (Ed S); gifted education (MS Ed); instructional leadership (MS Ed); secondary collaboration (MS Ed); M Div/MS Ed. *Accreditation:* NCATE. Part-time programs available. *Faculty:* 11 full-time (7 women), 9 part-time/adjunct (7 women). *Students:* 20 full-time (16 women), 169 part-time (122 women); includes 30 minority (26 Black or African American, non-Hispanic/Latino; 1 American Indian or Alaska Native, non-Hispanic/Latino; 1 Asian, non-Hispanic/Latino; 2 Hispanic/Latino), 1 international. Average age 39. 51 applicants, 92% accepted, 44 enrolled. In 2011, 57 master's, 9 doctorates, 35 other advanced degrees awarded. *Degree requirements:* For master's, comprehensive exam; for doctorate, comprehensive exam, thesis/dissertation. *Entrance requirements:* For master's, GRE or MAT, minimum GPA of 3.0; for doctorate, minimum GPA of 3.7; for Ed S, GRE, master's degree, teaching certificate, minimum GPA of 3.25. Additional exam requirements/recommendations for international students: Required—TOEFL (minimum score 550 paper-based; 213 computer-based). *Application deadline:* For fall admission, 7/15 for domestic students; for winter admission, 4/5 for domestic students; for spring admission, 12/4 for domestic students. Applications are processed on a rolling basis. Application fee: $25. *Expenses: Tuition:* Full-time $29,934; part-time $655 per credit. *Required fees:* $705. *Financial support:* Research assistantships, career-related internships or fieldwork, Federal Work-Study, scholarships/grants, and tuition waivers (partial) available. Support available to part-time students. Financial award applicants required to submit FAFSA. *Faculty research:* School law, the characteristics of beginning teachers, the nature of school reform, school culture, quality improvement in education, K-12 student achievement. *Unit head:* Dr. Jean Ann Box, Dean, 205-726-2565, E-mail: jabox@samford.edu. *Application contact:* Dr. Maurice Persall, Director, Graduate Office, 205-726-2019, E-mail: jmpersal@samford.edu. Web site: http://dlserver.samford.edu.

San Francisco State University, Division of Graduate Studies, College of Education, Department of Elementary Education, Program in Early Childhood Education, San Francisco, CA 94132-1722. Offers MA. *Accreditation:* NCATE. *Unit head:* Dr. Debra Luna, Chair, 415-338-1562, E-mail: dluna@sfsu.edu. *Application contact:* Dr. Barbara Henderson, Graduate Coordinator, 415-338-1319, E-mail: barbarah@sfsu.edu. Web site: http://www.coe.sfsu.edu/eed.

San Francisco State University, Division of Graduate Studies, College of Education, Department of Special Education, San Francisco, CA 94132-1722. Offers autism spectrum (AC); communicative disorders (MS); early childhood special education (AC); guide dog mobility (AC); orientation and mobility (MA, Credential); special education (MA, PhD). PhD offered jointly with University of California, Berkeley. *Accreditation:* NCATE. *Unit head:* Dr. Nicholas Certo, Chair, 415-338-1161, E-mail: ncerto@sfsu.edu. *Application contact:* Louise Guy, Office Coordinator, 415-338-1161, E-mail: lguy@sfsu.edu. Web site: http://coe.sfsu.edu/sped.

Shippensburg University of Pennsylvania, School of Graduate Studies, College of Education and Human Services, Department of Teacher Education, Shippensburg, PA 17257-2299. Offers curriculum and instruction (M Ed), including biology, early childhood education, elementary education, English, geography/earth science, history, mathematics, middle level education, modern languages; reading (M Ed). *Accreditation:* NCATE. Part-time and evening/weekend programs available. *Faculty:* 14 full-time (11 women), 8 part-time/adjunct (7 women). *Students:* 16 full-time (15 women), 143 part-time (130 women); includes 11 minority (4 Black or African American, non-Hispanic/Latino; 1 Asian, non-Hispanic/Latino; 4 Hispanic/Latino; 2 Two or more races, non-Hispanic/Latino), 1 international. Average age 30. 55 applicants, 55% accepted, 25 enrolled. In 2011, 76 master's awarded. *Degree requirements:* For master's, comprehensive exam (for some programs), thesis optional, practicum or internship; capstone seminar (for some programs). *Entrance requirements:* For master's, MAT (if GPA less than 2.75), interview, 3 letters of reference, questionnaire of teaching background and future goals. Additional exam requirements/recommendations for international students: Required—TOEFL (minimum score 580 paper-based; 237 computer-based); Recommended—IELTS (minimum score 6). *Application deadline:* For fall admission, 6/1 priority date for domestic students, 4/30 for international students; for spring admission, 9/1 priority date for domestic students, 9/30 for international students. Applications are processed on a rolling basis. Application fee: $30. Electronic applications accepted. *Expenses: Tuition, area resident:* Part-time $416 per credit. Tuition, state resident: part-time $416 per credit. Tuition, nonresident: part-time $624 per credit. *Required fees:* $119 per credit. *Financial support:* In 2011–12, 5 research assistantships with full tuition reimbursements (averaging $5,000 per year) were awarded; career-related internships or fieldwork, scholarships/grants, unspecified assistantships, and resident hall director and student payroll positions also available. Support available to part-time students. Financial award application deadline: 3/1; financial award applicants required to submit FAFSA. *Unit head:* Dr. Christine A. Royce, Chairperson, 717-477-1688, Fax: 717-477-4046, E-mail: caroyc@ship.edu. *Application contact:* Jeremy R. Goshorn, Assistant Dean of Graduate Admissions, 717-477-1231, Fax: 717-477-4016, E-mail: jrgoshorn@ship.edu. Web site: http://www.ship.edu/teacher/.

Siena Heights University, Graduate College, Program in Teacher Education, Concentration in Early Childhood Education, Adrian, MI 49221-1796. Offers Montessori education (MA). Part-time programs available. *Degree requirements:* For master's, thesis, presentation. *Entrance requirements:* For master's, interview, minimum GPA of 3.0. *Expenses: Tuition:* Full-time $11,400; part-time $475 per credit hour. *Required fees:* $1000; $500 $125 per term. Tuition and fees vary according to degree level.

South Carolina State University, School of Graduate Studies, Department of Education, Orangeburg, SC 29117-0001. Offers counseling education (M Ed); early childhood and special education (M Ed); early childhood education (MAT); educational leadership (Ed D, Ed S); elementary education (M Ed, MAT); engineering (MAT); general science (MAT); mathematics (MAT); secondary education (M Ed), including biology education, business education, counselor education, English education, home economics education, industrial education, mathematics education, science education, social studies education; special education (M Ed), including emotionally handicapped, learning disabilities, mentally handicapped. *Accreditation:* NCATE. Part-time and evening/weekend programs available. *Faculty:* 9 full-time (6 women), 6 part-time/adjunct (2 women). *Students:* 34 full-time (29 women), 50 part-time (40 women); includes 74 minority (72 Black or African American, non-Hispanic/Latino; 1 Asian, non-Hispanic/Latino; 1 Hispanic/Latino). Average age 34. 23 applicants, 91% accepted, 14 enrolled. In 2011, 11 master's awarded. *Degree requirements:* For master's, thesis optional, departmental qualifying exam. *Entrance requirements:* For master's, GRE General Test, NTE, interview, teaching certificate. *Application deadline:* For fall admission, 6/15 priority date for domestic students, 6/15 for international students; for spring admission, 11/1 for domestic and international students. Applications are processed on a rolling basis. Application fee: $25. Electronic applications accepted. *Expenses:* Tuition, state resident: full-time $8688; part-time $514 per credit hour. Tuition, nonresident: full-time $17,600; part-time $1009 per credit hour. *Required fees:* $570. *Financial support:* In 2011–12, 3 fellowships (averaging $5,020 per year) were awarded; career-related internships or fieldwork, Federal Work-Study, and institutionally sponsored loans also available. Financial award application deadline: 6/1. *Faculty research:* Critical thinking, child abuse, stress, test-taking skills, conflict resolution, mainstreaming. *Unit head:* Dr. Charlie Spell, Interim Chair, 803-536-7098, Fax: 803-516-4568, E-mail: cspell@scsu.edu. *Application contact:* Annette Hazzard-Jones, Program Coordinator II, 803-536-8809, Fax: 803-536-8812, E-mail: zs_ahazzard@scsu.edu.

Southern Oregon University, Graduate Studies, School of Education, Ashland, OR 97520. Offers elementary education (MA Ed, MS Ed), including classroom teacher, early childhood, handicapped learner, reading, supervision; secondary education (MA Ed, MS Ed), including classroom teacher, handicapped learner, reading, supervision; teaching (MAT). *Faculty:* 18 full-time (10 women), 10 part-time/adjunct (all women). *Students:* 128 full-time (88 women), 145 part-time (103 women); includes 32 minority (1 Black or African American, non-Hispanic/Latino; 3 American Indian or Alaska Native, non-Hispanic/Latino; 5 Asian, non-Hispanic/Latino; 13 Hispanic/Latino; 3 Native Hawaiian or other Pacific Islander, non-Hispanic/Latino; 7 Two or more races, non-Hispanic/Latino), 1 international. Average age 35. 48 applicants, 60% accepted, 23 enrolled. In 2011, 102 degrees awarded. *Degree requirements:* For master's, thesis optional. *Entrance requirements:* For master's, GRE General Test, minimum GPA of 3.0. *Application deadline:* For fall admission, 2/1 for domestic students. Application fee: $50. Electronic applications accepted. *Expenses:* Tuition, state resident: full-time $12,600; part-time $350 per credit. Tuition, nonresident: full-time $16,200; part-time $450 per credit. *Required fees:* $1590. *Financial support:* Research assistantships with partial tuition reimbursements available. *Unit head:* Dr. Geoff Mills, Dean, 541-552-6920, E-mail: mills@sou.edu. *Application contact:* Mark Bottorff, Director of Admissions, 541-552-6411, Fax: 541-552-8403, E-mail: admissions@sou.edu. Web site: http://www.sou.edu/education/.

Southwestern Oklahoma State University, College of Professional and Graduate Studies, School of Behavioral Sciences and Education, Specialization in Early Childhood Education, Weatherford, OK 73096-3098. Offers M Ed. M Ed distance learning degree program offered to Oklahoma residents only. *Accreditation:* NCATE. Part-time and evening/weekend programs available. *Degree requirements:* For master's, exam. *Entrance requirements:* For master's, GRE General Test or minimum undergraduate GPA of 3.0. Additional exam requirements/recommendations for international students: Required—TOEFL.

Southwest Minnesota State University, Department of Education, Marshall, MN 56258. Offers ESL (MS); math (MS); reading (MS); special education (MS), including developmental disabilities, early childhood education, emotional behavioral disorders, learning disabilities; teaching, learning and leadership (MS). Part-time and evening/weekend programs available. Postbaccalaureate distance learning degree programs offered (no on-campus study). *Entrance requirements:* Additional exam requirements/recommendations for international students: Required—TOEFL or IELTS; Recommended—TOEFL (minimum score 550 paper-based; 213 computer-based; 80 iBT), IELTS.

Springfield College, Graduate Programs, Program in Education, Springfield, MA 01109-3797. Offers counseling and secondary education (M Ed, MS); early childhood education (M Ed, MS); education (M Ed, MS); educational administration (M Ed, MS); educational studies (M Ed, MS); elementary education (M Ed, MS); secondary education (M Ed, MS); special education (M Ed, MS). Part-time and evening/weekend programs available. *Entrance requirements:* Additional exam requirements/recommendations for international students: Required—TOEFL (minimum score 550 paper-based; 213 computer-based). Electronic applications accepted.

Spring Hill College, Graduate Programs, Program in Education, Mobile, AL 36608-1791. Offers early childhood education (MAT, MS Ed); educational theory (MS Ed); elementary education (MAT, MS Ed); secondary education (MAT, MS Ed). Part-time programs available. *Faculty:* 3 full-time (2 women), 3 part-time/adjunct (all women). *Students:* 7 full-time (6 women), 21 part-time (18 women); includes 7 minority (6 Black or African American, non-Hispanic/Latino; 1 Asian, non-Hispanic/Latino). Average age 31.

In 2011, 13 master's awarded. *Degree requirements:* For master's, comprehensive exam, completion of program within 6 calendar years of entrance into graduate studies at Spring Hill; documentation of course field assignments (MS) or completion of internship (MAT). *Entrance requirements:* For master's, GRE, MAT, or PRAXIS (varies by program), bachelor's degree with minimum undergraduate GPA of 3.0; class B certificate (MS) or minimum number of hours in specific fields (MAT). Additional exam requirements/recommendations for international students: Required—TOEFL (minimum score 550 paper-based; 213 computer-based; 80 iBT), IELTS (minimum score 6.5), CPE or CAE (minimum score C),Michigan English Language Assessment Battery (minimum score 90). *Application deadline:* For fall admission, 8/1 priority date for domestic students, 8/1 for international students; for spring admission, 12/1 priority date for domestic students, 12/1 for international students. Applications are processed on a rolling basis. Application fee: $25 ($35 for international students). Electronic applications accepted. *Expenses:* Contact institution. *Financial support:* Applicants required to submit FAFSA. *Unit head:* Dr. Ann A. Adams, Chair of Teacher Education, 251-380-3479, Fax: 251-460-2184, E-mail: aadams@shc.edu. *Application contact:* Donna B. Tarasavage, Director of Admissions, Graduate and Continuing Studies, 251-380-3067, Fax: 251-460-2190, E-mail: dtarasavage@shc.edu. Web site: http://www.shc.edu/grad/academics/teaching.

State University of New York at Binghamton, Graduate School, School of Education, Program in Childhood Education, Binghamton, NY 13902-6000. Offers MS Ed. *Accreditation:* Teacher Education Accreditation Council. Part-time and evening/weekend programs available. *Students:* 2 applicants, 50% accepted, 0 enrolled. *Entrance requirements:* For master's, GRE General Test. Additional exam requirements/recommendations for international students: Required—TOEFL (minimum score 550 paper-based; 213 computer-based; 80 iBT). *Application deadline:* For fall admission, 2/1 priority date for domestic students, 2/1 for international students; for spring admission, 10/15 priority date for domestic students, 10/15 for international students. Applications are processed on a rolling basis. Application fee: $60. Electronic applications accepted. *Financial support:* Fellowships, research assistantships, teaching assistantships, career-related internships or fieldwork, Federal Work-Study, institutionally sponsored loans, scholarships/grants, health care benefits, tuition waivers (full), and unspecified assistantships available. Financial award application deadline: 2/15; financial award applicants required to submit FAFSA. *Unit head:* Dr. Jenny Gordon, Coordinator, 607-777-4184, E-mail: gordon@binghamton.edu. *Application contact:* Catherine Smith, Recruiting and Admissions Coordinator, 607-777-2151, Fax: 607-777-2501, E-mail: cmsmith@binghamton.edu.

State University of New York at New Paltz, Graduate School, School of Education, Department of Educational Studies, Program in Special Education, New Paltz, NY 12561. Offers adolescence (7-12) (MS Ed); adolescence special education and literacy education (MS Ed); childhood (1-6) (MS Ed); childhood special education and literacy education (MS Ed); early childhood (B-2) (MS Ed). *Accreditation:* NCATE. Part-time and evening/weekend programs available. *Faculty:* 6 full-time (4 women), 4 part-time/adjunct (all women). *Students:* 36 full-time (33 women), 54 part-time (44 women); includes 8 minority (5 Black or African American, non-Hispanic/Latino; 2 Asian, non-Hispanic/Latino; 1 Native Hawaiian or other Pacific Islander, non-Hispanic/Latino). Average age 29. 67 applicants, 73% accepted, 40 enrolled. In 2011, 44 master's awarded. *Degree requirements:* For master's, portfolio. *Entrance requirements:* For master's, minimum GPA of 3.0 (3.2 for special education and literacy programs), New York state teaching certificate. Additional exam requirements/recommendations for international students: Required—TOEFL (minimum score 550 paper-based; 213 computer-based; 80 iBT), IELTS (minimum score 6.5). *Application deadline:* For fall admission, 3/15 priority date for domestic students, 3/15 for international students; for spring admission, 11/1 for domestic and international students. Application fee: $50. Electronic applications accepted. *Expenses:* Tuition, state resident: full-time $8870; part-time $370 per credit. Tuition, nonresident: full-time $15,160; part-time $632 per credit. *Required fees:* $1188; $34 per credit. $184 per semester. *Financial support:* In 2011–12, 2 students received support, including 2 fellowships (averaging $3,750 per year); career-related internships or fieldwork, Federal Work-Study, institutionally sponsored loans, and tuition waivers (full) also available. Financial award application deadline: 8/1; financial award applicants required to submit FAFSA. *Unit head:* Dr. Spencer Salend, Coordinator, 845-257-2831, E-mail: salends@newpaltz.edu. *Application contact:* Dr. Catherine Whittaker, Coordinator, 845-257-2831, E-mail: whittakc@newpaltz.edu.

State University of New York at Oswego, Graduate Studies, School of Education, Department of Curriculum and Instruction, Oswego, NY 13126. Offers adolescence education (MST); art education (MAT); childhood education (MST); elementary education (MS Ed); literacy education (MS Ed); secondary education (MS Ed); special education (MS Ed). Part-time and evening/weekend programs available. *Degree requirements:* For master's, comprehensive exam (for some programs), thesis optional. *Entrance requirements:* For master's, GRE General Test, minimum GPA of 2.7, provisional teaching certificate. Additional exam requirements/recommendations for international students: Required—TOEFL (minimum score 560 paper-based; 220 computer-based). *Faculty research:* Classroom applications for microcomputers; classroom questioning, wait-time, and achievement; values clarification and academic achievement.

State University of New York at Plattsburgh, Division of Education, Health, and Human Services, Program in Early Childhood Education, Plattsburgh, NY 12901-2681. Offers Advanced Certificate. *Unit head:* Dr. Heidi Schnackenberg, Coordinator, 518-564-5143, E-mail: schnachl@msplattsburgh.edu. *Application contact:* Marguerite Adelman, Assistant Director, Graduate Admissions, 518-564-4723, Fax: 518-564-4722, E-mail: adelmaml@plattsburgh.edu.

State University of New York College at Cortland, Graduate Studies, School of Education, Program in Childhood/Early Child Education, Cortland, NY 13045. Offers MS Ed, MST. *Accreditation:* NCATE.

State University of New York College at Geneseo, Graduate Studies, School of Education, Program in Early Childhood Education, Geneseo, NY 14454-1401. Offers MS Ed. Part-time and evening/weekend programs available. *Degree requirements:* For master's, thesis optional.

State University of New York College at Potsdam, School of Education and Professional Studies, Program in Special Education, Potsdam, NY 13676. Offers adolescence (grades 7-12) (MS Ed); childhood (grades 1-6) (MS Ed); early childhood (birth-grade 2) (MS Ed). *Accreditation:* NCATE. Part-time programs available. *Faculty:* 2 full-time (1 woman), 5 part-time/adjunct (4 women). *Students:* 19 full-time (15 women), 3 part-time (all women); includes 4 minority (2 American Indian or Alaska Native, non-Hispanic/Latino; 1 Hispanic/Latino; 1 Two or more races, non-Hispanic/Latino). 27 applicants, 100% accepted, 15 enrolled. In 2011, 18 master's awarded. *Degree requirements:* For master's, culminating experience. *Entrance requirements:* For master's, minimum GPA of 3.0 in last 60 hours of course work. Additional exam requirements/recommendations for international students: Required—TOEFL (minimum score 550 paper-based; 213 computer-based; 80 iBT), IELTS (minimum score 6). *Application deadline:* For fall admission, 4/1 for domestic and international students. Applications are processed on a rolling basis. Application fee: $50. *Expenses:* Tuition, state resident: full-time $8870; part-time $370 per credit hour. Tuition, nonresident: full-time $15,160; part-time $632 per credit hour. *Required fees:* $1066; $44.10 per credit hour. One-time fee: $3. *Financial support:* Unspecified assistantships available. Financial award application deadline: 3/1; financial award applicants required to submit FAFSA. *Unit head:* Dr. Dennis Conrad, Chairperson, 315-267-2916, Fax: 315-267-4802, E-mail: conradda@potsdam.edu. *Application contact:* Peter Cutler, Graduate Admissions Counselor, 315-267-2165, Fax: 315-267-4802, E-mail: graduate@potsdam.edu. Web site: http://www.potsdam.edu/academics/SOEPS/SpecialEd/msedspecialed.cfm.

Stephen F. Austin State University, Graduate School, College of Education, Department of Elementary Education, Program in Early Childhood Education, Nacogdoches, TX 75962. Offers M Ed. *Accreditation:* NCATE. *Degree requirements:* For master's, comprehensive exam. *Entrance requirements:* For master's, GRE General Test. Additional exam requirements/recommendations for international students: Required—TOEFL (minimum score 550 paper-based; 213 computer-based).

Syracuse University, School of Education, Program in Childhood Education: (1-6) Preparation, Syracuse, NY 13244. Offers MS. *Students:* 8 full-time (7 women), 1 (woman) part-time. Average age 26. 27 applicants, 59% accepted, 7 enrolled. In 2011, 6 degrees awarded. *Entrance requirements:* For master's, interview. Additional exam requirements/recommendations for international students: Required—TOEFL (minimum score 100 iBT). *Application deadline:* For fall admission, 2/1 priority date for domestic students, 2/1 for international students. Application fee: $75. Electronic applications accepted. *Expenses: Tuition:* Part-time $1206 per credit. *Financial support:* Fellowships with full tuition reimbursements and teaching assistantships with tuition reimbursements available. Financial award application deadline: 1/1; financial award applicants required to submit FAFSA. *Unit head:* Dr. Patricia Tinto, Program Director, 315-443-2684, E-mail: pptinto@syr.edu. *Application contact:* Laurie Deyo, Graduate Recruiter, School of Education, 315-443-2505, E-mail: e-gradrcrt@syr.edu. Web site: http://soeweb.syr.edu/.

Syracuse University, School of Education, Program in Early Childhood Special Education, Syracuse, NY 13244. Offers MS. Part-time programs available. *Students:* 15 full-time (12 women), 19 part-time (18 women); includes 6 minority (3 Black or African American, non-Hispanic/Latino; 2 American Indian or Alaska Native, non-Hispanic/Latino; 1 Asian, non-Hispanic/Latino). Average age 32. 14 applicants, 86% accepted, 9 enrolled. In 2011, 7 degrees awarded. *Entrance requirements:* For master's, interview. Additional exam requirements/recommendations for international students: Required—TOEFL (minimum score 100 iBT). *Application deadline:* For fall admission, 2/1 for domestic and international students; for spring admission, 10/15 priority date for domestic students, 10/15 for international students. Applications are processed on a rolling basis. Application fee: $75. Electronic applications accepted. *Expenses: Tuition:* Part-time $1206 per credit. *Financial support:* Fellowships with full tuition reimbursements and teaching assistantships with full and partial tuition reimbursements available. Financial award application deadline: 1/1; financial award applicants required to submit FAFSA. *Unit head:* Dr. Gail Ensher, Director, 315-443-9650. *Application contact:* Laurie Deyo, Graduate Recruiter, School of Education, 315-443-2505, E-mail: e-gradrcrt@syr.edu. Web site: http://www.soeweb.syr.edu/.

Teachers College, Columbia University, Graduate Faculty of Education, Department of Curriculum and Teaching, Program in Early Childhood Education, New York, NY 10027. Offers Ed M, MA, Ed D. *Accreditation:* NCATE. *Faculty:* 4 full-time (all women). *Students:* 10 full-time (all women), 43 part-time (42 women); includes 14 minority (1 Black or African American, non-Hispanic/Latino; 7 Asian, non-Hispanic/Latino; 6 Hispanic/Latino), 8 international. Average age 30. In 2011, 12 master's, 1 doctorate awarded. *Degree requirements:* For master's, culminating project; for doctorate, thesis/dissertation. *Entrance requirements:* For doctorate, GRE General Test or MAT. *Application deadline:* For fall admission, 1/2 priority date for domestic students. Application fee: $65. Electronic applications accepted. *Financial support:* Career-related internships or fieldwork, Federal Work-Study, institutionally sponsored loans, and tuition waivers (full and partial) available. Support available to part-time students. Financial award applicants required to submit FAFSA. *Faculty research:* Infancy, child development, children and family, policy and program, childhood bilingualism. *Unit head:* Prof. Celia Genishi, Program Coordinator, 212-678-3860, E-mail: genishi@tc.edu. *Application contact:* Peter Shon, Assistant Director of Admission, 212-678-3305, Fax: 212-678-4171, E-mail: shon@exchange.tc.columbia.edu. Web site: http://www.tc.columbia.edu/c&t/childEd/.

Teachers College, Columbia University, Graduate Faculty of Education, Department of Curriculum and Teaching, Program in Early Childhood Special Education, New York, NY 10027-6696. Offers Ed M, MA. *Accreditation:* NCATE. *Faculty:* 4 full-time (all women). *Students:* 59 full-time (48 women), 159 part-time (147 women); includes 69 minority (17 Black or African American, non-Hispanic/Latino; 37 Asian, non-Hispanic/Latino; 15 Hispanic/Latino), 16 international. Average age 26. 337 applicants, 51% accepted, 80 enrolled. In 2011, 91 master's awarded. *Degree requirements:* For master's, culminating project. *Application deadline:* For fall admission, 1/15 priority date for domestic students. Application fee: $65. *Financial support:* Research assistantships, teaching assistantships, career-related internships or fieldwork, Federal Work-Study, institutionally sponsored loans, and tuition waivers (full and partial) available. Support available to part-time students. Financial award application deadline: 2/1; financial award applicants required to submit FAFSA. *Faculty research:* Curriculum development, infants, urban education, visually-impaired infants. *Unit head:* Prof. Susan Recchia, Program Coordinator, 212-678-3860, E-mail: recchia@tc.edu. *Application contact:* Peter Shon, Assistant Director of Admission, 212-678-3305, Fax: 212-678-4171, E-mail: shon@exchange.tc.columbia.edu.

Temple University, College of Education, Department of Curriculum, Instruction, and Technology in Education, Philadelphia, PA 19122-6096. Offers applied behavioral analysis (MS Ed); career and technical education (MS Ed); early childhood education and elementary education (MS Ed); English education (MS Ed); language arts education (Ed D); math/science education (Ed D); mathematics education (MS Ed); science education (MS Ed); second and foreign language education (MS Ed); special education (MS Ed); teaching English as a second language (MS Ed). Part-time and evening/weekend programs available. *Faculty:* 19 full-time (12 women). *Students:* 30 full-time (23 women), 86 part-time (69 women); includes 12 minority (4 Black or African American, non-Hispanic/Latino; 2 Asian, non-Hispanic/Latino; 5 Hispanic/Latino; 1 Two or more races, non-Hispanic/Latino), 5 international. 82 applicants, 71% accepted, 51 enrolled. In 2011, 181 master's, 16 doctorates awarded. Terminal master's awarded for partial completion of doctoral program. *Degree requirements:* For master's, thesis or alternative; for doctorate, thesis/dissertation. *Entrance requirements:* For master's and doctorate, GRE General Test or MAT, minimum GPA of 3.0. Additional exam requirements/recommendations for international students: Required—TOEFL (minimum score 550 paper-based; 213 computer-based; 79 iBT). *Application deadline:* For fall admission, 4/1 for domestic students, 12/15 for international students; for spring admission, 10/1 for domestic students, 8/1 for international students. Application fee: $50. Electronic applications accepted. *Expenses:* Tuition, state resident: full-time $12,366; part-time $687 per credit hour. Tuition, nonresident: full-time $17,298; part-time $961 per credit hour. *Required fees:* $590; $213 per year. *Financial support:* Fellowships, research assistantships with full tuition reimbursements, and teaching assistantships with full tuition reimbursements available. Financial award application deadline: 1/15; financial award applicants required to submit FAFSA. *Faculty research:* School improvement, problem-solving, literacy, language development. *Unit head:* Dr. Michael W. Smith, Chair, 215-204-6387, Fax: 215-204-1414, E-mail: mwsmith@temple.edu. *Application contact:* Dr. Margo Greicar, Director for Graduate Academic and Student Affairs, 215-204-8011, Fax: 215-204-4383, E-mail: margo.greicar@temple.edu. Web site: http://www.temple.edu/education/cite/.

Tennessee Technological University, Graduate School, College of Education, Department of Curriculum and Instruction, Program in Early Childhood Education, Cookeville, TN 38505. Offers MA, Ed S. *Accreditation:* NCATE. Part-time and evening/weekend programs available. *Faculty:* 2 full-time (both women). *Students:* 5 full-time (all women), 17 part-time (all women). Average age 27. 9 applicants, 89% accepted, 5 enrolled. In 2011, 3 master's, 3 other advanced degrees awarded. *Degree requirements:* For master's and Ed S, comprehensive exam, thesis or alternative. *Entrance requirements:* For master's and Ed S, MAT or GRE. Additional exam requirements/recommendations for international students: Required—TOEFL (minimum score 550 paper-based; 71 iBT), IELTS (minimum score 5.5), Pearson Test of English. *Application deadline:* For fall admission, 8/1 priority date for domestic students, 5/1 for international students; for spring admission, 12/1 for domestic students, 10/1 for international students. Application fee: $25 ($30 for international students). Electronic applications accepted. *Expenses:* Tuition, state resident: full-time $8094; part-time $422 per credit hour. Tuition, nonresident: full-time $20,574; part-time $1046 per credit hour. *Financial support:* In 2011–12, research assistantships (averaging $4,000 per year), teaching assistantships (averaging $4,000 per year) were awarded; fellowships and career-related internships or fieldwork also available. Financial award application deadline: 4/1. *Unit head:* Dr. Susan Gore, Interim Chairperson, 931-372-3181, Fax: 931-372-6270, E-mail: sgore@tntech.edu. *Application contact:* Shelia K. Kendrick, Coordinator of Graduate Admissions, 931-372-3808, Fax: 931-372-3497, E-mail: skendrick@tntech.edu.

Texas A&M University–Commerce, Graduate School, College of Education and Human Services, Department of Curriculum and Instruction, Commerce, TX 75429-3011. Offers bilingual/ESL education (M Ed, MS); early childhood education (M Ed, MS); elementary education (M Ed, MS); reading (M Ed, MS); secondary education (M Ed, MS); supervision, curriculum and instruction: elementary education (Ed D). MS and M Ed programs in early childhood education offered jointly with Texas Woman's University and University of North Texas. Part-time programs available. Terminal master's awarded for partial completion of doctoral program. *Degree requirements:* For master's, comprehensive exam, thesis (for some programs); for doctorate, 2 foreign languages, thesis/dissertation, departmental qualifying exam. *Entrance requirements:* For master's and doctorate, GRE General Test. Electronic applications accepted. *Faculty research:* Literacy and learning, early childhood, preservice teacher education, technology.

Texas A&M University–Corpus Christi, Graduate Studies and Research, College of Education, Corpus Christi, TX 78412-5503. Offers counseling (MS, PhD), including counseling (MS), counselor education (PhD); curriculum and instruction (MS, Ed D); early childhood education (MS); educational administration (MS); educational leadership (Ed D); educational technology (MS); elementary education (MS); kinesiology (MS); reading (MS); secondary education (MS); special education (MS). Part-time and evening/weekend programs available. *Degree requirements:* For master's, comprehensive exam, thesis (for some programs); for doctorate, comprehensive exam, thesis/dissertation. *Entrance requirements:* For master's, GRE General Test. Additional exam requirements/recommendations for international students: Required—TOEFL. Electronic applications accepted.

Texas A&M University–Kingsville, College of Graduate Studies, College of Education, Department of Education, Program in Early Childhood Education, Kingsville, TX 78363. Offers M Ed. Part-time and evening/weekend programs available. *Degree requirements:* For master's, comprehensive exam, mini-thesis. *Entrance requirements:* For master's, GRE General Test, MAT, minimum GPA of 3.0.

Texas A&M University–San Antonio, Department of Curriculum and Kinesiology, San Antonio, TX 78224. Offers bilingual education (MA); early childhood education (M Ed); kinesiology (MS); reading (MS); special education (M Ed), including educational diagnostician, instructional specialist. Part-time and evening/weekend programs available. *Students:* 76 full-time (51 women), 240 part-time (180 women). Average age 37. *Degree requirements:* For master's, comprehensive exam, thesis or alternative. *Entrance requirements:* For master's, MAT. Additional exam requirements/recommendations for international students: Required—TOEFL (minimum score 550 paper-based; 213 computer-based; 80 iBT), IELTS (minimum score 6). *Application deadline:* For fall admission, 8/15 priority date for domestic students, 6/1 for international students; for spring admission, 12/15 priority date for domestic students, 10/1 for international students. Applications are processed on a rolling basis. Application fee: $35 ($50 for international students). Electronic applications accepted. *Expenses:* Tuition, state resident: part-time $691.11 per course. Tuition, nonresident: part-time $1621.11 per course. *Financial support:* Application deadline: 3/31; applicants required to submit FAFSA. *Unit head:* Dr. Samuel Garcia, Department Chair, 210-784-2505, E-mail: samuel.garcia@tamusa.tamus.edu. *Application contact:* Jennifer M. Dovalina, Graduate Admissions Specialist, 210-784-1380, E-mail: graduateadmissions@tamusa.tamus.edu. Web site: http://www.tamusa.tamus.edu/education/index.html.

Texas Woman's University, Graduate School, College of Professional Education, Department of Family Sciences, Denton, TX 76201. Offers child development (MS); counseling and development (MS); early childhood development and education (PhD); early childhood education (M Ed, MA, MS); family studies (MS, PhD); family therapy (MS, PhD). *Accreditation:* ACA (one or more programs are accredited). Part-time and evening/weekend programs available. *Faculty:* 24 full-time (18 women), 2 part-time/adjunct (both women). *Students:* 135 full-time (129 women), 313 part-time (286 women); includes 185 minority (125 Black or African American, non-Hispanic/Latino; 1 American Indian or Alaska Native, non-Hispanic/Latino; 15 Asian, non-Hispanic/Latino; 44 Hispanic/Latino), 15 international. Average age 36. 220 applicants, 56% accepted, 101 enrolled. In 2011, 77 master's, 26 doctorates awarded. Terminal master's awarded for partial completion of doctoral program. *Degree requirements:* For master's, comprehensive exam (for some programs), thesis (for some programs); for doctorate, comprehensive exam, thesis/dissertation. *Entrance requirements:* Additional exam requirements/recommendations for international students: Required—TOEFL (minimum score 550 paper-based; 213 computer-based; 79 iBT). *Application deadline:* For fall admission, 7/1 priority date for domestic students, 2/15 for international students; for spring admission, 9/15 priority date for domestic students, 7/1 for international students. Applications are processed on a rolling basis. Application fee: $50 ($75 for international students). Electronic applications accepted. *Expenses:* Tuition, state resident: full-time $3834; part-time $213 per credit hour. Tuition, nonresident: full-time $9468; part-time $526 per credit hour. *Required fees:* $213 per credit hour. Tuition and fees vary according to course load. *Financial support:* In 2011–12, 137 students received support, including 15 research assistantships (averaging $12,942 per year), 8 teaching assistantships (averaging $12,942 per year); career-related internships or fieldwork, Federal Work-Study, institutionally sponsored loans, scholarships/grants, traineeships, health care benefits, and unspecified assistantships also available. Support available to part-time students. Financial award application deadline: 3/1; financial award applicants required to submit FAFSA. *Faculty research:* Parenting/parent education, military families, play therapy, family sexuality, diversity, healthy relationships/healthy marriages, childhood obesity, male communication. *Total annual research expenditures:* $24,151. *Unit head:* Dr. Larry LeFlore, Chair, 940-898-2685, Fax: 940-898-2676, E-mail: famsci@twu.edu. *Application contact:* Dr. Samuel Wheeler, Assistant Director of Admissions, 940-898-3188, Fax: 940-898-3081, E-mail: wheelersr@twu.edu. Web site: http://www.twu.edu/family-sciences/.

Towson University, Program in Early Childhood Education, Towson, MD 21252-0001. Offers M Ed, CAS. *Accreditation:* NCATE. Part-time and evening/weekend programs available. *Students:* 7 full-time (all women), 186 part-time (181 women); includes 42 minority (31 Black or African American, non-Hispanic/Latino; 4 American Indian or Alaska Native, non-Hispanic/Latino; 3 Asian, non-Hispanic/Latino; 2 Hispanic/Latino; 1 Native Hawaiian or other Pacific Islander, non-Hispanic/Latino; 1 Two or more races, non-Hispanic/Latino), 2 international. *Degree requirements:* For master's, thesis optional. *Entrance requirements:* For master's, minimum GPA of 3.0, teacher certification, work experience or course work in early childhood education. *Application deadline:* Applications are processed on a rolling basis. Application fee: $50. Electronic applications accepted. *Expenses:* Tuition, state resident: part-time $337 per credit. Tuition, nonresident: part-time $709 per credit. *Required fees:* $99 per credit. *Financial support:* Application deadline: 4/1; applicants required to submit FAFSA. *Faculty research:* Developmental programs, training caregivers for HIV/AIDS children. *Unit head:* Dr. Edyth Wheeler, Graduate Program Director, 410-704-2460, Fax: 410-704-2733, E-mail: ejwheeler@towson.edu.

Trident University International, College of Education, Program in Education, Cypress, CA 90630. Offers adult education (MA Ed); aviation education (MA Ed); children's literacy development (MA Ed); e-learning (MA Ed); early childhood education (MA Ed); enrollment management (MA Ed); higher education (MA Ed); teaching and instruction (MA Ed); training and development (MA Ed). Part-time and evening/weekend programs available. Postbaccalaureate distance learning degree programs offered (no on-campus study). *Degree requirements:* For master's, capstone project with integrative paper. *Entrance requirements:* For master's, minimum GPA of 2.5 (students with GPA 3.0 or greater may transfer up to 30% of graduate level credits). Additional exam requirements/recommendations for international students: Required—TOEFL (minimum score 525 paper-based). Electronic applications accepted.

Trinity Washington University, School of Education, Washington, DC 20017-1094. Offers counseling (MA); early childhood education (MAT); educating for change (M Ed); educational administration (MSA); elementary education (MAT); school counseling (MA); secondary education (MAT), including English, social studies; special education (MAT); teaching English as a second language (MAT); teaching English to speakers of other languages (M Ed); the teaching of reading (M Ed). *Accreditation:* NCATE. Part-time and evening/weekend programs available. *Degree requirements:* For master's, thesis (for some programs), capstone project(s). *Entrance requirements:* For master's, PRAXIS I, minimum GPA of 2.8. Additional exam requirements/recommendations for international students: Required—TOEFL (minimum score 550 paper-based; 213 computer-based). *Faculty research:* Technology, literacy, special education, organizations, inclusion models.

Troy University, Graduate School, College of Education, Program in Early Childhood Education, Troy, AL 36082. Offers 5th year early childhood (MS); early childhood education (Ed S); traditional early childhood (MS). Part-time and evening/weekend programs available. Postbaccalaureate distance learning degree programs offered. *Faculty:* 4 full-time (all women), 1 (woman) part-time/adjunct. *Students:* 4 full-time (all women), 6 part-time (all women); includes 3 minority (1 Black or African American, non-Hispanic/Latino; 2 Two or more races, non-Hispanic/Latino). Average age 27. 5 applicants, 60% accepted, 1 enrolled. In 2011, 8 master's awarded. *Entrance requirements:* For master's, GRE, MAT, or GMAT, bachelor's degree. Additional exam requirements/recommendations for international students: Required—TOEFL (minimum score 523 paper-based; 193 computer-based; 70 iBT), IELTS (minimum score 6), or ACT COMPASS ESL (minimum listening, reading, and grammar score 270). Application fee: $50. *Expenses:* Tuition, state resident: full-time $6960; part-time $290 per credit hour. Tuition, nonresident: full-time $13,920; part-time $580 per credit hour. *Required fees:* $386 per term. *Unit head:* Dr. Victoria Morin, Professor, 334-983-6556 Ext. 351, E-mail: vmorin@troy.edu. *Application contact:* Brenda K. Campbell, Director of Graduate Admissions, 334-670-3178, Fax: 334-670-3733, E-mail: bcamp@troy.edu.

Tufts University, Graduate School of Arts and Sciences, Department of Child Development, Medford, MA 02155. Offers child development (MA, PhD, CAGS); early childhood education (MAT). Part-time programs available. *Faculty:* 16 full-time, 12 part-time/adjunct. *Students:* 118 full-time (106 women); includes 21 minority (9 Black or African American, non-Hispanic/Latino; 6 Asian, non-Hispanic/Latino; 6 Hispanic/Latino), 19 international. Average age 27. 126 applicants, 67% accepted, 32 enrolled. In 2011, 32 master's, 7 doctorates awarded. *Degree requirements:* For master's, thesis (for some programs); for doctorate, thesis/dissertation. *Entrance requirements:* For master's and doctorate, GRE General Test. Additional exam requirements/recommendations for international students: Required—TOEFL (minimum score 550 paper-based; 213 computer-based; 80 iBT). *Application deadline:* For fall admission, 1/15 for domestic students, 12/15 for international students. Applications are processed on a rolling basis. Application fee: $75. Electronic applications accepted. *Expenses: Tuition:* Full-time $41,208; part-time $1030 per credit hour. Full-time tuition and fees vary according to degree level, program and student level. Part-time tuition and fees vary according to course load. *Financial support:* Fellowships, research assistantships with full and partial tuition reimbursements, teaching assistantships with full and partial tuition reimbursements, Federal Work-Study, scholarships/grants, tuition waivers (partial), and unspecified assistantships available. Support available to part-time students. Financial award application deadline: 1/15; financial award applicants required to submit FAFSA. *Unit head:* Jayanthi Mistry, Chair, 617-627-3355. *Application contact:* Ellen Pinderhughes, Graduate Advisor, 617-627-3355. Web site: http://ase.tufts.edu/epcd.

United States University, School of Education, Cypress, CA 90630. Offers administration (MA Ed); early childhood education (MA Ed); general (MA Ed); higher education administration (MA Ed); Spanish language education (MA Ed); special education (MA Ed). *Degree requirements:* For master's, portfolio. *Entrance requirements:* For master's, minimum undergraduate GPA of 2.5. Additional exam requirements/recommendations for international students: Required—TOEFL (minimum score 500 paper-based; 173 computer-based; 61 iBT).

Universidad del Turabo, Graduate Programs, Programs in Education, Program in Teaching at Primary Level, Gurabo, PR 00778-3030. Offers M Ed. *Students:* 7 full-time (all women), 7 part-time (6 women); includes 11 minority (all Hispanic/Latino). Average age 37. 10 applicants, 40% accepted, 2 enrolled. In 2011, 19 master's awarded. *Unit head:* Angela Candelario, Dean, 787-743-7979 Ext. 4126. *Application contact:* Virginia Gonzalez, Admissions Officer, 787-746-3009.

University at Buffalo, the State University of New York, Graduate School, Graduate School of Education, Department of Learning and Instruction, Buffalo, NY 14260. Offers biology education (Ed M, Certificate); chemistry education (Ed M, Certificate); childhood education (Ed M); childhood education with bilingual extension (Ed M); early childhood education (Ed M); early childhood education with bilingual extension (birth-grade 2) (Ed M); earth science education (Ed M, Certificate); educational technology and new literacies (Certificate); educational technology and new literacies (online) (Certificate); elementary education (Ed D, PhD); English education (Ed M, PhD, Certificate); English for speakers of other languages (Ed M); foreign and second language education (PhD); French education (Ed M, Certificate); general education (Ed M); German education (Ed M, Certificate); gifted education (online) (Certificate); Latin education (Ed M, Certificate); literacy teaching and learning (Certificate); literary specialist (Ed M); mathematics education (Ed M, PhD, Certificate); music education (Ed M, Certificate); physics education (Ed M, Certificate); reading education (PhD); science and the public (online) (Ed M); science education (PhD); social studies education (Ed M, Certificate); Spanish education (Ed M, Certificate); special education (PhD); teaching and leading for diversity (Certificate); teaching English to speakers of other languages (Ed M). Part-time and evening/weekend programs available. Postbaccalaureate distance learning degree programs offered (no on-campus study). *Faculty:* 32 full-time (23 women), 54 part-time/adjunct (43 women). *Students:* 294 full-time (222 women), 350 part-time (261 women); includes 75 minority (19 Black or African American, non-Hispanic/Latino; 6 American Indian or Alaska Native, non-Hispanic/Latino; 40 Asian, non-Hispanic/Latino; 10 Hispanic/Latino), 76 international. Average age 29. 548 applicants, 52% accepted, 253 enrolled. In 2011, 225 master's, 17 doctorates, 37 other advanced degrees awarded. *Degree requirements:* For master's, comprehensive exam; for doctorate, thesis/dissertation, research analysis exam, research experience component. *Entrance requirements:* For doctorate, GRE General Test or MAT, interview, writing sample, letters of recommendation. Additional exam requirements/recommendations for international students: Required—TOEFL (minimum score 600 paper-based; 96 iBT). *Application deadline:* For fall admission, 2/1 priority date for domestic students, 2/1 for international students; for spring admission, 11/15 priority date for domestic students, 10/1 for international students. Applications are processed on a rolling basis. Application fee: $50. Electronic applications accepted. *Financial support:* In 2011–12, 40 fellowships (averaging $12,991 per year), 46 research assistantships (averaging $10,986 per year) were awarded; teaching assistantships with full tuition reimbursements, career-related internships or fieldwork, Federal Work-Study, institutionally sponsored loans, scholarships/grants, and unspecified assistantships also available. Financial award application deadline: 2/28; financial award applicants required to submit FAFSA. *Faculty research:* Science assessment, foreign language teaching and learning, early learning, new literacies, gender and education. *Unit head:* Dr. Julie Sarama, Chair, 716-645-2455, Fax: 716-645-3161, E-mail: jcollins@buffalo.edu. *Application contact:* Cathy Dimino, Admissions Assistant, 716-645-2110, Fax: 716-645-7937, E-mail: cadimino@buffalo.edu.

The University of Alabama at Birmingham, College of Arts and Sciences, School of Education, Program in Early Childhood Education, Birmingham, AL 35294. Offers MA Ed, PhD. *Accreditation:* NCATE. *Degree requirements:* For master's, comprehensive exam, thesis optional; for doctorate, thesis/dissertation. *Entrance requirements:* For master's, GRE General Test, MAT, or NTE, minimum GPA of 3.0; for doctorate, GRE General Test, MAT, minimum GPA of 3.25. *Application deadline:* Applications are processed on a rolling basis. Application fee: $35 ($60 for international students). Electronic applications accepted. *Expenses:* Tuition, state resident: full-time $5922; part-time $309 per hour. Tuition, nonresident: full-time $13,428; part-time $726 per hour. Tuition and fees vary according to program. *Unit head:* Dr. Lynn Kirkland, Chair, 205-934-8358. Web site: http://www.uab.edu/ci/early-childhood-education.

University of Alaska Anchorage, College of Education, Program in Special Education, Anchorage, AK 99508. Offers early childhood special education (M Ed); special education (M Ed, Certificate). Part-time programs available. *Degree requirements:* For master's, comprehensive exam (for some programs), thesis or alternative. *Entrance requirements:* For master's, GRE or MAT, interview, minimum GPA of 2.75. Additional exam requirements/recommendations for international students: Required—TOEFL (minimum score 550 paper-based; 213 computer-based). *Faculty research:* Mild disabilities, substance abuse issues for educators, partnerships to improve at-risk youth, analysis of planning models for teachers in special education.

University of Alaska Southeast, Graduate Programs, Program in Education, Juneau, AK 99801. Offers early childhood education (M Ed, MAT); educational technology (M Ed); elementary education (MAT); reading (M Ed); secondary education (MAT). *Accreditation:* NCATE. Part-time and evening/weekend programs available. Postbaccalaureate distance learning degree programs offered (minimal on-campus study). *Degree requirements:* For master's, comprehensive exam or project, portfolio. *Entrance requirements:* For master's, PRAXIS, minimum GPA of 3.0, writing sample, letters of recommendation. Electronic applications accepted. *Faculty research:* Applied classroom research, culturally responsive practices, action research, teaching effectiveness.

University of Arkansas, Graduate School, College of Education and Health Professions, Department of Curriculum and Instruction, Program in Childhood Education, Fayetteville, AR 72701-1201. Offers MAT. *Accreditation:* NCATE. *Students:* 63 full-time (62 women); includes 9 minority (1 Black or African American, non-Hispanic/Latino; 1 American Indian or Alaska Native, non-Hispanic/Latino; 1 Asian, non-Hispanic/Latino; 5 Hispanic/Latino; 1 Two or more races, non-Hispanic/Latino). In 2011, 72 master's awarded. *Application deadline:* For fall admission, 4/1 for international students; for spring admission, 10/1 for international students. Applications are processed on a rolling basis. Application fee: $40 ($50 for international students). Electronic applications accepted. *Financial support:* Fellowships, research assistantships, and teaching assistantships available. *Unit head:* Dr. Michael Daugherty, Unit Head, 479-575-4201, E-mail: mkd03@uark.edu. *Application contact:* Dr. Barbara Gartin, Graduate Coordinator, 479-575-7525, Fax: 479-575-6676, E-mail: bgartin@uark.edu. Web site: http://cied.uark.edu/.

University of Arkansas at Little Rock, Graduate School, College of Education, Department of Teacher Education, Program in Early Childhood Education, Little Rock, AR 72204-1099. Offers M Ed.

University of Arkansas at Pine Bluff, School of Education, Pine Bluff, AR 71601-2799. Offers early childhood education (M Ed); secondary education (M Ed), including English education, mathematics education, physical education, science education, social studies education; teaching (MAT). *Accreditation:* NCATE. Part-time and evening/weekend programs available. *Degree requirements:* For master's, comprehensive exam. *Entrance requirements:* For master's, GRE, minimum GPA of 2.75, NTE or Standard Arkansas Teaching Certificate. *Faculty research:* Teacher certification, accreditation, assessment, standards, portfolio development, rehabilitation, technology.

University of Bridgeport, School of Education, Department of Education, Bridgeport, CT 06604. Offers education (MS); educational management (Ed D, Diploma), including intermediate administrator or supervisor (Diploma), leadership (Ed D); elementary education (MS, Diploma), including early childhood education, elementary education; middle school education (MS); music education (MS); remedial reading and language arts (Diploma); secondary education (MS, Diploma), including computer specialist (Diploma), international education (Diploma), reading specialist, secondary education. Part-time and evening/weekend programs available. *Faculty:* 12 full-time (5 women), 108 part-time/adjunct (60 women). *Students:* 232 full-time (161 women), 216 part-time (160 women); includes 61 minority (21 Black or African American, non-Hispanic/Latino; 8 Asian, non-Hispanic/Latino; 22 Hispanic/Latino; 10 Two or more races, non-Hispanic/Latino), 34 international. Average age 30. 412 applicants, 63% accepted, 147 enrolled. In 2011, 216 master's, 7 other advanced degrees awarded. *Degree requirements:* For master's, final exam, final project, or thesis; for doctorate, comprehensive exam, thesis/dissertation; for Diploma, thesis or alternative, final project. *Entrance requirements:* For master's, minimum undergraduate QPA of 2.67; for doctorate, GRE, MAT; for Diploma, GRE General Test or MAT, minimum graduate QPA of 3.0. Additional exam requirements/recommendations for international students: Recommended—TOEFL (minimum score 550 paper-based; 213 computer-based; 80 iBT), IELTS (minimum score 6.5). *Application deadline:* For fall admission, 8/1 priority date for domestic students, 8/1 for international students; for spring admission, 12/1 priority date for domestic students, 12/1 for international students. Applications are processed on a rolling basis. Application fee: $50. Electronic applications accepted. *Expenses: Tuition:* Full-time $22,880; part-time $700 per credit. *Required fees:* $1870; $95 per semester. Tuition and fees vary according to course load and program. *Financial support:* In 2011–12, 120 students received support. Fellowships, research assistantships, teaching assistantships, career-related internships or fieldwork, Federal Work-Study, and institutionally sponsored loans available. Support available to part-time students. Financial award application deadline: 6/1; financial award applicants required to submit FAFSA. *Faculty research:* Self-concept, internship assessment, stress and situational development, follow-up of graduation, trend analysis. *Unit head:* Dr. Allen P. Cook, Dean, 203-576-4192, Fax: 203-576-4200, E-mail: acook@bridgeport.edu. *Application contact:* Karissa Peckham, Dean of Admissions, 203-576-4552, Fax: 203-576-4941, E-mail: admit@bridgeport.edu.

The University of British Columbia, Faculty of Education, Centre for Cross-Faculty Inquiry in Education, Vancouver, BC V6T 1Z1, Canada. Offers curriculum and instruction (M Ed, MA, PhD); early childhood education (M Ed, MA). Part-time and evening/weekend programs available. Terminal master's awarded for partial completion of doctoral program. *Degree requirements:* For master's, thesis (MA); for doctorate, thesis/dissertation. *Entrance requirements:* Additional exam requirements/recommendations for international students: Required—TOEFL (minimum score 567 paper-based; 227 computer-based). Electronic applications accepted.

University of Central Florida, College of Education, Department of Child, Family and Community Sciences, Early Childhood Development and Education, Orlando, FL 32816. Offers MS. *Accreditation:* NCATE. *Students:* 6 full-time (all women), 11 part-time (10 women); includes 3 minority (1 Black or African American, non-Hispanic/Latino; 1 Asian, non-Hispanic/Latino; 1 Hispanic/Latino), 1 international. Average age 28. 17 applicants, 59% accepted, 7 enrolled. In 2011, 8 master's awarded. Application fee: $30. Electronic applications accepted. *Expenses:* Tuition, state resident: part-time $277.08 per credit hour. Tuition, nonresident: part-time $277.08 per credit hour. Part-time tuition and fees vary according to degree level and program. *Financial support:* In 2011–12, 2 students received support, including 1 fellowship (averaging $300 per year), 1 research assistantship (averaging $7,100 per year); teaching assistantships also available. *Unit head:* Dr. Judit Szente, Program Coordinator, 407-823-3656, E-mail: judit.szente@ .ucf.edu. *Application contact:* Barbara Rodriguez, Director, Admissions and Registration, 407-823-2766, Fax: 407-823-6442, E-mail: gradadmissions@ucf.edu.

University of Central Oklahoma, College of Graduate Studies and Research, College of Education and Professional Studies, Department of Curriculum and Instruction, Edmond, OK 73034-5209. Offers early childhood education (M Ed); elementary education (M Ed). Part-time programs available. Postbaccalaureate distance learning degree programs offered (minimal on-campus study). *Faculty:* 13 full-time (11 women), 10 part-time/adjunct (9 women). *Students:* 55 full-time (52 women), 89 part-time (81 women); includes 28 minority (6 Black or African American, non-Hispanic/Latino; 4 American Indian or Alaska Native, non-Hispanic/Latino; 1 Asian, non-Hispanic/Latino; 12 Hispanic/Latino; 5 Two or more races, non-Hispanic/Latino), 44 international. Average age 34. In 2011, 61 master's awarded. *Entrance requirements:* For master's, GRE General Test. Additional exam requirements/recommendations for international students: Required—TOEFL (minimum score 550 paper-based; 213 computer-based). *Application deadline:* Applications are processed on a rolling basis. Application fee: $50. Electronic applications accepted. *Expenses:* Tuition, state resident: full-time $3901; part-time $218.30 per credit hour. Tuition, nonresident: full-time $9198; part-time $511.20 per credit hour. Tuition and fees vary according to program. *Financial support:* Unspecified assistantships available. Financial award application deadline: 3/31; financial award applicants required to submit FAFSA. *Faculty research:* Tourette's syndrome, bilingual education, science education, language development/disorders. *Unit head:* Dr. Paulette Shreck, Chairperson, 405-974-5721. *Application contact:* Dr. Richard Bernard, Dean, Graduate College, 405-974-3493, Fax: 405-974-3852, E-mail: gradcoll@uco.edu.

University of Cincinnati, Graduate School, College of Education, Criminal Justice, and Human Services, Division of Teacher Education, Program in Early Childhood Education, Cincinnati, OH 45221. Offers M Ed. *Accreditation:* NCATE. Part-time programs available. *Degree requirements:* For master's, thesis or alternative. *Entrance requirements:* For master's, GRE General Test. Additional exam requirements/recommendations for international students: Required—TOEFL (minimum score 610 paper-based), TWE (minimum score 5), OEPT. Electronic applications accepted.

University of Colorado Denver, School of Education and Human Development, Early Childhood Education Program, Denver, CO 80217. Offers early childhood education (MA); special education (MA). *Accreditation:* NCATE. Part-time and evening/weekend programs available. Postbaccalaureate distance learning degree programs offered (no on-campus study). *Students:* 59 full-time (57 women), 38 part-time (all women); includes 11 minority (2 Black or African American, non-Hispanic/Latino; 2 Asian, non-Hispanic/Latino; 7 Hispanic/Latino), 5 international. Average age 32. 21 applicants, 86% accepted, 15 enrolled. In 2011, 42 master's awarded. *Degree requirements:* For master's, comprehensive exam, fieldwork, practica, 40 credit hours. *Entrance requirements:* For master's, GRE or MAT (if GPA is below 2.75), minimum GPA of 2.75, resume, three letters of recommendation. Additional exam requirements/recommendations for international students: Required—TOEFL (minimum score 525 paper-based; 197 computer-based; 71 iBT). *Application deadline:* For fall admission, 4/15 for domestic students, 4/1 for international students; for spring admission, 9/15 for domestic students, 9/1 for international students. Application fee: $50 ($75 for international students). Electronic applications accepted. *Expenses:* Contact institution. *Financial support:* Research assistantships, teaching assistantships, and Federal Work-Study available. Financial award application deadline: 4/1; financial award applicants required to submit FAFSA. *Faculty research:* Early childhood growth and development, faculty development, adult learning, gender and equity issues, research methodology. *Unit head:* William Goodwin, Professor, 303-315-6323, E-mail: bill.goodwin@ucdenver.edu. *Application contact:* Hans Broers, Academic Advisor, 303-315-6351, Fax: 303-315-6311, E-mail: hans.broers@ucdenver.edu. Web site: http://www.ucdenver.edu/academics/colleges/SchoolOfEducation/Academics/MASTERS/ECE/Pages/EarlyChildhoodEducation.aspx.

Early Childhood Education

University of Colorado Denver, School of Education and Human Development, Program in Educational Leadership and Innovation, Denver, CO 80217-3364. Offers educational studies and research (PhD), including administrative leadership and policy, early childhood special education, math education, research, assessment and evaluation, science education, urban ecologies. Part-time and evening/weekend programs available. *Students:* 21 full-time (15 women), 25 part-time (17 women); includes 10 minority (5 Black or African American, non-Hispanic/Latino; 1 American Indian or Alaska Native, non-Hispanic/Latino; 3 Asian, non-Hispanic/Latino; 1 Hispanic/Latino), 1 international. Average age 43. 11 applicants, 45% accepted, 3 enrolled. In 2011, 11 doctorates awarded. *Degree requirements:* For doctorate, comprehensive exam, thesis/dissertation, 75 credit hours (for PhD). *Entrance requirements:* For doctorate, GRE or equivalent, resume or curriculum vitae, written statement, letters of recommendation, master's degree or equivalent, completion of basic or advanced statistics course with minimum B grade. Additional exam requirements/recommendations for international students: Required—TOEFL (minimum score 525 paper-based; 197 computer-based). *Application deadline:* Applications are processed on a rolling basis. Application fee: $50 ($75 for international students). Electronic applications accepted. *Expenses:* Contact institution. *Financial support:* Fellowships, research assistantships, teaching assistantships, scholarships/grants, and unspecified assistantships available. Financial award application deadline: 4/1; financial award applicants required to submit FAFSA. *Faculty research:* Administrative leadership and policy studies, early childhood education, research in diversity, paraprofessionals in education, urban schools lab. *Unit head:* Dr. Deanna Sands, Associate Dean, Research and Professional Development, 303-315-4931, E-mail: deanna.sands@ucdenver.edu. *Application contact:* Student Services Center, 303-315-6300, Fax: 303-315-6311, E-mail: education@ucdenver.edu. Web site: http://www.ucdenver.edu/ACADEMICS/COLLEGES/SCHOOLOFEDUCATION/ACADEMICS/Pages/AcademicPrograms.aspx.

University of Dayton, Department of Teacher Education, Dayton, OH 45469-1300. Offers adolescent/young adult (MS Ed); art education (MS Ed); early childhood education (MS Ed); early childhood leadership advocacy (MS Ed); inclusive early childhood (MS Ed); interdisciplinary education (MS Ed); intervention specialist education, mild/moderate (MS Ed); literacy (MS Ed); middle childhood (MS Ed); multi-age education (MS Ed); music education (MS Ed); teacher as leader (MS Ed); technology in education (MS Ed). Part-time and evening/weekend programs available. Postbaccalaureate distance learning degree programs offered (no on-campus study). *Faculty:* 15 full-time (11 women), 22 part-time/adjunct (20 women). *Students:* 41 full-time (29 women), 95 part-time (87 women); includes 13 minority (9 Black or African American, non-Hispanic/Latino; 1 Asian, non-Hispanic/Latino; 3 Hispanic/Latino), 9 international. Average age 32. 111 applicants, 55% accepted, 38 enrolled. In 2011, 97 degrees awarded. *Degree requirements:* For master's, thesis, capstone research project. *Entrance requirements:* For master's, GRE General Test, minimum GPA of 2.75. Additional exam requirements/recommendations for international students: Required—TOEFL (minimum score 550 paper-based; 213 computer-based; 80 iBT). *Application deadline:* For fall admission, 3/1 priority date for domestic students, 3/1 for international students; for winter admission, 7/1 for international students; for spring admission, 1/1 for international students. Applications are processed on a rolling basis. Application fee: $0 ($50 for international students). Electronic applications accepted. *Expenses:* Contact institution. *Financial support:* In 2011–12, 5 research assistantships with full and partial tuition reimbursements (averaging $8,470 per year) were awarded; career-related internships or fieldwork, institutionally sponsored loans, health care benefits, and unspecified assistantships also available. Financial award applicants required to submit FAFSA. *Faculty research:* Diversity, literacy, art representation by young children, preservice teacher preparation. *Unit head:* Dr. Katie A. Kinnucan-Welsch, Chair, 937-229-3346. *Application contact:* Alexsandar Popovski, Enrollment Management Administrator, 937-229-2357, Fax: 937-229-4729, E-mail: alex.popovski@notes.udayton.edu.

The University of Findlay, Graduate and Professional Studies, College of Education, Findlay, OH 45840-3653. Offers administration (MA Ed); children's literature (MA Ed); early childhood (MA Ed); human resource development (MA Ed); reading endorsement (MA Ed); science (MA Ed); special education (MA Ed); technology (MA Ed). *Accreditation:* NCATE. Part-time and evening/weekend programs available. Postbaccalaureate distance learning degree programs offered (no on-campus study). *Faculty:* 16 full-time (12 women), 5 part-time/adjunct (2 women). *Students:* 72 full-time (49 women), 198 part-time (119 women); includes 10 minority (7 Black or African American, non-Hispanic/Latino; 1 Asian, non-Hispanic/Latino; 2 Hispanic/Latino), 16 international. Average age 30. 75 applicants, 88% accepted, 36 enrolled. In 2011, 76 master's awarded. *Degree requirements:* For master's, thesis, cumulative project. *Entrance requirements:* For master's, bachelor's degree from accredited institution, minimum undergraduate GPA of 2.75 in last 62 hours of course work. Additional exam requirements/recommendations for international students: Required—TOEFL (minimum score 550 paper-based; 213 computer-based; 80 iBT). *Application deadline:* Applications are processed on a rolling basis. Application fee: $25. Electronic applications accepted. *Expenses:* Contact institution. *Financial support:* In 2011–12, 5 research assistantships with full and partial tuition reimbursements (averaging $4,200 per year) were awarded; Federal Work-Study, health care benefits, and unspecified assistantships also available. Financial award application deadline: 4/1; financial award applicants required to submit FAFSA. *Faculty research:* Children's literature, books and artwork, educational technology, professional development. *Unit head:* Dr. Julie McIntosh, Dean, 419-434-4862, Fax: 419-434-4822. *Application contact:* Heather Riffle, Assistant Director, Graduate and Professional Studies, 419-434-4640, Fax: 419-434-5517, E-mail: riffle@findlay.edu. Web site: http://www.findlay.edu.

University of Florida, Graduate School, College of Education, Department of Special Education, School Psychology and Early Childhood Studies, Gainesville, FL 32611. Offers early childhood education (M Ed, MAE); school psychology (M Ed, MAE, Ed D, PhD, Ed S); special education (M Ed, MAE, Ed D, PhD, Ed S). *Accreditation:* NCATE. Part-time and evening/weekend programs available. Postbaccalaureate distance learning degree programs offered (no on-campus study). *Faculty:* 21 full-time (17 women). *Students:* 151 full-time (134 women), 62 part-time (56 women); includes 61 minority (26 Black or African American, non-Hispanic/Latino; 1 American Indian or Alaska Native, non-Hispanic/Latino; 10 Asian, non-Hispanic/Latino; 24 Hispanic/Latino), 11 international. Average age 31. 189 applicants, 38% accepted, 40 enrolled. In 2011, 60 master's, 10 doctorates, 6 other advanced degrees awarded. *Degree requirements:* For master's, comprehensive exam (for some programs), thesis (MAE); for doctorate, comprehensive exam, thesis/dissertation. *Entrance requirements:* For master's and doctorate, GRE General Test, minimum GPA of 3.0; for Ed S, GRE General Test. Additional exam requirements/recommendations for international students: Required—TOEFL (minimum score 550 paper-based; 213 computer-based; 80 iBT), IELTS (minimum score 6). *Application deadline:* For fall admission, 11/1 priority date for domestic students. Applications are processed on a rolling basis. Application fee: $30. Electronic applications accepted. *Financial support:* Fellowships, research assistantships, teaching assistantships, career-related internships or fieldwork, and unspecified assistantships available. Financial award application deadline: 11/15; financial award applicants required to submit FAFSA. *Faculty research:* Teacher quality/teacher education, early childhood, autism, instructional interventions in reading and mathematics, behavioral interventions. *Unit head:* Dr. Jean Crockett, Chair, 352-273-4292, Fax: 352-392-2655, E-mail: crocketj@ufl.edu. *Application contact:* Dr. Penny R. Cox, Coordinator, 352-273-4280, Fax: 352-392-2655, E-mail: contact-sespecs@coe.ufl.edu. Web site: http://education.ufl.edu/sespecs/.

University of Georgia, College of Education, Department of Elementary and Social Studies Education, Athens, GA 30602. Offers early childhood education (M Ed, MAT, PhD, Ed S), including child and family development (MAT); elementary education (PhD); middle school education (M Ed, PhD, Ed S); social studies education (M Ed, Ed D, PhD, Ed S). *Faculty:* 17 full-time (10 women). *Students:* 119 full-time (96 women), 110 part-time (96 women); includes 42 minority (22 Black or African American, non-Hispanic/Latino; 1 American Indian or Alaska Native, non-Hispanic/Latino; 11 Asian, non-Hispanic/Latino; 6 Hispanic/Latino; 2 Two or more races, non-Hispanic/Latino), 12 international. Average age 30. 68 applicants, 72% accepted, 22 enrolled. In 2011, 92 master's, 12 doctorates, 2 other advanced degrees awarded. *Entrance requirements:* For master's and Ed S, GRE General Test or MAT; for doctorate, GRE General Test. *Application deadline:* For fall admission, 7/1 priority date for domestic students; for spring admission, 11/15 for domestic students. Application fee: $50. Electronic applications accepted. *Financial support:* Fellowships, research assistantships, teaching assistantships, and unspecified assistantships available. *Unit head:* Dr. Ronald Butchart, Interim Head, 706-542-6490, E-mail: butchart@uga.edu. *Application contact:* Dr. Stephanie R. Jones, Graduate Coordinator, 706-542-4283, Fax: 706-542-8996, E-mail: essegrad@uga.edu. Web site: http://www.coe.uga.edu/esse/.

University of Hartford, College of Education, Nursing, and Health Professions, Program in Early Childhood Education, West Hartford, CT 06117-1599. Offers M Ed. *Accreditation:* NCATE. Part-time and evening/weekend programs available. *Degree requirements:* For master's, comprehensive exam. *Entrance requirements:* For master's, PRAXIS I or waiver, interview, 2 letters of recommendation. Additional exam requirements/recommendations for international students: Required—TOEFL (minimum score 550 paper-based; 213 computer-based). Electronic applications accepted.

University of Hawaii at Manoa, Graduate Division, College of Education, Department of Curriculum Studies, Program in Early Childhood Education, Honolulu, HI 96822. Offers M Ed. *Accreditation:* NCATE. Part-time programs available. *Degree requirements:* For master's, thesis optional. *Entrance requirements:* Additional exam requirements/recommendations for international students: Required—TOEFL (minimum score 580 paper-based; 237 computer-based; 92 iBT), IELTS (minimum score 5).

University of Houston–Clear Lake, School of Education, Program in Curriculum and Instruction, Houston, TX 77058-1098. Offers curriculum and instruction (MS); early childhood education (MS); reading (MS); school library and information science (MS). Part-time and evening/weekend programs available. *Degree requirements:* For master's, thesis (for some programs). *Entrance requirements:* For master's, GRE or minimum GPA of 3.0 in last 60 hours. Additional exam requirements/recommendations for international students: Required—TOEFL (minimum score 550 paper-based; 213 computer-based). Electronic applications accepted.

The University of Iowa, Graduate College, College of Education, Department of Teaching and Learning, Program in Elementary Education, Iowa City, IA 52242-1316. Offers curriculum and supervision (MA, PhD); developmental reading (MA); early childhood education and care (MA); elementary education (MA, PhD); language, literature and culture (PhD). *Degree requirements:* For master's, thesis optional, exam; for doctorate, comprehensive exam, thesis/dissertation. *Entrance requirements:* For master's and doctorate, GRE General Test, minimum GPA of 3.0. Additional exam requirements/recommendations for international students: Required—TOEFL (minimum score 550 paper-based; 213 computer-based; 81 iBT). Electronic applications accepted.

University of Kentucky, Graduate School, College of Education, Program in Special Education, Lexington, KY 40506-0032. Offers early childhood special education (MS Ed); rehabilitation counseling (MRC); special education (MS Ed); special education leadership personnel preparation (Ed D). *Accreditation:* CORE; NCATE. Terminal master's awarded for partial completion of doctoral program. *Degree requirements:* For master's, comprehensive exam, thesis optional; for doctorate, comprehensive exam, thesis/dissertation. *Entrance requirements:* For master's, GRE General Test, minimum undergraduate GPA of 2.75; for doctorate, GRE General Test, minimum graduate GPA of 3.0. Additional exam requirements/recommendations for international students: Required—TOEFL (minimum score 550 paper-based; 213 computer-based). Electronic applications accepted. *Faculty research:* Applied behavior analysis applications in special education, single subject research design in classroom settings, transition research across life span, rural special education personnel.

University of Louisville, Graduate School, College of Education and Human Development, Department of Teaching and Learning, Louisville, KY 40292-0001. Offers art education (MAT); curriculum and instruction (PhD); early elementary education (MAT); instructional technology (M Ed); interdisciplinary early childhood education (MAT); middle school education (MAT); music education (MAT); reading education (M Ed); secondary education (MAT); special education (M Ed, MAT); teacher leadership (M Ed). Part-time and evening/weekend programs available. *Degree requirements:* For doctorate, comprehensive exam, thesis/dissertation. *Entrance requirements:* For master's, GRE General Test, PRAXIS II (for some programs); for doctorate, GRE General Test. Additional exam requirements/recommendations for international students: Required—TOEFL (minimum score 560 paper-based; 210 computer-based; 83 iBT). Electronic applications accepted. *Expenses:* Tuition, state resident: full-time $9692; part-time $539 per credit hour. Tuition, nonresident: full-time $20,168; part-time $1121 per credit hour. Tuition and fees vary according to program and reciprocity agreements. *Faculty research:* Mathematics teacher education and ongoing professional development in pedagogy and content knowledge; development of literacy, including early literacy in science and mathematics and literacy development for English language learners; immersive visualizations for promoting STEM education from nanoscience to cosmic scales; evidence-based practices for students with disabilities; urban education, including teacher response to intervention systems in schools and cross-cultural competence.

University of Maine at Farmington, Program in Education, Farmington, ME 04938-1990. Offers early childhood education (MS Ed); educational leadership (MS Ed). *Accreditation:* NCATE. Part-time and evening/weekend programs available. Postbaccalaureate distance learning degree programs offered (minimal on-campus study). *Degree requirements:* For master's, capstone project (for educational leadership). *Entrance requirements:* For master's, baccalaureate degree from accredited institution, valid teaching certificate or professional experience in education, professional employment by school district or other educational institution (exceptions may be made by the Assistant Dean), minimum of two years experience in professional education. *Faculty research:* School improvement strategies, technology integration.

University of Mary, School of Education and Behavioral Sciences, Department of Education, Bismarck, ND 58504-9652. Offers college teaching (M Ed); curriculum, instruction and assessment (M Ed); early childhood education (M Ed); early childhood special education (M Ed); elementary administration (M Ed); emotional disorders (M Ed); learning disabilities (M Ed); reading (M Ed); secondary administration (M Ed); special education strategist (M Ed). Part-time programs available. *Faculty:* 6 full-time (5 women), 12 part-time/adjunct (8 women). *Students:* 5 full-time (4 women), 77 part-time (56 women); includes 9 minority (1 Black or African American, non-Hispanic/Latino; 4 American Indian or Alaska Native, non-Hispanic/Latino; 1 Asian, non-Hispanic/Latino; 3 Hispanic/Latino), 1 international. Average age 30. 58 applicants, 55% accepted, 29 enrolled. In 2011, 16 master's awarded. *Degree requirements:* For master's, portfolio or thesis. *Entrance requirements:* For master's, interview, letters of reference, minimum GPA of 2.5. Additional exam requirements/recommendations for international students: Required—TOEFL (minimum score 500 paper-based; 197 computer-based; 71 iBT). *Application deadline:* Applications are processed on a rolling basis. Application fee: $40. Electronic applications accepted. *Financial support:* In 2011–12, 1 teaching assistantship with full tuition reimbursement was awarded; career-related internships or fieldwork also available. Financial award application deadline: 8/1; financial award applicants required to submit FAFSA. *Faculty research:* Innovative pedagogy in higher education, technology in education, content standards, children of poverty, children with diverse learning needs. *Unit head:* Dr. Rebecca Yunker Salveson, Director, 701-355-8186, E-mail: rysalves@umary.edu. *Application contact:* Leona Friedig, Administrative Secretary, 701-355-8058, E-mail: lfriedig@umary.edu.

University of Maryland, Baltimore County, Graduate School, College of Arts, Humanities and Social Sciences, Department of Education, Program in Teaching, Baltimore, MD 21250. Offers early childhood education (MAT); elementary education (MAT); secondary education (MAT), including social studies; secondary education (MAT), including art, biology, chemistry, dance, earth/space science, English, foreign language, mathematics, music, physics, theatre. Part-time and evening/weekend programs available. *Faculty:* 24 full-time (18 women), 25 part-time/adjunct (19 women). *Students:* 46 full-time (35 women), 64 part-time (39 women); includes 24 minority (8 Black or African American, non-Hispanic/Latino; 7 Asian, non-Hispanic/Latino; 6 Hispanic/Latino; 1 Native Hawaiian or other Pacific Islander, non-Hispanic/Latino; 2 Two or more races, non-Hispanic/Latino), 4 international. Average age 31. 88 applicants, 57% accepted, 39 enrolled. In 2011, 106 master's awarded. *Degree requirements:* For master's, comprehensive exam (for some programs), thesis (for some programs). *Entrance requirements:* For master's, PRAXIS I or GRE (minimum score of 1000), minimum GPA of 3.0. Additional exam requirements/recommendations for international students: Required—TOEFL. *Application deadline:* For fall admission, 6/1 for domestic students; for spring admission, 11/1 for domestic students. Applications are processed on a rolling basis. Application fee: $50. Electronic applications accepted. *Financial support:* In 2011–12, 6 students received support, including teaching assistantships with full and partial tuition reimbursements available (averaging $12,000 per year); career-related internships or fieldwork, Federal Work-Study, scholarships/grants, tuition waivers, and unspecified assistantships also available. Financial award application deadline: 3/1. *Faculty research:* STEM teacher education, culturally sensitive pedagogy, ESOL/bilingual education, early childhood education, language, literacy and culture. *Unit head:* Dr. Susan M. Blunck, Graduate Program Director, 410-455-2869, Fax: 410-455-3986, E-mail: blunck@umbc.edu. *Application contact:* Cheryl Johnson, 410-455-3388, E-mail: blackwel@umbc.edu. Web site: http://www.umbc.edu/education/.

University of Maryland, College Park, Academic Affairs, College of Education, Department of Human Development, College Park, MD 20742. Offers early childhood/elementary education (M Ed, MA, Ed D, PhD); human development (M Ed, MA, Ed D, PhD). *Accreditation:* NCATE. Part-time and evening/weekend programs available. Postbaccalaureate distance learning degree programs offered. *Faculty:* 50 full-time (43 women), 18 part-time/adjunct (16 women). *Students:* 58 full-time (52 women), 23 part-time (20 women); includes 23 minority (7 Black or African American, non-Hispanic/Latino; 7 Asian, non-Hispanic/Latino; 7 Hispanic/Latino; 1 Native Hawaiian or other Pacific Islander, non-Hispanic/Latino; 1 Two or more races, non-Hispanic/Latino), 7 international. 108 applicants, 22% accepted, 21 enrolled. In 2011, 21 master's, 6 doctorates awarded. *Degree requirements:* For master's, comprehensive exam, thesis optional; for doctorate, comprehensive exam, thesis/dissertation, essay, exam, research paper. *Entrance requirements:* For master's, GRE General Test, minimum GPA of 3.0, 3 letters of recommendation; for doctorate, GRE General Test or MAT, minimum undergraduate GPA of 3.0, graduate 3.5; 3 letters of recommendation. Additional exam requirements/recommendations for international students: Required—TOEFL. *Application deadline:* For fall admission, 3/15 for domestic students, 12/15 for international students; for spring admission, 10/1 priority date for domestic students, 6/1 for international students. Applications are processed on a rolling basis. Application fee: $75. Electronic applications accepted. *Expenses: Tuition, area resident:* Part-time $525 per credit hour. Tuition, state resident: part-time $525 per credit hour. Tuition, nonresident: part-time $1131 per credit hour. *Required fees:* $386.31 per term. Tuition and fees vary according to program. *Financial support:* In 2011–12, 5 fellowships with full and partial tuition reimbursements (averaging $16,476 per year), 38 teaching assistantships (averaging $17,258 per year) were awarded; Federal Work-Study and scholarships/grants also available. Support available to part-time students. Financial award applicants required to submit FAFSA. *Faculty research:* Developmental science, educational psychology, cognitive development, language development. *Total annual research expenditures:* $3.4 million. *Unit head:* Dr. Kathryn Wentzel, Interim Chair, 301-405-1659, Fax: 301-405-2891, E-mail: wentzel@umd.edu. *Application contact:* Dr. Charles A. Caramello, Dean of Graduate School, 301-405-0358, Fax: 301-314-9305.

University of Massachusetts Amherst, Graduate School, School of Education, Program in Education, Amherst, MA 01003. Offers bilingual, English as a second language, and multicultural education (M Ed, CAGS); child study and early education (M Ed); children, families and schools (Ed D, CAGS); early childhood and elementary teacher education (M Ed); educational leadership (M Ed, CAGS); educational policy and leadership (Ed D); higher education (M Ed, CAGS); international education (M Ed); language, literacy and culture (Ed D); learning, media and technology (M Ed, CAGS); mathematics, science, and learning technologies (Ed D); policy studies in education (CAGS); psychometric methods, educational statistics and research methods (Ed D); reading and writing (M Ed); school counselor education (M Ed, CAGS); science education (CAGS); secondary teacher education (M Ed); social justice education (M Ed, Ed D, CAGS); special education (M Ed, Ed D, CAGS). *Accreditation:* NCATE. Part-time programs available. Postbaccalaureate distance learning degree programs offered (minimal on-campus study). *Faculty:* 81 full-time (46 women). *Students:* 341 full-time (240 women), 333 part-time (226 women); includes 113 minority (36 Black or African American, non-Hispanic/Latino; 1 American Indian or Alaska Native, non-Hispanic/Latino; 14 Asian, non-Hispanic/Latino; 51 Hispanic/Latino; 1 Native Hawaiian or other Pacific Islander, non-Hispanic/Latino; 10 Two or more races, non-Hispanic/Latino), 98 international. Average age 36. 721 applicants, 57% accepted, 202 enrolled. In 2011, 166 master's, 33 doctorates, 25 CAGSs awarded. Terminal master's awarded for partial completion of doctoral program. *Degree requirements:* For doctorate, comprehensive exam, thesis/dissertation. *Entrance requirements:* Additional exam requirements/recommendations for international students: Required—TOEFL (minimum score 550 paper-based; 213 computer-based; 80 iBT), IELTS (minimum score 6.5). *Application deadline:* For fall admission, 1/15 for domestic and international students. Applications are processed on a rolling basis. Application fee: $50 ($65 for international students). Electronic applications accepted. Tuition and fees vary according to course load, campus/location and program. *Financial support:* Fellowships with full and partial tuition reimbursements, research assistantships with full and partial tuition reimbursements, teaching assistantships with full and partial tuition reimbursements, career-related internships or fieldwork, Federal Work-Study, scholarships/grants, traineeships, health care benefits, tuition waivers (full and partial), and unspecified assistantships available. Support available to part-time students. Financial award application deadline: 1/15. *Unit head:* Dr. Linda L. Griffin, Graduate Program Director, 413-545-6984, Fax: 413-545-1523. *Application contact:* Lindsay DeSantis, Interim Supervisor of Admissions, 413-545-0722, Fax: 413-577-0010, E-mail: gradadm@grad.umass.edu. Web site: http://www.umass.edu/education/.

University of Memphis, Graduate School, College of Education, Department of Instruction and Curriculum Leadership, Memphis, TN 38152. Offers early childhood education (MAT, MS, Ed D); elementary education (MAT); instruction and curriculum (MS, Ed D); instruction design and technology (MS, Ed D); middle grades education (MAT); reading (MS, Ed D); secondary education (MAT); special education (MAT, MS, Ed D). *Accreditation:* NCATE (one or more programs are accredited). Part-time programs available. Terminal master's awarded for partial completion of doctoral program. *Degree requirements:* For master's, comprehensive exam, thesis or alternative; for doctorate, comprehensive exam, thesis/dissertation. *Entrance requirements:* For master's, GRE General Test, minimum GPA of 2.5; for doctorate, GRE General Test, GRE Subject Test, 2 years of teaching experience. Electronic applications accepted. *Faculty research:* Effective urban teachers, preparation and retention of urban teachers, technology utilization in schools, field-based teacher preparation programs, effective use of online instruction.

University of Miami, Graduate School, School of Education and Human Development, Department of Teaching and Learning, Program in Early Childhood Special Education, Coral Gables, FL 33124. Offers MS Ed, Ed S. Part-time and evening/weekend programs available. *Students:* 16 part-time (all women); includes 12 minority (3 Black or African American, non-Hispanic/Latino; 9 Hispanic/Latino). Average age 38. *Degree requirements:* For master's, electronic portfolio. *Entrance requirements:* For master's, GRE General Test. Additional exam requirements/recommendations for international students: Required—TOEFL (minimum score 550 paper-based; 80 iBT); Recommended—IELTS (minimum score 6.5). Application fee: $65. Electronic applications accepted. *Financial support:* Application deadline: 3/1; applicants required to submit FAFSA. *Unit head:* Dr. Elizabeth Harry, Department Chairperson and Program Director, 305-284-4961, Fax: 305-284-6998, E-mail: bharry@miami.edu. *Application contact:* Maria Papazian, Graduate Admissions Coordinator, 305-284-2963, Fax: 305-284-6998, E-mail: m.papazian@miami.edu.

University of Minnesota, Twin Cities Campus, Graduate School, College of Education and Human Development, Department of Curriculum and Instruction, Minneapolis, MN 55455-0213. Offers art education (M Ed, MA, PhD); children's literature (M Ed, MA, PhD); curriculum and instruction (MA, PhD); early childhood education (M Ed, PhD); elementary education (M Ed, MA, PhD); English education (MA, PhD); environmental education (M Ed); family education (M Ed, MA, Ed D, PhD); instructional systems and technology (M Ed, MA, PhD); language arts (MA, PhD); language immersion education (Certificate); literacy education (MA); mathematics education (MA, PhD); reading education (MA, PhD); science education (MA, PhD); second languages and cultures education (MA, PhD); social studies education (MA, PhD); teaching (M Ed), including Chinese, earth science, elementary special education, English, English as a second language, French, German, Hebrew, Japanese, life sciences, mathematics, middle school science, science, second languages and cultures, social studies, Spanish; technology enhanced learning (Certificate); writing education (M Ed, MA, PhD). *Faculty:* 34 full-time (22 women). *Students:* 433 full-time (319 women), 310 part-time (239 women); includes 97 minority (34 Black or African American, non-Hispanic/Latino; 6 American Indian or Alaska Native, non-Hispanic/Latino; 35 Asian, non-Hispanic/Latino; 22 Hispanic/Latino), 47 international. Average age 33. 660 applicants, 68% accepted, 395 enrolled. In 2011, 518 master's, 19 doctorates, 14 other advanced degrees awarded. Application fee: $55. *Financial support:* In 2011–12, 6 fellowships (averaging $9,308 per year), 39 research assistantships with full tuition reimbursements (averaging $8,301 per year), 61 teaching assistantships with full tuition reimbursements (averaging $9,206 per year) were awarded. *Faculty research:* Teaching and learning; quality of education; influence of cultural, linguistic, social, political, technological and economic factors on teaching, learning and educational research; relationship between educational practice and a democratic and just society. *Total annual research expenditures:* $943,365. *Unit head:* Dr. Nina Asher, Chair, 612-624-4772, Fax: 612-624-1357, E-mail: nasher@umn.edu. *Application contact:* Dr. Jennifer Engler, Assistant Dean, 612-626-2887, Fax: 612-626-7496, E-mail: engle009@umn.edu. Web site: http://www.cehd.umn.edu/ci.

University of Minnesota, Twin Cities Campus, Graduate School, College of Education and Human Development, Department of Educational Psychology, Minneapolis, MN 55455-0213. Offers counseling and student personnel psychology (MA, PhD, Ed S); early childhood education (M Ed, MA, PhD); educational psychology (PhD); psychological foundations of education (MA, PhD, Ed S); school psychology (MA, PhD, Ed S); special education (M Ed, MA, PhD, Ed S); talent development and gifted education (Certificate). *Accreditation:* APA (one or more programs are accredited). *Faculty:* 31 full-time (13 women). *Students:* 312 full-time (231 women), 88 part-time (67 women); includes 54 minority (20 Black or African American, non-Hispanic/Latino; 5 American Indian or Alaska Native, non-Hispanic/Latino; 18 Asian, non-Hispanic/Latino; 11 Hispanic/Latino), 5,149 international. Average age 30. 440 applicants, 48% accepted, 127 enrolled. In 2011, 98 master's, 21 doctorates, 22 other advanced degrees awarded. *Financial support:* In 2011–12, 4 fellowships (averaging $20,729 per year), 62 research assistantships (averaging $10,014 per year), 36 teaching assistantships (averaging $10,014 per year) were awarded. *Faculty research:* Learning, cognitive and social processes; multicultural education and counseling; measurement and statistical processes; performance assessment; instructional design/strategies for students with special needs. *Total annual research expenditures:* $4 million. *Unit head:* Dr. Susan Hupp, Chair, 612-624-1003, Fax: 612-624-8241, E-mail: shupp@umn.edu. *Application contact:* Dr. Jennifer Engler, Assistant Dean, 612-626-2887, Fax: 612-626-7496, E-mail: engle009@umn.edu. Web site: http://www.cehd.umn.edu/EdPsych.

University of Minnesota, Twin Cities Campus, Graduate School, College of Education and Human Development, Institute of Child Development, Minneapolis, MN 55455-0213. Offers child psychology (MA, PhD); early childhood education (M Ed, MA, PhD); school psychology (MA, PhD). *Faculty:* 15 full-time (8 women). *Students:* 84 full-time (78 women), 26 part-time (25 women); includes 12 minority (2 Black or African American, non-Hispanic/Latino; 1 American Indian or Alaska Native, non-Hispanic/Latino; 5 Asian, non-Hispanic/Latino; 4 Hispanic/Latino), 9 international. Average age 29. 143 applicants, 20% accepted, 25 enrolled. In 2011, 52 master's, 7 doctorates awarded. Application fee: $55. *Financial support:* In 2011–12, 22 fellowships (averaging $21,299 per year), 26 research assistantships with full tuition reimbursements (averaging $8,070 per year), 28 teaching assistantships with full tuition reimbursements (averaging $7,110 per year) were awarded. *Faculty research:* Developmental affective and cognitive neuroscience; developmental psychopathology; intervention and prevention science; social and emotional development; cognitive, language, and perceptual development. *Total annual research expenditures:* $5.7 million. *Unit head:*

Early Childhood Education

Dr. Megan Gunnar, Director, 612-624-2846, Fax: 612-624-6373, E-mail: gunnar@umn.edu. *Application contact:* Dr. Jennifer Engler, Assistant Dean, 612-626-2887, Fax: 612-626-7496, E-mail: engle009@umn.edu. Web site: http://www.cehd.umn.edu/ICD.

University of Missouri, Graduate School, College of Education, Department of Learning, Teaching and Curriculum, Columbia, MO 65211. Offers agricultural education (M Ed, PhD, Ed S); art education (M Ed, PhD, Ed S); business and office education (M Ed, PhD, Ed S); early childhood education (M Ed, PhD, Ed S); elementary education (M Ed, PhD, Ed S); English education (M Ed, PhD, Ed S); foreign language education (M Ed, PhD, Ed S); health education and promotion (M Ed, PhD); learning and instruction (M Ed); marketing education (M Ed, PhD, Ed S); mathematics education (M Ed, PhD, Ed S); music education (M Ed, PhD, Ed S); reading education (M Ed, PhD, Ed S); science education (M Ed, PhD, Ed S); social studies education (M Ed, PhD, Ed S); vocational education (M Ed, PhD, Ed S). Part-time programs available. *Faculty:* 26 full-time (16 women), 3 part-time/adjunct (2 women). *Students:* 184 full-time (145 women), 276 part-time (215 women); includes 34 minority (10 Black or African American, non-Hispanic/Latino; 1 American Indian or Alaska Native, non-Hispanic/Latino; 7 Asian, non-Hispanic/Latino; 8 Hispanic/Latino; 8 Two or more races, non-Hispanic/Latino), 39 international. Average age 32. 309 applicants, 76% accepted, 204 enrolled. In 2011, 232 master's, 8 doctorates, 2 other advanced degrees awarded. Terminal master's awarded for partial completion of doctoral program. *Degree requirements:* For doctorate, thesis/dissertation. *Entrance requirements:* For master's and Ed S, GRE General Test or MAT, minimum GPA of 3.0; for doctorate, GRE General Test, minimum GPA of 3.0. Additional exam requirements/recommendations for international students: Required—TOEFL (minimum score 600 paper-based; 250 computer-based; 100 iBT). Application fee: $55 ($75 for international students). Electronic applications accepted. *Expenses:* Tuition, state resident: full-time $5881. Tuition, nonresident: full-time $15,183. *Required fees:* $952. Tuition and fees vary according to campus/location and program. *Financial support:* Fellowships, research assistantships, teaching assistantships, and institutionally sponsored loans available. *Application contact:* Fran Colley, 573-882-6462, E-mail: colleyf@missouri.edu. Web site: http://education.missouri.edu/LTC/.

University of Missouri–St. Louis, College of Education, Division of Teaching and Learning, St. Louis, MO 63121. Offers autism studies (Certificate); elementary education (M Ed), including early childhood, general, reading; secondary education (M Ed), including curriculum and instruction, general, middle level education, reading, teaching English to speakers of other languages (TESOL); secondary school teaching (Certificate); special education (M Ed), including autism and developmental disabilities, early childhood special education, general; teaching English to speakers of other languages (Certificate). Part-time and evening/weekend programs available. *Faculty:* 32 full-time (16 women), 51 part-time/adjunct (36 women). *Students:* 95 full-time (63 women), 703 part-time (541 women); includes 176 minority (125 Black or African American, non-Hispanic/Latino; 1 American Indian or Alaska Native, non-Hispanic/Latino; 16 Asian, non-Hispanic/Latino; 26 Hispanic/Latino; 8 Two or more races, non-Hispanic/Latino), 11 international. Average age 29. 379 applicants, 90% accepted, 263 enrolled. In 2011, 190 master's, 9 Certificates awarded. *Degree requirements:* For master's, comprehensive exam. *Entrance requirements:* Additional exam requirements/recommendations for international students: Recommended—TOEFL (minimum score 550 paper-based; 213 computer-based). *Application deadline:* For fall admission, 7/1 priority date for domestic students, 7/1 for international students; for spring admission, 12/1 priority date for domestic students, 12/1 for international students. Application fee: $35 ($40 for international students). Electronic applications accepted. *Expenses:* Tuition, state resident: full-time $6273; part-time $3866 per year. Tuition, nonresident: full-time $14,969; part-time $9980 per year. *Required fees:* $315 per year. *Financial support:* In 2011–12, 6 research assistantships with full and partial tuition reimbursements (averaging $9,500 per year), 2 teaching assistantships with full and partial tuition reimbursements (averaging $10,500 per year) were awarded. Financial award application deadline: 4/1; financial award applicants required to submit FAFSA. *Unit head:* Dr. Joseph Polman, Chair, 314-516-5791. *Application contact:* 314-516-5458, Fax: 314-516-6996, E-mail: gadadm@umsl.edu. Web site: http://coe.umsl.edu/web/divisions/teach-learn/index.html.

University of Nebraska–Lincoln, Graduate College, College of Education and Human Sciences, Department of Child, Youth and Family Studies, Lincoln, NE 68588. Offers child development/early childhood education (MS, PhD); child, youth and family studies (MS); family and consumer sciences education (MS, PhD); family financial planning (MS); family science (MS, PhD); gerontology (PhD); human sciences (PhD), including child, youth and family studies, gerontology, medical family therapy; marriage and family therapy (MS); medical family therapy (PhD); youth development (MS). *Accreditation:* AAMFT/COAMFTE (one or more programs are accredited). Postbaccalaureate distance learning degree programs offered. *Degree requirements:* For master's, thesis optional. *Entrance requirements:* For master's, GRE. Additional exam requirements/recommendations for international students: Required—TOEFL (minimum score 550 paper-based; 213 computer-based). Electronic applications accepted. *Faculty research:* Marriage and family therapy, child development/early childhood education, family financial management.

University of Nevada, Las Vegas, Graduate College, College of Education, Department of Educational and Clinical Studies, Las Vegas, NV 89154-3066. Offers addiction studies (Advanced Certificate); counselor education (M Ed, MS), including clinical mental health counseling (MS), school counseling (M Ed); mental health counseling (Advanced Certificate); rehabilitation counseling (Advanced Certificate); special education (M Ed, MS, PhD), including early childhood education (M Ed), special education (M Ed); PhD/JD. *Faculty:* 21 full-time (13 women), 20 part-time/adjunct (14 women). *Students:* 166 full-time (137 women), 203 part-time (161 women); includes 109 minority (42 Black or African American, non-Hispanic/Latino; 1 American Indian or Alaska Native, non-Hispanic/Latino; 6 Asian, non-Hispanic/Latino; 47 Hispanic/Latino; 1 Native Hawaiian or other Pacific Islander, non-Hispanic/Latino; 12 Two or more races, non-Hispanic/Latino), 7 international. Average age 35. 204 applicants, 71% accepted, 111 enrolled. In 2011, 218 master's, 3 doctorates, 8 other advanced degrees awarded. *Degree requirements:* For master's, comprehensive exam (for some programs), thesis (for some programs); for other advanced degree, thesis (for some programs). *Entrance requirements:* Additional exam requirements/recommendations for international students: Required—TOEFL (minimum score 550 paper-based; 213 computer-based; 80 iBT), IELTS (minimum score 7). *Application deadline:* For fall admission, 3/1 priority date for domestic students, 5/1 for international students; for spring admission, 9/1 for domestic students, 10/1 for international students. Applications are processed on a rolling basis. Application fee: $60 ($95 for international students). Electronic applications accepted. *Financial support:* In 2011–12, 42 students received support, including 1 fellowship with full tuition reimbursement available (averaging $25,000 per year), 17 research assistantships with partial tuition reimbursements available (averaging $8,703 per year), 24 teaching assistantships with partial tuition reimbursements available (averaging $10,686 per year); institutionally sponsored loans, scholarships/grants, health care benefits, and unspecified assistantships also available. Financial award application deadline: 3/1. *Faculty research:* Multicultural issues in counseling, academic interventions for students with disabilities, rough and tumble play in early childhood, inclusive strategies for students with disabilities, addictions. *Total annual research expenditures:* $614,125. *Unit head:* Dr. Thomas Pierce, Interim Chair/Associate Professor, 702-895-1104, Fax: 702-895-5550, E-mail: tom.pierce@unlv.edu. *Application contact:* Graduate College Admissions Evaluator, 702-895-3320, Fax: 702-895-4180, E-mail: gradcollege@unlv.edu. Web site: http://education.unlv.edu/ecs/.

University of New Hampshire, Graduate School, College of Liberal Arts, Department of Education, Program in Early Childhood Education, Durham, NH 03824. Offers early childhood education (M Ed); special needs (M Ed). Part-time programs available. *Faculty:* 32 full-time. *Students:* 10 full-time (all women), 5 part-time (all women); includes 1 minority (Black or African American, non-Hispanic/Latino). Average age 30. 8 applicants, 38% accepted, 3 enrolled. In 2011, 6 master's awarded. *Degree requirements:* For master's, thesis or alternative. *Entrance requirements:* For master's, GRE General Test. Additional exam requirements/recommendations for international students: Required—TOEFL (minimum score 550 paper-based; 213 computer-based; 80 iBT). *Application deadline:* For fall admission, 2/1 priority date for domestic students, 2/1 for international students; for spring admission, 12/1 for domestic students. Applications are processed on a rolling basis. Application fee: $65. Electronic applications accepted. *Expenses:* Tuition, state resident: full-time $12,360; part-time $687 per credit hour. Tuition, nonresident: full-time $25,680; part-time $1058 per credit hour. *International tuition:* $29,550 full-time. *Required fees:* $1666; $833 per course. $416.50 per semester. Tuition and fees vary according to course load and degree level. *Financial support:* In 2011–12, 14 students received support. Fellowships, research assistantships, teaching assistantships, career-related internships or fieldwork, Federal Work-Study, scholarships/grants, and tuition waivers (full and partial) available. Support available to part-time students. Financial award application deadline: 2/15. *Faculty research:* Young children with special needs. *Unit head:* Dr. Todd Demitchell, Coordinator, 603-862-5043, E-mail: education.department@unh.edu. *Application contact:* Lisa Wilder, Graduate Coordinator, 603-862-2310, E-mail: education.department@unh.edu. Web site: http://www.unh.edu/education.

University of New Mexico, Graduate School, College of Education, Department of Teacher Education, Program in Multicultural Teacher and Childhood Education, Albuquerque, NM 87131-2039. Offers Ed D, PhD. *Accreditation:* NCATE. Part-time programs available. *Faculty:* 1 (woman) full-time. *Students:* 5 full-time (4 women), 24 part-time (17 women); includes 11 minority (1 Black or African American, non-Hispanic/Latino; 1 American Indian or Alaska Native, non-Hispanic/Latino; 8 Hispanic/Latino; 1 Two or more races, non-Hispanic/Latino). Average age 47. 11 applicants, 73% accepted, 6 enrolled. In 2011, 2 degrees awarded. *Degree requirements:* For doctorate, comprehensive exam, thesis/dissertation (for some programs). *Entrance requirements:* For doctorate, GRE, master's degree, minimum GPA of 3.0, 3 years teaching experience, 3-5 letters of reference, 1 letter of intent, professional writing sample. Additional exam requirements/recommendations for international students: Required—TOEFL (minimum score 550 paper-based; 213 computer-based). *Application deadline:* For fall admission, 3/1 priority date for domestic students, 3/1 for international students; for spring admission, 10/30 for domestic and international students. Application fee: $50. Electronic applications accepted. *Financial support:* In 2011–12, 10 students received support, including 2 research assistantships (averaging $22,000 per year), 3 teaching assistantships with partial tuition reimbursements available (averaging $8,628 per year); fellowships, career-related internships or fieldwork, scholarships/grants, and unspecified assistantships also available. Financial award application deadline: 4/15; financial award applicants required to submit FAFSA. *Faculty research:* Mathematics/science/technology education, diversity, curriculum development, reflective practice, social justice, student learning, teacher education. *Unit head:* Dr. Rosalita Mitchell, Department Chair, 505-277-9611, Fax: 505-277-0455, E-mail: ted@unm.edu. *Application contact:* Robert Romero, Program Coordinator, 505-277-0513, Fax: 505-277-0455, E-mail: ted@unm.edu. Web site: http://coe.unm.edu/departments/teacher-ed/grad-degrees-certs/mctc-edd-phd.html.

The University of North Carolina at Chapel Hill, Graduate School, School of Education, Master of Education Program for Experienced Teachers: Early Childhood Intervention and Family Support, Chapel Hill, NC 27599. Offers M Ed. *Accreditation:* NCATE. Part-time programs available. *Degree requirements:* For master's, comprehensive exam. *Entrance requirements:* For master's, minimum GPA of 3.0 during last 2 years of undergraduate course work. Electronic applications accepted.

The University of North Carolina at Chapel Hill, Graduate School, School of Education, Program in Education, Chapel Hill, NC 27599. Offers culture, curriculum and change (MA, PhD); early childhood, intervention and literacy (MA, PhD); educational psychology, measurement and evaluation (MA, PhD). *Accreditation:* NCATE. *Degree requirements:* For master's, thesis; for doctorate, comprehensive exam, thesis/dissertation. *Entrance requirements:* For master's, GRE General Test, minimum GPA of 3.0 during last 2 years of undergraduates course work; for doctorate, GRE General Test, minimum GPA of 3.0 during last 2 years of undergraduate course work. Additional exam requirements/recommendations for international students: Required—TOEFL (minimum score 550 paper-based; 213 computer-based). Electronic applications accepted.

The University of North Carolina at Greensboro, Graduate School, School of Education, Department of Specialized Education Services, Greensboro, NC 27412-5001. Offers cross-categorical special education (M Ed); interdisciplinary studies in special education (M Ed); leadership early care and education (Certificate); special education (M Ed, PhD). *Degree requirements:* For master's, thesis or alternative. *Entrance requirements:* For master's, GRE General Test. Additional exam requirements/recommendations for international students: Required—TOEFL. Electronic applications accepted.

University of North Dakota, Graduate School, College of Education and Human Development, Program in Early Childhood Education, Grand Forks, ND 58202. Offers MS. *Accreditation:* NCATE. Part-time programs available. *Degree requirements:* For master's, comprehensive exam, thesis or alternative. *Entrance requirements:* For master's, minimum GPA of 3.0. Additional exam requirements/recommendations for international students: Required—TOEFL (minimum score 550 paper-based; 213 computer-based; 79 iBT), IELTS (minimum score 6.5). Electronic applications accepted.

University of Northern Colorado, Graduate School, College of Education and Behavioral Sciences, School of Psychological Sciences, Program in Educational Psychology, Greeley, CO 80639. Offers early childhood education (MA); educational psychology (MA, PhD). *Accreditation:* NCATE. Part-time programs available. *Degree requirements:* For master's, comprehensive exam, thesis or alternative; for doctorate, comprehensive exam, thesis/dissertation. *Entrance requirements:* For master's, GRE General Test, letters of recommendation; for doctorate, GRE General Test, letters of recommendation, resume. Electronic applications accepted.

University of Northern Iowa, Graduate College, College of Education, Department of Curriculum and Instruction, Program in Early Childhood Education, Cedar Falls, IA 50614. Offers curriculum and instruction (MAE). *Students:* 18 part-time (all women). 4 applicants, 25% accepted, 0 enrolled. In 2011, 1 master's awarded. *Degree requirements:* For master's, comprehensive exam, thesis or alternative. *Entrance requirements:* For master's, minimum GPA of 3.0. Additional exam requirements/recommendations for international students: Required—TOEFL (minimum score 500 paper-based; 180 computer-based; 61 iBT). *Application deadline:* For fall admission, 8/1 priority date for domestic students. Applications are processed on a rolling basis. Application fee: $50 ($70 for international students). Electronic applications accepted. *Expenses:* Tuition, state resident: full-time $7476. Tuition, nonresident: full-time $16,410. *Required fees:* $942. *Financial support:* Application deadline: 2/1. *Unit head:* Dr. Gloria Kirkland-Holmes, Coordinator, 319-273-2007, Fax: 319-273-5886, E-mail: gloria.holmes@uni.edu. *Application contact:* Laurie S. Russell, Record Analyst, 319-273-2623, Fax: 319-273-2885, E-mail: laurie.russell@uni.edu. Web site: http://www.uni.edu/coe/ci/.

University of North Texas, Toulouse Graduate School, College of Education, Department of Educational Psychology, Program in Development and Family Studies, Denton, TX 76203. Offers MS, Certificate. Evening/weekend programs available. *Degree requirements:* For master's, comprehensive exam, thesis optional. *Entrance requirements:* For master's, GRE General Test, resume, references. Additional exam requirements/recommendations for international students: Recommended—TOEFL (minimum score 550 paper-based; 213 computer-based). Electronic applications accepted. *Expenses:* Tuition, state resident: part-time $100 per credit hour. Tuition, nonresident: part-time $413 per credit hour. *Faculty research:* Parent-child issues, cognitive development, social development.

University of North Texas, Toulouse Graduate School, College of Education, Department of Teacher Education and Administration, Program in Early Childhood Education, Denton, TX 76203. Offers MS, Ed D. Part-time programs available. Terminal master's awarded for partial completion of doctoral program. *Degree requirements:* For master's, comprehensive exam, thesis optional; for doctorate, comprehensive exam, thesis/dissertation. *Entrance requirements:* For master's, GRE General Test, 3 letters of reference, goal statement; for doctorate, GRE General Test, minimum graduate GPA of 3.5, 3 letters of reference, goal statement. Additional exam requirements/recommendations for international students: Recommended—TOEFL (minimum score 550 paper-based; 213 computer-based; 79 iBT). Electronic applications accepted. *Expenses:* Tuition, state resident: part-time $100 per credit hour. Tuition, nonresident: part-time $413 per credit hour. *Faculty research:* Early literacy programs, African-American student achievement in the early grades, cross-cultural approaches to early childhood education.

University of Oklahoma, Jeannine Rainbolt College of Education, Department of Instructional Leadership and Academic Curriculum, Norman, OK 73072. Offers communication, culture and pedagogy for Hispanic populations in educational settings (Graduate Certificate); instructional leadership and academic curriculum (M Ed, PhD), including bilingual education, early childhood education, elementary education, English education, instructional leadership, mathematics education, reading education, science education, science, technology, engineering and mathematics education (M Ed), secondary education, social studies education, teacher education (M Ed). *Accreditation:* NCATE. Part-time and evening/weekend programs available. *Faculty:* 19 full-time (13 women), 1 (woman) part-time/adjunct. *Students:* 73 full-time (63 women), 114 part-time (87 women); includes 29 minority (5 Black or African American, non-Hispanic/Latino; 12 American Indian or Alaska Native, non-Hispanic/Latino; 5 Asian, non-Hispanic/Latino; 3 Hispanic/Latino; 1 Native Hawaiian or other Pacific Islander, non-Hispanic/Latino; 3 Two or more races, non-Hispanic/Latino), 7 international. Average age 33. 87 applicants, 86% accepted, 68 enrolled. In 2011, 36 master's, 6 doctorates awarded. Terminal master's awarded for partial completion of doctoral program. *Degree requirements:* For doctorate, thesis/dissertation. *Entrance requirements:* For master's, 12 hours of course work in education; for doctorate, GRE General Test, master's degree, minimum graduate GPA of 3.0. Additional exam requirements/recommendations for international students: Required—TOEFL (minimum score 550 paper-based; 79 iBT). *Application deadline:* For fall admission, 6/1 priority date for domestic students, 3/1 for international students; for spring admission, 11/1 for domestic students, 9/1 for international students. Applications are processed on a rolling basis. Application fee: $40 ($90 for international students). Electronic applications accepted. *Expenses:* Tuition, state resident: full-time $4087; part-time $170.30 per credit hour. Tuition, nonresident: full-time $14,875; part-time $619.80 per credit hour. *Required fees:* $2659; $100.25 per credit hour. Tuition and fees vary according to course load and degree level. *Financial support:* In 2011–12, 128 students received support, including 2 research assistantships with partial tuition reimbursements available (averaging $12,431 per year), 12 teaching assistantships with partial tuition reimbursements available (averaging $10,161 per year); institutionally sponsored loans, scholarships/grants, and unspecified assistantships also available. Financial award applicants required to submit FAFSA. *Faculty research:* Engineering in practice for sustainable future, no child left behind (reading), early childhood learning games impact study, Educare randomized control startup, Oklahoma mentoring professional development. *Total annual research expenditures:* $1.1 million. *Unit head:* Lawrence Baines, Chair, 405-325-1498, Fax: 405-325-4061, E-mail: lbaines@ou.edu. *Application contact:* Lynn Crussel, Graduate Programs Officer, 405-325-4843, Fax: 405-325-4061, E-mail: lcrussel@ou.edu. Web site: http://education.ou.edu/departments/ilac.

University of Phoenix–Bay Area Campus, College of Education, San Jose, CA 95134-1805. Offers administration and supervision (MA Ed); adult education and training (MA Ed); early childhood education (MA Ed); education (Ed S); educational leadership (Ed D); elementary teacher education (MA Ed); higher education administration (PhD); secondary teacher education (MA Ed); special education (MA Ed); teacher leadership (MA Ed). Evening/weekend programs available. Postbaccalaureate distance learning degree programs offered (no on-campus study). *Degree requirements:* For master's, thesis (for some programs). *Entrance requirements:* For master's, minimum undergraduate GPA of 2.5, 3 years of work experience. Additional exam requirements/recommendations for international students: Required—TOEFL (minimum score 550 paper-based; 213 computer-based; 79 iBT). Electronic applications accepted.

University of Phoenix–Central Florida Campus, College of Education, Maitland, FL 32751-7057. Offers administration and supervision (MA Ed); curriculum and instruction (MA Ed); curriculum and instruction-computer education (MA Ed); curriculum and instruction-mathematics education (MA Ed); early childhood education (MA Ed); elementary teacher education (MA Ed); secondary teacher education (MA Ed). Evening/weekend programs available. *Degree requirements:* For master's, thesis (for some programs). *Entrance requirements:* For master's, 3 years of work experience, minimum undergraduate GPA of 2.5. Additional exam requirements/recommendations for international students: Required—TOEFL (minimum score 550 paper-based; 213 computer-based; 79 iBT). Electronic applications accepted.

University of Phoenix–Louisiana Campus, College of Education, Metairie, LA 70001-2082. Offers curriculum and instruction (MA Ed); early childhood education (MA Ed). Postbaccalaureate distance learning degree programs offered. *Degree requirements:* For master's, thesis. *Entrance requirements:* For master's, minimum undergraduate GPA of 2.5, 3 years work experience. Additional exam requirements/recommendations for international students: Required—TOEFL (minimum score 550 paper-based; 213 computer-based; 79 iBT).

University of Phoenix–North Florida Campus, College of Education, Jacksonville, FL 32216-0959. Offers administration and supervision (MA Ed); curriculum and instruction (MA Ed), including computer education, mathematics education; early childhood education (MA Ed); elementary teacher education (MA Ed); secondary teacher education (MA Ed). Evening/weekend programs available. *Degree requirements:* For master's, thesis (for some programs). *Entrance requirements:* For master's, 3 years of work experience, minimum undergraduate GPA of 2.5. Additional exam requirements/recommendations for international students: Required—TOEFL (minimum score 550 paper-based; 213 computer-based; 49 iBT). Electronic applications accepted.

University of Phoenix–Online Campus, College of Education, Phoenix, AZ 85034-7209. Offers administration and supervision (MAEd, Graduate Certificate); adult education and training (MAEd); curriculum and instruction (MAEd); curriculum and instruction reading (MAEd); curriculum and instruction-computer education (MAEd); curriculum and instruction-language arts (MAEd); curriculum and instruction-mathematics (MAEd); early childhood education (MAEd); educational studies (MAEd); elementary teacher education (MAEd); elementary teacher education-early childhood (MAEd); secondary teacher education (MAEd); special education (MAEd); teacher education - elementary/middle level (MAEd); teacher education middle level generalist (MAEd); teacher education middle level mathematics (MAEd); teacher education middle level science (MAEd); teacher education secondary mathematics (MAEd); teacher education secondary science (MAEd); teacher leadership (MAEd). *Accreditation:* Teacher Education Accreditation Council. Evening/weekend programs available. Postbaccalaureate distance learning degree programs offered. *Students:* 9,180 full-time (7,178 women); includes 2,913 minority (2,069 Black or African American, non-Hispanic/Latino; 50 American Indian or Alaska Native, non-Hispanic/Latino; 100 Asian, non-Hispanic/Latino; 542 Hispanic/Latino; 48 Native Hawaiian or other Pacific Islander, non-Hispanic/Latino; 104 Two or more races, non-Hispanic/Latino), 147 international. Average age 36. *Entrance requirements:* Additional exam requirements/recommendations for international students: Required—TOEFL, TOEIC (Test of English as an International Communication), Berlitz Online English Proficiency Exam, Pearson Test of English, or IELTS. *Application deadline:* Applications are processed on a rolling basis. Application fee: $45. Electronic applications accepted. *Expenses:* Contact institution. *Financial support:* Scholarships/grants available. Financial award applicants required to submit FAFSA. *Application contact:* 866-766-0766. Web site: http://www.phoenix.edu/colleges_divisions/education.html.

University of Phoenix–Oregon Campus, College of Education, Tigard, OR 97223. Offers curriculum and instruction (MA Ed); early childhood education (MA Ed); elementary education (MA Ed), including early childhood specialization, middle level specialization; secondary education (MA Ed), including middle level specialization. Evening/weekend programs available. *Degree requirements:* For master's, thesis (for some programs). *Entrance requirements:* For master's, minimum undergraduate GPA of 2.5, 3 years work experience. Additional exam requirements/recommendations for international students: Required—TOEFL (minimum score 550 paper-based; 213 computer-based; 79 iBT). Electronic applications accepted.

University of Phoenix–Phoenix Main Campus, College of Education, Tempe, AZ 85282-2371. Offers administration and supervision (MA Ed); adult education and training (MA Ed); curriculum and instruction reading (MA Ed); curriculum instruction (MA Ed); early childhood education (MA Ed); education studies (MA Ed); elementary teacher education (MA Ed); secondary teacher education (MA Ed); special education (MA Ed); teacher leadership (MA Ed). Evening/weekend programs available. Postbaccalaureate distance learning degree programs offered. *Students:* 297 full-time (203 women); includes 53 minority (19 Black or African American, non-Hispanic/Latino; 1 American Indian or Alaska Native, non-Hispanic/Latino; 6 Asian, non-Hispanic/Latino; 21 Hispanic/Latino; 2 Native Hawaiian or other Pacific Islander, non-Hispanic/Latino; 4 Two or more races, non-Hispanic/Latino), 3 international. Average age 35. *Entrance requirements:* Additional exam requirements/recommendations for international students: Required—TOEFL, TOEIC (Test of English as an International Communication), Berlitz Online English Proficiency Exam, Pearson Test of English, or IELTS. *Application deadline:* Applications are processed on a rolling basis. Application fee: $45. Electronic applications accepted. *Expenses:* Contact institution. *Financial support:* Scholarships/grants available. Financial award applicants required to submit FAFSA. *Application contact:* 866-766-0766. Web site: http://www.phoenix.edu/colleges_divisions/education.html.

University of Phoenix–Puerto Rico Campus, College of Education, Guaynabo, PR 00968. Offers administration and supervision (MA Ed); early childhood education (MA Ed); school counselor (MSC). Evening/weekend programs available. *Degree requirements:* For master's, thesis (for some programs). *Entrance requirements:* For master's, minimum undergraduate GPA of 2.5, 3 years work experience. Additional exam requirements/recommendations for international students: Required—TOEFL (minimum score 550 paper-based; 213 computer-based; 79 iBT). Electronic applications accepted.

University of Phoenix–South Florida Campus, College of Education, Fort Lauderdale, FL 33309. Offers administration and supervision (MA Ed); curriculum and instruction (MA Ed), including computer education, curriculum and instruction, mathematics education; early childhood education (MA Ed); elementary teacher education (MA Ed); secondary teacher education (MA Ed). Evening/weekend programs available. *Degree requirements:* For master's, thesis (for some programs). *Entrance requirements:* For master's, 3 years of work experience, minimum undergraduate GPA of 2.5. Additional exam requirements/recommendations for international students: Required—TOEFL (minimum score 550 paper-based; 213 computer-based; 79 iBT). Electronic applications accepted.

University of Phoenix–Washington D.C. Campus, College of Education, Washington, DC 20001. Offers administration and supervision (MA Ed); adult education and training (MA Ed); computer education (MA Ed); curriculum and instruction (MA Ed, Ed D); early childhood education (MA Ed); education (Ed S); educational leadership (Ed D); educational technology (Ed D); elementary teacher education (MA Ed); English and language arts education (MA Ed); English as a second language (MA Ed); higher education administration (PhD); mathematics education (MA Ed); secondary teacher education (MA Ed); special education (MA Ed); teacher leadership (MA Ed).

University of Phoenix–West Florida Campus, College of Education, Temple Terrace, FL 33637. Offers administration and supervision (MA Ed); curriculum and instruction (MA Ed), including computer education, curriculum and instruction, mathematics education; curriculum and technology (MA Ed); early childhood education (MA Ed); elementary teacher education (MA Ed); secondary teacher education (MA Ed). Evening/weekend programs available. *Degree requirements:* For master's, thesis (for some programs). *Entrance requirements:* For master's, 3 years of work experience, minimum undergraduate GPA of 2.5. Additional exam requirements/recommendations for international students: Required—TOEFL (minimum score 550 paper-based; 213 computer-based; 79 iBT).

University of Pittsburgh, School of Education, Department of Instruction and Learning, Program in Early Childhood Education, Pittsburgh, PA 15260. Offers M Ed. Part-time and evening/weekend programs available. *Students:* 14 full-time (13 women), 5 part-time (all women); includes 1 minority (Two or more races, non-Hispanic/Latino), 1 international. Average age 29. 16 applicants, 56% accepted, 5 enrolled. In 2011, 2 degrees awarded. *Degree requirements:* For master's, thesis. *Entrance requirements:* For master's, PRAXIS I. Additional exam requirements/recommendations for international students: Required—TOEFL. *Application deadline:* For fall admission, 2/1 for domestic students. Application fee: $50. Electronic applications accepted. *Expenses:* Tuition, state resident: full-time $18,774; part-time $760 per credit. Tuition, nonresident: full-time $30,736; part-time $1258 per credit. *Required fees:* $740; $200 per term. Tuition and fees vary according to program. *Financial support:* Career-related internships or fieldwork, Federal Work-Study, institutionally sponsored loans, and tuition waivers (partial) available. Support available to part-time students. Financial award application deadline: 3/15; financial award applicants required to submit FAFSA. *Unit head:* Dr. Richard Donato, Chairman, 412-624-7248, Fax: 412-648-7081, E-mail: donato@pitt.edu. *Application contact:* Dr. Marjie Schermer, Graduate Enrollment Manager, 412-648-2230, Fax: 412-648-1899, E-mail: soeinfo@pitt.edu. Web site: http://www.education.pitt.edu/.

University of Pittsburgh, School of Education, Department of Instruction and Learning, Program in Special Education, Pittsburgh, PA 15260. Offers combined studies in early childhood and special education (M Ed); early education of disabled students (M Ed); education of students with mental and physical disabilities (M Ed); general special education (M Ed); special education (Ed D, PhD); special education teacher preparation K-8 (M Ed); vision studies (M Ed). Part-time and evening/weekend programs available. *Students:* 65 full-time (57 women), 87 part-time (76 women); includes 9 minority (3 Black or African American, non-Hispanic/Latino; 2 Asian, non-Hispanic/Latino; 2 Hispanic/Latino; 2 Two or more races, non-Hispanic/Latino), 4 international. Average age 32. 58 applicants, 86% accepted, 45 enrolled. In 2011, 62 degrees awarded. *Degree requirements:* For master's, thesis; for doctorate, thesis/dissertation. *Entrance requirements:* For master's, PRAXIS I; for doctorate, GRE General Test. Additional exam requirements/recommendations for international students: Required—TOEFL. *Application deadline:* For fall admission, 2/1 priority date for domestic students; for spring admission, 11/1 priority date for domestic students. Applications are processed on a rolling basis. Application fee: $50. *Expenses:* Tuition, state resident: full-time $18,774; part-time $760 per credit. Tuition, nonresident: full-time $30,736; part-time $1258 per credit. *Required fees:* $740; $200 per term. Tuition and fees vary according to program. *Financial support:* Research assistantships, teaching assistantships, career-related internships or fieldwork, Federal Work-Study, and tuition waivers (partial) available. Support available to part-time students. Financial award application deadline: 3/15; financial award applicants required to submit FAFSA. *Unit head:* Dr. Richard Donato, Chairman, 412-624-7248, Fax: 412-648-7081, E-mail: donato@pitt.edu. *Application contact:* Lauren Spadafora, Graduate Enrollment Manager, 412-648-2230, Fax: 412-648-1899, E-mail: soeinfo@pitt.edu. Web site: http://www.education.pitt.edu/AcademicDepartments/InstructionLearning/Programs/GeneralSpecialEducation.aspx.

University of Puerto Rico, Río Piedras, College of Education, Program in Early Child Education, San Juan, PR 00931-3300. Offers M Ed. Part-time programs available. *Degree requirements:* For master's, thesis. *Entrance requirements:* For master's, EXADEP, GRE General Test or PAEG, interview, minimum GPA of 3.0, letter of recommendation.

University of St. Thomas, Graduate Studies, School of Education, Department of Special Education and Gifted Education, St. Paul, MN 55105-1096. Offers autism spectrum disorders (MA, Certificate); developmental disabilities (MA); director of special education (Ed S); early childhood special education (MA); emotional behavioral disorders (MA); gifted, creative, and talented education (MA); learning disabilities (MA); Orton-Gillingham reading (Certificate); special education (MA). *Accreditation:* NCATE. Part-time and evening/weekend programs available. *Faculty:* 7 full-time (5 women), 31 part-time/adjunct (25 women). *Students:* 23 full-time (19 women), 253 part-time (205 women); includes 31 minority (17 Black or African American, non-Hispanic/Latino; 3 Asian, non-Hispanic/Latino; 5 Hispanic/Latino; 2 Native Hawaiian or other Pacific Islander, non-Hispanic/Latino; 4 Two or more races, non-Hispanic/Latino), 2 international. Average age 36. 123 applicants, 88% accepted, 98 enrolled. In 2011, 57 master's, 2 other advanced degrees awarded. *Degree requirements:* For master's, thesis; for other advanced degree, professional portfolio. *Entrance requirements:* For master's, minimum GPA of 3.0 or MAT; for other advanced degree, MAT or minimum GPA of 2.75. Additional exam requirements/recommendations for international students: Required—TOEFL (minimum score 550 paper-based; 213 computer-based; 80 iBT). *Application deadline:* For fall admission, 6/1 priority date for domestic students; for spring admission, 11/1 priority date for domestic students. Applications are processed on a rolling basis. Application fee: $50. *Financial support:* Fellowships, research assistantships, institutionally sponsored loans, and scholarships/grants available. Support available to part-time students. Financial award applicants required to submit FAFSA. *Faculty research:* Reading and math fluency, inclusion curriculum for developmental disorders, parent involvement in positive behavior supports, children's friendships, preschool inclusion. *Unit head:* Dr. Terri L. Vandercook, Chair, 651-962-4389, Fax: 651-962-4169, E-mail: tlvandercook@stthomas.edu. *Application contact:* Patricia L. Thomas, Department Assistant, 651-962-4980, Fax: 651-962-4169, E-mail: thom2319@stthomas.edu. Web site: http://www.stthomas.edu/education.

The University of Scranton, College of Graduate and Continuing Education, Department of Education, Program in Early Childhood Education, Scranton, PA 18510. Offers MA, MS. Part-time and evening/weekend programs available. *Students:* 1 (woman) part-time. Average age 29. 1 applicant, 100% accepted. In 2011, 1 master's awarded. *Degree requirements:* For master's, comprehensive exam, thesis (for some programs), capstone experience. *Entrance requirements:* For master's, minimum GPA of 2.75. Additional exam requirements/recommendations for international students: Required—TOEFL (minimum score 500 paper-based; 173 computer-based), IELTS (minimum score 5.5). *Application deadline:* Applications are processed on a rolling basis. Application fee: $0. *Financial support:* Unspecified assistantships available. Financial award application deadline: 3/1. *Unit head:* Dr. Art Chambers, Director, 570-941-4668, Fax: 570-941-5515, E-mail: chambersa2@scranton.edu. *Application contact:* Joseph M. Roback, Director of Admissions, 570-941-4385, Fax: 570-941-5928, E-mail: robackj2@scranton.edu.

University of South Alabama, Graduate School, College of Education, Department of Leadership and Teacher Education, Mobile, AL 36688-0002. Offers early childhood education (M Ed); educational administration (Ed S); educational leadership (M Ed); elementary education (M Ed); reading education (M Ed); science education (M Ed); secondary education (M Ed); special education (M Ed, Ed S). *Accreditation:* NCATE. Part-time programs available. *Faculty:* 20 full-time (14 women). *Students:* 135 full-time (106 women), 75 part-time (62 women); includes 50 minority (40 Black or African American, non-Hispanic/Latino; 3 American Indian or Alaska Native, non-Hispanic/Latino; 3 Asian, non-Hispanic/Latino; 3 Hispanic/Latino; 1 Two or more races, non-Hispanic/Latino), 1 international. 89 applicants, 49% accepted, 36 enrolled. In 2011, 88 master's, 13 Ed Ss awarded. *Degree requirements:* For master's, comprehensive exam. *Entrance requirements:* For master's, GRE General Test or MAT, minimum GPA of 3.0. *Application deadline:* For fall admission, 7/15 priority date for domestic students, 6/15 for international students; for spring admission, 12/1 priority date for domestic students, 11/1 for international students. Applications are processed on a rolling basis. Application fee: $35. *Expenses:* Tuition, state resident: full-time $7968; part-time $332 per credit hour. Tuition, nonresident: full-time $15,936; part-time $664 per credit hour. *Financial support:* Research assistantships and career-related internships or fieldwork available. Support available to part-time students. Financial award application deadline: 4/1. *Unit head:* Dr. Harold Dodge, Jr., Chair, 251-380-2894. *Application contact:* Dr. Abigail Baxter, Director of Graduate Studies, 251-460-6310, Fax: 251-461-1513, E-mail: kharriso@usouthal.edu. Web site: http://www.southalabama.edu/coe/lted.

University of South Carolina, The Graduate School, College of Education, Department of Instruction and Teacher Education, Program in Early Childhood Education, Columbia, SC 29208. Offers M Ed, Ed D, PhD. *Accreditation:* NCATE. *Degree requirements:* For master's, comprehensive exam; for doctorate, one foreign language, comprehensive exam, thesis/dissertation. *Entrance requirements:* For master's, GRE General Test, MAT, interview; for doctorate, GRE General Test, MAT, interview, teaching experience. *Faculty research:* Parent involvement, play, multicultural education, global education.

University of South Carolina Upstate, Graduate Programs, Spartanburg, SC 29303-4999. Offers early childhood education (M Ed); elementary education (M Ed); special education: visual impairment (M Ed). *Accreditation:* NCATE. Part-time and evening/weekend programs available. *Faculty:* 8 full-time (6 women), 4 part-time/adjunct (2 women). *Students:* 6 full-time (all women), 69 part-time (63 women); includes 16 minority (14 Black or African American, non-Hispanic/Latino; 2 Two or more races, non-Hispanic/Latino), 2 international. Average age 33. In 2011, 8 master's awarded. *Degree requirements:* For master's, professional portfolio. *Entrance requirements:* For master's, GRE General Test or MAT, interview, minimum undergraduate GPA of 2.5, teaching certificate, 2 letters of recommendation. *Application deadline:* Applications are processed on a rolling basis. Application fee: $40. *Expenses:* Tuition, state resident: full-time $10,916; part-time $455 per credit hour. Tuition, nonresident: full-time $23,444; part-time $977 per credit hour. *Required fees:* $450 per semester. Tuition and fees vary according to course load and program. *Financial support:* Institutionally sponsored loans and institutional work-study available. Financial award application deadline: 7/15; financial award applicants required to submit FAFSA. *Faculty research:* Rough and tumble play, social justice education, American Indian literatures and cultures, diversity and multicultural education, science teaching strategy. *Unit head:* Dr. Tina Herzberg, Director of Graduate Programs, 864-503-5572, Fax: 864-503-5573, E-mail: rstevens@uscupstate.edu. *Application contact:* Donette Stewart, Associate Vice Chancellor for Enrollment Services, 864-503-5280, E-mail: dstewart@uscupstate.edu. Web site: http://www.uscupstate.edu/graduate/.

University of Southern Mississippi, Graduate School, College of Education and Psychology, Department of Curriculum, Instruction, and Special Education, Hattiesburg, MS 39406-0001. Offers alternative secondary teacher education (MAT); early childhood education (M Ed, Ed S); education (Ed D); education of the gifted (M Ed, PhD, Ed S); elementary education (M Ed, PhD, Ed S); reading (M Ed, MS); secondary education (M Ed, MS, PhD); special education (M Ed, PhD, Ed S). Part-time programs available. *Faculty:* 23 full-time (17 women), 3 part-time/adjunct (2 women). *Students:* 39 full-time (34 women), 92 part-time (77 women); includes 36 minority (31 Black or African American, non-Hispanic/Latino; 3 Hispanic/Latino; 2 Two or more races, non-Hispanic/Latino), 3 international. Average age 37. 56 applicants, 55% accepted, 29 enrolled. In 2011, 45 master's, 5 doctorates awarded. *Degree requirements:* For master's and Ed S, comprehensive exam, thesis (for some programs); for doctorate, comprehensive exam, thesis/dissertation. *Entrance requirements:* For master's, GRE General Test, MAT, minimum GPA of 3.0; for doctorate, GRE General Test, minimum GPA of 3.5; for Ed S, GRE General Test, MAT, minimum GPA of 3.25. Additional exam requirements/recommendations for international students: Required—TOEFL, IELTS. *Application deadline:* For fall admission, 3/1 priority date for domestic students, 3/1 for international students; for spring admission, 1/10 priority date for domestic students, 1/10 for international students. Applications are processed on a rolling basis. Application fee: $50. *Financial support:* In 2011–12, 9 research assistantships with tuition reimbursements (averaging $18,316 per year), 2 teaching assistantships with full tuition reimbursements (averaging $8,500 per year) were awarded; Federal Work-Study, institutionally sponsored loans, scholarships/grants, health care benefits, tuition waivers (partial), and unspecified assistantships also available. Financial award application deadline: 3/15; financial award applicants required to submit FAFSA. *Faculty research:* Mathematical problem solving, integrative curriculum, writing process, teacher education models. *Total annual research expenditures:* $100,000. *Unit head:* Dr. David Daves, Chair, 601-266-4547, Fax: 601-266-4175, E-mail: david.daves@usm.edu. *Application contact:* Dr. Marie Crowe, Director of Graduate Studies, 601-266-6005, Fax: 601-266-4548, E-mail: margie.crowe@usm.edu. Web site: http://www.usm.edu/graduateschool/table.php.

University of South Florida, Graduate School, College of Education, Department of Childhood Education, Tampa, FL 33620-9951. Offers early childhood education (M Ed, MA, PhD); elementary education (MA, MAT, PhD); reading/language arts (MA, PhD, Ed S). *Accreditation:* NCATE. Part-time and evening/weekend programs available. *Faculty:* 24 full-time (21 women), 2 part-time/adjunct (both women). *Students:* 88 full-time (81 women), 116 part-time (110 women); includes 48 minority (21 Black or African American, non-Hispanic/Latino; 6 Asian, non-Hispanic/Latino; 19 Hispanic/Latino; 2 Two or more races, non-Hispanic/Latino), 7 international. Average age 33. 200 applicants, 67% accepted, 76 enrolled. In 2011, 87 master's, 8 doctorates, 1 other advanced degree awarded. *Degree requirements:* For master's, comprehensive exam; for doctorate, comprehensive exam, thesis/dissertation, philosophies of inquiry; multiple research methods. *Entrance requirements:* For master's, GRE (if GPA less than 3.0), minimum GPA of 3.0 in last 60 hours of course work; for doctorate, GRE General Test, minimum GPA of 3.0 undergraduate, 3.5 graduate; interview; for Ed S, GRE General Test, interview. Additional exam requirements/recommendations for international students: Required—TOEFL (minimum score 550 paper-based; 213 computer-based). *Application deadline:* For fall admission, 2/15 for domestic students, 1/2 for international students; for winter admission, 2/15 for domestic students, 1/2 for international students; for spring admission, 10/15 for domestic students, 6/1 for international students. Application fee: $30. Electronic applications accepted. *Financial support:* In 2011–12, 7 teaching assistantships with full tuition reimbursements (averaging $10,300 per year) were awarded; institutionally sponsored loans, scholarships/grants, and unspecified assistantships also available. Financial award applicants required to submit FAFSA. *Faculty research:* Evaluating interventions for struggling readers, prevention and intervention services for young children at risk for behavioral and mental health challenges, preservice teacher education and young adolescent middle school experience, art and inquiry-based approaches to teaching and learning, study of children's writing development. *Total annual research expenditures:* $381,048. *Unit head:* Dr. Diane Yendol-Hoppey, Chairperson, 813-974-3460, Fax: 813-974-0938. *Application contact:* Dr. Diane Briscoe, Coordinator of Graduate Studies, 813-974-1804, Fax: 813-974-3391, E-mail: briscoe@usf.edu. Web site: http://www.coedu.usf.edu/main/departments/ce/ce.html.

The University of Tennessee, Graduate School, College of Education, Health and Human Sciences, Department of Child and Family Studies, Knoxville, TN 37996. Offers child and family studies (MS); early childhood education (MS). Part-time programs available. *Degree requirements:* For master's, thesis or alternative. *Entrance requirements:* For master's, GRE General Test, minimum GPA of 2.7. Additional exam requirements/recommendations for international students: Required—TOEFL. Electronic applications accepted. *Expenses:* Tuition, state resident: full-time $8332; part-time $464 per credit hour. Tuition, nonresident: full-time $25,174; part-time $1400 per credit hour. *Required fees:* $1162; $56 per credit hour. Tuition and fees vary according to program.

The University of Tennessee, Graduate School, College of Education, Health and Human Sciences, Program in Education, Knoxville, TN 37996. Offers art education (MS); counseling education (PhD); cultural studies in education (PhD); curriculum (MS, Ed S); curriculum, educational research and evaluation (Ed D, PhD); early childhood education (PhD); early childhood special education (MS); education of deaf and hard of hearing (MS); educational administration and policy studies (Ed D, PhD); educational administration and supervision (Ed S); educational psychology (Ed D, PhD); elementary education (MS, Ed S); elementary teaching (MS); English education (MS, Ed S); exercise science (PhD); foreign language/ESL education (MS, Ed S); instructional technology (MS, Ed D, PhD, Ed S); literacy, language and ESL education (PhD); literacy, language education, and ESL education (Ed D); mathematics education (MS, Ed S); modified and comprehensive special education (MS); reading education (MS, Ed S); school counseling (Ed S); school psychology (PhD, Ed S); science education (MS, Ed S); secondary teaching (MS); social foundations (MS); social science education (MS, Ed S); socio-cultural foundations of sports and education (PhD); special education (Ed S); teacher education (Ed D, PhD). *Accreditation:* NCATE. Part-time and evening/weekend programs available. *Degree requirements:* For master's and Ed S, thesis optional; for doctorate, variable foreign language requirement, thesis/dissertation. *Entrance requirements:* For master's, minimum GPA of 2.7; for doctorate and Ed S, GRE General Test, minimum GPA of 2.7. Additional exam requirements/recommendations for international students: Required—TOEFL. Electronic applications accepted. *Expenses:* Tuition, state resident: full-time $8332; part-time $464 per credit hour. Tuition, nonresident: full-time $25,174; part-time $1400 per credit hour. *Required fees:* $1162; $56 per credit hour. Tuition and fees vary according to program.

The University of Texas at Austin, Graduate School, College of Education, Department of Curriculum and Instruction, Austin, TX 78712-1111. Offers bilingual/bicultural education (M Ed, MA, PhD); cultural studies in education (M Ed, MA, PhD); early childhood education (M Ed, MA, PhD); language and literacy studies (M Ed, PhD); learning technologies (M Ed, MA, PhD); physical education (M Ed, MA, PhD). Terminal master's awarded for partial completion of doctoral program. *Degree requirements:* For doctorate, thesis/dissertation. *Entrance requirements:* For master's and doctorate, GRE General Test. *Application deadline:* For fall admission, 3/1 for domestic students; for spring admission, 10/1 for domestic students. Applications are processed on a rolling basis. Application fee: $50 ($75 for international students). Electronic applications accepted. *Financial support:* Fellowships and teaching assistantships with partial tuition reimbursements available. Financial award application deadline: 2/1. *Unit head:* Betty Maloch, Chair, 512-232-4262, E-mail: bmaloch@austin.utexas.edu. *Application contact:* Stephen Flynn, Graduate Coordinator, 512-471-3747, E-mail: sflynn@austin.utexas.edu. Web site: http://www.edb.utexas.edu/coe/depts/ci/cti.html.

The University of Texas at Austin, Graduate School, College of Education, Department of Special Education, Austin, TX 78712-1111. Offers autism and developmental disabilities (Ed D, PhD); autism and developmental disability (M Ed, MA); early childhood special education (M Ed, MA, Ed D, PhD); learning disabilities (Ed D, PhD); learning disabilities/behavior disorders (M Ed, MA); multicultural special education (M Ed, MA, Ed D, PhD); rehabilitation counselor (M Ed); rehabilitation counselor education (Ed D, PhD); special education administration (Ed D, PhD). *Accreditation:* CORE. Part-time and evening/weekend programs available. Postbaccalaureate distance learning degree programs offered (no on-campus study). *Degree requirements:* For master's, thesis or alternative; for doctorate, thesis/dissertation. *Entrance requirements:* For master's and doctorate, GRE General Test. *Application deadline:* For fall admission, 2/1 priority date for domestic students; for spring admission, 10/1 priority date for domestic students. Applications are processed on a rolling basis. Application fee: $50 ($75 for international students). *Financial support:* Fellowships with tuition reimbursements, research assistantships with partial tuition reimbursements, teaching assistantships with partial tuition reimbursements, career-related internships or fieldwork, Federal Work-Study, institutionally sponsored loans, scholarships/grants, tuition waivers (full and partial), and unspecified assistantships available. Financial award application deadline: 2/1. *Faculty research:* Anchored instruction, reading disabilities, multicultural/bilingual. *Unit head:* Herbert J. Rieth, Jr., Chairman, 512-475-6552, Fax: 512-471-2471, E-mail: rieth.herb@mail.utexas.edu. *Application contact:* James Schaller, Graduate Adviser, 512-475-6543, E-mail: jschaller@mail.utexas.edu. Web site: http://www.edb.utexas.edu/coe/depts/sped.html.

The University of Texas at Brownsville, Graduate Studies, School of Education, Brownsville, TX 78520-4991. Offers bilingual education (M Ed); counseling and guidance (M Ed); curriculum and instruction (M Ed); early childhood education (M Ed); educational administration (M Ed); educational technology (M Ed); English as a second language (M Ed); reading specialist (M Ed); special education/educational diagnostician (M Ed). Part-time and evening/weekend programs available. Postbaccalaureate distance learning degree programs offered (minimal on-campus study). *Degree requirements:* For master's, thesis optional. *Entrance requirements:* For master's, GRE General Test. Additional exam requirements/recommendations for international students: Required—TOEFL.

The University of Texas at San Antonio, College of Education and Human Development, Department of Interdisciplinary Learning and Teaching, San Antonio, TX 78249-0617. Offers adult learning and teaching (MA); education (MA), including curriculum and instruction, early childhood and elementary education, educational psychology/special education, instructional technology, reading and literacy education; interdisciplinary learning and teaching (PhD). Part-time and evening/weekend programs available. *Faculty:* 26 full-time (21 women), 1 (woman) part-time/adjunct. *Students:* 131 full-time (100 women), 357 part-time (283 women); includes 275 minority (31 Black or African American, non-Hispanic/Latino; 9 Asian, non-Hispanic/Latino; 227 Hispanic/Latino; 8 Two or more races, non-Hispanic/Latino), 31 international. Average age 33. 239 applicants, 75% accepted, 120 enrolled. In 2011, 119 master's awarded. *Degree requirements:* For master's, comprehensive exam, thesis optional, 36 hours of course work without thesis (33 with thesis); for doctorate, comprehensive exam, thesis/dissertation, minimum of 60 semester credit hours. *Entrance requirements:* For master's, GRE General Test, bachelor's degree with minimum GPA of 3.0 in last 60 hours of coursework; resume; two letters of recommendation; statement of purpose; for doctorate, GRE, transcripts from all colleges and universities attended, professional vitae demonstrating experience in work environment where education was primary professional emphasis, 3 letters of recommendation, statement of purpose, master's degree transcript documenting minimum GPA of 3.5. Additional exam requirements/recommendations for international students: Required—TOEFL (minimum score 500 paper-based; 61 iBT), IELTS (minimum score 5). *Application deadline:* For fall admission, 7/1 for domestic students, 4/1 for international students; for spring admission, 11/1 for domestic students, 9/1 for international students. Application fee: $45 ($85 for international students). *Expenses:* Tuition, state resident: full-time $3148; part-time $2176 per semester. Tuition, nonresident: full-time $8782; part-time $5932 per semester. *Required fees:* $719 per semester. *Financial support:* In 2011–12, 9 fellowships with partial tuition reimbursements (averaging $27,000 per year) were awarded; career-related internships or fieldwork, Federal Work-Study, and scholarships/grants also available. Support available to part-time students. *Faculty research:* Explorations of science, learning and teaching, family Involvement in early childhood, culturally-responsive literacy instruction in diverse settings, STEM education, autism spectrum disorders. *Total annual research expenditures:* $5.9 million. *Unit head:* Dr. Maria R. Cortez, Department Chair, 210-458-5969, Fax: 210-458-7281, E-mail: mari.cortez@utsa.edu. *Application contact:* Erin Doran, Student Development Specialist, 210-458-7443, Fax: 210-458-7281, E-mail: erin.doran@utsa.edu.

The University of Texas at Tyler, College of Education and Psychology, School of Education, Tyler, TX 75799-0001. Offers early childhood education (M Ed, MA); reading (M Ed, MA); special education (M Ed, MA). Part-time and evening/weekend programs available. *Degree requirements:* For master's, comprehensive exam, thesis (for some programs), research project. *Entrance requirements:* For master's, GRE General Test. Additional exam requirements/recommendations for international students: Required—TOEFL (minimum score 79 computer-based). Electronic applications accepted. *Faculty research:* Improving quality in childcare settings, play and creativity, teacher interactions, effects of modeling on early childhood teachers, biofeedback, literacy instruction.

The University of Texas of the Permian Basin, Office of Graduate Studies, School of Education, Program in Early Childhood Education, Odessa, TX 79762-0001. Offers MA. *Degree requirements:* For master's, comprehensive exam (for some programs), thesis (for some programs). *Entrance requirements:* For master's, GRE General Test. Additional exam requirements/recommendations for international students: Required—TOEFL (minimum score 550 paper-based; 213 computer-based).

The University of Texas–Pan American, College of Education, Department of Curriculum and Instruction: Elementary and Secondary, Edinburg, TX 78539. Offers bilingual education (M Ed); early childhood education (M Ed); elementary education (M Ed); reading (M Ed); secondary education (M Ed). Part-time programs available. *Degree requirements:* For master's, comprehensive exam, thesis optional. *Entrance requirements:* For master's, GRE. Additional exam requirements/recommendations for international students: Required—TOEFL, IELTS. *Application deadline:* For fall admission, 7/17 for domestic and international students; for spring admission, 11/16 for domestic and international students. Application fee: $0. Tuition and fees vary according to course load, program and student level. *Financial support:* Research assistantships with tuition reimbursements, Federal Work-Study, institutionally sponsored loans, scholarships/grants, and unspecified assistantships available. Financial award application deadline: 4/15. *Faculty research:* Dual language instruction, literacy and technology, teacher education in diverse populations, mathematics and science education. *Unit head:* Dr. Veronica L. Estrada, Chair, 956-665-2431, Fax: 956-665-2434, E-mail: vlestradaa@utpa.edu. Web site: http://www.utpa.edu/dept/curr_ins/graduat.html.

University of the District of Columbia, College of Arts and Sciences, Department of Education, Program in Early Childhood Education, Washington, DC 20008-1175. Offers MA. *Accreditation:* NCATE. Part-time programs available. *Degree requirements:* For master's, comprehensive exam, research paper. *Entrance requirements:* For master's, GRE General Test, writing proficiency exam, minimum GPA of 3.0. *Expenses: Tuition, area resident:* Full-time $7580; part-time $421 per credit hour. Tuition, state resident: full-time $8580; part-time $477 per credit hour. Tuition, nonresident: full-time $14,580; part-time $810 per credit hour. *Required fees:* $620; $30 per credit hour. $310 per semester.

University of the Incarnate Word, School of Graduate Studies and Research, Dreeben School of Education, Programs in Education, San Antonio, TX 78209-6397. Offers adult education (M Ed, MA); cross-cultural education (M Ed, MA); early childhood literacy (M Ed, MA); general education (M Ed, MA); higher education (PhD); instructional technology (M Ed, MA); international education and entrepreneurship (PhD); kinesiology (M Ed, MA); literacy (M Ed, MA); organizational leadership (PhD); organizational learning and learning (M Ed, MA); reading (M Ed, MA); special education (M Ed, MA); teacher leadership (M Ed, MA). Part-time and evening/weekend programs available. *Faculty:* 14 full-time (8 women), 10 part-time/adjunct (9 women). *Students:* 13 full-time (7 women), 197 part-time (129 women); includes 111 minority (23 Black or African American, non-Hispanic/Latino; 2 American Indian or Alaska Native, non-Hispanic/Latino; 1 Asian, non-Hispanic/Latino; 85 Hispanic/Latino), 26 international. Average age 41. 78 applicants, 79% accepted, 34 enrolled. In 2011, 21 master's, 12 doctorates awarded. *Degree requirements:* For master's, capstone; for doctorate, thesis/dissertation, qualifying exam. *Entrance requirements:* For master's, baccalaureate degree; minimum foundation GPA of 2.5; interview; for doctorate, master's degree; interview; supervised writing sample. Additional exam requirements/recommendations for international students: Required—TOEFL (minimum score 560 paper-based; 220 computer-based; 83 iBT). *Application deadline:* Applications are processed on a rolling basis. Application fee: $20. Electronic applications accepted. *Expenses: Tuition:* Part-time $725 per credit hour. Tuition and fees vary according to degree level. *Financial support:* In 2011–12, 5 research assistantships were awarded; Federal Work-Study and scholarships/grants also available. Financial award applicants required to submit FAFSA. *Unit head:* Dr. Denise Staudt, Dean, Dreeben School of Education, 210-829-2762, E-mail: staudt@uiwtx.edu. *Application contact:* Andrea Cyterski-Acosta, Dean of Enrollment, 210-829-6005, Fax: 210-829-3921, E-mail: admis@uiwtx.edu. Web site: http://www.uiw.edu/education/index.htm.

University of the Sacred Heart, Graduate Programs, Department of Education, San Juan, PR 00914-0383. Offers early childhood education (M Ed); information technology and multimedia (Certificate); instruction systems and education technology (M Ed), including English, information technology and multimedia, instructional design, mathematics, Spanish. Part-time and evening/weekend programs available. *Degree requirements:* For master's, thesis. *Entrance requirements:* For master's, EXADEP, minimum undergraduate GPA of 2.75, interview.

University of the Southwest, Graduate Programs, Hobbs, NM 88240-9129. Offers business administration (MBA); curriculum and instruction (MSE); curriculum and instruction: bilingual (MSE); curriculum and instruction: TESOL (MSE); early childhood education (MSE); educational administration (MSE); mental health counseling (MSE); school counseling (MSE); special education (MSE); sports management (MBA). Part-time and evening/weekend programs available. Postbaccalaureate distance learning degree programs offered (no on-campus study). *Faculty:* 13 full-time (6 women), 28 part-time/adjunct (17 women). *Students:* 76 full-time (63 women), 229 part-time (194 women); includes 104 minority (50 Black or African American, non-Hispanic/Latino; 2 American Indian or Alaska Native, non-Hispanic/Latino; 8 Asian, non-Hispanic/Latino; 44 Hispanic/Latino). Average age 38. 173 applicants, 71% accepted, 101 enrolled. In 2011, 75 master's awarded. *Degree requirements:* For master's, comprehensive exam, thesis (for some programs). *Entrance requirements:* Additional exam requirements/recommendations for international students: Recommended—TOEFL. *Application deadline:* Applications are processed on a rolling basis. Application fee: $50. Electronic applications accepted. *Expenses: Tuition:* Full-time $12,288; part-time $512 per credit hour. One-time fee: $50. Tuition and fees vary according to course load. *Financial support:* In 2011–12, 47 students received support. Federal Work-Study available. Financial award application deadline: 4/1; financial award applicants required to submit FAFSA. *Unit head:* Dr. Mary Harris, Dean of Education, 575-492-2162, Fax: 575-392-

6006, E-mail: mharris@usw.edu. *Application contact:* Melissa Mitchell, Senior Online Program Advisor, 575-492-2142, Fax: 575-392-6006, E-mail: mmitchell@usw.edu. Web site: http://www.usw.edu/admissions/graduate_admission/graduate_admissions.

The University of Toledo, College of Graduate Studies, Judith Herb College of Education, Health Science and Human Service, Department of Early Childhood, Physical and Special Education, Toledo, OH 43606-3390. Offers early childhood education (ME, PhD); physical education (ME); special education (ME, PhD). Part-time programs available. *Faculty:* 15. *Students:* 29 full-time (20 women), 125 part-time (102 women); includes 15 minority (10 Black or African American, non-Hispanic/Latino; 2 Asian, non-Hispanic/Latino; 3 Hispanic/Latino), 3 international. Average age 32. 61 applicants, 67% accepted, 34 enrolled. In 2011, 55 master's awarded. *Degree requirements:* For master's, thesis. *Entrance requirements:* For master's, minimum cumulative GPA of 2.7 for all previous academic work, letters of recommendation. Additional exam requirements/recommendations for international students: Required—TOEFL (minimum score 550 paper-based; 213 computer-based; 80 iBT), IELTS (minimum score 6.5). *Application deadline:* For fall admission, 1/15 priority date for domestic students, 1/15 for international students. Applications are processed on a rolling basis. Application fee: $45 ($75 for international students). Electronic applications accepted. *Financial support:* In 2011–12, 13 teaching assistantships with full and partial tuition reimbursements (averaging $4,974 per year) were awarded; career-related internships or fieldwork, Federal Work-Study, institutionally sponsored loans, scholarships/grants, tuition waivers (full and partial), and unspecified assistantships also available. Support available to part-time students. *Unit head:* Dr. Richard Welsch, Interim Chair, 419-530-2468, E-mail: richard.welsch@utoledo.edu. *Application contact:* Graduate School Office, 419-530-4723, Fax: 419-530-4724, E-mail: grdsch@utnet.utoledo.edu. Web site: http://www.utoledo.edu/eduhshs/.

University of Utah, Graduate School, College of Education, Department of Special Education, Salt Lake City, UT 84112. Offers early childhood hearing impairments (M Ed, MS); early childhood special education (M Ed, PhD); early childhood vision impairments (M Ed, MS); hearing impairments (M Ed, MS); mild/moderate disabilities (M Ed, MS, PhD); professional practice (M Ed); research in special education (MS); severe disabilities (M Ed, MS, PhD); vision impairments (M Ed). Part-time and evening/weekend programs available. Postbaccalaureate distance learning degree programs offered (no on-campus study). *Faculty:* 16 full-time (11 women). *Students:* 34 full-time (26 women), 25 part-time (22 women); includes 11 minority (1 Black or African American, non-Hispanic/Latino; 3 American Indian or Alaska Native, non-Hispanic/Latino; 4 Hispanic/Latino; 1 Native Hawaiian or other Pacific Islander, non-Hispanic/Latino; 2 Two or more races, non-Hispanic/Latino), 1 international. Average age 35. 37 applicants, 54% accepted, 16 enrolled. In 2011, 26 degrees awarded. Terminal master's awarded for partial completion of doctoral program. *Degree requirements:* For master's, comprehensive exam, thesis (for some programs), qualifying exam; for doctorate, thesis/dissertation, qualifying exam. *Entrance requirements:* For master's, GRE or Analytical/Writing portion of GRE plus PRAXIS I, minimum GPA of 3.0; for doctorate, GRE General Test (minimum scores: Verbal 600; Quantitative 600; Analytical/Writing 4), minimum GPA of 3.0, 3.5 (recommended). Additional exam requirements/recommendations for international students: Required—TOEFL (minimum score 600 paper-based; 250 computer-based; 100 iBT); Recommended—IELTS (minimum score 7). *Application deadline:* For fall admission, 3/1 for domestic and international students; for spring admission, 11/1 for domestic and international students. Applications are processed on a rolling basis. Application fee: $55 ($65 for international students). Electronic applications accepted. *Expenses:* Contact institution. *Financial support:* In 2011–12, 25 students received support, including 25 fellowships with full tuition reimbursements available (averaging $7,124 per year), 3 teaching assistantships with full tuition reimbursements available (averaging $10,750 per year); research assistantships and career-related internships or fieldwork also available. Support available to part-time students. Financial award application deadline: 3/1; financial award applicants required to submit FAFSA. *Faculty research:* Inclusive education, positive behavior support, reading, instruction and intervention strategies. *Total annual research expenditures:* $5,926. *Unit head:* Dr. Robert E. O'Neill, Chair, 801-581-8121, Fax: 801-585-6476, E-mail: rob.oneill@utah.edu. *Application contact:* Patty Davis, Academic Advisor, 801-581-4764, Fax: 801-585-6476, E-mail: patty.davis@utah.edu. Web site: http://www.ed.utah.edu/sped/.

University of Utah, Graduate School, College of Social and Behavioral Science, Department of Family and Consumer Studies, Salt Lake City, UT 84112-0080. Offers early childhood education (M Ed); human development and social policy (MS). Part-time programs available. *Faculty:* 17 full-time (9 women). *Students:* 19 full-time (18 women), 17 part-time (15 women); includes 3 minority (2 Hispanic/Latino; 1 Native Hawaiian or other Pacific Islander, non-Hispanic/Latino), 1 international. Average age 32. 25 applicants, 72% accepted, 18 enrolled. In 2011, 8 degrees awarded. *Degree requirements:* For master's, comprehensive exam (for some programs), thesis or alternative. *Entrance requirements:* For master's, GRE General Test, minimum undergraduate GPA of 3.0, courses in research methods and statistics. Additional exam requirements/recommendations for international students: Required—TOEFL (minimum score 500 paper-based; 173 computer-based). *Application deadline:* For fall admission, 2/1 priority date for domestic students, 2/1 for international students. Application fee: $55 ($65 for international students). Electronic applications accepted. *Financial support:* In 2011–12, 9 students received support, including 9 teaching assistantships with partial tuition reimbursements available (averaging $5,500 per year). Financial award application deadline: 2/1. *Faculty research:* Social, physical, educational and economic contexts of families and communities. *Total annual research expenditures:* $53,635. *Unit head:* Dr. Russell A. Isabella, Chair, 801-581-7712, Fax: 801-581-5156, E-mail: russ@fcs.utah.edu. *Application contact:* Dr. Marissa Diener, Graduate Director, 801-581-6521, E-mail: marissa.diener@fcs.utah.edu. Web site: http://www.fcs.utah.edu/index.html.

University of Victoria, Faculty of Graduate Studies, Faculty of Education, Department of Curriculum and Instruction, Victoria, BC V8W 2Y2, Canada. Offers art education (M Ed, PhD); curriculum studies (M Ed, MA, PhD); early childhood education (M Ed, PhD); educational studies (PhD); language and literacy (M Ed, MA, PhD); mathematics (M Ed, MA, PhD); music education (M Ed, MA, PhD); science (M Ed, MA, PhD); social studies (M Ed, MA); social, cultural and foundational studies (MA, PhD); technology and environmental education (PhD). Part-time programs available. *Degree requirements:* For master's, thesis, project (M Ed); for doctorate, comprehensive exam, thesis/dissertation. *Entrance requirements:* For master's, minimum B average. Additional exam requirements/recommendations for international students: Required—TOEFL (minimum score 575 paper-based; 233 computer-based), IELTS (minimum score 7). Electronic applications accepted. *Faculty research:* Elementary and secondary English, language arts, curriculum theory and practice, educational media and technology, educational administration and leadership, history and philosophy of education.

University of Virginia, Curry School of Education, Program in Education, Charlottesville, VA 22903. Offers administration and supervision (PhD); applied developmental science (PhD); counselor education (PhD); curriculum and instruction (PhD); early childhood-developmental risk (MT); education evaluation (PhD); educational psychology (PhD); educational research (PhD); elementary (MT, PhD); English education (MT, PhD); foreign language education (MT); higher education (PhD); instructional technology (PhD); kinesiology (MT, PhD); math education (PhD); reading education (PhD); research statistics and evaluation (PhD); school psychology (PhD); science education (PhD); social studies education (MT, PhD); special education (PhD); world languages education (MT). *Students:* 299 full-time (216 women), 60 part-time (33 women); includes 46 minority (18 Black or African American, non-Hispanic/Latino; 17 Asian, non-Hispanic/Latino; 7 Hispanic/Latino; 4 Two or more races, non-Hispanic/Latino), 23 international. Average age 30. 307 applicants, 42% accepted, 80 enrolled. In 2011, 113 master's, 62 doctorates awarded. *Degree requirements:* For master's, comprehensive exam (for some programs), field project; for doctorate, comprehensive exam, thesis/dissertation. *Entrance requirements:* For doctorate, GRE General Test. Additional exam requirements/recommendations for international students: Required—TOEFL (minimum score 600 paper-based; 250 computer-based; 90 iBT), IELTS (minimum score 7). *Application deadline:* Applications are processed on a rolling basis. Application fee: $60. Electronic applications accepted. *Financial support:* Fellowships, research assistantships, and teaching assistantships available. Financial award application deadline: 1/5; financial award applicants required to submit FAFSA. *Unit head:* Robert C. Pianta, Dean, 434-924-3334. *Application contact:* Joanne McNergney, Assistant Dean for Admissions and Student Services, 434-924-3334, E-mail: curry-admissions@virginia.edu.

The University of West Alabama, School of Graduate Studies, College of Education, Departments of Instructional Leadership and Support/Curriculum and Instruction, Program in Early Childhood Education, Livingston, AL 35470. Offers M Ed. *Accreditation:* NCATE. Part-time programs available. *Faculty:* 8 full-time (7 women). *Students:* 96 (92 women); includes 56 minority (55 Black or African American, non-Hispanic/Latino; 1 Asian, non-Hispanic/Latino). In 2011, 20 master's awarded. *Degree requirements:* For master's, comprehensive exam. *Entrance requirements:* For master's, GRE General Test, MAT, minimum GPA of 2.75. Additional exam requirements/recommendations for international students: Required—TOEFL (minimum score 61 computer-based). *Application deadline:* For fall admission, 9/10 priority date for domestic students; for spring admission, 3/24 for domestic students. Applications are processed on a rolling basis. Application fee: $25 ($50 for international students). *Expenses:* Tuition, state resident: full-time $5112; part-time $284 per credit hour. Tuition, nonresident: full-time $10,224; part-time $568 per credit hour. *Required fees:* $180; $40 per semester. One-time fee: $65. Tuition and fees vary according to class time, course load, campus/location and program. *Financial support:* Teaching assistantships, career-related internships or fieldwork, Federal Work-Study, scholarships/grants, and unspecified assistantships available. Support available to part-time students. *Unit head:* Dr. Esther Howard, Chair of Curriculum and Instruction, 205-652-3428, Fax: 205-652-3706, E-mail: ehoward@uwa.edu. *Application contact:* Dr. Kathy Chandler, Dean of Graduate Studies, 205-652-3421, Fax: 205-652-3706, E-mail: kchandler@uwa.edu. Web site: http://www.uwa.edu/earlychildhoodeducationp3.aspx.

University of West Florida, College of Professional Studies, School of Education, Program in Curriculum and Instruction, Pensacola, FL 32514-5750. Offers curriculum and instruction: special education (M Ed); elementary education (M Ed); primary education (M Ed). Part-time and evening/weekend programs available. *Students:* 10 full-time (all women), 62 part-time (56 women); includes 16 minority (9 Black or African American, non-Hispanic/Latino; 1 American Indian or Alaska Native, non-Hispanic/Latino; 1 Asian, non-Hispanic/Latino; 3 Hispanic/Latino; 1 Native Hawaiian or other Pacific Islander, non-Hispanic/Latino; 1 Two or more races, non-Hispanic/Latino). Average age 35. 67 applicants, 70% accepted, 37 enrolled. In 2011, 62 master's awarded. *Entrance requirements:* For master's, GRE (minimum score 450 verbal) or MAT (minimum score 396) if bachelor's GPA less than 3.0, state teaching certification; letter of intent; two professional references. Additional exam requirements/recommendations for international students: Required—TOEFL (minimum score 550 paper-based; 213 computer-based). *Application deadline:* For fall admission, 6/1 for domestic and international students; for spring admission, 10/1 for domestic and international students. Applications are processed on a rolling basis. Application fee: $30. *Expenses:* Tuition, state resident: full-time $5729; part-time $302 per credit hour. Tuition, nonresident: full-time $20,059; part-time $961 per credit hour. *Required fees:* $1509; $63 per credit hour. *Financial support:* Career-related internships or fieldwork, Federal Work-Study, scholarships/grants, and tuition waivers (partial) available. Support available to part-time students. Financial award application deadline: 4/15; financial award applicants required to submit FAFSA. *Unit head:* Dr. William H. Evans, Acting Director, 850-474-2892, Fax: 850-474-2844, E-mail: wevans@uwf.edu. *Application contact:* Terry McCray, Assistant Director of Graduate Admissions, 850-473-7718, Fax: 850-473-7714, E-mail: gradadmissions@uwf.edu.

University of West Georgia, College of Education, Department of Early Learning and Childhood Education, Carrollton, GA 30118. Offers early childhood education (M Ed, Ed S). *Accreditation:* ACA; NCATE. Part-time and evening/weekend programs available. *Faculty:* 7 full-time (6 women). *Students:* 43 full-time (39 women), 92 part-time (86 women); includes 25 minority (19 Black or African American, non-Hispanic/Latino; 5 Hispanic/Latino; 1 Two or more races, non-Hispanic/Latino). Average age 32. 52 applicants, 83% accepted, 8 enrolled. In 2011, 77 master's, 22 Ed Ss awarded. *Entrance requirements:* For master's, undergraduate degree in early childhood or elementary education; minimum overall GPA of 2.7; clear and renewable level 4 teaching certificate; for Ed S, master's degree in early childhood or elementary education; minimum overall GPA of 3.0 in graduate work; level 5 teaching certificate. Additional exam requirements/recommendations for international students: Required—TOEFL (minimum score 523 paper-based; 193 computer-based; 69 iBT); Recommended—IELTS (minimum score 6). *Application deadline:* For fall admission, 7/21 for domestic students, 6/1 for international students; for spring admission, 11/30 for domestic students, 10/15 for international students. Applications are processed on a rolling basis. Application fee: $30. Electronic applications accepted. *Expenses:* Tuition, state resident: full-time $4336; part-time $181 per credit hour. Tuition, nonresident: full-time $17,362; part-time $724 per credit hour. Tuition and fees vary according to course load, degree level, campus/location and program. *Financial support:* In 2011–12, 1 research assistantship with full tuition reimbursement (averaging $2,963 per year) was awarded; scholarships/grants and unspecified assistantships also available. Support available to part-time students. Financial award application deadline: 7/1; financial award applicants required to submit FAFSA. *Faculty research:* Early childhood education, social justice. *Unit head:* Dr. Donna Harkins, Chair, 678-839-6066, Fax: 678-839-6063, E-mail: dharkins@westga.edu. *Application contact:* Deanna Richards, Coordinator, Graduate Studies, 678-839-5946, E-mail: drichard@westga.edu. Web site: http://www.westga.edu/coeelce.

University of Wisconsin–Milwaukee, Graduate School, School of Education, Department of Curriculum and Instruction, Milwaukee, WI 53201-0413. Offers curriculum planning and instruction improvement (MS); early childhood education (MS); elementary education (MS); junior high/middle school education (MS); reading education (MS); secondary education (MS); teaching in an urban setting (MS). Part-time programs available. *Faculty:* 18 full-time (13 women). *Students:* 29 full-time (23 women), 54 part-time (44 women); includes 21 minority (10 Black or African American, non-Hispanic/Latino; 4 Asian, non-Hispanic/Latino; 3 Hispanic/Latino; 4 Two or more races, non-Hispanic/Latino). Average age 32. 43 applicants, 65% accepted, 13 enrolled. In 2011, 23 degrees awarded. *Degree requirements:* For master's, thesis or alternative.

Entrance requirements: Additional exam requirements/recommendations for international students: Required—TOEFL (minimum score 550 paper-based; 79 iBT), IELTS (minimum score 6.5). *Application deadline:* For fall admission, 1/1 priority date for domestic students; for spring admission, 9/1 for domestic students. Applications are processed on a rolling basis. Application fee: $56 ($96 for international students). Electronic applications accepted. One-time fee: $506.10 full-time. Tuition and fees vary according to course load and reciprocity agreements. *Financial support:* In 2011–12, 1 fellowship was awarded; research assistantships, teaching assistantships, career-related internships or fieldwork, health care benefits, unspecified assistantships, and project assistantships also available. Support available to part-time students. Financial award application deadline: 4/15; financial award applicants required to submit FAFSA. *Total annual research expenditures:* $21,843. *Unit head:* Hope Longwell-Grice, Department Chair, 414-229-3059, Fax: 414-229-5571, E-mail: hope@uwm.edu. *Application contact:* General Information Contact, 414-229-4982, Fax: 414-229-6967, E-mail: gradschool@uwm.edu. Web site: http://www.uwm.edu/SOE/.

University of Wisconsin–Oshkosh, Graduate Studies, College of Education and Human Services, Department of Special Education, Oshkosh, WI 54901. Offers cross-categorical (MSE); early childhood: exceptional education needs (MSE); non-licensure (MSE). Part-time and evening/weekend programs available. *Degree requirements:* For master's, comprehensive exam (for some programs), thesis or alternative, field report. *Entrance requirements:* For master's, interview, minimum GPA of 3.0, teaching license, letters of recommendation. Additional exam requirements/recommendations for international students: Required—TOEFL (minimum score 550 paper-based; 213 computer-based; 79 iBT). Electronic applications accepted. *Faculty research:* Private agency contributions to the disabled, graduation requirements for exceptional education needs students, direct instruction in spelling for learning disabled, effects of behavioral parent training, secondary education programming issues.

Ursuline College, School of Graduate Studies, Program in Education, Pepper Pike, OH 44124-4398. Offers art education (MA); early childhood education (MA); language arts education (MA); life science education (MA); math education (MA); middle school education (MA); social studies education (MA); special education (MA). *Accreditation:* NCATE. *Faculty:* 3 full-time (all women), 8 part-time/adjunct (6 women). *Students:* 28 full-time (22 women), 1 (woman) part-time; includes 11 minority (7 Black or African American, non-Hispanic/Latino; 2 Asian, non-Hispanic/Latino; 1 Hispanic/Latino; 1 Native Hawaiian or other Pacific Islander, non-Hispanic/Latino). Average age 32. In 2011, 29 master's awarded. *Degree requirements:* For master's, comprehensive exam. *Entrance requirements:* For master's, minimum undergraduate GPA of 3.0. Additional exam requirements/recommendations for international students: Required—TOEFL (minimum score 500 paper-based; 173 computer-based). *Application deadline:* For fall admission, 8/1 priority date for domestic students. Applications are processed on a rolling basis. Application fee: $25. *Expenses:* Contact institution. *Financial support:* Federal Work-Study available. Financial award application deadline: 3/1. *Unit head:* Dr. Edna West, Director, Master's Apprentice Program, 440-646-6134, Fax: 440-684-6088, E-mail: ewest@ursuline.edu. *Application contact:* Melanie Steele, Graduate Admission Assistant, 440-646-8199, Fax: 440-684-6138, E-mail: graduateadmissions@ursuline.edu.

Valdosta State University, Department of Early Childhood and Special Education, Valdosta, GA 31698. Offers early childhood (M Ed); special education (M Ed, Ed S). *Accreditation:* ASHA (one or more programs are accredited); NCATE. Part-time and evening/weekend programs available. Postbaccalaureate distance learning degree programs offered (no on-campus study). *Faculty:* 17 full-time (14 women). *Students:* 37 full-time (30 women), 110 part-time (78 women); includes 37 minority (33 Black or African American, non-Hispanic/Latino; 2 American Indian or Alaska Native, non-Hispanic/Latino; 2 Asian, non-Hispanic/Latino). Average age 25. 27 applicants, 81% accepted, 22 enrolled. In 2011, 48 master's awarded. *Degree requirements:* For master's, thesis (for some programs), comprehensive written and/or oral exams; for Ed S, thesis. *Entrance requirements:* For master's, GRE General Test or MAT, minimum GPA of 2.5; for Ed S, GRE General Test or MAT, minimum GPA of 3.0. Additional exam requirements/recommendations for international students: Required—TOEFL (minimum score 523 paper-based; 193 computer-based). *Application deadline:* For fall and spring admission, 7/1 for domestic and international students. Applications are processed on a rolling basis. Application fee: $35. Electronic applications accepted. *Expenses:* Tuition, state resident: full-time $7098; part-time $217 per hour. Tuition, nonresident: full-time $20,630; part-time $780 per hour. *Financial support:* In 2011–12, 5 students received support, including 5 research assistantships with full tuition reimbursements available (averaging $3,252 per year); institutionally sponsored loans, scholarships/grants, and unspecified assistantships also available. Support available to part-time students. Financial award application deadline: 7/1; financial award applicants required to submit FAFSA. *Unit head:* Dr. Shirley Andrews, Acting Head, 229-333-5929, E-mail: spandrew@valdosta.edu. *Application contact:* Shantae Lynn, Admissions Specialist, 229-333-5694, Fax: 229-245-3853, E-mail: smlynn@valdosta.edu.

Virginia Commonwealth University, Graduate School, School of Education, Program in Special Education, Richmond, VA 23284-9005. Offers autism spectrum disorders (Certificate); disability leadership (Certificate); early childhood (M Ed); general education (M Ed); severe disabilities (M Ed). *Accreditation:* NCATE. *Degree requirements:* For master's, comprehensive exam. *Entrance requirements:* For master's, GRE General Test or MAT. Additional exam requirements/recommendations for international students: Required—TOEFL (minimum score 600 paper-based; 250 computer-based; 100 iBT). Electronic applications accepted. *Expenses:* Tuition, state resident: full-time $9133; part-time $507 per credit. Tuition, nonresident: full-time $18,777; part-time $1043 per credit. *Required fees:* $77 per credit. Tuition and fees vary according to degree level, campus/location, program and student level.

Virginia Commonwealth University, Graduate School, School of Education, Program in Teaching and Learning, Richmond, VA 23284-9005. Offers early and elementary education (MT); health and physical education (MT); secondary 6-12 education (MT); secondary education (Certificate). *Accreditation:* NCATE. Part-time programs available. *Entrance requirements:* For master's, GRE General Test or MAT. Additional exam requirements/recommendations for international students: Required—TOEFL (minimum score 600 paper-based; 250 computer-based; 100 iBT). Electronic applications accepted. *Expenses:* Tuition, state resident: full-time $9133; part-time $507 per credit. Tuition, nonresident: full-time $18,777; part-time $1043 per credit. *Required fees:* $77 per credit. Tuition and fees vary according to degree level, campus/location, program and student level.

Wagner College, Division of Graduate Studies, Department of Education, Program in Early Childhood Education (Birth-Grade 2), Staten Island, NY 10301-4495. Offers MS Ed. Part-time and evening/weekend programs available. *Faculty:* 4 full-time (3 women), 2 part-time/adjunct (both women). *Students:* 8 full-time (all women), 2 part-time (both women); includes 2 minority (1 Asian, non-Hispanic/Latino; 1 Hispanic/Latino). Average age 24. 8 applicants, 88% accepted, 3 enrolled. In 2011, 4 master's awarded. *Degree requirements:* For master's, thesis. *Entrance requirements:* For master's, minimum GPA of 2.75. Additional exam requirements/recommendations for international students: Required—TOEFL (minimum score 550 paper-based; 217 computer-based; 79 iBT). *Application deadline:* For fall admission, 5/1 priority date for domestic students, 3/1 for international students; for spring admission, 11/1 priority date for domestic students, 10/1 for international students. Applications are processed on a rolling basis. Application fee: $50 ($85 for international students). *Expenses: Tuition:* Full-time $16,200; part-time $890 per credit. *Financial support:* Career-related internships or fieldwork, tuition waivers (partial), unspecified assistantships, and alumni fellowship grant available. Financial award applicants required to submit FAFSA. *Unit head:* Dr. Stephen Preskill, Graduate Coordinator, 718-420-4070, Fax: 718-390-3456, E-mail: jkraus@wagner.edu. *Application contact:* Patricia Clancy, Administrative Assistant, Admissions, 718-420-4464, Fax: 718-390-3105, E-mail: patricia.clancy@wagner.edu.

Walden University, Graduate Programs, Richard W. Riley College of Education and Leadership, Minneapolis, MN 55401. Offers administrator leadership for teaching and learning (Ed D, Ed S); adult education (Ed D, Ed S); adult learning (MS, Postbaccalaureate Certificate), including developmental education (MS), online teaching (MS), teaching adults English as a second language (MS), training and performance management (MS); college teaching and learning (Ed D, Ed S, Postbaccalaureate Certificate); curriculum, instruction and assessment (Ed D, Postbaccalaureate Certificate); curriculum, instruction, and professional development (Ed S); developmental education (Postbaccalaureate Certificate); early childhood administration, management, and leadership (Postbaccalaureate Certificate); early childhood education (birth-grade 3) (MAT); early childhood public policy and advocacy (Postbaccalaureate Certificate); early childhood studies (MS), including administration, management and leadership, early childhood public policy and advocacy, teaching adults in the early childhood field, teaching and diversity; education (MS, PhD), including adolescent literacy and technology (grades 6-12) (MS), adult education leadership (PhD), assessment, evaluation, and accountability (PhD), community college leadership (PhD), curriculum, instruction, and assessment, early childhood education (PhD), educational technology (PhD), elementary reading and literacy (MS), elementary reading and mathematics (MS), general program, global and comparative education (PhD), higher education (PhD), integrating technology in the classroom (MS), K-12 educational leadership (PhD), leadership, policy and change (PhD), learning, instruction and innovation (PhD), literacy and learning in the content areas (MS), mathematics (grades 6-8) (MS), mathematics (grades K-5) (MS), middle level education (grades 5-8) (MS), professional development (MS), science (grades K-8) (MS), self-designed (PhD), special education (PhD), special education (non-licensure) (MS), teacher leadership (grades K-12) (MS), teaching English language learners (grades K-12) (MS); educational leadership and administration (principal preparation) (Ed S); educational technology (Ed S); elementary reading and literacy (Postbaccalaureate Certificate); engaging culturally diverse learners (Postbaccalaureate Certificate); enrollment management and institutional marketing (Postbaccalaureate Certificate); higher education (MS), including college teaching and learning, enrollment management and institutional planning, global higher education, leadership for student success, online and distance learning; higher education leadership (Ed D); instructional design (Postbaccalaureate Certificate); instructional design and technology (MS), including general program (MS, PhD), online learning, training and performance improvement; integrating technology in the classroom (Postbaccalaureate Certificate); online teaching for adult learners (Postbaccalaureate Certificate); professional development (Postbaccalaureate Certificate); reading and literacy leadership (Ed D); science K-8 (Postbaccalaureate Certificate); special education (Ed D, Ed S); special education: emotional/behavioral disorders (K-12) (MAT); special education: learning disabilities (K-12) (MAT); teacher leadership (Ed D, Ed S, Postbaccalaureate Certificate); training and performance management (Postbaccalaureate Certificate). Part-time and evening/weekend programs available. Postbaccalaureate distance learning degree programs offered (minimal on-campus study). *Faculty:* 71 full-time (48 women), 853 part-time/adjunct (585 women). *Students:* 11,326 full-time (9,212 women), 2,148 part-time (1,795 women); includes 5,346 minority (4,403 Black or African American, non-Hispanic/Latino; 76 American Indian or Alaska Native, non-Hispanic/Latino; 140 Asian, non-Hispanic/Latino; 561 Hispanic/Latino; 21 Native Hawaiian or other Pacific Islander, non-Hispanic/Latino; 145 Two or more races, non-Hispanic/Latino), 322 international. Average age 39. In 2011, 3,477 master's, 318 doctorates, 471 other advanced degrees awarded. *Degree requirements:* For doctorate, thesis/dissertation (for some programs), residency; for other advanced degree, residency (for some programs). *Entrance requirements:* For master's, bachelor's degree or equivalent in related field; minimum GPA of 2.5; official transcripts; goal statement; access to computer and Internet; for doctorate, master's degree or equivalent in related field; minimum GPA of 3.0; official transcripts; three years' related professional/academic experience (preferred); access to computer and Internet; for other advanced degree, master's degree or equivalent in related field; minimum GPA of 3.0; 3 years related professional/academic experience (preferred); access to computer and Internet (Ed S). Additional exam requirements/recommendations for international students: Required—TOEFL (minimum score 550 paper-based; 213 computer-based), IELTS (minimum score 6.5), or Michigan English Language Assessment Battery (minimum score 82). *Application deadline:* Applications are processed on a rolling basis. Application fee: $50. Electronic applications accepted. *Financial support:* Federal Work-Study, scholarships/grants, unspecified assistantships, and family tuition reduction, active duty/veteran tuition reduction, group tuition reduction, interest-free payment plans, employee tuition reduction available. Support available to part-time students. Financial award applicants required to submit FAFSA. *Unit head:* Dr. Kate Steffens, Dean, 800-925-3368. *Application contact:* Jennifer Hall, Vice President of Enrollment Management, 866-4-WALDEN, E-mail: info@waldenu.edu. Web site: http://www.waldenu.edu/Colleges-and-Schools/College-of-Education-and-Leadership.htm.

Wayne State College, School of Education and Counseling, Department of Educational Foundations and Leadership, Program in Curriculum and Instruction, Wayne, NE 68787. Offers alternative education (MSE); business and information technology education (MSE); communication arts education (MSE); early childhood education (MSE); elementary education (MSE); English as a second language (MSE); English education (MSE); family and consumer sciences education (MSE); industrial technology and vocational education (MSE); learning communities (MSE); mathematics education (MSE); music education (MSE); science education (MSE); social science education (MSE). *Accreditation:* NCATE. Part-time and evening/weekend programs available. *Degree requirements:* For master's, comprehensive exam, thesis optional. *Entrance requirements:* For master's, GRE General Test. Additional exam requirements/recommendations for international students: Required—TOEFL (minimum score 550 paper-based; 213 computer-based).

Wayne State University, College of Education, Division of Teacher Education, Detroit, MI 48202. Offers art education (M Ed), including art therapy; bilingual/bicultural education (M Ed); career and technical education (M Ed); curriculum and instruction (Ed D, PhD, Ed S), including art education (PhD), bilingual education (Ed D, Ed S), bilingual-bicultural education (PhD), career and technical education (MAT, Ed D, PhD, Ed S), early childhood education (MAT, Ed D, PhD, Ed S), elementary education, English as a second language (MAT, Ed D, Ed S), English education (MAT, Ed D, PhD, Ed S), foreign language education (MAT, PhD), K-12 curriculum, mathematics education (MAT, Ed D, PhD, Ed S), science education (MAT, Ed D, PhD, Ed S), secondary education, social studies education (MAT, Ed S), social studies education: secondary (Ed D, PhD); elementary education (MAT), including special education; elementary education (M Ed, MAT), including children's literature (MAT), early childhood education

(MAT, Ed D, PhD, Ed S), general elementary education (MAT); elementary or secondary education (MAT), including bilingual/bicultural education, English as a second language (MAT, Ed D, Ed S), mathematics education (MAT, Ed D, PhD, Ed S), science education (MAT, Ed D, PhD, Ed S), social studies education (MAT, Ed S); English education-secondary (M Ed); foreign language education (M Ed); mathematics education (M Ed); reading (M Ed, Ed S); reading, languages and literature (Ed D); science education (M Ed); secondary education (MAT), including art education (K-12), career and technical education (MAT, Ed D, PhD, Ed S), English education (MAT, Ed D, PhD, Ed S), foreign language education (MAT, PhD), kinesiology; social studies education secondary (M Ed); special education (M Ed, Ed D, PhD, Ed S). *Students:* 216 full-time (154 women), 626 part-time (478 women); includes 289 minority (227 Black or African American, non-Hispanic/Latino; 4 American Indian or Alaska Native, non-Hispanic/Latino; 27 Asian, non-Hispanic/Latino; 21 Hispanic/Latino; 1 Native Hawaiian or other Pacific Islander, non-Hispanic/Latino; 9 Two or more races, non-Hispanic/Latino), 14 international. Average age 37. 347 applicants, 37% accepted, 93 enrolled. In 2011, 226 master's, 12 doctorates, 46 other advanced degrees awarded. *Degree requirements:* For master's, thesis (for some programs), thesis, essay or project (for some M Ed programs), professional field experience (for MAT programs); for doctorate, thesis/dissertation. *Entrance requirements:* For master's, Michigan Basic Skills Test (MA in teaching); for doctorate, minimum undergraduate GPA of 3.0, graduate 3.5; interview, curriculum vitae; references. Additional exam requirements/recommendations for international students: Required—TOEFL (minimum score 550 paper-based; 213 computer-based), TWE (minimum score 5.5). *Application deadline:* For fall admission, 6/1 priority date for domestic students, 5/1 for international students; for winter admission, 10/1 priority date for domestic students, 9/1 for international students; for spring admission, 2/1 priority date for domestic students, 1/1 for international students. Applications are processed on a rolling basis. Application fee: $50. Electronic applications accepted. *Expenses:* Tuition, state resident: part-time $512.85 per credit. Tuition, nonresident: part-time $1132.65 per credit. *Required fees:* $26.60 per credit. $199.65 per semester. Tuition and fees vary according to course load and program. *Financial support:* In 2011–12, 42 students received support. Fellowships, research assistantships with tuition reimbursements available, teaching assistantships, scholarships/grants, and unspecified assistantships available. *Faculty research:* Reading and writing literacy and literature. *Total annual research expenditures:* $264,016. *Unit head:* Dr. Craig Roney, Assistant Dean, 313-577-0902, E-mail: rroney@wayne.edu. Web site: http://coe.wayne.edu/ted/index.php.

Webster University, School of Education, Department of Communication Arts, Reading and Early Childhood, St. Louis, MO 63119-3194. Offers communications (MAT); early childhood education (MAT). *Entrance requirements:* For master's, minimum GPA of 2.5. Additional exam requirements/recommendations for international students: Required—TOEFL. *Expenses: Tuition:* Full-time $10,890; part-time $605 per credit hour. Tuition and fees vary according to campus/location and program.

Wesleyan College, Department of Education, Program in Early Childhood Education, Macon, GA 31210-4462. Offers MA. Part-time programs available. *Degree requirements:* For master's, thesis or alternative, practicum, professional portfolio. *Entrance requirements:* For master's, GRE or MAT, interview, teaching certificate, 3 letters of recommendation. Additional exam requirements/recommendations for international students: Required—TOEFL.

West Chester University of Pennsylvania, College of Education, Department of Early and Middle Grades, West Chester, PA 19383. Offers applied studies in teaching and learning (M Ed); early childhood education (M Ed, Teaching Certificate); early grades preparation (Teaching Certificate); elementary education (Teaching Certificate); middle grades preparation (Teaching Certificate). *Accreditation:* NCATE. Part-time and evening/weekend programs available. *Faculty:* 7 part-time/adjunct (6 women). *Students:* 54 full-time (41 women), 100 part-time (84 women); includes 14 minority (8 Black or African American, non-Hispanic/Latino; 1 Asian, non-Hispanic/Latino; 2 Hispanic/Latino; 3 Two or more races, non-Hispanic/Latino). Average age 32. 78 applicants, 63% accepted, 32 enrolled. In 2011, 22 degrees awarded. *Degree requirements:* For master's, teacher research project, portfolio (for M Ed). *Entrance requirements:* For master's, minimum GPA of 3.0, teacher certification, one year of full-time teaching experience; for Teaching Certificate, PRAXIS I and II, minimum GPA of 3.0. Additional exam requirements/recommendations for international students: Required—TOEFL (minimum score 550 paper-based; 213 computer-based; 80 iBT). *Application deadline:* For fall admission, 4/15 priority date for domestic students, 3/15 for international students; for spring admission, 10/15 priority date for domestic students. Applications are processed on a rolling basis. Application fee: $45. Electronic applications accepted. *Expenses:* Tuition, state resident: full-time $7488; part-time $416 per credit. Tuition, nonresident: full-time $11,232; part-time $624 per credit. *Required fees:* $1784.64; $67.59 per credit. Tuition and fees vary according to program. *Financial support:* Unspecified assistantships available. Support available to part-time students. Financial award application deadline: 2/15; financial award applicants required to submit FAFSA. *Faculty research:* Cooperative learning, creative expression and critical thinking, teacher research, learning styles, middle school education. *Unit head:* Dr. Heather Leaman, Chair, 610-436-2944, Fax: 610-436-3102, E-mail: hleaman@wcupa.edu. *Application contact:* Dr. Connie DiLucchio, Graduate Coordinator, 610-436-3323, Fax: 610-436-3102, E-mail: cdilucchio@wcupa.edu. Web site: http://www.wcupa.edu/_academics/sch_sed.elementaryed/.

Western Kentucky University, Graduate Studies, College of Education and Behavioral Sciences, School of Teacher Education, Bowling Green, KY 42101. Offers elementary education (MAE, Ed S); exceptional education: learning and behavioral disorders (MAE); exceptional education: moderate and severe disabilities (MAE); instructional design (MS); interdisciplinary early childhood education (MAE); library media education (MS); literacy education (MAE); middle grades education (MAE); secondary education (MAE, Ed S). Part-time and evening/weekend programs available. Postbaccalaureate distance learning degree programs offered (minimal on-campus study). *Degree requirements:* For master's, comprehensive exam. *Entrance requirements:* For master's, GRE General Test. Additional exam requirements/recommendations for international students: Required—TOEFL (minimum score 555 paper-based; 213 computer-based; 79 iBT). *Faculty research:* Teacher preparation in moderate/severe disabilities.

Western Oregon University, Graduate Programs, College of Education, Division of Special Education, Program in Early Childhood Special Education, Monmouth, OR 97361-1394. Offers MS Ed. *Accreditation:* NCATE. Part-time and evening/weekend programs available. *Degree requirements:* For master's, thesis optional, written exam, portfolio. *Entrance requirements:* For master's, CBEST, PRAXIS or GRE General Test, minimum GPA of 3.0, teaching license. Additional exam requirements/recommendations for international students: Required—TOEFL (minimum score 550 paper-based; 213 computer-based; 79 iBT), IELTS (minimum score 6.5). *Faculty research:* High school through university articulation, career development for early childhood educators professional collaboration/cooperation.

Westfield State University, Division of Graduate and Continuing Education, Department of Education, Program in Early Childhood Education, Westfield, MA 01086. Offers M Ed. *Accreditation:* NCATE. Part-time and evening/weekend programs available. *Degree requirements:* For master's, comprehensive exam, practicum. *Entrance requirements:* For master's, GRE General Test or MAT, minimum undergraduate GPA of 2.7.

West Virginia University, College of Human Resources and Education, Department of Special Education, Morgantown, WV 26506. Offers autism spectrum disorder (5-adult) (MA); autism spectrum disorder (K-6) (MA); early intervention/early childhood special education (MA); gifted education (1-12) (MA); low vision (PreK-adult) (MA); multicategorical special education (5-adult) (MA); multicategorical special education (K-6) (MA); severe/multiple disabilities (K-adult) (MA); special education (MA, Ed D); vision impairments (PreK-adult) (MA). *Accreditation:* NCATE. Part-time and evening/weekend programs available. Postbaccalaureate distance learning degree programs offered (no on-campus study). *Degree requirements:* For master's, thesis optional; for doctorate, comprehensive exam, thesis/dissertation. *Entrance requirements:* For master's, minimum GPA of 2.75 passing scores on PRAXIS PPST; for doctorate, GRE General Test or MAT. Additional exam requirements/recommendations for international students: Required—TOEFL.

Wheelock College, Graduate Programs, Division of Education, Boston, MA 02215-4176. Offers early childhood education (MS); education leadership (MS); elementary education (MS); language, literacy, and reading (MS); teaching students with moderate disabilities (MS). *Accreditation:* NCATE. Postbaccalaureate distance learning degree programs offered (minimal on-campus study). *Degree requirements:* For master's, comprehensive exam. *Entrance requirements:* Additional exam requirements/recommendations for international students: Required—TOEFL. Electronic applications accepted. *Faculty research:* Symbolic learning, emergent literacy, diversity inclusion, beginning reading language and culture, math education.

Wichita State University, Graduate School, College of Education, Department of Curriculum and Instruction, Wichita, KS 67260. Offers curriculum and instruction (M Ed); special education (M Ed), including adaptive, early childhood unified (M Ed, MAT), functional, gifted; teaching (MAT), including curriculum and instruction, early childhood unified (M Ed, MAT). *Accreditation:* NCATE. Part-time and evening/weekend programs available. *Entrance requirements:* For master's, MAT, minimum GPA of 2.75. *Expenses:* Tuition, state resident: full-time $4746; part-time $263.65 per credit. Tuition, nonresident: full-time $11,669; part-time $648.30 per credit. *Unit head:* Dr. Janice Ewing, Chairperson, 316-978-3322, E-mail: janice.ewing@wichita.edu. *Application contact:* Dr. Kay Gibson, Graduate Coordinator, 316-978-3322, E-mail: kay.gibson@wichita.edu. Web site: http://www.wichita.edu/.

Widener University, School of Human Service Professions, Center for Education, Chester, PA 19013-5792. Offers adult education (M Ed); counseling in higher education (M Ed); counselor education (M Ed); early childhood education (M Ed); educational foundations (M Ed); educational leadership (M Ed); educational psychology (M Ed); elementary education (M Ed); English and language arts (M Ed); health education (M Ed); higher education leadership (Ed D); home and school visitor (M Ed); human sexuality (M Ed, PhD); mathematics education (M Ed); middle school education (M Ed); principalship (M Ed); reading and language arts (Ed D); reading education (M Ed); school administration (Ed D); science education (M Ed); social studies education (M Ed); special education (M Ed); technology education (M Ed). *Accreditation:* NCATE. Part-time and evening/weekend programs available. Terminal master's awarded for partial completion of doctoral program. *Degree requirements:* For doctorate, thesis/dissertation. *Entrance requirements:* For master's, minimum GPA of 2.5; for doctorate, GRE or MAT, minimum GPA of 2.0 (undergraduate), 3.5 (graduate). Electronic applications accepted. *Expenses:* Contact institution. *Faculty research:* Reading and cognition, adult education, technology education, educational leadership, special education.

Wilkes University, College of Graduate and Professional Studies, School of Education, Wilkes-Barre, PA 18766-0002. Offers art and science of teaching (MS Ed); classroom technology (MS Ed); early childhood literacy (MS Ed); educational computing (MS Ed); educational development and strategies (MS Ed); educational leadership (MS Ed); educational technology (Ed D); higher education administration (Ed D); instructional media (MS Ed); instructional technology (MS Ed); K-12 administration (Ed D); online teaching (MS Ed); reading (MS Ed); school business leadership (MS Ed); secondary education (MS Ed), including biology, chemistry, English, history, mathematics; special education (MS Ed); teaching English as a second language (MS Ed); twenty-first century teaching and learning (MS Ed). Part-time and evening/weekend programs available. Postbaccalaureate distance learning degree programs offered (minimal on-campus study). *Students:* 92 full-time (63 women), 2,005 part-time (1,459 women); includes 89 minority (23 Black or African American, non-Hispanic/Latino; 1 American Indian or Alaska Native, non-Hispanic/Latino; 14 Asian, non-Hispanic/Latino; 33 Hispanic/Latino; 1 Native Hawaiian or other Pacific Islander, non-Hispanic/Latino; 17 Two or more races, non-Hispanic/Latino), 6 international. Average age 33. In 2011, 1,150 master's, 3 doctorates awarded. *Entrance requirements:* Additional exam requirements/recommendations for international students: Required—TOEFL (minimum score 550 paper-based; 213 computer-based; 79 iBT). *Application deadline:* Applications are processed on a rolling basis. Application fee: $45. Electronic applications accepted. *Expenses:* Contact institution. *Financial support:* Federal Work-Study and unspecified assistantships available. Financial award application deadline: 3/1; financial award applicants required to submit FAFSA. *Unit head:* Dr. Michael Speziale, Dean, 570-408-4679, Fax: 570-408-4905, E-mail: michael.speziale@wilkes.edu. *Application contact:* Erin Sutzko, Director of Extended Learning, 570-408-4253, Fax: 570-408-7846, E-mail: erin.sutzko@wilkes.edu. Web site: http://www.wilkes.edu/pages/383.asp.

Worcester State University, Graduate Studies, Department of Education, Program in Early Childhood Education, Worcester, MA 01602-2597. Offers M Ed. Part-time and evening/weekend programs available. *Faculty:* 12 full-time (9 women), 22 part-time/adjunct (10 women). *Students:* 15 part-time (all women); includes 1 minority (Hispanic/Latino). Average age 33. 15 applicants, 67% accepted, 6 enrolled. In 2011, 8 master's awarded. *Degree requirements:* For master's, comprehensive exam (for some programs), thesis optional. *Entrance requirements:* For master's, GRE General Test or MAT, teaching certificate. Additional exam requirements/recommendations for international students: Required—TOEFL (minimum score 500 paper-based; 61 iBT). *Application deadline:* For fall admission, 6/15 for domestic and international students; for spring admission, 4/1 for domestic and international students. Applications are processed on a rolling basis. Application fee: $40. Electronic applications accepted. *Expenses:* Tuition, state resident: full-time $2700; part-time $150 per credit. Tuition, nonresident: full-time $2700; part-time $150 per credit. *Required fees:* $2016; $112 per credit. *Financial support:* Career-related internships or fieldwork, scholarships/grants, and unspecified assistantships available. Financial award application deadline: 3/1; financial award applicants required to submit FAFSA. *Unit head:* Dr. Carol Donnelly, Coordinator, 508-929-8667, Fax: 508-929-8164, E-mail: cdonnelly@worcester.edu. *Application contact:* Sara Grady, Assistant Dean of Graduate and Continuing Education, 508-929-8787, Fax: 508-929-8100, E-mail: sara.grady@worcester.edu.

Wright State University, School of Graduate Studies, College of Education and Human Services, Department of Teacher Education, Program in Early Childhood Education, Dayton, OH 45435. Offers M Ed, MA. *Accreditation:* NCATE. *Degree requirements:* For master's, thesis (for some programs). *Entrance requirements:* For master's, GRE General Test, MAT. Additional exam requirements/recommendations for international students: Required—TOEFL.

Xavier University, College of Social Sciences, Health and Education, School of Education, Department of Childhood Education and Literacy, Program in Montessori Education, Cincinnati, OH 45207. Offers M Ed. Part-time programs available. *Faculty:* 2 full-time (both women), 5 part-time/adjunct (4 women). *Students:* 24 full-time (21 women), 23 part-time (18 women); includes 7 minority (2 Black or African American, non-Hispanic/Latino; 1 Asian, non-Hispanic/Latino; 3 Hispanic/Latino; 1 Two or more races, non-Hispanic/Latino), 1 international. Average age 37. 15 applicants, 100% accepted, 8 enrolled. In 2011, 21 master's awarded. *Degree requirements:* For master's, comprehensive exam, research project or thesis. *Entrance requirements:* For master's, MAT or GRE. Additional exam requirements/recommendations for international students: Required—TOEFL (minimum score 550 paper-based; 213 computer-based; 79 iBT). *Application deadline:* Applications are processed on a rolling basis. Application fee: $35. Electronic applications accepted. *Expenses: Tuition:* Part-time $576 per credit hour. *Financial support:* In 2011–12, 27 students received support. Unspecified assistantships available. Financial award applicants required to submit FAFSA. *Faculty research:* First-year teacher retention, teaching efficacy of science educators, adolescents' literacy practices, family resiliency, preparing culturally responsive teachers. *Unit head:* Gina Taliaferro Lofquist, Director, 513-745-3424, Fax: 513-745-4378, E-mail: lofquistgm@xavier.edu. *Application contact:* Roger Bosse, Graduate Services Director, 513-745-3357, Fax: 513-745-1048, E-mail: bosse@xavier.edu. Web site: http://www.xavier.edu/montessori-grad/.

Youngstown State University, Graduate School, Beeghly College of Education, Department of Teacher Education, Program in Early Childhood Education, Youngstown, OH 44555-0001. Offers MS Ed. *Accreditation:* NCATE. Part-time and evening/weekend programs available. *Degree requirements:* For master's, comprehensive exam. *Entrance requirements:* For master's, GRE, MAT, or teaching certificate; minimum GPA of 2.7. Additional exam requirements/recommendations for international students: Required—TOEFL.

Elementary Education

Adelphi University, Ruth S. Ammon School of Education, Program in Childhood Education, Garden City, NY 11530-0701. Offers elementary teachers pre K-6 (MA); grades 1-6 (MA). Part-time and evening/weekend programs available. *Students:* 70 full-time (68 women), 28 part-time (23 women); includes 18 minority (10 Black or African American, non-Hispanic/Latino; 1 Asian, non-Hispanic/Latino; 5 Hispanic/Latino; 2 Two or more races, non-Hispanic/Latino). Average age 26. In 2011, 68 master's awarded. *Entrance requirements:* For master's, 2 letters of recommendation, resume. Additional exam requirements/recommendations for international students: Required—TOEFL (minimum score 550 paper-based; 213 computer-based; 80 iBT). *Application deadline:* For fall admission, 4/1 for international students; for spring admission, 11/1 for international students. Application fee: $50. Electronic applications accepted. *Expenses: Tuition:* Full-time $29,600; part-time $930 per credit. *Required fees:* $1100. *Financial support:* Fellowships, research assistantships with partial tuition reimbursements, teaching assistantships, career-related internships or fieldwork, Federal Work-Study, institutionally sponsored loans, and tuition waivers (full) available. Support available to part-time students. Financial award application deadline: 2/15; financial award applicants required to submit FAFSA. *Faculty research:* Diversity; parental involvement; teacher education; psychoanalytic understanding of racial formation; relationships between ideology, language, culture and individual subject formation. *Unit head:* Dr. Carl Mirra, Director, 516-877-4137, E-mail: mirra@adelphi.edu. *Application contact:* Christine Murphy, Director of Admissions, 516-877-3050, Fax: 516-877-3039, E-mail: graduateadmissions@adelphi.edu.

Alabama Agricultural and Mechanical University, School of Graduate Studies, School of Education, Area in Elementary and Early Childhood Education, Huntsville, AL 35811. Offers early childhood education (MS Ed, Ed S); elementary education (MS Ed, Ed S). *Accreditation:* NCATE. Evening/weekend programs available. *Degree requirements:* For master's, comprehensive exam; for Ed S, thesis. *Entrance requirements:* For master's, GRE General Test. Additional exam requirements/recommendations for international students: Required—TOEFL (minimum score 500 paper-based; 173 computer-based; 61 iBT). Electronic applications accepted. *Faculty research:* Multicultural education, learning styles, diagnostic-prescriptive instruction.

Alabama State University, Department of Curriculum and Instruction, Program in Elementary Education, Montgomery, AL 36101-0271. Offers M Ed, Ed S. Part-time programs available. *Students:* 9 full-time (7 women), 72 part-time (65 women); includes 79 minority (all Black or African American, non-Hispanic/Latino). Average age 33. 36 applicants, 72% accepted, 12 enrolled. In 2011, 1 master's awarded. *Degree requirements:* For master's, comprehensive exam, thesis optional; for Ed S, comprehensive exam, thesis. *Entrance requirements:* For master's, GRE General Test, MAT, graduate writing competency test; for Ed S, graduate writing competency test, GRE, MAT. Additional exam requirements/recommendations for international students: Required—TOEFL (minimum score 500 paper-based; 173 computer-based). *Application deadline:* For fall admission, 7/15 for domestic students; for spring admission, 12/15 for domestic students. Applications are processed on a rolling basis. Application fee: $10. *Unit head:* Dr. Daniel Lucas, Coordinator, 334-229-4167, Fax: 334-229-4904, E-mail: dlucas@alasu.edu. *Application contact:* Dr. Allen Stewart, Chair, 334-229-6882, Fax: 334-229-6904, E-mail: astewart@alasu.edu. Web site: http://www.alasu.edu/academics/colleges—departments/college-of-education/curriculum—instruction/degree-programs/elementary-education/index.aspx.

Alaska Pacific University, Graduate Programs, Education Department, Program in Teaching, Anchorage, AK 99508-4672. Offers teaching (K-8) (MAT). *Degree requirements:* For master's, research project. *Entrance requirements:* For master's, GRE or MAT, PRAXIS, minimum GPA of 3.0.

Albright College, Graduate Division, Reading, PA 19612-5234. Offers early childhood education (MS); elementary education (MS); English as a second language (MA); general education (MA); special education (MS). Part-time and evening/weekend programs available. *Degree requirements:* For master's, thesis. *Entrance requirements:* For master's, GRE General Test or MAT, minimum undergraduate GPA of 3.0, 2 letters of recommendation, interview. Additional exam requirements/recommendations for international students: Recommended—TOEFL (minimum score 525 paper-based; 197 computer-based). Electronic applications accepted.

Alcorn State University, School of Graduate Studies, School of Psychology and Education, Alcorn State, MS 39096-7500. Offers agricultural education (MS Ed); elementary education (MS Ed, Ed S); guidance and counseling (MS Ed); industrial education (MS Ed); secondary education (MS Ed), including health and physical education; special education (MS Ed). *Accreditation:* NCATE. *Degree requirements:* For master's, thesis optional.

American International College, School of Arts, Education and Sciences, Department of Education, Springfield, MA 01109-3189. Offers early childhood education (M Ed, CAGS); educational leadership and supervision (Ed D); elementary education (M Ed, CAGS); middle/secondary education (M Ed, CAGS); moderate disabilities (M Ed, CAGS); reading (M Ed, CAGS); school adjustment counseling (MA, CAGS); school administration (M Ed, CAGS); school guidance counseling (MA, CAGS); teaching (MA, MS); teaching and learning (Ed D). Part-time and evening/weekend programs available. Terminal master's awarded for partial completion of doctoral program. *Degree requirements:* For master's, comprehensive exam (for some programs), thesis (for some programs), practicum; for doctorate, comprehensive exam (for some programs), thesis/dissertation; for CAGS, practicum. *Entrance requirements:* For master's, minimum B-average in undergraduate course work; for doctorate, GRE General Test, interview. Additional exam requirements/recommendations for international students: Required—TOEFL. Electronic applications accepted.

American Public University System, AMU/APU Graduate Programs, Charles Town, WV 25414. Offers accounting (MBA, MS); administration and supervision (M Ed); criminal justice (MA); emergency and disaster management (MA); entrepreneurship (MBA); environmental policy and management (MS), including environmental planning, environmental sustainability, fish and wildlife management, general (MA, MS), global environmental management; finance (MBA); general (MBA); global business management (MBA); guidance and counseling (M Ed); history (MA), including American history, ancient and classical history, European history, global history, military and diplomatic history, public history; homeland security (MA); homeland security resource allocation (MBA); humanities (MA); information technology (MS), including digital forensics, enterprise software development, information assurance and security, IT project management; information technology management (MBA); intelligence studies (MA), including criminal intelligence, general (MA, MS), homeland security, intelligence analysis, intelligence collection, intelligence operations, terrorism studies; international relations and conflict resolution (MA), including comparative and security issues, conflict resolution, international and transnational security issues, peacekeeping; legal studies (MA); management (MA), including defense management, general (MA, MS), human resource management, organizational leadership, public administration, reverse logistics, strategic consulting; marketing (MBA); military history (MA), including American military history, American revolution, civil war, war since 1946, World War II; military studies (MA), including air warfare, asymmetrical warfare, joint warfare, land warfare, naval warfare, strategic leadership; national security studies (MA), including general (MA, MS), homeland security, regional security studies, security and intelligence analysis, terrorism studies; nonprofit management (MBA); political science (MA), including American politics and government, comparative government and development, public policy; psychology (MA); public administration (MA, MPA), including disaster management (MPA), environmental policy (MA), health policy (MPA), human resources (MPA), national security (MPA), organizational management (MPA), security management (MPA); public health (MA, MPH), including emergency management (MPH), environmental health (MPH), public administration (MA); reverse logistics management (MA); security management (MA); space studies (MS), including aerospace science, planetary science; sports and health sciences (MS); sports management (MS), including coaching theory and strategy, sports administration; teaching (M Ed), including curriculum and instruction for elementary teachers, elementary, elementary reading, English language learners, instructional leadership, online learning, secondary social sciences, special education; transportation and logistics management (MA), including maritime engineering management. Programs offered via distance learning only. Part-time and evening/weekend programs available. Postbaccalaureate distance learning degree programs offered (no on-campus study). *Faculty:* 445 full-time (241 women), 1,360 part-time/adjunct (617 women). *Students:* 688 full-time (338 women), 10,168 part-time (3,706 women); includes 3,130 minority (1,007 Black or African American, non-Hispanic/Latino; 103 American Indian or Alaska Native, non-Hispanic/Latino; 825 Asian, non-Hispanic/Latino; 810 Hispanic/Latino; 51 Native Hawaiian or other Pacific Islander, non-Hispanic/Latino; 334 Two or more races, non-Hispanic/Latino), 134 international. Average age 35. In 2011, 2,386 master's awarded. *Degree requirements:* For master's, comprehensive exam or practicum. *Entrance requirements:* For master's, official transcript showing earned bachelor's degree from institution accredited by recognized accrediting body. Additional exam requirements/recommendations for international students: Required—TOEFL (minimum score 550 paper-based; 213 computer-based), IELTS (minimum score 6.5). *Application deadline:* Applications are processed on a rolling basis. Application fee: $0. Electronic applications accepted. *Expenses: Tuition:* Part-time $325 per credit hour. *Financial support:* Applicants required to submit FAFSA. *Faculty research:* Military history, criminal justice, management performance, national security. *Unit head:* Dr. Karan Powell, Executive Vice President and Provost, 877-468-6268, Fax: 304-724-3780. *Application contact:* Terry Grant, Vice President of Enrollment Management, 877-468-6268, Fax: 304-724-3780, E-mail: info@apus.edu. Web site: http://www.apus.edu.

American University, College of Arts and Sciences, School of Education, Teaching, and Health, Program in Elementary Education, Washington, DC 20016-8001. Offers MAT, Certificate. *Students:* 5 full-time (all women), 40 part-time (35 women); includes 12 minority (11 Black or African American, non-Hispanic/Latino; 1 Two or more races, non-Hispanic/Latino). Average age 29. 26 applicants, 85% accepted, 14 enrolled. In 2011, 50 master's awarded. *Degree requirements:* For master's, comprehensive exam, PRAXIS II; for Certificate, PRAXIS II. *Entrance requirements:* For master's, GRE, PRAXIS I, minimum GPA of 3.0, 2 recommendations; for Certificate, PRAXIS I, bachelor's degree, two letters of recommendation. Additional exam requirements/recommendations for international students: Required—TOEFL (minimum score 600 paper-based; 250 computer-based; 100 iBT). *Application deadline:* For fall admission, 2/1 priority date for domestic students; for spring admission, 10/1 priority date for domestic students. Applications are processed on a rolling basis. Application fee: $80. *Expenses: Tuition:* Full-time $24,264; part-time $1348 per credit hour. *Required fees:* $430. Tuition and fees vary according to course load and program. *Financial support:* Research assistantships with partial tuition reimbursements available. Financial award application deadline: 2/1. *Unit head:* Sarah Irvine-Belson, Dean, 202-885-3727, Fax: 202-885-1187,

Elementary Education

E-mail: sirvine@american.edu. *Application contact:* Kathleen Clowery, Director, Graduate Admissions, 202-885-3621, Fax: 202-885-1505, E-mail: clowery@american.edu. Web site: http://www.american.edu/cas/seth/.

American University of Puerto Rico, Program in Education, Bayamón, PR 00960-2037. Offers art education (M Ed); elementary education 4-6 (M Ed); elementary education K-3 (M Ed); general science education (M Ed); physical education (M Ed); special education (M Ed). *Entrance requirements:* For master's, EXADEP, GRE, or MAT, 2 letters of recommendation, minimum GPA of 2.5. *Application deadline:* For fall admission, 8/1 for domestic students; for winter admission, 10/18 for domestic students; for spring admission, 3/15 for domestic students. Applications are processed on a rolling basis. Application fee: $50. *Expenses: Tuition:* Part-time $190 per credit. *Required fees:* $48.33 per credit. Tuition and fees vary according to course load and program. *Application contact:* Information Contact, 787-620-2040, E-mail: oficnaadmisiones@aupr.edu.

Andrews University, School of Graduate Studies, School of Education, Department of Teaching, Learning, and Curriculum, Berrien Springs, MI 49104. Offers curriculum and instruction (MA, Ed D, PhD, Ed S); elementary education (MAT); secondary education (MAT), including biology, education, English, English as a second language, French, history, physics; teacher education (MAT). *Students:* 15 full-time (10 women), 27 part-time (22 women); includes 18 minority (12 Black or African American, non-Hispanic/Latino; 1 Asian, non-Hispanic/Latino; 3 Hispanic/Latino; 1 Native Hawaiian or other Pacific Islander, non-Hispanic/Latino; 1 Two or more races, non-Hispanic/Latino), 10 international. Average age 42. 48 applicants, 48% accepted, 10 enrolled. In 2011, 5 master's, 2 doctorates, 2 other advanced degrees awarded. *Entrance requirements:* For master's, GRE Subject Test. Additional exam requirements/recommendations for international students: Required—TOEFL (minimum score 550 paper-based). *Application deadline:* For fall admission, 8/15 for domestic students. Applications are processed on a rolling basis. Application fee: $40. *Unit head:* Dr. Lee C. Davidson, Chair, 269-471-6364. *Application contact:* Carolyn Hurst, Supervisor of Graduate Admission, 800-253-2874, Fax: 269-471-6321, E-mail: graduate@andrews.edu.

Anna Maria College, Graduate Division, Program in Education, Paxton, MA 01612. Offers early childhood education (M Ed); education (CAGS); elementary education (M Ed); English language arts (M Ed); visual arts (M Ed). Part-time and evening/weekend programs available. *Entrance requirements:* For master's, bachelor's degree in liberal arts or sciences, minimum GPA of 3.0. Additional exam requirements/recommendations for international students: Required—TOEFL (minimum score 500 paper-based). Electronic applications accepted.

Antioch University New England, Graduate School, Department of Education, Keene, NH 03431-3552. Offers experienced educators (M Ed); integrated learning (M Ed), including early childhood education, elementary education; Waldorf teacher training (M Ed). *Degree requirements:* For master's, thesis (for some programs), internship. *Entrance requirements:* Additional exam requirements/recommendations for international students: Required—TOEFL (minimum score 600 paper-based; 250 computer-based). *Expenses:* Contact institution. *Faculty research:* Classroom and school restructuring, problem-based learning, Waldorf collaborative leadership, ecological literacy.

Antioch University New England, Graduate School, Department of Education, Integrated Learning Program, Concentration in Elementary Education, Keene, NH 03431-3552. Offers M Ed.

Appalachian State University, Cratis D. Williams Graduate School, Department of Curriculum and Instruction, Boone, NC 28608. Offers curriculum specialist (MA); educational media (MA); elementary education (MA); middle grades education (MA), including language arts, mathematics, science, social studies. *Accreditation:* NCATE. Part-time and evening/weekend programs available. Postbaccalaureate distance learning degree programs offered (no on-campus study). *Faculty:* 33 full-time (23 women), 5 part-time/adjunct (2 women). *Students:* 23 full-time (18 women), 110 part-time (90 women); includes 7 minority (4 Black or African American, non-Hispanic/Latino; 1 Asian, non-Hispanic/Latino; 2 Hispanic/Latino). 79 applicants, 94% accepted, 64 enrolled. In 2011, 87 master's awarded. *Degree requirements:* For master's, comprehensive exam, thesis or alternative. *Entrance requirements:* For master's, GRE General Test or MAT, 3 letters of recommendation. Additional exam requirements/recommendations for international students: Required—TOEFL (minimum score 570 paper-based; 230 computer-based; 79 iBT), IELTS (minimum score 6.5). *Application deadline:* For fall admission, 3/14 for domestic students, 2/1 for international students; for spring admission, 11/1 for domestic students, 7/1 for international students. Applications are processed on a rolling basis. Application fee: $55. Electronic applications accepted. *Expenses:* Tuition, state resident: full-time $4040; part-time $180 per semester hour. Tuition, nonresident: full-time $15,900; part-time $760 per semester hour. *Required fees:* $2500; $20 per semester hour. Tuition and fees vary according to campus/location. *Financial support:* In 2011–12, 6 teaching assistantships (averaging $8,000 per year) were awarded; fellowships, research assistantships, career-related internships or fieldwork, Federal Work-Study, scholarships/grants, and unspecified assistantships also available. Financial award application deadline: 4/1; financial award applicants required to submit FAFSA. *Faculty research:* Media literacy, elementary teaching, curriculum development, online learning environments. *Total annual research expenditures:* $480,000. *Unit head:* Dr. Michael Jacobson, Chairperson, 828-262-2224. *Application contact:* Sandy Krause, Director of Admissions and Recruiting, 828-262-2130, Fax: 828-262-2709, E-mail: krausesl@appstate.edu. Web site: http://www.ced.appstate.edu/departments/ci.

Arcadia University, Graduate Studies, Department of Education, Glenside, PA 19038-3295. Offers art education (M Ed); computer education (CAS); curriculum (CAS); curriculum studies (M Ed); early childhood education (M Ed, CAS), including individualized (M Ed), master teacher (M Ed), research in child development (M Ed); educational leadership (M Ed, Ed D, CAS); elementary education (M Ed, CAS); English education (MA Ed); environmental education (MA Ed, CAS); history education (MA Ed); instructional technology (M Ed); language arts (M Ed, CAS); library science (M Ed); mathematics education (M Ed, MA Ed, CAS); music education (MA Ed); psychology (MA Ed); reading (M Ed, CAS); science education (M Ed, CAS); secondary education (M Ed, CAS); special education (M Ed, Ed D, CAS); theater arts (MA Ed); written communication (MA Ed). *Accreditation:* NASAD. Part-time and evening/weekend programs available. Postbaccalaureate distance learning degree programs offered (minimal on-campus study). *Faculty:* 12 full-time (8 women), 38 part-time/adjunct (26 women). *Students:* 66 full-time (48 women), 590 part-time (477 women); includes 65 minority (53 Black or African American, non-Hispanic/Latino; 6 Asian, non-Hispanic/Latino; 3 Hispanic/Latino; 3 Two or more races, non-Hispanic/Latino), 4 international. Average age 36. In 2011, 229 master's, 5 doctorates awarded. *Application deadline:* Applications are processed on a rolling basis. Application fee: $50. Electronic applications accepted. *Expenses:* Contact institution. *Financial support:* Career-related internships or fieldwork, tuition waivers (partial), and unspecified assistantships available. *Unit head:* Dr. Steven P. Gulkus, Associate Professor, 215-572-2120, E-mail: gulkus@arcadia.edu. *Application contact:* 215-572-2925, Fax: 215-572-2126, E-mail: grad@arcadia.edu.

Argosy University, Atlanta, College of Education, Atlanta, GA 30328. Offers educational leadership (MAEd, Ed D, Ed S), including higher education administration (Ed D), K-12 education (Ed D); teaching and learning (MAEd, Ed D, Ed S), including education technology (Ed D), higher education (Ed D), K-12 education (Ed D).

See Close-Up on page 1017.

Argosy University, Chicago, College of Education, Chicago, IL 60601. Offers adult education and training (MA Ed); community college executive leadership (Ed D); educational leadership (MA Ed, Ed D, Ed S), including district leadership (Ed D), higher education administration (Ed D), K-12 education (Ed D); instructional leadership (Ed D, Ed S), including higher education (Ed D), K-12 education (Ed D). Postbaccalaureate distance learning degree programs offered (minimal on-campus study).

See Close-Up on page 769.

Argosy University, Denver, College of Education, Denver, CO 80231. Offers community college executive leadership (Ed D); educational leadership (MA Ed, Ed D), including higher education (Ed D), K-12 education (Ed D); instructional leadership (MA Ed, Ed D), including higher education administration (Ed D), K-12 education (Ed D).

See Close-Up on page 773.

Argosy University, Hawai`i, College of Education, Honolulu, HI 96813. Offers adult education and training (MAEd); educational leadership (Ed D), including higher education administration, K-12 education; instructional leadership (Ed D), including higher education, K-12 education; school psychology (MA).

See Close-Up on page 775.

Argosy University, Inland Empire, College of Education, San Bernardino, CA 92408. Offers community college executive leadership (Ed D); educational leadership (MA Ed, Ed D), including higher education administration (Ed D), K-12 education (Ed D); instructional leadership (MA Ed, Ed D), including higher education (Ed D), K-12 education (Ed D), multiple subject teacher preparation (MA Ed), single subject teacher preparation (MA Ed).

See Close-Up on page 1019.

Argosy University, Los Angeles, College of Education, Santa Monica, CA 90045. Offers community college executive leadership (Ed D); educational leadership (MA Ed, Ed D), including higher education administration (Ed D), K-12 education (Ed D); instructional leadership (MA Ed, Ed D), including higher education (Ed D), K-12 education (Ed D), multiple subject teacher preparation (MA Ed), single subject teacher preparation (MA Ed).

See Close-Up on page 777.

Argosy University, Nashville, College of Education, Program in Educational Leadership, Nashville, TN 37214. Offers educational leadership (MA Ed, Ed S); higher education administration (Ed D); K-12 education (Ed D).

See Close-Up on page 1021.

Argosy University, Nashville, College of Education, Program in Instructional Leadership, Nashville, TN 37214. Offers education technology (Ed D); higher education administration (Ed D); instructional leadership (MA Ed, Ed S); K-12 education (Ed D).

See Close-Up on page 1021.

Argosy University, Orange County, College of Education, Orange, CA 92868. Offers community college executive leadership (Ed D); educational leadership (MA Ed, Ed D), including higher education administration (Ed D), K-12 education (Ed D); instructional leadership (MA Ed, Ed D), including education technology (Ed D), higher education (Ed D), K-12 education (Ed D), multiple subject teacher preparation (MA Ed), single subject teacher preparation (MA Ed).

See Close-Up on page 779.

Argosy University, Phoenix, College of Education, Phoenix, AZ 85021. Offers adult education and training (MA Ed); advanced educational administration (Ed D, Ed S); community college executive leadership (Ed D); educational administration (MA Ed); educational leadership (MA Ed, Ed D, Ed S), including education technology (Ed D), higher education administration (Ed D), K-12 education (Ed D); higher and postsecondary education (MA Ed); initial educational administration (Ed D, Ed S); school psychology (MA); teaching and learning (MA Ed, Ed D, Ed S), including education technology (Ed D), higher education (Ed D), K-12 education (Ed D).

See Close-Up on page 781.

Argosy University, San Diego, College of Education, San Diego, CA 92108. Offers community college executive leadership (Ed D); educational leadership (MA Ed, Ed D), including higher education administration (Ed D), K-12 education (Ed D); instructional leadership (MA Ed, Ed D), including higher education (Ed D), K-12 education (Ed D).

See Close-Up on page 785.

Argosy University, San Francisco Bay Area, College of Education, Alameda, CA 94501. Offers community college executive leadership (Ed D); educational leadership (MA Ed, Ed D), including education technology (Ed D), higher education administration (Ed D), K-12 education (Ed D); instructional leadership (MA Ed, Ed D), including education technology (Ed D), higher education (Ed D), K-12 education (Ed D), multiple subject teacher preparation (MA Ed), single subject teacher preparation (MA Ed).

See Close-Up on page 787.

Argosy University, Sarasota, College of Education, Sarasota, FL 34235. Offers community college executive leadership (Ed D); educational leadership (MA Ed, Ed D, Ed S), including higher education administration (Ed D), K-12 education (Ed D); school counseling (MA, Ed S); school psychology (MA); teaching and learning (MA Ed, Ed D, Ed S), including education technology (Ed D), higher education (Ed D), K-12 education (Ed D).

See Close-Up on page 789.

Argosy University, Schaumburg, College of Education, Schaumburg, IL 60173-5403. Offers community college executive leadership (Ed D); educational leadership (MA Ed, Ed D, Ed S), including district leadership (Ed D), higher education administration (Ed D), K-12 education (Ed D); instructional leadership (Ed D, Ed S), including higher education (Ed D), K-12 education (Ed D).

See Close-Up on page 791.

Argosy University, Seattle, College of Education, Seattle, WA 98121. Offers adult education and training (MA Ed); community college executive leadership (Ed D); educational leadership (MA Ed, Ed D), including higher education administration (Ed D), K-12 education (Ed D); higher and postsecondary education (MA Ed); instructional leadership (MA Ed, Ed D), including education technology (Ed D), higher education (Ed D), K-12 education (Ed D).

See Close-Up on page 793.

Argosy University, Tampa, College of Education, Tampa, FL 33607. Offers community college executive leadership (Ed D); educational leadership (MA Ed, Ed D, Ed S), including higher education administration (Ed D), K-12 education (Ed D); school counseling (MA); teaching and learning (MA Ed, Ed D, Ed S), including higher education (Ed D), K-12 education (Ed D).

See Close-Up on page 795.

Argosy University, Twin Cities, College of Education, Eagan, MN 55121. Offers advanced educational administration (Ed D, Ed S); educational leadership (MA Ed, Ed D, Ed S), including higher education administration (Ed D), K-12 education (Ed D); higher and postsecondary education (MA Ed); initial educational administration (Ed D, Ed S); instructional leadership (MA Ed, Ed D, Ed S), including education technology (Ed D), higher education (Ed D), K-12 education (Ed D).

See Close-Up on page 797.

Argosy University, Washington DC, College of Education, Arlington, VA 22209. Offers community college executive leadership (Ed D); educational leadership (MA Ed, Ed D, Ed S), including higher education administration (Ed D), K-12 education (Ed D); instructional leadership (MA Ed, Ed D, Ed S), including higher education (Ed D), K-12 education (Ed D).

See Close-Up on page 799.

Arizona State University, Mary Lou Fulton Teachers College, Program in Curriculum and Instruction, Phoenix, AZ 85069. Offers curriculum and instruction (M Ed, MA, PhD); elementary education (M Ed); physical education (MPE); secondary education (M Ed). Part-time and evening/weekend programs available. Postbaccalaureate distance learning degree programs offered (minimal on-campus study). Terminal master's awarded for partial completion of doctoral program. *Degree requirements:* For master's, thesis or alternative, applied project, interactive Program of Study (iPOS) submitted before completing 50 percent of required credit hours; for doctorate, comprehensive exam, thesis/dissertation, interactive Program of Study (iPOS) submitted before completing 50 percent of required credit hours. *Entrance requirements:* For master's, GRE or GMAT (for some programs), minimum GPA of 3.0 or equivalent in last 2 years of work leading to bachelor's degree, 3 letters of recommendation, personal statement describing research and career goals, curriculum vitae or resume, IVP fingerprint clearance card (for those seeking Arizona certification); for doctorate, GRE or GMAT (depending on program), minimum GPA of 3.0 or equivalent in last 2 years of work leading to bachelor's degree, 3 letters of recommendation, personal statement describing research and career goals, curriculum vitae or resume. Additional exam requirements/recommendations for international students: Required—TOEFL, IELTS, or Pearson Test of English. Electronic applications accepted. *Expenses:* Contact institution. *Faculty research:* Early childhood, media and computers, elementary education, secondary education, English education, bilingual education, language and literacy, science education, engineering education, exercise and wellness education.

Arkansas State University, Graduate School, College of Education, Department of Teacher Education, Jonesboro, State University, AR 72467. Offers early childhood education (MAT, MSE); early childhood services (MS); middle level education (MAT, MSE); reading (MSE, Ed S). *Accreditation:* NCATE. Part-time programs available. *Faculty:* 16 full-time (11 women). *Students:* 47 full-time (44 women), 81 part-time (76 women); includes 52 minority (49 Black or African American, non-Hispanic/Latino; 1 Hispanic/Latino; 2 Two or more races, non-Hispanic/Latino), 2 international. Average age 33. 114 applicants, 58% accepted, 57 enrolled. In 2011, 35 master's awarded. *Degree requirements:* For master's, comprehensive exam, thesis or alternative; for Ed S, comprehensive exam. *Entrance requirements:* For master's, GRE General Test or MAT, appropriate bachelor's degree, official transcripts, immunization records; for Ed S, GRE General Test or MAT, interview, master's degree, official transcript, immunization records. Additional exam requirements/recommendations for international students: Required—TOEFL (minimum score 550 paper-based; 213 computer-based; 79 iBT), IELTS (minimum score 6), Pearson Test of English Academic (minimum score 56). *Application deadline:* For fall admission, 7/1 for domestic and international students; for spring admission, 11/15 for domestic students, 11/14 for international students. Applications are processed on a rolling basis. Application fee: $30 ($40 for international students). Electronic applications accepted. *Expenses:* Tuition, state resident: full-time $4044; part-time $225 per credit hour. Tuition, nonresident: full-time $8087; part-time $449 per credit hour. *Required fees:* $936; $52 per credit hour. $25 per term. One-time fee: $30. Tuition and fees vary according to course load and program. *Financial support:* In 2011–12, 5 students received support. Teaching assistantships, career-related internships or fieldwork, scholarships/grants, and unspecified assistantships available. Financial award application deadline: 7/1; financial award applicants required to submit FAFSA. *Unit head:* Dr. Lina Owens, Chair, 870-972-3059, Fax: 870-972-3344, E-mail: llowens@astate.edu. *Application contact:* Dr. Andrew Sustich, Dean of the Graduate School, 870-972-3029, Fax: 870-972-3857, E-mail: sustich@astate.edu. Web site: http://www.astate.edu/a/education/teachered/.

Arkansas Tech University, Center for Leadership and Learning, College of Education, Russellville, AR 72801. Offers college student personnel (MS); educational leadership (Ed S); elementary education (M Ed); instructional improvement (M Ed); instructional technology (M Ed); physical education (M Ed); school counseling and leadership (M Ed); teaching (MAT). *Accreditation:* NCATE. Part-time and evening/weekend programs available. Postbaccalaureate distance learning degree programs offered (no on-campus study). *Students:* 70 full-time (44 women), 247 part-time (189 women); includes 57 minority (38 Black or African American, non-Hispanic/Latino; 1 American Indian or Alaska Native, non-Hispanic/Latino; 8 Asian, non-Hispanic/Latino; 4 Hispanic/Latino; 6 Two or more races, non-Hispanic/Latino), 3 international. Average age 31. In 2011, 58 master's awarded. *Degree requirements:* For master's, comprehensive exam, thesis optional, action research project. *Entrance requirements:* Additional exam requirements/recommendations for international students: Required—TOEFL (minimum score 550 paper-based; 213 computer-based; 79 iBT), IELTS (minimum score 6.5). *Application deadline:* For fall admission, 3/1 priority date for domestic students, 5/1 for international students; for spring admission, 10/1 priority date for domestic students, 10/1 for international students. Applications are processed on a rolling basis. Application fee: $25 ($75 for international students). Electronic applications accepted. *Expenses:* Tuition, state resident: full-time $4968; part-time $207 per credit hour. Tuition, nonresident: full-time $9936; part-time $414 per credit hour. *Required fees:* $375 per semester. Tuition and fees vary according to course load. *Financial support:* In 2011–12, teaching assistantships with full tuition reimbursements (averaging $4,800 per year) were awarded; research assistantships with full tuition reimbursements, career-related internships or fieldwork, Federal Work-Study, scholarships/grants, health care benefits, and unspecified assistantships also available. Support available to part-time students. Financial award application deadline: 4/15; financial award applicants required to submit FAFSA. *Unit head:* Dr. Eldon G. Clary, Jr., Dean, 479-968-0350, Fax: 479-968-0350, E-mail: eclary@atu.edu. *Application contact:* Dr. Mary B. Gunter, Dean of Graduate College, 479-968-0398, Fax: 479-964-0542, E-mail: gradcollege@atu.edu. Web site: http://www.atu.edu/education/.

Armstrong Atlantic State University, School of Graduate Studies, Program in Education, Savannah, GA 31419-1997. Offers adult education (M Ed); curriculum and instruction (M Ed); early childhood education (M Ed); education (M Ed); elementary education (M Ed); middle grades education (M Ed); secondary education (M Ed), including business education, English education, mathematics education, science education, social science education; special education (M Ed), including behavioral disorders, learning disabilities, speech-language pathology. *Accreditation:* NCATE. Part-time and evening/weekend programs available. Postbaccalaureate distance learning degree programs offered (minimal on-campus study). *Faculty:* 33 full-time (23 women), 3 part-time/adjunct (2 women). *Students:* 97 full-time (91 women), 262 part-time (227 women); includes 83 minority (70 Black or African American, non-Hispanic/Latino; 3 Asian, non-Hispanic/Latino; 8 Hispanic/Latino; 2 Two or more races, non-Hispanic/Latino), 5 international. Average age 34. 169 applicants, 69% accepted, 102 enrolled. In 2011, 227 master's awarded. *Degree requirements:* For master's, comprehensive exam, portfolio. *Entrance requirements:* For master's, GRE General Test or MAT, minimum GPA of 2.5, letters of recommendation. Additional exam requirements/recommendations for international students: Required—TOEFL (minimum score 523 paper-based; 193 computer-based). *Application deadline:* For fall admission, 7/1 priority date for domestic students, 5/1 for international students; for spring admission, 11/15 priority date for domestic students, 9/15 for international students. Applications are processed on a rolling basis. Application fee: $30. Electronic applications accepted. *Expenses:* Tuition, state resident: full-time $3402. Tuition, nonresident: full-time $12,636. *Financial support:* In 2011–12, research assistantships with full tuition reimbursements (averaging $5,000 per year) were awarded; career-related internships or fieldwork, Federal Work-Study, scholarships/grants, and unspecified assistantships also available. Support available to part-time students. Financial award applicants required to submit FAFSA. *Unit head:* Dr. Patricia Wachholz, Dean, College of Education, 912-344-2797, E-mail: patricia.wachholz@armstrong.edu. *Application contact:* Jill Bell, Director, Graduate Enrollment Services, 912-344-2798, Fax: 912-344-3488, E-mail: graduate@armstrong.edu. Web site: http://www.armstrong.edu/Education/coe_deans_office/coe_education_welcome.

Auburn University, Graduate School, College of Education, Department of Curriculum and Teaching, Auburn University, AL 36849. Offers business education (M Ed, MS, PhD); early childhood education (M Ed, MS, PhD, Ed S); elementary education (M Ed, MS, PhD, Ed S); foreign languages (M Ed, MS); music education (M Ed, MS, PhD, Ed S); postsecondary education (PhD); reading education (PhD, Ed S); secondary education (M Ed, MS, PhD, Ed S), including English language arts, mathematics, science, social studies. *Accreditation:* NASM (one or more programs are accredited); NCATE. Part-time programs available. *Faculty:* 22 full-time (17 women), 3 part-time/adjunct (all women). *Students:* 80 full-time (58 women), 181 part-time (126 women); includes 42 minority (28 Black or African American, non-Hispanic/Latino; 7 Asian, non-Hispanic/Latino; 7 Hispanic/Latino). Average age 34. 184 applicants, 53% accepted, 60 enrolled. In 2011, 77 master's, 10 doctorates, 35 other advanced degrees awarded. *Degree requirements:* For master's, thesis (for some programs); for doctorate, thesis/dissertation; for Ed S, field project. *Entrance requirements:* For master's, doctorate, and Ed S, GRE General Test. *Application deadline:* For fall admission, 7/7 for domestic students; for spring admission, 11/24 for domestic students. Applications are processed on a rolling basis. Application fee: $50 ($60 for international students). Electronic applications accepted. *Expenses:* Tuition, state resident: full-time $7290; part-time $405 per credit hour. Tuition, nonresident: full-time $21,870; part-time $1215 per credit hour. *International tuition:* $22,000 full-time. *Required fees:* $1402. *Financial support:* Fellowships, teaching assistantships, career-related internships or fieldwork, and Federal Work-Study available. Support available to part-time students. Financial award application deadline: 3/15; financial award applicants required to submit FAFSA. *Faculty research:* Emerging literacy, reading attitudes, music for at-risk youth, portfolio assessment. *Unit head:* Dr. Kimberly Walls, Head, 334-844-4434. *Application contact:* Dr. George Flowers, Dean of the Graduate School, 334-844-2125. Web site: http://education.auburn.edu/academic_departments/curr/.

Auburn University Montgomery, School of Education, Department of Early Childhood, Elementary, and Reading Education, Montgomery, AL 36124-4023. Offers early childhood education (M Ed, Ed S); elementary education (M Ed, Ed S); reading education (M Ed, Ed S). *Accreditation:* NCATE. Part-time and evening/weekend programs available. *Degree requirements:* For master's and Ed S, comprehensive exam. *Entrance requirements:* For master's, GRE General Test or MAT, certification, BS in teaching; for Ed S, GRE General Test or MAT, certification. Electronic applications accepted. *Expenses:* Tuition, state resident: full-time $5076. Tuition, nonresident: full-time $15,228.

Aurora University, College of Education, Aurora, IL 60506-4892. Offers curriculum and instruction (MA, Ed D); early childhood and special education (MA); education (MAT), including elementary certification; education and administration (Ed D); educational leadership (MEL); educational technology (MATL); reading instruction (MA); special education (MA). *Accreditation:* NCATE. Part-time and evening/weekend programs available. *Degree requirements:* For doctorate, comprehensive exam, thesis/dissertation. *Entrance requirements:* For master's, 2 years of teaching experience, valid teaching certificate. Additional exam requirements/recommendations for international students: Required—TOEFL (minimum score 550 paper-based; 213 computer-based). Electronic applications accepted. *Expenses:* Contact institution.

Austin College, Program in Education, Sherman, TX 75090-4400. Offers art education (MA); elementary education (MA); middle school education (MA); music education (MA); physical education and coaching (MA); secondary education (MA); theatre education (MA). Part-time programs available. *Faculty:* 5 full-time (4 women). *Students:* 21 full-time (13 women), 2 part-time (both women). Average age 23. In 2011, 24 master's awarded. *Degree requirements:* For master's, one foreign language, thesis or alternative. *Entrance requirements:* For master's, Texas Academic Skills Program Test. *Application deadline:* For fall admission, 5/1 priority date for domestic students; for spring admission, 1/15 priority date for domestic students. Applications are processed on a rolling basis. Application fee: $35. Electronic applications accepted. *Expenses: Tuition:* Full-time $38,445. *Required fees:* $160. *Financial support:* Career-related internships or fieldwork, Federal Work-Study, scholarships/grants, and unspecified assistantships available. Support available to part-time students. Financial award application deadline: 4/1; financial award applicants required to submit FAFSA. *Unit head:* Dr. Barbara Sylvester, Director of Teaching Program, 903-813-2327, E-mail: bsylvester@austincollege.edu. *Application contact:* Dr. Barbara Sylvester, Director of Teaching Program, 903-813-2327, E-mail: bsylvester@austincollege.edu. Web site: http://www.austincollege.edu/.

Austin Peay State University, College of Graduate Studies, College of Education, Department of Educational Specialties, Clarksville, TN 37044. Offers administration and supervision (Ed S); curriculum and instruction (MA Ed); education leadership (MA Ed); elementary education (Ed S); secondary education (Ed S); special education (MA Ed). Part-time and evening/weekend programs available. Postbaccalaureate distance learning degree programs offered. *Faculty:* 7 full-time (4 women), 4 part-time/adjunct (3 women). *Students:* 6 full-time (4 women), 86 part-time (66 women); includes 11 minority (6 Black or African American, non-Hispanic/Latino; 1 American Indian or Alaska Native, non-Hispanic/Latino; 4 Hispanic/Latino). Average age 37. 33 applicants, 100% accepted, 23 enrolled. In 2011, 32 master's, 7 Ed Ss awarded. *Degree requirements:* For master's, comprehensive exam, thesis optional. *Entrance requirements:* For master's, GRE General Test, 3 letters of recommendation, minimum undergraduate GPA of 2.75. Additional exam requirements/recommendations for international students: Required—TOEFL (minimum score 500 paper-based; 173 computer-based). *Application deadline:* For fall admission, 8/1 priority date for domestic students. Applications are processed on a rolling basis. Application fee: $25. Electronic applications accepted. *Expenses:* Tuition, state resident: part-time $350 per credit hour. Tuition, nonresident: full-time $20,644; part-time $971 per credit hour. *Required fees:* $1224; $61.20 per credit hour. *Financial support:* Career-related internships or fieldwork, Federal Work-Study, institutionally sponsored loans, scholarships/grants, and unspecified assistantships available. Support available to part-time students. Financial award application deadline: 3/1; financial award applicants required to submit FAFSA. *Unit head:* Dr. Moniqueka Gold, Chair, 931-221-7696, Fax: 931-221-1292, E-mail: goldm@apsu.edu. *Application contact:* Kendra Bryant, Graduate Admissions, 800-844-2778, Fax: 931-221-6188, E-mail: admissionsweb@apsu.edu.

Austin Peay State University, College of Graduate Studies, College of Education, Department of Teaching and Learning, Clarksville, TN 37044. Offers elementary education K-6 (MAT); reading (MA Ed); secondary education 7-12 (MAT); special education K-12 (MAT). Part-time and evening/weekend programs available. Postbaccalaureate distance learning degree programs offered. *Faculty:* 14 full-time (11 women), 3 part-time/adjunct (2 women). *Students:* 84 full-time (67 women), 97 part-time (81 women); includes 27 minority (12 Black or African American, non-Hispanic/Latino; 2 American Indian or Alaska Native, non-Hispanic/Latino; 2 Asian, non-Hispanic/Latino; 4 Hispanic/Latino; 1 Native Hawaiian or other Pacific Islander, non-Hispanic/Latino; 6 Two or more races, non-Hispanic/Latino). Average age 33. 61 applicants, 98% accepted, 51 enrolled. In 2011, 55 master's awarded. *Degree requirements:* For master's, comprehensive exam, thesis optional. *Entrance requirements:* For master's, GRE General Test, 3 letters of recommendation, minimum undergraduate GPA of 2.75. Additional exam requirements/recommendations for international students: Required—TOEFL (minimum score 500 paper-based; 173 computer-based). *Application deadline:* For fall admission, 8/1 priority date for domestic students. Applications are processed on a rolling basis. Application fee: $25. Electronic applications accepted. *Expenses:* Tuition, state resident: part-time $350 per credit hour. Tuition, nonresident: full-time $20,644; part-time $971 per credit hour. *Required fees:* $1224; $61.20 per credit hour. *Financial support:* Career-related internships or fieldwork, Federal Work-Study, institutionally sponsored loans, scholarships/grants, and unspecified assistantships available. Support available to part-time students. Financial award application deadline: 3/1; financial award applicants required to submit FAFSA. *Unit head:* Dr. Rebecca McMahan, Chair, 931-221-7513, Fax: 931-221-1292, E-mail: mcmahanb@apsu.edu. *Application contact:* Kendra Bryant, Graduate Admissions, 800-844-2778, Fax: 931-221-6188, E-mail: admissionsweb@apsu.edu.

Ball State University, Graduate School, Teachers College, Department of Elementary Education, Muncie, IN 47306-1099. Offers MAE, Ed D, PhD. *Accreditation:* NCATE. *Faculty:* 19 full-time (15 women). *Students:* 32 full-time (31 women), 433 part-time (400 women); includes 12 minority (6 Black or African American, non-Hispanic/Latino; 1 American Indian or Alaska Native, non-Hispanic/Latino; 2 Asian, non-Hispanic/Latino; 2 Hispanic/Latino; 1 Two or more races, non-Hispanic/Latino). Average age 25. 82 applicants, 80% accepted, 47 enrolled. In 2011, 150 master's, 3 doctorates awarded. *Degree requirements:* For doctorate, thesis/dissertation. *Entrance requirements:* For doctorate, GRE General Test, interview, minimum graduate GPA of 3.2. Application fee: $50. Tuition and fees vary according to program and reciprocity agreements. *Financial support:* In 2011–12, 10 students received support, including 4 teaching assistantships (averaging $6,762 per year); research assistantships with full tuition reimbursements available also available. Financial award application deadline: 3/1. *Unit head:* Dr. Thomas Schroeder, Chairperson, 765-285-8560, Fax: 765-285-8793. *Application contact:* Harold Roberts, Associate Provost for Research and Dean of the Graduate School, 765-285-9046, E-mail: hroberts@bsu.edu. Web site: http://www.bsu.edu/elementaryeducation/.

Bank Street College of Education, Graduate School, Program in Elementary/Childhood Education, New York, NY 10025. Offers early childhood and elementary/childhood education (MS Ed); elementary/childhood education (MS Ed). *Students:* 39 full-time (29 women), 77 part-time (65 women); includes 23 minority (7 Black or African American, non-Hispanic/Latino; 8 Asian, non-Hispanic/Latino; 5 Hispanic/Latino; 1 Native Hawaiian or other Pacific Islander, non-Hispanic/Latino; 2 Two or more races, non-Hispanic/Latino), 2 international. Average age 28. 73 applicants, 84% accepted, 40 enrolled. In 2011, 36 master's awarded. *Degree requirements:* For master's, thesis. *Entrance requirements:* For master's, interview, essays. Additional exam requirements/recommendations for international students: Required—TOEFL (minimum score 600 paper-based; 250 computer-based; 100 iBT), IELTS (minimum score 7). *Application deadline:* For fall admission, 2/15 priority date for domestic students, 2/15 for international students; for spring admission, 11/1 priority date for domestic students, 11/1 for international students. Applications are processed on a rolling basis. Application fee: $65. Electronic applications accepted. *Expenses: Required fees:* $1240 per credit. $100 per term. One-time fee: $250 part-time. *Financial support:* Career-related internships or fieldwork, Federal Work-Study, scholarships/grants, and unspecified assistantships available. Support available to part-time students. Financial award application deadline: 4/15; financial award applicants required to submit FAFSA. *Faculty research:* Social studies in the elementary grades, urban education, experiential learning, child-centered classrooms. *Unit head:* Dr. Peggy McNamara, Chairperson, 212-875-4586, Fax: 212-875-4753, E-mail: mam@bankstreet.edu. *Application contact:* Seena Berg, Associate Director of Graduate Admissions, 212-875-4402, Fax: 212-875-4678, E-mail: sberg@bankstreet.edu. Web site: http://bankstreet.edu/graduate-school/academics/programs/general-teacher-education-programs-overview/.

Barry University, School of Education, Program in Curriculum and Instruction, Miami Shores, FL 33161-6695. Offers accomplished teacher (Ed S); culture, language and literacy (TESOL) (PhD); curriculum evaluation and research (PhD); early childhood (Ed S); early childhood education (PhD); elementary (Ed S); elementary education (PhD); ESOL (Ed S); gifted (Ed S); Montessori (Ed S); PKP/elementary (Ed S); reading (Ed S); reading, language and cognition (PhD). *Entrance requirements:* For doctorate, GRE, minimum GPA of 3.25.

Barry University, School of Education, Program in Elementary Education, Miami Shores, FL 33161-6695. Offers elementary education (MS); elementary education/ESOL (MS). Part-time and evening/weekend programs available. *Degree requirements:* For master's, comprehensive exam, practicum. *Entrance requirements:* For master's, GRE General Test or MAT, minimum GPA of 3.0. Electronic applications accepted.

Bayamón Central University, Graduate Programs, Program in Education, Bayamón, PR 00960-1725. Offers administration and supervision (MA Ed); commercial education (MA Ed); elementary education (K–3) (MA Ed); family counseling (Graduate Certificate); guidance and counseling (MA Ed); pre-elementary teacher (MA Ed); rehabilitation counseling (MA Ed); special education (MA Ed), including attention deficit disorder, education of the autistic, learning disabilities. Part-time and evening/weekend programs available. *Degree requirements:* For master's, comprehensive exam. *Entrance requirements:* For master's, EXADEP, bachelor's degree in education or related field.

Belhaven University, School of Education, Jackson, MS 39202-1789. Offers elementary education (M Ed, MAT); secondary education (M Ed, MAT). Part-time and evening/weekend programs available. *Faculty:* 7 full-time (6 women), 15 part-time/adjunct (10 women). *Students:* 167 full-time (133 women), 124 part-time (97 women); includes 205 minority (193 Black or African American, non-Hispanic/Latino; 7 Hispanic/Latino; 5 Two or more races, non-Hispanic/Latino). Average age 33. 446 applicants, 64% accepted, 210 enrolled. In 2011, 94 master's awarded. *Degree requirements:* For master's, comprehensive exam, portfolio. *Entrance requirements:* For master's, PRAXIS I and II, minimum GPA of 2.8. *Application deadline:* Applications are processed on a rolling basis. Application fee: $25. Electronic applications accepted. *Expenses: Tuition:* Part-time $545 per contact hour. *Financial support:* Federal Work-Study, scholarships/grants, tuition waivers (full), and unspecified assistantships available. Support available to part-time students. Financial award applicants required to submit FAFSA. *Unit head:* Dr. Sandra L. Rasberry, Dean, 601-968-8703, Fax: 601-974-6461, E-mail: srasberry@belhaven.edu. *Application contact:* Jenny Mixon, Director of Graduate and Online Admission, 601-968-8947, Fax: 601-968-5953, E-mail: gradadmission@belhaven.edu. Web site: http://graduateed.belhaven.edu.

Belmont University, College of Arts and Sciences, Department of Education, Nashville, TN 37212-3757. Offers education (M Ed); elementary education (MAT), including early childhood education, elementary education, language arts education; English (MAT); history (MAT); mathematics (MAT); middle grade education (MAT); science (MAT); secondary education (MAT); special education (MAT); sports administration (MSA). *Accreditation:* NCATE. Part-time and evening/weekend programs available. *Faculty:* 11 full-time (8 women), 23 part-time/adjunct (12 women). *Students:* 83 full-time (77 women), 205 part-time (162 women); includes 50 minority (36 Black or African American, non-Hispanic/Latino; 1 American Indian or Alaska Native, non-Hispanic/Latino; 1 Asian, non-Hispanic/Latino; 7 Hispanic/Latino; 5 Two or more races, non-Hispanic/Latino), 2 international. Average age 30. 83 applicants, 67% accepted, 35 enrolled. In 2011, 169 master's awarded. *Degree requirements:* For master's, thesis (for some programs). *Entrance requirements:* For master's, MAT or GRE and/or GMAT, minimum GPA of 2.75. Additional exam requirements/recommendations for international students: Required—TOEFL. *Application deadline:* For fall admission, 8/1 priority date for domestic students, 6/1 for international students; for spring admission, 12/1 priority date for domestic students, 10/1 for international students. Applications are processed on a rolling basis. Application fee: $50. *Expenses:* Contact institution. *Financial support:* In 2011–12, 30 students received support. Fellowships with partial tuition reimbursements available, teaching assistantships with partial tuition reimbursements available, institutionally sponsored loans, tuition waivers (partial), and unspecified assistantships available. Financial award application deadline: 4/15; financial award applicants required to submit FAFSA. *Faculty research:* Improving secondary literacy, Montessori, classroom management strategies, teacher residency programs, online professional development, mentoring, leadership, faculty development. *Total annual research expenditures:* $2,500. *Unit head:* Dr. Cynthia R. Watkins, Associate Dean, 615-460-6053, Fax: 615-460-5556, E-mail: cynthia.watkins@belmont.edu. *Application contact:* Andrea McClain, Admission/Licensure Officer, 615-460-5483, Fax: 615-460-5556, E-mail: andrea.mcclain@belmont.edu.

Benedictine University, Graduate Programs, Program in Education, Lisle, IL 60532-0900. Offers curriculum and instruction and collaborative teaching (M Ed); elementary education (MA Ed); leadership and administration (M Ed); reading and literacy (M Ed); secondary education (MA Ed); special education (MA Ed). Part-time and evening/weekend programs available. *Faculty:* 4 full-time (2 women), 52 part-time/adjunct (30 women). *Students:* 178 full-time (157 women), 239 part-time (211 women); includes 41 minority (29 Black or African American, non-Hispanic/Latino; 4 Asian, non-Hispanic/Latino; 8 Hispanic/Latino), 2 international. Average age 33. 177 applicants, 44% accepted, 68 enrolled. In 2011, 278 master's awarded. *Degree requirements:* For master's, comprehensive exam, thesis (for some programs). *Entrance requirements:* For master's, GRE or MAT. Additional exam requirements/recommendations for international students: Required—TOEFL (minimum score 550 paper-based; 213 computer-based). *Application deadline:* For fall admission, 9/1 for domestic students; for winter admission, 12/1 for domestic students; for spring admission, 2/15 for domestic students. Applications are processed on a rolling basis. Application fee: $40. Electronic applications accepted. *Expenses:* Contact institution. *Financial support:* Career-related internships or fieldwork and health care benefits available. Support available to part-time students. *Unit head:* MeShelda Jackson, Director, 630-829-6282, E-mail: mjackson@ben.edu. *Application contact:* Kari Gibbons, Associate Vice President, Enrollment Center, 630-829-6200, Fax: 630-829-6584, E-mail: kgibbons@ben.edu.

Benedictine University at Springfield, Program in Elementary Education, Springfield, IL 62702. Offers MA Ed. *Degree requirements:* For master's, student teaching. *Entrance requirements:* For master's, official transcript, minimum cumulative GPA of 3.0, 3 letters of recommendation, statement of goals.

Bethel University, Graduate School, St. Paul, MN 55112-6999. Offers autism spectrum disorders (Certificate); business administration (MBA); communication (MA); counseling psychology (MA); education (M Ed); educational leadership (Ed D); gerontology (MA, Certificate); international baccalaureate education (Certificate); K-12 education (MA); literacy education (MA); nursing (MA); nursing education (Certificate); nursing leadership (Certificate); organizational leadership (MA); postsecondary teaching (Certificate); special education (MA); teaching (MA). Part-time and evening/weekend programs available. Postbaccalaureate distance learning degree programs offered (minimal on-campus study). *Faculty:* 8 full-time (3 women), 98 part-time/adjunct (46 women). *Students:* 651 full-time (419 women), 312 part-time (212 women); includes 79 minority (35 Black or African American, non-Hispanic/Latino; 2 American Indian or Alaska Native, non-Hispanic/Latino; 19 Asian, non-Hispanic/Latino; 17 Hispanic/Latino; 6 Two or more races, non-Hispanic/Latino), 6 international. Average age 36. In 2011, 245 master's, 4 doctorates, 32 other advanced degrees awarded. *Degree requirements:* For master's, comprehensive exam (for some programs), thesis (for some programs); for doctorate, comprehensive exam, thesis/dissertation. *Entrance requirements:* Additional exam requirements/recommendations for international students: Required—TOEFL (minimum score 550 paper-based; 213 computer-based; 80 iBT). *Application deadline:* Applications are processed on a rolling basis. Electronic applications accepted. Tuition and fees vary according to course load, degree level and program. *Financial support:* Applicants required to submit FAFSA. *Unit head:* Dick Crombie, Vice-President/Dean, 651-635-8000, Fax: 651-635-8004, E-mail: gs@bethel.edu. *Application contact:* Paul Ives, Director of Admissions, 651-635-8000, Fax: 651-635-8004, E-mail: gs@bethel.edu. Web site: http://gs.bethel.edu/.

Bloomsburg University of Pennsylvania, School of Graduate Studies, College of Education, Department of Early Childhood and Adolescent Education, Program in Adolescent Education, Bloomsburg, PA 17815-1301. Offers M Ed. *Accreditation:* NCATE. *Degree requirements:* For master's, thesis or alternative. *Entrance requirements:* For master's, MAT or PRAXIS, minimum QPA of 3.0, teaching certificate. Additional exam requirements/recommendations for international students: Required—TOEFL (minimum score 550 paper-based; 213 computer-based; 79 iBT). Electronic applications accepted. *Faculty research:* Supervision, computing, measurement, mathematics, school law.

Blue Mountain College, Program in Elementary Education, Blue Mountain, MS 38610-9509. Offers M Ed. *Entrance requirements:* For master's, PRAXIS, GRE or MAT, official transcripts; bachelors degree in elementary education from accredited university or college; teaching certificate; three recommendations. Additional exam requirements/recommendations for international students: Required—TOEFL (minimum score 550 paper-based). Electronic applications accepted.

Bob Jones University, Graduate Programs, Greenville, SC 29614. Offers accountancy (MS); Bible (MA); Bible translation (MA); Biblical studies (Certificate); broadcast management (MS); business administration (MBA); church history (MA, PhD); church ministries (MA); church music (MM); cinema and video production (MA); counseling (MS); curriculum and instruction (Ed D); divinity (M Div); dramatic production (MA); educational leadership (MS, Ed D, Ed S); elementary education (M Ed, MAT); English (M Ed, MA, MAT); fine arts (MA); graphic design (MA); history (M Ed, MA); illustration (MA); interpretative speech (MA); mathematics (M Ed, MAT); medical missions (Certificate); ministry (MM, D Min); multi-categorical special education (M Ed, MAT); music (M Ed); New Testament interpretation (PhD); Old Testament interpretation (PhD); orchestral instrument performance (MM); organ performance (MM); pastoral studies (MA); personnel services (MS, Ed S); piano pedagogy (MM); piano performance (MM); platform arts (MA); radio and television broadcasting (MS); rhetoric and public address (MA); secondary education (M Ed); studio art (MA); teaching Bible (MA); theology (MA, PhD); voice performance (MM); youth ministries (MA); M Div/MM.

Boston College, Lynch Graduate School of Education, Program in Elementary Education, Chestnut Hill, MA 02467-3800. Offers M Ed, MAT. *Accreditation:* Teacher Education Accreditation Council. Part-time and evening/weekend programs available. *Students:* 33 full-time (29 women), 9 part-time (8 women); includes 11 minority (6 Black or African American, non-Hispanic/Latino; 4 Asian, non-Hispanic/Latino; 1 Hispanic/Latino), 1 international. 122 applicants, 61% accepted, 33 enrolled. In 2011, 27 degrees awarded. *Degree requirements:* For master's, comprehensive exam. *Entrance requirements:* For master's, GRE General Test or MAT. Additional exam requirements/recommendations for international students: Required—TOEFL (minimum score 550 paper-based; 213 computer-based; 79 iBT). *Application deadline:* For fall admission, 1/1 priority date for domestic students. Application fee: $65. Electronic applications accepted. *Financial support:* Fellowships with full and partial tuition reimbursements, research assistantships with full and partial tuition reimbursements, teaching assistantships with full and partial tuition reimbursements, career-related internships or fieldwork, Federal Work-Study, scholarships/grants, traineeships, health care benefits, tuition waivers (full and partial), and unspecified assistantships available. Support available to part-time students. Financial award applicants required to submit FAFSA. *Faculty research:* Cross-cultural studies in teaching, learning or supervision, curriculum design, teacher research. *Unit head:* Dr. Maria E. Brisk, Chairperson, 617-552-4214, Fax: 617-552-0398. *Application contact:* Adam Poluzzi, Director, Graduate Admission and Financial Aid, 617-552-4214, Fax: 617-552-0398, E-mail: poluzzi@bc.edu.

Bowie State University, Graduate Programs, Program in Elementary Education, Bowie, MD 20715-9465. Offers M Ed. *Accreditation:* NCATE. Part-time and evening/weekend programs available. *Faculty:* 1 (woman) full-time. *Students:* 1 (woman) full-time, 7 part-time (6 women); includes 5 minority (all Black or African American, non-Hispanic/Latino), 1 international. Average age 33. 3 applicants, 100% accepted, 3 enrolled. In 2011, 6 master's awarded. *Degree requirements:* For master's, comprehensive exam, thesis optional, research paper. *Entrance requirements:* For master's, minimum GPA of 2.5, teaching certificate, teaching experience. *Application deadline:* For fall admission, 4/1 priority date for domestic students, 4/1 for international students; for spring admission, 11/1 priority date for domestic students, 11/1 for international students. Applications are processed on a rolling basis. Application fee: $40. Electronic applications accepted. *Expenses:* Tuition, state resident: full-time $4140; part-time $3105 per semester. Tuition, nonresident: full-time $7836; part-time $5877 per semester. *Required fees:* $1715; $648 per semester. *Financial support:* Application deadline: 4/1. *Unit head:* Dr. Marion Amory, Coordinator, 301-860-3139, E-mail: mamory@bowiestate.edu. *Application contact:* Angela Issac, Information Contact, 301-860-4000.

Brandeis University, Graduate School of Arts and Sciences, Teaching Program, Waltham, MA 02454-9110. Offers elementary education (public) (MAT); Jewish day school (MAT); secondary education (MAT), including Bible, biology, chemistry, Chinese, English, history, math, physics. *Faculty:* 5 full-time (3 women), 9 part-time/adjunct (6 women). *Students:* 31 full-time (23 women); includes 3 minority (2 Asian, non-Hispanic/Latino; 1 Hispanic/Latino), 3 international. 76 applicants, 67% accepted, 31 enrolled. In 2011, 23 master's awarded. *Degree requirements:* For master's, internship; research project. *Entrance requirements:* For master's, GRE General Test or Miller Analogies Test, official transcript(s), 3 letters of recommendation, resume, statement of purpose. Additional exam requirements/recommendations for international students: Required—TOEFL (minimum score 600 paper-based; 250 computer-based; 100 iBT); Recommended—IELTS (minimum score 7). *Application deadline:* Applications are processed on a rolling basis. Application fee: $75. Electronic applications accepted. *Expenses:* Contact institution. *Financial support:* Scholarships/grants and tuition waivers (partial) available. Financial award applicants required to submit FAFSA. *Faculty research:* Teacher education, education, teaching, elementary education, secondary education, Jewish education, English, history, biology, chemistry, physics, math, Chinese, Bible/Tanakh. *Unit head:* Prof. Marya Levenson, Director, 781-736-2020, Fax: 781-736-5020, E-mail: mlevenso@brandeis.edu. *Application contact:* Manuel Tuan, Department Administrator, 781-736-2633, Fax: 781-736-5020, E-mail: tuan@brandeis.edu. Web site: http://www.brandeis.edu/programs/mat.

Bridgewater State University, School of Graduate Studies, School of Education and Allied Studies, Department of Elementary and Early Childhood Education, Program in Elementary Education, Bridgewater, MA 02325-0001. Offers M Ed. *Accreditation:* NCATE. Part-time and evening/weekend programs available. *Entrance requirements:* For master's, GRE General Test or Massachusetts Test for Educator Licensure.

Brooklyn College of the City University of New York, Division of Graduate Studies, School of Education, Program in Childhood Education, Brooklyn, NY 11210-2889. Offers bilingual education (MS Ed); liberal arts (MS Ed); mathematics (MS Ed); science/environmental education (MS Ed). Part-time and evening/weekend programs available. *Entrance requirements:* For master's, LAST, interview, previous course work in education, writing sample, resume, 2 letters of recommendation. Additional exam requirements/recommendations for international students: Required—TOEFL (minimum score 500 paper-based; 173 computer-based; 61 iBT). Electronic applications accepted. *Faculty research:* Emotional intelligence, multiculturalism, arts immersion, the Holocaust.

Brown University, Graduate School, Department of Education, Providence, RI 02912. Offers teaching (MAT), including biology, elementary education, English, history/social studies; urban education policy (AM). *Degree requirements:* For master's, student teaching, portfolio. *Entrance requirements:* For master's, GRE General Test, letters of recommendation, interview. Additional exam requirements/recommendations for international students: Recommended—TOEFL.

Buffalo State College, State University of New York, The Graduate School, Faculty of Applied Science and Education, Department of Elementary Education and Reading, Program in Elementary Education, Buffalo, NY 14222-1095. Offers childhood education (grades 1-6) (MS Ed); early childhood and childhood curriculum and instruction (MS Ed); early childhood education (birth-grade 2) (MS Ed). *Accreditation:* NCATE. Part-time programs available. *Degree requirements:* For master's, thesis or project. *Entrance requirements:* For master's, minimum GPA of 2.5 in last 60 hours, New York teaching certificate. Additional exam requirements/recommendations for international students: Required—TOEFL (minimum score 550 paper-based; 213 computer-based).

Butler University, College of Education, Indianapolis, IN 46208-3485. Offers administration (MS); elementary education (MS); reading (MS); school counseling (MS); secondary education (MS); special education (MS). *Accreditation:* ACA; NCATE. Part-time and evening/weekend programs available. *Faculty:* 7 full-time (4 women), 5 part-time/adjunct (all women). *Students:* 9 full-time (6 women), 136 part-time (105 women); includes 21 minority (14 Black or African American, non-Hispanic/Latino; 5 Asian, non-Hispanic/Latino; 1 Hispanic/Latino; 1 Two or more races, non-Hispanic/Latino), 1 international. Average age 31. 69 applicants, 94% accepted, 24 enrolled. In 2011, 66 master's awarded. *Entrance requirements:* For master's, GRE General Test, MAT, interview. *Application deadline:* For fall admission, 8/15 priority date for domestic students. Applications are processed on a rolling basis. Application fee: $35. Electronic applications accepted. *Expenses: Tuition:* Part-time $466 per credit. *Financial support:* Institutionally sponsored loans available. Support available to part-time students. Financial award application deadline: 7/15; financial award applicants required to submit FAFSA. *Faculty research:* Ethics in cybercounseling, history of sports for disabled, effect of fetal alcohol syndrome on perceptual learning, reading recovery's theoretical framework in teacher education. *Unit head:* Dr. Ena Shelley, Dean, 317-940-9752, Fax: 317-940-6481. *Application contact:* Karen Farrell, Department Secretary, 317-940-9220, E-mail: kfarrell@butler.edu.

California Lutheran University, Graduate Studies, Graduate School of Education, Thousand Oaks, CA 91360-2787. Offers counseling and guidance (MS), including college student personnel, counseling and guidance; educational leadership (MA, Ed D), including educational leadership (K-12) (Ed D), higher education leadership (Ed D); special education (MS); teacher leadership (M Ed); teaching (M Ed). *Accreditation:* NCATE. Part-time and evening/weekend programs available. *Entrance requirements:* For master's, GRE General Test, interview, minimum GPA of 3.0.

California State University, Fullerton, Graduate Studies, College of Education, Department of Elementary and Bilingual Education, Fullerton, CA 92834-9480. Offers bilingual/bicultural education (MS); elementary curriculum and instruction (MS). *Accreditation:* NCATE. Part-time programs available. *Students:* 121 full-time (115 women), 123 part-time (112 women); includes 121 minority (3 Black or African American, non-Hispanic/Latino; 1 American Indian or Alaska Native, non-Hispanic/Latino; 44 Asian, non-Hispanic/Latino; 67 Hispanic/Latino; 6 Two or more races, non-Hispanic/Latino), 1 international. Average age 28. 183 applicants, 51% accepted, 82 enrolled. In 2011, 81 master's awarded. *Degree requirements:* For master's, comprehensive exam, project or thesis. *Entrance requirements:* For master's, minimum GPA of 2.5, teaching certificate. Application fee: $55. *Financial support:* Career-related internships or fieldwork, Federal Work-Study, institutionally sponsored loans, and scholarships/grants available. Support available to part-time students. Financial award application deadline: 3/1; financial award applicants required to submit FAFSA. *Faculty research:* Teacher training and tracking, model for improvement of teaching. *Unit head:* Dr. Karen Ivers, Chair, 657-278-2470. *Application contact:* Admissions/Applications, 657-278-2371.

California State University, Long Beach, Graduate Studies, College of Education, Department of Teacher Education, Long Beach, CA 90840. Offers elementary education (MA); secondary education (MA). Part-time and evening/weekend programs available. *Faculty:* 13 full-time (10 women), 2 part-time/adjunct (1 woman). *Students:* 27 full-time (24 women), 217 part-time (186 women); includes 156 minority (13 Black or African American, non-Hispanic/Latino; 12 American Indian or Alaska Native, non-Hispanic/Latino; 26 Asian, non-Hispanic/Latino; 91 Hispanic/Latino; 10 Native Hawaiian or other Pacific Islander, non-Hispanic/Latino; 4 Two or more races, non-Hispanic/Latino), 4 international. Average age 33. 145 applicants, 66% accepted, 89 enrolled. In 2011, 122 master's awarded. *Degree requirements:* For master's, comprehensive exam or thesis. *Entrance requirements:* For master's, GRE General Test, minimum GPA of 2.75. *Application deadline:* For fall admission, 7/1 for domestic students; for spring admission, 12/1 for domestic students. Applications are processed on a rolling basis. Application fee: $55. Electronic applications accepted. *Financial support:* Federal Work-Study, institutionally sponsored loans, and scholarships/grants available. Financial award application deadline: 3/2. *Faculty research:* Teacher stress and burnout, new teacher induction. *Unit head:* Dr. Catherine DuCharme, Chair, 562-985-4506, Fax: 562-985-1774, E-mail: ducharme@csulb.edu. *Application contact:* Nancy L. McGlothin, Coordinator for Graduate Studies and Research, 562-985-8476, Fax: 562-985-4951, E-mail: nmcgloth@csulb.edu.

California State University, Los Angeles, Graduate Studies, Charter College of Education, Division of Curriculum and Instruction, Los Angeles, CA 90032-8530. Offers elementary teaching (MA); reading (MA); secondary teaching (MA). Part-time and evening/weekend programs available. *Faculty:* 12 full-time (7 women), 5 part-time/adjunct (3 women). *Students:* 218 full-time (157 women), 156 part-time (118 women); includes 305 minority (20 Black or African American, non-Hispanic/Latino; 1 American Indian or Alaska Native, non-Hispanic/Latino; 59 Asian, non-Hispanic/Latino; 216 Hispanic/Latino; 9 Two or more races, non-Hispanic/Latino), 5 international. Average age 31. 93 applicants, 59% accepted, 52 enrolled. In 2011, 117 master's awarded. *Entrance requirements:* For master's, minimum GPA of 2.75 in last 90 units of course work, teaching certificate. Additional exam requirements/recommendations for international students: Required—TOEFL (minimum score 500 paper-based; 173 computer-based). *Application deadline:* For fall admission, 5/1 for domestic and international students. Applications are processed on a rolling basis. Application fee: $55. Electronic applications accepted. *Expenses:* Tuition, state resident: full-time $8225. *Financial support:* Federal Work-Study available. Support available to part-time students. Financial award application deadline: 3/1. *Faculty research:* Media, language arts, mathematics, computers, drug-free schools. *Unit head:* Dr. Robert Land, Chair, 323-343-4350, Fax: 323-343-5458, E-mail: rland@calstatela.edu. *Application contact:* Dr. Karin Brown, Acting Associate Dean of Graduate Studies, 323-343-3820 Ext. 3827, Fax: 323-343-5653, E-mail: kbrown5@calstatela.edu. Web site: http://www.calstatela.edu/academic/ccoe/index_edci.htm.

California State University, Northridge, Graduate Studies, College of Education, Department of Elementary Education, Northridge, CA 91330. Offers curriculum and instruction (MA); language and literacy (MA); multilingual/multicultural education (MA); teaching and learning (MA). *Accreditation:* NCATE. Part-time and evening/weekend programs available. *Degree requirements:* For master's, comprehensive exam. *Entrance requirements:* For master's, GRE General Test or minimum GPA of 3.0.

Elementary Education

Additional exam requirements/recommendations for international students: Required—TOEFL.

California State University, Stanislaus, College of Education, Program in Education (MA), Turlock, CA 95382. Offers curriculum and instruction (MA), including education technology, elementary education, multilingual education, physical education, reading, secondary education, special education; school administration (MA); school counseling (MA). Part-time and evening/weekend programs available. *Degree requirements:* For master's, comprehensive exam (for some programs), thesis (for some programs). *Entrance requirements:* For master's, MAT, GRE, or CBEST (varies by concentration), 3 letters of recommendation, personal statement. Additional exam requirements/ recommendations for international students: Required—TOEFL (minimum score 550 paper-based; 213 computer-based). *Application deadline:* For fall admission, 5/1 for domestic students; for spring admission, 1/7 for domestic students. Application fee: $55. Electronic applications accepted. *Expenses: Required fees:* $4616 per year. *Financial support:* Federal Work-Study available. Financial award application deadline: 3/1; financial award applicants required to submit FAFSA. *Faculty research:* Children's perspectives on historical events, method elementary schools dual language education, K-12 reading and CYRM programs. *Unit head:* Dr. Kathy Norman, Dean, College of Education, 209-667-3652, Fax: 209-664-6613, E-mail: coe@csustan.edu. *Application contact:* Graduate School, 209-667-3129, Fax: 209-664-7025, E-mail: graduate_school@csustan.edu. Web site: http://www.csustan.edu/COE/.

California University of Pennsylvania, School of Graduate Studies and Research, College of Education and Human Services, Department of Elementary Education, California, PA 15419-1394. Offers reading specialist (M Ed). *Accreditation:* NCATE. Part-time and evening/weekend programs available. *Degree requirements:* For master's, comprehensive exam, thesis optional. *Entrance requirements:* For master's, MAT, PRAXIS, minimum GPA of 3.0, state police clearances. Additional exam requirements/recommendations for international students: Required—TOEFL (minimum score 550 paper-based; 213 computer-based; 80 iBT). Electronic applications accepted. *Faculty research:* English as a second language, adult literacy, emerging literacy, diagnosis and remediation, phonemic awareness.

Cambridge College, School of Education, Cambridge, MA 02138-5304. Offers autism specialist (M Ed); autism/behavior analyst (M Ed); behavior analyst (Post-Master's Certificate); behavioral management (M Ed); early childhood teacher (M Ed); education specialist in curriculum and instruction (CAGS); educational leadership (Ed D); elementary teacher (M Ed); English as a second language (M Ed, Certificate); general science (M Ed); health education (Post-Master's Certificate); health/family and consumer sciences (M Ed); history (M Ed); individualized (M Ed); information technology literacy (M Ed); instructional technology (M Ed); interdisciplinary studies (M Ed); library teacher (M Ed); literacy education (M Ed); mathematics (M Ed); mathematics specialist (Certificate); middle school mathematics and science (M Ed); school administration (M Ed, CAGS); school guidance counselor (M Ed); school nurse education (M Ed); school social worker/school adjustment counselor (M Ed); special education administrator (CAGS); special education/moderate disabilities (M Ed); teaching skills and methodologies (M Ed). Part-time and evening/weekend programs available. Postbaccalaureate distance learning degree programs offered (minimal on-campus study). *Degree requirements:* For master's, thesis, internship/practicum (licensure program only); for doctorate, thesis/dissertation; for other advanced degree, thesis. *Entrance requirements:* For master's, interview, resume, documentation of licensure, 2 professional references; for doctorate, official transcripts, interview, resume, documentation of licensure (if any), written personal statement/essay, portfolio of scholarly and professional work, qualifying assessment, 2 professional references, health insurance, immunizations form; for other advanced degree, official transcripts, interview, resume, documentation of licensure (if any), written personal statement/ essay, 2 professional references, health insurance, immunizations form. Additional exam requirements/recommendations for international students: Required—TOEFL (minimum score 550 paper-based; 213 computer-based; 79 iBT); Recommended—IELTS (minimum score 6). Electronic applications accepted. *Expenses:* Contact institution. *Faculty research:* Adult education, accelerated learning, mathematics education, brain compatible learning, special education and law.

Campbell University, Graduate and Professional Programs, School of Education, Buies Creek, NC 27506. Offers administration (MSA); community counseling (MA); elementary education (M Ed); English education (M Ed); interdisciplinary studies (M Ed); mathematics education (M Ed); middle grades education (M Ed); physical education (M Ed); school counseling (M Ed); secondary education (M Ed); social science education (M Ed). *Accreditation:* NCATE. Part-time and evening/weekend programs available. *Degree requirements:* For master's, comprehensive exam. *Entrance requirements:* For master's, GRE General Test, minimum GPA of 2.7. *Faculty research:* Spiritual values and wellness issues in counseling, stress and professional burnout among counselors, thinking strategies, leadership, adaptive technology.

Canisius College, Graduate Division, School of Education and Human Services, Department of Adolescence Education, Buffalo, NY 14208-1098. Offers adolescence education (MS Ed); business and marketing education (MS Ed). Part-time and evening/ weekend programs available. *Faculty:* 11 full-time (8 women), 26 part-time/adjunct (14 women). *Students:* 73 full-time (37 women), 17 part-time (9 women); includes 4 minority (3 Black or African American, non-Hispanic/Latino; 1 Hispanic/Latino), 27 international. Average age 29. 48 applicants, 71% accepted, 17 enrolled. In 2011, 65 master's awarded. *Degree requirements:* For master's, thesis, project internship. *Entrance requirements:* For master's, GRE if cumulative GPA less than 2.7, transcripts, two letters of recommendation. Additional exam requirements/recommendations for international students: Required—TOEFL. *Application deadline:* Applications are processed on a rolling basis. Application fee: $25. Electronic applications accepted. *Financial support:* Career-related internships or fieldwork, Federal Work-Study, scholarships/grants, tuition waivers (partial), and unspecified assistantships available. Support available to part-time students. Financial award application deadline: 4/30; financial award applicants required to submit FAFSA. *Faculty research:* Culturally congruent pedagogy in physical education, information processing and perceptual styles of athletes, qualities of effective coaches, student perceptions of online courses, teaching effectiveness. *Unit head:* Dr. Barbera A. Burns, Chair of Adolescence Education, 716-888-3291, E-mail: burns1@ canisius.edu. *Application contact:* Jim Bagwell, Director of Graduate Recruitment and Admissions, 716-888-2544, Fax: 716-888-3290, E-mail: bagwellj@canisius.edu. Web site: http://www.canisius.edu/catalog/teachcert6.asp.

Canisius College, Graduate Division, School of Education and Human Services, Department of Graduate Education and Leadership, Buffalo, NY 14208-1098. Offers college student personnel (MS Ed); deaf education (MS Ed); deaf/adolescent education, grades 7-12 (MS Ed); deaf/childhood education, grades 1-6 (MS Ed); differential instruction (MS Ed); education administration (MS Ed); gifted education extention (Certificate); literacy (MS Ed); reading (Certificate); school building leadership (MS Ed, Certificate); school district leadership (Certificate). *Accreditation:* NCATE. Part-time and evening/weekend programs available. Postbaccalaureate distance learning degree programs offered (minimal on-campus study). *Faculty:* 7 full-time (6 women), 36 part-time/adjunct (22 women). *Students:* 149 full-time (114 women), 242 part-time (177 women); includes 42 minority (29 Black or African American, non-Hispanic/Latino; 2 American Indian or Alaska Native, non-Hispanic/Latino; 3 Asian, non-Hispanic/Latino; 6 Hispanic/Latino; 2 Two or more races, non-Hispanic/Latino), 3 international. Average age 30. 250 applicants, 84% accepted, 124 enrolled. In 2011, 135 degrees awarded. *Entrance requirements:* For master's, GRE if cumulative GPA less than 2.7, transcripts, two letters of recommendation. Additional exam requirements/recommendations for international students: Required—TOEFL. *Application deadline:* Applications are processed on a rolling basis. Application fee: $25. Electronic applications accepted. *Financial support:* Career-related internships or fieldwork, Federal Work-Study, scholarships/grants, tuition waivers (partial), and unspecified assistantships available. Support available to part-time students. Financial award application deadline: 4/30; financial award applicants required to submit FAFSA. *Faculty research:* Asperger's disease, autism, private higher education, reading strategies. *Unit head:* Dr. Rosemary K. Murray, Chair/Associate Professor of Graduate Education and Leadership, 716-888-3723, E-mail: murray1@canisius.edu. *Application contact:* Jim Bagwell, Director of Graduate Recruitment and Admissions, 716-888-2544, Fax: 716-888-3290, E-mail: bagwellj@canisius.edu. Web site: http://www.canisius.edu/education/graduate.asp.

Canisius College, Graduate Division, School of Education and Human Services, Education Department, Buffalo, NY 14208-1098. Offers general education non-matriculated (MS Ed); middle childhood (MS Ed); special education/adolescent (MS Ed); special education/advanced (MS Ed); special education/childhood (MS Ed); special education/childhood education grades 1-6 (MS Ed). Part-time and evening/weekend programs available. Postbaccalaureate distance learning degree programs offered (minimal on-campus study). *Faculty:* 17 full-time (13 women), 23 part-time/adjunct (11 women). *Students:* 139 full-time (103 women), 62 part-time (47 women); includes 10 minority (9 Black or African American, non-Hispanic/Latino; 1 Hispanic/Latino), 67 international. Average age 30. 135 applicants, 70% accepted, 53 enrolled. In 2011, 125 master's awarded. *Degree requirements:* For master's, research project or thesis. *Entrance requirements:* For master's, GRE if cumulative GPA less than 2.7, transcripts, two letters of recommendation. Additional exam requirements/recommendations for international students: Required—TOEFL. *Application deadline:* Applications are processed on a rolling basis. Application fee: $25. Electronic applications accepted. *Financial support:* Career-related internships or fieldwork, Federal Work-Study, scholarships/grants, tuition waivers (partial), and unspecified assistantships available. Support available to part-time students. Financial award application deadline: 4/30; financial award applicants required to submit FAFSA. *Faculty research:* Family as faculty, tutorial experiences in modern math, integrating digital technologies in the classroom. *Unit head:* Dr. Julie Henry, Chair/Professor, 716-888-3729, E-mail: henry1@ canisius.edu. *Application contact:* Jim Bagwell, Director of Graduate Recruitment and Admissions, 716-888-2544, Fax: 716-888-3290, E-mail: bagwellj@canisius.edu. Web site: http://www.canisius.edu/education/facultystaff.asp.

Capella University, School of Education, Minneapolis, MN 55402. Offers college teaching (Certificate); curriculum and instruction (MS, PhD); education (MS); enrollment management (MS); instructional design for online learning (MS, PhD); k-12 studies in education (MS, PhD); leadership for higher education (MS, PhD); leadership in education administration (Certificate); leadership in educational administration (MS, PhD); postsecondary and adult education (MS, PhD); professional studies in education (MS, PhD); reading and literacy (MS); training and performance improvement (MS, PhD). Part-time and evening/weekend programs available. Postbaccalaureate distance learning degree programs offered (minimal on-campus study). Terminal master's awarded for partial completion of doctoral program. *Degree requirements:* For master's, thesis optional, integrative project; for doctorate, comprehensive exam, thesis/ dissertation. *Entrance requirements:* Additional exam requirements/recommendations for international students: Required—TOEFL (minimum score 550 paper-based; 213 computer-based), TWE (minimum score 4). Electronic applications accepted. *Faculty research:* Higher education administration, distance learning, adult education, training and curriculum design.

Caribbean University, Graduate School, Bayamón, PR 00960-0493. Offers administration and supervision (MA Ed); criminal justice (MA); curriculum and instruction (MA Ed, PhD), including elementary education (MA Ed), English education (MA Ed), history education (MA Ed), mathematics education (MA Ed), primary education (MA Ed), science education (MA Ed), Spanish education (MA Ed); educational technology in instructional systems (MA Ed); gerontology (MSN); human resources (MBA); museology, archiving and art history (MA Ed); neonatal pediatrics (MSN); physical education (MA Ed); special education (MA Ed). *Entrance requirements:* For master's, interview, minimum GPA of 2.5.

Carson-Newman College, Graduate Program in Education, Jefferson City, TN 37760. Offers curriculum and instruction (M Ed); educational leadership (M Ed); elementary education (MAT); school counseling (MS); secondary education (MAT); teaching English as a second language (MATESL). *Accreditation:* NCATE. Part-time and evening/ weekend programs available. *Faculty:* 5 full-time (2 women), 10 part-time/adjunct (3 women). *Students:* 85 full-time (55 women), 76 part-time (53 women); includes 8 minority (5 Black or African American, non-Hispanic/Latino; 2 Asian, non-Hispanic/ Latino; 1 Two or more races, non-Hispanic/Latino), 23 international. Average age 32. 80 applicants, 96% accepted. In 2011, 90 master's awarded. *Degree requirements:* For master's, thesis or alternative. *Entrance requirements:* For master's, NTE, minimum GPA of 3.0 in major, 2.5 overall. *Application deadline:* For fall admission, 7/15 priority date for domestic students. Applications are processed on a rolling basis. Application fee: $25 ($50 for international students). *Expenses: Tuition:* Full-time $6750; part-time $375 per credit hour. *Required fees:* $200. *Financial support:* In 2011–12, 41 students received support. Federal Work-Study and unspecified assistantships available. Financial award application deadline: 4/1; financial award applicants required to submit FAFSA. *Unit head:* Dr. Sharon Teets, Chair, 865-471-3461. *Application contact:* Graduate Admissions and Services Adviser, 865-471-3460, Fax: 865-471-3875.

Catawba College, Program in Education, Salisbury, NC 28144-2488. Offers elementary education (M Ed). *Accreditation:* NCATE. Part-time and evening/weekend programs available. *Faculty:* 4 full-time (3 women). *Students:* 35 part-time (34 women). Average age 36. In 2011, 17 master's awarded. *Degree requirements:* For master's, portfolio. *Entrance requirements:* For master's, NTE, PRAXIS II, minimum undergraduate GPA of 3.0, valid teaching license, official transcripts, 3 references, essay, interview, practicing teacher. *Application deadline:* For fall admission, 7/1 for domestic students; for spring admission, 12/1 for domestic students. Applications are processed on a rolling basis. Application fee: $25. *Expenses: Tuition:* Part-time $160 per credit hour. *Financial support:* Scholarships/grants available. Financial award applicants required to submit FAFSA. *Unit head:* Dr. Rhonda Truitt, Chair, Department of Teacher Education, 704-637-4468, Fax: 704-637-4732, E-mail: rltruitt@catawba.edu. *Application contact:* Dr. Lou W. Kasias, Director, Graduate Program, 704-637-4462, Fax: 704-637-4732, E-mail: lakasias@catawba.edu. Web site: http://www.catawba.edu/academic/ teachereducation/grad/.

Centenary College of Louisiana, Graduate Programs, Department of Education, Shreveport, LA 71104. Offers administration (M Ed); elementary education (MAT); secondary education (MAT); supervision of instruction (M Ed). Part-time and evening/ weekend programs available. *Degree requirements:* For master's, comprehensive exam. *Entrance requirements:* For master's, GRE General Test (M Ed), PRAXIS I and

PRAXIS II (MAT), teacher certification (M Ed), minimum GPA of 2.5. *Expenses:* Contact institution. *Faculty research:* Teachers as advocates for teachers, portfolio assessment, disabled readers.

Central Connecticut State University, School of Graduate Studies, School of Education and Professional Studies, Department of Teacher Education, Program in Elementary Education, New Britain, CT 06050-4010. Offers MS, Certificate. Part-time and evening/weekend programs available. *Students:* 15 full-time (14 women), 18 part-time (15 women); includes 3 minority (2 Black or African American, non-Hispanic/Latino; 1 Hispanic/Latino). Average age 30. 25 applicants, 64% accepted, 8 enrolled. In 2011, 11 master's, 3 other advanced degrees awarded. *Degree requirements:* For master's, comprehensive exam, thesis or alternative; for Certificate, qualifying exam. *Entrance requirements:* For master's, minimum undergraduate GPA of 2.7. Additional exam requirements/recommendations for international students: Required—TOEFL (minimum score 550 paper-based; 213 computer-based). *Application deadline:* For fall admission, 6/1 for domestic students, 5/1 for international students; for spring admission, 11/1 for domestic and international students. Applications are processed on a rolling basis. Application fee: $50. Electronic applications accepted. *Expenses: Tuition, area resident:* Full-time $5137; part-time $482 per credit. Tuition, state resident: full-time $7707; part-time $494 per credit. Tuition, nonresident: full-time $14,311; part-time $494 per credit. *Required fees:* $3865. One-time fee: $62 part-time. *Faculty research:* Elementary school curriculum, changing school populations, multicultural education, professional development. *Unit head:* Dr. Ronnie Casella, Chair, 860-832-2415, E-mail: casellar@ccsu.edu. *Application contact:* Patricia Gardner, Associate Director of Graduate Studies, 860-832-2350, Fax: 860-832-2352, E-mail: graduateadmissions@ccsu.edu.

Central Michigan University, College of Graduate Studies, College of Education and Human Services, Department of Teacher Education and Professional Development, Mount Pleasant, MI 48859. Offers educational technology (MA, Graduate Certificate); elementary education (MA), including classroom teaching, early childhood; middle level education (MA); reading and literacy K-12 (MA); secondary education (MA). Part-time and evening/weekend programs available. *Degree requirements:* For master's, thesis or alternative. Electronic applications accepted. *Faculty research:* Integrating literacy across the curriculum, science teaching and aesthetic learning in science, diversity education, educational technology, educational psychology and child development.

Chadron State College, School of Professional and Graduate Studies, Department of Education, Chadron, NE 69337. Offers business (MA Ed); community counseling (MA Ed); educational administration (MS Ed, Sp Ed); elementary education (MS Ed); history (MA Ed); language and literature (MA Ed); secondary administration (MS Ed); secondary education (MS Ed). *Accreditation:* NCATE. Part-time and evening/weekend programs available. Postbaccalaureate distance learning degree programs offered. *Degree requirements:* For master's, thesis optional. *Entrance requirements:* For master's, GRE General Test, GRE Writing Test, minimum GPA of 2.75 or 12 graduate hours at CSC with minimum GPA of 3.25. Additional exam requirements/recommendations for international students: Required—TOEFL. Electronic applications accepted. *Faculty research:* Rural education, technology, mental health.

Chaminade University of Honolulu, Graduate Services, Program in Education, Honolulu, HI 96816-1578. Offers child development (M Ed); educational leadership (M Ed); elementary education with licensure (MAT); instructional leadership (M Ed); Montessori credential (M Ed); Montessori emphasis (M Ed); secondary education with licensure (MAT), including English, math, science, social studies; special education with licensure (MAT). Part-time and evening/weekend programs available. Postbaccalaureate distance learning degree programs offered (minimal on-campus study). *Faculty:* 2 full-time (both women), 32 part-time/adjunct (25 women). *Students:* 53 full-time (38 women), 88 part-time (67 women); includes 77 minority (6 Black or African American, non-Hispanic/Latino; 1 American Indian or Alaska Native, non-Hispanic/Latino; 44 Asian, non-Hispanic/Latino; 5 Hispanic/Latino; 17 Native Hawaiian or other Pacific Islander, non-Hispanic/Latino; 4 Two or more races, non-Hispanic/Latino), 1 international. Average age 35. 40 applicants, 88% accepted, 30 enrolled. In 2011, 105 master's awarded. *Degree requirements:* For master's, thesis or alternative. *Entrance requirements:* For master's, PRAXIS (for MAT only), minimum GPA of 2.75, 3 letters of recommendation. Additional exam requirements/recommendations for international students: Required—TOEFL (minimum score 550 paper-based). *Application deadline:* For fall admission, 9/1 priority date for domestic students, 9/1 for international students; for winter admission, 12/1 priority date for domestic students, 12/1 for international students; for spring admission, 3/1 priority date for domestic students, 3/1 for international students. Applications are processed on a rolling basis. Application fee: $50. Electronic applications accepted. *Expenses: Required fees:* $600 per credit hour. One-time fee: $93 part-time. *Financial support:* In 2011–12, 172 students received support. Career-related internships or fieldwork, Federal Work-Study, institutionally sponsored loans, scholarships/grants, and tuition waivers (partial) available. Support available to part-time students. Financial award application deadline: 3/1; financial award applicants required to submit FAFSA. *Faculty research:* Peace and curriculum education. *Unit head:* Dr. Joseph Peters, Dean, 808-440-4251, Fax: 808-739-4607, E-mail: joseph.peters@chaminade.edu. *Application contact:* 808-739-4663, Fax: 808-739-8329, E-mail: gradserv@chaminade.edu. Web site: http://www.chaminade.edu/education/grad.php.

Chapman University, College of Educational Studies, Orange, CA 92866. Offers communication sciences and disorders (MS); counseling (MA), including school counseling (MA, Credential); education (MA, PhD), including cultural and curricular studies (PhD), disability studies (PhD), school psychology (PhD, Credential); educational psychology (MA); professional clear (Credential); pupil personnel services (Credential), including school counseling (MA, Credential), school psychology (PhD, Credential); school psychology (Ed S); single subject (Credential); special education (MA); special education (level ii) (Credential), including mild/moderate, moderate/severe; special education (preliminary) (Credential), including mild/moderate, moderate/severe; speech language pathology (Credential); teaching (MA), including elementary education, secondary education. *Accreditation:* Teacher Education Accreditation Council. Part-time and evening/weekend programs available. *Faculty:* 27 full-time (18 women), 35 part-time/adjunct (24 women). *Students:* 220 full-time (188 women), 164 part-time (128 women); includes 140 minority (12 Black or African American, non-Hispanic/Latino; 1 American Indian or Alaska Native, non-Hispanic/Latino; 44 Asian, non-Hispanic/Latino; 73 Hispanic/Latino; 4 Native Hawaiian or other Pacific Islander, non-Hispanic/Latino; 6 Two or more races, non-Hispanic/Latino), 1 international. Average age 29. 436 applicants, 38% accepted, 126 enrolled. In 2011, 130 master's, 5 doctorates awarded. *Entrance requirements:* Additional exam requirements/recommendations for international students: Required—TOEFL (minimum score 550 paper-based; 213 computer-based; 80 iBT). *Application deadline:* Applications are processed on a rolling basis. Application fee: $60. Electronic applications accepted. Tuition and fees vary according to degree level and program. *Financial support:* Fellowships and scholarships/grants available. Financial award application deadline: 6/30; financial award applicants required to submit FAFSA. *Unit head:* Dr. Don Cardinal, Dean, 714-997-6781, E-mail: cardinal@chapman.edu. *Application contact:* Admissions Coordinator, 714-997-6714. Web site: http://www.chapman.edu/CES/.

Charleston Southern University, School of Education, Charleston, SC 29423-8087. Offers administration and supervision (M Ed), including elementary, secondary; elementary education (M Ed); secondary education (M Ed). *Accreditation:* NCATE. Part-time and evening/weekend programs available. *Degree requirements:* For master's, thesis optional. *Entrance requirements:* For master's, GRE or MAT. Additional exam requirements/recommendations for international students: Required—TOEFL (minimum score 550 paper-based; 213 computer-based; 79 iBT). *Expenses:* Contact institution.

Chatham University, Program in Education, Pittsburgh, PA 15232-2826. Offers early childhood education (MAT); elementary education (MAT); environmental education (K-12) (MAT); secondary art (MAT); secondary biology education (MAT); secondary chemistry education (MAT); secondary English education (MAT); secondary math education (MAT); secondary physics education (MAT); secondary social studies education (MAT); special education (MAT). *Students:* 52 full-time (42 women), 17 part-time (16 women); includes 2 minority (1 Black or African American, non-Hispanic/Latino; 1 Hispanic/Latino). Average age 29. 39 applicants, 82% accepted, 23 enrolled. In 2011, 37 master's awarded. *Degree requirements:* For master's, thesis, teaching experience. *Entrance requirements:* For master's, minimum GPA of 3.0, sample of written work, recommendation letters. Additional exam requirements/recommendations for international students: Required—TOEFL (minimum score 600 paper-based; 250 computer-based; 100 iBT), IELTS (minimum score 7), TWE. *Application deadline:* For fall admission, 4/1 priority date for domestic students, 4/1 for international students; for spring admission, 11/1 priority date for domestic students, 10/1 for international students. Applications are processed on a rolling basis. Application fee: $45. Electronic applications accepted. Application fee is waived when completed online. *Expenses: Tuition:* Full-time $13,896. Tuition and fees vary according to program. *Financial support:* Career-related internships or fieldwork available. Financial award applicants required to submit FAFSA. *Faculty research:* Gifted education, environmental education, technology in education, writing as learning, class size and achievement. *Unit head:* Dr. Elvira Sanatullova-Allison, Director of Education Programs, 412-365-2773, E-mail: esanatullovaallison@chatham.edu. *Application contact:* Dory Perry, Associate Director of Graduate Admission, 412-365-2758, Fax: 412-365-1609, E-mail: gradadmissions@chatham.edu. Web site: http://www.chatham.edu/mat.

Cheyney University of Pennsylvania, School of Education and Professional Studies, Program in Elementary Education, Cheyney, PA 19319. Offers M Ed, MAT. *Accreditation:* NCATE. Part-time and evening/weekend programs available. *Degree requirements:* For master's, thesis or alternative. *Entrance requirements:* For master's, GRE General Test, MAT, minimum GPA of 2.75. Electronic applications accepted.

Chicago State University, School of Graduate and Professional Studies, College of Education, Department of Reading, Elementary Education, Library Information and Media Studies, Program in Elementary Education, Chicago, IL 60628. Offers MAT. *Accreditation:* NCATE. *Degree requirements:* For master's, comprehensive exam, thesis optional. *Entrance requirements:* For master's, minimum GPA of 3.0 in last 60 hours.

Christopher Newport University, Graduate Studies, Department of Teacher Preparation, Newport News, VA 23606-2998. Offers art (PK-12) (MAT); biology (6-12) (MAT); chemistry (6-12) (MAT); computer science (6-12) (MAT); elementary (PK-6) (MAT); English (6-12) (MAT); English as second language (PK-12) (MAT); French (PK-12) (MAT); history and social science (6-12) (MAT); mathematics (6-12) (MAT); music (PK-12) (MAT), including choral, instrumental; physics (6-12) (MAT); Spanish (PK-12) (MAT). Part-time and evening/weekend programs available. *Degree requirements:* For master's, comprehensive exam, thesis or alternative. *Entrance requirements:* For master's, PRAXIS I, minimum GPA of 3.0. Additional exam requirements/recommendations for international students: Required—TOEFL (minimum score 580 paper-based; 237 computer-based; 92 iBT). Electronic applications accepted. *Faculty research:* Early literacy development, instructional innovations, professional teaching standards, multicultural issues, aesthetic education.

The Citadel, The Military College of South Carolina, Citadel Graduate College, School of Education, Program in Guidance and Counseling, Charleston, SC 29409. Offers elementary/secondary school counseling (M Ed); student affairs and college counseling (M Ed). *Accreditation:* ACA; NCATE. Part-time and evening/weekend programs available. *Faculty:* 12 full-time (8 women), 9 part-time/adjunct (4 women). *Students:* 24 full-time (22 women), 36 part-time (31 women); includes 9 minority (8 Black or African American, non-Hispanic/Latino; 1 Hispanic/Latino). Average age 31. In 2011, 22 master's awarded. *Degree requirements:* For master's, comprehensive exam, practicum or internship. *Entrance requirements:* For master's, GRE (minimum score 900) or MAT (minimum score 396), minimum undergraduate GPA of 3.0, 3 letters of reference, group interview. Additional exam requirements/recommendations for international students: Required—TOEFL (minimum score 550 paper-based; 213 computer-based; 79 iBT). *Application deadline:* For fall admission, 6/1 for domestic students; for spring admission, 10/1 for domestic students. Application fee: $30. Electronic applications accepted. *Expenses: Tuition, area resident:* Part-time $501 per credit hour. Tuition, state resident: part-time $501 per credit hour. Tuition, nonresident: part-time $824 per credit hour. *Required fees:* $40 per term. One-time fee: $30. *Financial support:* Career-related internships or fieldwork, health care benefits, and unspecified assistantships available. Support available to part-time students. Financial award application deadline: 7/1; financial award applicants required to submit FAFSA. *Unit head:* Dr. George T. Williams, Director, 843-953-2205, Fax: 843-953-7258, E-mail: williamsg@citadel.edu. *Application contact:* Dr. Steve A. Nida, Associate Provost, The Citadel Graduate College, 843-953-5089, Fax: 843-953-7630, E-mail: cgc@citadel.edu. Web site: http://www.citadel.edu/education/counselor.html.

City University of Seattle, Graduate Division, Albright School of Education, Bellevue, WA 98005. Offers administrator certification (Certificate); curriculum and instruction (M Ed); educational leadership (Ed D); elementary education (MIT); guidance and counseling (M Ed); higher education leadership (Ed D); leadership (M Ed); leadership and school counseling (M Ed); organizational leadership (Ed D); reading and literacy (M Ed); special education (MIT); superintendent certification (Certificate). Part-time and evening/weekend programs available. Postbaccalaureate distance learning degree programs offered (no on-campus study). *Faculty:* 23 full-time (15 women), 123 part-time/adjunct (82 women). *Students:* 353 full-time (263 women), 75 part-time (50 women); includes 40 minority (12 Black or African American, non-Hispanic/Latino; 5 American Indian or Alaska Native, non-Hispanic/Latino; 7 Asian, non-Hispanic/Latino; 8 Hispanic/Latino; 5 Native Hawaiian or other Pacific Islander, non-Hispanic/Latino; 3 Two or more races, non-Hispanic/Latino). Average age 36. 129 applicants, 98% accepted, 126 enrolled. In 2011, 351 master's, 30 Certificates awarded. *Degree requirements:* For master's, comprehensive exam (for some programs), thesis (for some programs); for doctorate, comprehensive exam, thesis/dissertation. *Entrance requirements:* Additional exam requirements/recommendations for international students: Required—TOEFL (minimum score 567 paper-based; 227 computer-based; 87 iBT); Recommended—IELTS. *Application deadline:* For fall admission, 9/1 for international students; for winter admission, 12/1 for international students; for spring admission, 3/1 for international students. Applications are processed on a rolling basis. Application fee: $50. Electronic applications accepted. *Expenses:* Contact institution. *Financial support:* In 2011–12, 40 students received support. Federal Work-Study and scholarships/grants available. Support available to part-time students. Financial award applicants required to submit

FAFSA. *Unit head:* Craig Schieber, Dean, 425-637-101 Ext. 5460, Fax: 425-709-5363, E-mail: schieber@cityu.edu. *Application contact:* Alysa Borelli, 888-422-4898, Fax: 425-709-5363, E-mail: info@cityu.edu. Web site: http://www.cityu.edu/programs/soe/index.aspx.

Clemson University, Graduate School, College of Health, Education, and Human Development, Eugene T. Moore School of Education, Program in Early Childhood Education, Clemson, SC 29634. Offers early childhood education (M Ed); elementary education (M Ed); secondary English (M Ed); secondary math (M Ed); secondary science (M Ed); secondary social studies (M Ed). Part-time and evening/weekend programs available. *Students:* 5 applicants, 0% accepted, 0 enrolled. In 2011, 3 master's awarded. *Degree requirements:* For master's, comprehensive exam. *Entrance requirements:* For master's, GRE, valid teaching certificate. Additional exam requirements/recommendations for international students: Required—TOEFL; Recommended—IELTS. *Application deadline:* Applications are processed on a rolling basis. Application fee: $70 ($80 for international students). Electronic applications accepted. *Expenses:* Contact institution. *Financial support:* Institutionally sponsored loans, health care benefits, and unspecified assistantships available. Financial award application deadline: 3/1; financial award applicants required to submit FAFSA. *Faculty research:* Elementary education, mathematics education, social studies education, English education, science education. *Unit head:* Dr. Michael J. Padilla, Director/Associate Dean, 864-656-4444, Fax: 864-656-0311, E-mail: padilla@clemson.edu. *Application contact:* Dr. David Fleming, Graduate Programs Coordinator, 864-656-1881, Fax: 864-656-0311, E-mail: dflemin@clemson.edu.

Clemson University, Graduate School, College of Health, Education, and Human Development, Eugene T. Moore School of Education, Program in Teaching and Learning, Clemson, SC 29634. Offers elementary education (M Ed); English education (M Ed); mathematics education (M Ed); science education (M Ed); social studies education (M Ed). *Entrance requirements:* For master's, GRE, baccalaureate degree from regionally-accredited institution, official transcripts, copy of valid teaching certificate, two letters of recommendation. *Application contact:* Dr. David Fleming, Graduate Programs Coordinator, 864-656-1881, Fax: 864-656-0311, E-mail: dflemin@clemson.edu. Web site: http://www.clemson.edu/hehd/departments/education/academics/graduate/MEd-teach-learn.html.

College of Charleston, Graduate School, School of Education, Health, and Human Performance, Department of Elementary and Early Childhood Education, Program in Elementary Education, Charleston, SC 29424-0001. Offers MAT. *Accreditation:* NCATE. Part-time and evening/weekend programs available. *Faculty:* 34 full-time (25 women), 9 part-time/adjunct (all women). *Students:* 29 full-time (26 women), 4 part-time (all women); includes 1 minority (Asian, non-Hispanic/Latino). Average age 26. 24 applicants, 38% accepted, 6 enrolled. In 2011, 13 degrees awarded. *Degree requirements:* For master's, thesis or alternative, written qualifying exam, student teaching experience. *Entrance requirements:* For master's, GRE, 2 letters of recommendation. Additional exam requirements/recommendations for international students: Required—TOEFL (minimum score 81 iBT). *Application deadline:* For fall admission, 4/1 for domestic students; for spring admission, 11/1 for domestic students. Applications are processed on a rolling basis. Application fee: $45. Electronic applications accepted. *Expenses:* Tuition, state resident: full-time $5455; part-time $455 per credit. Tuition, nonresident: full-time $13,917; part-time $1160 per credit. *Financial support:* In 2011–12, research assistantships (averaging $12,400 per year), teaching assistantships (averaging $13,300 per year) were awarded; Federal Work-Study, scholarships/grants, and unspecified assistantships also available. Support available to part-time students. Financial award application deadline: 4/1; financial award applicants required to submit FAFSA. *Unit head:* Dr. Angela Cozart, Director, 843-953-6353, Fax: 843-953-5407, E-mail: cozarta@cofc.edu. *Application contact:* Susan Hallatt, Director of Graduate Admissions, 843-953-5614, Fax: 843-953-1434, E-mail: hallatts@cofc.edu.

The College of New Jersey, Graduate Studies, School of Education, Department of Elementary and Early Childhood Education, Program in Elementary Education, Ewing, NJ 08628. Offers M Ed, MAT. *Accreditation:* NCATE. Part-time programs available. *Degree requirements:* For master's, comprehensive exam. *Entrance requirements:* For master's, GRE General Test, minimum GPA of 3.0 in field or 2.75 overall. Additional exam requirements/recommendations for international students: Required—TOEFL. Electronic applications accepted.

The College of New Rochelle, Graduate School, Division of Education, Program in Elementary Education/Early Childhood Education, New Rochelle, NY 10805-2308. Offers MS Ed. Part-time programs available. *Degree requirements:* For master's, comprehensive exam (for some programs), thesis (for some programs), practicum. *Entrance requirements:* For master's, interview, minimum GPA of 3.0 in field, 2.7 overall.

College of St. Joseph, Graduate Programs, Division of Education, Program in Elementary Education, Rutland, VT 05701-3899. Offers M Ed. Part-time and evening/weekend programs available. *Faculty:* 4 full-time (3 women), 8 part-time/adjunct (6 women). *Students:* 2 full-time (both women), 4 part-time (3 women). Average age 35. 2 applicants, 100% accepted, 1 enrolled. In 2011, 1 master's awarded. *Degree requirements:* For master's, comprehensive exam. *Entrance requirements:* For master's, PRAXIS I (for initial licensure), official college transcripts; 2 letters of reference; minimum GPA of 3.0 (initial licensure) or 2.7 (nonlicensure); interview. Additional exam requirements/recommendations for international students: Required—TOEFL (minimum score 550 paper-based). *Application deadline:* Applications are processed on a rolling basis. Application fee: $35. Electronic applications accepted. *Expenses: Tuition:* Full-time $15,200; part-time $400 per credit. *Required fees:* $45 per semester. *Financial support:* Career-related internships or fieldwork, Federal Work-Study, and unspecified assistantships available. Support available to part-time students. Financial award application deadline: 3/1. *Unit head:* Dr. Maria Bove, Chair, 802-773-5900 Ext. 3243, Fax: 802-776-5258, E-mail: mbove@csj.edu. *Application contact:* Alan Young, Dean of Admissions, 802-773-5900 Ext. 3227, Fax: 802-776-5310, E-mail: alanyoung@csj.edu.

The College of Saint Rose, Graduate Studies, School of Education, Teacher Education Department, Albany, NY 12203-1419. Offers business and marketing (MS Ed); childhood education (MS Ed); curriculum and instruction (MS Ed); early childhood education (MS Ed); elementary education (K-6) (MS Ed); secondary education (MS Ed, Certificate); teacher education (MS Ed, Certificate), including bilingual pupil personnel services (Certificate), teacher education (MS Ed). Part-time and evening/weekend programs available. *Entrance requirements:* For master's, minimum undergraduate GPA of 3.0. Additional exam requirements/recommendations for international students: Required—TOEFL (minimum score 550 paper-based; 213 computer-based). Electronic applications accepted.

College of Staten Island of the City University of New York, Graduate Programs, Department of Education, Program in Childhood Education, Staten Island, NY 10314-6600. Offers MS Ed. Part-time and evening/weekend programs available. *Faculty:* 5 full-time (4 women), 8 part-time/adjunct (4 women). *Students:* 22 full-time, 153 part-time. Average age 30. 49 applicants, 73% accepted, 29 enrolled. In 2011, 80 master's awarded. *Degree requirements:* For master's, research project. *Entrance requirements:* For master's, minimum GPA of 3.0, 2 letters of recommendation, letter of intent, N.Y. State Initial Certification. Additional exam requirements/recommendations for international students: Required—TOEFL (minimum score 550 paper-based; 213 computer-based; 79 iBT), IELTS (minimum score 6.5). *Application deadline:* For fall admission, 4/25 for domestic and international students; for spring admission, 11/15 for domestic and international students. Applications are processed on a rolling basis. Application fee: $125. Electronic applications accepted. *Expenses:* Tuition, state resident: full-time $8210; part-time $345 per credit. Tuition, nonresident: part-time $640 per credit. *Required fees:* $128 per semester. *Financial support:* In 2011–12, 1 student received support. Career-related internships or fieldwork, Federal Work-Study, and scholarships/grants available. Support available to part-time students. Financial award applicants required to submit FAFSA. *Unit head:* Dr. Vivian Shulman, Coordinator, 718-982-4086, Fax: 718-982-3743, E-mail: vivian.shulman@csi.cuny.edu. *Application contact:* Sasha Spence, Assistant Director for Graduate Admissions, 718-982-2699, Fax: 718-982-2500, E-mail: sasha.spence@csi.cuny.edu. Web site: http://www.library.csi.cuny.edu/~education/.

The College of William and Mary, School of Education, Program in Curriculum and Instruction, Williamsburg, VA 23187-8795. Offers elementary education (MA Ed); gifted education (MA Ed); math specialist (MA Ed); reading education (MA Ed); secondary education (MA Ed), including English education, mathematics education, modern foreign languages education, science education, social studies education; special education (MA Ed), including collaborating master educator, general curriculum. *Accreditation:* NCATE. Part-time programs available. *Faculty:* 15 full-time (10 women), 39 part-time/adjunct (32 women). *Students:* 80 full-time (69 women), 13 part-time (11 women); includes 11 minority (3 Black or African American, non-Hispanic/Latino; 1 American Indian or Alaska Native, non-Hispanic/Latino; 2 Hispanic/Latino; 5 Two or more races, non-Hispanic/Latino), 1 international. Average age 25. 220 applicants, 56% accepted, 85 enrolled. In 2011, 78 master's awarded. *Degree requirements:* For master's, project. *Entrance requirements:* For master's, GRE or MAT, minimum GPA of 2.5. Additional exam requirements/recommendations for international students: Required—TOEFL. *Application deadline:* For fall admission, 1/15 for domestic and international students; for spring admission, 10/1 for domestic and international students. Application fee: $50. Electronic applications accepted. *Expenses:* Tuition, state resident: full-time $6400; part-time $365 per credit hour. Tuition, nonresident: full-time $19,720; part-time $985 per credit hour. *Required fees:* $4562. *Financial support:* In 2011–12, 53 students received support, including 10 research assistantships with full and partial tuition reimbursements available (averaging $7,000 per year); career-related internships or fieldwork, Federal Work-Study, institutionally sponsored loans, scholarships/grants, and unspecified assistantships also available. Financial award application deadline: 1/15; financial award applicants required to submit FAFSA. *Faculty research:* National Council of Teachers of Mathematics Standards, counseling, self-concept and self-esteem, special education, curriculum development. *Unit head:* Dr. Margie Mason, Area Coordinator, 757-221-2327, E-mail: mmmaso@wm.edu. *Application contact:* Dorothy Smith Osborne, Assistant Dean for Admission, 757-221-2317, Fax: 757-221-2293, E-mail: dsosbo@wm.edu. Web site: http://education.wm.edu.

Colorado Christian University, Program in Curriculum and Instruction, Lakewood, CO 80226. Offers corporate education (MACI); early childhood educator (MACI); elementary educator (MACI); instructional technology (MACI); master educator (MACI); online course developer (MACI); online teaching and learning (MACI); special education generalist (MACI). Part-time and evening/weekend programs available. *Degree requirements:* For master's, thesis optional, practicum. *Entrance requirements:* For master's, interviews, letters of recommendation. Additional exam requirements/recommendations for international students: Required—TOEFL. Electronic applications accepted. *Expenses:* Contact institution.

The Colorado College, Education Department, Program in Elementary Education, Colorado Springs, CO 80903-3294. Offers elementary school teaching (MAT). *Faculty:* 4 full-time (3 women), 5 part-time/adjunct (4 women). *Students:* 9 full-time (8 women). Average age 26. 17 applicants, 82% accepted, 9 enrolled. In 2011, 9 master's awarded. *Degree requirements:* For master's, thesis, internship. *Application deadline:* For fall admission, 12/1 for domestic and international students. Applications are processed on a rolling basis. Application fee: $50. Electronic applications accepted. *Expenses: Tuition:* Full-time $29,313. *Required fees:* $2000. *Financial support:* In 2011–12, 8 students received support. Career-related internships or fieldwork, institutionally sponsored loans, scholarships/grants, and health care benefits available. Financial award application deadline: 2/15; financial award applicants required to submit FAFSA. *Unit head:* Dr. Charlotte Mendoza, Director, 719-389-6474, Fax: 719-389-6473, E-mail: cmendoza@coloradocollege.edu. *Application contact:* Debra Yazulla Mortenson, Education Services Manager, 719-389-6472, Fax: 719-389-6473, E-mail: debra.mortenson@coloradocollege.edu. Web site: http://www.coloradocollege.edu/academics/dept/education/graduate-programs/elementary-mat.dot.

Columbia College, Graduate Programs, Department of Education, Columbia, SC 29203-5998. Offers divergent learning (M Ed). *Accreditation:* NCATE. Part-time and evening/weekend programs available. Postbaccalaureate distance learning degree programs offered (minimal on-campus study). *Faculty:* 3 full-time (1 woman), 18 part-time/adjunct (10 women). *Students:* 93 full-time (89 women), 18 part-time (16 women); includes 33 minority (32 Black or African American, non-Hispanic/Latino; 1 Asian, non-Hispanic/Latino). Average age 27. 53 applicants, 96% accepted, 43 enrolled. In 2011, 197 master's awarded. *Degree requirements:* For master's, thesis. *Entrance requirements:* For master's, GRE General Test, MAT, 2 recommendations, current South Carolina teaching certificate, minimum GPA of 3.2. *Application deadline:* For fall admission, 8/22 for domestic students. Application fee: $50. *Expenses:* Contact institution. *Financial support:* Available to part-time students. Application deadline: 7/1; applicants required to submit FAFSA. *Unit head:* Dr. Mary Steppling, Chair, 803-786-3782, Fax: 803-786-3034, E-mail: msteppling@colacoll.edu. *Application contact:* Carolyn Emeneker, Director of Graduate School and Evening College Admissions, 803-786-3766, Fax: 803-786-3674, E-mail: emeneker@colacoll.edu.

Columbia College Chicago, Graduate School, Department of Educational Studies, Chicago, IL 60605-1996. Offers elementary education (MAT); English (MAT); interdisciplinary arts (MAT); multicultural education (MA); urban teaching (MA). Part-time and evening/weekend programs available. *Degree requirements:* For master's, thesis, student teaching experience, 100 pre-clinical hours. *Entrance requirements:* For master's, supplemental recommendation form. Additional exam requirements/recommendations for international students: Required—TOEFL (minimum score 550 paper-based; 213 computer-based). Electronic applications accepted.

Columbia International University, Columbia Graduate School, Columbia, SC 29230-3122. Offers Bible teaching (MABT); Christian higher education leadership (Ed D); Christian school educational leadership (Ed D); counseling (MACN); curriculum and instruction (M Ed), including Christian school guidance, English as a second language, learning disabilities, school technology; early childhood and elementary education (MAT); educational administration (M Ed); teaching English as a foreign language (Certificate); teaching English as a foreign language and intercultural studies (MATF). Part-time and evening/weekend programs available. *Degree requirements:* For master's, internships, professional project. *Entrance requirements:* For master's,

Minnesota Multiphasic Personality Inventory, MAT, minimum GPA of 2.7. Additional exam requirements/recommendations for international students: Required—TOEFL. Electronic applications accepted.

Concordia University, College of Education, Portland, OR 97211-6099. Offers curriculum and instruction (elementary) (M Ed); educational administration (M Ed); elementary education (MAT); secondary education (MAT). Part-time programs available. Postbaccalaureate distance learning degree programs offered (no on-campus study). *Degree requirements:* For master's, comprehensive exam, work samples/ portfolio. *Entrance requirements:* For master's, California Basic Educational Skills Test or PRAXIS I, minimum undergraduate GPA of 2.8, graduate 3.0; 2 letters of recommendation. Additional exam requirements/recommendations for international students: Required—TOEFL (minimum score 525 paper-based; 195 computer-based). Electronic applications accepted. *Faculty research:* Learner centered classroom, brain-based learning future of on-line learning.

Concordia University Chicago, College of Education, Program in Teaching, River Forest, IL 60305-1499. Offers early childhood education (MAT); elementary education (MAT); secondary education (MAT). *Degree requirements:* For master's, thesis or alternative. *Entrance requirements:* For master's, minimum GPA of 2.9. Additional exam requirements/recommendations for international students: Required—TOEFL (minimum score 550 paper-based; 195 computer-based). Electronic applications accepted.

Concordia University, Nebraska, Graduate Programs in Education, Program in Educational Administration, Seward, NE 68434-1599. Offers elementary and secondary education (M Ed); elementary education (M Ed); secondary education (M Ed). *Accreditation:* NCATE. Part-time programs available. *Degree requirements:* For master's, thesis or alternative. *Entrance requirements:* For master's, GRE, MAT, or NTE, BS in education or equivalent, minimum GPA of 3.0.

Converse College, School of Education and Graduate Studies, Program in Elementary Education, Spartanburg, SC 29302-0006. Offers M Ed, MAT. Part-time programs available. *Degree requirements:* For master's, capstone paper. *Entrance requirements:* For master's, NTE or PRAXIS II (M Ed), minimum GPA of 2.75, 2 recommendations. Electronic applications accepted.

Creighton University, Graduate School, College of Arts and Sciences, Department of Education, Program in Teaching, Omaha, NE 68178-0001. Offers elementary teaching (M Ed); secondary teaching (M Ed). Part-time and evening/weekend programs available. *Faculty:* 14 full-time (8 women). *Students:* 11 full-time (5 women), 30 part-time (19 women); includes 4 minority (1 Black or African American, non-Hispanic/Latino; 1 American Indian or Alaska Native, non-Hispanic/Latino; 2 Hispanic/Latino), 1 international. Average age 27. 6 applicants, 67% accepted, 4 enrolled. In 2011, 21 master's awarded. *Entrance requirements:* For master's, 3 letters of recommendation, 2 writing samples. Additional exam requirements/recommendations for international students: Required—TOEFL (minimum score 550 paper-based; 213 computer-based; 80 iBT). *Application deadline:* For fall admission, 7/1 priority date for domestic students, 3/1 for international students; for winter admission, 12/1 priority date for domestic students, 6/1 for international students; for spring admission, 3/1 priority date for domestic students, 3/1 for international students. Applications are processed on a rolling basis. Application fee: $50. Electronic applications accepted. *Expenses: Tuition:* Full-time $12,672; part-time $704 per credit hour. *Required fees:* $1410; $136 per semester. Tuition and fees vary according to campus/location and reciprocity agreements. *Financial support:* Scholarships/grants and tuition waivers (partial) available. Support available to part-time students. Financial award applicants required to submit FAFSA. *Unit head:* Dr. Lynne Houtz, Director, 402-280-2247, E-mail: lhoutz@creighton.edu. *Application contact:* Taunya Plater, Senior Program Coordinator, 402-280-2870, Fax: 402-280-2423, E-mail: taunyaplater@creighton.edu.

Curry College, Graduate Studies, Program in Education, Milton, MA 02186-9984. Offers elementary education (M Ed); foundations (non-license) (M Ed); reading (M Ed, Certificate); special education (M Ed). Part-time and evening/weekend programs available. *Degree requirements:* For master's, project or thesis. *Entrance requirements:* For master's, interview, recommendations, resume, written statement. Additional exam requirements/recommendations for international students: Required—TOEFL (minimum score 550 paper-based; 213 computer-based; 80 iBT). *Expenses:* Contact institution. *Faculty research:* Classroom trauma, therapeutic writing, inclusionary practices.

Dallas Baptist University, Dorothy M. Bush College of Education, Teaching Program, Dallas, TX 75211-9299. Offers all-level (MAT); distance learning (MAT); elementary (MAT); English as a second language (MAT); Montessori (MAT); multisensory (MAT); secondary (MAT). Part-time and evening/weekend programs available. *Entrance requirements:* For master's, GRE General Test, minimum GPA of 3.0. Additional exam requirements/recommendations for international students: Required—TOEFL, IELTS. *Application deadline:* Applications are processed on a rolling basis. Application fee: $25. Electronic applications accepted. *Expenses: Tuition:* Full-time $12,060; part-time $670 per credit hour. *Required fees:* $100; $50 per semester. *Financial support:* Federal Work-Study, institutionally sponsored loans, scholarships/grants, and tuition waivers (full and partial) available. Support available to part-time students. Financial award applicants required to submit FAFSA. *Unit head:* Dara Owen, Acting Director, 214-333-5413, Fax: 214-333-5551, E-mail: graduate@dbu.edu. *Application contact:* Kit P. Montgomery, Director of Graduate Programs, 214-333-5242, Fax: 214-333-5579, E-mail: graduate@dbu.edu. Web site: http://www3.dbu.edu/graduate/mat.asp.

Delta State University, Graduate Programs, College of Education, Division of Teacher Education, Programs in Elementary Education, Cleveland, MS 38733-0001. Offers elementary education (M Ed, Ed S); teaching (alternate route) (MAT). *Accreditation:* NCATE. Part-time and evening/weekend programs available. *Degree requirements:* For master's, thesis optional. *Entrance requirements:* For master's, GRE General Test; for Ed S, master's degree, teaching certificate. *Expenses:* Tuition, state resident: full-time $4702; part-time $294 per credit hour. Tuition, nonresident: full-time $12,516; part-time $760 per credit hour. *Required fees:* $586.

Delta State University, Graduate Programs, College of Education, Thad Cochran Center for Rural School Leadership and Research, Program in Professional Studies, Cleveland, MS 38733-0001. Offers counselor education (Ed D); educational leadership (Ed D); elementary education (Ed D); higher education (Ed D). Part-time and evening/weekend programs available. *Degree requirements:* For doctorate, thesis/dissertation. *Entrance requirements:* For doctorate, GRE General Test. *Expenses:* Tuition, state resident: full-time $4702; part-time $294 per credit hour. Tuition, nonresident: full-time $12,516; part-time $760 per credit hour. *Required fees:* $586.

DePaul University, College of Education, Chicago, IL 60106. Offers bilingual bicultural education (M Ed, MA); counseling (M Ed, MA), including college student development, community counseling, school counseling; curriculum studies (M Ed, MA, Ed D); early childhood education (M Ed, MA); educational leadership (M Ed, MA, Ed D), including administration and supervision (M Ed, MA), physical education (M Ed, MA); middle school mathematics education (MS); reading specialist (M Ed, MA); social and cultural foundations in education (M Ed, MA), including curriculum studies/development (MA); special education (M Ed, MA); teaching and learning (M Ed, MA), including elementary education, secondary education; world languages education (M Ed, MA). Part-time and evening/weekend programs available. *Faculty:* 49 full-time (28 women), 94 part-time/adjunct (60 women). *Students:* 894 full-time (707 women), 473 part-time (361 women); includes 349 minority (159 Black or African American, non-Hispanic/Latino; 3 American Indian or Alaska Native, non-Hispanic/Latino; 45 Asian, non-Hispanic/Latino; 115 Hispanic/Latino; 2 Native Hawaiian or other Pacific Islander, non-Hispanic/Latino; 25 Two or more races, non-Hispanic/Latino), 21 international. Average age 30. 872 applicants, 64% accepted, 325 enrolled. In 2011, 499 master's, 10 doctorates awarded. *Median time to degree:* Of those who began their doctoral program in fall 2003, 32% received their degree in 8 years or less. *Degree requirements:* For master's, thesis/ dissertation (for MA); capstone course or paper (for M Ed); for doctorate, thesis/ dissertation. *Entrance requirements:* For master's, interview, minimum GPA of 2.75, 2 letters of recommendation, bachelor's degree conferred by accredited college or university; for doctorate, interview, master's degree, writing sample, 3 letters of recommendation. Additional exam requirements/recommendations for international students: Required—TOEFL (minimum score 550 paper-based; 213 computer-based; 80 iBT). *Application deadline:* For fall admission, 8/15 priority date for domestic students; for winter admission, 12/1 priority date for domestic students; for spring admission, 3/1 priority date for domestic students. Applications are processed on a rolling basis. Application fee: $40. Electronic applications accepted. *Financial support:* In 2011–12, 163 students received support, including 15 research assistantships with full tuition reimbursements available (averaging $6,375 per year); career-related internships or fieldwork, Federal Work-Study, scholarships/grants, and unspecified assistantships also available. Support available to part-time students. Financial award application deadline: 12/31; financial award applicants required to submit FAFSA. *Faculty research:* Reflective teaching, children at risk, loss, ethnicity, urban education. *Total annual research expenditures:* $916,310. *Unit head:* Dr. Paul Zionts, Dean, 773-325-7581, Fax: 773-325-7713, E-mail: pzionts@depaul.edu. *Application contact:* Brandon Washington, Enrollment Management Coordinator, 773-325-1152, Fax: 773-325-2270, E-mail: bwashin3@depaul.edu. Web site: http://education.depaul.edu.

Dominican College, Division of Teacher Education, Department of Teacher Education, Orangeburg, NY 10962-1210. Offers childhood education (MS Ed); teacher of students with disabilities (MS Ed); teacher of visually impaired (MS Ed). *Accreditation:* Teacher Education Accreditation Council. Part-time and evening/weekend programs available. Postbaccalaureate distance learning degree programs offered (minimal on-campus study). *Degree requirements:* For master's, practicum, research project. *Entrance requirements:* For master's, interview, 3 letters of recommendation, minimum undergraduate GPA of 3.0. Additional exam requirements/recommendations for international students: Required—TOEFL (minimum score 550 paper-based; 213 computer-based).

Dominican University, School of Education, River Forest, IL 60305-1099. Offers curriculum and instruction (MA Ed); early childhood education (MS); education (MAT); educational administration (MA); elementary (online) (MS); English as a second language (online) (MS); reading (online) (MS); special education (MS). Part-time and evening/weekend programs available. Postbaccalaureate distance learning degree programs offered (no on-campus study). *Faculty:* 19 full-time (13 women), 53 part-time/ adjunct (41 women). *Students:* 24 full-time (19 women), 434 part-time (357 women); includes 95 minority (27 Black or African American, non-Hispanic/Latino; 1 American Indian or Alaska Native, non-Hispanic/Latino; 12 Asian, non-Hispanic/Latino; 48 Hispanic/Latino; 7 Two or more races, non-Hispanic/Latino), 1 international. Average age 33. 92 applicants, 99% accepted, 91 enrolled. In 2011, 267 master's awarded. *Entrance requirements:* For master's, Illinois certification test of basic skills. Additional exam requirements/recommendations for international students: Required—TOEFL (minimum score 550 paper-based; 213 computer-based; 79 iBT). *Application deadline:* Applications are processed on a rolling basis. Application fee: $25. *Expenses:* Contact institution. *Financial support:* Career-related internships or fieldwork, scholarships/ grants, and tuition waivers (partial) available. Support available to part-time students. Financial award application deadline: 8/15; financial award applicants required to submit FAFSA. *Faculty research:* Governance of private education institutions, reading and language arts, inclusion, organizational planning, leadership and vision. *Unit head:* Dr. Colleen Reardon, Dean, 718-524-6643, Fax: 708-524-6665, E-mail: creardon@ dom.edu. *Application contact:* Keven Hansen, Coordinator of Recruitment and Admissions, 708-524-6921, Fax: 708-524-6665, E-mail: educate@dom.edu. Web site: http://www.dom.edu/soe.

Drury University, Graduate Programs in Education, Springfield, MO 65802. Offers elementary education (M Ed); gifted education (M Ed); human services (M Ed); instructional mathematics K-8 (M Ed); instructional technology (M Ed); middle school teaching (M Ed); secondary education (M Ed); special education (M Ed); special reading (M Ed). *Accreditation:* NCATE. Part-time and evening/weekend programs available. *Degree requirements:* For master's, thesis. *Entrance requirements:* For master's, GRE or MAT, minimum GPA of 2.75. Additional exam requirements/recommendations for international students: Required—TOEFL. Electronic applications accepted. *Faculty research:* Cultural enrichment, research skills, parental involvement relating to reading skills, reading strategies for mainstreaming children.

D'Youville College, Department of Education, Buffalo, NY 14201-1084. Offers elementary education (MS Ed, Teaching Certificate); secondary education (MS Ed, Teaching Certificate); special education (MS Ed). Part-time and evening/weekend programs available. *Faculty:* 29 full-time (18 women), 29 part-time/adjunct (17 women). *Students:* 198 full-time (133 women), 52 part-time (41 women); includes 12 minority (7 Black or African American, non-Hispanic/Latino; 1 American Indian or Alaska Native, non-Hispanic/Latino; 1 Asian, non-Hispanic/Latino; 3 Hispanic/Latino), 161 international. Average age 29. 245 applicants, 46% accepted, 57 enrolled. In 2011, 235 master's awarded. *Degree requirements:* For master's, one foreign language, comprehensive exam, project or thesis. *Entrance requirements:* For master's, GRE (if GPA less than 2.75), minimum GPA of 3.0. Additional exam requirements/recommendations for international students: Required—TOEFL (minimum score 500 paper-based; 173 computer-based). *Application deadline:* For fall admission, 5/1 for international students; for spring admission, 9/1 for international students. Applications are processed on a rolling basis. Application fee: $25. Electronic applications accepted. *Expenses: Tuition:* Full-time $18,960; part-time $790 per credit hour. *Required fees:* $310. Tuition and fees vary according to degree level and program. *Financial support:* In 2011–12, 1 research assistantship with partial tuition reimbursement (averaging $3,000 per year) was awarded; career-related internships or fieldwork, Federal Work-Study, institutionally sponsored loans, scholarships/grants, tuition waivers (full and partial), and unspecified assistantships also available. Support available to part-time students. Financial award application deadline: 3/1; financial award applicants required to submit FAFSA. *Faculty research:* Developmental disabilities, multiculturalism, early childhood education. *Unit head:* Dr. Hilary Lochte, Chair, 716-829-8110, Fax: 716-829-7660. *Application contact:* Linda Fisher, Graduate Admissions Director, 716-829-8400, Fax: 716-829-7900, E-mail: graduateadmissions@dyc.edu.

East Carolina University, Graduate School, College of Education, Department of Business and Information Technologies Education, Greenville, NC 27858-4353. Offers business education (MA Ed); elementary education (MAT); English education (MAT); family and consumer science (MAT); health education (MAT); Hispanic studies (MAT); history education (MAT); marketing education (MA Ed); middle grades education (MAT);

music education (MAT); physical education (MAT); science education (MAT); special education (MAT), including general curriculum; vocation education (MS). *Accreditation:* NCATE. Part-time and evening/weekend programs available. Postbaccalaureate distance learning degree programs offered (no on-campus study). *Degree requirements:* For master's, comprehensive exam, thesis optional. *Entrance requirements:* For master's, GRE or MAT, minimum GPA of 2.5, bachelor's degree in related field, teaching license (MA Ed). Additional exam requirements/recommendations for international students: Required—TOEFL. *Application deadline:* For fall admission, 6/1 priority date for domestic students. Applications are processed on a rolling basis. Application fee: $50. *Expenses:* Tuition, state resident: full-time $3557; part-time $444.63 per semester hour. Tuition, nonresident: full-time $14,351; part-time $1793.88 per semester hour. *Required fees:* $2016; $252 per semester hour. Part-time tuition and fees vary according to course load, campus/location and program. *Financial support:* Federal Work-Study available. Support available to part-time students. Financial award application deadline: 6/1. *Unit head:* Dr. Ivan G. Wallace, Chair, 252-328-6983, Fax: 252-328-6835, E-mail: wallacei@ecu.edu. *Application contact:* Dean of Graduate School, 252-328-6012, Fax: 252-328-6071, E-mail: gradschool@ecu.edu. Web site: http://www.ecu.edu/cs-educ/bite/index.cfm.

East Carolina University, Graduate School, College of Education, Department of Curriculum and Instruction, Greenville, NC 27858-4353. Offers assistive technology (Certificate); autism (Certificate); deaf/blindness (Certificate); elementary education (MA Ed); English education (MA Ed); history (MA Ed); middle grade education (MA Ed); reading education (MA Ed); special education (MA Ed); teaching (MAT). Part-time programs available. Postbaccalaureate distance learning degree programs offered. *Degree requirements:* For master's, comprehensive exam, thesis optional. *Entrance requirements:* For master's, GRE General Test or MAT, interview, bachelor's degree in related field, minimum GPA of 2.5, teaching license. Additional exam requirements/recommendations for international students: Required—TOEFL. *Application deadline:* For fall admission, 6/1 priority date for domestic students. Applications are processed on a rolling basis. Application fee: $50. *Expenses:* Tuition, state resident: full-time $3557; part-time $444.63 per semester hour. Tuition, nonresident: full-time $14,351; part-time $1793.88 per semester hour. *Required fees:* $2016; $252 per semester hour. Part-time tuition and fees vary according to course load, campus/location and program. *Financial support:* Research assistantships, teaching assistantships, and Federal Work-Study available. Support available to part-time students. Financial award application deadline: 6/1; financial award applicants required to submit FAFSA. *Unit head:* Carolyn C. Ledford, Interim Chair, 252-328-1100, E-mail: ledfordc@ecu.edu. *Application contact:* Dean of Graduate School, 252-328-6012, Fax: 252-328-6071, E-mail: gradschool@ecu.edu. Web site: http://www.ecu.edu/cs-educ/ci/Graduate.cfm.

Eastern Connecticut State University, School of Education and Professional Studies/Graduate Division, Program in Elementary Education, Willimantic, CT 06226-2295. Offers MS. *Accreditation:* NCATE. Part-time and evening/weekend programs available. *Degree requirements:* For master's, comprehensive exam or thesis. *Entrance requirements:* For master's, PRAXIS I, minimum GPA of 2.7, teaching certificate. Additional exam requirements/recommendations for international students: Required—TOEFL (minimum score 550 paper-based; 213 computer-based).

Eastern Illinois University, Graduate School, College of Education and Professional Studies, Department of Early Childhood, Elementary and Middle Level Education, Charleston, IL 61920-3099. Offers elementary education (MS Ed). *Accreditation:* NCATE. Part-time programs available. *Degree requirements:* For master's, comprehensive exam. *Expenses:* Tuition, state resident: part-time $279 per credit hour. Tuition, nonresident: part-time $670 per credit hour. *Required fees:* $179.07 per credit hour. $1253 per semester.

Eastern Kentucky University, The Graduate School, College of Education, Department of Curriculum and Instruction, Richmond, KY 40475-3102. Offers elementary education (MA Ed), including early elementary education, reading; library science (MA Ed); music education (MA Ed); secondary and higher education (MA Ed), including secondary education; teaching (MAT). *Accreditation:* NCATE. Part-time programs available. *Degree requirements:* For master's, portfolio is part of exam. *Entrance requirements:* For master's, GRE General Test, PRAXIS II (KY), minimum GPA of 2.5. *Faculty research:* Technology in education, reading instruction, e-portfolios, induction to teacher education, dispositions of teachers.

Eastern Michigan University, Graduate School, College of Education, Department of Teacher Education, Program in K–12 Education, Ypsilanti, MI 48197. Offers curriculum and instruction (MA); elementary education (MA); K-12 education (MA); middle school education (MA); secondary school education (MA). *Accreditation:* NCATE. Part-time and evening/weekend programs available. Postbaccalaureate distance learning degree programs offered (minimal on-campus study). *Students:* 14 full-time (9 women), 87 part-time (62 women); includes 12 minority (7 Black or African American, non-Hispanic/Latino; 1 American Indian or Alaska Native, non-Hispanic/Latino; 1 Asian, non-Hispanic/Latino; 2 Hispanic/Latino; 1 Two or more races, non-Hispanic/Latino). Average age 37. 57 applicants, 74% accepted, 25 enrolled. In 2011, 6 master's awarded. *Entrance requirements:* For master's, GRE. Additional exam requirements/recommendations for international students: Required—TOEFL. *Application deadline:* Applications are processed on a rolling basis. Application fee: $35. *Expenses:* Tuition, state resident: full-time $10,367; part-time $432 per credit hour. Tuition, nonresident: full-time $20,435; part-time $851 per credit hour. *Required fees:* $39 per credit hour. $46 per semester. One-time fee: $100. Tuition and fees vary according to course level, degree level and reciprocity agreements. *Financial support:* Fellowships, research assistantships with full tuition reimbursements, teaching assistantships with full tuition reimbursements, career-related internships or fieldwork, Federal Work-Study, institutionally sponsored loans, scholarships/grants, tuition waivers (partial), and unspecified assistantships available. Support available to part-time students. Financial award applicants required to submit FAFSA. *Unit head:* Dr. Wendy Burke, Coordinator, 734-487-3260, Fax: 734-487-2101, E-mail: wendy.burke@emich.edu. *Application contact:* Dr. Anne Bednar, Advisor, 734-487-3260, Fax: 734-487-2101, E-mail: anne.bednar@emich.edu.

Eastern Nazarene College, Adult and Graduate Studies, Division of Teacher Education, Quincy, MA 02170. Offers administration (M Ed); early childhood education (M Ed, Certificate); elementary education (M Ed, Certificate); English as a second language (Certificate); instructional enrichment and development (Certificate); middle school education (M Ed, Certificate); moderate special needs education (Certificate); principal (Certificate); program development and supervision (Certificate); secondary education (M Ed, Certificate); special education administrator (Certificate); special needs (M Ed); supervisor (Certificate); teacher of reading (M Ed, Certificate). M Ed also available through weekend program for administration, special needs, and teacher of reading only. Part-time and evening/weekend programs available. *Entrance requirements:* Additional exam requirements/recommendations for international students: Required—TOEFL (minimum score 550 paper-based).

Eastern New Mexico University, Graduate School, College of Education and Technology, Department of Curriculum and Instruction, Portales, NM 88130. Offers bilingual education (M Ed); educational technology (M Ed); elementary education (M Ed); English as a second language (M Ed); pedagogy and learning (M Ed); professional technical education (M Ed); reading/literacy (M Ed). Part-time programs available. Postbaccalaureate distance learning degree programs offered (minimal on-campus study). *Degree requirements:* For master's, comprehensive exam, thesis optional. *Entrance requirements:* For master's, minimum GPA of 3.0, photocopy of teaching license, writing assessment, letter of recommendation. Additional exam requirements/recommendations for international students: Required—TOEFL (minimum score 550 paper-based; 213 computer-based; 79 iBT), IELTS (minimum score 6). Electronic applications accepted.

Eastern Oregon University, Program in Elementary Education, La Grande, OR 97850-2899. Offers MAT. Part-time programs available. Postbaccalaureate distance learning degree programs offered (minimal on-campus study). *Degree requirements:* For master's, thesis. *Entrance requirements:* For master's, NTE.

Eastern Washington University, Graduate Studies, College of Arts, Letters and Education, Department of Education, Program in Elementary Teaching, Cheney, WA 99004-2431. Offers M Ed. *Degree requirements:* For master's, comprehensive exam. *Entrance requirements:* For master's, minimum GPA of 3.0. *Application deadline:* For fall admission, 4/1 priority date for domestic students; for spring admission, 1/15 for domestic students. Applications are processed on a rolling basis. Application fee: $50. *Financial support:* In 2011–12, teaching assistantships with partial tuition reimbursements (averaging $7,000 per year) were awarded; career-related internships or fieldwork, Federal Work-Study, institutionally sponsored loans, scholarships/grants, health care benefits, tuition waivers (partial), and unspecified assistantships also available. Support available to part-time students. Financial award application deadline: 2/1; financial award applicants required to submit FAFSA. *Unit head:* Robin Showalter, Program Coordinator, 509-359-6492, E-mail: rshowalter@mail.ewu.edu. *Application contact:* Dr. Judy Leach, Adviser, 509-359-2500, Fax: 509-359-4822.

East Stroudsburg University of Pennsylvania, Graduate School, College of Education, Program in Elementary Education, East Stroudsburg, PA 18301-2999. Offers M Ed. Part-time and evening/weekend programs available. *Degree requirements:* For master's, comprehensive exam, professional portfolio, curriculum project or action research. *Entrance requirements:* For master's, PRAXIS/teacher certification, letter of recommendation, Pennsylvania Department of Education requirements. Additional exam requirements/recommendations for international students: Required—TOEFL (minimum score 560 paper-based; 220 computer-based; 83 iBT).

East Tennessee State University, School of Graduate Studies, College of Education, Department of Curriculum and Instruction, Johnson City, TN 37614. Offers educational media/educational technology (M Ed), including educational communications and technology, school library media; elementary education (M Ed); reading (MA), including reading education, storytelling; school library professional (Post-Master's Certificate); secondary education (M Ed), including classroom technology, secondary education (M Ed, MAT); storytelling (Postbaccalaureate Certificate); teacher education with multiple levels (initial licensure) (MAT), including elementary education, middle grades education, secondary education (M Ed, MAT). *Accreditation:* NCATE. Part-time and evening/weekend programs available. Postbaccalaureate distance learning degree programs offered (no on-campus study). *Faculty:* 20 full-time (13 women), 3 part-time/adjunct (all women). *Students:* 108 full-time (76 women), 107 part-time (97 women); includes 9 minority (4 Black or African American, non-Hispanic/Latino; 1 Asian, non-Hispanic/Latino; 2 Hispanic/Latino; 2 Two or more races, non-Hispanic/Latino), 2 international. Average age 33. 141 applicants, 57% accepted, 79 enrolled. In 2011, 129 master's awarded. *Degree requirements:* For master's, comprehensive exam, thesis optional, student teaching, practicum; for other advanced degree, field work (school library); culminating experience (storytelling). *Entrance requirements:* For master's, GRE, SAT, ACT, PRAXIS, minimum GPA of 3.0; for other advanced degree, master's degree, TN teaching license (school library professional post-master's certificate); three letters of recommendation (storytelling certificate). Additional exam requirements/recommendations for international students: Required—TOEFL (minimum score 550 paper-based; 213 computer-based; 79 iBT). *Application deadline:* For fall admission, 6/1 for domestic students, 4/30 for international students; for spring admission, 11/1 for domestic students, 4/30 for international students. Application fee: $35 ($45 for international students). Electronic applications accepted. *Expenses:* Tuition, state resident: full-time $7312; part-time $350 per credit hour. Tuition, nonresident: full-time $18,490; part-time $621 per credit hour. *Required fees:* $63 per credit hour. Tuition and fees vary according to course load and program. *Financial support:* In 2011–12, 60 students received support, including 7 research assistantships with full tuition reimbursements available (averaging $6,000 per year), 11 teaching assistantships with full tuition reimbursements available (averaging $6,000 per year); career-related internships or fieldwork, institutionally sponsored loans, scholarships/grants, and unspecified assistantships also available. Financial award application deadline: 7/1; financial award applicants required to submit FAFSA. *Faculty research:* Critical thinking; curriculum development in reading, math, and science education; cultural diversity; cognitive processes; effective teaching strategies. *Unit head:* Dr. Rhona Hurwitz, Chair, 423-439-7598, Fax: 423-439-8362, E-mail: hurwitz@etsu.edu. *Application contact:* Fiona Goodyear, Graduate Specialist, 423-439-6148, Fax: 423-439-5624, E-mail: goodyear@etsu.edu.

Edinboro University of Pennsylvania, School of Education, Department of Elementary, Middle and Secondary Education, Edinboro, PA 16444. Offers elementary education (M Ed); middle/secondary instruction (M Ed). Part-time and evening/weekend programs available. *Faculty:* 4 full-time (2 women). *Students:* 104 full-time (58 women), 131 part-time (95 women); includes 5 minority (3 Black or African American, non-Hispanic/Latino; 2 Hispanic/Latino). Average age 30. In 2011, 82 master's awarded. *Degree requirements:* For master's, comprehensive exam, thesis or alternative, project. *Entrance requirements:* For master's, GRE or MAT, minimum QPA of 2.5. *Application deadline:* Applications are processed on a rolling basis. Application fee: $30. Electronic applications accepted. *Financial support:* In 2011–12, 14 research assistantships with full and partial tuition reimbursements (averaging $4,050 per year) were awarded; career-related internships or fieldwork, Federal Work-Study, scholarships/grants, and unspecified assistantships also available. Support available to part-time students. Financial award application deadline: 2/15; financial award applicants required to submit FAFSA. *Unit head:* Dr. Jo Ann Holtz, Program Head, Middle and Secondary Instruction, 814-732-2794, E-mail: jholtz@edinboro.edu. *Application contact:* Dr. Alan Biel, Dean of Graduate Studies and Research, 814-732-2856, Fax: 814-732-2611, E-mail: abiel@edinboro.edu.

Edinboro University of Pennsylvania, School of Education, Department of Professional Studies, Edinboro, PA 16444. Offers counseling (MA), including community counseling, elementary guidance, rehabilitation counseling, secondary guidance, student personnel services; educational leadership (M Ed), including elementary school administration, secondary school administration; educational psychology (M Ed); educational specialist school psychology (MS); elementary principal (Certificate); elementary school guidance counselor (Certificate); K-12 school administration (Certificate); letter of eligibility (Certificate); reading (M Ed); reading specialist (Certificate); school psychology (Certificate); school supervision (Certificate), including music, special education. Part-time and evening/weekend programs available. *Faculty:* 13 full-time (8 women). *Students:* 171 full-time (134 women), 563 part-time (441 women); includes 26 minority (20 Black or African American, non-Hispanic/Latino; 1

American Indian or Alaska Native, non-Hispanic/Latino; 1 Asian, non-Hispanic/Latino; 4 Hispanic/Latino). Average age 31. In 2011, 297 master's, 49 other advanced degrees awarded. *Degree requirements:* For master's, thesis or alternative, competency exam; for Certificate, thesis or alternative. *Entrance requirements:* For master's and Certificate, GRE or MAT, minimum QPA of 2.5. *Application deadline:* Applications are processed on a rolling basis. Application fee: $30. Electronic applications accepted. *Financial support:* In 2011–12, 60 research assistantships with full and partial tuition reimbursements (averaging $4,050 per year) were awarded; career-related internships or fieldwork, Federal Work-Study, scholarships/grants, and unspecified assistantships also available. Support available to part-time students. Financial award application deadline: 2/15; financial award applicants required to submit FAFSA. *Unit head:* Dr. Susan Norton, 814-732-2260, E-mail: scnorton@edinboro.edu. *Application contact:* Dr. Andrew Pushchack, Program Head, Educational Leadership, 814-732-1548, E-mail: apushchack@edinboro.edu.

Elizabeth City State University, School of Education and Psychology, Program in Elementary Education, Elizabeth City, NC 27909-7806. Offers M Ed. *Accreditation:* NCATE. Part-time and evening/weekend programs available. *Degree requirements:* For master's, comprehensive exam, thesis. *Entrance requirements:* For master's, GRE and/or MAT, full-time teacher employment in elementary classroom. Additional exam requirements/recommendations for international students: Recommended—TOEFL. Electronic applications accepted. *Faculty research:* Diverse learners, disproportionality, inclusionary classrooms, international curriculum development.

Elms College, Division of Education, Chicopee, MA 01013-2839. Offers early childhood education (MAT); education (M Ed, CAGS); elementary education (MAT); English as a second language (MAT); reading (MAT); secondary education (MAT), including biology education, English education, Spanish education; special education (MAT). Part-time and evening/weekend programs available. *Degree requirements:* For master's, thesis (for some programs). *Entrance requirements:* For master's, Massachusetts Educators Certification Test, minimum GPA of 3.0; for CAGS, master's degree in education. Additional exam requirements/recommendations for international students: Required—TOEFL.

Elon University, Program in Education, Elon, NC 27244-2010. Offers elementary education (M Ed); gifted education (M Ed); special education (M Ed). *Accreditation:* NCATE. Part-time programs available. *Faculty:* 19 full-time (15 women). *Students:* 47 part-time (41 women); includes 8 minority (7 Black or African American, non-Hispanic/Latino; 1 Asian, non-Hispanic/Latino). Average age 33. 29 applicants, 86% accepted, 22 enrolled. In 2011, 39 master's awarded. *Entrance requirements:* For master's, GRE, MAT. Additional exam requirements/recommendations for international students: Required—TOEFL (minimum score 550 paper-based; 213 computer-based; 79 iBT). *Application deadline:* For winter admission, 6/1 priority date for domestic students. Applications are processed on a rolling basis. Application fee: $50. Electronic applications accepted. *Expenses:* Contact institution. *Financial support:* In 2011–12, 5 students received support. Federal Work-Study and scholarships/grants available. Support available to part-time students. Financial award application deadline: 6/1; financial award applicants required to submit FAFSA. *Faculty research:* Teaching reading to low-achieving second and third graders, pre- and post-student teaching attitudes , children's writing, whole language methodology, critical creative thinking. *Unit head:* Dr. Angela Owusu-Ansah, Director and Associate Dean of Education, 336-278-5885, Fax: 336-278-5919, E-mail: aansah@elon.edu. *Application contact:* Art Fadde, Director of Graduate Admissions, 800-334-8448 Ext. 3, Fax: 336-278-7699, E-mail: afadde@elon.edu. Web site: http://www.elon.edu/med/.

Emmanuel College, Graduate and Professional Programs, Graduate Programs in Education, Boston, MA 02115. Offers educational leadership (CAGS); elementary education (MAT); school administration (M Ed); secondary education (MAT). Part-time and evening/weekend programs available. *Faculty:* 3 full-time (all women), 11 part-time/adjunct (3 women). *Students:* 12 full-time (11 women), 28 part-time (21 women); includes 9 minority (6 Black or African American, non-Hispanic/Latino; 1 American Indian or Alaska Native, non-Hispanic/Latino; 2 Hispanic/Latino). Average age 30. 9 applicants, 78% accepted, 6 enrolled. In 2011, 14 degrees awarded. *Degree requirements:* For master's, 36 credits, including 6-credit practicum. *Entrance requirements:* For master's and CAGS, transcripts from all regionally-accredited institutions attended (showing proof of bachelor's degree completion), 2 letters of recommendation, essay, resume, interview. Additional exam requirements/recommendations for international students: Required—TOEFL (minimum score 600 paper-based; 250 computer-based; 106 iBT) or IELTS (minimum score 6.5). *Application deadline:* For fall admission, 7/31 priority date for domestic students; for spring admission, 11/30 priority date for domestic students. Applications are processed on a rolling basis. Application fee: $0. Electronic applications accepted. *Expenses: Tuition:* Part-time $2139 per course. Tuition and fees vary according to program and reciprocity agreements. *Financial support:* Applicants required to submit FAFSA. *Faculty research:* Literature/reading, history of education, multicultural education, special education. *Unit head:* Dr. Joyce DeLeo, Vice President of Academic Affairs, 617-735-9700, Fax: 617-507-0434, E-mail: gpp@emmanuel.edu. *Application contact:* Enrollment Counselor, 617-735-9700, Fax: 617-507-0434, E-mail: gpp@emmanuel.edu. Web site: http://gpp.emmanuel.edu.

Emporia State University, Graduate School, Teachers College, Department of Elementary Education, Early Childhood, and Special Education, Program in Master Teacher, Emporia, KS 66801-5087. Offers elementary subject matter (MS); reading (MS). *Accreditation:* NCATE. Part-time programs available. *Students:* 83 part-time (80 women); includes 6 minority (3 Black or African American, non-Hispanic/Latino; 1 Asian, non-Hispanic/Latino; 2 Hispanic/Latino). 21 applicants, 86% accepted, 15 enrolled. In 2011, 31 master's awarded. *Degree requirements:* For master's, comprehensive exam or thesis, practicum. *Entrance requirements:* For master's, GRE General Test or MAT, graduate essay exam, appropriate bachelor's degree, letters of recommendation. Additional exam requirements/recommendations for international students: Required—TOEFL (minimum score 520 paper-based; 133 computer-based; 68 iBT). *Application deadline:* For fall admission, 8/15 priority date for domestic students. Applications are processed on a rolling basis. Application fee: $30 ($75 for international students). Electronic applications accepted. *Expenses:* Tuition, state resident: full-time $2342; part-time $195 per credit hour. Tuition, nonresident: full-time $7254; part-time $605 per credit hour. *Required fees:* $66 per credit hour. Tuition and fees vary according to campus/location. *Financial support:* Federal Work-Study, institutionally sponsored loans, health care benefits, and unspecified assistantships available. Financial award application deadline: 3/15; financial award applicants required to submit FAFSA. *Unit head:* Dr. Jean Morrow, Chair, 620-341-5766, E-mail: jmorrow@emporia.edu. *Application contact:* Mary Sewell, Admissions Coordinator, 800-950-GRAD, Fax: 620-341-5909, E-mail: msewell@emporia.edu.

Endicott College, Van Loan School of Graduate and Professional Studies, Program in Elementary Education, Beverly, MA 01915-2096. Offers initial and professional licensure (M Ed). Part-time and evening/weekend programs available. *Faculty:* 1 full-time (0 women). *Students:* 1 (woman) full-time, 4 part-time (all women). Average age 41. 4 applicants, 25% accepted, 0 enrolled. In 2011, 2 master's awarded. *Degree requirements:* For master's, comprehensive exam. *Entrance requirements:* For master's, MAT or GRE, Massachusetts teaching certificate, 2 professional letters of recommendation. Additional exam requirements/recommendations for international students: Required—TOEFL. *Application deadline:* Applications are processed on a rolling basis. Application fee: $50. Electronic applications accepted. Tuition and fees vary according to degree level and program. *Financial support:* Career-related internships or fieldwork, Federal Work-Study, and institutionally sponsored loans available. Financial award applicants required to submit FAFSA. *Unit head:* Dr. John D. MacLean, Jr., Director of Licensure Programs, 978-232-2408, E-mail: jmaclean@endicott.edu. *Application contact:* Vice President and Dean of the School of Graduate and Professional Studies. Web site: http://www.endicott.edu/GradProf/GPSGradMEd.aspx.

Fairfield University, Graduate School of Education and Allied Professions, Fairfield, CT 06824-5195. Offers applied psychology (MA); bilingual education (CAS); clinical mental health counseling (MA, CAS); educational technology (MA); elementary education (MA); family studies (MA); marriage and family therapy (MA); school counseling (MA, CAS); school psychology (MA, CAS); special education (MA); teaching (Certificate); teaching and foundations (MA, CAS); TESOL foreign language and bilingual/multicultural education (MA, CAS). *Accreditation:* NCATE. Part-time and evening/weekend programs available. *Faculty:* 24 full-time (19 women). *Students:* 147 full-time (120 women), 391 part-time (321 women); includes 60 minority (13 Black or African American, non-Hispanic/Latino; 8 Asian, non-Hispanic/Latino; 35 Hispanic/Latino; 4 Two or more races, non-Hispanic/Latino), 1 international. Average age 34. 319 applicants, 48% accepted, 80 enrolled. In 2011, 185 master's, 20 other advanced degrees awarded. *Degree requirements:* For master's, comprehensive exam. *Entrance requirements:* For master's, PRAXIS I (for certification programs), minimum QPA of 3.0, 2 recommendations, resume. Additional exam requirements/recommendations for international students: Required—TOEFL (minimum score 550 paper-based; 213 computer-based; 84 iBT) or IELTS (minimum score 7.5). *Application deadline:* For fall admission, 2/15 for international students; for spring admission, 10/1 for international students. Application fee: $60. Electronic applications accepted. *Expenses: Tuition:* Part-time $600 per credit hour. *Required fees:* $25 per term. *Financial support:* In 2011–12, 45 students received support. Career-related internships or fieldwork and unspecified assistantships available. Financial award applicants required to submit FAFSA. *Faculty research:* Literacy, adolescent psychology, special education, early childhood education, teaching development. *Unit head:* Dr. Susan D. Franzosa, Dean, 203-254-4000 Ext. 4250, Fax: 203-254-4241, E-mail: sfranzosa@fairfield.edu. *Application contact:* Marianne Gumpper, Director of Graduate and Continuing Studies Admission, 203-254-4184, Fax: 203-254-4073, E-mail: gradadmis@fairfield.edu. Web site: http://www.fairfield.edu/gseap/gseap_grad_1.html.

Fayetteville State University, Graduate School, Program in Elementary Education, Fayetteville, NC 28301-4298. Offers MA Ed. *Accreditation:* NCATE. Part-time and evening/weekend programs available. *Faculty:* 9 full-time (7 women), 1 (woman) part-time/adjunct. In 2011, 2 master's awarded. *Degree requirements:* For master's, comprehensive exam, internships. *Entrance requirements:* For master's, GRE or MAT, minimum GPA of 2.5, professional certification or waiver permission. *Application deadline:* For fall admission, 4/15 for domestic students; for spring admission, 10/15 for domestic students. Applications are processed on a rolling basis. Application fee: $35. Electronic applications accepted. *Faculty research:* Outdoor play, early literacy, math, professional development, accreditation. *Unit head:* Dr. Saundra Shorter, Chairperson, 910-672-1257, E-mail: sshorter@uncfsu.edu. *Application contact:* Katrina Hoffman, Graduate Admission Officer, 910-672-1374, Fax: 910-672-1470, E-mail: khoffma1@uncfsu.edu.

Ferris State University, College of Education and Human Services, School of Education, Big Rapids, MI 49307. Offers administration (MSCTE); curriculum and instruction (M Ed), including administration, elementary education, experiential education, philanthropic education, reading, secondary education, special education, subject matter option; education technology (MSCTE); instructor (MSCTE); post-secondary administration (MSCTE); training and development (MSCTE). Part-time and evening/weekend programs available. Postbaccalaureate distance learning degree programs offered (minimal on-campus study). *Faculty:* 9 full-time (7 women), 9 part-time/adjunct (6 women). *Students:* 8 full-time (7 women), 132 part-time (75 women); includes 13 minority (11 Black or African American, non-Hispanic/Latino; 1 American Indian or Alaska Native, non-Hispanic/Latino; 1 Hispanic/Latino), 5 international. Average age 36. 20 applicants, 100% accepted, 8 enrolled. In 2011, 51 master's awarded. *Degree requirements:* For master's, thesis, research paper. *Entrance requirements:* For master's, 2 years of work experience for vocational setting, minimum GPA of 2.75. Additional exam requirements/recommendations for international students: Recommended—TOEFL (minimum score 500 paper-based; 173 computer-based; 61 iBT). *Application deadline:* For fall admission, 7/1 priority date for domestic students, 7/1 for international students; for spring admission, 11/1 priority date for domestic students, 11/1 for international students. Applications are processed on a rolling basis. Application fee: $30. Electronic applications accepted. Application fee is waived when completed online. *Financial support:* Career-related internships or fieldwork and scholarships/grants available. Support available to part-time students. Financial award applicants required to submit FAFSA. *Faculty research:* Suicide prevention, reading, women in education, special needs, administration. *Unit head:* Dr. James Powell, Director, 231-591-5362, Fax: 231-591-2043, E-mail: powelj20@ferris.edu. *Application contact:* Kimisue Worrall, Secretary, 231-591-5361, Fax: 231-591-2043. Web site: http://www.ferris.edu/education/education/.

Fitchburg State University, Division of Graduate and Continuing Education, Program in Elementary Education, Fitchburg, MA 01420-2697. Offers M Ed. *Accreditation:* NCATE. Part-time and evening/weekend programs available. *Students:* 45 part-time (39 women). Average age 33. 7 applicants, 100% accepted, 6 enrolled. In 2011, 18 master's awarded. *Entrance requirements:* Additional exam requirements/recommendations for international students: Required—TOEFL (minimum score 550 paper-based; 213 computer-based; 79 iBT). *Application deadline:* For fall admission, 7/15 for international students; for spring admission, 12/1 for international students. Applications are processed on a rolling basis. Application fee: $25 ($50 for international students). Electronic applications accepted. *Expenses:* Tuition, state resident: full-time $2700; part-time $150 per credit. Tuition, nonresident: full-time $2700; part-time $150 per credit. *Required fees:* $2286; $127 per credit. *Financial support:* In 2011–12, research assistantships with partial tuition reimbursements (averaging $5,500 per year) were awarded; Federal Work-Study, scholarships/grants, and unspecified assistantships also available. Support available to part-time students. Financial award application deadline: 3/1; financial award applicants required to submit FAFSA. *Unit head:* Richard Beardmore, Chair, 978-665-3193, Fax: 978-665-3658, E-mail: gce@fitchburgstate.edu. *Application contact:* Kay Reynolds, Director of Admissions, 978-665-3144, Fax: 978-665-4540, E-mail: admissions@fitchburgstate.edu. Web site: http://www.fitchburgstate.edu.

Florida Agricultural and Mechanical University, Division of Graduate Studies, Research, and Continuing Education, College of Education, Department of Elementary Education, Tallahassee, FL 32307-3200. Offers early childhood and elementary education (M Ed, MS Ed). *Accreditation:* NCATE. *Degree requirements:* For master's, thesis (for some programs). *Entrance requirements:* For master's, GRE General Test, minimum GPA of 3.0. Additional exam requirements/recommendations for international students: Required—TOEFL.

Florida Atlantic University, College of Education, Department of Teaching and Learning, Boca Raton, FL 33431-0991. Offers curriculum and instruction (M Ed); elementary education (M Ed); environmental education (M Ed); reading education (M Ed); social foundations of education (M Ed). *Accreditation:* NCATE. Part-time and evening/weekend programs available. *Faculty:* 32 full-time (25 women), 90 part-time/adjunct (68 women). *Students:* 34 full-time (30 women), 103 part-time (96 women); includes 29 minority (8 Black or African American, non-Hispanic/Latino; 7 Asian, non-Hispanic/Latino; 11 Hispanic/Latino; 3 Two or more races, non-Hispanic/Latino), 1 international. Average age 32. 96 applicants, 66% accepted, 24 enrolled. In 2011, 71 master's awarded. *Entrance requirements:* For master's, GRE General Test, minimum GPA of 3.0 in last 2 years of undergraduate course work. Additional exam requirements/recommendations for international students: Required—TOEFL. *Application deadline:* For fall admission, 7/1 for domestic students, 2/15 for international students; for spring admission, 11/1 for domestic students, 7/15 for international students. Applications are processed on a rolling basis. Application fee: $30. *Expenses: Tuition, area resident:* Part-time $343.02 per credit hour. Tuition, state resident: full-time $8232. Tuition, nonresident: full-time $23,931; part-time $997.14 per credit hour. *Financial support:* Fellowships with partial tuition reimbursements, research assistantships with partial tuition reimbursements, teaching assistantships with partial tuition reimbursements, career-related internships or fieldwork, scholarships/grants, and unspecified assistantships available. *Faculty research:* Technology, teaching English to speakers of other languages, math teaching, electronic portfolio assessment, global perspectives through social studies. *Unit head:* Dr. Barbara Ridener, Chairperson, 561-297-3588. *Application contact:* Dr. Eliah Watlington, Associate Dean, 561-296-8520, Fax: 261-297-2991, E-mail: ewatling@fau.edu. Web site: http://www.coe.fau.edu/academicdepartments/tl/.

Florida Institute of Technology, Graduate Programs, College of Science, Department of Education and Interdisciplinary Studies, Melbourne, FL 32901-6975. Offers computer education (MS); elementary science education (M Ed); environmental education (MS); interdisciplinary science (MS); mathematics education (MS, PhD, Ed S); science education (MS, PhD, Ed S), including informal science education (MS); teaching (MAT). Part-time and evening/weekend programs available. *Faculty:* 4 full-time (1 woman), 3 part-time/adjunct (2 women). *Students:* 22 full-time (16 women), 27 part-time (18 women); includes 8 minority (2 Black or African American, non-Hispanic/Latino; 4 Asian, non-Hispanic/Latino; 2 Hispanic/Latino), 9 international. Average age 34. 57 applicants, 70% accepted, 19 enrolled. In 2011, 5 master's, 1 doctorate awarded. Terminal master's awarded for partial completion of doctoral program. *Median time to degree:* Of those who began their doctoral program in fall 2003, 50% received their degree in 8 years or less. *Degree requirements:* For master's, comprehensive exam (for some programs), thesis optional; for doctorate, comprehensive exam, thesis/dissertation; for Ed S, comprehensive exam. *Entrance requirements:* For master's, minimum GPA of 3.0, resume, 3 letters of recommendation (elementary science education), statement of objectives; for doctorate, minimum GPA of 3.2, resume, 3 letters of recommendation, statement of objectives, 3 years teaching experience (recommended); for Ed S, minimum GPA of 3.0, resume, 3 letters of recommendation, statement of objectives. Additional exam requirements/recommendations for international students: Required—TOEFL (minimum score 550 paper-based; 213 computer-based; 79 iBT). *Application deadline:* For fall admission, 4/1 for international students; for spring admission, 9/30 for international students. Applications are processed on a rolling basis. Electronic applications accepted. *Expenses: Tuition:* Full-time $19,620; part-time $1090 per credit hour. Tuition and fees vary according to campus/location. *Financial support:* In 2011–12, 1 teaching assistantship with full and partial tuition reimbursement (averaging $797 per year) was awarded; research assistantships with full and partial tuition reimbursements, career-related internships or fieldwork, institutionally sponsored loans, tuition waivers (partial), unspecified assistantships, and tuition remissions also available. Support available to part-time students. Financial award application deadline: 3/1; financial award applicants required to submit FAFSA. *Faculty research:* Measurement and evaluation, computers in education, educational technology. *Total annual research expenditures:* $1. *Unit head:* Dr. Lazlo A. Baksay, Department Head, 321-674-7205, Fax: 321-674-7598, E-mail: baksay@fit.edu. *Application contact:* Cheryl A. Brown, Associate Director of Graduate Admissions, 321-674-7581, Fax: 321-723-9468, E-mail: cbrown@fit.edu. Web site: http://cos.fit.edu/education/.

Florida International University, College of Education, Department of Curriculum and Instruction, Miami, FL 33199. Offers art education (MAT, MS, Ed D); curriculum and instruction (Ed S); curriculum development (MS); curriculum studies (PhD); early childhood education (MS, Ed D); elementary education (MS, Ed D); English education (MAT, MS, Ed D); foreign language education - teaching English to speakers of other languages (TESOL) (MS, Certificate), including foreign language education (Certificate), teaching English (MS); French education - initial teacher preparation (MAT); international and intercultural development education (Ed D); international and intercultural developmental education (MS); language, literacy and culture (PhD); learning technologies (MS, Ed D, PhD); mathematics education (MAT, MS, Ed D, PhD); modern language education/bilingual education (MS, Ed D); physical education (MS); reading education (MS, Ed D); science education (MAT, MS, Ed D, PhD); social studies education (MAT, MS, Ed D); Spanish education - initial teacher preparation (MAT); special education (MS). Part-time and evening/weekend programs available. *Degree requirements:* For doctorate, comprehensive exam, thesis/dissertation. *Entrance requirements:* For master's, GRE General Test, Florida General Knowledge Test or Florida College Level Academic Skills Test; for doctorate and other advanced degree, GRE General Test. Additional exam requirements/recommendations for international students: Required—TOEFL (minimum score 550 paper-based; 213 computer-based; 80 iBT), IELTS (minimum score 6.3). Electronic applications accepted.

Florida Memorial University, School of Education, Miami-Dade, FL 33054. Offers elementary education (MS); exceptional student education (MS); reading (MS). *Degree requirements:* For master's, comprehensive exam or thesis, field and clinical experiences, exit exam. *Entrance requirements:* For master's, GRE, CLAST, PRAXIS I, baccalaureate or graduate degree with minimum GPA of 3.0 in last 60 hours, 3 recommendations. Additional exam requirements/recommendations for international students: Recommended—TOEFL.

Florida State University, The Graduate School, College of Education, School of Teacher Education, Program in Elementary Education, Tallahassee, FL 32306. Offers MS, Ed D, PhD, Ed S. Part-time programs available. *Faculty:* 4 full-time (3 women). *Students:* 19 full-time (18 women), 17 part-time (13 women); includes 13 minority (10 Black or African American, non-Hispanic/Latino; 3 American Indian or Alaska Native, non-Hispanic/Latino), 3 international. Average age 31. 15 applicants, 53% accepted, 3 enrolled. In 2011, 16 master's, 2 doctorates awarded. *Degree requirements:* For master's and Ed S, comprehensive exam, thesis optional; for doctorate, comprehensive exam, thesis/dissertation. *Entrance requirements:* For master's, doctorate, and Ed S, GRE General Test, minimum GPA of 3.0. Additional exam requirements/recommendations for international students: Required—TOEFL (minimum score 550 paper-based; 213 computer-based; 80 iBT); Recommended—TWE. *Application deadline:* For fall admission, 7/1 for domestic and international students; for winter admission, 11/1 for domestic and international students; for spring admission, 3/1 for domestic and international students. Applications are processed on a rolling basis. Application fee: $30. Electronic applications accepted. *Expenses:* Tuition, state resident: full-time $9474; part-time $350.88 per credit hour. Tuition, nonresident: full-time $16,236; part-time $601.34 per credit hour. *Required fees:* $630 per semester. One-time fee: $20. Tuition and fees vary according to course load and campus/location. *Financial support:* Fellowships with full and partial tuition reimbursements, research assistantships with full and partial tuition reimbursements, teaching assistantships with full and partial tuition reimbursements, career-related internships or fieldwork, scholarships/grants, health care benefits, and unspecified assistantships available. Financial award applicants required to submit FAFSA. *Unit head:* Dr. Diana Rice, Head, 850-644-6553, Fax: 850-644-8715, E-mail: drice@fsu.edu. *Application contact:* Harriet Kasper, Program Assistant, 850-644-2122, Fax: 850-644-7736, E-mail: hkasper@fsu.edu. Web site: http://www.coe.fsu.edu/Academic-Programs/Departments/School-of-Teacher-Education-STE/Degree-Programs/Elementary-Education.

Fordham University, Graduate School of Education, Division of Curriculum and Teaching, New York, NY 10023. Offers adult education (MS, MSE); bilingual teacher education (MSE); curriculum and teaching (MSE); early childhood education (MSE); elementary education (MST); language, literacy, and learning (PhD); reading education (MSE, Adv C); secondary education (MAT, MSE); special education (MSE, Adv C); teaching English as a second language (MSE). *Accreditation:* NCATE. *Degree requirements:* For doctorate, thesis/dissertation; for Adv C, thesis. *Entrance requirements:* For doctorate, MAT, GRE General Test. *Expenses: Tuition:* Full-time $30,480; part-time $1270 per credit. *Required fees:* $586; $293 per semester.

Framingham State University, Division of Graduate and Continuing Education, Program in Elementary Education, Framingham, MA 01701-9101. Offers M Ed.

Francis Marion University, Graduate Programs, School of Education, Florence, SC 29502-0547. Offers early childhood education (M Ed); elementary education (M Ed); learning disabilities (M Ed, MAT); remedial education (M Ed); secondary education (M Ed). *Accreditation:* NCATE. Part-time programs available. *Faculty:* 20 full-time (16 women), 1 (woman) part-time/adjunct. *Students:* 10 full-time (8 women), 115 part-time (88 women); includes 30 minority (26 Black or African American, non-Hispanic/Latino; 3 Asian, non-Hispanic/Latino; 1 Hispanic/Latino), 1 international. Average age 32. 249 applicants, 33% accepted, 77 enrolled. In 2011, 41 master's awarded. *Degree requirements:* For master's, comprehensive exam. *Entrance requirements:* For master's, GRE General Test, MAT, NTE, or PRAXIS II. *Application deadline:* For fall admission, 3/15 priority date for domestic students; for spring admission, 10/15 priority date for domestic students. Applications are processed on a rolling basis. Application fee: $31. *Expenses:* Tuition, state resident: full-time $8467; part-time $443.35 per credit hour. Tuition, nonresident: full-time $16,934; part-time $866.70 per credit hour. *Required fees:* $335; $12.25 per credit hour. $30 per semester. *Financial support:* In 2011–12, 3 research assistantships (averaging $6,000 per year) were awarded; scholarships/grants and unspecified assistantships also available. Support available to part-time students. Financial award application deadline: 3/1; financial award applicants required to submit FAFSA. *Faculty research:* Identification and alternate assessment of at-risk students. *Unit head:* Dr. James R. Faulkenberry, Dean, 843-661-1460, Fax: 843-661-4647. *Application contact:* Rannie Gamble, Administrative Manager, 843-661-1286, Fax: 843-661-4688, E-mail: rgamble@fmarion.edu.

Fresno Pacific University, Graduate Programs, School of Education, Division of Mathematics/Science/Computer Education, Program in Mathematics Education, Fresno, CA 93702-4709. Offers elementary and middle school mathematics (MA Ed); secondary school mathematics (MA Ed). Part-time and evening/weekend programs available. *Degree requirements:* For master's, thesis or alternative. *Entrance requirements:* Additional exam requirements/recommendations for international students: Required—TOEFL (minimum score 550 paper-based; 213 computer-based).

Frostburg State University, Graduate School, College of Education, Department of Educational Professions, Program in Curriculum and Instruction, Frostburg, MD 21532-1099. Offers educational technology (M Ed); elementary education (M Ed); secondary education (M Ed). Part-time and evening/weekend programs available. *Degree requirements:* For master's, thesis or alternative. *Entrance requirements:* For master's, teaching certificate. Additional exam requirements/recommendations for international students: Required—TOEFL. Electronic applications accepted.

Frostburg State University, Graduate School, College of Education, Department of Educational Professions, Program in Elementary Teaching, Frostburg, MD 21532-1099. Offers MAT. *Accreditation:* NCATE. *Degree requirements:* For master's, thesis or alternative, PRAXIS II. *Entrance requirements:* For master's, PRAXIS I, entry portfolio. Additional exam requirements/recommendations for international students: Required—TOEFL. Electronic applications accepted.

Gallaudet University, The Graduate School, Washington, DC 20002-3625. Offers audiology (Au D); clinical psychology (PhD); critical studies in the education of deaf learners (PhD); deaf and hard of hearing infants, toddlers, and their families (Certificate); deaf education (Ed S); deaf education: advanced studies (MA); deaf education: special programs in deaf education (MA); deaf history (Certificate); deaf studies (MA, Certificate); education deaf students with disabilities (Certificate); education: teacher preparation (MA), including deaf education, early childhood education and deaf education, elementary education and deaf education, secondary education and deaf education; hearing, speech and language sciences (MS, PhD); international development (MA); interpretation (MA, PhD); linguistics (MA, PhD); mental health counseling (MA); public administration (MA); school counseling (MA); school psychology (Psy S); sign language teaching (MA); social work (MSW); speech-language pathology (MS). Part-time programs available. *Faculty:* 62 full-time (44 women). *Students:* 300 full-time (246 women), 110 part-time (82 women); includes 80 minority (27 Black or African American, non-Hispanic/Latino; 1 American Indian or Alaska Native, non-Hispanic/Latino; 11 Asian, non-Hispanic/Latino; 25 Hispanic/Latino; 1 Native Hawaiian or other Pacific Islander, non-Hispanic/Latino; 15 Two or more races, non-Hispanic/Latino), 24 international. Average age 30. 498 applicants, 45% accepted, 168 enrolled. In 2011, 129 master's, 24 doctorates, 19 other advanced degrees awarded. Terminal master's awarded for partial completion of doctoral program. *Degree requirements:* For master's, comprehensive exam (for some programs), thesis optional; for doctorate, comprehensive exam, thesis/dissertation. *Entrance requirements:* For master's and doctorate, GRE General Test or MAT, letters of recommendation, interviews, goals statement, ASL proficiency interview, written English competency. Additional exam requirements/recommendations for international students: Required—TOEFL. *Application deadline:* For fall admission, 2/15 for domestic students. Applications are processed on a rolling basis. Application fee: $50. Electronic applications accepted. *Expenses: Tuition:* Full-time $12,770; part-time $710 per credit. *Required fees:* $376. *Financial support:* In 2011–12, 287 students received support. Fellowships, research assistantships, teaching assistantships, career-related internships or fieldwork, Federal Work-Study, scholarships/grants, tuition waivers (partial), and unspecified assistantships available. Support available to part-time students. Financial award applicants required to submit FAFSA. *Faculty research:* Bimodal bilingualism development, audiology, telecommunications access, early childhood education, linguistics, visual language and visual learning, rehabilitation and hearing enhancement. *Unit head:* Dr. Carol J. Erting, Dean, 202-651-5520, Fax: 202-651-5027, E-mail: carol.erting@gallaudet.edu. *Application contact:* Wednesday Luria, Coordinator of Prospective Graduate Student Services, 202-651-5400, Fax: 202-651-5295, E-mail: graduate.school@gallaudet.edu. Web site: http://www.gallaudet.edu/x26696.xml.

Gardner-Webb University, Graduate School, School of Education, Program in Elementary Education, Boiling Springs, NC 28017. Offers MA. *Accreditation:* NCATE. Part-time and evening/weekend programs available. *Faculty:* 9 full-time (3 women), 20 part-time/adjunct (7 women). *Students:* 2 full-time (both women), 259 part-time (252 women); includes 45 minority (39 Black or African American, non-Hispanic/Latino; 2 American Indian or Alaska Native, non-Hispanic/Latino; 3 Asian, non-Hispanic/Latino; 1 Hispanic/Latino). Average age 35. 12 applicants, 100% accepted, 12 enrolled. In 2011, 12 master's awarded. *Degree requirements:* For master's, comprehensive exam. *Entrance requirements:* For master's, GRE General Test or NTE, PRAXIS, minimum GPA of 2.5. *Application deadline:* For fall admission, 8/1 priority date for domestic students. Applications are processed on a rolling basis. Application fee: $40. Electronic applications accepted. *Expenses: Tuition:* Full-time $6300; part-time $350 per credit hour. *Financial support:* Unspecified assistantships available. *Unit head:* Dr. Alan D. Eury, Chair, 704-406-4402, Fax: 704-406-3921, E-mail: dsimmons@gardner-webb.edu. *Application contact:* Office of Graduate Admissions, 877-498-4723, Fax: 704-406-3895, E-mail: gradinfo@gardner-webb.edu.

The George Washington University, Graduate School of Education and Human Development, Department of Curriculum and Pedagogy, Program in Elementary Education, Washington, DC 20052. Offers M Ed. *Accreditation:* NCATE. Part-time programs available. *Students:* 30 full-time (26 women), 2 part-time (1 woman); includes 8 minority (5 Black or African American, non-Hispanic/Latino; 3 Hispanic/Latino). Average age 29. 57 applicants, 95% accepted, 25 enrolled. In 2011, 36 master's awarded. *Degree requirements:* For master's, comprehensive exam. *Entrance requirements:* For master's, GRE General Test or MAT, minimum GPA of 2.75. *Application deadline:* For fall admission, 1/15 priority date for domestic students; for spring admission, 10/1 for domestic students. Applications are processed on a rolling basis. Application fee: $75. *Financial support:* In 2011–12, 27 students received support. Fellowships, career-related internships or fieldwork, Federal Work-Study, and tuition waivers (partial) available. Financial award application deadline: 1/15; financial award applicants required to submit FAFSA. *Faculty research:* Issues in teacher training. *Unit head:* Dr. Sylven S. Beck, Director, 202-994-3365, E-mail: sbeck@gwu.edu. *Application contact:* Sarah Lang, Director of Graduate Admissions, 202-994-1447, Fax: 202-994-7207, E-mail: slang@gwu.edu.

Grand Canyon University, College of Education, Phoenix, AZ 85017-1097. Offers curriculum and instruction (M Ed); education administration (M Ed); elementary education (M Ed); secondary education (M Ed); special education (M Ed); teaching (MA). Part-time and evening/weekend programs available. Postbaccalaureate distance learning degree programs offered (no on-campus study). *Degree requirements:* For master's, publishable research paper (M Ed), e-portfolio. *Entrance requirements:* For master's, undergraduate degree from accredited, GCU-approved college, university, or program with minimum GPA 2.8. Additional exam requirements/recommendations for international students: Required—TOEFL (minimum score 550 paper-based; 213 computer-based; 79 iBT), IELTS (minimum score 6). Electronic applications accepted.

Grand Valley State University, College of Education, Programs in General Education, Allendale, MI 49401-9403. Offers adult and higher education (M Ed); early childhood education (M Ed); educational differentiation (M Ed); educational leadership (M Ed); educational technology integration (M Ed); elementary education (M Ed); middle level education (M Ed); school library media services (M Ed); secondary level education (M Ed); teaching English to speakers of other languages (M Ed). Part-time and evening/weekend programs available. Postbaccalaureate distance learning degree programs offered (minimal on-campus study). *Degree requirements:* For master's, thesis. *Entrance requirements:* For master's, GRE General Test or minimum GPA of 3.0. Additional exam requirements/recommendations for international students: Required—TOEFL. Electronic applications accepted. *Faculty research:* Effectiveness of technology in education, parental involvement, effective teaching, effective schools research.

Greensboro College, Program in Education, Greensboro, NC 27401-1875. Offers elementary education (M Ed); special education (M Ed). Part-time and evening/weekend programs available. *Degree requirements:* For master's, thesis. *Entrance requirements:* For master's, GRE, teacher license, 2 years of teaching experience, 2 letters of recommendation. Additional exam requirements/recommendations for international students: Required—TOEFL (minimum score 550 paper-based; 213 computer-based). Electronic applications accepted.

Greenville College, Program in Education, Greenville, IL 62246-0159. Offers education (MAT); elementary education (MAE); secondary education (MAE). *Degree requirements:* For master's, thesis (for some programs). *Entrance requirements:* For master's, GRE, Illinois Basic Skills Test, teacher certification. Electronic applications accepted.

Hampton University, Graduate College, College of Education and Continuing Studies, Program in Elementary Education, Hampton, VA 23668. Offers MA. *Accreditation:* NCATE. Part-time and evening/weekend programs available. *Entrance requirements:* For master's, GRE General Test.

Harding University, College of Education, Searcy, AR 72149-0001. Offers advanced studies in teaching and learning (M Ed); art (MSE); behavioral science (MSE); counseling (MS, Ed S); early childhood special education (M Ed, MSE); education (MSE); educational leadership (M Ed, Ed S); elementary education (M Ed); English (MSE); French (MSE); history/social science (MSE); kinesiology (MSE); math (MSE); reading (M Ed); secondary education (M Ed); Spanish (MSE); teaching (MAT); teaching English as a second language (MSE). *Accreditation:* NCATE. Part-time and evening/weekend programs available. *Faculty:* 9 full-time (2 women), 48 part-time/adjunct (26 women). *Students:* 100 full-time (77 women), 333 part-time (239 women); includes 76 minority (59 Black or African American, non-Hispanic/Latino; 1 Asian, non-Hispanic/Latino; 10 Hispanic/Latino; 6 Two or more races, non-Hispanic/Latino), 2 international. Average age 36. 93 applicants, 91% accepted, 83 enrolled. In 2011, 159 master's, 10 other advanced degrees awarded. *Degree requirements:* For master's, comprehensive exam (for some programs), thesis optional, portfolio(s); for Ed S, comprehensive exam, portfolio, project. *Entrance requirements:* For master's, GRE, MAT, PRAXIS; for Ed S, MAT or GRE. Additional exam requirements/recommendations for international students: Required—TOEFL (minimum score 550 paper-based; 79 iBT). *Application deadline:* For fall admission, 8/1 for domestic and international students; for spring admission, 1/1 for domestic and international students. Applications are processed on a rolling basis. Application fee: $35. *Expenses: Tuition:* Full-time $10,512; part-time $584 per credit hour. *Required fees:* $500; $25 per credit hour. Tuition and fees vary according to course load, degree level and program. *Financial support:* In 2011–12, 37 students received support. Unspecified assistantships available. *Faculty research:* Reading, comprehension, school violence, educational technology, behavior, college choice, differentiated instruction, brain-based teaching. *Unit head:* Dr. Clara Carroll, Chair, 501-279-4501, Fax: 501-279-4083, E-mail: ccarroll@harding.edu. *Application contact:* Information Contact, 501-279-4315, E-mail: gradstudiesedu@harding.edu. Web site: http://www.harding.edu/education/grad.html.

Hawai`i Pacific University, College of Humanities and Social Sciences, Program in Elementary Education, Honolulu, HI 96813. Offers M Ed. Part-time and evening/weekend programs available. *Students:* 42 full-time (27 women), 13 part-time (10 women); includes 33 minority (13 Asian, non-Hispanic/Latino; 9 Hispanic/Latino; 1 Native Hawaiian or other Pacific Islander, non-Hispanic/Latino; 10 Two or more races, non-Hispanic/Latino). 13 applicants, 62% accepted, 7 enrolled. In 2011, 141 master's awarded. *Expenses: Tuition:* Full-time $13,230; part-time $735 per credit. Tuition and fees vary according to course load and program. *Financial support:* In 2011–12, 15 students received support. Career-related internships or fieldwork, Federal Work-Study, scholarships/grants, and tuition waivers available. *Unit head:* Dr. William Potter, Associate Vice President and Dean, 808-544-0228, Fax: 808-544-1424, E-mail: wpotter@hpu.edu. *Application contact:* Chad Schempp, Director of Graduate Admissions, 808-543-8035, Fax: 808-544-0280, E-mail: graduate@hpu.edu. Web site: http://www.hpu.edu/CHSS/Education/MEDEE/index.html.

See Display on next page and Close-Up on page 1195.

High Point University, Norcross Graduate School, High Point, NC 27262-3598. Offers business administration (MBA); educational leadership (M Ed); elementary education (M Ed); history (MA); nonprofit management (MA); secondary math (M Ed); special education (M Ed); strategic communication (MA); teaching elementary education k-6 (MAT); teaching secondary mathematics 9-12 (MAT). *Accreditation:* ACBSP; NCATE. Part-time and evening/weekend programs available. *Degree requirements:* For master's, comprehensive exam (for some programs), thesis (for some programs). *Entrance requirements:* For master's, GMAT (MBA), GRE, MAT, minimum GPA of 3.0. Additional exam requirements/recommendations for international students: Required—TOEFL (minimum score 550 paper-based). Electronic applications accepted.

Hofstra University, School of Education, Health, and Human Services, Department of Foundations, Leadership, and Policy Studies, Hempstead, NY 11549. Offers educational and policy leadership (MS Ed, Ed D), including higher education (MS Ed), K-12 (MS Ed); educational policy and leadership (Advanced Certificate), including school district business leader; foundations of education (MA, Advanced Certificate); Advanced Certificate/Advanced Certificate. Part-time and evening/weekend programs available. Postbaccalaureate distance learning degree programs offered (minimal on-campus study). *Students:* 22 full-time (16 women), 105 part-time (65 women); includes 45 minority (33 Black or African American, non-Hispanic/Latino; 1 Asian, non-Hispanic/Latino; 11 Hispanic/Latino), 2 international. Average age 37. 78 applicants, 94% accepted, 42 enrolled. In 2011, 12 master's, 6 doctorates, 12 other advanced degrees awarded. *Degree requirements:* For master's, one foreign language, comprehensive exam (for some programs), thesis or alternative, minimum GPA of 3.0; for doctorate, comprehensive exam (for some programs), thesis/dissertation (for some programs), minimum GPA of 3.0. *Entrance requirements:* For master's and Advanced Certificate, interview, writing sample, essay; for doctorate, GMAT, GRE, LSAT, or MAT, interview, 3 letters of recommendation, resume, essay. Additional exam requirements/recommendations for international students: Required—TOEFL (minimum score 550 paper-based; 213 computer-based; 80 iBT). *Application deadline:* Applications are processed on a rolling basis. Application fee: $70 ($75 for international students). Electronic applications accepted. *Expenses: Tuition:* Full-time $18,990; part-time $1055 per credit hour. *Required fees:* $970. Tuition and fees vary according to program. *Financial support:* In 2011–12, 66 students received support, including 44 fellowships with full and partial tuition reimbursements available (averaging $3,788 per year), 3 research assistantships with full and partial tuition reimbursements available (averaging $12,125 per year); Federal Work-Study, institutionally sponsored loans, scholarships/grants, tuition waivers (full and partial), and unspecified assistantships also available. Support available to part-time students. Financial award applicants required to submit FAFSA. *Faculty research:* School improvement, professional assessment - APPR, educational policy, professional development, race/gender in education. *Unit head:* Dr. Esther Fusco, Chairperson, 516-463-7704, Fax: 516-463-6196, E-mail: catezf@hofstra.edu. *Application contact:* Carol Drummer, Dean of Graduate Admissions, 516-463-4876, Fax: 516-463-4664, E-mail: gradstudent@hofstra.edu. Web site: http://www.hofstra.edu/education/.

Hofstra University, School of Education, Health, and Human Services, Department of Literacy Studies, Hempstead, NY 11549. Offers advanced literacy studies (PD), including birth-grade 6 (MA, MS Ed, PD); advanced literary studies (PD), including grades 5-12 (MA, PD); birth-grade 6 (MS Ed, Advanced Certificate); grades 5-12 (Advanced Certificate); literacy studies (Ed D, PhD); special education (MS Ed), including birth-grade 2, birth-grade 6 (MA, MS Ed, PD); special education (MS Ed), including birth-grade 2; teaching of writing (MA), including birth-grade 6 (MA, MS Ed, PD), grades 5-12 (MA, PD). Part-time and evening/weekend programs available. *Students:* 43 full-time (42 women), 70 part-time (63 women); includes 15 minority (7 Black or African American, non-Hispanic/Latino; 1 Asian, non-Hispanic/Latino; 7 Hispanic/Latino). Average age 33. 67 applicants, 81% accepted, 32 enrolled. In 2011, 47 master's, 1 doctorate, 10 other advanced degrees awarded. *Degree requirements:* For master's, comprehensive exam, portfolio, minimum GPA of 3.0; for doctorate, one foreign language, comprehensive exam, thesis/dissertation, qualifying hearing, minimum GPA of 3.0. *Entrance requirements:* For master's, interview, teaching certificate, 2 letters of recommendation; for doctorate, GRE or MAT, interview, resume, essay, master's degree, 3 letters of recommendation, writing sample; for other advanced degree, 2 letters of recommendation, interview, teaching certificate, essay, master's degree. Additional exam requirements/recommendations for international students: Required—TOEFL (minimum score 550 paper-based; 213 computer-based; 80 iBT). *Application deadline:* Applications are processed on a rolling basis. Application fee: $70 ($75 for international students). Electronic applications accepted. *Expenses: Tuition:* Full-time $18,990; part-time $1055 per credit hour. *Required fees:* $970. Tuition and fees vary according to program. *Financial support:* In 2011–12, 78 students received support, including 36 fellowships with full and partial tuition reimbursements available (averaging $3,622 per year); research assistantships with full and partial tuition reimbursements available, career-related internships or fieldwork, Federal Work-Study, institutionally sponsored loans, scholarships/grants, tuition waivers (full and partial), and unspecified assistantships also available. Support available to part-time students. Financial award applicants required to submit FAFSA. *Faculty research:* Research literacy practices of immigrant and urban youth, literature for children and adolescents, eye movement/miscue analysis, literacy strategies for effective instruction, transnational literacies. *Unit head:* Dr. Esther Fusco, Chairperson, 516-463-7704, Fax: 516-463-6196, E-mail: catezf@hofstra.edu. *Application contact:* Carol Drummer, Dean of Graduate Admissions, 516-463-4876, Fax: 516-463-4664, E-mail: gradstudent@hofstra.edu. Web site: http://www.hofstra.edu/education/.

Hofstra University, School of Education, Health, and Human Services, Program in Elementary Education, Hempstead, NY 11549. Offers early childhood and childhood education (MS Ed); early childhood education (MA, MS Ed); educational technology (MA); elementary education (MS Ed); literacy (MA); math specialist (Advanced Certificate); math, science, technology (MA); multiculturalism (MA). Part-time and evening/weekend programs available. Postbaccalaureate distance learning degree programs offered (minimal on-campus study). *Students:* 54 full-time (48 women), 43 part-time (37 women); includes 17 minority (10 Black or African American, non-Hispanic/Latino; 2 Asian, non-Hispanic/Latino; 5 Hispanic/Latino), 2 international. Average age 29. 65 applicants, 88% accepted, 18 enrolled. In 2011, 58 master's awarded. *Degree requirements:* For master's, comprehensive exam, thesis (for some programs), 35 semester hours (for MA); 38-41 semester hours (for MS Ed), minimum GPA of 3.0. *Entrance requirements:* For master's, 2 letters of recommendation, teacher certification (MA), interview, essay. Additional exam requirements/recommendations for international students: Required—TOEFL (minimum score 550 paper-based; 213 computer-based; 80 iBT). *Application deadline:* Applications are processed on a rolling basis. Application fee: $70 ($75 for international students). Electronic applications accepted. *Expenses: Tuition:* Full-time $18,990; part-time $1055 per credit hour. *Required fees:* $970. Tuition and fees vary according to program. *Financial support:* In 2011–12, 45 students received support, including 22 fellowships with full and partial tuition reimbursements available (averaging $2,560 per year), 2 research assistantships with full and partial tuition reimbursements available (averaging $21,993 per year); career-related internships or fieldwork, Federal Work-Study, institutionally sponsored loans, scholarships/grants, tuition waivers (full and partial), and unspecified assistantships also available. Support available to part-time students. Financial award applicants required to submit FAFSA. *Faculty research:* Dynamic-themes curriculum/complexity theory, joyful learning, teacher education, multicultural education, multiple authentic assessments. *Unit head:* Dr. Esther Fusco, Chairperson, 516-463-7704, Fax: 516-463-6196, E-mail: catezf@hofstra.edu. *Application contact:* Carol Drummer, Dean of Graduate Admissions, 516-463-4876, Fax: 516-463-4664, E-mail: gradstudent@hofstra.edu. Web site: http://www.hofstra.edu/education/.

Holy Family University, Graduate School, School of Education, Philadelphia, PA 19114. Offers education (M Ed); education leadership (M Ed); elementary education (M Ed); reading specialist (M Ed); secondary education (M Ed); special education (M Ed). Part-time and evening/weekend programs available. *Degree requirements:* For master's, thesis optional. *Entrance requirements:* For master's, GRE or MAT, interview. Electronic applications accepted. *Faculty research:* Cognition, developmental issues, sociological issues in education.

See Display on page 707 and Close-Up on page 803.

Hood College, Graduate School, Department of Education, Frederick, MD 21701-8575. Offers curriculum and instruction (MS), including early childhood education, elementary education, elementary school science and mathematics, secondary education, special education; educational leadership (MS, Certificate); reading specialization (MS). Part-time and evening/weekend programs available. *Degree requirements:* For master's, action research project, portfolio (reading). *Entrance requirements:* For master's, minimum GPA of 2.75, teaching certification. Additional exam requirements/recommendations for international students: Required—TOEFL (minimum score 575 paper-based; 231 computer-based; 89 iBT). Electronic applications accepted. *Faculty research:* Leadership, action research, brain research, learning styles.

Hope International University, School of Graduate and Professional Studies, Program in Education, Fullerton, CA 92831-3138. Offers education administration (MA); elementary education (ME); secondary education (ME). Part-time and evening/weekend programs available. *Degree requirements:* For master's, comprehensive exam (for some programs), thesis. *Entrance requirements:* For master's, minimum GPA of 3.0, 2 references. Additional exam requirements/recommendations for international students: Required—TOEFL (minimum score 550 paper-based; 213 computer-based; 86 iBT); Recommended—IELTS (minimum score 6.5). Electronic applications accepted. *Expenses:* Contact institution. *Faculty research:* Distance education.

Howard University, School of Education, Department of Curriculum and Instruction, Program in Elementary Education, Washington, DC 20059-0002. Offers M Ed. *Accreditation:* NCATE. *Faculty:* 3 full-time (2 women), 1 (woman) part-time/adjunct. *Students:* 26 full-time (21 women), 8 part-time (5 women); all minorities (all Black or African American, non-Hispanic/Latino). Average age 28. 32 applicants, 88% accepted, 22 enrolled. In 2011, 4 master's awarded. *Degree requirements:* For master's, comprehensive exam, expository writing exam, internships, seminar paper. *Entrance requirements:* For master's, PRAXIS I, minimum GPA of 2.7. Additional exam requirements/recommendations for international students: Required—TOEFL (minimum score 550 paper-based). *Application deadline:* For fall admission, 2/15 priority date for domestic students; for spring admission, 11/1 for domestic students. Applications are processed on a rolling basis. Application fee: $45. Electronic applications accepted. *Financial support:* In 2011–12, 4 students received support, including 2 fellowships with full and partial tuition reimbursements available (averaging $16,000 per year), 2 research assistantships (averaging $2,225 per year); career-related internships or fieldwork, Federal Work-Study, scholarships/grants, and unspecified assistantships also available. Financial award application deadline: 3/15. *Unit head:* Dr. James T. Jackson, Chair, Department of Curriculum and Instruction, 202-806-5300, Fax: 202-806-5297, E-mail: jt_jackson@howard.edu. *Application contact:* June L. Harris, Administrative Assistant, Department of Curriculum and Instruction, 202-806-7343, Fax: 202-806-5297, E-mail: jlharris@howard.edu.

Hunter College of the City University of New York, Graduate School, School of Education, Department of Curriculum and Teaching and Department of Educational Foundations and Counseling Programs, Program in Elementary Education, New York, NY 10021-5085. Offers MS. *Accreditation:* NCATE. *Faculty:* 7 full-time (2 women), 24 part-time/adjunct (10 women). *Students:* 53 full-time (47 women), 342 part-time (287 women); includes 115 minority (30 Black or African American, non-Hispanic/Latino; 5 American Indian or Alaska Native, non-Hispanic/Latino; 34 Asian, non-Hispanic/Latino; 46 Hispanic/Latino), 3 international. Average age 28. 271 applicants, 64% accepted, 116 enrolled. In 2011, 230 master's awarded. *Degree requirements:* For master's, thesis, integrative seminar, New York State Teacher Certification Exams, student teaching. *Entrance requirements:* For master's, minimum undergraduate GPA of 2.8, writing sample. Additional exam requirements/recommendations for international students: Required—TOEFL, TWE. *Application deadline:* For fall admission, 4/1 for domestic students, 2/1 for international students; for spring admission, 11/1 for domestic students, 9/1 for international students. Application fee: $125. *Expenses:* Tuition, state resident: full-time $8210; part-time $345 per credit. Tuition, nonresident: full-time $15,360; part-time $640 per credit. *Required fees:* $280 per semester. One-time fee: $125. Tuition and fees vary according to class time, campus/location and program. *Financial support:* Federal Work-Study, scholarships/grants, and tuition waivers (partial) available. Support available to part-time students. *Faculty research:* Urban education, multicultural education, gifted education, educational technology, cultural cognition. *Unit head:* Dr. Patrick Burke, Education Adviser, 212-396-6043, E-mail: patrick.burke@hunter.cuny.edu. *Application contact:* William Zlata, Director for Graduate Admissions, 212-772-4482, Fax: 212-650-3336, E-mail: admissions@hunter.cuny.edu. Web site: http://www.hunter.cuny.edu/school-of-education/programs/graduate/childhood-math-science.

Idaho State University, Office of Graduate Studies, College of Education, Department of Educational Foundations, Pocatello, ID 83209-8059. Offers child and family studies (M Ed); curriculum leadership (M Ed); education (M Ed); educational administration (M Ed); educational foundations (5th Year Certificate); elementary education (M Ed), including K-12 education, literacy, secondary education. Part-time programs available. *Degree requirements:* For master's, comprehensive exam, thesis optional, oral exam, written exam; for 5th Year Certificate, comprehensive exam, thesis (for some programs), oral exam, written exam. *Entrance requirements:* For master's, GRE General Test or MAT, minimum undergraduate GPA of 3.0; for 5th Year Certificate, GRE General Test, minimum undergraduate GPA of 3.0, master's degree. Additional exam requirements/recommendations for international students: Required—TOEFL (minimum score 550 paper-based; 213 computer-based; 80 iBT). Electronic applications accepted. *Faculty research:* Child and families studies; business education; special education; math, science, and technology education.

Immaculata University, College of Graduate Studies, Program in Educational Leadership and Administration, Immaculata, PA 19345. Offers educational leadership and administration (MA, Ed D); elementary education (Certificate); school principal (Certificate); school superintendent (Certificate); secondary education (Certificate); special education (Certificate). Part-time and evening/weekend programs available. *Degree requirements:* For master's, comprehensive exam, thesis optional; for doctorate, comprehensive exam, thesis/dissertation. *Entrance requirements:* For master's, GRE or MAT, minimum GPA of 3.0; for doctorate, GRE General Test or MAT, minimum GPA of 3.5. Additional exam requirements/recommendations for international students: Required—TOEFL. Electronic applications accepted. *Faculty research:* Cooperative learning, school-based management, whole language, performance assessment.

Indiana State University, College of Graduate and Professional Studies, College of Education, Department of Elementary, Early and Special Education, Terre Haute, IN 47809. Offers early childhood education (M Ed); elementary education (M Ed); MA/MS. *Accreditation:* NCATE. Electronic applications accepted.

Indiana University Bloomington, School of Education, Department of Curriculum and Instruction, Bloomington, IN 47405-7000. Offers art education (MS, Ed D, PhD); curriculum studies (Ed D, PhD); elementary education (MS, Ed D, PhD, Ed S); mathematics education (MS, Ed D, PhD); science education (MS, Ed D, PhD); secondary education (MS, Ed D, PhD); social studies education (MS, PhD); special education (PhD, Ed S). *Accreditation:* NCATE. Part-time and evening/weekend programs available. Terminal master's awarded for partial completion of doctoral program. *Degree requirements:* For doctorate, thesis/dissertation; for Ed S, comprehensive exam or project. *Entrance requirements:* For master's, doctorate, and Ed S, GRE General Test. Electronic applications accepted.

Indiana University Kokomo, Division of Education, Kokomo, IN 46904-9003. Offers elementary education (MS Ed). *Accreditation:* NCATE. Part-time and evening/weekend programs available. *Faculty:* 1 full-time (0 women). *Students:* 13 full-time (10 women), 6 part-time (4 women); includes 1 minority (Hispanic/Latino). Average age 36. 9 applicants, 100% accepted, 8 enrolled. In 2011, 14 master's awarded. *Degree requirements:* For master's, thesis optional, research project. *Entrance requirements:* For master's, GRE General Test, minimum GPA of 2.5. *Application deadline:* For fall admission, 8/1 for domestic students; for spring admission, 12/1 for domestic students. Applications are processed on a rolling basis. Application fee: $40 ($50 for international students). *Financial support:* In 2011–12, 2 fellowships (averaging $375 per year) were awarded; minority teacher scholarships also available. *Faculty research:* Reading, teaching effectiveness, portfolio, curriculum development. *Unit head:* D. Antonio Cantu, Dean, 765-455-9441, Fax: 765-455-9503. *Application contact:* Charlotte Miller, Coordinator, Educational and Student Resources, 765-455-9367, Fax: 765-455-9503, E-mail: cmiller@iuk.edu.

Indiana University Northwest, School of Education, Gary, IN 46408-1197. Offers elementary education (MS Ed); secondary education (MS Ed). *Accreditation:* NCATE. Part-time and evening/weekend programs available. *Faculty:* 5 full-time (2 women). *Students:* 49 full-time (37 women), 204 part-time (164 women); includes 119 minority (84 Black or African American, non-Hispanic/Latino; 1 American Indian or Alaska Native, non-Hispanic/Latino; 1 Asian, non-Hispanic/Latino; 30 Hispanic/Latino; 3 Two or more races, non-Hispanic/Latino). Average age 37. 32 applicants, 100% accepted, 25 enrolled. In 2011, 44 master's awarded. *Entrance requirements:* For master's, GRE General Test or MAT, minimum GPA of 3.0. *Application deadline:* For fall admission, 7/15 priority date for domestic students; for spring admission, 11/15 for domestic students. Application fee: $25. *Unit head:* Dr. Stanley E. Wigle, Dean, 219-980-6510, Fax: 219-981-4208, E-mail: amsanche@iun.edu. *Application contact:* Admissions Counselor, 219-980-6760, Fax: 219-980-7103. Web site: http://www.iun.edu/~edu/.

Indiana University of Pennsylvania, School of Graduate Studies and Research, College of Education and Educational Technology, Department of Professional Studies in Education, Program in Elementary Education, Indiana, PA 15705-1087. Offers M Ed. *Accreditation:* NCATE. Part-time programs available. *Faculty:* 19 full-time (13 women), 1 (woman) part-time/adjunct. *Students:* 1 applicant, 0% accepted, 0 enrolled. In 2011, 8 master's awarded. *Degree requirements:* For master's, thesis optional. *Entrance requirements:* For master's, 2 letters of recommendation. Additional exam requirements/recommendations for international students: Required—TOEFL (minimum score 540 paper-based; 207 computer-based). Application fee: $50. *Expenses:* Tuition, state resident: full-time $7488; part-time $416 per credit. Tuition, nonresident: full-time $11,232; part-time $624 per credit. *Required fees:* $2070; $192.20 per credit. $90 per semester. *Financial support:* Fellowships, research assistantships with full and partial tuition reimbursements, teaching assistantships with partial tuition reimbursements, career-related internships or fieldwork, and Federal Work-Study available. Financial award application deadline: 4/15; financial award applicants required to submit FAFSA. *Unit head:* Dr. Mary R. Jalongo, Graduate Coordinator, 724-357-2417, E-mail: mjalongo@iup.edu. *Application contact:* Dr. Edward Nardi, Associate Dean, 724-357-2480, Fax: 724-357-5595, E-mail: ewnardi@iup.edu.

Indiana University–Purdue University Fort Wayne, College of Education and Public Policy, Department of Educational Studies, Fort Wayne, IN 46805-1499. Offers elementary education (MS Ed); secondary education (MS Ed). *Accreditation:* NCATE. Part-time programs available. *Faculty:* 14 full-time (6 women). *Students:* 1 (woman) full-time, 30 part-time (23 women); includes 5 minority (4 Black or African American, non-Hispanic/Latino; 1 Asian, non-Hispanic/Latino). Average age 38. 7 applicants, 100% accepted, 4 enrolled. In 2011, 16 master's awarded. *Entrance requirements:* For master's, minimum GPA of 2.5, three professional letters of recommendation. Additional exam requirements/recommendations for international students: Required—TOEFL (minimum score 550 paper-based; 213 computer-based; 77 iBT). *Application deadline:* For fall admission, 4/1 priority date for domestic students, 4/1 for international students. Applications are processed on a rolling basis. Application fee: $55. *Financial support:* Scholarships/grants available. Support available to part-time students. Financial award application deadline: 3/1; financial award applicants required to submit FAFSA. *Faculty research:* Ethnic minority higher education, South Korea and higher education reform, Turkish-American parents' experience and U. S. elementary education. *Total annual research expenditures:* $77,627. *Unit head:* Dr. Joe Nichols, Chair, 260-481-6445, Fax: 260-481-5408, E-mail: nicholsj@ipfw.edu. *Application contact:* Vicky L. Schmidt, Graduate Recorder, 260-481-6450, Fax: 260-481-5408, E-mail: schmidt@ipfw.edu. Web site: http://www.ipfw.edu/education.

Indiana University South Bend, School of Education, South Bend, IN 46634-7111. Offers counseling and human services (MS Ed); elementary education (MS Ed); secondary education (MS Ed); special education (MS Ed). *Accreditation:* NCATE. Part-time and evening/weekend programs available. *Faculty:* 21 full-time (11 women), 9 part-time/adjunct (3 women). *Students:* 70 full-time (45 women), 262 part-time (206 women); includes 39 minority (15 Black or African American, non-Hispanic/Latino; 3 American Indian or Alaska Native, non-Hispanic/Latino; 5 Asian, non-Hispanic/Latino; 14 Hispanic/Latino; 2 Two or more races, non-Hispanic/Latino), 15 international. Average age 36. 52 applicants, 75% accepted, 28 enrolled. In 2011, 75 master's awarded. *Degree requirements:* For master's, thesis or alternative, exit project. *Entrance requirements:* For master's, letters of recommendation, GRE or minimum GPA of 3.0. Additional exam requirements/recommendations for international students: Required—TOEFL. *Application deadline:* For fall admission, 7/1 for domestic students; for spring admission, 11/1 for domestic students. Applications are processed on a rolling basis. Application fee: $50 ($60 for international students). Electronic applications accepted. *Financial support:* Career-related internships or fieldwork available. Support available to part-time students. Financial award application deadline: 3/1; financial award applicants required to submit FAFSA. *Faculty research:* Professional dispositions, early childhood literacy, online learning, program assessments, problem-based learning. *Unit head:* Dr. Michael Horvath, Professor/Dean, 574-520-4339, Fax: 574-520-4550. *Application contact:* Dr. Todd Norris, Director of Education Student Services, 574-520-4845, E-mail: toanorri@iusb.edu. Web site: http://www.iusb.edu/~edud/.

Indiana University Southeast, School of Education, New Albany, IN 47150-6405. Offers counselor education (MS Ed); elementary education (MS Ed); secondary education (MS Ed). *Accreditation:* NCATE. Part-time and evening/weekend programs available. *Students:* 31 full-time (24 women), 622 part-time (497 women); includes 83 minority (63 Black or African American, non-Hispanic/Latino; 2 American Indian or Alaska Native, non-Hispanic/Latino; 5 Asian, non-Hispanic/Latino; 8 Hispanic/Latino; 5 Two or more races, non-Hispanic/Latino). Average age 33. 99 applicants, 93% accepted, 75 enrolled. In 2011, 143 master's awarded. *Entrance requirements:* For master's, minimum undergraduate GPA of 2.5, graduate 3.0. *Application deadline:* Applications are processed on a rolling basis. Application fee: $35. *Financial support:* Career-related internships or fieldwork, Federal Work-Study, and institutionally sponsored loans available. Support available to part-time students. Financial award applicants required to submit FAFSA. *Faculty research:* Learning styles, technology, constructivism, group process, innovative math strategies. *Unit head:* Dr. Gloria Murray, Dean, 812-941-2169, Fax: 812-941-2667, E-mail: soeinfo@ius.edu. *Application contact:* Admissions Counselor, 812-941-2212, Fax: 812-941-2595, E-mail: admissions@ius.edu. Web site: http://www.ius.edu/education/.

Inter American University of Puerto Rico, Aguadilla Campus, Graduate School, Aguadilla, PR 00605. Offers accounting (MBA); counseling psychology specializing in family (MS); criminal justice (MA); educative management and leadership (MA); elementary education (M Ed); finance (MBA); human resources (MBA); industrial management (MBA); management information systems (MBA); marketing (MBA). Part-time and evening/weekend programs available. *Degree requirements:* For master's, comprehensive exam. *Entrance requirements:* For master's, EXADEP, 2 letters of recommendation, minimum GPA of 2.5. Electronic applications accepted.

Inter American University of Puerto Rico, Arecibo Campus, Programs in Education, Arecibo, PR 00614-4050. Offers administration and educational supervision (MA Ed); counseling and guidance (MA Ed); curriculum and teaching (MA Ed), including biology education, English as a second language, history education, math education, Spanish; elementary education (MA Ed). *Degree requirements:* For master's, comprehensive exam, thesis optional. *Entrance requirements:* For master's, GRE, EXADEP, bachelor's degree in education or teaching license (administration and supervision) or courses in education and psychology (counseling and guidance), minimum GPA of 2.5 in last 60 credits.

Inter American University of Puerto Rico, Barranquitas Campus, Program in Education, Barranquitas, PR 00794. Offers curriculum and teaching (M Ed), including biology education, English as a second language, history education, mathematics education, Spanish; educational leadership and management (MA); elementary education (M Ed); information and library service technology (M Ed); special education (MA). *Degree requirements:* For master's, comprehensive exam, thesis optional. *Entrance requirements:* For master's, EXADEP, letter of recommendation. Electronic applications accepted.

Inter American University of Puerto Rico, Guayama Campus, Department of Education and Social Sciences, Guayama, PR 00785. Offers early childhood education (0-4 years) (M Ed); elementary education (M Ed). Part-time programs available. *Entrance requirements:* For master's, GRE, MAT, EXADEP, letters of recommendation, minimum GPA of 2.5. Electronic applications accepted.

Inter American University of Puerto Rico, Metropolitan Campus, Graduate Programs, Program in Elementary Education, San Juan, PR 00919-1293. Offers MA. *Degree requirements:* For master's, comprehensive exam. *Entrance requirements:* For master's, GRE or EXADEP, interview. Electronic applications accepted.

Inter American University of Puerto Rico, Ponce Campus, Graduate School, Mercedita, PR 00715-1602. Offers accounting (MBA); biology (M Ed); chemistry (M Ed); criminal justice (MA); elementary education (M Ed); English as a Second Language (M Ed); finance (MBA); history (M Ed); human resources (MBA); marketing (MBA); mathematics (M Ed); Spanish (M Ed). *Entrance requirements:* For master's, minimum GPA of 2.5.

Inter American University of Puerto Rico, San Germán Campus, Graduate Studies Center, Program in Elementary Education, San Germán, PR 00683-5008. Offers MA. Part-time and evening/weekend programs available. *Degree requirements:* For master's, comprehensive exam. *Entrance requirements:* For master's, GRE General Test or EXADEP, minimum GPA of 3.0. Application fee: $31. *Expenses: Required fees:* $213 per semester. *Financial support:* Teaching assistantships, Federal Work-Study, and unspecified assistantships available. *Unit head:* Dr. Elba T. Irizarry, Director of Graduate Studies Center, 787-264-1912 Ext. 7357, Fax: 787-892-6350, E-mail: elbat@sg.inter.edu.

Iona College, School of Arts and Science, Program in Education, New Rochelle, NY 10801-1890. Offers adolescence education: biology (MS Ed, MST); adolescence education: English (MS Ed, MST); adolescence education: Italian (MS Ed, MST); adolescence education: mathematics (MS Ed, MST); adolescence education: social studies (MS Ed, MST); adolescence education: Spanish (MS Ed, MST); adolescence special education 5-12 (MST); adolescence special education/literacy 5-12 (MS Ed); childhood 1-6/special education 1-6 (MST); childhood education (MST); early childhood/childhood (MST); educational leadership (MS Ed); literacy birth-grade 6/special education 1-6 (MS Ed); literacy education: birth-grade 6 (MS Ed). *Accreditation:* NCATE. Part-time and evening/weekend programs available. *Faculty:* 21 full-time (13 women), 13 part-time/adjunct (8 women). *Students:* 59 full-time (45 women), 101 part-time (78 women); includes 11 minority (2 Black or African American, non-Hispanic/Latino; 2 Asian, non-Hispanic/Latino; 7 Hispanic/Latino). Average age 26. 74 applicants, 66% accepted, 35 enrolled. In 2011, 46 master's awarded. *Degree requirements:* For master's, thesis or alternative. *Entrance requirements:* For master's, minimum GPA of 2.5 (MST), New York teaching certificate (MS Ed). Additional exam requirements/recommendations for international students: Required—TOEFL (minimum score 550 paper-based; 213 computer-based). *Application deadline:* Applications are processed on a rolling basis. Application fee: $50. Electronic applications accepted. *Expenses: Tuition:* Part-time $872 per credit. *Required fees:* $225 per term. *Financial support:* Unspecified assistantships available. Support available to part-time students. Financial award application deadline: 4/15; financial award applicants required to submit FAFSA. *Faculty research:* Reading/writing, educational technology, administration, early literacy assessment, literacy development. *Unit head:* Dr. Catherine O'Callaghan, Chair, 914-633-2210, Fax: 914-633-2608, E-mail: cocallaghan@iona.edu. *Application contact:* Dr. Jeanne Zaino, Interim Dean, School of Arts and Science, 914-633-2112, Fax: 914-633-2023, E-mail: jzaino@iona.edu.

Iowa State University of Science and Technology, Department of Curriculum and Instruction, Ames, IA 50011. Offers curriculum and instructional technology (M Ed, MS, PhD); elementary education (M Ed, MS); historical, philosophical, and comparative studies in education (M Ed, MS); special education (M Ed, MS, PhD). *Degree requirements:* For master's, thesis or alternative; for doctorate, thesis/dissertation. *Entrance requirements:* For master's and doctorate, GRE General Test. Additional exam requirements/recommendations for international students: Required—TOEFL (minimum score 560 paper-based; 83 iBT), IELTS (minimum score 6.5). *Application deadline:* For fall admission, 1/1 priority date for domestic students, 1/1 for international students; for spring admission, 9/1 for domestic and international students. Application fee: $40 ($90 for international students). Electronic applications accepted. *Unit head:* Dr. Anne Foegen, Director of Graduate Education, 515-294-7021, Fax: 515-294-6206, E-mail: cigrad@iastate.edu. *Application contact:* Phyllis Kendall, Director of Graduate Education, 515-294-7021, Fax: 515-294-6206, E-mail: cigrad@iastate.edu. Web site: http://www.ci.hs.iastate.edu.

Ithaca College, Division of Graduate and Professional Studies, School of Humanities and Sciences, Program in Childhood Education, Grades 1-6, Ithaca, NY 14850. Offers MS. Part-time programs available. *Faculty:* 23 full-time (7 women). *Students:* 9 full-time (7 women); includes 2 minority (1 Hispanic/Latino; 1 Two or more races, non-Hispanic/Latino). Average age 26. 23 applicants, 39% accepted, 9 enrolled. In 2011, 11 master's awarded. *Degree requirements:* For master's, thesis or alternative, student teaching. *Entrance requirements:* For master's, minimum GPA of 3.0. Additional exam requirements/recommendations for international students: Required—TOEFL (minimum score 550 paper-based; 213 computer-based; 80 iBT). *Application deadline:* For fall admission, 2/15 for domestic and international students; for spring admission, 12/1 for domestic and international students. Applications are processed on a rolling basis. Application fee: $40. Electronic applications accepted. *Expenses:* Contact institution. *Financial support:* In 2011–12, 7 students received support, including 7 teaching assistantships (averaging $10,314 per year); career-related internships or fieldwork, Federal Work-Study, scholarships/grants, and unspecified assistantships also available. Support available to part-time students. Financial award application deadline: 2/15; financial award applicants required to submit CSS PROFILE or FAFSA. *Faculty research:* Bilingual education, socio-linguistic perspectives on literacy. *Unit head:* Dr. Linda Hanrahan, Chairperson, 607-274-3143, Fax: 607-274-1263, E-mail: gps@ithaca.edu. *Application contact:* Gerard Turbide, Director, Office of Admission, 607-274-3143, Fax: 607-274-1263, E-mail: gps@ithaca.edu. Web site: http://www.ithaca.edu/gps/gradprograms/overview/school/hs/childhooded.

Jackson State University, Graduate School, College of Education and Human Development, Department of Elementary and Early Childhood Education, Jackson, MS 39217. Offers early childhood education (MS Ed, Ed D); elementary education (MS Ed, Ed S). *Accreditation:* NCATE. Evening/weekend programs available. Terminal master's awarded for partial completion of doctoral program. *Degree requirements:* For master's, comprehensive exam, thesis or alternative; for doctorate, comprehensive exam, thesis/dissertation. *Entrance requirements:* For master's, GRE General Test; for doctorate, MAT, teaching experience. Additional exam requirements/recommendations for international students: Required—TOEFL (minimum score 520 paper-based; 195 computer-based; 67 iBT).

Jacksonville State University, College of Graduate Studies and Continuing Education, College of Education and Professional Studies, Program in Elementary Education, Jacksonville, AL 36265-1602. Offers MS Ed. *Accreditation:* NCATE. Part-time and evening/weekend programs available. *Degree requirements:* For master's, comprehensive exam, thesis (for some programs). *Entrance requirements:* For master's, GRE General Test or MAT. Electronic applications accepted. *Expenses:* Tuition, state resident: part-time $336 per hour. Tuition, nonresident: part-time $672 per hour. Part-time tuition and fees vary according to degree level.

James Madison University, The Graduate School, College of Education, Early, Elementary, and Reading Education Department, Program in Elementary Education, Harrisonburg, VA 22807. Offers M Ed. *Students:* Average age 27. *Entrance requirements:* For master's, GRE General Test, PRAXIS II, minimum undergraduate GPA of 2.75, 2-page essay, interview. Additional exam requirements/recommendations for international students: Required—TOEFL. *Application deadline:* For fall admission, 5/1 for domestic students; for spring admission, 9/1 for domestic students. Applications are processed on a rolling basis. Application fee: $55. Electronic applications accepted. *Expenses:* Tuition, state resident: full-time $8016; part-time $334 per credit hour. Tuition, nonresident: full-time $22,656; part-time $944 per credit hour. *Unit head:* Dr. Martha Ross, Academic Unit Head, 540-568-6255. *Application contact:* Lynette M. Bible, Director of Graduate Admissions, 540-568-6395, Fax: 540-568-7860, E-mail: biblelm@jmu.edu.

The Johns Hopkins University, School of Education, Department of Teacher Preparation, Baltimore, MD 21218. Offers early childhood education (MAT); education (MS), including educational studies; elementary education (MAT); English for speakers of other languages (MAT); K-8 mathematics lead-teacher (Certificate); K-8 science lead-teacher (Certificate); secondary education (MAT), including biology, chemistry, earth/space/environmental science, English, French, mathematics, physics, social studies, Spanish. Part-time and evening/weekend programs available. *Degree requirements:* For master's, portfolio, PRAXIS II, internship. *Entrance requirements:* For master's, PRAXIS I, SAT, ACT, or GRE (MAT), minimum undergraduate GPA of 3.0, interview, 1 letter of recommendation, curriculum vitae/resume; for Certificate, bachelor's degree, minimum undergraduate GPA of 3.0, essay/statement of goals, interview. Additional exam requirements/recommendations for international students: Required—TOEFL (minimum score 600 paper-based; 250 computer-based; 100 iBT). Electronic applications accepted. *Faculty research:* Teacher retention, STEM education reform, alternative certification programs, school-university partnerships, urban education, action research/data-informed instruction, family engagement.

Johnson & Wales University, The Alan Shawn Feinstein Graduate School, Ed D Program, Providence, RI 02903-3703. Offers higher education (Ed D); K-12 (Ed D). Part-time programs available. *Degree requirements:* For doctorate, thesis/dissertation. *Entrance requirements:* For doctorate, MAT, minimum GPA of 3.25; master's degree in appropriate field from accredited institution. Additional exam requirements/recommendations for international students: Required—TOEFL (minimum score 550 paper-based; 210 computer-based); Recommended—IELTS, TWE. *Faculty research:* Site-based management, collaborative learning, technology and education, K-16 education.

Johnson & Wales University, The Alan Shawn Feinstein Graduate School, MAT Program in Teacher Education, Providence, RI 02903-3703. Offers business education and secondary special education (MAT); elementary education and elementary special education (MAT); elementary education and elementary/secondary special education (MAT); elementary education and secondary special education (MAT); food service education (MAT). Part-time and evening/weekend programs available. *Entrance requirements:* For master's, MAT, minimum GPA of 2.75. Additional exam requirements/recommendations for international students: Required—TOEFL (minimum score 550 paper-based; 210 computer-based) or IELTS (recommended). *Faculty research:* Secondary education, student teaching, educational reform, evaluation procedures.

Jones International University, School of Education, Centennial, CO 80112. Offers adult education (M Ed); corporate training and knowledge management (M Ed); curriculum and instruction (M Ed), including elementary teacher licensure, secondary teacher licensure; e-learning technology and design (M Ed); educational leadership and administration (M Ed); educational leadership and administration: principal and administrator licensure (M Ed); elementary curriculum instruction and assessment (M Ed); higher education leadership and administration (M Ed); K-12 instructional technology (M Ed); K-12 instructional technology: teacher licensure (M Ed); secondary curriculum instruction and assessment (M Ed); technology and design (M Ed). Part-time and evening/weekend programs available. Postbaccalaureate distance learning degree programs offered (no on-campus study). *Entrance requirements:* For master's, minimum cumulative GPA of 2.5. Additional exam requirements/recommendations for international students: Recommended—TOEFL (minimum score 550 paper-based; 213 computer-based). Electronic applications accepted.

Kansas State University, Graduate School, College of Education, Department of Curriculum and Instruction, Manhattan, KS 66506. Offers career and technical education (Ed D, PhD); curriculum studies (Ed D, PhD); digital teaching and learning (MS); educational computing, design and online learning (MS); educational technology (Ed D, PhD); elementary/middle level (MS); English as a second language (MS); language/diversity education (Ed D, PhD); literacy education (Ed D, PhD); mathematics education (Ed D, PhD); middle level/secondary (MS); reading and language arts (MS); reading specialist endorsement (MS); science education (Ed D, PhD); social science education (Ed D, PhD); teacher education (Ed D, PhD); teacher leader/school improvement (MS, Ed D). *Accreditation:* NCATE. Part-time programs available. Postbaccalaureate distance learning degree programs offered (minimal on-campus study). *Faculty:* 15 full-time (12 women), 3 part-time/adjunct (2 women). *Students:* 37 full-time (30 women), 113 part-time (91 women); includes 14 minority (4 Black or African American, non-Hispanic/Latino; 1 American Indian or Alaska Native, non-Hispanic/Latino; 1 Asian, non-Hispanic/Latino; 7 Hispanic/Latino; 1 Two or more races, non-Hispanic/Latino), 15 international. Average age 37. 75 applicants, 51% accepted, 9 enrolled. In 2011, 48 master's, 14 doctorates awarded. *Degree requirements:* For master's, comprehensive exam, portfolio, project, report or thesis; for doctorate, comprehensive exam, thesis/dissertation, preliminary exam. *Entrance requirements:* For master's, minimum GPA of 3.0; for doctorate, GRE, minimum GPA of 3.0. Additional exam requirements/recommendations for international students: Required—TOEFL. *Application deadline:* For fall admission, 2/1 priority date for domestic students, 2/1 for international students; for spring admission, 8/1 priority date for domestic students, 8/1 for international students. Applications are processed on a rolling basis. Application fee: $40 ($55 for international students). Electronic applications accepted. *Financial support:* In 2011–12, 1 research assistantship (averaging $16,900 per year), 8 teaching assistantships (averaging $12,466 per year) were awarded; career-related internships or fieldwork, institutionally sponsored loans, and scholarships/grants also available. Support available to part-time students. Financial award application deadline: 3/1; financial award applicants required to submit FAFSA. *Faculty research:* Literacy and technology, critical race theory and diversity, achievement gaps, school improvement, teacher education. *Total annual research expenditures:* $510,907. *Unit head:* Dr. Gail Shroyer, Chair, 785-532-5550, Fax: 785-532-7304, E-mail: gshroyer@ksu.edu. *Application contact:* Dona Deam, Application Contact, 785-532-5595, Fax: 785-532-7304, E-mail: ddeam@ksu.edu. Web site: http://coe.k-state.edu/departments/currin/curringrad.htm.

Kennesaw State University, Leland and Clarice C. Bagwell College of Education, Program in Graduate Education, Kennesaw, GA 30144-5591. Offers adolescent education (M Ed); educational leadership (M Ed); educational leadership technology (M Ed); elementary and early childhood education (M Ed); special education (M Ed); teaching English to speakers of other languages (M Ed). *Accreditation:* NCATE. Part-time programs available. *Students:* 42 full-time (39 women), 132 part-time (105 women); includes 31 minority (20 Black or African American, non-Hispanic/Latino; 4 Asian, non-Hispanic/Latino; 5 Hispanic/Latino; 2 Two or more races, non-Hispanic/Latino). Average age 34. 48 applicants, 79% accepted, 38 enrolled. In 2011, 117 master's awarded. *Degree requirements:* For master's, thesis or alternative. *Entrance requirements:* For master's, GRE General Test, T-4 state certification, minimum GPA of 2.75. Additional exam requirements/recommendations for international students: Required—TOEFL (minimum score 550 paper-based; 213 computer-based; 80 iBT), IELTS (minimum score 6). *Application deadline:* For fall admission, 7/1 for domestic and international students; for spring admission, 10/1 for domestic and international students. Application fee: $60. Electronic applications accepted. *Expenses:* Tuition, state resident: full-time $3000; part-time $250 per semester hour. Tuition, nonresident: full-time $10,836; part-time $903 per semester hour. *Required fees:* $774 per semester. *Financial support:* Federal Work-Study and unspecified assistantships available. Support available to part-time students. Financial award application deadline: 4/1; financial award applicants required to submit FAFSA. *Unit head:* Dr. Nita Paris, Associate Dean for Graduate Programs, 770-423-6636, E-mail: nparis@kennesaw.edu. *Application contact:* Alisha Bello, Administrative Coordinator, 770-423-6043, Fax: 770-420-4435, E-mail: abello1@kennesaw.edu. Web site: http://www.kennesaw.edu/education/grad/.

Kutztown University of Pennsylvania, College of Education, Program in Elementary Education, Kutztown, PA 19530-0730. Offers M Ed. *Accreditation:* NCATE. Part-time and evening/weekend programs available. *Faculty:* 7 full-time (all women), 1 (woman) part-time/adjunct. *Students:* 16 part-time (15 women). Average age 29. 2 applicants, 50% accepted, 1 enrolled. In 2011, 5 master's awarded. *Degree requirements:* For master's, comprehensive exam, thesis optional, comprehensive project. *Entrance requirements:* For master's, GRE General Test. Additional exam requirements/recommendations for international students: Required—TOEFL (minimum score 550 paper-based; 79 iBT). *Application deadline:* For fall admission, 8/1 priority date for domestic students, 8/1 for international students; for spring admission, 12/1 priority date for domestic students, 12/1 for international students. Applications are processed on a rolling basis. Application fee: $35. Electronic applications accepted. *Expenses:* Tuition, state resident: full-time $7488; part-time $416 per credit. Tuition, nonresident: full-time $11,232; part-time $624 per credit. *Financial support:* Career-related internships or fieldwork, Federal Work-Study, scholarships/grants, and unspecified assistantships available. Financial award application deadline: 3/1; financial award applicants required to submit FAFSA. *Faculty research:* Whole language, middle schools, cooperative learning discussion techniques, oral reading techniques, hemisphericity. *Unit head:* Dr. Jeanie Burnett, Chairperson, 610-683-4286, Fax: 610-683-1327, E-mail: burnett@kutztown.edu. *Application contact:* Kelly D. Burr, Associate Director, Graduate Admissions, 610-683-4200, Fax: 610-683-1393, E-mail: graduate@kutztown.edu.

Lancaster Bible College, Graduate School, Lancaster, PA 17601-5036. Offers adult ministries (MA); Bible (MA); children and family ministry (MA); consulting resource teacher (M Ed); elementary school counseling (M Ed); leadership (PhD); leadership studies (MA); marriage and family counseling (MA); mental health counseling (MA); pastoral studies (MA); secondary school counseling (M Ed); student ministry (MA). Part-time and evening/weekend programs available. *Degree requirements:* For master's, comprehensive exam (for some programs), thesis (for some programs). *Entrance requirements:* For master's, bachelor's degree with a minimum of 30 credits of course work in Bible, minimum undergraduate GPA of 3.0, interview. Additional exam requirements/recommendations for international students: Required—TOEFL.

Lander University, School of Education, Greenwood, SC 29649-2099. Offers elementary education (M Ed); teaching (MAT). *Accreditation:* NCATE. Part-time programs available. *Degree requirements:* For master's, comprehensive exam, thesis or alternative. *Entrance requirements:* For master's, GRE General Test. Additional exam requirements/recommendations for international students: Required—TOEFL (minimum score 550 paper-based; 213 computer-based). Electronic applications accepted.

Langston University, School of Education and Behavioral Sciences, Langston, OK 73050. Offers bilingual/multicultural (M Ed); elementary education (M Ed); English as a second language (M Ed); rehabilitation counseling (M Sc); urban education (M Ed). *Accreditation:* CORE; NCATE (one or more programs are accredited). Part-time programs available. *Degree requirements:* For master's, comprehensive exam, thesis optional. *Entrance requirements:* For master's, GRE, writing skills test, minimum GPA of 2.5, 3 letters of recommendation. Additional exam requirements/recommendations for international students: Required—TOEFL, TWE. *Faculty research:* Bilingual/multicultural education, financing post-secondary education.

Lasell College, Graduate and Professional Studies in Education, Newton, MA 02466-2709. Offers elementary education - grades 1-6 (M Ed); special education: moderate disabilities (pre-K-8) (M Ed). Part-time and evening/weekend programs available. Postbaccalaureate distance learning degree programs offered. *Faculty:* 2 full-time (both women). *Students:* 9 part-time (8 women); includes 2 minority (1 Black or African American, non-Hispanic/Latino; 1 Hispanic/Latino). Average age 26. 12 applicants, 42% accepted, 5 enrolled. *Degree requirements:* For master's, 18 credits in licensure requirements for initial licensure; 12 in licensure requirements plus 6 credits selected with advisor and department approval for professional licensure. *Entrance requirements:* For master's, bachelor's degree from an accredited institution. Additional exam requirements/recommendations for international students: Required—TOEFL (minimum score 550 paper-based; 213 computer-based; 79 iBT), IELTS. *Application deadline:* For fall admission, 8/31 priority date for domestic students, 6/30 for international students; for spring admission, 12/31 priority date for domestic students, 10/31 for international students. Applications are processed on a rolling basis. Electronic applications accepted. *Expenses: Tuition:* Part-time $575 per credit. *Required fees:* $70 per semester. *Financial support:* Available to part-time students. Application deadline: 8/31; applicants required to submit FAFSA. *Unit head:* Dr. Joan Dolamore, Dean of Graduate and Professional Studies, 617-243-2485, Fax: 617-243-2450, E-mail: gradinfo@lasell.edu. *Application contact:* Adrienne Franciosi, Director of Graduate Admission, 617-243-2214, Fax: 617-243-2450, E-mail: gradinfo@lasell.edu. Web site: http://www.lasell.edu/Academics/Graduate-and-Professional-Studies/Master-of-Education.html.

Lee University, Program in Education, Cleveland, TN 37320-3450. Offers classroom teaching (M Ed, Ed S); educational leadership (M Ed, Ed S); elementary/secondary education (MAT); secondary education (MAT); special education (M Ed); special education (secondary) (MAT). Part-time programs available. *Faculty:* 14 full-time (6 women), 5 part-time/adjunct (3 women). *Students:* 43 full-time (27 women), 176 part-time (107 women); includes 19 minority (4 Black or African American, non-Hispanic/Latino; 3 American Indian or Alaska Native, non-Hispanic/Latino; 1 Asian, non-Hispanic/Latino; 8 Hispanic/Latino; 3 Two or more races, non-Hispanic/Latino), 4 international. Average age 33. 52 applicants, 100% accepted, 38 enrolled. In 2011, 90 master's, 14 other advanced degrees awarded. *Degree requirements:* For master's, variable foreign language requirement, comprehensive exam, thesis, internship. *Entrance requirements:* For master's, MAT or GRE General Test, minimum GPA of 2.75, 3 letters of recommendation, interview, writing sample. Additional exam requirements/recommendations for international students: Required—TOEFL (minimum score 450 paper-based; 45 computer-based). *Application deadline:* For fall admission, 4/1 priority date for domestic students; for spring admission, 10/1 priority date for domestic students. Applications are processed on a rolling basis. Application fee: $25. *Expenses: Tuition:* Full-time $12,120; part-time $506 per credit hour. *Required fees:* $560; $305 per term. Part-time tuition and fees vary according to course load. *Financial support:* In 2011–12, 18 teaching assistantships (averaging $1,966 per year) were awarded; career-related internships or fieldwork, Federal Work-Study, institutionally sponsored loans, scholarships/grants, and unspecified assistantships also available. Financial award application deadline: 3/1; financial award applicants required to submit FAFSA. *Unit head:* Dr. Gary Riggins, Director, 423-614-8193. *Application contact:* Vicki Glasscock, Graduate Admissions Director, 423-614-8059, E-mail: vglasscock@leeuniversity.edu. Web site: http://www.leeuniversity.edu/academics/graduate/education.

Lehigh University, College of Education, Program in Teaching, Learning and Technology, Bethlehem, PA 18015. Offers elementary education with certification (M Ed); instructional technology (MS); learning sciences and technology (PhD); teaching and learning (M Ed, MA); technology use in the schools (Graduate Certificate); M Ed/MA. Part-time programs available. *Faculty:* 5 full-time (2 women), 9 part-time/adjunct (5 women). *Students:* 49 full-time (37 women), 48 part-time (38 women); includes 12 minority (2 Black or African American, non-Hispanic/Latino; 6 Asian, non-Hispanic/Latino; 3 Hispanic/Latino; 1 Native Hawaiian or other Pacific Islander, non-Hispanic/Latino), 4 international. Average age 31. 72 applicants, 76% accepted, 18 enrolled. In 2011, 46 master's, 2 doctorates awarded. Terminal master's awarded for partial completion of doctoral program. *Degree requirements:* For master's, comprehensive exam and thesis/dissertation (for M Ed); for doctorate, comprehensive exam, thesis/dissertation. *Entrance requirements:* For master's, minimum GPA of 3.0, 2 letters of recommendation, essay, transcript; for doctorate, GRE General Test, minimum graduate GPA of 3.0, writing sample, 2 letters of recommendation, essay, transcript. Additional exam requirements/recommendations for international students: Required—TOEFL (minimum score 600 paper-based; 250 computer-based; 93 iBT). *Application deadline:* For fall admission, 2/1 for domestic and international students; for spring admission, 11/1 for domestic and international students. Applications are processed on a rolling basis. Application fee: $65. Electronic applications accepted. *Financial support:* In 2011–12, 18 students received support, including 1 fellowship with full and partial tuition reimbursement available (averaging $16,000 per year), 2 research assistantships with full and partial tuition reimbursements available (averaging $18,000 per year); career-related internships or fieldwork, institutionally sponsored loans, scholarships/grants, and tuition waivers (full and partial) also available. Financial award application deadline: 1/31. *Faculty research:* Instructional media and delivery systems, technologies to enhance education, technical and informal education, Web-based learning. *Unit head:* Dr. M. J. Bishop, Director, 610-758-3235, Fax: 610-758-3243, E-mail: mjba@lehigh.edu. *Application contact:* Donna M. Johnson, Coordinator, 610-758-3231, Fax: 610-758-6223, E-mail: dmj4@lehigh.edu.

Lehman College of the City University of New York, Division of Education, Department of Early Childhood and Elementary Education, Program in Elementary Education, Bronx, NY 10468-1589. Offers MS Ed. *Accreditation:* NCATE. Part-time and evening/weekend programs available. *Degree requirements:* For master's, thesis. *Entrance requirements:* For master's, minimum GPA of 3.0. *Faculty research:* POS network, emotional and intellectual learning, realistic picture books.

Le Moyne College, Department of Education, Syracuse, NY 13214. Offers adolescent education (MS Ed, MST); adolescent education/special education (MS Ed, MST); adolescent English (grades 7-12) (MST); adolescent history (grades 7-12) (MST); childhood education (MS Ed); childhood education/special education (MS Ed); elementary education (MS Ed); general professional education (MS Ed); inclusive childhood education (MST); literacy education (birth to grade 6) (MS Ed); literacy education (grades 5-12) (MS Ed); school building leadership (MS Ed, CAS); school district business leader (MS Ed, CAS); school district leadership (MS Ed, CAS); secondary education (MS Ed); special education (MS Ed); students with disabilities-generalist (grades 7-12) (MS Ed); TESOL (teaching English to speakers of other languages) (MS Ed); urban studies (MS Ed). *Accreditation:* Teacher Education Accreditation Council. Part-time and evening/weekend programs available. *Faculty:* 9 full-time (6 women), 51 part-time/adjunct (28 women). *Students:* 61 full-time (47 women), 311 part-time (222 women); includes 31 minority (19 Black or African American, non-Hispanic/Latino; 3 American Indian or Alaska Native, non-Hispanic/Latino; 4 Asian, non-Hispanic/Latino; 5 Hispanic/Latino), 2 international. Average age 30. 242 applicants, 90% accepted, 180 enrolled. In 2011, 168 master's, 23 CASs awarded. *Degree requirements:* For master's, thesis. *Entrance requirements:* For master's, GRE General Test, bachelor's degree, 2 letters of recommendation, written statement, transcripts. Additional exam requirements/recommendations for international students: Required—TOEFL (minimum score 550 paper-based; 213 computer-based; 79 iBT). *Application deadline:* For fall admission, 4/1 priority date for domestic students, 4/1 for international students; for spring admission, 10/1 priority date for domestic students, 10/1 for international students. Applications are processed on a rolling basis. Application fee: $50. *Expenses:* Contact institution. *Financial support:* In 2011–12, 32 students received support. Career-related internships or fieldwork and health care benefits available. Support available to part-time students. Financial award applicants required to submit FAFSA. *Faculty research:* Minority teachers, special education, multiculturalism, literacy, technology, video games learning, autism, school district organization, service-learning, higher level problem solving, teacher leadership. *Unit head:* Dr. Suzanne L. Gilmour, Chair, Department of Education and Director of Graduate Education Programs, 315-445-4376, Fax: 315-445-4744, E-mail: gilmous@lemoyne.edu. *Application contact:* Kristen P. Trapasso, Director of Graduate Admission, 315-445-4265, Fax: 315-445-6027, E-mail: trapaskp@lemoyne.edu. Web site: http://www.lemoyne.edu/education.

Lesley University, School of Education, Cambridge, MA 02138-2790. Offers curriculum and instruction (M Ed, CAGS); early childhood education (M Ed); educational studies (PhD); elementary education (M Ed); individually designed (M Ed); middle school education (M Ed); moderate special needs (M Ed); reading (M Ed, CAGS); science in education (M Ed); severe special needs (M Ed); special needs (CAGS); technology in education (M Ed, CAGS). *Accreditation:* Teacher Education Accreditation Council. Part-time and evening/weekend programs available. Postbaccalaureate distance learning degree programs offered (no on-campus study). *Faculty:* 36 full-time (27 women), 170 part-time/adjunct (129 women). *Students:* 552 full-time (437 women), 1,971 part-time (1,697 women); includes 364 minority (189 Black or African American, non-Hispanic/Latino; 19 American Indian or Alaska Native, non-Hispanic/Latino; 45 Asian, non-Hispanic/Latino; 83 Hispanic/Latino; 2 Native Hawaiian or other Pacific Islander, non-Hispanic/Latino; 26 Two or more races, non-Hispanic/Latino), 28 international. Average age 37. In 2011, 1,390 master's, 8 doctorates, 42 other advanced degrees awarded. *Degree requirements:* For master's, practicum; for doctorate, thesis/dissertation. *Entrance requirements:* For doctorate, GRE General Test or MAT, interview, master's degree, resume; for CAGS, interview, master's degree. Additional exam requirements/recommendations for international students: Required—TOEFL (minimum score 550 paper-based; 213 computer-based; 80 iBT). *Application deadline:* Applications are processed on a rolling basis. Application fee: $50. Electronic applications accepted. *Financial support:* In 2011–12, research assistantships (averaging $3,400 per year), teaching assistantships (averaging $3,400 per year) were awarded; career-related internships or fieldwork, Federal Work-Study, scholarships/grants, and unspecified assistantships also available. Support available to part-time students. Financial award application deadline: 4/15; financial award applicants required to submit FAFSA. *Faculty research:* Assessment in literacy, mathematics and science; autism spectrum disorders; instructional technology and online learning; multicultural education and ELL. *Unit head:* Dr. Mario Borunda, Dean, 617-349-8375, Fax: 617-349-8607, E-mail: mborunda@lesley.edu. *Application contact:* Rosie Davis, Senior Assistant Director of Admissions, 617-349-8851, Fax: 617-349-8313, E-mail: rdavis4@lesley.edu. Web site: http://www.lesley.edu/soe.html.

Lewis & Clark College, Graduate School of Education and Counseling, Department of Teacher Education, Program in Early Childhood/Elementary Education, Portland, OR 97219-7899. Offers MAT. *Accreditation:* NCATE. *Faculty:* 5 full-time (4 women), 2 part-time/adjunct (1 woman). *Students:* 54 full-time (47 women), 4 part-time (1 woman); includes 12 minority (1 Black or African American, non-Hispanic/Latino; 3 American Indian or Alaska Native, non-Hispanic/Latino; 4 Asian, non-Hispanic/Latino; 2 Hispanic/Latino; 2 Two or more races, non-Hispanic/Latino), 1 international. Average age 29. 98 applicants, 85% accepted, 55 enrolled. In 2011, 69 master's awarded. *Entrance requirements:* For master's, minimum undergraduate GPA of 2.75; history of work, either volunteer or paid, with children in grades K-6. Additional exam requirements/recommendations for international students: Required—TOEFL (minimum score 575 paper-based; 233 computer-based). *Application deadline:* For fall admission, 12/1 priority date for domestic students, 12/1 for international students. Application fee: $50. Electronic applications accepted. *Expenses: Tuition:* Part-time $738 per semester hour. Tuition and fees vary according to course level and campus/location. *Financial support:* In 2011–12, 11 students received support. Career-related internships or fieldwork, Federal Work-Study, institutionally sponsored loans, scholarships/grants, health care benefits, and tuition waivers (partial) available. Support available to part-time students. Financial award application deadline: 3/1; financial award applicants required to submit FAFSA. *Faculty research:* Classroom ethnography, assessing student learning, reading, moral development, language arts. *Unit head:* Dr. Linda Griffin, Program Director, 503-768-6100, Fax: 503-768-6115, E-mail: lcteach@lclark.edu. *Application contact:* Becky Haas, Director of Admissions, 503-768-6200, Fax: 503-768-6205, E-mail: gseadmit@lclark.edu. Web site: http://graduate.lclark.edu/departments/teacher_education/prospective_teachers/early_childhood_elementary/.

Lewis University, College of Education, Program in Elementary Education, Romeoville, IL 60446. Offers MA. *Students:* 14 full-time (13 women), 57 part-time (51 women); includes 28 minority (9 Black or African American, non-Hispanic/Latino; 1 Asian, non-Hispanic/Latino; 16 Hispanic/Latino; 2 Two or more races, non-Hispanic/Latino), 1 international. Average age 32. In 2011, 19 master's awarded. *Entrance requirements:* For master's, departmental qualifying exam, writing exam, minimum GPA of 2.75, 2 letters of recommendation, interview. Additional exam requirements/recommendations for international students: Required—TOEFL (minimum score 550 paper-based; 213 computer-based; 80 iBT). *Application deadline:* For fall admission, 5/1 for international students; for spring admission, 11/15 for international students. Application fee: $40. Electronic applications accepted. *Financial support:* Federal Work-Study, scholarships/grants, and unspecified assistantships available. Financial award application deadline: 5/1; financial award applicants required to submit FAFSA. *Unit head:* Dr. Suzanne O'Brien, Program Director, 815-836-5632, E-mail: obriensu@lewisu.edu. *Application contact:* Anne Czech, Graduate Admission Counselor, 815-838-5610 Ext. 5027, E-mail: czechan@lewisu.edu.

Liberty University, School of Education, Lynchburg, VA 24502. Offers administration and supervision (M Ed); curriculum and instruction (M Ed); early childhood education (M Ed); educational leadership (Ed D, Ed S); educational technology and online instruction (M Ed); elementary education (M Ed, MAT); gifted education (M Ed); math specialist (M Ed); middle grades (M Ed); outdoor adventure sport (MS); reading specialist (M Ed); school counseling (M Ed); secondary education (M Ed, MAT); special education (M Ed, MAT); sports administration (MS); teaching and learning (Ed D, Ed S). *Accreditation:* NCATE. Part-time programs available. Postbaccalaureate distance learning degree programs offered (minimal on-campus study). *Students:* 2,245 full-time (1,572 women), 3,500 part-time (2,558 women); includes 1,141 minority (888 Black or African American, non-Hispanic/Latino; 19 American Indian or Alaska Native, non-Hispanic/Latino; 21 Asian, non-Hispanic/Latino; 123 Hispanic/Latino; 9 Native Hawaiian or other Pacific Islander, non-Hispanic/Latino; 81 Two or more races, non-Hispanic/Latino), 76 international. Average age 37. In 2011, 760 master's, 48 doctorates, 321 other advanced degrees awarded. *Degree requirements:* For doctorate, comprehensive exam, thesis/dissertation. *Entrance requirements:* For master's, GRE General Test or MAT (if taken in or before 1999), 2 letters of recommendation, minimum undergraduate GPA of 3.0, curriculum vitae; for doctorate, GRE General Test or MAT (if taken before 1999), minimum master's GPA of 3.0, 3 years of teacher experience; for Ed S, GRE General Test or MAT (if taken before 1999), minimum master's GPA of 3.0, 3 years of teaching experience. Additional exam requirements/recommendations for international students: Required—TOEFL (minimum score 600 paper-based; 250 computer-based). *Application deadline:* For fall admission, 6/1 priority date for domestic students; for spring admission, 11/1 for domestic students. Applications are processed on a rolling basis. Application fee: $50. Electronic applications accepted. *Expenses:* Contact institution. *Financial support:* Federal Work-Study and tuition waivers (partial) available. *Faculty research:* Self-determination, character education, bibliotherapy, learning styles, distance education. *Unit head:* Dr. Karen L. Parker, Dean, 434-582-2195, Fax: 434-582-2468, E-mail: kparker@liberty.edu. *Application contact:* Jay Bridge, Director of Graduate Admissions, 800-424-9595, Fax: 800-628-7977, E-mail: gradadmissions@liberty.edu. Web site: http://www.liberty.edu/academics/education/graduate/.

Lincoln University, Graduate Center, Lincoln University, PA 19352. Offers administration (MSA), including finance, human resources management; early childhood education (M Ed); elementary education (M Ed); human services (M Hum Svcs); reading (MSR). Evening/weekend programs available. *Degree requirements:* For master's, thesis. *Entrance requirements:* For master's, 5 years of work experience in human services. *Faculty research:* Gerontology/minority aging, computers in composition instruction.

Lincoln University, School of Graduate Studies and Continuing Education, Jefferson City, MO 65102. Offers business administration (MBA), including accounting, entrepreneurship, management, public administration and policy; educational leadership (Ed S), including elementary leadership, secondary leadership, superintendency; guidance and counseling (M Ed), including community/agency counseling, elementary school, secondary school; history (MA); school administration and supervision (M Ed), including elementary school administration, secondary school administration, special education administration; school teaching (M Ed), including elementary school teaching, secondary school teaching; social science (MA), including history, political science, sociology; sociology (MA); sociology/criminal justice (MA). Part-time and evening/weekend programs available. *Degree requirements:* For master's and Ed S, comprehensive exam, thesis optional. *Entrance requirements:* For master's and Ed S, GRE, MAT or GMAT, minimum GPA of 2.75 in major, 2.5 overall; 3 letters of recommendation; minimum C average in English composition; personal statement of purpose. Additional exam requirements/recommendations for international students: Required—TOEFL (minimum score 500 paper-based; 173 computer-based; 61 iBT). *Faculty research:* Suicide prevention.

Lock Haven University of Pennsylvania, Department of Education, Lock Haven, PA 17745-2390. Offers alternative education (M Ed); teaching and learning (M Ed). *Accreditation:* NCATE. Part-time and evening/weekend programs available. Postbaccalaureate distance learning degree programs offered. *Degree requirements:* For master's, thesis. *Entrance requirements:* For master's, minimum undergraduate GPA of 3.0. Additional exam requirements/recommendations for international students: Required—TOEFL. Electronic applications accepted.

Long Island University–Brooklyn Campus, School of Education, Department of Teaching and Learning, Program in Elementary Education, Brooklyn, NY 11201-8423. Offers MS Ed. Part-time and evening/weekend programs available. *Degree requirements:* For master's, thesis optional. *Entrance requirements:* For master's, 2 letters of recommendation. Additional exam requirements/recommendations for international students: Required—TOEFL (minimum score 500 paper-based; 173 computer-based). Electronic applications accepted.

Long Island University–C. W. Post Campus, School of Education, Department of Curriculum and Instruction, Brookville, NY 11548-1300. Offers adolescence education (MS); adolescence education: biology (MS); adolescence education: earth science (MS); adolescence education: English (MS); adolescence education: mathematics (MS); adolescence education: social studies (MS); adolescence education: Spanish (MS); art education (MS); bilingual education (MS); childhood education (MS); early childhood education (MS); middle childhood education (MS); music education (MS); teaching English to speakers of other languages (MS). Part-time and evening/weekend programs available. *Degree requirements:* For master's, comprehensive exam or thesis, student teaching. *Entrance requirements:* For master's, minimum GPA of 2.75 in major, 2.5 overall. Electronic applications accepted. *Faculty research:* Ethics and education, teaching strategies.

Long Island University–Hudson at Rockland, Graduate School, Program in Curriculum and Instruction, Orangeburg, NY 10962. Offers adolescence education (MS Ed); childhood education (MS Ed). Part-time and evening/weekend programs available. *Degree requirements:* For master's, LAST and CST exams. *Entrance requirements:* For master's, college transcripts, letters of recommendation, personal statement.

Long Island University–Hudson at Westchester, Programs in Education-Teaching, Purchase, NY 10577. Offers early childhood education (MS Ed, Advanced Certificate); elementary education (MS Ed, Advanced Certificate); literacy education (MS Ed, Advanced Certificate); second language, TESOL, bilingual education (MS Ed, Advanced Certificate); special education and secondary education (MS Ed, Advanced Certificate). *Accreditation:* Teacher Education Accreditation Council. Part-time and evening/weekend programs available. *Degree requirements:* For master's, comprehensive exam.

Long Island University–Riverhead, Education Division, Program in Childhood Education, Riverhead, NY 11901. Offers childhood education (MS Ed); elementary education (MS Ed). *Accreditation:* Teacher Education Accreditation Council. *Faculty:* 1 full-time (0 women), 11 part-time/adjunct (7 women). *Students:* 19 full-time (17 women), 17 part-time (16 women); includes 4 minority (2 Black or African American, non-Hispanic/Latino; 2 Hispanic/Latino). Average age 30. In 2011, 22 master's awarded. *Degree requirements:* For master's, thesis. *Entrance requirements:* For master's, minimum undergraduate GPA of 2.75, on-campus writing sample. Additional exam requirements/recommendations for international students: Required—TOEFL (minimum score 550 paper-based; 250 computer-based). *Application deadline:* Applications are processed on a rolling basis. Application fee: $30. Electronic applications accepted. *Expenses: Tuition:* Part-time $1028 per credit. *Financial support:* In 2011–12, 1 research assistantship with full tuition reimbursement was awarded; scholarships/grants and unspecified assistantships also available. Support available to part-time students. Financial award applicants required to submit FAFSA. *Unit head:* Prof. David S. Schultz, Head, 631-287-8010, Fax: 631-287-8253. *Application contact:* Andrea Borra, Admissions Counselor, 631-287-8010, Fax: 631-287-8253, E-mail: andrea.borra@liu.edu.

Longwood University, Office of Graduate Studies, College of Education and Human Services, Farmville, VA 23909. Offers communication sciences and disorders (MS); community and college counseling (MS); curriculum and instruction specialist-elementary (MS), including mild disabilities, modern languages; curriculum and instruction specialist-secondary (MS), including English, mild disabilities, modern languages; educational leadership (MS); guidance and counseling (MS); literacy and culture (MS); school library media (MS). *Accreditation:* NCATE. Part-time and evening/weekend programs available. *Degree requirements:* For master's, comprehensive exam, thesis optional. *Entrance requirements:* For master's, GRE (communication sciences and disorders), minimum GPA of 2.75. Additional exam requirements/recommendations for international students: Required—TOEFL (minimum score 550 paper-based; 213 computer-based).

Louisiana State University and Agricultural and Mechanical College, Graduate School, College of Education, Department of Educational Theory, Policy and Practice, Baton Rouge, LA 70803. Offers counseling (M Ed, MA, Ed S); educational administration (M Ed, MA, PhD, Ed S); educational technology (MA); elementary education (M Ed, MAT); higher education (PhD); research methodology (PhD); secondary education (M Ed, MAT). PhD programs offered jointly with Louisiana State University in Shreveport. *Accreditation:* ACA (one or more programs are accredited); NCATE. Part-time and evening/weekend programs available. *Faculty:* 17 full-time (all women). *Students:* 188 full-time (145 women), 161 part-time (130 women); includes 104 minority (88 Black or African American, non-Hispanic/Latino; 1 American Indian or Alaska Native, non-Hispanic/Latino; 6 Asian, non-Hispanic/Latino; 5 Hispanic/Latino; 4 Two or more races, non-Hispanic/Latino), 9 international. Average age 31. 151 applicants, 61% accepted, 58 enrolled. In 2011, 129 master's, 17 doctorates, 11 other advanced degrees awarded. Terminal master's awarded for partial completion of doctoral program. *Degree requirements:* For doctorate, thesis/dissertation; for Ed S, thesis optional. *Entrance requirements:* For master's and doctorate, GRE General Test, minimum GPA of 3.0. Additional exam requirements/recommendations for international students: Required—TOEFL (minimum score 550 paper-based; 213 computer-based; 79 iBT) or IELTS (minimum score 6.5). *Application deadline:* For fall admission, 1/25 priority date for domestic students, 5/15 for international students; for spring admission, 10/15 for international students. Applications are processed on a rolling basis. Application fee: $50 ($70 for international students). Electronic applications accepted. *Financial support:* In 2011–12, 230 students received support, including 2 fellowships (averaging $19,353 per year), 24 research assistantships with full and partial tuition reimbursements available (averaging $10,052 per year), 53 teaching assistantships with full and partial tuition reimbursements available (averaging $12,218 per year); career-related internships or fieldwork, Federal Work-Study, institutionally sponsored loans, health care benefits, and unspecified assistantships also available. Support available to part-time students. Financial award applicants required to submit FAFSA. *Faculty research:* Literary, curriculum studies, science education, K-12 leadership, higher education. *Total annual research expenditures:* $774,887. *Unit head:* Dr. Earl Cheek, Jr., Chair, 225-578-6867, Fax: 225-578-9135, E-mail: echeek@lsu.edu. *Application contact:* Dr. Rita Culross, Graduate Coordinator, 225-578-6867, Fax: 225-578-9135, E-mail: acrita@lsu.edu.

Loyola Marymount University, School of Education, Department of Elementary and Secondary Education, Program in Elementary Education, Los Angeles, CA 90045. Offers MA. Part-time and evening/weekend programs available. *Faculty:* 7 full-time (6 women), 17 part-time/adjunct (10 women). *Students:* 91 full-time (84 women), 35 part-time (30 women); includes 75 minority (2 Black or African American, non-Hispanic/Latino; 1 American Indian or Alaska Native, non-Hispanic/Latino; 10 Asian, non-Hispanic/Latino; 59 Hispanic/Latino; 3 Two or more races, non-Hispanic/Latino). Average age 29. 68 applicants, 79% accepted, 46 enrolled. In 2011, 51 master's awarded. *Degree requirements:* For master's, comprehensive exam. *Entrance requirements:* For master's, CBEST, CSET, RICA, 3 letters of recommendation. Additional exam requirements/recommendations for international students: Required—TOEFL (minimum score 600 paper-based; 250 computer-based; 100 iBT). *Application deadline:* For fall admission, 6/15 for domestic students; for spring admission, 11/15 for domestic students. Application fee: $50. Electronic applications accepted. *Financial support:* In 2011–12, 93 students received support. Scholarships/grants and unspecified assistantships available. Support available to part-time students. Financial award application deadline: 6/15; financial award applicants required to submit FAFSA. *Unit head:* Dr. Irene Oliver, Chair/Director, 310-338-7302, E-mail: ioliver@lmu.edu. *Application contact:* Chake H. Kouyoumjian, Director, Graduate Admissions, 310-338-2721, E-mail: ckouyoum@lmu.edu. Web site: http://soe.lmu.edu/admissions/programs/tcp/elem.htm.

Loyola University Chicago, School of Education, Program in Teaching and Learning, Chicago, IL 60660. Offers elementary education (M Ed); English as a second language (Certificate); math education (M Ed); reading specialist (M Ed); reading teacher endorsement (Certificate); school technology (M Ed); science education (M Ed); secondary education (M Ed); special education (M Ed). *Accreditation:* NCATE. *Faculty:* 12 full-time (9 women), 12 part-time/adjunct (6 women). *Students:* 131. Average age 28. 115 applicants, 65% accepted, 30 enrolled. In 2011, 80 master's awarded. *Degree requirements:* For master's, comprehensive exam. *Entrance requirements:* For master's, Illinois Basic Skills Test, 3 letters of recommendation, minimum GPA of 3.0, resume. Additional exam requirements/recommendations for international students: Required—TOEFL (minimum score 550 paper-based; 213 computer-based; 79 iBT). *Application deadline:* For fall admission, 7/1 priority date for domestic students, 7/1 for international students; for spring admission, 11/1 priority date for domestic students, 11/1 for international students. Applications are processed on a rolling basis. Application fee: $50. Electronic applications accepted. Application fee is waived when completed online. *Expenses: Tuition:* Full-time $15,660; part-time $870 per credit hour. *Required fees:* $125 per semester. Tuition and fees vary according to course load and program. *Financial support:* Institutionally sponsored loans, scholarships/grants, and unspecified assistantships available. Support available to part-time students. Financial award application deadline: 2/1; financial award applicants required to submit FAFSA. *Faculty research:* Positive behavior support, school reform, school improvement. *Unit head:* Dr. Dorothy Giroux, Director, 312-915-7027, E-mail: dgiroux@luc.edu. *Application contact:* Marie Rosin-Dittmar, Information Contact, 312-915-6800, E-mail: schleduc@luc.edu.

Loyola University Maryland, Graduate Programs, Department of Education, Program in Montessori Education, Baltimore, MD 21210-2699. Offers elementary education (M Ed); infant education (M Ed); Montessori education (CAS); primary education (M Ed). *Accreditation:* NCATE. *Faculty:* 11 full-time (all women). *Students:* 35 full-time (31 women), 1 (woman) part-time; includes 4 minority (1 Asian, non-Hispanic/Latino; 2 Hispanic/Latino; 1 Two or more races, non-Hispanic/Latino), 6 international. Average age 29. In 2011, 98 master's awarded. *Entrance requirements:* Additional exam requirements/recommendations for international students: Required—TOEFL (minimum score 550 paper-based; 213 computer-based). *Application deadline:* For fall admission, 10/1 priority date for domestic students. Application fee: $50. Electronic applications accepted. *Financial support:* Research assistantships and unspecified assistantships available. Financial award application deadline: 4/15; financial award applicants required to submit FAFSA. *Unit head:* Dr. Sharon Dubble, Director, 410-617-7772, E-mail: sdubble@loyola.edu. *Application contact:* Maureen Faux, Executive Director, Graduate Admissions, 410-617-5020, Fax: 410-617-2002, E-mail: graduate@loyola.edu.

Loyola University Maryland, Graduate Programs, Department of Education, Program in Special Education, Baltimore, MD 21210-2699. Offers early childhood education (M Ed, CAS); elementary/middle education (M Ed, CAS); secondary education (M Ed, CAS). *Accreditation:* NCATE. Part-time programs available. *Faculty:* 57 full-time (32 women), 21 part-time/adjunct (10 women). *Students:* 6 full-time (5 women), 33 part-time (31 women); includes 3 minority (all Black or African American, non-Hispanic/Latino). Average age 29. In 2011, 11 master's awarded. *Entrance requirements:* For master's and CAS, PRAXIS, SAT, ACT, or GRE. Additional exam requirements/recommendations for international students: Required—TOEFL (minimum score 550 paper-based; 213 computer-based). *Application deadline:* For fall admission, 6/15 priority date for domestic students; for spring admission, 11/1 priority date for domestic students. Application fee: $50. Electronic applications accepted. *Financial support:* Research assistantships and unspecified assistantships available. Financial award application deadline: 4/15; financial award applicants required to submit FAFSA. *Unit head:* Monica J. Phelps, Director, 410-617-2671, E-mail: mphelps@loyola.edu. *Application contact:* Maureen Faux, Executive Director, Graduate Admissions, 410-617-5020, Fax: 410-617-2002, E-mail: graduate@loyola.edu.

Loyola University Maryland, Graduate Programs, Department of Education, Program in Teacher Education, Baltimore, MD 21210-2699. Offers elementary/middle education (MAT); secondary education (MAT); secondary education: biology (MAT); secondary education: chemistries (MAT); secondary education: earth science (MAT); secondary education: English (MAT); secondary education: mathematics (MAT); secondary education: physics (MAT). Part-time programs available. *Faculty:* 25 full-time (21 women), 14 part-time/adjunct (11 women). *Students:* 28 full-time (19 women), 58 part-time (45 women); includes 5 minority (1 Black or African American, non-Hispanic/Latino; 2 Asian, non-Hispanic/Latino; 2 Two or more races, non-Hispanic/Latino), 4 international. Average age 28. In 2011, 37 master's awarded. *Entrance requirements:* For master's, PRAXIS, SAT, ACT, or GRE. Additional exam requirements/recommendations for international students: Required—TOEFL (minimum score 550 paper-based; 213 computer-based). *Application deadline:* For fall admission, 6/15 for domestic students; for spring admission, 11/1 for domestic students. Electronic applications accepted. *Financial support:* Research assistantships and unspecified assistantships available. Financial award application deadline: 4/15. *Unit head:* Wendy Smith, Chair, 410-617-2194, E-mail: wmsmith@loyola.edu. *Application contact:* Maureen Faux, Executive Director, Graduate Admissions, 410-617-5020, Fax: 410-617-2002, E-mail: graduate@loyola.edu. Web site: http://www.loyola.edu/academics/theology/.

Maharishi University of Management, Graduate Studies, Department of Education, Fairfield, IA 52557. Offers teaching elementary education (MA); teaching secondary education (MA). *Degree requirements:* For master's, thesis or alternative. *Entrance requirements:* For master's, GRE, minimum GPA of 3.0. Additional exam requirements/recommendations for international students: Required—TOEFL. *Faculty research:* Unified field-based approach to education, moral climate, scientific study of teaching.

Manhattanville College, Graduate Studies, School of Education, Program in Child and Early Childhood Education, Purchase, NY 10577-2132. Offers MAT, MPS. Part-time and evening/weekend programs available. *Degree requirements:* For master's, comprehensive exam or research project, field experience. *Entrance requirements:* For master's, minimum undergraduate GPA of 3.0, 2 letters of recommendation. Additional exam requirements/recommendations for international students: Required—TOEFL. Electronic applications accepted.

Manhattanville College, Graduate Studies, School of Education, Program in Childhood Education, Purchase, NY 10577-2132. Offers childhood and special education (MPS); childhood education (MAT); special education childhood (MPS). Part-time and evening/weekend programs available. *Degree requirements:* For master's, comprehensive exam or research project, field experience. *Entrance requirements:* For master's, minimum undergraduate GPA of 3.0, 2 letters of recommendation. Additional exam requirements/recommendations for international students: Required—TOEFL.

Mansfield University of Pennsylvania, Graduate Studies, Department of Education and Special Education, Mansfield, PA 16933. Offers elementary education (M Ed); secondary education (MS); special education (M Ed). *Accreditation:* NCATE (one or more programs are accredited). Part-time and evening/weekend programs available. Postbaccalaureate distance learning degree programs offered (no on-campus study). *Degree requirements:* For master's, comprehensive exam, thesis optional. *Entrance requirements:* For master's, minimum GPA of 3.0. Additional exam requirements/recommendations for international students: Required—TOEFL (minimum score 550 paper-based; 220 computer-based). Electronic applications accepted. *Expenses:* Tuition, state resident: full-time $7488; part-time $416 per credit. Tuition, nonresident: full-time $11,232; part-time $624 per credit.

Marquette University, Graduate School, College of Education, Department of Educational Policy and Leadership, Milwaukee, WI 53201-1881. Offers college student personnel administration (M Ed); curriculum and instruction (MA); education (MA); educational administration (M Ed); educational policy and foundations (MA); elementary education (Certificate); literacy (MA); principal (Certificate); reading specialist (Certificate); reading teacher (Certificate); secondary education (Certificate); superintendent (Certificate). Part-time and evening/weekend programs available. *Faculty:* 14 full-time (9 women). *Students:* 40 full-time (34 women), 137 part-time (80 women); includes 25 minority (14 Black or African American, non-Hispanic/Latino; 1 American Indian or Alaska Native, non-Hispanic/Latino; 2 Asian, non-Hispanic/Latino; 8 Hispanic/Latino), 2 international. Average age 32. 132 applicants, 73% accepted, 67 enrolled. In 2011, 46 master's, 3 doctorates, 5 other advanced degrees awarded. Terminal master's awarded for partial completion of doctoral program. *Degree requirements:* For master's, comprehensive exam, thesis (for some programs); for doctorate, thesis/dissertation, qualifying exam, supporting minor. *Entrance requirements:* For master's, GRE General Test or MAT, official transcripts from all current and previous colleges/universities except Marquette, three letters of recommendation, statement of purpose; for doctorate, GRE General Test, MAT, sample of written work, official transcripts from all current and previous colleges/universities except Marquette, three letters of recommendation, statement of purpose, resume/curriculum vitae; for Certificate, GRE General Test or MAT, master's degree. Additional exam requirements/recommendations for international students: Required—TOEFL (minimum score 530 paper-based; 78 computer-based). *Application deadline:* For fall admission, 1/15 for domestic and international students. Application fee: $50. *Expenses:* Contact institution. *Financial support:* In 2011–12, 130 students received support, including 1 fellowship with full tuition reimbursement available (averaging $18,780 per year), 5 research assistantships with full tuition reimbursements available (averaging $13,404 per year); health care benefits, tuition waivers (partial), and unspecified assistantships also available. Support available to part-time students. Financial award application deadline: 2/15. *Faculty research:* Leadership; social justice in education; development of lifelong learners; race, class, and schooling in historical perspective; urban teacher education. *Unit head:* Dr. Ellen Eckman, Chair, 414-288-1561, E-mail: ellen.eckman@marquette.edu. *Application contact:* Craig Pierce, Assistant Dean of the Graduate School, 414-288-5740, Fax: 414-288-1902, E-mail: craig.pierce@marquette.edu.

Marshall University, Academic Affairs Division, Graduate School of Education and Professional Development, Program in Elementary Education, Huntington, WV 25755. Offers MA. *Accreditation:* NCATE. Part-time and evening/weekend programs available. *Students:* 19 full-time (17 women), 87 part-time (83 women), 1 international. Average age 34. In 2011, 33 master's awarded. *Degree requirements:* For master's, thesis optional, comprehensive or oral assessment, research project. *Entrance requirements:* For master's, GRE General Test or MAT. Application fee: $40. *Financial support:* Federal Work-Study, tuition waivers (full and partial), and unspecified assistantships available. Support available to part-time students. Financial award applicants required to submit FAFSA. *Unit head:* Dr. Lisa Heaton, Director, 304-7462026, E-mail: heaton@marshall.edu. *Application contact:* Information Contact, Graduate Admissions, 304-746-1900, Fax: 304-746-1902, E-mail: services@marshall.edu.

Mary Baldwin College, Graduate Studies, Program in Teaching, Staunton, VA 24401-3610. Offers elementary education (MAT); middle grades education (MAT). *Accreditation:* Teacher Education Accreditation Council.

Marygrove College, Graduate Division, Sage Program, Detroit, MI 48221-2599. Offers M Ed. *Entrance requirements:* For master's, Michigan Teacher Test for Certification.

Marymount University, School of Education and Human Services, Program in Education, Arlington, VA 22207-4299. Offers elementary education (M Ed); English as a second language (M Ed); professional studies (M Ed); secondary education (M Ed); special education, general curriculum (M Ed). *Accreditation:* NCATE. Part-time and evening/weekend programs available. *Faculty:* 9 full-time (7 women), 7 part-time/adjunct (5 women). *Students:* 62 full-time (57 women), 103 part-time (86 women); includes 22 minority (3 Black or African American, non-Hispanic/Latino; 4 Asian, non-Hispanic/Latino; 10 Hispanic/Latino; 5 Two or more races, non-Hispanic/Latino), 13 international. Average age 31. 69 applicants, 100% accepted, 52 enrolled. In 2011, 79 master's awarded. *Degree requirements:* For master's, thesis or alternative. *Entrance requirements:* For master's, GRE or MAT and PRAXIS I or SAT/ACT and VCLA, 2 letters of recommendation, resume, interview. Additional exam requirements/recommendations for international students: Required—TOEFL (minimum score 600 paper-based; 250 computer-based; 96 iBT), IELTS (minimum score 6.5). *Application deadline:* For fall admission, 7/1 for international students. Applications are processed on a rolling basis. Application fee: $40. Electronic applications accepted. *Expenses: Tuition:* Part-time $770 per credit hour. *Required fees:* $8 per credit hour. One-time fee: $180 full-time. *Financial support:* In 2011–12, 27 students received support. Research assistantships with full tuition reimbursements available, career-related internships or fieldwork, Federal Work-Study, scholarships/grants, and unspecified assistantships available. Support available to part-time students. Financial award applicants required to submit FAFSA. *Unit head:* Dr. Shelly Haser, Chair, 703-526-6855, Fax: 703-284-1631, E-mail: shelly.haser@marymount.edu. *Application contact:* Francesca Reed, Director, Graduate Admissions, 703-284-5901, Fax: 703-527-3815, E-mail: grad.admissions@marymount.edu. Web site: http://www.marymount.edu/academics/schools/sehs/grad.aspx.

Maryville University of Saint Louis, School of Education, St. Louis, MO 63141-7299. Offers art education (MA Ed); early childhood education (MA Ed); educational leadership (Ed D); educational leadership: principal certification (MA Ed); elementary education (MA Ed); gifted education (MA Ed); higher education leadership (Ed D); literacy specialist (MA Ed); middle grades education (MA Ed); secondary teaching and inquiry (MA Ed); teacher as leader (MA Ed). *Accreditation:* NCATE. Part-time and evening/weekend programs available. *Faculty:* 10 full-time (6 women), 19 part-time/adjunct (15 women). *Students:* 33 full-time (25 women), 251 part-time (190 women); includes 42 minority (32 Black or African American, non-Hispanic/Latino; 1 American Indian or Alaska Native, non-Hispanic/Latino; 4 Asian, non-Hispanic/Latino; 2 Hispanic/Latino; 3 Two or more races, non-Hispanic/Latino). Average age 38. In 2011, 69 master's, 43 doctorates awarded. *Degree requirements:* For master's, thesis, project. *Entrance requirements:* For master's, minimum cumulative GPA of 3.0, 3 professional recommendations, essays, interview with program faculty; for doctorate, minimum GPA of 3.0, 3 professional recommendations, essay, interview, on-site writing sample. Additional exam requirements/recommendations for international students: Required—TOEFL (minimum score 550 paper-based). *Application deadline:* Applications are processed on a rolling basis. Application fee: $40 ($60 for international students). Electronic applications accepted. *Expenses: Tuition:* Full-time $21,922; part-time $675 per credit hour. *Required fees:* $233.75 per semester. *Financial support:* Career-related internships or fieldwork, Federal Work-Study, tuition waivers (partial), and professional educator discounts available. Financial award application deadline: 3/1; financial award applicants required to submit FAFSA. *Faculty research:* Collaboration with public schools, pre-service program development, mathematics, diversity, literacy. *Unit head:* Dr. Sam Hausfather, Dean, 314-529-9466, Fax: 314-529-9921, E-mail: shausfather@maryville.edu. *Application contact:* Holly Stanwich, Graduate Admissions Coordinator, 314-529-9542, Fax: 314-529-9921, E-mail: teachered@maryville.edu. Web site: http://www.maryville.edu/academics-ed-graduate.

Marywood University, Academic Affairs, Reap College of Education and Human Development, Department of Education, Program in Elementary Education, Scranton, PA 18509-1598. Offers MAT. *Accreditation:* NCATE. *Entrance requirements:* Additional exam requirements/recommendations for international students: Required—TOEFL (minimum score 550 paper-based; 213 computer-based; 79 iBT). *Application deadline:* For fall admission, 4/1 priority date for domestic students, 3/31 for international students; for spring admission, 11/1 priority date for domestic students, 8/31 for international students. Applications accepted. Applications are processed on a rolling basis. Application fee: $35. Electronic applications accepted. *Financial support:* Research assistantships, career-related internships or fieldwork, scholarships/grants, and unspecified assistantships available. Support available to part-time students. Financial award application deadline: 6/30; financial award applicants required to submit FAFSA. *Unit head:* Dr. Patricia S. Arter, Chairperson, 570-348-6211 Ext. 2511, E-mail: psarter@marywood.edu. *Application contact:* Tammy Manka, Assistant Director of Graduate Admissions, 570-348-6211 Ext. 2322, E-mail: tmanka@marywood.edu. Web site: http://www.marywood.edu/education/graduate-programs/mat-elementary.html.

McDaniel College, Graduate and Professional Studies, Program in Elementary and Secondary Education, Westminster, MD 21157-4390. Offers elementary education (MS); secondary education (MS). *Accreditation:* NCATE. Part-time and evening/weekend programs available. *Degree requirements:* For master's, comprehensive exam (for some programs), thesis optional. *Entrance requirements:* For master's, GRE General Test, MAT, or NTE/PRAXIS I, letters of reference (3). Additional exam requirements/recommendations for international students: Required—TOEFL (minimum score 213 computer-based).

McNeese State University, Doré School of Graduate Studies, Burton College of Education, Department of Education Professions, Program in Curriculum and Instruction, Lake Charles, LA 70609. Offers early childhood education (M Ed); elementary education (M Ed); reading (M Ed); secondary education (M Ed). Evening/weekend programs available. *Faculty:* 10 full-time (5 women). *Students:* 8 full-time (7 women), 11 part-time (all women); includes 6 minority (all Black or African American, non-Hispanic/Latino), 1 international. In 2011, 6 master's awarded. *Entrance requirements:* For master's, GRE, teaching certificate. *Application deadline:* For fall admission, 5/15 priority date for domestic students, 5/15 for international students; for spring admission, 10/15 priority date for domestic students, 10/15 for international students. Applications are processed on a rolling basis. Application fee: $20 ($30 for international students). *Expenses:* Tuition, state resident: part-time $519 per credit hour. Tuition and fees vary according to course load. *Financial support:* Application deadline: 5/1. *Unit head:* Dr. Dustin M. Hebert, Director, 337-475-5424, Fax: 337-475-5272, E-mail: dhebert@mcneese.edu. *Application contact:* Dr. George F. Mead, Jr., Interim Dean of Dore' School of Graduate Studies, 337-475-5396, Fax: 337-475-5397, E-mail: admissions@mcneese.edu.

McNeese State University, Doré School of Graduate Studies, Burton College of Education, Department of Education Professions, Program in Teaching, Lake Charles, LA 70609. Offers elementary education grades 1-5 (MAT); secondary education grades 6-12 (MAT); special education (MAT), including mild/moderate grades 1-5. *Faculty:* 10 full-time (5 women). *Students:* 49 full-time (37 women), 89 part-time (69 women); includes 20 minority (16 Black or African American, non-Hispanic/Latino; 4 Hispanic/Latino), 1 international. In 2011, 61 master's awarded. *Entrance requirements:* For master's, GRE, PRAXIS, 2 letters of recommendation; autobiography. *Application deadline:* For fall admission, 5/15 priority date for domestic students, 5/15 for international students; for spring admission, 10/15 priority date for domestic students, 10/15 for international students. Applications are processed on a rolling basis. Application fee: $20 ($30 for international students). *Expenses:* Tuition, state resident: part-time $519 per credit hour. Tuition and fees vary according to course load. *Financial support:* Application deadline: 5/1. *Unit head:* Dr. Dustin M. Hebert, Director, 337-475-5424, Fax: 337-475-5272, E-mail: dhebert@mcneese.edu. *Application contact:* Dr. George F. Mead, Jr., Interim Dean of Dore' School of Graduate Studies, 337-475-5396, Fax: 337-475-5397, E-mail: admissions@mcneese.edu.

Medaille College, Program in Education, Buffalo, NY 14214-2695. Offers adolescent education (MS Ed); curriculum and instruction (MS Ed); education preparation (MS Ed); literacy (MS Ed); special education (MS). *Accreditation:* Teacher Education Accreditation Council. Part-time and evening/weekend programs available. *Faculty:* 15 full-time (11 women), 31 part-time/adjunct (21 women). *Students:* 371 full-time (281 women), 37 part-time (29 women); includes 75 minority (11 Black or African American, non-Hispanic/Latino; 6 Asian, non-Hispanic/Latino; 3 Hispanic/Latino; 55 Native Hawaiian or other Pacific Islander, non-Hispanic/Latino), 264 international. Average age 29. 354 applicants, 99% accepted, 163 enrolled. In 2011, 457 master's awarded. *Degree requirements:* For master's, comprehensive exam (for some programs), thesis or alternative. *Entrance requirements:* For master's, minimum undergraduate GPA of 2.7. Additional exam requirements/recommendations for international students: Required—TOEFL (minimum score 550 paper-based; 213 computer-based). *Application deadline:* For fall admission, 8/15 priority date for domestic students; for spring admission, 1/15 priority date for domestic students. Applications are processed on a rolling basis. Application fee: $35. Electronic applications accepted. Tuition and fees vary according to program. *Financial support:* Federal Work-Study available. Financial award applicants required to submit FAFSA. *Faculty research:* Curriculum planning, truancy, tracking minority students, curriculum design, mentoring students. *Unit head:* Dr. Robert DiSibio, Director of Graduate Programs, 716-932-2548, Fax: 716-631-1380, E-mail: rdisibio@medaille.edu. *Application contact:* Jacqueline Matheny, Executive Director of Marketing and Enrollment, 716-932-2541, Fax: 716-632-1811, E-mail: jmatheny@medaille.edu. Web site: http://www.medaille.edu.

Mercy College, School of Education, Program in Childhood Education, Grade 1-6, Dobbs Ferry, NY 10522-1189. Offers MS. Part-time and evening/weekend programs available. Postbaccalaureate distance learning degree programs offered (no on-campus study). *Degree requirements:* For master's, comprehensive exam. *Entrance requirements:* For master's, interview, resume, minimum undergraduate GPA of 3.0 (writing sample for those with GPA lower than 3.0), assessment by specific program director or designee. Additional exam requirements/recommendations for international students: Required—TOEFL (minimum score 600 paper-based; 250 computer-based; 100 iBT), IELTS (minimum score 8). Electronic applications accepted. *Faculty research:* Teaching literacy, behavior management applications, assistive technology.

Merrimack College, School of Education, North Andover, MA 01845-5800. Offers community engagement (M Ed); early childhood education (M Ed); elementary education (M Ed); elementary education plus moderate disabilities-dual license (M Ed); English as a second language (M Ed); general studies (M Ed); higher education (M Ed); middle (M Ed); moderate disabilities (preK-8) (M Ed); reading (M Ed); secondary (M Ed); teacher leadership (CAGS). Part-time and evening/weekend programs available. *Faculty:* 4 full-time (all women), 9 part-time/adjunct (7 women). *Students:* 70 full-time (60 women), 39 part-time (33 women); includes 2 minority (1 Asian, non-Hispanic/Latino; 1 Hispanic/Latino). Average age 27. In 2011, 26 master's awarded. *Degree requirements:* For master's, portfolio. *Entrance requirements:* Additional exam requirements/recommendations for international students: Required—TOEFL (minimum score 80 iBT). *Application deadline:* For fall admission, 8/1 priority date for domestic students, 7/15 for international students; for winter admission, 12/1 priority date for domestic students, 11/15 for international students; for spring admission, 3/1 priority date for domestic students, 2/15 for international students. Applications are processed on a rolling basis. Electronic applications accepted. *Expenses: Tuition:* Part-time $475 per credit. *Required fees:* $62.50 per semester. *Financial support:* In 2011–12, 50 fellowships were awarded; career-related internships or fieldwork and scholarships/grants also available. Financial award applicants required to submit FAFSA. *Faculty research:* Higher education, community engagement, literacy, leadership. *Unit head:* Dr. Theresa Kirk, Chair, 978-837-5436, E-mail: kirkt@merrimack.edu. *Application contact:* Jessica McCarthy, Program Coordinator, 978-837-5443, E-mail: mccarthyj@merrimack.edu. Web site: http://www.merrimack.edu/academics/education/med/.

Metropolitan College of New York, Program in Childhood Education, New York, NY 10013. Offers MS. *Degree requirements:* For master's, one foreign language. *Entrance requirements:* For master's, Liberal Arts and Sciences Test (LAST) recommended, minimum GPA of 3.0, 2 letters of reference, writing sample, interview. Additional exam requirements/recommendations for international students: Required—TOEFL (minimum score 600 paper-based; 250 computer-based). *Expenses:* Contact institution. *Faculty research:* Classroom management, learner autonomy, teacher research, math and gender, intelligence.

Miami University, School of Education and Allied Professions, Department of Teacher Education, Oxford, OH 45056. Offers elementary education (M Ed, MAT); reading education (M Ed); secondary education (M Ed, MAT), including adolescent education (MAT), elementary mathematics education (M Ed), secondary education. Part-time programs available. *Students:* 32 full-time (19 women), 40 part-time (37 women); includes 6 minority (3 Black or African American, non-Hispanic/Latino; 2 Hispanic/Latino; 1 Two or more races, non-Hispanic/Latino), 3 international. Average age 28. In 2011, 42 master's awarded. *Entrance requirements:* For master's, GRE (for MAT), minimum undergraduate GPA of 3.0 during previous 2 years or 2.75 overall. *Application deadline:* Applications are processed on a rolling basis. Application fee: $50. Electronic applications accepted. *Expenses:* Tuition, state resident: full-time $12,023; part-time $501 per credit hour. Tuition, nonresident: full-time $26,554; part-time $1107 per credit hour. *Required fees:* $528. *Financial support:* Fellowships with full tuition reimbursements, research assistantships, teaching assistantships, career-related internships or fieldwork, Federal Work-Study, scholarships/grants, health care benefits, tuition waivers (full), and unspecified assistantships available. Financial award application deadline: 2/15. *Unit head:* Dr. James Shiveley, Chair, 513-529-6443, Fax: 513-529-4931, E-mail: shiveljm@muohio.edu. *Application contact:* Linda Dennett, Program Associate, 513-529-5708, E-mail: dennetlg@muohio.edu. Web site: http://www.units.muohio.edu/eap/departments/edt/.

Middle Tennessee State University, College of Graduate Studies, College of Education, Department of Elementary and Special Education, Major in Curriculum and Instruction, Murfreesboro, TN 37132. Offers early childhood education (M Ed); elementary education (M Ed, Ed S); middle school education (M Ed). *Accreditation:* NCATE. Part-time and evening/weekend programs available. Postbaccalaureate distance learning degree programs offered. *Faculty:* 14 full-time (9 women), 7 part-time/adjunct (all women). *Students:* 16 full-time (13 women), 144 part-time (129 women); includes 18 minority (16 Black or African American, non-Hispanic/Latino; 1 Asian, non-Hispanic/Latino; 1 Hispanic/Latino). 110 applicants, 73% accepted. In 2011, 55 master's awarded. *Degree requirements:* For master's, comprehensive exam; for Ed S, comprehensive exam, thesis or alternative. *Entrance requirements:* For master's and Ed S, GRE, MAT or PRAXIS. Additional exam requirements/recommendations for international students: Required—TOEFL (minimum score 525 paper-based; 195 computer-based; 71 iBT) or IELTS (minimum score 6). *Application deadline:* For fall admission, 8/1 priority date for domestic students. Applications are processed on a rolling basis. Application fee: $25. Electronic applications accepted. *Expenses:* Tuition, state resident: full-time $10,008. Tuition, nonresident: full-time $25,056. *Financial support:* Tuition waivers available. Support available to part-time students. Financial award application deadline: 5/1. *Unit head:* Dr. Kathleen Burriss, Interim Chair, 615-898-2323, Fax: 615-898-5309, E-mail: kathleen.burris@mtsu.edu. *Application contact:* Dr. Michael D. Allen, Dean and Vice Provost for Research, 615-898-2840, Fax: 615-904-8020, E-mail: michael.allen@mtsu.edu.

Millersville University of Pennsylvania, College of Graduate and Professional Studies, School of Education, Department of Elementary and Early Childhood Education, Program in Elementary Education, Millersville, PA 17551-0302. Offers M Ed. *Accreditation:* NCATE. Part-time and evening/weekend programs available. *Faculty:* 16 full-time (12 women), 8 part-time/adjunct (5 women). *Students:* 14 full-time (12 women), 14 part-time (13 women); includes 1 minority (Hispanic/Latino). Average age 29. 10 applicants, 100% accepted, 5 enrolled. In 2011, 10 master's awarded. *Degree requirements:* For master's, comprehensive exam, thesis optional. *Entrance requirements:* For master's, GRE or MAT, 3 letters of recommendation, copy of teaching certificate. Additional exam requirements/recommendations for international students: Required—TOEFL (minimum score 500 paper-based; 183 computer-based; 65 iBT). *Application deadline:* For fall admission, 1/15 priority date for domestic students, 1/15 for international students; for winter admission, 10/1 priority date for domestic students, 10/1 for international students; for spring admission, 10/1 priority date for domestic students, 10/1 for international students. Applications are processed on a rolling basis. Application fee: $40 ($50 for international students). Electronic applications accepted. *Expenses:* Tuition, state resident: full-time $3744; part-time $416 per credit. Tuition, nonresident: full-time $5616; part-time $624 per credit. *Required fees:* $1130; $125.50 per credit. Tuition and fees vary according to course load. *Financial support:* In 2011–12, 4 students received support, including 4 research assistantships with full tuition reimbursements available (averaging $4,256 per year); institutionally sponsored loans and unspecified assistantships also available. Support available to part-time students. Financial award application deadline: 3/15; financial award applicants required to submit FAFSA. *Faculty research:* Longitudinal study of teacher development. *Unit head:* Dr. Kazi I. Hossain, Coordinator, 717-871-2265, Fax: 717-871-5462, E-mail: kazi.hossain@millersville.edu. *Application contact:* Dr. Victor S. DeSantis, Dean, College of Graduate and Professional Studies, 717-872-3099, Fax: 717-872-3453, E-mail: victor.desantis@millersville.edu. Web site: http://www.millersville.edu/academics/educ/eled/graduate.php.

Mills College, Graduate Studies, School of Education, Oakland, CA 94613-1000. Offers child life in hospitals (MA); early childhood education (MA); education (MA), including art education, curriculum and instruction, elementary education, English education, foreign language education, mathematics education, science education, secondary education, social studies education, teaching; educational leadership (MA, Ed D). Part-time and evening/weekend programs available. *Faculty:* 13 full-time (10 women), 14 part-time/adjunct (10 women). *Students:* 149 full-time (133 women), 69 part-time (61 women); includes 85 minority (32 Black or African American, non-Hispanic/Latino; 1 American Indian or Alaska Native, non-Hispanic/Latino; 16 Asian, non-Hispanic/Latino; 24 Hispanic/Latino; 1 Native Hawaiian or other Pacific Islander, non-Hispanic/Latino; 11 Two or more races, non-Hispanic/Latino), 3 international. Average age 28. 238 applicants, 84% accepted, 106 enrolled. In 2011, 41 master's, 2 doctorates awarded. Terminal master's awarded for partial completion of doctoral program. *Degree requirements:* For master's, comprehensive exam. *Entrance requirements:* For master's, statement of purpose, official transcript, 3 recommendations; for doctorate, GRE General Test. Additional exam requirements/recommendations for international students: Required—TOEFL (minimum score 550 paper-based; 80 iBT) or IELTS (minimum score 6). *Application deadline:* For fall admission, 12/31 priority date for domestic students, 12/15 for international students; for spring admission, 11/1 priority date for domestic students, 10/1 for international students. Applications are processed on a rolling basis. Application fee: $50. Electronic applications accepted. *Expenses: Tuition:* Full-time $28,280; part-time $15,640 per year. *Required fees:* $958. Tuition and fees vary according to program. *Financial support:* In 2011–12, 43 students received support, including 225 fellowships with full and partial tuition reimbursements available (averaging $6,020 per year), 43 teaching assistantships with full and partial tuition reimbursements available (averaging $6,782 per year); career-related internships or fieldwork and scholarships/grants also available. Support available to part-time students. Financial award application deadline: 2/1; financial award applicants required to submit FAFSA. *Faculty research:* Early childhood education, teacher preparation, educational leadership. *Total annual research expenditures:* $2.3 million. *Unit head:* Katherine Schultz, Chairperson, 510-430-3170, Fax: 510-430-3379, E-mail: grad-studies@mills.edu. *Application contact:* Tiana Kozoil, Graduate Admission Specialist, 510-430-3305, Fax: 510-430-2159, E-mail: grad-studies@mills.edu. Web site: http://www.mills.edu/education.

Minnesota State University Mankato, College of Graduate Studies, College of Education, Department of Elementary and Early Childhood Education, Mankato, MN 56001. Offers MS, Certificate. *Accreditation:* NCATE. Part-time programs available. *Students:* 12 full-time (all women), 77 part-time (73 women). *Degree requirements:* For master's, comprehensive exam, thesis or alternative. *Entrance requirements:* For master's, GRE General Test or MAT, minimum GPA of 3.0 during previous 2 years. Additional exam requirements/recommendations for international students: Required—TOEFL. *Application deadline:* For fall admission, 7/1 priority date for domestic students; for spring admission, 11/1 for domestic students. Applications are processed on a rolling basis. Application fee: $40. Electronic applications accepted. *Financial support:* Application deadline: 3/15; applicants required to submit FAFSA. *Unit head:* Dr. Peggy Ballard, Graduate Coordinator, 507-389-1516. *Application contact:* 507-389-2321, E-mail: grad@mnsu.edu. Web site: http://ed.mnsu.edu/eec/.

Minot State University, Graduate School, Teacher Education and Human Performance Department, Minot, ND 58707-0002. Offers elementary education (M Ed). *Accreditation:* NCATE. *Degree requirements:* For master's, thesis. *Entrance requirements:* For master's, 2 years of teaching experience, bachelor's degree in education, minimum GPA of 2.75. Additional exam requirements/recommendations for international students: Required—TOEFL. *Faculty research:* Technology, personnel-teaching efficacy, reflective teaching.

Mississippi College, Graduate School, School of Education, Department of Teacher Education and Leadership, Clinton, MS 39058. Offers art (M Ed); biological science (M Ed); business education (M Ed); computer science (M Ed); dyslexia therapy (M Ed); educational leadership (M Ed, Ed D, Ed S); elementary education (M Ed, Ed S); English (M Ed); higher education administration (MS); mathematics (M Ed); secondary education (M Ed); social studies (history) (M Ed); teaching arts (M Ed). Part-time programs available. Postbaccalaureate distance learning degree programs offered (no on-campus study). *Degree requirements:* For master's, comprehensive exam, thesis optional. *Entrance requirements:* For master's, NTE. Additional exam requirements/recommendations for international students: Recommended—TOEFL, IELTS. Electronic applications accepted.

Mississippi State University, College of Education, Department of Curriculum, Instruction and Special Education, Mississippi State, MS 39762. Offers elementary education (MS, PhD, Ed S); middle level education (MAT); secondary education (MAT, MS, Ed S); special education (MS, Ed S). *Accreditation:* NCATE. Part-time and evening/weekend programs available. *Faculty:* 12 full-time (10 women), 2 part-time/adjunct (1 woman). *Students:* 57 full-time (41 women), 104 part-time (81 women); includes 54 minority (52 Black or African American, non-Hispanic/Latino; 1 Hispanic/Latino; 1 Two or more races, non-Hispanic/Latino). Average age 33. 100 applicants, 60% accepted, 48 enrolled. In 2011, 38 master's, 5 doctorates, 5 other advanced degrees awarded. *Degree requirements:* For master's, comprehensive exam; for doctorate, thesis/dissertation; for Ed S, comprehensive exam, thesis or alternative. *Entrance requirements:* For master's, GRE, minimum GPA of 2.75 in junior and senior year, eligibility for initial teacher certification; for doctorate, GRE, minimum graduate GPA of 3.4; for Ed S, GRE, minimum graduate GPA of 3.2. Additional exam requirements/recommendations for international students: Required—TOEFL (minimum score 600 paper-based; 250 computer-based; 100 iBT); Recommended—IELTS (minimum score 7.5). *Application deadline:* For fall admission, 3/1 priority date for domestic students, 5/1 for international students; for spring admission, 9/1 priority date for domestic students, 9/1 for international students. Applications are processed on a rolling basis. Application fee: $40. Electronic applications accepted. *Expenses:* Tuition, state resident: full-time $5805; part-time $322.50 per credit hour. Tuition, nonresident: full-time $14,670; part-time $815 per credit hour. *Financial support:* In 2011–12, 7 research assistantships with full and partial tuition reimbursements (averaging $9,264 per year), 4 teaching assistantships (averaging $8,937 per year) were awarded; Federal Work-Study, institutionally sponsored loans, scholarships/grants, and unspecified assistantships also available. Financial award application deadline: 4/1; financial award applicants required to submit FAFSA. *Faculty research:* Early childhood education, reading, rural schools, multicultural education, use of technology in instruction. *Unit head:* Dr. Devon Brenner, Professor and Interim Head, 662-325-7119, Fax: 662-325-7857, E-mail: devon@ra.msstate.edu. *Application contact:* Dr. C. Susie Burroughs, Professor and Graduate Coordinator, 662-325-3747, Fax: 662-325-7857, E-mail: susie.burroughs@msstate.edu. Web site: http://www.cise.msstate.edu/.

Mississippi Valley State University, Department of Education, Itta Bena, MS 38941-1400. Offers education (MAT); elementary education (MA). *Accreditation:* NCATE.

Missouri State University, Graduate College, College of Education, Department of Childhood Education and Family Studies, Program in Elementary Education, Springfield, MO 65897. Offers MS Ed. Part-time and evening/weekend programs available. Postbaccalaureate distance learning degree programs offered (minimal on-campus study). *Students:* 8 full-time (7 women), 34 part-time (29 women); includes 3 minority (1 Black or African American, non-Hispanic/Latino; 2 Hispanic/Latino). Average age 34. 13 applicants, 100% accepted, 10 enrolled. In 2011, 21 master's awarded. *Degree requirements:* For master's, comprehensive exam, thesis or alternative. *Entrance requirements:* For master's, GRE (if GPA less than 3.0), minimum GPA of 2.75, teaching certificate. Additional exam requirements/recommendations for international students: Required—TOEFL (minimum score 550 paper-based; 213 computer-based; 79 iBT). *Application deadline:* For fall admission, 7/20 priority date for domestic students, 5/1 for international students; for spring admission, 12/20 priority date for domestic students, 9/1 for international students. Applications are processed on a rolling basis. Application fee: $35 ($50 for international students). Electronic applications accepted. *Expenses:* Tuition, state resident: full-time $4086; part-time $227 per credit hour. Tuition, nonresident: full-time $8172; part-time $454 per credit hour. *Required fees:* $275 per semester. Tuition and fees vary according to course load, campus/location and program. *Financial support:* Federal Work-Study, institutionally sponsored loans, and scholarships/grants available. Financial award application deadline: 3/31; financial award applicants required to submit FAFSA. *Unit head:* Dr. Cynthia Wilson-Hail, Program Coordinator, 417-836-6065, E-mail: cindywilson@missouristate.edu. *Application contact:* Misty Stewart, Coordinator of Graduate Recruitment, 417-836-6079, Fax: 417-836-6200, E-mail: mistystewart@missouristate.edu. Web site: http://education.missouristate.edu/ele/.

Missouri State University, Graduate College, College of Education, Department of Counseling, Leadership, and Special Education, Program in Educational Administration, Springfield, MO 65897. Offers educational administration (MS Ed, Ed S); elementary education (MS Ed); elementary principal (Ed S); secondary education (MS Ed); secondary principal (Ed S); superintendent (Ed S). Part-time and evening/weekend programs available. *Students:* 20 full-time (13 women), 109 part-time (73 women); includes 6 minority (1 Black or African American, non-Hispanic/Latino; 2 American Indian or Alaska Native, non-Hispanic/Latino; 1 Hispanic/Latino; 2 Two or more races, non-Hispanic/Latino), 5 international. Average age 35. 60 applicants, 98% accepted, 43 enrolled. In 2011, 51 master's, 16 Ed Ss awarded. *Degree requirements:* For master's and Ed S, comprehensive exam, thesis or alternative. *Entrance requirements:* For master's, minimum GPA of 2.75; for Ed S, GRE General Test, MAT, minimum GPA of 2.75. Additional exam requirements/recommendations for international students: Required—TOEFL (minimum score 550 paper-based; 213 computer-based; 79 iBT). *Application deadline:* For fall admission, 7/20 priority date for domestic students, 5/1 for international students; for spring admission, 12/20 priority date for domestic students, 9/1 for international students. Applications are processed on a rolling basis. Application fee: $35 ($50 for international students). Electronic applications accepted. *Expenses:* Tuition, state resident: full-time $4086; part-time $227 per credit hour. Tuition, nonresident: full-time $8172; part-time $454 per credit hour. *Required fees:* $275 per semester. Tuition and fees vary according to course load, campus/location and program. *Financial support:* Career-related internships or fieldwork, Federal Work-Study, institutionally sponsored loans, scholarships/grants, and unspecified assistantships available. Financial award application deadline: 3/31; financial award applicants required to submit FAFSA. *Unit head:* Dr. Kim Finch, Program Coordinator, 417-836-5192, Fax: 417-836-4918, E-mail: clse@missouristate.edu. *Application contact:* Misty Stewart, Coordinator of Admissions and Recruitment, 417-836-6079, Fax: 417-836-6200, E-mail: mistystewart@missouristate.edu. Web site: http://education.missouristate.edu/edadmin/.

Monmouth University, The Graduate School, School of Education, West Long Branch, NJ 07764-1898. Offers education (M Ed); initial certification (MAT), including elementary level, K-12, secondary level; learning disabilities-teacher consultant (Certificate); principal (MS Ed); principal/school administrator (MS Ed); reading specialist (MS Ed, Certificate); school counseling (MS Ed); special education (MS Ed), including autism, learning disabilities teacher consultant, teacher of students with disabilities, teaching in inclusive settings; supervisor (Certificate); teacher of the handicapped (Certificate); teaching English to speakers of other languages (TESOL) (Certificate). *Accreditation:* NCATE. Part-time and evening/weekend programs available. *Faculty:* 16 full-time (12 women), 24 part-time/adjunct (17 women). *Students:* 134 full-time (104 women), 293 part-time (246 women); includes 34 minority (11 Black or African American, non-Hispanic/Latino; 2 Asian, non-Hispanic/Latino; 18 Hispanic/Latino; 3 Two or more races, non-Hispanic/Latino), 2 international. Average age 29. 288 applicants, 92% accepted, 182 enrolled. In 2011, 173 master's awarded. *Entrance requirements:* For master's, minimum GPA of 3.0 in major, 2.75 overall; 2 letters of recommendation (for some programs). Additional exam requirements/recommendations for international students: Required—TOEFL (minimum score 550 paper-based; 213 computer-based; 79 iBT), IELTS (minimum score 5), Michigan English Language Assessment Battery (minimum score 77), Cambridge A, B, C. *Application deadline:* For fall admission, 7/15 priority date for domestic students, 7/1 for international students; for spring admission, 11/15 priority date for domestic students, 11/1 for international students. Applications are processed on a rolling basis. Application fee: $50. Electronic applications accepted. *Financial support:* In 2011–12, 274 students received support, including 291 fellowships (averaging $1,783 per year), 21 research assistantships (averaging $8,792 per year); career-related internships or fieldwork, scholarships/grants, and unspecified assistantships also available. Support available to part-time students. Financial award applicants required to submit FAFSA. *Faculty research:* Multicultural literacy, science and mathematics teaching strategies, teacher as reflective practitioner, children with disabilities. *Unit head:* Dr. Jason Barr, Program Director, 732-263-5238, Fax: 732-263-5277, E-mail: jbarr@monmouth.edu. *Application contact:* Kevin Roane, Director, Office of Graduate Admission, 732-571-3452, Fax: 732-263-5123, E-mail: gradadm@monmouth.edu. Web site: http://www.monmouth.edu/academics/schools/education/default.asp.

Montclair State University, The Graduate School, College of Education and Human Services, Department of Early Childhood, Elementary and Literacy Education, Program in Early Childhood and Elementary Education, Montclair, NJ 07043-1624. Offers M Ed. Part-time and evening/weekend programs available. *Students:* 14 part-time (all women); includes 2 minority (both Black or African American, non-Hispanic/Latino). 8 applicants, 13% accepted, 0 enrolled. In 2011, 7 master's awarded. *Degree requirements:* For master's, comprehensive exam, thesis or alternative. *Entrance requirements:* For master's, GRE General Test, interview, 2 letters of recommendation. Additional exam requirements/recommendations for international students: Required—TOEFL (minimum score 83 iBT), IELTS (minimum score 6.5). *Application deadline:* Applications are processed on a rolling basis. Application fee: $60. Electronic applications accepted. *Financial support:* Federal Work-Study, scholarships/grants, and unspecified assistantships available. Support available to part-time students. Financial award application deadline: 3/1; financial award applicants required to submit FAFSA. *Unit head:* Dr. Tina Jacobowitz, Chairperson, 973-655-7191. *Application contact:* Amy Aiello, Director of Graduate Admissions and Operations, 973-655-5147, Fax: 973-655-7869, E-mail: graduate.school@montclair.edu. Web site: http://cehs.montclair.edu/academic/ecele/programs/masterspecial1.shtml.

Montclair State University, The Graduate School, College of Education and Human Services, Department of Early Childhood, Elementary and Literacy Education, Program in Teaching Elementary Education, Montclair, NJ 07043-1624. Offers MAT. *Students:* 33 full-time (31 women), 81 part-time (69 women); includes 38 minority (11 Black or African American, non-Hispanic/Latino; 7 Asian, non-Hispanic/Latino; 19 Hispanic/Latino; 1 Native Hawaiian or other Pacific Islander, non-Hispanic/Latino), 1 international. Average age 31. 52 applicants, 54% accepted, 27 enrolled. *Degree requirements:* For master's, comprehensive exam, thesis or alternative. *Entrance requirements:* For master's, GRE General Test, interview, essay, 2 letters of recommendation. Additional exam requirements/recommendations for international students: Required—TOEFL (minimum score 83 iBT), IELTS (minimum score 6.5). *Application deadline:* Applications are processed on a rolling basis. Application fee: $60. Electronic applications accepted. *Financial support:* Federal Work-Study, scholarships/grants, and unspecified assistantships available. Support available to part-time students. Financial award application deadline: 3/1; financial award applicants required to submit FAFSA. *Unit head:* Dr. Tina Jacobowitz, Chairperson, 973-655-7191. *Application contact:* Amy Aiello, Executive Director of The Graduate School, 973-655-5147, Fax: 973-655-7869, E-mail: graduate.school@montclair.edu. Web site: http://cehs.montclair.edu/academic/ecele/programs/masterelem.shtml.

Morehead State University, Graduate Programs, College of Education, Department of Curriculum and Instruction, Morehead, KY 40351. Offers curriculum and instruction

(Ed S); elementary education (MA Ed), including elementary education, international education, middle school education, reading; secondary education (MA Ed); special education (MA Ed); teaching (MAT). Part-time and evening/weekend programs available. *Degree requirements:* For master's, comprehensive exam, thesis optional; for Ed S, thesis, oral exam. *Entrance requirements:* For master's, GRE General Test, minimum GPA of 2.75, teaching certificate; for Ed S, GRE General Test, interview, master's degree, minimum GPA of 3.5, work experience. Additional exam requirements/recommendations for international students: Required—TOEFL (minimum score 500 paper-based; 173 computer-based). Electronic applications accepted. *Faculty research:* Communicative competence of learning-disabled students, teaching social studies in elementary schools, ungraded primary school organization, study skills.

Morehead State University, Graduate Programs, College of Education, Department of Foundational and Graduate Studies in Education, Morehead, KY 40351. Offers adult and higher education (MA, Ed S); certified professional counselor (Ed S); counseling P-12 (MA); curriculum and instruction (Ed S); educational technology (MA Ed); instructional leadership (Ed S); school administration (MA); school counseling (Ed S); teacher leader business and marketing content (MA Ed); teacher leader business and marketing technology (MA Ed); teacher leader educational technology (MA Ed); teacher leader English (MA Ed); teacher leader gifted education (MA Ed); teacher leader IECE certification (MA Ed); teacher leader interdisciplinary education P-5 (MA Ed); teacher leader middle grades (MA Ed); teacher leader non IECE certification (MA Ed); teacher leader reading/writing - non-certification (MA Ed); teacher leader reading/writing certification (MA Ed); teacher leader school communication - certification (MA Ed); teacher leader school communication - non-certification (MA Ed); teacher leader social studies (MA Ed); teacher leader special education (MA Ed). *Accreditation:* NCATE. Part-time and evening/weekend programs available. *Degree requirements:* For master's, thesis optional, oral and/or written comprehensive exams; for Ed S, thesis, oral exam. *Entrance requirements:* For master's, GRE General Test, minimum overall undergraduate GPA of 2.5; for Ed S, GRE General Test, interview, master's degree, minimum GPA of 3.5, work experience. Additional exam requirements/recommendations for international students: Required—TOEFL (minimum score 500 paper-based; 173 computer-based). Electronic applications accepted. *Faculty research:* Character education, school accountability, computer applications for school administrators.

Morgan State University, School of Graduate Studies, School of Education and Urban Studies, Department of Advanced Studies, Leadership and Policy, Program in Elementary and Middle School Education, Baltimore, MD 21251. Offers elementary education (MS). *Accreditation:* NCATE. Part-time and evening/weekend programs available. *Degree requirements:* For master's, comprehensive exam, thesis optional. *Faculty research:* Multicultural education, cooperative learning, psychology of cognition.

Morgan State University, School of Graduate Studies, School of Education and Urban Studies, MAT Program, Baltimore, MD 21251. Offers elementary education (MAT); high school education (MAT); middle school education (MAT). Part-time programs available. *Degree requirements:* For master's, comprehensive exam. *Entrance requirements:* For master's, GRE General Test or MAT. *Faculty research:* Multicultural education, cooperative learning, psychology of cognition.

Mount Saint Mary College, Division of Education, Newburgh, NY 12550-3494. Offers adolescence and special education (MS Ed); adolescence education (MS Ed); childhood and special education (MS Ed); childhood education (MS Ed); literacy (5-12) (Advanced Certificate); literacy (birth-6) (Advanced Certificate); literacy and special education (MS Ed); literacy/childhood (MS Ed); middle school (5-6) (MS Ed); middle school (7-9) (MS Ed); special education (1-6) (MS Ed); special education (7-12) (MS Ed). *Accreditation:* NCATE. Part-time and evening/weekend programs available. *Faculty:* 14 full-time (12 women), 14 part-time/adjunct (8 women). *Students:* 55 full-time (42 women), 158 part-time (125 women); includes 23 minority (4 Black or African American, non-Hispanic/Latino; 1 Asian, non-Hispanic/Latino; 18 Hispanic/Latino). Average age 29. 119 applicants, 45% accepted, 24 enrolled. In 2011, 107 master's awarded. *Application deadline:* Applications are processed on a rolling basis. Application fee: $45. Application fee is waived when completed online. *Expenses: Tuition:* Full-time $13,356; part-time $742 per credit. *Required fees:* $70 per semester. *Financial support:* In 2011–12, 99 students received support. Unspecified assistantships available. Financial award application deadline: 4/15; financial award applicants required to submit FAFSA. *Faculty research:* Learning and teaching styles, computers in special education, language development. *Unit head:* Dr. Theresa Lewis, Coordinator, 845-569-3149, Fax: 845-569-3535, E-mail: tlewis@msmc.edu. *Application contact:* Courtney McDermott, Graduate Recruiter, 845-569-3402, Fax: 845-569-3450, E-mail: courtney.mcdermott@msmc.edu. Web site: http://www.msmc.edu/Academics/Graduate_Programs/Master_of_Science_in_Education.

Mount St. Mary's College, Graduate Division, Department of Education, Specialization in Elementary Education, Los Angeles, CA 90049-1599. Offers MS. *Degree requirements:* For master's, thesis, research project. *Entrance requirements:* For master's, MAT, minimum GPA of 3.0. *Application deadline:* For fall admission, 7/15 priority date for domestic students; for spring admission, 11/15 priority date for domestic students. Application fee: $50 ($75 for international students). *Expenses: Tuition:* Part-time $752 per unit. Part-time tuition and fees vary according to degree level and program. *Financial support:* Career-related internships or fieldwork and scholarships/grants available. Financial award application deadline: 3/15; financial award applicants required to submit FAFSA. *Unit head:* Dr. Julie Feldman-Abe, Director, 213-477-2625, E-mail: jabe@msmc.la.edu.

Mount Saint Vincent University, Graduate Programs, Faculty of Education, Program in Elementary Education, Halifax, NS B3M 2J6, Canada. Offers M Ed, MA Ed, MA-R. Part-time and evening/weekend programs available. Postbaccalaureate distance learning degree programs offered (minimal on-campus study). *Degree requirements:* For master's, thesis (for some programs). *Entrance requirements:* For master's, bachelor's degree in education, 1 year of teaching experience. Electronic applications accepted. *Faculty research:* Curriculum theory, mathematics education, philosophy in teacher education, science education, literacy education.

Murray State University, College of Education, Department of Early Childhood and Elementary Education, Programs in Elementary Education/Reading and Writing, Murray, KY 42071. Offers elementary education (MA Ed, Ed S); reading and writing (MA Ed). *Accreditation:* NCATE. Part-time programs available. *Degree requirements:* For master's, comprehensive exam, thesis optional; for Ed S, comprehensive exam. *Entrance requirements:* For master's, minimum GPA of 2.5 for conditional admittance, 3.0 for unconditional; for Ed S, GRE General Test or MAT. Additional exam requirements/recommendations for international students: Required—TOEFL.

National Louis University, National College of Education, Chicago, IL 60603. Offers administration and supervision (M Ed, Ed D, CAS, Ed S); curriculum and instruction (M Ed, MS Ed, CAS); early childhood administration (M Ed, CAS); early childhood education (M Ed, MAT, MS Ed, CAS); education (Ed D); educational psychology/human learning and development (M Ed, MS Ed, CAS, Ed S); elementary education (MAT); interdisciplinary curriculum and instruction (M Ed); mathematics education (M Ed, MS Ed, CAS); reading and language (M Ed, MS Ed, CAS); school psychology (M Ed, Ed S); science education (M Ed, MS Ed, CAS); secondary education (MAT); special education (M Ed, MAT, CAS); technology in education (M Ed, CAS). *Accreditation:* NCATE. Part-time and evening/weekend programs available. *Students:* 224 full-time (162 women), 2,336 part-time (1,767 women); includes 677 minority (366 Black or African American, non-Hispanic/Latino; 8 American Indian or Alaska Native, non-Hispanic/Latino; 68 Asian, non-Hispanic/Latino; 218 Hispanic/Latino; 2 Native Hawaiian or other Pacific Islander, non-Hispanic/Latino; 15 Two or more races, non-Hispanic/Latino), 2 international. Average age 34. In 2011, 1,711 master's, 76 doctorates, 86 other advanced degrees awarded. *Degree requirements:* For doctorate, comprehensive exam, thesis/dissertation. *Entrance requirements:* For master's, MAT or GRE, minimum GPA of 3.0; for doctorate, GRE General Test, minimum GPA of 3.25, interview, resume, writing sample, 4 recommendations. Additional exam requirements/recommendations for international students: Required—TOEFL (minimum score 550 paper-based; 213 computer-based; 79 iBT). *Application deadline:* Applications are processed on a rolling basis. Application fee: $40. *Financial support:* Fellowships, research assistantships, teaching assistantships, career-related internships or fieldwork, Federal Work-Study, institutionally sponsored loans, and scholarships/grants available. Support available to part-time students. Financial award applicants required to submit FAFSA. *Unit head:* Dr. Alison Hilsabeck, Dean, 312-361-3580, Fax: 312-261-2580, E-mail: ahilsabeck@nl.edu. *Application contact:* Ken Kasprzak, Director of Admission, 888-658-8632, Fax: 847-947-5575, E-mail: kkasprzak@nl.edu.

National University, Academic Affairs, School of Education, Department of Teacher Education, La Jolla, CA 92037-1011. Offers best practices (Certificate); early childhood education (Certificate); educational technology (Certificate); elementary education (M Ed); instructional technology (MS Ed); multiple or single subjects teaching (M Ed); national board certified teacher leadership (Certificate); secondary education (M Ed); teaching (MA). Part-time and evening/weekend programs available. Postbaccalaureate distance learning degree programs offered (no on-campus study). *Degree requirements:* For master's, thesis. *Entrance requirements:* For master's, interview, minimum GPA of 2.5. Additional exam requirements/recommendations for international students: Required—TOEFL (minimum score 550 paper-based; 213 computer-based; 79 iBT), IELTS (minimum score 6). *Application deadline:* Applications are processed on a rolling basis. Application fee: $60 ($65 for international students). Electronic applications accepted. *Financial support:* Career-related internships or fieldwork, institutionally sponsored loans, scholarships/grants, and tuition waivers (partial) available. Support available to part-time students. Financial award application deadline: 6/30; financial award applicants required to submit FAFSA. *Unit head:* Dr. Cynthia Schubert-Irastroza, Chair, 858-642-8339, Fax: 858-642-8724, E-mail: cshubert@nu.edu. *Application contact:* Dominick Giovanniello, Associate Regional Dean, 800-NAT-UNIV, Fax: 858-541-7792, E-mail: dgiovann@nu.edu. Web site: http://www.nu.edu/OurPrograms/SchoolOfEducation/TeacherEducation.html.

Nazareth College of Rochester, Graduate Studies, Department of Education, Program in Inclusive Education-Childhood Level, Rochester, NY 14618-3790. Offers MS Ed. *Accreditation:* Teacher Education Accreditation Council. *Entrance requirements:* For master's, minimum GPA of 3.0.

New Jersey City University, Graduate Studies and Continuing Education, Debra Cannon Partridge Wolfe College of Education, Department of Elementary and Secondary Education, Jersey City, NJ 07305-1597. Offers elementary education (MAT); secondary education (MAT). Part-time and evening/weekend programs available. *Students:* 24 full-time (14 women), 53 part-time (31 women); includes 27 minority (7 Black or African American, non-Hispanic/Latino; 8 Asian, non-Hispanic/Latino; 12 Hispanic/Latino). Average age 32. In 2011, 18 master's awarded. *Entrance requirements:* Additional exam requirements/recommendations for international students: Required—TOEFL. *Application deadline:* For fall admission, 8/1 priority date for domestic students; for spring admission, 12/1 for domestic students. Applications are processed on a rolling basis. Application fee: $0. *Expenses:* Tuition, state resident: part-time $494 per credit. Tuition, nonresident: part-time $911.30 per credit. *Required fees:* $95.90 per year. *Financial support:* Teaching assistantships, career-related internships or fieldwork, and unspecified assistantships available. *Unit head:* Dr. Althea Hall, Coordinator, 201-200-2101, E-mail: ahall@njcu.edu. *Application contact:* Dr. William Bajor, Dean of Graduate Studies, 201-200-3409, Fax: 201-200-3411, E-mail: wbajor@njcu.edu.

New York Institute of Technology, Graduate Division, School of Education, Program in Childhood Education, Old Westbury, NY 11568-8000. Offers MS. Part-time and evening/weekend programs available. Postbaccalaureate distance learning degree programs offered. *Students:* 6 full-time (5 women), 21 part-time (18 women); includes 7 minority (4 Black or African American, non-Hispanic/Latino; 1 Asian, non-Hispanic/Latino; 2 Two or more races, non-Hispanic/Latino). Average age 32. In 2011, 3 master's awarded. *Entrance requirements:* Additional exam requirements/recommendations for international students: Required—TOEFL (minimum score 550 paper-based; 213 computer-based). *Application deadline:* For fall admission, 7/1 priority date for domestic students; for spring admission, 12/1 priority date for domestic students. Applications are processed on a rolling basis. Application fee: $50. Electronic applications accepted. *Expenses: Tuition:* Part-time $930 per credit hour. *Financial support:* Research assistantships with partial tuition reimbursements, career-related internships or fieldwork, institutionally sponsored loans, and tuition waivers (full and partial) available. Support available to part-time students. Financial award applicants required to submit FAFSA. *Unit head:* Dr. Michael Uttendorfer, Dean, 516-686-7706, Fax: 516-686-7655, E-mail: muttendo@nyit.edu. *Application contact:* Dr. Jacquelyn Nealon, Vice President for Enrollment Services, 516-686-7925, Fax: 516-686-7597, E-mail: jnealon@nyit.edu. Web site: http://www.nyit.edu/education/childhood_education.

New York University, Steinhardt School of Culture, Education, and Human Development, Department of Teaching and Learning, Program in Early Childhood and Childhood Education, New York, NY 10012-1019. Offers childhood education (MA); childhood education/special education: childhood (MA); early childhood education (MA); positions of leadership: early childhood and elementary education (PhD). *Accreditation:* Teacher Education Accreditation Council. Part-time programs available. *Degree requirements:* For master's, thesis (for some programs); for doctorate, thesis/dissertation. *Entrance requirements:* For doctorate, GRE General Test, interview. Additional exam requirements/recommendations for international students: Required—TOEFL. Electronic applications accepted. *Faculty research:* Teacher evaluation and beliefs about teaching, early literacy development, language arts, child development and education, cultural differences.

Niagara University, Graduate Division of Education, Concentration in Teacher Education, Niagara Falls, Niagara University, NY 14109. Offers early childhood and childhood education (MS Ed); middle and adolescence education (MS Ed); special education (grades 1-12) (MS Ed). *Accreditation:* NCATE. *Faculty:* 4 full-time (1 woman), 6 part-time/adjunct (4 women). *Students:* 249 full-time (162 women), 56 part-time (39 women); includes 11 minority (5 Black or African American, non-Hispanic/Latino; 1 American Indian or Alaska Native, non-Hispanic/Latino; 1 Asian, non-Hispanic/Latino; 2 Hispanic/Latino; 2 Two or more races, non-Hispanic/Latino), 176 international. Average age 24. In 2011, 233 master's, 1 Certificate awarded. *Entrance requirements:* For master's, GRE General Test or MAT. *Application deadline:* For fall admission, 8/1 for domestic students. Applications are processed on a rolling basis. Application fee: $30. *Expenses:* Contact institution. *Financial support:* Career-related internships or fieldwork, Federal Work-Study, and scholarships/grants available. Financial award application deadline: 3/15. *Unit head:* Dr. Chandra Foote, Chair, 716-286-8549. *Application contact:* Dr. Debra A. Colley, Dean of Education, 716-286-8560, Fax: 716-286-8561, E-mail: dcolley@niagara.edu.

North Carolina Agricultural and Technical State University, School of Graduate Studies, School of Education, Department of Curriculum and Instruction, Program in Elementary Education, Greensboro, NC 27411. Offers MA Ed. *Accreditation:* NCATE. Part-time and evening/weekend programs available. *Degree requirements:* For master's, comprehensive exam, research project or comprehensive portfolio. *Entrance requirements:* For master's, GRE General Test, minimum GPA of 3.0.

North Carolina Central University, Division of Academic Affairs, School of Education, Department of Curriculum, Instruction and Professional Studies, Durham, NC 27707-3129. Offers curriculum and instruction (MA), including elementary education, middle grades education. *Accreditation:* NCATE. Part-time and evening/weekend programs available. *Degree requirements:* For master's, comprehensive exam, thesis or alternative. *Entrance requirements:* For master's, minimum GPA of 3.0 in major, 2.5 overall. Additional exam requirements/recommendations for international students: Required—TOEFL. *Faculty research:* Simulation of decision-making behavior of school boards.

North Carolina State University, Graduate School, College of Education, Department of Elementary Education, Raleigh, NC 27695. Offers M Ed. *Entrance requirements:* For master's, MAT or GRE, 3 letters of reference.

Northern Arizona University, Graduate College, College of Education, Department of Teaching and Learning, Flagstaff , AZ 86011. Offers early childhood education (M Ed); elementary education - certification (M Ed); elementary education - continuing professional (M Ed); secondary education - certification (M Ed); secondary education - continuing professional (M Ed). Part-time programs available. *Faculty:* 32 full-time (23 women). *Students:* 297 full-time (238 women), 368 part-time (333 women); includes 193 minority (16 Black or African American, non-Hispanic/Latino; 43 American Indian or Alaska Native, non-Hispanic/Latino; 11 Asian, non-Hispanic/Latino; 113 Hispanic/Latino; 10 Two or more races, non-Hispanic/Latino), 8 international. Average age 29. 182 applicants, 91% accepted, 118 enrolled. In 2011, 415 master's awarded. *Degree requirements:* For master's, comprehensive exam (for some programs), thesis (for some programs). *Entrance requirements:* For master's, minimum GPA of 3.0. Additional exam requirements/recommendations for international students: Required—TOEFL (minimum score 550 paper-based; 213 computer-based; 80 iBT), IELTS (minimum score 7). *Application deadline:* For fall admission, 3/1 for international students; for spring admission, 9/15 for international students. Applications are processed on a rolling basis. Application fee: $65. Electronic applications accepted. *Expenses:* Tuition, state resident: full-time $7190; part-time $355 per credit hour. Tuition, nonresident: full-time $18,092; part-time $1005 per credit hour. *Required fees:* $818; $328 per semester. *Financial support:* In 2011–12, 7 teaching assistantships with partial tuition reimbursements (averaging $10,000 per year) were awarded; Federal Work-Study, scholarships/grants, health care benefits, tuition waivers (full and partial), and unspecified assistantships also available. Financial award applicants required to submit FAFSA. *Unit head:* Dr. Sandra J. Stone, Chair, 928-523-4280, Fax: 928-523-1929, E-mail: sandra.stone@nau.edu. *Application contact:* Kay Quillen, Administrative Assistant, 928-523-9316, Fax: 928-523-1929, E-mail: kay.quillen@nau.edu. Web site: http://nau.edu/coe/teaching-and-learning/.

Northern Illinois University, Graduate School, College of Education, Department of Special and Early Education, De Kalb, IL 60115-2854. Offers curriculum and instruction (MS Ed, Ed D), including curriculum leadership (Ed D), elementary education (Ed D), secondary education (Ed D); early childhood education (MS Ed); elementary education (MS Ed); special education (MS Ed). Part-time and evening/weekend programs available. *Faculty:* 22 full-time (14 women), 2 part-time/adjunct (both women). *Students:* 58 full-time (46 women), 241 part-time (189 women); includes 35 minority (17 Black or African American, non-Hispanic/Latino; 7 Asian, non-Hispanic/Latino; 9 Hispanic/Latino; 2 Two or more races, non-Hispanic/Latino), 3 international. Average age 35. 100 applicants, 65% accepted, 45 enrolled. In 2011, 186 master's, 7 doctorates awarded. *Degree requirements:* For master's, comprehensive exam, thesis optional; for doctorate, thesis/dissertation, candidacy exam, dissertation defense. *Entrance requirements:* For master's, GRE General Test or MAT, minimum undergraduate GPA of 2.75; for doctorate, GRE General Test or MAT, minimum undergraduate GPA of 2.75, graduate 3.2. Additional exam requirements/recommendations for international students: Required—TOEFL (minimum score 550 paper-based; 213 computer-based). *Application deadline:* For fall admission, 6/1 for domestic students, 5/1 for international students; for spring admission, 11/1 for domestic students, 10/1 for international students. Applications are processed on a rolling basis. Application fee: $40. Electronic applications accepted. *Financial support:* In 2011–12, 34 research assistantships with full tuition reimbursements were awarded; fellowships with full tuition reimbursements, teaching assistantships with full tuition reimbursements, career-related internships or fieldwork, Federal Work-Study, scholarships/grants, tuition waivers (full), and unspecified assistantships also available. Support available to part-time students. Financial award applicants required to submit FAFSA. *Faculty research:* Teacher certification, stress reduction during student teaching, teaching history, portfolios in student teaching. *Unit head:* Dr. Connie Fox, Interim Chair, 815-753-1619, E-mail: seed@niu.edu. *Application contact:* Gail Myers, 815-753-0381, E-mail: gmyers@niu.edu. Web site: http://www.cedu.niu.edu/seed/.

Northern Michigan University, College of Graduate Studies, College of Professional Studies, School of Education, Program in Elementary Education, Marquette, MI 49855-5301. Offers MA Ed. Part-time programs available. *Degree requirements:* For master's, thesis or alternative. *Entrance requirements:* For master's, minimum GPA of 3.0. *Faculty research:* Whole language research, literature-based reading, essential elements of instruction, supervision and improvement of instruction.

Northern State University, Division of Graduate Studies in Education, Program in Teaching and Learning, Aberdeen, SD 57401-7198. Offers educational studies (MS Ed); elementary classroom teaching (MS Ed); health, physical education, and coaching (MS Ed); secondary classroom teaching (MS Ed). *Accreditation:* NCATE. Part-time and evening/weekend programs available. *Degree requirements:* For master's, thesis optional. *Entrance requirements:* For master's, minimum GPA of 2.75. Additional exam requirements/recommendations for international students: Required—TOEFL (minimum score 550 paper-based; 213 computer-based; 76 iBT), IELTS (minimum score 6). Electronic applications accepted.

Northwestern Oklahoma State University, School of Professional Studies, Program in Elementary Education, Alva, OK 73717-2799. Offers M Ed. *Accreditation:* NCATE. Part-time programs available. *Faculty:* 10 full-time (7 women). *Students:* 1 full-time (0 women), 4 part-time (all women); includes 1 minority (American Indian or Alaska Native, non-Hispanic/Latino). 5 applicants, 60% accepted, 3 enrolled. In 2011, 2 master's awarded. *Degree requirements:* For master's, thesis optional, portfolio. *Entrance requirements:* For master's, GRE General Test or MAT, minimum GPA of 2.75. *Application deadline:* Applications are processed on a rolling basis. Application fee: $15. *Financial support:* Federal Work-Study available. Support available to part-time students. Financial award application deadline: 5/1; financial award applicants required to submit FAFSA. *Unit head:* Dr. Beverly Warden, Chair, Education Division, 580-327-8451. *Application contact:* Sabrina Watson, Coordinator of Graduate Studies, 580-327-8410, E-mail: sdhaines@nwosu.edu. Web site: http://www.nwosu.edu/education.

Northwestern State University of Louisiana, Graduate Studies and Research, College of Education and Human Development, Program in Elementary Education, Natchitoches, LA 71497. Offers MAT. *Students:* 8 full-time (all women), 36 part-time (all women); includes 8 minority (6 Black or African American, non-Hispanic/Latino; 1 American Indian or Alaska Native, non-Hispanic/Latino; 1 Two or more races, non-Hispanic/Latino). Average age 31. 14 applicants, 100% accepted, 10 enrolled. In 2011, 5 master's awarded. *Degree requirements:* For master's, comprehensive exam, thesis or alternative. *Entrance requirements:* For master's, GRE General Test, minimum undergraduate GPA of 2.5. Additional exam requirements/recommendations for international students: Required—TOEFL. *Application deadline:* For fall admission, 3/15 priority date for domestic students; for spring admission, 10/15 priority date for domestic students. Applications are processed on a rolling basis. Application fee: $20 ($30 for international students). Electronic applications accepted. *Expenses:* Tuition, state resident: full-time $3440. Tuition, nonresident: full-time $12,010. *Financial support:* Application deadline: 5/1; applicants required to submit FAFSA. *Unit head:* Dr. Vickie Gentry, Chair, 318-357-6288, Fax: 318-357-6275, E-mail: education@nsula.edu. *Application contact:* Dr. Steven G. Horton, Associate Provost/Dean, Graduate Studies, Research, and Information Systems, 318-357-5851, Fax: 318-357-5019, E-mail: grad_school@nsula.edu.

Northwestern State University of Louisiana, Graduate Studies and Research, College of Education and Human Development, Programs in Educational Leadership and Instruction, Natchitoches, LA 71497. Offers counseling (Ed S); educational leadership (M Ed, Ed S); educational technology (Ed S); elementary teaching (Ed S); reading (Ed S); secondary teaching (Ed S); special education (Ed S). *Accreditation:* NASAD. *Students:* 7 full-time (6 women), 75 part-time (59 women); includes 22 minority (18 Black or African American, non-Hispanic/Latino; 2 American Indian or Alaska Native, non-Hispanic/Latino; 2 Hispanic/Latino). Average age 36. 30 applicants, 97% accepted, 15 enrolled. In 2011, 31 master's, 16 Ed Ss awarded. *Degree requirements:* For master's, comprehensive exam, thesis (for some programs). *Entrance requirements:* For master's and Ed S, GRE General Test. Additional exam requirements/recommendations for international students: Required—TOEFL. *Application deadline:* For fall admission, 3/15 priority date for domestic students; for spring admission, 10/15 priority date for domestic students. Applications are processed on a rolling basis. Application fee: $20 ($30 for international students). Electronic applications accepted. *Expenses:* Tuition, state resident: full-time $3440. Tuition, nonresident: full-time $12,010. *Unit head:* Dr. Vickie Gentry, Chair, 318-357-6288, Fax: 318-357-6275, E-mail: education@nsula.edu. *Application contact:* Dr. Steven G. Horton, Associate Provost/Dean, Graduate Studies, Research, and Information Systems, 318-357-5851, Fax: 318-357-5019, E-mail: grad_school@nsula.edu.

Northwestern University, The Graduate School, School of Education and Social Policy, Program in Education, Evanston, IL 60035. Offers advanced teaching (MS); elementary teaching (MS); higher education administration (MS); secondary teaching (MS). Part-time and evening/weekend programs available. *Degree requirements:* For master's, research project. *Entrance requirements:* For master's, GRE General Test, Illinois State Board of Education Basic Skills Exam (secondary and elementary), bachelor's degree. Additional exam requirements/recommendations for international students: Recommended—TOEFL. Electronic applications accepted. *Faculty research:* Cultural context and literacy, philosophy of education and interpretive discussion, productivity, enhancing research and teaching, motivation, new and junior faculty issues, professional development for K-12 teachers to improve math and science teaching, female/underrepresented students/faculty in STEM disciplines.

Northwest Missouri State University, Graduate School, College of Education and Human Services, Department of Curriculum and Instruction, Program in Teaching: Elementary Self Contained, Maryville, MO 64468-6001. Offers MS Ed. *Accreditation:* NCATE. Part-time programs available. *Faculty:* 17 full-time (all women). *Students:* 1 (woman) full-time, 5 part-time (all women). 1 applicant, 0% accepted. In 2011, 2 master's awarded. *Degree requirements:* For master's, comprehensive exam. *Entrance requirements:* For master's, GRE General Test, minimum undergraduate GPA of 2.75, teaching certificate, writing sample. Additional exam requirements/recommendations for international students: Required—TOEFL (minimum score 550 paper-based; 213 computer-based). *Application deadline:* For fall admission, 7/1 for domestic and international students; for spring admission, 11/15 for domestic and international students. Applications are processed on a rolling basis. Application fee: $0 ($50 for international students). Electronic applications accepted. *Financial support:* Application deadline: 4/1; applicants required to submit FAFSA. *Unit head:* Dr. Carolyn McCall, Director, 660-562-1236. *Application contact:* Dr. Gregory Haddock, Dean of Graduate School, 660-562-1145, Fax: 660-562-1096, E-mail: gradsch@nwmissouri.edu.

Northwest Missouri State University, Graduate School, College of Education and Human Services, Department of Educational Leadership, Program in Educational Leadership, Maryville, MO 64468-6001. Offers educational leadership: elementary (MS Ed); educational leadership: K-12 (MS Ed); educational leadership: secondary (MS Ed); elementary principalship (Ed S); secondary principalship (Ed S); superintendency (Ed S). *Accreditation:* NCATE. Part-time programs available. *Faculty:* 14 full-time (6 women). *Students:* 11 full-time (6 women), 86 part-time (58 women); includes 6 minority (all Black or African American, non-Hispanic/Latino). 20 applicants, 100% accepted, 7 enrolled. In 2011, 56 degrees awarded. *Degree requirements:* For master's, comprehensive exam; for Ed S, comprehensive exam, thesis. *Entrance requirements:* For master's, GRE General Test, minimum undergraduate GPA of 2.75, teaching certificate, writing sample; for Ed S, minimum graduate GPA of 3.25. Additional exam requirements/recommendations for international students: Required—TOEFL (minimum score 550 paper-based; 213 computer-based). *Application deadline:* For fall admission, 7/1 for domestic and international students; for spring admission, 11/15 for domestic and international students. Application fee: $0 ($50 for international students). *Financial support:* In 2011–12, research assistantships with full tuition reimbursements (averaging $6,000 per year), 5 teaching assistantships with full tuition reimbursements (averaging $6,000 per year) were awarded; unspecified assistantships also available. Financial award application deadline: 4/1; financial award applicants required to submit FAFSA. *Unit head:* Dr. Jan Glenn, Chairperson, 660-562-1064. *Application contact:* Dr. Gregory Haddock, Dean of Graduate School, 660-562-1145, Fax: 660-562-1096, E-mail: gradsch@nwmissouri.edu.

Nyack College, School of Education, Nyack, NY 10960-3698. Offers childhood education (MS); childhood special education (MS). Part-time and evening/weekend programs available. *Students:* 3 full-time (all women), 29 part-time (24 women); includes 16 minority (5 Black or African American, non-Hispanic/Latino; 2 Asian, non-Hispanic/Latino; 8 Hispanic/Latino; 1 Two or more races, non-Hispanic/Latino), 1 international. Average age 29. In 2011, 4 master's awarded. *Degree requirements:* For master's, comprehensive exam, field experience. *Entrance requirements:* For master's, LAST

(Liberal Arts and Sciences Test), transcripts, autobiography and statement on reasons for pursuing graduate study in education, recommendations, 6 credits of language, evidence of computer literacy, introductory course in psychology. Additional exam requirements/recommendations for international students: Required—TOEFL (minimum score 550 paper-based), TWE (minimum score 4). *Application deadline:* Applications are processed on a rolling basis. Application fee: $30. Electronic applications accepted. *Expenses:* Contact institution. *Financial support:* Scholarships/grants and state aid (for NY residents) available. Financial award applicants required to submit FAFSA. *Unit head:* Dr. JoAnn Looney, Dean, 845-675-4538, Fax: 845-358-0874. *Application contact:* Traci Piescki, Director of Admissions, 800-541-6891, Fax: 845-348-3912, E-mail: admissions.grad@nyack.edu. Web site: http://www.nyack.edu/education.

Occidental College, Graduate Studies, Department of Education, Program in Elementary Education, Los Angeles, CA 90041-3314. Offers liberal studies (MAT). Part-time programs available. *Degree requirements:* For master's, comprehensive exam, graduate synthesis paper. *Entrance requirements:* For master's, GRE General Test, minimum GPA of 3.0. Additional exam requirements/recommendations for international students: Required—TOEFL (minimum score 625 paper-based; 263 computer-based). *Expenses:* Contact institution.

Oklahoma City University, Petree College of Arts and Sciences, Programs in Education, Oklahoma City, OK 73106-1402. Offers applied behavioral studies (M Ed); early childhood education (M Ed); elementary education (M Ed). Part-time and evening/weekend programs available. *Faculty:* 4 full-time (2 women), 2 part-time/adjunct (1 woman). *Students:* 34 full-time (31 women), 14 part-time (11 women); includes 14 minority (11 Black or African American, non-Hispanic/Latino; 2 Hispanic/Latino; 1 Two or more races, non-Hispanic/Latino), 6 international. Average age 30. 34 applicants, 79% accepted, 18 enrolled. In 2011, 21 master's awarded. *Entrance requirements:* For master's, minimum GPA of 3.0. Additional exam requirements/recommendations for international students: Required—TOEFL (minimum score 550 paper-based). *Application deadline:* Applications are processed on a rolling basis. Application fee: $50 ($70 for international students). Electronic applications accepted. *Expenses: Tuition:* Full-time $16,848; part-time $936 per credit hour. *Required fees:* $2070; $115 per credit hour. One-time fee: $300. *Financial support:* Career-related internships or fieldwork, Federal Work-Study, and tuition waivers available. Support available to part-time students. Financial award application deadline: 6/1; financial award applicants required to submit FAFSA. *Faculty research:* Adult literacy, cognition, reading strategies. *Unit head:* Dr. Lois Lawler-Brown, Chair, 405-208-5374, Fax: 405-208-6012, E-mail: llbrown@okcu.edu. *Application contact:* Michelle Cook, Director, Admissions, 800-633-7242, Fax: 405-208-5916, E-mail: gadmissions@okcu.edu. Web site: http://www.okcu.edu/petree/education/graduate.aspx.

Old Dominion University, Darden College of Education, Program in Elementary/Middle Education, Norfolk, VA 23529. Offers elementary education (MS Ed); instructional technology (MS Ed); library science (MS Ed); middle school education (MS Ed). *Accreditation:* NCATE. Part-time and evening/weekend programs available. Postbaccalaureate distance learning degree programs offered (no on-campus study). *Faculty:* 18 full-time (16 women), 34 part-time/adjunct (27 women). *Students:* 151 full-time (140 women), 118 part-time (96 women); includes 53 minority (27 Black or African American, non-Hispanic/Latino; 3 Asian, non-Hispanic/Latino; 10 Hispanic/Latino; 2 Native Hawaiian or other Pacific Islander, non-Hispanic/Latino; 11 Two or more races, non-Hispanic/Latino). Average age 31. 291 applicants, 50% accepted, 123 enrolled. In 2011, 167 master's awarded. *Degree requirements:* For master's, comprehensive exam. *Entrance requirements:* For master's, GRE General Test or MAT; PRAXIS I, SAT or ACT, minimum GPA of 2.8. Additional exam requirements/recommendations for international students: Required—TOEFL (minimum score 600 paper-based; 250 computer-based). *Application deadline:* For fall admission, 6/1 priority date for domestic students; for winter admission, 11/1 priority date for domestic students; for spring admission, 3/1 priority date for domestic students. Applications are processed on a rolling basis. Application fee: $50. Electronic applications accepted. *Expenses:* Tuition, state resident: full-time $9096; part-time $379 per credit. Tuition, nonresident: full-time $23,064; part-time $961 per credit. *Required fees:* $127 per semester. One-time fee: $50. *Financial support:* In 2011–12, 180 students received support, including teaching assistantships (averaging $9,000 per year); career-related internships or fieldwork, Federal Work-Study, institutionally sponsored loans, and scholarships/grants also available. Support available to part-time students. Financial award application deadline: 2/15; financial award applicants required to submit FAFSA. *Faculty research:* Education pre-K to 6, school librarianship. *Unit head:* Dr. Lea Lee, Graduate Program Director, 757-683-4801, Fax: 757-683-5862, E-mail: lxlee@odu.edu. *Application contact:* William Heffelfinger, Director of Graduate Admissions, 757-683-5554, Fax: 757-683-3255, E-mail: gradadmit@odu.edu. Web site: http://education.odu.edu/eci/.

Olivet Nazarene University, Graduate School, Division of Education, Program in Elementary Education, Bourbonnais, IL 60914. Offers MAT. *Accreditation:* NCATE. Evening/weekend programs available. *Degree requirements:* For master's, thesis or alternative.

Oregon State University, Graduate School, College of Education, Program in Elementary Education, Corvallis, OR 97331. Offers MAT. *Accreditation:* NCATE. *Entrance requirements:* For master's, NTE, minimum GPA of 3.0 in last 90 hours of course work. Additional exam requirements/recommendations for international students: Required—TOEFL. *Faculty research:* Kindergarten curriculum, the reading-writing connection, authentic assessment, classroom management.

Ottawa University, Graduate Studies-Arizona, Program in Education, Ottawa, KS 66067-3399. Offers community college counseling (MA); curriculum and instruction (MA); early childhood (MA); education intervention (MA); education leadership (MA); education technology (MA); Montessori early childhood education (MA); Montessori elementary education (MA); professional development (MA); school guidance counseling (MA); special education - cross categorical (MA). Programs offered in Mesa, Phoenix, Tempe and West Valley, AZ. *Accreditation:* NCATE. Part-time programs available. *Degree requirements:* For master's, thesis or alternative. *Entrance requirements:* For master's, minimum undergraduate GPA of 3.0, copy of current state certification or teaching license. Additional exam requirements/recommendations for international students: Required—TOEFL (minimum score 550 paper-based; 213 computer-based). Electronic applications accepted. *Expenses:* Contact institution.

Our Lady of the Lake University of San Antonio, School of Professional Studies, Program in Early Elementary Education, San Antonio, TX 78207-4689. Offers M Ed. Part-time programs available.

Our Lady of the Lake University of San Antonio, School of Professional Studies, Program in Generic Special Education, San Antonio, TX 78207-4689. Offers elementary education (M Ed). Part-time and evening/weekend programs available. *Degree requirements:* For master's, comprehensive exam, thesis optional, examination for the Certification of Education in Texas. *Entrance requirements:* For master's, GRE General Test or MAT, interview. Additional exam requirements/recommendations for international students: Required—TOEFL. Electronic applications accepted.

Pace University, School of Education, New York, NY 10038. Offers adolescent education (MST); childhood education (MST); educational leadership (MS Ed); educational technology studies (MS); literacy (MSE); school business management (Certificate); special education (MS Ed); teaching students with disabilities (MSE). *Accreditation:* NCATE. Part-time and evening/weekend programs available. *Students:* 164 full-time (131 women), 533 part-time (396 women); includes 157 minority (59 Black or African American, non-Hispanic/Latino; 2 American Indian or Alaska Native, non-Hispanic/Latino; 26 Asian, non-Hispanic/Latino; 54 Hispanic/Latino; 1 Native Hawaiian or other Pacific Islander, non-Hispanic/Latino; 15 Two or more races, non-Hispanic/Latino), 10 international. Average age 29. 256 applicants, 79% accepted, 114 enrolled. In 2011, 334 master's, 34 other advanced degrees awarded. *Degree requirements:* For master's, internship. *Entrance requirements:* For master's, interview, teaching certificate. Additional exam requirements/recommendations for international students: Required—TOEFL. *Application deadline:* For fall admission, 7/31 priority date for domestic students; for spring admission, 11/30 for domestic students. Applications are processed on a rolling basis. Application fee: $70. Electronic applications accepted. *Expenses:* Contact institution. *Financial support:* Research assistantships, career-related internships or fieldwork, and Federal Work-Study available. Support available to part-time students. Financial award applicants required to submit FAFSA. *Unit head:* Dr. Andrea M. Spencer, Dean, 212-346-1345, E-mail: aspencer@pace.edu. *Application contact:* Susan Ford-Goldschein, Director of Admissions, 212-346-1660, Fax: 212-346-1585, E-mail: gradnyc@pace.edu. Web site: http://www.pace.edu/.

Pacific Union College, Education Department, Angwin, CA 94508-9707. Offers education (M Ed); elementary teaching (MAT); secondary teaching (MAT). Part-time programs available. *Faculty:* 3 full-time (1 woman), 3 part-time/adjunct (all women). *Students:* 14 part-time (9 women). *Degree requirements:* For master's, thesis, action research project, field experiences. *Entrance requirements:* For master's, GRE, two interviews, teaching credential, letters of recommendation. *Application deadline:* Applications are processed on a rolling basis. Application fee: $0. *Expenses: Tuition:* Full-time $25,740; part-time $750 per quarter hour. Tuition and fees vary according to student's religious affiliation. *Financial support:* Available to part-time students. *Unit head:* Prof. Thomas Lee, Chair, 707-965-6646, Fax: 707-965-6645, E-mail: tdlee@puc.edu. *Application contact:* Marsha Crow, Assistant Chair/Accreditation and Certification Specialist, 707-965-6643, Fax: 707-965-6645, E-mail: mcrow@puc.edu. Web site: http://www.puc.edu/academics/departments/education/.

Pacific University, College of Education, Forest Grove, OR 97116-1797. Offers early childhood education (MAT); education (MAE); elementary education (MAT); high school education (MAT); middle school education (MAT); special education (MAT); visual function in learning (M Ed). *Accreditation:* NCATE. Part-time and evening/weekend programs available. *Degree requirements:* For master's, research project. *Entrance requirements:* For master's, California Basic Educational Skills Test, PRAXIS II, minimum undergraduate GPA of 2.75, 3.0 graduate. Additional exam requirements/recommendations for international students: Required—TOEFL. Electronic applications accepted. *Expenses:* Contact institution. *Faculty research:* Defining a culturally competent classroom, technology in the k-12 classroom, Socratic seminars, social studies education.

Pfeiffer University, Program in Elementary Education, Misenheimer, NC 28109-0960. Offers MAT, MS. *Accreditation:* NCATE. *Entrance requirements:* For master's, GRE, MAT, minimum GPA of 2.75.

Pittsburg State University, Graduate School, College of Education, Department of Curriculum and Instruction, Pittsburg, KS 66762. Offers classroom reading teacher (MS); early childhood education (MS); elementary education (MS); reading (MS); reading specialist (MS); secondary education (MS); teaching (MAT). *Accreditation:* NCATE. *Degree requirements:* For master's, thesis or alternative. *Entrance requirements:* For master's, GRE or MAT.

Plymouth State University, College of Graduate Studies, Graduate Studies in Education, Program in Elementary Education, Plymouth, NH 03264-1595. Offers M Ed. *Accreditation:* NCATE. Part-time and evening/weekend programs available. *Entrance requirements:* For master's, MAT, minimum GPA of 3.0.

Plymouth State University, College of Graduate Studies, Graduate Studies in Education, Program in K-12 Education, Plymouth, NH 03264-1595. Offers M Ed. *Accreditation:* NCATE. Part-time and evening/weekend programs available. *Degree requirements:* For master's, PRAXIS. *Entrance requirements:* For master's, MAT, minimum GPA of 3.0.

Portland State University, Graduate Studies, School of Education, Department of Curriculum and Instruction, Portland, OR 97207-0751. Offers early childhood education (MA, MS); education (M Ed, MA, MS); educational leadership: curriculum and instruction (Ed D); educational media/school librarianship (MA, MS); elementary education (M Ed, MAT, MST); reading (MA, MS); secondary education (M Ed, MAT, MST). *Accreditation:* NCATE. Part-time programs available. *Degree requirements:* For master's, comprehensive exam, thesis or alternative; for doctorate, thesis/dissertation. *Entrance requirements:* For master's, California Basic Educational Skills Test, minimum GPA of 3.0 in upper-division course work or 2.75 overall. Additional exam requirements/recommendations for international students: Required—TOEFL (minimum score 550 paper-based; 213 computer-based). *Faculty research:* Early literacy, characteristics of successful teachers of at-risk students, participation of women/minorities in technology courses, selection of cooperating teachers.

Prescott College, Graduate Programs, Program in Education, Prescott, AZ 86301. Offers early childhood education (MA); early childhood special education (MA); education (MA); elementary education (MA); environmental education leadership and administration (MA); equine-assisted experiential learning (MA); school guidance counseling (MA); secondary education (MA); special education, learning disability (MA); special education, mental retardation (MA); special education, serious emotional disability (MA); student-directed independent study (MA); sustainability education (PhD). Part-time programs available. Postbaccalaureate distance learning degree programs offered (minimal on-campus study). *Faculty:* 2 full-time (both women), 47 part-time/adjunct (31 women). *Students:* 59 full-time (36 women), 48 part-time (30 women); includes 16 minority (3 Black or African American, non-Hispanic/Latino; 1 American Indian or Alaska Native, non-Hispanic/Latino; 1 Asian, non-Hispanic/Latino; 8 Hispanic/Latino; 3 Two or more races, non-Hispanic/Latino), 2 international. Average age 40. 75 applicants, 76% accepted, 36 enrolled. In 2011, 14 master's, 8 doctorates awarded. *Degree requirements:* For master's, thesis, fieldwork or internship, practicum; for doctorate, thesis/dissertation. *Entrance requirements:* For master's, 2 letters of recommendation, resume; for doctorate, 3 letters of recommendation, resume, official transcripts, personal statement, program proposal. Additional exam requirements/recommendations for international students: Required—TOEFL (minimum score 500 paper-based; 173 computer-based). *Application deadline:* For fall admission, 4/15 priority date for domestic students, 4/15 for international students; for spring admission, 9/15 priority date for domestic students, 9/15 for international students. Applications are processed on a rolling basis. Application fee: $40. Electronic applications accepted. *Expenses: Tuition:* Full-time $16,440; part-time $685 per credit. *Required fees:* $150 per semester. One-time fee: $350. *Financial support:* Career-related internships or fieldwork and Federal Work-Study available. Financial award applicants required to submit FAFSA. *Unit head:* Noel Caniglia, Chair, 928-358-3201, Fax: 928-776-5151,

E-mail: ncaniglia@prescott.edu. *Application contact:* Kerstin Alicki, Admissions Counselor, 928-350-2100, Fax: 928-776-5242, E-mail: admissions@prescott.edu.

Providence College, Program in Special Education, Providence, RI 02918. Offers elementary special education (M Ed), including elementary, secondary. Part-time and evening/weekend programs available. *Faculty:* 7 part-time/adjunct (5 women). *Students:* 7 full-time (all women), 36 part-time (25 women); includes 2 minority (1 Black or African American, non-Hispanic/Latino; 1 Hispanic/Latino). Average age 31. 21 applicants, 100% accepted, 5 enrolled. In 2011, 33 master's awarded. *Degree requirements:* For master's, comprehensive exam. *Entrance requirements:* For master's, GRE General Test. Additional exam requirements/recommendations for international students: Required—TOEFL (minimum score 550 paper-based; 213 computer-based; 80 iBT). *Application deadline:* For fall admission, 8/1 priority date for domestic students, 8/1 for international students; for spring admission, 12/1 priority date for domestic students, 12/1 for international students. Applications are processed on a rolling basis. Application fee: $55. *Expenses: Tuition:* Part-time $404 per credit. *Required fees:* $404 per credit. *Financial support:* In 2011–12, 1 research assistantship with full tuition reimbursement (averaging $8,400 per year) was awarded; career-related internships or fieldwork and unspecified assistantships also available. Support available to part-time students. Financial award application deadline: 8/1; financial award applicants required to submit FAFSA. *Unit head:* Diane LaMontagne, Director, 401-865-2912, Fax: 401-865-1147, E-mail: dlamonta@providence.edu. *Application contact:* Carol A. Daniels, Coordinator of Graduate Faculty and Administrative Services, 401-865-2247, Fax: 401-865-1147, E-mail: daniels@providence.edu. Web site: http://www.providence.edu/professional-studies/graduate-degrees/Pages/master-education-specialed.aspx.

Providence College, Programs in Administration, Providence, RI 02918. Offers elementary administration (M Ed); secondary administration (M Ed). Part-time and evening/weekend programs available. *Faculty:* 11 part-time/adjunct (4 women). *Students:* 4 full-time (2 women), 81 part-time (45 women). Average age 36. 31 applicants, 94% accepted, 10 enrolled. In 2011, 18 master's awarded. *Degree requirements:* For master's, comprehensive exam. *Entrance requirements:* For master's, GRE General Test. Additional exam requirements/recommendations for international students: Required—TOEFL (minimum score 550 paper-based; 213 computer-based; 80 iBT). *Application deadline:* For fall admission, 8/1 priority date for domestic students, 8/1 for international students; for spring admission, 12/1 priority date for domestic students, 12/1 for international students. Applications are processed on a rolling basis. Application fee: $55. *Expenses: Tuition:* Part-time $404 per credit. *Required fees:* $404 per credit. *Financial support:* In 2011–12, research assistantships with full tuition reimbursements (averaging $8,400 per year) were awarded; career-related internships or fieldwork, institutionally sponsored loans, and unspecified assistantships also available. Support available to part-time students. Financial award application deadline: 8/1; financial award applicants required to submit FAFSA. *Unit head:* Francis J. Leary, Director, 401-865-2247, Fax: 401-865-1147, E-mail: fleary@providence.edu. *Application contact:* Carol A. Daniels, Coordinator of Graduate Faculty and Administrative Services, 401-865-2247, Fax: 401-865-1147, E-mail: daniels@providence.edu.

Purdue University, Graduate School, College of Education, Department of Curriculum and Instruction, West Lafayette, IN 47907. Offers agricultural and extension education (PhD, Ed S); agriculture and extension education (MS, MS Ed); art education (PhD); consumer and family sciences and extension education (MS Ed, PhD, Ed S); curriculum studies (MS Ed, PhD, Ed S); educational technology (MS Ed, PhD, Ed S); elementary education (MS Ed); foreign language education (MS Ed, PhD, Ed S); industrial technology (PhD, Ed S); language arts (MS Ed, PhD, Ed S); literacy (MS Ed, PhD, Ed S); mathematics/science education (MS, MS Ed, PhD, Ed S); social studies (MS Ed, PhD); social studies education (Ed S); vocational/industrial education (MS Ed, PhD, Ed S); vocational/technical education (MS Ed, PhD, Ed S). *Accreditation:* NCATE. Part-time and evening/weekend programs available. *Faculty:* 30 full-time (21 women), 1 (woman) part-time/adjunct. *Students:* 89 full-time (64 women), 134 part-time (84 women); includes 31 minority (12 Black or African American, non-Hispanic/Latino; 3 American Indian or Alaska Native, non-Hispanic/Latino; 7 Asian, non-Hispanic/Latino; 9 Hispanic/Latino), 49 international. Average age 36. 136 applicants, 83% accepted, 72 enrolled. In 2011, 26 master's, 13 doctorates awarded. *Degree requirements:* For master's, thesis optional; for doctorate, thesis/dissertation, oral and written exams; for Ed S, oral presentation, project. *Entrance requirements:* For master's, GRE general test is required if undergraduate GPA is below 3.0, minimum undergraduate GPA of 3.0 or equivalent; for doctorate, GRE General Test, a combined GRE verbal and quantitative score of 1000 (300 for revised GRE Test) or more is expected, minimum undergraduate GPA of 3.0 or equivalent; master's degree with minimum GPA of 3.0 or equivalent; for Ed S, GRE general test, a combined GRE verbal and quantitative score of 1000 (300 for revised GRE Test) or more is expected, minimum undergraduate GPA of 3.0 or equivalent; master's degree. Additional exam requirements/recommendations for international students: Required—TOEFL (minimum score 550 paper-based; 77 iBT). *Application deadline:* For fall admission, 12/15 priority date for domestic students, 3/1 for international students; for spring admission, 9/15 for domestic students, 8/1 for international students. Application fee: $60 ($75 for international students). Electronic applications accepted. *Financial support:* Fellowships with full tuition reimbursements, research assistantships with full tuition reimbursements, teaching assistantships with full tuition reimbursements, career-related internships or fieldwork, and tuition waivers (full) available. Support available to part-time students. Financial award application deadline: 3/1; financial award applicants required to submit FAFSA. *Faculty research:* Literacy acquisition and development, teacher beliefs and knowledge, recruitment and retention of underrepresented students, economic education, literacy discourse. *Unit head:* Dr. Philip J. VanFossen, Head, 765-494-7935, Fax: 765-496-1622, E-mail: vanfoss@purdue.edu. *Application contact:* Sarah N. Prater, Graduate Contact, 765-494-2345, Fax: 765-494-5832, E-mail: prater0@purdue.edu. Web site: http://www.edci.purdue.edu/.

Purdue University North Central, Program in Education, Westville, IN 46391-9542. Offers elementary education (MS Ed). *Accreditation:* NCATE. Part-time and evening/weekend programs available. *Degree requirements:* For master's, one foreign language. *Entrance requirements:* For master's, GRE, minimum GPA of 3.0. Electronic applications accepted. *Faculty research:* Diversity, integration.

Queens College of the City University of New York, Division of Graduate Studies, Division of Education, Department of Elementary and Early Childhood Education, Flushing, NY 11367-1597. Offers bilingual education (MS Ed); childhood education (MA); early childhood education (MA); elementary education (MS Ed, AC); literacy (MS Ed). Part-time and evening/weekend programs available. *Faculty:* 31 full-time (25 women). *Students:* 87 full-time (74 women), 561 part-time (522 women); includes 226 minority (49 Black or African American, non-Hispanic/Latino; 68 Asian, non-Hispanic/Latino; 109 Hispanic/Latino), 5 international. 436 applicants, 64% accepted, 212 enrolled. In 2011, 229 master's, 1 other advanced degree awarded. *Degree requirements:* For master's, research project; for AC, thesis optional. *Entrance requirements:* For master's, minimum GPA of 3.0. Additional exam requirements/recommendations for international students: Required—TOEFL. *Application deadline:* For fall admission, 4/1 for domestic students; for spring admission, 11/1 for domestic students. Applications are processed on a rolling basis. Application fee: $125. *Expenses:* Tuition, state resident: part-time $345 per credit. Tuition, nonresident: part-time $640 per credit. *Required fees:* $145.25 per semester. *Financial support:* Career-related internships or fieldwork, Federal Work-Study, institutionally sponsored loans, and tuition waivers (partial) available. Support available to part-time students. Financial award application deadline: 4/1; financial award applicants required to submit FAFSA. *Unit head:* Dr. Myra Zarnowski, Chairperson, 718-997-5328. *Application contact:* Mario Caruso, Director of Graduate Admissions, 718-997-5200, Fax: 718-997-5193, E-mail: graduate_admissions@qc.edu.

Queens University of Charlotte, Wayland H. Cato, Jr. School of Education, Charlotte, NC 28274-0002. Offers education in literacy (M Ed); elementary education (MAT); school administration (MSA). *Accreditation:* NCATE. Part-time and evening/weekend programs available. *Degree requirements:* For master's, comprehensive exam. *Entrance requirements:* For master's, GRE General Test. *Expenses:* Contact institution.

Quinnipiac University, School of Education, Program in Elementary Education, Hamden, CT 06518-1940. Offers MAT. *Accreditation:* NCATE. *Faculty:* 7 full-time (5 women), 41 part-time/adjunct (24 women). *Students:* 73 full-time (66 women); includes 7 minority (1 Black or African American, non-Hispanic/Latino; 2 Asian, non-Hispanic/Latino; 4 Hispanic/Latino). 71 applicants, 97% accepted, 61 enrolled. In 2011, 59 master's awarded. *Entrance requirements:* For master's, PRAXIS I, minimum GPA of 2.67, interview. *Application deadline:* For fall admission, 3/31 priority date for domestic students. Applications are processed on a rolling basis. Application fee: $45. Electronic applications accepted. *Expenses: Tuition:* Part-time $855 per credit. *Required fees:* $35 per credit. *Financial support:* In 2011–12, 3 students received support. Career-related internships or fieldwork, scholarships/grants, and tuition waivers (full and partial) available. Financial award application deadline: 4/15; financial award applicants required to submit FAFSA. *Faculty research:* Multicultural and urban education/leadership, challenges of teaching diverse learners, scholarship of teaching and learning, technology and teaching, humor and education. *Unit head:* Mordechai Gordon, Program Director, 203-582-8442, Fax: 203-582-3473, E-mail: mordechai.gordon@quinnipiac.edu. *Application contact:* Jennifer Boutin, Associate Director of Graduate Admissions, 203-582-8672, Fax: 203-582-3443, E-mail: jennifer.boutin@quinnipiac.edu. Web site: http://www.quinnipiac.edu/academics/colleges-schools-and-departments/school-of-education/graduate-programs/five-semester-mat-programs/elementary-educa.

Regent University, Graduate School, School of Education, Virginia Beach, VA 23464-9800. Offers adult education (Ed D); adult/staff development (Ed D, PhD); career switcher with licensure (M Ed), including alternative licensure; character education (Ed D, PhD); Christian education leadership (Ed D, PhD); Christian education specialist (Ed S); Christian school program (M Ed), including ACSI licensure; distance education (Ed D, PhD); education licensure (M Ed), including preK-6th grade; educational leadership (M Ed, PhD); educational leadership - special education (Ed S), including administration and supervision; educational psychology (Ed D, PhD), including learning and development, research and evaluation, special education; higher education (Ed D, PhD), including administration, research and institutional planning, teaching; higher education leadership (Ed D); individualized degree plan (M Ed), including behavior disorders, learning disabilities, mental retardation, reading specialist; K-12 school leadership (Ed D, PhD); leadership in character education (M Ed); master teacher (M Ed), including TESOL; mathematics education (M Ed); special education (PhD); student affairs (M Ed); TESOL (M Ed), including adult education, ESL: preK-12. *Accreditation:* Teacher Education Accreditation Council. Part-time and evening/weekend programs available. Postbaccalaureate distance learning degree programs offered (minimal on-campus study). *Faculty:* 26 full-time (13 women), 54 part-time/adjunct (34 women). *Students:* 140 full-time (109 women), 786 part-time (626 women); includes 218 minority (189 Black or African American, non-Hispanic/Latino; 2 American Indian or Alaska Native, non-Hispanic/Latino; 11 Asian, non-Hispanic/Latino; 16 Hispanic/Latino), 42 international. Average age 39. 673 applicants, 57% accepted, 298 enrolled. In 2011, 178 master's, 15 doctorates awarded. *Degree requirements:* For master's, thesis or alternative; for doctorate, comprehensive exam, thesis/dissertation. *Entrance requirements:* For master's, MAT, minimum undergraduate GPA of 2.75, writing sample, resume, recommendations, interview; for doctorate, GRE, writing sample, 3 years of relevant professional experience, master's-level paper, copies of published work, resume, transcripts, interview, recommendations. Additional exam requirements/recommendations for international students: Required—TOEFL (minimum score 577 paper-based; 233 computer-based). *Application deadline:* For fall admission, 4/1 priority date for domestic students; for spring admission, 10/15 priority date for domestic students. Applications are processed on a rolling basis. Application fee: $50. Electronic applications accepted. *Expenses:* Contact institution. *Financial support:* Fellowships, career-related internships or fieldwork, scholarships/grants, tuition waivers (full and partial), and unspecified assistantships available. Support available to part-time students. Financial award application deadline: 4/1; financial award applicants required to submit FAFSA. *Faculty research:* Character development and discipline for children, education leadership development, diversity in schools, classroom management, technology in education settings. *Unit head:* Dr. Alan A. Arroyo, Dean, 757-352-4261, Fax: 757-352-4318, E-mail: alanarr@regent.edu. *Application contact:* Matthew Chadwick, Director of Enrollment Support Services, 800-373-5504, Fax: 757-352-4381, E-mail: admissions@regent.edu. Web site: http://www.regent.edu/education/.

Regis College, Programs in Education, Weston, MA 02493. Offers elementary teacher (MAT); reading (MAT); special education (MAT). Part-time and evening/weekend programs available. *Degree requirements:* For master's, thesis. *Entrance requirements:* For master's, GRE or MAT. Additional exam requirements/recommendations for international students: Required—TOEFL. Electronic applications accepted. *Faculty research:* Reflective teaching, gender-based education, integrated teaching.

Rhode Island College, School of Graduate Studies, Feinstein School of Education and Human Development, Department of Elementary Education, Providence, RI 02908-1991. Offers early childhood education (M Ed); elementary education (M Ed, MAT); reading (M Ed). *Accreditation:* NCATE. Part-time and evening/weekend programs available. *Faculty:* 11 full-time (7 women), 2 part-time/adjunct (both women). *Students:* 23 full-time (20 women), 37 part-time (36 women); includes 3 minority (1 Black or African American, non-Hispanic/Latino; 1 Asian, non-Hispanic/Latino; 1 Hispanic/Latino). Average age 31. In 2011, 30 master's awarded. *Degree requirements:* For master's, comprehensive exam (for some programs), comprehensive assessment. *Entrance requirements:* For master's, GRE General Test or MAT, PRAXIS II (elementary content knowledge), undergraduate transcripts; minimum undergraduate GPA of 3.0; 3 letters of recommendation. Additional exam requirements/recommendations for international students: Recommended—TOEFL (minimum score 550 paper-based; 213 computer-based; 79 iBT). *Application deadline:* For fall admission, 3/1 for domestic students; for spring admission, 11/1 for domestic students. Applications are processed on a rolling basis. Application fee: $50. *Expenses:* Tuition, state resident: full-time $8592; part-time $358 per credit hour. Tuition, nonresident: full-time $16,800; part-time $700 per credit hour. *Required fees:* $602; $22 per credit. $72 per term. *Financial support:* Teaching assistantships with full tuition reimbursements, Federal Work-Study, scholarships/grants, and health care benefits available. Support available to part-time students.

Elementary Education

Financial award application deadline: 5/15; financial award applicants required to submit FAFSA. *Unit head:* Dr. Patricia Cordeiro, Chair, 401-456-8016. *Application contact:* Graduate Studies, 401-456-8700. Web site: http://www.ric.edu/elementaryEducation/.

Rider University, Department of Graduate Education, Leadership and Counseling, Teacher Certification Program, Lawrenceville, NJ 08648-3001. Offers business education (Certificate); elementary education (Certificate); English as a second language (Certificate); English education (Certificate); mathematics education (Certificate); preschool to grade 3 (Certificate); science education (Certificate); social studies education (Certificate); world languages (Certificate), including French, German, Spanish. Part-time programs available. *Degree requirements:* For Certificate, internship, professional portfolio. *Entrance requirements:* For degree, PRAXIS, resume. Additional exam requirements/recommendations for international students: Required—TOEFL (minimum score 550 paper-based; 213 computer-based). Electronic applications accepted. *Expenses: Tuition:* Full-time $32,820; part-time $710 per credit. *Required fees:* $350; $35 per course. Tuition and fees vary according to campus/location and program. *Faculty research:* Conceptual foundations for optimal development of creativity; creative theory, cognitive processes in mathematics learning, teacher collaboration.

Rivier University, School of Graduate Studies, Department of Education, Nashua, NH 03060. Offers curriculum and instruction (M Ed); early childhood education (M Ed); educational administration (M Ed); educational studies (M Ed); elementary education (M Ed); elementary education and general special education (M Ed); emotional and behavioral disorders (M Ed); general social education (M Ed); leadership and learning (Ed D, CAGS); learning disabilities (M Ed); learning disabilities and reading (M Ed); mental health counseling (MA); reading (M Ed); school counseling (M Ed). Part-time and evening/weekend programs available. *Degree requirements:* For master's, comprehensive exam (for some programs), internships. *Entrance requirements:* For master's, GRE General Test or MAT.

Rockford College, Graduate Studies, Department of Education, Program in Elementary Education, Rockford, IL 61108-2393. Offers MAT. Part-time and evening/weekend programs available. *Degree requirements:* For master's, thesis optional. *Entrance requirements:* For master's, GRE General Test, basic skills test (for students seeking certification), 3 letters of recommendation. Additional exam requirements/recommendations for international students: Required—TOEFL (minimum score 550 paper-based; 213 computer-based; 79 iBT). *Application deadline:* Applications are processed on a rolling basis. Application fee: $50. Electronic applications accepted. *Expenses: Tuition:* Full-time $16,200; part-time $675 per credit. *Required fees:* $80; $40 per semester. Tuition and fees vary according to class time, course level, course load, degree level, campus/location and program. *Financial support:* Scholarships/grants and unspecified assistantships available. Support available to part-time students. Financial award application deadline: 3/1; financial award applicants required to submit FAFSA. *Unit head:* Dr. Michelle McReynolds, MAT Director, 815-226-3390, Fax: 815-394-3706, E-mail: mmcreynolds@rockford.edu. *Application contact:* Michele Mehren, Office Manager for Graduate Studies, 815-226-4041, Fax: 815-394-3706, E-mail: mmehren@rockford.edu. Web site: http://www.rockford.edu/?page=MAT.

Roger Williams University, School of Education, Program in Elementary Education, Bristol, RI 02809. Offers MAT. Part-time and evening/weekend programs available. *Degree requirements:* For master's, state-mandated exams. *Entrance requirements:* For master's, resume, 3 letters of recommendation. Additional exam requirements/recommendations for international students: Recommended—TOEFL, IELTS. Electronic applications accepted. *Expenses:* Contact institution. *Faculty research:* Assistive technology; standards-based curricular development; professional development strategies, instruction, and assessment.

Rollins College, Hamilton Holt School, Graduate Studies in Education, Winter Park, FL 32789. Offers elementary education (M Ed, MAT). Part-time and evening/weekend programs available. *Faculty:* 6 full-time (3 women), 5 part-time/adjunct (2 women). *Students:* 9 full-time (7 women), 19 part-time (18 women); includes 4 minority (1 Black or African American, non-Hispanic/Latino; 3 Hispanic/Latino), 2 international. Average age 33. 10 applicants, 70% accepted, 7 enrolled. In 2011, 10 master's awarded. *Degree requirements:* For master's, comprehensive exam, Professional Education Test (PED) and Subject Area Examination (SAE) of the Florida Teacher Certification Examinations (FTCE), successful review of the Expanded Teacher Education Portfolio (ETEP), successful completion of all required coursework. *Entrance requirements:* For master's, General Knowledge Test of the Florida Teacher Certification Examination (FTCE), official transcripts, letter(s) of recommendation, essay. Additional exam requirements/recommendations for international students: Required—TOEFL (minimum score 550 paper-based; 213 computer-based; 80 iBT). *Application deadline:* For fall admission, 8/11 for domestic students; for spring admission, 12/10 for domestic students. Applications are processed on a rolling basis. Application fee: $50. *Expenses:* Contact institution. *Financial support:* In 2011–12, 12 students received support. Federal Work-Study, scholarships/grants, and unspecified assistantships available. Support available to part-time students. Financial award applicants required to submit FAFSA. *Unit head:* Dr. J. Scott Hewit, Faculty Director, 407-646-2300, E-mail: shewit@rollins.edu. *Application contact:* Rebecca Cordray, Coordinator of Records and Registration, 407-646-1568, Fax: 407-975-6430, E-mail: rcordray@rollins.edu. Web site: http://www.rollins.edu/holt/graduate/gse.html.

Roosevelt University, Graduate Division, College of Education, Department of Teaching and Learning, Program in Elementary Education, Chicago, IL 60605. Offers MA.

Rosemont College, Schools of Graduate and Professional Studies, Graduate Education Program, Rosemont, PA 19010-1699. Offers elementary certification (MA). Part-time and evening/weekend programs available. *Faculty:* 8 part-time/adjunct (4 women). *Students:* 9 full-time (7 women), 13 part-time (10 women); includes 3 minority (all Black or African American, non-Hispanic/Latino). Average age 29. 18 applicants, 89% accepted, 16 enrolled. In 2011, 36 master's awarded. *Degree requirements:* For master's, thesis optional. *Entrance requirements:* For master's, minimum college GPA of 3.0, 3 letters of recommendation. Additional exam requirements/recommendations for international students: Required—TOEFL. *Application deadline:* Applications are processed on a rolling basis. Application fee: $50. Electronic applications accepted. Application fee is waived when completed online. *Expenses: Tuition:* Part-time $650 per credit. *Financial support:* Career-related internships or fieldwork, institutionally sponsored loans, and unspecified assistantships available. Support available to part-time students. Financial award applicants required to submit FAFSA. *Unit head:* Dr. Ann S. Hartsock, Director, 610-527-0200 Ext. 3108, E-mail: ahartsock@rosemont.edu. *Application contact:* Meghan Mellinger, Director, Enrollment and Student Services, 610-527-0200 Ext. 2596, Fax: 610-520-4399, E-mail: gpsadmissions@rosemont.edu. Web site: http://www.rosemont.edu/.

Rowan University, Graduate School, College of Education, Department of Teacher Education, Program in Elementary Education, Glassboro, NJ 08028-1701. Offers MST. Part-time and evening/weekend programs available. *Degree requirements:* For master's, thesis. *Entrance requirements:* For master's, GRE General Test, minimum GPA of 2.8, 1 year of teaching experience. Additional exam requirements/recommendations for international students: Required—TOEFL. Electronic applications accepted.

Rowan University, Graduate School, College of Education, Department of Teacher Education, Program in Elementary School Teaching, Glassboro, NJ 08028-1701. Offers MA. Part-time and evening/weekend programs available. *Degree requirements:* For master's, thesis. *Entrance requirements:* For master's, GRE General Test, minimum GPA of 2.8, 1 year of teaching experience. Additional exam requirements/recommendations for international students: Required—TOEFL. Electronic applications accepted.

Rutgers, The State University of New Jersey, New Brunswick, Graduate School of Education, Department of Learning and Teaching, Program in Early Childhood/Elementary Education, Piscataway, NJ 08854-8097. Offers Ed M, Ed D. Part-time programs available. Terminal master's awarded for partial completion of doctoral program. *Degree requirements:* For master's, comprehensive exam (for some programs); for doctorate, thesis/dissertation, qualifying exam. *Entrance requirements:* For master's, GRE General Test, minimum GPA of 3.0; for doctorate, GRE General Test, minimum GPA of 3.5. Additional exam requirements/recommendations for international students: Required—TOEFL. Electronic applications accepted.

Sacred Heart University, Graduate Programs, Isabelle Farrington College of Education, Fairfield, CT 06825-1000. Offers administration (CAS); educational technology (MAT); elementary education (MAT); reading (CAS); secondary education (MAT); teaching (CAS). Part-time and evening/weekend programs available. Postbaccalaureate distance learning degree programs offered (minimal on-campus study). *Degree requirements:* For master's, thesis or alternative. *Entrance requirements:* For master's, PRAXIS (teacher certification/MAT); for CAS, PRAXIS I. Additional exam requirements/recommendations for international students: Required—TOEFL (minimum score 550 paper-based; 213 computer-based). Electronic applications accepted. *Expenses:* Contact institution. *Faculty research:* Reading education, learning theory, teacher preparation, education of underachievers.

Sage Graduate School, Esteves School of Education, Program in Childhood Education, Troy, NY 12180-4115. Offers MS Ed. *Accreditation:* NCATE. Part-time and evening/weekend programs available. *Faculty:* 10 full-time (6 women), 27 part-time/adjunct (23 women). *Students:* 6 full-time (all women), 10 part-time (7 women). Average age 27. 22 applicants, 41% accepted, 5 enrolled. In 2011, 14 master's awarded. *Degree requirements:* For master's, thesis. *Entrance requirements:* For master's, minimum GPA of 2.75, resume, 2 letters of recommendation, interview, assessment of writing skills. Additional exam requirements/recommendations for international students: Required—TOEFL (minimum score 550 paper-based; 213 computer-based). *Application deadline:* Applications are processed on a rolling basis. Application fee: $40. *Expenses: Tuition:* Full-time $11,880; part-time $660 per credit hour. Tuition and fees vary according to program. *Financial support:* Federal Work-Study, scholarships/grants, and unspecified assistantships available. Support available to part-time students. Financial award application deadline: 3/1; financial award applicants required to submit FAFSA. *Faculty research:* The effects of teachers' personal characteristics on the instructional process. *Unit head:* Dr. Lori Quigley, Dean, Esteves School of Education, 518-244-2326, Fax: 518-244-4571, E-mail: l.quigley@sage.edu. *Application contact:* Mary Grace Luibrand, Professional Advisor for Teacher Education Programs, 518-244-4578, Fax: 518-244-4571, E-mail: luibrm@sage.edu.

Sage Graduate School, Esteves School of Education, Program in Childhood Education/Literacy, Troy, NY 12180-4115. Offers MS. Part-time and evening/weekend programs available. *Faculty:* 10 full-time (6 women), 27 part-time/adjunct (23 women). *Students:* 5 full-time (all women), 13 part-time (all women); includes 1 minority (Asian, non-Hispanic/Latino). Average age 28. 12 applicants, 33% accepted, 4 enrolled. In 2011, 7 master's awarded. *Degree requirements:* For master's, thesis optional. *Entrance requirements:* For master's, minimum GPA of 2.75, resume, 2 letters of recommendation, interview, assessment of writing skills. Additional exam requirements/recommendations for international students: Required—TOEFL (minimum score 550 paper-based; 213 computer-based). *Application deadline:* Applications are processed on a rolling basis. Application fee: $40. *Expenses: Tuition:* Full-time $11,880; part-time $660 per credit hour. Tuition and fees vary according to program. *Financial support:* Fellowships, research assistantships, Federal Work-Study, scholarships/grants, and unspecified assistantships available. Support available to part-time students. Financial award application deadline: 3/1. *Unit head:* Dr. Lori Quigley, Dean, Esteves School of Education, 518-244-2326, Fax: 518-244-4571, E-mail: l.quigley@sage.edu. *Application contact:* Mary Grace Luibrand, Director, 518-244-4578, Fax: 518-244-4571, E-mail: luibrm@sage.edu.

Sage Graduate School, Esteves School of Education, Program in Childhood Special Education, Troy, NY 12180-4115. Offers MS Ed. *Accreditation:* NCATE. Part-time and evening/weekend programs available. *Faculty:* 10 full-time (6 women), 27 part-time/adjunct (23 women). *Students:* 15 full-time (14 women), 18 part-time (16 women). Average age 27. 12 applicants, 75% accepted, 7 enrolled. In 2011, 4 master's awarded. *Degree requirements:* For master's, thesis optional. *Entrance requirements:* For master's, minimum GPA of 2.75, resume, 2 letters of recommendation, interview, assessment of writing skills. Additional exam requirements/recommendations for international students: Required—TOEFL (minimum score 550 paper-based; 213 computer-based). *Application deadline:* Applications are processed on a rolling basis. Application fee: $40. *Expenses: Tuition:* Full-time $11,880; part-time $660 per credit hour. Tuition and fees vary according to program. *Financial support:* Fellowships, research assistantships, Federal Work-Study, scholarships/grants, and unspecified assistantships available. Support available to part-time students. Financial award application deadline: 3/1; financial award applicants required to submit FAFSA. *Faculty research:* Effective behavioral strategies for classroom instruction. *Unit head:* Dr. Lori Quigley, Dean, Esteves School of Education, 518-244-2326, Fax: 518-244-4571, E-mail: l.quigley@sage.edu. *Application contact:* Mary Grace Luibrand, Director, 518-244-4578, Fax: 518-244-4571, E-mail: luibrm@sage.edu.

Saginaw Valley State University, College of Education, Program in Elementary Classroom Teaching, University Center, MI 48710. Offers MAT. *Accreditation:* NCATE. Part-time and evening/weekend programs available. *Students:* 23 part-time (20 women); includes 2 minority (both Black or African American, non-Hispanic/Latino), 1 international. Average age 33. 5 applicants, 80% accepted, 2 enrolled. In 2011, 18 master's awarded. *Degree requirements:* For master's, capstone course. *Entrance requirements:* For master's, minimum GPA of 3.0, teaching certificate. Additional exam requirements/recommendations for international students: Required—TOEFL (minimum score 525 paper-based; 197 computer-based; 71 iBT). *Application deadline:* Applications are processed on a rolling basis. Application fee: $25. Electronic applications accepted. *Expenses:* Tuition, state resident: full-time $8300; part-time $5333 per year. Tuition, nonresident: full-time $15,613; part-time $10,209 per year. *International tuition:* $15,631 full-time. *Financial support:* Federal Work-Study and scholarships/grants available. Support available to part-time students. Financial award applicants required to submit FAFSA. *Unit head:* Dr. Steve P. Barbus, Jr., Dean, 989-964-6067, Fax: 989-790-4385, E-mail: barbus@svsu.edu. *Application contact:* Kathy Lopez, Certification Officer, 989-964-4661, Fax: 989-964-4385, E-mail: klopez@svsu.edu.

Saginaw Valley State University, College of Education, Program in Natural Science Teaching, University Center, MI 48710. Offers elementary (MAT); middle school (MAT); secondary school (MAT). *Accreditation:* NCATE. Part-time and evening/weekend programs available. *Students:* 9 part-time (7 women); includes 1 minority (Black or African American, non-Hispanic/Latino). Average age 35. 1 applicant, 100% accepted, 0 enrolled. In 2011, 14 master's awarded. *Degree requirements:* For master's, capstone course. *Entrance requirements:* For master's, minimum GPA of 3.0, teaching certificate. Additional exam requirements/recommendations for international students: Required—TOEFL (minimum score 525 paper-based; 197 computer-based; 71 iBT). *Application deadline:* Applications are processed on a rolling basis. Application fee: $25. Electronic applications accepted. *Expenses:* Tuition, state resident: full-time $8300; part-time $5333 per year. Tuition, nonresident: full-time $15,613; part-time $10,209 per year. *International tuition:* $15,631 full-time. *Financial support:* Federal Work-Study and scholarships/grants available. Support available to part-time students. Financial award applicants required to submit FAFSA. *Unit head:* Dr. Steve P. Barbus, Jr., Dean, 989-964-6067, Fax: 989-790-4385, E-mail: barbus@svsu.edu. *Application contact:* Kathy Lopez, Certification Officer, 989-964-4661, Fax: 989-964-4385, E-mail: klopez@svsu.edu.

St. John Fisher College, Ralph C. Wilson Jr. School of Education, Program in Childhood Education/Special Education, Rochester, NY 14618-3597. Offers MS. Part-time and evening/weekend programs available. *Faculty:* 5 full-time (3 women), 2 part-time/adjunct (both women). *Students:* 47 full-time (36 women), 4 part-time (all women); includes 9 minority (4 Black or African American, non-Hispanic/Latino; 1 Asian, non-Hispanic/Latino; 4 Hispanic/Latino). Average age 29. 38 applicants, 87% accepted, 16 enrolled. In 2011, 35 master's awarded. *Degree requirements:* For master's, field experience, student teaching, LAST. *Entrance requirements:* For master's, 2 letters of recommendation, personal statement, current resume. Additional exam requirements/recommendations for international students: Required—TOEFL (minimum score 575 paper-based; 233 computer-based; 80 iBT). *Application deadline:* Applications are processed on a rolling basis. Application fee: $30. Electronic applications accepted. *Expenses: Tuition:* Part-time $735 per credit. One-time fee: $50 part-time. Tuition and fees vary according to course load, degree level and program. *Financial support:* In 2011–12, 10 students received support. Scholarships/grants available. Financial award applicants required to submit FAFSA. *Faculty research:* Professional development, science assessment, multi-cultural; educational technology. *Unit head:* Dr. Susan Schultz, Program Director, 585-385-7296, E-mail: sschultz@sjfc.edu. *Application contact:* Jose Perales, Director of Graduate Admissions, 585-385-8067, E-mail: jperales@sjfc.edu. Web site: http://www.sjfc.edu/admissions/graduate/programs/childhood.dot.

St. John's University, The School of Education, Department of Curriculum and Instruction, Program in Childhood Education, Queens, NY 11439. Offers MS Ed. *Students:* 23 full-time (18 women), 73 part-time (61 women); includes 30 minority (11 Black or African American, non-Hispanic/Latino; 4 Asian, non-Hispanic/Latino; 13 Hispanic/Latino; 1 Native Hawaiian or other Pacific Islander, non-Hispanic/Latino; 1 Two or more races, non-Hispanic/Latino), 5 international. Average age 31. 46 applicants, 72% accepted, 11 enrolled. In 2011, 48 master's awarded. *Degree requirements:* For master's, comprehensive exam. *Entrance requirements:* For master's, minimum GPA of 3.0, qualification for New York State provisional (initial) teaching certificate, 2 letters of recommendation. Additional exam requirements/recommendations for international students: Required—TOEFL (minimum score 600 paper-based; 250 computer-based; 100 iBT), IELTS (minimum score 5.5). *Application deadline:* For fall admission, 8/17 for domestic students, 5/1 for international students; for spring admission, 1/5 for domestic students, 11/1 for international students. Applications are processed on a rolling basis. Application fee: $70. Electronic applications accepted. *Expenses: Tuition:* Full-time $18,000; part-time $1000 per credit. *Required fees:* $170 per semester. Tuition and fees vary according to program. *Financial support:* Research assistantships available. *Faculty research:* Self determination in the special education setting; parent, teacher, and student views on testing in elementary school. *Unit head:* Dr. Judith McVarish, Chair, 718-990-2334, E-mail: mcvarisj@stjohns.edu. *Application contact:* Dr. Kelly K. Ronayne, Associate Dean of Graduate Admissions, 718-990-2304, Fax: 718-990-2343, E-mail: graded@stjohns.edu.

Saint Joseph's University, College of Arts and Sciences, Department of Education, Philadelphia, PA 19131-1395. Offers curriculum supervisor of instruction (Certificate); educational leadership (MS, Ed D); elementary education (MS, Certificate); elementary/middle years (Certificate); English second language specialist online (Certificate); hearing impaired: N-12th grade (Certificate); instructional technology (MS, Certificate); principal certification (Certificate); professional education (MS); reading specialist (MS, Certificate); reading supervisory (Certificate); secondary education (MS, Certificate); special education (MS, Certificate); superintendent's letter of eligibility (Certificate); supervisor of special education (Certificate); Wilson reading certificate online (Certificate). Part-time and evening/weekend programs available. Postbaccalaureate distance learning degree programs offered (no on-campus study). *Faculty:* 26 full-time (24 women), 83 part-time/adjunct (52 women). *Students:* 112 full-time (92 women), 923 part-time (709 women); includes 147 minority (92 Black or African American, non-Hispanic/Latino; 4 American Indian or Alaska Native, non-Hispanic/Latino; 19 Asian, non-Hispanic/Latino; 28 Hispanic/Latino; 4 Two or more races, non-Hispanic/Latino), 8 international. Average age 31. 285 applicants, 77% accepted, 176 enrolled. In 2011, 276 master's, 13 doctorates, 2 other advanced degrees awarded. *Entrance requirements:* For master's, 2 letters of recommendation, minimum GPA of 3.0, official transcripts, personal statement; for doctorate, GRE, master's degree from accredited institution, minimum graduate GPA of 3.5, computer competence, commitment to participate in cohort, interview with program director. Additional exam requirements/recommendations for international students: Required—TOEFL (minimum score 550 paper-based; 213 computer-based; 79 iBT). *Application deadline:* For fall admission, 7/15 priority date for domestic students, 4/15 for international students; for winter admission, 11/15 for domestic students, 1/15 for international students; for spring admission, 11/15 priority date for domestic students, 10/15 for international students. Applications are processed on a rolling basis. Application fee: $35. Electronic applications accepted. *Expenses:* Contact institution. *Financial support:* Unspecified assistantships available. Financial award applicants required to submit FAFSA. *Faculty research:* Public education professional development, factors predicting early mathematics skills for low income children. *Total annual research expenditures:* $92,975. *Unit head:* Dr. Jeanne Brady, Associate Dean, Education, 610-660-1580, E-mail: jebrady@sju.edu. *Application contact:* Kate McConnell, Director, Graduate College of Arts and Sciences Admissions and Retention, 610-660-3184, Fax: 610-660-3230, E-mail: kate.mcconnell@sju.edu.

Saint Mary's University of Minnesota, Schools of Graduate and Professional Programs, Graduate School of Education, Instruction Program, Winona, MN 55987-1399. Offers MA, Certificate. *Unit head:* Matthew Klebe, Director, 507-457-6619, E-mail: mklebe@smumn.edu. *Application contact:* Yasin Alsaidi, Director of Admissions for Graduate and Professional Programs, 612-728-5207, Fax: 612-728-5121, E-mail: yalsaidi@smumn.edu. Web site: http://www.smumn.edu/graduate-home/areas-of-study/graduate-school-of-education/ma-in-instruction.

Saint Peter's University, Graduate Programs in Education, Program in Teaching, Jersey City, NJ 07306-5997. Offers 6-8 middle school education (MA Ed, Certificate); K-12 secondary education (MA Ed, Certificate); K-5 elementary education (MA Ed, Certificate). Part-time and evening/weekend programs available. *Degree requirements:* For master's, comprehensive exam. *Entrance requirements:* For master's, GRE or MAT. Additional exam requirements/recommendations for international students: Required—TOEFL (minimum score 79 computer-based). Electronic applications accepted.

St. Thomas Aquinas College, Division of Teacher Education, Sparkill, NY 10976. Offers adolescence education (MST); childhood and special education (MST); childhood education (MST); educational leadership (MS Ed); reading (MS Ed, PMC); special education (MS Ed, PMC); teaching (MS Ed), including elementary education, middle school education, secondary education. *Accreditation:* NCATE. Part-time and evening/weekend programs available. *Degree requirements:* For master's, comprehensive exam, comprehensive professional portfolio; for PMC, action research project. *Entrance requirements:* For master's, New York State Qualifying Exam, GRE General Test or minimum GPA of 3.0, teaching certificate; for PMC, GRE General Test or minimum GPA of 3.0. Electronic applications accepted. *Faculty research:* Computer applications in education, adolescent special education students, literacy development, inclusive practices for special education students.

St. Thomas University, School of Leadership Studies, Institute for Education, Miami Gardens, FL 33054-6459. Offers earth/space science (Certificate); educational administration (MS, Certificate); educational leadership (Ed D); elementary education (MS); ESOL (Certificate); gifted education (Certificate); instructional technology (MS, Certificate); professional/studies (Certificate); reading (MS, Certificate); special education (MS). Part-time and evening/weekend programs available. *Degree requirements:* For master's, comprehensive exam; for doctorate, comprehensive exam, thesis/dissertation. *Entrance requirements:* For master's, interview, minimum GPA of 3.0 or GRE; for doctorate, GRE or MAT. Additional exam requirements/recommendations for international students: Required—TOEFL (minimum score 550 paper-based; 213 computer-based; 79 iBT). Electronic applications accepted.

Saint Xavier University, Graduate Studies, School of Education, Chicago, IL 60655-3105. Offers counseling (MA); curriculum and instruction (MA); early childhood education (MA); educational administration (MA); elementary education (MA); individualized studies (MA), including educational technology, English as a second language (ESL), ISTEM (integrative science, technology, engineering, and math), science education; music education (MA); reading (MA); secondary education (MA); Spanish education (MA); special education (MA); teaching and leadership (MA). *Accreditation:* NCATE. Part-time and evening/weekend programs available. *Degree requirements:* For master's, thesis or project. *Entrance requirements:* For master's, minimum GPA of 3.0. *Application deadline:* For fall admission, 8/15 priority date for domestic students. Applications are processed on a rolling basis. Application fee: $35. *Expenses:* Contact institution. *Financial support:* Career-related internships or fieldwork available. Support available to part-time students. Financial award applicants required to submit FAFSA. *Unit head:* Dr. Beverly Gulley, Dean, 773-298-3221, Fax: 773-779-9061, E-mail: gulley@sxu.edu. *Application contact:* Beth Gierach, Managing Director of Admission, 773-298-3053, Fax: 773-298-3076, E-mail: gierach@sxu.edu.

Salem College, Department of Teacher Education, Winston-Salem, NC 27101. Offers art education (MAT); elementary education (M Ed, MAT); language and literacy (M Ed); middle school education (MAT); music education (MAT); school counseling (M Ed); second language studies (MAT); secondary education (MAT); special education (M Ed, MAT). *Accreditation:* NCATE. Part-time and evening/weekend programs available. Postbaccalaureate distance learning degree programs offered (minimal on-campus study). *Degree requirements:* For master's, comprehensive exam, practicum (MAT), project (M Ed), oral and written comprehensive exams. *Entrance requirements:* For master's, GRE, minimum GPA of 2.5. *Faculty research:* Content area reading strategies, literacy development, brain compatible instruction.

Salem State University, School of Graduate Studies, Program in Elementary Education, Salem, MA 01970-5353. Offers M Ed. *Accreditation:* NCATE. Part-time and evening/weekend programs available. *Entrance requirements:* For master's, GRE or MAT. Additional exam requirements/recommendations for international students: Required—TOEFL (minimum score 550 paper-based; 80 iBT) or IELTS (minimum score 5.5).

Salem State University, School of Graduate Studies, Program in Spanish, Salem, MA 01970-5353. Offers MAT. Part-time and evening/weekend programs available. *Entrance requirements:* For master's, GRE or MAT. Additional exam requirements/recommendations for international students: Required—TOEFL (minimum score 550 paper-based; 80 iBT) or IELTS (minimum score 5.5).

Samford University, Orlean Bullard Beeson School of Education and Professional Studies, Birmingham, AL 35229. Offers early childhood education (Ed S); early childhood/elementary education (MS Ed); educational administration (Ed S); educational leadership (Ed D); elementary education (Ed S); gifted education (MS Ed); instructional leadership (MS Ed); secondary collaboration (MS Ed); M Div/MS Ed. *Accreditation:* NCATE. Part-time programs available. *Faculty:* 11 full-time (7 women), 9 part-time/adjunct (7 women). *Students:* 20 full-time (16 women), 169 part-time (122 women); includes 30 minority (26 Black or African American, non-Hispanic/Latino; 1 American Indian or Alaska Native, non-Hispanic/Latino; 1 Asian, non-Hispanic/Latino; 2 Hispanic/Latino), 1 international. Average age 39. 51 applicants, 92% accepted, 44 enrolled. In 2011, 57 master's, 9 doctorates, 35 other advanced degrees awarded. *Degree requirements:* For master's, comprehensive exam; for doctorate, comprehensive exam, thesis/dissertation. *Entrance requirements:* For master's, GRE or MAT, minimum GPA of 3.0; for doctorate, minimum GPA of 3.7; for Ed S, GRE, master's degree, teaching certificate, minimum GPA of 3.25. Additional exam requirements/recommendations for international students: Required—TOEFL (minimum score 550 paper-based; 213 computer-based). *Application deadline:* For fall admission, 7/15 for domestic students; for winter admission, 4/5 for domestic students; for spring admission, 12/4 for domestic students. Applications are processed on a rolling basis. Application fee: $25. *Expenses: Tuition:* Full-time $29,934; part-time $655 per credit. *Required fees:* $705. *Financial support:* Research assistantships, career-related internships or fieldwork, Federal Work-Study, scholarships/grants, and tuition waivers (partial) available. Support available to part-time students. Financial award applicants required to submit FAFSA. *Faculty research:* School law, the characteristics of beginning teachers, the nature of school reform, school culture, quality improvement in education, K-12 student achievement. *Unit head:* Dr. Jean Ann Box, Dean, 205-726-2565, E-mail: jabox@samford.edu. *Application contact:* Dr. Maurice Persall, Director, Graduate Office, 205-726-2019, E-mail: jmpersal@samford.edu. Web site: http://dlserver.samford.edu.

San Diego State University, Graduate and Research Affairs, College of Education, School of Teacher Education, Program in Elementary Curriculum and Instruction, San Diego, CA 92182. Offers MA. *Accreditation:* NCATE. Evening/weekend programs available. *Entrance requirements:* For master's, GRE General Test, letters of reference. Additional exam requirements/recommendations for international students: Required—TOEFL. Electronic applications accepted.

Elementary Education

San Francisco State University, Division of Graduate Studies, College of Education, Department of Elementary Education, Program in Elementary Education, San Francisco, CA 94132-1722. Offers MA. *Accreditation:* NCATE. *Unit head:* Dr. Debra Luna, Chair, 415-338-1562, E-mail: dluna@sfsu.edu. *Application contact:* Dr. Barbara Ford, Graduate Coordinator, 415-338-2156, E-mail: barbara@sfsu.edu. Web site: http://coe.sfsu.edu/eed.

San Jose State University, Graduate Studies and Research, Connie L. Lurie College of Education, Department of Elementary Education, San Jose, CA 95192-0001. Offers curriculum and instruction (MA); reading (Certificate). *Accreditation:* NCATE. *Degree requirements:* For master's, thesis or alternative. Electronic applications accepted.

Seton Hill University, Program in Elementary Education/Middle Level Education, Greensburg, PA 15601. Offers MA, Certificate. *Accreditation:* Teacher Education Accreditation Council. Part-time and evening/weekend programs available. Postbaccalaureate distance learning degree programs offered (minimal on-campus study). *Faculty:* 3 full-time (2 women), 4 part-time/adjunct (2 women). *Students:* 15 full-time (14 women), 3 part-time (all women). In 2011, 10 degrees awarded. *Entrance requirements:* For master's, teacher's certification, 3 letters of recommendation, personal statement, transcripts, resume. Additional exam requirements/recommendations for international students: Required—TOEFL (minimum score 600 paper-based; 250 computer-based; 100 iBT), IELTS (minimum score 6.5). *Application deadline:* Applications are processed on a rolling basis. Application fee: $0. Electronic applications accepted. *Expenses: Tuition:* Full-time $13,446; part-time $747 per credit. *Required fees:* $700; $25 per credit. $50 per term. *Financial support:* Tuition discounts available. *Faculty research:* Autism spectrum disorder. *Unit head:* Dr. Audrey Quinlan, Director, 724-830-4734, E-mail: quinlan@setonhill.edu. *Application contact:* Laurel Komarny, Program Counselor, 724-838-4209, E-mail: komarny@setonhill.edu.

Shippensburg University of Pennsylvania, School of Graduate Studies, College of Education and Human Services, Department of Teacher Education, Shippensburg, PA 17257-2299. Offers curriculum and instruction (M Ed), including biology, early childhood education, elementary education, English, geography/earth science, history, mathematics, middle level education, modern languages; reading (M Ed). *Accreditation:* NCATE. Part-time and evening/weekend programs available. *Faculty:* 14 full-time (11 women), 8 part-time/adjunct (7 women). *Students:* 16 full-time (15 women), 143 part-time (130 women); includes 11 minority (4 Black or African American, non-Hispanic/Latino; 1 Asian, non-Hispanic/Latino; 4 Hispanic/Latino; 2 Two or more races, non-Hispanic/Latino), 1 international. Average age 30. 55 applicants, 55% accepted, 25 enrolled. In 2011, 76 master's awarded. *Degree requirements:* For master's, comprehensive exam (for some programs), thesis optional, practicum or internship; capstone seminar (for some programs). *Entrance requirements:* For master's, MAT (if GPA less than 2.75), interview, 3 letters of reference, questionnaire of teaching background and future goals. Additional exam requirements/recommendations for international students: Required—TOEFL (minimum score 580 paper-based; 237 computer-based); Recommended—IELTS (minimum score 6). *Application deadline:* For fall admission, 6/1 priority date for domestic students, 4/30 for international students; for spring admission, 9/1 priority date for domestic students, 9/30 for international students. Applications are processed on a rolling basis. Application fee: $30. Electronic applications accepted. *Expenses: Tuition, area resident:* Part-time $416 per credit. Tuition, state resident: part-time $416 per credit. Tuition, nonresident: part-time $624 per credit. *Required fees:* $119 per credit. *Financial support:* In 2011–12, 5 research assistantships with full tuition reimbursements (averaging $5,000 per year) were awarded; career-related internships or fieldwork, scholarships/grants, unspecified assistantships, and resident hall director and student payroll positions also available. Support available to part-time students. Financial award application deadline: 3/1; financial award applicants required to submit FAFSA. *Unit head:* Dr. Christine A. Royce, Chairperson, 717-477-1688, Fax: 717-477-4046, E-mail: caroyc@ship.edu. *Application contact:* Jeremy R. Goshorn, Assistant Dean of Graduate Admissions, 717-477-1231, Fax: 717-477-4016, E-mail: jrgoshorn@ship.edu. Web site: http://www.ship.edu/teacher/.

Siena Heights University, Graduate College, Program in Teacher Education, Concentration in Elementary Education, Adrian, MI 49221-1796. Offers elementary education/reading (MA). Part-time programs available. *Degree requirements:* For master's, thesis, presentation. *Entrance requirements:* For master's, interview, minimum GPA of 3.0. *Expenses: Tuition:* Full-time $11,400; part-time $475 per credit hour. *Required fees:* $1000; $500 $125 per term. Tuition and fees vary according to degree level.

Sierra Nevada College, Teacher Education Program, Incline Village, NV 89451. Offers advanced teaching and leadership (M Ed); elementary education (MAT); secondary education (MAT). Part-time and evening/weekend programs available. Postbaccalaureate distance learning degree programs offered (minimal on-campus study). *Faculty:* 2 full-time (both women), 26 part-time/adjunct (16 women). *Students:* 247 full-time (192 women), 240 part-time (162 women); includes 234 minority (44 Black or African American, non-Hispanic/Latino; 8 American Indian or Alaska Native, non-Hispanic/Latino; 132 Asian, non-Hispanic/Latino; 38 Hispanic/Latino; 12 Native Hawaiian or other Pacific Islander, non-Hispanic/Latino). Average age 35. 147 applicants, 84% accepted, 124 enrolled. In 2011, 146 master's awarded. *Degree requirements:* For master's, comprehensive exam, thesis, PRAXIS I and II. *Entrance requirements:* For master's, 2 letters of recommendation, minimum GPA of 3.0. *Application deadline:* For fall admission, 8/6 priority date for domestic students; for winter admission, 1/7 priority date for domestic students; for spring admission, 5/6 priority date for domestic students. Applications are processed on a rolling basis. Application fee: $50. Electronic applications accepted. *Expenses: Tuition:* Full-time $7138; part-time $397 per credit. *Required fees:* $100 per semester. *Financial support:* In 2011–12, 334 students received support. Federal Work-Study available. Support available to part-time students. Financial award application deadline: 8/15; financial award applicants required to submit FAFSA. *Unit head:* Beth Bouchard, Chair of Education Department, 775-831-1314, Fax: 775-832-1686, E-mail: bbouchard@sierranevada.edu. *Application contact:* Katrina Midgley, Director of Graduate Admission, 775-831-1314 Ext. 7517, Fax: 775-832-1686, E-mail: kmidgley@sierranevada.edu. Web site: http://www.sierranevada.edu/.

Sinte Gleska University, Graduate Education Program, Mission, SD 57555. Offers elementary education (M Ed). Part-time and evening/weekend programs available. *Degree requirements:* For master's, thesis. *Entrance requirements:* For master's, 2 years of experience in elementary education, minimum GPA of 2.5, South Dakota elementary education certification. *Faculty research:* American Indian graduate education, teaching of Native American students.

Slippery Rock University of Pennsylvania, Graduate Studies (Recruitment), College of Education, Department of Elementary Education and Early Childhood, Slippery Rock, PA 16057-1383. Offers math/science (K-8) (M Ed); reading (M Ed). *Accreditation:* NCATE. Part-time and evening/weekend programs available. Postbaccalaureate distance learning degree programs offered. *Faculty:* 3 full-time (all women). *Students:* 2 full-time (both women), 33 part-time (all women); includes 1 minority (Two or more races, non-Hispanic/Latino). Average age 28. 55 applicants, 69% accepted, 11 enrolled. In 2011, 33 degrees awarded. *Entrance requirements:* For master's, GRE General Test, MAT, minimum GPA of 3.0, resume, teaching certification, letters of recommendation, transcripts (depending on program). Additional exam requirements/recommendations for international students: Required—TOEFL (minimum score 550 paper-based; 213 computer-based; 80 iBT). *Application deadline:* For fall admission, 3/1 priority date for domestic students, 5/1 for international students; for spring admission, 10/1 priority date for domestic students, 9/1 for international students. Applications are processed on a rolling basis. Application fee: $25 ($30 for international students). Electronic applications accepted. *Expenses:* Contact institution. *Financial support:* Career-related internships or fieldwork, Federal Work-Study, institutionally sponsored loans, scholarships/grants, tuition waivers (partial), and unspecified assistantships available. Support available to part-time students. Financial award application deadline: 5/1; financial award applicants required to submit FAFSA. *Unit head:* Dr. Suzanne Rose, Graduate Coordinator, 724-738-2863, Fax: 724-738-4987, E-mail: suzanne.rose@sru.edu. *Application contact:* Angela Barrett, Director of Graduate Admissions, 724-738-2051, Fax: 724-738-2146, E-mail: graduate.admissions@sru.edu.

Smith College, Graduate and Special Programs, Department of Education and Child Study, Program in Elementary Education, Northampton, MA 01063. Offers MAT. Part-time programs available. *Faculty:* 6 full-time (4 women), 3 part-time/adjunct (2 women). *Students:* 11 full-time (8 women), 3 part-time (all women); includes 1 minority (Asian, non-Hispanic/Latino). Average age 31. 22 applicants, 55% accepted, 11 enrolled. In 2011, 16 master's awarded. *Entrance requirements:* For master's, GRE. Additional exam requirements/recommendations for international students: Required—TOEFL (minimum score 590 paper-based; 243 computer-based; 97 iBT). *Application deadline:* For fall admission, 4/1 for domestic students, 1/15 for international students; for spring admission, 12/1 for domestic students. Application fee: $60. *Expenses: Tuition:* Full-time $14,925; part-time $1245 per credit. *Financial support:* In 2011–12, 12 students received support. Career-related internships or fieldwork, institutionally sponsored loans, and scholarships/grants available. Support available to part-time students. Financial award application deadline: 1/15. *Unit head:* Alan Rudnitsky, Graduate Student Adviser, 413-585-3261, E-mail: arudnits@smith.edu. *Application contact:* Ruth Morgan, Administrative Assistant, 413-585-3050, Fax: 413-585-3054, E-mail: gradstdy@smith.edu. Web site: http://www.smith.edu/educ/.

South Carolina State University, School of Graduate Studies, Department of Education, Orangeburg, SC 29117-0001. Offers counseling education (M Ed); early childhood and special education (M Ed); early childhood education (MAT); educational leadership (Ed D, Ed S); elementary education (M Ed, MAT); engineering (MAT); general science (MAT); mathematics (MAT); secondary education (M Ed), including biology education, business education, counselor education, English education, home economics education, industrial education, mathematics education, science education, social studies education; special education (M Ed), including emotionally handicapped, learning disabilities, mentally handicapped. *Accreditation:* NCATE. Part-time and evening/weekend programs available. *Faculty:* 9 full-time (6 women), 6 part-time/adjunct (2 women). *Students:* 34 full-time (29 women), 50 part-time (40 women); includes 74 minority (72 Black or African American, non-Hispanic/Latino; 1 Asian, non-Hispanic/Latino; 1 Hispanic/Latino). Average age 34. 23 applicants, 91% accepted, 14 enrolled. In 2011, 11 master's awarded. *Degree requirements:* For master's, thesis optional, departmental qualifying exam. *Entrance requirements:* For master's, GRE General Test, NTE, interview, teaching certificate. *Application deadline:* For fall admission, 6/15 priority date for domestic students, 6/15 for international students; for spring admission, 11/1 for domestic and international students. Applications are processed on a rolling basis. Application fee: $25. Electronic applications accepted. *Expenses:* Tuition, state resident: full-time $8688; part-time $514 per credit hour. Tuition, nonresident: full-time $17,600; part-time $1009 per credit hour. *Required fees:* $570. *Financial support:* In 2011–12, 3 fellowships (averaging $5,020 per year) were awarded; career-related internships or fieldwork, Federal Work-Study, and institutionally sponsored loans also available. Financial award application deadline: 6/1. *Faculty research:* Critical thinking, child abuse, stress, test-taking skills, conflict resolution, mainstreaming. *Unit head:* Dr. Charlie Spell, Interim Chair, 803-536-7098, Fax: 803-516-4568, E-mail: cspell@scsu.edu. *Application contact:* Annette Hazzard-Jones, Program Coordinator II, 803-536-8809, Fax: 803-536-8812, E-mail: zs_ahazzard@scsu.edu.

Southeastern Louisiana University, College of Education and Human Development, Department of Teaching and Learning, Hammond, LA 70402. Offers curriculum and instruction (M Ed); elementary education (MAT); special education (M Ed); special education: early interventionist (MAT). *Accreditation:* NCATE. Part-time and evening/weekend programs available. *Faculty:* 13 full-time (11 women). *Students:* 30 full-time (all women), 84 part-time (78 women); includes 15 minority (10 Black or African American, non-Hispanic/Latino; 2 Asian, non-Hispanic/Latino; 3 Hispanic/Latino). Average age 32. 20 applicants, 100% accepted, 14 enrolled. In 2011, 37 degrees awarded. *Degree requirements:* For master's, comprehensive exam (for some programs), thesis (for some programs), action research project, oral defense of research project, portfolio, teaching certificate, minimum cumulative GPA of 3.0. *Entrance requirements:* For master's, GRE (verbal and quantitative), PRAXIS (MAT). Additional exam requirements/recommendations for international students: Required—TOEFL (minimum score 500 paper-based; 173 computer-based; 61 iBT). *Application deadline:* For fall admission, 7/15 priority date for domestic students, 6/1 for international students; for spring admission, 12/1 priority date for domestic students, 10/1 for international students. Applications are processed on a rolling basis. Application fee: $20 ($30 for international students). Electronic applications accepted. *Expenses:* Tuition, state resident: full-time $3977; part-time $283 per semester hour. Tuition, nonresident: full-time $13,482; part-time $811 per semester hour. *Financial support:* Career-related internships or fieldwork, Federal Work-Study, institutionally sponsored loans, scholarships/grants, and unspecified assistantships available. Support available to part-time students. Financial award application deadline: 5/1; financial award applicants required to submit FAFSA. *Faculty research:* ESL, dyslexia, pre-service teachers, inclusion, early childhood education. *Total annual research expenditures:* $356,182. *Unit head:* Dr. Cynthia Elliott, Interim Department Head, 985-549-2221, Fax: 985-549-5009, E-mail: celliott@selu.edu. *Application contact:* Sandra Meyers, Graduate Admissions Analyst, 985-549-5620, Fax: 985-549-5632, E-mail: admissions@selu.edu. Web site: http://www.selu.edu/acad_research/depts/teach_lrn/index.html.

Southeastern University, College of Education, Lakeland, FL 33801-6099. Offers educational leadership (M Ed); elementary education (M Ed); teaching and learning (M Ed).

Southeast Missouri State University, School of Graduate Studies, Department of Educational Leadership and Counseling, Program in Educational Administration, Cape Girardeau, MO 63701-4799. Offers educational administration (Ed S); educational leadership development (Ed S); elementary administration and supervision (MA); higher education administration (MA); secondary administration and supervision (MA); teacher leadership (MA). *Accreditation:* NCATE. Part-time and evening/weekend programs available. Postbaccalaureate distance learning degree programs offered (minimal on-campus study). *Faculty:* 12 full-time (7 women). *Students:* 32 full-time (23 women), 172 part-time (122 women); includes 10 minority (6 Black or African American, non-Hispanic/Latino; 3 Asian, non-Hispanic/Latino; 1 Hispanic/Latino), 1 international. Average age 34. 62 applicants, 95% accepted, 51 enrolled. In 2011, 34 master's, 13 other advanced degrees awarded. *Degree requirements:* For master's, comprehensive exam (for some programs), thesis (for some programs), minimum GPA of 3.25; paper, portfolio or oral exam (for some programs); for Ed S, comprehensive exam. *Entrance requirements:* For master's, minimum undergraduate GPA of 2.75, valid teacher certification; for Ed S, GRE General Test, PRAXIS or MAT, minimum graduate GPA of 3.5; master's degree; valid teaching certificate. Additional exam requirements/recommendations for international students: Required—TOEFL (minimum score 550 paper-based; 213 computer-based; 79 iBT); Recommended—IELTS (minimum score 6). *Application deadline:* For fall admission, 8/1 for domestic students, 7/1 for international students; for spring admission, 11/21 for domestic students, 11/1 for international students. Applications are processed on a rolling basis. Application fee: $30 ($40 for international students). Electronic applications accepted. *Expenses:* Tuition, state resident: full-time $4896; part-time $272 per credit hour. Tuition, nonresident: full-time $8649; part-time $480.50 per credit hour. *Financial support:* In 2011–12, 16 students received support. Career-related internships or fieldwork, Federal Work-Study, scholarships/grants, tuition waivers (full), and unspecified assistantships available. Financial award application deadline: 6/30; financial award applicants required to submit FAFSA. *Faculty research:* Teacher leadership, organizational leadership effectiveness, state assessment and accountability systems. *Unit head:* Dr. David Stader, 573-651-2417, E-mail: dstader@semo.edu. *Application contact:* Alisa Aleen McFerron, Assistant Director of Admissions for Operations, 573-651-5937, Fax: 573-651-5936, E-mail: amcferron@semo.edu. Web site: http://www4.semo.edu/edadmin/admin.

Southeast Missouri State University, School of Graduate Studies, Department of Elementary, Early and Special Education, Program in Elementary Education, Cape Girardeau, MO 63701-4799. Offers MA. *Accreditation:* NCATE. Part-time and evening/weekend programs available. Postbaccalaureate distance learning degree programs offered (no on-campus study). *Faculty:* 8 full-time (6 women). *Students:* 2 full-time (both women), 26 part-time (all women); includes 1 minority (Black or African American, non-Hispanic/Latino). Average age 37. 4 applicants, 75% accepted, 3 enrolled. In 2011, 7 master's awarded. *Degree requirements:* For master's, comprehensive exam, minimum GPA of 3.25; teaching certificate or qualifying score on PRAXIS or 50th percentile on GRE or MAT. *Entrance requirements:* For master's, GRE General Test, MAT, or PRAXIS, minimum undergraduate GPA of 2.75; valid teaching certificate. Additional exam requirements/recommendations for international students: Required—TOEFL (minimum score 550 paper-based; 213 computer-based; 79 iBT); Recommended—IELTS (minimum score 6). *Application deadline:* For fall admission, 8/1 for domestic students, 7/1 for international students; for spring admission, 11/21 for domestic students, 11/1 for international students. Applications are processed on a rolling basis. Application fee: $30 ($40 for international students). Electronic applications accepted. *Expenses:* Tuition, state resident: full-time $4896; part-time $272 per credit hour. Tuition, nonresident: full-time $8649; part-time $480.50 per credit hour. *Financial support:* In 2011–12, 5 students received support. Career-related internships or fieldwork, Federal Work-Study, scholarships/grants, tuition waivers (full), and unspecified assistantships available. Financial award application deadline: 6/30; financial award applicants required to submit FAFSA. *Unit head:* Dr. Julie Ray, Interim Chairperson and Professor, 573-651-2444, E-mail: jaray@semo.edu. *Application contact:* Gail Amick, Administrative Secretary, 573-651-2049, Fax: 573-651-2001, E-mail: gamick@semo.edu. Web site: http://www.semo.edu/eese/.

Southern Arkansas University–Magnolia, Graduate Programs, Magnolia, AR 71754. Offers agriculture (MS); business administration (MBA); computer and information sciences (MS); education (M Ed), including counseling and development, curriculum and instruction, educational administration and supervision, elementary education, middle level, reading, secondary education, TESOL; kinesiology (M Ed); library media and information specialist (M Ed); mental health and clinical counseling (MS); public administration (MPA); school counseling (M Ed); teaching (MAT). *Accreditation:* NCATE. Part-time and evening/weekend programs available. Postbaccalaureate distance learning degree programs offered. *Faculty:* 34 full-time (15 women), 8 part-time/adjunct (5 women). *Students:* 87 full-time (62 women), 320 part-time (224 women); includes 116 minority (111 Black or African American, non-Hispanic/Latino; 2 American Indian or Alaska Native, non-Hispanic/Latino; 2 Asian, non-Hispanic/Latino; 1 Hispanic/Latino), 25 international. Average age 33. 201 applicants, 98% accepted, 156 enrolled. In 2011, 162 master's awarded. *Degree requirements:* For master's, comprehensive exam (for some programs), thesis optional. *Entrance requirements:* For master's, GRE, MAT or GMAT, minimum GPA of 2.5. Additional exam requirements/recommendations for international students: Required—TOEFL (minimum score 173 computer-based). *Application deadline:* For fall admission, 7/15 for domestic and international students; for winter admission, 12/1 for domestic and international students; for spring admission, 12/1 for domestic and international students. Applications are processed on a rolling basis. Application fee: $25 ($35 for international students). Electronic applications accepted. *Expenses:* Tuition, state resident: part-time $232 per credit. Tuition, nonresident: part-time $339 per credit. *Required fees:* $44 per credit. Part-time tuition and fees vary according to course load. *Financial support:* Career-related internships or fieldwork, Federal Work-Study, scholarships/grants, tuition waivers (full), and unspecified assistantships available. Financial award applicants required to submit FAFSA. *Faculty research:* Alternative certification for teachers, supervision of instruction, instructional leadership, counseling. *Unit head:* Dr. Kim Bloss, Dean, School of Graduate Studies, 870-235-4150, Fax: 870-235-5227, E-mail: kkbloss@saumag.edu. *Application contact:* Gaye Calhoun, Admissions Specialist, 870-235-4150, Fax: 870-235-5227, E-mail: glcalhoun@saumag.edu. Web site: http://www.saumag.edu/graduate.

Southern Connecticut State University, School of Graduate Studies, School of Education, Department of Education, New Haven, CT 06515-1355. Offers classroom teacher specialist (Diploma); elementary education (MS). *Accreditation:* NCATE. Part-time and evening/weekend programs available. *Faculty:* 8 full-time (4 women), 3 part-time/adjunct (2 women). *Students:* 61 full-time (54 women), 58 part-time (49 women); includes 10 minority (3 Black or African American, non-Hispanic/Latino; 3 Asian, non-Hispanic/Latino; 2 Hispanic/Latino; 2 Two or more races, non-Hispanic/Latino). 369 applicants, 8% accepted, 22 enrolled. In 2011, 66 master's, 7 other advanced degrees awarded. *Degree requirements:* For master's, thesis or alternative. *Entrance requirements:* For master's, interview, minimum QPA of 2.5; for Diploma, master's degree. *Application deadline:* For fall admission, 7/15 priority date for domestic students. Applications are processed on a rolling basis. Application fee: $50. Electronic applications accepted. *Expenses:* Tuition, state resident: full-time $5137; part-time $413 per credit. *Required fees:* $4008; $55 per term. *Financial support:* Application deadline: 4/15; applicants required to submit FAFSA. *Unit head:* Dr. Maria Diamantis, Chairperson, 203-392-6143, Fax: 203-392-6473, E-mail: diamantism1@southernct.edu. *Application contact:* Dr. Adam Goldberg, Graduate Coordinator, 203-392-6442, E-mail: goldberga2@southernct.edu.

Southern New Hampshire University, School of Education, Manchester, NH 03106-1045. Offers business education (MS); child development (M Ed); computer technology education (Certificate); curriculum and instruction (M Ed); education (M Ed, CAS); elementary education (M Ed); general special education (Certificate); school business administrator (Certificate); secondary education (M Ed); training and development (Certificate). Part-time and evening/weekend programs available. Postbaccalaureate distance learning degree programs offered (no on-campus study). *Degree requirements:* For master's, comprehensive exam (for some programs), thesis or alternative. *Entrance requirements:* For master's, PRAXIS I, minimum GPA of 2.75. Additional exam requirements/recommendations for international students: Required—TOEFL (minimum score 550 paper-based; 213 computer-based). Electronic applications accepted. *Expenses:* Contact institution.

Southern Oregon University, Graduate Studies, School of Education, Ashland, OR 97520. Offers elementary education (MA Ed, MS Ed), including classroom teacher, early childhood, handicapped learner, reading, supervision; secondary education (MA Ed, MS Ed), including classroom teacher, handicapped learner, reading, supervision; teaching (MAT). *Faculty:* 18 full-time (10 women), 10 part-time/adjunct (all women). *Students:* 128 full-time (88 women), 145 part-time (103 women); includes 32 minority (1 Black or African American, non-Hispanic/Latino; 3 American Indian or Alaska Native, non-Hispanic/Latino; 5 Asian, non-Hispanic/Latino; 13 Hispanic/Latino; 3 Native Hawaiian or other Pacific Islander, non-Hispanic/Latino; 7 Two or more races, non-Hispanic/Latino), 1 international. Average age 35. 48 applicants, 60% accepted, 23 enrolled. In 2011, 102 degrees awarded. *Degree requirements:* For master's, thesis optional. *Entrance requirements:* For master's, GRE General Test, minimum GPA of 3.0. *Application deadline:* For fall admission, 2/1 for domestic students. Application fee: $50. Electronic applications accepted. *Expenses:* Tuition, state resident: full-time $12,600; part-time $350 per credit. Tuition, nonresident: full-time $16,200; part-time $450 per credit. *Required fees:* $1590. *Financial support:* Research assistantships with partial tuition reimbursements available. *Unit head:* Dr. Geoff Mills, Dean, 541-552-6920, E-mail: mills@sou.edu. *Application contact:* Mark Bottorff, Director of Admissions, 541-552-6411, Fax: 541-552-8403, E-mail: admissions@sou.edu. Web site: http://www.sou.edu/education/.

Southern University and Agricultural and Mechanical College, Graduate School, College of Education, Department of Curriculum and Instruction, Baton Rouge, LA 70813. Offers elementary education (M Ed); media (M Ed); secondary education (M Ed). *Degree requirements:* For master's, comprehensive exam, thesis optional. *Entrance requirements:* For master's, GMAT or GRE General Test. Additional exam requirements/recommendations for international students: Required—TOEFL (minimum score 525 paper-based; 193 computer-based).

Southwestern Oklahoma State University, College of Professional and Graduate Studies, School of Behavioral Sciences and Education, Specialization in Elementary Education, Weatherford, OK 73096-3098. Offers M Ed. M Ed distance learning degree program offered to Oklahoma residents only. *Accreditation:* NCATE. Part-time and evening/weekend programs available. *Degree requirements:* For master's, exam. *Entrance requirements:* For master's, GRE General Test or minimum undergraduate GPA of 3.0. Additional exam requirements/recommendations for international students: Required—TOEFL.

Spalding University, Graduate Studies, College of Education, Programs in Education, Louisville, KY 40203-2188. Offers elementary school education (MAT); general education (MA); high school education (MAT); middle school education (MAT); school administration (MA); special education (learning and behavioral disorders) (MAT); student guidance counselor (MA). MAT programs offered for first teaching certificate/license students. *Accreditation:* NCATE. Part-time and evening/weekend programs available. *Faculty:* 9 full-time (6 women), 32 part-time/adjunct (20 women). *Students:* 142 full-time (100 women), 71 part-time (53 women); includes 75 minority (65 Black or African American, non-Hispanic/Latino; 1 American Indian or Alaska Native, non-Hispanic/Latino; 6 Hispanic/Latino; 3 Two or more races, non-Hispanic/Latino). Average age 36. 96 applicants, 44% accepted, 41 enrolled. In 2011, 69 master's awarded. *Degree requirements:* For master's, portfolio, final project, clinical experience. *Entrance requirements:* For master's, GRE General Test or MAT, interview, recommendations, resume. Additional exam requirements/recommendations for international students: Required—TOEFL (minimum score 535 paper-based; 203 computer-based). *Application deadline:* Applications are processed on a rolling basis. Application fee: $30. Electronic applications accepted. *Expenses: Tuition:* Full-time $12,438. Tuition and fees vary according to course load, degree level and program. *Financial support:* In 2011–12, 72 students received support, including 3 research assistantships with partial tuition reimbursements available (averaging $4,490 per year); scholarships/grants, traineeships, and unspecified assistantships also available. Financial award application deadline: 3/15; financial award applicants required to submit FAFSA. *Faculty research:* Instructional technology, achievement gap, classroom management, assessment. *Unit head:* Dr. Beverly Keepers, Dean, 502-588-7121, Fax: 502-585-7123, E-mail: bkeepers@spalding.edu. *Application contact:* Bonnie Caughron, 502-873-4262, E-mail: bcaughron@spalding.edu.

Springfield College, Graduate Programs, Program in Education, Springfield, MA 01109-3797. Offers counseling and secondary education (M Ed, MS); early childhood education (M Ed, MS); education (M Ed, MS); educational administration (M Ed, MS); educational studies (M Ed, MS); elementary education (M Ed, MS); secondary education (M Ed, MS); special education (M Ed, MS). Part-time and evening/weekend programs available. *Entrance requirements:* Additional exam requirements/recommendations for international students: Required—TOEFL (minimum score 550 paper-based; 213 computer-based). Electronic applications accepted.

Spring Hill College, Graduate Programs, Program in Education, Mobile, AL 36608-1791. Offers early childhood education (MAT, MS Ed); educational theory (MS Ed); elementary education (MAT, MS Ed); secondary education (MAT, MS Ed). Part-time programs available. *Faculty:* 3 full-time (2 women), 3 part-time/adjunct (all women). *Students:* 7 full-time (6 women), 21 part-time (18 women); includes 7 minority (6 Black or African American, non-Hispanic/Latino; 1 Asian, non-Hispanic/Latino). Average age 31. In 2011, 13 master's awarded. *Degree requirements:* For master's, comprehensive exam, completion of program within 6 calendar years of entrance into graduate studies at Spring Hill; documentation of course field assignments (MS) or completion of internship (MAT). *Entrance requirements:* For master's, GRE, MAT, or PRAXIS (varies by program), bachelor's degree with minimum undergraduate GPA of 3.0; class B certificate (MS) or minimum number of hours in specific fields (MAT). Additional exam requirements/recommendations for international students: Required—TOEFL (minimum score 550 paper-based; 213 computer-based; 80 iBT), IELTS (minimum score 6.5), CPE or CAE (minimum score C),Michigan English Language Assessment Battery (minimum score 90). *Application deadline:* For fall admission, 8/1 priority date for domestic students, 8/1 for international students; for spring admission, 12/1 priority date for domestic students, 12/1 for international students. Applications are processed on a rolling basis. Application fee: $25 ($35 for international students). Electronic applications accepted. *Expenses:* Contact institution. *Financial support:* Applicants required to submit FAFSA. *Unit head:* Dr. Ann A. Adams, Chair of Teacher Education, 251-380-3479, Fax: 251-460-2184, E-mail: aadams@shc.edu. *Application contact:* Donna B. Tarasavage, Director of Admissions, Graduate and Continuing Studies, 251-380-3067, Fax: 251-460-2190, E-mail: dtarasavage@shc.edu. Web site: http://www.shc.edu/grad/academics/teaching.

State University of New York at Fredonia, Graduate Studies, College of Education, Program in Elementary Education, Fredonia, NY 14063-1136. Offers MS Ed. *Accreditation:* NCATE. Part-time and evening/weekend programs available. *Degree requirements:* For master's, thesis optional. *Expenses:* Tuition, state resident: full-time

$6666; part-time $370 per credit hour. Tuition, nonresident: full-time $11,376; part-time $632 per credit hour. *Required fees:* $1059.30; $58.85 per credit hour. Tuition and fees vary according to course load.

State University of New York at New Paltz, Graduate School, School of Education, Department of Elementary Education, New Paltz, NY 12561. Offers childhood education (1-6) (MS Ed, MST); literacy education (5-12) (MS Ed); literacy education (B-6) (MS Ed); literacy education and adolescence special education (MS Ed); literacy education and childhood education and childhood special education (MS Ed). *Accreditation:* NCATE. Part-time and evening/weekend programs available. *Faculty:* 9 full-time (8 women), 6 part-time/adjunct (5 women). *Students:* 66 full-time (61 women), 129 part-time (115 women); includes 14 minority (3 Black or African American, non-Hispanic/Latino; 1 Asian, non-Hispanic/Latino; 7 Hispanic/Latino; 3 Two or more races, non-Hispanic/Latino). Average age 28. 121 applicants, 64% accepted, 66 enrolled. In 2011, 95 master's awarded. *Degree requirements:* For master's, comprehensive exam (for some programs), portfolio. *Entrance requirements:* For master's, GRE and MAT (MST), minimum GPA of 3.0 (3.2 for literacy and special education), New York state teaching certificate (MS Ed). Additional exam requirements/recommendations for international students: Required—TOEFL (minimum score 550 paper-based; 213 computer-based; 80 iBT), IELTS (minimum score 6.5). *Application deadline:* For fall admission, 4/1 for domestic and international students; for spring admission, 11/15 for domestic and international students. Application fee: $50. Electronic applications accepted. *Expenses:* Tuition, state resident: full-time $8870; part-time $370 per credit. Tuition, nonresident: full-time $15,160; part-time $632 per credit. *Required fees:* $1188; $34 per credit. $184 per semester. *Financial support:* In 2011–12, 1 fellowship (averaging $5,000 per year) was awarded; Federal Work-Study and institutionally sponsored loans also available. Financial award application deadline: 8/1; financial award applicants required to submit FAFSA. *Faculty research:* Multi-sensory teaching methods, volunteer tutoring programs for struggling readers, school readiness and transition, math/science/technology, university-school partnerships. *Unit head:* Dr. Andrea Noel, Chair, 845-257-2860, E-mail: noela@newpaltz.edu. *Application contact:* Caroline Murphy, Graduate Admissions Advisor, 845-257-3285, Fax: 845-257-3284, E-mail: gradschool@newpaltz.edu. Web site: http://www.newpaltz.edu/elementaryed/.

State University of New York at Oswego, Graduate Studies, School of Education, Department of Curriculum and Instruction, Oswego, NY 13126. Offers adolescence education (MST); art education (MAT); childhood education (MST); elementary education (MS Ed); literacy education (MS Ed); secondary education (MS Ed); special education (MS Ed). Part-time and evening/weekend programs available. *Degree requirements:* For master's, comprehensive exam (for some programs), thesis optional. *Entrance requirements:* For master's, GRE General Test, minimum GPA of 2.7, provisional teaching certificate. Additional exam requirements/recommendations for international students: Required—TOEFL (minimum score 560 paper-based; 220 computer-based). *Faculty research:* Classroom applications for microcomputers; classroom questioning, wait-time, and achievement; values clarification and academic achievement.

State University of New York at Plattsburgh, Division of Education, Health, and Human Services, Program in Teacher Education: Adolescence MST, Plattsburgh, NY 12901-2681. Offers adolescence education (MST); biology 7-12 (MST); chemistry 7-12 (MST); earth science 7-12 (MST); English 7-12 (MST); French 7-12 (MST); mathematics 7-12 (MST); physics 7-12 (MST); social studies 7-12 (MST); Spanish 7-12 (MST). *Accreditation:* Teacher Education Accreditation Council. Part-time and evening/weekend programs available. *Students:* 53 full-time (26 women), 5 part-time (4 women). Average age 29. *Entrance requirements:* For master's, minimum GPA of 2.75. Additional exam requirements/recommendations for international students: Required—TOEFL. *Application deadline:* For fall admission, 2/15 priority date for domestic students. Applications are processed on a rolling basis. Application fee: $75. *Financial support:* Application deadline: 4/15; applicants required to submit FAFSA. *Unit head:* Dr. Robert Ackland, Coordinator, 518-564-5131, E-mail: acklanrt@plattsburgh.edu. *Application contact:* Marguerite Adelman, Assistant Director, Graduate Admissions, 518-564-4723, Fax: 518-564-4722, E-mail: adelmaml@plattsburgh.edu.

State University of New York at Plattsburgh, Division of Education, Health, and Human Services, Program in Teacher Education: Childhood MST, Plattsburgh, NY 12901-2681. Offers childhood education (grades 1-6) (MST). *Accreditation:* Teacher Education Accreditation Council. Part-time and evening/weekend programs available. *Students:* 21 full-time (17 women), 2 part-time (both women). Average age 31. *Entrance requirements:* For master's, minimum GPA of 2.75. Additional exam requirements/recommendations for international students: Required—TOEFL. *Application deadline:* For fall admission, 2/15 priority date for domestic students. Applications are processed on a rolling basis. Application fee: $75. *Financial support:* Federal Work-Study available. Support available to part-time students. Financial award application deadline: 4/15; financial award applicants required to submit FAFSA. *Unit head:* Dr. Robert Ackland, Coordinator, 518-564-5131, E-mail: acklanrt@plattsburgh.edu. *Application contact:* Marguerite Adelman, Assistant Director, Graduate Admissions, 518-564-4723, Fax: 518-564-4722, E-mail: adelmaml@plattsburgh.edu.

State University of New York College at Geneseo, Graduate Studies, School of Education, Program in Elementary Education, Geneseo, NY 14454-1401. Offers MS Ed. Part-time and evening/weekend programs available. *Degree requirements:* For master's, thesis optional.

State University of New York College at Oneonta, Graduate Education, Division of Education, Department of Elementary Education and Reading, Oneonta, NY 13820-4015. Offers childhood education (MS Ed); literacy education (MS Ed). *Accreditation:* NCATE. Part-time and evening/weekend programs available. *Entrance requirements:* For master's, GRE General Test.

State University of New York College at Potsdam, School of Education and Professional Studies, Program in Curriculum and Instruction, Potsdam, NY 13676. Offers childhood education (MST); curriculum and instruction (MS Ed). *Accreditation:* NCATE. Postbaccalaureate distance learning degree programs offered (minimal on-campus study). *Faculty:* 14 full-time (12 women), 8 part-time/adjunct (4 women). *Students:* 136 full-time (105 women), 44 part-time (34 women); includes 9 minority (5 Black or African American, non-Hispanic/Latino; 1 American Indian or Alaska Native, non-Hispanic/Latino; 3 Hispanic/Latino), 75 international. 100 applicants, 99% accepted, 69 enrolled. In 2011, 146 master's awarded. *Degree requirements:* For master's, thesis (for some programs). *Entrance requirements:* For master's, minimum GPA of 2.75 in last 60 credit hours of undergraduate study. Additional exam requirements/recommendations for international students: Required—TOEFL (minimum score 550 paper-based; 213 computer-based; 80 iBT), IELTS (minimum score 6). *Application deadline:* For fall admission, 4/1 for domestic and international students; for winter admission, 10/15 for domestic and international students; for spring admission, 3/1 for domestic and international students. Applications are processed on a rolling basis. Application fee: $50. *Expenses:* Tuition, state resident: full-time $8870; part-time $370 per credit hour. Tuition, nonresident: full-time $15,160; part-time $632 per credit hour. *Required fees:* $1066; $44.10 per credit hour. One-time fee: $3. *Financial support:* Federal Work-Study, scholarships/grants, and unspecified assistantships available. Support available to part-time students. Financial award application deadline: 3/1; financial award applicants required to submit FAFSA. *Unit head:* Dr. Sandy Chadwick, Chairperson, 315-267-2502, Fax: 315-267-4802, E-mail: chadwisc@potsdam.edu. *Application contact:* Peter Cutler, Graduate Admissions Counselor, 315-267-2165, Fax: 315-267-4802, E-mail: graduate@potsdam.edu. Web site: http://www.potsdam.edu/academics/SOEPS/Curriculum/.

State University of New York College at Potsdam, School of Education and Professional Studies, Program in Special Education, Potsdam, NY 13676. Offers adolescence (grades 7-12) (MS Ed); childhood (grades 1-6) (MS Ed); early childhood (birth-grade 2) (MS Ed). *Accreditation:* NCATE. Part-time programs available. *Faculty:* 2 full-time (1 woman), 5 part-time/adjunct (4 women). *Students:* 19 full-time (15 women), 3 part-time (all women); includes 4 minority (2 American Indian or Alaska Native, non-Hispanic/Latino; 1 Hispanic/Latino; 1 Two or more races, non-Hispanic/Latino). 27 applicants, 100% accepted, 15 enrolled. In 2011, 18 master's awarded. *Degree requirements:* For master's, culminating experience. *Entrance requirements:* For master's, minimum GPA of 3.0 in last 60 hours of course work. Additional exam requirements/recommendations for international students: Required—TOEFL (minimum score 550 paper-based; 213 computer-based; 80 iBT), IELTS (minimum score 6). *Application deadline:* For fall admission, 4/1 for domestic and international students. Applications are processed on a rolling basis. Application fee: $50. *Expenses:* Tuition, state resident: full-time $8870; part-time $370 per credit hour. Tuition, nonresident: full-time $15,160; part-time $632 per credit hour. *Required fees:* $1066; $44.10 per credit hour. One-time fee: $3. *Financial support:* Unspecified assistantships available. Financial award application deadline: 3/1; financial award applicants required to submit FAFSA. *Unit head:* Dr. Dennis Conrad, Chairperson, 315-267-2916, Fax: 315-267-4802, E-mail: conradda@potsdam.edu. *Application contact:* Peter Cutler, Graduate Admissions Counselor, 315-267-2165, Fax: 315-267-4802, E-mail: graduate@potsdam.edu. Web site: http://www.potsdam.edu/academics/SOEPS/SpecialEd/msedspecialed.cfm.

Stephen F. Austin State University, Graduate School, College of Education, Department of Elementary Education, Program in Elementary Education, Nacogdoches, TX 75962. Offers M Ed. *Accreditation:* NCATE. *Degree requirements:* For master's, comprehensive exam. *Entrance requirements:* For master's, GRE General Test. Additional exam requirements/recommendations for international students: Required—TOEFL.

Sul Ross State University, Rio Grande College of Sul Ross State University, Alpine, TX 79832. Offers business administration (MBA); teacher education (M Ed), including bilingual education, counseling, educational diagnostics, elementary education, general education, reading, school administration, secondary education. Part-time and evening/weekend programs available. Postbaccalaureate distance learning degree programs offered (no on-campus study). *Faculty:* 11 full-time (3 women), 4 part-time/adjunct (3 women). *Students:* 45 full-time (36 women), 255 part-time (168 women); includes 218 minority (2 Black or African American, non-Hispanic/Latino; 1 American Indian or Alaska Native, non-Hispanic/Latino; 215 Hispanic/Latino), 1 international. Average age 36. In 2011, 47 master's awarded. *Degree requirements:* For master's, comprehensive exam, thesis optional, minimum GPA of 3.0. *Entrance requirements:* For master's, GMAT or GRE General Test, minimum GPA of 2.5 in last 60 hours of undergraduate work. Additional exam requirements/recommendations for international students: Required—TOEFL. *Application deadline:* Applications are processed on a rolling basis. Application fee: $0 ($50 for international students). *Financial support:* Career-related internships or fieldwork, Federal Work-Study, and institutionally sponsored loans available. Support available to part-time students. Financial award application deadline: 5/1; financial award applicants required to submit FAFSA. *Unit head:* Dr. Paul Sorrels, Associate Provost/Dean, 512-278-3339, Fax: 512-278-3330. *Application contact:* Claudia R. Wright, Director of Admissions and Records, 915-837-8050, Fax: 915-837-8431, E-mail: rcullins@sulross.edu.

Sul Ross State University, School of Professional Studies, Department of Teacher Education, Program in Elementary Education, Alpine, TX 79832. Offers M Ed. Part-time and evening/weekend programs available. *Degree requirements:* For master's, thesis optional. *Entrance requirements:* For master's, GMAT or GRE General Test, minimum GPA of 2.5 in last 60 hours of undergraduate work.

Teacher Education University, Graduate Programs, Winter Park, FL 32789. Offers educational leadership (MA); educational technology (MA); elementary education K-6 (MA); instructional strategies (MA Ed); school guidance and counseling (MA).

Teachers College, Columbia University, Graduate Faculty of Education, Department of Curriculum and Teaching, New York, NY 10027-6696. Offers childhood/disabilities (Certificate); curriculum and teaching (Ed M, MA, Ed D); early childhood education (Ed M, MA, Ed D); early childhood special education (Ed M, MA); elementary/childhood education, preservice (MA); giftedness (MA, Ed D); learning disabilities (Ed M, MA, Ed D); literacy specialist (MA). Part-time and evening/weekend programs available. *Students:* 168 full-time (140 women), 406 part-time (369 women); includes 170 minority (41 Black or African American, non-Hispanic/Latino; 1 American Indian or Alaska Native, non-Hispanic/Latino; 77 Asian, non-Hispanic/Latino; 51 Hispanic/Latino), 52 international. Average age 30. 541 applicants, 58% accepted, 130 enrolled. In 2011, 180 master's, 14 doctorates awarded. Terminal master's awarded for partial completion of doctoral program. *Degree requirements:* For doctorate, thesis/dissertation. *Entrance requirements:* For doctorate, GRE General Test or MAT. Application fee: $65. *Financial support:* Fellowships, research assistantships, teaching assistantships, career-related internships or fieldwork, Federal Work-Study, institutionally sponsored loans, tuition waivers (full and partial), and instructorships available. Support available to part-time students. Financial award application deadline: 2/1. *Faculty research:* Multicultural education, school improvement, reading in effective schools, urban education. *Unit head:* Marjorie Siegel, Chair, 212-678-3765. *Application contact:* Peter Shon, Assistant Director of Admission, 212-678-3305, Fax: 212-678-4171, E-mail: shon@exchange.tc.columbia.edu.

Temple University, College of Education, Department of Curriculum, Instruction, and Technology in Education, Philadelphia, PA 19122-6096. Offers applied behavioral analysis (MS Ed); career and technical education (MS Ed); early childhood education and elementary education (MS Ed); English education (MS Ed); language arts education (Ed D); math/science education (Ed D); mathematics education (MS Ed); science education (MS Ed); second and foreign language education (MS Ed); special education (MS Ed); teaching English as a second language (MS Ed). Part-time and evening/weekend programs available. *Faculty:* 19 full-time (12 women). *Students:* 30 full-time (23 women), 86 part-time (69 women); includes 12 minority (4 Black or African American, non-Hispanic/Latino; 2 Asian, non-Hispanic/Latino; 5 Hispanic/Latino; 1 Two or more races, non-Hispanic/Latino), 5 international. 82 applicants, 71% accepted, 51 enrolled. In 2011, 181 master's, 16 doctorates awarded. Terminal master's awarded for partial completion of doctoral program. *Degree requirements:* For master's, thesis or alternative; for doctorate, thesis/dissertation. *Entrance requirements:* For master's and doctorate, GRE General Test or MAT, minimum GPA of 3.0. Additional exam requirements/recommendations for international students: Required—TOEFL (minimum score 550 paper-based; 213 computer-based; 79 iBT). *Application deadline:* For fall admission, 4/1 for domestic students, 12/15 for international students; for spring admission, 10/1 for domestic students, 8/1 for international students. Application fee:

$50. Electronic applications accepted. *Expenses:* Tuition, state resident: full-time $12,366; part-time $687 per credit hour. Tuition, nonresident: full-time $17,298; part-time $961 per credit hour. *Required fees:* $590; $213 per year. *Financial support:* Fellowships, research assistantships with full tuition reimbursements, and teaching assistantships with full tuition reimbursements available. Financial award application deadline: 1/15; financial award applicants required to submit FAFSA. *Faculty research:* School improvement, problem-solving, literacy, language development. *Unit head:* Dr. Michael W. Smith, Chair, 215-204-6387, Fax: 215-204-1414, E-mail: mwsmith@temple.edu. *Application contact:* Dr. Margo Greicar, Director for Graduate Academic and Student Affairs, 215-204-8011, Fax: 215-204-4383, E-mail: margo.greicar@temple.edu. Web site: http://www.temple.edu/education/cite/.

Tennessee State University, The School of Graduate Studies and Research, College of Education, Department of Teaching and Learning, Nashville, TN 37209-1561. Offers curriculum and instruction (M Ed, Ed D); elementary education (M Ed, MA Ed, Ed D); special education (M Ed, MA Ed, Ed D). *Accreditation:* NCATE. *Degree requirements:* For doctorate, thesis/dissertation. *Entrance requirements:* For master's, GRE General Test, GRE Subject Test, or MAT, minimum GPA of 2.5; for doctorate, GRE General Test, GRE Subject Test, or MAT, minimum GPA of 3.25. Electronic applications accepted. *Faculty research:* Multicultural education, teacher education reform, whole language, interactive video teaching, English as a second language.

Tennessee Technological University, Graduate School, College of Education, Department of Curriculum and Instruction, Program in Elementary Education, Cookeville, TN 38505. Offers MA, Ed S. *Accreditation:* NCATE. Part-time and evening/weekend programs available. *Faculty:* 8 full-time (2 women). *Students:* 18 full-time (14 women), 21 part-time (15 women); includes 1 minority (Hispanic/Latino). Average age 27. 13 applicants, 85% accepted, 6 enrolled. In 2011, 8 degrees awarded. *Degree requirements:* For master's and Ed S, comprehensive exam, thesis or alternative. *Entrance requirements:* For master's and Ed S, MAT or GRE. Additional exam requirements/recommendations for international students: Required—TOEFL (minimum score 550 paper-based; 71 iBT), IELTS (minimum score 5.5), Pearson Test of English Academic. *Application deadline:* For fall admission, 8/1 for domestic students, 5/1 for international students; for spring admission, 12/1 for domestic students, 10/1 for international students. Application fee: $25 ($30 for international students). Electronic applications accepted. *Expenses:* Tuition, state resident: full-time $8094; part-time $422 per credit hour. Tuition, nonresident: full-time $20,574; part-time $1046 per credit hour. *Financial support:* In 2011–12, 1 fellowship (averaging $8,000 per year), research assistantships (averaging $4,000 per year), 1 teaching assistantship (averaging $4,000 per year) were awarded; career-related internships or fieldwork also available. Financial award application deadline: 4/1. *Faculty research:* Educational television art program. *Unit head:* Dr. Susan Gore, Interim Chairperson, 931-372-3181, Fax: 931-372-6270, E-mail: sgore@tntech.edu. *Application contact:* Shelia K. Kendrick, Coordinator of Graduate Admissions, 931-372-3808, Fax: 931-372-3497, E-mail: skendrick@tntech.edu.

Texas A&M University–Commerce, Graduate School, College of Education and Human Services, Department of Curriculum and Instruction, Commerce, TX 75429-3011. Offers bilingual/ESL education (M Ed, MS); early childhood education (M Ed, MS); elementary education (M Ed, MS); reading (M Ed, MS); secondary education (M Ed, MS); supervision, curriculum and instruction: elementary education (Ed D). MS and M Ed programs in early childhood education offered jointly with Texas Woman's University and University of North Texas. Part-time programs available. Terminal master's awarded for partial completion of doctoral program. *Degree requirements:* For master's, comprehensive exam, thesis (for some programs); for doctorate, 2 foreign languages, thesis/dissertation, departmental qualifying exam. *Entrance requirements:* For master's and doctorate, GRE General Test. Electronic applications accepted. *Faculty research:* Literacy and learning, early childhood, preservice teacher education, technology.

Texas A&M University–Corpus Christi, Graduate Studies and Research, College of Education, Program in Elementary Education, Corpus Christi, TX 78412-5503. Offers MS. Part-time and evening/weekend programs available. *Degree requirements:* For master's, comprehensive exam, thesis (for some programs). *Entrance requirements:* For master's, GRE General Test. Additional exam requirements/recommendations for international students: Required—TOEFL. Electronic applications accepted.

Texas A&M University–Kingsville, College of Graduate Studies, College of Education, Department of Education, Program in Elementary Education, Kingsville, TX 78363. Offers MA, MS. Part-time and evening/weekend programs available. *Degree requirements:* For master's, comprehensive exam, thesis or alternative. *Entrance requirements:* For master's, GRE General Test, MAT, minimum GPA of 3.0. *Faculty research:* Strategies in elementary science, manipulatives in the classroom, latest developments.

Texas Christian University, College of Education, Program in Elementary Education, Fort Worth, TX 76129-0002. Offers M Ed. Part-time and evening/weekend programs available. *Faculty:* 27 full-time (21 women), 1 part-time/adjunct. *Students:* 1 (woman) full-time, 3 part-time (all women); includes 1 minority (Black or African American, non-Hispanic/Latino). Average age 28. 15 applicants, 40% accepted, 4 enrolled. *Degree requirements:* For master's, comprehensive exam, thesis. *Entrance requirements:* Additional exam requirements/recommendations for international students: Required—TOEFL (minimum score 550 paper-based; 213 computer-based; 80 iBT). *Application deadline:* For fall admission, 11/15 for domestic and international students; for spring admission, 3/1 for domestic and international students. Application fee: $60. Electronic applications accepted. *Expenses: Tuition:* Full-time $20,250; part-time $1125 per credit hour. Part-time tuition and fees vary according to course load and program. *Financial support:* Teaching assistantships with full tuition reimbursements, career-related internships or fieldwork, scholarships/grants, and unspecified assistantships available. Financial award application deadline: 3/1. *Unit head:* Dr. Jan Lacina, Associate Dean, 817-257-6786, E-mail: j.lacina@tcu.edu. *Application contact:* Patricia Garcia, Academic Program Specialist, 817-257-7661, E-mail: p.m.garcia@tcu.edu.

Texas Christian University, College of Education, Program in Elementary (Four-One Option), Fort Worth, TX 76129-0002. Offers M Ed. Part-time and evening/weekend programs available. *Faculty:* 27 full-time (21 women), 1 part-time/adjunct. *Students:* 9 full-time (all women); includes 1 minority (Black or African American, non-Hispanic/Latino). Average age 22. 10 applicants, 90% accepted, 9 enrolled. In 2011, 7 master's awarded. *Degree requirements:* For master's, oral exam. *Entrance requirements:* Additional exam requirements/recommendations for international students: Required—TOEFL (minimum score 550 paper-based; 213 computer-based; 80 iBT). *Application deadline:* For fall admission, 11/16 for domestic and international students; for spring admission, 3/1 for domestic and international students. Application fee: $60. Electronic applications accepted. *Expenses: Tuition:* Full-time $20,250; part-time $1125 per credit hour. Part-time tuition and fees vary according to course load and program. *Financial support:* Teaching assistantships with full tuition reimbursements, career-related internships or fieldwork, scholarships/grants, and unspecified assistantships available. Financial award application deadline: 3/1. *Unit head:* Dr. Jan Lacina, Associate Dean, 817-257-6786, E-mail: j.lacina@tcu.edu. *Application contact:* Patricia Garcia, Academic Program Specialist, 817-257-7661, E-mail: p.m.garcia@tcu.edu.

Texas State University–San Marcos, Graduate School, College of Education, Department of Curriculum and Instruction, Program in Elementary Education, San Marcos, TX 78666. Offers M Ed, MA. Part-time and evening/weekend programs available. *Faculty:* 19 full-time (15 women), 11 part-time/adjunct (all women). *Students:* 108 full-time (95 women), 159 part-time (149 women); includes 71 minority (13 Black or African American, non-Hispanic/Latino; 8 Asian, non-Hispanic/Latino; 47 Hispanic/Latino; 3 Two or more races, non-Hispanic/Latino), 1 international. Average age 32. 106 applicants, 80% accepted, 43 enrolled. In 2011, 173 master's awarded. *Degree requirements:* For master's, comprehensive exam, thesis (for some programs). *Entrance requirements:* For master's, minimum GPA of 2.75 in last 60 hours of course work, teaching experience. Additional exam requirements/recommendations for international students: Required—TOEFL (minimum score 550 paper-based; 213 computer-based; 78 iBT). *Application deadline:* For fall admission, 6/15 priority date for domestic students, 6/1 for international students; for spring admission, 10/15 priority date for domestic students, 10/1 for international students. Applications are processed on a rolling basis. Application fee: $40 ($90 for international students). Electronic applications accepted. *Expenses:* Tuition, state resident: full-time $6408; part-time $3204 per semester. Tuition, nonresident: full-time $14,832; part-time $7416 per semester. *Required fees:* $1824; $912 per semester. Tuition and fees vary according to course load. *Financial support:* In 2011–12, 135 students received support, including 11 research assistantships (averaging $10,152 per year), 5 teaching assistantships (averaging $12,366 per year); career-related internships or fieldwork, Federal Work-Study, and institutionally sponsored loans also available. Support available to part-time students. Financial award application deadline: 4/1; financial award applicants required to submit FAFSA. *Faculty research:* Bilingual, general elementary, and early childhood education; gifted and talented education. *Unit head:* Dr. Priscilla Crawford, Graduate Advisor, 512-245-2041, Fax: 512-245-7911, E-mail: ph12@txstate.edu. *Application contact:* Dr. J. Michael Willoughby, Dean of Graduate School, 512-245-2581, Fax: 512-245-8365, E-mail: gradcollege@txstate.edu. Web site: http://www.education.txstate.edu/ci/degrees-programs/graduate/elementary-education.html.

Texas State University–San Marcos, Graduate School, College of Education, Department of Curriculum and Instruction, Program in Elementary Education-Bilingual/Bicultural, San Marcos, TX 78666. Offers M Ed, MA. Part-time programs available. *Faculty:* 5 full-time (all women). *Students:* 7 full-time (6 women), 14 part-time (11 women); includes 15 minority (all Hispanic/Latino), 2 international. Average age 29. 24 applicants, 58% accepted, 7 enrolled. In 2011, 11 master's awarded. *Degree requirements:* For master's, comprehensive exam, thesis optional. *Entrance requirements:* For master's, minimum GPA of 2.75 in last 60 hours of course work, teaching experience. Additional exam requirements/recommendations for international students: Required—TOEFL (minimum score 550 paper-based; 213 computer-based; 78 iBT). *Application deadline:* For fall admission, 6/15 priority date for domestic students, 6/1 for international students; for spring admission, 10/15 priority date for domestic students, 10/1 for international students. Applications are processed on a rolling basis. Application fee: $40 ($90 for international students). Electronic applications accepted. *Expenses:* Tuition, state resident: full-time $6408; part-time $3204 per semester. Tuition, nonresident: full-time $14,832; part-time $7416 per semester. *Required fees:* $1824; $912 per semester. Tuition and fees vary according to course load. *Financial support:* In 2011–12, 11 students received support, including 1 teaching assistantship (averaging $10,152 per year); career-related internships or fieldwork, Federal Work-Study, institutionally sponsored loans, and unspecified assistantships also available. Support available to part-time students. Financial award application deadline: 4/1; financial award applicants required to submit FAFSA. *Unit head:* Dr. Roxanne Allsup, Graduate Advisor, 512-245-2041, Fax: 512-245-7911, E-mail: ra17@txstate.edu. *Application contact:* Dr. J. Michael Willoughby, Dean of Graduate School, 512-245-2581, Fax: 512-245-8365, E-mail: gradcollege@txstate.edu. Web site: http://www.education.txstate.edu/ci/degrees-programs/graduate/elementary-education.html.

Texas State University–San Marcos, Graduate School, Interdisciplinary Studies Program in Elementary Mathematics, Science, and Technology, San Marcos, TX 78666. Offers MSIS. *Students:* 2 full-time (both women), 2 part-time (both women). Average age 32. 5 applicants, 40% accepted, 2 enrolled. *Degree requirements:* For master's, comprehensive exam, thesis optional. *Entrance requirements:* For master's, minimum GPA of 2.75 in the last 60 hours of undergraduate work. Additional exam requirements/recommendations for international students: Required—TOEFL (minimum score 550 paper-based; 213 computer-based; 78 iBT). *Application deadline:* For fall admission, 6/15 priority date for domestic students, 6/1 for international students; for spring admission, 10/15 priority date for domestic students, 10/1 for international students. Applications are processed on a rolling basis. Application fee: $40 ($90 for international students). Electronic applications accepted. *Expenses:* Tuition, state resident: full-time $6408; part-time $3204 per semester. Tuition, nonresident: full-time $14,832; part-time $7416 per semester. *Required fees:* $1824; $912 per semester. Tuition and fees vary according to course load. *Financial support:* Research assistantships, teaching assistantships, Federal Work-Study, institutionally sponsored loans, scholarships/grants, health care benefits, and unspecified assistantships available. Support available to part-time students. Financial award application deadline: 4/1; financial award applicants required to submit FAFSA. *Unit head:* Dr. Sandra Mody, Acting Dean, 512-245-3360, Fax: 512-245-8095, E-mail: sw04@txstate.edu. *Application contact:* Dr. J. Michael Willoughby, Dean of Graduate School, 512-245-2581, Fax: 512-245-8365, E-mail: gradcollege@txstate.edu.

Texas Tech University, Graduate School, College of Education, Department of Curriculum and Instruction, Lubbock, TX 79409. Offers bilingual education (M Ed); curriculum and instruction (M Ed, PhD); elementary education (M Ed); language/literacy education (M Ed); secondary education (M Ed). *Accreditation:* NCATE. Part-time programs available. *Students:* 69 full-time (50 women), 115 part-time (91 women); includes 62 minority (9 Black or African American, non-Hispanic/Latino; 3 Asian, non-Hispanic/Latino; 47 Hispanic/Latino; 3 Two or more races, non-Hispanic/Latino), 18 international. Average age 34. 95 applicants, 41% accepted, 26 enrolled. In 2011, 62 master's, 9 doctorates awarded. *Degree requirements:* For master's, comprehensive written exam with 36 hours of course credit or thesis (6 hours) with 30 hours of course credit; for doctorate, thesis/dissertation. *Entrance requirements:* For doctorate, GRE General Test. Additional exam requirements/recommendations for international students: Required—TOEFL (minimum score 550 paper-based; 213 computer-based; 79 iBT). *Application deadline:* For fall admission, 6/1 priority date for domestic students, 1/15 for international students; for spring admission, 9/1 priority date for domestic students, 6/15 for international students. Applications are processed on a rolling basis. Application fee: $50 ($75 for international students). Electronic applications accepted. *Expenses:* Tuition, state resident: full-time $5899; part-time $245.80 per credit hour. Tuition, nonresident: full-time $13,411; part-time $558.80 per credit hour. *Required fees:* $2680.60; $86.50 per credit hour. $920.30 per semester. *Financial support:* In 2011–12, 58 students received support. Application deadline: 4/15; applicants required to submit FAFSA. *Faculty research:* Multicultural foundations of education, teacher education, instruction and pedagogy in subject areas, curriculum theory, language and literary. *Total annual research expenditures:* $948,943. *Unit head:* Dr. Margaret A. Price, Interim Chair, 806-742-1997 Ext. 318, Fax: 806-742-2179, E-mail: peggie.price@ttu.edu.

Application contact: Stephenie Allyn McDaniel, Administrative Assistant, 806-742-1988 Ext. 434, Fax: 806-742-2179, E-mail: stephenie.mcdaniel@ttu.edu.

Towson University, Program in Elementary Education, Towson, MD 21252-0001. Offers M Ed. *Accreditation:* NCATE. Part-time and evening/weekend programs available. *Students:* 60 part-time (58 women); includes 9 minority (5 Black or African American, non-Hispanic/Latino; 3 Hispanic/Latino; 1 Native Hawaiian or other Pacific Islander, non-Hispanic/Latino). *Degree requirements:* For master's, capstone project or thesis. *Entrance requirements:* For master's, minimum GPA of 3.0, bachelor's degree in education, certified in teaching or eligibility for certification. Additional exam requirements/recommendations for international students: Required—TOEFL. *Application deadline:* Applications are processed on a rolling basis. Application fee: $50. Electronic applications accepted. *Expenses:* Tuition, state resident: part-time $337 per credit. Tuition, nonresident: part-time $709 per credit. *Required fees:* $99 per credit. *Financial support:* Federal Work-Study and unspecified assistantships available. Financial award application deadline: 4/1; financial award applicants required to submit FAFSA. *Unit head:* Linda Emerick, Graduate Program Director, 410-704-4251, Fax: 410-704-2733, E-mail: eledmed@towson.edu.

Trevecca Nazarene University, College of Lifelong Learning, School of Education, Major in Teaching, Nashville, TN 37210-2877. Offers teaching 7-12 (MAT); teaching K-6 (MAT). Part-time and evening/weekend programs available. *Students:* 207 full-time (159 women), 11 part-time (9 women); includes 34 minority (29 Black or African American, non-Hispanic/Latino; 3 Hispanic/Latino; 2 Two or more races, non-Hispanic/Latino), 1 international. In 2011, 104 master's awarded. *Degree requirements:* For master's, exit assessment, student teaching. *Entrance requirements:* For master's, GRE General Test, MAT, PRAXIS I: Pre-Professional Skills Test, minimum GPA of 2.7, 2 letters of reference. Additional exam requirements/recommendations for international students: Required—TOEFL (minimum score 550 paper-based; 213 computer-based). *Application deadline:* Applications are processed on a rolling basis. Application fee: $25. *Expenses:* Contact institution. *Financial support:* Applicants required to submit FAFSA. *Unit head:* Dr. Esther Swink, Dean, School of Education/Director of Graduate Education Programs, 615-248-1201, Fax: 615-248-1597, E-mail: admissions_ged@trevecca.edu. *Application contact:* Melanie Eaton, Admissions, 615-248-1498, E-mail: admissions_ged@trevecca.edu. Web site: http://www.trevecca.edu/soe.

Trinity Washington University, School of Education, Washington, DC 20017-1094. Offers counseling (MA); early childhood education (MAT); educating for change (M Ed); educational administration (MSA); elementary education (MAT); school counseling (MA); secondary education (MAT), including English, social studies; special education (MAT); teaching English as a second language (MAT); teaching English to speakers of other languages (M Ed); the teaching of reading (M Ed). *Accreditation:* NCATE. Part-time and evening/weekend programs available. *Degree requirements:* For master's, thesis (for some programs), capstone project(s). *Entrance requirements:* For master's, PRAXIS I, minimum GPA of 2.8. Additional exam requirements/recommendations for international students: Required—TOEFL (minimum score 550 paper-based; 213 computer-based). *Faculty research:* Technology, literacy, special education, organizations, inclusion models.

Troy University, Graduate School, College of Education, Program in K–6 Elementary and Collaborative Education, Troy, AL 36082. Offers alternative K-6 elementary (MS); elementary education (Ed S); traditional K-6 elementary (MS). *Accreditation:* NCATE. Part-time and evening/weekend programs available. *Students:* 83 full-time (80 women), 133 part-time (123 women); includes 77 minority (69 Black or African American, non-Hispanic/Latino; 2 American Indian or Alaska Native, non-Hispanic/Latino; 4 Hispanic/Latino; 2 Two or more races, non-Hispanic/Latino). Average age 31. 104 applicants, 87% accepted, 39 enrolled. In 2011, 119 master's, 22 other advanced degrees awarded. *Degree requirements:* For master's, comprehensive exam, thesis. *Entrance requirements:* For master's, minimum GPA of 2.5, bachelor's degree; for Ed S, GRE General Test or MAT, Alabama Class A certificate or equivalent, minimum graduate GPA of 3.0. Additional exam requirements/recommendations for international students: Required—TOEFL (minimum score 523 paper-based; 193 computer-based; 70 iBT), IELTS (minimum score 6). *Application deadline:* Applications are processed on a rolling basis. Application fee: $50. Electronic applications accepted. *Expenses:* Tuition, state resident: full-time $6960; part-time $290 per credit hour. Tuition, nonresident: full-time $13,920; part-time $580 per credit hour. *Required fees:* $386 per term. *Financial support:* Available to part-time students. Applicants required to submit FAFSA. *Unit head:* Dr. Jan Oliver, Professor, 334-670-3444, Fax: 334-670-3474, E-mail: oliverj@troy.edu. *Application contact:* Brenda K. Campbell, Director of Graduate Admissions, 334-670-3178, Fax: 334-670-3733, E-mail: bcamp@troy.edu.

Union College, Graduate Programs, Department of Education, Program in Elementary Education, Barbourville, KY 40906-1499. Offers MA. *Degree requirements:* For master's, thesis optional. *Entrance requirements:* For master's, GRE General Test, NTE.

Universidad del Este, Graduate School, Carolina, PR 00984. Offers accounting (MBA); adult education (M Ed); agribusiness (MBA); criminal justice and criminology (MA); curriculum and instruction - early education (M Ed); curriculum and instruction - elementary (M Ed); curriculum and instruction - English (M Ed); curriculum and instruction - Spanish (M Ed); human resources (MBA); information security management (MBA); information technology and Web business development (MBA); management (MBA); public policy (MPA); social work (MA), including clinical social work; special education (M Ed); strategic leadership (MBA).

Universidad Metropolitana, School of Education, Program in Teaching of Physical Education, San Juan, PR 00928-1150. Offers teaching of adult physical education (M Ed); teaching of elementary physical education (M Ed); teaching of secondary physical education (M Ed). *Degree requirements:* For master's, thesis or alternative. *Entrance requirements:* For master's, EXADEP, interview. Electronic applications accepted.

Université de Sherbrooke, Faculty of Education, Program in Elementary Education, Sherbrooke, QC J1K 2R1, Canada. Offers M Ed, Diploma. Part-time and evening/weekend programs available. *Degree requirements:* For master's, thesis.

University at Buffalo, the State University of New York, Graduate School, Graduate School of Education, Department of Learning and Instruction, Buffalo, NY 14260. Offers biology education (Ed M, Certificate); chemistry education (Ed M, Certificate); childhood education (Ed M); childhood education with bilingual extension (Ed M); early childhood education (Ed M); early childhood education with bilingual extension (birth-grade 2) (Ed M); earth science education (Ed M, Certificate); educational technology and new literacies (Certificate); educational technology and new literacies (online) (Certificate); elementary education (Ed D, PhD); English education (Ed M, PhD, Certificate); English for speakers of other languages (Ed M); foreign and second language education (PhD); French education (Ed M, Certificate); general education (Ed M); German education (Ed M, Certificate); gifted education (online) (Certificate); Latin education (Ed M, Certificate); literacy teaching and learning (Certificate); literary specialist (Ed M); mathematics education (Ed M, PhD, Certificate); music education (Ed M, Certificate); physics education (Ed M, Certificate); reading education (PhD); science and the public (online) (Ed M); science education (PhD); social studies education (Ed M, Certificate); Spanish education (Ed M, Certificate); special education (PhD); teaching and leading for diversity (Certificate); teaching English to speakers of other languages (Ed M). Part-time and evening/weekend programs available. Postbaccalaureate distance learning degree programs offered (no on-campus study). *Faculty:* 32 full-time (23 women), 54 part-time/adjunct (43 women). *Students:* 294 full-time (222 women), 350 part-time (261 women); includes 75 minority (19 Black or African American, non-Hispanic/Latino; 6 American Indian or Alaska Native, non-Hispanic/Latino; 40 Asian, non-Hispanic/Latino; 10 Hispanic/Latino), 76 international. Average age 29. 548 applicants, 52% accepted, 253 enrolled. In 2011, 225 master's, 17 doctorates, 37 other advanced degrees awarded. *Degree requirements:* For master's, comprehensive exam; for doctorate, thesis/dissertation, research analysis exam, research experience component. *Entrance requirements:* For doctorate, GRE General Test or MAT, interview, writing sample, letters of recommendation. Additional exam requirements/recommendations for international students: Required—TOEFL (minimum score 600 paper-based; 96 iBT). *Application deadline:* For fall admission, 2/1 priority date for domestic students, 2/1 for international students; for spring admission, 11/15 priority date for domestic students, 10/1 for international students. Applications are processed on a rolling basis. Application fee: $50. Electronic applications accepted. *Financial support:* In 2011–12, 40 fellowships (averaging $12,991 per year), 46 research assistantships (averaging $10,986 per year) were awarded; teaching assistantships with full tuition reimbursements, career-related internships or fieldwork, Federal Work-Study, institutionally sponsored loans, scholarships/grants, and unspecified assistantships also available. Financial award application deadline: 2/28; financial award applicants required to submit FAFSA. *Faculty research:* Science assessment, foreign language teaching and learning, early learning, new literacies, gender and education. *Unit head:* Dr. Julie Sarama, Chair, 716-645-2455, Fax: 716-645-3161, E-mail: jcollins@buffalo.edu. *Application contact:* Cathy Dimino, Admissions Assistant, 716-645-2110, Fax: 716-645-7937, E-mail: cadimino@buffalo.edu.

The University of Akron, Graduate School, College of Education, Department of Curricular and Instructional Studies, Program in Elementary Education, Akron, OH 44325. Offers elementary education (PhD); elementary education - literacy (MA); elementary education with licensure (MS). *Accreditation:* NCATE. *Students:* 13 full-time (12 women), 76 part-time (67 women); includes 9 minority (3 Black or African American, non-Hispanic/Latino; 3 Asian, non-Hispanic/Latino; 1 Hispanic/Latino; 2 Two or more races, non-Hispanic/Latino), 2 international. Average age 37. 23 applicants, 65% accepted, 10 enrolled. In 2011, 46 master's, 1 doctorate awarded. *Degree requirements:* For master's, comprehensive exam, thesis optional; for doctorate, variable foreign language requirement, comprehensive exam, thesis/dissertation, written and oral exams. *Entrance requirements:* For master's, minimum GPA of 2.75, valid teaching license; for doctorate, MAT or GRE, minimum GPA of 3.5, three letters of recommendation, statement of purpose indicating career goals and research interest, controlled department writing sample, completion of Agreement to Advise Form, current curriculum vitae, at least three years of teaching experience. Additional exam requirements/recommendations for international students: Required—TOEFL (minimum score 550 paper-based; 213 computer-based; 79 iBT). *Application deadline:* For fall admission, 3/1 for domestic and international students; for spring admission, 10/1 for domestic and international students. Applications are processed on a rolling basis. Application fee: $30 ($40 for international students). Electronic applications accepted. *Expenses:* Tuition, state resident: full-time $7038; part-time $391 per credit hour. Tuition, nonresident: full-time $12,051; part-time $670 per credit hour. *Required fees:* $1274; $34 per credit hour. *Unit head:* Dr. Bridgie Ford, Chair, 330-972-6967, E-mail: alexis2@uakron.edu. *Application contact:* Dr. Mark Tausig, Associate Dean, 330-972-6266, Fax: 330-972-6475, E-mail: mtausig@uakron.edu.

The University of Alabama, Graduate School, College of Education, Department of Curriculum and Instruction, Tuscaloosa, AL 35487. Offers elementary education (MA, Ed D, PhD, Ed S); secondary education (MA, Ed D, PhD, Ed S). Evening/weekend programs available. Postbaccalaureate distance learning degree programs offered (minimal on-campus study). *Faculty:* 21 full-time (14 women). *Students:* 94 full-time (65 women), 138 part-time (117 women); includes 39 minority (23 Black or African American, non-Hispanic/Latino; 2 Asian, non-Hispanic/Latino; 9 Hispanic/Latino; 5 Two or more races, non-Hispanic/Latino), 7 international. Average age 33. 110 applicants, 72% accepted, 46 enrolled. In 2011, 65 master's, 12 doctorates, 12 other advanced degrees awarded. *Degree requirements:* For master's, comprehensive exam, thesis (for some programs); for doctorate, comprehensive exam, thesis/dissertation; for Ed S, comprehensive exam, thesis optional. *Entrance requirements:* For master's, doctorate, and Ed S, MAT and/or GRE. Additional exam requirements/recommendations for international students: Recommended—TOEFL (minimum score 550 paper-based; 213 computer-based), IELTS (minimum score 6.5). *Application deadline:* For fall admission, 7/1 priority date for domestic students, 1/15 for international students; for spring admission, 11/1 priority date for domestic students, 6/1 for international students. Application fee: $50 ($60 for international students). Electronic applications accepted. *Expenses:* Tuition, state resident: full-time $8600. Tuition, nonresident: full-time $21,900. *Financial support:* In 2011–12, 14 students received support, including 10 research assistantships with tuition reimbursements available (averaging $9,844 per year), 4 teaching assistantships with tuition reimbursements available (averaging $9,844 per year); institutionally sponsored loans, traineeships, and unspecified assistantships also available. *Faculty research:* Teacher education, diversity, integration of curriculum, technology. *Total annual research expenditures:* $458,059. *Unit head:* Dr. Miguel Mantero, Chair, 205-348-1402, Fax: 205-348-9863, E-mail: mmantero@bamaed.ua.edu. *Application contact:* Dr. Kathy S. Wetzel, Assistant Dean for Student Services, 205-348-1154, Fax: 205-348-0080, E-mail: kwetzel@bamaed.ua.edu.

The University of Alabama at Birmingham, College of Arts and Sciences, School of Education, Program in Elementary Education, Birmingham, AL 35294. Offers MA Ed. *Accreditation:* NCATE. *Degree requirements:* For master's, thesis optional. *Entrance requirements:* For master's, GRE General Test, MAT, or NTE, minimum GPA of 3.0. *Application deadline:* Applications are processed on a rolling basis. Electronic applications accepted. *Expenses:* Tuition, state resident: full-time $5922; part-time $309 per hour. Tuition, nonresident: full-time $13,428; part-time $726 per hour. Tuition and fees vary according to program. *Unit head:* Dr. Lynn Kirkland, Chair, 205-934-8358. Web site: http://www.uab.edu/ci/ele.

University of Alaska Fairbanks, School of Education, Program in Education, Fairbanks, AK 99775. Offers curriculum and instruction (M Ed); education (M Ed, Graduate Certificate); elementary education (M Ed); language and literacy (M Ed); reading (M Ed); secondary education (M Ed); special education (M Ed). *Faculty:* 25 full-time (15 women). *Students:* 30 full-time (23 women), 69 part-time (50 women); includes 17 minority (7 American Indian or Alaska Native, non-Hispanic/Latino; 1 Asian, non-Hispanic/Latino; 2 Hispanic/Latino; 1 Native Hawaiian or other Pacific Islander, non-Hispanic/Latino; 6 Two or more races, non-Hispanic/Latino), 1 international. Average age 33. 68 applicants, 76% accepted, 37 enrolled. In 2011, 26 master's, 22 other advanced degrees awarded. *Degree requirements:* For master's, comprehensive exam, thesis, oral defense. *Entrance requirements:* Additional exam requirements/recommendations for international students: Required—TOEFL (minimum score 550 paper-based; 213 computer-based; 80 iBT). *Application deadline:* For fall admission, 5/1 for domestic students, 3/1 for international students; for spring admission, 10/15 for domestic students, 8/1 for international students. Applications are processed on a rolling basis. Application fee: $60. Electronic applications accepted. *Expenses:* Tuition, state resident: full-time $6696; part-time $372 per credit. Tuition, nonresident: full-time $13,680; part-time $760 per credit. Tuition and fees vary according to course load and reciprocity agreements. *Financial support:* Fellowships with tuition reimbursements, research assistantships with tuition reimbursements, teaching assistantships with tuition reimbursements, career-related internships or fieldwork, Federal Work-Study, scholarships/grants, health care benefits, and unspecified assistantships available. Support available to part-time students. Financial award application deadline: 6/1; financial award applicants required to submit FAFSA. *Unit head:* Allan Morotti, Interim Dean, 907-474-7341, Fax: 907-474-5451, E-mail: uaf-soe-school@alaska.edu. *Application contact:* Mike Earnest, Director of Admissions, 907-474-7500, Fax: 907-474-5379, E-mail: admissions@uaf.edu. Web site: http://www.uaf.edu/educ/graduate/counseling.html.

University of Alaska Southeast, Graduate Programs, Program in Education, Juneau, AK 99801. Offers early childhood education (M Ed, MAT); educational technology (M Ed); elementary education (MAT); reading (M Ed); secondary education (MAT). *Accreditation:* NCATE. Part-time and evening/weekend programs available. Postbaccalaureate distance learning degree programs offered (minimal on-campus study). *Degree requirements:* For master's, comprehensive exam or project, portfolio. *Entrance requirements:* For master's, PRAXIS, minimum GPA of 3.0, writing sample, letters of recommendation. Electronic applications accepted. *Faculty research:* Applied classroom research, culturally responsive practices, action research, teaching effectiveness.

University of Alberta, Faculty of Graduate Studies and Research, Department of Elementary Education, Edmonton, AB T6G 2E1, Canada. Offers M Ed, Ed D, PhD. Part-time and evening/weekend programs available. Postbaccalaureate distance learning degree programs offered (minimal on-campus study). *Degree requirements:* For master's, thesis (for some programs); for doctorate, thesis/dissertation. *Entrance requirements:* For master's and doctorate, 1 year of teaching experience, minimum GPA of 6.5 on a 9.0 scale. *Faculty research:* Literacy education, early childhood education, teacher education, curriculum studies, instructional studies.

University of Arkansas, Graduate School, College of Education and Health Professions, Department of Curriculum and Instruction, Program in Elementary Education, Fayetteville, AR 72701-1201. Offers M Ed, Ed S. *Accreditation:* NCATE. *Students:* 5 full-time (all women), 8 part-time (all women); includes 2 minority (both Black or African American, non-Hispanic/Latino), 1 international. In 2011, 4 master's awarded. *Application deadline:* For fall admission, 4/1 for international students; for spring admission, 10/1 for international students. Applications are processed on a rolling basis. Application fee: $40 ($50 for international students). Electronic applications accepted. *Financial support:* Fellowships, research assistantships, teaching assistantships, career-related internships or fieldwork, and Federal Work-Study available. Support available to part-time students. Financial award application deadline: 4/1; financial award applicants required to submit FAFSA. *Unit head:* Dr. Michael Daugherty, Unit Head, 479-575-4201, E-mail: mkd03@uark.edu. *Application contact:* Dr. Barbara Gartin, Graduate Coordinator, 479-575-7525, Fax: 479-575-6676, E-mail: bgartin@uark.edu. Web site: http://cied.uark.edu/.

University of Bridgeport, School of Education, Department of Education, Bridgeport, CT 06604. Offers education (MS); educational management (Ed D, Diploma), including intermediate administrator or supervisor (Diploma), leadership (Ed D); elementary education (MS, Diploma), including early childhood education, elementary education; middle school education (MS); music education (MS); remedial reading and language arts (Diploma); secondary education (MS, Diploma), including computer specialist (Diploma), international education (Diploma), reading specialist, secondary education. Part-time and evening/weekend programs available. *Faculty:* 12 full-time (5 women), 108 part-time/adjunct (60 women). *Students:* 232 full-time (161 women), 216 part-time (160 women); includes 61 minority (21 Black or African American, non-Hispanic/Latino; 8 Asian, non-Hispanic/Latino; 22 Hispanic/Latino; 10 Two or more races, non-Hispanic/Latino), 34 international. Average age 30. 412 applicants, 63% accepted, 147 enrolled. In 2011, 216 master's, 7 other advanced degrees awarded. *Degree requirements:* For master's, final exam, final project, or thesis; for doctorate, comprehensive exam, thesis/dissertation; for Diploma, thesis or alternative, final project. *Entrance requirements:* For master's, minimum undergraduate QPA of 2.67; for doctorate, GRE, MAT; for Diploma, GRE General Test or MAT, minimum graduate QPA of 3.0. Additional exam requirements/recommendations for international students: Recommended—TOEFL (minimum score 550 paper-based; 213 computer-based; 80 iBT), IELTS (minimum score 6.5). *Application deadline:* For fall admission, 8/1 priority date for domestic students, 8/1 for international students; for spring admission, 12/1 priority date for domestic students, 12/1 for international students. Applications are processed on a rolling basis. Application fee: $50. Electronic applications accepted. *Expenses: Tuition:* Full-time $22,880; part-time $700 per credit. *Required fees:* $1870; $95 per semester. Tuition and fees vary according to course load and program. *Financial support:* In 2011–12, 120 students received support. Fellowships, research assistantships, teaching assistantships, career-related internships or fieldwork, Federal Work-Study, and institutionally sponsored loans available. Support available to part-time students. Financial award application deadline: 6/1; financial award applicants required to submit FAFSA. *Faculty research:* Self-concept, internship assessment, stress and situational development, follow-up of graduation, trend analysis. *Unit head:* Dr. Allen P. Cook, Dean, 203-576-4192, Fax: 203-576-4200, E-mail: acook@bridgeport.edu. *Application contact:* Karissa Peckham, Dean of Admissions, 203-576-4552, Fax: 203-576-4941, E-mail: admit@bridgeport.edu.

University of California, Irvine, Department of Education, Irvine, CA 92697. Offers educational administration (Ed D); educational administration and leadership (Ed D); elementary and secondary education (MAT). Part-time and evening/weekend programs available. *Students:* 246 full-time (185 women), 8 part-time (5 women); includes 121 minority (4 Black or African American, non-Hispanic/Latino; 1 American Indian or Alaska Native, non-Hispanic/Latino; 65 Asian, non-Hispanic/Latino; 37 Hispanic/Latino; 2 Native Hawaiian or other Pacific Islander, non-Hispanic/Latino; 12 Two or more races, non-Hispanic/Latino), 7 international. Average age 28. 455 applicants, 75% accepted, 185 enrolled. In 2011, 146 master's, 12 doctorates awarded. *Degree requirements:* For doctorate, thesis/dissertation. *Entrance requirements:* For master's, GRE, minimum GPA of 3.0; for doctorate, GRE General Test, minimum GPA of 3.0. Additional exam requirements/recommendations for international students: Required—TOEFL (minimum score 550 paper-based; 213 computer-based). *Application deadline:* For fall admission, 1/2 priority date for domestic students, 1/2 for international students. Application fee: $80 ($100 for international students). Electronic applications accepted. *Financial support:* Fellowships, research assistantships with full tuition reimbursements, institutionally sponsored loans, traineeships, health care benefits, and unspecified assistantships available. Financial award application deadline: 3/1; financial award applicants required to submit FAFSA. *Faculty research:* Education technology, learning theory, social theory, cultural diversity, postmodernism. *Unit head:* Deborah L. Vandell, Chair, 949-824-8026, Fax: 949-824-3968, E-mail: dvandell@uci.edu. *Application contact:* Sarah K. Singh, Credential Program Counselor, 949-824-6673, Fax: 949-824-9103, E-mail: sksingh@uci.edu. Web site: http://www.gse.uci.edu/.

University of Central Florida, College of Education, Education Doctoral Programs, Orlando, FL 32816. Offers communication sciences and disorders (PhD); counselor education (PhD); education (Ed D); elementary education (PhD); exceptional education (PhD); exercise physiology (PhD); higher education (PhD); hospitality education (PhD); instructional technology (PhD); mathematics education (PhD); reading education (PhD); science education (PhD); social science education (PhD); TESOL (PhD). *Students:* 135 full-time (87 women), 73 part-time (51 women); includes 49 minority (21 Black or African American, non-Hispanic/Latino; 4 Asian, non-Hispanic/Latino; 20 Hispanic/Latino; 4 Two or more races, non-Hispanic/Latino), 18 international. Average age 39. 125 applicants, 46% accepted, 46 enrolled. In 2011, 43 doctorates awarded. Application fee: $30. Electronic applications accepted. *Expenses:* Tuition, state resident: part-time $277.08 per credit hour. Tuition, nonresident: part-time $277.08 per credit hour. Part-time tuition and fees vary according to degree level and program. *Financial support:* In 2011–12, 85 students received support, including 48 fellowships with partial tuition reimbursements available (averaging $5,900 per year), 36 research assistantships with partial tuition reimbursements available (averaging $6,900 per year), 59 teaching assistantships with partial tuition reimbursements available (averaging $6,900 per year). *Unit head:* Dr. Rex Culp, Associate Dean, 407-823-5391, E-mail: rex.culp@ucf.edu. *Application contact:* Barbara Rodriguez, Associate Director, Admissions and Registration, 407-823-2766, Fax: 407-823-6442, E-mail: gradadmissions@ucf.edu. Web site: http://education.ucf.edu/departments.cfm.

University of Central Florida, College of Education, School of Teaching, Learning, and Leadership, Program in Elementary Education, Orlando, FL 32816. Offers M Ed, MA. *Accreditation:* NCATE. *Students:* 46 full-time (40 women), 78 part-time (72 women); includes 24 minority (6 Black or African American, non-Hispanic/Latino; 4 Asian, non-Hispanic/Latino; 12 Hispanic/Latino; 2 Two or more races, non-Hispanic/Latino), 2 international. Average age 30. 68 applicants, 68% accepted, 27 enrolled. In 2011, 32 master's awarded. *Degree requirements:* For master's, thesis or alternative. *Application deadline:* For fall admission, 7/15 for domestic students; for spring admission, 12/15 for domestic students. Application fee: $30. Electronic applications accepted. *Expenses:* Tuition, state resident: part-time $277.08 per credit hour. Tuition, nonresident: part-time $277.08 per credit hour. Part-time tuition and fees vary according to degree level and program. *Financial support:* In 2011–12, 1 student received support, including 1 research assistantship with tuition reimbursement available (averaging $7,200 per year); fellowships with tuition reimbursements available, teaching assistantships, career-related internships or fieldwork, Federal Work-Study, institutionally sponsored loans, tuition waivers (partial), and unspecified assistantships also available. *Unit head:* Dr. Karri J. Williams, Program Coordinator, 407-433-7922, E-mail: karri.williams@ucf.edu. *Application contact:* Barbara Rodriguez, Director, Admissions and Registration, 321-823-2766, Fax: 407-823-6442, E-mail: gradadmissions@ucf.edu.

University of Central Missouri, The Graduate School, College of Education, Warrensburg, MO 64093. Offers career and technical education administration (MS); career and technical education industry training (MS); career and technical education leadership/teaching (MS); college student personnel administration (MS); counseling (MS); curriculum and instruction (Ed S); educational leadership (Ed D); educational technology (MS); elementary education/educational foundations and literacy (MSE); elementary school administration (MSE); elementary school principalship (Ed S); human services/learning resources (Ed S); human services/professional counseling (Ed S); human services/special education (Ed S); human services/technology and occupational education (Ed S); K-12 education/educational foundations and literacy (MSE); K-12 special education (MSE); library science and information services (MS); literacy education (MSE); secondary education/educational foundations & literacy (MSE); secondary school administration (MSE); secondary school principalship (Ed S); superintendency (Ed S); teaching (MAT). Ed D offered jointly with University of Missouri. Part-time programs available. Postbaccalaureate distance learning degree programs offered. *Entrance requirements:* Additional exam requirements/recommendations for international students: Required—TOEFL (minimum score 550 paper-based; 79 computer-based). Electronic applications accepted.

University of Central Oklahoma, College of Graduate Studies and Research, College of Education and Professional Studies, Department of Curriculum and Instruction, Edmond, OK 73034-5209. Offers early childhood education (M Ed); elementary education (M Ed). Part-time programs available. Postbaccalaureate distance learning degree programs offered (minimal on-campus study). *Faculty:* 13 full-time (11 women), 10 part-time/adjunct (9 women). *Students:* 55 full-time (52 women), 89 part-time (81 women); includes 28 minority (6 Black or African American, non-Hispanic/Latino; 4 American Indian or Alaska Native, non-Hispanic/Latino; 1 Asian, non-Hispanic/Latino; 12 Hispanic/Latino; 5 Two or more races, non-Hispanic/Latino), 44 international. Average age 34. In 2011, 61 master's awarded. *Entrance requirements:* For master's, GRE General Test. Additional exam requirements/recommendations for international students: Required—TOEFL (minimum score 550 paper-based; 213 computer-based). *Application deadline:* Applications are processed on a rolling basis. Application fee: $50. Electronic applications accepted. *Expenses:* Tuition, state resident: full-time $3901; part-time $218.30 per credit hour. Tuition, nonresident: full-time $9198; part-time $511.20 per credit hour. Tuition and fees vary according to program. *Financial support:* Unspecified assistantships available. Financial award application deadline: 3/31; financial award applicants required to submit FAFSA. *Faculty research:* Tourette's syndrome, bilingual education, science education, language development/disorders. *Unit head:* Dr. Paulette Shreck, Chairperson, 405-974-5721. *Application contact:* Dr. Richard Bernard, Dean, Graduate College, 405-974-3493, Fax: 405-974-3852, E-mail: gradcoll@uco.edu.

University of Cincinnati, Graduate School, College of Education, Criminal Justice, and Human Services, Division of Teacher Education, Program in Middle Childhood Education, Cincinnati, OH 45221. Offers M Ed. *Accreditation:* NCATE. Part-time programs available. *Degree requirements:* For master's, thesis or alternative. *Entrance requirements:* For master's, GRE General Test. Additional exam requirements/recommendations for international students: Required—TOEFL (minimum score 550 paper-based; 213 computer-based), TWE (minimum score 4.5), OEPT. Electronic applications accepted.

University of Colorado Denver, School of Education and Human Development, Information and Learning Technologies Program, Denver, CO 80217-3364. Offers e-learning design and implementation (MA); instructional design and adult learning (MA); K-12 teaching (MA). Part-time and evening/weekend programs available. Postbaccalaureate distance learning degree programs offered (no on-campus study). *Students:* 82 full-time (65 women), 46 part-time (38 women); includes 13 minority (2 Black or African American, non-Hispanic/Latino; 3 Asian, non-Hispanic/Latino; 8 Hispanic/Latino), 3 international. Average age 38. 35 applicants, 89% accepted, 27 enrolled. In 2011, 79 master's awarded. *Degree requirements:* For master's, comprehensive exam (for some programs), comprehensive exam or online portfolio; 30 credit hours. *Entrance requirements:* For master's, GRE or MAT (if GPA is below 2.75), resume, statement of intent, three letters of recommendation. Additional exam requirements/recommendations for international students: Required—TOEFL (minimum score 525 paper-based; 197 computer-based). *Application deadline:* For fall admission, 5/15 for domestic students; for spring admission, 11/15 for domestic students. Application fee: $50 ($75 for international students). *Expenses:* Contact institution. *Financial support:* Scholarships/grants available. Financial award application deadline: 4/1; financial award applicants required to submit FAFSA. *Faculty research:* Technology for educational management, instructional design foundations, e-Learning, educational design. *Unit head:* Brent Wilson, Professor, 303-315-4963, E-mail: brent.wilson@ucdenver.edu. *Application contact:* Hans Broers, Academic Advisor, 303-315-6351, Fax: 303-315-6311, E-mail: hans.broers@ucdenver.edu. Web site: http://www.ucdenver.edu/ACADEMICS/COLLEGES/SCHOOLOFEDUCATION/ACADEMICS/Pages/AcademicPrograms.aspx.

University of Colorado Denver, School of Education and Human Development, Teacher Education Programs, Denver, CO 80217. Offers elementary linguistically diverse education (MA); elementary math and science education (MA); elementary math education (MA); elementary reading and writing (MA); elementary science education (MA); secondary English education (MA); secondary linguistically diverse education (MA); secondary math education (MA); secondary reading and writing (MA); secondary science education (MA); special education (MA). *Accreditation:* NCATE. Part-time and evening/weekend programs available. *Students:* 419 full-time (325 women), 238 part-time (196 women); includes 83 minority (11 Black or African American, non-Hispanic/Latino; 1 American Indian or Alaska Native, non-Hispanic/Latino; 15 Asian, non-Hispanic/Latino; 53 Hispanic/Latino; 3 Two or more races, non-Hispanic/Latino), 9 international. Average age 30. 206 applicants, 88% accepted, 85 enrolled. In 2011, 278 master's awarded. *Degree requirements:* For master's, comprehensive exam. *Entrance requirements:* For master's, GRE or MAT (for those with GPA below 2.75), transcripts, resume, letters of recommendation. Additional exam requirements/recommendations for international students: Required—TOEFL (minimum score 525 paper-based; 197 computer-based). *Application deadline:* For fall admission, 4/15 priority date for domestic students; for spring admission, 9/15 priority date for domestic students. Applications are processed on a rolling basis. Application fee: $50 ($75 for international students). Electronic applications accepted. *Expenses:* Contact institution. *Financial support:* Research assistantships, teaching assistantships, and Federal Work-Study available. Financial award application deadline: 4/1; financial award applicants required to submit FAFSA. *Faculty research:* Linguistically diverse education/ESL, elementary reading and writing, elementary teacher education, secondary teacher education, special education. *Unit head:* Cindy Gutierrez, Director, 303-315-4982, E-mail: cindy.gutierrez@ucdenver.edu. *Application contact:* Lori Sisneros, Student Services Center, 303-315-4979, E-mail: education@ucdenver.edu. Web site: http://www.ucdenver.edu/academics/colleges/SchoolOfEducation/Academics/MASTERS/Pages/default.aspx.

University of Connecticut, Graduate School, Neag School of Education, Department of Curriculum and Instruction, Program in Elementary Education, Storrs, CT 06269. Offers MA, PhD, Post-Master's Certificate. *Accreditation:* NCATE. Terminal master's awarded for partial completion of doctoral program. *Degree requirements:* For master's, comprehensive exam, thesis or alternative; for doctorate, thesis/dissertation. *Entrance requirements:* For doctorate, GRE General Test. Additional exam requirements/recommendations for international students: Required—TOEFL (minimum score 550 paper-based; 214 computer-based). Electronic applications accepted.

University of Florida, Graduate School, College of Education, School of Teaching and Learning, Gainesville, FL 32611. Offers bilingual/ESOL education (M Ed, MAE, Ed D, PhD, Ed S); curriculum and instruction (M Ed, MAE, Ed D, PhD, Ed S); elementary education (M Ed, MAE); English education (M Ed, MAE); mathematics education (M Ed, MAE); reading education (M Ed, MAE); science education (M Ed, MAE); social foundations of education (M Ed, MAE, Ed D, PhD); social studies education (M Ed, MAE). *Accreditation:* NCATE. Part-time and evening/weekend programs available. Postbaccalaureate distance learning degree programs offered (no on-campus study). *Faculty:* 26 full-time (19 women). *Students:* 247 full-time (201 women), 236 part-time (196 women); includes 100 minority (32 Black or African American, non-Hispanic/Latino; 2 American Indian or Alaska Native, non-Hispanic/Latino; 15 Asian, non-Hispanic/Latino; 51 Hispanic/Latino), 32 international. Average age 33. 290 applicants, 60% accepted, 122 enrolled. In 2011, 284 master's, 19 doctorates, 29 other advanced degrees awarded. Terminal master's awarded for partial completion of doctoral program. *Degree requirements:* For master's, comprehensive exam (for some programs), thesis (for some programs); for doctorate, comprehensive exam (for some programs), thesis/dissertation (for some programs). *Entrance requirements:* For master's and doctorate, GRE General Test, minimum GPA of 3.0; for Ed S, GRE General Test. Additional exam requirements/recommendations for international students: Required—TOEFL (minimum score 550 paper-based; 213 computer-based; 80 iBT), IELTS (minimum score 6). *Application deadline:* For fall admission, 2/15 for domestic students, 12/1 for international students; for spring admission, 9/15 for domestic students, 3/1 for international students. Applications are processed on a rolling basis. Application fee: $30. Electronic applications accepted. *Financial support:* Fellowships, research assistantships, teaching assistantships, career-related internships or fieldwork, and unspecified assistantships available. Financial award applicants required to submit FAFSA. *Faculty research:* Early childhood, child and adolescents, diverse learners, race/ethnicity issues, teacher education, professional development, language and literacy development, policy development. *Unit head:* Dr. Elizabeth Bondy, Chair, 352-273-4242, Fax: 352-392-9193, E-mail: bondy@coe.ufl.edu. *Application contact:* Wevan Terzian, Graduate Coordinator, 352-273-4216, Fax: 352-392-9193, E-mail: sterzian@coe.ufl.edu. Web site: http://education.ufl.edu/school-teaching-learning/.

University of Georgia, College of Education, Department of Elementary and Social Studies Education, Athens, GA 30602. Offers early childhood education (M Ed, MAT, PhD, Ed S), including child and family development (MAT); elementary education (PhD); middle school education (M Ed, PhD, Ed S); social studies education (M Ed, Ed D, PhD, Ed S). *Faculty:* 17 full-time (10 women). *Students:* 119 full-time (96 women), 110 part-time (96 women); includes 42 minority (22 Black or African American, non-Hispanic/Latino; 1 American Indian or Alaska Native, non-Hispanic/Latino; 11 Asian, non-Hispanic/Latino; 6 Hispanic/Latino; 2 Two or more races, non-Hispanic/Latino), 12 international. Average age 30. 68 applicants, 72% accepted, 22 enrolled. In 2011, 92 master's, 12 doctorates, 2 other advanced degrees awarded. *Entrance requirements:* For master's and Ed S, GRE General Test or MAT; for doctorate, GRE General Test. *Application deadline:* For fall admission, 7/1 priority date for domestic students; for spring admission, 11/15 for domestic students. Application fee: $50. Electronic applications accepted. *Financial support:* Fellowships, research assistantships, teaching assistantships, and unspecified assistantships available. *Unit head:* Dr. Ronald Butchart, Interim Head, 706-542-6490, E-mail: butchart@uga.edu. *Application contact:* Dr. Stephanie R. Jones, Graduate Coordinator, 706-542-4283, Fax: 706-542-8996, E-mail: essegrad@uga.edu. Web site: http://www.coe.uga.edu/esse/.

University of Hartford, College of Education, Nursing, and Health Professions, Program in Elementary and Special Education, West Hartford, CT 06117-1599. Offers elementary education (M Ed). *Accreditation:* NCATE. Part-time and evening/weekend programs available. *Degree requirements:* For master's, comprehensive exam. *Entrance requirements:* For master's, PRAXIS I or waiver, interview, 2 letters of recommendation. Additional exam requirements/recommendations for international students: Required—TOEFL (minimum score 550 paper-based; 213 computer-based). Electronic applications accepted.

University of Houston–Downtown, College of Public Service, Department of Urban Education, Houston, TX 77002. Offers bilingual education (MAT); curriculum and instruction (MAT); elementary education (MAT); secondary education (MAT). Part-time and evening/weekend programs available. *Faculty:* 12 full-time (8 women). *Students:* 13 full-time (10 women), 25 part-time (22 women); includes 30 minority (15 Black or African American, non-Hispanic/Latino; 3 Asian, non-Hispanic/Latino; 11 Hispanic/Latino; 1 Two or more races, non-Hispanic/Latino). Average age 35. 17 applicants, 100% accepted, 16 enrolled. In 2011, 5 master's awarded. *Degree requirements:* For master's, capstone course with completed project, position paper, grant proposal, empirical study, curriculum development/revision, or advanced technology project presented at annual Graduate Project Exhibition. *Entrance requirements:* For master's, GRE, personal statement, 3 recommendation forms. Additional exam requirements/recommendations for international students: Required—TOEFL (minimum score 550 paper-based; 213 computer-based; 80 iBT). *Application deadline:* For fall admission, 7/15 for domestic and international students; for spring admission, 11/15 for domestic and international students. Applications are processed on a rolling basis. Application fee: $35 ($60 for international students). Electronic applications accepted. *Expenses:* Tuition, state resident: full-time $3420; part-time $2280 per year. Tuition, nonresident: full-time $8424; part-time $5616 per year. *Required fees:* $1018; $840 per year. Tuition and fees vary according to program. *Financial support:* Scholarships/grants available. Financial award applicants required to submit FAFSA. *Unit head:* Dr. Myrna Cohen, Department Chair, 713-221-2759, Fax: 713-226-5294, E-mail: cohenm@uhd.edu. *Application contact:* Traneshia Parker, Associate Director of International Student Services and Graduate Admissions, 713-221-8093, Fax: 713-221-8157, E-mail: parkert@uhd.edu. Web site: http://www.uhd.edu/academic/colleges/publicservice/urbaned/mat.htm.

University of Illinois at Chicago, Graduate College, College of Education, Department of Curriculum and Instruction, Chicago, IL 60607-7128. Offers curriculum studies (PhD); educational studies (M Ed); elementary education (M Ed); literacy, language and culture (M Ed, PhD); secondary education (M Ed). Part-time and evening/weekend programs available. *Degree requirements:* For doctorate, thesis/dissertation. *Entrance requirements:* For master's, minimum GPA of 2.75; for doctorate, GRE General Test, minimum GPA of 2.75. Additional exam requirements/recommendations for international students: Required—TOEFL. Electronic applications accepted. *Faculty research:* Curriculum theory, curriculum development, research on teaching, curriculum and context, reading/literacy.

University of Indianapolis, Graduate Programs, School of Education, Indianapolis, IN 46227-3697. Offers art education (MAT); biology (MAT); chemistry (MAT); curriculum and instruction (MA); earth sciences (MAT); education (MA, MAT); educational leadership (MA); elementary education (MA); English (MAT); French (MAT); math (MAT); physical education (MAT); physics (MAT); secondary education (MA), including art education, education, English education, social studies education; social studies (MAT); Spanish (MAT). *Accreditation:* NCATE. Part-time and evening/weekend programs available. *Faculty:* 3 full-time (2 women), 3 part-time/adjunct (2 women). *Students:* 32 full-time (18 women), 97 part-time (56 women); includes 22 minority (20 Black or African American, non-Hispanic/Latino; 1 Asian, non-Hispanic/Latino; 1 Hispanic/Latino), 3 international. Average age 33. In 2011, 78 master's awarded. *Entrance requirements:* For master's, GRE Subject Test, PRAXIS I, minimum GPA of 2.5, 3 letters of recommendation, interview, writing exercise. Additional exam requirements/recommendations for international students: Required—TOEFL (minimum score 550 paper-based; 213 computer-based). *Application deadline:* Applications are processed on a rolling basis. Application fee: $50. Tuition and fees vary according to degree level and program. *Financial support:* Federal Work-Study available. Financial award application deadline: 5/1; financial award applicants required to submit FAFSA. *Faculty research:* Assessment of teacher education, perceptions of prospective teachers by parents. *Unit head:* Dr. Kathy Moran, Dean, 317-788-3285, Fax: 317-788-3300, E-mail: kmoran@uindy.edu. *Application contact:* Jeni Kirby, 317-788-2113, E-mail: kirbyj@uindy.edu. Web site: http://education.uindy.edu/.

The University of Iowa, Graduate College, College of Education, Department of Teaching and Learning, Program in Elementary Education, Iowa City, IA 52242-1316. Offers curriculum and supervision (MA, PhD); developmental reading (MA); early childhood education and care (MA); elementary education (MA, PhD); language, literature and culture (PhD). *Degree requirements:* For master's, thesis optional, exam; for doctorate, comprehensive exam, thesis/dissertation. *Entrance requirements:* For master's and doctorate, GRE General Test, minimum GPA of 3.0. Additional exam requirements/recommendations for international students: Required—TOEFL (minimum score 550 paper-based; 213 computer-based; 81 iBT). Electronic applications accepted.

University of Louisiana at Monroe, Graduate School, College of Education and Human Development, Department of Curriculum and Instruction, Program in Curriculum and Instruction, Monroe, LA 71209-0001. Offers curriculum and instruction (Ed D); elementary education (1-5) (M Ed); reading education (K-12) (M Ed); SPED-academically gifted education (K-12) (M Ed); SPED-early intervention education (birth-3) (M Ed); SPED-educational diagnostics education (PreK-12) (M Ed). *Accreditation:* NCATE. *Students:* 42 full-time (37 women), 54 part-time (47 women); includes 20 minority (18 Black or African American, non-Hispanic/Latino; 1 Asian, non-Hispanic/Latino; 1 Hispanic/Latino), 12 international. Average age 36. 55 applicants, 95% accepted, 38 enrolled. In 2011, 27 master's, 1 doctorate awarded. *Degree requirements:* For master's, comprehensive exam (for some programs), thesis; for doctorate, thesis/dissertation, internships. *Entrance requirements:* For master's, GRE General Test; for doctorate, GRE General Test, minimum undergraduate GPA of 2.75, graduate 3.25. Additional exam requirements/recommendations for international students: Required—TOEFL (minimum score 500 paper-based; 173 computer-based; 61 iBT). *Application deadline:* For fall admission, 8/24 priority date for domestic students, 7/1 for international students; for winter admission, 12/14 priority date for domestic students; for spring admission, 1/19 for domestic students, 11/1 for international students. Applications are processed on a rolling basis. Application fee: $20 ($30 for international students). Electronic applications accepted. *Expenses:* Tuition, state resident: full-time $3436; part-time $240 per credit hour. Tuition, nonresident: full-time $3436; part-time $240 per credit hour. *International tuition:* $10,733 full-time. *Required fees:* $1460.90. *Financial support:* In 2011–12, 12 research assistantships with full tuition reimbursements (averaging $2,500 per year) were awarded; career-related internships or fieldwork, Federal Work-Study, and unspecified assistantships also available. Financial award application deadline: 4/1; financial award applicants required to submit FAFSA. *Unit head:* Dr. Dorothy Schween, Coordinator, 318-342-1269, Fax: 318-342-3131, E-mail: schween@ulm.edu. *Application contact:* Whitney Sutherland, Administrative Assistant to the Department Head, 318-342-1266, Fax: 318-342-3131, E-mail: sutherland@ulm.edu. Web site: http://www.ulm.edu/ci/.

University of Louisiana at Monroe, Graduate School, College of Education and Human Development, Department of Curriculum and Instruction, Program in Elementary Education, Monroe, LA 71209-0001. Offers elementary education (MAT); grades 1-5

(M Ed). *Accreditation:* NCATE. Part-time and evening/weekend programs available. *Faculty:* 2 full-time (both women). *Students:* 15 full-time (all women), 51 part-time (44 women); includes 14 minority (13 Black or African American, non-Hispanic/Latino; 1 American Indian or Alaska Native, non-Hispanic/Latino). Average age 32. 12 applicants, 67% accepted, 7 enrolled. In 2011, 29 master's awarded. *Degree requirements:* For master's, thesis optional. *Entrance requirements:* For master's, GRE General Test, minimum GPA of 2.5. Additional exam requirements/recommendations for international students: Required—TOEFL (minimum score 500 paper-based; 173 computer-based; 61 iBT). *Application deadline:* For fall admission, 8/24 for domestic students, 7/1 for international students; for winter admission, 12/14 priority date for domestic students; for spring admission, 1/19 for domestic students, 11/1 for international students. Applications are processed on a rolling basis. Application fee: $20 ($30 for international students). Electronic applications accepted. *Expenses:* Tuition, state resident: full-time $3436; part-time $240 per credit hour. Tuition, nonresident: full-time $3436; part-time $240 per credit hour. *International tuition:* $10,733 full-time. *Required fees:* $1460.90. *Financial support:* Career-related internships or fieldwork, Federal Work-Study, and unspecified assistantships available. Financial award application deadline: 4/1; financial award applicants required to submit FAFSA. *Faculty research:* Student attitudes. *Unit head:* Dr. Dorothy Schween, Department Head, 318-342-1266, E-mail: schween@ulm.edu. *Application contact:* Whitney Sutherland, Administrative Assistant to Department Head, 318-342-1266, E-mail: sutherland@ulm.edu. Web site: http://www.ulm.edu/ci/.

University of Louisville, Graduate School, College of Education and Human Development, Department of Teaching and Learning, Louisville, KY 40292-0001. Offers art education (MAT); curriculum and instruction (PhD); early elementary education (MAT); instructional technology (M Ed); interdisciplinary early childhood education (MAT); middle school education (MAT); music education (MAT); reading education (M Ed); secondary education (MAT); special education (M Ed, MAT); teacher leadership (M Ed). Part-time and evening/weekend programs available. *Degree requirements:* For doctorate, comprehensive exam, thesis/dissertation. *Entrance requirements:* For master's, GRE General Test, PRAXIS II (for some programs); for doctorate, GRE General Test. Additional exam requirements/recommendations for international students: Required—TOEFL (minimum score 560 paper-based; 210 computer-based; 83 iBT). Electronic applications accepted. *Expenses:* Tuition, state resident: full-time $9692; part-time $539 per credit hour. Tuition, nonresident: full-time $20,168; part-time $1121 per credit hour. Tuition and fees vary according to program and reciprocity agreements. *Faculty research:* Mathematics teacher education and ongoing professional development in pedagogy and content knowledge; development of literacy, including early literacy in science and mathematics and literacy development for English language learners; immersive visualizations for promoting STEM education from nanoscience to cosmic scales; evidence-based practices for students with disabilities; urban education, including teacher response to intervention systems in schools and cross-cultural competence.

University of Maine, Graduate School, College of Education and Human Development, Program in Elementary Education, Orono, ME 04469. Offers M Ed, MAT, MS, CAS. *Accreditation:* NCATE. Part-time and evening/weekend programs available. *Students:* 1 full-time (0 women), 2 part-time (both women); includes 2 minority (1 American Indian or Alaska Native, non-Hispanic/Latino; 1 Hispanic/Latino), 1 international. Average age 26. 2 applicants, 50% accepted, 1 enrolled. In 2011, 10 degrees awarded. *Degree requirements:* For master's, thesis or alternative. *Entrance requirements:* For master's, MAT; for CAS, MA, M Ed, or MS. Additional exam requirements/recommendations for international students: Required—TOEFL. *Application deadline:* For fall admission, 2/1 priority date for domestic students. Applications are processed on a rolling basis. Application fee: $65. Electronic applications accepted. *Expenses:* Tuition, state resident: full-time $5016. Tuition, nonresident: full-time $14,424. *Financial support:* Career-related internships or fieldwork, Federal Work-Study, institutionally sponsored loans, tuition waivers (full and partial), and unspecified assistantships available. Financial award application deadline: 3/1. *Unit head:* Dr. Janet Spector, Coordinator, 207-581-2444, Fax: 207-581-2423. *Application contact:* Scott G. Delcourt, Associate Dean of the Graduate School, 207-581-3291, Fax: 207-581-3232, E-mail: graduate@maine.edu. Web site: http://www2.umaine.edu/graduate/.

University of Maryland, Baltimore County, Graduate School, College of Arts, Humanities and Social Sciences, Department of Education, Program in Teaching, Baltimore, MD 21250. Offers early childhood education (MAT); elementary education (MAT); secondary education (MAT), including social studies; secondary education (MAT), including art, biology, chemistry, dance, earth/space science, English, foreign language, mathematics, music, physics, theatre. Part-time and evening/weekend programs available. *Faculty:* 24 full-time (18 women), 25 part-time/adjunct (19 women). *Students:* 46 full-time (35 women), 64 part-time (39 women); includes 24 minority (8 Black or African American, non-Hispanic/Latino; 7 Asian, non-Hispanic/Latino; 6 Hispanic/Latino; 1 Native Hawaiian or other Pacific Islander, non-Hispanic/Latino; 2 Two or more races, non-Hispanic/Latino), 4 international. Average age 31. 88 applicants, 57% accepted, 39 enrolled. In 2011, 106 master's awarded. *Degree requirements:* For master's, comprehensive exam (for some programs), thesis (for some programs). *Entrance requirements:* For master's, PRAXIS I or GRE (minimum score of 1000), minimum GPA of 3.0. Additional exam requirements/recommendations for international students: Required—TOEFL. *Application deadline:* For fall admission, 6/1 for domestic students; for spring admission, 11/1 for domestic students. Applications are processed on a rolling basis. Application fee: $50. Electronic applications accepted. *Financial support:* In 2011–12, 6 students received support, including teaching assistantships with full and partial tuition reimbursements available (averaging $12,000 per year); career-related internships or fieldwork, Federal Work-Study, scholarships/grants, tuition waivers, and unspecified assistantships also available. Financial award application deadline: 3/1. *Faculty research:* STEM teacher education, culturally sensitive pedagogy, ESOL/bilingual education, early childhood education, language, literacy and culture. *Unit head:* Dr. Susan M. Blunck, Graduate Program Director, 410-455-2869, Fax: 410-455-3986, E-mail: blunck@umbc.edu. *Application contact:* Cheryl Johnson, 410-455-3388, E-mail: blackwel@umbc.edu. Web site: http://www.umbc.edu/education/.

University of Massachusetts Amherst, Graduate School, School of Education, Program in Education, Amherst, MA 01003. Offers bilingual, English as a second language, and multicultural education (M Ed, CAGS); child study and early education (M Ed); children, families and schools (Ed D, CAGS); early childhood and elementary teacher education (M Ed); educational leadership (M Ed, CAGS); educational policy and leadership (Ed D); higher education (M Ed, CAGS); international education (M Ed); language, literacy and culture (Ed D); learning, media and technology (M Ed, CAGS); mathematics, science, and learning technologies (Ed D); policy studies in education (CAGS); psychometric methods, educational statistics and research methods (Ed D); reading and writing (M Ed); school counselor education (M Ed, CAGS); science education (CAGS); secondary teacher education (M Ed); social justice education (M Ed, Ed D, CAGS); special education (M Ed, Ed D, CAGS). *Accreditation:* NCATE. Part-time programs available. Postbaccalaureate distance learning degree programs offered (minimal on-campus study). *Faculty:* 81 full-time (46 women). *Students:* 341 full-time (240 women), 333 part-time (226 women); includes 113 minority (36 Black or African American, non-Hispanic/Latino; 1 American Indian or Alaska Native, non-Hispanic/Latino; 14 Asian, non-Hispanic/Latino; 51 Hispanic/Latino; 1 Native Hawaiian or other Pacific Islander, non-Hispanic/Latino; 10 Two or more races, non-Hispanic/Latino), 98 international. Average age 36. 721 applicants, 57% accepted, 202 enrolled. In 2011, 166 master's, 33 doctorates, 25 CAGSs awarded. Terminal master's awarded for partial completion of doctoral program. *Degree requirements:* For doctorate, comprehensive exam, thesis/dissertation. *Entrance requirements:* Additional exam requirements/recommendations for international students: Required—TOEFL (minimum score 550 paper-based; 213 computer-based; 80 iBT), IELTS (minimum score 6.5). *Application deadline:* For fall admission, 1/15 for domestic and international students. Applications are processed on a rolling basis. Application fee: $50 ($65 for international students). Electronic applications accepted. Tuition and fees vary according to course load, campus/location and program. *Financial support:* Fellowships with full and partial tuition reimbursements, research assistantships with full and partial tuition reimbursements, teaching assistantships with full and partial tuition reimbursements, career-related internships or fieldwork, Federal Work-Study, scholarships/grants, traineeships, health care benefits, tuition waivers (full and partial), and unspecified assistantships available. Support available to part-time students. Financial award application deadline: 1/15. *Unit head:* Dr. Linda L. Griffin, Graduate Program Director, 413-545-6984, Fax: 413-545-1523. *Application contact:* Lindsay DeSantis, Interim Supervisor of Admissions, 413-545-0722, Fax: 413-577-0010, E-mail: gradadm@grad.umass.edu. Web site: http://www.umass.edu/education/.

University of Massachusetts Boston, Office of Graduate Studies, Graduate College of Education, School Organization, Curriculum and Instruction Department, Boston, MA 02125-3393. Offers education (M Ed, Ed D), including elementary and secondary education/certification (M Ed), higher education administration (Ed D), teacher certification (M Ed), urban school leadership (Ed D); educational administration (M Ed, CAGS); special education (M Ed). *Degree requirements:* For master's and CAGS, comprehensive exam; for doctorate, comprehensive exam, thesis/dissertation. *Entrance requirements:* For master's, GRE General Test or MAT; for doctorate, GRE General Test or MAT, minimum GPA of 2.75; for CAGS, minimum GPA of 2.75.

University of Massachusetts Boston, Office of Graduate Studies, Graduate College of Education, School Organization, Curriculum and Instruction Department, Program in Education, Track in Elementary and Secondary Education/Certification, Boston, MA 02125-3393. Offers M Ed. Part-time and evening/weekend programs available. *Degree requirements:* For master's, comprehensive exam, thesis optional, practicum. *Entrance requirements:* For master's, GRE General Test or MAT, minimum GPA of 3.0, 2 years of teaching experience. *Faculty research:* Anti-bias education, inclusionary curriculum and instruction, creativity and learning, science, technology and society, teaching of reading.

University of Massachusetts Dartmouth, Graduate School, School of Education, Public Policy, and Civic Engagement, Department of Teaching and Learning, North Dartmouth, MA 02747-2300. Offers elementary education (MAT, Postbaccalaureate Certificate); middle school education (MAT); principal initial licensure (Postbaccalaureate Certificate); secondary school education (MAT). *Faculty:* 5 full-time (4 women), 9 part-time/adjunct (4 women). *Students:* 15 full-time (10 women), 180 part-time (119 women); includes 17 minority (7 Black or African American, non-Hispanic/Latino; 1 Asian, non-Hispanic/Latino; 5 Hispanic/Latino; 4 Two or more races, non-Hispanic/Latino). Average age 34. 110 applicants, 98% accepted, 85 enrolled. In 2011, 88 master's, 28 other advanced degrees awarded. *Degree requirements:* For master's, thesis or alternative. *Entrance requirements:* For master's, Massachusetts Tests for Educator Licensure (MTEL), minimum undergraduate GPA of 2.7, teacher certification, 3 letters of recommendation, resume, statement of intent; for Postbaccalaureate Certificate, Massachusetts Tests for Educator Licensure (MTEL), 3 letters of recommendation, resume, statement of intent. Additional exam requirements/recommendations for international students: Required—TOEFL (minimum score 533 paper-based; 200 computer-based; 72 iBT). *Application deadline:* For fall admission, 7/15 priority date for domestic students, 6/15 for international students; for spring admission, 12/15 priority date for domestic students, 11/15 for international students. Applications are processed on a rolling basis. Application fee: $40 ($60 for international students). *Expenses:* Tuition, state resident: full-time $2071; part-time $86.29 per credit. Tuition, nonresident: full-time $8099; part-time $337.46 per credit. *Required fees:* $438.58 per credit. Part-time tuition and fees vary according to class time, course load, degree level and reciprocity agreements. *Financial support:* Federal Work-Study available. Financial award application deadline: 3/1. *Total annual research expenditures:* $92,694. *Unit head:* Sheila Macrine, Graduate Program Director, 508-999-9234, Fax: 508-910-6916, E-mail: smacrine@umassd.edu. *Application contact:* Elan Turcotte-Shamski, Graduate Admissions Officer, 508-999-8604, Fax: 508-999-8183, E-mail: graduate@umassd.edu. Web site: http://www.umassd.edu/seppce/teachingandlearning/index.html.

University of Memphis, Graduate School, College of Education, Department of Instruction and Curriculum Leadership, Memphis, TN 38152. Offers early childhood education (MAT, MS, Ed D); elementary education (MAT); instruction and curriculum (MS, Ed D); instruction design and technology (MS, Ed D); middle grades education (MAT); reading (MS, Ed D); secondary education (MAT); special education (MAT, MS, Ed D). *Accreditation:* NCATE (one or more programs are accredited). Part-time programs available. Terminal master's awarded for partial completion of doctoral program. *Degree requirements:* For master's, comprehensive exam, thesis or alternative; for doctorate, comprehensive exam, thesis/dissertation. *Entrance requirements:* For master's, GRE General Test, minimum GPA of 2.5; for doctorate, GRE General Test, GRE Subject Test, 2 years of teaching experience. Electronic applications accepted. *Faculty research:* Effective urban teachers, preparation and retention of urban teachers, technology utilization in schools, field-based teacher preparation programs, effective use of online instruction.

University of Michigan–Flint, School of Education and Human Services, Department of Education, Flint, MI 48502-1950. Offers education (MA); elementary education with teaching certification (MA); literacy (K-12) (MA); special education (MA); technology in education (MA). Part-time programs available. *Entrance requirements:* For master's, BS with minimum GPA of 3.0. Additional exam requirements/recommendations for international students: Required—TOEFL (minimum score 560 paper-based; 220 computer-based; 84 iBT), IELTS (minimum score 6.5). *Expenses:* Contact institution.

University of Minnesota, Twin Cities Campus, Graduate School, College of Education and Human Development, Department of Curriculum and Instruction, Minneapolis, MN 55455-0213. Offers art education (M Ed, MA, PhD); children's literature (M Ed, MA, PhD); curriculum and instruction (MA, PhD); early childhood education (M Ed, PhD); elementary education (M Ed, MA, PhD); English education (MA, PhD); environmental education (M Ed); family education (M Ed, MA, Ed D, PhD); instructional systems and technology (M Ed, MA, PhD); language arts (MA, PhD); language immersion education (Certificate); literacy education (MA); mathematics education (MA, PhD); reading education (MA, PhD); science education (MA, PhD); second languages and cultures education (MA, PhD); social studies education (MA, PhD); teaching (M Ed), including Chinese, earth science, elementary special education, English, English as a second language, French, German, Hebrew, Japanese, life sciences, mathematics, middle school science, science, second languages and cultures, social studies, Spanish; technology enhanced learning (Certificate); writing education

(M Ed, MA, PhD). *Faculty:* 34 full-time (22 women). *Students:* 433 full-time (319 women), 310 part-time (239 women); includes 97 minority (34 Black or African American, non-Hispanic/Latino; 6 American Indian or Alaska Native, non-Hispanic/Latino; 35 Asian, non-Hispanic/Latino; 22 Hispanic/Latino), 47 international. Average age 33. 660 applicants, 68% accepted, 395 enrolled. In 2011, 518 master's, 19 doctorates, 14 other advanced degrees awarded. Application fee: $55. *Financial support:* In 2011–12, 6 fellowships (averaging $9,308 per year), 39 research assistantships with full tuition reimbursements (averaging $8,301 per year), 61 teaching assistantships with full tuition reimbursements (averaging $9,206 per year) were awarded. *Faculty research:* Teaching and learning; quality of education; influence of cultural, linguistic, social, political, technological and economic factors on teaching, learning and educational research; relationship between educational practice and a democratic and just society. *Total annual research expenditures:* $943,365. *Unit head:* Dr. Nina Asher, Chair, 612-624-4772, Fax: 612-624-1357, E-mail: nasher@umn.edu. *Application contact:* Dr. Jennifer Engler, Assistant Dean, 612-626-2887, Fax: 612-626-7496, E-mail: engle009@umn.edu. Web site: http://www.cehd.umn.edu/ci.

University of Missouri, Graduate School, College of Education, Department of Learning, Teaching and Curriculum, Columbia, MO 65211. Offers agricultural education (M Ed, PhD, Ed S); art education (M Ed, PhD, Ed S); business and office education (M Ed, PhD, Ed S); early childhood education (M Ed, PhD, Ed S); elementary education (M Ed, PhD, Ed S); English education (M Ed, PhD, Ed S); foreign language education (M Ed, PhD, Ed S); health education and promotion (M Ed, PhD); learning and instruction (M Ed); marketing education (M Ed, PhD, Ed S); mathematics education (M Ed, PhD, Ed S); music education (M Ed, PhD, Ed S); reading education (M Ed, PhD, Ed S); science education (M Ed, PhD, Ed S); social studies education (M Ed, PhD, Ed S); vocational education (M Ed, PhD, Ed S). Part-time programs available. *Faculty:* 26 full-time (16 women), 3 part-time/adjunct (2 women). *Students:* 184 full-time (145 women), 276 part-time (215 women); includes 34 minority (10 Black or African American, non-Hispanic/Latino; 1 American Indian or Alaska Native, non-Hispanic/Latino; 7 Asian, non-Hispanic/Latino; 8 Hispanic/Latino; 8 Two or more races, non-Hispanic/Latino), 39 international. Average age 32. 309 applicants, 76% accepted, 204 enrolled. In 2011, 232 master's, 8 doctorates, 2 other advanced degrees awarded. Terminal master's awarded for partial completion of doctoral program. *Degree requirements:* For doctorate, thesis/dissertation. *Entrance requirements:* For master's and Ed S, GRE General Test or MAT, minimum GPA of 3.0; for doctorate, GRE General Test, minimum GPA of 3.0. Additional exam requirements/recommendations for international students: Required—TOEFL (minimum score 600 paper-based; 250 computer-based; 100 iBT). Application fee: $55 ($75 for international students). Electronic applications accepted. *Expenses:* Tuition, state resident: full-time $5881. Tuition, nonresident: full-time $15,183. *Required fees:* $952. Tuition and fees vary according to campus/location and program. *Financial support:* Fellowships, research assistantships, teaching assistantships, and institutionally sponsored loans available. *Application contact:* Fran Colley, 573-882-6462, E-mail: colleyf@missouri.edu. Web site: http://education.missouri.edu/LTC/.

University of Missouri–St. Louis, College of Education, Division of Counseling, St. Louis, MO 63121. Offers community counseling (M Ed); elementary school counseling (M Ed); secondary school counseling (M Ed). *Accreditation:* ACA; NCATE. Part-time and evening/weekend programs available. *Faculty:* 6 full-time (3 women), 11 part-time/adjunct (8 women). *Students:* 44 full-time (38 women), 162 part-time (134 women); includes 54 minority (42 Black or African American, non-Hispanic/Latino; 3 Asian, non-Hispanic/Latino; 7 Hispanic/Latino; 2 Two or more races, non-Hispanic/Latino), 2 international. Average age 32. 106 applicants, 48% accepted, 31 enrolled. In 2011, 60 master's awarded. *Degree requirements:* For master's, comprehensive exam. *Entrance requirements:* For master's, 3 letters of recommendation. Additional exam requirements/recommendations for international students: Required—TOEFL (minimum score 550 paper-based; 213 computer-based). *Application deadline:* For fall admission, 6/1 for domestic and international students; for spring admission, 10/1 for domestic and international students. Application fee: $35 ($40 for international students). Electronic applications accepted. *Expenses:* Tuition, state resident: full-time $6273; part-time $3866 per year. Tuition, nonresident: full-time $14,969; part-time $9980 per year. *Required fees:* $315 per year. *Financial support:* In 2011–12, 2 research assistantships with full and partial tuition reimbursements (averaging $12,500 per year), 2 teaching assistantships with full and partial tuition reimbursements (averaging $10,500 per year) were awarded. Financial award application deadline: 4/1; financial award applicants required to submit FAFSA. *Faculty research:* Vocational interests, self-concept, decision-making factors, developmental differences. *Unit head:* Dr. Mark Pope, Chair, 314-516-5782. *Application contact:* 314-516-5458, Fax: 314-516-6996, E-mail: gradadm@umsl.edu.

University of Missouri–St. Louis, College of Education, Division of Teaching and Learning, St. Louis, MO 63121. Offers autism studies (Certificate); elementary education (M Ed), including early childhood, general, reading; secondary education (M Ed), including curriculum and instruction, general, middle level education, reading, teaching English to speakers of other languages (TESOL); secondary school teaching (Certificate); special education (M Ed), including autism and developmental disabilities, early childhood special education, general; teaching English to speakers of other languages (Certificate). Part-time and evening/weekend programs available. *Faculty:* 32 full-time (16 women), 51 part-time/adjunct (36 women). *Students:* 95 full-time (63 women), 703 part-time (541 women); includes 176 minority (125 Black or African American, non-Hispanic/Latino; 1 American Indian or Alaska Native, non-Hispanic/Latino; 16 Asian, non-Hispanic/Latino; 26 Hispanic/Latino; 8 Two or more races, non-Hispanic/Latino), 11 international. Average age 29. 379 applicants, 90% accepted, 263 enrolled. In 2011, 190 master's, 9 Certificates awarded. *Degree requirements:* For master's, comprehensive exam. *Entrance requirements:* Additional exam requirements/recommendations for international students: Recommended—TOEFL (minimum score 550 paper-based; 213 computer-based). *Application deadline:* For fall admission, 7/1 priority date for domestic students, 7/1 for international students; for spring admission, 12/1 priority date for domestic students, 12/1 for international students. Application fee: $35 ($40 for international students). Electronic applications accepted. *Expenses:* Tuition, state resident: full-time $6273; part-time $3866 per year. Tuition, nonresident: full-time $14,969; part-time $9980 per year. *Required fees:* $315 per year. *Financial support:* In 2011–12, 6 research assistantships with full and partial tuition reimbursements (averaging $9,500 per year), 2 teaching assistantships with full and partial tuition reimbursements (averaging $10,500 per year) were awarded. Financial award application deadline: 4/1; financial award applicants required to submit FAFSA. *Unit head:* Dr. Joseph Polman, Chair, 314-516-5791. *Application contact:* 314-516-5458, Fax: 314-516-6996, E-mail: gadadm@umsl.edu. Web site: http://coe.umsl.edu/web/divisions/teach-learn/index.html.

University of Montevallo, College of Education, Program in Elementary Education, Montevallo, AL 35115. Offers M Ed. *Accreditation:* NCATE. Part-time programs available. *Students:* 29 full-time (25 women), 48 part-time (47 women); includes 11 minority (all Black or African American, non-Hispanic/Latino). In 2011, 35 master's awarded. *Degree requirements:* For master's, comprehensive exam. *Entrance requirements:* For master's, GRE General Test, MAT, minimum undergraduate GPA of 2.5. Additional exam requirements/recommendations for international students: Required—TOEFL (minimum score 550 paper-based). *Application deadline:* For fall admission, 7/15 for domestic students; for spring admission, 11/15 for domestic students. Application fee: $25. *Financial support:* Federal Work-Study, scholarships/grants, and unspecified assistantships available. *Unit head:* Dr. Anna E. McEwan, Dean, 205-665-6360, E-mail: mcewanae@montevallo.edu. *Application contact:* Rebecca Hartley, Coordinator for Graduate Studies, 205-665-6350, Fax: 205-665-6353, E-mail: hartleyrs@montevallo.edu.

University of Nebraska at Omaha, Graduate Studies, College of Education, Department of Teacher Education, Program in Elementary Education, Omaha, NE 68182. Offers MA, MS. *Accreditation:* NCATE. Part-time and evening/weekend programs available. *Faculty:* 9 full-time (6 women). *Students:* 3 full-time (2 women), 103 part-time (96 women); includes 6 minority (2 Black or African American, non-Hispanic/Latino; 2 Asian, non-Hispanic/Latino; 2 Hispanic/Latino). Average age 34. 24 applicants, 79% accepted, 12 enrolled. In 2011, 42 master's awarded. *Degree requirements:* For master's, comprehensive exam (for some programs), thesis (for some programs). *Entrance requirements:* For master's, minimum GPA of 3.0. Additional exam requirements/recommendations for international students: Required—TOEFL (minimum score 550 paper-based; 213 computer-based; 80 iBT). *Application deadline:* For fall admission, 8/1 priority date for domestic students; for spring admission, 12/1 priority date for domestic students. Applications are processed on a rolling basis. Application fee: $45. Electronic applications accepted. *Financial support:* In 2011–12, 52 students received support, including 1 research assistantship with tuition reimbursement available; fellowships, teaching assistantships with tuition reimbursements available, Federal Work-Study, institutionally sponsored loans, scholarships/grants, tuition waivers (full), and unspecified assistantships also available. Support available to part-time students. Financial award application deadline: 3/1. *Unit head:* Dr. Lana Danielson, Advisor, 402-554-2212. *Application contact:* Dr. Wilma Kuhlman, Student Contact, 402-554-2212.

University of Nevada, Reno, Graduate School, College of Education, Department of Curriculum, Teaching and Learning, Program in Elementary Education, Reno, NV 89557. Offers M Ed, MA, MS. *Degree requirements:* For master's, thesis optional. *Entrance requirements:* For master's, GRE General Test, minimum GPA of 2.75. Additional exam requirements/recommendations for international students: Required—TOEFL (minimum score 500 paper-based; 173 computer-based; 61 iBT), IELTS (minimum score 6). Electronic applications accepted. *Faculty research:* Child development, educational trends.

University of New Hampshire, Graduate School, College of Liberal Arts, Department of Education, Program in Elementary Education, Durham, NH 03824. Offers M Ed, MAT. Part-time programs available. *Faculty:* 32 full-time. *Students:* 28 full-time (23 women), 43 part-time (37 women); includes 3 minority (2 Black or African American, non-Hispanic/Latino; 1 Two or more races, non-Hispanic/Latino). Average age 25. 30 applicants, 67% accepted, 15 enrolled. In 2011, 64 master's awarded. *Degree requirements:* For master's, thesis or alternative. *Entrance requirements:* For master's, GRE General Test. Additional exam requirements/recommendations for international students: Required—TOEFL (minimum score 550 paper-based; 213 computer-based; 80 iBT). *Application deadline:* For fall admission, 4/1 priority date for domestic students, 4/1 for international students; for spring admission, 11/1 for domestic students. Applications are processed on a rolling basis. Application fee: $65. *Expenses:* Tuition, state resident: full-time $12,360; part-time $687 per credit hour. Tuition, nonresident: full-time $25,680; part-time $1058 per credit hour. *International tuition:* $29,550 full-time. *Required fees:* $1666; $833 per course. $416.50 per semester. Tuition and fees vary according to course load and degree level. *Financial support:* In 2011–12, 3 students received support. Fellowships, research assistantships, teaching assistantships, career-related internships or fieldwork, Federal Work-Study, scholarships/grants, and tuition waivers (full and partial) available. Support available to part-time students. Financial award application deadline: 2/15. *Faculty research:* Pre-service teacher education. *Unit head:* Dr. Michael Middleton, Coordinator, 603-862-7054, E-mail: education.department@unh.edu. *Application contact:* Lisa Wilder, Graduate Coordinator, 603-862-2310, E-mail: education.department@unh.edu. Web site: http://www.unh.edu/education.

University of New Mexico, Graduate School, College of Education, Department of Teacher Education, Program in Elementary Education, Albuquerque, NM 87131-2039. Offers math, science, environmental and technology education (MA). Part-time programs available. *Students:* 40 full-time (37 women), 184 part-time (150 women); includes 86 minority (5 Black or African American, non-Hispanic/Latino; 11 American Indian or Alaska Native, non-Hispanic/Latino; 9 Asian, non-Hispanic/Latino; 55 Hispanic/Latino; 1 Native Hawaiian or other Pacific Islander, non-Hispanic/Latino; 5 Two or more races, non-Hispanic/Latino), 3 international. Average age 36. 87 applicants, 68% accepted, 47 enrolled. In 2011, 104 degrees awarded. *Degree requirements:* For master's, comprehensive exam, thesis optional. *Entrance requirements:* For master's, minimum overall GPA of 3.0, some experience working with students, NMTA or teacher's license, 3 letters of reference, 1 letter of intent. Additional exam requirements/recommendations for international students: Required—TOEFL (minimum score 550 paper-based; 213 computer-based). *Application deadline:* For fall admission, 3/1 for domestic students; for spring admission, 10/30 for domestic students. Application fee: $50. Electronic applications accepted. *Financial support:* In 2011–12, 127 students received support, including 1 fellowship (averaging $2,000 per year); career-related internships or fieldwork, scholarships/grants, and unspecified assistantships also available. Financial award application deadline: 4/15; financial award applicants required to submit FAFSA. *Faculty research:* Elementary education, science education, technology education, reflective practice, teacher education. *Unit head:* Dr. Rosalita Mitchell, Chair, 505-277-9611, Fax: 505-277-0455, E-mail: ted@unm.edu. *Application contact:* Mary Francis, Administrative Assistant, 505-277-9439, Fax: 505-277-0455, E-mail: ted@unm.edu. Web site: http://ted.unm.edu.

University of North Alabama, College of Education, Department of Elementary Education, Program in Elementary Education, Florence, AL 35632-0001. Offers MA Ed. *Accreditation:* NCATE. Part-time and evening/weekend programs available. *Faculty:* 4 part-time/adjunct (all women). *Students:* 5 full-time (all women), 36 part-time (34 women); includes 4 minority (3 Black or African American, non-Hispanic/Latino; 1 Two or more races, non-Hispanic/Latino). Average age 31. In 2011, 13 master's awarded. *Degree requirements:* For master's, comprehensive exam. *Entrance requirements:* For master's, GRE, MAT, or NTE, minimum GPA of 2.5, Alabama Class B Certificate or equivalent, teaching experience. *Application deadline:* For fall admission, 7/1 priority date for domestic students; for spring admission, 12/1 for domestic students. Applications are processed on a rolling basis. Application fee: $25. Electronic applications accepted. *Financial support:* Federal Work-Study available. Support available to part-time students. Financial award application deadline: 4/1. *Unit head:* Dr. Linda Armstrong, Chair, 256-765-4251, Fax: 256-765-4664, E-mail: ljarmstrong@una.edu. *Application contact:* Kim Mauldin, Director of Admissions, 256-765-4608, Fax: 256-765-4960, E-mail: komauldin@una.edu.

The University of North Carolina at Charlotte, Graduate School, College of Education, Department of Reading and Elementary Education, Charlotte, NC 28223-0001. Offers elementary education (M Ed); reading, language and literacy (M Ed). Part-time and evening/weekend programs available. Postbaccalaureate distance learning degree programs offered (no on-campus study). *Faculty:* 26 full-time (13 women), 6 part-time/adjunct (5 women). *Students:* 5 full-time (4 women), 58 part-time (all women); includes 3 minority (2 Hispanic/Latino; 1 Two or more races, non-Hispanic/Latino). Average age 30. 45 applicants, 98% accepted, 35 enrolled. In 2011, 63 master's awarded. *Degree requirements:* For master's, thesis or alternative. *Entrance requirements:* For master's, GRE or MAT. Additional exam requirements/ recommendations for international students: Required—TOEFL (minimum score 557 paper-based; 220 computer-based; 83 iBT). *Application deadline:* For fall admission, 7/1 for domestic students, 5/1 for international students; for spring admission, 11/1 for domestic students, 10/1 for international students. Applications are processed on a rolling basis. Application fee: $65 ($75 for international students). Electronic applications accepted. *Expenses:* Tuition, state resident: full-time $3689. Tuition, nonresident: full-time $15,226. *Required fees:* $2198. Tuition and fees vary according to course load and program. *Financial support:* In 2011–12, 2 students received support, including 1 research assistantship (averaging $13,500 per year); career-related internships or fieldwork, institutionally sponsored loans, scholarships/grants, unspecified assistantships, and administrative assistantship also available. Support available to part-time students. Financial award application deadline: 4/1; financial award applicants required to submit FAFSA. *Total annual research expenditures:* $8,327. *Unit head:* Dr. Robert J. Rickelman, Chair, 704-687-8890, Fax: 704-687-3749, E-mail: rjrickel@uncc.edu. *Application contact:* Kathy B. Giddings, Director of Graduate Admissions, 704-687-5503, Fax: 704-687-3279, E-mail: gradadm@uncc.edu. Web site: http://education.uncc.edu/reel.

The University of North Carolina at Greensboro, Graduate School, School of Education, Department of Curriculum and Instruction, Program in Curriculum and Teaching, Greensboro, NC 27412-5001. Offers higher education (PhD); teacher education and development (PhD). *Accreditation:* NCATE. *Degree requirements:* For doctorate, comprehensive exam, thesis/dissertation. *Entrance requirements:* For doctorate, GRE General Test. Additional exam requirements/recommendations for international students: Required—TOEFL. Electronic applications accepted.

The University of North Carolina at Pembroke, Graduate Studies, School of Education, Program in Elementary Education, Pembroke, NC 28372-1510. Offers MA Ed. *Accreditation:* NCATE. Part-time and evening/weekend programs available. *Degree requirements:* For master's, comprehensive exam, thesis optional. *Entrance requirements:* For master's, GRE General Test or MAT, minimum GPA of 3.0 in major, 2.5 overall; teaching license. Additional exam requirements/recommendations for international students: Required—TOEFL.

The University of North Carolina Wilmington, Watson School of Education, Department of Elementary, Middle Level and Literacy Education, Program in Elementary Education, Wilmington, NC 28403-3297. Offers M Ed. *Accreditation:* NCATE. Part-time and evening/weekend programs available. *Degree requirements:* For master's, comprehensive exam. *Entrance requirements:* For master's, GRE General Test, MAT, minimum B average in upper-division undergraduate course work, bachelor's degree in elementary education.

University of North Dakota, Graduate School, College of Education and Human Development, Program in Elementary Education, Grand Forks, ND 58202. Offers M Ed, MS. *Accreditation:* NCATE. Part-time programs available. Postbaccalaureate distance learning degree programs offered (minimal on-campus study). *Degree requirements:* For master's, comprehensive exam, thesis or alternative. *Entrance requirements:* For master's, minimum GPA of 3.0. Additional exam requirements/recommendations for international students: Required—TOEFL (minimum score 550 paper-based; 213 computer-based; 79 iBT), IELTS (minimum score 6.5). Electronic applications accepted. *Faculty research:* Whole language, multicultural education, child-focused learning, experiential science, cooperative learning.

University of North Dakota, Graduate School, College of Education and Human Development, Teaching and Learning Program, Grand Forks, ND 58202. Offers elementary education (Ed D, PhD); measurement and statistics (Ed D, PhD); secondary education (Ed D, PhD); special education (Ed D, PhD). *Accreditation:* NCATE. Postbaccalaureate distance learning degree programs offered (minimal on-campus study). *Degree requirements:* For doctorate, comprehensive exam, thesis/dissertation, final exam. *Entrance requirements:* For doctorate, minimum GPA of 3.5. Additional exam requirements/recommendations for international students: Required—TOEFL (minimum score 550 paper-based; 213 computer-based; 79 iBT), IELTS (minimum score 6.5). Electronic applications accepted.

University of Northern Iowa, Graduate College, College of Education, Department of Curriculum and Instruction, Program in Elementary Education, Cedar Falls, IA 50614. Offers curriculum and instruction (MAE). Part-time and evening/weekend programs available. *Students:* 15 part-time (12 women). 31 applicants, 71% accepted, 15 enrolled. In 2011, 1 master's awarded. *Degree requirements:* For master's, comprehensive exam, thesis or alternative. *Entrance requirements:* For master's, minimum GPA of 3.0. Additional exam requirements/recommendations for international students: Required—TOEFL (minimum score 500 paper-based; 180 computer-based; 61 iBT). *Application deadline:* For fall admission, 8/1 priority date for domestic students. Applications are processed on a rolling basis. Application fee: $50 ($70 for international students). *Expenses:* Tuition, state resident: full-time $7476. Tuition, nonresident: full-time $16,410. *Required fees:* $942. *Financial support:* Career-related internships or fieldwork, Federal Work-Study, and tuition waivers (full and partial) available. Support available to part-time students. Financial award application deadline: 2/1. *Unit head:* Dr. Lynn E. Nielsen, Coordinator, 319-273-7759, Fax: 319-273-5886, E-mail: lynn.nielsen@uni.edu. *Application contact:* Laurie S. Russell, Record Analyst, 319-273-2623, Fax: 319-273-2885, E-mail: laurie.russell@uni.edu. Web site: http://www.uni.edu/coe/ci/elem/index.shtml.

University of North Florida, College of Education and Human Services, Department of Childhood Education, Jacksonville, FL 32224. Offers literacy K-12 (M Ed); professional education - elementary education (M Ed); TESOL K-12 (M Ed). *Accreditation:* NCATE. Part-time and evening/weekend programs available. *Faculty:* 11 full-time (9 women). *Students:* 16 full-time (15 women), 38 part-time (37 women); includes 9 minority (3 Black or African American, non-Hispanic/Latino; 1 American Indian or Alaska Native, non-Hispanic/Latino; 1 Asian, non-Hispanic/Latino; 4 Hispanic/Latino), 3 international. Average age 29. 24 applicants, 67% accepted, 12 enrolled. In 2011, 17 master's awarded. *Entrance requirements:* For master's, GRE General Test, minimum GPA of 3.0 in last 60 hours, 3 letters of recommendation, interview. Additional exam requirements/recommendations for international students: Required—TOEFL (minimum score 500 paper-based; 173 computer-based). *Application deadline:* For fall admission, 7/1 priority date for domestic students, 5/1 for international students; for spring admission, 11/1 priority date for domestic students, 10/1 for international students. Applications are processed on a rolling basis. Application fee: $30. Electronic applications accepted. *Expenses:* Tuition, state resident: full-time $8793; part-time $366.38 per credit hour. Tuition, nonresident: full-time $23,502; part-time $979.24 per credit hour. *Required fees:* $1384; $57.66 per credit hour. Tuition and fees vary according to course load and program. *Financial support:* In 2011–12, 16 students received support, including 1 research assistantship (averaging $5,700 per year); Federal Work-Study, tuition waivers (partial), and unspecified assistantships also available. Support available to part-time students. Financial award application deadline: 4/1; financial award applicants required to submit FAFSA. *Faculty research:* The social context of and processes in learning, inter-disciplinary instruction, cross-cultural conflict resolution, the Vygotskian perspective on literacy diagnosis and instruction, performance poetry and teaching the language arts through drama. *Total annual research expenditures:* $118,609. *Unit head:* Dr. Ronghua Ouyang, Chair, 904-620-2611, Fax: 904-620-1025, E-mail: ronghua.ouyang@unf.edu. *Application contact:* Lillith Richardson, Assistant Director, The Graduate School, 904-620-1360, Fax: 904-620-1362, E-mail: graduateschool@unf.edu. Web site: http://www.unf.edu/coehs/childhood/.

University of Oklahoma, Jeannine Rainbolt College of Education, Department of Instructional Leadership and Academic Curriculum, Norman, OK 73072. Offers communication, culture and pedagogy for Hispanic populations in educational settings (Graduate Certificate); instructional leadership and academic curriculum (M Ed, PhD), including bilingual education, early childhood education, elementary education, English education, instructional leadership, mathematics education, reading education, science education, science, technology, engineering and mathematics education (M Ed), secondary education, social studies education, teacher education (M Ed). *Accreditation:* NCATE. Part-time and evening/weekend programs available. *Faculty:* 19 full-time (13 women), 1 (woman) part-time/adjunct. *Students:* 73 full-time (63 women), 114 part-time (87 women); includes 29 minority (5 Black or African American, non-Hispanic/Latino; 12 American Indian or Alaska Native, non-Hispanic/Latino; 5 Asian, non-Hispanic/Latino; 3 Hispanic/Latino; 1 Native Hawaiian or other Pacific Islander, non-Hispanic/Latino; 3 Two or more races, non-Hispanic/Latino), 7 international. Average age 33. 87 applicants, 86% accepted, 68 enrolled. In 2011, 36 master's, 6 doctorates awarded. Terminal master's awarded for partial completion of doctoral program. *Degree requirements:* For doctorate, thesis/dissertation. *Entrance requirements:* For master's, 12 hours of course work in education; for doctorate, GRE General Test, master's degree, minimum graduate GPA of 3.0. Additional exam requirements/recommendations for international students: Required—TOEFL (minimum score 550 paper-based; 79 iBT). *Application deadline:* For fall admission, 6/1 priority date for domestic students, 3/1 for international students; for spring admission, 11/1 for domestic students, 9/1 for international students. Applications are processed on a rolling basis. Application fee: $40 ($90 for international students). Electronic applications accepted. *Expenses:* Tuition, state resident: full-time $4087; part-time $170.30 per credit hour. Tuition, nonresident: full-time $14,875; part-time $619.80 per credit hour. *Required fees:* $2659; $100.25 per credit hour. Tuition and fees vary according to course load and degree level. *Financial support:* In 2011–12, 128 students received support, including 2 research assistantships with partial tuition reimbursements available (averaging $12,431 per year), 12 teaching assistantships with partial tuition reimbursements available (averaging $10,161 per year); institutionally sponsored loans, scholarships/grants, and unspecified assistantships also available. Financial award applicants required to submit FAFSA. *Faculty research:* Engineering in practice for sustainable future, no child left behind (reading), early childhood learning games impact study, Educare randomized control startup, Oklahoma mentoring professional development. *Total annual research expenditures:* $1.1 million. *Unit head:* Lawrence Baines, Chair, 405-325-1498, Fax: 405-325-4061, E-mail: lbaines@ou.edu. *Application contact:* Lynn Crussel, Graduate Programs Officer, 405-325-4843, Fax: 405-325-4061, E-mail: lcrussel@ou.edu. Web site: http://education.ou.edu/departments/ilac.

University of Pennsylvania, Graduate School of Education, Division of Teaching, Learning, and Leadership, Teacher Education Program, Philadelphia, PA 19104. Offers elementary education (MS Ed); secondary education (MS Ed). *Students:* 76 full-time (55 women), 1 (woman) part-time; includes 22 minority (9 Black or African American, non-Hispanic/Latino; 4 Asian, non-Hispanic/Latino; 5 Hispanic/Latino; 4 Two or more races, non-Hispanic/Latino). 207 applicants, 72% accepted, 77 enrolled. In 2011, 113 degrees awarded. *Degree requirements:* For master's, comprehensive exam or portfolio. *Entrance requirements:* For master's, GRE General Test, MAT. *Application deadline:* For fall admission, 12/15 priority date for domestic students. Applications are processed on a rolling basis. Application fee: $70. Electronic applications accepted. *Expenses:* Contact institution. *Financial support:* Fellowships available. Financial award applicants required to submit FAFSA. *Unit head:* Dr. Andrew Porter, Dean, 215-898-7014. *Application contact:* Maureen Cotterill, 215-898-7364, E-mail: maureenc@gse.upenn.edu. Web site: http://tep.gse.upenn.edu/join/join_ms-ed.html.

University of Phoenix–Bay Area Campus, College of Education, San Jose, CA 95134-1805. Offers administration and supervision (MA Ed); adult education and training (MA Ed); early childhood education (MA Ed); education (Ed S); educational leadership (Ed D); elementary teacher education (MA Ed); higher education administration (PhD); secondary teacher education (MA Ed); special education (MA Ed); teacher leadership (MA Ed). Evening/weekend programs available. Postbaccalaureate distance learning degree programs offered (no on-campus study). *Degree requirements:* For master's, thesis (for some programs). *Entrance requirements:* For master's, minimum undergraduate GPA of 2.5, 3 years of work experience. Additional exam requirements/recommendations for international students: Required—TOEFL (minimum score 550 paper-based; 213 computer-based; 79 iBT). Electronic applications accepted.

University of Phoenix–Central Florida Campus, College of Education, Maitland, FL 32751-7057. Offers administration and supervision (MA Ed); curriculum and instruction (MA Ed); curriculum and instruction-computer education (MA Ed); curriculum and instruction-mathematics education (MA Ed); early childhood education (MA Ed); elementary teacher education (MA Ed); secondary teacher education (MA Ed). Evening/weekend programs available. *Degree requirements:* For master's, thesis (for some programs). *Entrance requirements:* For master's, 3 years of work experience, minimum undergraduate GPA of 2.5. Additional exam requirements/recommendations for international students: Required—TOEFL (minimum score 550 paper-based; 213 computer-based; 79 iBT). Electronic applications accepted.

University of Phoenix–Central Valley Campus, College of Education, Fresno, CA 93720-1562. Offers curriculum and instruction (MA Ed); curriculum and instruction-computer education (MA Ed); elementary teacher education (MA Ed); secondary teacher education (MA Ed).

University of Phoenix–Chattanooga Campus, College of Education, Chattanooga, TN 37421-3707. Offers administration and supervision (MA Ed); curriculum and instruction (MA Ed); elementary teacher education (MA Ed); secondary teacher education (MA Ed).

University of Phoenix–Denver Campus, College of Education, Lone Tree, CO 80124-5453. Offers administration and supervision (MAEd); curriculum instruction (MAEd); elementary teacher education (MAEd); school counseling (MSC); secondary teacher education (MAEd). Evening/weekend programs available. *Degree requirements:* For master's, thesis (for some programs). *Entrance requirements:* For master's, minimum undergraduate GPA of 2.5, 3 years work experience. Additional exam requirements/recommendations for international students: Required—TOEFL (minimum score 550 paper-based; 213 computer-based; 79 iBT). Electronic applications accepted.

University of Phoenix–Hawaii Campus, College of Education, Honolulu, HI 96813-4317. Offers administration and supervision (MA Ed); curriculum and instruction (MA Ed); elementary education (MA Ed); secondary education (MA Ed); special education (MA Ed); teacher education for elementary licensure (MA Ed). Evening/weekend programs available. *Degree requirements:* For master's, thesis (for some programs). *Entrance requirements:* For master's, minimum undergraduate GPA of 2.5, 3 years of work experience. Additional exam requirements/recommendations for international students: Required—TOEFL (minimum score 550 paper-based; 213 computer-based; 79 iBT). Electronic applications accepted.

University of Phoenix–Idaho Campus, College of Education, Meridian, ID 83642-5114. Offers administration and supervision (MA Ed); curriculum and instruction (MA Ed); elementary teacher education (MA Ed); secondary teacher education (MA Ed). Evening/weekend programs available. *Degree requirements:* For master's, thesis (for some programs). *Entrance requirements:* For master's, minimum undergraduate GPA of 2.5, 3 years of work experience. Additional exam requirements/recommendations for international students: Required—TOEFL (minimum score 550 paper-based; 213 computer-based). Electronic applications accepted.

University of Phoenix–Indianapolis Campus, College of Education, Indianapolis, IN 46250-932. Offers elementary teacher education (MA Ed); secondary teacher education (MA Ed).

University of Phoenix–Las Vegas Campus, College of Education, Las Vegas, NV 89128. Offers administration and supervision (MA Ed); curriculum and instruction (MA Ed); school counseling (MSC); teacher education-elementary licensure (MA Ed). Evening/weekend programs available. *Degree requirements:* For master's, thesis (for some programs). *Entrance requirements:* For master's, minimum undergraduate GPA of 2.5, 3 years of work experience. Additional exam requirements/recommendations for international students: Required—TOEFL (minimum score 550 paper-based; 213 computer-based; 79 iBT). Electronic applications accepted.

University of Phoenix–Memphis Campus, College of Education, Cordova, TN 38018. Offers administration and supervision (MA Ed); curriculum and instruction (MA Ed); elementary teacher education (MA Ed); secondary teacher education (MA Ed).

University of Phoenix–Metro Detroit Campus, College of Education, Troy, MI 48098-2623. Offers administration and supervision (MA Ed); elementary teacher education (MA Ed); secondary teacher education (MA Ed); special education (MA Ed). Evening/weekend programs available. *Degree requirements:* For master's, thesis (for some programs). *Entrance requirements:* For master's, 3 years of work experience, minimum undergraduate GPA of 2.5. Additional exam requirements/recommendations for international students: Required—TOEFL (minimum score 550 paper-based; 213 computer-based; 79 iBT). Electronic applications accepted.

University of Phoenix–Nashville Campus, College of Education, Nashville, TN 37214-5048. Offers administration and supervision (MA Ed); curriculum and instruction (MA Ed); elementary teacher education (MA Ed); secondary teacher education (MA Ed). Evening/weekend programs available. *Degree requirements:* For master's, thesis (for some programs). *Entrance requirements:* For master's, minimum undergraduate GPA of 2.5, 3 years work experience. Additional exam requirements/recommendations for international students: Required—TOEFL (minimum score 500 paper-based; 213 computer-based; 79 iBT). Electronic applications accepted.

University of Phoenix–New Mexico Campus, College of Education, Albuquerque, NM 87113-1570. Offers administration and supervision (MAEd); curriculum and instruction (MAEd); elementary teacher education (MAEd); school counseling (MSC); secondary teacher education (MAEd). Evening/weekend programs available. *Degree requirements:* For master's, thesis (for some programs). *Entrance requirements:* For master's, minimum undergraduate GPA of 2.5, 3 years of work experience. Additional exam requirements/recommendations for international students: Required—TOEFL (minimum score 550 paper-based; 213 computer-based; 79 iBT). Electronic applications accepted.

University of Phoenix–Northern Nevada Campus, College of Education, Reno, NV 89521-5862. Offers administration and supervision (MA Ed); curriculum and instruction (MA Ed); elementary teacher education (MA Ed); secondary teacher education (MA Ed).

University of Phoenix–North Florida Campus, College of Education, Jacksonville, FL 32216-0959. Offers administration and supervision (MA Ed); curriculum and instruction (MA Ed), including computer education, mathematics education; early childhood education (MA Ed); elementary teacher education (MA Ed); secondary teacher education (MA Ed). Evening/weekend programs available. *Degree requirements:* For master's, thesis (for some programs). *Entrance requirements:* For master's, 3 years of work experience, minimum undergraduate GPA of 2.5. Additional exam requirements/recommendations for international students: Required—TOEFL (minimum score 550 paper-based; 213 computer-based; 49 iBT). Electronic applications accepted.

University of Phoenix–Omaha Campus, College of Education, Omaha, NE 68154-5240. Offers administration and supervision (MA Ed); curriculum and instruction (MA Ed), including adult education, computer education, curriculum and instruction, English and language arts education, English as a second language, mathematics education; elementary teacher education (MA Ed); secondary teacher education (MA Ed); special education (MA Ed).

University of Phoenix–Online Campus, College of Education, Phoenix, AZ 85034-7209. Offers administration and supervision (MAEd, Graduate Certificate); adult education and training (MAEd); curriculum and instruction (MAEd); curriculum and instruction reading (MAEd); curriculum and instruction-computer education (MAEd); curriculum and instruction-language arts (MAEd); curriculum and instruction-mathematics (MAEd); early childhood education (MAEd); educational studies (MAEd); elementary teacher education (MAEd); elementary teacher education-early childhood (MAEd); secondary teacher education (MAEd); special education (MAEd); teacher education - elementary/middle level (MAEd); teacher education middle level generalist (MAEd); teacher education middle level mathematics (MAEd); teacher education middle level science (MAEd); teacher education secondary mathematics (MAEd); teacher education secondary science (MAEd); teacher leadership (MAEd). *Accreditation:* Teacher Education Accreditation Council. Evening/weekend programs available. Postbaccalaureate distance learning degree programs offered. *Students:* 9,180 full-time (7,178 women); includes 2,913 minority (2,069 Black or African American, non-Hispanic/Latino; 50 American Indian or Alaska Native, non-Hispanic/Latino; 100 Asian, non-Hispanic/Latino; 542 Hispanic/Latino; 48 Native Hawaiian or other Pacific Islander, non-Hispanic/Latino; 104 Two or more races, non-Hispanic/Latino), 147 international. Average age 36. *Entrance requirements:* Additional exam requirements/recommendations for international students: Required—TOEFL, TOEIC (Test of English as an International Communication), Berlitz Online English Proficiency Exam, Pearson Test of English, or IELTS. *Application deadline:* Applications are processed on a rolling basis. Application fee: $45. Electronic applications accepted. *Expenses:* Contact institution. *Financial support:* Scholarships/grants available. Financial award applicants required to submit FAFSA. *Application contact:* 866-766-0766. Web site: http://www.phoenix.edu/colleges_divisions/education.html.

University of Phoenix–Oregon Campus, College of Education, Tigard, OR 97223. Offers curriculum and instruction (MA Ed); early childhood education (MA Ed); elementary education (MA Ed), including early childhood specialization, middle level specialization; secondary education (MA Ed), including middle level specialization. Evening/weekend programs available. *Degree requirements:* For master's, thesis (for some programs). *Entrance requirements:* For master's, minimum undergraduate GPA of 2.5, 3 years work experience. Additional exam requirements/recommendations for international students: Required—TOEFL (minimum score 550 paper-based; 213 computer-based; 79 iBT). Electronic applications accepted.

University of Phoenix–Phoenix Main Campus, College of Education, Tempe, AZ 85282-2371. Offers administration and supervision (MA Ed); adult education and training (MA Ed); curriculum and instruction reading (MA Ed); curriculum instruction (MA Ed); early childhood education (MA Ed); education studies (MA Ed); elementary teacher education (MA Ed); secondary teacher education (MA Ed); special education (MA Ed); teacher leadership (MA Ed). Evening/weekend programs available. Postbaccalaureate distance learning degree programs offered. *Students:* 297 full-time (203 women); includes 53 minority (19 Black or African American, non-Hispanic/Latino; 1 American Indian or Alaska Native, non-Hispanic/Latino; 6 Asian, non-Hispanic/Latino; 21 Hispanic/Latino; 2 Native Hawaiian or other Pacific Islander, non-Hispanic/Latino; 4 Two or more races, non-Hispanic/Latino), 3 international. Average age 35. *Entrance requirements:* Additional exam requirements/recommendations for international students: Required—TOEFL, TOEIC (Test of English as an International Communication), Berlitz Online English Proficiency Exam, Pearson Test of English, or IELTS. *Application deadline:* Applications are processed on a rolling basis. Application fee: $45. Electronic applications accepted. *Expenses:* Contact institution. *Financial support:* Scholarships/grants available. Financial award applicants required to submit FAFSA. *Application contact:* 866-766-0766. Web site: http://www.phoenix.edu/colleges_divisions/education.html.

University of Phoenix–Sacramento Valley Campus, College of Education, Sacramento, CA 95833-3632. Offers adult education (MA Ed); curriculum instruction (MA Ed); elementary teacher education (MA Ed); secondary teacher education (MA Ed); teacher education (Certificate). Evening/weekend programs available. *Degree requirements:* For master's, thesis (for some programs). *Entrance requirements:* For master's, 3 years of work experience, minimum undergraduate GPA of 2.5. Additional exam requirements/recommendations for international students: Required—TOEFL (minimum score 550 paper-based; 213 computer-based; 79 iBT). Electronic applications accepted.

University of Phoenix–San Diego Campus, College of Education, San Diego, CA 92123. Offers curriculum and instruction (MA Ed), including computer education, curriculum and instruction, English as a second language; elementary teacher education (MA Ed); secondary teacher education (MA Ed). Evening/weekend programs available. *Degree requirements:* For master's, thesis (for some programs). *Entrance requirements:* For master's, 3 years of work experience, minimum undergraduate GPA of 3.0. Additional exam requirements/recommendations for international students: Required—TOEFL (minimum score 550 paper-based; 213 computer-based; 79 iBT). Electronic applications accepted.

University of Phoenix–Southern Arizona Campus, College of Education, Tucson, AZ 85711. Offers administration and supervision (MA Ed); adult education and training (MA Ed); curriculum instruction (MA Ed); educational counseling (MA Ed); elementary teacher education (MA Ed); school counseling (MSC); secondary teacher education (MA Ed); special education (MA Ed, Certificate). Evening/weekend programs available. *Degree requirements:* For master's, thesis (for some programs). *Entrance requirements:* For master's, minimum undergraduate GPA of 2.5, 3 years of work experience. Additional exam requirements/recommendations for international students: Required—TOEFL (minimum score 550 paper-based; 213 computer-based; 79 iBT). Electronic applications accepted.

University of Phoenix–Southern Colorado Campus, College of Education, Colorado Springs, CO 80919-2335. Offers administration and supervision (MA Ed); curriculum and instruction (MA Ed); elementary teacher education (MA Ed); principal licensure certification (Certificate); school counseling (MSC); secondary teacher education (MA Ed). Evening/weekend programs available. *Degree requirements:* For master's, thesis (for some programs). *Entrance requirements:* For master's, minimum undergraduate GPA of 2.5, 3 years of work experience. Additional exam requirements/recommendations for international students: Required—TOEFL (minimum score 550 paper-based; 213 computer-based; 79 iBT). Electronic applications accepted.

University of Phoenix–South Florida Campus, College of Education, Fort Lauderdale, FL 33309. Offers administration and supervision (MA Ed); curriculum and instruction (MA Ed), including computer education, curriculum and instruction, mathematics education; early childhood education (MA Ed); elementary teacher education (MA Ed); secondary teacher education (MA Ed). Evening/weekend programs available. *Degree requirements:* For master's, thesis (for some programs). *Entrance requirements:* For master's, 3 years of work experience, minimum undergraduate GPA of 2.5. Additional exam requirements/recommendations for international students: Required—TOEFL (minimum score 550 paper-based; 213 computer-based; 79 iBT). Electronic applications accepted.

University of Phoenix–Utah Campus, College of Education, Salt Lake City, UT 84123-4617. Offers administration and supervision (MA Ed); curriculum and instruction (MA Ed); elementary teacher education (MA Ed); school counseling (MSC); secondary teacher education (MA Ed); special education (MA Ed). Evening/weekend programs available. *Degree requirements:* For master's, thesis (for some programs). *Entrance requirements:* For master's, minimum undergraduate GPA of 2.5, 3 years work experience. Additional exam requirements/recommendations for international students: Required—TOEFL (minimum score 550 paper-based; 213 computer-based; 79 iBT). Electronic applications accepted.

University of Phoenix–Washington D.C. Campus, College of Education, Washington, DC 20001. Offers administration and supervision (MA Ed); adult education and training (MA Ed); computer education (MA Ed); curriculum and instruction (MA Ed, Ed D); early childhood education (MA Ed); education (Ed S); educational leadership (Ed D); educational technology (Ed D); elementary teacher education (MA Ed); English and language arts education (MA Ed); English as a second language (MA Ed); higher education administration (PhD); mathematics education (MA Ed); secondary teacher education (MA Ed); special education (MA Ed); teacher leadership (MA Ed).

University of Phoenix–West Florida Campus, College of Education, Temple Terrace, FL 33637. Offers administration and supervision (MA Ed); curriculum and instruction (MA Ed), including computer education, curriculum and instruction, mathematics education; curriculum and technology (MA Ed); early childhood education (MA Ed); elementary teacher education (MA Ed); secondary teacher education (MA Ed). Evening/weekend programs available. *Degree requirements:* For master's, thesis (for some programs). *Entrance requirements:* For master's, 3 years of work experience, minimum undergraduate GPA of 2.5. Additional exam requirements/recommendations for international students: Required—TOEFL (minimum score 550 paper-based; 213 computer-based; 79 iBT).

University of Pittsburgh, School of Education, Department of Instruction and Learning, Program in Elementary Education, Pittsburgh, PA 15260. Offers M Ed, MAT. *Students:* 67 full-time (51 women), 24 part-time (22 women); includes 7 minority (2 Black or African American, non-Hispanic/Latino; 2 Asian, non-Hispanic/Latino; 1 Hispanic/Latino; 2 Two or more races, non-Hispanic/Latino). Average age 26. 45 applicants, 89% accepted, 38 enrolled. In 2011, 61 degrees awarded. *Degree requirements:* For master's, thesis. *Entrance requirements:* For master's, PRAXIS I. Additional exam requirements/recommendations for international students: Required—TOEFL. *Application deadline:* For fall admission, 2/1 for domestic students. Application fee: $50. Electronic applications accepted. *Expenses:* Tuition, state resident: full-time $18,774; part-time $760 per credit. Tuition, nonresident: full-time $30,736; part-time $1258 per credit. *Required fees:* $740; $200 per term. Tuition and fees vary according to program. *Financial support:* In 2011–12, fellowships (averaging $1,000 per year) were awarded; career-related internships or fieldwork, Federal Work-Study, traineeships, and tuition waivers (partial) also available. Support available to part-time students. Financial award application deadline: 3/15; financial award applicants required to submit FAFSA. *Unit head:* Dr. Richard Donato, Chairman, 412-624-7248, Fax: 412-648-7081, E-mail: donato@pitt.edu. *Application contact:* Dr. Marjie Schermer, Graduate Enrollment Manager, 412-648-2230, Fax: 412-648-1899, E-mail: soeinfo@pitt.edu.

University of Pittsburgh, School of Education, Department of Instruction and Learning, Program in Special Education, Pittsburgh, PA 15260. Offers combined studies in early childhood and special education (M Ed); early education of disabled students (M Ed); education of students with mental and physical disabilities (M Ed); general special education (M Ed); special education (Ed D, PhD); special education teacher preparation K-8 (M Ed); vision studies (M Ed). Part-time and evening/weekend programs available. *Students:* 65 full-time (57 women), 87 part-time (76 women); includes 9 minority (3 Black or African American, non-Hispanic/Latino; 2 Asian, non-Hispanic/Latino; 2 Hispanic/Latino; 2 Two or more races, non-Hispanic/Latino), 4 international. Average age 32. 58 applicants, 86% accepted, 45 enrolled. In 2011, 62 degrees awarded. *Degree requirements:* For master's, thesis; for doctorate, thesis/dissertation. *Entrance requirements:* For master's, PRAXIS I; for doctorate, GRE General Test. Additional exam requirements/recommendations for international students: Required—TOEFL. *Application deadline:* For fall admission, 2/1 priority date for domestic students; for spring admission, 11/1 priority date for domestic students. Applications are processed on a rolling basis. Application fee: $50. *Expenses:* Tuition, state resident: full-time $18,774; part-time $760 per credit. Tuition, nonresident: full-time $30,736; part-time $1258 per credit. *Required fees:* $740; $200 per term. Tuition and fees vary according to program. *Financial support:* Research assistantships, teaching assistantships, career-related internships or fieldwork, Federal Work-Study, and tuition waivers (partial) available. Support available to part-time students. Financial award application deadline: 3/15; financial award applicants required to submit FAFSA. *Unit head:* Dr. Richard Donato, Chairman, 412-624-7248, Fax: 412-648-7081, E-mail: donato@pitt.edu. *Application contact:* Lauren Spadafora, Graduate Enrollment Manager, 412-648-2230, Fax: 412-648-1899, E-mail: soeinfo@pitt.edu. Web site: http://www.education.pitt.edu/AcademicDepartments/InstructionLearning/Programs/GeneralSpecialEducation.aspx.

University of Puget Sound, Graduate Studies, School of Education, Program in Teaching, Tacoma, WA 98416. Offers elementary education (MAT); secondary education (MAT). *Accreditation:* NASM; NCATE. *Faculty:* 6 full-time (3 women). *Students:* 27 full-time (17 women); includes 3 minority (all Hispanic/Latino). Average age 25. 53 applicants, 74% accepted, 27 enrolled. In 2011, 33 master's awarded. *Degree requirements:* For master's, capstone course. *Entrance requirements:* For master's, GRE General Test, WEST-B, WEST-E in content area, minimum GPA of 3.0. Additional exam requirements/recommendations for international students: Required—TOEFL (minimum score 550 paper-based; 213 computer-based; 80 iBT). *Application deadline:* For fall admission, 3/1 priority date for domestic students, 3/1 for international students. Applications are processed on a rolling basis. Application fee: $60. Electronic applications accepted. *Financial support:* In 2011–12, 24 students received support. Career-related internships or fieldwork and scholarships/grants available. Financial award application deadline: 3/31; financial award applicants required to submit FAFSA. *Faculty research:* Math education, social studies education, professional development, international education, classroom discourse, equity education. *Unit head:* Dr. John Woodward, Dean, 253-879-3375, E-mail: woodward@pugetsound.edu. *Application contact:* Dr. George H. Mills, Jr., Vice President for Enrollment, 253-879-3211, Fax: 253-879-3993, E-mail: admission@pugetsound.edu. Web site: http://www.pugetsound.edu/academics/departments-and-programs/graduate/school-of-education/mat/.

University of Rhode Island, Graduate School, College of Human Science and Services, School of Education, Kingston, RI 02881. Offers adult education (MA); education (PhD); elementary education (MA); music education (MM); reading education (MA); secondary education (MA); special education (MA); MS/PhD. *Accreditation:* NCATE. Part-time and evening/weekend programs available. *Faculty:* 21 full-time (13 women), 3 part-time/adjunct (1 woman). *Students:* 54 full-time (48 women), 108 part-time (86 women); includes 14 minority (3 Black or African American, non-Hispanic/Latino; 4 Asian, non-Hispanic/Latino; 7 Hispanic/Latino), 4 international. In 2011, 56 master's, 8 doctorates awarded. *Degree requirements:* For master's, comprehensive exam (for some programs), thesis optional; for doctorate, comprehensive exam, thesis/dissertation. *Entrance requirements:* For master's, 2 letters of recommendation; interview (for special education applicants); for doctorate, GRE, 3 letters of recommendation, resume. Additional exam requirements/recommendations for international students: Required—TOEFL (minimum score 600 paper-based; 250 computer-based; 100 iBT). *Application deadline:* For fall admission, 1/31 for international students. Application fee: $65. Electronic applications accepted. *Expenses:* Tuition, state resident: full-time $10,432; part-time $580 per credit hour. Tuition, nonresident: full-time $23,130; part-time $1285 per credit hour. *Required fees:* $1362; $36 per credit hour. $35 per semester. One-time fee: $130. *Financial support:* In 2011–12, 4 teaching assistantships with full and partial tuition reimbursements (averaging $12,157 per year) were awarded; career-related internships or fieldwork also available. Financial award applicants required to submit FAFSA. *Unit head:* Dr. David Byrd, Director, 401-874-5484, Fax: 401-874-5471, E-mail: dbyrd@uri.edu. *Application contact:* Dr. John Boulmetis, Coordinator of Graduate Studies, 401-874-4159, Fax: 401-874-7610, E-mail: johnb@uri.edu. Web site: http://www.uri.edu/hss/education/.

University of St. Francis, College of Education, Joliet, IL 60435-6169. Offers educational leadership (MS, Ed D); elementary education certification (M Ed); reading (MS); secondary education certification (M Ed), including English education, math education, science education, social studies education, visual arts education; special education (M Ed); teaching and learning (MS). *Accreditation:* NCATE. Part-time and evening/weekend programs available. Postbaccalaureate distance learning degree programs offered (no on-campus study). *Faculty:* 7 full-time (5 women), 21 part-time/adjunct (14 women). *Students:* 32 full-time (21 women), 230 part-time (175 women); includes 23 minority (7 Black or African American, non-Hispanic/Latino; 2 Asian, non-Hispanic/Latino; 13 Hispanic/Latino; 1 Two or more races, non-Hispanic/Latino), 1 international. Average age 32. 147 applicants, 60% accepted, 57 enrolled. In 2011, 156 master's awarded. *Entrance requirements:* For doctorate, master's degree, IL Type 75 or Principal's endorsement, interview. Additional exam requirements/recommendations for international students: Required—TOEFL (minimum score 550 paper-based; 213 computer-based). *Application deadline:* Applications are processed on a rolling basis. Application fee: $30. Electronic applications accepted. *Expenses:* Contact institution. *Financial support:* In 2011–12, 23 students received support. Federal Work-Study, scholarships/grants, tuition waivers (partial), and unspecified assistantships available. Support available to part-time students. Financial award applicants required to submit FAFSA. *Unit head:* Dr. John Gambro, Dean, 815-740-3829, Fax: 815-740-2264, E-mail: jgambro@stfrancis.edu. *Application contact:* Sandra Sloka, Director of Admissions for Graduate and Degree Completion Programs, 800-735-7500, Fax: 815-740-5032, E-mail: ssloka@stfrancis.edu. Web site: http://www.stfrancis.edu/academics/college-of-education/.

University of St. Thomas, Graduate Studies, School of Education, Department of Teacher Education, St. Paul, MN 55105-1096. Offers curriculum and instruction (MA), including elementary, individualized, K-12, secondary; elementary (MAT); engineering education (Certificate); English as a second language (MA); math education (Certificate); multicultural education (Certificate); reading (MA, Certificate), including elementary (MA), K-12 (MA). *Accreditation:* NCATE. Part-time and evening/weekend programs available. *Faculty:* 7 full-time (4 women), 26 part-time/adjunct (20 women). *Students:* 19 full-time (14 women), 161 part-time (113 women); includes 28 minority (3 Black or African American, non-Hispanic/Latino; 7 American Indian or Alaska Native, non-Hispanic/Latino; 6 Asian, non-Hispanic/Latino; 9 Hispanic/Latino; 3 Two or more races, non-Hispanic/Latino), 5 international. Average age 35. 150 applicants, 79% accepted, 88 enrolled. In 2011, 83 master's awarded. *Entrance requirements:* For master's, minimum GPA of 3.0 or MAT. Additional exam requirements/recommendations for international students: Required—TOEFL (minimum score 550 paper-based; 210 computer-based; 80 iBT). *Application deadline:* For fall admission, 6/1 for domestic students; for spring admission, 11/1 for domestic students. Applications are processed on a rolling basis. Application fee: $50. *Financial support:* Fellowships, research assistantships, institutionally sponsored loans, and scholarships/grants available. Support available to part-time students. Financial award applicants required to submit FAFSA. *Unit head:* Dr. Jan L. H. Frank, Department Chair, 651-962-4446, Fax: 651-962-4169, E-mail: jlhfrank@stthomas.edu. *Application contact:* Rosemary R. Barreto, Department Assistant, 651-962-4420, Fax: 651-962-4169, E-mail: barr7879@stthomas.edu. Web site: http://www.stthomas.edu/education.

University of St. Thomas, School of Education, Houston, TX 77006-4696. Offers all level teaching (M Ed); bilingual/dual language (M Ed); Catholic school teaching (M Ed); Catholic/private school leadership (M Ed); counselor education (M Ed); curriculum and instruction (M Ed); educational leadership (M Ed); elementary teaching (M Ed); English as a second language (M Ed); exceptionality/ educational diagnostician (M Ed); exceptionality/special education (M Ed); generalist (M Ed); reading (M Ed); secondary teaching (M Ed). Part-time and evening/weekend programs available. Postbaccalaureate distance learning degree programs offered (no on-campus study). *Faculty:* 30 full-time (17 women), 54 part-time/adjunct (37 women). *Students:* 66 full-time (43 women), 1,178 part-time (1,044 women); includes 777 minority (313 Black or African American, non-Hispanic/Latino; 5 American Indian or Alaska Native, non-Hispanic/Latino; 29 Asian, non-Hispanic/Latino; 395 Hispanic/Latino; 2 Native Hawaiian or other Pacific Islander, non-Hispanic/Latino; 33 Two or more races, non-Hispanic/Latino), 26 international. Average age 36. 551 applicants, 94% accepted, 416 enrolled. In 2011, 72 master's awarded. *Degree requirements:* For master's, thesis, field experience. *Entrance requirements:* For master's, GRE or MAT if GPA is below 3.0, bachelor's degree; minimum GPA of 2.75 in bachelor's degree or last 60 credit hours; official transcripts from all institutions; goal statement of 250-300 words; 1 reference. Additional exam requirements/recommendations for international students: Required—TOEFL. *Application deadline:* Applications are processed on a rolling basis. Application fee: $35. Electronic applications accepted. *Expenses:* Contact institution. *Financial support:* In 2011–12, 9 students received support. Federal Work-Study, scholarships/grants, and state work-study, institutional employment available. Support available to part-time students. Financial award application deadline: 4/15; financial award applicants required to submit FAFSA. *Faculty research:* Leadership, diversity, personality traits, second language acquisition. *Unit head:* Dr. Nora Hutto, Dean, 713-525-3540, Fax: 713-525-3871, E-mail: education@stthom.edu. *Application contact:* Paula C. Hollis, Administrative Assistant, 713-525-3540, Fax: 713-525-3871, E-mail: education@stthom.edu. Web site: http://www.stthom.edu/Schools_Centers_of_Excellence/Schools_of_Study/School_of_Education/Index.aqf.

The University of Scranton, College of Graduate and Continuing Education, Department of Education, Program in Elementary Education, Scranton, PA 18510. Offers MS. *Accreditation:* NCATE. Part-time and evening/weekend programs available. *Students:* 5 full-time (3 women). Average age 26. In 2011, 2 master's awarded. *Degree requirements:* For master's, comprehensive exam, capstone experience. *Entrance requirements:* For master's, minimum GPA of 2.75. Additional exam requirements/recommendations for international students: Required—TOEFL (minimum score 500 paper-based; 173 computer-based), IELTS (minimum score 5.5). *Application deadline:* Applications are processed on a rolling basis. Application fee: $0. *Financial support:* Fellowships, teaching assistantships, career-related internships or fieldwork, Federal Work-Study, and unspecified assistantships available. Support available to part-time students. Financial award application deadline: 3/1. *Unit head:* Dr. Art Chambers, Director, 570-941-4668, Fax: 570-941-5515, E-mail: stufftda@scranton.edu. *Application contact:* Joseph M. Roback, Director of Admissions, 570-941-4385, Fax: 570-941-5928, E-mail: robackj2@scranton.edu.

University of South Alabama, Graduate School, College of Education, Department of Leadership and Teacher Education, Mobile, AL 36688-0002. Offers early childhood education (M Ed); educational administration (Ed S); educational leadership (M Ed); elementary education (M Ed); reading education (M Ed); science education (M Ed); secondary education (M Ed); special education (M Ed, Ed S). *Accreditation:* NCATE. Part-time programs available. *Faculty:* 20 full-time (14 women). *Students:* 135 full-time (106 women), 75 part-time (62 women); includes 50 minority (40 Black or African American, non-Hispanic/Latino; 3 American Indian or Alaska Native, non-Hispanic/Latino; 3 Asian, non-Hispanic/Latino; 3 Hispanic/Latino; 1 Two or more races, non-Hispanic/Latino), 1 international. 89 applicants, 49% accepted, 36 enrolled. In 2011, 88 master's, 13 Ed Ss awarded. *Degree requirements:* For master's, comprehensive exam. *Entrance requirements:* For master's, GRE General Test or MAT, minimum GPA of 3.0. *Application deadline:* For fall admission, 7/15 priority date for domestic students, 6/15 for international students; for spring admission, 12/1 priority date for domestic students, 11/1 for international students. Applications are processed on a rolling basis. Application fee: $35. *Expenses:* Tuition, state resident: full-time $7968; part-time $332 per credit hour. Tuition, nonresident: full-time $15,936; part-time $664 per credit hour. *Financial support:* Research assistantships and career-related internships or fieldwork available. Support available to part-time students. Financial award application deadline: 4/1. *Unit head:* Dr. Harold Dodge, Jr., Chair, 251-380-2894. *Application contact:* Dr. Abigail Baxter, Director of Graduate Studies, 251-460-6310, Fax: 251-461-1513, E-mail: kharriso@usouthal.edu. Web site: http://www.southalabama.edu/coe/lted.

University of South Carolina, The Graduate School, College of Education, Department of Instruction and Teacher Education, Program in Elementary Education, Columbia, SC 29208. Offers MAT, Ed D, PhD. *Accreditation:* NCATE. *Degree requirements:* For master's, comprehensive exam; for doctorate, one foreign language, comprehensive exam, thesis/dissertation. *Entrance requirements:* For master's, GRE General Test, MAT, interview, letters of reference, resume; for doctorate, GRE General Test, MAT, interview, letters of reference, letters of intent, resum&e, transcript. *Faculty research:* Children's conception of science, whole language, middle school curriculum.

Elementary Education

University of South Carolina Upstate, Graduate Programs, Spartanburg, SC 29303-4999. Offers early childhood education (M Ed); elementary education (M Ed); special education: visual impairment (M Ed). *Accreditation:* NCATE. Part-time and evening/weekend programs available. *Faculty:* 8 full-time (6 women), 4 part-time/adjunct (2 women). *Students:* 6 full-time (all women), 69 part-time (63 women); includes 16 minority (14 Black or African American, non-Hispanic/Latino; 2 Two or more races, non-Hispanic/Latino), 2 international. Average age 33. In 2011, 8 master's awarded. *Degree requirements:* For master's, professional portfolio. *Entrance requirements:* For master's, GRE General Test or MAT, interview, minimum undergraduate GPA of 2.5, teaching certificate, 2 letters of recommendation. *Application deadline:* Applications are processed on a rolling basis. Application fee: $40. *Expenses:* Tuition, state resident: full-time $10,916; part-time $455 per credit hour. Tuition, nonresident: full-time $23,444; part-time $977 per credit hour. *Required fees:* $450 per semester. Tuition and fees vary according to course load and program. *Financial support:* Institutionally sponsored loans and institutional work-study available. Financial award application deadline: 7/15; financial award applicants required to submit FAFSA. *Faculty research:* Rough and tumble play, social justice education, American Indian literatures and cultures, diversity and multicultural education, science teaching strategy. *Unit head:* Dr. Tina Herzberg, Director of Graduate Programs, 864-503-5572, Fax: 864-503-5573, E-mail: rstevens@uscupstate.edu. *Application contact:* Donette Stewart, Associate Vice Chancellor for Enrollment Services, 864-503-5280, E-mail: dstewart@uscupstate.edu. Web site: http://www.uscupstate.edu/graduate/.

The University of South Dakota, Graduate School, School of Education, Division of Curriculum and Instruction, Program in Elementary Education, Vermillion, SD 57069-2390. Offers MA. *Accreditation:* NCATE. Part-time programs available. Postbaccalaureate distance learning degree programs offered. *Degree requirements:* For master's, comprehensive exam, thesis or alternative. *Entrance requirements:* For master's, GRE General Test, MAT, minimum GPA of 2.7. Additional exam requirements/recommendations for international students: Required—TOEFL (minimum score 550 paper-based; 213 computer-based; 79 iBT). Electronic applications accepted. *Expenses:* Tuition, state resident: full-time $3118.50; part-time $173.25 per credit hour. Tuition, nonresident: full-time $6601; part-time $366.70 per credit hour. *Required fees:* $2268; $126 per credit hour. Tuition and fees vary according to program.

University of Southern Indiana, Graduate Studies, College of Science, Engineering, and Education, Department of Teacher Education, Program in Elementary Education, Evansville, IN 47712-3590. Offers MS. *Accreditation:* NCATE. Part-time and evening/weekend programs available. *Faculty:* 8 full-time (4 women), 1 part-time/adjunct (0 women). *Students:* 62 part-time (56 women); includes 2 minority (both Black or African American, non-Hispanic/Latino). Average age 31. 40 applicants, 100% accepted, 23 enrolled. In 2011, 21 master's awarded. *Entrance requirements:* For master's, GRE General Test, NTE or PRAXIS I, minimum GPA of 3.0, teaching license. Additional exam requirements/recommendations for international students: Required—TOEFL (minimum score 550 paper-based; 213 computer-based; 79 iBT), IELTS (minimum score 6). *Application deadline:* For fall admission, 7/1 priority date for domestic students. Applications are processed on a rolling basis. Application fee: $35. Electronic applications accepted. *Expenses:* Tuition, state resident: full-time $5044; part-time $280.21 per credit hour. Tuition, nonresident: full-time $9949; part-time $552.71 per credit hour. *Required fees:* $240; $22.75 per term. Tuition and fees vary according to course load and reciprocity agreements. *Financial support:* In 2011–12, 2 students received support. Federal Work-Study, scholarships/grants, tuition waivers (full and partial), and unspecified assistantships available. Financial award application deadline: 3/1; financial award applicants required to submit FAFSA. *Unit head:* Dr. Vella Goebel, Coordinator, 812-461-5306, E-mail: vgoebel@usi.edu. *Application contact:* Dr. Wes Durham, Director, Graduate Studies, 812-465-7015, Fax: 812-464-1956, E-mail: wdurham@usi.edu. Web site: http://www.usi.edu/science/teachered/mse-objectives.asp.

University of Southern Mississippi, Graduate School, College of Education and Psychology, Department of Curriculum, Instruction, and Special Education, Hattiesburg, MS 39406-0001. Offers alternative secondary teacher education (MAT); early childhood education (M Ed, Ed S); education (Ed D); education of the gifted (M Ed, PhD, Ed S); elementary education (M Ed, PhD, Ed S); reading (M Ed, MS); secondary education (M Ed, MS, PhD); special education (M Ed, PhD, Ed S). Part-time programs available. *Faculty:* 23 full-time (17 women), 3 part-time/adjunct (2 women). *Students:* 39 full-time (34 women), 92 part-time (77 women); includes 36 minority (31 Black or African American, non-Hispanic/Latino; 3 Hispanic/Latino; 2 Two or more races, non-Hispanic/Latino), 3 international. Average age 37. 56 applicants, 55% accepted, 29 enrolled. In 2011, 45 master's, 5 doctorates awarded. *Degree requirements:* For master's and Ed S, comprehensive exam, thesis (for some programs); for doctorate, comprehensive exam, thesis/dissertation. *Entrance requirements:* For master's, GRE General Test, MAT, minimum GPA of 3.0; for doctorate, GRE General Test, minimum GPA of 3.5; for Ed S, GRE General Test, MAT, minimum GPA of 3.25. Additional exam requirements/recommendations for international students: Required—TOEFL, IELTS. *Application deadline:* For fall admission, 3/1 priority date for domestic students, 3/1 for international students; for spring admission, 1/10 priority date for domestic students, 1/10 for international students. Applications are processed on a rolling basis. Application fee: $50. *Financial support:* In 2011–12, 9 research assistantships with tuition reimbursements (averaging $18,316 per year), 2 teaching assistantships with full tuition reimbursements (averaging $8,500 per year) were awarded; Federal Work-Study, institutionally sponsored loans, scholarships/grants, health care benefits, tuition waivers (partial), and unspecified assistantships also available. Financial award application deadline: 3/15; financial award applicants required to submit FAFSA. *Faculty research:* Mathematical problem solving, integrative curriculum, writing process, teacher education models. *Total annual research expenditures:* $100,000. *Unit head:* Dr. David Daves, Chair, 601-266-4547, Fax: 601-266-4175, E-mail: david.daves@usm.edu. *Application contact:* Dr. Marie Crowe, Director of Graduate Studies, 601-266-6005, Fax: 601-266-4548, E-mail: margie.crowe@usm.edu. Web site: http://www.usm.edu/graduateschool/table.php.

University of South Florida, Graduate School, College of Education, Department of Childhood Education, Tampa, FL 33620-9951. Offers early childhood education (M Ed, MA, PhD); elementary education (MA, MAT, PhD); reading/language arts (MA, PhD, Ed S). *Accreditation:* NCATE. Part-time and evening/weekend programs available. *Faculty:* 24 full-time (21 women), 2 part-time/adjunct (both women). *Students:* 88 full-time (81 women), 116 part-time (110 women); includes 48 minority (21 Black or African American, non-Hispanic/Latino; 6 Asian, non-Hispanic/Latino; 19 Hispanic/Latino; 2 Two or more races, non-Hispanic/Latino), 7 international. Average age 33. 200 applicants, 67% accepted, 76 enrolled. In 2011, 87 master's, 8 doctorates, 1 other advanced degree awarded. *Degree requirements:* For master's, comprehensive exam; for doctorate, comprehensive exam, thesis/dissertation, philosophies of inquiry; multiple research methods. *Entrance requirements:* For master's, GRE (if GPA less than 3.0), minimum GPA of 3.0 in last 60 hours of course work; for doctorate, GRE General Test, minimum GPA of 3.0 undergraduate, 3.5 graduate; interview; for Ed S, GRE General Test, interview. Additional exam requirements/recommendations for international students: Required—TOEFL (minimum score 550 paper-based; 213 computer-based). *Application deadline:* For fall admission, 2/15 for domestic students, 1/2 for international students; for winter admission, 2/15 for domestic students, 1/2 for international students; for spring admission, 10/15 for domestic students, 6/1 for international students. Application fee: $30. Electronic applications accepted. *Financial support:* In 2011–12, 7 teaching assistantships with full tuition reimbursements (averaging $10,300 per year) were awarded; institutionally sponsored loans, scholarships/grants, and unspecified assistantships also available. Financial award applicants required to submit FAFSA. *Faculty research:* Evaluating interventions for struggling readers, prevention and intervention services for young children at risk for behavioral and mental health challenges, preservice teacher education and young adolescent middle school experience, art and inquiry-based approaches to teaching and learning, study of children's writing development. *Total annual research expenditures:* $381,048. *Unit head:* Dr. Diane Yendol-Hoppey, Chairperson, 813-974-3460, Fax: 813-974-0938. *Application contact:* Dr. Diane Briscoe, Coordinator of Graduate Studies, 813-974-1804, Fax: 813-974-3391, E-mail: briscoe@usf.edu. Web site: http://www.coedu.usf.edu/main/departments/ce/ce.html.

University of South Florida–St. Petersburg Campus, College of Education, St. Petersburg, FL 33701. Offers educational leadership development (M Ed); elementary education (MA), including math/science; English education (MA); middle grades STEM education (MS); reading education (MA). Part-time programs available. *Students:* 30 full-time (27 women), 130 part-time (109 women); includes 28 minority (14 Black or African American, non-Hispanic/Latino; 4 Asian, non-Hispanic/Latino; 9 Hispanic/Latino; 1 Two or more races, non-Hispanic/Latino). Average age 34. 63 applicants, 70% accepted, 36 enrolled. In 2011, 74 master's awarded. *Degree requirements:* For master's, comprehensive exam, practicum, internship, comprehensive portfolio. *Entrance requirements:* For master's, State of Florida General Knowledge Test (GKT), Florida Teaching Certificate (for non-initial certification programs), letters of recommendation. Additional exam requirements/recommendations for international students: Required—TOEFL (minimum score 550 paper-based; 79 iBT); Recommended—IELTS. *Application deadline:* For fall admission, 6/1 priority date for domestic students, 6/1 for international students; for spring admission, 10/15 priority date for domestic students, 10/15 for international students. Applications are processed on a rolling basis. Application fee: $30. Electronic applications accepted. *Expenses:* Tuition, state resident: full-time $8847. Tuition, nonresident: full-time $18,423. One-time fee: $35 full-time. Full-time tuition and fees vary according to course load and program. *Financial support:* Applicants required to submit FAFSA. *Unit head:* Dr. Harold W. Heller, Dean, 727-873-4155, Fax: 727-873-4191, E-mail: hheller@usfsp.edu. *Application contact:* Eric Douthirt, Enrollment Management Specialist, 727-873-4450, E-mail: douthirt@usfsp.edu. Web site: http://www1.usfsp.edu/coe/index.asp.

University of South Florida Sarasota-Manatee, College of Education, Sarasota, FL 34243. Offers educational leadership (M Ed), including curriculum leadership, K-12, non-public/charter school leadership; elementary education K-6 (MA); K-6 with ESOL endorsement (MAT); reading education K-12 (MA); MAT/MA. Part-time and evening/weekend programs available. *Faculty:* 12 full-time (8 women), 4 part-time/adjunct (3 women). *Students:* 19 full-time (17 women), 64 part-time (50 women); includes 7 minority (1 Black or African American, non-Hispanic/Latino; 1 Asian, non-Hispanic/Latino; 4 Hispanic/Latino; 1 Two or more races, non-Hispanic/Latino). Average age 33. 50 applicants, 62% accepted, 21 enrolled. In 2011, 41 master's awarded. *Degree requirements:* For master's, comprehensive exam (for some programs). *Entrance requirements:* For master's, GRE. Additional exam requirements/recommendations for international students: Required—TOEFL (minimum score 213 computer-based; 79 iBT) or IELTS. *Application deadline:* For fall admission, 2/15 for domestic students, 1/2 for international students; for spring admission, 10/15 for domestic students, 6/1 for international students. Applications are processed on a rolling basis. Application fee: $30. Electronic applications accepted. *Expenses:* Tuition, state resident: full-time $9301; part-time $387.55 per credit hour. Tuition, nonresident: full-time $19,412; part-time $808.85 per credit hour. *Required fees:* $15; $5 per semester. One-time fee: $30. *Financial support:* Federal Work-Study, scholarships/grants, health care benefits, and unspecified assistantships available. Support available to part-time students. Financial award application deadline: 3/1; financial award applicants required to submit FAFSA. *Faculty research:* Child development, student achievement, intergenerational studies. *Unit head:* Dr. Terry A. Osborn, Dean, 941-359-4531, E-mail: terryosborn@sar.usf.edu. *Application contact:* Jo Lynn Raudebaugh, Graduate Admissions Advisor, 941-359-4587, E-mail: jraudeba@sar.usf.edu. Web site: http://www.sarasota.usf.edu/Academics/COE/.

The University of Tennessee, Graduate School, College of Education, Health and Human Sciences, Program in Education, Knoxville, TN 37996. Offers art education (MS); counseling education (PhD); cultural studies in education (PhD); curriculum (MS, Ed S); curriculum, educational research and evaluation (Ed D, PhD); early childhood education (PhD); early childhood special education (MS); education of deaf and hard of hearing (MS); educational administration and policy studies (Ed D, PhD); educational administration and supervision (Ed S); educational psychology (Ed D, PhD); elementary education (MS, Ed S); elementary teaching (MS); English education (MS, Ed S); exercise science (PhD); foreign language/ESL education (MS, Ed S); instructional technology (MS, Ed D, PhD, Ed S); literacy, language and ESL education (PhD); literacy, language education, and ESL education (Ed D); mathematics education (MS, Ed S); modified and comprehensive special education (MS); reading education (MS, Ed S); school counseling (Ed S); school psychology (PhD, Ed S); science education (MS, Ed S); secondary teaching (MS); social foundations (MS); social science education (MS, Ed S); socio-cultural foundations of sports and education (PhD); special education (Ed S); teacher education (Ed D, PhD). *Accreditation:* NCATE. Part-time and evening/weekend programs available. *Degree requirements:* For master's and Ed S, thesis optional; for doctorate, variable foreign language requirement, thesis/dissertation. *Entrance requirements:* For master's, minimum GPA of 2.7; for doctorate and Ed S, GRE General Test, minimum GPA of 2.7. Additional exam requirements/recommendations for international students: Required—TOEFL. Electronic applications accepted. *Expenses:* Tuition, state resident: full-time $8332; part-time $464 per credit hour. Tuition, nonresident: full-time $25,174; part-time $1400 per credit hour. *Required fees:* $1162; $56 per credit hour. Tuition and fees vary according to program.

The University of Tennessee at Chattanooga, Graduate School, College of Health, Education and Professional Studies, School of Education, Chattanooga, TN 37403-2598. Offers counseling (M Ed), including community counseling, school counseling; education (M Ed, Post-Master's Certificate), including elementary education (M Ed), school leadership, secondary education (M Ed), special education (M Ed); educational specialist (Ed S), including educational technology, school psychology; learning and leadership (Ed D), including educational leadership. *Accreditation:* ACA; NCATE. Part-time and evening/weekend programs available. Postbaccalaureate distance learning degree programs offered (no on-campus study). *Faculty:* 25 full-time (17 women), 10 part-time/adjunct (3 women). *Students:* 145 full-time (104 women), 319 part-time (236 women); includes 63 minority (43 Black or African American, non-Hispanic/Latino; 4 American Indian or Alaska Native, non-Hispanic/Latino; 2 Asian, non-Hispanic/Latino; 6 Hispanic/Latino; 8 Two or more races, non-Hispanic/Latino), 2 international. Average age 34. 226 applicants, 79% accepted, 111 enrolled. In 2011, 120 master's, 9 doctorates, 17 other advanced degrees awarded. *Degree requirements:* For master's, comprehensive exam, thesis optional, culminating experience; for doctorate, comprehensive exam, thesis/dissertation; for other advanced degree, internship. *Entrance requirements:* For master's, GRE General Test, PPST 1, teaching certificate; for doctorate, GRE General Test, master's degree, two years of practical work experience in organizational environment; for other advanced degree, GRE General Test, letters of reference. Additional exam requirements/recommendations for international students: Required—TOEFL (minimum score 550 paper-based; 213 computer-based; 79 iBT), IELTS (minimum score 6). *Application deadline:* For fall admission, 8/1 for domestic students, 6/1 for international students; for spring admission, 12/1 for domestic students, 10/1 for international students. Applications are processed on a rolling basis. Application fee: $35. Electronic applications accepted. *Expenses:* Tuition, state resident: full-time $6472; part-time $359 per credit hour. Tuition, nonresident: full-time $20,006; part-time $1111 per credit hour. *Required fees:* $1320; $160 per credit hour. *Financial support:* Career-related internships or fieldwork, institutionally sponsored loans, scholarships/grants, and unspecified assistantships available. Support available to part-time students. Financial award applicants required to submit FAFSA. *Faculty research:* School counseling, community counseling, elementary and secondary education, school leadership and administration. *Total annual research expenditures:* $675,479. *Unit head:* Dr. John Freeman, Head, 423-425-4133, Fax: 423-425-5380, E-mail: john-freeman@utc.edu. *Application contact:* Dr. Jerald Ainsworth, Dean of Graduate Studies, 423-425-4478, Fax: 423-425-5223, E-mail: jerald-ainsworth@utc.edu. Web site: http://www.utc.edu/Administration/HealthEducationAndProfessionalStudies/Graduate_Studies/graduate_studies.html.

The University of Texas–Pan American, College of Education, Department of Curriculum and Instruction: Elementary and Secondary, Edinburg, TX 78539. Offers bilingual education (M Ed); early childhood education (M Ed); elementary education (M Ed); reading (M Ed); secondary education (M Ed). Part-time programs available. *Degree requirements:* For master's, comprehensive exam, thesis optional. *Entrance requirements:* For master's, GRE. Additional exam requirements/recommendations for international students: Required—TOEFL, IELTS. *Application deadline:* For fall admission, 7/17 for domestic and international students; for spring admission, 11/16 for domestic and international students. Application fee: $0. Tuition and fees vary according to course load, program and student level. *Financial support:* Research assistantships with tuition reimbursements, Federal Work-Study, institutionally sponsored loans, scholarships/grants, and unspecified assistantships available. Financial award application deadline: 4/15. *Faculty research:* Dual language instruction, literacy and technology, teacher education in diverse populations, mathematics and science education. *Unit head:* Dr. Veronica L. Estrada, Chair, 956-665-2431, Fax: 956-665-2434, E-mail: vlestradaa@utpa.edu. Web site: http://www.utpa.edu/dept/curr_ins/graduat.html.

University of the Cumberlands, Graduate Programs in Education, Williamsburg, KY 40769-1372. Offers all grades (P-12) (M Ed); business and marketing (MA Ed, MAT); director of pupil personnel (Certificate); director of special education (Certificate); educational administration and supervision (Ed S); educational leadership (Ed D); elementary education (MA Ed, MAT); instructional leadership - principalship (MA Ed); instructional leadership - school principal (Certificate); middle school education (MA Ed, MAT); reading and writing (MA Ed); school counseling (MA Ed); school superintendent (Certificate); secondary education (MA Ed, MAT); special education (MAT); supervisor of instruction (Certificate); teacher leader (MA Ed). Part-time and evening/weekend programs available. Postbaccalaureate distance learning degree programs offered. *Degree requirements:* For master's, comprehensive exam. Electronic applications accepted.

University of the Incarnate Word, School of Graduate Studies and Research, Dreeben School of Education, Program in Teaching, San Antonio, TX 78209-6397. Offers all-level teaching (MAT); elementary teaching (MAT); secondary teaching (MAT). Part-time and evening/weekend programs available. *Faculty:* 14 full-time (8 women), 10 part-time/adjunct (9 women). *Students:* 2 full-time (1 woman), 29 part-time (25 women); includes 20 minority (2 Black or African American, non-Hispanic/Latino; 18 Hispanic/Latino). Average age 33. 11 applicants, 91% accepted, 7 enrolled. In 2011, 9 degrees awarded. *Degree requirements:* For master's, internship. *Entrance requirements:* For master's, GRE, Texas Higher Education Assessment test (THEA), interview. Additional exam requirements/recommendations for international students: Required—TOEFL (minimum score 560 paper-based; 220 computer-based; 83 iBT). *Application deadline:* Applications are processed on a rolling basis. Application fee: $20. Electronic applications accepted. *Expenses: Tuition:* Part-time $725 per credit hour. Tuition and fees vary according to degree level. *Financial support:* Federal Work-Study and scholarships/grants available. Financial award applicants required to submit FAFSA. *Unit head:* Dr. Elda Martinez, Director of Teacher Education, 210-832-3297, Fax: 210-829-3134, E-mail: eemartin@uiwtx.edu. *Application contact:* Andrea Cyterski-Acosta, Dean of Enrollment, 210-829-6005, Fax: 210-829-3921, E-mail: admis@uiwtx.edu. Web site: http://www.uiw.edu/education/graduate.html.

University of Tulsa, Graduate School, College of Arts and Sciences, School of Education, Program in Education, Tulsa, OK 74104-3189. Offers education (MA); elementary certification (M Ed); secondary certification (M Ed). Part-time programs available. *Faculty:* 7 full-time (3 women). *Students:* 16 full-time (11 women), 4 part-time (3 women); includes 5 minority (1 Black or African American, non-Hispanic/Latino; 2 American Indian or Alaska Native, non-Hispanic/Latino; 1 Asian, non-Hispanic/Latino; 1 Hispanic/Latino), 2 international. Average age 27. 17 applicants, 76% accepted, 10 enrolled. In 2011, 7 master's awarded. *Degree requirements:* For master's, thesis optional. *Entrance requirements:* For master's, GRE General Test. Additional exam requirements/recommendations for international students: Required—TOEFL (minimum score 577 paper-based; 233 computer-based; 91 iBT), IELTS (minimum score 6.5). *Application deadline:* Applications are processed on a rolling basis. Application fee: $40. Electronic applications accepted. *Expenses: Tuition:* Full-time $17,748; part-time $986 per hour. *Required fees:* $5 per contact hour. $75 per semester. Tuition and fees vary according to program. *Financial support:* In 2011–12, 12 students received support, including 1 research assistantship with full and partial tuition reimbursement available (averaging $6,051 per year), 11 teaching assistantships with full and partial tuition reimbursements available (averaging $11,264 per year); fellowships with full and partial tuition reimbursements available, Federal Work-Study, scholarships/grants, health care benefits, tuition waivers (full and partial), and unspecified assistantships also available. Support available to part-time students. Financial award application deadline: 2/1; financial award applicants required to submit FAFSA. *Faculty research:* Elementary and secondary education; educational foundations; language, discourse and development. *Total annual research expenditures:* $362,470. *Unit head:* Dr. David Brown, Advisor, 918-631-2719, Fax: 918-631-2133, E-mail: david-brown@utulsa.edu. *Application contact:* Dr. David Brown, Advisor, 918-631-2719, Fax: 918-631-2133, E-mail: david-brown@utulsa.edu.

University of Utah, Graduate School, College of Education, Department of Educational Psychology, Salt Lake City, UT 84112. Offers counseling psychology (PhD); educational psychology (MA); elementary education (M Ed); instructional design and educational technology (M Ed); instructional design and technology (M Ed, MS); learning and cognition (MS, PhD); learning sciences (MA); professional counseling (MS); professional psychology (M Ed); reading and literacy (M Ed, PhD); school counseling (M Ed, MS); school psychology (M Ed, MS, PhD); statistics (M Stat). *Accreditation:* APA (one or more programs are accredited). Evening/weekend programs available. Postbaccalaureate distance learning degree programs offered (minimal on-campus study). *Faculty:* 23 full-time (12 women), 9 part-time/adjunct (7 women). *Students:* 104 full-time (85 women), 107 part-time (78 women); includes 26 minority (1 American Indian or Alaska Native, non-Hispanic/Latino; 4 Asian, non-Hispanic/Latino; 17 Hispanic/Latino; 1 Native Hawaiian or other Pacific Islander, non-Hispanic/Latino; 3 Two or more races, non-Hispanic/Latino), 4 international. Average age 32. 213 applicants, 27% accepted, 48 enrolled. In 2011, 39 master's, 9 doctorates awarded. *Median time to degree:* Of those who began their doctoral program in fall 2003, 50% received their degree in 8 years or less. *Degree requirements:* For master's, variable foreign language requirement, comprehensive exam, thesis (for some programs); for doctorate, variable foreign language requirement, thesis/dissertation, oral exam. *Entrance requirements:* For master's and doctorate, GRE General Test, minimum GPA of 3.0. Additional exam requirements/recommendations for international students: Required—TOEFL (minimum score 500 paper-based; 173 computer-based). *Application deadline:* For fall admission, 4/1 for domestic and international students; for spring admission, 11/1 for domestic and international students. Application fee: $55 ($65 for international students). *Expenses:* Contact institution. *Financial support:* In 2011–12, 59 students received support, including 25 fellowships with full and partial tuition reimbursements available (averaging $12,000 per year), 7 research assistantships with full and partial tuition reimbursements available (averaging $12,000 per year), 27 teaching assistantships with full and partial tuition reimbursements available (averaging $12,000 per year); career-related internships or fieldwork, Federal Work-Study, institutionally sponsored loans, scholarships/grants, and unspecified assistantships also available. Financial award application deadline: 2/1; financial award applicants required to submit FAFSA. *Faculty research:* Autism, computer technology and instruction, cognitive behavior, aging, group counseling. *Total annual research expenditures:* $371,256. *Unit head:* Dr. Elaine Clark, Chair, 801-581-7148, Fax: 801-581-5566, E-mail: clark@ed.utah.edu. *Application contact:* Kendra Lee Wiebke, Academic Program Specialist, 801-581-7148, Fax: 801-581-5566, E-mail: kendra.wiebke@utah.edu. Web site: http://www.ed.utah.edu/edps/.

University of Utah, Graduate School, College of Education, Department of Teaching and Learning, Salt Lake City, UT 84112-1107. Offers elementary education (MAT); secondary education (MAT); teaching and learning (M Ed, M Phil, MA, MS, PhD). Part-time and evening/weekend programs available. *Faculty:* 4 full-time (2 women). *Students:* 14 full-time (11 women), 25 part-time (16 women); includes 3 minority (1 Asian, non-Hispanic/Latino; 1 Hispanic/Latino; 1 Native Hawaiian or other Pacific Islander, non-Hispanic/Latino), 1 international. Average age 33. 10 applicants, 0% accepted. In 2011, 26 master's, 2 doctorates awarded. *Degree requirements:* For master's, comprehensive exam (for some programs), thesis optional; for doctorate, thesis/dissertation. *Entrance requirements:* For master's, GRE General Test or MAT, GRE Subject Test, minimum GPA of 3.0; for doctorate, GRE General Test, minimum graduate GPA of 3.5, undergraduate 3.0. Additional exam requirements/recommendations for international students: Required—TOEFL (minimum score 500 paper-based; 173 computer-based). *Application deadline:* For fall admission, 3/1 for domestic students, 4/1 for international students; for spring admission, 10/15 for domestic students, 11/1 for international students. Applications are processed on a rolling basis. Application fee: $55 ($65 for international students). *Financial support:* Fellowships, research assistantships with full and partial tuition reimbursements, teaching assistantships with full and partial tuition reimbursements, career-related internships or fieldwork, and tuition waivers (partial) available. Financial award application deadline: 2/1; financial award applicants required to submit FAFSA. *Faculty research:* Teacher development, teacher education, reading instruction, math instruction, technology. *Unit head:* Doug Hacker, Department Chair, 801-581-5080, Fax: 801-581-3609, E-mail: douglas.hacker@utah.edu. *Application contact:* Jan Dole, Graduate Program Director, 801-587-7991, Fax: 801-581-3609, E-mail: jan.dole@utah.edu.

University of Virginia, Curry School of Education, Department of Curriculum, Instruction, and Special Education, Program in Curriculum and Instruction, Charlottesville, VA 22903. Offers curriculum and instruction (M Ed, Ed S); elementary (M Ed, Ed D); English (M Ed, Ed D); foreign language (M Ed); mathematics (M Ed, Ed D); reading (M Ed, Ed D, Ed S); science (Ed D); social studies (M Ed). *Students:* 22 full-time (17 women), 29 part-time (27 women); includes 4 minority (1 Black or African American, non-Hispanic/Latino; 1 Asian, non-Hispanic/Latino; 2 Two or more races, non-Hispanic/Latino), 1 international. Average age 33. 67 applicants, 75% accepted, 33 enrolled. In 2011, 78 master's, 2 doctorates, 12 other advanced degrees awarded. *Degree requirements:* For master's, comprehensive exam (for some programs); for doctorate, comprehensive exam, thesis/dissertation; for Ed S, comprehensive exam. *Entrance requirements:* For master's, doctorate, and Ed S, GRE General Test, 2 letters of recommendation. Additional exam requirements/recommendations for international students: Required—TOEFL (minimum score 600 paper-based; 250 computer-based; 90 iBT), IELTS (minimum score 7). *Application deadline:* Applications are processed on a rolling basis. Application fee: $60. Electronic applications accepted. *Financial support:* Fellowships with tuition reimbursements, research assistantships with tuition reimbursements, and teaching assistantships with tuition reimbursements available. Financial award application deadline: 1/5; financial award applicants required to submit FAFSA. *Unit head:* Laura Smolkin, Chair, 434-924-0831. *Application contact:* Karen Dwier, Information Contact, 434-924-0831, E-mail: kgd9g@virginia.edu.

University of Virginia, Curry School of Education, Program in Education, Charlottesville, VA 22903. Offers administration and supervision (PhD); applied developmental science (PhD); counselor education (PhD); curriculum and instruction (PhD); early childhood-developmental risk (MT); education evaluation (PhD); educational psychology (PhD); educational research (PhD); elementary (MT, PhD); English education (MT, PhD); foreign language education (MT); higher education (PhD); instructional technology (PhD); kinesiology (MT, PhD); math education (PhD); reading education (PhD); research statistics and evaluation (PhD); school psychology (PhD); science education (PhD); social studies education (MT, PhD); special education (PhD); world languages education (MT). *Students:* 299 full-time (216 women), 60 part-time (33 women); includes 46 minority (18 Black or African American, non-Hispanic/Latino; 17 Asian, non-Hispanic/Latino; 7 Hispanic/Latino; 4 Two or more races, non-Hispanic/Latino), 23 international. Average age 30. 307 applicants, 42% accepted, 80 enrolled. In 2011, 113 master's, 62 doctorates awarded. *Degree requirements:* For master's, comprehensive exam (for some programs), field project; for doctorate, comprehensive exam, thesis/dissertation. *Entrance requirements:* For doctorate, GRE General Test. Additional exam requirements/recommendations for international students: Required—TOEFL (minimum score 600 paper-based; 250 computer-based; 90 iBT), IELTS (minimum score 7). *Application deadline:* Applications are processed on a rolling basis. Application fee: $60. Electronic applications accepted. *Financial support:* Fellowships, research assistantships, and teaching assistantships available. Financial award application deadline: 1/5; financial award applicants required to submit FAFSA. *Unit head:* Robert C. Pianta, Dean, 434-924-3334. *Application contact:* Joanne McNergney, Assistant Dean for Admissions and Student Services, 434-924-3334, E-mail: curry-admissions@virginia.edu.

University of Washington, Tacoma, Graduate Programs, Program in Education, Tacoma, WA 98402-3100. Offers education (M Ed); educational administration (principal or program administrator certification) (M Ed); elementary education teacher certification (M Ed); elementary education/special education teacher certification (M Ed); secondary science or math teacher certification (M Ed). Part-time and evening/weekend programs available. *Degree requirements:* For master's, culminating project. *Entrance requirements:* For master's, WEST-B, WEST-E (teacher certification programs only), official sealed transcript from every college/university attended, personal goal statement, letters of recommendation, copy of valid teaching certificate. Additional exam requirements/recommendations for international students: Required—TOEFL (minimum score 580 paper-based; 237 computer-based; 92 iBT). Electronic applications accepted. *Faculty research:* Global learning communities for English/Chinese languages, evaluation of mathematics and reading intervention programs, response to intervention, school-wide behavioral and emotional support, mathematics education and culturally responsive mathematics education.

The University of West Alabama, School of Graduate Studies, College of Education, Departments of Instructional Leadership and Support/Curriculum and Instruction, Program in Elementary Education, Livingston, AL 35470. Offers M Ed. *Accreditation:* NCATE. Part-time programs available. *Faculty:* 29 full-time (13 women). *Students:* 652 (618 women); includes 379 minority (368 Black or African American, non-Hispanic/Latino; 4 American Indian or Alaska Native, non-Hispanic/Latino; 4 Asian, non-Hispanic/Latino; 2 Hispanic/Latino; 1 Native Hawaiian or other Pacific Islander, non-Hispanic/Latino). In 2011, 196 master's awarded. *Degree requirements:* For master's, comprehensive exam. *Entrance requirements:* For master's, GRE General Test, MAT, minimum GPA of 2.75. Additional exam requirements/recommendations for international students: Required—TOEFL (minimum score 61 computer-based). *Application deadline:* For fall admission, 9/10 priority date for domestic students; for spring admission, 3/24 for domestic students. Applications are processed on a rolling basis. Application fee: $25 ($50 for international students). *Expenses:* Tuition, state resident: full-time $5112; part-time $284 per credit hour. Tuition, nonresident: full-time $10,224; part-time $568 per credit hour. *Required fees:* $180; $40 per semester. One-time fee: $65. Tuition and fees vary according to class time, course load, campus/location and program. *Financial support:* Teaching assistantships, career-related internships or fieldwork, Federal Work-Study, scholarships/grants, and unspecified assistantships available. Support available to part-time students. Financial award application deadline: 3/1. *Unit head:* Dr. Esther Howard, Chair of Curriculum and Instruction, 205-652-3428, Fax: 205-652-3706, E-mail: ehoward@uwa.edu. *Application contact:* Dr. Kathy Chandler, Dean of Graduate Studies, 205-652-3421, Fax: 205-652-3706, E-mail: kchandler@uwa.edu. Web site: http://www.uwa.edu/elementaryeducationk6.aspx.

University of West Florida, College of Professional Studies, School of Education, Program in Curriculum and Instruction, Pensacola, FL 32514-5750. Offers curriculum and instruction: special education (M Ed); elementary education (M Ed); primary education (M Ed). Part-time and evening/weekend programs available. *Students:* 10 full-time (all women), 62 part-time (56 women); includes 16 minority (9 Black or African American, non-Hispanic/Latino; 1 American Indian or Alaska Native, non-Hispanic/Latino; 1 Asian, non-Hispanic/Latino; 3 Hispanic/Latino; 1 Native Hawaiian or other Pacific Islander, non-Hispanic/Latino; 1 Two or more races, non-Hispanic/Latino). Average age 35. 67 applicants, 70% accepted, 37 enrolled. In 2011, 62 master's awarded. *Entrance requirements:* For master's, GRE (minimum score 450 verbal) or MAT (minimum score 396) if bachelor's GPA less than 3.0, state teaching certification; letter of intent; two professional references. Additional exam requirements/recommendations for international students: Required—TOEFL (minimum score 550 paper-based; 213 computer-based). *Application deadline:* For fall admission, 6/1 for domestic and international students; for spring admission, 10/1 for domestic and international students. Applications are processed on a rolling basis. Application fee: $30. *Expenses:* Tuition, state resident: full-time $5729; part-time $302 per credit hour. Tuition, nonresident: full-time $20,059; part-time $961 per credit hour. *Required fees:* $1509; $63 per credit hour. *Financial support:* Career-related internships or fieldwork, Federal Work-Study, scholarships/grants, and tuition waivers (partial) available. Support available to part-time students. Financial award application deadline: 4/15; financial award applicants required to submit FAFSA. *Unit head:* Dr. William H. Evans, Acting Director, 850-474-2892, Fax: 850-474-2844, E-mail: wevans@uwf.edu. *Application contact:* Terry McCray, Assistant Director of Graduate Admissions, 850-473-7718, Fax: 850-473-7714, E-mail: gradadmissions@uwf.edu.

University of Wisconsin–Eau Claire, College of Education and Human Sciences, Program in Elementary Education, Eau Claire, WI 54702-4004. Offers MST. Part-time programs available. *Faculty:* 13 full-time (9 women). *Students:* 1 applicant, 100% accepted, 0 enrolled. *Degree requirements:* For master's, comprehensive exam, written exam, portfolio, research paper or thesis; oral exam. *Entrance requirements:* For master's, GRE, minimum undergraduate GPA of 2.75, certification to teach. Additional exam requirements/recommendations for international students: Required—TOEFL (minimum score 550 paper-based; 213 computer-based; 79 iBT); Recommended—IELTS (minimum score 7). *Application deadline:* For fall admission, 7/1 priority date for domestic students, 6/1 for international students; for spring admission, 12/1 priority date for domestic students, 11/1 for international students. Applications are processed on a rolling basis. Application fee: $56. *Expenses:* Tuition, state resident: full-time $7312; part-time $406 per credit. Tuition, nonresident: full-time $16,771; part-time $932 per credit. *Required fees:* $1101; $61 per credit. *Financial support:* Federal Work-Study and unspecified assistantships available. Financial award application deadline: 3/1; financial award applicants required to submit FAFSA. *Unit head:* Dr. Jill Pastrana, Chair, 715-836-2013, Fax: 715-836-4868, E-mail: pastrajp@uwec.edu. *Application contact:* Dr. Sherry Macaul, Coordinator, 715-836-5735, E-mail: macaulsl@uwec.edu. Web site: http://www.uwec.edu/Admissions/facts/graduate/mst-elem.htm.

University of Wisconsin–La Crosse, Office of University Graduate Studies, College of Liberal Studies, Department of Educational Studies, MEPD Initial Certification and Professional Development Program, La Crosse, WI 54601. Offers elementary education (MEPD), including grades 1 through 6, grades 1 through 9; K-12 (MEPD); professional development (MEPD); secondary education (MEPD), including grades 6 through 12. Part-time programs available. *Students:* 13 full-time (8 women), 2 part-time (0 women); includes 4 minority (1 American Indian or Alaska Native, non-Hispanic/Latino; 3 Asian, non-Hispanic/Latino). Average age 28. 10 applicants, 80% accepted, 5 enrolled. In 2011, 7 master's awarded. *Degree requirements:* For master's, thesis optional. *Entrance requirements:* For master's, PPST, minimum GPA of 3.0 cumulative and in subject area. Additional exam requirements/recommendations for international students: Required—TOEFL (minimum score 550 paper-based; 213 computer-based; 79 iBT). *Application deadline:* Applications are processed on a rolling basis. Application fee: $56. Electronic applications accepted. *Expenses:* Tuition, state resident: full-time $8391; part-time $481.17 per credit. Tuition, nonresident: full-time $17,850; part-time $1006.68 per credit. *Required fees:* $2 per credit. $18.25 per semester. Tuition and fees vary according to course load, program, reciprocity agreements and student level. *Financial support:* In 2011–12, 6 research assistantships (averaging $5,568 per year) were awarded; Federal Work-Study, scholarships/grants, health care benefits, and tuition waivers (partial) also available. Support available to part-time students. Financial award application deadline: 3/15; financial award applicants required to submit FAFSA. *Faculty research:* Professional development schools, technology in education, critical literacy, self-efficacy of teaching, digital storytelling. *Unit head:* Dr. Gary L. Willhite, Director, 608-785-8130, Fax: 608-785-8137, E-mail: gwillhite@uwlax.edu. *Application contact:* Dr. Gary L. Willhite, Director, 608-785-8130, Fax: 608-785-8137, E-mail: admissions@uwlax.edu. Web site: http://www.uwlax.edu/MEPD/.

University of Wisconsin–Milwaukee, Graduate School, School of Education, Department of Curriculum and Instruction, Milwaukee, WI 53201-0413. Offers curriculum planning and instruction improvement (MS); early childhood education (MS); elementary education (MS); junior high/middle school education (MS); reading education (MS); secondary education (MS); teaching in an urban setting (MS). Part-time programs available. *Faculty:* 18 full-time (13 women). *Students:* 29 full-time (23 women), 54 part-time (44 women); includes 21 minority (10 Black or African American, non-Hispanic/Latino; 4 Asian, non-Hispanic/Latino; 3 Hispanic/Latino; 4 Two or more races, non-Hispanic/Latino). Average age 32. 43 applicants, 65% accepted, 13 enrolled. In 2011, 23 degrees awarded. *Degree requirements:* For master's, thesis or alternative. *Entrance requirements:* Additional exam requirements/recommendations for international students: Required—TOEFL (minimum score 550 paper-based; 79 iBT), IELTS (minimum score 6.5). *Application deadline:* For fall admission, 1/1 priority date for domestic students; for spring admission, 9/1 for domestic students. Applications are processed on a rolling basis. Application fee: $56 ($96 for international students). Electronic applications accepted. One-time fee: $506.10 full-time. Tuition and fees vary according to course load and reciprocity agreements. *Financial support:* In 2011–12, 1 fellowship was awarded; research assistantships, teaching assistantships, career-related internships or fieldwork, health care benefits, unspecified assistantships, and project assistantships also available. Support available to part-time students. Financial award application deadline: 4/15; financial award applicants required to submit FAFSA. *Total annual research expenditures:* $21,843. *Unit head:* Hope Longwell-Grice, Department Chair, 414-229-3059, Fax: 414-229-5571, E-mail: hope@uwm.edu. *Application contact:* General Information Contact, 414-229-4982, Fax: 414-229-6967, E-mail: gradschool@uwm.edu. Web site: http://www.uwm.edu/SOE/.

University of Wisconsin–Platteville, School of Graduate Studies, College of Liberal Arts and Education, School of Education, Platteville, WI 53818-3099. Offers adult education (MSE); elementary education (MSE); English education (MSE); middle school education (MSE); secondary education (MSE). *Accreditation:* NCATE. Part-time programs available. *Faculty:* 8 part-time/adjunct (3 women). *Students:* 62 full-time (47 women), 86 part-time (69 women); includes 22 minority (20 Black or African American, non-Hispanic/Latino; 2 Hispanic/Latino), 55 international. 17 applicants, 76% accepted. In 2011, 82 master's awarded. *Degree requirements:* For master's, comprehensive exam, thesis or alternative. *Entrance requirements:* Additional exam requirements/recommendations for international students: Required—TOEFL (minimum score 500 paper-based; 61 iBT), IELTS (minimum score 6). *Application deadline:* For fall admission, 7/1 priority date for domestic students; for spring admission, 11/1 for domestic students. Applications are processed on a rolling basis. Application fee: $56. Electronic applications accepted. *Financial support:* Research assistantships with partial tuition reimbursements, career-related internships or fieldwork, Federal Work-Study, institutionally sponsored loans, scholarships/grants, and unspecified assistantships available. Support available to part-time students. Financial award applicants required to submit FAFSA. *Unit head:* Dr. Karen Stinson, Director, 608-342-1131, Fax: 608-342-1133, E-mail: stinsonk@uwplatt.edu. *Application contact:* Lisa Popp, School of Graduate Studies, 608-342-1322, Fax: 608-342-1389, E-mail: poppl@uwplatt.edu. Web site: http://www.uwplatt.edu/.

University of Wisconsin–River Falls, Outreach and Graduate Studies, College of Education and Professional Studies, Department of Teacher Education, River Falls, WI 54022. Offers elementary education (MSE); professional development shared inquiry communities (MSE); reading (MSE). Part-time programs available. *Degree requirements:* For master's, comprehensive exam, thesis or alternative. *Entrance requirements:* For master's, minimum GPA of 2.75. Additional exam requirements/recommendations for international students: Required—TOEFL (minimum score 500 paper-based; 65 iBT), IELTS (minimum score 5.5). Electronic applications accepted.

University of Wisconsin–Stevens Point, College of Professional Studies, School of Education, Program in Elementary Education, Stevens Point, WI 54481-3897. Offers MSE. Part-time programs available. *Degree requirements:* For master's, comprehensive exam, thesis or alternative. *Entrance requirements:* For master's, teacher certification, minimum undergraduate GPA of 3.0. Additional exam requirements/recommendations for international students: Required—TOEFL (minimum score 523 paper-based). *Faculty research:* Gifted education, early childhood special education, curriculum and instruction, standards-based education.

Utah State University, School of Graduate Studies, Emma Eccles Jones College of Education and Human Services, Program in Elementary Education, Logan, UT 84322. Offers M Ed, MA, MS. Part-time programs available. Postbaccalaureate distance learning degree programs offered (no on-campus study). *Degree requirements:* For master's, comprehensive exam (for some programs), thesis (for some programs). *Entrance requirements:* For master's, GRE General Test or MAT, minimum GPA of 3.0, teaching certificate, 3 recommendations, 1 year teaching department record. Additional exam requirements/recommendations for international students: Required—TOEFL. *Faculty research:* Teacher education, supervision, gifted and talented education, language arts/writing, early childhood education.

Vanderbilt University, Peabody College, Department of Teaching and Learning, Nashville, TN 37240-1001. Offers elementary education (M Ed); English language learners (M Ed); learning and instruction (M Ed); learning, diversity, and urban studies (M Ed); reading education (M Ed); secondary education (M Ed). *Accreditation:* NCATE. *Faculty:* 35 full-time (24 women), 19 part-time/adjunct (14 women). *Students:* 123 full-time (96 women), 38 part-time (34 women); includes 26 minority (6 Black or African American, non-Hispanic/Latino; 3 Asian, non-Hispanic/Latino; 7 Hispanic/Latino; 10 Two or more races, non-Hispanic/Latino), 12 international. Average age 26. 251 applicants, 56% accepted, 60 enrolled. In 2011, 80 master's awarded. *Degree requirements:* For master's, comprehensive exam, thesis optional. *Entrance requirements:* For master's, GRE General Test, MAT. Additional exam requirements/recommendations for international students: Required—TOEFL (minimum score 550 paper-based; 213 computer-based). *Application deadline:* For fall admission, 12/31 priority date for domestic students, 12/31 for international students; for spring admission, 11/1 priority date for domestic students, 11/1 for international students. Applications are processed on a rolling basis. Application fee: $0. Electronic applications accepted. *Financial support:* Fellowships with full and partial tuition reimbursements, research assistantships with full and partial tuition reimbursements, teaching assistantships with full and partial tuition reimbursements, Federal Work-Study, institutionally sponsored loans, scholarships/grants, tuition waivers (partial), and unspecified assistantships available. Support available to part-time students. Financial award application deadline: 2/1; financial award applicants required to submit FAFSA. *Faculty research:* Learning environments for mathematics of space and motion, visual programming tools for children's learning of basic science concepts, pathways for elementary and middle school children's learning about measurement and statistics, early reading intervention, professional development for ambitious mathematics teaching. *Unit head:* Dr. David Dickinson, Acting Chair, 615-322-8100, Fax: 615-322-8999, E-mail: david.k.dickinson@

vanderbilt.edu. *Application contact:* Angela Saylor, Educational Coordinator, 615-322-8092, Fax: 615-322-8999, E-mail: angela.saylor@vanderbilt.edu.

Virginia Commonwealth University, Graduate School, School of Education, Program in Teaching and Learning, Richmond, VA 23284-9005. Offers early and elementary education (MT); health and physical education (MT); secondary 6-12 education (MT); secondary education (Certificate). *Accreditation:* NCATE. Part-time programs available. *Entrance requirements:* For master's, GRE General Test or MAT. Additional exam requirements/recommendations for international students: Required—TOEFL (minimum score 600 paper-based; 250 computer-based; 100 iBT). Electronic applications accepted. *Expenses:* Tuition, state resident: full-time $9133; part-time $507 per credit. Tuition, nonresident: full-time $18,777; part-time $1043 per credit. *Required fees:* $77 per credit. Tuition and fees vary according to degree level, campus/location, program and student level.

Wagner College, Division of Graduate Studies, Department of Education, Program in Childhood Education, Staten Island, NY 10301-4495. Offers MS Ed. Part-time and evening/weekend programs available. *Faculty:* 2 full-time (both women), 12 part-time/adjunct (9 women). *Students:* 32 full-time (28 women), 2 part-time (both women); includes 4 minority (3 Black or African American, non-Hispanic/Latino; 1 Hispanic/Latino), 1 international. Average age 25. 23 applicants, 87% accepted, 16 enrolled. In 2011, 24 master's awarded. *Degree requirements:* For master's, thesis (for some programs). *Entrance requirements:* For master's, New York State Teacher Certification Examinations (NYSTCE), Liberal Arts and Sciences Test (LAST), minimum GPA of 2.75. Additional exam requirements/recommendations for international students: Required—TOEFL (minimum score 550 paper-based; 217 computer-based; 79 iBT). *Application deadline:* For fall admission, 5/1 priority date for domestic students, 3/1 for international students; for spring admission, 11/1 priority date for domestic students, 10/1 for international students. Applications are processed on a rolling basis. Application fee: $50 ($80 for international students). *Expenses: Tuition:* Full-time $16,200; part-time $890 per credit. *Financial support:* Career-related internships or fieldwork, tuition waivers (partial), unspecified assistantships, and alumni fellowship grant available. Financial award applicants required to submit FAFSA. *Unit head:* Dr. Stephen Preskill, Graduate Coordinator, 718-420-4070, Fax: 718-390-3456, E-mail: stephen.preskill@wagner.edu. *Application contact:* Patricia Clancy, Administrative Assistant, Admissions, 718-420-4464, Fax: 718-390-3105, E-mail: patricia.clancy@wagner.edu.

Walden University, Graduate Programs, Richard W. Riley College of Education and Leadership, Minneapolis, MN 55401. Offers administrator leadership for teaching and learning (Ed D, Ed S); adult education (Ed D, Ed S); adult learning (MS, Postbaccalaureate Certificate), including developmental education (MS), online teaching (MS), teaching adults English as a second language (MS), training and performance management (MS); college teaching and learning (Ed D, Ed S, Postbaccalaureate Certificate); curriculum, instruction and assessment (Ed D, Postbaccalaureate Certificate); curriculum, instruction, and professional development (Ed S); developmental education (Postbaccalaureate Certificate); early childhood administration, management, and leadership (Postbaccalaureate Certificate); early childhood education (birth-grade 3) (MAT); early childhood public policy and advocacy (Postbaccalaureate Certificate); early childhood studies (MS), including administration, management and leadership, early childhood public policy and advocacy, teaching adults in the early childhood field, teaching and diversity; education (MS, PhD), including adolescent literacy and technology (grades 6-12) (MS), adult education leadership (PhD), assessment, evaluation, and accountability (PhD), community college leadership (PhD), curriculum, instruction, and assessment, early childhood education (PhD), educational technology (PhD), elementary reading and literacy (MS), elementary reading and mathematics (MS), general program, global and comparative education (PhD), higher education (PhD), integrating technology in the classroom (MS), K-12 educational leadership (PhD), leadership, policy and change (PhD), learning, instruction and innovation (PhD), literacy and learning in the content areas (MS), mathematics (grades 6-8) (MS), mathematics (grades K-5) (MS), middle level education (grades 5-8) (MS), professional development (MS), science (grades K-8) (MS), self-designed (PhD), special education (PhD), special education (non-licensure) (MS), teacher leadership (grades K-12) (MS), teaching English language learners (grades K-12) (MS); educational leadership and administration (principal preparation) (Ed S); educational technology (Ed S); elementary reading and literacy (Postbaccalaureate Certificate); engaging culturally diverse learners (Postbaccalaureate Certificate); enrollment management and institutional marketing (Postbaccalaureate Certificate); higher education (MS), including college teaching and learning, enrollment management and institutional planning, global higher education, leadership for student success, online and distance learning; higher education leadership (Ed D); instructional design (Postbaccalaureate Certificate); instructional design and technology (MS), including general program (MS, PhD), online learning, training and performance improvement; integrating technology in the classroom (Postbaccalaureate Certificate); online teaching for adult learners (Postbaccalaureate Certificate); professional development (Postbaccalaureate Certificate); reading and literacy leadership (Ed D); science K-8 (Postbaccalaureate Certificate); special education (Ed D, Ed S); special education: emotional/behavioral disorders (K-12) (MAT); special education: learning disabilities (K-12) (MAT); teacher leadership (Ed D, Ed S, Postbaccalaureate Certificate); training and performance management (Postbaccalaureate Certificate). Part-time and evening/weekend programs available. Postbaccalaureate distance learning degree programs offered (minimal on-campus study). *Faculty:* 71 full-time (48 women), 853 part-time/adjunct (585 women). *Students:* 11,326 full-time (9,212 women), 2,148 part-time (1,795 women); includes 5,346 minority (4,403 Black or African American, non-Hispanic/Latino; 76 American Indian or Alaska Native, non-Hispanic/Latino; 140 Asian, non-Hispanic/Latino; 561 Hispanic/Latino; 21 Native Hawaiian or other Pacific Islander, non-Hispanic/Latino; 145 Two or more races, non-Hispanic/Latino), 322 international. Average age 39. In 2011, 3,477 master's, 318 doctorates, 471 other advanced degrees awarded. *Degree requirements:* For doctorate, thesis/dissertation (for some programs), residency; for other advanced degree, residency (for some programs). *Entrance requirements:* For master's, bachelor's degree or equivalent in related field; minimum GPA of 2.5; official transcripts; goal statement; access to computer and Internet; for doctorate, master's degree or equivalent in related field; minimum GPA of 3.0; official transcripts; three years' related professional/academic experience (preferred); access to computer and Internet; for other advanced degree, master's degree or equivalent in related field; minimum GPA of 3.0; 3 years related professional/academic experience (preferred); access to computer and Internet (Ed S). Additional exam requirements/recommendations for international students: Required—TOEFL (minimum score 550 paper-based; 213 computer-based), IELTS (minimum score 6.5), or Michigan English Language Assessment Battery (minimum score 82). *Application deadline:* Applications are processed on a rolling basis. Application fee: $50. Electronic applications accepted. *Financial support:* Federal Work-Study, scholarships/grants, unspecified assistantships, and family tuition reduction, active duty/veteran tuition reduction, group tuition reduction, interest-free payment plans, employee tuition reduction available. Support available to part-time students. Financial award applicants required to submit FAFSA. *Unit head:* Dr. Kate Steffens, Dean, 800-925-3368. *Application contact:* Jennifer Hall, Vice President of Enrollment Management, 866-4-WALDEN, E-mail: info@waldenu.edu. Web site: http://www.waldenu.edu/Colleges-and-Schools/College-of-Education-and-Leadership.htm.

Washington State University, Graduate School, College of Education, Department of Teaching and Learning, Pullman, WA 99164. Offers curriculum and instruction (Ed D, PhD); diverse languages (M Ed, MA); elementary education (M Ed, MA, MIT); exercise science (MS); literacy education (M Ed, MA, PhD); math education (PhD); secondary education (M Ed, MA). *Accreditation:* NCATE. *Faculty:* 20. *Students:* 79 full-time (51 women), 40 part-time (31 women); includes 24 minority (3 Black or African American, non-Hispanic/Latino; 5 Asian, non-Hispanic/Latino; 13 Hispanic/Latino; 1 Native Hawaiian or other Pacific Islander, non-Hispanic/Latino; 2 Two or more races, non-Hispanic/Latino), 43 international. Average age 34. 106 applicants, 47% accepted, 43 enrolled. In 2011, 34 master's, 3 doctorates awarded. *Degree requirements:* For master's, comprehensive exam (for some programs), thesis (for some programs), oral or written exam; for doctorate, comprehensive exam, thesis/dissertation, oral and written exam. *Entrance requirements:* For master's and doctorate, GRE General Test, minimum GPA of 3.0, 3 letters of recommendation. Additional exam requirements/recommendations for international students: Required—TOEFL. *Application deadline:* For fall admission, 2/1 for domestic students, 3/1 for international students; for spring admission, 9/1 for domestic students, 7/1 for international students. Applications are processed on a rolling basis. Application fee: $75. *Financial support:* In 2011–12, 130 teaching assistantships with partial tuition reimbursements (averaging $18,204 per year) were awarded; career-related internships or fieldwork, Federal Work-Study, institutionally sponsored loans, tuition waivers (partial), unspecified assistantships, and staff assistantships, teaching associateships also available. Financial award application deadline: 4/1. *Faculty research:* Evolution of middle school education, issues in special education, computer-assisted language learning. *Total annual research expenditures:* $324,000. *Unit head:* Dr. Dawn Shinew, Interim Chair, 509-335-5027, E-mail: dshinew@wsu.edu. *Application contact:* Graduate School Admissions, 800-GRADWSU, Fax: 509-335-1949, E-mail: gradsch@wsu.edu. Web site: http://www.educ.wsu.edu/TL/overview.htm.

Washington University in St. Louis, Graduate School of Arts and Sciences, Department of Education, Program in Elementary Education, St. Louis, MO 63130-4899. Offers MA Ed. *Degree requirements:* For master's, thesis or alternative. *Entrance requirements:* For master's, GRE General Test or MAT. Electronic applications accepted.

Wayne State College, School of Education and Counseling, Department of Educational Foundations and Leadership, Program in Curriculum and Instruction, Wayne, NE 68787. Offers alternative education (MSE); business and information technology education (MSE); communication arts education (MSE); early childhood education (MSE); elementary education (MSE); English as a second language (MSE); English education (MSE); family and consumer sciences education (MSE); industrial technology and vocational education (MSE); learning communities (MSE); mathematics education (MSE); music education (MSE); science education (MSE); social science education (MSE). *Accreditation:* NCATE. Part-time and evening/weekend programs available. *Degree requirements:* For master's, comprehensive exam, thesis optional. *Entrance requirements:* For master's, GRE General Test. Additional exam requirements/recommendations for international students: Required—TOEFL (minimum score 550 paper-based; 213 computer-based).

Wayne State University, College of Education, Division of Teacher Education, Detroit, MI 48202. Offers art education (M Ed), including art therapy; bilingual/bicultural education (M Ed); career and technical education (M Ed); curriculum and instruction (Ed D, PhD, Ed S), including art education (PhD), bilingual education (Ed D, Ed S), bilingual-bicultural education (PhD), career and technical education (MAT, Ed D, PhD, Ed S), early childhood education (MAT, Ed D, PhD, Ed S), elementary education, English as a second language (MAT, Ed D, Ed S), English education (MAT, Ed D, PhD, Ed S), foreign language education (MAT, PhD), K-12 curriculum, mathematics education (MAT, Ed D, PhD, Ed S), science education (MAT, Ed D, PhD, Ed S), secondary education, social studies education (MAT, Ed S), social studies education: secondary (Ed D, PhD); elementary education (MAT), including special education; elementary education (M Ed, MAT), including children's literature (MAT), early childhood education (MAT, Ed D, PhD, Ed S), general elementary education (MAT); elementary or secondary education (MAT), including bilingual/bicultural education, English as a second language (MAT, Ed D, Ed S), mathematics education (MAT, Ed D, PhD, Ed S), science education (MAT, Ed D, PhD, Ed S), social studies education (MAT, Ed S); English education-secondary (M Ed); foreign language education (M Ed); mathematics education (M Ed); reading (M Ed, Ed S); reading, languages and literature (Ed D); science education (M Ed); secondary education (MAT), including art education (K-12), career and technical education (MAT, Ed D, PhD, Ed S), English education (MAT, Ed D, PhD, Ed S), foreign language education (MAT, PhD), kinesiology; social studies education secondary (M Ed); special education (M Ed, Ed D, PhD, Ed S). *Students:* 216 full-time (154 women), 626 part-time (478 women); includes 289 minority (227 Black or African American, non-Hispanic/Latino; 4 American Indian or Alaska Native, non-Hispanic/Latino; 27 Asian, non-Hispanic/Latino; 21 Hispanic/Latino; 1 Native Hawaiian or other Pacific Islander, non-Hispanic/Latino; 9 Two or more races, non-Hispanic/Latino), 14 international. Average age 37. 347 applicants, 37% accepted, 93 enrolled. In 2011, 226 master's, 12 doctorates, 46 other advanced degrees awarded. *Degree requirements:* For master's, thesis (for some programs), thesis, essay or project (for some M Ed programs), professional field experience (for MAT programs); for doctorate, thesis/dissertation. *Entrance requirements:* For master's, Michigan Basic Skills Test (MA in teaching); for doctorate, minimum undergraduate GPA of 3.0, graduate 3.5; interview, curriculum vitae; references. Additional exam requirements/recommendations for international students: Required—TOEFL (minimum score 550 paper-based; 213 computer-based), TWE (minimum score 5.5). *Application deadline:* For fall admission, 6/1 priority date for domestic students, 5/1 for international students; for winter admission, 10/1 priority date for domestic students, 9/1 for international students; for spring admission, 2/1 priority date for domestic students, 1/1 for international students. Applications are processed on a rolling basis. Application fee: $50. Electronic applications accepted. *Expenses:* Tuition, state resident: part-time $512.85 per credit. Tuition, nonresident: part-time $1132.65 per credit. *Required fees:* $26.60 per credit. $199.65 per semester. Tuition and fees vary according to course load and program. *Financial support:* In 2011–12, 42 students received support. Fellowships, research assistantships with tuition reimbursements available, teaching assistantships, scholarships/grants, and unspecified assistantships available. *Faculty research:* Reading and writing literacy and literature. *Total annual research expenditures:* $264,016. *Unit head:* Dr. Craig Roney, Assistant Dean, 313-577-0902, E-mail: rroney@wayne.edu. Web site: http://coe.wayne.edu/ted/index.php.

West Chester University of Pennsylvania, College of Education, Department of Early and Middle Grades, West Chester, PA 19383. Offers applied studies in teaching and learning (M Ed); early childhood education (M Ed, Teaching Certificate); early grades preparation (Teaching Certificate); elementary education (Teaching Certificate); middle grades preparation (Teaching Certificate). *Accreditation:* NCATE. Part-time and evening/weekend programs available. *Faculty:* 7 part-time/adjunct (6 women). *Students:* 54 full-time (41 women), 100 part-time (84 women); includes 14 minority (8 Black or African American, non-Hispanic/Latino; 1 Asian, non-Hispanic/Latino; 2 Hispanic/Latino; 3 Two or more races, non-Hispanic/Latino). Average age 32. 78 applicants, 63% accepted, 32 enrolled. In 2011, 22 degrees awarded. *Degree requirements:* For

Elementary Education

master's, teacher research project, portfolio (for M Ed). *Entrance requirements:* For master's, minimum GPA of 3.0, teacher certification, one year of full-time teaching experience; for Teaching Certificate, PRAXIS I and II, minimum GPA of 3.0. Additional exam requirements/recommendations for international students: Required—TOEFL (minimum score 550 paper-based; 213 computer-based; 80 iBT). *Application deadline:* For fall admission, 4/15 priority date for domestic students, 3/15 for international students; for spring admission, 10/15 priority date for domestic students. Applications are processed on a rolling basis. Application fee: $45. Electronic applications accepted. *Expenses:* Tuition, state resident: full-time $7488; part-time $416 per credit. Tuition, nonresident: full-time $11,232; part-time $624 per credit. *Required fees:* $1784.64; $67.59 per credit. Tuition and fees vary according to program. *Financial support:* Unspecified assistantships available. Support available to part-time students. Financial award application deadline: 2/15; financial award applicants required to submit FAFSA. *Faculty research:* Cooperative learning, creative expression and critical thinking, teacher research, learning styles, middle school education. *Unit head:* Dr. Heather Leaman, Chair, 610-436-2944, Fax: 610-436-3102, E-mail: hleaman@wcupa.edu. *Application contact:* Dr. Connie DiLucchio, Graduate Coordinator, 610-436-3323, Fax: 610-436-3102, E-mail: cdilucchio@wcupa.edu. Web site: http://www.wcupa.edu/_academics/sch_sed.elementaryed/.

Western Governors University, Teachers College, Salt Lake City, UT 84107. Offers curriculum and instruction (MS); educational leadership (MS); educational studies (MA); educational studies (5-12) (MA), including mathematics; elementary education (k-8) (Postbaccalaureate Certificate); English language learning (K-12) (MA); instructional design (MAT); learning and technology (M Ed, MA); management and innovation (M Ed); mathematics (5-12) (Postbaccalaureate Certificate); mathematics (5-9) (Postbaccalaureate Certificate); mathematics education (5-12) (MA); mathematics education (5-9) (MA); mathematics education (K-6) (MA); measurement and evaluation (M Ed); science (5-12) (Postbaccalaureate Certificate); science (5-9) (Postbaccalaureate Certificate); science education (5-12) (MA), including biology, chemistry, geology, physics; science education (5-9) (MA); social science (5-12) (MAT); special education (MAT). *Accreditation:* NCATE. Evening/weekend programs available. Postbaccalaureate distance learning degree programs offered (no on-campus study). *Students:* 3,746 full-time (2,811 women); includes 652 minority (332 Black or African American, non-Hispanic/Latino; 37 American Indian or Alaska Native, non-Hispanic/Latino; 74 Asian, non-Hispanic/Latino; 139 Hispanic/Latino; 70 Two or more races, non-Hispanic/Latino), 12 international. Average age 37. In 2011, 1,080 master's, 242 other advanced degrees awarded. *Degree requirements:* For master's, capstone project. *Entrance requirements:* For master's and Postbaccalaureate Certificate, Readiness Assessment, commitment counseling discussion, transcript submissions, completion of orientation. Additional exam requirements/recommendations for international students: Required—TOEFL (minimum score 450 paper-based; 80 iBT). *Application deadline:* Applications are processed on a rolling basis. Application fee: $65. Electronic applications accepted. *Expenses:* Contact institution. *Financial support:* Scholarships/grants and tuition waivers (partial) available. Financial award applicants required to submit FAFSA. *Unit head:* Dr. Philip Schmidt, Dean of the Teachers College, 845-255-4656. *Application contact:* Enrollment Department, 866-225-5948, Fax: 801-274-3306, E-mail: info@wgu.edu.

Western Illinois University, School of Graduate Studies, College of Education and Human Services, Department of Curriculum and Instruction, Program in Elementary Education, Macomb, IL 61455-1390. Offers MS Ed. *Accreditation:* NCATE. Part-time programs available. *Students:* 70 part-time (65 women); includes 2 minority (both Hispanic/Latino). Average age 35. 6 applicants, 67% accepted. In 2011, 38 master's awarded. *Degree requirements:* For master's, thesis or alternative. *Entrance requirements:* Additional exam requirements/recommendations for international students: Required—TOEFL (minimum score 550 paper-based; 213 computer-based; 80 iBT). *Application deadline:* Applications are processed on a rolling basis. Application fee: $30. Electronic applications accepted. *Expenses:* Tuition, state resident: part-time $281.16 per credit hour. Tuition, nonresident: part-time $562.32 per credit hour. Part-time tuition and fees vary according to campus/location and reciprocity agreements. *Financial support:* In 2011–12, research assistantships with full tuition reimbursements (averaging $7,360 per year) were awarded. Financial award applicants required to submit FAFSA. *Unit head:* Dr. Cindy Dooley, Graduate Committee Chairperson, 309-298-1961. *Application contact:* Dr. Nancy Parsons, Assistant Director of Graduate Studies, 309-298-1806, Fax: 309-298-2345, E-mail: grad-office@wiu.edu. Web site: http://wiu.edu/curriculum.

Western Kentucky University, Graduate Studies, College of Education and Behavioral Sciences, School of Teacher Education, Bowling Green, KY 42101. Offers elementary education (MAE, Ed S); exceptional education: learning and behavioral disorders (MAE); exceptional education: moderate and severe disabilities (MAE); instructional design (MS); interdisciplinary early childhood education (MAE); library media education (MS); literacy education (MAE); middle grades education (MAE); secondary education (MAE, Ed S). Part-time and evening/weekend programs available. Postbaccalaureate distance learning degree programs offered (minimal on-campus study). *Degree requirements:* For master's, comprehensive exam. *Entrance requirements:* For master's, GRE General Test. Additional exam requirements/recommendations for international students: Required—TOEFL (minimum score 555 paper-based; 213 computer-based; 79 iBT). *Faculty research:* Teacher preparation in moderate/severe disabilities.

Western New England University, College of Arts and Sciences, Program in Elementary Education, Springfield, MA 01119. Offers M Ed. Part-time and evening/weekend programs available. *Students:* 25 part-time (all women); includes 1 minority (Hispanic/Latino). In 2011, 16 master's awarded. *Entrance requirements:* For master's, initial license for elementary teaching, recommendations, resume, personal statement. *Application deadline:* Applications are processed on a rolling basis. Application fee: $30. *Financial support:* Available to part-time students. Application deadline: 4/1; applicants required to submit FAFSA. *Unit head:* Dr. Saeed Ghahramani, Dean, 413-782-1218, Fax: 413-796-2118, E-mail: sghahram@wne.edu. *Application contact:* Matt Fox, Director of Recruiting and Marketing for Adult Learners, 413-782-1249, Fax: 413-782-1779, E-mail: learn@wne.edu. Web site: http://www1.wnec.edu/artsandsciences/index.cfm?selection-doc.1672.

Western New Mexico University, Graduate Division, School of Education, Silver City, NM 88062-0680. Offers bilingual education (MAT); counseling (MA); educational leadership (MA); elementary education (MAT); reading (MAT); school psychology (MA); secondary education (MAT); special education (MAT); TESOL (teaching English to speakers of other languages) (MAT). *Accreditation:* NCATE. *Degree requirements:* For master's, comprehensive exam. *Entrance requirements:* For master's, GRE General Test, GRE Subject Test, minimum GPA of 3.2 in last 64 hours of undergraduate study. Additional exam requirements/recommendations for international students: Required—TOEFL (minimum score 550 paper-based; 213 computer-based). Electronic applications accepted.

Western Washington University, Graduate School, Woodring College of Education, Department of Elementary Education, Bellingham, WA 98225-5996. Offers M Ed. *Accreditation:* NCATE. Part-time programs available. *Degree requirements:* For master's, comprehensive exam, thesis optional. *Entrance requirements:* For master's, GRE General Test or MAT, minimum GPA of 3.0 in last 60 semester hours or last 90 quarter hours, elementary teaching certificate. Additional exam requirements/recommendations for international students: Required—TOEFL (minimum score 567 paper-based; 227 computer-based). Electronic applications accepted. *Faculty research:* Teacher learning through National Board certification.

Westfield State University, Division of Graduate and Continuing Education, Department of Education, Program in Elementary Education, Westfield, MA 01086. Offers M Ed. *Accreditation:* NCATE. Part-time and evening/weekend programs available. *Degree requirements:* For master's, comprehensive exam, practicum. *Entrance requirements:* For master's, GRE General Test or MAT, minimum undergraduate GPA of 2.7.

West Virginia University, College of Human Resources and Education, Department of Curriculum and Instruction/Literacy Studies, Program in Elementary Education, Morgantown, WV 26506. Offers MA. Students enter program as undergraduates. *Accreditation:* NCATE. Part-time programs available. *Degree requirements:* For master's, thesis optional, content exams. *Entrance requirements:* For master's, minimum GPA of 2.75. Additional exam requirements/recommendations for international students: Required—TOEFL. Electronic applications accepted. *Faculty research:* Teacher education, school reform, teacher and student attitudes, curriculum development, education technology.

Wheaton College, Graduate School, Department of Education, Wheaton, IL 60187-5593. Offers elementary level (MAT); secondary level (MAT). *Accreditation:* NCATE. *Students:* 17 full-time (12 women), 24 part-time (21 women); includes 5 minority (4 Asian, non-Hispanic/Latino; 1 Hispanic/Latino). Average age 24. 8 applicants, 100% accepted, 2 enrolled. In 2011, 4 master's awarded. *Degree requirements:* For master's, thesis or alternative. *Entrance requirements:* For master's, GRE General Test or MAT. Additional exam requirements/recommendations for international students: Required—TOEFL (minimum score 550 paper-based; 80 iBT), IELTS (minimum score 6.5). *Application deadline:* For fall admission, 5/1 for domestic students, 1/1 for international students; for spring admission, 11/1 for domestic students. Applications are processed on a rolling basis. Application fee: $30. Electronic applications accepted. *Expenses: Tuition:* Full-time $16,440; part-time $685 per credit hour. Tuition and fees vary according to degree level and program. *Financial support:* Career-related internships or fieldwork and Federal Work-Study available. Financial award application deadline: 3/1; financial award applicants required to submit FAFSA. *Unit head:* Dr. Jillian Lederhouse, Chair, 630-752-5764, E-mail: jillian.lederhouse@wheaton.edu. *Application contact:* Julie A. Huebner, Director of Graduate Admissions, 630-752-5195, Fax: 630-752-5935, E-mail: gradadm@wheaton.edu. Web site: http://www.wheaton.edu/academics/departments/education.

Wheelock College, Graduate Programs, Division of Education, Boston, MA 02215-4176. Offers early childhood education (MS); education leadership (MS); elementary education (MS); language, literacy, and reading (MS); teaching students with moderate disabilities (MS). *Accreditation:* NCATE. Postbaccalaureate distance learning degree programs offered (minimal on-campus study). *Degree requirements:* For master's, comprehensive exam. *Entrance requirements:* Additional exam requirements/recommendations for international students: Required—TOEFL. Electronic applications accepted. *Faculty research:* Symbolic learning, emergent literacy, diversity inclusion, beginning reading language and culture, math education.

Whittier College, Graduate Programs, Department of Education and Child Development, Program in Elementary Education, Whittier, CA 90608-0634. Offers MA Ed. Part-time and evening/weekend programs available. *Degree requirements:* For master's, thesis. *Entrance requirements:* For master's, GRE General Test, MAT.

Whitworth University, School of Education, Graduate Studies in Education, Spokane, WA 99251-0001. Offers administration (M Ed); counseling (M Ed), including school counselors, social agency/church setting; elementary education (M Ed); gifted and talented (MAT); secondary education (M Ed); special education (MAT); teaching (MIT). *Accreditation:* NCATE. Part-time and evening/weekend programs available. *Degree requirements:* For master's, comprehensive exam, thesis (for some programs). *Entrance requirements:* For master's, GRE General Test, MAT. Additional exam requirements/recommendations for international students: Required—TOEFL. Tuition and fees vary according to program. *Faculty research:* Rural program development, mainstreaming, special needs learners.

Widener University, School of Human Service Professions, Center for Education, Chester, PA 19013-5792. Offers adult education (M Ed); counseling in higher education (M Ed); counselor education (M Ed); early childhood education (M Ed); educational foundations (M Ed); educational leadership (M Ed); educational psychology (M Ed); elementary education (M Ed); English and language arts (M Ed); health education (M Ed); higher education leadership (Ed D); home and school visitor (M Ed); human sexuality (M Ed, PhD); mathematics education (M Ed); middle school education (M Ed); principalship (M Ed); reading and language arts (Ed D); reading education (M Ed); school administration (Ed D); science education (M Ed); social studies education (M Ed); special education (M Ed); technology education (M Ed). *Accreditation:* NCATE. Part-time and evening/weekend programs available. Terminal master's awarded for partial completion of doctoral program. *Degree requirements:* For doctorate, thesis/dissertation. *Entrance requirements:* For master's, minimum GPA of 2.5; for doctorate, GRE or MAT, minimum GPA of 2.0 (undergraduate), 3.5 (graduate). Electronic applications accepted. *Expenses:* Contact institution. *Faculty research:* Reading and cognition, adult education, technology education, educational leadership, special education.

William Carey University, School of Education, Hattiesburg, MS 39401-5499. Offers art education (M Ed); art of teaching (M Ed); elementary education (M Ed, Ed S); English education (M Ed); gifted education (M Ed); history and social science (M Ed); mild/moderate disabilities (M Ed); secondary education (M Ed). Part-time programs available. *Degree requirements:* For master's, comprehensive exam. *Entrance requirements:* For master's, GRE, MAT, minimum GPA of 2.5, Class A teacher's license. Additional exam requirements/recommendations for international students: Required—TOEFL (minimum score 550 paper-based; 213 computer-based).

William Woods University, Graduate and Adult Studies, Fulton, MO 65251-1098. Offers administration (Ed S); agriculture (MBA); athletic/activities administration (M Ed); curriculum and instruction (M Ed); curriculum leadership (Ed S); elementary administration (M Ed); health management (MBA); human resources (MBA); principalship (Ed S); secondary administration (M Ed); special education director (M Ed). Evening/weekend programs available. *Degree requirements:* For master's, capstone course (MBA), action research (M Ed); for Ed S, field experience. *Entrance requirements:* For master's, 2 recommendations, resumé, BA/BS; teaching certification (M Ed); course work in economics and accounting (MBA); for Ed S, M Ed, 2 letters of recommendation, resume, teaching certification. Additional exam requirements/recommendations for international students: Required—TOEFL (minimum score 550 paper-based). Electronic applications accepted.

Wilmington University, College of Education, New Castle, DE 19720-6491. Offers applied technology in education (M Ed); career and technical education (M Ed);

educational leadership (Ed D); elementary and secondary school counseling (M Ed); elementary studies (M Ed); ESOL literacy (M Ed); higher education leadership (Ed D); instruction: gifted and talented (M Ed); instruction: teacher of reading (M Ed); instruction: teaching and learning (M Ed); organizational leadership (Ed D); school leadership (M Ed); secondary education (MAT); special education (M Ed). *Accreditation:* NCATE. Part-time and evening/weekend programs available. *Faculty:* 7 full-time (4 women). *Students:* 638 full-time (425 women), 2,014 part-time (1,635 women). Average age 33. *Entrance requirements:* For master's, 2 letters of recommendation, interview. Additional exam requirements/recommendations for international students: Required—TOEFL (minimum score 500 paper-based; 173 computer-based). *Application deadline:* For fall admission, 4/30 for domestic students. Applications are processed on a rolling basis. Application fee: $35. Electronic applications accepted. *Expenses: Tuition:* Part-time $534 per credit hour. *Required fees:* $25 per term. *Financial support:* Applicants required to submit FAFSA. *Unit head:* Dr. John C. Gray, Dean, 302-295-1139. *Application contact:* Chris Ferguson, Director of Admissions, 302-356-4636 Ext. 256, Fax: 302-328-5164, E-mail: inquire@wilmcoll.edu. Web site: http://www.wilmu.edu/education/.

Wilson College, Program in Education, Chambersburg, PA 17201-1285. Offers M Ed. Evening/weekend programs available. *Degree requirements:* For master's, project. *Entrance requirements:* For master's, PRAXIS, minimum undergraduate cumulative GPA of 3.0, 2 letters of recommendation, current certification for eligibility to teach in grades K-12, resume, personal interview. Electronic applications accepted.

Wingate University, Thayer School of Education, Wingate, NC 28174-0159. Offers community college leadership (Ed D); educational leadership (MA Ed, Ed D); elementary education (MA Ed, MAT); health and physical education (MA Ed); sport administration (MA Ed). *Accreditation:* NCATE. Part-time and evening/weekend programs available. *Faculty:* 5 full-time (3 women), 10 part-time/adjunct (3 women). *Students:* 7 full-time (4 women), 251 part-time (152 women); includes 68 minority (63 Black or African American, non-Hispanic/Latino; 1 American Indian or Alaska Native, non-Hispanic/Latino; 1 Asian, non-Hispanic/Latino; 3 Hispanic/Latino), 2 international. Average age 35. In 2011, 29 master's awarded. *Degree requirements:* For master's, portfolio. *Entrance requirements:* For master's, GRE General Test or MAT, teaching certificate (MA Ed). *Application deadline:* For fall admission, 8/15 priority date for domestic students; for spring admission, 12/15 for domestic students. Applications are processed on a rolling basis. Application fee: $0. *Expenses: Tuition:* Part-time $455 per credit hour. Part-time tuition and fees vary according to degree level and program. *Financial support:* In 2011–12, 20 students received support. Scholarships/grants available. Support available to part-time students. Financial award applicants required to submit FAFSA. *Unit head:* Dr. Sarah Harrison-Burns, Dean, 704-233-8128, E-mail: shburns@wingate.edu. *Application contact:* Theresa Hopkins, Secretary, 704-321-1470, Fax: 704-233-8273, E-mail: t.hopkins@wingate.edu.

Winston-Salem State University, Program in Elementary Education, Winston-Salem, NC 27110-0003. Offers M Ed. *Accreditation:* NCATE. Part-time and evening/weekend programs available. Postbaccalaureate distance learning degree programs offered (minimal on-campus study). *Entrance requirements:* For master's, GRE, MAT, NC teacher licensure. Electronic applications accepted. *Faculty research:* Action research on issues in elementary classroom.

Worcester State University, Graduate Studies, Department of Education, Program in Elementary Education, Worcester, MA 01602-2597. Offers M Ed. Part-time and evening/weekend programs available. *Faculty:* 12 full-time (9 women), 22 part-time/adjunct (10 women). *Students:* 4 full-time (all women), 21 part-time (18 women); includes 2 minority (1 Hispanic/Latino; 1 Two or more races, non-Hispanic/Latino). Average age 30. 12 applicants, 75% accepted, 7 enrolled. In 2011, 9 master's awarded. *Degree requirements:* For master's, comprehensive exam (for some programs), thesis optional. *Entrance requirements:* For master's, GRE General Test or MAT, elementary teaching certificate. Additional exam requirements/recommendations for international students: Required—TOEFL (minimum score 500 paper-based; 61 iBT). *Application deadline:* For fall admission, 6/15 for domestic and international students; for spring admission, 4/1 for domestic and international students. Applications are processed on a rolling basis. Application fee: $40. Electronic applications accepted. *Expenses:* Tuition, state resident: full-time $2700; part-time $150 per credit. Tuition, nonresident: full-time $2700; part-time $150 per credit. *Required fees:* $2016; $112 per credit. *Financial support:* Career-related internships or fieldwork, scholarships/grants, and unspecified assistantships available. Financial award application deadline: 3/1; financial award applicants required to submit FAFSA. *Faculty research:* Contemporary elementary education, social studies in the elementary school. *Unit head:* Dr. Elaine Tateronis, Coordinator, 508-929-8823, Fax: 508-929-8164, E-mail: etateronis@worcester.edu. *Application contact:* Sara Grady, Assistant Dean of Graduate and Continuing Education, 508-929-8787, Fax: 508-929-8100, E-mail: sara.grady@worcester.edu.

Wright State University, School of Graduate Studies, College of Education and Human Services, Department of Teacher Education, Programs in Classroom Teacher Education, Dayton, OH 45435. Offers M Ed, MA. *Accreditation:* NCATE. *Degree requirements:* For master's, thesis (for some programs). *Entrance requirements:* For master's, GRE General Test, MAT, PRAXIS II. Additional exam requirements/recommendations for international students: Required—TOEFL.

Xavier University, College of Social Sciences, Health and Education, School of Education, Department of Childhood Education and Literacy, Program in Elementary Education, Cincinnati, OH 45207. Offers M Ed. Part-time programs available. *Faculty:* 2 full-time (1 woman). *Students:* 67 full-time (53 women), 36 part-time (30 women); includes 13 minority (10 Black or African American, non-Hispanic/Latino; 1 Asian, non-Hispanic/Latino; 2 Hispanic/Latino). Average age 30. 22 applicants, 95% accepted, 20 enrolled. In 2011, 33 master's awarded. *Degree requirements:* For master's, comprehensive exam, research project or thesis. *Entrance requirements:* For master's, GRE or MAT. Additional exam requirements/recommendations for international students: Required—TOEFL (minimum score 550 paper-based; 213 computer-based; 79 iBT). *Application deadline:* Applications are processed on a rolling basis. Application fee: $35. Electronic applications accepted. *Expenses: Tuition:* Part-time $576 per credit hour. *Financial support:* In 2011–12, 70 students received support. Unspecified assistantships available. Financial award applicants required to submit FAFSA. *Faculty research:* First-year teacher retention, teaching efficacy of science educators, adolescents' literacy practices, family resiliency, preparing culturally responsive teachers. *Unit head:* Dr. Cynthia Geer, Department Chairperson/Professor, 513-745-3262, Fax: 513-745-3504, E-mail: geer@xavier.edu. *Application contact:* Roger Bosse, Graduate Services Director, 513-745-3357, Fax: 513-745-1048, E-mail: bosse@xavier.edu. Web site: http://www.xavier.edu/elementary-grad/.

Higher Education

Abilene Christian University, Graduate School, College of Education and Human Services, Graduate Studies in Education, Program in Higher Education, Abilene, TX 79699-9100. Offers M Ed. Postbaccalaureate distance learning degree programs offered (minimal on-campus study). *Faculty:* 1 full-time (0 women), 3 part-time/adjunct (1 woman). *Students:* 8 full-time (5 women), 37 part-time (23 women); includes 18 minority (11 Black or African American, non-Hispanic/Latino; 5 Hispanic/Latino; 2 Two or more races, non-Hispanic/Latino), 3 international. 39 applicants, 31% accepted, 7 enrolled. In 2011, 28 master's awarded. *Degree requirements:* For master's, internship. *Entrance requirements:* Additional exam requirements/recommendations for international students: Required—TOEFL (minimum score 550 paper-based; 213 computer-based; 80 iBT), IELTS (minimum score 6). *Application deadline:* For fall admission, 8/15 priority date for domestic students; for winter admission, 10/1 priority date for domestic students; for spring admission, 12/15 priority date for domestic students. Applications are processed on a rolling basis. Application fee: $100. Electronic applications accepted. *Expenses: Tuition:* Full-time $14,168; part-time $787 per hour. *Required fees:* $82 per hour. $10 per term. *Financial support:* In 2011–12, 12 students received support. Application deadline: 4/1; applicants required to submit FAFSA. *Unit head:* Dr. Jason Morris, Graduate Advisor, 325-674-2838, Fax: 325-674-2123, E-mail: morrisj@acu.edu. *Application contact:* David Pittman, Graduate Admissions Counselor, 325-674-2656, Fax: 325-674-6717, E-mail: gradinfo@acu.edu. Web site: http://www.acu.edu/hied.

Alliant International University–Irvine, Shirley M. Hufstedler School of Education, Educational Leadership Programs, Irvine, CA 92612. Offers educational administration (MA, Credential); educational leadership and management (K-12) (Ed D); higher education (Ed D); preliminary administrative services (Credential). Part-time programs available. *Students:* 11. In 2011, 8 master's, 4 doctorates awarded. *Entrance requirements:* For master's and doctorate, minimum GPA of 3.0, letters of recommendation. Additional exam requirements/recommendations for international students: Required—TOEFL (minimum score 550 paper-based; 213 computer-based), TWE (minimum score 5). *Application deadline:* For fall admission, 7/1 priority date for domestic students, 7/1 for international students; for spring admission, 12/1 priority date for domestic students, 12/1 for international students. Applications are processed on a rolling basis. Application fee: $55. Electronic applications accepted. *Financial support:* Federal Work-Study, institutionally sponsored loans, and scholarships/grants available. Financial award application deadline: 2/15. *Unit head:* Dr. Suzanne Power, Acting Director, 866-825-5426, Fax: 949-833-3507, E-mail: admissions@alliant.edu. *Application contact:* Alliant International University Central Contact Center, 866-U-ALLIANT, Fax: 858-635-4555, E-mail: admissions@alliant.edu. Web site: http://www.alliant.edu/gsoe/.

Alliant International University–San Diego, Shirley M. Hufstedler School of Education, Educational Leadership Programs, San Diego, CA 92131-1799. Offers educational administration (MA); educational leadership and management (K-12) (Ed D); higher education (Ed D, Certificate); preliminary administrative services (Credential). Part-time programs available. *Faculty:* 4 full-time (2 women), 3 part-time/adjunct (2 women). *Students:* 11 full-time (8 women), 32 part-time (21 women); includes 19 minority (10 Black or African American, non-Hispanic/Latino; 5 Asian, non-Hispanic/Latino; 4 Hispanic/Latino), 4 international. Average age 45. In 2011, 1 master's, 5 doctorates awarded. *Degree requirements:* For doctorate, comprehensive exam, thesis/dissertation. *Entrance requirements:* For master's, minimum GPA of 2.5, letters of recommendation; for doctorate, minimum GPA of 3.0, letters of recommendation. Additional exam requirements/recommendations for international students: Required—TOEFL (minimum score 550 paper-based; 213 computer-based), TWE (minimum score 5). *Application deadline:* For fall admission, 7/1 priority date for domestic students, 7/1 for international students; for spring admission, 12/1 priority date for domestic students, 12/1 for international students. Applications are processed on a rolling basis. Application fee: $55. Electronic applications accepted. Tuition and fees vary according to degree level and program. *Financial support:* Federal Work-Study, institutionally sponsored loans, and scholarships/grants available. Financial award application deadline: 2/15; financial award applicants required to submit FAFSA. *Faculty research:* Global education, women and international educational opportunities. *Unit head:* Dr. Trudy Day, Program Director, Educational Policy and Practice Programs, 415-955-2102, Fax: 415-955-2179, E-mail: admissions@alliant.edu. *Application contact:* Alliant International University Central Contact Center, 866-U-ALLIANT, Fax: 858-635-4555, E-mail: admissions@alliant.edu.

Alliant International University–San Francisco, Shirley M. Hufstedler School of Education, Educational Leadership Programs, San Francisco, CA 94133-1221. Offers community college administration (Ed D); educational administration (MA); educational leadership and management (K-12) (Ed D); higher education (Ed D); preliminary administrative services (Credential). Part-time programs available. *Faculty:* 5 full-time (2 women), 2 part-time/adjunct (both women). *Students:* 11 part-time (5 women). Average age 46. In 2011, 2 doctorates awarded. *Degree requirements:* For doctorate, comprehensive exam, thesis/dissertation. *Entrance requirements:* For master's and doctorate, minimum GPA of 3.0, letters of recommendation. Additional exam requirements/recommendations for international students: Required—TOEFL (minimum score 550 paper-based; 213 computer-based; 80 iBT), TWE (minimum score 5). *Application deadline:* For fall admission, 7/1 priority date for domestic students, 7/1 for international students; for spring admission, 12/1 priority date for domestic students, 12/1 for international students. Applications are processed on a rolling basis. Application fee: $65. Electronic applications accepted. *Financial support:* Federal Work-Study, institutionally sponsored loans, and scholarships/grants available. Financial award application deadline: 2/15; financial award applicants required to submit FAFSA. *Faculty research:* Leadership in higher education, community colleges. *Unit head:* Dr. Trudy Day, Educational Policy and Practice Director, 415-955-2102, Fax: 415-955-2179, E-mail: admissions@alliant.edu. *Application contact:* Alliant International University Central Contact Center, 866-U-ALLIANT, Fax: 858-635-4555, E-mail: admissions@alliant.edu. Web site: http://www.alliant.edu/gsoe/.

Andrews University, School of Graduate Studies, School of Education, Department of Leadership and Educational Administration, Berrien Springs, MI 49104. Offers educational administration and leadership (MA, Ed D, PhD, Ed S); higher education administration (MA, Ed D, PhD, Ed S); leadership (MA, Ed D, PhD, Ed S). *Students:* 2 full-time (1 woman), 118 part-time (50 women); includes 30 minority (18 Black or African

American, non-Hispanic/Latino; 1 American Indian or Alaska Native, non-Hispanic/Latino; 3 Asian, non-Hispanic/Latino; 7 Hispanic/Latino; 1 Two or more races, non-Hispanic/Latino), 23 international. Average age 47. 57 applicants, 44% accepted, 14 enrolled. In 2011, 8 master's, 9 doctorates awarded. *Degree requirements:* For doctorate, thesis/dissertation. *Entrance requirements:* For master's, GRE. Additional exam requirements/recommendations for international students: Required—TOEFL (minimum score 550 paper-based). *Application deadline:* Applications are processed on a rolling basis. Application fee: $40. *Unit head:* Dr. Robson Marinho, Chair, 269-471-3487. *Application contact:* Carolyn Hurst, Supervisor of Graduate Admission, 800-253-2874, Fax: 269-471-6321, E-mail: graduate@andrews.edu.

Angelo State University, College of Graduate Studies, College of Education, Department of Curriculum and Instruction, Program in Student Development and Leadership in Higher Education, San Angelo, TX 76909. Offers M Ed. Part-time and evening/weekend programs available. *Faculty:* 17 full-time (12 women). *Students:* 18 full-time (12 women), 41 part-time (31 women); includes 24 minority (7 Black or African American, non-Hispanic/Latino; 1 Asian, non-Hispanic/Latino; 16 Hispanic/Latino). Average age 32. 25 applicants, 84% accepted, 15 enrolled. In 2011, 7 master's awarded. *Degree requirements:* For master's, comprehensive exam. *Entrance requirements:* Additional exam requirements/recommendations for international students: Required—TOEFL or IELTS. *Application deadline:* For fall admission, 7/15 priority date for domestic students, 6/10 for international students; for spring admission, 12/1 priority date for domestic students, 11/1 for international students. Applications are processed on a rolling basis. Application fee: $40 ($50 for international students). Electronic applications accepted. *Financial support:* In 2011–12, 7 students received support. Federal Work-Study, scholarships/grants, and unspecified assistantships available. Support available to part-time students. Financial award application deadline: 3/1; financial award applicants required to submit FAFSA. *Unit head:* Dr. Alaric Williams, Graduate Advisor, 325-942-2052 Ext. 262, Fax: 325-942-2039, E-mail: alaric.williams@angelo.edu. *Application contact:* Aly Hunter, Graduate Admissions Assistant, 325-942-2169, Fax: 325-942-2194, E-mail: aly.hunter@angelo.edu.

Appalachian State University, Cratis D. Williams Graduate School, Department of Leadership and Educational Studies, Boone, NC 28608. Offers educational administration (Ed S); educational media (MA); higher education (MA, Ed S); library science (MLS); school administration (MSA). Part-time and evening/weekend programs available. Postbaccalaureate distance learning degree programs offered (no on-campus study). *Faculty:* 35 full-time (15 women), 1 (woman) part-time/adjunct. *Students:* 35 full-time (27 women), 369 part-time (293 women); includes 31 minority (26 Black or African American, non-Hispanic/Latino; 1 Asian, non-Hispanic/Latino; 4 Hispanic/Latino). 196 applicants, 83% accepted, 117 enrolled. In 2011, 195 master's, 32 other advanced degrees awarded. *Degree requirements:* For master's and Ed S, comprehensive exam, thesis optional. *Entrance requirements:* For master's and Ed S, GRE or MAT, 3 letters of recommendation. Additional exam requirements/recommendations for international students: Required—TOEFL (minimum score 570 paper-based; 230 computer-based; 79 iBT), IELTS (minimum score 6.5). *Application deadline:* For fall admission, 3/14 priority date for domestic students, 2/1 for international students; for spring admission, 11/1 for domestic students, 7/1 for international students. Applications are processed on a rolling basis. Application fee: $55. Electronic applications accepted. *Expenses:* Tuition, state resident: full-time $4040; part-time $180 per semester hour. Tuition, nonresident: full-time $15,900; part-time $760 per semester hour. *Required fees:* $2500; $20 per semester hour. Tuition and fees vary according to campus/location. *Financial support:* In 2011–12, 10 research assistantships (averaging $8,000 per year) were awarded; career-related internships or fieldwork, scholarships/grants, and unspecified assistantships also available. Financial award application deadline: 4/1; financial award applicants required to submit FAFSA. *Faculty research:* Brain, learning and meditation; leadership of teaching and learning. *Total annual research expenditures:* $515,000. *Unit head:* Dr. Robert Sanders, Interim Director, 828-262-3112, E-mail: sandersrl@appstate.edu. *Application contact:* Lori Dean, Graduate Student Coordinator, 828-262-6041, E-mail: deanlk@appstate.edu. Web site: http://www.les.appstate.edu.

Argosy University, Atlanta, College of Education, Atlanta, GA 30328. Offers educational leadership (MAEd, Ed D, Ed S), including higher education administration (Ed D), K-12 education (Ed D); teaching and learning (MAEd, Ed D, Ed S), including education technology (Ed D), higher education (Ed D), K-12 education (Ed D).

See Close-Up on page 1017.

Argosy University, Chicago, College of Education, Chicago, IL 60601. Offers adult education and training (MA Ed); community college executive leadership (Ed D); educational leadership (MA Ed, Ed D, Ed S), including district leadership (Ed D), higher education administration (Ed D), K-12 education (Ed D); instructional leadership (Ed D, Ed S), including higher education (Ed D), K-12 education (Ed D). Postbaccalaureate distance learning degree programs offered (minimal on-campus study).

See Close-Up on page 769.

Argosy University, Dallas, College of Education, Farmers Branch, TX 75244. Offers educational administration (MA Ed); educational leadership (Ed D); higher and postsecondary education (MA Ed); instructional leadership (MA Ed); school psychology (MA).

See Close-Up on page 771.

Argosy University, Denver, College of Education, Denver, CO 80231. Offers community college executive leadership (Ed D); educational leadership (MA Ed, Ed D), including higher education (Ed D), K-12 education (Ed D); instructional leadership (MA Ed, Ed D), including higher education administration (Ed D), K-12 education (Ed D).

See Close-Up on page 773.

Argosy University, Hawai`i, College of Education, Honolulu, HI 96813. Offers adult education and training (MAEd); educational leadership (Ed D), including higher education administration, K-12 education; instructional leadership (Ed D), including higher education, K-12 education; school psychology (MA).

See Close-Up on page 775.

Argosy University, Inland Empire, College of Education, San Bernardino, CA 92408. Offers community college executive leadership (Ed D); educational leadership (MA Ed, Ed D), including higher education administration (Ed D), K-12 education (Ed D); instructional leadership (MA Ed, Ed D), including higher education (Ed D), K-12 education (Ed D), multiple subject teacher preparation (MA Ed), single subject teacher preparation (MA Ed).

See Close-Up on page 1019.

Argosy University, Los Angeles, College of Education, Santa Monica, CA 90045. Offers community college executive leadership (Ed D); educational leadership (MA Ed, Ed D), including higher education administration (Ed D), K-12 education (Ed D); instructional leadership (MA Ed, Ed D), including higher education (Ed D), K-12 education (Ed D), multiple subject teacher preparation (MA Ed), single subject teacher preparation (MA Ed).

See Close-Up on page 777.

Argosy University, Nashville, College of Education, Program in Educational Leadership, Nashville, TN 37214. Offers educational leadership (MA Ed, Ed S); higher education administration (Ed D); K-12 education (Ed D).

See Close-Up on page 1021.

Argosy University, Nashville, College of Education, Program in Instructional Leadership, Nashville, TN 37214. Offers education technology (Ed D); higher education administration (Ed D); instructional leadership (MA Ed, Ed S); K-12 education (Ed D).

See Close-Up on page 1021.

Argosy University, Orange County, College of Education, Orange, CA 92868. Offers community college executive leadership (Ed D); educational leadership (MA Ed, Ed D), including higher education administration (Ed D), K-12 education (Ed D); instructional leadership (MA Ed, Ed D), including education technology (Ed D), higher education (Ed D), K-12 education (Ed D), multiple subject teacher preparation (MA Ed), single subject teacher preparation (MA Ed).

See Close-Up on page 779.

Argosy University, Phoenix, College of Education, Phoenix, AZ 85021. Offers adult education and training (MA Ed); advanced educational administration (Ed D, Ed S); community college executive leadership (Ed D); educational administration (MA Ed); educational leadership (MA Ed, Ed D, Ed S), including education technology (Ed D), higher education administration (Ed D), K-12 education (Ed D); higher and postsecondary education (MA Ed); initial educational administration (Ed D, Ed S); school psychology (MA); teaching and learning (MA Ed, Ed D, Ed S), including education technology (Ed D), higher education (Ed D), K-12 education (Ed D).

See Close-Up on page 781.

Argosy University, San Diego, College of Education, San Diego, CA 92108. Offers community college executive leadership (Ed D); educational leadership (MA Ed, Ed D), including higher education administration (Ed D), K-12 education (Ed D); instructional leadership (MA Ed, Ed D), including higher education (Ed D), K-12 education (Ed D).

See Close-Up on page 785.

Argosy University, San Francisco Bay Area, College of Education, Alameda, CA 94501. Offers community college executive leadership (Ed D); educational leadership (MA Ed, Ed D), including education technology (Ed D), higher education administration (Ed D), K-12 education (Ed D); instructional leadership (MA Ed, Ed D), including education technology (Ed D), higher education (Ed D), K-12 education (Ed D), multiple subject teacher preparation (MA Ed), single subject teacher preparation (MA Ed).

See Close-Up on page 787.

Argosy University, Sarasota, College of Education, Sarasota, FL 34235. Offers community college executive leadership (Ed D); educational leadership (MA Ed, Ed D, Ed S), including higher education administration (Ed D), K-12 education (Ed D); school counseling (MA, Ed S); school psychology (MA); teaching and learning (MA Ed, Ed D, Ed S), including education technology (Ed D), higher education (Ed D), K-12 education (Ed D).

See Close-Up on page 789.

Argosy University, Schaumburg, College of Education, Schaumburg, IL 60173-5403. Offers community college executive leadership (Ed D); educational leadership (MA Ed, Ed D, Ed S), including district leadership (Ed D), higher education administration (Ed D), K-12 education (Ed D); instructional leadership (Ed D, Ed S), including higher education (Ed D), K-12 education (Ed D).

See Close-Up on page 791.

Argosy University, Seattle, College of Education, Seattle, WA 98121. Offers adult education and training (MA Ed); community college executive leadership (Ed D); educational leadership (MA Ed, Ed D), including higher education administration (Ed D), K-12 education (Ed D); higher and postsecondary education (MA Ed); instructional leadership (MA Ed, Ed D), including education technology (Ed D), higher education (Ed D), K-12 education (Ed D).

See Close-Up on page 793.

Argosy University, Tampa, College of Education, Tampa, FL 33607. Offers community college executive leadership (Ed D); educational leadership (MA Ed, Ed D, Ed S), including higher education administration (Ed D), K-12 education (Ed D); school counseling (MA); teaching and learning (MA Ed, Ed D, Ed S), including higher education (Ed D), K-12 education (Ed D).

See Close-Up on page 795.

Argosy University, Twin Cities, College of Education, Eagan, MN 55121. Offers advanced educational administration (Ed D, Ed S); educational leadership (MA Ed, Ed D, Ed S), including higher education administration (Ed D), K-12 education (Ed D); higher and postsecondary education (MA Ed); initial educational administration (Ed D, Ed S); instructional leadership (MA Ed, Ed D, Ed S), including education technology (Ed D), higher education (Ed D), K-12 education (Ed D).

See Close-Up on page 797.

Argosy University, Washington DC, College of Education, Arlington, VA 22209. Offers community college executive leadership (Ed D); educational leadership (MA Ed, Ed D, Ed S), including higher education administration (Ed D), K-12 education (Ed D); instructional leadership (MA Ed, Ed D, Ed S), including higher education (Ed D), K-12 education (Ed D).

See Close-Up on page 799.

Arizona State University, Mary Lou Fulton Teachers College, Program in Higher and Post-Secondary Education, Phoenix, AZ 85069. Offers M Ed. Part-time and evening/weekend programs available. *Degree requirements:* For master's, thesis or alternative, applied project, interactive Program of Study (iPOS) submitted before completing 50 percent of required credit hours. *Entrance requirements:* For master's, minimum GPA of 3.0 or equivalent in last 2 years of work leading to bachelor's degree, 3 letters of recommendation, personal statement describing research and career goals, curriculum vitae or resume. Additional exam requirements/recommendations for international students: Required—TOEFL (minimum score 80 iBT), TOEFL, IELTS, or Pearson Test of English. Electronic applications accepted.

Auburn University, Graduate School, College of Education, Department of Curriculum and Teaching, Auburn University, AL 36849. Offers business education (M Ed, MS, PhD); early childhood education (M Ed, MS, PhD, Ed S); elementary education (M Ed, MS, PhD, Ed S); foreign languages (M Ed, MS); music education (M Ed, MS, PhD, Ed S); postsecondary education (PhD); reading education (PhD, Ed S); secondary education (M Ed, MS, PhD, Ed S), including English language arts, mathematics, science, social studies. *Accreditation:* NASM (one or more programs are accredited); NCATE. Part-time programs available. *Faculty:* 22 full-time (17 women), 3 part-time/adjunct (all women). *Students:* 80 full-time (58 women), 181 part-time (126 women); includes 42 minority (28 Black or African American, non-Hispanic/Latino; 7 Asian, non-Hispanic/Latino; 7 Hispanic/Latino). Average age 34. 184 applicants, 53% accepted, 60 enrolled. In 2011, 77 master's, 10 doctorates, 35 other advanced degrees awarded. *Degree requirements:* For master's, thesis (for some programs); for doctorate, thesis/dissertation; for Ed S, field project. *Entrance requirements:* For master's, doctorate, and Ed S, GRE General Test. *Application deadline:* For fall admission, 7/7 for domestic students; for spring admission, 11/24 for domestic students. Applications are processed on a rolling basis. Application fee: $50 ($60 for international students). Electronic applications accepted. *Expenses:* Tuition, state resident: full-time $7290; part-time $405 per credit hour. Tuition, nonresident: full-time $21,870; part-time $1215 per credit hour. *International tuition:* $22,000 full-time. *Required fees:* $1402. *Financial support:* Fellowships, teaching assistantships, career-related internships or fieldwork, and Federal Work-Study available. Support available to part-time students. Financial award application deadline: 3/15; financial award applicants required to submit FAFSA. *Faculty research:* Emerging literacy, reading attitudes, music for at-risk youth, portfolio assessment. *Unit head:* Dr. Kimberly Walls, Head, 334-844-4434. *Application contact:* Dr. George Flowers, Dean of the Graduate School, 334-844-2125. Web site: http://education.auburn.edu/academic_departments/curr/.

Auburn University, Graduate School, College of Education, Department of Educational Foundations, Leadership, and Technology, Auburn University, AL 36849. Offers adult education (M Ed, MS, Ed D); curriculum and instruction (M Ed, MS, Ed D, Ed S); curriculum supervision (M Ed, MS, Ed D, Ed S); educational psychology (PhD); higher education administration (M Ed, MS, Ed D, Ed S); media instructional design (MS); media specialist (M Ed); school administration (M Ed, MS, Ed D, Ed S). *Accreditation:* NCATE. Part-time programs available. *Faculty:* 26 full-time (16 women), 3 part-time/adjunct (all women). *Students:* 58 full-time (28 women), 215 part-time (135 women); includes 89 minority (82 Black or African American, non-Hispanic/Latino; 1 American Indian or Alaska Native, non-Hispanic/Latino; 4 Asian, non-Hispanic/Latino; 2 Hispanic/Latino), 13 international. Average age 35. 140 applicants, 61% accepted, 56 enrolled. In 2011, 37 master's, 29 doctorates, 9 other advanced degrees awarded. *Degree requirements:* For master's, thesis (for some programs); for doctorate, thesis/dissertation; for Ed S, field project. *Entrance requirements:* For master's, doctorate, and Ed S, GRE General Test. *Application deadline:* For fall admission, 7/7 for domestic students; for spring admission, 11/24 for domestic students. Applications are processed on a rolling basis. Application fee: $50 ($60 for international students). Electronic applications accepted. *Expenses:* Tuition, state resident: full-time $7290; part-time $405 per credit hour. Tuition, nonresident: full-time $21,870; part-time $1215 per credit hour. *International tuition:* $22,000 full-time. *Required fees:* $1402. *Financial support:* Teaching assistantships and Federal Work-Study available. Support available to part-time students. Financial award application deadline: 3/15; financial award applicants required to submit FAFSA. *Unit head:* Dr. Sherida Downer, Head, 334-844-4460. *Application contact:* Dr. George Flowers, Dean of the Graduate School, 334-844-4700. Web site: http://www.education.auburn.edu/academic_departments/eflt/.

Azusa Pacific University, School of Behavioral and Applied Sciences, Department of Doctoral Higher Education, Azusa, CA 91702-7000. Offers educational leadership (Ed D); higher education leadership (Ed D).

Azusa Pacific University, School of Behavioral and Applied Sciences, Department of Higher Education and Organizational Leadership, Program in College Student Affairs, Azusa, CA 91702-7000. Offers M Ed. Part-time and evening/weekend programs available. *Degree requirements:* For master's, exam. *Entrance requirements:* For master's, 12 units of course work in social science, minimum GPA of 3.0.

Ball State University, Graduate School, Teachers College, Department of Educational Studies, Program in Adult Education, Muncie, IN 47306-1099. Offers adult and community education (MA); adult, community, and higher education (Ed D). *Accreditation:* NCATE. *Students:* 31 full-time (21 women), 82 part-time (57 women); includes 19 minority (13 Black or African American, non-Hispanic/Latino; 1 Asian, non-Hispanic/Latino; 2 Hispanic/Latino; 3 Two or more races, non-Hispanic/Latino), 2 international. Average age 34. 39 applicants, 67% accepted, 21 enrolled. In 2011, 19 master's, 7 doctorates awarded. *Degree requirements:* For doctorate, thesis/dissertation. *Entrance requirements:* For doctorate, GRE General Test, minimum graduate GPA of 3.2. Application fee: $50. Tuition and fees vary according to program and reciprocity agreements. *Financial support:* In 2011–12, 37 students received support, including 22 teaching assistantships with full tuition reimbursements available (averaging $6,202 per year); career-related internships or fieldwork also available. Financial award application deadline: 3/1. *Faculty research:* Community education, executive development for public services, applied gerontology. *Unit head:* Jayne Beilke, Director of Doctoral Program, 765-285-5348, Fax: 765-285-5489. *Application contact:* Dr. Thalia Mulvihill, Associate Provost for Research and Dean of the Graduate School. Web site: http://www.bsu.edu/teachers/departments/edstudies/.

Ball State University, Graduate School, Teachers College, Department of Educational Studies, Program in Student Affairs Administration in Higher Education, Muncie, IN 47306-1099. Offers MA. *Accreditation:* NCATE. *Students:* 36 full-time (25 women), 7 part-time (4 women); includes 15 minority (13 Black or African American, non-Hispanic/Latino; 1 Hispanic/Latino; 1 Two or more races, non-Hispanic/Latino), 1 international. Average age 22. 178 applicants, 22% accepted, 31 enrolled. In 2011, 23 master's awarded. *Entrance requirements:* For master's, GRE General Test, interview. Application fee: $50. Tuition and fees vary according to program and reciprocity agreements. *Financial support:* In 2011–12, 41 students received support, including 40 research assistantships with full tuition reimbursements available (averaging $15,978 per year). Financial award application deadline: 3/1. *Unit head:* Dr. Jayne Beilke, Director, 765-285-5486, Fax: 765-285-2464. *Application contact:* Dr. Roger Wessel, Associate Provost for Research and Dean of the Graduate School, 765-285-8290, E-mail: rwessel@bsu.edu. Web site: http://www.bsu.edu/teachers/departments/edstudies/.

Barry University, School of Education, Program in Higher Education Administration, Miami Shores, FL 33161-6695. Offers MS. Part-time and evening/weekend programs available. *Degree requirements:* For master's, comprehensive exam. *Entrance requirements:* For master's, GRE General Test or MAT, minimum GPA of 3.0. Electronic applications accepted.

Barry University, School of Education, Program in Leadership and Education, Miami Shores, FL 33161-6695. Offers educational technology (PhD); exceptional student education (PhD); higher education administration (PhD); human resource development (PhD); leadership (PhD). Part-time and evening/weekend programs available. *Degree requirements:* For doctorate, thesis/dissertation. *Entrance requirements:* For doctorate, GRE General Test, minimum GPA of 3.25. Electronic applications accepted.

Bay Path College, Program in Higher Education Administration, Longmeadow, MA 01106-2292. Offers enrollment management (MS); general administration (MS); institutional advancement (MS). Part-time programs available. Postbaccalaureate distance learning degree programs offered (no on-campus study). *Students:* 7 full-time (6 women), 39 part-time (32 women); includes 9 minority (6 Black or African American, non-Hispanic/Latino; 1 Asian, non-Hispanic/Latino; 2 Hispanic/Latino). Average age 35. 46 applicants, 74% accepted, 25 enrolled. In 2011, 10 master's awarded. *Application deadline:* Applications are processed on a rolling basis. Application fee: $45. Electronic applications accepted. Application fee is waived when completed online. *Expenses: Tuition:* Part-time $665 per credit. Tuition and fees vary according to program. *Financial support:* In 2011–12, 12 students received support. Scholarships/grants available. Financial award applicants required to submit FAFSA. *Application contact:* Lisa Adams, Director of Graduate Admissions, 413-565-1317, Fax: 413-565-1250, E-mail: ladams@baypath.edu.

Bay Path College, Program in Strategic Fundraising and Philanthropy, Longmeadow, MA 01106-2292. Offers higher education (MS); non-profit fundraising administration (MS). Part-time and evening/weekend programs available. Postbaccalaureate distance learning degree programs offered (no on-campus study). *Students:* 3 full-time (all women), 9 part-time (7 women), 1 international. Average age 30. 22 applicants, 73% accepted, 12 enrolled. In 2011, 4 master's awarded. *Application deadline:* Applications are processed on a rolling basis. Application fee: $45. Electronic applications accepted. Application fee is waived when completed online. *Expenses: Tuition:* Part-time $665 per credit. Tuition and fees vary according to program. *Financial support:* In 2011–12, 2 students received support. Scholarships/grants available. Financial award applicants required to submit FAFSA. *Application contact:* Lisa Adams, Director of Graduate Admissions, 413-565-1317, Fax: 413-565-1250, E-mail: ladams@baypath.edu.

Benedictine University, Graduate Programs, Program in Higher Education and Organizational Change, Lisle, IL 60532-0900. Offers Ed D. *Faculty:* 2 full-time (1 woman). *Students:* 35 full-time (24 women), 65 part-time (38 women); includes 34 minority (24 Black or African American, non-Hispanic/Latino; 1 American Indian or Alaska Native, non-Hispanic/Latino; 2 Asian, non-Hispanic/Latino; 7 Hispanic/Latino), 2 international. 34 applicants, 71% accepted, 22 enrolled. In 2011, 7 degrees awarded. Application fee: $40. *Unit head:* Dr. Sunil Chand, Director, 630-829-1930, E-mail: schand@ben.edu. *Application contact:* Kari Gibbons, Associate Vice President, Enrollment Center, 630-829-6200, Fax: 630-829-6584, E-mail: kgibbons@ben.edu.

Bernard M. Baruch College of the City University of New York, School of Public Affairs, Program in Higher Education Administration, New York, NY 10010-5585. Offers MS Ed. Part-time and evening/weekend programs available. *Faculty:* 45 full-time (17 women), 34 part-time/adjunct (12 women). *Students:* 6 full-time (5 women), 115 part-time (83 women); includes 66 minority (31 Black or African American, non-Hispanic/Latino; 5 Asian, non-Hispanic/Latino; 27 Hispanic/Latino; 3 Two or more races, non-Hispanic/Latino). Average age 34. *Entrance requirements:* For master's, GRE General Test. Additional exam requirements/recommendations for international students: Required—TOEFL. *Application deadline:* For fall admission, 4/1 priority date for domestic students, 4/1 for international students; for spring admission, 11/15 priority date for domestic students, 11/15 for international students. Applications are processed on a rolling basis. Application fee: $125. Electronic applications accepted. *Expenses:* Contact institution. *Financial support:* In 2011–12, fellowships (averaging $3,000 per year) were awarded; research assistantships, teaching assistantships, career-related internships or fieldwork, Federal Work-Study, scholarships/grants, tuition waivers (partial), and unspecified assistantships also available. Support available to part-time students. Financial award application deadline: 5/15; financial award applicants required to submit FAFSA. *Unit head:* David S. Birdsell, Dean, 646-660-6700, Fax: 646-660-6721, E-mail: david.birdsell@baruch.cuny.edu. *Application contact:* Michael J. Lovaglio, Director of Student Affairs and Graduate Admissions, 646-660-6760, Fax: 646-660-6751, E-mail: michael.lovaglio@baruch.cuny.edu. Web site: http://www.baruch.cuny.edu/spa/academics/graduatedegrees/highereducationadmin.php.

Bethel University, Graduate School, St. Paul, MN 55112-6999. Offers autism spectrum disorders (Certificate); business administration (MBA); communication (MA); counseling psychology (MA); education (M Ed); educational leadership (Ed D); gerontology (MA, Certificate); international baccalaureate education (Certificate); K-12 education (MA); literacy education (MA); nursing (MA); nursing education (Certificate); nursing leadership (Certificate); organizational leadership (MA); postsecondary teaching (Certificate); special education (MA); teaching (MA). Part-time and evening/weekend programs available. Postbaccalaureate distance learning degree programs offered (minimal on-campus study). *Faculty:* 8 full-time (3 women), 98 part-time/adjunct (46 women). *Students:* 651 full-time (419 women), 312 part-time (212 women); includes 79 minority (35 Black or African American, non-Hispanic/Latino; 2 American Indian or Alaska Native, non-Hispanic/Latino; 19 Asian, non-Hispanic/Latino; 17 Hispanic/Latino; 6 Two or more races, non-Hispanic/Latino), 6 international. Average age 36. In 2011, 245 master's, 4 doctorates, 32 other advanced degrees awarded. *Degree requirements:* For master's, comprehensive exam (for some programs), thesis (for some programs); for doctorate, comprehensive exam, thesis/dissertation. *Entrance requirements:* Additional exam requirements/recommendations for international students: Required—TOEFL (minimum score 550 paper-based; 213 computer-based; 80 iBT). *Application deadline:* Applications are processed on a rolling basis. Electronic applications accepted. Tuition and fees vary according to course load, degree level and program. *Financial support:* Applicants required to submit FAFSA. *Unit head:* Dick Crombie, Vice-President/Dean, 651-635-8000, Fax: 651-635-8004, E-mail: gs@bethel.edu. *Application contact:* Paul Ives, Director of Admissions, 651-635-8000, Fax: 651-635-8004, E-mail: gs@bethel.edu. Web site: http://gs.bethel.edu/.

Boston College, Lynch Graduate School of Education, Program in Higher Education, Chestnut Hill, MA 02467-3800. Offers MA, PhD, JD/MA, MBA/MA. *Accreditation:* Teacher Education Accreditation Council. Part-time and evening/weekend programs available. *Students:* 73 full-time (51 women), 57 part-time (39 women); includes 27 minority (3 Black or African American, non-Hispanic/Latino; 9 Asian, non-Hispanic/Latino; 12 Hispanic/Latino; 3 Two or more races, non-Hispanic/Latino), 6 international. 248 applicants, 39% accepted, 57 enrolled. In 2011, 45 master's, 11 doctorates awarded. Terminal master's awarded for partial completion of doctoral program. *Degree requirements:* For master's, comprehensive exam; for doctorate, comprehensive exam, thesis/dissertation. *Entrance requirements:* For master's, GRE General Test or MAT; for doctorate, GRE General Test. Additional exam requirements/recommendations for international students: Required—TOEFL (minimum score 550 paper-based; 213 computer-based; 79 iBT). Application fee: $65. Electronic applications accepted. *Financial support:* Fellowships with full and partial tuition reimbursements, research assistantships with full and partial tuition reimbursements, teaching assistantships with full and partial tuition reimbursements, career-related internships or fieldwork, Federal Work-Study, scholarships/grants, traineeships, health care benefits, tuition waivers (full and partial), and unspecified assistantships available. Support available to part-time students. Financial award applicants required to submit FAFSA. *Faculty research:* Race, culture and gender in higher education; international education; college student development; Catholic higher education; organizational analysis. *Unit head:* Dr. Ana M. Martinez-Aleman, Chairperson, 617-552-4214, Fax: 617-552-0398. *Application contact:* Adam Poluzzi, Director, Graduate Admission and Financial Aid, 617-552-4214, Fax: 617-552-0398, E-mail: poluzzi@bc.edu.

Higher Education

Bowling Green State University, Graduate College, College of Education and Human Development, School of Leadership and Policy Studies, Program in Higher Education Administration, Bowling Green, OH 43403. Offers PhD. *Accreditation:* NCATE. Part-time programs available. *Degree requirements:* For doctorate, comprehensive exam, thesis/dissertation. *Entrance requirements:* For doctorate, GRE General Test. Additional exam requirements/recommendations for international students: Required—TOEFL. Electronic applications accepted. *Faculty research:* Adult learners, legal issues, intellectual development.

California Lutheran University, Graduate Studies, Graduate School of Education, Thousand Oaks, CA 91360-2787. Offers counseling and guidance (MS), including college student personnel, counseling and guidance; educational leadership (MA, Ed D), including educational leadership (K-12) (Ed D), higher education leadership (Ed D); special education (MS); teacher leadership (M Ed); teaching (M Ed). *Accreditation:* NCATE. Part-time and evening/weekend programs available. *Entrance requirements:* For master's, GRE General Test, interview, minimum GPA of 3.0.

California State University, Long Beach, Graduate Studies, College of Education, Department of Advanced Studies in Education and Counseling, Master of Science in Counseling Program, Long Beach, CA 90840. Offers marriage and family therapy (MS); school counseling (MS); student development in higher education (MS). *Accreditation:* NCATE. *Students:* 150 full-time (114 women), 65 part-time (48 women); includes 153 minority (23 Black or African American, non-Hispanic/Latino; 3 American Indian or Alaska Native, non-Hispanic/Latino; 32 Asian, non-Hispanic/Latino; 86 Hispanic/Latino; 1 Native Hawaiian or other Pacific Islander, non-Hispanic/Latino; 8 Two or more races, non-Hispanic/Latino), 3 international. Average age 28. 488 applicants, 18% accepted, 68 enrolled. In 2011, 59 master's awarded. *Degree requirements:* For master's, comprehensive exam or thesis. *Application deadline:* For fall admission, 3/1 for domestic students. Applications are processed on a rolling basis. Application fee: $55. Electronic applications accepted. *Financial support:* Federal Work-Study, institutionally sponsored loans, and scholarships/grants available. Financial award application deadline: 3/2. *Unit head:* Dr. Jennifer Coots, Chair, 562-985-4517, Fax: 562-985-4534, E-mail: jcoots@csulb.edu. *Application contact:* Dr. Bita Ghafoori, Assistant Chair, 562-985-7864, Fax: 562-985-4534, E-mail: bghafoor@csulb.edu.

Capella University, School of Education, Minneapolis, MN 55402. Offers college teaching (Certificate); curriculum and instruction (MS, PhD); education (MS); enrollment management (MS); instructional design for online learning (MS, PhD); k-12 studies in education (MS, PhD); leadership for higher education (MS, PhD); leadership in education administration (Certificate); leadership in educational administration (MS, PhD); postsecondary and adult education (MS, PhD); professional studies in education (MS, PhD); reading and literacy (MS); training and performance improvement (MS, PhD). Part-time and evening/weekend programs available. Postbaccalaureate distance learning degree programs offered (minimal on-campus study). Terminal master's awarded for partial completion of doctoral program. *Degree requirements:* For master's, thesis optional, integrative project; for doctorate, comprehensive exam, thesis/dissertation. *Entrance requirements:* Additional exam requirements/recommendations for international students: Required—TOEFL (minimum score 550 paper-based; 213 computer-based), TWE (minimum score 4). Electronic applications accepted. *Faculty research:* Higher education administration, distance learning, adult education, training and curriculum design.

Central Michigan University, Central Michigan University Global Campus, Program in Education, Mount Pleasant, MI 48859. Offers adult education (MA); college teaching (Graduate Certificate); community college (MA); educational leadership (MA), including charter school leadership; educational technology (MA); guidance and development (MA); instruction (MA); reading and literacy K-12 (MA); school principalship (MA); teacher leadership (MA). *Accreditation:* Teacher Education Accreditation Council. Part-time and evening/weekend programs available. *Entrance requirements:* For master's, minimum GPA of 2.7 in major. Additional exam requirements/recommendations for international students: Required—TOEFL. *Application deadline:* Applications are processed on a rolling basis. Application fee: $50. Electronic applications accepted. *Financial support:* Scholarships/grants available. Support available to part-time students. *Unit head:* Dr. Peter Ross, Director, 989-774-4456, E-mail: ross1pg@cmich.edu. *Application contact:* 877-268-4636, E-mail: cmuglobal@cmich.edu.

Central Michigan University, College of Graduate Studies, College of Education and Human Services, Department of Educational Leadership, Mount Pleasant, MI 48859. Offers educational leadership (MA, Ed D), including charter school leadership (MA), educational technology (Ed D, Ed S), general educational leadership (MA), higher education administration (MA, Ed S), higher education leadership (Ed D), K-12 curriculum (Ed D), K-12 leadership (Ed D), student affairs administration (MA); general educational administration (Ed S), including administrative leadership K-12, educational technology (Ed D, Ed S), higher education administration (MA, Ed S), instructional leadership K-12; school principalship (MA); teacher leadership (MA). Part-time and evening/weekend programs available. *Degree requirements:* For master's and other advanced degree, thesis or alternative; for doctorate, thesis/dissertation. *Entrance requirements:* For doctorate, GRE or MAT, master's degree, minimum GPA of 3.5, 3 years of professional education experience. Electronic applications accepted. *Faculty research:* Elementary administration, secondary administration, student achievement, in-service training, internships in administration.

Chicago State University, School of Graduate and Professional Studies, College of Education, Department of Educational Leadership, Curriculum and Foundations, Program in Educational Leadership, Chicago, IL 60628. Offers educational leadership (Ed D); general administration (MA); higher education administration (MA). *Accreditation:* NCATE. *Degree requirements:* For master's, comprehensive exam, thesis optional. *Entrance requirements:* For master's, minimum GPA of 2.75.

City University of Seattle, Graduate Division, Albright School of Education, Bellevue, WA 98005. Offers administrator certification (Certificate); curriculum and instruction (M Ed); educational leadership (Ed D); elementary education (MIT); guidance and counseling (M Ed); higher education leadership (Ed D); leadership (M Ed); leadership and school counseling (M Ed); organizational leadership (Ed D); reading and literacy (M Ed); special education (MIT); superintendent certification (Certificate). Part-time and evening/weekend programs available. Postbaccalaureate distance learning degree programs offered (no on-campus study). *Faculty:* 23 full-time (15 women), 123 part-time/adjunct (82 women). *Students:* 353 full-time (263 women), 75 part-time (50 women); includes 40 minority (12 Black or African American, non-Hispanic/Latino; 5 American Indian or Alaska Native, non-Hispanic/Latino; 7 Asian, non-Hispanic/Latino; 8 Hispanic/Latino; 5 Native Hawaiian or other Pacific Islander, non-Hispanic/Latino; 3 Two or more races, non-Hispanic/Latino). Average age 36. 129 applicants, 98% accepted, 126 enrolled. In 2011, 351 master's, 30 Certificates awarded. *Degree requirements:* For master's, comprehensive exam (for some programs), thesis (for some programs); for doctorate, comprehensive exam, thesis/dissertation. *Entrance requirements:* Additional exam requirements/recommendations for international students: Required—TOEFL (minimum score 567 paper-based; 227 computer-based; 87 iBT); Recommended—IELTS. *Application deadline:* For fall admission, 9/1 for international students; for winter admission, 12/1 for international students; for spring admission, 3/1 for international students. Applications are processed on a rolling basis. Application fee: $50. Electronic applications accepted. *Expenses:* Contact institution. *Financial support:* In 2011–12, 40 students received support. Federal Work-Study and scholarships/grants available. Support available to part-time students. Financial award applicants required to submit FAFSA. *Unit head:* Craig Schieber, Dean, 425-637-101 Ext. 5460, Fax: 425-709-5363, E-mail: schieber@cityu.edu. *Application contact:* Alysa Borelli, 888-422-4898, Fax: 425-709-5363, E-mail: info@cityu.edu. Web site: http://www.cityu.edu/programs/soe/index.aspx.

Claremont Graduate University, Graduate Programs, School of Educational Studies, Claremont, CA 91711-6160. Offers Africana education (Certificate); education and policy (MA, PhD); higher education/student affairs (MA, PhD); human development (MA, PhD); public school administration (MA, PhD); quantitative evaluation (MA, PhD); special education (MA, PhD); teacher education (MA); teaching and learning (MA, PhD); urban leadership (PhD); MBA/PhD. PhD program offered jointly with San Diego State University. Part-time programs available. *Faculty:* 18 full-time (10 women), 2 part-time/adjunct (1 woman). *Students:* 307 full-time (220 women), 134 part-time (96 women); includes 228 minority (59 Black or African American, non-Hispanic/Latino; 3 American Indian or Alaska Native, non-Hispanic/Latino; 37 Asian, non-Hispanic/Latino; 110 Hispanic/Latino; 2 Native Hawaiian or other Pacific Islander, non-Hispanic/Latino; 17 Two or more races, non-Hispanic/Latino), 13 international. Average age 38. In 2011, 93 master's, 23 doctorates, 10 other advanced degrees awarded. Terminal master's awarded for partial completion of doctoral program. *Entrance requirements:* For master's and doctorate, GRE General Test. Additional exam requirements/recommendations for international students: Required—TOEFL (minimum score 550 paper-based; 213 computer-based; 80 iBT). *Application deadline:* For fall admission, 2/1 priority date for domestic students. Applications are processed on a rolling basis. Application fee: $60. Electronic applications accepted. *Expenses: Tuition:* Full-time $36,374; part-time $1581 per unit. *Required fees:* $165 per semester. *Financial support:* Fellowships, research assistantships, Federal Work-Study, institutionally sponsored loans, and scholarships/grants available. Support available to part-time students. Financial award application deadline: 2/15; financial award applicants required to submit FAFSA. *Faculty research:* Education administration, K-12 and higher education, multicultural education, education policy, diversity in higher education, faculty issues. *Unit head:* Margaret Grogan, Dean, 909-621-8075, Fax: 909-621-8734, E-mail: margaret.grogan@cgu.edu. *Application contact:* Julia Evans, Director of Central Recruitment, 909-607-3689, Fax: 909-607-7285, E-mail: admiss@cgu.edu. Web site: http://www.cgu.edu/pages/267.asp.

Clemson University, Graduate School, College of Health, Education, and Human Development, Eugene T. Moore School of Education, Program in Educational Leadership, Clemson, SC 29634. Offers higher education (PhD); K-12 (PhD). *Accreditation:* NCATE. Part-time and evening/weekend programs available. *Students:* 28 full-time (14 women), 66 part-time (38 women); includes 23 minority (19 Black or African American, non-Hispanic/Latino; 2 Hispanic/Latino; 2 Two or more races, non-Hispanic/Latino), 3 international. Average age 38. 37 applicants, 57% accepted, 13 enrolled. In 2011, 10 doctorates awarded. *Degree requirements:* For doctorate, comprehensive exam, thesis/dissertation, preliminary exam. *Entrance requirements:* For doctorate, GRE General Test, master's degree in related field. Additional exam requirements/recommendations for international students: Required—TOEFL; Recommended—IELTS. *Application deadline:* For fall admission, 3/1 for domestic and international students; for spring admission, 10/1 for domestic and international students. Application fee: $70 ($80 for international students). Electronic applications accepted. *Financial support:* In 2011–12, 19 students received support, including 1 fellowship with full and partial tuition reimbursement available (averaging $8,000 per year), 11 research assistantships with partial tuition reimbursements available (averaging $16,075 per year), 3 teaching assistantships with partial tuition reimbursements available (averaging $15,333 per year); institutionally sponsored loans, health care benefits, and unspecified assistantships also available. Financial award application deadline: 6/1; financial award applicants required to submit FAFSA. *Faculty research:* Higher education leadership, P-12 educational leadership. *Unit head:* Dr. Michael J. Padilla, Director/Associate Dean, 864-656-4444, Fax: 864-656-0311, E-mail: padilla@clemson.edu. *Application contact:* Dr. David Fleming, Graduate Coordinator, 864-656-1881, Fax: 864-656-0311, E-mail: dflemin@clemson.edu.

College of Saint Elizabeth, Department of Psychology, Morristown, NJ 07960-6989. Offers counseling psychology (MA); forensic psychology (MA); mental health counseling (Certificate); student affairs in higher education (Certificate). Part-time and evening/weekend programs available. *Faculty:* 5 full-time (3 women), 5 part-time/adjunct (4 women). *Students:* 28 full-time (23 women), 72 part-time (67 women); includes 28 minority (18 Black or African American, non-Hispanic/Latino; 2 Asian, non-Hispanic/Latino; 8 Hispanic/Latino), 2 international. Average age 29. 85 applicants, 47% accepted, 29 enrolled. In 2011, 26 master's, 1 other advanced degree awarded. *Degree requirements:* For master's, thesis or alternative, portfolio. *Entrance requirements:* For master's, minimum GPA of 3.0, BA in psychology (preferred), 12 credits of course work in psychology. Additional exam requirements/recommendations for international students: Required—TOEFL (minimum score 550 paper-based). *Application deadline:* For fall admission, 4/1 priority date for domestic students; for spring admission, 11/15 for domestic students. Applications are processed on a rolling basis. Application fee: $35. Electronic applications accepted. *Expenses: Tuition:* Part-time $899 per credit. *Required fees:* $73 per credit. *Financial support:* Career-related internships or fieldwork, tuition waivers (partial), and unspecified assistantships available. Support available to part-time students. Financial award application deadline: 3/15; financial award applicants required to submit FAFSA. *Faculty research:* Family systems, dissociative identity disorder, multicultural counseling, outcomes assessment. *Unit head:* Dr. Valerie Scott, Director of the Graduate Program in Counseling Psychology, 973-290-4102, Fax: 973-290-4676, E-mail: vscott@cse.edu. *Application contact:* Donna Tatarka, Dean of Admission, 973-290-4705, Fax: 973-290-4710, E-mail: dtatarka@cse.edu. Web site: http://www.cse.edu/academics/academic-areas/human-social-dev/psychology/?tabID-tabGraduate&divID-progGraduate.

Columbia International University, Columbia Graduate School, Columbia, SC 29230-3122. Offers Bible teaching (MABT); Christian higher education leadership (Ed D); Christian school educational leadership (Ed D); counseling (MACN); curriculum and instruction (M Ed), including Christian school guidance, English as a second language, learning disabilities, school technology; early childhood and elementary education (MAT); educational administration (M Ed); teaching English as a foreign language (Certificate); teaching English as a foreign language and intercultural studies (MATF). Part-time and evening/weekend programs available. *Degree requirements:* For master's, internships, professional project. *Entrance requirements:* For master's, Minnesota Multiphasic Personality Inventory, MAT, minimum GPA of 2.7. Additional exam requirements/recommendations for international students: Required—TOEFL. Electronic applications accepted.

Columbus State University, Graduate Studies, College of Education and Health Professions, Department of Counseling, Foundations, and Leadership, Columbus, GA 31907-5645. Offers community counseling (MS); curriculum and leadership (Ed D); educational leadership (M Ed, Ed S); higher education (M Ed); school counseling (M Ed, Ed S). *Accreditation:* ACA; NCATE. Part-time and evening/weekend programs available.

Postbaccalaureate distance learning degree programs offered (minimal on-campus study). *Degree requirements:* For master's, thesis, exit exam; for Ed S, thesis or alternative. *Entrance requirements:* For master's, GRE General Test, minimum GPA of 2.75; for doctorate, minimum graduate GPA of 3.5, four years of professional service; for Ed S, GRE General Test. Additional exam requirements/recommendations for international students: Required—TOEFL (minimum score 550 paper-based; 213 computer-based; 79 iBT). Electronic applications accepted.

Dallas Baptist University, Gary Cook School of Leadership, Program in Education in Higher Education, Dallas, TX 75211-9299. Offers M Ed, MA/MA. Part-time and evening/weekend programs available. *Entrance requirements:* For master's, GRE General Test, minimum GPA of 3.0. Additional exam requirements/recommendations for international students: Required—TOEFL, IELTS. *Application deadline:* Applications are processed on a rolling basis. Application fee: $25. Electronic applications accepted. *Expenses: Tuition:* Full-time $12,060; part-time $670 per credit hour. *Required fees:* $100; $50 per semester. *Financial support:* Federal Work-Study, institutionally sponsored loans, scholarships/grants, and tuition waivers (full and partial) available. Support available to part-time students. Financial award applicants required to submit FAFSA. *Faculty research:* Enrollment management, portfolio assessment, servant leadership. *Unit head:* Mark Hale, Director, 214-333-5246, Fax: 214-333-5115, E-mail: graduate@dbu.edu. *Application contact:* Kit P. Montgomery, Director of Graduate Programs, 214-333-5242, Fax: 214-333-5579, E-mail: graduate@dbu.edu. Web site: http://www3.dbu.edu/leadership/hied/.

Dallas Baptist University, Professional Development Program, Dallas, TX 75211-9299. Offers accounting (MA); church leadership (MA); counseling (MA); criminal justice (MA); English as a second language (MA); finance (MA); higher education (MA); leadership studies (MA); management (MA); management information systems (MA); marketing (MA); missions (MA); professional life coaching (MA). Part-time and evening/weekend programs available. *Entrance requirements:* For master's, minimum GPA of 3.0. Additional exam requirements/recommendations for international students: Required—TOEFL, IELTS. Application fee: $25. *Expenses: Tuition:* Full-time $12,060; part-time $670 per credit hour. *Required fees:* $100; $50 per semester. *Financial support:* Federal Work-Study, institutionally sponsored loans, scholarships/grants, and tuition waivers (full and partial) available. Support available to part-time students. Financial award applicants required to submit FAFSA. *Unit head:* Angela Fogle, Acting Director, 214-333-6830, Fax: 214-333-5558, E-mail: graduate@dbu.edu. *Application contact:* Kit P. Montgomery, Director of Graduate Programs, 214-333-5242, Fax: 214-333-5579, E-mail: graduate@dbu.edu. Web site: http://www3.dbu.edu/graduate/mapd.asp.

Delta State University, Graduate Programs, College of Education, Thad Cochran Center for Rural School Leadership and Research, Program in Professional Studies, Cleveland, MS 38733-0001. Offers counselor education (Ed D); educational leadership (Ed D); elementary education (Ed D); higher education (Ed D). Part-time and evening/weekend programs available. *Degree requirements:* For doctorate, thesis/dissertation. *Entrance requirements:* For doctorate, GRE General Test. *Expenses:* Tuition, state resident: full-time $4702; part-time $294 per credit hour. Tuition, nonresident: full-time $12,516; part-time $760 per credit hour. *Required fees:* $586.

Drexel University, Goodwin College of Professional Studies, School of Education, Program in Higher Education, Philadelphia, PA 19104-2875. Offers MS. Postbaccalaureate distance learning degree programs offered (no on-campus study). *Degree requirements:* For master's, co-op experience. *Entrance requirements:* For master's, bachelor's degree from an accredited institution, minimum GPA of 3.0 or GRE. Additional exam requirements/recommendations for international students: Required—TOEFL (minimum score 550 paper-based). *Faculty research:* Governance and administration, financial management, enrollment management, institutional research, strategic planning, advancement, academic development, technology, and instruction.

East Carolina University, Graduate School, College of Education, Department of Higher, Adult, and Counselor Education, Greenville, NC 27858-4353. Offers adult education (MA Ed); counselor education (MS); higher education administration (Ed D). *Accreditation:* NCATE. Part-time and evening/weekend programs available. *Degree requirements:* For master's, comprehensive exam, thesis optional. *Entrance requirements:* For master's, GRE General Test or MAT, interview, minimum GPA of 2.5, bachelor's degree in related field, teaching license (MA Ed). Additional exam requirements/recommendations for international students: Required—TOEFL. *Application deadline:* For fall admission, 5/15 priority date for domestic students. Applications are processed on a rolling basis. Application fee: $50. *Expenses:* Tuition, state resident: full-time $3557; part-time $444.63 per semester hour. Tuition, nonresident: full-time $14,351; part-time $1793.88 per semester hour. *Required fees:* $2016; $252 per semester hour. Part-time tuition and fees vary according to course load, campus/location and program. *Financial support:* Research assistantships with partial tuition reimbursements, teaching assistantships with partial tuition reimbursements, and Federal Work-Study available. Support available to part-time students. Financial award application deadline: 6/1. *Unit head:* Dr. Vivian W. Mott, Chair, 252-328-6177, Fax: 252-328-4368, E-mail: mottv@ecu.edu. *Application contact:* Dean of Graduate School, 252-328-6012, Fax: 252-328-6071, E-mail: gradschool@ecu.edu. Web site: http://www.ecu.edu/cs-educ/hace/index.cfm.

Eastern Kentucky University, The Graduate School, College of Education, Department of Curriculum and Instruction, Program in Secondary and Higher Education, Richmond, KY 40475-3102. Offers secondary education (MA Ed), including agricultural education, art education, biological sciences education, business education, English education, geography education, history education, home economics education, industrial education, mathematical sciences education, physical education, school health education. *Accreditation:* NCATE. Part-time programs available. *Entrance requirements:* For master's, GRE General Test, minimum GPA of 2.5.

East Tennessee State University, School of Graduate Studies, College of Education, Department of Human Development and Learning, Johnson City, TN 37614. Offers counseling (MA), including community agency counseling, elementary and secondary (school counseling), higher education counseling, marriage and family therapy; early childhood education (MA, PhD), including initial licensure in PreK-3 (MA), master teacher (MA), researcher (MA); special education (MA), including advanced practitioner, early childhood special education, special education. *Accreditation:* ACA; NCATE. Part-time programs available. *Faculty:* 31 full-time (22 women), 5 part-time/adjunct (all women). *Students:* 112 full-time (90 women), 41 part-time (36 women); includes 8 minority (5 Black or African American, non-Hispanic/Latino; 3 Two or more races, non-Hispanic/Latino), 4 international. Average age 32. 145 applicants, 34% accepted, 46 enrolled. In 2011, 34 master's awarded. Terminal master's awarded for partial completion of doctoral program. *Degree requirements:* For master's, comprehensive exam, thesis optional, internship, student teaching, culminating experience; for doctorate, comprehensive exam, thesis/dissertation, research apprenticeship. *Entrance requirements:* For master's, GRE General Test, minimum GPA of 3.0; for doctorate, GRE General Test, professional resume, master's degree in early childhood or related field, interview. Additional exam requirements/recommendations for international students: Required—TOEFL (minimum score 550 paper-based; 213 computer-based; 79 iBT). *Application deadline:* For fall admission, 2/1 for domestic and international students. Application fee: $35 ($45 for international students). Electronic applications accepted. *Expenses:* Tuition, state resident: full-time $7312; part-time $350 per credit hour. Tuition, nonresident: full-time $18,490; part-time $621 per credit hour. *Required fees:* $63 per credit hour. Tuition and fees vary according to course load and program. *Financial support:* In 2011–12, 86 students received support, including 6 fellowships with full tuition reimbursements available (averaging $18,000 per year), 28 research assistantships with full tuition reimbursements available (averaging $6,000 per year), 10 teaching assistantships with full tuition reimbursements available (averaging $6,000 per year); career-related internships or fieldwork, institutionally sponsored loans, scholarships/grants, traineeships, and unspecified assistantships also available. Financial award application deadline: 7/1; financial award applicants required to submit FAFSA. *Faculty research:* Drug and alcohol abuse, marriage and family counseling, severe mental retardation, parenting of children with disabilities. *Total annual research expenditures:* $2,600. *Unit head:* Dr. Pamela Evanshen, Chair, 423-439-7694, Fax: 423-439-7790, E-mail: evanshep@etsu.edu. *Application contact:* Fiona Goodyear, Graduate Specialist, 423-439-6148, Fax: 423-439-5624, E-mail: goodyear@etsu.edu.

Fielding Graduate University, Graduate Programs, School of Educational Leadership and Change, Santa Barbara, CA 93105-3538. Offers collaborative educational leadership (MA); educational leadership and change (Ed D), including community college leadership and change, grounded theory/grounded action, leadership of higher education systems, media studies; teaching in the virtual classroom (Graduate Certificate). Postbaccalaureate distance learning degree programs offered (minimal on-campus study). *Faculty:* 15 full-time (8 women), 5 part-time/adjunct (3 women). *Students:* 201 full-time (141 women), 9 part-time (8 women); includes 108 minority (64 Black or African American, non-Hispanic/Latino; 6 American Indian or Alaska Native, non-Hispanic/Latino; 7 Asian, non-Hispanic/Latino; 21 Hispanic/Latino; 1 Native Hawaiian or other Pacific Islander, non-Hispanic/Latino; 9 Two or more races, non-Hispanic/Latino), 2 international. Average age 47. 27 applicants, 93% accepted, 19 enrolled. In 2011, 44 master's, 45 doctorates, 7 other advanced degrees awarded. *Degree requirements:* For master's, capstone research project; for doctorate, comprehensive exam, thesis/dissertation. *Entrance requirements:* For master's, minimum GPA of 2.5; for doctorate, resume, 2 letters of recommendation, writing sample. *Application deadline:* For fall admission, 6/10 for domestic and international students; for spring admission, 11/19 for domestic and international students. Application fee: $75. Electronic applications accepted. *Expenses:* Contact institution. *Financial support:* In 2011–12, 21 students received support. Scholarships/grants, health care benefits, and tuition waivers (partial) available. Support available to part-time students. Financial award applicants required to submit FAFSA. *Unit head:* Dr. Mario R. Borunda, Dean, 805-898-2940, E-mail: mborunda@fielding.edu. *Application contact:* Admission Counselor, 800-340-1099 Ext. 4098, Fax: 805-687-9793, E-mail: elcadmissions@fielding.edu. Web site: http://www.fielding.edu/programs/elc/default.aspx.

Fitchburg State University, Division of Graduate and Continuing Education, Program in Educational Leadership and Management, Fitchburg, MA 01420-2697. Offers educational technology (Certificate); higher education administration (CAGS); non-licensure (M Ed, CAGS); school principal (M Ed, CAGS); supervisor/director (M Ed, CAGS); technology leader (M Ed, CAGS). *Accreditation:* NCATE. Part-time and evening/weekend programs available. *Students:* 26 full-time (14 women), 49 part-time (22 women); includes 2 minority (1 Black or African American, non-Hispanic/Latino; 1 Hispanic/Latino). Average age 41. 10 applicants, 100% accepted, 9 enrolled. In 2011, 11 master's, 30 CAGSs awarded. *Entrance requirements:* Additional exam requirements/recommendations for international students: Required—TOEFL (minimum score 550 paper-based; 213 computer-based; 79 iBT). *Application deadline:* For fall admission, 7/15 for international students; for spring admission, 12/1 for international students. Applications are processed on a rolling basis. Application fee: $25 ($50 for international students). Electronic applications accepted. *Expenses:* Tuition, state resident: full-time $2700; part-time $150 per credit. Tuition, nonresident: full-time $2700; part-time $150 per credit. *Required fees:* $2286; $127 per credit. *Financial support:* In 2011–12, research assistantships with partial tuition reimbursements (averaging $5,500 per year) were awarded; Federal Work-Study, scholarships/grants, and unspecified assistantships also available. Support available to part-time students. Financial award application deadline: 3/1; financial award applicants required to submit FAFSA. *Unit head:* Dr. Randy Howe, Chair, 978-665-3544, Fax: 978-665-3658, E-mail: gce@fitchburgstate.edu. *Application contact:* Kay Reynolds, Director of Admissions, 978-665-3144, Fax: 978-665-4540, E-mail: admissions@fitchburgstate.edu. Web site: http://www.fitchburgstate.edu.

Florida Atlantic University, College of Education, Department of Educational Leadership and Research Methodology, Boca Raton, FL 33431-0991. Offers adult and community education (M Ed, PhD, Ed S); educational leadership (M Ed, PhD, Ed S); higher education (M Ed, PhD); K-12 school leadership (M Ed, PhD, Ed S). *Accreditation:* NCATE. Part-time and evening/weekend programs available. Postbaccalaureate distance learning degree programs offered (minimal on-campus study). *Faculty:* 20 full-time (11 women), 17 part-time/adjunct (7 women). *Students:* 100 full-time (75 women), 245 part-time (173 women); includes 126 minority (59 Black or African American, non-Hispanic/Latino; 15 Asian, non-Hispanic/Latino; 47 Hispanic/Latino; 5 Two or more races, non-Hispanic/Latino), 4 international. Average age 36. 253 applicants, 47% accepted, 66 enrolled. In 2011, 122 master's, 11 doctorates awarded. *Degree requirements:* For doctorate, comprehensive exam, thesis/dissertation, departmental qualifying exam; for Ed S, departmental qualifying exam. *Entrance requirements:* For master's, GRE General Test, minimum GPA of 3.0 during previous 2 years; for doctorate, GRE General Test, minimum GPA of 3.5; for Ed S, GRE General Test. *Application deadline:* For fall admission, 7/1 for domestic students, 2/15 for international students; for spring admission, 9/15 for domestic students, 7/15 for international students. Applications are processed on a rolling basis. Application fee: $30. Electronic applications accepted. *Expenses: Tuition, area resident:* Part-time $343.02 per credit hour. Tuition, state resident: full-time $8232. Tuition, nonresident: full-time $23,931; part-time $997.14 per credit hour. *Financial support:* Fellowships, research assistantships, teaching assistantships, career-related internships or fieldwork, and tuition waivers (partial) available. *Faculty research:* Self-directed learning, school reform issues, legal issues, mentoring, school leadership. *Unit head:* Dr. Robert Shockley, Chair, 561-297-3550, Fax: 561-297-3618, E-mail: shockley@fau.edu. *Application contact:* Catherine Politi, Senior Secretary, 561-297-3550, Fax: 561-297-3618, E-mail: edleadership@fau.edu. Web site: http://www.coe.fau.edu/academicdepartments/el/.

Florida International University, College of Education, Department of Educational Leadership and Policy Studies, Miami, FL 33199. Offers adult education (MS); adult education in human resource development (Ed D); clinical mental health counseling (MS); conflict resolution and consensus building (Certificate); counselor education (MS); educational administration and supervision (Ed D); educational leadership (MS, Certificate, Ed S); higher education (Ed D); higher education administration (MS); human resource development (MS); instruction in urban settings (MS); international/intercultural education (MS); learning technologies (MS); multicultural-bilingual (MS); multicultural-TESOL (MS); recreation and sport management (MS); recreation therapy (MS); rehabilitation counseling (MS); school counseling (MS); school psychology (Ed S); urban education (MS). Part-time and evening/weekend programs available. *Degree* *requirements:* For doctorate, thesis/dissertation. *Entrance requirements:* For master's, minimum GPA of 3.0; for doctorate and other advanced degree, GRE General Test. Additional exam requirements/recommendations for international students: Required—TOEFL (minimum score 550 paper-based; 213 computer-based; 80 iBT), IELTS (minimum score 6.3). Electronic applications accepted.

Florida State University, The Graduate School, College of Education, Department of Educational Leadership and Policy Studies, Program in Higher Education, Tallahassee, FL 32306. Offers MS, Ed D, PhD, Ed S. *Faculty:* 7 full-time (1 woman), 5 part-time/adjunct (2 women). *Students:* 90 full-time (64 women), 32 part-time (17 women); includes 33 minority (24 Black or African American, non-Hispanic/Latino; 2 American Indian or Alaska Native, non-Hispanic/Latino; 3 Asian, non-Hispanic/Latino; 4 Hispanic/Latino), 6 international. Average age 28. 147 applicants, 58% accepted, 39 enrolled. In 2011, 31 master's, 10 doctorates, 5 other advanced degrees awarded. Terminal master's awarded for partial completion of doctoral program. *Degree requirements:* For master's and Ed S, comprehensive exam, thesis optional; for doctorate, comprehensive exam, thesis/dissertation. *Entrance requirements:* For master's, GRE General Test, minimum GPA of 3.0; for doctorate and Ed S, GRE General Test, minimum graduate GPA of 3.0. Additional exam requirements/recommendations for international students: Required—TOEFL (minimum score 550 paper-based; 213 computer-based; 80 iBT). *Application deadline:* For fall admission, 7/1 for domestic and international students; for winter admission, 11/1 for domestic and international students; for spring admission, 3/1 for domestic and international students. Application fee: $30. Electronic applications accepted. *Expenses:* Tuition, state resident: full-time $9474; part-time $350.88 per credit hour. Tuition, nonresident: full-time $16,236; part-time $601.34 per credit hour. *Required fees:* $630 per semester. One-time fee: $20. Tuition and fees vary according to course load and campus/location. *Financial support:* Fellowships with full and partial tuition reimbursements, research assistantships with full and partial tuition reimbursements, teaching assistantships with full and partial tuition reimbursements, career-related internships or fieldwork, scholarships/grants, health care benefits, and unspecified assistantships available. Financial award applicants required to submit FAFSA. *Faculty research:* Higher education laws, public policy, organizational theory. *Unit head:* Dr. Shouping Hu, Associate Professor/Program Coordinator, 850-644-6777, Fax: 850-644-1258, E-mail: shu@fsu.edu. *Application contact:* Jimmy Pastrano, Program Assistant, 850-644-6777, Fax: 850-644-1258, E-mail: jpastrano@fsu.edu. Web site: http://www.coe.fsu/HE.

Geneva College, Master of Arts in Higher Education Program, Beaver Falls, PA 15010-3599. Offers campus ministry (MA); college teaching (MA); educational leadership (MA); student affairs administration (MA). Part-time and evening/weekend programs available. Postbaccalaureate distance learning degree programs offered (minimal on-campus study). *Faculty:* 1 full-time (0 women), 4 part-time/adjunct (0 women). *Students:* 30 full-time (13 women), 34 part-time (21 women); includes 5 minority (3 Black or African American, non-Hispanic/Latino; 1 Native Hawaiian or other Pacific Islander, non-Hispanic/Latino; 1 Two or more races, non-Hispanic/Latino). Average age 25. 39 applicants, 90% accepted, 24 enrolled. In 2011, 23 master's awarded. *Degree requirements:* For master's, 36 hours (27 in core courses) including a capstone research project. *Entrance requirements:* For master's, minimum GPA of 3.0, writing sample, 3 letters of recommendation, essay on motivation for participation in the HED program. Additional exam requirements/recommendations for international students: Required—TOEFL. *Application deadline:* For fall admission, 9/1 priority date for domestic students; for winter admission, 1/2 priority date for domestic students; for spring admission, 3/11 priority date for domestic students. Applications are processed on a rolling basis. Electronic applications accepted. *Expenses: Tuition:* Part-time $625 per credit hour. Tuition and fees vary according to program. *Financial support:* In 2011–12, 45 students received support. Unspecified assistantships available. Financial award application deadline: 8/1; financial award applicants required to submit FAFSA. *Faculty research:* Student development, learning theories, church-related higher education, assessment, organizational culture. *Unit head:* Dr. David Guthrie, Program Director, 724-847-5565, Fax: 724-847-6107, E-mail: hed@geneva.edu. *Application contact:* Jerryn S. Carson, Program Coordinator, 724-847-6510, Fax: 724-847-6696, E-mail: hed@geneva.edu. Web site: http://www.geneva.edu/.

George Fox University, School of Education, Educational Foundations and Leadership Program, Newberg, OR 97132-2697. Offers continuing administrator license (Certificate); curriculum and instruction (M Ed); educational leadership (M Ed, Ed D); ESOL (Certificate); higher education (M Ed); initial administrator license (Certificate); instructional leadership (Ed S); library media (M Ed, Certificate); literacy (M Ed); reading (M Ed); secondary education (M Ed). *Accreditation:* NCATE. Part-time and evening/weekend programs available. Postbaccalaureate distance learning degree programs offered (minimal on-campus study). *Faculty:* 10 full-time (3 women), 6 part-time/adjunct (3 women). *Students:* 2 full-time (both women), 111 part-time (83 women); includes 16 minority (2 American Indian or Alaska Native, non-Hispanic/Latino; 6 Asian, non-Hispanic/Latino; 7 Hispanic/Latino; 1 Native Hawaiian or other Pacific Islander, non-Hispanic/Latino), 3 international. Average age 39. 44 applicants, 98% accepted, 43 enrolled. In 2011, 34 master's, 7 doctorates, 76 Certificates awarded. *Degree requirements:* For master's, thesis (for some programs); for doctorate, comprehensive exam, thesis/dissertation, project. *Entrance requirements:* For master's, minimum undergraduate GPA of 3.0 during previous 2 years of course work, resume, 3 professional recommendations on university forms, official transcripts; for doctorate, GRE, master's degree with minimum GPA of 3.25, 3 years of relevant professional experience, interview, personal essay, scholarly work, 3 professional recommendations on university forms along with 3 written letters of recommendation, official transcripts. Additional exam requirements/recommendations for international students: Required—TOEFL (minimum score 577 paper-based; 233 computer-based; 90 iBT). *Application deadline:* For fall admission, 7/15 for domestic and international students; for winter admission, 11/1 for domestic and international students; for spring admission, 4/1 for domestic and international students. Applications are processed on a rolling basis. Application fee: $40. Electronic applications accepted. *Expenses:* Contact institution. *Financial support:* Career-related internships or fieldwork available. Financial award applicants required to submit FAFSA. *Unit head:* Dr. Scot Headley, Professor/Chair, 503-554-2836, E-mail: sheadley@georgefox.edu. *Application contact:* Alex Martin, Admissions Counselor, 800-631-0921, Fax: 503-554-3110, E-mail: amartin@georgefox.edu. Web site: http://www.georgefox.edu/education/index.html.

George Mason University, College of Humanities and Social Sciences, Higher Education Program, Fairfax, VA 22030. Offers college teaching (Certificate); community college education (DA Ed); higher education administration (Certificate). *Faculty:* 4 full-time (3 women), 2 part-time/adjunct (0 women). *Students:* 5 full-time (4 women), 47 part-time (28 women); includes 15 minority (9 Black or African American, non-Hispanic/Latino; 2 Asian, non-Hispanic/Latino; 4 Hispanic/Latino). Average age 47. 23 applicants, 48% accepted, 6 enrolled. In 2011, 5 doctorates, 7 Certificates awarded. *Degree requirements:* For doctorate, thesis/dissertation, internship. *Entrance requirements:* For doctorate, GRE, 3 letters of recommendation; writing sample; resume; master's degree; expanded goals statement; official transcripts; for Certificate, official transcripts; expanded goals statement; 3 letters of recommendation; resume. Additional exam requirements/recommendations for international students: Required—TOEFL (minimum score 570 paper-based; 230 computer-based; 88 iBT), IELTS, Pearson Test of English. *Application deadline:* For fall admission, 4/15 priority date for domestic students; for spring admission, 11/1 priority date for domestic students. Application fee: $65 ($80 for international students). Electronic applications accepted. *Expenses:* Tuition, state resident: full-time $8750; part-time $364.58 per credit. Tuition, nonresident: full-time $24,092; part-time $1003.83 per credit. *Required fees:* $2514; $104.75 per credit. *Financial support:* In 2011–12, 3 students received support, including 1 research assistantship with full and partial tuition reimbursement available (averaging $14,500 per year), 2 teaching assistantships with full and partial tuition reimbursements available (averaging $6,504 per year); career-related internships or fieldwork, Federal Work-Study, scholarships/grants, unspecified assistantships, and health care benefits (full-time research or teaching assistantship recipients) also available. Support available to part-time students. Financial award application deadline: 3/1; financial award applicants required to submit FAFSA. *Faculty research:* Leadership, the scholarship of teaching, learning, and assessment; ethical leadership; assessment; information technology; diversity. *Unit head:* John S. O'Connor, Director, 703-993-1455, Fax: 703-993-2307, E-mail: joconnor@gmu.edu. *Application contact:* Nina Joshi, Administrative Coordinator, 703-993-2310, Fax: 703-993-2307, E-mail: njoshi@gmu.edu. Web site: http://highered.gmu.edu/.

The George Washington University, Graduate School of Education and Human Development, Department of Educational Leadership, Program in Higher Education Administration, Washington, DC 20052. Offers MA Ed, Ed D, Ed S. *Accreditation:* NCATE. *Students:* 19 full-time (11 women), 115 part-time (69 women); includes 48 minority (31 Black or African American, non-Hispanic/Latino; 5 Asian, non-Hispanic/Latino; 8 Hispanic/Latino; 4 Two or more races, non-Hispanic/Latino). Average age 34. 163 applicants, 78% accepted. In 2011, 22 master's, 9 doctorates, 2 other advanced degrees awarded. *Degree requirements:* For master's and Ed S, comprehensive exam; for doctorate, comprehensive exam, thesis/dissertation. *Entrance requirements:* For master's, GRE General Test or MAT, minimum GPA of 2.75; for doctorate, GRE General Test or MAT, interview, minimum GPA of 3.3; for Ed S, GRE General Test or MAT, minimum GPA of 3.3. *Application deadline:* For fall admission, 1/15 priority date for domestic students; for spring admission, 10/1 for domestic students. Applications are processed on a rolling basis. Application fee: $75. *Financial support:* In 2011–12, 17 students received support. Fellowships, research assistantships, career-related internships or fieldwork, Federal Work-Study, and tuition waivers (partial) available. Financial award application deadline: 1/15; financial award applicants required to submit FAFSA. *Faculty research:* Technology in higher education administration. *Unit head:* Virginia Roach, Chair, 202-994-3094, E-mail: vroach@gwu.edu. *Application contact:* Sarah Lang, Director of Graduate Admissions, 202-994-1447, Fax: 202-994-7207, E-mail: slang@gwu.edu.

Georgia Southern University, Jack N. Averitt College of Graduate Studies, College of Education, Department of Leadership, Technology, and Human Development, Program in Higher Education, Statesboro, GA 30460. Offers M Ed. *Accreditation:* NCATE. Part-time and evening/weekend programs available. *Students:* 43 full-time (29 women), 54 part-time (44 women); includes 42 minority (34 Black or African American, non-Hispanic/Latino; 2 Asian, non-Hispanic/Latino; 6 Hispanic/Latino), 3 international. Average age 30. 39 applicants, 95% accepted, 27 enrolled. In 2011, 15 master's awarded. *Degree requirements:* For master's, portfolio, practicum, transition point assessments. *Entrance requirements:* For master's, GRE General Test or MAT, minimum GPA of 2.5. Additional exam requirements/recommendations for international students: Required—TOEFL (minimum score 550 paper-based; 213 computer-based; 80 iBT). *Application deadline:* For fall admission, 3/1 priority date for domestic students, 3/1 for international students; for spring admission, 10/1 priority date for domestic students, 10/1 for international students. Applications are processed on a rolling basis. Application fee: $50. Electronic applications accepted. *Expenses:* Tuition, state resident: full-time $6300; part-time $263 per semester hour. Tuition, nonresident: full-time $25,174; part-time $1049 per semester hour. *Required fees:* $1872. *Financial support:* In 2011–12, 26 students received support, including research assistantships with partial tuition reimbursements available (averaging $7,200 per year), teaching assistantships with partial tuition reimbursements available (averaging $7,200 per year); career-related internships or fieldwork, Federal Work-Study, scholarships/grants, tuition waivers (partial), and unspecified assistantships also available. Support available to part-time students. Financial award application deadline: 4/15; financial award applicants required to submit FAFSA. *Faculty research:* Global issues in higher education, leadership and identity development in higher education. *Unit head:* Dr. Brenda Marina, Coordinator, 912-478-5600, Fax: 912-478-7140, E-mail: dmarina@georgiasouthern.edu. *Application contact:* Amanda Gilliland, Coordinator for Graduate Student Recruitment, 912-478-5384, Fax: 912-478-0740, E-mail: gradadmissions@georgiasouthern.edu. Web site: http://coe.georgiasouthern.edu/ithd/leadership.html.

Grambling State University, School of Graduate Studies and Research, College of Education, Department of Educational Leadership, Grambling, LA 71245. Offers curriculum and instruction (Ed D); developmental education (MS, Ed D), including curriculum and instruction: reading (Ed D), English (MS), guidance and counseling (MS), higher education administration (Ed D), instructional systems and technology (Ed D), mathematics (MS), reading (MS), science (MS), student development and personnel services (Ed D); educational leadership (MS, Ed D). Part-time and evening/weekend programs available. *Degree requirements:* For master's, comprehensive exam, thesis (for some programs); for doctorate, comprehensive exam, thesis/dissertation. *Entrance requirements:* For master's, GRE, minimum GPA of 2.5 on last degree; for doctorate, GRE (minimum 1000, 500 on Verbal), master's degree, minimum GPA of 3.0 on last degree. Additional exam requirements/recommendations for international students: Required—TOEFL (minimum score 500 paper-based; 173 computer-based; 61 iBT). Electronic applications accepted. *Expenses:* Tuition, state resident: full-time $3546; part-time $192 per credit hour. Tuition, nonresident: full-time $3456; part-time $192 per credit hour. *Required fees:* $1829; $1829 per semester hour.

Grand Canyon University, College of Doctoral Studies, Phoenix, AZ 85017-1097. Offers business administration (DBA); general psychology (PhD), including cognition and instruction, industrial and organizational psychology; organizational leadership (Ed D, PhD), including behavioral health (PhD), education and effective schools (PhD), higher education (PhD), instructional leadership (PhD), organizational development (Ed D). *Degree requirements:* For doctorate, comprehensive exam, thesis/dissertation. *Entrance requirements:* For doctorate, minimum GPA of 3.4 on earned advanced degree from regionally-accredited institution; transcripts; goals statement.

Grand Valley State University, College of Education, Program in College Student Affairs Leadership, Allendale, MI 49401-9403. Offers M Ed. Part-time programs available. *Entrance requirements:* For master's, GRE General Test or minimum GPA of 3.0. *Faculty research:* Adult learners, diversity and multiculturalism.

Grand Valley State University, College of Education, Program in Higher Education, Allendale, MI 49401-9403. Offers M Ed.

Grand Valley State University, College of Education, Programs in General Education, Allendale, MI 49401-9403. Offers adult and higher education (M Ed); early childhood education (M Ed); educational differentiation (M Ed); educational leadership (M Ed); educational technology integration (M Ed); elementary education (M Ed); middle level education (M Ed); school library media services (M Ed); secondary level education

(M Ed); teaching English to speakers of other languages (M Ed). Part-time and evening/weekend programs available. Postbaccalaureate distance learning degree programs offered (minimal on-campus study). *Degree requirements:* For master's, thesis. *Entrance requirements:* For master's, GRE General Test or minimum GPA of 3.0. Additional exam requirements/recommendations for international students: Required—TOEFL. Electronic applications accepted. *Faculty research:* Effectiveness of technology in education, parental involvement, effective teaching, effective schools research.

Harvard University, Harvard Graduate School of Education, Doctoral Program in Education, Cambridge, MA 02138. Offers culture, communities and education (Ed D); education policy, leadership and instructional practice (Ed D); higher education (Ed D); human development and education (Ed D); quantitative policy analysis in education (Ed D). *Faculty:* 83 full-time (44 women), 67 part-time/adjunct (29 women). *Students:* 251 full-time (172 women), 16 part-time (7 women); includes 87 minority (32 Black or African American, non-Hispanic/Latino; 1 American Indian or Alaska Native, non-Hispanic/Latino; 26 Asian, non-Hispanic/Latino; 22 Hispanic/Latino; 1 Native Hawaiian or other Pacific Islander, non-Hispanic/Latino; 5 Two or more races, non-Hispanic/Latino), 30 international. Average age 34. 545 applicants, 7% accepted, 28 enrolled. In 2011, 47 doctorates awarded. Terminal master's awarded for partial completion of doctoral program. *Degree requirements:* For doctorate, thesis/dissertation. *Entrance requirements:* For doctorate, GRE General Test, statement of purpose, 3 letters of recommendation, resume, official transcripts. Additional exam requirements/recommendations for international students: Required—TOEFL (minimum score 613 paper-based; 104 computer-based; 100 iBT), TWE (minimum score 5). *Application deadline:* For fall admission, 12/14 for domestic and international students. Application fee: $85. Electronic applications accepted. *Expenses:* Contact institution. *Financial support:* In 2011–12, 203 students received support, including 62 fellowships with full and partial tuition reimbursements available (averaging $13,939 per year), 35 research assistantships (averaging $9,534 per year), 134 teaching assistantships (averaging $10,748 per year); career-related internships or fieldwork, Federal Work-Study, institutionally sponsored loans, scholarships/grants, health care benefits, tuition waivers (full and partial), and unspecified assistantships also available. Support available to part-time students. Financial award application deadline: 2/1; financial award applicants required to submit FAFSA. *Faculty research:* Learning and development, educational leadership and organizations, education policy analysis. *Total annual research expenditures:* $26 million. *Unit head:* Dr. Shu-Ling Chen, Assistant Dean, 617-496-4406. *Application contact:* Information Contact, 617-495-3414, Fax: 617-496-3577, E-mail: gseadmissions@harvard.edu. Web site: http://gse.harvard.edu/.

Hofstra University, School of Education, Health, and Human Services, Department of Foundations, Leadership, and Policy Studies, Hempstead, NY 11549. Offers educational and policy leadership (MS Ed, Ed D), including higher education (MS Ed), K-12 (MS Ed); educational policy and leadership (Advanced Certificate), including school district business leader; foundations of education (MA, Advanced Certificate); Advanced Certificate/Advanced Certificate. Part-time and evening/weekend programs available. Postbaccalaureate distance learning degree programs offered (minimal on-campus study). *Students:* 22 full-time (16 women), 105 part-time (65 women); includes 45 minority (33 Black or African American, non-Hispanic/Latino; 1 Asian, non-Hispanic/Latino; 11 Hispanic/Latino), 2 international. Average age 37. 78 applicants, 94% accepted, 42 enrolled. In 2011, 12 master's, 6 doctorates, 12 other advanced degrees awarded. *Degree requirements:* For master's, one foreign language, comprehensive exam (for some programs), thesis or alternative, minimum GPA of 3.0; for doctorate, comprehensive exam (for some programs), thesis/dissertation (for some programs), minimum GPA of 3.0. *Entrance requirements:* For master's and Advanced Certificate, interview, writing sample, essay; for doctorate, GMAT, GRE, LSAT, or MAT, interview, 3 letters of recommendation, resume, essay. Additional exam requirements/recommendations for international students: Required—TOEFL (minimum score 550 paper-based; 213 computer-based; 80 iBT). *Application deadline:* Applications are processed on a rolling basis. Application fee: $70 ($75 for international students). Electronic applications accepted. *Expenses: Tuition:* Full-time $18,990; part-time $1055 per credit hour. *Required fees:* $970. Tuition and fees vary according to program. *Financial support:* In 2011–12, 66 students received support, including 44 fellowships with full and partial tuition reimbursements available (averaging $3,788 per year), 3 research assistantships with full and partial tuition reimbursements available (averaging $12,125 per year); Federal Work-Study, institutionally sponsored loans, scholarships/grants, tuition waivers (full and partial), and unspecified assistantships also available. Support available to part-time students. Financial award applicants required to submit FAFSA. *Faculty research:* School improvement, professional assessment - APPR, educational policy, professional development, race/gender in education. *Unit head:* Dr. Esther Fusco, Chairperson, 516-463-7704, Fax: 516-463-6196, E-mail: catezf@hofstra.edu. *Application contact:* Carol Drummer, Dean of Graduate Admissions, 516-463-4876, Fax: 516-463-4664, E-mail: gradstudent@hofstra.edu. Web site: http://www.hofstra.edu/education/.

Illinois State University, Graduate School, College of Education, Department of Curriculum and Instruction, Normal, IL 61790-2200. Offers curriculum and instruction (MS, MS Ed, Ed D); educational policies (Ed D); postsecondary education (Ed D); reading (MS Ed); supervision (Ed D). *Accreditation:* NCATE. *Degree requirements:* For master's, variable foreign language requirement, thesis or alternative; for doctorate, variable foreign language requirement, thesis/dissertation, 2 terms of residency, internship. *Entrance requirements:* For master's, GRE General Test, minimum GPA of 3.0 in last 60 hours of course work; for doctorate, GRE General Test. *Faculty research:* In-service and pre-service teacher education for teachers of English language learners; teachers for all children: developing a model for alternative, bilingual elementary certification for paraprofessionals in Illinois; Illinois Geographic Alliance, Connections Project.

Indiana State University, College of Graduate and Professional Studies, College of Education, Department of Educational Leadership, Administration, and Foundations, Terre Haute, IN 47809. Offers educational administration (PhD); leadership in higher education (PhD); school administration (Ed S); school administration and supervision (M Ed); student affairs in higher education (MS). *Accreditation:* NCATE. Part-time and evening/weekend programs available. Terminal master's awarded for partial completion of doctoral program. *Degree requirements:* For master's, thesis; for doctorate, thesis/dissertation. *Entrance requirements:* For master's, GRE General Test, minimum undergraduate GPA of 2.5; for doctorate, GRE General Test, minimum undergraduate GPA of 3.5; for Ed S, GRE General Test, minimum graduate GPA of 3.25. Electronic applications accepted.

Indiana University Bloomington, School of Education, Department of Educational Leadership and Policy Studies, Bloomington, IN 47405-7000. Offers education policy studies (PhD); educational leadership (MS, Ed D, Ed S); higher education (MS, Ed D, PhD); history and philosophy of education (MS); history of education (PhD); international and comparative education (MS, PhD); philosophy of education (PhD); student affairs administration (MS). *Accreditation:* NCATE. Part-time and evening/weekend programs available. *Degree requirements:* For master's, thesis optional; for doctorate, comprehensive exam, thesis/dissertation; for Ed S, comprehensive exam or project. *Entrance requirements:* For master's, doctorate, and Ed S, GRE General Test. Additional exam requirements/recommendations for international students: Required—TOEFL (minimum score 213 computer-based; 79 iBT). Electronic applications accepted. *Faculty research:* Student engagement at higher education institutions in the nation, Reading First professional development initiative, state finance policy on financial access to higher education, school reform, special needs studies.

Indiana University of Pennsylvania, School of Graduate Studies and Research, College of Education and Educational Technology, Department of Student Affairs in Higher Education, Indiana, PA 15705-1087. Offers MA. *Accreditation:* NCATE. Part-time programs available. *Faculty:* 4 full-time (2 women). *Students:* 57 full-time (40 women), 6 part-time (4 women); includes 5 minority (4 Black or African American, non-Hispanic/Latino; 1 Two or more races, non-Hispanic/Latino). Average age 24. 136 applicants, 52% accepted, 35 enrolled. In 2011, 26 master's awarded. *Degree requirements:* For master's, comprehensive exam, thesis optional. *Entrance requirements:* For master's, resume, interview, 2 letters of recommendation, writing sample. Additional exam requirements/recommendations for international students: Required—TOEFL (minimum score 540 paper-based; 207 computer-based). *Application deadline:* For fall admission, 1/15 priority date for domestic students. Application fee: $50. Electronic applications accepted. *Expenses:* Tuition, state resident: full-time $7488; part-time $416 per credit. Tuition, nonresident: full-time $11,232; part-time $624 per credit. *Required fees:* $2070; $192.20 per credit. $90 per semester. *Financial support:* In 2011–12, 1 fellowship (averaging $500 per year), 17 research assistantships with full and partial tuition reimbursements (averaging $5,284 per year) were awarded; career-related internships or fieldwork and Federal Work-Study also available. Support available to part-time students. Financial award application deadline: 4/15; financial award applicants required to submit FAFSA. *Unit head:* Dr. Linda W. Hall, Chairperson and Graduate Coordinator, 724-357-4535, E-mail: linda.hall@iup.edu. *Application contact:* Dr. Edward Nardi, Interim Associate Dean, 724-357-2480, Fax: 724-357-5595, E-mail: ewnardi@iup.edu. Web site: http://www.iup.edu/upper.aspx?id=216.

Indiana University–Purdue University Indianapolis, School of Education, Indianapolis, IN 46202-2896. Offers computer education (Certificate); curriculum and instruction (MS); early childhood (MS); educational leadership (MS, Certificate); English as a second language (Certificate); higher education and student affairs (MS); kindergarten (Certificate); language education (MS); reading (Certificate); school counseling (MS); special education (MS, Certificate). Part-time and evening/weekend programs available. *Faculty:* 41 full-time, 80 part-time/adjunct. *Students:* 67 full-time (52 women), 467 part-time (360 women); includes 82 minority (44 Black or African American, non-Hispanic/Latino; 3 American Indian or Alaska Native, non-Hispanic/Latino; 8 Asian, non-Hispanic/Latino; 13 Hispanic/Latino; 14 Two or more races, non-Hispanic/Latino), 10 international. Average age 33. 63 applicants, 57% accepted, 29 enrolled. In 2011, 167 master's awarded. *Degree requirements:* For master's, thesis optional. *Entrance requirements:* For master's, GRE General Test, minimum GPA of 3.0. Additional exam requirements/recommendations for international students: Required—TOEFL. *Application deadline:* For fall admission, 5/1 priority date for domestic students; for spring admission, 11/1 for domestic students. Application fee: $55 ($65 for international students). *Financial support:* Fellowships, research assistantships with partial tuition reimbursements, teaching assistantships, Federal Work-Study, institutionally sponsored loans, scholarships/grants, and tuition waivers (partial) available. Support available to part-time students. *Faculty research:* Teachers in the process of change, learning cycles, children's concepts of science. *Total annual research expenditures:* $614,458. *Unit head:* Dr. Chris Leland, Interim Executive Associate Dean, 317-274-6801, Fax: 317-274-6864. *Application contact:* Sarah Brandenburg, Graduate Advisor, 317-274-6801, Fax: 317-274-6864, E-mail: edugrad@iupui.edu. Web site: http://education.iupui.edu/.

Indiana Wesleyan University, Graduate School, College of Arts and Sciences, Marion, IN 46953. Offers addictions counseling (MS); clinical mental health counseling (MS); community counseling (MS); marriage and family therapy (MS); school counseling (MS); student development counseling and administration (MS). *Accreditation:* ACA. Part-time programs available. *Degree requirements:* For master's, thesis or alternative. *Entrance requirements:* For master's, GRE General Test. Additional exam requirements/recommendations for international students: Required—TOEFL. Electronic applications accepted. *Expenses:* Contact institution. *Faculty research:* Community counseling, multicultural counseling, addictions.

Inter American University of Puerto Rico, Metropolitan Campus, Graduate Programs, Program in Higher Education Administration, San Juan, PR 00919-1293. Offers MA. *Degree requirements:* For master's, comprehensive exam. *Entrance requirements:* For master's, GRE or EXADEP, interview. Electronic applications accepted.

Iowa State University of Science and Technology, Department of Educational Leadership and Policy Studies, Ames, IA 50011. Offers counselor education (M Ed, MS); educational administration (M Ed, MS); educational leadership (PhD); higher education (M Ed, MS); organizational learning and human resource development (M Ed, MS); research and evaluation (MS); student affairs (MS). *Degree requirements:* For master's, thesis or alternative; for doctorate, thesis/dissertation. *Entrance requirements:* For master's and doctorate, GRE General Test. Additional exam requirements/recommendations for international students: Required—TOEFL (minimum score 560 paper-based; 83 iBT), IELTS (minimum score 6.5). *Application deadline:* For fall admission, 1/1 priority date for domestic students, 1/1 for international students. Application fee: $40 ($90 for international students). Electronic applications accepted. *Unit head:* Dr. Daniel Robinson, Director of Graduate Education, 515-294-1241, Fax: 515-294-4942, E-mail: edldrshp@iastate.edu. *Application contact:* Judy Weiland, Application Contact, 515-294-1241, Fax: 515-294-4942, E-mail: eldrshp@iastate.edu. Web site: http://www.elps.hs.iastate.edu/.

John Brown University, Graduate Business Programs, Siloam Springs, AR 72761-2121. Offers global continuous improvement (MBA); international community development leadership (MS); leadership and ethics (MBA, MS); leadership and higher education (MS). Part-time and evening/weekend programs available. Postbaccalaureate distance learning degree programs offered (minimal on-campus study). *Faculty:* 6 full-time (2 women), 31 part-time/adjunct (7 women). *Students:* 29 full-time (13 women), 185 part-time (90 women); includes 33 minority (12 Black or African American, non-Hispanic/Latino; 3 American Indian or Alaska Native, non-Hispanic/Latino; 4 Asian, non-Hispanic/Latino; 11 Hispanic/Latino; 3 Two or more races, non-Hispanic/Latino), 7 international. 75 applicants, 88% accepted. *Entrance requirements:* For master's, MAT, GMAT or GRE if undergraduate GPA is less than 3.0, recommendation forms from three people, 200-word essay describing professional plans and reason for seeking acceptance. Additional exam requirements/recommendations for international students: Required—TOEFL (minimum score 550 paper-based; 213 computer-based; 70 iBT). *Application deadline:* Applications are processed on a rolling basis. Application fee: $35 ($100 for international students). Electronic applications accepted. *Expenses: Tuition:* Part-time $470 per credit hour. *Financial support:* Fellowships, institutionally sponsored loans, and scholarships/grants available. *Unit head:* Dr. Joe Walenciak, Program Director, 479-524-7431, E-mail: jwalenci@jbu.edu. *Application contact:* Brent Young, Graduate Business Representative, 479-524-7450, E-mail: byoung@jbu.edu. Web site: http://www.jbu.edu/grad/business/.

Higher Education

Johnson & Wales University, The Alan Shawn Feinstein Graduate School, Ed D Program, Providence, RI 02903-3703. Offers higher education (Ed D); K-12 (Ed D). Part-time programs available. *Degree requirements:* For doctorate, thesis/dissertation. *Entrance requirements:* For doctorate, MAT, minimum GPA of 3.25; master's degree in appropriate field from accredited institution. Additional exam requirements/recommendations for international students: Required—TOEFL (minimum score 550 paper-based; 210 computer-based); Recommended—IELTS, TWE. *Faculty research:* Site-based management, collaborative learning, technology and education, K-16 education.

Jones International University, School of Education, Centennial, CO 80112. Offers adult education (M Ed); corporate training and knowledge management (M Ed); curriculum and instruction (M Ed), including elementary teacher licensure, secondary teacher licensure; e-learning technology and design (M Ed); educational leadership and administration (M Ed); educational leadership and administration: principal and administrator licensure (M Ed); elementary curriculum instruction and assessment (M Ed); higher education leadership and administration (M Ed); K-12 instructional technology (M Ed); K-12 instructional technology: teacher licensure (M Ed); secondary curriculum instruction and assessment (M Ed); technology and design (M Ed). Part-time and evening/weekend programs available. Postbaccalaureate distance learning degree programs offered (no on-campus study). *Entrance requirements:* For master's, minimum cumulative GPA of 2.5. Additional exam requirements/recommendations for international students: Recommended—TOEFL (minimum score 550 paper-based; 213 computer-based). Electronic applications accepted.

Kansas State University, Graduate School, College of Education, Department of Special Education, Counseling and Student Affairs, Manhattan, KS 66506. Offers academic advising (MS); counseling and student development (MS, Ed D, PhD), including college student development (MS), counselor education and supervision (PhD), school counseling (MS), student affairs in higher education (PhD); special education (MS, Ed D). *Accreditation:* ACA; NCATE. Part-time programs available. *Faculty:* 8 full-time (4 women), 4 part-time/adjunct (1 woman). *Students:* 87 full-time (64 women), 323 part-time (251 women); includes 62 minority (27 Black or African American, non-Hispanic/Latino; 4 American Indian or Alaska Native, non-Hispanic/Latino; 5 Asian, non-Hispanic/Latino; 19 Hispanic/Latino; 2 Native Hawaiian or other Pacific Islander, non-Hispanic/Latino; 5 Two or more races, non-Hispanic/Latino), 4 international. Average age 34. 236 applicants, 70% accepted, 83 enrolled. In 2011, 111 master's, 2 doctorates awarded. *Degree requirements:* For master's, comprehensive exam; for doctorate, comprehensive exam, thesis/dissertation. *Entrance requirements:* For master's, minimum undergraduate GPA of 3.0; for doctorate, GRE General Test, minimum GPA of 3.0 in last 60 hours. Additional exam requirements/recommendations for international students: Required—TOEFL. *Application deadline:* For fall admission, 2/1 priority date for domestic students, 2/1 for international students; for spring admission, 8/1 priority date for domestic students, 8/1 for international students. Applications are processed on a rolling basis. Application fee: $40 ($55 for international students). Electronic applications accepted. *Financial support:* In 2011–12, 3 teaching assistantships (averaging $18,090 per year) were awarded; career-related internships or fieldwork, institutionally sponsored loans, and scholarships/grants also available. Financial award application deadline: 3/1; financial award applicants required to submit FAFSA. *Faculty research:* Counseling supervision, academic advising, career development, student development, universal design for learning, autism, learning disabilities. *Total annual research expenditures:* $2,678. *Unit head:* Kenneth Hughey, Head, 785-532-6445, Fax: 785-532-7304, E-mail: khughey@ksu.edu. *Application contact:* Dona Deam, Application Contact, 785-532-5595, Fax: 785-532-7304, E-mail: ddeam@ksu.edu. Web site: http://coe.ksu.edu/departments/secsa/index.htm.

Kaplan University, Davenport Campus, School of Higher Education Studies, Davenport, IA 52807-2095. Offers college administration and leadership (MS); college teaching and learning (MS); student services (MS). Part-time and evening/weekend programs available. Postbaccalaureate distance learning degree programs offered (no on-campus study). *Entrance requirements:* Additional exam requirements/recommendations for international students: Required—TOEFL (minimum score 550 paper-based; 218 computer-based; 80 iBT).

Kent State University, Graduate School of Education, Health, and Human Services, School of Foundations, Leadership and Administration, Program in Higher Education, Kent, OH 44242-0001. Offers PhD, Ed S. *Accreditation:* NCATE. Part-time and evening/weekend programs available. *Faculty:* 5 full-time (3 women), 6 part-time/adjunct (4 women). *Students:* 18 full-time (11 women), 24 part-time (17 women); includes 7 minority (5 Black or African American, non-Hispanic/Latino; 1 Asian, non-Hispanic/Latino; 1 Hispanic/Latino). 23 applicants, 22% accepted. In 2011, 2 degrees awarded. *Median time to degree:* Of those who began their doctoral program in fall 2003, 60% received their degree in 8 years or less. *Degree requirements:* For doctorate, comprehensive exam, thesis/dissertation. *Entrance requirements:* For doctorate, GRE General Test, 2 letters of reference, resume, interview, goals statement. Additional exam requirements/recommendations for international students: Required—TOEFL (minimum score 550 paper-based; 213 computer-based; 80 iBT). *Application deadline:* Applications are processed on a rolling basis. Application fee: $30 ($60 for international students). Electronic applications accepted. *Expenses:* Tuition, state resident: full-time $8136; part-time $452 per credit hour. Tuition, nonresident: full-time $14,292; part-time $794 per credit hour. *Financial support:* In 2011–12, 2 fellowships with full tuition reimbursements (averaging $12,000 per year), 4 research assistantships with full tuition reimbursements (averaging $12,000 per year) were awarded; teaching assistantships with full tuition reimbursements, career-related internships or fieldwork, Federal Work-Study, institutionally sponsored loans, scholarships/grants, health care benefits, unspecified assistantships, and 1 administrative assistantship (averaging $12,000 per year) also available. Support available to part-time students. Financial award application deadline: 4/1; financial award applicants required to submit FAFSA. *Faculty research:* Leadership. *Unit head:* Dr. Mark Kretovics, Coordinator, 330-672-0642, E-mail: mkretov1@kent.edu. *Application contact:* Nancy Miller, Academic Program Coordinator, Office of Graduate Student Services, 330-672-2576, Fax: 330-672-9162, E-mail: ogs@kent.edu.

Kent State University, Graduate School of Education, Health, and Human Services, School of Foundations, Leadership and Administration, Program in Higher Education and Student Personnel, Kent, OH 44242-0001. Offers M Ed. *Accreditation:* NCATE. Part-time and evening/weekend programs available. *Faculty:* 5 full-time (3 women), 6 part-time/adjunct (4 women). *Students:* 75 full-time (58 women), 31 part-time (23 women); includes 10 minority (4 Black or African American, non-Hispanic/Latino; 2 Asian, non-Hispanic/Latino; 4 Hispanic/Latino). 112 applicants, 39% accepted. In 2011, 35 master's awarded. *Entrance requirements:* For master's, GRE required if undergraduate GPA is below 3.0, resume, interview, 2 letters of recommendation, goals statement. Additional exam requirements/recommendations for international students: Required—TOEFL (minimum score 550 paper-based; 213 computer-based; 80 iBT). *Application deadline:* Applications are processed on a rolling basis. Application fee: $30 ($60 for international students). Electronic applications accepted. *Expenses:* Tuition, state resident: full-time $8136; part-time $452 per credit hour. Tuition, nonresident: full-time $14,292; part-time $794 per credit hour. *Financial support:* In 2011–12, 2 research assistantships with full tuition reimbursements (averaging $8,500 per year) were awarded; teaching assistantships with full tuition reimbursements, Federal Work-Study, scholarships/grants, unspecified assistantships, and 5 administrative assistantships (averaging $8,500 per year) also available. Financial award application deadline: 4/1; financial award applicants required to submit FAFSA. *Faculty research:* History/sociology of higher education, organization and administration in higher education. *Unit head:* Dr. Mark Kretovics, Coordinator, 330-672-0642, E-mail: mkretov1@kent.edu. *Application contact:* Nancy Miller, Academic Program Coordinator, Office of Graduate Student Services, 330-672-2576, Fax: 330-672-9162, E-mail: ogs@kent.edu.

Lewis University, College of Arts and Sciences, Program in Organizational Leadership, Romeoville, IL 60446. Offers higher education/student services (MA); non-for-profit management (MA); organizational management (MA); public administration (MA); training and development (MA). Part-time and evening/weekend programs available. Postbaccalaureate distance learning degree programs offered (no on-campus study). *Faculty:* 2 full-time (0 women), 9 part-time/adjunct (2 women). *Students:* 15 full-time (14 women), 193 part-time (143 women); includes 61 minority (50 Black or African American, non-Hispanic/Latino; 2 Asian, non-Hispanic/Latino; 9 Hispanic/Latino). Average age 36. In 2011, 46 master's awarded. *Entrance requirements:* For master's, bachelor's degree, at least 25 years of age, minimum of 3 years of work experience, minimum GPA of 3.0, letter of recommendation, interview. Additional exam requirements/recommendations for international students: Required—TOEFL (minimum score 550 paper-based; 213 computer-based). *Application deadline:* For fall admission, 5/1 for international students; for spring admission, 11/15 for international students. Applications are processed on a rolling basis. Application fee: $40. Electronic applications accepted. *Financial support:* Federal Work-Study, scholarships/grants, tuition waivers, and unspecified assistantships available. Financial award application deadline: 5/1; financial award applicants required to submit FAFSA. *Unit head:* Dr. Rich Walsh, Director, 815-838-0500, E-mail: walshri@lewisu.edu. *Application contact:* Julie Branchaw, Assistant Director, Graduate and Adult Admission, 815-836-5574, Fax: 815-836-5578, E-mail: branchju@lewisu.edu.

Lincoln Memorial University, Carter and Moyers School of Education, Harrogate, TN 37752-1901. Offers administration and supervision (M Ed, Ed S); counseling and guidance (M Ed); curriculum and instruction (M Ed, Ed D, Ed S); English (M Ed); executive leadership (Ed D); higher education administration (Ed D); human resource development (Ed D); leadership and administration (Ed D). Part-time and evening/weekend programs available. Postbaccalaureate distance learning degree programs offered. *Degree requirements:* For master's, comprehensive exam, thesis optional; for Ed S, comprehensive exam. *Entrance requirements:* For master's, PRAXIS, NTE, GRE, MAT, letters of recommendation; for Ed S, graduate transcripts. Additional exam requirements/recommendations for international students: Recommended—TOEFL. *Faculty research:* Brain compatible teaching and learning; poverty in Appalachia; leadership for change; ethics, moral responsibility and social justice; human and organizational learning.

Louisiana State University and Agricultural and Mechanical College, Graduate School, College of Education, Department of Educational Theory, Policy and Practice, Baton Rouge, LA 70803. Offers counseling (M Ed, MA, Ed S); educational administration (M Ed, MA, PhD, Ed S); educational technology (MA); elementary education (M Ed, MAT); higher education (PhD); research methodology (PhD); secondary education (M Ed, MAT). PhD programs offered jointly with Louisiana State University in Shreveport. *Accreditation:* ACA (one or more programs are accredited); NCATE. Part-time and evening/weekend programs available. *Faculty:* 17 full-time (all women). *Students:* 188 full-time (145 women), 161 part-time (130 women); includes 104 minority (88 Black or African American, non-Hispanic/Latino; 1 American Indian or Alaska Native, non-Hispanic/Latino; 6 Asian, non-Hispanic/Latino; 5 Hispanic/Latino; 4 Two or more races, non-Hispanic/Latino), 9 international. Average age 31. 151 applicants, 61% accepted, 58 enrolled. In 2011, 129 master's, 17 doctorates, 11 other advanced degrees awarded. Terminal master's awarded for partial completion of doctoral program. *Degree requirements:* For doctorate, thesis/dissertation; for Ed S, thesis optional. *Entrance requirements:* For master's and doctorate, GRE General Test, minimum GPA of 3.0. Additional exam requirements/recommendations for international students: Required—TOEFL (minimum score 550 paper-based; 213 computer-based; 79 iBT) or IELTS (minimum score 6.5). *Application deadline:* For fall admission, 1/25 priority date for domestic students, 5/15 for international students; for spring admission, 10/15 for international students. Applications are processed on a rolling basis. Application fee: $50 ($70 for international students). Electronic applications accepted. *Financial support:* In 2011–12, 230 students received support, including 2 fellowships (averaging $19,353 per year), 24 research assistantships with full and partial tuition reimbursements available (averaging $10,052 per year), 53 teaching assistantships with full and partial tuition reimbursements available (averaging $12,218 per year); career-related internships or fieldwork, Federal Work-Study, institutionally sponsored loans, health care benefits, and unspecified assistantships also available. Support available to part-time students. Financial award applicants required to submit FAFSA. *Faculty research:* Literary, curriculum studies, science education, K-12 leadership, higher education. *Total annual research expenditures:* $774,887. *Unit head:* Dr. Earl Cheek, Jr., Chair, 225-578-6867, Fax: 225-578-9135, E-mail: echeek@lsu.edu. *Application contact:* Dr. Rita Culross, Graduate Coordinator, 225-578-6867, Fax: 225-578-9135, E-mail: acrita@lsu.edu.

Loyola University Chicago, School of Education, Program in Higher Education, Chicago, IL 60660. Offers M Ed, PhD. PhD offered through the Graduate School. *Accreditation:* NCATE. Part-time programs available. *Faculty:* 5 full-time (2 women), 4 part-time/adjunct (2 women). *Students:* 122. Average age 38. 187 applicants, 72% accepted, 38 enrolled. In 2011, 52 master's, 5 doctorates awarded. *Degree requirements:* For master's, comprehensive exam; for doctorate, comprehensive exam, thesis/dissertation. *Entrance requirements:* For master's, letters of recommendation, minimum GPA of 3.0, resume, transcripts; for doctorate, GMAT, GRE General Test, or MAT, 5 years of higher education work experience, interview. Additional exam requirements/recommendations for international students: Required—TOEFL (minimum score 550 paper-based; 213 computer-based; 79 iBT). *Application deadline:* For fall admission, 1/1 for domestic and international students; for spring admission, 11/1 for domestic and international students. Applications are processed on a rolling basis. Application fee: $50. Electronic applications accepted. Application fee is waived when completed online. *Expenses: Tuition:* Full-time $15,660; part-time $870 per credit hour. *Required fees:* $125 per semester. Tuition and fees vary according to course load and program. *Financial support:* In 2011–12, 3 fellowships with full tuition reimbursements (averaging $14,000 per year), 10 research assistantships with full tuition reimbursements (averaging $12,000 per year) were awarded; career-related internships or fieldwork, institutionally sponsored loans, scholarships/grants, traineeships, health care benefits, and unspecified assistantships also available. Support available to part-time students. Financial award application deadline: 2/1; financial award applicants required to submit FAFSA. *Faculty research:* Church-affiliated higher education, enrollment management, academic programs, program evaluation/quality. *Unit head:* Dr. Bridget Kelly, Director, 312-915-6855, Fax: 312-915-6660, E-mail: bkelly4@luc.edu. *Application contact:* Marie Rosin-Dittmar, Information Contact, 312-915-6800, E-mail: schleduc@luc.edu.

Maryville University of Saint Louis, School of Education, St. Louis, MO 63141-7299. Offers art education (MA Ed); early childhood education (MA Ed); educational leadership (Ed D); educational leadership: principal certification (MA Ed); elementary education (MA Ed); gifted education (MA Ed); higher education leadership (Ed D); literacy specialist (MA Ed); middle grades education (MA Ed); secondary teaching and inquiry (MA Ed); teacher as leader (MA Ed). *Accreditation:* NCATE. Part-time and evening/weekend programs available. *Faculty:* 10 full-time (6 women), 19 part-time/adjunct (15 women). *Students:* 33 full-time (25 women), 251 part-time (190 women); includes 42 minority (32 Black or African American, non-Hispanic/Latino; 1 American Indian or Alaska Native, non-Hispanic/Latino; 4 Asian, non-Hispanic/Latino; 2 Hispanic/Latino; 3 Two or more races, non-Hispanic/Latino). Average age 38. In 2011, 69 master's, 43 doctorates awarded. *Degree requirements:* For master's, thesis, project. *Entrance requirements:* For master's, minimum cumulative GPA of 3.0, 3 professional recommendations, essays, interview with program faculty; for doctorate, minimum GPA of 3.0, 3 professional recommendations, essay, interview, on-site writing sample. Additional exam requirements/recommendations for international students: Required—TOEFL (minimum score 550 paper-based). *Application deadline:* Applications are processed on a rolling basis. Application fee: $40 ($60 for international students). Electronic applications accepted. *Expenses: Tuition:* Full-time $21,922; part-time $675 per credit hour. *Required fees:* $233.75 per semester. *Financial support:* Career-related internships or fieldwork, Federal Work-Study, tuition waivers (partial), and professional educator discounts available. Financial award application deadline: 3/1; financial award applicants required to submit FAFSA. *Faculty research:* Collaboration with public schools, pre-service program development, mathematics, diversity, literacy. *Unit head:* Dr. Sam Hausfather, Dean, 314-529-9466, Fax: 314-529-9921, E-mail: shausfather@maryville.edu. *Application contact:* Holly Stanwich, Graduate Admissions Coordinator, 314-529-9542, Fax: 314-529-9921, E-mail: teachered@maryville.edu. Web site: http://www.maryville.edu/academics-ed-graduate.

Marywood University, Academic Affairs, Reap College of Education and Human Development, Department of Education, Program in Higher Education Administration, Scranton, PA 18509-1598. Offers MS. Part-time and evening/weekend programs available. *Entrance requirements:* Additional exam requirements/recommendations for international students: Required—TOEFL (minimum score 550 paper-based; 213 computer-based; 79 iBT). *Application deadline:* For fall admission, 4/1 priority date for domestic students, 3/31 for international students; for spring admission, 11/1 priority date for domestic students, 8/31 for international students. Applications are processed on a rolling basis. Application fee: $30. Electronic applications accepted. *Financial support:* Research assistantships with tuition reimbursements, career-related internships or fieldwork, scholarships/grants, and unspecified assistantships available. Support available to part-time students. Financial award application deadline: 6/30; financial award applicants required to submit FAFSA. *Faculty research:* Integrated thematic instruction. *Unit head:* Patricia S. Arter, Chairperson, 570-348-6211 Ext. 2511, E-mail: psarter@marywood.edu. *Application contact:* Tammy Manka, Assistant Director of Graduate Admissions, 570-348-6211 Ext. 2322, E-mail: tmanka@marywood.edu. Web site: http://www.marywood.edu/education/graduate-programs/ms_higher_education_administration.html.

Marywood University, Academic Affairs, Reap College of Education and Human Development, Department of Human Development, Emphasis in Higher Education Administration, Scranton, PA 18509-1598. Offers PhD. *Entrance requirements:* Additional exam requirements/recommendations for international students: Required—TOEFL (minimum score 550 paper-based; 213 computer-based; 79 iBT). *Application deadline:* For fall admission, 1/30 for domestic and international students. Application fee: $35. Electronic applications accepted. *Expenses:* Contact institution. *Financial support:* Career-related internships or fieldwork, scholarships/grants, and unspecified assistantships available. Support available to part-time students. Financial award application deadline: 6/30; financial award applicants required to submit FAFSA. *Unit head:* Dr. Brook Cannon, Director, 570-348-6211 Ext. 2324, E-mail: cannonb@marywood.edu. *Application contact:* Tammy Manka, Assistant Director of Graduate Admissions, 570-348-6211 Ext. 2322, E-mail: tmanka@marywood.edu. Web site: http://www.marywood.edu/phd/specializations.html.

McKendree University, Graduate Programs, Master of Arts in Education Program, Lebanon, IL 62254-1299. Offers certification (MA Ed); educational administration and leadership (MA Ed); educational studies (MA Ed); higher education administrative services (MA Ed); music education (MA Ed); special education (MA Ed); teacher leadership (MA Ed); transition to teaching (MA Ed). *Accreditation:* NCATE. Part-time and evening/weekend programs available. Postbaccalaureate distance learning degree programs offered (no on-campus study). *Entrance requirements:* For master's, official transcripts from institutions attended, minimum GPA of 3.0, resume, references. Additional exam requirements/recommendations for international students: Required—TOEFL. Electronic applications accepted.

Mercer University, Graduate Studies, Cecil B. Day Campus, Tift College of Education (Atlanta), Macon, GA 31207-0003. Offers curriculum and instruction (PhD); early childhood education (M Ed, MAT); educational leadership (PhD, Ed S); higher education leadership (M Ed); middle grades education (M Ed, MAT); reading education (M Ed); school counseling (Ed S); secondary education (M Ed, MAT); teacher leadership (Ed S). *Accreditation:* NCATE. Part-time and evening/weekend programs available. *Faculty:* 31 full-time (17 women), 6 part-time/adjunct (3 women). *Students:* 249 full-time (207 women), 413 part-time (326 women); includes 349 minority (322 Black or African American, non-Hispanic/Latino; 1 American Indian or Alaska Native, non-Hispanic/Latino; 18 Asian, non-Hispanic/Latino; 6 Hispanic/Latino; 2 Two or more races, non-Hispanic/Latino), 6 international. Average age 34. 204 applicants, 76% accepted, 125 enrolled. In 2011, 235 master's, 8 doctorates, 27 other advanced degrees awarded. *Degree requirements:* For master's and Ed S, research project; for doctorate, thesis/dissertation. *Entrance requirements:* For master's, GRE or MAT, minimum undergraduate GPA of 2.75; for doctorate, GRE; for Ed S, GRE or MAT, minimum GPA of 3.25, 3 years of teaching experience. Additional exam requirements/recommendations for international students: Required—TOEFL. *Application deadline:* For fall admission, 8/1 for domestic and international students; for spring admission, 12/1 for domestic and international students. Applications are processed on a rolling basis. Application fee: $25. *Expenses:* Contact institution. *Financial support:* Federal Work-Study available. Support available to part-time students. Financial award application deadline: 5/1. *Faculty research:* Educational technology, multicultural and minority issues in education, educational leadership (P-12 and higher education), school discipline and school bullying, standards-based mathematics education. *Unit head:* Dr. Carl R. Martray, Dean, 478-301-5397, Fax: 478-301-2280, E-mail: martray_cr@mercer.edu. *Application contact:* Dr. Allison Gilmore, Associate Dean for Graduate Teacher Education, 678-547-6333, Fax: 678-547-6055, E-mail: gilmore_a@mercer.edu. Web site: http://www.mercer.edu/education/.

Mercer University, Graduate Studies, Macon Campus, Tift College of Education (Macon), Macon, GA 31207-0003. Offers curriculum and instruction (PhD); early childhood education (M Ed); education leadership (PhD), including higher education, P-12; educational leadership (Ed S); higher education (M Ed); teacher leadership (Ed S). *Accreditation:* NCATE. Part-time and evening/weekend programs available. Postbaccalaureate distance learning degree programs offered (minimal on-campus study). *Faculty:* 26 full-time (17 women), 2 part-time/adjunct (0 women). *Students:* 87 full-time (78 women), 147 part-time (124 women); includes 92 minority (83 Black or African American, non-Hispanic/Latino; 3 American Indian or Alaska Native, non-Hispanic/Latino; 3 Asian, non-Hispanic/Latino; 3 Hispanic/Latino), 1 international. Average age 36. 122 applicants, 66% accepted, 72 enrolled. In 2011, 51 master's, 5 doctorates, 37 other advanced degrees awarded. *Degree requirements:* For master's, research project report; for doctorate, comprehensive exam, thesis/dissertation. *Entrance requirements:* For master's, GRE or MAT, minimum GPA of 2.75; for doctorate, GRE, minimum GPA of 3.5; interview; writing sample; 3 recommendations; for Ed S, GRE or MAT, minimum GPA of 3.5 (for Ed S in teacher leadership), 3.0 (for Ed S in educational leadership). Additional exam requirements/recommendations for international students: Required—TOEFL. *Application deadline:* For fall admission, 8/1 for domestic students; for spring admission, 12/1 for domestic students. Applications are processed on a rolling basis. Application fee: $35. *Expenses:* Contact institution. *Financial support:* Federal Work-Study and institutionally sponsored loans available. Support available to part-time students. Financial award application deadline: 5/1. *Faculty research:* Teacher effectiveness, specific learning disabilities, inclusion. *Unit head:* Dr. Carl R. Martray, Dean, 478-301-5397, Fax: 478-301-2280, E-mail: martray_cr@mercer.edu. *Application contact:* Tracey Wofford, Associate Director of Admissions, 678-547-6422, Fax: 678-547-6367, E-mail: wofford_tm@mercer.edu. Web site: http://education.mercer.edu.

Mercyhurst College, Graduate Studies, Program in Organizational Leadership, Erie, PA 16546. Offers accounting (MS); entrepreneurship (MS); higher education administration (MS); human resources (MS); nonprofit management (MS); organizational leadership (Certificate); sports leadership (MS). Part-time and evening/weekend programs available. *Faculty:* 1 full-time (0 women), 11 part-time/adjunct (4 women). *Students:* 42 full-time (16 women), 22 part-time (15 women); includes 5 minority (3 Black or African American, non-Hispanic/Latino; 1 American Indian or Alaska Native, non-Hispanic/Latino; 1 Hispanic/Latino), 9 international. Average age 30. 60 applicants, 62% accepted, 25 enrolled. In 2011, 27 master's, 2 other advanced degrees awarded. *Degree requirements:* For master's, thesis. *Entrance requirements:* For master's, GRE General Test or MAT, interview, resume, essay, three professional references, transcripts. Additional exam requirements/recommendations for international students: Required—TOEFL. *Application deadline:* For fall admission, 8/1 priority date for domestic students, 7/1 for international students; for winter admission, 11/1 for domestic students, 10/1 for international students; for spring admission, 2/1 for domestic students, 1/1 for international students. Applications are processed on a rolling basis. Application fee: $35. Electronic applications accepted. *Expenses: Tuition:* Part-time $570 per credit. *Required fees:* $90 per term. Tuition and fees vary according to program. *Financial support:* In 2011–12, 16 students received support, including 112 research assistantships with full and partial tuition reimbursements available (averaging $6,000 per year); career-related internships or fieldwork and unspecified assistantships also available. Support available to part-time students. Financial award application deadline: 5/1; financial award applicants required to submit FAFSA. *Faculty research:* Leadership training, organizational communication, leadership pedagogy. *Unit head:* Dr. Gilbert Jacobs, Director, 814-824-2390, E-mail: gjacobs@mercyhurst.edu. *Application contact:* Sarah Murphy, Academic Coordinator, 814-824-2297, Fax: 814-824-2055, E-mail: smurphy@mercyhurst.edu.

Merrimack College, School of Education, North Andover, MA 01845-5800. Offers community engagement (M Ed); early childhood education (M Ed); elementary education (M Ed); elementary education plus moderate disabilities-dual license (M Ed); English as a second language (M Ed); general studies (M Ed); higher education (M Ed); middle (M Ed); moderate disabilities (preK-8) (M Ed); reading (M Ed); secondary (M Ed); teacher leadership (CAGS). Part-time and evening/weekend programs available. *Faculty:* 4 full-time (all women), 9 part-time/adjunct (7 women). *Students:* 70 full-time (60 women), 39 part-time (33 women); includes 2 minority (1 Asian, non-Hispanic/Latino; 1 Hispanic/Latino). Average age 27. In 2011, 26 master's awarded. *Degree requirements:* For master's, portfolio. *Entrance requirements:* Additional exam requirements/recommendations for international students: Required—TOEFL (minimum score 80 iBT). *Application deadline:* For fall admission, 8/1 priority date for domestic students, 7/15 for international students; for winter admission, 12/1 priority date for domestic students, 11/15 for international students; for spring admission, 3/1 priority date for domestic students, 2/15 for international students. Applications are processed on a rolling basis. Electronic applications accepted. *Expenses: Tuition:* Part-time $475 per credit. *Required fees:* $62.50 per semester. *Financial support:* In 2011–12, 50 fellowships were awarded; career-related internships or fieldwork and scholarships/grants also available. Financial award applicants required to submit FAFSA. *Faculty research:* Higher education, community engagement, literacy, leadership. *Unit head:* Dr. Theresa Kirk, Chair, 978-837-5436, E-mail: kirkt@merrimack.edu. *Application contact:* Jessica McCarthy, Program Coordinator, 978-837-5443, E-mail: mccarthyj@merrimack.edu. Web site: http://www.merrimack.edu/academics/education/med/.

Messiah College, Program in Higher Education, Mechanicsburg, PA 17055. Offers college athletics management (MA); self-designed concentration (MA); student affairs (MA). Part-time programs available. *Faculty:* 2 full-time (1 woman), 3 part-time/adjunct (2 women). *Students:* 2 full-time (1 woman), 2 part-time (both women). Average age 25. *Application deadline:* For fall admission, 6/1 priority date for domestic students; for winter admission, 11/1 priority date for domestic students; for spring admission, 11/1 priority date for domestic students. Applications are processed on a rolling basis. Application fee: $30. Electronic applications accepted. *Expenses: Tuition:* Full-time $9648; part-time $536 per credit hour. *Required fees:* $150; $25 per course. *Financial support:* Federal Work-Study and unspecified assistantships available. Financial award applicants required to submit FAFSA. *Faculty research:* College athletics management, assessment and student learning outcomes, the life and legacy of Ernest L. Boyer, common learning, student affairs practice. *Unit head:* Dr. Cynthia Wells, Assistant Professor of Higher Education/Program Coordinator, 717-766-2511 Ext. 7378, E-mail: cwells@messiah.edu. *Application contact:* Jackie Gehman, Graduate Enrollment Coordinator, 717-796-5061, Fax: 717-691-2386, E-mail: jgehman@messiah.edu. Web site: http://www.messiah.edu/academics/graduate_studies/Higher-Ed/.

Miami University, School of Education and Allied Professions, Department of Educational Leadership, Oxford, OH 45056. Offers curriculum and teacher leadership (M Ed); educational administration (Ed D, PhD); school leadership (MS); student affairs in higher education (MS, PhD). *Accreditation:* NCATE. Part-time programs available. *Students:* 102 full-time (63 women), 96 part-time (73 women); includes 45 minority (34 Black or African American, non-Hispanic/Latino; 1 American Indian or Alaska Native, non-Hispanic/Latino; 3 Asian, non-Hispanic/Latino; 2 Hispanic/Latino; 5 Two or more races, non-Hispanic/Latino), 7 international. Average age 32. In 2011, 52 master's, 7 doctorates awarded. *Entrance requirements:* For master's, MAT or GRE, minimum undergraduate GPA of 3.0 during previous 2 years or 2.75 overall; for doctorate, GRE, minimum GPA of 2.75 (undergraduate), 3.0 (graduate). Additional exam requirements/recommendations for international students: Required—TOEFL. Application fee: $50. *Expenses:* Tuition, state resident: full-time $12,023; part-time $501 per credit hour. Tuition, nonresident: full-time $26,554; part-time $1107 per credit hour. *Required fees:* $528. *Financial support:* Fellowships with full tuition reimbursements, research assistantships with full tuition reimbursements, teaching assistantships with full tuition reimbursements, career-related internships or fieldwork, Federal Work-Study, health care benefits, tuition waivers (full), and unspecified assistantships available. Financial award application deadline: 2/15; financial award applicants required to submit FAFSA. *Unit head:* Dr. Kate Rousmaniere, Chair, 513-529-6843, Fax: 513-529-1729, E-mail: rousmak@muohio.edu. Web site: http://www.units.muohio.edu/eap/edl/index.html.

Michigan State University, The Graduate School, College of Education, Department of Educational Administration, East Lansing, MI 48824. Offers higher, adult and lifelong education (MA, PhD); K–12 educational administration (MA, PhD, Ed S); student affairs administration (MA). Part-time programs available. *Entrance requirements:* Additional exam requirements/recommendations for international students: Required—TOEFL. Electronic applications accepted.

Minnesota State University Mankato, College of Graduate Studies, College of Social and Behavioral Sciences, Department of Sociology and Corrections, Mankato, MN 56001. Offers sociology (MA); sociology: college teaching option (MA); sociology: corrections (MS); sociology: human services planning and administration (MS). Part-time programs available. *Students:* 12 full-time (9 women), 33 part-time (20 women). *Degree requirements:* For master's, comprehensive exam, thesis or alternative. *Entrance requirements:* For master's, minimum GPA of 3.0 during previous 2 years, 3 letters of reference, resume. Additional exam requirements/recommendations for international students: Required—TOEFL. *Application deadline:* For fall admission, 7/1 priority date for domestic students; for spring admission, 11/1 for domestic students. Applications are processed on a rolling basis. Application fee: $40. Electronic applications accepted. *Financial support:* Research assistantships with full tuition reimbursements, teaching assistantships with full tuition reimbursements, career-related internships or fieldwork, Federal Work-Study, institutionally sponsored loans, and unspecified assistantships available. Support available to part-time students. Financial award application deadline: 3/15; financial award applicants required to submit FAFSA. *Faculty research:* Women's suffrage movements. *Unit head:* Dr. Barbara Carson, Chairperson, 507-389-1562. *Application contact:* 507-389-2321, E-mail: grad@mnsu.edu. Web site: http://sbs.mnsu.edu/soccorr/.

Mississippi College, Graduate School, School of Education, Department of Teacher Education and Leadership, Clinton, MS 39058. Offers art (M Ed); biological science (M Ed); business education (M Ed); computer science (M Ed); dyslexia therapy (M Ed); educational leadership (M Ed, Ed D, Ed S); elementary education (M Ed, Ed S); English (M Ed); higher education administration (MS); mathematics (M Ed); secondary education (M Ed); social studies (history) (M Ed); teaching arts (M Ed). Part-time programs available. Postbaccalaureate distance learning degree programs offered (no on-campus study). *Degree requirements:* For master's, comprehensive exam, thesis optional. *Entrance requirements:* For master's, NTE. Additional exam requirements/recommendations for international students: Recommended—TOEFL, IELTS. Electronic applications accepted.

Mississippi College, Graduate School, School of Education, Program in Higher Education Administration, Clinton, MS 39058. Offers MS. Part-time programs available. Postbaccalaureate distance learning degree programs offered (no on-campus study). *Degree requirements:* For master's, comprehensive exam, thesis optional. *Entrance requirements:* For master's, GRE or GMAT, minimum GPA of 3.0. Additional exam requirements/recommendations for international students: Recommended—TOEFL, IELTS.

Missouri State University, Graduate College, College of Education, Department of Counseling, Leadership, and Special Education, Program in Student Affairs in Higher Education, Springfield, MO 65897. Offers MS. Part-time programs available. *Students:* 29 full-time (17 women), 13 part-time (12 women); includes 10 minority (4 Black or African American, non-Hispanic/Latino; 3 Asian, non-Hispanic/Latino; 2 Hispanic/Latino; 1 Two or more races, non-Hispanic/Latino). Average age 27. 36 applicants, 83% accepted, 21 enrolled. In 2011, 18 master's awarded. *Degree requirements:* For master's, comprehensive exam, thesis or alternative. *Entrance requirements:* For master's, statement of purpose; three references. Additional exam requirements/recommendations for international students: Required—TOEFL (minimum score 550 paper-based; 213 computer-based; 79 iBT). *Application deadline:* For fall admission, 7/20 priority date for domestic students, 5/1 for international students; for spring admission, 12/20 priority date for domestic students, 9/1 for international students. Applications are processed on a rolling basis. Application fee: $35 ($50 for international students). Electronic applications accepted. *Expenses:* Tuition, state resident: full-time $4086; part-time $227 per credit hour. Tuition, nonresident: full-time $8172; part-time $454 per credit hour. *Required fees:* $275 per semester. Tuition and fees vary according to course load, campus/location and program. *Financial support:* Federal Work-Study, institutionally sponsored loans, scholarships/grants, and unspecified assistantships available. Financial award application deadline: 3/31; financial award applicants required to submit FAFSA. *Unit head:* Dr. Gilbert Brown, Program Director, 417-836-4428, E-mail: gilbertbrown@missouristate.edu. *Application contact:* Misty Stewart, Coordinator of Graduate Recruitment, 417-836-6079, Fax: 417-836-6200, E-mail: mistystewart@missouristate.edu. Web site: http://education.missouristate.edu/edadmin/MSEDSA.htm.

Montana State University, College of Graduate Studies, College of Education, Health, and Human Development, Department of Education, Bozeman, MT 59717. Offers adult and higher education (Ed D); curriculum and instruction (M Ed, Ed D), including professional educator (M Ed), technology education (M Ed); education (M Ed), including adult and higher education, educational leadership, school counseling; educational leadership (Ed D, Ed S). *Accreditation:* Teacher Education Accreditation Council. Part-time programs available. Postbaccalaureate distance learning degree programs offered (minimal on-campus study). *Degree requirements:* For master's, comprehensive exam; for doctorate, comprehensive exam, thesis/dissertation. *Entrance requirements:* For master's, GRE, 3 letters of reference, essays, BA transcripts; for doctorate, GRE, MAT, 3 letters of reference, essay, BA and M Ed transcripts; for Ed S, PRAXIS. Additional exam requirements/recommendations for international students: Required—TOEFL (minimum score 550 paper-based; 213 computer-based). Electronic applications accepted. *Faculty research:* Critical literacy; standards-based education; school Improvement, organizational change, leadership in rural education, leadership in Indian education; student Learning; multicultural/culturally responsive education for social justice Native American indigenous education, community-centered education teacher preparation.

Morehead State University, Graduate Programs, College of Education, Department of Foundational and Graduate Studies in Education, Morehead, KY 40351. Offers adult and higher education (MA, Ed S); certified professional counselor (Ed S); counseling P-12 (MA); curriculum and instruction (Ed S); educational technology (MA Ed); instructional leadership (Ed S); school administration (MA); school counseling (Ed S); teacher leader business and marketing content (MA Ed); teacher leader business and marketing technology (MA Ed); teacher leader educational technology (MA Ed); teacher leader English (MA Ed); teacher leader gifted education (MA Ed); teacher leader IECE certification (MA Ed); teacher leader interdisciplinary education P-5 (MA Ed); teacher leader middle grades (MA Ed); teacher leader non IECE certification (MA Ed); teacher leader reading/writing - non-certification (MA Ed); teacher leader reading/writing certification (MA Ed); teacher leader school communication - certification (MA Ed); teacher leader school communication - non-certification (MA Ed); teacher leader social studies (MA Ed); teacher leader special education (MA Ed). *Accreditation:* NCATE. Part-time and evening/weekend programs available. *Degree requirements:* For master's, thesis optional, oral and/or written comprehensive exams; for Ed S, thesis, oral exam. *Entrance requirements:* For master's, GRE General Test, minimum overall undergraduate GPA of 2.5; for Ed S, GRE General Test, interview, master's degree, minimum GPA of 3.5, work experience. Additional exam requirements/recommendations for international students: Required—TOEFL (minimum score 500 paper-based; 173 computer-based). Electronic applications accepted. *Faculty research:* Character education, school accountability, computer applications for school administrators.

Morgan State University, School of Graduate Studies, School of Education and Urban Studies, Department of Advanced Studies, Leadership and Policy, Program in Higher Education Administration, Baltimore, MD 21251. Offers PhD. *Degree requirements:* For doctorate, comprehensive exam, thesis/dissertation. *Entrance requirements:* For doctorate, GRE General Test or MAT, minimum GPA of 3.0.

Morgan State University, School of Graduate Studies, School of Education and Urban Studies, Department of Advanced Studies, Leadership and Policy, Program in Higher Education-Community College Leadership, Baltimore, MD 21251. Offers Ed D. *Accreditation:* NCATE. Part-time and evening/weekend programs available. *Degree requirements:* For doctorate, comprehensive exam, thesis/dissertation. *Entrance requirements:* For doctorate, GRE General Test or MAT. Additional exam requirements/recommendations for international students: Required—TOEFL (minimum score 550 paper-based; 213 computer-based). *Faculty research:* Multicultural education, cooperative learning, psychology of cognition.

National University, Academic Affairs, School of Education, Department of Educational Administration and School Counseling/Psychology, La Jolla, CA 92037-1011. Offers accomplished collaborative leadership (MA); applied behavior analysis (MS); applied school leadership (MS); educational administration (MS); educational counseling (MS); higher education administration (MS); innovative school leadership (MS); instructional leadership (MS); school psychology (MS). Part-time and evening/weekend programs available. Postbaccalaureate distance learning degree programs offered (no on-campus study). *Degree requirements:* For master's, thesis. *Entrance requirements:* For master's, interview, minimum GPA of 2.5. Additional exam requirements/recommendations for international students: Required—TOEFL (minimum score 550 paper-based; 213 computer-based; 79 iBT), IELTS (minimum score 6). *Application deadline:* Applications are processed on a rolling basis. Application fee: $60 ($65 for international students). Electronic applications accepted. *Financial support:* Career-related internships or fieldwork, institutionally sponsored loans, scholarships/grants, and tuition waivers (partial) available. Support available to part-time students. Financial award application deadline: 6/30; financial award applicants required to submit FAFSA. *Unit head:* Dr. Rollin Nordgren, Chair and Professor, 858-642-8144, Fax: 858-642-8724, E-mail: rnordgren@nu.edu. *Application contact:* Dominick Giovanniello, Associate Regional Dean, 800-NAT-UNIV, Fax: 858-541-7792, E-mail: dgiovann@nu.edu. Web site: http://www.nu.edu/OurPrograms/SchoolOfEducation/EducationalAdministration.html.

New England College, Program in Education, Henniker, NH 03242-3293. Offers higher education administration (MS, Ed D); K-12 leadership (Ed D); literacy and language arts (M Ed); meeting the needs of all learners/special education (M Ed); teacher leadership/school reform (M Ed). Part-time and evening/weekend programs available.

New York University, Steinhardt School of Culture, Education, and Human Development, Department of Administration, Leadership, and Technology, Program in Higher Education, New York, NY 10012-1019. Offers higher and postsecondary education (PhD); higher education administration (Ed D); student personnel administration in higher education (MA). *Accreditation:* Teacher Education Accreditation Council. Part-time programs available. *Faculty:* 8 full-time (5 women). *Students:* 29 full-time (22 women), 104 part-time (73 women); includes 62 minority (27 Black or African American, non-Hispanic/Latino; 9 Asian, non-Hispanic/Latino; 19 Hispanic/Latino; 1 Native Hawaiian or other Pacific Islander, non-Hispanic/Latino; 6 Two or more races, non-Hispanic/Latino), 3 international. Average age 31. 235 applicants, 18% accepted, 38 enrolled. In 2011, 42 master's, 7 doctorates awarded. *Degree requirements:* For master's, thesis (for some programs); for doctorate, thesis/dissertation. *Entrance requirements:* For master's, interview, 2 letters of recommendation; for doctorate, GRE General Test, interview. Additional exam requirements/recommendations for international students: Required—TOEFL. *Application deadline:* For fall admission, 12/1 priority date for domestic students, 12/1 for international students; for spring admission, 11/1 for domestic and international students. Applications are processed on a rolling basis. Application fee: $75. Electronic applications accepted. *Financial support:* Fellowships with full and partial tuition reimbursements, career-related internships or fieldwork, Federal Work-Study, institutionally sponsored loans, scholarships/grants, tuition waivers (partial), and unspecified assistantships available. Support available to part-time students. Financial award application deadline: 2/1; financial award applicants required to submit FAFSA. *Faculty research:* Organizational theory and culture, systemic change, leadership development, access, equity and diversity. *Unit head:* Dr. Ann Marcus, Head, 212-998-4041, Fax: 212-995-4041. *Application contact:* 212-998-5030, Fax: 212-995-4328, E-mail: steinhardt.gradadmissions@nyu.edu. Web site: http://steinhardt.nyu.edu/alt/highered.

North Carolina State University, Graduate School, College of Education, Department of Adult and Higher Education, Program in Higher Education Administration, Raleigh, NC 27695. Offers M Ed, MS, Ed D. *Degree requirements:* For master's, thesis (for some programs); for doctorate, thesis/dissertation. *Entrance requirements:* For master's and doctorate, GRE General Test or MAT, minimum GPA of 3.0 in major. Electronic applications accepted.

North Dakota State University, College of Graduate and Interdisciplinary Studies, Program in College Teaching, Fargo, ND 58108. Offers Certificate. *Students:* 1 (woman) part-time, all international. 1 applicant, 100% accepted, 0 enrolled. In 2011, 7 Certificates awarded. *Entrance requirements:* For degree, minimum cumulative GPA of 3.0. Application fee: $35. Electronic applications accepted. *Unit head:* Dr. Donald Schwert, Director, 701-231-7496, Fax: 701-231-5924, E-mail: donald.schwert@ndsu.edu. *Application contact:* Sonya Goergen, Marketing, Recruitment, and Public Relations Coordinator, 701-231-7033, Fax: 701-231-6524. Web site: http://www.ndsu.edu/csme/college_teaching_certificate/.

Northeastern State University, Graduate College, College of Education, Department of Educational Foundations and Leadership, Program in Collegiate Scholarship and Services, Tahlequah, OK 74464-2399. Offers MS. Part-time and evening/weekend programs available. In 2011, 3 master's awarded. *Degree requirements:* For master's, thesis. *Entrance requirements:* For master's, MAT or GRE, minimum GPA of 3.0. Additional exam requirements/recommendations for international students: Required—TOEFL (minimum score 213 computer-based). *Application deadline:* For fall admission, 6/1 priority date for domestic students. Applications are processed on a rolling basis. Application fee: $0 ($25 for international students). Electronic applications accepted. *Financial support:* Federal Work-Study available. Financial award application deadline: 3/1. *Unit head:* Dr. Swen Digranes, Coordinator, 918-456-5511 Ext. 3719, E-mail:

digranes@nsuok.edu. *Application contact:* Margie Railey, Administrative Assistant, 918-456-5511 Ext. 2093, Fax: 918-458-2061, E-mail: railey@nsouk.edu.

Northern Arizona University, Graduate College, College of Education, Department of Educational Leadership, Flagstaff , AZ 86011. Offers community college/higher education (M Ed); educational foundations (M Ed); educational leadership (M Ed, Ed D); principal (Certificate); principal K-12 (M Ed); school leadership K-12 (M Ed); superintendent (Certificate). Part-time programs available. *Faculty:* 18 full-time (8 women). *Students:* 249 full-time (148 women), 737 part-time (460 women); includes 291 minority (51 Black or African American, non-Hispanic/Latino; 65 American Indian or Alaska Native, non-Hispanic/Latino; 14 Asian, non-Hispanic/Latino; 143 Hispanic/Latino; 2 Native Hawaiian or other Pacific Islander, non-Hispanic/Latino; 16 Two or more races, non-Hispanic/Latino), 1 international. Average age 32. 251 applicants, 94% accepted, 196 enrolled. In 2011, 356 master's, 12 doctorates, 74 Certificates awarded. *Degree requirements:* For master's, comprehensive exam, thesis (for some programs); for doctorate, comprehensive exam, thesis/dissertation. *Entrance requirements:* For master's, minimum GPA of 3.0; for doctorate, GRE or MAT, minimum GPA of 3.5. Additional exam requirements/recommendations for international students: Required—TOEFL (minimum score 550 paper-based; 213 computer-based; 80 iBT), IELTS (minimum score 7). *Application deadline:* For fall admission, 3/1 for international students; for spring admission, 9/15 for international students. Applications are processed on a rolling basis. Application fee: $65. Electronic applications accepted. *Expenses:* Tuition, state resident: full-time $7190; part-time $355 per credit hour. Tuition, nonresident: full-time $18,092; part-time $1005 per credit hour. *Required fees:* $818; $328 per semester. *Financial support:* In 2011–12, 1 research assistantship with partial tuition reimbursement (averaging $10,000 per year) was awarded. Financial award applicants required to submit FAFSA. *Unit head:* Dr. Michael Schwanenberger, Chair, 928-523-4212, Fax: 928-523-1929, E-mail: michael.schwanenberger@nau.edu. *Application contact:* Jennifer Offutt, Administrative Assistant, 928-523-5098, Fax: 928-523-1929, E-mail: jennifer.offutt@nau.edu. Web site: http://nau.edu/coe/ed-leadership/.

Northern Illinois University, Graduate School, College of Education, Department of Counseling, Adult and Higher Education, De Kalb, IL 60115-2854. Offers adult and higher education (MS Ed, Ed D); counseling (MS Ed, Ed D). *Accreditation:* ACA. Part-time and evening/weekend programs available. *Faculty:* 19 full-time (11 women), 2 part-time/adjunct (1 woman). *Students:* 122 full-time (84 women), 292 part-time (215 women); includes 149 minority (109 Black or African American, non-Hispanic/Latino; 1 American Indian or Alaska Native, non-Hispanic/Latino; 14 Asian, non-Hispanic/Latino; 20 Hispanic/Latino; 5 Two or more races, non-Hispanic/Latino), 14 international. Average age 36. 115 applicants, 55% accepted, 42 enrolled. In 2011, 58 master's, 21 doctorates awarded. Terminal master's awarded for partial completion of doctoral program. *Degree requirements:* For master's, comprehensive exam, thesis optional; for doctorate, thesis/dissertation, candidacy exam, dissertation defense. *Entrance requirements:* For master's, GRE General Test or MAT, minimum undergraduate GPA of 2.75, interview (counseling); for doctorate, GRE General Test, minimum undergraduate GPA of 2.75, 3.2 graduate, interview (counseling). Additional exam requirements/recommendations for international students: Required—TOEFL (minimum score 550 paper-based; 213 computer-based). *Application deadline:* For fall admission, 6/1 for domestic students, 5/1 for international students; for spring admission, 11/1 for domestic students, 10/1 for international students. Applications are processed on a rolling basis. Application fee: $40. Electronic applications accepted. *Financial support:* In 2011–12, 5 research assistantships with full tuition reimbursements, 1 teaching assistantship with full tuition reimbursement were awarded; fellowships with full tuition reimbursements, career-related internships or fieldwork, Federal Work-Study, scholarships/grants, tuition waivers (full), and staff assistantships also available. Support available to part-time students. Financial award applicants required to submit FAFSA. *Unit head:* Dr. Barbara Johnson, Interim Chair, 815-753-1448, E-mail: cahe@niu.edu. *Application contact:* Graduate School Office, 815-753-0395, E-mail: gradsch@niu.edu. Web site: http://www.cedu.niu.edu/cahe/index.html.

Northwestern University, The Graduate School, School of Education and Social Policy, Program in Education, Evanston, IL 60035. Offers advanced teaching (MS); elementary teaching (MS); higher education administration (MS); secondary teaching (MS). Part-time and evening/weekend programs available. *Degree requirements:* For master's, research project. *Entrance requirements:* For master's, GRE General Test, Illinois State Board of Education Basic Skills Exam (secondary and elementary), bachelor's degree. Additional exam requirements/recommendations for international students: Recommended—TOEFL. Electronic applications accepted. *Faculty research:* Cultural context and literacy, philosophy of education and interpretive discussion, productivity, enhancing research and teaching, motivation, new and junior faculty issues, professional development for K-12 teachers to improve math and science teaching, female/underrepresented students/faculty in STEM disciplines.

Northwest Missouri State University, Graduate School, College of Education and Human Services, Department of Educational Leadership, Maryville, MO 64468-6001. Offers educational leadership (MS Ed, Ed S), including educational leadership: elementary (MS Ed), educational leadership: K-12 (MS Ed), educational leadership: secondary (MS Ed), elementary principalship (Ed S), secondary principalship (Ed S), superintendency (Ed S); higher education leadership (MS); secondary individualized prescribed programs (MS Ed), including teacher leadership, teaching secondary. Part-time programs available. *Faculty:* 14 full-time (6 women). *Students:* 17 full-time (9 women), 111 part-time (76 women); includes 10 minority (6 Black or African American, non-Hispanic/Latino; 2 Asian, non-Hispanic/Latino; 2 Hispanic/Latino), 1 international. 46 applicants, 100% accepted, 28 enrolled. In 2011, 65 master's, 25 other advanced degrees awarded. *Degree requirements:* For master's, comprehensive exam; for Ed S, comprehensive exam, thesis. *Entrance requirements:* For master's, GRE General Test, minimum undergraduate GPA of 2.75, teaching certificate, writing sample; for Ed S, minimum graduate GPA of 3.25. Additional exam requirements/recommendations for international students: Required—TOEFL (minimum score 550 paper-based; 213 computer-based). *Application deadline:* For fall admission, 7/1 for domestic and international students; for spring admission, 11/15 for domestic and international students. Application fee: $0 ($50 for international students). *Financial support:* In 2011–12, research assistantships with full tuition reimbursements (averaging $6,000 per year), 6 teaching assistantships with full tuition reimbursements (averaging $6,000 per year) were awarded; unspecified assistantships also available. Financial award application deadline: 4/1; financial award applicants required to submit FAFSA. *Unit head:* Dr. Jan Glenn, Chairperson, 660-562-1064. *Application contact:* Dr. Gregory Haddock, Dean of Graduate School, 660-562-1145, Fax: 660-562-1096, E-mail: gradsch@nwmissouri.edu.

Oakland University, Graduate Study and Lifelong Learning, School of Education and Human Services, Department of Educational Leadership, Rochester, MI 48309-4401. Offers educational leadership (M Ed, PhD); higher education (Certificate); higher education administration (Certificate); school administration (Ed S). *Entrance requirements:* Additional exam requirements/recommendations for international students: Required—TOEFL (minimum score 550 paper-based; 213 computer-based).

Ohio University, Graduate College, Gladys W. and David H. Patton College of Education and Human Services, Department of Counseling and Higher Education, Athens, OH 45701-2979. Offers college student personnel (M Ed); community/agency counseling (M Ed); counselor education (PhD); higher education (PhD); rehabilitation counseling (M Ed); school counseling (M Ed). *Accreditation:* ACA; CORE. Part-time and evening/weekend programs available. *Students:* 174 full-time (133 women), 40 part-time (25 women); includes 38 minority (21 Black or African American, non-Hispanic/Latino; 2 American Indian or Alaska Native, non-Hispanic/Latino; 2 Asian, non-Hispanic/Latino; 7 Hispanic/Latino; 6 Two or more races, non-Hispanic/Latino), 9 international. 130 applicants, 59% accepted, 62 enrolled. In 2011, 45 master's, 7 doctorates awarded. *Degree requirements:* For master's, comprehensive exam (for some programs), thesis or alternative; for doctorate, comprehensive exam, thesis/dissertation. *Entrance requirements:* For master's, GRE General Test or MAT (if GPA less than 2.9), 3 letters of reference; for doctorate, GRE General Test, work experience, minimum GPA of 3.4. Additional exam requirements/recommendations for international students: Required—TOEFL (minimum score 550 paper-based; 80 iBT) or IELTS (minimum score 6.5). *Application deadline:* For fall admission, 1/15 for domestic and international students. Application fee: $50 ($55 for international students). Electronic applications accepted. *Financial support:* Research assistantships with full tuition reimbursements, teaching assistantships with full tuition reimbursements, Federal Work-Study, institutionally sponsored loans, tuition waivers (partial), and unspecified assistantships available. Financial award application deadline: 1/15. *Faculty research:* Youth violence, gender studies, student affairs, chemical dependency, disabilities issues. *Total annual research expenditures:* $527,983. *Unit head:* Dr. Tracy Leinbaugh, Chair, 740-593-0846, Fax: 740-593-0477, E-mail: leinbaug@ohio.edu. *Application contact:* Floyd J. Doney, Director of Student Affairs, 740-593-4400, Fax: 740-593-9310, E-mail: doney@ohio.edu. Web site: http://www.cehs.ohio.edu/academics/che/.

Oklahoma State University, College of Education, School of Educational Studies, Stillwater, OK 74078. Offers higher education (Ed D). Part-time programs available. *Faculty:* 28 full-time (12 women), 27 part-time/adjunct (7 women). *Students:* 45 full-time (18 women), 270 part-time (165 women); includes 57 minority (18 Black or African American, non-Hispanic/Latino; 22 American Indian or Alaska Native, non-Hispanic/Latino; 1 Asian, non-Hispanic/Latino; 7 Hispanic/Latino; 9 Two or more races, non-Hispanic/Latino), 28 international. Average age 39. 76 applicants, 39% accepted, 21 enrolled. In 2011, 47 master's, 18 doctorates awarded. *Degree requirements:* For master's, thesis (for some programs); for doctorate, comprehensive exam, thesis/dissertation. *Entrance requirements:* For master's and doctorate, GRE or GMAT. Additional exam requirements/recommendations for international students: Required—TOEFL (minimum score 550 paper-based; 79 iBT). *Application deadline:* For fall admission, 3/1 for international students; for spring admission, 8/1 for international students. Applications are processed on a rolling basis. Application fee: $40 ($75 for international students). Electronic applications accepted. *Expenses:* Tuition, state resident: full-time $4044; part-time $168.50 per credit hour. Tuition, nonresident: full-time $16,008; part-time $667 per credit hour. *Required fees:* $2122; $88.45 per credit hour. One-time fee: $50. Tuition and fees vary according to course load and campus/location. *Financial support:* In 2011–12, 15 research assistantships (averaging $10,164 per year), 8 teaching assistantships (averaging $8,506 per year) were awarded; career-related internships or fieldwork, Federal Work-Study, scholarships/grants, health care benefits, tuition waivers (partial), and unspecified assistantships also available. Support available to part-time students. Financial award application deadline: 3/1; financial award applicants required to submit FAFSA. *Unit head:* Dr. Katye Perry, Interim Head, 405-744-6275, Fax: 405-744-7758. *Application contact:* Dr. Sheryl Tucker, Dean, 405-744-7099, Fax: 405-744-0355, E-mail: grad-i@okstate.edu. Web site: http://education.okstate.edu/index.php/academic-units/school-of-educational-studies.

Old Dominion University, Darden College of Education, Doctoral Program in Higher Education, Norfolk, VA 23529. Offers PhD. Part-time programs available. Postbaccalaureate distance learning degree programs offered (minimal on-campus study). *Faculty:* 3 full-time (1 woman), 10 part-time/adjunct (5 women). *Students:* 12 full-time (8 women), 14 part-time (8 women); includes 7 minority (4 Black or African American, non-Hispanic/Latino; 1 American Indian or Alaska Native, non-Hispanic/Latino; 1 Asian, non-Hispanic/Latino; 1 Hispanic/Latino). Average age 37. 13 applicants, 54% accepted, 5 enrolled. In 2011, 1 doctorate awarded. *Degree requirements:* For doctorate, comprehensive exam, thesis/dissertation. *Entrance requirements:* For doctorate, GRE, master's degree, minimum graduate GPA of 3.5. Additional exam requirements/recommendations for international students: Required—TOEFL. *Application deadline:* For spring admission, 2/1 for domestic and international students. Application fee: $50. Electronic applications accepted. *Expenses:* Tuition, state resident: full-time $9096; part-time $379 per credit. Tuition, nonresident: full-time $23,064; part-time $961 per credit. *Required fees:* $127 per semester. One-time fee: $50. *Financial support:* In 2011–12, 2 fellowships with tuition reimbursements (averaging $15,000 per year), research assistantships with full tuition reimbursements (averaging $15,000 per year), 6 teaching assistantships with full tuition reimbursements (averaging $15,000 per year) were awarded; career-related internships or fieldwork, tuition waivers (full), and unspecified assistantships also available. Financial award application deadline: 2/1. *Faculty research:* Law leadership, student development, research administration, international higher education administration, academic integrity, leadership. *Unit head:* Dr. Dennis Gregory, Graduate Program Director, 757-683-5163, E-mail: dgregory@odu.edu. *Application contact:* William Heffelfinger, Director of Graduate Admissions, 757-683-5554, Fax: 757-683-3255, E-mail: gradadmit@odu.edu.

Old Dominion University, Darden College of Education, Programs in Higher Education, Norfolk, VA 23529. Offers educational leadership (MS Ed, Ed S), including higher education. Part-time programs available. *Faculty:* 3 full-time (1 woman), 10 part-time/adjunct (5 women). *Students:* 35 full-time (28 women), 20 part-time (13 women); includes 33 minority (28 Black or African American, non-Hispanic/Latino; 2 Asian, non-Hispanic/Latino; 2 Hispanic/Latino; 1 Two or more races, non-Hispanic/Latino). Average age 28. 43 applicants, 63% accepted, 20 enrolled. In 2011, 19 master's, 3 Ed Ss awarded. *Degree requirements:* For master's, comprehensive exam. *Entrance requirements:* For master's, GRE, minimum undergraduate GPA of 2.8; for Ed S, GRE, 2 letters of reference, minimum GPA of 3.5, master's degree. Additional exam requirements/recommendations for international students: Required—TOEFL. *Application deadline:* For fall admission, 3/1 priority date for domestic students, 3/1 for international students; for winter admission, 10/1 for domestic and international students; for spring admission, 3/1 for domestic and international students. Applications are processed on a rolling basis. Application fee: $50. Electronic applications accepted. *Expenses:* Tuition, state resident: full-time $9096; part-time $379 per credit. Tuition, nonresident: full-time $23,064; part-time $961 per credit. *Required fees:* $127 per semester. One-time fee: $50. *Financial support:* Research assistantships with partial tuition reimbursements, career-related internships or fieldwork, scholarships/grants, and unspecified assistantships available. *Faculty research:* Law leadership, student development, research administration, international higher education administration. *Unit head:* Dr. Dennis Gregory, Graduate Program Director, 757-683-5163, E-mail: hied@odu.edu. *Application contact:* William Heffelfinger, Director of Graduate Admissions, 757-683-5554, Fax: 757-683-3255, E-mail: gradadmit@odu.edu. Web site: http://education.odu.edu/efl/academics/highered/msed/msed_international_2.shtml.

Higher Education

Oral Roberts University, School of Education, Tulsa, OK 74171. Offers Christian school administration (K-12) (MA Ed, Ed D); Christian school curriculum development (MA Ed); college and higher education administration (Ed D); public school administration (K-12) (MA Ed, Ed D); public school teaching (MA Ed). *Accreditation:* NCATE. Part-time programs available. Postbaccalaureate distance learning degree programs offered (minimal on-campus study). *Degree requirements:* For master's, comprehensive exam, thesis optional; for doctorate, comprehensive exam, thesis/dissertation. *Entrance requirements:* For master's, GRE General Test or MAT, minimum GPA of 3.0; for doctorate, minimum GPA of 3.0. Additional exam requirements/recommendations for international students: Required—TOEFL (minimum score 500 paper-based; 173 computer-based). *Expenses:* Contact institution. *Faculty research:* Teacher effectiveness, college success in high achieving African-Americans, professional development practices.

Penn State University Park, Graduate School, College of Education, Department of Education Policy Studies, State College, University Park, PA 16802-1503. Offers college student affairs (M Ed); educational leadership (M Ed); educational theory and policy (MA, PhD); higher education (D Ed, PhD). *Accreditation:* NCATE. *Unit head:* Dr. David H. Monk, Dean, 814-865-2526, Fax: 814-865-0555, E-mail: dhm6@psu.edu. *Application contact:* Cynthia E. Nicosia, Director, Graduate Enrollment Services, 814-865-1834, E-mail: cey1@psu.edu. Web site: http://www.ed.psu.edu/educ/eps/.

Phillips Theological Seminary, Programs in Theology, Tulsa, OK 74116. Offers administration of church agencies (M Div); campus ministry (M Div); church-related social work (M Div); college and seminary teaching (M Div); global mission work (M Div); institutional chaplaincy (M Div); ministerial vocations in Christian education (M Div); ministry (D Min), including parish ministry, pastoral counseling, practices of ministry; ministry and culture (MAMC), including Christian education, congregational leadership, history and practice of Christian spirituality, theology, ethics, and culture; ministry of music (M Div); pastoral care and counseling (M Div); pastoral ministry (M Div); theological studies (MTS). *Accreditation:* ATS. Part-time programs available. Postbaccalaureate distance learning degree programs offered (minimal on-campus study). *Degree requirements:* For master's, thesis (for some programs); for doctorate, thesis/dissertation. *Entrance requirements:* For master's, minimum GPA of 2.5; for doctorate, M Div, minimum GPA of 3.0. *Faculty research:* Biblical studies, historical studies, theology and culture, practical theology, theology and film.

Pittsburg State University, Graduate School, College of Education, Department of Special Services and Leadership Studies, Pittsburg, KS 66762. Offers community college and higher education (Ed S); educational leadership (MS), including educational technology; educational technology (MS); general school administration (Ed S); special education (MS), including behavioral disorders, learning disabilities, mentally retarded. *Degree requirements:* For master's, thesis or alternative. *Entrance requirements:* For master's, GRE General Test or MAT.

Portland State University, Graduate Studies, School of Education, Department of Educational Policy, Foundations, and Administrative Studies, Portland, OR 97207-0751. Offers educational leadership (MA, MS, Ed D); postsecondary, adult and continuing education (Ed D). *Accreditation:* NCATE. Part-time and evening/weekend programs available. *Degree requirements:* For master's, thesis or alternative, written exam or research project; for doctorate, comprehensive exam, thesis/dissertation. *Entrance requirements:* For master's, California Basic Educational Skills Test, minimum GPA of 3.0 in upper-division course work or 2.75 overall; for doctorate, GRE General Test or MAT. Additional exam requirements/recommendations for international students: Required—TOEFL (minimum score 550 paper-based; 213 computer-based). *Faculty research:* Leadership development and research, principals and urban schools, accelerated schools, cooperative learning, family involvement in schools.

Purdue University, Graduate School, College of Education, Department of Educational Studies, West Lafayette, IN 47907. Offers administration (MS Ed, PhD, Ed S); counseling and development (MS Ed, PhD); education of the gifted (MS Ed); educational psychology (MS Ed, PhD); foundations of education (MS Ed, PhD); higher education administration (MS Ed, PhD); special education (MS Ed, PhD). *Accreditation:* ACA (one or more programs are accredited); NCATE (one or more programs are accredited). Part-time and evening/weekend programs available. *Faculty:* 23 full-time (17 women), 1 part-time/adjunct (0 women). *Students:* 111 full-time (79 women), 93 part-time (58 women); includes 34 minority (19 Black or African American, non-Hispanic/Latino; 1 American Indian or Alaska Native, non-Hispanic/Latino; 4 Asian, non-Hispanic/Latino; 6 Hispanic/Latino; 4 Two or more races, non-Hispanic/Latino), 30 international. Average age 35. 249 applicants, 37% accepted, 46 enrolled. In 2011, 39 master's, 20 doctorates, 4 other advanced degrees awarded. *Degree requirements:* For master's, thesis optional; for doctorate, thesis/dissertation, oral and written exams; for Ed S, oral presentation, project. *Entrance requirements:* For master's, GRE General Test required for all Educational Studies program areas, except for Special Education if undergraduate GPA is higher than a 3.0, minimum undergraduate GPA of 3.0; for doctorate and Ed S, GRE general test is required, a combined score of 1000 (300 for revised GRE test) or more is expected., minimum undergraduate GPA of 3.0. Additional exam requirements/recommendations for international students: Required—TOEFL (minimum score 550 paper-based; 77 iBT), TWE (minimum score 5). *Application deadline:* Applications are processed on a rolling basis. Application fee: $60 ($75 for international students). Electronic applications accepted. *Financial support:* Fellowships with full tuition reimbursements, research assistantships with full tuition reimbursements, teaching assistantships with full tuition reimbursements, career-related internships or fieldwork, and tuition waivers (full) available. Support available to part-time students. Financial award application deadline: 3/1; financial award applicants required to submit FAFSA. *Faculty research:* Motivation, learning disabilities, school learning, group processes, cognitive development. *Unit head:* Dr. Ala Samrapungavan, Head, 765-494-9170, Fax: 765-496-1228, E-mail: ala@purdue.edu. *Application contact:* Sarah N. Prater, Graduate Contact, 765-494-2345, Fax: 765-494-5832, E-mail: prater0@purdue.edu. Web site: http://www.edst.purdue.edu/.

Regent University, Graduate School, School of Education, Virginia Beach, VA 23464-9800. Offers adult education (Ed D); adult/staff development (Ed D, PhD); career switcher with licensure (M Ed), including alternative licensure; character education (Ed D, PhD); Christian education leadership (Ed D, PhD); Christian education specialist (Ed S); Christian school program (M Ed), including ACSI licensure; distance education (Ed D, PhD); education licensure (M Ed), including preK-6th grade; educational leadership (M Ed, PhD); educational leadership - special education (Ed S), including administration and supervision; educational psychology (Ed D, PhD), including learning and development, research and evaluation, special education; higher education (Ed D, PhD), including administration, research and institutional planning, teaching; higher education leadership (Ed D); individualized degree plan (M Ed), including behavior disorders, learning disabilities, mental retardation, reading specialist; K-12 school leadership (Ed D, PhD); leadership in character education (M Ed); master teacher (M Ed), including TESOL; mathematics education (M Ed); special education (PhD); student affairs (M Ed); TESOL (M Ed), including adult education, ESL: preK-12. *Accreditation:* Teacher Education Accreditation Council. Part-time and evening/weekend programs available. Postbaccalaureate distance learning degree programs offered (minimal on-campus study). *Faculty:* 26 full-time (13 women), 54 part-time/adjunct (34 women). *Students:* 140 full-time (109 women), 786 part-time (626 women); includes 218 minority (189 Black or African American, non-Hispanic/Latino; 2 American Indian or Alaska Native, non-Hispanic/Latino; 11 Asian, non-Hispanic/Latino; 16 Hispanic/Latino), 42 international. Average age 39. 673 applicants, 57% accepted, 298 enrolled. In 2011, 178 master's, 15 doctorates awarded. *Degree requirements:* For master's, thesis or alternative; for doctorate, comprehensive exam, thesis/dissertation. *Entrance requirements:* For master's, MAT, minimum undergraduate GPA of 2.75, writing sample, resume, recommendations, interview; for doctorate, GRE, writing sample, 3 years of relevant professional experience, master's-level paper, copies of published work, resume, transcripts, interview, recommendations. Additional exam requirements/recommendations for international students: Required—TOEFL (minimum score 577 paper-based; 233 computer-based). *Application deadline:* For fall admission, 4/1 priority date for domestic students; for spring admission, 10/15 priority date for domestic students. Applications are processed on a rolling basis. Application fee: $50. Electronic applications accepted. *Expenses:* Contact institution. *Financial support:* Fellowships, career-related internships or fieldwork, scholarships/grants, tuition waivers (full and partial), and unspecified assistantships available. Support available to part-time students. Financial award application deadline: 4/1; financial award applicants required to submit FAFSA. *Faculty research:* Character development and discipline for children, education leadership development, diversity in schools, classroom management, technology in education settings. *Unit head:* Dr. Alan A. Arroyo, Dean, 757-352-4261, Fax: 757-352-4318, E-mail: alanarr@regent.edu. *Application contact:* Matthew Chadwick, Director of Enrollment Support Services, 800-373-5504, Fax: 757-352-4381, E-mail: admissions@regent.edu. Web site: http://www.regent.edu/education/.

Robert Morris University Illinois, Morris Graduate School of Management, Chicago, IL 60605. Offers accounting (MBA); accounting/finance (MBA); design and media (MM); health care administration (MM); higher education administration (MM); human resource management (MBA); information systems (MIS); law enforcement administration (MM); management (MBA); management/finance (MIS); management/human resource management (MBA); sports administration (MM). Part-time and evening/weekend programs available. *Faculty:* 7 full-time (1 woman), 21 part-time/adjunct (5 women). *Students:* 296 full-time (172 women), 216 part-time (136 women); includes 273 minority (160 Black or African American, non-Hispanic/Latino; 1 American Indian or Alaska Native, non-Hispanic/Latino; 32 Asian, non-Hispanic/Latino; 78 Hispanic/Latino; 2 Two or more races, non-Hispanic/Latino), 28 international. Average age 32. 247 applicants, 69% accepted, 152 enrolled. In 2011, 244 master's awarded. *Entrance requirements:* Additional exam requirements/recommendations for international students: Required—TOEFL (minimum score 550 paper-based; 173 computer-based). *Application deadline:* Applications are processed on a rolling basis. Application fee: $20 ($100 for international students). Electronic applications accepted. *Expenses: Tuition:* Full-time $13,800; part-time $2300 per course. *Financial support:* In 2011–12, 643 students received support. Federal Work-Study, scholarships/grants, tuition waivers, and leadership and athletic scholarships available. Support available to part-time students. Financial award applicants required to submit FAFSA. *Unit head:* Kayed Akkawi, Dean, 312-935-6025, Fax: 312-935-6020, E-mail: kakkawi@robertmorris.edu. *Application contact:* Fernando Villeda, Dean of Morris Graduate School of Management, 312-935-6050, Fax: 312-935-6020, E-mail: fvilleda@robertmorris.edu.

Rowan University, Graduate School, College of Education, Department of Educational Leadership, Program in Higher Education Administration, Glassboro, NJ 08028-1701. Offers MA. *Accreditation:* NCATE. Part-time and evening/weekend programs available. *Degree requirements:* For master's, comprehensive exam, thesis. *Entrance requirements:* For master's, GRE General Test, minimum GPA of 2.8, 2 years of teaching experience. Additional exam requirements/recommendations for international students: Required—TOEFL. Electronic applications accepted.

St. Cloud State University, School of Graduate Studies, School of Education, Department of Educational Leadership and Higher Education, Program in Higher Education Administration, St. Cloud, MN 56301-4498. Offers MS, Ed D.

Saint Leo University, Graduate Studies in Education, Saint Leo, FL 33574-6665. Offers educational leadership (M Ed); exceptional student education (M Ed); higher education leadership (Ed S); instructional design (MS); instructional leadership (M Ed); reading (M Ed); school leadership (Ed S). Part-time and evening/weekend programs available. Postbaccalaureate distance learning degree programs offered (minimal on-campus study). *Faculty:* 14 full-time (10 women), 21 part-time/adjunct (16 women). *Students:* 523 full-time (427 women), 20 part-time (17 women); includes 65 minority (43 Black or African American, non-Hispanic/Latino; 2 Asian, non-Hispanic/Latino; 16 Hispanic/Latino; 4 Two or more races, non-Hispanic/Latino), 3 international. Average age 37. In 2011, 153 master's, 18 other advanced degrees awarded. *Degree requirements:* For master's, comprehensive exam, appropriate State of Florida certification tests. *Entrance requirements:* For master's, GRE (minimum score of 1000) or MAT (minimum score of 410) if undergraduate GPA for last 60 hours of coursework was below 3.0 (for M Ed), bachelor's degree with minimum GPA of 3.0 for last 60 hours of coursework from regionally-accredited college or university, 2 recommendations, resume, statement of professional goals, copy of valid teaching certificate (for M Ed); for Ed S, GRE (minimum score 1000) or MAT (minimum score 410) if undergraduate GPA for last 60 hours of coursework less than 3.0, bachelor's degree with minimum GPA of 3.0 for last 60 hours of coursework from regionally-accredited college or university, 2 recommendations, resume, valid teaching certificate. Additional exam requirements/recommendations for international students: Required—TOEFL (minimum score 550 paper-based; 213 computer-based; 80 iBT). *Application deadline:* For fall admission, 7/1 priority date for domestic students, 7/1 for international students; for winter admission, 7/1 for international students; for spring admission, 11/1 priority date for domestic students. Applications are processed on a rolling basis. Application fee: $80. Electronic applications accepted. *Expenses:* Contact institution. *Financial support:* In 2011–12, 20 students received support. Career-related internships or fieldwork, Federal Work-Study, scholarships/grants, and health care benefits available. Financial award application deadline: 3/1; financial award applicants required to submit FAFSA. *Faculty research:* The role of the school leader in data analysis of student achievement, teacher recruitment, teacher effectiveness. *Unit head:* Dr. Sharyn Disabato, Director, 352-588-8309, Fax: 352-588-8861, E-mail: med@saintleo.edu. *Application contact:* Jared Welling, Director of Graduate Admission, 800-707-8846, Fax: 352-588-7873, E-mail: grad.admissions@saintleo.edu. Web site: http://www.saintleo.edu/Academics/School-of-Education-Social-Services/Graduate-Degree-Programs.

Saint Louis University, Graduate Education, College of Education and Public Service and Graduate Education, Department of Educational Leadership and Higher Education, St. Louis, MO 63103-2097. Offers Catholic school leadership (MA); educational administration (MA, Ed D, PhD, Ed S); higher education (MA, Ed D, PhD); student personnel administration (MA). *Accreditation:* NCATE. Part-time programs available. *Degree requirements:* For master's, comprehensive written and oral exam; for doctorate, comprehensive exam, thesis/dissertation, preliminary oral and written exams. *Entrance requirements:* For master's, GRE General Test, MAT, LSAT, GMAT or MCAT, letters of recommendation, resume; for doctorate and Ed S, GRE General Test, LSAT, GMAT or MCAT, letters of recommendation, resumé, goal statement, transcripts. Additional exam requirements/recommendations for international students: Required—

TOEFL (minimum score 525 paper-based; 194 computer-based). Electronic applications accepted. *Faculty research:* Superintendent of schools, school finance, school facilities, student personal administration, building leadership.

Salem State University, School of Graduate Studies, Program in Higher Education in Student Affairs, Salem, MA 01970-5353. Offers M Ed. Part-time and evening/weekend programs available. *Entrance requirements:* For master's, GRE or MAT. Additional exam requirements/recommendations for international students: Required—TOEFL (minimum score 550 paper-based; 80 iBT) or IELTS (minimum score 5.5).

Sam Houston State University, College of Education, Department of Educational Leadership and Counseling, Huntsville, TX 77341. Offers administration (M Ed); counseling (M Ed, MA); counselor education (PhD); developmental education administration (Ed D); educational leadership (Ed D); higher education administration (MA); instructional leadership (M Ed, MA). Part-time programs available. *Faculty:* 27 full-time (17 women), 27 part-time/adjunct (14 women). *Students:* 98 full-time (78 women), 474 part-time (378 women); includes 182 minority (101 Black or African American, non-Hispanic/Latino; 10 American Indian or Alaska Native, non-Hispanic/Latino; 8 Asian, non-Hispanic/Latino; 63 Hispanic/Latino), 8 international. Average age 37. 407 applicants, 61% accepted, 194 enrolled. In 2011, 166 master's, 25 doctorates awarded. *Entrance requirements:* For master's, GRE General Test. Additional exam requirements/recommendations for international students: Required—TOEFL (minimum score 550 paper-based; 213 computer-based; 79 iBT). *Application deadline:* For fall admission, 8/1 for domestic students, 6/25 for international students; for spring admission, 12/1 for domestic students, 11/12 for international students. Applications are processed on a rolling basis. Application fee: $45 ($75 for international students). Electronic applications accepted. *Expenses:* Tuition, state resident: full-time $4420; part-time $221 per credit hour. Tuition, nonresident: full-time $10,680; part-time $534 per credit hour. *Required fees:* $329 per credit hour. *Financial support:* Career-related internships or fieldwork, Federal Work-Study, and institutionally sponsored loans available. Support available to part-time students. Financial award application deadline: 5/31; financial award applicants required to submit FAFSA. *Unit head:* Dr. Stacey Edmonson, Chair, 936-294-1752, Fax: 936-294-3886, E-mail: edu_sle01@shsu.edu. *Application contact:* Dr. Stacey Edmondson, Advisor, 936-294-1752, E-mail: sedmonson@shsu.edu. Web site: http://www.shsu.edu/~edu_elc/.

San Diego State University, Graduate and Research Affairs, College of Education, Department of Administration, Rehabilitation and Post-Secondary Education, San Diego, CA 92182. Offers educational leadership in post-secondary education (MA); rehabilitation counseling (MS), including deafness. Evening/weekend programs available. Postbaccalaureate distance learning degree programs offered. *Degree requirements:* For master's, comprehensive exam (for some programs), thesis (for some programs). *Entrance requirements:* For master's, GRE General Test, letters of reference. Additional exam requirements/recommendations for international students: Required—TOEFL. Electronic applications accepted. *Faculty research:* Rehabilitation in cultural diversity, distance learning technology.

San Jose State University, Graduate Studies and Research, Connie L. Lurie College of Education, Department of Educational Leadership, San Jose, CA 95192-0001. Offers educational administration (K-12) (MA); higher education administration (MA). *Accreditation:* NCATE. *Degree requirements:* For master's, thesis or alternative. Electronic applications accepted.

Seton Hall University, College of Education and Human Services, Department of Education Leadership, Management and Policy, Program in Higher Education Administration, South Orange, NJ 07079-2697. Offers Ed D, PhD. *Accreditation:* NCATE. Part-time and evening/weekend programs available. *Faculty:* 12 full-time (4 women), 1 part-time/adjunct (0 women). *Students:* 14 full-time (8 women), 62 part-time (39 women); includes 19 minority (13 Black or African American, non-Hispanic/Latino; 6 Hispanic/Latino), 9 international. Average age 41. 26 applicants, 81% accepted, 16 enrolled. In 2011, 6 doctorates awarded. *Degree requirements:* For doctorate, comprehensive exam, thesis/dissertation, internship. *Entrance requirements:* For doctorate, GRE or MAT, interview, minimum GPA of 3.5. Additional exam requirements/recommendations for international students: Required—TOEFL. *Application deadline:* For fall admission, 2/1 priority date for domestic students; for spring admission, 10/1 for domestic students. Applications are processed on a rolling basis. Application fee: $50. *Expenses: Tuition:* Part-time $1033 per credit hour. *Required fees:* $85 per semester. *Financial support:* In 2011–12, 7 research assistantships with tuition reimbursements (averaging $5,000 per year) were awarded. Financial award application deadline: 2/1. *Unit head:* Dr. Michael Osnato, Chair, 973-275-2446, E-mail: osnatomi@shu.edu. *Application contact:* Dr. Manina Urgolo Huckvale, Associate Dean, 973-761-9668, Fax: 973-275-2187, E-mail: manina.urgolo-huckvale@shu.edu. Web site: http://www.shu.edu.

Shippensburg University of Pennsylvania, School of Graduate Studies, College of Arts and Sciences, Department of Sociology and Anthropology, Shippensburg, PA 17257-2299. Offers organizational development and leadership (MS), including business, communications, environmental management, higher education structure and policy, historical administration, individual and organizational development, management information systems, public organizations, social structures and organizations. Part-time and evening/weekend programs available. *Faculty:* 3 full-time (all women). *Students:* 12 full-time (6 women), 40 part-time (34 women); includes 6 minority (3 Black or African American, non-Hispanic/Latino; 2 Asian, non-Hispanic/Latino; 1 Two or more races, non-Hispanic/Latino), 2 international. Average age 33. 52 applicants, 46% accepted, 16 enrolled. In 2011, 34 master's awarded. *Degree requirements:* For master's, capstone experience including internship. *Entrance requirements:* For master's, interview (if GPA less than 2.75), resume, personal goals statement. Additional exam requirements/recommendations for international students: Required—TOEFL (minimum score 580 paper-based; 237 computer-based); Recommended—IELTS (minimum score 6). *Application deadline:* For fall admission, 4/30 for international students; for spring admission, 9/30 for international students. Applications are processed on a rolling basis. Application fee: $30. Electronic applications accepted. *Expenses: Tuition, area resident:* Part-time $416 per credit. Tuition, state resident: part-time $416 per credit. Tuition, nonresident: part-time $624 per credit. *Required fees:* $119 per credit. *Financial support:* In 2011–12, 9 research assistantships with full tuition reimbursements (averaging $5,000 per year) were awarded; career-related internships or fieldwork, scholarships/grants, unspecified assistantships, and resident hall director and student payroll positions also available. Support available to part-time students. Financial award applicants required to submit FAFSA. *Unit head:* Dr. Barbara Denison, Program Coordinator, 717-477-1735, Fax: 717-477-4011, E-mail: bjdeni@ship.edu. *Application contact:* Jeremy R. Goshorn, Assistant Dean of Graduate Admissions, 717-477-1231, Fax: 717-477-4016, E-mail: jrgoshorn@ship.edu. Web site: http://www.ship.edu/odl/.

Southeast Missouri State University, School of Graduate Studies, Department of Educational Leadership and Counseling, Program in Educational Administration, Cape Girardeau, MO 63701-4799. Offers educational administration (Ed S); educational leadership development (Ed S); elementary administration and supervision (MA); higher education administration (MA); secondary administration and supervision (MA); teacher leadership (MA). *Accreditation:* NCATE. Part-time and evening/weekend programs available. Postbaccalaureate distance learning degree programs offered (minimal on-campus study). *Faculty:* 12 full-time (7 women). *Students:* 32 full-time (23 women), 172 part-time (122 women); includes 10 minority (6 Black or African American, non-Hispanic/Latino; 3 Asian, non-Hispanic/Latino; 1 Hispanic/Latino), 1 international. Average age 34. 62 applicants, 95% accepted, 51 enrolled. In 2011, 34 master's, 13 other advanced degrees awarded. *Degree requirements:* For master's, comprehensive exam (for some programs), thesis (for some programs), minimum GPA of 3.25; paper, portfolio or oral exam (for some programs); for Ed S, comprehensive exam. *Entrance requirements:* For master's, minimum undergraduate GPA of 2.75, valid teacher certification; for Ed S, GRE General Test, PRAXIS or MAT, minimum graduate GPA of 3.5; master's degree; valid teaching certificate. Additional exam requirements/recommendations for international students: Required—TOEFL (minimum score 550 paper-based; 213 computer-based; 79 iBT); Recommended—IELTS (minimum score 6). *Application deadline:* For fall admission, 8/1 for domestic students, 7/1 for international students; for spring admission, 11/21 for domestic students, 11/1 for international students. Applications are processed on a rolling basis. Application fee: $30 ($40 for international students). Electronic applications accepted. *Expenses:* Tuition, state resident: full-time $4896; part-time $272 per credit hour. Tuition, nonresident: full-time $8649; part-time $480.50 per credit hour. *Financial support:* In 2011–12, 16 students received support. Career-related internships or fieldwork, Federal Work-Study, scholarships/grants, tuition waivers (full), and unspecified assistantships available. Financial award application deadline: 6/30; financial award applicants required to submit FAFSA. *Faculty research:* Teacher leadership, organizational leadership effectiveness, state assessment and accountability systems. *Unit head:* Dr. David Stader, 573-651-2417, E-mail: dstader@semo.edu. *Application contact:* Alisa Aleen McFerron, Assistant Director of Admissions for Operations, 573-651-5937, Fax: 573-651-5936, E-mail: amcferron@semo.edu. Web site: http://www4.semo.edu/edadmin/admin.

Southern Baptist Theological Seminary, School of Church Ministries, Louisville, KY 40280-0004. Offers Biblical counseling (M Div, MA); children's and family ministry (M Div, MA); Christian education (MA); Christian worship (PhD); church ministries (M Div); church music (MCM); college ministry (M Div, MA); discipleship and family ministry (M Div, MA); education (Ed D); family ministry (D Min, PhD); higher education (PhD); leadership (M Div, MA, D Min, PhD); ministry (D Ed Min); missions and ethnodoxology (M Div); women's leadership (M Div, MA); worship leadership (M Div, MA); worship leadership and church ministry (MA); youth and family ministry (M Div, MA). Part-time programs available. Postbaccalaureate distance learning degree programs offered (minimal on-campus study). *Faculty:* 10 full-time (2 women), 5 part-time/adjunct (2 women). *Students:* 393. *Degree requirements:* For doctorate, thesis/dissertation. *Entrance requirements:* For doctorate, GRE General Test, interview, M Div or MACE. Additional exam requirements/recommendations for international students: Required—TWE. *Application deadline:* For fall admission, 7/15 priority date for domestic students; for spring admission, 12/1 for domestic students. Applications are processed on a rolling basis. Application fee: $35. *Financial support:* Research assistantships, teaching assistantships, career-related internships or fieldwork, institutionally sponsored loans, and tuition waivers (partial) available. Financial award application deadline: 4/1. *Faculty research:* Gerontology, creative teaching methods, faith development in children, faith development in youth, transformational learning. *Unit head:* Dr. Randy Stinson, Dean, 800-626-5525, E-mail: rstinson@sbts.edu. *Application contact:* John Powell, Director of Admissions and Recruiting, 800-626-5525 Ext. 4617. Web site: http://www.sbts.edu/church-ministries/.

Southern Illinois University Carbondale, Graduate School, College of Education and Human Services, Department of Educational Administration and Higher Education, Program in Higher Education, Carbondale, IL 62901-4701. Offers MS Ed. *Accreditation:* NCATE. Part-time programs available. *Faculty:* 9 full-time (3 women). *Students:* 25 full-time (17 women), 5 part-time (3 women); includes 7 minority (6 Black or African American, non-Hispanic/Latino; 1 Hispanic/Latino), 1 international. Average age 26. 18 applicants, 83% accepted, 7 enrolled. In 2011, 20 master's awarded. *Degree requirements:* For master's, thesis. *Entrance requirements:* For master's, GRE General Test or MAT, minimum GPA of 2.7. Additional exam requirements/recommendations for international students: Required—TOEFL. *Application deadline:* For fall admission, 5/15 for domestic students; for spring admission, 9/15 for domestic students. Applications are processed on a rolling basis. Application fee: $20. *Financial support:* In 2011–12, 15 students received support. Fellowships with full tuition reimbursements available, research assistantships with full tuition reimbursements available, teaching assistantships with full tuition reimbursements available, Federal Work-Study, institutionally sponsored loans, tuition waivers (full), and unspecified assistantships available. Support available to part-time students. Financial award application deadline: 4/1. *Faculty research:* Student affairs administration, international education, community college teaching. *Unit head:* Dr. W. Bradley Colwell, Chair, 618-536-4434, Fax: 618-453-4338, E-mail: bcolwell@siu.edu. *Application contact:* Debra Mibb, Admissions Secretary, 618-536-4434, Fax: 618-453-4338, E-mail: dmibb@siu.edu.

Southern Illinois University Edwardsville, Graduate School, College of Arts and Sciences, Department of Mathematics and Statistics, Edwardsville, IL 62026. Offers mathematics (MS), including computational mathematics, postsecondary mathematics education, pure math, statistics and operations research. Part-time programs available. *Faculty:* 19 full-time (5 women). *Students:* 13 full-time (2 women), 30 part-time (17 women); includes 2 minority (both Black or African American, non-Hispanic/Latino), 12 international. 34 applicants, 47% accepted. In 2011, 14 master's awarded. *Degree requirements:* For master's, thesis (for some programs), research paper/project. *Entrance requirements:* Additional exam requirements/recommendations for international students: Required—TOEFL (minimum score 550 paper-based; 213 computer-based; 79 iBT), IELTS (minimum score 6.5). *Application deadline:* For fall admission, 7/22 for domestic students, 6/1 for international students; for spring admission, 12/9 for domestic students, 10/1 for international students. Applications are processed on a rolling basis. Application fee: $30. Electronic applications accepted. Tuition and fees vary according to course load and program. *Financial support:* In 2011–12, 3 research assistantships with full tuition reimbursements (averaging $9,927 per year), 22 teaching assistantships with full tuition reimbursements (averaging $9,927 per year) were awarded; fellowships with full tuition reimbursements, institutionally sponsored loans, scholarships/grants, and unspecified assistantships also available. Financial award application deadline: 3/1; financial award applicants required to submit FAFSA. *Unit head:* Dr. Krzysztof Jarosz, Chair, 618-650-2354, E-mail: kjarosz@siue.edu. *Application contact:* Dr. Adam Weyhaupt, Director, 618-650-2220, E-mail: aweyhau@siue.edu. Web site: http://www.siue.edu/artsandsciences/math/.

Stanford University, School of Education, Program in Social Sciences, Policy, and Educational Practice, Stanford, CA 94305-9991. Offers administration and policy analysis (Ed D, PhD); anthropology of education (PhD); economics of education (PhD); educational linguistics (PhD); evaluation (MA), including interdisciplinary studies; higher education (PhD); history of education (PhD); interdisciplinary studies (PhD); international comparative education (MA, PhD); international education administration and policy analysis (MA); philosophy of education (PhD); policy analysis (MA); prospective principal's program (MA); sociology of education (PhD). *Degree requirements:* For master's, thesis (for some programs); for doctorate, thesis/dissertation. *Entrance requirements:* For master's and doctorate, GRE General Test.

Electronic applications accepted. *Expenses: Tuition:* Full-time $40,050; part-time $890 per credit.

Syracuse University, College of Arts and Sciences, Program in College Science Teaching, Syracuse, NY 13244. Offers PhD. Part-time programs available. *Students:* 5 full-time (3 women), 3 part-time (2 women). Average age 39. 2 applicants, 100% accepted, 1 enrolled. In 2011, 1 degree awarded. *Entrance requirements:* For doctorate, GRE General Test, GRE Subject Test. Additional exam requirements/recommendations for international students: Required—TOEFL (minimum score 100 iBT). *Application deadline:* For fall admission, 2/1 for international students. Applications are processed on a rolling basis. Application fee: $75. Electronic applications accepted. *Expenses: Tuition:* Part-time $1206 per credit. *Financial support:* Fellowships with full tuition reimbursements and teaching assistantships with full and partial tuition reimbursements available. Financial award application deadline: 1/1; financial award applicants required to submit FAFSA. *Unit head:* Dr. Joanna Masingila, Chair, 315-443-1483, E-mail: jomasing@syr.edu. *Application contact:* Cynthia Daley, Information Contact, 315-443-2586, E-mail: cyndaley@syr.edu. Web site: http://sciteach.syr.edu/.

Syracuse University, School of Education, Program in Higher Education, Syracuse, NY 13244. Offers MS, PhD. Part-time programs available. *Students:* 34 full-time (22 women), 33 part-time (23 women); includes 11 minority (6 Black or African American, non-Hispanic/Latino; 2 Asian, non-Hispanic/Latino; 3 Hispanic/Latino), 4 international. Average age 32. 75 applicants, 75% accepted, 18 enrolled. In 2011, 17 master's, 2 doctorates awarded. *Degree requirements:* For master's, thesis or alternative; for doctorate, thesis/dissertation. *Entrance requirements:* For master's, resume; for doctorate, GRE, resume, interview, writing sample, 3-5 years of experience in higher education administration. Additional exam requirements/recommendations for international students: Required—TOEFL (minimum score 100 iBT). *Application deadline:* For fall admission, 2/1 priority date for domestic students, 2/1 for international students; for spring admission, 10/15 for domestic and international students. Applications are processed on a rolling basis. Application fee: $75. Electronic applications accepted. *Expenses: Tuition:* Part-time $1206 per credit. *Financial support:* Fellowships with full tuition reimbursements, research assistantships with full and partial tuition reimbursements, and teaching assistantships with full and partial tuition reimbursements available. Financial award application deadline: 1/1; financial award applicants required to submit FAFSA. *Faculty research:* Faculty evaluation, teaching portfolios, student culture, college student personnel development, organizational culture. *Unit head:* Dr. Catherine Engstrom, Chair, 315-443-4763, E-mail: cmengstr@syr.edu. *Application contact:* Laurie Deyo, Graduate Recruiter, School of Education, 315-443-2505, E-mail: e-gradrcrt@syr.edu. Web site: http://soeweb.syr.edu/highered/HIGHEREDU/.

Taylor University, Master of Arts in Higher Education Program, Upland, IN 46989-1001. Offers MA. *Accreditation:* NCATE. Part-time programs available. *Faculty:* 1 full-time (0 women), 6 part-time/adjunct (1 woman). *Students:* 35 full-time (19 women), 3 part-time (1 woman); includes 1 minority (Asian, non-Hispanic/Latino), 1 international. Average age 27. 34 applicants, 68% accepted, 19 enrolled. In 2011, 14 master's awarded. *Degree requirements:* For master's, thesis. *Application deadline:* For fall admission, 2/1 for domestic students, 1/1 for international students. Applications are processed on a rolling basis. Application fee: $100. *Expenses: Tuition:* Full-time $9800; part-time $570 per credit hour. *Required fees:* $72 per semester. One-time fee: $100. Tuition and fees vary according to program. *Financial support:* In 2011–12, 12 students received support, including 37 fellowships (averaging $5,800 per year). Financial award applicants required to submit FAFSA. *Unit head:* Dr. Tim Herrmann, Chair, 765-998-5142, E-mail: tmherrmann@taylor.edu. *Application contact:* Cindi Carder, Program Assistant, 765-998-5373, Fax: 765-998-4577, E-mail: jccarder@taylor.edu. Web site: http://www.taylor.edu/mahe.

Teachers College, Columbia University, Graduate Faculty of Education, Department of Organization and Leadership, Program in Higher Education, New York, NY 10027-6696. Offers Ed M, MA, Ed D. *Accreditation:* NCATE. *Faculty:* 2 full-time (1 woman), 11 part-time/adjunct (8 women). *Students:* 36 full-time (27 women), 91 part-time (68 women); includes 49 minority (14 Black or African American, non-Hispanic/Latino; 9 Asian, non-Hispanic/Latino; 24 Hispanic/Latino; 2 Two or more races, non-Hispanic/Latino), 4 international. Average age 30. 183 applicants, 74% accepted, 41 enrolled. In 2011, 66 master's, 5 doctorates awarded. *Degree requirements:* For master's, culminating essay/integrative paper; for doctorate, comprehensive exam, thesis/dissertation. *Entrance requirements:* For doctorate, master's degree, 2 years of professional experience. *Application deadline:* For fall admission, 1/15 priority date for domestic students. Application fee: $65. Electronic applications accepted. *Financial support:* Career-related internships or fieldwork, Federal Work-Study, institutionally sponsored loans, and tuition waivers (full and partial) available. Support available to part-time students. Financial award application deadline: 2/1. *Faculty research:* Educational leadership, general management issues, finance and planning, organizational analysis and development, higher education issues. *Unit head:* Prof. Anna Neumann, Program Coordinator, 212-678-3750, E-mail: highered@tc.edu. *Application contact:* Debbie Lesperance, Assistant Director of Admission, 212-678-3710, Fax: 212-678-4171.

Texas A&M University, College of Education and Human Development, Department of Educational Administration and Human Resource Development, College Station, TX 77843. Offers adult education (PhD); higher education administration (MS, PhD); human resource development (MS, PhD); public school administration (M Ed, Ed D, PhD). Part-time programs available. *Faculty:* 31. *Students:* 126 full-time (88 women), 270 part-time (156 women); includes 162 minority (65 Black or African American, non-Hispanic/Latino; 2 American Indian or Alaska Native, non-Hispanic/Latino; 15 Asian, non-Hispanic/Latino; 77 Hispanic/Latino; 3 Two or more races, non-Hispanic/Latino), 23 international. Average age 37. In 2011, 91 master's, 30 doctorates awarded. *Degree requirements:* For master's, thesis optional; for doctorate, thesis/dissertation. *Entrance requirements:* For master's, GRE General Test, writing exam, interview, professional experience; for doctorate, GRE General Test, writing exam, interview/presentation, professional experience. Additional exam requirements/recommendations for international students: Required—TOEFL. *Application deadline:* For fall admission, 12/1 for domestic and international students; for spring admission, 8/15 for domestic and international students. Application fee: $50 ($75 for international students). Electronic applications accepted. *Expenses:* Tuition, state resident: full-time $5437; part-time $226.55 per credit hour. Tuition, nonresident: full-time $12,949; part-time $539.55 per credit hour. *Required fees:* $2741. *Financial support:* In 2011–12, fellowships (averaging $20,000 per year), research assistantships (averaging $12,000 per year) were awarded; career-related internships or fieldwork and institutionally sponsored loans also available. Support available to part-time students. Financial award application deadline: 3/1; financial award applicants required to submit FAFSA. *Faculty research:* Higher education administration, public school administration, student affairs. *Unit head:* Dr. Fred M. Nafukho, Head, 979-862-3395, Fax: 979-862-4347, E-mail: fnafukho@tamu.edu. *Application contact:* Joyce Nelson, Director of Academic Advising, 979-847-9098, Fax: 979-862-4347, E-mail: jnelson@tamu.edu. Web site: http://eahr.tamu.edu.

Texas A&M University–Commerce, Graduate School, College of Education and Human Services, Department of Educational Leadership, Commerce, TX 75429-3011. Offers educational administration (M Ed, Ed D); educational technology (M Ed, MS); higher education (MS, Ed D); training and development (MS). Part-time programs available. Terminal master's awarded for partial completion of doctoral program. *Degree requirements:* For master's, comprehensive exam, thesis (for some programs); for doctorate, thesis/dissertation, departmental qualifying exam. *Entrance requirements:* For master's, GRE General Test; for doctorate, GRE General Test, writing skills exam, interview. Electronic applications accepted. *Faculty research:* Property tax reform, politics of education, administrative stress.

Texas A&M University–Kingsville, College of Graduate Studies, College of Education, Department of Education, Program in Higher Education Administration Leadership, Kingsville, TX 78363. Offers PhD. Program offered jointly with Texas A&M University. *Degree requirements:* For doctorate, one foreign language, comprehensive exam, thesis/dissertation. *Entrance requirements:* For doctorate, GRE General Test, MAT, minimum GPA of 3.25.

Texas Christian University, College of Education, Ed D in Educational Leadership Program, Fort Worth, TX 76129-0002. Offers educational leadership (Ed D); higher education (Ed D). Part-time and evening/weekend programs available. *Faculty:* 27 full-time (21 women), 1 part-time/adjunct. *Students:* 8 full-time (7 women), 16 part-time (7 women); includes 8 minority (5 Black or African American, non-Hispanic/Latino; 1 American Indian or Alaska Native, non-Hispanic/Latino; 1 Asian, non-Hispanic/Latino; 1 Hispanic/Latino). Average age 37. 15 applicants, 40% accepted, 6 enrolled. In 2011, 7 doctorates awarded. *Degree requirements:* For doctorate, comprehensive exam, thesis/dissertation. *Entrance requirements:* For doctorate, GRE or MAT. Additional exam requirements/recommendations for international students: Required—TOEFL (minimum score 550 paper-based; 213 computer-based; 80 iBT). *Application deadline:* For winter admission, 2/1 for domestic and international students. Application fee: $60. Electronic applications accepted. *Expenses: Tuition:* Full-time $20,250; part-time $1125 per credit hour. Part-time tuition and fees vary according to course load and program. *Financial support:* Teaching assistantships with full tuition reimbursements, career-related internships or fieldwork, scholarships/grants, and unspecified assistantships available. Financial award application deadline: 2/1. *Unit head:* Dr. Jan Lacina, Associate Dean, 817-257-6786, E-mail: j.lacina@tcu.edu. *Application contact:* Patricia Garcia, Academic Program Specialist, 817-257-7661, E-mail: p.m.garcia@tcu.edu. Web site: http://www.coe.tcu.edu/187.asp.

Texas Southern University, College of Education, Department of Educational Administration and Foundation, Houston, TX 77004-4584. Offers educational administration (M Ed, Ed D). Part-time and evening/weekend programs available. *Degree requirements:* For master's, comprehensive exam; for doctorate, comprehensive exam, thesis/dissertation. *Entrance requirements:* For master's, GRE General Test, minimum GPA of 2.5; for doctorate, GRE General Test or MAT, master's degree, minimum B+ average. Additional exam requirements/recommendations for international students: Required—TOEFL. Electronic applications accepted.

Texas State University–San Marcos, Graduate School, College of Education, Department of Counseling, Leadership, Adult Education, and School Psychology, Program of Student Affairs in Higher Education, San Marcos, TX 78666. Offers M Ed. *Accreditation:* ACA. Part-time and evening/weekend programs available. *Faculty:* 2 full-time (1 woman), 3 part-time/adjunct (1 woman). *Students:* 29 full-time (22 women), 13 part-time (all women); includes 12 minority (3 Black or African American, non-Hispanic/Latino; 2 Asian, non-Hispanic/Latino; 5 Hispanic/Latino; 2 Two or more races, non-Hispanic/Latino), 1 international. Average age 29. 39 applicants, 49% accepted, 11 enrolled. In 2011, 41 master's awarded. *Degree requirements:* For master's, comprehensive exam, thesis (for some programs). *Entrance requirements:* For master's, GRE General Test, minimum GPA of 3.0 in last 60 hours of course work. Additional exam requirements/recommendations for international students: Required—TOEFL (minimum score 550 paper-based; 213 computer-based; 78 iBT). *Application deadline:* For fall admission, 4/15 for domestic students, 3/15 for international students; for spring admission, 10/1 for domestic and international students. Applications are processed on a rolling basis. Application fee: $40 ($90 for international students). Electronic applications accepted. *Expenses:* Tuition, state resident: full-time $6408; part-time $3204 per semester. Tuition, nonresident: full-time $14,832; part-time $7416 per semester. *Required fees:* $1824; $912 per semester. Tuition and fees vary according to course load. *Financial support:* In 2011–12, 26 students received support, including 22 research assistantships (averaging $9,720 per year), 1 teaching assistantship (averaging $5,076 per year); career-related internships or fieldwork, Federal Work-Study, and institutionally sponsored loans also available. Support available to part-time students. Financial award application deadline: 4/1; financial award applicants required to submit FAFSA. *Unit head:* Dr. Paige Haber, Graduate Advisor, 512-245-7628, Fax: 512-245-8872, E-mail: ph31@txstate.edu. *Application contact:* Dr. J. Michael Willoughby, Dean of Graduate School, 512-245-2581, Fax: 512-245-8365, E-mail: gradcollege@txstate.edu. Web site: http://www.txstate.edu/clas/Student-Affairs/student-affairs-in-higher-ed2.html.

Texas Tech University, Graduate School, College of Education, Department of Educational Psychology and Leadership, Lubbock, TX 79409. Offers counselor education (M Ed, PhD); educational leadership (M Ed, Ed D); educational psychology (M Ed, PhD); higher education (M Ed, Ed D); higher education: higher education research (PhD); instructional technology (M Ed, Ed D); instructional technology: distance education (M Ed); special education (M Ed, Ed D). *Accreditation:* ACA; NCATE. Part-time programs available. Postbaccalaureate distance learning degree programs offered (no on-campus study). *Students:* 180 full-time (133 women), 418 part-time (297 women); includes 127 minority (34 Black or African American, non-Hispanic/Latino; 3 American Indian or Alaska Native, non-Hispanic/Latino; 6 Asian, non-Hispanic/Latino; 76 Hispanic/Latino; 8 Two or more races, non-Hispanic/Latino), 41 international. Average age 36. 478 applicants, 42% accepted, 134 enrolled. In 2011, 139 master's, 30 doctorates awarded. *Degree requirements:* For master's, thesis optional; for doctorate, thesis/dissertation. *Entrance requirements:* For master's and doctorate, GRE General Test. Additional exam requirements/recommendations for international students: Required—TOEFL (minimum score 550 paper-based; 213 computer-based; 79 iBT). *Application deadline:* For fall admission, 6/1 priority date for domestic students, 1/15 for international students; for spring admission, 9/1 priority date for domestic students, 6/15 for international students. Applications are processed on a rolling basis. Application fee: $50 ($75 for international students). Electronic applications accepted. *Expenses:* Tuition, state resident: full-time $5899; part-time $245.80 per credit hour. Tuition, nonresident: full-time $13,411; part-time $558.80 per credit hour. *Required fees:* $2680.60; $86.50 per credit hour. $920.30 per semester. *Financial support:* In 2011–12, 142 students received support. Application deadline: 4/15; applicants required to submit FAFSA. *Faculty research:* Psychological processes of teaching and learning, teaching populations with special needs, instructional technology, educational administration in education, theories and practice in counseling and counselor education K-12 and higher. *Total annual research expenditures:* $1.4 million. *Unit head:* Dr. William Lan, Chair, 806-742-1998 Ext. 436, Fax: 806-742-2179, E-mail: william.lan@ttu.edu. *Application contact:* Dr. Hansel Burley, Associate Academic Dean, 806-742-1998 Ext. 447, Fax: 806-742-2179, E-mail: hansel.burley@ttu.edu.

Trident University International, College of Education, Program in Education, Cypress, CA 90630. Offers adult education (MA Ed); aviation education (MA Ed); children's literacy development (MA Ed); e-learning (MA Ed); early childhood education (MA Ed); enrollment management (MA Ed); higher education (MA Ed); teaching and instruction (MA Ed); training and development (MA Ed). Part-time and evening/weekend programs available. Postbaccalaureate distance learning degree programs offered (no on-campus study). *Degree requirements:* For master's, capstone project with integrative paper. *Entrance requirements:* For master's, minimum GPA of 2.5 (students with GPA 3.0 or greater may transfer up to 30% of graduate level credits). Additional exam requirements/recommendations for international students: Required—TOEFL (minimum score 525 paper-based). Electronic applications accepted.

Trident University International, College of Education, Program in Educational Leadership, Cypress, CA 90630. Offers e-learning leadership (MA Ed, PhD); educational leadership (MA Ed); higher education leadership (PhD); K-12 leadership (PhD). Part-time and evening/weekend programs available. Postbaccalaureate distance learning degree programs offered (no on-campus study). *Degree requirements:* For doctorate, comprehensive exam, thesis/dissertation, defense of dissertation. *Entrance requirements:* For master's, minimum GPA of 2.5 (students with GPA 3.0 or greater may transfer up to 30% of graduate level credits); for doctorate, minimum GPA of 3.4, course work in research methods or statistics. Additional exam requirements/recommendations for international students: Required—TOEFL. Electronic applications accepted.

Troy University, Graduate School, College of Education, Program in Postsecondary Education, Troy, AL 36082. Offers adult education (M Ed); biology (M Ed); criminal justice (M Ed); English (M Ed); foundations of education (M Ed); general science (M Ed); higher education administration (M Ed); history (M Ed); instructional technology (M Ed); mathematics (M Ed); music industry (M Ed); physical fitness (M Ed); political science (M Ed); public administration (M Ed); social science (M Ed); teaching English (M Ed). *Accreditation:* NCATE. Part-time and evening/weekend programs available. *Faculty:* 53 full-time (21 women), 22 part-time/adjunct (8 women). *Students:* 74 full-time (51 women), 166 part-time (121 women); includes 148 minority (143 Black or African American, non-Hispanic/Latino; 1 American Indian or Alaska Native, non-Hispanic/Latino; 2 Hispanic/Latino; 2 Two or more races, non-Hispanic/Latino). Average age 34. 174 applicants, 82% accepted, 88 enrolled. In 2011, 221 master's awarded. *Degree requirements:* For master's, comprehensive exam, thesis. *Entrance requirements:* For master's, MAT (minimum score 385), minimum GPA of 2.5. Additional exam requirements/recommendations for international students: Required—TOEFL (minimum score 523 paper-based; 193 computer-based; 70 iBT), IELTS (minimum score 6), or ACT COMPASS ESL (minimum listening, reading, and grammar score 270). *Application deadline:* Applications are processed on a rolling basis. Application fee: $50. Electronic applications accepted. *Expenses:* Tuition, state resident: full-time $6960; part-time $290 per credit hour. Tuition, nonresident: full-time $13,920; part-time $580 per credit hour. *Required fees:* $386 per term. *Financial support:* Available to part-time students. Applicants required to submit FAFSA. *Unit head:* Dr. Jan Oliver, Associate Professor, 334-670-3444, Fax: 334-670-3296, E-mail: oliver@troy.edu. *Application contact:* Brenda K. Campbell, Director of Graduate Admissions, 334-670-3178, Fax: 334-670-3733, E-mail: bcamp@troy.edu.

Union Institute & University, Education Programs, Cincinnati, OH 45206-1925. Offers adult and higher education (M Ed); curriculum and instruction (M Ed); educational leadership (M Ed, Ed D); guidance and counseling (Ed S); higher education (Ed D); issues in education (M Ed); reading (Ed S). M Ed offered online and in Vermont and Florida, concentrations vary by location; Ed S offered in Florida; Ed D program is a hybrid (online with limited residency) offered in Ohio. Postbaccalaureate distance learning degree programs offered (minimal on-campus study). *Degree requirements:* For master's, comprehensive exam (for some programs), thesis (for some programs), electronic portfolio; for doctorate, comprehensive exam, thesis/dissertation, electronic portfolio.

Union University, School of Education, Jackson, TN 38305-3697. Offers education (M Ed, MA Ed); education administration generalist (Ed S); educational leadership (Ed D); educational supervision (Ed S); higher education (Ed D). M Ed also available at Germantown campus. *Accreditation:* NCATE. Part-time and evening/weekend programs available. *Degree requirements:* For master's, thesis (for some programs), capstone research course; for doctorate, comprehensive exam, thesis/dissertation; for Ed S, thesis or alternative. *Entrance requirements:* For master's, MAT, PRAXIS II or GRE, minimum GPA of 3.0, teaching license, writing sample; for doctorate, GRE, minimum graduate GPA of 3.2, writing sample; for Ed S, PRAXIS II, minimum graduate GPA of 3.2, writing sample. *Faculty research:* Mathematics education, direct instruction, language disorders and special education, brain compatible learning, empathy and school leadership.

United States University, School of Education, Cypress, CA 90630. Offers administration (MA Ed); early childhood education (MA Ed); general (MA Ed); higher education administration (MA Ed); Spanish language education (MA Ed); special education (MA Ed). *Degree requirements:* For master's, portfolio. *Entrance requirements:* For master's, minimum undergraduate GPA of 2.5. Additional exam requirements/recommendations for international students: Required—TOEFL (minimum score 500 paper-based; 173 computer-based; 61 iBT).

Universidad Central del Este, Graduate School, San Pedro de Macoris, Dominican Republic. Offers environmental engineering (ME); financial management (M Ad); higher education (M Ed), including higher education management, higher education pedagogy; human resources (M Ad). *Entrance requirements:* For master's, letters of recommendation.

Université de Sherbrooke, Faculty of Education, Program in Postsecondary Education Training, Sherbrooke, QC J1K 2R1, Canada. Offers M Ed, Diploma. *Degree requirements:* For master's, thesis.

University at Buffalo, the State University of New York, Graduate School, Graduate School of Education, Department of Educational Leadership and Policy, Buffalo, NY 14260. Offers educational administration (Ed M, PhD); educational culture, policy and society (PhD); general education (Ed M); higher education administration (Ed M, PhD); school building leadership (LIFTS) (Certificate); school business and human resource administration (Certificate); school district business leadership (LIFTS) (Certificate); school district leadership (LIFTS) (Certificate). Part-time and evening/weekend programs available. *Faculty:* 12 full-time (7 women), 9 part-time/adjunct (7 women). *Students:* 79 full-time (55 women), 136 part-time (76 women); includes 47 minority (24 Black or African American, non-Hispanic/Latino; 1 American Indian or Alaska Native, non-Hispanic/Latino; 9 Asian, non-Hispanic/Latino; 13 Hispanic/Latino), 17 international. Average age 35. 194 applicants, 40% accepted, 73 enrolled. In 2011, 44 master's, 18 doctorates, 25 other advanced degrees awarded. *Degree requirements:* For master's, comprehensive exam (for some programs), thesis optional; for doctorate, comprehensive exam, thesis/dissertation. *Entrance requirements:* For doctorate, GRE General Test or MAT, writing sample. Additional exam requirements/recommendations for international students: Required—TOEFL (minimum score 550 paper-based; 213 computer-based; 79 iBT). *Application deadline:* For fall admission, 3/1 priority date for domestic students, 3/1 for international students; for spring admission, 11/15 priority date for domestic students, 10/1 for international students. Applications are processed on a rolling basis. Application fee: $50. Electronic applications accepted. *Financial support:* In 2011–12, 21 fellowships (averaging $10,298 per year), 9 research assistantships (averaging $11,955 per year) were awarded; career-related internships or fieldwork, Federal Work-Study, institutionally sponsored loans, health care benefits, and unspecified assistantships also available. Financial award application deadline: 3/15; financial award applicants required to submit FAFSA. *Faculty research:* College access and choice, school leadership preparation and practice, public policy, curriculum and pedagogy, comparative and international education. *Unit head:* Dr. William C. Barba, Chairman, 716-645-2471, Fax: 716-645-2481, E-mail: barba@buffalo.edu. *Application contact:* Bonnie Reed, Admissions Assistant, 716-645-2110, Fax: 716-645-7937, E-mail: brfisher@buffalo.edu. Web site: http://gse.buffalo.edu/elp.

The University of Akron, Graduate School, College of Education, Department of Educational Foundations and Leadership, Program in Higher Education Administration, Akron, OH 44325. Offers MA, MS. *Accreditation:* NCATE. *Students:* 45 full-time (28 women), 40 part-time (26 women); includes 19 minority (15 Black or African American, non-Hispanic/Latino; 2 Hispanic/Latino; 2 Two or more races, non-Hispanic/Latino), 1 international. Average age 32. 43 applicants, 65% accepted, 15 enrolled. In 2011, 42 master's awarded. *Degree requirements:* For master's, comprehensive exam. *Entrance requirements:* For master's, GRE, minimum GPA of 2.75, declaration of intent that includes statement of professional goals and reasons for choosing the field of higher education administration and The University of Akron. Additional exam requirements/recommendations for international students: Required—TOEFL (minimum score 550 paper-based; 213 computer-based; 79 iBT). *Application deadline:* Applications are processed on a rolling basis. Application fee: $30 ($40 for international students). Electronic applications accepted. *Expenses:* Tuition, state resident: full-time $7038; part-time $391 per credit hour. Tuition, nonresident: full-time $12,051; part-time $670 per credit hour. *Required fees:* $1274; $34 per credit hour. *Financial support:* Fellowships, research assistantships, and teaching assistantships available. *Unit head:* Dr. Sharon Kruse, Coordinator, 330-972-8177, E-mail: skruse@uakron.edu. *Application contact:* Dr. Mark Tausig, Associate Dean, 330-972-6266, Fax: 330-972-6475, E-mail: mtausig@uakron.edu.

The University of Alabama, Graduate School, College of Education, Department of Educational Leadership, Policy, and Technology Studies, Higher Education Administration Program, Tuscaloosa, AL 35487. Offers MA, Ed D, PhD. Evening/weekend programs available. *Faculty:* 8 full-time (3 women), 1 part-time/adjunct (0 women). *Students:* 54 full-time (25 women), 89 part-time (53 women); includes 28 minority (21 Black or African American, non-Hispanic/Latino; 2 American Indian or Alaska Native, non-Hispanic/Latino; 2 Asian, non-Hispanic/Latino; 1 Hispanic/Latino; 2 Two or more races, non-Hispanic/Latino), 1 international. Average age 37. 62 applicants, 61% accepted, 22 enrolled. In 2011, 13 master's, 11 doctorates awarded. Terminal master's awarded for partial completion of doctoral program. *Degree requirements:* For master's, comprehensive exam; for doctorate, comprehensive exam, thesis/dissertation. *Entrance requirements:* For master's, GRE, MAT or GMAT; for doctorate, GRE or MAT. Application fee: $50 ($60 for international students). Electronic applications accepted. *Expenses:* Tuition, state resident: full-time $8600. Tuition, nonresident: full-time $21,900. *Financial support:* In 2011–12, 5 students received support. Career-related internships or fieldwork, scholarships/grants, and unspecified assistantships available. *Unit head:* Dr. Claire H. Major, Coordinator and Associate Professor, 205-348-6871, Fax: 205-348-2161, E-mail: bea@bamaed.ua.edu. *Application contact:* Donna Smith, Administration Assistant, 205-348-6871, Fax: 205-348-2161, E-mail: dbsmith@bamaed.ua.edu.

The University of Arizona, College of Education, Department of Educational Policy Studies and Practice, Program in Higher Education, Tucson, AZ 85721. Offers MA, PhD. *Faculty:* 9 full-time (4 women). *Students:* 71 full-time (48 women), 24 part-time (13 women); includes 38 minority (9 Black or African American, non-Hispanic/Latino; 1 American Indian or Alaska Native, non-Hispanic/Latino; 2 Asian, non-Hispanic/Latino; 14 Hispanic/Latino; 12 Two or more races, non-Hispanic/Latino), 4 international. Average age 35. 88 applicants, 40% accepted, 18 enrolled. In 2011, 10 master's, 4 doctorates awarded. Terminal master's awarded for partial completion of doctoral program. *Degree requirements:* For master's, comprehensive exam, thesis; for doctorate, comprehensive exam, thesis/dissertation. *Entrance requirements:* For master's, GRE General Test or MAT, minimum undergraduate GPA of 3.0; for doctorate, GRE General Test or MAT, minimum undergraduate GPA of 3.0, graduate 3.5. Additional exam requirements/recommendations for international students: Required—TOEFL (minimum score 550 paper-based; 213 computer-based; 79 iBT). *Application deadline:* For fall admission, 1/15 for domestic and international students. Applications are processed on a rolling basis. Application fee: $75. Electronic applications accepted. *Expenses:* Tuition, state resident: full-time $10,840. Tuition, nonresident: full-time $25,802. *Financial support:* Research assistantships with full tuition reimbursements, teaching assistantships with full tuition reimbursements, career-related internships or fieldwork, scholarships/grants, health care benefits, tuition waivers (partial), and unspecified assistantships available. Financial award application deadline: 4/30. *Faculty research:* Technology transfer, higher education policy, finance, curricular change. *Total annual research expenditures:* $112,593. *Unit head:* Dr. John Cheslock, Professor and Interim Department Head, 520-626-7313, Fax: 520-621-1875, E-mail: grhoades@mail.ed.arizona.edu. *Application contact:* Sara J. Kersels, Administrative Assistant, 520-626-7313, Fax: 520-621-1875, E-mail: skersels@email.arizona.edu. Web site: http://grad.arizona.edu/live/programs/description/76.

University of Arkansas, Graduate School, College of Education and Health Professions, Department of Rehabilitation, Human Resources and Communication Disorders, Program in Higher Education, Fayetteville, AR 72701-1201. Offers M Ed, Ed D, Ed S. *Accreditation:* NCATE. Part-time and evening/weekend programs available. *Students:* 32 full-time (24 women), 69 part-time (42 women); includes 25 minority (17 Black or African American, non-Hispanic/Latino; 1 American Indian or Alaska Native, non-Hispanic/Latino; 1 Asian, non-Hispanic/Latino; 3 Hispanic/Latino; 3 Two or more races, non-Hispanic/Latino), 4 international. In 2011, 21 master's, 14 doctorates awarded. *Degree requirements:* For master's, thesis optional; for doctorate, thesis/dissertation. *Entrance requirements:* For master's, GRE General Test, MAT or minimum GPA of 3.0; for doctorate, GRE General Test or MAT. *Application deadline:* For fall admission, 4/1 for international students; for spring admission, 10/1 for international students. Applications are processed on a rolling basis. Application fee: $40 ($50 for international students). Electronic applications accepted. *Financial support:* In 2011–12, 30 research assistantships, 1 teaching assistantship were awarded; fellowships with tuition reimbursements, career-related internships or fieldwork, and Federal Work-Study also available. Support available to part-time students. Financial award application deadline: 4/1; financial award applicants required to submit FAFSA. *Unit head:* Dr. Fran Hagstrom, Departmental Chairperson, 479-575-4758, Fax: 479-575-2492, E-mail: fhagstr@uark.edu. *Application contact:* Dr. Brent Williams, Graduate Coordinator, 479-575-4758, E-mail: btwilli@uark.edu. Web site: http://hied.uark.edu.

University of Arkansas at Little Rock, Graduate School, College of Education, Department of Educational Leadership, Program in Higher Education Administration, Little Rock, AR 72204-1099. Offers Ed D. *Degree requirements:* For doctorate, comprehensive exam, oral defense of dissertation, residency. *Entrance requirements:* For doctorate, GRE General Test or MAT, interview, minimum graduate GPA of 3.0, teaching certificate, work experience.

The University of British Columbia, Faculty of Education, Department of Educational Studies, Vancouver, BC V6T 1Z1, Canada. Offers adult education (M Ed, MA); adult learning and global change (M Ed); educational administration (M Ed, MA); educational leadership and policy (Ed D); educational studies (PhD); higher education (M Ed, MA); society, culture and politics in education (M Ed, MA). Part-time and evening/weekend programs available. Terminal master's awarded for partial completion of doctoral program. *Degree requirements:* For master's, thesis; for doctorate, comprehensive exam, thesis/dissertation, master's thesis. *Entrance requirements:* For master's, minimum B+ average, 4-year undergraduate degree, field-related experience; for doctorate, minimum B+ average, 4-year undergraduate degree, master's degree, field-related experience. Additional exam requirements/recommendations for international students: Required—TOEFL (minimum score 600 paper-based; 250 computer-based; 100 iBT) or IELTS (minimum score 6.5). Electronic applications accepted. *Faculty research:* Educational leadership educational administration adult education politics in education, global change and adult learning.

University of Calgary, Faculty of Graduate Studies, Faculty of Education, Graduate Division of Educational Research, Calgary, AB T2N 1N4, Canada. Offers community rehabilitation and disability studies (M Ed, M Sc, Ed D, PhD, Graduate Certificate, Graduate Diploma); curriculum, teaching and learning (M Ed, M Sc, MA, Ed D, PhD, Graduate Certificate, Graduate Diploma); educational contexts (M Ed, MA, Ed D, PhD, Graduate Certificate, Graduate Diploma); educational leadership (M Ed, MA, Ed D, PhD, Graduate Certificate, Graduate Diploma); educational technology (M Ed, M Sc, MA, Ed D, PhD, Graduate Certificate, Graduate Diploma); gifted education (M Sc, MA, Ed D, PhD, Graduate Certificate, Graduate Diploma); higher education administration (Ed D); interpretive studies in education (M Ed, M Sc, MA, Ed D, PhD, Graduate Certificate, Graduate Diploma); second language teaching (M Ed, Ed D, PhD, Graduate Certificate, Graduate Diploma); teaching English as a second language (M Ed, M Sc, MA, Ed D, PhD, Graduate Certificate, Graduate Diploma); workplace and adult learning (M Ed, MA, Ed D, PhD, Graduate Certificate, Graduate Diploma). Ed D in both higher education administration and educational leadership offered via distance delivery. Part-time and evening/weekend programs available. Postbaccalaureate distance learning degree programs offered (minimal on-campus study). *Degree requirements:* For master's, thesis (for some programs); for doctorate, thesis/dissertation, candidacy exam. *Entrance requirements:* For master's, minimum GPA of 3.0, 3 letters of reference; for doctorate, minimum GPA of 3.5, 3 letters of reference; for other advanced degree, minimum GPA of 3.0. Additional exam requirements/recommendations for international students: Required—TOEFL, IELTS. Electronic applications accepted. *Faculty research:* Curriculum, leadership, technology, contexts, gifted, second language teaching, work place and adult learning.

University of California, Riverside, Graduate Division, Graduate School of Education, Riverside, CA 92521-0102. Offers autism (M Ed); diversity and equity (M Ed); education, society and culture (MA, PhD); educational psychology (MA, PhD); general education (M Ed); higher education administration and policy (M Ed, PhD); reading (M Ed); school psychology (PhD); special education (M Ed, MA, PhD). *Faculty:* 19 full-time (9 women), 9 part-time/adjunct (6 women). *Students:* 181 full-time (128 women); includes 79 minority (8 Black or African American, non-Hispanic/Latino; 1 American Indian or Alaska Native, non-Hispanic/Latino; 26 Asian, non-Hispanic/Latino; 34 Hispanic/Latino; 10 Two or more races, non-Hispanic/Latino), 5 international. Average age 31. 200 applicants, 48% accepted, 76 enrolled. In 2011, 67 master's, 12 doctorates awarded. Terminal master's awarded for partial completion of doctoral program. *Degree requirements:* For master's, thesis optional, comprehensive exams or thesis (MA), case study or analytical report (M Ed); for doctorate, thesis/dissertation, written and oral qualifying exams, college teaching practicum. *Entrance requirements:* For master's, GRE General Test, CBEST, CSET, minimum GPA of 3.2; for doctorate, GRE General Test, master's degree (desirable), minimum GPA of 3.2. Additional exam requirements/recommendations for international students: Required—TOEFL (minimum score 550 paper-based; 213 computer-based; 80 iBT), IELTS (minimum score 7). *Application deadline:* For fall admission, 9/1 for domestic students, 4/1 for international students; for winter admission, 12/1 for domestic students, 7/1 for international students; for spring admission, 3/1 for domestic students, 10/1 for international students. Applications are processed on a rolling basis. Application fee: $80 ($100 for international students). Electronic applications accepted. *Financial support:* In 2011–12, 59 students received support, including 9 fellowships with full and partial tuition reimbursements available (averaging $26,587 per year), 21 research assistantships with full and partial tuition reimbursements available (averaging $14,517 per year), 1 teaching assistantship with full and partial tuition reimbursement available (averaging $17,307 per year); career-related internships or fieldwork, Federal Work-Study, institutionally sponsored loans, scholarships/grants, and unspecified assistantships also available. Financial award application deadline: 1/5. *Faculty research:* Responsiveness to intervention, faculty core, response to intervention of English language learners, advanced modeling techniques, study on social capital, trust, and motivation. *Total annual research expenditures:* $2.8 million. *Unit head:* Prof. Douglas Mitchell, Interim Dean, 951-827-5802, Fax: 951-827-3942, E-mail: douglas.mitchell@ucr.edu. *Application contact:* Prof. Robert Ream, Graduate Advisor for Admission, 951-827-6362, Fax: 951-827-3291, E-mail: edgrad@ucr.edu. Web site: http://www.education.ucr.edu/.

University of Central Florida, College of Education, Department of Educational and Human Sciences, Program in Educational Leadership, Orlando, FL 32816. Offers educational leadership (MA, Ed D), including community college education (MA), higher education (Ed D), student personnel (MA). Part-time and evening/weekend programs available. *Students:* 82 full-time (55 women), 179 part-time (126 women); includes 53 minority (27 Black or African American, non-Hispanic/Latino; 3 Asian, non-Hispanic/Latino; 19 Hispanic/Latino; 4 Two or more races, non-Hispanic/Latino), 1 international. Average age 35. 142 applicants, 69% accepted, 62 enrolled. In 2011, 60 master's, 26 doctorates awarded. *Degree requirements:* For master's, thesis or alternative; for doctorate, thesis/dissertation, candidacy exam. *Entrance requirements:* For master's, GRE General Test; for doctorate, GRE General Test, GRE Subject Test, minimum GPA of 3.0, resume. Additional exam requirements/recommendations for international students: Required—TOEFL. *Application deadline:* For fall admission, 2/20 priority date for domestic students; for spring admission, 9/20 priority date for domestic students. Application fee: $30. Electronic applications accepted. *Expenses:* Tuition, state resident: part-time $277.08 per credit hour. Tuition, nonresident: part-time $277.08 per credit hour. Part-time tuition and fees vary according to degree level and program. *Financial support:* In 2011–12, 17 students received support, including 4 fellowships with partial tuition reimbursements available (averaging $8,300 per year), 14 research assistantships with partial tuition reimbursements available (averaging $7,000 per year), 2 teaching assistantships with partial tuition reimbursements available (averaging $1,000 per year); career-related internships or fieldwork, Federal Work-Study, institutionally sponsored loans, tuition waivers (partial), and unspecified assistantships also available. Financial award application deadline: 3/1; financial award applicants required to submit FAFSA. *Unit head:* Dr. Rosa Cintron, Program Coordinator, 407-832-1248, E-mail: rosa.cintrondelgado@ucf.edu. *Application contact:* Barbara Rodriguez, Director, Admissions and Registration, 407-823-2766, Fax: 407-823-6442, E-mail: gradadmissions@ucf.edu. Web site: http://education.ucf.edu/departments.cfm.

University of Central Florida, College of Education, Education Doctoral Programs, Orlando, FL 32816. Offers communication sciences and disorders (PhD); counselor education (PhD); education (Ed D); elementary education (PhD); exceptional education (PhD); exercise physiology (PhD); higher education (PhD); hospitality education (PhD); instructional technology (PhD); mathematics education (PhD); reading education (PhD); science education (PhD); social science education (PhD); TESOL (PhD). *Students:* 135 full-time (87 women), 73 part-time (51 women); includes 49 minority (21 Black or African American, non-Hispanic/Latino; 4 Asian, non-Hispanic/Latino; 20 Hispanic/Latino; 4 Two or more races, non-Hispanic/Latino), 18 international. Average age 39. 125 applicants, 46% accepted, 46 enrolled. In 2011, 43 doctorates awarded. Application fee: $30. Electronic applications accepted. *Expenses:* Tuition, state resident: part-time $277.08 per credit hour. Tuition, nonresident: part-time $277.08 per credit hour. Part-time tuition and fees vary according to degree level and program. *Financial support:* In 2011–12, 85 students received support, including 48 fellowships with partial tuition reimbursements available (averaging $5,900 per year), 36 research assistantships with partial tuition reimbursements available (averaging $6,900 per year), 59 teaching assistantships with partial tuition reimbursements available (averaging $6,900 per year). *Unit head:* Dr. Rex Culp, Associate Dean, 407-823-5391, E-mail: rex.culp@ucf.edu. *Application contact:* Barbara Rodriguez, Associate Director, Admissions and Registration, 407-823-2766, Fax: 407-823-6442, E-mail: gradadmissions@ucf.edu. Web site: http://education.ucf.edu/departments.cfm.

University of Central Oklahoma, College of Graduate Studies and Research, College of Education and Professional Studies, Department of Occupational and Technical Education, Edmond, OK 73034-5209. Offers adult education (M Ed), including community services, gerontology; general education (M Ed); professional health occupations (M Ed). Part-time programs available. *Faculty:* 11 full-time (5 women), 11 part-time/adjunct (6 women). *Students:* 23 full-time (17 women), 76 part-time (59 women); includes 28 minority (15 Black or African American, non-Hispanic/Latino; 4 American Indian or Alaska Native, non-Hispanic/Latino; 6 Hispanic/Latino; 3 Two or more races, non-Hispanic/Latino), 3 international. Average age 40. In 2011, 64 master's awarded. *Entrance requirements:* For master's, GRE General Test. Additional exam requirements/recommendations for international students: Required—TOEFL (minimum score 550 paper-based; 213 computer-based). *Application deadline:* Applications are processed on a rolling basis. Application fee: $50. Electronic applications accepted. *Expenses:* Tuition, state resident: full-time $3901; part-time $218.30 per credit hour. Tuition, nonresident: full-time $9198; part-time $511.20 per credit hour. Tuition and fees vary according to program. *Financial support:* Unspecified assistantships available. Financial award application deadline: 3/31; financial award applicants required to submit FAFSA. *Faculty research:* Violence in the workplace/schools, aging issues, trade and industrial education. *Unit head:* Dr. Candy Sebert, Chairman, 405-974-5780, Fax: 405-974-3822. *Application contact:* Dr. Richard Bernard, Dean, Graduate College, 405-974-3493, Fax: 405-974-3852, E-mail: gradcoll@uco.edu.

University of Connecticut, Graduate School, Neag School of Education, Department of Educational Leadership, Field of Higher Education and Student Affairs, Storrs, CT 06269. Offers MA. *Accreditation:* NCATE. *Degree requirements:* For master's, comprehensive exam, thesis or alternative. *Entrance requirements:* Additional exam requirements/recommendations for international students: Required—TOEFL (minimum score 550 paper-based; 213 computer-based). Electronic applications accepted.

University of Delaware, College of Education and Human Development, School of Education, Newark, DE 19716. Offers education (PhD); educational leadership (Ed D); higher education (M Ed); instruction (MI); reading (M Ed); school leadership (M Ed); school psychology (MA, Ed S); teaching English as a second language (TESL) (MA). *Accreditation:* NCATE. Part-time and evening/weekend programs available. Terminal master's awarded for partial completion of doctoral program. *Degree requirements:* For master's, comprehensive exam (for some programs), thesis (for some programs); for doctorate, comprehensive exam (for some programs), thesis/dissertation. *Entrance requirements:* For master's and doctorate, GRE, 3 letters of recommendation. Additional exam requirements/recommendations for international students: Required—TOEFL (minimum score 600 paper-based; 250 computer-based). Electronic applications accepted. *Faculty research:* Teacher education; curriculum theory and development; community based education models, educational leadership.

University of Denver, Morgridge College of Education, Denver, CO 80208. Offers advanced study in law librarianship (Certificate); child and family studies (MA, PhD); counseling psychology (MA, PhD); curriculum and instruction (MA, PhD, Certificate); educational leadership (Ed D, PhD); educational leadership and policy studies (MA, Certificate); higher education (MA, PhD); library and information science (MLIS); research methods and statistics (MA, PhD); school administration (PhD); school psychology (Ed S). *Accreditation:* ALA; APA (one or more programs are accredited). Part-time and evening/weekend programs available. Postbaccalaureate distance learning degree programs offered (no on-campus study). *Faculty:* 34 full-time (25 women), 70 part-time/adjunct (54 women). *Students:* 385 full-time (289 women), 386 part-time (303 women); includes 168 minority (49 Black or African American, non-Hispanic/Latino; 8 American Indian or Alaska Native, non-Hispanic/Latino; 25 Asian, non-Hispanic/Latino; 71 Hispanic/Latino; 1 Native Hawaiian or other Pacific Islander, non-Hispanic/Latino; 14 Two or more races, non-Hispanic/Latino), 17 international. Average age 33. 668 applicants, 72% accepted, 256 enrolled. In 2011, 308 master's, 43 doctorates, 55 other advanced degrees awarded. Terminal master's awarded for partial completion of doctoral program. *Degree requirements:* For master's, comprehensive exam; for doctorate, 2 foreign languages, comprehensive exam, thesis/dissertation. *Entrance requirements:* For master's and doctorate, GRE General Test or GMAT. Additional exam requirements/recommendations for international students: Required—TOEFL (minimum score 550 paper-based; 80 iBT). *Application deadline:* Applications are processed on a rolling basis. Application fee: $60. Electronic applications accepted. *Financial support:* In 2011–12, 72 teaching assistantships with full and partial tuition reimbursements (averaging $9,049 per year) were awarded; career-related internships or fieldwork, Federal Work-Study, institutionally sponsored loans, scholarships/grants, and unspecified assistantships also available. Support available to part-time students. Financial award application deadline: 2/15; financial award applicants required to submit FAFSA. *Faculty research:* Parkinson's disease, personnel training, development and assessments, gifted education, service-learning, transportation, public schools. *Unit head:* Dr. Gregory M. Anderson, Dean, 303-871-3665, E-mail: gregory.m.anderson@du.edu. *Application contact:* Chris Dowen, Director, MCE Admission Office, 303-871-2783, E-mail: chris.dowen@du.edu. Web site: http://www.du.edu/education/.

University of Florida, Graduate School, College of Education, Department of Educational Administration and Policy, Gainesville, FL 32611. Offers curriculum and instruction (Ed D, PhD); educational leadership (M Ed, MAE, Ed D, PhD, Ed S); higher education administration (Ed D, PhD, Ed S); student personnel in higher education (M Ed, MAE); PhD/JD. *Accreditation:* NCATE. Part-time and evening/weekend programs available. Postbaccalaureate distance learning degree programs offered. Terminal master's awarded for partial completion of doctoral program. *Degree requirements:* For master's, thesis (for some programs); for doctorate, comprehensive exam (for some programs), thesis/dissertation (for some programs). *Entrance requirements:* For master's, GRE General Test, minimum GPA of 3.0, teaching experience; for doctorate and Ed S, GRE General Test, minimum GPA of 3.0. Additional exam requirements/recommendations for international students: Required—TOEFL (minimum score 550 paper-based; 213 computer-based; 80 iBT), IELTS (minimum score 6). *Application deadline:* For fall admission, 2/15 for domestic students, 12/1 for international students; for spring admission, 9/15 for domestic students, 3/1 for international students. Applications are processed on a rolling basis. Application fee: $30. Electronic applications accepted. *Financial support:* Career-related internships or fieldwork and unspecified assistantships available. Financial award applicants required to submit FAFSA.

University of Georgia, College of Education, Program in Higher Education, Athens, GA 30602. Offers PhD. *Accreditation:* NCATE. *Faculty:* 6 full-time (3 women). *Students:* 19 full-time (10 women), 38 part-time (15 women); includes 10 minority (7 Black or African American, non-Hispanic/Latino; 3 Hispanic/Latino), 2 international. Average age 38. 30 applicants, 37% accepted, 4 enrolled. In 2011, 27 doctorates awarded. *Degree requirements:* For doctorate, thesis/dissertation. *Entrance requirements:* For doctorate, GRE General Test. *Application deadline:* For fall admission, 7/1 priority date for domestic students; for spring admission, 11/15 for domestic students. Application fee: $50. Electronic applications accepted. *Financial support:* Fellowships, research assistantships, teaching assistantships, and unspecified assistantships available. *Unit head:* Dr. Libby V. Morris, Director, 706-542-3464, E-mail: lvmorris@uga.edu. *Application contact:* Dr. Eric C. Ness, Graduate Coordinator, 706-542-05731, E-mail: eness@uga.edu. Web site: http://www.uga.edu/ihe.

University of Houston, College of Education, Department of Educational Leadership and Cultural Studies, Houston, TX 77204. Offers administration and supervision (M Ed, Ed D); higher education (M Ed); historical, social, and cultural foundations of education (M Ed). *Accreditation:* NCATE. Part-time and evening/weekend programs available. *Degree requirements:* For master's, comprehensive exam or thesis; for doctorate, comprehensive exam, thesis/dissertation. *Entrance requirements:* For master's, GRE General Test, minimum cumulative GPA of 2.6, 3 letters of recommendation, resume/vitae, goal statement; for doctorate, GRE General Test, minimum cumulative GPA of 2.6, 3 letters of recommendation, resume/vitae, goal statement, writing sample, interview. Additional exam requirements/recommendations for international students: Required—TOEFL (minimum score 550 paper-based; 79 iBT). Electronic applications accepted. *Faculty research:* Change, supervision, multiculturalism, evaluation, policy.

University of Houston, College of Education, Department of Educational Psychology, Houston, TX 77204. Offers administration and supervision - higher education (M Ed); counseling (M Ed); counseling psychology (PhD); educational psychology (M Ed); school psychology (PhD); school psychology and individual differences (PhD); special education (M Ed). *Accreditation:* NCATE. Part-time and evening/weekend programs available. Postbaccalaureate distance learning degree programs offered. *Degree requirements:* For master's, comprehensive exam or thesis; for doctorate, comprehensive exam, thesis/dissertation. *Entrance requirements:* For master's, GRE, transcripts, 3 letters of recommendation, curriculum vita, goal statement; for doctorate, GRE, transcripts, 3 letters of recommendation, curriculum vita, goal statement, writing sample, interview. Additional exam requirements/recommendations for international students: Required—TOEFL (minimum score 550 paper-based; 79 iBT), IELTS (minimum score 6.5). Electronic applications accepted. *Faculty research:* Evidence-based assessment and intervention, multicultural issues in psychology, social and cultural context of learning, systemic barriers to college, motivational aspects of self-regulated learning.

The University of Iowa, Graduate College, College of Education, Department of Educational Policy and Leadership Studies, Program in Higher Education, Iowa City, IA 52242-1316. Offers MA, PhD, Ed S, JD/PhD. *Degree requirements:* For master's and Ed S, exam; for doctorate, comprehensive exam, thesis/dissertation. *Entrance requirements:* For master's, doctorate, and Ed S, GRE General Test, minimum GPA of 3.0. Additional exam requirements/recommendations for international students: Required—TOEFL (minimum score 550 paper-based; 213 computer-based; 81 iBT). Electronic applications accepted.

The University of Kansas, Graduate Studies, School of Education, Department of Educational Leadership and Policy Studies, Education Leadership and Policy Program, Lawrence, KS 66045-3101. Offers educational administration (Ed D, PhD); foundations (PhD); higher education (Ed D, PhD); policy studies (PhD). Part-time and evening/weekend programs available. *Faculty:* 16. *Students:* 99 full-time (65 women), 52 part-time (28 women); includes 31 minority (10 Black or African American, non-Hispanic/Latino; 5 American Indian or Alaska Native, non-Hispanic/Latino; 5 Asian, non-Hispanic/Latino; 7 Hispanic/Latino; 4 Two or more races, non-Hispanic/Latino), 10 international. Average age 38. 44 applicants, 73% accepted, 22 enrolled. In 2011, 26 degrees awarded. *Degree requirements:* For doctorate, comprehensive exam, thesis/dissertation. *Entrance requirements:* For doctorate, GRE General Test, minimum graduate GPA of 3.5. Additional exam requirements/recommendations for international students: Required—TOEFL (minimum score 570 paper-based; 230 computer-based; 80 iBT). *Application deadline:* For fall admission, 7/1 for domestic and international students; for spring admission, 11/1 for domestic and international students. Applications are processed on a rolling basis. Application fee: $55 ($65 for international students). Electronic applications accepted. Tuition and fees vary according to course load, campus/location, program and reciprocity agreements. *Financial support:* Fellowships, research assistantships with full and partial tuition reimbursements, teaching assistantships with full and partial tuition reimbursements, scholarships/grants, and unspecified assistantships available. Financial award application deadline: 3/15. *Faculty research:* Historical and philosophical issues in education, education policy and leadership, higher education faculty, research on college students, education technology. *Unit head:* Dr. Susan Twombly, Chair, 785-864-9721, Fax: 785-864-4697, E-mail: stwombly@ku.edu. *Application contact:* Denise Brubaker, Admissions Coordinator, 785-864-4458, Fax: 785-864-4697, E-mail: elps@ku.edu. Web site: http://soe.ku.edu/elps/.

The University of Kansas, Graduate Studies, School of Education, Department of Educational Leadership and Policy Studies, Program in Higher Education Administration, Lawrence, KS 66045-3101. Offers higher education (MS Ed). Part-time and evening/weekend programs available. *Faculty:* 4. *Students:* 50 full-time (31 women), 16 part-time (11 women); includes 12 minority (7 Black or African American, non-Hispanic/Latino; 1 American Indian or Alaska Native, non-Hispanic/Latino; 3 Hispanic/Latino; 1 Two or more races, non-Hispanic/Latino), 3 international. Average age 26. 84 applicants, 39% accepted, 29 enrolled. In 2011, 26 master's awarded. *Degree requirements:* For master's, comprehensive exam. *Entrance requirements:* For master's, minimum GPA of 3.0. Additional exam requirements/recommendations for international students: Required—TOEFL (minimum score 570 paper-based; 230 computer-based; 80 iBT). *Application deadline:* For fall admission, 2/1 priority date for domestic students, 2/1 for international students. Application fee: $55 ($65 for international students). Electronic applications accepted. Tuition and fees vary according to course load, campus/location, program and reciprocity agreements. *Financial support:* Fellowships, career-related internships or fieldwork, and scholarships/grants available. Financial award application deadline: 2/1; financial award applicants required to submit FAFSA. *Faculty research:* Higher education policy, faculty issues, research on college students, financial aid, access to higher education. *Unit head:* Dr. Susan Twombly, Chair, 785-864-9721, Fax: 785-864-4697, E-mail: stwombly@ku.edu. *Application contact:* Denise Brubaker, Admissions Coordinator, 785-864-4458, Fax: 785-864-4697, E-mail: elps@ku.edu. Web site: http://soe.ku.edu/elps/academics/highered/mse.

University of Kentucky, Graduate School, College of Education, Program in Educational Policy Studies and Evaluation, Lexington, KY 40506-0032. Offers educational policy studies and evaluation (Ed D); higher education (MS Ed, PhD). *Accreditation:* NCATE. Terminal master's awarded for partial completion of doctoral program. *Degree requirements:* For master's, comprehensive exam, thesis optional; for doctorate, comprehensive exam, thesis/dissertation. *Entrance requirements:* For master's, GRE General Test, minimum undergraduate GPA of 2.75; for doctorate, GRE General Test, minimum graduate GPA of 3.0. Additional exam requirements/recommendations for international students: Required—TOEFL (minimum score 550 paper-based; 213 computer-based). Electronic applications accepted. *Faculty research:* Studies in higher education; comparative and international education; evaluation of educational programs, policies, and reform; student, teacher, and faculty cultures; gender and education.

University of Louisville, Graduate School, College of Education and Human Development, Department of Leadership, Foundations and Human Resource Education, Louisville, KY 40292-0001. Offers educational leadership and organizational development (Ed D, PhD); higher education (MA); human resource education (MS); P-12 educational administration (M Ed, Ed S). *Accreditation:* NCATE. Part-time and evening/weekend programs available. Postbaccalaureate distance learning degree programs offered. *Degree requirements:* For doctorate, comprehensive exam, thesis/dissertation. *Entrance requirements:* For master's, doctorate, and Ed S, GRE General Test. Additional exam requirements/recommendations for international students: Required—TOEFL (minimum score 560 paper-based; 210 computer-based; 83 iBT). Electronic applications accepted. *Expenses:* Tuition, state resident: full-time $9692; part-time $539 per credit hour. Tuition, nonresident: full-time $20,168; part-time $1121 per credit hour. Tuition and fees vary according to program and reciprocity agreements. *Faculty research:* Evaluation of methods and programs to improve elementary and secondary education; research on organizational and human resource development; student access, retention and success in post-secondary education; educational policy analysis; multivariate quantitative research methods.

University of Maine, Graduate School, College of Education and Human Development, Program in Higher Education, Orono, ME 04469. Offers M Ed, MA, MS, Ed D, CAS. *Accreditation:* NCATE. Part-time and evening/weekend programs available. *Students:* 27 full-time (16 women), 15 part-time (10 women); includes 3 minority (1 American Indian or Alaska Native, non-Hispanic/Latino; 1 Asian, non-Hispanic/Latino; 1 Hispanic/Latino), 3 international. Average age 35. 39 applicants, 69% accepted, 20 enrolled. In 2011, 11 master's, 1 other advanced degree awarded. *Degree requirements:* For master's, thesis or alternative. *Entrance requirements:* For master's, MAT; for doctorate, GRE General Test, MA, M Ed, or MS; for CAS, MA, M Ed, or MS. Additional exam requirements/recommendations for international students: Required—TOEFL. *Application deadline:* For fall admission, 2/1 priority date for domestic students. Applications are processed on a rolling basis. Application fee: $65. Electronic applications accepted. *Expenses:* Tuition, state resident: full-time $5016. Tuition, nonresident: full-time $14,424. *Financial support:* Federal Work-Study, institutionally sponsored loans, tuition waivers (full and partial), and unspecified assistantships available. Financial award application deadline: 3/1. *Unit head:* Dr. Janet Spector, Coordinator, 207-581-2444, Fax: 207-581-2423. *Application contact:* Scott G. Delcourt, Associate Dean of the Graduate School, 207-581-3291, Fax: 207-581-3232, E-mail: graduate@maine.edu. Web site: http://2.umaine.edu/graduate/.

University of Manitoba, Faculty of Graduate Studies, Faculty of Education, Department of Educational Administration, Foundations and Psychology, Winnipeg, MB R3T 2N2, Canada. Offers adult and post-secondary education (M Ed); educational administration (M Ed); guidance and counseling (M Ed); inclusive special education (M Ed); social foundations of education (M Ed). *Degree requirements:* For master's, thesis or alternative.

University of Mary, School of Education and Behavioral Sciences, Department of Education, Bismarck, ND 58504-9652. Offers college teaching (M Ed); curriculum, instruction and assessment (M Ed); early childhood education (M Ed); early childhood special education (M Ed); elementary administration (M Ed); emotional disorders (M Ed); learning disabilities (M Ed); reading (M Ed); secondary administration (M Ed); special education strategist (M Ed). Part-time programs available. *Faculty:* 6 full-time (5 women), 12 part-time/adjunct (8 women). *Students:* 5 full-time (4 women), 77 part-time (56 women); includes 9 minority (1 Black or African American, non-Hispanic/Latino; 4 American Indian or Alaska Native, non-Hispanic/Latino; 1 Asian, non-Hispanic/Latino; 3 Hispanic/Latino), 1 international. Average age 30. 58 applicants, 55% accepted, 29 enrolled. In 2011, 16 master's awarded. *Degree requirements:* For master's, portfolio or thesis. *Entrance requirements:* For master's, interview, letters of reference, minimum GPA of 2.5. Additional exam requirements/recommendations for international students: Required—TOEFL (minimum score 500 paper-based; 197 computer-based; 71 iBT). *Application deadline:* Applications are processed on a rolling basis. Application fee: $40. Electronic applications accepted. *Financial support:* In 2011–12, 1 teaching assistantship with full tuition reimbursement was awarded; career-related internships or fieldwork also available. Financial award application deadline: 8/1; financial award applicants required to submit FAFSA. *Faculty research:* Innovative pedagogy in higher education, technology in education, content standards, children of poverty, children with diverse learning needs. *Unit head:* Dr. Rebecca Yunker Salveson, Director, 701-355-8186, E-mail: rysalves@umary.edu. *Application contact:* Leona Friedig, Administrative Secretary, 701-355-8058, E-mail: lfriedig@umary.edu.

University of Maryland, College Park, Academic Affairs, College of Education, Department of Education Leadership, Higher Education and International Education, College Park, MD 20742. Offers MA, Ed D, PhD. *Faculty:* 13 full-time (8 women), 3 part-time/adjunct (2 women). *Students:* 56 full-time (43 women), 21 part-time (12 women); includes 25 minority (13 Black or African American, non-Hispanic/Latino; 2 Asian, non-Hispanic/Latino; 8 Hispanic/Latino; 2 Two or more races, non-Hispanic/Latino), 8 international. 235 applicants, 11% accepted, 15 enrolled. In 2011, 25 master's, 1 doctorate awarded. *Entrance requirements:* Additional exam requirements/recommendations for international students: Required—TOEFL. *Application deadline:* For fall admission, 12/15 for domestic and international students. Application fee: $75. *Expenses: Tuition, area resident:* Part-time $525 per credit hour. Tuition, state resident: part-time $525 per credit hour. Tuition, nonresident: part-time $1131 per credit hour. *Required fees:* $386.31 per term. Tuition and fees vary according to program. *Financial support:* In 2011–12, 6 fellowships with full and partial tuition reimbursements (averaging $11,552 per year), 46 teaching assistantships (averaging $16,671 per year) were awarded. *Total annual research expenditures:* $250,238. *Unit head:* Dennis Kivlighan, Chair, 301-405-2858, E-mail: dennisk@umd.edu. *Application contact:* Dr. Charles A. Caramello, Dean of Graduate School, 301-405-0358, Fax: 301-314-9305. Web site: http://www.education.umd.edu/EDHI/.

Higher Education

University of Massachusetts Amherst, Graduate School, School of Education, Program in Education, Amherst, MA 01003. Offers bilingual, English as a second language, and multicultural education (M Ed, CAGS); child study and early education (M Ed); children, families and schools (Ed D, CAGS); early childhood and elementary teacher education (M Ed); educational leadership (M Ed, CAGS); educational policy and leadership (Ed D); higher education (M Ed, CAGS); international education (M Ed); language, literacy and culture (Ed D); learning, media and technology (M Ed, CAGS); mathematics, science, and learning technologies (Ed D); policy studies in education (CAGS); psychometric methods, educational statistics and research methods (Ed D); reading and writing (M Ed); school counselor education (M Ed, CAGS); science education (CAGS); secondary teacher education (M Ed); social justice education (M Ed, Ed D, CAGS); special education (M Ed, Ed D, CAGS). *Accreditation:* NCATE. Part-time programs available. Postbaccalaureate distance learning degree programs offered (minimal on-campus study). *Faculty:* 81 full-time (46 women). *Students:* 341 full-time (240 women), 333 part-time (226 women); includes 113 minority (36 Black or African American, non-Hispanic/Latino; 1 American Indian or Alaska Native, non-Hispanic/Latino; 14 Asian, non-Hispanic/Latino; 51 Hispanic/Latino; 1 Native Hawaiian or other Pacific Islander, non-Hispanic/Latino; 10 Two or more races, non-Hispanic/Latino), 98 international. Average age 36. 721 applicants, 57% accepted, 202 enrolled. In 2011, 166 master's, 33 doctorates, 25 CAGSs awarded. Terminal master's awarded for partial completion of doctoral program. *Degree requirements:* For doctorate, comprehensive exam, thesis/dissertation. *Entrance requirements:* Additional exam requirements/recommendations for international students: Required—TOEFL (minimum score 550 paper-based; 213 computer-based; 80 iBT), IELTS (minimum score 6.5). *Application deadline:* For fall admission, 1/15 for domestic and international students. Applications are processed on a rolling basis. Application fee: $50 ($65 for international students). Electronic applications accepted. Tuition and fees vary according to course load, campus/location and program. *Financial support:* Fellowships with full and partial tuition reimbursements, research assistantships with full and partial tuition reimbursements, teaching assistantships with full and partial tuition reimbursements, career-related internships or fieldwork, Federal Work-Study, scholarships/grants, traineeships, health care benefits, tuition waivers (full and partial), and unspecified assistantships available. Support available to part-time students. Financial award application deadline: 1/15. *Unit head:* Dr. Linda L. Griffin, Graduate Program Director, 413-545-6984, Fax: 413-545-1523. *Application contact:* Lindsay DeSantis, Interim Supervisor of Admissions, 413-545-0722, Fax: 413-577-0010, E-mail: gradadm@grad.umass.edu. Web site: http://www.umass.edu/education/.

University of Massachusetts Boston, Office of Graduate Studies, Graduate College of Education, School Organization, Curriculum and Instruction Department, Boston, MA 02125-3393. Offers education (M Ed, Ed D), including elementary and secondary education/certification (M Ed), higher education administration (Ed D), teacher certification (M Ed), urban school leadership (Ed D); educational administration (M Ed, CAGS); special education (M Ed). *Degree requirements:* For master's and CAGS, comprehensive exam; for doctorate, comprehensive exam, thesis/dissertation. *Entrance requirements:* For master's, GRE General Test or MAT; for doctorate, GRE General Test or MAT, minimum GPA of 2.75; for CAGS, minimum GPA of 2.75.

University of Massachusetts Boston, Office of Graduate Studies, Graduate College of Education, School Organization, Curriculum and Instruction Department, Program in Education, Track in Higher Education Administration, Boston, MA 02125-3393. Offers Ed D. Part-time and evening/weekend programs available. *Degree requirements:* For doctorate, comprehensive exam, thesis/dissertation. *Entrance requirements:* For doctorate, GRE General Test or MAT, minimum GPA of 2.75. *Faculty research:* Women, higher education and professionalization, school reform, urban classroom, higher education policy.

University of Memphis, Graduate School, College of Education, Department of Leadership, Memphis, TN 38152. Offers adult education (Ed D); educational leadership (Ed D); higher education (Ed D); leadership (MS); policy studies (Ed D); school administration and supervision (MS). *Accreditation:* NCATE. Part-time and evening/weekend programs available. Postbaccalaureate distance learning degree programs offered (minimal on-campus study). *Degree requirements:* For master's, comprehensive exam, thesis optional; for doctorate, comprehensive exam, thesis/dissertation. *Entrance requirements:* For master's and doctorate, GRE. Electronic applications accepted. *Faculty research:* School improvement, social justice, online learning, adult learning, diversity.

University of Miami, Graduate School, School of Education and Human Development, Department of Educational and Psychological Studies, Program in Higher Education Administration, Coral Gables, FL 33124. Offers enrollment management (MS Ed, Certificate); higher education leadership (Ed D); student life and development (MS Ed, Certificate). Part-time and evening/weekend programs available. *Faculty:* 2 full-time (both women). *Students:* 28 full-time (18 women), 10 part-time (4 women); includes 21 minority (5 Black or African American, non-Hispanic/Latino; 2 Asian, non-Hispanic/Latino; 14 Hispanic/Latino), 5 international. Average age 35. 40 applicants, 73% accepted, 19 enrolled. In 2011, 13 master's awarded. Terminal master's awarded for partial completion of doctoral program. *Degree requirements:* For master's, comprehensive exam; for doctorate, thesis/dissertation, qualifying exam. *Entrance requirements:* For master's and doctorate, GRE General Test. Additional exam requirements/recommendations for international students: Required—TOEFL (minimum score 550 paper-based; 80 iBT); Recommended—IELTS (minimum score 6.5). *Application deadline:* Applications are processed on a rolling basis. Application fee: $65. Electronic applications accepted. *Financial support:* In 2011–12, 11 students received support. Institutionally sponsored loans and scholarships/grants available. Support available to part-time students. Financial award application deadline: 3/1; financial award applicants required to submit FAFSA. *Unit head:* Dr. Carol Anne Phekoo, Lecturer/Director, 305-284-5013, Fax: 305-284-3003, E-mail: cphekoo@miami.edu. *Application contact:* Lois Heffernan, Graduate Admissions Coordinator, 305-284-2167, Fax: 305-284-9395, E-mail: lheffernan@miami.edu.

University of Minnesota, Twin Cities Campus, Graduate School, College of Education and Human Development, Department of Organizational Leadership, Policy and Development, Program in Higher Education, Minneapolis, MN 55455-0213. Offers MA, PhD. *Students:* 51 full-time (34 women), 126 part-time (74 women); includes 24 minority (13 Black or African American, non-Hispanic/Latino; 1 American Indian or Alaska Native, non-Hispanic/Latino; 6 Asian, non-Hispanic/Latino; 4 Hispanic/Latino), 10 international. Average age 38. 61 applicants, 69% accepted, 30 enrolled. In 2011, 8 master's, 10 doctorates awarded. Application fee: $55. *Unit head:* Dr. Rebecca Ropers-Huilman, Chair, 612-624-1006, Fax: 612-624-3377, E-mail: ropers@umn.edu. *Application contact:* Dr. Jennifer Engler, Assistant Dean, 612-626-2887, Fax: 612-626-7496, E-mail: engle009@umn.edu. Web site: http://www.cehd.umn.edu/EdPA/HigherEd/.

University of Mississippi, Graduate School, School of Education, Department of Educational Leadership and Counselor Education, Oxford, University, MS 38677. Offers counselor education (M Ed, PhD, Specialist); educational leadership (PhD); educational leadership and counselor education (M Ed, MA, Ed D, Ed S); higher education/student personnel (MA). *Accreditation:* ACA; NCATE. *Students:* 155 full-time (106 women), 177 part-time (110 women); includes 100 minority (91 Black or African American, non-Hispanic/Latino; 1 Asian, non-Hispanic/Latino; 5 Hispanic/Latino; 3 Two or more races, non-Hispanic/Latino), 7 international. In 2011, 82 master's, 13 doctorates, 36 other advanced degrees awarded. *Degree requirements:* For doctorate, thesis/dissertation. *Entrance requirements:* For master's, GRE General Test, minimum GPA of 3.0; for doctorate, GRE General Test. Additional exam requirements/recommendations for international students: Required—TOEFL. *Application deadline:* For fall admission, 4/1 for domestic students; for spring admission, 10/1 for domestic students. Applications are processed on a rolling basis. Application fee: $25. Electronic applications accepted. *Financial support:* Scholarships/grants available. Financial award application deadline: 3/1; financial award applicants required to submit FAFSA. *Unit head:* Dr. Timothy Letzring, Acting Chair, 662-915-7063, Fax: 662-915-7249. *Application contact:* Dr. Christy M. Wyandt, Associate Dean, 662-915-7474, Fax: 662-915-7577, E-mail: cwyandt@olemiss.edu.

University of Missouri, Graduate School, College of Education, Department of Educational Leadership and Policy Analysis, Columbia, MO 65211. Offers education administration (M Ed, MA, Ed D, PhD, Ed S); higher and adult education (M Ed, MA, Ed D, PhD, Ed S). Part-time programs available. *Faculty:* 15 full-time (8 women), 5 part-time/adjunct (4 women). *Students:* 139 full-time (85 women), 273 part-time (158 women); includes 55 minority (38 Black or African American, non-Hispanic/Latino; 1 American Indian or Alaska Native, non-Hispanic/Latino; 6 Asian, non-Hispanic/Latino; 6 Hispanic/Latino; 4 Two or more races, non-Hispanic/Latino), 13 international. Average age 38. 186 applicants, 74% accepted, 91 enrolled. In 2011, 19 master's, 56 doctorates, 16 other advanced degrees awarded. *Degree requirements:* For doctorate, variable foreign language requirement, comprehensive exam (for some programs), thesis/dissertation. *Entrance requirements:* For master's, doctorate, and Ed S, minimum GPA of 3.0. Additional exam requirements/recommendations for international students: Required—TOEFL (minimum score 500 paper-based; 173 computer-based; 61 iBT), IELTS (minimum score 5.5). *Application deadline:* For fall admission, 2/15 priority date for domestic students; for spring admission, 10/15 for domestic students. Applications are processed on a rolling basis. Application fee: $55 ($75 for international students). Electronic applications accepted. *Expenses:* Tuition, state resident: full-time $5881. Tuition, nonresident: full-time $15,183. *Required fees:* $952. Tuition and fees vary according to campus/location and program. *Financial support:* In 2011–12, 2 fellowships with full tuition reimbursements, 32 research assistantships with full tuition reimbursements, 4 teaching assistantships with full tuition reimbursements were awarded; institutionally sponsored loans, scholarships/grants, health care benefits, and unspecified assistantships also available. *Faculty research:* Administrative communication and behavior, middle schools leadership, administration of special education. *Unit head:* Dr. Jay Scribner, Department Chair, E-mail: scribnerj@missouri.edu. *Application contact:* Betty Kissane, 573-882-8231, E-mail: kissaneb@missouri.edu. Web site: http://education.missouri.edu/ELPA/index.php.

University of Missouri–St. Louis, College of Education, Division of Educational Leadership and Policy Studies, St. Louis, MO 63121. Offers adult and higher education (M Ed), including adult education, higher education; educational administration (M Ed, Ed S), including community education (M Ed), elementary education (M Ed), secondary education (M Ed); institutional research (Certificate). *Accreditation:* NCATE. Part-time and evening/weekend programs available. *Faculty:* 17 full-time (8 women), 7 part-time/adjunct (5 women). *Students:* 23 full-time (15 women), 187 part-time (137 women); includes 103 minority (96 Black or African American, non-Hispanic/Latino; 2 Asian, non-Hispanic/Latino; 4 Hispanic/Latino; 1 Two or more races, non-Hispanic/Latino), 4 international. Average age 35. 95 applicants, 86% accepted, 68 enrolled. In 2011, 57 master's, 19 Certificates awarded. *Degree requirements:* For master's, comprehensive exam (for some programs). *Entrance requirements:* Additional exam requirements/recommendations for international students: Required—TOEFL (minimum score 550 paper-based; 213 computer-based). *Application deadline:* For fall admission, 7/1 priority date for domestic students, 7/1 for international students; for spring admission, 12/1 priority date for domestic students, 12/1 for international students. Applications are processed on a rolling basis. Application fee: $35 ($40 for international students). Electronic applications accepted. *Expenses:* Tuition, state resident: full-time $6273; part-time $3866 per year. Tuition, nonresident: full-time $14,969; part-time $9980 per year. *Required fees:* $315 per year. *Financial support:* In 2011–12, 12 research assistantships (averaging $12,000 per year), 1 teaching assistantship (averaging $10,500 per year) were awarded. Financial award application deadline: 4/1; financial award applicants required to submit FAFSA. *Faculty research:* Educational policy research; philosophy of education; higher, adult, and vocational education; school initiatives, change, and reform. *Unit head:* Dr. E. Paulette Savage, Chair, 514-516-5944. *Application contact:* 314-516-5458, Fax: 314-516-6996, E-mail: gradadm@umsl.edu. Web site: http://coe.umsl.edu/web/divisions/elaps/index.html.

University of Missouri–St. Louis, College of Education, Interdisciplinary Doctoral Programs, St. Louis, MO 63121. Offers adult and higher education (Ed D); counseling (PhD); counselor education (Ed D); educational administration (Ed D); educational leadership and policy studies (PhD); educational psychology (PhD); teaching-learning processes (Ed D, PhD). *Faculty:* 72 full-time (33 women). *Students:* 44 full-time (29 women), 199 part-time (138 women); includes 65 minority (52 Black or African American, non-Hispanic/Latino; 3 American Indian or Alaska Native, non-Hispanic/Latino; 5 Asian, non-Hispanic/Latino; 5 Hispanic/Latino), 6 international. Average age 43. 47 applicants, 34% accepted, 11 enrolled. In 2011, 27 doctorates awarded. *Degree requirements:* For doctorate, thesis/dissertation. *Entrance requirements:* For doctorate, GRE General Test, 3 letters of recommendation; personal interview. Additional exam requirements/recommendations for international students: Recommended—TOEFL (minimum score 550 paper-based; 230 computer-based). *Application deadline:* For fall admission, 3/1 for domestic and international students; for spring admission, 10/1 for domestic and international students. Application fee: $35 ($40 for international students). Electronic applications accepted. *Expenses:* Tuition, state resident: full-time $6273; part-time $3866 per year. Tuition, nonresident: full-time $14,969; part-time $9980 per year. *Required fees:* $315 per year. *Financial support:* In 2011–12, 15 research assistantships (averaging $12,240 per year), 8 teaching assistantships (averaging $12,240 per year) were awarded. Financial award application deadline: 4/1; financial award applicants required to submit FAFSA. *Faculty research:* Higher education law and policy, gender and higher education, student retention, lifelong learning orientation, school counselor's role in violence prevention. *Unit head:* Dr. Kathleen Haywood, Director of Graduate Studies, 314-516-5483, Fax: 314-516-5227, E-mail: kathleen_haywood@umsl.edu. *Application contact:* 314-516-5458, Fax: 314-516-6996, E-mail: gradadm@umsl.edu.

University of Nevada, Las Vegas, Graduate College, College of Education, Department of Educational Research, Cognition, and Development, Las Vegas, NV 89154-3002. Offers educational leadership (M Ed, MS, Ed D, PhD); educational leadership-executive (Ed D); educational psychology (MS, PhD, Ed S); higher education leadership (PhD); learning and technology (PhD); school psychology (PhD); PhD/JD. *Accreditation:* NCATE. Part-time and evening/weekend programs available. *Faculty:* 28 full-time (14 women), 13 part-time/adjunct (9 women). *Students:* 54 full-time (40 women), 184 part-time (124 women); includes 68 minority (26 Black or African American, non-Hispanic/Latino; 1 American Indian or Alaska Native, non-Hispanic/

Latino; 9 Asian, non-Hispanic/Latino; 21 Hispanic/Latino; 2 Native Hawaiian or other Pacific Islander, non-Hispanic/Latino; 9 Two or more races, non-Hispanic/Latino), 4 international. Average age 37. 70 applicants, 69% accepted, 41 enrolled. In 2011, 94 master's, 34 doctorates, 12 other advanced degrees awarded. *Degree requirements:* For master's, comprehensive exam (for some programs), thesis (for some programs); for doctorate, comprehensive exam (for some programs), thesis/dissertation; for Ed S, comprehensive exam, thesis. *Entrance requirements:* For master's, GMAT or GRE General Test; for doctorate, GRE General Test, writing exam; for Ed S, GRE General Test. Additional exam requirements/recommendations for international students: Required—TOEFL (minimum score 550 paper-based; 213 computer-based; 80 iBT), IELTS (minimum score 7). *Application deadline:* For fall admission, 2/1 for domestic students, 5/1 for international students; for spring admission, 10/1 for international students. Application fee: $60 ($95 for international students). Electronic applications accepted. *Financial support:* In 2011–12, 44 students received support, including 16 research assistantships with partial tuition reimbursements available (averaging $9,428 per year), 28 teaching assistantships with partial tuition reimbursements available (averaging $10,783 per year); institutionally sponsored loans, scholarships/grants, health care benefits, and unspecified assistantships also available. Financial award application deadline: 3/1. *Faculty research:* Innovation and change in educational settings; educational policy, finance, and marketing; psycho-educational assessment; student retention, persistence, development, language, and culture; statistical modeling, program evaluation, qualitative and quantitative research methods. *Total annual research expenditures:* $269,710. *Unit head:* Dr. LeAnn Putney, Chair/Professor, 702-895-4879, Fax: 702-895-3492, E-mail: leann.putney@unlv.edu. *Application contact:* Graduate College Admissions Evaluator, 702-895-3320, Fax: 702-895-4180, E-mail: gradcollege@unlv.edu. Web site: http://education.unlv.edu/ercd/.

University of New Hampshire, Graduate School, Interdisciplinary Programs, Program in College Teaching, Durham, NH 03824. Offers MST. Program offered in summer only. Part-time programs available. *Faculty:* 17 full-time (7 women). *Students:* 2 part-time (1 woman); includes 1 minority (Asian, non-Hispanic/Latino). Average age 45. 1 applicant, 0% accepted, 0 enrolled. In 2011, 4 master's awarded. *Entrance requirements:* Additional exam requirements/recommendations for international students: Required—TOEFL (minimum score 550 paper-based; 213 computer-based; 80 iBT). *Application deadline:* For fall admission, 6/1 priority date for domestic students, 4/1 for international students; for spring admission, 12/1 for domestic students. Applications are processed on a rolling basis. Application fee: $65. Electronic applications accepted. *Expenses:* Tuition, state resident: full-time $12,360; part-time $687 per credit hour. Tuition, nonresident: full-time $25,680; part-time $1058 per credit hour. *International tuition:* $29,550 full-time. *Required fees:* $1666; $833 per course. $416.50 per semester. Tuition and fees vary according to course load and degree level. *Financial support:* Fellowships, research assistantships, and teaching assistantships available. Financial award application deadline: 2/15. *Unit head:* Dr. Harry J. Richards, Dean, 603-862-3005, Fax: 603-862-0275, E-mail: harry.richards@unh.edu. *Application contact:* Sharon Andrews, Senior Administrative Assistant, 603-862-3005, E-mail: college.teaching@unh.edu. Web site: http://www.unh.edu/teaching-excellence/Academic_prog_in_coll_teach/index.html.

University of New Mexico, Health Sciences Center Graduate Programs, Program in Biomedical Sciences, Program in University Science Teaching, Albuquerque, NM 87131-2039. Offers Certificate. In 2011, 3 Certificates awarded. *Unit head:* Dr. Sherry Rogers, Program Director, 505-272-0007, E-mail: srogers@salud.unm.edu. *Application contact:* Dr. Angela Wandinger-Ness, Coordinator, 505-272-1459, Fax: 505-272-8738, E-mail: awandinger@salud.unm.edu.

The University of North Carolina at Greensboro, Graduate School, School of Education, Department of Curriculum and Instruction, Program in Curriculum and Teaching, Greensboro, NC 27412-5001. Offers higher education (PhD); teacher education and development (PhD). *Accreditation:* NCATE. *Degree requirements:* For doctorate, comprehensive exam, thesis/dissertation. *Entrance requirements:* For doctorate, GRE General Test. Additional exam requirements/recommendations for international students: Required—TOEFL. Electronic applications accepted.

University of Northern Colorado, Graduate School, College of Education and Behavioral Sciences, Department of Leadership, Policy and Development: Higher Education and P-12 Education, Program in Higher Education and Student Affairs Leadership, Greeley, CO 80639. Offers PhD. Part-time programs available. *Entrance requirements:* For doctorate, GRE General Test, transcripts, 3 letters of recommendation. Electronic applications accepted.

University of Northern Iowa, Graduate College, College of Education, Department of Educational Leadership, Counseling, and Postsecondary Education, Program in Postsecondary Education, Cedar Falls, IA 50614. Offers student affairs (MAE). *Students:* 26 full-time (19 women), 13 part-time (11 women); includes 10 minority (5 Black or African American, non-Hispanic/Latino; 1 Asian, non-Hispanic/Latino; 4 Hispanic/Latino). 48 applicants, 50% accepted, 17 enrolled. In 2011, 6 master's awarded. *Degree requirements:* For master's, comprehensive exam, thesis or alternative. *Entrance requirements:* For master's, minimum GPA of 3.0. Additional exam requirements/recommendations for international students: Required—TOEFL (minimum score 500 paper-based; 180 computer-based; 61 iBT). *Application deadline:* For fall admission, 8/1 priority date for domestic students. Applications are processed on a rolling basis. Application fee: $50 ($70 for international students). Electronic applications accepted. *Expenses:* Tuition, state resident: full-time $7476. Tuition, nonresident: full-time $16,410. *Required fees:* $942. *Financial support:* Career-related internships or fieldwork, Federal Work-Study, scholarships/grants, and tuition waivers (full) available. Financial award application deadline: 2/1. *Unit head:* Dr. Michael Waggoner, Professor, 319-273-2605, Fax: 319-273-5175, E-mail: mike.waggoner@uni.edu. *Application contact:* Laurie S. Russell, Record Analyst, 319-273-2623, Fax: 319-273-2885, E-mail: laurie.russell@uni.edu. Web site: http://www.uni.edu/coe/elpe/.

University of North Texas, Toulouse Graduate School, College of Education, Department of Counseling and Higher Education, Program in Higher Education, Denton, TX 76203. Offers M Ed, MS, Ed D, PhD, Certificate. *Accreditation:* NCATE. Part-time and evening/weekend programs available. *Degree requirements:* For master's, internship; for doctorate, comprehensive exam, thesis/dissertation. *Entrance requirements:* For master's, GRE General Test, recommendations; for doctorate, GRE General Test, admissions exam, recommendations, interview. Additional exam requirements/recommendations for international students: Recommended—TOEFL (minimum score 550 paper-based; 213 computer-based; 79 iBT). *Expenses:* Tuition, state resident: part-time $100 per credit hour. Tuition, nonresident: part-time $413 per credit hour. *Faculty research:* Access to higher education, transfer issues, student development, community colleges, diversity in higher education.

University of Oklahoma, Jeannine Rainbolt College of Education, Department of Educational Leadership and Policy Studies, Program in Adult and Higher Education, Norman, OK 73019. Offers M Ed, PhD. *Accreditation:* NCATE. Part-time and evening/weekend programs available. *Students:* 131 full-time (71 women), 88 part-time (47 women); includes 64 minority (32 Black or African American, non-Hispanic/Latino; 12 American Indian or Alaska Native, non-Hispanic/Latino; 4 Asian, non-Hispanic/Latino; 7 Hispanic/Latino; 9 Two or more races, non-Hispanic/Latino), 6 international. Average age 29. 134 applicants, 67% accepted, 59 enrolled. In 2011, 65 master's, 3 doctorates awarded. Terminal master's awarded for partial completion of doctoral program. *Degree requirements:* For master's, comprehensive exam; for doctorate, variable foreign language requirement, thesis/dissertation, general exam. *Entrance requirements:* For master's, minimum GPA of 3.0 in last 60 hours of undergraduate course work; for doctorate, GRE General Test, resume, 3 letters of reference, scholarly writing sample. Additional exam requirements/recommendations for international students: Required—TOEFL (minimum score 550 paper-based; 79 iBT). *Application deadline:* For fall admission, 6/1 for domestic students, 3/1 for international students; for spring admission, 10/1 for domestic students, 9/1 for international students. Application fee: $40 ($90 for international students). Electronic applications accepted. *Expenses:* Tuition, state resident: full-time $4087; part-time $170.30 per credit hour. Tuition, nonresident: full-time $14,875; part-time $619.80 per credit hour. *Required fees:* $2659; $100.25 per credit hour. Tuition and fees vary according to course load and degree level. *Financial support:* In 2011–12, 201 students received support. Unspecified assistantships available. Financial award applicants required to submit FAFSA. *Faculty research:* Spirituality and identity; academic performance, persistence and graduation of college athletes; autobiography as a movement toward possibility; virtual learning; leadership, policy, and public good. *Unit head:* David Tan, Chair, 405-325-4202, Fax: 405-325-2403, E-mail: dtan@ou.edu. *Application contact:* Geri Evans, Graduate Programs Representative, 405-325-5978, Fax: 405-325-2403, E-mail: gevans@ou.edu. Web site: http://education.ou.edu/departments_1/edah_1.

University of Oklahoma, Jeannine Rainbolt College of Education, Department of Instructional Leadership and Academic Curriculum, Program in Education, Norman, OK 73019. Offers college teaching (Graduate Certificate). *Students:* 56 full-time (49 women), 10 part-time (8 women); includes 8 minority (3 American Indian or Alaska Native, non-Hispanic/Latino; 1 Asian, non-Hispanic/Latino; 3 Hispanic/Latino; 1 Two or more races, non-Hispanic/Latino). Average age 28. 53 applicants, 96% accepted, 51 enrolled. *Application deadline:* For fall admission, 6/1 for domestic students, 3/1 for international students; for spring admission, 11/1 for domestic students, 9/1 for international students. Applications are processed on a rolling basis. Application fee: $40 ($90 for international students). Electronic applications accepted. *Expenses:* Tuition, state resident: full-time $4087; part-time $170.30 per credit hour. Tuition, nonresident: full-time $14,875; part-time $619.80 per credit hour. *Required fees:* $2659; $100.25 per credit hour. Tuition and fees vary according to course load and degree level. *Unit head:* Lawrence Baines, Chair, 405-325-1498, Fax: 405-325-4061, E-mail: lbaines@ou.edu. *Application contact:* Lynn Crussel, Graduate Programs Officer, 405-325-4843, Fax: 405-325-4061, E-mail: lcrussel@ou.edu. Web site: http://education.ou.edu.

University of Pennsylvania, Graduate School of Education, Division of Higher Education, Executive Doctorate Program in Higher Education Management, Philadelphia, PA 19104. Offers Ed D. *Students:* 49 full-time (25 women), 1 (woman) part-time; includes 13 minority (6 Black or African American, non-Hispanic/Latino; 1 American Indian or Alaska Native, non-Hispanic/Latino; 3 Asian, non-Hispanic/Latino; 3 Hispanic/Latino), 3 international. 74 applicants, 38% accepted, 26 enrolled. In 2011, 24 doctorates awarded. *Expenses: Tuition:* Full-time $26,660; part-time $4944 per course. *Required fees:* $2318; $291 per course. Tuition and fees vary according to course load, degree level and program. *Application contact:* Alyssa D'Alconzo, Associate Director, Admissions, 215-898-6415, Fax: 215-746-6884, E-mail: admissions@gse.upenn.edu. Web site: http://www.gse.upenn.edu/execdoc.

University of Pennsylvania, Graduate School of Education, Division of Higher Education, Program in Higher Education, Philadelphia, PA 19104. Offers MS Ed, Ed D, PhD. *Students:* 73 full-time (50 women), 37 part-time (26 women); includes 26 minority (14 Black or African American, non-Hispanic/Latino; 1 American Indian or Alaska Native, non-Hispanic/Latino; 5 Asian, non-Hispanic/Latino; 3 Hispanic/Latino; 3 Two or more races, non-Hispanic/Latino), 5 international. 276 applicants, 48% accepted, 70 enrolled. In 2011, 46 master's, 10 doctorates awarded. *Degree requirements:* For doctorate, thesis/dissertation (for some programs). *Expenses: Tuition:* Full-time $26,660; part-time $4944 per course. *Required fees:* $2318; $291 per course. Tuition and fees vary according to course load, degree level and program. *Financial support:* Research assistantships available. *Unit head:* Dr. Andrew Porter, Dean, 215-898-7014. *Application contact:* Karen Carter, Coordinator, 215-898-2444, E-mail: karen@gse.upenn.edu.

University of Phoenix–Bay Area Campus, College of Education, San Jose, CA 95134-1805. Offers administration and supervision (MA Ed); adult education and training (MA Ed); early childhood education (MA Ed); education (Ed S); educational leadership (Ed D); elementary teacher education (MA Ed); higher education administration (PhD); secondary teacher education (MA Ed); special education (MA Ed); teacher leadership (MA Ed). Evening/weekend programs available. Postbaccalaureate distance learning degree programs offered (no on-campus study). *Degree requirements:* For master's, thesis (for some programs). *Entrance requirements:* For master's, minimum undergraduate GPA of 2.5, 3 years of work experience. Additional exam requirements/recommendations for international students: Required—TOEFL (minimum score 550 paper-based; 213 computer-based; 79 iBT). Electronic applications accepted.

University of Phoenix–Madison Campus, College of Education, Madison, WI 53718-2416. Offers education (Ed S); educational leadership (Ed D); educational leadership: curriculum and instruction (Ed D); higher education administration (PhD).

University of Phoenix–Milwaukee Campus, College of Education, Milwaukee, WI 53045. Offers curriculum and instruction (MA Ed, Ed D); education (Ed S); educational leadership (Ed D); English as a second language (MA Ed); higher education administration (PhD).

University of Phoenix–Online Campus, School of Advanced Studies, Phoenix, AZ 85034-7209. Offers business administration (DBA); education (Ed S); educational leadership (Ed D), including curriculum and instruction, education technology, educational leadership; health administration (DHA); higher education administration (PhD); industrial/organizational psychology (PhD); nursing (PhD); organizational leadership (DM), including information systems and technology, organizational leadership. Evening/weekend programs available. Postbaccalaureate distance learning degree programs offered. *Students:* 7,581 full-time (5,042 women); includes 3,199 minority (2,505 Black or African American, non-Hispanic/Latino; 68 American Indian or Alaska Native, non-Hispanic/Latino; 158 Asian, non-Hispanic/Latino; 395 Hispanic/Latino; 46 Native Hawaiian or other Pacific Islander, non-Hispanic/Latino; 27 Two or more races, non-Hispanic/Latino), 397 international. Average age 44. *Degree requirements:* For doctorate, thesis/dissertation. *Entrance requirements:* Additional exam requirements/recommendations for international students: Required—TOEFL, TOEIC (Test of English as an International Communication), Berlitz Online English Proficiency Exam, Pearson Test of English, or IELTS. *Application deadline:* Applications are processed on a rolling basis. Application fee: $45. Electronic applications accepted. *Expenses:* Contact institution. *Financial support:* Scholarships/grants available. Financial award applicants required to submit FAFSA. *Unit head:* Dr. Jeremy Moreland, Executive Dean. *Application contact:* 866-766-0766. Web site: http://www.phoenix.edu/colleges_divisions/doctoral.html.

Higher Education

University of Phoenix–Washington D.C. Campus, College of Education, Washington, DC 20001. Offers administration and supervision (MA Ed); adult education and training (MA Ed); computer education (MA Ed); curriculum and instruction (MA Ed, Ed D); early childhood education (MA Ed); education (Ed S); educational leadership (Ed D); educational technology (Ed D); elementary teacher education (MA Ed); English and language arts education (MA Ed); English as a second language (MA Ed); higher education administration (PhD); mathematics education (MA Ed); secondary teacher education (MA Ed); special education (MA Ed); teacher leadership (MA Ed).

University of Pittsburgh, School of Education, Department of Administrative and Policy Studies, Program in Higher Education Management, Pittsburgh, PA 15260. Offers higher education (M Ed, Ed D, PhD). Part-time and evening/weekend programs available. *Students:* 50 full-time (33 women), 70 part-time (48 women); includes 17 minority (13 Black or African American, non-Hispanic/Latino; 1 Asian, non-Hispanic/Latino; 2 Hispanic/Latino; 1 Two or more races, non-Hispanic/Latino), 18 international. Average age 34. 80 applicants, 86% accepted, 48 enrolled. In 2011, 23 master's, 3 doctorates awarded. *Degree requirements:* For master's, thesis; for doctorate, thesis/dissertation. *Entrance requirements:* For doctorate, GRE General Test. Additional exam requirements/recommendations for international students: Required—TOEFL (minimum score 213 computer-based; 80 iBT). *Application deadline:* For fall admission, 2/1 priority date for domestic students, 2/1 for international students; for spring admission, 11/1 priority date for domestic students, 7/1 for international students. Applications are processed on a rolling basis. Application fee: $50. Electronic applications accepted. *Expenses:* Tuition, state resident: full-time $18,774; part-time $760 per credit. Tuition, nonresident: full-time $30,736; part-time $1258 per credit. *Required fees:* $740; $200 per term. Tuition and fees vary according to program. *Financial support:* Fellowships, Federal Work-Study, institutionally sponsored loans, scholarships/grants, health care benefits, tuition waivers (partial), and unspecified assistantships available. Support available to part-time students. Financial award application deadline: 3/15; financial award applicants required to submit FAFSA. *Unit head:* Dr. Mary Margaret Kerr, Chair, 412-648-7205, Fax: 412-648-1784, E-mail: mmkerr@pitt.edu. *Application contact:* Lauren Spadafora, Enrollment Manager, 412-648-2230, Fax: 412-648-1899, E-mail: soeinfo@pitt.edu. Web site: http://www.education.pitt.edu/.

University of Rochester, Margaret Warner Graduate School of Education and Human Development, Doctoral Programs in Education, Rochester, NY 14627. Offers counseling (Ed D); educational administration (Ed D); educational policy and theory (PhD); higher education (PhD); human development in educational context (PhD); teaching, curriculum, and change (PhD). *Expenses: Tuition:* Full-time $41,040.

University of Rochester, Margaret Warner Graduate School of Education and Human Development, Master's Program in Higher Education, Rochester, NY 14627. Offers higher education (MS); higher education student affairs (MS). *Expenses: Tuition:* Full-time $41,040.

University of San Diego, School of Leadership and Education Sciences, Department of Leadership Studies, San Diego, CA 92110-2492. Offers higher education leadership (MA); leadership studies (MA, PhD); nonprofit leadership and management (MA, Certificate). Part-time and evening/weekend programs available. *Faculty:* 11 full-time (6 women), 16 part-time/adjunct (8 women). *Students:* 14 full-time (9 women), 202 part-time (139 women); includes 65 minority (16 Black or African American, non-Hispanic/Latino; 11 Asian, non-Hispanic/Latino; 30 Hispanic/Latino; 3 Native Hawaiian or other Pacific Islander, non-Hispanic/Latino; 5 Two or more races, non-Hispanic/Latino), 8 international. Average age 35. 236 applicants, 51% accepted, 75 enrolled. In 2011, 53 master's, 11 doctorates awarded. *Degree requirements:* For master's, thesis (for some programs), portfolio; for doctorate, comprehensive exam, thesis/dissertation. *Entrance requirements:* For master's, minimum GPA of 3.0, interview; for doctorate, GRE, master's degree, minimum GPA of 3.5 (recommended), interview, writing sample, resume. Additional exam requirements/recommendations for international students: Required—TOEFL (minimum score 580 paper-based; 237 computer-based; 83 iBT), TWE. *Application deadline:* For fall admission, 1/15 for domestic and international students. Application fee: $45. Electronic applications accepted. *Expenses: Tuition:* Full-time $22,482; part-time $1249 per unit. *Required fees:* $224. Full-time tuition and fees vary according to course load and degree level. *Financial support:* In 2011–12, 161 students received support. Career-related internships or fieldwork, Federal Work-Study, institutionally sponsored loans, unspecified assistantships, and stipends available. Support available to part-time students. Financial award application deadline: 4/1; financial award applicants required to submit FAFSA. *Faculty research:* Higher education administration policy and relations, organizational leadership, nonprofits and philanthropy, student affairs leadership. *Unit head:* Dr. Cheryl Getz, Graduate Program Director, 619-260-4289, Fax: 619-260-6835, E-mail: cgetz@sandiego.edu. *Application contact:* Monica Mahon, Associate Director of Graduate Admissions, 619-260-4524, Fax: 619-260-4158, E-mail: grads@sandiego.edu. Web site: http://www.sandiego.edu/soles/programs/leadership_studies/.

University of South Carolina, The Graduate School, College of Education, Department of Educational Leadership and Policies, Program in Higher Education and Student Affairs, Columbia, SC 29208. Offers M Ed. *Accreditation:* NCATE. Part-time programs available. *Degree requirements:* For master's, comprehensive exam, thesis (for some programs). *Entrance requirements:* For master's, GRE General Test or MAT, letters of reference. Electronic applications accepted. *Faculty research:* Minorities in higher education, community college transfer problem, federal role in educational research.

University of Southern California, Graduate School, Rossier School of Education, Doctor of Education Programs, Los Angeles, CA 90089. Offers educational psychology (Ed D); higher education administration (Ed D); K-12 leadership in urban school settings (Ed D); teacher education in multicultural societies (Ed D). Part-time and evening/weekend programs available. *Degree requirements:* For doctorate, thesis/dissertation. *Entrance requirements:* For doctorate, GRE. Additional exam requirements/recommendations for international students: Required—TOEFL (minimum score 250 computer-based; 100 iBT). Electronic applications accepted. *Faculty research:* Data-driven decision-making in K-12 schools and districts; examination of college and university leadership and management in U. S. and Asia; studies in facilitating student learning; organizational change and the role of leaders; leadership, diversity, learning and accountability.

University of Southern California, Graduate School, Rossier School of Education, Doctor of Philosophy in Education Programs, Los Angeles, CA 90089. Offers educational psychology (PhD); higher education administration and policy (PhD); K-12 policy and practice (PhD). *Degree requirements:* For doctorate, thesis/dissertation, 63 units; qualifying exam; dissertation proposal and defense. *Entrance requirements:* For doctorate, GRE. Additional exam requirements/recommendations for international students: Required—TOEFL (minimum score 250 computer-based; 100 iBT). Electronic applications accepted. *Faculty research:* Diversity in higher education, organizational change, educational psychology, policy and politics of educational reform, economics of education and education policy.

University of Southern Maine, School of Education and Human Development, Program in Adult Education, Portland, ME 04104-9300. Offers adult and higher education (MS); adult learning (CAS). *Accreditation:* Teacher Education Accreditation Council. Part-time and evening/weekend programs available. Postbaccalaureate distance learning degree programs offered (minimal on-campus study). *Degree requirements:* For master's and CAS, thesis or alternative. *Entrance requirements:* For master's, interview; for CAS, master's degree. Additional exam requirements/recommendations for international students: Required—TOEFL (minimum score 550 paper-based; 213 computer-based; 79 iBT). Electronic applications accepted. *Faculty research:* Workplace education, gerontology.

University of Southern Mississippi, Graduate School, College of Education and Psychology, Department of Educational Studies and Research, Hattiesburg, MS 39406-0001. Offers adult education (Graduate Certificate); community college leadership (Graduate Certificate); counseling and personnel services (college) (M Ed); education (PhD, Ed S), including adult education, research, evaluation and statistics (PhD); education (Ed D), including educational administration, educational research; education: educational leadership and research (Ed S), including higher education administration; educational administration and supervision (M Ed); higher education administration (Ed D, PhD); institutional research (Graduate Certificate). *Faculty:* 7 full-time (1 woman), 5 part-time/adjunct (1 woman). *Students:* 33 full-time (25 women), 104 part-time (25 women); includes 46 minority (40 Black or African American, non-Hispanic/Latino; 1 Asian, non-Hispanic/Latino; 3 Hispanic/Latino; 2 Two or more races, non-Hispanic/Latino), 1 international. Average age 36. 27 applicants, 48% accepted, 1 enrolled. In 2011, 27 master's, 13 doctorates, 1 other advanced degree awarded. *Degree requirements:* For master's and other advanced degree, comprehensive exam, thesis (for some programs); for doctorate, comprehensive exam, thesis/dissertation. *Entrance requirements:* For master's, doctorate, and other advanced degree, GRE General Test, minimum GPA of 2.75. Additional exam requirements/recommendations for international students: Required—TOEFL. *Application deadline:* For fall admission, 2/1 for domestic students, 3/1 for international students. Applications are processed on a rolling basis. Application fee: $35. *Financial support:* Career-related internships or fieldwork, Federal Work-Study, and institutionally sponsored loans available. Financial award application deadline: 3/15; financial award applicants required to submit FAFSA. *Total annual research expenditures:* $88,500. *Unit head:* Dr. Thomas V. O'Brien, Chair, 601-266-6093, E-mail: thomas.obrien@usm.edu. *Application contact:* Shonna Breland, Manager of Graduate Admissions, 601-266-6563, Fax: 601-266-5138. Web site: http://www.usm.edu/cep/esr/.

University of South Florida, Graduate School, College of Education, Department of Adult, Career and Higher Education, Tampa, FL 33620-9951. Offers adult education (MA, Ed D, PhD, Ed S); career and technical education (MA); career and workforce education (PhD); higher education/community college teaching (MA, Ed D, PhD); vocational education (Ed S). Part-time programs available. Postbaccalaureate distance learning degree programs offered (minimal on-campus study). *Faculty:* 9 full-time (3 women), 4 part-time/adjunct (3 women). *Students:* 38 full-time (21 women), 169 part-time (115 women); includes 59 minority (37 Black or African American, non-Hispanic/Latino; 5 Asian, non-Hispanic/Latino; 14 Hispanic/Latino; 3 Two or more races, non-Hispanic/Latino), 6 international. Average age 44. 98 applicants, 70% accepted, 42 enrolled. In 2011, 33 master's, 13 doctorates awarded. *Median time to degree:* Of those who began their doctoral program in fall 2003, 50% received their degree in 8 years or less. *Degree requirements:* For master's, comprehensive exam; for doctorate, comprehensive exam, thesis/dissertation, philosophies of inquiry; multiple research methods; for Ed S, comprehensive exam, thesis. *Entrance requirements:* For master's, minimum GPA of 3.0 in last 60 hours of course work; for doctorate and Ed S, GRE General Test, GRE Writing Test. Additional exam requirements/recommendations for international students: Required—TOEFL (minimum score 500 paper-based; 213 computer-based; 91 iBT). *Application deadline:* For fall admission, 2/15 for domestic students, 1/2 for international students; for spring admission, 10/15 for domestic students, 6/1 for international students. Applications are processed on a rolling basis. Application fee: $30. Electronic applications accepted. *Financial support:* In 2011–12, 5 students received support, including 5 teaching assistantships with full tuition reimbursements available (averaging $15,000 per year); career-related internships or fieldwork, scholarships/grants, and unspecified assistantships also available. Financial award applicants required to submit FAFSA. *Faculty research:* Community college leadership; integration of academic, career and technical education; competency-based education; continuing education administration; adult learning and development. *Total annual research expenditures:* $9,807. *Unit head:* Dr. Ann Cranston-Gingras, Chairperson, 813-974-6036, Fax: 813-974-3366, E-mail: cranston@usf.edu. *Application contact:* Dr. William Young, Program Director, 813-974-1861, Fax: 813-974-3366, E-mail: williamyoung@usf.edu.

The University of Texas at Arlington, Graduate School, College of Education and Health Professions, Department of Educational Leadership and Policy Studies, Arlington, TX 76019. Offers dual language (M Ed); education leadership and policy studies (PhD); higher education (M Ed); principal certification (M Ed). Part-time and evening/weekend programs available. Postbaccalaureate distance learning degree programs offered (no on-campus study). *Faculty:* 12 full-time (9 women). *Students:* 31 full-time (25 women), 749 part-time (523 women); includes 334 minority (165 Black or African American, non-Hispanic/Latino; 5 American Indian or Alaska Native, non-Hispanic/Latino; 11 Asian, non-Hispanic/Latino; 140 Hispanic/Latino; 13 Two or more races, non-Hispanic/Latino), 9 international. 342 applicants, 84% accepted, 247 enrolled. In 2011, 183 master's, 1 doctorate awarded. *Degree requirements:* For master's, 2 field-based practica; for doctorate, comprehensive exam, thesis/dissertation, 2 research-based practica. *Entrance requirements:* For master's, GRE, 3 references forms, minimum undergraduate GPA of 3.0 in the last 60 hours of course work; for doctorate, GRE, resume, statement of intent, 3 reference forms, applicable master's degree. Application fee: $50. *Financial support:* In 2011–12, 6 students received support, including 4 fellowships (averaging $6,700 per year), 2 research assistantships (averaging $8,000 per year). Financial award applicants required to submit FAFSA. *Faculty research:* Lived realities of students of color in K-16 contexts, K-16 faculty, K-16 policy and law, K-16 student access, K-16 student success. *Unit head:* Dr. Adrienne E. Hyle, Chair, 817-272-2841, Fax: 817-272-2127, E-mail: ahyle@uta.edu. *Application contact:* Paige Cordor, Graduate Advisor, 817-272-5051, Fax: 817-272-2127, E-mail: paigec@uta.edu. Web site: http://www.uta.edu/coehp/educleadership/.

The University of Texas at San Antonio, College of Education and Human Development, Department of Educational Leadership and Policy Studies, San Antonio, TX 78249-0617. Offers educational leadership (Ed D); educational leadership and policy studies (M Ed), including educational leadership, higher education administration; higher education administration (M Ed). Part-time programs available. *Faculty:* 17 full-time (8 women), 26 part-time/adjunct (13 women). *Students:* 71 full-time (52 women), 269 part-time (185 women); includes 213 minority (33 Black or African American, non-Hispanic/Latino; 3 Asian, non-Hispanic/Latino; 171 Hispanic/Latino; 6 Two or more races, non-Hispanic/Latino), 4 international. Average age 36. 155 applicants, 77% accepted, 95 enrolled. In 2011, 102 master's, 8 doctorates awarded. *Degree requirements:* For master's, comprehensive exam, thesis or alternative; for doctorate, comprehensive exam, thesis/dissertation. *Entrance requirements:* For master's, bachelor's degree with 18 credit hours in field of study or in another appropriate field of study, resume, letter of recommendation; for doctorate, GRE General Test, minimum GPA of 3.5 in a master's program, resume, three letters of recommendation, statement of purpose. Additional exam requirements/recommendations for international students: Required—TOEFL (minimum score 550 paper-based; 61 iBT), IELTS (minimum score 5). *Application deadline:* For fall admission, 7/1 for domestic students, 4/1 for international students; for spring admission, 11/1 for domestic students, 9/1 for international students. Application fee: $45 ($85 for international students). *Expenses:* Tuition, state resident: full-time $3148; part-time $2176 per semester. Tuition, nonresident: full-time $8782; part-time $5932 per semester. *Required fees:* $719 per semester. *Financial support:* In 2011–12, 6 students received support, including 6 fellowships with full and partial tuition reimbursements available (averaging $40,000 per year). Financial award application deadline: 2/1. *Faculty research:* Urban and international school leadership, student success, college access, higher education policy, multiculturalism, minority student achievement. *Unit head:* Dr. David P. Thompson, Department Chair, 210-458-5404, Fax: 210-458-5848, E-mail: david.thompson@utsa.edu. *Application contact:* Elisha Reynolds, Student Development Specialist, 210-458-6620, Fax: 210-458-5848, E-mail: grelisha.reynolds@utsa.edu.

University of the Incarnate Word, School of Graduate Studies and Research, Dreeben School of Education, Programs in Education, San Antonio, TX 78209-6397. Offers adult education (M Ed, MA); cross-cultural education (M Ed, MA); early childhood literacy (M Ed, MA); general education (M Ed, MA); higher education (PhD); instructional technology (M Ed, MA); international education and entrepreneurship (PhD); kinesiology (M Ed, MA); literacy (M Ed, MA); organizational leadership (PhD); organizational learning and learning (M Ed, MA); reading (M Ed, MA); special education (M Ed, MA); teacher leadership (M Ed, MA). Part-time and evening/weekend programs available. *Faculty:* 14 full-time (8 women), 10 part-time/adjunct (9 women). *Students:* 13 full-time (7 women), 197 part-time (129 women); includes 111 minority (23 Black or African American, non-Hispanic/Latino; 2 American Indian or Alaska Native, non-Hispanic/Latino; 1 Asian, non-Hispanic/Latino; 85 Hispanic/Latino), 26 international. Average age 41. 78 applicants, 79% accepted, 34 enrolled. In 2011, 21 master's, 12 doctorates awarded. *Degree requirements:* For master's, capstone; for doctorate, thesis/dissertation, qualifying exam. *Entrance requirements:* For master's, baccalaureate degree; minimum foundation GPA of 2.5; interview; for doctorate, master's degree; interview; supervised writing sample. Additional exam requirements/recommendations for international students: Required—TOEFL (minimum score 560 paper-based; 220 computer-based; 83 iBT). *Application deadline:* Applications are processed on a rolling basis. Application fee: $20. Electronic applications accepted. *Expenses: Tuition:* Part-time $725 per credit hour. Tuition and fees vary according to degree level. *Financial support:* In 2011–12, 5 research assistantships were awarded; Federal Work-Study and scholarships/grants also available. Financial award applicants required to submit FAFSA. *Unit head:* Dr. Denise Staudt, Dean, Dreeben School of Education, 210-829-2762, E-mail: staudt@uiwtx.edu. *Application contact:* Andrea Cyterski-Acosta, Dean of Enrollment, 210-829-6005, Fax: 210-829-3921, E-mail: admis@uiwtx.edu. Web site: http://www.uiw.edu/education/index.htm.

The University of Toledo, College of Graduate Studies, Judith Herb College of Education, Health Science and Human Service, Department of Educational Foundations and Leadership, Toledo, OH 43606-3390. Offers educational administration and supervision (ME, DE, Ed S); educational psychology (ME, DE, PhD); educational research and measurement (ME, PhD); educational sociology (DE, PhD); educational theory and social foundations (ME); foundations of education (DE, PhD); higher education (ME, PhD); history of education (PhD); philosophy of education (PhD). *Accreditation:* NCATE. Part-time and evening/weekend programs available. *Faculty:* 32. *Students:* 26 full-time (14 women), 222 part-time (134 women); includes 78 minority (57 Black or African American, non-Hispanic/Latino; 5 Asian, non-Hispanic/Latino; 15 Hispanic/Latino; 1 Two or more races, non-Hispanic/Latino), 5 international. Average age 40. 85 applicants, 61% accepted, 34 enrolled. In 2011, 37 master's, 7 doctorates, 18 other advanced degrees awarded. *Degree requirements:* For master's, comprehensive exam, thesis or alternative; for doctorate, comprehensive exam, thesis/dissertation; for Ed S, thesis optional. *Entrance requirements:* For master's, doctorate, and Ed S, minimum cumulative GPA of 2.7 for all previous academic work, letters of recommendation. Additional exam requirements/recommendations for international students: Required—TOEFL (minimum score 550 paper-based; 213 computer-based; 80 iBT), IELTS (minimum score 6.5). *Application deadline:* For fall admission, 1/15 priority date for domestic students, 1/15 for international students. Applications are processed on a rolling basis. Application fee: $45 ($75 for international students). Electronic applications accepted. *Financial support:* In 2011–12, 10 research assistantships with full and partial tuition reimbursements (averaging $6,734 per year), 8 teaching assistantships with full and partial tuition reimbursements (averaging $9,000 per year) were awarded; career-related internships or fieldwork, Federal Work-Study, institutionally sponsored loans, scholarships/grants, tuition waivers (full and partial), unspecified assistantships, and administrative assistantships also available. Support available to part-time students. *Unit head:* Dr. William Gray, Interim Chair, 419-530-2565, Fax: 419-530-8447, E-mail: william.gray@utoledo.edu. *Application contact:* Graduate School Office, 419-530-4723, Fax: 419-530-4724, E-mail: grdsch@utnet.utoledo.edu. Web site: http://www.utoledo.edu/eduhshs/.

University of Virginia, Curry School of Education, Department of Leadership, Foundations and Policy, Program in Higher Education, Charlottesville, VA 22903. Offers higher education (Ed S); student affairs practice (M Ed). *Students:* 23 full-time (12 women), 18 part-time (9 women); includes 6 minority (5 Black or African American, non-Hispanic/Latino; 1 Asian, non-Hispanic/Latino). Average age 31. 15 applicants, 60% accepted, 8 enrolled. In 2011, 16 master's awarded. *Entrance requirements:* For master's, doctorate, and Ed S, GRE General Test, 2 letters of recommendation. Additional exam requirements/recommendations for international students: Required—TOEFL (minimum score 600 paper-based; 250 computer-based; 90 iBT), IELTS (minimum score 7). *Application deadline:* Applications are processed on a rolling basis. Application fee: $60. Electronic applications accepted. *Financial support:* Fellowships, research assistantships, and teaching assistantships available. Financial award applicants required to submit FAFSA. *Unit head:* Brian Pusser, Associate Professor and Director, 434-924-7782, E-mail: highered@virginia.edu. *Application contact:* Lisa Miller, Assistant to the Chair, 434-982-2849, E-mail: lam3v@virgnina.edu. Web site: http://curry.virginia.edu/academics/areas-of-study/higher-education.

University of Virginia, Curry School of Education, Program in Education, Charlottesville, VA 22903. Offers administration and supervision (PhD); applied developmental science (PhD); counselor education (PhD); curriculum and instruction (PhD); early childhood-developmental risk (MT); education evaluation (PhD); educational psychology (PhD); educational research (PhD); elementary (MT, PhD); English education (MT, PhD); foreign language education (MT); higher education (PhD); instructional technology (PhD); kinesiology (MT, PhD); math education (PhD); reading education (PhD); research statistics and evaluation (PhD); school psychology (PhD); science education (PhD); social studies education (MT, PhD); special education (PhD); world languages education (MT). *Students:* 299 full-time (216 women), 60 part-time (33 women); includes 46 minority (18 Black or African American, non-Hispanic/Latino; 17 Asian, non-Hispanic/Latino; 7 Hispanic/Latino; 4 Two or more races, non-Hispanic/Latino), 23 international. Average age 30. 307 applicants, 42% accepted, 80 enrolled. In 2011, 113 master's, 62 doctorates awarded. *Degree requirements:* For master's, comprehensive exam (for some programs), field project; for doctorate, comprehensive exam, thesis/dissertation. *Entrance requirements:* For doctorate, GRE General Test. Additional exam requirements/recommendations for international students: Required—TOEFL (minimum score 600 paper-based; 250 computer-based; 90 iBT), IELTS (minimum score 7). *Application deadline:* Applications are processed on a rolling basis. Application fee: $60. Electronic applications accepted. *Financial support:* Fellowships, research assistantships, and teaching assistantships available. Financial award application deadline: 1/5; financial award applicants required to submit FAFSA. *Unit head:* Robert C. Pianta, Dean, 434-924-3334. *Application contact:* Joanne McNergney, Assistant Dean for Admissions and Student Services, 434-924-3334, E-mail: curry-admissions@virginia.edu.

University of Washington, Graduate School, College of Education, Seattle, WA 98195. Offers curriculum and instruction (M Ed, Ed D, PhD), including educational technology, general curriculum (Ed D, PhD), language, literacy, and culture, mathematics education, multicultural education, reading and language arts education (Ed D), science education, social studies education, teaching and curriculum (M Ed); educational leadership and policy studies (M Ed, Ed D, PhD), including administration (Ed D), educational policy, organization, and leadership (M Ed, PhD), higher education, leadership for learning (Ed D), social and cultural foundations of education (M Ed, PhD); educational psychology (M Ed, PhD), including educational psychology (PhD), human development and cognition (M Ed), learning sciences, measurement, statistics and research design (M Ed), school psychology (M Ed); instructional leadership (M Ed); intercollegiate athletic leadership (M Ed); special education (M Ed, Ed D, PhD), including early childhood special education (M Ed), emotional and behavioral disabilities (M Ed), learning disabilities (M Ed), low-incidence disabilities (M Ed), severe disabilities (M Ed), special education (Ed D, PhD); teacher education (MIT). *Accreditation:* APA. Part-time and evening/weekend programs available. *Degree requirements:* For master's, thesis optional; for doctorate, thesis/dissertation. *Entrance requirements:* For master's and doctorate, GRE General Test, minimum GPA of 3.0. Additional exam requirements/recommendations for international students: Required—TOEFL. Electronic applications accepted. *Faculty research:* School restructuring/effective schools, special education interventions, literacy and writing, technology, school partnerships, teacher preparation.

University of Wisconsin–La Crosse, Office of University Graduate Studies, College of Liberal Studies, Department of Student Affairs Administration in Higher Education, La Crosse, WI 54601-3742. Offers MS Ed. Part-time programs available. Postbaccalaureate distance learning degree programs offered (no on-campus study). *Faculty:* 1 full-time (0 women), 11 part-time/adjunct (5 women). *Students:* 34 full-time (25 women), 42 part-time (30 women); includes 8 minority (2 Black or African American, non-Hispanic/Latino; 1 American Indian or Alaska Native, non-Hispanic/Latino; 2 Asian, non-Hispanic/Latino; 2 Hispanic/Latino; 1 Two or more races, non-Hispanic/Latino). Average age 29. 71 applicants, 55% accepted, 16 enrolled. In 2011, 36 master's awarded. *Degree requirements:* For master's, comprehensive exam (for some programs), thesis optional, electronic portfolio, applied research project. *Entrance requirements:* For master's, interview, writing sample, references, experience in the field. Additional exam requirements/recommendations for international students: Required—TOEFL (minimum score 550 paper-based; 213 computer-based; 79 iBT). *Application deadline:* For fall admission, 2/1 priority date for domestic students, 2/1 for international students. Application fee: $56. Electronic applications accepted. *Expenses:* Tuition, state resident: full-time $8391; part-time $481.17 per credit. Tuition, nonresident: full-time $17,850; part-time $1006.68 per credit. *Required fees:* $2 per credit. $18.25 per semester. Tuition and fees vary according to course load, program, reciprocity agreements and student level. *Financial support:* In 2011–12, 32 research assistantships with partial tuition reimbursements (averaging $10,016 per year) were awarded; Federal Work-Study, scholarships/grants, and health care benefits also available. Support available to part-time students. Financial award application deadline: 3/15; financial award applicants required to submit FAFSA. *Unit head:* Dr. Jodie Rindt, Director, 608-785-6450, E-mail: rindt.jodi@uwlax.edu. *Application contact:* Kathryn Kiefer, Director of Admissions, 608-785-8939, E-mail: admissions@uwlax.edu. Web site: http://www.uwlax.edu/saa/.

University of Wisconsin–Milwaukee, Graduate School, School of Education, Department of Administrative Leadership, Milwaukee, WI 53201-0413. Offers administrative leadership and supervision in education (MS); specialist in administrative leadership (Certificate); teaching and learning in higher education (Certificate). Part-time programs available. *Faculty:* 9 full-time (6 women), 1 part-time/adjunct (0 women). *Students:* 29 full-time (21 women), 122 part-time (87 women); includes 37 minority (22 Black or African American, non-Hispanic/Latino; 5 Asian, non-Hispanic/Latino; 2 Hispanic/Latino; 8 Two or more races, non-Hispanic/Latino), 3 international. Average age 34. 79 applicants, 68% accepted, 30 enrolled. In 2011, 44 degrees awarded. *Degree requirements:* For master's, comprehensive exam, thesis or alternative. *Entrance requirements:* For master's, GRE General Test. Additional exam requirements/recommendations for international students: Required—TOEFL (minimum score 550 paper-based; 79 iBT), IELTS (minimum score 6.5). *Application deadline:* For fall admission, 1/1 priority date for domestic students; for spring admission, 9/1 for domestic students. Applications are processed on a rolling basis. Application fee: $56 ($96 for international students). Electronic applications accepted. One-time fee: $506.10 full-time. Tuition and fees vary according to course load and reciprocity agreements. *Financial support:* In 2011–12, 2 fellowships were awarded; research assistantships, teaching assistantships, career-related internships or fieldwork, health care benefits, unspecified assistantships, and project assistantships also available. Support available to part-time students. Financial award application deadline: 4/15; financial award applicants required to submit FAFSA. *Total annual research expenditures:* $31,569. *Unit head:* Larry Martin, Department Chair, 414-229-5754, Fax: 414-229-5300, E-mail: lmartin@uwm.edu. *Application contact:* General Information Contact, 414-229-4982, Fax: 414-229-6967, E-mail: gradschool@uwm.edu. Web site: http://www.uwm.edu/Dept/Ad_Ldsp/.

University of Wisconsin–Whitewater, School of Graduate Studies, College of Business and Economics, Department of Business Education, Whitewater, WI 53190-1790. Offers business and marketing education (MS), including general, post secondary, secondary. *Accreditation:* NCATE. Part-time and evening/weekend programs available. Postbaccalaureate distance learning degree programs offered (no on-campus study). *Students:* 2 full-time (1 woman), 19 part-time (8 women); includes 1 minority (Hispanic/Latino). Average age 35. 5 applicants, 80% accepted, 2 enrolled. In 2011, 7 master's awarded. *Degree requirements:* For master's, thesis or alternative. *Entrance requirements:* For master's, interview, teaching license. Additional exam requirements/recommendations for international students: Required—TOEFL (minimum score 550 paper-based; 213 computer-based; 80 iBT), IELTS (minimum score 6). *Application deadline:* For fall admission, 7/15 priority date for domestic students, 7/15 for international students; for spring admission, 12/1 priority date for domestic students, 12/1 for international students. Applications are processed on a rolling basis. Application fee: $56. Electronic applications accepted. *Expenses:* Tuition, state resident: full-time $4088. Tuition, nonresident: full-time $8817. Tuition and fees vary according to program. *Financial support:* In 2011–12, 2 research assistantships (averaging $7,245 per year) were awarded; Federal Work-Study, unspecified assistantships, and out of state fee waiver also available. Support available to part-time students. Financial award application deadline: 3/15; financial award applicants required to submit FAFSA. *Faculty* *research:* Active learning and performance strategies, technology-enhanced formative assessment, computer-supported cooperative work, privacy surveillance. *Unit head:* Dr. Lila Waldman, Coordinator, 262-472-5475. *Application contact:* Sally A. Lange, School of Graduate Studies, 262-472-1006, Fax: 262-472-5027, E-mail: gradschl@uww.edu.

University of Wisconsin–Whitewater, School of Graduate Studies, College of Education and Professional Studies, Department of Counselor Education, Whitewater, WI 53190-1790. Offers community counseling (MS Ed); higher education (MS Ed); school (MS Ed). *Accreditation:* ACA; NCATE. Part-time and evening/weekend programs available. *Students:* 86 full-time (72 women), 63 part-time (55 women); includes 17 minority (10 Black or African American, non-Hispanic/Latino; 1 Asian, non-Hispanic/Latino; 6 Hispanic/Latino). Average age 30. 44 applicants, 77% accepted, 16 enrolled. In 2011, 27 master's awarded. *Degree requirements:* For master's, thesis or alternative. *Entrance requirements:* For master's, resume, 2 letters of reference, goal statement, autobiography. Additional exam requirements/recommendations for international students: Required—TOEFL (minimum score 550 paper-based; 213 computer-based; 80 iBT), IELTS (minimum score 6). *Application deadline:* For fall admission, 2/1 for domestic and international students. Application fee: $56. Electronic applications accepted. *Expenses:* Tuition, state resident: full-time $4088. Tuition, nonresident: full-time $8817. Tuition and fees vary according to program. *Financial support:* In 2011–12, 1 research assistantship (averaging $5,175 per year) was awarded; Federal Work-Study, unspecified assistantships, and out of state fee waiver also available. Support available to part-time students. Financial award application deadline: 3/15; financial award applicants required to submit FAFSA. *Faculty research:* Alcohol and other drugs, counseling effectiveness, teacher mentoring. *Unit head:* Dr. Brenda O'Beirne, Coordinator, 262-472-1452, Fax: 262-472-2841, E-mail: obeirneneb@uww.edu. *Application contact:* Sally A. Lange, School of Graduate Studies, 262-472-1006, Fax: 262-472-5027, E-mail: gradschl@uww.edu.

Upper Iowa University, Online Master's Programs, Fayette, IA 52142-1857. Offers accounting (MBA); corporate financial management (MBA); global business (MBA); health and human services (MPA); higher education administration (MHEA); homeland security (MPA); human resources management (MBA); justice administration (MPA); organizational development (MBA); public personnel management (MPA); quality management (MBA). MBA also available at Madison, WI campus. Part-time programs available. Postbaccalaureate distance learning degree programs offered (no on-campus study). *Degree requirements:* For master's, research project. *Entrance requirements:* For master's, GMAT, GRE, or minimum GPA of 2.7 during last 60 hours. Additional exam requirements/recommendations for international students: Required—TOEFL (minimum score 570 paper-based; 230 computer-based). Electronic applications accepted. *Faculty research:* Total quality management, CQI, teams, organization culture and climate, management.

Vanderbilt University, Peabody College, Department of Leadership, Policy, and Organizations, Nashville, TN 37240-1001. Offers education policy (MPP); educational leadership and policy (Ed D); higher education (M Ed); higher education, leadership and policy (Ed D); international education policy and management (M Ed); leadership and organizational performance (M Ed). Part-time and evening/weekend programs available. *Faculty:* 27 full-time (12 women), 10 part-time/adjunct (3 women). *Students:* 165 full-time (117 women), 98 part-time (46 women); includes 35 minority (15 Black or African American, non-Hispanic/Latino; 4 Asian, non-Hispanic/Latino; 10 Hispanic/Latino; 6 Two or more races, non-Hispanic/Latino), 30 international. Average age 28. 465 applicants, 54% accepted, 87 enrolled. In 2011, 102 master's, 25 doctorates awarded. *Degree requirements:* For master's, comprehensive exam, thesis optional; for doctorate, thesis/dissertation, qualifying exams, residency. *Entrance requirements:* For master's and doctorate, GRE General Test. Additional exam requirements/recommendations for international students: Required—TOEFL (minimum score 550 paper-based; 213 computer-based). *Application deadline:* For fall admission, 12/31 priority date for domestic students, 12/31 for international students; for spring admission, 11/1 priority date for domestic students, 11/1 for international students. Applications are processed on a rolling basis. Application fee: $0. Electronic applications accepted. *Financial support:* Fellowships with full and partial tuition reimbursements, research assistantships with full and partial tuition reimbursements, teaching assistantships with full and partial tuition reimbursements, Federal Work-Study, institutionally sponsored loans, scholarships/grants, tuition waivers (partial), and unspecified assistantships available. Support available to part-time students. Financial award application deadline: 2/1; financial award applicants required to submit FAFSA. *Faculty research:* Education policy, education reform, school choice, equity and diversity, higher education. *Unit head:* Dr. Ellen B. Goldring, Chair, 615-322-8000, Fax: 615-343-7094, E-mail: ellen.b.goldring@vanderbilt.edu. *Application contact:* Rosie Moody, Educational Coordinator, 615-322-8019, Fax: 615-343-7094, E-mail: rosie.moody@vanderbilt.edu.

Virginia Polytechnic Institute and State University, Graduate School, College of Liberal Arts and Human Sciences, School of Education, Department of Educational Leadership and Policy Studies, Blacksburg, VA 24061. Offers administration and supervision of special education (Ed D, PhD); counselor education (MA, PhD); educational leadership and policy studies (MA, Ed D, PhD, Ed S); educational research and evaluation (PhD); higher education (MA, PhD). *Accreditation:* ACA; NCATE. *Degree requirements:* For master's, comprehensive exam (for some programs), thesis (for some programs); for doctorate, comprehensive exam (for some programs), thesis/dissertation (for some programs). *Entrance requirements:* For master's and doctorate, GRE. Additional exam requirements/recommendations for international students: Required—TOEFL (minimum score 550 paper-based; 213 computer-based). *Application deadline:* For fall admission, 7/1 for domestic and international students; for spring admission, 12/1 for domestic and international students. Applications are processed on a rolling basis. Application fee: $65. Electronic applications accepted. *Expenses:* Tuition, state resident: full-time $10,048; part-time $558.25 per credit hour. Tuition, nonresident: full-time $19,497; part-time $1083.25 per credit hour. *Required fees:* $405 per semester. Tuition and fees vary according to course load, campus/location and program. *Financial support:* Career-related internships or fieldwork, Federal Work-Study, scholarships/grants, health care benefits, and unspecified assistantships available. Financial award application deadline: 1/15. *Unit head:* Dr. M. David Alexander, Unit Head, 540-231-9723, Fax: 540-231-7845, E-mail: mdavid@vt.edu. *Application contact:* Daisy Stewart, Information Contact, 540-231-8180, Fax: 540-231-7845, E-mail: daisys@vt.edu. Web site: http://www.soe.vt.edu/elps/index.html.

Virginia Polytechnic Institute and State University, Graduate School, College of Liberal Arts and Human Sciences, School of Education, Department of Teaching and Learning, Blacksburg, VA 24061. Offers career and technical education (MS Ed, Ed D, PhD, Ed S); cognition and education (Certificate); counselor education (MA, PhD); curriculum and instruction (MA Ed, Ed D, PhD, Ed S); educational research, evaluation (PhD); higher education administration (Certificate); integrative STEM education (Certificate). *Accreditation:* NCATE. Postbaccalaureate distance learning degree programs offered (no on-campus study). Terminal master's awarded for partial completion of doctoral program. *Degree requirements:* For master's, comprehensive exam (for some programs), thesis (for some programs); for doctorate, comprehensive exam (for some programs), thesis/dissertation (for some programs). *Entrance requirements:* For master's and doctorate, GRE. Additional exam requirements/recommendations for international students: Required—TOEFL (minimum score 550 paper-based; 213 computer-based). *Application deadline:* For fall admission, 7/1 for domestic and international students; for spring admission, 12/1 for domestic and international students. Applications are processed on a rolling basis. Application fee: $65. Electronic applications accepted. *Expenses:* Tuition, state resident: full-time $10,048; part-time $558.25 per credit hour. Tuition, nonresident: full-time $19,497; part-time $1083.25 per credit hour. *Required fees:* $405 per semester. Tuition and fees vary according to course load, campus/location and program. *Financial support:* Career-related internships or fieldwork, Federal Work-Study, scholarships/grants, health care benefits, and unspecified assistantships available. Financial award application deadline: 1/15. *Faculty research:* Instructional technology, teacher evaluation, school change, literacy, teaching strategies. *Unit head:* Dr. Daisy L. Stewart, Unit Head, 540-231-8180, Fax: 540-231-3717, E-mail: daisys@vt.edu. *Application contact:* Daisy Stewart, Contact, 540-231-8180, Fax: 540-231-3717, E-mail: daisys@vt.edu. Web site: http://www.soe.vt.edu/.

Walden University, Graduate Programs, Richard W. Riley College of Education and Leadership, Minneapolis, MN 55401. Offers administrator leadership for teaching and learning (Ed D, Ed S); adult education (Ed D, Ed S); adult learning (MS, Postbaccalaureate Certificate), including developmental education (MS), online teaching (MS), teaching adults English as a second language (MS), training and performance management (MS); college teaching and learning (Ed D, Ed S, Postbaccalaureate Certificate); curriculum, instruction and assessment (Ed D, Postbaccalaureate Certificate); curriculum, instruction, and professional development (Ed S); developmental education (Postbaccalaureate Certificate); early childhood administration, management, and leadership (Postbaccalaureate Certificate); early childhood education (birth-grade 3) (MAT); early childhood public policy and advocacy (Postbaccalaureate Certificate); early childhood studies (MS), including administration, management and leadership, early childhood public policy and advocacy, teaching adults in the early childhood field, teaching and diversity; education (MS, PhD), including adolescent literacy and technology (grades 6-12) (MS), adult education leadership (PhD), assessment, evaluation, and accountability (PhD), community college leadership (PhD), curriculum, instruction, and assessment, early childhood education (PhD), educational technology (PhD), elementary reading and literacy (MS), elementary reading and mathematics (MS), general program, global and comparative education (PhD), higher education (PhD), integrating technology in the classroom (MS), K-12 educational leadership (PhD), leadership, policy and change (PhD), learning, instruction and innovation (PhD), literacy and learning in the content areas (MS), mathematics (grades 6-8) (MS), mathematics (grades K-5) (MS), middle level education (grades 5-8) (MS), professional development (MS), science (grades K-8) (MS), self-designed (PhD), special education (PhD), special education (non-licensure) (MS), teacher leadership (grades K-12) (MS), teaching English language learners (grades K-12) (MS); educational leadership and administration (principal preparation) (Ed S); educational technology (Ed S); elementary reading and literacy (Postbaccalaureate Certificate); engaging culturally diverse learners (Postbaccalaureate Certificate); enrollment management and institutional marketing (Postbaccalaureate Certificate); higher education (MS), including college teaching and learning, enrollment management and institutional planning, global higher education, leadership for student success, online and distance learning; higher education leadership (Ed D); instructional design (Postbaccalaureate Certificate); instructional design and technology (MS), including general program (MS, PhD), online learning, training and performance improvement; integrating technology in the classroom (Postbaccalaureate Certificate); online teaching for adult learners (Postbaccalaureate Certificate); professional development (Postbaccalaureate Certificate); reading and literacy leadership (Ed D); science K-8 (Postbaccalaureate Certificate); special education (Ed D, Ed S); special education: emotional/behavioral disorders (K-12) (MAT); special education: learning disabilities (K-12) (MAT); teacher leadership (Ed D, Ed S, Postbaccalaureate Certificate); training and performance management (Postbaccalaureate Certificate). Part-time and evening/weekend programs available. Postbaccalaureate distance learning degree programs offered (minimal on-campus study). *Faculty:* 71 full-time (48 women), 853 part-time/adjunct (585 women). *Students:* 11,326 full-time (9,212 women), 2,148 part-time (1,795 women); includes 5,346 minority (4,403 Black or African American, non-Hispanic/Latino; 76 American Indian or Alaska Native, non-Hispanic/Latino; 140 Asian, non-Hispanic/Latino; 561 Hispanic/Latino; 21 Native Hawaiian or other Pacific Islander, non-Hispanic/Latino; 145 Two or more races, non-Hispanic/Latino), 322 international. Average age 39. In 2011, 3,477 master's, 318 doctorates, 471 other advanced degrees awarded. *Degree requirements:* For doctorate, thesis/dissertation (for some programs), residency; for other advanced degree, residency (for some programs). *Entrance requirements:* For master's, bachelor's degree or equivalent in related field; minimum GPA of 2.5; official transcripts; goal statement; access to computer and Internet; for doctorate, master's degree or equivalent in related field; minimum GPA of 3.0; official transcripts; three years' related professional/academic experience (preferred); access to computer and Internet; for other advanced degree, master's degree or equivalent in related field; minimum GPA of 3.0; 3 years related professional/academic experience (preferred); access to computer and Internet (Ed S). Additional exam requirements/recommendations for international students: Required—TOEFL (minimum score 550 paper-based; 213 computer-based), IELTS (minimum score 6.5), or Michigan English Language Assessment Battery (minimum score 82). *Application deadline:* Applications are processed on a rolling basis. Application fee: $50. Electronic applications accepted. *Financial support:* Federal Work-Study, scholarships/grants, unspecified assistantships, and family tuition reduction, active duty/veteran tuition reduction, group tuition reduction, interest-free payment plans, employee tuition reduction available. Support available to part-time students. Financial award applicants required to submit FAFSA. *Unit head:* Dr. Kate Steffens, Dean, 800-925-3368. *Application contact:* Jennifer Hall, Vice President of Enrollment Management, 866-4-WALDEN, E-mail: info@waldenu.edu. Web site: http://www.waldenu.edu/Colleges-and-Schools/College-of-Education-and-Leadership.htm.

Washington State University, Graduate School, College of Education, Department of Educational Leadership and Counseling Psychology, Pullman, WA 99164. Offers counseling psychology (Ed M, MA, PhD, Certificate), including counseling psychology (Ed M, MA, PhD), school psychologist (Certificate); educational leadership (M Ed, MA, Ed D, PhD); educational psychology (Ed M, MA, PhD); higher education (Ed M, MA, Ed D, PhD), including higher education administration (PhD), sport management (PhD), student affairs (PhD); higher education with sport management (Ed M). *Accreditation:* NCATE. *Faculty:* 12. *Students:* 103 full-time (68 women), 59 part-time (29 women); includes 36 minority (6 Black or African American, non-Hispanic/Latino; 10 Asian, non-Hispanic/Latino; 16 Hispanic/Latino; 4 Two or more races, non-Hispanic/Latino), 18 international. Average age 30. 244 applicants, 29% accepted, 45 enrolled. In 2011, 44 master's, 11 doctorates awarded. Terminal master's awarded for partial completion of doctoral program. *Degree requirements:* For master's, comprehensive exam (for some programs), thesis (for some programs), oral or written exam; for doctorate, comprehensive exam, thesis/dissertation, oral and written exams. *Entrance requirements:* For master's and doctorate, GRE General Test, minimum GPA of 3.0, 3 letters of recommendation. Additional exam requirements/recommendations for international students: Required—TOEFL (minimum score 550 paper-based; 213 computer-based). *Application deadline:* For fall admission, 3/1 for domestic and international students; for spring admission, 10/1 for domestic students, 7/1 for international students. Application fee: $75. *Financial support:* In 2011–12, 1 research assistantship (averaging $18,204 per year), 4 teaching assistantships (averaging $18,204 per year) were awarded; career-related internships or fieldwork, Federal Work-Study, institutionally sponsored loans, scholarships/grants, tuition waivers (partial), and unspecified assistantships also available. Financial award application deadline: 4/1; financial award applicants required to submit FAFSA. *Faculty research:* Attentional processes, cross-cultural psychology, faculty development in higher education. *Total annual research expenditures:* $554,000. *Unit head:* Dr. Phyllis Erdman, Associate Dean, 509-335-9117, E-mail: perdman@wsu.edu. *Application contact:* Graduate School Admissions, 800-GRADWSU, Fax: 509-335-1949, E-mail: gradsch@wsu.edu. Web site: http://www.educ.wsu.edu/elcp/.

Wayland Baptist University, Graduate Programs, Program in Education, Plainview, TX 79072-6998. Offers education administration (M Ed); higher education administration (M Ed); instructional leadership (M Ed); instructional technology (M Ed); special education (M Ed). Part-time and evening/weekend programs available. Postbaccalaureate distance learning degree programs offered (no on-campus study). *Degree requirements:* For master's, comprehensive exam, capstone course. *Entrance requirements:* For master's, GRE, GMAT or MAT. Additional exam requirements/recommendations for international students: Required—TOEFL (minimum score 500 paper-based; 173 computer-based; 61 iBT). Electronic applications accepted.

Wayne State University, College of Education, Division of Administrative and Organizational Studies, Detroit, MI 48202. Offers college and university teaching (Certificate); educational leadership (M Ed); educational leadership and policy studies (Ed D, PhD); general administration and supervision (Ed S); instructional technology (M Ed, Ed D, PhD, Ed S); online teaching (Certificate); secondary curriculum and instruction (Ed S). *Students:* 86 full-time (62 women), 261 part-time (172 women); includes 171 minority (145 Black or African American, non-Hispanic/Latino; 1 American Indian or Alaska Native, non-Hispanic/Latino; 8 Asian, non-Hispanic/Latino; 16 Hispanic/Latino; 1 Two or more races, non-Hispanic/Latino), 8 international. Average age 39. 122 applicants, 40% accepted, 28 enrolled. In 2011, 73 master's, 9 doctorates, 50 other advanced degrees awarded. *Degree requirements:* For doctorate, thesis/dissertation. *Entrance requirements:* For doctorate, GRE or MAT, interview; autobiography or curriculum vitae; references; master's degree; minimum undergraduate GPA of 3.0, graduate 3.75; 3 years relevant experience; foundational course work; for other advanced degree, minimum GPA of 3.4. Additional exam requirements/recommendations for international students: Required—TOEFL (minimum score 550 paper-based; 213 computer-based), TWE (minimum score 5.5). *Application deadline:* For fall admission, 6/1 priority date for domestic students, 5/1 for international students; for winter admission, 10/1 priority date for domestic students, 9/1 for international students; for spring admission, 2/1 priority date for domestic students, 1/1 for international students. Applications are processed on a rolling basis. Application fee: $50. Electronic applications accepted. *Expenses:* Tuition, state resident: part-time $512.85 per credit. Tuition, nonresident: part-time $1132.65 per credit. *Required fees:* $26.60 per credit. $199.65 per semester. Tuition and fees vary according to course load and program. *Financial support:* In 2011–12, 59 students received support, including 1 fellowship with tuition reimbursement available (averaging $17,347 per year), 4 research assistantships with tuition reimbursements available (averaging $15,713 per year); career-related internships or fieldwork, Federal Work-Study, institutionally sponsored loans, scholarships/grants, health care benefits, and unspecified assistantships also available. Support available to part-time students. *Faculty research:* Total quality management, participatory management, administering educational technology, school improvement, principalship. *Total annual research expenditures:* $22,232. *Unit head:* Dr. Alan Hoffman, Interim Assistant Dean, 313-577-5235, E-mail: alanhoffman@wayne.edu. *Application contact:* Janice Green, Assistant Dean, 313-577-1605, E-mail: jwgreen@wayne.edu. Web site: http://coe.wayne.edu/aos/index.php.

Western Carolina University, Graduate School, College of Education and Allied Professions, School of Teaching and Learning, Cullowhee, NC 28723. Offers community college and higher education (MA Ed), including community college administration, community college teaching; comprehensive education (MA Ed, MAT); educational leadership (MA Ed, MSA, Ed D, Ed S), including educational leadership (MSA, Ed D, Ed S), educational supervision (MA Ed); teaching (MA Ed, MAT), including comprehensive education (MA Ed), physical education (MA Ed), teaching (MAT). *Accreditation:* NCATE. Part-time and evening/weekend programs available. Postbaccalaureate distance learning degree programs offered. *Students:* 40 full-time (24 women), 150 part-time (133 women); includes 13 minority (6 Black or African American, non-Hispanic/Latino; 2 American Indian or Alaska Native, non-Hispanic/Latino; 4 Hispanic/Latino; 1 Two or more races, non-Hispanic/Latino), 9 international. Average age 32. 96 applicants, 90% accepted, 71 enrolled. In 2011, 86 master's, 13 doctorates, 5 other advanced degrees awarded. *Degree requirements:* For master's, comprehensive exam; for doctorate, comprehensive exam, thesis/dissertation. *Entrance requirements:* For master's, GRE, appropriate undergraduate degree, 3 letters of recommendation; for doctorate, GRE General Test, minimum graduate GPA of 3.5, appropriate master's degree; for other advanced degree, GRE General Test, minimum graduate GPA of 3.5, work experience, appropriate master's degree. Additional exam requirements/recommendations for international students: Required—TOEFL (minimum score 550 paper-based; 270 computer-based; 79 iBT). *Application deadline:* For fall admission, 2/1 for domestic students; for spring admission, 9/1 priority date for domestic students. Applications are processed on a rolling basis. Application fee: $50. *Expenses:* Tuition, state resident: full-time $3348. Tuition, nonresident: full-time $12,933. *Required fees:* $3155. *Financial support:* In 2011–12, 2 fellowships were awarded; research assistantships with full and partial tuition reimbursements, teaching assistantships with full and partial tuition reimbursements, career-related internships or fieldwork, institutionally sponsored loans, scholarships/grants, and unspecified assistantships also available. Financial award application deadline: 3/31; financial award applicants required to submit FAFSA. *Faculty research:* Educational leadership, special education, rural education, organizational theory and practice, interinstitutional partnership, program evaluation. *Unit head:* Dr. William Dee Nichols, Department Head, 828-227-7108, Fax: 828-227-7607, E-mail: wdnichols@wcu.edu. *Application contact:* Admissions Specialist for Educational Leadership and Foundations, 828-227-7398, Fax: 828-227-7480, E-mail: gradsch@email.wcu.edu. Web site: http://www.wcu.edu/3067.asp.

Western Governors University, Teachers College, Salt Lake City, UT 84107. Offers curriculum and instruction (MS); educational leadership (MS); educational studies (MA); educational studies (5-12) (MA), including mathematics; elementary education (k-8) (Postbaccalaureate Certificate); English language learning (K-12) (MA); instructional design (MAT); learning and technology (M Ed, MA); management and innovation (M Ed); mathematics (5-12) (Postbaccalaureate Certificate); mathematics (5-9) (Postbaccalaureate Certificate); mathematics education (5-12) (MA); mathematics education (5-9) (MA); mathematics education (K-6) (MA); measurement and evaluation (M Ed); science (5-12) (Postbaccalaureate Certificate); science (5-9) (Postbaccalaureate Certificate); science education (5-12) (MA), including biology, chemistry, geology, physics; science education (5-9) (MA); social science (5-12) (MAT); special education (MAT). *Accreditation:* NCATE. Evening/weekend programs available. Postbaccalaureate distance learning degree programs offered (no on-campus study). *Students:* 3,746 full-time (2,811 women); includes 652 minority (332 Black or African American, non-Hispanic/Latino; 37 American Indian or Alaska Native, non-Hispanic/Latino; 74 Asian, non-Hispanic/Latino; 139 Hispanic/Latino; 70 Two or more races, non-Hispanic/Latino), 12 international. Average age 37. In 2011, 1,080 master's, 242 other advanced degrees awarded. *Degree requirements:* For master's, capstone project. *Entrance requirements:* For master's and Postbaccalaureate Certificate, Readiness Assessment, commitment counseling discussion, transcript submissions, completion of orientation. Additional exam requirements/recommendations for international students: Required—TOEFL (minimum score 450 paper-based; 80 iBT). *Application deadline:* Applications are processed on a rolling basis. Application fee: $65. Electronic applications accepted. *Expenses:* Contact institution. *Financial support:* Scholarships/grants and tuition waivers (partial) available. Financial award applicants required to submit FAFSA. *Unit head:* Dr. Philip Schmidt, Dean of the Teachers College, 845-255-4656. *Application contact:* Enrollment Department, 866-225-5948, Fax: 801-274-3306, E-mail: info@wgu.edu.

Western Kentucky University, Graduate Studies, College of Education and Behavioral Sciences, Department of Counseling and Student Affairs, Bowling Green, KY 42101. Offers counseling (MA Ed), including marriage and family therapy, mental health counseling; school counseling (P-12) (MA Ed); student affairs in higher education (MA Ed). *Accreditation:* ACA; NCATE. Part-time and evening/weekend programs available. *Degree requirements:* For master's, comprehensive exam, thesis optional. *Entrance requirements:* For master's, GRE General Test. Additional exam requirements/recommendations for international students: Required—TOEFL (minimum score 555 paper-based; 213 computer-based; 79 iBT). *Faculty research:* Counselor education, research for residential workers.

Western Washington University, Graduate School, Woodring College of Education, Department of Educational Leadership, Program in Continuing and College Education, Bellingham, WA 98225-5996. Offers M Ed. Part-time and evening/weekend programs available. Postbaccalaureate distance learning degree programs offered (minimal on-campus study). *Degree requirements:* For master's, comprehensive exam, thesis optional. *Entrance requirements:* For master's, GRE General Test or MAT, minimum GPA of 3.0 in last 60 semester hours or last 90 quarter hours. Additional exam requirements/recommendations for international students: Required—TOEFL (minimum score 567 paper-based; 227 computer-based). Electronic applications accepted. *Faculty research:* Transfer of learning, postsecondary faculty development, action research as professional development, literacy education in community colleges, adult education in the Middle East, distance learning tools for graduate students.

West Virginia University, College of Human Resources and Education, Department of Curriculum and Instruction/Literacy Studies, Program in Secondary Education, Morgantown, WV 26506. Offers higher education curriculum and teaching (MA); secondary education (MA). Students enter program as undergraduates. *Accreditation:* NCATE. Part-time programs available. *Degree requirements:* For master's, thesis optional, content exams. *Entrance requirements:* For master's, minimum GPA of 2.75. Additional exam requirements/recommendations for international students: Required—TOEFL. Electronic applications accepted. *Faculty research:* Teacher education, school reform, curriculum development, education technology.

West Virginia University, College of Human Resources and Education, Department of Educational Leadership Studies, Morgantown, WV 26506. Offers educational leadership (Ed D); higher education administration (MA); public school administration (MA). *Accreditation:* NCATE. Part-time programs available. *Degree requirements:* For master's, content exams; for doctorate, comprehensive exam, thesis/dissertation. *Entrance requirements:* For master's, minimum GPA of 2.75 or MA Degree or MAT of 4107; for doctorate, GRE General Test or MAT, minimum GPA of 3.25. Additional exam requirements/recommendations for international students: Required—TOEFL. Electronic applications accepted. *Faculty research:* Evaluation, collective bargaining, educational law, international higher education, superintendency.

Wilkes University, College of Graduate and Professional Studies, School of Education, Wilkes-Barre, PA 18766-0002. Offers art and science of teaching (MS Ed); classroom technology (MS Ed); early childhood literacy (MS Ed); educational computing (MS Ed); educational development and strategies (MS Ed); educational leadership (MS Ed); educational technology (Ed D); higher education administration (Ed D); instructional media (MS Ed); instructional technology (MS Ed); K-12 administration (Ed D); online teaching (MS Ed); reading (MS Ed); school business leadership (MS Ed); secondary education (MS Ed), including biology, chemistry, English, history, mathematics; special education (MS Ed); teaching English as a second language (MS Ed); twenty-first century teaching and learning (MS Ed). Part-time and evening/weekend programs available. Postbaccalaureate distance learning degree programs offered (minimal on-campus study). *Students:* 92 full-time (63 women), 2,005 part-time (1,459 women); includes 89 minority (23 Black or African American, non-Hispanic/Latino; 1 American Indian or Alaska Native, non-Hispanic/Latino; 14 Asian, non-Hispanic/Latino; 33 Hispanic/Latino; 1 Native Hawaiian or other Pacific Islander, non-Hispanic/Latino; 17 Two or more races, non-Hispanic/Latino), 6 international. Average age 33. In 2011, 1,150 master's, 3 doctorates awarded. *Entrance requirements:* Additional exam requirements/recommendations for international students: Required—TOEFL (minimum score 550 paper-based; 213 computer-based; 79 iBT). *Application deadline:* Applications are processed on a rolling basis. Application fee: $45. Electronic applications accepted. *Expenses:* Contact institution. *Financial support:* Federal Work-Study and unspecified assistantships available. Financial award application deadline: 3/1; financial award applicants required to submit FAFSA. *Unit head:* Dr. Michael Speziale, Dean, 570-408-4679, Fax: 570-408-4905, E-mail: michael.speziale@wilkes.edu. *Application contact:* Erin Sutzko, Director of Extended Learning, 570-408-4253, Fax: 570-408-7846, E-mail: erin.sutzko@wilkes.edu. Web site: http://www.wilkes.edu/pages/383.asp.

Wilmington University, College of Education, New Castle, DE 19720-6491. Offers applied technology in education (M Ed); career and technical education (M Ed); educational leadership (Ed D); elementary and secondary school counseling (M Ed); elementary studies (M Ed); ESOL literacy (M Ed); higher education leadership (Ed D); instruction: gifted and talented (M Ed); instruction: teacher of reading (M Ed); instruction: teaching and learning (M Ed); organizational leadership (Ed D); school leadership (M Ed); secondary education (MAT); special education (M Ed). *Accreditation:* NCATE. Part-time and evening/weekend programs available. *Faculty:* 7 full-time (4 women). *Students:* 638 full-time (425 women), 2,014 part-time (1,635 women). Average age 33. *Entrance requirements:* For master's, 2 letters of recommendation, interview. Additional exam requirements/recommendations for international students: Required—TOEFL (minimum score 500 paper-based; 173 computer-based). *Application deadline:* For fall admission, 4/30 for domestic students. Applications are processed on a rolling basis. Application fee: $35. Electronic applications accepted. *Expenses: Tuition:* Part-time $534 per credit hour. *Required fees:* $25 per term. *Financial support:* Applicants required to submit FAFSA. *Unit head:* Dr. John C. Gray, Dean, 302-295-1139. *Application contact:* Chris Ferguson, Director of Admissions, 302-356-4636 Ext. 256, Fax: 302-328-5164, E-mail: inquire@wilmcoll.edu. Web site: http://www.wilmu.edu/education/.

Wright State University, School of Graduate Studies, College of Education and Human Services, Department of Educational Leadership, Program in Advanced Educational Leadership, Dayton, OH 45435. Offers advanced curriculum and instruction (Ed S); higher education-adult education (Ed S); superintendent (Ed S). *Accreditation:* NCATE. *Degree requirements:* For Ed S, thesis. *Entrance requirements:* For degree, GRE General Test, MAT. Additional exam requirements/recommendations for international students: Required—TOEFL.

Wright State University, School of Graduate Studies, College of Education and Human Services, Department of Educational Leadership, Programs in Educational Leadership, Dayton, OH 45435. Offers curriculum and instruction: teacher leader (MA); educational administrative specialist: teacher leader (M Ed); educational administrative specialist: vocational education administration (M Ed, MA); student affairs in higher education-administration (M Ed, MA). *Accreditation:* NCATE. *Degree requirements:* For master's, thesis (for some programs). *Entrance requirements:* For master's, GRE General Test, MAT. Additional exam requirements/recommendations for international students: Required—TOEFL.

Middle School Education

Alaska Pacific University, Graduate Programs, Education Department, Program in Teaching, Anchorage, AK 99508-4672. Offers teaching (K-8) (MAT). *Degree requirements:* For master's, research project. *Entrance requirements:* For master's, GRE or MAT, PRAXIS, minimum GPA of 3.0.

Albany State University, College of Education, Albany, GA 31705-2717. Offers early childhood education (M Ed); education specialist (Ed S); educational leadership and administration (M Ed); health, physical education and recreation (M Ed); middle grades education (M Ed); school counseling (M Ed); special education (M Ed). *Accreditation:* NCATE. Part-time and evening/weekend programs available. Postbaccalaureate distance learning degree programs offered (minimal on-campus study). *Faculty:* 19 full-time (13 women), 7 part-time/adjunct (5 women). *Students:* 90 full-time (69 women), 118 part-time (92 women); includes 152 minority (151 Black or African American, non-Hispanic/Latino; 1 American Indian or Alaska Native, non-Hispanic/Latino), 1 international. Average age 35. 93 applicants, 78% accepted, 38 enrolled. In 2011, 43 master's, 8 Ed Ss awarded. *Degree requirements:* For master's, comprehensive exam, internship, GACE Content Exam. *Entrance requirements:* For master's, GRE or MAT. *Application deadline:* For fall admission, 6/1 for domestic students, 5/1 for international students; for spring admission, 11/1 for domestic students, 10/1 for international students. Applications are processed on a rolling basis. Application fee: $20. Electronic applications accepted. *Expenses:* Tuition, state resident: full-time $3204; part-time $178 per credit hour. Tuition, nonresident: full-time $12,816; part-time $712 per credit hour. *Required fees:* $379 per semester. *Financial support:* Scholarships/grants available. Financial award application deadline: 4/15; financial award applicants required to submit FAFSA. *Faculty research:* GACE preparation, STEM (science, technology, engineering, and mathematics), technology education, special education, professional teacher development, health implications liberation philosophy, NET-Q, learning community, disabled or at-risk students. *Total annual research expenditures:* $252,502. *Unit head:* Dr. Kimberly King-Jupiter, Dean, 229-430-1718, Fax: 229-430-4993, E-mail: kimberly.king-jupiter@asurams.edu. *Application contact:* Jeffrey Pierce, II, Graduate Admissions Counselor, 229-430-4646, Fax: 229-430-4105, E-mail: jeffrey.pierce@asurams.edu. Web site: http://asu-sacs.asurams.edu/ASUCatalog/Graduate/index.html.

American International College, School of Arts, Education and Sciences, Department of Education, Springfield, MA 01109-3189. Offers early childhood education (M Ed, CAGS); educational leadership and supervision (Ed D); elementary education (M Ed, CAGS); middle/secondary education (M Ed, CAGS); moderate disabilities (M Ed, CAGS); reading (M Ed, CAGS); school adjustment counseling (MA, CAGS); school administration (M Ed, CAGS); school guidance counseling (MA, CAGS); teaching (MA, MS); teaching and learning (Ed D). Part-time and evening/weekend programs available. Terminal master's awarded for partial completion of doctoral program. *Degree requirements:* For master's, comprehensive exam (for some programs), thesis (for some programs), practicum; for doctorate, comprehensive exam (for some programs), thesis/dissertation; for CAGS, practicum. *Entrance requirements:* For master's, minimum B-average in undergraduate course work; for doctorate, GRE General Test, interview. Additional exam requirements/recommendations for international students: Required—TOEFL. Electronic applications accepted.

Appalachian State University, Cratis D. Williams Graduate School, Department of Curriculum and Instruction, Boone, NC 28608. Offers curriculum specialist (MA); educational media (MA); elementary education (MA); middle grades education (MA), including language arts, mathematics, science, social studies. *Accreditation:* NCATE. Part-time and evening/weekend programs available. Postbaccalaureate distance learning degree programs offered (no on-campus study). *Faculty:* 33 full-time (23 women), 5 part-time/adjunct (2 women). *Students:* 23 full-time (18 women), 110 part-time (90 women); includes 7 minority (4 Black or African American, non-Hispanic/Latino; 1 Asian, non-Hispanic/Latino; 2 Hispanic/Latino). 79 applicants, 94% accepted, 64 enrolled. In 2011, 87 master's awarded. *Degree requirements:* For master's, comprehensive exam, thesis or alternative. *Entrance requirements:* For master's, GRE General Test or MAT, 3 letters of recommendation. Additional exam requirements/recommendations for international students: Required—TOEFL (minimum score 570 paper-based; 230 computer-based; 79 iBT), IELTS (minimum score 6.5). *Application deadline:* For fall admission, 3/14 for domestic students, 2/1 for international students; for spring admission, 11/1 for domestic students, 7/1 for international students. Applications are processed on a rolling basis. Application fee: $55. Electronic applications accepted. *Expenses:* Tuition, state resident: full-time $4040; part-time $180 per semester hour. Tuition, nonresident: full-time $15,900; part-time $760 per semester hour. *Required fees:* $2500; $20 per semester hour. Tuition and fees vary according to campus/location. *Financial support:* In 2011–12, 6 teaching assistantships (averaging $8,000 per year) were awarded; fellowships, research assistantships, career-related internships or fieldwork, Federal Work-Study, scholarships/grants, and unspecified assistantships also available. Financial award application deadline: 4/1; financial award applicants required to submit FAFSA. *Faculty research:* Media literacy, elementary teaching, curriculum development, online learning environments. *Total annual research expenditures:* $480,000. *Unit head:* Dr. Michael Jacobson, Chairperson, 828-262-2224. *Application contact:* Sandy Krause, Director of Admissions and Recruiting, 828-262-2130, Fax: 828-262-2709, E-mail: krausesl@appstate.edu. Web site: http://www.ced.appstate.edu/departments/ci.

Arkansas State University, Graduate School, College of Education, Department of Teacher Education, Jonesboro, State University, AR 72467. Offers early childhood education (MAT, MSE); early childhood services (MS); middle level education (MAT, MSE); reading (MSE, Ed S). *Accreditation:* NCATE. Part-time programs available. *Faculty:* 16 full-time (11 women). *Students:* 47 full-time (44 women), 81 part-time (76 women); includes 52 minority (49 Black or African American, non-Hispanic/Latino; 1 Hispanic/Latino; 2 Two or more races, non-Hispanic/Latino), 2 international. Average age 33. 114 applicants, 58% accepted, 57 enrolled. In 2011, 35 master's awarded. *Degree requirements:* For master's, comprehensive exam, thesis or alternative; for Ed S, comprehensive exam. *Entrance requirements:* For master's, GRE General Test or MAT, appropriate bachelor's degree, official transcripts, immunization records; for Ed S, GRE General Test or MAT, interview, master's degree, official transcript, immunization records. Additional exam requirements/recommendations for international students: Required—TOEFL (minimum score 550 paper-based; 213 computer-based; 79 iBT), IELTS (minimum score 6), Pearson Test of English Academic (minimum score 56). *Application deadline:* For fall admission, 7/1 for domestic and international students; for spring admission, 11/15 for domestic students, 11/14 for international students. Applications are processed on a rolling basis. Application fee: $30 ($40 for international students). Electronic applications accepted. *Expenses:* Tuition, state resident: full-time $4044; part-time $225 per credit hour. Tuition, nonresident: full-time $8087; part-time $449 per credit hour. *Required fees:* $936; $52 per credit hour. $25 per term. One-time fee: $30. Tuition and fees vary according to course load and program. *Financial support:* In 2011–12, 5 students received support. Teaching assistantships, career-related internships or fieldwork, scholarships/grants, and unspecified assistantships available. Financial award application deadline: 7/1; financial award applicants required to submit FAFSA. *Unit head:* Dr. Lina Owens, Chair, 870-972-3059, Fax: 870-972-3344, E-mail: llowens@astate.edu. *Application contact:* Dr. Andrew Sustich, Dean of the Graduate School, 870-972-3029, Fax: 870-972-3857, E-mail: sustich@astate.edu. Web site: http://www.astate.edu/a/education/teachered/.

Armstrong Atlantic State University, School of Graduate Studies, Program in Education, Savannah, GA 31419-1997. Offers adult education (M Ed); curriculum and instruction (M Ed); early childhood education (M Ed); education (M Ed); elementary education (M Ed); middle grades education (M Ed); secondary education (M Ed), including business education, English education, mathematics education, science education, social science education; special education (M Ed), including behavioral disorders, learning disabilities, speech-language pathology. *Accreditation:* NCATE. Part-time and evening/weekend programs available. Postbaccalaureate distance learning degree programs offered (minimal on-campus study). *Faculty:* 33 full-time (23 women), 3 part-time/adjunct (2 women). *Students:* 97 full-time (91 women), 262 part-time (227 women); includes 83 minority (70 Black or African American, non-Hispanic/Latino; 3 Asian, non-Hispanic/Latino; 8 Hispanic/Latino; 2 Two or more races, non-Hispanic/Latino), 5 international. Average age 34. 169 applicants, 69% accepted, 102 enrolled. In 2011, 227 master's awarded. *Degree requirements:* For master's, comprehensive exam, portfolio. *Entrance requirements:* For master's, GRE General Test or MAT, minimum GPA of 2.5, letters of recommendation. Additional exam requirements/recommendations for international students: Required—TOEFL (minimum score 523 paper-based; 193 computer-based). *Application deadline:* For fall admission, 7/1 priority date for domestic students, 5/1 for international students; for spring admission, 11/15 priority date for domestic students, 9/15 for international students. Applications are processed on a rolling basis. Application fee: $30. Electronic applications accepted. *Expenses:* Tuition, state resident: full-time $3402. Tuition, nonresident: full-time $12,636. *Financial support:* In 2011–12, research assistantships with full tuition reimbursements (averaging $5,000 per year) were awarded; career-related internships or fieldwork, Federal Work-Study, scholarships/grants, and unspecified assistantships also available. Support available to part-time students. Financial award applicants required to submit FAFSA. *Unit head:* Dr. Patricia Wachholz, Dean, College of Education, 912-344-2797, E-mail: patricia.wachholz@armstrong.edu. *Application contact:* Jill Bell, Director, Graduate Enrollment Services, 912-344-2798, Fax: 912-344-3488, E-mail: graduate@armstrong.edu. Web site: http://www.armstrong.edu/Education/coe_deans_office/coe_education_welcome.

Austin College, Program in Education, Sherman, TX 75090-4400. Offers art education (MA); elementary education (MA); middle school education (MA); music education (MA); physical education and coaching (MA); secondary education (MA); theatre education (MA). Part-time programs available. *Faculty:* 5 full-time (4 women). *Students:* 21 full-time (13 women), 2 part-time (both women). Average age 23. In 2011, 24 master's awarded. *Degree requirements:* For master's, one foreign language, thesis or alternative. *Entrance requirements:* For master's, Texas Academic Skills Program Test. *Application deadline:* For fall admission, 5/1 priority date for domestic students; for spring admission, 1/15 priority date for domestic students. Applications are processed on a rolling basis. Application fee: $35. Electronic applications accepted. *Expenses: Tuition:* Full-time $38,445. *Required fees:* $160. *Financial support:* Career-related internships or fieldwork, Federal Work-Study, scholarships/grants, and unspecified assistantships available. Support available to part-time students. Financial award application deadline: 4/1; financial award applicants required to submit FAFSA. *Unit head:* Dr. Barbara Sylvester, Director of Teaching Program, 903-813-2327, E-mail: bsylvester@austincollege.edu. *Application contact:* Dr. Barbara Sylvester, Director of Teaching Program, 903-813-2327, E-mail: bsylvester@austincollege.edu. Web site: http://www.austincollege.edu/.

Bellarmine University, Annsley Frazier Thornton School of Education, Louisville, KY 40205-0671. Offers early elementary education (MA Ed, MAT); education and social change (PhD); learning and behavior disorders (MA Ed, MAT); middle school education (MA Ed, MAT); principalship (Ed S); reading and writing endorsement (MA Ed); secondary school education (MAT); teacher leadership, grades P-12 (MA Ed). *Accreditation:* NCATE. Part-time and evening/weekend programs available. *Faculty:* 13 full-time (6 women), 12 part-time/adjunct (10 women). *Students:* 85 full-time (65 women), 186 part-time (144 women); includes 30 minority (22 Black or African American, non-Hispanic/Latino; 1 American Indian or Alaska Native, non-Hispanic/Latino; 6 Asian, non-Hispanic/Latino; 1 Hispanic/Latino). Average age 33. In 2011, 105 master's awarded. *Degree requirements:* For master's, comprehensive exam, thesis (for some programs); for doctorate, comprehensive exam, thesis/dissertation. *Entrance requirements:* For master's, GRE, baccalaureate degree from accredited institution; minimum overall GPA of 2.75, 3.0 in major; letters of recommendation; valid Kentucky provisional or professional certificate; for doctorate, GRE, minimum GPA of 3.5 in all graduate coursework completed at time of application; baccalaureate and master's degrees in education (MA, MS) or fields directly relevant to education; three letters of recommendation; two essays (no more than 1,000 words each); interview. Additional exam requirements/recommendations for international students: Required—TOEFL (minimum score 550 paper-based; 213 computer-based; 80 iBT). *Application deadline:* Applications are processed on a rolling basis. Application fee: $25. *Expenses:* Contact institution. *Financial support:* Scholarships/grants available. Financial award applicants required to submit FAFSA. *Faculty research:* Literacy, service-learning, dispositions, educational technology, special education. *Unit head:* Dr. Robert Cooter, Dean, 502-272-8191, Fax: 502-272-8189, E-mail: rcooter@bellarmine.edu. *Application contact:* Theresa Klapheke, Administrative Director of Graduate Programs, 502-272-8271, Fax: 502-272-8002, E-mail: tklapheke@bellarmine.edu. Web site: http://www.bellarmine.edu/education/graduate.

Belmont University, College of Arts and Sciences, Department of Education, Nashville, TN 37212-3757. Offers education (M Ed); elementary education (MAT), including early childhood education, elementary education, language arts education; English (MAT); history (MAT); mathematics (MAT); middle grade education (MAT); science (MAT); secondary education (MAT); special education (MAT); sports administration (MSA). *Accreditation:* NCATE. Part-time and evening/weekend programs available. *Faculty:* 11 full-time (8 women), 23 part-time/adjunct (12 women). *Students:* 83 full-time (77 women), 205 part-time (162 women); includes 50 minority (36 Black or African American, non-Hispanic/Latino; 1 American Indian or Alaska Native, non-Hispanic/Latino; 1 Asian, non-Hispanic/Latino; 7 Hispanic/Latino; 5 Two or more races, non-Hispanic/Latino), 2 international. Average age 30. 83 applicants, 67% accepted, 35 enrolled. In 2011, 169 master's awarded. *Degree requirements:* For master's, thesis (for some programs). *Entrance requirements:* For master's, MAT or GRE and/or GMAT, minimum GPA of 2.75. Additional exam requirements/recommendations for international students: Required—TOEFL. *Application deadline:* For fall admission, 8/1 priority date for domestic students, 6/1 for international students; for spring admission, 12/1 priority date for domestic students, 10/1 for international students. Applications are processed on a rolling basis. Application fee: $50. *Expenses:* Contact institution. *Financial support:* In 2011–12, 30 students received support. Fellowships with partial tuition reimbursements available, teaching assistantships with partial tuition reimbursements available, institutionally sponsored loans, tuition waivers (partial), and unspecified assistantships available. Financial award application deadline: 4/15; financial award applicants required to submit FAFSA. *Faculty research:* Improving secondary literacy, Montessori, classroom management strategies, teacher residency programs, online professional development, mentoring, leadership, faculty development. *Total annual research expenditures:* $2,500. *Unit head:* Dr. Cynthia R. Watkins, Associate Dean, 615-460-6053, Fax: 615-460-5556, E-mail: cynthia.watkins@belmont.edu. *Application contact:* Andrea McClain, Admission/Licensure Officer, 615-460-5483, Fax: 615-460-5556, E-mail: andrea.mcclain@belmont.edu.

Berry College, Graduate Programs, Graduate Programs in Education, Program in Middle Grades Education and Reading, Mount Berry, GA 30149-0159. Offers middle grades education (MAT); middle grades education and reading (M Ed). *Accreditation:* NCATE. Part-time programs available. *Faculty:* 12 part-time/adjunct (8 women). *Students:* 2 full-time (1 woman), 17 part-time (14 women). Average age 32. In 2011, 7 master's awarded. *Degree requirements:* For master's, thesis optional, oral exams. *Entrance requirements:* For master's, GRE General Test, MAT, or NTE, minimum GPA of 2.5. Additional exam requirements/recommendations for international students: Required—TOEFL (minimum score 550 paper-based; 213 computer-based). *Application deadline:* For fall admission, 5/1 for domestic and international students; for spring admission, 10/1 for domestic and international students. Applications are processed on a rolling basis. Application fee: $25 ($30 for international students). Electronic applications accepted. *Expenses:* Contact institution. *Financial support:* In 2011–12, 5 students received support, including 1 research assistantship with full tuition reimbursement available (averaging $2,440 per year); scholarships/grants, tuition waivers (partial), and unspecified assistantships also available. Support available to part-time students. Financial award application deadline: 3/1; financial award applicants required to submit FAFSA. *Faculty research:* Curriculum development, teacher training, pedagogy, ESOL and immigrant student literacy development. *Unit head:* Dr. Jacqueline McDowell, 706-236-1717, Fax: 706-238-5827, E-mail: jmcdowell@berry.edu. *Application contact:* Brett Kennedy, Director of Admissions, 706-236-2215, Fax: 706-290-2178, E-mail: admissions@berry.edu. Web site: http://www.berry.edu/academics/education/graduate/.

Brenau University, Sydney O. Smith Graduate School, School of Education, Gainesville, GA 30501. Offers early childhood (Ed S); early childhood education (M Ed, MAT); middle grades (Ed S); middle grades education (M Ed, MAT); secondary education (MAT); special education (M Ed, MAT). *Accreditation:* NCATE. Part-time and evening/weekend programs available. Postbaccalaureate distance learning degree programs offered (no on-campus study). *Degree requirements:* For master's, thesis optional, comprehensive exam or applied research project, effective portfolio; for Ed S, thesis, applied research project. *Entrance requirements:* For master's, GRE, MAT, interview, minimum GPA of 3.0, 3 references, writing samples; for Ed S, GRE, MAT, master's degree, minimum GPA of 3.0, writing sample, letters of reference. Additional exam requirements/recommendations for international students: Required—TOEFL (minimum score 500 paper-based; 173 computer-based; 61 iBT); Recommended—IELTS (minimum score 5). Electronic applications accepted. *Expenses:* Contact institution.

Brooklyn College of the City University of New York, Division of Graduate Studies, School of Education, Program in Middle Childhood Education (Math), Brooklyn, NY 11210-2889. Offers MS Ed. *Entrance requirements:* For master's, LAST, 2 letters of recommendation, essay, resume. Additional exam requirements/recommendations for international students: Required—TOEFL (minimum score 500 paper-based; 173 computer-based; 61 iBT). Electronic applications accepted.

Brooklyn College of the City University of New York, Division of Graduate Studies, School of Education, Program in Middle Childhood Education (Science), Brooklyn, NY 11210-2889. Offers biology (MA); chemistry (MA); earth science (MA); general science (MA); physics (MA). Part-time and evening/weekend programs available. *Entrance requirements:* For master's, LAST, interview, previous course work in education and mathematics, resume, 2 letters of recommendation, essay. Additional exam requirements/recommendations for international students: Required—TOEFL (minimum score 500 paper-based; 173 computer-based; 61 iBT). Electronic applications accepted. *Faculty research:* Geometric thinking, mastery of basic facts, problem-solving strategies, history of mathematics.

California Lutheran University, Graduate Studies, Graduate School of Education, Thousand Oaks, CA 91360-2787. Offers counseling and guidance (MS), including college student personnel, counseling and guidance; educational leadership (MA, Ed D), including educational leadership (K-12) (Ed D), higher education leadership (Ed D); special education (MS); teacher leadership (M Ed); teaching (M Ed). *Accreditation:* NCATE. Part-time and evening/weekend programs available. *Entrance requirements:* For master's, GRE General Test, interview, minimum GPA of 3.0.

California State University, Bakersfield, Division of Graduate Studies, School of Natural Sciences, Mathematics, and Engineering, Program in Teaching Mathematics, Bakersfield, CA 93311. Offers MA. *Entrance requirements:* For master's, minimum GPA of 2.5 for last 90 quarter units. *Expenses: Required fees:* $1302 per unit. Part-time tuition and fees vary according to course load and program. *Unit head:* Dr. Joseph Fiedler, Head, 661-654-2058, Fax: 661-664-2039. Web site: http://www.csub.edu/math/GradProgram.shtml.

California State University, Fullerton, Graduate Studies, College of Education, Department of Secondary Education, Fullerton, CA 92834-9480. Offers middle school mathematics (MS); secondary education (MS); teacher induction (MS). Part-time programs available. *Students:* 1 (woman) full-time, 39 part-time (34 women); includes 17 minority (1 Black or African American, non-Hispanic/Latino; 6 Asian, non-Hispanic/Latino; 10 Hispanic/Latino). Average age 30. 17 applicants, 65% accepted, 9 enrolled. In 2011, 16 master's awarded. Application fee: $55. *Financial support:* Career-related internships or fieldwork, Federal Work-Study, institutionally sponsored loans, and scholarships/grants available. Support available to part-time students. Financial award application deadline: 3/1; financial award applicants required to submit FAFSA. *Unit head:* Dr. Mark Ellis, Chair, 657-278-2745. *Application contact:* Admissions/Applications, 657-278-2371.

Cambridge College, School of Education, Cambridge, MA 02138-5304. Offers autism specialist (M Ed); autism/behavior analyst (M Ed); behavior analyst (Post-Master's Certificate); behavioral management (M Ed); early childhood teacher (M Ed); education specialist in curriculum and instruction (CAGS); educational leadership (Ed D); elementary teacher (M Ed); English as a second language (M Ed, Certificate); general science (M Ed); health education (Post-Master's Certificate); health/family and consumer sciences (M Ed); history (M Ed); individualized (M Ed); information technology literacy (M Ed); instructional technology (M Ed); interdisciplinary studies (M Ed); library teacher (M Ed); literacy education (M Ed); mathematics (M Ed); mathematics specialist (Certificate); middle school mathematics and science (M Ed); school administration (M Ed, CAGS); school guidance counselor (M Ed); school nurse education (M Ed); school social worker/school adjustment counselor (M Ed); special education administrator (CAGS); special education/moderate disabilities (M Ed); teaching skills and methodologies (M Ed). Part-time and evening/weekend programs available. Postbaccalaureate distance learning degree programs offered (minimal on-campus study). *Degree requirements:* For master's, thesis, internship/practicum (licensure program only); for doctorate, thesis/dissertation; for other advanced degree, thesis. *Entrance requirements:* For master's, interview, resume, documentation of licensure, 2 professional references; for doctorate, official transcripts, interview, resume, documentation of licensure (if any), written personal statement/essay, portfolio of scholarly and professional work, qualifying assessment, 2 professional references, health insurance, immunizations form; for other advanced degree, official transcripts, interview, resume, documentation of licensure (if any), written personal statement/essay, 2 professional references, health insurance, immunizations form. Additional exam requirements/recommendations for international students: Required—TOEFL (minimum score 550 paper-based; 213 computer-based; 79 iBT); Recommended—IELTS (minimum score 6). Electronic applications accepted. *Expenses:* Contact institution. *Faculty research:* Adult education, accelerated learning, mathematics education, brain compatible learning, special education and law.

Campbell University, Graduate and Professional Programs, School of Education, Buies Creek, NC 27506. Offers administration (MSA); community counseling (MA); elementary education (M Ed); English education (M Ed); interdisciplinary studies (M Ed); mathematics education (M Ed); middle grades education (M Ed); physical education (M Ed); school counseling (M Ed); secondary education (M Ed); social science education (M Ed). *Accreditation:* NCATE. Part-time and evening/weekend programs available. *Degree requirements:* For master's, comprehensive exam. *Entrance requirements:* For master's, GRE General Test, minimum GPA of 2.7. *Faculty research:* Spiritual values and wellness issues in counseling, stress and professional burnout among counselors, thinking strategies, leadership, adaptive technology.

Canisius College, Graduate Division, School of Education and Human Services, Education Department, Buffalo, NY 14208-1098. Offers general education non-matriculated (MS Ed); middle childhood (MS Ed); special education/adolescent (MS Ed); special education/advanced (MS Ed); special education/childhood (MS Ed); special education/childhood education grades 1-6 (MS Ed). Part-time and evening/weekend programs available. Postbaccalaureate distance learning degree programs offered (minimal on-campus study). *Faculty:* 17 full-time (13 women), 23 part-time/adjunct (11 women). *Students:* 139 full-time (103 women), 62 part-time (47 women); includes 10 minority (9 Black or African American, non-Hispanic/Latino; 1 Hispanic/Latino), 67 international. Average age 30. 135 applicants, 70% accepted, 53 enrolled. In 2011, 125 master's awarded. *Degree requirements:* For master's, research project or thesis. *Entrance requirements:* For master's, GRE if cumulative GPA less than 2.7, transcripts, two letters of recommendation. Additional exam requirements/recommendations for international students: Required—TOEFL. *Application deadline:* Applications are processed on a rolling basis. Application fee: $25. Electronic applications accepted. *Financial support:* Career-related internships or fieldwork, Federal Work-Study, scholarships/grants, tuition waivers (partial), and unspecified assistantships available. Support available to part-time students. Financial award application deadline: 4/30; financial award applicants required to submit FAFSA. *Faculty research:* Family as faculty, tutorial experiences in modern math, integrating digital technologies in the classroom. *Unit head:* Dr. Julie Henry, Chair/Professor, 716-888-3729, E-mail: henry1@canisius.edu. *Application contact:* Jim Bagwell, Director of Graduate Recruitment and Admissions, 716-888-2544, Fax: 716-888-3290, E-mail: bagwellj@canisius.edu. Web site: http://www.canisius.edu/education/facultystaff.asp.

Capella University, School of Education, Minneapolis, MN 55402. Offers college teaching (Certificate); curriculum and instruction (MS, PhD); education (MS); enrollment management (MS); instructional design for online learning (MS, PhD); k-12 studies in education (MS, PhD); leadership for higher education (MS, PhD); leadership in education administration (Certificate); leadership in educational administration (MS, PhD); postsecondary and adult education (MS, PhD); professional studies in education (MS, PhD); reading and literacy (MS); training and performance improvement (MS, PhD). Part-time and evening/weekend programs available. Postbaccalaureate distance learning degree programs offered (minimal on-campus study). Terminal master's awarded for partial completion of doctoral program. *Degree requirements:* For master's, thesis optional, integrative project; for doctorate, comprehensive exam, thesis/dissertation. *Entrance requirements:* Additional exam requirements/recommendations for international students: Required—TOEFL (minimum score 550 paper-based; 213 computer-based), TWE (minimum score 4). Electronic applications accepted. *Faculty research:* Higher education administration, distance learning, adult education, training and curriculum design.

Carlow University, School of Education, Program in Education, Pittsburgh, PA 15213-3165. Offers art education (M Ed); early childhood education (M Ed); instructional technology specialist (M Ed); middle level education (M Ed); secondary education (M Ed); special education (M Ed). Part-time and evening/weekend programs available. *Students:* 72 full-time (58 women), 16 part-time (13 women); includes 16 minority (15

Black or African American, non-Hispanic/Latino; 1 Hispanic/Latino). Average age 32. 68 applicants, 28% accepted, 11 enrolled. In 2011, 41 master's awarded. *Entrance requirements:* For master's, resume, 3 letters of recommendation, minimum GPA of 3.0, interview. Additional exam requirements/recommendations for international students: Required—TOEFL. *Application deadline:* For fall admission, 6/15 priority date for domestic students, 6/15 for international students; for spring admission, 11/15 priority date for domestic students, 11/15 for international students. Applications are processed on a rolling basis. Application fee: $20. Electronic applications accepted. *Expenses: Tuition:* Full-time $10,290; part-time $686 per credit. Tuition and fees vary according to course load, degree level and program. *Financial support:* Applicants required to submit FAFSA. *Unit head:* Dr. Marilyn J. Llewellyn, Director, 412-578-6011, Fax: 412-578-0816, E-mail: llewellynmj@carlow.edu. *Application contact:* Jo Danhires, Administrative Assistant, Admissions, 412-578-6089, Fax: 412-578-6321, E-mail: gradstudies@carlow.edu. Web site: http://www.carlow.edu.

Central Michigan University, College of Graduate Studies, College of Education and Human Services, Department of Teacher Education and Professional Development, Program in Middle Level Education, Mount Pleasant, MI 48859. Offers MA. *Accreditation:* Teacher Education Accreditation Council. Part-time and evening/weekend programs available. *Degree requirements:* For master's, thesis or alternative. *Entrance requirements:* For master's, bachelor's degree with a minimum GPA of 2.7, Michigan elementary or secondary teaching certificate or equivalent. Electronic applications accepted.

Chestnut Hill College, School of Graduate Studies, Department of Education, Program in Middle Education, Philadelphia, PA 19118-2693. Offers M Ed. Part-time and evening/weekend programs available. *Faculty:* 6 full-time (4 women), 50 part-time/adjunct (33 women). *Students:* 25 full-time (18 women), 105 part-time (93 women); includes 26 minority (22 Black or African American, non-Hispanic/Latino; 2 Asian, non-Hispanic/Latino; 2 Hispanic/Latino). Average age 34. 27 applicants, 96% accepted. In 2011, 60 master's awarded. *Degree requirements:* For master's, thesis optional. *Entrance requirements:* For master's, PRAXIS I or proof of teaching certification, letters of recommendation, writing sample, 6 graduate credits with minimum B grade if undergraduate GPA less than 3.0. Additional exam requirements/recommendations for international students: Required—TOEFL (minimum score 500 paper-based; 213 computer-based). *Application deadline:* For fall admission, 7/17 priority date for domestic students, 7/15 for international students; for spring admission, 12/15 priority date for domestic students, 12/15 for international students. Applications are processed on a rolling basis. Application fee: $55. *Expenses:* Contact institution. *Financial support:* Unspecified assistantships available. *Faculty research:* Inclusive education, cultural issues in education. *Unit head:* Dr. Carol Pate, Chair, Education Department, 215-248-7127, Fax: 215-248-7155, E-mail: cmpate@chc.edu. *Application contact:* Amy Boorse, Administrative Assistant, School of Graduate Studies Office, 215-248-7170, Fax: 215-248-7161, E-mail: gradadmissions@chc.edu. Web site: http://www.chc.edu/Graduate/Programs/Masters/Education/.

Chicago State University, School of Graduate and Professional Studies, College of Education, Department of Reading, Elementary Education, Library Information and Media Studies, Program in Middle School Education, Chicago, IL 60628. Offers MAT.

City College of the City University of New York, Graduate School, School of Education, Department of Secondary Education, New York, NY 10031-9198. Offers adolescent mathematics education (MA, AC); English education (MA); middle school mathematics education (MS); science education (MA); social studies education (AC). *Accreditation:* NCATE. *Entrance requirements:* For master's, Liberal Arts and Sciences Test (LAST), Content Specialty Test (CST). Additional exam requirements/recommendations for international students: Required—TOEFL.

Clemson University, Graduate School, College of Health, Education, and Human Development, Eugene T. Moore School of Education, Program in Middle Grades Education, Clemson, SC 29634. Offers MAT. *Students:* 44 full-time (24 women), 5 part-time (3 women); includes 7 minority (4 Black or African American, non-Hispanic/Latino; 1 Asian, non-Hispanic/Latino; 1 Hispanic/Latino; 1 Two or more races, non-Hispanic/Latino). Average age 33. 26 applicants, 77% accepted, 14 enrolled. In 2011, 34 master's awarded. *Degree requirements:* For master's, student teaching. *Entrance requirements:* For master's, PRAXIS II. Additional exam requirements/recommendations for international students: Required—TOEFL; Recommended—IELTS. *Application deadline:* Applications are processed on a rolling basis. Application fee: $70 ($80 for international students). Electronic applications accepted. *Expenses:* Contact institution. *Financial support:* In 2011–12, 1 student received support, including 1 teaching assistantship with partial tuition reimbursement available (averaging $13,624 per year); research assistantships with partial tuition reimbursements available, institutionally sponsored loans, scholarships/grants, health care benefits, and unspecified assistantships also available. *Faculty research:* Language arts in the middle school, equity and social justice pedagogies in mathematics education, acquisition of scientific discourse. *Unit head:* Dr. Michael J. Padilla, Director/Associate Dean, 864-656-4444, Fax: 864-656-0311, E-mail: padilla@clemson.edu. *Application contact:* Dr. David Fleming, Graduate Coordinator, 864-656-1881, Fax: 864-656-0311, E-mail: dflemin@clemson.edu. Web site: http://www.grad.clemson.edu/programs/Middle-Level-Education/.

Cleveland State University, College of Graduate Studies, College of Education and Human Services, Department of Teacher Education, Cleveland, OH 44115. Offers art education (M Ed); early childhood education (M Ed); foreign language education (M Ed); mathematics and science education (M Ed); middle childhood education (M Ed); special education (M Ed), including mild/moderate disabilities, moderate/intensive disabilities; teaching English to speakers of other languages (M Ed). Part-time and evening/weekend programs available. *Faculty:* 20 full-time (12 women), 26 part-time/adjunct (20 women). *Students:* 108 full-time (77 women), 388 part-time (306 women); includes 126 minority (100 Black or African American, non-Hispanic/Latino; 8 Asian, non-Hispanic/Latino; 15 Hispanic/Latino; 1 Native Hawaiian or other Pacific Islander, non-Hispanic/Latino; 2 Two or more races, non-Hispanic/Latino), 25 international. Average age 33. 249 applicants, 73% accepted, 118 enrolled. In 2011, 286 master's awarded. *Degree requirements:* For master's, comprehensive exam (for some programs), thesis or alternative. *Entrance requirements:* For master's, GRE General Test or MAT, minimum GPA of 2.75. Additional exam requirements/recommendations for international students: Required—TOEFL (minimum score 525 paper-based; 197 computer-based), IELTS (minimum score 6). *Application deadline:* For fall admission, 7/15 priority date for domestic students. Applications are processed on a rolling basis. Application fee: $30. *Expenses:* Tuition, state resident: full-time $6416; part-time $494 per credit hour. Tuition, nonresident: full-time $12,074; part-time $929 per credit hour. *Financial support:* In 2011–12, 12 research assistantships with full tuition reimbursements (averaging $3,480 per year) were awarded; tuition waivers (partial) and unspecified assistantships also available. *Faculty research:* Early literacy, professional development in reading, reading recovery, dual language, induction programs. *Total annual research expenditures:* $6.2 million. *Unit head:* Dr. Clifford T. Bennett, Chairperson, 216-523-7105, Fax: 216-687-5379, E-mail: c.t.bennett@csuohio.edu. *Application contact:* Deborah L. Brown, Interim Assistant Director, Graduate Admissions, 216-523-7572, E-mail: d.l.brown@csuohio.edu. Web site: http://www.csuohio.edu/coehs/departments/te.

The College at Brockport, State University of New York, School of Education and Human Services, Department of Education and Human Development, Program in Adolescence Education, Brockport, NY 14420-2997. Offers adolescence biology education (MS Ed); adolescence chemistry education (MS Ed); adolescence earth science education (MS Ed); adolescence English education (MS Ed); adolescence mathematics education (MS Ed); adolescence physics education (MS Ed); adolescence social studies education (MS Ed). *Accreditation:* NCATE. Part-time programs available. *Students:* 12 full-time (9 women), 60 part-time (28 women); includes 6 minority (1 American Indian or Alaska Native, non-Hispanic/Latino; 3 Asian, non-Hispanic/Latino; 1 Hispanic/Latino; 1 Native Hawaiian or other Pacific Islander, non-Hispanic/Latino). 26 applicants, 81% accepted, 17 enrolled. In 2011, 47 master's awarded. *Degree requirements:* For master's, thesis or alternative. *Entrance requirements:* For master's, minimum GPA of 3.0, letters of recommendation; statement of objectives, current resume. Additional exam requirements/recommendations for international students: Required—TOEFL (minimum score 550 paper-based; 213 computer-based; 79 iBT). *Application deadline:* For fall admission, 2/15 priority date for domestic students, 2/15 for international students; for spring admission, 9/15 priority date for domestic students, 9/15 for international students. Application fee: $80. Electronic applications accepted. *Financial support:* Federal Work-Study, scholarships/grants, and unspecified assistantships available. Support available to part-time students. Financial award application deadline: 3/15; financial award applicants required to submit FAFSA. *Unit head:* Dr. Don Halquist, Chairperson, 585-395-5550, Fax: 585-395-2172, E-mail: dhalquis@brockport.edu. *Application contact:* Michael Harrison, Coordinator of Certification and Graduate Advisement, 585-395-2326, Fax: 585-395-2172, E-mail: mharriso@brockport.edu. Web site: http://www.brockport.edu/graduate/.

The College at Brockport, State University of New York, School of Education and Human Services, Department of Education and Human Development, Program in Adolescence Inclusive Education, Brockport, NY 14420-2997. Offers English (MS Ed); mathematics (MS Ed); science (MS Ed); social studies (MS Ed). *Students:* 42 full-time (22 women), 21 part-time (10 women); includes 4 minority (2 Black or African American, non-Hispanic/Latino; 2 Hispanic/Latino). 50 applicants, 64% accepted, 19 enrolled. In 2011, 2 master's awarded. *Degree requirements:* For master's, thesis or alternative. *Entrance requirements:* For master's, minimum GPA of 3.0, letters of recommendation, statement of objectives, academic major (or equivalent) in program discipline; current resume. Additional exam requirements/recommendations for international students: Required—TOEFL (minimum score 550 paper-based; 213 computer-based; 79 iBT). *Application deadline:* For fall admission, 2/15 priority date for domestic students, 2/15 for international students; for spring admission, 9/15 priority date for domestic students, 9/15 for international students. Application fee: $80. Electronic applications accepted. *Financial support:* Federal Work-Study, scholarships/grants, and unspecified assistantships available. Support available to part-time students. Financial award application deadline: 3/15; financial award applicants required to submit FAFSA. *Unit head:* Dr. Don Halquist, Chairperson, 585-395-2205, Fax: 585-395-2171, E-mail: dhalquis@brockport.edu. *Application contact:* Michael Harrison, Coordinator of Certification and Graduate Advisement, 585-395-2326, Fax: 585-395-2172, E-mail: mharriso@brockport.edu.

College of Mount St. Joseph, Graduate Education Program, Cincinnati, OH 45233-1670. Offers adolescent young adult education (MA); art (MA); inclusive early childhood education (MA); instructional leadership (MA); middle childhood education (MA); multi-age education (MA); multicultural special education (MA); music (MA); reading (MA). *Accreditation:* Teacher Education Accreditation Council. Part-time and evening/weekend programs available. *Faculty:* 22 full-time (12 women), 11 part-time/adjunct (8 women). *Students:* 51 full-time (40 women), 92 part-time (72 women); includes 17 minority (14 Black or African American, non-Hispanic/Latino; 1 American Indian or Alaska Native, non-Hispanic/Latino; 1 Asian, non-Hispanic/Latino; 1 Hispanic/Latino). Average age 34. 87 applicants, 44% accepted, 29 enrolled. In 2011, 61 master's awarded. *Degree requirements:* For master's, research project, student teaching, clinical and field-based experiences. *Entrance requirements:* For master's, GRE, PRAXIS II in teaching content area (math or science), 2 letters of recommendation, interview, resume. Additional exam requirements/recommendations for international students: Required—TOEFL (minimum score 560 paper-based; 220 computer-based; 83 iBT). *Application deadline:* Applications are processed on a rolling basis. Application fee: $50. Electronic applications accepted. *Expenses: Tuition:* Full-time $24,200; part-time $540 per credit hour. *Required fees:* $112.50 per semester. One-time fee: $200. *Financial support:* In 2011–12, 22 students received support. Scholarships/grants available. Financial award applicants required to submit FAFSA. *Faculty research:* Foreign and second language learning problems/reading disabilities/hyperlexia, multicultural/bilingual special education, alternative educator licensure, science education, pedagogical content knowledge. *Unit head:* Dr. Mary West, Chair, 513-244-3263, Fax: 513-244-4867, E-mail: mary_west@mail.msj.edu. *Application contact:* Marilyn Hoskins, Assistant Director of Graduate Recruitment, 513-244-4723, Fax: 513-244-4629, E-mail: marilyn_hoskins@mail.msj.edu. Web site: http://www.msj.edu/view/academics/graduate-programs/education.aspx.

College of Mount Saint Vincent, School of Professional and Continuing Studies, Department of Teacher Education, Riverdale, NY 10471-1093. Offers instructional technology and global perspectives (Certificate); middle level education (Certificate); multicultural studies (Certificate); urban and multicultural education (MS Ed). *Accreditation:* Teacher Education Accreditation Council. Part-time programs available. *Degree requirements:* For master's, comprehensive exam. *Entrance requirements:* For master's, interview, New York teaching certificate. Additional exam requirements/recommendations for international students: Required—TOEFL.

Columbus State University, Graduate Studies, College of Education and Health Professions, Department of Teacher Education, Columbus, GA 31907-5645. Offers accomplished teaching (M Ed); early childhood education (M Ed, MAT, Ed S); health and physical education (M Ed, MAT); middle grades education (M Ed, MAT, Ed S); school library media (M Ed, MAT); secondary education (M Ed, MAT, Ed S), including English/language arts (M Ed, Ed S), general science (M Ed), mathematics (M Ed), social science (M Ed); special education (M Ed, Ed S), including general curriculum (M Ed). *Accreditation:* NCATE. Part-time and evening/weekend programs available. Postbaccalaureate distance learning degree programs offered (minimal on-campus study). *Degree requirements:* For master's, thesis, exit exam; for Ed S, thesis or alternative. *Entrance requirements:* For master's, GRE General Test, minimum GPA of 2.75; for Ed S, GRE General Test. Additional exam requirements/recommendations for international students: Required—TOEFL (minimum score 550 paper-based; 213 computer-based; 79 iBT). Electronic applications accepted.

Daemen College, Education Department, Amherst, NY 14226-3592. Offers adolescence education (MS); childhood education (MS); childhood special education (MS); childhood special-alternative certification (MS); early childhood special-alternative certification (MS). Part-time programs available. *Degree requirements:* For master's, thesis optional, research thesis in lieu of comprehensive exam; completion of degree within 5 years. *Entrance requirements:* For master's, 2 letters of recommendation (professional and character), proof of initial certificate of license for professional programs, resume. Additional exam requirements/recommendations for international students: Required—TOEFL (minimum score 500 paper-based; 173 computer-based; 63 iBT), IELTS (minimum score 5.5). Electronic applications accepted. *Faculty research:* Transition for students with disabilities, early childhood special education, traumatic brain injury (TBI), reading assessment.

Dowling College, Graduate Programs in Education, Oakdale, NY 11769-1999. Offers adolescence education with middle childhood extension (MS); advanced certificate in gifted education (AC); childhood and early childhood education (MS); childhood and gifted education (MS); computers in education (AC); early childhood education (MS); educational administration (Ed D); educational technology leadership (MS); educational technology specialist (AC); literacy education (MS); literary education (AC); school building leader (AC); school district business leader (MBA, AC); school district leader (AC); special education (MS); sports management (MS). *Accreditation:* NCATE. Part-time and evening/weekend programs available. Postbaccalaureate distance learning degree programs offered (minimal on-campus study). *Faculty:* 23 full-time (12 women), 70 part-time/adjunct (44 women). *Students:* 336 full-time (245 women), 631 part-time (485 women); includes 83 minority (29 Black or African American, non-Hispanic/Latino; 2 American Indian or Alaska Native, non-Hispanic/Latino; 7 Asian, non-Hispanic/Latino; 45 Hispanic/Latino). Average age 32. 280 applicants, 85% accepted, 167 enrolled. In 2011, 425 master's, 27 doctorates, 40 other advanced degrees awarded. *Degree requirements:* For master's and AC, comprehensive exam; for doctorate, thesis/dissertation. *Entrance requirements:* For master's, minimum GPA of 3.0; for doctorate, GRE, master's degree; for AC, teaching certificate. Additional exam requirements/recommendations for international students: Required—TOEFL (minimum score 550 paper-based). *Application deadline:* For fall admission, 9/1 priority date for domestic students; for winter admission, 1/1 priority date for domestic students; for spring admission, 2/1 priority date for domestic students. Applications are processed on a rolling basis. Application fee: $50. Electronic applications accepted. *Expenses: Tuition:* Full-time $19,162; part-time $933 per credit. *Required fees:* $1330; $700 per year. Tuition and fees vary according to course load. *Financial support:* Career-related internships or fieldwork and Federal Work-Study available. Support available to part-time students. Financial award application deadline: 6/30; financial award applicants required to submit FAFSA. *Faculty research:* Natural readers, Korean styles and learning strategies, mothers of children with disabilities, computers in instruction, cultural background and organizational roadblocks to problem solving. *Unit head:* Carol Pulsonetti, Director of Operations, School of Education, 631-244-3243, E-mail: pulsonec@dowling.edu. *Application contact:* Ronnie S. Macdonald, Assistant Vice President for Enrollment Services/Dean of Admissions, 631-244-3357, Fax: 631-244-1059, E-mail: macdonar@dowling.edu.

Drury University, Graduate Programs in Education, Springfield, MO 65802. Offers elementary education (M Ed); gifted education (M Ed); human services (M Ed); instructional mathematics K-8 (M Ed); instructional technology (M Ed); middle school teaching (M Ed); secondary education (M Ed); special education (M Ed); special reading (M Ed). *Accreditation:* NCATE. Part-time and evening/weekend programs available. *Degree requirements:* For master's, thesis. *Entrance requirements:* For master's, GRE or MAT, minimum GPA of 2.75. Additional exam requirements/recommendations for international students: Required—TOEFL. Electronic applications accepted. *Faculty research:* Cultural enrichment, research skills, parental involvement relating to reading skills, reading strategies for mainstreaming children.

East Carolina University, Graduate School, College of Education, Department of Business and Information Technologies Education, Greenville, NC 27858-4353. Offers business education (MA Ed); elementary education (MAT); English education (MAT); family and consumer science (MAT); health education (MAT); Hispanic studies (MAT); history education (MAT); marketing education (MA Ed); middle grades education (MAT); music education (MAT); physical education (MAT); science education (MAT); special education (MAT), including general curriculum; vocation education (MS). *Accreditation:* NCATE. Part-time and evening/weekend programs available. Postbaccalaureate distance learning degree programs offered (no on-campus study). *Degree requirements:* For master's, comprehensive exam, thesis optional. *Entrance requirements:* For master's, GRE or MAT, minimum GPA of 2.5, bachelor's degree in related field, teaching license (MA Ed). Additional exam requirements/recommendations for international students: Required—TOEFL. *Application deadline:* For fall admission, 6/1 priority date for domestic students. Applications are processed on a rolling basis. Application fee: $50. *Expenses:* Tuition, state resident: full-time $3557; part-time $444.63 per semester hour. Tuition, nonresident: full-time $14,351; part-time $1793.88 per semester hour. *Required fees:* $2016; $252 per semester hour. Part-time tuition and fees vary according to course load, campus/location and program. *Financial support:* Federal Work-Study available. Support available to part-time students. Financial award application deadline: 6/1. *Unit head:* Dr. Ivan G. Wallace, Chair, 252-328-6983, Fax: 252-328-6835, E-mail: wallacei@ecu.edu. *Application contact:* Dean of Graduate School, 252-328-6012, Fax: 252-328-6071, E-mail: gradschool@ecu.edu. Web site: http://www.ecu.edu/cs-educ/bite/index.cfm.

East Carolina University, Graduate School, College of Education, Department of Curriculum and Instruction, Greenville, NC 27858-4353. Offers assistive technology (Certificate); autism (Certificate); deaf/blindness (Certificate); elementary education (MA Ed); English education (MA Ed); history (MA Ed); middle grade education (MA Ed); reading education (MA Ed); special education (MA Ed); teaching (MAT). Part-time programs available. Postbaccalaureate distance learning degree programs offered. *Degree requirements:* For master's, comprehensive exam, thesis optional. *Entrance requirements:* For master's, GRE General Test or MAT, interview, bachelor's degree in related field, minimum GPA of 2.5, teaching license. Additional exam requirements/recommendations for international students: Required—TOEFL. *Application deadline:* For fall admission, 6/1 priority date for domestic students. Applications are processed on a rolling basis. Application fee: $50. *Expenses:* Tuition, state resident: full-time $3557; part-time $444.63 per semester hour. Tuition, nonresident: full-time $14,351; part-time $1793.88 per semester hour. *Required fees:* $2016; $252 per semester hour. Part-time tuition and fees vary according to course load, campus/location and program. *Financial support:* Research assistantships, teaching assistantships, and Federal Work-Study available. Support available to part-time students. Financial award application deadline: 6/1; financial award applicants required to submit FAFSA. *Unit head:* Carolyn C. Ledford, Interim Chair, 252-328-1100, E-mail: ledfordc@ecu.edu. *Application contact:* Dean of Graduate School, 252-328-6012, Fax: 252-328-6071, E-mail: gradschool@ecu.edu. Web site: http://www.ecu.edu/cs-educ/ci/Graduate.cfm.

Eastern Illinois University, Graduate School, College of Education and Professional Studies, Department of Early Childhood, Elementary and Middle Level Education, Charleston, IL 61920-3099. Offers elementary education (MS Ed). *Accreditation:* NCATE. Part-time programs available. *Degree requirements:* For master's, comprehensive exam. *Expenses:* Tuition, state resident: part-time $279 per credit hour. Tuition, nonresident: part-time $670 per credit hour. *Required fees:* $179.07 per credit hour. $1253 per semester.

Eastern Michigan University, Graduate School, College of Education, Department of Teacher Education, Program in K–12 Education, Ypsilanti, MI 48197. Offers curriculum and instruction (MA); elementary education (MA); K-12 education (MA); middle school education (MA); secondary school education (MA). *Accreditation:* NCATE. Part-time and evening/weekend programs available. Postbaccalaureate distance learning degree programs offered (minimal on-campus study). *Students:* 14 full-time (9 women), 87 part-time (62 women); includes 12 minority (7 Black or African American, non-Hispanic/Latino; 1 American Indian or Alaska Native, non-Hispanic/Latino; 1 Asian, non-Hispanic/Latino; 2 Hispanic/Latino; 1 Two or more races, non-Hispanic/Latino). Average age 37. 57 applicants, 74% accepted, 25 enrolled. In 2011, 6 master's awarded. *Entrance requirements:* For master's, GRE. Additional exam requirements/recommendations for international students: Required—TOEFL. *Application deadline:* Applications are processed on a rolling basis. Application fee: $35. *Expenses:* Tuition, state resident: full-time $10,367; part-time $432 per credit hour. Tuition, nonresident: full-time $20,435; part-time $851 per credit hour. *Required fees:* $39 per credit hour. $46 per semester. One-time fee: $100. Tuition and fees vary according to course level, degree level and reciprocity agreements. *Financial support:* Fellowships, research assistantships with full tuition reimbursements, teaching assistantships with full tuition reimbursements, career-related internships or fieldwork, Federal Work-Study, institutionally sponsored loans, scholarships/grants, tuition waivers (partial), and unspecified assistantships available. Support available to part-time students. Financial award applicants required to submit FAFSA. *Unit head:* Dr. Wendy Burke, Coordinator, 734-487-3260, Fax: 734-487-2101, E-mail: wendy.burke@emich.edu. *Application contact:* Dr. Anne Bednar, Advisor, 734-487-3260, Fax: 734-487-2101, E-mail: anne.bednar@emich.edu.

Eastern Nazarene College, Adult and Graduate Studies, Division of Teacher Education, Quincy, MA 02170. Offers administration (M Ed); early childhood education (M Ed, Certificate); elementary education (M Ed, Certificate); English as a second language (Certificate); instructional enrichment and development (Certificate); middle school education (M Ed, Certificate); moderate special needs education (Certificate); principal (Certificate); program development and supervision (Certificate); secondary education (M Ed, Certificate); special education administrator (Certificate); special needs (M Ed); supervisor (Certificate); teacher of reading (M Ed, Certificate). M Ed also available through weekend program for administration, special needs, and teacher of reading only. Part-time and evening/weekend programs available. *Entrance requirements:* Additional exam requirements/recommendations for international students: Required—TOEFL (minimum score 550 paper-based).

East Tennessee State University, School of Graduate Studies, College of Education, Department of Curriculum and Instruction, Johnson City, TN 37614. Offers educational media/educational technology (M Ed), including educational communications and technology, school library media; elementary education (M Ed); reading (MA), including reading education, storytelling; school library professional (Post-Master's Certificate); secondary education (M Ed), including classroom technology, secondary education (M Ed, MAT); storytelling (Postbaccalaureate Certificate); teacher education with multiple levels (initial licensure) (MAT), including elementary education, middle grades education, secondary education (M Ed, MAT). *Accreditation:* NCATE. Part-time and evening/weekend programs available. Postbaccalaureate distance learning degree programs offered (no on-campus study). *Faculty:* 20 full-time (13 women), 3 part-time/adjunct (all women). *Students:* 108 full-time (76 women), 107 part-time (97 women); includes 9 minority (4 Black or African American, non-Hispanic/Latino; 1 Asian, non-Hispanic/Latino; 2 Hispanic/Latino; 2 Two or more races, non-Hispanic/Latino), 2 international. Average age 33. 141 applicants, 57% accepted, 79 enrolled. In 2011, 129 master's awarded. *Degree requirements:* For master's, comprehensive exam, thesis optional, student teaching, practicum; for other advanced degree, field work (school library); culminating experience (storytelling). *Entrance requirements:* For master's, GRE, SAT, ACT, PRAXIS, minimum GPA of 3.0; for other advanced degree, master's degree, TN teaching license (school library professional post-master's certificate); three letters of recommendation (storytelling certificate). Additional exam requirements/recommendations for international students: Required—TOEFL (minimum score 550 paper-based; 213 computer-based; 79 iBT). *Application deadline:* For fall admission, 6/1 for domestic students, 4/30 for international students; for spring admission, 11/1 for domestic students, 4/30 for international students. Application fee: $35 ($45 for international students). Electronic applications accepted. *Expenses:* Tuition, state resident: full-time $7312; part-time $350 per credit hour. Tuition, nonresident: full-time $18,490; part-time $621 per credit hour. *Required fees:* $63 per credit hour. Tuition and fees vary according to course load and program. *Financial support:* In 2011–12, 60 students received support, including 7 research assistantships with full tuition reimbursements available (averaging $6,000 per year), 11 teaching assistantships with full tuition reimbursements available (averaging $6,000 per year); career-related internships or fieldwork, institutionally sponsored loans, scholarships/grants, and unspecified assistantships also available. Financial award application deadline: 7/1; financial award applicants required to submit FAFSA. *Faculty research:* Critical thinking; curriculum development in reading, math, and science education; cultural diversity; cognitive processes; effective teaching strategies. *Unit head:* Dr. Rhona Hurwitz, Chair, 423-439-7598, Fax: 423-439-8362, E-mail: hurwitz@etsu.edu. *Application contact:* Fiona Goodyear, Graduate Specialist, 423-439-6148, Fax: 423-439-5624, E-mail: goodyear@etsu.edu.

Edinboro University of Pennsylvania, School of Education, Department of Elementary, Middle and Secondary Education, Edinboro, PA 16444. Offers elementary education (M Ed); middle/secondary instruction (M Ed). Part-time and evening/weekend programs available. *Faculty:* 4 full-time (2 women). *Students:* 104 full-time (58 women), 131 part-time (95 women); includes 5 minority (3 Black or African American, non-Hispanic/Latino; 2 Hispanic/Latino). Average age 30. In 2011, 82 master's awarded. *Degree requirements:* For master's, comprehensive exam, thesis or alternative, project. *Entrance requirements:* For master's, GRE or MAT, minimum QPA of 2.5. *Application deadline:* Applications are processed on a rolling basis. Application fee: $30. Electronic applications accepted. *Financial support:* In 2011–12, 14 research assistantships with full and partial tuition reimbursements (averaging $4,050 per year) were awarded; career-related internships or fieldwork, Federal Work-Study, scholarships/grants, and unspecified assistantships also available. Support available to part-time students. Financial award application deadline: 2/15; financial award applicants required to submit FAFSA. *Unit head:* Dr. Jo Ann Holtz, Program Head, Middle and Secondary Instruction, 814-732-2794, E-mail: jholtz@edinboro.edu. *Application contact:* Dr. Alan Biel, Dean of Graduate Studies and Research, 814-732-2856, Fax: 814-732-2611, E-mail: abiel@edinboro.edu.

Emory University, Laney Graduate School, Division of Educational Studies, Atlanta, GA 30322-1100. Offers educational studies (MA, PhD); middle grades teaching (MAT); secondary teaching (MAT). *Accreditation:* NCATE. *Faculty:* 10 full-time (4 women), 3 part-time/adjunct (2 women). *Students:* 56 full-time (48 women); includes 20 minority (18 Black or African American, non-Hispanic/Latino; 2 Asian, non-Hispanic/Latino), 2 international. 86 applicants, 42% accepted, 26 enrolled. In 2011, 16 master's, 4 doctorates awarded. Terminal master's awarded for partial completion of doctoral program. *Degree requirements:* For master's, thesis; for doctorate, comprehensive exam, thesis/dissertation. *Entrance requirements:* For master's and doctorate, GRE General Test, minimum GPA of 3.0. Additional exam requirements/recommendations for international students: Required—TOEFL. *Application deadline:* For fall admission, 1/3 for domestic students. Application fee: $45. Electronic applications accepted. *Expenses:*

Tuition: Full-time $34,800. *Required fees:* $1300. *Financial support:* In 2011–12, 50 students received support, including 10 fellowships; research assistantships, teaching assistantships, career-related internships or fieldwork, scholarships/grants, tuition waivers (full and partial), and unspecified assistantships also available. Financial award application deadline: 1/3. *Faculty research:* Educational policy, educational measurement, urban and multicultural education, mathematics and science education, comparative education. *Total annual research expenditures:* $130,000. *Unit head:* Prof. George Engelhard, Director of Graduate Studies, 404-727-0607, E-mail: gengelh@emory.edu. *Application contact:* Dr. Glen Avant, Graduate Program Administrator, 404-727-0612, E-mail: gavant@emory.edu. Web site: http://des.emory.edu/.

Fayetteville State University, Graduate School, Program in Middle Grades, Secondary and Special Education, Fayetteville, NC 28301-4298. Offers biology (MA Ed); history (MA Ed); mathematics (MA Ed); middle grades (MA Ed); political science (MA Ed); reading (MA Ed); sociology (MA Ed); special education (MA Ed), including behavioral-emotional handicaps, mentally handicapped, specific training disability. *Accreditation:* NCATE. Part-time and evening/weekend programs available. *Faculty:* 12 full-time (8 women), 4 part-time/adjunct (3 women). *Students:* 37 full-time (31 women), 66 part-time (57 women); includes 75 minority (68 Black or African American, non-Hispanic/Latino; 1 American Indian or Alaska Native, non-Hispanic/Latino; 3 Hispanic/Latino; 3 Two or more races, non-Hispanic/Latino). Average age 35. 18 applicants, 100% accepted, 18 enrolled. In 2011, 35 master's awarded. *Degree requirements:* For master's, comprehensive exam, internship. *Application deadline:* For fall admission, 4/15 for domestic students; for spring admission, 10/15 for domestic students. Applications are processed on a rolling basis. Application fee: $35. Electronic applications accepted. *Faculty research:* Students with disabilities and selected leadership behaviors, new vision for professional development, gifted and talented studentsm emotional and behavioral disabilities, professional development for high school biology teachers. *Unit head:* Dr. Kimberly Smith-Burton, Interim Chair, 910-672-1182, E-mail: cbarringerbrown@uncfsu.edu. *Application contact:* Katrina Hoffman, Graduate Admission Officer, 910-672-1374, Fax: 910-672-1470, E-mail: khoffma1@uncfsu.edu.

Fitchburg State University, Division of Graduate and Continuing Education, Program in Middle School Education, Fitchburg, MA 01420-2697. Offers M Ed. *Accreditation:* NCATE. Part-time and evening/weekend programs available. *Students:* 1 (woman) full-time, 31 part-time (20 women); includes 3 minority (all Hispanic/Latino). Average age 37. 3 applicants, 100% accepted, 2 enrolled. In 2011, 12 master's awarded. *Entrance requirements:* Additional exam requirements/recommendations for international students: Required—TOEFL (minimum score 550 paper-based; 213 computer-based; 79 iBT). *Application deadline:* For fall admission, 7/15 for international students; for spring admission, 12/1 for international students. Applications are processed on a rolling basis. Application fee: $25 ($50 for international students). Electronic applications accepted. *Expenses:* Tuition, state resident: full-time $2700; part-time $150 per credit. Tuition, nonresident: full-time $2700; part-time $150 per credit. *Required fees:* $2286; $127 per credit. *Financial support:* In 2011–12, research assistantships with partial tuition reimbursements (averaging $5,500 per year) were awarded; Federal Work-Study, scholarships/grants, and unspecified assistantships also available. Support available to part-time students. Financial award application deadline: 3/1; financial award applicants required to submit FAFSA. *Unit head:* Richard Beardmore, Chair, 978-665-3193, Fax: 978-665-3658, E-mail: gce@fitchburgstate.edu. *Application contact:* Kay Reynolds, Director of Admissions, 978-665-3144, Fax: 978-665-4540, E-mail: admissions@fitchburgstate.edu. Web site: http://www.fitchburgstate.edu.

Fresno Pacific University, Graduate Programs, School of Education, Division of Mathematics/Science/Computer Education, Program in Mathematics Education, Fresno, CA 93702-4709. Offers elementary and middle school mathematics (MA Ed); secondary school mathematics (MA Ed). Part-time and evening/weekend programs available. *Degree requirements:* For master's, thesis or alternative. *Entrance requirements:* Additional exam requirements/recommendations for international students: Required—TOEFL (minimum score 550 paper-based; 213 computer-based).

Gardner-Webb University, Graduate School, School of Education, Program in Middle Grades Education, Boiling Springs, NC 28017. Offers MA. *Accreditation:* NCATE. Part-time and evening/weekend programs available. *Faculty:* 10 full-time (4 women), 20 part-time/adjunct (7 women). *Students:* 70 part-time (59 women); includes 18 minority (all Black or African American, non-Hispanic/Latino). Average age 37. 6 applicants, 100% accepted, 6 enrolled. In 2011, 4 master's awarded. *Degree requirements:* For master's, comprehensive exam. *Entrance requirements:* For master's, GRE General Test or NTE, PRAXIS, minimum GPA of 2.5. *Application deadline:* For fall admission, 8/1 priority date for domestic students. Applications are processed on a rolling basis. Application fee: $40. Electronic applications accepted. *Expenses: Tuition:* Full-time $6300; part-time $350 per credit hour. *Financial support:* Unspecified assistantships available. *Unit head:* Dr. Alan D. Eury, Chair, 704-406-4402, Fax: 704-406-3921, E-mail: dsimmons@gardner-webb.edu. *Application contact:* Office of Graduate Admissions, 877-498-4723, Fax: 704-406-3895, E-mail: gradinfo@gardner-webb.edu.

Georgia College & State University, Graduate School, The John H. Lounsbury College of Education, Department of Early Childhood and Middle Grades Education, Milledgeville, GA 31061. Offers early childhood education (M Ed, Ed S); middle grades education (M Ed, Ed S). *Accreditation:* NCATE. Part-time and evening/weekend programs available. *Students:* 6 full-time (5 women), 38 part-time (33 women); includes 10 minority (7 Black or African American, non-Hispanic/Latino; 2 Hispanic/Latino; 1 Two or more races, non-Hispanic/Latino). Average age 34. 23 applicants, 52% accepted, 8 enrolled. In 2011, 26 master's awarded. *Degree requirements:* For master's, comprehensive exam, exit portfolio; for Ed S, comprehensive exam, electronic portfolio presentation. *Entrance requirements:* For master's, on-site writing assessment, level 4 teaching certificate, 2 recommendations; for Ed S, on-site writing assessment, master's degree, 2 years of teaching experience, 2 professional recommendations, level 5 teacher certification. Additional exam requirements/recommendations for international students: Recommended—TOEFL (minimum score 550 paper-based; 213 computer-based; 79 iBT). *Application deadline:* For fall admission, 7/1 priority date for domestic students; for spring admission, 11/15 priority date for domestic students. Applications are processed on a rolling basis. Application fee: $40. Electronic applications accepted. *Expenses:* Tuition, state resident: full-time $4806; part-time $267 per credit hour. Tuition, nonresident: full-time $17,802; part-time $989 per credit hour. *Required fees:* $936 per semester. Tuition and fees vary according to course load and campus/location. *Financial support:* In 2011–12, 2 research assistantships were awarded; career-related internships or fieldwork, Federal Work-Study, and unspecified assistantships also available. Support available to part-time students. Financial award applicants required to submit FAFSA. *Unit head:* Dr. Nancy Mizelle, Chair, 478-445-5479, Fax: 478-445-6695, E-mail: nancy.mizelle@gcsu.edu. *Application contact:* Shanda Brand, Graduate Coordinator, 478-445-1383, E-mail: shanda.brand@gcsu.edu.

Georgia Southern University, Jack N. Averitt College of Graduate Studies, College of Education, Department of Teaching and Learning, Program in Middle Grades Education, Statesboro, GA 30460. Offers M Ed, MAT. *Accreditation:* NCATE. Part-time and evening/weekend programs available. *Students:* 10 full-time (9 women), 1 (woman) part-time; includes 2 minority (both Black or African American, non-Hispanic/Latino). Average age 30. 2 applicants, 100% accepted, 1 enrolled. In 2011, 4 master's awarded. *Degree requirements:* For master's, portfolio, transition point assessments, exit assessment. *Entrance requirements:* For master's, GRE General Test or MAT; GACE Basic Skills and Content Assessments (MAT), minimum cumulative GPA of 2.5. Additional exam requirements/recommendations for international students: Required—TOEFL (minimum score 550 paper-based; 213 computer-based; 80 iBT). *Application deadline:* For fall admission, 3/1 priority date for domestic students, 3/1 for international students; for spring admission, 10/1 priority date for domestic students, 10/1 for international students. Applications are processed on a rolling basis. Application fee: $50. Electronic applications accepted. *Expenses:* Tuition, state resident: full-time $6300; part-time $263 per semester hour. Tuition, nonresident: full-time $25,174; part-time $1049 per semester hour. *Required fees:* $1872. *Financial support:* In 2011–12, 2 students received support, including research assistantships with partial tuition reimbursements available (averaging $7,200 per year), teaching assistantships with partial tuition reimbursements available (averaging $7,200 per year); career-related internships or fieldwork, Federal Work-Study, and tuition waivers (partial) also available. Support available to part-time students. Financial award application deadline: 4/15; financial award applicants required to submit FAFSA. *Faculty research:* Teacher teams, gender, technology applications. *Unit head:* Dr. Ronnie Sheppard, Department Chair, 912-478-5203, Fax: 912-478-0026, E-mail: sheppard@georgiasouthern.edu. *Application contact:* Amanda Gilliland, Coordinator for Graduate Student Recruitment, 912-478-5384, Fax: 912-478-0740, E-mail: gradadmissions@georgiasouthern.edu. Web site: http://coe.georgiasouthern.edu/tandl/index.html.

Georgia Southwestern State University, Graduate Studies, School of Education, Americus, GA 31709-4693. Offers early childhood education (M Ed, Ed S); health and physical education (M Ed); middle grades education (M Ed, Ed S); reading (M Ed); secondary education (M Ed); special education (M Ed). *Accreditation:* NCATE. *Degree requirements:* For master's, comprehensive exam. *Entrance requirements:* For master's, GRE General Test or MAT, minimum GPA of 2.5; for Ed S, GRE General Test or MAT, minimum graduate GPA of 3.25, M Ed from accredited college or university, 3 years teaching experience. Electronic applications accepted.

Georgia State University, College of Education, Department of Middle-Secondary Education and Instructional Technology, Program in Middle Childhood Education, Atlanta, GA 30302-3083. Offers M Ed, Ed S. *Accreditation:* NCATE. Part-time and evening/weekend programs available. *Degree requirements:* For master's, comprehensive exam; for Ed S, project/exam. *Entrance requirements:* For master's, GRE General Test, minimum GPA of 2.5; for Ed S, GRE General Test or MAT, minimum graduate GPA of 3.25.

Grand Valley State University, College of Education, Programs in General Education, Allendale, MI 49401-9403. Offers adult and higher education (M Ed); early childhood education (M Ed); educational differentiation (M Ed); educational leadership (M Ed); educational technology integration (M Ed); elementary education (M Ed); middle level education (M Ed); school library media services (M Ed); secondary level education (M Ed); teaching English to speakers of other languages (M Ed). Part-time and evening/weekend programs available. Postbaccalaureate distance learning degree programs offered (minimal on-campus study). *Degree requirements:* For master's, thesis. *Entrance requirements:* For master's, GRE General Test or minimum GPA of 3.0. Additional exam requirements/recommendations for international students: Required—TOEFL. Electronic applications accepted. *Faculty research:* Effectiveness of technology in education, parental involvement, effective teaching, effective schools research.

Hampton University, Graduate College, College of Education and Continuing Studies, Program in Teaching, Hampton, VA 23668. Offers early childhood education (MT); middle school education (MT); music education (MT); secondary education (MT); special education (MT). *Entrance requirements:* For master's, GRE General Test.

Hebrew College, Shoolman Graduate School of Jewish Education, Newton Centre, MA 02459. Offers early childhood Jewish education (Certificate); Jewish day school education (Certificate); Jewish education (MJ Ed); Jewish family education (Certificate); Jewish special education (Certificate); Jewish youth education, informal education and camping (Certificate). Part-time and evening/weekend programs available. Postbaccalaureate distance learning degree programs offered. *Degree requirements:* For master's, one foreign language. *Entrance requirements:* For master's, GRE, interview. Additional exam requirements/recommendations for international students: Required—TOEFL.

Henderson State University, Graduate Studies, Teachers College, Department of Advanced Instructional Studies, Arkadelphia, AR 71999-0001. Offers early childhood (P-4) (MSE); education (MAT); middle school (MSE); reading (MSE); special education (MSE). *Accreditation:* NCATE. Part-time programs available. *Entrance requirements:* For master's, GRE General Test or MAT, minimum GPA of 2.7, teacher certification. Additional exam requirements/recommendations for international students: Required—TOEFL (minimum score 550 paper-based; 213 computer-based); Recommended—IELTS (minimum score 6). Electronic applications accepted.

Hofstra University, School of Education, Health, and Human Services, Programs in Teaching (K-12), Hempstead, NY 11549. Offers bilingual education (MA); bilingual extension (Advanced Certificate), including education/speech language pathology, intensive teacher institute; family and consumer science (MS Ed); fine art and music education (Advanced Certificate); fine arts education (MA, MS Ed); mentoring and coaching for teachers (Advanced Certificate); middle childhood extension (Advanced Certificate), including grades 5-6 or 7-9; music education (MA, MS Ed); teaching languages other than English and TESOL (MS Ed); TESOL (MS Ed, Advanced Certificate), including intensive teacher institute (Advanced Certificate), TESOL (Advanced Certificate); wind conducting (MA). Part-time and evening/weekend programs available. *Students:* 54 full-time (48 women), 60 part-time (53 women); includes 30 minority (10 Black or African American, non-Hispanic/Latino; 9 Asian, non-Hispanic/Latino; 11 Hispanic/Latino), 8 international. Average age 29. 109 applicants, 76% accepted, 43 enrolled. In 2011, 71 master's, 42 other advanced degrees awarded. *Degree requirements:* For master's, one foreign language, thesis (for some programs), electronic portfolio, Tk20 portfolios, minimum GPA of 3.0. *Entrance requirements:* For master's, 2 letters of recommendation, portfolio, teacher certification (MA), essay; for Advanced Certificate, 2 letters of recommendation, interview, teaching certificate, essay. Additional exam requirements/recommendations for international students: Required—TOEFL (minimum score 550 paper-based; 213 computer-based; 80 iBT). *Application deadline:* Applications are processed on a rolling basis. Application fee: $70 ($75 for international students). Electronic applications accepted. *Expenses: Tuition:* Full-time $18,990; part-time $1055 per credit hour. *Required fees:* $970. Tuition and fees vary according to program. *Financial support:* In 2011–12, 39 students received support, including 13 fellowships with full and partial tuition reimbursements available (averaging $3,347 per year), 2 research assistantships with full and partial tuition reimbursements available (averaging $7,363 per year); career-related internships or fieldwork, Federal Work-Study, institutionally sponsored loans, scholarships/grants, tuition waivers (full and partial), and unspecified assistantships also available. Support available to part-time students. Financial award applicants required to submit FAFSA. *Faculty research:* The teacher/artist, interdisciplinary curriculum, applied linguistics, structural inequalities, creativity. *Unit head:* Dr. Esther Fusco, Chairperson, 516-463-7704, Fax: 516-463-6196, E-mail: catezf@hofstra.edu. *Application contact:* Carol Drummer, Dean of Graduate

Admissions, 516-463-4876, Fax: 516-463-4664, E-mail: gradstudent@hofstra.edu. Web site: http://www.hofstra.edu/education/.

Hood College, Graduate School, Program in Secondary Mathematics Education, Frederick, MD 21701-8575. Offers mathematics education (MS), including high school, middle school; secondary mathematics education (Certificate). Part-time and evening/weekend programs available. *Degree requirements:* For master's, capstone/research project. *Entrance requirements:* For master's, minimum GPA of 2.75. Additional exam requirements/recommendations for international students: Required—TOEFL (minimum score 575 paper-based; 231 computer-based; 89 iBT). Electronic applications accepted.

James Madison University, The Graduate School, College of Education, Middle, Secondary, and Mathematics Education Department, Program in Middle Education, Harrisonburg, VA 22807. Offers MAT. *Accreditation:* NCATE. Part-time and evening/weekend programs available. *Students:* Average age 27. *Entrance requirements:* For master's, GRE General Test, minimum undergraduate GPA of 2.5. Additional exam requirements/recommendations for international students: Required—TOEFL. *Application deadline:* For fall admission, 5/1 priority date for domestic students; for spring admission, 9/1 priority date for domestic students. Applications are processed on a rolling basis. Application fee: $55. Electronic applications accepted. *Expenses:* Tuition, state resident: full-time $8016; part-time $334 per credit hour. Tuition, nonresident: full-time $22,656; part-time $944 per credit hour. *Financial support:* Federal Work-Study and unspecified assistantships available. Financial award application deadline: 3/1; financial award applicants required to submit FAFSA. *Unit head:* Dr. Steven L. Purcell, Academic Unit Head, 540-568-6793. *Application contact:* Lynette M. Bible, Director of Graduate Admissions, 540-568-6395, Fax: 540-568-7860, E-mail: biblelm@jmu.edu.

John Carroll University, Graduate School, Department of Education and Allied Studies, Program in School Based Middle Childhood Education, University Heights, OH 44118-4581. Offers M Ed. *Accreditation:* NCATE. *Degree requirements:* For master's, comprehensive exam. *Entrance requirements:* For master's, GRE General Test or MAT, minimum GPA of 2.75, interview. Additional exam requirements/recommendations for international students: Required—TOEFL. Electronic applications accepted.

John Carroll University, Graduate School, Program in Integrated Science, University Heights, OH 44118-4581. Offers MA. Part-time programs available. *Degree requirements:* For master's, thesis optional. *Entrance requirements:* For master's, minimum GPA of 2.5, teachers license. Electronic applications accepted.

Kansas State University, Graduate School, College of Education, Department of Curriculum and Instruction, Manhattan, KS 66506. Offers career and technical education (Ed D, PhD); curriculum studies (Ed D, PhD); digital teaching and learning (MS); educational computing, design and online learning (MS); educational technology (Ed D, PhD); elementary/middle level (MS); English as a second language (MS); language/diversity education (Ed D, PhD); literacy education (Ed D, PhD); mathematics education (Ed D, PhD); middle level/secondary (MS); reading and language arts (MS); reading specialist endorsement (MS); science education (Ed D, PhD); social science education (Ed D, PhD); teacher education (Ed D, PhD); teacher leader/school improvement (MS, Ed D). *Accreditation:* NCATE. Part-time programs available. Postbaccalaureate distance learning degree programs offered (minimal on-campus study). *Faculty:* 15 full-time (12 women), 3 part-time/adjunct (2 women). *Students:* 37 full-time (30 women), 113 part-time (91 women); includes 14 minority (4 Black or African American, non-Hispanic/Latino; 1 American Indian or Alaska Native, non-Hispanic/Latino; 1 Asian, non-Hispanic/Latino; 7 Hispanic/Latino; 1 Two or more races, non-Hispanic/Latino), 15 international. Average age 37. 75 applicants, 51% accepted, 9 enrolled. In 2011, 48 master's, 14 doctorates awarded. *Degree requirements:* For master's, comprehensive exam, portfolio, project, report or thesis; for doctorate, comprehensive exam, thesis/dissertation, preliminary exam. *Entrance requirements:* For master's, minimum GPA of 3.0; for doctorate, GRE, minimum GPA of 3.0. Additional exam requirements/recommendations for international students: Required—TOEFL. *Application deadline:* For fall admission, 2/1 priority date for domestic students, 2/1 for international students; for spring admission, 8/1 priority date for domestic students, 8/1 for international students. Applications are processed on a rolling basis. Application fee: $40 ($55 for international students). Electronic applications accepted. *Financial support:* In 2011–12, 1 research assistantship (averaging $16,900 per year), 8 teaching assistantships (averaging $12,466 per year) were awarded; career-related internships or fieldwork, institutionally sponsored loans, and scholarships/grants also available. Support available to part-time students. Financial award application deadline: 3/1; financial award applicants required to submit FAFSA. *Faculty research:* Literacy and technology, critical race theory and diversity, achievement gaps, school improvement, teacher education. *Total annual research expenditures:* $510,907. *Unit head:* Dr. Gail Shroyer, Chair, 785-532-5550, Fax: 785-532-7304, E-mail: gshroyer@ksu.edu. *Application contact:* Dona Deam, Application Contact, 785-532-5595, Fax: 785-532-7304, E-mail: ddeam@ksu.edu. Web site: http://coe.k-state.edu/departments/currin/curringrad.htm.

Kennesaw State University, Leland and Clarice C. Bagwell College of Education, Program in Graduate Education, Kennesaw, GA 30144-5591. Offers adolescent education (M Ed); educational leadership (M Ed); educational leadership technology (M Ed); elementary and early childhood education (M Ed); special education (M Ed); teaching English to speakers of other languages (M Ed). *Accreditation:* NCATE. Part-time programs available. *Students:* 42 full-time (39 women), 132 part-time (105 women); includes 31 minority (20 Black or African American, non-Hispanic/Latino; 4 Asian, non-Hispanic/Latino; 5 Hispanic/Latino; 2 Two or more races, non-Hispanic/Latino). Average age 34. 48 applicants, 79% accepted, 38 enrolled. In 2011, 117 master's awarded. *Degree requirements:* For master's, thesis or alternative. *Entrance requirements:* For master's, GRE General Test, T-4 state certification, minimum GPA of 2.75. Additional exam requirements/recommendations for international students: Required—TOEFL (minimum score 550 paper-based; 213 computer-based; 80 iBT), IELTS (minimum score 6). *Application deadline:* For fall admission, 7/1 for domestic and international students; for spring admission, 10/1 for domestic and international students. Application fee: $60. Electronic applications accepted. *Expenses:* Tuition, state resident: full-time $3000; part-time $250 per semester hour. Tuition, nonresident: full-time $10,836; part-time $903 per semester hour. *Required fees:* $774 per semester. *Financial support:* Federal Work-Study and unspecified assistantships available. Support available to part-time students. Financial award application deadline: 4/1; financial award applicants required to submit FAFSA. *Unit head:* Dr. Nita Paris, Associate Dean for Graduate Programs, 770-423-6636, E-mail: nparis@kennesaw.edu. *Application contact:* Alisha Bello, Administrative Coordinator, 770-423-6043, Fax: 770-420-4435, E-mail: abello1@kennesaw.edu. Web site: http://www.kennesaw.edu/education/grad/.

Kent State University, Graduate School of Education, Health, and Human Services, School of Teaching, Learning and Curriculum Studies, Program in Junior High/Middle School, Kent, OH 44242-0001. Offers M Ed, MA. Part-time programs available. *Faculty:* 6 full-time (5 women), 1 part-time/adjunct. *Students:* 5 full-time (all women), 1 (woman) part-time; includes 1 minority (Black or African American, non-Hispanic/Latino). 4 applicants, 75% accepted. In 2011, 1 master's awarded. *Degree requirements:* For master's, thesis (for some programs). *Entrance requirements:* For master's, 2 letters of reference, goals statement. Additional exam requirements/recommendations for international students: Required—TOEFL (minimum score 550 paper-based; 213 computer-based; 80 iBT). *Application deadline:* Applications are processed on a rolling basis. Application fee: $30 ($60 for international students). Electronic applications accepted. *Expenses:* Tuition, state resident: full-time $8136; part-time $452 per credit hour. Tuition, nonresident: full-time $14,292; part-time $794 per credit hour. *Financial support:* Research assistantships with full tuition reimbursements, Federal Work-Study, scholarships/grants, and unspecified assistantships available. Financial award applicants required to submit FAFSA. *Faculty research:* Middle school reform, teacher action research. *Unit head:* Dr. Bette Brooks, Coordinator, 330-672-0536, E-mail: ebrooks@kent.edu. *Application contact:* Nancy Miller, Academic Program Coordinator, Office of Graduate Student Services, 330-672-2576, Fax: 330-672-9162, E-mail: ogs@kent.edu.

LaGrange College, Graduate Programs, Department of Education, LaGrange, GA 30240-2999. Offers curriculum and instruction (M Ed, Ed S); middle grades (MAT); secondary education (MAT). Part-time and evening/weekend programs available. *Degree requirements:* For master's, comprehensive exam. *Entrance requirements:* For master's, GRE, MAT, minimum GPA of 2.5. Additional exam requirements/recommendations for international students: Required—TOEFL (minimum score 550 paper-based).

Le Moyne College, Department of Education, Syracuse, NY 13214. Offers adolescent education (MS Ed, MST); adolescent education/special education (MS Ed, MST); adolescent English (grades 7-12) (MST); adolescent history (grades 7-12) (MST); childhood education (MS Ed); childhood education/special education (MS Ed); elementary education (MS Ed); general professional education (MS Ed); inclusive childhood education (MST); literacy education (birth to grade 6) (MS Ed); literacy education (grades 5-12) (MS Ed); school building leadership (MS Ed, CAS); school district business leader (MS Ed, CAS); school district leadership (MS Ed, CAS); secondary education (MS Ed); special education (MS Ed); students with disabilities-generalist (grades 7-12) (MS Ed); TESOL (teaching English to speakers of other languages) (MS Ed); urban studies (MS Ed). *Accreditation:* Teacher Education Accreditation Council. Part-time and evening/weekend programs available. *Faculty:* 9 full-time (6 women), 51 part-time/adjunct (28 women). *Students:* 61 full-time (47 women), 311 part-time (222 women); includes 31 minority (19 Black or African American, non-Hispanic/Latino; 3 American Indian or Alaska Native, non-Hispanic/Latino; 4 Asian, non-Hispanic/Latino; 5 Hispanic/Latino), 2 international. Average age 30. 242 applicants, 90% accepted, 180 enrolled. In 2011, 168 master's, 23 CASs awarded. *Degree requirements:* For master's, thesis. *Entrance requirements:* For master's, GRE General Test, bachelor's degree, 2 letters of recommendation, written statement, transcripts. Additional exam requirements/recommendations for international students: Required—TOEFL (minimum score 550 paper-based; 213 computer-based; 79 iBT). *Application deadline:* For fall admission, 4/1 priority date for domestic students, 4/1 for international students; for spring admission, 10/1 priority date for domestic students, 10/1 for international students. Applications are processed on a rolling basis. Application fee: $50. *Expenses:* Contact institution. *Financial support:* In 2011–12, 32 students received support. Career-related internships or fieldwork and health care benefits available. Support available to part-time students. Financial award applicants required to submit FAFSA. *Faculty research:* Minority teachers, special education, multiculturalism, literacy, technology, video games learning, autism, school district organization, service-learning, higher level problem solving, teacher leadership. *Unit head:* Dr. Suzanne L. Gilmour, Chair, Department of Education and Director of Graduate Education Programs, 315-445-4376, Fax: 315-445-4744, E-mail: gilmous@lemoyne.edu. *Application contact:* Kristen P. Trapasso, Director of Graduate Admission, 315-445-4265, Fax: 315-445-6027, E-mail: trapaskp@lemoyne.edu. Web site: http://www.lemoyne.edu/education.

Lesley University, School of Education, Cambridge, MA 02138-2790. Offers curriculum and instruction (M Ed, CAGS); early childhood education (M Ed); educational studies (PhD); elementary education (M Ed); individually designed (M Ed); middle school education (M Ed); moderate special needs (M Ed); reading (M Ed, CAGS); science in education (M Ed); severe special needs (M Ed); special needs (CAGS); technology in education (M Ed, CAGS). *Accreditation:* Teacher Education Accreditation Council. Part-time and evening/weekend programs available. Postbaccalaureate distance learning degree programs offered (no on-campus study). *Faculty:* 36 full-time (27 women), 170 part-time/adjunct (129 women). *Students:* 552 full-time (437 women), 1,971 part-time (1,697 women); includes 364 minority (189 Black or African American, non-Hispanic/Latino; 19 American Indian or Alaska Native, non-Hispanic/Latino; 45 Asian, non-Hispanic/Latino; 83 Hispanic/Latino; 2 Native Hawaiian or other Pacific Islander, non-Hispanic/Latino; 26 Two or more races, non-Hispanic/Latino), 28 international. Average age 37. In 2011, 1,390 master's, 8 doctorates, 42 other advanced degrees awarded. *Degree requirements:* For master's, practicum; for doctorate, thesis/dissertation. *Entrance requirements:* For doctorate, GRE General Test or MAT, interview, master's degree, resume; for CAGS, interview, master's degree. Additional exam requirements/recommendations for international students: Required—TOEFL (minimum score 550 paper-based; 213 computer-based; 80 iBT). *Application deadline:* Applications are processed on a rolling basis. Application fee: $50. Electronic applications accepted. *Financial support:* In 2011–12, research assistantships (averaging $3,400 per year), teaching assistantships (averaging $3,400 per year) were awarded; career-related internships or fieldwork, Federal Work-Study, scholarships/grants, and unspecified assistantships also available. Support available to part-time students. Financial award application deadline: 4/15; financial award applicants required to submit FAFSA. *Faculty research:* Assessment in literacy, mathematics and science; autism spectrum disorders; instructional technology and online learning; multicultural education and ELL. *Unit head:* Dr. Mario Borunda, Dean, 617-349-8375, Fax: 617-349-8607, E-mail: mborunda@lesley.edu. *Application contact:* Rosie Davis, Senior Assistant Director of Admissions, 617-349-8851, Fax: 617-349-8313, E-mail: rdavis4@lesley.edu. Web site: http://www.lesley.edu/soe.html.

Lewis & Clark College, Graduate School of Education and Counseling, Department of Teacher Education, Program in Middle Level/High School Education, Portland, OR 97219-7899. Offers MAT. *Accreditation:* NCATE. *Faculty:* 6 full-time (5 women), 6 part-time/adjunct (4 women). *Students:* 57 full-time (37 women); includes 7 minority (2 American Indian or Alaska Native, non-Hispanic/Latino; 2 Asian, non-Hispanic/Latino; 2 Hispanic/Latino; 1 Two or more races, non-Hispanic/Latino). Average age 28. 110 applicants, 79% accepted, 57 enrolled. In 2011, 71 master's awarded. *Entrance requirements:* For master's, prior experience working with children and/or youth; minimum undergraduate GPA of 2.75. Additional exam requirements/recommendations for international students: Required—TOEFL (minimum score 575 paper-based; 233 computer-based). *Application deadline:* For fall admission, 12/1 priority date for domestic students, 12/1 for international students. Application fee: $50. Electronic applications accepted. *Expenses: Tuition:* Part-time $738 per semester hour. Tuition and fees vary according to course level and campus/location. *Financial support:* In 2011–12, 12 students received support. Career-related internships or fieldwork, Federal Work-Study, institutionally sponsored loans, scholarships/grants, health care benefits, and tuition waivers (partial) available. Support available to part-time students. Financial award application deadline: 3/1; financial award applicants required to submit FAFSA. *Faculty research:* Classroom management, classroom assessment, science education, classroom ethnography, moral development. *Unit head:* Dr. Kasi Allen, Coordinator,

503-768-6100, Fax: 503-768-7715, E-mail: lcteach@lclark.edu. *Application contact:* Becky Haas, Director of Admissions, 503-768-6200, Fax: 503-768-6205, E-mail: gseadmit@lclark.edu. Web site: http://graduate.lclark.edu/departments/teacher_education/prospective_teachers/middle_high_school/.

Liberty University, School of Education, Lynchburg, VA 24502. Offers administration and supervision (M Ed); curriculum and instruction (M Ed); early childhood education (M Ed); educational leadership (Ed D, Ed S); educational technology and online instruction (M Ed); elementary education (M Ed, MAT); gifted education (M Ed); math specialist (M Ed); middle grades (M Ed); outdoor adventure sport (MS); reading specialist (M Ed); school counseling (M Ed); secondary education (M Ed, MAT); special education (M Ed, MAT); sports administration (MS); teaching and learning (Ed D, Ed S). *Accreditation:* NCATE. Part-time programs available. Postbaccalaureate distance learning degree programs offered (minimal on-campus study). *Students:* 2,245 full-time (1,572 women), 3,500 part-time (2,558 women); includes 1,141 minority (888 Black or African American, non-Hispanic/Latino; 19 American Indian or Alaska Native, non-Hispanic/Latino; 21 Asian, non-Hispanic/Latino; 123 Hispanic/Latino; 9 Native Hawaiian or other Pacific Islander, non-Hispanic/Latino; 81 Two or more races, non-Hispanic/Latino), 76 international. Average age 37. In 2011, 760 master's, 48 doctorates, 321 other advanced degrees awarded. *Degree requirements:* For doctorate, comprehensive exam, thesis/dissertation. *Entrance requirements:* For master's, GRE General Test or MAT (if taken in or before 1999), 2 letters of recommendation, minimum undergraduate GPA of 3.0, curriculum vitae; for doctorate, GRE General Test or MAT (if taken before 1999), minimum master's GPA of 3.0, 3 years of teacher experience; for Ed S, GRE General Test or MAT (if taken before 1999), minimum master's GPA of 3.0, 3 years of teaching experience. Additional exam requirements/recommendations for international students: Required—TOEFL (minimum score 600 paper-based; 250 computer-based). *Application deadline:* For fall admission, 6/1 priority date for domestic students; for spring admission, 11/1 for domestic students. Applications are processed on a rolling basis. Application fee: $50. Electronic applications accepted. *Expenses:* Contact institution. *Financial support:* Federal Work-Study and tuition waivers (partial) available. *Faculty research:* Self-determination, character education, bibliotherapy, learning styles, distance education. *Unit head:* Dr. Karen L. Parker, Dean, 434-582-2195, Fax: 434-582-2468, E-mail: kparker@liberty.edu. *Application contact:* Jay Bridge, Director of Graduate Admissions, 800-424-9595, Fax: 800-628-7977, E-mail: gradadmissions@liberty.edu. Web site: http://www.liberty.edu/academics/education/graduate/.

Long Island University–C. W. Post Campus, School of Education, Department of Curriculum and Instruction, Brookville, NY 11548-1300. Offers adolescence education (MS); adolescence education: biology (MS); adolescence education: earth science (MS); adolescence education: English (MS); adolescence education: mathematics (MS); adolescence education: social studies (MS); adolescence education: Spanish (MS); art education (MS); bilingual education (MS); childhood education (MS); early childhood education (MS); middle childhood education (MS); music education (MS); teaching English to speakers of other languages (MS). Part-time and evening/weekend programs available. *Degree requirements:* For master's, comprehensive exam or thesis, student teaching. *Entrance requirements:* For master's, minimum GPA of 2.75 in major, 2.5 overall. Electronic applications accepted. *Faculty research:* Ethics and education, teaching strategies.

Loyola University Maryland, Graduate Programs, Department of Education, Program in Special Education, Baltimore, MD 21210-2699. Offers early childhood education (M Ed, CAS); elementary/middle education (M Ed, CAS); secondary education (M Ed, CAS). *Accreditation:* NCATE. Part-time programs available. *Faculty:* 57 full-time (32 women), 21 part-time/adjunct (10 women). *Students:* 6 full-time (5 women), 33 part-time (31 women); includes 3 minority (all Black or African American, non-Hispanic/Latino). Average age 29. In 2011, 11 master's awarded. *Entrance requirements:* For master's and CAS, PRAXIS, SAT, ACT, or GRE. Additional exam requirements/recommendations for international students: Required—TOEFL (minimum score 550 paper-based; 213 computer-based). *Application deadline:* For fall admission, 6/15 priority date for domestic students; for spring admission, 11/1 priority date for domestic students. Application fee: $50. Electronic applications accepted. *Financial support:* Research assistantships and unspecified assistantships available. Financial award application deadline: 4/15; financial award applicants required to submit FAFSA. *Unit head:* Monica J. Phelps, Director, 410-617-2671, E-mail: mphelps@loyola.edu. *Application contact:* Maureen Faux, Executive Director, Graduate Admissions, 410-617-5020, Fax: 410-617-2002, E-mail: graduate@loyola.edu.

Loyola University Maryland, Graduate Programs, Department of Education, Program in Teacher Education, Baltimore, MD 21210-2699. Offers elementary/middle education (MAT); secondary education (MAT); secondary education: biology (MAT); secondary education: chemistries (MAT); secondary education: earth science (MAT); secondary education: English (MAT); secondary education: mathematics (MAT); secondary education: physics (MAT). Part-time programs available. *Faculty:* 25 full-time (21 women), 14 part-time/adjunct (11 women). *Students:* 28 full-time (19 women), 58 part-time (45 women); includes 5 minority (1 Black or African American, non-Hispanic/Latino; 2 Asian, non-Hispanic/Latino; 2 Two or more races, non-Hispanic/Latino), 4 international. Average age 28. In 2011, 37 master's awarded. *Entrance requirements:* For master's, PRAXIS, SAT, ACT, or GRE. Additional exam requirements/recommendations for international students: Required—TOEFL (minimum score 550 paper-based; 213 computer-based). *Application deadline:* For fall admission, 6/15 for domestic students; for spring admission, 11/1 for domestic students. Electronic applications accepted. *Financial support:* Research assistantships and unspecified assistantships available. Financial award application deadline: 4/15. *Unit head:* Wendy Smith, Chair, 410-617-2194, E-mail: wmsmith@loyola.edu. *Application contact:* Maureen Faux, Executive Director, Graduate Admissions, 410-617-5020, Fax: 410-617-2002, E-mail: graduate@loyola.edu. Web site: http://www.loyola.edu/academics/theology/.

Manhattanville College, Graduate Studies, School of Education, Program in Middle Childhood/Adolescence Education (Grades 5-12), Purchase, NY 10577-2132. Offers biology (MAT); biology and special education (MPS); chemistry (MAT); chemistry and special education (MPS); English (MAT); English and special education (MPS); literacy (MPS), including reading and writing, writing; literacy and special education (MPS); math (MAT); math and special education (MPS); second language (MAT), including French, Italian, Latin, Spanish; social studies (MAT); social studies and special education (MPS); special education (MPS). Part-time and evening/weekend programs available. *Degree requirements:* For master's, comprehensive exam or research project, field experience. *Entrance requirements:* For master's, minimum undergraduate GPA of 3.0, 2 letters of recommendation. Additional exam requirements/recommendations for international students: Required—TOEFL. Electronic applications accepted.

Mary Baldwin College, Graduate Studies, Program in Teaching, Staunton, VA 24401-3610. Offers elementary education (MAT); middle grades education (MAT). *Accreditation:* Teacher Education Accreditation Council.

Maryville University of Saint Louis, School of Education, St. Louis, MO 63141-7299. Offers art education (MA Ed); early childhood education (MA Ed); educational leadership (Ed D); educational leadership: principal certification (MA Ed); elementary education (MA Ed); gifted education (MA Ed); higher education leadership (Ed D); literacy specialist (MA Ed); middle grades education (MA Ed); secondary teaching and inquiry (MA Ed); teacher as leader (MA Ed). *Accreditation:* NCATE. Part-time and evening/weekend programs available. *Faculty:* 10 full-time (6 women), 19 part-time/adjunct (15 women). *Students:* 33 full-time (25 women), 251 part-time (190 women); includes 42 minority (32 Black or African American, non-Hispanic/Latino; 1 American Indian or Alaska Native, non-Hispanic/Latino; 4 Asian, non-Hispanic/Latino; 2 Hispanic/Latino; 3 Two or more races, non-Hispanic/Latino). Average age 38. In 2011, 69 master's, 43 doctorates awarded. *Degree requirements:* For master's, thesis, project. *Entrance requirements:* For master's, minimum cumulative GPA of 3.0, 3 professional recommendations, essays, interview with program faculty; for doctorate, minimum GPA of 3.0, 3 professional recommendations, essay, interview, on-site writing sample. Additional exam requirements/recommendations for international students: Required—TOEFL (minimum score 550 paper-based). *Application deadline:* Applications are processed on a rolling basis. Application fee: $40 ($60 for international students). Electronic applications accepted. *Expenses: Tuition:* Full-time $21,922; part-time $675 per credit hour. *Required fees:* $233.75 per semester. *Financial support:* Career-related internships or fieldwork, Federal Work-Study, tuition waivers (partial), and professional educator discounts available. Financial award application deadline: 3/1; financial award applicants required to submit FAFSA. *Faculty research:* Collaboration with public schools, pre-service program development, mathematics, diversity, literacy. *Unit head:* Dr. Sam Hausfather, Dean, 314-529-9466, Fax: 314-529-9921, E-mail: shausfather@maryville.edu. *Application contact:* Holly Stanwich, Graduate Admissions Coordinator, 314-529-9542, Fax: 314-529-9921, E-mail: teachered@maryville.edu. Web site: http://www.maryville.edu/academics-ed-graduate.

Mercer University, Graduate Studies, Cecil B. Day Campus, Tift College of Education (Atlanta), Macon, GA 31207-0003. Offers curriculum and instruction (PhD); early childhood education (M Ed, MAT); educational leadership (PhD, Ed S); higher education leadership (M Ed); middle grades education (M Ed, MAT); reading education (M Ed); school counseling (Ed S); secondary education (M Ed, MAT); teacher leadership (Ed S). *Accreditation:* NCATE. Part-time and evening/weekend programs available. *Faculty:* 31 full-time (17 women), 6 part-time/adjunct (3 women). *Students:* 249 full-time (207 women), 413 part-time (326 women); includes 349 minority (322 Black or African American, non-Hispanic/Latino; 1 American Indian or Alaska Native, non-Hispanic/Latino; 18 Asian, non-Hispanic/Latino; 6 Hispanic/Latino; 2 Two or more races, non-Hispanic/Latino), 6 international. Average age 34. 204 applicants, 76% accepted, 125 enrolled. In 2011, 235 master's, 8 doctorates, 27 other advanced degrees awarded. *Degree requirements:* For master's and Ed S, research project; for doctorate, thesis/dissertation. *Entrance requirements:* For master's, GRE or MAT, minimum undergraduate GPA of 2.75; for doctorate, GRE; for Ed S, GRE or MAT, minimum GPA of 3.25, 3 years of teaching experience. Additional exam requirements/recommendations for international students: Required—TOEFL. *Application deadline:* For fall admission, 8/1 for domestic and international students; for spring admission, 12/1 for domestic and international students. Applications are processed on a rolling basis. Application fee: $25. *Expenses:* Contact institution. *Financial support:* Federal Work-Study available. Support available to part-time students. Financial award application deadline: 5/1. *Faculty research:* Educational technology, multicultural and minority issues in education, educational leadership (P-12 and higher education), school discipline and school bullying, standards-based mathematics education. *Unit head:* Dr. Carl R. Martray, Dean, 478-301-5397, Fax: 478-301-2280, E-mail: martray_cr@mercer.edu. *Application contact:* Dr. Allison Gilmore, Associate Dean for Graduate Teacher Education, 678-547-6333, Fax: 678-547-6055, E-mail: gilmore_a@mercer.edu. Web site: http://www.mercer.edu/education/.

Mercy College, School of Education, Program in Middle Childhood Education, Grades 5-9, Dobbs Ferry, NY 10522-1189. Offers MS. Part-time and evening/weekend programs available. Postbaccalaureate distance learning degree programs offered (no on-campus study). *Degree requirements:* For master's, comprehensive exam, thesis. *Entrance requirements:* For master's, interview, resume, minimum undergraduate GPA of 3.0 (writing sample for those with GPA lower than 3.0), assessment by specific program director or designee. Additional exam requirements/recommendations for international students: Required—TOEFL (minimum score 600 paper-based; 250 computer-based; 100 iBT), IELTS (minimum score 8). Electronic applications accepted. *Faculty research:* Behavior management application, assistive technology, educational psychology.

Merrimack College, School of Education, North Andover, MA 01845-5800. Offers community engagement (M Ed); early childhood education (M Ed); elementary education (M Ed); elementary education plus moderate disabilities-dual license (M Ed); English as a second language (M Ed); general studies (M Ed); higher education (M Ed); middle (M Ed); moderate disabilities (preK-8) (M Ed); reading (M Ed); secondary (M Ed); teacher leadership (CAGS). Part-time and evening/weekend programs available. *Faculty:* 4 full-time (all women), 9 part-time/adjunct (7 women). *Students:* 70 full-time (60 women), 39 part-time (33 women); includes 2 minority (1 Asian, non-Hispanic/Latino; 1 Hispanic/Latino). Average age 27. In 2011, 26 master's awarded. *Degree requirements:* For master's, portfolio. *Entrance requirements:* Additional exam requirements/recommendations for international students: Required—TOEFL (minimum score 80 iBT). *Application deadline:* For fall admission, 8/1 priority date for domestic students, 7/15 for international students; for winter admission, 12/1 priority date for domestic students, 11/15 for international students; for spring admission, 3/1 priority date for domestic students, 2/15 for international students. Applications are processed on a rolling basis. Electronic applications accepted. *Expenses: Tuition:* Part-time $475 per credit. *Required fees:* $62.50 per semester. *Financial support:* In 2011–12, 50 fellowships were awarded; career-related internships or fieldwork and scholarships/grants also available. Financial award applicants required to submit FAFSA. *Faculty research:* Higher education, community engagement, literacy, leadership. *Unit head:* Dr. Theresa Kirk, Chair, 978-837-5436, E-mail: kirkt@merrimack.edu. *Application contact:* Jessica McCarthy, Program Coordinator, 978-837-5443, E-mail: mccarthyj@merrimack.edu. Web site: http://www.merrimack.edu/academics/education/med/.

Middle Tennessee State University, College of Graduate Studies, College of Education, Department of Elementary and Special Education, Major in Curriculum and Instruction, Murfreesboro, TN 37132. Offers early childhood education (M Ed); elementary education (M Ed, Ed S); middle school education (M Ed). *Accreditation:* NCATE. Part-time and evening/weekend programs available. Postbaccalaureate distance learning degree programs offered. *Faculty:* 14 full-time (9 women), 7 part-time/adjunct (all women). *Students:* 16 full-time (13 women), 144 part-time (129 women); includes 18 minority (16 Black or African American, non-Hispanic/Latino; 1 Asian, non-Hispanic/Latino; 1 Hispanic/Latino). 110 applicants, 73% accepted. In 2011, 55 master's awarded. *Degree requirements:* For master's, comprehensive exam; for Ed S, comprehensive exam, thesis or alternative. *Entrance requirements:* For master's and Ed S, GRE, MAT or PRAXIS. Additional exam requirements/recommendations for international students: Required—TOEFL (minimum score 525 paper-based; 195 computer-based; 71 iBT) or IELTS (minimum score 6). *Application deadline:* For fall admission, 8/1 priority date for domestic students. Applications are processed on a rolling basis. Application fee: $25. Electronic applications accepted. *Expenses:* Tuition, state resident: full-time $10,008. Tuition, nonresident: full-time $25,056. *Financial support:* Tuition waivers available. Support available to part-time students. Financial award application deadline: 5/1. *Unit head:* Dr. Kathleen Burriss, Interim Chair, 615-898-2323, Fax: 615-898-5309, E-mail: kathleen.burris@mtsu.edu. *Application contact:* Dr. Michael D. Allen, Dean and Vice Provost for Research, 615-898-2840, Fax: 615-904-8020, E-mail: michael.allen@mtsu.edu.

Mississippi State University, College of Education, Department of Curriculum, Instruction and Special Education, Mississippi State, MS 39762. Offers elementary education (MS, PhD, Ed S); middle level education (MAT); secondary education (MAT, MS, Ed S); special education (MS, Ed S). *Accreditation:* NCATE. Part-time and evening/weekend programs available. *Faculty:* 12 full-time (10 women), 2 part-time/adjunct (1 woman). *Students:* 57 full-time (41 women), 104 part-time (81 women); includes 54 minority (52 Black or African American, non-Hispanic/Latino; 1 Hispanic/Latino; 1 Two or more races, non-Hispanic/Latino). Average age 33. 100 applicants, 60% accepted, 48 enrolled. In 2011, 38 master's, 5 doctorates, 5 other advanced degrees awarded. *Degree requirements:* For master's, comprehensive exam; for doctorate, thesis/dissertation; for Ed S, comprehensive exam, thesis or alternative. *Entrance requirements:* For master's, GRE, minimum GPA of 2.75 in junior and senior year, eligibility for initial teacher certification; for doctorate, GRE, minimum graduate GPA of 3.4; for Ed S, GRE, minimum graduate GPA of 3.2. Additional exam requirements/recommendations for international students: Required—TOEFL (minimum score 600 paper-based; 250 computer-based; 100 iBT); Recommended—IELTS (minimum score 7.5). *Application deadline:* For fall admission, 3/1 priority date for domestic students, 5/1 for international students; for spring admission, 9/1 priority date for domestic students, 9/1 for international students. Applications are processed on a rolling basis. Application fee: $40. Electronic applications accepted. *Expenses:* Tuition, state resident: full-time $5805; part-time $322.50 per credit hour. Tuition, nonresident: full-time $14,670; part-time $815 per credit hour. *Financial support:* In 2011–12, 7 research assistantships with full and partial tuition reimbursements (averaging $9,264 per year), 4 teaching assistantships (averaging $8,937 per year) were awarded; Federal Work-Study, institutionally sponsored loans, scholarships/grants, and unspecified assistantships also available. Financial award application deadline: 4/1; financial award applicants required to submit FAFSA. *Faculty research:* Early childhood education, reading, rural schools, multicultural education, use of technology in instruction. *Unit head:* Dr. Devon Brenner, Professor and Interim Head, 662-325-7119, Fax: 662-325-7857, E-mail: devon@ra.msstate.edu. *Application contact:* Dr. C. Susie Burroughs, Professor and Graduate Coordinator, 662-325-3747, Fax: 662-325-7857, E-mail: susie.burroughs@msstate.edu. Web site: http://www.cise.msstate.edu/.

Morehead State University, Graduate Programs, College of Education, Department of Curriculum and Instruction, Morehead, KY 40351. Offers curriculum and instruction (Ed S); elementary education (MA Ed), including elementary education, international education, middle school education, reading; secondary education (MA Ed); special education (MA Ed); teaching (MAT). Part-time and evening/weekend programs available. *Degree requirements:* For master's, comprehensive exam, thesis optional; for Ed S, thesis, oral exam. *Entrance requirements:* For master's, GRE General Test, minimum GPA of 2.75, teaching certificate; for Ed S, GRE General Test, interview, master's degree, minimum GPA of 3.5, work experience. Additional exam requirements/recommendations for international students: Required—TOEFL (minimum score 500 paper-based; 173 computer-based). Electronic applications accepted. *Faculty research:* Communicative competence of learning-disabled students, teaching social studies in elementary schools, ungraded primary school organization, study skills.

Morehead State University, Graduate Programs, College of Education, Department of Foundational and Graduate Studies in Education, Morehead, KY 40351. Offers adult and higher education (MA, Ed S); certified professional counselor (Ed S); counseling P-12 (MA); curriculum and instruction (Ed S); educational technology (MA Ed); instructional leadership (Ed S); school administration (MA); school counseling (Ed S); teacher leader business and marketing content (MA Ed); teacher leader business and marketing technology (MA Ed); teacher leader educational technology (MA Ed); teacher leader English (MA Ed); teacher leader gifted education (MA Ed); teacher leader IECE certification (MA Ed); teacher leader interdisciplinary education P-5 (MA Ed); teacher leader middle grades (MA Ed); teacher leader non IECE certification (MA Ed); teacher leader reading/writing - non-certification (MA Ed); teacher leader reading/writing certification (MA Ed); teacher leader school communication - certification (MA Ed); teacher leader school communication - non-certification (MA Ed); teacher leader social studies (MA Ed); teacher leader special education (MA Ed). *Accreditation:* NCATE. Part-time and evening/weekend programs available. *Degree requirements:* For master's, thesis optional, oral and/or written comprehensive exams; for Ed S, thesis, oral exam. *Entrance requirements:* For master's, GRE General Test, minimum overall undergraduate GPA of 2.5; for Ed S, GRE General Test, interview, master's degree, minimum GPA of 3.5, work experience. Additional exam requirements/recommendations for international students: Required—TOEFL (minimum score 500 paper-based; 173 computer-based). Electronic applications accepted. *Faculty research:* Character education, school accountability, computer applications for school administrators.

Morehead State University, Graduate Programs, College of Education, Department of Middle Grades and Secondary Education, Morehead, KY 40351. Offers business and marketing education (MAT); English/language arts 5-9 (MAT); French (MAT); health P-12 (MAT); mathematics 5-9 (MAT); physical education P-12 (MAT); science 5-9 (MAT); secondary biology (MAT); secondary chemistry (MAT); secondary earth science (MAT); secondary English (MAT); secondary math (MAT); secondary physics (MAT); secondary social studies (MAT); social studies 5-9 (MAT); Spanish (MAT). Part-time and evening/weekend programs available. *Degree requirements:* For master's, portfolio. *Entrance requirements:* For master's, GRE or PRAXIS II content exam, minimum overall undergraduate GPA of 2.5. Additional exam requirements/recommendations for international students: Required—TOEFL (minimum score 500 paper-based; 173 computer-based). Electronic applications accepted.

Morgan State University, School of Graduate Studies, School of Education and Urban Studies, MAT Program, Baltimore, MD 21251. Offers elementary education (MAT); high school education (MAT); middle school education (MAT). Part-time programs available. *Degree requirements:* For master's, comprehensive exam. *Entrance requirements:* For master's, GRE General Test or MAT. *Faculty research:* Multicultural education, cooperative learning, psychology of cognition.

Mount Saint Mary College, Division of Education, Newburgh, NY 12550-3494. Offers adolescence and special education (MS Ed); adolescence education (MS Ed); childhood and special education (MS Ed); childhood education (MS Ed); literacy (5-12) (Advanced Certificate); literacy (birth-6) (Advanced Certificate); literacy and special education (MS Ed); literacy/childhood (MS Ed); middle school (5-6) (MS Ed); middle school (7-9) (MS Ed); special education (1-6) (MS Ed); special education (7-12) (MS Ed). *Accreditation:* NCATE. Part-time and evening/weekend programs available. *Faculty:* 14 full-time (12 women), 14 part-time/adjunct (8 women). *Students:* 55 full-time (42 women), 158 part-time (125 women); includes 23 minority (4 Black or African American, non-Hispanic/Latino; 1 Asian, non-Hispanic/Latino; 18 Hispanic/Latino). Average age 29. 119 applicants, 45% accepted, 24 enrolled. In 2011, 107 master's awarded. *Application deadline:* Applications are processed on a rolling basis. Application fee: $45. Application fee is waived when completed online. *Expenses:* Tuition: Full-time $13,356; part-time $742 per credit. *Required fees:* $70 per semester. *Financial support:* In 2011–12, 99 students received support. Unspecified assistantships available. Financial award application deadline: 4/15; financial award applicants required to submit FAFSA. *Faculty research:* Learning and teaching styles, computers in special education, language development. *Unit head:* Dr. Theresa Lewis, Coordinator, 845-569-3149, Fax: 845-569-3535, E-mail: tlewis@msmc.edu. *Application contact:* Courtney McDermott, Graduate Recruiter, 845-569-3402, Fax: 845-569-3450, E-mail: courtney.mcdermott@msmc.edu. Web site: http://www.msmc.edu/Academics/Graduate_Programs/Master_of_Science_in_Education.

Mount Saint Vincent University, Graduate Programs, Faculty of Education, Program in Curriculum Studies, Halifax, NS B3M 2J6, Canada. Offers education of young adolescents (M Ed, MA Ed, MA-R); general studies (M Ed, MA Ed, MA-R); teaching English as a second language (M Ed, MA Ed, MA-R). Part-time and evening/weekend programs available. Postbaccalaureate distance learning degree programs offered (minimal on-campus study). *Degree requirements:* For master's, thesis (for some programs). *Entrance requirements:* For master's, bachelor's degree in related field, minimum B average, 1 year of teaching experience. Electronic applications accepted. *Faculty research:* Science education, cultural studies, international education, curriculum development.

Murray State University, College of Education, Department of Adolescent, Career and Special Education, Program in Middle School Education, Murray, KY 42071. Offers MA Ed, Ed S. *Accreditation:* NCATE. *Degree requirements:* For master's, comprehensive exam, thesis optional. *Entrance requirements:* Additional exam requirements/recommendations for international students: Required—TOEFL.

Nazareth College of Rochester, Graduate Studies, Department of Education, Program in Inclusive Education-Adolescence Level, Rochester, NY 14618-3790. Offers MS Ed. *Accreditation:* Teacher Education Accreditation Council. *Entrance requirements:* For master's, minimum GPA of 3.0.

Niagara University, Graduate Division of Education, Concentration in Teacher Education, Niagara Falls, Niagara University, NY 14109. Offers early childhood and childhood education (MS Ed); middle and adolescence education (MS Ed); special education (grades 1-12) (MS Ed). *Accreditation:* NCATE. *Faculty:* 4 full-time (1 woman), 6 part-time/adjunct (4 women). *Students:* 249 full-time (162 women), 56 part-time (39 women); includes 11 minority (5 Black or African American, non-Hispanic/Latino; 1 American Indian or Alaska Native, non-Hispanic/Latino; 1 Asian, non-Hispanic/Latino; 2 Hispanic/Latino; 2 Two or more races, non-Hispanic/Latino), 176 international. Average age 24. In 2011, 233 master's, 1 Certificate awarded. *Entrance requirements:* For master's, GRE General Test or MAT. *Application deadline:* For fall admission, 8/1 for domestic students. Applications are processed on a rolling basis. Application fee: $30. *Expenses:* Contact institution. *Financial support:* Career-related internships or fieldwork, Federal Work-Study, and scholarships/grants available. Financial award application deadline: 3/15. *Unit head:* Dr. Chandra Foote, Chair, 716-286-8549. *Application contact:* Dr. Debra A. Colley, Dean of Education, 716-286-8560, Fax: 716-286-8561, E-mail: dcolley@niagara.edu.

North Carolina Central University, Division of Academic Affairs, School of Education, Department of Curriculum, Instruction and Professional Studies, Durham, NC 27707-3129. Offers curriculum and instruction (MA), including elementary education, middle grades education. *Accreditation:* NCATE. Part-time and evening/weekend programs available. *Degree requirements:* For master's, comprehensive exam, thesis or alternative. *Entrance requirements:* For master's, minimum GPA of 3.0 in major, 2.5 overall. Additional exam requirements/recommendations for international students: Required—TOEFL. *Faculty research:* Simulation of decision-making behavior of school boards.

North Carolina State University, Graduate School, College of Education, Department of Curriculum and Instruction, Program in Middle Grades Education, Raleigh, NC 27695. Offers M Ed, MS. *Accreditation:* NCATE. *Degree requirements:* For master's, thesis optional. *Entrance requirements:* For master's, GRE General Test or MAT, minimum GPA of 3.0 in major.

North Georgia College & State University, School of Education, Dahlonega, GA 30597. Offers art education (MAT); early childhood education (M Ed); English education (MAT); history education (MAT); math education (MAT); middle grades education (M Ed, MAT); physical education (MS); school leadership (Ed S); secondary education (M Ed), including English education, history education, mathematics education, physical education; teacher education (MAT). *Accreditation:* NCATE. Part-time and evening/weekend programs available. Postbaccalaureate distance learning degree programs offered (no on-campus study). *Faculty:* 23 full-time (14 women), 16 part-time/adjunct (11 women). *Students:* 19 full-time (17 women), 199 part-time (147 women); includes 7 minority (3 Black or African American, non-Hispanic/Latino; 1 Asian, non-Hispanic/Latino; 3 Hispanic/Latino), 1 international. Average age 34. 259 applicants, 66% accepted, 112 enrolled. In 2011, 100 master's, 16 other advanced degrees awarded. *Degree requirements:* For master's, comprehensive exam, thesis optional. *Entrance requirements:* For master's, GRE or MAT, GACE, minimum GPA of 2.75; for Ed S, GRE General Test or MAT, 3 years of teaching experience, master's degree, minimum graduate GPA of 3.25, leadership position in the school. Additional exam requirements/recommendations for international students: Required—TOEFL (minimum score 550 paper-based; 213 computer-based; 79 iBT), IELTS (minimum score 6.5). *Application deadline:* For fall admission, 8/1 priority date for domestic students, 7/1 for international students; for spring admission, 12/1 priority date for domestic students, 11/1 for international students. Applications are processed on a rolling basis. Application fee: $40. Electronic applications accepted. *Expenses:* Tuition, state resident: full-time $3528; part-time $196 per credit hour. Tuition, nonresident: full-time $14,094; part-time $783 per credit hour. *Required fees:* $1718; $859 per semester. Tuition and fees vary according to course load, campus/location and program. *Financial support:* Teaching assistantships, career-related internships or fieldwork, scholarships/grants, and unspecified assistantships available. Financial award application deadline: 5/1; financial award applicants required to submit CSS PROFILE or FAFSA. *Faculty research:* Identification of professional development school structures supporting P-12 student achievement, impact of diverse field placement settings in teacher belief development among preservice teachers, use of inquiry methodology in social studies teaching with English language learners, use of instructional differentiation in the middle grades classroom, effects of international school placements on preservice teacher beliefs and attitudes. *Unit head:* Dr. Bob Michael, Dean, School of Education, 706-864-1998, Fax: 706-867-2850, E-mail: bmichael@northgeorgia.edu. *Application contact:* Susan L. Perry, Graduate Admissions Coordinator, 706-864-1543, Fax: 706-867-2795, E-mail: slperry@northgeorgia.edu. Web site: http://www.northgeorgia.edu/soe/.

Northwestern State University of Louisiana, Graduate Studies and Research, College of Education and Human Development, Program in Middle School Education, Natchitoches, LA 71497. Offers MAT. *Students:* 3 full-time (1 woman), 29 part-time (25 women); includes 7 minority (all Black or African American, non-Hispanic/Latino). Average age 34. 7 applicants, 100% accepted, 7 enrolled. In 2011, 9 master's awarded. *Degree requirements:* For master's, comprehensive exam, thesis or alternative. *Entrance requirements:* For master's, GRE General Test, minimum undergraduate GPA of 2.5. Additional exam requirements/recommendations for international students: Required—TOEFL. *Application deadline:* For fall admission, 3/15 priority date for domestic students; for spring admission, 10/15 priority date for domestic students. Applications are processed on a rolling basis. Application fee: $20 ($30 for international students). Electronic applications accepted. *Expenses:* Tuition, state resident: full-time $3440. Tuition, nonresident: full-time $12,010. *Unit head:* Dr. Vickie Gentry, Chair, 318-357-6288, Fax: 318-357-6275, E-mail: education@nsula.edu. *Application contact:* Dr. Steven G. Horton, Associate Provost/Dean, Graduate Studies, Research, and Information Systems, 318-357-5851, Fax: 318-357-5019, E-mail: grad_school@nsula.edu.

Northwest Missouri State University, Graduate School, College of Education and Human Services, Department of Curriculum and Instruction, Program in Teaching: Middle School, Maryville, MO 64468-6001. Offers MS Ed. *Accreditation:* NCATE. *Faculty:* 17 full-time (all women). *Students:* 1 (woman) part-time. In 2011, 1 master's awarded. *Degree requirements:* For master's, comprehensive exam. *Entrance requirements:* For master's, GRE General Test, minimum undergraduate GPA of 2.75, teaching certificate, writing sample. Additional exam requirements/recommendations for international students: Required—TOEFL. *Application deadline:* For fall admission, 7/1 for domestic and international students; for spring admission, 11/15 for domestic and international students. Applications are processed on a rolling basis. Application fee: $0 ($50 for international students). *Financial support:* Application deadline: 4/1; applicants required to submit FAFSA. *Unit head:* Pat Thompson, Director, 660-562-1775. *Application contact:* Dr. Gregory Haddock, Dean of Graduate School, 660-562-1145, Fax: 660-562-1096, E-mail: gradsch@nwmissouri.edu.

The Ohio State University at Lima, Graduate Programs, Lima, OH 45804. Offers early childhood education (M Ed); education (MA); middle childhood education (M Ed); social work (MSW). Part-time programs available. *Faculty:* 41. *Students:* 27 full-time (13 women), 39 part-time (33 women); includes 3 minority (1 Black or African American, non-Hispanic/Latino; 2 Two or more races, non-Hispanic/Latino). Average age 34. Terminal master's awarded for partial completion of doctoral program. *Degree requirements:* For master's, comprehensive exam (for some programs), thesis (for some programs). *Entrance requirements:* For master's, GRE, minimum GPA of 3.0. Additional exam requirements/recommendations for international students: Required—TOEFL (minimum score 550 paper-based; 79 iBT), Michigan English Language Assessment Battery (minimum score 82); Recommended—IELTS (minimum score 7), TWE. *Application deadline:* For fall admission, 6/1 priority date for domestic students, 6/1 for international students; for spring admission, 10/15 priority date for domestic students, 10/15 for international students. Applications are processed on a rolling basis. Application fee: $40 ($50 for international students). Electronic applications accepted. *Expenses:* Tuition, state resident: full-time $11,130. Tuition, nonresident: full-time $27,855. *Financial support:* Application deadline: 2/1. *Unit head:* Dr. John Snyder, Dean/Director, 419-995-8481, E-mail: snyder.4@osu.edu. *Application contact:* Graduate Admissions, 614-292-9444, Fax: 614-292-3895, E-mail: domestic.grad@osu.edu.

The Ohio State University at Marion, Graduate Programs, Marion, OH 43302-5695. Offers early childhood education (pre-K to grade 3) (M Ed); education - teaching and learning (MA); middle childhood education (grades 4-9) (M Ed). Part-time programs available. *Faculty:* 38. *Students:* 67 full-time (49 women), 13 part-time (9 women); includes 2 minority (1 American Indian or Alaska Native, non-Hispanic/Latino; 1 Hispanic/Latino). Average age 32. *Degree requirements:* For master's, comprehensive exam (for some programs), thesis (for some programs). *Entrance requirements:* For master's, GRE, minimum undergraduate GPA of 3.0. Additional exam requirements/recommendations for international students: Required—Michigan English Language Assessment Battery (minimum score 82); Recommended—TOEFL (minimum score 650 paper-based; 79 iBT), IELTS (minimum score 7). *Application deadline:* For fall admission, 6/1 priority date for domestic students, 6/1 for international students; for spring admission, 10/15 priority date for domestic students, 10/15 for international students. Applications are processed on a rolling basis. Application fee: $40 ($50 for international students). Electronic applications accepted. *Expenses:* Tuition, state resident: full-time $11,130. Tuition, nonresident: full-time $27,855. Tuition and fees vary according to course load. *Financial support:* Application deadline: 1/15; applicants required to submit FAFSA. *Unit head:* Dr. Gregory S. Rose, Dean/Director, 740-389-6786 Ext. 6218, E-mail: rose.9@osu.edu. *Application contact:* Graduate Admissions, 614-292-9444, Fax: 614-292-3895, E-mail: domestic.grad@osu.edu.

The Ohio State University–Mansfield Campus, Graduate Programs, Mansfield, OH 44906-1599. Offers early childhood education (M Ed); education (MA); middle childhood education (M Ed); social work (MSW). Part-time programs available. *Faculty:* 41. *Students:* 21 full-time (15 women), 57 part-time (48 women); includes 5 minority (2 Black or African American, non-Hispanic/Latino; 1 Asian, non-Hispanic/Latino; 1 Hispanic/Latino; 1 Two or more races, non-Hispanic/Latino), 1 international. Average age 33. *Degree requirements:* For master's, comprehensive exam (for some programs), thesis (for some programs). *Entrance requirements:* For master's, GRE, minimum GPA of 3.0. Additional exam requirements/recommendations for international students: Required—TOEFL (minimum score 550 paper-based; 79 iBT), Michigan English Language Assessment Battery (minimum score 82); Recommended—IELTS (minimum score 7). *Application deadline:* For fall admission, 6/1 priority date for domestic students, 6/1 for international students; for spring admission, 10/15 priority date for domestic students, 10/15 for international students. Applications are processed on a rolling basis. Application fee: $40 ($50 for international students). Electronic applications accepted. *Expenses:* Tuition, state resident: full-time $11,130. Tuition, nonresident: full-time $27,855. Tuition and fees vary according to course load. *Financial support:* Teaching assistantships with full tuition reimbursements, Federal Work-Study, and scholarships/grants available. Support available to part-time students. Financial award application deadline: 2/1. *Unit head:* Dr. Stephen M. Gavazzi, Dean and Director, 419-755-4221, Fax: 419-755-4241, E-mail: gavazzi.1@osu.edu. *Application contact:* Graduate Admissions, 614-292-9444, Fax: 614-292-3895, E-mail: domestic.grad@osu.edu.

The Ohio State University–Newark Campus, Graduate Programs, Newark, OH 43055-1797. Offers early/middle childhood education (M Ed); education - teaching and learning (MA); social work (MSW). Part-time programs available. *Faculty:* 56. *Students:* 63 full-time (55 women), 46 part-time (39 women); includes 6 minority (1 Black or African American, non-Hispanic/Latino; 1 Asian, non-Hispanic/Latino; 3 Hispanic/Latino; 1 Two or more races, non-Hispanic/Latino). Average age 31. Terminal master's awarded for partial completion of doctoral program. *Degree requirements:* For master's, comprehensive exam (for some programs), thesis (for some programs). *Entrance requirements:* For master's, GRE, minimum GPA of 3.0. Additional exam requirements/recommendations for international students: Required—Michigan English Language Assessment Battery (minimum score 82); Recommended—TOEFL (minimum score 550 paper-based; 79 iBT), IELTS (minimum score 7). *Application deadline:* For fall admission, 6/1 priority date for domestic students, 6/1 for international students; for spring admission, 10/15 priority date for domestic students, 2/1 for international students. Applications are processed on a rolling basis. Application fee: $40 ($50 for international students). Electronic applications accepted. *Unit head:* Dr. William L. MacDonald, Dean/Director, 740-366-9333 Ext. 330, E-mail: macdonald.24@osu.edu. *Application contact:* Graduate Admissions, 614-292-9444, Fax: 614-292-3985, E-mail: domestic.grad@osu.edu.

Ohio University, Graduate College, Gladys W. and David H. Patton College of Education and Human Services, Department of Teacher Education, Athens, OH 45701-2979. Offers adolescent to young adult education (M Ed); curriculum and instruction (M Ed, PhD); early childhood/special education (M Ed); intervention specialist/mild-moderate needs (M Ed); intervention specialist/moderate-intensive needs (M Ed); mathematics education (PhD); middle child education (M Ed); reading education (M Ed); social studies education (PhD). Part-time and evening/weekend programs available. *Students:* 131 full-time (92 women), 82 part-time (62 women); includes 9 minority (4 Black or African American, non-Hispanic/Latino; 2 American Indian or Alaska Native, non-Hispanic/Latino; 1 Asian, non-Hispanic/Latino; 1 Hispanic/Latino; 1 Two or more races, non-Hispanic/Latino), 11 international. 136 applicants, 70% accepted, 65 enrolled. In 2011, 58 master's, 8 doctorates awarded. *Degree requirements:* For master's, thesis or alternative; for doctorate, comprehensive exam, thesis/dissertation. *Entrance requirements:* For master's, GRE General Test or MAT (if GPA is below 2.9); for doctorate, GRE General Test, minimum GPA of 3.4, work experience. Additional exam requirements/recommendations for international students: Required—TOEFL (minimum score 550 paper-based; 80 iBT) or IELTS (minimum score 6.5). *Application deadline:* For fall admission, 5/1 priority date for domestic students, 4/1 for international students; for winter admission, 11/1 priority date for domestic students, 10/1 for international students; for spring admission, 2/15 priority date for domestic students, 1/1 for international students. Applications are processed on a rolling basis. Application fee: $50 ($55 for international students). Electronic applications accepted. *Financial support:* Research assistantships with full tuition reimbursements, teaching assistantships with full tuition reimbursements, Federal Work-Study, institutionally sponsored loans, tuition waivers (partial), and unspecified assistantships available. Financial award application deadline: 3/1. *Faculty research:* Cognition literacy, character education, teacher's education reform, disabilities. *Total annual research expenditures:* $46,933. *Unit head:* Dr. John Henning, Chair, 740-597-1830, Fax: 740-593-0477, E-mail: henningj@ohio.edu. *Application contact:* Floyd J. Doney, Director of Student Affairs, 740-593-4400, Fax: 740-593-9310, E-mail: doney@ohio.edu. Web site: http://www.cehs.ohio.edu/academics/te/index.htm.

Old Dominion University, Darden College of Education, Program in Elementary/Middle Education, Norfolk, VA 23529. Offers elementary education (MS Ed); instructional technology (MS Ed); library science (MS Ed); middle school education (MS Ed). *Accreditation:* NCATE. Part-time and evening/weekend programs available. Postbaccalaureate distance learning degree programs offered (no on-campus study). *Faculty:* 18 full-time (16 women), 34 part-time/adjunct (27 women). *Students:* 151 full-time (140 women), 118 part-time (96 women); includes 53 minority (27 Black or African American, non-Hispanic/Latino; 3 Asian, non-Hispanic/Latino; 10 Hispanic/Latino; 2 Native Hawaiian or other Pacific Islander, non-Hispanic/Latino; 11 Two or more races, non-Hispanic/Latino). Average age 31. 291 applicants, 50% accepted, 123 enrolled. In 2011, 167 master's awarded. *Degree requirements:* For master's, comprehensive exam. *Entrance requirements:* For master's, GRE General Test or MAT; PRAXIS I, SAT or ACT, minimum GPA of 2.8. Additional exam requirements/recommendations for international students: Required—TOEFL (minimum score 600 paper-based; 250 computer-based). *Application deadline:* For fall admission, 6/1 priority date for domestic students; for winter admission, 11/1 priority date for domestic students; for spring admission, 3/1 priority date for domestic students. Applications are processed on a rolling basis. Application fee: $50. Electronic applications accepted. *Expenses:* Tuition, state resident: full-time $9096; part-time $379 per credit. Tuition, nonresident: full-time $23,064; part-time $961 per credit. *Required fees:* $127 per semester. One-time fee: $50. *Financial support:* In 2011–12, 180 students received support, including teaching assistantships (averaging $9,000 per year); career-related internships or fieldwork, Federal Work-Study, institutionally sponsored loans, and scholarships/grants also available. Support available to part-time students. Financial award application deadline: 2/15; financial award applicants required to submit FAFSA. *Faculty research:* Education pre-K to 6, school librarianship. *Unit head:* Dr. Lea Lee, Graduate Program Director, 757-683-4801, Fax: 757-683-5862, E-mail: lxlee@odu.edu. *Application contact:* William Heffelfinger, Director of Graduate Admissions, 757-683-5554, Fax: 757-683-3255, E-mail: gradadmit@odu.edu. Web site: http://education.odu.edu/eci/.

Our Lady of the Lake University of San Antonio, School of Professional Studies, Program in Intermediate Education, San Antonio, TX 78207-4689. Offers math/science education (M Ed); professional studies (M Ed). Part-time and evening/weekend programs available.

Pacific University, College of Education, Forest Grove, OR 97116-1797. Offers early childhood education (MAT); education (MAE); elementary education (MAT); high school education (MAT); middle school education (MAT); special education (MAT); visual function in learning (M Ed). *Accreditation:* NCATE. Part-time and evening/weekend programs available. *Degree requirements:* For master's, research project. *Entrance requirements:* For master's, California Basic Educational Skills Test, PRAXIS II, minimum undergraduate GPA of 2.75, 3.0 graduate. Additional exam requirements/recommendations for international students: Required—TOEFL. Electronic applications accepted. *Expenses:* Contact institution. *Faculty research:* Defining a culturally competent classroom, technology in the k-12 classroom, Socratic seminars, social studies education.

Park University, College of Graduate and Professional Studies, Kansas City, MO 54105. Offers adult education (M Ed); at-risk students (M Ed); disaster and emergency management (MPA); educational administration (M Ed); entrepreneurship (MBA); general business (MBA); general education (M Ed); government/business relations (MPA); healthcare/services management (MBA, MPA); international business (MBA); K-12 certification (MAT); management information systems (MBA); management of information systems (MPA); middle school certification (MAT); multi-cultural education (M Ed); nonprofit management (MPA); public management (MPA); school law (M Ed); secondary school certification (MAT); special education (M Ed). Part-time and evening/weekend programs available. Postbaccalaureate distance learning degree programs offered (no on-campus study). *Degree requirements:* For master's, comprehensive exam, thesis (for some programs). *Entrance requirements:* For master's, GRE, GMAT, teacher certification (M Ed). Additional exam requirements/recommendations for international students: Required—TOEFL (minimum score 550 paper-based). Electronic applications accepted. *Faculty research:* Literacy, leadership, brain based research, multicultural education, diversity.

Piedmont College, School of Education, Demorest, GA 30535-0010. Offers early childhood education (MA, MAT); middle grades education (MA); secondary education (MA, MAT); special education (MA, MAT); teacher leadership (Ed S). Part-time and evening/weekend programs available. *Students:* 546 full-time (433 women), 809 part-time (698 women); includes 172 minority (139 Black or African American, non-Hispanic/Latino; 2 American Indian or Alaska Native, non-Hispanic/Latino; 6 Asian, non-Hispanic/Latino; 18 Hispanic/Latino; 7 Two or more races, non-Hispanic/Latino), 17 international. Average age 37. 342 applicants, 83% accepted, 234 enrolled. In 2011, 444 master's, 510 other advanced degrees awarded. *Degree requirements:* For master's, thesis, field experience in the classroom teaching ; for doctorate, thesis/dissertation. *Entrance* *requirements:* For master's, GRE General Test, MAT, minimum undergraduate GPA of 2.5; for Ed S, minimum graduate GPA of 3.5, valid teaching certificate. Additional exam requirements/recommendations for international students: Required—TOEFL (minimum score 550 paper-based; 213 computer-based). *Application deadline:* For fall admission, 7/15 for domestic students; for spring admission, 12/1 for domestic students. Applications are processed on a rolling basis. Application fee: $0. Electronic applications accepted. *Expenses: Tuition:* Part-time $407 per credit hour. Tuition and fees vary according to program. *Financial support:* Career-related internships or fieldwork, Federal Work-Study, and unspecified assistantships available. Support available to part-time students. Financial award applicants required to submit FAFSA. *Unit head:* Dr. Bob Cummings, Dean, 706-778-3000 Ext. 1201, Fax: 706-776-9608, E-mail: bcummings@piedmont.edu. *Application contact:* Penny Loggins, Director of Graduate Admissions, 706-778-8500 Ext. 1181, Fax: 706-778-0150, E-mail: ploggins@piedmont.edu.

Plymouth State University, College of Graduate Studies, Graduate Studies in Education, Program in K-12 Education, Plymouth, NH 03264-1595. Offers M Ed. *Accreditation:* NCATE. Part-time and evening/weekend programs available. *Degree requirements:* For master's, PRAXIS. *Entrance requirements:* For master's, MAT, minimum GPA of 3.0.

Quinnipiac University, School of Education, Program in Secondary Education, Hamden, CT 06518-1940. Offers biology (MAT); English (MAT); history/social studies (MAT); mathematics (MAT); Spanish (MAT). *Accreditation:* NCATE. *Faculty:* 7 full-time (5 women), 41 part-time/adjunct (24 women). *Students:* 56 full-time (38 women), 1 (woman) part-time; includes 5 minority (1 Black or African American, non-Hispanic/Latino; 1 Asian, non-Hispanic/Latino; 3 Hispanic/Latino). 51 applicants, 96% accepted, 44 enrolled. In 2011, 49 master's awarded. *Entrance requirements:* For master's, PRAXIS I, minimum GPA of 2.67, interview. *Application deadline:* For fall admission, 3/31 priority date for domestic students. Applications are processed on a rolling basis. Application fee: $45. Electronic applications accepted. *Expenses: Tuition:* Part-time $855 per credit. *Required fees:* $35 per credit. *Financial support:* In 2011–12, 1 student received support. Career-related internships or fieldwork, scholarships/grants, and tuition waivers (full and partial) available. Financial award application deadline: 4/15; financial award applicants required to submit FAFSA. *Faculty research:* Multicultural and urban education/leadership, challenges of teaching diverse learners, scholarship of teaching and learning, technology and teaching, humor and education. *Unit head:* Mordechai Gordon, Program Director, 203-582-8442, Fax: 203-582-3473, E-mail: mordechai.gordon@quinnipiac.edu. *Application contact:* Jennifer Boutin, Associate Director of Graduate Admissions, 800-462-1944, Fax: 203-582-3443, E-mail: jennifer.boutin@quinnipiac.edu. Web site: http://www.quinnipiac.edu/academics/colleges-schools-and-departments/school-of-education/graduate-programs/five-semester-mat-programs/secondary-educat.

Roberts Wesleyan College, Division of Teacher Education, Rochester, NY 14624-1997. Offers adolescence education (M Ed); childhood and special education (M Ed); literacy education (M Ed); urban education (M Ed). Part-time and evening/weekend programs available. *Degree requirements:* For master's, thesis.

Saginaw Valley State University, College of Education, Program in Middle School Classroom Teaching, University Center, MI 48710. Offers MAT. *Accreditation:* NCATE. Part-time and evening/weekend programs available. *Students:* 12 part-time (11 women). Average age 31. 2 applicants, 100% accepted, 1 enrolled. In 2011, 4 master's awarded. *Degree requirements:* For master's, capstone course. *Entrance requirements:* For master's, minimum GPA of 3.0, teaching certificate. Additional exam requirements/recommendations for international students: Required—TOEFL (minimum score 525 paper-based; 197 computer-based; 71 iBT). *Application deadline:* Applications are processed on a rolling basis. Application fee: $25. Electronic applications accepted. *Expenses:* Tuition, state resident: full-time $8300; part-time $5333 per year. Tuition, nonresident: full-time $15,613; part-time $10,209 per year. *International tuition:* $15,631 full-time. *Financial support:* Federal Work-Study and scholarships/grants available. Support available to part-time students. Financial award applicants required to submit FAFSA. *Faculty research:* Pre-service, middle school, secondary teacher, literacy education. *Unit head:* Dr. Steve P. Barbus, Jr., Dean, 989-964-6067, Fax: 989-790-4385, E-mail: barbus@svsu.edu. *Application contact:* Jeanne Chipman, Certification Officer, 989-964-4083, Fax: 989-964-4385, E-mail: jdc@svsu.edu.

Saginaw Valley State University, College of Education, Program in Natural Science Teaching, University Center, MI 48710. Offers elementary (MAT); middle school (MAT); secondary school (MAT). *Accreditation:* NCATE. Part-time and evening/weekend programs available. *Students:* 9 part-time (7 women); includes 1 minority (Black or African American, non-Hispanic/Latino). Average age 35. 1 applicant, 100% accepted, 0 enrolled. In 2011, 14 master's awarded. *Degree requirements:* For master's, capstone course. *Entrance requirements:* For master's, minimum GPA of 3.0, teaching certificate. Additional exam requirements/recommendations for international students: Required—TOEFL (minimum score 525 paper-based; 197 computer-based; 71 iBT). *Application deadline:* Applications are processed on a rolling basis. Application fee: $25. Electronic applications accepted. *Expenses:* Tuition, state resident: full-time $8300; part-time $5333 per year. Tuition, nonresident: full-time $15,613; part-time $10,209 per year. *International tuition:* $15,631 full-time. *Financial support:* Federal Work-Study and scholarships/grants available. Support available to part-time students. Financial award applicants required to submit FAFSA. *Unit head:* Dr. Steve P. Barbus, Jr., Dean, 989-964-6067, Fax: 989-790-4385, E-mail: barbus@svsu.edu. *Application contact:* Kathy Lopez, Certification Officer, 989-964-4661, Fax: 989-964-4385, E-mail: klopez@svsu.edu.

St. Bonaventure University, School of Graduate Studies, School of Education, Adolescence Education Program, St. Bonaventure, NY 14778-2284. Offers MS Ed. *Faculty:* 2 full-time (both women), 1 (woman) part-time/adjunct. *Students:* 10 full-time (5 women), 7 part-time (2 women). Average age 24. 3 applicants, 67% accepted, 2 enrolled. In 2011, 7 master's awarded. *Degree requirements:* For master's, comprehensive exam, electronic portfolio, completion of student teaching. *Entrance requirements:* For master's, New York State Teacher Certification Exam (L.A.S.T and Content Exam); PRAXIS I and appropriate content exam (for PA applicants), undergraduate degree in teachable content area; minimum GPA of 3.0, personal interview, writing sample. Additional exam requirements/recommendations for international students: Required—TOEFL (minimum score 550 paper-based; 213 computer-based; 79 iBT). *Application deadline:* For fall admission, 3/15 priority date for domestic students, 2/1 for international students; for spring admission, 11/1 for domestic students. Applications are processed on a rolling basis. Application fee: $30. Electronic applications accepted. *Expenses: Tuition:* Part-time $670 per credit. *Financial support:* Research assistantships, Federal Work-Study, scholarships/grants, health care benefits, tuition waivers (partial), and unspecified assistantships available. Support available to part-time students. Financial award application deadline: 4/15; financial award applicants required to submit FAFSA. *Unit head:* Dr. Paula Kenneson, Director, 716-375-2177, E-mail: pkenneso@sbu.edu. *Application contact:* Bruce Campbell, Director of Graduate Admissions, 716-375-2429, Fax: 716-375-4015, E-mail: gradsch@sbu.edu.

St. Bonaventure University, School of Graduate Studies, School of Education, Literacy Programs, St. Bonaventure, NY 14778-2284. Offers adolescent literacy 5-12 (MS Ed); childhood literacy B-6 (MS Ed). *Accreditation:* NCATE. Part-time and evening/weekend programs available. *Faculty:* 2 full-time (both women). *Students:* 18 full-time (16 women), 33 part-time (32 women). Average age 24. 33 applicants, 67% accepted, 15 enrolled. In 2011, 50 master's awarded. *Degree requirements:* For master's, comprehensive exam, thesis optional, literacy coaching internship, portfolio. *Entrance requirements:* For master's, interview, writing sample, minimum undergraduate GPA of 3.0, references, teaching certificate in matching area. Additional exam requirements/recommendations for international students: Required—TOEFL (minimum score 550 paper-based; 213 computer-based; 80 iBT). *Application deadline:* For fall admission, 6/15 priority date for domestic students, 2/1 for international students; for spring admission, 11/15 priority date for domestic students, 7/1 for international students. Applications are processed on a rolling basis. Application fee: $30. Electronic applications accepted. *Expenses: Tuition:* Part-time $670 per credit. *Financial support:* In 2011–12, 4 research assistantships with full and partial tuition reimbursements were awarded; Federal Work-Study, scholarships/grants, health care benefits, and unspecified assistantships also available. Support available to part-time students. Financial award application deadline: 4/15; financial award applicants required to submit FAFSA. *Unit head:* Dr. Pamela Sharp Crawford, Director, 716-375-2387, E-mail: pcrawfor@sbu.edu. *Application contact:* Bruce Campbell, 716-375-2429, Fax: 716-375-4015, E-mail: gradsch@sbu.edu. Web site: http://www.sbu.edu/education.aspx?id=2994.

St. John Fisher College, Ralph C. Wilson Jr. School of Education, Program in Adolescence Education/Special Education, Rochester, NY 14618-3597. Offers adolescence English (MS Ed); adolescence French (MS Ed); adolescence social studies (MS Ed); adolescence Spanish (MS Ed). Part-time and evening/weekend programs available. *Faculty:* 5 full-time (3 women), 2 part-time/adjunct (both women). *Students:* 25 full-time (13 women), 1 (woman) part-time. Average age 22. 19 applicants, 79% accepted, 11 enrolled. In 2011, 18 master's awarded. *Degree requirements:* For master's, field experiences, student teaching, LAST. *Entrance requirements:* For master's, 2 letters of recommendation, personal statement, current resume. Additional exam requirements/recommendations for international students: Required—TOEFL (minimum score 575 paper-based; 233 computer-based; 80 iBT). *Application deadline:* Applications are processed on a rolling basis. Application fee: $30. Electronic applications accepted. *Expenses: Tuition:* Part-time $735 per credit. One-time fee: $50 part-time. Tuition and fees vary according to course load, degree level and program. *Financial support:* In 2011–12, 5 students received support. Scholarships/grants available. Financial award applicants required to submit FAFSA. *Faculty research:* Arts and humanities, urban schools, constructivist learning, at risk students, mentoring. *Unit head:* Dr. Susan Schultz, Program Director, 585-385-7296, E-mail: sschultz@sjfc.edu. *Application contact:* Jose Perales, Director of Graduate Admissions, 585-385-8067, E-mail: jperales@sjfc.edu. Web site: http://www.sjfc.edu/academics/education/departments/ms-special-ed/options/initial-adolescence.dot.

St. John's University, The School of Education, Department of Curriculum and Instruction, Queens, NY 11439. Offers adolescent education (MS Ed); childhood education (MS Ed); early childhood education (MS Ed), including early childhood; middle school education (Adv C). Part-time programs available. *Students:* 122 full-time (90 women), 293 part-time (197 women); includes 141 minority (52 Black or African American, non-Hispanic/Latino; 27 Asian, non-Hispanic/Latino; 55 Hispanic/Latino; 1 Native Hawaiian or other Pacific Islander, non-Hispanic/Latino; 6 Two or more races, non-Hispanic/Latino), 10 international. Average age 30. 266 applicants, 88% accepted, 145 enrolled. In 2011, 178 master's awarded. *Degree requirements:* For master's, comprehensive exam. *Entrance requirements:* For master's, minimum GPA of 3.0, 2 letters of recommendation, qualification for the New York State provisional (initial) teaching certificate. Additional exam requirements/recommendations for international students: Required—TOEFL (minimum score 600 paper-based; 250 computer-based; 100 iBT), IELTS (minimum score 5.5). *Application deadline:* For fall admission, 8/17 for domestic students, 5/1 for international students; for spring admission, 1/5 for domestic students, 11/1 for international students. Applications are processed on a rolling basis. Application fee: $70. Electronic applications accepted. *Expenses: Tuition:* Full-time $18,000; part-time $1000 per credit. *Required fees:* $170 per semester. Tuition and fees vary according to program. *Financial support:* Research assistantships available. *Faculty research:* Student learning and satisfaction in online courses, online collaboration needs, female education in south and east Asia, e-portfolio assessment, pedagogical practices in mathematics education. *Unit head:* Dr. Judith McVarish, Chair, 718-990-2334, E-mail: mcvarisj@stjohns.edu. *Application contact:* Dr. Kelly K. Ronayne, Associate Dean for Graduate Admissions, 718-990-2304, Fax: 718-990-2343, E-mail: graded@stjohns.edu.

Saint Joseph's University, College of Arts and Sciences, Department of Education, Philadelphia, PA 19131-1395. Offers curriculum supervisor of instruction (Certificate); educational leadership (MS, Ed D); elementary education (MS, Certificate); elementary/middle years (Certificate); English second language specialist online (Certificate); hearing impaired: N-12th grade (Certificate); instructional technology (MS, Certificate); principal certification (Certificate); professional education (MS); reading specialist (MS, Certificate); reading supervisory (Certificate); secondary education (MS, Certificate); special education (MS, Certificate); superintendent's letter of eligibility (Certificate); supervisor of special education (Certificate); Wilson reading certificate online (Certificate). Part-time and evening/weekend programs available. Postbaccalaureate distance learning degree programs offered (no on-campus study). *Faculty:* 26 full-time (24 women), 83 part-time/adjunct (52 women). *Students:* 112 full-time (92 women), 923 part-time (709 women); includes 147 minority (92 Black or African American, non-Hispanic/Latino; 4 American Indian or Alaska Native, non-Hispanic/Latino; 19 Asian, non-Hispanic/Latino; 28 Hispanic/Latino; 4 Two or more races, non-Hispanic/Latino), 8 international. Average age 31. 285 applicants, 77% accepted, 176 enrolled. In 2011, 276 master's, 13 doctorates, 2 other advanced degrees awarded. *Entrance requirements:* For master's, 2 letters of recommendation, minimum GPA of 3.0, official transcripts, personal statement; for doctorate, GRE, master's degree from accredited institution, minimum graduate GPA of 3.5, computer competence, commitment to participate in cohort, interview with program director. Additional exam requirements/recommendations for international students: Required—TOEFL (minimum score 550 paper-based; 213 computer-based; 79 iBT). *Application deadline:* For fall admission, 7/15 priority date for domestic students, 4/15 for international students; for winter admission, 11/15 for domestic students, 1/15 for international students; for spring admission, 11/15 priority date for domestic students, 10/15 for international students. Applications are processed on a rolling basis. Application fee: $35. Electronic applications accepted. *Expenses:* Contact institution. *Financial support:* Unspecified assistantships available. Financial award applicants required to submit FAFSA. *Faculty research:* Public education professional development, factors predicting early mathematics skills for low income children. *Total annual research expenditures:* $92,975. *Unit head:* Dr. Jeanne Brady, Associate Dean, Education, 610-660-1580, E-mail: jebrady@sju.edu. *Application contact:* Kate McConnell, Director, Graduate College of Arts and Sciences Admissions and Retention, 610-660-3184, Fax: 610-660-3230, E-mail: kate.mcconnell@sju.edu.

Saint Peter's University, Graduate Programs in Education, Program in Teaching, Jersey City, NJ 07306-5997. Offers 6-8 middle school education (MA Ed, Certificate); K-12 secondary education (MA Ed, Certificate); K-5 elementary education (MA Ed, Certificate). Part-time and evening/weekend programs available. *Degree requirements:*

For master's, comprehensive exam. *Entrance requirements:* For master's, GRE or MAT. Additional exam requirements/recommendations for international students: Required—TOEFL (minimum score 79 computer-based). Electronic applications accepted.

St. Thomas Aquinas College, Division of Teacher Education, Sparkill, NY 10976. Offers adolescence education (MST); childhood and special education (MST); childhood education (MST); educational leadership (MS Ed); reading (MS Ed, PMC); special education (MS Ed, PMC); teaching (MS Ed), including elementary education, middle school education, secondary education. *Accreditation:* NCATE. Part-time and evening/weekend programs available. *Degree requirements:* For master's, comprehensive exam, comprehensive professional portfolio; for PMC, action research project. *Entrance requirements:* For master's, New York State Qualifying Exam, GRE General Test or minimum GPA of 3.0, teaching certificate; for PMC, GRE General Test or minimum GPA of 3.0. Electronic applications accepted. *Faculty research:* Computer applications in education, adolescent special education students, literacy development, inclusive practices for special education students.

Salem College, Department of Teacher Education, Winston-Salem, NC 27101. Offers art education (MAT); elementary education (M Ed, MAT); language and literacy (M Ed); middle school education (MAT); music education (MAT); school counseling (M Ed); second language studies (MAT); secondary education (MAT); special education (M Ed, MAT). *Accreditation:* NCATE. Part-time and evening/weekend programs available. Postbaccalaureate distance learning degree programs offered (minimal on-campus study). *Degree requirements:* For master's, comprehensive exam, practicum (MAT), project (M Ed), oral and written comprehensive exams. *Entrance requirements:* For master's, GRE, minimum GPA of 2.5. *Faculty research:* Content area reading strategies, literacy development, brain compatible instruction.

Salem State University, School of Graduate Studies, Program in Middle School Education, Salem, MA 01970-5353. Offers humanities (M Ed); math/science (MAT). Part-time and evening/weekend programs available. *Entrance requirements:* For master's, GRE or MAT. Additional exam requirements/recommendations for international students: Required—TOEFL (minimum score 550 paper-based; 80 iBT) or IELTS (minimum score 5.5).

Salem State University, School of Graduate Studies, Program in Middle School General Science, Salem, MA 01970-5353. Offers MAT. Part-time and evening/weekend programs available. *Entrance requirements:* For master's, GRE or MAT. Additional exam requirements/recommendations for international students: Required—TOEFL (minimum score 550 paper-based; 80 iBT) or IELTS (minimum score 5.5).

Salem State University, School of Graduate Studies, Program in Middle School Math, Salem, MA 01970-5353. Offers MAT. Part-time and evening/weekend programs available. *Entrance requirements:* For master's, GRE or MAT. Additional exam requirements/recommendations for international students: Required—TOEFL (minimum score 550 paper-based; 80 iBT) or IELTS (minimum score 5.5).

Seton Hill University, Program in Elementary Education/Middle Level Education, Greensburg, PA 15601. Offers MA, Certificate. *Accreditation:* Teacher Education Accreditation Council. Part-time and evening/weekend programs available. Postbaccalaureate distance learning degree programs offered (minimal on-campus study). *Faculty:* 3 full-time (2 women), 4 part-time/adjunct (2 women). *Students:* 15 full-time (14 women), 3 part-time (all women). In 2011, 10 degrees awarded. *Entrance requirements:* For master's, teacher's certification, 3 letters of recommendation, personal statement, transcripts, resume. Additional exam requirements/recommendations for international students: Required—TOEFL (minimum score 600 paper-based; 250 computer-based; 100 iBT), IELTS (minimum score 6.5). *Application deadline:* Applications are processed on a rolling basis. Application fee: $0. Electronic applications accepted. *Expenses: Tuition:* Full-time $13,446; part-time $747 per credit. *Required fees:* $700; $25 per credit. $50 per term. *Financial support:* Tuition discounts available. *Faculty research:* Autism spectrum disorder. *Unit head:* Dr. Audrey Quinlan, Director, 724-830-4734, E-mail: quinlan@setonhill.edu. *Application contact:* Laurel Komarny, Program Counselor, 724-838-4209, E-mail: komarny@setonhill.edu.

Shippensburg University of Pennsylvania, School of Graduate Studies, College of Education and Human Services, Department of Teacher Education, Shippensburg, PA 17257-2299. Offers curriculum and instruction (M Ed), including biology, early childhood education, elementary education, English, geography/earth science, history, mathematics, middle level education, modern languages; reading (M Ed). *Accreditation:* NCATE. Part-time and evening/weekend programs available. *Faculty:* 14 full-time (11 women), 8 part-time/adjunct (7 women). *Students:* 16 full-time (15 women), 143 part-time (130 women); includes 11 minority (4 Black or African American, non-Hispanic/Latino; 1 Asian, non-Hispanic/Latino; 4 Hispanic/Latino; 2 Two or more races, non-Hispanic/Latino), 1 international. Average age 30. 55 applicants, 55% accepted, 25 enrolled. In 2011, 76 master's awarded. *Degree requirements:* For master's, comprehensive exam (for some programs), thesis optional, practicum or internship; capstone seminar (for some programs). *Entrance requirements:* For master's, MAT (if GPA less than 2.75), interview, 3 letters of reference, questionnaire of teaching background and future goals. Additional exam requirements/recommendations for international students: Required—TOEFL (minimum score 580 paper-based; 237 computer-based); Recommended—IELTS (minimum score 6). *Application deadline:* For fall admission, 6/1 priority date for domestic students, 4/30 for international students; for spring admission, 9/1 priority date for domestic students, 9/30 for international students. Applications are processed on a rolling basis. Application fee: $30. Electronic applications accepted. *Expenses: Tuition, area resident:* Part-time $416 per credit. Tuition, state resident: part-time $416 per credit. Tuition, nonresident: part-time $624 per credit. *Required fees:* $119 per credit. *Financial support:* In 2011–12, 5 research assistantships with full tuition reimbursements (averaging $5,000 per year) were awarded; career-related internships or fieldwork, scholarships/grants, unspecified assistantships, and resident hall director and student payroll positions also available. Support available to part-time students. Financial award application deadline: 3/1; financial award applicants required to submit FAFSA. *Unit head:* Dr. Christine A. Royce, Chairperson, 717-477-1688, Fax: 717-477-4046, E-mail: caroyc@ship.edu. *Application contact:* Jeremy R. Goshorn, Assistant Dean of Graduate Admissions, 717-477-1231, Fax: 717-477-4016, E-mail: jrgoshorn@ship.edu. Web site: http://www.ship.edu/teacher/.

Siena Heights University, Graduate College, Program in Teacher Education, Concentration in Middle School Education, Adrian, MI 49221-1796. Offers MA. Part-time programs available. *Degree requirements:* For master's, thesis, presentation. *Entrance requirements:* For master's, minimum GPA of 3.0, interview. *Expenses: Tuition:* Full-time $11,400; part-time $475 per credit hour. *Required fees:* $1000; $500 $125 per term. Tuition and fees vary according to degree level.

Smith College, Graduate and Special Programs, Department of Education and Child Study, Northampton, MA 01063. Offers education of the deaf (MED); elementary education (MAT); middle school education (MAT); secondary education (MAT), including biological sciences education, chemistry education, English education, French education, geology education, government education, history education, mathematics education, physics education, Spanish education. Part-time programs available. *Faculty:* 6 full-time (4 women), 3 part-time/adjunct (2 women). *Students:* 34 full-time (28 women), 7 part-time (all women); includes 3 minority (2 Asian, non-Hispanic/Latino; 1 Hispanic/Latino). Average age 29. 72 applicants, 64% accepted, 34 enrolled. In 2011, 30 master's awarded. *Entrance requirements:* For master's, GRE. Additional exam requirements/recommendations for international students: Required—TOEFL (minimum score 590 paper-based; 243 computer-based; 97 iBT). *Application deadline:* For fall admission, 4/1 for domestic students, 1/15 for international students; for spring admission, 12/1 for domestic students. Application fee: $60. *Expenses: Tuition:* Full-time $14,925; part-time $1245 per credit. *Financial support:* In 2011–12, 38 students received support, including 7 fellowships; career-related internships or fieldwork, institutionally sponsored loans, and scholarships/grants also available. Support available to part-time students. Financial award application deadline: 1/15; financial award applicants required to submit CSS PROFILE or FAFSA. *Unit head:* Sam Intrator, Chair, 413-585-3242, Fax: 413-585-3268, E-mail: sintrato@smith.edu. *Application contact:* Ruth Morgan, Administrative Assistant, 413-585-3050, Fax: 413-585-3054, E-mail: gradstdy@smith.edu.

Southeast Missouri State University, School of Graduate Studies, Department of Middle and Secondary Education, Cape Girardeau, MO 63701-4799. Offers secondary education (MA), including education studies, education technology. *Accreditation:* NCATE. Part-time and evening/weekend programs available. *Faculty:* 4 full-time (3 women). *Students:* 3 full-time (2 women), 18 part-time (14 women); includes 2 minority (both Black or African American, non-Hispanic/Latino), 1 international. Average age 30. 7 applicants, 86% accepted, 6 enrolled. In 2011, 12 master's awarded. *Degree requirements:* For master's, comprehensive exam, research paper. *Entrance requirements:* For master's, minimum undergraduate GPA of 2.75. Additional exam requirements/recommendations for international students: Required—TOEFL (minimum score 550 paper-based; 213 computer-based; 79 iBT); Recommended—IELTS (minimum score 6). *Application deadline:* For fall admission, 8/1 for domestic students, 7/1 for international students; for spring admission, 11/21 for domestic students, 11/1 for international students. Applications are processed on a rolling basis. Application fee: $30 ($40 for international students). Electronic applications accepted. *Expenses:* Tuition, state resident: full-time $4896; part-time $272 per credit hour. Tuition, nonresident: full-time $8649; part-time $480.50 per credit hour. *Financial support:* In 2011–12, 4 students received support. Career-related internships or fieldwork, Federal Work-Study, scholarships/grants, tuition waivers (full), and unspecified assistantships available. Financial award application deadline: 6/30; financial award applicants required to submit FAFSA. *Faculty research:* Pedagogy of teaching, multicultural education, reading and writing strategies, use of technology in the classroom. *Unit head:* Dr. Simin L. Cwick, Chairperson and Graduate Coordinator, 573-651-5965, Fax: 573-986-6141, E-mail: scwick@semo.edu. *Application contact:* Alisa Aleen McFerron, Assistant Director of Admissions for Operations, 573-651-5937, Fax: 573-651-5936, E-mail: amcferron@semo.edu. Web site: http://www5.semo.edu/middleandsec/.

Southern Arkansas University–Magnolia, Graduate Programs, Magnolia, AR 71754. Offers agriculture (MS); business administration (MBA); computer and information sciences (MS); education (M Ed), including counseling and development, curriculum and instruction, educational administration and supervision, elementary education, middle level, reading, secondary education, TESOL; kinesiology (M Ed); library media and information specialist (M Ed); mental health and clinical counseling (MS); public administration (MPA); school counseling (M Ed); teaching (MAT). *Accreditation:* NCATE. Part-time and evening/weekend programs available. Postbaccalaureate distance learning degree programs offered. *Faculty:* 34 full-time (15 women), 8 part-time/adjunct (5 women). *Students:* 87 full-time (62 women), 320 part-time (224 women); includes 116 minority (111 Black or African American, non-Hispanic/Latino; 2 American Indian or Alaska Native, non-Hispanic/Latino; 2 Asian, non-Hispanic/Latino; 1 Hispanic/Latino), 25 international. Average age 33. 201 applicants, 98% accepted, 156 enrolled. In 2011, 162 master's awarded. *Degree requirements:* For master's, comprehensive exam (for some programs), thesis optional. *Entrance requirements:* For master's, GRE, MAT or GMAT, minimum GPA of 2.5. Additional exam requirements/recommendations for international students: Required—TOEFL (minimum score 173 computer-based). *Application deadline:* For fall admission, 7/15 for domestic and international students; for winter admission, 12/1 for domestic and international students; for spring admission, 12/1 for domestic and international students. Applications are processed on a rolling basis. Application fee: $25 ($35 for international students). Electronic applications accepted. *Expenses:* Tuition, state resident: part-time $232 per credit. Tuition, nonresident: part-time $339 per credit. *Required fees:* $44 per credit. Part-time tuition and fees vary according to course load. *Financial support:* Career-related internships or fieldwork, Federal Work-Study, scholarships/grants, tuition waivers (full), and unspecified assistantships available. Financial award applicants required to submit FAFSA. *Faculty research:* Alternative certification for teachers, supervision of instruction, instructional leadership, counseling. *Unit head:* Dr. Kim Bloss, Dean, School of Graduate Studies, 870-235-4150, Fax: 870-235-5227, E-mail: kkbloss@saumag.edu. *Application contact:* Gaye Calhoun, Admissions Specialist, 870-235-4150, Fax: 870-235-5227, E-mail: glcalhoun@saumag.edu. Web site: http://www.saumag.edu/graduate.

Spalding University, Graduate Studies, College of Education, Programs in Education, Louisville, KY 40203-2188. Offers elementary school education (MAT); general education (MA); high school education (MAT); middle school education (MAT); school administration (MA); special education (learning and behavioral disorders) (MAT); student guidance counselor (MA). MAT programs offered for first teaching certificate/license students. *Accreditation:* NCATE. Part-time and evening/weekend programs available. *Faculty:* 9 full-time (6 women), 32 part-time/adjunct (20 women). *Students:* 142 full-time (100 women), 71 part-time (53 women); includes 75 minority (65 Black or African American, non-Hispanic/Latino; 1 American Indian or Alaska Native, non-Hispanic/Latino; 6 Hispanic/Latino; 3 Two or more races, non-Hispanic/Latino). Average age 36. 96 applicants, 44% accepted, 41 enrolled. In 2011, 69 master's awarded. *Degree requirements:* For master's, portfolio, final project, clinical experience. *Entrance requirements:* For master's, GRE General Test or MAT, interview, recommendations, resume. Additional exam requirements/recommendations for international students: Required—TOEFL (minimum score 535 paper-based; 203 computer-based). *Application deadline:* Applications are processed on a rolling basis. Application fee: $30. Electronic applications accepted. *Expenses: Tuition:* Full-time $12,438. Tuition and fees vary according to course load, degree level and program. *Financial support:* In 2011–12, 72 students received support, including 3 research assistantships with partial tuition reimbursements available (averaging $4,490 per year); scholarships/grants, traineeships, and unspecified assistantships also available. Financial award application deadline: 3/15; financial award applicants required to submit FAFSA. *Faculty research:* Instructional technology, achievement gap, classroom management, assessment. *Unit head:* Dr. Beverly Keepers, Dean, 502-588-7121, Fax: 502-585-7123, E-mail: bkeepers@spalding.edu. *Application contact:* Bonnie Caughron, 502-873-4262, E-mail: bcaughron@spalding.edu.

State University of New York at Oswego, Graduate Studies, School of Education, Department of Curriculum and Instruction, Oswego, NY 13126. Offers adolescence education (MST); art education (MAT); childhood education (MST); elementary education (MS Ed); literacy education (MS Ed); secondary education (MS Ed); special education (MS Ed). Part-time and evening/weekend programs available. *Degree requirements:* For master's, comprehensive exam (for some programs), thesis optional. *Entrance requirements:* For master's, GRE General Test, minimum GPA of 2.7, provisional teaching certificate. Additional exam requirements/recommendations for international students: Required—TOEFL (minimum score 560 paper-based; 220 computer-based). *Faculty research:* Classroom applications for microcomputers; classroom questioning, wait-time, and achievement; values clarification and academic achievement.

State University of New York College at Oneonta, Graduate Education, Division of Education, Department of Secondary Education, Oneonta, NY 13820-4015. Offers adolescence education (MS Ed); family and consumer science education (MS Ed). *Accreditation:* NCATE. Part-time and evening/weekend programs available. *Entrance requirements:* For master's, GRE General Test.

State University of New York College at Potsdam, School of Education and Professional Studies, Program in Special Education, Potsdam, NY 13676. Offers adolescence (grades 7-12) (MS Ed); childhood (grades 1-6) (MS Ed); early childhood (birth-grade 2) (MS Ed). *Accreditation:* NCATE. Part-time programs available. *Faculty:* 2 full-time (1 woman), 5 part-time/adjunct (4 women). *Students:* 19 full-time (15 women), 3 part-time (all women); includes 4 minority (2 American Indian or Alaska Native, non-Hispanic/Latino; 1 Hispanic/Latino; 1 Two or more races, non-Hispanic/Latino). 27 applicants, 100% accepted, 15 enrolled. In 2011, 18 master's awarded. *Degree requirements:* For master's, culminating experience. *Entrance requirements:* For master's, minimum GPA of 3.0 in last 60 hours of course work. Additional exam requirements/recommendations for international students: Required—TOEFL (minimum score 550 paper-based; 213 computer-based; 80 iBT), IELTS (minimum score 6). *Application deadline:* For fall admission, 4/1 for domestic and international students. Applications are processed on a rolling basis. Application fee: $50. *Expenses:* Tuition, state resident: full-time $8870; part-time $370 per credit hour. Tuition, nonresident: full-time $15,160; part-time $632 per credit hour. *Required fees:* $1066; $44.10 per credit hour. One-time fee: $3. *Financial support:* Unspecified assistantships available. Financial award application deadline: 3/1; financial award applicants required to submit FAFSA. *Unit head:* Dr. Dennis Conrad, Chairperson, 315-267-2916, Fax: 315-267-4802, E-mail: conradda@potsdam.edu. *Application contact:* Peter Cutler, Graduate Admissions Counselor, 315-267-2165, Fax: 315-267-4802, E-mail: graduate@potsdam.edu. Web site: http://www.potsdam.edu/academics/SOEPS/SpecialEd/msedspecialed.cfm.

Suffolk University, College of Arts and Sciences, Department of Education and Human Services, Boston, MA 02108-2770. Offers administration of higher education (M Ed, CAGS), including administration of higher education (M Ed), leadership (CAGS); human resource, learning and performance (MS, CAGS, Graduate Certificate), including global human resources (Graduate Certificate), human resources (MS, Graduate Certificate), organizational development (CAGS, Graduate Certificate), organizational learning and development (MS, Graduate Certificate); mental health counseling (MS, CAGS); school counseling (M Ed, CAGS); school teaching (M Ed, CAGS), including foundations of education (M Ed), middle school teaching (M Ed), secondary school teaching (M Ed); MPA/MSMHC; MS/Certificate. Part-time and evening/weekend programs available. *Faculty:* 10 full-time (6 women), 7 part-time/adjunct (3 women). *Students:* 53 full-time (39 women), 131 part-time (112 women); includes 21 minority (7 Black or African American, non-Hispanic/Latino; 2 American Indian or Alaska Native, non-Hispanic/Latino; 5 Asian, non-Hispanic/Latino; 5 Hispanic/Latino; 2 Two or more races, non-Hispanic/Latino), 9 international. Average age 28. 158 applicants, 73% accepted, 60 enrolled. In 2011, 72 master's, 8 other advanced degrees awarded. *Entrance requirements:* For master's, GRE General Test or MAT, 2 letters of recommendation, resume. Additional exam requirements/recommendations for international students: Required—TOEFL (minimum score 550 paper-based; 213 computer-based; 80 iBT). *Application deadline:* For fall admission, 6/15 priority date for domestic students, 6/15 for international students; for spring admission, 11/1 priority date for domestic students, 11/1 for international students. Applications are processed on a rolling basis. Application fee: $50. Electronic applications accepted. *Expenses:* Contact institution. *Financial support:* In 2011–12, 102 students received support, including 30 fellowships with full and partial tuition reimbursements available (averaging $10,664 per year); career-related internships or fieldwork, Federal Work-Study, and institutionally sponsored loans also available. Support available to part-time students. Financial award application deadline: 4/1; financial award applicants required to submit FAFSA. *Faculty research:* Predicting competent Head Start preschools, cultural differences. *Unit head:* Dr. Krisanne Bursik, Associate Dean and Acting Chair, 617-573-8261, Fax: 617-305-1743, E-mail: kbursik@suffolk.edu. *Application contact:* Ellen Driscoll, Director of Graduate Admissions, 617-573-8302, Fax: 617-305-1733, E-mail: grad.admission@suffolk.edu. Web site: http://www.suffolk.edu/college/9785.html.

Texas Christian University, College of Education, Program in Middle School Education (Four-One Option), Fort Worth, TX 76129-0002. Offers M Ed. Part-time and evening/weekend programs available. *Faculty:* 27 full-time (21 women), 1 part-time/adjunct. *Students:* 5 full-time (all women); includes 1 minority (Hispanic/Latino). Average age 22. 5 applicants, 100% accepted, 3 enrolled. In 2011, 8 master's awarded. *Degree requirements:* For master's, oral exam. *Entrance requirements:* Additional exam requirements/recommendations for international students: Required—TOEFL (minimum score 550 paper-based; 213 computer-based; 80 iBT). *Application deadline:* For fall admission, 11/15 for domestic and international students; for spring admission, 3/1 for domestic and international students. Application fee: $60. Electronic applications accepted. *Expenses: Tuition:* Full-time $20,250; part-time $1125 per credit hour. Part-time tuition and fees vary according to course load and program. *Financial support:* Teaching assistantships with full tuition reimbursements, career-related internships or fieldwork, scholarships/grants, and unspecified assistantships available. Financial award application deadline: 3/1; financial award applicants required to submit FAFSA. *Unit head:* Dr. Jan Lacina, Associate Dean, 817-257-6786, E-mail: j.lacina@tcu.edu. *Application contact:* Patricia Garcia, Academic Program Specialist, 817-257-7661, E-mail: p.m.garcia@tcu.edu.

Tufts University, Graduate School of Arts and Sciences, Department of Education, Program in Education, Medford, MA 02155. Offers education (MS, PhD); middle and secondary education (MA, MAT); secondary education (MA). *Faculty:* 13 full-time, 9 part-time/adjunct. *Students:* 111 full-time (80 women); includes 20 minority (8 Black or African American, non-Hispanic/Latino; 3 American Indian or Alaska Native, non-Hispanic/Latino; 3 Asian, non-Hispanic/Latino; 6 Hispanic/Latino), 4 international. Average age 27. 193 applicants, 76% accepted, 82 enrolled. In 2011, 81 master's, 7 doctorates awarded. *Degree requirements:* For master's, thesis optional; for doctorate, thesis/dissertation. *Entrance requirements:* For master's, GRE General Test. Additional exam requirements/recommendations for international students: Required—TOEFL (minimum score 550 paper-based; 213 computer-based; 80 iBT). *Application deadline:* For fall admission, 2/1 for domestic students, 12/15 for international students; for spring admission, 10/15 for domestic students, 9/15 for international students. Applications are processed on a rolling basis. Application fee: $75. Electronic applications accepted. *Expenses: Tuition:* Full-time $41,208; part-time $1030 per credit hour. Full-time tuition and fees vary according to degree level, program and student level. Part-time tuition and fees vary according to course load. *Financial support:* Teaching assistantships with full and partial tuition reimbursements, Federal Work-Study, scholarships/grants, and tuition waivers (full and partial) available. Support available to part-time students. Financial award application deadline: 2/1. *Unit head:* Barbara Brizuela, Chair, 617-627-3244, Fax: 617-627-3901. *Application contact:* Patricia Romeo, Information Contact, 617-627-3244.

Union College, Graduate Programs, Department of Education, Program in Middle Grades, Barbourville, KY 40906-1499. Offers MA. *Degree requirements:* For master's, thesis optional. *Entrance requirements:* For master's, GRE General Test, NTE.

Union Graduate College, School of Education, Schenectady, NY 12308-3107. Offers biology (MAT, MS); chemistry (MAT); Chinese (MAT); earth science (MAT); English (MAT); French (MAT); general science (MAT); German (MAT); Greek (MAT); languages (MAT); Latin (MAT); mathematics (MAT); mathematics and technology (MS); mentoring and teacher leadership (AC); middle childhood extension (AC); national board certificate and teacher leadership (AC); physical science (MS); physics (MAT); social studies (MAT); Spanish (MAT). *Accreditation:* Teacher Education Accreditation Council. *Faculty:* 3 full-time (1 woman), 51 part-time/adjunct (24 women). *Students:* 37 full-time (26 women), 25 part-time (16 women); includes 4 minority (3 Asian, non-Hispanic/Latino; 1 Hispanic/Latino). Average age 32. 66 applicants, 83% accepted, 41 enrolled. In 2011, 47 master's, 29 other advanced degrees awarded. *Degree requirements:* For master's, thesis or project. *Entrance requirements:* For master's, minimum GPA of 3.0, letters of recommendation. Additional exam requirements/recommendations for international students: Required—TOEFL (minimum score 550 paper-based; 213 computer-based). *Application deadline:* Applications are processed on a rolling basis. Application fee: $60. Electronic applications accepted. *Expenses:* Contact institution. *Financial support:* In 2011–12, 22 students received support. Career-related internships or fieldwork, Federal Work-Study, scholarships/grants, health care benefits, and tuition waivers (partial) available. Support available to part-time students. Financial award applicants required to submit FAFSA. *Faculty research:* Transformative learning, science education, National Board Certification, teacher leadership, teacher quality. *Unit head:* Dr. Patrick Allen, Dean, 518-631-9870, Fax: 518-631-9901. *Application contact:* Christine Angley, Assistant, 518-631-9871, Fax: 518-631-9903, E-mail: angleyc@uniongraduatecollege.edu.

University of Arkansas, Graduate School, College of Education and Health Professions, Department of Curriculum and Instruction, Fayetteville, AR 72701-1201. Offers childhood education (MAT); curriculum and instruction (PhD); education policy (PhD); educational leadership (M Ed, Ed D, Ed S); educational statistics and research methods (MS, PhD); educational technology (M Ed); elementary education (M Ed, Ed S); middle-level education (MAT); secondary education (M Ed, MAT, Ed S); special education (M Ed, MAT). *Accreditation:* NCATE. *Students:* 175 full-time (137 women), 216 part-time (161 women); includes 49 minority (18 Black or African American, non-Hispanic/Latino; 5 American Indian or Alaska Native, non-Hispanic/Latino; 4 Asian, non-Hispanic/Latino; 10 Hispanic/Latino; 12 Two or more races, non-Hispanic/Latino), 19 international. In 2011, 171 master's, 14 doctorates, 5 other advanced degrees awarded. *Degree requirements:* For doctorate, thesis/dissertation. *Entrance requirements:* For doctorate, GRE General Test or MAT. *Application deadline:* For fall admission, 4/1 for international students; for spring admission, 10/1 for international students. Applications are processed on a rolling basis. Application fee: $40 ($50 for international students). Electronic applications accepted. *Financial support:* In 2011–12, 41 research assistantships, 2 teaching assistantships were awarded; fellowships with tuition reimbursements, career-related internships or fieldwork, and Federal Work-Study also available. Support available to part-time students. Financial award application deadline: 4/1; financial award applicants required to submit FAFSA. *Unit head:* Dr. Michael Daugherty, Departmental Chairperson, 479-575-4209, Fax: 479-575-5119, E-mail: mkd03@uark.edu. *Application contact:* Dr. Barbara Gartin, Graduate Coordinator, 479-575-7525, Fax: 479-575-6676, E-mail: bgartin@uark.edu. Web site: http://cied.uark.edu/.

University of Arkansas at Little Rock, Graduate School, College of Education, Department of Teacher Education, Program in Middle Childhood Education, Little Rock, AR 72204-1099. Offers M Ed.

University of Bridgeport, School of Education, Department of Education, Bridgeport, CT 06604. Offers education (MS); educational management (Ed D, Diploma), including intermediate administrator or supervisor (Diploma), leadership (Ed D); elementary education (MS, Diploma), including early childhood education, elementary education; middle school education (MS); music education (MS); remedial reading and language arts (Diploma); secondary education (MS, Diploma), including computer specialist (Diploma), international education (Diploma), reading specialist, secondary education. Part-time and evening/weekend programs available. *Faculty:* 12 full-time (5 women), 108 part-time/adjunct (60 women). *Students:* 232 full-time (161 women), 216 part-time (160 women); includes 61 minority (21 Black or African American, non-Hispanic/Latino; 8 Asian, non-Hispanic/Latino; 22 Hispanic/Latino; 10 Two or more races, non-Hispanic/Latino), 34 international. Average age 30. 412 applicants, 63% accepted, 147 enrolled. In 2011, 216 master's, 7 other advanced degrees awarded. *Degree requirements:* For master's, final exam, final project, or thesis; for doctorate, comprehensive exam, thesis/dissertation; for Diploma, thesis or alternative, final project. *Entrance requirements:* For master's, minimum undergraduate QPA of 2.67; for doctorate, GRE, MAT; for Diploma, GRE General Test or MAT, minimum graduate QPA of 3.0. Additional exam requirements/recommendations for international students: Recommended—TOEFL (minimum score 550 paper-based; 213 computer-based; 80 iBT), IELTS (minimum score 6.5). *Application deadline:* For fall admission, 8/1 priority date for domestic students, 8/1 for international students; for spring admission, 12/1 priority date for domestic students, 12/1 for international students. Applications are processed on a rolling basis. Application fee: $50. Electronic applications accepted. *Expenses: Tuition:* Full-time $22,880; part-time $700 per credit. *Required fees:* $1870; $95 per semester. Tuition and fees vary according to course load and program. *Financial support:* In 2011–12, 120 students received support. Fellowships, research assistantships, teaching assistantships, career-related internships or fieldwork, Federal Work-Study, and institutionally sponsored loans available. Support available to part-time students. Financial award application deadline: 6/1; financial award applicants required to submit FAFSA. *Faculty research:* Self-concept, internship assessment, stress and situational development, follow-up of graduation, trend analysis. *Unit head:* Dr. Allen P. Cook, Dean, 203-576-4192, Fax: 203-576-4200, E-mail: acook@bridgeport.edu. *Application contact:* Karissa Peckham, Dean of Admissions, 203-576-4552, Fax: 203-576-4941, E-mail: admit@bridgeport.edu.

University of Central Florida, College of Education, School of Teaching, Learning, and Leadership, Program in Mathematics Education, Orlando, FL 32816. Offers teacher education (MAT), including mathematics education, middle school mathematics; teacher leadership (M Ed). *Accreditation:* NCATE. Part-time and evening/weekend programs available. *Students:* 10 full-time (9 women), 32 part-time (23 women); includes 11 minority (4 Black or African American, non-Hispanic/Latino; 3 Asian, non-Hispanic/Latino; 4 Hispanic/Latino). Average age 35. 16 applicants, 63% accepted, 7 enrolled. In 2011, 16 master's awarded. *Entrance requirements:* For master's, GRE General Test. Additional exam requirements/recommendations for international students: Required—TOEFL. *Application deadline:* For fall admission, 7/15 for domestic students; for spring admission, 12/1 for domestic students. Application fee: $30. Electronic applications accepted. *Expenses:* Tuition, state resident: part-time $277.08 per credit hour. Tuition, nonresident: part-time $277.08 per credit hour. Part-time tuition and fees vary according to degree level and program. *Financial support:* In 2011–12, 1 student received support, including 1 research assistantship with partial tuition reimbursement available (averaging $6,900 per year); fellowships with partial tuition reimbursements available, teaching assistantships with partial tuition reimbursements available, career-related internships or fieldwork, Federal Work-Study, institutionally sponsored loans, tuition waivers (partial), and unspecified assistantships also available. Financial award application deadline: 3/1; financial award applicants required to submit FAFSA. *Unit head:* Dr. Janet B. Andreasen, Program Coordinator, 407-823-5430, E-mail: janet.andreasen@ucf.edu. *Application contact:* Barbara Rodriguez, Director, Admissions and Registration, 407-823-2766, Fax: 407-823-6442, E-mail: gradadmissions@ucf.edu.

University of Central Florida, College of Education, School of Teaching, Learning, and Leadership, Program in Science Education, Orlando, FL 32816. Offers teacher education (MAT), including biology, middle school science, physics; teacher leadership (M Ed), including science education. *Accreditation:* NCATE. Part-time and evening/weekend programs available. *Students:* 9 full-time (6 women), 19 part-time (12 women); includes 5 minority (1 Asian, non-Hispanic/Latino; 3 Hispanic/Latino; 1 Two or more races, non-Hispanic/Latino). Average age 33. 19 applicants, 58% accepted, 7 enrolled. In 2011, 21 master's awarded. *Entrance requirements:* For master's, GRE General Test. Additional exam requirements/recommendations for international students: Required—TOEFL. *Application deadline:* For fall admission, 7/15 for domestic students; for spring admission, 12/1 for domestic students. Application fee: $30. Electronic applications accepted. *Expenses:* Tuition, state resident: part-time $277.08 per credit hour. Tuition, nonresident: part-time $277.08 per credit hour. Part-time tuition and fees vary according to degree level and program. *Financial support:* Career-related internships or fieldwork, Federal Work-Study, institutionally sponsored loans, tuition waivers (partial), and unspecified assistantships available. Financial award application deadline: 3/1; financial award applicants required to submit FAFSA. *Unit head:* Dr. Janet B. Andreasen, Program Coordinator, 407-823-5430, E-mail: janet.andreasen@ucf.edu. *Application contact:* Barbara Rodriguez, Director, Admissions and Registration, 407-823-2766, Fax: 407-823-6442, E-mail: gradadmissions@ucf.edu.

University of Dayton, Department of Teacher Education, Dayton, OH 45469-1300. Offers adolescent/young adult (MS Ed); art education (MS Ed); early childhood education (MS Ed); early childhood leadership advocacy (MS Ed); inclusive early childhood (MS Ed); interdisciplinary education (MS Ed); intervention specialist education, mild/moderate (MS Ed); literacy (MS Ed); middle childhood (MS Ed); multi-age education (MS Ed); music education (MS Ed); teacher as leader (MS Ed); technology in education (MS Ed). Part-time and evening/weekend programs available. Postbaccalaureate distance learning degree programs offered (no on-campus study). *Faculty:* 15 full-time (11 women), 22 part-time/adjunct (20 women). *Students:* 41 full-time (29 women), 95 part-time (87 women); includes 13 minority (9 Black or African American, non-Hispanic/Latino; 1 Asian, non-Hispanic/Latino; 3 Hispanic/Latino), 9 international. Average age 32. 111 applicants, 55% accepted, 38 enrolled. In 2011, 97 degrees awarded. *Degree requirements:* For master's, thesis, capstone research project. *Entrance requirements:* For master's, GRE General Test, minimum GPA of 2.75. Additional exam requirements/recommendations for international students: Required—TOEFL (minimum score 550 paper-based; 213 computer-based; 80 iBT). *Application deadline:* For fall admission, 3/1 priority date for domestic students, 3/1 for international students; for winter admission, 7/1 for international students; for spring admission, 1/1 for international students. Applications are processed on a rolling basis. Application fee: $0 ($50 for international students). Electronic applications accepted. *Expenses:* Contact institution. *Financial support:* In 2011–12, 5 research assistantships with full and partial tuition reimbursements (averaging $8,470 per year) were awarded; career-related internships or fieldwork, institutionally sponsored loans, health care benefits, and unspecified assistantships also available. Financial award applicants required to submit FAFSA. *Faculty research:* Diversity, literacy, art representation by young children, preservice teacher preparation. *Unit head:* Dr. Katie A. Kinnucan-Welsch, Chair, 937-229-3346. *Application contact:* Alexsandar Popovski, Enrollment Management Administrator, 937-229-2357, Fax: 937-229-4729, E-mail: alex.popovski@notes.udayton.edu.

University of Georgia, College of Education, Department of Elementary and Social Studies Education, Athens, GA 30602. Offers early childhood education (M Ed, MAT, PhD, Ed S), including child and family development (MAT); elementary education (PhD); middle school education (M Ed, PhD, Ed S); social studies education (M Ed, Ed D, PhD, Ed S). *Faculty:* 17 full-time (10 women). *Students:* 119 full-time (96 women), 110 part-time (96 women); includes 42 minority (22 Black or African American, non-Hispanic/Latino; 1 American Indian or Alaska Native, non-Hispanic/Latino; 11 Asian, non-Hispanic/Latino; 6 Hispanic/Latino; 2 Two or more races, non-Hispanic/Latino), 12 international. Average age 30. 68 applicants, 72% accepted, 22 enrolled. In 2011, 92 master's, 12 doctorates, 2 other advanced degrees awarded. *Entrance requirements:* For master's and Ed S, GRE General Test or MAT; for doctorate, GRE General Test. *Application deadline:* For fall admission, 7/1 priority date for domestic students; for spring admission, 11/15 for domestic students. Application fee: $50. Electronic applications accepted. *Financial support:* Fellowships, research assistantships, teaching assistantships, and unspecified assistantships available. *Unit head:* Dr. Ronald Butchart, Interim Head, 706-542-6490, E-mail: butchart@uga.edu. *Application contact:* Dr. Stephanie R. Jones, Graduate Coordinator, 706-542-4283, Fax: 706-542-8996, E-mail: essegrad@uga.edu. Web site: http://www.coe.uga.edu/esse/.

University of Kentucky, Graduate School, College of Education, Program in Curriculum and Instruction, Lexington, KY 40506-0032. Offers curriculum and instruction (MA Ed, Ed D); instruction and administration (Ed D); instruction system design (MS Ed); middle school education (MS Ed). *Accreditation:* NCATE. *Degree requirements:* For master's, comprehensive exam, thesis optional; for doctorate, comprehensive exam, thesis/dissertation. *Entrance requirements:* For master's, GRE General Test, minimum undergraduate GPA of 2.75; for doctorate, GRE General Test, minimum graduate GPA of 3.0. Additional exam requirements/recommendations for international students: Required—TOEFL (minimum score 550 paper-based; 213 computer-based). Electronic applications accepted. *Faculty research:* Educational reform, multicultural education, classroom instructional practices, performance based assessment, primary school programs.

University of Louisiana at Monroe, Graduate School, College of Education and Human Development, Department of Curriculum and Instruction, Program in Multiple Levels Grades K-12, Monroe, LA 71209-0001. Offers MAT. *Students:* 3 full-time (1 woman), 6 part-time (3 women); includes 1 minority (Black or African American, non-Hispanic/Latino). Average age 26. 5 applicants, 80% accepted, 4 enrolled. In 2011, 4 master's awarded. *Degree requirements:* For master's, thesis optional. *Entrance requirements:* For master's, GRE, PRAXIS, minimum GPA of 2.5. Additional exam requirements/recommendations for international students: Required—TOEFL (minimum score 500 paper-based; 173 computer-based; 61 iBT). *Application deadline:* For fall admission, 8/24 priority date for domestic students, 7/1 for international students; for winter admission, 12/14 priority date for domestic students; for spring admission, 1/19 priority date for domestic students, 11/1 for international students. Applications are processed on a rolling basis. Electronic applications accepted. *Expenses:* Tuition, state resident: full-time $3436; part-time $240 per credit hour. Tuition, nonresident: full-time $3436; part-time $240 per credit hour. *International tuition:* $10,733 full-time. *Required fees:* $1460.90. *Financial support:* Career-related internships or fieldwork, Federal Work-Study, and unspecified assistantships available. Financial award application deadline: 4/1; financial award applicants required to submit FAFSA. *Unit head:* Dr. Dorothy Schween, Department Head, 318-342-1266, E-mail: schween@ulm.edu. *Application contact:* Whitney Sutherland, Administrative Assistant to Department Head, 318-342-1266, E-mail: sutherland@ulm.edu. Web site: http://www.ulm.edu/ci/.

University of Louisville, Graduate School, College of Education and Human Development, Department of Teaching and Learning, Louisville, KY 40292-0001. Offers art education (MAT); curriculum and instruction (PhD); early elementary education (MAT); instructional technology (M Ed); interdisciplinary early childhood education (MAT); middle school education (MAT); music education (MAT); reading education (M Ed); secondary education (MAT); special education (M Ed, MAT); teacher leadership (M Ed). Part-time and evening/weekend programs available. *Degree requirements:* For doctorate, comprehensive exam, thesis/dissertation. *Entrance requirements:* For master's, GRE General Test, PRAXIS II (for some programs); for doctorate, GRE General Test. Additional exam requirements/recommendations for international students: Required—TOEFL (minimum score 560 paper-based; 210 computer-based; 83 iBT). Electronic applications accepted. *Expenses:* Tuition, state resident: full-time $9692; part-time $539 per credit hour. Tuition, nonresident: full-time $20,168; part-time $1121 per credit hour. Tuition and fees vary according to program and reciprocity agreements. *Faculty research:* Mathematics teacher education and ongoing professional development in pedagogy and content knowledge; development of literacy, including early literacy in science and mathematics and literacy development for English language learners; immersive visualizations for promoting STEM education from nanoscience to cosmic scales; evidence-based practices for students with disabilities; urban education, including teacher response to intervention systems in schools and cross-cultural competence.

University of Massachusetts Dartmouth, Graduate School, School of Education, Public Policy, and Civic Engagement, Department of Teaching and Learning, North Dartmouth, MA 02747-2300. Offers elementary education (MAT, Postbaccalaureate Certificate); middle school education (MAT); principal initial licensure (Postbaccalaureate Certificate); secondary school education (MAT). *Faculty:* 5 full-time (4 women), 9 part-time/adjunct (4 women). *Students:* 15 full-time (10 women), 180 part-time (119 women); includes 17 minority (7 Black or African American, non-Hispanic/Latino; 1 Asian, non-Hispanic/Latino; 5 Hispanic/Latino; 4 Two or more races, non-Hispanic/Latino). Average age 34. 110 applicants, 98% accepted, 85 enrolled. In 2011, 88 master's, 28 other advanced degrees awarded. *Degree requirements:* For master's, thesis or alternative. *Entrance requirements:* For master's, Massachusetts Tests for Educator Licensure (MTEL), minimum undergraduate GPA of 2.7, teacher certification, 3 letters of recommendation, resume, statement of intent; for Postbaccalaureate Certificate, Massachusetts Tests for Educator Licensure (MTEL), 3 letters of recommendation, resume, statement of intent. Additional exam requirements/recommendations for international students: Required—TOEFL (minimum score 533 paper-based; 200 computer-based; 72 iBT). *Application deadline:* For fall admission, 7/15 priority date for domestic students, 6/15 for international students; for spring admission, 12/15 priority date for domestic students, 11/15 for international students. Applications are processed on a rolling basis. Application fee: $40 ($60 for international students). *Expenses:* Tuition, state resident: full-time $2071; part-time $86.29 per credit. Tuition, nonresident: full-time $8099; part-time $337.46 per credit. *Required fees:* $438.58 per credit. Part-time tuition and fees vary according to class time, course load, degree level and reciprocity agreements. *Financial support:* Federal Work-Study available. Financial award application deadline: 3/1. *Total annual research expenditures:* $92,694. *Unit head:* Sheila Macrine, Graduate Program Director, 508-999-9234, Fax: 508-910-6916, E-mail: smacrine@umassd.edu. *Application contact:* Elan Turcotte-Shamski, Graduate Admissions Officer, 508-999-8604, Fax: 508-999-8183, E-mail: graduate@umassd.edu. Web site: http://www.umassd.edu/seppce/teachingandlearning/index.html.

University of Memphis, Graduate School, College of Education, Department of Instruction and Curriculum Leadership, Memphis, TN 38152. Offers early childhood education (MAT, MS, Ed D); elementary education (MAT); instruction and curriculum (MS, Ed D); instruction design and technology (MS, Ed D); middle grades education (MAT); reading (MS, Ed D); secondary education (MAT); special education (MAT, MS, Ed D). *Accreditation:* NCATE (one or more programs are accredited). Part-time programs available. Terminal master's awarded for partial completion of doctoral program. *Degree requirements:* For master's, comprehensive exam, thesis or alternative; for doctorate, comprehensive exam, thesis/dissertation. *Entrance requirements:* For master's, GRE General Test, minimum GPA of 2.5; for doctorate, GRE General Test, GRE Subject Test, 2 years of teaching experience. Electronic applications accepted. *Faculty research:* Effective urban teachers, preparation and retention of urban teachers, technology utilization in schools, field-based teacher preparation programs, effective use of online instruction.

University of Missouri–St. Louis, College of Education, Division of Teaching and Learning, St. Louis, MO 63121. Offers autism studies (Certificate); elementary education (M Ed), including early childhood, general, reading; secondary education (M Ed), including curriculum and instruction, general, middle level education, reading, teaching English to speakers of other languages (TESOL); secondary school teaching (Certificate); special education (M Ed), including autism and developmental disabilities, early childhood special education, general; teaching English to speakers of other languages (Certificate). Part-time and evening/weekend programs available. *Faculty:* 32 full-time (16 women), 51 part-time/adjunct (36 women). *Students:* 95 full-time (63 women), 703 part-time (541 women); includes 176 minority (125 Black or African American, non-Hispanic/Latino; 1 American Indian or Alaska Native, non-Hispanic/Latino; 16 Asian, non-Hispanic/Latino; 26 Hispanic/Latino; 8 Two or more races, non-Hispanic/Latino), 11 international. Average age 29. 379 applicants, 90% accepted, 263 enrolled. In 2011, 190 master's, 9 Certificates awarded. *Degree requirements:* For master's, comprehensive exam. *Entrance requirements:* Additional exam requirements/recommendations for international students: Recommended—TOEFL (minimum score 550 paper-based; 213 computer-based). *Application deadline:* For fall admission, 7/1 priority date for domestic students, 7/1 for international students; for spring admission, 12/1 priority date for domestic students, 12/1 for international students. Application fee: $35 ($40 for international students). Electronic applications accepted. *Expenses:* Tuition, state resident: full-time $6273; part-time $3866 per year. Tuition, nonresident: full-time $14,969; part-time $9980 per year. *Required fees:* $315 per year. *Financial support:* In 2011–12, 6 research assistantships with full and partial tuition reimbursements (averaging $9,500 per year), 2 teaching assistantships with full and partial tuition reimbursements (averaging $10,500 per year) were awarded. Financial award application deadline: 4/1; financial award applicants required to submit FAFSA. *Unit head:* Dr. Joseph Polman, Chair, 314-516-5791. *Application contact:* 314-516-5458, Fax: 314-516-6996, E-mail: gadadm@umsl.edu. Web site: http://coe.umsl.edu/web/divisions/teach-learn/index.html.

The University of North Carolina at Charlotte, Graduate School, College of Education, Department of Middle, Secondary and K-12 Education, Charlotte, NC 28223-0001. Offers art education (MAT); curriculum and instruction (PhD); dance education (MAT); foreign language education (MAT); middle grades education (M Ed, MAT); music education (MAT); secondary education (M Ed, MAT); teaching English as a second language (M Ed); theatre education (MAT). *Faculty:* 18 full-time (9 women), 6 part-time/adjunct (4 women). *Students:* 1 (woman) full-time, 57 part-time (44 women); includes 11 minority (5 Black or African American, non-Hispanic/Latino; 1 American Indian or Alaska Native, non-Hispanic/Latino; 2 Asian, non-Hispanic/Latino; 2 Hispanic/Latino; 1 Two or more races, non-Hispanic/Latino). Average age 33. 19 applicants, 100% accepted, 16 enrolled. In 2011, 12 master's awarded. *Entrance requirements:* For master's, GRE or MAT. Additional exam requirements/recommendations for international students: Required—TOEFL (minimum score 557 paper-based; 220 computer-based; 83 iBT). *Application deadline:* For fall admission, 7/1 for domestic students, 5/1 for international students; for spring admission, 11/1 for domestic students, 10/1 for international students. Applications are processed on a rolling basis. Application fee: $65 ($75 for international students). Electronic applications accepted. *Expenses:* Tuition, state resident: full-time $3689. Tuition, nonresident: full-time $15,226. *Required fees:* $2198. Tuition and fees vary according to course load and program. *Financial support:* In 2011–12, 5 students received support, including 5 research assistantships (averaging $4,290 per year); career-related internships or fieldwork, institutionally sponsored loans, scholarships/grants, and unspecified assistantships also available. Support available to part-time students. Financial award application deadline: 4/1; financial award applicants required to submit FAFSA. *Total annual research expenditures:* $126,589. *Unit head:* Melba Spooner, Chair, 704-687-8704, Fax: 704-687-6430, E-mail: mcspoone@uncc.edu. *Application contact:* Kathy B. Giddings, Director of Graduate Admissions, 704-687-5503, Fax: 704-687-3279, E-mail: gradadm@uncc.edu. Web site: http://education.uncc.edu/mdsk.

The University of North Carolina at Greensboro, Graduate School, School of Education, Department of Curriculum and Instruction, Greensboro, NC 27412-5001. Offers college teaching and adult learning (Certificate); curriculum and instruction (M Ed), including chemistry education, elementary education, English as a second language, French education, instructional technology, mathematics education, middle grades education, reading education, science education, social studies education, Spanish education; curriculum and teaching (PhD), including higher education, teacher education and development; English as a second language (Certificate); higher education (M Ed); supervision (M Ed). *Accreditation:* NCATE. Part-time programs available. *Degree requirements:* For doctorate, thesis/dissertation. *Entrance requirements:* For master's and doctorate, GRE General Test. Additional exam requirements/recommendations for international students: Required—TOEFL. Electronic applications accepted. *Faculty research:* Community college literacy program, middle school mathematics/computer mathematics.

The University of North Carolina at Pembroke, Graduate Studies, School of Education, Program in Middle Grades Education, Pembroke, NC 28372-1510. Offers MA Ed, MAT. *Accreditation:* NCATE. Part-time and evening/weekend programs available. *Degree requirements:* For master's, thesis optional. *Entrance requirements:* For master's, GRE General Test or MAT, minimum GPA of 3.0 in major, 2.5 overall. Additional exam requirements/recommendations for international students: Required—TOEFL.

The University of North Carolina Wilmington, Watson School of Education, Department of Elementary, Middle Level and Literacy Education, Program in Middle Grades Education, Wilmington, NC 28403-3297. Offers instructional technology (MS); secondary education (M Ed). *Degree requirements:* For master's, comprehensive exam.

University of Northern Iowa, Graduate College, College of Education, Department of Curriculum and Instruction, Program in Middle School/Junior High Education, Cedar Falls, IA 50614. Offers MAE. *Students:* 2 applicants, 0% accepted, 0 enrolled. In 2011, 1 master's awarded. *Degree requirements:* For master's, comprehensive exam (for some programs), thesis or alternative. *Entrance requirements:* For master's, minimum GPA of 3.0. Additional exam requirements/recommendations for international students: Required—TOEFL (minimum score 500 paper-based; 180 computer-based; 61 iBT). *Application deadline:* For fall admission, 8/1 priority date for domestic students. Applications are processed on a rolling basis. Application fee: $50 ($70 for international students). Electronic applications accepted. *Expenses:* Tuition, state resident: full-time $7476. Tuition, nonresident: full-time $16,410. *Required fees:* $942. *Financial support:* Application deadline: 2/1. *Unit head:* Dr. Jean Schneider, Coordinator, 319-273-3274, Fax: 319-273-5886, E-mail: jean.schneider@uni.edu. *Application contact:* Laurie S. Russell, Record Analyst, 319-273-2623, Fax: 319-273-2885, E-mail: laurie.russell@uni.edu. Web site: http://www.uni.edu/coe/ci/midlevel/index.shtml.

University of Northern Iowa, Graduate College, College of Humanities, Arts and Sciences, Department of Languages and Literatures, Program in English, Cedar Falls, IA 50614. Offers creative writing (MA); English (MA); literature (MA); teaching English in secondary schools (TESS) (MA), including middle/junior high and senior high; teaching English to speakers of other languages (MA). Part-time and evening/weekend programs available. *Students:* 12 full-time (6 women), 4 part-time (all women); includes 2 minority (1 Black or African American, non-Hispanic/Latino; 1 Hispanic/Latino). 16 applicants, 50% accepted, 5 enrolled. In 2011, 5 master's awarded. *Degree requirements:* For master's, one foreign language, comprehensive exam, thesis or alternative, portfolio. *Entrance requirements:* Additional exam requirements/recommendations for international students: Required—TOEFL (minimum score 600 paper-based; 250 computer-based; 100 iBT). *Application deadline:* For fall admission, 8/1 priority date for domestic students. Applications are processed on a rolling basis. Application fee: $50 ($70 for international students). Electronic applications accepted. *Expenses:* Tuition, state resident: full-time $7476. Tuition, nonresident: full-time $16,410. *Required fees:* $942. *Financial support:* Career-related internships or fieldwork, Federal Work-Study, scholarships/grants, and tuition waivers (full and partial) available. Support available to part-time students. Financial award application deadline: 2/1. *Unit head:* Dr. Julie Husband, Graduate Coordinator, 319-273-3849, Fax: 319-273-5807, E-mail: julie.husband@uni.edu. *Application contact:* Laurie S. Russell, Record Analyst, 319-273-2623, Fax: 319-273-2885, E-mail: laurie.russell@uni.edu. Web site: http://www.uni.edu/langlit/.

University of Phoenix–Online Campus, College of Education, Phoenix, AZ 85034-7209. Offers administration and supervision (MAEd, Graduate Certificate); adult education and training (MAEd); curriculum and instruction (MAEd); curriculum and instruction reading (MAEd); curriculum and instruction-computer education (MAEd); curriculum and instruction-language arts (MAEd); curriculum and instruction-mathematics (MAEd); early childhood education (MAEd); educational studies (MAEd); elementary teacher education (MAEd); elementary teacher education-early childhood (MAEd); secondary teacher education (MAEd); special education (MAEd); teacher education - elementary/middle level (MAEd); teacher education middle level generalist (MAEd); teacher education middle level mathematics (MAEd); teacher education middle level science (MAEd); teacher education secondary mathematics (MAEd); teacher education secondary science (MAEd); teacher leadership (MAEd). *Accreditation:* Teacher Education Accreditation Council. Evening/weekend programs available. Postbaccalaureate distance learning degree programs offered. *Students:* 9,180 full-time (7,178 women); includes 2,913 minority (2,069 Black or African American, non-Hispanic/Latino; 50 American Indian or Alaska Native, non-Hispanic/Latino; 100 Asian, non-Hispanic/Latino; 542 Hispanic/Latino; 48 Native Hawaiian or other Pacific Islander, non-Hispanic/Latino; 104 Two or more races, non-Hispanic/Latino), 147 international. Average age 36. *Entrance requirements:* Additional exam requirements/recommendations for international students: Required—TOEFL, TOEIC (Test of English as an International Communication), Berlitz Online English Proficiency Exam, Pearson Test of English, or IELTS. *Application deadline:* Applications are processed on a rolling basis. Application fee: $45. Electronic applications accepted. *Expenses:* Contact institution. *Financial support:* Scholarships/grants available. Financial award applicants required to submit FAFSA. *Application contact:* 866-766-0766. Web site: http://www.phoenix.edu/colleges_divisions/education.html.

University of Phoenix–Oregon Campus, College of Education, Tigard, OR 97223. Offers curriculum and instruction (MA Ed); early childhood education (MA Ed); elementary education (MA Ed), including early childhood specialization, middle level specialization; secondary education (MA Ed), including middle level specialization. Evening/weekend programs available. *Degree requirements:* For master's, thesis (for some programs). *Entrance requirements:* For master's, minimum undergraduate GPA of 2.5, 3 years work experience. Additional exam requirements/recommendations for international students: Required—TOEFL (minimum score 550 paper-based; 213 computer-based; 79 iBT). Electronic applications accepted.

University of Southern Maine, School of Education and Human Development, Educational Leadership Program, Portland, ME 04104-9300. Offers assistant principal (Certificate); athletic administration (Certificate); educational leadership (MS Ed, CAS); middle-level education (Certificate). Part-time and evening/weekend programs available. Postbaccalaureate distance learning degree programs offered (minimal on-campus study). *Degree requirements:* For master's, thesis or alternative, practicum, internship; for other advanced degree, thesis or alternative. *Entrance requirements:* For master's, three years of documented teaching; for other advanced degree, master's degree. Additional exam requirements/recommendations for international students: Required—TOEFL (minimum score 550 paper-based; 213 computer-based; 79 iBT). Electronic applications accepted.

University of South Florida–St. Petersburg Campus, College of Education, St. Petersburg, FL 33701. Offers educational leadership development (M Ed); elementary education (MA), including math/science; English education (MA); middle grades STEM education (MS); reading education (MA). Part-time programs available. *Students:* 30 full-time (27 women), 130 part-time (109 women); includes 28 minority (14 Black or African American, non-Hispanic/Latino; 4 Asian, non-Hispanic/Latino; 9 Hispanic/Latino; 1 Two or more races, non-Hispanic/Latino). Average age 34. 63 applicants, 70% accepted, 36 enrolled. In 2011, 74 master's awarded. *Degree requirements:* For master's, comprehensive exam, practicum, internship, comprehensive portfolio. *Entrance requirements:* For master's, State of Florida General Knowledge Test (GKT), Florida Teaching Certificate (for non-initial certification programs), letters of recommendation. Additional exam requirements/recommendations for international students: Required—TOEFL (minimum score 550 paper-based; 79 iBT); Recommended—IELTS. *Application deadline:* For fall admission, 6/1 priority date for domestic students, 6/1 for international students; for spring admission, 10/15 priority date for domestic students, 10/15 for international students. Applications are processed on a rolling basis. Application fee: $30. Electronic applications accepted. *Expenses:* Tuition, state resident: full-time $8847. Tuition, nonresident: full-time $18,423. One-time fee: $35 full-time. Full-time tuition and fees vary according to course load and program. *Financial support:* Applicants required to submit FAFSA. *Unit head:* Dr. Harold W. Heller, Dean, 727-873-4155, Fax: 727-873-4191, E-mail: hheller@usfsp.edu. *Application contact:* Eric Douthirt, Enrollment Management Specialist, 727-873-4450, E-mail: douthirt@usfsp.edu. Web site: http://www1.usfsp.edu/coe/index.asp.

University of the Cumberlands, Graduate Programs in Education, Williamsburg, KY 40769-1372. Offers all grades (P-12) (M Ed); business and marketing (MA Ed, MAT); director of pupil personnel (Certificate); director of special education (Certificate); educational administration and supervision (Ed S); educational leadership (Ed D); elementary education (MA Ed, MAT); instructional leadership - principalship (MA Ed); instructional leadership - school principal (Certificate); middle school education (MA Ed, MAT); reading and writing (MA Ed); school counseling (MA Ed); school superintendent (Certificate); secondary education (MA Ed, MAT); special education (MAT); supervisor of instruction (Certificate); teacher leader (MA Ed). Part-time and evening/weekend programs available. Postbaccalaureate distance learning degree programs offered. *Degree requirements:* For master's, comprehensive exam. Electronic applications accepted.

The University of Toledo, College of Graduate Studies, Judith Herb College of Education, Health Science and Human Service, Department of Curriculum and Instruction, Toledo, OH 43606-3390. Offers art education (ME); career and technical education (ME); curriculum and instruction (ME, PhD, Ed S); education and anthropology (MAE); education and biology (MES); education and chemistry (MES); education and classics (MAE); education and economics (MAE); education and English (MAE); education and French (MAE); education and geography (MAE); education and geology (MES); education and German (MAE); education and history (MAE); education and mathematics (MAE, MES); education and physics (MES); education and political science (MAE); education and sociology (MAE); education and Spanish (MAE); educational media (PhD); educational technology (ME); English as a second language (MAE); gifted and talented (PhD); middle childhood education licensure (ME); music education (MME); secondary education (PhD); secondary education licensure (ME). *Accreditation:* NCATE. Part-time and evening/weekend programs available. *Faculty:* 24. *Students:* 60 full-time (31 women), 211 part-time (161 women); includes 23 minority (21 Black or African American, non-Hispanic/Latino; 2 Hispanic/Latino), 20 international. Average age 35. 115 applicants, 73% accepted, 74 enrolled. In 2011, 105 master's, 3 doctorates, 4 other advanced degrees awarded. *Degree requirements:* For master's, comprehensive exam, thesis or alternative; for doctorate, comprehensive exam, thesis/dissertation; for Ed S, thesis optional. *Entrance requirements:* For master's, doctorate, and Ed S, minimum cumulative GPA of 2.7 for all previous academic work, letters of recommendation. Additional exam requirements/recommendations for international students: Required—TOEFL (minimum score 550 paper-based; 213 computer-based; 80 iBT), IELTS (minimum score 6.5). *Application deadline:* For fall admission, 1/15 priority date for domestic students, 1/15 for international students. Applications are processed on a rolling basis. Application fee: $45 ($75 for international students). Electronic applications accepted. *Financial support:* In 2011–12, 9 research assistantships with full and partial tuition reimbursements (averaging $7,184 per year), 12 teaching assistantships with full and partial tuition reimbursements (averaging $8,425 per year) were awarded; career-related internships or fieldwork, Federal Work-Study, institutionally sponsored loans, scholarships/grants, tuition waivers (full and partial), unspecified assistantships, and administrative assistantships also available. Support available to part-time students. *Unit head:* Dr. Leigh Chiarelott, Chair, 419-530-5371, E-mail: eigh.chiarelott@utoledo.edu. *Application contact:* Graduate School Office, 419-

530-4723, Fax: 419-530-4724, E-mail: grdsch@utnet.utoledo.edu. Web site: http://www.utoledo.edu/eduhshs/.

University of Washington, Bothell, Program in Education, Bothell, WA 98011-8246. Offers education (M Ed); leadership development for educators (M Ed); secondary/middle level endorsement (M Ed). Part-time and evening/weekend programs available. *Faculty:* 14 full-time (10 women), 1 (woman) part-time/adjunct. *Students:* 52 full-time (40 women), 115 part-time (94 women); includes 19 minority (3 Black or African American, non-Hispanic/Latino; 9 Asian, non-Hispanic/Latino; 4 Hispanic/Latino; 3 Two or more races, non-Hispanic/Latino). Average age 35. 76 applicants, 80% accepted, 57 enrolled. In 2011, 74 master's awarded. *Degree requirements:* For master's, thesis. *Entrance requirements:* Additional exam requirements/recommendations for international students: Required—TOEFL. *Application deadline:* For fall admission, 8/14 priority date for domestic students, 8/14 for international students; for spring admission, 4/7 priority date for domestic students, 11/1 for international students. Applications are processed on a rolling basis. Application fee: $75. Electronic applications accepted. *Financial support:* In 2011–12, 2 students received support. Federal Work-Study and unspecified assistantships available. Financial award application deadline: 5/2. *Faculty research:* Multicultural education in citizenship education, intercultural education, knowledge and practice in the principalship, educational public policy, national board certification for teachers, teacher learning in literacy, technology and its impact on teaching and learning of mathematics, reading assessments, professional development in literacy education and mobility, digital media, education and class. *Unit head:* Dr. Bradley S. Portin, Director/Professor, 425-352-3482, Fax: 425-352-5234, E-mail: bportin@uwb.edu. *Application contact:* Nick Brownlee, Advisor, 425-352-5369, Fax: 425-352-5369, E-mail: nbrownlee@uwb.edu.

University of West Florida, College of Professional Studies, Department of Research and Applied Studies, Pensacola, FL 32514-5750. Offers administration (MSA), including acquisition and contract administration, biomedical/pharmaceutical, criminal justice administration, database administration, education leadership, healthcare administration, human performance technology, leadership, nursing administration, public administration, software engineering and administration; college student personnel administration (M Ed), including college personnel administration, guidance and counseling; curriculum and instruction (M Ed, Ed S); educational leadership (M Ed); middle and secondary level education and ESOL (M Ed). Part-time and evening/weekend programs available. *Faculty:* 2 full-time (both women), 3 part-time/adjunct (2 women). *Students:* 26 full-time (15 women), 13 part-time (9 women); includes 8 minority (4 Black or African American, non-Hispanic/Latino; 2 American Indian or Alaska Native, non-Hispanic/Latino; 1 Hispanic/Latino; 1 Two or more races, non-Hispanic/Latino), 1 international. Average age 26. 51 applicants, 51% accepted, 16 enrolled. In 2011, 17 master's, 49 Ed Ss awarded. *Entrance requirements:* For master's, GRE or MAT, official transcripts; minimum undergraduate GPA of 3.0; letter of intent; three letters of recommendation; resume. Additional exam requirements/recommendations for international students: Required—TOEFL (minimum score 550 paper-based; 213 computer-based). *Application deadline:* For fall admission, 6/1 for domestic and international students; for spring admission, 10/1 for domestic and international students. Applications are processed on a rolling basis. Application fee: $30. *Expenses:* Tuition, state resident: full-time $5729; part-time $302 per credit hour. Tuition, nonresident: full-time $20,059; part-time $961 per credit hour. *Required fees:* $1509; $63 per credit hour. *Financial support:* In 2011–12, 33 fellowships (averaging $860 per year), 10 research assistantships (averaging $3,280 per year), 2 teaching assistantships (averaging $3,760 per year) were awarded; unspecified assistantships also available. Financial award application deadline: 4/15; financial award applicants required to submit FAFSA. *Unit head:* Dr. Joyce Nichols, Chairperson, 850-857-6042, E-mail: jcoleman0@uwf.edu. *Application contact:* Terry McCray, Assistant Director of Graduate Admissions, 850-473-7718, Fax: 850-473-7714, E-mail: gradadmissions@uwf.edu. Web site: http://uwf.edu/pcl/.

University of West Georgia, College of Education, Department of Leadership and Applied Instruction, Carrollton, GA 30118. Offers art education (M Ed); art teacher education (Ed S); biology - secondary education (M Ed); biology/secondary education (Ed S); business education (M Ed, Ed S); chemistry/secondary education (Ed S); earth science/secondary education (Ed S); economics/secondary education (Ed S); educational leadership (M Ed, Ed S); English teacher education (M Ed, Ed S); French teacher education (M Ed, Ed S); history teacher education (Ed S); mathematics teacher education (M Ed, Ed S); middle grades education (M Ed, Ed S); physical education and recreation (Ed S); physical education teaching and coaching (M Ed); physics/secondary education (Ed S); science teacher education (M Ed, Ed S); secondary education (M Ed); social science - secondary education (M Ed); social science teacher education (M Ed); Spanish (M Ed); Spanish teacher education (M Ed, Ed S); sports management (M Ed). *Accreditation:* NCATE. Part-time and evening/weekend programs available. *Faculty:* 18 full-time (9 women). *Students:* 75 full-time (49 women), 169 part-time (109 women); includes 90 minority (85 Black or African American, non-Hispanic/Latino; 3 Hispanic/Latino; 2 Two or more races, non-Hispanic/Latino), 1 international. Average age 36. 115 applicants, 67% accepted, 19 enrolled. In 2011, 73 master's, 53 Ed Ss awarded. *Degree requirements:* For master's, internship; for Ed S, research project. *Entrance requirements:* For master's, GRE General Test, minimum GPA of 2.7; for Ed S, GRE General Test, master's degree, minimum graduate GPA of 3.0, district appointment. Additional exam requirements/recommendations for international students: Required—TOEFL (minimum score 523 paper-based; 193 computer-based; 69 iBT); Recommended—IELTS (minimum score 6). *Application deadline:* For fall admission, 7/21 for domestic students, 6/1 for international students; for spring admission, 11/30 for domestic students, 10/15 for international students. Applications are processed on a rolling basis. Application fee: $30. Electronic applications accepted. *Expenses:* Tuition, state resident: full-time $4336; part-time $181 per credit hour. Tuition, nonresident: full-time $17,362; part-time $724 per credit hour. Tuition and fees vary according to course load, degree level, campus/location and program. *Financial support:* In 2011–12, 1 research assistantship with full tuition reimbursement (averaging $7,444 per year) was awarded; career-related internships or fieldwork, scholarships/grants, and unspecified assistantships also available. Support available to part-time students. Financial award application deadline: 7/1; financial award applicants required to submit FAFSA. *Total annual research expenditures:* $5,000. *Unit head:* Dr. Frank Butts, Chair, 678-839-6530, Fax: 678-839-6195, E-mail: fbutts@westga.edu. *Application contact:* Deanna Richards, Coordinator, Graduate Studies, 678-839-5946, E-mail: drichard@westga.edu. Web site: http://www.westga.edu/coelai.

University of Wisconsin–Milwaukee, Graduate School, School of Education, Department of Curriculum and Instruction, Milwaukee, WI 53201-0413. Offers curriculum planning and instruction improvement (MS); early childhood education (MS); elementary education (MS); junior high/middle school education (MS); reading education (MS); secondary education (MS); teaching in an urban setting (MS). Part-time programs available. *Faculty:* 18 full-time (13 women). *Students:* 29 full-time (23 women), 54 part-time (44 women); includes 21 minority (10 Black or African American, non-Hispanic/Latino; 4 Asian, non-Hispanic/Latino; 3 Hispanic/Latino; 4 Two or more races, non-Hispanic/Latino). Average age 32. 43 applicants, 65% accepted, 13 enrolled. In 2011, 23 degrees awarded. *Degree requirements:* For master's, thesis or alternative. *Entrance requirements:* Additional exam requirements/recommendations for international students: Required—TOEFL (minimum score 550 paper-based; 79 iBT), IELTS (minimum score 6.5). *Application deadline:* For fall admission, 1/1 priority date for domestic students; for spring admission, 9/1 for domestic students. Applications are processed on a rolling basis. Application fee: $56 ($96 for international students). Electronic applications accepted. One-time fee: $506.10 full-time. Tuition and fees vary according to course load and reciprocity agreements. *Financial support:* In 2011–12, 1 fellowship was awarded; research assistantships, teaching assistantships, career-related internships or fieldwork, health care benefits, unspecified assistantships, and project assistantships also available. Support available to part-time students. Financial award application deadline: 4/15; financial award applicants required to submit FAFSA. *Total annual research expenditures:* $21,843. *Unit head:* Hope Longwell-Grice, Department Chair, 414-229-3059, Fax: 414-229-5571, E-mail: hope@uwm.edu. *Application contact:* General Information Contact, 414-229-4982, Fax: 414-229-6967, E-mail: gradschool@uwm.edu. Web site: http://www.uwm.edu/SOE/.

University of Wisconsin–Platteville, School of Graduate Studies, College of Liberal Arts and Education, School of Education, Platteville, WI 53818-3099. Offers adult education (MSE); elementary education (MSE); English education (MSE); middle school education (MSE); secondary education (MSE). *Accreditation:* NCATE. Part-time programs available. *Faculty:* 8 part-time/adjunct (3 women). *Students:* 62 full-time (47 women), 86 part-time (69 women); includes 22 minority (20 Black or African American, non-Hispanic/Latino; 2 Hispanic/Latino), 55 international. 17 applicants, 76% accepted. In 2011, 82 master's awarded. *Degree requirements:* For master's, comprehensive exam, thesis or alternative. *Entrance requirements:* Additional exam requirements/recommendations for international students: Required—TOEFL (minimum score 500 paper-based; 61 iBT), IELTS (minimum score 6). *Application deadline:* For fall admission, 7/1 priority date for domestic students; for spring admission, 11/1 for domestic students. Applications are processed on a rolling basis. Application fee: $56. Electronic applications accepted. *Financial support:* Research assistantships with partial tuition reimbursements, career-related internships or fieldwork, Federal Work-Study, institutionally sponsored loans, scholarships/grants, and unspecified assistantships available. Support available to part-time students. Financial award applicants required to submit FAFSA. *Unit head:* Dr. Karen Stinson, Director, 608-342-1131, Fax: 608-342-1133, E-mail: stinsonk@uwplatt.edu. *Application contact:* Lisa Popp, School of Graduate Studies, 608-342-1322, Fax: 608-342-1389, E-mail: poppl@uwplatt.edu. Web site: http://www.uwplatt.edu/.

Ursuline College, School of Graduate Studies, Program in Education, Pepper Pike, OH 44124-4398. Offers art education (MA); early childhood education (MA); language arts education (MA); life science education (MA); math education (MA); middle school education (MA); social studies education (MA); special education (MA). *Accreditation:* NCATE. *Faculty:* 3 full-time (all women), 8 part-time/adjunct (6 women). *Students:* 28 full-time (22 women), 1 (woman) part-time; includes 11 minority (7 Black or African American, non-Hispanic/Latino; 2 Asian, non-Hispanic/Latino; 1 Hispanic/Latino; 1 Native Hawaiian or other Pacific Islander, non-Hispanic/Latino). Average age 32. In 2011, 29 master's awarded. *Degree requirements:* For master's, comprehensive exam. *Entrance requirements:* For master's, minimum undergraduate GPA of 3.0. Additional exam requirements/recommendations for international students: Required—TOEFL (minimum score 500 paper-based; 173 computer-based). *Application deadline:* For fall admission, 8/1 priority date for domestic students. Applications are processed on a rolling basis. Application fee: $25. *Expenses:* Contact institution. *Financial support:* Federal Work-Study available. Financial award application deadline: 3/1. *Unit head:* Dr. Edna West, Director, Master's Apprentice Program, 440-646-6134, Fax: 440-684-6088, E-mail: ewest@ursuline.edu. *Application contact:* Melanie Steele, Graduate Admission Assistant, 440-646-8199, Fax: 440-684-6138, E-mail: graduateadmissions@ursuline.edu.

Valdosta State University, Department of Middle, Secondary, Reading and Deaf Education, Valdosta, GA 31698. Offers middle grades education (M Ed, Ed S); secondary education (M Ed, Ed S). *Accreditation:* NCATE. Part-time and evening/weekend programs available. *Faculty:* 12 full-time (9 women). *Students:* 1 (woman) full-time, 22 part-time (20 women); includes 1 minority (Native Hawaiian or other Pacific Islander, non-Hispanic/Latino). Average age 25. 18 applicants, 78% accepted, 6 enrolled. In 2011, 24 master's, 5 Ed Ss awarded. *Degree requirements:* For master's, thesis (for some programs), comprehensive written and/or oral exams; for Ed S, thesis. *Entrance requirements:* For master's, GRE General Test or MAT, minimum GPA of 2.5; for Ed S, GRE General Test or MAT, minimum GPA of 3.0. Additional exam requirements/recommendations for international students: Required—TOEFL (minimum score 523 paper-based; 193 computer-based). *Application deadline:* For fall admission, 7/1 for domestic and international students; for spring admission, 11/15 for domestic and international students. Applications are processed on a rolling basis. Application fee: $35. Electronic applications accepted. *Expenses:* Tuition, state resident: full-time $7098; part-time $217 per hour. Tuition, nonresident: full-time $20,630; part-time $780 per hour. *Financial support:* In 2011–12, 4 students received support, including 4 research assistantships with full tuition reimbursements available (averaging $3,652 per year); institutionally sponsored loans, scholarships/grants, and unspecified assistantships also available. Support available to part-time students. Financial award application deadline: 7/1; financial award applicants required to submit FAFSA. *Faculty research:* Distance education, learning styles, alternative assessment methods, interactive teaching strategies, learning styles of pre-service teachers. *Unit head:* Dr. Barbara Stanley, Head, 229-333-5611, Fax: 229-333-7167. *Application contact:* Meg Moore, Director of GOML Programs, 229-333-5694, Fax: 229-245-3853, E-mail: mhgiddin@valdosta.edu.

Wagner College, Division of Graduate Studies, Department of Education, Program in Adolescent Education, Staten Island, NY 10301-4495. Offers MS Ed. Part-time and evening/weekend programs available. *Faculty:* 3 full-time (2 women), 14 part-time/adjunct (10 women). *Students:* 19 full-time (5 women), 18 part-time (11 women); includes 3 minority (2 Black or African American, non-Hispanic/Latino; 1 Asian, non-Hispanic/Latino). Average age 24. 19 applicants, 95% accepted, 13 enrolled. In 2011, 14 master's awarded. *Degree requirements:* For master's, thesis (for some programs). *Entrance requirements:* For master's, Liberal Arts and Sciences Test (LAST), New York State Teacher Certification Examinations (NYSTCE), minimum GPA of 2.75. Additional exam requirements/recommendations for international students: Required—TOEFL (minimum score 550 paper-based; 217 computer-based; 79 iBT). *Application deadline:* For fall admission, 5/1 priority date for domestic students, 3/1 for international students; for spring admission, 11/1 priority date for domestic students, 10/1 for international students. Applications are processed on a rolling basis. Application fee: $50 ($85 for international students). *Expenses: Tuition:* Full-time $16,200; part-time $890 per credit. *Financial support:* Career-related internships or fieldwork, tuition waivers (partial), unspecified assistantships, and alumni fellowship grant available. Financial award applicants required to submit FAFSA. *Unit head:* Dr. Stephen Preskill, Graduate Coordinator, 718-420-4070, Fax: 718-390-3456, E-mail: stephen.preskill@wagner.edu. *Application contact:* Patricia Clancy, Assistant Coordinator of Graduate Studies, 718-420-4464, Fax: 718-390-3105, E-mail: patricia.clancy@wagner.edu.

Walden University, Graduate Programs, Richard W. Riley College of Education and Leadership, Minneapolis, MN 55401. Offers administrator leadership for teaching and

learning (Ed D, Ed S); adult education (Ed D, Ed S); adult learning (MS, Postbaccalaureate Certificate), including developmental education (MS), online teaching (MS), teaching adults English as a second language (MS), training and performance management (MS); college teaching and learning (Ed D, Ed S, Postbaccalaureate Certificate); curriculum, instruction and assessment (Ed D, Postbaccalaureate Certificate); curriculum, instruction, and professional development (Ed S); developmental education (Postbaccalaureate Certificate); early childhood administration, management, and leadership (Postbaccalaureate Certificate); early childhood education (birth-grade 3) (MAT); early childhood public policy and advocacy (Postbaccalaureate Certificate); early childhood studies (MS), including administration, management and leadership, early childhood public policy and advocacy, teaching adults in the early childhood field, teaching and diversity; education (MS, PhD), including adolescent literacy and technology (grades 6-12) (MS), adult education leadership (PhD), assessment, evaluation, and accountability (PhD), community college leadership (PhD), curriculum, instruction, and assessment, early childhood education (PhD), educational technology (PhD), elementary reading and literacy (MS), elementary reading and mathematics (MS), general program, global and comparative education (PhD), higher education (PhD), integrating technology in the classroom (MS), K-12 educational leadership (PhD), leadership, policy and change (PhD), learning, instruction and innovation (PhD), literacy and learning in the content areas (MS), mathematics (grades 6-8) (MS), mathematics (grades K-5) (MS), middle level education (grades 5-8) (MS), professional development (MS), science (grades K-8) (MS), self-designed (PhD), special education (PhD), special education (non-licensure) (MS), teacher leadership (grades K-12) (MS), teaching English language learners (grades K-12) (MS); educational leadership and administration (principal preparation) (Ed S); educational technology (Ed S); elementary reading and literacy (Postbaccalaureate Certificate); engaging culturally diverse learners (Postbaccalaureate Certificate); enrollment management and institutional marketing (Postbaccalaureate Certificate); higher education (MS), including college teaching and learning, enrollment management and institutional planning, global higher education, leadership for student success, online and distance learning; higher education leadership (Ed D); instructional design (Postbaccalaureate Certificate); instructional design and technology (MS), including general program (MS, PhD), online learning, training and performance improvement; integrating technology in the classroom (Postbaccalaureate Certificate); online teaching for adult learners (Postbaccalaureate Certificate); professional development (Postbaccalaureate Certificate); reading and literacy leadership (Ed D); science K-8 (Postbaccalaureate Certificate); special education (Ed D, Ed S); special education: emotional/behavioral disorders (K-12) (MAT); special education: learning disabilities (K-12) (MAT); teacher leadership (Ed D, Ed S, Postbaccalaureate Certificate); training and performance management (Postbaccalaureate Certificate). Part-time and evening/weekend programs available. Postbaccalaureate distance learning degree programs offered (minimal on-campus study). *Faculty:* 71 full-time (48 women), 853 part-time/adjunct (585 women). *Students:* 11,326 full-time (9,212 women), 2,148 part-time (1,795 women); includes 5,346 minority (4,403 Black or African American, non-Hispanic/Latino; 76 American Indian or Alaska Native, non-Hispanic/Latino; 140 Asian, non-Hispanic/Latino; 561 Hispanic/Latino; 21 Native Hawaiian or other Pacific Islander, non-Hispanic/Latino; 145 Two or more races, non-Hispanic/Latino), 322 international. Average age 39. In 2011, 3,477 master's, 318 doctorates, 471 other advanced degrees awarded. *Degree requirements:* For doctorate, thesis/dissertation (for some programs), residency; for other advanced degree, residency (for some programs). *Entrance requirements:* For master's, bachelor's degree or equivalent in related field; minimum GPA of 2.5; official transcripts; goal statement; access to computer and Internet; for doctorate, master's degree or equivalent in related field; minimum GPA of 3.0; official transcripts; three years' related professional/academic experience (preferred); access to computer and Internet; for other advanced degree, master's degree or equivalent in related field; minimum GPA of 3.0; 3 years related professional/academic experience (preferred); access to computer and Internet (Ed S). Additional exam requirements/recommendations for international students: Required—TOEFL (minimum score 550 paper-based; 213 computer-based), IELTS (minimum score 6.5), or Michigan English Language Assessment Battery (minimum score 82). *Application deadline:* Applications are processed on a rolling basis. Application fee: $50. Electronic applications accepted. *Financial support:* Federal Work-Study, scholarships/grants, unspecified assistantships, and family tuition reduction, active duty/veteran tuition reduction, group tuition reduction, interest-free payment plans, employee tuition reduction available. Support available to part-time students. Financial award applicants required to submit FAFSA. *Unit head:* Dr. Kate Steffens, Dean, 800-925-3368. *Application contact:* Jennifer Hall, Vice President of Enrollment Management, 866-4-WALDEN, E-mail: info@waldenu.edu. Web site: http://www.waldenu.edu/Colleges-and-Schools/College-of-Education-and-Leadership.htm.

West Chester University of Pennsylvania, College of Education, Department of Early and Middle Grades, West Chester, PA 19383. Offers applied studies in teaching and learning (M Ed); early childhood education (M Ed, Teaching Certificate); early grades preparation (Teaching Certificate); elementary education (Teaching Certificate); middle grades preparation (Teaching Certificate). *Accreditation:* NCATE. Part-time and evening/weekend programs available. *Faculty:* 7 part-time/adjunct (6 women). *Students:* 54 full-time (41 women), 100 part-time (84 women); includes 14 minority (8 Black or African American, non-Hispanic/Latino; 1 Asian, non-Hispanic/Latino; 2 Hispanic/Latino; 3 Two or more races, non-Hispanic/Latino). Average age 32. 78 applicants, 63% accepted, 32 enrolled. In 2011, 22 degrees awarded. *Degree requirements:* For master's, teacher research project, portfolio (for M Ed). *Entrance requirements:* For master's, minimum GPA of 3.0, teacher certification, one year of full-time teaching experience; for Teaching Certificate, PRAXIS I and II, minimum GPA of 3.0. Additional exam requirements/recommendations for international students: Required—TOEFL (minimum score 550 paper-based; 213 computer-based; 80 iBT). *Application deadline:* For fall admission, 4/15 priority date for domestic students, 3/15 for international students; for spring admission, 10/15 priority date for domestic students. Applications are processed on a rolling basis. Application fee: $45. Electronic applications accepted. *Expenses:* Tuition, state resident: full-time $7488; part-time $416 per credit. Tuition, nonresident: full-time $11,232; part-time $624 per credit. *Required fees:* $1784.64; $67.59 per credit. Tuition and fees vary according to program. *Financial support:* Unspecified assistantships available. Support available to part-time students. Financial award application deadline: 2/15; financial award applicants required to submit FAFSA. *Faculty research:* Cooperative learning, creative expression and critical thinking, teacher research, learning styles, middle school education. *Unit head:* Dr. Heather Leaman, Chair, 610-436-2944, Fax: 610-436-3102, E-mail: hleaman@wcupa.edu. *Application contact:* Dr. Connie DiLucchio, Graduate Coordinator, 610-436-3323, Fax: 610-436-3102, E-mail: cdilucchio@wcupa.edu. Web site: http://www.wcupa.edu/_academics/sch_sed.elementaryed/.

Western Kentucky University, Graduate Studies, College of Education and Behavioral Sciences, School of Teacher Education, Bowling Green, KY 42101. Offers elementary education (MAE, Ed S); exceptional education: learning and behavioral disorders (MAE); exceptional education: moderate and severe disabilities (MAE); instructional design (MS); interdisciplinary early childhood education (MAE); library media education (MS); literacy education (MAE); middle grades education (MAE); secondary education (MAE, Ed S). Part-time and evening/weekend programs available. Postbaccalaureate distance learning degree programs offered (minimal on-campus study). *Degree requirements:* For master's, comprehensive exam. *Entrance requirements:* For master's, GRE General Test. Additional exam requirements/recommendations for international students: Required—TOEFL (minimum score 555 paper-based; 213 computer-based; 79 iBT). *Faculty research:* Teacher preparation in moderate/severe disabilities.

Widener University, School of Human Service Professions, Center for Education, Chester, PA 19013-5792. Offers adult education (M Ed); counseling in higher education (M Ed); counselor education (M Ed); early childhood education (M Ed); educational foundations (M Ed); educational leadership (M Ed); educational psychology (M Ed); elementary education (M Ed); English and language arts (M Ed); health education (M Ed); higher education leadership (Ed D); home and school visitor (M Ed); human sexuality (M Ed, PhD); mathematics education (M Ed); middle school education (M Ed); principalship (M Ed); reading and language arts (Ed D); reading education (M Ed); school administration (Ed D); science education (M Ed); social studies education (M Ed); special education (M Ed); technology education (M Ed). *Accreditation:* NCATE. Part-time and evening/weekend programs available. Terminal master's awarded for partial completion of doctoral program. *Degree requirements:* For doctorate, thesis/dissertation. *Entrance requirements:* For master's, minimum GPA of 2.5; for doctorate, GRE or MAT, minimum GPA of 2.0 (undergraduate), 3.5 (graduate). Electronic applications accepted. *Expenses:* Contact institution. *Faculty research:* Reading and cognition, adult education, technology education, educational leadership, special education.

Winthrop University, College of Education, Program in Middle Level Education, Rock Hill, SC 29733. Offers M Ed. *Entrance requirements:* For master's, minimum GPA of 3.0, South Carolina Class III Teaching Certificate, 2 letters of recommendation. Electronic applications accepted.

Worcester State University, Graduate Studies, Department of Education, Program in Middle School Education, Worcester, MA 01602-2597. Offers M Ed, Postbaccalaureate Certificate. Part-time programs available. *Faculty:* 12 full-time (9 women), 22 part-time/adjunct (10 women). *Students:* 26 part-time (18 women); includes 2 minority (1 Black or African American, non-Hispanic/Latino; 1 Hispanic/Latino). Average age 34. 29 applicants, 79% accepted, 7 enrolled. In 2011, 1 degree awarded. *Degree requirements:* For master's, comprehensive exam (for some programs), thesis optional. *Entrance requirements:* For master's, GRE General Test or MAT. Additional exam requirements/recommendations for international students: Required—TOEFL (minimum score 500 paper-based; 61 iBT). *Application deadline:* For fall admission, 6/15 for domestic and international students; for spring admission, 4/1 for domestic and international students. Applications are processed on a rolling basis. Application fee: $40. Electronic applications accepted. *Expenses:* Tuition, state resident: full-time $2700; part-time $150 per credit. Tuition, nonresident: full-time $2700; part-time $150 per credit. *Required fees:* $2016; $112 per credit. *Financial support:* Career-related internships or fieldwork, scholarships/grants, and unspecified assistantships available. Financial award application deadline: 3/1; financial award applicants required to submit FAFSA. *Unit head:* Dr. Sara Young, Coordinator, 508-929-8246, E-mail: syoung3@worcester.edu. *Application contact:* Sara Grady, Assistant Dean of Graduate and Continuing Education, 508-929-8787, Fax: 508-929-8100, E-mail: sara.grady@worcester.edu.

Wright State University, School of Graduate Studies, College of Education and Human Services, Department of Teacher Education, Dayton, OH 45435. Offers adolescent young adult (M Ed, MA); classroom teacher education (M Ed, MA); early childhood education (M Ed, MA); intervention specialist (M Ed, MA), including gifted educational needs, mild to moderate educational needs, moderate to intensive educational needs; middle childhood education (M Ed, MA); multi-age (M Ed, MA); workforce education (M Ed, MA), including career, technology and vocational education, computer/technology education, library/media, vocational education. *Accreditation:* NCATE. *Entrance requirements:* For master's, GRE General Test, MAT, PRAXIS II. Additional exam requirements/recommendations for international students: Required—TOEFL. *Faculty research:* Reading recovery, early kindergarten birthdays, international children's literature, discipline models, university and public schools cooperation.

Youngstown State University, Graduate School, Beeghly College of Education, Department of Teacher Education, Program in Early Childhood Education, Youngstown, OH 44555-0001. Offers MS Ed. *Accreditation:* NCATE. Part-time and evening/weekend programs available. *Degree requirements:* For master's, comprehensive exam. *Entrance requirements:* For master's, GRE, MAT, or teaching certificate; minimum GPA of 2.7. Additional exam requirements/recommendations for international students: Required—TOEFL.

Youngstown State University, Graduate School, Beeghly College of Education, Department of Teacher Education, Program in Middle Childhood Education, Youngstown, OH 44555-0001. Offers MS Ed. *Accreditation:* NCATE. Part-time and evening/weekend programs available. *Degree requirements:* For master's, comprehensive exam, thesis optional. *Entrance requirements:* For master's, GRE, MAT, or teaching certificate; minimum GPA of 2.7. Additional exam requirements/recommendations for international students: Required—TOEFL. *Faculty research:* Critical reflectivity, gender issues in classroom instruction, collaborative research and analysis, literacy methodology.

Secondary Education

Adelphi University, Ruth S. Ammon School of Education, Program in Adolescent Education, Garden City, NY 11530-0701. Offers MA. Part-time and evening/weekend programs available. *Students:* 83 full-time (52 women), 25 part-time (15 women); includes 21 minority (6 Black or African American, non-Hispanic/Latino; 5 Asian, non-Hispanic/Latino; 10 Hispanic/Latino), 1 international. Average age 26. In 2011, 29 degrees awarded. *Entrance requirements:* For master's, 2 letters of recommendation, resume. Additional exam requirements/recommendations for international students: Required—TOEFL (minimum score 550 paper-based; 213 computer-based; 80 iBT). *Application deadline:* For fall admission, 4/1 for international students; for spring admission, 11/1 for international students. Applications are processed on a rolling basis. Application fee: $50. Electronic applications accepted. *Expenses: Tuition:* Full-time $29,600; part-time $930 per credit. *Required fees:* $1100. *Financial support:* Fellowships, research assistantships with partial tuition reimbursements, teaching assistantships, career-related internships or fieldwork, Federal Work-Study, institutionally sponsored loans, tuition waivers (full), and unspecified assistantships available. Support available to part-time students. Financial award application deadline: 2/15; financial award applicants required to submit FAFSA. *Faculty research:* Methods to enhance the development of teaching dispositions, ethical and moral issues in education. *Unit head:* Dr. Robert Linne, Director, 516-877-4411, E-mail: linne@adelphi.edu. *Application contact:* Christine Murphy, Director of Admissions, 516-877-3050, Fax: 516-877-3039, E-mail: graduateadmissions@adelphi.edu.

Alabama Agricultural and Mechanical University, School of Graduate Studies, School of Education, Area in Secondary Education, Huntsville, AL 35811. Offers education (M Ed, Ed S); higher administration (MS). *Accreditation:* NCATE. Evening/weekend programs available. *Degree requirements:* For master's, comprehensive exam; for Ed S, thesis. *Entrance requirements:* For master's, GRE General Test. Additional exam requirements/recommendations for international students: Required—TOEFL (minimum score 500 paper-based; 173 computer-based; 61 iBT). Electronic applications accepted. *Faculty research:* World peace through education, computer-assisted instruction.

Alabama State University, Department of Curriculum and Instruction, Program in Secondary Education, Montgomery, AL 36101-0271. Offers biology education (M Ed, Ed S); English/language arts (M Ed); history education (M Ed, Ed S); mathematics education (M Ed); secondary education (Ed S); social studies (Ed S). Part-time programs available. *Students:* 16 full-time (12 women), 13 part-time (9 women); includes 26 minority (all Black or African American, non-Hispanic/Latino). Average age 36. 48 applicants, 52% accepted, 5 enrolled. In 2011, 3 master's awarded. *Degree requirements:* For master's, comprehensive exam; for Ed S, comprehensive exam, thesis. *Entrance requirements:* For master's, GRE General Test, MAT, graduate writing competency test; for Ed S, graduate writing competency test, GRE, MAT. Additional exam requirements/recommendations for international students: Required—TOEFL (minimum score 500 paper-based; 173 computer-based). *Application deadline:* For fall admission, 7/15 for domestic students; for spring admission, 12/15 for domestic students. Applications are processed on a rolling basis. Application fee: $10. *Financial support:* In 2011–12, research assistantships (averaging $9,450 per year) were awarded. *Unit head:* Dr. Willa Bing Harris, Acting Chairperson, 334-229-4394, Fax: 334-229-4904, E-mail: wbharris@alasu.edu. *Application contact:* Dr. Doris Screws, Dean of Graduate Studies, 334-229-4274, Fax: 334-229-4928, E-mail: dscrews@alasu.edu. Web site: http://www.alasu.edu/academics/colleges—departments/college-of-education/curriculum—instruction/degree-programs/secondary-education/index.aspx.

Alcorn State University, School of Graduate Studies, School of Psychology and Education, Alcorn State, MS 39096-7500. Offers agricultural education (MS Ed); elementary education (MS Ed, Ed S); guidance and counseling (MS Ed); industrial education (MS Ed); secondary education (MS Ed), including health and physical education; special education (MS Ed). *Accreditation:* NCATE. *Degree requirements:* For master's, thesis optional.

American International College, School of Arts, Education and Sciences, Department of Education, Springfield, MA 01109-3189. Offers early childhood education (M Ed, CAGS); educational leadership and supervision (Ed D); elementary education (M Ed, CAGS); middle/secondary education (M Ed, CAGS); moderate disabilities (M Ed, CAGS); reading (M Ed, CAGS); school adjustment counseling (MA, CAGS); school administration (M Ed, CAGS); school guidance counseling (MA, CAGS); teaching (MA, MS); teaching and learning (Ed D). Part-time and evening/weekend programs available. Terminal master's awarded for partial completion of doctoral program. *Degree requirements:* For master's, comprehensive exam (for some programs), thesis (for some programs), practicum; for doctorate, comprehensive exam (for some programs), thesis/dissertation; for CAGS, practicum. *Entrance requirements:* For master's, minimum B-average in undergraduate course work; for doctorate, GRE General Test, interview. Additional exam requirements/recommendations for international students: Required—TOEFL. Electronic applications accepted.

American Public University System, AMU/APU Graduate Programs, Charles Town, WV 25414. Offers accounting (MBA, MS); administration and supervision (M Ed); criminal justice (MA); emergency and disaster management (MA); entrepreneurship (MBA); environmental policy and management (MS), including environmental planning, environmental sustainability, fish and wildlife management, general (MA, MS), global environmental management; finance (MBA); general (MBA); global business management (MBA); guidance and counseling (M Ed); history (MA), including American history, ancient and classical history, European history, global history, military and diplomatic history, public history; homeland security (MA); homeland security resource allocation (MBA); humanities (MA); information technology (MS), including digital forensics, enterprise software development, information assurance and security, IT project management; information technology management (MBA); intelligence studies (MA), including criminal intelligence, general (MA, MS), homeland security, intelligence analysis, intelligence collection, intelligence operations, terrorism studies; international relations and conflict resolution (MA), including comparative and security issues, conflict resolution, international and transnational security issues, peacekeeping; legal studies (MA); management (MA), including defense management, general (MA, MS), human resource management, organizational leadership, public administration, reverse logistics, strategic consulting; marketing (MBA); military history (MA), including American military history, American revolution, civil war, war since 1946, World War II; military studies (MA), including air warfare, asymmetrical warfare, joint warfare, land warfare, naval warfare, strategic leadership; national security studies (MA), including general (MA, MS), homeland security, regional security studies, security and intelligence analysis, terrorism studies; nonprofit management (MBA); political science (MA), including American politics and government, comparative government and development, public policy; psychology (MA); public administration (MA, MPA), including disaster management (MPA), environmental policy (MA), health policy (MPA), human resources (MPA), national security (MPA), organizational management (MPA), security management (MPA); public health (MA, MPH), including emergency management (MPH), environmental health (MPH), public administration (MA); reverse logistics management (MA); security management (MA); space studies (MS), including aerospace science, planetary science; sports and health sciences (MS); sports management (MS), including coaching theory and strategy, sports administration; teaching (M Ed), including curriculum and instruction for elementary teachers, elementary, elementary reading, English language learners, instructional leadership, online learning, secondary social sciences, special education; transportation and logistics management (MA), including maritime engineering management. Programs offered via distance learning only. Part-time and evening/weekend programs available. Postbaccalaureate distance learning degree programs offered (no on-campus study). *Faculty:* 445 full-time (241 women), 1,360 part-time/adjunct (617 women). *Students:* 688 full-time (338 women), 10,168 part-time (3,706 women); includes 3,130 minority (1,007 Black or African American, non-Hispanic/Latino; 103 American Indian or Alaska Native, non-Hispanic/Latino; 825 Asian, non-Hispanic/Latino; 810 Hispanic/Latino; 51 Native Hawaiian or other Pacific Islander, non-Hispanic/Latino; 334 Two or more races, non-Hispanic/Latino), 134 international. Average age 35. In 2011, 2,386 master's awarded. *Degree requirements:* For master's, comprehensive exam or practicum. *Entrance requirements:* For master's, official transcript showing earned bachelor's degree from institution accredited by recognized accrediting body. Additional exam requirements/recommendations for international students: Required—TOEFL (minimum score 550 paper-based; 213 computer-based), IELTS (minimum score 6.5). *Application deadline:* Applications are processed on a rolling basis. Application fee: $0. Electronic applications accepted. *Expenses: Tuition:* Part-time $325 per credit hour. *Financial support:* Applicants required to submit FAFSA. *Faculty research:* Military history, criminal justice, management performance, national security. *Unit head:* Dr. Karan Powell, Executive Vice President and Provost, 877-468-6268, Fax: 304-724-3780. *Application contact:* Terry Grant, Vice President of Enrollment Management, 877-468-6268, Fax: 304-724-3780, E-mail: info@apus.edu. Web site: http://www.apus.edu.

American University, College of Arts and Sciences, School of Education, Teaching, and Health, Program in Secondary Teaching, Washington, DC 20016-8001. Offers MAT, Certificate. *Students:* 12 full-time (7 women), 111 part-time (68 women); includes 21 minority (11 Black or African American, non-Hispanic/Latino; 2 American Indian or Alaska Native, non-Hispanic/Latino; 2 Asian, non-Hispanic/Latino; 6 Hispanic/Latino). Average age 27. 30 applicants, 83% accepted, 16 enrolled. In 2011, 124 master's awarded. *Degree requirements:* For master's, comprehensive exam, PRAXIS II; for Certificate, PRAXIS II. *Entrance requirements:* For master's, GRE General Test, PRAXIS I, minimum GPA of 3.0, 2 recommendations; for Certificate, PRAXIS I, bachelor's degree, 2 recommendation letters. *Application deadline:* For fall admission, 2/1 priority date for domestic students; for spring admission, 10/1 priority date for domestic students. Applications are processed on a rolling basis. Application fee: $80. *Expenses: Tuition:* Full-time $24,264; part-time $1348 per credit hour. *Required fees:* $430. Tuition and fees vary according to course load and program. *Financial support:* Research assistantships with partial tuition reimbursements available. Financial award application deadline: 2/1. *Unit head:* Sarah Irvine -Belson, Director, Teacher Education, 202-885-3727, Fax: 202-885-1187, E-mail: sirvine@american.edu. *Application contact:* Kathleen Clowery, Director, Graduate Admissions, 202-885-3621, Fax: 202-885-1505, E-mail: clowery@american.edu. Web site: http://www.american.edu/cas/seth/.

Andrews University, School of Graduate Studies, School of Education, Department of Teaching, Learning, and Curriculum, Berrien Springs, MI 49104. Offers curriculum and instruction (MA, Ed D, PhD, Ed S); elementary education (MAT); secondary education (MAT), including biology, education, English, English as a second language, French, history, physics; teacher education (MAT). *Students:* 15 full-time (10 women), 27 part-time (22 women); includes 18 minority (12 Black or African American, non-Hispanic/Latino; 1 Asian, non-Hispanic/Latino; 3 Hispanic/Latino; 1 Native Hawaiian or other Pacific Islander, non-Hispanic/Latino; 1 Two or more races, non-Hispanic/Latino), 10 international. Average age 42. 48 applicants, 48% accepted, 10 enrolled. In 2011, 5 master's, 2 doctorates, 2 other advanced degrees awarded. *Entrance requirements:* For master's, GRE Subject Test. Additional exam requirements/recommendations for international students: Required—TOEFL (minimum score 550 paper-based). *Application deadline:* For fall admission, 8/15 for domestic students. Applications are processed on a rolling basis. Application fee: $40. *Unit head:* Dr. Lee C. Davidson, Chair, 269-471-6364. *Application contact:* Carolyn Hurst, Supervisor of Graduate Admission, 800-253-2874, Fax: 269-471-6321, E-mail: graduate@andrews.edu.

Arcadia University, Graduate Studies, Department of Education, Glenside, PA 19038-3295. Offers art education (M Ed); computer education (CAS); curriculum (CAS); curriculum studies (M Ed); early childhood education (M Ed, CAS), including individualized (M Ed), master teacher (M Ed), research in child development (M Ed); educational leadership (M Ed, Ed D, CAS); elementary education (M Ed, CAS); English education (MA Ed); environmental education (MA Ed, CAS); history education (MA Ed); instructional technology (M Ed); language arts (M Ed, CAS); library science (M Ed); mathematics education (M Ed, MA Ed, CAS); music education (MA Ed); psychology (MA Ed); reading (M Ed, CAS); science education (M Ed, CAS); secondary education (M Ed, CAS); special education (M Ed, Ed D, CAS); theater arts (MA Ed); written communication (MA Ed). *Accreditation:* NASAD. Part-time and evening/weekend programs available. Postbaccalaureate distance learning degree programs offered (minimal on-campus study). *Faculty:* 12 full-time (8 women), 38 part-time/adjunct (26 women). *Students:* 66 full-time (48 women), 590 part-time (477 women); includes 65 minority (53 Black or African American, non-Hispanic/Latino; 6 Asian, non-Hispanic/Latino; 3 Hispanic/Latino; 3 Two or more races, non-Hispanic/Latino), 4 international. Average age 36. In 2011, 229 master's, 5 doctorates awarded. *Application deadline:* Applications are processed on a rolling basis. Application fee: $50. Electronic applications accepted. *Expenses:* Contact institution. *Financial support:* Career-related internships or fieldwork, tuition waivers (partial), and unspecified assistantships available. *Unit head:* Dr. Steven P. Gulkus, Associate Professor, 215-572-2120, E-mail: gulkus@arcadia.edu. *Application contact:* 215-572-2925, Fax: 215-572-2126, E-mail: grad@arcadia.edu.

Argosy University, Atlanta, College of Education, Atlanta, GA 30328. Offers educational leadership (MAEd, Ed D, Ed S), including higher education administration (Ed D), K-12 education (Ed D); teaching and learning (MAEd, Ed D, Ed S), including education technology (Ed D), higher education (Ed D), K-12 education (Ed D).

See Close-Up on page 1017.

Argosy University, Chicago, College of Education, Chicago, IL 60601. Offers adult education and training (MA Ed); community college executive leadership (Ed D); educational leadership (MA Ed, Ed D, Ed S), including district leadership (Ed D), higher education administration (Ed D), K-12 education (Ed D); instructional leadership (Ed D, Ed S), including higher education (Ed D), K-12 education (Ed D). Postbaccalaureate distance learning degree programs offered (minimal on-campus study).

See Close-Up on page 769.

Argosy University, Hawai`i, College of Education, Honolulu, HI 96813. Offers adult education and training (MAEd); educational leadership (Ed D), including higher education administration, K-12 education; instructional leadership (Ed D), including higher education, K-12 education; school psychology (MA).

See Close-Up on page 775.

Argosy University, Inland Empire, College of Education, San Bernardino, CA 92408. Offers community college executive leadership (Ed D); educational leadership (MA Ed, Ed D), including higher education administration (Ed D), K-12 education (Ed D); instructional leadership (MA Ed, Ed D), including higher education (Ed D), K-12 education (Ed D), multiple subject teacher preparation (MA Ed), single subject teacher preparation (MA Ed).

See Close-Up on page 1019.

Argosy University, Los Angeles, College of Education, Santa Monica, CA 90045. Offers community college executive leadership (Ed D); educational leadership (MA Ed, Ed D), including higher education administration (Ed D), K-12 education (Ed D); instructional leadership (MA Ed, Ed D), including higher education (Ed D), K-12 education (Ed D), multiple subject teacher preparation (MA Ed), single subject teacher preparation (MA Ed).

See Close-Up on page 777.

Argosy University, Nashville, College of Education, Program in Educational Leadership, Nashville, TN 37214. Offers educational leadership (MA Ed, Ed S); higher education administration (Ed D); K-12 education (Ed D).

See Close-Up on page 1021.

Argosy University, Nashville, College of Education, Program in Instructional Leadership, Nashville, TN 37214. Offers education technology (Ed D); higher education administration (Ed D); instructional leadership (MA Ed, Ed S); K-12 education (Ed D).

See Close-Up on page 1021.

Argosy University, Orange County, College of Education, Orange, CA 92868. Offers community college executive leadership (Ed D); educational leadership (MA Ed, Ed D), including higher education administration (Ed D), K-12 education (Ed D); instructional leadership (MA Ed, Ed D), including education technology (Ed D), higher education (Ed D), K-12 education (Ed D), multiple subject teacher preparation (MA Ed), single subject teacher preparation (MA Ed).

See Close-Up on page 779.

Argosy University, Phoenix, College of Education, Phoenix, AZ 85021. Offers adult education and training (MA Ed); advanced educational administration (Ed D, Ed S); community college executive leadership (Ed D); educational administration (MA Ed); educational leadership (MA Ed, Ed D, Ed S), including education technology (Ed D), higher education administration (Ed D), K-12 education (Ed D); higher and postsecondary education (MA Ed); initial educational administration (Ed D, Ed S); school psychology (MA); teaching and learning (MA Ed, Ed D, Ed S), including education technology (Ed D), higher education (Ed D), K-12 education (Ed D).

See Close-Up on page 781.

Argosy University, San Diego, College of Education, San Diego, CA 92108. Offers community college executive leadership (Ed D); educational leadership (MA Ed, Ed D), including higher education administration (Ed D), K-12 education (Ed D); instructional leadership (MA Ed, Ed D), including higher education (Ed D), K-12 education (Ed D).

See Close-Up on page 785.

Argosy University, San Francisco Bay Area, College of Education, Alameda, CA 94501. Offers community college executive leadership (Ed D); educational leadership (MA Ed, Ed D), including education technology (Ed D), higher education administration (Ed D), K-12 education (Ed D); instructional leadership (MA Ed, Ed D), including education technology (Ed D), higher education (Ed D), K-12 education (Ed D), multiple subject teacher preparation (MA Ed), single subject teacher preparation (MA Ed).

See Close-Up on page 787.

Argosy University, Sarasota, College of Education, Sarasota, FL 34235. Offers community college executive leadership (Ed D); educational leadership (MA Ed, Ed D, Ed S), including higher education administration (Ed D), K-12 education (Ed D); school counseling (MA, Ed S); school psychology (MA); teaching and learning (MA Ed, Ed D, Ed S), including education technology (Ed D), higher education (Ed D), K-12 education (Ed D).

See Close-Up on page 789.

Argosy University, Schaumburg, College of Education, Schaumburg, IL 60173-5403. Offers community college executive leadership (Ed D); educational leadership (MA Ed, Ed D, Ed S), including district leadership (Ed D), higher education administration (Ed D), K-12 education (Ed D); instructional leadership (Ed D, Ed S), including higher education (Ed D), K-12 education (Ed D).

See Close-Up on page 791.

Argosy University, Seattle, College of Education, Seattle, WA 98121. Offers adult education and training (MA Ed); community college executive leadership (Ed D); educational leadership (MA Ed, Ed D), including higher education administration (Ed D), K-12 education (Ed D); higher and postsecondary education (MA Ed); instructional leadership (MA Ed, Ed D), including education technology (Ed D), higher education (Ed D), K-12 education (Ed D).

See Close-Up on page 793.

Argosy University, Tampa, College of Education, Tampa, FL 33607. Offers community college executive leadership (Ed D); educational leadership (MA Ed, Ed D, Ed S), including higher education administration (Ed D), K-12 education (Ed D); school counseling (MA); teaching and learning (MA Ed, Ed D, Ed S), including higher education (Ed D), K-12 education (Ed D).

See Close-Up on page 795.

Argosy University, Twin Cities, College of Education, Eagan, MN 55121. Offers advanced educational administration (Ed D, Ed S); educational leadership (MA Ed, Ed D, Ed S), including higher education administration (Ed D), K-12 education (Ed D); higher and postsecondary education (MA Ed); initial educational administration (Ed D, Ed S); instructional leadership (MA Ed, Ed D, Ed S), including education technology (Ed D), higher education (Ed D), K-12 education (Ed D).

See Close-Up on page 797.

Argosy University, Washington DC, College of Education, Arlington, VA 22209. Offers community college executive leadership (Ed D); educational leadership (MA Ed, Ed D, Ed S), including higher education administration (Ed D), K-12 education (Ed D); instructional leadership (MA Ed, Ed D, Ed S), including higher education (Ed D), K-12 education (Ed D).

See Close-Up on page 799.

Arizona State University, Mary Lou Fulton Teachers College, Program in Curriculum and Instruction, Phoenix, AZ 85069. Offers curriculum and instruction (M Ed, MA, PhD); elementary education (M Ed); physical education (MPE); secondary education (M Ed). Part-time and evening/weekend programs available. Postbaccalaureate distance learning degree programs offered (minimal on-campus study). Terminal master's awarded for partial completion of doctoral program. *Degree requirements:* For master's, thesis or alternative, applied project, interactive Program of Study (iPOS) submitted before completing 50 percent of required credit hours; for doctorate, comprehensive exam, thesis/dissertation, interactive Program of Study (iPOS) submitted before completing 50 percent of required credit hours. *Entrance requirements:* For master's, GRE or GMAT (for some programs), minimum GPA of 3.0 or equivalent in last 2 years of work leading to bachelor's degree, 3 letters of recommendation, personal statement describing research and career goals, curriculum vitae or resume, IVP fingerprint clearance card (for those seeking Arizona certification); for doctorate, GRE or GMAT (depending on program), minimum GPA of 3.0 or equivalent in last 2 years of work leading to bachelor's degree, 3 letters of recommendation, personal statement describing research and career goals, curriculum vitae or resume. Additional exam requirements/recommendations for international students: Required—TOEFL, IELTS, or Pearson Test of English. Electronic applications accepted. *Expenses:* Contact institution. *Faculty research:* Early childhood, media and computers, elementary education, secondary education, English education, bilingual education, language and literacy, science education, engineering education, exercise and wellness education.

Armstrong Atlantic State University, School of Graduate Studies, Program in Education, Savannah, GA 31419-1997. Offers adult education (M Ed); curriculum and instruction (M Ed); early childhood education (M Ed); education (M Ed); elementary education (M Ed); middle grades education (M Ed); secondary education (M Ed), including business education, English education, mathematics education, science education, social science education; special education (M Ed), including behavioral disorders, learning disabilities, speech-language pathology. *Accreditation:* NCATE. Part-time and evening/weekend programs available. Postbaccalaureate distance learning degree programs offered (minimal on-campus study). *Faculty:* 33 full-time (23 women), 3 part-time/adjunct (2 women). *Students:* 97 full-time (91 women), 262 part-time (227 women); includes 83 minority (70 Black or African American, non-Hispanic/Latino; 3 Asian, non-Hispanic/Latino; 8 Hispanic/Latino; 2 Two or more races, non-Hispanic/Latino), 5 international. Average age 34. 169 applicants, 69% accepted, 102 enrolled. In 2011, 227 master's awarded. *Degree requirements:* For master's, comprehensive exam, portfolio. *Entrance requirements:* For master's, GRE General Test or MAT, minimum GPA of 2.5, letters of recommendation. Additional exam requirements/recommendations for international students: Required—TOEFL (minimum score 523 paper-based; 193 computer-based). *Application deadline:* For fall admission, 7/1 priority date for domestic students, 5/1 for international students; for spring admission, 11/15 priority date for domestic students, 9/15 for international students. Applications are processed on a rolling basis. Application fee: $30. Electronic applications accepted. *Expenses:* Tuition, state resident: full-time $3402. Tuition, nonresident: full-time $12,636. *Financial support:* In 2011–12, research assistantships with full tuition reimbursements (averaging $5,000 per year) were awarded; career-related internships or fieldwork, Federal Work-Study, scholarships/grants, and unspecified assistantships also available. Support available to part-time students. Financial award applicants required to submit FAFSA. *Unit head:* Dr. Patricia Wachholz, Dean, College of Education, 912-344-2797, E-mail: patricia.wachholz@armstrong.edu. *Application contact:* Jill Bell, Director, Graduate Enrollment Services, 912-344-2798, Fax: 912-344-3488, E-mail: graduate@armstrong.edu. Web site: http://www.armstrong.edu/Education/coe_deans_office/coe_education_welcome.

Auburn University, Graduate School, College of Education, Department of Curriculum and Teaching, Auburn University, AL 36849. Offers business education (M Ed, MS, PhD); early childhood education (M Ed, MS, PhD, Ed S); elementary education (M Ed, MS, PhD, Ed S); foreign languages (M Ed, MS); music education (M Ed, MS, PhD, Ed S); postsecondary education (PhD); reading education (PhD, Ed S); secondary education (M Ed, MS, PhD, Ed S), including English language arts, mathematics, science, social studies. *Accreditation:* NASM (one or more programs are accredited); NCATE. Part-time programs available. *Faculty:* 22 full-time (17 women), 3 part-time/adjunct (all women). *Students:* 80 full-time (58 women), 181 part-time (126 women); includes 42 minority (28 Black or African American, non-Hispanic/Latino; 7 Asian, non-Hispanic/Latino; 7 Hispanic/Latino). Average age 34. 184 applicants, 53% accepted, 60 enrolled. In 2011, 77 master's, 10 doctorates, 35 other advanced degrees awarded. *Degree requirements:* For master's, thesis (for some programs); for doctorate, thesis/dissertation; for Ed S, field project. *Entrance requirements:* For master's, doctorate, and Ed S, GRE General Test. *Application deadline:* For fall admission, 7/7 for domestic students; for spring admission, 11/24 for domestic students. Applications are processed on a rolling basis. Application fee: $50 ($60 for international students). Electronic applications accepted. *Expenses:* Tuition, state resident: full-time $7290; part-time $405 per credit hour. Tuition, nonresident: full-time $21,870; part-time $1215 per credit hour. *International tuition:* $22,000 full-time. *Required fees:* $1402. *Financial support:* Fellowships, teaching assistantships, career-related internships or fieldwork, and Federal Work-Study. Support available to part-time students. Financial award application deadline: 3/15; financial award applicants required to submit FAFSA. *Faculty research:* Emerging literacy, reading attitudes, music for at-risk youth, portfolio assessment. *Unit head:* Dr. Kimberly Walls, Head, 334-844-4434. *Application contact:* Dr. George Flowers, Dean of the Graduate School, 334-844-2125. Web site: http://education.auburn.edu/academic_departments/curr/.

Auburn University Montgomery, School of Education, Department of Foundations, Secondary, and Physical Education, Montgomery, AL 36124-4023. Offers physical education (M Ed); secondary education (M Ed, Ed S). *Accreditation:* NCATE. Part-time and evening/weekend programs available. *Degree requirements:* For master's and Ed S, comprehensive exam, thesis optional. *Entrance requirements:* For master's, GRE General Test or MAT, certification, BS in teaching; for Ed S, GRE General Test or MAT, certification. Electronic applications accepted. *Expenses:* Tuition, state resident: full-time $5076. Tuition, nonresident: full-time $15,228.

Augusta State University, Graduate Studies, College of Education, Program in Teaching/Learning, Augusta, GA 30904-2200. Offers MAT, Ed S. *Faculty:* 11 full-time (6 women), 16 part-time/adjunct (14 women). *Students:* 222 full-time (179 women), 239 part-time (185 women); includes 158 minority (139 Black or African American, non-Hispanic/Latino; 2 American Indian or Alaska Native, non-Hispanic/Latino; 8 Asian, non-Hispanic/Latino; 9 Hispanic/Latino). 136 applicants, 94% accepted, 109 enrolled. In 2011, 70 master's, 50 other advanced degrees awarded. *Degree requirements:* For master's, thesis, portfolio. *Entrance requirements:* For master's, GRE, MAT, minimum GPA of 2.5. Application fee: $20. *Financial support:* Career-related internships or fieldwork, Federal Work-Study, institutionally sponsored loans, and unspecified assistantships available. Support available to part-time students. Financial award application deadline: 4/15. *Unit head:* Dr. J. Gordon Eisenman, Chair, 706-737-1496, Fax: 706-667-4706, E-mail: geisenman@aug.edu. *Application contact:* Andrea M. Scott, Secretary to the Dean, 706-737-1499, Fax: 706-667-4706, E-mail: ascott@aug.edu.

Austin College, Program in Education, Sherman, TX 75090-4400. Offers art education (MA); elementary education (MA); middle school education (MA); music education (MA); physical education and coaching (MA); secondary education (MA); theatre education (MA). Part-time programs available. *Faculty:* 5 full-time (4 women). *Students:* 21 full-time (13 women), 2 part-time (both women). Average age 23. In 2011, 24 master's awarded. *Degree requirements:* For master's, one foreign language, thesis or alternative. *Entrance requirements:* For master's, Texas Academic Skills Program Test. *Application deadline:* For fall admission, 5/1 priority date for domestic students; for spring admission, 1/15 priority date for domestic students. Applications are processed on a rolling basis. Application fee: $35. Electronic applications accepted. *Expenses: Tuition:* Full-time $38,445. *Required fees:* $160. *Financial support:* Career-related internships or fieldwork, Federal Work-Study, scholarships/grants, and unspecified assistantships available. Support available to part-time students. Financial award application deadline:

4/1; financial award applicants required to submit FAFSA. *Unit head:* Dr. Barbara Sylvester, Director of Teaching Program, 903-813-2327, E-mail: bsylvester@austincollege.edu. *Application contact:* Dr. Barbara Sylvester, Director of Teaching Program, 903-813-2327, E-mail: bsylvester@austincollege.edu. Web site: http://www.austincollege.edu/.

Austin Peay State University, College of Graduate Studies, College of Education, Department of Educational Specialties, Clarksville, TN 37044. Offers administration and supervision (Ed S); curriculum and instruction (MA Ed); education leadership (MA Ed); elementary education (Ed S); secondary education (Ed S); special education (MA Ed). Part-time and evening/weekend programs available. Postbaccalaureate distance learning degree programs offered. *Faculty:* 7 full-time (4 women), 4 part-time/adjunct (3 women). *Students:* 6 full-time (4 women), 86 part-time (66 women); includes 11 minority (6 Black or African American, non-Hispanic/Latino; 1 American Indian or Alaska Native, non-Hispanic/Latino; 4 Hispanic/Latino). Average age 37. 33 applicants, 100% accepted, 23 enrolled. In 2011, 32 master's, 7 Ed Ss awarded. *Degree requirements:* For master's, comprehensive exam, thesis optional. *Entrance requirements:* For master's, GRE General Test, 3 letters of recommendation, minimum undergraduate GPA of 2.75. Additional exam requirements/recommendations for international students: Required—TOEFL (minimum score 500 paper-based; 173 computer-based). *Application deadline:* For fall admission, 8/1 priority date for domestic students. Applications are processed on a rolling basis. Application fee: $25. Electronic applications accepted. *Expenses:* Tuition, state resident: part-time $350 per credit hour. Tuition, nonresident: full-time $20,644; part-time $971 per credit hour. *Required fees:* $1224; $61.20 per credit hour. *Financial support:* Career-related internships or fieldwork, Federal Work-Study, institutionally sponsored loans, scholarships/grants, and unspecified assistantships available. Support available to part-time students. Financial award application deadline: 3/1; financial award applicants required to submit FAFSA. *Unit head:* Dr. Moniqueka Gold, Chair, 931-221-7696, Fax: 931-221-1292, E-mail: goldm@apsu.edu. *Application contact:* Kendra Bryant, Graduate Admissions, 800-844-2778, Fax: 931-221-6188, E-mail: admissionsweb@apsu.edu.

Austin Peay State University, College of Graduate Studies, College of Education, Department of Teaching and Learning, Clarksville, TN 37044. Offers elementary education K-6 (MAT); reading (MA Ed); secondary education 7-12 (MAT); special education K-12 (MAT). Part-time and evening/weekend programs available. Postbaccalaureate distance learning degree programs offered. *Faculty:* 14 full-time (11 women), 3 part-time/adjunct (2 women). *Students:* 84 full-time (67 women), 97 part-time (81 women); includes 27 minority (12 Black or African American, non-Hispanic/Latino; 2 American Indian or Alaska Native, non-Hispanic/Latino; 2 Asian, non-Hispanic/Latino; 4 Hispanic/Latino; 1 Native Hawaiian or other Pacific Islander, non-Hispanic/Latino; 6 Two or more races, non-Hispanic/Latino). Average age 33. 61 applicants, 98% accepted, 51 enrolled. In 2011, 55 master's awarded. *Degree requirements:* For master's, comprehensive exam, thesis optional. *Entrance requirements:* For master's, GRE General Test, 3 letters of recommendation, minimum undergraduate GPA of 2.75. Additional exam requirements/recommendations for international students: Required—TOEFL (minimum score 500 paper-based; 173 computer-based). *Application deadline:* For fall admission, 8/1 priority date for domestic students. Applications are processed on a rolling basis. Application fee: $25. Electronic applications accepted. *Expenses:* Tuition, state resident: part-time $350 per credit hour. Tuition, nonresident: full-time $20,644; part-time $971 per credit hour. *Required fees:* $1224; $61.20 per credit hour. *Financial support:* Career-related internships or fieldwork, Federal Work-Study, institutionally sponsored loans, scholarships/grants, and unspecified assistantships available. Support available to part-time students. Financial award application deadline: 3/1; financial award applicants required to submit FAFSA. *Unit head:* Dr. Rebecca McMahan, Chair, 931-221-7513, Fax: 931-221-1292, E-mail: mcmahanb@apsu.edu. *Application contact:* Kendra Bryant, Graduate Admissions, 800-844-2778, Fax: 931-221-6188, E-mail: admissionsweb@apsu.edu.

Ball State University, Graduate School, Teachers College, Department of Educational Studies, Program in Secondary Education, Muncie, IN 47306-1099. Offers MA. *Accreditation:* NCATE. *Students:* 14 full-time (10 women), 50 part-time (33 women); includes 1 minority (Black or African American, non-Hispanic/Latino). Average age 30. 15 applicants, 80% accepted, 9 enrolled. In 2011, 28 master's awarded. Application fee: $50. Tuition and fees vary according to program and reciprocity agreements. *Financial support:* In 2011–12, 11 students received support, including 3 teaching assistantships (averaging $8,786 per year). Financial award application deadline: 3/1. *Unit head:* Jayne Beilke, Head, 785-285-5460, Fax: 785-285-5489. *Application contact:* Dr. Nicole Bell, Associate Provost for Research and Dean of the Graduate School. Web site: http://www.bsu.edu/teachers/departments/edstudies/.

Belhaven University, School of Education, Jackson, MS 39202-1789. Offers elementary education (M Ed, MAT); secondary education (M Ed, MAT). Part-time and evening/weekend programs available. *Faculty:* 7 full-time (6 women), 15 part-time/adjunct (10 women). *Students:* 167 full-time (133 women), 124 part-time (97 women); includes 205 minority (193 Black or African American, non-Hispanic/Latino; 7 Hispanic/Latino; 5 Two or more races, non-Hispanic/Latino). Average age 33. 446 applicants, 64% accepted, 210 enrolled. In 2011, 94 master's awarded. *Degree requirements:* For master's, comprehensive exam, portfolio. *Entrance requirements:* For master's, PRAXIS I and II, minimum GPA of 2.8. *Application deadline:* Applications are processed on a rolling basis. Application fee: $25. Electronic applications accepted. *Expenses: Tuition:* Part-time $545 per contact hour. *Financial support:* Federal Work-Study, scholarships/grants, tuition waivers (full), and unspecified assistantships available. Support available to part-time students. Financial award applicants required to submit FAFSA. *Unit head:* Dr. Sandra L. Rasberry, Dean, 601-968-8703, Fax: 601-974-6461, E-mail: srasberry@belhaven.edu. *Application contact:* Jenny Mixon, Director of Graduate and Online Admission, 601-968-8947, Fax: 601-968-5953, E-mail: gradadmission@belhaven.edu. Web site: http://graduateed.belhaven.edu.

Bellarmine University, Annsley Frazier Thornton School of Education, Louisville, KY 40205-0671. Offers early elementary education (MA Ed, MAT); education and social change (PhD); learning and behavior disorders (MA Ed, MAT); middle school education (MA Ed, MAT); principalship (Ed S); reading and writing endorsement (MA Ed); secondary school education (MAT); teacher leadership, grades P-12 (MA Ed). *Accreditation:* NCATE. Part-time and evening/weekend programs available. *Faculty:* 13 full-time (6 women), 12 part-time/adjunct (10 women). *Students:* 85 full-time (65 women), 186 part-time (144 women); includes 30 minority (22 Black or African American, non-Hispanic/Latino; 1 American Indian or Alaska Native, non-Hispanic/Latino; 6 Asian, non-Hispanic/Latino; 1 Hispanic/Latino). Average age 33. In 2011, 105 master's awarded. *Degree requirements:* For master's, comprehensive exam, thesis (for some programs); for doctorate, comprehensive exam, thesis/dissertation. *Entrance requirements:* For master's, GRE, baccalaureate degree from accredited institution; minimum overall GPA of 2.75, 3.0 in major; letters of recommendation; valid Kentucky provisional or professional certificate; for doctorate, GRE, minimum GPA of 3.5 in all graduate coursework completed at time of application; baccalaureate and master's degrees in education (MA, MS) or fields directly relevant to education; three letters of recommendation; two essays (no more than 1,000 words each); interview. Additional exam requirements/recommendations for international students: Required—TOEFL (minimum score 550 paper-based; 213 computer-based; 80 iBT). *Application deadline:* Applications are processed on a rolling basis. Application fee: $25. *Expenses:* Contact institution. *Financial support:* Scholarships/grants available. Financial award applicants required to submit FAFSA. *Faculty research:* Literacy, service-learning, dispositions, educational technology, special education. *Unit head:* Dr. Robert Cooter, Dean, 502-272-8191, Fax: 502-272-8189, E-mail: rcooter@bellarmine.edu. *Application contact:* Theresa Klapheke, Administrative Director of Graduate Programs, 502-272-8271, Fax: 502-272-8002, E-mail: tklapheke@bellarmine.edu. Web site: http://www.bellarmine.edu/education/graduate.

Belmont University, College of Arts and Sciences, Department of Education, Nashville, TN 37212-3757. Offers education (M Ed); elementary education (MAT), including early childhood education, elementary education, language arts education; English (MAT); history (MAT); mathematics (MAT); middle grade education (MAT); science (MAT); secondary education (MAT); special education (MAT); sports administration (MSA). *Accreditation:* NCATE. Part-time and evening/weekend programs available. *Faculty:* 11 full-time (8 women), 23 part-time/adjunct (12 women). *Students:* 83 full-time (77 women), 205 part-time (162 women); includes 50 minority (36 Black or African American, non-Hispanic/Latino; 1 American Indian or Alaska Native, non-Hispanic/Latino; 1 Asian, non-Hispanic/Latino; 7 Hispanic/Latino; 5 Two or more races, non-Hispanic/Latino), 2 international. Average age 30. 83 applicants, 67% accepted, 35 enrolled. In 2011, 169 master's awarded. *Degree requirements:* For master's, thesis (for some programs). *Entrance requirements:* For master's, MAT or GRE and/or GMAT, minimum GPA of 2.75. Additional exam requirements/recommendations for international students: Required—TOEFL. *Application deadline:* For fall admission, 8/1 priority date for domestic students, 6/1 for international students; for spring admission, 12/1 priority date for domestic students, 10/1 for international students. Applications are processed on a rolling basis. Application fee: $50. *Expenses:* Contact institution. *Financial support:* In 2011–12, 30 students received support. Fellowships with partial tuition reimbursements available, teaching assistantships with partial tuition reimbursements available, institutionally sponsored loans, tuition waivers (partial), and unspecified assistantships available. Financial award application deadline: 4/15; financial award applicants required to submit FAFSA. *Faculty research:* Improving secondary literacy, Montessori, classroom management strategies, teacher residency programs, online professional development, mentoring, leadership, faculty development. *Total annual research expenditures:* $2,500. *Unit head:* Dr. Cynthia R. Watkins, Associate Dean, 615-460-6053, Fax: 615-460-5556, E-mail: cynthia.watkins@belmont.edu. *Application contact:* Andrea McClain, Admission/Licensure Officer, 615-460-5483, Fax: 615-460-5556, E-mail: andrea.mcclain@belmont.edu.

Benedictine University, Graduate Programs, Program in Education, Lisle, IL 60532-0900. Offers curriculum and instruction and collaborative teaching (M Ed); elementary education (MA Ed); leadership and administration (M Ed); reading and literacy (M Ed); secondary education (MA Ed); special education (MA Ed). Part-time and evening/weekend programs available. *Faculty:* 4 full-time (2 women), 52 part-time/adjunct (30 women). *Students:* 178 full-time (157 women), 239 part-time (211 women); includes 41 minority (29 Black or African American, non-Hispanic/Latino; 4 Asian, non-Hispanic/Latino; 8 Hispanic/Latino), 2 international. Average age 33. 177 applicants, 44% accepted, 68 enrolled. In 2011, 278 master's awarded. *Degree requirements:* For master's, comprehensive exam, thesis (for some programs). *Entrance requirements:* For master's, GRE or MAT. Additional exam requirements/recommendations for international students: Required—TOEFL (minimum score 550 paper-based; 213 computer-based). *Application deadline:* For fall admission, 9/1 for domestic students; for winter admission, 12/1 for domestic students; for spring admission, 2/15 for domestic students. Applications are processed on a rolling basis. Application fee: $40. Electronic applications accepted. *Expenses:* Contact institution. *Financial support:* Career-related internships or fieldwork and health care benefits available. Support available to part-time students. *Unit head:* MeShelda Jackson, Director, 630-829-6282, E-mail: mjackson@ben.edu. *Application contact:* Kari Gibbons, Associate Vice President, Enrollment Center, 630-829-6200, Fax: 630-829-6584, E-mail: kgibbons@ben.edu.

Berry College, Graduate Programs, Graduate Programs in Education, Program in Secondary Education, Mount Berry, GA 30149-0159. Offers M Ed, MAT. *Faculty:* 7 part-time/adjunct (4 women). *Students:* 3 full-time (1 woman), 24 part-time (15 women); includes 1 minority (Black or African American, non-Hispanic/Latino). Average age 30. In 2011, 7 master's awarded. *Degree requirements:* For master's, thesis optional, oral exams. *Entrance requirements:* For master's, GRE General Test, MAT, or NTE, minimum GPA of 2.5. Additional exam requirements/recommendations for international students: Required—TOEFL (minimum score 550 paper-based; 213 computer-based). *Application deadline:* For fall admission, 5/1 for domestic and international students; for spring admission, 10/1 for domestic and international students. Applications are processed on a rolling basis. Application fee: $25 ($30 for international students). Electronic applications accepted. *Expenses:* Contact institution. *Financial support:* In 2011–12, 12 students received support, including 9 research assistantships with full tuition reimbursements available (averaging $4,102 per year); scholarships/grants, tuition waivers (partial), and unspecified assistantships also available. Support available to part-time students. Financial award application deadline: 3/1; financial award applicants required to submit FAFSA. *Faculty research:* Curriculum development, teacher training, pedagogy. *Unit head:* Dr. Jacqueline McDowell, Dean, Charter School of Education and Human Sciences, 706-236-1717, Fax: 706-238-5827, E-mail: jmcdowell@berry.edu. *Application contact:* Brett Kennedy, Director of Admissions, 706-236-2215, Fax: 706-290-2178, E-mail: admissions@berry.edu. Web site: http://www.berry.edu/academics/education/graduate/.

Bethel University, Graduate School, St. Paul, MN 55112-6999. Offers autism spectrum disorders (Certificate); business administration (MBA); communication (MA); counseling psychology (MA); education (M Ed); educational leadership (Ed D); gerontology (MA, Certificate); international baccalaureate education (Certificate); K-12 education (MA); literacy education (MA); nursing (MA); nursing education (Certificate); nursing leadership (Certificate); organizational leadership (MA); postsecondary teaching (Certificate); special education (MA); teaching (MA). Part-time and evening/weekend programs available. Postbaccalaureate distance learning degree programs offered (minimal on-campus study). *Faculty:* 8 full-time (3 women), 98 part-time/adjunct (46 women). *Students:* 651 full-time (419 women), 312 part-time (212 women); includes 79 minority (35 Black or African American, non-Hispanic/Latino; 2 American Indian or Alaska Native, non-Hispanic/Latino; 19 Asian, non-Hispanic/Latino; 17 Hispanic/Latino; 6 Two or more races, non-Hispanic/Latino), 6 international. Average age 36. In 2011, 245 master's, 4 doctorates, 32 other advanced degrees awarded. *Degree requirements:* For master's, comprehensive exam (for some programs), thesis (for some programs); for doctorate, comprehensive exam, thesis/dissertation. *Entrance requirements:* Additional exam requirements/recommendations for international students: Required—TOEFL (minimum score 550 paper-based; 213 computer-based; 80 iBT). *Application deadline:* Applications are processed on a rolling basis. Electronic applications accepted. Tuition and fees vary according to course load, degree level and program. *Financial support:* Applicants required to submit FAFSA. *Unit head:* Dick Crombie, Vice-President/Dean, 651-635-8000, Fax: 651-635-8004, E-mail: gs@bethel.edu. *Application contact:* Paul Ives, Director of Admissions, 651-635-8000, Fax: 651-635-8004, E-mail: gs@bethel.edu. Web site: http://gs.bethel.edu/.

Bob Jones University, Graduate Programs, Greenville, SC 29614. Offers accountancy (MS); Bible (MA); Bible translation (MA); Biblical studies (Certificate); broadcast management (MS); business administration (MBA); church history (MA, PhD); church ministries (MA); church music (MM); cinema and video production (MA); counseling (MS); curriculum and instruction (Ed D); divinity (M Div); dramatic production (MA); educational leadership (MS, Ed D, Ed S); elementary education (M Ed, MAT); English (M Ed, MA, MAT); fine arts (MA); graphic design (MA); history (M Ed, MA); illustration (MA); interpretative speech (MA); mathematics (M Ed, MAT); medical missions (Certificate); ministry (MM, D Min); multi-categorical special education (M Ed, MAT); music (M Ed); New Testament interpretation (PhD); Old Testament interpretation (PhD); orchestral instrument performance (MM); organ performance (MM); pastoral studies (MA); personnel services (MS, Ed S); piano pedagogy (MM); piano performance (MM); platform arts (MA); radio and television broadcasting (MS); rhetoric and public address (MA); secondary education (M Ed); studio art (MA); teaching Bible (MA); theology (MA, PhD); voice performance (MM); youth ministries (MA); M Div/MM.

Boston College, Lynch Graduate School of Education, Program in Secondary Education, Chestnut Hill, MA 02467-3800. Offers M Ed, MAT, MST. *Accreditation:* Teacher Education Accreditation Council. Part-time and evening/weekend programs available. *Students:* 76 full-time (52 women), 34 part-time (17 women); includes 21 minority (10 Black or African American, non-Hispanic/Latino; 2 Asian, non-Hispanic/Latino; 7 Hispanic/Latino; 2 Two or more races, non-Hispanic/Latino), 1 international. 308 applicants, 56% accepted, 74 enrolled. In 2011, 63 degrees awarded. *Degree requirements:* For master's, comprehensive exam. *Entrance requirements:* For master's, GRE General Test or MAT. Additional exam requirements/recommendations for international students: Required—TOEFL (minimum score 550 paper-based; 213 computer-based; 79 iBT). *Application deadline:* For fall admission, 1/1 priority date for domestic students. Application fee: $65. Electronic applications accepted. *Financial support:* Fellowships with full and partial tuition reimbursements, research assistantships with full and partial tuition reimbursements, teaching assistantships with full and partial tuition reimbursements, career-related internships or fieldwork, Federal Work-Study, institutionally sponsored loans, scholarships/grants, traineeships, health care benefits, tuition waivers (full and partial), and unspecified assistantships available. Support available to part-time students. Financial award applicants required to submit FAFSA. *Faculty research:* School reform, urban science education, teacher research, critical literacy, poverty and achievement. *Unit head:* Dr. Maria E. Brisk, Chairperson, 617-552-4214, Fax: 617-552-0398. *Application contact:* Adam Poluzzi, Director, Graduate Admission and Financial Aid, 617-552-4214, Fax: 617-552-0398, E-mail: poluzzi@bc.edu.

Bowie State University, Graduate Programs, Program in Secondary Education, Bowie, MD 20715-9465. Offers M Ed. *Accreditation:* NCATE. Part-time and evening/weekend programs available. *Faculty:* 1 full-time (0 women). *Students:* 16 part-time (10 women); includes 8 minority (all Black or African American, non-Hispanic/Latino), 4 international. Average age 37. 3 applicants, 100% accepted, 2 enrolled. In 2011, 6 master's awarded. *Degree requirements:* For master's, comprehensive exam, thesis optional, research paper. *Entrance requirements:* For master's, minimum undergraduate GPA of 3.0, bachelor's degree in education, teaching certificate, teaching experience. *Application deadline:* For fall admission, 4/1 priority date for domestic students, 4/1 for international students; for spring admission, 11/1 priority date for domestic students, 11/1 for international students. Applications are processed on a rolling basis. Application fee: $40. Electronic applications accepted. *Expenses:* Tuition, state resident: full-time $4140; part-time $3105 per semester. Tuition, nonresident: full-time $7836; part-time $5877 per semester. *Required fees:* $1715; $648 per semester. *Financial support:* Application deadline: 4/1. *Unit head:* Dr. Bruce Crim, Coordinator, 301-860-3127, E-mail: bcrim@bowiestate.edu. *Application contact:* Angela Issac, Information Contact, 301-860-4000.

Brandeis University, Graduate School of Arts and Sciences, Teaching Program, Waltham, MA 02454-9110. Offers elementary education (public) (MAT); Jewish day school (MAT); secondary education (MAT), including Bible, biology, chemistry, Chinese, English, history, math, physics. *Faculty:* 5 full-time (3 women), 9 part-time/adjunct (6 women). *Students:* 31 full-time (23 women); includes 3 minority (2 Asian, non-Hispanic/Latino; 1 Hispanic/Latino), 3 international. 76 applicants, 67% accepted, 31 enrolled. In 2011, 23 master's awarded. *Degree requirements:* For master's, internship; research project. *Entrance requirements:* For master's, GRE General Test or Miller Analogies Test, official transcript(s), 3 letters of recommendation, resume, statement of purpose. Additional exam requirements/recommendations for international students: Required—TOEFL (minimum score 600 paper-based; 250 computer-based; 100 iBT); Recommended—IELTS (minimum score 7). *Application deadline:* Applications are processed on a rolling basis. Application fee: $75. Electronic applications accepted. *Expenses:* Contact institution. *Financial support:* Scholarships/grants and tuition waivers (partial) available. Financial award applicants required to submit FAFSA. *Faculty research:* Teacher education, education, teaching, elementary education, secondary education, Jewish education, English, history, biology, chemistry, physics, math, Chinese, Bible/Tanakh. *Unit head:* Prof. Marya Levenson, Director, 781-736-2020, Fax: 781-736-5020, E-mail: mlevenso@brandeis.edu. *Application contact:* Manuel Tuan, Department Administrator, 781-736-2633, Fax: 781-736-5020, E-mail: tuan@brandeis.edu. Web site: http://www.brandeis.edu/programs/mat.

Brenau University, Sydney O. Smith Graduate School, School of Education, Gainesville, GA 30501. Offers early childhood (Ed S); early childhood education (M Ed, MAT); middle grades (Ed S); middle grades education (M Ed, MAT); secondary education (MAT); special education (M Ed, MAT). *Accreditation:* NCATE. Part-time and evening/weekend programs available. Postbaccalaureate distance learning degree programs offered (no on-campus study). *Degree requirements:* For master's, thesis optional, comprehensive exam or applied research project, effective portfolio; for Ed S, thesis, applied research project. *Entrance requirements:* For master's, GRE, MAT, interview, minimum GPA of 3.0, 3 references, writing samples; for Ed S, GRE, MAT, master's degree, minimum GPA of 3.0, writing sample, letters of reference. Additional exam requirements/recommendations for international students: Required—TOEFL (minimum score 500 paper-based; 173 computer-based; 61 iBT); Recommended—IELTS (minimum score 5). Electronic applications accepted. *Expenses:* Contact institution.

Bridgewater State University, School of Graduate Studies, School of Education and Allied Studies, Department of Secondary Education and Professional Programs, Program in Secondary Education, Bridgewater, MA 02325-0001. Offers MAT. *Accreditation:* NCATE. Part-time and evening/weekend programs available. *Entrance requirements:* For master's, GRE General Test.

Brooklyn College of the City University of New York, Division of Graduate Studies, School of Education, Program in Adolescence Education and Special Subjects, Brooklyn, NY 11210-2889. Offers adolescence science education (MAT); art teacher (MA); biology teacher (MA); chemistry teacher (MA); earth science teacher (MAT); English teacher (MA); French teacher (MA); health and nutrition sciences: health teacher (MS Ed); mathematics teacher (MA); music education (CAS); music teacher (MA); physical education teacher (MS Ed); physics teacher (MA); social studies teacher (MA); Spanish teacher (MA). Part-time and evening/weekend programs available. *Degree requirements:* For master's, comprehensive exam (for some programs), thesis (for some programs). *Entrance requirements:* For master's, LAST, previous course work in education, resume, 2 letters of recommendation, essay. Additional exam requirements/recommendations for international students: Required—TOEFL (minimum score 500 paper-based; 173 computer-based; 61 iBT). Electronic applications accepted. *Faculty research:* Interdisciplinary education, semiotics, discourse analysis, autobiography, teacher identity.

Brown University, Graduate School, Department of Education, Providence, RI 02912. Offers teaching (MAT), including biology, elementary education, English, history/social studies; urban education policy (AM). *Degree requirements:* For master's, student teaching, portfolio. *Entrance requirements:* For master's, GRE General Test, letters of recommendation, interview. Additional exam requirements/recommendations for international students: Recommended—TOEFL.

Butler University, College of Education, Indianapolis, IN 46208-3485. Offers administration (MS); elementary education (MS); reading (MS); school counseling (MS); secondary education (MS); special education (MS). *Accreditation:* ACA; NCATE. Part-time and evening/weekend programs available. *Faculty:* 7 full-time (4 women), 5 part-time/adjunct (all women). *Students:* 9 full-time (6 women), 136 part-time (105 women); includes 21 minority (14 Black or African American, non-Hispanic/Latino; 5 Asian, non-Hispanic/Latino; 1 Hispanic/Latino; 1 Two or more races, non-Hispanic/Latino), 1 international. Average age 31. 69 applicants, 94% accepted, 24 enrolled. In 2011, 66 master's awarded. *Entrance requirements:* For master's, GRE General Test, MAT, interview. *Application deadline:* For fall admission, 8/15 priority date for domestic students. Applications are processed on a rolling basis. Application fee: $35. Electronic applications accepted. *Expenses: Tuition:* Part-time $466 per credit. *Financial support:* Institutionally sponsored loans available. Support available to part-time students. Financial award application deadline: 7/15; financial award applicants required to submit FAFSA. *Faculty research:* Ethics in cybercounseling, history of sports for disabled, effect of fetal alcohol syndrome on perceptual learning, reading recovery's theoretical framework in teacher education. *Unit head:* Dr. Ena Shelley, Dean, 317-940-9752, Fax: 317-940-6481. *Application contact:* Karen Farrell, Department Secretary, 317-940-9220, E-mail: kfarrell@butler.edu.

California State University, Bakersfield, Division of Graduate Studies, School of Natural Sciences, Mathematics, and Engineering, Program in Teaching Mathematics, Bakersfield, CA 93311. Offers MA. *Entrance requirements:* For master's, minimum GPA of 2.5 for last 90 quarter units. *Expenses: Required fees:* $1302 per unit. Part-time tuition and fees vary according to course load and program. *Unit head:* Dr. Joseph Fiedler, Head, 661-654-2058, Fax: 661-664-2039. Web site: http://www.csub.edu/math/GradProgram.shtml.

California State University, Fullerton, Graduate Studies, College of Education, Department of Secondary Education, Fullerton, CA 92834-9480. Offers middle school mathematics (MS); secondary education (MS); teacher induction (MS). Part-time programs available. *Students:* 1 (woman) full-time, 39 part-time (34 women); includes 17 minority (1 Black or African American, non-Hispanic/Latino; 6 Asian, non-Hispanic/Latino; 10 Hispanic/Latino). Average age 30. 17 applicants, 65% accepted, 9 enrolled. In 2011, 16 master's awarded. Application fee: $55. *Financial support:* Career-related internships or fieldwork, Federal Work-Study, institutionally sponsored loans, and scholarships/grants available. Support available to part-time students. Financial award application deadline: 3/1; financial award applicants required to submit FAFSA. *Unit head:* Dr. Mark Ellis, Chair, 657-278-2745. *Application contact:* Admissions/Applications, 657-278-2371.

California State University, Long Beach, Graduate Studies, College of Education, Department of Teacher Education, Long Beach, CA 90840. Offers elementary education (MA); secondary education (MA). Part-time and evening/weekend programs available. *Faculty:* 13 full-time (10 women), 2 part-time/adjunct (1 woman). *Students:* 27 full-time (24 women), 217 part-time (186 women); includes 156 minority (13 Black or African American, non-Hispanic/Latino; 12 American Indian or Alaska Native, non-Hispanic/Latino; 26 Asian, non-Hispanic/Latino; 91 Hispanic/Latino; 10 Native Hawaiian or other Pacific Islander, non-Hispanic/Latino; 4 Two or more races, non-Hispanic/Latino), 4 international. Average age 33. 145 applicants, 66% accepted, 89 enrolled. In 2011, 122 master's awarded. *Degree requirements:* For master's, comprehensive exam or thesis. *Entrance requirements:* For master's, GRE General Test, minimum GPA of 2.75. *Application deadline:* For fall admission, 7/1 for domestic students; for spring admission, 12/1 for domestic students. Applications are processed on a rolling basis. Application fee: $55. Electronic applications accepted. *Financial support:* Federal Work-Study, institutionally sponsored loans, and scholarships/grants available. Financial award application deadline: 3/2. *Faculty research:* Teacher stress and burnout, new teacher induction. *Unit head:* Dr. Catherine DuCharme, Chair, 562-985-4506, Fax: 562-985-1774, E-mail: ducharme@csulb.edu. *Application contact:* Nancy L. McGlothin, Coordinator for Graduate Studies and Research, 562-985-8476, Fax: 562-985-4951, E-mail: nmcgloth@csulb.edu.

California State University, Long Beach, Graduate Studies, College of Natural Sciences and Mathematics, Department of Mathematics and Statistics, Long Beach, CA 90840. Offers mathematics (MS), including applied mathematics, applied statistics, mathematics education for secondary school teachers. Part-time programs available. *Faculty:* 21 full-time (5 women), 1 (woman) part-time/adjunct. *Students:* 67 full-time (31 women), 115 part-time (47 women); includes 95 minority (5 Black or African American, non-Hispanic/Latino; 1 American Indian or Alaska Native, non-Hispanic/Latino; 53 Asian, non-Hispanic/Latino; 29 Hispanic/Latino; 2 Native Hawaiian or other Pacific Islander, non-Hispanic/Latino; 5 Two or more races, non-Hispanic/Latino), 14 international. Average age 31. 162 applicants, 69% accepted, 58 enrolled. In 2011, 41 master's awarded. *Degree requirements:* For master's, comprehensive exam or thesis. *Application deadline:* For fall admission, 7/1 for domestic students; for spring admission, 12/1 for domestic students. Applications are processed on a rolling basis. Application fee: $55. Electronic applications accepted. *Financial support:* Teaching assistantships, Federal Work-Study, institutionally sponsored loans, scholarships/grants, and traineeships available. Financial award application deadline: 3/2. *Faculty research:* Algebra, functional analysis, partial differential equations, operator theory, numerical analysis. *Unit head:* Dr. Robert Mena, Chair, 562-985-4721, Fax: 562-985-8227, E-mail: rmena@csulb.edu. *Application contact:* Dr. Ngo Viet, Graduate Associate Chair, 562-985-4721, Fax: 562-985-8227, E-mail: viet@csulb.edu.

California State University, Los Angeles, Graduate Studies, Charter College of Education, Division of Curriculum and Instruction, Los Angeles, CA 90032-8530. Offers elementary teaching (MA); reading (MA); secondary teaching (MA). Part-time and evening/weekend programs available. *Faculty:* 12 full-time (7 women), 5 part-time/adjunct (3 women). *Students:* 218 full-time (157 women), 156 part-time (118 women); includes 305 minority (20 Black or African American, non-Hispanic/Latino; 1 American Indian or Alaska Native, non-Hispanic/Latino; 59 Asian, non-Hispanic/Latino; 216 Hispanic/Latino; 9 Two or more races, non-Hispanic/Latino), 5 international. Average age 31. 93 applicants, 59% accepted, 52 enrolled. In 2011, 117 master's awarded. *Entrance requirements:* For master's, minimum GPA of 2.75 in last 90 units of course work, teaching certificate. Additional exam requirements/recommendations for international students: Required—TOEFL (minimum score 500 paper-based; 173

computer-based). *Application deadline:* For fall admission, 5/1 for domestic and international students. Applications are processed on a rolling basis. Application fee: $55. Electronic applications accepted. *Expenses:* Tuition, state resident: full-time $8225. *Financial support:* Federal Work-Study available. Support available to part-time students. Financial award application deadline: 3/1. *Faculty research:* Media, language arts, mathematics, computers, drug-free schools. *Unit head:* Dr. Robert Land, Chair, 323-343-4350, Fax: 323-343-5458, E-mail: rland@calstatela.edu. *Application contact:* Dr. Karin Brown, Acting Associate Dean of Graduate Studies, 323-343-3820 Ext. 3827, Fax: 323-343-5653, E-mail: kbrown5@calstatela.edu. Web site: http://www.calstatela.edu/academic/ccoe/index_edci.htm.

California State University, Northridge, Graduate Studies, College of Education, Department of Secondary Education, Northridge, CA 91330. Offers educational technology (MA); English education (MA); mathematics education (MA); secondary science education (MA); teaching and learning (MA). *Accreditation:* NCATE. Part-time programs available. *Degree requirements:* For master's, thesis optional. *Entrance requirements:* For master's, GRE General Test or minimum GPA of 3.0. Additional exam requirements/recommendations for international students: Required—TOEFL.

California State University, San Bernardino, Graduate Studies, College of Education, San Bernardino, CA 92407-2397. Offers bilingual/cross-cultural education (MA); curriculum and instruction (MA); educational administration (MA); educational leadership and curriculum (Ed D); educational psychology and counseling (MA, MS), including correctional and alternative education (MA), counseling and guidance (MS), rehabilitation counseling (MA); English as a second language (MA); general education (MA); history and English for secondary teachers (MA); instructional technology (MA); reading (MA); secondary education (MA); special education and rehabilitation counseling (MA), including rehabilitation counseling, special education; teaching of science (MA); vocational and career education (MA). *Accreditation:* NCATE. Part-time and evening/weekend programs available. *Students:* 434 full-time (335 women), 188 part-time (139 women); includes 271 minority (54 Black or African American, non-Hispanic/Latino; 2 American Indian or Alaska Native, non-Hispanic/Latino; 29 Asian, non-Hispanic/Latino; 172 Hispanic/Latino; 2 Native Hawaiian or other Pacific Islander, non-Hispanic/Latino; 12 Two or more races, non-Hispanic/Latino), 28 international. Average age 32. 382 applicants, 61% accepted, 186 enrolled. In 2011, 279 master's awarded. *Degree requirements:* For master's, comprehensive exam (for some programs), thesis (for some programs), advancement to candidacy. *Entrance requirements:* For master's, minimum GPA of 3.0 in education. *Application deadline:* For fall admission, 8/31 priority date for domestic students. Application fee: $55. *Expenses:* Tuition, state resident: full-time $7356. Tuition, nonresident: full-time $7356. *Required fees:* $1077. Tuition and fees vary according to program. *Financial support:* Career-related internships or fieldwork and Federal Work-Study available. Support available to part-time students. *Faculty research:* Multicultural education, brain-based learning, science education, social studies/global education. *Unit head:* Dr. Patricia Arlin, Dean, 909-537-5600, Fax: 909-537-7011, E-mail: parlin@csusb.edu. *Application contact:* Olivia Rosas, Director of Admissions, 909-537-7577, Fax: 909-537-7034, E-mail: orosas@csusb.edu.

California State University, Stanislaus, College of Education, Program in Education (MA), Turlock, CA 95382. Offers curriculum and instruction (MA), including education technology, elementary education, multilingual education, physical education, reading, secondary education, special education; school administration (MA); school counseling (MA). Part-time and evening/weekend programs available. *Degree requirements:* For master's, comprehensive exam (for some programs), thesis (for some programs). *Entrance requirements:* For master's, MAT, GRE, or CBEST (varies by concentration), 3 letters of recommendation, personal statement. Additional exam requirements/recommendations for international students: Required—TOEFL (minimum score 550 paper-based; 213 computer-based). *Application deadline:* For fall admission, 5/1 for domestic students; for spring admission, 1/7 for domestic students. Application fee: $55. Electronic applications accepted. *Expenses: Required fees:* $4616 per year. *Financial support:* Federal Work-Study available. Financial award application deadline: 3/1; financial award applicants required to submit FAFSA. *Faculty research:* Children's perspectives on historical events, method elementary schools dual language education, K-12 reading and CYRM programs. *Unit head:* Dr. Kathy Norman, Dean, College of Education, 209-667-3652, Fax: 209-664-6613, E-mail: coe@csustan.edu. *Application contact:* Graduate School, 209-667-3129, Fax: 209-664-7025, E-mail: graduate_school@csustan.edu. Web site: http://www.csustan.edu/COE/.

California State University, Stanislaus, College of Humanities and Social Sciences, Program in History (MA), Turlock, CA 95382. Offers history (MA); international relations (MA); secondary school teachers (MA). Part-time programs available. *Degree requirements:* For master's, comprehensive exam, thesis or alternative. *Entrance requirements:* For master's, GRE, minimum GPA of 3.0, personal statement. Additional exam requirements/recommendations for international students: Required—TOEFL (minimum score 575 paper-based; 233 computer-based). *Application deadline:* For fall admission, 5/1 for domestic students; for spring admission, 1/7 for domestic students. Application fee: $55. Electronic applications accepted. *Expenses: Required fees:* $4616 per year. *Financial support:* Fellowships and Federal Work-Study available. Financial award application deadline: 3/1; financial award applicants required to submit FAFSA. *Faculty research:* History of Ancient Greece, history and ecology of the Central Valley, acculturation and gender. *Unit head:* Dr. Bret Carroll, Chair, 209-667-3238, Fax: 209-667-3132, E-mail: bcarroll@csustan.edu. *Application contact:* Graduate School, 209-667-3129, Fax: 209-664-7025. Web site: http://www.csustan.edu/history/.

California University of Pennsylvania, School of Graduate Studies and Research, College of Education and Human Services, Department of Secondary Education and Administrative Leadership, California, PA 15419-1394. Offers MAT. Part-time and evening/weekend programs available. Postbaccalaureate distance learning degree programs offered (no on-campus study). *Degree requirements:* For master's, comprehensive exam, thesis. *Entrance requirements:* For master's, PRAXIS, minimum GPA of 3.0, clearances. Additional exam requirements/recommendations for international students: Required—TOEFL (minimum score 550 paper-based; 213 computer-based; 80 iBT). Electronic applications accepted. *Faculty research:* The effectiveness of online instruction, student-centered instruction strategies in secondary education, computer technology in education, environmental education, multi-media in education.

Campbell University, Graduate and Professional Programs, School of Education, Buies Creek, NC 27506. Offers administration (MSA); community counseling (MA); elementary education (M Ed); English education (M Ed); interdisciplinary studies (M Ed); mathematics education (M Ed); middle grades education (M Ed); physical education (M Ed); school counseling (M Ed); secondary education (M Ed); social science education (M Ed). *Accreditation:* NCATE. Part-time and evening/weekend programs available. *Degree requirements:* For master's, comprehensive exam. *Entrance requirements:* For master's, GRE General Test, minimum GPA of 2.7. *Faculty research:* Spiritual values and wellness issues in counseling, stress and professional burnout among counselors, thinking strategies, leadership, adaptive technology.

Canisius College, Graduate Division, School of Education and Human Services, Department of Graduate Education and Leadership, Buffalo, NY 14208-1098. Offers college student personnel (MS Ed); deaf education (MS Ed); deaf/adolescent education, grades 7-12 (MS Ed); deaf/childhood education, grades 1-6 (MS Ed); differential instruction (MS Ed); education administration (MS Ed); gifted education extention (Certificate); literacy (MS Ed); reading (Certificate); school building leadership (MS Ed, Certificate); school district leadership (Certificate). *Accreditation:* NCATE. Part-time and evening/weekend programs available. Postbaccalaureate distance learning degree programs offered (minimal on-campus study). *Faculty:* 7 full-time (6 women), 36 part-time/adjunct (22 women). *Students:* 149 full-time (114 women), 242 part-time (177 women); includes 42 minority (29 Black or African American, non-Hispanic/Latino; 2 American Indian or Alaska Native, non-Hispanic/Latino; 3 Asian, non-Hispanic/Latino; 6 Hispanic/Latino; 2 Two or more races, non-Hispanic/Latino), 3 international. Average age 30. 250 applicants, 84% accepted, 124 enrolled. In 2011, 135 degrees awarded. *Entrance requirements:* For master's, GRE if cumulative GPA less than 2.7, transcripts, two letters of recommendation. Additional exam requirements/recommendations for international students: Required—TOEFL. *Application deadline:* Applications are processed on a rolling basis. Application fee: $25. Electronic applications accepted. *Financial support:* Career-related internships or fieldwork, Federal Work-Study, scholarships/grants, tuition waivers (partial), and unspecified assistantships available. Support available to part-time students. Financial award application deadline: 4/30; financial award applicants required to submit FAFSA. *Faculty research:* Asperger's disease, autism, private higher education, reading strategies. *Unit head:* Dr. Rosemary K. Murray, Chair/Associate Professor of Graduate Education and Leadership, 716-888-3723, E-mail: murray1@canisius.edu. *Application contact:* Jim Bagwell, Director of Graduate Recruitment and Admissions, 716-888-2544, Fax: 716-888-3290, E-mail: bagwellj@canisius.edu. Web site: http://www.canisius.edu/education/graduate.asp.

Carlow University, School of Education, Program in Education, Pittsburgh, PA 15213-3165. Offers art education (M Ed); early childhood education (M Ed); instructional technology specialist (M Ed); middle level education (M Ed); secondary education (M Ed); special education (M Ed). Part-time and evening/weekend programs available. *Students:* 72 full-time (58 women), 16 part-time (13 women); includes 16 minority (15 Black or African American, non-Hispanic/Latino; 1 Hispanic/Latino). Average age 32. 68 applicants, 28% accepted, 11 enrolled. In 2011, 41 master's awarded. *Entrance requirements:* For master's, resume, 3 letters of recommendation, minimum GPA of 3.0, interview. Additional exam requirements/recommendations for international students: Required—TOEFL. *Application deadline:* For fall admission, 6/15 priority date for domestic students, 6/15 for international students; for spring admission, 11/15 priority date for domestic students, 11/15 for international students. Applications are processed on a rolling basis. Application fee: $20. Electronic applications accepted. *Expenses: Tuition:* Full-time $10,290; part-time $686 per credit. Tuition and fees vary according to course load, degree level and program. *Financial support:* Applicants required to submit FAFSA. *Unit head:* Dr. Marilyn J. Llewellyn, Director, 412-578-6011, Fax: 412-578-0816, E-mail: llewellynmj@carlow.edu. *Application contact:* Jo Danhires, Administrative Assistant, Admissions, 412-578-6089, Fax: 412-578-6321, E-mail: gradstudies@carlow.edu. Web site: http://www.carlow.edu.

Carson-Newman College, Graduate Program in Education, Jefferson City, TN 37760. Offers curriculum and instruction (M Ed); educational leadership (M Ed); elementary education (MAT); school counseling (MS); secondary education (MAT); teaching English as a second language (MATESL). *Accreditation:* NCATE. Part-time and evening/weekend programs available. *Faculty:* 5 full-time (2 women), 10 part-time/adjunct (3 women). *Students:* 85 full-time (55 women), 76 part-time (53 women); includes 8 minority (5 Black or African American, non-Hispanic/Latino; 2 Asian, non-Hispanic/Latino; 1 Two or more races, non-Hispanic/Latino), 23 international. Average age 32. 80 applicants, 96% accepted. In 2011, 90 master's awarded. *Degree requirements:* For master's, thesis or alternative. *Entrance requirements:* For master's, NTE, minimum GPA of 3.0 in major, 2.5 overall. *Application deadline:* For fall admission, 7/15 priority date for domestic students. Applications are processed on a rolling basis. Application fee: $25 ($50 for international students). *Expenses: Tuition:* Full-time $6750; part-time $375 per credit hour. *Required fees:* $200. *Financial support:* In 2011–12, 41 students received support. Federal Work-Study and unspecified assistantships available. Financial award application deadline: 4/1; financial award applicants required to submit FAFSA. *Unit head:* Dr. Sharon Teets, Chair, 865-471-3461. *Application contact:* Graduate Admissions and Services Adviser, 865-471-3460, Fax: 865-471-3875.

The Catholic University of America, School of Arts and Sciences, Department of Education, Washington, DC 20064. Offers Catholic educational leadership and policy studies (PhD); Catholic school leadership (MA); education (Certificate); educational psychology (PhD); secondary education (MA); special education (MA). *Accreditation:* NCATE. Part-time programs available. *Faculty:* 10 full-time (8 women), 10 part-time/adjunct (8 women). *Students:* 4 full-time (all women), 44 part-time (34 women); includes 12 minority (6 Black or African American, non-Hispanic/Latino; 4 Hispanic/Latino; 2 Two or more races, non-Hispanic/Latino). Average age 39. 38 applicants, 24% accepted, 2 enrolled. In 2011, 5 master's, 4 doctorates, 3 other advanced degrees awarded. *Degree requirements:* For master's, comprehensive exam, thesis or alternative; for doctorate, comprehensive exam, thesis/dissertation; for Certificate, action research project. *Entrance requirements:* For master's and doctorate, GRE General Test or MAT, statement of purpose, official copies of academic transcripts, three letters of recommendation, interview; for Certificate, PRAXIS I, statement of purpose, official copies of academic transcripts, three letters of recommendation, interview. Additional exam requirements/recommendations for international students: Required—TOEFL (minimum score 580 paper-based; 237 computer-based). *Application deadline:* For fall admission, 8/1 priority date for domestic students, 7/15 for international students; for spring admission, 12/1 priority date for domestic students, 10/15 for international students. Applications are processed on a rolling basis. Application fee: $55. Electronic applications accepted. *Expenses: Tuition:* Full-time $35,260; part-time $1380 per credit. *Required fees:* $80; $40 per semester hour. One-time fee: $425. *Financial support:* Fellowships, research assistantships, teaching assistantships, Federal Work-Study, scholarships/grants, tuition waivers (full and partial), and unspecified assistantships available. Financial award application deadline: 2/1; financial award applicants required to submit FAFSA. *Faculty research:* Special education, early childhood education, educational psychology, Catholic school administration, leadership and policy studies, counseling, curriculum and instruction. *Total annual research expenditures:* $36,210. *Unit head:* Dr. Merylann J. Schuttloffel, Chair, 202-319-5805, Fax: 202-319-5815, E-mail: schuttloffel@cua.edu. *Application contact:* Andrew Woodall, Director of Graduate Admissions, 202-319-5057, Fax: 202-319-6533, E-mail: cua-admissions@cua.edu. Web site: http://education.cua.edu/.

Centenary College of Louisiana, Graduate Programs, Department of Education, Shreveport, LA 71104. Offers administration (M Ed); elementary education (MAT); secondary education (MAT); supervision of instruction (M Ed). Part-time and evening/weekend programs available. *Degree requirements:* For master's, comprehensive exam. *Entrance requirements:* For master's, GRE General Test (M Ed), PRAXIS I and PRAXIS II (MAT), teacher certification (M Ed), minimum GPA of 2.5. *Expenses:* Contact institution. *Faculty research:* Teachers as advocates for teachers, portfolio assessment, disabled readers.

Central Connecticut State University, School of Graduate Studies, School of Education and Professional Studies, Department of Teacher Education, Program in Educational Foundations Policy/Secondary Education, New Britain, CT 06050-4010. Offers MS. Part-time and evening/weekend programs available. *Students:* 11 part-time (7 women). Average age 37. In 2011, 8 master's awarded. *Degree requirements:* For master's, comprehensive exam, thesis or alternative. *Entrance requirements:* For master's, minimum undergraduate GPA of 2.7. Additional exam requirements/recommendations for international students: Required—TOEFL (minimum score 550 paper-based; 213 computer-based). *Application deadline:* For fall admission, 6/1 for domestic students, 5/1 for international students; for spring admission, 11/1 for domestic and international students. Applications are processed on a rolling basis. Application fee: $50. Electronic applications accepted. *Expenses: Tuition, area resident:* Full-time $5137; part-time $482 per credit. Tuition, state resident: full-time $7707; part-time $494 per credit. Tuition, nonresident: full-time $14,311; part-time $494 per credit. *Required fees:* $3865. One-time fee: $62 part-time. *Unit head:* Dr. Ronnie Casella, Chair, 860-832-2415, E-mail: casellar@ccsu.edu. *Application contact:* Patricia Gardner, Associate Director of Graduate Studies, 860-832-2350, Fax: 860-832-2352, E-mail: graduateadmissions@ccsu.edu.

Central Michigan University, College of Graduate Studies, College of Education and Human Services, Department of Teacher Education and Professional Development, Mount Pleasant, MI 48859. Offers educational technology (MA, Graduate Certificate); elementary education (MA), including classroom teaching, early childhood; middle level education (MA); reading and literacy K-12 (MA); secondary education (MA). Part-time and evening/weekend programs available. *Degree requirements:* For master's, thesis or alternative. Electronic applications accepted. *Faculty research:* Integrating literacy across the curriculum, science teaching and aesthetic learning in science, diversity education, educational technology, educational psychology and child development.

Central Michigan University, College of Graduate Studies, College of Science and Technology, Department of Chemistry, Mount Pleasant, MI 48859. Offers chemistry (MS); teaching chemistry (MA), including teaching college chemistry, teaching high school chemistry. Part-time programs available. *Degree requirements:* For master's, comprehensive exam, thesis or alternative. *Entrance requirements:* For master's, GRE. Electronic applications accepted. *Faculty research:* Analytical and organic-inorganic chemistry, biochemistry, catalysis, dendrimer and polymer studies, nanotechnology.

Chadron State College, School of Professional and Graduate Studies, Department of Education, Chadron, NE 69337. Offers business (MA Ed); community counseling (MA Ed); educational administration (MS Ed, Sp Ed); elementary education (MS Ed); history (MA Ed); language and literature (MA Ed); secondary administration (MS Ed); secondary education (MS Ed). *Accreditation:* NCATE. Part-time and evening/weekend programs available. Postbaccalaureate distance learning degree programs offered. *Degree requirements:* For master's, thesis optional. *Entrance requirements:* For master's, GRE General Test, GRE Writing Test, minimum GPA of 2.75 or 12 graduate hours at CSC with minimum GPA of 3.25. Additional exam requirements/recommendations for international students: Required—TOEFL. Electronic applications accepted. *Faculty research:* Rural education, technology, mental health.

Chaminade University of Honolulu, Graduate Services, Program in Education, Honolulu, HI 96816-1578. Offers child development (M Ed); educational leadership (M Ed); elementary education with licensure (MAT); instructional leadership (M Ed); Montessori credential (M Ed); Montessori emphasis (M Ed); secondary education with licensure (MAT), including English, math, science, social studies; special education with licensure (MAT). Part-time and evening/weekend programs available. Postbaccalaureate distance learning degree programs offered (minimal on-campus study). *Faculty:* 2 full-time (both women), 32 part-time/adjunct (25 women). *Students:* 53 full-time (38 women), 88 part-time (67 women); includes 77 minority (6 Black or African American, non-Hispanic/Latino; 1 American Indian or Alaska Native, non-Hispanic/Latino; 44 Asian, non-Hispanic/Latino; 5 Hispanic/Latino; 17 Native Hawaiian or other Pacific Islander, non-Hispanic/Latino; 4 Two or more races, non-Hispanic/Latino), 1 international. Average age 35. 40 applicants, 88% accepted, 30 enrolled. In 2011, 105 master's awarded. *Degree requirements:* For master's, thesis or alternative. *Entrance requirements:* For master's, PRAXIS (for MAT only), minimum GPA of 2.75, 3 letters of recommendation. Additional exam requirements/recommendations for international students: Required—TOEFL (minimum score 550 paper-based). *Application deadline:* For fall admission, 9/1 priority date for domestic students, 9/1 for international students; for winter admission, 12/1 priority date for domestic students, 12/1 for international students; for spring admission, 3/1 priority date for domestic students, 3/1 for international students. Applications are processed on a rolling basis. Application fee: $50. Electronic applications accepted. *Expenses: Required fees:* $600 per credit hour. One-time fee: $93 part-time. *Financial support:* In 2011–12, 172 students received support. Career-related internships or fieldwork, Federal Work-Study, institutionally sponsored loans, scholarships/grants, and tuition waivers (partial) available. Support available to part-time students. Financial award application deadline: 3/1; financial award applicants required to submit FAFSA. *Faculty research:* Peace and curriculum education. *Unit head:* Dr. Joseph Peters, Dean, 808-440-4251, Fax: 808-739-4607, E-mail: joseph.peters@chaminade.edu. *Application contact:* 808-739-4663, Fax: 808-739-8329, E-mail: gradserv@chaminade.edu. Web site: http://www.chaminade.edu/education/grad.php.

Chapman University, College of Educational Studies, Orange, CA 92866. Offers communication sciences and disorders (MS); counseling (MA), including school counseling (MA, Credential); education (MA, PhD), including cultural and curricular studies (PhD), disability studies (PhD), school psychology (PhD, Credential); educational psychology (MA); professional clear (Credential); pupil personnel services (Credential), including school counseling (MA, Credential), school psychology (PhD, Credential); school psychology (Ed S); single subject (Credential); special education (MA); special education (level ii) (Credential), including mild/moderate, moderate/severe; special education (preliminary) (Credential), including mild/moderate, moderate/severe; speech language pathology (Credential); teaching (MA), including elementary education, secondary education. *Accreditation:* Teacher Education Accreditation Council. Part-time and evening/weekend programs available. *Faculty:* 27 full-time (18 women), 35 part-time/adjunct (24 women). *Students:* 220 full-time (188 women), 164 part-time (128 women); includes 140 minority (12 Black or African American, non-Hispanic/Latino; 1 American Indian or Alaska Native, non-Hispanic/Latino; 44 Asian, non-Hispanic/Latino; 73 Hispanic/Latino; 4 Native Hawaiian or other Pacific Islander, non-Hispanic/Latino; 6 Two or more races, non-Hispanic/Latino), 1 international. Average age 29. 436 applicants, 38% accepted, 126 enrolled. In 2011, 130 master's, 5 doctorates awarded. *Entrance requirements:* Additional exam requirements/recommendations for international students: Required—TOEFL (minimum score 550 paper-based; 213 computer-based; 80 iBT). *Application deadline:* Applications are processed on a rolling basis. Application fee: $60. Electronic applications accepted. Tuition and fees vary according to degree level and program. *Financial support:* Fellowships and scholarships/grants available. Financial award application deadline: 6/30; financial award applicants required to submit FAFSA. *Unit head:* Dr. Don Cardinal, Dean, 714-997-6781, E-mail: cardinal@chapman.edu. *Application contact:* Admissions Coordinator, 714-997-6714. Web site: http://www.chapman.edu/CES/.

Charleston Southern University, School of Education, Charleston, SC 29423-8087. Offers administration and supervision (M Ed), including elementary, secondary; elementary education (M Ed); secondary education (M Ed). *Accreditation:* NCATE. Part-time and evening/weekend programs available. *Degree requirements:* For master's, thesis optional. *Entrance requirements:* For master's, GRE or MAT. Additional exam requirements/recommendations for international students: Required—TOEFL (minimum score 550 paper-based; 213 computer-based; 79 iBT). *Expenses:* Contact institution.

Chatham University, Program in Education, Pittsburgh, PA 15232-2826. Offers early childhood education (MAT); elementary education (MAT); environmental education (K-12) (MAT); secondary art (MAT); secondary biology education (MAT); secondary chemistry education (MAT); secondary English education (MAT); secondary math education (MAT); secondary physics education (MAT); secondary social studies education (MAT); special education (MAT). *Students:* 52 full-time (42 women), 17 part-time (16 women); includes 2 minority (1 Black or African American, non-Hispanic/Latino; 1 Hispanic/Latino). Average age 29. 39 applicants, 82% accepted, 23 enrolled. In 2011, 37 master's awarded. *Degree requirements:* For master's, thesis, teaching experience. *Entrance requirements:* For master's, minimum GPA of 3.0, sample of written work, recommendation letters. Additional exam requirements/recommendations for international students: Required—TOEFL (minimum score 600 paper-based; 250 computer-based; 100 iBT), IELTS (minimum score 7), TWE. *Application deadline:* For fall admission, 4/1 priority date for domestic students, 4/1 for international students; for spring admission, 11/1 priority date for domestic students, 10/1 for international students. Applications are processed on a rolling basis. Application fee: $45. Electronic applications accepted. Application fee is waived when completed online. *Expenses: Tuition:* Full-time $13,896. Tuition and fees vary according to program. *Financial support:* Career-related internships or fieldwork available. Financial award applicants required to submit FAFSA. *Faculty research:* Gifted education, environmental education, technology in education, writing as learning, class size and achievement. *Unit head:* Dr. Elvira Sanatullova-Allison, Director of Education Programs, 412-365-2773, E-mail: esanatullovaallison@chatham.edu. *Application contact:* Dory Perry, Associate Director of Graduate Admission, 412-365-2758, Fax: 412-365-1609, E-mail: gradadmissions@chatham.edu. Web site: http://www.chatham.edu/mat.

Chestnut Hill College, School of Graduate Studies, Department of Education, Program in Secondary Education, Philadelphia, PA 19118-2693. Offers M Ed. Part-time and evening/weekend programs available. *Faculty:* 6 full-time (4 women), 50 part-time/adjunct (33 women). *Students:* 12 full-time (8 women), 84 part-time (54 women); includes 13 minority (7 Black or African American, non-Hispanic/Latino; 2 Asian, non-Hispanic/Latino; 2 Hispanic/Latino; 2 Two or more races, non-Hispanic/Latino). Average age 30. 31 applicants, 100% accepted. In 2011, 65 master's awarded. *Degree requirements:* For master's, thesis optional. *Entrance requirements:* For master's, PRAXIS I or proof of teaching certification, letters of recommendation; writing sample; 6 graduate credits with minimum B average if undergraduate GPA less than 3.0. Additional exam requirements/recommendations for international students: Required—TOEFL (minimum score 500 paper-based; 213 computer-based). *Application deadline:* For fall admission, 7/17 priority date for domestic students; for spring admission, 12/15 priority date for domestic students. Applications are processed on a rolling basis. Application fee: $55. *Expenses: Tuition:* Part-time $555 per credit hour. One-time fee: $55 part-time. Part-time tuition and fees vary according to degree level and program. *Financial support:* Unspecified assistantships available. *Faculty research:* Science teaching. *Unit head:* Dr. Carol Pate, Chair, Education Department, 215-248-7127, Fax: 215-248-7155, E-mail: cpate@chc.edu. *Application contact:* Amy Boorse, Administrative Assistant, School of Graduate Studies Office, 215-248-7170, Fax: 215-248-7161, E-mail: gradadmissions@chc.edu. Web site: http://www.chc.edu/Graduate/Programs/Masters/Education/.

Chicago State University, School of Graduate and Professional Studies, College of Education, Department of Technology and Education, Chicago, IL 60628. Offers secondary education (MAT); technology and education (MS Ed). Postbaccalaureate distance learning degree programs offered. *Degree requirements:* For master's, thesis optional. *Entrance requirements:* For master's, minimum GPA of 2.75.

Christopher Newport University, Graduate Studies, Department of Teacher Preparation, Newport News, VA 23606-2998. Offers art (PK-12) (MAT); biology (6-12) (MAT); chemistry (6-12) (MAT); computer science (6-12) (MAT); elementary (PK-6) (MAT); English (6-12) (MAT); English as second language (PK-12) (MAT); French (PK-12) (MAT); history and social science (6-12) (MAT); mathematics (6-12) (MAT); music (PK-12) (MAT), including choral, instrumental; physics (6-12) (MAT); Spanish (PK-12) (MAT). Part-time and evening/weekend programs available. *Degree requirements:* For master's, comprehensive exam, thesis or alternative. *Entrance requirements:* For master's, PRAXIS I, minimum GPA of 3.0. Additional exam requirements/recommendations for international students: Required—TOEFL (minimum score 580 paper-based; 237 computer-based; 92 iBT). Electronic applications accepted. *Faculty research:* Early literacy development, instructional innovations, professional teaching standards, multicultural issues, aesthetic education.

The Citadel, The Military College of South Carolina, Citadel Graduate College, School of Education, Program in Guidance and Counseling, Charleston, SC 29409. Offers elementary/secondary school counseling (M Ed); student affairs and college counseling (M Ed). *Accreditation:* ACA; NCATE. Part-time and evening/weekend programs available. *Faculty:* 12 full-time (8 women), 9 part-time/adjunct (4 women). *Students:* 24 full-time (22 women), 36 part-time (31 women); includes 9 minority (8 Black or African American, non-Hispanic/Latino; 1 Hispanic/Latino). Average age 31. In 2011, 22 master's awarded. *Degree requirements:* For master's, comprehensive exam, practicum or internship. *Entrance requirements:* For master's, GRE (minimum score 900) or MAT (minimum score 396), minimum undergraduate GPA of 3.0, 3 letters of reference, group interview. Additional exam requirements/recommendations for international students: Required—TOEFL (minimum score 550 paper-based; 213 computer-based; 79 iBT). *Application deadline:* For fall admission, 6/1 for domestic students; for spring admission, 10/1 for domestic students. Application fee: $30. Electronic applications accepted. *Expenses: Tuition, area resident:* Part-time $501 per credit hour. Tuition, state resident: part-time $501 per credit hour. Tuition, nonresident: part-time $824 per credit hour. *Required fees:* $40 per term. One-time fee: $30. *Financial support:* Career-related internships or fieldwork, health care benefits, and unspecified assistantships available. Support available to part-time students. Financial award application deadline: 7/1; financial award applicants required to submit FAFSA. *Unit head:* Dr. George T. Williams, Director, 843-953-2205, Fax: 843-953-7258, E-mail: williamsg@citadel.edu. *Application contact:* Dr. Steve A. Nida, Associate Provost, The Citadel Graduate College, 843-953-5089, Fax: 843-953-7630, E-mail: cgc@citadel.edu. Web site: http://www.citadel.edu/education/counselor.html.

The Citadel, The Military College of South Carolina, Citadel Graduate College, School of Education, Program in Secondary Education, Charleston, SC 29409. Offers biology (MAT); English language arts (MAT); mathematics (MAT); mathematics education (MAE); physical education (MAT); social studies (MAT). *Accreditation:* NCATE. Part-time and evening/weekend programs available. *Faculty:* 12 full-time (8 women), 9 part-time/adjunct (4 women). *Students:* 21 full-time (11 women), 51 part-time (25 women); includes 10 minority (7 Black or African American, non-Hispanic/Latino; 2

Asian, non-Hispanic/Latino; 1 Hispanic/Latino). Average age 31. In 2011, 34 master's awarded. *Degree requirements:* For master's, comprehensive exam, internship. *Entrance requirements:* For master's, GRE (minimum score 900) or MAT (minimum score 396), minimum undergraduate GPA of 2.5. Additional exam requirements/recommendations for international students: Required—TOEFL (minimum score 550 paper-based; 213 computer-based). *Application deadline:* Applications are processed on a rolling basis. Application fee: $30. Electronic applications accepted. *Expenses: Tuition, area resident:* Part-time $501 per credit hour. Tuition, state resident: part-time $501 per credit hour. Tuition, nonresident: part-time $824 per credit hour. *Required fees:* $40 per term. One-time fee: $30. *Financial support:* Career-related internships or fieldwork, health care benefits, and unspecified assistantships available. Support available to part-time students. Financial award application deadline: 7/1; financial award applicants required to submit FAFSA. *Unit head:* Dr. Kathryn A. Richardson-Jones, Coordinator, 843-953-3163, Fax: 843-953-7258, E-mail: kathryn.jones@citadel.edu. *Application contact:* Dr. Steve A. Nida, Associate Provost, The Citadel Graduate College, 843-953-5089, Fax: 843-953-7630, E-mail: cgc@citadel.edu. Web site: http://www.citadel.edu/education/teacher-education/mat-master-of-arts-in-teaching.html.

City College of the City University of New York, Graduate School, School of Education, Department of Secondary Education, New York, NY 10031-9198. Offers adolescent mathematics education (MA, AC); English education (MA); middle school mathematics education (MS); science education (MA); social studies education (AC). *Accreditation:* NCATE. *Entrance requirements:* For master's, Liberal Arts and Sciences Test (LAST), Content Specialty Test (CST). Additional exam requirements/recommendations for international students: Required—TOEFL.

Clemson University, Graduate School, College of Health, Education, and Human Development, Eugene T. Moore School of Education, Program in Early Childhood Education, Clemson, SC 29634. Offers early childhood education (M Ed); elementary education (M Ed); secondary English (M Ed); secondary math (M Ed); secondary science (M Ed); secondary social studies (M Ed). Part-time and evening/weekend programs available. *Students:* 5 applicants, 0% accepted, 0 enrolled. In 2011, 3 master's awarded. *Degree requirements:* For master's, comprehensive exam. *Entrance requirements:* For master's, GRE, valid teaching certificate. Additional exam requirements/recommendations for international students: Required—TOEFL; Recommended—IELTS. *Application deadline:* Applications are processed on a rolling basis. Application fee: $70 ($80 for international students). Electronic applications accepted. *Expenses:* Contact institution. *Financial support:* Institutionally sponsored loans, health care benefits, and unspecified assistantships available. Financial award application deadline: 3/1; financial award applicants required to submit FAFSA. *Faculty research:* Elementary education, mathematics education, social studies education, English education, science education. *Unit head:* Dr. Michael J. Padilla, Director/Associate Dean, 864-656-4444, Fax: 864-656-0311, E-mail: padilla@clemson.edu. *Application contact:* Dr. David Fleming, Graduate Programs Coordinator, 864-656-1881, Fax: 864-656-0311, E-mail: dflemin@clemson.edu.

Clemson University, Graduate School, College of Health, Education, and Human Development, Eugene T. Moore School of Education, Program in Secondary Education: Math and Science, Clemson, SC 29634. Offers MAT. *Accreditation:* NCATE. *Students:* 9 full-time (6 women), 1 part-time; includes 1 minority (Black or African American, non-Hispanic/Latino). Average age 29. 15 applicants, 93% accepted, 9 enrolled. In 2011, 9 master's awarded. *Degree requirements:* For master's, digital portfolio. *Entrance requirements:* For master's, PRAXIS II. Additional exam requirements/recommendations for international students: Required—TOEFL; Recommended—IELTS. *Application deadline:* For fall admission, 4/1 for domestic students. Applications are processed on a rolling basis. Application fee: $70 ($80 for international students). Electronic applications accepted. *Expenses:* Contact institution. *Financial support:* Institutionally sponsored loans, scholarships/grants, health care benefits, and unspecified assistantships available. Financial award application deadline: 6/1; financial award applicants required to submit FAFSA. *Faculty research:* Science education, math education. *Unit head:* Dr. Michael J. Padilla, Director/Associate Dean, 864-656-4444, Fax: 864-656-0311, E-mail: padilla@clemson.edu. *Application contact:* Dr. David Fleming, Graduate Coordinator, 864-656-1881, Fax: 864-656-0311, E-mail: dflemin@clemson.edu. Web site: http://www.clemson.edu/hehd/departments/education/academics/graduate/MAT/secondary.html.

Colgate University, Master of Arts in Teaching Program, Hamilton, NY 13346-1386. Offers MAT. *Accreditation:* Teacher Education Accreditation Council. *Faculty:* 5 full-time (4 women), 2 part-time/adjunct (1 woman). *Students:* 7 full-time (5 women); includes 2 minority (1 American Indian or Alaska Native, non-Hispanic/Latino; 1 Two or more races, non-Hispanic/Latino). Average age 25. 11 applicants, 73% accepted, 4 enrolled. In 2011, 4 master's awarded. *Degree requirements:* For master's, special project or thesis. *Entrance requirements:* For master's, GRE General Test. *Application deadline:* For fall admission, 2/15 for domestic students. Application fee: $50. *Expenses: Tuition:* Full-time $42,625. *Required fees:* $295. Full-time tuition and fees vary according to course load. *Financial support:* In 2011–12, 7 students received support. Unspecified assistantships and Institutionally-sponsored grant available. Financial award application deadline: 2/15; financial award applicants required to submit FAFSA. *Faculty research:* Culturally responsive teaching, comparative education, moral development in education, politics in education, educational psychology. *Unit head:* Dr. Jeffrey Baldani, Associate Dean of the Faculty, 315-228-7220. *Application contact:* Ginger Babich, Administrative Assistant, 315-228-7256, Fax: 315-228-7857, E-mail: gbabich@colgate.edu. Web site: http://www.colgate.edu/academics/departments-and-programs/educational-studies/master-teaching.

College of Mount St. Joseph, Graduate Education Program, Cincinnati, OH 45233-1670. Offers adolescent young adult education (MA); art (MA); inclusive early childhood education (MA); instructional leadership (MA); middle childhood education (MA); multi-age education (MA); multicultural special education (MA); music (MA); reading (MA). *Accreditation:* Teacher Education Accreditation Council. Part-time and evening/weekend programs available. *Faculty:* 22 full-time (12 women), 11 part-time/adjunct (8 women). *Students:* 51 full-time (40 women), 92 part-time (72 women); includes 17 minority (14 Black or African American, non-Hispanic/Latino; 1 American Indian or Alaska Native, non-Hispanic/Latino; 1 Asian, non-Hispanic/Latino; 1 Hispanic/Latino). Average age 34. 87 applicants, 44% accepted, 29 enrolled. In 2011, 61 master's awarded. *Degree requirements:* For master's, research project, student teaching, clinical and field-based experiences. *Entrance requirements:* For master's, GRE, PRAXIS II in teaching content area (math or science), 2 letters of recommendation, interview, resume. Additional exam requirements/recommendations for international students: Required—TOEFL (minimum score 560 paper-based; 220 computer-based; 83 iBT). *Application deadline:* Applications are processed on a rolling basis. Application fee: $50. Electronic applications accepted. *Expenses: Tuition:* Full-time $24,200; part-time $540 per credit hour. *Required fees:* $112.50 per semester. One-time fee: $200. *Financial support:* In 2011–12, 22 students received support. Scholarships/grants available. Financial award applicants required to submit FAFSA. *Faculty research:* Foreign and second language learning problems/reading disabilities/hyperlexia, multicultural/bilingual special education, alternative educator licensure, science education, pedagogical content knowledge. *Unit head:* Dr. Mary West, Chair, 513-244-3263, Fax: 513-244-4867, E-mail: mary_west@mail.msj.edu. *Application contact:* Marilyn Hoskins, Assistant Director of Graduate Recruitment, 513-244-4723, Fax: 513-244-4629, E-mail: marilyn_hoskins@mail.msj.edu. Web site: http://www.msj.edu/view/academics/graduate-programs/education.aspx.

The College of New Jersey, Graduate Studies, School of Education, Department of Educational Administration and Secondary Education, Program in Secondary Education, Ewing, NJ 08628. Offers MAT. *Degree requirements:* For master's, comprehensive exam. *Entrance requirements:* For master's, GRE, minimum GPA of 3.0 in field or 2.75 overall. Additional exam requirements/recommendations for international students: Required—TOEFL. Electronic applications accepted.

College of St. Joseph, Graduate Programs, Division of Education, Program in Secondary Education, Rutland, VT 05701-3899. Offers English (M Ed); social studies (M Ed). Part-time and evening/weekend programs available. *Faculty:* 2 full-time (both women), 3 part-time/adjunct (1 woman). *Students:* 2 full-time (0 women), 4 part-time (2 women). Average age 29. 3 applicants, 67% accepted, 2 enrolled. *Degree requirements:* For master's, comprehensive exam. *Entrance requirements:* For master's, PRAXIS I, official college transcripts; 2 letters of reference; minimum GPA of 3.0 (initial licensure) or 2.7 (nonlicensure); interview. Additional exam requirements/recommendations for international students: Required—TOEFL (minimum score 550 paper-based). *Application deadline:* Applications are processed on a rolling basis. Application fee: $35. Electronic applications accepted. *Expenses: Tuition:* Full-time $15,200; part-time $400 per credit. *Required fees:* $45 per semester. *Financial support:* Career-related internships or fieldwork, Federal Work-Study, and unspecified assistantships available. Support available to part-time students. Financial award application deadline: 3/1. *Unit head:* Dr. Maria Bove, Chair, 802-773-5900 Ext. 3243, Fax: 802-776-5258, E-mail: mbove@csj.edu. *Application contact:* Alan Young, Director of Admissions, 802-773-5900 Ext. 3227, Fax: 802-776-5310, E-mail: alanyoung@csj.edu.

The College of Saint Rose, Graduate Studies, School of Education, Teacher Education Department, Albany, NY 12203-1419. Offers business and marketing (MS Ed); childhood education (MS Ed); curriculum and instruction (MS Ed); early childhood education (MS Ed); elementary education (K-6) (MS Ed); secondary education (MS Ed, Certificate); teacher education (MS Ed, Certificate), including bilingual pupil personnel services (Certificate), teacher education (MS Ed). Part-time and evening/weekend programs available. *Entrance requirements:* For master's, minimum undergraduate GPA of 3.0. Additional exam requirements/recommendations for international students: Required—TOEFL (minimum score 550 paper-based; 213 computer-based). Electronic applications accepted.

College of Staten Island of the City University of New York, Graduate Programs, Department of Education, Program in Adolescence Education, Staten Island, NY 10314-6600. Offers MS Ed. Part-time and evening/weekend programs available. *Faculty:* 15 full-time (7 women), 9 part-time/adjunct (3 women). *Students:* 10 full-time, 150 part-time. Average age 28. 68 applicants, 69% accepted, 38 enrolled. In 2011, 36 master's awarded. *Degree requirements:* For master's, research project. *Entrance requirements:* For master's, minimum GPA of 3.0, 2 letters of recommendation, New York State Initial Certification at secondary (adolescence) level. Additional exam requirements/recommendations for international students: Required—TOEFL (minimum score 550 paper-based; 213 computer-based; 79 iBT), IELTS (minimum score 6.5). *Application deadline:* For fall admission, 4/25 for domestic and international students; for spring admission, 11/15 for domestic and international students. Applications are processed on a rolling basis. Application fee: $125. Electronic applications accepted. *Expenses:* Tuition, state resident: full-time $8210; part-time $345 per credit. Tuition, nonresident: part-time $640 per credit. *Required fees:* $128 per semester. *Financial support:* In 2011–12, 2 students received support. Career-related internships or fieldwork, Federal Work-Study, and scholarships/grants available. Support available to part-time students. Financial award applicants required to submit FAFSA. *Unit head:* Dr. Kenneth Gold, Coordinator, 718-982-3737, Fax: 718-982-3743, E-mail: kenneth.gold@csi.cuny.edu. *Application contact:* Sasha Spence, Assistant Director for Graduate Admissions, 718-982-2699, Fax: 718-982-2500, E-mail: sasha.spence@csi.cuny.edu. Web site: http://www.csi.cuny.edu/catalog/graduate/graduate-programs-in-education.htm#o2608.

The College of William and Mary, School of Education, Program in Curriculum and Instruction, Williamsburg, VA 23187-8795. Offers elementary education (MA Ed); gifted education (MA Ed); math specialist (MA Ed); reading education (MA Ed); secondary education (MA Ed), including English education, mathematics education, modern foreign languages education, science education, social studies education; special education (MA Ed), including collaborating master educator, general curriculum. *Accreditation:* NCATE. Part-time programs available. *Faculty:* 15 full-time (10 women), 39 part-time/adjunct (32 women). *Students:* 80 full-time (69 women), 13 part-time (11 women); includes 11 minority (3 Black or African American, non-Hispanic/Latino; 1 American Indian or Alaska Native, non-Hispanic/Latino; 2 Hispanic/Latino; 5 Two or more races, non-Hispanic/Latino), 1 international. Average age 25. 220 applicants, 56% accepted, 85 enrolled. In 2011, 78 master's awarded. *Degree requirements:* For master's, project. *Entrance requirements:* For master's, GRE or MAT, minimum GPA of 2.5. Additional exam requirements/recommendations for international students: Required—TOEFL. *Application deadline:* For fall admission, 1/15 for domestic and international students; for spring admission, 10/1 for domestic and international students. Application fee: $50. Electronic applications accepted. *Expenses:* Tuition, state resident: full-time $6400; part-time $365 per credit hour. Tuition, nonresident: full-time $19,720; part-time $985 per credit hour. *Required fees:* $4562. *Financial support:* In 2011–12, 53 students received support, including 10 research assistantships with full and partial tuition reimbursements available (averaging $7,000 per year); career-related internships or fieldwork, Federal Work-Study, institutionally sponsored loans, scholarships/grants, and unspecified assistantships also available. Financial award application deadline: 1/15; financial award applicants required to submit FAFSA. *Faculty research:* National Council of Teachers of Mathematics Standards, counseling, self-concept and self-esteem, special education, curriculum development. *Unit head:* Dr. Margie Mason, Area Coordinator, 757-221-2327, E-mail: mmmaso@wm.edu. *Application contact:* Dorothy Smith Osborne, Assistant Dean for Admission, 757-221-2317, Fax: 757-221-2293, E-mail: dsosbo@wm.edu. Web site: http://education.wm.edu.

The Colorado College, Education Department, Program in Secondary Education, Colorado Springs, CO 80903-3294. Offers art teaching (K-12) (MAT); English teaching (MAT); foreign language teaching (MAT); mathematics teaching (MAT); music teaching (MAT); science teaching (MAT); social studies teaching (MAT). *Faculty:* 4 full-time (3 women), 6 part-time/adjunct (2 women). *Students:* 11 full-time (7 women); includes 3 minority (1 Asian, non-Hispanic/Latino; 2 Hispanic/Latino). Average age 27. 20 applicants, 85% accepted, 11 enrolled. In 2011, 15 master's awarded. *Degree requirements:* For master's, thesis, internship. *Application deadline:* For fall admission, 12/1 priority date for domestic students, 12/1 for international students. Applications are processed on a rolling basis. Application fee: $50. Electronic applications accepted. *Expenses: Tuition:* Full-time $29,313. *Required fees:* $2000. *Financial support:* In 2011–12, 15 students received support. Career-related internships or fieldwork, institutionally sponsored loans, scholarships/grants, and health care benefits available.

Financial award application deadline: 2/15; financial award applicants required to submit FAFSA. *Unit head:* Dr. Mike Taber, Director, 719-389-6026, Fax: 719-389-6473, E-mail: mike.taber@coloradocollege.edu. *Application contact:* Debra Yazulla Mortenson, Education Services Manager, 719-389-6472, Fax: 719-389-6473, E-mail: debra.mortenson@coloradocollege.edu. Web site: http://www.coloradocollege.edu/academics/dept/education/graduate-programs/secondary-mat.dot.

Columbus State University, Graduate Studies, College of Education and Health Professions, Department of Teacher Education, Columbus, GA 31907-5645. Offers accomplished teaching (M Ed); early childhood education (M Ed, MAT, Ed S); health and physical education (M Ed, MAT); middle grades education (M Ed, MAT, Ed S); school library media (M Ed, MAT); secondary education (M Ed, MAT, Ed S), including English/language arts (M Ed, Ed S), general science (M Ed), mathematics (M Ed), social science (M Ed); special education (M Ed, Ed S), including general curriculum (M Ed). *Accreditation:* NCATE. Part-time and evening/weekend programs available. Postbaccalaureate distance learning degree programs offered (minimal on-campus study). *Degree requirements:* For master's, thesis, exit exam; for Ed S, thesis or alternative. *Entrance requirements:* For master's, GRE General Test, minimum GPA of 2.75; for Ed S, GRE General Test. Additional exam requirements/recommendations for international students: Required—TOEFL (minimum score 550 paper-based; 213 computer-based; 79 iBT). Electronic applications accepted.

Concordia University, College of Education, Portland, OR 97211-6099. Offers curriculum and instruction (elementary) (M Ed); educational administration (M Ed); elementary education (MAT); secondary education (MAT). Part-time programs available. Postbaccalaureate distance learning degree programs offered (no on-campus study). *Degree requirements:* For master's, comprehensive exam, work samples/portfolio. *Entrance requirements:* For master's, California Basic Educational Skills Test or PRAXIS I, minimum undergraduate GPA of 2.8, graduate 3.0; 2 letters of recommendation. Additional exam requirements/recommendations for international students: Required—TOEFL (minimum score 525 paper-based; 195 computer-based). Electronic applications accepted. *Faculty research:* Learner centered classroom, brain-based learning future of on-line learning.

Concordia University Chicago, College of Education, Program in Teaching, River Forest, IL 60305-1499. Offers early childhood education (MAT); elementary education (MAT); secondary education (MAT). *Degree requirements:* For master's, thesis or alternative. *Entrance requirements:* For master's, minimum GPA of 2.9. Additional exam requirements/recommendations for international students: Required—TOEFL (minimum score 550 paper-based; 195 computer-based). Electronic applications accepted.

Concordia University, Nebraska, Graduate Programs in Education, Program in Educational Administration, Seward, NE 68434-1599. Offers elementary and secondary education (M Ed); elementary education (M Ed); secondary education (M Ed). *Accreditation:* NCATE. Part-time programs available. *Degree requirements:* For master's, thesis or alternative. *Entrance requirements:* For master's, GRE, MAT, or NTE, BS in education or equivalent, minimum GPA of 3.0.

Converse College, School of Education and Graduate Studies, Program in Secondary Education, Spartanburg, SC 29302-0006. Offers biology (MAT); chemistry (MAT); English (M Ed, MAT); mathematics (M Ed, MAT); natural sciences (M Ed); social sciences (M Ed, MAT). Part-time programs available. *Degree requirements:* For master's, capstone paper. *Entrance requirements:* For master's, NTE or PRAXIS II (M Ed), minimum GPA of 2.75, 2 recommendations. Electronic applications accepted.

Creighton University, Graduate School, College of Arts and Sciences, Department of Education, Program in Teaching, Omaha, NE 68178-0001. Offers elementary teaching (M Ed); secondary teaching (M Ed). Part-time and evening/weekend programs available. *Faculty:* 14 full-time (8 women). *Students:* 11 full-time (5 women), 30 part-time (19 women); includes 4 minority (1 Black or African American, non-Hispanic/Latino; 1 American Indian or Alaska Native, non-Hispanic/Latino; 2 Hispanic/Latino), 1 international. Average age 27. 6 applicants, 67% accepted, 4 enrolled. In 2011, 21 master's awarded. *Entrance requirements:* For master's, 3 letters of recommendation, 2 writing samples. Additional exam requirements/recommendations for international students: Required—TOEFL (minimum score 550 paper-based; 213 computer-based; 80 iBT). *Application deadline:* For fall admission, 7/1 priority date for domestic students, 3/1 for international students; for winter admission, 12/1 priority date for domestic students, 6/1 for international students; for spring admission, 3/1 priority date for domestic students, 3/1 for international students. Applications are processed on a rolling basis. Application fee: $50. Electronic applications accepted. *Expenses: Tuition:* Full-time $12,672; part-time $704 per credit hour. *Required fees:* $1410; $136 per semester. Tuition and fees vary according to campus/location and reciprocity agreements. *Financial support:* Scholarships/grants and tuition waivers (partial) available. Support available to part-time students. Financial award applicants required to submit FAFSA. *Unit head:* Dr. Lynne Houtz, Director, 402-280-2247, E-mail: lhoutz@creighton.edu. *Application contact:* Taunya Plater, Senior Program Coordinator, 402-280-2870, Fax: 402-280-2423, E-mail: taunyaplater@creighton.edu.

Dakota Wesleyan University, Program in Education, Mitchell, SD 57301-4398. Offers curriculum and instruction (MA Ed); educational policy and administration (MA Ed); preK-12 principal certification (MA Ed); secondary certification (MA Ed). Part-time and evening/weekend programs available. *Degree requirements:* For master's, comprehensive exam, thesis optional, electronic portfolio. *Entrance requirements:* For master's, minimum GPA of 2.7, elementary statistics course, statement of purpose, official transcripts, resume, three letters of recommendation. Additional exam requirements/recommendations for international students: Required—TOEFL (minimum score 500 paper-based; 71 computer-based), IELTS (minimum score 6.5). Electronic applications accepted. *Faculty research:* Math, political policy, technology in the classroom.

Dallas Baptist University, Dorothy M. Bush College of Education, Teaching Program, Dallas, TX 75211-9299. Offers all-level (MAT); distance learning (MAT); elementary (MAT); English as a second language (MAT); Montessori (MAT); multisensory (MAT); secondary (MAT). Part-time and evening/weekend programs available. *Entrance requirements:* For master's, GRE General Test, minimum GPA of 3.0. Additional exam requirements/recommendations for international students: Required—TOEFL, IELTS. *Application deadline:* Applications are processed on a rolling basis. Application fee: $25. Electronic applications accepted. *Expenses: Tuition:* Full-time $12,060; part-time $670 per credit hour. *Required fees:* $100; $50 per semester. *Financial support:* Federal Work-Study, institutionally sponsored loans, scholarships/grants, and tuition waivers (full and partial) available. Support available to part-time students. Financial award applicants required to submit FAFSA. *Unit head:* Dara Owen, Acting Director, 214-333-5413, Fax: 214-333-5551, E-mail: graduate@dbu.edu. *Application contact:* Kit P. Montgomery, Director of Graduate Programs, 214-333-5242, Fax: 214-333-5579, E-mail: graduate@dbu.edu. Web site: http://www3.dbu.edu/graduate/mat.asp.

Defiance College, Program in Education, Defiance, OH 43512-1610. Offers adolescent and young adult licensure (MA); mild and moderate intervention specialist (MA). Part-time programs available. *Faculty:* 7 full-time (4 women), 1 part-time/adjunct (0 women). *Students:* 34 part-time (25 women). *Degree requirements:* For master's, thesis (for some programs). *Entrance requirements:* For master's, teaching certificate. *Application deadline:* For fall admission, 8/1 for domestic students. Applications are processed on a rolling basis. Application fee: $25. *Expenses: Tuition:* Full-time $10,800; part-time $450 per credit hour. *Required fees:* $95; $35 per semester. *Unit head:* Dr. Suzanne McFarland, Coordinator, 419-783-2315, Fax: 419-784-0426, E-mail: smcfarland@defiance.edu. *Application contact:* Sally Bissell, Director of Continuing Education, 419-783-2350, Fax: 419-784-0426, E-mail: sbissell@defiance.edu.

Delta State University, Graduate Programs, College of Arts and Sciences, Department of History, Cleveland, MS 38733-0001. Offers secondary education (M Ed), including history. Part-time programs available. *Degree requirements:* For master's, thesis or alternative. *Entrance requirements:* For master's, GRE General Test or MAT. *Expenses:* Tuition, state resident: full-time $4702; part-time $294 per credit hour. Tuition, nonresident: full-time $12,516; part-time $760 per credit hour. *Required fees:* $586.

Delta State University, Graduate Programs, College of Arts and Sciences, Division of Languages and Literature, Cleveland, MS 38733-0001. Offers secondary education (M Ed), including English. Part-time programs available. *Degree requirements:* For master's, thesis or alternative. *Expenses:* Tuition, state resident: full-time $4702; part-time $294 per credit hour. Tuition, nonresident: full-time $12,516; part-time $760 per credit hour. *Required fees:* $586.

Delta State University, Graduate Programs, College of Arts and Sciences, Division of Social Sciences and History, Program in Social Science Secondary Education, Cleveland, MS 38733-0001. Offers secondary education (M Ed), including social science. Part-time programs available. *Degree requirements:* For master's, thesis or alternative. *Expenses:* Tuition, state resident: full-time $4702; part-time $294 per credit hour. Tuition, nonresident: full-time $12,516; part-time $760 per credit hour. *Required fees:* $586.

DePaul University, College of Education, Chicago, IL 60106. Offers bilingual bicultural education (M Ed, MA); counseling (M Ed, MA), including college student development, community counseling, school counseling; curriculum studies (M Ed, MA, Ed D); early childhood education (M Ed, MA); educational leadership (M Ed, MA, Ed D), including administration and supervision (M Ed, MA), physical education (M Ed, MA); middle school mathematics education (MS); reading specialist (M Ed, MA); social and cultural foundations in education (M Ed, MA), including curriculum studies/development (MA); special education (M Ed, MA); teaching and learning (M Ed, MA), including elementary education, secondary education; world languages education (M Ed, MA). Part-time and evening/weekend programs available. *Faculty:* 49 full-time (28 women), 94 part-time/adjunct (60 women). *Students:* 894 full-time (707 women), 473 part-time (361 women); includes 349 minority (159 Black or African American, non-Hispanic/Latino; 3 American Indian or Alaska Native, non-Hispanic/Latino; 45 Asian, non-Hispanic/Latino; 115 Hispanic/Latino; 2 Native Hawaiian or other Pacific Islander, non-Hispanic/Latino; 25 Two or more races, non-Hispanic/Latino), 21 international. Average age 30. 872 applicants, 64% accepted, 325 enrolled. In 2011, 499 master's, 10 doctorates awarded. *Median time to degree:* Of those who began their doctoral program in fall 2003, 32% received their degree in 8 years or less. *Degree requirements:* For master's, thesis/dissertation (for MA); capstone course or paper (for M Ed); for doctorate, thesis/dissertation. *Entrance requirements:* For master's, interview, minimum GPA of 2.75, 2 letters of recommendation, bachelor's degree conferred by accredited college or university; for doctorate, interview, master's degree, writing sample, 3 letters of recommendation. Additional exam requirements/recommendations for international students: Required—TOEFL (minimum score 550 paper-based; 213 computer-based; 80 iBT). *Application deadline:* For fall admission, 8/15 priority date for domestic students; for winter admission, 12/1 priority date for domestic students; for spring admission, 3/1 priority date for domestic students. Applications are processed on a rolling basis. Application fee: $40. Electronic applications accepted. *Financial support:* In 2011–12, 163 students received support, including 15 research assistantships with full tuition reimbursements available (averaging $6,375 per year); career-related internships or fieldwork, Federal Work-Study, scholarships/grants, and unspecified assistantships also available. Support available to part-time students. Financial award application deadline: 12/31; financial award applicants required to submit FAFSA. *Faculty research:* Reflective teaching, children at risk, loss, ethnicity, urban education. *Total annual research expenditures:* $916,310. *Unit head:* Dr. Paul Zionts, Dean, 773-325-7581, Fax: 773-325-7713, E-mail: pzionts@depaul.edu. *Application contact:* Brandon Washington, Enrollment Management Coordinator, 773-325-1152, Fax: 773-325-2270, E-mail: bwashin3@depaul.edu. Web site: http://education.depaul.edu.

Drury University, Graduate Programs in Education, Springfield, MO 65802. Offers elementary education (M Ed); gifted education (M Ed); human services (M Ed); instructional mathematics K-8 (M Ed); instructional technology (M Ed); middle school teaching (M Ed); secondary education (M Ed); special education (M Ed); special reading (M Ed). *Accreditation:* NCATE. Part-time and evening/weekend programs available. *Degree requirements:* For master's, thesis. *Entrance requirements:* For master's, GRE or MAT, minimum GPA of 2.75. Additional exam requirements/recommendations for international students: Required—TOEFL. Electronic applications accepted. *Faculty research:* Cultural enrichment, research skills, parental involvement relating to reading skills, reading strategies for mainstreaming children.

Duquesne University, School of Education, Department of Instruction and Leadership, Program in Secondary Education, Pittsburgh, PA 15282-0001. Offers biology (MS Ed). Part-time and evening/weekend programs available. *Faculty:* 4 full-time (3 women), 2 part-time/adjunct (0 women). *Students:* 50 full-time (28 women), 8 part-time (5 women); includes 2 minority (1 Asian, non-Hispanic/Latino; 1 Hispanic/Latino). Average age 26. 62 applicants, 34% accepted, 17 enrolled. In 2011, 32 master's awarded. *Degree requirements:* For master's, thesis optional. *Entrance requirements:* For master's, letters of recommendation, letter of intent, interview, bachelor's degree. Additional exam requirements/recommendations for international students: Required—TOEFL (minimum score 550 paper-based; 80 computer-based), IELTS (minimum score 7). *Application deadline:* For fall admission, 9/1 for domestic students; for spring admission, 1/1 for domestic students. Applications are processed on a rolling basis. Application fee: $0. Electronic applications accepted. Application fee is waived when completed online. *Expenses: Tuition:* Full-time $16,596; part-time $922 per credit. *Required fees:* $1584; $88 per credit. Tuition and fees vary according to program. *Financial support:* Research assistantships and Federal Work-Study available. Support available to part-time students. *Unit head:* Dr. Melissa Boston, Assistant Professor, 412-396-6109, E-mail: bostonm@duq.edu. *Application contact:* Michael Dolinger, Director of Student and Academic Services, 412-396-6647, Fax: 412-396-5585, E-mail: dolingerm@duq.edu. Web site: http://www.duq.edu/education.

D'Youville College, Department of Education, Buffalo, NY 14201-1084. Offers elementary education (MS Ed, Teaching Certificate); secondary education (MS Ed, Teaching Certificate); special education (MS Ed). Part-time and evening/weekend programs available. *Faculty:* 29 full-time (18 women), 29 part-time/adjunct (17 women). *Students:* 198 full-time (133 women), 52 part-time (41 women); includes 12 minority (7 Black or African American, non-Hispanic/Latino; 1 American Indian or Alaska Native, non-Hispanic/Latino; 1 Asian, non-Hispanic/Latino; 3 Hispanic/Latino), 161 international. Average age 29. 245 applicants, 46% accepted, 57 enrolled. In 2011, 235 master's awarded. *Degree requirements:* For master's, one foreign language, comprehensive exam, project or thesis. *Entrance requirements:* For master's, GRE (if GPA less than

2.75), minimum GPA of 3.0. Additional exam requirements/recommendations for international students: Required—TOEFL (minimum score 500 paper-based; 173 computer-based). *Application deadline:* For fall admission, 5/1 for international students; for spring admission, 9/1 for international students. Applications are processed on a rolling basis. Application fee: $25. Electronic applications accepted. *Expenses: Tuition:* Full-time $18,960; part-time $790 per credit hour. *Required fees:* $310. Tuition and fees vary according to degree level and program. *Financial support:* In 2011–12, 1 research assistantship with partial tuition reimbursement (averaging $3,000 per year) was awarded; career-related internships or fieldwork, Federal Work-Study, institutionally sponsored loans, scholarships/grants, tuition waivers (full and partial), and unspecified assistantships also available. Support available to part-time students. Financial award application deadline: 3/1; financial award applicants required to submit FAFSA. *Faculty research:* Developmental disabilities, multiculturalism, early childhood education. *Unit head:* Dr. Hilary Lochte, Chair, 716-829-8110, Fax: 716-829-7660. *Application contact:* Linda Fisher, Graduate Admissions Director, 716-829-8400, Fax: 716-829-7900, E-mail: graduateadmissions@dyc.edu.

Eastern Connecticut State University, School of Education and Professional Studies/Graduate Division, Program in Secondary Education, Willimantic, CT 06226-2295. Offers MS. *Accreditation:* NCATE. Part-time and evening/weekend programs available. *Degree requirements:* For master's, comprehensive exam or thesis. *Entrance requirements:* For master's, PRAXIS I and II, minimum GPA of 2.7. Additional exam requirements/recommendations for international students: Required—TOEFL (minimum score 550 paper-based; 213 computer-based).

Eastern Kentucky University, The Graduate School, College of Education, Department of Curriculum and Instruction, Program in Secondary and Higher Education, Richmond, KY 40475-3102. Offers secondary education (MA Ed), including agricultural education, art education, biological sciences education, business education, English education, geography education, history education, home economics education, industrial education, mathematical sciences education, physical education, school health education. *Accreditation:* NCATE. Part-time programs available. *Entrance requirements:* For master's, GRE General Test, minimum GPA of 2.5.

Eastern Michigan University, Graduate School, College of Education, Department of Teacher Education, Program in K–12 Education, Ypsilanti, MI 48197. Offers curriculum and instruction (MA); elementary education (MA); K-12 education (MA); middle school education (MA); secondary school education (MA). *Accreditation:* NCATE. Part-time and evening/weekend programs available. Postbaccalaureate distance learning degree programs offered (minimal on-campus study). *Students:* 14 full-time (9 women), 87 part-time (62 women); includes 12 minority (7 Black or African American, non-Hispanic/Latino; 1 American Indian or Alaska Native, non-Hispanic/Latino; 1 Asian, non-Hispanic/Latino; 2 Hispanic/Latino; 1 Two or more races, non-Hispanic/Latino). Average age 37. 57 applicants, 74% accepted, 25 enrolled. In 2011, 6 master's awarded. *Entrance requirements:* For master's, GRE. Additional exam requirements/recommendations for international students: Required—TOEFL. *Application deadline:* Applications are processed on a rolling basis. Application fee: $35. *Expenses:* Tuition, state resident: full-time $10,367; part-time $432 per credit hour. Tuition, nonresident: full-time $20,435; part-time $851 per credit hour. *Required fees:* $39 per credit hour. $46 per semester. One-time fee: $100. Tuition and fees vary according to course level, degree level and reciprocity agreements. *Financial support:* Fellowships, research assistantships with full tuition reimbursements, teaching assistantships with full tuition reimbursements, career-related internships or fieldwork, Federal Work-Study, institutionally sponsored loans, scholarships/grants, tuition waivers (partial), and unspecified assistantships available. Support available to part-time students. Financial award applicants required to submit FAFSA. *Unit head:* Dr. Wendy Burke, Coordinator, 734-487-3260, Fax: 734-487-2101, E-mail: wendy.burke@emich.edu. *Application contact:* Dr. Anne Bednar, Advisor, 734-487-3260, Fax: 734-487-2101, E-mail: anne.bednar@emich.edu.

Eastern Nazarene College, Adult and Graduate Studies, Division of Teacher Education, Quincy, MA 02170. Offers administration (M Ed); early childhood education (M Ed, Certificate); elementary education (M Ed, Certificate); English as a second language (Certificate); instructional enrichment and development (Certificate); middle school education (M Ed, Certificate); moderate special needs education (Certificate); principal (Certificate); program development and supervision (Certificate); secondary education (M Ed, Certificate); special education administrator (Certificate); special needs (M Ed); supervisor (Certificate); teacher of reading (M Ed, Certificate). M Ed also available through weekend program for administration, special needs, and teacher of reading only. Part-time and evening/weekend programs available. *Entrance requirements:* Additional exam requirements/recommendations for international students: Required—TOEFL (minimum score 550 paper-based).

Eastern New Mexico University, Graduate School, College of Education and Technology, Department of Educational Studies, Portales, NM 88130. Offers counseling (MA); education (M Ed), including educational adminstration, secondary education; school counseling (M Ed); special education (M Sp Ed), including early childhood special education, general. *Accreditation:* NCATE. Part-time and evening/weekend programs available. Postbaccalaureate distance learning degree programs offered (minimal on-campus study). *Degree requirements:* For master's, comprehensive exam, thesis optional. *Entrance requirements:* For master's, minimum GPA of 3.0, letter of recommendation, photocopy of teaching license, writing assessment, Level II teaching license (for M Ed in educational administration). Additional exam requirements/recommendations for international students: Required—TOEFL (minimum score 550 paper-based; 213 computer-based; 79 iBT), IELTS (minimum score 6). Electronic applications accepted.

Eastern Oregon University, Program in Secondary Education, La Grande, OR 97850-2899. Offers MAT. Part-time programs available. Postbaccalaureate distance learning degree programs offered (minimal on-campus study). *Degree requirements:* For master's, thesis. *Entrance requirements:* For master's, NTE.

Eastern Washington University, Graduate Studies, College of Arts, Letters and Education, Department of Education, Cheney, WA 99004-2431. Offers adult education (M Ed); curriculum development (M Ed); early childhood education (M Ed); education (M Ed); educational leadership (M Ed); elementary teaching (M Ed); foundations of education (M Ed); instructional media and technology (M Ed); literacy (M Ed); secondary teaching (M Ed); teaching K-8 (M Ed). Part-time programs available. *Faculty:* 25 full-time (16 women). *Students:* 40 full-time (27 women), 39 part-time (31 women); includes 4 minority (1 American Indian or Alaska Native, non-Hispanic/Latino; 3 Hispanic/Latino), 4 international. Average age 38. 48 applicants, 21% accepted, 8 enrolled. In 2011, 44 master's awarded. *Degree requirements:* For master's, comprehensive exam. *Entrance requirements:* For master's, minimum GPA of 3.0. *Application deadline:* For fall admission, 4/1 priority date for domestic students; for spring admission, 1/15 for domestic students. Applications are processed on a rolling basis. Application fee: $50. *Financial support:* In 2011–12, 2 teaching assistantships with partial tuition reimbursements (averaging $7,000 per year) were awarded; career-related internships or fieldwork, Federal Work-Study, institutionally sponsored loans, scholarships/grants, health care benefits, tuition waivers (partial), and unspecified assistantships also available. Support available to part-time students. Financial award application deadline: 2/1; financial award applicants required to submit FAFSA. *Unit head:* Dr. Kevin Pyatt, Assistant Professor, Science and Technology, 509-359-2831, E-mail: kpyatt@ewu.edu. *Application contact:* Dr. Robin Showalter, Graduate Program Coordinator, 509-359-6492, E-mail: rshowalter@ewu.edu. Web site: http://www.ewu.edu/CALE/Programs/Education.xml.

East Stroudsburg University of Pennsylvania, Graduate School, College of Education, Department of Professional and Secondary Education, East Stroudsburg, PA 18301-2999. Offers M Ed. *Accreditation:* NCATE. Part-time and evening/weekend programs available. *Degree requirements:* For master's, independent research problem or comprehensive assessment portfolio. *Entrance requirements:* For master's, PRAXIS/teacher certification, letter of recommendation, Pennsylvania Department of Education requirements. Additional exam requirements/recommendations for international students: Required—TOEFL (minimum score 560 paper-based; 220 computer-based; 83 iBT).

East Tennessee State University, School of Graduate Studies, College of Education, Department of Curriculum and Instruction, Johnson City, TN 37614. Offers educational media/educational technology (M Ed), including educational communications and technology, school library media; elementary education (M Ed); reading (MA), including reading education, storytelling; school library professional (Post-Master's Certificate); secondary education (M Ed), including classroom technology, secondary education (M Ed, MAT); storytelling (Postbaccalaureate Certificate); teacher education with multiple levels (initial licensure) (MAT), including elementary education, middle grades education, secondary education (M Ed, MAT). *Accreditation:* NCATE. Part-time and evening/weekend programs available. Postbaccalaureate distance learning degree programs offered (no on-campus study). *Faculty:* 20 full-time (13 women), 3 part-time/adjunct (all women). *Students:* 108 full-time (76 women), 107 part-time (97 women); includes 9 minority (4 Black or African American, non-Hispanic/Latino; 1 Asian, non-Hispanic/Latino; 2 Hispanic/Latino; 2 Two or more races, non-Hispanic/Latino), 2 international. Average age 33. 141 applicants, 57% accepted, 79 enrolled. In 2011, 129 master's awarded. *Degree requirements:* For master's, comprehensive exam, thesis optional, student teaching, practicum; for other advanced degree, field work (school library); culminating experience (storytelling). *Entrance requirements:* For master's, GRE, SAT, ACT, PRAXIS, minimum GPA of 3.0; for other advanced degree, master's degree, TN teaching license (school library professional post-master's certificate); three letters of recommendation (storytelling certificate). Additional exam requirements/recommendations for international students: Required—TOEFL (minimum score 550 paper-based; 213 computer-based; 79 iBT). *Application deadline:* For fall admission, 6/1 for domestic students, 4/30 for international students; for spring admission, 11/1 for domestic students, 4/30 for international students. Application fee: $35 ($45 for international students). Electronic applications accepted. *Expenses:* Tuition, state resident: full-time $7312; part-time $350 per credit hour. Tuition, nonresident: full-time $18,490; part-time $621 per credit hour. *Required fees:* $63 per credit hour. Tuition and fees vary according to course load and program. *Financial support:* In 2011–12, 60 students received support, including 7 research assistantships with full tuition reimbursements available (averaging $6,000 per year), 11 teaching assistantships with full tuition reimbursements available (averaging $6,000 per year); career-related internships or fieldwork, institutionally sponsored loans, scholarships/grants, and unspecified assistantships also available. Financial award application deadline: 7/1; financial award applicants required to submit FAFSA. *Faculty research:* Critical thinking; curriculum development in reading, math, and science education; cultural diversity; cognitive processes; effective teaching strategies. *Unit head:* Dr. Rhona Hurwitz, Chair, 423-439-7598, Fax: 423-439-8362, E-mail: hurwitz@etsu.edu. *Application contact:* Fiona Goodyear, Graduate Specialist, 423-439-6148, Fax: 423-439-5624, E-mail: goodyear@etsu.edu.

Edinboro University of Pennsylvania, School of Education, Department of Elementary, Middle and Secondary Education, Edinboro, PA 16444. Offers elementary education (M Ed); middle/secondary instruction (M Ed). Part-time and evening/weekend programs available. *Faculty:* 4 full-time (2 women). *Students:* 104 full-time (58 women), 131 part-time (95 women); includes 5 minority (3 Black or African American, non-Hispanic/Latino; 2 Hispanic/Latino). Average age 30. In 2011, 82 master's awarded. *Degree requirements:* For master's, comprehensive exam, thesis or alternative, project. *Entrance requirements:* For master's, GRE or MAT, minimum QPA of 2.5. *Application deadline:* Applications are processed on a rolling basis. Application fee: $30. Electronic applications accepted. *Financial support:* In 2011–12, 14 research assistantships with full and partial tuition reimbursements (averaging $4,050 per year) were awarded; career-related internships or fieldwork, Federal Work-Study, scholarships/grants, and unspecified assistantships also available. Support available to part-time students. Financial award application deadline: 2/15; financial award applicants required to submit FAFSA. *Unit head:* Dr. Jo Ann Holtz, Program Head, Middle and Secondary Instruction, 814-732-2794, E-mail: jholtz@edinboro.edu. *Application contact:* Dr. Alan Biel, Dean of Graduate Studies and Research, 814-732-2856, Fax: 814-732-2611, E-mail: abiel@edinboro.edu.

Elms College, Division of Education, Chicopee, MA 01013-2839. Offers early childhood education (MAT); education (M Ed, CAGS); elementary education (MAT); English as a second language (MAT); reading (MAT); secondary education (MAT), including biology education, English education, Spanish education; special education (MAT). Part-time and evening/weekend programs available. *Degree requirements:* For master's, thesis (for some programs). *Entrance requirements:* For master's, Massachusetts Educators Certification Test, minimum GPA of 3.0; for CAGS, master's degree in education. Additional exam requirements/recommendations for international students: Required—TOEFL.

Emmanuel College, Graduate and Professional Programs, Graduate Programs in Education, Boston, MA 02115. Offers educational leadership (CAGS); elementary education (MAT); school administration (M Ed); secondary education (MAT). Part-time and evening/weekend programs available. *Faculty:* 3 full-time (all women), 11 part-time/adjunct (3 women). *Students:* 12 full-time (11 women), 28 part-time (21 women); includes 9 minority (6 Black or African American, non-Hispanic/Latino; 1 American Indian or Alaska Native, non-Hispanic/Latino; 2 Hispanic/Latino). Average age 30. 9 applicants, 78% accepted, 6 enrolled. In 2011, 14 degrees awarded. *Degree requirements:* For master's, 36 credits, including 6-credit practicum. *Entrance requirements:* For master's and CAGS, transcripts from all regionally-accredited institutions attended (showing proof of bachelor's degree completion), 2 letters of recommendation, essay, resume, interview. Additional exam requirements/recommendations for international students: Required—TOEFL (minimum score 600 paper-based; 250 computer-based; 106 iBT) or IELTS (minimum score 6.5). *Application deadline:* For fall admission, 7/31 priority date for domestic students; for spring admission, 11/30 priority date for domestic students. Applications are processed on a rolling basis. Application fee: $0. Electronic applications accepted. *Expenses: Tuition:* Part-time $2139 per course. Tuition and fees vary according to program and reciprocity agreements. *Financial support:* Applicants required to submit FAFSA. *Faculty research:* Literature/reading, history of education, multicultural education, special education. *Unit head:* Dr. Joyce DeLeo, Vice President of Academic Affairs, 617-735-9700, Fax: 617-507-0434, E-mail: gpp@emmanuel.edu. *Application contact:* Enrollment Counselor,

617-735-9700, Fax: 617-507-0434, E-mail: gpp@emmanuel.edu. Web site: http://gpp.emmanuel.edu.

Emory University, Laney Graduate School, Division of Educational Studies, Atlanta, GA 30322-1100. Offers educational studies (MA, PhD); middle grades teaching (MAT); secondary teaching (MAT). *Accreditation:* NCATE. *Faculty:* 10 full-time (4 women), 3 part-time/adjunct (2 women). *Students:* 56 full-time (48 women); includes 20 minority (18 Black or African American, non-Hispanic/Latino; 2 Asian, non-Hispanic/Latino), 2 international. 86 applicants, 42% accepted, 26 enrolled. In 2011, 16 master's, 4 doctorates awarded. Terminal master's awarded for partial completion of doctoral program. *Degree requirements:* For master's, thesis; for doctorate, comprehensive exam, thesis/dissertation. *Entrance requirements:* For master's and doctorate, GRE General Test, minimum GPA of 3.0. Additional exam requirements/recommendations for international students: Required—TOEFL. *Application deadline:* For fall admission, 1/3 for domestic students. Application fee: $45. Electronic applications accepted. *Expenses: Tuition:* Full-time $34,800. *Required fees:* $1300. *Financial support:* In 2011–12, 50 students received support, including 10 fellowships; research assistantships, teaching assistantships, career-related internships or fieldwork, scholarships/grants, tuition waivers (full and partial), and unspecified assistantships also available. Financial award application deadline: 1/3. *Faculty research:* Educational policy, educational measurement, urban and multicultural education, mathematics and science education, comparative education. *Total annual research expenditures:* $130,000. *Unit head:* Prof. George Engelhard, Director of Graduate Studies, 404-727-0607, E-mail: gengelh@emory.edu. *Application contact:* Dr. Glen Avant, Graduate Program Administrator, 404-727-0612, E-mail: gavant@emory.edu. Web site: http://des.emory.edu/.

Endicott College, Van Loan School of Graduate and Professional Studies, Program in Secondary Education, Beverly, MA 01915-2096. Offers M Ed. Part-time and evening/weekend programs available. Postbaccalaureate distance learning degree programs offered. *Faculty:* 1 full-time (0 women), 3 part-time/adjunct (1 woman). *Students:* 14 full-time (all women). Average age 34. 42 applicants, 95% accepted, 14 enrolled. *Entrance requirements:* For master's, Massachusetts Tests for Educator Licensure (MTEL) Communication and Literacy Test, Massachusetts Tests for Educator Licensure (MTEL) Subject Matter Test (English, history, political science/philosophy, humanities, mathematics, biology, chemistry, earth science, physics, general science, mathematics/science), MAT or GRE, bachelor's degree from accredited college, transcript. Additional exam requirements/recommendations for international students: Required—TOEFL. *Application deadline:* Applications are processed on a rolling basis. Application fee: $50. Electronic applications accepted. Tuition and fees vary according to degree level and program. *Financial support:* Applicants required to submit FAFSA. *Unit head:* Dr. John D. MacLean, Jr., Director, 978-232-2408, E-mail: jmaclean@endicott.edu.

Evangel University, Department of Education, Springfield, MO 65802. Offers educational leadership (M Ed); reading education (M Ed); secondary teaching (M Ed); teaching (MA). *Accreditation:* NCATE. Part-time and evening/weekend programs available. *Faculty:* 4 full-time (1 woman), 2 part-time/adjunct (1 woman). *Students:* 10 full-time (5 women), 39 part-time (25 women). Average age 33. 14 applicants, 86% accepted, 11 enrolled. In 2011, 21 master's awarded. *Degree requirements:* For master's, comprehensive exam, thesis optional. *Entrance requirements:* For master's, PRAXIS II (preferred) or GRE. Additional exam requirements/recommendations for international students: Required—TOEFL (minimum score 550 paper-based; 213 computer-based). *Application deadline:* For fall admission, 7/15 priority date for domestic students; for spring admission, 11/15 priority date for domestic students. Applications are processed on a rolling basis. Application fee: $25. *Financial support:* In 2011–12, 3 students received support. Career-related internships or fieldwork, institutionally sponsored loans, and scholarships/grants available. Support available to part-time students. Financial award application deadline: 3/1; financial award applicants required to submit FAFSA. *Unit head:* Dr. Matt Stringer, Program Coordinator, 417-865-2815 Ext. 8563, E-mail: stringerm@evangel.edu. *Application contact:* Micah Hildreth, Admissions Representative, Graduate and Professional Studies, 417-865-2811 Ext. 7227, Fax: 417-865-9599, E-mail: hildrethm@evangel.edu. Web site: http://www.evangel.edu/departments/education/about-the-department/.

Fayetteville State University, Graduate School, Program in Middle Grades, Secondary and Special Education, Fayetteville, NC 28301-4298. Offers biology (MA Ed); history (MA Ed); mathematics (MA Ed); middle grades (MA Ed); political science (MA Ed); reading (MA Ed); sociology (MA Ed); special education (MA Ed), including behavioral-emotional handicaps, mentally handicapped, specific training disability. *Accreditation:* NCATE. Part-time and evening/weekend programs available. *Faculty:* 12 full-time (8 women), 4 part-time/adjunct (3 women). *Students:* 37 full-time (31 women), 66 part-time (57 women); includes 75 minority (68 Black or African American, non-Hispanic/Latino; 1 American Indian or Alaska Native, non-Hispanic/Latino; 3 Hispanic/Latino; 3 Two or more races, non-Hispanic/Latino). Average age 35. 18 applicants, 100% accepted, 18 enrolled. In 2011, 35 master's awarded. *Degree requirements:* For master's, comprehensive exam, internship. *Application deadline:* For fall admission, 4/15 for domestic students; for spring admission, 10/15 for domestic students. Applications are processed on a rolling basis. Application fee: $35. Electronic applications accepted. *Faculty research:* Students with disabilities and selected leadership behaviors, new vision for professional development, gifted and talented studentsm emotional and behavioral disabilities, professional development for high school biology teachers. *Unit head:* Dr. Kimberly Smith-Burton, Interim Chair, 910-672-1182, E-mail: cbarringerbrown@uncfsu.edu. *Application contact:* Katrina Hoffman, Graduate Admission Officer, 910-672-1374, Fax: 910-672-1470, E-mail: khoffma1@uncfsu.edu.

Fitchburg State University, Division of Graduate and Continuing Education, Program in Secondary Education, Fitchburg, MA 01420-2697. Offers M Ed. *Accreditation:* NCATE. Part-time and evening/weekend programs available. *Students:* 2 full-time (1 woman), 22 part-time (11 women); includes 1 minority (Hispanic/Latino), 1 international. Average age 39. 8 applicants, 100% accepted, 3 enrolled. In 2011, 13 master's awarded. *Entrance requirements:* Additional exam requirements/recommendations for international students: Required—TOEFL (minimum score 550 paper-based; 213 computer-based; 79 iBT). *Application deadline:* For fall admission, 7/15 for international students; for spring admission, 12/1 for international students. Applications are processed on a rolling basis. Application fee: $25 ($50 for international students). Electronic applications accepted. *Expenses:* Tuition, state resident: full-time $2700; part-time $150 per credit. Tuition, nonresident: full-time $2700; part-time $150 per credit. *Required fees:* $2286; $127 per credit. *Financial support:* In 2011–12, research assistantships with partial tuition reimbursements (averaging $5,500 per year) were awarded; Federal Work-Study, scholarships/grants, and unspecified assistantships also available. Support available to part-time students. Financial award application deadline: 3/1; financial award applicants required to submit FAFSA. *Unit head:* Dr. Nancy Kelly, Chair, 978-665-3447, Fax: 978-665-3658, E-mail: gce@fitchburgstate.edu. *Application contact:* Kay Reynolds, Director of Admissions, 978-665-3144, Fax: 978-665-4540, E-mail: admissions@fitchburgstate.edu. Web site: http://www.fitchburgstate.edu.

Florida Agricultural and Mechanical University, Division of Graduate Studies, Research, and Continuing Education, College of Education, Program in Secondary Education and Foundation, Tallahassee, FL 32307-3200. Offers biology (M Ed); chemistry (MS Ed); English (MS Ed); history (MS Ed); math (MS Ed); physics (MS Ed). *Accreditation:* NCATE. *Degree requirements:* For master's, thesis (for some programs). *Entrance requirements:* For master's, GRE General Test, minimum GPA of 3.0. Additional exam requirements/recommendations for international students: Required—TOEFL.

Fordham University, Graduate School of Education, Division of Curriculum and Teaching, New York, NY 10023. Offers adult education (MS, MSE); bilingual teacher education (MSE); curriculum and teaching (MSE); early childhood education (MSE); elementary education (MST); language, literacy, and learning (PhD); reading education (MSE, Adv C); secondary education (MAT, MSE); special education (MSE, Adv C); teaching English as a second language (MSE). *Accreditation:* NCATE. *Degree requirements:* For doctorate, thesis/dissertation; for Adv C, thesis. *Entrance requirements:* For doctorate, MAT, GRE General Test. *Expenses: Tuition:* Full-time $30,480; part-time $1270 per credit. *Required fees:* $586; $293 per semester.

Francis Marion University, Graduate Programs, School of Education, Florence, SC 29502-0547. Offers early childhood education (M Ed); elementary education (M Ed); learning disabilities (M Ed, MAT); remedial education (M Ed); secondary education (M Ed). *Accreditation:* NCATE. Part-time programs available. *Faculty:* 20 full-time (16 women), 1 (woman) part-time/adjunct. *Students:* 10 full-time (8 women), 115 part-time (88 women); includes 30 minority (26 Black or African American, non-Hispanic/Latino; 3 Asian, non-Hispanic/Latino; 1 Hispanic/Latino), 1 international. Average age 32. 249 applicants, 33% accepted, 77 enrolled. In 2011, 41 master's awarded. *Degree requirements:* For master's, comprehensive exam. *Entrance requirements:* For master's, GRE General Test, MAT, NTE, or PRAXIS II. *Application deadline:* For fall admission, 3/15 priority date for domestic students; for spring admission, 10/15 priority date for domestic students. Applications are processed on a rolling basis. Application fee: $31. *Expenses:* Tuition, state resident: full-time $8467; part-time $443.35 per credit hour. Tuition, nonresident: full-time $16,934; part-time $866.70 per credit hour. *Required fees:* $335; $12.25 per credit hour. $30 per semester. *Financial support:* In 2011–12, 3 research assistantships (averaging $6,000 per year) were awarded; scholarships/grants and unspecified assistantships also available. Support available to part-time students. Financial award application deadline: 3/1; financial award applicants required to submit FAFSA. *Faculty research:* Identification and alternate assessment of at-risk students. *Unit head:* Dr. James R. Faulkenberry, Dean, 843-661-1460, Fax: 843-661-4647. *Application contact:* Rannie Gamble, Administrative Manager, 843-661-1286, Fax: 843-661-4688, E-mail: rgamble@fmarion.edu.

Fresno Pacific University, Graduate Programs, School of Education, Division of Mathematics/Science/Computer Education, Program in Mathematics Education, Fresno, CA 93702-4709. Offers elementary and middle school mathematics (MA Ed); secondary school mathematics (MA Ed). Part-time and evening/weekend programs available. *Degree requirements:* For master's, thesis or alternative. *Entrance requirements:* Additional exam requirements/recommendations for international students: Required—TOEFL (minimum score 550 paper-based; 213 computer-based).

Frostburg State University, Graduate School, College of Education, Department of Educational Professions, Program in Curriculum and Instruction, Frostburg, MD 21532-1099. Offers educational technology (M Ed); elementary education (M Ed); secondary education (M Ed). Part-time and evening/weekend programs available. *Degree requirements:* For master's, thesis or alternative. *Entrance requirements:* For master's, teaching certificate. Additional exam requirements/recommendations for international students: Required—TOEFL. Electronic applications accepted.

Frostburg State University, Graduate School, College of Education, Department of Educational Professions, Program in Secondary Teaching, Frostburg, MD 21532-1099. Offers MAT. *Entrance requirements:* For master's, PRAXIS I, entry portfolio. Additional exam requirements/recommendations for international students: Required—TOEFL.

Gallaudet University, The Graduate School, Washington, DC 20002-3625. Offers audiology (Au D); clinical psychology (PhD); critical studies in the education of deaf learners (PhD); deaf and hard of hearing infants, toddlers, and their families (Certificate); deaf education (Ed S); deaf education: advanced studies (MA); deaf education: special programs in deaf education (MA); deaf history (Certificate); deaf studies (MA, Certificate); education deaf students with disabilities (Certificate); education: teacher preparation (MA), including deaf education, early childhood education and deaf education, elementary education and deaf education, secondary education and deaf education; hearing, speech and language sciences (MS, PhD); international development (MA); interpretation (MA, PhD); linguistics (MA, PhD); mental health counseling (MA); public administration (MA); school counseling (MA); school psychology (Psy S); sign language teaching (MA); social work (MSW); speech-language pathology (MS). Part-time programs available. *Faculty:* 62 full-time (44 women). *Students:* 300 full-time (246 women), 110 part-time (82 women); includes 80 minority (27 Black or African American, non-Hispanic/Latino; 1 American Indian or Alaska Native, non-Hispanic/Latino; 11 Asian, non-Hispanic/Latino; 25 Hispanic/Latino; 1 Native Hawaiian or other Pacific Islander, non-Hispanic/Latino; 15 Two or more races, non-Hispanic/Latino), 24 international. Average age 30. 498 applicants, 45% accepted, 168 enrolled. In 2011, 129 master's, 24 doctorates, 19 other advanced degrees awarded. Terminal master's awarded for partial completion of doctoral program. *Degree requirements:* For master's, comprehensive exam (for some programs), thesis optional; for doctorate, comprehensive exam, thesis/dissertation. *Entrance requirements:* For master's and doctorate, GRE General Test or MAT, letters of recommendation, interviews, goals statement, ASL proficiency interview, written English competency. Additional exam requirements/recommendations for international students: Required—TOEFL. *Application deadline:* For fall admission, 2/15 for domestic students. Applications are processed on a rolling basis. Application fee: $50. Electronic applications accepted. *Expenses: Tuition:* Full-time $12,770; part-time $710 per credit. *Required fees:* $376. *Financial support:* In 2011–12, 287 students received support. Fellowships, research assistantships, teaching assistantships, career-related internships or fieldwork, Federal Work-Study, scholarships/grants, tuition waivers (partial), and unspecified assistantships available. Support available to part-time students. Financial award applicants required to submit FAFSA. *Faculty research:* Bimodal bilingualism development, audiology, telecommunications access, early childhood education, linguistics, visual language and visual learning, rehabilitation and hearing enhancement. *Unit head:* Dr. Carol J. Erting, Dean, 202-651-5520, Fax: 202-651-5027, E-mail: carol.erting@gallaudet.edu. *Application contact:* Wednesday Luria, Coordinator of Prospective Graduate Student Services, 202-651-5400, Fax: 202-651-5295, E-mail: graduate.school@gallaudet.edu. Web site: http://www.gallaudet.edu/x26696.xml.

George Fox University, School of Education, Educational Foundations and Leadership Program, Newberg, OR 97132-2697. Offers continuing administrator license (Certificate); curriculum and instruction (M Ed); educational leadership (M Ed, Ed D); ESOL (Certificate); higher education (M Ed); initial administrator license (Certificate); instructional leadership (Ed S); library media (M Ed, Certificate); literacy (M Ed); reading (M Ed); secondary education (M Ed). *Accreditation:* NCATE. Part-time and evening/weekend programs available. Postbaccalaureate distance learning degree programs offered (minimal on-campus study). *Faculty:* 10 full-time (3 women), 6 part-time/adjunct (3 women). *Students:* 2 full-time (both women), 111 part-time (83 women); includes 16 minority (2 American Indian or Alaska Native, non-Hispanic/Latino; 6 Asian, non-Hispanic/Latino; 7 Hispanic/Latino; 1 Native Hawaiian or other Pacific Islander, non-

Hispanic/Latino), 3 international. Average age 39. 44 applicants, 98% accepted, 43 enrolled. In 2011, 34 master's, 7 doctorates, 76 Certificates awarded. *Degree requirements:* For master's, thesis (for some programs); for doctorate, comprehensive exam, thesis/dissertation, project. *Entrance requirements:* For master's, minimum undergraduate GPA of 3.0 during previous 2 years of course work, resume, 3 professional recommendations on university forms, official transcripts; for doctorate, GRE, master's degree with minimum GPA of 3.25, 3 years of relevant professional experience, interview, personal essay, scholarly work, 3 professional recommendations on university forms along with 3 written letters of recommendation, official transcripts. Additional exam requirements/recommendations for international students: Required—TOEFL (minimum score 577 paper-based; 233 computer-based; 90 iBT). *Application deadline:* For fall admission, 7/15 for domestic and international students; for winter admission, 11/1 for domestic and international students; for spring admission, 4/1 for domestic and international students. Applications are processed on a rolling basis. Application fee: $40. Electronic applications accepted. *Expenses:* Contact institution. *Financial support:* Career-related internships or fieldwork available. Financial award applicants required to submit FAFSA. *Unit head:* Dr. Scot Headley, Professor/Chair, 503-554-2836, E-mail: sheadley@georgefox.edu. *Application contact:* Alex Martin, Admissions Counselor, 800-631-0921, Fax: 503-554-3110, E-mail: amartin@georgefox.edu. Web site: http://www.georgefox.edu/education/index.html.

The George Washington University, Graduate School of Education and Human Development, Department of Curriculum and Pedagogy, Program in Secondary Education, Washington, DC 20052. Offers M Ed. Program also offered in Arlington and Ashburn, VA. *Accreditation:* NCATE. *Students:* 27 full-time (21 women), 71 part-time (59 women); includes 19 minority (6 Black or African American, non-Hispanic/Latino; 5 Asian, non-Hispanic/Latino; 8 Hispanic/Latino), 2 international. Average age 32. 56 applicants, 93% accepted, 26 enrolled. In 2011, 71 master's awarded. *Degree requirements:* For master's, comprehensive exam. *Entrance requirements:* For master's, GRE General Test or MAT, interview, minimum GPA of 2.75. *Application deadline:* For fall admission, 1/15 priority date for domestic students; for spring admission, 10/1 for domestic students. Applications are processed on a rolling basis. Application fee: $75. *Financial support:* Fellowships, career-related internships or fieldwork, Federal Work-Study, tuition waivers (full and partial), and stipends available. Financial award application deadline: 1/15; financial award applicants required to submit FAFSA. *Unit head:* Prof. Curtis Pyke, Chair, 202-994-4516, E-mail: cpyke@gwu.edu. *Application contact:* Sarah Lang, Director of Graduate Admissions, 202-994-1447, Fax: 202-994-7207, E-mail: slang@gwu.edu.

Georgia College & State University, Graduate School, The John H. Lounsbury College of Education, Department of Foundations and Secondary Education, Milledgeville, GA 31061. Offers curriculum and instruction (Ed S), including secondary education; educational technology (M Ed), including library media; educational technology (M Ed), including instructional technology; secondary education (M Ed, MAT). *Accreditation:* NCATE. Part-time and evening/weekend programs available. *Students:* 84 full-time (47 women), 120 part-time (98 women); includes 51 minority (43 Black or African American, non-Hispanic/Latino; 2 Asian, non-Hispanic/Latino; 4 Hispanic/Latino; 2 Two or more races, non-Hispanic/Latino), 1 international. Average age 31. 69 applicants, 51% accepted, 28 enrolled. In 2011, 105 master's, 33 other advanced degrees awarded. *Degree requirements:* For master's, comprehensive exam; for Ed S, comprehensive exam, electronic portfolio presentation. *Entrance requirements:* For master's, on-site writing assessment, 2 letters of recommendation, level 4 teaching certificate; for Ed S, on-site writing assessment, master's degree, 2 letters of recommendation, 2 years of teaching experience, level 5 teacher certification. Additional exam requirements/recommendations for international students: Recommended—TOEFL (minimum score 550 paper-based; 213 computer-based; 79 iBT). *Application deadline:* For fall admission, 7/1 priority date for domestic students, 4/1 for international students; for spring admission, 11/15 priority date for domestic students, 9/1 for international students. Applications are processed on a rolling basis. Application fee: $40. Electronic applications accepted. *Expenses:* Tuition, state resident: full-time $4806; part-time $267 per credit hour. Tuition, nonresident: full-time $17,802; part-time $989 per credit hour. *Required fees:* $936 per semester. Tuition and fees vary according to course load and campus/location. *Financial support:* In 2011–12, 12 research assistantships with full tuition reimbursements were awarded; career-related internships or fieldwork and Federal Work-Study also available. Support available to part-time students. Financial award applicants required to submit FAFSA. *Unit head:* Dr. Brian Mumma, Interim Chair, 478-445-2517, E-mail: brian.mumma@gcsu.edu. *Application contact:* Shanda Brand, Graduate Advisor, 478-445-1383, E-mail: shanda.brand@gcsu.edu.

Georgia Southwestern State University, Graduate Studies, School of Education, Americus, GA 31709-4693. Offers early childhood education (M Ed, Ed S); health and physical education (M Ed); middle grades education (M Ed, Ed S); reading (M Ed); secondary education (M Ed); special education (M Ed). *Accreditation:* NCATE. *Degree requirements:* For master's, comprehensive exam. *Entrance requirements:* For master's, GRE General Test or MAT, minimum GPA of 2.5; for Ed S, GRE General Test or MAT, minimum graduate GPA of 3.25, M Ed from accredited college or university, 3 years teaching experience. Electronic applications accepted.

Georgia State University, College of Education, Department of Middle-Secondary Education and Instructional Technology, Programs in Secondary Education, Atlanta, GA 30302-3083. Offers art education (Ed S); English education (M Ed, Ed S); mathematics education (M Ed, PhD, Ed S); music education (PhD); science education (M Ed, PhD, Ed S); social studies education (M Ed, PhD, Ed S). *Accreditation:* NASM (one or more programs are accredited); NCATE. Part-time and evening/weekend programs available. *Degree requirements:* For master's, comprehensive exam; for doctorate, comprehensive exam, thesis/dissertation; for Ed S, project/exam. *Entrance requirements:* For master's, GRE General Test, minimum GPA of 2.5; for doctorate, GRE General Test or MAT, minimum GPA of 3.3; for Ed S, GRE General Test or MAT, minimum graduate GPA of 3.25. *Faculty research:* Women and science, problem solving in mathematics, dialects, economic education.

Grand Canyon University, College of Education, Phoenix, AZ 85017-1097. Offers curriculum and instruction (M Ed); education administration (M Ed); elementary education (M Ed); secondary education (M Ed); special education (M Ed); teaching (MA). Part-time and evening/weekend programs available. Postbaccalaureate distance learning degree programs offered (no on-campus study). *Degree requirements:* For master's, publishable research paper (M Ed), e-portfolio. *Entrance requirements:* For master's, undergraduate degree from accredited, GCU-approved college, university, or program with minimum GPA 2.8. Additional exam requirements/recommendations for international students: Required—TOEFL (minimum score 550 paper-based; 213 computer-based; 79 iBT), IELTS (minimum score 6). Electronic applications accepted.

Grand Valley State University, College of Education, Programs in General Education, Allendale, MI 49401-9403. Offers adult and higher education (M Ed); early childhood education (M Ed); educational differentiation (M Ed); educational leadership (M Ed); educational technology integration (M Ed); elementary education (M Ed); middle level education (M Ed); school library media services (M Ed); secondary level education (M Ed); teaching English to speakers of other languages (M Ed). Part-time and evening/weekend programs available. Postbaccalaureate distance learning degree programs offered (minimal on-campus study). *Degree requirements:* For master's, thesis. *Entrance requirements:* For master's, GRE General Test or minimum GPA of 3.0. Additional exam requirements/recommendations for international students: Required—TOEFL. Electronic applications accepted. *Faculty research:* Effectiveness of technology in education, parental involvement, effective teaching, effective schools research.

Greenville College, Program in Education, Greenville, IL 62246-0159. Offers education (MAT); elementary education (MAE); secondary education (MAE). *Degree requirements:* For master's, thesis (for some programs). *Entrance requirements:* For master's, GRE, Illinois Basic Skills Test, teacher certification. Electronic applications accepted.

Hampton University, Graduate College, College of Education and Continuing Studies, Program in Teaching, Hampton, VA 23668. Offers early childhood education (MT); middle school education (MT); music education (MT); secondary education (MT); special education (MT). *Entrance requirements:* For master's, GRE General Test.

Harding University, College of Education, Searcy, AR 72149-0001. Offers advanced studies in teaching and learning (M Ed); art (MSE); behavioral science (MSE); counseling (MS, Ed S); early childhood special education (M Ed, MSE); education (MSE); educational leadership (M Ed, Ed S); elementary education (M Ed); English (MSE); French (MSE); history/social science (MSE); kinesiology (MSE); math (MSE); reading (M Ed); secondary education (M Ed); Spanish (MSE); teaching (MAT); teaching English as a second language (MSE). *Accreditation:* NCATE. Part-time and evening/weekend programs available. *Faculty:* 9 full-time (2 women), 48 part-time/adjunct (26 women). *Students:* 100 full-time (77 women), 333 part-time (239 women); includes 76 minority (59 Black or African American, non-Hispanic/Latino; 1 Asian, non-Hispanic/Latino; 10 Hispanic/Latino; 6 Two or more races, non-Hispanic/Latino), 2 international. Average age 36. 93 applicants, 91% accepted, 83 enrolled. In 2011, 159 master's, 10 other advanced degrees awarded. *Degree requirements:* For master's, comprehensive exam (for some programs), thesis optional, portfolio(s); for Ed S, comprehensive exam, portfolio, project. *Entrance requirements:* For master's, GRE, MAT, PRAXIS; for Ed S, MAT or GRE. Additional exam requirements/recommendations for international students: Required—TOEFL (minimum score 550 paper-based; 79 iBT). *Application deadline:* For fall admission, 8/1 for domestic and international students; for spring admission, 1/1 for domestic and international students. Applications are processed on a rolling basis. Application fee: $35. *Expenses:* *Tuition:* Full-time $10,512; part-time $584 per credit hour. *Required fees:* $500; $25 per credit hour. Tuition and fees vary according to course load, degree level and program. *Financial support:* In 2011–12, 37 students received support. Unspecified assistantships available. *Faculty research:* Reading, comprehension, school violence, educational technology, behavior, college choice, differentiated instruction, brain-based teaching. *Unit head:* Dr. Clara Carroll, Chair, 501-279-4501, Fax: 501-279-4083, E-mail: ccarroll@harding.edu. *Application contact:* Information Contact, 501-279-4315, E-mail: gradstudiesedu@harding.edu. Web site: http://www.harding.edu/education/grad.html.

Hawai`i Pacific University, College of Humanities and Social Sciences, Program in Secondary Education, Honolulu, HI 96813. Offers M Ed. Part-time and evening/weekend programs available. *Faculty:* 2 full-time (both women), 1 part-time/adjunct (0 women). *Students:* 16 full-time (13 women), 1 (woman) part-time; includes 12 minority (6 Asian, non-Hispanic/Latino; 1 Hispanic/Latino; 1 Native Hawaiian or other Pacific Islander, non-Hispanic/Latino; 4 Two or more races, non-Hispanic/Latino). Average age 31. 19 applicants, 74% accepted, 12 enrolled. In 2011, 16 master's awarded. *Degree requirements:* For master's, thesis. *Entrance requirements:* For master's, PRAXIS I and II. Additional exam requirements/recommendations for international students: Recommended—TOEFL (minimum score 550 paper-based; 213 computer-based; 80 iBT), TWE (minimum score 5). *Application deadline:* For fall admission, 2/15 priority date for domestic students; for spring admission, 10/15 priority date for domestic students. Applications are processed on a rolling basis. Application fee: $50. Electronic applications accepted. *Expenses:* *Tuition:* Full-time $13,230; part-time $735 per credit. Tuition and fees vary according to course load and program. *Financial support:* In 2011–12, 1 student received support. Career-related internships or fieldwork, Federal Work-Study, scholarships/grants, tuition waivers, and unspecified assistantships available. Financial award application deadline: 3/1. *Unit head:* Dr. Valentina Abordonado, Program Chair, 808-544-1143, Fax: 808-544-0841, E-mail: vabordonado@hpu.edu. *Application contact:* Chad Schempp, Director of Graduate Admissions, 808-543-8035, Fax: 808-544-0280, E-mail: graduate@hpu.edu. Web site: http://www.hpu.edu/MED.

See Display on next page and Close-Up on page 1197.

High Point University, Norcross Graduate School, High Point, NC 27262-3598. Offers business administration (MBA); educational leadership (M Ed); elementary education (M Ed); history (MA); nonprofit management (MA); secondary math (M Ed); special education (M Ed); strategic communication (MA); teaching elementary education k-6 (MAT); teaching secondary mathematics 9-12 (MAT). *Accreditation:* ACBSP; NCATE. Part-time and evening/weekend programs available. *Degree requirements:* For master's, comprehensive exam (for some programs), thesis (for some programs). *Entrance requirements:* For master's, GMAT (MBA), GRE, MAT, minimum GPA of 3.0. Additional exam requirements/recommendations for international students: Required—TOEFL (minimum score 550 paper-based). Electronic applications accepted.

Hofstra University, School of Education, Health, and Human Services, Department of Foundations, Leadership, and Policy Studies, Hempstead, NY 11549. Offers educational and policy leadership (MS Ed, Ed D), including higher education (MS Ed), K-12 (MS Ed); educational policy and leadership (Advanced Certificate), including school district business leader; foundations of education (MA, Advanced Certificate); Advanced Certificate/Advanced Certificate. Part-time and evening/weekend programs available. Postbaccalaureate distance learning degree programs offered (minimal on-campus study). *Students:* 22 full-time (16 women), 105 part-time (65 women); includes 45 minority (33 Black or African American, non-Hispanic/Latino; 1 Asian, non-Hispanic/Latino; 11 Hispanic/Latino), 2 international. Average age 37. 78 applicants, 94% accepted, 42 enrolled. In 2011, 12 master's, 6 doctorates, 12 other advanced degrees awarded. *Degree requirements:* For master's, one foreign language, comprehensive exam (for some programs), thesis or alternative, minimum GPA of 3.0; for doctorate, comprehensive exam (for some programs), thesis/dissertation (for some programs), minimum GPA of 3.0. *Entrance requirements:* For master's and Advanced Certificate, interview, writing sample, essay; for doctorate, GMAT, GRE, LSAT, or MAT, interview, 3 letters of recommendation, resume, essay. Additional exam requirements/recommendations for international students: Required—TOEFL (minimum score 550 paper-based; 213 computer-based; 80 iBT). *Application deadline:* Applications are processed on a rolling basis. Application fee: $70 ($75 for international students). Electronic applications accepted. *Expenses:* *Tuition:* Full-time $18,990; part-time $1055 per credit hour. *Required fees:* $970. Tuition and fees vary according to program. *Financial support:* In 2011–12, 66 students received support, including 44 fellowships with full and partial tuition reimbursements available (averaging $3,788 per year), 3 research assistantships with full and partial tuition reimbursements available (averaging $12,125 per year); Federal Work-Study, institutionally sponsored loans, scholarships/

grants, tuition waivers (full and partial), and unspecified assistantships also available. Support available to part-time students. Financial award applicants required to submit FAFSA. *Faculty research:* School improvement, professional assessment - APPR, educational policy, professional development, race/gender in education. *Unit head:* Dr. Esther Fusco, Chairperson, 516-463-7704, Fax: 516-463-6196, E-mail: catezf@hofstra.edu. *Application contact:* Carol Drummer, Dean of Graduate Admissions, 516-463-4876, Fax: 516-463-4664, E-mail: gradstudent@hofstra.edu. Web site: http://www.hofstra.edu/education/.

Hofstra University, School of Education, Health, and Human Services, Department of Literacy Studies, Hempstead, NY 11549. Offers advanced literacy studies (PD), including birth-grade 6 (MA, MS Ed, PD); advanced literary studies (PD), including grades 5-12 (MA, PD); birth-grade 6 (MS Ed, Advanced Certificate); grades 5-12 (Advanced Certificate); literacy studies (Ed D, PhD); special education (MS Ed), including birth-grade 2, birth-grade 6 (MA, MS Ed, PD); special education (MS Ed), including birth-grade 2; teaching of writing (MA), including birth-grade 6 (MA, MS Ed, PD), grades 5-12 (MA, PD). Part-time and evening/weekend programs available. *Students:* 43 full-time (42 women), 70 part-time (63 women); includes 15 minority (7 Black or African American, non-Hispanic/Latino; 1 Asian, non-Hispanic/Latino; 7 Hispanic/Latino). Average age 33. 67 applicants, 81% accepted, 32 enrolled. In 2011, 47 master's, 1 doctorate, 10 other advanced degrees awarded. *Degree requirements:* For master's, comprehensive exam, portfolio, minimum GPA of 3.0; for doctorate, one foreign language, comprehensive exam, thesis/dissertation, qualifying hearing, minimum GPA of 3.0. *Entrance requirements:* For master's, interview, teaching certificate, 2 letters of recommendation; for doctorate, GRE or MAT, interview, resume, essay, master's degree, 3 letters of recommendation, writing sample; for other advanced degree, 2 letters of recommendation, interview, teaching certificate, essay, master's degree. Additional exam requirements/recommendations for international students: Required—TOEFL (minimum score 550 paper-based; 213 computer-based; 80 iBT). *Application deadline:* Applications are processed on a rolling basis. Application fee: $70 ($75 for international students). Electronic applications accepted. *Expenses: Tuition:* Full-time $18,990; part-time $1055 per credit hour. *Required fees:* $970. Tuition and fees vary according to program. *Financial support:* In 2011–12, 78 students received support, including 36 fellowships with full and partial tuition reimbursements available (averaging $3,622 per year); research assistantships with full and partial tuition reimbursements available, career-related internships or fieldwork, Federal Work-Study, institutionally sponsored loans, scholarships/grants, tuition waivers (full and partial), and unspecified assistantships also available. Support available to part-time students. Financial award applicants required to submit FAFSA. *Faculty research:* Research literacy practices of immigrant and urban youth, literature for children and adolescents, eye movement/miscue analysis, literacy strategies for effective instruction, transnational literacies. *Unit head:* Dr. Esther Fusco, Chairperson, 516-463-7704, Fax: 516-463-6196, E-mail: catezf@hofstra.edu. *Application contact:* Carol Drummer, Dean of Graduate Admissions, 516-463-4876, Fax: 516-463-4664, E-mail: gradstudent@hofstra.edu. Web site: http://www.hofstra.edu/education/.

Hofstra University, School of Education, Health, and Human Services, Programs in Teaching - Secondary Education, Hempstead, NY 11549. Offers business education (MS Ed); education technology (Advanced Certificate); English education (MA, MS Ed); foreign language and TESOL (MS Ed); foreign language education (MA, MS Ed), including French, German, Russian, Spanish; mathematics education (MA, MS Ed); science education (MA, MS Ed), including biology, chemistry, earth science, geology, physics; secondary education (Advanced Certificate); social studies education (MA, MS Ed). Part-time and evening/weekend programs available. Postbaccalaureate distance learning degree programs offered (minimal on-campus study). *Students:* 72 full-time (47 women), 51 part-time (30 women); includes 21 minority (9 Black or African American, non-Hispanic/Latino; 7 Asian, non-Hispanic/Latino; 5 Hispanic/Latino). Average age 28. 103 applicants, 91% accepted, 41 enrolled. In 2011, 86 master's, 6 other advanced degrees awarded. *Degree requirements:* For master's, one foreign language, comprehensive exam (for some programs), thesis (for some programs), exit project, electronic portfolio, student teaching, fieldwork, curriculum project, minimum GPA of 3.0; for Advanced Certificate, 3 foreign languages, comprehensive exam (for some programs), thesis project, minimum GPA of 3.0. *Entrance requirements:* For master's, 2 letters of recommendation, teacher certification (MA), essay; for Advanced Certificate, 2 letters of recommendation, essay. Additional exam requirements/recommendations for international students: Required—TOEFL (minimum score 550 paper-based; 213 computer-based; 80 iBT). *Application deadline:* Applications are processed on a rolling basis. Application fee: $70 ($75 for international students). Electronic applications accepted. *Expenses: Tuition:* Full-time $18,990; part-time $1055 per credit hour. *Required fees:* $970. Tuition and fees vary according to program. *Financial support:* In 2011–12, 90 students received support, including 13 fellowships with full and partial tuition reimbursements available (averaging $3,202 per year), 1 research assistantship with full and partial tuition reimbursement available (averaging $11,645 per year); career-related internships or fieldwork, Federal Work-Study, institutionally sponsored loans, scholarships/grants, tuition waivers (full and partial), and unspecified assistantships also available. Support available to part-time students. Financial award applicants required to submit FAFSA. *Faculty research:* Appropriate content and pedagogy in secondary school disciplines, appropriate pedagogy in secondary school disciplines, adolescent development, secondary school organization, alternative secondary school programs. *Unit head:* Dr. Esther Fusco, Chairperson, 516-463-7704, Fax: 516-463-6196, E-mail: catezf@hofstra.edu. *Application contact:* Carol Drummer, Dean of Graduate Admissions, 516-463-4876, Fax: 516-463-4664, E-mail: gradstudent@hofstra.edu. Web site: http://www.hofstra.edu/education/.

Holy Family University, Graduate School, School of Education, Philadelphia, PA 19114. Offers education (M Ed); education leadership (M Ed); elementary education (M Ed); reading specialist (M Ed); secondary education (M Ed); special education (M Ed). Part-time and evening/weekend programs available. *Degree requirements:* For master's, thesis optional. *Entrance requirements:* For master's, GRE or MAT, interview. Electronic applications accepted. *Faculty research:* Cognition, developmental issues, sociological issues in education.

See Display on page 707 and Close-Up on page 803.

Hood College, Graduate School, Department of Education, Frederick, MD 21701-8575. Offers curriculum and instruction (MS), including early childhood education, elementary education, elementary school science and mathematics, secondary education, special education; educational leadership (MS, Certificate); reading specialization (MS). Part-time and evening/weekend programs available. *Degree requirements:* For master's, action research project, portfolio (reading). *Entrance requirements:* For master's, minimum GPA of 2.75, teaching certification. Additional exam requirements/recommendations for international students: Required—TOEFL (minimum score 575 paper-based; 231 computer-based; 89 iBT). Electronic applications accepted. *Faculty research:* Leadership, action research, brain research, learning styles.

Hood College, Graduate School, Program in Secondary Mathematics Education, Frederick, MD 21701-8575. Offers mathematics education (MS), including high school, middle school; secondary mathematics education (Certificate). Part-time and evening/weekend programs available. *Degree requirements:* For master's, capstone/research project. *Entrance requirements:* For master's, minimum GPA of 2.75. Additional exam requirements/recommendations for international students: Required—TOEFL (minimum score 575 paper-based; 231 computer-based; 89 iBT). Electronic applications accepted.

Secondary Education

Hope International University, School of Graduate and Professional Studies, Program in Education, Fullerton, CA 92831-3138. Offers education administration (MA); elementary education (ME); secondary education (ME). Part-time and evening/weekend programs available. *Degree requirements:* For master's, comprehensive exam (for some programs), thesis. *Entrance requirements:* For master's, minimum GPA of 3.0, 2 references. Additional exam requirements/recommendations for international students: Required—TOEFL (minimum score 550 paper-based; 213 computer-based; 86 iBT); Recommended—IELTS (minimum score 6.5). Electronic applications accepted. *Expenses:* Contact institution. *Faculty research:* Distance education.

Howard University, School of Education, Department of Curriculum and Instruction, Program in Secondary Education, Washington, DC 20059-0002. Offers M Ed. *Accreditation:* NCATE. *Faculty:* 2 full-time (both women), 1 (woman) part-time/adjunct. *Students:* 13 full-time (12 women), 11 part-time (6 women); includes 23 minority (all Black or African American, non-Hispanic/Latino). Average age 31. 24 applicants, 75% accepted, 12 enrolled. *Degree requirements:* For master's, comprehensive exam, thesis (for some programs), expository writing exam, internships, practicum. *Entrance requirements:* For master's, minimum GPA of 2.7. Additional exam requirements/ recommendations for international students: Required—TOEFL (minimum score 550 paper-based). *Application deadline:* For fall admission, 2/15 priority date for domestic students; for spring admission, 11/1 for domestic students. Applications are processed on a rolling basis. Application fee: $45. Electronic applications accepted. *Financial support:* Fellowships with full and partial tuition reimbursements, research assistantships, career-related internships or fieldwork, Federal Work-Study, institutionally sponsored loans, scholarships/grants, and unspecified assistantships available. Financial award application deadline: 2/15; financial award applicants required to submit FAFSA. *Unit head:* Dr. James T. Jackson, Chair, Department of Curriculum and Instruction, 202-806-5300, Fax: 202-806-5297, E-mail: jt_jackson@howard.edu. *Application contact:* June L. Harris, Administrative Assistant, Department of Curriculum and Instruction, 202-806-7343, Fax: 202-806-5297, E-mail: jlharris@howard.edu.

Hunter College of the City University of New York, Graduate School, School of Arts and Sciences, Department of Mathematics and Statistics, New York, NY 10021-5085. Offers applied mathematics (MA); mathematics for secondary education (MA); pure mathematics (MA). Part-time and evening/weekend programs available. *Faculty:* 8 full-time (1 woman), 2 part-time/adjunct (0 women). *Students:* 9 full-time (7 women), 71 part-time (34 women); includes 25 minority (7 Black or African American, non-Hispanic/ Latino; 16 Asian, non-Hispanic/Latino; 2 Hispanic/Latino), 11 international. Average age 28. 54 applicants, 56% accepted, 15 enrolled. In 2011, 30 master's awarded. *Degree requirements:* For master's, one foreign language, comprehensive exam, thesis (for some programs). *Entrance requirements:* For master's, GRE General Test, 24 credits in mathematics. Additional exam requirements/recommendations for international students: Required—TOEFL. *Application deadline:* For fall admission, 4/1 for domestic students, 2/1 for international students; for spring admission, 11/1 for domestic students, 9/1 for international students. Application fee: $125. *Expenses:* Tuition, state resident: full-time $8210; part-time $345 per credit. Tuition, nonresident: full-time $15,360; part-time $640 per credit. *Required fees:* $280 per semester. One-time fee: $125. Tuition and fees vary according to class time, campus/location and program. *Financial support:* Federal Work-Study, institutionally sponsored loans, scholarships/grants, and tuition waivers (partial) available. Support available to part-time students. *Faculty research:* Data analysis, dynamical systems, computer graphics, topology, statistical decision theory. *Unit head:* Ada Peluso, Chairperson, 212-772-5300, Fax: 212-772-4858, E-mail: peluso@math.hunter.cuny.edu. *Application contact:* William Zlata, Director for Graduate Admissions, 212-772-4482, Fax: 212-650-3336, E-mail: admissions@hunter.cuny.edu. Web site: http://math.hunter.cuny.edu/.

Hunter College of the City University of New York, Graduate School, School of Education, Programs in Secondary Education, New York, NY 10021-5085. Offers biology education (MA); chemistry education (MA); earth science (MA); English education (MA); French education (MA); Italian education (MA); mathematics education (MA); physics education (MA); social studies education (MA); Spanish education (MA). *Accreditation:* NCATE. *Faculty:* 49 full-time (31 women), 70 part-time/adjunct (55 women). *Students:* 15 full-time (7 women), 206 part-time (140 women); includes 68 minority (15 Black or African American, non-Hispanic/Latino; 1 American Indian or Alaska Native, non-Hispanic/Latino; 28 Asian, non-Hispanic/Latino; 24 Hispanic/Latino), 4 international. Average age 28. 701 applicants, 49% accepted, 182 enrolled. In 2011, 130 master's awarded. *Degree requirements:* For master's, thesis. *Entrance requirements:* Additional exam requirements/recommendations for international students: Required—TOEFL. *Application deadline:* For fall admission, 4/1 for domestic students, 2/1 for international students; for spring admission, 11/1 for domestic students, 9/1 for international students. Applications are processed on a rolling basis. Application fee: $125. *Expenses:* Tuition, state resident: full-time $8210; part-time $345 per credit. Tuition, nonresident: full-time $15,360; part-time $640 per credit. *Required fees:* $280 per semester. One-time fee: $125. Tuition and fees vary according to class time, campus/location and program. *Financial support:* Fellowships and tuition waivers (full and partial) available. Support available to part-time students. *Unit head:* Dr. Kate Garret, Coordinator, 212-772-4700, E-mail: kgarret@hunter.cuny.edu. *Application contact:* Milena Solo, Director for Graduate Admissions, 212-772-4482, Fax: 212-650-3336, E-mail: milena.solo@hunter.cuny.edu. Web site: http://www.hunter.cuny.edu/school-of-education/programs/graduate.

Idaho State University, Office of Graduate Studies, College of Education, Department of Educational Foundations, Pocatello, ID 83209-8059. Offers child and family studies (M Ed); curriculum leadership (M Ed); education (M Ed); educational administration (M Ed); educational foundations (5th Year Certificate); elementary education (M Ed), including K-12 education, literacy, secondary education. Part-time programs available. *Degree requirements:* For master's, comprehensive exam, thesis optional, oral exam, written exam; for 5th Year Certificate, comprehensive exam, thesis (for some programs), oral exam, written exam. *Entrance requirements:* For master's, GRE General Test or MAT, minimum undergraduate GPA of 3.0; for 5th Year Certificate, GRE General Test, minimum undergraduate GPA of 3.0, master's degree. Additional exam requirements/ recommendations for international students: Required—TOEFL (minimum score 550 paper-based; 213 computer-based; 80 iBT). Electronic applications accepted. *Faculty research:* Child and families studies; business education; special education; math, science, and technology education.

Immaculata University, College of Graduate Studies, Program in Educational Leadership and Administration, Immaculata, PA 19345. Offers educational leadership and administration (MA, Ed D); elementary education (Certificate); school principal (Certificate); school superintendent (Certificate); secondary education (Certificate); special education (Certificate). Part-time and evening/weekend programs available. *Degree requirements:* For master's, comprehensive exam, thesis optional; for doctorate, comprehensive exam, thesis/dissertation. *Entrance requirements:* For master's, GRE or MAT, minimum GPA of 3.0; for doctorate, GRE General Test or MAT, minimum GPA of 3.5. Additional exam requirements/recommendations for international students: Required—TOEFL. Electronic applications accepted. *Faculty research:* Cooperative learning, school-based management, whole language, performance assessment.

Indiana University Bloomington, School of Education, Department of Curriculum and Instruction, Bloomington, IN 47405-7000. Offers art education (MS, Ed D, PhD); curriculum studies (Ed D, PhD); elementary education (MS, Ed D, PhD, Ed S); mathematics education (MS, Ed D, PhD); science education (MS, Ed D, PhD); secondary education (MS, Ed D, PhD); social studies education (MS, PhD); special education (PhD, Ed S). *Accreditation:* NCATE. Part-time and evening/weekend programs available. Terminal master's awarded for partial completion of doctoral program. *Degree requirements:* For doctorate, thesis/dissertation; for Ed S, comprehensive exam or project. *Entrance requirements:* For master's, doctorate, and Ed S, GRE General Test. Electronic applications accepted.

Indiana University Northwest, School of Education, Gary, IN 46408-1197. Offers elementary education (MS Ed); secondary education (MS Ed). *Accreditation:* NCATE. Part-time and evening/weekend programs available. *Faculty:* 5 full-time (2 women). *Students:* 49 full-time (37 women), 204 part-time (164 women); includes 119 minority (84 Black or African American, non-Hispanic/Latino; 1 American Indian or Alaska Native, non-Hispanic/Latino; 1 Asian, non-Hispanic/Latino; 30 Hispanic/Latino; 3 Two or more races, non-Hispanic/Latino). Average age 37. 32 applicants, 100% accepted, 25 enrolled. In 2011, 44 master's awarded. *Entrance requirements:* For master's, GRE General Test or MAT, minimum GPA of 3.0. *Application deadline:* For fall admission, 7/15 priority date for domestic students; for spring admission, 11/15 for domestic students. Application fee: $25. *Unit head:* Dr. Stanley E. Wigle, Dean, 219-980-6510, Fax: 219-981-4208, E-mail: amsanche@iun.edu. *Application contact:* Admissions Counselor, 219-980-6760, Fax: 219-980-7103. Web site: http://www.iun.edu/~edu/.

Indiana University–Purdue University Fort Wayne, College of Education and Public Policy, Department of Educational Studies, Fort Wayne, IN 46805-1499. Offers elementary education (MS Ed); secondary education (MS Ed). *Accreditation:* NCATE. Part-time programs available. *Faculty:* 14 full-time (6 women). *Students:* 1 (woman) full-time, 30 part-time (23 women); includes 5 minority (4 Black or African American, non-Hispanic/Latino; 1 Asian, non-Hispanic/Latino). Average age 38. 7 applicants, 100% accepted, 4 enrolled. In 2011, 16 master's awarded. *Entrance requirements:* For master's, minimum GPA of 2.5, three professional letters of recommendation. Additional exam requirements/recommendations for international students: Required—TOEFL (minimum score 550 paper-based; 213 computer-based; 77 iBT). *Application deadline:* For fall admission, 4/1 priority date for domestic students, 4/1 for international students. Applications are processed on a rolling basis. Application fee: $55. *Financial support:* Scholarships/grants available. Support available to part-time students. Financial award application deadline: 3/1; financial award applicants required to submit FAFSA. *Faculty research:* Ethnic minority higher education, South Korea and higher education reform, Turkish-American parents' experience and U. S. elementary education. *Total annual research expenditures:* $77,627. *Unit head:* Dr. Joe Nichols, Chair, 260-481-6445, Fax: 260-481-5408, E-mail: nicholsj@ipfw.edu. *Application contact:* Vicky L. Schmidt, Graduate Recorder, 260-481-6450, Fax: 260-481-5408, E-mail: schmidt@ipfw.edu. Web site: http://www.ipfw.edu/education.

Indiana University South Bend, School of Education, South Bend, IN 46634-7111. Offers counseling and human services (MS Ed); elementary education (MS Ed); secondary education (MS Ed); special education (MS Ed). *Accreditation:* NCATE. Part-time and evening/weekend programs available. *Faculty:* 21 full-time (11 women), 9 part-time/adjunct (3 women). *Students:* 70 full-time (45 women), 262 part-time (206 women); includes 39 minority (15 Black or African American, non-Hispanic/Latino; 3 American Indian or Alaska Native, non-Hispanic/Latino; 5 Asian, non-Hispanic/Latino; 14 Hispanic/ Latino; 2 Two or more races, non-Hispanic/Latino), 15 international. Average age 36. 52 applicants, 75% accepted, 28 enrolled. In 2011, 75 master's awarded. *Degree requirements:* For master's, thesis or alternative, exit project. *Entrance requirements:* For master's, letters of recommendation, GRE or minimum GPA of 3.0. Additional exam requirements/recommendations for international students: Required—TOEFL. *Application deadline:* For fall admission, 7/1 for domestic students; for spring admission, 11/1 for domestic students. Applications are processed on a rolling basis. Application fee: $50 ($60 for international students). Electronic applications accepted. *Financial support:* Career-related internships or fieldwork available. Support available to part-time students. Financial award application deadline: 3/1; financial award applicants required to submit FAFSA. *Faculty research:* Professional dispositions, early childhood literacy, online learning, program assessments, problem-based learning. *Unit head:* Dr. Michael Horvath, Professor/Dean, 574-520-4339, Fax: 574-520-4550. *Application contact:* Dr. Todd Norris, Director of Education Student Services, 574-520-4845, E-mail: toanorri@iusb.edu. Web site: http://www.iusb.edu/~edud/.

Indiana University Southeast, School of Education, New Albany, IN 47150-6405. Offers counselor education (MS Ed); elementary education (MS Ed); secondary education (MS Ed). *Accreditation:* NCATE. Part-time and evening/weekend programs available. *Students:* 31 full-time (24 women), 622 part-time (497 women); includes 83 minority (63 Black or African American, non-Hispanic/Latino; 2 American Indian or Alaska Native, non-Hispanic/Latino; 5 Asian, non-Hispanic/Latino; 8 Hispanic/Latino; 5 Two or more races, non-Hispanic/Latino). Average age 33. 99 applicants, 93% accepted, 75 enrolled. In 2011, 143 master's awarded. *Entrance requirements:* For master's, minimum undergraduate GPA of 2.5, graduate 3.0. *Application deadline:* Applications are processed on a rolling basis. Application fee: $35. *Financial support:* Career-related internships or fieldwork, Federal Work-Study, and institutionally sponsored loans available. Support available to part-time students. Financial award applicants required to submit FAFSA. *Faculty research:* Learning styles, technology, constructivism, group process, innovative math strategies. *Unit head:* Dr. Gloria Murray, Dean, 812-941-2169, Fax: 812-941-2667, E-mail: soeinfo@ius.edu. *Application contact:* Admissions Counselor, 812-941-2212, Fax: 812-941-2595, E-mail: admissions@ius.edu. Web site: http://www.ius.edu/education/.

Instituto Tecnologico de Santo Domingo, Graduate School, Area of Humanities and Social Sciences, Santo Domingo, Dominican Republic. Offers accounting (Certificate); adult education (Certificate); applied linguistics (MA); economics (MA); education (M Ed); educational psychology (MA, Certificate); gender and development (MA, Certificate); humanistic studies (MA); international marketing management (Certificate); international relations in the Caribbean basin (Certificate); intervention systems in family therapy (MA); linguistic and literary communication (Certificate); pedagogical support (MA); social science education (M Ed); sustainable human development (MA); terminal illness and death psychology (Certificate); youth and adult education (M Ed).

Iona College, School of Arts and Science, Program in Education, New Rochelle, NY 10801-1890. Offers adolescence education: biology (MS Ed, MST); adolescence education: English (MS Ed, MST); adolescence education: Italian (MS Ed, MST); adolescence education: mathematics (MS Ed, MST); adolescence education: social studies (MS Ed, MST); adolescence education: Spanish (MS Ed, MST); adolescence special education 5-12 (MST); adolescence special education/literacy 5-12 (MS Ed); childhood 1-6/special education 1-6 (MST); childhood education (MST); early childhood/childhood (MST); educational leadership (MS Ed); literacy birth-grade 6/special education 1-6 (MS Ed); literacy education: birth-grade 6 (MS Ed). *Accreditation:* NCATE. Part-time and evening/weekend programs available. *Faculty:* 21 full-time (13 women), 13 part-time/adjunct (8 women). *Students:* 59 full-time (45 women), 101 part-time (78 women); includes 11 minority (2 Black or African American, non-Hispanic/Latino; 2

Asian, non-Hispanic/Latino; 7 Hispanic/Latino). Average age 26. 74 applicants, 66% accepted, 35 enrolled. In 2011, 46 master's awarded. *Degree requirements:* For master's, thesis or alternative. *Entrance requirements:* For master's, minimum GPA of 2.5 (MST), New York teaching certificate (MS Ed). Additional exam requirements/recommendations for international students: Required—TOEFL (minimum score 550 paper-based; 213 computer-based). *Application deadline:* Applications are processed on a rolling basis. Application fee: $50. Electronic applications accepted. *Expenses: Tuition:* Part-time $872 per credit. *Required fees:* $225 per term. *Financial support:* Unspecified assistantships available. Support available to part-time students. Financial award application deadline: 4/15; financial award applicants required to submit FAFSA. *Faculty research:* Reading/writing, educational technology, administration, early literacy assessment, literacy development. *Unit head:* Dr. Catherine O'Callaghan, Chair, 914-633-2210, Fax: 914-633-2608, E-mail: cocallaghan@iona.edu. *Application contact:* Dr. Jeanne Zaino, Interim Dean, School of Arts and Science, 914-633-2112, Fax: 914-633-2023, E-mail: jzaino@iona.edu.

Ithaca College, Division of Graduate and Professional Studies, School of Humanities and Sciences, Program in Adolescence Education, Ithaca, NY 14850. Offers biology 7-12 (MAT); chemistry 7-12 (MAT); English 7-12 (MAT); French 7-12 (MAT); math 7-12 (MAT); physics 7-12 (MAT); social studies 7-12 (MAT); Spanish (MAT). Part-time programs available. *Faculty:* 23 full-time (7 women). *Students:* 14 full-time (8 women), 1 part-time (0 women); includes 4 minority (1 Asian, non-Hispanic/Latino; 2 Hispanic/Latino; 1 Two or more races, non-Hispanic/Latino). Average age 27. 33 applicants, 64% accepted, 15 enrolled. In 2011, 15 master's awarded. *Degree requirements:* For master's, thesis or alternative, student teaching. *Entrance requirements:* For master's, minimum GPA of 3.0. Additional exam requirements/recommendations for international students: Required—TOEFL (minimum score 550 paper-based; 213 computer-based; 80 iBT). *Application deadline:* For fall admission, 2/15 priority date for domestic students, 2/15 for international students; for spring admission, 12/1 for domestic and international students. Applications are processed on a rolling basis. Application fee: $40. Electronic applications accepted. *Expenses:* Contact institution. *Financial support:* In 2011–12, 9 students received support, including 9 teaching assistantships (averaging $6,070 per year); career-related internships or fieldwork, Federal Work-Study, scholarships/grants, and unspecified assistantships also available. Support available to part-time students. Financial award application deadline: 2/15; financial award applicants required to submit CSS PROFILE or FAFSA. *Faculty research:* Bilingual education, socio-linguistic perspective on literacy. *Unit head:* Dr. Linda Hanrahan, Chairperson, 607-274-3143, Fax: 607-274-1263, E-mail: gps@ithaca.edu. *Application contact:* Gerard Turbide, Director, Office of Admission, 607-274-3143, Fax: 607-274-1263, E-mail: gps@ithaca.edu. Web site: http://www.ithaca.edu/gps/gradprograms/overview/school/hs/aded.

Jackson State University, Graduate School, College of Education and Human Development, Department of Educational Leadership, Jackson, MS 39217. Offers education administration (Ed S); educational administration (MS Ed, PhD); secondary education (MS Ed, Ed S), including educational technology (MS Ed). *Accreditation:* NCATE. Part-time and evening/weekend programs available. *Degree requirements:* For master's, comprehensive exam, thesis or alternative; for doctorate, comprehensive exam, thesis/dissertation; for Ed S, comprehensive exam, thesis. *Entrance requirements:* For master's, GRE General Test; for doctorate, MAT, GRE, teaching experience. Additional exam requirements/recommendations for international students: Required—TOEFL (minimum score 520 paper-based; 195 computer-based; 67 iBT).

Jacksonville State University, College of Graduate Studies and Continuing Education, College of Education and Professional Studies, Program in Secondary Education, Jacksonville, AL 36265-1602. Offers MS Ed. *Accreditation:* NCATE. Part-time and evening/weekend programs available. *Degree requirements:* For master's, comprehensive exam, thesis (for some programs). *Entrance requirements:* For master's, GRE General Test or MAT. Electronic applications accepted. *Expenses:* Tuition, state resident: part-time $336 per hour. Tuition, nonresident: part-time $672 per hour. Part-time tuition and fees vary according to degree level.

James Madison University, The Graduate School, College of Education, Middle, Secondary, and Mathematics Education Department, Program in Secondary Education, Harrisonburg, VA 22807. Offers MAT. *Accreditation:* NCATE. Part-time and evening/weekend programs available. *Students:* Average age 27. *Entrance requirements:* For master's, GRE General Test. Additional exam requirements/recommendations for international students: Required—TOEFL. *Application deadline:* For fall admission, 5/1 priority date for domestic students; for spring admission, 9/1 priority date for domestic students. Applications are processed on a rolling basis. Application fee: $55. Electronic applications accepted. *Expenses:* Tuition, state resident: full-time $8016; part-time $334 per credit hour. Tuition, nonresident: full-time $22,656; part-time $944 per credit hour. *Financial support:* Federal Work-Study and unspecified assistantships available. Financial award application deadline: 3/1; financial award applicants required to submit FAFSA. *Unit head:* Dr. Steven L. Purcell, Academic Unit Head, 540-568-6793. *Application contact:* Lynette M. Bible, Director of Graduate Admissions, 540-568-6395, Fax: 540-568-7860, E-mail: biblelm@jmu.edu.

John Carroll University, Graduate School, Department of Education and Allied Studies, Program in School Based Adolescent-Young Adult Education, University Heights, OH 44118-4581. Offers M Ed. *Degree requirements:* For master's, comprehensive exam. *Entrance requirements:* For master's, GRE General Test or MAT, minimum GPA of 2.75, interview. Electronic applications accepted.

The Johns Hopkins University, School of Education, Department of Teacher Preparation, Baltimore, MD 21218. Offers early childhood education (MAT); education (MS), including educational studies; elementary education (MAT); English for speakers of other languages (MAT); K-8 mathematics lead-teacher (Certificate); K-8 science lead-teacher (Certificate); secondary education (MAT), including biology, chemistry, earth/space/environmental science, English, French, mathematics, physics, social studies, Spanish. Part-time and evening/weekend programs available. *Degree requirements:* For master's, portfolio, PRAXIS II, internship. *Entrance requirements:* For master's, PRAXIS I, SAT, ACT, or GRE (MAT), minimum undergraduate GPA of 3.0, interview, 1 letter of recommendation, curriculum vitae/resume; for Certificate, bachelor's degree, minimum undergraduate GPA of 3.0, essay/statement of goals, interview. Additional exam requirements/recommendations for international students: Required—TOEFL (minimum score 600 paper-based; 250 computer-based; 100 iBT). Electronic applications accepted. *Faculty research:* Teacher retention, STEM education reform, alternative certification programs, school-university partnerships, urban education, action research/data-informed instruction, family engagement.

Johnson & Wales University, The Alan Shawn Feinstein Graduate School, Ed D Program, Providence, RI 02903-3703. Offers higher education (Ed D); K-12 (Ed D). Part-time programs available. *Degree requirements:* For doctorate, thesis/dissertation. *Entrance requirements:* For doctorate, MAT, minimum GPA of 3.25; master's degree in appropriate field from accredited institution. Additional exam requirements/recommendations for international students: Required—TOEFL (minimum score 550 paper-based; 210 computer-based); Recommended—IELTS, TWE. *Faculty research:* Site-based management, collaborative learning, technology and education, K-16 education.

Johnson & Wales University, The Alan Shawn Feinstein Graduate School, MAT Program in Teacher Education, Providence, RI 02903-3703. Offers business education and secondary special education (MAT); elementary education and elementary special education (MAT); elementary education and elementary/secondary special education (MAT); elementary education and secondary special education (MAT); food service education (MAT). Part-time and evening/weekend programs available. *Entrance requirements:* For master's, MAT, minimum GPA of 2.75. Additional exam requirements/recommendations for international students: Required—TOEFL (minimum score 550 paper-based; 210 computer-based) or IELTS (recommended). *Faculty research:* Secondary education, student teaching, educational reform, evaluation procedures.

Johnson State College, Graduate Program in Education, Program in Secondary Education, Johnson, VT 05656. Offers MA Ed. *Degree requirements:* For master's, internship. *Entrance requirements:* Additional exam requirements/recommendations for international students: Required—TOEFL. *Application deadline:* For fall admission, 4/1 priority date for domestic students, 4/15 for international students; for spring admission, 11/1 priority date for domestic students, 8/15 for international students. Applications are processed on a rolling basis. Application fee: $35. *Expenses: Tuition, area resident:* Part-time $459 per credit hour. Tuition, nonresident: part-time $990 per credit hour. *Unit head:* Kathleen Brinegar, Program Coordinator, 800-635-2356, E-mail: kathleen.brinegar@jsc.edu. *Application contact:* Catherine H. Higley, Administrative Assistant, 800-635-2356 Ext. 1244, Fax: 802-635-1248, E-mail: catherine.higley@jsc.edu.

Jones International University, School of Education, Centennial, CO 80112. Offers adult education (M Ed); corporate training and knowledge management (M Ed); curriculum and instruction (M Ed), including elementary teacher licensure, secondary teacher licensure; e-learning technology and design (M Ed); educational leadership and administration (M Ed); educational leadership and administration: principal and administrator licensure (M Ed); elementary curriculum instruction and assessment (M Ed); higher education leadership and administration (M Ed); K-12 instructional technology (M Ed); K-12 instructional technology: teacher licensure (M Ed); secondary curriculum instruction and assessment (M Ed); technology and design (M Ed). Part-time and evening/weekend programs available. Postbaccalaureate distance learning degree programs offered (no on-campus study). *Entrance requirements:* For master's, minimum cumulative GPA of 2.5. Additional exam requirements/recommendations for international students: Recommended—TOEFL (minimum score 550 paper-based; 213 computer-based). Electronic applications accepted.

Kansas State University, Graduate School, College of Education, Department of Curriculum and Instruction, Manhattan, KS 66506. Offers career and technical education (Ed D, PhD); curriculum studies (Ed D, PhD); digital teaching and learning (MS); educational computing, design and online learning (MS); educational technology (Ed D, PhD); elementary/middle level (MS); English as a second language (MS); language/diversity education (Ed D, PhD); literacy education (Ed D, PhD); mathematics education (Ed D, PhD); middle level/secondary (MS); reading and language arts (MS); reading specialist endorsement (MS); science education (Ed D, PhD); social science education (Ed D, PhD); teacher education (Ed D, PhD); teacher leader/school improvement (MS, Ed D). *Accreditation:* NCATE. Part-time programs available. Postbaccalaureate distance learning degree programs offered (minimal on-campus study). *Faculty:* 15 full-time (12 women), 3 part-time/adjunct (2 women). *Students:* 37 full-time (30 women), 113 part-time (91 women); includes 14 minority (4 Black or African American, non-Hispanic/Latino; 1 American Indian or Alaska Native, non-Hispanic/Latino; 1 Asian, non-Hispanic/Latino; 7 Hispanic/Latino; 1 Two or more races, non-Hispanic/Latino), 15 international. Average age 37. 75 applicants, 51% accepted, 9 enrolled. In 2011, 48 master's, 14 doctorates awarded. *Degree requirements:* For master's, comprehensive exam, portfolio, project, report or thesis; for doctorate, comprehensive exam, thesis/dissertation, preliminary exam. *Entrance requirements:* For master's, minimum GPA of 3.0; for doctorate, GRE, minimum GPA of 3.0. Additional exam requirements/recommendations for international students: Required—TOEFL. *Application deadline:* For fall admission, 2/1 priority date for domestic students, 2/1 for international students; for spring admission, 8/1 priority date for domestic students, 8/1 for international students. Applications are processed on a rolling basis. Application fee: $40 ($55 for international students). Electronic applications accepted. *Financial support:* In 2011–12, 1 research assistantship (averaging $16,900 per year), 8 teaching assistantships (averaging $12,466 per year) were awarded; career-related internships or fieldwork, institutionally sponsored loans, and scholarships/grants also available. Support available to part-time students. Financial award application deadline: 3/1; financial award applicants required to submit FAFSA. *Faculty research:* Literacy and technology, critical race theory and diversity, achievement gaps, school improvement, teacher education. *Total annual research expenditures:* $510,907. *Unit head:* Dr. Gail Shroyer, Chair, 785-532-5550, Fax: 785-532-7304, E-mail: gshroyer@ksu.edu. *Application contact:* Dona Deam, Application Contact, 785-532-5595, Fax: 785-532-7304, E-mail: ddeam@ksu.edu. Web site: http://coe.k-state.edu/departments/currin/curringrad.htm.

Kaplan University, Davenport Campus, School of Teacher Education, Davenport, IA 52807-2095. Offers education (M Ed); secondary education (M Ed); teaching and learning (MA); teaching literacy and language: grades 6-12 (MA); teaching literacy and language: grades K-6 (MA); teaching mathematics: grades 6-8 (MA); teaching mathematics: grades 9-12 (MA); teaching mathematics: grades K-5 (MA); teaching science: grades 6-12 (MA); teaching science: grades K-6 (MA); teaching students with special needs (MA); teaching with technology (MA). Part-time and evening/weekend programs available. Postbaccalaureate distance learning degree programs offered (no on-campus study). *Entrance requirements:* Additional exam requirements/recommendations for international students: Required—TOEFL (minimum score 550 paper-based; 218 computer-based; 80 iBT).

Kennesaw State University, Leland and Clarice C. Bagwell College of Education, Program in Teaching, Kennesaw, GA 30144-5591. Offers art education (MAT); secondary English or mathematics (MAT); secondary science education (MAT); teaching English to speakers of other languages (MAT). Program offered only in summer. Part-time and evening/weekend programs available. *Students:* 101 full-time (68 women), 20 part-time (15 women); includes 27 minority (14 Black or African American, non-Hispanic/Latino; 6 Asian, non-Hispanic/Latino; 4 Hispanic/Latino; 3 Two or more races, non-Hispanic/Latino), 3 international. Average age 33. 13 applicants, 62% accepted, 7 enrolled. In 2011, 81 master's awarded. *Entrance requirements:* For master's, GRE, GACE I (state certificate exam), minimum GPA of 2.75, 2 recommendations, resume. Additional exam requirements/recommendations for international students: Required—TOEFL (minimum score 550 paper-based; 213 computer-based; 80 iBT), IELTS (minimum score 6). *Application deadline:* For fall admission, 6/1 for domestic and international students; for spring admission, 3/1 for domestic and international students. Application fee: $60. Electronic applications accepted. *Expenses:* Tuition, state resident: full-time $3000; part-time $250 per semester hour. Tuition, nonresident: full-time $10,836; part-time $903 per semester hour. *Required fees:* $774 per semester. *Financial support:* In 2011–12, 2 research assistantships with tuition reimbursements (averaging $4,000 per year) were awarded; unspecified assistantships also available. Financial award application deadline: 4/1; financial award applicants required to submit FAFSA. *Unit head:* Dr. Lynn Stallings,

Director, 770-420-4477, E-mail: lstalling@kennesaw.edu. *Application contact:* Alisha Bello, Administrative Coordinator, 770-423-6043, Fax: 770-420-4435, E-mail: abello1@kennesaw.edu. Web site: http://www.kennesaw.edu.

Kent State University, Graduate School of Education, Health, and Human Services, School of Teaching, Learning and Curriculum Studies, Program in Secondary Education, Kent, OH 44242-0001. Offers MAT. *Accreditation:* NCATE. *Faculty:* 7 full-time (6 women), 1 part-time/adjunct. *Students:* 24 full-time (14 women), 1 part-time; includes 1 minority (Asian, non-Hispanic/Latino). 55 applicants, 58% accepted. In 2011, 32 master's awarded. *Entrance requirements:* For master's, GRE General Test, 2 letters of reference, moral character form. Additional exam requirements/recommendations for international students: Required—TOEFL (minimum score 550 paper-based; 213 computer-based; 80 iBT). Application fee: $30 ($60 for international students). Electronic applications accepted. *Expenses:* Tuition, state resident: full-time $8136; part-time $452 per credit hour. Tuition, nonresident: full-time $14,292; part-time $794 per credit hour. *Financial support:* Research assistantships with full tuition reimbursements, career-related internships or fieldwork, Federal Work-Study, institutionally sponsored loans, scholarships/grants, health care benefits, and unspecified assistantships available. Support available to part-time students. Financial award application deadline: 4/1; financial award applicants required to submit FAFSA. *Faculty research:* Creativity in science, women in science, teaching of writing, curriculum theory, mathematical reasoning. *Unit head:* Dr. Janice Hutchison, Coordinator, 330-672-0629, E-mail: jhutchi1@kent.edu. *Application contact:* Nancy Miller, Academic Program Coordinator, Office of Graduate Student Services, 330-672-2576, Fax: 330-672-9162, E-mail: ogs@kent.edu.

Kutztown University of Pennsylvania, College of Education, Program in Secondary Education, Kutztown, PA 19530-0730. Offers biology (M Ed); curriculum and instruction (M Ed); English (M Ed); mathematics (M Ed); social studies (M Ed). *Accreditation:* NCATE. Part-time and evening/weekend programs available. *Faculty:* 7 full-time (2 women). *Students:* 29 full-time (12 women), 73 part-time (43 women); includes 3 minority (1 Black or African American, non-Hispanic/Latino; 1 Asian, non-Hispanic/Latino; 1 Hispanic/Latino). Average age 28. 12 applicants, 100% accepted, 12 enrolled. In 2011, 29 master's awarded. *Degree requirements:* For master's, comprehensive exam, thesis optional. *Entrance requirements:* For master's, GRE General Test. Additional exam requirements/recommendations for international students: Required—TOEFL (minimum score 550 paper-based; 79 iBT). *Application deadline:* For fall admission, 8/1 priority date for domestic students, 8/1 for international students; for spring admission, 12/1 priority date for domestic students, 12/1 for international students. Applications are processed on a rolling basis. Application fee: $35. Electronic applications accepted. *Expenses:* Tuition, state resident: full-time $7488; part-time $416 per credit. Tuition, nonresident: full-time $11,232; part-time $624 per credit. *Financial support:* Career-related internships or fieldwork, Federal Work-Study, scholarships/grants, and unspecified assistantships available. Financial award application deadline: 3/1; financial award applicants required to submit FAFSA. *Unit head:* Dr. Theresa Stahler, Chairperson, 610-683-4259, Fax: 610-683-1338, E-mail: stahler@kutztown.edu. *Application contact:* Kelly D. Burr, Associate Director, Graduate Admissions, 610-683-4200, Fax: 610-683-1393, E-mail: graduate@kutztown.edu.

LaGrange College, Graduate Programs, Department of Education, LaGrange, GA 30240-2999. Offers curriculum and instruction (M Ed, Ed S); middle grades (MAT); secondary education (MAT). Part-time and evening/weekend programs available. *Degree requirements:* For master's, comprehensive exam. *Entrance requirements:* For master's, GRE, MAT, minimum GPA of 2.5. Additional exam requirements/recommendations for international students: Required—TOEFL (minimum score 550 paper-based).

Lancaster Bible College, Graduate School, Lancaster, PA 17601-5036. Offers adult ministries (MA); Bible (MA); children and family ministry (MA); consulting resource teacher (M Ed); elementary school counseling (M Ed); leadership (PhD); leadership studies (MA); marriage and family counseling (MA); mental health counseling (MA); pastoral studies (MA); secondary school counseling (M Ed); student ministry (MA). Part-time and evening/weekend programs available. *Degree requirements:* For master's, comprehensive exam (for some programs), thesis (for some programs). *Entrance requirements:* For master's, bachelor's degree with a minimum of 30 credits of course work in Bible, minimum undergraduate GPA of 3.0, interview. Additional exam requirements/recommendations for international students: Required—TOEFL.

Lee University, Program in Education, Cleveland, TN 37320-3450. Offers classroom teaching (M Ed, Ed S); educational leadership (M Ed, Ed S); elementary/secondary education (MAT); secondary education (MAT); special education (M Ed); special education (secondary) (MAT). Part-time programs available. *Faculty:* 14 full-time (6 women), 5 part-time/adjunct (3 women). *Students:* 43 full-time (27 women), 176 part-time (107 women); includes 19 minority (4 Black or African American, non-Hispanic/Latino; 3 American Indian or Alaska Native, non-Hispanic/Latino; 1 Asian, non-Hispanic/Latino; 8 Hispanic/Latino; 3 Two or more races, non-Hispanic/Latino), 4 international. Average age 33. 52 applicants, 100% accepted, 38 enrolled. In 2011, 90 master's, 14 other advanced degrees awarded. *Degree requirements:* For master's, variable foreign language requirement, comprehensive exam, thesis, internship. *Entrance requirements:* For master's, MAT or GRE General Test, minimum GPA of 2.75, 3 letters of recommendation, interview, writing sample. Additional exam requirements/recommendations for international students: Required—TOEFL (minimum score 450 paper-based; 45 computer-based). *Application deadline:* For fall admission, 4/1 priority date for domestic students; for spring admission, 10/1 priority date for domestic students. Applications are processed on a rolling basis. Application fee: $25. *Expenses: Tuition:* Full-time $12,120; part-time $506 per credit hour. *Required fees:* $560; $305 per term. Part-time tuition and fees vary according to course load. *Financial support:* In 2011–12, 18 teaching assistantships (averaging $1,966 per year) were awarded; career-related internships or fieldwork, Federal Work-Study, institutionally sponsored loans, scholarships/grants, and unspecified assistantships also available. Financial award application deadline: 3/1; financial award applicants required to submit FAFSA. *Unit head:* Dr. Gary Riggins, Director, 423-614-8193. *Application contact:* Vicki Glasscock, Graduate Admissions Director, 423-614-8059, E-mail: vglasscock@leeuniversity.edu. Web site: http://www.leeuniversity.edu/academics/graduate/education.

Le Moyne College, Department of Education, Syracuse, NY 13214. Offers adolescent education (MS Ed, MST); adolescent education/special education (MS Ed, MST); adolescent English (grades 7-12) (MST); adolescent history (grades 7-12) (MST); childhood education (MS Ed); childhood education/special education (MS Ed); elementary education (MS Ed); general professional education (MS Ed); inclusive childhood education (MST); literacy education (birth to grade 6) (MS Ed); literacy education (grades 5-12) (MS Ed); school building leadership (MS Ed, CAS); school district business leader (MS Ed, CAS); school district leadership (MS Ed, CAS); secondary education (MS Ed); special education (MS Ed); students with disabilities-generalist (grades 7-12) (MS Ed); TESOL (teaching English to speakers of other languages) (MS Ed); urban studies (MS Ed). *Accreditation:* Teacher Education Accreditation Council. Part-time and evening/weekend programs available. *Faculty:* 9 full-time (6 women), 51 part-time/adjunct (28 women). *Students:* 61 full-time (47 women), 311 part-time (222 women); includes 31 minority (19 Black or African American, non-Hispanic/Latino; 3 American Indian or Alaska Native, non-Hispanic/Latino; 4 Asian, non-Hispanic/Latino; 5 Hispanic/Latino), 2 international. Average age 30. 242 applicants, 90% accepted, 180 enrolled. In 2011, 168 master's, 23 CASs awarded. *Degree requirements:* For master's, thesis. *Entrance requirements:* For master's, GRE General Test, bachelor's degree, 2 letters of recommendation, written statement, transcripts. Additional exam requirements/recommendations for international students: Required—TOEFL (minimum score 550 paper-based; 213 computer-based; 79 iBT). *Application deadline:* For fall admission, 4/1 priority date for domestic students, 4/1 for international students; for spring admission, 10/1 priority date for domestic students, 10/1 for international students. Applications are processed on a rolling basis. Application fee: $50. *Expenses:* Contact institution. *Financial support:* In 2011–12, 32 students received support. Career-related internships or fieldwork and health care benefits available. Support available to part-time students. Financial award applicants required to submit FAFSA. *Faculty research:* Minority teachers, special education, multiculturalism, literacy, technology, video games learning, autism, school district organization, service-learning, higher level problem solving, teacher leadership. *Unit head:* Dr. Suzanne L. Gilmour, Chair, Department of Education and Director of Graduate Education Programs, 315-445-4376, Fax: 315-445-4744, E-mail: gilmous@lemoyne.edu. *Application contact:* Kristen P. Trapasso, Director of Graduate Admission, 315-445-4265, Fax: 315-445-6027, E-mail: trapaskp@lemoyne.edu. Web site: http://www.lemoyne.edu/education.

Lewis & Clark College, Graduate School of Education and Counseling, Department of Teacher Education, Program in Middle Level/High School Education, Portland, OR 97219-7899. Offers MAT. *Accreditation:* NCATE. *Faculty:* 6 full-time (5 women), 6 part-time/adjunct (4 women). *Students:* 57 full-time (37 women); includes 7 minority (2 American Indian or Alaska Native, non-Hispanic/Latino; 2 Asian, non-Hispanic/Latino; 2 Hispanic/Latino; 1 Two or more races, non-Hispanic/Latino). Average age 28. 110 applicants, 79% accepted, 57 enrolled. In 2011, 71 master's awarded. *Entrance requirements:* For master's, prior experience working with children and/or youth; minimum undergraduate GPA of 2.75. Additional exam requirements/recommendations for international students: Required—TOEFL (minimum score 575 paper-based; 233 computer-based). *Application deadline:* For fall admission, 12/1 priority date for domestic students, 12/1 for international students. Application fee: $50. Electronic applications accepted. *Expenses: Tuition:* Part-time $738 per semester hour. Tuition and fees vary according to course level and campus/location. *Financial support:* In 2011–12, 12 students received support. Career-related internships or fieldwork, Federal Work-Study, institutionally sponsored loans, scholarships/grants, health care benefits, and tuition waivers (partial) available. Support available to part-time students. Financial award application deadline: 3/1; financial award applicants required to submit FAFSA. *Faculty research:* Classroom management, classroom assessment, science education, classroom ethnography, moral development. *Unit head:* Dr. Kasi Allen, Coordinator, 503-768-6100, Fax: 503-768-7715, E-mail: lcteach@lclark.edu. *Application contact:* Becky Haas, Director of Admissions, 503-768-6200, Fax: 503-768-6205, E-mail: gseadmit@lclark.edu. Web site: http://graduate.lclark.edu/departments/teacher_education/prospective_teachers/middle_high_school/.

Lewis University, College of Education, Program in Secondary Education, Romeoville, IL 60446. Offers biology (MA); chemistry (MA); English (MA); history (MA); math (MA); physics (MA); psychology and social science (MA). Part-time programs available. *Students:* 17 full-time (11 women), 11 part-time (4 women); includes 4 minority (2 Black or African American, non-Hispanic/Latino; 2 Hispanic/Latino). Average age 30. In 2011, 7 master's awarded. *Entrance requirements:* For master's, departmental qualifying exam, writing exam, minimum GPA of 2.75, 2 letters of recommendation, interview. Additional exam requirements/recommendations for international students: Required—TOEFL (minimum score 550 paper-based; 213 computer-based; 80 iBT). *Application deadline:* For fall admission, 5/1 for international students; for spring admission, 11/15 for international students. Applications are processed on a rolling basis. Application fee: $40. Electronic applications accepted. *Financial support:* Federal Work-Study, scholarships/grants, and unspecified assistantships available. Financial award application deadline: 5/1; financial award applicants required to submit FAFSA. *Unit head:* Dr. Dorene Huvaere, Program Director, 815-838-0500 Ext. 5885, E-mail: huvaersdo@lewisu.edu. *Application contact:* Fran Welsh, Secretary, 815-838-0500 Ext. 5880, E-mail: welshfr@lewisu.edu.

Liberty University, School of Education, Lynchburg, VA 24502. Offers administration and supervision (M Ed); curriculum and instruction (M Ed); early childhood education (M Ed); educational leadership (Ed D, Ed S); educational technology and online instruction (M Ed); elementary education (M Ed, MAT); gifted education (M Ed); math specialist (M Ed); middle grades (M Ed); outdoor adventure sport (MS); reading specialist (M Ed); school counseling (M Ed); secondary education (M Ed, MAT); special education (M Ed, MAT); sports administration (MS); teaching and learning (Ed D, Ed S). *Accreditation:* NCATE. Part-time programs available. Postbaccalaureate distance learning degree programs offered (minimal on-campus study). *Students:* 2,245 full-time (1,572 women), 3,500 part-time (2,558 women); includes 1,141 minority (888 Black or African American, non-Hispanic/Latino; 19 American Indian or Alaska Native, non-Hispanic/Latino; 21 Asian, non-Hispanic/Latino; 123 Hispanic/Latino; 9 Native Hawaiian or other Pacific Islander, non-Hispanic/Latino; 81 Two or more races, non-Hispanic/Latino), 76 international. Average age 37. In 2011, 760 master's, 48 doctorates, 321 other advanced degrees awarded. *Degree requirements:* For doctorate, comprehensive exam, thesis/dissertation. *Entrance requirements:* For master's, GRE General Test or MAT (if taken in or before 1999), 2 letters of recommendation, minimum undergraduate GPA of 3.0, curriculum vitae; for doctorate, GRE General Test or MAT (if taken before 1999), minimum master's GPA of 3.0, 3 years of teacher experience; for Ed S, GRE General Test or MAT (if taken before 1999), minimum master's GPA of 3.0, 3 years of teaching experience. Additional exam requirements/recommendations for international students: Required—TOEFL (minimum score 600 paper-based; 250 computer-based). *Application deadline:* For fall admission, 6/1 priority date for domestic students; for spring admission, 11/1 for domestic students. Applications are processed on a rolling basis. Application fee: $50. Electronic applications accepted. *Expenses:* Contact institution. *Financial support:* Federal Work-Study and tuition waivers (partial) available. *Faculty research:* Self-determination, character education, bibliotherapy, learning styles, distance education. *Unit head:* Dr. Karen L. Parker, Dean, 434-582-2195, Fax: 434-582-2468, E-mail: kparker@liberty.edu. *Application contact:* Jay Bridge, Director of Graduate Admissions, 800-424-9595, Fax: 800-628-7977, E-mail: gradadmissions@liberty.edu. Web site: http://www.liberty.edu/academics/education/graduate/.

Lincoln University, School of Graduate Studies and Continuing Education, Jefferson City, MO 65102. Offers business administration (MBA), including accounting, entrepreneurship, management, public administration and policy; educational leadership (Ed S), including elementary leadership, secondary leadership, superintendency; guidance and counseling (M Ed), including community/agency counseling, elementary school, secondary school; history (MA); school administration and supervision (M Ed), including elementary school administration, secondary school administration, special education administration; school teaching (M Ed), including elementary school teaching, secondary school teaching; social science (MA), including history, political science, sociology; sociology (MA); sociology/criminal justice (MA). Part-time and evening/weekend programs available. *Degree requirements:* For master's and Ed S, comprehensive exam, thesis optional. *Entrance requirements:* For master's and Ed S, GRE, MAT or GMAT, minimum GPA of 2.75 in major, 2.5 overall; 3 letters of recommendation; minimum C average in English composition; personal statement of purpose. Additional exam requirements/recommendations for international students: Required—TOEFL (minimum score 500 paper-based; 173 computer-based; 61 iBT). *Faculty research:* Suicide prevention.

Long Island University–C. W. Post Campus, College of Liberal Arts and Sciences, Department of English, Brookville, NY 11548-1300. Offers English (MA); English for adolescence education (MS). Part-time and evening/weekend programs available. *Degree requirements:* For master's, comprehensive exam (for some programs), thesis (for some programs). *Entrance requirements:* For master's, minimum GPA of 3.5 in major, 3.0 overall; 21 credits of English. Electronic applications accepted. *Faculty research:* English Renaissance, Sinclair Lewis: The Early Years, puppetry archives, Irish-American Experiences: literature of memory, Henry James's anxiety of Poe's influence.

Long Island University–Hudson at Rockland, Graduate School, Program in Curriculum and Instruction, Orangeburg, NY 10962. Offers adolescence education (MS Ed); childhood education (MS Ed). Part-time and evening/weekend programs available. *Degree requirements:* For master's, LAST and CST exams. *Entrance requirements:* For master's, college transcripts, letters of recommendation, personal statement.

Long Island University–Hudson at Westchester, Programs in Education-Teaching, Program in Special Education and Secondary Education, Purchase, NY 10577. Offers MS Ed, Advanced Certificate. Part-time and evening/weekend programs available.

Longwood University, Office of Graduate Studies, College of Education and Human Services, Farmville, VA 23909. Offers communication sciences and disorders (MS); community and college counseling (MS); curriculum and instruction specialist-elementary (MS), including mild disabilities, modern languages; curriculum and instruction specialist-secondary (MS), including English, mild disabilities, modern languages; educational leadership (MS); guidance and counseling (MS); literacy and culture (MS); school library media (MS). *Accreditation:* NCATE. Part-time and evening/weekend programs available. *Degree requirements:* For master's, comprehensive exam, thesis optional. *Entrance requirements:* For master's, GRE (communication sciences and disorders), minimum GPA of 2.75. Additional exam requirements/recommendations for international students: Required—TOEFL (minimum score 550 paper-based; 213 computer-based).

Louisiana State University and Agricultural and Mechanical College, Graduate School, College of Education, Department of Educational Theory, Policy and Practice, Baton Rouge, LA 70803. Offers counseling (M Ed, MA, Ed S); educational administration (M Ed, MA, PhD, Ed S); educational technology (MA); elementary education (M Ed, MAT); higher education (PhD); research methodology (PhD); secondary education (M Ed, MAT). PhD programs offered jointly with Louisiana State University in Shreveport. *Accreditation:* ACA (one or more programs are accredited); NCATE. Part-time and evening/weekend programs available. *Faculty:* 17 full-time (all women). *Students:* 188 full-time (145 women), 161 part-time (130 women); includes 104 minority (88 Black or African American, non-Hispanic/Latino; 1 American Indian or Alaska Native, non-Hispanic/Latino; 6 Asian, non-Hispanic/Latino; 5 Hispanic/Latino; 4 Two or more races, non-Hispanic/Latino), 9 international. Average age 31. 151 applicants, 61% accepted, 58 enrolled. In 2011, 129 master's, 17 doctorates, 11 other advanced degrees awarded. Terminal master's awarded for partial completion of doctoral program. *Degree requirements:* For doctorate, thesis/dissertation; for Ed S, thesis optional. *Entrance requirements:* For master's and doctorate, GRE General Test, minimum GPA of 3.0. Additional exam requirements/recommendations for international students: Required—TOEFL (minimum score 550 paper-based; 213 computer-based; 79 iBT) or IELTS (minimum score 6.5). *Application deadline:* For fall admission, 1/25 priority date for domestic students, 5/15 for international students; for spring admission, 10/15 for international students. Applications are processed on a rolling basis. Application fee: $50 ($70 for international students). Electronic applications accepted. *Financial support:* In 2011–12, 230 students received support, including 2 fellowships (averaging $19,353 per year), 24 research assistantships with full and partial tuition reimbursements available (averaging $10,052 per year), 53 teaching assistantships with full and partial tuition reimbursements available (averaging $12,218 per year); career-related internships or fieldwork, Federal Work-Study, institutionally sponsored loans, health care benefits, and unspecified assistantships also available. Support available to part-time students. Financial award applicants required to submit FAFSA. *Faculty research:* Literary, curriculum studies, science education, K-12 leadership, higher education. *Total annual research expenditures:* $774,887. *Unit head:* Dr. Earl Cheek, Jr., Chair, 225-578-6867, Fax: 225-578-9135, E-mail: echeek@lsu.edu. *Application contact:* Dr. Rita Culross, Graduate Coordinator, 225-578-6867, Fax: 225-578-9135, E-mail: acrita@lsu.edu.

Louisiana Tech University, Graduate School, College of Education, Department of Curriculum, Instruction and Leadership, Ruston, LA 71272. Offers curriculum and instruction (MS, Ed D); educational leadership (Ed D); secondary education (M Ed), including business education, English education, foreign language education, health and physical education, mathematics education, science education, social studies education, speech education. *Accreditation:* NCATE. Part-time programs available. *Degree requirements:* For doctorate, thesis/dissertation. *Entrance requirements:* For master's and doctorate, GRE General Test.

Loyola Marymount University, School of Education, Department of Elementary and Secondary Education, Program in Secondary Education, Los Angeles, CA 90045. Offers MA. Part-time programs available. *Faculty:* 7 full-time (6 women), 17 part-time/adjunct (10 women). *Students:* 86 full-time (57 women), 31 part-time (14 women); includes 65 minority (13 Black or African American, non-Hispanic/Latino; 2 American Indian or Alaska Native, non-Hispanic/Latino; 7 Asian, non-Hispanic/Latino; 35 Hispanic/Latino; 8 Two or more races, non-Hispanic/Latino). Average age 30. 69 applicants, 74% accepted, 44 enrolled. In 2011, 61 master's awarded. *Degree requirements:* For master's, comprehensive exam. *Entrance requirements:* For master's, CBEST, CSET, 3 letters of recommendation. Additional exam requirements/recommendations for international students: Required—TOEFL (minimum score 600 paper-based; 250 computer-based; 100 iBT). *Application deadline:* For fall admission, 6/15 for domestic students; for spring admission, 11/15 for domestic students. Application fee: $50. Electronic applications accepted. *Financial support:* In 2011–12, 87 students received support, including 2 research assistantships (averaging $1,440 per year); scholarships/grants and unspecified assistantships also available. Support available to part-time students. Financial award application deadline: 6/15; financial award applicants required to submit FAFSA. *Unit head:* Dr. Irene Oliver, Chair/Director, 310-338-7302, E-mail: ioliver@lmu.edu. *Application contact:* Chake H. Kouyoumjian, Director, Graduate Admissions, 310-338-2721, E-mail: ckouyoum@lmu.edu. Web site: http://soe.lmu.edu/admissions/programs/tcp.htm.

Loyola University Chicago, School of Education, Program in Teaching and Learning, Chicago, IL 60660. Offers elementary education (M Ed); English as a second language (Certificate); math education (M Ed); reading specialist (M Ed); reading teacher endorsement (Certificate); school technology (M Ed); science education (M Ed); secondary education (M Ed); special education (M Ed). *Accreditation:* NCATE. *Faculty:* 12 full-time (9 women), 12 part-time/adjunct (6 women). *Students:* 131. Average age 28. 115 applicants, 65% accepted, 30 enrolled. In 2011, 80 master's awarded. *Degree requirements:* For master's, comprehensive exam. *Entrance requirements:* For master's, Illinois Basic Skills Test, 3 letters of recommendation, minimum GPA of 3.0, resume. Additional exam requirements/recommendations for international students: Required—TOEFL (minimum score 550 paper-based; 213 computer-based; 79 iBT). *Application deadline:* For fall admission, 7/1 priority date for domestic students, 7/1 for international students; for spring admission, 11/1 priority date for domestic students, 11/1 for international students. Applications are processed on a rolling basis. Application fee: $50. Electronic applications accepted. Application fee is waived when completed online. *Expenses: Tuition:* Full-time $15,660; part-time $870 per credit hour. *Required fees:* $125 per semester. Tuition and fees vary according to course load and program. *Financial support:* Institutionally sponsored loans, scholarships/grants, and unspecified assistantships available. Support available to part-time students. Financial award application deadline: 2/1; financial award applicants required to submit FAFSA. *Faculty research:* Positive behavior support, school reform, school improvement. *Unit head:* Dr. Dorothy Giroux, Director, 312-915-7027, E-mail: dgiroux@luc.edu. *Application contact:* Marie Rosin-Dittmar, Information Contact, 312-915-6800, E-mail: schleduc@luc.edu.

Loyola University Maryland, Graduate Programs, Department of Education, Program in Special Education, Baltimore, MD 21210-2699. Offers early childhood education (M Ed, CAS); elementary/middle education (M Ed, CAS); secondary education (M Ed, CAS). *Accreditation:* NCATE. Part-time programs available. *Faculty:* 57 full-time (32 women), 21 part-time/adjunct (10 women). *Students:* 6 full-time (5 women), 33 part-time (31 women); includes 3 minority (all Black or African American, non-Hispanic/Latino). Average age 29. In 2011, 11 master's awarded. *Entrance requirements:* For master's and CAS, PRAXIS, SAT, ACT, or GRE. Additional exam requirements/recommendations for international students: Required—TOEFL (minimum score 550 paper-based; 213 computer-based). *Application deadline:* For fall admission, 6/15 priority date for domestic students; for spring admission, 11/1 priority date for domestic students. Application fee: $50. Electronic applications accepted. *Financial support:* Research assistantships and unspecified assistantships available. Financial award application deadline: 4/15; financial award applicants required to submit FAFSA. *Unit head:* Monica J. Phelps, Director, 410-617-2671, E-mail: mphelps@loyola.edu. *Application contact:* Maureen Faux, Executive Director, Graduate Admissions, 410-617-5020, Fax: 410-617-2002, E-mail: graduate@loyola.edu.

Loyola University Maryland, Graduate Programs, Department of Education, Program in Teacher Education, Baltimore, MD 21210-2699. Offers elementary/middle education (MAT); secondary education (MAT); secondary education: biology (MAT); secondary education: chemistries (MAT); secondary education: earth science (MAT); secondary education: English (MAT); secondary education: mathematics (MAT); secondary education: physics (MAT). Part-time programs available. *Faculty:* 25 full-time (21 women), 14 part-time/adjunct (11 women). *Students:* 28 full-time (19 women), 58 part-time (45 women); includes 5 minority (1 Black or African American, non-Hispanic/Latino; 2 Asian, non-Hispanic/Latino; 2 Two or more races, non-Hispanic/Latino), 4 international. Average age 28. In 2011, 37 master's awarded. *Entrance requirements:* For master's, PRAXIS, SAT, ACT, or GRE. Additional exam requirements/recommendations for international students: Required—TOEFL (minimum score 550 paper-based; 213 computer-based). *Application deadline:* For fall admission, 6/15 for domestic students; for spring admission, 11/1 for domestic students. Electronic applications accepted. *Financial support:* Research assistantships and unspecified assistantships available. Financial award application deadline: 4/15. *Unit head:* Wendy Smith, Chair, 410-617-2194, E-mail: wmsmith@loyola.edu. *Application contact:* Maureen Faux, Executive Director, Graduate Admissions, 410-617-5020, Fax: 410-617-2002, E-mail: graduate@loyola.edu. Web site: http://www.loyola.edu/academics/theology/.

Maharishi University of Management, Graduate Studies, Department of Education, Fairfield, IA 52557. Offers teaching elementary education (MA); teaching secondary education (MA). *Degree requirements:* For master's, thesis or alternative. *Entrance requirements:* For master's, GRE, minimum GPA of 3.0. Additional exam requirements/recommendations for international students: Required—TOEFL. *Faculty research:* Unified field-based approach to education, moral climate, scientific study of teaching.

Manhattanville College, Graduate Studies, School of Education, Program in Middle Childhood/Adolescence Education (Grades 5-12), Purchase, NY 10577-2132. Offers biology (MAT); biology and special education (MPS); chemistry (MAT); chemistry and special education (MPS); English (MAT); English and special education (MPS); literacy (MPS), including reading and writing, writing; literacy and special education (MPS); math (MAT); math and special education (MPS); second language (MAT), including French, Italian, Latin, Spanish; social studies (MAT); social studies and special education (MPS); special education (MPS). Part-time and evening/weekend programs available. *Degree requirements:* For master's, comprehensive exam or research project, field experience. *Entrance requirements:* For master's, minimum undergraduate GPA of 3.0, 2 letters of recommendation. Additional exam requirements/recommendations for international students: Required—TOEFL. Electronic applications accepted.

Mansfield University of Pennsylvania, Graduate Studies, Department of Education and Special Education, Mansfield, PA 16933. Offers elementary education (M Ed); secondary education (MS); special education (M Ed). *Accreditation:* NCATE (one or more programs are accredited). Part-time and evening/weekend programs available. Postbaccalaureate distance learning degree programs offered (no on-campus study). *Degree requirements:* For master's, comprehensive exam, thesis optional. *Entrance requirements:* For master's, minimum GPA of 3.0. Additional exam requirements/recommendations for international students: Required—TOEFL (minimum score 550 paper-based; 220 computer-based). Electronic applications accepted. *Expenses:* Tuition, state resident: full-time $7488; part-time $416 per credit. Tuition, nonresident: full-time $11,232; part-time $624 per credit.

Marquette University, Graduate School, College of Education, Department of Educational Policy and Leadership, Milwaukee, WI 53201-1881. Offers college student personnel administration (M Ed); curriculum and instruction (MA); education (MA); educational administration (M Ed); educational policy and foundations (MA); elementary education (Certificate); literacy (MA); principal (Certificate); reading specialist (Certificate); reading teacher (Certificate); secondary education (Certificate); superintendent (Certificate). Part-time and evening/weekend programs available. *Faculty:* 14 full-time (9 women). *Students:* 40 full-time (34 women), 137 part-time (80 women); includes 25 minority (14 Black or African American, non-Hispanic/Latino; 1 American Indian or Alaska Native, non-Hispanic/Latino; 2 Asian, non-Hispanic/Latino; 8 Hispanic/Latino), 2 international. Average age 32. 132 applicants, 73% accepted, 67 enrolled. In 2011, 46 master's, 3 doctorates, 5 other advanced degrees awarded. Terminal master's awarded for partial completion of doctoral program. *Degree requirements:* For master's, comprehensive exam, thesis (for some programs); for doctorate, thesis/dissertation, qualifying exam, supporting minor. *Entrance requirements:* For master's, GRE General Test or MAT, official transcripts from all current and previous colleges/universities except Marquette, three letters of recommendation, statement of purpose; for doctorate, GRE General Test, MAT, sample of written work, official transcripts from all current and previous colleges/universities except Marquette, three letters of recommendation, statement of purpose, resume/ curriculum vitae; for Certificate, GRE General Test or MAT, master's degree. Additional exam requirements/recommendations for international students: Required—TOEFL (minimum score 530 paper-based; 78 computer-based). *Application deadline:* For fall admission, 1/15 for domestic and international students. Application fee: $50. *Expenses:* Contact institution. *Financial support:* In 2011–12, 130 students received support, including 1 fellowship with full tuition reimbursement available (averaging $18,780 per year), 5 research assistantships with full tuition reimbursements available (averaging $13,404 per year); health care benefits, tuition waivers (partial), and unspecified assistantships also available. Support available to part-time students. Financial award application deadline: 2/15. *Faculty research:* Leadership; social justice in education; development of lifelong learners; race, class, and schooling in historical perspective; urban teacher education. *Unit head:* Dr. Ellen Eckman, Chair, 414-288-1561, E-mail: ellen.eckman@marquette.edu. *Application contact:* Craig Pierce, Assistant Dean of the Graduate School, 414-288-5740, Fax: 414-288-1902, E-mail: craig.pierce@marquette.edu.

Marshall University, Academic Affairs Division, Graduate School of Education and Professional Development, Program in Secondary Education, Huntington, WV 25755. Offers MA. *Accreditation:* NCATE. Part-time and evening/weekend programs available. *Students:* 16 full-time (11 women), 65 part-time (52 women); includes 1 minority (Asian, non-Hispanic/Latino). Average age 33. In 2011, 25 master's awarded. *Degree requirements:* For master's, thesis optional, comprehensive or oral assessment. *Entrance requirements:* For master's, GRE General Test or MAT. Application fee: $40. *Financial support:* Federal Work-Study, tuition waivers (full), and unspecified assistantships available. Support available to part-time students. Financial award applicants required to submit FAFSA. *Unit head:* Dr. Lisa Heaton, Director, 304-746-2026, E-mail: heaton@marshall.edu. *Application contact:* Information Contact, Graduate Admissions, 304-746-1900, Fax: 304-746-1902, E-mail: services@marshall.edu.

Marygrove College, Graduate Division, Sage Program, Detroit, MI 48221-2599. Offers M Ed. *Entrance requirements:* For master's, Michigan Teacher Test for Certification.

Marymount University, School of Education and Human Services, Program in Education, Arlington, VA 22207-4299. Offers elementary education (M Ed); English as a second language (M Ed); professional studies (M Ed); secondary education (M Ed); special education, general curriculum (M Ed). *Accreditation:* NCATE. Part-time and evening/weekend programs available. *Faculty:* 9 full-time (7 women), 7 part-time/adjunct (5 women). *Students:* 62 full-time (57 women), 103 part-time (86 women); includes 22 minority (3 Black or African American, non-Hispanic/Latino; 4 Asian, non-Hispanic/ Latino; 10 Hispanic/Latino; 5 Two or more races, non-Hispanic/Latino), 13 international. Average age 31. 69 applicants, 100% accepted, 52 enrolled. In 2011, 79 master's awarded. *Degree requirements:* For master's, thesis or alternative. *Entrance requirements:* For master's, GRE or MAT and PRAXIS I or SAT/ACT and VCLA, 2 letters of recommendation, resume, interview. Additional exam requirements/ recommendations for international students: Required—TOEFL (minimum score 600 paper-based; 250 computer-based; 96 iBT), IELTS (minimum score 6.5). *Application deadline:* For fall admission, 7/1 for international students. Applications are processed on a rolling basis. Application fee: $40. Electronic applications accepted. *Expenses: Tuition:* Part-time $770 per credit hour. *Required fees:* $8 per credit hour. One-time fee: $180 full-time. *Financial support:* In 2011–12, 27 students received support. Research assistantships with full tuition reimbursements available, career-related internships or fieldwork, Federal Work-Study, scholarships/grants, and unspecified assistantships available. Support available to part-time students. Financial award applicants required to submit FAFSA. *Unit head:* Dr. Shelly Haser, Chair, 703-526-6855, Fax: 703-284-1631, E-mail: shelly.haser@marymount.edu. *Application contact:* Francesca Reed, Director, Graduate Admissions, 703-284-5901, Fax: 703-527-3815, E-mail: grad.admissions@marymount.edu. Web site: http://www.marymount.edu/academics/schools/sehs/grad.aspx.

Maryville University of Saint Louis, School of Education, St. Louis, MO 63141-7299. Offers art education (MA Ed); early childhood education (MA Ed); educational leadership (Ed D); educational leadership: principal certification (MA Ed); elementary education (MA Ed); gifted education (MA Ed); higher education leadership (Ed D); literacy specialist (MA Ed); middle grades education (MA Ed); secondary teaching and inquiry (MA Ed); teacher as leader (MA Ed). *Accreditation:* NCATE. Part-time and evening/weekend programs available. *Faculty:* 10 full-time (6 women), 19 part-time/ adjunct (15 women). *Students:* 33 full-time (25 women), 251 part-time (190 women); includes 42 minority (32 Black or African American, non-Hispanic/Latino; 1 American Indian or Alaska Native, non-Hispanic/Latino; 4 Asian, non-Hispanic/Latino; 2 Hispanic/ Latino; 3 Two or more races, non-Hispanic/Latino). Average age 38. In 2011, 69 master's, 43 doctorates awarded. *Degree requirements:* For master's, thesis, project. *Entrance requirements:* For master's, minimum cumulative GPA of 3.0, 3 professional recommendations, essays, interview with program faculty; for doctorate, minimum GPA of 3.0, 3 professional recommendations, essay, interview, on-site writing sample. Additional exam requirements/recommendations for international students: Required—TOEFL (minimum score 550 paper-based). *Application deadline:* Applications are processed on a rolling basis. Application fee: $40 ($60 for international students). Electronic applications accepted. *Expenses: Tuition:* Full-time $21,922; part-time $675 per credit hour. *Required fees:* $233.75 per semester. *Financial support:* Career-related internships or fieldwork, Federal Work-Study, tuition waivers (partial), and professional educator discounts available. Financial award application deadline: 3/1; financial award applicants required to submit FAFSA. *Faculty research:* Collaboration with public schools, pre-service program development, mathematics, diversity, literacy. *Unit head:* Dr. Sam Hausfather, Dean, 314-529-9466, Fax: 314-529-9921, E-mail: shausfather@maryville.edu. *Application contact:* Holly Stanwich, Graduate Admissions Coordinator, 314-529-9542, Fax: 314-529-9921, E-mail: teachered@maryville.edu. Web site: http://www.maryville.edu/academics-ed-graduate.

Marywood University, Academic Affairs, Reap College of Education and Human Development, Department of Education, Program in Secondary/K-12 Education, Scranton, PA 18509-1598. Offers MAT. *Entrance requirements:* Additional exam requirements/recommendations for international students: Required—TOEFL (minimum score 550 paper-based; 213 computer-based; 79 iBT). *Application deadline:* For fall admission, 4/1 priority date for domestic students, 3/31 for international students; for spring admission, 11/1 priority date for domestic students, 8/31 for international students. Applications are processed on a rolling basis. Application fee: $35. Electronic applications accepted. *Financial support:* Career-related internships or fieldwork, scholarships/grants, and unspecified assistantships available. Support available to part-time students. Financial award application deadline: 6/30; financial award applicants required to submit FAFSA. *Unit head:* Dr. Patricia S. Arter, Chairperson, 570-348-6211 Ext. 2511, E-mail: psarter@marywood.edu. *Application contact:* Tammy Manka, Assistant Director of Graduate Admissions, 570-348-6211 Ext. 2322, E-mail: tmanka@marywood.edu. Web site: http://www.marywood.edu/education/graduate-programs/mat-secondary-ed.html.

McDaniel College, Graduate and Professional Studies, Program in Elementary and Secondary Education, Westminster, MD 21157-4390. Offers elementary education (MS); secondary education (MS). *Accreditation:* NCATE. Part-time and evening/ weekend programs available. *Degree requirements:* For master's, comprehensive exam (for some programs), thesis optional. *Entrance requirements:* For master's, GRE General Test, MAT, or NTE/PRAXIS I, letters of reference (3). Additional exam requirements/recommendations for international students: Required—TOEFL (minimum score 213 computer-based).

McNeese State University, Doré School of Graduate Studies, Burton College of Education, Department of Education Professions, Program in Curriculum and Instruction, Lake Charles, LA 70609. Offers early childhood education (M Ed); elementary education (M Ed); reading (M Ed); secondary education (M Ed). Evening/ weekend programs available. *Faculty:* 10 full-time (5 women). *Students:* 8 full-time (7 women), 11 part-time (all women); includes 6 minority (all Black or African American, non-Hispanic/Latino), 1 international. In 2011, 6 master's awarded. *Entrance requirements:* For master's, GRE, teaching certificate. *Application deadline:* For fall admission, 5/15 priority date for domestic students, 5/15 for international students; for spring admission, 10/15 priority date for domestic students, 10/15 for international students. Applications are processed on a rolling basis. Application fee: $20 ($30 for international students). *Expenses:* Tuition, state resident: part-time $519 per credit hour. Tuition and fees vary according to course load. *Financial support:* Application deadline: 5/1. *Unit head:* Dr. Dustin M. Hebert, Director, 337-475-5424, Fax: 337-475-5272, E-mail: dhebert@mcneese.edu. *Application contact:* Dr. George F. Mead, Jr., Interim Dean of Dore' School of Graduate Studies, 337-475-5396, Fax: 337-475-5397, E-mail: admissions@mcneese.edu.

McNeese State University, Doré School of Graduate Studies, Burton College of Education, Department of Education Professions, Program in Teaching, Lake Charles, LA 70609. Offers elementary education grades 1-5 (MAT); secondary education grades 6-12 (MAT); special education (MAT), including mild/moderate grades 1-5. *Faculty:* 10 full-time (5 women). *Students:* 49 full-time (37 women), 89 part-time (69 women); includes 20 minority (16 Black or African American, non-Hispanic/Latino; 4 Hispanic/ Latino), 1 international. In 2011, 61 master's awarded. *Entrance requirements:* For master's, GRE, PRAXIS, 2 letters of recommendation; autobiography. *Application deadline:* For fall admission, 5/15 priority date for domestic students, 5/15 for international students; for spring admission, 10/15 priority date for domestic students, 10/15 for international students. Applications are processed on a rolling basis. Application fee: $20 ($30 for international students). *Expenses:* Tuition, state resident: part-time $519 per credit hour. Tuition and fees vary according to course load. *Financial support:* Application deadline: 5/1. *Unit head:* Dr. Dustin M. Hebert, Director, 337-475-5424, Fax: 337-475-5272, E-mail: dhebert@mcneese.edu. *Application contact:* Dr. George F. Mead, Jr., Interim Dean of Dore' School of Graduate Studies, 337-475-5396, Fax: 337-475-5397, E-mail: admissions@mcneese.edu.

Medaille College, Program in Education, Buffalo, NY 14214-2695. Offers adolescent education (MS Ed); curriculum and instruction (MS Ed); education preparation (MS Ed); literacy (MS Ed); special education (MS). *Accreditation:* Teacher Education Accreditation Council. Part-time and evening/weekend programs available. *Faculty:* 15 full-time (11 women), 31 part-time/adjunct (21 women). *Students:* 371 full-time (281 women), 37 part-time (29 women); includes 75 minority (11 Black or African American, non-Hispanic/Latino; 6 Asian, non-Hispanic/Latino; 3 Hispanic/Latino; 55 Native Hawaiian or other Pacific Islander, non-Hispanic/Latino), 264 international. Average age 29. 354 applicants, 99% accepted, 163 enrolled. In 2011, 457 master's awarded. *Degree requirements:* For master's, comprehensive exam (for some programs), thesis or alternative. *Entrance requirements:* For master's, minimum undergraduate GPA of 2.7. Additional exam requirements/recommendations for international students: Required—TOEFL (minimum score 550 paper-based; 213 computer-based). *Application deadline:* For fall admission, 8/15 priority date for domestic students; for spring admission, 1/15 priority date for domestic students. Applications are processed on a rolling basis. Application fee: $35. Electronic applications accepted. Tuition and fees vary according to program. *Financial support:* Federal Work-Study available. Financial award applicants required to submit FAFSA. *Faculty research:* Curriculum planning, truancy, tracking minority students, curriculum design, mentoring students. *Unit head:* Dr. Robert DiSibio, Director of Graduate Programs, 716-932-2548, Fax: 716-631-1380, E-mail: rdisibio@medaille.edu. *Application contact:* Jacqueline Matheny, Executive Director of Marketing and Enrollment, 716-932-2541, Fax: 716-632-1811, E-mail: jmatheny@medaille.edu. Web site: http://www.medaille.edu.

Mercer University, Graduate Studies, Cecil B. Day Campus, Tift College of Education (Atlanta), Macon, GA 31207-0003. Offers curriculum and instruction (PhD); early childhood education (M Ed, MAT); educational leadership (PhD, Ed S); higher education leadership (M Ed); middle grades education (M Ed, MAT); reading education (M Ed); school counseling (Ed S); secondary education (M Ed, MAT); teacher leadership (Ed S). *Accreditation:* NCATE. Part-time and evening/weekend programs available. *Faculty:* 31 full-time (17 women), 6 part-time/adjunct (3 women). *Students:* 249 full-time (207 women), 413 part-time (326 women); includes 349 minority (322 Black or African American, non-Hispanic/Latino; 1 American Indian or Alaska Native, non-Hispanic/ Latino; 18 Asian, non-Hispanic/Latino; 6 Hispanic/Latino; 2 Two or more races, non-Hispanic/Latino), 6 international. Average age 34. 204 applicants, 76% accepted, 125 enrolled. In 2011, 235 master's, 8 doctorates, 27 other advanced degrees awarded. *Degree requirements:* For master's and Ed S, research project; for doctorate, thesis/ dissertation. *Entrance requirements:* For master's, GRE or MAT, minimum undergraduate GPA of 2.75; for doctorate, GRE; for Ed S, GRE or MAT, minimum GPA of 3.25, 3 years of teaching experience. Additional exam requirements/ recommendations for international students: Required—TOEFL. *Application deadline:* For fall admission, 8/1 for domestic and international students; for spring admission, 12/1 for domestic and international students. Applications are processed on a rolling basis. Application fee: $25. *Expenses:* Contact institution. *Financial support:* Federal Work-Study available. Support available to part-time students. Financial award application deadline: 5/1. *Faculty research:* Educational technology, multicultural and minority issues in education, educational leadership (P-12 and higher education), school discipline and school bullying, standards-based mathematics education. *Unit head:* Dr. Carl R. Martray, Dean, 478-301-5397, Fax: 478-301-2280, E-mail: martray_cr@mercer.edu. *Application contact:* Dr. Allison Gilmore, Associate Dean for Graduate Teacher Education, 678-547-6333, Fax: 678-547-6055, E-mail: gilmore_a@mercer.edu. Web site: http://www.mercer.edu/education/.

Mercy College, School of Education, Program in Adolescence Education, Grades 7-12, Dobbs Ferry, NY 10522-1189. Offers MS. Part-time and evening/weekend programs available. Postbaccalaureate distance learning degree programs offered (no on-campus study). *Degree requirements:* For master's, comprehensive exam, thesis. *Entrance requirements:* For master's, resume, interview, assessment by specific program director or designee. Additional exam requirements/recommendations for international students: Required—TOEFL (minimum score 600 paper-based; 250 computer-based; 100 iBT), IELTS (minimum score 8). Electronic applications accepted. *Faculty research:* Teaching-learning process, adolescent development, literacy instruction.

Mercyhurst College, Graduate Studies, Program in Secondary Education: Pedagogy and Practice, Erie, PA 16546. Offers MS. Part-time and evening/weekend programs available. *Faculty:* 1 (woman) full-time, 4 part-time/adjunct (2 women). *Students:* 17 full-time (9 women), 4 part-time (3 women). Average age 24. 18 applicants, 56% accepted, 9 enrolled. In 2011, 6 master's awarded. *Entrance requirements:* For master's, GRE or PRAXIS I, resume, essay, three professional references, transcripts. Additional exam requirements/recommendations for international students: Required—TOEFL. *Application deadline:* For fall admission, 8/1 priority date for domestic students, 8/1 for international students; for winter admission, 11/1 priority date for domestic students, 10/1 for international students; for spring admission, 2/1 priority date for domestic students, 2/1 for international students. Applications are processed on a rolling basis. Application fee: $35. *Expenses: Tuition:* Part-time $570 per credit. *Required fees:* $90 per term. Tuition and fees vary according to program. *Financial support:* In 2011–12, 5 research assistantships with full and partial tuition reimbursements were awarded; unspecified assistantships also available. Financial award application deadline: 5/1; financial award applicants required to submit FAFSA. *Unit head:* Dr. Jane Blystone, Director, 814-824-3631, E-mail: jblystone@mercyhurst.edu. *Application contact:* Sarah Murphy, Academic Coordinator, 814-824-2297, Fax: 814-824-2055, E-mail: smurphy@mercyhurst.edu. Web site: http://graduate.mercyhurst.edu/academics/graduate-degrees/secondary-education-pedagogy-and-practice/.

Merrimack College, School of Education, North Andover, MA 01845-5800. Offers community engagement (M Ed); early childhood education (M Ed); elementary education (M Ed); elementary education plus moderate disabilities-dual license (M Ed); English as a second language (M Ed); general studies (M Ed); higher education (M Ed); middle (M Ed); moderate disabilities (preK-8) (M Ed); reading (M Ed); secondary (M Ed); teacher leadership (CAGS). Part-time and evening/weekend programs available. *Faculty:* 4 full-time (all women), 9 part-time/adjunct (7 women). *Students:* 70 full-time (60 women), 39 part-time (33 women); includes 2 minority (1 Asian, non-Hispanic/Latino; 1 Hispanic/Latino). Average age 27. In 2011, 26 master's awarded. *Degree requirements:* For master's, portfolio. *Entrance requirements:* Additional exam requirements/recommendations for international students: Required—TOEFL (minimum score 80 iBT). *Application deadline:* For fall admission, 8/1 priority date for domestic students, 7/15 for international students; for winter admission, 12/1 priority date for domestic students, 11/15 for international students; for spring admission, 3/1 priority date for domestic students, 2/15 for international students. Applications are processed on a rolling basis. Electronic applications accepted. *Expenses: Tuition:* Part-time $475 per credit. *Required fees:* $62.50 per semester. *Financial support:* In 2011–12, 50 fellowships were awarded; career-related internships or fieldwork and scholarships/grants also available. Financial award applicants required to submit FAFSA. *Faculty research:* Higher education, community engagement, literacy, leadership. *Unit head:* Dr. Theresa Kirk, Chair, 978-837-5436, E-mail: kirkt@merrimack.edu. *Application contact:* Jessica McCarthy, Program Coordinator, 978-837-5443, E-mail: mccarthyj@merrimack.edu. Web site: http://www.merrimack.edu/academics/education/med/.

Miami University, School of Education and Allied Professions, Department of Teacher Education, Oxford, OH 45056. Offers elementary education (M Ed, MAT); reading education (M Ed); secondary education (M Ed, MAT), including adolescent education (MAT), elementary mathematics education (M Ed), secondary education. Part-time programs available. *Students:* 32 full-time (19 women), 40 part-time (37 women); includes 6 minority (3 Black or African American, non-Hispanic/Latino; 2 Hispanic/Latino; 1 Two or more races, non-Hispanic/Latino), 3 international. Average age 28. In 2011, 42 master's awarded. *Entrance requirements:* For master's, GRE (for MAT), minimum undergraduate GPA of 3.0 during previous 2 years or 2.75 overall. *Application deadline:* Applications are processed on a rolling basis. Application fee: $50. Electronic applications accepted. *Expenses:* Tuition, state resident: full-time $12,023; part-time $501 per credit hour. Tuition, nonresident: full-time $26,554; part-time $1107 per credit hour. *Required fees:* $528. *Financial support:* Fellowships with full tuition reimbursements, research assistantships, teaching assistantships, career-related internships or fieldwork, Federal Work-Study, scholarships/grants, health care benefits, tuition waivers (full), and unspecified assistantships available. Financial award application deadline: 2/15. *Unit head:* Dr. James Shiveley, Chair, 513-529-6443, Fax: 513-529-4931, E-mail: shiveljm@muohio.edu. *Application contact:* Linda Dennett, Program Associate, 513-529-5708, E-mail: dennetlg@muohio.edu. Web site: http://www.units.muohio.edu/eap/departments/edt/.

Middle Tennessee State University, College of Graduate Studies, College of Education, Department of Educational Leadership, Program in Curriculum and Instruction, Murfreesboro, TN 37132. Offers curriculum and instruction (M Ed, Ed S); English as a second language (M Ed, Ed S); secondary education (M Ed); technology and curriculum design (Ed S). *Accreditation:* NCATE. Part-time and evening/weekend programs available. Postbaccalaureate distance learning degree programs offered. *Faculty:* 22 full-time (11 women), 22 part-time/adjunct (12 women). *Students:* 13 full-time (7 women), 208 part-time (167 women); includes 38 minority (29 Black or African American, non-Hispanic/Latino; 2 Asian, non-Hispanic/Latino; 2 Hispanic/Latino; 5 Two or more races, non-Hispanic/Latino). 154 applicants, 97% accepted. In 2011, 144 master's, 40 Ed Ss awarded. *Degree requirements:* For master's, comprehensive exam; for Ed S, comprehensive exam, thesis or alternative. *Entrance requirements:* For master's and Ed S, GRE, MAT or PRAXIS. Additional exam requirements/recommendations for international students: Required—TOEFL (minimum score 525 paper-based; 195 computer-based; 71 iBT) or IELTS (minimum score 6). *Application deadline:* For fall admission, 6/1 for domestic and international students. Applications are processed on a rolling basis. Application fee: $25 ($30 for international students). Electronic applications accepted. *Expenses:* Tuition, state resident: full-time $10,008. Tuition, nonresident: full-time $25,056. *Financial support:* Tuition waivers available. Support available to part-time students. Financial award application deadline: 5/1. *Unit head:* Dr. James Huffman, Chair, 615-898-2855, Fax: 615-898-2859. *Application contact:* Dr. Michael D. Allen, Dean and Vice Provost for Research, 615-898-2840, Fax: 615-904-8020, E-mail: michael.allen@mtsu.edu.

Mills College, Graduate Studies, School of Education, Oakland, CA 94613-1000. Offers child life in hospitals (MA); early childhood education (MA); education (MA), including art education, curriculum and instruction, elementary education, English education, foreign language education, mathematics education, science education, secondary education, social studies education, teaching; educational leadership (MA, Ed D). Part-time and evening/weekend programs available. *Faculty:* 13 full-time (10 women), 14 part-time/adjunct (10 women). *Students:* 149 full-time (133 women), 69 part-time (61 women); includes 85 minority (32 Black or African American, non-Hispanic/Latino; 1 American Indian or Alaska Native, non-Hispanic/Latino; 16 Asian, non-Hispanic/Latino; 24 Hispanic/Latino; 1 Native Hawaiian or other Pacific Islander, non-Hispanic/Latino; 11 Two or more races, non-Hispanic/Latino), 3 international. Average age 28. 238 applicants, 84% accepted, 106 enrolled. In 2011, 41 master's, 2 doctorates awarded. Terminal master's awarded for partial completion of doctoral program. *Degree requirements:* For master's, comprehensive exam. *Entrance requirements:* For master's, statement of purpose, official transcript, 3 recommendations; for doctorate, GRE General Test. Additional exam requirements/recommendations for international students: Required—TOEFL (minimum score 550 paper-based; 80 iBT) or IELTS (minimum score 6). *Application deadline:* For fall admission, 12/31 priority date for domestic students, 12/15 for international students; for spring admission, 11/1 priority date for domestic students, 10/1 for international students. Applications are processed on a rolling basis. Application fee: $50. Electronic applications accepted. *Expenses: Tuition:* Full-time $28,280; part-time $15,640 per year. *Required fees:* $958. Tuition and fees vary according to program. *Financial support:* In 2011–12, 43 students received support, including 225 fellowships with full and partial tuition reimbursements available (averaging $6,020 per year), 43 teaching assistantships with full and partial tuition reimbursements available (averaging $6,782 per year); career-related internships or fieldwork and scholarships/grants also available. Support available to part-time students. Financial award application deadline: 2/1; financial award applicants required to submit FAFSA. *Faculty research:* Early childhood education, teacher preparation, educational leadership. *Total annual research expenditures:* $2.3 million. *Unit head:* Katherine Schultz, Chairperson, 510-430-3170, Fax: 510-430-3379, E-mail: grad-studies@mills.edu. *Application contact:* Tiana Kozoil, Graduate Admission Specialist, 510-430-3305, Fax: 510-430-2159, E-mail: grad-studies@mills.edu. Web site: http://www.mills.edu/education.

Minnesota State University Mankato, College of Graduate Studies, College of Education, Department of Educational Studies: K–12 and Secondary Programs, Mankato, MN 56001. Offers curriculum and instruction (SP); educational technology (MS); library media education (MS, Certificate); teacher licensure program (MAT); teaching and learning (MS, Certificate). *Accreditation:* NCATE. *Students:* 34 full-time (19 women), 93 part-time (62 women). *Degree requirements:* For master's, comprehensive exam, thesis or alternative; for other advanced degree, comprehensive exam, thesis. *Entrance requirements:* For master's, GRE General Test or MAT, minimum GPA of 3.0 during previous 2 years; for other advanced degree, GRE, minimum GPA of 3.0. Additional exam requirements/recommendations for international students: Required—TOEFL. *Application deadline:* For fall admission, 7/1 priority date for domestic students, 5/1 for international students; for spring admission, 11/1 for domestic students, 10/1 for international students. Applications are processed on a rolling basis. Application fee: $40. Electronic applications accepted. *Financial support:* Application deadline: 3/15. *Unit head:* Dr. Kitty Foord, Chairperson, 507-389-1965. *Application contact:* 507-389-2321, E-mail: grad@mnsu.edu. Web site: http://ed.mnsu.edu/ksp/.

Mississippi College, Graduate School, School of Education, Department of Teacher Education and Leadership, Clinton, MS 39058. Offers art (M Ed); biological science (M Ed); business education (M Ed); computer science (M Ed); dyslexia therapy (M Ed); educational leadership (M Ed, Ed D, Ed S); elementary education (M Ed, Ed S); English (M Ed); higher education administration (MS); mathematics (M Ed); secondary education (M Ed); social studies (history) (M Ed); teaching arts (M Ed). Part-time programs available. Postbaccalaureate distance learning degree programs offered (no on-campus study). *Degree requirements:* For master's, comprehensive exam, thesis optional. *Entrance requirements:* For master's, NTE. Additional exam requirements/recommendations for international students: Recommended—TOEFL, IELTS. Electronic applications accepted.

Mississippi State University, College of Education, Department of Curriculum, Instruction and Special Education, Mississippi State, MS 39762. Offers elementary education (MS, PhD, Ed S); middle level education (MAT); secondary education (MAT, MS, Ed S); special education (MS, Ed S). *Accreditation:* NCATE. Part-time and evening/weekend programs available. *Faculty:* 12 full-time (10 women), 2 part-time/adjunct (1 woman). *Students:* 57 full-time (41 women), 104 part-time (81 women); includes 54 minority (52 Black or African American, non-Hispanic/Latino; 1 Hispanic/Latino; 1 Two or more races, non-Hispanic/Latino). Average age 33. 100 applicants, 60% accepted, 48 enrolled. In 2011, 38 master's, 5 doctorates, 5 other advanced degrees awarded. *Degree requirements:* For master's, comprehensive exam; for doctorate, thesis/dissertation; for Ed S, comprehensive exam, thesis or alternative. *Entrance requirements:* For master's, GRE, minimum GPA of 2.75 in junior and senior year, eligibility for initial teacher certification; for doctorate, GRE, minimum graduate GPA of 3.4; for Ed S, GRE, minimum graduate GPA of 3.2. Additional exam requirements/recommendations for international students: Required—TOEFL (minimum score 600 paper-based; 250 computer-based; 100 iBT); Recommended—IELTS (minimum score 7.5). *Application deadline:* For fall admission, 3/1 priority date for domestic students, 5/1 for international students; for spring admission, 9/1 priority date for domestic students, 9/1 for international students. Applications are processed on a rolling basis. Application fee: $40. Electronic applications accepted. *Expenses:* Tuition, state resident: full-time $5805; part-time $322.50 per credit hour. Tuition, nonresident: full-time $14,670; part-time $815 per credit hour. *Financial support:* In 2011–12, 7 research assistantships with full and partial tuition reimbursements (averaging $9,264 per year), 4 teaching assistantships (averaging $8,937 per year) were awarded; Federal Work-Study, institutionally sponsored loans, scholarships/grants, and unspecified assistantships also available. Financial award application deadline: 4/1; financial award applicants required to submit FAFSA. *Faculty research:* Early childhood education, reading, rural schools, multicultural education, use of technology in instruction. *Unit head:* Dr. Devon Brenner, Professor and Interim Head, 662-325-7119, Fax: 662-325-7857, E-mail: devon@ra.msstate.edu. *Application contact:* Dr. C. Susie Burroughs, Professor and Graduate Coordinator, 662-325-3747, Fax: 662-325-7857, E-mail: susie.burroughs@msstate.edu. Web site: http://www.cise.msstate.edu/.

Missouri State University, Graduate College, College of Arts and Letters, Department of English, Springfield, MO 65897. Offers English and writing (MA); secondary education (MS Ed), including English. Part-time and evening/weekend programs available. *Faculty:* 23 full-time (17 women), 3 part-time/adjunct (0 women). *Students:* 52 full-time (29 women), 33 part-time (19 women); includes 7 minority (2 Black or African American, non-Hispanic/Latino; 3 Hispanic/Latino; 2 Two or more races, non-Hispanic/Latino), 11 international. Average age 28. 50 applicants, 90% accepted, 28 enrolled. In 2011, 35 master's awarded. *Degree requirements:* For master's, one foreign language, comprehensive exam, thesis or alternative. *Entrance requirements:* For master's, GRE (MA), minimum GPA of 3.0 (MA), 9-12 teacher certification (MS Ed). Additional exam requirements/recommendations for international students: Required—TOEFL (minimum score 550 paper-based; 213 computer-based; 79 iBT). *Application deadline:* For fall admission, 7/20 for domestic students, 5/1 for international students; for spring admission, 12/20 for domestic students, 9/1 for international students. Applications are processed on a rolling basis. Application fee: $35 ($50 for international students). Electronic applications accepted. *Expenses:* Tuition, state resident: full-time $4086; part-time $227 per credit hour. Tuition, nonresident: full-time $8172; part-time $454 per credit hour. *Required fees:* $275 per semester. Tuition and fees vary according to course load, campus/location and program. *Financial support:* In 2011–12, 38 teaching assistantships with full tuition reimbursements (averaging $8,000 per year) were awarded; Federal Work-Study, institutionally sponsored loans, scholarships/grants, and unspecified assistantships also available. Support available to part-time students. Financial award application deadline: 3/31; financial award applicants required to submit FAFSA. *Faculty research:* Renaissance literature, William Blake, autobiography, Georgian theatre, TESOL. *Unit head:* Dr. W. D. Blackmon, Head, 417-836-5107, Fax: 417-836-6940, E-mail: wdblackon@missouristate.edu. *Application contact:* Misty Stewart, Coordinator of Graduate Recruitment, 417-836-5331, Fax: 417-836-6888, E-mail: ericeckert@missouristate.edu. Web site: http://english.missouristate.edu/.

Secondary Education

Missouri State University, Graduate College, College of Arts and Letters, Department of Modern and Classical Languages, Springfield, MO 65897. Offers secondary education (MS Ed), including Spanish. Part-time programs available. *Faculty:* 5 full-time (2 women). *Students:* 1 (woman) part-time. Average age 35. In 2011, 2 master's awarded. *Entrance requirements:* For master's, grades 9-12 teaching certification. Additional exam requirements/recommendations for international students: Required—TOEFL (minimum score 550 paper-based; 213 computer-based; 79 iBT), IELTS (minimum score 6). *Application deadline:* For fall admission, 7/20 priority date for domestic students, 5/1 for international students; for spring admission, 12/20 priority date for domestic students, 9/1 for international students. Applications are processed on a rolling basis. Application fee: $35 ($50 for international students). Electronic applications accepted. *Expenses:* Tuition, state resident: full-time $4086; part-time $227 per credit hour. Tuition, nonresident: full-time $8172; part-time $454 per credit hour. *Required fees:* $275 per semester. Tuition and fees vary according to course load, campus/location and program. *Financial support:* Federal Work-Study, scholarships/grants, and unspecified assistantships available. Financial award applicants required to submit FAFSA. *Unit head:* Dr. Madeleine Kernen, Head, 417-836-7626, E-mail: mcl@missouristate.edu. *Application contact:* Eric Eckert, Coordinator of Admissions and Recruitment, 417-836-5331, Fax: 417-836-6888, E-mail: ericeckert@missouristate.edu. Web site: http://www.missouristate.edu/MCL/.

Missouri State University, Graduate College, College of Arts and Letters, Department of Music, Springfield, MO 65897. Offers music (MM), including conducting, music education, music pedagogy, music theory and composition, performance; secondary education (MS Ed), including music. *Accreditation:* NASM. Part-time programs available. *Faculty:* 25 full-time (10 women). *Students:* 20 full-time (14 women), 19 part-time (10 women); includes 3 minority (2 Asian, non-Hispanic/Latino; 1 Hispanic/Latino), 8 international. Average age 27. 20 applicants, 100% accepted, 17 enrolled. In 2011, 17 master's awarded. *Degree requirements:* For master's, comprehensive exam, thesis or alternative. *Entrance requirements:* For master's, GRE, interview/audition (MM), 9-12 teaching certification (MS Ed). Additional exam requirements/recommendations for international students: Required—TOEFL (minimum score 550 paper-based; 213 computer-based; 79 iBT). *Application deadline:* For fall admission, 7/20 for domestic students, 5/1 for international students; for spring admission, 12/20 for domestic students, 9/1 for international students. Applications are processed on a rolling basis. Application fee: $35 ($50 for international students). Electronic applications accepted. *Expenses:* Tuition, state resident: full-time $4086; part-time $227 per credit hour. Tuition, nonresident: full-time $8172; part-time $454 per credit hour. *Required fees:* $275 per semester. Tuition and fees vary according to course load, campus/location and program. *Financial support:* In 2011–12, 11 teaching assistantships with full tuition reimbursements (averaging $8,000 per year) were awarded; Federal Work-Study, institutionally sponsored loans, scholarships/grants, tuition waivers (partial), and unspecified assistantships also available. Financial award application deadline: 3/31; financial award applicants required to submit FAFSA. *Faculty research:* Bulgarian violin literature, Ozarks fiddle music, carillon, nineteenth century piano. *Unit head:* Dr. Julie Combs, Head, 417-836-5648, Fax: 417-836-7665, E-mail: music@missouristate.edu. *Application contact:* Misty Stewart, Coordinator of Graduate Recruitment, 417-836-6079, Fax: 417-836-6200. Web site: http://www.missouristate.edu/music/.

Missouri State University, Graduate College, College of Arts and Letters, Department of Theatre and Dance, Springfield, MO 65897. Offers secondary education (MS Ed), including speech and theatre; theatre (MA). *Accreditation:* NAST. Part-time programs available. *Faculty:* 11 full-time (7 women). *Students:* 3 full-time (2 women), 8 part-time (7 women), 1 international. Average age 28. 8 applicants, 88% accepted, 3 enrolled. In 2011, 3 master's awarded. *Degree requirements:* For master's, comprehensive exam, thesis or alternative. *Entrance requirements:* For master's, minimum GPA of 3.0 (MA), 9-12 teaching certification (MS Ed). Additional exam requirements/recommendations for international students: Required—TOEFL (minimum score 550 paper-based; 213 computer-based; 79 iBT). *Application deadline:* For fall admission, 7/20 for domestic students, 5/1 for international students; for spring admission, 12/20 for domestic students, 9/1 for international students. Applications are processed on a rolling basis. Application fee: $35 ($50 for international students). Electronic applications accepted. *Expenses:* Tuition, state resident: full-time $4086; part-time $227 per credit hour. Tuition, nonresident: full-time $8172; part-time $454 per credit hour. *Required fees:* $275 per semester. Tuition and fees vary according to course load, campus/location and program. *Financial support:* Teaching assistantships, Federal Work-Study, institutionally sponsored loans, scholarships/grants, and unspecified assistantships available. Financial award application deadline: 3/31; financial award applicants required to submit FAFSA. *Unit head:* Bob Willenbrink, Department Head, 417-836-4156, Fax: 417-836-4234, E-mail: rwillenbrink@missouristate.edu. *Application contact:* Misty Stewart, Coordinator of Admissions and Recruitment, 417-836-6079, Fax: 417-836-6200, E-mail: mistystewart@missouristate.edu. Web site: http://theatreanddance.missouristate.edu/.

Missouri State University, Graduate College, College of Business Administration, Department of Computer Information Systems, Springfield, MO 65897. Offers computer information systems (MS); secondary education (MS Ed), including business. Part-time and evening/weekend programs available. Postbaccalaureate distance learning degree programs offered (no on-campus study). *Faculty:* 13 full-time (2 women), 5 part-time/adjunct (0 women). *Students:* 28 full-time (5 women), 2 part-time (1 woman); includes 2 minority (1 Asian, non-Hispanic/Latino; 1 Two or more races, non-Hispanic/Latino), 2 international. Average age 38. 20 applicants, 90% accepted, 11 enrolled. In 2011, 13 master's awarded. *Degree requirements:* For master's, thesis optional. *Entrance requirements:* For master's, GMAT, 3 years of work experience in computer information systems, minimum GPA of 2.75 (MS), 9-12 teaching certification (MS Ed). Additional exam requirements/recommendations for international students: Required—TOEFL (minimum score 550 paper-based; 213 computer-based; 79 iBT). *Application deadline:* For fall admission, 7/20 priority date for domestic students, 5/1 for international students; for spring admission, 12/20 priority date for domestic students, 9/1 for international students. Applications are processed on a rolling basis. Application fee: $35 ($50 for international students). Electronic applications accepted. *Expenses:* Contact institution. *Financial support:* Federal Work-Study, institutionally sponsored loans, scholarships/grants, and unspecified assistantships available. Support available to part-time students. Financial award application deadline: 3/31; financial award applicants required to submit FAFSA. *Faculty research:* Decision support systems, algorithms in Visual Basic, end-user satisfaction, information security. *Unit head:* Dr. Jerry Chin, Head, 417-836-4131, Fax: 417-836-6907, E-mail: jerrychin@missouristate.edu. *Application contact:* Misty Stewart, Coordinator of Graduate Admissions and Recruitment, 417-836-6079, Fax: 417-836-6200, E-mail: mistystewart@missouristate.edu. Web site: http://mscis.missouristate.edu.

Missouri State University, Graduate College, College of Business Administration, Department of Fashion and Interior Design, Springfield, MO 65897. Offers secondary education (MS Ed), including consumer sciences. Part-time programs available. *Faculty:* 1 (woman) full-time, 1 (woman) part-time/adjunct. *Students:* 2 part-time (both women). Average age 37. In 2011, 1 master's awarded. *Degree requirements:* For master's, comprehensive exam, thesis or alternative. *Entrance requirements:* For master's, 9-12 teaching certification (MS Ed), minimum GPA of 3.0 (MNAS). Additional exam requirements/recommendations for international students: Required—TOEFL (minimum score 550 paper-based; 213 computer-based; 79 iBT). *Application deadline:* For fall admission, 7/20 priority date for domestic students, 5/1 for international students; for spring admission, 12/20 priority date for domestic students, 9/1 for international students. Applications are processed on a rolling basis. Application fee: $35 ($50 for international students). Electronic applications accepted. *Expenses:* Tuition, state resident: full-time $4086; part-time $227 per credit hour. Tuition, nonresident: full-time $8172; part-time $454 per credit hour. *Required fees:* $275 per semester. Tuition and fees vary according to course load, campus/location and program. *Financial support:* Career-related internships or fieldwork, Federal Work-Study, institutionally sponsored loans, scholarships/grants, and unspecified assistantships available. Financial award application deadline: 3/31; financial award applicants required to submit FAFSA. *Unit head:* Dr. Shawn Strong, Head, 417-836-5136, Fax: 417-836-4341, E-mail: shawnstrong@missouristate.edu. *Application contact:* Misty Stewart, Coordinator of Graduate Admissions and Recruitment, 417-836-6079, Fax: 417-836-6200, E-mail: mistystewart@missouristate.edu. Web site: http://www.missouristate.edu/fid/.

Missouri State University, Graduate College, College of Education, Department of Counseling, Leadership, and Special Education, Program in Counseling, Springfield, MO 65897. Offers counseling and assessment (Ed S); secondary school counseling (MS). Part-time and evening/weekend programs available. *Students:* 45 full-time (36 women), 73 part-time (59 women); includes 8 minority (2 Black or African American, non-Hispanic/Latino; 1 American Indian or Alaska Native, non-Hispanic/Latino; 2 Asian, non-Hispanic/Latino; 3 Two or more races, non-Hispanic/Latino). Average age 33. 18 applicants, 94% accepted, 11 enrolled. In 2011, 45 master's awarded. *Degree requirements:* For master's, comprehensive exam, thesis or alternative. *Entrance requirements:* For master's, GRE or MAT, minimum GPA of 2.75. Additional exam requirements/recommendations for international students: Required—TOEFL (minimum score 550 paper-based; 213 computer-based; 79 iBT). *Application deadline:* For fall admission, 2/1 priority date for domestic students, 1/1 for international students; for spring admission, 10/1 priority date for domestic students, 9/1 for international students. Application fee: $35 ($50 for international students). Electronic applications accepted. *Expenses:* Tuition, state resident: full-time $4086; part-time $227 per credit hour. Tuition, nonresident: full-time $8172; part-time $454 per credit hour. *Required fees:* $275 per semester. Tuition and fees vary according to course load, campus/location and program. *Financial support:* Federal Work-Study, institutionally sponsored loans, scholarships/grants, and unspecified assistantships available. Financial award application deadline: 3/31; financial award applicants required to submit FAFSA. *Unit head:* Dr. Joseph Hulgus, Program Coordinator, 417-836-6522, Fax: 417-836-4918, E-mail: clse@missouristate.edu. *Application contact:* Misty Stewart, Coordinator of Admissions and Recruitment, 417-836-6079, Fax: 417-836-6200, E-mail: mistystewart@missouristate.edu. Web site: http://education.missouristate.edu/clse/.

Missouri State University, Graduate College, College of Education, Department of Counseling, Leadership, and Special Education, Program in Educational Administration, Springfield, MO 65897. Offers educational administration (MS Ed, Ed S); elementary education (MS Ed); elementary principal (Ed S); secondary education (MS Ed); secondary principal (Ed S); superintendent (Ed S). Part-time and evening/weekend programs available. *Students:* 20 full-time (13 women), 109 part-time (73 women); includes 6 minority (1 Black or African American, non-Hispanic/Latino; 2 American Indian or Alaska Native, non-Hispanic/Latino; 1 Hispanic/Latino; 2 Two or more races, non-Hispanic/Latino), 5 international. Average age 35. 60 applicants, 98% accepted, 43 enrolled. In 2011, 51 master's, 16 Ed Ss awarded. *Degree requirements:* For master's and Ed S, comprehensive exam, thesis or alternative. *Entrance requirements:* For master's, minimum GPA of 2.75; for Ed S, GRE General Test, MAT, minimum GPA of 2.75. Additional exam requirements/recommendations for international students: Required—TOEFL (minimum score 550 paper-based; 213 computer-based; 79 iBT). *Application deadline:* For fall admission, 7/20 priority date for domestic students, 5/1 for international students; for spring admission, 12/20 priority date for domestic students, 9/1 for international students. Applications are processed on a rolling basis. Application fee: $35 ($50 for international students). Electronic applications accepted. *Expenses:* Tuition, state resident: full-time $4086; part-time $227 per credit hour. Tuition, nonresident: full-time $8172; part-time $454 per credit hour. *Required fees:* $275 per semester. Tuition and fees vary according to course load, campus/location and program. *Financial support:* Career-related internships or fieldwork, Federal Work-Study, institutionally sponsored loans, scholarships/grants, and unspecified assistantships available. Financial award application deadline: 3/31; financial award applicants required to submit FAFSA. *Unit head:* Dr. Kim Finch, Program Coordinator, 417-836-5192, Fax: 417-836-4918, E-mail: clse@missouristate.edu. *Application contact:* Misty Stewart, Coordinator of Admissions and Recruitment, 417-836-6079, Fax: 417-836-6200, E-mail: mistystewart@missouristate.edu. Web site: http://education.missouristate.edu/edadmin/.

Missouri State University, Graduate College, College of Health and Human Services, Department of Health, Physical Education, and Recreation, Springfield, MO 65897. Offers health promotion and wellness management (MS); secondary education (MS Ed), including physical education. Part-time programs available. *Faculty:* 12 full-time (5 women). *Students:* 11 full-time (8 women), 8 part-time (5 women); includes 2 minority (1 Black or African American, non-Hispanic/Latino; 1 Asian, non-Hispanic/Latino). Average age 28. 14 applicants, 100% accepted, 9 enrolled. In 2011, 10 master's awarded. *Degree requirements:* For master's, comprehensive exam, thesis or alternative. *Entrance requirements:* For master's, GRE (MS), minimum GPA of 2.8 (MS); 9-12 teaching certification (MS Ed). Additional exam requirements/recommendations for international students: Required—TOEFL (minimum score 550 paper-based; 213 computer-based; 79 iBT). *Application deadline:* For fall admission, 7/20 priority date for domestic students, 5/1 for international students; for spring admission, 12/20 priority date for domestic students, 9/1 for international students. Applications are processed on a rolling basis. Application fee: $35 ($50 for international students). Electronic applications accepted. *Expenses:* Tuition, state resident: full-time $4086; part-time $227 per credit hour. Tuition, nonresident: full-time $8172; part-time $454 per credit hour. *Required fees:* $275 per semester. Tuition and fees vary according to course load, campus/location and program. *Financial support:* In 2011–12, 7 teaching assistantships with full tuition reimbursements (averaging $8,988 per year) were awarded; Federal Work-Study, institutionally sponsored loans, scholarships/grants, and unspecified assistantships also available. Financial award application deadline: 3/31; financial award applicants required to submit FAFSA. *Unit head:* Dr. Sarah McCallister, Acting Head, 417-836-6582, Fax: 417-836-5371, E-mail: sarahmccallister@missouristate.edu. *Application contact:* Misty Stewart, Coordinator of Graduate Admissions and Recruitment, 417-836-6079, Fax: 417-836-6200, E-mail: mistystewart@missouristate.edu. Web site: http://www.missouristate.edu/HPER/.

Missouri State University, Graduate College, College of Humanities and Public Affairs, Department of History, Springfield, MO 65897. Offers history (MA); secondary education (MS Ed), including history, social science. Part-time programs available. *Faculty:* 18 full-time (5 women). *Students:* 19 full-time (8 women), 46 part-time (14 women); includes 3 minority (2 American Indian or Alaska Native, non-Hispanic/Latino; 1 Two or more races, non-Hispanic/Latino). Average age 31. 23 applicants, 87% accepted, 18 enrolled. In 2011, 17 master's awarded. *Degree requirements:* For master's, comprehensive exam, thesis or alternative. *Entrance requirements:* For master's, minimum GPA of 2.75, 24 hours of undergraduate course work in history (MA), 9-12 teaching certification (MS Ed). Additional exam requirements/recommendations for international students: Required—TOEFL (minimum score 550 paper-based; 213 computer-based; 79 iBT). *Application deadline:* For fall admission, 7/20 priority date for domestic students, 5/1 for international students; for spring admission, 12/20 priority date for domestic students, 9/1 for international students. Applications are processed on a rolling basis. Application fee: $35 ($50 for international students). Electronic applications accepted. *Expenses:* Tuition, state resident: full-time $4086; part-time $227 per credit hour. Tuition, nonresident: full-time $8172; part-time $454 per credit hour. *Required fees:* $275 per semester. Tuition and fees vary according to course load, campus/location and program. *Financial support:* In 2011–12, 1 teaching assistantship with full tuition reimbursement (averaging $8,000 per year) was awarded; Federal Work-Study, scholarships/grants, and unspecified assistantships also available. Support available to part-time students. Financial award application deadline: 3/31; financial award applicants required to submit FAFSA. *Faculty research:* U. S. history, Native American history, Latin American history, women's history, ancient Near East. *Unit head:* Dr. Kathleen Kennedy, Head, 417-836-5511, Fax: 417-836-5523, E-mail: history@missouristate.edu. *Application contact:* Misty Stewart, Coordinator of Graduate Recruitment, 417-836-6079, Fax: 417-836-6200, E-mail: mistystewart@missouristate.edu. Web site: http://history.missouristate.edu/.

Missouri State University, Graduate College, College of Natural and Applied Sciences, Department of Biology, Springfield, MO 65897. Offers biology (MS); natural and applied science (MNAS), including biology (MNAS, MS Ed); secondary education (MS Ed), including biology (MNAS, MS Ed). *Faculty:* 19 full-time (4 women), 6 part-time/adjunct (1 woman). *Students:* 21 full-time (9 women), 37 part-time (18 women); includes 3 minority (all Two or more races, non-Hispanic/Latino), 2 international. Average age 28. 18 applicants, 94% accepted, 15 enrolled. In 2011, 14 master's awarded. *Degree requirements:* For master's, comprehensive exam, thesis or alternative. *Entrance requirements:* For master's, GRE (MS, MNAS), 24 hours of course work in biology (MS); minimum GPA of 3.0 (MS, MNAS), 9-12 teacher certification (MS Ed). Additional exam requirements/recommendations for international students: Required—TOEFL (minimum score 550 paper-based; 213 computer-based; 79 iBT). *Application deadline:* For fall admission, 7/20 priority date for domestic students, 5/1 for international students; for spring admission, 12/20 priority date for domestic students, 9/1 for international students. Applications are processed on a rolling basis. Application fee: $35 ($50 for international students). Electronic applications accepted. *Expenses:* Tuition, state resident: full-time $4086; part-time $227 per credit hour. Tuition, nonresident: full-time $8172; part-time $454 per credit hour. *Required fees:* $275 per semester. Tuition and fees vary according to course load, campus/location and program. *Financial support:* In 2011–12, 3 research assistantships with full tuition reimbursements (averaging $8,865 per year), 12 teaching assistantships with full tuition reimbursements (averaging $9,730 per year) were awarded; Federal Work-Study, institutionally sponsored loans, scholarships/grants, and unspecified assistantships also available. Financial award application deadline: 3/31; financial award applicants required to submit FAFSA. *Faculty research:* Hibernation physiology of bats, behavioral ecology of salamanders, mussel conservation, plant evolution and systematics, cellular/molecular mechanisms involved in migraine pathology. *Unit head:* Dr. S. Alicia Mathis, Head, 417-836-5126, Fax: 417-836-6934, E-mail: biology@missouristate.edu. *Application contact:* Misty Stewart, Coordinator of Graduate Recruitment, 417-836-6079, Fax: 417-836-6200, E-mail: mistystewart@missouristate.edu. Web site: http://biology.missouristate.edu/.

Missouri State University, Graduate College, College of Natural and Applied Sciences, Department of Chemistry, Springfield, MO 65897. Offers chemistry (MS); natural and applied science (MNAS), including chemistry (MNAS, MS Ed); secondary education (MS Ed), including chemistry (MNAS, MS Ed). Part-time programs available. *Faculty:* 15 full-time (2 women). *Students:* 18 full-time (6 women), 7 part-time (3 women); includes 1 minority (Black or African American, non-Hispanic/Latino), 6 international. Average age 31. 16 applicants, 38% accepted, 4 enrolled. In 2011, 5 master's awarded. *Degree requirements:* For master's, comprehensive exam, thesis. *Entrance requirements:* For master's, GRE General Test (MS, MNAS), minimum undergraduate GPA of 3.0 (MS and MNAS), 9-12 teacher certification (MS Ed). Additional exam requirements/recommendations for international students: Required—TOEFL (minimum score 550 paper-based; 213 computer-based; 79 iBT). *Application deadline:* For fall admission, 7/20 priority date for domestic students, 5/1 for international students; for spring admission, 12/20 priority date for domestic students, 9/1 for international students. Applications are processed on a rolling basis. Application fee: $35 ($50 for international students). Electronic applications accepted. *Expenses:* Tuition, state resident: full-time $4086; part-time $227 per credit hour. Tuition, nonresident: full-time $8172; part-time $454 per credit hour. *Required fees:* $275 per semester. Tuition and fees vary according to course load, campus/location and program. *Financial support:* In 2011–12, 1 research assistantship with full tuition reimbursement (averaging $8,865 per year), 4 teaching assistantships with full tuition reimbursements (averaging $9,730 per year) were awarded; Federal Work-Study, institutionally sponsored loans, scholarships/grants, and unspecified assistantships also available. Financial award application deadline: 3/31; financial award applicants required to submit FAFSA. *Faculty research:* Polyethylene glycol derivatives, electrochemiluminescence of environmental systems, enzymology, environmental organic pollutants, DNA repair via NMR. *Unit head:* Dr. Alan Schick, Department Head, 417-836-5506, Fax: 417-836-5507, E-mail: chemistry@missouristate.edu. *Application contact:* Misty Stewart, Coordinator of Graduate Recruitment, 417-836-6079, Fax: 417-836-6200, E-mail: mistystewart@missouristate.edu. Web site: http://chemistry.missouristate.edu/.

Missouri State University, Graduate College, College of Natural and Applied Sciences, Department of Geography, Geology, and Planning, Springfield, MO 65897. Offers geospatial sciences (MS, MS Ed), including earth science (MS Ed), geology (MS), human geography and planning (MS), physical geography (MS Ed); natural and applied science (MNAS), including geography, geology and planning; secondary education (MS Ed), including geography. Part-time and evening/weekend programs available. *Faculty:* 19 full-time (4 women). *Students:* 19 full-time (9 women), 12 part-time (7 women), 2 international. Average age 31. 20 applicants, 80% accepted, 11 enrolled. In 2011, 15 master's awarded. *Degree requirements:* For master's, comprehensive exam, thesis (for some programs). *Entrance requirements:* For master's, GRE General Test (MS, MNAS), minimum undergraduate GPA of 3.0 (MS, MNAS), 9-12 teacher certification (MS Ed). Additional exam requirements/recommendations for international students: Required—TOEFL (minimum score 550 paper-based; 213 computer-based; 79 iBT). *Application deadline:* For fall admission, 7/20 priority date for domestic students, 5/1 for international students; for spring admission, 12/20 priority date for domestic students, 9/1 for international students. Applications are processed on a rolling basis. Application fee: $35 ($50 for international students). Electronic applications accepted. *Expenses:* Tuition, state resident: full-time $4086; part-time $227 per credit hour. Tuition, nonresident: full-time $8172; part-time $454 per credit hour. *Required fees:* $275 per semester. Tuition and fees vary according to course load, campus/location and program. *Financial support:* In 2011–12, 3 research assistantships with full tuition reimbursements (averaging $8,000 per year), 9 teaching assistantships with full tuition reimbursements (averaging $8,000 per year) were awarded; career-related internships or fieldwork, Federal Work-Study, institutionally sponsored loans, scholarships/grants, and unspecified assistantships also available. Financial award application deadline: 3/31; financial award applicants required to submit FAFSA. *Faculty research:* Stratigraphy and ancient meteorite impacts, environmental geochemistry of karst, hyperspectral image processing, water quality, small town planning. *Unit head:* Dr. Thomas Plymate, Head, 417-836-5800, Fax: 417-836-6934, E-mail: tomplymate@missouristate.edu. *Application contact:* Misty Stewart, Coordinator of Graduate Recruitment, 417-836-6079, Fax: 417-836-6200, E-mail: mistystewart@missouristate.edu. Web site: http://geosciences.missouristate.edu/.

Missouri State University, Graduate College, College of Natural and Applied Sciences, Department of Mathematics, Springfield, MO 65897. Offers mathematics (MS); natural and applied science (MNAS), including mathematics (MNAS, MS Ed); secondary education (MS Ed), including mathematics (MNAS, MS Ed). Part-time programs available. *Faculty:* 21 full-time (6 women). *Students:* 18 full-time (8 women), 7 part-time (3 women); includes 2 minority (1 Black or African American, non-Hispanic/Latino; 1 Hispanic/Latino), 4 international. Average age 27. 11 applicants, 100% accepted, 8 enrolled. In 2011, 4 master's awarded. *Degree requirements:* For master's, comprehensive exam, thesis or alternative. *Entrance requirements:* For master's, GRE (MS, MNAS), minimum undergraduate GPA of 3.0 (MS, MNAS), 9-12 teacher certification (MS Ed). Additional exam requirements/recommendations for international students: Required—TOEFL (minimum score 550 paper-based; 213 computer-based; 79 iBT). *Application deadline:* For fall admission, 7/20 priority date for domestic students, 5/1 for international students; for spring admission, 12/20 priority date for domestic students, 9/1 for international students. Applications are processed on a rolling basis. Application fee: $35 ($50 for international students). Electronic applications accepted. *Expenses:* Tuition, state resident: full-time $4086; part-time $227 per credit hour. Tuition, nonresident: full-time $8172; part-time $454 per credit hour. *Required fees:* $275 per semester. Tuition and fees vary according to course load, campus/location and program. *Financial support:* In 2011–12, 4 teaching assistantships with full tuition reimbursements (averaging $9,730 per year) were awarded; Federal Work-Study, institutionally sponsored loans, scholarships/grants, and unspecified assistantships also available. Financial award application deadline: 3/31; financial award applicants required to submit FAFSA. *Faculty research:* Harmonic analysis, commutative algebra, number theory, K-theory, probability. *Unit head:* Dr. Kenneth Vollmar, Interim Head, 417-836-5112, Fax: 417-836-6966, E-mail: mathematics@missouristate.edu. *Application contact:* Misty Stewart, Coordinator of Graduate Recruitment, 417-836-6079, Fax: 417-836-6200, E-mail: mistystewart@missouristate.edu. Web site: http://math.missouristate.edu/.

Missouri State University, Graduate College, College of Natural and Applied Sciences, Department of Physics, Astronomy, and Materials Science, Springfield, MO 65897. Offers materials science (MS); physics, astronomy, and materials science (MNAS); secondary education (MS Ed), including physics. Part-time programs available. *Faculty:* 13 full-time (0 women). *Students:* 9 full-time (1 woman), 4 part-time (1 woman); includes 2 minority (1 Black or African American, non-Hispanic/Latino; 1 Hispanic/Latino), 8 international. Average age 29. 7 applicants, 100% accepted, 6 enrolled. In 2011, 6 master's awarded. *Degree requirements:* For master's, comprehensive exam, thesis. *Entrance requirements:* For master's, GRE (MS, MNAS), minimum undergraduate GPA of 3.0 (MS and MNAS), 9-12 teaching certification (MS Ed). Additional exam requirements/recommendations for international students: Required—TOEFL (minimum score 550 paper-based; 213 computer-based; 79 iBT). *Application deadline:* For fall admission, 7/20 priority date for domestic students, 5/1 for international students; for spring admission, 12/20 priority date for domestic students, 9/1 for international students. Applications are processed on a rolling basis. Application fee: $35 ($50 for international students). Electronic applications accepted. *Expenses:* Tuition, state resident: full-time $4086; part-time $227 per credit hour. Tuition, nonresident: full-time $8172; part-time $454 per credit hour. *Required fees:* $275 per semester. Tuition and fees vary according to course load, campus/location and program. *Financial support:* In 2011–12, 3 teaching assistantships with full tuition reimbursements (averaging $9,730 per year) were awarded; Federal Work-Study, institutionally sponsored loans, scholarships/grants, and unspecified assistantships also available. Financial award application deadline: 3/31; financial award applicants required to submit FAFSA. *Faculty research:* Nanocomposites, ferroelectricity, infrared focal plane array sensors, biosensors, pulsating stars. *Unit head:* Dr. David Cornelison, Head, 417-836-5131, Fax: 417-836-6226, E-mail: physics@missouristate.edu. *Application contact:* Misty Stewart, Coordinator of Admissions and Recruitment, 417-836-6079, Fax: 417-836-6200, E-mail: mistystewart@missouristate.edu. Web site: http://physics.missouristate.edu/.

Missouri State University, Graduate College, William H. Darr School of Agriculture, Springfield, MO 65897. Offers plant science (MS); secondary education (MS Ed), including agriculture. Part-time programs available. *Faculty:* 14 full-time (3 women), 1 part-time/adjunct (0 women). *Students:* 15 full-time (9 women), 15 part-time (8 women), 4 international. Average age 29. 19 applicants, 100% accepted, 14 enrolled. In 2011, 9 master's awarded. *Degree requirements:* For master's, comprehensive exam, thesis or alternative. *Entrance requirements:* For master's, GRE (MS in plant science, MNAS), 9-12 teacher certification (MS Ed), minimum GPA of 3.0 (MS plant science, MNAS). Additional exam requirements/recommendations for international students: Required—TOEFL (minimum score 550 paper-based; 213 computer-based; 79 iBT). *Application deadline:* For fall admission, 7/20 priority date for domestic students, 5/1 for international students; for spring admission, 12/20 priority date for domestic students, 9/1 for international students. Applications are processed on a rolling basis. Application fee: $35 ($50 for international students). Electronic applications accepted. *Expenses:* Tuition, state resident: full-time $4086; part-time $227 per credit hour. Tuition, nonresident: full-time $8172; part-time $454 per credit hour. *Required fees:* $275 per semester. Tuition and fees vary according to course load, campus/location and program. *Financial support:* In 2011–12, 6 research assistantships with full tuition reimbursements (averaging $8,288 per year), 3 teaching assistantships with full tuition reimbursements (averaging $8,576 per year) were awarded; Federal Work-Study, institutionally sponsored loans, scholarships/grants, and unspecified assistantships also available. Financial award application deadline: 3/31; financial award applicants required to submit FAFSA. *Faculty research:* Grapevine biotechnology, agricultural marketing, Asian elephant reproduction, poultry science, integrated pest management. *Unit head:* Dr. W. Anson Elliott, Head, 417-836-5638, E-mail: ansonelliot@missouristate.edu. *Application contact:* Misty Stewart, Coordinator of Graduate Recruitment, 417-836-6079, Fax: 417-836-6200, E-mail: mistystewart@missouristate.edu. Web site: http://ag.missouristate.edu/.

Monmouth University, The Graduate School, School of Education, West Long Branch, NJ 07764-1898. Offers education (M Ed); initial certification (MAT), including elementary level, K-12, secondary level; learning disabilities-teacher consultant (Certificate); principal (MS Ed); principal/school administrator (MS Ed); reading specialist (MS Ed, Certificate); school counseling (MS Ed); special education (MS Ed), including autism, learning disabilities teacher consultant, teacher of students with disabilities, teaching in inclusive settings; supervisor (Certificate); teacher of the handicapped (Certificate); teaching English to speakers of other languages (TESOL) (Certificate). *Accreditation:* NCATE. Part-time and evening/weekend programs available. *Faculty:* 16 full-time (12 women), 24 part-time/adjunct (17 women). *Students:* 134 full-time (104 women), 293 part-time (246 women); includes 34 minority (11 Black or African American, non-

Hispanic/Latino; 2 Asian, non-Hispanic/Latino; 18 Hispanic/Latino; 3 Two or more races, non-Hispanic/Latino), 2 international. Average age 29. 288 applicants, 92% accepted, 182 enrolled. In 2011, 173 master's awarded. *Entrance requirements:* For master's, minimum GPA of 3.0 in major, 2.75 overall; 2 letters of recommendation (for some programs). Additional exam requirements/recommendations for international students: Required—TOEFL (minimum score 550 paper-based; 213 computer-based; 79 iBT), IELTS (minimum score 5), Michigan English Language Assessment Battery (minimum score 77), Cambridge A, B, C. *Application deadline:* For fall admission, 7/15 priority date for domestic students, 7/1 for international students; for spring admission, 11/15 priority date for domestic students, 11/1 for international students. Applications are processed on a rolling basis. Application fee: $50. Electronic applications accepted. *Financial support:* In 2011–12, 274 students received support, including 291 fellowships (averaging $1,783 per year), 21 research assistantships (averaging $8,792 per year); career-related internships or fieldwork, scholarships/grants, and unspecified assistantships also available. Support available to part-time students. Financial award applicants required to submit FAFSA. *Faculty research:* Multicultural literacy, science and mathematics teaching strategies, teacher as reflective practitioner, children with disabilities. *Unit head:* Dr. Jason Barr, Program Director, 732-263-5238, Fax: 732-263-5277, E-mail: jbarr@monmouth.edu. *Application contact:* Kevin Roane, Director, Office of Graduate Admission, 732-571-3452, Fax: 732-263-5123, E-mail: gradadm@monmouth.edu. Web site: http://www.monmouth.edu/academics/schools/education/default.asp.

Montana State University Billings, College of Education, Department of Educational Theory and Practice, Option in Secondary Education, Billings, MT 59101-0298. Offers M Ed. *Accreditation:* NCATE. Part-time programs available. *Degree requirements:* For master's, professional paper or thesis. *Entrance requirements:* For master's, GRE General Test or MAT, minimum GPA of 3.0 (undergraduate), 3.25 (graduate).

Morehead State University, Graduate Programs, College of Education, Department of Curriculum and Instruction, Morehead, KY 40351. Offers curriculum and instruction (Ed S); elementary education (MA Ed), including elementary education, international education, middle school education, reading; secondary education (MA Ed); special education (MA Ed); teaching (MAT). Part-time and evening/weekend programs available. *Degree requirements:* For master's, comprehensive exam, thesis optional; for Ed S, thesis, oral exam. *Entrance requirements:* For master's, GRE General Test, minimum GPA of 2.75, teaching certificate; for Ed S, GRE General Test, interview, master's degree, minimum GPA of 3.5, work experience. Additional exam requirements/recommendations for international students: Required—TOEFL (minimum score 500 paper-based; 173 computer-based). Electronic applications accepted. *Faculty research:* Communicative competence of learning-disabled students, teaching social studies in elementary schools, ungraded primary school organization, study skills.

Morehead State University, Graduate Programs, College of Education, Department of Middle Grades and Secondary Education, Morehead, KY 40351. Offers business and marketing education (MAT); English/language arts 5-9 (MAT); French (MAT); health P-12 (MAT); mathematics 5-9 (MAT); physical education P-12 (MAT); science 5-9 (MAT); secondary biology (MAT); secondary chemistry (MAT); secondary earth science (MAT); secondary English (MAT); secondary math (MAT); secondary physics (MAT); secondary social studies (MAT); social studies 5-9 (MAT); Spanish (MAT). Part-time and evening/weekend programs available. *Degree requirements:* For master's, portfolio. *Entrance requirements:* For master's, GRE or PRAXIS II content exam, minimum overall undergraduate GPA of 2.5. Additional exam requirements/recommendations for international students: Required—TOEFL (minimum score 500 paper-based; 173 computer-based). Electronic applications accepted.

Morgan State University, School of Graduate Studies, School of Education and Urban Studies, MAT Program, Baltimore, MD 21251. Offers elementary education (MAT); high school education (MAT); middle school education (MAT). Part-time programs available. *Degree requirements:* For master's, comprehensive exam. *Entrance requirements:* For master's, GRE General Test or MAT. *Faculty research:* Multicultural education, cooperative learning, psychology of cognition.

Mount Saint Mary College, Division of Education, Newburgh, NY 12550-3494. Offers adolescence and special education (MS Ed); adolescence education (MS Ed); childhood and special education (MS Ed); childhood education (MS Ed); literacy (5-12) (Advanced Certificate); literacy (birth-6) (Advanced Certificate); literacy and special education (MS Ed); literacy/childhood (MS Ed); middle school (5-6) (MS Ed); middle school (7-9) (MS Ed); special education (1-6) (MS Ed); special education (7-12) (MS Ed). *Accreditation:* NCATE. Part-time and evening/weekend programs available. *Faculty:* 14 full-time (12 women), 14 part-time/adjunct (8 women). *Students:* 55 full-time (42 women), 158 part-time (125 women); includes 23 minority (4 Black or African American, non-Hispanic/Latino; 1 Asian, non-Hispanic/Latino; 18 Hispanic/Latino). Average age 29. 119 applicants, 45% accepted, 24 enrolled. In 2011, 107 master's awarded. *Application deadline:* Applications are processed on a rolling basis. Application fee: $45. Application fee is waived when completed online. *Expenses: Tuition:* Full-time $13,356; part-time $742 per credit. *Required fees:* $70 per semester. *Financial support:* In 2011–12, 99 students received support. Unspecified assistantships available. Financial award application deadline: 4/15; financial award applicants required to submit FAFSA. *Faculty research:* Learning and teaching styles, computers in special education, language development. *Unit head:* Dr. Theresa Lewis, Coordinator, 845-569-3149, Fax: 845-569-3535, E-mail: tlewis@msmc.edu. *Application contact:* Courtney McDermott, Graduate Recruiter, 845-569-3402, Fax: 845-569-3450, E-mail: courtney.mcdermott@msmc.edu. Web site: http://www.msmc.edu/Academics/Graduate_Programs/Master_of_Science_in_Education.

Mount St. Mary's College, Graduate Division, Department of Education, Specialization in Secondary Education, Los Angeles, CA 90049-1599. Offers MS. *Degree requirements:* For master's, thesis, research project. *Entrance requirements:* For master's, MAT, minimum GPA of 3.0. *Application deadline:* For fall admission, 7/15 priority date for domestic students; for spring admission, 11/15 priority date for domestic students. Application fee: $50 ($75 for international students). *Expenses: Tuition:* Part-time $752 per unit. Part-time tuition and fees vary according to degree level and program. *Financial support:* Scholarships/grants available. Financial award application deadline: 3/15; financial award applicants required to submit FAFSA. *Unit head:* Dr. Robin Gordon, Director, 213-477-2624. *Application contact:* Jessica M. Bibeau, Director of Graduate Admission, 213-477-2800 Ext. 2798, Fax: 213-477-2797, E-mail: jbibeau@msmc.la.edu.

Murray State University, College of Education, Department of Adolescent, Career and Special Education, Program in Secondary Education, Murray, KY 42071. Offers MA Ed, Ed S. *Accreditation:* NCATE. Part-time programs available. *Degree requirements:* For master's, comprehensive exam, thesis optional; for Ed S, comprehensive exam. *Entrance requirements:* Additional exam requirements/recommendations for international students: Required—TOEFL.

National Louis University, National College of Education, Chicago, IL 60603. Offers administration and supervision (M Ed, Ed D, CAS, Ed S); curriculum and instruction (M Ed, MS Ed, CAS); early childhood administration (M Ed, CAS); early childhood education (M Ed, MAT, MS Ed, CAS); education (Ed D); educational psychology/human learning and development (M Ed, MS Ed, CAS, Ed S); elementary education (MAT); interdisciplinary curriculum and instruction (M Ed); mathematics education (M Ed, MS Ed, CAS); reading and language (M Ed, MS Ed, CAS); school psychology (M Ed, Ed S); science education (M Ed, MS Ed, CAS); secondary education (MAT); special education (M Ed, MAT, CAS); technology in education (M Ed, CAS). *Accreditation:* NCATE. Part-time and evening/weekend programs available. *Students:* 224 full-time (162 women), 2,336 part-time (1,767 women); includes 677 minority (366 Black or African American, non-Hispanic/Latino; 8 American Indian or Alaska Native, non-Hispanic/Latino; 68 Asian, non-Hispanic/Latino; 218 Hispanic/Latino; 2 Native Hawaiian or other Pacific Islander, non-Hispanic/Latino; 15 Two or more races, non-Hispanic/Latino), 2 international. Average age 34. In 2011, 1,711 master's, 76 doctorates, 86 other advanced degrees awarded. *Degree requirements:* For doctorate, comprehensive exam, thesis/dissertation. *Entrance requirements:* For master's, MAT or GRE, minimum GPA of 3.0; for doctorate, GRE General Test, minimum GPA of 3.25, interview, resume, writing sample, 4 recommendations. Additional exam requirements/recommendations for international students: Required—TOEFL (minimum score 550 paper-based; 213 computer-based; 79 iBT). *Application deadline:* Applications are processed on a rolling basis. Application fee: $40. *Financial support:* Fellowships, research assistantships, teaching assistantships, career-related internships or fieldwork, Federal Work-Study, institutionally sponsored loans, and scholarships/grants available. Support available to part-time students. Financial award applicants required to submit FAFSA. *Unit head:* Dr. Alison Hilsabeck, Dean, 312-361-3580, Fax: 312-261-2580, E-mail: ahilsabeck@nl.edu. *Application contact:* Ken Kasprzak, Director of Admission, 888-658-8632, Fax: 847-947-5575, E-mail: kkasprzak@nl.edu.

National University, Academic Affairs, School of Education, Department of Teacher Education, La Jolla, CA 92037-1011. Offers best practices (Certificate); early childhood education (Certificate); educational technology (Certificate); elementary education (M Ed); instructional technology (MS Ed); multiple or single subjects teaching (M Ed); national board certified teacher leadership (Certificate); secondary education (M Ed); teaching (MA). Part-time and evening/weekend programs available. Postbaccalaureate distance learning degree programs offered (no on-campus study). *Degree requirements:* For master's, thesis. *Entrance requirements:* For master's, interview, minimum GPA of 2.5. Additional exam requirements/recommendations for international students: Required—TOEFL (minimum score 550 paper-based; 213 computer-based; 79 iBT), IELTS (minimum score 6). *Application deadline:* Applications are processed on a rolling basis. Application fee: $60 ($65 for international students). Electronic applications accepted. *Financial support:* Career-related internships or fieldwork, institutionally sponsored loans, scholarships/grants, and tuition waivers (partial) available. Support available to part-time students. Financial award application deadline: 6/30; financial award applicants required to submit FAFSA. *Unit head:* Dr. Cynthia Schubert-Irastroza, Chair, 858-642-8339, Fax: 858-642-8724, E-mail: cshubert@nu.edu. *Application contact:* Dominick Giovanniello, Associate Regional Dean, 800-NAT-UNIV, Fax: 858-541-7792, E-mail: dgiovann@nu.edu. Web site: http://www.nu.edu/OurPrograms/SchoolOfEducation/TeacherEducation.html.

New Jersey City University, Graduate Studies and Continuing Education, Debra Cannon Partridge Wolfe College of Education, Department of Elementary and Secondary Education, Jersey City, NJ 07305-1597. Offers elementary education (MAT); secondary education (MAT). Part-time and evening/weekend programs available. *Students:* 24 full-time (14 women), 53 part-time (31 women); includes 27 minority (7 Black or African American, non-Hispanic/Latino; 8 Asian, non-Hispanic/Latino; 12 Hispanic/Latino). Average age 32. In 2011, 18 master's awarded. *Entrance requirements:* Additional exam requirements/recommendations for international students: Required—TOEFL. *Application deadline:* For fall admission, 8/1 priority date for domestic students; for spring admission, 12/1 for domestic students. Applications are processed on a rolling basis. Application fee: $0. *Expenses:* Tuition, state resident: part-time $494 per credit. Tuition, nonresident: part-time $911.30 per credit. *Required fees:* $95.90 per year. *Financial support:* Teaching assistantships, career-related internships or fieldwork, and unspecified assistantships available. *Unit head:* Dr. Althea Hall, Coordinator, 201-200-2101, E-mail: ahall@njcu.edu. *Application contact:* Dr. William Bajor, Dean of Graduate Studies, 201-200-3409, Fax: 201-200-3411, E-mail: wbajor@njcu.edu.

New York University, Steinhardt School of Culture, Education, and Human Development, Department of Music and Performing Arts Professions, Program in Educational Theatre, New York, NY 10012-1019. Offers dual certification: educational theatre and English 7-12 (MA); dual certification: educational theatre and social studies (MA); educational theatre (Ed D, PhD, Advanced Certificate); educational theatre for colleges and communities (MA); teaching educational theatre, all grades (MA). Part-time programs available. *Degree requirements:* For master's, thesis (for some programs); for doctorate, thesis/dissertation. *Entrance requirements:* For master's, audition; for doctorate, GRE General Test, interview; for Advanced Certificate, master's degree. Additional exam requirements/recommendations for international students: Required—TOEFL. Electronic applications accepted. *Faculty research:* Theatre for young audiences, drama in education, applied theatre, arts education assessment, reflective praxis.

Niagara University, Graduate Division of Education, Concentration in Teacher Education, Niagara Falls, Niagara University, NY 14109. Offers early childhood and childhood education (MS Ed); middle and adolescence education (MS Ed); special education (grades 1-12) (MS Ed). *Accreditation:* NCATE. *Faculty:* 4 full-time (1 woman), 6 part-time/adjunct (4 women). *Students:* 249 full-time (162 women), 56 part-time (39 women); includes 11 minority (5 Black or African American, non-Hispanic/Latino; 1 American Indian or Alaska Native, non-Hispanic/Latino; 1 Asian, non-Hispanic/Latino; 2 Hispanic/Latino; 2 Two or more races, non-Hispanic/Latino), 176 international. Average age 24. In 2011, 233 master's, 1 Certificate awarded. *Entrance requirements:* For master's, GRE General Test or MAT. *Application deadline:* For fall admission, 8/1 for domestic students. Applications are processed on a rolling basis. Application fee: $30. *Expenses:* Contact institution. *Financial support:* Career-related internships or fieldwork, Federal Work-Study, and scholarships/grants available. Financial award application deadline: 3/15. *Unit head:* Dr. Chandra Foote, Chair, 716-286-8549. *Application contact:* Dr. Debra A. Colley, Dean of Education, 716-286-8560, Fax: 716-286-8561, E-mail: dcolley@niagara.edu.

Norfolk State University, School of Graduate Studies, School of Education, Department of Secondary Education and School Leadership, Norfolk, VA 23504. Offers principal preparation (MA); secondary education (MAT); urban education/administration (MA), including teaching. *Accreditation:* NCATE. Part-time programs available. *Entrance requirements:* For master's, GRE General Test, PRAXIS I, minimum GPA of 3.0 in major, 2.5 overall. Additional exam requirements/recommendations for international students: Required—TOEFL (minimum score 500 paper-based).

North Carolina Agricultural and Technical State University, School of Graduate Studies, College of Arts and Sciences, Department of Mathematics, Greensboro, NC 27411. Offers applied mathematics (MS), including secondary education. *Accreditation:* NCATE. Part-time and evening/weekend programs available. *Degree requirements:* For master's, comprehensive exam, thesis or alternative, qualifying exam. *Entrance requirements:* For master's, GRE General Test, minimum GPA of 3.0.

North Carolina State University, Graduate School, College of Education, Department of Curriculum and Instruction, Program in Secondary English Education, Raleigh, NC 27695. Offers M Ed, MS Ed. *Degree requirements:* For master's, thesis optional.

Northern Arizona University, Graduate College, College of Education, Department of Teaching and Learning, Flagstaff , AZ 86011. Offers early childhood education (M Ed); elementary education - certification (M Ed); elementary education - continuing professional (M Ed); secondary education - certification (M Ed); secondary education - continuing professional (M Ed). Part-time programs available. *Faculty:* 32 full-time (23 women). *Students:* 297 full-time (238 women), 368 part-time (333 women); includes 193 minority (16 Black or African American, non-Hispanic/Latino; 43 American Indian or Alaska Native, non-Hispanic/Latino; 11 Asian, non-Hispanic/Latino; 113 Hispanic/Latino; 10 Two or more races, non-Hispanic/Latino), 8 international. Average age 29. 182 applicants, 91% accepted, 118 enrolled. In 2011, 415 master's awarded. *Degree requirements:* For master's, comprehensive exam (for some programs), thesis (for some programs). *Entrance requirements:* For master's, minimum GPA of 3.0. Additional exam requirements/recommendations for international students: Required—TOEFL (minimum score 550 paper-based; 213 computer-based; 80 iBT), IELTS (minimum score 7). *Application deadline:* For fall admission, 3/1 for international students; for spring admission, 9/15 for international students. Applications are processed on a rolling basis. Application fee: $65. Electronic applications accepted. *Expenses:* Tuition, state resident: full-time $7190; part-time $355 per credit hour. Tuition, nonresident: full-time $18,092; part-time $1005 per credit hour. *Required fees:* $818; $328 per semester. *Financial support:* In 2011–12, 7 teaching assistantships with partial tuition reimbursements (averaging $10,000 per year) were awarded; Federal Work-Study, scholarships/grants, health care benefits, tuition waivers (full and partial), and unspecified assistantships also available. Financial award applicants required to submit FAFSA. *Unit head:* Dr. Sandra J. Stone, Chair, 928-523-4280, Fax: 928-523-1929, E-mail: sandra.stone@nau.edu. *Application contact:* Kay Quillen, Administrative Assistant, 928-523-9316, Fax: 928-523-1929, E-mail: kay.quillen@nau.edu. Web site: http://nau.edu/coe/teaching-and-learning/.

Northern Illinois University, Graduate School, College of Education, Department of Special and Early Education, De Kalb, IL 60115-2854. Offers curriculum and instruction (MS Ed, Ed D), including curriculum leadership (Ed D), elementary education (Ed D), secondary education (Ed D); early childhood education (MS Ed); elementary education (MS Ed); special education (MS Ed). Part-time and evening/weekend programs available. *Faculty:* 22 full-time (14 women), 2 part-time/adjunct (both women). *Students:* 58 full-time (46 women), 241 part-time (189 women); includes 35 minority (17 Black or African American, non-Hispanic/Latino; 7 Asian, non-Hispanic/Latino; 9 Hispanic/Latino; 2 Two or more races, non-Hispanic/Latino), 3 international. Average age 35. 100 applicants, 65% accepted, 45 enrolled. In 2011, 186 master's, 7 doctorates awarded. *Degree requirements:* For master's, comprehensive exam, thesis optional; for doctorate, thesis/dissertation, candidacy exam, dissertation defense. *Entrance requirements:* For master's, GRE General Test or MAT, minimum undergraduate GPA of 2.75; for doctorate, GRE General Test or MAT, minimum undergraduate GPA of 2.75, graduate 3.2. Additional exam requirements/recommendations for international students: Required—TOEFL (minimum score 550 paper-based; 213 computer-based). *Application deadline:* For fall admission, 6/1 for domestic students, 5/1 for international students; for spring admission, 11/1 for domestic students, 10/1 for international students. Applications are processed on a rolling basis. Application fee: $40. Electronic applications accepted. *Financial support:* In 2011–12, 34 research assistantships with full tuition reimbursements were awarded; fellowships with full tuition reimbursements, teaching assistantships with full tuition reimbursements, career-related internships or fieldwork, Federal Work-Study, scholarships/grants, tuition waivers (full), and unspecified assistantships also available. Support available to part-time students. Financial award applicants required to submit FAFSA. *Faculty research:* Teacher certification, stress reduction during student teaching, teaching history, portfolios in student teaching. *Unit head:* Dr. Connie Fox, Interim Chair, 815-753-1619, E-mail: seed@niu.edu. *Application contact:* Gail Myers, 815-753-0381, E-mail: gmyers@niu.edu. Web site: http://www.cedu.niu.edu/seed/.

Northern Michigan University, College of Graduate Studies, College of Professional Studies, School of Education, Program in Secondary Education, Marquette, MI 49855-5301. Offers MA Ed. Part-time programs available. *Degree requirements:* For master's, thesis or alternative. *Entrance requirements:* For master's, minimum GPA of 3.0. *Faculty research:* Supervision and improvement of instruction.

Northern State University, Division of Graduate Studies in Education, Program in Teaching and Learning, Aberdeen, SD 57401-7198. Offers educational studies (MS Ed); elementary classroom teaching (MS Ed); health, physical education, and coaching (MS Ed); secondary classroom teaching (MS Ed). *Accreditation:* NCATE. Part-time and evening/weekend programs available. *Degree requirements:* For master's, thesis optional. *Entrance requirements:* For master's, minimum GPA of 2.75. Additional exam requirements/recommendations for international students: Required—TOEFL (minimum score 550 paper-based; 213 computer-based; 76 iBT), IELTS (minimum score 6). Electronic applications accepted.

North Georgia College & State University, School of Education, Dahlonega, GA 30597. Offers art education (MAT); early childhood education (M Ed); English education (MAT); history education (MAT); math education (MAT); middle grades education (M Ed, MAT); physical education (MS); school leadership (Ed S); secondary education (M Ed), including English education, history education, mathematics education, physical education; teacher education (MAT). *Accreditation:* NCATE. Part-time and evening/weekend programs available. Postbaccalaureate distance learning degree programs offered (no on-campus study). *Faculty:* 23 full-time (14 women), 16 part-time/adjunct (11 women). *Students:* 19 full-time (17 women), 199 part-time (147 women); includes 7 minority (3 Black or African American, non-Hispanic/Latino; 1 Asian, non-Hispanic/Latino; 3 Hispanic/Latino), 1 international. Average age 34. 259 applicants, 66% accepted, 112 enrolled. In 2011, 100 master's, 16 other advanced degrees awarded. *Degree requirements:* For master's, comprehensive exam, thesis optional. *Entrance requirements:* For master's, GRE or MAT, GACE, minimum GPA of 2.75; for Ed S, GRE General Test or MAT, 3 years of teaching experience, master's degree, minimum graduate GPA of 3.25, leadership position in the school. Additional exam requirements/recommendations for international students: Required—TOEFL (minimum score 550 paper-based; 213 computer-based; 79 iBT), IELTS (minimum score 6.5). *Application deadline:* For fall admission, 8/1 priority date for domestic students, 7/1 for international students; for spring admission, 12/1 priority date for domestic students, 11/1 for international students. Applications are processed on a rolling basis. Application fee: $40. Electronic applications accepted. *Expenses:* Tuition, state resident: full-time $3528; part-time $196 per credit hour. Tuition, nonresident: full-time $14,094; part-time $783 per credit hour. *Required fees:* $1718; $859 per semester. Tuition and fees vary according to course load, campus/location and program. *Financial support:* Teaching assistantships, career-related internships or fieldwork, scholarships/grants, and unspecified assistantships available. Financial award application deadline: 5/1; financial award applicants required to submit CSS PROFILE or FAFSA. *Faculty research:* Identification of professional development school structures supporting P-12 student achievement, impact of diverse field placement settings in teacher belief development among preservice teachers, use of inquiry methodology in social studies teaching with English language learners, use of instructional differentiation in the middle grades classroom, effects of international school placements on preservice teacher beliefs and attitudes. *Unit head:* Dr. Bob Michael, Dean, School of Education, 706-864-1998, Fax: 706-867-2850, E-mail: bmichael@northgeorgia.edu. *Application contact:* Susan L. Perry, Graduate Admissions Coordinator, 706-864-1543, Fax: 706-867-2795, E-mail: slperry@northgeorgia.edu. Web site: http://www.northgeorgia.edu/soe/.

Northwestern Oklahoma State University, School of Professional Studies, Program in Secondary Education, Alva, OK 73717-2799. Offers M Ed. *Accreditation:* NCATE. Part-time programs available. *Faculty:* 10 full-time (7 women). *Students:* 5 part-time (1 woman). 2 applicants, 100% accepted, 2 enrolled. In 2011, 2 master's awarded. *Degree requirements:* For master's, thesis optional, portfolio. *Entrance requirements:* For master's, GRE General Test or MAT, minimum GPA of 2.75. *Application deadline:* Applications are processed on a rolling basis. Application fee: $15. *Financial support:* Federal Work-Study available. Support available to part-time students. Financial award application deadline: 5/1; financial award applicants required to submit FAFSA. *Faculty research:* Teacher education, professional school models of pedagogy, competency exams for teachers, teacher accreditation/certification. *Application contact:* Sabrina Watson, Coordinator of Graduate Studies, 580-327-8410, E-mail: sdwatson@nwosu.edu. Web site: http://www.nwosu.edu/education.

Northwestern State University of Louisiana, Graduate Studies and Research, College of Education and Human Development, Program in Secondary Education, Natchitoches, LA 71497. Offers MAT. *Students:* 10 full-time (9 women), 69 part-time (43 women); includes 13 minority (10 Black or African American, non-Hispanic/Latino; 1 American Indian or Alaska Native, non-Hispanic/Latino; 1 Hispanic/Latino; 1 Two or more races, non-Hispanic/Latino). Average age 31. 19 applicants, 100% accepted, 16 enrolled. In 2011, 11 master's awarded. *Degree requirements:* For master's, comprehensive exam, thesis or alternative. *Entrance requirements:* For master's, GRE General Test, minimum undergraduate GPA of 2.5. Additional exam requirements/recommendations for international students: Required—TOEFL. *Application deadline:* For fall admission, 3/15 priority date for domestic students; for spring admission, 10/15 priority date for domestic students. Applications are processed on a rolling basis. Application fee: $20 ($30 for international students). Electronic applications accepted. *Expenses:* Tuition, state resident: full-time $3440. Tuition, nonresident: full-time $12,010. *Financial support:* Application deadline: 5/1; applicants required to submit FAFSA. *Unit head:* Dr. Vickie Gentry, Chair, 318-357-6288, Fax: 318-357-6275, E-mail: education@nsula.edu. *Application contact:* Dr. Steven G. Horton, Associate Provost/Dean, Graduate Studies, Research, and Information Systems, 318-357-5851, Fax: 318-357-5019, E-mail: grad_school@nsula.edu.

Northwestern State University of Louisiana, Graduate Studies and Research, College of Education and Human Development, Programs in Educational Leadership and Instruction, Natchitoches, LA 71497. Offers counseling (Ed S); educational leadership (M Ed, Ed S); educational technology (Ed S); elementary teaching (Ed S); reading (Ed S); secondary teaching (Ed S); special education (Ed S). *Accreditation:* NASAD. *Students:* 7 full-time (6 women), 75 part-time (59 women); includes 22 minority (18 Black or African American, non-Hispanic/Latino; 2 American Indian or Alaska Native, non-Hispanic/Latino; 2 Hispanic/Latino). Average age 36. 30 applicants, 97% accepted, 15 enrolled. In 2011, 31 master's, 16 Ed Ss awarded. *Degree requirements:* For master's, comprehensive exam, thesis (for some programs). *Entrance requirements:* For master's and Ed S, GRE General Test. Additional exam requirements/recommendations for international students: Required—TOEFL. *Application deadline:* For fall admission, 3/15 priority date for domestic students; for spring admission, 10/15 priority date for domestic students. Applications are processed on a rolling basis. Application fee: $20 ($30 for international students). Electronic applications accepted. *Expenses:* Tuition, state resident: full-time $3440. Tuition, nonresident: full-time $12,010. *Unit head:* Dr. Vickie Gentry, Chair, 318-357-6288, Fax: 318-357-6275, E-mail: education@nsula.edu. *Application contact:* Dr. Steven G. Horton, Associate Provost/Dean, Graduate Studies, Research, and Information Systems, 318-357-5851, Fax: 318-357-5019, E-mail: grad_school@nsula.edu.

Northwestern University, The Graduate School, School of Education and Social Policy, Program in Education, Evanston, IL 60035. Offers advanced teaching (MS); elementary teaching (MS); higher education administration (MS); secondary teaching (MS). Part-time and evening/weekend programs available. *Degree requirements:* For master's, research project. *Entrance requirements:* For master's, GRE General Test, Illinois State Board of Education Basic Skills Exam (secondary and elementary), bachelor's degree. Additional exam requirements/recommendations for international students: Recommended—TOEFL. Electronic applications accepted. *Faculty research:* Cultural context and literacy, philosophy of education and interpretive discussion, productivity, enhancing research and teaching, motivation, new and junior faculty issues, professional development for K-12 teachers to improve math and science teaching, female/underrepresented students/faculty in STEM disciplines.

Northwest Missouri State University, Graduate School, College of Education and Human Services, Department of Educational Leadership, Program in Educational Leadership, Maryville, MO 64468-6001. Offers educational leadership: elementary (MS Ed); educational leadership: K-12 (MS Ed); educational leadership: secondary (MS Ed); elementary principalship (Ed S); secondary principalship (Ed S); superintendency (Ed S). *Accreditation:* NCATE. Part-time programs available. *Faculty:* 14 full-time (6 women). *Students:* 11 full-time (6 women), 86 part-time (58 women); includes 6 minority (all Black or African American, non-Hispanic/Latino). 20 applicants, 100% accepted, 7 enrolled. In 2011, 56 degrees awarded. *Degree requirements:* For master's, comprehensive exam; for Ed S, comprehensive exam, thesis. *Entrance requirements:* For master's, GRE General Test, minimum undergraduate GPA of 2.75, teaching certificate, writing sample; for Ed S, minimum graduate GPA of 3.25. Additional exam requirements/recommendations for international students: Required—TOEFL (minimum score 550 paper-based; 213 computer-based). *Application deadline:* For fall admission, 7/1 for domestic and international students; for spring admission, 11/15 for domestic and international students. Application fee: $0 ($50 for international students). *Financial support:* In 2011–12, research assistantships with full tuition reimbursements (averaging $6,000 per year), 5 teaching assistantships with full tuition reimbursements (averaging $6,000 per year) were awarded; unspecified assistantships also available. Financial award application deadline: 4/1; financial award applicants required to submit FAFSA. *Unit head:* Dr. Jan Glenn, Chairperson, 660-562-1064. *Application contact:* Dr. Gregory Haddock, Dean of Graduate School, 660-562-1145, Fax: 660-562-1096, E-mail: gradsch@nwmissouri.edu.

Northwest Missouri State University, Graduate School, College of Education and Human Services, Department of Educational Leadership, Program in Secondary Individualized Prescribed Programs, Maryville, MO 64468-6001. Offers teaching secondary (MS Ed). *Faculty:* 14 full-time (6 women). *Students:* 19 part-time (14 women); includes 2 minority (1 Asian, non-Hispanic/Latino; 1 Hispanic/Latino), 1 international. 14 applicants, 100% accepted, 14 enrolled. In 2011, 2 master's awarded. *Entrance requirements:* Additional exam requirements/recommendations for international students: Required—TOEFL (minimum score 550 paper-based; 213 computer-based). *Application deadline:* For fall admission, 7/1 for domestic and international students; for spring admission, 11/15 for domestic and international students. Application fee: $0 ($50 for international students). *Financial support:* Application deadline: 4/1. *Unit head:* Dr. Matt Symonds, Director, 660-562-1069. *Application contact:* Dr. Gregory Haddock, Dean of Graduate School, 660-562-1145, Fax: 660-562-1096, E-mail: gradsch@nwmissouri.edu.

Oakland University, Graduate Study and Lifelong Learning, School of Education and Human Services, Department of Teacher Development and Educational Studies, Rochester, MI 48309-4401. Offers education studies (M Ed); secondary education (MAT). *Entrance requirements:* For master's, minimum GPA of 3.0 for unconditional admission. Electronic applications accepted. *Faculty research:* Earth science for middle and high school teachers through real world connections, learning communities, content enrichment.

Occidental College, Graduate Studies, Department of Education, Program in Secondary Education, Los Angeles, CA 90041-3314. Offers English and comparative literary studies (MAT); history (MAT); life science (MAT); mathematics (MAT); physical science (MAT); social science (MAT); Spanish (MAT). Part-time programs available. *Degree requirements:* For master's, comprehensive exam, graduate synthesis paper. *Entrance requirements:* For master's, GRE General Test, minimum GPA of 3.0. Additional exam requirements/recommendations for international students: Required—TOEFL (minimum score 625 paper-based; 263 computer-based). *Expenses:* Contact institution.

Ohio University, Graduate College, Gladys W. and David H. Patton College of Education and Human Services, Department of Teacher Education, Athens, OH 45701-2979. Offers adolescent to young adult education (M Ed); curriculum and instruction (M Ed, PhD); early childhood/special education (M Ed); intervention specialist/mild-moderate needs (M Ed); intervention specialist/moderate-intensive needs (M Ed); mathematics education (PhD); middle child education (M Ed); reading education (M Ed); social studies education (PhD). Part-time and evening/weekend programs available. *Students:* 131 full-time (92 women), 82 part-time (62 women); includes 9 minority (4 Black or African American, non-Hispanic/Latino; 2 American Indian or Alaska Native, non-Hispanic/Latino; 1 Asian, non-Hispanic/Latino; 1 Hispanic/Latino; 1 Two or more races, non-Hispanic/Latino), 11 international. 136 applicants, 70% accepted, 65 enrolled. In 2011, 58 master's, 8 doctorates awarded. *Degree requirements:* For master's, thesis or alternative; for doctorate, comprehensive exam, thesis/dissertation. *Entrance requirements:* For master's, GRE General Test or MAT (if GPA is below 2.9); for doctorate, GRE General Test, minimum GPA of 3.4, work experience. Additional exam requirements/recommendations for international students: Required—TOEFL (minimum score 550 paper-based; 80 iBT) or IELTS (minimum score 6.5). *Application deadline:* For fall admission, 5/1 priority date for domestic students, 4/1 for international students; for winter admission, 11/1 priority date for domestic students, 10/1 for international students; for spring admission, 2/15 priority date for domestic students, 1/1 for international students. Applications are processed on a rolling basis. Application fee: $50 ($55 for international students). Electronic applications accepted. *Financial support:* Research assistantships with full tuition reimbursements, teaching assistantships with full tuition reimbursements, Federal Work-Study, institutionally sponsored loans, tuition waivers (partial), and unspecified assistantships available. Financial award application deadline: 3/1. *Faculty research:* Cognition literacy, character education, teacher's education reform, disabilities. *Total annual research expenditures:* $46,933. *Unit head:* Dr. John Henning, Chair, 740-597-1830, Fax: 740-593-0477, E-mail: henningj@ohio.edu. *Application contact:* Floyd J. Doney, Director of Student Affairs, 740-593-4400, Fax: 740-593-9310, E-mail: doney@ohio.edu. Web site: http://www.cehs.ohio.edu/academics/te/index.htm.

Old Dominion University, Darden College of Education, Programs in Secondary Education, Norfolk, VA 23529. Offers biology (MS Ed); chemistry (MS Ed); English (MS Ed); instructional technology (MS Ed); library science (MS Ed); secondary education (MS Ed). *Accreditation:* NCATE. Part-time and evening/weekend programs available. Postbaccalaureate distance learning degree programs offered (minimal on-campus study). *Faculty:* 20 full-time (16 women). *Students:* 82 full-time (49 women), 95 part-time (63 women); includes 37 minority (21 Black or African American, non-Hispanic/Latino; 3 Asian, non-Hispanic/Latino; 8 Hispanic/Latino; 5 Two or more races, non-Hispanic/Latino), 1 international. Average age 32. 67 applicants, 79% accepted, 53 enrolled. In 2011, 84 degrees awarded. *Degree requirements:* For master's, comprehensive exam, thesis. *Entrance requirements:* For master's, GRE General Test or MAT, PRAXIS I (for licensure), minimum GPA of 2.8, teaching certificate. Additional exam requirements/recommendations for international students: Required—TOEFL. *Application deadline:* For fall admission, 6/1 for domestic and international students; for winter admission, 11/1 for domestic and international students; for spring admission, 3/1 for domestic and international students. Applications are processed on a rolling basis. Application fee: $50. Electronic applications accepted. *Expenses:* Tuition, state resident: full-time $9096; part-time $379 per credit. Tuition, nonresident: full-time $23,064; part-time $961 per credit. *Required fees:* $127 per semester. One-time fee: $50. *Financial support:* In 2011–12, 56 students received support, including fellowships (averaging $15,000 per year), 2 research assistantships with tuition reimbursements available (averaging $9,000 per year), 3 teaching assistantships with tuition reimbursements available (averaging $12,500 per year); career-related internships or fieldwork, Federal Work-Study, institutionally sponsored loans, scholarships/grants, and tuition waivers (partial) also available. Support available to part-time students. Financial award application deadline: 2/15; financial award applicants required to submit FAFSA. *Faculty research:* Use of technology, writing project for teachers, geography teaching, reading. *Unit head:* Dr. Robert Lucking, Graduate Program Director, 757-683-5545, Fax: 757-683-5862, E-mail: rlucking@odu.edu. *Application contact:* William Heffelfinger, Director of Graduate Admissions, 757-683-5554, Fax: 757-683-3255, E-mail: gradadmit@odu.edu. Web site: http://education.odu.edu/eci/secondary/.

Olivet Nazarene University, Graduate School, Division of Education, Program in Secondary Education, Bourbonnais, IL 60914. Offers MAT. *Accreditation:* NCATE. Evening/weekend programs available. *Degree requirements:* For master's, thesis or alternative.

Our Lady of the Lake University of San Antonio, School of Professional Studies, Program in Secondary Education, San Antonio, TX 78207-4689. Offers M Ed.

Pacific Union College, Education Department, Angwin, CA 94508-9707. Offers education (M Ed); elementary teaching (MAT); secondary teaching (MAT). Part-time programs available. *Faculty:* 3 full-time (1 woman), 3 part-time/adjunct (all women). *Students:* 14 part-time (9 women). *Degree requirements:* For master's, thesis, action research project, field experiences. *Entrance requirements:* For master's, GRE, two interviews, teaching credential, letters of recommendation. *Application deadline:* Applications are processed on a rolling basis. Application fee: $0. *Expenses: Tuition:* Full-time $25,740; part-time $750 per quarter hour. Tuition and fees vary according to student's religious affiliation. *Financial support:* Available to part-time students. *Unit head:* Prof. Thomas Lee, Chair, 707-965-6646, Fax: 707-965-6645, E-mail: tdlee@puc.edu. *Application contact:* Marsha Crow, Assistant Chair/Accreditation and Certification Specialist, 707-965-6643, Fax: 707-965-6645, E-mail: mcrow@puc.edu. Web site: http://www.puc.edu/academics/departments/education/.

Pacific University, College of Education, Forest Grove, OR 97116-1797. Offers early childhood education (MAT); education (MAE); elementary education (MAT); high school education (MAT); middle school education (MAT); special education (MAT); visual function in learning (M Ed). *Accreditation:* NCATE. Part-time and evening/weekend programs available. *Degree requirements:* For master's, research project. *Entrance requirements:* For master's, California Basic Educational Skills Test, PRAXIS II, minimum undergraduate GPA of 2.75, 3.0 graduate. Additional exam requirements/recommendations for international students: Required—TOEFL. Electronic applications accepted. *Expenses:* Contact institution. *Faculty research:* Defining a culturally competent classroom, technology in the k-12 classroom, Socratic seminars, social studies education.

Park University, College of Graduate and Professional Studies, Kansas City, MO 54105. Offers adult education (M Ed); at-risk students (M Ed); disaster and emergency management (MPA); educational administration (M Ed); entrepreneurship (MBA); general business (MBA); general education (M Ed); government/business relations (MPA); healthcare/services management (MBA, MPA); international business (MBA); K-12 certification (MAT); management information systems (MBA); management of information systems (MPA); middle school certification (MAT); multi-cultural education (M Ed); nonprofit management (MPA); public management (MPA); school law (M Ed); secondary school certification (MAT); special education (M Ed). Part-time and evening/weekend programs available. Postbaccalaureate distance learning degree programs offered (no on-campus study). *Degree requirements:* For master's, comprehensive exam, thesis (for some programs). *Entrance requirements:* For master's, GRE, GMAT, teacher certification (M Ed). Additional exam requirements/recommendations for international students: Required—TOEFL (minimum score 550 paper-based). Electronic applications accepted. *Faculty research:* Literacy, leadership, brain based research, multicultural education, diversity.

Piedmont College, School of Education, Demorest, GA 30535-0010. Offers early childhood education (MA, MAT); middle grades education (MA); secondary education (MA, MAT); special education (MA, MAT); teacher leadership (Ed S). Part-time and evening/weekend programs available. *Students:* 546 full-time (433 women), 809 part-time (698 women); includes 172 minority (139 Black or African American, non-Hispanic/Latino; 2 American Indian or Alaska Native, non-Hispanic/Latino; 6 Asian, non-Hispanic/Latino; 18 Hispanic/Latino; 7 Two or more races, non-Hispanic/Latino), 17 international. Average age 37. 342 applicants, 83% accepted, 234 enrolled. In 2011, 444 master's, 510 other advanced degrees awarded. *Degree requirements:* For master's, thesis, field experience in the classroom teaching ; for doctorate, thesis/dissertation. *Entrance requirements:* For master's, GRE General Test, MAT, minimum undergraduate GPA of 2.5; for Ed S, minimum graduate GPA of 3.5, valid teaching certificate. Additional exam requirements/recommendations for international students: Required—TOEFL (minimum score 550 paper-based; 213 computer-based). *Application deadline:* For fall admission, 7/15 for domestic students; for spring admission, 12/1 for domestic students. Applications are processed on a rolling basis. Application fee: $0. Electronic applications accepted. *Expenses: Tuition:* Part-time $407 per credit hour. Tuition and fees vary according to program. *Financial support:* Career-related internships or fieldwork, Federal Work-Study, and unspecified assistantships available. Support available to part-time students. Financial award applicants required to submit FAFSA. *Unit head:* Dr. Bob Cummings, Dean, 706-778-3000 Ext. 1201, Fax: 706-776-9608, E-mail: bcummings@piedmont.edu. *Application contact:* Penny Loggins, Director of Graduate Admissions, 706-778-8500 Ext. 1181, Fax: 706-778-0150, E-mail: ploggins@piedmont.edu.

Pittsburg State University, Graduate School, College of Education, Department of Curriculum and Instruction, Pittsburg, KS 66762. Offers classroom reading teacher (MS); early childhood education (MS); elementary education (MS); reading (MS); reading specialist (MS); secondary education (MS); teaching (MAT). *Accreditation:* NCATE. *Degree requirements:* For master's, thesis or alternative. *Entrance requirements:* For master's, GRE or MAT.

Plymouth State University, College of Graduate Studies, Graduate Studies in Education, Program in K-12 Education, Plymouth, NH 03264-1595. Offers M Ed. *Accreditation:* NCATE. Part-time and evening/weekend programs available. *Degree requirements:* For master's, PRAXIS. *Entrance requirements:* For master's, MAT, minimum GPA of 3.0.

Plymouth State University, College of Graduate Studies, Graduate Studies in Education, Program in Secondary Education, Plymouth, NH 03264-1595. Offers M Ed. Part-time and evening/weekend programs available. *Entrance requirements:* For master's, MAT.

Portland State University, Graduate Studies, School of Education, Department of Curriculum and Instruction, Portland, OR 97207-0751. Offers early childhood education (MA, MS); education (M Ed, MA, MS); educational leadership: curriculum and instruction (Ed D); educational media/school librarianship (MA, MS); elementary education (M Ed, MAT, MST); reading (MA, MS); secondary education (M Ed, MAT, MST). *Accreditation:* NCATE. Part-time programs available. *Degree requirements:* For master's, comprehensive exam, thesis or alternative; for doctorate, thesis/dissertation. *Entrance requirements:* For master's, California Basic Educational Skills Test, minimum GPA of 3.0 in upper-division course work or 2.75 overall. Additional exam requirements/recommendations for international students: Required—TOEFL (minimum score 550 paper-based; 213 computer-based). *Faculty research:* Early literacy, characteristics of successful teachers of at-risk students, participation of women/minorities in technology courses, selection of cooperating teachers.

Prescott College, Graduate Programs, Program in Education, Prescott, AZ 86301. Offers early childhood education (MA); early childhood special education (MA); education (MA); elementary education (MA); environmental education leadership and administration (MA); equine-assisted experiential learning (MA); school guidance counseling (MA); secondary education (MA); special education, learning disability (MA); special education, mental retardation (MA); special education, serious emotional disability (MA); student-directed independent study (MA); sustainability education (PhD). Part-time programs available. Postbaccalaureate distance learning degree programs offered (minimal on-campus study). *Faculty:* 2 full-time (both women), 47 part-time/adjunct (31 women). *Students:* 59 full-time (36 women), 48 part-time (30 women); includes 16 minority (3 Black or African American, non-Hispanic/Latino; 1 American Indian or Alaska Native, non-Hispanic/Latino; 1 Asian, non-Hispanic/Latino; 8 Hispanic/Latino; 3 Two or more races, non-Hispanic/Latino), 2 international. Average age 40. 75 applicants, 76% accepted, 36 enrolled. In 2011, 14 master's, 8 doctorates awarded. *Degree requirements:* For master's, thesis, fieldwork or internship, practicum; for doctorate, thesis/dissertation. *Entrance requirements:* For master's, 2 letters of recommendation, resume; for doctorate, 3 letters of recommendation, resume, official transcripts, personal statement, program proposal. Additional exam requirements/recommendations for international students: Required—TOEFL (minimum score 500 paper-based; 173 computer-based). *Application deadline:* For fall admission, 4/15 priority date for domestic students, 4/15 for international students; for spring admission, 9/15 priority date for domestic students, 9/15 for international students. Applications are processed on a rolling basis. Application fee: $40. Electronic applications accepted. *Expenses: Tuition:* Full-time $16,440; part-time $685 per credit. *Required fees:* $150 per semester. One-time fee: $350. *Financial support:* Career-related internships or fieldwork and Federal Work-Study available. Financial award applicants required to submit FAFSA. *Unit head:* Noel Caniglia, Chair, 928-358-3201, Fax: 928-776-5151, E-mail: ncaniglia@prescott.edu. *Application contact:* Kerstin Alicki, Admissions Counselor, 928-350-2100, Fax: 928-776-5242, E-mail: admissions@prescott.edu.

Providence College, Program in Special Education, Providence, RI 02918. Offers elementary special education (M Ed), including elementary, secondary. Part-time and evening/weekend programs available. *Faculty:* 7 part-time/adjunct (5 women). *Students:* 7 full-time (all women), 36 part-time (25 women); includes 2 minority (1 Black or African American, non-Hispanic/Latino; 1 Hispanic/Latino). Average age 31. 21 applicants, 100% accepted, 5 enrolled. In 2011, 33 master's awarded. *Degree requirements:* For master's, comprehensive exam. *Entrance requirements:* For master's, GRE General Test. Additional exam requirements/recommendations for international students: Required—TOEFL (minimum score 550 paper-based; 213 computer-based; 80 iBT). *Application deadline:* For fall admission, 8/1 priority date for domestic students, 8/1 for international students; for spring admission, 12/1 priority date for domestic students, 12/1 for international students. Applications are processed on a rolling basis. Application fee: $55. *Expenses: Tuition:* Part-time $404 per credit. *Required fees:* $404 per credit. *Financial support:* In 2011–12, 1 research assistantship with full tuition reimbursement (averaging $8,400 per year) was awarded; career-related internships or fieldwork and unspecified assistantships also available. Support available to part-time students. Financial award application deadline: 8/1; financial award applicants required to submit FAFSA. *Unit head:* Diane LaMontagne, Director, 401-865-2912, Fax: 401-865-1147, E-mail: dlamonta@providence.edu. *Application contact:* Carol A. Daniels, Coordinator of Graduate Faculty and Administrative Services, 401-865-2247, Fax: 401-865-1147, E-mail: daniels@providence.edu. Web site: http://www.providence.edu/professional-studies/graduate-degrees/Pages/master-education-specialed.aspx.

Providence College, Programs in Administration, Providence, RI 02918. Offers elementary administration (M Ed); secondary administration (M Ed). Part-time and evening/weekend programs available. *Faculty:* 11 part-time/adjunct (4 women). *Students:* 4 full-time (2 women), 81 part-time (45 women). Average age 36. 31 applicants, 94% accepted, 10 enrolled. In 2011, 18 master's awarded. *Degree requirements:* For master's, comprehensive exam. *Entrance requirements:* For master's, GRE General Test. Additional exam requirements/recommendations for international students: Required—TOEFL (minimum score 550 paper-based; 213 computer-based; 80 iBT). *Application deadline:* For fall admission, 8/1 priority date for domestic students, 8/1 for international students; for spring admission, 12/1 priority date for domestic students, 12/1 for international students. Applications are processed on a rolling basis. Application fee: $55. *Expenses: Tuition:* Part-time $404 per credit. *Required fees:* $404 per credit. *Financial support:* In 2011–12, research assistantships with full tuition reimbursements (averaging $8,400 per year) were awarded; career-related internships or fieldwork, institutionally sponsored loans, and unspecified assistantships also available. Support available to part-time students. Financial award application deadline: 8/1; financial award applicants required to submit FAFSA. *Unit head:* Francis J. Leary, Director, 401-865-2247, Fax: 401-865-1147, E-mail: fleary@providence.edu. *Application contact:* Carol A. Daniels, Coordinator of Graduate Faculty and Administrative Services, 401-865-2247, Fax: 401-865-1147, E-mail: daniels@providence.edu.

Providence College, Providence Alliance for Catholic Teachers (PACT) Program, Providence, RI 02918. Offers secondary education (M Ed). *Faculty:* 45 full-time (26 women). *Students:* 33 full-time (20 women). Average age 23. 55 applicants, 33% accepted, 13 enrolled. In 2011, 12 master's awarded. *Degree requirements:* For master's, comprehensive exam. *Entrance requirements:* For master's, GRE/MAT. Additional exam requirements/recommendations for international students: Required—TOEFL (minimum score 550 paper-based; 213 computer-based; 80 iBT). *Application deadline:* For fall admission, 2/1 priority date for domestic students, 2/1 for international students. Applications are processed on a rolling basis. Application fee: $55. *Expenses: Tuition:* Part-time $404 per credit. *Required fees:* $404 per credit. *Financial support:* In 2011–12, teaching assistantships (averaging $14,500 per year) were awarded. Financial award application deadline: 8/1; financial award applicants required to submit FAFSA. *Unit head:* Br. Patrick Carey, Director, 401-865-2657, E-mail: pcarey@providence.edu. *Application contact:* Carol A. Daniels, Coordinator of Graduate Faculty and Administrative Services, 401-865-2247, Fax: 401-865-1147, E-mail: daniels@providence.edu. Web site: http://www.providence.edu/pact/Pages/default.aspx.

Queens College of the City University of New York, Division of Graduate Studies, Division of Education, Department of Secondary Education, Flushing, NY 11367-1597. Offers art (MS Ed); biology (MS Ed, AC); chemistry (MS Ed, AC); earth sciences (MS Ed, AC); English (MS Ed, AC); French (MS Ed, AC); Italian (MS Ed, AC); mathematics (MS Ed, AC); music (MS Ed, AC); physics (MS Ed, AC); social studies (MS Ed, AC); Spanish (MS Ed, AC). Part-time and evening/weekend programs available. *Faculty:* 22 full-time (14 women). *Students:* 46 full-time (23 women), 727 part-time (442 women); includes 234 minority (41 Black or African American, non-Hispanic/Latino; 78 Asian, non-Hispanic/Latino; 115 Hispanic/Latino), 5 international. 591 applicants, 60% accepted, 250 enrolled. In 2011, 170 master's awarded. *Degree requirements:* For master's, research project; for AC, thesis optional. *Entrance requirements:* For master's, minimum GPA of 3.0. Additional exam requirements/recommendations for international students: Required—TOEFL. *Application deadline:* For fall admission, 4/1 for domestic students; for spring admission, 11/1 for domestic students. Applications are processed on a rolling basis. Application fee: $125. *Expenses:* Tuition, state resident: part-time $345 per credit. Tuition, nonresident: part-time $640 per credit. *Required fees:* $145.25 per semester. *Financial support:* Career-related internships or fieldwork, Federal Work-Study, institutionally sponsored loans, and tuition waivers (partial) available. Support available to part-time students. Financial award application deadline: 4/1; financial award applicants required to submit FAFSA. *Unit head:* Dr. Eleanor Armour-Thomas, Chairperson, 718-997-5150, E-mail: armourthomas@yahoo.com. *Application contact:* Mario Caruso, Director of Graduate Admissions, 718-997-5200, Fax: 718-997-5193, E-mail: graduate_admissions@qc.edu.

Quinnipiac University, School of Education, Program in Secondary Education, Hamden, CT 06518-1940. Offers biology (MAT); English (MAT); history/social studies (MAT); mathematics (MAT); Spanish (MAT). *Accreditation:* NCATE. *Faculty:* 7 full-time (5 women), 41 part-time/adjunct (24 women). *Students:* 56 full-time (38 women), 1 (woman) part-time; includes 5 minority (1 Black or African American, non-Hispanic/Latino; 1 Asian, non-Hispanic/Latino; 3 Hispanic/Latino). 51 applicants, 96% accepted, 44 enrolled. In 2011, 49 master's awarded. *Entrance requirements:* For master's, PRAXIS I, minimum GPA of 2.67, interview. *Application deadline:* For fall admission, 3/31 priority date for domestic students. Applications are processed on a rolling basis. Application fee: $45. Electronic applications accepted. *Expenses: Tuition:* Part-time $855 per credit. *Required fees:* $35 per credit. *Financial support:* In 2011–12, 1 student received support. Career-related internships or fieldwork, scholarships/grants, and tuition waivers (full and partial) available. Financial award application deadline: 4/15; financial award applicants required to submit FAFSA. *Faculty research:* Multicultural and urban education/leadership, challenges of teaching diverse learners, scholarship of teaching and learning, technology and teaching, humor and education. *Unit head:* Mordechai Gordon, Program Director, 203-582-8442, Fax: 203-582-3473, E-mail: mordechai.gordon@quinnipiac.edu. *Application contact:* Jennifer Boutin, Associate Director of Graduate Admissions, 800-462-1944, Fax: 203-582-3443, E-mail: jennifer.boutin@quinnipiac.edu. Web site: http://www.quinnipiac.edu/academics/colleges-schools-and-departments/school-of-education/graduate-programs/five-semester-mat-programs/secondary-educat.

Rhode Island College, School of Graduate Studies, Feinstein School of Education and Human Development, Department of Educational Studies, Providence, RI 02908-1991. Offers advanced studies in teaching and learning (M Ed); English (MAT); French (MAT); history (MAT); math (MAT); secondary education (MAT); Spanish (MAT); teaching English as a second language (M Ed). *Accreditation:* NCATE. Part-time and evening/weekend programs available. *Faculty:* 14 full-time (7 women), 4 part-time/adjunct (2 women). *Students:* 10 full-time (all women), 61 part-time (51 women); includes 8 minority (1 Black or African American, non-Hispanic/Latino; 4 Asian, non-Hispanic/Latino; 3 Hispanic/Latino). Average age 33. In 2011, 32 master's awarded. *Degree requirements:* For master's, capstone or comprehensive assessment. *Entrance requirements:* For master's, GRE or MAT (for most programs), minimum undergraduate GPA of 3.0; baccalaureate degree in English, French, history, math or Spanish; evaluation of content area knowledge; 3 letters of recommendation; interview. Additional exam requirements/recommendations for international students: Recommended—TOEFL (minimum score 550 paper-based; 213 computer-based; 79 iBT). *Application deadline:* For fall admission, 3/1 for domestic students; for spring admission, 11/1 for domestic students. Applications are processed on a rolling basis. Application fee: $50. *Expenses:* Tuition, state resident: full-time $8592; part-time $358 per credit hour. Tuition, nonresident: full-time $16,800; part-time $700 per credit hour. *Required fees:* $602; $22 per credit. $72 per term. *Financial support:* Teaching assistantships with full tuition reimbursements, career-related internships or fieldwork, Federal Work-Study, scholarships/grants, health care benefits, and unspecified assistantships available. Support available to part-time students. Financial award application deadline: 5/15; financial award applicants required to submit FAFSA. *Faculty research:* School administration, school/college articulation. *Unit head:* Dr. Ellen Bigler, Chair, 401-456-8170. *Application contact:* Graduate Studies, 401-456-8700. Web site: http://www.ric.edu/educationalStudies/.

Roberts Wesleyan College, Division of Teacher Education, Rochester, NY 14624-1997. Offers adolescence education (M Ed); childhood and special education (M Ed); literacy education (M Ed); urban education (M Ed). Part-time and evening/weekend programs available. *Degree requirements:* For master's, thesis.

Rochester Institute of Technology, Graduate Enrollment Services, National Technical Institute for the Deaf, Department of Research and Teacher Education, Rochester, NY 14623-5603. Offers MS. *Accreditation:* Teacher Education Accreditation Council. *Students:* 54 full-time (38 women), 5 part-time (all women); includes 7 minority (4 Black or African American, non-Hispanic/Latino; 1 Asian, non-Hispanic/Latino; 2 Hispanic/Latino), 1 international. Average age 28. 43 applicants, 60% accepted, 23 enrolled. In 2011, 21 degrees awarded. *Degree requirements:* For master's, thesis or alternative. *Entrance requirements:* For master's, minimum GPA of 3.0. Additional exam requirements/recommendations for international students: Required—TOEFL (minimum score 550 paper-based; 213 computer-based; 88 iBT) or IELTS (minimum score 6.5). *Application deadline:* For fall admission, 2/15 priority date for domestic students, 2/15 for international students. Applications are processed on a rolling basis. Application fee: $50. Electronic applications accepted. *Expenses: Tuition:* Full-time $34,659; part-time $963 per credit hour. *Required fees:* $228; $76 per quarter. *Financial support:* Fellowships with full and partial tuition reimbursements, research assistantships with partial tuition reimbursements, teaching assistantships with partial tuition reimbursements, career-related internships or fieldwork, institutionally sponsored loans, scholarships/grants, and unspecified assistantships available. Support available to part-time students. Financial award applicants required to submit FAFSA. *Faculty research:* Applied research on the effective use of access and support services to enhance learning for deaf and hard-of-hearing students in the mainstreamed classroom, STEM research and instruction. *Unit head:* Gerald Bateman, Director, 585-475-6480, Fax: 585-475-2525, E-mail: gcbnmp@rit.edu. *Application contact:* Diane Ellison, Assistant Vice President, Graduate Enrollment Services, 585-475-2229, Fax: 585-475-7164, E-mail: gradinfo@rit.edu. Web site: http://www.ntid.rit.edu/research/department/.

Rockford College, Graduate Studies, Department of Education, Program in Secondary Education, Rockford, IL 61108-2393. Offers MAT. Part-time and evening/weekend programs available. *Degree requirements:* For master's, thesis optional. *Entrance requirements:* For master's, GRE General Test, basic skills test (for students seeking certification), 3 letters of recommendation. Additional exam requirements/recommendations for international students: Required—TOEFL (minimum score 550 paper-based; 213 computer-based; 79 iBT). *Application deadline:* Applications are processed on a rolling basis. Application fee: $50. Electronic applications accepted. *Expenses: Tuition:* Full-time $16,200; part-time $675 per credit. *Required fees:* $80; $40 per semester. Tuition and fees vary according to class time, course level, course load, degree level, campus/location and program. *Financial support:* Scholarships/grants and unspecified assistantships available. Support available to part-time students. Financial award application deadline: 3/1; financial award applicants required to submit FAFSA. *Unit head:* Dr. Michelle McReynolds, MAT Director, 815-226-3390, Fax: 815-394-3706, E-mail: mmcreynolds@rockford.edu. *Application contact:* Michele Mehren, Office Manager for Graduate Studies, 815-226-4041, Fax: 815-394-3706, E-mail: mmehren@rockford.edu. Web site: http://www.rockford.edu/?page=MAT.

Roosevelt University, Graduate Division, College of Education, Department of Secondary Education, Chicago, IL 60605. Offers MA.

Rowan University, Graduate School, College of Education, Department of Teacher Education, Program in Secondary Education, Glassboro, NJ 08028-1701. Offers MST. *Degree requirements:* For master's, thesis. *Entrance requirements:* For master's, GRE General Test. Additional exam requirements/recommendations for international students: Required—TOEFL. Electronic applications accepted.

Sacred Heart University, Graduate Programs, Isabelle Farrington College of Education, Fairfield, CT 06825-1000. Offers administration (CAS); educational technology (MAT); elementary education (MAT); reading (CAS); secondary education (MAT); teaching (CAS). Part-time and evening/weekend programs available. Postbaccalaureate distance learning degree programs offered (minimal on-campus study). *Degree requirements:* For master's, thesis or alternative. *Entrance requirements:* For master's, PRAXIS (teacher certification/MAT); for CAS, PRAXIS I. Additional exam requirements/recommendations for international students: Required—TOEFL (minimum score 550 paper-based; 213 computer-based). Electronic applications accepted. *Expenses:* Contact institution. *Faculty research:* Reading education, learning theory, teacher preparation, education of underachievers.

Saginaw Valley State University, College of Education, Program in Natural Science Teaching, University Center, MI 48710. Offers elementary (MAT); middle school (MAT); secondary school (MAT). *Accreditation:* NCATE. Part-time and evening/weekend programs available. *Students:* 9 part-time (7 women); includes 1 minority (Black or African American, non-Hispanic/Latino). Average age 35. 1 applicant, 100% accepted, 0 enrolled. In 2011, 14 master's awarded. *Degree requirements:* For master's, capstone course. *Entrance requirements:* For master's, minimum GPA of 3.0, teaching certificate. Additional exam requirements/recommendations for international students: Required—TOEFL (minimum score 525 paper-based; 197 computer-based; 71 iBT). *Application deadline:* Applications are processed on a rolling basis. Application fee: $25. Electronic applications accepted. *Expenses:* Tuition, state resident: full-time $8300; part-time $5333 per year. Tuition, nonresident: full-time $15,613; part-time $10,209 per year. *International tuition:* $15,631 full-time. *Financial support:* Federal Work-Study and scholarships/grants available. Support available to part-time students. Financial award applicants required to submit FAFSA. *Unit head:* Dr. Steve P. Barbus, Jr., Dean, 989-964-6067, Fax: 989-790-4385, E-mail: barbus@svsu.edu. *Application contact:* Kathy Lopez, Certification Officer, 989-964-4661, Fax: 989-964-4385, E-mail: klopez@svsu.edu.

Saginaw Valley State University, College of Education, Program in Secondary Classroom Teaching, University Center, MI 48710. Offers MAT. *Accreditation:* NCATE. Part-time and evening/weekend programs available. *Students:* 2 full-time (1 woman), 36 part-time (23 women); includes 3 minority (1 Black or African American, non-Hispanic/Latino; 1 Asian, non-Hispanic/Latino; 1 Hispanic/Latino). Average age 32. 14 applicants, 100% accepted, 10 enrolled. In 2011, 20 master's awarded. *Degree requirements:* For master's, capstone course. *Entrance requirements:* For master's, minimum GPA of 3.0, teaching certificate. Additional exam requirements/recommendations for international students: Required—TOEFL (minimum score 525 paper-based; 197 computer-based; 71 iBT). *Application deadline:* Applications are processed on a rolling basis. Application fee: $25. Electronic applications accepted. *Expenses:* Tuition, state resident: full-time $8300; part-time $5333 per year. Tuition, nonresident: full-time $15,613; part-time $10,209 per year. *International tuition:* $15,631 full-time. *Financial support:* Federal Work-Study and scholarships/grants available. Support available to part-time students. Financial award applicants required to submit FAFSA. *Unit head:* Dr. Steve P. Barbus, Jr., Dean, 989-964-6067, Fax: 989-790-4385, E-mail: barbus@svsu.edu. *Application contact:* Kathy Lopez, Certification Officer, 989-964-4661, Fax: 989-964-4385, E-mail: klopez@svsu.edu.

St. Bonaventure University, School of Graduate Studies, School of Education, Literacy Programs, St. Bonaventure, NY 14778-2284. Offers adolescent literacy 5-12 (MS Ed); childhood literacy B-6 (MS Ed). *Accreditation:* NCATE. Part-time and evening/weekend programs available. *Faculty:* 2 full-time (both women). *Students:* 18 full-time (16 women), 33 part-time (32 women). Average age 24. 33 applicants, 67% accepted, 15 enrolled. In 2011, 50 master's awarded. *Degree requirements:* For master's, comprehensive exam, thesis optional, literacy coaching internship, portfolio. *Entrance requirements:* For master's, interview, writing sample, minimum undergraduate GPA of 3.0, references, teaching certificate in matching area. Additional exam requirements/recommendations for international students: Required—TOEFL (minimum score 550 paper-based; 213 computer-based; 80 iBT). *Application deadline:* For fall admission, 6/15 priority date for domestic students, 2/1 for international students; for spring admission, 11/15 priority date for domestic students, 7/1 for international students. Applications are processed on a rolling basis. Application fee: $30. Electronic applications accepted. *Expenses: Tuition:* Part-time $670 per credit. *Financial support:* In 2011–12, 4 research assistantships with full and partial tuition reimbursements were awarded; Federal Work-Study, scholarships/grants, health care benefits, and unspecified assistantships also available. Support available to part-time students. Financial award application deadline: 4/15; financial award applicants required to submit FAFSA. *Unit head:* Dr. Pamela Sharp Crawford, Director, 716-375-2387, E-mail: pcrawfor@sbu.edu. *Application contact:* Bruce Campbell, 716-375-2429, Fax: 716-375-4015, E-mail: gradsch@sbu.edu. Web site: http://www.sbu.edu/education.aspx?id=2994.

St. John's University, The School of Education, Department of Curriculum and Instruction, Program in Adolescent Education, Queens, NY 11439. Offers MS Ed. Part-time and evening/weekend programs available. *Students:* 72 full-time (45 women), 192 part-time (109 women); includes 85 minority (32 Black or African American, non-Hispanic/Latino; 18 Asian, non-Hispanic/Latino; 31 Hispanic/Latino; 4 Two or more races, non-Hispanic/Latino), 3 international. Average age 30. 176 applicants, 95% accepted, 116 enrolled. In 2011, 116 master's awarded. *Degree requirements:* For master's, variable foreign language requirement, comprehensive exam. *Entrance requirements:* For master's, minimum GPA of 3.0, 2 letters of recommendation, qualification for the New York State provisional (initial) teaching certificate. Additional exam requirements/recommendations for international students: Required—TOEFL (minimum score 600 paper-based; 250 computer-based; 100 iBT), IELTS (minimum score 5.5). *Application deadline:* For fall admission, 8/17 for domestic students, 5/1 for international students; for spring admission, 1/5 for domestic students, 11/1 for international students. Applications are processed on a rolling basis. Application fee: $70. Electronic applications accepted. *Expenses: Tuition:* Full-time $18,000; part-time $1000 per credit. *Required fees:* $170 per semester. Tuition and fees vary according to program. *Financial support:* Research assistantships, career-related internships or fieldwork, and scholarships/grants available. Support available to part-time students. Financial award application deadline: 3/1; financial award applicants required to submit FAFSA. *Faculty research:* Investigating self-efficacy in literacy learning, using problem solving as an approach for math learning. *Unit head:* Dr. Judith McVarish, Chair, 718-990-2334, E-mail: mcvarisj@stjohns.edu. *Application contact:* Dr. Kelly K. Ronayne, Associate Dean for Graduate Admissions, 718-990-2304, Fax: 718-990-2343, E-mail: graded@stjohns.edu.

Saint Joseph's University, College of Arts and Sciences, Department of Education, Philadelphia, PA 19131-1395. Offers curriculum supervisor of instruction (Certificate); educational leadership (MS, Ed D); elementary education (MS, Certificate); elementary/middle years (Certificate); English second language specialist online (Certificate); hearing impaired: N-12th grade (Certificate); instructional technology (MS, Certificate); principal certification (Certificate); professional education (MS); reading specialist (MS, Certificate); reading supervisory (Certificate); secondary education (MS, Certificate); special education (MS, Certificate); superintendent's letter of eligibility (Certificate); supervisor of special education (Certificate); Wilson reading certificate online (Certificate). Part-time and evening/weekend programs available. Postbaccalaureate distance learning degree programs offered (no on-campus study). *Faculty:* 26 full-time (24 women), 83 part-time/adjunct (52 women). *Students:* 112 full-time (92 women), 923 part-time (709 women); includes 147 minority (92 Black or African American, non-Hispanic/Latino; 4 American Indian or Alaska Native, non-Hispanic/Latino; 19 Asian, non-Hispanic/Latino; 28 Hispanic/Latino; 4 Two or more races, non-Hispanic/Latino), 8 international. Average age 31. 285 applicants, 77% accepted, 176 enrolled. In 2011, 276 master's, 13 doctorates, 2 other advanced degrees awarded. *Entrance requirements:* For master's, 2 letters of recommendation, minimum GPA of 3.0, official transcripts, personal statement; for doctorate, GRE, master's degree from accredited institution, minimum graduate GPA of 3.5, computer competence, commitment to participate in cohort, interview with program director. Additional exam requirements/recommendations for international students: Required—TOEFL (minimum score 550 paper-based; 213 computer-based; 79 iBT). *Application deadline:* For fall admission, 7/15 priority date for domestic students, 4/15 for international students; for winter admission, 11/15 for domestic students, 1/15 for international students; for spring admission, 11/15 priority date for domestic students, 10/15 for international students. Applications are processed on a rolling basis. Application fee: $35. Electronic applications accepted. *Expenses:* Contact institution. *Financial support:* Unspecified assistantships available. Financial award applicants required to submit FAFSA. *Faculty research:* Public education professional development, factors predicting early mathematics skills for low income children. *Total annual research expenditures:* $92,975. *Unit head:* Dr. Jeanne Brady, Associate Dean, Education, 610-660-1580, E-mail: jebrady@sju.edu. *Application contact:* Kate McConnell, Director, Graduate College of Arts and Sciences Admissions and Retention, 610-660-3184, Fax: 610-660-3230, E-mail: kate.mcconnell@sju.edu.

Saint Mary's University of Minnesota, Schools of Graduate and Professional Programs, Graduate School of Education, Instruction Program, Winona, MN 55987-1399. Offers MA, Certificate. *Unit head:* Matthew Klebe, Director, 507-457-6619, E-mail: mklebe@smumn.edu. *Application contact:* Yasin Alsaidi, Director of Admissions for Graduate and Professional Programs, 612-728-5207, Fax: 612-728-5121, E-mail: yalsaidi@smumn.edu. Web site: http://www.smumn.edu/graduate-home/areas-of-study/graduate-school-of-education/ma-in-instruction.

Saint Peter's University, Graduate Programs in Education, Program in Teaching, Jersey City, NJ 07306-5997. Offers 6-8 middle school education (MA Ed, Certificate); K-12 secondary education (MA Ed, Certificate); K-5 elementary education (MA Ed, Certificate). Part-time and evening/weekend programs available. *Degree requirements:* For master's, comprehensive exam. *Entrance requirements:* For master's, GRE or MAT. Additional exam requirements/recommendations for international students: Required—TOEFL (minimum score 79 computer-based). Electronic applications accepted.

St. Thomas Aquinas College, Division of Teacher Education, Sparkill, NY 10976. Offers adolescence education (MST); childhood and special education (MST); childhood education (MST); educational leadership (MS Ed); reading (MS Ed, PMC); special education (MS Ed, PMC); teaching (MS Ed), including elementary education, middle school education, secondary education. *Accreditation:* NCATE. Part-time and evening/weekend programs available. *Degree requirements:* For master's, comprehensive exam, comprehensive professional portfolio; for PMC, action research project. *Entrance requirements:* For master's, New York State Qualifying Exam, GRE General Test or minimum GPA of 3.0, teaching certificate; for PMC, GRE General Test or minimum GPA of 3.0. Electronic applications accepted. *Faculty research:* Computer applications in education, adolescent special education students, literacy development, inclusive practices for special education students.

Saint Xavier University, Graduate Studies, School of Education, Chicago, IL 60655-3105. Offers counseling (MA); curriculum and instruction (MA); early childhood education (MA); educational administration (MA); elementary education (MA); individualized studies (MA), including educational technology, English as a second language (ESL), ISTEM (integrative science, technology, engineering, and math), science education; music education (MA); reading (MA); secondary education (MA); Spanish education (MA); special education (MA); teaching and leadership (MA). *Accreditation:* NCATE. Part-time and evening/weekend programs available. *Degree requirements:* For master's, thesis or project. *Entrance requirements:* For master's, minimum GPA of 3.0. *Application deadline:* For fall admission, 8/15 priority date for domestic students. Applications are processed on a rolling basis. Application fee: $35. *Expenses:* Contact institution. *Financial support:* Career-related internships or fieldwork available. Support available to part-time students. Financial award applicants required to submit FAFSA. *Unit head:* Dr. Beverly Gulley, Dean, 773-298-3221, Fax: 773-779-9061, E-mail: gulley@sxu.edu. *Application contact:* Beth Gierach, Managing Director of Admission, 773-298-3053, Fax: 773-298-3076, E-mail: gierach@sxu.edu.

Salem College, Department of Teacher Education, Winston-Salem, NC 27101. Offers art education (MAT); elementary education (M Ed, MAT); language and literacy (M Ed); middle school education (MAT); music education (MAT); school counseling (M Ed); second language studies (MAT); secondary education (MAT); special education (M Ed, MAT). *Accreditation:* NCATE. Part-time and evening/weekend programs available. Postbaccalaureate distance learning degree programs offered (minimal on-campus study). *Degree requirements:* For master's, comprehensive exam, practicum (MAT), project (M Ed); oral and written comprehensive exams. *Entrance requirements:* For master's, GRE, minimum GPA of 2.5. *Faculty research:* Content area reading strategies, literacy development, brain compatible instruction.

Salem State University, School of Graduate Studies, Program in Secondary Education, Salem, MA 01970-5353. Offers M Ed. Part-time and evening/weekend programs available. *Entrance requirements:* For master's, GRE or MAT. Additional exam requirements/recommendations for international students: Required—TOEFL (minimum score 550 paper-based; 80 iBT) or IELTS (minimum score 5.5).

Salem State University, School of Graduate Studies, Program in Spanish, Salem, MA 01970-5353. Offers MAT. Part-time and evening/weekend programs available. *Entrance requirements:* For master's, GRE or MAT. Additional exam requirements/recommendations for international students: Required—TOEFL (minimum score 550 paper-based; 80 iBT) or IELTS (minimum score 5.5).

Samford University, Orlean Bullard Beeson School of Education and Professional Studies, Birmingham, AL 35229. Offers early childhood education (Ed S); early childhood/elementary education (MS Ed); educational administration (Ed S); educational leadership (Ed D); elementary education (Ed S); gifted education (MS Ed); instructional leadership (MS Ed); secondary collaboration (MS Ed); M Div/MS Ed. *Accreditation:* NCATE. Part-time programs available. *Faculty:* 11 full-time (7 women), 9 part-time/adjunct (7 women). *Students:* 20 full-time (16 women), 169 part-time (122 women); includes 30 minority (26 Black or African American, non-Hispanic/Latino; 1 American Indian or Alaska Native, non-Hispanic/Latino; 1 Asian, non-Hispanic/Latino; 2 Hispanic/Latino), 1 international. Average age 39. 51 applicants, 92% accepted, 44 enrolled. In 2011, 57 master's, 9 doctorates, 35 other advanced degrees awarded. *Degree requirements:* For master's, comprehensive exam; for doctorate, comprehensive exam, thesis/dissertation. *Entrance requirements:* For master's, GRE or MAT, minimum GPA of 3.0; for doctorate, minimum GPA of 3.7; for Ed S, GRE, master's degree, teaching certificate, minimum GPA of 3.25. Additional exam requirements/recommendations for international students: Required—TOEFL (minimum score 550 paper-based; 213 computer-based). *Application deadline:* For fall admission, 7/15 for domestic students; for winter admission, 4/5 for domestic students; for spring admission, 12/4 for domestic students. Applications are processed on a rolling basis. Application fee: $25. *Expenses: Tuition:* Full-time $29,934; part-time $655 per credit. *Required fees:* $705. *Financial support:* Research assistantships, career-related internships or fieldwork, Federal Work-Study, scholarships/grants, and tuition waivers (partial) available. Support available to part-time students. Financial award applicants required to submit FAFSA. *Faculty research:* School law, the characteristics of beginning teachers, the nature of school reform, school culture, quality improvement in education, K-12 student achievement. *Unit head:* Dr. Jean Ann Box, Dean, 205-726-2565, E-mail: jabox@samford.edu. *Application contact:* Dr. Maurice Persall, Director, Graduate Office, 205-726-2019, E-mail: jmpersal@samford.edu. Web site: http://dlserver.samford.edu.

San Diego State University, Graduate and Research Affairs, College of Education, School of Teacher Education, Program in Secondary Curriculum and Instruction, San Diego, CA 92182. Offers MA. *Accreditation:* NCATE. *Entrance requirements:* For master's, GRE General Test, letters of reference. Additional exam requirements/

recommendations for international students: Required—TOEFL. Electronic applications accepted.

San Francisco State University, Division of Graduate Studies, College of Education, Department of Secondary Education, San Francisco, CA 94132-1722. Offers MA. *Accreditation:* NCATE. *Unit head:* Dr. Nathan Avani, Chair, 415-338-1202, E-mail: natalio@sfsu.edu. *Application contact:* Dr. Jamal Cooks, Graduate Coordinator, 415-338-1202, E-mail: jcooks@sfsu.edu. Web site: http://coe.sfsu.edu/sed.

San Jose State University, Graduate Studies and Research, Connie L. Lurie College of Education, Department of Secondary Education, San Jose, CA 95192-0001. Offers Certificate. *Accreditation:* NCATE. Evening/weekend programs available. Electronic applications accepted.

Seattle Pacific University, Master of Arts in Teaching Program, Seattle, WA 98119-1997. Offers alternate routes to certification (Certificate); teaching (MAT). *Accreditation:* NCATE. Part-time and evening/weekend programs available. *Degree requirements:* For master's, field experience, internship. *Entrance requirements:* For master's, GRE General Test or MAT, minimum GPA of 3.0. Electronic applications accepted. *Expenses:* Contact institution.

Siena Heights University, Graduate College, Program in Teacher Education, Concentration in Secondary Education, Adrian, MI 49221-1796. Offers secondary education/reading (MA). Part-time programs available. *Degree requirements:* For master's, thesis, presentation. *Entrance requirements:* For master's, minimum GPA of 3.0, interview. *Expenses: Tuition:* Full-time $11,400; part-time $475 per credit hour. *Required fees:* $1000; $500 $125 per term. Tuition and fees vary according to degree level.

Sierra Nevada College, Teacher Education Program, Incline Village, NV 89451. Offers advanced teaching and leadership (M Ed); elementary education (MAT); secondary education (MAT). Part-time and evening/weekend programs available. Postbaccalaureate distance learning degree programs offered (minimal on-campus study). *Faculty:* 2 full-time (both women), 26 part-time/adjunct (16 women). *Students:* 247 full-time (192 women), 240 part-time (162 women); includes 234 minority (44 Black or African American, non-Hispanic/Latino; 8 American Indian or Alaska Native, non-Hispanic/Latino; 132 Asian, non-Hispanic/Latino; 38 Hispanic/Latino; 12 Native Hawaiian or other Pacific Islander, non-Hispanic/Latino). Average age 35. 147 applicants, 84% accepted, 124 enrolled. In 2011, 146 master's awarded. *Degree requirements:* For master's, comprehensive exam, thesis, PRAXIS I and II. *Entrance requirements:* For master's, 2 letters of recommendation, minimum GPA of 3.0. *Application deadline:* For fall admission, 8/6 priority date for domestic students; for winter admission, 1/7 priority date for domestic students; for spring admission, 5/6 priority date for domestic students. Applications are processed on a rolling basis. Application fee: $50. Electronic applications accepted. *Expenses: Tuition:* Full-time $7138; part-time $397 per credit. *Required fees:* $100 per semester. *Financial support:* In 2011–12, 334 students received support. Federal Work-Study available. Support available to part-time students. Financial award application deadline: 8/15; financial award applicants required to submit FAFSA. *Unit head:* Beth Bouchard, Chair of Education Department, 775-831-1314, Fax: 775-832-1686, E-mail: bbouchard@sierranevada.edu. *Application contact:* Katrina Midgley, Director of Graduate Admission, 775-831-1314 Ext. 7517, Fax: 775-832-1686, E-mail: kmidgley@sierranevada.edu. Web site: http://www.sierranevada.edu/.

Simpson College, Department of Education, Indianola, IA 50125-1297. Offers secondary education (MAT). *Degree requirements:* For master's, PRAXIS II, electronic portfolio. *Entrance requirements:* For master's, bachelor's degree; minimum cumulative GPA of 2.75, 3.0 in major; 3 letters of recommendation.

Slippery Rock University of Pennsylvania, Graduate Studies (Recruitment), College of Education, Department of Secondary Education/Foundations of Education, Slippery Rock, PA 16057-1383. Offers educational leadership (M Ed); secondary education in English (M Ed); secondary education in math/science (M Ed); secondary education in social studies (M Ed). *Accreditation:* NCATE. Part-time and evening/weekend programs available. *Faculty:* 9 full-time (4 women), 3 part-time/adjunct (0 women). *Students:* 64 full-time (34 women), 16 part-time (8 women); includes 2 minority (1 Asian, non-Hispanic/Latino; 1 Two or more races, non-Hispanic/Latino). Average age 28. 68 applicants, 76% accepted, 27 enrolled. In 2011, 54 degrees awarded. *Degree requirements:* For master's, comprehensive exam, thesis (for some programs). *Entrance requirements:* For master's, GRE General Test, MAT, minimum GPA of 2.8 (depending on program). Additional exam requirements/recommendations for international students: Required—TOEFL (minimum score 550 paper-based; 213 computer-based; 80 iBT). *Application deadline:* For fall admission, 3/1 priority date for domestic students, 5/1 for international students; for spring admission, 10/1 priority date for domestic students, 9/1 for international students. Applications are processed on a rolling basis. Application fee: $25 ($30 for international students). Electronic applications accepted. *Expenses:* Tuition, state resident: full-time $7488; part-time $416 per credit. Tuition, nonresident: full-time $11,232; part-time $624 per credit. *International tuition:* $11,146 full-time. *Required fees:* $2722; $140 per credit. Tuition and fees vary according to degree level and program. *Financial support:* Career-related internships or fieldwork, Federal Work-Study, institutionally sponsored loans, scholarships/grants, tuition waivers (partial), and unspecified assistantships available. Support available to part-time students. Financial award application deadline: 5/1; financial award applicants required to submit FAFSA. *Unit head:* Dr. Jeffrey Lehman, Graduate Coordinator, 724-738-2311, Fax: 724-738-4987, E-mail: jeffrey.lehman@sru.edu. *Application contact:* Angela Barrett, Interim Director of Graduate Studies, 724-738-2051, Fax: 724-738-2146, E-mail: graduate.admissions@sru.edu.

Smith College, Graduate and Special Programs, Department of Education and Child Study, Program in Secondary Education, Northampton, MA 01063. Offers biological sciences education (MAT); chemistry education (MAT); English education (MAT); French education (MAT); geology education (MAT); government education (MAT); history education (MAT); mathematics education (MAT); physics education (MAT); Spanish education (MAT). Part-time programs available. *Faculty:* 6 full-time (4 women), 3 part-time/adjunct (2 women). *Students:* 11 full-time (8 women), 3 part-time (all women); includes 2 minority (1 Asian, non-Hispanic/Latino; 1 Hispanic/Latino). Average age 26. 21 applicants, 95% accepted, 12 enrolled. In 2011, 2 master's awarded. *Entrance requirements:* For master's, GRE. Additional exam requirements/recommendations for international students: Required—TOEFL (minimum score 590 paper-based; 243 computer-based; 97 iBT). *Application deadline:* For fall admission, 4/1 for domestic students, 1/15 for international students; for spring admission, 12/1 for domestic students. Application fee: $60. *Expenses: Tuition:* Full-time $14,925; part-time $1245 per credit. *Financial support:* In 2011–12, 13 students received support. Career-related internships or fieldwork, institutionally sponsored loans, and scholarships/grants available. Support available to part-time students. Financial award application deadline: 1/15; financial award applicants required to submit CSS PROFILE or FAFSA. *Unit head:* Rosetta Cohen, Graduate Student Advisor, 413-585-3266, E-mail: rcohen@smith.edu. *Application contact:* Ruth Morgan, Administrative Assistant, 413-585-3050, Fax: 413-585-3054, E-mail: gradstdy@smith.edu. Web site: http://www.smith.edu/educ/.

South Carolina State University, School of Graduate Studies, Department of Education, Orangeburg, SC 29117-0001. Offers counseling education (M Ed); early childhood and special education (M Ed); early childhood education (MAT); educational leadership (Ed D, Ed S); elementary education (M Ed, MAT); engineering (MAT); general science (MAT); mathematics (MAT); secondary education (M Ed), including biology education, business education, counselor education, English education, home economics education, industrial education, mathematics education, science education, social studies education; special education (M Ed), including emotionally handicapped, learning disabilities, mentally handicapped. *Accreditation:* NCATE. Part-time and evening/weekend programs available. *Faculty:* 9 full-time (6 women), 6 part-time/adjunct (2 women). *Students:* 34 full-time (29 women), 50 part-time (40 women); includes 74 minority (72 Black or African American, non-Hispanic/Latino; 1 Asian, non-Hispanic/Latino; 1 Hispanic/Latino). Average age 34. 23 applicants, 91% accepted, 14 enrolled. In 2011, 11 master's awarded. *Degree requirements:* For master's, thesis optional, departmental qualifying exam. *Entrance requirements:* For master's, GRE General Test, NTE, interview, teaching certificate. *Application deadline:* For fall admission, 6/15 priority date for domestic students, 6/15 for international students; for spring admission, 11/1 for domestic and international students. Applications are processed on a rolling basis. Application fee: $25. Electronic applications accepted. *Expenses:* Tuition, state resident: full-time $8688; part-time $514 per credit hour. Tuition, nonresident: full-time $17,600; part-time $1009 per credit hour. *Required fees:* $570. *Financial support:* In 2011–12, 3 fellowships (averaging $5,020 per year) were awarded; career-related internships or fieldwork, Federal Work-Study, and institutionally sponsored loans also available. Financial award application deadline: 6/1. *Faculty research:* Critical thinking, child abuse, stress, test-taking skills, conflict resolution, mainstreaming. *Unit head:* Dr. Charlie Spell, Interim Chair, 803-536-7098, Fax: 803-516-4568, E-mail: cspell@scsu.edu. *Application contact:* Annette Hazzard-Jones, Program Coordinator II, 803-536-8809, Fax: 803-536-8812, E-mail: zs_ahazzard@scsu.edu.

Southeast Missouri State University, School of Graduate Studies, Department of Educational Leadership and Counseling, Program in Educational Administration, Cape Girardeau, MO 63701-4799. Offers educational administration (Ed S); educational leadership development (Ed S); elementary administration and supervision (MA); higher education administration (MA); secondary administration and supervision (MA); teacher leadership (MA). *Accreditation:* NCATE. Part-time and evening/weekend programs available. Postbaccalaureate distance learning degree programs offered (minimal on-campus study). *Faculty:* 12 full-time (7 women). *Students:* 32 full-time (23 women), 172 part-time (122 women); includes 10 minority (6 Black or African American, non-Hispanic/Latino; 3 Asian, non-Hispanic/Latino; 1 Hispanic/Latino), 1 international. Average age 34. 62 applicants, 95% accepted, 51 enrolled. In 2011, 34 master's, 13 other advanced degrees awarded. *Degree requirements:* For master's, comprehensive exam (for some programs), thesis (for some programs), minimum GPA of 3.25; paper, portfolio or oral exam (for some programs); for Ed S, comprehensive exam. *Entrance requirements:* For master's, minimum undergraduate GPA of 2.75, valid teacher certification; for Ed S, GRE General Test, PRAXIS or MAT, minimum graduate GPA of 3.5; master's degree; valid teaching certificate. Additional exam requirements/recommendations for international students: Required—TOEFL (minimum score 550 paper-based; 213 computer-based; 79 iBT); Recommended—IELTS (minimum score 6). *Application deadline:* For fall admission, 8/1 for domestic students, 7/1 for international students; for spring admission, 11/21 for domestic students, 11/1 for international students. Applications are processed on a rolling basis. Application fee: $30 ($40 for international students). Electronic applications accepted. *Expenses:* Tuition, state resident: full-time $4896; part-time $272 per credit hour. Tuition, nonresident: full-time $8649; part-time $480.50 per credit hour. *Financial support:* In 2011–12, 16 students received support. Career-related internships or fieldwork, Federal Work-Study, scholarships/grants, tuition waivers (full), and unspecified assistantships available. Financial award application deadline: 6/30; financial award applicants required to submit FAFSA. *Faculty research:* Teacher leadership, organizational leadership effectiveness, state assessment and accountability systems. *Unit head:* Dr. David Stader, 573-651-2417, E-mail: dstader@semo.edu. *Application contact:* Alisa Aleen McFerron, Assistant Director of Admissions for Operations, 573-651-5937, Fax: 573-651-5936, E-mail: amcferron@semo.edu. Web site: http://www4.semo.edu/edadmin/admin.

Southeast Missouri State University, School of Graduate Studies, Department of Middle and Secondary Education, Cape Girardeau, MO 63701-4799. Offers secondary education (MA), including education studies, education technology. *Accreditation:* NCATE. Part-time and evening/weekend programs available. *Faculty:* 4 full-time (3 women). *Students:* 3 full-time (2 women), 18 part-time (14 women); includes 2 minority (both Black or African American, non-Hispanic/Latino), 1 international. Average age 30. 7 applicants, 86% accepted, 6 enrolled. In 2011, 12 master's awarded. *Degree requirements:* For master's, comprehensive exam, research paper. *Entrance requirements:* For master's, minimum undergraduate GPA of 2.75. Additional exam requirements/recommendations for international students: Required—TOEFL (minimum score 550 paper-based; 213 computer-based; 79 iBT); Recommended—IELTS (minimum score 6). *Application deadline:* For fall admission, 8/1 for domestic students, 7/1 for international students; for spring admission, 11/21 for domestic students, 11/1 for international students. Applications are processed on a rolling basis. Application fee: $30 ($40 for international students). Electronic applications accepted. *Expenses:* Tuition, state resident: full-time $4896; part-time $272 per credit hour. Tuition, nonresident: full-time $8649; part-time $480.50 per credit hour. *Financial support:* In 2011–12, 4 students received support. Career-related internships or fieldwork, Federal Work-Study, scholarships/grants, tuition waivers (full), and unspecified assistantships available. Financial award application deadline: 6/30; financial award applicants required to submit FAFSA. *Faculty research:* Pedagogy of teaching, multicultural education, reading and writing strategies, use of technology in the classroom. *Unit head:* Dr. Simin L. Cwick, Chairperson and Graduate Coordinator, 573-651-5965, Fax: 573-986-6141, E-mail: scwick@semo.edu. *Application contact:* Alisa Aleen McFerron, Assistant Director of Admissions for Operations, 573-651-5937, Fax: 573-651-5936, E-mail: amcferron@semo.edu. Web site: http://www5.semo.edu/middleandsec/.

Southern Arkansas University–Magnolia, Graduate Programs, Magnolia, AR 71754. Offers agriculture (MS); business administration (MBA); computer and information sciences (MS); education (M Ed), including counseling and development, curriculum and instruction, educational administration and supervision, elementary education, middle level, reading, secondary education, TESOL; kinesiology (M Ed); library media and information specialist (M Ed); mental health and clinical counseling (MS); public administration (MPA); school counseling (M Ed); teaching (MAT). *Accreditation:* NCATE. Part-time and evening/weekend programs available. Postbaccalaureate distance learning degree programs offered. *Faculty:* 34 full-time (15 women), 8 part-time/adjunct (5 women). *Students:* 87 full-time (62 women), 320 part-time (224 women); includes 116 minority (111 Black or African American, non-Hispanic/Latino; 2 American Indian or Alaska Native, non-Hispanic/Latino; 2 Asian, non-Hispanic/Latino; 1 Hispanic/Latino), 25 international. Average age 33. 201 applicants, 98% accepted, 156 enrolled. In 2011, 162 master's awarded. *Degree requirements:* For master's, comprehensive exam (for some programs), thesis optional. *Entrance requirements:* For master's, GRE, MAT or GMAT, minimum GPA of 2.5. Additional exam requirements/recommendations for international students: Required—TOEFL (minimum score 173 computer-based).

Secondary Education

Application deadline: For fall admission, 7/15 for domestic and international students; for winter admission, 12/1 for domestic and international students; for spring admission, 12/1 for domestic and international students. Applications are processed on a rolling basis. Application fee: $25 ($35 for international students). Electronic applications accepted. *Expenses:* Tuition, state resident: part-time $232 per credit. Tuition, nonresident: part-time $339 per credit. *Required fees:* $44 per credit. Part-time tuition and fees vary according to course load. *Financial support:* Career-related internships or fieldwork, Federal Work-Study, scholarships/grants, tuition waivers (full), and unspecified assistantships available. Financial award applicants required to submit FAFSA. *Faculty research:* Alternative certification for teachers, supervision of instruction, instructional leadership, counseling. *Unit head:* Dr. Kim Bloss, Dean, School of Graduate Studies, 870-235-4150, Fax: 870-235-5227, E-mail: kkbloss@saumag.edu. *Application contact:* Gaye Calhoun, Admissions Specialist, 870-235-4150, Fax: 870-235-5227, E-mail: glcalhoun@saumag.edu. Web site: http://www.saumag.edu/graduate.

Southern Illinois University Edwardsville, Graduate School, School of Education, Department of Curriculum and Instruction, Program in Secondary Education, Edwardsville, IL 62026. Offers art (MS Ed); biology (MS Ed); chemistry (MS Ed); earth and space sciences (MS Ed); English/language arts (MS Ed); foreign languages (MS Ed); history (MS Ed); mathematics (MS Ed); physics (MS Ed). *Accreditation:* NCATE. Part-time and evening/weekend programs available. *Students:* 1 full-time (0 women), 42 part-time (33 women); includes 2 minority (both Black or African American, non-Hispanic/Latino). 16 applicants, 31% accepted. In 2011, 8 master's awarded. *Degree requirements:* For master's, comprehensive exam (for some programs), final exam/paper. *Entrance requirements:* Additional exam requirements/recommendations for international students: Required—TOEFL (minimum score 550 paper-based; 213 computer-based; 79 iBT), IELTS (minimum score 6.5). *Application deadline:* For fall admission, 7/22 for domestic students, 6/1 for international students; for spring admission, 12/9 for domestic students, 10/1 for international students. Applications are processed on a rolling basis. Application fee: $30. Electronic applications accepted. Tuition and fees vary according to course load and program. *Financial support:* Fellowships, research assistantships, teaching assistantships, institutionally sponsored loans, scholarships/grants, and unspecified assistantships available. Financial award application deadline: 3/1; financial award applicants required to submit FAFSA. *Unit head:* Dr. Susan Breck, Director, 618-650-3444, E-mail: sbreck@siue.edu. *Application contact:* Dr. Michelle Robinson, Coordinator of Graduate Recruitment, 618-650-2811, Fax: 618-650-3523, E-mail: michero@siue.edu. Web site: http://www.siue.edu/education/ci/.

Southern New Hampshire University, School of Education, Manchester, NH 03106-1045. Offers business education (MS); child development (M Ed); computer technology education (Certificate); curriculum and instruction (M Ed); education (M Ed, CAS); elementary education (M Ed); general special education (Certificate); school business administrator (Certificate); secondary education (M Ed); training and development (Certificate). Part-time and evening/weekend programs available. Postbaccalaureate distance learning degree programs offered (no on-campus study). *Degree requirements:* For master's, comprehensive exam (for some programs), thesis or alternative. *Entrance requirements:* For master's, PRAXIS I, minimum GPA of 2.75. Additional exam requirements/recommendations for international students: Required—TOEFL (minimum score 550 paper-based; 213 computer-based). Electronic applications accepted. *Expenses:* Contact institution.

Southern Oregon University, Graduate Studies, School of Education, Ashland, OR 97520. Offers elementary education (MA Ed, MS Ed), including classroom teacher, early childhood, handicapped learner, reading, supervision; secondary education (MA Ed, MS Ed), including classroom teacher, handicapped learner, reading, supervision; teaching (MAT). *Faculty:* 18 full-time (10 women), 10 part-time/adjunct (all women). *Students:* 128 full-time (88 women), 145 part-time (103 women); includes 32 minority (1 Black or African American, non-Hispanic/Latino; 3 American Indian or Alaska Native, non-Hispanic/Latino; 5 Asian, non-Hispanic/Latino; 13 Hispanic/Latino; 3 Native Hawaiian or other Pacific Islander, non-Hispanic/Latino; 7 Two or more races, non-Hispanic/Latino), 1 international. Average age 35. 48 applicants, 60% accepted, 23 enrolled. In 2011, 102 degrees awarded. *Degree requirements:* For master's, thesis optional. *Entrance requirements:* For master's, GRE General Test, minimum GPA of 3.0. *Application deadline:* For fall admission, 2/1 for domestic students. Application fee: $50. Electronic applications accepted. *Expenses:* Tuition, state resident: full-time $12,600; part-time $350 per credit. Tuition, nonresident: full-time $16,200; part-time $450 per credit. *Required fees:* $1590. *Financial support:* Research assistantships with partial tuition reimbursements available. *Unit head:* Dr. Geoff Mills, Dean, 541-552-6920, E-mail: mills@sou.edu. *Application contact:* Mark Bottorff, Director of Admissions, 541-552-6411, Fax: 541-552-8403, E-mail: admissions@sou.edu. Web site: http://www.sou.edu/education/.

Southern University and Agricultural and Mechanical College, Graduate School, College of Education, Department of Curriculum and Instruction, Baton Rouge, LA 70813. Offers elementary education (M Ed); media (M Ed); secondary education (M Ed). *Degree requirements:* For master's, comprehensive exam, thesis optional. *Entrance requirements:* For master's, GMAT or GRE General Test. Additional exam requirements/recommendations for international students: Required—TOEFL (minimum score 525 paper-based; 193 computer-based).

Southwestern Assemblies of God University, Thomas F. Harrison School of Graduate Studies, Program in Education, Waxahachie, TX 75165-5735. Offers Christian school administration (MS); curriculum development (MS); early education administration (M Ed); middle and secondary education (M Ed). *Degree requirements:* For master's, comprehensive written and oral exams. *Entrance requirements:* For master's, GRE General Test, minimum GPA of 2.5. Electronic applications accepted.

Southwestern Oklahoma State University, College of Professional and Graduate Studies, School of Behavioral Sciences and Education, Weatherford, OK 73096-3098. Offers community counseling (M Ed); early childhood education (M Ed); educational administration (M Ed); elementary education (M Ed); health sciences and microbiology (M Ed); kinesiology (M Ed); parks and recreation management (M Ed); school counseling (M Ed); school psychology (MS); school psychometry (M Ed); secondary education (M Ed); special education (M Ed). *Accreditation:* NCATE. Part-time and evening/weekend programs available. Postbaccalaureate distance learning degree programs offered (minimal on-campus study). *Degree requirements:* For master's, exam. *Entrance requirements:* For master's, GRE General Test or minimum undergraduate GPA of 3.0. Additional exam requirements/recommendations for international students: Required—TOEFL.

Spalding University, Graduate Studies, College of Education, Programs in Education, Louisville, KY 40203-2188. Offers elementary school education (MAT); general education (MA); high school education (MAT); middle school education (MAT); school administration (MA); special education (learning and behavioral disorders) (MAT); student guidance counselor (MA). MAT programs offered for first teaching certificate/license students. *Accreditation:* NCATE. Part-time and evening/weekend programs available. *Faculty:* 9 full-time (6 women), 32 part-time/adjunct (20 women). *Students:* 142 full-time (100 women), 71 part-time (53 women); includes 75 minority (65 Black or African American, non-Hispanic/Latino; 1 American Indian or Alaska Native, non-Hispanic/Latino; 6 Hispanic/Latino; 3 Two or more races, non-Hispanic/Latino). Average age 36. 96 applicants, 44% accepted, 41 enrolled. In 2011, 69 master's awarded. *Degree requirements:* For master's, portfolio, final project, clinical experience. *Entrance requirements:* For master's, GRE General Test or MAT, interview, recommendations, resume. Additional exam requirements/recommendations for international students: Required—TOEFL (minimum score 535 paper-based; 203 computer-based). *Application deadline:* Applications are processed on a rolling basis. Application fee: $30. Electronic applications accepted. *Expenses: Tuition:* Full-time $12,438. Tuition and fees vary according to course load, degree level and program. *Financial support:* In 2011–12, 72 students received support, including 3 research assistantships with partial tuition reimbursements available (averaging $4,490 per year); scholarships/grants, traineeships, and unspecified assistantships also available. Financial award application deadline: 3/15; financial award applicants required to submit FAFSA. *Faculty research:* Instructional technology, achievement gap, classroom management, assessment. *Unit head:* Dr. Beverly Keepers, Dean, 502-588-7121, Fax: 502-585-7123, E-mail: bkeepers@spalding.edu. *Application contact:* Bonnie Caughron, 502-873-4262, E-mail: bcaughron@spalding.edu.

Springfield College, Graduate Programs, Program in Education, Springfield, MA 01109-3797. Offers counseling and secondary education (M Ed, MS); early childhood education (M Ed, MS); education (M Ed, MS); educational administration (M Ed, MS); educational studies (M Ed, MS); elementary education (M Ed, MS); secondary education (M Ed, MS); special education (M Ed, MS). Part-time and evening/weekend programs available. *Entrance requirements:* Additional exam requirements/recommendations for international students: Required—TOEFL (minimum score 550 paper-based; 213 computer-based). Electronic applications accepted.

Spring Hill College, Graduate Programs, Program in Education, Mobile, AL 36608-1791. Offers early childhood education (MAT, MS Ed); educational theory (MS Ed); elementary education (MAT, MS Ed); secondary education (MAT, MS Ed). Part-time programs available. *Faculty:* 3 full-time (2 women), 3 part-time/adjunct (all women). *Students:* 7 full-time (6 women), 21 part-time (18 women); includes 7 minority (6 Black or African American, non-Hispanic/Latino; 1 Asian, non-Hispanic/Latino). Average age 31. In 2011, 13 master's awarded. *Degree requirements:* For master's, comprehensive exam, completion of program within 6 calendar years of entrance into graduate studies at Spring Hill; documentation of course field assignments (MS) or completion of internship (MAT). *Entrance requirements:* For master's, GRE, MAT, or PRAXIS (varies by program), bachelor's degree with minimum undergraduate GPA of 3.0; class B certificate (MS) or minimum number of hours in specific fields (MAT). Additional exam requirements/recommendations for international students: Required—TOEFL (minimum score 550 paper-based; 213 computer-based; 80 iBT), IELTS (minimum score 6.5), CPE or CAE (minimum score C),Michigan English Language Assessment Battery (minimum score 90). *Application deadline:* For fall admission, 8/1 priority date for domestic students, 8/1 for international students; for spring admission, 12/1 priority date for domestic students, 12/1 for international students. Applications are processed on a rolling basis. Application fee: $25 ($35 for international students). Electronic applications accepted. *Expenses:* Contact institution. *Financial support:* Applicants required to submit FAFSA. *Unit head:* Dr. Ann A. Adams, Chair of Teacher Education, 251-380-3479, Fax: 251-460-2184, E-mail: aadams@shc.edu. *Application contact:* Donna B. Tarasavage, Director of Admissions, Graduate and Continuing Studies, 251-380-3067, Fax: 251-460-2190, E-mail: dtarasavage@shc.edu. Web site: http://www.shc.edu/grad/academics/teaching.

State University of New York at Binghamton, Graduate School, School of Education, Program in Adolescence Education, Binghamton, NY 13902-6000. Offers biology education (MAT, MS Ed, MST); earth science education (MAT, MS Ed, MST); English education (MAT, MS Ed, MST); French education (MAT, MST); mathematical sciences education (MAT, MS Ed, MST); physics (MAT, MS Ed, MST); social studies (MAT, MS Ed, MST); Spanish education (MAT, MST). *Accreditation:* Teacher Education Accreditation Council. Part-time and evening/weekend programs available. *Students:* 98 full-time (66 women), 13 part-time (11 women); includes 2 minority (1 Black or African American, non-Hispanic/Latino; 1 Hispanic/Latino). Average age 26. 73 applicants, 70% accepted, 35 enrolled. In 2011, 58 master's awarded. *Entrance requirements:* For master's, GRE General Test. Additional exam requirements/recommendations for international students: Required—TOEFL (minimum score 550 paper-based; 213 computer-based; 80 iBT). *Application deadline:* For fall admission, 2/1 priority date for domestic students, 2/1 for international students; for spring admission, 10/15 priority date for domestic students, 10/15 for international students. Applications are processed on a rolling basis. Application fee: $60. Electronic applications accepted. *Financial support:* In 2011–12, 4 students received support, including 1 fellowship with partial tuition reimbursement available (averaging $12,000 per year); career-related internships or fieldwork, Federal Work-Study, institutionally sponsored loans, scholarships/grants, health care benefits, tuition waivers (full), and unspecified assistantships also available. Financial award application deadline: 2/15; financial award applicants required to submit FAFSA. *Unit head:* Dr. S. G. Grant, Dean of School of Education, 607-777-7329, E-mail: sggrant@binghamton.edu. *Application contact:* Catherine Smith, Recruiting and Admissions Coordinator, 607-777-2151, Fax: 607-777-2501, E-mail: cmsmith@binghamton.edu.

State University of New York at Fredonia, Graduate Studies, College of Education, Program in Secondary Education, Fredonia, NY 14063-1136. Offers MS Ed. *Accreditation:* NCATE. Part-time and evening/weekend programs available. *Degree requirements:* For master's, thesis optional. *Expenses:* Tuition, state resident: full-time $6666; part-time $370 per credit hour. Tuition, nonresident: full-time $11,376; part-time $632 per credit hour. *Required fees:* $1059.30; $58.85 per credit hour. Tuition and fees vary according to course load.

State University of New York at New Paltz, Graduate School, School of Education, Department of Educational Studies, Program in Special Education, New Paltz, NY 12561. Offers adolescence (7-12) (MS Ed); adolescence special education and literacy education (MS Ed); childhood (1-6) (MS Ed); childhood special education and literacy education (MS Ed); early childhood (B-2) (MS Ed). *Accreditation:* NCATE. Part-time and evening/weekend programs available. *Faculty:* 6 full-time (4 women), 4 part-time/adjunct (all women). *Students:* 36 full-time (33 women), 54 part-time (44 women); includes 8 minority (5 Black or African American, non-Hispanic/Latino; 2 Asian, non-Hispanic/Latino; 1 Native Hawaiian or other Pacific Islander, non-Hispanic/Latino). Average age 29. 67 applicants, 73% accepted, 40 enrolled. In 2011, 44 master's awarded. *Degree requirements:* For master's, portfolio. *Entrance requirements:* For master's, minimum GPA of 3.0 (3.2 for special education and literacy programs), New York state teaching certificate. Additional exam requirements/recommendations for international students: Required—TOEFL (minimum score 550 paper-based; 213 computer-based; 80 iBT), IELTS (minimum score 6.5). *Application deadline:* For fall admission, 3/15 priority date for domestic students, 3/15 for international students; for spring admission, 11/1 for domestic and international students. Application fee: $50. Electronic applications accepted. *Expenses:* Tuition, state resident: full-time $8870; part-time $370 per credit. Tuition, nonresident: full-time $15,160; part-time $632 per credit. *Required fees:* $1188; $34 per credit. $184 per semester. *Financial support:* In 2011–12, 2 students received support, including 2 fellowships (averaging $3,750 per year); career-related internships or fieldwork, Federal Work-Study, institutionally sponsored loans, and tuition waivers (full) also available. Financial award application deadline: 8/1; financial award applicants required to submit FAFSA. *Unit head:* Dr. Spencer Salend, Coordinator, 845-257-2831, E-mail: salends@newpaltz.edu. *Application contact:* Dr. Catherine Whittaker, Coordinator, 845-257-2831, E-mail: whittakc@newpaltz.edu.

State University of New York at New Paltz, Graduate School, School of Education, Department of Secondary Education, New Paltz, NY 12561. Offers adolescence education: biology (MAT, MS Ed); adolescence education: chemistry (MAT, MS Ed); adolescence education: earth science (MAT, MS Ed); adolescence education: English (MAT, MS Ed); adolescence education: French (MAT, MS Ed); adolescence education: social studies (MAT, MS Ed); adolescence education: Spanish (MAT, MS Ed); second language education (MS Ed). *Accreditation:* NCATE. Part-time and evening/weekend programs available. *Faculty:* 18 full-time (10 women), 2 part-time/adjunct (both women). *Students:* 79 full-time (48 women), 76 part-time (55 women); includes 30 minority (3 Black or African American, non-Hispanic/Latino; 2 Asian, non-Hispanic/Latino; 22 Hispanic/Latino; 3 Two or more races, non-Hispanic/Latino), 1 international. Average age 32. 127 applicants, 69% accepted, 64 enrolled. In 2011, 73 master's awarded. *Degree requirements:* For master's, comprehensive exam (for some programs), portfolio. *Entrance requirements:* For master's, minimum GPA of 3.0, New York state teaching certificate (MS Ed). Additional exam requirements/recommendations for international students: Required—TOEFL (minimum score 550 paper-based; 213 computer-based; 80 iBT), IELTS (minimum score 6.5). *Application deadline:* For fall admission, 3/1 priority date for domestic students, 3/1 for international students; for spring admission, 10/1 priority date for domestic students, 10/1 for international students. Application fee: $50. Electronic applications accepted. *Expenses:* Tuition, state resident: full-time $8870; part-time $370 per credit. Tuition, nonresident: full-time $15,160; part-time $632 per credit. *Required fees:* $1188; $34 per credit. $184 per semester. *Financial support:* In 2011–12, 13 students received support, including 3 fellowships with partial tuition reimbursements available (averaging $7,000 per year); Federal Work-Study, institutionally sponsored loans, and tuition waivers (full) also available. Financial award application deadline: 8/1; financial award applicants required to submit FAFSA. *Unit head:* Dr. Devon Duhaney, Chair, 845-257-2850, E-mail: duhaneyd@newpaltz.edu. *Application contact:* Caroline Murphy, Graduate Admissions Advisor, 845-257-3285, Fax: 845-257-3284, E-mail: gradschool@newpaltz.edu. Web site: http://www.newpaltz.edu/secondaryed/.

State University of New York at Oswego, Graduate Studies, School of Education, Department of Curriculum and Instruction, Oswego, NY 13126. Offers adolescence education (MST); art education (MAT); childhood education (MST); elementary education (MS Ed); literacy education (MS Ed); secondary education (MS Ed); special education (MS Ed). Part-time and evening/weekend programs available. *Degree requirements:* For master's, comprehensive exam (for some programs), thesis optional. *Entrance requirements:* For master's, GRE General Test, minimum GPA of 2.7, provisional teaching certificate. Additional exam requirements/recommendations for international students: Required—TOEFL (minimum score 560 paper-based; 220 computer-based). *Faculty research:* Classroom applications for microcomputers; classroom questioning, wait-time, and achievement; values clarification and academic achievement.

State University of New York at Plattsburgh, Division of Education, Health, and Human Services, Program in Teacher Education: Adolescence MST, Plattsburgh, NY 12901-2681. Offers adolescence education (MST); biology 7-12 (MST); chemistry 7-12 (MST); earth science 7-12 (MST); English 7-12 (MST); French 7-12 (MST); mathematics 7-12 (MST); physics 7-12 (MST); social studies 7-12 (MST); Spanish 7-12 (MST). *Accreditation:* Teacher Education Accreditation Council. Part-time and evening/weekend programs available. *Students:* 53 full-time (26 women), 5 part-time (4 women). Average age 29. *Entrance requirements:* For master's, minimum GPA of 2.75. Additional exam requirements/recommendations for international students: Required—TOEFL. *Application deadline:* For fall admission, 2/15 priority date for domestic students. Applications are processed on a rolling basis. Application fee: $75. *Financial support:* Application deadline: 4/15; applicants required to submit FAFSA. *Unit head:* Dr. Robert Ackland, Coordinator, 518-564-5131, E-mail: acklanrt@plattsburgh.edu. *Application contact:* Marguerite Adelman, Assistant Director, Graduate Admissions, 518-564-4723, Fax: 518-564-4722, E-mail: adelmaml@plattsburgh.edu.

State University of New York College at Cortland, Graduate Studies, School of Arts and Sciences, Programs in Adolescence Education, Cortland, NY 13045. Offers biology (MAT, MS Ed); chemistry (MAT, MS Ed); earth science (MAT, MS Ed); English (MS Ed); French (MS Ed); mathematics (MAT, MS Ed); physics (MAT, MS Ed); social studies (MS Ed); Spanish (MS Ed). *Accreditation:* NCATE. Part-time and evening/weekend programs available. *Degree requirements:* For master's, one foreign language, comprehensive exam (for some programs), thesis (for some programs). *Entrance requirements:* For master's, GRE General Test.

State University of New York College at Geneseo, Graduate Studies, School of Education, Program in Secondary Education, Geneseo, NY 14454-1401. Offers MS Ed. Part-time and evening/weekend programs available. *Degree requirements:* For master's, thesis optional.

State University of New York College at Oneonta, Graduate Education, Division of Education, Department of Secondary Education, Oneonta, NY 13820-4015. Offers adolescence education (MS Ed); family and consumer science education (MS Ed). *Accreditation:* NCATE. Part-time and evening/weekend programs available. *Entrance requirements:* For master's, GRE General Test.

State University of New York College at Potsdam, School of Education and Professional Studies, Program in Secondary Education, Potsdam, NY 13676. Offers English (MST); mathematics (with grades 5-6 extension) (MST); science (MST), including biology, chemistry, earth science, physics; Social Studies (with grades 5-6 extension) (MST). *Accreditation:* NCATE. *Faculty:* 9 full-time (3 women), 3 part-time/adjunct (2 women). *Students:* 32 full-time (17 women), 1 part-time (0 women); includes 2 minority (1 Black or African American, non-Hispanic/Latino; 1 Asian, non-Hispanic/Latino), 3 international. 43 applicants, 88% accepted, 24 enrolled. In 2011, 43 master's awarded. *Degree requirements:* For master's, culminating experience. *Entrance requirements:* For master's, minimum GPA of 2.75 in last 60 hours of course work (3.0 for English program). Additional exam requirements/recommendations for international students: Required—TOEFL (minimum score 550 paper-based; 213 computer-based; 80 iBT), IELTS (minimum score 6). *Application deadline:* For spring admission, 3/1 for domestic and international students. Applications are processed on a rolling basis. Application fee: $50. *Expenses:* Tuition, state resident: full-time $8870; part-time $370 per credit hour. Tuition, nonresident: full-time $15,160; part-time $632 per credit hour. *Required fees:* $1066; $44.10 per credit hour. One-time fee: $3. *Financial support:* Fellowships, teaching assistantships, career-related internships or fieldwork, Federal Work-Study, scholarships/grants, and unspecified assistantships available. Support available to part-time students. Financial award application deadline: 3/1; financial award applicants required to submit FAFSA. *Unit head:* Donald C. Straight, Chairperson, 315-267-2553, Fax: 315-267-4802, E-mail: straigdc@potsdam.edu. *Application contact:* Peter Cutler, Graduate Admissions Counselor, 315-267-2165, Fax: 315-267-4802, E-mail: graduate@potsdam.edu. Web site: http://www.potsdam.edu/academics/SOEPS/SecondaryEd/index.cfm.

Stephen F. Austin State University, Graduate School, College of Education, Department of Secondary Education and Educational Leadership, Nacogdoches, TX 75962. Offers educational leadership (Ed D); secondary education (M Ed). *Accreditation:* NCATE. *Degree requirements:* For master's, comprehensive exam; for doctorate, thesis/dissertation. *Entrance requirements:* For master's, GRE General Test; for doctorate, GRE General Test, interview, writing sample. Additional exam requirements/recommendations for international students: Required—TOEFL. Electronic applications accepted.

Suffolk University, College of Arts and Sciences, Department of Education and Human Services, Boston, MA 02108-2770. Offers administration of higher education (M Ed, CAGS), including administration of higher education (M Ed), leadership (CAGS); human resource, learning and performance (MS, CAGS, Graduate Certificate), including global human resources (Graduate Certificate), human resources (MS, Graduate Certificate), organizational development (CAGS, Graduate Certificate), organizational learning and development (MS, Graduate Certificate); mental health counseling (MS, CAGS); school counseling (M Ed, CAGS); school teaching (M Ed, CAGS), including foundations of education (M Ed), middle school teaching (M Ed), secondary school teaching (M Ed); MPA/MSMHC; MS/Certificate. Part-time and evening/weekend programs available. *Faculty:* 10 full-time (6 women), 7 part-time/adjunct (3 women). *Students:* 53 full-time (39 women), 131 part-time (112 women); includes 21 minority (7 Black or African American, non-Hispanic/Latino; 2 American Indian or Alaska Native, non-Hispanic/Latino; 5 Asian, non-Hispanic/Latino; 5 Hispanic/Latino; 2 Two or more races, non-Hispanic/Latino), 9 international. Average age 28. 158 applicants, 73% accepted, 60 enrolled. In 2011, 72 master's, 8 other advanced degrees awarded. *Entrance requirements:* For master's, GRE General Test or MAT, 2 letters of recommendation, resume. Additional exam requirements/recommendations for international students: Required—TOEFL (minimum score 550 paper-based; 213 computer-based; 80 iBT). *Application deadline:* For fall admission, 6/15 priority date for domestic students, 6/15 for international students; for spring admission, 11/1 priority date for domestic students, 11/1 for international students. Applications are processed on a rolling basis. Application fee: $50. Electronic applications accepted. *Expenses:* Contact institution. *Financial support:* In 2011–12, 102 students received support, including 30 fellowships with full and partial tuition reimbursements available (averaging $10,664 per year); career-related internships or fieldwork, Federal Work-Study, and institutionally sponsored loans also available. Support available to part-time students. Financial award application deadline: 4/1; financial award applicants required to submit FAFSA. *Faculty research:* Predicting competent Head Start preschools, cultural differences. *Unit head:* Dr. Krisanne Bursik, Associate Dean and Acting Chair, 617-573-8261, Fax: 617-305-1743, E-mail: kbursik@suffolk.edu. *Application contact:* Ellen Driscoll, Director of Graduate Admissions, 617-573-8302, Fax: 617-305-1733, E-mail: grad.admission@suffolk.edu. Web site: http://www.suffolk.edu/college/9785.html.

Sul Ross State University, Rio Grande College of Sul Ross State University, Alpine, TX 79832. Offers business administration (MBA); teacher education (M Ed), including bilingual education, counseling, educational diagnostics, elementary education, general education, reading, school administration, secondary education. Part-time and evening/weekend programs available. Postbaccalaureate distance learning degree programs offered (no on-campus study). *Faculty:* 11 full-time (3 women), 4 part-time/adjunct (3 women). *Students:* 45 full-time (36 women), 255 part-time (168 women); includes 218 minority (2 Black or African American, non-Hispanic/Latino; 1 American Indian or Alaska Native, non-Hispanic/Latino; 215 Hispanic/Latino), 1 international. Average age 36. In 2011, 47 master's awarded. *Degree requirements:* For master's, comprehensive exam, thesis optional, minimum GPA of 3.0. *Entrance requirements:* For master's, GMAT or GRE General Test, minimum GPA of 2.5 in last 60 hours of undergraduate work. Additional exam requirements/recommendations for international students: Required—TOEFL. *Application deadline:* Applications are processed on a rolling basis. Application fee: $0 ($50 for international students). *Financial support:* Career-related internships or fieldwork, Federal Work-Study, and institutionally sponsored loans available. Support available to part-time students. Financial award application deadline: 5/1; financial award applicants required to submit FAFSA. *Unit head:* Dr. Paul Sorrels, Associate Provost/Dean, 512-278-3339, Fax: 512-278-3330. *Application contact:* Claudia R. Wright, Director of Admissions and Records, 915-837-8050, Fax: 915-837-8431, E-mail: rcullins@sulross.edu.

Sul Ross State University, School of Professional Studies, Department of Teacher Education, Program in Secondary Education, Alpine, TX 79832. Offers M Ed. Part-time and evening/weekend programs available. *Degree requirements:* For master's, thesis optional. *Entrance requirements:* For master's, GMAT or GRE General Test, minimum GPA of 2.5 in last 60 hours of undergraduate work.

Tarleton State University, College of Graduate Studies, College of Education, Department of Psychology and Counseling, Stephenville, TX 76402. Offers counseling and psychology (M Ed), including counseling, counseling psychology, educational psychology; educational administration (M Ed); secondary education (Certificate); special education (Certificate). Part-time and evening/weekend programs available. Postbaccalaureate distance learning degree programs offered (minimal on-campus study). *Faculty:* 8 full-time (5 women), 13 part-time/adjunct (6 women). *Students:* 73 full-time (62 women), 219 part-time (186 women); includes 55 minority (25 Black or African American, non-Hispanic/Latino; 1 American Indian or Alaska Native, non-Hispanic/Latino; 1 Asian, non-Hispanic/Latino; 22 Hispanic/Latino; 1 Native Hawaiian or other Pacific Islander, non-Hispanic/Latino; 5 Two or more races, non-Hispanic/Latino), 1 international. Average age 35. 92 applicants, 91% accepted, 62 enrolled. In 2011, 65 master's awarded. *Degree requirements:* For master's, comprehensive exam, thesis optional. *Entrance requirements:* For master's, GRE General Test, minimum GPA of 3.0. Additional exam requirements/recommendations for international students: Required—TOEFL (minimum score 550 paper-based; 213 computer-based; 80 iBT). *Application deadline:* For fall admission, 8/5 priority date for domestic students; for spring admission, 12/1 for domestic students. Applications are processed on a rolling basis. Application fee: $30 ($130 for international students). Electronic applications accepted. *Expenses:* Tuition, state resident: full-time $3131.46; part-time $174 per credit hour. Tuition, nonresident: full-time $8225; part-time $457 per credit hour. *Required fees:* $1446. Tuition and fees vary according to course load and campus/location. *Financial support:* Research assistantships, teaching assistantships, career-related internships or fieldwork, Federal Work-Study, institutionally sponsored loans, and tuition waivers (partial) available. Support available to part-time students. Financial award application deadline: 5/1; financial award applicants required to submit FAFSA. *Unit head:* Dr. Bob Newby, Interim Department Head, 254-968-9813, Fax: 254-968-1991, E-mail: newby@tarleton.edu. *Application contact:* Information Contact, 254-968-9104, Fax: 254-968-9670, E-mail: gradoffice@tarleton.edu. Web site: http://www.tarleton.edu/~dpc.

Tennessee Technological University, Graduate School, College of Education, Department of Curriculum and Instruction, Program in Secondary Education, Cookeville, TN 38505. Offers MA, Ed S. *Accreditation:* NCATE. Part-time and evening/weekend programs available. *Faculty:* 7 full-time (0 women). *Students:* 28 full-time (13 women), 43 part-time (23 women); includes 6 minority (4 Black or African American, non-

Hispanic/Latino; 2 Hispanic/Latino), 1 international. Average age 27. 26 applicants, 96% accepted, 20 enrolled. In 2011, 16 master's, 3 other advanced degrees awarded. *Degree requirements:* For master's and Ed S, comprehensive exam, thesis or alternative. *Entrance requirements:* For master's and Ed S, MAT or GRE. Additional exam requirements/recommendations for international students: Required—TOEFL (minimum score 550 paper-based; 71 iBT), IELTS (minimum score 5.5), Pearson Test of English Academic. *Application deadline:* For fall admission, 8/1 for domestic students, 5/1 for international students; for spring admission, 12/1 for domestic students, 10/1 for international students. Application fee: $25 ($30 for international students). Electronic applications accepted. *Expenses:* Tuition, state resident: full-time $8094; part-time $422 per credit hour. Tuition, nonresident: full-time $20,574; part-time $1046 per credit hour. *Financial support:* In 2011–12, 1 fellowship (averaging $8,000 per year), 1 research assistantship (averaging $4,000 per year), 1 teaching assistantship (averaging $4,000 per year) were awarded; career-related internships or fieldwork also available. Financial award application deadline: 4/1. *Unit head:* Dr. Susan Gore, Interim Chairperson, 931-372-3181, Fax: 931-372-6270, E-mail: sgore@tntech.edu. *Application contact:* Shelia K. Kendrick, Coordinator of Graduate Admissions, 931-372-3808, Fax: 931-372-3497, E-mail: skendrick@tntech.edu.

Texas A&M University–Commerce, Graduate School, College of Education and Human Services, Department of Curriculum and Instruction, Commerce, TX 75429-3011. Offers bilingual/ESL education (M Ed, MS); early childhood education (M Ed, MS); elementary education (M Ed, MS); reading (M Ed, MS); secondary education (M Ed, MS); supervision, curriculum and instruction: elementary education (Ed D). MS and M Ed programs in early childhood education offered jointly with Texas Woman's University and University of North Texas. Part-time programs available. Terminal master's awarded for partial completion of doctoral program. *Degree requirements:* For master's, comprehensive exam, thesis (for some programs); for doctorate, 2 foreign languages, thesis/dissertation, departmental qualifying exam. *Entrance requirements:* For master's and doctorate, GRE General Test. Electronic applications accepted. *Faculty research:* Literacy and learning, early childhood, preservice teacher education, technology.

Texas A&M University–Corpus Christi, Graduate Studies and Research, College of Education, Program in Secondary Education, Corpus Christi, TX 78412-5503. Offers MS. Part-time and evening/weekend programs available. *Degree requirements:* For master's, comprehensive exam, thesis (for some programs). *Entrance requirements:* For master's, GRE General Test. Additional exam requirements/recommendations for international students: Required—TOEFL. Electronic applications accepted.

Texas A&M University–Kingsville, College of Graduate Studies, College of Education, Department of Education, Program in Secondary Education, Kingsville, TX 78363. Offers MA, MS. Part-time and evening/weekend programs available. *Degree requirements:* For master's, comprehensive exam, thesis or alternative, research report. *Entrance requirements:* For master's, GRE General Test, MAT, minimum GPA of 3.0. *Faculty research:* Professional development/technology, interdisciplinary teaming, educational restructuring.

Texas Christian University, College of Education, Program in Secondary Education (Four-One Option), Fort Worth, TX 76129-0002. Offers M Ed. Part-time and evening/weekend programs available. *Faculty:* 27 full-time (21 women), 1 part-time/adjunct. *Students:* 6 full-time (4 women); includes 1 minority (Asian, non-Hispanic/Latino). Average age 22. 2 applicants, 100% accepted, 2 enrolled. In 2011, 3 master's awarded. *Degree requirements:* For master's, oral exam. *Entrance requirements:* Additional exam requirements/recommendations for international students: Required—TOEFL (minimum score 550 paper-based; 213 computer-based; 80 iBT). *Application deadline:* For fall admission, 11/15 for domestic and international students; for spring admission, 3/1 for domestic and international students. Application fee: $60. Electronic applications accepted. *Expenses: Tuition:* Full-time $20,250; part-time $1125 per credit hour. Part-time tuition and fees vary according to course load and program. *Financial support:* Teaching assistantships with full tuition reimbursements, career-related internships or fieldwork, scholarships/grants, and unspecified assistantships available. Financial award application deadline: 3/1; financial award applicants required to submit FAFSA. *Unit head:* Dr. Jan Lacina, Associate Dean, 817-257-6786, E-mail: j.lacina@tcu.edu. *Application contact:* Patricia Garcia, Academic Program Specialist, 817-257-7661, E-mail: p.m.garcia@tcu.edu.

Texas Southern University, College of Education, Area of Curriculum and Instruction, Houston, TX 77004-4584. Offers bilingual education (M Ed); curriculum and instruction (Ed D); secondary education (M Ed). Part-time and evening/weekend programs available. *Degree requirements:* For master's, comprehensive exam; for doctorate, comprehensive exam, thesis/dissertation. *Entrance requirements:* For master's, GRE General Test, minimum GPA of 2.5; for doctorate, GRE General Test or MAT, master's degree, minimum B+ average. Additional exam requirements/recommendations for international students: Required—TOEFL. Electronic applications accepted.

Texas State University–San Marcos, Graduate School, College of Education, Department of Curriculum and Instruction, Program in Secondary Education, San Marcos, TX 78666. Offers M Ed, MA. Part-time and evening/weekend programs available. *Faculty:* 18 full-time (14 women), 10 part-time/adjunct (all women). *Students:* 61 full-time (38 women), 68 part-time (49 women); includes 31 minority (6 Black or African American, non-Hispanic/Latino; 1 American Indian or Alaska Native, non-Hispanic/Latino; 5 Asian, non-Hispanic/Latino; 17 Hispanic/Latino; 2 Two or more races, non-Hispanic/Latino), 1 international. Average age 32. 73 applicants, 75% accepted, 37 enrolled. In 2011, 64 master's awarded. *Degree requirements:* For master's, comprehensive exam, thesis (for some programs). *Entrance requirements:* For master's, GRE General Test, minimum GPA of 2.75 in last 60 hours of course work, teaching experience. Additional exam requirements/recommendations for international students: Required—TOEFL (minimum score 550 paper-based; 213 computer-based; 78 iBT). *Application deadline:* For fall admission, 6/15 priority date for domestic students, 6/1 for international students; for spring admission, 10/15 priority date for domestic students, 10/1 for international students. Applications are processed on a rolling basis. Application fee: $40 ($90 for international students). Electronic applications accepted. *Expenses:* Tuition, state resident: full-time $6408; part-time $3204 per semester. Tuition, nonresident: full-time $14,832; part-time $7416 per semester. *Required fees:* $1824; $912 per semester. Tuition and fees vary according to course load. *Financial support:* In 2011–12, 104 students received support, including 14 research assistantships (averaging $21,627 per year), 4 teaching assistantships (averaging $9,171 per year); career-related internships or fieldwork, Federal Work-Study, and institutionally sponsored loans also available. Support available to part-time students. Financial award application deadline: 4/1; financial award applicants required to submit FAFSA. *Faculty research:* Gifted and talented education, general secondary education, induction of first-year teachers. *Unit head:* Dr. Gene Martin, Graduate Advisor, 512-245-2157, Fax: 512-245-7911, E-mail: gm01@txstate.edu. *Application contact:* Dr. J. Michael Willoughby, Dean of Graduate School, 512-245-2581, Fax: 512-245-8365, E-mail: gradcollege@txstate.edu. Web site: http://www.education.txstate.edu/ci/degrees-programs/graduate.html.

Texas Tech University, Graduate School, College of Education, Department of Curriculum and Instruction, Lubbock, TX 79409. Offers bilingual education (M Ed); curriculum and instruction (M Ed, PhD); elementary education (M Ed); language/literacy education (M Ed); secondary education (M Ed). *Accreditation:* NCATE. Part-time programs available. *Students:* 69 full-time (50 women), 115 part-time (91 women); includes 62 minority (9 Black or African American, non-Hispanic/Latino; 3 Asian, non-Hispanic/Latino; 47 Hispanic/Latino; 3 Two or more races, non-Hispanic/Latino), 18 international. Average age 34. 95 applicants, 41% accepted, 26 enrolled. In 2011, 62 master's, 9 doctorates awarded. *Degree requirements:* For master's, comprehensive written exam with 36 hours of course credit or thesis (6 hours) with 30 hours of course credit; for doctorate, thesis/dissertation. *Entrance requirements:* For doctorate, GRE General Test. Additional exam requirements/recommendations for international students: Required—TOEFL (minimum score 550 paper-based; 213 computer-based; 79 iBT). *Application deadline:* For fall admission, 6/1 priority date for domestic students, 1/15 for international students; for spring admission, 9/1 priority date for domestic students, 6/15 for international students. Applications are processed on a rolling basis. Application fee: $50 ($75 for international students). Electronic applications accepted. *Expenses:* Tuition, state resident: full-time $5899; part-time $245.80 per credit hour. Tuition, nonresident: full-time $13,411; part-time $558.80 per credit hour. *Required fees:* $2680.60; $86.50 per credit hour. $920.30 per semester. *Financial support:* In 2011–12, 58 students received support. Application deadline: 4/15; applicants required to submit FAFSA. *Faculty research:* Multicultural foundations of education, teacher education, instruction and pedagogy in subject areas, curriculum theory, language and literary. *Total annual research expenditures:* $948,943. *Unit head:* Dr. Margaret A. Price, Interim Chair, 806-742-1997 Ext. 318, Fax: 806-742-2179, E-mail: peggie.price@ttu.edu. *Application contact:* Stephenie Allyn McDaniel, Administrative Assistant, 806-742-1988 Ext. 434, Fax: 806-742-2179, E-mail: stephenie.mcdaniel@ttu.edu.

Towson University, Program in Secondary Education, Towson, MD 21252-0001. Offers M Ed. *Accreditation:* NCATE. Part-time and evening/weekend programs available. *Students:* 1 (woman) full-time, 36 part-time (27 women); includes 7 minority (5 Black or African American, non-Hispanic/Latino; 2 Two or more races, non-Hispanic/Latino), 1 international. *Degree requirements:* For master's, thesis optional. *Entrance requirements:* For master's, Maryland teaching certification or permission of program director, minimum GPA of 3.0. *Application deadline:* Applications are processed on a rolling basis. Application fee: $50. Electronic applications accepted. *Expenses:* Tuition, state resident: part-time $337 per credit. Tuition, nonresident: part-time $709 per credit. *Required fees:* $99 per credit. *Financial support:* Application deadline: 4/1; applicants required to submit FAFSA. *Unit head:* Todd Kenreich, Graduate Program Director, 410-704-5897, E-mail: tkenreich@towson.edu.

Trevecca Nazarene University, College of Lifelong Learning, School of Education, Major in Teaching, Nashville, TN 37210-2877. Offers teaching 7-12 (MAT); teaching K-6 (MAT). Part-time and evening/weekend programs available. *Students:* 207 full-time (159 women), 11 part-time (9 women); includes 34 minority (29 Black or African American, non-Hispanic/Latino; 3 Hispanic/Latino; 2 Two or more races, non-Hispanic/Latino), 1 international. In 2011, 104 master's awarded. *Degree requirements:* For master's, exit assessment, student teaching. *Entrance requirements:* For master's, GRE General Test, MAT, PRAXIS I: Pre-Professional Skills Test, minimum GPA of 2.7, 2 letters of reference. Additional exam requirements/recommendations for international students: Required—TOEFL (minimum score 550 paper-based; 213 computer-based). *Application deadline:* Applications are processed on a rolling basis. Application fee: $25. *Expenses:* Contact institution. *Financial support:* Applicants required to submit FAFSA. *Unit head:* Dr. Esther Swink, Dean, School of Education/Director of Graduate Education Programs, 615-248-1201, Fax: 615-248-1597, E-mail: admissions_ged@trevecca.edu. *Application contact:* Melanie Eaton, Admissions, 615-248-1498, E-mail: admissions_ged@trevecca.edu. Web site: http://www.trevecca.edu/soe.

Trinity Washington University, School of Education, Washington, DC 20017-1094. Offers counseling (MA); early childhood education (MAT); educating for change (M Ed); educational administration (MSA); elementary education (MAT); school counseling (MA); secondary education (MAT), including English, social studies; special education (MAT); teaching English as a second language (MAT); teaching English to speakers of other languages (M Ed); the teaching of reading (M Ed). *Accreditation:* NCATE. Part-time and evening/weekend programs available. *Degree requirements:* For master's, thesis (for some programs), capstone project(s). *Entrance requirements:* For master's, PRAXIS I, minimum GPA of 2.8. Additional exam requirements/recommendations for international students: Required—TOEFL (minimum score 550 paper-based; 213 computer-based). *Faculty research:* Technology, literacy, special education, organizations, inclusion models.

Troy University, Graduate School, College of Education, Program in Secondary Education, Troy, AL 36082. Offers 5th year biology (MS); 5th year computer science (MS); 5th year history (MS); 5th year language arts (MS); 5th year mathematics (MS); 5th year social science (MS); traditional biology (MS); traditional computer science (MS); traditional history (MS); traditional language arts (MS); traditional mathematics (MS); traditional social science (MS). *Accreditation:* NCATE. Part-time and evening/weekend programs available. *Faculty:* 4 full-time (3 women). *Students:* 14 full-time (8 women), 29 part-time (21 women); includes 9 minority (all Black or African American, non-Hispanic/Latino). Average age 28. 11 applicants, 100% accepted, 5 enrolled. In 2011, 16 master's awarded. *Degree requirements:* For master's, comprehensive exam, thesis. *Entrance requirements:* For master's, minimum GPA of 2.5, bachelor's degree. Additional exam requirements/recommendations for international students: Required—TOEFL (minimum score 523 paper-based; 193 computer-based; 70 iBT), IELTS (minimum score 6). *Application deadline:* Applications are processed on a rolling basis. Application fee: $50. Electronic applications accepted. *Expenses:* Tuition, state resident: full-time $6960; part-time $290 per credit hour. Tuition, nonresident: full-time $13,920; part-time $580 per credit hour. *Required fees:* $386 per term. *Financial support:* Career-related internships or fieldwork available. Support available to part-time students. Financial award applicants required to submit FAFSA. *Unit head:* Dr. Jan Oliver, Associate Professor, 334-670-3444, Fax: 334-670-3548, E-mail: oliver@troy.edu. *Application contact:* Brenda K. Campbell, Director of Graduate Admissions, 334-670-3178, Fax: 334-670-3733, E-mail: bcamp@troy.edu.

Tufts University, Graduate School of Arts and Sciences, Department of Education, Program in Education, Medford, MA 02155. Offers education (MS, PhD); middle and secondary education (MA, MAT); secondary education (MA). *Faculty:* 13 full-time, 9 part-time/adjunct. *Students:* 111 full-time (80 women); includes 20 minority (8 Black or African American, non-Hispanic/Latino; 3 American Indian or Alaska Native, non-Hispanic/Latino; 3 Asian, non-Hispanic/Latino; 6 Hispanic/Latino), 4 international. Average age 27. 193 applicants, 76% accepted, 82 enrolled. In 2011, 81 master's, 7 doctorates awarded. *Degree requirements:* For master's, thesis optional; for doctorate, thesis/dissertation. *Entrance requirements:* For master's, GRE General Test. Additional exam requirements/recommendations for international students: Required—TOEFL (minimum score 550 paper-based; 213 computer-based; 80 iBT). *Application deadline:* For fall admission, 2/1 for domestic students, 12/15 for international students; for spring admission, 10/15 for domestic students, 9/15 for international students. Applications are processed on a rolling basis. Application fee: $75. Electronic applications accepted. *Expenses: Tuition:* Full-time $41,208; part-time $1030 per credit hour. Full-time tuition and fees vary according to degree level, program and student level. Part-time tuition and fees vary according to course load. *Financial support:* Teaching assistantships with full and partial tuition reimbursements, Federal Work-Study, scholarships/grants, and tuition waivers (full and partial) available. Support available to part-time students. Financial award application deadline: 2/1. *Unit head:* Barbara Brizuela, Chair, 617-627-3244, Fax: 617-627-3901. *Application contact:* Patricia Romeo, Information Contact, 617-627-3244.

Union College, Graduate Programs, Department of Education, Program in Secondary Education, Barbourville, KY 40906-1499. Offers MA. *Degree requirements:* For master's, thesis optional. *Entrance requirements:* For master's, GRE General Test, NTE.

Universidad Metropolitana, School of Education, Program in Teaching of Physical Education, San Juan, PR 00928-1150. Offers teaching of adult physical education (M Ed); teaching of elementary physical education (M Ed); teaching of secondary physical education (M Ed). *Degree requirements:* For master's, thesis or alternative. *Entrance requirements:* For master's, EXADEP, interview. Electronic applications accepted.

The University of Akron, Graduate School, College of Education, Department of Curricular and Instructional Studies, Program in Secondary Education, Akron, OH 44325. Offers secondary education (MA, PhD); secondary education with licensure (MS). *Accreditation:* NCATE. *Students:* 35 full-time (23 women), 51 part-time (40 women); includes 18 minority (11 Black or African American, non-Hispanic/Latino; 2 Asian, non-Hispanic/Latino; 4 Hispanic/Latino; 1 Two or more races, non-Hispanic/Latino), 4 international. Average age 39. 17 applicants, 53% accepted, 9 enrolled. In 2011, 9 master's, 1 doctorate awarded. *Degree requirements:* For master's, comprehensive exam, portfolio; for doctorate, variable foreign language requirement, comprehensive exam, thesis/dissertation, written and oral exams. *Entrance requirements:* For master's, minimum GPA of 2.75, valid teaching license; for doctorate, MAT or GRE, minimum GPA of 3.5, three letters of recommendation, statement of purpose indicating career goals and research interest, controlled department writing sample, completion of Agreement to Advise Form, current curriculum vitae, at least three years of teaching experience. Additional exam requirements/recommendations for international students: Required—TOEFL (minimum score 550 paper-based; 213 computer-based; 79 iBT). *Application deadline:* For fall admission, 3/31 for domestic and international students; for spring admission, 10/31 for domestic and international students. Applications are processed on a rolling basis. Application fee: $30 ($40 for international students). Electronic applications accepted. *Expenses:* Tuition, state resident: full-time $7038; part-time $391 per credit hour. Tuition, nonresident: full-time $12,051; part-time $670 per credit hour. *Required fees:* $1274; $34 per credit hour. *Unit head:* Dr. Bridgie Ford, Chair, 330-972-6967, E-mail: alexis2@uakron.edu. *Application contact:* Dr. Mark Tausig, Associate Dean, 330-972-6266, Fax: 330-972-6475, E-mail: mtausig@uakron.edu.

The University of Alabama, Graduate School, College of Education, Department of Curriculum and Instruction, Tuscaloosa, AL 35487. Offers elementary education (MA, Ed D, PhD, Ed S); secondary education (MA, Ed D, PhD, Ed S). Evening/weekend programs available. Postbaccalaureate distance learning degree programs offered (minimal on-campus study). *Faculty:* 21 full-time (14 women). *Students:* 94 full-time (65 women), 138 part-time (117 women); includes 39 minority (23 Black or African American, non-Hispanic/Latino; 2 Asian, non-Hispanic/Latino; 9 Hispanic/Latino; 5 Two or more races, non-Hispanic/Latino), 7 international. Average age 33. 110 applicants, 72% accepted, 46 enrolled. In 2011, 65 master's, 12 doctorates, 12 other advanced degrees awarded. *Degree requirements:* For master's, comprehensive exam, thesis (for some programs); for doctorate, comprehensive exam, thesis/dissertation; for Ed S, comprehensive exam, thesis optional. *Entrance requirements:* For master's, doctorate, and Ed S, MAT and/or GRE. Additional exam requirements/recommendations for international students: Recommended—TOEFL (minimum score 550 paper-based; 213 computer-based), IELTS (minimum score 6.5). *Application deadline:* For fall admission, 7/1 priority date for domestic students, 1/15 for international students; for spring admission, 11/1 priority date for domestic students, 6/1 for international students. Application fee: $50 ($60 for international students). Electronic applications accepted. *Expenses:* Tuition, state resident: full-time $8600. Tuition, nonresident: full-time $21,900. *Financial support:* In 2011–12, 14 students received support, including 10 research assistantships with tuition reimbursements available (averaging $9,844 per year), 4 teaching assistantships with tuition reimbursements available (averaging $9,844 per year); institutionally sponsored loans, traineeships, and unspecified assistantships also available. *Faculty research:* Teacher education, diversity, integration of curriculum, technology. *Total annual research expenditures:* $458,059. *Unit head:* Dr. Miguel Mantero, Chair, 205-348-1402, Fax: 205-348-9863, E-mail: mmantero@bamaed.ua.edu. *Application contact:* Dr. Kathy S. Wetzel, Assistant Dean for Student Services, 205-348-1154, Fax: 205-348-0080, E-mail: kwetzel@bamaed.ua.edu.

The University of Alabama at Birmingham, College of Arts and Sciences, School of Education, Program in High School Education, Birmingham, AL 35294. Offers MA Ed. *Accreditation:* NCATE. *Degree requirements:* For master's, thesis optional. *Entrance requirements:* For master's, GRE General Test, MAT, or NTE, minimum GPA of 3.0. *Application deadline:* Applications are processed on a rolling basis. Electronic applications accepted. *Expenses:* Tuition, state resident: full-time $5922; part-time $309 per hour. Tuition, nonresident: full-time $13,428; part-time $726 per hour. Tuition and fees vary according to program. *Faculty research:* Soviet education, religious education, cultural pluralism. *Unit head:* Dr. Lynn Kirkland, Chair, 205-934-8358. Web site: http://www.uab.edu/ci/ehs.

University of Alaska Fairbanks, School of Education, Program in Education, Fairbanks, AK 99775. Offers curriculum and instruction (M Ed); education (M Ed, Graduate Certificate); elementary education (M Ed); language and literacy (M Ed); reading (M Ed); secondary education (M Ed); special education (M Ed). *Faculty:* 25 full-time (15 women). *Students:* 30 full-time (23 women), 69 part-time (50 women); includes 17 minority (7 American Indian or Alaska Native, non-Hispanic/Latino; 1 Asian, non-Hispanic/Latino; 2 Hispanic/Latino; 1 Native Hawaiian or other Pacific Islander, non-Hispanic/Latino; 6 Two or more races, non-Hispanic/Latino), 1 international. Average age 33. 68 applicants, 76% accepted, 37 enrolled. In 2011, 26 master's, 22 other advanced degrees awarded. *Degree requirements:* For master's, comprehensive exam, thesis, oral defense. *Entrance requirements:* Additional exam requirements/recommendations for international students: Required—TOEFL (minimum score 550 paper-based; 213 computer-based; 80 iBT). *Application deadline:* For fall admission, 5/1 for domestic students, 3/1 for international students; for spring admission, 10/15 for domestic students, 8/1 for international students. Applications are processed on a rolling basis. Application fee: $60. Electronic applications accepted. *Expenses:* Tuition, state resident: full-time $6696; part-time $372 per credit. Tuition, nonresident: full-time $13,680; part-time $760 per credit. Tuition and fees vary according to course load and reciprocity agreements. *Financial support:* Fellowships with tuition reimbursements, research assistantships with tuition reimbursements, teaching assistantships with tuition reimbursements, career-related internships or fieldwork, Federal Work-Study, scholarships/grants, health care benefits, and unspecified assistantships available. Support available to part-time students. Financial award application deadline: 6/1; financial award applicants required to submit FAFSA. *Unit head:* Allan Morotti, Interim Dean, 907-474-7341, Fax: 907-474-5451, E-mail: uaf-soe-school@alaska.edu. *Application contact:* Mike Earnest, Director of Admissions, 907-474-7500, Fax: 907-474-5379, E-mail: admissions@uaf.edu. Web site: http://www.uaf.edu/educ/graduate/counseling.html.

University of Alaska Southeast, Graduate Programs, Program in Education, Juneau, AK 99801. Offers early childhood education (M Ed, MAT); educational technology (M Ed); elementary education (MAT); reading (M Ed); secondary education (MAT). *Accreditation:* NCATE. Part-time and evening/weekend programs available. Postbaccalaureate distance learning degree programs offered (minimal on-campus study). *Degree requirements:* For master's, comprehensive exam or project, portfolio. *Entrance requirements:* For master's, PRAXIS, minimum GPA of 3.0, writing sample, letters of recommendation. Electronic applications accepted. *Faculty research:* Applied classroom research, culturally responsive practices, action research, teaching effectiveness.

University of Alberta, Faculty of Graduate Studies and Research, Department of Secondary Education, Edmonton, AB T6G 2E1, Canada. Offers M Ed, Ed D, PhD. Part-time programs available. *Degree requirements:* For master's, thesis or alternative, 1 year of residency; for doctorate, thesis/dissertation, 2 years of residency (PhD), 1 year of residency (Ed D). *Entrance requirements:* For master's, teaching certificate, 2 years of teaching experience; for doctorate, master's degree. *Faculty research:* Curriculum studies, teacher education, subject area specializations.

University of Arkansas, Graduate School, College of Education and Health Professions, Department of Curriculum and Instruction, Program in Secondary Education, Fayetteville, AR 72701-1201. Offers M Ed, MAT, Ed S. *Accreditation:* NCATE. *Students:* 54 full-time (33 women), 15 part-time (11 women); includes 5 minority (1 Black or African American, non-Hispanic/Latino; 1 American Indian or Alaska Native, non-Hispanic/Latino; 1 Asian, non-Hispanic/Latino; 1 Hispanic/Latino; 1 Two or more races, non-Hispanic/Latino), 2 international. In 2011, 64 master's awarded. *Application deadline:* For fall admission, 4/1 for international students; for spring admission, 10/1 for international students. Applications are processed on a rolling basis. Application fee: $40 ($50 for international students). Electronic applications accepted. *Financial support:* Fellowships with tuition reimbursements, research assistantships, teaching assistantships, career-related internships or fieldwork, and Federal Work-Study available. Support available to part-time students. Financial award application deadline: 4/1; financial award applicants required to submit FAFSA. *Faculty research:* Mathematics. *Unit head:* Dr. Michael Daugherty, Unit Head, 479-575-4209, E-mail: mkd03@uark.edu. *Application contact:* Dr. Barbara Gartin, Graduate Coordinator, 479-575-7525, Fax: 479-575-6676, E-mail: bgartin@uark.edu. Web site: http://cied.uark.edu/.

University of Arkansas at Little Rock, Graduate School, College of Education, Department of Teacher Education, Program in Secondary Education, Little Rock, AR 72204-1099. Offers M Ed. *Accreditation:* NCATE. Part-time programs available. *Degree requirements:* For master's, comprehensive exam. *Entrance requirements:* For master's, interview, minimum GPA of 2.75, GRE General Test or teaching certificate.

University of Arkansas at Pine Bluff, School of Education, Pine Bluff, AR 71601-2799. Offers early childhood education (M Ed); secondary education (M Ed), including English education, mathematics education, physical education, science education, social studies education; teaching (MAT). *Accreditation:* NCATE. Part-time and evening/weekend programs available. *Degree requirements:* For master's, comprehensive exam. *Entrance requirements:* For master's, GRE, minimum GPA of 2.75, NTE or Standard Arkansas Teaching Certificate. *Faculty research:* Teacher certification, accreditation, assessment, standards, portfolio development, rehabilitation, technology.

University of Bridgeport, School of Education, Department of Education, Bridgeport, CT 06604. Offers education (MS); educational management (Ed D, Diploma), including intermediate administrator or supervisor (Diploma), leadership (Ed D); elementary education (MS, Diploma), including early childhood education, elementary education; middle school education (MS); music education (MS); remedial reading and language arts (Diploma); secondary education (MS, Diploma), including computer specialist (Diploma), international education (Diploma), reading specialist, secondary education. Part-time and evening/weekend programs available. *Faculty:* 12 full-time (5 women), 108 part-time/adjunct (60 women). *Students:* 232 full-time (161 women), 216 part-time (160 women); includes 61 minority (21 Black or African American, non-Hispanic/Latino; 8 Asian, non-Hispanic/Latino; 22 Hispanic/Latino; 10 Two or more races, non-Hispanic/Latino), 34 international. Average age 30. 412 applicants, 63% accepted, 147 enrolled. In 2011, 216 master's, 7 other advanced degrees awarded. *Degree requirements:* For master's, final exam, final project, or thesis; for doctorate, comprehensive exam, thesis/dissertation; for Diploma, thesis or alternative, final project. *Entrance requirements:* For master's, minimum undergraduate QPA of 2.67; for doctorate, GRE, MAT; for Diploma, GRE General Test or MAT, minimum graduate QPA of 3.0. Additional exam requirements/recommendations for international students: Recommended—TOEFL (minimum score 550 paper-based; 213 computer-based; 80 iBT), IELTS (minimum score 6.5). *Application deadline:* For fall admission, 8/1 priority date for domestic students, 8/1 for international students; for spring admission, 12/1 priority date for domestic students, 12/1 for international students. Applications are processed on a rolling basis. Application fee: $50. Electronic applications accepted. *Expenses: Tuition:* Full-time $22,880; part-time $700 per credit. *Required fees:* $1870; $95 per semester. Tuition and fees vary according to course load and program. *Financial support:* In 2011–12, 120 students received support. Fellowships, research assistantships, teaching assistantships, career-related internships or fieldwork, Federal Work-Study, and institutionally sponsored loans available. Support available to part-time students. Financial award application deadline: 6/1; financial award applicants required to submit FAFSA. *Faculty research:* Self-concept, internship assessment, stress and situational development, follow-up of graduation, trend analysis. *Unit head:* Dr. Allen P. Cook, Dean, 203-576-4192, Fax: 203-576-4200, E-mail: acook@bridgeport.edu. *Application contact:* Karissa Peckham, Dean of Admissions, 203-576-4552, Fax: 203-576-4941, E-mail: admit@bridgeport.edu.

University of California, Irvine, Department of Education, Irvine, CA 92697. Offers educational administration (Ed D); educational administration and leadership (Ed D); elementary and secondary education (MAT). Part-time and evening/weekend programs available. *Students:* 246 full-time (185 women), 8 part-time (5 women); includes 121 minority (4 Black or African American, non-Hispanic/Latino; 1 American Indian or Alaska Native, non-Hispanic/Latino; 65 Asian, non-Hispanic/Latino; 37 Hispanic/Latino; 2 Native Hawaiian or other Pacific Islander, non-Hispanic/Latino; 12 Two or more races, non-Hispanic/Latino), 7 international. Average age 28. 455 applicants, 75% accepted, 185 enrolled. In 2011, 146 master's, 12 doctorates awarded. *Degree requirements:* For doctorate, thesis/dissertation. *Entrance requirements:* For master's, GRE, minimum GPA of 3.0; for doctorate, GRE General Test, minimum GPA of 3.0. Additional exam requirements/recommendations for international students: Required—TOEFL (minimum score 550 paper-based; 213 computer-based). *Application deadline:* For fall admission, 1/2 priority date for domestic students, 1/2 for international students. Application fee: $80 ($100 for international students). Electronic applications accepted. *Financial support:* Fellowships, research assistantships with full tuition reimbursements, institutionally sponsored loans, traineeships, health care benefits, and unspecified assistantships available. Financial award application deadline: 3/1; financial award applicants required to submit FAFSA. *Faculty research:* Education technology, learning theory, social theory, cultural diversity, postmodernism. *Unit head:* Deborah L. Vandell, Chair, 949-824-8026, Fax: 949-824-3968, E-mail: dvandell@uci.edu. *Application contact:* Sarah K. Singh, Credential Program Counselor, 949-824-6673, Fax: 949-824-9103, E-mail: sksingh@uci.edu. Web site: http://www.gse.uci.edu/.

University of Central Missouri, The Graduate School, College of Education, Warrensburg, MO 64093. Offers career and technical education administration (MS); career and technical education industry training (MS); career and technical education leadership/teaching (MS); college student personnel administration (MS); counseling (MS); curriculum and instruction (Ed S); educational leadership (Ed D); educational technology (MS); elementary education/educational foundations and literacy (MSE); elementary school administration (MSE); elementary school principalship (Ed S); human services/learning resources (Ed S); human services/professional counseling (Ed S); human services/special education (Ed S); human services/technology and occupational education (Ed S); K-12 education/educational foundations and literacy (MSE); K-12 special education (MSE); library science and information services (MS); literacy education (MSE); secondary education/educational foundations & literacy (MSE); secondary school administration (MSE); secondary school principalship (Ed S); superintendency (Ed S); teaching (MAT). Ed D offered jointly with University of Missouri. Part-time programs available. Postbaccalaureate distance learning degree programs offered. *Entrance requirements:* Additional exam requirements/recommendations for international students: Required—TOEFL (minimum score 550 paper-based; 79 computer-based). Electronic applications accepted.

University of Central Oklahoma, College of Graduate Studies and Research, College of Education and Professional Studies, Department of Professional Teacher Education, Program in Secondary Education, Edmond, OK 73034-5209. Offers M Ed. *Accreditation:* NCATE. Part-time programs available. *Faculty:* 7 full-time (4 women). *Students:* 16 full-time (10 women), 67 part-time (46 women); includes 12 minority (5 Black or African American, non-Hispanic/Latino; 2 American Indian or Alaska Native, non-Hispanic/Latino; 2 Asian, non-Hispanic/Latino; 2 Hispanic/Latino; 1 Two or more races, non-Hispanic/Latino), 1 international. Average age 30. In 2011, 13 master's awarded. *Entrance requirements:* For master's, GRE General Test. Additional exam requirements/recommendations for international students: Required—TOEFL (minimum score 550 paper-based; 213 computer-based). *Application deadline:* Applications are processed on a rolling basis. Application fee: $50. Electronic applications accepted. *Expenses:* Tuition, state resident: full-time $3901; part-time $218.30 per credit hour. Tuition, nonresident: full-time $9198; part-time $511.20 per credit hour. Tuition and fees vary according to program. *Financial support:* Unspecified assistantships available. Financial award application deadline: 3/31; financial award applicants required to submit FAFSA. *Unit head:* Dr. Mike Nelson, Director, 405-974-5411, E-mail: mnelson1@uco.edu.

University of Cincinnati, Graduate School, College of Education, Criminal Justice, and Human Services, Division of Teacher Education, Program in Secondary Education, Cincinnati, OH 45221. Offers M Ed. *Accreditation:* NCATE. Part-time programs available. *Degree requirements:* For master's, thesis or alternative. *Entrance requirements:* For master's, GRE General Test. Additional exam requirements/recommendations for international students: Required—TOEFL (minimum score 550 paper-based), TWE (minimum score 4.5), OEPT. Electronic applications accepted.

University of Colorado Denver, School of Education and Human Development, Information and Learning Technologies Program, Denver, CO 80217-3364. Offers e-learning design and implementation (MA); instructional design and adult learning (MA); K-12 teaching (MA). Part-time and evening/weekend programs available. Postbaccalaureate distance learning degree programs offered (no on-campus study). *Students:* 82 full-time (65 women), 46 part-time (38 women); includes 13 minority (2 Black or African American, non-Hispanic/Latino; 3 Asian, non-Hispanic/Latino; 8 Hispanic/Latino), 3 international. Average age 38. 35 applicants, 89% accepted, 27 enrolled. In 2011, 79 master's awarded. *Degree requirements:* For master's, comprehensive exam (for some programs), comprehensive exam or online portfolio; 30 credit hours. *Entrance requirements:* For master's, GRE or MAT (if GPA is below 2.75), resume, statement of intent, three letters of recommendation. Additional exam requirements/recommendations for international students: Required—TOEFL (minimum score 525 paper-based; 197 computer-based). *Application deadline:* For fall admission, 5/15 for domestic students; for spring admission, 11/15 for domestic students. Application fee: $50 ($75 for international students). *Expenses:* Contact institution. *Financial support:* Scholarships/grants available. Financial award application deadline: 4/1; financial award applicants required to submit FAFSA. *Faculty research:* Technology for educational management, instructional design foundations, e-Learning, educational design. *Unit head:* Brent Wilson, Professor, 303-315-4963, E-mail: brent.wilson@ucdenver.edu. *Application contact:* Hans Broers, Academic Advisor, 303-315-6351, Fax: 303-315-6311, E-mail: hans.broers@ucdenver.edu. Web site: http://www.ucdenver.edu/ACADEMICS/COLLEGES/SCHOOLOFEDUCATION/ACADEMICS/Pages/AcademicPrograms.aspx.

University of Colorado Denver, School of Education and Human Development, Teacher Education Programs, Denver, CO 80217. Offers elementary linguistically diverse education (MA); elementary math and science education (MA); elementary math education (MA); elementary reading and writing (MA); elementary science education (MA); secondary English education (MA); secondary linguistically diverse education (MA); secondary math education (MA); secondary reading and writing (MA); secondary science education (MA); special education (MA). *Accreditation:* NCATE. Part-time and evening/weekend programs available. *Students:* 419 full-time (325 women), 238 part-time (196 women); includes 83 minority (11 Black or African American, non-Hispanic/Latino; 1 American Indian or Alaska Native, non-Hispanic/Latino; 15 Asian, non-Hispanic/Latino; 53 Hispanic/Latino; 3 Two or more races, non-Hispanic/Latino), 9 international. Average age 30. 206 applicants, 88% accepted, 85 enrolled. In 2011, 278 master's awarded. *Degree requirements:* For master's, comprehensive exam. *Entrance requirements:* For master's, GRE or MAT (for those with GPA below 2.75), transcripts, resume, letters of recommendation. Additional exam requirements/recommendations for international students: Required—TOEFL (minimum score 525 paper-based; 197 computer-based). *Application deadline:* For fall admission, 4/15 priority date for domestic students; for spring admission, 9/15 priority date for domestic students. Applications are processed on a rolling basis. Application fee: $50 ($75 for international students). Electronic applications accepted. *Expenses:* Contact institution. *Financial support:* Research assistantships, teaching assistantships, and Federal Work-Study available. Financial award application deadline: 4/1; financial award applicants required to submit FAFSA. *Faculty research:* Linguistically diverse education/ESL, elementary reading and writing, elementary teacher education, secondary teacher education, special education. *Unit head:* Cindy Gutierrez, Director, 303-315-4982, E-mail: cindy.gutierrez@ucdenver.edu. *Application contact:* Lori Sisneros, Student Services Center, 303-315-4979, E-mail: education@ucdenver.edu. Web site: http://www.ucdenver.edu/academics/colleges/SchoolOfEducation/Academics/MASTERS/Pages/default.aspx.

University of Connecticut, Graduate School, Neag School of Education, Department of Curriculum and Instruction, Program in Secondary Education, Storrs, CT 06269. Offers MA, PhD, Post-Master's Certificate. *Accreditation:* NCATE. Terminal master's awarded for partial completion of doctoral program. *Degree requirements:* For master's, comprehensive exam, thesis or alternative; for doctorate, thesis/dissertation. *Entrance requirements:* For doctorate, GRE General Test. Additional exam requirements/recommendations for international students: Required—TOEFL (minimum score 550 paper-based; 213 computer-based). Electronic applications accepted.

University of Dayton, Department of Teacher Education, Dayton, OH 45469-1300. Offers adolescent/young adult (MS Ed); art education (MS Ed); early childhood education (MS Ed); early childhood leadership advocacy (MS Ed); inclusive early childhood (MS Ed); interdisciplinary education (MS Ed); intervention specialist education, mild/moderate (MS Ed); literacy (MS Ed); middle childhood (MS Ed); multi-age education (MS Ed); music education (MS Ed); teacher as leader (MS Ed); technology in education (MS Ed). Part-time and evening/weekend programs available. Postbaccalaureate distance learning degree programs offered (no on-campus study). *Faculty:* 15 full-time (11 women), 22 part-time/adjunct (20 women). *Students:* 41 full-time (29 women), 95 part-time (87 women); includes 13 minority (9 Black or African American, non-Hispanic/Latino; 1 Asian, non-Hispanic/Latino; 3 Hispanic/Latino), 9 international. Average age 32. 111 applicants, 55% accepted, 38 enrolled. In 2011, 97 degrees awarded. *Degree requirements:* For master's, thesis, capstone research project. *Entrance requirements:* For master's, GRE General Test, minimum GPA of 2.75. Additional exam requirements/recommendations for international students: Required—TOEFL (minimum score 550 paper-based; 213 computer-based; 80 iBT). *Application deadline:* For fall admission, 3/1 priority date for domestic students, 3/1 for international students; for winter admission, 7/1 for international students; for spring admission, 1/1 for international students. Applications are processed on a rolling basis. Application fee: $0 ($50 for international students). Electronic applications accepted. *Expenses:* Contact institution. *Financial support:* In 2011–12, 5 research assistantships with full and partial tuition reimbursements (averaging $8,470 per year) were awarded; career-related internships or fieldwork, institutionally sponsored loans, health care benefits, and unspecified assistantships also available. Financial award applicants required to submit FAFSA. *Faculty research:* Diversity, literacy, art representation by young children, preservice teacher preparation. *Unit head:* Dr. Katie A. Kinnucan-Welsch, Chair, 937-229-3346. *Application contact:* Alexsandar Popovski, Enrollment Management Administrator, 937-229-2357, Fax: 937-229-4729, E-mail: alex.popovski@notes.udayton.edu.

University of Great Falls, Graduate Studies, Secondary Teaching Program, Great Falls, MT 59405. Offers MAT. Part-time programs available. Postbaccalaureate distance learning degree programs offered (no on-campus study). *Degree requirements:* For master's, comprehensive exam, thesis optional, extensive portfolio. *Entrance requirements:* For master's, GRE General Test or MAT, bachelor's degree in teaching, teaching certificate, interview, 3 letters of recommendation, minimum undergraduate GPA of 3.0. Additional exam requirements/recommendations for international students: Required—TOEFL (minimum score 500 paper-based; 205 computer-based). Electronic applications accepted. *Faculty research:* Gifted, curriculum design, administration.

University of Guam, Office of Graduate Studies, School of Education, Program in Secondary Education, Mangilao, GU 96923. Offers M Ed. *Degree requirements:* For master's, thesis, comprehensive oral and written exams. *Entrance requirements:* For master's, GRE General Test. Additional exam requirements/recommendations for international students: Required—TOEFL.

University of Houston–Downtown, College of Public Service, Department of Urban Education, Houston, TX 77002. Offers bilingual education (MAT); curriculum and instruction (MAT); elementary education (MAT); secondary education (MAT). Part-time and evening/weekend programs available. *Faculty:* 12 full-time (8 women). *Students:* 13 full-time (10 women), 25 part-time (22 women); includes 30 minority (15 Black or African American, non-Hispanic/Latino; 3 Asian, non-Hispanic/Latino; 11 Hispanic/Latino; 1 Two or more races, non-Hispanic/Latino). Average age 35. 17 applicants, 100% accepted, 16 enrolled. In 2011, 5 master's awarded. *Degree requirements:* For master's, capstone course with completed project, position paper, grant proposal, empirical study, curriculum development/revision, or advanced technology project presented at annual Graduate Project Exhibition. *Entrance requirements:* For master's, GRE, personal statement, 3 recommendation forms. Additional exam requirements/recommendations for international students: Required—TOEFL (minimum score 550 paper-based; 213 computer-based; 80 iBT). *Application deadline:* For fall admission, 7/15 for domestic and international students; for spring admission, 11/15 for domestic and international students. Applications are processed on a rolling basis. Application fee: $35 ($60 for international students). Electronic applications accepted. *Expenses:* Tuition, state resident: full-time $3420; part-time $2280 per year. Tuition, nonresident: full-time $8424; part-time $5616 per year. *Required fees:* $1018; $840 per year. Tuition and fees vary according to program. *Financial support:* Scholarships/grants available. Financial award applicants required to submit FAFSA. *Unit head:* Dr. Myrna Cohen, Department Chair, 713-221-2759, Fax: 713-226-5294, E-mail: cohenm@uhd.edu. *Application contact:* Traneshia Parker, Associate Director of International Student Services and Graduate Admissions, 713-221-8093, Fax: 713-221-8157, E-mail: parkert@uhd.edu. Web site: http://www.uhd.edu/academic/colleges/publicservice/urbaned/mat.htm.

University of Illinois at Chicago, Graduate College, College of Education, Department of Curriculum and Instruction, Chicago, IL 60607-7128. Offers curriculum studies (PhD); educational studies (M Ed); elementary education (M Ed); literacy, language and culture (M Ed, PhD); secondary education (M Ed). Part-time and evening/weekend programs available. *Degree requirements:* For doctorate, thesis/dissertation. *Entrance requirements:* For master's, minimum GPA of 2.75; for doctorate, GRE General Test, minimum GPA of 2.75. Additional exam requirements/recommendations for international students: Required—TOEFL. Electronic applications accepted. *Faculty research:* Curriculum theory, curriculum development, research on teaching, curriculum and context, reading/literacy.

University of Indianapolis, Graduate Programs, School of Education, Indianapolis, IN 46227-3697. Offers art education (MAT); biology (MAT); chemistry (MAT); curriculum and instruction (MA); earth sciences (MAT); education (MA, MAT); educational leadership (MA); elementary education (MA); English (MAT); French (MAT); math (MAT); physical education (MAT); physics (MAT); secondary education (MA), including art education, education, English education, social studies education; social studies (MAT); Spanish (MAT). *Accreditation:* NCATE. Part-time and evening/weekend programs available. *Faculty:* 3 full-time (2 women), 3 part-time/adjunct (2 women). *Students:* 32 full-time (18 women), 97 part-time (56 women); includes 22 minority (20 Black or African American, non-Hispanic/Latino; 1 Asian, non-Hispanic/Latino; 1 Hispanic/Latino), 3 international. Average age 33. In 2011, 78 master's awarded. *Entrance requirements:* For master's, GRE Subject Test, PRAXIS I, minimum GPA of 2.5, 3 letters of recommendation, interview, writing exercise. Additional exam requirements/recommendations for international students: Required—TOEFL (minimum score 550 paper-based; 213 computer-based). *Application deadline:* Applications are processed on a rolling basis. Application fee: $50. Tuition and fees vary according to degree level and program. *Financial support:* Federal Work-Study available. Financial award application deadline: 5/1; financial award applicants required to submit FAFSA. *Faculty research:* Assessment of teacher education, perceptions of prospective teachers by parents. *Unit head:* Dr. Kathy Moran, Dean, 317-788-3285, Fax: 317-788-3300,

E-mail: kmoran@uindy.edu. *Application contact:* Jeni Kirby, 317-788-2113, E-mail: kirbyj@uindy.edu. Web site: http://education.uindy.edu/.

The University of Iowa, Graduate College, College of Education, Department of Teaching and Learning, Program in Secondary Education, Iowa City, IA 52242-1316. Offers art education (PhD); curriculum and supervision (PhD); curriculum supervision (MA); developmental reading (MA); English education (MA, MAT); foreign language education (MA, MAT); foreign language/ESL education (PhD); language, literature and culture (PhD); math education (PhD); mathematics education (MA); social studies (MA, PhD). *Degree requirements:* For master's, thesis optional, exam; for doctorate, comprehensive exam, thesis/dissertation. *Entrance requirements:* For master's and doctorate, GRE General Test, minimum GPA of 3.0. Additional exam requirements/ recommendations for international students: Required—TOEFL (minimum score 550 paper-based; 213 computer-based; 81 iBT). Electronic applications accepted.

University of Louisiana at Monroe, Graduate School, College of Education and Human Development, Department of Curriculum and Instruction, Program in Secondary Education 6-12, Monroe, LA 71209-0001. Offers M Ed, MAT. *Accreditation:* NCATE. Part-time and evening/weekend programs available. *Faculty:* 1 (woman) full-time. *Students:* 7 full-time (6 women), 29 part-time (15 women); includes 5 minority (4 Black or African American, non-Hispanic/Latino; 1 Two or more races, non-Hispanic/Latino). Average age 32. 9 applicants, 44% accepted, 4 enrolled. In 2011, 22 master's awarded. *Entrance requirements:* For master's, GRE General Test, PRAXIS, minimum GPA of 2.5. Additional exam requirements/recommendations for international students: Required—TOEFL (minimum score 500 paper-based; 173 computer-based; 61 iBT). *Application deadline:* For fall admission, 8/24 priority date for domestic students, 7/1 for international students; for winter admission, 12/14 priority date for domestic students; for spring admission, 1/19 for domestic students, 11/1 for international students. Applications are processed on a rolling basis. Application fee: $20 ($30 for international students). Electronic applications accepted. *Expenses:* Tuition, state resident: full-time $3436; part-time $240 per credit hour. Tuition, nonresident: full-time $3436; part-time $240 per credit hour. *International tuition:* $10,733 full-time. *Required fees:* $1460.90. *Financial support:* Career-related internships or fieldwork, Federal Work-Study, and unspecified assistantships available. Financial award application deadline: 4/1; financial award applicants required to submit FAFSA. *Unit head:* Dr. Dorothy Schween, Department Head, 318-342-1266, E-mail: schween@ulm.edu. *Application contact:* Whitney Sutherland, Administrative Assistant to Department Head, 318-342-1266, E-mail: sutherland@ulm.edu.

University of Louisville, Graduate School, College of Education and Human Development, Department of Teaching and Learning, Louisville, KY 40292-0001. Offers art education (MAT); curriculum and instruction (PhD); early elementary education (MAT); instructional technology (M Ed); interdisciplinary early childhood education (MAT); middle school education (MAT); music education (MAT); reading education (M Ed); secondary education (MAT); special education (M Ed, MAT); teacher leadership (M Ed). Part-time and evening/weekend programs available. *Degree requirements:* For doctorate, comprehensive exam, thesis/dissertation. *Entrance requirements:* For master's, GRE General Test, PRAXIS II (for some programs); for doctorate, GRE General Test. Additional exam requirements/recommendations for international students: Required—TOEFL (minimum score 560 paper-based; 210 computer-based; 83 iBT). Electronic applications accepted. *Expenses:* Tuition, state resident: full-time $9692; part-time $539 per credit hour. Tuition, nonresident: full-time $20,168; part-time $1121 per credit hour. Tuition and fees vary according to program and reciprocity agreements. *Faculty research:* Mathematics teacher education and ongoing professional development in pedagogy and content knowledge; development of literacy, including early literacy in science and mathematics and literacy development for English language learners; immersive visualizations for promoting STEM education from nanoscience to cosmic scales; evidence-based practices for students with disabilities; urban education, including teacher response to intervention systems in schools and cross-cultural competence.

University of Maine, Graduate School, College of Education and Human Development, Program in Secondary Education, Orono, ME 04469. Offers M Ed, MA, MAT, MS, CAS. *Accreditation:* NCATE. Part-time and evening/weekend programs available. *Students:* 11 full-time (8 women), 1 (woman) part-time; includes 1 minority (Two or more races, non-Hispanic/Latino). Average age 28. 4 applicants, 50% accepted, 2 enrolled. In 2011, 11 degrees awarded. *Degree requirements:* For master's, thesis or alternative. *Entrance requirements:* For master's, MAT; for CAS, MAT, MA, M Ed, or MS. Additional exam requirements/recommendations for international students: Required—TOEFL. *Application deadline:* For fall admission, 2/1 priority date for domestic students. Applications are processed on a rolling basis. Application fee: $65. Electronic applications accepted. *Expenses:* Tuition, state resident: full-time $5016. Tuition, nonresident: full-time $14,424. *Financial support:* Career-related internships or fieldwork, Federal Work-Study, tuition waivers (full and partial), and unspecified assistantships available. Support available to part-time students. Financial award application deadline: 3/1. *Unit head:* Dr. Janet Spector, Coordinator, 207-581-2444, Fax: 207-581-2423. *Application contact:* Scott G. Delcourt, Associate Dean of the Graduate School, 207-581-3291, Fax: 207-581-3232, E-mail: graduate@maine.edu. Web site: http://www2.umaine.edu/graduate/.

University of Maryland, Baltimore County, Graduate School, College of Arts, Humanities and Social Sciences, Department of Education, Program in Teaching, Baltimore, MD 21250. Offers early childhood education (MAT); elementary education (MAT); secondary education (MAT), including social studies; secondary education (MAT), including art, biology, chemistry, dance, earth/space science, English, foreign language, mathematics, music, physics, theatre. Part-time and evening/weekend programs available. *Faculty:* 24 full-time (18 women), 25 part-time/adjunct (19 women). *Students:* 46 full-time (35 women), 64 part-time (39 women); includes 24 minority (8 Black or African American, non-Hispanic/Latino; 7 Asian, non-Hispanic/Latino; 6 Hispanic/Latino; 1 Native Hawaiian or other Pacific Islander, non-Hispanic/Latino; 2 Two or more races, non-Hispanic/Latino), 4 international. Average age 31. 88 applicants, 57% accepted, 39 enrolled. In 2011, 106 master's awarded. *Degree requirements:* For master's, comprehensive exam (for some programs), thesis (for some programs). *Entrance requirements:* For master's, PRAXIS I or GRE (minimum score of 1000), minimum GPA of 3.0. Additional exam requirements/recommendations for international students: Required—TOEFL. *Application deadline:* For fall admission, 6/1 for domestic students; for spring admission, 11/1 for domestic students. Applications are processed on a rolling basis. Application fee: $50. Electronic applications accepted. *Financial support:* In 2011–12, 6 students received support, including teaching assistantships with full and partial tuition reimbursements available (averaging $12,000 per year); career-related internships or fieldwork, Federal Work-Study, scholarships/grants, tuition waivers, and unspecified assistantships also available. Financial award application deadline: 3/1. *Faculty research:* STEM teacher education, culturally sensitive pedagogy, ESOL/bilingual education, early childhood education, language, literacy and culture. *Unit head:* Dr. Susan M. Blunck, Graduate Program Director, 410-455-2869, Fax: 410-455-3986, E-mail: blunck@umbc.edu. *Application contact:* Cheryl Johnson, 410-455-3388, E-mail: blackwel@umbc.edu. Web site: http://www.umbc.edu/education/.

University of Maryland, College Park, Academic Affairs, College of Education, Department of Curriculum and Instruction, College Park, MD 20742. Offers reading (M Ed, MA, PhD, CAGS); secondary education (M Ed, MA, Ed D, PhD, CAGS); teaching English to speakers of other languages (M Ed). *Accreditation:* NCATE. Part-time and evening/weekend programs available. Postbaccalaureate distance learning degree programs offered (no on-campus study). *Faculty:* 51 full-time (38 women), 23 part-time/ adjunct (18 women). *Students:* 252 full-time (177 women), 178 part-time (134 women); includes 121 minority (51 Black or African American, non-Hispanic/Latino; 37 Asian, non-Hispanic/Latino; 24 Hispanic/Latino; 9 Two or more races, non-Hispanic/Latino), 41 international. 264 applicants, 48% accepted, 80 enrolled. In 2011, 176 master's, 17 doctorates awarded. *Degree requirements:* For master's, comprehensive exam, seminar paper; for doctorate, comprehensive exam, thesis/dissertation, published paper, oral exam. *Entrance requirements:* For master's, GRE General Test or MAT, minimum GPA of 3.0, 3 letters of recommendation; for doctorate, GRE General Test or MAT, minimum undergraduate GPA of 3.0, graduate 3.5; 3 letters of recommendation. *Application deadline:* For fall admission, 11/15 priority date for domestic students, 11/15 for international students. Applications are processed on a rolling basis. Application fee: $75. Electronic applications accepted. *Expenses: Tuition, area resident:* Part-time $525 per credit hour. Tuition, state resident: part-time $525 per credit hour. Tuition, nonresident: part-time $1131 per credit hour. *Required fees:* $386.31 per term. Tuition and fees vary according to program. *Financial support:* In 2011–12, 11 research assistantships (averaging $17,535 per year), 79 teaching assistantships (averaging $17,270 per year) were awarded; Federal Work-Study and scholarships/grants also available. Support available to part-time students. Financial award applicants required to submit FAFSA. *Faculty research:* Teacher preparation, curriculum study, in-service education. *Total annual research expenditures:* $3.6 million. *Unit head:* Francine Hultgren, Interim Chair, 301-405-3117, E-mail: fh@umd.edu. *Application contact:* Dr. Charles A. Caramello, Dean of Graduate School, 301-405-0358, Fax: 301-314-9305.

University of Massachusetts Amherst, Graduate School, School of Education, Program in Education, Amherst, MA 01003. Offers bilingual, English as a second language, and multicultural education (M Ed, CAGS); child study and early education (M Ed); children, families and schools (Ed D, CAGS); early childhood and elementary teacher education (M Ed); educational leadership (M Ed, CAGS); educational policy and leadership (Ed D); higher education (M Ed, CAGS); international education (M Ed); language, literacy and culture (Ed D); learning, media and technology (M Ed, CAGS); mathematics, science, and learning technologies (Ed D); policy studies in education (CAGS); psychometric methods, educational statistics and research methods (Ed D); reading and writing (M Ed); school counselor education (M Ed, CAGS); science education (CAGS); secondary teacher education (M Ed); social justice education (M Ed, Ed D, CAGS); special education (M Ed, Ed D, CAGS). *Accreditation:* NCATE. Part-time programs available. Postbaccalaureate distance learning degree programs offered (minimal on-campus study). *Faculty:* 81 full-time (46 women). *Students:* 341 full-time (240 women), 333 part-time (226 women); includes 113 minority (36 Black or African American, non-Hispanic/Latino; 1 American Indian or Alaska Native, non-Hispanic/ Latino; 14 Asian, non-Hispanic/Latino; 51 Hispanic/Latino; 1 Native Hawaiian or other Pacific Islander, non-Hispanic/Latino; 10 Two or more races, non-Hispanic/Latino), 98 international. Average age 36. 721 applicants, 57% accepted, 202 enrolled. In 2011, 166 master's, 33 doctorates, 25 CAGSs awarded. Terminal master's awarded for partial completion of doctoral program. *Degree requirements:* For doctorate, comprehensive exam, thesis/dissertation. *Entrance requirements:* Additional exam requirements/ recommendations for international students: Required—TOEFL (minimum score 550 paper-based; 213 computer-based; 80 iBT), IELTS (minimum score 6.5). *Application deadline:* For fall admission, 1/15 for domestic and international students. Applications are processed on a rolling basis. Application fee: $50 ($65 for international students). Electronic applications accepted. Tuition and fees vary according to course load, campus/location and program. *Financial support:* Fellowships with full and partial tuition reimbursements, research assistantships with full and partial tuition reimbursements, teaching assistantships with full and partial tuition reimbursements, career-related internships or fieldwork, Federal Work-Study, scholarships/grants, traineeships, health care benefits, tuition waivers (full and partial), and unspecified assistantships available. Support available to part-time students. Financial award application deadline: 1/15. *Unit head:* Dr. Linda L. Griffin, Graduate Program Director, 413-545-6984, Fax: 413-545-1523. *Application contact:* Lindsay DeSantis, Interim Supervisor of Admissions, 413-545-0722, Fax: 413-577-0010, E-mail: gradadm@grad.umass.edu. Web site: http://www.umass.edu/education/.

University of Massachusetts Boston, Office of Graduate Studies, Graduate College of Education, School Organization, Curriculum and Instruction Department, Boston, MA 02125-3393. Offers education (M Ed, Ed D), including elementary and secondary education/certification (M Ed), higher education administration (Ed D), teacher certification (M Ed), urban school leadership (Ed D); educational administration (M Ed, CAGS); special education (M Ed). *Degree requirements:* For master's and CAGS, comprehensive exam; for doctorate, comprehensive exam, thesis/dissertation. *Entrance requirements:* For master's, GRE General Test or MAT; for doctorate, GRE General Test or MAT, minimum GPA of 2.75; for CAGS, minimum GPA of 2.75.

University of Massachusetts Boston, Office of Graduate Studies, Graduate College of Education, School Organization, Curriculum and Instruction Department, Program in Education, Track in Elementary and Secondary Education/Certification, Boston, MA 02125-3393. Offers M Ed. Part-time and evening/weekend programs available. *Degree requirements:* For master's, comprehensive exam, thesis optional, practicum. *Entrance requirements:* For master's, GRE General Test or MAT, minimum GPA of 3.0, 2 years of teaching experience. *Faculty research:* Anti-bias education, inclusionary curriculum and instruction, creativity and learning, science, technology and society, teaching of reading.

University of Massachusetts Dartmouth, Graduate School, School of Education, Public Policy, and Civic Engagement, Department of Teaching and Learning, North Dartmouth, MA 02747-2300. Offers elementary education (MAT, Postbaccalaureate Certificate); middle school education (MAT); principal initial licensure (Postbaccalaureate Certificate); secondary school education (MAT). *Faculty:* 5 full-time (4 women), 9 part-time/adjunct (4 women). *Students:* 15 full-time (10 women), 180 part-time (119 women); includes 17 minority (7 Black or African American, non-Hispanic/ Latino; 1 Asian, non-Hispanic/Latino; 5 Hispanic/Latino; 4 Two or more races, non-Hispanic/Latino). Average age 34. 110 applicants, 98% accepted, 85 enrolled. In 2011, 88 master's, 28 other advanced degrees awarded. *Degree requirements:* For master's, thesis or alternative. *Entrance requirements:* For master's, Massachusetts Tests for Educator Licensure (MTEL), minimum undergraduate GPA of 2.7, teacher certification, 3 letters of recommendation, resume, statement of intent; for Postbaccalaureate Certificate, Massachusetts Tests for Educator Licensure (MTEL), 3 letters of recommendation, resume, statement of intent. Additional exam requirements/ recommendations for international students: Required—TOEFL (minimum score 533 paper-based; 200 computer-based; 72 iBT). *Application deadline:* For fall admission, 7/ 15 priority date for domestic students, 6/15 for international students; for spring admission, 12/15 priority date for domestic students, 11/15 for international students. Applications are processed on a rolling basis. Application fee: $40 ($60 for international students). *Expenses:* Tuition, state resident: full-time $2071; part-time $86.29 per credit. Tuition, nonresident: full-time $8099; part-time $337.46 per credit. *Required fees:*

$438.58 per credit. Part-time tuition and fees vary according to class time, course load, degree level and reciprocity agreements. *Financial support:* Federal Work-Study available. Financial award application deadline: 3/1. *Total annual research expenditures:* $92,694. *Unit head:* Sheila Macrine, Graduate Program Director, 508-999-9234, Fax: 508-910-6916, E-mail: smacrine@umassd.edu. *Application contact:* Elan Turcotte-Shamski, Graduate Admissions Officer, 508-999-8604, Fax: 508-999-8183, E-mail: graduate@umassd.edu. Web site: http://www.umassd.edu/seppce/teachingandlearning/index.html.

University of Memphis, Graduate School, College of Education, Department of Instruction and Curriculum Leadership, Memphis, TN 38152. Offers early childhood education (MAT, MS, Ed D); elementary education (MAT); instruction and curriculum (MS, Ed D); instruction design and technology (MS, Ed D); middle grades education (MAT); reading (MS, Ed D); secondary education (MAT); special education (MAT, MS, Ed D). *Accreditation:* NCATE (one or more programs are accredited). Part-time programs available. Terminal master's awarded for partial completion of doctoral program. *Degree requirements:* For master's, comprehensive exam, thesis or alternative; for doctorate, comprehensive exam, thesis/dissertation. *Entrance requirements:* For master's, GRE General Test, minimum GPA of 2.5; for doctorate, GRE General Test, GRE Subject Test, 2 years of teaching experience. Electronic applications accepted. *Faculty research:* Effective urban teachers, preparation and retention of urban teachers, technology utilization in schools, field-based teacher preparation programs, effective use of online instruction.

University of Missouri–St. Louis, College of Education, Division of Counseling, St. Louis, MO 63121. Offers community counseling (M Ed); elementary school counseling (M Ed); secondary school counseling (M Ed). *Accreditation:* ACA; NCATE. Part-time and evening/weekend programs available. *Faculty:* 6 full-time (3 women), 11 part-time/adjunct (8 women). *Students:* 44 full-time (38 women), 162 part-time (134 women); includes 54 minority (42 Black or African American, non-Hispanic/Latino; 3 Asian, non-Hispanic/Latino; 7 Hispanic/Latino; 2 Two or more races, non-Hispanic/Latino), 2 international. Average age 32. 106 applicants, 48% accepted, 31 enrolled. In 2011, 60 master's awarded. *Degree requirements:* For master's, comprehensive exam. *Entrance requirements:* For master's, 3 letters of recommendation. Additional exam requirements/recommendations for international students: Required—TOEFL (minimum score 550 paper-based; 213 computer-based). *Application deadline:* For fall admission, 6/1 for domestic and international students; for spring admission, 10/1 for domestic and international students. Application fee: $35 ($40 for international students). Electronic applications accepted. *Expenses:* Tuition, state resident: full-time $6273; part-time $3866 per year. Tuition, nonresident: full-time $14,969; part-time $9980 per year. *Required fees:* $315 per year. *Financial support:* In 2011–12, 2 research assistantships with full and partial tuition reimbursements (averaging $12,500 per year), 2 teaching assistantships with full and partial tuition reimbursements (averaging $10,500 per year) were awarded. Financial award application deadline: 4/1; financial award applicants required to submit FAFSA. *Faculty research:* Vocational interests, self-concept, decision-making factors, developmental differences. *Unit head:* Dr. Mark Pope, Chair, 314-516-5782. *Application contact:* 314-516-5458, Fax: 314-516-6996, E-mail: gradadm@umsl.edu.

University of Missouri–St. Louis, College of Education, Division of Teaching and Learning, St. Louis, MO 63121. Offers autism studies (Certificate); elementary education (M Ed), including early childhood, general, reading; secondary education (M Ed), including curriculum and instruction, general, middle level education, reading, teaching English to speakers of other languages (TESOL); secondary school teaching (Certificate); special education (M Ed), including autism and developmental disabilities, early childhood special education, general; teaching English to speakers of other languages (Certificate). Part-time and evening/weekend programs available. *Faculty:* 32 full-time (16 women), 51 part-time/adjunct (36 women). *Students:* 95 full-time (63 women), 703 part-time (541 women); includes 176 minority (125 Black or African American, non-Hispanic/Latino; 1 American Indian or Alaska Native, non-Hispanic/Latino; 16 Asian, non-Hispanic/Latino; 26 Hispanic/Latino; 8 Two or more races, non-Hispanic/Latino), 11 international. Average age 29. 379 applicants, 90% accepted, 263 enrolled. In 2011, 190 master's, 9 Certificates awarded. *Degree requirements:* For master's, comprehensive exam. *Entrance requirements:* Additional exam requirements/recommendations for international students: Recommended—TOEFL (minimum score 550 paper-based; 213 computer-based). *Application deadline:* For fall admission, 7/1 priority date for domestic students, 7/1 for international students; for spring admission, 12/1 priority date for domestic students, 12/1 for international students. Application fee: $35 ($40 for international students). Electronic applications accepted. *Expenses:* Tuition, state resident: full-time $6273; part-time $3866 per year. Tuition, nonresident: full-time $14,969; part-time $9980 per year. *Required fees:* $315 per year. *Financial support:* In 2011–12, 6 research assistantships with full and partial tuition reimbursements (averaging $9,500 per year), 2 teaching assistantships with full and partial tuition reimbursements (averaging $10,500 per year) were awarded. Financial award application deadline: 4/1; financial award applicants required to submit FAFSA. *Unit head:* Dr. Joseph Polman, Chair, 314-516-5791. *Application contact:* 314-516-5458, Fax: 314-516-6996, E-mail: gadadm@umsl.edu. Web site: http://coe.umsl.edu/web/divisions/teach-learn/index.html.

University of Montevallo, College of Education, Program in Secondary/High School Education, Montevallo, AL 35115. Offers M Ed. *Accreditation:* NCATE. *Students:* 64 full-time (47 women), 83 part-time (48 women); includes 26 minority (22 Black or African American, non-Hispanic/Latino; 2 American Indian or Alaska Native, non-Hispanic/Latino; 2 Hispanic/Latino), 1 international. In 2011, 57 master's awarded. *Degree requirements:* For master's, comprehensive exam. *Entrance requirements:* For master's, GRE General Test, MAT, minimum undergraduate GPA of 2.5. Additional exam requirements/recommendations for international students: Required—TOEFL (minimum score 550 paper-based). *Application deadline:* For fall admission, 7/15 for domestic students; for spring admission, 11/15 for domestic students. Application fee: $25. *Financial support:* Federal Work-Study, scholarships/grants, and unspecified assistantships available. *Unit head:* Dr. Anna E. McEwan, Dean, 205-665-6360, E-mail: mcewanae@montevallo.edu. *Application contact:* Rebecca Hartley, Coordinator for Graduate Studies, 205-665-6350, Fax: 205-665-6353, E-mail: hartleyrs@montevallo.edu.

University of Nebraska at Omaha, Graduate Studies, College of Education, Department of Teacher Education, Program in Secondary Education, Omaha, NE 68182. Offers MA, MS. *Accreditation:* NCATE. Part-time and evening/weekend programs available. *Faculty:* 7 full-time (5 women). *Students:* 17 full-time (15 women), 98 part-time (69 women); includes 5 minority (1 Black or African American, non-Hispanic/Latino; 1 American Indian or Alaska Native, non-Hispanic/Latino; 3 Hispanic/Latino), 1 international. Average age 34. 26 applicants, 73% accepted, 16 enrolled. In 2011, 44 master's awarded. *Degree requirements:* For master's, comprehensive exam, thesis (for some programs). *Entrance requirements:* For master's, minimum GPA of 3.0. Additional exam requirements/recommendations for international students: Required—TOEFL (minimum score 550 paper-based; 213 computer-based; 80 iBT). *Application deadline:* For fall admission, 8/1 priority date for domestic students; for spring admission, 12/1 priority date for domestic students. Applications are processed on a rolling basis. Application fee: $45. Electronic applications accepted. *Financial support:* In 2011–12, 66 students received support, including 3 research assistantships with tuition reimbursements available; fellowships, teaching assistantships with tuition reimbursements available, Federal Work-Study, institutionally sponsored loans, scholarships/grants, tuition waivers (full), and unspecified assistantships also available. Support available to part-time students. Financial award application deadline: 3/1. *Unit head:* Dr. Lana Danielson, Advisor, 402-554-2212. *Application contact:* Dr. Wilma Kuhlman, Student Contact, 402-554-2212.

University of Nevada, Reno, Graduate School, College of Education, Department of Curriculum, Teaching and Learning, Program in Secondary Education, Reno, NV 89557. Offers M Ed, MA, MS. *Degree requirements:* For master's, thesis optional. *Entrance requirements:* For master's, GRE General Test, minimum GPA of 2.75. Additional exam requirements/recommendations for international students: Required—TOEFL (minimum score 500 paper-based; 173 computer-based; 61 iBT), IELTS (minimum score 6). Electronic applications accepted. *Faculty research:* Educational trends, pedagogy.

University of New Hampshire, Graduate School, College of Liberal Arts, Department of Education, Program in Secondary Education, Durham, NH 03824. Offers M Ed, MAT. Part-time programs available. *Faculty:* 32 full-time. *Students:* 44 full-time (29 women), 61 part-time (42 women); includes 3 minority (2 Asian, non-Hispanic/Latino; 1 Hispanic/Latino). Average age 25. 59 applicants, 71% accepted, 21 enrolled. In 2011, 89 master's awarded. *Degree requirements:* For master's, thesis or alternative. *Entrance requirements:* For master's, GRE General Test. Additional exam requirements/recommendations for international students: Required—TOEFL (minimum score 550 paper-based; 213 computer-based; 80 iBT). *Application deadline:* For fall admission, 6/1 priority date for domestic students, 4/1 for international students; for spring admission, 12/1 for domestic students. Applications are processed on a rolling basis. Application fee: $65. Electronic applications accepted. *Expenses:* Tuition, state resident: full-time $12,360; part-time $687 per credit hour. Tuition, nonresident: full-time $25,680; part-time $1058 per credit hour. *International tuition:* $29,550 full-time. *Required fees:* $1666; $833 per course. $416.50 per semester. Tuition and fees vary according to course load and degree level. *Financial support:* In 2011–12, 8 students received support, including 4 teaching assistantships; fellowships, research assistantships, career-related internships or fieldwork, Federal Work-Study, scholarships/grants, and tuition waivers (full and partial) also available. Support available to part-time students. Financial award application deadline: 2/15. *Faculty research:* Pre-service teacher education. *Unit head:* Dr. Michael Middleton, Coordinator, 603-862-7054, E-mail: education.department@unh.edu. *Application contact:* Lisa Wilder, Graduate Coordinator, 603-862-2310, E-mail: education.department@unh.edu. Web site: http://www.unh.edu/education.

University of New Mexico, Graduate School, College of Education, Department of Teacher Education, Program in Secondary Education, Albuquerque, NM 87131-2039. Offers mathematics, science, and educational technology education (MA). Part-time programs available. *Students:* 36 full-time (18 women), 49 part-time (32 women); includes 30 minority (2 Black or African American, non-Hispanic/Latino; 6 American Indian or Alaska Native, non-Hispanic/Latino; 3 Asian, non-Hispanic/Latino; 19 Hispanic/Latino), 1 international. Average age 33. 35 applicants, 57% accepted, 16 enrolled. In 2011, 41 degrees awarded. *Degree requirements:* For master's, comprehensive exam, thesis optional. *Entrance requirements:* For master's, minimum overall GPA of 3.0, some experience working with students, NMTA or teacher's licensure, 3 letters of reference, 1 letter of intent. Additional exam requirements/recommendations for international students: Required—TOEFL (minimum score 550 paper-based; 213 computer-based). *Application deadline:* For fall admission, 3/1 for domestic students; for spring admission, 10/1 for domestic students. Applications are processed on a rolling basis. Application fee: $50. Electronic applications accepted. *Financial support:* In 2011–12, 74 students received support, including 2 teaching assistantships with partial tuition reimbursements available (averaging $8,713 per year); career-related internships or fieldwork, scholarships/grants, and unspecified assistantships also available. Financial award application deadline: 4/15. *Faculty research:* Secondary education, teacher education, reflective practice, teacher leadership, student learning. *Unit head:* Dr. Rosalita Mitchell, Chair, 505-277-9611, Fax: 505-277-0455, E-mail: ted@unm.edu. *Application contact:* Robert Romero, Administrative Assistant, 505-277-0513, Fax: 505-277-0455, E-mail: ted@unm.edu. Web site: http://ted.unm.edu.

University of North Alabama, College of Education, Department of Secondary Education, Program in Secondary Education, Florence, AL 35632-0001. Offers MA Ed. *Accreditation:* NCATE. Part-time and evening/weekend programs available. *Faculty:* 2 full-time (0 women), 8 part-time/adjunct (5 women). *Students:* 71 full-time (45 women), 72 part-time (54 women); includes 17 minority (10 Black or African American, non-Hispanic/Latino; 1 American Indian or Alaska Native, non-Hispanic/Latino; 2 Asian, non-Hispanic/Latino; 2 Hispanic/Latino; 2 Two or more races, non-Hispanic/Latino). Average age 31. In 2011, 32 master's awarded. *Degree requirements:* For master's, comprehensive exam. *Entrance requirements:* For master's, GRE, MAT, or NTE, minimum GPA of 2.5, Alabama Class B Certificate or equivalent, teaching experience. *Application deadline:* For fall admission, 7/1 priority date for domestic students; for spring admission, 12/1 for domestic students. Applications are processed on a rolling basis. Application fee: $25. Electronic applications accepted. *Financial support:* Federal Work-Study available. Support available to part-time students. Financial award application deadline: 4/1. *Unit head:* Dr. Lee Hurren, Chair, 256-765-4575, Fax: 256-765-4159, E-mail: blhurren@una.edu. *Application contact:* Kim Mauldin, Director of Admissions, 256-765-4608, Fax: 256-765-4960, E-mail: komauldin@una.edu.

The University of North Carolina at Chapel Hill, Graduate School, School of Education, Program in Secondary Education, Chapel Hill, NC 27599. Offers English (Grades 9-12) (MAT); English as a second language (MAT); French (Grades K-12) (MAT); German (Grades K-12) (MAT); Japanese (Grades K-12) (MAT); Latin (Grades 9-12) (MAT); mathematics (Grades 9-12) (MAT); music (Grades K-12) (MAT); science (Grades 9-12) (MAT); social studies (Grades 9-12) (MAT); Spanish (Grades K-12) (MAT). *Accreditation:* NCATE. *Degree requirements:* For master's, comprehensive exam. *Entrance requirements:* For master's, GRE General Test, minimum GPA of 3.0 during last 2 years of undergraduate course work. Additional exam requirements/recommendations for international students: Required—TOEFL (minimum score 550 paper-based; 79 computer-based). Electronic applications accepted.

The University of North Carolina at Charlotte, Graduate School, College of Education, Department of Middle, Secondary and K-12 Education, Charlotte, NC 28223-0001. Offers art education (MAT); curriculum and instruction (PhD); dance education (MAT); foreign language education (MAT); middle grades education (M Ed, MAT); music education (MAT); secondary education (M Ed, MAT); teaching English as a second language (M Ed); theatre education (MAT). *Faculty:* 18 full-time (9 women), 6 part-time/adjunct (4 women). *Students:* 1 (woman) full-time, 57 part-time (44 women); includes 11 minority (5 Black or African American, non-Hispanic/Latino; 1 American Indian or Alaska Native, non-Hispanic/Latino; 2 Asian, non-Hispanic/Latino; 2 Hispanic/Latino; 1 Two or more races, non-Hispanic/Latino). Average age 33. 19 applicants, 100% accepted, 16 enrolled. In 2011, 12 master's awarded. *Entrance requirements:* For master's, GRE or MAT. Additional exam requirements/recommendations for international students: Required—TOEFL (minimum score 557 paper-based; 220 computer-based; 83 iBT). *Application deadline:* For fall admission, 7/1 for domestic students, 5/1 for international students; for spring admission, 11/1 for domestic students, 10/1 for international students. Applications are processed on a rolling basis. Application fee: $65 ($75 for international students). Electronic applications accepted. *Expenses:* Tuition, state resident: full-time $3689. Tuition, nonresident: full-time $15,226. *Required fees:* $2198. Tuition and fees vary according to course load and program. *Financial support:* In 2011–12, 5 students received support, including 5 research assistantships (averaging $4,290 per year); career-related internships or fieldwork, institutionally sponsored loans, scholarships/grants, and unspecified assistantships also available. Support available to part-time students. Financial award application deadline: 4/1; financial award applicants required to submit FAFSA. *Total annual research expenditures:* $126,589. *Unit head:* Melba Spooner, Chair, 704-687-8704, Fax: 704-687-6430, E-mail: mcspoone@uncc.edu. *Application contact:* Kathy B. Giddings, Director of Graduate Admissions, 704-687-5503, Fax: 704-687-3279, E-mail: gradadm@uncc.edu. Web site: http://education.uncc.edu/mdsk.

The University of North Carolina Wilmington, Watson School of Education, Department of Elementary, Middle Level and Literacy Education, Program in Middle Grades Education, Wilmington, NC 28403-3297. Offers instructional technology (MS); secondary education (M Ed). *Degree requirements:* For master's, comprehensive exam.

The University of North Carolina Wilmington, Watson School of Education, Department of Instructional Technology, Foundations and Secondary Education, Wilmington, NC 28403-3297. Offers instructional technology (MS); secondary education (M Ed); teaching (MAT). *Degree requirements:* For master's, comprehensive exam, thesis or alternative. *Entrance requirements:* Additional exam requirements/recommendations for international students: Required—TOEFL (minimum score 550 paper-based; 217 computer-based; 79 iBT), IELTS (minimum score 6.5).

University of North Dakota, Graduate School, College of Education and Human Development, Teaching and Learning Program, Grand Forks, ND 58202. Offers elementary education (Ed D, PhD); measurement and statistics (Ed D, PhD); secondary education (Ed D, PhD); special education (Ed D, PhD). *Accreditation:* NCATE. Postbaccalaureate distance learning degree programs offered (minimal on-campus study). *Degree requirements:* For doctorate, comprehensive exam, thesis/dissertation, final exam. *Entrance requirements:* For doctorate, minimum GPA of 3.5. Additional exam requirements/recommendations for international students: Required—TOEFL (minimum score 550 paper-based; 213 computer-based; 79 iBT), IELTS (minimum score 6.5). Electronic applications accepted.

University of Northern Iowa, Graduate College, College of Humanities, Arts and Sciences, Department of Languages and Literatures, Program in English, Cedar Falls, IA 50614. Offers creative writing (MA); English (MA); literature (MA); teaching English in secondary schools (TESS) (MA), including middle/junior high and senior high; teaching English to speakers of other languages (MA). Part-time and evening/weekend programs available. *Students:* 12 full-time (6 women), 4 part-time (all women); includes 2 minority (1 Black or African American, non-Hispanic/Latino; 1 Hispanic/Latino). 16 applicants, 50% accepted, 5 enrolled. In 2011, 5 master's awarded. *Degree requirements:* For master's, one foreign language, comprehensive exam, thesis or alternative, portfolio. *Entrance requirements:* Additional exam requirements/recommendations for international students: Required—TOEFL (minimum score 600 paper-based; 250 computer-based; 100 iBT). *Application deadline:* For fall admission, 8/1 priority date for domestic students. Applications are processed on a rolling basis. Application fee: $50 ($70 for international students). Electronic applications accepted. *Expenses:* Tuition, state resident: full-time $7476. Tuition, nonresident: full-time $16,410. *Required fees:* $942. *Financial support:* Career-related internships or fieldwork, Federal Work-Study, scholarships/grants, and tuition waivers (full and partial) available. Support available to part-time students. Financial award application deadline: 2/1. *Unit head:* Dr. Julie Husband, Graduate Coordinator, 319-273-3849, Fax: 319-273-5807, E-mail: julie.husband@uni.edu. *Application contact:* Laurie S. Russell, Record Analyst, 319-273-2623, Fax: 319-273-2885, E-mail: laurie.russell@uni.edu. Web site: http://www.uni.edu/langlit/.

University of Northern Iowa, Graduate College, College of Humanities, Arts and Sciences, Department of Mathematics, Cedar Falls, IA 50614. Offers industrial mathematics (PSM), including actuarial science, continuous quality improvement, mathematical computing and modeling; mathematics (MA), including mathematics, secondary; mathematics for middle grades 4-8 (MA). Part-time programs available. *Students:* 13 full-time (6 women), 23 part-time (17 women); includes 2 minority (1 Black or African American, non-Hispanic/Latino; 1 Asian, non-Hispanic/Latino), 6 international. 35 applicants, 74% accepted, 11 enrolled. In 2011, 19 master's awarded. *Degree requirements:* For master's, comprehensive exam (for some programs), thesis or alternative. *Entrance requirements:* For master's, minimum GPA of 3.0. Additional exam requirements/recommendations for international students: Required—TOEFL (minimum score 600 paper-based; 250 computer-based; 100 iBT). *Application deadline:* For fall admission, 8/1 priority date for domestic students. Applications are processed on a rolling basis. Application fee: $50 ($70 for international students). Electronic applications accepted. *Expenses:* Tuition, state resident: full-time $7476. Tuition, nonresident: full-time $16,410. *Required fees:* $942. *Financial support:* Career-related internships or fieldwork, Federal Work-Study, scholarships/grants, and tuition waivers (full and partial) available. Support available to part-time students. Financial award application deadline: 2/1. *Unit head:* Dr. Douglas Mupasiri, Interim Head, 319-273-2012, Fax: 319-273-2546, E-mail: douglas.mupasiri@uni.edu. *Application contact:* Laurie S. Russell, Record Analyst, 319-273-2623, Fax: 319-273-2885, E-mail: laurie.russell@uni.edu. Web site: http://www.math.uni.edu/.

University of North Florida, College of Education and Human Services, Department of Foundations and Secondary Education, Jacksonville, FL 32224. Offers adult learning (M Ed); professional education (M Ed). *Accreditation:* NCATE. Part-time and evening/weekend programs available. *Faculty:* 11 full-time (4 women). *Students:* 9 full-time (8 women), 19 part-time (12 women); includes 2 minority (1 Black or African American, non-Hispanic/Latino; 1 Asian, non-Hispanic/Latino), 5 international. Average age 33. 13 applicants, 38% accepted, 5 enrolled. In 2011, 12 master's awarded. *Entrance requirements:* For master's, GRE General Test, minimum GPA of 3.0 in last 60 hours, interview, 3 letters of recommendation. Additional exam requirements/recommendations for international students: Required—TOEFL (minimum score 500 paper-based; 173 computer-based; 61 iBT). *Application deadline:* For fall admission, 7/1 priority date for domestic students, 5/1 for international students; for spring admission, 11/1 priority date for domestic students, 10/1 for international students. Applications are processed on a rolling basis. Application fee: $30. Electronic applications accepted. *Expenses:* Tuition, state resident: full-time $8793; part-time $366.38 per credit hour. Tuition, nonresident: full-time $23,502; part-time $979.24 per credit hour. *Required fees:* $1384; $57.66 per credit hour. Tuition and fees vary according to course load and program. *Financial support:* In 2011–12, 6 students received support. Teaching assistantships, career-related internships or fieldwork, Federal Work-Study, and tuition waivers (partial) available. Support available to part-time students. Financial award application deadline: 4/1; financial award applicants required to submit FAFSA. *Faculty research:* Using children's literature to enhance metalinguistic awareness, education, oral language diagnosis of middle-schoolers, science inquiry teaching and learning. *Total annual research expenditures:* $429. *Unit head:* Dr. Jeffery Cornett, Chair, 904-620-2610, Fax: 904-620-1821, E-mail: jcornett@unf.edu. *Application contact:* Lillith Richardson, Assistant Director, The Graduate School, 904-620-1360, Fax: 904-620-1362, E-mail: graduateschool@unf.edu. Web site: http://www.unf.edu/coehs/fse/.

University of North Texas, Toulouse Graduate School, College of Education, Department of Teacher Education and Administration, Program in Secondary Education, Denton, TX 76203. Offers M Ed, Certificate. *Accreditation:* NCATE. *Degree requirements:* For master's, portfolio. *Entrance requirements:* For master's, GRE General Test, resume. Additional exam requirements/recommendations for international students: Recommended—TOEFL (minimum score 550 paper-based; 213 computer-based; 79 iBT). Electronic applications accepted. *Expenses:* Tuition, state resident: part-time $100 per credit hour. Tuition, nonresident: part-time $413 per credit hour. *Faculty research:* Geography instruction and digital technology, multicultural education teacher development.

University of Oklahoma, Jeannine Rainbolt College of Education, Department of Instructional Leadership and Academic Curriculum, Norman, OK 73072. Offers communication, culture and pedagogy for Hispanic populations in educational settings (Graduate Certificate); instructional leadership and academic curriculum (M Ed, PhD), including bilingual education, early childhood education, elementary education, English education, instructional leadership, mathematics education, reading education, science education, science, technology, engineering and mathematics education (M Ed), secondary education, social studies education, teacher education (M Ed). *Accreditation:* NCATE. Part-time and evening/weekend programs available. *Faculty:* 19 full-time (13 women), 1 (woman) part-time/adjunct. *Students:* 73 full-time (63 women), 114 part-time (87 women); includes 29 minority (5 Black or African American, non-Hispanic/Latino; 12 American Indian or Alaska Native, non-Hispanic/Latino; 5 Asian, non-Hispanic/Latino; 3 Hispanic/Latino; 1 Native Hawaiian or other Pacific Islander, non-Hispanic/Latino; 3 Two or more races, non-Hispanic/Latino), 7 international. Average age 33. 87 applicants, 86% accepted, 68 enrolled. In 2011, 36 master's, 6 doctorates awarded. Terminal master's awarded for partial completion of doctoral program. *Degree requirements:* For doctorate, thesis/dissertation. *Entrance requirements:* For master's, 12 hours of course work in education; for doctorate, GRE General Test, master's degree, minimum graduate GPA of 3.0. Additional exam requirements/recommendations for international students: Required—TOEFL (minimum score 550 paper-based; 79 iBT). *Application deadline:* For fall admission, 6/1 priority date for domestic students, 3/1 for international students; for spring admission, 11/1 for domestic students, 9/1 for international students. Applications are processed on a rolling basis. Application fee: $40 ($90 for international students). Electronic applications accepted. *Expenses:* Tuition, state resident: full-time $4087; part-time $170.30 per credit hour. Tuition, nonresident: full-time $14,875; part-time $619.80 per credit hour. *Required fees:* $2659; $100.25 per credit hour. Tuition and fees vary according to course load and degree level. *Financial support:* In 2011–12, 128 students received support, including 2 research assistantships with partial tuition reimbursements available (averaging $12,431 per year), 12 teaching assistantships with partial tuition reimbursements available (averaging $10,161 per year); institutionally sponsored loans, scholarships/grants, and unspecified assistantships also available. Financial award applicants required to submit FAFSA. *Faculty research:* Engineering in practice for sustainable future, no child left behind (reading), early childhood learning games impact study, Educare randomized control startup, Oklahoma mentoring professional development. *Total annual research expenditures:* $1.1 million. *Unit head:* Lawrence Baines, Chair, 405-325-1498, Fax: 405-325-4061, E-mail: lbaines@ou.edu. *Application contact:* Lynn Crussel, Graduate Programs Officer, 405-325-4843, Fax: 405-325-4061, E-mail: lcrussel@ou.edu. Web site: http://education.ou.edu/departments/ilac.

University of Pennsylvania, Graduate School of Education, Division of Teaching, Learning, and Leadership, Teacher Education Program, Philadelphia, PA 19104. Offers elementary education (MS Ed); secondary education (MS Ed). *Students:* 76 full-time (55 women), 1 (woman) part-time; includes 22 minority (9 Black or African American, non-Hispanic/Latino; 4 Asian, non-Hispanic/Latino; 5 Hispanic/Latino; 4 Two or more races, non-Hispanic/Latino). 207 applicants, 72% accepted, 77 enrolled. In 2011, 113 degrees awarded. *Degree requirements:* For master's, comprehensive exam or portfolio. *Entrance requirements:* For master's, GRE General Test, MAT. *Application deadline:* For fall admission, 12/15 priority date for domestic students. Applications are processed on a rolling basis. Application fee: $70. Electronic applications accepted. *Expenses:* Contact institution. *Financial support:* Fellowships available. Financial award applicants required to submit FAFSA. *Unit head:* Dr. Andrew Porter, Dean, 215-898-7014. *Application contact:* Maureen Cotterill, 215-898-7364, E-mail: maureenc@gse.upenn.edu. Web site: http://tep.gse.upenn.edu/join/join_ms-ed.html.

University of Phoenix–Bay Area Campus, College of Education, San Jose, CA 95134-1805. Offers administration and supervision (MA Ed); adult education and training (MA Ed); early childhood education (MA Ed); education (Ed S); educational leadership (Ed D); elementary teacher education (MA Ed); higher education administration (PhD); secondary teacher education (MA Ed); special education (MA Ed); teacher leadership (MA Ed). Evening/weekend programs available. Postbaccalaureate distance learning degree programs offered (no on-campus study). *Degree requirements:* For master's, thesis (for some programs). *Entrance requirements:* For master's, minimum undergraduate GPA of 2.5, 3 years of work experience. Additional exam requirements/recommendations for international students: Required—TOEFL (minimum score 550 paper-based; 213 computer-based; 79 iBT). Electronic applications accepted.

University of Phoenix–Central Florida Campus, College of Education, Maitland, FL 32751-7057. Offers administration and supervision (MA Ed); curriculum and instruction (MA Ed); curriculum and instruction-computer education (MA Ed); curriculum and instruction-mathematics education (MA Ed); early childhood education (MA Ed); elementary teacher education (MA Ed); secondary teacher education (MA Ed). Evening/weekend programs available. *Degree requirements:* For master's, thesis (for some programs). *Entrance requirements:* For master's, 3 years of work experience, minimum undergraduate GPA of 2.5. Additional exam requirements/recommendations for international students: Required—TOEFL (minimum score 550 paper-based; 213 computer-based; 79 iBT). Electronic applications accepted.

University of Phoenix–Central Valley Campus, College of Education, Fresno, CA 93720-1562. Offers curriculum and instruction (MA Ed); curriculum and instruction-computer education (MA Ed); elementary teacher education (MA Ed); secondary teacher education (MA Ed).

University of Phoenix–Chattanooga Campus, College of Education, Chattanooga, TN 37421-3707. Offers administration and supervision (MA Ed); curriculum and instruction (MA Ed); elementary teacher education (MA Ed); secondary teacher education (MA Ed).

University of Phoenix–Denver Campus, College of Education, Lone Tree, CO 80124-5453. Offers administration and supervision (MAEd); curriculum instruction (MAEd); elementary teacher education (MAEd); school counseling (MSC); secondary teacher education (MAEd). Evening/weekend programs available. *Degree requirements:* For master's, thesis (for some programs). *Entrance requirements:* For master's, minimum undergraduate GPA of 2.5, 3 years work experience. Additional exam requirements/recommendations for international students: Required—TOEFL (minimum score 550 paper-based; 213 computer-based; 79 iBT). Electronic applications accepted.

Secondary Education

University of Phoenix–Hawaii Campus, College of Education, Honolulu, HI 96813-4317. Offers administration and supervision (MA Ed); curriculum and instruction (MA Ed); elementary education (MA Ed); secondary education (MA Ed); special education (MA Ed); teacher education for elementary licensure (MA Ed). Evening/weekend programs available. *Degree requirements:* For master's, thesis (for some programs). *Entrance requirements:* For master's, minimum undergraduate GPA of 2.5, 3 years of work experience. Additional exam requirements/recommendations for international students: Required—TOEFL (minimum score 550 paper-based; 213 computer-based; 79 iBT). Electronic applications accepted.

University of Phoenix–Idaho Campus, College of Education, Meridian, ID 83642-5114. Offers administration and supervision (MA Ed); curriculum and instruction (MA Ed); elementary teacher education (MA Ed); secondary teacher education (MA Ed). Evening/weekend programs available. *Degree requirements:* For master's, thesis (for some programs). *Entrance requirements:* For master's, minimum undergraduate GPA of 2.5, 3 years of work experience. Additional exam requirements/recommendations for international students: Required—TOEFL (minimum score 550 paper-based; 213 computer-based). Electronic applications accepted.

University of Phoenix–Indianapolis Campus, College of Education, Indianapolis, IN 46250-932. Offers elementary teacher education (MA Ed); secondary teacher education (MA Ed).

University of Phoenix–Memphis Campus, College of Education, Cordova, TN 38018. Offers administration and supervision (MA Ed); curriculum and instruction (MA Ed); elementary teacher education (MA Ed); secondary teacher education (MA Ed).

University of Phoenix–Metro Detroit Campus, College of Education, Troy, MI 48098-2623. Offers administration and supervision (MA Ed); elementary teacher education (MA Ed); secondary teacher education (MA Ed); special education (MA Ed). Evening/weekend programs available. *Degree requirements:* For master's, thesis (for some programs). *Entrance requirements:* For master's, 3 years of work experience, minimum undergraduate GPA of 2.5. Additional exam requirements/recommendations for international students: Required—TOEFL (minimum score 550 paper-based; 213 computer-based; 79 iBT). Electronic applications accepted.

University of Phoenix–Nashville Campus, College of Education, Nashville, TN 37214-5048. Offers administration and supervision (MA Ed); curriculum and instruction (MA Ed); elementary teacher education (MA Ed); secondary teacher education (MA Ed). Evening/weekend programs available. *Degree requirements:* For master's, thesis (for some programs). *Entrance requirements:* For master's, minimum undergraduate GPA of 2.5, 3 years work experience. Additional exam requirements/recommendations for international students: Required—TOEFL (minimum score 500 paper-based; 213 computer-based; 79 iBT). Electronic applications accepted.

University of Phoenix–New Mexico Campus, College of Education, Albuquerque, NM 87113-1570. Offers administration and supervision (MAEd); curriculum and instruction (MAEd); elementary teacher education (MAEd); school counseling (MSC); secondary teacher education (MAEd). Evening/weekend programs available. *Degree requirements:* For master's, thesis (for some programs). *Entrance requirements:* For master's, minimum undergraduate GPA of 2.5, 3 years of work experience. Additional exam requirements/recommendations for international students: Required—TOEFL (minimum score 550 paper-based; 213 computer-based; 79 iBT). Electronic applications accepted.

University of Phoenix–Northern Nevada Campus, College of Education, Reno, NV 89521-5862. Offers administration and supervision (MA Ed); curriculum and instruction (MA Ed); elementary teacher education (MA Ed); secondary teacher education (MA Ed).

University of Phoenix–North Florida Campus, College of Education, Jacksonville, FL 32216-0959. Offers administration and supervision (MA Ed); curriculum and instruction (MA Ed), including computer education, mathematics education; early childhood education (MA Ed); elementary teacher education (MA Ed); secondary teacher education (MA Ed). Evening/weekend programs available. *Degree requirements:* For master's, thesis (for some programs). *Entrance requirements:* For master's, 3 years of work experience, minimum undergraduate GPA of 2.5. Additional exam requirements/recommendations for international students: Required—TOEFL (minimum score 550 paper-based; 213 computer-based; 49 iBT). Electronic applications accepted.

University of Phoenix–Omaha Campus, College of Education, Omaha, NE 68154-5240. Offers administration and supervision (MA Ed); curriculum and instruction (MA Ed), including adult education, computer education, curriculum and instruction, English and language arts education, English as a second language, mathematics education; elementary teacher education (MA Ed); secondary teacher education (MA Ed); special education (MA Ed).

University of Phoenix–Online Campus, College of Education, Phoenix, AZ 85034-7209. Offers administration and supervision (MAEd, Graduate Certificate); adult education and training (MAEd); curriculum and instruction (MAEd); curriculum and instruction reading (MAEd); curriculum and instruction-computer education (MAEd); curriculum and instruction-language arts (MAEd); curriculum and instruction-mathematics (MAEd); early childhood education (MAEd); educational studies (MAEd); elementary teacher education (MAEd); elementary teacher education-early childhood (MAEd); secondary teacher education (MAEd); special education (MAEd); teacher education - elementary/middle level (MAEd); teacher education middle level generalist (MAEd); teacher education middle level mathematics (MAEd); teacher education middle level science (MAEd); teacher education secondary mathematics (MAEd); teacher education secondary science (MAEd); teacher leadership (MAEd). *Accreditation:* Teacher Education Accreditation Council. Evening/weekend programs available. Postbaccalaureate distance learning degree programs offered. *Students:* 9,180 full-time (7,178 women); includes 2,913 minority (2,069 Black or African American, non-Hispanic/Latino; 50 American Indian or Alaska Native, non-Hispanic/Latino; 100 Asian, non-Hispanic/Latino; 542 Hispanic/Latino; 48 Native Hawaiian or other Pacific Islander, non-Hispanic/Latino; 104 Two or more races, non-Hispanic/Latino), 147 international. Average age 36. *Entrance requirements:* Additional exam requirements/recommendations for international students: Required—TOEFL, TOEIC (Test of English as an International Communication), Berlitz Online English Proficiency Exam, Pearson Test of English, or IELTS. *Application deadline:* Applications are processed on a rolling basis. Application fee: $45. Electronic applications accepted. *Expenses:* Contact institution. *Financial support:* Scholarships/grants available. Financial award applicants required to submit FAFSA. *Application contact:* 866-766-0766. Web site: http://www.phoenix.edu/colleges_divisions/education.html.

University of Phoenix–Oregon Campus, College of Education, Tigard, OR 97223. Offers curriculum and instruction (MA Ed); early childhood education (MA Ed); elementary education (MA Ed), including early childhood specialization, middle level specialization; secondary education (MA Ed), including middle level specialization. Evening/weekend programs available. *Degree requirements:* For master's, thesis (for some programs). *Entrance requirements:* For master's, minimum undergraduate GPA of 2.5, 3 years work experience. Additional exam requirements/recommendations for international students: Required—TOEFL (minimum score 550 paper-based; 213 computer-based; 79 iBT). Electronic applications accepted.

University of Phoenix–Phoenix Main Campus, College of Education, Tempe, AZ 85282-2371. Offers administration and supervision (MA Ed); adult education and training (MA Ed); curriculum and instruction reading (MA Ed); curriculum instruction (MA Ed); early childhood education (MA Ed); education studies (MA Ed); elementary teacher education (MA Ed); secondary teacher education (MA Ed); special education (MA Ed); teacher leadership (MA Ed). Evening/weekend programs available. Postbaccalaureate distance learning degree programs offered. *Students:* 297 full-time (203 women); includes 53 minority (19 Black or African American, non-Hispanic/Latino; 1 American Indian or Alaska Native, non-Hispanic/Latino; 6 Asian, non-Hispanic/Latino; 21 Hispanic/Latino; 2 Native Hawaiian or other Pacific Islander, non-Hispanic/Latino; 4 Two or more races, non-Hispanic/Latino), 3 international. Average age 35. *Entrance requirements:* Additional exam requirements/recommendations for international students: Required—TOEFL, TOEIC (Test of English as an International Communication), Berlitz Online English Proficiency Exam, Pearson Test of English, or IELTS. *Application deadline:* Applications are processed on a rolling basis. Application fee: $45. Electronic applications accepted. *Expenses:* Contact institution. *Financial support:* Scholarships/grants available. Financial award applicants required to submit FAFSA. *Application contact:* 866-766-0766. Web site: http://www.phoenix.edu/colleges_divisions/education.html.

University of Phoenix–Sacramento Valley Campus, College of Education, Sacramento, CA 95833-3632. Offers adult education (MA Ed); curriculum instruction (MA Ed); elementary teacher education (MA Ed); secondary teacher education (MA Ed); teacher education (Certificate). Evening/weekend programs available. *Degree requirements:* For master's, thesis (for some programs). *Entrance requirements:* For master's, 3 years of work experience, minimum undergraduate GPA of 2.5. Additional exam requirements/recommendations for international students: Required—TOEFL (minimum score 550 paper-based; 213 computer-based; 79 iBT). Electronic applications accepted.

University of Phoenix–San Diego Campus, College of Education, San Diego, CA 92123. Offers curriculum and instruction (MA Ed), including computer education, curriculum and instruction, English as a second language; elementary teacher education (MA Ed); secondary teacher education (MA Ed). Evening/weekend programs available. *Degree requirements:* For master's, thesis (for some programs). *Entrance requirements:* For master's, 3 years of work experience, minimum undergraduate GPA of 3.0. Additional exam requirements/recommendations for international students: Required—TOEFL (minimum score 550 paper-based; 213 computer-based; 79 iBT). Electronic applications accepted.

University of Phoenix–Southern Arizona Campus, College of Education, Tucson, AZ 85711. Offers administration and supervision (MA Ed); adult education and training (MA Ed); curriculum instruction (MA Ed); educational counseling (MA Ed); elementary teacher education (MA Ed); school counseling (MSC); secondary teacher education (MA Ed); special education (MA Ed, Certificate). Evening/weekend programs available. *Degree requirements:* For master's, thesis (for some programs). *Entrance requirements:* For master's, minimum undergraduate GPA of 2.5, 3 years of work experience. Additional exam requirements/recommendations for international students: Required—TOEFL (minimum score 550 paper-based; 213 computer-based; 79 iBT). Electronic applications accepted.

University of Phoenix–Southern Colorado Campus, College of Education, Colorado Springs, CO 80919-2335. Offers administration and supervision (MA Ed); curriculum and instruction (MA Ed); elementary teacher education (MA Ed); principal licensure certification (Certificate); school counseling (MSC); secondary teacher education (MA Ed). Evening/weekend programs available. *Degree requirements:* For master's, thesis (for some programs). *Entrance requirements:* For master's, minimum undergraduate GPA of 2.5, 3 years of work experience. Additional exam requirements/recommendations for international students: Required—TOEFL (minimum score 550 paper-based; 213 computer-based; 79 iBT). Electronic applications accepted.

University of Phoenix–South Florida Campus, College of Education, Fort Lauderdale, FL 33309. Offers administration and supervision (MA Ed); curriculum and instruction (MA Ed), including computer education, curriculum and instruction, mathematics education; early childhood education (MA Ed); elementary teacher education (MA Ed); secondary teacher education (MA Ed). Evening/weekend programs available. *Degree requirements:* For master's, thesis (for some programs). *Entrance requirements:* For master's, 3 years of work experience, minimum undergraduate GPA of 2.5. Additional exam requirements/recommendations for international students: Required—TOEFL (minimum score 550 paper-based; 213 computer-based; 79 iBT). Electronic applications accepted.

University of Phoenix–Utah Campus, College of Education, Salt Lake City, UT 84123-4617. Offers administration and supervision (MA Ed); curriculum and instruction (MA Ed); elementary teacher education (MA Ed); school counseling (MSC); secondary teacher education (MA Ed); special education (MA Ed). Evening/weekend programs available. *Degree requirements:* For master's, thesis (for some programs). *Entrance requirements:* For master's, minimum undergraduate GPA of 2.5, 3 years work experience. Additional exam requirements/recommendations for international students: Required—TOEFL (minimum score 550 paper-based; 213 computer-based; 79 iBT). Electronic applications accepted.

University of Phoenix–Washington D.C. Campus, College of Education, Washington, DC 20001. Offers administration and supervision (MA Ed); adult education and training (MA Ed); computer education (MA Ed); curriculum and instruction (MA Ed, Ed D); early childhood education (MA Ed); education (Ed S); educational leadership (Ed D); educational technology (Ed D); elementary teacher education (MA Ed); English and language arts education (MA Ed); English as a second language (MA Ed); higher education administration (PhD); mathematics education (MA Ed); secondary teacher education (MA Ed); special education (MA Ed); teacher leadership (MA Ed).

University of Phoenix–West Florida Campus, College of Education, Temple Terrace, FL 33637. Offers administration and supervision (MA Ed); curriculum and instruction (MA Ed), including computer education, curriculum and instruction, mathematics education; curriculum and technology (MA Ed); early childhood education (MA Ed); elementary teacher education (MA Ed); secondary teacher education (MA Ed). Evening/weekend programs available. *Degree requirements:* For master's, thesis (for some programs). *Entrance requirements:* For master's, 3 years of work experience, minimum undergraduate GPA of 2.5. Additional exam requirements/recommendations for international students: Required—TOEFL (minimum score 550 paper-based; 213 computer-based; 79 iBT).

University of Pittsburgh, School of Education, Department of Instruction and Learning, Program in Secondary Education, Pittsburgh, PA 15260. Offers English/communications education (M Ed, MAT); foreign languages education (M Ed, MAT); mathematics education (M Ed, MAT, Ed D); science education (M Ed, MAT, Ed D); social studies education (M Ed, MAT). Part-time and evening/weekend programs available. *Students:* 154 full-time (92 women), 68 part-time (47 women); includes 18 minority (6 Black or African American, non-Hispanic/Latino; 3 Asian, non-Hispanic/Latino; 7 Hispanic/Latino; 2 Two or more races, non-Hispanic/Latino), 6 international. Average age 30. 208 applicants, 48% accepted, 72 enrolled. In 2011, 116 master's, 6 doctorates awarded.

Degree requirements: For master's, thesis; for doctorate, thesis/dissertation. *Entrance requirements:* For master's, PRAXIS I; for doctorate, GRE General Test. Additional exam requirements/recommendations for international students: Required—TOEFL. *Application deadline:* For fall admission, 2/1 priority date for domestic students; for spring admission, 11/15 priority date for domestic students. Applications are processed on a rolling basis. Application fee: $50. Electronic applications accepted. *Expenses:* Tuition, state resident: full-time $18,774; part-time $760 per credit. Tuition, nonresident: full-time $30,736; part-time $1258 per credit. *Required fees:* $740; $200 per term. Tuition and fees vary according to program. *Financial support:* Fellowships, teaching assistantships, career-related internships or fieldwork, Federal Work-Study, tuition waivers (partial), and unspecified assistantships available. Support available to part-time students. Financial award application deadline: 3/15; financial award applicants required to submit FAFSA. *Unit head:* Dr. Richard Donato, Chairman, 412-624-7248, Fax: 412-648-7081, E-mail: donato@pitt.edu. *Application contact:* Marianne L. Budziszewski, Director of Admissions and Enrollment Services, 412-648-2230, Fax: 412-648-1899, E-mail: soeinfo@pitt.edu. Web site: http://www.education.pitt.edu/.

University of Puget Sound, Graduate Studies, School of Education, Program in Teaching, Tacoma, WA 98416. Offers elementary education (MAT); secondary education (MAT). *Accreditation:* NASM; NCATE. *Faculty:* 6 full-time (3 women). *Students:* 27 full-time (17 women); includes 3 minority (all Hispanic/Latino). Average age 25. 53 applicants, 74% accepted, 27 enrolled. In 2011, 33 master's awarded. *Degree requirements:* For master's, capstone course. *Entrance requirements:* For master's, GRE General Test, WEST-B, WEST-E in content area, minimum GPA of 3.0. Additional exam requirements/recommendations for international students: Required—TOEFL (minimum score 550 paper-based; 213 computer-based; 80 iBT). *Application deadline:* For fall admission, 3/1 priority date for domestic students, 3/1 for international students. Applications are processed on a rolling basis. Application fee: $60. Electronic applications accepted. *Financial support:* In 2011–12, 24 students received support. Career-related internships or fieldwork and scholarships/grants available. Financial award application deadline: 3/31; financial award applicants required to submit FAFSA. *Faculty research:* Math education, social studies education, professional development, international education, classroom discourse, equity education. *Unit head:* Dr. John Woodward, Dean, 253-879-3375, E-mail: woodward@pugetsound.edu. *Application contact:* Dr. George H. Mills, Jr., Vice President for Enrollment, 253-879-3211, Fax: 253-879-3993, E-mail: admission@pugetsound.edu. Web site: http://www.pugetsound.edu/academics/departments-and-programs/graduate/school-of-education/mat/.

University of Rhode Island, Graduate School, College of Human Science and Services, School of Education, Kingston, RI 02881. Offers adult education (MA); education (PhD); elementary education (MA); music education (MM); reading education (MA); secondary education (MA); special education (MA); MS/PhD. *Accreditation:* NCATE. Part-time and evening/weekend programs available. *Faculty:* 21 full-time (13 women), 3 part-time/adjunct (1 woman). *Students:* 54 full-time (48 women), 108 part-time (86 women); includes 14 minority (3 Black or African American, non-Hispanic/Latino; 4 Asian, non-Hispanic/Latino; 7 Hispanic/Latino), 4 international. In 2011, 56 master's, 8 doctorates awarded. *Degree requirements:* For master's, comprehensive exam (for some programs), thesis optional; for doctorate, comprehensive exam, thesis/dissertation. *Entrance requirements:* For master's, 2 letters of recommendation; interview (for special education applicants); for doctorate, GRE, 3 letters of recommendation, resume. Additional exam requirements/recommendations for international students: Required—TOEFL (minimum score 600 paper-based; 250 computer-based; 100 iBT). *Application deadline:* For fall admission, 1/31 for international students. Application fee: $65. Electronic applications accepted. *Expenses:* Tuition, state resident: full-time $10,432; part-time $580 per credit hour. Tuition, nonresident: full-time $23,130; part-time $1285 per credit hour. *Required fees:* $1362; $36 per credit hour. $35 per semester. One-time fee: $130. *Financial support:* In 2011–12, 4 teaching assistantships with full and partial tuition reimbursements (averaging $12,157 per year) were awarded; career-related internships or fieldwork also available. Financial award applicants required to submit FAFSA. *Unit head:* Dr. David Byrd, Director, 401-874-5484, Fax: 401-874-5471, E-mail: dbyrd@uri.edu. *Application contact:* Dr. John Boulmetis, Coordinator of Graduate Studies, 401-874-4159, Fax: 401-874-7610, E-mail: johnb@uri.edu. Web site: http://www.uri.edu/hss/education/.

University of St. Francis, College of Education, Joliet, IL 60435-6169. Offers educational leadership (MS, Ed D); elementary education certification (M Ed); reading (MS); secondary education certification (M Ed), including English education, math education, science education, social studies education, visual arts education; special education (M Ed); teaching and learning (MS). *Accreditation:* NCATE. Part-time and evening/weekend programs available. Postbaccalaureate distance learning degree programs offered (no on-campus study). *Faculty:* 7 full-time (5 women), 21 part-time/adjunct (14 women). *Students:* 32 full-time (21 women), 230 part-time (175 women); includes 23 minority (7 Black or African American, non-Hispanic/Latino; 2 Asian, non-Hispanic/Latino; 13 Hispanic/Latino; 1 Two or more races, non-Hispanic/Latino), 1 international. Average age 32. 147 applicants, 60% accepted, 57 enrolled. In 2011, 156 master's awarded. *Entrance requirements:* For doctorate, master's degree, IL Type 75 or Principal's endorsement, interview. Additional exam requirements/recommendations for international students: Required—TOEFL (minimum score 550 paper-based; 213 computer-based). *Application deadline:* Applications are processed on a rolling basis. Application fee: $30. Electronic applications accepted. *Expenses:* Contact institution. *Financial support:* In 2011–12, 23 students received support. Federal Work-Study, scholarships/grants, tuition waivers (partial), and unspecified assistantships available. Support available to part-time students. Financial award applicants required to submit FAFSA. *Unit head:* Dr. John Gambro, Dean, 815-740-3829, Fax: 815-740-2264, E-mail: jgambro@stfrancis.edu. *Application contact:* Sandra Sloka, Director of Admissions for Graduate and Degree Completion Programs, 800-735-7500, Fax: 815-740-5032, E-mail: ssloka@stfrancis.edu. Web site: http://www.stfrancis.edu/academics/college-of-education/.

University of St. Thomas, Graduate Studies, School of Education, Department of Teacher Education, St. Paul, MN 55105-1096. Offers curriculum and instruction (MA), including elementary, individualized, K-12, secondary; elementary (MAT); engineering education (Certificate); English as a second language (MA); math education (Certificate); multicultural education (Certificate); reading (MA, Certificate), including elementary (MA), K-12 (MA). *Accreditation:* NCATE. Part-time and evening/weekend programs available. *Faculty:* 7 full-time (4 women), 26 part-time/adjunct (20 women). *Students:* 19 full-time (14 women), 161 part-time (113 women); includes 28 minority (3 Black or African American, non-Hispanic/Latino; 7 American Indian or Alaska Native, non-Hispanic/Latino; 6 Asian, non-Hispanic/Latino; 9 Hispanic/Latino; 3 Two or more races, non-Hispanic/Latino), 5 international. Average age 35. 150 applicants, 79% accepted, 88 enrolled. In 2011, 83 master's awarded. *Entrance requirements:* For master's, minimum GPA of 3.0 or MAT. Additional exam requirements/recommendations for international students: Required—TOEFL (minimum score 550 paper-based; 210 computer-based; 80 iBT). *Application deadline:* For fall admission, 6/1 for domestic students; for spring admission, 11/1 for domestic students. Applications are processed on a rolling basis. Application fee: $50. *Financial support:* Fellowships, research assistantships, institutionally sponsored loans, and scholarships/grants available. Support available to part-time students. Financial award applicants required to submit FAFSA. *Unit head:* Dr. Jan L. H. Frank, Department Chair, 651-962-4446, Fax: 651-962-4169, E-mail: jlhfrank@stthomas.edu. *Application contact:* Rosemary R. Barreto, Department Assistant, 651-962-4420, Fax: 651-962-4169, E-mail: barr7879@stthomas.edu. Web site: http://www.stthomas.edu/education.

University of St. Thomas, School of Education, Houston, TX 77006-4696. Offers all level teaching (M Ed); bilingual/dual language (M Ed); Catholic school teaching (M Ed); Catholic/private school leadership (M Ed); counselor education (M Ed); curriculum and instruction (M Ed); educational leadership (M Ed); elementary teaching (M Ed); English as a second language (M Ed); exceptionality/ educational diagnostician (M Ed); exceptionality/special education (M Ed); generalist (M Ed); reading (M Ed); secondary teaching (M Ed). Part-time and evening/weekend programs available. Postbaccalaureate distance learning degree programs offered (no on-campus study). *Faculty:* 30 full-time (17 women), 54 part-time/adjunct (37 women). *Students:* 66 full-time (43 women), 1,178 part-time (1,044 women); includes 777 minority (313 Black or African American, non-Hispanic/Latino; 5 American Indian or Alaska Native, non-Hispanic/Latino; 29 Asian, non-Hispanic/Latino; 395 Hispanic/Latino; 2 Native Hawaiian or other Pacific Islander, non-Hispanic/Latino; 33 Two or more races, non-Hispanic/Latino), 26 international. Average age 36. 551 applicants, 94% accepted, 416 enrolled. In 2011, 72 master's awarded. *Degree requirements:* For master's, thesis, field experience. *Entrance requirements:* For master's, GRE or MAT if GPA is below 3.0, bachelor's degree; minimum GPA of 2.75 in bachelor's degree or last 60 credit hours; official transcripts from all institutions; goal statement of 250-300 words; 1 reference. Additional exam requirements/recommendations for international students: Required—TOEFL. *Application deadline:* Applications are processed on a rolling basis. Application fee: $35. Electronic applications accepted. *Expenses:* Contact institution. *Financial support:* In 2011–12, 9 students received support. Federal Work-Study, scholarships/grants, and state work-study, institutional employment available. Support available to part-time students. Financial award application deadline: 4/15; financial award applicants required to submit FAFSA. *Faculty research:* Leadership, diversity, personality traits, second language acquisition. *Unit head:* Dr. Nora Hutto, Dean, 713-525-3540, Fax: 713-525-3871, E-mail: education@stthom.edu. *Application contact:* Paula C. Hollis, Administrative Assistant, 713-525-3540, Fax: 713-525-3871, E-mail: education@stthom.edu. Web site: http://www.stthom.edu/Schools_Centers_of_Excellence/Schools_of_Study/School_of_Education/Index.aqf.

The University of Scranton, College of Graduate and Continuing Education, Department of Education, Program in Secondary Education, Scranton, PA 18510. Offers MS. *Accreditation:* NCATE. Part-time and evening/weekend programs available. *Students:* 11 full-time (2 women), 17 part-time (15 women); includes 2 minority (1 Asian, non-Hispanic/Latino; 1 Hispanic/Latino), 2 international. Average age 28. 29 applicants, 93% accepted. In 2011, 11 master's awarded. *Degree requirements:* For master's, comprehensive exam, capstone experience. *Entrance requirements:* For master's, minimum GPA of 2.75. Additional exam requirements/recommendations for international students: Required—TOEFL (minimum score 500 paper-based; 173 computer-based), IELTS (minimum score 5.5). *Application deadline:* Applications are processed on a rolling basis. Application fee: $0. *Financial support:* Teaching assistantships, career-related internships or fieldwork, Federal Work-Study, and unspecified assistantships available. Support available to part-time students. Financial award application deadline: 3/1. *Unit head:* Dr. Art Chambers, Director, 570-941-4668, Fax: 570-941-5515, E-mail: chambera2@scranton.edu. *Application contact:* Joseph M. Roback, Director of Admissions, 570-941-4385, Fax: 570-941-5928, E-mail: robackj2@scranton.edu.

University of South Alabama, Graduate School, College of Education, Department of Leadership and Teacher Education, Mobile, AL 36688-0002. Offers early childhood education (M Ed); educational administration (Ed S); educational leadership (M Ed); elementary education (M Ed); reading education (M Ed); science education (M Ed); secondary education (M Ed); special education (M Ed, Ed S). *Accreditation:* NCATE. Part-time programs available. *Faculty:* 20 full-time (14 women). *Students:* 135 full-time (106 women), 75 part-time (62 women); includes 50 minority (40 Black or African American, non-Hispanic/Latino; 3 American Indian or Alaska Native, non-Hispanic/Latino; 3 Asian, non-Hispanic/Latino; 3 Hispanic/Latino; 1 Two or more races, non-Hispanic/Latino), 1 international. 89 applicants, 49% accepted, 36 enrolled. In 2011, 88 master's, 13 Ed Ss awarded. *Degree requirements:* For master's, comprehensive exam. *Entrance requirements:* For master's, GRE General Test or MAT, minimum GPA of 3.0. *Application deadline:* For fall admission, 7/15 priority date for domestic students, 6/15 for international students; for spring admission, 12/1 priority date for domestic students, 11/1 for international students. Applications are processed on a rolling basis. Application fee: $35. *Expenses:* Tuition, state resident: full-time $7968; part-time $332 per credit hour. Tuition, nonresident: full-time $15,936; part-time $664 per credit hour. *Financial support:* Research assistantships and career-related internships or fieldwork available. Support available to part-time students. Financial award application deadline: 4/1. *Unit head:* Dr. Harold Dodge, Jr., Chair, 251-380-2894. *Application contact:* Dr. Abigail Baxter, Director of Graduate Studies, 251-460-6310, Fax: 251-461-1513, E-mail: kharriso@usouthal.edu. Web site: http://www.southalabama.edu/coe/lted.

University of South Carolina, The Graduate School, College of Education, Department of Instruction and Teacher Education, Program in Secondary Education, Columbia, SC 29208. Offers art education (IMA, MAT); business education (IMA, MAT); English (MAT); foreign language (MAT); health education (MAT); mathematics (MAT); science (IMA, MAT); secondary (Ed D); secondary education (MT, PhD); social studies (MAT); theatre and speech (MAT). IMA and MT offered jointly with the subject areas. *Accreditation:* NCATE. *Degree requirements:* For master's, comprehensive exam, thesis (for some programs), foreign language (MA); for doctorate, one foreign language, comprehensive exam, thesis/dissertation. *Entrance requirements:* For master's, GRE General Test or MAT, teaching certificate (IMA, M Ed), interview; for doctorate, GRE General Test or MAT, interview. *Faculty research:* Middle school programs, professional development, school collaboration.

The University of South Dakota, Graduate School, School of Education, Division of Curriculum and Instruction, Program in Secondary Education, Vermillion, SD 57069-2390. Offers MA. *Accreditation:* NCATE. Part-time programs available. Postbaccalaureate distance learning degree programs offered. *Degree requirements:* For master's, comprehensive exam, thesis or alternative. *Entrance requirements:* For master's, GRE General Test, MAT, minimum GPA of 2.7. Additional exam requirements/recommendations for international students: Required—TOEFL (minimum score 550 paper-based; 213 computer-based; 79 iBT). Electronic applications accepted. *Expenses:* Tuition, state resident: full-time $3118.50; part-time $173.25 per credit hour. Tuition, nonresident: full-time $6601; part-time $366.70 per credit hour. *Required fees:* $2268; $126 per credit hour. Tuition and fees vary according to program.

University of Southern Indiana, Graduate Studies, College of Science, Engineering, and Education, Department of Teacher Education, Program in Secondary Education, Evansville, IN 47712-3590. Offers MS. *Accreditation:* NCATE. Part-time and evening/weekend programs available. *Faculty:* 8 full-time (4 women), 1 part-time/adjunct (0 women). *Students:* 1 (woman) full-time, 62 part-time (39 women); includes 5 minority (3 Black or African American, non-Hispanic/Latino; 1 Asian, non-Hispanic/Latino; 1 Hispanic/Latino), 2 international. Average age 34. 28 applicants, 96% accepted, 24 enrolled. In 2011, 14 master's awarded. *Entrance requirements:* For master's, GRE

General Test, NTE or PRAXIS I, minimum GPA of 3.0, teaching license. Additional exam requirements/recommendations for international students: Required—TOEFL (minimum score 550 paper-based; 213 computer-based; 79 iBT), IELTS (minimum score 6). *Application deadline:* For fall admission, 7/1 priority date for domestic students, 1/1 for international students. Applications are processed on a rolling basis. Application fee: $35. Electronic applications accepted. *Expenses:* Tuition, state resident: full-time $5044; part-time $280.21 per credit hour. Tuition, nonresident: full-time $9949; part-time $552.71 per credit hour. *Required fees:* $240; $22.75 per term. Tuition and fees vary according to course load and reciprocity agreements. *Financial support:* In 2011–12, 1 student received support. Federal Work-Study, institutionally sponsored loans, scholarships/grants, tuition waivers (full and partial), and unspecified assistantships available. Financial award application deadline: 3/1; financial award applicants required to submit FAFSA. *Unit head:* Dr. Vella Goebel, Coordinator, 812-461-5306, E-mail: vgoebel@usi.edu. *Application contact:* Dr. Wes Durham, Interim Director, Graduate Studies, 812-465-7015, Fax: 812-464-1956, E-mail: wdurham@usi.edu. Web site: http://www.usi.edu/science/teachered/mse-secondaryeducation.asp.

University of Southern Mississippi, Graduate School, College of Education and Psychology, Department of Curriculum, Instruction, and Special Education, Hattiesburg, MS 39406-0001. Offers alternative secondary teacher education (MAT); early childhood education (M Ed, Ed S); education (Ed D); education of the gifted (M Ed, PhD, Ed S); elementary education (M Ed, PhD, Ed S); reading (M Ed, MS); secondary education (M Ed, MS, PhD); special education (M Ed, PhD, Ed S). Part-time programs available. *Faculty:* 23 full-time (17 women), 3 part-time/adjunct (2 women). *Students:* 39 full-time (34 women), 92 part-time (77 women); includes 36 minority (31 Black or African American, non-Hispanic/Latino; 3 Hispanic/Latino; 2 Two or more races, non-Hispanic/Latino), 3 international. Average age 37. 56 applicants, 55% accepted, 29 enrolled. In 2011, 45 master's, 5 doctorates awarded. *Degree requirements:* For master's and Ed S, comprehensive exam, thesis (for some programs); for doctorate, comprehensive exam, thesis/dissertation. *Entrance requirements:* For master's, GRE General Test, MAT, minimum GPA of 3.0; for doctorate, GRE General Test, minimum GPA of 3.5; for Ed S, GRE General Test, MAT, minimum GPA of 3.25. Additional exam requirements/recommendations for international students: Required—TOEFL, IELTS. *Application deadline:* For fall admission, 3/1 priority date for domestic students, 3/1 for international students; for spring admission, 1/10 priority date for domestic students, 1/10 for international students. Applications are processed on a rolling basis. Application fee: $50. *Financial support:* In 2011–12, 9 research assistantships with tuition reimbursements (averaging $18,316 per year), 2 teaching assistantships with full tuition reimbursements (averaging $8,500 per year) were awarded; Federal Work-Study, institutionally sponsored loans, scholarships/grants, health care benefits, tuition waivers (partial), and unspecified assistantships also available. Financial award application deadline: 3/15; financial award applicants required to submit FAFSA. *Faculty research:* Mathematical problem solving, integrative curriculum, writing process, teacher education models. *Total annual research expenditures:* $100,000. *Unit head:* Dr. David Daves, Chair, 601-266-4547, Fax: 601-266-4175, E-mail: david.daves@usm.edu. *Application contact:* Dr. Marie Crowe, Director of Graduate Studies, 601-266-6005, Fax: 601-266-4548, E-mail: margie.crowe@usm.edu. Web site: http://www.usm.edu/graduateschool/table.php.

University of South Florida, Graduate School, College of Education, Department of Secondary Education, Tampa, FL 33620-9951. Offers English education (M Ed, MA, MAT, PhD); foreign language education/ESOL (M Ed, MA, MAT); instructional technology (M Ed, PhD, Ed S); mathematics education (M Ed, MA, MAT, PhD, Ed S); science education (M Ed, MA, MAT, PhD); second language acquisition/instructional technology (PhD); secondary education (M Ed, PhD); secondary education/TESOL (M Ed); social science education (M Ed, MA, MAT); teaching and learning in the content area (PhD). *Accreditation:* NCATE. Part-time and evening/weekend programs available. *Faculty:* 28 full-time (17 women), 3 part-time/adjunct (1 woman). *Students:* 174 full-time (116 women), 268 part-time (184 women); includes 103 minority (26 Black or African American, non-Hispanic/Latino; 10 Asian, non-Hispanic/Latino; 58 Hispanic/Latino; 9 Two or more races, non-Hispanic/Latino), 32 international. Average age 37. 229 applicants, 73% accepted, 141 enrolled. In 2011, 115 master's, 16 doctorates, 5 other advanced degrees awarded. *Degree requirements:* For master's, variable foreign language requirement, comprehensive exam, project (for some programs); for doctorate, variable foreign language requirement, comprehensive exam, thesis/dissertation, philosophies of inquiry; multiple research methods. *Entrance requirements:* For master's, GRE General Test or General Knowledge Test, minimum GPA of 3.0; for doctorate, GRE General Test, minimum GPA of 3.5; for Ed S, GRE General Test. Additional exam requirements/recommendations for international students: Required—TOEFL (minimum score 550 paper-based; 213 computer-based; 79 iBT). *Application deadline:* For fall admission, 2/15 for domestic students, 1/2 for international students; for spring admission, 10/15 for domestic students, 6/1 for international students. Application fee: $30. Electronic applications accepted. *Financial support:* In 2011–12, 7 students received support, including 1 research assistantship with full tuition reimbursement available (averaging $10,000 per year), 55 teaching assistantships with full and partial tuition reimbursements available (averaging $7,900 per year); scholarships/grants and unspecified assistantships also available. Financial award application deadline: 4/15; financial award applicants required to submit FAFSA. *Faculty research:* English language learners/multicultural, social science education, mathematics education, science education, instructional technology. *Total annual research expenditures:* $336,023. *Unit head:* Dr. Stephen Thornton, Chairperson, 813-974-3533, Fax: 813-974-3837, E-mail: thornton@usf.edu. *Application contact:* Dr. Diane Briscoe, Coordinator of Graduate Studies, 813-974-1804, Fax: 813-974-3391, E-mail: briscoe@usf.edu. Web site: http://www.coedu.usf.edu/main/departments/seced/seced.html.

The University of Tennessee, Graduate School, College of Education, Health and Human Sciences, Program in Education, Knoxville, TN 37996. Offers art education (MS); counseling education (PhD); cultural studies in education (PhD); curriculum (MS, Ed S); curriculum, educational research and evaluation (Ed D, PhD); early childhood education (PhD); early childhood special education (MS); education of deaf and hard of hearing (MS); educational administration and policy studies (Ed D, PhD); educational administration and supervision (Ed S); educational psychology (Ed D, PhD); elementary education (MS, Ed S); elementary teaching (MS); English education (MS, Ed S); exercise science (PhD); foreign language/ESL education (MS, Ed S); instructional technology (MS, Ed D, PhD, Ed S); literacy, language and ESL education (PhD); literacy, language education, and ESL education (Ed D); mathematics education (MS, Ed S); modified and comprehensive special education (MS); reading education (MS, Ed S); school counseling (Ed S); school psychology (PhD, Ed S); science education (MS, Ed S); secondary teaching (MS); social foundations (MS); social science education (MS, Ed S); socio-cultural foundations of sports and education (PhD); special education (Ed S); teacher education (Ed D, PhD). *Accreditation:* NCATE. Part-time and evening/weekend programs available. *Degree requirements:* For master's and Ed S, thesis optional; for doctorate, variable foreign language requirement, thesis/dissertation. *Entrance requirements:* For master's, minimum GPA of 2.7; for doctorate and Ed S, GRE General Test, minimum GPA of 2.7. Additional exam requirements/recommendations for international students: Required—TOEFL. Electronic applications accepted. *Expenses:* Tuition, state resident: full-time $8332; part-time $464 per credit hour. Tuition, nonresident: full-time $25,174; part-time $1400 per credit hour. *Required fees:* $1162; $56 per credit hour. Tuition and fees vary according to program.

The University of Tennessee at Chattanooga, Graduate School, College of Health, Education and Professional Studies, School of Education, Chattanooga, TN 37403-2598. Offers counseling (M Ed), including community counseling, school counseling; education (M Ed, Post-Master's Certificate), including elementary education (M Ed), school leadership, secondary education (M Ed), special education (M Ed); educational specialist (Ed S), including educational technology, school psychology; learning and leadership (Ed D), including educational leadership. *Accreditation:* ACA; NCATE. Part-time and evening/weekend programs available. Postbaccalaureate distance learning degree programs offered (no on-campus study). *Faculty:* 25 full-time (17 women), 10 part-time/adjunct (3 women). *Students:* 145 full-time (104 women), 319 part-time (236 women); includes 63 minority (43 Black or African American, non-Hispanic/Latino; 4 American Indian or Alaska Native, non-Hispanic/Latino; 2 Asian, non-Hispanic/Latino; 6 Hispanic/Latino; 8 Two or more races, non-Hispanic/Latino), 2 international. Average age 34. 226 applicants, 79% accepted, 111 enrolled. In 2011, 120 master's, 9 doctorates, 17 other advanced degrees awarded. *Degree requirements:* For master's, comprehensive exam, thesis optional, culminating experience; for doctorate, comprehensive exam, thesis/dissertation; for other advanced degree, internship. *Entrance requirements:* For master's, GRE General Test, PPST 1, teaching certificate; for doctorate, GRE General Test, master's degree, two years of practical work experience in organizational environment; for other advanced degree, GRE General Test, letters of reference. Additional exam requirements/recommendations for international students: Required—TOEFL (minimum score 550 paper-based; 213 computer-based; 79 iBT), IELTS (minimum score 6). *Application deadline:* For fall admission, 8/1 for domestic students, 6/1 for international students; for spring admission, 12/1 for domestic students, 10/1 for international students. Applications are processed on a rolling basis. Application fee: $35. Electronic applications accepted. *Expenses:* Tuition, state resident: full-time $6472; part-time $359 per credit hour. Tuition, nonresident: full-time $20,006; part-time $1111 per credit hour. *Required fees:* $1320; $160 per credit hour. *Financial support:* Career-related internships or fieldwork, institutionally sponsored loans, scholarships/grants, and unspecified assistantships available. Support available to part-time students. Financial award applicants required to submit FAFSA. *Faculty research:* School counseling, community counseling, elementary and secondary education, school leadership and administration. *Total annual research expenditures:* $675,479. *Unit head:* Dr. John Freeman, Head, 423-425-4133, Fax: 423-425-5380, E-mail: john-freeman@utc.edu. *Application contact:* Dr. Jerald Ainsworth, Dean of Graduate Studies, 423-425-4478, Fax: 423-425-5223, E-mail: jerald-ainsworth@utc.edu. Web site: http://www.utc.edu/Administration/HealthEducationAndProfessionalStudies/Graduate_Studies/graduate_studies.html.

The University of Texas–Pan American, College of Education, Department of Curriculum and Instruction: Elementary and Secondary, Edinburg, TX 78539. Offers bilingual education (M Ed); early childhood education (M Ed); elementary education (M Ed); reading (M Ed); secondary education (M Ed). Part-time programs available. *Degree requirements:* For master's, comprehensive exam, thesis optional. *Entrance requirements:* For master's, GRE. Additional exam requirements/recommendations for international students: Required—TOEFL, IELTS. *Application deadline:* For fall admission, 7/17 for domestic and international students; for spring admission, 11/16 for domestic and international students. Application fee: $0. Tuition and fees vary according to course load, program and student level. *Financial support:* Research assistantships with tuition reimbursements, Federal Work-Study, institutionally sponsored loans, scholarships/grants, and unspecified assistantships available. Financial award application deadline: 4/15. *Faculty research:* Dual language instruction, literacy and technology, teacher education in diverse populations, mathematics and science education. *Unit head:* Dr. Veronica L. Estrada, Chair, 956-665-2431, Fax: 956-665-2434, E-mail: vlestradaa@utpa.edu. Web site: http://www.utpa.edu/dept/curr_ins/graduat.html.

University of the Cumberlands, Graduate Programs in Education, Williamsburg, KY 40769-1372. Offers all grades (P-12) (M Ed); business and marketing (MA Ed, MAT); director of pupil personnel (Certificate); director of special education (Certificate); educational administration and supervision (Ed S); educational leadership (Ed D); elementary education (MA Ed, MAT); instructional leadership - principalship (MA Ed); instructional leadership - school principal (Certificate); middle school education (MA Ed, MAT); reading and writing (MA Ed); school counseling (MA Ed); school superintendent (Certificate); secondary education (MA Ed, MAT); special education (MAT); supervisor of instruction (Certificate); teacher leader (MA Ed). Part-time and evening/weekend programs available. Postbaccalaureate distance learning degree programs offered. *Degree requirements:* For master's, comprehensive exam. Electronic applications accepted.

University of the Incarnate Word, School of Graduate Studies and Research, Dreeben School of Education, Program in Teaching, San Antonio, TX 78209-6397. Offers all-level teaching (MAT); elementary teaching (MAT); secondary teaching (MAT). Part-time and evening/weekend programs available. *Faculty:* 14 full-time (8 women), 10 part-time/adjunct (9 women). *Students:* 2 full-time (1 woman), 29 part-time (25 women); includes 20 minority (2 Black or African American, non-Hispanic/Latino; 18 Hispanic/Latino). Average age 33. 11 applicants, 91% accepted, 7 enrolled. In 2011, 9 degrees awarded. *Degree requirements:* For master's, internship. *Entrance requirements:* For master's, GRE, Texas Higher Education Assessment test (THEA), interview. Additional exam requirements/recommendations for international students: Required—TOEFL (minimum score 560 paper-based; 220 computer-based; 83 iBT). *Application deadline:* Applications are processed on a rolling basis. Application fee: $20. Electronic applications accepted. *Expenses: Tuition:* Part-time $725 per credit hour. Tuition and fees vary according to degree level. *Financial support:* Federal Work-Study and scholarships/grants available. Financial award applicants required to submit FAFSA. *Unit head:* Dr. Elda Martinez, Director of Teacher Education, 210-832-3297, Fax: 210-829-3134, E-mail: eemartin@uiwtx.edu. *Application contact:* Andrea Cyterski-Acosta, Dean of Enrollment, 210-829-6005, Fax: 210-829-3921, E-mail: admis@uiwtx.edu. Web site: http://www.uiw.edu/education/graduate.html.

The University of Toledo, College of Graduate Studies, Judith Herb College of Education, Health Science and Human Service, Department of Curriculum and Instruction, Toledo, OH 43606-3390. Offers art education (ME); career and technical education (ME); curriculum and instruction (ME, PhD, Ed S); education and anthropology (MAE); education and biology (MES); education and chemistry (MES); education and classics (MAE); education and economics (MAE); education and English (MAE); education and French (MAE); education and geography (MAE); education and geology (MES); education and German (MAE); education and history (MAE); education and mathematics (MAE, MES); education and physics (MES); education and political science (MAE); education and sociology (MAE); education and Spanish (MAE); educational media (PhD); educational technology (ME); English as a second language (MAE); gifted and talented (PhD); middle childhood education licensure (ME); music education (MME); secondary education (PhD); secondary education licensure (ME). *Accreditation:* NCATE. Part-time and evening/weekend programs available. *Faculty:* 24.

Students: 60 full-time (31 women), 211 part-time (161 women); includes 23 minority (21 Black or African American, non-Hispanic/Latino; 2 Hispanic/Latino), 20 international. Average age 35. 115 applicants, 73% accepted, 74 enrolled. In 2011, 105 master's, 3 doctorates, 4 other advanced degrees awarded. *Degree requirements:* For master's, comprehensive exam, thesis or alternative; for doctorate, comprehensive exam, thesis/dissertation; for Ed S, thesis optional. *Entrance requirements:* For master's, doctorate, and Ed S, minimum cumulative GPA of 2.7 for all previous academic work, letters of recommendation. Additional exam requirements/recommendations for international students: Required—TOEFL (minimum score 550 paper-based; 213 computer-based; 80 iBT), IELTS (minimum score 6.5). *Application deadline:* For fall admission, 1/15 priority date for domestic students, 1/15 for international students. Applications are processed on a rolling basis. Application fee: $45 ($75 for international students). Electronic applications accepted. *Financial support:* In 2011–12, 9 research assistantships with full and partial tuition reimbursements (averaging $7,184 per year), 12 teaching assistantships with full and partial tuition reimbursements (averaging $8,425 per year) were awarded; career-related internships or fieldwork, Federal Work-Study, institutionally sponsored loans, scholarships/grants, tuition waivers (full and partial), unspecified assistantships, and administrative assistantships also available. Support available to part-time students. *Unit head:* Dr. Leigh Chiarelott, Chair, 419-530-5371, E-mail: eigh.chiarelott@utoledo.edu. *Application contact:* Graduate School Office, 419-530-4723, Fax: 419-530-4724, E-mail: grdsch@utnet.utoledo.edu. Web site: http://www.utoledo.edu/eduhshs/.

University of Tulsa, Graduate School, College of Arts and Sciences, School of Education, Program in Education, Tulsa, OK 74104-3189. Offers education (MA); elementary certification (M Ed); secondary certification (M Ed). Part-time programs available. *Faculty:* 7 full-time (3 women). *Students:* 16 full-time (11 women), 4 part-time (3 women); includes 5 minority (1 Black or African American, non-Hispanic/Latino; 2 American Indian or Alaska Native, non-Hispanic/Latino; 1 Asian, non-Hispanic/Latino; 1 Hispanic/Latino), 2 international. Average age 27. 17 applicants, 76% accepted, 10 enrolled. In 2011, 7 master's awarded. *Degree requirements:* For master's, thesis optional. *Entrance requirements:* For master's, GRE General Test. Additional exam requirements/recommendations for international students: Required—TOEFL (minimum score 577 paper-based; 233 computer-based; 91 iBT), IELTS (minimum score 6.5). *Application deadline:* Applications are processed on a rolling basis. Application fee: $40. Electronic applications accepted. *Expenses: Tuition:* Full-time $17,748; part-time $986 per hour. *Required fees:* $5 per contact hour. $75 per semester. Tuition and fees vary according to program. *Financial support:* In 2011–12, 12 students received support, including 1 research assistantship with full and partial tuition reimbursement available (averaging $6,051 per year), 11 teaching assistantships with full and partial tuition reimbursements available (averaging $11,264 per year); fellowships with full and partial tuition reimbursements available, Federal Work-Study, scholarships/grants, health care benefits, tuition waivers (full and partial), and unspecified assistantships also available. Support available to part-time students. Financial award application deadline: 2/1; financial award applicants required to submit FAFSA. *Faculty research:* Elementary and secondary education; educational foundations; language, discourse and development. *Total annual research expenditures:* $362,470. *Unit head:* Dr. David Brown, Advisor, 918-631-2719, Fax: 918-631-2133, E-mail: david-brown@utulsa.edu. *Application contact:* Dr. David Brown, Advisor, 918-631-2719, Fax: 918-631-2133, E-mail: david-brown@utulsa.edu.

University of Utah, Graduate School, College of Education, Department of Teaching and Learning, Salt Lake City, UT 84112-1107. Offers elementary education (MAT); secondary education (MAT); teaching and learning (M Ed, M Phil, MA, MS, PhD). Part-time and evening/weekend programs available. *Faculty:* 4 full-time (2 women). *Students:* 14 full-time (11 women), 25 part-time (16 women); includes 3 minority (1 Asian, non-Hispanic/Latino; 1 Hispanic/Latino; 1 Native Hawaiian or other Pacific Islander, non-Hispanic/Latino), 1 international. Average age 33. 10 applicants, 0% accepted. In 2011, 26 master's, 2 doctorates awarded. *Degree requirements:* For master's, comprehensive exam (for some programs), thesis optional; for doctorate, thesis/dissertation. *Entrance requirements:* For master's, GRE General Test or MAT, GRE Subject Test, minimum GPA of 3.0; for doctorate, GRE General Test, minimum graduate GPA of 3.5, undergraduate 3.0. Additional exam requirements/recommendations for international students: Required—TOEFL (minimum score 500 paper-based; 173 computer-based). *Application deadline:* For fall admission, 3/1 for domestic students, 4/1 for international students; for spring admission, 10/15 for domestic students, 11/1 for international students. Applications are processed on a rolling basis. Application fee: $55 ($65 for international students). *Financial support:* Fellowships, research assistantships with full and partial tuition reimbursements, teaching assistantships with full and partial tuition reimbursements, career-related internships or fieldwork, and tuition waivers (partial) available. Financial award application deadline: 2/1; financial award applicants required to submit FAFSA. *Faculty research:* Teacher development, teacher education, reading instruction, math instruction, technology. *Unit head:* Doug Hacker, Department Chair, 801-581-5080, Fax: 801-581-3609, E-mail: douglas.hacker@utah.edu. *Application contact:* Jan Dole, Graduate Program Director, 801-587-7991, Fax: 801-581-3609, E-mail: jan.dole@utah.edu.

University of Washington, Bothell, Program in Education, Bothell, WA 98011-8246. Offers education (M Ed); leadership development for educators (M Ed); secondary/middle level endorsement (M Ed). Part-time and evening/weekend programs available. *Faculty:* 14 full-time (10 women), 1 (woman) part-time/adjunct. *Students:* 52 full-time (40 women), 115 part-time (94 women); includes 19 minority (3 Black or African American, non-Hispanic/Latino; 9 Asian, non-Hispanic/Latino; 4 Hispanic/Latino; 3 Two or more races, non-Hispanic/Latino). Average age 35. 76 applicants, 80% accepted, 57 enrolled. In 2011, 74 master's awarded. *Degree requirements:* For master's, thesis. *Entrance requirements:* Additional exam requirements/recommendations for international students: Required—TOEFL. *Application deadline:* For fall admission, 8/14 priority date for domestic students, 8/14 for international students; for spring admission, 4/7 priority date for domestic students, 11/1 for international students. Applications are processed on a rolling basis. Application fee: $75. Electronic applications accepted. *Financial support:* In 2011–12, 2 students received support. Federal Work-Study and unspecified assistantships available. Financial award application deadline: 5/2. *Faculty research:* Multicultural education in citizenship education, intercultural education, knowledge and practice in the principalship, educational public policy, national board certification for teachers, teacher learning in literacy, technology and its impact on teaching and learning of mathematics, reading assessments, professional development in literacy education and mobility, digital media, education and class. *Unit head:* Dr. Bradley S. Portin, Director/Professor, 425-352-3482, Fax: 425-352-5234, E-mail: bportin@uwb.edu. *Application contact:* Nick Brownlee, Advisor, 425-352-5369, Fax: 425-352-5369, E-mail: nbrownlee@uwb.edu.

The University of West Alabama, School of Graduate Studies, College of Education, Departments of Instructional Leadership and Support/Curriculum and Instruction, Program in Secondary Education, Livingston, AL 35470. Offers MAT. Part-time programs available. *Faculty:* 8 full-time (7 women). In 2011, 29 master's awarded. *Degree requirements:* For master's, comprehensive exam. *Entrance requirements:* For master's, GRE General Test, MAT, minimum GPA of 2.75. Additional exam requirements/recommendations for international students: Required—TOEFL (minimum score 61 computer-based). *Application deadline:* For fall admission, 9/10 priority date for domestic students; for spring admission, 3/24 for domestic students. Applications are processed on a rolling basis. Application fee: $25 ($50 for international students). *Expenses:* Tuition, state resident: full-time $5112; part-time $284 per credit hour. Tuition, nonresident: full-time $10,224; part-time $568 per credit hour. *Required fees:* $180; $40 per semester. One-time fee: $65. Tuition and fees vary according to class time, course load, campus/location and program. *Financial support:* Teaching assistantships, career-related internships or fieldwork, Federal Work-Study, scholarships/grants, and unspecified assistantships available. Support available to part-time students. Financial award application deadline: 3/1. *Faculty research:* Integrated arts into the curriculum, moral development of children. *Unit head:* Dr. Esther Howard, Chair of Curriculum and Instruction, 205-652-3428, Fax: 205-652-3706, E-mail: ehoward@uwa.edu. *Application contact:* Dr. Kathy Chandler, Dean of Graduate Studies, 205-652-3421, Fax: 205-652-3706, E-mail: kchandler@uwa.edu. Web site: http://www.uwa.edu/highschool612.aspx.

University of West Florida, College of Professional Studies, Department of Research and Applied Studies, Pensacola, FL 32514-5750. Offers administration (MSA), including acquisition and contract administration, biomedical/pharmaceutical, criminal justice administration, database administration, education leadership, healthcare administration, human performance technology, leadership, nursing administration, public administration, software engineering and administration; college student personnel administration (M Ed), including college personnel administration, guidance and counseling; curriculum and instruction (M Ed, Ed S); educational leadership (M Ed); middle and secondary level education and ESOL (M Ed). Part-time and evening/weekend programs available. *Faculty:* 2 full-time (both women), 3 part-time/adjunct (2 women). *Students:* 26 full-time (15 women), 13 part-time (9 women); includes 8 minority (4 Black or African American, non-Hispanic/Latino; 2 American Indian or Alaska Native, non-Hispanic/Latino; 1 Hispanic/Latino; 1 Two or more races, non-Hispanic/Latino), 1 international. Average age 26. 51 applicants, 51% accepted, 16 enrolled. In 2011, 17 master's, 49 Ed Ss awarded. *Entrance requirements:* For master's, GRE or MAT, official transcripts; minimum undergraduate GPA of 3.0; letter of intent; three letters of recommendation; resume. Additional exam requirements/recommendations for international students: Required—TOEFL (minimum score 550 paper-based; 213 computer-based). *Application deadline:* For fall admission, 6/1 for domestic and international students; for spring admission, 10/1 for domestic and international students. Applications are processed on a rolling basis. Application fee: $30. *Expenses:* Tuition, state resident: full-time $5729; part-time $302 per credit hour. Tuition, nonresident: full-time $20,059; part-time $961 per credit hour. *Required fees:* $1509; $63 per credit hour. *Financial support:* In 2011–12, 33 fellowships (averaging $860 per year), 10 research assistantships (averaging $3,280 per year), 2 teaching assistantships (averaging $3,760 per year) were awarded; unspecified assistantships also available. Financial award application deadline: 4/15; financial award applicants required to submit FAFSA. *Unit head:* Dr. Joyce Nichols, Chairperson, 850-857-6042, E-mail: jcoleman0@uwf.edu. *Application contact:* Terry McCray, Assistant Director of Graduate Admissions, 850-473-7718, Fax: 850-473-7714, E-mail: gradadmissions@uwf.edu. Web site: http://uwf.edu/pcl/.

University of West Georgia, College of Education, Department of Leadership and Applied Instruction, Carrollton, GA 30118. Offers art education (M Ed); art teacher education (Ed S); biology - secondary education (M Ed); biology/secondary education (Ed S); business education (M Ed, Ed S); chemistry/secondary education (Ed S); earth science/secondary education (Ed S); economics/secondary education (Ed S); educational leadership (M Ed, Ed S); English teacher education (M Ed, Ed S); French teacher education (M Ed, Ed S); history teacher education (Ed S); mathematics teacher education (M Ed, Ed S); middle grades education (M Ed, Ed S); physical education and recreation (Ed S); physical education teaching and coaching (M Ed); physics/secondary education (Ed S); science teacher education (M Ed, Ed S); secondary education (M Ed); social science - secondary education (M Ed); social science teacher education (M Ed); Spanish (M Ed); Spanish teacher education (M Ed, Ed S); sports management (M Ed). *Accreditation:* NCATE. Part-time and evening/weekend programs available. *Faculty:* 18 full-time (9 women). *Students:* 75 full-time (49 women), 169 part-time (109 women); includes 90 minority (85 Black or African American, non-Hispanic/Latino; 3 Hispanic/Latino; 2 Two or more races, non-Hispanic/Latino), 1 international. Average age 36. 115 applicants, 67% accepted, 19 enrolled. In 2011, 73 master's, 53 Ed Ss awarded. *Degree requirements:* For master's, internship; for Ed S, research project. *Entrance requirements:* For master's, GRE General Test, minimum GPA of 2.7; for Ed S, GRE General Test, master's degree, minimum graduate GPA of 3.0, district appointment. Additional exam requirements/recommendations for international students: Required—TOEFL (minimum score 523 paper-based; 193 computer-based; 69 iBT); Recommended—IELTS (minimum score 6). *Application deadline:* For fall admission, 7/21 for domestic students, 6/1 for international students; for spring admission, 11/30 for domestic students, 10/15 for international students. Applications are processed on a rolling basis. Application fee: $30. Electronic applications accepted. *Expenses:* Tuition, state resident: full-time $4336; part-time $181 per credit hour. Tuition, nonresident: full-time $17,362; part-time $724 per credit hour. Tuition and fees vary according to course load, degree level, campus/location and program. *Financial support:* In 2011–12, 1 research assistantship with full tuition reimbursement (averaging $7,444 per year) was awarded; career-related internships or fieldwork, scholarships/grants, and unspecified assistantships also available. Support available to part-time students. Financial award application deadline: 7/1; financial award applicants required to submit FAFSA. *Total annual research expenditures:* $5,000. *Unit head:* Dr. Frank Butts, Chair, 678-839-6530, Fax: 678-839-6195, E-mail: fbutts@westga.edu. *Application contact:* Deanna Richards, Coordinator, Graduate Studies, 678-839-5946, E-mail: drichard@westga.edu. Web site: http://www.westga.edu/coelai.

University of Wisconsin–Eau Claire, College of Education and Human Sciences, Program in Secondary Education, Eau Claire, WI 54702-4004. Offers professional development (MEPD), including initial teacher, library science, professional development, professional educator. Part-time and evening/weekend programs available. Postbaccalaureate distance learning degree programs offered (minimal on-campus study). *Faculty:* 13 full-time (9 women). *Students:* 3 full-time (1 woman), 34 part-time (29 women); includes 5 minority (2 American Indian or Alaska Native, non-Hispanic/Latino; 1 Asian, non-Hispanic/Latino; 2 Hispanic/Latino). Average age 34. 8 applicants, 88% accepted, 6 enrolled. In 2011, 10 master's awarded. *Degree requirements:* For master's, comprehensive exam, thesis, research paper, portfolio or written exam; oral exam. *Entrance requirements:* For master's, certification to teach, minimum GPA of 2.75. Additional exam requirements/recommendations for international students: Required—TOEFL (minimum score 550 paper-based; 213 computer-based; 79 iBT); Recommended—IELTS (minimum score 7). *Application deadline:* For fall admission, 7/1 priority date for domestic students, 6/1 for international students; for spring admission, 12/1 priority date for domestic students, 11/1 for international students. Applications are processed on a rolling basis. Application fee: $56. *Expenses:* Tuition, state resident: full-time $7312; part-time $406 per credit. Tuition, nonresident: full-time $16,771; part-time $932 per credit. *Required fees:* $1101; $61 per credit. *Financial support:* In 2011–12, 8 students received support. Federal Work-Study and unspecified assistantships available. Financial award application deadline: 3/1; financial award applicants required to submit FAFSA. *Unit head:* Dr. Jill Pastrana, Chair, 715-836-2013, Fax: 715-836-4868, E-mail: pastrajp@uwec.edu. *Application contact:* Dr. Sherry Macaul, Coordinator, 715-836-5735, E-mail: macaulsl@uwec.edu. Web site: http://www.uwec.edu/ES/programs/graduateprograms.htm.

University of Wisconsin–La Crosse, Office of University Graduate Studies, College of Liberal Studies, Department of Educational Studies, MEPD Initial Certification and Professional Development Program, La Crosse, WI 54601. Offers elementary education (MEPD), including grades 1 through 6, grades 1 through 9; K-12 (MEPD); professional development (MEPD); secondary education (MEPD), including grades 6 through 12. Part-time programs available. *Students:* 13 full-time (8 women), 2 part-time (0 women); includes 4 minority (1 American Indian or Alaska Native, non-Hispanic/Latino; 3 Asian, non-Hispanic/Latino). Average age 28. 10 applicants, 80% accepted, 5 enrolled. In 2011, 7 master's awarded. *Degree requirements:* For master's, thesis optional. *Entrance requirements:* For master's, PPST, minimum GPA of 3.0 cumulative and in subject area. Additional exam requirements/recommendations for international students: Required—TOEFL (minimum score 550 paper-based; 213 computer-based; 79 iBT). *Application deadline:* Applications are processed on a rolling basis. Application fee: $56. Electronic applications accepted. *Expenses:* Tuition, state resident: full-time $8391; part-time $481.17 per credit. Tuition, nonresident: full-time $17,850; part-time $1006.68 per credit. *Required fees:* $2 per credit. $18.25 per semester. Tuition and fees vary according to course load, program, reciprocity agreements and student level. *Financial support:* In 2011–12, 6 research assistantships (averaging $5,568 per year) were awarded; Federal Work-Study, scholarships/grants, health care benefits, and tuition waivers (partial) also available. Support available to part-time students. Financial award application deadline: 3/15; financial award applicants required to submit FAFSA. *Faculty research:* Professional development schools, technology in education, critical literacy, self-efficacy of teaching, digital storytelling. *Unit head:* Dr. Gary L. Willhite, Director, 608-785-8130, Fax: 608-785-8137, E-mail: gwillhite@uwlax.edu. *Application contact:* Dr. Gary L. Willhite, Director, 608-785-8130, Fax: 608-785-8137, E-mail: admissions@uwlax.edu. Web site: http://www.uwlax.edu/MEPD/.

University of Wisconsin–Milwaukee, Graduate School, School of Education, Department of Curriculum and Instruction, Milwaukee, WI 53201-0413. Offers curriculum planning and instruction improvement (MS); early childhood education (MS); elementary education (MS); junior high/middle school education (MS); reading education (MS); secondary education (MS); teaching in an urban setting (MS). Part-time programs available. *Faculty:* 18 full-time (13 women). *Students:* 29 full-time (23 women), 54 part-time (44 women); includes 21 minority (10 Black or African American, non-Hispanic/Latino; 4 Asian, non-Hispanic/Latino; 3 Hispanic/Latino; 4 Two or more races, non-Hispanic/Latino). Average age 32. 43 applicants, 65% accepted, 13 enrolled. In 2011, 23 degrees awarded. *Degree requirements:* For master's, thesis or alternative. *Entrance requirements:* Additional exam requirements/recommendations for international students: Required—TOEFL (minimum score 550 paper-based; 79 iBT), IELTS (minimum score 6.5). *Application deadline:* For fall admission, 1/1 priority date for domestic students; for spring admission, 9/1 for domestic students. Applications are processed on a rolling basis. Application fee: $56 ($96 for international students). Electronic applications accepted. One-time fee: $506.10 full-time. Tuition and fees vary according to course load and reciprocity agreements. *Financial support:* In 2011–12, 1 fellowship was awarded; research assistantships, teaching assistantships, career-related internships or fieldwork, health care benefits, unspecified assistantships, and project assistantships also available. Support available to part-time students. Financial award application deadline: 4/15; financial award applicants required to submit FAFSA. *Total annual research expenditures:* $21,843. *Unit head:* Hope Longwell-Grice, Department Chair, 414-229-3059, Fax: 414-229-5571, E-mail: hope@uwm.edu. *Application contact:* General Information Contact, 414-229-4982, Fax: 414-229-6967, E-mail: gradschool@uwm.edu. Web site: http://www.uwm.edu/SOE/.

University of Wisconsin–Platteville, School of Graduate Studies, College of Liberal Arts and Education, School of Education, Platteville, WI 53818-3099. Offers adult education (MSE); elementary education (MSE); English education (MSE); middle school education (MSE); secondary education (MSE). *Accreditation:* NCATE. Part-time programs available. *Faculty:* 8 part-time/adjunct (3 women). *Students:* 62 full-time (47 women), 86 part-time (69 women); includes 22 minority (20 Black or African American, non-Hispanic/Latino; 2 Hispanic/Latino), 55 international. 17 applicants, 76% accepted. In 2011, 82 master's awarded. *Degree requirements:* For master's, comprehensive exam, thesis or alternative. *Entrance requirements:* Additional exam requirements/recommendations for international students: Required—TOEFL (minimum score 500 paper-based; 61 iBT), IELTS (minimum score 6). *Application deadline:* For fall admission, 7/1 priority date for domestic students; for spring admission, 11/1 for domestic students. Applications are processed on a rolling basis. Application fee: $56. Electronic applications accepted. *Financial support:* Research assistantships with partial tuition reimbursements, career-related internships or fieldwork, Federal Work-Study, institutionally sponsored loans, scholarships/grants, and unspecified assistantships available. Support available to part-time students. Financial award applicants required to submit FAFSA. *Unit head:* Dr. Karen Stinson, Director, 608-342-1131, Fax: 608-342-1133, E-mail: stinsonk@uwplatt.edu. *Application contact:* Lisa Popp, School of Graduate Studies, 608-342-1322, Fax: 608-342-1389, E-mail: poppl@uwplatt.edu. Web site: http://www.uwplatt.edu/.

University of Wisconsin–Whitewater, School of Graduate Studies, College of Business and Economics, Department of Business Education, Whitewater, WI 53190-1790. Offers business and marketing education (MS), including general, post secondary, secondary. *Accreditation:* NCATE. Part-time and evening/weekend programs available. Postbaccalaureate distance learning degree programs offered (no on-campus study). *Students:* 2 full-time (1 woman), 19 part-time (8 women); includes 1 minority (Hispanic/Latino). Average age 35. 5 applicants, 80% accepted, 2 enrolled. In 2011, 7 master's awarded. *Degree requirements:* For master's, thesis or alternative. *Entrance requirements:* For master's, interview, teaching license. Additional exam requirements/recommendations for international students: Required—TOEFL (minimum score 550 paper-based; 213 computer-based; 80 iBT), IELTS (minimum score 6). *Application deadline:* For fall admission, 7/15 priority date for domestic students, 7/15 for international students; for spring admission, 12/1 priority date for domestic students, 12/1 for international students. Applications are processed on a rolling basis. Application fee: $56. Electronic applications accepted. *Expenses:* Tuition, state resident: full-time $4088. Tuition, nonresident: full-time $8817. Tuition and fees vary according to program. *Financial support:* In 2011–12, 2 research assistantships (averaging $7,245 per year) were awarded; Federal Work-Study, unspecified assistantships, and out of state fee waiver also available. Support available to part-time students. Financial award application deadline: 3/15; financial award applicants required to submit FAFSA. *Faculty research:* Active learning and performance strategies, technology-enhanced formative assessment, computer-supported cooperative work, privacy surveillance. *Unit head:* Dr. Lila Waldman, Coordinator, 262-472-5475. *Application contact:* Sally A. Lange, School of Graduate Studies, 262-472-1006, Fax: 262-472-5027, E-mail: gradschl@uww.edu.

Utah State University, School of Graduate Studies, Emma Eccles Jones College of Education and Human Services, Program in Secondary Education, Logan, UT 84322. Offers M Ed, MA, MS. Part-time and evening/weekend programs available. *Degree requirements:* For master's, thesis (for some programs). *Entrance requirements:* For master's, GRE General Test or MAT, minimum GPA of 3.0, 1 year teaching, teaching license, letters of recommendation. Additional exam requirements/recommendations for international students: Required—TOEFL. Electronic applications accepted. *Faculty research:* Character education, science education, reading/writing skills, mathematics education, pre-service teacher education.

Valdosta State University, Department of Middle, Secondary, Reading and Deaf Education, Valdosta, GA 31698. Offers middle grades education (M Ed, Ed S); secondary education (M Ed, Ed S). *Accreditation:* NCATE. Part-time and evening/weekend programs available. *Faculty:* 12 full-time (9 women). *Students:* 1 (woman) full-time, 22 part-time (20 women); includes 1 minority (Native Hawaiian or other Pacific Islander, non-Hispanic/Latino). Average age 25. 18 applicants, 78% accepted, 6 enrolled. In 2011, 24 master's, 5 Ed Ss awarded. *Degree requirements:* For master's, thesis (for some programs), comprehensive written and/or oral exams; for Ed S, thesis. *Entrance requirements:* For master's, GRE General Test or MAT, minimum GPA of 2.5; for Ed S, GRE General Test or MAT, minimum GPA of 3.0. Additional exam requirements/recommendations for international students: Required—TOEFL (minimum score 523 paper-based; 193 computer-based). *Application deadline:* For fall admission, 7/1 for domestic and international students; for spring admission, 11/15 for domestic and international students. Applications are processed on a rolling basis. Application fee: $35. Electronic applications accepted. *Expenses:* Tuition, state resident: full-time $7098; part-time $217 per hour. Tuition, nonresident: full-time $20,630; part-time $780 per hour. *Financial support:* In 2011–12, 4 students received support, including 4 research assistantships with full tuition reimbursements available (averaging $3,652 per year); institutionally sponsored loans, scholarships/grants, and unspecified assistantships also available. Support available to part-time students. Financial award application deadline: 7/1; financial award applicants required to submit FAFSA. *Faculty research:* Distance education, learning styles, alternative assessment methods, interactive teaching strategies, learning styles of pre-service teachers. *Unit head:* Dr. Barbara Stanley, Head, 229-333-5611, Fax: 229-333-7167. *Application contact:* Meg Moore, Director of GOML Programs, 229-333-5694, Fax: 229-245-3853, E-mail: mhgiddin@valdosta.edu.

Vanderbilt University, Peabody College, Department of Teaching and Learning, Nashville, TN 37240-1001. Offers elementary education (M Ed); English language learners (M Ed); learning and instruction (M Ed); learning, diversity, and urban studies (M Ed); reading education (M Ed); secondary education (M Ed). *Accreditation:* NCATE. *Faculty:* 35 full-time (24 women), 19 part-time/adjunct (14 women). *Students:* 123 full-time (96 women), 38 part-time (34 women); includes 26 minority (6 Black or African American, non-Hispanic/Latino; 3 Asian, non-Hispanic/Latino; 7 Hispanic/Latino; 10 Two or more races, non-Hispanic/Latino), 12 international. Average age 26. 251 applicants, 56% accepted, 60 enrolled. In 2011, 80 master's awarded. *Degree requirements:* For master's, comprehensive exam, thesis optional. *Entrance requirements:* For master's, GRE General Test, MAT. Additional exam requirements/recommendations for international students: Required—TOEFL (minimum score 550 paper-based; 213 computer-based). *Application deadline:* For fall admission, 12/31 priority date for domestic students, 12/31 for international students; for spring admission, 11/1 priority date for domestic students, 11/1 for international students. Applications are processed on a rolling basis. Application fee: $0. Electronic applications accepted. *Financial support:* Fellowships with full and partial tuition reimbursements, research assistantships with full and partial tuition reimbursements, teaching assistantships with full and partial tuition reimbursements, Federal Work-Study, institutionally sponsored loans, scholarships/grants, tuition waivers (partial), and unspecified assistantships available. Support available to part-time students. Financial award application deadline: 2/1; financial award applicants required to submit FAFSA. *Faculty research:* Learning environments for mathematics of space and motion, visual programming tools for children's learning of basic science concepts, pathways for elementary and middle school children's learning about measurement and statistics, early reading intervention, professional development for ambitious mathematics teaching. *Unit head:* Dr. David Dickinson, Acting Chair, 615-322-8100, Fax: 615-322-8999, E-mail: david.k.dickinson@vanderbilt.edu. *Application contact:* Angela Saylor, Educational Coordinator, 615-322-8092, Fax: 615-322-8999, E-mail: angela.saylor@vanderbilt.edu.

Villanova University, Graduate School of Liberal Arts and Sciences, Department of Education and Counseling, Program in Secondary Education, Villanova, PA 19085-1699. Offers MA. Part-time and evening/weekend programs available. *Students:* 17 full-time (11 women); includes 2 minority (1 Black or African American, non-Hispanic/Latino; 1 Asian, non-Hispanic/Latino). Average age 30. In 2011, 17 master's awarded. *Degree requirements:* For master's, comprehensive exam. *Entrance requirements:* For master's, GRE or MAT, minimum GPA of 3.0. *Application deadline:* Applications are processed on a rolling basis. Application fee: $50. Electronic applications accepted. *Expenses: Tuition:* Part-time $675 per credit. Part-time tuition and fees vary according to degree level and program. *Financial support:* Career-related internships or fieldwork and Federal Work-Study available. Financial award applicants required to submit FAFSA. *Unit head:* Dr. Edward Fierros, Coordinator, 610-519-4620. *Application contact:* Dean, Graduate School of Liberal Arts and Sciences.

Virginia Commonwealth University, Graduate School, School of Education, Program in Teaching and Learning, Richmond, VA 23284-9005. Offers early and elementary education (MT); health and physical education (MT); secondary 6-12 education (MT); secondary education (Certificate). *Accreditation:* NCATE. Part-time programs available. *Entrance requirements:* For master's, GRE General Test or MAT. Additional exam requirements/recommendations for international students: Required—TOEFL (minimum score 600 paper-based; 250 computer-based; 100 iBT). Electronic applications accepted. *Expenses:* Tuition, state resident: full-time $9133; part-time $507 per credit. Tuition, nonresident: full-time $18,777; part-time $1043 per credit. *Required fees:* $77 per credit. Tuition and fees vary according to degree level, campus/location, program and student level.

Wagner College, Division of Graduate Studies, Department of Education, Program in Adolescent Education, Staten Island, NY 10301-4495. Offers MS Ed. Part-time and evening/weekend programs available. *Faculty:* 3 full-time (2 women), 14 part-time/adjunct (10 women). *Students:* 19 full-time (5 women), 18 part-time (11 women); includes 3 minority (2 Black or African American, non-Hispanic/Latino; 1 Asian, non-Hispanic/Latino). Average age 24. 19 applicants, 95% accepted, 13 enrolled. In 2011, 14 master's awarded. *Degree requirements:* For master's, thesis (for some programs). *Entrance requirements:* For master's, Liberal Arts and Sciences Test (LAST), New York State Teacher Certification Examinations (NYSTCE), minimum GPA of 2.75. Additional exam requirements/recommendations for international students: Required—TOEFL (minimum score 550 paper-based; 217 computer-based; 79 iBT). *Application deadline:* For fall admission, 5/1 priority date for domestic students, 3/1 for international students; for spring admission, 11/1 priority date for domestic students, 10/1 for international students. Applications are processed on a rolling basis. Application fee: $50 ($85 for international students). *Expenses: Tuition:* Full-time $16,200; part-time $890 per credit. *Financial support:* Career-related internships or fieldwork, tuition waivers (partial), unspecified assistantships, and alumni fellowship grant available. Financial award applicants required to submit FAFSA. *Unit head:* Dr. Stephen Preskill, Graduate

Coordinator, 718-420-4070, Fax: 718-390-3456, E-mail: stephen.preskill@wagner.edu. *Application contact:* Patricia Clancy, Assistant Coordinator of Graduate Studies, 718-420-4464, Fax: 718-390-3105, E-mail: patricia.clancy@wagner.edu.

Wake Forest University, Graduate School of Arts and Sciences, Department of Education, Winston-Salem, NC 27109. Offers secondary education (MA Ed). *Accreditation:* ACA; NCATE. Part-time programs available. *Faculty:* 7 full-time (4 women), 6 part-time/adjunct (3 women). *Students:* 24 full-time (14 women), 17 part-time (14 women); includes 10 minority (3 Black or African American, non-Hispanic/Latino; 1 Asian, non-Hispanic/Latino; 6 Hispanic/Latino). Average age 26. 46 applicants, 59% accepted, 26 enrolled. In 2011, 36 master's awarded. *Degree requirements:* For master's, thesis optional. *Entrance requirements:* For master's, GRE General Test. Additional exam requirements/recommendations for international students: Required—TOEFL (minimum score 550 paper-based; 213 computer-based). *Application deadline:* For fall admission, 1/15 for domestic and international students. Application fee: $60. Electronic applications accepted. *Expenses:* Contact institution. *Financial support:* In 2011–12, 24 fellowships with full tuition reimbursements (averaging $48,000 per year) were awarded; teaching assistantships with full tuition reimbursements, scholarships/grants, and tuition waivers (full) also available. Support available to part-time students. Financial award application deadline: 2/15. *Faculty research:* Teaching and learning. *Unit head:* Dr. MaryLynn Redmond, Chair, 336-758-5341, Fax: 336-758-4591, E-mail: redmond@wfu.edu. *Application contact:* Dr. Leah McCoy, Program Director, 336-758-5998, Fax: 336-758-4591, E-mail: mccoy@wfu.edu. Web site: http://college.wfu.edu/education/graduate-program/overview-of-graduate-programs/.

Walden University, Graduate Programs, Richard W. Riley College of Education and Leadership, Minneapolis, MN 55401. Offers administrator leadership for teaching and learning (Ed D, Ed S); adult education (Ed D, Ed S); adult learning (MS, Postbaccalaureate Certificate), including developmental education (MS), online teaching (MS), teaching adults English as a second language (MS), training and performance management (MS); college teaching and learning (Ed D, Ed S, Postbaccalaureate Certificate); curriculum, instruction and assessment (Ed D, Postbaccalaureate Certificate); curriculum, instruction, and professional development (Ed S); developmental education (Postbaccalaureate Certificate); early childhood administration, management, and leadership (Postbaccalaureate Certificate); early childhood education (birth-grade 3) (MAT); early childhood public policy and advocacy (Postbaccalaureate Certificate); early childhood studies (MS), including administration, management and leadership, early childhood public policy and advocacy, teaching adults in the early childhood field, teaching and diversity; education (MS, PhD), including adolescent literacy and technology (grades 6-12) (MS), adult education leadership (PhD), assessment, evaluation, and accountability (PhD), community college leadership (PhD), curriculum, instruction, and assessment, early childhood education (PhD), educational technology (PhD), elementary reading and literacy (MS), elementary reading and mathematics (MS), general program, global and comparative education (PhD), higher education (PhD), integrating technology in the classroom (MS), K-12 educational leadership (PhD), leadership, policy and change (PhD), learning, instruction and innovation (PhD), literacy and learning in the content areas (MS), mathematics (grades 6-8) (MS), mathematics (grades K-5) (MS), middle level education (grades 5-8) (MS), professional development (MS), science (grades K-8) (MS), self-designed (PhD), special education (PhD), special education (non-licensure) (MS), teacher leadership (grades K-12) (MS), teaching English language learners (grades K-12) (MS); educational leadership and administration (principal preparation) (Ed S); educational technology (Ed S); elementary reading and literacy (Postbaccalaureate Certificate); engaging culturally diverse learners (Postbaccalaureate Certificate); enrollment management and institutional marketing (Postbaccalaureate Certificate); higher education (MS), including college teaching and learning, enrollment management and institutional planning, global higher education, leadership for student success, online and distance learning; higher education leadership (Ed D); instructional design (Postbaccalaureate Certificate); instructional design and technology (MS), including general program (MS, PhD), online learning, training and performance improvement; integrating technology in the classroom (Postbaccalaureate Certificate); online teaching for adult learners (Postbaccalaureate Certificate); professional development (Postbaccalaureate Certificate); reading and literacy leadership (Ed D); science K-8 (Postbaccalaureate Certificate); special education (Ed D, Ed S); special education: emotional/behavioral disorders (K-12) (MAT); special education: learning disabilities (K-12) (MAT); teacher leadership (Ed D, Ed S, Postbaccalaureate Certificate); training and performance management (Postbaccalaureate Certificate). Part-time and evening/weekend programs available. Postbaccalaureate distance learning degree programs offered (minimal on-campus study). *Faculty:* 71 full-time (48 women), 853 part-time/adjunct (585 women). *Students:* 11,326 full-time (9,212 women), 2,148 part-time (1,795 women); includes 5,346 minority (4,403 Black or African American, non-Hispanic/Latino; 76 American Indian or Alaska Native, non-Hispanic/Latino; 140 Asian, non-Hispanic/Latino; 561 Hispanic/Latino; 21 Native Hawaiian or other Pacific Islander, non-Hispanic/Latino; 145 Two or more races, non-Hispanic/Latino), 322 international. Average age 39. In 2011, 3,477 master's, 318 doctorates, 471 other advanced degrees awarded. *Degree requirements:* For doctorate, thesis/dissertation (for some programs), residency; for other advanced degree, residency (for some programs). *Entrance requirements:* For master's, bachelor's degree or equivalent in related field; minimum GPA of 2.5; official transcripts; goal statement; access to computer and Internet; for doctorate, master's degree or equivalent in related field; minimum GPA of 3.0; official transcripts; three years' related professional/academic experience (preferred); access to computer and Internet; for other advanced degree, master's degree or equivalent in related field; minimum GPA of 3.0; 3 years related professional/academic experience (preferred); access to computer and Internet (Ed S). Additional exam requirements/recommendations for international students: Required—TOEFL (minimum score 550 paper-based; 213 computer-based), IELTS (minimum score 6.5), or Michigan English Language Assessment Battery (minimum score 82). *Application deadline:* Applications are processed on a rolling basis. Application fee: $50. Electronic applications accepted. *Financial support:* Federal Work-Study, scholarships/grants, unspecified assistantships, and family tuition reduction, active duty/veteran tuition reduction, group tuition reduction, interest-free payment plans, employee tuition reduction available. Support available to part-time students. Financial award applicants required to submit FAFSA. *Unit head:* Dr. Kate Steffens, Dean, 800-925-3368. *Application contact:* Jennifer Hall, Vice President of Enrollment Management, 866-4-WALDEN, E-mail: info@waldenu.edu. Web site: http://www.waldenu.edu/Colleges-and-Schools/College-of-Education-and-Leadership.htm.

Washington State University, Graduate School, College of Education, Department of Teaching and Learning, Pullman, WA 99164. Offers curriculum and instruction (Ed D, PhD); diverse languages (M Ed, MA); elementary education (M Ed, MA, MIT); exercise science (MS); literacy education (M Ed, MA, PhD); math education (PhD); secondary education (M Ed, MA). *Accreditation:* NCATE. *Faculty:* 20. *Students:* 79 full-time (51 women), 40 part-time (31 women); includes 24 minority (3 Black or African American, non-Hispanic/Latino; 5 Asian, non-Hispanic/Latino; 13 Hispanic/Latino; 1 Native Hawaiian or other Pacific Islander, non-Hispanic/Latino; 2 Two or more races, non-Hispanic/Latino), 43 international. Average age 34. 106 applicants, 47% accepted, 43 enrolled. In 2011, 34 master's, 3 doctorates awarded. *Degree requirements:* For master's, comprehensive exam (for some programs), thesis (for some programs), oral or written exam; for doctorate, comprehensive exam, thesis/dissertation, oral and written exam. *Entrance requirements:* For master's and doctorate, GRE General Test, minimum GPA of 3.0, 3 letters of recommendation. Additional exam requirements/recommendations for international students: Required—TOEFL. *Application deadline:* For fall admission, 2/1 for domestic students, 3/1 for international students; for spring admission, 9/1 for domestic students, 7/1 for international students. Applications are processed on a rolling basis. Application fee: $75. *Financial support:* In 2011–12, 130 teaching assistantships with partial tuition reimbursements (averaging $18,204 per year) were awarded; career-related internships or fieldwork, Federal Work-Study, institutionally sponsored loans, tuition waivers (partial), unspecified assistantships, and staff assistantships, teaching associateships also available. Financial award application deadline: 4/1. *Faculty research:* Evolution of middle school education, issues in special education, computer-assisted language learning. *Total annual research expenditures:* $324,000. *Unit head:* Dr. Dawn Shinew, Interim Chair, 509-335-5027, E-mail: dshinew@wsu.edu. *Application contact:* Graduate School Admissions, 800-GRADWSU, Fax: 509-335-1949, E-mail: gradsch@wsu.edu. Web site: http://www.educ.wsu.edu/TL/overview.htm.

Washington State University Tri-Cities, Graduate Programs, Program in Education, Richland, WA 99352-1671. Offers counseling (Ed M); educational leadership (Ed M, Ed D); literacy (Ed M); secondary certification (Ed M); teaching (MIT). Part-time programs available. *Faculty:* 24. *Students:* 19 full-time (14 women), 73 part-time (46 women); includes 18 minority (1 Black or African American, non-Hispanic/Latino; 3 Asian, non-Hispanic/Latino; 14 Hispanic/Latino). Average age 34. 26 applicants, 69% accepted, 18 enrolled. In 2011, 31 master's awarded. *Degree requirements:* For master's, comprehensive exam, thesis or alternative; for doctorate, comprehensive exam, thesis/dissertation. *Entrance requirements:* For master's, GRE, minimum GPA of 3.0, Working with Youth form, Character and Fitness form, 3 letters of recommendation. Additional exam requirements/recommendations for international students: Required—TOEFL. *Application deadline:* For fall admission, 1/10 priority date for domestic students, 1/10 for international students; for spring admission, 7/1 priority date for domestic students, 7/1 for international students. Applications are processed on a rolling basis. Application fee: $75. Electronic applications accepted. *Financial support:* In 2011–12, 59 students received support, including research assistantships (averaging $14,634 per year), teaching assistantships (averaging $13,383 per year); Federal Work-Study, scholarships/grants, and unspecified assistantships also available. Financial award application deadline: 2/15. *Faculty research:* Multicultural counseling, socio-cultural influences in schools, diverse learners, teacher education, K-12 educational leadership. *Unit head:* Dr. Elizabeth Nagel, Director, 509-372-7398, E-mail: elizabeth_nagel@tricity.wsu.edu. *Application contact:* Helen Berry, Academic Coordinator, 800-GRADWSU, Fax: 509-372-3796, E-mail: hberry@tricity.wsu.edu. Web site: http://www.tricity.wsu.edu/education/graduate.html.

Washington University in St. Louis, Graduate School of Arts and Sciences, Department of Education, Program in Secondary Education, St. Louis, MO 63130-4899. Offers MA Ed, MAT. *Degree requirements:* For master's, thesis or alternative. *Entrance requirements:* For master's, GRE General Test or MAT. Electronic applications accepted.

Wayne State University, College of Education, Division of Administrative and Organizational Studies, Detroit, MI 48202. Offers college and university teaching (Certificate); educational leadership (M Ed); educational leadership and policy studies (Ed D, PhD); general administration and supervision (Ed S); instructional technology (M Ed, Ed D, PhD, Ed S); online teaching (Certificate); secondary curriculum and instruction (Ed S). *Students:* 86 full-time (62 women), 261 part-time (172 women); includes 171 minority (145 Black or African American, non-Hispanic/Latino; 1 American Indian or Alaska Native, non-Hispanic/Latino; 8 Asian, non-Hispanic/Latino; 16 Hispanic/Latino; 1 Two or more races, non-Hispanic/Latino), 8 international. Average age 39. 122 applicants, 40% accepted, 28 enrolled. In 2011, 73 master's, 9 doctorates, 50 other advanced degrees awarded. *Degree requirements:* For doctorate, thesis/dissertation. *Entrance requirements:* For doctorate, GRE or MAT, interview; autobiography or curriculum vitae; references; master's degree; minimum undergraduate GPA of 3.0, graduate 3.75; 3 years relevant experience; foundational course work; for other advanced degree, minimum GPA of 3.4. Additional exam requirements/recommendations for international students: Required—TOEFL (minimum score 550 paper-based; 213 computer-based), TWE (minimum score 5.5). *Application deadline:* For fall admission, 6/1 priority date for domestic students, 5/1 for international students; for winter admission, 10/1 priority date for domestic students, 9/1 for international students; for spring admission, 2/1 priority date for domestic students, 1/1 for international students. Applications are processed on a rolling basis. Application fee: $50. Electronic applications accepted. *Expenses:* Tuition, state resident: part-time $512.85 per credit. Tuition, nonresident: part-time $1132.65 per credit. *Required fees:* $26.60 per credit. $199.65 per semester. Tuition and fees vary according to course load and program. *Financial support:* In 2011–12, 59 students received support, including 1 fellowship with tuition reimbursement available (averaging $17,347 per year), 4 research assistantships with tuition reimbursements available (averaging $15,713 per year); career-related internships or fieldwork, Federal Work-Study, institutionally sponsored loans, scholarships/grants, health care benefits, and unspecified assistantships also available. Support available to part-time students. *Faculty research:* Total quality management, participatory management, administering educational technology, school improvement, principalship. *Total annual research expenditures:* $22,232. *Unit head:* Dr. Alan Hoffman, Interim Assistant Dean, 313-577-5235, E-mail: alanhoffman@wayne.edu. *Application contact:* Janice Green, Assistant Dean, 313-577-1605, E-mail: jwgreen@wayne.edu. Web site: http://coe.wayne.edu/aos/index.php.

Wayne State University, College of Education, Division of Teacher Education, Detroit, MI 48202. Offers art education (M Ed), including art therapy; bilingual/bicultural education (M Ed); career and technical education (M Ed); curriculum and instruction (Ed D, PhD, Ed S), including art education (PhD), bilingual education (Ed D, Ed S), bilingual-bicultural education (PhD), career and technical education (MAT, Ed D, PhD, Ed S), early childhood education (MAT, Ed D, PhD, Ed S), elementary education, English as a second language (MAT, Ed D, Ed S), English education (MAT, Ed D, PhD, Ed S), foreign language education (MAT, PhD), K-12 curriculum, mathematics education (MAT, Ed D, PhD, Ed S), science education (MAT, Ed D, PhD, Ed S), secondary education, social studies education (MAT, Ed S), social studies education: secondary (Ed D, PhD); elementary education (MAT), including special education; elementary education (M Ed, MAT), including children's literature (MAT), early childhood education (MAT, Ed D, PhD, Ed S), general elementary education (MAT); elementary or secondary education (MAT), including bilingual/bicultural education, English as a second language (MAT, Ed D, Ed S), mathematics education (MAT, Ed D, PhD, Ed S), science education (MAT, Ed D, PhD, Ed S), social studies education (MAT, Ed S); English education-secondary (M Ed); foreign language education (M Ed); mathematics education (M Ed); reading (M Ed, Ed S); reading, languages and literature (Ed D); science education (M Ed); secondary education (MAT), including art education (K-12), career and technical education (MAT, Ed D, PhD, Ed S), English education (MAT, Ed D, PhD, Ed S), foreign language education (MAT, PhD), kinesiology; social studies education secondary (M Ed); special education (M Ed, Ed D, PhD, Ed S). *Students:* 216 full-time (154 women), 626 part-time (478 women); includes 289 minority (227 Black or

African American, non-Hispanic/Latino; 4 American Indian or Alaska Native, non-Hispanic/Latino; 27 Asian, non-Hispanic/Latino; 21 Hispanic/Latino; 1 Native Hawaiian or other Pacific Islander, non-Hispanic/Latino; 9 Two or more races, non-Hispanic/Latino), 14 international. Average age 37. 347 applicants, 37% accepted, 93 enrolled. In 2011, 226 master's, 12 doctorates, 46 other advanced degrees awarded. *Degree requirements:* For master's, thesis (for some programs), thesis, essay or project (for some M Ed programs), professional field experience (for MAT programs); for doctorate, thesis/dissertation. *Entrance requirements:* For master's, Michigan Basic Skills Test (MA in teaching); for doctorate, minimum undergraduate GPA of 3.0, graduate 3.5; interview, curriculum vitae; references. Additional exam requirements/recommendations for international students: Required—TOEFL (minimum score 550 paper-based; 213 computer-based), TWE (minimum score 5.5). *Application deadline:* For fall admission, 6/1 priority date for domestic students, 5/1 for international students; for winter admission, 10/1 priority date for domestic students, 9/1 for international students; for spring admission, 2/1 priority date for domestic students, 1/1 for international students. Applications are processed on a rolling basis. Application fee: $50. Electronic applications accepted. *Expenses:* Tuition, state resident: part-time $512.85 per credit. Tuition, nonresident: part-time $1132.65 per credit. *Required fees:* $26.60 per credit. $199.65 per semester. Tuition and fees vary according to course load and program. *Financial support:* In 2011–12, 42 students received support. Fellowships, research assistantships with tuition reimbursements available, teaching assistantships, scholarships/grants, and unspecified assistantships available. *Faculty research:* Reading and writing literacy and literature. *Total annual research expenditures:* $264,016. *Unit head:* Dr. Craig Roney, Assistant Dean, 313-577-0902, E-mail: rroney@wayne.edu. Web site: http://coe.wayne.edu/ted/index.php.

West Chester University of Pennsylvania, College of Education, Department of Professional and Secondary Education, West Chester, PA 19383. Offers education for sustainability (Certificate); entrepreneurial education (Certificate); secondary education (M Ed, Teaching Certificate); teaching and learning with technology (Certificate). Part-time programs available. *Faculty:* 1 (woman) full-time, 9 part-time/adjunct (7 women). *Students:* 5 full-time (all women), 26 part-time (11 women); includes 4 minority (2 Black or African American, non-Hispanic/Latino; 1 Asian, non-Hispanic/Latino; 1 Two or more races, non-Hispanic/Latino). Average age 33. 34 applicants, 56% accepted, 10 enrolled. In 2011, 6 master's, 4 Certificates awarded. *Degree requirements:* For master's, comprehensive exam, thesis (for some programs). *Entrance requirements:* For master's, teaching certification (strongly recommended). Additional exam requirements/recommendations for international students: Required—TOEFL (minimum score 550 paper-based; 213 computer-based; 80 iBT). *Application deadline:* For fall admission, 4/15 priority date for domestic students, 3/15 for international students; for spring admission, 10/15 priority date for domestic students, 9/1 for international students. Applications are processed on a rolling basis. Application fee: $45. Electronic applications accepted. *Expenses:* Tuition, state resident: full-time $7488; part-time $416 per credit. Tuition, nonresident: full-time $11,232; part-time $624 per credit. *Required fees:* $1784.64; $67.59 per credit. Tuition and fees vary according to program. *Financial support:* Unspecified assistantships available. Support available to part-time students. Financial award application deadline: 2/15; financial award applicants required to submit FAFSA. *Faculty research:* Technology integration: preparing our teachers for the twenty-first century, critical pedagogy. *Unit head:* Dr. John Elmore, Chair, 610-436-6934, Fax: 610-436-3102, E-mail: jelmore@wcupa.edu. *Application contact:* Dr. David Bolton, Graduate Coordinator, 610-436-6914, Fax: 610-436-3102, E-mail: dbolton@wcupa.edu. Web site: http://www.wcupa.edu/_academics/sch_sed.prof&seced/.

Western Connecticut State University, Division of Graduate Studies, School of Professional Studies, Department of Education and Educational Psychology, Program in Secondary Education, Danbury, CT 06810-6885. Offers biology (MAT); mathematics (MAT). Part-time programs available. *Faculty:* 4 full-time (all women). *Students:* 10 full-time (4 women), 2 part-time (1 woman); includes 3 minority (all Hispanic/Latino). Average age 36. 27 applicants, 41% accepted, 9 enrolled. In 2011, 14 degrees awarded. *Entrance requirements:* For master's, PRAXIS I Pre-Professional Skills Tests, PRAXIS II subject assessment(s), minimum combined undergraduate GPA of 2.8 or MAT (minimum score in 35th percentile). Additional exam requirements/recommendations for international students: Recommended—TOEFL (minimum score 550 paper-based; 213 computer-based; 79 iBT), IELTS (minimum score 6). *Application deadline:* For fall admission, 8/5 priority date for domestic students; for spring admission, 1/5 priority date for domestic students. Application fee: $50. Tuition and fees vary according to course level, course load, degree level and program. *Financial support:* Application deadline: 5/1; applicants required to submit FAFSA. *Faculty research:* Differentiated instruction, the transition of teacher learning, teacher retention, relationship building through the evaluation process and leadership development, culture development, differentiated instruction, scheduling, transitioning teacher learning and curriculum. *Unit head:* Dr. Bonnie Rabe, Chairperson, Department of Education and Educational Psychology, 203-837-3206. *Application contact:* Chris Shankle, Associate Director of Graduate Studies, 203-837-9005, Fax: 203-837-8326, E-mail: shanklec@wcsu.edu.

Western Kentucky University, Graduate Studies, College of Education and Behavioral Sciences, School of Teacher Education, Bowling Green, KY 42101. Offers elementary education (MAE, Ed S); exceptional education: learning and behavioral disorders (MAE); exceptional education: moderate and severe disabilities (MAE); instructional design (MS); interdisciplinary early childhood education (MAE); library media education (MS); literacy education (MAE); middle grades education (MAE); secondary education (MAE, Ed S). Part-time and evening/weekend programs available. Postbaccalaureate distance learning degree programs offered (minimal on-campus study). *Degree requirements:* For master's, comprehensive exam. *Entrance requirements:* For master's, GRE General Test. Additional exam requirements/recommendations for international students: Required—TOEFL (minimum score 555 paper-based; 213 computer-based; 79 iBT). *Faculty research:* Teacher preparation in moderate/severe disabilities.

Western New Mexico University, Graduate Division, School of Education, Silver City, NM 88062-0680. Offers bilingual education (MAT); counseling (MA); educational leadership (MA); elementary education (MAT); reading (MAT); school psychology (MA); secondary education (MAT); special education (MAT); TESOL (teaching English to speakers of other languages) (MAT). *Accreditation:* NCATE. *Degree requirements:* For master's, comprehensive exam. *Entrance requirements:* For master's, GRE General Test, GRE Subject Test, minimum GPA of 3.2 in last 64 hours of undergraduate study. Additional exam requirements/recommendations for international students: Required—TOEFL (minimum score 550 paper-based; 213 computer-based). Electronic applications accepted.

Western Oregon University, Graduate Programs, College of Education, Division of Teacher Education, Program in Secondary Education, Monmouth, OR 97361-1394. Offers bilingual education (MS Ed); health (MS Ed); humanities (MAT, MS Ed); initial licensure (MAT); mathematics (MAT, MS Ed); science (MAT, MS Ed); social science (MAT, MS Ed). *Accreditation:* NCATE. Part-time and evening/weekend programs available. *Degree requirements:* For master's, thesis optional, written exam. *Entrance requirements:* For master's, minimum GPA of 3.0, teaching license. Additional exam requirements/recommendations for international students: Required—TOEFL (minimum score 550 paper-based; 213 computer-based; 79 iBT), IELTS (minimum score 6.5). *Faculty research:* Literacy, science in primary grades, geography education, retention, teacher burnout.

Western Washington University, Graduate School, Woodring College of Education, Department of Secondary Education, Bellingham, WA 98225-5996. Offers MIT. *Accreditation:* NCATE. Part-time programs available. *Degree requirements:* For master's, comprehensive exam, thesis optional. *Entrance requirements:* For master's, GRE General Test or MAT, minimum GPA of 3.0 in last 60 semester hours or last 90 quarter hours, secondary teaching certification. Additional exam requirements/recommendations for international students: Required—TOEFL (minimum score 567 paper-based; 227 computer-based). Electronic applications accepted. *Faculty research:* Service learning, controversial issues in classroom, trauma-sensitive teaching-learning, measuring a teacher's "withitness".

Westfield State University, Division of Graduate and Continuing Education, Department of Education, Program in Secondary Education, Westfield, MA 01086. Offers M Ed. *Accreditation:* NCATE. Part-time and evening/weekend programs available. *Degree requirements:* For master's, comprehensive exam, practicum. *Entrance requirements:* For master's, GRE General Test or MAT, minimum undergraduate GPA of 2.7.

West Virginia University, College of Human Resources and Education, Department of Curriculum and Instruction/Literacy Studies, Program in Secondary Education, Morgantown, WV 26506. Offers higher education curriculum and teaching (MA); secondary education (MA). Students enter program as undergraduates. *Accreditation:* NCATE. Part-time programs available. *Degree requirements:* For master's, thesis optional, content exams. *Entrance requirements:* For master's, minimum GPA of 2.75. Additional exam requirements/recommendations for international students: Required—TOEFL. Electronic applications accepted. *Faculty research:* Teacher education, school reform, curriculum development, education technology.

West Virginia University, Eberly College of Arts and Sciences, Department of Mathematics, Morgantown, WV 26506. Offers applied mathematics (MS, PhD); discrete mathematics (PhD); interdisciplinary mathematics (MS); mathematics for secondary education (MS); pure mathematics (MS). Part-time programs available. Terminal master's awarded for partial completion of doctoral program. *Degree requirements:* For master's, comprehensive exam (for some programs), thesis optional; for doctorate, one foreign language, comprehensive exam, thesis/dissertation. *Entrance requirements:* For master's, GRE Subject Test (recommended), minimum GPA of 2.5; for doctorate, GRE Subject Test (recommended), master's degree in mathematics. Additional exam requirements/recommendations for international students: Required—TOEFL (paper-based 550; computer-based 213) or IELTS (paper-based 6). *Faculty research:* Combinatorics and graph theory, differential equations, applied and computational mathematics.

Wheaton College, Graduate School, Department of Education, Wheaton, IL 60187-5593. Offers elementary level (MAT); secondary level (MAT). *Accreditation:* NCATE. *Students:* 17 full-time (12 women), 24 part-time (21 women); includes 5 minority (4 Asian, non-Hispanic/Latino; 1 Hispanic/Latino). Average age 24. 8 applicants, 100% accepted, 2 enrolled. In 2011, 4 master's awarded. *Degree requirements:* For master's, thesis or alternative. *Entrance requirements:* For master's, GRE General Test or MAT. Additional exam requirements/recommendations for international students: Required—TOEFL (minimum score 550 paper-based; 80 iBT), IELTS (minimum score 6.5). *Application deadline:* For fall admission, 5/1 for domestic students, 1/1 for international students; for spring admission, 11/1 for domestic students. Applications are processed on a rolling basis. Application fee: $30. Electronic applications accepted. *Expenses: Tuition:* Full-time $16,440; part-time $685 per credit hour. Tuition and fees vary according to degree level and program. *Financial support:* Career-related internships or fieldwork and Federal Work-Study available. Financial award application deadline: 3/1; financial award applicants required to submit FAFSA. *Unit head:* Dr. Jillian Lederhouse, Chair, 630-752-5764, E-mail: jillian.lederhouse@wheaton.edu. *Application contact:* Julie A. Huebner, Director of Graduate Admissions, 630-752-5195, Fax: 630-752-5935, E-mail: gradadm@wheaton.edu. Web site: http://www.wheaton.edu/academics/departments/education.

Whittier College, Graduate Programs, Department of Education and Child Development, Program in Secondary Education, Whittier, CA 90608-0634. Offers MA Ed. Part-time and evening/weekend programs available. *Degree requirements:* For master's, thesis. *Entrance requirements:* For master's, GRE General Test, MAT.

Whitworth University, School of Education, Graduate Studies in Education, Spokane, WA 99251-0001. Offers administration (M Ed); counseling (M Ed), including school counselors, social agency/church setting; elementary education (M Ed); gifted and talented (MAT); secondary education (M Ed); special education (MAT); teaching (MIT). *Accreditation:* NCATE. Part-time and evening/weekend programs available. *Degree requirements:* For master's, comprehensive exam, thesis (for some programs). *Entrance requirements:* For master's, GRE General Test, MAT. Additional exam requirements/recommendations for international students: Required—TOEFL. Tuition and fees vary according to program. *Faculty research:* Rural program development, mainstreaming, special needs learners.

Wilkes University, College of Graduate and Professional Studies, School of Education, Wilkes-Barre, PA 18766-0002. Offers art and science of teaching (MS Ed); classroom technology (MS Ed); early childhood literacy (MS Ed); educational computing (MS Ed); educational development and strategies (MS Ed); educational leadership (MS Ed); educational technology (Ed D); higher education administration (Ed D); instructional media (MS Ed); instructional technology (MS Ed); K-12 administration (Ed D); online teaching (MS Ed); reading (MS Ed); school business leadership (MS Ed); secondary education (MS Ed), including biology, chemistry, English, history, mathematics; special education (MS Ed); teaching English as a second language (MS Ed); twenty-first century teaching and learning (MS Ed). Part-time and evening/weekend programs available. Postbaccalaureate distance learning degree programs offered (minimal on-campus study). *Students:* 92 full-time (63 women), 2,005 part-time (1,459 women); includes 89 minority (23 Black or African American, non-Hispanic/Latino; 1 American Indian or Alaska Native, non-Hispanic/Latino; 14 Asian, non-Hispanic/Latino; 33 Hispanic/Latino; 1 Native Hawaiian or other Pacific Islander, non-Hispanic/Latino; 17 Two or more races, non-Hispanic/Latino), 6 international. Average age 33. In 2011, 1,150 master's, 3 doctorates awarded. *Entrance requirements:* Additional exam requirements/recommendations for international students: Required—TOEFL (minimum score 550 paper-based; 213 computer-based; 79 iBT). *Application deadline:* Applications are processed on a rolling basis. Application fee: $45. Electronic applications accepted. *Expenses:* Contact institution. *Financial support:* Federal Work-Study and unspecified assistantships available. Financial award application deadline: 3/1; financial award applicants required to submit FAFSA. *Unit head:* Dr. Michael Speziale, Dean, 570-408-4679, Fax: 570-408-4905, E-mail: michael.speziale@wilkes.edu. *Application contact:* Erin Sutzko, Director of Extended Learning, 570-408-4253, Fax: 570-408-7846, E-mail: erin.sutzko@wilkes.edu. Web site: http://www.wilkes.edu/pages/383.asp.

William Carey University, School of Education, Hattiesburg, MS 39401-5499. Offers art education (M Ed); art of teaching (M Ed); elementary education (M Ed, Ed S); English education (M Ed); gifted education (M Ed); history and social science (M Ed); mild/moderate disabilities (M Ed); secondary education (M Ed). Part-time programs available. *Degree requirements:* For master's, comprehensive exam. *Entrance requirements:* For master's, GRE, MAT, minimum GPA of 2.5, Class A teacher's license. Additional exam requirements/recommendations for international students: Required—TOEFL (minimum score 550 paper-based; 213 computer-based).

William Woods University, Graduate and Adult Studies, Fulton, MO 65251-1098. Offers administration (Ed S); agriculture (MBA); athletic/activities administration (M Ed); curriculum and instruction (M Ed); curriculum leadership (Ed S); elementary administration (M Ed); health management (MBA); human resources (MBA); principalship (Ed S); secondary administration (M Ed); special education director (M Ed). Evening/weekend programs available. *Degree requirements:* For master's, capstone course (MBA), action research (M Ed); for Ed S, field experience. *Entrance requirements:* For master's, 2 recommendations, resumé, BA/BS; teaching certification (M Ed); course work in economics and accounting (MBA); for Ed S, M Ed, 2 letters of recommendation, resume, teaching certification. Additional exam requirements/ recommendations for international students: Required—TOEFL (minimum score 550 paper-based). Electronic applications accepted.

Wilmington University, College of Education, New Castle, DE 19720-6491. Offers applied technology in education (M Ed); career and technical education (M Ed); educational leadership (Ed D); elementary and secondary school counseling (M Ed); elementary studies (M Ed); ESOL literacy (M Ed); higher education leadership (Ed D); instruction: gifted and talented (M Ed); instruction: teacher of reading (M Ed); instruction: teaching and learning (M Ed); organizational leadership (Ed D); school leadership (M Ed); secondary education (MAT); special education (M Ed). *Accreditation:* NCATE. Part-time and evening/weekend programs available. *Faculty:* 7 full-time (4 women). *Students:* 638 full-time (425 women), 2,014 part-time (1,635 women). Average age 33. *Entrance requirements:* For master's, 2 letters of recommendation, interview. Additional exam requirements/recommendations for international students: Required—TOEFL (minimum score 500 paper-based; 173 computer-based). *Application deadline:* For fall admission, 4/30 for domestic students. Applications are processed on a rolling basis. Application fee: $35. Electronic applications accepted. *Expenses: Tuition:* Part-time $534 per credit hour. *Required fees:* $25 per term. *Financial support:* Applicants required to submit FAFSA. *Unit head:* Dr. John C. Gray, Dean, 302-295-1139. *Application contact:* Chris Ferguson, Director of Admissions, 302-356-4636 Ext. 256, Fax: 302-328-5164, E-mail: inquire@wilmcoll.edu. Web site: http://www.wilmu.edu/ education/.

Wilson College, Program in Education, Chambersburg, PA 17201-1285. Offers M Ed. Evening/weekend programs available. *Degree requirements:* For master's, project. *Entrance requirements:* For master's, PRAXIS, minimum undergraduate cumulative GPA of 3.0, 2 letters of recommendation, current certification for eligibility to teach in grades K-12, resume, personal interview. Electronic applications accepted.

Winthrop University, College of Education, Program in Secondary Education, Rock Hill, SC 29733. Offers M Ed, MAT. *Accreditation:* NCATE. Part-time programs available. *Entrance requirements:* For master's, PRAXIS, minimum GPA of 3.0, South Carolina Class III Teaching Certificate. Electronic applications accepted.

Worcester State University, Graduate Studies, Department of Education, Program in Secondary Education, Worcester, MA 01602-2597. Offers M Ed. Part-time programs available. *Faculty:* 12 full-time (9 women), 22 part-time/adjunct (10 women). *Students:* 5 full-time (3 women), 69 part-time (40 women); includes 3 minority (1 Hispanic/Latino; 2 Two or more races, non-Hispanic/Latino). Average age 34. 74 applicants, 77% accepted, 28 enrolled. In 2011, 20 master's awarded. *Degree requirements:* For master's, comprehensive exam (for some programs), thesis optional. *Entrance requirements:* For master's, GRE General Test or MAT, initial license in middle school education or secondary school license from Commonwealth of Massachusetts; evidence of course in adolescent developmental psychology with minimum grade of B or CLEP exam in human growth and development (minimum score of 50). Additional exam requirements/recommendations for international students: Required—TOEFL (minimum score 500 paper-based; 61 iBT). *Application deadline:* For fall admission, 6/15 for domestic and international students; for spring admission, 4/1 for domestic and international students. Applications are processed on a rolling basis. Application fee: $40. Electronic applications accepted. *Expenses:* Tuition, state resident: full-time $2700; part-time $150 per credit. Tuition, nonresident: full-time $2700; part-time $150 per credit. *Required fees:* $2016; $112 per credit. *Financial support:* Career-related internships or fieldwork, scholarships/grants, and unspecified assistantships available. Financial award application deadline: 3/1; financial award applicants required to submit FAFSA. *Unit head:* Dr. Sara Young, Coordinator, 508-929-8246, E-mail: syoung3@ worcester.edu. *Application contact:* Sara Grady, Assistant Dean of Continuing Education, 508-929-8787, Fax: 508-929-8100, E-mail: sara.grady@worcester.edu.

Wright State University, School of Graduate Studies, College of Education and Human Services, Department of Teacher Education, Programs in Classroom Teacher Education, Dayton, OH 45435. Offers M Ed, MA. *Accreditation:* NCATE. *Degree requirements:* For master's, thesis (for some programs). *Entrance requirements:* For master's, GRE General Test, MAT, PRAXIS II. Additional exam requirements/ recommendations for international students: Required—TOEFL.

Xavier University, College of Social Sciences, Health and Education, School of Education, Department of Secondary and Special Education, Program in Secondary Education, Cincinnati, OH 45207. Offers M Ed. Part-time and evening/weekend programs available. *Faculty:* 6 full-time (1 woman), 1 (woman) part-time/adjunct. *Students:* 83 full-time (51 women), 73 part-time (45 women); includes 14 minority (4 Black or African American, non-Hispanic/Latino; 6 Asian, non-Hispanic/Latino; 4 Hispanic/Latino). Average age 31. 25 applicants, 96% accepted, 23 enrolled. In 2011, 45 master's awarded. *Degree requirements:* For master's, comprehensive exam, thesis. *Entrance requirements:* For master's, MAT. *Expenses: Tuition:* Part-time $576 per credit hour. *Financial support:* In 2011–12, 93 students received support. Applicants required to submit FAFSA. *Unit head:* Dr. Michael Flick, Chair, Department of Secondary and Special Education, 513-745-3225, Fax: 513-745-3410, E-mail: flick@xavier.edu. *Application contact:* Jeff Hutton, Director, 513-745-3702, Fax: 513-745-3410, E-mail: hutton@xavier.edu. Web site: http://www.xavier.edu/education/secondary-special-education/index.cfm.

Youngstown State University, Graduate School, Beeghly College of Education, Department of Teacher Education, Program in Middle Childhood Education, Youngstown, OH 44555-0001. Offers MS Ed. *Accreditation:* NCATE. Part-time and evening/weekend programs available. *Degree requirements:* For master's, comprehensive exam, thesis optional. *Entrance requirements:* For master's, GRE, MAT, or teaching certificate; minimum GPA of 2.7. Additional exam requirements/ recommendations for international students: Required—TOEFL. *Faculty research:* Critical reflectivity, gender issues in classroom instruction, collaborative research and analysis, literacy methodology.

HAWAI'I PACIFIC UNIVERSITY

Master of Education in Elementary Education

Programs of Study

The School of Education at Hawai'i Pacific University (HPU) offers a Master's of Education (M.Ed.) in Elementary Education. Graduates leave fully prepared to pass licensure examinations in Hawai'i and 46 other states.

The program provides field-based, inquiry-oriented, and standards-based curricula that prepare future teachers for the challenges they will face in the classroom. Students gain experience in culturally diverse classrooms and work with faculty mentors with expertise in specific content areas. Faculty members and students are also active collaborators on research and community development programs.

In addition to receiving their teaching licensure for kindergarten through 6th grade, graduates have taken positions as school librarians, curriculum specialists, school counselors, corporate trainers, and chief academic officers. Private and public school teaching mentors guide HPU teacher candidates as they complete field experiences at partner schools.

HPU's M.Ed. in Elementary Education requires a minimum of 42 semester hours that include seminar and field experience courses, teaching internships, research, and concentration courses in elementary instruction, curriculum, and assessment. Students use their field experiences to create portfolios of proficiencies and relevant experience. The M.Ed. in Elementary Education program offers convenient evening courses and Web-based courses.

Research Facilities

To support graduate studies, HPU's Meader and Atherton Libraries hold more than 110,000 bound volumes, 350,000 microfiche items, and periodical subscriptions to 1,500 print titles and 30,000 electronic journals. Databases of public and state university libraries, legislative information, and business-oriented statistical data are also available in the library or online. Students can access HPU's library databases, course information, their academic information, and an e-mail account through Pipeline, the University's internal Web site for students. The University's accessible on-campus computer center houses more than 420 computers with specialized software to support graduate academic programs. HPU also provides free Wi-Fi so that students can access Pipeline resources anywhere on campus using laptops. A significant number of online courses are available.

Financial Aid

The University participates in all federal financial aid programs designated for graduate students. These programs provide aid in the form of subsidized (need-based) and unsubsidized (non-need-based) Federal Stafford Student Loans. Through these loans, funds may be available to cover a student's entire cost of education. To apply for aid, students must submit the Free Application for Federal Student Aid (FAFSA) beginning January 1.

The University also offers several types of institutional graduate scholarships to new full-time, degree-seeking students. U.S. citizens, permanent residents, and international students who have a demonstrated financial need may apply. HPU's graduate scholarships include the Graduate Trustee Scholarship of $6000 ($3000 for two semesters), the Graduate Dean Scholarship of $4000 ($2000 for two semesters), and the Graduate Kokua Scholarship of $2000 ($1000 for two semesters). Factors that may be considered when evaluating requests are previous academic record, community involvement and service, and professional work experience and achievement.

In order to be eligible for the best award package, students should apply by HPU's priority deadline of March 1. Applications received after the priority deadline will be awarded on a funds-availability basis. Mailing of student award letters usually begins by the end of March. Applicants will be notified by mail as decisions are made.

Cost of Study

Tuition for graduate students enrolled in fall and spring semesters is determined on a per-credit basis; full-time status for a graduate student is 9 credits. Tuition for the optional winter and summer sessions is also determined on a per-credit basis. For the 2012–13 academic year (excluding winter and summer sessions), full-time tuition is $13,590 for most graduate degree programs, including the M.Ed. in Elementary Education. Other expenses, including books, personal expenses, fees, and a student bus pass are estimated at $3285.

Living and Housing Costs

The University has off-campus housing for graduate students and an apartment referral service. The cost of living in off-campus apartments is approximately $12,482 for a double occupancy room. Additional housing information is available online at www.hpu.edu/housing.

Student Group

University enrollment currently stands at more than 8,200. HPU is one of the most culturally diverse universities in America, with students from all fifty U.S. states and more than 100 countries.

Location

Hawai'i Pacific University combines the excitement of an urban, downtown campus with the serenity of a residential campus. The urban campus is ideally located in downtown Honolulu, the business and financial center of the Pacific. The downtown campus is composed of seven buildings in the center of Honolulu's business district and is home to the College of Business Administration and the College of Humanities and Social Sciences.

Eight miles away, situated on 135 acres in Kaneohe, the windward Hawai'i Loa campus is the site of the College of Nursing and Health Sciences and the College of Natural and Computational Sciences. The Hawai'i Loa campus has residence halls; dining commons; the Educational Technology Center; a student center; and outdoor recreational facilities including a soccer field, tennis courts, a softball field, and an exercise room.

Hawai'i Pacific University

HPU is affiliated with the Oceanic Institute, an aquaculture research facility located on a 56-acre site at Makapu'u Point on the windward coast of Oahu, Hawaii. All three sites are conveniently linked by a free HPU shuttle and easily accessible by public transportation as well.

Notably, the downtown campus location is within walking distance of shopping and dining. 'Iolani Palace, the only royal palace in the United States, is a few blocks away, as are the State Capitol, City Hall, and the Blaisdell Concert Hall. The Honolulu Academy of Arts, Museum of Contemporary Art, Waikiki Aquarium, Honolulu Zoo, and many other cultural attractions are located nearby.

The University

HPU is a private, nonprofit university with approximately 8,200 students. Founded in 1965, HPU prides itself on maintaining strong academic programs, small class sizes, individual attention to students, and a diverse faculty and student population. Students may choose from more than fifty acclaimed undergraduate programs and fourteen distinguished graduate programs.

HPU is recognized as a Best in the West college by The Princeton Review and *U.S. News & World Report* and a Best Buy by *Barron's* business magazine.

HPU boasts more than 500 full- and part-time faculty members from around the world with outstanding academic and professional credentials. HPU's student-centered approach and low student-to-faculty ratio of 15:1 results in personal attention and one-on-one guidance. The average class size is under 25.

A wide range of counseling and other student support services are available. There are more than fifty student organizations on campus, including the Graduate Student Organization.

Applying

Students must have a baccalaureate degree from an accredited college or university in the United States or an equivalent degree from another country. Applicants should complete and forward a graduate admissions application, send in the $50 nonrefundable application fee, have official transcripts sent from all colleges or universities previously attended, and forward two letters of recommendation. A resume and personal statement about the applicant's academic and career goals is required. Elementary and Secondary Education graduate programs require the successful completion of the PRAXIS I (PPST) exam to be accepted into the program. International students should submit scores of a recognized English proficiency test such as TOEFL. Admissions decisions are made on a rolling basis, and applicants are notified between one and two weeks after all documents have been submitted. Applicants are encouraged to submit their applications online.

Correspondence and Information

Graduate Admissions
Hawai'i Pacific University
1164 Bishop Street, #911
Honolulu, Hawai'i 96813
Phone: 808-544-1135
866-GRAD-HPU (toll-free)
Fax: 808-544-0280
E-mail: graduate@hpu.edu
Web site: http://www.hpu.edu/hpumed

THE FACULTY

Valentina M. Abordonado, Associate Professor of English and Director of Teacher Education Program, Ph.D., Arizona.

Edwin, Van Gorder, Associate Professor of Education, Ph.D., Standford University

Kathleen J. Cassity, Assistant Professor of English, Ph.D., Hawaii at Manoa

Jaime Simpson Steele, Assistant Professor of Education, Hawai'i at Manoa

Leslie Correa, Vice President/Associate Professor of Education, Ed.D., Hawaii at Manoa

Mani Sehgal, Instructor of Education, Ph.D., University of Victoria,

Jon Davidann, Director/Professor of History, Ph.D., Minnesota.

Dorothy Douthit, Visiting Assistant Professor of Education, Ph.D., Texas at Austin.

Gordon L. Jones, Professor of Computer Science and Information Systems, Ph.D., New Mexico.

Kenneth Rossi, Assistant Professor of Information Systems, Ed.D., USC.

Linda Wheeler, Assistant Professor of Education and TEP Field Coordinator, Ed.D., Hawai'i at Manoa.

HAWAI'I PACIFIC UNIVERSITY

Master of Education in Secondary Education

Programs of Study

The Master of Education in Secondary Education (MEdSE) degree program at Hawai'i Pacific University develops professional educators who are reflective practitioners dedicated to the scholarship of teaching and school renewal. The program is based on an innovative, standards-driven, field-based curriculum that employs cutting-edge educational technology to integrate content and pedagogy. Upon completing the program, each teacher candidate is able to demonstrate knowledge of his or her content area and will have the ability to develop and modify instruction plans to meet learner needs. Teacher candidates will be committed to the education profession by engaging in appropriate professional practices and will have the desire to collaborate with colleagues, families, and community members. The program is accredited by the Accrediting Commission for Senior Colleges and Universities of the Western Association of Schools and Colleges. The MEdSE degree program prepares candidates for licensure in secondary education in forty-six states.

Research Facilities

To support graduate studies, HPU's Meader and Atherton Libraries hold more than 110,000 bound volumes, 350,000 microfiche items, and periodical subscriptions to 1,500 print titles and 30,000 electronic journals. Databases of public and state university libraries, legislative information, and business-oriented statistical data are also available in the library or online. Students can access HPU's library databases, course information, their academic information, and an e-mail account through Pipeline, the university's internal Web site for students. The University's accessible on-campus computer center houses more than 420 computers with specialized software to support graduate academic programs. HPU also provides free Wi-Fi so that students can access Pipeline resources anywhere on campus using laptops. A significant number of online courses are available.

Financial Aid

The University participates in all federal financial aid programs designated for graduate students. These programs provide aid in the form of subsidized (need-based) and unsubsidized (non-need-based) Federal Stafford Student Loans. Through these loans, funds may be available to cover a student's entire cost of education. To apply for aid, students must submit the Free Application for Federal Student Aid (FAFSA) beginning January 1.

The University also offers several types of institutional graduate scholarships to new full-time, degree-seeking students. U.S. citizens, permanent residents, and international students who have a demonstrated financial need may apply. HPU's graduate scholarships include the Graduate Trustee Scholarship of $6000 ($3000/semester), the Graduate Dean Scholarship of $4000 ($2000/semester), and the Graduate Kokua Scholarship of $2000 ($1000/semester). Factors that may be considered when evaluating requests are previous academic record, community involvement and service, and professional work experience and achievement.

In order to be eligible for the best award package, students should apply by HPU's priority deadline of March 1. Applications received after the priority deadline will be awarded on a funds-available basis. Mailing of student award letters usually begins by the end of March. Applicants will be notified by mail as decisions are made.

Cost of Study

Tuition for graduate students enrolled in fall and spring semesters is determined on a per-credit basis; full-time status for a graduate student is 9 credits. Tuition for the optional winter and summer sessions is also determined on a per-credit basis. For the 2012–13 academic year, full-time tuition is $13,590 for most graduate degree programs, including the MEdSE program. Other expenses, including books, personal expenses, fees, and a student bus pass, are estimated at $3285.

Living and Housing Costs

The University has off-campus housing and an apartment referral service for graduate students. The cost of living in off-campus apartments is approximately $12,482 for a double-occupancy room. Additional graduate housing information is available online at www.hpu.edu/housing.

Student Group

University enrollment currently stands at more than 8,200. HPU is one of the most culturally diverse universities in America, with students from all fifty U.S. states and more than 100 countries.

Location

Hawai'i Pacific University combines the excitement of an urban, downtown campus with the serenity of a residential campus. The urban campus is ideally located in downtown Honolulu, the business and financial center of the Pacific. The downtown campus comprises seven buildings in the center of Honolulu's business district and is home to the College of Business Administration and the College of Humanities and Social Sciences.

Eight miles away, situated on 135 acres in Kaneohe, the windward Hawai'i Loa campus is the site of the College of Nursing and Health Sciences and the College of Natural and Computational Sciences. The Hawai'i Loa campus has residence halls, dining commons, the Educational Technology Center, a student center, and outdoor recreational facilities, including a soccer field, tennis courts, a softball field, and an exercise room.

HPU is affiliated with the Oceanic Institute, an aquaculture research facility located on a 56-acre site at Makapu'u Point on the windward coast of Oahu, Hawaii. All three sites are linked by HPU shuttle and easily accessed by public transportation as well.

Notably, the downtown campus location is within walking distance of shopping and dining. Iolani Palace, the only royal palace in the United States, is a few blocks away, as are the State Capitol, City Hall, and the Blaisdell Concert Hall. The Honolulu Academy of Arts, Museum of Contemporary Art, Waikiki Aquarium, Honolulu Zoo, and many other cultural attractions are located nearby.

The University

HPU is a private, nonprofit university with approximately 8,200 students. Founded in 1965, HPU prides itself on maintaining strong academic programs, small class sizes, individual attention to students, and a diverse faculty and student population. HPU is recognized as a Best in the West college by the Princeton Review and *U.S. News & World Report*, and a Best Buy by *Barron's* business magazine. HPU offers more than fifty acclaimed undergraduate programs and fourteen distinguished graduate programs. The

Hawai'i Pacific University

University has a faculty of more than 500, a student-faculty ratio of 15:1, and an average class size of fewer than 25 students. A wide range of counseling and other student support services are available. There are more than fifty student organizations on campus, including the Graduate Student Organization.

Applying

Students must have a baccalaureate degree from an accredited college or university in the United States or an equivalent degree from another country. Applicants should complete and forward a graduate admissions application, send in the $50 nonrefundable application fee, have official transcripts sent from all colleges or universities previously attended, and forward two letters of recommendation. A resume and personal statement about the applicant's academic and career goals is required. Elementary and secondary education graduate programs require the successful completion of the PRAXIS I (PPST) exam. International students should submit scores of a recognized English proficiency test such as TOEFL. Admissions decisions are made on a rolling basis and applicants are notified between one and two weeks after all documents have been submitted. Applicants are encouraged to submit their applications online.

Correspondence and Information

Graduate Admissions
Hawai'i Pacific University
1164 Bishop Street, #911
Honolulu, Hawai'i 96813
Phone: 808-544-1135
866-GRAD-HPU (toll-free)
Fax: 808-544-0280
E-mail: graduate@hpu.edu
Web site: http://www.hpu.edu/hpumed

THE FACULTY

Valentina M. Abordonado, Director, School of Education; Ph.D., Arizona.

Kathleen J. Cassity, Assistant Professor of English; Ph.D., Hawaii.

Leslie Correa, Vice President/Associate Professor or Education; Ed.D., Hawaii.

Jon Davidann, Director/Professor of History; Ph.D., Minnesota.

Dorothy Douthit, Visiting Assistant Professor of Education; Ph.D., Texas at Austin.

Gordon L. Jones, Professor of Computer Science and Information Systems; Ph.D., New Mexico.

Kenneth Rossi, Assistant Professor of Information Systems; Ed.D., USC.

Edwin Van Gorder, Associate Professor of Education; Ph.D., Stanford.

Linda Wheeler, Field Services Director for Secondary Education; Ed.D., Hawai'i at Manoa.

Section 25
Special Focus

This section contains a directory of institutions offering graduate work in special focus, followed by an in-depth entry submitted by an institution that chose to prepare a detailed program description. Additional information about programs listed in the directory but not augmented by an in-depth entry may be obtained by writing directly to the dean of a graduate school or chair of a department at the address given in the directory.

For programs offering related work, see also in this book *Administration, Instruction, and Theory; Education; Instructional Levels; Leisure Studies and Recreation; Physical Education and Kinesiology;* and *Subject Areas.* In other guides in this series:

Graduate Programs in the Humanities, Arts & Social Sciences

See *Psychology and Counseling (School Psychology)* and *Public, Regional, and Industrial Affairs (Urban Studies)*

Graduate Programs in the Biological/Biomedical Sciences & Health-Related Medical Professions

See *Health-Related Professions*

CONTENTS

Program Directories

Displays and Close-Ups

Education of Students with Severe/Multiple Disabilities

Cleveland State University, College of Graduate Studies, College of Education and Human Services, Department of Teacher Education, Cleveland, OH 44115. Offers art education (M Ed); early childhood education (M Ed); foreign language education (M Ed); mathematics and science education (M Ed); middle childhood education (M Ed); special education (M Ed), including mild/moderate disabilities, moderate/intensive disabilities; teaching English to speakers of other languages (M Ed). Part-time and evening/weekend programs available. *Faculty:* 20 full-time (12 women), 26 part-time/adjunct (20 women). *Students:* 108 full-time (77 women), 388 part-time (306 women); includes 126 minority (100 Black or African American, non-Hispanic/Latino; 8 Asian, non-Hispanic/Latino; 15 Hispanic/Latino; 1 Native Hawaiian or other Pacific Islander, non-Hispanic/Latino; 2 Two or more races, non-Hispanic/Latino), 25 international. Average age 33. 249 applicants, 73% accepted, 118 enrolled. In 2011, 286 master's awarded. *Degree requirements:* For master's, comprehensive exam (for some programs), thesis or alternative. *Entrance requirements:* For master's, GRE General Test or MAT, minimum GPA of 2.75. Additional exam requirements/recommendations for international students: Required—TOEFL (minimum score 525 paper-based; 197 computer-based), IELTS (minimum score 6). *Application deadline:* For fall admission, 7/15 priority date for domestic students. Applications are processed on a rolling basis. Application fee: $30. *Expenses:* Tuition, state resident: full-time $6416; part-time $494 per credit hour. Tuition, nonresident: full-time $12,074; part-time $929 per credit hour. *Financial support:* In 2011–12, 12 research assistantships with full tuition reimbursements (averaging $3,480 per year) were awarded; tuition waivers (partial) and unspecified assistantships also available. *Faculty research:* Early literacy, professional development in reading, reading recovery, dual language, induction programs. *Total annual research expenditures:* $6.2 million. *Unit head:* Dr. Clifford T. Bennett, Chairperson, 216-523-7105, Fax: 216-687-5379, E-mail: c.t.bennett@csuohio.edu. *Application contact:* Deborah L. Brown, Interim Assistant Director, Graduate Admissions, 216-523-7572, E-mail: d.l.brown@csuohio.edu. Web site: http://www.csuohio.edu/coehs/departments/te.

Fresno Pacific University, Graduate Programs, School of Education, Division of Special Education, Fresno, CA 93702-4709. Offers mild/moderate (MA Ed); moderate/severe (MA Ed); physical and health impairments (MA Ed). Part-time and evening/weekend programs available. *Degree requirements:* For master's, thesis or alternative. *Entrance requirements:* Additional exam requirements/recommendations for international students: Required—TOEFL (minimum score 550 paper-based; 213 computer-based).

Georgia State University, College of Education, Department of Educational Psychology and Special Education, Program in Multiple and Severe Disabilities, Atlanta, GA 30302-3083. Offers M Ed, MAT. *Accreditation:* NCATE. *Degree requirements:* For master's, comprehensive exam. *Entrance requirements:* For master's, GRE General Test, minimum GPA of 2.5. *Faculty research:* Cognition, discipline, curriculum development, social maladjustment.

Hunter College of the City University of New York, Graduate School, School of Education, Department of Special Education, New York, NY 10021-5085. Offers blind or visually impaired (MS Ed); deaf or hard of hearing (MS Ed); severe/multiple disabilities (MS Ed); special education (MS Ed). *Accreditation:* NCATE. *Faculty:* 11 full-time (7 women), 63 part-time/adjunct (52 women). *Students:* 96 full-time (84 women), 730 part-time (621 women); includes 221 minority (60 Black or African American, non-Hispanic/Latino; 5 American Indian or Alaska Native, non-Hispanic/Latino; 54 Asian, non-Hispanic/Latino; 102 Hispanic/Latino), 12 international. Average age 28. 560 applicants, 34% accepted, 101 enrolled. In 2011, 281 master's awarded. *Degree requirements:* For master's, comprehensive exam, thesis, student teaching practica, clinical teaching lab courses, New York State Teacher Certification Exams. *Entrance requirements:* For master's, minimum GPA of 2.8. Additional exam requirements/recommendations for international students: Required—TOEFL, TWE. *Application deadline:* For fall admission, 4/1 for domestic students, 2/1 for international students; for spring admission, 11/1 for domestic students, 9/1 for international students. Applications are processed on a rolling basis. Application fee: $50. *Expenses:* Tuition, state resident: full-time $8210; part-time $345 per credit. Tuition, nonresident: full-time $15,360; part-time $640 per credit. *Required fees:* $280 per semester. One-time fee: $125. Tuition and fees vary according to class time, campus/location and program. *Financial support:* Career-related internships or fieldwork, Federal Work-Study, institutionally sponsored loans, and tuition waivers (partial) available. Support available to part-time students. *Faculty research:* Mathematics learning disabilities; street behavior; assessment; bilingual special education; families, diversity, and disabilities. *Unit head:* Dr. Kate Garnett, Chairperson, 212-772-4700, E-mail: kgarnett@hunter.cuny.edu. *Application contact:* William Zlata, Director for Graduate Admissions, 212-772-4482, Fax: 212-650-3336, E-mail: admissions@hunter.cuny.edu. Web site: http://www.hunter.cuny.edu/school-of-education/programs/graduate/special-education.

Minot State University, Graduate School, Program in Special Education, Minot, ND 58707-0002. Offers education of the deaf (MS); learning disabilities (MS); special education strategist (MS), including early childhood special education, severe multiple handicaps. *Accreditation:* NCATE. *Degree requirements:* For master's, comprehensive exam (for some programs), thesis (for some programs). *Entrance requirements:* For master's, GRE General Test or minimum GPA of 3.0. Additional exam requirements/recommendations for international students: Required—TOEFL. *Faculty research:* Special education team diagnostic unit; individual diagnostic assessments of mentally retarded, learning-disabled, hearing-impaired, and speech-impaired youth; educational programming for the hearing impaired.

Norfolk State University, School of Graduate Studies, School of Education, Department of Special Education, Program in Severe Disabilities, Norfolk, VA 23504. Offers MA. *Accreditation:* NCATE. Part-time programs available. *Degree requirements:* For master's, thesis or alternative. *Entrance requirements:* For master's, GRE, minimum GPA of 3.0 in major, 2.5 overall.

Syracuse University, School of Education, Program in Inclusive Special Education: Severe/Multiple Disabilities, Syracuse, NY 13244. Offers MS. Part-time programs available. *Students:* 5 full-time (all women), 4 part-time (3 women). Average age 25. 4 applicants, 50% accepted, 2 enrolled. In 2011, 2 master's awarded. *Entrance requirements:* For master's, New York state initial certification in students with disabilities (Birth-2, 1-6, 5-9, or 7-12). Additional exam requirements/recommendations for international students: Required—TOEFL (minimum score 100 iBT). *Application deadline:* For fall admission, 2/1 priority date for domestic students, 2/1 for international students; for spring admission, 10/15 priority date for domestic students, 10/15 for international students. Applications are processed on a rolling basis. Application fee: $75. Electronic applications accepted. *Expenses: Tuition:* Part-time $1206 per credit. *Financial support:* Fellowships with full tuition reimbursements and teaching assistantships with full and partial tuition reimbursements available. Financial award application deadline: 1/1. *Unit head:* Dr. Gail Ensher, Program Coordinator, 315-443-9650, E-mail: glensher@syr.edu. *Application contact:* Laurie Deyo, Graduate Recruiter, School of Education, 315-443-2505, E-mail: e-gradrcrt@syr.edu. Web site: http://soeweb.syr.edu/.

Teachers College, Columbia University, Graduate Faculty of Education, Department of Health and Behavioral Studies, Program in Severe or Multiple Disabilities, New York, NY 10027-6696. Offers MA. *Faculty:* 7 full-time (4 women), 11 part-time/adjunct (10 women). *Students:* 7 full-time (6 women), 4 part-time (all women); includes 1 minority (Asian, non-Hispanic/Latino). Average age 25. 9 applicants, 100% accepted, 5 enrolled. In 2011, 4 master's awarded. *Degree requirements:* For master's, integrative project. *Entrance requirements:* For master's, minimum GPA of 3.0, evidence of New York State initial teacher certification in one of the required areas. *Application deadline:* For fall admission, 1/15 priority date for domestic students; for spring admission, 11/1 for domestic students. Applications are processed on a rolling basis. Application fee: $65. Electronic applications accepted. *Financial support:* Career-related internships or fieldwork, Federal Work-Study, institutionally sponsored loans, and tuition waivers (partial) available. Support available to part-time students. Financial award application deadline: 2/1; financial award applicants required to submit FAFSA. *Faculty research:* Reading and spelling disorders, workplace literacy, reading and writing among children and adults. *Unit head:* Prof. Linda Hickson, Program Coordinator, 212-678-3854, E-mail: lh76@columbia.edu. *Application contact:* Peter Shon, Assistant Director of Admission, 212-678-3305, Fax: 212-678-4171, E-mail: shon@exchange.tc.columbia.edu. Web site: http://www.tc.edu/hbs/specialed/.

University of Illinois at Urbana–Champaign, Graduate College, College of Education, Department of Special Education, Champaign, IL 61820. Offers Ed M, MS, Ed D, PhD, CAS. Part-time programs available. Postbaccalaureate distance learning degree programs offered (minimal on-campus study). *Faculty:* 9 full-time (7 women). *Students:* 44 full-time (39 women), 24 part-time (18 women); includes 13 minority (8 Black or African American, non-Hispanic/Latino; 1 Asian, non-Hispanic/Latino; 4 Hispanic/Latino), 4 international. 44 applicants, 39% accepted, 15 enrolled. In 2011, 15 master's, 5 doctorates awarded. *Entrance requirements:* For master's and doctorate, minimum GPA of 3.0. Additional exam requirements/recommendations for international students: Required—TOEFL (minimum score 102 iBT). *Application deadline:* Applications are processed on a rolling basis. Application fee: $75 ($90 for international students). Electronic applications accepted. *Financial support:* In 2011–12, 35 fellowships, 9 research assistantships, 7 teaching assistantships were awarded; tuition waivers (full and partial) also available. *Unit head:* Michaelene Ostrosky, Interim Head, 217-333-0260, Fax: 217-333-6555, E-mail: ostrosky@illinois.edu. *Application contact:* Laura Ketchum, Manager I, 217-333-2155, Fax: 217-333-6555, E-mail: ketchum@illinois.edu. Web site: http://education.illinois.edu/SPED/.

West Virginia University, College of Human Resources and Education, Department of Special Education, Morgantown, WV 26506. Offers autism spectrum disorder (5-adult) (MA); autism spectrum disorder (K-6) (MA); early intervention/early childhood special education (MA); gifted education (1-12) (MA); low vision (PreK-adult) (MA); multicategorical special education (5-adult) (MA); multicategorical special education (K-6) (MA); severe/multiple disabilities (K-adult) (MA); special education (MA, Ed D); vision impairments (PreK-adult) (MA). *Accreditation:* NCATE. Part-time and evening/weekend programs available. Postbaccalaureate distance learning degree programs offered (no on-campus study). *Degree requirements:* For master's, thesis optional; for doctorate, comprehensive exam, thesis/dissertation. *Entrance requirements:* For master's, minimum GPA of 2.75 passing scores on PRAXIS PPST; for doctorate, GRE General Test or MAT. Additional exam requirements/recommendations for international students: Required—TOEFL.

Education of the Gifted

Arkansas State University, Graduate School, College of Education, Department of Educational Leadership, Curriculum, and Special Education, Jonesboro, State University, AR 72467. Offers community college administration education (SCCT); curriculum and instruction (MSE); educational leadership (MSE, Ed D, PhD, Ed S), including curriculum and instruction (MSE, Ed S); special education (MSE), including gifted, talented, and creative, instructional specialist 4-12, instructional specialist P-4. *Accreditation:* NCATE. Part-time programs available. Postbaccalaureate distance learning degree programs offered (no on-campus study). *Faculty:* 12 full-time (5 women). *Students:* 11 full-time (6 women), 2,240 part-time (1,686 women); includes 374 minority (278 Black or African American, non-Hispanic/Latino; 14 American Indian or Alaska Native, non-Hispanic/Latino; 12 Asian, non-Hispanic/Latino; 46 Hispanic/Latino; 2 Native Hawaiian or other Pacific Islander, non-Hispanic/Latino; 22 Two or more races, non-Hispanic/Latino), 1 international. Average age 37. 1,519 applicants, 76% accepted, 790 enrolled. In 2011, 827 master's, 8 doctorates, 30 other advanced degrees awarded.

Degree requirements: For master's, comprehensive exam, thesis or alternative; for doctorate, comprehensive exam, thesis/dissertation; for other advanced degree, comprehensive exam. *Entrance requirements:* For master's, GRE General Test or MAT, appropriate bachelor's degree, letters of reference, interview, official transcript, immunization records; for doctorate, GRE General Test or MAT, interview, master's degree, letters of reference, official transcript, personal statement, writing sample, immunization records; for other advanced degree, GRE General Test or MAT, interview, master's degree, letters of reference, official transcript, 3 years teaching experience, mentor, teaching license, immunization records. Additional exam requirements/recommendations for international students: Required—TOEFL (minimum score 550 paper-based; 213 computer-based; 79 iBT), IELTS (minimum score 6), Pearson Test of English Academic (minimum score 56). *Application deadline:* Applications are processed on a rolling basis. Application fee: $50. Electronic applications accepted. *Expenses:* Tuition, state resident: full-time $4044; part-time $225 per credit hour. Tuition, nonresident: full-time $8087; part-time $449 per credit hour. *Required fees:* $936; $52 per credit hour. $25 per term. One-time fee: $30. Tuition and fees vary according to course load and program. *Financial support:* In 2011–12, 6 students received support. Fellowships, teaching assistantships, career-related internships or fieldwork, scholarships/grants, and unspecified assistantships available. Financial award application deadline: 7/1; financial award applicants required to submit FAFSA. *Unit head:* Dr. Mitchell Holifield, Chair, 870-972-3062, Fax: 870-680-8130, E-mail: hfield@astate.edu. *Application contact:* Dr. Andrew Sustich, Dean of the Graduate School, 870-972-3029, Fax: 870-972-3857, E-mail: sustich@astate.edu. Web site: http://www.astate.edu/a/education/elcse/.

Ashland University, Dwight Schar College of Education, Department of Inclusive Services and Exceptional Learners, Ashland, OH 44805-3702. Offers intervention specialist, mild/moderate (M Ed); intervention specialist, moderate/intensive (M Ed); talented and gifted (M Ed). Part-time and evening/weekend programs available. *Faculty:* 10 full-time (8 women), 36 part-time/adjunct (23 women). *Students:* 74 full-time (57 women), 108 part-time (92 women); includes 12 minority (6 Black or African American, non-Hispanic/Latino; 1 American Indian or Alaska Native, non-Hispanic/Latino; 4 Hispanic/Latino; 1 Two or more races, non-Hispanic/Latino). Average age 33. 31 applicants, 100% accepted, 29 enrolled. In 2011, 74 master's awarded. *Degree requirements:* For master's, thesis or alternative, internship, practicum, inquiry seminar. *Entrance requirements:* Additional exam requirements/recommendations for international students: Required—TOEFL. *Application deadline:* For fall admission, 8/15 for domestic students; for spring admission, 1/15 for domestic students. Applications are processed on a rolling basis. Application fee: $30. Electronic applications accepted. *Expenses: Tuition:* Full-time $5580; part-time $465 per credit hour. *Financial support:* Teaching assistantships with partial tuition reimbursements and scholarships/grants available. Financial award application deadline: 4/15. *Unit head:* Dr. Allison Dickey, Chair, 419-289-5376, Fax: 419-207-4949, E-mail: adickey@ashland.edu. *Application contact:* Dr. Linda Billman, Associate Dean, 419-289-5369, Fax: 419-289-5331, E-mail: lbillman@ashland.edu.

Barry University, School of Education, Program in Curriculum and Instruction, Miami Shores, FL 33161-6695. Offers accomplished teacher (Ed S); culture, language and literacy (TESOL) (PhD); curriculum evaluation and research (PhD); early childhood (Ed S); early childhood education (PhD); elementary (Ed S); elementary education (PhD); ESOL (Ed S); gifted (Ed S); Montessori (Ed S); PKP/elementary (Ed S); reading (Ed S); reading, language and cognition (PhD). *Entrance requirements:* For doctorate, GRE, minimum GPA of 3.25.

Barry University, School of Education, Program in Exceptional Student Education, Miami Shores, FL 33161-6695. Offers MS, Ed S. Part-time and evening/weekend programs available. *Degree requirements:* For master's, comprehensive exam; for Ed S, practicum. *Entrance requirements:* For master's, GRE General Test or MAT, minimum GPA of 3.0; for Ed S, GRE General Test, minimum GPA of 3.0. Electronic applications accepted.

Barry University, School of Education, Program in Leadership and Education, Miami Shores, FL 33161-6695. Offers educational technology (PhD); exceptional student education (PhD); higher education administration (PhD); human resource development (PhD); leadership (PhD). Part-time and evening/weekend programs available. *Degree requirements:* For doctorate, thesis/dissertation. *Entrance requirements:* For doctorate, GRE General Test, minimum GPA of 3.25. Electronic applications accepted.

Baylor University, Graduate School, School of Education, Department of Educational Psychology, Waco, TX 76798-7301. Offers applied behavior analysis (MS Ed); educational psychology (MA); exceptionalities (PhD); gifted (PhD); quantitative (PhD); school psychology (PhD, Ed S). *Accreditation:* NCATE. Part-time programs available. *Faculty:* 7 full-time (4 women), 2 part-time/adjunct (1 woman). *Students:* 42 full-time (34 women), 11 part-time (9 women); includes 15 minority (5 Black or African American, non-Hispanic/Latino; 5 Asian, non-Hispanic/Latino; 3 Hispanic/Latino; 2 Two or more races, non-Hispanic/Latino), 2 international. Average age 28. 31 applicants, 48% accepted, 13 enrolled. In 2011, 3 master's, 5 doctorates, 7 other advanced degrees awarded. *Degree requirements:* For master's, thesis optional; for doctorate, comprehensive exam, thesis/dissertation; for Ed S, comprehensive exam, thesis or alternative. *Entrance requirements:* For master's and Ed S, GRE General Test; for doctorate, GRE General Test, master's degree. Additional exam requirements/recommendations for international students: Required—TOEFL. *Application deadline:* For fall admission, 2/1 priority date for domestic students, 2/1 for international students. Application fee: $50. Electronic applications accepted. *Financial support:* In 2011–12, 20 students received support, including 20 research assistantships with full and partial tuition reimbursements available; career-related internships or fieldwork, Federal Work-Study, institutionally sponsored loans, scholarships/grants, health care benefits, tuition waivers (full and partial), unspecified assistantships, and stipends also available. Financial award application deadline: 2/1. *Faculty research:* Individual differences, quantitative methods, gifted and talented, special education, school psychology, autism, applied behavior analysis. *Unit head:* Dr. Marley W. Watkins, Professor and Chairman, 254-710-4234, Fax: 254-710-3987, E-mail: marley_watkins@baylor.edu. *Application contact:* Lisa Rowe, Administrative Assistant, 254-710-3112, Fax: 254-710-3112, E-mail: lisa_rowe@baylor.edu. Web site: http://www.baylor.edu/soe/EDP/.

Bowling Green State University, Graduate College, College of Education and Human Development, School of Education and Intervention Services, Intervention Services Division, Program in Special Education, Bowling Green, OH 43403. Offers assistive technology (M Ed); early childhood intervention (M Ed); gifted education (M Ed); hearing impaired intervention (M Ed); mild/moderate intervention (M Ed); moderate/intensive intervention (M Ed). *Accreditation:* NCATE. Part-time programs available. *Degree requirements:* For master's, thesis or alternative. *Entrance requirements:* For master's, GRE General Test. Additional exam requirements/recommendations for international students: Required—TOEFL. Electronic applications accepted. *Faculty research:* Reading and special populations, deafness, early childhood, gifted and talented, behavior disorders.

Canisius College, Graduate Division, School of Education and Human Services, Department of Graduate Education and Leadership, Buffalo, NY 14208-1098. Offers college student personnel (MS Ed); deaf education (MS Ed); deaf/adolescent education, grades 7-12 (MS Ed); deaf/childhood education, grades 1-6 (MS Ed); differential instruction (MS Ed); education administration (MS Ed); gifted education extention (Certificate); literacy (MS Ed); reading (Certificate); school building leadership (MS Ed, Certificate); school district leadership (Certificate). *Accreditation:* NCATE. Part-time and evening/weekend programs available. Postbaccalaureate distance learning degree programs offered (minimal on-campus study). *Faculty:* 7 full-time (6 women), 36 part-time/adjunct (22 women). *Students:* 149 full-time (114 women), 242 part-time (177 women); includes 42 minority (29 Black or African American, non-Hispanic/Latino; 2 American Indian or Alaska Native, non-Hispanic/Latino; 3 Asian, non-Hispanic/Latino; 6 Hispanic/Latino; 2 Two or more races, non-Hispanic/Latino), 3 international. Average age 30. 250 applicants, 84% accepted, 124 enrolled. In 2011, 135 degrees awarded. *Entrance requirements:* For master's, GRE if cumulative GPA less than 2.7, transcripts, two letters of recommendation. Additional exam requirements/recommendations for international students: Required—TOEFL. *Application deadline:* Applications are processed on a rolling basis. Application fee: $25. Electronic applications accepted. *Financial support:* Career-related internships or fieldwork, Federal Work-Study, scholarships/grants, tuition waivers (partial), and unspecified assistantships available. Support available to part-time students. Financial award application deadline: 4/30; financial award applicants required to submit FAFSA. *Faculty research:* Asperger's disease, autism, private higher education, reading strategies. *Unit head:* Dr. Rosemary K. Murray, Chair/Associate Professor of Graduate Education and Leadership, 716-888-3723, E-mail: murray1@canisius.edu. *Application contact:* Jim Bagwell, Director of Graduate Recruitment and Admissions, 716-888-2544, Fax: 716-888-3290, E-mail: bagwellj@canisius.edu. Web site: http://www.canisius.edu/education/graduate.asp.

Carlos Albizu University, Miami Campus, Graduate Programs, Miami, FL 33172-2209. Offers clinical psychology (Psy D); entrepreneurship (MBA); exceptional student education (MS); industrial/organizational psychology (MS); marriage and family therapy (MS); mental health counseling (MS); nonprofit management (MBA); organizational management (MBA); psychology (MS); school counseling (MS); teaching English as a second language (MS). *Accreditation:* APA. Part-time and evening/weekend programs available. *Faculty:* 19 full-time (12 women), 53 part-time/adjunct (27 women). *Students:* 524 full-time (431 women), 216 part-time (169 women); includes 563 minority (50 Black or African American, non-Hispanic/Latino; 1 American Indian or Alaska Native, non-Hispanic/Latino; 4 Asian, non-Hispanic/Latino; 492 Hispanic/Latino; 16 Native Hawaiian or other Pacific Islander, non-Hispanic/Latino), 17 international. Average age 31. 174 applicants, 67% accepted, 116 enrolled. In 2011, 157 master's, 21 doctorates awarded. Terminal master's awarded for partial completion of doctoral program. *Degree requirements:* For master's, one foreign language, comprehensive exam, integrative project (MBA), research project (exceptional student education, teaching English as a second language); for doctorate, one foreign language, comprehensive exam, internship, project. *Entrance requirements:* For master's, 3 letters of recommendation, interview, minimum GPA of 3.0, resume, statement of purpose, official transcripts; for doctorate, 3 letters of recommendation, minimum GPA of 3.0, resume, interview, statement of purpose, official transcripts. Additional exam requirements/recommendations for international students: Required—Michigan Test of English Language Proficiency. *Application deadline:* For fall admission, 4/1 priority date for domestic students, 5/1 for international students; for spring admission, 11/1 priority date for domestic students, 9/1 for international students. Applications are processed on a rolling basis. Application fee: $50. Electronic applications accepted. *Expenses: Tuition:* Full-time $9360; part-time $520 per credit. *Required fees:* $298 per term. Tuition and fees vary according to course load, degree level and program. *Financial support:* In 2011–12, 106 students received support. Federal Work-Study, scholarships/grants, and tuition discounts available. Financial award application deadline: 6/1; financial award applicants required to submit FAFSA. *Faculty research:* Psychotherapy, forensic psychology, neuropsychology, marketing strategy, entrepreneurship, special education. *Unit head:* Dr. Carmen S. Roca, Chancellor, 305-593-1223 Ext. 120, Fax: 305-629-8052, E-mail: croca@albizu.edu. *Application contact:* Vanessa Almendarez, Administrative Assistant, 305-593-1223 Ext. 137, Fax: 305-593-1854, E-mail: valmendarez@albizu.edu.

Carthage College, Division of Teacher Education, Kenosha, WI 53140. Offers classroom guidance and counseling (M Ed); creative arts (M Ed); gifted and talented children (M Ed); language arts (M Ed); modern language (M Ed); natural sciences (M Ed); reading (M Ed, Certificate); social sciences (M Ed); teacher leadership (M Ed). Part-time and evening/weekend programs available. *Degree requirements:* For master's, thesis optional. *Entrance requirements:* For master's, MAT, minimum B average, letters of reference.

The College of New Rochelle, Graduate School, Division of Education, Program in Creative Teaching and Learning, New Rochelle, NY 10805-2308. Offers MS Ed, Certificate. Part-time programs available. *Degree requirements:* For master's, practicum. *Entrance requirements:* For master's, interview, minimum GPA of 3.0 in field, 2.7 overall.

The College of William and Mary, School of Education, Program in Curriculum and Instruction, Williamsburg, VA 23187-8795. Offers elementary education (MA Ed); gifted education (MA Ed); math specialist (MA Ed); reading education (MA Ed); secondary education (MA Ed), including English education, mathematics education, modern foreign languages education, science education, social studies education; special education (MA Ed), including collaborating master educator, general curriculum. *Accreditation:* NCATE. Part-time programs available. *Faculty:* 15 full-time (10 women), 39 part-time/adjunct (32 women). *Students:* 80 full-time (69 women), 13 part-time (11 women); includes 11 minority (3 Black or African American, non-Hispanic/Latino; 1 American Indian or Alaska Native, non-Hispanic/Latino; 2 Hispanic/Latino; 5 Two or more races, non-Hispanic/Latino), 1 international. Average age 25. 220 applicants, 56% accepted, 85 enrolled. In 2011, 78 master's awarded. *Degree requirements:* For master's, project. *Entrance requirements:* For master's, GRE or MAT, minimum GPA of 2.5. Additional exam requirements/recommendations for international students: Required—TOEFL. *Application deadline:* For fall admission, 1/15 for domestic and international students; for spring admission, 10/1 for domestic and international students. Application fee: $50. Electronic applications accepted. *Expenses:* Tuition, state resident: full-time $6400; part-time $365 per credit hour. Tuition, nonresident: full-time $19,720; part-time $985 per credit hour. *Required fees:* $4562. *Financial support:* In 2011–12, 53 students received support, including 10 research assistantships with full and partial tuition reimbursements available (averaging $7,000 per year); career-related internships or fieldwork, Federal Work-Study, institutionally sponsored loans, scholarships/grants, and unspecified assistantships also available. Financial award application deadline: 1/15; financial award applicants required to submit FAFSA. *Faculty research:* National Council of Teachers of Mathematics Standards, counseling, self-concept and self-esteem, special education, curriculum development. *Unit head:* Dr. Margie Mason, Area Coordinator, 757-221-2327, E-mail: mmmaso@wm.edu. *Application contact:* Dorothy Smith Osborne, Assistant Dean for Admission, 757-221-2317, Fax: 757-221-2293, E-mail: dsosbo@wm.edu. Web site: http://education.wm.edu.

Converse College, School of Education and Graduate Studies, Program in Gifted Education, Spartanburg, SC 29302-0006. Offers M Ed. Part-time programs available.

Education of the Gifted

Degree requirements: For master's, capstone paper. *Entrance requirements:* For master's, NTE or PRAXIS II, minimum GPA of 2.75, teaching certificate, 2 recommendations. Electronic applications accepted. *Faculty research:* Identification of gifted minorities, arts in gifted education.

Dowling College, Graduate Programs in Education, Oakdale, NY 11769-1999. Offers adolescence education with middle childhood extension (MS); advanced certificate in gifted education (AC); childhood and early childhood education (MS); childhood and gifted education (MS); computers in education (AC); early childhood education (MS); educational administration (Ed D); educational technology leadership (MS); educational technology specialist (AC); literacy education (MS); literary education (AC); school building leader (AC); school district business leader (MBA, AC); school district leader (AC); special education (MS); sports management (MS). *Accreditation:* NCATE. Part-time and evening/weekend programs available. Postbaccalaureate distance learning degree programs offered (minimal on-campus study). *Faculty:* 23 full-time (12 women), 70 part-time/adjunct (44 women). *Students:* 336 full-time (245 women), 631 part-time (485 women); includes 83 minority (29 Black or African American, non-Hispanic/Latino; 2 American Indian or Alaska Native, non-Hispanic/Latino; 7 Asian, non-Hispanic/Latino; 45 Hispanic/Latino). Average age 32. 280 applicants, 85% accepted, 167 enrolled. In 2011, 425 master's, 27 doctorates, 40 other advanced degrees awarded. *Degree requirements:* For master's and AC, comprehensive exam; for doctorate, thesis/dissertation. *Entrance requirements:* For master's, minimum GPA of 3.0; for doctorate, GRE, master's degree; for AC, teaching certificate. Additional exam requirements/recommendations for international students: Required—TOEFL (minimum score 550 paper-based). *Application deadline:* For fall admission, 9/1 priority date for domestic students; for winter admission, 1/1 priority date for domestic students; for spring admission, 2/1 priority date for domestic students. Applications are processed on a rolling basis. Application fee: $50. Electronic applications accepted. *Expenses: Tuition:* Full-time $19,162; part-time $933 per credit. *Required fees:* $1330; $700 per year. Tuition and fees vary according to course load. *Financial support:* Career-related internships or fieldwork and Federal Work-Study available. Support available to part-time students. Financial award application deadline: 6/30; financial award applicants required to submit FAFSA. *Faculty research:* Natural readers, Korean styles and learning strategies, mothers of children with disabilities, computers in instruction, cultural background and organizational roadblocks to problem solving. *Unit head:* Carol Pulsonetti, Director of Operations, School of Education, 631-244-3243, E-mail: pulsonec@dowling.edu. *Application contact:* Ronnie S. Macdonald, Assistant Vice President for Enrollment Services/Dean of Admissions, 631-244-3357, Fax: 631-244-1059, E-mail: macdonar@dowling.edu.

Drury University, Graduate Programs in Education, Springfield, MO 65802. Offers elementary education (M Ed); gifted education (M Ed); human services (M Ed); instructional mathematics K-8 (M Ed); instructional technology (M Ed); middle school teaching (M Ed); secondary education (M Ed); special education (M Ed); special reading (M Ed). *Accreditation:* NCATE. Part-time and evening/weekend programs available. *Degree requirements:* For master's, thesis. *Entrance requirements:* For master's, GRE or MAT, minimum GPA of 2.75. Additional exam requirements/recommendations for international students: Required—TOEFL. Electronic applications accepted. *Faculty research:* Cultural enrichment, research skills, parental involvement relating to reading skills, reading strategies for mainstreaming children.

Elon University, Program in Education, Elon, NC 27244-2010. Offers elementary education (M Ed); gifted education (M Ed); special education (M Ed). *Accreditation:* NCATE. Part-time programs available. *Faculty:* 19 full-time (15 women). *Students:* 47 part-time (41 women); includes 8 minority (7 Black or African American, non-Hispanic/Latino; 1 Asian, non-Hispanic/Latino). Average age 33. 29 applicants, 86% accepted, 22 enrolled. In 2011, 39 master's awarded. *Entrance requirements:* For master's, GRE, MAT. Additional exam requirements/recommendations for international students: Required—TOEFL (minimum score 550 paper-based; 213 computer-based; 79 iBT). *Application deadline:* For winter admission, 6/1 priority date for domestic students. Applications are processed on a rolling basis. Application fee: $50. Electronic applications accepted. *Expenses:* Contact institution. *Financial support:* In 2011–12, 5 students received support. Federal Work-Study and scholarships/grants available. Support available to part-time students. Financial award application deadline: 6/1; financial award applicants required to submit FAFSA. *Faculty research:* Teaching reading to low-achieving second and third graders, pre- and post-student teaching attitudes , children's writing, whole language methodology, critical creative thinking. *Unit head:* Dr. Angela Owusu-Ansah, Director and Associate Dean of Education, 336-278-5885, Fax: 336-278-5919, E-mail: aansah@elon.edu. *Application contact:* Art Fadde, Director of Graduate Admissions, 800-334-8448 Ext. 3, Fax: 336-278-7699, E-mail: afadde@elon.edu. Web site: http://www.elon.edu/med/.

Emporia State University, Graduate School, Teachers College, Department of Elementary Education, Early Childhood, and Special Education, Program in Special Education, Emporia, KS 66801-5087. Offers behavior disorders (MS); gifted, talented, and creative (MS); interrelated special education (MS); learning disabilities (MS); mental retardation (MS). *Accreditation:* NCATE. Part-time programs available. *Students:* 7 full-time (6 women), 183 part-time (130 women); includes 12 minority (4 Black or African American, non-Hispanic/Latino; 1 American Indian or Alaska Native, non-Hispanic/Latino; 1 Hispanic/Latino; 2 Native Hawaiian or other Pacific Islander, non-Hispanic/Latino; 4 Two or more races, non-Hispanic/Latino), 1 international. 44 applicants, 84% accepted, 31 enrolled. In 2011, 55 master's awarded. *Degree requirements:* For master's, comprehensive exam or thesis, practicum. *Entrance requirements:* For master's, GRE General Test or MAT, graduate essay exam, appropriate bachelor's degree, teacher certification, letters of recommendation. Additional exam requirements/recommendations for international students: Required—TOEFL (minimum score 520 paper-based; 133 computer-based; 68 iBT). *Application deadline:* For fall admission, 8/15 priority date for domestic students. Applications are processed on a rolling basis. Application fee: $30 ($75 for international students). Electronic applications accepted. *Expenses:* Tuition, state resident: full-time $2342; part-time $195 per credit hour. Tuition, nonresident: full-time $7254; part-time $605 per credit hour. *Required fees:* $66 per credit hour. Tuition and fees vary according to campus/location. *Financial support:* Federal Work-Study, institutionally sponsored loans, health care benefits, and unspecified assistantships available. Financial award application deadline: 3/15; financial award applicants required to submit FAFSA. *Unit head:* Dr. Jean Morrow, Chair, 620-341-5317, E-mail: jmorrow@emporia.edu. *Application contact:* Mary Sewell, Admissions Coordinator, 800-950-GRAD, Fax: 620-341-5909, E-mail: msewell@emporia.edu.

Hampton University, Graduate College, College of Education and Continuing Studies, Program in Gifted Education, Hampton, VA 23668. Offers MA. *Accreditation:* NCATE. Part-time and evening/weekend programs available. *Entrance requirements:* For master's, GRE General Test.

Hardin-Simmons University, Graduate School, Irvin School of Education, Department of Educational Studies, Program in Gifted Education, Abilene, TX 79698-0001. Offers M Ed. Part-time programs available. *Faculty:* 2 full-time (both women). *Students:* 2 full-time (both women), 37 part-time (34 women); includes 4 minority (1 Black or African American, non-Hispanic/Latino; 1 Asian, non-Hispanic/Latino; 2 Hispanic/Latino). Average age 37. 29 applicants, 93% accepted, 21 enrolled. In 2011, 5 master's awarded. *Degree requirements:* For master's, comprehensive exam. *Entrance requirements:* For master's, minimum undergraduate GPA of 3.0 in major, 2.7 overall. Additional exam requirements/recommendations for international students: Required—TOEFL (minimum score 550 paper-based; 213 computer-based; 75 iBT). *Application deadline:* For fall admission, 8/15 priority date for domestic students, 4/1 for international students; for spring admission, 1/5 priority date for domestic students, 9/1 for international students. Applications are processed on a rolling basis. Application fee: $50. *Expenses: Tuition:* Full-time $12,870; part-time $715 per credit hour. *Required fees:* $650; $110 per semester. Tuition and fees vary according to degree level. *Financial support:* In 2011–12, 7 students received support, including 4 fellowships (averaging $2,475 per year); scholarships/grants also available. Support available to part-time students. Financial award application deadline: 6/30; financial award applicants required to submit FAFSA. *Faculty research:* Experiences of gifted learners in college, use of authentic assessment, brain research and how it works in learning, theories of multiple intelligence beyond Gardner. *Unit head:* Dr. Mary Christopher, Director, 325-670-1510, Fax: 325-670-1397, E-mail: mchris@hsutx.edu. *Application contact:* Dr. Nancy Kucinski, Dean of Graduate Studies, 325-670-1298, Fax: 325-670-1564, E-mail: gradoff@hsutx.edu. Web site: http://www.hsutx.edu/academics/irvin/graduate/gifted.

The Johns Hopkins University, School of Education, Department of Teacher Development and Leadership, Baltimore, MD 21218-2699. Offers adolescent literacy education (Certificate); data-based decision making and organizational improvement (Certificate); education (MS), including reading, school administration and supervision, technology for educators; educational leadership for independent schools (Certificate); effective teaching of reading (Certificate); emergent literacy education (Certificate); English as a second language instruction (Certificate); gifted education (Certificate); leadership for school, family, and community collaboration (Certificate); leadership in technology integration (Certificate); school administration and supervision (Certificate); teacher development and leadership (Ed D); teacher leadership (Certificate). Part-time and evening/weekend programs available. Postbaccalaureate distance learning degree programs offered (minimal on-campus study). *Degree requirements:* For master's and Certificate, portfolio; for doctorate, comprehensive exam (for some programs), thesis/dissertation, portfolio or comprehensive exam. *Entrance requirements:* For master's and Certificate, bachelor's degree; minimum undergraduate GPA of 3.0; essay/statement of goals; for doctorate, GRE, essay/statement of goals; three letters of recommendation; curriculum vitae/resume; K-12 professional experience; interview; writing assessment. Additional exam requirements/recommendations for international students: Required—TOEFL (minimum score 600 paper-based; 250 computer-based; 100 iBT). Electronic applications accepted. *Faculty research:* Application of psychoanalytic concepts to teaching, schools, and education reform; adolescent literacies; use of emerging technologies for teaching, learning, and school leadership; quantitative analyses of the social contexts of education; school, family, and community collaboration; program evaluation methodologies.

Johnson State College, Graduate Program in Education, Program in Gifted and Talented, Johnson, VT 05656. Offers MA Ed. Part-time programs available. *Degree requirements:* For master's, comprehensive exam, thesis or alternative. *Entrance requirements:* For master's, interview. Additional exam requirements/recommendations for international students: Required—TOEFL. *Application deadline:* For fall admission, 7/15 priority date for domestic students, 4/15 for international students; for spring admission, 11/1 priority date for domestic students, 8/15 for international students. Applications are processed on a rolling basis. Application fee: $35. *Expenses: Tuition, area resident:* Part-time $459 per credit hour. Tuition, nonresident: part-time $990 per credit hour. *Financial support:* Career-related internships or fieldwork, Federal Work-Study, and institutionally sponsored loans available. Support available to part-time students. Financial award application deadline: 3/1; financial award applicants required to submit FAFSA. *Application contact:* Catherine H. Higley, Administrative Assistant, 800-635-2356 Ext. 1244, Fax: 802-635-1248, E-mail: catherine.higley@jsc.edu.

Kent State University, Graduate School of Education, Health, and Human Services, School of Lifespan Development and Educational Sciences, Program in Special Education, Kent, OH 44242-0001. Offers deaf education (M Ed); general special education (M Ed); gifted education (M Ed); mild/moderate intervention (M Ed); moderate/intensive intervention (M Ed); special education (PhD, Ed S). *Accreditation:* NCATE. *Faculty:* 24 full-time (18 women), 21 part-time/adjunct (20 women). *Students:* 96 full-time (76 women), 81 part-time (64 women); includes 8 minority (5 Black or African American, non-Hispanic/Latino; 2 Asian, non-Hispanic/Latino; 1 Hispanic/Latino). 66 applicants, 56% accepted. In 2011, 48 master's, 3 doctorates awarded. *Degree requirements:* For doctorate, comprehensive exam, thesis/dissertation. *Entrance requirements:* For master's, minimum undergraduate GPA of 2.75, moral character form, 2 letters of reference, goals statement; for doctorate and Ed S, GRE General Test, goals statement, 2 letter of reference, interview, resume. Additional exam requirements/recommendations for international students: Required—TOEFL (minimum score 550 paper-based; 213 computer-based; 80 iBT). *Application deadline:* Applications are processed on a rolling basis. Application fee: $30 ($60 for international students). Electronic applications accepted. *Expenses:* Tuition, state resident: full-time $8136; part-time $452 per credit hour. Tuition, nonresident: full-time $14,292; part-time $794 per credit hour. *Financial support:* In 2011–12, 1 fellowship with full tuition reimbursement (averaging $12,000 per year), 4 research assistantships with full tuition reimbursements (averaging $9,375 per year) were awarded; teaching assistantships with full tuition reimbursements, career-related internships or fieldwork, Federal Work-Study, institutionally sponsored loans, scholarships/grants, health care benefits, unspecified assistantships, and 5 administrative assistantships (averaging $10,600 per year) also available. Support available to part-time students. Financial award application deadline: 4/1; financial award applicants required to submit FAFSA. *Faculty research:* Social/emotional needs of gifted, inclusion transition services, early intervention/ecobehavioral assessments, applied behavioral analysis. *Unit head:* Lyle Barton, Coordinator, 330-672-0578, E-mail: lbarton@kent.edu. *Application contact:* Nancy Miller, Academic Program Coordinator, Office of Graduate Student Services, 330-672-2576, Fax: 330-672-9162, E-mail: ogs@kent.edu. Web site: http://www.kent.edu/ehhs/sped/.

Liberty University, School of Education, Lynchburg, VA 24502. Offers administration and supervision (M Ed); curriculum and instruction (M Ed); early childhood education (M Ed); educational leadership (Ed D, Ed S); educational technology and online instruction (M Ed); elementary education (M Ed, MAT); gifted education (M Ed); math specialist (M Ed); middle grades (M Ed); outdoor adventure sport (MS); reading specialist (M Ed); school counseling (M Ed); secondary education (M Ed, MAT); special education (M Ed, MAT); sports administration (MS); teaching and learning (Ed D, Ed S). *Accreditation:* NCATE. Part-time programs available. Postbaccalaureate distance learning degree programs offered (minimal on-campus study). *Students:* 2,245 full-time (1,572 women), 3,500 part-time (2,558 women); includes 1,141 minority (888 Black or African American, non-Hispanic/Latino; 19 American Indian or Alaska Native, non-Hispanic/Latino; 21 Asian, non-Hispanic/Latino; 123 Hispanic/Latino; 9 Native Hawaiian or other Pacific Islander, non-Hispanic/Latino; 81 Two or more races, non-Hispanic/Latino), 76 international. Average age 37. In 2011, 760 master's, 48 doctorates, 321 other advanced degrees awarded. *Degree requirements:* For doctorate, comprehensive exam, thesis/dissertation. *Entrance requirements:* For master's, GRE General Test or MAT (if taken in or before 1999), 2 letters of recommendation, minimum undergraduate GPA of 3.0, curriculum vitae; for doctorate, GRE General Test or MAT (if taken before 1999), minimum master's GPA of 3.0, 3 years of teacher experience; for Ed S, GRE General Test or MAT (if taken before 1999), minimum master's GPA of 3.0, 3 years of teaching experience. Additional exam requirements/recommendations for international students: Required—TOEFL (minimum score 600 paper-based; 250 computer-based). *Application deadline:* For fall admission, 6/1 priority date for domestic students; for spring admission, 11/1 for domestic students. Applications are processed on a rolling basis. Application fee: $50. Electronic applications accepted. *Expenses:* Contact institution. *Financial support:* Federal Work-Study and tuition waivers (partial) available. *Faculty research:* Self-determination, character education, bibliotherapy, learning styles, distance education. *Unit head:* Dr. Karen L. Parker, Dean, 434-582-2195, Fax: 434-582-2468, E-mail: kparker@liberty.edu. *Application contact:* Jay Bridge, Director of Graduate Admissions, 800-424-9595, Fax: 800-628-7977, E-mail: gradadmissions@liberty.edu. Web site: http://www.liberty.edu/academics/education/graduate/.

Lynn University, Donald and Helen Ross College of Education, Boca Raton, FL 33431-5598. Offers educational leadership (M Ed, PhD); exceptional student education (M Ed); teacher preparation (PhD). Part-time and evening/weekend programs available. *Degree requirements:* For master's, thesis (for some programs); for doctorate, thesis/dissertation, qualifying paper. *Entrance requirements:* For master's, GRE, minimum undergraduate GPA of 3.0, resume, 2 letters of recommendation; for doctorate, GRE or GMAT, minimum GPA of 3.25, resume, 2 letters of recommendation. Additional exam requirements/recommendations for international students: Required—TOEFL (minimum score 550 paper-based; 213 computer-based). Electronic applications accepted. *Faculty research:* Non-traditional education, innovative curricula, multicultural education, simulation games.

Maryville University of Saint Louis, School of Education, St. Louis, MO 63141-7299. Offers art education (MA Ed); early childhood education (MA Ed); educational leadership (Ed D); educational leadership: principal certification (MA Ed); elementary education (MA Ed); gifted education (MA Ed); higher education leadership (Ed D); literacy specialist (MA Ed); middle grades education (MA Ed); secondary teaching and inquiry (MA Ed); teacher as leader (MA Ed). *Accreditation:* NCATE. Part-time and evening/weekend programs available. *Faculty:* 10 full-time (6 women), 19 part-time/adjunct (15 women). *Students:* 33 full-time (25 women), 251 part-time (190 women); includes 42 minority (32 Black or African American, non-Hispanic/Latino; 1 American Indian or Alaska Native, non-Hispanic/Latino; 4 Asian, non-Hispanic/Latino; 2 Hispanic/Latino; 3 Two or more races, non-Hispanic/Latino). Average age 38. In 2011, 69 master's, 43 doctorates awarded. *Degree requirements:* For master's, thesis, project. *Entrance requirements:* For master's, minimum cumulative GPA of 3.0, 3 professional recommendations, essays, interview with program faculty; for doctorate, minimum GPA of 3.0, 3 professional recommendations, essay, interview, on-site writing sample. Additional exam requirements/recommendations for international students: Required—TOEFL (minimum score 550 paper-based). *Application deadline:* Applications are processed on a rolling basis. Application fee: $40 ($60 for international students). Electronic applications accepted. *Expenses: Tuition:* Full-time $21,922; part-time $675 per credit hour. *Required fees:* $233.75 per semester. *Financial support:* Career-related internships or fieldwork, Federal Work-Study, tuition waivers (partial), and professional educator discounts available. Financial award application deadline: 3/1; financial award applicants required to submit FAFSA. *Faculty research:* Collaboration with public schools, pre-service program development, mathematics, diversity, literacy. *Unit head:* Dr. Sam Hausfather, Dean, 314-529-9466, Fax: 314-529-9921, E-mail: shausfather@maryville.edu. *Application contact:* Holly Stanwich, Graduate Admissions Coordinator, 314-529-9542, Fax: 314-529-9921, E-mail: teachered@maryville.edu. Web site: http://www.maryville.edu/academics-ed-graduate.

Millersville University of Pennsylvania, College of Graduate and Professional Studies, School of Education, Department of Elementary and Early Childhood Education, Program in Gifted Education, Millersville, PA 17551-0302. Offers M Ed. Part-time and evening/weekend programs available. *Faculty:* 16 full-time (12 women), 8 part-time/adjunct (5 women). *Students:* 6 part-time (all women). Average age 40. 3 applicants, 100% accepted, 1 enrolled. In 2011, 8 master's awarded. *Degree requirements:* For master's, thesis optional. *Entrance requirements:* For master's, GRE or MAT, 3 letters of recommendation, copy of teaching certificate. Additional exam requirements/recommendations for international students: Required—TOEFL (minimum score 500 paper-based; 183 computer-based; 65 iBT). *Application deadline:* For fall admission, 1/15 priority date for domestic students, 1/15 for international students; for winter admission, 10/1 priority date for domestic students, 10/1 for international students; for spring admission, 10/1 priority date for domestic students, 10/1 for international students. Applications are processed on a rolling basis. Application fee: $40 ($50 for international students). Electronic applications accepted. *Expenses:* Tuition, state resident: full-time $3744; part-time $416 per credit. Tuition, nonresident: full-time $5616; part-time $624 per credit. *Required fees:* $1130; $125.50 per credit. Tuition and fees vary according to course load. *Financial support:* Research assistantships with full tuition reimbursements, institutionally sponsored loans, and unspecified assistantships available. Support available to part-time students. Financial award application deadline: 3/15; financial award applicants required to submit FAFSA. *Faculty research:* Social and emotional development in gifted children, identification of gifted children, gifted friendly classrooms and curriculum, psychological development of gifted children, culturally diverse gifted students. *Unit head:* Dr. Kimberly S. Heilshorn, Coordinator, 717-871-5146, Fax: 717-871-5462, E-mail: kimberly.heilshorn@millersville.edu. *Application contact:* Dr. Victor S. DeSantis, Dean, College of Graduate and Professional Studies, 717-872-3099, Fax: 717-872-3453, E-mail: victor.desantis@millersville.edu. Web site: http://www.millersville.edu/academics/educ/eled/graduate.php.

Mississippi University for Women, Graduate School, College of Education and Human Sciences, Columbus, MS 39701-9998. Offers differentiated instruction (M Ed); educational leadership (M Ed); gifted studies (M Ed); reading/literacy (M Ed); teaching (MAT). *Accreditation:* ASHA; NCATE. Part-time programs available. *Degree requirements:* For master's, comprehensive exam, thesis optional. *Entrance requirements:* For master's, GRE General Test or NTE (M Ed in gifted education or MS in speech/language pathology), MAT (M Ed in instructional management), minimum QPA of 3.0.

Morehead State University, Graduate Programs, College of Education, Department of Foundational and Graduate Studies in Education, Morehead, KY 40351. Offers adult and higher education (MA, Ed S); certified professional counselor (Ed S); counseling P-12 (MA); curriculum and instruction (Ed S); educational technology (MA Ed); instructional leadership (Ed S); school administration (MA); school counseling (Ed S); teacher leader business and marketing content (MA Ed); teacher leader business and marketing technology (MA Ed); teacher leader educational technology (MA Ed); teacher leader English (MA Ed); teacher leader gifted education (MA Ed); teacher leader IECE certification (MA Ed); teacher leader interdisciplinary education P-5 (MA Ed); teacher leader middle grades (MA Ed); teacher leader non IECE certification (MA Ed); teacher leader reading/writing - non-certification (MA Ed); teacher leader reading/writing certification (MA Ed); teacher leader school communication - certification (MA Ed); teacher leader school communication - non-certification (MA Ed); teacher leader social studies (MA Ed); teacher leader special education (MA Ed). *Accreditation:* NCATE. Part-time and evening/weekend programs available. *Degree requirements:* For master's, thesis optional, oral and/or written comprehensive exams; for Ed S, thesis, oral exam. *Entrance requirements:* For master's, GRE General Test, minimum overall undergraduate GPA of 2.5; for Ed S, GRE General Test, interview, master's degree, minimum GPA of 3.5, work experience. Additional exam requirements/recommendations for international students: Required—TOEFL (minimum score 500 paper-based; 173 computer-based). Electronic applications accepted. *Faculty research:* Character education, school accountability, computer applications for school administrators.

Northeastern Illinois University, Graduate College, College of Education, Department of Special Education, Program in Gifted Education, Chicago, IL 60625-4699. Offers MA. Part-time and evening/weekend programs available. *Degree requirements:* For master's, comprehensive exam, thesis or alternative. *Entrance requirements:* For master's, teaching certificate or previous course work in history or philosophy of education, minimum GPA of 2.75. Additional exam requirements/recommendations for international students: Required—TOEFL (minimum score 550 paper-based; 213 computer-based; 79 iBT). Electronic applications accepted. *Faculty research:* Effect of inclusion in public school gifted programs, social and emotional needs of gifted children, problem-based learning strategies.

Purdue University, Graduate School, College of Education, Department of Educational Studies, West Lafayette, IN 47907. Offers administration (MS Ed, PhD, Ed S); counseling and development (MS Ed, PhD); education of the gifted (MS Ed); educational psychology (MS Ed, PhD); foundations of education (MS Ed, PhD); higher education administration (MS Ed, PhD); special education (MS Ed, PhD). *Accreditation:* ACA (one or more programs are accredited); NCATE (one or more programs are accredited). Part-time and evening/weekend programs available. *Faculty:* 23 full-time (17 women), 1 part-time/adjunct (0 women). *Students:* 111 full-time (79 women), 93 part-time (58 women); includes 34 minority (19 Black or African American, non-Hispanic/Latino; 1 American Indian or Alaska Native, non-Hispanic/Latino; 4 Asian, non-Hispanic/Latino; 6 Hispanic/Latino; 4 Two or more races, non-Hispanic/Latino), 30 international. Average age 35. 249 applicants, 37% accepted, 46 enrolled. In 2011, 39 master's, 20 doctorates, 4 other advanced degrees awarded. *Degree requirements:* For master's, thesis optional; for doctorate, thesis/dissertation, oral and written exams; for Ed S, oral presentation, project. *Entrance requirements:* For master's, GRE General Test required for all Educational Studies program areas, except for Special Education if undergraduate GPA is higher than a 3.0, minimum undergraduate GPA of 3.0; for doctorate and Ed S, GRE general test is required, a combined score of 1000 (300 for revised GRE test) or more is expected., minimum undergraduate GPA of 3.0. Additional exam requirements/recommendations for international students: Required—TOEFL (minimum score 550 paper-based; 77 iBT), TWE (minimum score 5). *Application deadline:* Applications are processed on a rolling basis. Application fee: $60 ($75 for international students). Electronic applications accepted. *Financial support:* Fellowships with full tuition reimbursements, research assistantships with full tuition reimbursements, teaching assistantships with full tuition reimbursements, career-related internships or fieldwork, and tuition waivers (full) available. Support available to part-time students. Financial award application deadline: 3/1; financial award applicants required to submit FAFSA. *Faculty research:* Motivation, learning disabilities, school learning, group processes, cognitive development. *Unit head:* Dr. Ala Samrapungavan, Head, 765-494-9170, Fax: 765-496-1228, E-mail: ala@purdue.edu. *Application contact:* Sarah N. Prater, Graduate Contact, 765-494-2345, Fax: 765-494-5832, E-mail: prater0@purdue.edu. Web site: http://www.edst.purdue.edu/.

St. Bonaventure University, School of Graduate Studies, School of Education, Program in Advanced Inclusive Processes, St. Bonaventure, NY 14778-2284. Offers gifted education (MS Ed); gifted education and students with disabilities (MS Ed). Part-time and evening/weekend programs available. *Faculty:* 3 full-time (all women), 2 part-time/adjunct (both women). *Students:* 29 full-time (27 women), 5 part-time (4 women); includes 2 minority (1 Hispanic/Latino; 1 Two or more races, non-Hispanic/Latino). Average age 25. 22 applicants, 82% accepted, 15 enrolled. In 2011, 19 master's awarded. *Degree requirements:* For master's, comprehensive exam, internship, portfolio. *Entrance requirements:* For master's, teaching certification, interview, references, writing sample, transcripts. Additional exam requirements/recommendations for international students: Required—TOEFL (minimum score 550 paper-based; 213 computer-based; 80 iBT). *Application deadline:* For fall admission, 6/15 priority date for domestic students, 2/1 for international students; for spring admission, 11/15 priority date for domestic students, 7/1 for international students. Applications are processed on a rolling basis. Application fee: $30. Electronic applications accepted. *Expenses: Tuition:* Part-time $670 per credit. *Financial support:* In 2011–12, 3 research assistantships with full and partial tuition reimbursements were awarded; Federal Work-Study, scholarships/grants, health care benefits, tuition waivers (partial), and unspecified assistantships also available. Support available to part-time students. Financial award application deadline: 4/15; financial award applicants required to submit FAFSA. *Unit head:* Dr. Rene Garrison, Director, 716-375-4078, E-mail: rgarriso@sbu.edu. *Application contact:* Bruce Campbell, Director of Graduate Admissions, 716-375-2429, Fax: 716-375-4015, E-mail: gradsch@sbu.edu.

Saint Leo University, Graduate Studies in Education, Saint Leo, FL 33574-6665. Offers educational leadership (M Ed); exceptional student education (M Ed); higher education leadership (Ed S); instructional design (MS); instructional leadership (M Ed); reading (M Ed); school leadership (Ed S). Part-time and evening/weekend programs available. Postbaccalaureate distance learning degree programs offered (minimal on-campus study). *Faculty:* 14 full-time (10 women), 21 part-time/adjunct (16 women). *Students:* 523 full-time (427 women), 20 part-time (17 women); includes 65 minority (43 Black or African American, non-Hispanic/Latino; 2 Asian, non-Hispanic/Latino; 16 Hispanic/Latino; 4 Two or more races, non-Hispanic/Latino), 3 international. Average age 37. In 2011, 153 master's, 18 other advanced degrees awarded. *Degree requirements:* For master's, comprehensive exam, appropriate State of Florida certification tests. *Entrance requirements:* For master's, GRE (minimum score of 1000) or MAT (minimum score of 410) if undergraduate GPA for last 60 hours of coursework was below 3.0 (for M Ed), bachelor's degree with minimum GPA of 3.0 for last 60 hours of coursework from regionally-accredited college or university, 2 recommendations, resume, statement of professional goals, copy of valid teaching certificate (for M Ed); for Ed S, GRE (minimum score 1000) or MAT (minimum score 410) if undergraduate GPA for last 60 hours of coursework less than 3.0, bachelor's degree with minimum GPA of 3.0 for last 60 hours of coursework from regionally-accredited college or university, 2 recommendations, resume, valid teaching certificate. Additional exam requirements/recommendations for international students: Required—TOEFL (minimum score 550 paper-based; 213 computer-based; 80 iBT). *Application deadline:* For fall admission, 7/1 priority date for domestic students, 7/1 for international students; for winter admission, 7/1 for international students; for spring admission, 11/1 priority date for domestic students. Applications are processed on a rolling basis. Application fee: $80. Electronic applications accepted. *Expenses:* Contact institution. *Financial support:* In 2011–12, 20 students received support. Career-related internships or fieldwork, Federal Work-Study, scholarships/grants, and health care benefits available. Financial award application deadline: 3/1; financial award applicants required to submit FAFSA. *Faculty research:* The role of the school leader in data analysis of student achievement, teacher recruitment, teacher effectiveness. *Unit head:* Dr. Sharyn Disabato, Director, 352-588-8309, Fax: 352-588-8861, E-mail: med@saintleo.edu. *Application contact:* Jared Welling, Director of Graduate Admission, 800-707-8846, Fax: 352-588-7873, E-mail: grad.admissions@saintleo.edu. Web site: http://www.saintleo.edu/Academics/School-of-Education-Social-Services/Graduate-Degree-Programs.

Saint Mary's University of Minnesota, Schools of Graduate and Professional Programs, Graduate School of Education, Education Program, Winona, MN 55987-1399. Offers education (MA); gifted and talented instruction (Certificate). *Unit head:* Sandra Nicholson, Director, 612-728-5179, Fax: 612-728-5121, E-mail: snichols@smumn.edu. *Application contact:* Yasin Alsaidi, Director of Admissions for Graduate and Professional Programs, 612-728-5207, Fax: 612-728-5121, E-mail: yalsaidi@smumn.edu. Web site: http://www.smumn.edu/graduate-home/areas-of-study/graduate-school-of-education/ma-in-education.

St. Thomas University, School of Leadership Studies, Institute for Education, Miami Gardens, FL 33054-6459. Offers earth/space science (Certificate); educational administration (MS, Certificate); educational leadership (Ed D); elementary education (MS); ESOL (Certificate); gifted education (Certificate); instructional technology (MS, Certificate); professional/studies (Certificate); reading (MS, Certificate); special education (MS). Part-time and evening/weekend programs available. *Degree requirements:* For master's, comprehensive exam; for doctorate, comprehensive exam, thesis/dissertation. *Entrance requirements:* For master's, interview, minimum GPA of 3.0 or GRE; for doctorate, GRE or MAT. Additional exam requirements/recommendations for international students: Required—TOEFL (minimum score 550 paper-based; 213 computer-based; 79 iBT). Electronic applications accepted.

Samford University, Orlean Bullard Beeson School of Education and Professional Studies, Birmingham, AL 35229. Offers early childhood education (Ed S); early childhood/elementary education (MS Ed); educational administration (Ed S); educational leadership (Ed D); elementary education (Ed S); gifted education (MS Ed); instructional leadership (MS Ed); secondary collaboration (MS Ed); M Div/MS Ed. *Accreditation:* NCATE. Part-time programs available. *Faculty:* 11 full-time (7 women), 9 part-time/adjunct (7 women). *Students:* 20 full-time (16 women), 169 part-time (122 women); includes 30 minority (26 Black or African American, non-Hispanic/Latino; 1 American Indian or Alaska Native, non-Hispanic/Latino; 1 Asian, non-Hispanic/Latino; 2 Hispanic/Latino), 1 international. Average age 39. 51 applicants, 92% accepted, 44 enrolled. In 2011, 57 master's, 9 doctorates, 35 other advanced degrees awarded. *Degree requirements:* For master's, comprehensive exam; for doctorate, comprehensive exam, thesis/dissertation. *Entrance requirements:* For master's, GRE or MAT, minimum GPA of 3.0; for doctorate, minimum GPA of 3.7; for Ed S, GRE, master's degree, teaching certificate, minimum GPA of 3.25. Additional exam requirements/recommendations for international students: Required—TOEFL (minimum score 550 paper-based; 213 computer-based). *Application deadline:* For fall admission, 7/15 for domestic students; for winter admission, 4/5 for domestic students; for spring admission, 12/4 for domestic students. Applications are processed on a rolling basis. Application fee: $25. *Expenses: Tuition:* Full-time $29,934; part-time $655 per credit. *Required fees:* $705. *Financial support:* Research assistantships, career-related internships or fieldwork, Federal Work-Study, scholarships/grants, and tuition waivers (partial) available. Support available to part-time students. Financial award applicants required to submit FAFSA. *Faculty research:* School law, the characteristics of beginning teachers, the nature of school reform, school culture, quality improvement in education, K-12 student achievement. *Unit head:* Dr. Jean Ann Box, Dean, 205-726-2565, E-mail: jabox@samford.edu. *Application contact:* Dr. Maurice Persall, Director, Graduate Office, 205-726-2019, E-mail: jmpersal@samford.edu. Web site: http://dlserver.samford.edu.

Southern Methodist University, Annette Caldwell Simmons School of Education and Human Development, Department of Teaching and Learning, Dallas, TX 75275. Offers bilingual/ESL education (MBE); education (M Ed, PhD); educational preparation (Certificate); gifted and talented focus (MBE); learning therapist (Certificate). Part-time and evening/weekend programs available. Terminal master's awarded for partial completion of doctoral program. *Degree requirements:* For master's, comprehensive exam, minimum GPA of 3.0; for doctorate, thesis/dissertation, qualifying exams, major area paper, evidence of teaching competency, dissemination of research (e.g., conference presentation), professional portfolio. *Entrance requirements:* For master's, minimum GPA of 3.0 or GRE, 3 letters of recommendation; for doctorate, GRE, minimum GPA of 3.3, 3 years of full-time teaching, 3 letters of recommendation, interview. Additional exam requirements/recommendations for international students: Required—TOEFL. Electronic applications accepted. *Faculty research:* Reading intervention, mathematics intervention, bilingual education, new literacies.

Teachers College, Columbia University, Graduate Faculty of Education, Department of Curriculum and Teaching, Program in Giftedness, New York, NY 10027. Offers MA, Ed D. Part-time programs available. *Faculty:* 1 full-time (0 women), 1 (woman) part-time/adjunct. *Students:* 4 full-time (all women), 5 part-time (4 women); includes 3 minority (2 Asian, non-Hispanic/Latino; 1 Hispanic/Latino), 2 international. Average age 37. 6 applicants, 83% accepted, 2 enrolled. In 2011, 2 master's, 2 doctorates awarded. Terminal master's awarded for partial completion of doctoral program. *Degree requirements:* For master's, culminating project; for doctorate, thesis/dissertation. *Entrance requirements:* For doctorate, GRE General Test or MAT. *Application deadline:* For fall admission, 1/15 priority date for domestic students; for spring admission, 11/1 for domestic students. Application fee: $65. Electronic applications accepted. *Financial support:* Research assistantships, career-related internships or fieldwork, Federal Work-Study, institutionally sponsored loans, and tuition waivers (full and partial) available. Support available to part-time students. Financial award application deadline: 2/1; financial award applicants required to submit FAFSA. *Faculty research:* Urban and economically disadvantaged gifted children, identification issues with regard to gifted and early childhood giftedness. *Unit head:* Prof. James Borland, Program Coordinator, 212-678-3765, E-mail: borland@tc.edu. *Application contact:* Peter Shon, Assistant Director of Admission, 212-678-3305, Fax: 212-678-4171, E-mail: shon@exchange.tc.columbia.edu. Web site: http://www.tc.edu/c%26t/GiftedEd/.

Tennessee Technological University, Graduate School, College of Education, Department of Curriculum and Instruction, Program in Exceptional Learning, Cookeville, TN 38505. Offers applied behavior and learning (PhD); literacy (PhD); program planning and evaluation (PhD); STEM education (PhD). Part-time and evening/weekend programs available. *Students:* 11 full-time (7 women), 12 part-time (9 women); includes 2 minority (both Black or African American, non-Hispanic/Latino), 1 international. 18 applicants, 50% accepted, 8 enrolled. In 2011, 7 doctorates awarded. *Degree requirements:* For doctorate, comprehensive exam, thesis/dissertation. *Entrance requirements:* For doctorate, GRE, minimum GPA of 3.0. Additional exam requirements/recommendations for international students: Required—TOEFL (minimum score 550 paper-based; 71 iBT), IELTS (minimum score 5.5), Pearson Test of English Academic. *Application deadline:* For fall admission, 8/1 for domestic students, 5/1 for international students; for spring admission, 12/1 for domestic students, 10/1 for international students. Application fee: $25 ($30 for international students). Electronic applications accepted. *Expenses:* Tuition, state resident: full-time $8094; part-time $422 per credit hour. Tuition, nonresident: full-time $20,574; part-time $1046 per credit hour. *Financial support:* In 2011–12, 4 fellowships (averaging $8,000 per year), 10 research assistantships (averaging $12,000 per year), 1 teaching assistantship (averaging $12,000 per year) were awarded. Financial award application deadline: 4/1. *Unit head:* Dr. Lisa Zagumny, Director, 931-372-3078, Fax: 931-372-3517, E-mail: lzagumny@tntech.edu. *Application contact:* Shelia K. Kendrick, Coordinator of Graduate Admissions, 931-372-3808, Fax: 931-372-3497, E-mail: skendrick@tntech.edu.

Touro College, Graduate School of Education, New York, NY 10010. Offers bilingual programs (Advanced Certificate); education and special education (MS); gifted and talented education (Advanced Certificate); instructional technology (MS); mathematics education (MS); school leadership (MS); teaching children with autism and other severe or multiple disabilities (Advanced Certificate); teaching English to speakers of other languages (MS, Advanced Certificate); teaching literacy (MS). Part-time and evening/weekend programs available. Postbaccalaureate distance learning degree programs offered (no on-campus study). *Faculty:* 75 full-time, 131 part-time/adjunct. *Students:* 382 full-time (324 women), 3,790 part-time (3,196 women); includes 1,211 minority (537 Black or African American, non-Hispanic/Latino; 4 American Indian or Alaska Native, non-Hispanic/Latino; 187 Asian, non-Hispanic/Latino; 472 Hispanic/Latino; 3 Native Hawaiian or other Pacific Islander, non-Hispanic/Latino; 8 Two or more races, non-Hispanic/Latino), 1 international. 1,422 applicants, 50% accepted, 675 enrolled. In 2011, 6 master's, 4 other advanced degrees awarded. *Application deadline:* For fall admission, 8/26 for domestic students, 7/15 for international students; for spring admission, 12/31 for domestic students, 12/15 for international students. Applications are processed on a rolling basis. Application fee: $50. *Financial support:* Federal Work-Study available. Financial award applicants required to submit FAFSA. *Faculty research:* Equity assistance, language development, scholar communications, Latin American studies and cultural sensitivity, behavior management techniques and strategies in special education. *Unit head:* Dr. LaMar Miller, Dean, 212-463-0400 Ext. 5561, Fax: 212-462-4889, E-mail: lpmiller@touro.edu. *Application contact:* Natalie Arroyo, Admissions Assistant, 212-463-0400 Ext. 5119, E-mail: natalie.arroyo@touro.edu.

Troy University, Graduate School, College of Education, Program in Teacher Education-Multiple Levels, Troy, AL 36082. Offers art education (MS); gifted education (MS); instrumental (MS); physical education (MS); reading specialist (MS); vocal/choral (MS). Part-time and evening/weekend programs available. *Faculty:* 6 full-time (4 women). *Students:* 6 full-time (4 women), 20 part-time (10 women); includes 3 minority (all Black or African American, non-Hispanic/Latino). Average age 30. 12 applicants, 83% accepted, 5 enrolled. In 2011, 13 master's awarded. *Degree requirements:* For master's, comprehensive exam, thesis. *Entrance requirements:* For master's, minimum GPA of 2.5. Additional exam requirements/recommendations for international students: Required—TOEFL (minimum score 523 paper-based; 193 computer-based; 70 iBT), IELTS (minimum score 6). *Application deadline:* Applications are processed on a rolling basis. Application fee: $50. Electronic applications accepted. *Expenses:* Tuition, state resident: full-time $6960; part-time $290 per credit hour. Tuition, nonresident: full-time $13,920; part-time $580 per credit hour. *Required fees:* $386 per term. *Financial support:* Available to part-time students. Applicants required to submit FAFSA. *Unit head:* Dr. Charlotte S. Minnick, Director, Teacher Education, 334-670-3544, Fax: 334-670-3548, E-mail: csminnick@troy.edu. *Application contact:* Brenda K. Campbell, Director of Graduate Admissions, 334-670-3178, Fax: 334-670-3733, E-mail: bcamp@troy.edu.

University at Buffalo, the State University of New York, Graduate School, Graduate School of Education, Department of Learning and Instruction, Buffalo, NY 14260. Offers biology education (Ed M, Certificate); chemistry education (Ed M, Certificate); childhood education (Ed M); childhood education with bilingual extension (Ed M); early childhood education (Ed M); early childhood education with bilingual extension (birth-grade 2) (Ed M); earth science education (Ed M, Certificate); educational technology and new literacies (Certificate); educational technology and new literacies (online) (Certificate); elementary education (Ed D, PhD); English education (Ed M, PhD, Certificate); English for speakers of other languages (Ed M); foreign and second language education (PhD); French education (Ed M, Certificate); general education (Ed M); German education (Ed M, Certificate); gifted education (online) (Certificate); Latin education (Ed M, Certificate); literacy teaching and learning (Certificate); literary specialist (Ed M); mathematics education (Ed M, PhD, Certificate); music education (Ed M, Certificate); physics education (Ed M, Certificate); reading education (PhD); science and the public (online) (Ed M); science education (PhD); social studies education (Ed M, Certificate); Spanish education (Ed M, Certificate); special education (PhD); teaching and leading for diversity (Certificate); teaching English to speakers of other languages (Ed M). Part-time and evening/weekend programs available. Postbaccalaureate distance learning degree programs offered (no on-campus study). *Faculty:* 32 full-time (23 women), 54 part-time/adjunct (43 women). *Students:* 294 full-time (222 women), 350 part-time (261 women); includes 75 minority (19 Black or African American, non-Hispanic/Latino; 6 American Indian or Alaska Native, non-Hispanic/Latino; 40 Asian, non-Hispanic/Latino; 10 Hispanic/Latino), 76 international. Average age 29. 548 applicants, 52% accepted, 253 enrolled. In 2011, 225 master's, 17 doctorates, 37 other advanced degrees awarded. *Degree requirements:* For master's, comprehensive exam; for doctorate, thesis/dissertation, research analysis exam, research experience component. *Entrance requirements:* For doctorate, GRE General Test or MAT, interview, writing sample, letters of recommendation. Additional exam requirements/recommendations for international students: Required—TOEFL (minimum score 600 paper-based; 96 iBT). *Application deadline:* For fall admission, 2/1 priority date for domestic students, 2/1 for international students; for spring admission, 11/15 priority date for domestic students, 10/1 for international students. Applications are processed on a rolling basis. Application fee: $50. Electronic applications accepted. *Financial support:* In 2011–12, 40 fellowships (averaging $12,991 per year), 46 research assistantships (averaging $10,986 per year) were awarded; teaching assistantships with full tuition reimbursements, career-related internships or fieldwork, Federal Work-Study, institutionally sponsored loans, scholarships/grants, and unspecified assistantships also available. Financial award application deadline: 2/28; financial award applicants required to submit FAFSA. *Faculty research:* Science assessment, foreign language teaching and learning, early learning, new literacies, gender and education. *Unit head:* Dr. Julie Sarama, Chair, 716-645-2455, Fax: 716-645-3161, E-mail: jcollins@buffalo.edu. *Application contact:* Cathy Dimino, Admissions Assistant, 716-645-2110, Fax: 716-645-7937, E-mail: cadimino@buffalo.edu.

The University of Alabama, Graduate School, College of Education, Department of Special Education and Multiple Abilities, Tuscaloosa, AL 35487. Offers collaborative teacher program (M Ed, Ed S); early intervention (M Ed, Ed S); gifted education (M Ed, Ed S); multiple abilities program (M Ed); special education (Ed D, PhD). Part-time and evening/weekend programs available. *Faculty:* 10 full-time (7 women), 1 (woman) part-time/adjunct. *Students:* 26 full-time (21 women), 53 part-time (47 women); includes 10 minority (7 Black or African American, non-Hispanic/Latino; 1 American Indian or Alaska Native, non-Hispanic/Latino; 2 Hispanic/Latino). Average age 32. 32 applicants, 69% accepted, 17 enrolled. In 2011, 14 master's, 7 other advanced degrees awarded. Terminal master's awarded for partial completion of doctoral program. *Degree* *requirements:* For master's, comprehensive exam, thesis optional; for doctorate, one foreign language, comprehensive exam, thesis/dissertation. *Entrance requirements:* For master's, GRE or MAT, minimum undergraduate GPA of 3.0, teaching certificate, 3 letters of recommendation; for doctorate, GRE or MAT, 3 years of teaching experience, minimum undergraduate GPA of 3.25. Additional exam requirements/recommendations for international students: Required—TOEFL. *Application deadline:* For fall admission, 7/1 for domestic students; for spring admission, 11/1 for domestic students. Applications are processed on a rolling basis. Application fee: $50 ($60 for international students). Electronic applications accepted. *Expenses:* Tuition, state resident: full-time $8600. Tuition, nonresident: full-time $21,900. *Financial support:* In 2011–12, 8 students received support, including 4 research assistantships with tuition reimbursements available (averaging $9,000 per year), 4 teaching assistantships with tuition reimbursements available (averaging $9,000 per year); health care benefits and unspecified assistantships also available. Financial award application deadline: 7/1; financial award applicants required to submit FAFSA. *Faculty research:* Gifted education, mild disabilities, early intervention, severe disabilities. *Unit head:* James A. Siders, Associate Professor and Head, 205-348-5577, Fax: 205-348-6782, E-mail: jsiders@bama.ua.edu. *Application contact:* April Zark, Office Support, 205-348-6093, Fax: 205-348-6782, E-mail: azark@bamaed.ua.edu.

University of Arkansas at Little Rock, Graduate School, College of Education, Department of Teacher Education, Program in Teaching the Gifted and Talented, Little Rock, AR 72204-1099. Offers M Ed. *Accreditation:* NCATE. Part-time and evening/weekend programs available. *Degree requirements:* For master's, comprehensive exam. *Entrance requirements:* For master's, interview, minimum GPA of 2.75, GRE General Test or teaching certificate.

University of Calgary, Faculty of Graduate Studies, Faculty of Education, Graduate Division of Educational Research, Calgary, AB T2N 1N4, Canada. Offers community rehabilitation and disability studies (M Ed, M Sc, Ed D, PhD, Graduate Certificate, Graduate Diploma); curriculum, teaching and learning (M Ed, M Sc, MA, Ed D, PhD, Graduate Certificate, Graduate Diploma); educational contexts (M Ed, MA, Ed D, PhD, Graduate Certificate, Graduate Diploma); educational leadership (M Ed, MA, Ed D, PhD, Graduate Certificate, Graduate Diploma); educational technology (M Ed, M Sc, MA, Ed D, PhD, Graduate Certificate, Graduate Diploma); gifted education (M Sc, MA, Ed D, PhD, Graduate Certificate, Graduate Diploma); higher education administration (Ed D); interpretive studies in education (M Ed, M Sc, MA, Ed D, PhD, Graduate Certificate, Graduate Diploma); second language teaching (M Ed, Ed D, PhD, Graduate Certificate, Graduate Diploma); teaching English as a second language (M Ed, M Sc, MA, Ed D, PhD, Graduate Certificate, Graduate Diploma); workplace and adult learning (M Ed, MA, Ed D, PhD, Graduate Certificate, Graduate Diploma). Ed D in both higher education administration and educational leadership offered via distance delivery. Part-time and evening/weekend programs available. Postbaccalaureate distance learning degree programs offered (minimal on-campus study). *Degree requirements:* For master's, thesis (for some programs); for doctorate, thesis/dissertation, candidacy exam. *Entrance requirements:* For master's, minimum GPA of 3.0, 3 letters of reference; for doctorate, minimum GPA of 3.5, 3 letters of reference; for other advanced degree, minimum GPA of 3.0. Additional exam requirements/recommendations for international students: Required—TOEFL, IELTS. Electronic applications accepted. *Faculty research:* Curriculum, leadership, technology, contexts, gifted, second language teaching, work place and adult learning.

University of Central Florida, College of Education, School of Teaching, Learning, and Leadership, Applied Learning and Instruction Program, Orlando, FL 32816. Offers applied learning and instruction (MA); community college education (Certificate); gifted education (Certificate); global and comparative education (Certificate); initial teacher professional preparation (Certificate); urban education (Certificate). *Accreditation:* NCATE. Part-time and evening/weekend programs available. *Students:* 12 full-time (10 women), 79 part-time (65 women); includes 23 minority (6 Black or African American, non-Hispanic/Latino; 1 American Indian or Alaska Native, non-Hispanic/Latino; 3 Asian, non-Hispanic/Latino; 12 Hispanic/Latino; 1 Two or more races, non-Hispanic/Latino), 1 international. Average age 31. 53 applicants, 72% accepted, 24 enrolled. In 2011, 11 master's, 24 other advanced degrees awarded. *Degree requirements:* For Certificate, thesis or alternative, final exam. *Entrance requirements:* For degree, GRE General Test, minimum GPA of 3.0, resume. Additional exam requirements/recommendations for international students: Required—TOEFL. *Application deadline:* For fall admission, 2/20 for domestic students; for spring admission, 9/20 for domestic students. Application fee: $30. Electronic applications accepted. *Expenses:* Tuition, state resident: part-time $277.08 per credit hour. Tuition, nonresident: part-time $277.08 per credit hour. Part-time tuition and fees vary according to degree level and program. *Financial support:* In 2011–12, 3 students received support, including 2 research assistantships with partial tuition reimbursements available (averaging $7,100 per year), 1 teaching assistantship with partial tuition reimbursement available (averaging $6,900 per year); fellowships with partial tuition reimbursements available, career-related internships or fieldwork, Federal Work-Study, institutionally sponsored loans, and unspecified assistantships also available. Financial award application deadline: 3/1; financial award applicants required to submit FAFSA. *Unit head:* Dr. Bobby Hoffman, Program Coordinator, 407-823-1770, E-mail: bobby.hoffman@ucf.edu. *Application contact:* Barbara Rodriguez, Director, Admissions and Registration, 407-823-2766, Fax: 407-823-6442, E-mail: gradadmissions@ucf.edu. Web site: http://education.ucf.edu/departments.cfm.

University of Connecticut, Graduate School, Neag School of Education, Department of Educational Psychology, Program in Gifted and Talented Education, Storrs, CT 06269. Offers MA, PhD, Post-Master's Certificate. *Accreditation:* NCATE. Terminal master's awarded for partial completion of doctoral program. *Degree requirements:* For master's, comprehensive exam, thesis or alternative; for doctorate, thesis/dissertation. *Entrance requirements:* For master's and doctorate, GRE General Test. Additional exam requirements/recommendations for international students: Required—TOEFL (minimum score 550 paper-based; 213 computer-based). Electronic applications accepted.

University of Louisiana at Lafayette, College of Education, Graduate Studies and Research in Education, Program in Education of the Gifted, Lafayette, LA 70504. Offers M Ed. *Accreditation:* NCATE. *Degree requirements:* For master's, thesis or alternative. *Entrance requirements:* For master's, GRE General Test, teaching certificate. Additional exam requirements/recommendations for international students: Required—TOEFL (minimum score 550 paper-based; 213 computer-based). Electronic applications accepted.

University of Louisiana at Monroe, Graduate School, College of Education and Human Development, Department of Curriculum and Instruction, Program in Curriculum and Instruction, Monroe, LA 71209-0001. Offers curriculum and instruction (Ed D); elementary education (1-5) (M Ed); reading education (K-12) (M Ed); SPED-academically gifted education (K-12) (M Ed); SPED-early intervention education (birth-3) (M Ed); SPED-educational diagnostics education (PreK-12) (M Ed). *Accreditation:* NCATE. *Students:* 42 full-time (37 women), 54 part-time (47 women); includes 20 minority (18 Black or African American, non-Hispanic/Latino; 1 Asian, non-Hispanic/Latino; 1 Hispanic/Latino), 12 international. Average age 36. 55 applicants, 95% accepted, 38 enrolled. In 2011, 27 master's, 1 doctorate awarded. *Degree requirements:* For master's, comprehensive exam (for some programs), thesis; for doctorate, thesis/dissertation, internships. *Entrance requirements:* For master's, GRE General Test; for doctorate, GRE General Test, minimum undergraduate GPA of 2.75, graduate 3.25. Additional exam requirements/recommendations for international students: Required—TOEFL (minimum score 500 paper-based; 173 computer-based; 61 iBT). *Application deadline:* For fall admission, 8/24 priority date for domestic students, 7/1 for international students; for winter admission, 12/14 priority date for domestic students; for spring admission, 1/19 for domestic students, 11/1 for international students. Applications are processed on a rolling basis. Application fee: $20 ($30 for international students). Electronic applications accepted. *Expenses:* Tuition, state resident: full-time $3436; part-time $240 per credit hour. Tuition, nonresident: full-time $3436; part-time $240 per credit hour. *International tuition:* $10,733 full-time. *Required fees:* $1460.90. *Financial support:* In 2011–12, 12 research assistantships with full tuition reimbursements (averaging $2,500 per year) were awarded; career-related internships or fieldwork, Federal Work-Study, and unspecified assistantships also available. Financial award application deadline: 4/1; financial award applicants required to submit FAFSA. *Unit head:* Dr. Dorothy Schween, Coordinator, 318-342-1269, Fax: 318-342-3131, E-mail: schween@ulm.edu. *Application contact:* Whitney Sutherland, Administrative Assistant to the Department Head, 318-342-1266, Fax: 318-342-3131, E-mail: sutherland@ulm.edu. Web site: http://www.ulm.edu/ci/.

University of Minnesota, Twin Cities Campus, Graduate School, College of Education and Human Development, Department of Educational Psychology, Minneapolis, MN 55455-0213. Offers counseling and student personnel psychology (MA, PhD, Ed S); early childhood education (M Ed, MA, PhD); educational psychology (PhD); psychological foundations of education (MA, PhD, Ed S); school psychology (MA, PhD, Ed S); special education (M Ed, MA, PhD, Ed S); talent development and gifted education (Certificate). *Accreditation:* APA (one or more programs are accredited). *Faculty:* 31 full-time (13 women). *Students:* 312 full-time (231 women), 88 part-time (67 women); includes 54 minority (20 Black or African American, non-Hispanic/Latino; 5 American Indian or Alaska Native, non-Hispanic/Latino; 18 Asian, non-Hispanic/Latino; 11 Hispanic/Latino), 5,149 international. Average age 30. 440 applicants, 48% accepted, 127 enrolled. In 2011, 98 master's, 21 doctorates, 22 other advanced degrees awarded. *Financial support:* In 2011–12, 4 fellowships (averaging $20,729 per year), 62 research assistantships (averaging $10,014 per year), 36 teaching assistantships (averaging $10,014 per year) were awarded. *Faculty research:* Learning, cognitive and social processes; multicultural education and counseling; measurement and statistical processes; performance assessment; instructional design/strategies for students with special needs. *Total annual research expenditures:* $4 million. *Unit head:* Dr. Susan Hupp, Chair, 612-624-1003, Fax: 612-624-8241, E-mail: shupp@umn.edu. *Application contact:* Dr. Jennifer Engler, Assistant Dean, 612-626-2887, Fax: 612-626-7496, E-mail: engle009@umn.edu. Web site: http://www.cehd.umn.edu/EdPsych.

University of Missouri, Graduate School, College of Education, Department of Special Education, Columbia, MO 65211. Offers administration and supervision of special education (PhD); behavior disorders (M Ed, PhD); curriculum development of exceptional students (M Ed, PhD); early childhood special education (M Ed, PhD); general special education (M Ed, MA, PhD); learning and instruction (M Ed); learning disabilities (M Ed, PhD); mental retardation (M Ed, PhD). Part-time and evening/weekend programs available. Postbaccalaureate distance learning degree programs offered (no on-campus study). *Faculty:* 11 full-time (8 women), 1 (woman) part-time/adjunct. *Students:* 26 full-time (23 women), 65 part-time (60 women); includes 7 minority (2 Black or African American, non-Hispanic/Latino; 4 Hispanic/Latino; 1 Two or more races, non-Hispanic/Latino). Average age 33. 56 applicants, 64% accepted, 32 enrolled. In 2011, 31 master's, 3 doctorates awarded. *Degree requirements:* For master's, comprehensive exam, thesis or alternative; for doctorate, comprehensive exam, thesis/dissertation. *Entrance requirements:* For master's and doctorate, GRE General Test, letters of recommendation. Additional exam requirements/recommendations for international students: Required—TOEFL (minimum score 500 paper-based; 173 computer-based; 61 iBT). *Application deadline:* For fall admission, 7/1 priority date for domestic students, 7/1 for international students; for winter admission, 11/1 priority date for domestic students, 11/1 for international students; for spring admission, 4/1 priority date for domestic students, 4/1 for international students. Application fee: $55 ($75 for international students). Electronic applications accepted. *Expenses:* Tuition, state resident: full-time $5881. Tuition, nonresident: full-time $15,183. *Required fees:* $952. Tuition and fees vary according to campus/location and program. *Financial support:* Fellowships with full and partial tuition reimbursements, research assistantships with full and partial tuition reimbursements, teaching assistantships with full and partial tuition reimbursements, career-related internships or fieldwork, scholarships/grants, health care benefits, and unspecified assistantships available. *Faculty research:* Positive behavior support, applied behavior analysis, attention deficit disorder, pre-linguistic development, school discipline. *Total annual research expenditures:* $1.4 million. *Unit head:* Dr. Mike Pullis, Department Chair, E-mail: pullism@missouri.edu. *Application contact:* Glenda Rice, 573-882-4421, E-mail: riceg@missouri.edu. Web site: http://education.missouri.edu/SPED/.

The University of North Carolina at Charlotte, Graduate School, College of Education, Department of Special Education and Child Development, Charlotte, NC 28223-0001. Offers academically gifted (Graduate Certificate); child and family studies (M Ed); special education (M Ed, PhD), including academically gifted (M Ed), behavioral - emotional handicaps (M Ed), cross-categorical disabilities (M Ed), learning disabilities (M Ed), mental handicaps (M Ed), severe and profound handicaps (M Ed). Part-time programs available. *Faculty:* 25 full-time (18 women), 7 part-time/adjunct (all women). *Students:* 19 full-time (all women), 107 part-time (100 women); includes 20 minority (16 Black or African American, non-Hispanic/Latino; 1 American Indian or Alaska Native, non-Hispanic/Latino; 2 Hispanic/Latino; 1 Native Hawaiian or other Pacific Islander, non-Hispanic/Latino). Average age 34. 26 applicants, 77% accepted, 16 enrolled. In 2011, 29 master's, 4 doctorates awarded. Terminal master's awarded for partial completion of doctoral program. *Degree requirements:* For master's, thesis or alternative; for doctorate, comprehensive exam, thesis/dissertation, portfolio, qualifying exam. *Entrance requirements:* For master's, GRE or MAT; for doctorate, GRE or MAT, 3 letters of reference, resume or curriculum vitae, minimum GPA of 3.5, master's degree in special education or related field, 3 years of teaching experience. Additional exam requirements/recommendations for international students: Required—TOEFL (minimum score 557 paper-based; 220 computer-based; 83 iBT). *Application deadline:* For fall admission, 7/15 for domestic students, 5/1 for international students; for spring admission, 11/15 for domestic students, 10/1 for international students. Application fee: $65 ($75 for international students). *Expenses:* Tuition, state resident: full-time $3689. Tuition, nonresident: full-time $15,226. *Required fees:* $2198. Tuition and fees vary according to course load and program. *Financial support:* In 2011–12, 12 students received support, including 12 research assistantships (averaging $12,144 per year). Financial award application deadline: 4/1; financial award applicants required to submit FAFSA. *Faculty research:* Transition to adulthood and self-determination, teaching reading and other academic skills to students with disabilities, alternate assessment, early intervention, preschool education. *Total annual research expenditures:* $2.7 million. *Unit head:* David Gilmore, Unit Head, 704-687-8186, Fax: 704-687-2916. *Application contact:* Kathy B. Giddings, Director of Graduate Admissions, 704-687-5503,

Fax: 704-687-3279, E-mail: gradadm@uncc.edu. Web site: http://education.uncc.edu/spcd/sped/special_ed.htm.

University of Northern Iowa, Graduate College, College of Education, Department of Curriculum and Instruction, Program in Education of the Gifted, Cedar Falls, IA 50614. Offers MAE. Part-time and evening/weekend programs available. Postbaccalaureate distance learning degree programs offered. *Students:* 5 part-time (4 women). *Degree requirements:* For master's, comprehensive exam (for some programs), thesis (for some programs). *Entrance requirements:* Additional exam requirements/recommendations for international students: Required—TOEFL (minimum score 550 paper-based; 213 computer-based; 79 iBT). *Application deadline:* For fall admission, 2/1 for domestic students, 4/1 for international students; for winter admission, 10/1 for international students. Applications are processed on a rolling basis. Application fee: $50 ($70 for international students). Electronic applications accepted. *Expenses:* Tuition, state resident: full-time $7476. Tuition, nonresident: full-time $16,410. *Required fees:* $942. *Financial support:* Unspecified assistantships available. Financial award application deadline: 2/1; financial award applicants required to submit FAFSA. *Unit head:* Audrey Rule, Coordinator, 319-273-7829, Fax: 319-273-5886, E-mail: audrey.rule@uni.edu. *Application contact:* Laurie S. Russell, Record Analyst, 319-273-2623, Fax: 319-273-2885, E-mail: laurie.russell@uni.edu. Web site: http://www.uni.edu/coe/ci/gifted/.

University of St. Thomas, Graduate Studies, School of Education, Department of Special Education and Gifted Education, St. Paul, MN 55105-1096. Offers autism spectrum disorders (MA, Certificate); developmental disabilities (MA); director of special education (Ed S); early childhood special education (MA); emotional behavioral disorders (MA); gifted, creative, and talented education (MA); learning disabilities (MA); Orton-Gillingham reading (Certificate); special education (MA). *Accreditation:* NCATE. Part-time and evening/weekend programs available. *Faculty:* 7 full-time (5 women), 31 part-time/adjunct (25 women). *Students:* 23 full-time (19 women), 253 part-time (205 women); includes 31 minority (17 Black or African American, non-Hispanic/Latino; 3 Asian, non-Hispanic/Latino; 5 Hispanic/Latino; 2 Native Hawaiian or other Pacific Islander, non-Hispanic/Latino; 4 Two or more races, non-Hispanic/Latino), 2 international. Average age 36. 123 applicants, 88% accepted, 98 enrolled. In 2011, 57 master's, 2 other advanced degrees awarded. *Degree requirements:* For master's, thesis; for other advanced degree, professional portfolio. *Entrance requirements:* For master's, minimum GPA of 3.0 or MAT; for other advanced degree, MAT or minimum GPA of 2.75. Additional exam requirements/recommendations for international students: Required—TOEFL (minimum score 550 paper-based; 213 computer-based; 80 iBT). *Application deadline:* For fall admission, 6/1 priority date for domestic students; for spring admission, 11/1 priority date for domestic students. Applications are processed on a rolling basis. Application fee: $50. *Financial support:* Fellowships, research assistantships, institutionally sponsored loans, and scholarships/grants available. Support available to part-time students. Financial award applicants required to submit FAFSA. *Faculty research:* Reading and math fluency, inclusion curriculum for developmental disorders, parent involvement in positive behavior supports, children's friendships, preschool inclusion. *Unit head:* Dr. Terri L. Vandercook, Chair, 651-962-4389, Fax: 651-962-4169, E-mail: tlvandercook@stthomas.edu. *Application contact:* Patricia L. Thomas, Department Assistant, 651-962-4980, Fax: 651-962-4169, E-mail: thom2319@stthomas.edu. Web site: http://www.stthomas.edu/education.

University of Southern Maine, School of Education and Human Development, Abilities and Disabilities Studies Program, Portland, ME 04104-9300. Offers gifted and talented (MS); self-design in special education (MS); teaching all students (MS); teaching all students (Certificate). *Accreditation:* Teacher Education Accreditation Council. Part-time and evening/weekend programs available. *Degree requirements:* For master's, thesis or alternative, portfolio. *Entrance requirements:* For master's, proof of teacher certification. Additional exam requirements/recommendations for international students: Required—TOEFL (minimum score 550 paper-based; 213 computer-based; 79 iBT). Electronic applications accepted. *Faculty research:* Moderate-to-severe disabilities, gifted and talented.

University of Southern Mississippi, Graduate School, College of Education and Psychology, Department of Curriculum, Instruction, and Special Education, Hattiesburg, MS 39406-0001. Offers alternative secondary teacher education (MAT); early childhood education (M Ed, Ed S); education (Ed D); education of the gifted (M Ed, PhD, Ed S); elementary education (M Ed, PhD, Ed S); reading (M Ed, MS); secondary education (M Ed, MS, PhD); special education (M Ed, PhD, Ed S). Part-time programs available. *Faculty:* 23 full-time (17 women), 3 part-time/adjunct (2 women). *Students:* 39 full-time (34 women), 92 part-time (77 women); includes 36 minority (31 Black or African American, non-Hispanic/Latino; 3 Hispanic/Latino; 2 Two or more races, non-Hispanic/Latino), 3 international. Average age 37. 56 applicants, 55% accepted, 29 enrolled. In 2011, 45 master's, 5 doctorates awarded. *Degree requirements:* For master's and Ed S, comprehensive exam, thesis (for some programs); for doctorate, comprehensive exam, thesis/dissertation. *Entrance requirements:* For master's, GRE General Test, MAT, minimum GPA of 3.0; for doctorate, GRE General Test, minimum GPA of 3.5; for Ed S, GRE General Test, MAT, minimum GPA of 3.25. Additional exam requirements/recommendations for international students: Required—TOEFL, IELTS. *Application deadline:* For fall admission, 3/1 priority date for domestic students, 3/1 for international students; for spring admission, 1/10 priority date for domestic students, 1/10 for international students. Applications are processed on a rolling basis. Application fee: $50. *Financial support:* In 2011–12, 9 research assistantships with tuition reimbursements (averaging $18,316 per year), 2 teaching assistantships with full tuition reimbursements (averaging $8,500 per year) were awarded; Federal Work-Study, institutionally sponsored loans, scholarships/grants, health care benefits, tuition waivers (partial), and unspecified assistantships also available. Financial award application deadline: 3/15; financial award applicants required to submit FAFSA. *Faculty research:* Mathematical problem solving, integrative curriculum, writing process, teacher education models. *Total annual research expenditures:* $100,000. *Unit head:* Dr. David Daves, Chair, 601-266-4547, Fax: 601-266-4175, E-mail: david.daves@usm.edu. *Application contact:* Dr. Marie Crowe, Director of Graduate Studies, 601-266-6005, Fax: 601-266-4548, E-mail: margie.crowe@usm.edu. Web site: http://www.usm.edu/graduateschool/table.php.

University of South Florida, Graduate School, College of Education, Department of Special Education, Tampa, FL 33620-9951. Offers autism spectrum disorders and severe intellectual disabilities (MA); behavior disorders (MA); exceptional student education (MA, MAT); gifted education (MA); mental retardation (MA); special education (PhD); specific learning disabilities (MA). *Accreditation:* NCATE. Part-time and evening/weekend programs available. *Faculty:* 12 full-time (9 women), 2 part-time/adjunct (1 woman). *Students:* 62 full-time (49 women), 104 part-time (94 women); includes 44 minority (22 Black or African American, non-Hispanic/Latino; 2 American Indian or Alaska Native, non-Hispanic/Latino; 4 Asian, non-Hispanic/Latino; 15 Hispanic/Latino; 1 Two or more races, non-Hispanic/Latino), 3 international. Average age 36. 131 applicants, 62% accepted, 60 enrolled. In 2011, 34 master's, 2 doctorates awarded. *Median time to degree:* Of those who began their doctoral program in fall 2003, 14% received their degree in 8 years or less. *Degree requirements:* For master's, comprehensive exam; for doctorate, comprehensive exam, thesis/dissertation, philosophies of inquiry; multiple research methods. *Entrance requirements:* For master's, GRE General Test (if undergraduate GPA less than 3.0), minimum GPA of 3.0 in last 60 hours of course work; for doctorate, GRE General Test, minimum GPA of 3.0 undergraduate, 3.5 graduate; interview. Additional exam requirements/recommendations for international students: Required—TOEFL (minimum score 500 paper-based; 213 computer-based). *Application deadline:* For fall admission, 2/15 for domestic students, 1/2 for international students; for winter admission, 2/15 for domestic students, 1/2 for international students; for spring admission, 10/15 for domestic students, 6/1 for international students. Application fee: $30. Electronic applications accepted. *Financial support:* In 2011–12, 3 fellowships with full tuition reimbursements (averaging $10,000 per year), 4 research assistantships with full tuition reimbursements (averaging $10,000 per year), 7 teaching assistantships with full tuition reimbursements (averaging $10,000 per year) were awarded; scholarships/grants and unspecified assistantships also available. Financial award application deadline: 6/1; financial award applicants required to submit FAFSA. *Faculty research:* Instruction methods for students with learning and behavioral disabilities; teacher preparation, experiential learning, and participatory action research; public policy research; personal preparation for transitional services; case-based instruction, partnerships and mentor development; inclusion and voices of teachers and students with disabilities; narrative ethics and philosophies of research. *Total annual research expenditures:* $2.9 million. *Unit head:* Dr. Daphne Thomas, Chairperson, 813-974-1383, Fax: 813-974-5542, E-mail: dthomas@usf.edu. *Application contact:* Dr. Diane Briscoe, Coordinator of Graduate Studies, 813-974-1804, Fax: 813-974-3391, E-mail: briscoe@usf.edu. Web site: http://www.coedu.usf.edu/main/departments/sped/sped.html.

The University of Texas–Pan American, College of Education, Department of Educational Psychology, Edinburg, TX 78539. Offers educational diagnostician (M Ed); gifted education (M Ed); guidance and counseling (M Ed); school psychology (MA); special education (M Ed). Part-time and evening/weekend programs available. *Degree requirements:* For master's, comprehensive exam (for some programs), thesis (for some programs). *Entrance requirements:* For master's, GRE General Test, interview. *Application deadline:* For fall admission, 7/17 for domestic students; for spring admission, 11/16 for domestic students. Application fee: $0. Tuition and fees vary according to course load, program and student level. *Financial support:* Research assistantships, career-related internships or fieldwork, Federal Work-Study, and institutionally sponsored loans available. Support available to part-time students. Financial award application deadline: 4/15. *Faculty research:* Reading instruction, assessment practice, behavior interventions consultation, mental retardation. *Unit head:* Dr. Paul Sale, Chair, 956-665-2433, E-mail: psale@utpa.edu. *Application contact:* Dr. Sylvia Ramirez, Associate Dean of Graduate Studies, 956-665-3488, E-mail: ramirezs@utpa.edu. Web site: http://portal.utpa.edu/utpa_main/daa_home/coed_home/edpsy_home.

The University of Toledo, College of Graduate Studies, Judith Herb College of Education, Health Science and Human Service, Department of Curriculum and Instruction, Toledo, OH 43606-3390. Offers art education (ME); career and technical education (ME); curriculum and instruction (ME, PhD, Ed S); education and anthropology (MAE); education and biology (MES); education and chemistry (MES); education and classics (MAE); education and economics (MAE); education and English (MAE); education and French (MAE); education and geography (MAE); education and geology (MES); education and German (MAE); education and history (MAE); education and mathematics (MAE, MES); education and physics (MES); education and political science (MAE); education and sociology (MAE); education and Spanish (MAE); educational media (PhD); educational technology (ME); English as a second language (MAE); gifted and talented (PhD); middle childhood education licensure (ME); music education (MME); secondary education (PhD); secondary education licensure (ME). *Accreditation:* NCATE. Part-time and evening/weekend programs available. *Faculty:* 24. *Students:* 60 full-time (31 women), 211 part-time (161 women); includes 23 minority (21 Black or African American, non-Hispanic/Latino; 2 Hispanic/Latino), 20 international. Average age 35. 115 applicants, 73% accepted, 74 enrolled. In 2011, 105 master's, 3 doctorates, 4 other advanced degrees awarded. *Degree requirements:* For master's, comprehensive exam, thesis or alternative; for doctorate, comprehensive exam, thesis/dissertation; for Ed S, thesis optional. *Entrance requirements:* For master's, doctorate, and Ed S, minimum cumulative GPA of 2.7 for all previous academic work, letters of recommendation. Additional exam requirements/recommendations for international students: Required—TOEFL (minimum score 550 paper-based; 213 computer-based; 80 iBT), IELTS (minimum score 6.5). *Application deadline:* For fall admission, 1/15 priority date for domestic students, 1/15 for international students. Applications are processed on a rolling basis. Application fee: $45 ($75 for international students). Electronic applications accepted. *Financial support:* In 2011–12, 9 research assistantships with full and partial tuition reimbursements (averaging $7,184 per year), 12 teaching assistantships with full and partial tuition reimbursements (averaging $8,425 per year) were awarded; career-related internships or fieldwork, Federal Work-Study, institutionally sponsored loans, scholarships/grants, tuition waivers (full and partial), unspecified assistantships, and administrative assistantships also available. Support available to part-time students. *Unit head:* Dr. Leigh Chiarelott, Chair, 419-530-5371, E-mail: eigh.chiarelott@utoledo.edu. *Application contact:* Graduate School Office, 419-530-4723, Fax: 419-530-4724, E-mail: grdsch@utnet.utoledo.edu. Web site: http://www.utoledo.edu/eduhshs/.

University of Virginia, Curry School of Education, Department of Leadership, Foundations and Policy, Program in Educational Psychology, Charlottesville, VA 22903. Offers applied developmental science (M Ed); educational evaluation (M Ed); educational psychology (M Ed, Ed D, Ed S); educational research (Ed D); gifted education (M Ed); instructional technology (M Ed, Ed S); research statistics and evaluation (Ed D); school psychology (Ed D). *Students:* 17 full-time (12 women), 10 part-time (7 women); includes 2 minority (1 Black or African American, non-Hispanic/Latino; 1 Hispanic/Latino), 1 international. Average age 29. 56 applicants, 77% accepted, 23 enrolled. In 2011, 40 master's, 1 doctorate awarded. *Degree requirements:* For master's, comprehensive exam. *Entrance requirements:* For master's and doctorate, GRE General Test, 2 letters of recommendation. Additional exam requirements/recommendations for international students: Required—TOEFL (minimum score 600 paper-based; 250 computer-based; 90 iBT), IELTS (minimum score 7). *Application deadline:* Applications are processed on a rolling basis. Application fee: $60. Electronic applications accepted. *Financial support:* Fellowships, research assistantships, and teaching assistantships available. Financial award application deadline: 1/5; financial award applicants required to submit FAFSA. *Unit head:* Christopher De La Cerda, Program Coordinator, 434-243-2021, E-mail: cjd8kn@virginia.edu. *Application contact:* Lisa Miller, Assistant to the Chair, 434-982-2849, E-mail: lam3v@virgnina.edu.

University of Wisconsin–Whitewater, School of Graduate Studies, College of Education and Professional Studies, Department of Curriculum and Instruction, Whitewater, WI 53190-1790. Offers professional development (MS), including bilingual education, challenging advanced learners, curriculum and instruction, educational leadership, health, human performance and recreation, health, physical education and coaching, information technologies and libraries, reading. *Accreditation:* NCATE. Part-time and evening/weekend programs available. Postbaccalaureate distance learning degree programs offered. *Students:* 25 full-time (12 women), 68 part-time (51 women); includes 26 minority (15 Black or African American, non-Hispanic/Latino; 3 Asian, non-

Hispanic/Latino; 8 Hispanic/Latino). Average age 33. 29 applicants, 86% accepted, 16 enrolled. In 2011, 44 master's awarded. *Degree requirements:* For master's, thesis or integrated project. *Entrance requirements:* Additional exam requirements/recommendations for international students: Required—TOEFL (minimum score 550 paper-based; 213 computer-based; 80 iBT), IELTS (minimum score 6). *Application deadline:* For fall admission, 7/15 priority date for domestic students, 7/15 for international students; for spring admission, 12/1 priority date for domestic students, 12/1 for international students. Applications are processed on a rolling basis. Application fee: $56. Electronic applications accepted. *Expenses:* Tuition, state resident: full-time $4088. Tuition, nonresident: full-time $8817. Tuition and fees vary according to program. *Financial support:* Research assistantships, Federal Work-Study, unspecified assistantships, and out-of-state fee waivers available. Support available to part-time students. Financial award application deadline: 3/15; financial award applicants required to submit FAFSA. *Faculty research:* Hybrid of exercise physiology and psychology; gender equity; education, pedagogy, and technology; comprehensive school health education. *Unit head:* Dr. John Zbikowski, Coordinator, 262-472-4860, Fax: 262-472-1988, E-mail: zbikowskij@uww.edu. *Application contact:* Sally A. Lange, School of Graduate Studies, 262-472-1006, Fax: 262-472-5027, E-mail: gradschl@uww.edu.

Western Washington University, Graduate School, Woodring College of Education, Department of Special Education, Bellingham, WA 98225-5996. Offers M Ed. *Accreditation:* NCATE. Part-time programs available. *Degree requirements:* For master's, comprehensive exam, thesis optional. *Entrance requirements:* For master's, GRE General Test or MAT, minimum GPA of 3.0 in last 60 semester hours or last 90 quarter hours. Additional exam requirements/recommendations for international students: Required—TOEFL (minimum score 567 paper-based; 227 computer-based). Electronic applications accepted. *Faculty research:* Applied behavioral analysis, controversial practices, infant/toddler social-emotional interventions, reflective practices in teacher education.

West Virginia University, College of Human Resources and Education, Department of Special Education, Morgantown, WV 26506. Offers autism spectrum disorder (5-adult) (MA); autism spectrum disorder (K-6) (MA); early intervention/early childhood special education (MA); gifted education (1-12) (MA); low vision (PreK-adult) (MA); multicategorical special education (5-adult) (MA); multicategorical special education (K-6) (MA); severe/multiple disabilities (K-adult) (MA); special education (MA, Ed D); vision impairments (PreK-adult) (MA). *Accreditation:* NCATE. Part-time and evening/weekend programs available. Postbaccalaureate distance learning degree programs offered (no on-campus study). *Degree requirements:* For master's, thesis optional; for doctorate, comprehensive exam, thesis/dissertation. *Entrance requirements:* For master's, minimum GPA of 2.75 passing scores on PRAXIS PPST; for doctorate, GRE General Test or MAT. Additional exam requirements/recommendations for international students: Required—TOEFL.

Whitworth University, School of Education, Graduate Studies in Education, Program in Gifted and Talented, Spokane, WA 99251-0001. Offers MAT. *Accreditation:* NCATE. Part-time and evening/weekend programs available. *Degree requirements:* For master's, comprehensive exam, thesis (for some programs). *Entrance requirements:* For master's, GRE General Test, MAT. Tuition and fees vary according to program.

Wichita State University, Graduate School, College of Education, Department of Curriculum and Instruction, Wichita, KS 67260. Offers curriculum and instruction (M Ed); special education (M Ed), including adaptive, early childhood unified (M Ed, MAT), functional, gifted; teaching (MAT), including curriculum and instruction, early childhood unified (M Ed, MAT). *Accreditation:* NCATE. Part-time and evening/weekend programs available. *Entrance requirements:* For master's, MAT, minimum GPA of 2.75. *Expenses:* Tuition, state resident: full-time $4746; part-time $263.65 per credit. Tuition, nonresident: full-time $11,669; part-time $648.30 per credit. *Unit head:* Dr. Janice Ewing, Chairperson, 316-978-3322, E-mail: janice.ewing@wichita.edu. *Application contact:* Dr. Kay Gibson, Graduate Coordinator, 316-978-3322, E-mail: kay.gibson@wichita.edu. Web site: http://www.wichita.edu/.

William Carey University, School of Education, Hattiesburg, MS 39401-5499. Offers art education (M Ed); art of teaching (M Ed); elementary education (M Ed, Ed S); English education (M Ed); gifted education (M Ed); history and social science (M Ed); mild/moderate disabilities (M Ed); secondary education (M Ed). Part-time programs available. *Degree requirements:* For master's, comprehensive exam. *Entrance requirements:* For master's, GRE, MAT, minimum GPA of 2.5, Class A teacher's license. Additional exam requirements/recommendations for international students: Required—TOEFL (minimum score 550 paper-based; 213 computer-based).

Wilmington University, College of Education, New Castle, DE 19720-6491. Offers applied technology in education (M Ed); career and technical education (M Ed); educational leadership (Ed D); elementary and secondary school counseling (M Ed); elementary studies (M Ed); ESOL literacy (M Ed); higher education leadership (Ed D); instruction: gifted and talented (M Ed); instruction: teacher of reading (M Ed); instruction: teaching and learning (M Ed); organizational leadership (Ed D); school leadership (M Ed); secondary education (MAT); special education (M Ed). *Accreditation:* NCATE. Part-time and evening/weekend programs available. *Faculty:* 7 full-time (4 women). *Students:* 638 full-time (425 women), 2,014 part-time (1,635 women). Average age 33. *Entrance requirements:* For master's, 2 letters of recommendation, interview. Additional exam requirements/recommendations for international students: Required—TOEFL (minimum score 500 paper-based; 173 computer-based). *Application deadline:* For fall admission, 4/30 for domestic students. Applications are processed on a rolling basis. Application fee: $35. Electronic applications accepted. *Expenses: Tuition:* Part-time $534 per credit hour. *Required fees:* $25 per term. *Financial support:* Applicants required to submit FAFSA. *Unit head:* Dr. John C. Gray, Dean, 302-295-1139. *Application contact:* Chris Ferguson, Director of Admissions, 302-356-4636 Ext. 256, Fax: 302-328-5164, E-mail: inquire@wilmcoll.edu. Web site: http://www.wilmu.edu/education/.

Wright State University, School of Graduate Studies, College of Education and Human Services, Department of Teacher Education, Programs in Intervention Specialist, Dayton, OH 45435. Offers gifted educational needs (M Ed, MA); mild to moderate educational needs (M Ed, MA); moderate to intensive educational needs (M Ed, MA). *Accreditation:* NCATE. *Degree requirements:* For master's, thesis (for some programs). *Entrance requirements:* For master's, GRE General Test, MAT. Additional exam requirements/recommendations for international students: Required—TOEFL.

Youngstown State University, Graduate School, Beeghly College of Education, Department of Teacher Education, Program in Special Education, Youngstown, OH 44555-0001. Offers gifted and talented education (MS Ed); special education (MS Ed). *Accreditation:* NCATE. Part-time and evening/weekend programs available. *Degree requirements:* For master's, comprehensive exam. *Entrance requirements:* For master's, GRE, MAT, or teaching certificate; interview; minimum GPA of 2.7. Additional exam requirements/recommendations for international students: Required—TOEFL. *Faculty research:* Learning disabilities, learning styles, developing self-esteem and social skills of severe behaviorally handicapped students, inclusion.

English as a Second Language

Adelphi University, Ruth S. Ammon School of Education, Program in Teaching English to Speakers of Other Languages, Garden City, NY 11530-0701. Offers MA, Certificate. Part-time and evening/weekend programs available. *Students:* 20 full-time (18 women), 18 part-time (17 women); includes 9 minority (3 Black or African American, non-Hispanic/Latino; 2 Asian, non-Hispanic/Latino; 4 Hispanic/Latino), 5 international. Average age 29. In 2011, 12 master's, 5 other advanced degrees awarded. *Entrance requirements:* For master's, 2 letters of recommendation, resume. Additional exam requirements/recommendations for international students: Required—TOEFL (minimum score 550 paper-based; 213 computer-based; 80 iBT). *Application deadline:* For fall admission, 4/1 priority date for domestic students; for spring admission, 11/1 priority date for domestic students. Applications are processed on a rolling basis. Application fee: $50. Electronic applications accepted. *Expenses: Tuition:* Full-time $29,600; part-time $930 per credit. *Required fees:* $1100. *Financial support:* Fellowships, research assistantships with partial tuition reimbursements, teaching assistantships, career-related internships or fieldwork, Federal Work-Study, institutionally sponsored loans, tuition waivers (full), and unspecified assistantships available. Support available to part-time students. Financial award application deadline: 2/15; financial award applicants required to submit FAFSA. *Faculty research:* Theories of language acquisition, English as a second language in the content areas, apprenticeship in English as a second language instruction. *Unit head:* Eva Roca, Director, 516-877-4072, E-mail: rocaz@adelphi.edu. *Application contact:* Christine Murphy, Director of Admissions, 516-877-3050, Fax: 516-877-3039, E-mail: graduateadmissions@adelphi.edu.

Albright College, Graduate Division, Reading, PA 19612-5234. Offers early childhood education (MS); elementary education (MS); English as a second language (MA); general education (MA); special education (MS). Part-time and evening/weekend programs available. *Degree requirements:* For master's, thesis. *Entrance requirements:* For master's, GRE General Test or MAT, minimum undergraduate GPA of 3.0, 2 letters of recommendation, interview. Additional exam requirements/recommendations for international students: Recommended—TOEFL (minimum score 525 paper-based; 197 computer-based). Electronic applications accepted.

Alliant International University–Fresno, Shirley M. Hufstedler School of Education, Program in Teaching English to Speakers of Other Languages, Fresno, CA 93727. Offers MA, Certificate. Part-time programs available. *Faculty:* 2 full-time (both women). *Students:* 3. *Entrance requirements:* For master's, minimum GPA of 3.0, letters of recommendation. Additional exam requirements/recommendations for international students: Required—TOEFL (minimum score 550 paper-based; 213 computer-based), TWE. *Application deadline:* For fall admission, 7/1 priority date for domestic students, 7/1 for international students; for spring admission, 12/1 priority date for domestic students, 12/1 for international students. Applications are processed on a rolling basis. Application fee: $55. Electronic applications accepted. Tuition and fees vary according to course load. *Financial support:* Federal Work-Study, institutionally sponsored loans, and scholarships/grants available. Financial award application deadline: 2/15; financial award applicants required to submit FAFSA. *Faculty research:* Technology and second language instruction, curriculum design, sociolinguistics, TESOL teaching training, bilingualism. *Unit head:* Dr. Mary Ellen Butler-Pascoe, Systemwide Program Director for TESOL Programs, 858-635-4507, Fax: 559-253-2267, E-mail: admissions@alliant.edu. *Application contact:* Alliant International University Central Contact Center, 866-U-ALLIANT, Fax: 858-635-4555, E-mail: admissions@alliant.edu. Web site: http://www.alliant.edu/gsic/.

Alliant International University–Irvine, Shirley M. Hufstedler School of Education, Program in Teaching English to Speakers of Other Languages, Irvine, CA 92612. Offers MA, Ed D. Part-time programs available. *Students:* 7. In 2011, 4 master's, 1 doctorate awarded. *Degree requirements:* For doctorate, thesis/dissertation. *Entrance requirements:* For master's and doctorate, minimum GPA of 3.0, letters of recommendation. Additional exam requirements/recommendations for international students: Required—TOEFL (minimum score 550 paper-based; 213 computer-based), TWE. *Application deadline:* For fall admission, 7/1 priority date for domestic students, 7/1 for international students; for spring admission, 12/1 priority date for domestic students, 12/1 for international students. Applications are processed on a rolling basis. Application fee: $70. Electronic applications accepted. *Financial support:* Federal Work-Study, institutionally sponsored loans, and scholarships/grants available. Financial award applicants required to submit FAFSA. *Unit head:* Dr. Ellen Butler-Pascoe, Systemwide Program Director for International Teacher Education, 866-825-5426, Fax: 949-833-3507, E-mail: admissions@alliant.edu. *Application contact:* Alliant International University Central Contact Center, 866-U-ALLIANT, Fax: 858-635-4555, E-mail: admissions@alliant.edu. Web site: http://www.alliant.edu/gsoe/.

Alliant International University–San Diego, Shirley M. Hufstedler School of Education, Program in Teaching English to Speakers of Other Languages, San Diego, CA 92131-1799. Offers MA, Ed D, Certificate. Part-time programs available. *Faculty:* 4 full-time (2 women), 4 part-time/adjunct (3 women). *Students:* 51 full-time (47 women), 33 part-time (29 women); includes 8 minority (4 Asian, non-Hispanic/Latino; 4 Hispanic/Latino), 24 international. Average age 38. In 2011, 21 master's, 10 doctorates awarded. *Degree requirements:* For doctorate, thesis/dissertation. *Entrance requirements:* For master's, minimum GPA of 2.5, letters of recommendation; for doctorate, minimum GPA of 3.0, letters of recommendation. Additional exam requirements/recommendations for international students: Required—TOEFL (minimum score 575 paper-based; 233 computer-based; 83 iBT), TWE (minimum score 5). *Application deadline:* For fall admission, 7/1 priority date for domestic students, 7/1 for international students; for spring admission, 12/1 priority date for domestic students, 12/1 for international students. Applications are processed on a rolling basis. Application fee: $55. Electronic applications accepted. Tuition and fees vary according to degree level and program. *Financial support:* Federal Work-Study, institutionally sponsored loans, and scholarships/grants available. Financial award applicants required to submit FAFSA. *Faculty research:* Global education, psycho-linguistics, bilingualism and education, curriculum and instruction. *Unit head:* Dr. Mary Ellen Butler-Pascoe, Systemwide Program Director for International Teacher Education, 858-635-4791, Fax: 858-635-

4739, E-mail: admissions@alliant.edu. *Application contact:* Alliant International University Central Contact Center, 866-U-ALLIANT, Fax: 858-635-4555, E-mail: admissions@alliant.edu. Web site: http://www.alliant.edu/.

American College of Education, Graduate Programs, Chicago, IL 60606. Offers curriculum and instruction (M Ed), including bilingual, ESL; educational leadership (M Ed); educational technology (M Ed).

American Public University System, AMU/APU Graduate Programs, Charles Town, WV 25414. Offers accounting (MBA, MS); administration and supervision (M Ed); criminal justice (MA); emergency and disaster management (MA); entrepreneurship (MBA); environmental policy and management (MS), including environmental planning, environmental sustainability, fish and wildlife management, general (MA, MS), global environmental management; finance (MBA); general (MBA); global business management (MBA); guidance and counseling (M Ed); history (MA), including American history, ancient and classical history, European history, global history, military and diplomatic history, public history; homeland security (MA); homeland security resource allocation (MBA); humanities (MA); information technology (MS), including digital forensics, enterprise software development, information assurance and security, IT project management; information technology management (MBA); intelligence studies (MA), including criminal intelligence, general (MA, MS), homeland security, intelligence analysis, intelligence collection, intelligence operations, terrorism studies; international relations and conflict resolution (MA), including comparative and security issues, conflict resolution, international and transnational security issues, peacekeeping; legal studies (MA); management (MA), including defense management, general (MA, MS), human resource management, organizational leadership, public administration, reverse logistics, strategic consulting; marketing (MBA); military history (MA), including American military history, American revolution, civil war, war since 1946, World War II; military studies (MA), including air warfare, asymmetrical warfare, joint warfare, land warfare, naval warfare, strategic leadership; national security studies (MA), including general (MA, MS), homeland security, regional security studies, security and intelligence analysis, terrorism studies; nonprofit management (MBA); political science (MA), including American politics and government, comparative government and development, public policy; psychology (MA); public administration (MA, MPA), including disaster management (MPA), environmental policy (MA), health policy (MPA), human resources (MPA), national security (MPA), organizational management (MPA), security management (MPA); public health (MA, MPH), including emergency management (MPH), environmental health (MPH), public administration (MA); reverse logistics management (MA); security management (MA); space studies (MS), including aerospace science, planetary science; sports and health sciences (MS); sports management (MS), including coaching theory and strategy, sports administration; teaching (M Ed), including curriculum and instruction for elementary teachers, elementary, elementary reading, English language learners, instructional leadership, online learning, secondary social sciences, special education; transportation and logistics management (MA), including maritime engineering management. Programs offered via distance learning only. Part-time and evening/weekend programs available. Postbaccalaureate distance learning degree programs offered (no on-campus study). *Faculty:* 445 full-time (241 women), 1,360 part-time/adjunct (617 women). *Students:* 688 full-time (338 women), 10,168 part-time (3,706 women); includes 3,130 minority (1,007 Black or African American, non-Hispanic/Latino; 103 American Indian or Alaska Native, non-Hispanic/Latino; 825 Asian, non-Hispanic/Latino; 810 Hispanic/Latino; 51 Native Hawaiian or other Pacific Islander, non-Hispanic/Latino; 334 Two or more races, non-Hispanic/Latino), 134 international. Average age 35. In 2011, 2,386 master's awarded. *Degree requirements:* For master's, comprehensive exam or practicum. *Entrance requirements:* For master's, official transcript showing earned bachelor's degree from institution accredited by recognized accrediting body. Additional exam requirements/recommendations for international students: Required—TOEFL (minimum score 550 paper-based; 213 computer-based), IELTS (minimum score 6.5). *Application deadline:* Applications are processed on a rolling basis. Application fee: $0. Electronic applications accepted. *Expenses: Tuition:* Part-time $325 per credit hour. *Financial support:* Applicants required to submit FAFSA. *Faculty research:* Military history, criminal justice, management performance, national security. *Unit head:* Dr. Karan Powell, Executive Vice President and Provost, 877-468-6268, Fax: 304-724-3780. *Application contact:* Terry Grant, Vice President of Enrollment Management, 877-468-6268, Fax: 304-724-3780, E-mail: info@apus.edu. Web site: http://www.apus.edu.

American University, College of Arts and Sciences, School of Education, Teaching, and Health, Program in English for Speakers of Other Languages, Washington, DC 20016-8001. Offers MAT, Certificate. *Students:* 3 full-time (all women), 8 part-time (5 women), 1 international. Average age 31. 11 applicants, 91% accepted, 4 enrolled. In 2011, 12 master's awarded. *Degree requirements:* For master's, comprehensive exam, PRAXIS II. *Entrance requirements:* For master's, GRE General Test, PRAXIS I, minimum GPA of 3.0, 2 recommendations; for Certificate, bachelor's degree. Additional exam requirements/recommendations for international students: Required—TOEFL (minimum score 600 paper-based; 200 computer-based; 100 iBT), IELTS (minimum score 7). *Application deadline:* For fall admission, 2/1 priority date for domestic students; for spring admission, 10/1 priority date for domestic students. Applications are processed on a rolling basis. Application fee: $80. Electronic applications accepted. *Expenses: Tuition:* Full-time $24,264; part-time $1348 per credit hour. *Required fees:* $430. Tuition and fees vary according to course load and program. *Financial support:* Research assistantships with partial tuition reimbursements available. Financial award application deadline: 2/1. *Unit head:* Sarah Irvine-Belson, Director, Teacher Education, 202-885-3727, Fax: 202-885-1187, E-mail: sirvine@american.edu. *Application contact:* Kathleen Clowery, Director, Graduate Admissions, 202-885-3621, Fax: 202-885-1505, E-mail: clowery@american.edu.

The American University in Cairo, School of Humanities and Social Sciences, English Language Institute, Cairo, Egypt. Offers teaching English as a foreign language (MA, Diploma). Part-time programs available. *Degree requirements:* For master's, one foreign language, thesis optional. *Entrance requirements:* Additional exam requirements/recommendations for international students: Required—English entrance exam and/or TOEFL. *Application deadline:* For fall admission, 3/31 priority date for domestic students; for spring admission, 1/10 priority date for domestic students. Applications are processed on a rolling basis. Application fee: $45. Electronic applications accepted. *Expenses: Tuition:* Part-time $932 per credit hour. Tuition and fees vary according to course load, degree level and program. *Financial support:* Fellowships, teaching assistantships, career-related internships or fieldwork, and tuition waivers (partial) available. *Faculty research:* Teacher education, social linguistics, teaching methodology pragmatics. *Unit head:* Dr. Paul Stevens, Director, 202-357-5080, Fax: 202-355-7565, E-mail: pstevens@aucegypt.edu. *Application contact:* Mary Davidson, Coordinator of Student Affairs, 212-730-8800, Fax: 212-730-1600, E-mail: mdavidson@aucnyo.edu. Web site: http://www.aucegypt.edu/huss/eli/.

American University of Sharjah, Graduate Programs, Sharjah, United Arab Emirates. Offers business (EMBA, GEMPA, MBA); chemical engineering (MS Ch E); civil engineering (MSCE); computer engineering (MS); electrical engineering (MSEE); mechanical engineering (MSME); mechatronics engineering (MS); public administration (MPA); teaching English to speakers of other languages (MA); translation and interpreting (MA); urban planning (MUP). Part-time and evening/weekend programs available. *Entrance requirements:* For master's, GMAT (MBA). Additional exam requirements/recommendations for international students: Required—TOEFL (minimum score 550 paper-based; 213 computer-based; 80 iBT), TWE (minimum score 5). Electronic applications accepted. *Faculty research:* Chemical engineering, civil engineering, computer engineering, electrical engineering, linguistics, translation.

Anaheim University, Program in Teaching English to Speakers of Other Languages, Anaheim, CA 92806-5150. Offers MA, Certificate. Postbaccalaureate distance learning degree programs offered (no on-campus study).

Andrews University, School of Graduate Studies, School of Education, Department of Teaching, Learning, and Curriculum, Berrien Springs, MI 49104. Offers curriculum and instruction (MA, Ed D, PhD, Ed S); elementary education (MAT); secondary education (MAT), including biology, education, English, English as a second language, French, history, physics; teacher education (MAT). *Students:* 15 full-time (10 women), 27 part-time (22 women); includes 18 minority (12 Black or African American, non-Hispanic/Latino; 1 Asian, non-Hispanic/Latino; 3 Hispanic/Latino; 1 Native Hawaiian or other Pacific Islander, non-Hispanic/Latino; 1 Two or more races, non-Hispanic/Latino), 10 international. Average age 42. 48 applicants, 48% accepted, 10 enrolled. In 2011, 5 master's, 2 doctorates, 2 other advanced degrees awarded. *Entrance requirements:* For master's, GRE Subject Test. Additional exam requirements/recommendations for international students: Required—TOEFL (minimum score 550 paper-based). *Application deadline:* For fall admission, 8/15 for domestic students. Applications are processed on a rolling basis. Application fee: $40. *Unit head:* Dr. Lee C. Davidson, Chair, 269-471-6364. *Application contact:* Carolyn Hurst, Supervisor of Graduate Admission, 800-253-2874, Fax: 269-471-6321, E-mail: graduate@andrews.edu.

Arizona State University, College of Liberal Arts and Sciences, Department of English, Tempe, AZ 85287-0302. Offers applied linguistics (PhD); creative writing (MFA); English (MA, PhD), including comparative literature (MA), linguistics (MA), literature, rhetoric and composition (MA), rhetoric/composition and linguistics (PhD); linguistics (Graduate Certificate); teaching English to speakers of other languages (MTESOL). Terminal master's awarded for partial completion of doctoral program. *Degree requirements:* For master's, variable foreign language requirement, comprehensive exam (for some programs), thesis (for some programs), interactive Program of Study (iPOS) submitted before completing 50 percent of required credit hours; for doctorate, variable foreign language requirement, comprehensive exam, thesis/dissertation, interactive Program of Study (iPOS) submitted before completing 50 percent of required credit hours. *Entrance requirements:* For master's and doctorate, GRE, minimum GPA of 3.0 or equivalent in last 2 years of work leading to bachelor's degree. Additional exam requirements/recommendations for international students: Required—TOEFL (minimum score 80 iBT), TOEFL, IELTS, or Pearson Test of English. Electronic applications accepted.

Arkansas Tech University, Center for Leadership and Learning, College of Arts and Humanities, Russellville, AR 72801. Offers English (M Ed, MA); history (MA); liberal arts (MLA); multi-media journalism (MA); psychology (MS); Spanish (MA); teaching English as a second language (MA). Part-time programs available. *Students:* 51 full-time (33 women), 74 part-time (55 women); includes 15 minority (5 Black or African American, non-Hispanic/Latino; 3 American Indian or Alaska Native, non-Hispanic/Latino; 1 Asian, non-Hispanic/Latino; 5 Hispanic/Latino; 1 Two or more races, non-Hispanic/Latino), 22 international. Average age 32. In 2011, 54 master's awarded. *Degree requirements:* For master's, comprehensive exam (for some programs), thesis (for some programs), project. *Entrance requirements:* For master's, GRE General Test or GMAT. Additional exam requirements/recommendations for international students: Required—TOEFL (minimum score 550 paper-based; 213 computer-based; 79 iBT), IELTS (minimum score 6). *Application deadline:* For fall admission, 3/1 priority date for domestic students, 5/1 for international students; for spring admission, 10/1 priority date for domestic students, 10/1 for international students. Applications are processed on a rolling basis. Application fee: $25 ($75 for international students). Electronic applications accepted. *Expenses:* Tuition, state resident: full-time $4968; part-time $207 per credit hour. Tuition, nonresident: full-time $9936; part-time $414 per credit hour. *Required fees:* $375 per semester. Tuition and fees vary according to course load. *Financial support:* In 2011–12, teaching assistantships with full tuition reimbursements (averaging $4,000 per year) were awarded; research assistantships with full tuition reimbursements, career-related internships or fieldwork, Federal Work-Study, scholarships/grants, health care benefits, and unspecified assistantships also available. Support available to part-time students. Financial award application deadline: 4/15; financial award applicants required to submit FAFSA. *Unit head:* Dr. Micheal Tarver, Dean, 479-968-0274, Fax: 479-964-0812, E-mail: mtarver@atu.edu. *Application contact:* Dr. Mary B. Gunter, Dean of Graduate College, 479-968-0398, Fax: 479-964-0542, E-mail: gradcollege@atu.edu. Web site: http://www.atu.edu/lfa/.

Asbury University, School of Graduate and Professional Studies, Wilmore, KY 40390-1198. Offers biology: alternative certificate (MA Ed); chemistry: alternative certificate (MA Ed); English (MA Ed); English as a second language (MA Ed); ESL (MA Ed); French (MA Ed); Latin: alternative certificate (MA Ed); mathematics: alternative certificate (MA Ed); reading/writing endorsement (MA Ed); social studies (MA Ed); social work (MSW), including child and family services; Spanish (MA Ed); special education (MA Ed); special education: alternative certificate (MA Ed); teacher as leader endorsement (MA Ed). *Accreditation:* NCATE. Part-time programs available. *Degree requirements:* For master's, action research project, portfolio. *Entrance requirements:* For master's, PRAXIS/NTE, minimum GPA of 2.75, letters of recommendation. Additional exam requirements/recommendations for international students: Required—TOEFL (minimum score 550 paper-based). Electronic applications accepted.

Avila University, School of Education, Kansas City, MO 64145-1698. Offers education (MA); English for speakers of other languages (Advanced Certificate). Part-time and evening/weekend programs available. *Faculty:* 6 full-time (5 women), 5 part-time/adjunct (3 women). *Students:* 113 full-time (84 women), 33 part-time (28 women); includes 25 minority (15 Black or African American, non-Hispanic/Latino; 4 American Indian or Alaska Native, non-Hispanic/Latino; 4 Hispanic/Latino; 2 Two or more races, non-Hispanic/Latino), 2 international. Average age 34. 66 applicants, 79% accepted, 47 enrolled. In 2011, 20 master's awarded. *Entrance requirements:* For master's, minimum GPA of 3.0, writing sample, recommendation, interview; for Advanced Certificate, foreign language. Additional exam requirements/recommendations for international students: Required—TOEFL (minimum score 580 paper-based; 237 computer-based; 92 iBT). *Application deadline:* Applications are processed on a rolling basis. Electronic applications accepted. *Expenses:* Contact institution. *Financial support:* In 2011–12, 64 students received support, including 1 research assistantship; career-related internships or fieldwork also available. Support available to part-time students. Financial award applicants required to submit FAFSA. *Unit head:* Deana Angotti, Director of Graduate Education, 816-501-2446, Fax: 816-501-2915, E-mail: deana.angotti@avila.edu. *Application contact:* Margaret Longstreet, 816-501-2464, E-mail: margaret.longstreet@avila.edu.

Azusa Pacific University, College of Liberal Arts and Sciences, Program in Teaching English to Speakers of Other Languages, Azusa, CA 91702-7000. Offers MA.

Ball State University, Graduate School, College of Sciences and Humanities, Department of English, Muncie, IN 47306-1099. Offers English (MA, PhD), including composition, creative writing (MA), general (MA), literature; linguistics (MA, PhD), including applied linguistics (PhD), linguistics (MA); linguistics and teaching English to speakers of other languages (MA); teaching English to speakers of other languages (MA). *Faculty:* 28 full-time (14 women). *Students:* 41 full-time (24 women), 52 part-time (34 women); includes 3 minority (1 Asian, non-Hispanic/Latino; 2 Two or more races, non-Hispanic/Latino), 18 international. Average age 27. 90 applicants, 37% accepted, 20 enrolled. In 2011, 13 master's, 4 doctorates awarded. *Degree requirements:* For doctorate, variable foreign language requirement, thesis/dissertation. *Entrance requirements:* For master's, GRE General Test, writing sample; for doctorate, GRE General Test, GRE Subject Test, minimum graduate GPA of 3.2, writing sample. Application fee: $25 ($35 for international students). Tuition and fees vary according to program and reciprocity agreements. *Financial support:* In 2011–12, 71 students received support, including 63 teaching assistantships with full tuition reimbursements available (averaging $8,672 per year); fellowships, career-related internships or fieldwork, and unspecified assistantships also available. Financial award application deadline: 3/1. *Faculty research:* American literature; literary editing; medieval, Renaissance, and eighteenth century British literature; rhetoric. *Unit head:* Dr. Elizabeth Riddle, Chairperson, 765-285-8535, Fax: 765-285-3765. *Application contact:* Dr. Jill Christman. Web site: http://www.bsu.edu/english/.

Barry University, School of Education, Program in Curriculum and Instruction, Miami Shores, FL 33161-6695. Offers accomplished teacher (Ed S); culture, language and literacy (TESOL) (PhD); curriculum evaluation and research (PhD); early childhood (Ed S); early childhood education (PhD); elementary (Ed S); elementary education (PhD); ESOL (Ed S); gifted (Ed S); Montessori (Ed S); PKP/elementary (Ed S); reading (Ed S); reading, language and cognition (PhD). *Entrance requirements:* For doctorate, GRE, minimum GPA of 3.25.

Barry University, School of Education, Program in Technology and TESOL, Miami Shores, FL 33161-6695. Offers MS, Ed S.

Barry University, School of Education, Program in TESOL, Miami Shores, FL 33161-6695. Offers TESOL (MS); TESOL international (MS). *Entrance requirements:* For master's, GRE or MAT.

Biola University, Cook School of Intercultural Studies, La Mirada, CA 90639-0001. Offers anthropology (MA); applied linguistics (MA); intercultural education (PhD); intercultural studies (MA, PhD); linguistics (Certificate); linguistics and Biblical languages (MA); missions (MA); teaching English to speakers of other languages (MA, Certificate). Part-time programs available. *Faculty:* 19. *Students:* 82 full-time (48 women), 128 part-time (72 women); includes 56 minority (6 Black or African American, non-Hispanic/Latino; 45 Asian, non-Hispanic/Latino; 5 Two or more races, non-Hispanic/Latino), 22 international. In 2011, 41 master's, 10 doctorates awarded. *Entrance requirements:* For master's, minimum undergraduate GPA of 3.0; for doctorate, master's degree or equivalent, 3 years of cross-cultural experience, minimum graduate GPA of 3.3. Additional exam requirements/recommendations for international students: Required—TOEFL (minimum score 600 paper-based; 250 computer-based; 100 iBT). *Application deadline:* For fall admission, 7/1 for domestic students, 6/1 for international students; for spring admission, 12/1 for domestic students. Application fee: $55. Electronic applications accepted. *Financial support:* Institutionally sponsored loans and scholarships/grants available. Financial award applicants required to submit FAFSA. *Faculty research:* Linguistics, anthropology, intercultural studies, teaching English to speakers of other languages. *Unit head:* Dr. F. Douglas Pennoyer, Dean, 562-903-4844. *Application contact:* Graduate Admissions Office, 562-903-4752, E-mail: graduate.admissions@biola.edu. Web site: http://cook.biola.edu.

Bishop's University, School of Education, Sherbrooke, QC J1M 0C8, Canada. Offers advanced studies in education (Diploma); education (M Ed, MA); teaching English as a second language (Certificate). Part-time programs available. Postbaccalaureate distance learning degree programs offered (minimal on-campus study). *Degree requirements:* For master's, thesis (for some programs). *Entrance requirements:* For master's, teaching license, 2 years of teaching experience. *Faculty research:* Integration of special needs students, multigrade classes/small schools, leadership in organizational development, second language acquisition.

Brigham Young University, Graduate Studies, College of Humanities, Department of Linguistics and English Language, Provo, UT 84602. Offers general linguistics (MA); teaching English as a second language (MA). Part-time programs available. *Faculty:* 24 full-time (6 women), 10 part-time/adjunct (9 women). *Students:* 54 full-time (34 women); includes 3 minority (all Hispanic/Latino), 11 international. Average age 28. 46 applicants, 83% accepted, 34 enrolled. In 2011, 14 master's awarded. *Degree requirements:* For master's, 2 foreign languages, thesis. *Entrance requirements:* For master's, GRE General Test, minimum GPA of 3.6 in last 60 hours of course work. Additional exam requirements/recommendations for international students: Required—TOEFL (minimum score 580 paper-based; 237 computer-based; 90 iBT), TWE. *Application deadline:* 1/15 for domestic and international students. Application fee: $50. Electronic applications accepted. *Expenses: Tuition:* Full-time $5760; part-time $320 per credit. Tuition and fees vary according to student's religious affiliation. *Financial support:* In 2011–12, 9 research assistantships with partial tuition reimbursements (averaging $2,908 per year), 10 teaching assistantships with partial tuition reimbursements (averaging $1,751 per year) were awarded; fellowships with partial tuition reimbursements, career-related internships or fieldwork, institutionally sponsored loans, scholarships/grants, tuition waivers (partial), unspecified assistantships, and student instructorships also available. Support available to part-time students. Financial award application deadline: 5/1. *Faculty research:* Teaching English to speakers of other languages, second language acquisition, computational linguistics, semiotics and semantics, computer-assisted language instruction. *Total annual research expenditures:* $46,000. *Unit head:* Dr. William G. Eggington, Chair, 801-422-2937, Fax: 801-422-0906, E-mail: bill_eggington@byu.edu. *Application contact:* LoriAnne Spear, Secretary, 801-422-9010, Fax: 801-422-0906, E-mail: lorianne_spear@byu.edu. Web site: http://linguistics.byu.edu/.

Brock University, Faculty of Graduate Studies, Faculty of Humanities, Program in Applied Linguistics, St. Catharines, ON L2S 3A1, Canada. Offers MA. Part-time programs available. *Degree requirements:* For master's, thesis optional. *Entrance requirements:* For master's, honours degree with a background in English, English linguistics, teaching English as a second language, or a comparable field. Additional exam requirements/recommendations for international students: Required—TOEFL (minimum score 630 paper-based; 267 computer-based; 109 iBT), IELTS (minimum score 8), TWE (minimum score 5.5). Electronic applications accepted. *Expenses:* Contact institution. *Faculty research:* Metalinguistic ability in subsequent language learning, language teaching methodology, forensic linguistics, philosophy of education, culturally appropriate pedagogy.

Buena Vista University, School of Education, Storm Lake, IA 50588. Offers curriculum and instruction (M Ed), including effective teaching, TESL; school guidance and counseling (MS Ed). Program offered in summer only. Part-time and evening/weekend programs available. Postbaccalaureate distance learning degree programs offered (minimal on-campus study). *Degree requirements:* For master's, thesis, fieldwork/practicum, capstone portfolio. *Entrance requirements:* For master's, Analytical Writing Assessment (in-house), minimum undergraduate GPA of 2.75. Electronic applications accepted. *Faculty research:* Reading, curriculum, educational psychology, special education.

California Baptist University, Program in English, Riverside, CA 92504-3206. Offers English pedagogy (MA); literature (MA); teaching English to speakers of other languages (TESOL) (MA). Part-time and evening/weekend programs available. *Faculty:* 8 full-time (5 women). *Students:* 27 full-time (20 women); includes 6 minority (all Hispanic/Latino), 5 international. Average age 30. 15 applicants, 53% accepted, 8 enrolled. In 2011, 6 master's awarded. *Degree requirements:* For master's, comprehensive exam or thesis. *Entrance requirements:* For master's, minimum undergraduate GPA of 3.0; 18 semester hours of course work in English beyond freshman level; three recommendations; essay; demonstration of writing; interview. Additional exam requirements/recommendations for international students: Required—TOEFL (minimum score 575 paper-based; 230 computer-based; 89 iBT). *Application deadline:* For fall admission, 8/1 priority date for domestic students, 7/1 for international students; for spring admission, 12/1 priority date for domestic students, 11/1 for international students. Applications are processed on a rolling basis. Application fee: $45. Electronic applications accepted. *Expenses:* Contact institution. *Financial support:* Federal Work-Study and institutionally sponsored loans available. Financial award applicants required to submit FAFSA. *Faculty research:* Science fiction and fantasy literature, Latin American literature, mythology and folklore, Native American literature, comparative literature. *Unit head:* Dr. James Lu, Chair, Department of Modern Languages and Literature, 951-343-4277, E-mail: jlu@calbaptist.edu. *Application contact:* Dr. Jennifer Newton, Director, Master of Art Program in English, 951-343-4276, Fax: 951-343-4661, E-mail: jnewton@calbaptist.edu. Web site: http://www.calbaptist.edu/maenglish/.

California State University, Chico, Office of Graduate Studies, College of Communication and Education, School of Education, Teaching English Learners and Special Education Advising Patterns Program, Chico, CA 95929-0722. Offers special education (MA); teaching English learners (MA). Part-time and evening/weekend programs available. *Degree requirements:* For master's, comprehensive exam, thesis or project. *Entrance requirements:* Additional exam requirements/recommendations for international students: Required—TOEFL (minimum score 550 paper-based; 213 computer-based; 80 iBT), IELTS (minimum score 6.5), Pearson Test of English (minimum score 59). *Application deadline:* For fall admission, 3/1 priority date for domestic students, 3/1 for international students; for spring admission, 9/15 priority date for domestic students, 9/15 for international students. Application fee: $55. Electronic applications accepted. Tuition and fees vary according to class time, course load and degree level. *Financial support:* Fellowships, career-related internships or fieldwork, scholarships/grants, and stipends available. *Unit head:* Dr. Deborah Summers, Chair, 530-898-6421, Fax: 530-898-6177, E-mail: educ@csuchico.edu. *Application contact:* Judy I. Rice, Graduate Admissions Coordinator, 530-898-5416, Fax: 530-898-3342, E-mail: jlrice@csuchico.edu. Web site: http://www.csuchico.edu/soe/advanced/education/patterns.shtml.

California State University, Dominguez Hills, College of Arts and Humanities, Department of English, Carson, CA 90747-0001. Offers English (MA); rhetoric and composition (Certificate); teaching English as a second language (Certificate). Part-time and evening/weekend programs available. *Faculty:* 13 full-time (5 women). *Students:* 25 full-time (17 women), 65 part-time (40 women); includes 42 minority (12 Black or African American, non-Hispanic/Latino; 2 American Indian or Alaska Native, non-Hispanic/Latino; 9 Asian, non-Hispanic/Latino; 17 Hispanic/Latino; 2 Two or more races, non-Hispanic/Latino), 6 international. Average age 39. 56 applicants, 80% accepted, 29 enrolled. In 2011, 10 master's awarded. *Degree requirements:* For master's, comprehensive exam (for some programs), thesis or alternative. *Entrance requirements:* For master's, minimum GPA of 3.0 in last 60 units. Additional exam requirements/recommendations for international students: Required—TOEFL (minimum score 550 paper-based; 213 computer-based). *Application deadline:* Applications are processed on a rolling basis. Application fee: $55. Electronic applications accepted. *Faculty research:* Gender studies, transnationalism, discourse analysis, visual culture, Shakespeare. *Unit head:* Dr. Cyril Zoerner, Chair, 310-243-3322, E-mail: ezooerner@csudh.edu. *Application contact:* Brandy McLelland, Interim Director, Student Information Services, 310-243-3645, E-mail: bmclelland@csudh.edu. Web site: http://www.cah.csudh.edu.

California State University, East Bay, Office of Academic Programs and Graduate Studies, College of Letters, Arts, and Social Sciences, Department of English, Hayward, CA 94542-3000. Offers English (MA); teaching English to speakers of other languages (MA). Part-time programs available. *Faculty:* 5 full-time (4 women). *Students:* 11 full-time (10 women), 68 part-time (49 women); includes 28 minority (7 Black or African American, non-Hispanic/Latino; 1 American Indian or Alaska Native, non-Hispanic/Latino; 11 Asian, non-Hispanic/Latino; 7 Hispanic/Latino; 2 Two or more races, non-Hispanic/Latino), 11 international. Average age 34. 72 applicants, 71% accepted, 36 enrolled. In 2011, 27 master's awarded. *Degree requirements:* For master's, one foreign language, comprehensive exam, thesis optional. *Entrance requirements:* For master's, minimum GPA of 3.0 in field; 2 letters of recommendation; academic or professional writing sample; preferred teaching experience and some degree of bilingualism (for TESOL). Additional exam requirements/recommendations for international students: Required—TOEFL (minimum score 550 paper-based; 213 computer-based); Recommended—IELTS (minimum score 6.5). *Application deadline:* For fall admission, 6/30 for domestic and international students. Applications are processed on a rolling basis. Application fee: $55. Electronic applications accepted. *Expenses:* Tuition, state resident: full-time $6738; part-time $1302 per quarter. Tuition, nonresident: full-time $12,690; part-time $2294 per quarter. *Required fees:* $449 per quarter. Tuition and fees vary according to degree level, program and reciprocity agreements. *Financial support:* Fellowships, teaching assistantships, career-related internships or fieldwork, Federal Work-Study, institutionally sponsored loans, and scholarships/grants available. Support available to part-time students. Financial award application deadline: 3/2; financial award applicants required to submit FAFSA. *Unit head:* Dr. Dennis Chester, Chair/English Graduate Advisor, 510-885-3151, Fax: 510-885-4797, E-mail: dennis.chester@csueastbay.edu. Web site: http://www20.csueastbay.edu/class/departments/english/index.html.

California State University, Fresno, Division of Graduate Studies, College of Arts and Humanities, Department of Linguistics, Fresno, CA 93740-8027. Offers linguistics (MA), including Teaching English as a second language. Part-time and evening/weekend programs available. *Degree requirements:* For master's, comprehensive exam. *Entrance requirements:* For master's, GRE General Test, minimum GPA of 3.0. Additional exam requirements/recommendations for international students: Required—TOEFL. Electronic applications accepted. *Faculty research:* Communication systems, bilingual education, animal communication, conflict resolution, literacy programs.

California State University, Fullerton, Graduate Studies, College of Humanities and Social Sciences, Department of Modern Languages and Literatures, Fullerton, CA 92834-9480. Offers French (MA); German (MA); Spanish (MA); teaching English to speakers of other languages (MS). Part-time programs available. *Students:* 60 full-time (45 women), 44 part-time (34 women); includes 56 minority (18 Asian, non-Hispanic/Latino; 35 Hispanic/Latino; 3 Two or more races, non-Hispanic/Latino), 16 international. Average age 31. 128 applicants, 65% accepted, 41 enrolled. In 2011, 42 master's awarded. *Degree requirements:* For master's, comprehensive exam, thesis or alternative. *Entrance requirements:* For master's, minimum GPA of 2.5 in last 60 hours of course work, undergraduate major in a language. Application fee: $55. *Financial support:* Career-related internships or fieldwork, Federal Work-Study, institutionally sponsored loans, and scholarships/grants available. Support available to part-time students. Financial award application deadline: 3/1; financial award applicants required to submit FAFSA. *Unit head:* Dr. Janet Eyring, Chair, 657-278-3534. *Application contact:* Admissions/Applications, 657-278-2371.

California State University, Long Beach, Graduate Studies, College of Liberal Arts, Department of Linguistics, Long Beach, CA 90840. Offers general linguistics (MA); language and culture (MA); special concentration (MA); teaching English as a second language (MA). Part-time and evening/weekend programs available. *Faculty:* 9 full-time (7 women), 2 part-time/adjunct (1 woman). *Students:* 35 full-time (27 women), 24 part-time (13 women); includes 23 minority (1 Black or African American, non-Hispanic/Latino; 1 American Indian or Alaska Native, non-Hispanic/Latino; 10 Asian, non-Hispanic/Latino; 9 Hispanic/Latino; 1 Native Hawaiian or other Pacific Islander, non-Hispanic/Latino; 1 Two or more races, non-Hispanic/Latino), 14 international. Average age 31. 58 applicants, 57% accepted, 17 enrolled. In 2011, 19 master's awarded. *Degree requirements:* For master's, one foreign language, comprehensive exam, thesis optional. *Application deadline:* For fall admission, 5/1 for domestic students. Applications are processed on a rolling basis. Application fee: $55. Electronic applications accepted. *Financial support:* Teaching assistantships, career-related internships or fieldwork, Federal Work-Study, institutionally sponsored loans, and scholarships/grants available. Financial award application deadline: 3/2. *Faculty research:* Pedagogy of language instruction, role of language in society, Khmer language instruction. *Unit head:* Dr. Malcolm Awadajin Finney, Chair, 562-985-7425, Fax: 562-985-2593, E-mail: mfinney@csulb.edu. *Application contact:* Dr. Xiaoping Liang, Graduate Advisor, 562-985-8509, Fax: 562-985-5792, E-mail: xliang@csulb.edu.

California State University, Sacramento, Office of Graduate Studies, College of Arts and Letters, Department of English, Sacramento, CA 95819-6075. Offers creative writing (MA); teaching English to speakers of other languages (MA). Part-time programs available. *Faculty:* 23 full-time (12 women), 37 part-time/adjunct (32 women). *Students:* 56 full-time, 71 part-time; includes 23 minority (2 Black or African American, non-Hispanic/Latino; 1 American Indian or Alaska Native, non-Hispanic/Latino; 4 Asian, non-Hispanic/Latino; 12 Hispanic/Latino; 2 Native Hawaiian or other Pacific Islander, non-Hispanic/Latino; 2 Two or more races, non-Hispanic/Latino), 2 international. Average age 32. 91 applicants, 66% accepted, 39 enrolled. In 2011, 53 master's awarded. *Degree requirements:* For master's, thesis, project, or comprehensive exam; TESOL exam; writing proficiency exam. *Entrance requirements:* For master's, portfolio (creative writing); minimum GPA of 3.0 in English, 2.75 overall during previous 2 years. Additional exam requirements/recommendations for international students: Required—TOEFL. *Application deadline:* For fall admission, 2/15 for domestic students, 3/1 for international students; for spring admission, 9/30 for international students. Applications are processed on a rolling basis. Application fee: $55. Electronic applications accepted. *Financial support:* Research assistantships, teaching assistantships, career-related internships or fieldwork, and Federal Work-Study available. Support available to part-time students. Financial award application deadline: 3/1; financial award applicants required to submit FAFSA. *Faculty research:* Teaching composition, remedial writing. *Unit head:* Bradley Buchanan, Chair, 916-278-6586, Fax: 916-278-4588, E-mail: buchanan@csus.edu. *Application contact:* Jose Martinez, Outreach and Graduate Diversity Coordinator, 916-278-6470, Fax: 916-278-5669, E-mail: martinj@skymail.csus.edu. Web site: http://www.csus.edu/engl.

California State University, San Bernardino, Graduate Studies, College of Education, San Bernardino, CA 92407-2397. Offers bilingual/cross-cultural education (MA); curriculum and instruction (MA); educational administration (MA); educational leadership and curriculum (Ed D); educational psychology and counseling (MA, MS), including correctional and alternative education (MA), counseling and guidance (MS), rehabilitation counseling (MA); English as a second language (MA); general education (MA); history and English for secondary teachers (MA); instructional technology (MA); reading (MA); secondary education (MA); special education and rehabilitation counseling (MA), including rehabilitation counseling, special education; teaching of science (MA); vocational and career education (MA). *Accreditation:* NCATE. Part-time and evening/weekend programs available. *Students:* 434 full-time (335 women), 188 part-time (139 women); includes 271 minority (54 Black or African American, non-Hispanic/Latino; 2 American Indian or Alaska Native, non-Hispanic/Latino; 29 Asian, non-Hispanic/Latino; 172 Hispanic/Latino; 2 Native Hawaiian or other Pacific Islander, non-Hispanic/Latino; 12 Two or more races, non-Hispanic/Latino), 28 international. Average age 32. 382 applicants, 61% accepted, 186 enrolled. In 2011, 279 master's awarded. *Degree requirements:* For master's, comprehensive exam (for some programs), thesis (for some programs), advancement to candidacy. *Entrance requirements:* For master's, minimum GPA of 3.0 in education. *Application deadline:* For fall admission, 8/31 priority date for domestic students. Application fee: $55. *Expenses:* Tuition, state resident: full-time $7356. Tuition, nonresident: full-time $7356. *Required fees:* $1077. Tuition and fees vary according to program. *Financial support:* Career-related internships or fieldwork and Federal Work-Study available. Support available to part-time students. *Faculty research:* Multicultural education, brain-based learning, science education, social studies/global education. *Unit head:* Dr. Patricia Arlin, Dean, 909-537-5600, Fax: 909-537-7011, E-mail: parlin@csusb.edu. *Application contact:* Olivia Rosas, Director of Admissions, 909-537-7577, Fax: 909-537-7034, E-mail: orosas@csusb.edu.

California State University, San Bernardino, Graduate Studies, College of Extended Learning, San Bernardino, CA 92407-2397. Offers executive business administration (MBA); TESOL (MA Ed). Part-time and evening/weekend programs available. *Expenses:* Tuition, state resident: full-time $7356. Tuition, nonresident: full-time $7356. *Required fees:* $1077. Tuition and fees vary according to program.

California State University, Stanislaus, College of Humanities and Social Sciences, Program in English (MA), Turlock, CA 95382. Offers literature (Certificate); rhetoric and teaching writing (MA); teaching English to speakers of other languages (MA). Part-time programs available. *Degree requirements:* For master's, comprehensive exam, thesis or alternative. *Entrance requirements:* For master's, GRE, minimum GPA of 3.0, 2 letters of reference, personal statement. Additional exam requirements/recommendations for international students: Required—TOEFL (minimum score 575 paper-based; 233 computer-based), TWE (minimum score 4). *Application deadline:* For fall admission, 5/1 for domestic students; for spring admission, 9/15 for domestic students. Application fee: $55. Electronic applications accepted. *Expenses: Required fees:* $4616 per year. *Financial support:* Fellowships, research assistantships, teaching assistantships, career-related internships or fieldwork, and Federal Work-Study available. Financial award application deadline: 3/1; financial award applicants required to submit FAFSA. *Faculty research:* Transnational literacies, Renaissance and medieval literature, abolition writings and slave narratives, qualitative writing. *Unit head:* Dr. Scott Davis, Chair, 209-667-3361, Fax: 209-667-3720, E-mail: english@csustan.edu. *Application contact:* Graduate School, 209-667-3129, Fax: 209-664-7025, E-mail: graduate_school@csustan.edu. Web site: http://www.csustan.edu/english/.

Cambridge College, School of Education, Cambridge, MA 02138-5304. Offers autism specialist (M Ed); autism/behavior analyst (M Ed); behavior analyst (Post-Master's Certificate); behavioral management (M Ed); early childhood teacher (M Ed); education specialist in curriculum and instruction (CAGS); educational leadership (Ed D); elementary teacher (M Ed); English as a second language (M Ed, Certificate); general science (M Ed); health education (Post-Master's Certificate); health/family and consumer sciences (M Ed); history (M Ed); individualized (M Ed); information technology literacy (M Ed); instructional technology (M Ed); interdisciplinary studies (M Ed); library teacher (M Ed); literacy education (M Ed); mathematics (M Ed); mathematics specialist (Certificate); middle school mathematics and science (M Ed); school administration (M Ed, CAGS); school guidance counselor (M Ed); school nurse education (M Ed); school social worker/school adjustment counselor (M Ed); special education administrator (CAGS); special education/moderate disabilities (M Ed); teaching skills and methodologies (M Ed). Part-time and evening/weekend programs available. Postbaccalaureate distance learning degree programs offered (minimal on-campus study). *Degree requirements:* For master's, thesis, internship/practicum (licensure program only); for doctorate, thesis/dissertation; for other advanced degree, thesis. *Entrance requirements:* For master's, interview, resume, documentation of licensure, 2 professional references; for doctorate, official transcripts, interview, resume, documentation of licensure (if any), written personal statement/essay, portfolio of scholarly and professional work, qualifying assessment, 2 professional references, health insurance, immunizations form; for other advanced degree, official transcripts, interview, resume, documentation of licensure (if any), written personal statement/essay, 2 professional references, health insurance, immunizations form. Additional exam requirements/recommendations for international students: Required—TOEFL (minimum score 550 paper-based; 213 computer-based; 79 iBT); Recommended—IELTS (minimum score 6). Electronic applications accepted. *Expenses:* Contact institution. *Faculty research:* Adult education, accelerated learning, mathematics education, brain compatible learning, special education and law.

Cardinal Stritch University, College of Education, Department of Literacy, Milwaukee, WI 53217-3985. Offers literacy/English as a second language (MA); reading/language arts (MA); reading/learning disability (MA). *Accreditation:* NCATE. Part-time and evening/weekend programs available. *Degree requirements:* For master's, comprehensive exam, thesis, faculty recommendation, research project. *Entrance requirements:* For master's, letters of recommendation (2), minimum GPA of 2.75.

Carlos Albizu University, Miami Campus, Graduate Programs, Miami, FL 33172-2209. Offers clinical psychology (Psy D); entrepreneurship (MBA); exceptional student education (MS); industrial/organizational psychology (MS); marriage and family therapy (MS); mental health counseling (MS); nonprofit management (MBA); organizational management (MBA); psychology (MS); school counseling (MS); teaching English as a second language (MS). *Accreditation:* APA. Part-time and evening/weekend programs available. *Faculty:* 19 full-time (12 women), 53 part-time/adjunct (27 women). *Students:* 524 full-time (431 women), 216 part-time (169 women); includes 563 minority (50 Black or African American, non-Hispanic/Latino; 1 American Indian or Alaska Native, non-Hispanic/Latino; 4 Asian, non-Hispanic/Latino; 492 Hispanic/Latino; 16 Native Hawaiian or other Pacific Islander, non-Hispanic/Latino), 17 international. Average age 31. 174 applicants, 67% accepted, 116 enrolled. In 2011, 157 master's, 21 doctorates awarded. Terminal master's awarded for partial completion of doctoral program. *Degree requirements:* For master's, one foreign language, comprehensive exam, integrative project (MBA), research project (exceptional student education, teaching English as a second language); for doctorate, one foreign language, comprehensive exam, internship, project. *Entrance requirements:* For master's, 3 letters of recommendation, interview, minimum GPA of 3.0, resume, statement of purpose, official transcripts; for doctorate, 3 letters of recommendation, minimum GPA of 3.0, resume, interview, statement of purpose, official transcripts. Additional exam requirements/recommendations for international students: Required—Michigan Test of English Language Proficiency. *Application deadline:* For fall admission, 4/1 priority date for domestic students, 5/1 for international students; for spring admission, 11/1 priority date for domestic students, 9/1 for international students. Applications are processed on a rolling basis. Application fee: $50. Electronic applications accepted. *Expenses: Tuition:* Full-time $9360; part-time $520 per credit. *Required fees:* $298 per term. Tuition and fees vary according to course load, degree level and program. *Financial support:* In 2011–12, 106 students received support. Federal Work-Study, scholarships/grants, and tuition discounts available. Financial award application deadline: 6/1; financial award applicants required to submit FAFSA. *Faculty research:* Psychotherapy, forensic psychology, neuropsychology, marketing strategy, entrepreneurship, special education. *Unit head:* Dr. Carmen S. Roca, Chancellor, 305-593-1223 Ext. 120, Fax: 305-629-8052, E-mail: croca@albizu.edu. *Application contact:* Vanessa Almendarez, Administrative Assistant, 305-593-1223 Ext. 137, Fax: 305-593-1854, E-mail: valmendarez@albizu.edu.

Carson-Newman College, Graduate Program in Education, Jefferson City, TN 37760. Offers curriculum and instruction (M Ed); educational leadership (M Ed); elementary education (MAT); school counseling (MS); secondary education (MAT); teaching English as a second language (MATESL). *Accreditation:* NCATE. Part-time and evening/weekend programs available. *Faculty:* 5 full-time (2 women), 10 part-time/adjunct (3 women). *Students:* 85 full-time (55 women), 76 part-time (53 women); includes 8 minority (5 Black or African American, non-Hispanic/Latino; 2 Asian, non-Hispanic/Latino; 1 Two or more races, non-Hispanic/Latino), 23 international. Average age 32. 80 applicants, 96% accepted. In 2011, 90 master's awarded. *Degree requirements:* For master's, thesis or alternative. *Entrance requirements:* For master's, NTE, minimum GPA of 3.0 in major, 2.5 overall. *Application deadline:* For fall admission, 7/15 priority date for domestic students. Applications are processed on a rolling basis. Application fee: $25 ($50 for international students). *Expenses: Tuition:* Full-time $6750; part-time $375 per credit hour. *Required fees:* $200. *Financial support:* In 2011–12, 41 students received support. Federal Work-Study and unspecified assistantships available. Financial award application deadline: 4/1; financial award applicants required to submit FAFSA. *Unit head:* Dr. Sharon Teets, Chair, 865-471-3461. *Application contact:* Graduate Admissions and Services Adviser, 865-471-3460, Fax: 865-471-3875.

Central Connecticut State University, School of Graduate Studies, School of Arts and Sciences, Department of English, Program in Teaching English to Speakers of Other Languages, New Britain, CT 06050-4010. Offers MS, Certificate. Part-time and evening/weekend programs available. *Students:* 21 full-time (14 women), 25 part-time (22 women); includes 9 minority (1 American Indian or Alaska Native, non-Hispanic/Latino; 3 Asian, non-Hispanic/Latino; 2 Hispanic/Latino; 3 Two or more races, non-Hispanic/Latino). Average age 36. 37 applicants, 68% accepted, 16 enrolled. In 2011, 5 master's, 5 other advanced degrees awarded. *Degree requirements:* For master's, comprehensive exam, thesis or alternative; for Certificate, qualifying exam. *Entrance requirements:* For master's, 3 semester hours of study of a second language. Additional exam requirements/recommendations for international students: Required—TOEFL (minimum score 550 paper-based; 213 computer-based). *Application deadline:* For fall admission, 6/1 for domestic students, 5/1 for international students; for spring admission, 11/1 for domestic and international students. Applications are processed on a rolling basis. Application fee: $50. Electronic applications accepted. *Expenses: Tuition, area resident:* Full-time $5137; part-time $482 per credit. Tuition, state resident: full-time $7707; part-time $494 per credit. Tuition, nonresident: full-time $14,311; part-time $494 per credit. *Required fees:* $3865. One-time fee: $62 part-time. *Faculty research:* Phonology, general linguistics, second language writing, East Asian languages, English language structure. *Unit head:* Dr. Stephen Cohen, Chair, 860-832-2795, E-mail: cohens@mail.ccsu.edu. *Application contact:* Patricia Gardner, Associate Director of Graduate Studies, 860-832-2350, Fax: 860-832-2352, E-mail: graduateadmissions@ccsu.edu.

Central Michigan University, College of Graduate Studies, College of Humanities and Social and Behavioral Sciences, Department of English Language and Literature, Mount Pleasant, MI 48859. Offers English composition and communication (MA); English language and literature (MA), including children's and young adult literature, creative writing, general concentration; teaching English to speakers of other languages (MA). Part-time and evening/weekend programs available. *Degree requirements:* For master's, thesis or alternative. Electronic applications accepted. *Faculty research:* Composition theory, science fiction history and bibliography, children's and young adult literature, nineteenth-century American literature, applied linguistics.

Central Washington University, Graduate Studies and Research, College of Arts and Humanities, Department of English, Ellensburg, WA 98926. Offers English (MA); teaching English as a second language (MA). Part-time programs available. *Faculty:* 17 full-time (11 women). *Students:* 22 full-time (9 women); includes 3 minority (all Hispanic/Latino). 40 applicants, 83% accepted, 24 enrolled. In 2011, 10 master's awarded. *Degree requirements:* For master's, thesis or alternative. *Entrance requirements:* For master's, GRE General Test, minimum GPA of 3.0, writing sample. Additional exam requirements/recommendations for international students: Required—TOEFL (minimum score 550 paper-based; 213 computer-based; 79 iBT) or IELTS (minimum score 6.5). *Application deadline:* For fall admission, 2/1 priority date for domestic students; for winter admission, 10/1 for domestic students; for spring admission, 1/1 for domestic students. Applications are processed on a rolling basis. Application fee: $50. Electronic applications accepted. *Expenses:* Tuition, state resident: full-time $8112; part-time $270 per credit. Tuition, nonresident: full-time $18,069; part-time $602 per credit. *Required fees:* $924. *Financial support:* In 2011–12, 14 teaching assistantships with partial tuition reimbursements (averaging $9,234 per year) were awarded; research assistantships with partial tuition reimbursements, Federal Work-Study, health care benefits, and unspecified assistantships also available. Financial award application deadline: 3/1; financial award applicants required to submit FAFSA. *Unit head:* Dr. Laila Abdalla, Graduate Coordinator, 509-963-1546, Fax: 509-963-1561, E-mail: abdallal@cwu.edu. *Application contact:* Justine Eason, Admissions Program Coordinator, 509-963-3103, Fax: 509-963-1799, E-mail: masters@cwu.edu. Web site: http://www.cwu.edu/~english/

Christopher Newport University, Graduate Studies, Department of Teacher Preparation, Newport News, VA 23606-2998. Offers art (PK-12) (MAT); biology (6-12) (MAT); chemistry (6-12) (MAT); computer science (6-12) (MAT); elementary (PK-6) (MAT); English (6-12) (MAT); English as second language (PK-12) (MAT); French (PK-12) (MAT); history and social science (6-12) (MAT); mathematics (6-12) (MAT); music (PK-12) (MAT), including choral, instrumental; physics (6-12) (MAT); Spanish (PK-12) (MAT). Part-time and evening/weekend programs available. *Degree requirements:* For master's, comprehensive exam, thesis or alternative. *Entrance requirements:* For master's, PRAXIS I, minimum GPA of 3.0. Additional exam requirements/recommendations for international students: Required—TOEFL (minimum score 580 paper-based; 237 computer-based; 92 iBT). Electronic applications accepted. *Faculty research:* Early literacy development, instructional innovations, professional teaching standards, multicultural issues, aesthetic education.

Cleveland State University, College of Graduate Studies, College of Education and Human Services, Department of Teacher Education, Cleveland, OH 44115. Offers art education (M Ed); early childhood education (M Ed); foreign language education (M Ed); mathematics and science education (M Ed); middle childhood education (M Ed); special education (M Ed), including mild/moderate disabilities, moderate/intensive disabilities; teaching English to speakers of other languages (M Ed). Part-time and evening/weekend programs available. *Faculty:* 20 full-time (12 women), 26 part-time/adjunct (20 women). *Students:* 108 full-time (77 women), 388 part-time (306 women); includes 126 minority (100 Black or African American, non-Hispanic/Latino; 8 Asian, non-Hispanic/Latino; 15 Hispanic/Latino; 1 Native Hawaiian or other Pacific Islander, non-Hispanic/Latino; 2 Two or more races, non-Hispanic/Latino), 25 international. Average age 33. 249 applicants, 73% accepted, 118 enrolled. In 2011, 286 master's awarded. *Degree requirements:* For master's, comprehensive exam (for some programs), thesis or alternative. *Entrance requirements:* For master's, GRE General Test or MAT, minimum GPA of 2.75. Additional exam requirements/recommendations for international students: Required—TOEFL (minimum score 525 paper-based; 197 computer-based), IELTS (minimum score 6). *Application deadline:* For fall admission, 7/15 priority date for domestic students. Applications are processed on a rolling basis. Application fee: $30. *Expenses:* Tuition, state resident: full-time $6416; part-time $494 per credit hour. Tuition, nonresident: full-time $12,074; part-time $929 per credit hour. *Financial support:* In 2011–12, 12 research assistantships with full tuition reimbursements (averaging $3,480 per year) were awarded; tuition waivers (partial) and unspecified assistantships also available. *Faculty research:* Early literacy, professional development in reading, reading recovery, dual language, induction programs. *Total annual research expenditures:* $6.2 million. *Unit head:* Dr. Clifford T. Bennett, Chairperson, 216-523-7105, Fax: 216-687-5379, E-mail: c.t.bennett@csuohio.edu. *Application contact:* Deborah L. Brown, Interim Assistant Director, Graduate Admissions, 216-523-7572, E-mail: d.l.brown@csuohio.edu. Web site: http://www.csuohio.edu/coehs/departments/te.

College of Charleston, Graduate School, School of Education, Health, and Human Performance, Program in English to Speakers of Other Languages, Charleston, SC 29424-0001. Offers Certificate. Part-time programs available. Postbaccalaureate distance learning degree programs offered (minimal on-campus study). *Students:* 1 (woman) part-time. Average age 27. *Entrance requirements:* Additional exam requirements/recommendations for international students: Required—TOEFL (minimum score 81 iBT). *Application deadline:* For fall admission, 7/1 for domestic students; for spring admission, 11/1 for domestic students. Application fee: $45. Electronic applications accepted. *Expenses:* Tuition, state resident: full-time $5455; part-time $455 per credit. Tuition, nonresident: full-time $13,917; part-time $1160 per credit. *Unit head:* Dr. Angela Crespo Cozart, Director, 843-953-6353, E-mail: cozarta@cofc.edu. *Application contact:* Susan Hallatt, Director of Graduate Admissions, 843-953-5614, Fax: 843-953-1434, E-mail: hallatts@cofc.edu.

The College of New Jersey, Graduate Studies, School of Education, Department of Special Education, Language and Literacy, Program in Teaching English as a Second Language, Ewing, NJ 08628. Offers English as a second language (M Ed); teaching English as a second language (Certificate). *Accreditation:* NCATE. Part-time programs available. *Degree requirements:* For master's, comprehensive exam. *Entrance requirements:* For master's, GRE General Test, minimum GPA of 3.0 in field or 2.75 overall. Additional exam requirements/recommendations for international students: Required—TOEFL. Electronic applications accepted.

The College of New Rochelle, Graduate School, Division of Education, Program in Teaching English as a Second Language and Multilingual/Multicultural Education, New Rochelle, NY 10805-2308. Offers bilingual education (Certificate); teaching English as a second language (MS Ed). Part-time and evening/weekend programs available. *Degree requirements:* For master's, practicum. *Entrance requirements:* For master's, interview, minimum GPA of 3.0 in field, 2.7 overall.

College of Saint Mary, Program in Education, Omaha, NE 68106. Offers assessment leadership (MSE); English as a second language (MSE). Part-time programs available. *Entrance requirements:* For master's, technology competency test or equivalent, minimum cumulative GPA of 3.0, teaching certificate, 2 letters of reference, resume.

Colorado Mesa University, Center for Teacher Education, Grand Junction, CO 81501-3122. Offers educational leadership (MAEd); English for speakers of other languages (MAEd). *Accreditation:* NCATE. Part-time programs available. Postbaccalaureate distance learning degree programs offered (minimal on-campus study). *Degree requirements:* For master's, comprehensive exam, capstone presentation. *Entrance requirements:* For master's, GRE, 2 professional letters of recommendation. Additional exam requirements/recommendations for international students: Required—TOEFL (minimum score 550 paper-based; 207 computer-based). Electronic applications accepted.

Columbia International University, Columbia Graduate School, Columbia, SC 29230-3122. Offers Bible teaching (MABT); Christian higher education leadership (Ed D); Christian school educational leadership (Ed D); counseling (MACN); curriculum and instruction (M Ed), including Christian school guidance, English as a second language, learning disabilities, school technology; early childhood and elementary education (MAT); educational administration (M Ed); teaching English as a foreign language (Certificate); teaching English as a foreign language and intercultural studies (MATF). Part-time and evening/weekend programs available. *Degree requirements:* For master's, internships, professional project. *Entrance requirements:* For master's, Minnesota Multiphasic Personality Inventory, MAT, minimum GPA of 2.7. Additional exam requirements/recommendations for international students: Required—TOEFL. Electronic applications accepted.

Concordia University, School of Graduate Studies, Faculty of Arts and Science, Department of Education, Program in Applied Linguistics, Montréal, QC H3G 1M8, Canada. Offers applied linguistics (MA); teaching English as a second language (Certificate).

Cornerstone University, Graduate Programs, Grand Rapids, MI 49525-5897. Offers business administration (MBA); education (MA Ed); management (MSM); teaching English to speakers of other languages (MA, Graduate Certificate). Programs also offered at Holland, Kalamazoo, and Troy, MI campuses. Part-time programs available. Postbaccalaureate distance learning degree programs offered. *Degree requirements:* For master's, comprehensive exam (for some programs), thesis (for some programs). *Entrance requirements:* For master's, minimum GPA of 2.5, 2 letters of reference. Additional exam requirements/recommendations for international students: Required—TOEFL (minimum score 575 paper-based; 235 computer-based). Electronic applications accepted.

Dallas Baptist University, Dorothy M. Bush College of Education, Program in Reading and English as a Second Language, Dallas, TX 75211-9299. Offers English as a second language (M Ed); master reading teacher (M Ed); reading specialist (M Ed). Part-time and evening/weekend programs available. *Entrance requirements:* For master's, GRE General Test, minimum GPA of 3.0. Additional exam requirements/recommendations for international students: Required—TOEFL, IELTS. Application fee: $25. *Expenses: Tuition:* Full-time $12,060; part-time $670 per credit hour. *Required fees:* $100; $50 per semester. *Financial support:* Federal Work-Study, institutionally sponsored loans, scholarships/grants, and tuition waivers (full and partial) available. Support available to part-time students. Financial award applicants required to submit FAFSA. *Unit head:* Amie Sarker, Director, 214-333-5200, Fax: 214-333-5551, E-mail: graduate@dbu.edu. *Application contact:* Kit P. Montgomery, Director of Graduate Programs, 214-333-5242, Fax: 214-333-5579, E-mail: graduate@dbu.edu. Web site: http://www3.dbu.edu/graduate/english_reading.asp.

Dallas Baptist University, Dorothy M. Bush College of Education, Teaching Program, Dallas, TX 75211-9299. Offers all-level (MAT); distance learning (MAT); elementary (MAT); English as a second language (MAT); Montessori (MAT); multisensory (MAT); secondary (MAT). Part-time and evening/weekend programs available. *Entrance requirements:* For master's, GRE General Test, minimum GPA of 3.0. Additional exam requirements/recommendations for international students: Required—TOEFL, IELTS. *Application deadline:* Applications are processed on a rolling basis. Application fee: $25. Electronic applications accepted. *Expenses: Tuition:* Full-time $12,060; part-time $670 per credit hour. *Required fees:* $100; $50 per semester. *Financial support:* Federal Work-Study, institutionally sponsored loans, scholarships/grants, and tuition waivers (full and partial) available. Support available to part-time students. Financial award applicants required to submit FAFSA. *Unit head:* Dara Owen, Acting Director, 214-333-5413, Fax: 214-333-5551, E-mail: graduate@dbu.edu. *Application contact:* Kit P. Montgomery, Director of Graduate Programs, 214-333-5242, Fax: 214-333-5579, E-mail: graduate@dbu.edu. Web site: http://www3.dbu.edu/graduate/mat.asp.

Dallas Baptist University, Gary Cook School of Leadership, Program in Global Leadership, Dallas, TX 75211-9299. Offers business communication (MA); East Asian studies (MA); ESL (MA); general studies (MA); global leadership (MA); global studies (MA); international business (MA); leading the nonprofit organization (MA); missions (MA); small group ministry (MA); MA/MA. Part-time and evening/weekend programs available. *Entrance requirements:* For master's, minimum GPA of 3.0. Additional exam requirements/recommendations for international students: Required—TOEFL, IELTS. Application fee: $25. *Expenses: Tuition:* Full-time $12,060; part-time $670 per credit hour. *Required fees:* $100; $50 per semester. *Financial support:* Federal Work-Study, institutionally sponsored loans, scholarships/grants, and tuition waivers (full and partial) available. Support available to part-time students. Financial award applicants required to submit FAFSA. *Unit head:* Dr. Bob Garrett, Director, 214-333-5508, Fax: 214-333-5689, E-mail: graduate@dbu.edu. *Application contact:* Kit P. Montgomery, Director of Graduate Programs, 214-333-5242, Fax: 214-333-5579, E-mail: graduate@dbu.edu. Web site: http://www3.dbu.edu/leadership/globalleadership.asp.

Dallas Baptist University, Liberal Arts Program, Dallas, TX 75211-9299. Offers arts (MLA); Christian ministry (MLA); East Asian studies (MLA); English (MLA); English as a second language (MLA); fine arts (MLA); history (MLA); missions (MLA); political science (MLA). Part-time and evening/weekend programs available. *Entrance requirements:* For master's, minimum GPA of 3.0. Additional exam requirements/recommendations for international students: Required—TOEFL. *Application deadline:* Applications are processed on a rolling basis. Application fee: $25. Electronic applications accepted. *Expenses: Tuition:* Full-time $12,060; part-time $670 per credit hour. *Required fees:* $100; $50 per semester. *Financial support:* Federal Work-Study, institutionally sponsored loans, scholarships/grants, and tuition waivers (full and partial) available. Support available to part-time students. Financial award applicants required to submit FAFSA. *Faculty research:* Milton and seventeenth century Puritans, inter-Biblical years, nineteenth century literature, Latin American and Texas history. *Unit head:* Angel Fogle, Director, 214-333-6830, Fax: 214-333-5558, E-mail: graduate@dbu.edu. *Application contact:* Kit P. Montgomery, Director of Graduate Programs, 214-333-5242, Fax: 214-333-5579, E-mail: graduate@dbu.edu. Web site: http://www3.dbu.edu/graduate/mla.asp.

Dallas Baptist University, Professional Development Program, Dallas, TX 75211-9299. Offers accounting (MA); church leadership (MA); counseling (MA); criminal justice (MA); English as a second language (MA); finance (MA); higher education (MA); leadership studies (MA); management (MA); management information systems (MA); marketing (MA); missions (MA); professional life coaching (MA). Part-time and evening/weekend programs available. *Entrance requirements:* For master's, minimum GPA of 3.0. Additional exam requirements/recommendations for international students: Required—TOEFL, IELTS. Application fee: $25. *Expenses: Tuition:* Full-time $12,060; part-time $670 per credit hour. *Required fees:* $100; $50 per semester. *Financial support:* Federal Work-Study, institutionally sponsored loans, scholarships/grants, and tuition waivers (full and partial) available. Support available to part-time students. Financial award applicants required to submit FAFSA. *Unit head:* Angela Fogle, Acting Director, 214-333-6830, Fax: 214-333-5558, E-mail: graduate@dbu.edu. *Application contact:* Kit P. Montgomery, Director of Graduate Programs, 214-333-5242, Fax: 214-333-5579, E-mail: graduate@dbu.edu. Web site: http://www3.dbu.edu/graduate/mapd.asp.

DePaul University, College of Liberal Arts and Sciences, Department of English, Chicago, IL 60614. Offers English (MA); teaching English to speakers of other languages (Certificate); writing and publishing (MA). Part-time and evening/weekend programs available. *Faculty:* 29 full-time (12 women). *Students:* 113 full-time (74 women), 73 part-time (58 women); includes 32 minority (12 Black or African American, non-Hispanic/Latino; 5 Asian, non-Hispanic/Latino; 11 Hispanic/Latino; 4 Two or more races, non-Hispanic/Latino), 5 international. Average age 28. 95 applicants, 56% accepted. In 2011, 100 master's awarded. *Degree requirements:* For master's, written exam. *Entrance requirements:* Additional exam requirements/recommendations for international students: Required—TOEFL. *Application deadline:* For fall admission, 7/1 priority date for domestic students; for winter admission, 10/1 priority date for domestic students; for spring admission, 2/1 priority date for domestic students. Applications are processed on a rolling basis. Application fee: $40. Electronic applications accepted. *Financial support:* In 2011–12, 2 research assistantships with full tuition reimbursements, 7 teaching assistantships with full tuition reimbursements (averaging $7,500 per year) were awarded; fellowships with partial tuition reimbursements, career-related internships or fieldwork, institutionally sponsored loans, scholarships/grants, tuition waivers (partial), and unspecified assistantships also available. Support available to part-time students. Financial award application deadline: 4/1. *Faculty research:* Rhetoric and composition, technical writing, creative writing, linguistics, literacy theory. *Unit head:* Dr. Janet Hickey, Chairperson, 773-325-4635, E-mail: jhicke11@depaul.edu. *Application contact:* Dr. Lesley Kordecki, Director, 773-325-1786, Fax: 773-325-8607, E-mail: lkordeck@depaul.edu.

DeSales University, Graduate Division, Program in Education, Center Valley, PA 18034-9568. Offers academic standards and reform (M Ed); academic standards for K-6 (M Ed); English as a second language (M Ed); instructional technology for K-12 (M Ed); special education (M Ed); teaching English to speakers of other languages (M Ed). Part-time and evening/weekend programs available. Postbaccalaureate distance learning degree programs offered (no on-campus study). *Degree requirements:* For master's, thesis project. *Entrance requirements:* Additional exam requirements/recommendations for international students: Required—TOEFL. *Application deadline:* Applications are processed on a rolling basis. Electronic applications accepted. Tuition and fees vary according to degree level. *Financial support:* Application deadline: 5/1. *Unit head:* Dr. Judith Rance-Roney, Interim Director, 610-282-1100 Ext. 1323, E-mail: judith.rance-roney@desales.edu. *Application contact:* Caryn Stopper, Director of Graduate Admissions, 610-282-1100 Ext. 1768, Fax: 610-282-0525, E-mail: caryn.stopper@desales.edu.

Dominican University, School of Education, River Forest, IL 60305-1099. Offers curriculum and instruction (MA Ed); early childhood education (MS); education (MAT); educational administration (MA); elementary (online) (MS); English as a second language (online) (MS); reading (online) (MS); special education (MS). Part-time and evening/weekend programs available. Postbaccalaureate distance learning degree programs offered (no on-campus study). *Faculty:* 19 full-time (13 women), 53 part-time/adjunct (41 women). *Students:* 24 full-time (19 women), 434 part-time (357 women); includes 95 minority (27 Black or African American, non-Hispanic/Latino; 1 American Indian or Alaska Native, non-Hispanic/Latino; 12 Asian, non-Hispanic/Latino; 48 Hispanic/Latino; 7 Two or more races, non-Hispanic/Latino), 1 international. Average age 33. 92 applicants, 99% accepted, 91 enrolled. In 2011, 267 master's awarded. *Entrance requirements:* For master's, Illinois certification test of basic skills. Additional exam requirements/recommendations for international students: Required—TOEFL (minimum score 550 paper-based; 213 computer-based; 79 iBT). *Application deadline:* Applications are processed on a rolling basis. Application fee: $25. *Expenses:* Contact institution. *Financial support:* Career-related internships or fieldwork, scholarships/grants, and tuition waivers (partial) available. Support available to part-time students. Financial award application deadline: 8/15; financial award applicants required to submit FAFSA. *Faculty research:* Governance of private education institutions, reading and language arts, inclusion, organizational planning, leadership and vision. *Unit head:* Dr. Colleen Reardon, Dean, 718-524-6643, Fax: 708-524-6665, E-mail: creardon@dom.edu. *Application contact:* Keven Hansen, Coordinator of Recruitment and Admissions, 708-524-6921, Fax: 708-524-6665, E-mail: educate@dom.edu. Web site: http://www.dom.edu/soe.

Duquesne University, School of Education, Department of Instruction and Leadership, Program in English as a Second Language, Pittsburgh, PA 15282-0001. Offers MS Ed. Part-time and evening/weekend programs available. *Faculty:* 3 full-time (1 woman), 2 part-time/adjunct (1 woman). *Students:* 13 full-time (12 women), 6 part-time (5 women); includes 4 minority (2 Black or African American, non-Hispanic/Latino; 1 Asian, non-Hispanic/Latino; 1 Two or more races, non-Hispanic/Latino), 7 international. Average age 30. 26 applicants, 73% accepted, 9 enrolled. In 2011, 8 degrees awarded. *Degree requirements:* For master's, thesis optional. *Entrance requirements:* For master's, bachelor's degree. Additional exam requirements/recommendations for international students: Required—TOEFL (minimum score 550 paper-based; 80 computer-based), IELTS (minimum score 7). *Application deadline:* For fall admission, 9/1 for domestic students; for spring admission, 1/1 for domestic students. Applications are processed on a rolling basis. Electronic applications accepted. Application fee is waived when completed online. *Expenses: Tuition:* Full-time $16,596; part-time $922 per credit. *Required fees:* $1584; $88 per credit. Tuition and fees vary according to program. *Unit head:* Dr. Nihat Polat, Assistant Professor, 412-396-4464, Fax: 412-396-1997, E-mail: polatn@duq.edu. *Application contact:* Michael Dolinger, Director of Student and Academic Services, 412-396-6647, Fax: 412-396-5585, E-mail: dolingerm@duq.edu. Web site: http://www.duq.edu/education/esl/index.cfm.

East Carolina University, Graduate School, Thomas Harriot College of Arts and Sciences, Department of English, Greenville, NC 27858-4353. Offers creative writing (MA); English studies (MA); linguistics (MA); literature (MA); multicultural and transnational literatures (MA, Certificate); rhetoric and composition (MA); teaching English to speakers of other languages (MA); teaching English to speaks of other languages (Certificate); technical and professional communication (MA); technical and professional discourse (PhD). Part-time and evening/weekend programs available. *Degree requirements:* For master's, one foreign language, comprehensive exam, thesis optional. *Entrance requirements:* For master's, GRE General Test, MAT (MA Ed). Additional exam requirements/recommendations for international students: Required—TOEFL. *Application deadline:* For fall admission, 6/1 priority date for domestic students; for spring admission, 10/15 for domestic students. Applications are processed on a rolling basis. Application fee: $50. *Expenses:* Tuition, state resident: full-time $3557; part-time $444.63 per semester hour. Tuition, nonresident: full-time $14,351; part-time $1793.88 per semester hour. *Required fees:* $2016; $252 per semester hour. Part-time tuition and fees vary according to course load, campus/location and program. *Financial support:* Research assistantships with partial tuition reimbursements, teaching assistantships with partial tuition reimbursements, and Federal Work-Study available. Support available to part-time students. Financial award application deadline: 6/1. *Unit head:* Dr. Jeffrey Johnson, Chair, 252-328-6041, E-mail: johnsonj@ecu.edu. *Application contact:* Dean of Graduate School, 252-328-6012, Fax: 252-328-6071, E-mail: gradschool@ecu.edu. Web site: http://www.ecu.edu/cs-cas/engl/graduate/.

Eastern Michigan University, Graduate School, College of Arts and Sciences, Department of World Languages, Program in Teaching English to Speakers of Other Languages, Ypsilanti, MI 48197. Offers MA, Graduate Certificate. Part-time and evening/weekend programs available. Postbaccalaureate distance learning degree programs offered (minimal on-campus study). *Students:* 6 full-time (5 women), 45 part-time (37 women); includes 5 minority (3 Black or African American, non-Hispanic/Latino; 2 Asian, non-Hispanic/Latino), 11 international. Average age 35. 54 applicants, 65% accepted, 18 enrolled. In 2011, 18 master's, 3 other advanced degrees awarded. *Degree requirements:* For master's, one foreign language. *Entrance requirements:* Additional exam requirements/recommendations for international students: Required—TOEFL. *Application deadline:* Applications are processed on a rolling basis. Application fee: $35. *Expenses:* Tuition, state resident: full-time $10,367; part-time $432 per credit hour. Tuition, nonresident: full-time $20,435; part-time $851 per credit hour. *Required fees:* $39 per credit hour. $46 per semester. One-time fee: $100. Tuition and fees vary according to course level, degree level and reciprocity agreements. *Financial support:* Fellowships, research assistantships with full tuition reimbursements, teaching assistantships with full tuition reimbursements, career-related internships or fieldwork, Federal Work-Study, institutionally sponsored loans, scholarships/grants, tuition waivers (partial), and unspecified assistantships available. Support available to part-time students. Financial award applicants required to submit FAFSA. *Unit head:* Dr. Rosemary Weston-Gil, Department Head, 734-487-0130, Fax: 734-487-3411, E-mail: rweston3@emich.edu. *Application contact:* Dr. Jo Ann Aebersold, Program Advisor, 734-487-0130, Fax: 734-487-3411, E-mail: jaebersol@emich.edu.

Eastern Nazarene College, Adult and Graduate Studies, Division of Teacher Education, Quincy, MA 02170. Offers administration (M Ed); early childhood education (M Ed, Certificate); elementary education (M Ed, Certificate); English as a second language (Certificate); instructional enrichment and development (Certificate); middle school education (M Ed, Certificate); moderate special needs education (Certificate); principal (Certificate); program development and supervision (Certificate); secondary education (M Ed, Certificate); special education administrator (Certificate); special needs (M Ed); supervisor (Certificate); teacher of reading (M Ed, Certificate). M Ed also available through weekend program for administration, special needs, and teacher of reading only. Part-time and evening/weekend programs available. *Entrance requirements:* Additional exam requirements/recommendations for international students: Required—TOEFL (minimum score 550 paper-based).

Eastern New Mexico University, Graduate School, College of Education and Technology, Department of Curriculum and Instruction, Portales, NM 88130. Offers bilingual education (M Ed); educational technology (M Ed); elementary education (M Ed); English as a second language (M Ed); pedagogy and learning (M Ed); professional technical education (M Ed); reading/literacy (M Ed). Part-time programs available. Postbaccalaureate distance learning degree programs offered (minimal on-campus study). *Degree requirements:* For master's, comprehensive exam, thesis optional. *Entrance requirements:* For master's, minimum GPA of 3.0, photocopy of teaching license, writing assessment, letter of recommendation. Additional exam requirements/recommendations for international students: Required—TOEFL (minimum score 550 paper-based; 213 computer-based; 79 iBT), IELTS (minimum score 6). Electronic applications accepted.

Eastern Washington University, Graduate Studies, College of Arts, Letters and Education, Department of English, Cheney, WA 99004-2431. Offers literature (MA); rhetoric, composition, and technical communication (MA); teaching English as a second language (MA). *Students:* 80 full-time (47 women), 6 part-time (4 women); includes 7 minority (1 Asian, non-Hispanic/Latino; 6 Hispanic/Latino), 1 international. 39 applicants, 46% accepted, 13 enrolled. In 2011, 16 master's awarded. *Degree requirements:* For master's, comprehensive exam, thesis or alternative. *Entrance requirements:* For master's, GRE General Test, minimum GPA of 3.0. *Application deadline:* For fall admission, 4/1 priority date for domestic students; for spring admission, 1/15 for domestic students. Applications are processed on a rolling basis. Application fee: $50. *Financial support:* In 2011–12, 25 teaching assistantships with partial tuition reimbursements (averaging $7,000 per year) were awarded; career-related internships or fieldwork, Federal Work-Study, institutionally sponsored loans, scholarships/grants, health care benefits, tuition waivers (partial), and unspecified assistantships also available. Support available to part-time students. Financial award application deadline: 2/1; financial award applicants required to submit FAFSA. *Unit head:* Dr. Teena Carnegie, Chair, 509-359-2400, E-mail: tcarnegie@ewu.edu. *Application contact:* Julie Marr, Advisor/Recruiter for Graduate Studies, 509-359-2491, E-mail: gradprograms@ewu.edu. Web site: http://www.ewu.edu/CALE/Programs/English.xml.

East Tennessee State University, School of Graduate Studies, College of Arts and Sciences, Department of Literature and Language, Johnson City, TN 37614. Offers English (MA); teaching English to speakers of other languages (Postbaccalaureate Certificate). Part-time and evening/weekend programs available. *Faculty:* 28 full-time (13 women). *Students:* 19 full-time (12 women), 2 part-time (1 woman); includes 4 minority (1 Black or African American, non-Hispanic/Latino; 2 Hispanic/Latino; 1 Two or more races, non-Hispanic/Latino). Average age 29. 32 applicants, 56% accepted, 13 enrolled. In 2011, 10 master's, 2 other advanced degrees awarded. *Degree requirements:* For master's, comprehensive exam, thesis optional. *Entrance requirements:* For master's, GRE General Test, minimum undergraduate GPA of 3.0 in English, writing samples. Additional exam requirements/recommendations for international students: Required—TOEFL (minimum score 550 paper-based; 213 computer-based; 79 iBT). *Application deadline:* For fall admission, 6/1 for domestic students, 4/30 for international students; for spring admission, 11/1 for domestic students, 9/30 for international students. Application fee: $35 ($45 for international students). Electronic applications accepted. *Expenses:* Tuition, state resident: full-time $7312; part-time $350 per credit hour. Tuition, nonresident: full-time $18,490; part-time $621 per credit hour. *Required fees:* $63 per credit hour. Tuition and fees vary according to course load and program. *Financial support:* In 2011–12, 19 students received support, including 10 research assistantships with full tuition reimbursements available (averaging $7,000 per year), 7 teaching assistantships with full tuition reimbursements available (averaging $7,000 per year); career-related internships or fieldwork, institutionally sponsored loans, scholarships/grants, and unspecified assistantships also available. Financial award application deadline: 7/1; financial award applicants required to submit FAFSA. *Faculty research:* Appalachian studies, women's studies, sports images in religion, British and American literature. *Total annual research expenditures:* $8,000. *Unit head:* Dr. Judith B. Slagle, Chair, 423-439-4339, Fax: 423-439-7193, E-mail: slagle@etsu.edu. *Application contact:* Bethany Glassbrenner, Graduate Specialist, 423-439-6165, Fax: 423-439-5624, E-mail: glassbrenner@etsu.edu.

Edgewood College, Program in Education, Madison, WI 53711-1997. Offers adult learning (MA Ed); bilingual teaching and learning (MA Ed); director of instruction (Certificate); director of special education and pupil services (Certificate); education (MA Ed); educational administration (MA Ed); educational leadership (Ed D); professional studies (MA Ed); program coordinator (Certificate); reading administration (MA Ed); school business administration (Certificate); school principalship K-12 (Certificate); special education (MA Ed); sustainability leadership (MA Ed); teaching and learning (MA Ed); teaching English to speakers of other languages (TESOL) (MA Ed). *Accreditation:* NCATE (one or more programs are accredited). Part-time and evening/weekend programs available. *Students:* 155 full-time (93 women), 152 part-time (116 women); includes 39 minority (13 Black or African American, non-Hispanic/Latino; 5 Asian, non-Hispanic/Latino; 17 Hispanic/Latino; 4 Two or more races, non-Hispanic/Latino), 9 international. Average age 36. In 2011, 39 master's, 32 doctorates awarded. *Degree requirements:* For master's, practicum, research project; for doctorate, comprehensive exam, thesis/dissertation. *Entrance requirements:* For master's, minimum GPA of 2.75, 2 letters of recommendation, personal statement; for doctorate, resume, letter of intent, 2 letters of recommendation, interview, writing sample. Additional exam requirements/recommendations for international students: Required—TOEFL (minimum score 525 paper-based; 197 computer-based; 72 iBT). *Application deadline:* For fall admission, 8/15 for domestic students, 5/1 for international students; for spring admission, 1/8 for domestic students, 11/1 for international students. Applications are processed on a rolling basis. Application fee: $25. Electronic applications accepted. *Expenses: Tuition:* Part-time $747 per credit. Part-time tuition and fees vary according to program. *Unit head:* Dr. Jane Belmore, Dean, 608-663-8336, Fax: 608-663-3291, E-mail: jbelmore@edgewood.edu. *Application contact:* Joann Eastman, Admissions Counselor, 608-663-3250, Fax: 608-663-2214, E-mail: gps@edgewood.edu. Web site: http://education.edgewood.edu/graduate.html.

Elms College, Division of Education, Chicopee, MA 01013-2839. Offers early childhood education (MAT); education (M Ed, CAGS); elementary education (MAT); English as a second language (MAT); reading (MAT); secondary education (MAT), including biology education, English education, Spanish education; special education (MAT). Part-time and evening/weekend programs available. *Degree requirements:* For master's, thesis (for some programs). *Entrance requirements:* For master's, Massachusetts Educators Certification Test, minimum GPA of 3.0; for CAGS, master's degree in education. Additional exam requirements/recommendations for international students: Required—TOEFL.

Emporia State University, Graduate School, College of Liberal Arts and Sciences, Department of English, Modern Languages and Journalism, Program in Teaching English to Speakers of Other Languages, Emporia, KS 66801-5087. Offers MA. Part-time programs available. *Students:* 2 full-time (both women), 19 part-time (12 women); includes 2 minority (1 Asian, non-Hispanic/Latino; 1 Two or more races, non-Hispanic/Latino), 3 international. 5 applicants, 40% accepted, 1 enrolled. In 2011, 12 master's awarded. *Degree requirements:* For master's, comprehensive exam, thesis optional. *Entrance requirements:* For master's, minimum undergraduate GPA of 2.75 over last 60 hours. Additional exam requirements/recommendations for international students: Required—TOEFL (minimum score 520 paper-based; 133 computer-based; 68 iBT). *Application deadline:* For fall admission, 8/15 priority date for domestic students. Applications are processed on a rolling basis. Application fee: $30 ($75 for international students). Electronic applications accepted. *Expenses:* Tuition, state resident: full-time $2342; part-time $195 per credit hour. Tuition, nonresident: full-time $7254; part-time $605 per credit hour. *Required fees:* $66 per credit hour. Tuition and fees vary according to campus/location. *Financial support:* Federal Work-Study, institutionally sponsored loans, health care benefits, and unspecified assistantships available. Financial award application deadline: 2/15. *Unit head:* Dr. Abdelilah Salim Sehlaoui, Associate Professor, 620-341-5237, E-mail: asehlaou@emporia.edu. *Application contact:* Mary Sewell, Admissions Coordinator, 800-950-GRAD, Fax: 620-341-5909, E-mail: msewell@emporia.edu.

Erikson Institute, Academic Programs, Chicago, IL 60654. Offers administration (Certificate); bilingual/ESL (Certificate); child development (MS); early childhood education (MS); infant mental health (Certificate); infant studies (Certificate); MS/MSW. MS/MSW offered jointly with Loyola University Chicago. Part-time and evening/weekend programs available. *Degree requirements:* For master's, comprehensive exam, internship; for Certificate, internship. *Entrance requirements:* For master's and Certificate, minimum GPA of 2.75. Additional exam requirements/recommendations for international students: Required—TOEFL. *Faculty research:* Assessment strategies from early childhood through elementary years; language, literacy, and the arts in children's development; inclusive special education; parent-child relationships; cognitive development.

Fairfield University, Graduate School of Education and Allied Professions, Fairfield, CT 06824-5195. Offers applied psychology (MA); bilingual education (CAS); clinical mental health counseling (MA, CAS); educational technology (MA); elementary education (MA); family studies (MA); marriage and family therapy (MA); school counseling (MA, CAS); school psychology (MA, CAS); special education (MA); teaching (Certificate); teaching and foundations (MA, CAS); TESOL foreign language and bilingual/multicultural education (MA, CAS). *Accreditation:* NCATE. Part-time and evening/weekend programs available. *Faculty:* 24 full-time (19 women). *Students:* 147 full-time (120 women), 391 part-time (321 women); includes 60 minority (13 Black or African American, non-Hispanic/Latino; 8 Asian, non-Hispanic/Latino; 35 Hispanic/Latino; 4 Two or more races, non-Hispanic/Latino), 1 international. Average age 34. 319 applicants, 48% accepted, 80 enrolled. In 2011, 185 master's, 20 other advanced degrees awarded. *Degree requirements:* For master's, comprehensive exam. *Entrance requirements:* For master's, PRAXIS I (for certification programs), minimum QPA of 3.0, 2 recommendations, resume. Additional exam requirements/recommendations for international students: Required—TOEFL (minimum score 550 paper-based; 213 computer-based; 84 iBT) or IELTS (minimum score 7.5). *Application deadline:* For fall admission, 2/15 for international students; for spring admission, 10/1 for international students. Application fee: $60. Electronic applications accepted. *Expenses: Tuition:* Part-time $600 per credit hour. *Required fees:* $25 per term. *Financial support:* In 2011–12, 45 students received support. Career-related internships or fieldwork and unspecified assistantships available. Financial award applicants required to submit FAFSA. *Faculty research:* Literacy, adolescent psychology, special education, early childhood education, teaching development. *Unit head:* Dr. Susan D. Franzosa, Dean, 203-254-4000 Ext. 4250, Fax: 203-254-4241, E-mail: sfranzosa@fairfield.edu. *Application contact:* Marianne Gumpper, Director of Graduate and Continuing Studies Admission, 203-254-4184, Fax: 203-254-4073, E-mail: gradadmis@fairfield.edu. Web site: http://www.fairfield.edu/gseap/gseap_grad_1.html.

Florida Atlantic University, College of Education, Department of Curriculum, Culture, and Educational Inquiry, Boca Raton, FL 33431-0991. Offers curriculum and instruction (Ed D, Ed S); early childhood education (M Ed); multicultural education (M Ed); teaching English to speakers of other languages (TESOL) (M Ed). *Faculty:* 14 full-time (11 women), 16 part-time/adjunct (13 women). *Students:* 28 full-time (21 women), 138 part-time (106 women); includes 46 minority (18 Black or African American, non-Hispanic/Latino; 1 American Indian or Alaska Native, non-Hispanic/Latino; 3 Asian, non-Hispanic/Latino; 23 Hispanic/Latino; 1 Two or more races, non-Hispanic/Latino), 7 international. Average age 36. 120 applicants, 53% accepted, 32 enrolled. In 2011, 33 master's, 2 doctorates awarded. *Application deadline:* For fall admission, 7/1 for domestic students, 2/15 for international students; for spring admission, 11/1 for domestic students, 7/15 for international students. *Expenses: Tuition, area resident:* Part-time $343.02 per credit hour. Tuition, state resident: full-time $8232. Tuition, nonresident: full-time $23,931; part-time $997.14 per credit hour. *Faculty research:* Multicultural education, early intervention strategies, family literacy, religious diversity in schools, early childhood curriculum. *Unit head:* Dr. James McLaughlin, Interim Chair, 561-297-3965, E-mail: jmclau17@fau.edu. *Application contact:* Dr. Eliah Watlington, Associate Dean, 561-296-8520, Fax: 261-297-2991, E-mail: ewatling@fau.edu. Web site: http://www.coe.fau.edu/academicdepartments/ccei/.

Florida International University, College of Education, Department of Curriculum and Instruction, Miami, FL 33199. Offers art education (MAT, MS, Ed D); curriculum and instruction (Ed S); curriculum development (MS); curriculum studies (PhD); early childhood education (MS, Ed D); elementary education (MS, Ed D); English education (MAT, MS, Ed D); foreign language education - teaching English to speakers of other languages (TESOL) (MS, Certificate), including foreign language education (Certificate), teaching English (MS); French education - initial teacher preparation (MAT); international and intercultural development education (Ed D); international and intercultural developmental education (MS); language, literacy and culture (PhD); learning technologies (MS, Ed D, PhD); mathematics education (MAT, MS, Ed D, PhD); modern language education/bilingual education (MS, Ed D); physical education (MS); reading education (MS, Ed D); science education (MAT, MS, Ed D, PhD); social studies education (MAT, MS, Ed D); Spanish education - initial teacher preparation (MAT); special education (MS). Part-time and evening/weekend programs available. *Degree requirements:* For doctorate, comprehensive exam, thesis/dissertation. *Entrance requirements:* For master's, GRE General Test, Florida General Knowledge Test or Florida College Level Academic Skills Test; for doctorate and other advanced degree, GRE General Test. Additional exam requirements/recommendations for international students: Required—TOEFL (minimum score 550 paper-based; 213 computer-based; 80 iBT), IELTS (minimum score 6.3). Electronic applications accepted.

Florida International University, College of Education, Department of Educational Leadership and Policy Studies, Miami, FL 33199. Offers adult education (MS); adult education in human resource development (Ed D); clinical mental health counseling (MS); conflict resolution and consensus building (Certificate); counselor education (MS); educational administration and supervision (Ed D); educational leadership (MS, Certificate, Ed S); higher education (Ed D); higher education administration (MS); human resource development (MS); instruction in urban settings (MS); international/intercultural education (MS); learning technologies (MS); multicultural-bilingual (MS); multicultural-TESOL (MS); recreation and sport management (MS); recreation therapy (MS); rehabilitation counseling (MS); school counseling (MS); school psychology (Ed S); urban education (MS). Part-time and evening/weekend programs available. *Degree requirements:* For doctorate, thesis/dissertation. *Entrance requirements:* For master's, minimum GPA of 3.0; for doctorate and other advanced degree, GRE General Test. Additional exam requirements/recommendations for international students: Required—TOEFL (minimum score 550 paper-based; 213 computer-based; 80 iBT), IELTS (minimum score 6.3). Electronic applications accepted.

Fordham University, Graduate School of Education, Division of Curriculum and Teaching, New York, NY 10023. Offers adult education (MS, MSE); bilingual teacher education (MSE); curriculum and teaching (MSE); early childhood education (MSE); elementary education (MST); language, literacy, and learning (PhD); reading education (MSE, Adv C); secondary education (MAT, MSE); special education (MSE, Adv C); teaching English as a second language (MSE). *Accreditation:* NCATE. *Degree requirements:* For doctorate, thesis/dissertation; for Adv C, thesis. *Entrance requirements:* For doctorate, MAT, GRE General Test. *Expenses: Tuition:* Full-time $30,480; part-time $1270 per credit. *Required fees:* $586; $293 per semester.

Framingham State University, Division of Graduate and Continuing Education, Program in the Teaching of English as a Second Language, Framingham, MA 01701-9101. Offers M Ed.

Fresno Pacific University, Graduate Programs, School of Education, Division of Language, Literacy, and Culture, Program in Reading, Fresno, CA 93702-4709. Offers reading/English as a second language (MA Ed); reading/language arts (MA Ed). Part-time and evening/weekend programs available. *Degree requirements:* For master's, thesis or alternative. *Entrance requirements:* Additional exam requirements/recommendations for international students: Required—TOEFL (minimum score 550 paper-based; 213 computer-based). Electronic applications accepted.

Fresno Pacific University, Graduate Programs, School of Education, Division of Language, Literacy, and Culture, Program in Teaching English to Speakers of Other Languages, Fresno, CA 93702-4709. Offers MA. Part-time and evening/weekend programs available. *Degree requirements:* For master's, thesis. *Entrance requirements:* For master's, GMAT, MAT, GRE, interview, 2 writing samples. Additional exam requirements/recommendations for international students: Required—TOEFL (minimum score 550 paper-based; 213 computer-based). Electronic applications accepted.

Furman University, Graduate Division, Department of Education, Greenville, SC 29613. Offers curriculum and instruction (MA); early childhood education (MA); educational leadership (Ed S); English as a second language (MA); literacy (MA); school leadership (MA); special education (MA). *Accreditation:* NCATE. Part-time programs available. Postbaccalaureate distance learning degree programs offered (minimal on-campus study). *Faculty:* 14 full-time (8 women), 6 part-time/adjunct (4 women). *Students:* 237 part-time (188 women); includes 27 minority (22 Black or African American, non-Hispanic/Latino; 1 Asian, non-Hispanic/Latino; 3 Hispanic/Latino; 1 Native Hawaiian or other Pacific Islander, non-Hispanic/Latino). Average age 29. 97 applicants, 100% accepted, 90 enrolled. In 2011, 34 master's awarded. *Degree requirements:* For master's, comprehensive exam (for some programs), thesis or alternative. *Entrance requirements:* For master's, PRAXIS II. *Application deadline:* For fall admission, 8/1 priority date for domestic students, 7/15 for international students; for spring admission, 12/1 priority date for domestic students, 12/1 for international students. Applications are processed on a rolling basis. Application fee: $50. *Financial support:* Scholarships/grants available. Financial award application deadline: 5/15; financial award applicants required to submit FAFSA. *Faculty research:* Literacy, pedagogy and practice, social justice, advanced leadership, achievement in high poverty schools. *Unit head:* Dr. Nelly Hecker, Head, 864-294-3385. *Application contact:* Helen Reynolds, Department Assistant, 864-294-2213, Fax: 864-294-3579, E-mail: helen.reynolds@furman.edu. Web site: http://www.furman.edu/gradstudies/.

Gannon University, School of Graduate Studies, College of Humanities, Education, and Social Sciences, School of Education, Program in English as a Second Language, Erie, PA 16541-0001. Offers Certificate. Part-time and evening/weekend programs available. *Students:* 4 part-time (all women). Average age 30. 5 applicants, 100% accepted, 2 enrolled. *Degree requirements:* For Certificate, comprehensive exam. *Entrance requirements:* For degree, valid instructional certificate, letters of recommendation, minimum GPA of 3.0, bachelor's degree. Additional exam requirements/recommendations for international students: Required—TOEFL (minimum score 79 iBT). *Application deadline:* Applications are processed on a rolling basis. Application fee: $25. Electronic applications accepted. *Expenses:* Contact institution. *Financial support:* Application deadline: 7/1; applicants required to submit FAFSA. *Faculty research:* Academic transition of ESL students, international education models, international teacher training, program evaluation, instructional leadership. *Unit head:* Dr. Kathleen Kingston, Director, 814-871-5626, E-mail: kingston002@gannon.edu. *Application contact:* Kara Morgan, Director of Graduate Admissions, 814-871-5831, Fax: 814-871-5827, E-mail: graduate@gannon.edu.

George Fox University, School of Education, Educational Foundations and Leadership Program, Newberg, OR 97132-2697. Offers continuing administrator license (Certificate); curriculum and instruction (M Ed); educational leadership (M Ed, Ed D); ESOL (Certificate); higher education (M Ed); initial administrator license (Certificate); instructional leadership (Ed S); library media (M Ed, Certificate); literacy (M Ed); reading (M Ed); secondary education (M Ed). *Accreditation:* NCATE. Part-time and evening/weekend programs available. Postbaccalaureate distance learning degree programs offered (minimal on-campus study). *Faculty:* 10 full-time (3 women), 6 part-time/adjunct (3 women). *Students:* 2 full-time (both women), 111 part-time (83 women); includes 16 minority (2 American Indian or Alaska Native, non-Hispanic/Latino; 6 Asian, non-Hispanic/Latino; 7 Hispanic/Latino; 1 Native Hawaiian or other Pacific Islander, non-Hispanic/Latino), 3 international. Average age 39. 44 applicants, 98% accepted, 43 enrolled. In 2011, 34 master's, 7 doctorates, 76 Certificates awarded. *Degree requirements:* For master's, thesis (for some programs); for doctorate, comprehensive exam, thesis/dissertation, project. *Entrance requirements:* For master's, minimum undergraduate GPA of 3.0 during previous 2 years of course work, resume, 3 professional recommendations on university forms, official transcripts; for doctorate, GRE, master's degree with minimum GPA of 3.25, 3 years of relevant professional experience, interview, personal essay, scholarly work, 3 professional recommendations on university forms along with 3 written letters of recommendation, official transcripts. Additional exam requirements/recommendations for international students: Required—TOEFL (minimum score 577 paper-based; 233 computer-based; 90 iBT). *Application deadline:* For fall admission, 7/15 for domestic and international students; for winter admission, 11/1 for domestic and international students; for spring admission, 4/1 for domestic and international students. Applications are processed on a rolling basis. Application fee: $40. Electronic applications accepted. *Expenses:* Contact institution. *Financial support:* Career-related internships or fieldwork available. Financial award applicants required to submit FAFSA. *Unit head:* Dr. Scot Headley, Professor/Chair, 503-554-2836, E-mail: sheadley@georgefox.edu. *Application contact:* Alex Martin, Admissions Counselor, 800-631-0921, Fax: 503-554-3110, E-mail: amartin@georgefox.edu. Web site: http://www.georgefox.edu/education/index.html.

George Fox University, School of Education, Master of Arts in Teaching Program, Newberg, OR 97132-2697. Offers teaching (MAT); teaching plus ESOL (MAT); teaching plus ESOL/bilingual (MAT); teaching plus reading (MAT). Program offered in Oregon and Idaho. Part-time and evening/weekend programs available. *Faculty:* 17 full-time (13 women), 19 part-time/adjunct (16 women). *Students:* 115 full-time (75 women), 55 part-time (36 women); includes 16 minority (1 Black or African American, non-Hispanic/Latino; 11 Asian, non-Hispanic/Latino; 3 Hispanic/Latino; 1 Two or more races, non-Hispanic/Latino). Average age 31. 55 applicants, 76% accepted, 32 enrolled. In 2011, 156 master's awarded. *Entrance requirements:* For master's, CBEST, PRAXIS PPST, or EAS, bachelor's degree with minimum GPA of 3.0 in last two years of course work from regionally-accredited college or university, official transcripts. Additional exam requirements/recommendations for international students: Required—TOEFL (minimum score 577 paper-based; 233 computer-based; 90 iBT), IELTS (minimum score 7). *Application deadline:* For fall admission, 6/1 for domestic and international students; for winter admission, 10/1 for domestic and international students; for spring admission, 2/1 for domestic and international students. Applications are processed on a rolling basis. Application fee: $40. Electronic applications accepted. *Expenses:* Contact institution. *Financial support:* In 2011–12, 20 students received support. Scholarships/grants available. Financial award application deadline: 2/1; financial award applicants required to submit FAFSA. *Unit head:* Carol Brazo, Chair, 503-554-6115, E-mail: cbrazo@georgefox.edu. *Application contact:* Beth Molzahn, Admissions Counselor, 800-631-0921, Fax: 503-554-3110, E-mail: mat@georgefox.edu. Web site: http://www.georgefox.edu/soe/mat/.

George Mason University, College of Humanities and Social Sciences, Department of English, Fairfax, VA 22030. Offers creative writing (MFA); English (MA); folklore studies (Certificate); linguistics (PhD); professional writing and rhetoric (Certificate); teaching English as a second language (Certificate). *Faculty:* 81 full-time (45 women), 36 part-time/adjunct (23 women). *Students:* 111 full-time (69 women), 159 part-time (116 women); includes 38 minority (10 Black or African American, non-Hispanic/Latino; 1 American Indian or Alaska Native, non-Hispanic/Latino; 13 Asian, non-Hispanic/Latino; 9 Hispanic/Latino; 5 Two or more races, non-Hispanic/Latino), 12 international. Average age 31. 391 applicants, 51% accepted, 87 enrolled. In 2011, 82 master's, 14 other advanced degrees awarded. *Degree requirements:* For master's, thesis (for some programs), proficiency in a foreign language by course work or translation test. *Entrance requirements:* For master's, official transcripts; expanded goals statement; writing sample; portfolio; 2 letters of recommendation; for doctorate, GRE, expanded goals statement; 3 letters of recommendation; writing sample; introductory course in linguistics; official transcripts; for Certificate, official transcripts; expanded goals statement; 3 letters of recommendation; portfolio and writing sample (professional writing and rhetoric); resume and writing sample (folklore). Additional exam requirements/recommendations for international students: Required—TOEFL (minimum score 570 paper-based; 230 computer-based; 88 iBT), IELTS, Pearson Test of English. *Application deadline:* For fall admission, 3/15 priority date for domestic students; for spring admission, 10/15 priority date for domestic students. Application fee: $65 ($80 for international students). Electronic applications accepted. *Expenses:* Tuition, state resident: full-time $8750; part-time $364.58 per credit. Tuition, nonresident: full-time $24,092; part-time $1003.83 per credit. *Required fees:* $2514; $104.75 per credit. *Financial support:* In 2011–12, 57 students received support, including 3 fellowships with full tuition reimbursements available (averaging $18,000 per year), 6 research assistantships with full and partial tuition reimbursements available (averaging $10,896 per year), 49 teaching assistantships with full and partial tuition reimbursements available (averaging $11,099 per year); career-related internships or fieldwork, Federal Work-Study, scholarships/grants, unspecified assistantships, and health care benefits (full-time research or teaching assistantship recipients) also available. Support available to part-time students. Financial award application deadline: 3/1; financial award applicants required to submit FAFSA. *Faculty research:* Literature, professional writing and editing, writing of fiction or poetry. *Total annual research expenditures:* $1.1 million. *Unit head:* Robert Matz, Chair, 703-993-1170, Fax: 703-993-1161, E-mail: rmatz@gmu.edu. *Application contact:* Diane Swain, Graduate Program Admissions, 703-993-1185, Fax: 703-993-1161, E-mail: dswain6@gmu.edu. Web site: http://english.gmu.edu.

Georgetown University, Graduate School of Arts and Sciences, Department of Linguistics, Washington, DC 20057. Offers bilingual education (Certificate); language and communication (MA); linguistics (MS, PhD), including applied linguistics, computational linguistics, sociolinguistics, theoretical linguistics; teaching English as a second language (MAT, Certificate); teaching English as a second language and bilingual education (MAT). Terminal master's awarded for partial completion of doctoral program. *Degree requirements:* For master's, one foreign language, comprehensive exam, optional research project; for doctorate, 2 foreign languages, comprehensive exam, thesis/dissertation. *Entrance requirements:* For master's and doctorate, 18 undergraduate credits in a foreign language. Additional exam requirements/recommendations for international students: Required—TOEFL.

Georgia State University, College of Education, Department of Middle-Secondary Education and Instructional Technology, Program in Reading Instruction, Atlanta, GA 30302-3083. Offers reading, language and literacy (M Ed); reading, language, and literacy (PhD, Ed S); teaching English as a second language (M Ed). *Accreditation:* NCATE. Part-time and evening/weekend programs available. *Degree requirements:* For master's, comprehensive exam; for Ed S, project/exam. *Entrance requirements:* For master's, GRE General Test, minimum GPA of 2.5; for Ed S, GRE General Test or MAT, minimum graduate GPA of 3.25. *Faculty research:* Language development, attribution theory, linguistics.

Gonzaga University, Program in Teaching English as a Second Language, Spokane, WA 99258. Offers MATESL. Electronic applications accepted.

Grand Valley State University, College of Education, Programs in General Education, Allendale, MI 49401-9403. Offers adult and higher education (M Ed); early childhood education (M Ed); educational differentiation (M Ed); educational leadership (M Ed); educational technology integration (M Ed); elementary education (M Ed); middle level education (M Ed); school library media services (M Ed); secondary level education (M Ed); teaching English to speakers of other languages (M Ed). Part-time and evening/weekend programs available. Postbaccalaureate distance learning degree programs offered (minimal on-campus study). *Degree requirements:* For master's, thesis. *Entrance requirements:* For master's, GRE General Test or minimum GPA of 3.0. Additional exam requirements/recommendations for international students: Required—TOEFL. Electronic applications accepted. *Faculty research:* Effectiveness of technology in education, parental involvement, effective teaching, effective schools research.

Greensboro College, Program in Teaching English to Speakers of Other Languages, Greensboro, NC 27401-1875. Offers MA. *Accreditation:* NCATE. Part-time and evening/weekend programs available. *Degree requirements:* For master's, thesis, portfolio. *Entrance requirements:* For master's, GRE or MAT, 2 letters of reference. Additional exam requirements/recommendations for international students: Required—TOEFL (minimum score 550 paper-based; 213 computer-based). Electronic applications accepted.

Hamline University, School of Education, St. Paul, MN 55104-1284. Offers education (MA Ed, Ed D); English as a second language (MA); literacy education (MA); natural science and environmental education (MA Ed); teaching (MAT). *Accreditation:* NCATE (one or more programs are accredited). Part-time and evening/weekend programs available. Postbaccalaureate distance learning degree programs offered (no on-campus study). *Faculty:* 33 full-time (24 women), 106 part-time/adjunct (77 women). *Students:* 319 full-time (221 women), 717 part-time (524 women); includes 88 minority (30 Black or African American, non-Hispanic/Latino; 2 American Indian or Alaska Native, non-Hispanic/Latino; 26 Asian, non-Hispanic/Latino; 27 Hispanic/Latino; 3 Two or more races, non-Hispanic/Latino), 21 international. Average age 32. 468 applicants, 76% accepted, 259 enrolled. In 2011, 197 master's, 10 doctorates awarded. *Degree requirements:* For master's, thesis, foreign language (for MA in English as a second language only); for doctorate, comprehensive exam, thesis/dissertation. *Entrance requirements:* For master's, written essay, official transcripts, 2 letters of recommendation, minimum GPA of 2.5 from bachelor's work; for doctorate, personal statement, master's degree, 3 years experience, 3 letters of recommendation, writing sample, interview. Additional exam requirements/recommendations for international students: Required—TOEFL (minimum score 625 paper-based; 107 computer-based; 75 iBT) or IELTS. *Application deadline:* Applications are processed on a rolling basis. Application fee: $0 ($100 for international students). Electronic applications accepted. *Expenses:* *Tuition:* Full-time $3720; part-time $465 per credit. *Required fees:* $28 per year. Tuition and fees vary according to degree level, campus/location and program. *Financial support:* Federal Work-Study and scholarships/grants available. Support available to part-time students. Financial award applicants required to submit FAFSA. *Faculty research:* Adult basic education, service-learning, teacher dispositions, diversity, technology. *Unit head:* Dr. Larry Harris, Interim Dean, 651-523-2600, Fax: 651-523-2489, E-mail: lharris02@gw.hamline.edu. *Application contact:* Michael Hand, Assistant Director, Graduate Admission, 651-523-2900, Fax: 651-523-3058, E-mail: mhand01@gw.hamline.edu. Web site: http://www.hamline.edu/education.

Harding University, College of Education, Searcy, AR 72149-0001. Offers advanced studies in teaching and learning (M Ed); art (MSE); behavioral science (MSE); counseling (MS, Ed S); early childhood special education (M Ed, MSE); education (MSE); educational leadership (M Ed, Ed S); elementary education (M Ed); English (MSE); French (MSE); history/social science (MSE); kinesiology (MSE); math (MSE); reading (M Ed); secondary education (M Ed); Spanish (MSE); teaching (MAT); teaching English as a second language (MSE). *Accreditation:* NCATE. Part-time and evening/weekend programs available. *Faculty:* 9 full-time (2 women), 48 part-time/adjunct (26 women). *Students:* 100 full-time (77 women), 333 part-time (239 women); includes 76 minority (59 Black or African American, non-Hispanic/Latino; 1 Asian, non-Hispanic/Latino; 10 Hispanic/Latino; 6 Two or more races, non-Hispanic/Latino), 2 international. Average age 36. 93 applicants, 91% accepted, 83 enrolled. In 2011, 159 master's, 10 other advanced degrees awarded. *Degree requirements:* For master's, comprehensive exam (for some programs), thesis optional, portfolio(s); for Ed S, comprehensive exam, portfolio, project. *Entrance requirements:* For master's, GRE, MAT, PRAXIS; for Ed S, MAT or GRE. Additional exam requirements/recommendations for international students: Required—TOEFL (minimum score 550 paper-based; 79 iBT). *Application deadline:* For fall admission, 8/1 for domestic and international students; for spring admission, 1/1 for domestic and international students. Applications are processed on a rolling basis. Application fee: $35. *Expenses:* *Tuition:* Full-time $10,512; part-time $584 per credit hour. *Required fees:* $500; $25 per credit hour. Tuition and fees vary according to course load, degree level and program. *Financial support:* In 2011–12, 37 students received support. Unspecified assistantships available. *Faculty research:* Reading, comprehension, school violence, educational technology, behavior, college choice, differentiated instruction, brain-based teaching. *Unit head:* Dr. Clara Carroll, Chair, 501-279-4501, Fax: 501-279-4083, E-mail: ccarroll@harding.edu. *Application contact:* Information Contact, 501-279-4315, E-mail: gradstudiesedu@harding.edu. Web site: http://www.harding.edu/education/grad.html.

Hawai`i Pacific University, College of Humanities and Social Sciences, Program in Teaching English to Speakers of Other Languages, Honolulu, HI 96813. Offers MA. Part-time and evening/weekend programs available. *Faculty:* 7 full-time (5 women), 2 part-time/adjunct (both women). *Students:* 39 full-time (32 women), 12 part-time (9 women); includes 35 minority (3 Black or African American, non-Hispanic/Latino; 18 Asian, non-Hispanic/Latino; 2 Hispanic/Latino; 1 Native Hawaiian or other Pacific Islander, non-Hispanic/Latino; 11 Two or more races, non-Hispanic/Latino). Average age 33. 42 applicants, 95% accepted, 26 enrolled. In 2011, 13 master's awarded. *Entrance requirements:* Additional exam requirements/recommendations for international students: Recommended—TOEFL (minimum score 550 paper-based; 213 computer-based; 80 iBT), TWE (minimum score 5). *Application deadline:* For fall admission, 2/15 priority date for domestic students; for spring admission, 10/15 priority date for domestic students. Applications are processed on a rolling basis. Application fee: $50. Electronic applications accepted. *Expenses: Tuition:* Full-time $13,230; part-time $735 per credit. Tuition and fees vary according to course load and program. *Financial support:* In 2011–12, 24 students received support. Career-related internships or fieldwork, Federal Work-Study, scholarships/grants, tuition waivers, and unspecified assistantships available. Financial award application deadline: 3/1; financial award applicants required to submit FAFSA. *Unit head:* Dr. Carlos Juarez, Dean, 808-566-2493, Fax: 808-544-0834, E-mail: cjuarez@hpu.edu. *Application contact:* Chad Schempp, Director of Graduate Admissions, 808-543-8035, Fax: 808-544-0280, E-mail: graduate@hpu.edu. Web site: http://www.hpu.edu/MATESL/.

See Display below and Close-Up on page 1309.

Heritage University, Graduate Programs in Education, Program in Professional Studies, Toppenish, WA 98948-9599. Offers bilingual education/ESL (M Ed); biology (M Ed); English and literature (M Ed); reading/literacy (M Ed); special education (M Ed). Part-time and evening/weekend programs available. *Degree requirements:* For master's, comprehensive exam (for some programs), thesis (for some programs).

Hofstra University, College of Liberal Arts and Sciences, Programs in Forensic and Applied Linguistics, Hempstead, NY 11549. Offers applied linguistics (TESOL) (MA); linguistics (MA), including forensic linguistics. Part-time and evening/weekend programs available. *Faculty:* 1 full-time (0 women), 8 part-time/adjunct (4 women). *Students:* 21 full-time (14 women), 4 part-time (all women); includes 5 minority (1 Black or African American, non-Hispanic/Latino; 1 Asian, non-Hispanic/Latino; 3 Hispanic/Latino), 2 international. Average age 30. 34 applicants, 76% accepted, 14 enrolled. In 2011, 3 master's awarded. *Degree requirements:* For master's, thesis, 36 credits; capstone; minimum GPA of 3.0. *Entrance requirements:* For master's, bachelor's degree in related area; interview; 2 letters of recommendation. Additional exam requirements/recommendations for international students: Required—TOEFL (minimum score 550 paper-based; 213 computer-based; 80 iBT). *Application deadline:* Applications are processed on a rolling basis. Application fee: $70 ($75 for international students). Electronic applications accepted. *Expenses: Tuition:* Full-time $18,990; part-time $1055 per credit hour. *Required fees:* $970. Tuition and fees vary according to program. *Financial support:* In 2011–12, 14 students received support, including 1 fellowship with full and partial tuition reimbursement available (averaging $3,000 per year), 1 research assistantship with full and partial tuition reimbursement available (averaging $12,550 per year); Federal Work-Study, institutionally sponsored loans, scholarships/grants, tuition waivers (full and partial), and unspecified assistantships also available. Support available to part-time students. Financial award applicants required to submit FAFSA. *Faculty research:* Application of linguistics to forensic data, interrogation techniques and invalid confessions, authorship analysis, forensic linguistically-enhanced threat assessment, second language acquisition and writing. *Unit head:* Dr. George L. Greaney, Program Director, 516-463-5651, E-mail: cllglg@hofstra.edu. *Application contact:* Carol Drummer, Dean of Graduate Admissions, 516-463-4876, Fax: 516-463-4664, E-mail: gradstudent@hofstra.edu. Web site: http://www.hofstra.edu/hclas.

Hofstra University, School of Education, Health, and Human Services, Programs in Teaching (K-12), Hempstead, NY 11549. Offers bilingual education (MA); bilingual extension (Advanced Certificate), including education/speech language pathology, intensive teacher institute; family and consumer science (MS Ed); fine art and music education (Advanced Certificate); fine arts education (MA, MS Ed); mentoring and coaching for teachers (Advanced Certificate); middle childhood extension (Advanced Certificate), including grades 5-6 or 7-9; music education (MA, MS Ed); teaching languages other than English and TESOL (MS Ed); TESOL (MS Ed, Advanced Certificate), including intensive teacher institute (Advanced Certificate), TESOL (Advanced Certificate); wind conducting (MA). Part-time and evening/weekend programs available. *Students:* 54 full-time (48 women), 60 part-time (53 women); includes 30 minority (10 Black or African American, non-Hispanic/Latino; 9 Asian, non-Hispanic/Latino; 11 Hispanic/Latino), 8 international. Average age 29. 109 applicants, 76% accepted, 43 enrolled. In 2011, 71 master's, 42 other advanced degrees awarded. *Degree requirements:* For master's, one foreign language, thesis (for some programs), electronic portfolio, Tk20 portfolios, minimum GPA of 3.0. *Entrance requirements:* For master's, 2 letters of recommendation, portfolio, teacher certification (MA), essay; for Advanced Certificate, 2 letters of recommendation, interview, teaching certificate, essay. Additional exam requirements/recommendations for international students: Required—TOEFL (minimum score 550 paper-based; 213 computer-based; 80 iBT). *Application deadline:* Applications are processed on a rolling basis. Application fee: $70 ($75 for international students). Electronic applications accepted. *Expenses: Tuition:* Full-time $18,990; part-time $1055 per credit hour. *Required fees:* $970. Tuition and fees vary according to program. *Financial support:* In 2011–12, 39 students received support, including 13 fellowships with full and partial tuition reimbursements available (averaging $3,347 per year), 2 research assistantships with full and partial tuition reimbursements available (averaging $7,363 per year); career-related internships or fieldwork, Federal Work-Study, institutionally sponsored loans, scholarships/grants, tuition waivers (full and partial), and unspecified assistantships also available. Support available to part-time students. Financial award applicants required to submit FAFSA. *Faculty research:* The teacher/artist, interdisciplinary curriculum, applied linguistics, structural inequalities, creativity. *Unit head:* Dr. Esther Fusco, Chairperson, 516-463-7704, Fax: 516-463-6196, E-mail: catezf@hofstra.edu. *Application contact:* Carol Drummer, Dean of Graduate Admissions, 516-463-4876, Fax: 516-463-4664, E-mail: gradstudent@hofstra.edu. Web site: http://www.hofstra.edu/education/.

Hofstra University, School of Education, Health, and Human Services, Programs in Teaching - Secondary Education, Hempstead, NY 11549. Offers business education (MS Ed); education technology (Advanced Certificate); English education (MA, MS Ed); foreign language and TESOL (MS Ed); foreign language education (MA, MS Ed), including French, German, Russian, Spanish; mathematics education (MA, MS Ed); science education (MA, MS Ed), including biology, chemistry, earth science, geology, physics; secondary education (Advanced Certificate); social studies education (MA, MS Ed). Part-time and evening/weekend programs available. Postbaccalaureate distance learning degree programs offered (minimal on-campus study). *Students:* 72

full-time (47 women), 51 part-time (30 women); includes 21 minority (9 Black or African American, non-Hispanic/Latino; 7 Asian, non-Hispanic/Latino; 5 Hispanic/Latino). Average age 28. 103 applicants, 91% accepted, 41 enrolled. In 2011, 86 master's, 6 other advanced degrees awarded. *Degree requirements:* For master's, one foreign language, comprehensive exam (for some programs), thesis (for some programs), exit project, electronic portfolio, student teaching, fieldwork, curriculum project, minimum GPA of 3.0; for Advanced Certificate, 3 foreign languages, comprehensive exam (for some programs), thesis project, minimum GPA of 3.0. *Entrance requirements:* For master's, 2 letters of recommendation, teacher certification (MA), essay; for Advanced Certificate, 2 letters of recommendation, essay. Additional exam requirements/recommendations for international students: Required—TOEFL (minimum score 550 paper-based; 213 computer-based; 80 iBT). *Application deadline:* Applications are processed on a rolling basis. Application fee: $70 ($75 for international students). Electronic applications accepted. *Expenses: Tuition:* Full-time $18,990; part-time $1055 per credit hour. *Required fees:* $970. Tuition and fees vary according to program. *Financial support:* In 2011–12, 90 students received support, including 13 fellowships with full and partial tuition reimbursements available (averaging $3,202 per year), 1 research assistantship with full and partial tuition reimbursement available (averaging $11,645 per year); career-related internships or fieldwork, Federal Work-Study, institutionally sponsored loans, scholarships/grants, tuition waivers (full and partial), and unspecified assistantships also available. Support available to part-time students. Financial award applicants required to submit FAFSA. *Faculty research:* Appropriate content and pedagogy in secondary school disciplines, appropriate pedagogy in secondary school disciplines, adolescent development, secondary school organization, alternative secondary school programs. *Unit head:* Dr. Esther Fusco, Chairperson, 516-463-7704, Fax: 516-463-6196, E-mail: catezf@hofstra.edu. *Application contact:* Carol Drummer, Dean of Graduate Admissions, 516-463-4876, Fax: 516-463-4664, E-mail: gradstudent@hofstra.edu. Web site: http://www.hofstra.edu/education/.

Holy Names University, Graduate Division, Department of Education, Oakland, CA 94619-1699. Offers educational therapy (Certificate); level 1 education specialist mild/moderate disabilities (Credential); level 2 education specialist mild/moderate disabilities (Credential); multiple subject teaching credential (Credential); single subject teaching credential (Credential); teaching English as a second language (TESL) (M Ed); urban education: educational therapy (M Ed); urban education: K-12 education (M Ed); urban education: special education (M Ed). Part-time programs available. *Degree requirements:* For master's, comprehensive exam, research paper, thesis or project. *Entrance requirements:* For master's, minimum undergraduate GPA of 2.6 overall, 3.0 in major. Additional exam requirements/recommendations for international students: Required—TOEFL (minimum score 550 paper-based; 213 computer-based; 80 iBT). *Faculty research:* Cognitive development, language development, learning handicaps.

Houston Baptist University, College of Education and Behavioral Sciences, Programs in Education, Houston, TX 77074-3298. Offers bilingual education (M Ed); counselor education (M Ed); curriculum and instruction (M Ed); educational administration (M Ed); educational diagnostician (M Ed); reading education (M Ed). Part-time programs available. *Entrance requirements:* For master's, GRE General Test or MAT. Additional exam requirements/recommendations for international students: Required—TOEFL (minimum score 550 paper-based; 213 computer-based).

Hunter College of the City University of New York, Graduate School, School of Education, Department of Curriculum and Teaching, Program in Teaching English as a Second Language, New York, NY 10021-5085. Offers MA. *Accreditation:* NCATE. *Faculty:* 11 full-time (4 women), 25 part-time/adjunct (11 women). *Students:* 42 full-time (29 women), 187 part-time (155 women); includes 68 minority (13 Black or African American, non-Hispanic/Latino; 2 American Indian or Alaska Native, non-Hispanic/Latino; 26 Asian, non-Hispanic/Latino; 27 Hispanic/Latino), 7 international. Average age 32. 181 applicants, 57% accepted, 68 enrolled. In 2011, 70 master's awarded. *Degree requirements:* For master's, one foreign language, thesis, comprehensive exam or essay, New York state teacher certification exams. *Entrance requirements:* For master's, minimum GPA of 2.8, 2 letters of recommendation, interview. Additional exam requirements/recommendations for international students: Required—TOEFL (minimum score 600 paper-based), TWE (minimum score 5). *Application deadline:* For fall admission, 4/1 for domestic students, 2/1 for international students; for spring admission, 11/1 for domestic students, 9/1 for international students. Applications are processed on a rolling basis. Application fee: $125. *Expenses:* Tuition, state resident: full-time $8210; part-time $345 per credit. Tuition, nonresident: full-time $15,360; part-time $640 per credit. *Required fees:* $280 per semester. One-time fee: $125. Tuition and fees vary according to class time, campus/location and program. *Financial support:* Federal Work-Study, scholarships/grants, and tuition waivers (partial) available. Support available to part-time students. *Unit head:* Dr. Bede McCormack, Coordinator, 212-777-4665, E-mail: bmccorma@hunter.cuny.edu. *Application contact:* William Zlata, Director for Graduate Admissions, 212-772-4482, Fax: 212-650-3336, E-mail: admissions@hunter.cuny.edu. Web site: http://www.hunter.cuny.edu/school-of-education/programs/graduate/tesol.

Idaho State University, Office of Graduate Studies, College of Arts and Letters, Department of English, Pocatello, ID 83209-8056. Offers English (MA, DA); English and the teaching of English (PhD); TESOL (Post-Master's Certificate). Part-time programs available. *Degree requirements:* For master's, one foreign language, comprehensive exam, thesis optional; for doctorate, one foreign language, comprehensive exam, thesis/dissertation, 2 papers, 2 teaching internships; for Post-Master's Certificate, 6 credits of elective linguistics, practicum. *Entrance requirements:* For master's, GRE General Test (minimum 50th percentile verbal), general literature exam, minimum GPA of 3.0, 3 letters of recommendation, 5-page writing sample; for doctorate, GRE General Test, GRE Subject Test, minimum GPA of 3.5, writing examples, 3 letters of recommendation, master's degree in English; for Post-Master's Certificate, GRE (minimum 35th percentile on verbal section), bachelor's degree, minimum undergraduate GPA of 3.0 in last 2 years, 3 letters of recommendation, knowledge of second language. Additional exam requirements/recommendations for international students: Required—TOEFL (minimum score 550 paper-based; 213 computer-based; 80 iBT). Electronic applications accepted. *Faculty research:* American literature, Renaissance literature, composition and rhetoric, Intermountain West studies, ethics.

Indiana State University, College of Graduate and Professional Studies, College of Arts and Sciences, Department of Languages, Literatures, and Linguistics, Terre Haute, IN 47809. Offers linguistics/teaching English as a second language (MA); TESL/TEFL (CAS). *Degree requirements:* For master's, comprehensive exam. Electronic applications accepted.

Indiana University Bloomington, University Graduate School, College of Arts and Sciences, Department of Second Language Studies, Bloomington, IN 47405-7000. Offers second language studies (MA, PhD); TESOL and applied linguistics (MA). *Faculty:* 1 (woman) full-time. *Students:* 36 full-time (24 women), 3 part-time (1 woman); includes 7 minority (2 Black or African American, non-Hispanic/Latino; 4 Hispanic/Latino; 1 Two or more races, non-Hispanic/Latino), 17 international. Average age 31. 102 applicants, 35% accepted, 19 enrolled. In 2011, 8 master's awarded. *Entrance requirements:* Additional exam requirements/recommendations for international students: Required—TOEFL (minimum score 100 iBT). *Application deadline:* For fall admission, 1/15 for domestic students, 12/1 for international students. Application fee: $55 ($65 for international students). *Financial support:* In 2011–12, 12 teaching assistantships with tuition reimbursements (averaging $13,456 per year) were awarded; fellowships with tuition reimbursements also available. *Unit head:* Kathleen Bardovi-Harlig, Chair, 812-855-7951, E-mail: bardovi@indiana.edu. *Application contact:* Julie Abrams, Graduate Secretary, 812-855-7951, E-mail: abramsj@indiana.edu. Web site: http://www.indiana.edu/~dsls/.

Indiana University of Pennsylvania, School of Graduate Studies and Research, College of Humanities and Social Sciences, Department of English, Program in Composition and Teaching English to Speakers of Other Languages, Indiana, PA 15705-1087. Offers composition and teaching English to speakers of other languages (PhD); teaching English (MAT); teaching English to speakers of other languages (MA). *Faculty:* 27 full-time (11 women). *Students:* 24 full-time (15 women), 119 part-time (76 women); includes 8 minority (3 Black or African American, non-Hispanic/Latino; 4 Asian, non-Hispanic/Latino; 1 Hispanic/Latino), 38 international. Average age 40. 184 applicants, 24% accepted, 17 enrolled. In 2011, 31 doctorates awarded. *Degree requirements:* For master's, thesis optional; for doctorate, one foreign language, comprehensive exam, thesis/dissertation. *Entrance requirements:* For master's and doctorate, 2 letters of recommendation. Additional exam requirements/recommendations for international students: Required—TOEFL (minimum score 540 paper-based; 207 computer-based). *Application deadline:* Applications are processed on a rolling basis. Application fee: $50. Electronic applications accepted. *Expenses:* Tuition, state resident: full-time $7488; part-time $416 per credit. Tuition, nonresident: full-time $11,232; part-time $624 per credit. *Required fees:* $2070; $192.20 per credit. $90 per semester. *Financial support:* In 2011–12, 19 research assistantships with full and partial tuition reimbursements (averaging $6,699 per year), 10 teaching assistantships with partial tuition reimbursements (averaging $14,558 per year) were awarded; fellowships also available. Financial award application deadline: 4/15; financial award applicants required to submit FAFSA. *Unit head:* Dr. Ben Rafoth, Graduate Coordinator, 724-357-2272. *Application contact:* Paula Stossel, Assistant Dean, 724-357-4511, E-mail: graduate-admissions@iup.edu. Web site: http://www.iup.edu/upper.aspx?id=216.

Indiana University of Pennsylvania, School of Graduate Studies and Research, College of Humanities and Social Sciences, Department of English, Program in English: TESOL and Applied Linguistics, Indiana, PA 15705-1087. Offers MA. *Faculty:* 27 full-time (11 women). *Students:* 35 full-time (21 women), 2 part-time (both women), 36 international. Average age 28. 78 applicants, 46% accepted, 15 enrolled. In 2011, 14 master's awarded. *Entrance requirements:* Additional exam requirements/recommendations for international students: Required—TOEFL (minimum score 540 paper-based; 207 computer-based). *Application deadline:* Applications are processed on a rolling basis. Application fee: $50. Electronic applications accepted. *Expenses:* Tuition, state resident: full-time $7488; part-time $416 per credit. Tuition, nonresident: full-time $11,232; part-time $624 per credit. *Required fees:* $2070; $192.20 per credit. $90 per semester. *Financial support:* In 2011–12, 6 research assistantships with full and partial tuition reimbursements (averaging $3,434 per year) were awarded. Financial award application deadline: 4/15; financial award applicants required to submit FAFSA. *Unit head:* Dr. Gloria Park, Director, 724-357-3095, E-mail: gloria.park@iup.edu. *Application contact:* Paula Stossel, Assistant Dean, 724-357-2222, Fax: 724-357-4862, E-mail: graduate-admissions@iup.edu. Web site: http://www.iup.edu/english/matesol/.

Indiana University–Purdue University Fort Wayne, College of Arts and Sciences, Department of English and Linguistics, Fort Wayne, IN 46805-1499. Offers English (MA, MAT); TENL (teaching English as a new language) (Certificate). Part-time programs available. *Faculty:* 23 full-time (10 women), 1 (woman) part-time/adjunct. *Students:* 7 full-time (3 women), 26 part-time (19 women); includes 1 minority (Hispanic/Latino). Average age 34. 7 applicants, 71% accepted, 4 enrolled. In 2011, 11 master's, 5 other advanced degrees awarded. *Degree requirements:* For master's, one foreign language, thesis (for some programs), teaching certificate (MAT). *Entrance requirements:* For master's, GRE General Test, minimum GPA of 3.0, major or minor in English, 3 letters of recommendation; for Certificate, bachelor's degree with minimum GPA of 2.5. Additional exam requirements/recommendations for international students: Required—TOEFL (minimum score 600 paper-based; 260 computer-based; 77 iBT). *Application deadline:* For fall admission, 8/1 for domestic students; for spring admission, 10/15 for domestic students. Applications are processed on a rolling basis. Application fee: $50. *Financial support:* In 2011–12, 11 teaching assistantships with partial tuition reimbursements (averaging $12,930 per year) were awarded; career-related internships or fieldwork, scholarships/grants, and unspecified assistantships also available. Support available to part-time students. Financial award application deadline: 3/1; financial award applicants required to submit FAFSA. *Faculty research:* Generosity, basic writers at open-admission universities, three-volume novel. *Total annual research expenditures:* $60,146. *Unit head:* Dr. Hardin Aasand, Chair and Professor, 260-481-6750, Fax: 260-481-6985, E-mail: aasandh@ipfw.edu. *Application contact:* Dr. Lewis Roberts, Graduate Program Director, 260-481-6754, Fax: 260-481-6985, E-mail: robertlc@ipfw.edu. Web site: http://www.ipfw.edu/english.

Indiana University–Purdue University Indianapolis, School of Education, Indianapolis, IN 46202-2896. Offers computer education (Certificate); curriculum and instruction (MS); early childhood (MS); educational leadership (MS, Certificate); English as a second language (Certificate); higher education and student affairs (MS); kindergarten (Certificate); language education (MS); reading (Certificate); school counseling (MS); special education (MS, Certificate). Part-time and evening/weekend programs available. *Faculty:* 41 full-time, 80 part-time/adjunct. *Students:* 67 full-time (52 women), 467 part-time (360 women); includes 82 minority (44 Black or African American, non-Hispanic/Latino; 3 American Indian or Alaska Native, non-Hispanic/Latino; 8 Asian, non-Hispanic/Latino; 13 Hispanic/Latino; 14 Two or more races, non-Hispanic/Latino), 10 international. Average age 33. 63 applicants, 57% accepted, 29 enrolled. In 2011, 167 master's awarded. *Degree requirements:* For master's, thesis optional. *Entrance requirements:* For master's, GRE General Test, minimum GPA of 3.0. Additional exam requirements/recommendations for international students: Required—TOEFL. *Application deadline:* For fall admission, 5/1 priority date for domestic students; for spring admission, 11/1 for domestic students. Application fee: $55 ($65 for international students). *Financial support:* Fellowships, research assistantships with partial tuition reimbursements, teaching assistantships, Federal Work-Study, institutionally sponsored loans, scholarships/grants, and tuition waivers (partial) available. Support available to part-time students. *Faculty research:* Teachers in the process of change, learning cycles, children's concepts of science. *Total annual research expenditures:* $614,458. *Unit head:* Dr. Chris Leland, Interim Executive Associate Dean, 317-274-6801, Fax: 317-274-6864. *Application contact:* Sarah Brandenburg, Graduate Advisor, 317-274-6801, Fax: 317-274-6864, E-mail: edugrad@iupui.edu. Web site: http://education.iupui.edu/.

Indiana University–Purdue University Indianapolis, School of Liberal Arts, Department of English, Indianapolis, IN 46202-2896. Offers English (MA); teaching English (MA); teaching English as a second language (TESOL) (Certificate); teaching writing (Certificate). *Faculty:* 22 full-time (11 women). *Students:* 21 full-time (13 women), 14 part-time (9 women); includes 2 minority (1 Black or African American, non-Hispanic/

Latino; 1 Two or more races, non-Hispanic/Latino). Average age 32. 28 applicants, 68% accepted, 14 enrolled. In 2011, 25 master's, 7 other advanced degrees awarded. *Entrance requirements:* For master's, GRE. Additional exam requirements/ recommendations for international students: Required—TOEFL. *Application deadline:* For fall admission, 1/15 priority date for domestic students, 1/15 for international students; for spring admission, 10/15 priority date for domestic students, 10/15 for international students. Application fee: $55 ($65 for international students). *Financial support:* In 2011–12, 2 fellowships (averaging $10,000 per year), 4 research assistantships (averaging $9,500 per year), 12 teaching assistantships (averaging $7,103 per year) were awarded; career-related internships or fieldwork also available. *Unit head:* Dr. Thomas Upton, Chair, 317-274-4226, Fax: 317-278-1287, E-mail: tupton@iupui.edu. *Application contact:* Dr. Robert Rebein, Director of Graduate Studies in English, 317-274-1405, Fax: 317-278-1287, E-mail: rrebein@iupui.edu. Web site: http://liberalarts.iupui.edu/english/.

Inter American University of Puerto Rico, Arecibo Campus, Programs in Education, Arecibo, PR 00614-4050. Offers administration and educational supervision (MA Ed); counseling and guidance (MA Ed); curriculum and teaching (MA Ed), including biology education, English as a second language, history education, math education, Spanish; elementary education (MA Ed). *Degree requirements:* For master's, comprehensive exam, thesis optional. *Entrance requirements:* For master's, GRE, EXADEP, bachelor's degree in education or teaching license (administration and supervision) or courses in education and psychology (counseling and guidance), minimum GPA of 2.5 in last 60 credits.

Inter American University of Puerto Rico, Barranquitas Campus, Program in Education, Barranquitas, PR 00794. Offers curriculum and teaching (M Ed), including biology education, English as a second language, history education, mathematics education, Spanish; educational leadership and management (MA); elementary education (M Ed); information and library service technology (M Ed); special education (MA). *Degree requirements:* For master's, comprehensive exam, thesis optional. *Entrance requirements:* For master's, EXADEP, letter of recommendation. Electronic applications accepted.

Inter American University of Puerto Rico, Metropolitan Campus, Graduate Programs, Program in Teaching English as a Second Language, San Juan, PR 00919-1293. Offers MA. Part-time and evening/weekend programs available. *Degree requirements:* For master's, comprehensive exam, thesis or alternative. *Entrance requirements:* For master's, GRE General Test or EXADEP, interview, minimum GPA of 2.5. Electronic applications accepted.

Inter American University of Puerto Rico, Ponce Campus, Graduate School, Mercedita, PR 00715-1602. Offers accounting (MBA); biology (M Ed); chemistry (M Ed); criminal justice (MA); elementary education (M Ed); English as a Second Language (M Ed); finance (MBA); history (M Ed); human resources (MBA); marketing (MBA); mathematics (M Ed); Spanish (M Ed). *Entrance requirements:* For master's, minimum GPA of 2.5.

Inter American University of Puerto Rico, San Germán Campus, Graduate Studies Center, Program in Teaching English as a Second Language, San Germán, PR 00683-5008. Offers MA. Part-time and evening/weekend programs available. *Degree requirements:* For master's, comprehensive exam. *Entrance requirements:* For master's, GRE General Test or EXADEP, minimum GPA of 3.0. *Application deadline:* For fall admission, 4/30 priority date for domestic students; for spring admission, 11/15 for domestic students. Applications are processed on a rolling basis. Application fee: $31. *Expenses: Required fees:* $213 per semester. *Financial support:* Teaching assistantships and unspecified assistantships available. *Unit head:* Dr. Elba T. Irizarry, Director of Graduate Studies Center, 787-264-1912 Ext. 7357, Fax: 787-892-6350, E-mail: elbat@sg.inter.edu. Web site: http://www.sg.inter.edu/tesl/.

Iowa State University of Science and Technology, Program in Teaching English as a Second Language/Applied Linguistics, Ames, IA 50011-1201. Offers MA. *Entrance requirements:* For master's, GRE, official academic transcripts, resume, three letters of recommendation, statement of personal goals, writing sample. Additional exam requirements/recommendations for international students: Required—TOEFL (minimum score 600 paper-based; 100 iBT), IELTS (minimum score 7). *Application deadline:* For fall admission, 1/5 for domestic students. Electronic applications accepted. *Unit head:* John Levis, Director of Graduate Education, 515-294-2477, Fax: 515-294-6814, E-mail: englgrad@iastate.edu. *Application contact:* Teresa Smiley, Application Contact, 515-294-2477, Fax: 515-294-6814, E-mail: grad_admissions@iastate.edu. Web site: http://www.public.iastate.edu/~apling/MA_homepage.html.

The Johns Hopkins University, School of Education, Department of Teacher Development and Leadership, Baltimore, MD 21218-2699. Offers adolescent literacy education (Certificate); data-based decision making and organizational improvement (Certificate); education (MS), including reading, school administration and supervision, technology for educators; educational leadership for independent schools (Certificate); effective teaching of reading (Certificate); emergent literacy education (Certificate); English as a second language instruction (Certificate); gifted education (Certificate); leadership for school, family, and community collaboration (Certificate); leadership in technology integration (Certificate); school administration and supervision (Certificate); teacher development and leadership (Ed D); teacher leadership (Certificate). Part-time and evening/weekend programs available. Postbaccalaureate distance learning degree programs offered (minimal on-campus study). *Degree requirements:* For master's and Certificate, portfolio; for doctorate, comprehensive exam (for some programs), thesis/dissertation, portfolio or comprehensive exam. *Entrance requirements:* For master's and Certificate, bachelor's degree; minimum undergraduate GPA of 3.0; essay/statement of goals; for doctorate, GRE, essay/statement of goals; three letters of recommendation; curriculum vitae/resume; K-12 professional experience; interview; writing assessment. Additional exam requirements/recommendations for international students: Required—TOEFL (minimum score 600 paper-based; 250 computer-based; 100 iBT). Electronic applications accepted. *Faculty research:* Application of psychoanalytic concepts to teaching, schools, and education reform; adolescent literacies; use of emerging technologies for teaching, learning, and school leadership; quantitative analyses of the social contexts of education; school, family, and community collaboration; program evaluation methodologies.

The Johns Hopkins University, School of Education, Department of Teacher Preparation, Baltimore, MD 21218. Offers early childhood education (MAT); education (MS), including educational studies; elementary education (MAT); English for speakers of other languages (MAT); K-8 mathematics lead-teacher (Certificate); K-8 science lead-teacher (Certificate); secondary education (MAT), including biology, chemistry, earth/space/environmental science, English, French, mathematics, physics, social studies, Spanish. Part-time and evening/weekend programs available. *Degree requirements:* For master's, portfolio, PRAXIS II, internship. *Entrance requirements:* For master's, PRAXIS I, SAT, ACT, or GRE (MAT), minimum undergraduate GPA of 3.0, interview, 1 letter of recommendation, curriculum vitae/resume; for Certificate, bachelor's degree, minimum undergraduate GPA of 3.0, essay/statement of goals, interview. Additional exam requirements/recommendations for international students: Required—TOEFL (minimum score 600 paper-based; 250 computer-based; 100 iBT). Electronic applications accepted. *Faculty research:* Teacher retention, STEM education reform, alternative certification programs, school-university partnerships, urban education, action research/data-informed instruction, family engagement.

Judson University, Graduate Programs, Program in Education with ESL/Bilingual Endorsement, Elgin, IL 60123-1498. Offers M Ed. Part-time programs available. *Degree requirements:* For master's, thesis, portfolio. *Entrance requirements:* For master's, bachelor's degree with minimum GPA of 3.0; letters of reference. Additional exam requirements/recommendations for international students: Required—TOEFL (minimum score 550 paper-based; 213 computer-based). Application fee: $40. Electronic applications accepted. *Expenses: Tuition:* Full-time $9500. *Required fees:* $350. Tuition and fees vary according to course load and program. *Financial support:* Partial tuition reimbursement from some school districts available. Financial award applicants required to submit FAFSA. *Faculty research:* Bilingual education, multicultural policies and subject integration, legal issues in the classroom, curriculum planning and design, differentiated instruction, inclusive classrooms, cross-curricular integration. *Unit head:* Dr. Kathy Miller, Dean, School of Education, 847-628-1088, E-mail: dsimmons@judsonu.edu. *Application contact:* Maria Aguirre, Assistant to the Registrar for Graduate Programs, 847-628-1160, E-mail: maguirre@judsonu.edu. Web site: http://www.judsonu.edu/MEDESLBilingual/.

Kansas State University, Graduate School, College of Arts and Sciences, Department of Modern Languages, Manhattan, KS 66506. Offers French (MA); German (MA); Spanish (MA); teaching English as a foreign language (MA). Part-time and evening/weekend programs available. Postbaccalaureate distance learning degree programs offered (minimal on-campus study). *Faculty:* 11 full-time (7 women), 3 part-time/adjunct (1 woman). *Students:* 20 full-time (13 women), 14 part-time (9 women); includes 6 minority (1 Black or African American, non-Hispanic/Latino; 5 Hispanic/Latino), 5 international. Average age 30. 22 applicants, 68% accepted, 5 enrolled. In 2011, 14 master's awarded. *Degree requirements:* For master's, thesis optional. *Entrance requirements:* For master's, teaching certificate. Additional exam requirements/recommendations for international students: Required—TOEFL (minimum score 560 paper-based). *Application deadline:* For fall admission, 2/1 priority date for domestic students, 2/1 for international students; for spring admission, 8/1 priority date for domestic students, 8/1 for international students. Applications are processed on a rolling basis. Application fee: $40 ($55 for international students). Electronic applications accepted. *Financial support:* In 2011–12, 18 teaching assistantships with full tuition reimbursements (averaging $10,938 per year) were awarded; Federal Work-Study, institutionally sponsored loans, and scholarships/grants also available. Support available to part-time students. Financial award application deadline: 3/1; financial award applicants required to submit FAFSA. *Faculty research:* Second language acquisitions; Chicano literature; Francophone literature; cultural studies; German, French, Spanish, and Spanish-American literature from the Middle Ages to the modern era; teaching English as a foreign language. *Unit head:* Salvador Oropesa, Head, 785-532-1987, Fax: 785-532-7004, E-mail: oropesa@ksu.edu. *Application contact:* Claire Dehon, Coordinator, 785-532-1929, Fax: 785-532-7004, E-mail: dehoncl@ksu.edu. Web site: http://www.k-state.edu/mlangs/.

Kansas State University, Graduate School, College of Education, Department of Curriculum and Instruction, Manhattan, KS 66506. Offers career and technical education (Ed D, PhD); curriculum studies (Ed D, PhD); digital teaching and learning (MS); educational computing, design and online learning (MS); educational technology (Ed D, PhD); elementary/middle level (MS); English as a second language (MS); language/diversity education (Ed D, PhD); literacy education (Ed D, PhD); mathematics education (Ed D, PhD); middle level/secondary (MS); reading and language arts (MS); reading specialist endorsement (MS); science education (Ed D, PhD); social science education (Ed D, PhD); teacher education (Ed D, PhD); teacher leader/school improvement (MS, Ed D). *Accreditation:* NCATE. Part-time programs available. Postbaccalaureate distance learning degree programs offered (minimal on-campus study). *Faculty:* 15 full-time (12 women), 3 part-time/adjunct (2 women). *Students:* 37 full-time (30 women), 113 part-time (91 women); includes 14 minority (4 Black or African American, non-Hispanic/Latino; 1 American Indian or Alaska Native, non-Hispanic/Latino; 1 Asian, non-Hispanic/Latino; 7 Hispanic/Latino; 1 Two or more races, non-Hispanic/Latino), 15 international. Average age 37. 75 applicants, 51% accepted, 9 enrolled. In 2011, 48 master's, 14 doctorates awarded. *Degree requirements:* For master's, comprehensive exam, portfolio, project, report or thesis; for doctorate, comprehensive exam, thesis/dissertation, preliminary exam. *Entrance requirements:* For master's, minimum GPA of 3.0; for doctorate, GRE, minimum GPA of 3.0. Additional exam requirements/recommendations for international students: Required—TOEFL. *Application deadline:* For fall admission, 2/1 priority date for domestic students, 2/1 for international students; for spring admission, 8/1 priority date for domestic students, 8/1 for international students. Applications are processed on a rolling basis. Application fee: $40 ($55 for international students). Electronic applications accepted. *Financial support:* In 2011–12, 1 research assistantship (averaging $16,900 per year), 8 teaching assistantships (averaging $12,466 per year) were awarded; career-related internships or fieldwork, institutionally sponsored loans, and scholarships/grants also available. Support available to part-time students. Financial award application deadline: 3/1; financial award applicants required to submit FAFSA. *Faculty research:* Literacy and technology, critical race theory and diversity, achievement gaps, school improvement, teacher education. *Total annual research expenditures:* $510,907. *Unit head:* Dr. Gail Shroyer, Chair, 785-532-5550, Fax: 785-532-7304, E-mail: gshroyer@ksu.edu. *Application contact:* Dona Deam, Application Contact, 785-532-5595, Fax: 785-532-7304, E-mail: ddeam@ksu.edu. Web site: http://coe.k-state.edu/departments/currin/curringrad.htm.

Kean University, College of Education, Program in Instruction and Curriculum, Union, NJ 07083. Offers bilingual (MA); classroom instruction (MA); mathematics/science/computer education (MA); teaching (MA); teaching English as a second language (MA); teaching physics (MA); world languages (Spanish) (MA). *Accreditation:* NCATE. *Faculty:* 22 full-time (12 women). *Students:* 56 full-time (33 women), 139 part-time (103 women); includes 87 minority (27 Black or African American, non-Hispanic/Latino; 8 Asian, non-Hispanic/Latino; 52 Hispanic/Latino), 1 international. Average age 34. 85 applicants, 100% accepted, 72 enrolled. In 2011, 78 master's awarded. *Degree requirements:* For master's, comprehensive exam, two-semester advanced seminar. *Entrance requirements:* For master's, GRE General Test or MAT, PRAXIS, minimum GPA of 3.0, 2 letters of recommendation, interview, teacher certification (for some programs), transcripts, resume. Additional exam requirements/recommendations for international students: Required—TOEFL (minimum score 79 iBT). *Application deadline:* For fall admission, 6/1 for domestic and international students; for spring admission, 12/1 for domestic and international students. Applications are processed on a rolling basis. Application fee: $75 ($150 for international students). Electronic applications accepted. *Expenses:* Tuition, state resident: full-time $11,302; part-time $550 per credit. Tuition, nonresident: full-time $15,318; part-time $674 per credit. *Required fees:* $2849; $130 per credit. Tuition and fees vary according to degree level. *Financial support:* In 2011–12, 3 research assistantships with full tuition reimbursements (averaging $3,263 per year) were awarded; unspecified assistantships also available. Financial award applicants required to submit FAFSA. *Unit head:* Dr. Thomas Walsh, Program Coordinator, 908-737-4003, E-mail: tpwalsh@kean.edu. *Application contact:* Ann-Marie Kay, Assistant Director for Graduate Admissions, 908-737-5922, Fax: 908-737-5925,

E-mail: akay@kean.edu. Web site: http://www.kean.edu/KU/Bilingual-Bicultural-Education-Instruction-and-Curriculum.

Kennesaw State University, Leland and Clarice C. Bagwell College of Education, Program in Graduate Education, Kennesaw, GA 30144-5591. Offers adolescent education (M Ed); educational leadership (M Ed); educational leadership technology (M Ed); elementary and early childhood education (M Ed); special education (M Ed); teaching English to speakers of other languages (M Ed). *Accreditation:* NCATE. Part-time programs available. *Students:* 42 full-time (39 women), 132 part-time (105 women); includes 31 minority (20 Black or African American, non-Hispanic/Latino; 4 Asian, non-Hispanic/Latino; 5 Hispanic/Latino; 2 Two or more races, non-Hispanic/Latino). Average age 34. 48 applicants, 79% accepted, 38 enrolled. In 2011, 117 master's awarded. *Degree requirements:* For master's, thesis or alternative. *Entrance requirements:* For master's, GRE General Test, T-4 state certification, minimum GPA of 2.75. Additional exam requirements/recommendations for international students: Required—TOEFL (minimum score 550 paper-based; 213 computer-based; 80 iBT), IELTS (minimum score 6). *Application deadline:* For fall admission, 7/1 for domestic and international students; for spring admission, 10/1 for domestic and international students. Application fee: $60. Electronic applications accepted. *Expenses:* Tuition, state resident: full-time $3000; part-time $250 per semester hour. Tuition, nonresident: full-time $10,836; part-time $903 per semester hour. *Required fees:* $774 per semester. *Financial support:* Federal Work-Study and unspecified assistantships available. Support available to part-time students. Financial award application deadline: 4/1; financial award applicants required to submit FAFSA. *Unit head:* Dr. Nita Paris, Associate Dean for Graduate Programs, 770-423-6636, E-mail: nparis@kennesaw.edu. *Application contact:* Alisha Bello, Administrative Coordinator, 770-423-6043, Fax: 770-420-4435, E-mail: abello1@kennesaw.edu. Web site: http://www.kennesaw.edu/education/grad/.

Kennesaw State University, Leland and Clarice C. Bagwell College of Education, Program in Teaching, Kennesaw, GA 30144-5591. Offers art education (MAT); secondary English or mathematics (MAT); secondary science education (MAT); teaching English to speakers of other languages (MAT). Program offered only in summer. Part-time and evening/weekend programs available. *Students:* 101 full-time (68 women), 20 part-time (15 women); includes 27 minority (14 Black or African American, non-Hispanic/Latino; 6 Asian, non-Hispanic/Latino; 4 Hispanic/Latino; 3 Two or more races, non-Hispanic/Latino), 3 international. Average age 33. 13 applicants, 62% accepted, 7 enrolled. In 2011, 81 master's awarded. *Entrance requirements:* For master's, GRE, GACE I (state certificate exam), minimum GPA of 2.75, 2 recommendations, resume. Additional exam requirements/recommendations for international students: Required—TOEFL (minimum score 550 paper-based; 213 computer-based; 80 iBT), IELTS (minimum score 6). *Application deadline:* For fall admission, 6/1 for domestic and international students; for spring admission, 3/1 for domestic and international students. Application fee: $60. Electronic applications accepted. *Expenses:* Tuition, state resident: full-time $3000; part-time $250 per semester hour. Tuition, nonresident: full-time $10,836; part-time $903 per semester hour. *Required fees:* $774 per semester. *Financial support:* In 2011–12, 2 research assistantships with tuition reimbursements (averaging $4,000 per year) were awarded; unspecified assistantships also available. Financial award application deadline: 4/1; financial award applicants required to submit FAFSA. *Unit head:* Dr. Lynn Stallings, Director, 770-420-4477, E-mail: lstalling@kennesaw.edu. *Application contact:* Alisha Bello, Administrative Coordinator, 770-423-6043, Fax: 770-420-4435, E-mail: abello1@kennesaw.edu. Web site: http://www.kennesaw.edu.

Kent State University, College of Arts and Sciences, Department of English, Kent, OH 44242-0001. Offers comparative literature (MA); creative writing (MFA); English (PhD); English for teachers (MA); literature and writing (MA); rhetoric and composition (PhD); teaching English as a second language (MA). MFA program offered jointly with Cleveland State University, The University of Akron, and Youngstown State University. Part-time programs available. Terminal master's awarded for partial completion of doctoral program. *Degree requirements:* For master's, one foreign language, thesis optional; for doctorate, one foreign language, thesis/dissertation, qualifying exams. *Entrance requirements:* For master's and doctorate, GRE General Test, writing sample, letters of recommendation. Additional exam requirements/recommendations for international students: Required—TOEFL (minimum score 600 paper-based). Electronic applications accepted. *Expenses:* Tuition, state resident: full-time $8136; part-time $452 per credit hour. Tuition, nonresident: full-time $14,292; part-time $794 per credit hour. *Faculty research:* British and American literature, textual editing, rhetoric and composition, cultural studies, linguistic and critical theories.

Langston University, School of Education and Behavioral Sciences, Langston, OK 73050. Offers bilingual/multicultural (M Ed); elementary education (M Ed); English as a second language (M Ed); rehabilitation counseling (M Sc); urban education (M Ed). *Accreditation:* CORE; NCATE (one or more programs are accredited). Part-time programs available. *Degree requirements:* For master's, comprehensive exam, thesis optional. *Entrance requirements:* For master's, GRE, writing skills test, minimum GPA of 2.5, 3 letters of recommendation. Additional exam requirements/recommendations for international students: Required—TOEFL, TWE. *Faculty research:* Bilingual/multicultural education, financing post-secondary education.

Lehigh University, College of Education, Program in Comparative and International Education, Bethlehem, PA 18015. Offers comparative and international education (MA); globalization and educational change (M Ed); international counseling (Certificate); international development in education (Certificate); special education (Certificate); technology use in schools (Certificate); TESOL (Certificate). Part-time programs available. Postbaccalaureate distance learning degree programs offered (no on-campus study). *Faculty:* 4 full-time (2 women). *Students:* 25 full-time (10 women), 45 part-time (31 women); includes 5 minority (all Asian, non-Hispanic/Latino), 16 international. Average age 34. 45 applicants, 71% accepted, 12 enrolled. In 2011, 21 master's awarded. *Degree requirements:* For master's, thesis (MA). *Entrance requirements:* For master's, 2 letters of recommendation. Additional exam requirements/recommendations for international students: Required—TOEFL (minimum score 600 paper-based; 250 computer-based; 93 iBT). *Application deadline:* For fall and spring admission, 2/1 for domestic and international students. Application fee: $65. Electronic applications accepted. *Financial support:* In 2011–12, 8 students received support, including 3 research assistantships with full and partial tuition reimbursements available (averaging $13,000 per year). Financial award application deadline: 3/15. *Faculty research:* Comparative education, rural education, gender equity in education, post-socialist education transformation, educational borrowing, comparing education systems, education policy an globalization, family-school relationships, China, international testing, social inequities. *Unit head:* Dr. Iveta Silova, Program Director and Associate Professor, 610-758-5750, Fax: 610-758-6223, E-mail: ism207@lehigh.edu. *Application contact:* Donna M. Johnson, Coordinator, 610-758-3231, Fax: 610-758-6223, E-mail: dmj4@lehigh.edu. Web site: http://www.lehigh.edu/education/cie.

Lehman College of the City University of New York, Division of Education, Department of Middle and High School Education, Program in Teaching English to Speakers of Other Languages, Bronx, NY 10468-1589. Offers MS Ed. *Accreditation:* NCATE. *Degree requirements:* For master's, thesis. *Entrance requirements:* For master's, minimum GPA of 3.0.

Le Moyne College, Department of Education, Syracuse, NY 13214. Offers adolescent education (MS Ed, MST); adolescent education/special education (MS Ed, MST); adolescent English (grades 7-12) (MST); adolescent history (grades 7-12) (MST); childhood education (MS Ed); childhood education/special education (MS Ed); elementary education (MS Ed); general professional education (MS Ed); inclusive childhood education (MST); literacy education (birth to grade 6) (MS Ed); literacy education (grades 5-12) (MS Ed); school building leadership (MS Ed, CAS); school district business leader (MS Ed, CAS); school district leadership (MS Ed, CAS); secondary education (MS Ed); special education (MS Ed); students with disabilities-generalist (grades 7-12) (MS Ed); TESOL (teaching English to speakers of other languages) (MS Ed); urban studies (MS Ed). *Accreditation:* Teacher Education Accreditation Council. Part-time and evening/weekend programs available. *Faculty:* 9 full-time (6 women), 51 part-time/adjunct (28 women). *Students:* 61 full-time (47 women), 311 part-time (222 women); includes 31 minority (19 Black or African American, non-Hispanic/Latino; 3 American Indian or Alaska Native, non-Hispanic/Latino; 4 Asian, non-Hispanic/Latino; 5 Hispanic/Latino), 2 international. Average age 30. 242 applicants, 90% accepted, 180 enrolled. In 2011, 168 master's, 23 CASs awarded. *Degree requirements:* For master's, thesis. *Entrance requirements:* For master's, GRE General Test, bachelor's degree, 2 letters of recommendation, written statement, transcripts. Additional exam requirements/recommendations for international students: Required—TOEFL (minimum score 550 paper-based; 213 computer-based; 79 iBT). *Application deadline:* For fall admission, 4/1 priority date for domestic students, 4/1 for international students; for spring admission, 10/1 priority date for domestic students, 10/1 for international students. Applications are processed on a rolling basis. Application fee: $50. *Expenses:* Contact institution. *Financial support:* In 2011–12, 32 students received support. Career-related internships or fieldwork and health care benefits available. Support available to part-time students. Financial award applicants required to submit FAFSA. *Faculty research:* Minority teachers, special education, multiculturalism, literacy, technology, video games learning, autism, school district organization, service-learning, higher level problem solving, teacher leadership. *Unit head:* Dr. Suzanne L. Gilmour, Chair, Department of Education and Director of Graduate Education Programs, 315-445-4376, Fax: 315-445-4744, E-mail: gilmous@lemoyne.edu. *Application contact:* Kristen P. Trapasso, Director of Graduate Admission, 315-445-4265, Fax: 315-445-6027, E-mail: trapaskp@lemoyne.edu. Web site: http://www.lemoyne.edu/education.

Lewis University, College of Education, Program in English as a Second Language, Romeoville, IL 60446. Offers M Ed. Part-time and evening/weekend programs available. *Students:* 37 part-time (34 women); includes 5 minority (1 Black or African American, non-Hispanic/Latino; 4 Hispanic/Latino). Average age 35. In 2011, 9 master's awarded. *Entrance requirements:* For master's, departmental qualifying exam, writing exam, minimum GPA of 2.75, 2 letters of recommendation, interview. Additional exam requirements/recommendations for international students: Required—TOEFL (minimum score 550 paper-based; 213 computer-based; 80 iBT). *Application deadline:* For fall admission, 5/1 for international students; for spring admission, 11/15 for international students. Application fee: $40. *Financial support:* Federal Work-Study, scholarships/grants, and unspecified assistantships available. Financial award application deadline: 5/1; financial award applicants required to submit FAFSA. *Unit head:* Dr. Barbara Mackey, Program Director, 815-838-0500 Ext. 5962, E-mail: mackeyba@lewisu.edu. *Application contact:* Pat Levenda, Secretary, 815-838-0500 Ext. 5769, E-mail: levendpa@lewisu.edu.

Lindenwood University, Graduate Programs, School of Education, St. Charles, MO 63301-1695. Offers education (MA); educational administration (MA, Ed D, Ed S); human performance (MS); instructional leadership (Ed D, Ed S); library media (MA); professional and school counseling (MA); professional counseling (MA); school administration (Ed S); school counseling (MA); teaching (MA); teaching English to speakers of other languages (MA). Part-time and evening/weekend programs available. *Faculty:* 33 full-time (13 women), 176 part-time/adjunct (83 women). *Students:* 472 full-time (353 women), 1,772 part-time (1,373 women); includes 666 minority (605 Black or African American, non-Hispanic/Latino; 15 American Indian or Alaska Native, non-Hispanic/Latino; 5 Asian, non-Hispanic/Latino; 2 Hispanic/Latino; 4 Native Hawaiian or other Pacific Islander, non-Hispanic/Latino; 35 Two or more races, non-Hispanic/Latino), 24 international. Average age 36. 472 applicants, 87% accepted, 366 enrolled. In 2011, 747 master's, 42 doctorates, 69 other advanced degrees awarded. *Degree requirements:* For master's, thesis (for some programs), minimum GPA of 3.0; for doctorate, thesis/dissertation, minimum GPA of 3.0; for Ed S, comprehensive exam, project, minimum GPA of 3.0. *Entrance requirements:* For master's, interview, minimum GPA of 3.0, writing sample, letter of recommendation; for doctorate, GRE, minimum graduate GPA of 3.4, resume, interview, writing sample, 4 letters of recommendation; for Ed S, master's degree in education, relevant work experience. Additional exam requirements/recommendations for international students: Required—TOEFL (minimum score 550 paper-based; 213 computer-based; 80 iBT). *Application deadline:* For fall admission, 8/26 priority date for domestic students, 8/26 for international students; for spring admission, 1/27 priority date for domestic students, 1/27 for international students. Applications are processed on a rolling basis. Application fee: $30 ($100 for international students). Electronic applications accepted. *Expenses: Tuition:* Full-time $13,650; part-time $395 per credit hour. *Required fees:* $150 per semester. Tuition and fees vary according to course level and course load. *Financial support:* In 2011–12, 153 students received support. Career-related internships or fieldwork, institutionally sponsored loans, tuition waivers (partial), and unspecified assistantships available. Financial award application deadline: 6/30; financial award applicants required to submit FAFSA. *Unit head:* Dr. Cynthia Bice, Dean, 636-949-4618, Fax: 636-949-4197, E-mail: cbice@lindenwood.edu. *Application contact:* Brett Barger, Dean of Evening Admissions and Extension Campuses, 636-949-4934, Fax: 636-949-4109, E-mail: adultadmissions@lindenwood.edu.

Long Island University–Brooklyn Campus, School of Education, Department of Teaching and Learning, Program in Teaching English to Speakers of Other Languages, Brooklyn, NY 11201-8423. Offers MS Ed. Part-time and evening/weekend programs available. *Degree requirements:* For master's, thesis optional. *Entrance requirements:* For master's, 2 letters of recommendation. Additional exam requirements/recommendations for international students: Required—TOEFL (minimum score 500 paper-based; 173 computer-based). Electronic applications accepted.

Long Island University–C. W. Post Campus, School of Education, Department of Curriculum and Instruction, Brookville, NY 11548-1300. Offers adolescence education (MS); adolescence education: biology (MS); adolescence education: earth science (MS); adolescence education: English (MS); adolescence education: mathematics (MS); adolescence education: social studies (MS); adolescence education: Spanish (MS); art education (MS); bilingual education (MS); childhood education (MS); early childhood education (MS); middle childhood education (MS); music education (MS); teaching English to speakers of other languages (MS). Part-time and evening/weekend programs available. *Degree requirements:* For master's, comprehensive exam or thesis, student teaching. *Entrance requirements:* For master's, minimum GPA of 2.75 in major, 2.5 overall. Electronic applications accepted. *Faculty research:* Ethics and education, teaching strategies.

Long Island University–Hudson at Westchester, Programs in Education-Teaching, Program in Second Language, TESOL, Bilingual Education, Purchase, NY 10577. Offers MS Ed, Advanced Certificate. Part-time and evening/weekend programs available.

Loyola University Chicago, School of Education, Program in Teaching and Learning, Chicago, IL 60660. Offers elementary education (M Ed); English as a second language (Certificate); math education (M Ed); reading specialist (M Ed); reading teacher endorsement (Certificate); school technology (M Ed); science education (M Ed); secondary education (M Ed); special education (M Ed). *Accreditation:* NCATE. *Faculty:* 12 full-time (9 women), 12 part-time/adjunct (6 women). *Students:* 131. Average age 28. 115 applicants, 65% accepted, 30 enrolled. In 2011, 80 master's awarded. *Degree requirements:* For master's, comprehensive exam. *Entrance requirements:* For master's, Illinois Basic Skills Test, 3 letters of recommendation, minimum GPA of 3.0, resume. Additional exam requirements/recommendations for international students: Required—TOEFL (minimum score 550 paper-based; 213 computer-based; 79 iBT). *Application deadline:* For fall admission, 7/1 priority date for domestic students, 7/1 for international students; for spring admission, 11/1 priority date for domestic students, 11/1 for international students. Applications are processed on a rolling basis. Application fee: $50. Electronic applications accepted. Application fee is waived when completed online. *Expenses: Tuition:* Full-time $15,660; part-time $870 per credit hour. *Required fees:* $125 per semester. Tuition and fees vary according to course load and program. *Financial support:* Institutionally sponsored loans, scholarships/grants, and unspecified assistantships available. Support available to part-time students. Financial award application deadline: 2/1; financial award applicants required to submit FAFSA. *Faculty research:* Positive behavior support, school reform, school improvement. *Unit head:* Dr. Dorothy Giroux, Director, 312-915-7027, E-mail: dgiroux@luc.edu. *Application contact:* Marie Rosin-Dittmar, Information Contact, 312-915-6800, E-mail: schleduc@luc.edu.

Madonna University, Program in Teaching English to Speakers of Other Languages, Livonia, MI 48150-1173. Offers MATESOL. Part-time and evening/weekend programs available. *Degree requirements:* For master's, one foreign language, thesis or alternative. Electronic applications accepted.

Manhattanville College, Graduate Studies, School of Education, Program in English as a Second Language, Purchase, NY 10577-2132. Offers English as a second language (MAT); teaching English as a second language (MPS). Part-time and evening/weekend programs available. *Degree requirements:* For master's, comprehensive exam or research project, field experience. *Entrance requirements:* For master's, minimum undergraduate GPA of 3.0. Additional exam requirements/recommendations for international students: Required—TOEFL. Electronic applications accepted.

Marymount University, School of Education and Human Services, Program in Education, Arlington, VA 22207-4299. Offers elementary education (M Ed); English as a second language (M Ed); professional studies (M Ed); secondary education (M Ed); special education, general curriculum (M Ed). *Accreditation:* NCATE. Part-time and evening/weekend programs available. *Faculty:* 9 full-time (7 women), 7 part-time/adjunct (5 women). *Students:* 62 full-time (57 women), 103 part-time (86 women); includes 22 minority (3 Black or African American, non-Hispanic/Latino; 4 Asian, non-Hispanic/Latino; 10 Hispanic/Latino; 5 Two or more races, non-Hispanic/Latino), 13 international. Average age 31. 69 applicants, 100% accepted, 52 enrolled. In 2011, 79 master's awarded. *Degree requirements:* For master's, thesis or alternative. *Entrance requirements:* For master's, GRE or MAT and PRAXIS I or SAT/ACT and VCLA, 2 letters of recommendation, resume, interview. Additional exam requirements/recommendations for international students: Required—TOEFL (minimum score 600 paper-based; 250 computer-based; 96 iBT), IELTS (minimum score 6.5). *Application deadline:* For fall admission, 7/1 for international students. Applications are processed on a rolling basis. Application fee: $40. Electronic applications accepted. *Expenses: Tuition:* Part-time $770 per credit hour. *Required fees:* $8 per credit hour. One-time fee: $180 full-time. *Financial support:* In 2011–12, 27 students received support. Research assistantships with full tuition reimbursements available, career-related internships or fieldwork, Federal Work-Study, scholarships/grants, and unspecified assistantships available. Support available to part-time students. Financial award applicants required to submit FAFSA. *Unit head:* Dr. Shelly Haser, Chair, 703-526-6855, Fax: 703-284-1631, E-mail: shelly.haser@marymount.edu. *Application contact:* Francesca Reed, Director, Graduate Admissions, 703-284-5901, Fax: 703-527-3815, E-mail: grad.admissions@marymount.edu. Web site: http://www.marymount.edu/academics/schools/sehs/grad.aspx.

Mercy College, School of Education, Program in Teaching English to Speakers of Other Languages (TESOL), Dobbs Ferry, NY 10522-1189. Offers MS, Advanced Certificate. Part-time and evening/weekend programs available. Postbaccalaureate distance learning degree programs offered (no on-campus study). *Degree requirements:* For master's, comprehensive exam (for some programs). *Entrance requirements:* For master's, resume, interview, minimum undergraduate GPA of 3.0. Additional exam requirements/recommendations for international students: Required—TOEFL (minimum score 600 paper-based; 250 computer-based; 100 iBT), IELTS (minimum score 8). Electronic applications accepted. *Faculty research:* Multicultural literature, literacy assessment, literacy acquisition.

Merrimack College, School of Education, North Andover, MA 01845-5800. Offers community engagement (M Ed); early childhood education (M Ed); elementary education (M Ed); elementary education plus moderate disabilities-dual license (M Ed); English as a second language (M Ed); general studies (M Ed); higher education (M Ed); middle (M Ed); moderate disabilities (preK-8) (M Ed); reading (M Ed); secondary (M Ed); teacher leadership (CAGS). Part-time and evening/weekend programs available. *Faculty:* 4 full-time (all women), 9 part-time/adjunct (7 women). *Students:* 70 full-time (60 women), 39 part-time (33 women); includes 2 minority (1 Asian, non-Hispanic/Latino; 1 Hispanic/Latino). Average age 27. In 2011, 26 master's awarded. *Degree requirements:* For master's, portfolio. *Entrance requirements:* Additional exam requirements/recommendations for international students: Required—TOEFL (minimum score 80 iBT). *Application deadline:* For fall admission, 8/1 priority date for domestic students, 7/15 for international students; for winter admission, 12/1 priority date for domestic students, 11/15 for international students; for spring admission, 3/1 priority date for domestic students, 2/15 for international students. Applications are processed on a rolling basis. Electronic applications accepted. *Expenses: Tuition:* Part-time $475 per credit. *Required fees:* $62.50 per semester. *Financial support:* In 2011–12, 50 fellowships were awarded; career-related internships or fieldwork and scholarships/grants also available. Financial award applicants required to submit FAFSA. *Faculty research:* Higher education, community engagement, literacy, leadership. *Unit head:* Dr. Theresa Kirk, Chair, 978-837-5436, E-mail: kirkt@merrimack.edu. *Application contact:* Jessica McCarthy, Program Coordinator, 978-837-5443, E-mail: mccarthyj@merrimack.edu. Web site: http://www.merrimack.edu/academics/education/med/.

Messiah College, Program in Education, Mechanicsburg, PA 17055. Offers special education (M Ed); teaching English to speakers of other languages (M Ed). Part-time programs available. Postbaccalaureate distance learning degree programs offered (no on-campus study). *Faculty:* 5 full-time (3 women). *Students:* 3 full-time (all women), 4 part-time (all women). Average age 30. *Application deadline:* For fall admission, 6/1 priority date for domestic students; for winter admission, 11/1 priority date for domestic students; for spring admission, 11/1 priority date for domestic students. Applications are processed on a rolling basis. Application fee: $30. Electronic applications accepted. *Expenses: Tuition:* Full-time $9648; part-time $536 per credit hour. *Required fees:* $150; $25 per course. *Financial support:* Federal Work-Study available. Financial award applicants required to submit FAFSA. *Faculty research:* Socio-cultural perspectives on education, TESOL, autism, special education. *Unit head:* Dr. Nancy Patric, Faculty Member and Director of the Graduate Program in Education, 717-766-2511 Ext. 7239, E-mail: npatrick@messiah.edu. *Application contact:* Jackie Gehman, Graduate Enrollment Coordinator, 717-796-5061, Fax: 717-691-2386, E-mail: jgehman@messiah.edu. Web site: http://www.messiah.edu/academics/graduate_studies/Education/.

Michigan State University, The Graduate School, College of Arts and Letters, Department of Linguistics and Germanic, Slavic, Asian, and African Languages, East Lansing, MI 48824. Offers German studies (MA, PhD); linguistics (MA, PhD); teaching English to speakers of other languages (MA). Part-time and evening/weekend programs available. *Entrance requirements:* For master's, GRE General Test, minimum GPA of 3.2 in last 2 undergraduate years, 2 years of college-level foreign language, 3 letters of recommendation, portfolio (German studies); for doctorate, GRE General Test, minimum graduate GPA of 3.5, 3 letters of recommendation, master's degree or sufficient graduate course work in linguistics or language of study, master's thesis or major research paper. Additional exam requirements/recommendations for international students: Required—TOEFL. Electronic applications accepted.

MidAmerica Nazarene University, Graduate Studies in Education, Olathe, KS 66062-1899. Offers ESOL (M Ed); professional teaching (M Ed); special education (MA); technology enhanced teaching (M Ed). *Accreditation:* NCATE. Part-time and evening/weekend programs available. Postbaccalaureate distance learning degree programs offered (no on-campus study). *Degree requirements:* For master's, thesis or alternative, creative project, technology leadership practicum. *Entrance requirements:* For master's, minimum undergraduate GPA of 2.8, 2 years of teaching experience. *Expenses:* Contact institution.

Middle Tennessee State University, College of Graduate Studies, College of Education, Department of Educational Leadership, Program in Curriculum and Instruction, Murfreesboro, TN 37132. Offers curriculum and instruction (M Ed, Ed S); English as a second language (M Ed, Ed S); secondary education (M Ed); technology and curriculum design (Ed S). *Accreditation:* NCATE. Part-time and evening/weekend programs available. Postbaccalaureate distance learning degree programs offered. *Faculty:* 22 full-time (11 women), 22 part-time/adjunct (12 women). *Students:* 13 full-time (7 women), 208 part-time (167 women); includes 38 minority (29 Black or African American, non-Hispanic/Latino; 2 Asian, non-Hispanic/Latino; 2 Hispanic/Latino; 5 Two or more races, non-Hispanic/Latino). 154 applicants, 97% accepted. In 2011, 144 master's, 40 Ed Ss awarded. *Degree requirements:* For master's, comprehensive exam; for Ed S, comprehensive exam, thesis or alternative. *Entrance requirements:* For master's and Ed S, GRE, MAT or PRAXIS. Additional exam requirements/recommendations for international students: Required—TOEFL (minimum score 525 paper-based; 195 computer-based; 71 iBT) or IELTS (minimum score 6). *Application deadline:* For fall admission, 6/1 for domestic and international students. Applications are processed on a rolling basis. Application fee: $25 ($30 for international students). Electronic applications accepted. *Expenses:* Tuition, state resident: full-time $10,008. Tuition, nonresident: full-time $25,056. *Financial support:* Tuition waivers available. Support available to part-time students. Financial award application deadline: 5/1. *Unit head:* Dr. James Huffman, Chair, 615-898-2855, Fax: 615-898-2859. *Application contact:* Dr. Michael D. Allen, Dean and Vice Provost for Research, 615-898-2840, Fax: 615-904-8020, E-mail: michael.allen@mtsu.edu.

Middle Tennessee State University, College of Graduate Studies, College of Liberal Arts, Department of Foreign Languages and Literatures, Murfreesboro, TN 37132. Offers English as a second language (M Ed); foreign language (MAT). Part-time and evening/weekend programs available. Postbaccalaureate distance learning degree programs offered. *Faculty:* 16 full-time (12 women). *Students:* 3 full-time (all women), 14 part-time (11 women); includes 3 minority (1 Black or African American, non-Hispanic/Latino; 2 Hispanic/Latino). Average age 29. 15 applicants, 80% accepted. In 2011, 6 master's awarded. *Degree requirements:* For master's, one foreign language, comprehensive exam, thesis optional. *Entrance requirements:* For master's, GRE. Additional exam requirements/recommendations for international students: Required—TOEFL (minimum score 525 paper-based; 195 computer-based; 71 iBT) or IELTS (minimum score 6). *Application deadline:* For fall admission, 6/1 for domestic and international students. Applications are processed on a rolling basis. Application fee: $25 ($30 for international students). Electronic applications accepted. *Expenses:* Tuition, state resident: full-time $10,008. Tuition, nonresident: full-time $25,056. *Financial support:* In 2011–12, 15 students received support. Tuition waivers available. Support available to part-time students. Financial award application deadline: 5/1; financial award applicants required to submit FAFSA. *Faculty research:* Linguistics, holocaust studies, foreign language pedagogy. *Unit head:* Dr. Joan McRae, Chair, 615-898-2981, Fax: 615-898-5735, E-mail: joan.mcrae@mtsu.edu. *Application contact:* Dr. Michael D. Allen, Dean and Vice Provost for Research, 615-898-2840, Fax: 615-904-8020, E-mail: michael.allen@mtsu.edu.

Minnesota State University Mankato, College of Graduate Studies, College of Arts and Humanities, Department of English, Mankato, MN 56001. Offers creative writing (MFA); English (MAT); English studies (MA); teaching English as a second language (MA, Certificate); technical communication (MA, Certificate). Part-time programs available. *Students:* 57 full-time (30 women), 153 part-time (96 women). *Degree requirements:* For master's, one foreign language, comprehensive exam, thesis or alternative. *Entrance requirements:* For master's, minimum GPA of 3.0 during previous 2 years, writing sample (MFA). Additional exam requirements/recommendations for international students: Required—TOEFL (minimum score 500 paper-based; 61 iBT). *Application deadline:* For fall admission, 7/1 for domestic students, 5/1 for international students. Applications are processed on a rolling basis. Application fee: $40. Electronic applications accepted. *Financial support:* Research assistantships with full tuition reimbursements, teaching assistantships with full tuition reimbursements, career-related internships or fieldwork, Federal Work-Study, and unspecified assistantships available. Financial award application deadline: 3/15; financial award applicants required to submit FAFSA. *Faculty research:* Keats and Christianity. *Unit head:* Dr. John Banschbach, Chairperson, 507-389-2117. *Application contact:* 507-389-2321, E-mail: grad@mnsu.edu. Web site: http://english.mnsu.edu/.

Mississippi College, Graduate School, College of Arts and Sciences, School of Humanities and Social Sciences, Department of Modern Languages, Clinton, MS 39058. Offers teaching English to speakers of other languages (MA, MS). Part-time programs available. *Degree requirements:* For master's, thesis (for some programs). *Entrance requirements:* For master's, GRE or NTE. Additional exam requirements/recommendations for international students: Recommended—TOEFL, IELTS. Electronic applications accepted.

Missouri Western State University, Program in Assessment, St. Joseph, MO 64507-2294. Offers autism spectrum disorders (MAS); learning improvement (MAS); TESOL (MAS); writing (MAS). Part-time programs available. In 2011, 10 degrees awarded.

Application deadline: Applications are processed on a rolling basis. Application fee: $45 ($50 for international students). Electronic applications accepted. *Expenses:* Tuition, state resident: full-time $4697; part-time $261 per credit hour. Tuition, nonresident: full-time $9355; part-time $520 per credit hour. *Required fees:* $343; $19.10 per credit hour. $30 per semester. Tuition and fees vary according to course load. *Application contact:* Dr. Brian C. Cronk, Dean of the Graduate School, 816-271-4394, E-mail: graduate@missouriwestern.edu.

Monmouth University, The Graduate School, School of Education, West Long Branch, NJ 07764-1898. Offers education (M Ed); initial certification (MAT), including elementary level, K-12, secondary level; learning disabilities-teacher consultant (Certificate); principal (MS Ed); principal/school administrator (MS Ed); reading specialist (MS Ed, Certificate); school counseling (MS Ed); special education (MS Ed), including autism, learning disabilities teacher consultant, teacher of students with disabilities, teaching in inclusive settings; supervisor (Certificate); teacher of the handicapped (Certificate); teaching English to speakers of other languages (TESOL) (Certificate). *Accreditation:* NCATE. Part-time and evening/weekend programs available. *Faculty:* 16 full-time (12 women), 24 part-time/adjunct (17 women). *Students:* 134 full-time (104 women), 293 part-time (246 women); includes 34 minority (11 Black or African American, non-Hispanic/Latino; 2 Asian, non-Hispanic/Latino; 18 Hispanic/Latino; 3 Two or more races, non-Hispanic/Latino), 2 international. Average age 29. 288 applicants, 92% accepted, 182 enrolled. In 2011, 173 master's awarded. *Entrance requirements:* For master's, minimum GPA of 3.0 in major, 2.75 overall; 2 letters of recommendation (for some programs). Additional exam requirements/recommendations for international students: Required—TOEFL (minimum score 550 paper-based; 213 computer-based; 79 iBT), IELTS (minimum score 5), Michigan English Language Assessment Battery (minimum score 77), Cambridge A, B, C. *Application deadline:* For fall admission, 7/15 priority date for domestic students, 7/1 for international students; for spring admission, 11/15 priority date for domestic students, 11/1 for international students. Applications are processed on a rolling basis. Application fee: $50. Electronic applications accepted. *Financial support:* In 2011–12, 274 students received support, including 291 fellowships (averaging $1,783 per year), 21 research assistantships (averaging $8,792 per year); career-related internships or fieldwork, scholarships/grants, and unspecified assistantships also available. Support available to part-time students. Financial award applicants required to submit FAFSA. *Faculty research:* Multicultural literacy, science and mathematics teaching strategies, teacher as reflective practitioner, children with disabilities. *Unit head:* Dr. Jason Barr, Program Director, 732-263-5238, Fax: 732-263-5277, E-mail: jbarr@monmouth.edu. *Application contact:* Kevin Roane, Director, Office of Graduate Admission, 732-571-3452, Fax: 732-263-5123, E-mail: gradadm@monmouth.edu. Web site: http://www.monmouth.edu/academics/schools/education/default.asp.

Montclair State University, The Graduate School, College of Education and Human Services, Department of Curriculum and Teaching, Program in Teaching in Content Area, Montclair, NJ 07043-1624. Offers art (MAT); biology (MAT); chemistry (MAT); earth science (MAT); English (MAT); French (MAT); health and physical education (MAT); health education (MAT); mathematics (MAT); music (MAT); physical education (MAT); physical science (MAT); social studies (MAT); Spanish (MAT); teacher of English as a second language (MAT). *Students:* 162 full-time (90 women), 47 part-time (29 women); includes 37 minority (4 Black or African American, non-Hispanic/Latino; 11 Asian, non-Hispanic/Latino; 18 Hispanic/Latino; 4 Two or more races, non-Hispanic/Latino), 5 international. Average age 31. 145 applicants, 41% accepted, 56 enrolled. In 2011, 229 master's awarded. *Degree requirements:* For master's, comprehensive exam, thesis or alternative. *Entrance requirements:* For master's, GRE General Test, interview, 2 letters of recommendation. Additional exam requirements/recommendations for international students: Required—TOEFL (minimum score 83 iBT), IELTS (minimum score 6.5). *Application deadline:* Applications are processed on a rolling basis. Application fee: $60. Electronic applications accepted. *Financial support:* Federal Work-Study, scholarships/grants, and unspecified assistantships available. Support available to part-time students. Financial award application deadline: 3/1; financial award applicants required to submit FAFSA. *Unit head:* Dr. David Schwarzer, Chairperson, 973-655-5187. *Application contact:* Amy Aiello, Executive Director of The Graduate School, 973-655-5147, Fax: 973-655-7869, E-mail: graduate.school@montclair.edu.

Montclair State University, The Graduate School, College of Humanities and Social Sciences, Department of Linguistics, Program in Teaching English as a Second Language, Montclair, NJ 07043-1624. Offers MAT. *Students:* 17 part-time (16 women); includes 2 minority (both Hispanic/Latino). Average age 31. 5 applicants, 0% accepted, 0 enrolled. *Degree requirements:* For master's, comprehensive exam. *Entrance requirements:* For master's, GRE General Test, 2 letters of recommendation, essay. Additional exam requirements/recommendations for international students: Required—TOEFL (minimum score 83 iBT), IELTS (minimum score 6.5). *Application deadline:* Applications are processed on a rolling basis. Application fee: $60. Electronic applications accepted. *Financial support:* Applicants required to submit FAFSA. *Faculty research:* Cultural factors in bilingualism, emergent technologies in language learning. *Unit head:* Dr. Eileen Fitzpatrick, Chairperson, 973-655-4480. *Application contact:* Amy Aiello, Executive Director of The Graduate School, 973-655-5147, Fax: 973-655-7869, E-mail: graduate.school@montclair.edu.

Montclair State University, The Graduate School, College of Humanities and Social Sciences, Department of Linguistics, Teaching English to Speakers of Other Languages Certificate Program, Montclair, NJ 07043-1624. Offers Certificate. Part-time and evening/weekend programs available. *Students:* 2 full-time (1 woman), 5 part-time (4 women); includes 2 minority (both Asian, non-Hispanic/Latino). Average age 31. 10 applicants, 60% accepted, 3 enrolled. In 2011, 8 Certificates awarded. *Degree requirements:* For Certificate, comprehensive exam. *Entrance requirements:* For degree, 2 letters of recommendation, essay. Additional exam requirements/recommendations for international students: Required—TOEFL (minimum score 83 iBT), IELTS (minimum score 6.5). *Application deadline:* Applications are processed on a rolling basis. Application fee: $60. Electronic applications accepted. *Financial support:* Federal Work-Study, scholarships/grants, and unspecified assistantships available. Support available to part-time students. Financial award application deadline: 3/1; financial award applicants required to submit FAFSA. *Faculty research:* Language learning and technology research, interlanguage, bilingual pragmatics. *Unit head:* Dr. Eileen Fitzpatrick, Chairperson, 973-655-4480. *Application contact:* Amy Aiello, Executive Director of The Graduate School, 973-655-5147, E-mail: graduate.school@montclair.edu.

Monterey Institute of International Studies, Graduate School of Translation, Interpretation and Language Education, Program in Teaching English to Speakers of Other Languages, Monterey, CA 93940-2691. Offers MATESOL. *Degree requirements:* For master's, portfolio, oral defense. *Entrance requirements:* For master's, minimum GPA of 3.0. Additional exam requirements/recommendations for international students: Required—TOEFL (minimum score 600 paper-based; 250 computer-based; 100 iBT). Electronic applications accepted. *Expenses: Tuition:* Full-time $32,800; part-time $1560 per credit. *Required fees:* $28 per semester.

Mount Saint Vincent University, Graduate Programs, Faculty of Education, Program in Curriculum Studies, Halifax, NS B3M 2J6, Canada. Offers education of young adolescents (M Ed, MA Ed, MA-R); general studies (M Ed, MA Ed, MA-R); teaching English as a second language (M Ed, MA Ed, MA-R). Part-time and evening/weekend programs available. Postbaccalaureate distance learning degree programs offered (minimal on-campus study). *Degree requirements:* For master's, thesis (for some programs). *Entrance requirements:* For master's, bachelor's degree in related field, minimum B average, 1 year of teaching experience. Electronic applications accepted. *Faculty research:* Science education, cultural studies, international education, curriculum development.

Multnomah University, Multnomah Bible College Graduate Degree Programs, Portland, OR 97220-5898. Offers counseling (MA); teaching (MA); TESOL (MA). *Faculty:* 5 full-time (all women), 25 part-time/adjunct (12 women). *Students:* 126 full-time (84 women), 21 part-time (13 women); includes 24 minority (5 Black or African American, non-Hispanic/Latino; 1 American Indian or Alaska Native, non-Hispanic/Latino; 8 Asian, non-Hispanic/Latino; 7 Hispanic/Latino; 3 Two or more races, non-Hispanic/Latino). Average age 35. 73 applicants, 81% accepted, 45 enrolled. In 2011, 13 master's awarded. *Degree requirements:* For master's, variable foreign language requirement, comprehensive exam (for some programs), thesis optional. *Entrance requirements:* For master's, CBEST or WEST-B (for MAT), interview; references (4 for teaching); writing sample (for counseling). Additional exam requirements/recommendations for international students: Required—TOEFL (minimum score 550 paper-based; 213 computer-based). *Application deadline:* For fall admission, 8/1 for domestic students, 12/1 for international students; for spring admission, 12/1 for domestic and international students. Application fee: $40. *Expenses: Tuition:* Part-time $485 per credit hour. *Required fees:* $25 per semester. Tuition and fees vary according to campus/location and program. *Financial support:* Career-related internships or fieldwork and scholarships/grants available. Support available to part-time students. Financial award application deadline: 7/1; financial award applicants required to submit FAFSA. *Unit head:* Dr. Rex Koivisto, Academic Dean, 503-251-6401. *Application contact:* Jennifer Hancock, Assistant Director of Graduate and Seminary Admissions, 503-251-6481, Fax: 503-254-1268, E-mail: admiss@multnomah.edu.

Murray State University, College of Humanities and Fine Arts, Department of English and Philosophy, Program in Teaching English to Speakers of Other Languages, Murray, KY 42071. Offers MA. Part-time programs available. Postbaccalaureate distance learning degree programs offered (no on-campus study). *Degree requirements:* For master's, one foreign language, comprehensive exam, 12 hours for portfolio. *Entrance requirements:* For master's, minimum GPA of 2.25. Additional exam requirements/recommendations for international students: Required—TOEFL (minimum score 525 paper-based), IELTS (minimum score 5.5). *Faculty research:* Methods, integrated skills, intercultural communication, assessment.

Nazareth College of Rochester, Graduate Studies, Department of Education, Program in Teaching English to Speakers of Other Languages, Rochester, NY 14618-3790. Offers MS Ed. *Accreditation:* Teacher Education Accreditation Council. *Entrance requirements:* For master's, minimum GPA of 3.0.

New Jersey City University, Graduate Studies and Continuing Education, Debra Cannon Partridge Wolfe College of Education, Department of Educational Leadership, Jersey City, NJ 07305-1597. Offers basics and urban studies (MA); bilingual/bicultural education and English as a second language (MA); educational administration and supervision (MA). Part-time and evening/weekend programs available. *Students:* 16 full-time (12 women), 167 part-time (113 women); includes 72 minority (18 Black or African American, non-Hispanic/Latino; 3 Asian, non-Hispanic/Latino; 51 Hispanic/Latino), 6 international. Average age 34. In 2011, 126 master's awarded. *Entrance requirements:* Additional exam requirements/recommendations for international students: Required—TOEFL. *Application deadline:* For fall admission, 8/1 priority date for domestic students; for spring admission, 12/1 for domestic students. Applications are processed on a rolling basis. Application fee: $0. *Expenses:* Tuition, state resident: part-time $494 per credit. Tuition, nonresident: part-time $911.30 per credit. *Required fees:* $95.90 per year. *Financial support:* Fellowships, teaching assistantships, career-related internships or fieldwork, and unspecified assistantships available. *Unit head:* Dr. Catherine Rogers, Chairperson, 201-200-3012, E-mail: cshevey@njcu.edu. *Application contact:* Dr. William Bajor, Dean of Graduate Studies, 201-200-3409, Fax: 201-200-3411, E-mail: wbajor@njcu.edu.

Newman University, Master of Education Program, Wichita, KS 67213-2097. Offers building leadership (MS Ed); curriculum and instruction (MS Ed), including accountability, English as a second language, reading specialist. *Accreditation:* NCATE. Part-time and evening/weekend programs available. Postbaccalaureate distance learning degree programs offered (no on-campus study). *Faculty:* 4 full-time (2 women), 38 part-time/adjunct (all women). *Students:* 47 full-time (40 women), 414 part-time (318 women); includes 62 minority (20 Black or African American, non-Hispanic/Latino; 8 Asian, non-Hispanic/Latino; 30 Hispanic/Latino; 3 Native Hawaiian or other Pacific Islander, non-Hispanic/Latino; 1 Two or more races, non-Hispanic/Latino), 3 international. Average age 35. 42 applicants, 76% accepted, 27 enrolled. In 2011, 46 master's awarded. *Degree requirements:* For master's, thesis optional. *Entrance requirements:* For master's, interview, minimum GPA of 3.0, writing sample, 2 letters of recommendation, evidence of teaching certification. Additional exam requirements/recommendations for international students: Required—TOEFL (minimum score 600 paper-based; 250 computer-based; 100 iBT). *Application deadline:* For fall admission, 8/15 priority date for domestic students, 7/15 for international students; for spring admission, 1/10 priority date for domestic students, 11/15 for international students. Applications are processed on a rolling basis. Application fee: $25 ($40 for international students). Electronic applications accepted. *Expenses:* Contact institution. *Financial support:* In 2011–12, 18 students received support. Federal Work-Study available. Financial award application deadline: 8/15; financial award applicants required to submit FAFSA. *Unit head:* Dr. Guy Glidden, Director, Graduate Education, 316-942-4291 Ext. 2331, Fax: 316-942-4483, E-mail: gliddeng@newmanu.edu. *Application contact:* Linda Kay Sabala, Director of Graduate Admissions, 316-942-4291 Ext. 2230, Fax: 316-942-4483, E-mail: sabalal@newmanu.edu.

The New School, The New School for Public Engagement, Program in Teaching English to Speakers of Other Languages, New York, NY 10011. Offers MA. Part-time and evening/weekend programs available. Postbaccalaureate distance learning degree programs offered (no on-campus study). *Entrance requirements:* Additional exam requirements/recommendations for international students: Required—TOEFL (minimum score 600 paper-based; 250 computer-based; 100 iBT), IELTS (minimum score 7), TWE. Electronic applications accepted.

New York University, Steinhardt School of Culture, Education, and Human Development, Department of Teaching and Learning, Program in Multilingual/Multicultural Studies, New York, NY 10012-1019. Offers bilingual education (MA, PhD, Advanced Certificate); foreign language education (MA, Advanced Certificate); foreign language education/TESOL (MA); teaching English to speakers of other languages (MA, PhD, Advanced Certificate); teaching French as a foreign language (MA). *Accreditation:* Teacher Education Accreditation Council. Part-time and evening/weekend programs available. *Degree requirements:* For master's, thesis (for some programs); for doctorate, thesis/dissertation. *Entrance requirements:* For doctorate, GRE General Test, interview; for Advanced Certificate, master's degree. Additional exam requirements/

recommendations for international students: Required—TOEFL. Electronic applications accepted. *Faculty research:* Second language acquisition, cross-cultural communication, technology-enhanced language learning, language variation, action learning.

Northeastern Illinois University, Graduate College, College of Arts and Sciences, Department of Linguistics, Program in Linguistics, Chicago, IL 60625-4699. Offers linguistics (MA); TESL (MA). Part-time and evening/weekend programs available. *Degree requirements:* For master's, one foreign language, comprehensive exam, thesis optional. *Entrance requirements:* For master's, 9 undergraduate hours in a foreign language or equivalent, minimum GPA of 2.75. Additional exam requirements/recommendations for international students: Required—TOEFL (minimum score 550 paper-based; 213 computer-based; 79 iBT). Electronic applications accepted. *Faculty research:* Acquisition of literacy, Mayan language, Rotuman language, English as a second language methodology, Farsi language.

Northern Arizona University, Graduate College, College of Arts and Letters, Department of English, Flagstaff, AZ 86011. Offers applied linguistics (PhD); English (MA, MFA), including creative writing (MFA), general English studies (MA), literacy, technology and professional writing (MA), literature (MA), secondary English education (MA); professional writing (Certificate); teaching English as a second language (MA, Certificate). Part-time programs available. *Faculty:* 52 full-time (35 women). *Students:* 107 full-time (70 women), 100 part-time (77 women); includes 41 minority (9 Black or African American, non-Hispanic/Latino; 3 American Indian or Alaska Native, non-Hispanic/Latino; 2 Asian, non-Hispanic/Latino; 20 Hispanic/Latino; 7 Two or more races, non-Hispanic/Latino), 30 international. Average age 31. 209 applicants, 62% accepted, 78 enrolled. In 2011, 115 master's, 5 doctorates, 14 other advanced degrees awarded. *Degree requirements:* For master's, comprehensive exam (for some programs), thesis (for some programs), departmental qualifying exam; for doctorate, comprehensive exam, thesis/dissertation, departmental qualifying exam. *Entrance requirements:* For master's, minimum GPA of 3.0 or GRE; for doctorate, GRE General Test. Additional exam requirements/recommendations for international students: Required—TOEFL (minimum score 550 paper-based; 213 computer-based; 80 iBT), IELTS (minimum score 7), TOEFL (minimum score 600 paper-based; 250 computer-based; 100 iBT) for PhD; TOEFL (minimum score 570 paper-based; 237 computer-based; 89 iBT) for MA. *Application deadline:* For fall admission, 4/15 priority date for domestic students, 2/15 for international students; for spring admission, 11/15 priority date for domestic students, 11/15 for international students. Applications are processed on a rolling basis. Application fee: $65. Electronic applications accepted. *Expenses:* Tuition, state resident: full-time $7190; part-time $355 per credit hour. Tuition, nonresident: full-time $18,092; part-time $1005 per credit hour. *Required fees:* $818; $328 per semester. *Financial support:* In 2011–12, 72 teaching assistantships with partial tuition reimbursements (averaging $11,623 per year) were awarded; Federal Work-Study, scholarships/grants, health care benefits, tuition waivers (full and partial), and unspecified assistantships also available. Financial award applicants required to submit FAFSA. *Unit head:* Dr. John Rothfork, Chair, 928-523-0559, Fax: 928-523-4911, E-mail: john.rothfork@nau.edu. *Application contact:* Yvette Loeffler-Schmelzle, Secretary, 928-523-6842, Fax: 928-523-4911, E-mail: yvette.schmelzle@nau.edu. Web site: http://nau.edu/cal/english/.

Northern Arizona University, Graduate College, College of Education, Department of Educational Specialties, Flagstaff , AZ 86011. Offers autism spectrum disorders (Certificate); bilingual/multicultural education (M Ed), including bilingual education, ESL education; career and technical education (M Ed, Certificate); curriculum and instruction (Ed D); early childhood special education (M Ed); early intervention (Certificate); educational technology (M Ed, Certificate); special education (M Ed). *Faculty:* 28 full-time (19 women). *Students:* 113 full-time (91 women), 206 part-time (158 women); includes 104 minority (8 Black or African American, non-Hispanic/Latino; 17 American Indian or Alaska Native, non-Hispanic/Latino; 6 Asian, non-Hispanic/Latino; 65 Hispanic/Latino; 2 Native Hawaiian or other Pacific Islander, non-Hispanic/Latino; 6 Two or more races, non-Hispanic/Latino), 3 international. Average age 30. 141 applicants, 75% accepted, 76 enrolled. In 2011, 167 master's, 7 Certificates awarded. *Degree requirements:* For master's, comprehensive exam (for some programs), thesis (for some programs). *Entrance requirements:* For master's, minimum GPA of 3.0. Additional exam requirements/recommendations for international students: Required—TOEFL (minimum score 550 paper-based; 213 computer-based; 80 iBT), IELTS (minimum score 7). *Application deadline:* For fall admission, 3/1 for international students; for spring admission, 9/15 for international students. Applications are processed on a rolling basis. Application fee: $65. Electronic applications accepted. *Expenses:* Tuition, state resident: full-time $7190; part-time $355 per credit hour. Tuition, nonresident: full-time $18,092; part-time $1005 per credit hour. *Required fees:* $818; $328 per semester. *Financial support:* Applicants required to submit FAFSA. *Unit head:* Dr. Jennifer Prior, Chair, 928-523-5064, Fax: 928-523-1929, E-mail: jennifer.prior@nau.edu. *Application contact:* Shirley Robinson, Coordinator, 928-523-4348, Fax: 928-523-8950, E-mail: shirley.robinson@nau.edu. Web site: http://nau.edu/coe/ed-specialties/.

Northwest Missouri State University, Graduate School, College of Education and Human Services, Department of Curriculum and Instruction, Maryville, MO 64468-6001. Offers English language learners (Certificate); reading (MS Ed); special education (MS Ed); teaching: early childhood (MS Ed); teaching: elementary self contained (MS Ed); teaching: English language learners (MS Ed); teaching: middle school (MS Ed). *Accreditation:* NCATE. Part-time programs available. *Faculty:* 11 full-time (all women). *Students:* 9 full-time (all women), 74 part-time (68 women); includes 6 minority (1 Black or African American, non-Hispanic/Latino; 3 Hispanic/Latino; 2 Two or more races, non-Hispanic/Latino). 31 applicants, 100% accepted, 17 enrolled. In 2011, 38 master's awarded. *Degree requirements:* For master's, comprehensive exam. *Entrance requirements:* For master's, GRE General Test, minimum undergraduate GPA of 2.75, teaching certificate, writing sample. Additional exam requirements/recommendations for international students: Required—TOEFL (minimum score 550 paper-based; 213 computer-based). *Application deadline:* For fall admission, 7/1 for domestic and international students; for spring admission, 11/15 for domestic and international students. Applications are processed on a rolling basis. Application fee: $0 ($50 for international students). Electronic applications accepted. *Financial support:* In 2011–12, research assistantships with full tuition reimbursements (averaging $6,000 per year), 3 teaching assistantships with full tuition reimbursements (averaging $6,000 per year) were awarded; unspecified assistantships also available. Financial award application deadline: 4/1; financial award applicants required to submit FAFSA. *Unit head:* Dr. Barbara Crossland, Head, 660-562-1776, E-mail: barbara@mail.nwmissouri.edu. *Application contact:* Dr. Gregory Haddock, Dean of Graduate School, 660-562-1145, Fax: 660-562-1096, E-mail: gradsch@nwmissouri.edu.

Notre Dame de Namur University, Division of Academic Affairs, College of Arts and Sciences, Department of English, Belmont, CA 94002-1908. Offers English (MA); teaching English to speakers of other languages (Certificate). Part-time and evening/weekend programs available. *Faculty:* 5 full-time (2 women), 5 part-time/adjunct (3 women). *Students:* 4 full-time (3 women), 20 part-time (15 women); includes 1 minority (Hispanic/Latino). Average age 28. 6 applicants, 100% accepted, 4 enrolled. In 2011, 6 master's awarded. *Degree requirements:* For master's, thesis optional, exam. *Entrance requirements:* For master's, minimum GPA of 2.5, writing sample. Additional exam requirements/recommendations for international students: Required—TOEFL (minimum score 550 paper-based; 213 computer-based; 79 iBT). *Application deadline:* For fall admission, 8/1 priority date for domestic students; for spring admission, 12/1 priority date for domestic students. Applications are processed on a rolling basis. Application fee: $50 ($500 for international students). Electronic applications accepted. *Expenses: Tuition:* Full-time $14,220; part-time $790 per credit. *Required fees:* $35 per semester. Tuition and fees vary according to program. *Financial support:* Career-related internships or fieldwork available. Support available to part-time students. Financial award applicants required to submit FAFSA. *Unit head:* Jacqueline Berger, Director, 650-508-3730. *Application contact:* Candace Hallmark, Associate Director of Admissions, 650-508-3600, Fax: 650-508-3426, E-mail: grad.admit@ndnu.edu.

Notre Dame of Maryland University, Graduate Studies, Program in Teaching English to Speakers of Other Languages, Baltimore, MD 21210-2476. Offers MA. *Accreditation:* NCATE. Part-time and evening/weekend programs available. *Entrance requirements:* Additional exam requirements/recommendations for international students: Required—TOEFL (minimum score 500 paper-based; 173 computer-based; 61 iBT). Electronic applications accepted.

Oakland University, Graduate Study and Lifelong Learning, College of Arts and Sciences, Department of Linguistics, Rochester, MI 48309-4401. Offers linguistics (MA); teaching English as a second language (Certificate). Part-time and evening/weekend programs available. *Entrance requirements:* For master's, minimum GPA of 3.0 for unconditional admission. Additional exam requirements/recommendations for international students: Required—TOEFL (minimum score 550 paper-based; 213 computer-based).

Ohio Dominican University, Graduate Programs, TESOL Program, Columbus, OH 43219-2099. Offers MA. Part-time and evening/weekend programs available. *Degree requirements:* For master's, thesis. *Entrance requirements:* For master's, minimum undergraduate GPA of 3.0, 3 letters of recommendation, interview. Additional exam requirements/recommendations for international students: Required—TOEFL (minimum score 550 paper-based; 213 computer-based), IELTS (minimum score 6.5).

Ohio University, Graduate College, College of Arts and Sciences, Department of Linguistics, Athens, OH 45701-2979. Offers applied linguistics/TESOL (MA). Part-time programs available. *Students:* 32 full-time (16 women), 3 part-time (2 women), 19 international. 80 applicants, 39% accepted, 12 enrolled. In 2011, 16 master's awarded. *Degree requirements:* For master's, one foreign language, thesis or alternative. *Entrance requirements:* For master's, minimum GPA of 3.0. Additional exam requirements/recommendations for international students: Required—TOEFL (minimum score 600 paper-based; 100 iBT) or IELTS (minimum score 7). *Application deadline:* For fall admission, 2/15 priority date for domestic students, 2/15 for international students. Application fee: $50 ($55 for international students). Electronic applications accepted. *Financial support:* In 2011–12, 2 fellowships with tuition reimbursements were awarded; research assistantships with tuition reimbursements, teaching assistantships with tuition reimbursements, Federal Work-Study, institutionally sponsored loans, tuition waivers (partial), and unspecified assistantships also available. Financial award application deadline: 2/15. *Faculty research:* Syntax, language learning, language teaching, computers for teaching, sociolinguistics. *Unit head:* Dr. Chris Thompson, Chair, 740-593-0666, E-mail: thompsoc@ohio.edu. *Application contact:* Dr. Hiroyuki Oshita, Graduate Chair, 740-593-4570, Fax: 740-593-2967, E-mail: oshita@ohio.edu. Web site: http://www.ohiou.edu/linguistics/dept/welcome.html.

Oklahoma City University, Petree College of Arts and Sciences, Program in Teaching English to Speakers of Other Languages, Oklahoma City, OK 73106-1402. Offers MA. Part-time and evening/weekend programs available. *Faculty:* 4 full-time (2 women), 2 part-time/adjunct (both women). *Students:* 44 full-time (35 women), 23 part-time (19 women); includes 5 minority (2 Black or African American, non-Hispanic/Latino; 1 Asian, non-Hispanic/Latino; 2 Hispanic/Latino), 61 international. Average age 34. In 2011, 47 master's awarded. *Degree requirements:* For master's, comprehensive exam, thesis optional. *Entrance requirements:* For master's, minimum GPA of 3.0. Additional exam requirements/recommendations for international students: Required—TOEFL (minimum score 600 paper-based; 260 computer-based). *Application deadline:* Applications are processed on a rolling basis. Application fee: $50 ($70 for international students). Electronic applications accepted. *Expenses: Tuition:* Full-time $16,848; part-time $936 per credit hour. *Required fees:* $2070; $115 per credit hour. One-time fee: $300. *Financial support:* Career-related internships or fieldwork and Federal Work-Study available. Support available to part-time students. Financial award application deadline: 6/1. *Faculty research:* L2 language acquisition, L2 writing language. *Unit head:* Dr. Robert Griffin, Acting Director, 405-208-5941, Fax: 405-208-6012, E-mail: rgriffin@okcu.edu. *Application contact:* Michelle Cook, Director, Graduate Admissions, 800-633-7242, Fax: 405-208-5916, E-mail: gadmissions@okcu.edu. Web site: http://www.okcu.edu/petree/graduate/tesol/.

Our Lady of the Lake University of San Antonio, School of Professional Studies, Program in Curriculum and Instruction, San Antonio, TX 78207-4689. Offers bilingual (M Ed); early childhood education (M Ed); English as a second language (M Ed); integrated math teaching (M Ed); integrated science teaching (M Ed); master reading teacher (M Ed); master technology teacher (M Ed); reading specialist (M Ed).

Pontifical Catholic University of Puerto Rico, College of Education, Program in English as a Second Language, Ponce, PR 00717-0777. Offers M Ed. *Degree requirements:* For master's, comprehensive exam, thesis (for some programs). *Entrance requirements:* For master's, GRE, 2 letters of recommendation, interview, minimum GPA of 2.75.

Portland State University, Graduate Studies, College of Liberal Arts and Sciences, Department of Applied Linguistics, Portland, OR 97207-0751. Offers teaching English to speakers of other languages (MA). Part-time programs available. *Degree requirements:* For master's, one foreign language, comprehensive exam, thesis. *Entrance requirements:* For master's, minimum GPA of 3.0 in upper-division course work or 2.75 overall, proficiency in at least 1 foreign language. Additional exam requirements/recommendations for international students: Required—TOEFL (minimum score 600 paper-based; 250 computer-based). *Faculty research:* Sociolinguistics, linguistics and cognitive science, language proficiency testing, lexical phrases and language teaching, teaching English as a second language methodology.

Providence College and Theological Seminary, Theological Seminary, Otterburne, MB R0A 1G0, Canada. Offers children's ministry (Certificate); Christian studies (MA, Certificate); counseling (MA); cross-cultural discipleship (Certificate); divinity (M Div); educational studies (MA), including counseling psychology, educational ministries, student development, teaching English to speakers of other languages, training teachers of English to speakers of other languages; global studies (MA); lay counseling (Diploma); ministry (D Min); teaching English to speakers of other languages (Certificate); theological studies (MA); training teacher of English to speakers of other languages (Certificate); youth ministry (Certificate). *Accreditation:* ATS. Part-time programs available. *Degree requirements:* For master's, variable foreign language requirement, thesis (for some programs); for doctorate, thesis/dissertation. *Entrance requirements:* Additional exam requirements/recommendations for international students: Recommended—TOEFL (minimum score 550 paper-based; 213 computer-based). *Faculty research:* Studies in Isaiah, theology of sin.

Queens College of the City University of New York, Division of Graduate Studies, Arts and Humanities Division, Department of Linguistics and Communication Disorders, Program in Teaching English to Speakers of Other Languages, Flushing, NY 11367-1597. Offers MS Ed. Part-time and evening/weekend programs available. *Faculty:* 8 full-time (5 women). *Students:* 10 full-time (all women), 107 part-time (96 women); includes 45 minority (1 Black or African American, non-Hispanic/Latino; 20 Asian, non-Hispanic/Latino; 24 Hispanic/Latino), 1 international. 110 applicants, 52% accepted, 42 enrolled. In 2011, 36 master's awarded. *Degree requirements:* For master's, thesis optional. *Entrance requirements:* For master's, minimum GPA of 3.0. Additional exam requirements/recommendations for international students: Required—TOEFL. *Application deadline:* For fall admission, 4/1 for domestic students; for spring admission, 11/1 for domestic students. Applications are processed on a rolling basis. Application fee: $125. *Expenses:* Tuition, state resident: part-time $345 per credit. Tuition, nonresident: part-time $640 per credit. *Required fees:* $145.25 per semester. *Financial support:* Career-related internships or fieldwork, Federal Work-Study, institutionally sponsored loans, and tuition waivers (partial) available. Support available to part-time students. Financial award application deadline: 4/1; financial award applicants required to submit FAFSA. *Unit head:* Dr. Robert M. Vago, Chairperson, 718-997-2875. *Application contact:* Mario Caruso, Director of Graduate Admissions, 718-997-5200, Fax: 718-997-5193, E-mail: graduate_admissions@qc.edu.

Regent University, Graduate School, School of Divinity, Virginia Beach, VA 23464-9800. Offers Biblical studies (MA), including Biblical interpretation, Christian doctrine and history, English Bible, New Testament, Old Testament; leadership and renewal (D Min), including Christian leadership and renewal, clinical pastoral education, community transformation, military ministry, ministry leadership coaching; missiology (M Div, MA), including Biblical languages (M Div), Biblical studies (M Div), church and ministry, interdisciplinary studies, TESOL, worship and renewal; practical theology (M Div, MA), including Biblical studies (M Div), church and ministry, interdisciplinary studies, military chaplaincy (MA), worship and renewal; renewal studies (PhD), including history, theology. *Accreditation:* ACIPE; ATS. Part-time programs available. Postbaccalaureate distance learning degree programs offered (minimal on-campus study). *Faculty:* 20 full-time (4 women), 16 part-time/adjunct (4 women). *Students:* 124 full-time (64 women), 529 part-time (209 women); includes 298 minority (260 Black or African American, non-Hispanic/Latino; 5 American Indian or Alaska Native, non-Hispanic/Latino; 13 Asian, non-Hispanic/Latino; 20 Hispanic/Latino), 41 international. Average age 41. 506 applicants, 60% accepted, 179 enrolled. In 2011, 94 master's, 14 doctorates awarded. *Degree requirements:* For master's, comprehensive exam, thesis or alternative, internship; for doctorate, thesis/dissertation or alternative. *Entrance requirements:* For master's, GRE General Test or MAT, minimum undergraduate GPA of 2.75, writing sample, clergy recommendation; for doctorate, M Div or theological master's degree; minimum graduate GPA of 3.5 (PhD), 3.0 (D Min); recommendations; writing sample; transcripts. Additional exam requirements/recommendations for international students: Required—TOEFL (minimum score 577 paper-based; 233 computer-based). *Application deadline:* For fall admission, 5/1 priority date for domestic students. Applications are processed on a rolling basis. Application fee: $50. Electronic applications accepted. *Expenses:* Contact institution. *Financial support:* Fellowships with full and partial tuition reimbursements, career-related internships or fieldwork, scholarships/grants, tuition waivers (full and partial), and unspecified assistantships available. Support available to part-time students. Financial award application deadline: 9/1; financial award applicants required to submit FAFSA. *Faculty research:* Greek and Hebrew, theology, spiritual formation, global missions and world Christianity, women's studies. *Unit head:* Dr. Michael Palmer, Dean, 757-352-4406, Fax: 757-352-4597, E-mail: mpalmer@regent.edu. *Application contact:* Matthew Chadwick, Director of Enrollment Support Services, 800-373-5504, Fax: 757-352-4381, E-mail: admissions@regent.edu. Web site: http://www.regent.edu/acad/schdiv/home.shtml?r=home.cfm.

Regent University, Graduate School, School of Education, Virginia Beach, VA 23464-9800. Offers adult education (Ed D); adult/staff development (Ed D, PhD); career switcher with licensure (M Ed), including alternative licensure; character education (Ed D, PhD); Christian education leadership (Ed D, PhD); Christian education specialist (Ed S); Christian school program (M Ed), including ACSI licensure; distance education (Ed D, PhD); education licensure (M Ed), including preK-6th grade; educational leadership (M Ed, PhD); educational leadership - special education (Ed S), including administration and supervision; educational psychology (Ed D, PhD), including learning and development, research and evaluation, special education; higher education (Ed D, PhD), including administration, research and institutional planning, teaching; higher education leadership (Ed D); individualized degree plan (M Ed), including behavior disorders, learning disabilities, mental retardation, reading specialist; K-12 school leadership (Ed D, PhD); leadership in character education (M Ed); master teacher (M Ed), including TESOL; mathematics education (M Ed); special education (PhD); student affairs (M Ed); TESOL (M Ed), including adult education, ESL: preK-12. *Accreditation:* Teacher Education Accreditation Council. Part-time and evening/weekend programs available. Postbaccalaureate distance learning degree programs offered (minimal on-campus study). *Faculty:* 26 full-time (13 women), 54 part-time/adjunct (34 women). *Students:* 140 full-time (109 women), 786 part-time (626 women); includes 218 minority (189 Black or African American, non-Hispanic/Latino; 2 American Indian or Alaska Native, non-Hispanic/Latino; 11 Asian, non-Hispanic/Latino; 16 Hispanic/Latino), 42 international. Average age 39. 673 applicants, 57% accepted, 298 enrolled. In 2011, 178 master's, 15 doctorates awarded. *Degree requirements:* For master's, thesis or alternative; for doctorate, comprehensive exam, thesis/dissertation. *Entrance requirements:* For master's, MAT, minimum undergraduate GPA of 2.75, writing sample, resume, recommendations, interview; for doctorate, GRE, writing sample, 3 years of relevant professional experience, master's-level paper, copies of published work, resume, transcripts, interview, recommendations. Additional exam requirements/recommendations for international students: Required—TOEFL (minimum score 577 paper-based; 233 computer-based). *Application deadline:* For fall admission, 4/1 priority date for domestic students; for spring admission, 10/15 priority date for domestic students. Applications are processed on a rolling basis. Application fee: $50. Electronic applications accepted. *Expenses:* Contact institution. *Financial support:* Fellowships, career-related internships or fieldwork, scholarships/grants, tuition waivers (full and partial), and unspecified assistantships available. Support available to part-time students. Financial award application deadline: 4/1; financial award applicants required to submit FAFSA. *Faculty research:* Character development and discipline for children, education leadership development, diversity in schools, classroom management, technology in education settings. *Unit head:* Dr. Alan A. Arroyo, Dean, 757-352-4261, Fax: 757-352-4318, E-mail: alanarr@regent.edu. *Application contact:* Matthew Chadwick, Director of Enrollment Support Services, 800-373-5504, Fax: 757-352-4381, E-mail: admissions@regent.edu. Web site: http://www.regent.edu/education/.

Rhode Island College, School of Graduate Studies, Feinstein School of Education and Human Development, Department of Educational Studies, Providence, RI 02908-1991. Offers advanced studies in teaching and learning (M Ed); English (MAT); French (MAT); history (MAT); math (MAT); secondary education (MAT); Spanish (MAT); teaching English as a second language (M Ed). *Accreditation:* NCATE. Part-time and evening/weekend programs available. *Faculty:* 14 full-time (7 women), 4 part-time/adjunct (2 women). *Students:* 10 full-time (all women), 61 part-time (51 women); includes 8 minority (1 Black or African American, non-Hispanic/Latino; 4 Asian, non-Hispanic/Latino; 3 Hispanic/Latino). Average age 33. In 2011, 32 master's awarded. *Degree requirements:* For master's, capstone or comprehensive assessment. *Entrance requirements:* For master's, GRE or MAT (for most programs), minimum undergraduate GPA of 3.0; baccalaureate degree in English, French, history, math or Spanish; evaluation of content area knowledge; 3 letters of recommendation; interview. Additional exam requirements/recommendations for international students: Recommended—TOEFL (minimum score 550 paper-based; 213 computer-based; 79 iBT). *Application deadline:* For fall admission, 3/1 for domestic students; for spring admission, 11/1 for domestic students. Applications are processed on a rolling basis. Application fee: $50. *Expenses:* Tuition, state resident: full-time $8592; part-time $358 per credit hour. Tuition, nonresident: full-time $16,800; part-time $700 per credit hour. *Required fees:* $602; $22 per credit. $72 per term. *Financial support:* Teaching assistantships with full tuition reimbursements, career-related internships or fieldwork, Federal Work-Study, scholarships/grants, health care benefits, and unspecified assistantships available. Support available to part-time students. Financial award application deadline: 5/15; financial award applicants required to submit FAFSA. *Faculty research:* School administration, school/college articulation. *Unit head:* Dr. Ellen Bigler, Chair, 401-456-8170. *Application contact:* Graduate Studies, 401-456-8700. Web site: http://www.ric.edu/educationalStudies/.

Rider University, Department of Graduate Education, Leadership and Counseling, Teacher Certification Program, Lawrenceville, NJ 08648-3001. Offers business education (Certificate); elementary education (Certificate); English as a second language (Certificate); English education (Certificate); mathematics education (Certificate); preschool to grade 3 (Certificate); science education (Certificate); social studies education (Certificate); world languages (Certificate), including French, German, Spanish. Part-time programs available. *Degree requirements:* For Certificate, internship, professional portfolio. *Entrance requirements:* For degree, PRAXIS, resume. Additional exam requirements/recommendations for international students: Required—TOEFL (minimum score 550 paper-based; 213 computer-based). Electronic applications accepted. *Expenses: Tuition:* Full-time $32,820; part-time $710 per credit. *Required fees:* $350; $35 per course. Tuition and fees vary according to campus/location and program. *Faculty research:* Conceptual foundations for optimal development of creativity; creative theory, cognitive processes in mathematics learning, teacher collaboration.

Rowan University, Graduate School, College of Education, Department of Teacher Education, Program in ESL/Bilingual Education, Glassboro, NJ 08028-1701. Offers Graduate Certificate. Part-time and evening/weekend programs available. *Entrance requirements:* Additional exam requirements/recommendations for international students: Required—TOEFL. Electronic applications accepted.

Rutgers, The State University of New Jersey, New Brunswick, Graduate School of Education, Department of Learning and Teaching, Program in Language Education, Piscataway, NJ 08854-8097. Offers English as a second language education (Ed M); language education (Ed M, Ed D). Part-time programs available. Terminal master's awarded for partial completion of doctoral program. *Degree requirements:* For master's, comprehensive exam; for doctorate, thesis/dissertation, concept paper, qualifying exam. *Entrance requirements:* For master's, GRE General Test, minimum GPA of 3.0; for doctorate, GRE General Test, minimum GPA of 3.5. Additional exam requirements/recommendations for international students: Required—TOEFL. Electronic applications accepted. *Faculty research:* Linguistics, sociolinguistics, cross-cultural/international communication.

St. Cloud State University, School of Graduate Studies, College of Liberal Arts, Department of English, St. Cloud, MN 56301-4498. Offers English (MA, MS); teaching English as a second language (MA). Part-time programs available. *Degree requirements:* For master's, thesis or alternative. *Entrance requirements:* For master's, GRE General Test, minimum GPA of 2.75. Additional exam requirements/recommendations for international students: Required—Michigan English Language Assessment Battery; Recommended—TOEFL (minimum score 550 paper-based; 213 computer-based), IELTS (minimum score 6.5). Electronic applications accepted.

St. John's University, The School of Education, Department of Human Services and Counseling, Program in Teaching English to Speakers of Other Languages, Queens, NY 11439. Offers MS Ed, Adv C. Part-time and evening/weekend programs available. Postbaccalaureate distance learning degree programs offered. *Students:* 73 full-time (69 women), 183 part-time (160 women); includes 92 minority (8 Black or African American, non-Hispanic/Latino; 16 Asian, non-Hispanic/Latino; 65 Hispanic/Latino; 1 Native Hawaiian or other Pacific Islander, non-Hispanic/Latino; 2 Two or more races, non-Hispanic/Latino), 28 international. Average age 32. 221 applicants, 92% accepted, 104 enrolled. In 2011, 61 master's awarded. *Degree requirements:* For master's, comprehensive exam, fieldwork. *Entrance requirements:* For master's, minimum GPA of 3.0, eligibility for teacher certification, 2 letters of recommendation; for Adv C, New York State initial teaching certification or eligibility for teaching certification. Additional exam requirements/recommendations for international students: Required—TOEFL (minimum score 600 paper-based; 250 computer-based; 100 iBT), IELTS (minimum score 5.5). *Application deadline:* For fall admission, 8/17 for domestic students, 5/1 for international students; for spring admission, 1/5 for domestic students, 11/1 for international students. Applications are processed on a rolling basis. Application fee: $70. Electronic applications accepted. *Expenses: Tuition:* Full-time $18,000; part-time $1000 per credit. *Required fees:* $170 per semester. Tuition and fees vary according to program. *Financial support:* Research assistantships, career-related internships or fieldwork, and scholarships/grants available. Support available to part-time students. Financial award application deadline: 3/1; financial award applicants required to submit FAFSA. *Faculty research:* Second language learning and academic achievement, heritage language education, assessing the progress of English language learners towards English acquisition, dual language acquisition, study of English Creoles and dialects of other Englishes. *Unit head:* Dr. Francine Guastello, Chair, 718-990-1475, E-mail: guastelf@stjohns.edu. *Application contact:* Dr. Kelly K. Ronayne, Associate Dean of Graduate Admissions, 718-990-2304, Fax: 718-990-2343, E-mail: graded@stjohns.edu.

Saint Joseph's University, College of Arts and Sciences, Department of Education, Philadelphia, PA 19131-1395. Offers curriculum supervisor of instruction (Certificate); educational leadership (MS, Ed D); elementary education (MS, Certificate); elementary/middle years (Certificate); English second language specialist online (Certificate); hearing impaired: N-12th grade (Certificate); instructional technology (MS, Certificate); principal certification (Certificate); professional education (MS); reading specialist (MS, Certificate); reading supervisory (Certificate); secondary education (MS, Certificate); special education (MS, Certificate); superintendent's letter of eligibility (Certificate); supervisor of special education (Certificate); Wilson reading certificate online (Certificate). Part-time and evening/weekend programs available. Postbaccalaureate distance learning degree programs offered (no on-campus study). *Faculty:* 26 full-time (24 women), 83 part-time/adjunct (52 women). *Students:* 112 full-time (92 women), 923 part-time (709 women); includes 147 minority (92 Black or African American, non-Hispanic/Latino; 4 American Indian or Alaska Native, non-Hispanic/Latino; 19 Asian, non-Hispanic/Latino; 28 Hispanic/Latino; 4 Two or more races, non-Hispanic/Latino), 8 international. Average age 31. 285 applicants, 77% accepted, 176 enrolled. In 2011, 276 master's, 13 doctorates, 2 other advanced degrees awarded. *Entrance requirements:* For master's, 2 letters of recommendation, minimum GPA of 3.0, official transcripts, personal statement; for doctorate, GRE, master's degree from accredited institution, minimum graduate GPA of 3.5, computer competence, commitment to participate in cohort, interview with program director. Additional exam requirements/recommendations for international students: Required—TOEFL (minimum score 550 paper-based; 213 computer-based; 79 iBT). *Application deadline:* For fall admission, 7/15 priority date for domestic students, 4/15 for international students; for winter admission, 11/15 for domestic students, 1/15 for international students; for spring admission, 11/15 priority date for domestic students, 10/15 for international students. Applications are processed on a rolling basis. Application fee: $35. Electronic applications accepted. *Expenses:* Contact institution. *Financial support:* Unspecified assistantships available. Financial award applicants required to submit FAFSA. *Faculty research:* Public education professional development, factors predicting early mathematics skills for low income children. *Total annual research expenditures:* $92,975. *Unit head:* Dr. Jeanne Brady, Associate Dean, Education, 610-660-1580, E-mail: jebrady@sju.edu. *Application contact:* Kate McConnell, Director, Graduate College of Arts and Sciences Admissions and Retention, 610-660-3184, Fax: 610-660-3230, E-mail: kate.mcconnell@sju.edu.

Saint Martin's University, Graduate Programs, College of Education, Lacey, WA 98503. Offers administration (M Ed); English as a second language (M Ed); guidance and counseling (M Ed); reading (M Ed); special education (M Ed); teaching (MIT). *Accreditation:* Teacher Education Accreditation Council. Part-time and evening/weekend programs available. *Faculty:* 12 full-time (8 women), 9 part-time/adjunct (7 women). *Students:* 68 full-time (38 women), 28 part-time (20 women); includes 15 minority (2 Black or African American, non-Hispanic/Latino; 2 American Indian or Alaska Native, non-Hispanic/Latino; 7 Asian, non-Hispanic/Latino; 2 Hispanic/Latino; 2 Two or more races, non-Hispanic/Latino), 4 international. Average age 35. 17 applicants, 94% accepted, 15 enrolled. In 2011, 12 master's awarded. *Degree requirements:* For master's, comprehensive exam (for some programs), thesis or alternative, project or comprehensives. *Entrance requirements:* For master's, GRE General Test or MAT, resume. Additional exam requirements/recommendations for international students: Required—TOEFL (minimum score 560 paper-based; 220 computer-based; 83 iBT). *Application deadline:* For fall admission, 6/1 priority date for domestic students, 6/1 for international students; for spring admission, 10/1 priority date for domestic students, 10/1 for international students. Applications are processed on a rolling basis. Application fee: $35. *Expenses: Tuition:* Part-time $910 per credit hour. Tuition and fees vary according to course level, campus/location and program. *Financial support:* Career-related internships or fieldwork, Federal Work-Study, institutionally sponsored loans, and unspecified assistantships available. Support available to part-time students. Financial award application deadline: 3/1; financial award applicants required to submit FAFSA. *Faculty research:* Reader's theatre and reader/writer workshops, curriculum and assessment integration, gender and equity, classroom evaluations, organizational leadership. *Unit head:* Dr. Joyce Westgard, Dean, College of Education and Professional Psychology, 360-438-4509, Fax: 360-438-4486, E-mail: westgard@stmartin.edu. *Application contact:* Ryan M. Smith, Administrative Assistant, 360-438-4333, Fax: 360-438-4486, E-mail: ryan.smith@stmartin.edu. Web site: http://www.stmartin.edu/CEPP/.

Saint Michael's College, Graduate Programs, Program in Teaching English as a Second Language, Colchester, VT 05439. Offers MATESL, Certificate. Part-time and evening/weekend programs available. *Degree requirements:* For master's, one foreign language, comprehensive exam, thesis or alternative. *Entrance requirements:* For master's, minimum GPA of 3.0. Additional exam requirements/recommendations for international students: Required—TOEFL (minimum score 550 paper-based; 213 computer-based; 80 iBT). *Faculty research:* Language teaching methodology, discourse analysis, second language acquisition, language assessment, sociolinguistics, K–12 English as a second language for children.

St. Thomas University, School of Leadership Studies, Institute for Education, Miami Gardens, FL 33054-6459. Offers earth/space science (Certificate); educational administration (MS, Certificate); educational leadership (Ed D); elementary education (MS); ESOL (Certificate); gifted education (Certificate); instructional technology (MS, Certificate); professional/studies (Certificate); reading (MS, Certificate); special education (MS). Part-time and evening/weekend programs available. *Degree requirements:* For master's, comprehensive exam; for doctorate, comprehensive exam, thesis/dissertation. *Entrance requirements:* For master's, interview, minimum GPA of 3.0 or GRE; for doctorate, GRE or MAT. Additional exam requirements/recommendations for international students: Required—TOEFL (minimum score 550 paper-based; 213 computer-based; 79 iBT). Electronic applications accepted.

Saint Xavier University, Graduate Studies, School of Education, Chicago, IL 60655-3105. Offers counseling (MA); curriculum and instruction (MA); early childhood education (MA); educational administration (MA); elementary education (MA); individualized studies (MA), including educational technology, English as a second language (ESL), ISTEM (integrative science, technology, engineering, and math), science education; music education (MA); reading (MA); secondary education (MA); Spanish education (MA); special education (MA); teaching and leadership (MA). *Accreditation:* NCATE. Part-time and evening/weekend programs available. *Degree requirements:* For master's, thesis or project. *Entrance requirements:* For master's, minimum GPA of 3.0. *Application deadline:* For fall admission, 8/15 priority date for domestic students. Applications are processed on a rolling basis. Application fee: $35. *Expenses:* Contact institution. *Financial support:* Career-related internships or fieldwork available. Support available to part-time students. Financial award applicants required to submit FAFSA. *Unit head:* Dr. Beverly Gulley, Dean, 773-298-3221, Fax: 773-779-9061, E-mail: gulley@sxu.edu. *Application contact:* Beth Gierach, Managing Director of Admission, 773-298-3053, Fax: 773-298-3076, E-mail: gierach@sxu.edu.

Salem College, Department of Teacher Education, Winston-Salem, NC 27101. Offers art education (MAT); elementary education (M Ed, MAT); language and literacy (M Ed); middle school education (MAT); music education (MAT); school counseling (M Ed); second language studies (MAT); secondary education (MAT); special education (M Ed, MAT). *Accreditation:* NCATE. Part-time and evening/weekend programs available. Postbaccalaureate distance learning degree programs offered (minimal on-campus study). *Degree requirements:* For master's, comprehensive exam, practicum (MAT), project (M Ed), oral and written comprehensive exams. *Entrance requirements:* For master's, GRE, minimum GPA of 2.5. *Faculty research:* Content area reading strategies, literacy development, brain compatible instruction.

Salem State University, School of Graduate Studies, Program in Teaching English as a Second Language, Salem, MA 01970-5353. Offers MAT. Part-time and evening/weekend programs available. *Entrance requirements:* Additional exam requirements/recommendations for international students: Required—TOEFL (minimum score 550 paper-based; 80 iBT) or IELTS (minimum score 5.5).

Salisbury University, Graduate Division, Program in English, Salisbury, MD 21801-6837. Offers composition, language and rhetoric (MA); literature (MA); teaching English to speakers of other languages (MA). Part-time and evening/weekend programs available. *Faculty:* 14 full-time (6 women). *Students:* 18 full-time (13 women), 13 part-time (9 women); includes 2 minority (both Two or more races, non-Hispanic/Latino). Average age 28. 16 applicants, 88% accepted, 11 enrolled. In 2011, 18 master's awarded. *Degree requirements:* For master's, comprehensive exam (for some programs), thesis optional. *Entrance requirements:* For master's, GRE General Test, MAT or PRAXIS, minimum GPA of 3.0, 2 letters of recommendation, personal statement. Additional exam requirements/recommendations for international students: Required—TOEFL (minimum score 550 paper-based; 79 iBT). *Application deadline:* For fall admission, 8/1 for domestic students; for spring admission, 1/1 for domestic students. Applications are processed on a rolling basis. Application fee: $45. Electronic applications accepted. *Expenses: Tuition, area resident:* Part-time $306 per credit hour. Tuition, state resident: part-time $306 per credit hour. Tuition, nonresident: part-time $595 per credit hour. *Required fees:* $68 per credit hour. *Financial support:* In 2011–12, 11 students received support, including 13 teaching assistantships with full tuition reimbursements available (averaging $10,250 per year); career-related internships or fieldwork, institutionally sponsored loans, and unspecified assistantships also available. Support available to part-time students. Financial award application deadline: 3/1; financial award applicants required to submit FAFSA. *Faculty research:* Training and retraining grades K through 12 Eastern Shore. *Total annual research expenditures:* $300,000. *Unit head:* Dr. John D. Kalb, Director, 410-543-6049, Fax: 410-548-2142, E-mail: jdkalb@salisbury.edu. Web site: http://www.salisbury.edu/english/grad/.

San Diego State University, Graduate and Research Affairs, College of Arts and Letters, Department of Linguistics and Oriental Languages, San Diego, CA 92182. Offers applied linguistics and English as a second language (CAL); computational linguistics (MA); English as a second language/applied linguistics (MA); general linguistics (MA). *Degree requirements:* For master's, one foreign language, comprehensive exam, thesis optional. *Entrance requirements:* For master's, GRE General Test, 2 letters of recommendation. Additional exam requirements/recommendations for international students: Required—TOEFL (minimum score 570 paper-based). Electronic applications accepted. *Faculty research:* Cross-cultural linguistic studies of semantics.

San Francisco State University, Division of Graduate Studies, College of Liberal and Creative Arts, Department of English Language and Literature, Program in Teaching English to Speakers of Other Languages, San Francisco, CA 94132-1722. Offers MA. Part-time programs available. *Degree requirements:* For master's, comprehensive exam (for some programs), thesis (for some programs). *Application deadline:* Applications are processed on a rolling basis. Electronic applications accepted. *Unit head:* Beverly Voloshin, Chair, 415-338-2264, E-mail: english@sfsu.edu. *Application contact:* Maricel Santos, 415-338-7445, E-mail: matesol@sfsu.edu. Web site: http://www.sfsu.edu/~matesol/.

San Jose State University, Graduate Studies and Research, College of Humanities and the Arts, Department of Linguistics and Language Development, San Jose, CA 95192-0001. Offers computational linguistics (Certificate); linguistics (MA); teaching English to speakers of other languages (MA, Certificate). *Entrance requirements:* Additional exam requirements/recommendations for international students: Required—TOEFL (minimum score 570 paper-based; 230 computer-based). Electronic applications accepted.

Seattle Pacific University, MA in Teaching English to Speakers of Other Languages Program, Seattle, WA 98119-1997. Offers K-12 certification (MA); teaching English to speakers of other languages (MA). Part-time programs available. *Degree requirements:* For master's, one foreign language, practicum. *Entrance requirements:* For master's, GRE General Test or MAT, minimum GPA of 3.0 in last 45 quarter credits. Additional exam requirements/recommendations for international students: Required—TOEFL (minimum score 600 paper-based; 250 computer-based). Electronic applications accepted. *Expenses:* Contact institution. *Faculty research:* Second language acquisition.

Seattle University, College of Education, Program in Teaching English to Speakers of Other Languages, Seattle, WA 98122-1090. Offers M Ed, MA, Certificate. *Accreditation:* NCATE. Part-time programs available. *Students:* 12 full-time (8 women), 36 part-time (28 women); includes 7 minority (3 Black or African American, non-Hispanic/Latino; 3 Asian, non-Hispanic/Latino; 1 Hispanic/Latino), 10 international. Average age 34. 41 applicants, 63% accepted, 11 enrolled. In 2011, 21 master's, 1 other advanced degree awarded. *Degree requirements:* For master's, comprehensive exam, thesis, internship. *Entrance requirements:* For master's, GRE, MAT, or minimum GPA of 3.0. Additional exam requirements/recommendations for international students: Required—TOEFL. *Application deadline:* For fall admission, 8/20 priority date for domestic students; for winter admission, 11/20 for domestic students; for spring admission, 2/20 for domestic students. Applications are processed on a rolling basis. Application fee: $55. *Financial support:* Career-related internships or fieldwork and Federal Work-Study available. Support available to part-time students. Financial award applicants required to submit FAFSA. *Unit head:* Dr. Jian Yang, Coordinator, 209-296-5908. *Application contact:* Janet Shandley, Associate Dean of Graduate Admissions, 206-296-5900, Fax: 206-298-5656, E-mail: grad_admissions@seattleu.edu.

Simmons College, College of Arts and Sciences Graduate Studies, Boston, MA 02115. Offers applied behavior analysis (PhD); behavior analysis (MS, Ed S); children's literature (MA); education (MS, CAGS, Ed S); educational leadership (PhD, CAGS); English (MA); gender and cultural studies (MA); health professions education (PhD); history (MA); Spanish (MA); special education moderate licensure (Certificate); special needs administration (Ed D); special needs education (Ed S); teaching (MAT); teaching English as a second language (MA, CAGS); urban education (CAGS); writing for children (MFA); MA/MA; MA/MS; MAT/MA. *Unit head:* Renee White, Dean. *Application contact:* Kristen Haack, Director, Graduate Studies Admission, 617-521-2917, Fax: 617-521-3058, E-mail: gsa@simmons.edu. Web site: http://www.simmons.edu/gradstudies/.

Simon Fraser University, Graduate Studies, Faculty of Education, Program in Teaching English as a Second/Foreign Language, Burnaby, BC V5A 1S6, Canada. Offers M Ed. *Degree requirements:* For master's, comprehensive exam.

SIT Graduate Institute, Graduate Programs, Program in English for Speakers of Other Languages, Brattleboro, VT 05302-0676. Offers MAT. *Degree requirements:* For master's, one foreign language, thesis, teaching practice. *Entrance requirements:* For master's, 4 letters of reference. Additional exam requirements/recommendations for international students: Required—TOEFL.

Soka University of America, Graduate School, Aliso Viejo, CA 92656. Offers teaching Japanese as a foreign language (Certificate). Evening/weekend programs available. *Entrance requirements:* For degree, bachelor's degree with minimum GPA of 3.0, proficiency in Japanese. Additional exam requirements/recommendations for international students: Required—TOEFL (minimum score 600 paper-based; 100 iBT).

Southeast Missouri State University, School of Graduate Studies, Department of English, Cape Girardeau, MO 63701-4799. Offers English (MA); teaching English to speakers of other languages (MA). Part-time and evening/weekend programs available. Postbaccalaureate distance learning degree programs offered (no on-campus study). *Faculty:* 13 full-time (8 women). *Students:* 38 full-time (21 women), 50 part-time (39 women); includes 8 minority (5 Black or African American, non-Hispanic/Latino; 2

American Indian or Alaska Native, non-Hispanic/Latino; 1 Hispanic/Latino), 11 international. Average age 33. 41 applicants, 90% accepted, 34 enrolled. In 2011, 18 master's awarded. *Degree requirements:* For master's, paper and comprehensive exam or thesis and oral defense. *Entrance requirements:* For master's, minimum undergraduate GPA of 2.5; 24 undergraduate credit hours in field (for English); valid teaching certificate and minimum undergraduate GPA of 2.75 or master's degree (for ESOL certification). Additional exam requirements/recommendations for international students: Required—TOEFL (minimum score 550 paper-based; 213 computer-based; 79 iBT); Recommended—IELTS (minimum score 6). *Application deadline:* For fall admission, 8/1 for domestic students, 7/1 for international students; for spring admission, 11/21 for domestic students, 11/1 for international students. Applications are processed on a rolling basis. Application fee: $30 ($40 for international students). Electronic applications accepted. *Expenses:* Tuition, state resident: full-time $4896; part-time $272 per credit hour. Tuition, nonresident: full-time $8649; part-time $480.50 per credit hour. *Financial support:* In 2011–12, 30 students received support, including 17 teaching assistantships with full tuition reimbursements available (averaging $7,600 per year); career-related internships or fieldwork, Federal Work-Study, scholarships/grants, tuition waivers (full), and unspecified assistantships also available. Financial award application deadline: 6/30; financial award applicants required to submit FAFSA. *Faculty research:* Literature, writing, linguistics, education, TESOL. *Unit head:* Dr. Carol Scates, Chairperson and Graduate Program Coordinator, 573-651-2156, E-mail: cscates@semo.edu. *Application contact:* Gail Amick, Administrative Secretary, 573-651-2049, Fax: 573-651-2001, E-mail: gamick@semo.edu. Web site: http://www.semo.edu/english/.

Southern Arkansas University–Magnolia, Graduate Programs, Magnolia, AR 71754. Offers agriculture (MS); business administration (MBA); computer and information sciences (MS); education (M Ed), including counseling and development, curriculum and instruction, educational administration and supervision, elementary education, middle level, reading, secondary education, TESOL; kinesiology (M Ed); library media and information specialist (M Ed); mental health and clinical counseling (MS); public administration (MPA); school counseling (M Ed); teaching (MAT). *Accreditation:* NCATE. Part-time and evening/weekend programs available. Postbaccalaureate distance learning degree programs offered. *Faculty:* 34 full-time (15 women), 8 part-time/adjunct (5 women). *Students:* 87 full-time (62 women), 320 part-time (224 women); includes 116 minority (111 Black or African American, non-Hispanic/Latino; 2 American Indian or Alaska Native, non-Hispanic/Latino; 2 Asian, non-Hispanic/Latino; 1 Hispanic/Latino), 25 international. Average age 33. 201 applicants, 98% accepted, 156 enrolled. In 2011, 162 master's awarded. *Degree requirements:* For master's, comprehensive exam (for some programs), thesis optional. *Entrance requirements:* For master's, GRE, MAT or GMAT, minimum GPA of 2.5. Additional exam requirements/recommendations for international students: Required—TOEFL (minimum score 173 computer-based). *Application deadline:* For fall admission, 7/15 for domestic and international students; for winter admission, 12/1 for domestic and international students; for spring admission, 12/1 for domestic and international students. Applications are processed on a rolling basis. Application fee: $25 ($35 for international students). Electronic applications accepted. *Expenses:* Tuition, state resident: part-time $232 per credit. Tuition, nonresident: part-time $339 per credit. *Required fees:* $44 per credit. Part-time tuition and fees vary according to course load. *Financial support:* Career-related internships or fieldwork, Federal Work-Study, scholarships/grants, tuition waivers (full), and unspecified assistantships available. Financial award applicants required to submit FAFSA. *Faculty research:* Alternative certification for teachers, supervision of instruction, instructional leadership, counseling. *Unit head:* Dr. Kim Bloss, Dean, School of Graduate Studies, 870-235-4150, Fax: 870-235-5227, E-mail: kkbloss@saumag.edu. *Application contact:* Gaye Calhoun, Admissions Specialist, 870-235-4150, Fax: 870-235-5227, E-mail: glcalhoun@saumag.edu. Web site: http://www.saumag.edu/graduate.

Southern Connecticut State University, School of Graduate Studies, School of Arts and Sciences, Department of Foreign Languages, New Haven, CT 06515-1355. Offers multicultural-bilingual education/teaching English to speakers of other languages (MS). Part-time and evening/weekend programs available. *Faculty:* 6 full-time (4 women), 1 (woman) part-time/adjunct. *Students:* 9 full-time (6 women), 40 part-time (35 women); includes 15 minority (14 Hispanic/Latino; 1 Two or more races, non-Hispanic/Latino). 93 applicants, 28% accepted, 19 enrolled. In 2011, 18 master's awarded. *Degree requirements:* For master's, one foreign language, thesis or alternative. *Entrance requirements:* For master's, interview, minimum undergraduate GPA of 2.7. *Application deadline:* For fall admission, 7/15 priority date for domestic students. Applications are processed on a rolling basis. Application fee: $50. Electronic applications accepted. *Expenses:* Tuition, state resident: full-time $5137; part-time $413 per credit. *Required fees:* $4008; $55 per term. *Financial support:* Application deadline: 4/15; applicants required to submit FAFSA. *Unit head:* Dr. Elena Schmitt, Chairperson, 203-392-6138, Fax: 203-392-6136, E-mail: schmitte1@southernct.edu. *Application contact:* Dr. Luisa Piemontese, Graduate Coordinator, 203-392-6751, E-mail: piemontesel1@southernct.edu.

Southern Illinois University Carbondale, Graduate School, College of Liberal Arts, Department of Applied Linguistics, Program in Teaching English to Speakers of Other Languages, Carbondale, IL 62901-4701. Offers MA. *Students:* 42 full-time (24 women), 13 part-time (9 women); includes 3 minority (2 Asian, non-Hispanic/Latino; 1 Hispanic/Latino), 26 international. 46 applicants, 50% accepted, 9 enrolled. In 2011, 25 master's awarded. *Unit head:* Peggy Stockdale, Chair, 618-453-8331, E-mail: pstock@siu.edu. *Application contact:* Diane Korando, Office Specialist, 618-536-3385, E-mail: ling@siu.edu.

Southern Illinois University Edwardsville, Graduate School, College of Arts and Sciences, Department of English Language and Literature, Program in Teaching English as a Second Language, Edwardsville, IL 62026-0001. Offers MA, Postbaccalaureate Certificate. Part-time and evening/weekend programs available. *Students:* 10 full-time (9 women), 14 part-time (12 women); includes 4 minority (2 Asian, non-Hispanic/Latino; 1 Hispanic/Latino; 1 Two or more races, non-Hispanic/Latino), 5 international. 20 applicants, 60% accepted. In 2011, 8 master's, 1 other advanced degree awarded. *Degree requirements:* For master's, one foreign language, thesis (for some programs), final exam. *Entrance requirements:* Additional exam requirements/recommendations for international students: Required—TOEFL (minimum score 550 paper-based; 213 computer-based; 79 iBT), IELTS (minimum score 6.5). *Application deadline:* For fall admission, 7/22 for domestic students, 6/1 for international students; for spring admission, 12/9 for domestic students, 10/1 for international students. Applications are processed on a rolling basis. Application fee: $30. Electronic applications accepted. Tuition and fees vary according to course load and program. *Financial support:* Fellowships with full tuition reimbursements, research assistantships with full tuition reimbursements, teaching assistantships with full tuition reimbursements, institutionally sponsored loans, scholarships/grants, and unspecified assistantships available. Financial award application deadline: 3/1; financial award applicants required to submit FAFSA. *Unit head:* Dr. Joel Hardman, Director, 618-650-5978, E-mail: jhardma@siue.edu. *Application contact:* Dr. Joel Hardman, Director, 618-650-5978, E-mail: jhardma@siue.edu.

Southern New Hampshire University, School of Liberal Arts, Manchester, NH 03106-1045. Offers clinical services for adults psychiatric disabilities (Certificate); clinical services for children and adolescents with psychiatric disabilities (Certificate); clinical services for persons with co-occurring substance abuse and psychiatric disabilities (Certificate); community mental health (MS); fiction writing (MFA); non-fiction writing (MFA); teaching English as a foreign language (MS). Part-time and evening/weekend programs available. *Degree requirements:* For master's, one foreign language, thesis. *Entrance requirements:* For master's, minimum GPA of 2.75: MS-TEFL, 3.0: MFA. Additional exam requirements/recommendations for international students: Required—TOEFL (minimum score 550 paper-based; 213 computer-based; 79 iBT), IELTS (minimum score 6.5), TWE (minimum score 5). Electronic applications accepted. *Expenses:* Contact institution. *Faculty research:* Action research, state of the art practice in behavioral health services, wraparound approaches to working with youth, learning styles.

Southwest Minnesota State University, Department of Education, Marshall, MN 56258. Offers ESL (MS); math (MS); reading (MS); special education (MS), including developmental disabilities, early childhood education, emotional behavioral disorders, learning disabilities; teaching, learning and leadership (MS). Part-time and evening/weekend programs available. Postbaccalaureate distance learning degree programs offered (no on-campus study). *Entrance requirements:* Additional exam requirements/recommendations for international students: Required—TOEFL or IELTS; Recommended—TOEFL (minimum score 550 paper-based; 213 computer-based; 80 iBT), IELTS.

State University of New York at Fredonia, Graduate Studies, College of Education, Program in Teaching English to Speakers of Other Languages, Fredonia, NY 14063-1136. Offers MS Ed. *Expenses:* Tuition, state resident: full-time $6666; part-time $370 per credit hour. Tuition, nonresident: full-time $11,376; part-time $632 per credit hour. *Required fees:* $1059.30; $58.85 per credit hour. Tuition and fees vary according to course load.

State University of New York at New Paltz, Graduate School, School of Education, Department of Secondary Education, Program in Second Language Education, New Paltz, NY 12561. Offers MS Ed. *Accreditation:* NCATE. Part-time and evening/weekend programs available. *Students:* 19 full-time (17 women), 31 part-time (30 women); includes 17 minority (1 Black or African American, non-Hispanic/Latino; 14 Hispanic/Latino; 2 Two or more races, non-Hispanic/Latino), 1 international. Average age 35. 41 applicants, 78% accepted, 25 enrolled. In 2011, 20 master's awarded. *Degree requirements:* For master's, practicum. *Entrance requirements:* For master's, minimum GPA of 3.0, 12 credits of a foreign language. Additional exam requirements/recommendations for international students: Required—TOEFL (minimum score 575 paper-based; 233 computer-based; 90 iBT), IELTS (minimum score 7). *Application deadline:* For fall admission, 4/15 priority date for domestic students, 4/15 for international students. Application fee: $50. Electronic applications accepted. *Expenses:* Tuition, state resident: full-time $8870; part-time $370 per credit. Tuition, nonresident: full-time $15,160; part-time $632 per credit. *Required fees:* $1188; $34 per credit. $184 per semester. *Financial support:* In 2011–12, 4 students received support, including 1 fellowship (averaging $8,000 per year); tuition waivers (full) also available. Financial award application deadline: 8/1; financial award applicants required to submit FAFSA. *Unit head:* Prof. Vern Todd, Coordinator, 845-257-2818, E-mail: toddv@newpaltz.edu. *Application contact:* Caroline Murphy, Graduate Admissions Advisor, 845-257-3285, Fax: 845-257-3284, E-mail: gradschool@newpaltz.edu.

State University of New York College at Cortland, Graduate Studies, School of Arts and Sciences, Department of Second Language Education, Cortland, NY 13045. Offers MS Ed. *Accreditation:* NCATE.

Stony Brook University, State University of New York, Graduate School, College of Arts and Sciences, Department of Linguistics, Program in Teaching English to Speakers of Other Languages, Stony Brook, NY 11794. Offers MA. *Accreditation:* NCATE.

Syracuse University, College of Arts and Sciences, Program in Language Teaching: TESOL/TLOTE, Syracuse, NY 13244. Offers CAS. Part-time programs available. *Students:* 14 applicants, 100% accepted. *Entrance requirements:* Additional exam requirements/recommendations for international students: Required—TOEFL (minimum score 100 iBT). *Application deadline:* For fall admission, 2/1 priority date for domestic students, 2/1 for international students. Applications are processed on a rolling basis. Electronic applications accepted. *Expenses: Tuition:* Part-time $1206 per credit. *Unit head:* Dr. George M. Langford, Dean, 315-443-2201, E-mail: dean@cas.syr.edu. *Application contact:* Prof. Amanda Brown, 315-443-2244, E-mail: abrown08@syr.edu. Web site: http://thecollege.syr.edu/.

Syracuse University, School of Education, Program in Teaching English Language Learners, Syracuse, NY 13244. Offers MS. Part-time programs available. *Students:* 9 full-time (8 women), 4 part-time (all women); includes 1 minority (Hispanic/Latino). Average age 32. 15 applicants, 60% accepted, 9 enrolled. In 2011, 5 degrees awarded. *Entrance requirements:* For master's, New York State Teacher Certification or eligibility. Additional exam requirements/recommendations for international students: Required—TOEFL (minimum score 100 iBT). *Application deadline:* For fall admission, 2/1 for domestic and international students. Application fee: $75. Electronic applications accepted. *Expenses: Tuition:* Part-time $1206 per credit. *Financial support:* Fellowships with full tuition reimbursements, teaching assistantships with full and partial tuition reimbursements, and tuition waivers available. Financial award application deadline: 1/1; financial award applicants required to submit FAFSA. *Unit head:* Dr. Zaline Roy-Campbell, Program Coordinator, 315-443-8194, E-mail: zmroycam@syr.edu. *Application contact:* Laurie Deyo, Graduate Recruiter, School of Education, 315-443-2505, E-mail: e-gradrcrt@syr.edu. Web site: http://soeweb.syr.edu/.

Taylor College and Seminary, Graduate and Professional Programs, Edmonton, AB T6J 4T3, Canada. Offers Christian studies (Diploma); intercultural studies (MA, Diploma), including intercultural studies (Diploma), TESOL; theology (M Div, MTS). *Accreditation:* ATS. Part-time programs available. Postbaccalaureate distance learning degree programs offered (minimal on-campus study). *Degree requirements:* For master's, thesis optional. *Entrance requirements:* Additional exam requirements/recommendations for international students: Required—TOEFL (minimum score 550 paper-based; 80 iBT), IELTS (minimum score 6.5). *Faculty research:* Biblical studies, administration and organization, world religions, ethics, missiology.

Teachers College, Columbia University, Graduate Faculty of Education, Department of Arts and Humanities, Program in Teaching English to Speakers of Other Languages, New York, NY 10027-6696. Offers Ed M, MA, Ed D. *Accreditation:* NCATE. Part-time programs available. *Faculty:* 5 full-time (3 women), 7 part-time/adjunct (3 women). *Students:* 24 full-time (22 women), 180 part-time (128 women); includes 51 minority (4 Black or African American, non-Hispanic/Latino; 36 Asian, non-Hispanic/Latino; 11 Hispanic/Latino), 75 international. Average age 32. 259 applicants, 50% accepted, 50 enrolled. In 2011, 70 degrees awarded. *Degree requirements:* For master's, project; for doctorate, comprehensive exam, thesis/dissertation. *Entrance requirements:* For master's, MA in related field (for Ed M); for doctorate, MA in teaching English to speakers of other languages. Additional exam requirements/recommendations for international students: Required—TOEFL (minimum score 102 iBT), IELTS (minimum score 7). *Application deadline:* For fall admission, 1/15 priority date for domestic students. Application fee: $65. Electronic applications accepted. *Financial support:* Career-related internships or fieldwork, Federal Work-Study, institutionally sponsored loans, and tuition waivers (full and partial) available. Support available to part-time students. Financial award application deadline: 2/1. *Faculty research:* Classroom-centered research, electronic media, K-12 English as a second language, second language acquisition. *Unit head:* Prof. James E. Purpura, Program Coordinator, 212-678-3795, E-mail: jp248@columbia.edu. *Application contact:* Thomas P. Rock, Director of Admissions, 212-678-3083, Fax: 212-678-4171, E-mail: rock@tc.edu.

Temple University, College of Education, Department of Curriculum, Instruction, and Technology in Education, Philadelphia, PA 19122-6096. Offers applied behavioral analysis (MS Ed); career and technical education (MS Ed); early childhood education and elementary education (MS Ed); English education (MS Ed); language arts education (Ed D); math/science education (Ed D); mathematics education (MS Ed); science education (MS Ed); second and foreign language education (MS Ed); special education (MS Ed); teaching English as a second language (MS Ed). Part-time and evening/weekend programs available. *Faculty:* 19 full-time (12 women). *Students:* 30 full-time (23 women), 86 part-time (69 women); includes 12 minority (4 Black or African American, non-Hispanic/Latino; 2 Asian, non-Hispanic/Latino; 5 Hispanic/Latino; 1 Two or more races, non-Hispanic/Latino), 5 international. 82 applicants, 71% accepted, 51 enrolled. In 2011, 181 master's, 16 doctorates awarded. Terminal master's awarded for partial completion of doctoral program. *Degree requirements:* For master's, thesis or alternative; for doctorate, thesis/dissertation. *Entrance requirements:* For master's and doctorate, GRE General Test or MAT, minimum GPA of 3.0. Additional exam requirements/recommendations for international students: Required—TOEFL (minimum score 550 paper-based; 213 computer-based; 79 iBT). *Application deadline:* For fall admission, 4/1 for domestic students, 12/15 for international students; for spring admission, 10/1 for domestic students, 8/1 for international students. Application fee: $50. Electronic applications accepted. *Expenses:* Tuition, state resident: full-time $12,366; part-time $687 per credit hour. Tuition, nonresident: full-time $17,298; part-time $961 per credit hour. *Required fees:* $590; $213 per year. *Financial support:* Fellowships, research assistantships with full tuition reimbursements, and teaching assistantships with full tuition reimbursements available. Financial award application deadline: 1/15; financial award applicants required to submit FAFSA. *Faculty research:* School improvement, problem-solving, literacy, language development. *Unit head:* Dr. Michael W. Smith, Chair, 215-204-6387, Fax: 215-204-1414, E-mail: mwsmith@temple.edu. *Application contact:* Dr. Margo Greicar, Director for Graduate Academic and Student Affairs, 215-204-8011, Fax: 215-204-4383, E-mail: margo.greicar@temple.edu. Web site: http://www.temple.edu/education/cite/.

Texas A&M University, College of Education and Human Development, Department of Teaching, Learning, and Culture, College Station, TX 77843. Offers culture and curriculum (M Ed, MS); curriculum and instruction (PhD); English as a second language (M Ed, MS, PhD); mathematics education (M Ed, MS, PhD); reading and language arts education (M Ed, MS, PhD); science education (M Ed, MS, PhD); urban education (M Ed, MS, PhD). Part-time programs available. *Faculty:* 30. *Students:* 163 full-time (119 women), 226 part-time (185 women); includes 108 minority (56 Black or African American, non-Hispanic/Latino; 2 American Indian or Alaska Native, non-Hispanic/Latino; 6 Asian, non-Hispanic/Latino; 37 Hispanic/Latino; 7 Two or more races, non-Hispanic/Latino), 62 international. Average age 36. In 2011, 107 master's, 44 doctorates awarded. *Degree requirements:* For master's, comprehensive exam, thesis (for some programs); for doctorate, comprehensive exam, thesis/dissertation. *Entrance requirements:* For master's, GRE General Test, minimum GPA of 3.0; for doctorate, GRE General Test, 3 years of teaching experience. Additional exam requirements/recommendations for international students: Required—TOEFL (minimum score 550 paper-based; 213 computer-based). *Application deadline:* For fall admission, 1/15 priority date for domestic students, 1/15 for international students; for spring admission, 9/15 priority date for domestic students, 9/15 for international students. Applications are processed on a rolling basis. Application fee: $50 ($75 for international students). Electronic applications accepted. *Expenses:* Tuition, state resident: full-time $5437; part-time $226.55 per credit hour. Tuition, nonresident: full-time $12,949; part-time $539.55 per credit hour. *Required fees:* $2741. *Financial support:* In 2011–12, fellowships with partial tuition reimbursements (averaging $3,000 per year), teaching assistantships with partial tuition reimbursements (averaging $7,200 per year) were awarded; research assistantships with partial tuition reimbursements, career-related internships or fieldwork, Federal Work-Study, institutionally sponsored loans, scholarships/grants, tuition waivers (partial), and unspecified assistantships also available. Support available to part-time students. Financial award application deadline: 4/1; financial award applicants required to submit FAFSA. *Unit head:* Dr. Yeping Li, Head, 979-845-8384, Fax: 979-845-9663, E-mail: yepingli@tamu.edu. *Application contact:* Kerri Smith, Senior Academic Advisor II, 979-845-8382, Fax: 979-845-9663, E-mail: krsmith@tamu.edu. Web site: http://tlac.tamu.edu.

Texas A&M University–Commerce, Graduate School, College of Education and Human Services, Department of Curriculum and Instruction, Commerce, TX 75429-3011. Offers bilingual/ESL education (M Ed, MS); early childhood education (M Ed, MS); elementary education (M Ed, MS); reading (M Ed, MS); secondary education (M Ed, MS); supervision, curriculum and instruction: elementary education (Ed D). MS and M Ed programs in early childhood education offered jointly with Texas Woman's University and University of North Texas. Part-time programs available. Terminal master's awarded for partial completion of doctoral program. *Degree requirements:* For master's, comprehensive exam, thesis (for some programs); for doctorate, 2 foreign languages, thesis/dissertation, departmental qualifying exam. *Entrance requirements:* For master's and doctorate, GRE General Test. Electronic applications accepted. *Faculty research:* Literacy and learning, early childhood, preservice teacher education, technology.

Texas A&M University–Kingsville, College of Graduate Studies, College of Education, Department of Education, Program in English as a Second Language, Kingsville, TX 78363. Offers M Ed. *Degree requirements:* For master's, comprehensive exam. *Entrance requirements:* For master's, GRE General Test, MAT, minimum GPA of 3.0.

Touro College, Graduate School of Education, New York, NY 10010. Offers bilingual programs (Advanced Certificate); education and special education (MS); gifted and talented education (Advanced Certificate); instructional technology (MS); mathematics education (MS); school leadership (MS); teaching children with autism and other severe or multiple disabilities (Advanced Certificate); teaching English to speakers of other languages (MS, Advanced Certificate); teaching literacy (MS). Part-time and evening/weekend programs available. Postbaccalaureate distance learning degree programs offered (no on-campus study). *Faculty:* 75 full-time, 131 part-time/adjunct. *Students:* 382 full-time (324 women), 3,790 part-time (3,196 women); includes 1,211 minority (537 Black or African American, non-Hispanic/Latino; 4 American Indian or Alaska Native, non-Hispanic/Latino; 187 Asian, non-Hispanic/Latino; 472 Hispanic/Latino; 3 Native Hawaiian or other Pacific Islander, non-Hispanic/Latino; 8 Two or more races, non-Hispanic/Latino), 1 international. 1,422 applicants, 50% accepted, 675 enrolled. In 2011, 6 master's, 4 other advanced degrees awarded. *Application deadline:* For fall admission, 8/26 for domestic students, 7/15 for international students; for spring admission, 12/31 for domestic students, 12/15 for international students. Applications are processed on a rolling basis. Application fee: $50. *Financial support:* Federal Work-Study available. Financial award applicants required to submit FAFSA. *Faculty research:* Equity assistance, language development, scholar communications, Latin American studies and cultural sensitivity, behavior management techniques and strategies in special education. *Unit head:* Dr. LaMar Miller, Dean, 212-463-0400 Ext. 5561, Fax: 212-462-4889, E-mail: lpmiller@touro.edu. *Application contact:* Natalie Arroyo, Admissions Assistant, 212-463-0400 Ext. 5119, E-mail: natalie.arroyo@touro.edu.

Trevecca Nazarene University, College of Lifelong Learning, School of Education, Major in English Language Learners (PreK-12), Nashville, TN 37210-2877. Offers M Ed. *Accreditation:* NCATE. Part-time and evening/weekend programs available. *Students:* 21 full-time (19 women), 3 part-time (all women); includes 4 minority (3 Black or African American, non-Hispanic/Latino; 1 Asian, non-Hispanic/Latino), 1 international. In 2011, 12 master's awarded. *Degree requirements:* For master's, exit assessment. *Entrance requirements:* For master's, GRE General Test, MAT, minimum GPA of 2.7, 2 reference forms. Additional exam requirements/recommendations for international students: Required—TOEFL (minimum score 550 paper-based; 213 computer-based). *Application deadline:* Applications are processed on a rolling basis. Application fee: $25. *Expenses:* Contact institution. *Financial support:* Applicants required to submit FAFSA. *Unit head:* Dr. Esther Swink, Dean/Director of Graduate Education Programs, 615-248-1201, Fax: 615-248-1597, E-mail: admissions_ged@trevecca.edu. *Application contact:* Melanie Eaton, Admissions, 615-248-1498, E-mail: cll@trevecca.edu.

Trinity Washington University, School of Education, Washington, DC 20017-1094. Offers counseling (MA); early childhood education (MAT); educating for change (M Ed); educational administration (MSA); elementary education (MAT); school counseling (MA); secondary education (MAT), including English, social studies; special education (MAT); teaching English as a second language (MAT); teaching English to speakers of other languages (M Ed); the teaching of reading (M Ed). *Accreditation:* NCATE. Part-time and evening/weekend programs available. *Degree requirements:* For master's, thesis (for some programs), capstone project(s). *Entrance requirements:* For master's, PRAXIS I, minimum GPA of 2.8. Additional exam requirements/recommendations for international students: Required—TOEFL (minimum score 550 paper-based; 213 computer-based). *Faculty research:* Technology, literacy, special education, organizations, inclusion models.

Trinity Western University, School of Graduate Studies, Program in Teaching English to Speakers of Other Languages (TESOL), Langley, BC V2Y 1Y1, Canada. Offers MA. Part-time programs available. Postbaccalaureate distance learning degree programs offered (minimal on-campus study). *Degree requirements:* For master's, project. *Entrance requirements:* For master's, minimum GPA of 3.0. Additional exam requirements/recommendations for international students: Required—TOEFL (minimum score 600 paper-based; 250 computer-based). *Faculty research:* ESL methodology, second language acquisition, computer assisted language learning.

Universidad del Este, Graduate School, Carolina, PR 00984. Offers accounting (MBA); adult education (M Ed); agribusiness (MBA); criminal justice and criminology (MA); curriculum and instruction - early education (M Ed); curriculum and instruction - elementary (M Ed); curriculum and instruction - English (M Ed); curriculum and instruction - Spanish (M Ed); human resources (MBA); information security management (MBA); information technology and Web business development (MBA); management (MBA); public policy (MPA); social work (MA), including clinical social work; special education (M Ed); strategic leadership (MBA).

Universidad del Turabo, Graduate Programs, Programs in Education, Program in Teaching English as a Second Language, Gurabo, PR 00778-3030. Offers M Ed. *Students:* 16 full-time (11 women), 134 part-time (107 women); includes 81 minority (all Hispanic/Latino). Average age 35. 80 applicants, 95% accepted, 60 enrolled. In 2011, 52 master's awarded. *Entrance requirements:* For master's, GRE, EXADEP, interview. *Application deadline:* For fall admission, 8/5 for domestic students. Application fee: $25. *Financial support:* Institutionally sponsored loans available. *Unit head:* Angela Candelario, Dean, 787-743-7979 Ext. 4126. *Application contact:* Virginia Gonzalez, Admissions Officer, 787-746-3009.

University at Buffalo, the State University of New York, Graduate School, Graduate School of Education, Department of Learning and Instruction, Buffalo, NY 14260. Offers biology education (Ed M, Certificate); chemistry education (Ed M, Certificate); childhood education (Ed M); childhood education with bilingual extension (Ed M); early childhood education (Ed M); early childhood education with bilingual extension (birth-grade 2) (Ed M); earth science education (Ed M, Certificate); educational technology and new literacies (Certificate); educational technology and new literacies (online) (Certificate); elementary education (Ed D, PhD); English education (Ed M, PhD, Certificate); English for speakers of other languages (Ed M); foreign and second language education (PhD); French education (Ed M, Certificate); general education (Ed M); German education (Ed M, Certificate); gifted education (online) (Certificate); Latin education (Ed M, Certificate); literacy teaching and learning (Certificate); literary specialist (Ed M); mathematics education (Ed M, PhD, Certificate); music education (Ed M, Certificate); physics education (Ed M, Certificate); reading education (PhD); science and the public (online) (Ed M); science education (PhD); social studies education (Ed M, Certificate); Spanish education (Ed M, Certificate); special education (PhD); teaching and leading for diversity (Certificate); teaching English to speakers of other languages (Ed M). Part-time and evening/weekend programs available. Postbaccalaureate distance learning degree programs offered (no on-campus study). *Faculty:* 32 full-time (23 women), 54 part-time/adjunct (43 women). *Students:* 294 full-time (222 women), 350 part-time (261 women); includes 75 minority (19 Black or African American, non-Hispanic/Latino; 6 American Indian or Alaska Native, non-Hispanic/Latino; 40 Asian, non-Hispanic/Latino; 10 Hispanic/Latino), 76 international. Average age 29. 548 applicants, 52% accepted, 253 enrolled. In 2011, 225 master's, 17 doctorates, 37 other advanced degrees awarded. *Degree requirements:* For master's, comprehensive exam; for doctorate, thesis/dissertation, research analysis exam, research experience component. *Entrance requirements:* For doctorate, GRE General Test or MAT, interview, writing sample, letters of recommendation. Additional exam requirements/recommendations for international students: Required—TOEFL (minimum score 600 paper-based; 96 iBT). *Application deadline:* For fall admission, 2/1 priority date for domestic students, 2/1 for international students; for spring admission, 11/15 priority date for domestic students, 10/1 for international students. Applications are processed on a rolling basis. Application fee: $50. Electronic applications accepted. *Financial support:* In 2011–12, 40 fellowships (averaging $12,991 per year), 46 research assistantships (averaging $10,986 per year) were awarded; teaching assistantships with full tuition reimbursements, career-related internships or fieldwork, Federal Work-Study, institutionally sponsored loans, scholarships/grants, and unspecified assistantships also available. Financial award application deadline: 2/28; financial award applicants required to submit FAFSA. *Faculty research:* Science assessment, foreign language teaching and learning, early learning, new literacies, gender and education. *Unit head:* Dr. Julie Sarama, Chair, 716-645-2455, Fax: 716-645-3161, E-mail: jcollins@buffalo.edu. *Application contact:* Cathy Dimino, Admissions Assistant, 716-645-2110, Fax: 716-645-7937, E-mail: cadimino@buffalo.edu.

English as a Second Language

The University of Alabama, Graduate School, College of Arts and Sciences, Department of English, Tuscaloosa, AL 35487. Offers composition and rhetoric (PhD); creative writing (MFA), including fiction, poetry; literature (MA, PhD); rhetoric and composition (MA); teaching English as a second language (MATESOL). *Faculty:* 31 full-time (15 women). *Students:* 125 full-time (77 women), 15 part-time (11 women); includes 15 minority (10 Black or African American, non-Hispanic/Latino; 1 Asian, non-Hispanic/Latino; 2 Hispanic/Latino; 1 Native Hawaiian or other Pacific Islander, non-Hispanic/Latino; 1 Two or more races, non-Hispanic/Latino), 7 international. Average age 28. 364 applicants, 16% accepted, 39 enrolled. In 2011, 30 master's, 3 doctorates awarded. *Degree requirements:* For master's, one foreign language, comprehensive exam, thesis (for some programs); for doctorate, 2 foreign languages, comprehensive exam, thesis/dissertation. *Entrance requirements:* For master's and doctorate, GRE, minimum GPA of 3.0, critical writing sample. Additional exam requirements/recommendations for international students: Required—TOEFL. *Application deadline:* For fall admission, 1/15 priority date for domestic students, 1/15 for international students. Application fee: $50 ($60 for international students). Electronic applications accepted. *Expenses:* Tuition, state resident: full-time $8600. Tuition, nonresident: full-time $21,900. *Financial support:* In 2011–12, 7 fellowships with full tuition reimbursements (averaging $15,000 per year), 1 research assistantship (averaging $11,708 per year), 106 teaching assistantships with full tuition reimbursements (averaging $11,708 per year) were awarded; career-related internships or fieldwork, scholarships/grants, health care benefits, and unspecified assistantships also available. Financial award application deadline: 1/15. *Faculty research:* Critical theory; modern, Renaissance, and African-American literature. *Unit head:* Dr. Catherine E. Davies, Director of Graduate Studies, 205-348-8499, E-mail: cdavies@bama.ua.edu. *Application contact:* Vernita W. James, Office Assistant II, 205-348-0766, Fax: 205-348-1388, E-mail: vwjames@bama.ua.edu.

University of Alberta, Faculty of Graduate Studies and Research, Department of Educational Psychology, Edmonton, AB T6G 2E1, Canada. Offers counseling psychology (M Ed, PhD); educational psychology (M Ed, PhD); instructional technology (M Ed); school counseling (M Ed); school psychology (M Ed, PhD); special education (M Ed, PhD); special education-deafness studies (M Ed); teaching English as a second language (M Ed). Part-time programs available. *Degree requirements:* For master's, thesis optional; for doctorate, comprehensive exam, thesis/dissertation. *Entrance requirements:* For master's and doctorate, minimum GPA of 3.0. Additional exam requirements/recommendations for international students: Required—TOEFL. *Faculty research:* Human learning, development and assessment.

The University of Arizona, College of Humanities, Department of English, English Language/Linguistics Program, Tucson, AZ 85721. Offers ESL (MA). *Faculty:* 42 full-time (16 women), 2 part-time/adjunct (1 woman). *Students:* 72 full-time (43 women), 10 part-time (6 women); includes 17 minority (1 American Indian or Alaska Native, non-Hispanic/Latino; 4 Hispanic/Latino; 12 Two or more races, non-Hispanic/Latino), 8 international. Average age 34. 25 applicants, 68% accepted, 9 enrolled. In 2011, 18 master's awarded. *Application deadline:* For fall admission, 1/15 priority date for domestic students, 1/15 for international students. Application fee: $75. *Expenses:* Tuition, state resident: full-time $10,840. Tuition, nonresident: full-time $25,802. *Total annual research expenditures:* $252,020. *Unit head:* Dr. Jun Liu, Department Head, 520-621-3287, E-mail: junliu@email.arizona.edu. *Application contact:* Marcia Marma, Graduate Secretary, 520-621-1358, Fax: 520-621-7397, E-mail: mmarma@u.arizona.edu.

The University of Arizona, Graduate Interdisciplinary Programs, Graduate Interdisciplinary Program in Second Language Acquisition and Teaching, Tucson, AZ 85721. Offers PhD. *Students:* 56 full-time (37 women), 6 part-time (4 women); includes 8 minority (3 Black or African American, non-Hispanic/Latino; 3 Hispanic/Latino; 2 Two or more races, non-Hispanic/Latino), 25 international. Average age 36. 58 applicants, 47% accepted, 13 enrolled. In 2011, 8 degrees awarded. *Degree requirements:* For doctorate, one foreign language, comprehensive exam, thesis/dissertation. *Entrance requirements:* For doctorate, GRE, 3 letters of recommendation, writing sample. Additional exam requirements/recommendations for international students: Required—TOEFL (minimum score 550 paper-based; 213 computer-based; 79 iBT); Recommended—TWE. *Application deadline:* For fall admission, 2/1 for domestic students, 1/15 for international students. Applications are processed on a rolling basis. Application fee: $75. Electronic applications accepted. *Expenses:* Tuition, state resident: full-time $10,840. Tuition, nonresident: full-time $25,802. *Financial support:* Scholarships/grants, health care benefits, tuition waivers (full and partial), and unspecified assistantships available. Financial award application deadline: 2/1; financial award applicants required to submit FAFSA. *Unit head:* Dr. Linda Waugh, Chair, 520-621-7391, E-mail: lwaugh@u.arizona.edu. *Application contact:* Shaun O'Connor, Senior Program Coordinator, 520-621-7391, E-mail: azslat@u.arizona.edu. Web site: http://slat.arizona.edu/.

University of Arkansas at Little Rock, Graduate School, College of Arts, Humanities, and Social Science, Department of International and Second Language Studies, Little Rock, AR 72204-1099. Offers second languages (MA).

The University of British Columbia, Faculty of Education, Program in Language and Literacy Education, Vancouver, BC V6T 1Z1, Canada. Offers library education (M Ed); literacy education (M Ed, MA, PhD); modern language education (M Ed, MA, PhD); teaching English as a second language (M Ed, MA, PhD). Part-time and evening/weekend programs available. *Degree requirements:* For master's, thesis (MA); for doctorate, thesis/dissertation. *Entrance requirements:* For master's and doctorate, minimum B+ average in last 2 years with minimum 2 courses at A standing. Additional exam requirements/recommendations for international students: Required—TOEFL (minimum score 580 paper-based; 237 computer-based; 92 iBT), TWE (minimum score 5). Electronic applications accepted. *Faculty research:* Language and literacy development, second language acquisition, Asia Pacific language curriculum, children's literature, whole language instruction.

University of Calgary, Faculty of Graduate Studies, Faculty of Education, Graduate Division of Educational Research, Calgary, AB T2N 1N4, Canada. Offers community rehabilitation and disability studies (M Ed, M Sc, Ed D, PhD, Graduate Certificate, Graduate Diploma); curriculum, teaching and learning (M Ed, M Sc, MA, Ed D, PhD, Graduate Certificate, Graduate Diploma); educational contexts (M Ed, MA, Ed D, PhD, Graduate Certificate, Graduate Diploma); educational leadership (M Ed, MA, Ed D, PhD, Graduate Certificate, Graduate Diploma); educational technology (M Ed, M Sc, MA, Ed D, PhD, Graduate Certificate, Graduate Diploma); gifted education (M Sc, MA, Ed D, PhD, Graduate Certificate, Graduate Diploma); higher education administration (Ed D); interpretive studies in education (M Ed, M Sc, MA, Ed D, PhD, Graduate Certificate, Graduate Diploma); second language teaching (M Ed, Ed D, PhD, Graduate Certificate, Graduate Diploma); teaching English as a second language (M Ed, M Sc, MA, Ed D, PhD, Graduate Certificate, Graduate Diploma); workplace and adult learning (M Ed, MA, Ed D, PhD, Graduate Certificate, Graduate Diploma). Ed D in both higher education administration and educational leadership offered via distance delivery. Part-time and evening/weekend programs available. Postbaccalaureate distance learning degree programs offered (minimal on-campus study). *Degree requirements:* For master's, thesis (for some programs); for doctorate, thesis/dissertation, candidacy exam. *Entrance requirements:* For master's, minimum GPA of 3.0, 3 letters of reference; for doctorate, minimum GPA of 3.5, 3 letters of reference; for other advanced degree, minimum GPA of 3.0. Additional exam requirements/recommendations for international students: Required—TOEFL, IELTS. Electronic applications accepted. *Faculty research:* Curriculum, leadership, technology, contexts, gifted, second language teaching, work place and adult learning.

University of California, Berkeley, UC Berkeley Extension, Certificate Programs in Education, Berkeley, CA 94720-1500. Offers college admissions and career planning (Certificate); teaching English as a second language (Certificate).

University of California, Los Angeles, Graduate Division, College of Letters and Science, Department of Applied Linguistics and Teaching English as a Second Language, Los Angeles, CA 90095. Offers applied linguistics (PhD); applied linguistics and teaching English as a second language (MA); teaching English as a second language (Certificate). *Faculty:* 6 full-time (3 women). *Students:* 49 full-time (39 women); includes 15 minority (1 Black or African American, non-Hispanic/Latino; 6 Asian, non-Hispanic/Latino; 7 Hispanic/Latino; 1 Two or more races, non-Hispanic/Latino), 14 international. Average age 33. 97 applicants, 12% accepted, 11 enrolled. In 2011, 3 master's, 1 doctorate awarded. *Degree requirements:* For master's, one foreign language, thesis; for doctorate, one foreign language, thesis/dissertation, oral and written exams. *Entrance requirements:* For master's, minimum GPA of 3.0, sample of research writing; for doctorate, minimum GPA of 3.0, MA in relevant field. *Application deadline:* For fall admission, 12/15 for domestic and international students. Application fee: $70 ($90 for international students). Electronic applications accepted. *Financial support:* In 2011–12, 32 fellowships with full and partial tuition reimbursements, 21 research assistantships with full and partial tuition reimbursements, 28 teaching assistantships with full and partial tuition reimbursements were awarded; Federal Work-Study, institutionally sponsored loans, scholarships/grants, health care benefits, tuition waivers (full and partial), and unspecified assistantships also available. Financial award application deadline: 3/1; financial award applicants required to submit FAFSA. *Unit head:* Dr. Shoichi Iwasaki, Chair, 310-794-8933, E-mail: iwasaki@humnet.ucla.edu. *Application contact:* Jessika Herrera, Graduate Advisor, 310-825-4631, Fax: 310-206-4118, E-mail: jherrera@humnet.ucla.edu. Web site: http://www.appling.ucla.edu/.

University of Central Florida, College of Arts and Humanities, Department of Modern Languages and Literatures, Program in Teaching English to Speakers of Other Languages, Orlando, FL 32816. Offers ESOL endorsement K-12 (Certificate); teaching English to speakers of other languages (MA); TEFL (Certificate). *Accreditation:* NCATE. Part-time and evening/weekend programs available. *Students:* 12 full-time (11 women), 41 part-time (34 women); includes 15 minority (2 Black or African American, non-Hispanic/Latino; 1 Asian, non-Hispanic/Latino; 9 Hispanic/Latino; 3 Two or more races, non-Hispanic/Latino), 1 international. Average age 35. 38 applicants, 74% accepted, 17 enrolled. In 2011, 19 master's, 14 other advanced degrees awarded. *Degree requirements:* For master's, comprehensive exam, thesis or alternative. *Entrance requirements:* For master's, GRE General Test, minimum GPA of 3.0 in last 60 hours. Additional exam requirements/recommendations for international students: Required—TOEFL. *Application deadline:* For fall admission, 6/15 for domestic students; for spring admission, 11/1 for domestic students. Application fee: $30. Electronic applications accepted. *Expenses:* Tuition, state resident: part-time $277.08 per credit hour. Tuition, nonresident: part-time $277.08 per credit hour. Part-time tuition and fees vary according to degree level and program. *Financial support:* In 2011–12, 2 students received support, including 1 fellowship (averaging $4,000 per year), 2 teaching assistantships with partial tuition reimbursements available (averaging $8,300 per year); career-related internships or fieldwork, Federal Work-Study, institutionally sponsored loans, tuition waivers (partial), and unspecified assistantships also available. Financial award application deadline: 3/1; financial award applicants required to submit FAFSA. *Unit head:* Dr. Kerry Purmensky, Program Coordinator, 407-823-0110, E-mail: lerry.purmensky@ucf.edu. *Application contact:* Barbara Rodriguez Lamas, Director, Admissions and Registration, 407-823-2766, Fax: 407-823-6442, E-mail: gradadmissions@ucf.edu. Web site: http://mll.cah.ucf.edu/graduate/index.php#TESOL.

University of Central Florida, College of Education, Education Doctoral Programs, Orlando, FL 32816. Offers communication sciences and disorders (PhD); counselor education (PhD); education (Ed D); elementary education (PhD); exceptional education (PhD); exercise physiology (PhD); higher education (PhD); hospitality education (PhD); instructional technology (PhD); mathematics education (PhD); reading education (PhD); science education (PhD); social science education (PhD); TESOL (PhD). *Students:* 135 full-time (87 women), 73 part-time (51 women); includes 49 minority (21 Black or African American, non-Hispanic/Latino; 4 Asian, non-Hispanic/Latino; 20 Hispanic/Latino; 4 Two or more races, non-Hispanic/Latino), 18 international. Average age 39. 125 applicants, 46% accepted, 46 enrolled. In 2011, 43 doctorates awarded. Application fee: $30. Electronic applications accepted. *Expenses:* Tuition, state resident: part-time $277.08 per credit hour. Tuition, nonresident: part-time $277.08 per credit hour. Part-time tuition and fees vary according to degree level and program. *Financial support:* In 2011–12, 85 students received support, including 48 fellowships with partial tuition reimbursements available (averaging $5,900 per year), 36 research assistantships with partial tuition reimbursements available (averaging $6,900 per year), 59 teaching assistantships with partial tuition reimbursements available (averaging $6,900 per year). *Unit head:* Dr. Rex Culp, Associate Dean, 407-823-5391, E-mail: rex.culp@ucf.edu. *Application contact:* Barbara Rodriguez, Associate Director, Admissions and Registration, 407-823-2766, Fax: 407-823-6442, E-mail: gradadmissions@ucf.edu. Web site: http://education.ucf.edu/departments.cfm.

University of Central Florida, College of Education, School of Teaching, Learning, and Leadership, Program in English Language Arts Education, Orlando, FL 32816. Offers teacher education (MAT), including ESOL endorsement; teacher leadership (M Ed). *Accreditation:* NCATE. Part-time and evening/weekend programs available. *Students:* 18 full-time (15 women), 30 part-time (25 women); includes 14 minority (5 Black or African American, non-Hispanic/Latino; 2 Asian, non-Hispanic/Latino; 6 Hispanic/Latino; 1 Two or more races, non-Hispanic/Latino). Average age 29. 14 applicants, 71% accepted, 9 enrolled. In 2011, 14 master's awarded. *Degree requirements:* For master's, thesis or alternative, research project. *Entrance requirements:* For master's, GRE General Test. Additional exam requirements/recommendations for international students: Required—TOEFL. *Application deadline:* For fall admission, 7/15 for domestic students; for spring admission, 12/1 for domestic students. Application fee: $30. Electronic applications accepted. *Expenses:* Tuition, state resident: part-time $277.08 per credit hour. Tuition, nonresident: part-time $277.08 per credit hour. Part-time tuition and fees vary according to degree level and program. *Financial support:* In 2011–12, 1 student received support. Fellowships with partial tuition reimbursements available, research assistantships with partial tuition reimbursements available, teaching assistantships with partial tuition reimbursements available, career-related internships or fieldwork, Federal Work-Study, institutionally sponsored loans, tuition waivers (partial), and unspecified assistantships available. Financial award application deadline: 3/1; financial award applicants required to submit FAFSA. *Unit head:* Dr. Janet B. Andreasen, Program Coordinator, 407-823-5430, E-mail: janet.andreasen@ucf.edu. *Application contact:* Barbara Rodriguez, Director, Admissions and Registration, 407-823-2766, Fax: 407-823-6442, E-mail: gradadmissions@ucf.edu.

University of Central Missouri, The Graduate School, College of Arts, Humanities and Social Sciences, Warrensburg, MO 64093. Offers English (MA); history (MA); mass communication (MA); music (MA); psychology (MS); speech communication (MA); teaching English as a second language (MA); theatre (MA). Part-time programs available. *Entrance requirements:* Additional exam requirements/recommendations for international students: Required—TOEFL (minimum score 550 paper-based; 79 computer-based). Electronic applications accepted.

University of Central Oklahoma, College of Graduate Studies and Research, College of Liberal Arts, Department of English, Edmond, OK 73034-5209. Offers composition skills (MA); contemporary literature (MA); creative writing (MA); teaching English as a second language (MA); traditional studies (MA). Part-time programs available. *Faculty:* 20 full-time (9 women), 7 part-time/adjunct (2 women). *Students:* 58 full-time (42 women), 68 part-time (48 women); includes 14 minority (1 Black or African American, non-Hispanic/Latino; 5 American Indian or Alaska Native, non-Hispanic/Latino; 1 Asian, non-Hispanic/Latino; 4 Hispanic/Latino; 3 Two or more races, non-Hispanic/Latino), 23 international. Average age 32. In 2011, 34 master's awarded. *Degree requirements:* For master's, one foreign language. *Entrance requirements:* For master's, 24 hours of course work in English language and literature. Additional exam requirements/recommendations for international students: Required—TOEFL (minimum score 550 paper-based; 213 computer-based). *Application deadline:* Applications are processed on a rolling basis. Application fee: $50. Electronic applications accepted. *Expenses:* Tuition, state resident: full-time $3901; part-time $218.30 per credit hour. Tuition, nonresident: full-time $9198; part-time $511.20 per credit hour. Tuition and fees vary according to program. *Financial support:* In 2011–12, 6 teaching assistantships with partial tuition reimbursements were awarded; career-related internships or fieldwork, Federal Work-Study, and unspecified assistantships also available. Financial award application deadline: 3/31; financial award applicants required to submit FAFSA. *Faculty research:* John Milton, Harriet Beecher Stowe. *Unit head:* Dr. Amy Carrell, 405-974-5609, E-mail: acarrell@uco.edu.

University of Cincinnati, Graduate School, College of Education, Criminal Justice, and Human Services, Division of Teacher Education, Program in Teaching English as a Second Language, Cincinnati, OH 45221. Offers M Ed, Ed D, Certificate. *Entrance requirements:* For master's and doctorate, GRE General Test. Additional exam requirements/recommendations for international students: Required—TOEFL (minimum score 550 paper-based; 213 computer-based), TWE (minimum score 5), Test of Spoken English (minimum score: 50).

University of Delaware, College of Education and Human Development, School of Education, Newark, DE 19716. Offers education (PhD); educational leadership (Ed D); higher education (M Ed); instruction (MI); reading (M Ed); school leadership (M Ed); school psychology (MA, Ed S); teaching English as a second language (TESL) (MA). *Accreditation:* NCATE. Part-time and evening/weekend programs available. Terminal master's awarded for partial completion of doctoral program. *Degree requirements:* For master's, comprehensive exam (for some programs), thesis (for some programs); for doctorate, comprehensive exam (for some programs), thesis/dissertation. *Entrance requirements:* For master's and doctorate, GRE, 3 letters of recommendation. Additional exam requirements/recommendations for international students: Required—TOEFL (minimum score 600 paper-based; 250 computer-based). Electronic applications accepted. *Faculty research:* Teacher education; curriculum theory and development; community based education models, educational leadership.

The University of Findlay, Graduate and Professional Studies, College of Liberal Arts, Master of Arts in Teaching English to Speakers of Other Languages (TESOL) and Bilingual Education Program, Findlay, OH 45840-3653. Offers bilingual education (MA); teaching English to speakers of other languages (MA). Part-time and evening/weekend programs available. *Faculty:* 11 full-time (6 women). *Students:* 19 full-time (13 women), 15 part-time (11 women), 17 international. Average age 35. 13 applicants, 85% accepted, 7 enrolled. In 2011, 6 master's awarded. *Degree requirements:* For master's, cumulative project. *Entrance requirements:* For master's, bachelor's degree from accredited institution, minimum undergraduate GPA of 2.75 in last 64 hours of course work, 3 letters of recommendation. Additional exam requirements/recommendations for international students: Required—TOEFL (minimum score 550 paper-based; 213 computer-based; 80 iBT). *Application deadline:* Applications are processed on a rolling basis. Application fee: $25. Electronic applications accepted. *Expenses: Tuition:* Full-time $6300; part-time $700 per semester hour. *Required fees:* $35 per semester hour. One-time fee: $25. Tuition and fees vary according to course load, degree level and program. *Financial support:* In 2011–12, 2 teaching assistantships with full and partial tuition reimbursements (averaging $3,600 per year) were awarded; Federal Work-Study, health care benefits, and unspecified assistantships also available. Financial award application deadline: 4/1; financial award applicants required to submit FAFSA. *Unit head:* Dr. Hiroaki Kawamura, Chair, Department of Language and Culture, 419-434-4619, Fax: 419-434-4822, E-mail: kawamura@findlay.edu. *Application contact:* Heather Riffle, Assistant Director, Graduate and Professional Studies, 419-434-4640, Fax: 419-434-5517, E-mail: riffle@findlay.edu. Web site: http://www.findlay.edu.

University of Florida, Graduate School, College of Liberal Arts and Sciences, Linguistics Department, Gainesville, FL 32611. Offers linguistics (MA, PhD); teaching English as a second language (Certificate). Part-time programs available. *Faculty:* 11 full-time (8 women), 1 (woman) part-time/adjunct. *Students:* 48 full-time (25 women), 1 (woman) part-time; includes 1 minority (Asian, non-Hispanic/Latino), 30 international. Average age 31. 84 applicants, 30% accepted, 9 enrolled. In 2011, 10 master's, 1 doctorate awarded. Terminal master's awarded for partial completion of doctoral program. *Degree requirements:* For master's, one foreign language, comprehensive exam, thesis (for some programs); for doctorate, 2 foreign languages, comprehensive exam, thesis/dissertation. *Entrance requirements:* For master's and doctorate, GRE General Test, minimum GPA of 3.0. Additional exam requirements/recommendations for international students: Required—TOEFL (minimum score 550 paper-based; 213 computer-based; 80 iBT), IELTS (minimum score 6). *Application deadline:* For fall admission, 12/15 priority date for domestic students, 12/15 for international students. Applications are processed on a rolling basis. Application fee: $30. Electronic applications accepted. *Financial support:* Fellowships with tuition reimbursements, research assistantships, teaching assistantships with tuition reimbursements, institutionally sponsored loans, and unspecified assistantships available. Financial award application deadline: 12/15; financial award applicants required to submit FAFSA. *Faculty research:* Theoretical, applied, and descriptive linguistics. *Unit head:* Dr. Caroline R. Wiltshire, Chair, 352-392-0639 Ext. 224, Fax: 352-392-8480, E-mail: wiltshir@ufl.edu. *Application contact:* Dr. Ratree Wayland, Graduate Coordinator, 352-392-0639 Ext. 225, Fax: 352-392-8480, E-mail: ratree@ufl.edu. Web site: http://web.lin.ufl.edu/.

University of Guam, Office of Graduate Studies, School of Education, Program in Teaching English to Speakers of Other Languages, Mangilao, GU 96923. Offers M Ed. *Degree requirements:* For master's, comprehensive oral and written exams, special project or thesis. *Entrance requirements:* For master's, GRE General Test. Additional exam requirements/recommendations for international students: Required—TOEFL.

University of Hawaii at Manoa, Graduate Division, College of Languages, Linguistics and Literature, Department of Second Language Studies, Honolulu, HI 96822. Offers English as a second language (MA, Graduate Certificate); second language acquisition (PhD). Part-time programs available. *Degree requirements:* For master's, 2 foreign languages, thesis optional; for doctorate, 2 foreign languages, comprehensive exam, thesis/dissertation. *Entrance requirements:* For master's, GRE General Test, minimum GPA of 3.0; for doctorate, GRE General Test, MA, scholarly publications. Additional exam requirements/recommendations for international students: Required—TOEFL (minimum score 600 paper-based; 250 computer-based; 100 iBT), IELTS (minimum score 7). *Faculty research:* Second language use, second language analysis, second language pedagogy and testing, second language learning, qualitative and quantitative research methods for second languages.

University of Idaho, College of Graduate Studies, College of Letters, Arts and Social Sciences, Department of English, Program in Teaching English as a Second Language, Moscow, ID 83844-2282. Offers MA. *Students:* 10 full-time, 8 part-time. Average age 32. In 2011, 5 master's awarded. *Entrance requirements:* For master's, minimum GPA of 2.8. *Application deadline:* For fall admission, 8/1 for domestic students; for spring admission, 12/15 for domestic students. Applications are processed on a rolling basis. Application fee: $60. Electronic applications accepted. *Expenses:* Tuition, state resident: full-time $3874; part-time $334 per credit hour. Tuition, nonresident: full-time $16,394; part-time $861 per credit hour. *Required fees:* $2808; $99 per credit hour. Tuition and fees vary according to program. *Financial support:* Applicants required to submit FAFSA. *Unit head:* Dr. Gary Williams, Chair, 208-883-6156. *Application contact:* Erick Larson, Director of Graduate Admissions, 208-885-4723, E-mail: gadms@uidaho.edu. Web site: http://www.uidaho.edu/class/english/graduate/mateachingenglishasasecondlanguage.

University of Illinois at Chicago, Graduate College, College of Liberal Arts and Sciences, Department of English, Program in Linguistics, Chicago, IL 60607-7128. Offers teaching English to speakers of other languages/applied linguistics (MA). Part-time programs available. *Degree requirements:* For master's, one foreign language, comprehensive exam, thesis (for some programs). *Entrance requirements:* For master's, minimum GPA of 3.0. Additional exam requirements/recommendations for international students: Required—TOEFL. Electronic applications accepted. *Faculty research:* Second language acquisition, methodology of second language teaching, lexicography, language, sex and gender.

University of Illinois at Urbana–Champaign, Graduate College, College of Liberal Arts and Sciences, School of Literatures, Cultures and Linguistics, Department of Linguistics, Champaign, IL 61820. Offers linguistics (MA, PhD); teaching of English as a second language (MA). *Faculty:* 16 full-time (5 women). *Students:* 65 full-time (47 women), 35 part-time (26 women); includes 16 minority (2 Black or African American, non-Hispanic/Latino; 11 Asian, non-Hispanic/Latino; 3 Hispanic/Latino), 48 international. 174 applicants, 24% accepted, 25 enrolled. In 2011, 32 master's, 12 doctorates awarded. *Entrance requirements:* For master's, GRE, minimum GPA of 3.0; writing sample; for doctorate, GRE, minimum GPA of 3.5; writing sample. Additional exam requirements/recommendations for international students: Required—TOEFL (minimum score 88 iBT). *Application deadline:* Applications are processed on a rolling basis. Application fee: $75 ($90 for international students). Electronic applications accepted. *Financial support:* In 2011–12, 17 fellowships, 26 research assistantships, 65 teaching assistantships were awarded; tuition waivers (full and partial) also available. *Unit head:* Hye Suk James Yoon, Acting Head, 217-244-3340, E-mail: jyoon@illinois.edu. *Application contact:* Lynn Stanke, Office Support Specialist, 217-333-6269, Fax: 217-244-3050, E-mail: stanke@illinois.edu. Web site: http://www.linguistics.illinois.edu/.

The University of Manchester, School of Languages, Linguistics and Cultures, Manchester, United Kingdom. Offers Arab world studies (PhD); Chinese studies (M Phil, PhD); East Asian studies (M Phil, PhD); English language (PhD); French studies (M Phil, PhD); German studies (M Phil, PhD); interpreting studies (PhD); Italian studies (M Phil, PhD); Japanese studies (M Phil, PhD); Latin American cultural studies (M Phil, PhD); linguistics (M Phil, PhD); Middle Eastern studies (M Phil, PhD); Polish studies (M Phil, PhD); Portuguese studies (M Phil, PhD); Russian studies (M Phil, PhD); Spanish studies (M Phil, PhD); translation and intercultural studies (M Phil, PhD).

University of Manitoba, Faculty of Graduate Studies, Faculty of Education, Department of Curriculum, Teaching and Learning, Winnipeg, MB R3T 2N2, Canada. Offers language and literacy (M Ed); second language education (M Ed); studies in curriculum, teaching and learning (M Ed). *Degree requirements:* For master's, thesis or alternative.

University of Maryland, Baltimore County, Graduate School, College of Arts, Humanities and Social Sciences, Department of Education, Program in Teaching English for Speakers of Other Languages, Baltimore, MD 21250. Offers MA, Postbaccalaureate Certificate. Part-time and evening/weekend programs available. Postbaccalaureate distance learning degree programs offered (no on-campus study). *Faculty:* 5 full-time (4 women), 13 part-time/adjunct (10 women). *Students:* 25 full-time (20 women), 93 part-time (82 women); includes 18 minority (3 Black or African American, non-Hispanic/Latino; 5 Asian, non-Hispanic/Latino; 9 Hispanic/Latino; 1 Native Hawaiian or other Pacific Islander, non-Hispanic/Latino), 11 international. Average age 36. 57 applicants, 82% accepted, 42 enrolled. In 2011, 29 master's, 13 other advanced degrees awarded. *Degree requirements:* For master's, comprehensive exam, thesis optional, internship (for certification). *Entrance requirements:* For master's, GRE (minimum score 500 verbal or 150 on the new version), 3 letters of reference. Additional exam requirements/recommendations for international students: Required—TOEFL (minimum score 550 paper-based; 213 computer-based; 80 iBT). *Application deadline:* For fall admission, 4/15 priority date for domestic students, 3/1 for international students; for spring admission, 10/31 priority date for domestic students, 10/31 for international students. Application fee: $50. Electronic applications accepted. *Financial support:* In 2011–12, 14 students received support, including research assistantships with full tuition reimbursements available (averaging $12,000 per year); career-related internships or fieldwork, Federal Work-Study, scholarships/grants, and unspecified assistantships also available. *Faculty research:* Adult education, bilingual language learning, online instruction, English grammar, cross-culture communication. *Unit head:* Dr. John Nelson, Director, 410-455-2379, E-mail: jnelson@umbc.edu. *Application contact:* Alexander Sheffrin, Graduate Assistant, 410-455-3061, E-mail: esol@umbc.edu. Web site: http://www.umbc.edu/education/.

University of Maryland, College Park, Academic Affairs, College of Education, Department of Curriculum and Instruction, College Park, MD 20742. Offers reading (M Ed, MA, PhD, CAGS); secondary education (M Ed, MA, Ed D, PhD, CAGS); teaching English to speakers of other languages (M Ed). *Accreditation:* NCATE. Part-time and evening/weekend programs available. Postbaccalaureate distance learning degree programs offered (no on-campus study). *Faculty:* 51 full-time (38 women), 23 part-time/adjunct (18 women). *Students:* 252 full-time (177 women), 178 part-time (134 women); includes 121 minority (51 Black or African American, non-Hispanic/Latino; 37 Asian, non-Hispanic/Latino; 24 Hispanic/Latino; 9 Two or more races, non-Hispanic/Latino), 41 international. 264 applicants, 48% accepted, 80 enrolled. In 2011, 176 master's, 17 doctorates awarded. *Degree requirements:* For master's, comprehensive exam, seminar paper; for doctorate, comprehensive exam, thesis/dissertation, published paper, oral exam. *Entrance requirements:* For master's, GRE General Test or MAT, minimum GPA of 3.0, 3 letters of recommendation; for doctorate, GRE General Test or MAT, minimum undergraduate GPA of 3.0, graduate 3.5; 3 letters of recommendation. *Application* *deadline:* For fall admission, 11/15 priority date for domestic students, 11/15 for international students. Applications are processed on a rolling basis. Application fee: $75. Electronic applications accepted. *Expenses: Tuition, area resident:* Part-time $525 per credit hour. Tuition, state resident: part-time $525 per credit hour. Tuition, nonresident: part-time $1131 per credit hour. *Required fees:* $386.31 per term. Tuition and fees vary according to program. *Financial support:* In 2011–12, 11 research assistantships (averaging $17,535 per year), 79 teaching assistantships (averaging $17,270 per year) were awarded; Federal Work-Study and scholarships/grants also available. Support available to part-time students. Financial award applicants required to submit FAFSA. *Faculty research:* Teacher preparation, curriculum study, in-service education. *Total annual research expenditures:* $3.6 million. *Unit head:* Francine Hultgren, Interim Chair, 301-405-3117, E-mail: fh@umd.edu. *Application contact:* Dr. Charles A. Caramello, Dean of Graduate School, 301-405-0358, Fax: 301-314-9305.

University of Massachusetts Amherst, Graduate School, School of Education, Program in Education, Amherst, MA 01003. Offers bilingual, English as a second language, and multicultural education (M Ed, CAGS); child study and early education (M Ed); children, families and schools (Ed D, CAGS); early childhood and elementary teacher education (M Ed); educational leadership (M Ed, CAGS); educational policy and leadership (Ed D); higher education (M Ed, CAGS); international education (M Ed); language, literacy and culture (Ed D); learning, media and technology (M Ed, CAGS); mathematics, science, and learning technologies (Ed D); policy studies in education (CAGS); psychometric methods, educational statistics and research methods (Ed D); reading and writing (M Ed); school counselor education (M Ed, CAGS); science education (CAGS); secondary teacher education (M Ed); social justice education (M Ed, Ed D, CAGS); special education (M Ed, Ed D, CAGS). *Accreditation:* NCATE. Part-time programs available. Postbaccalaureate distance learning degree programs offered (minimal on-campus study). *Faculty:* 81 full-time (46 women). *Students:* 341 full-time (240 women), 333 part-time (226 women); includes 113 minority (36 Black or African American, non-Hispanic/Latino; 1 American Indian or Alaska Native, non-Hispanic/Latino; 14 Asian, non-Hispanic/Latino; 51 Hispanic/Latino; 1 Native Hawaiian or other Pacific Islander, non-Hispanic/Latino; 10 Two or more races, non-Hispanic/Latino), 98 international. Average age 36. 721 applicants, 57% accepted, 202 enrolled. In 2011, 166 master's, 33 doctorates, 25 CAGSs awarded. Terminal master's awarded for partial completion of doctoral program. *Degree requirements:* For doctorate, comprehensive exam, thesis/dissertation. *Entrance requirements:* Additional exam requirements/recommendations for international students: Required—TOEFL (minimum score 550 paper-based; 213 computer-based; 80 iBT), IELTS (minimum score 6.5). *Application deadline:* For fall admission, 1/15 for domestic and international students. Applications are processed on a rolling basis. Application fee: $50 ($65 for international students). Electronic applications accepted. Tuition and fees vary according to course load, campus/location and program. *Financial support:* Fellowships with full and partial tuition reimbursements, research assistantships with full and partial tuition reimbursements, teaching assistantships with full and partial tuition reimbursements, career-related internships or fieldwork, Federal Work-Study, scholarships/grants, traineeships, health care benefits, tuition waivers (full and partial), and unspecified assistantships available. Support available to part-time students. Financial award application deadline: 1/15. *Unit head:* Dr. Linda L. Griffin, Graduate Program Director, 413-545-6984, Fax: 413-545-1523. *Application contact:* Lindsay DeSantis, Interim Supervisor of Admissions, 413-545-0722, Fax: 413-577-0010, E-mail: gradadm@grad.umass.edu. Web site: http://www.umass.edu/education/.

University of Massachusetts Boston, Office of Graduate Studies, College of Liberal Arts, Program in Applied Linguistics, Boston, MA 02125-3393. Offers bilingual education (MA); English as a second language (MA); foreign language pedagogy (MA). Part-time and evening/weekend programs available. *Degree requirements:* For master's, one foreign language, comprehensive exam. *Entrance requirements:* For master's, minimum GPA of 2.75. *Faculty research:* Multicultural theory and curriculum development, foreign language pedagogy, language and culture, applied psycholinguistics, bilingual education.

University of Memphis, Graduate School, College of Arts and Sciences, Department of English, Memphis, TN 38152. Offers African-American literature (Graduate Certificate); applied linguistics (PhD); composition studies (PhD); creative writing (MFA); English as a second language (MA); linguistics (MA); literary and cultural studies (PhD), including African-American literature; literature (MA); professional writing (MA, PhD); teaching English as a second language (Graduate Certificate). Part-time and evening/weekend programs available. Postbaccalaureate distance learning degree programs offered (no on-campus study). Terminal master's awarded for partial completion of doctoral program. *Degree requirements:* For master's, one foreign language, comprehensive exam, thesis optional; for doctorate, 2 foreign languages, comprehensive exam, thesis/dissertation. *Entrance requirements:* For master's and doctorate, GRE. Additional exam requirements/recommendations for international students: Required—TOEFL. Electronic applications accepted. *Faculty research:* Applied linguistics, British and American literature, professional writing, composition studies.

University of Minnesota, Twin Cities Campus, Graduate School, College of Education and Human Development, Department of Curriculum and Instruction, Program in Teaching, Minneapolis, MN 55455-0213. Offers Chinese (M Ed); earth science (M Ed); elementary special education (M Ed); English (M Ed); English as a second language (M Ed); French (M Ed); German (M Ed); Hebrew (M Ed); Japanese (M Ed); life sciences (M Ed); mathematics (M Ed); middle school science (M Ed); science (M Ed); second languages and cultures (M Ed); social studies (M Ed); Spanish (M Ed). *Students:* 375 full-time (319 women), 72 part-time (56 women); includes 34 minority (8 Black or African American, non-Hispanic/Latino; 16 Asian, non-Hispanic/Latino; 10 Hispanic/Latino), 5 international. Average age 27. 317 applicants, 70% accepted, 215 enrolled. In 2011, 443 master's awarded. Application fee: $55. *Unit head:* Dr. Nina Asher, Chair, 612-624-1357, Fax: 612-624-8277, E-mail: nasher@umn.edu. *Application contact:* Dr. Jennifer Engler, Assistant Dean, 612-626-2887, Fax: 612-626-7496, E-mail: engle009@umn.edu. Web site: http://www.cehd.umn.edu/ci/.

University of Minnesota, Twin Cities Campus, Graduate School, College of Liberal Arts, Institute of Linguistics, English as a Second Language, and Slavic Languages and Literatures (ILES), English as a Second Language Program, Minneapolis, MN 55455-0213. Offers MA. *Degree requirements:* For master's, one foreign language, comprehensive exam, thesis. *Entrance requirements:* For master's, GRE, 3 letters of recommendation. Additional exam requirements/recommendations for international students: Required—TOEFL (minimum score 600 paper-based; 250 computer-based). Electronic applications accepted. *Faculty research:* Second language acquisitions, communication strategies, English for specific purposes, literacy, speech act, proymatics in general, language assessment, discourse analysis, research methods.

University of Missouri–St. Louis, College of Education, Division of Teaching and Learning, St. Louis, MO 63121. Offers autism studies (Certificate); elementary education (M Ed), including early childhood, general, reading; secondary education (M Ed), including curriculum and instruction, general, middle level education, reading, teaching English to speakers of other languages (TESOL); secondary school teaching (Certificate); special education (M Ed), including autism and developmental disabilities, early childhood special education, general; teaching English to speakers of other languages (Certificate). Part-time and evening/weekend programs available. *Faculty:* 32 full-time (16 women), 51 part-time/adjunct (36 women). *Students:* 95 full-time (63 women), 703 part-time (541 women); includes 176 minority (125 Black or African American, non-Hispanic/Latino; 1 American Indian or Alaska Native, non-Hispanic/Latino; 16 Asian, non-Hispanic/Latino; 26 Hispanic/Latino; 8 Two or more races, non-Hispanic/Latino), 11 international. Average age 29. 379 applicants, 90% accepted, 263 enrolled. In 2011, 190 master's, 9 Certificates awarded. *Degree requirements:* For master's, comprehensive exam. *Entrance requirements:* Additional exam requirements/recommendations for international students: Recommended—TOEFL (minimum score 550 paper-based; 213 computer-based). *Application deadline:* For fall admission, 7/1 priority date for domestic students, 7/1 for international students; for spring admission, 12/1 priority date for domestic students, 12/1 for international students. Application fee: $35 ($40 for international students). Electronic applications accepted. *Expenses:* Tuition, state resident: full-time $6273; part-time $3866 per year. Tuition, nonresident: full-time $14,969; part-time $9980 per year. *Required fees:* $315 per year. *Financial support:* In 2011–12, 6 research assistantships with full and partial tuition reimbursements (averaging $9,500 per year), 2 teaching assistantships with full and partial tuition reimbursements (averaging $10,500 per year) were awarded. Financial award application deadline: 4/1; financial award applicants required to submit FAFSA. *Unit head:* Dr. Joseph Polman, Chair, 314-516-5791. *Application contact:* 314-516-5458, Fax: 314-516-6996, E-mail: gadadm@umsl.edu. Web site: http://coe.umsl.edu/web/divisions/teach-learn/index.html.

University of Nebraska at Omaha, Graduate Studies, College of Arts and Sciences, Department of English, Omaha, NE 68182. Offers advanced writing (Certificate); English (MA); teaching English to speakers of other languages (Certificate); technical communication (Certificate). Part-time and evening/weekend programs available. *Faculty:* 18 full-time (9 women). *Students:* 13 full-time (8 women), 78 part-time (52 women); includes 11 minority (2 Black or African American, non-Hispanic/Latino; 4 Asian, non-Hispanic/Latino; 3 Hispanic/Latino; 2 Two or more races, non-Hispanic/Latino), 1 international. Average age 32. 50 applicants, 90% accepted, 34 enrolled. In 2011, 15 master's, 16 other advanced degrees awarded. *Degree requirements:* For master's, comprehensive exam, thesis (for some programs). *Entrance requirements:* For master's, minimum GPA of 3.0, 3 letters of recommendation, statement of purpose. Additional exam requirements/recommendations for international students: Required—TOEFL (minimum score 600 paper-based; 250 computer-based; 100 iBT). *Application deadline:* For fall admission, 8/1 priority date for domestic students; for spring admission, 12/1 priority date for domestic students. Applications are processed on a rolling basis. Application fee: $45. Electronic applications accepted. *Financial support:* In 2011–12, 28 students received support, including 23 teaching assistantships with tuition reimbursements available; fellowships, Federal Work-Study, institutionally sponsored loans, scholarships/grants, tuition waivers (partial), and unspecified assistantships also available. Support available to part-time students. Financial award application deadline: 3/1; financial award applicants required to submit FAFSA. *Unit head:* Dr. Robert Darcy, Chairperson, 402-554-3636. *Application contact:* Dr. Tracy Bridgeford, Student Contact, 402-554-3636.

University of Nevada, Reno, Graduate School, College of Education, Department of Educational Specialties, Program in Teaching English to Speakers of Other Languages, Reno, NV 89557. Offers MA. Terminal master's awarded for partial completion of doctoral program. *Degree requirements:* For master's, thesis optional. *Entrance requirements:* For master's, minimum GPA of 2.75. Additional exam requirements/recommendations for international students: Required—TOEFL (minimum score 500 paper-based; 173 computer-based; 61 iBT), IELTS (minimum score 6). Electronic applications accepted. *Faculty research:* Bilingualism, multicultural education.

University of New Mexico, Graduate School, College of Education, Department of Language, Literacy and Sociocultural Studies, Program in Language, Literacy and Sociocultural Studies, Albuquerque, NM 87131. Offers American Indian education (MA); bilingual education (MA, PhD); educational linguistics (PhD); educational thought and sociocultural studies (MA, PhD); literacy/language arts (MA, PhD); social studies (MA); TESOL (MA, PhD). *Faculty:* 19 full-time (12 women), 12 part-time/adjunct (10 women). *Students:* 40 full-time (30 women), 47 part-time (17 women); includes 85 minority (4 Black or African American, non-Hispanic/Latino; 14 American Indian or Alaska Native, non-Hispanic/Latino; 4 Asian, non-Hispanic/Latino; 59 Hispanic/Latino; 4 Two or more races, non-Hispanic/Latino), 14 international. Average age 41. 63 applicants, 57% accepted, 22 enrolled. In 2011, 44 master's, 8 doctorates awarded. *Degree requirements:* For master's, comprehensive exam, thesis optional; for doctorate, comprehensive exam, thesis/dissertation, research skills. *Entrance requirements:* For master's, letter of intent, 3 letters of recommendation, resume, BA/BS, department demographic form, transcripts; for doctorate, writing sample, letter of intent, 3 letters of recommendation, resume, BA/BS, department demographic form, transcripts. Additional exam requirements/recommendations for international students: Required—TOEFL. *Application deadline:* For fall admission, 12/1 for domestic and international students; for spring admission, 9/15 for domestic and international students. Application fee: $50. Electronic applications accepted. *Financial support:* In 2011–12, 7 students received support, including 7 fellowships (averaging $3,170 per year), 1,318 teaching assistantships with tuition reimbursements available (averaging $3,789 per year); research assistantships, career-related internships or fieldwork, institutionally sponsored loans, scholarships/grants, and unspecified assistantships also available. Support available to part-time students. Financial award application deadline: 3/1; financial award applicants required to submit FAFSA. *Faculty research:* School reform, professional development, history of education, Native American education, politics of education, feminism and issues of sexual identity, critical race theory, bilingualism, literacy reading, adolescent literature, second language acquisition, critical theory and schooling, indigenous languages. *Unit head:* Dr. Lois M. Meyer, Chair, 505-277-7244, Fax: 505-277-8362, E-mail: lsmeyer@unm.edu. *Application contact:* Debra Schaffer, Administrative Assistant, 505-277-0437, Fax: 505-277-8362, E-mail: schaffer@unm.edu. Web site: http://coe.unm.edu/departments/department-of-language-literacy-and-sociocultural-studies/llss-program.html.

The University of North Carolina at Chapel Hill, Graduate School, School of Education, Program in Secondary Education, Chapel Hill, NC 27599. Offers English (Grades 9-12) (MAT); English as a second language (MAT); French (Grades K-12) (MAT); German (Grades K-12) (MAT); Japanese (Grades K-12) (MAT); Latin (Grades 9-12) (MAT); mathematics (Grades 9-12) (MAT); music (Grades K-12) (MAT); science (Grades 9-12) (MAT); social studies (Grades 9-12) (MAT); Spanish (Grades K-12) (MAT). *Accreditation:* NCATE. *Degree requirements:* For master's, comprehensive exam. *Entrance requirements:* For master's, GRE General Test, minimum GPA of 3.0 during last 2 years of undergraduate course work. Additional exam requirements/recommendations for international students: Required—TOEFL (minimum score 550 paper-based; 79 computer-based). Electronic applications accepted.

The University of North Carolina at Greensboro, Graduate School, School of Education, Department of Curriculum and Instruction, Greensboro, NC 27412-5001. Offers college teaching and adult learning (Certificate); curriculum and instruction (M Ed), including chemistry education, elementary education, English as a second language, French education, instructional technology, mathematics education, middle grades education, reading education, science education, social studies education, Spanish education; curriculum and teaching (PhD), including higher education, teacher education and development; English as a second language (Certificate); higher education (M Ed); supervision (M Ed). *Accreditation:* NCATE. Part-time programs available. *Degree requirements:* For doctorate, thesis/dissertation. *Entrance requirements:* For master's and doctorate, GRE General Test. Additional exam requirements/recommendations for international students: Required—TOEFL. Electronic applications accepted. *Faculty research:* Community college literacy program, middle school mathematics/computer mathematics.

University of Northern Iowa, Graduate College, College of Humanities, Arts and Sciences, Department of Languages and Literatures, Program in English, Cedar Falls, IA 50614. Offers creative writing (MA); English (MA); literature (MA); teaching English in secondary schools (TESS) (MA), including middle/junior high and senior high; teaching English to speakers of other languages (MA). Part-time and evening/weekend programs available. *Students:* 12 full-time (6 women), 4 part-time (all women); includes 2 minority (1 Black or African American, non-Hispanic/Latino; 1 Hispanic/Latino). 16 applicants, 50% accepted, 5 enrolled. In 2011, 5 master's awarded. *Degree requirements:* For master's, one foreign language, comprehensive exam, thesis or alternative, portfolio. *Entrance requirements:* Additional exam requirements/recommendations for international students: Required—TOEFL (minimum score 600 paper-based; 250 computer-based; 100 iBT). *Application deadline:* For fall admission, 8/1 priority date for domestic students. Applications are processed on a rolling basis. Application fee: $50 ($70 for international students). Electronic applications accepted. *Expenses:* Tuition, state resident: full-time $7476. Tuition, nonresident: full-time $16,410. *Required fees:* $942. *Financial support:* Career-related internships or fieldwork, Federal Work-Study, scholarships/grants, and tuition waivers (full and partial) available. Support available to part-time students. Financial award application deadline: 2/1. *Unit head:* Dr. Julie Husband, Graduate Coordinator, 319-273-3849, Fax: 319-273-5807, E-mail: julie.husband@uni.edu. *Application contact:* Laurie S. Russell, Record Analyst, 319-273-2623, Fax: 319-273-2885, E-mail: laurie.russell@uni.edu. Web site: http://www.uni.edu/langlit/.

University of Northern Iowa, Graduate College, College of Humanities, Arts and Sciences, Department of Languages and Literatures, Program in French, Cedar Falls, IA 50614. Offers French (MA); teaching English to speakers of other languages/French (MA). Part-time and evening/weekend programs available. *Students:* 4 full-time (all women), 1 (woman) part-time; includes 1 minority (Asian, non-Hispanic/Latino), 3 international. 4 applicants, 50% accepted, 1 enrolled. In 2011, 2 master's awarded. *Degree requirements:* For master's, one foreign language, comprehensive exam, thesis or alternative. *Entrance requirements:* For master's, minimum GPA of 3.0, valid teaching license, documentation of successful teaching experience. Additional exam requirements/recommendations for international students: Required—TOEFL (minimum score 600 paper-based; 250 computer-based; 100 iBT). *Application deadline:* For fall admission, 8/1 priority date for domestic students. Applications are processed on a rolling basis. Application fee: $50 ($70 for international students). Electronic applications accepted. *Expenses:* Tuition, state resident: full-time $7476. Tuition, nonresident: full-time $16,410. *Required fees:* $942. *Financial support:* Career-related internships or fieldwork, Federal Work-Study, and tuition waivers (full and partial) available. Support available to part-time students. Financial award application deadline: 2/1. *Unit head:* Dr. Gabriela Olivares, Coordinator, 319-273-6102, Fax: 319-273-5807, E-mail: gabriela.olivares@uni.edu. *Application contact:* Laurie S. Russell, Record Analyst, 319-273-2623, Fax: 319-273-2885, E-mail: laurie.russell@uni.edu. Web site: http://www.uni.edu/langlit/.

University of Northern Iowa, Graduate College, College of Humanities, Arts and Sciences, Department of Languages and Literatures, Program in German, Cedar Falls, IA 50614. Offers German (MA); teaching English to speakers of other languages/German (MA). Part-time and evening/weekend programs available. *Students:* 5 full-time (3 women), 1 (woman) part-time, 4 international. 3 applicants, 100% accepted, 3 enrolled. In 2011, 3 master's awarded. *Degree requirements:* For master's, one foreign language, comprehensive exam, thesis or alternative. *Entrance requirements:* For master's, minimum GPA of 3.0, valid teaching license, documentation of successful teaching experience. Additional exam requirements/recommendations for international students: Required—TOEFL (minimum score 600 paper-based; 250 computer-based; 100 iBT). *Application deadline:* For fall admission, 8/1 priority date for domestic students. Applications are processed on a rolling basis. Application fee: $50 ($70 for international students). *Expenses:* Tuition, state resident: full-time $7476. Tuition, nonresident: full-time $16,410. *Required fees:* $942. *Financial support:* Career-related internships or fieldwork, Federal Work-Study, and tuition waivers (full and partial) available. Support available to part-time students. Financial award application deadline: 2/1. *Unit head:* Dr. Gabriela Olivares, Coordinator, 319-273-6102, Fax: 319-273-5807, E-mail: gabriela.olivares@uni.edu. *Application contact:* Laurie S. Russell, Record Analyst, 319-273-2623, Fax: 319-273-2885, E-mail: laurie.russell@uni.edu. Web site: http://www.uni.edu/langlit/.

University of Northern Iowa, Graduate College, College of Humanities, Arts and Sciences, Department of Languages and Literatures, Program in Spanish, Cedar Falls, IA 50614. Offers Spanish (MA); teaching English to speakers of other languages/Spanish (MA). Part-time and evening/weekend programs available. *Students:* 15 full-time (12 women), 10 part-time (7 women); includes 6 minority (all Hispanic/Latino), 2 international. 14 applicants, 64% accepted, 3 enrolled. In 2011, 10 master's awarded. *Degree requirements:* For master's, one foreign language, comprehensive exam, thesis or alternative. *Entrance requirements:* For master's, minimum GPA of 3.0, valid teaching license, documentation of successful teaching experience. Additional exam requirements/recommendations for international students: Required—TOEFL (minimum score 600 paper-based; 250 computer-based; 100 iBT). *Application deadline:* For fall admission, 8/1 priority date for domestic students. Applications are processed on a rolling basis. Application fee: $50 ($70 for international students). Electronic applications accepted. *Expenses:* Tuition, state resident: full-time $7476. Tuition, nonresident: full-time $16,410. *Required fees:* $942. *Financial support:* Career-related internships or fieldwork, Federal Work-Study, and tuition waivers (full and partial) available. Support available to part-time students. Financial award application deadline: 2/1. *Unit head:* Dr. Juan C. Castillo, Coordinator, 319-273-6200, Fax: 319-273-5807, E-mail: juan.castillo@uni.edu. *Application contact:* Laurie S. Russell, Record Analyst, 319-273-2623, Fax: 319-273-2885, E-mail: laurie.russell@uni.edu. Web site: http://www.uni.edu/langlit/.

University of North Florida, College of Education and Human Services, Department of Childhood Education, Jacksonville, FL 32224. Offers literacy K-12 (M Ed); professional education - elementary education (M Ed); TESOL K-12 (M Ed). *Accreditation:* NCATE. Part-time and evening/weekend programs available. *Faculty:* 11 full-time (9 women). *Students:* 16 full-time (15 women), 38 part-time (37 women); includes 9 minority (3 Black or African American, non-Hispanic/Latino; 1 American Indian or Alaska Native, non-Hispanic/Latino; 1 Asian, non-Hispanic/Latino; 4 Hispanic/Latino), 3 international. Average age 29. 24 applicants, 67% accepted, 12 enrolled. In 2011, 17 master's awarded. *Entrance requirements:* For master's, GRE General Test, minimum GPA of 3.0 in last 60 hours, 3 letters of recommendation, interview. Additional exam requirements/recommendations for international students: Required—TOEFL (minimum score 500 paper-based; 173 computer-based). *Application deadline:* For fall admission, 7/1 priority date for domestic students, 5/1 for international students; for spring admission, 11/1 priority date for domestic students, 10/1 for international students. Applications are processed on a rolling basis. Application fee: $30. Electronic applications accepted. *Expenses:* Tuition, state resident: full-time $8793; part-time $366.38 per credit hour. Tuition, nonresident: full-time $23,502; part-time $979.24 per credit hour. *Required fees:* $1384; $57.66 per credit hour. Tuition and fees vary according to course load and program. *Financial support:* In 2011–12, 16 students received support, including 1 research assistantship (averaging $5,700 per year); Federal Work-Study, tuition waivers (partial), and unspecified assistantships also available. Support available to part-time students. Financial award application deadline: 4/1; financial award applicants required to submit FAFSA. *Faculty research:* The social context of and processes in learning, inter-disciplinary instruction, cross-cultural conflict resolution, the Vygotskian perspective on literacy diagnosis and instruction, performance poetry and teaching the language arts through drama. *Total annual research expenditures:* $118,609. *Unit head:* Dr. Ronghua Ouyang, Chair, 904-620-2611, Fax: 904-620-1025, E-mail: ronghua.ouyang@unf.edu. *Application contact:* Lillith Richardson, Assistant Director, The Graduate School, 904-620-1360, Fax: 904-620-1362, E-mail: graduateschool@unf.edu. Web site: http://www.unf.edu/coehs/childhood/.

University of Pennsylvania, Graduate School of Education, Division of Educational Linguistics, Program in Teaching English to Speakers of Other Languages, Philadelphia, PA 19104. Offers MS Ed, PhD. Part-time programs available. Postbaccalaureate distance learning degree programs offered (minimal on-campus study). *Students:* 117 full-time (103 women), 11 part-time (9 women); includes 11 minority (9 Asian, non-Hispanic/Latino; 1 Hispanic/Latino; 1 Two or more races, non-Hispanic/Latino), 109 international. 294 applicants, 56% accepted, 96 enrolled. In 2011, 69 master's awarded. Terminal master's awarded for partial completion of doctoral program. *Degree requirements:* For master's, comprehensive exam, thesis (for some programs). *Entrance requirements:* For master's, GRE General Test or MAT. Additional exam requirements/recommendations for international students: Required—TOEFL. *Application deadline:* For fall admission, 12/15 priority date for domestic students. Applications are processed on a rolling basis. Application fee: $70. Electronic applications accepted. *Expenses:* Contact institution. *Financial support:* Fellowships, research assistantships, institutionally sponsored loans, scholarships/grants, traineeships, health care benefits, and unspecified assistantships available. *Faculty research:* Second language acquisition, social linguistics, English as a second language. *Unit head:* Dr. Andrew Porter, Dean, 215-898-7014. *Application contact:* Penny Creedon, 215-898-3245, E-mail: pennyc@gse.upenn.edu. Web site: http://www.gse.upenn.edu/degrees_programs/tesol.

University of Phoenix–Milwaukee Campus, College of Education, Milwaukee, WI 53045. Offers curriculum and instruction (MA Ed, Ed D); education (Ed S); educational leadership (Ed D); English as a second language (MA Ed); higher education administration (PhD).

University of Phoenix–Omaha Campus, College of Education, Omaha, NE 68154-5240. Offers administration and supervision (MA Ed); curriculum and instruction (MA Ed), including adult education, computer education, curriculum and instruction, English and language arts education, English as a second language, mathematics education; elementary teacher education (MA Ed); secondary teacher education (MA Ed); special education (MA Ed).

University of Phoenix–San Diego Campus, College of Education, San Diego, CA 92123. Offers curriculum and instruction (MA Ed), including computer education, curriculum and instruction, English as a second language; elementary teacher education (MA Ed); secondary teacher education (MA Ed). Evening/weekend programs available. *Degree requirements:* For master's, thesis (for some programs). *Entrance requirements:* For master's, 3 years of work experience, minimum undergraduate GPA of 3.0. Additional exam requirements/recommendations for international students: Required—TOEFL (minimum score 550 paper-based; 213 computer-based; 79 iBT). Electronic applications accepted.

University of Phoenix–Springfield Campus, College of Education, Springfield, MO 65804-7211. Offers administration and supervision (MA Ed); curriculum and instruction (MA Ed), including computer education, curriculum and instruction, English and language arts education, English as a second language, mathematics education; English and language arts education (MA Ed).

University of Phoenix–Washington D.C. Campus, College of Education, Washington, DC 20001. Offers administration and supervision (MA Ed); adult education and training (MA Ed); computer education (MA Ed); curriculum and instruction (MA Ed, Ed D); early childhood education (MA Ed); education (Ed S); educational leadership (Ed D); educational technology (Ed D); elementary teacher education (MA Ed); English and language arts education (MA Ed); English as a second language (MA Ed); higher education administration (PhD); mathematics education (MA Ed); secondary teacher education (MA Ed); special education (MA Ed); teacher leadership (MA Ed).

University of Pittsburgh, Dietrich School of Arts and Sciences, TESOL - Teaching English to Speakers of Other Languages Certificate Program, Pittsburgh, PA 15260. Offers Certificate. Part-time programs available. *Faculty:* 10 full-time (4 women). *Students:* 7 full-time (4 women), 2 part-time (1 woman), 3 international. Average age 28. 7 applicants, 71% accepted, 5 enrolled. *Entrance requirements:* Additional exam requirements/recommendations for international students: Required—TOEFL (minimum score 600 paper-based; 250 computer-based; 100 iBT). *Application deadline:* For spring admission, 3/15 for domestic and international students. Application fee: $50. *Expenses:* Tuition, state resident: full-time $18,774; part-time $760 per credit. Tuition, nonresident: full-time $30,736; part-time $1258 per credit. *Required fees:* $740; $200 per term. Tuition and fees vary according to program. *Faculty research:* Language contact, second language acquisition, applied linguistics, sociolinguistics. *Unit head:* Dr. Yasuhiro Shirai, Chair, 412-624-5933, Fax: 412-624-6130, E-mail: yshirai@pitt.edu. *Application contact:* Dr. Dawn E. McCormick, Lecturer/Associate Director, 412-624-5902, Fax: 412-624-6130, E-mail: mccormic@pitt.edu. Web site: http://www.linguistics.pitt.edu/.

University of Puerto Rico, Río Piedras, College of Education, Program in Teaching English as a Second Language, San Juan, PR 00931-3300. Offers M Ed. Part-time programs available. *Degree requirements:* For master's, thesis. *Entrance requirements:* For master's, PAEG or GRE, minimum GPA of 3.0, letter of recommendation. *Faculty research:* Second language acquisition, bilingual education.

University of St. Thomas, Graduate Studies, School of Education, Department of Teacher Education, St. Paul, MN 55105-1096. Offers curriculum and instruction (MA), including elementary, individualized, K-12, secondary; elementary (MAT); engineering education (Certificate); English as a second language (MA); math education (Certificate); multicultural education (Certificate); reading (MA, Certificate), including elementary (MA), K-12 (MA). *Accreditation:* NCATE. Part-time and evening/weekend programs available. *Faculty:* 7 full-time (4 women), 26 part-time/adjunct (20 women). *Students:* 19 full-time (14 women), 161 part-time (113 women); includes 28 minority (3 Black or African American, non-Hispanic/Latino; 7 American Indian or Alaska Native, non-Hispanic/Latino; 6 Asian, non-Hispanic/Latino; 9 Hispanic/Latino; 3 Two or more races, non-Hispanic/Latino), 5 international. Average age 35. 150 applicants, 79% accepted, 88 enrolled. In 2011, 83 master's awarded. *Entrance requirements:* For master's, minimum GPA of 3.0 or MAT. Additional exam requirements/recommendations for international students: Required—TOEFL (minimum score 550 paper-based; 210 computer-based; 80 iBT). *Application deadline:* For fall admission, 6/1 for domestic students; for spring admission, 11/1 for domestic students. Applications are processed on a rolling basis. Application fee: $50. *Financial support:* Fellowships, research assistantships, institutionally sponsored loans, and scholarships/grants available. Support available to part-time students. Financial award applicants required to submit FAFSA. *Unit head:* Dr. Jan L. H. Frank, Department Chair, 651-962-4446, Fax: 651-962-4169, E-mail: jlhfrank@stthomas.edu. *Application contact:* Rosemary R. Barreto, Department Assistant, 651-962-4420, Fax: 651-962-4169, E-mail: barr7879@stthomas.edu. Web site: http://www.stthomas.edu/education.

University of St. Thomas, School of Education, Houston, TX 77006-4696. Offers all level teaching (M Ed); bilingual/dual language (M Ed); Catholic school teaching (M Ed); Catholic/private school leadership (M Ed); counselor education (M Ed); curriculum and instruction (M Ed); educational leadership (M Ed); elementary teaching (M Ed); English as a second language (M Ed); exceptionality/ educational diagnostician (M Ed); exceptionality/special education (M Ed); generalist (M Ed); reading (M Ed); secondary teaching (M Ed). Part-time and evening/weekend programs available. Postbaccalaureate distance learning degree programs offered (no on-campus study). *Faculty:* 30 full-time (17 women), 54 part-time/adjunct (37 women). *Students:* 66 full-time (43 women), 1,178 part-time (1,044 women); includes 777 minority (313 Black or African American, non-Hispanic/Latino; 5 American Indian or Alaska Native, non-Hispanic/Latino; 29 Asian, non-Hispanic/Latino; 395 Hispanic/Latino; 2 Native Hawaiian or other Pacific Islander, non-Hispanic/Latino; 33 Two or more races, non-Hispanic/Latino), 26 international. Average age 36. 551 applicants, 94% accepted, 416 enrolled. In 2011, 72 master's awarded. *Degree requirements:* For master's, thesis, field experience. *Entrance requirements:* For master's, GRE or MAT if GPA is below 3.0, bachelor's degree; minimum GPA of 2.75 in bachelor's degree or last 60 credit hours; official transcripts from all institutions; goal statement of 250-300 words; 1 reference. Additional exam requirements/recommendations for international students: Required—TOEFL. *Application deadline:* Applications are processed on a rolling basis. Application fee: $35. Electronic applications accepted. *Expenses:* Contact institution. *Financial support:* In 2011–12, 9 students received support. Federal Work-Study, scholarships/grants, and state work-study, institutional employment available. Support available to part-time students. Financial award application deadline: 4/15; financial award applicants required to submit FAFSA. *Faculty research:* Leadership, diversity, personality traits, second language acquisition. *Unit head:* Dr. Nora Hutto, Dean, 713-525-3540, Fax: 713-525-3871, E-mail: education@stthom.edu. *Application contact:* Paula C. Hollis, Administrative Assistant, 713-525-3540, Fax: 713-525-3871, E-mail: education@stthom.edu. Web site: http://www.stthom.edu/Schools_Centers_of_Excellence/Schools_of_Study/School_of_Education/Index.aqf.

University of San Diego, School of Leadership and Education Sciences, Department of Learning and Teaching, San Diego, CA 92110-2492. Offers curriculum and instruction (M Ed); special education (M Ed); special education with deaf and hard of hearing (M Ed); teaching (MAT); TESOL, literacy and culture (M Ed). Part-time and evening/weekend programs available. *Faculty:* 11 full-time (8 women), 41 part-time/adjunct (32 women). *Students:* 86 full-time (69 women), 73 part-time (62 women); includes 54 minority (7 Black or African American, non-Hispanic/Latino; 1 American Indian or Alaska Native, non-Hispanic/Latino; 7 Asian, non-Hispanic/Latino; 27 Hispanic/Latino; 1 Native Hawaiian or other Pacific Islander, non-Hispanic/Latino; 11 Two or more races, non-Hispanic/Latino), 12 international. Average age 28. 177 applicants, 60% accepted, 61 enrolled. In 2011, 57 master's awarded. *Degree requirements:* For master's, thesis (for some programs). *Entrance requirements:* For master's, minimum GPA of 3.0. Additional exam requirements/recommendations for international students: Required—TOEFL (minimum score 580 paper-based; 237 computer-based; 83 iBT), TWE. *Application deadline:* For fall admission, 3/1 priority date for domestic students, 3/1 for international students; for spring admission, 10/15 priority date for domestic students, 10/15 for international students. Application fee: $45. Electronic applications accepted. *Expenses: Tuition:* Full-time $22,482; part-time $1249 per unit. *Required fees:* $224. Full-time tuition and fees vary according to course load and degree level. *Financial support:* In 2011–12, 77 students received support. Career-related internships or fieldwork, Federal Work-Study, institutionally sponsored loans, and stipends available. Support available to part-time students. Financial award application deadline: 4/1; financial award applicants required to submit FAFSA. *Faculty research:* Action research methodology, cultural studies, instructional theories and practices, second language acquisition, school reform. *Unit head:* Dr. Heather Lattimer, Director, 619-260-7616, Fax: 619-260-8159, E-mail: hlattimer@sandiego.edu. *Application contact:* Monica Mahon, Associate Director of Graduate Admissions, 619-260-4524, Fax: 619-260-4158, E-mail: grads@sandiego.edu. Web site: http://www.sandiego.edu/soles/programs/learning_and_teaching/.

University of San Francisco, School of Education, Department of International and Multicultural Education, San Francisco, CA 94117-1080. Offers international and multicultural education (MA, Ed D); multicultural literature for children and young adults (MA); teaching English as a second language (MA). *Faculty:* 3 full-time (all women), 6 part-time/adjunct (3 women). *Students:* 128 full-time (105 women), 52 part-time (43 women); includes 84 minority (15 Black or African American, non-Hispanic/Latino; 21 Asian, non-Hispanic/Latino; 39 Hispanic/Latino; 9 Two or more races, non-Hispanic/Latino), 26 international. Average age 36. 203 applicants, 58% accepted, 50 enrolled. In 2011, 35 master's, 5 doctorates awarded. *Degree requirements:* For doctorate, thesis/dissertation. Application fee: $55 ($65 for international students). *Expenses: Tuition:* Full-time $20,070; part-time $1115 per unit. Tuition and fees vary according to course load, campus/location and program. *Financial support:* In 2011–12, 11 students received support. Fellowships, research assistantships, and teaching assistantships available. Financial award application deadline: 3/2; financial award applicants required to submit FAFSA. *Unit head:* Dr. Katz Susan, Chair, 415-422-6878. *Application contact:* Beth Teague, Associate Director of Graduate Outreach, 415-422-5467, E-mail: schoolofeducation@usfca.edu.

The University of Scranton, College of Graduate and Continuing Education, Department of Education, Program in English as a Second Language, Scranton, PA 18510. Offers MS. Part-time and evening/weekend programs available. *Students:* 2 full-time (both women), 1 international. Average age 25. In 2011, 2 master's awarded. *Degree requirements:* For master's, comprehensive exam, capstone experience. *Entrance requirements:* For master's, minimum GPA of 2.75. Additional exam requirements/recommendations for international students: Required—TOEFL (minimum score 500 paper-based; 173 computer-based), IELTS (minimum score 5.5). *Application deadline:* Applications are processed on a rolling basis. Application fee: $0. *Financial support:* Application deadline: 3/1. *Unit head:* Dr. Art Chambers, Director, 570-941-4668, Fax: 570-941-5515, E-mail: chambersa2@scranton.edu. *Application contact:* Joseph M. Roback, Director of Admissions, 570-941-4385, Fax: 570-941-5928, E-mail: robackj2@scranton.edu.

University of South Africa, College of Human Sciences, Pretoria, South Africa. Offers adult education (M Ed); African languages (MA, PhD); African politics (MA, PhD); Afrikaans (MA, PhD); ancient history (MA, PhD); ancient Near Eastern studies (MA, PhD); anthropology (MA, PhD); applied linguistics (MA); Arabic (MA, PhD); archaeology (MA); art history (MA); Biblical archaeology (MA); Biblical studies (M Th, D Th, PhD); Christian spirituality (M Th, D Th); church history (M Th, D Th); classical studies (MA, PhD); clinical psychology (MA); communication (MA, PhD); comparative education (M Ed, Ed D); consulting psychology (D Admin, D Com, PhD); curriculum studies (M Ed, Ed D); development studies (M Admin, MA, D Admin, PhD); didactics (M Ed, Ed D); education (M Tech); education management (M Ed, Ed D); educational psychology (M Ed); English (MA); environmental education (M Ed); French (MA, PhD); German (MA, PhD); Greek (MA); guidance and counseling (M Ed); health studies (MA, PhD), including health sciences education (MA), health services management (MA), medical and surgical nursing science (critical care general) (MA), midwifery and neonatal nursing science (MA), trauma and emergency care (MA); history (MA, PhD); history of education (Ed D); inclusive education (M Ed, Ed D); information and communications technology policy and regulation (MA); information science (MA, MIS, PhD); international politics (MA, PhD); Islamic studies (MA, PhD); Italian (MA, PhD); Judaica (MA, PhD); linguistics (MA, PhD); mathematical education (M Ed); mathematics education (MA); missiology (M Th, D Th); modern Hebrew (MA, PhD); musicology (MA, MMus, D Mus, PhD); natural science education (M Ed); New Testament (M Th, D Th); Old Testament (D Th); pastoral therapy (M Th, D Th); philosophy (MA); philosophy of education (M Ed, Ed D); politics (MA, PhD); Portuguese (MA, PhD); practical theology (M Th, D Th); psychology (MA, MS, PhD); psychology of education (M Ed, Ed D); public health (MA); religious studies (MA, D Th, PhD); Romance languages (MA); Russian (MA, PhD); Semitic languages (MA, PhD); social behavior studies in HIV/AIDS (MA); social science (mental health) (MA); social science in development studies (MA); social science in psychology (MA); social science in social work (MA); social science in sociology (MA); social work (MSW, DSW, PhD); socio-education (M Ed, Ed D); sociolinguistics (MA); sociology (MA, PhD); Spanish (MA, PhD); systematic theology (M Th, D Th); TESOL (teaching English to speakers of other languages) (MA); theological ethics (M Th, D Th); theory of literature (MA, PhD); urban ministries (D Th); urban ministry (M Th).

University of South Carolina, The Graduate School, College of Arts and Sciences, Linguistics Program, Columbia, SC 29208. Offers linguistics (MA, PhD); teaching English to speakers of other languages (Certificate). Part-time programs available. Terminal master's awarded for partial completion of doctoral program. *Degree requirements:* For master's, one foreign language, comprehensive exam, thesis optional; for doctorate, 3 foreign languages, comprehensive exam, thesis/dissertation. *Entrance requirements:* For master's and Certificate, GRE General Test, minimum GPA of 3.0; for doctorate, GRE General Test, minimum GPA of 3.5. Additional exam requirements/recommendations for international students: Required—TOEFL. Electronic applications accepted. *Faculty research:* Second language acquisition, sociolinguistics, syntax, historical linguistics and phonology.

University of Southern California, Graduate School, Rossier School of Education, Master's Programs in Education, Los Angeles, CA 90089-4038. Offers educational counseling (ME); marriage, family and child counseling (MMFT); postsecondary administration and student affairs [PASA] (ME); school counseling (ME); teaching (online) (MAT); teaching and teaching credential (MAT); teaching English to speakers of other languages (MAT). Part-time and evening/weekend programs available. Postbaccalaureate distance learning degree programs offered (no on-campus study). *Degree requirements:* For master's, thesis optional. *Entrance requirements:* For master's, GRE (for all programs except MAT). Additional exam requirements/recommendations for international students: Required—TOEFL (minimum score 250 computer-based; 100 iBT). Electronic applications accepted. *Faculty research:* College access and equity, preparing teachers for culturally diverse populations, sociocultural basis of learning as mediated by instruction with focus on reading and literacy in English learners, social and political aspects of teaching and learning English, school counselor development and training.

University of Southern Maine, School of Education and Human Development, Program in Literacy Education, Portland, ME 04104-9300. Offers applied literacy (MS Ed); early language and literacy (Certificate); English as a second language (MS Ed, CAS); literacy education (MS Ed, CAS, Certificate). *Accreditation:* Teacher Education Accreditation Council. Part-time and evening/weekend programs available. *Degree requirements:* For master's, comprehensive exam, thesis or alternative; for other advanced degree, thesis or alternative. *Entrance requirements:* For master's, teacher certification; for other advanced degree, master's degree. Additional exam requirements/recommendations for international students: Required—TOEFL (minimum score 550 paper-based; 213 computer-based; 79 iBT). Electronic applications accepted.

University of South Florida, Graduate School, College of Arts and Sciences, World Languages Department, Tampa, FL 33620-9951. Offers French (MA); linguistics: ESL (MA); Spanish (MA). Part-time and evening/weekend programs available. *Faculty:* 19 full-time (13 women), 13 part-time/adjunct (9 women). *Students:* 38 full-time (27 women), 18 part-time (12 women); includes 28 minority (5 Black or African American, non-Hispanic/Latino; 1 Asian, non-Hispanic/Latino; 22 Hispanic/Latino), 6 international. Average age 34. 60 applicants, 50% accepted, 17 enrolled. In 2011, 20 master's awarded. *Degree requirements:* For master's, one foreign language, comprehensive exam, thesis optional. *Entrance requirements:* For master's, GRE General Test, minimum GPA of 3.0, statement of purpose; oral interview (for MA in Spanish and French); writing sample (for MA in French). Additional exam requirements/recommendations for international students: Required—TOEFL (minimum score 600 paper-based; 250 computer-based). *Application deadline:* For fall admission, 2/15 for domestic students, 1/2 for international students; for spring admission, 10/15 for domestic students, 6/1 for international students. Application fee: $30. Electronic applications accepted. *Financial support:* In 2011–12, 43 students received support, including 43 teaching assistantships with full and partial tuition reimbursements available (averaging $10,152 per year); tuition waivers (partial) and unspecified assistantships also available. Financial award application deadline: 6/30. *Faculty research:* Second language writing, academic literacy. *Unit head:* Dr. Stephan Schindler, Chair, 813-974-2548, Fax: 813-974-1718, E-mail: skschindler@.usf.edu. *Application contact:* Dr. Camilla Vasquez, Program Director, 813-974-7378, Fax: 813-974-5911, E-mail: cvasquez@usf.edu. Web site: http://www.cas.usf.edu/classics/degree.html.

University of South Florida, Graduate School, College of Education, Department of Secondary Education, Tampa, FL 33620-9951. Offers English education (M Ed, MA, MAT, PhD); foreign language education/ESOL (M Ed, MA, MAT); instructional technology (M Ed, PhD, Ed S); mathematics education (M Ed, MA, MAT, PhD, Ed S); science education (M Ed, MA, MAT, PhD); second language acquisition/instructional technology (PhD); secondary education (M Ed, PhD); secondary education/TESOL (M Ed); social science education (M Ed, MA, MAT); teaching and learning in the content area (PhD). *Accreditation:* NCATE. Part-time and evening/weekend programs available. *Faculty:* 28 full-time (17 women), 3 part-time/adjunct (1 woman). *Students:* 174 full-time (116 women), 268 part-time (184 women); includes 103 minority (26 Black or African American, non-Hispanic/Latino; 10 Asian, non-Hispanic/Latino; 58 Hispanic/Latino; 9

Two or more races, non-Hispanic/Latino), 32 international. Average age 37. 229 applicants, 73% accepted, 141 enrolled. In 2011, 115 master's, 16 doctorates, 5 other advanced degrees awarded. *Degree requirements:* For master's, variable foreign language requirement, comprehensive exam, project (for some programs); for doctorate, variable foreign language requirement, comprehensive exam, thesis/dissertation, philosophies of inquiry; multiple research methods. *Entrance requirements:* For master's, GRE General Test or General Knowledge Test, minimum GPA of 3.0; for doctorate, GRE General Test, minimum GPA of 3.5; for Ed S, GRE General Test. Additional exam requirements/recommendations for international students: Required—TOEFL (minimum score 550 paper-based; 213 computer-based; 79 iBT). *Application deadline:* For fall admission, 2/15 for domestic students, 1/2 for international students; for spring admission, 10/15 for domestic students, 6/1 for international students. Application fee: $30. Electronic applications accepted. *Financial support:* In 2011–12, 7 students received support, including 1 research assistantship with full tuition reimbursement available (averaging $10,000 per year), 55 teaching assistantships with full and partial tuition reimbursements available (averaging $7,900 per year); scholarships/grants and unspecified assistantships also available. Financial award application deadline: 4/15; financial award applicants required to submit FAFSA. *Faculty research:* English language learners/multicultural, social science education, mathematics education, science education, instructional technology. *Total annual research expenditures:* $336,023. *Unit head:* Dr. Stephen Thornton, Chairperson, 813-974-3533, Fax: 813-974-3837, E-mail: thornton@usf.edu. *Application contact:* Dr. Diane Briscoe, Coordinator of Graduate Studies, 813-974-1804, Fax: 813-974-3391, E-mail: briscoe@usf.edu. Web site: http://www.coedu.usf.edu/main/departments/seced/seced.html.

University of South Florida Sarasota-Manatee, College of Education, Sarasota, FL 34243. Offers educational leadership (M Ed), including curriculum leadership, K-12, non-public/charter school leadership; elementary education K-6 (MA); K-6 with ESOL endorsement (MAT); reading education K-12 (MA); MAT/MA. Part-time and evening/weekend programs available. *Faculty:* 12 full-time (8 women), 4 part-time/adjunct (3 women). *Students:* 19 full-time (17 women), 64 part-time (50 women); includes 7 minority (1 Black or African American, non-Hispanic/Latino; 1 Asian, non-Hispanic/Latino; 4 Hispanic/Latino; 1 Two or more races, non-Hispanic/Latino). Average age 33. 50 applicants, 62% accepted, 21 enrolled. In 2011, 41 master's awarded. *Degree requirements:* For master's, comprehensive exam (for some programs). *Entrance requirements:* For master's, GRE. Additional exam requirements/recommendations for international students: Required—TOEFL (minimum score 213 computer-based; 79 iBT) or IELTS. *Application deadline:* For fall admission, 2/15 for domestic students, 1/2 for international students; for spring admission, 10/15 for domestic students, 6/1 for international students. Applications are processed on a rolling basis. Application fee: $30. Electronic applications accepted. *Expenses:* Tuition, state resident: full-time $9301; part-time $387.55 per credit hour. Tuition, nonresident: full-time $19,412; part-time $808.85 per credit hour. *Required fees:* $15; $5 per semester. One-time fee: $30. *Financial support:* Federal Work-Study, scholarships/grants, health care benefits, and unspecified assistantships available. Support available to part-time students. Financial award application deadline: 3/1; financial award applicants required to submit FAFSA. *Faculty research:* Child development, student achievement, intergenerational studies. *Unit head:* Dr. Terry A. Osborn, Dean, 941-359-4531, E-mail: terryosborn@sar.usf.edu. *Application contact:* Jo Lynn Raudebaugh, Graduate Admissions Advisor, 941-359-4587, E-mail: jraudeba@sar.usf.edu. Web site: http://www.sarasota.usf.edu/Academics/COE/.

The University of Tennessee, Graduate School, College of Education, Health and Human Sciences, Program in Education, Knoxville, TN 37996. Offers art education (MS); counseling education (PhD); cultural studies in education (PhD); curriculum (MS, Ed S); curriculum, educational research and evaluation (Ed D, PhD); early childhood education (PhD); early childhood special education (MS); education of deaf and hard of hearing (MS); educational administration and policy studies (Ed D, PhD); educational administration and supervision (Ed S); educational psychology (Ed D, PhD); elementary education (MS, Ed S); elementary teaching (MS); English education (MS, Ed S); exercise science (PhD); foreign language/ESL education (MS, Ed S); instructional technology (MS, Ed D, PhD, Ed S); literacy, language and ESL education (PhD); literacy, language education, and ESL education (Ed D); mathematics education (MS, Ed S); modified and comprehensive special education (MS); reading education (MS, Ed S); school counseling (Ed S); school psychology (PhD, Ed S); science education (MS, Ed S); secondary teaching (MS); social foundations (MS); social science education (MS, Ed S); socio-cultural foundations of sports and education (PhD); special education (Ed S); teacher education (Ed D, PhD). *Accreditation:* NCATE. Part-time and evening/weekend programs available. *Degree requirements:* For master's and Ed S, thesis optional; for doctorate, variable foreign language requirement, thesis/dissertation. *Entrance requirements:* For master's, minimum GPA of 2.7; for doctorate and Ed S, GRE General Test, minimum GPA of 2.7. Additional exam requirements/recommendations for international students: Required—TOEFL. Electronic applications accepted. *Expenses:* Tuition, state resident: full-time $8332; part-time $464 per credit hour. Tuition, nonresident: full-time $25,174; part-time $1400 per credit hour. *Required fees:* $1162; $56 per credit hour. Tuition and fees vary according to program.

The University of Texas at Arlington, Graduate School, College of Liberal Arts, Department of Linguistics and TESOL, Program in Teaching English to Speakers of Other Languages, Arlington, TX 76019. Offers MA. *Accreditation:* NCATE. Part-time and evening/weekend programs available. *Students:* 4 full-time (all women), 6 part-time (4 women); includes 2 minority (both Hispanic/Latino), 3 international. In 2011, 3 degrees awarded. *Degree requirements:* For master's, comprehensive exam (for some programs), thesis optional. *Entrance requirements:* For master's, GRE General Test, minimum undergraduate GPA of 3.0, 6 credits of undergraduate foundation courses, the equivalent of 2 years of university level foreign language study. Additional exam requirements/recommendations for international students: Required—TOEFL (minimum score 550 paper-based; 213 computer-based). *Application deadline:* For fall admission, 6/1 priority date for domestic students. Applications are processed on a rolling basis. Application fee: $35 ($50 for international students). Electronic applications accepted. *Unit head:* Dr. Laurel Stvan, Chair, 817-272-3133, Fax: 817-272-2731, E-mail: stvan@uta.edu. *Application contact:* Dr. Laurel Stvan, Graduate Advisor, 817-272-3133, Fax: 817-272-2731, E-mail: stvan@uta.edu.

The University of Texas at Brownsville, Graduate Studies, School of Education, Brownsville, TX 78520-4991. Offers bilingual education (M Ed); counseling and guidance (M Ed); curriculum and instruction (M Ed); early childhood education (M Ed); educational administration (M Ed); educational technology (M Ed); English as a second language (M Ed); reading specialist (M Ed); special education/educational diagnostician (M Ed). Part-time and evening/weekend programs available. Postbaccalaureate distance learning degree programs offered (minimal on-campus study). *Degree requirements:* For master's, thesis optional. *Entrance requirements:* For master's, GRE General Test. Additional exam requirements/recommendations for international students: Required—TOEFL.

The University of Texas at El Paso, Graduate School, College of Liberal Arts, Department of Languages and Linguistics, El Paso, TX 79968-0001. Offers linguistics (MA); Spanish (MA); teaching English to speakers of other languages (Certificate). Part-time and evening/weekend programs available. *Students:* 26 (17 women); includes 18 minority (all Hispanic/Latino), 6 international. Average age 34. 10 applicants, 90% accepted, 6 enrolled. In 2011, 3 master's awarded. *Degree requirements:* For master's, thesis optional. *Entrance requirements:* For master's, GRE General Test, departmental exam, minimum GPA of 3.0, letters of recommendation. Additional exam requirements/recommendations for international students: Required—TOEFL; Recommended—IELTS. *Application deadline:* For fall admission, 8/1 for domestic students, 3/1 for international students; for spring admission, 11/1 for domestic students, 9/1 for international students. Applications are processed on a rolling basis. Application fee: $45 ($80 for international students). Electronic applications accepted. *Financial support:* In 2011–12, research assistantships with partial tuition reimbursements (averaging $18,625 per year), teaching assistantships with partial tuition reimbursements (averaging $14,900 per year) were awarded; fellowships with partial tuition reimbursements, institutionally sponsored loans, scholarships/grants, health care benefits, tuition waivers (partial), and unspecified assistantships also available. Support available to part-time students. Financial award application deadline: 3/15; financial award applicants required to submit FAFSA. *Unit head:* Dr. Kirsten F. Nigro, Chair, 915-747-5767, Fax: 915-747-5292, E-mail: kfnigro@utep.edu. *Application contact:* Dr. Benjamin Flores, Interim Dean of the Graduate School, 915-747-5491, Fax: 915-747-5788, E-mail: bflores@utep.edu.

The University of Texas at San Antonio, College of Education and Human Development, Department of Bicultural and Bilingual Studies, San Antonio, TX 78249-0617. Offers bicultural studies (MA); bicultural/bilingual education (MA); culture, literacy, and language (PhD); teaching English as a second language (MA). Part-time and evening/weekend programs available. *Faculty:* 13 full-time (8 women). *Students:* 61 full-time (51 women), 113 part-time (91 women); includes 107 minority (8 Asian, non-Hispanic/Latino; 96 Hispanic/Latino; 1 Native Hawaiian or other Pacific Islander, non-Hispanic/Latino; 2 Two or more races, non-Hispanic/Latino), 29 international. Average age 35. 93 applicants, 78% accepted, 46 enrolled. In 2011, 38 master's, 4 doctorates awarded. *Degree requirements:* For master's, one foreign language, comprehensive exam, thesis optional; for doctorate, one foreign language, comprehensive exam, thesis/dissertation. *Entrance requirements:* For master's, GRE General Test if GPA is less than 3.0 for last 60 hours, bachelor's degree with 18 credit hours in field of study or in another appropriate field of study; for doctorate, GRE General Test, resume or curriculum vitae, 3 letters of recommendation, statement of purpose. Additional exam requirements/recommendations for international students: Required—TOEFL (minimum score 500 paper-based; 61 iBT), IELTS (minimum score 5). *Application deadline:* For fall admission, 7/1 for domestic students, 4/1 for international students; for spring admission, 11/1 for domestic students, 9/1 for international students. Applications are processed on a rolling basis. Application fee: $45 ($85 for international students). Electronic applications accepted. *Expenses:* Tuition, state resident: full-time $3148; part-time $2176 per semester. Tuition, nonresident: full-time $8782; part-time $5932 per semester. *Required fees:* $719 per semester. *Financial support:* In 2011–12, 28 students received support, including 14 fellowships with full tuition reimbursements available (averaging $25,385 per year), 2 research assistantships with full tuition reimbursements available (averaging $12,468 per year), 12 teaching assistantships with full tuition reimbursements available (averaging $11,000 per year). *Faculty research:* Bilingualism and biliteracy development, second language teaching and learning, language minority education, Mexican American studies, transnationalism and immigration. *Unit head:* Dr. Robert Milk, Chair, 210-458-4426, Fax: 210-458-5962, E-mail: robert.milk@utsa.edu. *Application contact:* Armando Trujillo, Assistant Dean of the Graduate School, 210-458-5576, Fax: 210-458-5576, E-mail: armando.trujillo@utsa.edu. Web site: http://coehd.utsa.edu/bicultural-bilingual_studies.

The University of Texas of the Permian Basin, Office of Graduate Studies, School of Education, Program in Bilingual/English as a Second Language Education, Odessa, TX 79762-0001. Offers MA. *Degree requirements:* For master's, comprehensive exam (for some programs), thesis (for some programs). *Entrance requirements:* For master's, GRE General Test. Additional exam requirements/recommendations for international students: Required—TOEFL (minimum score 550 paper-based; 213 computer-based).

The University of Texas–Pan American, College of Arts and Humanities, Department of English, Program in English as a Second Language, Edinburg, TX 78539. Offers MA. Part-time and evening/weekend programs available. *Degree requirements:* For master's, comprehensive exam, thesis optional. *Entrance requirements:* For master's, GRE General Test, minimum GPA of 3.0. *Application deadline:* For fall admission, 2/1 priority date for domestic students, 2/1 for international students; for spring admission, 9/1 priority date for domestic students, 9/1 for international students. Applications are processed on a rolling basis. Application fee: $0. Tuition and fees vary according to course load, program and student level. *Financial support:* Research assistantships, teaching assistantships, institutionally sponsored loans, scholarships/grants, and unspecified assistantships available. Financial award application deadline: 4/15. *Faculty research:* Oral versus literary culture discourse analysis, language shift among Hispanics. *Unit head:* Dr. Steven Schneider, Director, 956-380-8775, E-mail: schneiders@panam.edu. *Application contact:* Dr. Pamela L. Anderson Mejias, Professor/Chair, 956-665-3426, E-mail: pla66f5@utpa.edu. Web site: http://portal.utpa.edu/utpa_main/daa_home/coah_home/english_home/english_grad/grad_maesl.

University of the Southwest, Graduate Programs, Hobbs, NM 88240-9129. Offers business administration (MBA); curriculum and instruction (MSE); curriculum and instruction: bilingual (MSE); curriculum and instruction: TESOL (MSE); early childhood education (MSE); educational administration (MSE); mental health counseling (MSE); school counseling (MSE); special education (MSE); sports management (MBA). Part-time and evening/weekend programs available. Postbaccalaureate distance learning degree programs offered (no on-campus study). *Faculty:* 13 full-time (6 women), 28 part-time/adjunct (17 women). *Students:* 76 full-time (63 women), 229 part-time (194 women); includes 104 minority (50 Black or African American, non-Hispanic/Latino; 2 American Indian or Alaska Native, non-Hispanic/Latino; 8 Asian, non-Hispanic/Latino; 44 Hispanic/Latino). Average age 38. 173 applicants, 71% accepted, 101 enrolled. In 2011, 75 master's awarded. *Degree requirements:* For master's, comprehensive exam, thesis (for some programs). *Entrance requirements:* Additional exam requirements/recommendations for international students: Recommended—TOEFL. *Application deadline:* Applications are processed on a rolling basis. Application fee: $50. Electronic applications accepted. *Expenses: Tuition:* Full-time $12,288; part-time $512 per credit hour. One-time fee: $50. Tuition and fees vary according to course load. *Financial support:* In 2011–12, 47 students received support. Federal Work-Study available. Financial award application deadline: 4/1; financial award applicants required to submit FAFSA. *Unit head:* Dr. Mary Harris, Dean of Education, 575-492-2162, Fax: 575-392-6006, E-mail: mharris@usw.edu. *Application contact:* Melissa Mitchell, Senior Online Program Advisor, 575-492-2142, Fax: 575-392-6006, E-mail: mmitchell@usw.edu. Web site: http://www.usw.edu/admissions/graduate_admission/graduate_admissions.

The University of Toledo, College of Graduate Studies, College of Language, Literature and Social Sciences, Department of English, Toledo, OH 43606-3390. Offers English as a second language (MA); literature (MA); teaching of writing (Certificate).

Part-time programs available. *Faculty:* 17. *Students:* 36 full-time (25 women), 11 part-time (7 women); includes 4 minority (2 Black or African American, non-Hispanic/Latino; 1 Asian, non-Hispanic/Latino; 1 Hispanic/Latino), 7 international. Average age 27. 45 applicants, 73% accepted, 26 enrolled. In 2011, 16 master's, 6 other advanced degrees awarded. *Degree requirements:* For master's, thesis. *Entrance requirements:* For master's, GRE if GPA is less than 3.0, minimum cumulative point-hour ratio of 2.7 for all previous academic work, three letters of recommendation, transcripts from all prior institutions attended, critical essay; for Certificate, statement of purpose, transcripts from all prior institutions attended, 2 letters of recommendation. Additional exam requirements/recommendations for international students: Required—TOEFL (minimum score 550 paper-based; 213 computer-based; 80 iBT), IELTS (minimum score 6.5). *Application deadline:* For fall admission, 1/15 priority date for domestic students, 1/15 for international students. Applications are processed on a rolling basis. Application fee: $45 ($75 for international students). Electronic applications accepted. *Financial support:* In 2011–12, 4 research assistantships with full and partial tuition reimbursements (averaging $7,812 per year), 31 teaching assistantships with full and partial tuition reimbursements (averaging $7,858 per year) were awarded; Federal Work-Study, institutionally sponsored loans, scholarships/grants, tuition waivers (full), and unspecified assistantships also available. Support available to part-time students. *Faculty research:* Literary criticism, linguistics, creative writing, folklore and cultural studies. *Unit head:* Dr. Sara Lundquist, Chair, 419-530-2506, Fax: 419-530-2590, E-mail: sara.lundquist@utoledo.edu. *Application contact:* Graduate School Office, 419-530-4723, Fax: 419-530-4724, E-mail: grdsch@utoledo.edu. Web site: http://www.utoledo.edu/llss/.

The University of Toledo, College of Graduate Studies, Judith Herb College of Education, Health Science and Human Service, Department of Curriculum and Instruction, Toledo, OH 43606-3390. Offers art education (ME); career and technical education (ME); curriculum and instruction (ME, PhD, Ed S); education and anthropology (MAE); education and biology (MES); education and chemistry (MES); education and classics (MAE); education and economics (MAE); education and English (MAE); education and French (MAE); education and geography (MAE); education and geology (MES); education and German (MAE); education and history (MAE); education and mathematics (MAE, MES); education and physics (MES); education and political science (MAE); education and sociology (MAE); education and Spanish (MAE); educational media (PhD); educational technology (ME); English as a second language (MAE); gifted and talented (PhD); middle childhood education licensure (ME); music education (MME); secondary education (PhD); secondary education licensure (ME). *Accreditation:* NCATE. Part-time and evening/weekend programs available. *Faculty:* 24. *Students:* 60 full-time (31 women), 211 part-time (161 women); includes 23 minority (21 Black or African American, non-Hispanic/Latino; 2 Hispanic/Latino), 20 international. Average age 35. 115 applicants, 73% accepted, 74 enrolled. In 2011, 105 master's, 3 doctorates, 4 other advanced degrees awarded. *Degree requirements:* For master's, comprehensive exam, thesis or alternative; for doctorate, comprehensive exam, thesis/dissertation; for Ed S, thesis optional. *Entrance requirements:* For master's, doctorate, and Ed S, minimum cumulative GPA of 2.7 for all previous academic work, letters of recommendation. Additional exam requirements/recommendations for international students: Required—TOEFL (minimum score 550 paper-based; 213 computer-based; 80 iBT), IELTS (minimum score 6.5). *Application deadline:* For fall admission, 1/15 priority date for domestic students, 1/15 for international students. Applications are processed on a rolling basis. Application fee: $45 ($75 for international students). Electronic applications accepted. *Financial support:* In 2011–12, 9 research assistantships with full and partial tuition reimbursements (averaging $7,184 per year), 12 teaching assistantships with full and partial tuition reimbursements (averaging $8,425 per year) were awarded; career-related internships or fieldwork, Federal Work-Study, institutionally sponsored loans, scholarships/grants, tuition waivers (full and partial), unspecified assistantships, and administrative assistantships also available. Support available to part-time students. *Unit head:* Dr. Leigh Chiarelott, Chair, 419-530-5371, E-mail: eigh.chiarelott@utoledo.edu. *Application contact:* Graduate School Office, 419-530-4723, Fax: 419-530-4724, E-mail: grdsch@utnet.utoledo.edu. Web site: http://www.utoledo.edu/eduhshs/.

University of Washington, Graduate School, College of Arts and Sciences, Department of English, Seattle, WA 98195. Offers creative writing (MFA); English as a second language (MAT); English literature and language (MA, MAT, PhD). Part-time programs available. Terminal master's awarded for partial completion of doctoral program. *Degree requirements:* For master's, one foreign language, thesis (for some programs); for doctorate, one foreign language, thesis/dissertation. *Entrance requirements:* For master's, GRE General Test, GRE Subject Test (MA and MAT in English), minimum GPA of 3.0; for doctorate, GRE General Test, GRE Subject Test. Additional exam requirements/recommendations for international students: Required—TOEFL. Electronic applications accepted. *Faculty research:* English and American literature, critical theory, creative writing, language theory.

University of West Georgia, College of Education, Department of Collaborative Support and Intervention, Carrollton, GA 30118. Offers English to speakers of other languages (Ed S); guidance and counseling (M Ed, Ed S); professional counseling (M Ed, Ed S); professional counseling and supervision (Ed D, Ed S); reading education (M Ed, Ed S); reading endorsement (Ed S); special education-general (M Ed, Ed S); speech-language pathology (M Ed). Part-time and evening/weekend programs available. *Faculty:* 22 full-time (13 women), 6 part-time/adjunct (4 women). *Students:* 174 full-time (140 women), 253 part-time (228 women); includes 155 minority (127 Black or African American, non-Hispanic/Latino; 3 Asian, non-Hispanic/Latino; 14 Hispanic/Latino; 11 Two or more races, non-Hispanic/Latino), 2 international. Average age 33. 282 applicants, 49% accepted, 50 enrolled. In 2011, 98 master's, 27 other advanced degrees awarded. *Degree requirements:* For master's, comprehensive exam; for Ed S, research project. *Entrance requirements:* For master's, minimum GPA of 2.7; for Ed S, master's degree, minimum graduate GPA of 2.7. Additional exam requirements/recommendations for international students: Required—TOEFL (minimum score 523 paper-based; 193 computer-based; 69 iBT); Recommended—IELTS (minimum score 6). *Application deadline:* For fall admission, 6/3 for domestic students, 6/1 for international students; for spring admission, 10/7 for domestic students, 10/15 for international students. Applications are processed on a rolling basis. Application fee: $30. Electronic applications accepted. *Expenses:* Tuition, state resident: full-time $4336; part-time $181 per credit hour. Tuition, nonresident: full-time $17,362; part-time $724 per credit hour. Tuition and fees vary according to course load, degree level, campus/location and program. *Financial support:* In 2011–12, 5 research assistantships with full tuition reimbursements (averaging $3,000 per year) were awarded; career-related internships or fieldwork and scholarships/grants also available. Support available to part-time students. Financial award applicants required to submit FAFSA. *Unit head:* Dr. Michael Garrett, Chair, 678-839-6567, Fax: 678-839-6162, E-mail: mgarrett@westga.edu. *Application contact:* Deanna Richards, Coordinator, Graduate Studies, 678-839-5946, E-mail: drichard@westga.edu. Web site: http://www.westga.edu/coecsi.

University of Wisconsin–Milwaukee, Graduate School, College of Letters and Sciences, Department of Linguistics, Milwaukee, WI 53201-0413. Offers linguistics (MA, PhD); TESOL (Graduate Certificate). *Faculty:* 7 full-time (2 women). *Students:* 22 full-time (14 women), 5 part-time (all women); includes 5 minority (2 Asian, non-Hispanic/Latino; 1 Hispanic/Latino; 2 Two or more races, non-Hispanic/Latino), 12 international. Average age 33. 23 applicants, 48% accepted, 5 enrolled. One-time fee: $506.10 full-time. Tuition and fees vary according to course load and reciprocity agreements. *Total annual research expenditures:* $131,509. *Unit head:* Hamid Ouali, Department Chair, 414-229-1113, E-mail: ouali@uwm.edu. *Application contact:* General Information Contact, 414-229-4982, Fax: 414-229-6967, E-mail: gradschool@uwm.edu. Web site: http://www4.uwm.edu/letsci/linguistics/.

University of Wisconsin–River Falls, Outreach and Graduate Studies, College of Arts and Science, Program in Teaching English to Speakers of Other Languages, River Falls, WI 54022. Offers MA.

Valley City State University, Online Master of Education Program, Valley City, ND 58072. Offers library and information technologies (M Ed); teaching and technology (M Ed); teaching English language learners (ELL) (M Ed); technology education (M Ed). *Accreditation:* NCATE. Part-time and evening/weekend programs available. Postbaccalaureate distance learning degree programs offered (no on-campus study). *Faculty:* 25 full-time (18 women), 2 part-time/adjunct (both women). *Students:* 4 full-time (3 women), 147 part-time (99 women); includes 6 minority (1 Black or African American, non-Hispanic/Latino; 1 American Indian or Alaska Native, non-Hispanic/Latino; 2 Asian, non-Hispanic/Latino; 2 Hispanic/Latino). Average age 34. 40 applicants, 83% accepted, 30 enrolled. In 2011, 30 master's awarded. *Degree requirements:* For master's, action research report, comprehensive portfolio. *Entrance requirements:* For master's, GRE, MAT, PRAXIS II or National Teaching Board for Professional Standards (if GPA less than 3.0). Additional exam requirements/recommendations for international students: Required—TOEFL (minimum score 525 paper-based; 70 iBT). *Application deadline:* For fall admission, 5/23 priority date for domestic students, 5/23 for international students; for spring admission, 4/20 priority date for domestic students, 4/23 for international students. Applications are processed on a rolling basis. Application fee: $35. Electronic applications accepted. *Expenses:* Tuition, state resident: full-time $4533.30; part-time $251.85 per credit hour. Tuition, nonresident: full-time $4533; part-time $251.85 per credit hour. *Required fees:* $1239.48; $68.86 per credit hour. *Financial support:* In 2011–12, 27 students received support. Tuition waivers (full and partial) available. Financial award application deadline: 5/15; financial award applicants required to submit FAFSA. *Faculty research:* Academically at-risk students in higher education, communication pedagogy and technology, gender communication, computer-mediated communication, creativity in music. *Total annual research expenditures:* $26,000. *Unit head:* Dr. Gary Thompson, Dean, 701-845-7197, E-mail: gary.thompson@vcsu.edu. *Application contact:* Misty Lindgren, 701-845-7303, Fax: 701-845-7305, E-mail: misty.lindgren@vcsu.edu. Web site: http://www.vcsu.edu/graduate.

Valparaiso University, Graduate School, Program in English Studies and Communication, Valparaiso, IN 46383. Offers English studies and communication (MA); teaching of English to speakers of other languages (MA); teaching of English to speakers of other languages (TESOL) (Certificate). Part-time and evening/weekend programs available. *Students:* 12 full-time (10 women), 5 part-time (4 women); includes 2 minority (1 Black or African American, non-Hispanic/Latino; 1 Hispanic/Latino), 9 international. Average age 30. In 2011, 12 master's, 11 other advanced degrees awarded. *Entrance requirements:* For master's, minimum GPA of 3.0. Additional exam requirements/recommendations for international students: Required—TOEFL (minimum score 550 paper-based; 213 computer-based; 80 iBT). *Application deadline:* Applications are processed on a rolling basis. Application fee: $30 ($50 for international students). Electronic applications accepted. *Expenses: Tuition:* Part-time $560 per credit hour. Tuition and fees vary according to course load and program. *Financial support:* Available to part-time students. Applicants required to submit FAFSA. *Unit head:* Dr. David L. Rowland, Dean, Graduate School and Continuing Education/Associate Provost, 219-464-5313, Fax: 219-464-5381, E-mail: david.rowland@valpo.edu. *Application contact:* Dustin Jesch, Coordinator, U.S. Student Engagement, 219-464-5313, Fax: 219-464-5381, E-mail: dustin.jesch@valpo.edu. Web site: http://valpo.edu/grad/esc/.

Virginia International University, School of English Language Studies, Fairfax, VA 22030. Offers teaching English to speakers of other languages (MA, Graduate Certificate). Part-time programs available. *Entrance requirements:* For master's and Graduate Certificate, bachelor's degree. Additional exam requirements/recommendations for international students: Required—TOEFL (minimum score 550 paper-based; 213 computer-based; 80 iBT), IELTS (minimum score 6). Electronic applications accepted.

Walden University, Graduate Programs, Richard W. Riley College of Education and Leadership, Minneapolis, MN 55401. Offers administrator leadership for teaching and learning (Ed D, Ed S); adult education (Ed D, Ed S); adult learning (MS, Postbaccalaureate Certificate), including developmental education (MS), online teaching (MS), teaching adults English as a second language (MS), training and performance management (MS); college teaching and learning (Ed D, Ed S, Postbaccalaureate Certificate); curriculum, instruction and assessment (Ed D, Postbaccalaureate Certificate); curriculum, instruction, and professional development (Ed S); developmental education (Postbaccalaureate Certificate); early childhood administration, management, and leadership (Postbaccalaureate Certificate); early childhood education (birth-grade 3) (MAT); early childhood public policy and advocacy (Postbaccalaureate Certificate); early childhood studies (MS), including administration, management and leadership, early childhood public policy and advocacy, teaching adults in the early childhood field, teaching and diversity; education (MS, PhD), including adolescent literacy and technology (grades 6-12) (MS), adult education leadership (PhD), assessment, evaluation, and accountability (PhD), community college leadership (PhD), curriculum, instruction, and assessment, early childhood education (PhD), educational technology (PhD), elementary reading and literacy (MS), elementary reading and mathematics (MS), general program, global and comparative education (PhD), higher education (PhD), integrating technology in the classroom (MS), K-12 educational leadership (PhD), leadership, policy and change (PhD), learning, instruction and innovation (PhD), literacy and learning in the content areas (MS), mathematics (grades 6-8) (MS), mathematics (grades K-5) (MS), middle level education (grades 5-8) (MS), professional development (MS), science (grades K-8) (MS), self-designed (PhD), special education (PhD), special education (non-licensure) (MS), teacher leadership (grades K-12) (MS), teaching English language learners (grades K-12) (MS); educational leadership and administration (principal preparation) (Ed S); educational technology (Ed S); elementary reading and literacy (Postbaccalaureate Certificate); engaging culturally diverse learners (Postbaccalaureate Certificate); enrollment management and institutional marketing (Postbaccalaureate Certificate); higher education (MS), including college teaching and learning, enrollment management and institutional planning, global higher education, leadership for student success, online and distance learning; higher education leadership (Ed D); instructional design (Postbaccalaureate Certificate); instructional design and technology (MS), including general program (MS, PhD), online learning, training and performance improvement; integrating technology in the classroom (Postbaccalaureate Certificate); online teaching for adult learners (Postbaccalaureate Certificate); professional development (Postbaccalaureate Certificate); reading and literacy leadership (Ed D); science K-8 (Postbaccalaureate Certificate); special education (Ed D, Ed S); special education:

emotional/behavioral disorders (K-12) (MAT); special education: learning disabilities (K-12) (MAT); teacher leadership (Ed D, Ed S, Postbaccalaureate Certificate); training and performance management (Postbaccalaureate Certificate). Part-time and evening/weekend programs available. Postbaccalaureate distance learning degree programs offered (minimal on-campus study). *Faculty:* 71 full-time (48 women), 853 part-time/adjunct (585 women). *Students:* 11,326 full-time (9,212 women), 2,148 part-time (1,795 women); includes 5,346 minority (4,403 Black or African American, non-Hispanic/Latino; 76 American Indian or Alaska Native, non-Hispanic/Latino; 140 Asian, non-Hispanic/Latino; 561 Hispanic/Latino; 21 Native Hawaiian or other Pacific Islander, non-Hispanic/Latino; 145 Two or more races, non-Hispanic/Latino), 322 international. Average age 39. In 2011, 3,477 master's, 318 doctorates, 471 other advanced degrees awarded. *Degree requirements:* For doctorate, thesis/dissertation (for some programs), residency; for other advanced degree, residency (for some programs). *Entrance requirements:* For master's, bachelor's degree or equivalent in related field; minimum GPA of 2.5; official transcripts; goal statement; access to computer and Internet; for doctorate, master's degree or equivalent in related field; minimum GPA of 3.0; official transcripts; three years' related professional/academic experience (preferred); access to computer and Internet; for other advanced degree, master's degree or equivalent in related field; minimum GPA of 3.0; 3 years related professional/academic experience (preferred); access to computer and Internet (Ed S). Additional exam requirements/recommendations for international students: Required—TOEFL (minimum score 550 paper-based; 213 computer-based), IELTS (minimum score 6.5), or Michigan English Language Assessment Battery (minimum score 82). *Application deadline:* Applications are processed on a rolling basis. Application fee: $50. Electronic applications accepted. *Financial support:* Federal Work-Study, scholarships/grants, unspecified assistantships, and family tuition reduction, active duty/veteran tuition reduction, group tuition reduction, interest-free payment plans, employee tuition reduction available. Support available to part-time students. Financial award applicants required to submit FAFSA. *Unit head:* Dr. Kate Steffens, Dean, 800-925-3368. *Application contact:* Jennifer Hall, Vice President of Enrollment Management, 866-4-WALDEN, E-mail: info@waldenu.edu. Web site: http://www.waldenu.edu/Colleges-and-Schools/College-of-Education-and-Leadership.htm.

Wayne State College, School of Education and Counseling, Department of Educational Foundations and Leadership, Program in Curriculum and Instruction, Wayne, NE 68787. Offers alternative education (MSE); business and information technology education (MSE); communication arts education (MSE); early childhood education (MSE); elementary education (MSE); English as a second language (MSE); English education (MSE); family and consumer sciences education (MSE); industrial technology and vocational education (MSE); learning communities (MSE); mathematics education (MSE); music education (MSE); science education (MSE); social science education (MSE). *Accreditation:* NCATE. Part-time and evening/weekend programs available. *Degree requirements:* For master's, comprehensive exam, thesis optional. *Entrance requirements:* For master's, GRE General Test. Additional exam requirements/recommendations for international students: Required—TOEFL (minimum score 550 paper-based; 213 computer-based).

Wayne State University, College of Education, Division of Teacher Education, Detroit, MI 48202. Offers art education (M Ed), including art therapy; bilingual/bicultural education (M Ed); career and technical education (M Ed); curriculum and instruction (Ed D, PhD, Ed S), including art education (PhD), bilingual education (Ed D, Ed S), bilingual-bicultural education (PhD), career and technical education (MAT, Ed D, PhD, Ed S), early childhood education (MAT, Ed D, PhD, Ed S), elementary education, English as a second language (MAT, Ed D, Ed S), English education (MAT, Ed D, PhD, Ed S), foreign language education (MAT, PhD), K-12 curriculum, mathematics education (MAT, Ed D, PhD, Ed S), science education (MAT, Ed D, PhD, Ed S), secondary education, social studies education (MAT, Ed S), social studies education: secondary (Ed D, PhD); elementary education (MAT), including special education; elementary education (M Ed, MAT), including children's literature (MAT), early childhood education (MAT, Ed D, PhD, Ed S), general elementary education (MAT); elementary or secondary education (MAT), including bilingual/bicultural education, English as a second language (MAT, Ed D, Ed S), mathematics education (MAT, Ed D, PhD, Ed S), science education (MAT, Ed D, PhD, Ed S), social studies education (MAT, Ed S); English education-secondary (M Ed); foreign language education (M Ed); mathematics education (M Ed); reading (M Ed, Ed S); reading, languages and literature (Ed D); science education (M Ed); secondary education (MAT), including art education (K-12), career and technical education (MAT, Ed D, PhD, Ed S), English education (MAT, Ed D, PhD, Ed S), foreign language education (MAT, PhD), kinesiology; social studies education secondary (M Ed); special education (M Ed, Ed D, PhD, Ed S). *Students:* 216 full-time (154 women), 626 part-time (478 women); includes 289 minority (227 Black or African American, non-Hispanic/Latino; 4 American Indian or Alaska Native, non-Hispanic/Latino; 27 Asian, non-Hispanic/Latino; 21 Hispanic/Latino; 1 Native Hawaiian or other Pacific Islander, non-Hispanic/Latino; 9 Two or more races, non-Hispanic/Latino), 14 international. Average age 37. 347 applicants, 37% accepted, 93 enrolled. In 2011, 226 master's, 12 doctorates, 46 other advanced degrees awarded. *Degree requirements:* For master's, thesis (for some programs), thesis, essay or project (for some M Ed programs), professional field experience (for MAT programs); for doctorate, thesis/dissertation. *Entrance requirements:* For master's, Michigan Basic Skills Test (MA in teaching); for doctorate, minimum undergraduate GPA of 3.0, graduate 3.5; interview, curriculum vitae; references. Additional exam requirements/recommendations for international students: Required—TOEFL (minimum score 550 paper-based; 213 computer-based), TWE (minimum score 5.5). *Application deadline:* For fall admission, 6/1 priority date for domestic students, 5/1 for international students; for winter admission, 10/1 priority date for domestic students, 9/1 for international students; for spring admission, 2/1 priority date for domestic students, 1/1 for international students. Applications are processed on a rolling basis. Application fee: $50. Electronic applications accepted. *Expenses:* Tuition, state resident: part-time $512.85 per credit. Tuition, nonresident: part-time $1132.65 per credit. *Required fees:* $26.60 per credit. $199.65 per semester. Tuition and fees vary according to course load and program. *Financial support:* In 2011–12, 42 students received support. Fellowships, research assistantships with tuition reimbursements available, teaching assistantships, scholarships/grants, and unspecified assistantships available. *Faculty research:* Reading and writing literacy and literature. *Total annual research expenditures:* $264,016. *Unit head:* Dr. Craig Roney, Assistant Dean, 313-577-0902, E-mail: rroney@wayne.edu. Web site: http://coe.wayne.edu/ted/index.php.

Webster University, School of Education, Department of Communication Arts, Reading and Early Childhood, St. Louis, MO 63119-3194. Offers communications (MAT); early childhood education (MAT). *Entrance requirements:* For master's, minimum GPA of 2.5. Additional exam requirements/recommendations for international students: Required—TOEFL. *Expenses: Tuition:* Full-time $10,890; part-time $605 per credit hour. Tuition and fees vary according to campus/location and program.

West Chester University of Pennsylvania, College of Arts and Sciences, Department of English, West Chester, PA 19383. Offers English (MA, Teaching Certificate); English (non-thesis) (MA); TESL (MA, Certificate). Part-time and evening/weekend programs available. *Faculty:* 14 part-time/adjunct (7 women). *Students:* 48 full-time (32 women), 84 part-time (67 women); includes 11 minority (7 Black or African American, non-Hispanic/Latino; 1 Asian, non-Hispanic/Latino; 2 Hispanic/Latino; 1 Two or more races, non-Hispanic/Latino), 1 international. Average age 30. 55 applicants, 62% accepted, 27 enrolled. In 2011, 14 degrees awarded. *Degree requirements:* For master's, thesis optional, capstone experience (for English). *Entrance requirements:* For master's, minimum GPA of 2.8 and writing sample; two letters of recommendation, completed application with goals statement, and official transcripts (for English); three letters of recommendation and interview (for TESL); for other advanced degree, goals statement (for Certificate). Additional exam requirements/recommendations for international students: Required—TOEFL (minimum score 550 paper-based; 213 computer-based; 80 iBT). *Application deadline:* For fall admission, 4/15 priority date for domestic students, 3/15 for international students; for spring admission, 10/15 priority date for domestic students, 9/1 for international students. Applications are processed on a rolling basis. Application fee: $45. Electronic applications accepted. *Expenses:* Tuition, state resident: full-time $7488; part-time $416 per credit. Tuition, nonresident: full-time $11,232; part-time $624 per credit. *Required fees:* $1784.64; $67.59 per credit. Tuition and fees vary according to program. *Financial support:* Unspecified assistantships available. Support available to part-time students. Financial award application deadline: 2/15; financial award applicants required to submit FAFSA. *Faculty research:* Critical theory, cultural studies, literature, composition, rhetoric, second language acquisition and teaching, second language writing, phonology, language teacher development. *Unit head:* Dr. Vicki Tischio, Chair, 610-436-2822, Fax: 610-738-0516, E-mail: vtischio@wcupa.edu. *Application contact:* Dr. Carolyn Sorisio, Graduate Coordinator, 610-436-2745, Fax: 610-738-0516, E-mail: csorisio@wcupa.edu. Web site: http://www.wcupa.edu/_academics/sch_cas.eng/.

Western Carolina University, Graduate School, College of Arts and Sciences, Department of English, Cullowhee, NC 28723. Offers English (MA); teaching English as a second language or foreign language (MA). Part-time and evening/weekend programs available. *Students:* 26 full-time (16 women), 29 part-time (20 women); includes 2 minority (1 Black or African American, non-Hispanic/Latino; 1 Asian, non-Hispanic/Latino). Average age 34. 36 applicants, 89% accepted, 20 enrolled. In 2011, 17 master's awarded. *Degree requirements:* For master's, one foreign language, comprehensive exam, thesis (for some programs). *Entrance requirements:* For master's, GRE General Test, appropriate undergraduate degree, writing sample, 3 letters of recommendation. Additional exam requirements/recommendations for international students: Required—TOEFL (minimum score 550 paper-based; 270 computer-based; 79 iBT). *Application deadline:* For fall admission, 5/1 priority date for domestic students; for spring admission, 9/1 priority date for domestic students. Applications are processed on a rolling basis. Application fee: $50. *Expenses:* Tuition, state resident: full-time $3348. Tuition, nonresident: full-time $12,933. *Required fees:* $3155. *Financial support:* Fellowships with full and partial tuition reimbursements, research assistantships with full and partial tuition reimbursements, teaching assistantships with full and partial tuition reimbursements, career-related internships or fieldwork, institutionally sponsored loans, scholarships/grants, and unspecified assistantships available. Financial award application deadline: 3/31; financial award applicants required to submit FAFSA. *Faculty research:* TESOL, language assessment, applied linguistics, poetry, folk and fairy tales, post World War II British literature, Appalachian and southern literature. *Unit head:* Dr. Brian Gastle, Department Head, 828-227-7264, Fax: 828-227-7266, E-mail: bgastle@email.wcu.edu. *Application contact:* Admission Specialist for Department of English, 828-227-7398, Fax: 828-227-7480, E-mail: gradsch@email.wcu.edu. Web site: http://www.wcu.edu/as/english/.

Western Connecticut State University, Division of Graduate Studies, School of Arts and Sciences, Department of English, Danbury, CT 06810-6885. Offers English (MA); literature (MA); TESOL (MA); writing (MA). Part-time programs available. *Faculty:* 5 full-time (2 women). *Students:* 4 full-time (3 women), 23 part-time (15 women); includes 4 minority (2 Asian, non-Hispanic/Latino; 2 Hispanic/Latino). Average age 39. In 2011, 8 degrees awarded. *Degree requirements:* For master's, thesis (for writing option), completion of program in 6 years. *Entrance requirements:* For master's, minimum GPA of 2.5, writing sample. Additional exam requirements/recommendations for international students: Recommended—TOEFL (minimum score 550 paper-based; 213 computer-based; 79 iBT), IELTS (minimum score 6). *Application deadline:* For fall admission, 8/5 priority date for domestic students; for spring admission, 1/5 priority date for domestic students. Applications are processed on a rolling basis. Application fee: $50. Tuition and fees vary according to course level, course load, degree level and program. *Financial support:* Application deadline: 5/1; applicants required to submit FAFSA. *Faculty research:* Developing inquiry in teachers and students, encouraging talent development, analyzing program development and assessment techniques, developing student learning outcomes, encouraging teachers as researchers, assessing the impact of computer technologies. *Unit head:* Dr. Shouhua Qi, Co-Coordinator, 203-837-9048, Fax: 203-837-8525, E-mail: qis@wcsu.edu. *Application contact:* Chris Shankle, Associate Director of Graduate Studies, 203-837-9005, Fax: 203-837-8326, E-mail: shanklec@wcsu.edu. Web site: http://www.wcsu.edu/english/.

Western Illinois University, School of Graduate Studies, College of Education and Human Services, Department of Educational and Interdisciplinary Studies, Program in Educational and Interdisciplinary Studies, Macomb, IL 61455-1390. Offers educational and interdisciplinary studies (MS Ed); teaching English to speakers of other languages (Certificate). *Accreditation:* NCATE. Part-time programs available. *Students:* 13 full-time (10 women), 47 part-time (32 women); includes 9 minority (4 Black or African American, non-Hispanic/Latino; 1 Asian, non-Hispanic/Latino; 4 Hispanic/Latino). Average age 37. 12 applicants, 83% accepted. In 2011, 46 master's, 4 Certificates awarded. *Degree requirements:* For master's, thesis or alternative. *Entrance requirements:* For master's, minimum GPA of 2.75, interview. Additional exam requirements/recommendations for international students: Required—TOEFL (minimum score 550 paper-based; 213 computer-based; 80 iBT). *Application deadline:* Applications are processed on a rolling basis. Application fee: $30. Electronic applications accepted. *Expenses:* Tuition, state resident: part-time $281.16 per credit hour. Tuition, nonresident: part-time $562.32 per credit hour. Part-time tuition and fees vary according to campus/location and reciprocity agreements. *Financial support:* In 2011–12, 5 students received support, including 5 research assistantships with full tuition reimbursements available (averaging $7,360 per year). Financial award applicants required to submit FAFSA. *Unit head:* Dr. Tom Cody, Graduate Committee Chairperson, 309-298-1183. *Application contact:* Dr. Nancy Parsons, Interim Associate Provost and Director of Graduate Studies, 309-298-1806, Fax: 309-298-2345, E-mail: grad-office@wiu.edu. Web site: http://wiu.edu/eis.

Western Kentucky University, Graduate Studies, Potter College of Arts and Letters, Department of English, Bowling Green, KY 42101. Offers education (MA); English (MA Ed); literature (MA), including American literature, British literature, literary theory, women writers, world literature; teaching English as a second language (MA); writing (MA). Part-time and evening/weekend programs available. *Degree requirements:* For master's, comprehensive exam, thesis optional, final exam. *Entrance requirements:* For master's, GRE General Test, minimum GPA of 2.75. Additional exam requirements/recommendations for international students: Required—TOEFL (minimum score 555 paper-based; 213 computer-based; 79 iBT). *Faculty research:* Improving writing, linking teacher knowledge and performance, Victorian women writers, Kentucky women writers, Kentucky poets.

Western New Mexico University, Graduate Division, School of Education, Silver City, NM 88062-0680. Offers bilingual education (MAT); counseling (MA); educational leadership (MA); elementary education (MAT); reading (MAT); school psychology (MA); secondary education (MAT); special education (MAT); TESOL (teaching English to speakers of other languages) (MAT). *Accreditation:* NCATE. *Degree requirements:* For master's, comprehensive exam. *Entrance requirements:* For master's, GRE General Test, GRE Subject Test, minimum GPA of 3.2 in last 64 hours of undergraduate study. Additional exam requirements/recommendations for international students: Required—TOEFL (minimum score 550 paper-based; 213 computer-based). Electronic applications accepted.

West Virginia University, Eberly College of Arts and Sciences, Department of Foreign Languages, Morgantown, WV 26506. Offers French (MA); linguistics (MA); Spanish (MA); teaching English to speakers of other languages (MA). Part-time programs available. *Degree requirements:* For master's, one foreign language, comprehensive exam (for some programs), thesis optional. *Entrance requirements:* For master's, minimum GPA of 3.0. Electronic applications accepted. *Faculty research:* French, German, and Spanish literature; foreign language pedagogy; English as a second language; cultural studies; linguistics.

Wheaton College, Graduate School, Department of Intercultural Studies, Wheaton, IL 60187-5593. Offers evangelism and leadership (MA); intercultural studies (MA); intercultural studies/teaching English as a second language (MA); missions (MA); teaching English as a second language (Certificate). Part-time programs available. *Students:* 42 full-time (26 women), 42 part-time (20 women); includes 9 minority (3 Black or African American, non-Hispanic/Latino; 6 Asian, non-Hispanic/Latino), 12 international. Average age 32. 55 applicants, 87% accepted, 28 enrolled. In 2011, 46 master's awarded. *Degree requirements:* For master's, thesis or alternative. *Entrance requirements:* For master's, GRE General Test, MAT. Additional exam requirements/recommendations for international students: Required—TOEFL (minimum score 550 paper-based; 80 iBT), IELTS (minimum score 6.5), TOEFL (minimum score 600 paper-based; 90 iBT) or IELTS (minimum score 7.5) for MA in TESOL. *Application deadline:* For fall admission, 5/1 for domestic students, 1/1 for international students; for spring admission, 11/1 for domestic students. Applications are processed on a rolling basis. Application fee: $30. Electronic applications accepted. *Expenses: Tuition:* Full-time $16,440; part-time $685 per credit hour. Tuition and fees vary according to degree level and program. *Financial support:* Career-related internships or fieldwork, scholarships/grants, and unspecified assistantships available. Financial award application deadline: 3/1; financial award applicants required to submit FAFSA. *Unit head:* Dr. Scott Morea, Chair, 630-752-5949. *Application contact:* Julie A. Huebner, Director of Graduate Admissions, 630-752-5195, Fax: 630-752-5935, E-mail: gradadm@wheaton.edu. Web site: http://www.wheaton.edu/academics/departments/intr.

Wilkes University, College of Graduate and Professional Studies, School of Education, Wilkes-Barre, PA 18766-0002. Offers art and science of teaching (MS Ed); classroom technology (MS Ed); early childhood literacy (MS Ed); educational computing (MS Ed); educational development and strategies (MS Ed); educational leadership (MS Ed); educational technology (Ed D); higher education administration (Ed D); instructional media (MS Ed); instructional technology (MS Ed); K-12 administration (Ed D); online teaching (MS Ed); reading (MS Ed); school business leadership (MS Ed); secondary education (MS Ed), including biology, chemistry, English, history, mathematics; special education (MS Ed); teaching English as a second language (MS Ed); twenty-first century teaching and learning (MS Ed). Part-time and evening/weekend programs available. Postbaccalaureate distance learning degree programs offered (minimal on-campus study). *Students:* 92 full-time (63 women), 2,005 part-time (1,459 women); includes 89 minority (23 Black or African American, non-Hispanic/Latino; 1 American Indian or Alaska Native, non-Hispanic/Latino; 14 Asian, non-Hispanic/Latino; 33 Hispanic/Latino; 1 Native Hawaiian or other Pacific Islander, non-Hispanic/Latino; 17 Two or more races, non-Hispanic/Latino), 6 international. Average age 33. In 2011, 1,150 master's, 3 doctorates awarded. *Entrance requirements:* Additional exam requirements/recommendations for international students: Required—TOEFL (minimum score 550 paper-based; 213 computer-based; 79 iBT). *Application deadline:* Applications are processed on a rolling basis. Application fee: $45. Electronic applications accepted. *Expenses:* Contact institution. *Financial support:* Federal Work-Study and unspecified assistantships available. Financial award application deadline: 3/1; financial award applicants required to submit FAFSA. *Unit head:* Dr. Michael Speziale, Dean, 570-408-4679, Fax: 570-408-4905, E-mail: michael.speziale@wilkes.edu. *Application contact:* Erin Sutzko, Director of Extended Learning, 570-408-4253, Fax: 570-408-7846, E-mail: erin.sutzko@wilkes.edu. Web site: http://www.wilkes.edu/pages/383.asp.

Wilmington University, College of Education, New Castle, DE 19720-6491. Offers applied technology in education (M Ed); career and technical education (M Ed); educational leadership (Ed D); elementary and secondary school counseling (M Ed); elementary studies (M Ed); ESOL literacy (M Ed); higher education leadership (Ed D); instruction: gifted and talented (M Ed); instruction: teacher of reading (M Ed); instruction: teaching and learning (M Ed); organizational leadership (Ed D); school leadership (M Ed); secondary education (MAT); special education (M Ed). *Accreditation:* NCATE. Part-time and evening/weekend programs available. *Faculty:* 7 full-time (4 women). *Students:* 638 full-time (425 women), 2,014 part-time (1,635 women). Average age 33. *Entrance requirements:* For master's, 2 letters of recommendation, interview. Additional exam requirements/recommendations for international students: Required—TOEFL (minimum score 500 paper-based; 173 computer-based). *Application deadline:* For fall admission, 4/30 for domestic students. Applications are processed on a rolling basis. Application fee: $35. Electronic applications accepted. *Expenses: Tuition:* Part-time $534 per credit hour. *Required fees:* $25 per term. *Financial support:* Applicants required to submit FAFSA. *Unit head:* Dr. John C. Gray, Dean, 302-295-1139. *Application contact:* Chris Ferguson, Director of Admissions, 302-356-4636 Ext. 256, Fax: 302-328-5164, E-mail: inquire@wilmcoll.edu. Web site: http://www.wilmu.edu/education/.

Wright State University, School of Graduate Studies, College of Liberal Arts, Department of English Language and Literatures, Dayton, OH 45435. Offers composition and rhetoric (MA); English (MA); literature (MA); teaching English to speakers of other languages (MA). *Degree requirements:* For master's, thesis optional, portfolio. *Entrance requirements:* For master's, 20 hours in upper-level English. Additional exam requirements/recommendations for international students: Required—TOEFL. *Faculty research:* American literature, world literature in English, applied linguistics, writing theory and pedagogy.

Multilingual and Multicultural Education

Alliant International University–Irvine, Shirley M. Hufstedler School of Education, Teacher Education Programs, Irvine, CA 92612. Offers auditory oral education (Certificate); CLAD (Certificate); preliminary multiple subject (Credential); preliminary multiple subject with BCLAD (Credential); preliminary single subject (Credential); professional clear multiple subject (Credential); professional clear single subject (Credential); teaching (MA, Credential); technology and learning (MA). Part-time and evening/weekend programs available. *Students:* 4. In 2011, 6 master's awarded. *Entrance requirements:* For degree, California Basic Educational Skills Test, minimum GPA of 2.5. Additional exam requirements/recommendations for international students: Required—TOEFL (minimum score 550 paper-based; 213 computer-based), TWE. *Application deadline:* For fall admission, 7/1 priority date for domestic students, 7/1 for international students; for spring admission, 12/1 priority date for domestic students, 12/1 for international students. Applications are processed on a rolling basis. Application fee: $55. Electronic applications accepted. *Financial support:* Career-related internships or fieldwork, Federal Work-Study, institutionally sponsored loans, and scholarships/grants available. Financial award applicants required to submit FAFSA. *Unit head:* Dr. Trudy Day, Assistant Dean, 866-825-5426, Fax: 949-833-3507, E-mail: admissions@alliant.edu. *Application contact:* Alliant International University Central Contact Center, 866-U-ALLIANT, Fax: 858-635-4555, E-mail: admissions@alliant.edu. Web site: http://www.alliant.edu/gsoe.

Alliant International University–San Francisco, Shirley M. Hufstedler School of Education, Teacher Education Programs, San Francisco, CA 94133-1221. Offers auditory oral education (Certificate); CLAD (Certificate); education specialist: mild/moderate disabilities (Credential); preliminary multiple subject (Credential); preliminary single subject (Credential); professional clear multiple subject (Credential); professional clear single subject (Credential); special education (MA); teaching (MA). Part-time and evening/weekend programs available. *Faculty:* 6 full-time (4 women), 10 part-time/adjunct (8 women). *Students:* 46 full-time (30 women), 79 part-time (54 women); includes 35 minority (9 Black or African American, non-Hispanic/Latino; 15 Asian, non-Hispanic/Latino; 11 Hispanic/Latino). Average age 38. In 2011, 20 master's awarded. *Degree requirements:* For master's, thesis. *Entrance requirements:* For degree, California Basic Educational Skills Test, minimum GPA of 2.5. Additional exam requirements/recommendations for international students: Required—TOEFL (minimum score 550 paper-based; 213 computer-based), TWE (minimum score 5). *Application deadline:* For fall admission, 7/1 priority date for domestic students, 7/1 for international students; for spring admission, 12/1 priority date for domestic students, 12/1 for international students. Applications are processed on a rolling basis. Application fee: $55. Electronic applications accepted. *Financial support:* Career-related internships or fieldwork, Federal Work-Study, institutionally sponsored loans, and scholarships/grants available. Financial award application deadline: 2/15; financial award applicants required to submit FAFSA. *Faculty research:* Curriculum development, first year teachers, cross-cultural issues in teaching, biliteracy. *Unit head:* Dr. Trudy Day, Program Director, 415-955-2102, Fax: 415-955-2179, E-mail: admissions@alliant.edu. *Application contact:* Alliant International University Central Contact Center, 866-U-ALLIANT, Fax: 858-635-4555, E-mail: admissions@alliant.edu. Web site: http://www.alliant.edu/.

American College of Education, Graduate Programs, Chicago, IL 60606. Offers curriculum and instruction (M Ed), including bilingual, ESL; educational leadership (M Ed); educational technology (M Ed).

Azusa Pacific University, School of Education, Department of Foundations and Transdisciplinary Studies, Program in Curriculum and Instruction in Multicultural Contexts, Azusa, CA 91702-7000. Offers MA Ed. *Accreditation:* NCATE. Part-time and evening/weekend programs available. *Degree requirements:* For master's, core exams, oral presentation. *Entrance requirements:* For master's, 12 units of course work in education, minimum GPA of 3.0. *Faculty research:* Diversity in teacher education programs, teacher morale, student perception of school, case study instruction.

Bank Street College of Education, Graduate School, Program in Bilingual Education, New York, NY 10025. Offers bilingual childhood special education (Ed M); bilingual early childhood general education (MS Ed); bilingual early childhood special and general education (MS Ed); bilingual early childhood special education (Ed M, MS Ed); bilingual elementary/childhood general education (MS Ed); bilingual elementary/childhood special and general education (MS Ed); bilingual elementary/childhood special education (MS Ed). *Students:* 16 full-time (15 women), 21 part-time (16 women); includes 23 minority (1 American Indian or Alaska Native, non-Hispanic/Latino; 21 Hispanic/Latino; 1 Two or more races, non-Hispanic/Latino). Average age 28. 19 applicants, 63% accepted, 6 enrolled. In 2011, 13 master's awarded. *Degree requirements:* For master's, thesis. *Entrance requirements:* For master's, interview, fluency in Spanish and English, essays. Additional exam requirements/recommendations for international students: Required—TOEFL (minimum score 600 paper-based; 250 computer-based; 100 iBT), IELTS (minimum score 7). *Application deadline:* For fall admission, 2/15 priority date for domestic students, 2/15 for international students; for spring admission, 11/1 priority date for domestic students, 11/1 for international students. Applications are processed on a rolling basis. Application fee: $65. Electronic applications accepted. *Expenses: Required fees:* $1240 per credit. $100 per term. One-time fee: $250 part-time. *Financial support:* Career-related internships or fieldwork, Federal Work-Study, scholarships/grants, and unspecified assistantships available. Support available to part-time students. Financial award application deadline: 4/15; financial award applicants required to submit FAFSA. *Faculty research:* Dual language education, language immersion, bilingual education in the urban classroom, community and school partnerships. *Unit head:* Dr. Nilda Bayron-Resnick, Director, 212-875-4543, Fax: 212-875-4753, E-mail: nresnick@bankstreet.edu. *Application contact:* Seena Berg, Associate Director of Graduate Admissions, 212-875-4402, E-mail: sberg@bankstreet.edu. Web site: http://bankstreet.edu/graduate-school/academics/programs/bilingual-programs-overview/.

Belhaven University, School of Education, Jackson, MS 39202-1789. Offers elementary education (M Ed, MAT); secondary education (M Ed, MAT). Part-time and evening/weekend programs available. *Faculty:* 7 full-time (6 women), 15 part-time/adjunct (10 women). *Students:* 167 full-time (133 women), 124 part-time (97 women); includes 205 minority (193 Black or African American, non-Hispanic/Latino; 7 Hispanic/Latino; 5 Two or more races, non-Hispanic/Latino). Average age 33. 446 applicants, 64% accepted, 210 enrolled. In 2011, 94 master's awarded. *Degree requirements:* For master's, comprehensive exam, portfolio. *Entrance requirements:* For master's, PRAXIS

I and II, minimum GPA of 2.8. *Application deadline:* Applications are processed on a rolling basis. Application fee: $25. Electronic applications accepted. *Expenses: Tuition:* Part-time $545 per contact hour. *Financial support:* Federal Work-Study, scholarships/grants, tuition waivers (full), and unspecified assistantships available. Support available to part-time students. Financial award applicants required to submit FAFSA. *Unit head:* Dr. Sandra L. Rasberry, Dean, 601-968-8703, Fax: 601-974-6461, E-mail: srasberry@belhaven.edu. *Application contact:* Jenny Mixon, Director of Graduate and Online Admission, 601-968-8947, Fax: 601-968-5953, E-mail: gradadmission@belhaven.edu. Web site: http://graduateed.belhaven.edu.

Bennington College, Graduate Programs, MA in Teaching a Second Language Program, Bennington, VT 05201. Offers education (MATSL); foreign language education (MATSL); French (MATSL); Spanish (MATSL). Part-time programs available. *Faculty:* 2 full-time (both women), 5 part-time/adjunct (3 women). *Students:* 19 part-time (all women); includes 3 minority (1 Black or African American, non-Hispanic/Latino; 2 Hispanic/Latino). Average age 42. 13 applicants, 92% accepted, 9 enrolled. In 2011, 5 master's awarded. *Degree requirements:* For master's, one foreign language, 2 major projects and presentations. *Entrance requirements:* For master's, Oral Proficiency Interview (OPI). Additional exam requirements/recommendations for international students: Required—TOEFL (minimum score 577 paper-based; 233 computer-based; 91 iBT). *Application deadline:* For spring admission, 4/1 priority date for domestic students, 4/1 for international students. Applications are processed on a rolling basis. Application fee: $60. *Expenses:* Contact institution. *Financial support:* In 2011–12, 4 students received support. Scholarships/grants available. Financial award application deadline: 4/1; financial award applicants required to submit FAFSA. *Faculty research:* Acquisition, evaluation, assessment, conceptual teaching and learning, content-driven communication, applied linguistics. *Unit head:* Carol Meyer, Director, 802-440-4375, E-mail: cmeyer@bennington.edu. *Application contact:* Nancy Pearlman, Assistant Director, 802-440-4710, E-mail: matsl@bennington.edu. Web site: http://www.bennington.edu/Academics/GraduateCertificatePrograms/MATSL.aspx.

Brooklyn College of the City University of New York, Division of Graduate Studies, School of Education, Program in Childhood Education, Brooklyn, NY 11210-2889. Offers bilingual education (MS Ed); liberal arts (MS Ed); mathematics (MS Ed); science/environmental education (MS Ed). Part-time and evening/weekend programs available. *Entrance requirements:* For master's, LAST, interview, previous course work in education, writing sample, resume, 2 letters of recommendation. Additional exam requirements/recommendations for international students: Required—TOEFL (minimum score 500 paper-based; 173 computer-based; 61 iBT). Electronic applications accepted. *Faculty research:* Emotional intelligence, multiculturalism, arts immersion, the Holocaust.

Brown University, Graduate School, Center for Portuguese and Brazilian Studies, Providence, RI 02912. Offers Brazilian studies (AM); Portuguese and Brazilian studies (AM, PhD); Portuguese Bilingual Education and Cross-Cultural Studies (AM); MA/PhD. *Degree requirements:* For doctorate, thesis/dissertation.

Buffalo State College, State University of New York, The Graduate School, Faculty of Applied Science and Education, Department of Exceptional Education, Program in Teaching Bilingual Exceptional Individuals, Buffalo, NY 14222-1095. Offers MS Ed. *Accreditation:* NCATE. Part-time and evening/weekend programs available. *Degree requirements:* For master's, project. *Entrance requirements:* For master's, minimum GPA of 2.5. Additional exam requirements/recommendations for international students: Required—TOEFL (minimum score 550 paper-based; 213 computer-based).

California State University, Dominguez Hills, College of Professional Studies, School of Education, Division of Graduate Education, Program in Multicultural Education, Carson, CA 90747-0001. Offers MA. Part-time and evening/weekend programs available. *Faculty:* 2 full-time (1 woman). *Students:* 20 full-time (18 women), 24 part-time (19 women); includes 39 minority (15 Black or African American, non-Hispanic/Latino; 1 American Indian or Alaska Native, non-Hispanic/Latino; 1 Asian, non-Hispanic/Latino; 22 Hispanic/Latino). Average age 35. 18 applicants, 89% accepted, 7 enrolled. In 2011, 19 master's awarded. *Degree requirements:* For master's, comprehensive exam. *Entrance requirements:* For master's, minimum GPA of 2.75. *Application deadline:* For fall admission, 8/1 for domestic students; for spring admission, 10/1 for domestic students. Applications are processed on a rolling basis. Application fee: $55. *Faculty research:* English learning, intercultural communications. *Unit head:* Dr. Maximilian Contreras, Chairperson, 310-343-3918 Ext. 3524, E-mail: mcontreras@csudh.edu. *Application contact:* Admissions Office, 310-243-3530. Web site: http://www.csudh.edu/cps/soe/programsdegrees/graduate-programs-multicultural.shtml.

California State University, Fullerton, Graduate Studies, College of Education, Department of Elementary and Bilingual Education, Fullerton, CA 92834-9480. Offers bilingual/bicultural education (MS); elementary curriculum and instruction (MS). *Accreditation:* NCATE. Part-time programs available. *Students:* 121 full-time (115 women), 123 part-time (112 women); includes 121 minority (3 Black or African American, non-Hispanic/Latino; 1 American Indian or Alaska Native, non-Hispanic/Latino; 44 Asian, non-Hispanic/Latino; 67 Hispanic/Latino; 6 Two or more races, non-Hispanic/Latino), 1 international. Average age 28. 183 applicants, 51% accepted, 82 enrolled. In 2011, 81 master's awarded. *Degree requirements:* For master's, comprehensive exam, project or thesis. *Entrance requirements:* For master's, minimum GPA of 2.5, teaching certificate. Application fee: $55. *Financial support:* Career-related internships or fieldwork, Federal Work-Study, institutionally sponsored loans, and scholarships/grants available. Support available to part-time students. Financial award application deadline: 3/1; financial award applicants required to submit FAFSA. *Faculty research:* Teacher training and tracking, model for improvement of teaching. *Unit head:* Dr. Karen Ivers, Chair, 657-278-2470. *Application contact:* Admissions/Applications, 657-278-2371.

California State University, Northridge, Graduate Studies, College of Education, Department of Elementary Education, Northridge, CA 91330. Offers curriculum and instruction (MA); language and literacy (MA); multilingual/multicultural education (MA); teaching and learning (MA). *Accreditation:* NCATE. Part-time and evening/weekend programs available. *Degree requirements:* For master's, comprehensive exam. *Entrance requirements:* For master's, GRE General Test or minimum GPA of 3.0. Additional exam requirements/recommendations for international students: Required—TOEFL.

California State University, Sacramento, Office of Graduate Studies, College of Education, Department of Bilingual/Multicultural Education, Sacramento, CA 95819-6079. Offers MA. Part-time programs available. *Faculty:* 13 full-time (8 women), 6 part-time/adjunct (3 women). *Students:* 26 full-time, 9 part-time; includes 25 minority (2 Black or African American, non-Hispanic/Latino; 2 Asian, non-Hispanic/Latino; 18 Hispanic/Latino; 1 Native Hawaiian or other Pacific Islander, non-Hispanic/Latino; 2 Two or more races, non-Hispanic/Latino), 3 international. Average age 35. 26 applicants, 85% accepted, 19 enrolled. In 2011, 16 master's awarded. *Degree requirements:* For master's, thesis or alternative. *Entrance requirements:* For master's, minimum GPA of 2.5. Additional exam requirements/recommendations for international students: Required—TOEFL. *Application deadline:* For fall admission, 3/1 for domestic and international students; for spring admission, 9/15 for domestic students, 9/30 for international students. Applications are processed on a rolling basis. Application fee: $55. Electronic applications accepted. *Financial support:* Career-related internships or fieldwork and Federal Work-Study available. Support available to part-time students. Financial award application deadline: 3/1; financial award applicants required to submit FAFSA. *Unit head:* Nadeen Ruiz, Chair, 916-278-5942, Fax: 916-278-5993, E-mail: ntruiz@csus.edu. *Application contact:* Jose Martinez, Outreach and Graduate Diversity Coordinator, 916-278-6470, Fax: 916-278-5669, E-mail: martinj@skymail.csus.edu. Web site: http://www.edweb.csus.edu/bmed.

California State University, San Bernardino, Graduate Studies, College of Education, Program in Bilingual/Cross-Cultural Education, San Bernardino, CA 92407-2397. Offers MA. *Accreditation:* NCATE. *Students:* 12 full-time (8 women), 1 (woman) part-time; includes 11 minority (all Hispanic/Latino). Average age 40. 4 applicants, 50% accepted, 1 enrolled. In 2011, 2 master's awarded. *Expenses:* Tuition, state resident: full-time $7356. Tuition, nonresident: full-time $7356. *Required fees:* $1077. Tuition and fees vary according to program. *Unit head:* Dr. Jay Fiene, Dean, 909-537-7621, E-mail: jfience@csusb.edu. *Application contact:* Sandra Kamusikiri, Associate Vice-President/Dean of Graduate Studies, 909-537-5058, E-mail: skamusik@csusb.edu.

California State University, Stanislaus, College of Education, Program in Education (MA), Turlock, CA 95382. Offers curriculum and instruction (MA), including education technology, elementary education, multilingual education, physical education, reading, secondary education, special education; school administration (MA); school counseling (MA). Part-time and evening/weekend programs available. *Degree requirements:* For master's, comprehensive exam (for some programs), thesis (for some programs). *Entrance requirements:* For master's, MAT, GRE, or CBEST (varies by concentration), 3 letters of recommendation, personal statement. Additional exam requirements/recommendations for international students: Required—TOEFL (minimum score 550 paper-based; 213 computer-based). *Application deadline:* For fall admission, 5/1 for domestic students; for spring admission, 1/7 for domestic students. Application fee: $55. Electronic applications accepted. *Expenses: Required fees:* $4616 per year. *Financial support:* Federal Work-Study available. Financial award application deadline: 3/1; financial award applicants required to submit FAFSA. *Faculty research:* Children's perspectives on historical events, method elementary schools dual language education, K-12 reading and CYRM programs. *Unit head:* Dr. Kathy Norman, Dean, College of Education, 209-667-3652, Fax: 209-664-6613, E-mail: coe@csustan.edu. *Application contact:* Graduate School, 209-667-3129, Fax: 209-664-7025, E-mail: graduate_school@csustan.edu. Web site: http://www.csustan.edu/COE/.

Capella University, School of Human Services, Minneapolis, MN 55402. Offers addictions counseling (Certificate); counseling studies (MS, PhD); criminal justice (MS, PhD, Certificate); diversity studies (Certificate); general human services (MS, PhD); health care administration (MS, PhD, Certificate); management of nonprofit agencies (MS, PhD, Certificate); marital, couple and family counseling/therapy (MS); marriage and family services (Certificate); mental health counseling (MS); professional counseling (Certificate); social and community services (MS, PhD, Certificate). Part-time and evening/weekend programs available. Postbaccalaureate distance learning degree programs offered (minimal on-campus study). Terminal master's awarded for partial completion of doctoral program. *Degree requirements:* For master's, thesis optional, integrative project; for doctorate, comprehensive exam, thesis/dissertation. *Entrance requirements:* Additional exam requirements/recommendations for international students: Required—TOEFL (minimum score 550 paper-based; 213 computer-based), TWE (minimum score 4). Electronic applications accepted. *Faculty research:* Compulsive and addictive behaviors, substance abuse, assessment of psychopathology and neuropsychology.

Chicago State University, School of Graduate and Professional Studies, College of Education, Department of Special Education, Early Childhood Education and Bilingual Education, Program in Bilingual Education, Chicago, IL 60628. Offers M Ed. *Accreditation:* NCATE. *Degree requirements:* For master's, comprehensive exam, thesis optional. *Entrance requirements:* For master's, minimum GPA of 2.75.

City College of the City University of New York, Graduate School, School of Education, Program in Bilingual Education, New York, NY 10031-9198. Offers MS. *Accreditation:* NCATE. Part-time programs available. *Degree requirements:* For master's, thesis. *Entrance requirements:* For master's, Liberal Arts and Sciences Test (LAST), Content Specialty Test (CST). Additional exam requirements/recommendations for international students: Required—TOEFL.

The College at Brockport, State University of New York, School of Education and Human Services, Department of Education and Human Development, Program in Bilingual Education, Brockport, NY 14420-2997. Offers bilingual education (MS Ed). *Accreditation:* NCATE. Part-time programs available. *Students:* 2 full-time (both women), 6 part-time (5 women); includes 6 minority (all Hispanic/Latino). 4 applicants, 100% accepted, 3 enrolled. In 2011, 3 master's awarded. *Degree requirements:* For master's, thesis or alternative. *Entrance requirements:* For master's, minimum GPA of 3.0, letters of recommendation, statement of objectives, demonstrated proficiency in Spanish at the advanced level, appropriate provisional or initial teaching certificate; for AGC, minimum GPA of 3.0, appropriate New York state teaching certification, demonstrated proficiency in Spanish at the advanced level. Additional exam requirements/recommendations for international students: Required—TOEFL (minimum score 550 paper-based; 213 computer-based; 79 iBT). *Application deadline:* For fall admission, 2/15 priority date for domestic students, 2/15 for international students; for spring admission, 9/15 priority date for domestic students, 9/15 for international students. Application fee: $80. Electronic applications accepted. *Financial support:* Federal Work-Study, scholarships/grants, and unspecified assistantships available. Support available to part-time students. Financial award application deadline: 3/15; financial award applicants required to submit FAFSA. *Unit head:* Dr. Don Halquist, Chairperson, 585-395-5550, Fax: 585-395-2172, E-mail: dhalquis@brockport.edu. *Application contact:* Michael Harrison, Coordinator of Certification and Graduate Advisement, 585-395-2326, Fax: 585-395-2172, E-mail: mharriso@brockport.edu.

College of Mount St. Joseph, Graduate Education Program, Cincinnati, OH 45233-1670. Offers adolescent young adult education (MA); art (MA); inclusive early childhood education (MA); instructional leadership (MA); middle childhood education (MA); multi-age education (MA); multicultural special education (MA); music (MA); reading (MA). *Accreditation:* Teacher Education Accreditation Council. Part-time and evening/weekend programs available. *Faculty:* 22 full-time (12 women), 11 part-time/adjunct (8 women). *Students:* 51 full-time (40 women), 92 part-time (72 women); includes 17 minority (14 Black or African American, non-Hispanic/Latino; 1 American Indian or Alaska Native, non-Hispanic/Latino; 1 Asian, non-Hispanic/Latino; 1 Hispanic/Latino). Average age 34. 87 applicants, 44% accepted, 29 enrolled. In 2011, 61 master's awarded. *Degree requirements:* For master's, research project, student teaching, clinical and field-based experiences. *Entrance requirements:* For master's, GRE, PRAXIS II in teaching content area (math or science), 2 letters of recommendation, interview, resume. Additional exam requirements/recommendations for international students: Required—TOEFL (minimum score 560 paper-based; 220 computer-based; 83 iBT). *Application deadline:* Applications are processed on a rolling basis. Application fee: $50. Electronic applications accepted. *Expenses: Tuition:* Full-time $24,200; part-time $540 per credit hour. *Required fees:* $112.50 per semester. One-time fee: $200. *Financial support:* In

2011–12, 22 students received support. Scholarships/grants available. Financial award applicants required to submit FAFSA. *Faculty research:* Foreign and second language learning problems/reading disabilities/hyperlexia, multicultural/bilingual special education, alternative educator licensure, science education, pedagogical content knowledge. *Unit head:* Dr. Mary West, Chair, 513-244-3263, Fax: 513-244-4867, E-mail: mary_west@mail.msj.edu. *Application contact:* Marilyn Hoskins, Assistant Director of Graduate Recruitment, 513-244-4723, Fax: 513-244-4629, E-mail: marilyn_hoskins@mail.msj.edu. Web site: http://www.msj.edu/view/academics/graduate-programs/education.aspx.

College of Mount Saint Vincent, School of Professional and Continuing Studies, Department of Teacher Education, Riverdale, NY 10471-1093. Offers instructional technology and global perspectives (Certificate); middle level education (Certificate); multicultural studies (Certificate); urban and multicultural education (MS Ed). *Accreditation:* Teacher Education Accreditation Council. Part-time programs available. *Degree requirements:* For master's, comprehensive exam. *Entrance requirements:* For master's, interview, New York teaching certificate. Additional exam requirements/recommendations for international students: Required—TOEFL.

The College of New Rochelle, Graduate School, Division of Education, Program in Teaching English as a Second Language and Multilingual/Multicultural Education, New Rochelle, NY 10805-2308. Offers bilingual education (Certificate); teaching English as a second language (MS Ed). Part-time and evening/weekend programs available. *Degree requirements:* For master's, practicum. *Entrance requirements:* For master's, interview, minimum GPA of 3.0 in field, 2.7 overall.

The College of Saint Rose, Graduate Studies, School of Education, Teacher Education Department, Program in Teacher Education, Albany, NY 12203-1419. Offers bilingual pupil personnel services (Certificate); teacher education (MS Ed). Part-time and evening/weekend programs available. *Degree requirements:* For master's, comprehensive exam or thesis. *Entrance requirements:* For master's, minimum undergraduate GPA of 3.0, provisional or initial certification in a teaching area. Additional exam requirements/recommendations for international students: Required—TOEFL (minimum score 550 paper-based; 213 computer-based). Electronic applications accepted.

Columbia College Chicago, Graduate School, Department of Educational Studies, Chicago, IL 60605-1996. Offers elementary education (MAT); English (MAT); interdisciplinary arts (MAT); multicultural education (MA); urban teaching (MA). Part-time and evening/weekend programs available. *Degree requirements:* For master's, thesis, student teaching experience, 100 pre-clinical hours. *Entrance requirements:* For master's, supplemental recommendation form. Additional exam requirements/recommendations for international students: Required—TOEFL (minimum score 550 paper-based; 213 computer-based). Electronic applications accepted.

Columbia International University, Columbia Graduate School, Columbia, SC 29230-3122. Offers Bible teaching (MABT); Christian higher education leadership (Ed D); Christian school educational leadership (Ed D); counseling (MACN); curriculum and instruction (M Ed), including Christian school guidance, English as a second language, learning disabilities, school technology; early childhood and elementary education (MAT); educational administration (M Ed); teaching English as a foreign language (Certificate); teaching English as a foreign language and intercultural studies (MATF). Part-time and evening/weekend programs available. *Degree requirements:* For master's, internships, professional project. *Entrance requirements:* For master's, Minnesota Multiphasic Personality Inventory, MAT, minimum GPA of 2.7. Additional exam requirements/recommendations for international students: Required—TOEFL. Electronic applications accepted.

DePaul University, College of Education, Chicago, IL 60106. Offers bilingual bicultural education (M Ed, MA); counseling (M Ed, MA), including college student development, community counseling, school counseling; curriculum studies (M Ed, MA, Ed D); early childhood education (M Ed, MA); educational leadership (M Ed, MA, Ed D), including administration and supervision (M Ed, MA), physical education (M Ed, MA); middle school mathematics education (MS); reading specialist (M Ed, MA); social and cultural foundations in education (M Ed, MA), including curriculum studies/development (MA); special education (M Ed, MA); teaching and learning (M Ed, MA), including elementary education, secondary education; world languages education (M Ed, MA). Part-time and evening/weekend programs available. *Faculty:* 49 full-time (28 women), 94 part-time/adjunct (60 women). *Students:* 894 full-time (707 women), 473 part-time (361 women); includes 349 minority (159 Black or African American, non-Hispanic/Latino; 3 American Indian or Alaska Native, non-Hispanic/Latino; 45 Asian, non-Hispanic/Latino; 115 Hispanic/Latino; 2 Native Hawaiian or other Pacific Islander, non-Hispanic/Latino; 25 Two or more races, non-Hispanic/Latino), 21 international. Average age 30. 872 applicants, 64% accepted, 325 enrolled. In 2011, 499 master's, 10 doctorates awarded. *Median time to degree:* Of those who began their doctoral program in fall 2003, 32% received their degree in 8 years or less. *Degree requirements:* For master's, thesis/dissertation (for MA); capstone course or paper (for M Ed); for doctorate, thesis/dissertation. *Entrance requirements:* For master's, interview, minimum GPA of 2.75, 2 letters of recommendation, bachelor's degree conferred by accredited college or university; for doctorate, interview, master's degree, writing sample, 3 letters of recommendation. Additional exam requirements/recommendations for international students: Required—TOEFL (minimum score 550 paper-based; 213 computer-based; 80 iBT). *Application deadline:* For fall admission, 8/15 priority date for domestic students; for winter admission, 12/1 priority date for domestic students; for spring admission, 3/1 priority date for domestic students. Applications are processed on a rolling basis. Application fee: $40. Electronic applications accepted. *Financial support:* In 2011–12, 163 students received support, including 15 research assistantships with full tuition reimbursements available (averaging $6,375 per year); career-related internships or fieldwork, Federal Work-Study, scholarships/grants, and unspecified assistantships also available. Support available to part-time students. Financial award application deadline: 12/31; financial award applicants required to submit FAFSA. *Faculty research:* Reflective teaching, children at risk, loss, ethnicity, urban education. *Total annual research expenditures:* $916,310. *Unit head:* Dr. Paul Zionts, Dean, 773-325-7581, Fax: 773-325-7713, E-mail: pzionts@depaul.edu. *Application contact:* Brandon Washington, Enrollment Management Coordinator, 773-325-1152, Fax: 773-325-2270, E-mail: bwashin3@depaul.edu. Web site: http://education.depaul.edu.

Eastern Michigan University, Graduate School, College of Education, Department of Teacher Education, Ypsilanti, MI 48197. Offers culture and diversity (MA); curriculum and instruction (MA); early childhood education (MA); educational media and technology (MA, Graduate Certificate); educational psychology and assessment (MA, Graduate Certificate), including educational assessment (Graduate Certificate), educational psychology (MA); educational studies (PhD); K-12 education (MA), including curriculum and instruction, elementary education, K-12 education, middle school education, secondary school education; reading (MA); social foundations (MA). Part-time and evening/weekend programs available. Postbaccalaureate distance learning degree programs offered (minimal on-campus study). *Faculty:* 41 full-time (33 women). *Students:* 22 full-time (17 women), 444 part-time (380 women); includes 72 minority (51 Black or African American, non-Hispanic/Latino; 2 American Indian or Alaska Native, non-Hispanic/Latino; 8 Asian, non-Hispanic/Latino; 7 Hispanic/Latino; 1 Native Hawaiian or other Pacific Islander, non-Hispanic/Latino; 3 Two or more races, non-Hispanic/Latino), 7 international. Average age 35. 217 applicants, 71% accepted, 84 enrolled. In 2011, 113 master's, 450 other advanced degrees awarded. *Entrance requirements:* For master's, GRE. Additional exam requirements/recommendations for international students: Required—TOEFL. *Application deadline:* Applications are processed on a rolling basis. Application fee: $35. *Expenses:* Tuition, state resident: full-time $10,367; part-time $432 per credit hour. Tuition, nonresident: full-time $20,435; part-time $851 per credit hour. *Required fees:* $39 per credit hour. $46 per semester. One-time fee: $100. Tuition and fees vary according to course level, degree level and reciprocity agreements. *Financial support:* Fellowships, research assistantships with full tuition reimbursements, teaching assistantships with full tuition reimbursements, career-related internships or fieldwork, Federal Work-Study, institutionally sponsored loans, scholarships/grants, tuition waivers (partial), and unspecified assistantships available. Support available to part-time students. Financial award applicants required to submit FAFSA. *Unit head:* Dr. Donald Bennion, Department Head, 734-487-3260, Fax: 734-487-2101, E-mail: donald.bennion@emich.edu. *Application contact:* Dr. Anne Bednar, Advisor, 734-487-3260, Fax: 734-487-2101, E-mail: anne.bednar@emich.edu. Web site: http://www.emich.edu/coe/ted/.

Eastern New Mexico University, Graduate School, College of Education and Technology, Department of Curriculum and Instruction, Portales, NM 88130. Offers bilingual education (M Ed); educational technology (M Ed); elementary education (M Ed); English as a second language (M Ed); pedagogy and learning (M Ed); professional technical education (M Ed); reading/literacy (M Ed). Part-time programs available. Postbaccalaureate distance learning degree programs offered (minimal on-campus study). *Degree requirements:* For master's, comprehensive exam, thesis optional. *Entrance requirements:* For master's, minimum GPA of 3.0, photocopy of teaching license, writing assessment, letter of recommendation. Additional exam requirements/recommendations for international students: Required—TOEFL (minimum score 550 paper-based; 213 computer-based; 79 iBT), IELTS (minimum score 6). Electronic applications accepted.

Eastern University, Graduate Education Programs, Program in Multicultural Education, St. Davids, PA 19087-3696. Offers M Ed. *Entrance requirements:* For master's, minimum GPA of 2.5. Additional exam requirements/recommendations for international students: Required—TOEFL.

Edgewood College, Program in Education, Madison, WI 53711-1997. Offers adult learning (MA Ed); bilingual teaching and learning (MA Ed); director of instruction (Certificate); director of special education and pupil services (Certificate); education (MA Ed); educational administration (MA Ed); educational leadership (Ed D); professional studies (MA Ed); program coordinator (Certificate); reading administration (MA Ed); school business administration (Certificate); school principalship K-12 (Certificate); special education (MA Ed); sustainability leadership (MA Ed); teaching and learning (MA Ed); teaching English to speakers of other languages (TESOL) (MA Ed). *Accreditation:* NCATE (one or more programs are accredited). Part-time and evening/weekend programs available. *Students:* 155 full-time (93 women), 152 part-time (116 women); includes 39 minority (13 Black or African American, non-Hispanic/Latino; 5 Asian, non-Hispanic/Latino; 17 Hispanic/Latino; 4 Two or more races, non-Hispanic/Latino), 9 international. Average age 36. In 2011, 39 master's, 32 doctorates awarded. *Degree requirements:* For master's, practicum, research project; for doctorate, comprehensive exam, thesis/dissertation. *Entrance requirements:* For master's, minimum GPA of 2.75, 2 letters of recommendation, personal statement; for doctorate, resume, letter of intent, 2 letters of recommendation, interview, writing sample. Additional exam requirements/recommendations for international students: Required—TOEFL (minimum score 525 paper-based; 197 computer-based; 72 iBT). *Application deadline:* For fall admission, 8/15 for domestic students, 5/1 for international students; for spring admission, 1/8 for domestic students, 11/1 for international students. Applications are processed on a rolling basis. Application fee: $25. Electronic applications accepted. *Expenses: Tuition:* Part-time $747 per credit. Part-time tuition and fees vary according to program. *Unit head:* Dr. Jane Belmore, Dean, 608-663-8336, Fax: 608-663-3291, E-mail: jbelmore@edgewood.edu. *Application contact:* Joann Eastman, Admissions Counselor, 608-663-3250, Fax: 608-663-2214, E-mail: gps@edgewood.edu. Web site: http://education.edgewood.edu/graduate.html.

Fairfield University, Graduate School of Education and Allied Professions, Fairfield, CT 06824-5195. Offers applied psychology (MA); bilingual education (CAS); clinical mental health counseling (MA, CAS); educational technology (MA); elementary education (MA); family studies (MA); marriage and family therapy (MA); school counseling (MA, CAS); school psychology (MA, CAS); special education (MA); teaching (Certificate); teaching and foundations (MA, CAS); TESOL foreign language and bilingual/multicultural education (MA, CAS). *Accreditation:* NCATE. Part-time and evening/weekend programs available. *Faculty:* 24 full-time (19 women). *Students:* 147 full-time (120 women), 391 part-time (321 women); includes 60 minority (13 Black or African American, non-Hispanic/Latino; 8 Asian, non-Hispanic/Latino; 35 Hispanic/Latino; 4 Two or more races, non-Hispanic/Latino), 1 international. Average age 34. 319 applicants, 48% accepted, 80 enrolled. In 2011, 185 master's, 20 other advanced degrees awarded. *Degree requirements:* For master's, comprehensive exam. *Entrance requirements:* For master's, PRAXIS I (for certification programs), minimum QPA of 3.0, 2 recommendations, resume. Additional exam requirements/recommendations for international students: Required—TOEFL (minimum score 550 paper-based; 213 computer-based; 84 iBT) or IELTS (minimum score 7.5). *Application deadline:* For fall admission, 2/15 for international students; for spring admission, 10/1 for international students. Application fee: $60. Electronic applications accepted. *Expenses: Tuition:* Part-time $600 per credit hour. *Required fees:* $25 per term. *Financial support:* In 2011–12, 45 students received support. Career-related internships or fieldwork and unspecified assistantships available. Financial award applicants required to submit FAFSA. *Faculty research:* Literacy, adolescent psychology, special education, early childhood education, teaching development. *Unit head:* Dr. Susan D. Franzosa, Dean, 203-254-4000 Ext. 4250, Fax: 203-254-4241, E-mail: sfranzosa@fairfield.edu. *Application contact:* Marianne Gumpper, Director of Graduate and Continuing Studies Admission, 203-254-4184, Fax: 203-254-4073, E-mail: gradadmis@fairfield.edu. Web site: http://www.fairfield.edu/gseap/gseap_grad_1.html.

Fairleigh Dickinson University, Metropolitan Campus, University College: Arts, Sciences, and Professional Studies, Peter Sammartino School of Education, Program in Multilingual Education, Teaneck, NJ 07666-1914. Offers MA. *Accreditation:* Teacher Education Accreditation Council.

Florida Atlantic University, College of Education, Department of Curriculum, Culture, and Educational Inquiry, Boca Raton, FL 33431-0991. Offers curriculum and instruction (Ed D, Ed S); early childhood education (M Ed); multicultural education (M Ed); teaching English to speakers of other languages (TESOL) (M Ed). *Faculty:* 14 full-time (11 women), 16 part-time/adjunct (13 women). *Students:* 28 full-time (21 women), 138 part-time (106 women); includes 46 minority (18 Black or African American, non-Hispanic/Latino; 1 American Indian or Alaska Native, non-Hispanic/Latino; 3 Asian, non-Hispanic/Latino; 23 Hispanic/Latino; 1 Two or more races, non-Hispanic/Latino), 7 international. Average age 36. 120 applicants, 53% accepted, 32 enrolled. In 2011, 33 master's, 2 doctorates awarded. *Application deadline:* For fall admission, 7/1 for domestic students,

2/15 for international students; for spring admission, 11/1 for domestic students, 7/15 for international students. *Expenses: Tuition, area resident:* Part-time $343.02 per credit hour. Tuition, state resident: full-time $8232. Tuition, nonresident: full-time $23,931; part-time $997.14 per credit hour. *Faculty research:* Multicultural education, early intervention strategies, family literacy, religious diversity in schools, early childhood curriculum. *Unit head:* Dr. James McLaughlin, Interim Chair, 561-297-3965, E-mail: jmclau17@fau.edu. *Application contact:* Dr. Eliah Watlington, Associate Dean, 561-296-8520, Fax: 261-297-2991, E-mail: ewatling@fau.edu. Web site: http://www.coe.fau.edu/academicdepartments/ccei/.

Florida International University, College of Education, Department of Educational Leadership and Policy Studies, Miami, FL 33199. Offers adult education (MS); adult education in human resource development (Ed D); clinical mental health counseling (MS); conflict resolution and consensus building (Certificate); counselor education (MS); educational administration and supervision (Ed D); educational leadership (MS, Certificate, Ed S); higher education (Ed D); higher education administration (MS); human resource development (MS); instruction in urban settings (MS); international/intercultural education (MS); learning technologies (MS); multicultural-bilingual (MS); multicultural-TESOL (MS); recreation and sport management (MS); recreation therapy (MS); rehabilitation counseling (MS); school counseling (MS); school psychology (Ed S); urban education (MS). Part-time and evening/weekend programs available. *Degree requirements:* For doctorate, thesis/dissertation. *Entrance requirements:* For master's, minimum GPA of 3.0; for doctorate and other advanced degree, GRE General Test. Additional exam requirements/recommendations for international students: Required—TOEFL (minimum score 550 paper-based; 213 computer-based; 80 iBT), IELTS (minimum score 6.3). Electronic applications accepted.

Fordham University, Graduate School of Education, Division of Curriculum and Teaching, New York, NY 10023. Offers adult education (MS, MSE); bilingual teacher education (MSE); curriculum and teaching (MSE); early childhood education (MSE); elementary education (MST); language, literacy, and learning (PhD); reading education (MSE, Adv C); secondary education (MAT, MSE); special education (MSE, Adv C); teaching English as a second language (MSE). *Accreditation:* NCATE. *Degree requirements:* For doctorate, thesis/dissertation; for Adv C, thesis. *Entrance requirements:* For doctorate, MAT, GRE General Test. *Expenses: Tuition:* Full-time $30,480; part-time $1270 per credit. *Required fees:* $586; $293 per semester.

Fresno Pacific University, Graduate Programs, School of Education, Fresno, CA 93702-4709. Offers administration (MA Ed), including administrative services; foundations, curriculum and teaching (MA Ed), including curriculum and teaching, school library and information technology; language, literacy, and culture (MA Ed), including bilingual/cross-cultural education, language development, multilingual contexts, reading; mathematics/science/computer education (MA Ed), including educational technology, integrated mathematics/science education, mathematics education; pupil personnel services (MA Ed), including school counseling, school psychology; special education (MA Ed), including mild/moderate, moderate/severe, physical and health impairments. Part-time and evening/weekend programs available. *Degree requirements:* For master's, thesis (for some programs). *Entrance requirements:* For master's, interview; GMAT, GRE, MAT, or 6 units of course work with a faculty recommendation. Additional exam requirements/recommendations for international students: Required—TOEFL (minimum score 550 paper-based; 213 computer-based). Electronic applications accepted.

Fresno Pacific University, Graduate Programs, School of Education, Division of Language, Literacy, and Culture, Program in Bilingual/Cross-Cultural Education, Fresno, CA 93702-4709. Offers MA Ed. Part-time and evening/weekend programs available. *Degree requirements:* For master's, thesis or alternative. *Entrance requirements:* Additional exam requirements/recommendations for international students: Required—TOEFL (minimum score 550 paper-based; 213 computer-based). Electronic applications accepted.

Fresno Pacific University, Graduate Programs, School of Education, Division of Language, Literacy, and Culture, Program in Literacy in Multilingual Contexts, Fresno, CA 93702-4709. Offers MA Ed. Part-time and evening/weekend programs available. *Degree requirements:* For master's, thesis or alternative. *Entrance requirements:* Additional exam requirements/recommendations for international students: Required—TOEFL (minimum score 550 paper-based; 213 computer-based). Electronic applications accepted.

George Fox University, School of Education, Master of Arts in Teaching Program, Newberg, OR 97132-2697. Offers teaching (MAT); teaching plus ESOL (MAT); teaching plus ESOL/bilingual (MAT); teaching plus reading (MAT). Program offered in Oregon and Idaho. Part-time and evening/weekend programs available. *Faculty:* 17 full-time (13 women), 19 part-time/adjunct (16 women). *Students:* 115 full-time (75 women), 55 part-time (36 women); includes 16 minority (1 Black or African American, non-Hispanic/Latino; 11 Asian, non-Hispanic/Latino; 3 Hispanic/Latino; 1 Two or more races, non-Hispanic/Latino). Average age 31. 55 applicants, 76% accepted, 32 enrolled. In 2011, 156 master's awarded. *Entrance requirements:* For master's, CBEST, PRAXIS PPST, or EAS, bachelor's degree with minimum GPA of 3.0 in last two years of course work from regionally-accredited college or university, official transcripts. Additional exam requirements/recommendations for international students: Required—TOEFL (minimum score 577 paper-based; 233 computer-based; 90 iBT), IELTS (minimum score 7). *Application deadline:* For fall admission, 6/1 for domestic and international students; for winter admission, 10/1 for domestic and international students; for spring admission, 2/1 for domestic and international students. Applications are processed on a rolling basis. Application fee: $40. Electronic applications accepted. *Expenses:* Contact institution. *Financial support:* In 2011–12, 20 students received support. Scholarships/grants available. Financial award application deadline: 2/1; financial award applicants required to submit FAFSA. *Unit head:* Carol Brazo, Chair, 503-554-6115, E-mail: cbrazo@georgefox.edu. *Application contact:* Beth Molzahn, Admissions Counselor, 800-631-0921, Fax: 503-554-3110, E-mail: mat@georgefox.edu. Web site: http://www.georgefox.edu/soe/mat/.

Georgetown University, Graduate School of Arts and Sciences, Department of Linguistics, Washington, DC 20057. Offers bilingual education (Certificate); language and communication (MA); linguistics (MS, PhD), including applied linguistics, computational linguistics, sociolinguistics, theoretical linguistics; teaching English as a second language (MAT, Certificate); teaching English as a second language and bilingual education (MAT). Terminal master's awarded for partial completion of doctoral program. *Degree requirements:* For master's, one foreign language, comprehensive exam, optional research project; for doctorate, 2 foreign languages, comprehensive exam, thesis/dissertation. *Entrance requirements:* For master's and doctorate, 18 undergraduate credits in a foreign language. Additional exam requirements/recommendations for international students: Required—TOEFL.

The George Washington University, Graduate School of Education and Human Development, Department of Counseling and Human Development, Program in Counseling Culturally and Linguistically Diverse Persons, Washington, DC 20052. Offers Graduate Certificate.

The George Washington University, Graduate School of Education and Human Development, Department of Special Education and Disability Studies, Program in Bilingual Special Education, Washington, DC 20052. Offers MA, Ed D.

Graduate Institute of Applied Linguistics, Graduate Programs, Dallas, TX 75236. Offers applied linguistics (MA, Certificate); language development (MA). Part-time programs available. *Degree requirements:* For master's, one foreign language, comprehensive exam (for some programs), thesis (for some programs). *Entrance requirements:* For master's, GRE. Additional exam requirements/recommendations for international students: Required—TOEFL (minimum score 577 paper-based; 233 computer-based; 90 iBT). Electronic applications accepted. *Faculty research:* Minority languages, endangered languages, language documentation.

Harvard University, Harvard Graduate School of Education, Doctoral Program in Education, Cambridge, MA 02138. Offers culture, communities and education (Ed D); education policy, leadership and instructional practice (Ed D); higher education (Ed D); human development and education (Ed D); quantitative policy analysis in education (Ed D). *Faculty:* 83 full-time (44 women), 67 part-time/adjunct (29 women). *Students:* 251 full-time (172 women), 16 part-time (7 women); includes 87 minority (32 Black or African American, non-Hispanic/Latino; 1 American Indian or Alaska Native, non-Hispanic/Latino; 26 Asian, non-Hispanic/Latino; 22 Hispanic/Latino; 1 Native Hawaiian or other Pacific Islander, non-Hispanic/Latino; 5 Two or more races, non-Hispanic/Latino), 30 international. Average age 34. 545 applicants, 7% accepted, 28 enrolled. In 2011, 47 doctorates awarded. Terminal master's awarded for partial completion of doctoral program. *Degree requirements:* For doctorate, thesis/dissertation. *Entrance requirements:* For doctorate, GRE General Test, statement of purpose, 3 letters of recommendation, resume, official transcripts. Additional exam requirements/recommendations for international students: Required—TOEFL (minimum score 613 paper-based; 104 computer-based; 100 iBT), TWE (minimum score 5). *Application deadline:* For fall admission, 12/14 for domestic and international students. Application fee: $85. Electronic applications accepted. *Expenses:* Contact institution. *Financial support:* In 2011–12, 203 students received support, including 62 fellowships with full and partial tuition reimbursements available (averaging $13,939 per year), 35 research assistantships (averaging $9,534 per year), 134 teaching assistantships (averaging $10,748 per year); career-related internships or fieldwork, Federal Work-Study, institutionally sponsored loans, scholarships/grants, health care benefits, tuition waivers (full and partial), and unspecified assistantships also available. Support available to part-time students. Financial award application deadline: 2/1; financial award applicants required to submit FAFSA. *Faculty research:* Learning and development, educational leadership and organizations, education policy analysis. *Total annual research expenditures:* $26 million. *Unit head:* Dr. Shu-Ling Chen, Assistant Dean, 617-496-4406. *Application contact:* Information Contact, 617-495-3414, Fax: 617-496-3577, E-mail: gseadmissions@harvard.edu. Web site: http://gse.harvard.edu/.

Heritage University, Graduate Programs in Education, Program in Professional Studies, Toppenish, WA 98948-9599. Offers bilingual education/ESL (M Ed); biology (M Ed); English and literature (M Ed); reading/literacy (M Ed); special education (M Ed). Part-time and evening/weekend programs available. *Degree requirements:* For master's, comprehensive exam (for some programs), thesis (for some programs).

Hofstra University, School of Education, Health, and Human Services, Program in Elementary Education, Hempstead, NY 11549. Offers early childhood and childhood education (MS Ed); early childhood education (MA, MS Ed); educational technology (MA); elementary education (MS Ed); literacy (MA); math specialist (Advanced Certificate); math, science, technology (MA); multiculturalism (MA). Part-time and evening/weekend programs available. Postbaccalaureate distance learning degree programs offered (minimal on-campus study). *Students:* 54 full-time (48 women), 43 part-time (37 women); includes 17 minority (10 Black or African American, non-Hispanic/Latino; 2 Asian, non-Hispanic/Latino; 5 Hispanic/Latino), 2 international. Average age 29. 65 applicants, 88% accepted, 18 enrolled. In 2011, 58 master's awarded. *Degree requirements:* For master's, comprehensive exam, thesis (for some programs), 35 semester hours (for MA); 38-41 semester hours (for MS Ed), minimum GPA of 3.0. *Entrance requirements:* For master's, 2 letters of recommendation, teacher certification (MA), interview, essay. Additional exam requirements/recommendations for international students: Required—TOEFL (minimum score 550 paper-based; 213 computer-based; 80 iBT). *Application deadline:* Applications are processed on a rolling basis. Application fee: $70 ($75 for international students). Electronic applications accepted. *Expenses: Tuition:* Full-time $18,990; part-time $1055 per credit hour. *Required fees:* $970. Tuition and fees vary according to program. *Financial support:* In 2011–12, 45 students received support, including 22 fellowships with full and partial tuition reimbursements available (averaging $2,560 per year), 2 research assistantships with full and partial tuition reimbursements available (averaging $21,993 per year); career-related internships or fieldwork, Federal Work-Study, institutionally sponsored loans, scholarships/grants, tuition waivers (full and partial), and unspecified assistantships also available. Support available to part-time students. Financial award applicants required to submit FAFSA. *Faculty research:* Dynamic-themes curriculum/complexity theory, joyful learning, teacher education, multicultural education, multiple authentic assessments. *Unit head:* Dr. Esther Fusco, Chairperson, 516-463-7704, Fax: 516-463-6196, E-mail: catezf@hofstra.edu. *Application contact:* Carol Drummer, Dean of Graduate Admissions, 516-463-4876, Fax: 516-463-4664, E-mail: gradstudent@hofstra.edu. Web site: http://www.hofstra.edu/education/.

Hofstra University, School of Education, Health, and Human Services, Programs in Teaching (K-12), Hempstead, NY 11549. Offers bilingual education (MA); bilingual extension (Advanced Certificate), including education/speech language pathology, intensive teacher institute; family and consumer science (MS Ed); fine art and music education (Advanced Certificate); fine arts education (MA, MS Ed); mentoring and coaching for teachers (Advanced Certificate); middle childhood extension (Advanced Certificate), including grades 5-6 or 7-9; music education (MA, MS Ed); teaching languages other than English and TESOL (MS Ed); TESOL (MS Ed, Advanced Certificate), including intensive teacher institute (Advanced Certificate), TESOL (Advanced Certificate); wind conducting (MA). Part-time and evening/weekend programs available. *Students:* 54 full-time (48 women), 60 part-time (53 women); includes 30 minority (10 Black or African American, non-Hispanic/Latino; 9 Asian, non-Hispanic/Latino; 11 Hispanic/Latino), 8 international. Average age 29. 109 applicants, 76% accepted, 43 enrolled. In 2011, 71 master's, 42 other advanced degrees awarded. *Degree requirements:* For master's, one foreign language, thesis (for some programs), electronic portfolio, Tk20 portfolios, minimum GPA of 3.0. *Entrance requirements:* For master's, 2 letters of recommendation, portfolio, teacher certification (MA), essay; for Advanced Certificate, 2 letters of recommendation, interview, teaching certificate, essay. Additional exam requirements/recommendations for international students: Required—TOEFL (minimum score 550 paper-based; 213 computer-based; 80 iBT). *Application deadline:* Applications are processed on a rolling basis. Application fee: $70 ($75 for international students). Electronic applications accepted. *Expenses: Tuition:* Full-time $18,990; part-time $1055 per credit hour. *Required fees:* $970. Tuition and fees vary according to program. *Financial support:* In 2011–12, 39 students received support, including 13 fellowships with full and partial tuition reimbursements available (averaging $3,347 per year), 2 research assistantships with full and partial tuition reimbursements available (averaging $7,363 per year); career-related internships or fieldwork, Federal Work-Study, institutionally sponsored loans, scholarships/grants, tuition waivers (full and partial), and unspecified assistantships also available. Support available to part-time students. Financial award applicants required to submit FAFSA. *Faculty research:* The teacher/artist, interdisciplinary curriculum, applied linguistics, structural inequalities, creativity. *Unit head:* Dr. Esther Fusco, Chairperson, 516-463-7704, Fax: 516-463-6196, E-mail: catezf@hofstra.edu. *Application contact:* Carol Drummer, Dean of Graduate Admissions, 516-463-4876, Fax: 516-463-4664, E-mail: gradstudent@hofstra.edu. Web site: http://www.hofstra.edu/education/.

Howard University, School of Communications, Department of Communication and Culture, Washington, DC 20059-0002. Offers intercultural communication (MA, PhD); organizational communication (MA, PhD). Offered through the Graduate School of Arts and Sciences. Part-time programs available. Terminal master's awarded for partial completion of doctoral program. *Degree requirements:* For master's, comprehensive exam or thesis; for doctorate, one foreign language, comprehensive exam, thesis/dissertation. *Entrance requirements:* For master's, English proficiency exam, GRE General Test, minimum GPA of 3.0; for doctorate, English proficiency exam, GRE General Test, master's degree in related field, minimum GPA of 3.5. Additional exam requirements/recommendations for international students: Required—TOEFL. *Faculty research:* Media effects, black discourse, development communication, African-American organizations.

Hunter College of the City University of New York, Graduate School, School of Education, Department of Curriculum and Teaching, Program in Bilingual Education, New York, NY 10021-5085. Offers MS. *Accreditation:* NCATE. *Faculty:* 4 part-time/adjunct (all women). *Students:* 1 (woman) full-time, 25 part-time (all women); includes 17 minority (2 Black or African American, non-Hispanic/Latino; 15 Hispanic/Latino), 1 international. Average age 30. 14 applicants, 71% accepted, 5 enrolled. In 2011, 11 master's awarded. *Degree requirements:* For master's, one foreign language, thesis, research seminar, student teaching experience or practicum, New York State Teacher Certification Exams. *Entrance requirements:* For master's, interview, minimum GPA of 2.8, writing sample in English and Spanish. Additional exam requirements/recommendations for international students: Required—TOEFL, TWE. *Application deadline:* For fall admission, 4/1 for domestic students, 2/1 for international students; for spring admission, 11/1 for domestic students, 9/1 for international students. Applications are processed on a rolling basis. Application fee: $125. *Expenses:* Tuition, state resident: full-time $8210; part-time $345 per credit. Tuition, nonresident: full-time $15,360; part-time $640 per credit. *Required fees:* $280 per semester. One-time fee: $125. Tuition and fees vary according to class time, campus/location and program. *Financial support:* Federal Work-Study, scholarships/grants, and tuition waivers (partial) available. Support available to part-time students. *Faculty research:* Teacher effectiveness, language development, Spanish language and linguistics and multicultural education. *Unit head:* Yvonne DeGaetano, Coordinator, 212-772-4683, E-mail: ydegaetano@hunter.cuny.edu. *Application contact:* William Zlata, Director for Graduate Admissions, 212-772-4482, Fax: 212-650-3336, E-mail: admissions@hunter.cuny.edu. Web site: http://www.hunter.cuny.edu/school-of-education/programs/graduate/bilingual.

Hunter College of the City University of New York, Graduate School, School of Education, Department of Educational Foundations and Counseling Programs, Programs in School Counselor, New York, NY 10021-5085. Offers school counseling (MS Ed); school counseling with bilingual extension (MS Ed). *Accreditation:* ACA; NCATE. *Faculty:* 2 full-time (both women), 3 part-time/adjunct (0 women). *Students:* 41 full-time (37 women), 69 part-time (59 women); includes 47 minority (16 Black or African American, non-Hispanic/Latino; 6 Asian, non-Hispanic/Latino; 25 Hispanic/Latino), 2 international. Average age 29. 250 applicants, 15% accepted, 21 enrolled. In 2011, 33 master's awarded. *Degree requirements:* For master's, thesis, internship, practicum, research seminar. *Entrance requirements:* For master's, interview, minimum GPA of 2.7. Additional exam requirements/recommendations for international students: Required—TOEFL, TWE. *Application deadline:* For fall admission, 4/1 for domestic students, 2/1 for international students; for spring admission, 11/1 for domestic students, 9/1 for international students. Applications are processed on a rolling basis. Application fee: $125. *Expenses:* Tuition, state resident: full-time $8210; part-time $345 per credit. Tuition, nonresident: full-time $15,360; part-time $640 per credit. *Required fees:* $280 per semester. One-time fee: $125. Tuition and fees vary according to class time, campus/location and program. *Financial support:* Federal Work-Study and tuition waivers (partial) available. Support available to part-time students. *Unit head:* Dr. Tamara Buckley, Coordinator, 212-772-4758, E-mail: tamara.buckley@hunter.cuny.edu. *Application contact:* William Zlata, Director for Graduate Admissions, 212-772-4482, Fax: 212-650-3336, E-mail: admissions@hunter.cuny.edu. Web site: http://www.hunter.cuny.edu/school-of-education/programs/graduate/counseling/school-counseling.

Immaculata University, College of Graduate Studies, Program in Cultural and Linguistic Diversity, Immaculata, PA 19345. Offers MA. Part-time and evening/weekend programs available. *Degree requirements:* For master's, one foreign language, comprehensive exam, thesis optional, professional experience. *Entrance requirements:* For master's, GRE or MAT, proficiency in Spanish or Asian language, minimum GPA of 3.0. Additional exam requirements/recommendations for international students: Required—TOEFL, IELTS. Electronic applications accepted. *Faculty research:* Cognitive learning, Caribbean literature and culture, English as a second language, teaching English to speakers of other languages.

Indiana State University, College of Graduate and Professional Studies, College of Arts and Sciences, Department of Languages, Literatures, and Linguistics, Terre Haute, IN 47809. Offers linguistics/teaching English as a second language (MA); TESL/TEFL (CAS). *Degree requirements:* For master's, comprehensive exam. Electronic applications accepted.

Indiana University Bloomington, University Graduate School, College of Arts and Sciences, Department of Second Language Studies, Bloomington, IN 47405-7000. Offers second language studies (MA, PhD); TESOL and applied linguistics (MA). *Faculty:* 1 (woman) full-time. *Students:* 36 full-time (24 women), 3 part-time (1 woman); includes 7 minority (2 Black or African American, non-Hispanic/Latino; 4 Hispanic/Latino; 1 Two or more races, non-Hispanic/Latino), 17 international. Average age 31. 102 applicants, 35% accepted, 19 enrolled. In 2011, 8 master's awarded. *Entrance requirements:* Additional exam requirements/recommendations for international students: Required—TOEFL (minimum score 100 iBT). *Application deadline:* For fall admission, 1/15 for domestic students, 12/1 for international students. Application fee: $55 ($65 for international students). *Financial support:* In 2011–12, 12 teaching assistantships with tuition reimbursements (averaging $13,456 per year) were awarded; fellowships with tuition reimbursements also available. *Unit head:* Kathleen Bardovi-Harlig, Chair, 812-855-7951, E-mail: bardovi@indiana.edu. *Application contact:* Julie Abrams, Graduate Secretary, 812-855-7951, E-mail: abramsj@indiana.edu. Web site: http://www.indiana.edu/~dsls/.

Kean University, College of Education, Program in Instruction and Curriculum, Union, NJ 07083. Offers bilingual (MA); classroom instruction (MA); mathematics/science/computer education (MA); teaching (MA); teaching English as a second language (MA); teaching physics (MA); world languages (Spanish) (MA). *Accreditation:* NCATE. *Faculty:* 22 full-time (12 women). *Students:* 56 full-time (33 women), 139 part-time (103 women); includes 87 minority (27 Black or African American, non-Hispanic/Latino; 8 Asian, non-Hispanic/Latino; 52 Hispanic/Latino), 1 international. Average age 34. 85 applicants, 100% accepted, 72 enrolled. In 2011, 78 master's awarded. *Degree requirements:* For master's, comprehensive exam, two-semester advanced seminar. *Entrance requirements:* For master's, GRE General Test or MAT, PRAXIS, minimum GPA of 3.0, 2 letters of recommendation, interview, teacher certification (for some programs), transcripts, resume. Additional exam requirements/recommendations for international students: Required—TOEFL (minimum score 79 iBT). *Application deadline:* For fall admission, 6/1 for domestic and international students; for spring admission, 12/1 for domestic and international students. Applications are processed on a rolling basis. Application fee: $75 ($150 for international students). Electronic applications accepted. *Expenses:* Tuition, state resident: full-time $11,302; part-time $550 per credit. Tuition, nonresident: full-time $15,318; part-time $674 per credit. *Required fees:* $2849; $130 per credit. Tuition and fees vary according to degree level. *Financial support:* In 2011–12, 3 research assistantships with full tuition reimbursements (averaging $3,263 per year) were awarded; unspecified assistantships also available. Financial award applicants required to submit FAFSA. *Unit head:* Dr. Thomas Walsh, Program Coordinator, 908-737-4003, E-mail: tpwalsh@kean.edu. *Application contact:* Ann-Marie Kay, Assistant Director for Graduate Admissions, 908-737-5922, Fax: 908-737-5925, E-mail: akay@kean.edu. Web site: http://www.kean.edu/KU/Bilingual-Bicultural-Education-Instruction-and-Curriculum.

Langston University, School of Education and Behavioral Sciences, Langston, OK 73050. Offers bilingual/multicultural (M Ed); elementary education (M Ed); English as a second language (M Ed); rehabilitation counseling (M Sc); urban education (M Ed). *Accreditation:* CORE; NCATE (one or more programs are accredited). Part-time programs available. *Degree requirements:* For master's, comprehensive exam, thesis optional. *Entrance requirements:* For master's, GRE, writing skills test, minimum GPA of 2.5, 3 letters of recommendation. Additional exam requirements/recommendations for international students: Required—TOEFL, TWE. *Faculty research:* Bilingual/multicultural education, financing post-secondary education.

Lehman College of the City University of New York, Division of Education, Department of Specialized Services in Education, Bronx, NY 10468-1589. Offers guidance and counseling (MS Ed); reading teacher (MS Ed); teachers of special education (MS Ed), including bilingual special education, early special education, emotional handicaps, learning disabilities, mental retardation. Part-time and evening/weekend programs available. *Faculty research:* Battered women, whole language classrooms, parent education, mainstreaming.

Lehman College of the City University of New York, Division of Education, Department of Specialized Services in Education, Teachers of Special Education Program, Option in Bilingual Special Education, Bronx, NY 10468-1589. Offers MS Ed. *Accreditation:* NCATE. *Entrance requirements:* For master's, minimum GPA of 3.0.

Long Island University–Brooklyn Campus, School of Education, Department of Teaching and Learning, Program in Bilingual Education, Brooklyn, NY 11201-8423. Offers MS Ed. Part-time and evening/weekend programs available. *Degree requirements:* For master's, one foreign language, thesis optional. *Entrance requirements:* For master's, 2 letters of recommendation. Additional exam requirements/recommendations for international students: Required—TOEFL (minimum score 500 paper-based; 173 computer-based). Electronic applications accepted.

Long Island University–C. W. Post Campus, School of Education, Department of Curriculum and Instruction, Brookville, NY 11548-1300. Offers adolescence education (MS); adolescence education: biology (MS); adolescence education: earth science (MS); adolescence education: English (MS); adolescence education: mathematics (MS); adolescence education: social studies (MS); adolescence education: Spanish (MS); art education (MS); bilingual education (MS); childhood education (MS); early childhood education (MS); middle childhood education (MS); music education (MS); teaching English to speakers of other languages (MS). Part-time and evening/weekend programs available. *Degree requirements:* For master's, comprehensive exam or thesis, student teaching. *Entrance requirements:* For master's, minimum GPA of 2.75 in major, 2.5 overall. Electronic applications accepted. *Faculty research:* Ethics and education, teaching strategies.

Long Island University–Hudson at Westchester, Programs in Education-Teaching, Program in Second Language, TESOL, Bilingual Education, Purchase, NY 10577. Offers MS Ed, Advanced Certificate. Part-time and evening/weekend programs available.

Loyola Marymount University, School of Education, Department of Language and Culture in Education, Program in Bilingual Elementary Education, Los Angeles, CA 90045. Offers MA. Part-time and evening/weekend programs available. *Faculty:* 6 full-time (5 women), 1 part-time/adjunct (0 women). *Students:* 10 full-time (all women), 4 part-time (3 women); includes 7 minority (1 Asian, non-Hispanic/Latino; 6 Hispanic/Latino), 4 international. Average age 30. 5 applicants, 100% accepted, 5 enrolled. In 2011, 6 master's awarded. *Degree requirements:* For master's, comprehensive exam. *Entrance requirements:* For master's, CBEST, CSET, CSET LOTE Test 3, RICA, 3 letters of recommendation. Additional exam requirements/recommendations for international students: Required—TOEFL (minimum score 600 paper-based; 250 computer-based; 100 iBT). *Application deadline:* For fall admission, 6/15 for domestic students; for spring admission, 11/15 for domestic students. Application fee: $50. Electronic applications accepted. *Financial support:* In 2011–12, 8 students received support. Scholarships/grants and unspecified assistantships available. Support available to part-time students. Financial award application deadline: 6/15; financial award applicants required to submit FAFSA. *Total annual research expenditures:* $45,315. *Unit head:* Dr. Magaly Lavadenz, Program Director, 310-338-2924, E-mail: mlavaden@lmu.edu. *Application contact:* Chake H. Kouyoumjian, Director, Graduate Admissions, 310-338-2721, Fax: 310-338-6086, E-mail: ckouyoum@lmu.edu. Web site: http://soe.lmu.edu/admissions/programs/bilingual/elem2042.htm.

Loyola Marymount University, School of Education, Department of Language and Culture in Education, Program in Bilingual Secondary Education, Los Angeles, CA 90064. Offers MA. Part-time and evening/weekend programs available. *Faculty:* 6 full-time (5 women), 1 part-time/adjunct (0 women). *Students:* 10 full-time (8 women), 2 part-time (both women); includes 10 minority (6 Asian, non-Hispanic/Latino; 4 Hispanic/Latino), 2 international. Average age 34. 8 applicants, 75% accepted, 5 enrolled. In 2011, 12 master's awarded. *Degree requirements:* For master's, comprehensive exam. *Entrance requirements:* For master's, CBEST, CSET, CEST LOTE Test 3, RICA, 3 letters of recommendation. Additional exam requirements/recommendations for international students: Required—TOEFL (minimum score 600 paper-based; 250 computer-based; 100 iBT). *Application deadline:* For fall admission, 6/15 for domestic students; for spring admission, 11/15 for domestic students. Application fee: $50. Electronic applications accepted. *Financial support:* In 2011–12, 9 students received support, including 1 research assistantship (averaging $720 per year); scholarships/grants and unspecified assistantships also available. Support available to part-time students. Financial award application deadline: 6/15; financial award applicants required to submit FAFSA. *Total annual research expenditures:* $45,315. *Unit head:* Dr. Olga Moraga, Program Director, 310-338-3778, E-mail: olga.moraga@lmu.edu. *Application contact:* Chake H. Kouyoumjian, Director, Graduate Admissions, 310-338-2721, E-mail: ckouyoum@lmu.edu. Web site: http://soe.lmu.edu/admissions/programs/bilingual/secondary2042.htm.

Manhattan College, Graduate Division, School of Education, Program in Special Education, Riverdale, NY 10471. Offers autism spectrum disorder (Professional Diploma); bilingual special education (Certificate); dual childhood/special education (MS Ed); special education (MS Ed). Part-time and evening/weekend programs available. *Faculty:* 7 full-time (5 women), 22 part-time/adjunct (19 women). *Students:* 29 full-time (27 women), 59 part-time (50 women). Average age 24. 62 applicants, 92% accepted, 57 enrolled. In 2011, 30 master's awarded. *Degree requirements:* For master's, thesis, internship (if not certified). *Entrance requirements:* For master's, LAST, minimum GPA of 3.0. Additional exam requirements/recommendations for international students: Required—TOEFL (minimum score 550 paper-based). *Application deadline:* For fall admission, 8/10 priority date for domestic students; for spring admission, 1/7 priority date for domestic students. Applications are processed on a rolling basis. Application fee: $75. *Expenses:* Contact institution. *Financial support:* Federal Work-Study, scholarships/grants, and unspecified assistantships available. Financial award application deadline: 2/1. *Unit head:* Dr. Elizabeth Mary Kosky, Director of Childhood Special Education Programs, 718-862-7969, Fax: 718-862-7816, E-mail: elizabeth.kosky@manhattan.edu. *Application contact:* William Bisset, Information Contact, 718-862-8000.

Mercy College, School of Education, Program in Bilingual Education, Dobbs Ferry, NY 10522-1189. Offers MS. Part-time and evening/weekend programs available. *Degree requirements:* For master's, thesis or alternative, capstone. *Entrance requirements:* For master's, resume, interview by faculty advisor, minimum undergraduate GPA of 3.0. Additional exam requirements/recommendations for international students: Required—TOEFL (minimum score 600 paper-based; 250 computer-based; 100 iBT), IELTS (minimum score 8). Electronic applications accepted. *Faculty research:* Literacy construction, linguistics, education assessment.

Mercy College, School of Social and Behavioral Sciences, Dobbs Ferry, NY 10522-1189. Offers counseling (MS, Certificate), including alcohol and substance abuse counseling (Certificate), counseling (MS), family counseling (Certificate); health services management (MPA, MS); marriage and family therapy (MS); mental health counseling (MS); psychology (MS); school counseling (Certificate); school counseling and bilingual extension (Certificate); school psychology (MS). Part-time and evening/weekend programs available. Postbaccalaureate distance learning degree programs offered (minimal on-campus study). *Degree requirements:* For master's, comprehensive exam (for some programs), thesis (for some programs). *Entrance requirements:* For master's, 2 letters of recommendation, interview, resume, essay. Additional exam requirements/recommendations for international students: Required—TOEFL (minimum score 600 paper-based; 250 computer-based; 100 iBT), IELTS (minimum score 8). Electronic applications accepted.

Mercyhurst College, Graduate Studies, Program in Special Education, Erie, PA 16546. Offers bilingual/bicultural special education (MS); educational leadership (Certificate); special education (MS). Part-time and evening/weekend programs available. *Faculty:* 1 full-time (0 women), 13 part-time/adjunct (8 women). *Students:* 60 full-time (51 women), 19 part-time (14 women); includes 8 minority (3 Black or African American, non-Hispanic/Latino; 1 American Indian or Alaska Native, non-Hispanic/Latino; 1 Asian, non-Hispanic/Latino; 3 Hispanic/Latino), 1 international. Average age 30. 32 applicants, 84% accepted, 18 enrolled. In 2011, 52 master's awarded. *Degree requirements:* For master's, thesis optional. *Entrance requirements:* For master's, GRE or PRAXIS I, interview, resume, essay, three professional references, transcripts. Additional exam requirements/recommendations for international students: Required—TOEFL. *Application deadline:* For fall admission, 8/1 priority date for domestic students, 8/1 for international students; for winter admission, 11/1 for domestic and international students; for spring admission, 2/1 for domestic and international students. Applications are processed on a rolling basis. Application fee: $35. Electronic applications accepted. *Expenses: Tuition:* Part-time $570 per credit. *Required fees:* $90 per term. Tuition and fees vary according to program. *Financial support:* In 2011–12, 25 students received support, including 15 research assistantships with full and partial tuition reimbursements available (averaging $8,000 per year); institutionally sponsored loans and unspecified assistantships also available. Support available to part-time students. Financial award application deadline: 5/15; financial award applicants required to submit FAFSA. *Faculty research:* College-age learning disabled program, teacher preparation/collaboration, applied behavior analysis, special education policy issues. *Total annual research expenditures:* $278,141. *Unit head:* Dr. Phillip J. Belfiore, Coordinator, 814-824-2267, Fax: 814-824-2438, E-mail: belfiore@mercyhurst.edu. *Application contact:* Sarah Murphy, Academic Coordinator, 814-824-2297, Fax: 814-824-2055, E-mail: smurphy@mercyhurst.edu. Web site: http://graduate.mercyhurst.edu/academics/graduate-degrees/special-education/.

Minnesota State University Mankato, College of Graduate Studies, College of Social and Behavioral Sciences, Department of Ethnic Studies, Mankato, MN 56001. Offers MS, Certificate. *Students:* 8 full-time (4 women), 66 part-time (3 women). *Application deadline:* For fall admission, 7/1 for domestic students, 5/1 for international students; for winter admission, 11/1 for domestic students; for spring admission, 10/1 for international students. Applications are processed on a rolling basis. Electronic applications accepted. *Unit head:* Dr. Hanh Huy Phan, Graduate Coordinator, 507-389-1185. *Application contact:* 507-389-2321, E-mail: grad@mnsu.edu. Web site: http://sbs.mnsu.edu/ethnic/.

New Jersey City University, Graduate Studies and Continuing Education, Debra Cannon Partridge Wolfe College of Education, Department of Educational Leadership, Jersey City, NJ 07305-1597. Offers basics and urban studies (MA); bilingual/bicultural education and English as a second language (MA); educational administration and supervision (MA). Part-time and evening/weekend programs available. *Students:* 16 full-time (12 women), 167 part-time (113 women); includes 72 minority (18 Black or African American, non-Hispanic/Latino; 3 Asian, non-Hispanic/Latino; 51 Hispanic/Latino), 6 international. Average age 34. In 2011, 126 master's awarded. *Entrance requirements:* Additional exam requirements/recommendations for international students: Required—TOEFL. *Application deadline:* For fall admission, 8/1 priority date for domestic students; for spring admission, 12/1 for domestic students. Applications are processed on a rolling basis. Application fee: $0. *Expenses:* Tuition, state resident: part-time $494 per credit. Tuition, nonresident: part-time $911.30 per credit. *Required fees:* $95.90 per year. *Financial support:* Fellowships, teaching assistantships, career-related internships or fieldwork, and unspecified assistantships available. *Unit head:* Dr. Catherine Rogers, Chairperson, 201-200-3012, E-mail: cshevey@njcu.edu. *Application contact:* Dr. William Bajor, Dean of Graduate Studies, 201-200-3409, Fax: 201-200-3411, E-mail: wbajor@njcu.edu.

New Mexico State University, Graduate School, College of Education, Department of Special Education and Communication Disorders, Las Cruces, NM 88003-8001. Offers bilingual/multicultural special education (Ed D, PhD); communication disorders (MA); special education (MA, Ed D, PhD). *Accreditation:* ASHA (one or more programs are accredited); NCATE. Part-time and evening/weekend programs available. Postbaccalaureate distance learning degree programs offered. *Faculty:* 13 full-time (11 women), 1 part-time/adjunct (0 women). *Students:* 69 full-time (65 women), 56 part-time (41 women); includes 55 minority (2 American Indian or Alaska Native, non-Hispanic/Latino; 1 Asian, non-Hispanic/Latino; 51 Hispanic/Latino; 1 Two or more races, non-Hispanic/Latino), 4 international. Average age 37. 111 applicants, 32% accepted, 30 enrolled. In 2011, 41 master's, 3 doctorates awarded. *Degree requirements:* For master's, comprehensive exam, thesis optional; for doctorate, comprehensive exam, thesis/dissertation. *Entrance requirements:* For master's, GRE General Test or MAT. Additional exam requirements/recommendations for international students: Required—TOEFL (minimum score 550 paper-based; 79 iBT), IELTS (minimum score 6.5). *Application deadline:* For fall admission, 2/1 priority date for domestic students. Applications are processed on a rolling basis. Application fee: $40 ($50 for international students). Electronic applications accepted. *Expenses:* Tuition, state resident: full-time $5004; part-time $208.50 per credit. Tuition, nonresident: full-time $17,446; part-time $726.90 per credit. *Financial support:* In 2011–12, 1 research assistantship (averaging $1,975 per year), 16 teaching assistantships (averaging $10,248 per year) were awarded; fellowships, career-related internships or fieldwork, Federal Work-Study, and health care benefits also available. Support available to part-time students. Financial award application deadline: 3/1; financial award applicants required to submit FAFSA. *Faculty research:* Multicultural special education, multicultural communication disorders, mild disability, multicultural assessment, deaf education, early childhood, bilingual special education. *Unit head:* Dr. Eric Joseph Lopez, Interim Department Head, 575-646-2402, Fax: 575-646-7712, E-mail: leric@nmsu.edu. *Application contact:* Coordinator, 575-646-2736, Fax: 575-646-7721, E-mail: gradinfo@nmsu.edu. Web site: http://education.nmsu.edu/spedcd/.

New York University, Steinhardt School of Culture, Education, and Human Development, Department of Humanities and Social Sciences in the Professions, Program in Sociology of Education, New York, NY 10012-1019. Offers education and social policy (MA); sociology of education (MA, PhD), including education policy (MA), social and cultural studies of education (MA). Part-time programs available. *Faculty:* 14 full-time (7 women). *Students:* 43 full-time (35 women), 22 part-time (16 women); includes 19 minority (10 Black or African American, non-Hispanic/Latino; 3 Asian, non-Hispanic/Latino; 5 Hispanic/Latino; 1 Two or more races, non-Hispanic/Latino), 13 international. Average age 29. 127 applicants, 86% accepted, 33 enrolled. In 2011, 7 master's, 1 doctorate awarded. *Degree requirements:* For master's, thesis (for some programs); for doctorate, thesis/dissertation. *Entrance requirements:* For master's, letters of recommendation; for doctorate, GRE General Test, interview. Additional exam requirements/recommendations for international students: Required—TOEFL. *Application deadline:* For fall admission, 12/1 priority date for domestic students, 12/1 for international students; for spring admission, 11/1 for domestic and international students. Applications are processed on a rolling basis. Application fee: $75. Electronic applications accepted. *Financial support:* Fellowships with full and partial tuition reimbursements, Federal Work-Study, institutionally sponsored loans, scholarships/grants, and tuition waivers (partial) available. Support available to part-time students. Financial award application deadline: 2/1; financial award applicants required to submit FAFSA. *Faculty research:* Legal and institutional environments of schools; social inequality; high school reform and achievement; urban schooling, economics and education, educational policy. *Unit head:* Dr. Floyd M. Hammack, Program Director, 212-998-5542, Fax: 212-995-4832, E-mail: fmhl@nyu.edu. *Application contact:* 212-998-5030, Fax: 212-995-4328, E-mail: steinhardt.gradadmissions@nyu.edu. Web site: http://steinhardt.nyu.edu/humsocsci/sociology.

New York University, Steinhardt School of Culture, Education, and Human Development, Department of Teaching and Learning, Program in Multilingual/Multicultural Studies, New York, NY 10012-1019. Offers bilingual education (MA, PhD, Advanced Certificate); foreign language education (MA, Advanced Certificate); foreign language education/TESOL (MA); teaching English to speakers of other languages (MA, PhD, Advanced Certificate); teaching French as a foreign language (MA). *Accreditation:* Teacher Education Accreditation Council. Part-time and evening/weekend programs available. *Degree requirements:* For master's, thesis (for some programs); for doctorate, thesis/dissertation. *Entrance requirements:* For doctorate, GRE General Test, interview; for Advanced Certificate, master's degree. Additional exam requirements/recommendations for international students: Required—TOEFL. Electronic applications accepted. *Faculty research:* Second language acquisition, cross-cultural communication, technology-enhanced language learning, language variation, action learning.

Northeastern Illinois University, Graduate College, College of Education, School of Teacher Education, Program in Bilingual/Bicultural Education, Chicago, IL 60625-4699. Offers MAT, MSI. *Entrance requirements:* For master's, GRE, minimum GPA of 2.75. Additional exam requirements/recommendations for international students: Required—TOEFL (minimum score 550 paper-based; 213 computer-based; 79 iBT). Electronic applications accepted. *Faculty research:* Bilingual teacher preparation, linguistics and phonetics, Middle Eastern languages and cultures, TOEFL.

Northern Arizona University, Graduate College, College of Education, Department of Educational Specialties, Flagstaff , AZ 86011. Offers autism spectrum disorders (Certificate); bilingual/multicultural education (M Ed), including bilingual education, ESL education; career and technical education (M Ed, Certificate); curriculum and instruction (Ed D); early childhood special education (M Ed); early intervention (Certificate); educational technology (M Ed, Certificate); special education (M Ed). *Faculty:* 28 full-time (19 women). *Students:* 113 full-time (91 women), 206 part-time (158 women); includes 104 minority (8 Black or African American, non-Hispanic/Latino; 17 American Indian or Alaska Native, non-Hispanic/Latino; 6 Asian, non-Hispanic/Latino; 65 Hispanic/Latino; 2 Native Hawaiian or other Pacific Islander, non-Hispanic/Latino; 6 Two or more races, non-Hispanic/Latino), 3 international. Average age 30. 141 applicants, 75% accepted, 76 enrolled. In 2011, 167 master's, 7 Certificates awarded. *Degree requirements:* For master's, comprehensive exam (for some programs), thesis (for some programs). *Entrance requirements:* For master's, minimum GPA of 3.0. Additional exam requirements/recommendations for international students: Required—TOEFL (minimum score 550 paper-based; 213 computer-based; 80 iBT), IELTS (minimum score 7). *Application deadline:* For fall admission, 3/1 for international students; for spring admission, 9/15 for international students. Applications are processed on a rolling basis. Application fee: $65. Electronic applications accepted. *Expenses:* Tuition, state resident: full-time $7190; part-time $355 per credit hour. Tuition, nonresident: full-time $18,092; part-time $1005 per credit hour. *Required fees:* $818; $328 per semester. *Financial support:* Applicants required to submit FAFSA. *Unit head:* Dr. Jennifer Prior, Chair, 928-523-5064, Fax: 928-523-1929, E-mail: jennifer.prior@nau.edu. *Application contact:* Shirley Robinson, Coordinator, 928-523-4348, Fax: 928-523-8950, E-mail: shirley.robinson@nau.edu. Web site: http://nau.edu/coe/ed-specialties/.

Ohio University, Graduate College, Gladys W. and David H. Patton College of Education and Human Services, Department of Educational Studies, Athens, OH 45701-2979. Offers computer education and technology (M Ed); cultural studies (M Ed); educational administration (M Ed, Ed D); educational research and evaluation (M Ed, PhD); instructional technology (PhD). Part-time and evening/weekend programs available. Postbaccalaureate distance learning degree programs offered (minimal on-campus study). *Students:* 121 full-time (76 women), 94 part-time (57 women); includes 21 minority (15 Black or African American, non-Hispanic/Latino; 1 American Indian or Alaska Native, non-Hispanic/Latino; 2 Hispanic/Latino; 3 Two or more races, non-Hispanic/Latino), 35 international. 73 applicants, 67% accepted, 32 enrolled. In 2011, 52 master's, 13 doctorates awarded. *Degree requirements:* For master's, thesis or alternative; for doctorate, comprehensive exam, thesis/dissertation. *Entrance requirements:* For master's, GRE General Test (if GPA less than 2.9); for doctorate, GRE General Test, GRE Subject Test, minimum GPA of 2.9, work experience, 3 letters of reference, autobiography. Additional exam requirements/recommendations for international students: Required—TOEFL (minimum score 550 paper-based; 80 iBT) or IELTS (minimum score 6.5). *Application deadline:* For fall admission, 3/1 priority date for domestic students, 3/1 for international students; for winter admission, 10/1 priority date for domestic students, 10/1 for international students; for spring admission, 1/30 priority date for domestic students, 1/1 for international students. Applications are processed on a rolling basis. Application fee: $50 ($55 for international students). Electronic applications accepted. *Financial support:* Research assistantships with full tuition reimbursements, teaching assistantships with full tuition reimbursements, Federal Work-Study, institutionally sponsored loans, tuition waivers (partial), and unspecified assistantships available. Financial award application deadline: 3/1. *Faculty research:* Race, class and gender; computer programs; development and organization theory; evaluation/development of instruments, leadership. *Total annual research expenditures:* $158,037. *Unit head:* Dr. David Richard Moore, Chair, 740-597-1322, Fax: 740-593-0477, E-mail: moored3@ohio.edu. *Application contact:* Floyd J. Doney, Director of Student Affairs, 740-593-4400, Fax: 740-593-9310, E-mail: doney@ohio.edu. Web site: http://www.cehs.ohio.edu/academics/es/.

Our Lady of the Lake University of San Antonio, School of Professional Studies, Program in Curriculum and Instruction, San Antonio, TX 78207-4689. Offers bilingual (M Ed); early childhood education (M Ed); English as a second language (M Ed); integrated math teaching (M Ed); integrated science teaching (M Ed); master reading teacher (M Ed); master technology teacher (M Ed); reading specialist (M Ed).

Park University, College of Graduate and Professional Studies, Kansas City, MO 54105. Offers adult education (M Ed); at-risk students (M Ed); disaster and emergency management (MPA); educational administration (M Ed); entrepreneurship (MBA); general business (MBA); general education (M Ed); government/business relations (MPA); healthcare/services management (MBA, MPA); international business (MBA); K-12 certification (MAT); management information systems (MBA); management of information systems (MPA); middle school certification (MAT); multi-cultural education (M Ed); nonprofit management (MPA); public management (MPA); school law (M Ed); secondary school certification (MAT); special education (M Ed). Part-time and evening/weekend programs available. Postbaccalaureate distance learning degree programs offered (no on-campus study). *Degree requirements:* For master's, comprehensive exam, thesis (for some programs). *Entrance requirements:* For master's, GRE, GMAT, teacher certification (M Ed). Additional exam requirements/recommendations for international students: Required—TOEFL (minimum score 550 paper-based). Electronic applications accepted. *Faculty research:* Literacy, leadership, brain based research, multicultural education, diversity.

Queens College of the City University of New York, Division of Graduate Studies, Division of Education, Department of Elementary and Early Childhood Education, Flushing, NY 11367-1597. Offers bilingual education (MS Ed); childhood education (MA); early childhood education (MA); elementary education (MS Ed, AC); literacy (MS Ed). Part-time and evening/weekend programs available. *Faculty:* 31 full-time (25 women). *Students:* 87 full-time (74 women), 561 part-time (522 women); includes 226 minority (49 Black or African American, non-Hispanic/Latino; 68 Asian, non-Hispanic/Latino; 109 Hispanic/Latino), 5 international. 436 applicants, 64% accepted, 212 enrolled. In 2011, 229 master's, 1 other advanced degree awarded. *Degree requirements:* For master's, research project; for AC, thesis optional. *Entrance requirements:* For master's, minimum GPA of 3.0. Additional exam requirements/recommendations for international students: Required—TOEFL. *Application deadline:* For fall admission, 4/1 for domestic students; for spring admission, 11/1 for domestic students. Applications are processed on a rolling basis. Application fee: $125. *Expenses:* Tuition, state resident: part-time $345 per credit. Tuition, nonresident: part-time $640 per credit. *Required fees:* $145.25 per semester. *Financial support:* Career-related internships or fieldwork, Federal Work-Study, institutionally sponsored loans, and tuition waivers (partial) available. Support available to part-time students. Financial award application deadline: 4/1; financial award applicants required to submit FAFSA. *Unit head:* Dr. Myra Zarnowski, Chairperson, 718-997-5328. *Application contact:* Mario Caruso, Director of Graduate Admissions, 718-997-5200, Fax: 718-997-5193, E-mail: graduate_admissions@qc.edu.

Rowan University, Graduate School, College of Education, Department of Teacher Education, Program in ESL/Bilingual Education, Glassboro, NJ 08028-1701. Offers Graduate Certificate. Part-time and evening/weekend programs available. *Entrance requirements:* Additional exam requirements/recommendations for international students: Required—TOEFL. Electronic applications accepted.

Rutgers, The State University of New Jersey, New Brunswick, Graduate School-New Brunswick, Program in Spanish, Piscataway, NJ 08854-8097. Offers bilingualism and second language acquisition (MA, PhD); Spanish (MA, MAT, PhD); Spanish literature (MA, PhD); translation (MA). Part-time programs available. *Degree requirements:* For master's, comprehensive exam (for some programs), thesis (for some programs); for doctorate, 2 foreign languages, comprehensive exam, thesis/dissertation. *Entrance requirements:* For master's and doctorate, GRE General Test. Additional exam requirements/recommendations for international students: Required—TOEFL. Electronic applications accepted. *Faculty research:* Hispanic literature, Luso-Brazilian literature, Spanish linguistics, Spanish translation.

St. John's University, The School of Education, Department of Human Services and Counseling, Program in School Counseling with Bilingual Extension, Queens, NY 11439. Offers MS Ed. Part-time and evening/weekend programs available. *Students:* 12 full-time (all women), 7 part-time (all women); includes 15 minority (1 Asian, non-Hispanic/Latino; 14 Hispanic/Latino), 1 international. Average age 27. 8 applicants, 75% accepted, 2 enrolled. In 2011, 4 master's awarded. *Degree requirements:* For master's, comprehensive exam. *Entrance requirements:* For master's, GRE, New York State Bilingual Assessment (BEA), bachelor's degree from an accredited college or university, minimum GPA of 3.0, 2 letters of recommendation, interview, minimum of 18 credits in behavioral or social science. Additional exam requirements/recommendations for international students: Required—TOEFL (minimum score 600 paper-based; 250 computer-based; 100 iBT), IELTS (minimum score 5.5). *Application deadline:* For fall admission, 4/1 for domestic and international students; for spring admission, 11/1 for domestic and international students. Applications are processed on a rolling basis. Application fee: $70. Electronic applications accepted. *Expenses: Tuition:* Full-time $18,000; part-time $1000 per credit. *Required fees:* $170 per semester. Tuition and fees vary according to program. *Financial support:* Research assistantships, career-related internships or fieldwork, and scholarships/grants available. Support available to part-time students. Financial award application deadline: 3/1; financial award applicants required to submit FAFSA. *Faculty research:* Cross-cultural comparisons of predictors of active coping. *Unit head:* Dr. Francine Guastello, Chair, 718-990-1475, E-mail: guastelf@stjohns.edu. *Application contact:* Dr. Kelly K. Ronayne, Associate Dean for Graduate Admissions, 718-990-2304, Fax: 718-990-2343, E-mail: graded@stjohns.edu.

San Diego State University, Graduate and Research Affairs, College of Education, Department of Policy Studies in Language and Cross Cultural Education, San Diego, CA 92182. Offers multi-cultural emphasis (PhD); policy studies in language and cross cultural education (MA). *Accreditation:* NCATE. *Entrance requirements:* For master's, GRE General Test, letters of reference; for doctorate, GRE General Test, 3 letters of reference, resumé. Additional exam requirements/recommendations for international students: Required—TOEFL. Electronic applications accepted.

Southern Connecticut State University, School of Graduate Studies, School of Arts and Sciences, Department of Foreign Languages, New Haven, CT 06515-1355. Offers multicultural-bilingual education/teaching English to speakers of other languages (MS). Part-time and evening/weekend programs available. *Faculty:* 6 full-time (4 women), 1 (woman) part-time/adjunct. *Students:* 9 full-time (6 women), 40 part-time (35 women); includes 15 minority (14 Hispanic/Latino; 1 Two or more races, non-Hispanic/Latino). 93 applicants, 28% accepted, 19 enrolled. In 2011, 18 master's awarded. *Degree requirements:* For master's, one foreign language, thesis or alternative. *Entrance requirements:* For master's, interview, minimum undergraduate GPA of 2.7. *Application deadline:* For fall admission, 7/15 priority date for domestic students. Applications are processed on a rolling basis. Application fee: $50. Electronic applications accepted. *Expenses:* Tuition, state resident: full-time $5137; part-time $413 per credit. *Required fees:* $4008; $55 per term. *Financial support:* Application deadline: 4/15; applicants required to submit FAFSA. *Unit head:* Dr. Elena Schmitt, Chairperson, 203-392-6138, Fax: 203-392-6136, E-mail: schmitte1@southernct.edu. *Application contact:* Dr. Luisa Piemontese, Graduate Coordinator, 203-392-6751, E-mail: piemontesel1@southernct.edu.

Southern Methodist University, Annette Caldwell Simmons School of Education and Human Development, Department of Teaching and Learning, Dallas, TX 75275. Offers bilingual/ESL education (MBE); education (M Ed, PhD); educational preparation (Certificate); gifted and talented focus (MBE); learning therapist (Certificate). Part-time and evening/weekend programs available. Terminal master's awarded for partial completion of doctoral program. *Degree requirements:* For master's, comprehensive exam, minimum GPA of 3.0; for doctorate, thesis/dissertation, qualifying exams, major area paper, evidence of teaching competency, dissemination of research (e.g., conference presentation), professional portfolio. *Entrance requirements:* For master's, minimum GPA of 3.0 or GRE, 3 letters of recommendation; for doctorate, GRE, minimum GPA of 3.3, 3 years of full-time teaching, 3 letters of recommendation, interview. Additional exam requirements/recommendations for international students: Required—TOEFL. Electronic applications accepted. *Faculty research:* Reading intervention, mathematics intervention, bilingual education, new literacies.

State University of New York at New Paltz, Graduate School, School of Education, Department of Educational Studies, Program in Humanistic/Multicultural Education, New Paltz, NY 12561. Offers MPS. *Accreditation:* NCATE. Part-time and evening/weekend programs available. *Students:* 13 full-time (10 women), 41 part-time (28 women); includes 20 minority (8 Black or African American, non-Hispanic/Latino; 3 Asian, non-Hispanic/Latino; 5 Hispanic/Latino; 4 Two or more races, non-Hispanic/Latino), 2 international. Average age 32. 29 applicants, 69% accepted, 15 enrolled. In 2011, 16 master's awarded. *Degree requirements:* For master's, portfolio. *Entrance requirements:* For master's, minimum GPA of 3.0. Additional exam requirements/recommendations for international students: Required—TOEFL (minimum score 550 paper-based; 213 computer-based; 80 iBT), IELTS (minimum score 6.5). *Application deadline:* For fall admission, 3/15 priority date for domestic students, 3/15 for international students; for spring admission, 10/15 for domestic and international students. Application fee: $50. Electronic applications accepted. *Expenses:* Tuition, state resident: full-time $8870; part-time $370 per credit. Tuition, nonresident: full-time $15,160; part-time $632 per credit. *Required fees:* $1188; $34 per credit. $184 per semester. *Financial support:* In 2011–12, 3 students received support, including 4 fellowships with partial tuition reimbursements available (averaging $4,400 per year); tuition waivers (full) also available. Financial award application deadline: 8/1; financial award applicants required to submit FAFSA. *Unit head:* Dr. Nancy Schniedewind, Coordinator, 845-257-2827, E-mail: schniedn@newpaltz.edu. *Application contact:* Caroline Murphy, Graduate Admissions Advisor, 845-257-3285, E-mail: gradschool@newpaltz.edu.

State University of New York College at Geneseo, Graduate Studies, School of Education, Program in Childhood Multicultural Education (1-6), Geneseo, NY 14454-1401. Offers MS Ed. Part-time and evening/weekend programs available. *Degree requirements:* For master's, thesis optional, culminating experience.

Sul Ross State University, Rio Grande College of Sul Ross State University, Alpine, TX 79832. Offers business administration (MBA); teacher education (M Ed), including bilingual education, counseling, educational diagnostics, elementary education, general education, reading, school administration, secondary education. Part-time and evening/weekend programs available. Postbaccalaureate distance learning degree programs offered (no on-campus study). *Faculty:* 11 full-time (3 women), 4 part-time/adjunct (3 women). *Students:* 45 full-time (36 women), 255 part-time (168 women); includes 218 minority (2 Black or African American, non-Hispanic/Latino; 1 American Indian or Alaska Native, non-Hispanic/Latino; 215 Hispanic/Latino), 1 international. Average age 36. In 2011, 47 master's awarded. *Degree requirements:* For master's, comprehensive exam, thesis optional, minimum GPA of 3.0. *Entrance requirements:* For master's, GMAT or GRE General Test, minimum GPA of 2.5 in last 60 hours of undergraduate work. Additional exam requirements/recommendations for international students: Required—TOEFL. *Application deadline:* Applications are processed on a rolling basis. Application fee: $0 ($50 for international students). *Financial support:* Career-related internships or fieldwork, Federal Work-Study, and institutionally sponsored loans available. Support available to part-time students. Financial award application deadline: 5/1; financial award applicants required to submit FAFSA. *Unit head:* Dr. Paul Sorrels, Associate Provost/Dean, 512-278-3339, Fax: 512-278-3330. *Application contact:* Claudia R. Wright, Director of Admissions and Records, 915-837-8050, Fax: 915-837-8431, E-mail: rcullins@sulross.edu.

Sul Ross State University, School of Professional Studies, Department of Teacher Education, Program in Bilingual Education, Alpine, TX 79832. Offers M Ed. Part-time and evening/weekend programs available. *Degree requirements:* For master's, thesis optional. *Entrance requirements:* For master's, GMAT or GRE General Test, minimum GPA of 2.5 in last 60 hours of undergraduate work.

Teachers College, Columbia University, Graduate Faculty of Education, Department of International and Transcultural Studies, Program in Bilingual and Bicultural Education, New York, NY 10027-6696. Offers MA. *Accreditation:* NCATE. Part-time programs available. *Faculty:* 2 full-time (both women), 2 part-time/adjunct (both women). *Students:* 11 full-time (10 women), 82 part-time (74 women); includes 47 minority (2 Black or African American, non-Hispanic/Latino; 10 Asian, non-Hispanic/Latino; 33 Hispanic/Latino; 2 Two or more races, non-Hispanic/Latino), 12 international. Average age 27. 43 applicants, 72% accepted, 26 enrolled. In 2011, 26 master's awarded. *Degree* *requirements:* For master's, one foreign language. *Application deadline:* For fall admission, 5/15 for domestic students. Application fee: $65. *Financial support:* Research assistantships, career-related internships or fieldwork, Federal Work-Study, institutionally sponsored loans, scholarships/grants, and tuition waivers (full and partial) available. Support available to part-time students. Financial award application deadline: 2/1. *Faculty research:* Cross-cultural research in bilingual and bicultural school settings, diversity and teacher education. *Unit head:* Prof. Maria Torres-Guzman, Chair, 212-678-3758. *Application contact:* Deanna Ghozati, Associate Director of Admission, 212-678-3710, Fax: 212-678-4171, E-mail: tcinfo@tc.edu.

Texas A&M University, College of Education and Human Development, Department of Educational Psychology, College Station, TX 77843. Offers bilingual education (M Ed, PhD); cognition, creativity, instruction and development (MS, PhD); counseling psychology (PhD); educational psychology (PhD); educational technology (PhD); research, measurement and statistics (MS); research, measurement, and statistics (PhD); school psychology (PhD); special education (M Ed, PhD). *Accreditation:* APA (one or more programs are accredited). Part-time and evening/weekend programs available. Postbaccalaureate distance learning degree programs offered (no on-campus study). *Faculty:* 46. *Students:* 151 full-time (124 women), 123 part-time (101 women); includes 97 minority (20 Black or African American, non-Hispanic/Latino; 11 Asian, non-Hispanic/Latino; 59 Hispanic/Latino; 7 Two or more races, non-Hispanic/Latino), 50 international. In 2011, 58 master's, 33 doctorates awarded. *Degree requirements:* For master's, thesis optional; for doctorate, thesis/dissertation. *Entrance requirements:* For master's and doctorate, GRE General Test. Additional exam requirements/recommendations for international students: Required—TOEFL. Application fee: $50 ($75 for international students). Electronic applications accepted. *Expenses:* Tuition, state resident: full-time $5437; part-time $226.55 per credit hour. Tuition, nonresident: full-time $12,949; part-time $539.55 per credit hour. *Required fees:* $2741. *Financial support:* In 2011–12, fellowships (averaging $12,000 per year), research assistantships (averaging $9,000 per year), teaching assistantships (averaging $9,000 per year) were awarded; career-related internships or fieldwork, institutionally sponsored loans, scholarships/grants, and unspecified assistantships also available. Financial award applicants required to submit FAFSA. *Unit head:* Dr. Victor Willson, Head, 979-845-1800. *Application contact:* Carol A. Wagner, Director of Advising, 979-845-1833, Fax: 979-862-1256, E-mail: epsyadvisor@tamu.edu. Web site: http://epsy.tamu.edu.

Texas A&M University–Commerce, Graduate School, College of Education and Human Services, Department of Curriculum and Instruction, Commerce, TX 75429-3011. Offers bilingual/ESL education (M Ed, MS); early childhood education (M Ed, MS); elementary education (M Ed, MS); reading (M Ed, MS); secondary education (M Ed, MS); supervision, curriculum and instruction: elementary education (Ed D). MS and M Ed programs in early childhood education offered jointly with Texas Woman's University and University of North Texas. Part-time programs available. Terminal master's awarded for partial completion of doctoral program. *Degree requirements:* For master's, comprehensive exam, thesis (for some programs); for doctorate, 2 foreign languages, thesis/dissertation, departmental qualifying exam. *Entrance requirements:* For master's and doctorate, GRE General Test. Electronic applications accepted. *Faculty research:* Literacy and learning, early childhood, preservice teacher education, technology.

Texas A&M University–Kingsville, College of Graduate Studies, College of Education, Department of Bilingual Education, Kingsville, TX 78363. Offers MA, MS, Ed D. *Degree requirements:* For master's, one foreign language, comprehensive exam, thesis or alternative; for doctorate, one foreign language, comprehensive exam, thesis/dissertation. *Entrance requirements:* For master's, GRE General Test, minimum GPA of 3.0; for doctorate, GRE General Test, MAT, minimum GPA of 3.25. *Faculty research:* Language acquisition, acculturation in minority communities, English as a second language strategies.

Texas A&M University–San Antonio, Department of Curriculum and Kinesiology, San Antonio, TX 78224. Offers bilingual education (MA); early childhood education (M Ed); kinesiology (MS); reading (MS); special education (M Ed), including educational diagnostician, instructional specialist. Part-time and evening/weekend programs available. *Students:* 76 full-time (51 women), 240 part-time (180 women). Average age 37. *Degree requirements:* For master's, comprehensive exam, thesis or alternative. *Entrance requirements:* For master's, MAT. Additional exam requirements/recommendations for international students: Required—TOEFL (minimum score 550 paper-based; 213 computer-based; 80 iBT), IELTS (minimum score 6). *Application deadline:* For fall admission, 8/15 priority date for domestic students, 6/1 for international students; for spring admission, 12/15 priority date for domestic students, 10/1 for international students. Applications are processed on a rolling basis. Application fee: $35 ($50 for international students). Electronic applications accepted. *Expenses:* Tuition, state resident: part-time $691.11 per course. Tuition, nonresident: part-time $1621.11 per course. *Financial support:* Application deadline: 3/31; applicants required to submit FAFSA. *Unit head:* Dr. Samuel Garcia, Department Chair, 210-784-2505, E-mail: samuel.garcia@tamusa.tamus.edu. *Application contact:* Jennifer M. Dovalina, Graduate Admissions Specialist, 210-784-1380, E-mail: graduateadmissions@tamusa.tamus.edu. Web site: http://www.tamusa.tamus.edu/education/index.html.

Texas Southern University, College of Education, Area of Curriculum and Instruction, Houston, TX 77004-4584. Offers bilingual education (M Ed); curriculum and instruction (Ed D); secondary education (M Ed). Part-time and evening/weekend programs available. *Degree requirements:* For master's, comprehensive exam; for doctorate, comprehensive exam, thesis/dissertation. *Entrance requirements:* For master's, GRE General Test, minimum GPA of 2.5; for doctorate, GRE General Test or MAT, master's degree, minimum B+ average. Additional exam requirements/recommendations for international students: Required—TOEFL. Electronic applications accepted.

Texas State University–San Marcos, Graduate School, College of Education, Department of Curriculum and Instruction, Program in Elementary Education-Bilingual/Bicultural, San Marcos, TX 78666. Offers M Ed, MA. Part-time programs available. *Faculty:* 5 full-time (all women). *Students:* 7 full-time (6 women), 14 part-time (11 women); includes 15 minority (all Hispanic/Latino), 2 international. Average age 29. 24 applicants, 58% accepted, 7 enrolled. In 2011, 11 master's awarded. *Degree requirements:* For master's, comprehensive exam, thesis optional. *Entrance requirements:* For master's, minimum GPA of 2.75 in last 60 hours of course work, teaching experience. Additional exam requirements/recommendations for international students: Required—TOEFL (minimum score 550 paper-based; 213 computer-based; 78 iBT). *Application deadline:* For fall admission, 6/15 priority date for domestic students, 6/1 for international students; for spring admission, 10/15 priority date for domestic students, 10/1 for international students. Applications are processed on a rolling basis. Application fee: $40 ($90 for international students). Electronic applications accepted. *Expenses:* Tuition, state resident: full-time $6408; part-time $3204 per semester. Tuition, nonresident: full-time $14,832; part-time $7416 per semester. *Required fees:* $1824; $912 per semester. Tuition and fees vary according to course load. *Financial support:* In 2011–12, 11 students received support, including 1 teaching assistantship (averaging $10,152 per year); career-related internships or fieldwork, Federal Work-Study, institutionally sponsored loans, and unspecified assistantships also available. Support available to part-time students. Financial award application deadline: 4/1; financial award applicants required to submit FAFSA. *Unit head:* Dr. Roxanne Allsup, Graduate Advisor, 512-245-2041, Fax: 512-245-7911, E-mail: ra17@txstate.edu. *Application contact:* Dr. J. Michael Willoughby, Dean of Graduate School, 512-245-2581, Fax: 512-245-8365, E-mail: gradcollege@txstate.edu. Web site: http://www.education.txstate.edu/ci/degrees-programs/graduate/elementary-education.html.

Texas Tech University, Graduate School, College of Education, Department of Curriculum and Instruction, Lubbock, TX 79409. Offers bilingual education (M Ed); curriculum and instruction (M Ed, PhD); elementary education (M Ed); language/literacy education (M Ed); secondary education (M Ed). *Accreditation:* NCATE. Part-time programs available. *Students:* 69 full-time (50 women), 115 part-time (91 women); includes 62 minority (9 Black or African American, non-Hispanic/Latino; 3 Asian, non-Hispanic/Latino; 47 Hispanic/Latino; 3 Two or more races, non-Hispanic/Latino), 18 international. Average age 34. 95 applicants, 41% accepted, 26 enrolled. In 2011, 62 master's, 9 doctorates awarded. *Degree requirements:* For master's, comprehensive written exam with 36 hours of course credit or thesis (6 hours) with 30 hours of course credit; for doctorate, thesis/dissertation. *Entrance requirements:* For doctorate, GRE General Test. Additional exam requirements/recommendations for international students: Required—TOEFL (minimum score 550 paper-based; 213 computer-based; 79 iBT). *Application deadline:* For fall admission, 6/1 priority date for domestic students, 1/15 for international students; for spring admission, 9/1 priority date for domestic students, 6/15 for international students. Applications are processed on a rolling basis. Application fee: $50 ($75 for international students). Electronic applications accepted. *Expenses:* Tuition, state resident: full-time $5899; part-time $245.80 per credit hour. Tuition, nonresident: full-time $13,411; part-time $558.80 per credit hour. *Required fees:* $2680.60; $86.50 per credit hour. $920.30 per semester. *Financial support:* In 2011–12, 58 students received support. Application deadline: 4/15; applicants required to submit FAFSA. *Faculty research:* Multicultural foundations of education, teacher education, instruction and pedagogy in subject areas, curriculum theory, language and literary. *Total annual research expenditures:* $948,943. *Unit head:* Dr. Margaret A. Price, Interim Chair, 806-742-1997 Ext. 318, Fax: 806-742-2179, E-mail: peggie.price@ttu.edu. *Application contact:* Stephenie Allyn McDaniel, Administrative Assistant, 806-742-1988 Ext. 434, Fax: 806-742-2179, E-mail: stephenie.mcdaniel@ttu.edu.

Touro College, Graduate School of Education, New York, NY 10010. Offers bilingual programs (Advanced Certificate); education and special education (MS); gifted and talented education (Advanced Certificate); instructional technology (MS); mathematics education (MS); school leadership (MS); teaching children with autism and other severe or multiple disabilities (Advanced Certificate); teaching English to speakers of other languages (MS, Advanced Certificate); teaching literacy (MS). Part-time and evening/weekend programs available. Postbaccalaureate distance learning degree programs offered (no on-campus study). *Faculty:* 75 full-time, 131 part-time/adjunct. *Students:* 382 full-time (324 women), 3,790 part-time (3,196 women); includes 1,211 minority (537 Black or African American, non-Hispanic/Latino; 4 American Indian or Alaska Native, non-Hispanic/Latino; 187 Asian, non-Hispanic/Latino; 472 Hispanic/Latino; 3 Native Hawaiian or other Pacific Islander, non-Hispanic/Latino; 8 Two or more races, non-Hispanic/Latino), 1 international. 1,422 applicants, 50% accepted, 675 enrolled. In 2011, 6 master's, 4 other advanced degrees awarded. *Application deadline:* For fall admission, 8/26 for domestic students, 7/15 for international students; for spring admission, 12/31 for domestic students, 12/15 for international students. Applications are processed on a rolling basis. Application fee: $50. *Financial support:* Federal Work-Study available. Financial award applicants required to submit FAFSA. *Faculty research:* Equity assistance, language development, scholar communications, Latin American studies and cultural sensitivity, behavior management techniques and strategies in special education. *Unit head:* Dr. LaMar Miller, Dean, 212-463-0400 Ext. 5561, Fax: 212-462-4889, E-mail: lpmiller@touro.edu. *Application contact:* Natalie Arroyo, Admissions Assistant, 212-463-0400 Ext. 5119, E-mail: natalie.arroyo@touro.edu.

University at Buffalo, the State University of New York, Graduate School, Graduate School of Education, Department of Learning and Instruction, Buffalo, NY 14260. Offers biology education (Ed M, Certificate); chemistry education (Ed M, Certificate); childhood education (Ed M); childhood education with bilingual extension (Ed M); early childhood education (Ed M); early childhood education with bilingual extension (birth-grade 2) (Ed M); earth science education (Ed M, Certificate); educational technology and new literacies (Certificate); educational technology and new literacies (online) (Certificate); elementary education (Ed D, PhD); English education (Ed M, PhD, Certificate); English for speakers of other languages (Ed M); foreign and second language education (PhD); French education (Ed M, Certificate); general education (Ed M); German education (Ed M, Certificate); gifted education (online) (Certificate); Latin education (Ed M, Certificate); literacy teaching and learning (Certificate); literary specialist (Ed M); mathematics education (Ed M, PhD, Certificate); music education (Ed M, Certificate); physics education (Ed M, Certificate); reading education (PhD); science and the public (online) (Ed M); science education (PhD); social studies education (Ed M, Certificate); Spanish education (Ed M, Certificate); special education (PhD); teaching and leading for diversity (Certificate); teaching English to speakers of other languages (Ed M). Part-time and evening/weekend programs available. Postbaccalaureate distance learning degree programs offered (no on-campus study). *Faculty:* 32 full-time (23 women), 54 part-time/adjunct (43 women). *Students:* 294 full-time (222 women), 350 part-time (261 women); includes 75 minority (19 Black or African American, non-Hispanic/Latino; 6 American Indian or Alaska Native, non-Hispanic/Latino; 40 Asian, non-Hispanic/Latino; 10 Hispanic/Latino), 76 international. Average age 29. 548 applicants, 52% accepted, 253 enrolled. In 2011, 225 master's, 17 doctorates, 37 other advanced degrees awarded. *Degree requirements:* For master's, comprehensive exam; for doctorate, thesis/dissertation, research analysis exam, research experience component. *Entrance requirements:* For doctorate, GRE General Test or MAT, interview, writing sample, letters of recommendation. Additional exam requirements/recommendations for international students: Required—TOEFL (minimum score 600 paper-based; 96 iBT). *Application deadline:* For fall admission, 2/1 priority date for domestic students, 2/1 for international students; for spring admission, 11/15 priority date for domestic students, 10/1 for international students. Applications are processed on a rolling basis. Application fee: $50. Electronic applications accepted. *Financial support:* In 2011–12, 40 fellowships (averaging $12,991 per year), 46 research assistantships (averaging $10,986 per year) were awarded; teaching assistantships with full tuition reimbursements, career-related internships or fieldwork, Federal Work-Study, institutionally sponsored loans, scholarships/grants, and unspecified assistantships also available. Financial award application deadline: 2/28; financial award applicants required to submit FAFSA. *Faculty research:* Science assessment, foreign language teaching and learning, early learning, new literacies, gender and education. *Unit head:* Dr. Julie Sarama, Chair, 716-645-2455, Fax: 716-645-3161, E-mail: jcollins@buffalo.edu. *Application contact:* Cathy Dimino, Admissions Assistant, 716-645-2110, Fax: 716-645-7937, E-mail: cadimino@buffalo.edu.

University of Alaska Fairbanks, College of Liberal Arts, Department of Cross-Cultural Studies., Fairbanks, AK 99775-6300. Offers MA. *Faculty:* 2 full-time (0 women). *Students:* 2 full-time (both women), 4 part-time (2 women). Average age 38. 8 applicants, 63% accepted, 3 enrolled. In 2011, 4 degrees awarded. *Degree requirements:* For master's, comprehensive exam. *Entrance requirements:* Additional exam requirements/recommendations for international students: Required—TOEFL (minimum score 550 paper-based; 213 computer-based; 80 iBT). *Application deadline:* For fall admission, 6/1 for domestic students, 3/1 for international students; for spring admission, 10/15 for domestic students, 9/1 for international students. Applications are processed on a rolling basis. Application fee: $60. Electronic applications accepted. *Expenses:* Tuition, state resident: full-time $6696; part-time $372 per credit. Tuition, nonresident: full-time $13,680; part-time $760 per credit. Tuition and fees vary according to course load and reciprocity agreements. *Financial support:* Fellowships with tuition reimbursements, research assistantships with tuition reimbursements, teaching assistantships with tuition reimbursements, Federal Work-Study, scholarships/grants, health care benefits, and unspecified assistantships available. Support available to part-time students. Financial award application deadline: 7/1; financial award applicants required to submit FAFSA. *Faculty research:* Alaska native literature, oral traditions, history, law and policy; Alaska native cultures, art, native American religion and philosophy. *Unit head:* Raymond Barnhardt, Director, 907-474-1902, Fax: 907-474-1957, E-mail: fycxcs@uaf.edu. *Application contact:* Mike Earnest, Director of Admissions, 907-474-7500, Fax: 907-474-5379, E-mail: admissions@uaf.edu. Web site: http://www.uaf.edu/cxcs.

University of Alaska Fairbanks, College of Liberal Arts, Program in Linguistics, Fairbanks, AK 99775-6280. Offers applied linguistics (MA), including language documentation, second language acquisition teacher education. Part-time programs available. *Faculty:* 1 (woman) full-time. *Students:* 7 full-time (3 women); includes 3 minority (all American Indian or Alaska Native, non-Hispanic/Latino). Average age 35. 8 applicants, 63% accepted, 3 enrolled. In 2011, 3 master's awarded. *Degree requirements:* For master's, comprehensive exam, thesis or alternative. *Entrance requirements:* Additional exam requirements/recommendations for international students: Required—TOEFL (minimum score 550 paper-based; 213 computer-based; 80 iBT). *Application deadline:* For fall admission, 6/1 for domestic students, 3/1 for international students; for spring admission, 10/15 for domestic students, 9/1 for international students. Application fee: $60. *Expenses:* Tuition, state resident: full-time $6696; part-time $372 per credit. Tuition, nonresident: full-time $13,680; part-time $760 per credit. Tuition and fees vary according to course load and reciprocity agreements. *Financial support:* In 2011–12, 2 research assistantships with tuition reimbursements (averaging $4,677 per year), 4 teaching assistantships with tuition reimbursements (averaging $9,289 per year) were awarded; fellowships with tuition reimbursements, career-related internships or fieldwork, Federal Work-Study, scholarships/grants, health care benefits, and unspecified assistantships also available. Support available to part-time students. Financial award application deadline: 7/1; financial award applicants required to submit FAFSA. *Faculty research:* Second language acquisition/teaching, INUPIAQ, Athabaskan languages, language maintenance and shift, phonology, morphology. *Total annual research expenditures:* $130,000. *Unit head:* Dr. Siri Tuttle, Program Head, 907-474-7876, Fax: 907-474-6586, E-mail: ffamb@uaf.edu. *Application contact:* Mike Earnest, Director of Admissions, 907-474-7500, Fax: 907-474-5379, E-mail: admissions@uaf.edu. Web site: http://www.uaf.edu/linguist/.

University of Alaska Fairbanks, School of Education, Fairbanks, AK 99775. Offers counseling (M Ed), including counseling; education (M Ed, Graduate Certificate), including cross-cultural education (M Ed), curriculum and instruction (M Ed), education (M Ed), elementary education (M Ed), language and literacy (M Ed), reading (M Ed), secondary education (M Ed), special education (M Ed); guidance and counseling (M Ed). *Accreditation:* NCATE. Postbaccalaureate distance learning degree programs offered. *Faculty:* 26 full-time (15 women). *Students:* 61 full-time (46 women), 120 part-time (89 women); includes 35 minority (6 Black or African American, non-Hispanic/Latino; 10 American Indian or Alaska Native, non-Hispanic/Latino; 1 Asian, non-Hispanic/Latino; 8 Hispanic/Latino; 1 Native Hawaiian or other Pacific Islander, non-Hispanic/Latino; 9 Two or more races, non-Hispanic/Latino), 3 international. Average age 34. 111 applicants, 71% accepted, 62 enrolled. In 2011, 34 master's, 23 other advanced degrees awarded. *Degree requirements:* For master's, comprehensive exam, thesis or alternative, student teaching. *Entrance requirements:* For master's, GRE General Test, PRAXIS I, PRAXIS II, writing sample, evidence of technology competence, criminal background check. Additional exam requirements/recommendations for international students: Required—TOEFL (minimum score 550 paper-based; 213 computer-based; 80 iBT). *Application deadline:* For fall admission, 3/1 for domestic and international students; for spring admission, 10/15 for domestic students, 9/1 for international students. Application fee: $60. Electronic applications accepted. *Expenses:* Tuition, state resident: full-time $6696; part-time $372 per credit. Tuition, nonresident: full-time $13,680; part-time $760 per credit. Tuition and fees vary according to course load and reciprocity agreements. *Financial support:* In 2011–12, 4 teaching assistantships with tuition reimbursements (averaging $13,330 per year) were awarded; fellowships with tuition reimbursements, research assistantships with tuition reimbursements, career-related internships or fieldwork, Federal Work-Study, scholarships/grants, health care benefits, and unspecified assistantships also available. Support available to part-time students. Financial award application deadline: 2/15; financial award applicants required to submit FAFSA. *Faculty research:* Native ways of knowing, classroom research in methods of literacy instruction, multiple intelligence theory, geometry concept development, mathematics and science curriculum development. *Total annual research expenditures:* $6,000. *Unit head:* Allan Morotti, Dean, 907-474-7341, Fax: 907-474-5451, E-mail: uaf-soe-school@alaska.edu. *Application contact:* Mike Earnest, Director of Admissions, 907-474-7500, Fax: 907-474-5379, E-mail: admissions@uaf.edu. Web site: http://www.uaf.edu/educ/.

University of Alberta, Faculty of Graduate Studies and Research, Facultè Saint Jean, Edmonton, AB T6G 2E1, Canada. Offers M Ed. Part-time and evening/weekend programs available. Postbaccalaureate distance learning degree programs offered (minimal on-campus study). *Degree requirements:* For master's, thesis (for some programs). *Entrance requirements:* For master's, proficiency in French, 2 years of teaching experience. *Faculty research:* First and second language acquisition, first and second language learning through subject matter, cultural transmission.

The University of Arizona, College of Education, Department of Teaching, Learning and Sociocultural Studies, Tucson, AZ 85721. Offers bilingual education (M Ed); bilingual/multicultural education (MA); language, reading and culture (MA, Ed D, PhD, Ed S). Part-time programs available. *Faculty:* 23 full-time (18 women). *Students:* 162 full-time (108 women), 80 part-time (65 women); includes 71 minority (8 Black or African American, non-Hispanic/Latino; 3 American Indian or Alaska Native, non-Hispanic/Latino; 3 Asian, non-Hispanic/Latino; 38 Hispanic/Latino; 19 Two or more races, non-Hispanic/Latino), 23 international. Average age 37. 63 applicants, 71% accepted, 30 enrolled. In 2011, 89 master's, 19 doctorates awarded. Terminal master's awarded for partial completion of doctoral program. *Degree requirements:* For master's, thesis optional, thesis (MA); for doctorate, comprehensive exam, thesis/dissertation; for Ed S, thesis optional. *Entrance requirements:* For master's, 2 letters of recommendation, resume; for doctorate, GRE or MAT, 2 letters of recommendation, resume; for Ed S, GRE, MAT. Additional exam requirements/recommendations for international students: Required—TOEFL (minimum score 550 paper-based; 213 computer-based; 79 iBT). *Application deadline:* For fall admission, 2/1 for domestic and international students. Application fee: $75. Electronic applications accepted. *Expenses:* Tuition, state resident: full-time $10,840. Tuition, nonresident: full-time $25,802. *Financial support:* In 2011–12, 21 research assistantships with full tuition reimbursements (averaging $17,252 per year), 24 teaching assistantships with full tuition reimbursements (averaging $16,472 per year) were awarded; career-related internships or fieldwork, scholarships/grants, health care benefits, tuition waivers (full and partial), and unspecified assistantships also available. Financial award application deadline: 3/7; financial award applicants required to submit FAFSA. *Faculty research:* Reading, Native American education, language policy, children's literature, bilingual/bicultural literacy. *Total annual research expenditures:* $3.8 million. *Unit head:* Dr. Norma E. Gonzalez, Department Head, 520-621-1311, Fax: 520-621-1853, E-mail: ngonzale@email.arizona.edu. *Application contact:* Information Contact, 520-621-1311, Fax: 520-621-1853, E-mail: lrcinfo@email.arizona.edu. Web site: https://www.coe.arizona.edu/tls.

University of California, Riverside, Graduate Division, Graduate School of Education, Riverside, CA 92521-0102. Offers autism (M Ed); diversity and equity (M Ed); education, society and culture (MA, PhD); educational psychology (MA, PhD); general education (M Ed); higher education administration and policy (M Ed, PhD); reading (M Ed); school psychology (PhD); special education (M Ed, MA, PhD). *Faculty:* 19 full-time (9 women), 9 part-time/adjunct (6 women). *Students:* 181 full-time (128 women); includes 79 minority (8 Black or African American, non-Hispanic/Latino; 1 American Indian or Alaska Native, non-Hispanic/Latino; 26 Asian, non-Hispanic/Latino; 34 Hispanic/Latino; 10 Two or more races, non-Hispanic/Latino), 5 international. Average age 31. 200 applicants, 48% accepted, 76 enrolled. In 2011, 67 master's, 12 doctorates awarded. Terminal master's awarded for partial completion of doctoral program. *Degree requirements:* For master's, thesis optional, comprehensive exams or thesis (MA), case study or analytical report (M Ed); for doctorate, thesis/dissertation, written and oral qualifying exams, college teaching practicum. *Entrance requirements:* For master's, GRE General Test, CBEST, CSET, minimum GPA of 3.2; for doctorate, GRE General Test, master's degree (desirable), minimum GPA of 3.2. Additional exam requirements/recommendations for international students: Required—TOEFL (minimum score 550 paper-based; 213 computer-based; 80 iBT), IELTS (minimum score 7). *Application deadline:* For fall admission, 9/1 for domestic students, 4/1 for international students; for winter admission, 12/1 for domestic students, 7/1 for international students; for spring admission, 3/1 for domestic students, 10/1 for international students. Applications are processed on a rolling basis. Application fee: $80 ($100 for international students). Electronic applications accepted. *Financial support:* In 2011–12, 59 students received support, including 9 fellowships with full and partial tuition reimbursements available (averaging $26,587 per year), 21 research assistantships with full and partial tuition reimbursements available (averaging $14,517 per year), 1 teaching assistantship with full and partial tuition reimbursement available (averaging $17,307 per year); career-related internships or fieldwork, Federal Work-Study, institutionally sponsored loans, scholarships/grants, and unspecified assistantships also available. Financial award application deadline: 1/5. *Faculty research:* Responsiveness to intervention, faculty core, response to intervention of English language learners, advanced modeling techniques, study on social capital, trust, and motivation. *Total annual research expenditures:* $2.8 million. *Unit head:* Prof. Douglas Mitchell, Interim Dean, 951-827-5802, Fax: 951-827-3942, E-mail: douglas.mitchell@ucr.edu. *Application contact:* Prof. Robert Ream, Graduate Advisor for Admission, 951-827-6362, Fax: 951-827-3291, E-mail: edgrad@ucr.edu. Web site: http://www.education.ucr.edu/.

University of Colorado Boulder, Graduate School, School of Education, Division of Social Multicultural and Bilingual Foundations, Boulder, CO 80309. Offers MA, PhD. *Accreditation:* NCATE. *Students:* 63 full-time (58 women), 72 part-time (63 women); includes 45 minority (1 Black or African American, non-Hispanic/Latino; 4 Asian, non-Hispanic/Latino; 40 Hispanic/Latino), 3 international. Average age 35. 40 applicants, 58% accepted, 15 enrolled. In 2011, 96 master's, 3 doctorates awarded. Terminal master's awarded for partial completion of doctoral program. *Degree requirements:* For master's, comprehensive exam, thesis or alternative; for doctorate, one foreign language, comprehensive exam, thesis/dissertation. *Entrance requirements:* For master's, GRE General Test or MAT, minimum undergraduate GPA of 2.75; for doctorate, GRE General Test. *Application deadline:* For fall admission, 2/1 priority date for domestic students, 12/1 for international students; for spring admission, 9/1 for domestic students, 12/1 for international students. Application fee: $50 ($60 for international students). Electronic applications accepted. *Financial support:* In 2011–12, 72 students received support, including 96 fellowships (averaging $4,360 per year), 16 research assistantships with full and partial tuition reimbursements available (averaging $16,626 per year), 9 teaching assistantships with full and partial tuition reimbursements available (averaging $15,018 per year); institutionally sponsored loans, scholarships/grants, health care benefits, and unspecified assistantships also available. Financial award applicants required to submit FAFSA. *Faculty research:* Bilingual education, inclusion. *Application contact:* E-mail: edadvise@colorado.edu. Web site: http://www.colorado.edu/education/.

University of Colorado Denver, School of Education and Human Development, Teacher Education Programs, Denver, CO 80217. Offers elementary linguistically diverse education (MA); elementary math and science education (MA); elementary math education (MA); elementary reading and writing (MA); elementary science education (MA); secondary English education (MA); secondary linguistically diverse education (MA); secondary math education (MA); secondary reading and writing (MA); secondary science education (MA); special education (MA). *Accreditation:* NCATE. Part-time and evening/weekend programs available. *Students:* 419 full-time (325 women), 238 part-time (196 women); includes 83 minority (11 Black or African American, non-Hispanic/Latino; 1 American Indian or Alaska Native, non-Hispanic/Latino; 15 Asian, non-Hispanic/Latino; 53 Hispanic/Latino; 3 Two or more races, non-Hispanic/Latino), 9 international. Average age 30. 206 applicants, 88% accepted, 85 enrolled. In 2011, 278 master's awarded. *Degree requirements:* For master's, comprehensive exam. *Entrance requirements:* For master's, GRE or MAT (for those with GPA below 2.75), transcripts, resume, letters of recommendation. Additional exam requirements/recommendations for international students: Required—TOEFL (minimum score 525 paper-based; 197 computer-based). *Application deadline:* For fall admission, 4/15 priority date for domestic students; for spring admission, 9/15 priority date for domestic students. Applications are processed on a rolling basis. Application fee: $50 ($75 for international students). Electronic applications accepted. *Expenses:* Contact institution. *Financial support:* Research assistantships, teaching assistantships, and Federal Work-Study available. Financial award application deadline: 4/1; financial award applicants required to submit FAFSA. *Faculty research:* Linguistically diverse education/ESL, elementary reading and writing, elementary teacher education, secondary teacher education, special education. *Unit head:* Cindy Gutierrez, Director, 303-315-4982, E-mail: cindy.gutierrez@ucdenver.edu. *Application contact:* Lori Sisneros, Student Services Center, 303-315-4979, E-mail: education@ucdenver.edu. Web site: http://www.ucdenver.edu/academics/colleges/SchoolOfEducation/Academics/MASTERS/Pages/default.aspx.

University of Connecticut, Graduate School, Neag School of Education, Department of Curriculum and Instruction, Program in Bilingual and Bicultural Education, Storrs, CT 06269. Offers MA, PhD, Post-Master's Certificate. *Accreditation:* NCATE. Terminal master's awarded for partial completion of doctoral program. *Degree requirements:* For master's, comprehensive exam; for doctorate, thesis/dissertation. *Entrance requirements:* For doctorate, GRE General Test. Additional exam requirements/

recommendations for international students: Required—TOEFL (minimum score 550 paper-based; 213 computer-based). Electronic applications accepted.

University of Delaware, College of Education and Human Development, School of Education, Newark, DE 19716. Offers education (PhD); educational leadership (Ed D); higher education (M Ed); instruction (MI); reading (M Ed); school leadership (M Ed); school psychology (MA, Ed S); teaching English as a second language (TESL) (MA). *Accreditation:* NCATE. Part-time and evening/weekend programs available. Terminal master's awarded for partial completion of doctoral program. *Degree requirements:* For master's, comprehensive exam (for some programs), thesis (for some programs); for doctorate, comprehensive exam (for some programs), thesis/dissertation. *Entrance requirements:* For master's and doctorate, GRE, 3 letters of recommendation. Additional exam requirements/recommendations for international students: Required—TOEFL (minimum score 600 paper-based; 250 computer-based). Electronic applications accepted. *Faculty research:* Teacher education; curriculum theory and development; community based education models, educational leadership.

The University of Findlay, Graduate and Professional Studies, College of Liberal Arts, Master of Arts in Teaching English to Speakers of Other Languages (TESOL) and Bilingual Education Program, Findlay, OH 45840-3653. Offers bilingual education (MA); teaching English to speakers of other languages (MA). Part-time and evening/weekend programs available. *Faculty:* 11 full-time (6 women). *Students:* 19 full-time (13 women), 15 part-time (11 women), 17 international. Average age 35. 13 applicants, 85% accepted, 7 enrolled. In 2011, 6 master's awarded. *Degree requirements:* For master's, cumulative project. *Entrance requirements:* For master's, bachelor's degree from accredited institution, minimum undergraduate GPA of 2.75 in last 64 hours of course work, 3 letters of recommendation. Additional exam requirements/recommendations for international students: Required—TOEFL (minimum score 550 paper-based; 213 computer-based; 80 iBT). *Application deadline:* Applications are processed on a rolling basis. Application fee: $25. Electronic applications accepted. *Expenses: Tuition:* Full-time $6300; part-time $700 per semester hour. *Required fees:* $35 per semester hour. One-time fee: $25. Tuition and fees vary according to course load, degree level and program. *Financial support:* In 2011–12, 2 teaching assistantships with full and partial tuition reimbursements (averaging $3,600 per year) were awarded; Federal Work-Study, health care benefits, and unspecified assistantships also available. Financial award application deadline: 4/1; financial award applicants required to submit FAFSA. *Unit head:* Dr. Hiroaki Kawamura, Chair, Department of Language and Culture, 419-434-4619, Fax: 419-434-4822, E-mail: kawamura@findlay.edu. *Application contact:* Heather Riffle, Assistant Director, Graduate and Professional Studies, 419-434-4640, Fax: 419-434-5517, E-mail: riffle@findlay.edu. Web site: http://www.findlay.edu.

University of Florida, Graduate School, College of Education, School of Teaching and Learning, Gainesville, FL 32611. Offers bilingual/ESOL education (M Ed, MAE, Ed D, PhD, Ed S); curriculum and instruction (M Ed, MAE, Ed D, PhD, Ed S); elementary education (M Ed, MAE); English education (M Ed, MAE); mathematics education (M Ed, MAE); reading education (M Ed, MAE); science education (M Ed, MAE); social foundations of education (M Ed, MAE, Ed D, PhD); social studies education (M Ed, MAE). *Accreditation:* NCATE. Part-time and evening/weekend programs available. Postbaccalaureate distance learning degree programs offered (no on-campus study). *Faculty:* 26 full-time (19 women). *Students:* 247 full-time (201 women), 236 part-time (196 women); includes 100 minority (32 Black or African American, non-Hispanic/Latino; 2 American Indian or Alaska Native, non-Hispanic/Latino; 15 Asian, non-Hispanic/Latino; 51 Hispanic/Latino), 32 international. Average age 33. 290 applicants, 60% accepted, 122 enrolled. In 2011, 284 master's, 19 doctorates, 29 other advanced degrees awarded. Terminal master's awarded for partial completion of doctoral program. *Degree requirements:* For master's, comprehensive exam (for some programs), thesis (for some programs); for doctorate, comprehensive exam (for some programs), thesis/dissertation (for some programs). *Entrance requirements:* For master's and doctorate, GRE General Test, minimum GPA of 3.0; for Ed S, GRE General Test. Additional exam requirements/recommendations for international students: Required—TOEFL (minimum score 550 paper-based; 213 computer-based; 80 iBT), IELTS (minimum score 6). *Application deadline:* For fall admission, 2/15 for domestic students, 12/1 for international students; for spring admission, 9/15 for domestic students, 3/1 for international students. Applications are processed on a rolling basis. Application fee: $30. Electronic applications accepted. *Financial support:* Fellowships, research assistantships, teaching assistantships, career-related internships or fieldwork, and unspecified assistantships available. Financial award applicants required to submit FAFSA. *Faculty research:* Early childhood, child and adolescents, diverse learners, race/ethnicity issues, teacher education, professional development, language and literacy development, policy development. *Unit head:* Dr. Elizabeth Bondy, Chair, 352-273-4242, Fax: 352-392-9193, E-mail: bondy@coe.ufl.edu. *Application contact:* Wevan Terzian, Graduate Coordinator, 352-273-4216, Fax: 352-392-9193, E-mail: sterzian@coe.ufl.edu. Web site: http://education.ufl.edu/school-teaching-learning/.

University of Houston–Clear Lake, School of Education, Program in Foundations and Professional Studies, Houston, TX 77058-1098. Offers counseling (MS); instructional technology (MS); multicultural studies (MS). Part-time and evening/weekend programs available. *Degree requirements:* For master's, thesis optional. *Entrance requirements:* For master's, GRE or minimum GPA of 3.0 in last 60 hours. Additional exam requirements/recommendations for international students: Required—TOEFL (minimum score 550 paper-based; 213 computer-based). Electronic applications accepted.

University of Houston–Downtown, College of Public Service, Department of Urban Education, Houston, TX 77002. Offers bilingual education (MAT); curriculum and instruction (MAT); elementary education (MAT); secondary education (MAT). Part-time and evening/weekend programs available. *Faculty:* 12 full-time (8 women). *Students:* 13 full-time (10 women), 25 part-time (22 women); includes 30 minority (15 Black or African American, non-Hispanic/Latino; 3 Asian, non-Hispanic/Latino; 11 Hispanic/Latino; 1 Two or more races, non-Hispanic/Latino). Average age 35. 17 applicants, 100% accepted, 16 enrolled. In 2011, 5 master's awarded. *Degree requirements:* For master's, capstone course with completed project, position paper, grant proposal, empirical study, curriculum development/revision, or advanced technology project presented at annual Graduate Project Exhibition. *Entrance requirements:* For master's, GRE, personal statement, 3 recommendation forms. Additional exam requirements/recommendations for international students: Required—TOEFL (minimum score 550 paper-based; 213 computer-based; 80 iBT). *Application deadline:* For fall admission, 7/15 for domestic and international students; for spring admission, 11/15 for domestic and international students. Applications are processed on a rolling basis. Application fee: $35 ($60 for international students). Electronic applications accepted. *Expenses:* Tuition, state resident: full-time $3420; part-time $2280 per year. Tuition, nonresident: full-time $8424; part-time $5616 per year. *Required fees:* $1018; $840 per year. Tuition and fees vary according to program. *Financial support:* Scholarships/grants available. Financial award applicants required to submit FAFSA. *Unit head:* Dr. Myrna Cohen, Department Chair, 713-221-2759, Fax: 713-226-5294, E-mail: cohenm@uhd.edu. *Application contact:* Traneshia Parker, Associate Director of International Student Services and Graduate Admissions, 713-221-8093, Fax: 713-221-8157, E-mail: parkert@uhd.edu. Web site: http://www.uhd.edu/academic/colleges/publicservice/urbaned/mat.htm.

University of Illinois at Chicago, Graduate College, College of Education, Department of Curriculum and Instruction, Chicago, IL 60607-7128. Offers curriculum studies (PhD); educational studies (M Ed); elementary education (M Ed); literacy, language and culture (M Ed, PhD); secondary education (M Ed). Part-time and evening/weekend programs available. *Degree requirements:* For doctorate, thesis/dissertation. *Entrance requirements:* For master's, minimum GPA of 2.75; for doctorate, GRE General Test, minimum GPA of 2.75. Additional exam requirements/recommendations for international students: Required—TOEFL. Electronic applications accepted. *Faculty research:* Curriculum theory, curriculum development, research on teaching, curriculum and context, reading/literacy.

University of La Verne, Regional Campus Administration, Graduate Credential Program in Education, California Statewide Campus, La Verne, CA 91750-4443. Offers cross cultural language and academic development (Credential); multiple subject (Credential); single subject (Credential). *Entrance requirements:* For degree, California Basic Educational Skills Test, minimum undergraduate GPA of 2.75, 3 letters of recommendation, interview. *Expenses:* Contact institution.

University of Maryland, Baltimore County, Graduate School, College of Arts, Humanities and Social Sciences, Department of Modern Languages and Linguistics, Program in Intercultural Communication, Baltimore, MD 21250. Offers MA. Part-time and evening/weekend programs available. *Faculty:* 18 full-time (6 women), 3 part-time/adjunct (2 women). *Students:* 18 full-time (14 women), 10 part-time (9 women); includes 1 minority (Black or African American, non-Hispanic/Latino), 10 international. 17 applicants, 88% accepted, 12 enrolled. In 2011, 13 master's awarded. *Degree requirements:* For master's, one foreign language, comprehensive exam (for some programs), thesis (for some programs). *Entrance requirements:* For master's, GRE General Test, minimum GPA of 3.0, 3 letters of recommendation, self-evaluation and statement of support, resume. Additional exam requirements/recommendations for international students: Required—TOEFL (minimum score 550 paper-based; 213 computer-based; 80 iBT). *Application deadline:* For fall admission, 1/31 for domestic and international students. Application fee: $50. Electronic applications accepted. *Financial support:* In 2011–12, 8 students received support, including 5 teaching assistantships with full tuition reimbursements available (averaging $11,324 per year); Federal Work-Study, scholarships/grants, and tuition waivers (partial) also available. Financial award applicants required to submit FAFSA. *Faculty research:* Comparative television research-cross-cultural; cultural studies; social developments in Latin America; intercultural communication; French civilization and cultural studies; language, gender and sexuality; sociolinguistics; African linguistics; immigrants in U. S. and Latin American societies. *Unit head:* Dr. Denis Provencher, Director, 410-455-2109 Ext. 2636, Fax: 410-455-2636, E-mail: provench@umbc.edu. *Application contact:* Dr. Denis Provencher, Director, 410-455-2104, Fax: 410-455-2636, E-mail: provench@umbc.edu. Web site: http://www.umbc.edu/mll/incc/.

University of Maryland, Baltimore County, Graduate School, College of Arts, Humanities and Social Sciences, Program in Language, Literacy, and Culture, Baltimore, MD 21250. Offers PhD. Part-time and evening/weekend programs available. *Faculty:* 4 full-time (3 women), 41 part-time/adjunct (23 women). *Students:* 37 full-time (28 women), 35 part-time (25 women); includes 23 minority (18 Black or African American, non-Hispanic/Latino; 3 Asian, non-Hispanic/Latino; 2 Hispanic/Latino), 13 international. Average age 35. 55 applicants, 27% accepted, 13 enrolled. In 2011, 7 doctorates awarded. *Degree requirements:* For doctorate, comprehensive exam, thesis/dissertation, internship. *Entrance requirements:* For doctorate, research writing sample; resume or curriculum vitae; master's degree. Additional exam requirements/recommendations for international students: Required—TOEFL (minimum score 80 iBT). *Application deadline:* For fall admission, 12/1 for domestic and international students. Application fee: $50. Electronic applications accepted. *Financial support:* In 2011–12, 6 research assistantships with full and partial tuition reimbursements (averaging $14,000 per year), 6 teaching assistantships with full and partial tuition reimbursements (averaging $14,000 per year) were awarded; fellowships, Federal Work-Study, health care benefits, and unspecified assistantships also available. Financial award application deadline: 12/1. *Faculty research:* Public policy, educational equity, identity, intercultural communication, technology and communication. *Unit head:* Dr. Beverly Bickel, Director, 410-455-1305, Fax: 410-455-8947, E-mail: bickel@umbc.edu. *Application contact:* Liz Steenrod, Administrative Assistant, 410-455-2376, Fax: 410-455-8947, E-mail: llc@umbc.edu. Web site: http://www.umbc.edu/llc.

University of Massachusetts Amherst, Graduate School, School of Education, Program in Education, Amherst, MA 01003. Offers bilingual, English as a second language, and multicultural education (M Ed, CAGS); child study and early education (M Ed); children, families and schools (Ed D, CAGS); early childhood and elementary teacher education (M Ed); educational leadership (M Ed, CAGS); educational policy and leadership (Ed D); higher education (M Ed, CAGS); international education (M Ed); language, literacy and culture (Ed D); learning, media and technology (M Ed, CAGS); mathematics, science, and learning technologies (Ed D); policy studies in education (CAGS); psychometric methods, educational statistics and research methods (Ed D); reading and writing (M Ed); school counselor education (M Ed, CAGS); science education (CAGS); secondary teacher education (M Ed); social justice education (M Ed, Ed D, CAGS); special education (M Ed, Ed D, CAGS). *Accreditation:* NCATE. Part-time programs available. Postbaccalaureate distance learning degree programs offered (minimal on-campus study). *Faculty:* 81 full-time (46 women). *Students:* 341 full-time (240 women), 333 part-time (226 women); includes 113 minority (36 Black or African American, non-Hispanic/Latino; 1 American Indian or Alaska Native, non-Hispanic/Latino; 14 Asian, non-Hispanic/Latino; 51 Hispanic/Latino; 1 Native Hawaiian or other Pacific Islander, non-Hispanic/Latino; 10 Two or more races, non-Hispanic/Latino), 98 international. Average age 36. 721 applicants, 57% accepted, 202 enrolled. In 2011, 166 master's, 33 doctorates, 25 CAGSs awarded. Terminal master's awarded for partial completion of doctoral program. *Degree requirements:* For doctorate, comprehensive exam, thesis/dissertation. *Entrance requirements:* Additional exam requirements/recommendations for international students: Required—TOEFL (minimum score 550 paper-based; 213 computer-based; 80 iBT), IELTS (minimum score 6.5). *Application deadline:* For fall admission, 1/15 for domestic and international students. Applications are processed on a rolling basis. Application fee: $50 ($65 for international students). Electronic applications accepted. Tuition and fees vary according to course load, campus/location and program. *Financial support:* Fellowships with full and partial tuition reimbursements, research assistantships with full and partial tuition reimbursements, teaching assistantships with full and partial tuition reimbursements, career-related internships or fieldwork, Federal Work-Study, scholarships/grants, traineeships, health care benefits, tuition waivers (full and partial), and unspecified assistantships available. Support available to part-time students. Financial award application deadline: 1/15. *Unit head:* Dr. Linda L. Griffin, Graduate Program Director, 413-545-6984, Fax: 413-545-1523. *Application contact:* Lindsay DeSantis, Interim Supervisor of Admissions, 413-545-0722, Fax: 413-577-0010, E-mail: gradadm@grad.umass.edu. Web site: http://www.umass.edu/education/.

University of Massachusetts Boston, Office of Graduate Studies, College of Liberal Arts, Program in Applied Linguistics, Boston, MA 02125-3393. Offers bilingual education (MA); English as a second language (MA); foreign language pedagogy (MA). Part-time and evening/weekend programs available. *Degree requirements:* For master's, one foreign language, comprehensive exam. *Entrance requirements:* For master's, minimum GPA of 2.75. *Faculty research:* Multicultural theory and curriculum development, foreign language pedagogy, language and culture, applied psycholinguistics, bilingual education.

University of Miami, Graduate School, School of Education and Human Development, Department of Teaching and Learning, Program in Teaching and Learning, Coral Gables, FL 33124. Offers language and literacy learning in multilingual settings (PhD); science, technology, engineering and mathematics (PhD); special education (PhD). *Students:* 19 full-time (14 women); includes 10 minority (3 Black or African American, non-Hispanic/Latino; 7 Hispanic/Latino), 1 international. Average age 34. 12 applicants, 17% accepted, 2 enrolled. In 2011, 9 degrees awarded. *Degree requirements:* For doctorate, thesis/dissertation, qualifying exam. *Entrance requirements:* For doctorate, GRE General Test. Additional exam requirements/recommendations for international students: Required—TOEFL (minimum score 550 paper-based; 80 iBT); Recommended—IELTS (minimum score 6.5). *Application deadline:* For fall admission, 2/15 for domestic students, 10/15 for international students. Application fee: $65. Electronic applications accepted. *Financial support:* In 2011–12, 18 students received support, including 5 fellowships with full tuition reimbursements available (averaging $28,800 per year), 9 research assistantships with full and partial tuition reimbursements available (averaging $28,800 per year), 1 teaching assistantship with full and partial tuition reimbursement available (averaging $28,800 per year). Financial award application deadline: 3/1; financial award applicants required to submit FAFSA. *Faculty research:* Teacher education, multicultural education, technology, second language acquisition, math and science education. *Unit head:* Dr. Elizabeth Harry, Department Chairperson and Program Director, 305-284-4961, Fax: 305-284-6998, E-mail: bharry@miami.edu. *Application contact:* Lois Heffernan, Graduate Admission Coordinator, 305-284-2167, Fax: 305-284-9395, E-mail: lheffernan@miami.edu.

University of Minnesota, Twin Cities Campus, Graduate School, College of Education and Human Development, Department of Curriculum and Instruction, Program in Teaching, Minneapolis, MN 55455-0213. Offers Chinese (M Ed); earth science (M Ed); elementary special education (M Ed); English (M Ed); English as a second language (M Ed); French (M Ed); German (M Ed); Hebrew (M Ed); Japanese (M Ed); life sciences (M Ed); mathematics (M Ed); middle school science (M Ed); science (M Ed); second languages and cultures (M Ed); social studies (M Ed); Spanish (M Ed). *Students:* 375 full-time (319 women), 72 part-time (56 women); includes 34 minority (8 Black or African American, non-Hispanic/Latino; 16 Asian, non-Hispanic/Latino; 10 Hispanic/Latino), 5 international. Average age 27. 317 applicants, 70% accepted, 215 enrolled. In 2011, 443 master's awarded. Application fee: $55. *Unit head:* Dr. Nina Asher, Chair, 612-624-1357, Fax: 612-624-8277, E-mail: nasher@umn.edu. *Application contact:* Dr. Jennifer Engler, Assistant Dean, 612-626-2887, Fax: 612-626-7496, E-mail: engle009@umn.edu. Web site: http://www.cehd.umn.edu/ci/.

University of New Mexico, Graduate School, College of Education, Department of Language, Literacy and Sociocultural Studies, Program in Language, Literacy and Sociocultural Studies, Albuquerque, NM 87131. Offers American Indian education (MA); bilingual education (MA, PhD); educational linguistics (PhD); educational thought and sociocultural studies (MA, PhD); literacy/language arts (MA, PhD); social studies (MA); TESOL (MA, PhD). *Faculty:* 19 full-time (12 women), 12 part-time/adjunct (10 women). *Students:* 40 full-time (30 women), 47 part-time (17 women); includes 85 minority (4 Black or African American, non-Hispanic/Latino; 14 American Indian or Alaska Native, non-Hispanic/Latino; 4 Asian, non-Hispanic/Latino; 59 Hispanic/Latino; 4 Two or more races, non-Hispanic/Latino), 14 international. Average age 41. 63 applicants, 57% accepted, 22 enrolled. In 2011, 44 master's, 8 doctorates awarded. *Degree requirements:* For master's, comprehensive exam, thesis optional; for doctorate, comprehensive exam, thesis/dissertation, research skills. *Entrance requirements:* For master's, letter of intent, 3 letters of recommendation, resume, BA/BS, department demographic form, transcripts; for doctorate, writing sample, letter of intent, 3 letters of recommendation, resume, BA/BS, department demographic form, transcripts. Additional exam requirements/recommendations for international students: Required—TOEFL. *Application deadline:* For fall admission, 12/1 for domestic and international students; for spring admission, 9/15 for domestic and international students. Application fee: $50. Electronic applications accepted. *Financial support:* In 2011–12, 7 students received support, including 7 fellowships (averaging $3,170 per year), 1,318 teaching assistantships with tuition reimbursements available (averaging $3,789 per year); research assistantships, career-related internships or fieldwork, institutionally sponsored loans, scholarships/grants, and unspecified assistantships also available. Support available to part-time students. Financial award application deadline: 3/1; financial award applicants required to submit FAFSA. *Faculty research:* School reform, professional development, history of education, Native American education, politics of education, feminism and issues of sexual identity, critical race theory, bilingualism, literacy reading, adolescent literature, second language acquisition, critical theory and schooling, indigenous languages. *Unit head:* Dr. Lois M. Meyer, Chair, 505-277-7244, Fax: 505-277-8362, E-mail: lsmeyer@unm.edu. *Application contact:* Debra Schaffer, Administrative Assistant, 505-277-0437, Fax: 505-277-8362, E-mail: schaffer@unm.edu. Web site: http://coe.unm.edu/departments/department-of-language-literacy-and-sociocultural-studies/llss-program.html.

University of New Mexico, Graduate School, College of Education, Department of Teacher Education, Program in Multicultural Teacher and Childhood Education, Albuquerque, NM 87131-2039. Offers Ed D, PhD. *Accreditation:* NCATE. Part-time programs available. *Faculty:* 1 (woman) full-time. *Students:* 5 full-time (4 women), 24 part-time (17 women); includes 11 minority (1 Black or African American, non-Hispanic/Latino; 1 American Indian or Alaska Native, non-Hispanic/Latino; 8 Hispanic/Latino; 1 Two or more races, non-Hispanic/Latino). Average age 47. 11 applicants, 73% accepted, 6 enrolled. In 2011, 2 degrees awarded. *Degree requirements:* For doctorate, comprehensive exam, thesis/dissertation (for some programs). *Entrance requirements:* For doctorate, GRE, master's degree, minimum GPA of 3.0, 3 years teaching experience, 3-5 letters of reference, 1 letter of intent, professional writing sample. Additional exam requirements/recommendations for international students: Required—TOEFL (minimum score 550 paper-based; 213 computer-based). *Application deadline:* For fall admission, 3/1 priority date for domestic students, 3/1 for international students; for spring admission, 10/30 for domestic and international students. Application fee: $50. Electronic applications accepted. *Financial support:* In 2011–12, 10 students received support, including 2 research assistantships (averaging $22,000 per year), 3 teaching assistantships with partial tuition reimbursements available (averaging $8,628 per year); fellowships, career-related internships or fieldwork, scholarships/grants, and unspecified assistantships also available. Financial award application deadline: 4/15; financial award applicants required to submit FAFSA. *Faculty research:* Mathematics/science/technology education, diversity, curriculum development, reflective practice, social justice, student learning, teacher education. *Unit head:* Dr. Rosalita Mitchell, Department Chair, 505-277-9611, Fax: 505-277-0455, E-mail: ted@unm.edu. *Application contact:* Robert Romero, Program Coordinator, 505-277-0513, Fax: 505-277-0455, E-mail: ted@unm.edu. Web site: http://coe.unm.edu/departments/teacher-ed/grad-degrees-certs/mctc-edd-phd.html.

The University of North Carolina at Greensboro, Graduate School, School of Education, Department of Educational Leadership and Cultural Foundations, Greensboro, NC 27412-5001. Offers curriculum and teaching (PhD), including cultural studies; educational leadership (Ed D, Ed S); school administration (MSA). *Accreditation:* NCATE. *Degree requirements:* For doctorate, thesis/dissertation. *Entrance requirements:* For master's, doctorate, and Ed S, GRE General Test. Additional exam requirements/recommendations for international students: Required—TOEFL. Electronic applications accepted.

University of Oklahoma, Jeannine Rainbolt College of Education, Department of Instructional Leadership and Academic Curriculum, Norman, OK 73072. Offers communication, culture and pedagogy for Hispanic populations in educational settings (Graduate Certificate); instructional leadership and academic curriculum (M Ed, PhD), including bilingual education, early childhood education, elementary education, English education, instructional leadership, mathematics education, reading education, science education, science, technology, engineering and mathematics education (M Ed), secondary education, social studies education, teacher education (M Ed). *Accreditation:* NCATE. Part-time and evening/weekend programs available. *Faculty:* 19 full-time (13 women), 1 (woman) part-time/adjunct. *Students:* 73 full-time (63 women), 114 part-time (87 women); includes 29 minority (5 Black or African American, non-Hispanic/Latino; 12 American Indian or Alaska Native, non-Hispanic/Latino; 5 Asian, non-Hispanic/Latino; 3 Hispanic/Latino; 1 Native Hawaiian or other Pacific Islander, non-Hispanic/Latino; 3 Two or more races, non-Hispanic/Latino), 7 international. Average age 33. 87 applicants, 86% accepted, 68 enrolled. In 2011, 36 master's, 6 doctorates awarded. Terminal master's awarded for partial completion of doctoral program. *Degree requirements:* For doctorate, thesis/dissertation. *Entrance requirements:* For master's, 12 hours of course work in education; for doctorate, GRE General Test, master's degree, minimum graduate GPA of 3.0. Additional exam requirements/recommendations for international students: Required—TOEFL (minimum score 550 paper-based; 79 iBT). *Application deadline:* For fall admission, 6/1 priority date for domestic students, 3/1 for international students; for spring admission, 11/1 for domestic students, 9/1 for international students. Applications are processed on a rolling basis. Application fee: $40 ($90 for international students). Electronic applications accepted. *Expenses:* Tuition, state resident: full-time $4087; part-time $170.30 per credit hour. Tuition, nonresident: full-time $14,875; part-time $619.80 per credit hour. *Required fees:* $2659; $100.25 per credit hour. Tuition and fees vary according to course load and degree level. *Financial support:* In 2011–12, 128 students received support, including 2 research assistantships with partial tuition reimbursements available (averaging $12,431 per year), 12 teaching assistantships with partial tuition reimbursements available (averaging $10,161 per year); institutionally sponsored loans, scholarships/grants, and unspecified assistantships also available. Financial award applicants required to submit FAFSA. *Faculty research:* Engineering in practice for sustainable future, no child left behind (reading), early childhood learning games impact study, Educare randomized control startup, Oklahoma mentoring professional development. *Total annual research expenditures:* $1.1 million. *Unit head:* Lawrence Baines, Chair, 405-325-1498, Fax: 405-325-4061, E-mail: lbaines@ou.edu. *Application contact:* Lynn Crussel, Graduate Programs Officer, 405-325-4843, Fax: 405-325-4061, E-mail: lcrussel@ou.edu. Web site: http://education.ou.edu/departments/ilac.

University of Pennsylvania, Graduate School of Education, Division of Educational Linguistics, Program in Intercultural Communication, Philadelphia, PA 19104. Offers MS Ed. Part-time programs available. *Students:* 43 full-time (33 women), 9 part-time (8 women); includes 3 minority (all Asian, non-Hispanic/Latino), 34 international. 56 applicants, 54% accepted, 18 enrolled. In 2011, 18 master's awarded. *Degree requirements:* For master's, comprehensive exam, thesis. *Entrance requirements:* For master's, GRE General Test or MAT. *Application deadline:* For fall admission, 12/15 priority date for domestic students. Applications are processed on a rolling basis. Application fee: $70. Electronic applications accepted. *Expenses:* Contact institution. *Financial support:* Career-related internships or fieldwork, Federal Work-Study, and institutionally sponsored loans available. Support available to part-time students. Financial award applicants required to submit FAFSA. *Faculty research:* Anthropology of education, history of education, bicultural education, identity and gender education. *Unit head:* Dr. Andrew Porter, Dean, 215-898-7014. *Application contact:* Penny Creedon, 215-898-3245, E-mail: pennyc@gse.upenn.edu.

University of St. Thomas, Graduate Studies, School of Education, Department of Teacher Education, St. Paul, MN 55105-1096. Offers curriculum and instruction (MA), including elementary, individualized, K-12, secondary; elementary (MAT); engineering education (Certificate); English as a second language (MA); math education (Certificate); multicultural education (Certificate); reading (MA, Certificate), including elementary (MA), K-12 (MA). *Accreditation:* NCATE. Part-time and evening/weekend programs available. *Faculty:* 7 full-time (4 women), 26 part-time/adjunct (20 women). *Students:* 19 full-time (14 women), 161 part-time (113 women); includes 28 minority (3 Black or African American, non-Hispanic/Latino; 7 American Indian or Alaska Native, non-Hispanic/Latino; 6 Asian, non-Hispanic/Latino; 9 Hispanic/Latino; 3 Two or more races, non-Hispanic/Latino), 5 international. Average age 35. 150 applicants, 79% accepted, 88 enrolled. In 2011, 83 master's awarded. *Entrance requirements:* For master's, minimum GPA of 3.0 or MAT. Additional exam requirements/recommendations for international students: Required—TOEFL (minimum score 550 paper-based; 210 computer-based; 80 iBT). *Application deadline:* For fall admission, 6/1 for domestic students; for spring admission, 11/1 for domestic students. Applications are processed on a rolling basis. Application fee: $50. *Financial support:* Fellowships, research assistantships, institutionally sponsored loans, and scholarships/grants available. Support available to part-time students. Financial award applicants required to submit FAFSA. *Unit head:* Dr. Jan L. H. Frank, Department Chair, 651-962-4446, Fax: 651-962-4169, E-mail: jlhfrank@stthomas.edu. *Application contact:* Rosemary R. Barreto, Department Assistant, 651-962-4420, Fax: 651-962-4169, E-mail: barr7879@stthomas.edu. Web site: http://www.stthomas.edu/education.

University of St. Thomas, School of Education, Houston, TX 77006-4696. Offers all level teaching (M Ed); bilingual/dual language (M Ed); Catholic school teaching (M Ed); Catholic/private school leadership (M Ed); counselor education (M Ed); curriculum and instruction (M Ed); educational leadership (M Ed); elementary teaching (M Ed); English as a second language (M Ed); exceptionality/ educational diagnostician (M Ed); exceptionality/special education (M Ed); generalist (M Ed); reading (M Ed); secondary teaching (M Ed). Part-time and evening/weekend programs available. Postbaccalaureate distance learning degree programs offered (no on-campus study). *Faculty:* 30 full-time (17 women), 54 part-time/adjunct (37 women). *Students:* 66 full-time (43 women), 1,178 part-time (1,044 women); includes 777 minority (313 Black or African American, non-Hispanic/Latino; 5 American Indian or Alaska Native, non-Hispanic/Latino; 29 Asian, non-Hispanic/Latino; 395 Hispanic/Latino; 2 Native Hawaiian or other Pacific Islander, non-Hispanic/Latino; 33 Two or more races, non-Hispanic/Latino), 26 international. Average age 36. 551 applicants, 94% accepted, 416 enrolled. In 2011, 72 master's awarded. *Degree requirements:* For master's, thesis, field experience. *Entrance requirements:* For master's, GRE or MAT if GPA is below 3.0, bachelor's degree; minimum GPA of 2.75 in bachelor's degree or last 60 credit hours; official transcripts from all institutions; goal statement of 250-300 words; 1 reference. Additional exam requirements/recommendations for international students: Required—TOEFL. *Application deadline:* Applications are processed on a rolling basis. Application fee: $35.

Electronic applications accepted. *Expenses:* Contact institution. *Financial support:* In 2011–12, 9 students received support. Federal Work-Study, scholarships/grants, and state work-study, institutional employment available. Support available to part-time students. Financial award application deadline: 4/15; financial award applicants required to submit FAFSA. *Faculty research:* Leadership, diversity, personality traits, second language acquisition. *Unit head:* Dr. Nora Hutto, Dean, 713-525-3540, Fax: 713-525-3871, E-mail: education@stthom.edu. *Application contact:* Paula C. Hollis, Administrative Assistant, 713-525-3540, Fax: 713-525-3871, E-mail: education@stthom.edu. Web site: http://www.stthom.edu/Schools_Centers_of_Excellence/Schools_of_Study/School_of_Education/Index.aqf.

University of San Francisco, School of Education, Department of International and Multicultural Education, San Francisco, CA 94117-1080. Offers international and multicultural education (MA, Ed D); multicultural literature for children and young adults (MA); teaching English as a second language (MA). *Faculty:* 3 full-time (all women), 6 part-time/adjunct (3 women). *Students:* 128 full-time (105 women), 52 part-time (43 women); includes 84 minority (15 Black or African American, non-Hispanic/Latino; 21 Asian, non-Hispanic/Latino; 39 Hispanic/Latino; 9 Two or more races, non-Hispanic/Latino), 26 international. Average age 36. 203 applicants, 58% accepted, 50 enrolled. In 2011, 35 master's, 5 doctorates awarded. *Degree requirements:* For doctorate, thesis/dissertation. Application fee: $55 ($65 for international students). *Expenses:* Tuition: Full-time $20,070; part-time $1115 per unit. Tuition and fees vary according to course load, campus/location and program. *Financial support:* In 2011–12, 11 students received support. Fellowships, research assistantships, and teaching assistantships available. Financial award application deadline: 3/2; financial award applicants required to submit FAFSA. *Unit head:* Dr. Katz Susan, Chair, 415-422-6878. *Application contact:* Beth Teague, Associate Director of Graduate Outreach, 415-422-5467, E-mail: schoolofeducation@usfca.edu.

University of Southern California, Graduate School, Rossier School of Education, Doctor of Education Programs, Los Angeles, CA 90089. Offers educational psychology (Ed D); higher education administration (Ed D); K-12 leadership in urban school settings (Ed D); teacher education in multicultural societies (Ed D). Part-time and evening/weekend programs available. *Degree requirements:* For doctorate, thesis/dissertation. *Entrance requirements:* For doctorate, GRE. Additional exam requirements/recommendations for international students: Required—TOEFL (minimum score 250 computer-based; 100 iBT). Electronic applications accepted. *Faculty research:* Data-driven decision-making in K-12 schools and districts; examination of college and university leadership and management in U. S. and Asia; studies in facilitating student learning; organizational change and the role of leaders; leadership, diversity, learning and accountability.

The University of Tennessee, Graduate School, College of Education, Health and Human Sciences, Program in Education, Knoxville, TN 37996. Offers art education (MS); counseling education (PhD); cultural studies in education (PhD); curriculum (MS, Ed S); curriculum, educational research and evaluation (Ed D, PhD); early childhood education (PhD); early childhood special education (MS); education of deaf and hard of hearing (MS); educational administration and policy studies (Ed D, PhD); educational administration and supervision (Ed S); educational psychology (Ed D, PhD); elementary education (MS, Ed S); elementary teaching (MS); English education (MS, Ed S); exercise science (PhD); foreign language/ESL education (MS, Ed S); instructional technology (MS, Ed D, PhD, Ed S); literacy, language and ESL education (PhD); literacy, language education, and ESL education (Ed D); mathematics education (MS, Ed S); modified and comprehensive special education (MS); reading education (MS, Ed S); school counseling (Ed S); school psychology (PhD, Ed S); science education (MS, Ed S); secondary teaching (MS); social foundations (MS); social science education (MS, Ed S); socio-cultural foundations of sports and education (PhD); special education (Ed S); teacher education (Ed D, PhD). *Accreditation:* NCATE. Part-time and evening/weekend programs available. *Degree requirements:* For master's and Ed S, thesis optional; for doctorate, variable foreign language requirement, thesis/dissertation. *Entrance requirements:* For master's, minimum GPA of 2.7; for doctorate and Ed S, GRE General Test, minimum GPA of 2.7. Additional exam requirements/recommendations for international students: Required—TOEFL. Electronic applications accepted. *Expenses:* Tuition, state resident: full-time $8332; part-time $464 per credit hour. Tuition, nonresident: full-time $25,174; part-time $1400 per credit hour. *Required fees:* $1162; $56 per credit hour. Tuition and fees vary according to program.

The University of Texas at Arlington, Graduate School, College of Education and Health Professions, Department of Educational Leadership and Policy Studies, Arlington, TX 76019. Offers dual language (M Ed); education leadership and policy studies (PhD); higher education (M Ed); principal certification (M Ed). Part-time and evening/weekend programs available. Postbaccalaureate distance learning degree programs offered (no on-campus study). *Faculty:* 12 full-time (9 women). *Students:* 31 full-time (25 women), 749 part-time (523 women); includes 334 minority (165 Black or African American, non-Hispanic/Latino; 5 American Indian or Alaska Native, non-Hispanic/Latino; 11 Asian, non-Hispanic/Latino; 140 Hispanic/Latino; 13 Two or more races, non-Hispanic/Latino), 9 international. 342 applicants, 84% accepted, 247 enrolled. In 2011, 183 master's, 1 doctorate awarded. *Degree requirements:* For master's, 2 field-based practica; for doctorate, comprehensive exam, thesis/dissertation, 2 research-based practica. *Entrance requirements:* For master's, GRE, 3 references forms, minimum undergraduate GPA of 3.0 in the last 60 hours of course work; for doctorate, GRE, resume, statement of intent, 3 reference forms, applicable master's degree. Application fee: $50. *Financial support:* In 2011–12, 6 students received support, including 4 fellowships (averaging $6,700 per year), 2 research assistantships (averaging $8,000 per year). Financial award applicants required to submit FAFSA. *Faculty research:* Lived realities of students of color in K-16 contexts, K-16 faculty, K-16 policy and law, K-16 student access, K-16 student success. *Unit head:* Dr. Adrienne E. Hyle, Chair, 817-272-2841, Fax: 817-272-2127, E-mail: ahyle@uta.edu. *Application contact:* Paige Cordor, Graduate Advisor, 817-272-5051, Fax: 817-272-2127, E-mail: paigec@uta.edu. Web site: http://www.uta.edu/coehp/educleadership/.

The University of Texas at Austin, Graduate School, College of Education, Department of Curriculum and Instruction, Austin, TX 78712-1111. Offers bilingual/bicultural education (M Ed, MA, PhD); cultural studies in education (M Ed, MA, PhD); early childhood education (M Ed, MA, PhD); language and literacy studies (M Ed, PhD); learning technologies (M Ed, MA, PhD); physical education (M Ed, MA, PhD). Terminal master's awarded for partial completion of doctoral program. *Degree requirements:* For doctorate, thesis/dissertation. *Entrance requirements:* For master's and doctorate, GRE General Test. *Application deadline:* For fall admission, 3/1 for domestic students; for spring admission, 10/1 for domestic students. Applications are processed on a rolling basis. Application fee: $50 ($75 for international students). Electronic applications accepted. *Financial support:* Fellowships and teaching assistantships with partial tuition reimbursements available. Financial award application deadline: 2/1. *Unit head:* Betty Maloch, Chair, 512-232-4262, E-mail: bmaloch@austin.utexas.edu. *Application contact:* Stephen Flynn, Graduate Coordinator, 512-471-3747, E-mail: sflynn@austin.utexas.edu. Web site: http://www.edb.utexas.edu/coe/depts/ci/cti.html.

The University of Texas at Austin, Graduate School, College of Education, Department of Special Education, Austin, TX 78712-1111. Offers autism and developmental disabilities (Ed D, PhD); autism and developmental disability (M Ed, MA); early childhood special education (M Ed, MA, Ed D, PhD); learning disabilities (Ed D, PhD); learning disabilities/behavior disorders (M Ed, MA); multicultural special education (M Ed, MA, Ed D, PhD); rehabilitation counselor (M Ed); rehabilitation counselor education (Ed D, PhD); special education administration (Ed D, PhD). *Accreditation:* CORE. Part-time and evening/weekend programs available. Postbaccalaureate distance learning degree programs offered (no on-campus study). *Degree requirements:* For master's, thesis or alternative; for doctorate, thesis/dissertation. *Entrance requirements:* For master's and doctorate, GRE General Test. *Application deadline:* For fall admission, 2/1 priority date for domestic students; for spring admission, 10/1 priority date for domestic students. Applications are processed on a rolling basis. Application fee: $50 ($75 for international students). *Financial support:* Fellowships with tuition reimbursements, research assistantships with partial tuition reimbursements, teaching assistantships with partial tuition reimbursements, career-related internships or fieldwork, Federal Work-Study, institutionally sponsored loans, scholarships/grants, tuition waivers (full and partial), and unspecified assistantships available. Financial award application deadline: 2/1. *Faculty research:* Anchored instruction, reading disabilities, multicultural/bilingual. *Unit head:* Herbert J. Rieth, Jr., Chairman, 512-475-6552, Fax: 512-471-2471, E-mail: rieth.herb@mail.utexas.edu. *Application contact:* James Schaller, Graduate Adviser, 512-475-6543, E-mail: jschaller@mail.utexas.edu. Web site: http://www.edb.utexas.edu/coe/depts/sped.html.

The University of Texas at Brownsville, Graduate Studies, School of Education, Brownsville, TX 78520-4991. Offers bilingual education (M Ed); counseling and guidance (M Ed); curriculum and instruction (M Ed); early childhood education (M Ed); educational administration (M Ed); educational technology (M Ed); English as a second language (M Ed); reading specialist (M Ed); special education/educational diagnostician (M Ed). Part-time and evening/weekend programs available. Postbaccalaureate distance learning degree programs offered (minimal on-campus study). *Degree requirements:* For master's, thesis optional. *Entrance requirements:* For master's, GRE General Test. Additional exam requirements/recommendations for international students: Required—TOEFL.

The University of Texas at El Paso, Graduate School, College of Liberal Arts, Department of English, El Paso, TX 79968-0001. Offers bilingual professional writing (Certificate); English and American literature (MA); rhetoric and composition (PhD); rhetoric and writing studies (MA); teaching English (MAT). Part-time and evening/weekend programs available. *Students:* 115 (78 women); includes 68 minority (2 Black or African American, non-Hispanic/Latino; 1 American Indian or Alaska Native, non-Hispanic/Latino; 3 Asian, non-Hispanic/Latino; 62 Hispanic/Latino), 7 international. Average age 34. 52 applicants, 63% accepted, 31 enrolled. In 2011, 10 master's, 1 doctorate awarded. *Degree requirements:* For master's, thesis optional. *Entrance requirements:* For master's, GRE General Test, minimum GPA of 3.0. Additional exam requirements/recommendations for international students: Required—TOEFL. *Application deadline:* For fall admission, 7/1 priority date for domestic students, 3/1 for international students; for spring admission, 11/1 priority date for domestic students, 9/1 for international students. Applications are processed on a rolling basis. Application fee: $15 ($65 for international students). Electronic applications accepted. *Financial support:* In 2011–12, research assistantships with partial tuition reimbursements (averaging $20,555 per year), teaching assistantships with partial tuition reimbursements (averaging $16,444 per year) were awarded; Federal Work-Study, institutionally sponsored loans, scholarships/grants, and tuition waivers (partial) also available. Financial award application deadline: 3/15; financial award applicants required to submit FAFSA. *Faculty research:* Literature, creative writing, literary theory. *Unit head:* Dr. Evelyn Posey, Chair, 915-747-5731. *Application contact:* Dr. Benjamin Flores, Interim Dean of the Graduate School, 915-747-5491, Fax: 915-747-5788, E-mail: bflores@utep.edu.

The University of Texas at San Antonio, College of Education and Human Development, Department of Bicultural and Bilingual Studies, San Antonio, TX 78249-0617. Offers bicultural studies (MA); bicultural/bilingual education (MA); culture, literacy, and language (PhD); teaching English as a second language (MA). Part-time and evening/weekend programs available. *Faculty:* 13 full-time (8 women). *Students:* 61 full-time (51 women), 113 part-time (91 women); includes 107 minority (8 Asian, non-Hispanic/Latino; 96 Hispanic/Latino; 1 Native Hawaiian or other Pacific Islander, non-Hispanic/Latino; 2 Two or more races, non-Hispanic/Latino), 29 international. Average age 35. 93 applicants, 78% accepted, 46 enrolled. In 2011, 38 master's, 4 doctorates awarded. *Degree requirements:* For master's, one foreign language, comprehensive exam, thesis optional; for doctorate, one foreign language, comprehensive exam, thesis/dissertation. *Entrance requirements:* For master's, GRE General Test if GPA is less than 3.0 for last 60 hours, bachelor's degree with 18 credit hours in field of study or in another appropriate field of study; for doctorate, GRE General Test, resume or curriculum vitae, 3 letters of recommendation, statement of purpose. Additional exam requirements/recommendations for international students: Required—TOEFL (minimum score 500 paper-based; 61 iBT), IELTS (minimum score 5). *Application deadline:* For fall admission, 7/1 for domestic students, 4/1 for international students; for spring admission, 11/1 for domestic students, 9/1 for international students. Applications are processed on a rolling basis. Application fee: $45 ($85 for international students). Electronic applications accepted. *Expenses:* Tuition, state resident: full-time $3148; part-time $2176 per semester. Tuition, nonresident: full-time $8782; part-time $5932 per semester. *Required fees:* $719 per semester. *Financial support:* In 2011–12, 28 students received support, including 14 fellowships with full tuition reimbursements available (averaging $25,385 per year), 2 research assistantships with full tuition reimbursements available (averaging $12,468 per year), 12 teaching assistantships with full tuition reimbursements available (averaging $11,000 per year). *Faculty research:* Bilingualism and biliteracy development, second language teaching and learning, language minority education, Mexican American studies, transnationalism and immigration. *Unit head:* Dr. Robert Milk, Chair, 210-458-4426, Fax: 210-458-5962, E-mail: robert.milk@utsa.edu. *Application contact:* Armando Trujillo, Assistant Dean of the Graduate School, 210-458-5576, Fax: 210-458-5576, E-mail: armando.trujillo@utsa.edu. Web site: http://coehd.utsa.edu/bicultural-bilingual_studies.

The University of Texas–Pan American, College of Education, Department of Curriculum and Instruction: Elementary and Secondary, Edinburg, TX 78539. Offers bilingual education (M Ed); early childhood education (M Ed); elementary education (M Ed); reading (M Ed); secondary education (M Ed). Part-time programs available. *Degree requirements:* For master's, comprehensive exam, thesis optional. *Entrance requirements:* For master's, GRE. Additional exam requirements/recommendations for international students: Required—TOEFL, IELTS. *Application deadline:* For fall admission, 7/17 for domestic and international students; for spring admission, 11/16 for domestic and international students. Application fee: $0. Tuition and fees vary according to course load, program and student level. *Financial support:* Research assistantships with tuition reimbursements, Federal Work-Study, institutionally sponsored loans, scholarships/grants, and unspecified assistantships available. Financial award application deadline: 4/15. *Faculty research:* Dual language instruction, literacy and technology, teacher education in diverse populations, mathematics and science education. *Unit head:* Dr. Veronica L. Estrada, Chair, 956-665-2431, Fax: 956-665-

2434, E-mail: vlestradaa@utpa.edu. Web site: http://www.utpa.edu/dept/curr_ins/graduat.html.

University of the Incarnate Word, School of Graduate Studies and Research, Dreeben School of Education, Programs in Education, San Antonio, TX 78209-6397. Offers adult education (M Ed, MA); cross-cultural education (M Ed, MA); early childhood literacy (M Ed, MA); general education (M Ed, MA); higher education (PhD); instructional technology (M Ed, MA); international education and entrepreneurship (PhD); kinesiology (M Ed, MA); literacy (M Ed, MA); organizational leadership (PhD); organizational learning and learning (M Ed, MA); reading (M Ed, MA); special education (M Ed, MA); teacher leadership (M Ed, MA). Part-time and evening/weekend programs available. *Faculty:* 14 full-time (8 women), 10 part-time/adjunct (9 women). *Students:* 13 full-time (7 women), 197 part-time (129 women); includes 111 minority (23 Black or African American, non-Hispanic/Latino; 2 American Indian or Alaska Native, non-Hispanic/Latino; 1 Asian, non-Hispanic/Latino; 85 Hispanic/Latino), 26 international. Average age 41. 78 applicants, 79% accepted, 34 enrolled. In 2011, 21 master's, 12 doctorates awarded. *Degree requirements:* For master's, capstone; for doctorate, thesis/dissertation, qualifying exam. *Entrance requirements:* For master's, baccalaureate degree; minimum foundation GPA of 2.5; interview; for doctorate, master's degree; interview; supervised writing sample. Additional exam requirements/recommendations for international students: Required—TOEFL (minimum score 560 paper-based; 220 computer-based; 83 iBT). *Application deadline:* Applications are processed on a rolling basis. Application fee: $20. Electronic applications accepted. *Expenses: Tuition:* Part-time $725 per credit hour. Tuition and fees vary according to degree level. *Financial support:* In 2011–12, 5 research assistantships were awarded; Federal Work-Study and scholarships/grants also available. Financial award applicants required to submit FAFSA. *Unit head:* Dr. Denise Staudt, Dean, Dreeben School of Education, 210-829-2762, E-mail: staudt@uiwtx.edu. *Application contact:* Andrea Cyterski-Acosta, Dean of Enrollment, 210-829-6005, Fax: 210-829-3921, E-mail: admis@uiwtx.edu. Web site: http://www.uiw.edu/education/index.htm.

University of the Southwest, Graduate Programs, Hobbs, NM 88240-9129. Offers business administration (MBA); curriculum and instruction (MSE); curriculum and instruction: bilingual (MSE); curriculum and instruction: TESOL (MSE); early childhood education (MSE); educational administration (MSE); mental health counseling (MSE); school counseling (MSE); special education (MSE); sports management (MBA). Part-time and evening/weekend programs available. Postbaccalaureate distance learning degree programs offered (no on-campus study). *Faculty:* 13 full-time (6 women), 28 part-time/adjunct (17 women). *Students:* 76 full-time (63 women), 229 part-time (194 women); includes 104 minority (50 Black or African American, non-Hispanic/Latino; 2 American Indian or Alaska Native, non-Hispanic/Latino; 8 Asian, non-Hispanic/Latino; 44 Hispanic/Latino). Average age 38. 173 applicants, 71% accepted, 101 enrolled. In 2011, 75 master's awarded. *Degree requirements:* For master's, comprehensive exam, thesis (for some programs). *Entrance requirements:* Additional exam requirements/recommendations for international students: Recommended—TOEFL. *Application deadline:* Applications are processed on a rolling basis. Application fee: $50. Electronic applications accepted. *Expenses: Tuition:* Full-time $12,288; part-time $512 per credit hour. One-time fee: $50. Tuition and fees vary according to course load. *Financial support:* In 2011–12, 47 students received support. Federal Work-Study available. Financial award application deadline: 4/1; financial award applicants required to submit FAFSA. *Unit head:* Dr. Mary Harris, Dean of Education, 575-492-2162, Fax: 575-392-6006, E-mail: mharris@usw.edu. *Application contact:* Melissa Mitchell, Senior Online Program Advisor, 575-492-2142, Fax: 575-392-6006, E-mail: mmitchell@usw.edu. Web site: http://www.usw.edu/admissions/graduate_admission/graduate_admissions.

University of Washington, Graduate School, College of Education, Seattle, WA 98195. Offers curriculum and instruction (M Ed, Ed D, PhD), including educational technology, general curriculum (Ed D, PhD), language, literacy, and culture, mathematics education, multicultural education, reading and language arts education (Ed D), science education, social studies education, teaching and curriculum (M Ed); educational leadership and policy studies (M Ed, Ed D, PhD), including administration (Ed D), educational policy, organization, and leadership (M Ed, PhD), higher education, leadership for learning (Ed D), social and cultural foundations of education (M Ed, PhD); educational psychology (M Ed, PhD), including educational psychology (PhD), human development and cognition (M Ed), learning sciences, measurement, statistics and research design (M Ed), school psychology (M Ed); instructional leadership (M Ed); intercollegiate athletic leadership (M Ed); special education (M Ed, Ed D, PhD), including early childhood special education (M Ed), emotional and behavioral disabilities (M Ed), learning disabilities (M Ed), low-incidence disabilities (M Ed), severe disabilities (M Ed), special education (Ed D, PhD); teacher education (MIT). *Accreditation:* APA. Part-time and evening/weekend programs available. *Degree requirements:* For master's, thesis optional; for doctorate, thesis/dissertation. *Entrance requirements:* For master's and doctorate, GRE General Test, minimum GPA of 3.0. Additional exam requirements/recommendations for international students: Required—TOEFL. Electronic applications accepted. *Faculty research:* School restructuring/effective schools, special education interventions, literacy and writing, technology, school partnerships, teacher preparation.

University of West Florida, College of Professional Studies, Ed D Programs, Specialization in Curriculum and Instruction: Curriculum and Diversity Studies, Pensacola, FL 32514-5750. Offers Ed D. Part-time and evening/weekend programs available. *Students:* 1 full-time, 35 part-time (28 women); includes 15 minority (9 Black or African American, non-Hispanic/Latino; 3 Asian, non-Hispanic/Latino; 3 Hispanic/Latino). Average age 43. 16 applicants, 19% accepted, 3 enrolled. In 2011, 9 doctorates awarded. *Degree requirements:* For doctorate, comprehensive exam, thesis/dissertation. *Entrance requirements:* For doctorate, GRE, MAT, or GMAT, letter of intent; writing sample; three letters of recommendation; two completed disposition assessment forms; written statement of goals; interview with admissions committee. Additional exam requirements/recommendations for international students: Required—TOEFL (minimum score 550 paper-based; 213 computer-based). *Application deadline:* For fall admission, 6/1 for domestic and international students; for spring admission, 10/1 for domestic students. Applications are processed on a rolling basis. Application fee: $30. *Expenses:* Tuition, state resident: full-time $5729; part-time $302 per credit hour. Tuition, nonresident: full-time $20,059; part-time $961 per credit hour. *Required fees:* $1509; $63 per credit hour. *Unit head:* Dr. Pam Northrup, Interim Dean, 850-474-2769, Fax: 850-474-3205. *Application contact:* Terry McCray, Assistant Director of Graduate Admissions, 850-473-7718, Fax: 850-473-7714, E-mail: gradadmissions@uwf.edu. Web site: http://uwf.edu/edd/curriculum_diversity.cfm.

University of Wisconsin–Milwaukee, Graduate School, School of Education, Program in Urban Education, Milwaukee, WI 53201-0413. Offers adult and continuing education (PhD); curriculum and instruction (PhD); educational administration (PhD); educational and media technology (PhD); educational psychology (PhD); multicultural studies (PhD); social foundations of education (PhD). *Students:* 65 full-time (45 women), 37 part-time (25 women); includes 39 minority (18 Black or African American, non-Hispanic/Latino; 1 American Indian or Alaska Native, non-Hispanic/Latino; 6 Asian, non-Hispanic/Latino; 6 Hispanic/Latino; 8 Two or more races, non-Hispanic/Latino), 5 international. Average age 41. 26 applicants, 62% accepted, 2 enrolled. In 2011, 13 degrees awarded. *Degree requirements:* For doctorate, comprehensive exam, thesis/dissertation. *Entrance requirements:* For doctorate, GRE General Test, minimum undergraduate GPA of 2.85, graduate 3.5. Additional exam requirements/recommendations for international students: Required—TOEFL (minimum score 550 paper-based; 79 iBT), IELTS (minimum score 6.5). *Application deadline:* For fall admission, 1/1 priority date for domestic students; for spring admission, 9/1 for domestic students. Applications are processed on a rolling basis. Application fee: $56 ($96 for international students). Electronic applications accepted. One-time fee: $506.10 full-time. Tuition and fees vary according to course load and reciprocity agreements. *Financial support:* In 2011–12, 11 fellowships, 1 teaching assistantship were awarded; research assistantships, career-related internships or fieldwork, health care benefits, unspecified assistantships, and project assistantships also available. Support available to part-time students. Financial award application deadline: 4/15; financial award applicants required to submit FAFSA. *Unit head:* Larry Martin, Representative, 414-229-4729, Fax: 414-229-2920, E-mail: lmartin@uwm.edu. *Application contact:* General Information Contact, 414-229-4982, Fax: 414-229-6967, E-mail: gradschool@uwm.edu. Web site: http://www.uwm.edu/Dept/UrbanEd/.

University of Wisconsin–Whitewater, School of Graduate Studies, College of Education and Professional Studies, Department of Curriculum and Instruction, Whitewater, WI 53190-1790. Offers professional development (MS), including bilingual education, challenging advanced learners, curriculum and instruction, educational leadership, health, human performance and recreation, health, physical education and coaching, information technologies and libraries, reading. *Accreditation:* NCATE. Part-time and evening/weekend programs available. Postbaccalaureate distance learning degree programs offered. *Students:* 25 full-time (12 women), 68 part-time (51 women); includes 26 minority (15 Black or African American, non-Hispanic/Latino; 3 Asian, non-Hispanic/Latino; 8 Hispanic/Latino). Average age 33. 29 applicants, 86% accepted, 16 enrolled. In 2011, 44 master's awarded. *Degree requirements:* For master's, thesis or integrated project. *Entrance requirements:* Additional exam requirements/recommendations for international students: Required—TOEFL (minimum score 550 paper-based; 213 computer-based; 80 iBT), IELTS (minimum score 6). *Application deadline:* For fall admission, 7/15 priority date for domestic students, 7/15 for international students; for spring admission, 12/1 priority date for domestic students, 12/1 for international students. Applications are processed on a rolling basis. Application fee: $56. Electronic applications accepted. *Expenses:* Tuition, state resident: full-time $4088. Tuition, nonresident: full-time $8817. Tuition and fees vary according to program. *Financial support:* Research assistantships, Federal Work-Study, unspecified assistantships, and out-of-state fee waivers available. Support available to part-time students. Financial award application deadline: 3/15; financial award applicants required to submit FAFSA. *Faculty research:* Hybrid of exercise physiology and psychology; gender equity; education, pedagogy, and technology; comprehensive school health education. *Unit head:* Dr. John Zbikowski, Coordinator, 262-472-4860, Fax: 262-472-1988, E-mail: zbikowskij@uww.edu. *Application contact:* Sally A. Lange, School of Graduate Studies, 262-472-1006, Fax: 262-472-5027, E-mail: gradschl@uww.edu.

Utah State University, School of Graduate Studies, College of Humanities, Arts and Social Sciences, Department of Languages, Philosophy, and Speech Communication, Logan, UT 84322. Offers second language teaching (MSLT). *Entrance requirements:* For master's, GRE General Test or MAT, minimum GPA of 3.0. Additional exam requirements/recommendations for international students: Required—TOEFL.

Vanderbilt University, Graduate School, Program in Learning, Teaching and Diversity, Nashville, TN 37240-1001. Offers MS, PhD. *Faculty:* 21 full-time (11 women), 1 (woman) part-time/adjunct. *Students:* 54 full-time (35 women), 3 part-time (1 woman); includes 7 minority (2 Black or African American, non-Hispanic/Latino; 4 Asian, non-Hispanic/Latino; 1 Two or more races, non-Hispanic/Latino), 6 international. Average age 34. 147 applicants, 5% accepted, 6 enrolled. In 2011, 1 master's, 1 doctorate awarded. *Degree requirements:* For doctorate, comprehensive exam, thesis/dissertation. *Entrance requirements:* For doctorate, GRE General Test. Additional exam requirements/recommendations for international students: Required—TOEFL (minimum score 570 paper-based; 230 computer-based; 88 iBT). *Application deadline:* For fall admission, 12/31 for domestic and international students. Application fee: $0. Electronic applications accepted. *Financial support:* Fellowships with full and partial tuition reimbursements, research assistantships with full tuition reimbursements, teaching assistantships with full tuition reimbursements, Federal Work-Study, institutionally sponsored loans, scholarships/grants, traineeships, and health care benefits available. Financial award application deadline: 1/15; financial award applicants required to submit CSS PROFILE or FAFSA. *Faculty research:* New pedagogies for math, science, and language; the support of English language learners; the uses of new technology and media in the classroom; middle school mathematics and the institutional setting of teaching. *Unit head:* Dr. Paul Cobb, Chair, 615-343-1492, Fax: 615-322-8999, E-mail: paul.cobb@vanderbilt.edu. *Application contact:* Dr. Clifford Hofwolt, Director of Graduate Studies, 615-322-8227, Fax: 615-322-8014, E-mail: clifford.hofwolt@vanderbilt.edu. Web site: http://peabody.vanderbilt.edu/Admissions_and_Programs/PhD_Programs/PhD_Program_Choices.xml.

Vanderbilt University, Peabody College, Department of Teaching and Learning, Nashville, TN 37240-1001. Offers elementary education (M Ed); English language learners (M Ed); learning and instruction (M Ed); learning, diversity, and urban studies (M Ed); reading education (M Ed); secondary education (M Ed). *Accreditation:* NCATE. *Faculty:* 35 full-time (24 women), 19 part-time/adjunct (14 women). *Students:* 123 full-time (96 women), 38 part-time (34 women); includes 26 minority (6 Black or African American, non-Hispanic/Latino; 3 Asian, non-Hispanic/Latino; 7 Hispanic/Latino; 10 Two or more races, non-Hispanic/Latino), 12 international. Average age 26. 251 applicants, 56% accepted, 60 enrolled. In 2011, 80 master's awarded. *Degree requirements:* For master's, comprehensive exam, thesis optional. *Entrance requirements:* For master's, GRE General Test, MAT. Additional exam requirements/recommendations for international students: Required—TOEFL (minimum score 550 paper-based; 213 computer-based). *Application deadline:* For fall admission, 12/31 priority date for domestic students, 12/31 for international students; for spring admission, 11/1 priority date for domestic students, 11/1 for international students. Applications are processed on a rolling basis. Application fee: $0. Electronic applications accepted. *Financial support:* Fellowships with full and partial tuition reimbursements, research assistantships with full and partial tuition reimbursements, teaching assistantships with full and partial tuition reimbursements, Federal Work-Study, institutionally sponsored loans, scholarships/grants, tuition waivers (partial), and unspecified assistantships available. Support available to part-time students. Financial award application deadline: 2/1; financial award applicants required to submit FAFSA. *Faculty research:* Learning environments for mathematics of space and motion, visual programming tools for children's learning of basic science concepts, pathways for elementary and middle school children's learning about measurement and statistics, early reading intervention, professional development for ambitious mathematics teaching. *Unit head:* Dr. David Dickinson, Acting Chair, 615-322-8100, Fax: 615-322-8999, E-mail: david.k.dickinson@vanderbilt.edu. *Application contact:* Angela Saylor, Educational Coordinator, 615-322-8092, Fax: 615-322-8999, E-mail: angela.saylor@vanderbilt.edu.

Walden University, Graduate Programs, Richard W. Riley College of Education and Leadership, Minneapolis, MN 55401. Offers administrator leadership for teaching and

learning (Ed D, Ed S); adult education (Ed D, Ed S); adult learning (MS, Postbaccalaureate Certificate), including developmental education (MS), online teaching (MS), teaching adults English as a second language (MS), training and performance management (MS); college teaching and learning (Ed D, Ed S, Postbaccalaureate Certificate); curriculum, instruction and assessment (Ed D, Postbaccalaureate Certificate); curriculum, instruction, and professional development (Ed S); developmental education (Postbaccalaureate Certificate); early childhood administration, management, and leadership (Postbaccalaureate Certificate); early childhood education (birth-grade 3) (MAT); early childhood public policy and advocacy (Postbaccalaureate Certificate); early childhood studies (MS), including administration, management and leadership, early childhood public policy and advocacy, teaching adults in the early childhood field, teaching and diversity; education (MS, PhD), including adolescent literacy and technology (grades 6-12) (MS), adult education leadership (PhD), assessment, evaluation, and accountability (PhD), community college leadership (PhD), curriculum, instruction, and assessment, early childhood education (PhD), educational technology (PhD), elementary reading and literacy (MS), elementary reading and mathematics (MS), general program, global and comparative education (PhD), higher education (PhD), integrating technology in the classroom (MS), K-12 educational leadership (PhD), leadership, policy and change (PhD), learning, instruction and innovation (PhD), literacy and learning in the content areas (MS), mathematics (grades 6-8) (MS), mathematics (grades K-5) (MS), middle level education (grades 5-8) (MS), professional development (MS), science (grades K-8) (MS), self-designed (PhD), special education (PhD), special education (non-licensure) (MS), teacher leadership (grades K-12) (MS), teaching English language learners (grades K-12) (MS); educational leadership and administration (principal preparation) (Ed S); educational technology (Ed S); elementary reading and literacy (Postbaccalaureate Certificate); engaging culturally diverse learners (Postbaccalaureate Certificate); enrollment management and institutional marketing (Postbaccalaureate Certificate); higher education (MS), including college teaching and learning, enrollment management and institutional planning, global higher education, leadership for student success, online and distance learning; higher education leadership (Ed D); instructional design (Postbaccalaureate Certificate); instructional design and technology (MS), including general program (MS, PhD), online learning, training and performance improvement; integrating technology in the classroom (Postbaccalaureate Certificate); online teaching for adult learners (Postbaccalaureate Certificate); professional development (Postbaccalaureate Certificate); reading and literacy leadership (Ed D); science K-8 (Postbaccalaureate Certificate); special education (Ed D, Ed S); special education: emotional/behavioral disorders (K-12) (MAT); special education: learning disabilities (K-12) (MAT); teacher leadership (Ed D, Ed S, Postbaccalaureate Certificate); training and performance management (Postbaccalaureate Certificate). Part-time and evening/weekend programs available. Postbaccalaureate distance learning degree programs offered (minimal on-campus study). *Faculty:* 71 full-time (48 women), 853 part-time/adjunct (585 women). *Students:* 11,326 full-time (9,212 women), 2,148 part-time (1,795 women); includes 5,346 minority (4,403 Black or African American, non-Hispanic/Latino; 76 American Indian or Alaska Native, non-Hispanic/Latino; 140 Asian, non-Hispanic/Latino; 561 Hispanic/Latino; 21 Native Hawaiian or other Pacific Islander, non-Hispanic/Latino; 145 Two or more races, non-Hispanic/Latino), 322 international. Average age 39. In 2011, 3,477 master's, 318 doctorates, 471 other advanced degrees awarded. *Degree requirements:* For doctorate, thesis/dissertation (for some programs), residency; for other advanced degree, residency (for some programs). *Entrance requirements:* For master's, bachelor's degree or equivalent in related field; minimum GPA of 2.5; official transcripts; goal statement; access to computer and Internet; for doctorate, master's degree or equivalent in related field; minimum GPA of 3.0; official transcripts; three years' related professional/academic experience (preferred); access to computer and Internet; for other advanced degree, master's degree or equivalent in related field; minimum GPA of 3.0; 3 years related professional/academic experience (preferred); access to computer and Internet (Ed S). Additional exam requirements/recommendations for international students: Required—TOEFL (minimum score 550 paper-based; 213 computer-based), IELTS (minimum score 6.5), or Michigan English Language Assessment Battery (minimum score 82). *Application deadline:* Applications are processed on a rolling basis. Application fee: $50. Electronic applications accepted. *Financial support:* Federal Work-Study, scholarships/grants, unspecified assistantships, and family tuition reduction, active duty/veteran tuition reduction, group tuition reduction, interest-free payment plans, employee tuition reduction available. Support available to part-time students. Financial award applicants required to submit FAFSA. *Unit head:* Dr. Kate Steffens, Dean, 800-925-3368. *Application contact:* Jennifer Hall, Vice President of Enrollment Management, 866-4-WALDEN, E-mail: info@waldenu.edu. Web site: http://www.waldenu.edu/Colleges-and-Schools/College-of-Education-and-Leadership.htm.

Washington State University, Graduate School, College of Education, Department of Teaching and Learning, Pullman, WA 99164. Offers curriculum and instruction (Ed D, PhD); diverse languages (M Ed, MA); elementary education (M Ed, MA, MIT); exercise science (MS); literacy education (M Ed, MA, PhD); math education (PhD); secondary education (M Ed, MA). *Accreditation:* NCATE. *Faculty:* 20. *Students:* 79 full-time (51 women), 40 part-time (31 women); includes 24 minority (3 Black or African American, non-Hispanic/Latino; 5 Asian, non-Hispanic/Latino; 13 Hispanic/Latino; 1 Native Hawaiian or other Pacific Islander, non-Hispanic/Latino; 2 Two or more races, non-Hispanic/Latino), 43 international. Average age 34. 106 applicants, 47% accepted, 43 enrolled. In 2011, 34 master's, 3 doctorates awarded. *Degree requirements:* For master's, comprehensive exam (for some programs), thesis (for some programs), oral or written exam; for doctorate, comprehensive exam, thesis/dissertation, oral and written exam. *Entrance requirements:* For master's and doctorate, GRE General Test, minimum GPA of 3.0, 3 letters of recommendation. Additional exam requirements/recommendations for international students: Required—TOEFL. *Application deadline:* For fall admission, 2/1 for domestic students, 3/1 for international students; for spring admission, 9/1 for domestic students, 7/1 for international students. Applications are processed on a rolling basis. Application fee: $75. *Financial support:* In 2011–12, 130 teaching assistantships with partial tuition reimbursements (averaging $18,204 per year) were awarded; career-related internships or fieldwork, Federal Work-Study, institutionally sponsored loans, tuition waivers (partial), unspecified assistantships, and staff assistantships, teaching associateships also available. Financial award application deadline: 4/1. *Faculty research:* Evolution of middle school education, issues in special education, computer-assisted language learning. *Total annual research expenditures:* $324,000. *Unit head:* Dr. Dawn Shinew, Interim Chair, 509-335-5027, E-mail: dshinew@wsu.edu. *Application contact:* Graduate School Admissions, 800-GRADWSU, Fax: 509-335-1949, E-mail: gradsch@wsu.edu. Web site: http://www.educ.wsu.edu/TL/overview.htm.

Wayne State University, College of Education, Division of Teacher Education, Detroit, MI 48202. Offers art education (M Ed), including art therapy; bilingual/bicultural education (M Ed); career and technical education (M Ed); curriculum and instruction (Ed D, PhD, Ed S), including art education (PhD), bilingual education (Ed D, Ed S), bilingual-bicultural education (PhD), career and technical education (MAT, Ed D, PhD, Ed S), early childhood education (MAT, Ed D, PhD, Ed S), elementary education, English as a second language (MAT, Ed D, Ed S), English education (MAT, Ed D, PhD, Ed S), foreign language education (MAT, PhD), K-12 curriculum, mathematics education (MAT, Ed D, PhD, Ed S), science education (MAT, Ed D, PhD, Ed S), secondary education, social studies education (MAT, Ed S), social studies education: secondary (Ed D, PhD); elementary education (MAT), including special education; elementary education (M Ed, MAT), including children's literature (MAT), early childhood education (MAT, Ed D, PhD, Ed S), general elementary education (MAT); elementary or secondary education (MAT), including bilingual/bicultural education, English as a second language (MAT, Ed D, Ed S), mathematics education (MAT, Ed D, PhD, Ed S), science education (MAT, Ed D, PhD, Ed S), social studies education (MAT, Ed S); English education-secondary (M Ed); foreign language education (M Ed); mathematics education (M Ed); reading (M Ed, Ed S); reading, languages and literature (Ed D); science education (M Ed); secondary education (MAT), including art education (K-12), career and technical education (MAT, Ed D, PhD, Ed S), English education (MAT, Ed D, PhD, Ed S), foreign language education (MAT, PhD), kinesiology; social studies education secondary (M Ed); special education (M Ed, Ed D, PhD, Ed S). *Students:* 216 full-time (154 women), 626 part-time (478 women); includes 289 minority (227 Black or African American, non-Hispanic/Latino; 4 American Indian or Alaska Native, non-Hispanic/Latino; 27 Asian, non-Hispanic/Latino; 21 Hispanic/Latino; 1 Native Hawaiian or other Pacific Islander, non-Hispanic/Latino; 9 Two or more races, non-Hispanic/Latino), 14 international. Average age 37. 347 applicants, 37% accepted, 93 enrolled. In 2011, 226 master's, 12 doctorates, 46 other advanced degrees awarded. *Degree requirements:* For master's, thesis (for some programs), thesis, essay or project (for some M Ed programs), professional field experience (for MAT programs); for doctorate, thesis/dissertation. *Entrance requirements:* For master's, Michigan Basic Skills Test (MA in teaching); for doctorate, minimum undergraduate GPA of 3.0, graduate 3.5; interview, curriculum vitae; references. Additional exam requirements/recommendations for international students: Required—TOEFL (minimum score 550 paper-based; 213 computer-based), TWE (minimum score 5.5). *Application deadline:* For fall admission, 6/1 priority date for domestic students, 5/1 for international students; for winter admission, 10/1 priority date for domestic students, 9/1 for international students; for spring admission, 2/1 priority date for domestic students, 1/1 for international students. Applications are processed on a rolling basis. Application fee: $50. Electronic applications accepted. *Expenses:* Tuition, state resident: part-time $512.85 per credit. Tuition, nonresident: part-time $1132.65 per credit. *Required fees:* $26.60 per credit. $199.65 per semester. Tuition and fees vary according to course load and program. *Financial support:* In 2011–12, 42 students received support. Fellowships, research assistantships with tuition reimbursements available, teaching assistantships, scholarships/grants, and unspecified assistantships available. *Faculty research:* Reading and writing literacy and literature. *Total annual research expenditures:* $264,016. *Unit head:* Dr. Craig Roney, Assistant Dean, 313-577-0902, E-mail: rroney@wayne.edu. Web site: http://coe.wayne.edu/ted/index.php.

Western New Mexico University, Graduate Division, School of Education, Silver City, NM 88062-0680. Offers bilingual education (MAT); counseling (MA); educational leadership (MA); elementary education (MAT); reading (MAT); school psychology (MA); secondary education (MAT); special education (MAT); TESOL (teaching English to speakers of other languages) (MAT). *Accreditation:* NCATE. *Degree requirements:* For master's, comprehensive exam. *Entrance requirements:* For master's, GRE General Test, GRE Subject Test, minimum GPA of 3.2 in last 64 hours of undergraduate study. Additional exam requirements/recommendations for international students: Required—TOEFL (minimum score 550 paper-based; 213 computer-based). Electronic applications accepted.

Western Oregon University, Graduate Programs, College of Education, Division of Teacher Education, Program in Secondary Education, Monmouth, OR 97361-1394. Offers bilingual education (MS Ed); health (MS Ed); humanities (MAT, MS Ed); initial licensure (MAT); mathematics (MAT, MS Ed); science (MAT, MS Ed); social science (MAT, MS Ed). *Accreditation:* NCATE. Part-time and evening/weekend programs available. *Degree requirements:* For master's, thesis optional, written exam. *Entrance requirements:* For master's, minimum GPA of 3.0, teaching license. Additional exam requirements/recommendations for international students: Required—TOEFL (minimum score 550 paper-based; 213 computer-based; 79 iBT), IELTS (minimum score 6.5). *Faculty research:* Literacy, science in primary grades, geography education, retention, teacher burnout.

Xavier University, College of Social Sciences, Health and Education, School of Education, Department of Childhood Education and Literacy, Program in Multicultural Literature for Children, Cincinnati, OH 45207. Offers M Ed. Part-time programs available. *Faculty:* 4 part-time/adjunct (3 women). *Students:* 1 (woman) full-time, 2 part-time (both women). Average age 32. 1 applicant, 100% accepted, 1 enrolled. In 2011, 1 master's awarded. *Degree requirements:* For master's, comprehensive exam, thesis, research project. *Entrance requirements:* For master's, GRE or MAT. Additional exam requirements/recommendations for international students: Required—TOEFL (minimum score 550 paper-based; 213 computer-based; 79 iBT). *Application deadline:* Applications are processed on a rolling basis. Application fee: $35. Electronic applications accepted. *Expenses: Tuition:* Part-time $576 per credit hour. *Financial support:* In 2011–12, 2 students received support. Tuition waivers (partial) and unspecified assistantships available. Financial award applicants required to submit FAFSA. *Faculty research:* First-year teacher retention, teaching efficacy of science educators, adolescents' literacy practices, family resiliency, preparing culturally responsive teachers. *Unit head:* Dr. Cynthia Hayes Geer, Chair, 513-745-3262, Fax: 513-745-3504, E-mail: geer@xavier.edu. *Application contact:* Roger Bosse, Director of Graduate Studies, 513-745-3357, Fax: 513-745-1048, E-mail: bosse@xavier.edu. Web site: http://www.xavier.edu/multicultural-literature/.

Special Education

Acadia University, Faculty of Professional Studies, School of Education, Program in Inclusive Education, Wolfville, NS B4P 2R6, Canada. Offers M Ed. Part-time programs available. *Degree requirements:* For master's, thesis optional. *Entrance requirements:* For master's, bachelor's degree in education, minimum B average in undergraduate course work, course work in special education. Additional exam requirements/recommendations for international students: Required—TOEFL (minimum score 580 paper-based; 237 computer-based; 93 iBT), IELTS (minimum score 6.5). *Faculty research:* Technology and human interaction, inclusive education and community, accommodating diversity, program evaluation.

Adams State University, The Graduate School, Department of Teacher Education, Program in Special Education, Alamosa, CO 81102. Offers MA. *Accreditation:* Teacher Education Accreditation Council. Part-time programs available. Postbaccalaureate distance learning degree programs offered. *Degree requirements:* For master's, practicum, qualifying exam. *Entrance requirements:* For master's, GRE General Test or MAT, minimum undergraduate GPA of 3.0.

Adelphi University, Ruth S. Ammon School of Education, Program in Special Education, Garden City, NY 11530-0701. Offers MS, Certificate. Part-time and evening/weekend programs available. *Students:* 88 full-time (74 women), 105 part-time (101 women); includes 61 minority (32 Black or African American, non-Hispanic/Latino; 6 Asian, non-Hispanic/Latino; 22 Hispanic/Latino; 1 Native Hawaiian or other Pacific Islander, non-Hispanic/Latino), 4 international. Average age 30. In 2011, 72 master's, 58 other advanced degrees awarded. *Entrance requirements:* For master's, 2 letters of recommendation, resume detailing paid/volunteer experience and organizational membership. Additional exam requirements/recommendations for international students: Required—TOEFL (minimum score 550 paper-based; 213 computer-based; 80 iBT). *Application deadline:* For fall admission, 4/1 for international students; for spring admission, 11/1 for international students. Electronic applications accepted. *Expenses: Tuition:* Full-time $29,600; part-time $930 per credit. *Required fees:* $1100. *Financial support:* Fellowships, research assistantships with partial tuition reimbursements, teaching assistantships, career-related internships or fieldwork, Federal Work-Study, institutionally sponsored loans, tuition waivers (full), and unspecified assistantships available. Support available to part-time students. Financial award application deadline: 2/15; financial award applicants required to submit FAFSA. *Unit head:* Dr. Anne Mungai, Director, 516-877-4096, E-mail: mungai@adelphi.edu. *Application contact:* Christine Murphy, Director of Admissions, 516-877-3050, Fax: 516-877-3039, E-mail: graduateadmissions@adelphi.edu.

Alabama Agricultural and Mechanical University, School of Graduate Studies, School of Education, Department of Counseling and Special Education, Huntsville, AL 35811. Offers communicative disorders (M Ed, MS); psychology and counseling (MS, Ed S), including clinical psychology (MS), counseling and guidance, counseling psychology (MS), personnel management (MS), psychometry (MS), school psychology (MS); special education (M Ed, MS). *Accreditation:* CORE; NCATE. Part-time and evening/weekend programs available. *Degree requirements:* For master's, comprehensive exam. *Entrance requirements:* For master's, GRE General Test. Additional exam requirements/recommendations for international students: Required—TOEFL (minimum score 500 paper-based; 173 computer-based; 61 iBT). *Faculty research:* Increasing numbers of minorities in special education and speech-language pathology.

Alabama State University, Department of Curriculum and Instruction, Program in Special Education, Montgomery, AL 36101-0271. Offers M Ed. Part-time programs available. *Degree requirements:* For master's, comprehensive exam. *Entrance requirements:* For master's, GRE General Test, MAT, graduate writing competency test. Additional exam requirements/recommendations for international students: Required—TOEFL (minimum score 500 paper-based; 173 computer-based). *Application deadline:* For fall admission, 7/15 for domestic students; for spring admission, 12/15 for domestic students. Applications are processed on a rolling basis. Application fee: $10. *Financial support:* In 2011–12, research assistantships (averaging $9,450 per year) were awarded. *Unit head:* Dr. Willa Bing Harris, Acting Chairperson, 334-229-4394, Fax: 334-229-4904, E-mail: wbharris@alasu.edu. *Application contact:* Dr. Doris Screws, Dean of Graduate Studies, 334-229-4274, Fax: 334-229-4928, E-mail: dscrews@alasu.edu.

Albany State University, College of Education, Albany, GA 31705-2717. Offers early childhood education (M Ed); education specialist (Ed S); educational leadership and administration (M Ed); health, physical education and recreation (M Ed); middle grades education (M Ed); school counseling (M Ed); special education (M Ed). *Accreditation:* NCATE. Part-time and evening/weekend programs available. Postbaccalaureate distance learning degree programs offered (minimal on-campus study). *Faculty:* 19 full-time (13 women), 7 part-time/adjunct (5 women). *Students:* 90 full-time (69 women), 118 part-time (92 women); includes 152 minority (151 Black or African American, non-Hispanic/Latino; 1 American Indian or Alaska Native, non-Hispanic/Latino), 1 international. Average age 35. 93 applicants, 78% accepted, 38 enrolled. In 2011, 43 master's, 8 Ed Ss awarded. *Degree requirements:* For master's, comprehensive exam, internship, GACE Content Exam. *Entrance requirements:* For master's, GRE or MAT. *Application deadline:* For fall admission, 6/1 for domestic students, 5/1 for international students; for spring admission, 11/1 for domestic students, 10/1 for international students. Applications are processed on a rolling basis. Application fee: $20. Electronic applications accepted. *Expenses:* Tuition, state resident: full-time $3204; part-time $178 per credit hour. Tuition, nonresident: full-time $12,816; part-time $712 per credit hour. *Required fees:* $379 per semester. *Financial support:* Scholarships/grants available. Financial award application deadline: 4/15; financial award applicants required to submit FAFSA. *Faculty research:* GACE preparation, STEM (science, technology, engineering, and mathematics), technology education, special education, professional teacher development, health implications liberation philosophy, NET-Q, learning community, disabled or at-risk students. *Total annual research expenditures:* $252,502. *Unit head:* Dr. Kimberly King-Jupiter, Dean, 229-430-1718, Fax: 229-430-4993, E-mail: kimberly.king-jupiter@asurams.edu. *Application contact:* Jeffrey Pierce, II, Graduate Admissions Counselor, 229-430-4646, Fax: 229-430-4105, E-mail: jeffrey.pierce@asurams.edu. Web site: http://asu-sacs.asurams.edu/ASUCatalog/Graduate/index.html.

Albright College, Graduate Division, Reading, PA 19612-5234. Offers early childhood education (MS); elementary education (MS); English as a second language (MA); general education (MA); special education (MS). Part-time and evening/weekend programs available. *Degree requirements:* For master's, thesis. *Entrance requirements:* For master's, GRE General Test or MAT, minimum undergraduate GPA of 3.0, 2 letters of recommendation, interview. Additional exam requirements/recommendations for international students: Recommended—TOEFL (minimum score 525 paper-based; 197 computer-based). Electronic applications accepted.

Alcorn State University, School of Graduate Studies, School of Psychology and Education, Alcorn State, MS 39096-7500. Offers agricultural education (MS Ed); elementary education (MS Ed, Ed S); guidance and counseling (MS Ed); industrial education (MS Ed); secondary education (MS Ed), including health and physical education; special education (MS Ed). *Accreditation:* NCATE. *Degree requirements:* For master's, thesis optional.

Alliant International University–Irvine, Shirley M. Hufstedler School of Education, Teacher Education Programs, Irvine, CA 92612. Offers auditory oral education (Certificate); CLAD (Certificate); preliminary multiple subject (Credential); preliminary multiple subject with BCLAD (Credential); preliminary single subject (Credential); professional clear multiple subject (Credential); professional clear single subject (Credential); teaching (MA, Credential); technology and learning (MA). Part-time and evening/weekend programs available. *Students:* 4. In 2011, 6 master's awarded. *Entrance requirements:* For degree, California Basic Educational Skills Test, minimum GPA of 2.5. Additional exam requirements/recommendations for international students: Required—TOEFL (minimum score 550 paper-based; 213 computer-based), TWE. *Application deadline:* For fall admission, 7/1 priority date for domestic students, 7/1 for international students; for spring admission, 12/1 priority date for domestic students, 12/1 for international students. Applications are processed on a rolling basis. Application fee: $55. Electronic applications accepted. *Financial support:* Career-related internships or fieldwork, Federal Work-Study, institutionally sponsored loans, and scholarships/grants available. Financial award applicants required to submit FAFSA. *Unit head:* Dr. Trudy Day, Assistant Dean, 866-825-5426, Fax: 949-833-3507, E-mail: admissions@alliant.edu. *Application contact:* Alliant International University Central Contact Center, 866-U-ALLIANT, Fax: 858-635-4555, E-mail: admissions@alliant.edu. Web site: http://www.alliant.edu/gsoe.

Alliant International University–San Francisco, Shirley M. Hufstedler School of Education, Teacher Education Programs, San Francisco, CA 94133-1221. Offers auditory oral education (Certificate); CLAD (Certificate); education specialist: mild/moderate disabilities (Credential); preliminary multiple subject (Credential); preliminary single subject (Credential); professional clear multiple subject (Credential); professional clear single subject (Credential); special education (MA); teaching (MA). Part-time and evening/weekend programs available. *Faculty:* 6 full-time (4 women), 10 part-time/adjunct (8 women). *Students:* 46 full-time (30 women), 79 part-time (54 women); includes 35 minority (9 Black or African American, non-Hispanic/Latino; 15 Asian, non-Hispanic/Latino; 11 Hispanic/Latino). Average age 38. In 2011, 20 master's awarded. *Degree requirements:* For master's, thesis. *Entrance requirements:* For degree, California Basic Educational Skills Test, minimum GPA of 2.5. Additional exam requirements/recommendations for international students: Required—TOEFL (minimum score 550 paper-based; 213 computer-based), TWE (minimum score 5). *Application deadline:* For fall admission, 7/1 priority date for domestic students, 7/1 for international students; for spring admission, 12/1 priority date for domestic students, 12/1 for international students. Applications are processed on a rolling basis. Application fee: $55. Electronic applications accepted. *Financial support:* Career-related internships or fieldwork, Federal Work-Study, institutionally sponsored loans, and scholarships/grants available. Financial award application deadline: 2/15; financial award applicants required to submit FAFSA. *Faculty research:* Curriculum development, first year teachers, cross-cultural issues in teaching, biliteracy. *Unit head:* Dr. Trudy Day, Program Director, 415-955-2102, Fax: 415-955-2179, E-mail: admissions@alliant.edu. *Application contact:* Alliant International University Central Contact Center, 866-U-ALLIANT, Fax: 858-635-4555, E-mail: admissions@alliant.edu. Web site: http://www.alliant.edu/.

American International College, School of Arts, Education and Sciences, Department of Education, Springfield, MA 01109-3189. Offers early childhood education (M Ed, CAGS); educational leadership and supervision (Ed D); elementary education (M Ed, CAGS); middle/secondary education (M Ed, CAGS); moderate disabilities (M Ed, CAGS); reading (M Ed, CAGS); school adjustment counseling (MA, CAGS); school administration (M Ed, CAGS); school guidance counseling (MA, CAGS); teaching (MA, MS); teaching and learning (Ed D). Part-time and evening/weekend programs available. Terminal master's awarded for partial completion of doctoral program. *Degree requirements:* For master's, comprehensive exam (for some programs), thesis (for some programs), practicum; for doctorate, comprehensive exam (for some programs), thesis/dissertation; for CAGS, practicum. *Entrance requirements:* For master's, minimum B-average in undergraduate course work; for doctorate, GRE General Test, interview. Additional exam requirements/recommendations for international students: Required—TOEFL. Electronic applications accepted.

American Public University System, AMU/APU Graduate Programs, Charles Town, WV 25414. Offers accounting (MBA, MS); administration and supervision (M Ed); criminal justice (MA); emergency and disaster management (MA); entrepreneurship (MBA); environmental policy and management (MS), including environmental planning, environmental sustainability, fish and wildlife management, general (MA, MS), global environmental management; finance (MBA); general (MBA); global business management (MBA); guidance and counseling (M Ed); history (MA), including American history, ancient and classical history, European history, global history, military and diplomatic history, public history; homeland security (MA); homeland security resource allocation (MBA); humanities (MA); information technology (MS), including digital forensics, enterprise software development, information assurance and security, IT project management; information technology management (MBA); intelligence studies (MA), including criminal intelligence, general (MA, MS), homeland security, intelligence analysis, intelligence collection, intelligence operations, terrorism studies; international relations and conflict resolution (MA), including comparative and security issues, conflict resolution, international and transnational security issues, peacekeeping; legal studies (MA); management (MA), including defense management, general (MA, MS), human resource management, organizational leadership, public administration, reverse logistics, strategic consulting; marketing (MBA); military history (MA), including American military history, American revolution, civil war, war since 1946, World War II; military studies (MA), including air warfare, asymmetrical warfare, joint warfare, land warfare, naval warfare, strategic leadership; national security studies (MA), including general (MA, MS), homeland security, regional security studies, security and intelligence analysis, terrorism studies; nonprofit management (MBA); political science (MA), including American politics and government, comparative government and development, public policy; psychology (MA); public administration (MA, MPA), including disaster management (MPA), environmental policy (MA), health policy (MPA), human resources (MPA), national security (MPA), organizational management (MPA), security management (MPA); public health (MA, MPH), including emergency management (MPH), environmental health (MPH), public administration (MA); reverse logistics management (MA); security management (MA); space studies (MA), including aerospace science, planetary science; sports and health sciences (MS); sports management (MS), including coaching theory and strategy, sports administration; teaching (M Ed), including curriculum and instruction for elementary teachers, elementary, elementary reading, English language learners, instructional leadership, online learning, secondary social sciences, special education; transportation and logistics management (MA), including maritime engineering management. Programs offered via distance learning only. Part-time and evening/weekend programs available. Postbaccalaureate distance learning degree programs offered (no on-campus study). *Faculty:* 445 full-time (241 women), 1,360 part-time/adjunct (617 women). *Students:* 688 full-time (338 women), 10,168 part-time (3,706 women); includes 3,130 minority (1,007 Black or African American, non-Hispanic/Latino; 103 American Indian or Alaska Native, non-Hispanic/Latino; 825 Asian, non-Hispanic/Latino; 810 Hispanic/Latino; 51 Native Hawaiian or other Pacific Islander, non-Hispanic/Latino; 334 Two or more races, non-Hispanic/Latino), 134 international. Average age 35. In 2011, 2,386 master's awarded. *Degree requirements:* For master's, comprehensive exam or practicum. *Entrance requirements:* For master's, official transcript showing earned bachelor's degree from institution accredited by recognized accrediting body. Additional exam requirements/recommendations for international students: Required—TOEFL (minimum score 550 paper-based; 213 computer-based), IELTS (minimum score 6.5). *Application deadline:* Applications are processed on a rolling basis. Application fee: $0. Electronic applications accepted. *Expenses: Tuition:* Part-time $325 per credit hour. *Financial support:* Applicants required to submit FAFSA. *Faculty research:* Military history, criminal justice, management performance, national security. *Unit head:* Dr. Karan Powell, Executive Vice President and Provost, 877-468-6268, Fax: 304-724-3780. *Application contact:* Terry Grant, Vice President of Enrollment Management, 877-468-6268, Fax: 304-724-3780, E-mail: info@apus.edu. Web site: http://www.apus.edu.

American University, College of Arts and Sciences, School of Education, Teaching, and Health, Program in Special Education, Washington, DC 20016-8001. Offers special education: learning disabilities (MA). Part-time and evening/weekend programs available. *Students:* 9 full-time (all women), 17 part-time (15 women); includes 3 minority (all Black or African American, non-Hispanic/Latino), 1 international. Average age 33. 23 applicants, 87% accepted, 14 enrolled. In 2011, 8 master's awarded. *Degree requirements:* For master's, comprehensive exam, PRAXIS II. *Entrance requirements:* For master's, GRE General Test, PRAXIS I, minimum GPA of 3.0, 2 recommendations. *Application deadline:* For fall admission, 2/1 priority date for domestic students; for spring admission, 10/1 priority date for domestic students. Applications are processed on a rolling basis. Application fee: $80. Electronic applications accepted. *Expenses: Tuition:* Full-time $24,264; part-time $1348 per credit hour. *Required fees:* $430. Tuition and fees vary according to course load and program. *Financial support:* Fellowships with full tuition reimbursements, research assistantships, teaching assistantships, career-related internships or fieldwork, Federal Work-Study, and institutionally sponsored loans available. Support available to part-time students. Financial award application deadline: 2/1. *Unit head:* Sarah Irvine-Belson, Dean, 202-885-3727, Fax: 202-885-1187, E-mail: sirvine@american.edu. *Application contact:* Kathleen Clowery, Director, Graduate Admissions, 202-885-3621, Fax: 202-885-1505, E-mail: clowery@american.edu. Web site: http://www.american.edu/cas/seth/.

American University of Puerto Rico, Program in Education, Bayamón, PR 00960-2037. Offers art education (M Ed); elementary education 4-6 (M Ed); elementary education K-3 (M Ed); general science education (M Ed); physical education (M Ed); special education (M Ed). *Entrance requirements:* For master's, EXADEP, GRE, or MAT, 2 letters of recommendation, minimum GPA of 2.5. *Application deadline:* For fall admission, 8/1 for domestic students; for winter admission, 10/18 for domestic students; for spring admission, 3/15 for domestic students. Applications are processed on a rolling basis. Application fee: $50. *Expenses: Tuition:* Part-time $190 per credit. *Required fees:* $48.33 per credit. Tuition and fees vary according to course load and program. *Application contact:* Information Contact, 787-620-2040, E-mail: oficnaadmisiones@aupr.edu.

Andrews University, School of Graduate Studies, School of Education, Department of Educational and Counseling Psychology, Program in Special Education, Berrien Springs, MI 49104. Offers MS. *Students:* 5 full-time (4 women), 5 part-time (all women); includes 3 minority (1 Black or African American, non-Hispanic/Latino; 2 Hispanic/Latino), 3 international. Average age 36. 3 applicants, 100% accepted, 3 enrolled. *Entrance requirements:* Additional exam requirements/recommendations for international students: Required—TOEFL (minimum score 550 paper-based). Application fee: $40. *Unit head:* Dr. Nona Elmendorf-Steele, Dean, 269-471-6468. *Application contact:* Carolyn Hurst, Supervisor of Graduate Admission, 800-253-2874, Fax: 269-471-6321, E-mail: graduate@andrews.edu.

Angelo State University, College of Graduate Studies, College of Education, Department of Teacher Education, Program in Special Education, San Angelo, TX 76909. Offers M Ed. Part-time and evening/weekend programs available. *Faculty:* 17 full-time (12 women). *Students:* 2 full-time (both women), 27 part-time (23 women); includes 5 minority (1 Black or African American, non-Hispanic/Latino; 1 American Indian or Alaska Native, non-Hispanic/Latino; 3 Hispanic/Latino), 1 international. Average age 37. 12 applicants, 83% accepted, 6 enrolled. In 2011, 2 master's awarded. *Degree requirements:* For master's, comprehensive exam. *Entrance requirements:* Additional exam requirements/recommendations for international students: Required—TOEFL or IELTS. *Application deadline:* For fall admission, 7/15 priority date for domestic students, 6/10 for international students; for spring admission, 12/1 priority date for domestic students, 11/1 for international students. Applications are processed on a rolling basis. Application fee: $40 ($50 for international students). Electronic applications accepted. *Financial support:* In 2011–12, 3 students received support. Career-related internships or fieldwork, Federal Work-Study, scholarships/grants, and unspecified assistantships available. Support available to part-time students. Financial award application deadline: 3/1; financial award applicants required to submit FAFSA. *Unit head:* Dr. Mary E. Sanders, Graduate Advisor, 325-942-2052 Ext. 265, Fax: 325-942-2039, E-mail: mary.sanders@angelo.edu. *Application contact:* Aly Hunter, Graduate Admissions Assistant, 325-942-2169, Fax: 325-942-2194, E-mail: aly.hunter@angelo.edu. Web site: http://www.angelo.edu/dept/education/.

Appalachian State University, Cratis D. Williams Graduate School, Department of Reading Education and Special Education, Boone, NC 28608. Offers reading education (MA); special education (MA). *Accreditation:* ASHA. Part-time and evening/weekend programs available. Postbaccalaureate distance learning degree programs offered (no on-campus study). *Faculty:* 21 full-time (11 women), 3 part-time/adjunct (2 women). *Students:* 11 full-time (all women), 112 part-time (109 women); includes 7 minority (5 Black or African American, non-Hispanic/Latino; 1 American Indian or Alaska Native, non-Hispanic/Latino; 1 Hispanic/Latino). 40 applicants, 83% accepted, 27 enrolled. In 2011, 79 master's awarded. *Degree requirements:* For master's, comprehensive exam, thesis optional. *Entrance requirements:* For master's, GRE General Test or MAT, 3 letters of recommendation. Additional exam requirements/recommendations for international students: Required—TOEFL (minimum score 570 paper-based; 230 computer-based; 79 iBT), IELTS (minimum score 6.5). *Application deadline:* For fall admission, 3/15 priority date for domestic students, 2/1 for international students; for spring admission, 11/1 for domestic students, 7/1 for international students. Applications are processed on a rolling basis. Application fee: $55. Electronic applications accepted. *Expenses:* Tuition, state resident: full-time $4040; part-time $180 per semester hour. Tuition, nonresident: full-time $15,900; part-time $760 per semester hour. *Required fees:* $2500; $20 per semester hour. Tuition and fees vary according to campus/location. *Financial support:* In 2011–12, 4 research assistantships (averaging $8,000 per year) were awarded; Federal Work-Study, scholarships/grants, and unspecified assistantships also available. Financial award application deadline: 4/1; financial award applicants required to submit FAFSA. *Faculty research:* Special education, language arts, reading. *Total annual research expenditures:* $510,000. *Unit head:* Dr. Monica Lambert, Chairperson, 828-262-7173, Fax: 828-262-6767, E-mail: lambertma@appstate.edu. *Application contact:* Eveline Watts, Graduate Student Coordinator, 828-262-2182, E-mail: wattsem@appstate.edu. Web site: http://www.lre.appstate.edu/.

Arcadia University, Graduate Studies, Department of Education, Glenside, PA 19038-3295. Offers art education (M Ed); computer education (CAS); curriculum (CAS); curriculum studies (M Ed); early childhood education (M Ed, CAS), including individualized (M Ed), master teacher (M Ed), research in child development (M Ed); educational leadership (M Ed, Ed D, CAS); elementary education (M Ed, CAS); English education (MA Ed); environmental education (MA Ed, CAS); history education (MA Ed); instructional technology (M Ed); language arts (M Ed, CAS); library science (M Ed); mathematics education (M Ed, MA Ed, CAS); music education (MA Ed); psychology (MA Ed); reading (M Ed, CAS); science education (M Ed, CAS); secondary education (M Ed, CAS); special education (M Ed, Ed D, CAS); theater arts (MA Ed); written communication (MA Ed). *Accreditation:* NASAD. Part-time and evening/weekend programs available. Postbaccalaureate distance learning degree programs offered (minimal on-campus study). *Faculty:* 12 full-time (8 women), 38 part-time/adjunct (26 women). *Students:* 66 full-time (48 women), 590 part-time (477 women); includes 65 minority (53 Black or African American, non-Hispanic/Latino; 6 Asian, non-Hispanic/Latino; 3 Hispanic/Latino; 3 Two or more races, non-Hispanic/Latino), 4 international. Average age 36. In 2011, 229 master's, 5 doctorates awarded. *Application deadline:* Applications are processed on a rolling basis. Application fee: $50. Electronic applications accepted. *Expenses:* Contact institution. *Financial support:* Career-related internships or fieldwork, tuition waivers (partial), and unspecified assistantships available. *Unit head:* Dr. Steven P. Gulkus, Associate Professor, 215-572-2120, E-mail: gulkus@arcadia.edu. *Application contact:* 215-572-2925, Fax: 215-572-2126, E-mail: grad@arcadia.edu.

Arizona State University, Mary Lou Fulton Teachers College, Program in Special Education, Phoenix, AZ 85069. Offers autism spectrum disorder (Graduate Certificate); special education (M Ed, MA). Postbaccalaureate distance learning degree programs offered (minimal on-campus study). *Degree requirements:* For master's, thesis or alternative, applied project, student teaching, interactive Program of Study (iPOS) submitted before completing 50 percent of required credit hours. *Entrance requirements:* For master's, Arizona Educator Proficiency Assessments (AEPA), minimum GPA of 3.0 or equivalent in last 2 years of work leading to bachelor's degree, 3 letters of recommendation, personal statement, resume, IVP fingerprint clearance card (for those seeking Arizona certification). Additional exam requirements/recommendations for international students: Required—TOEFL (minimum score 80 iBT), TOEFL, IELTS, or Pearson Test of English. Electronic applications accepted.

Arkansas State University, Graduate School, College of Education, Department of Educational Leadership, Curriculum, and Special Education, Jonesboro, State University, AR 72467. Offers community college administration education (SCCT); curriculum and instruction (MSE); educational leadership (MSE, Ed D, PhD, Ed S), including curriculum and instruction (MSE, Ed S); special education (MSE), including gifted, talented, and creative, instructional specialist 4-12, instructional specialist P-4. *Accreditation:* NCATE. Part-time programs available. Postbaccalaureate distance learning degree programs offered (no on-campus study). *Faculty:* 12 full-time (5 women). *Students:* 11 full-time (6 women), 2,240 part-time (1,686 women); includes 374 minority (278 Black or African American, non-Hispanic/Latino; 14 American Indian or Alaska Native, non-Hispanic/Latino; 12 Asian, non-Hispanic/Latino; 46 Hispanic/Latino; 2 Native Hawaiian or other Pacific Islander, non-Hispanic/Latino; 22 Two or more races, non-Hispanic/Latino), 1 international. Average age 37. 1,519 applicants, 76% accepted, 790 enrolled. In 2011, 827 master's, 8 doctorates, 30 other advanced degrees awarded. *Degree requirements:* For master's, comprehensive exam, thesis or alternative; for doctorate, comprehensive exam, thesis/dissertation; for other advanced degree, comprehensive exam. *Entrance requirements:* For master's, GRE General Test or MAT, appropriate bachelor's degree, letters of reference, interview, official transcript, immunization records; for doctorate, GRE General Test or MAT, interview, master's degree, letters of reference, official transcript, personal statement, writing sample, immunization records; for other advanced degree, GRE General Test or MAT, interview, master's degree, letters of reference, official transcript, 3 years teaching experience, mentor, teaching license, immunization records. Additional exam requirements/recommendations for international students: Required—TOEFL (minimum score 550 paper-based; 213 computer-based; 79 iBT), IELTS (minimum score 6), Pearson Test of English Academic (minimum score 56). *Application deadline:* Applications are processed on a rolling basis. Application fee: $50. Electronic applications accepted. *Expenses:* Tuition, state resident: full-time $4044; part-time $225 per credit hour. Tuition, nonresident: full-time $8087; part-time $449 per credit hour. *Required fees:* $936; $52 per credit hour. $25 per term. One-time fee: $30. Tuition and fees vary according to course load and program. *Financial support:* In 2011–12, 6 students received support. Fellowships, teaching assistantships, career-related internships or fieldwork, scholarships/grants, and unspecified assistantships available. Financial award application deadline: 7/1; financial award applicants required to submit FAFSA. *Unit head:* Dr. Mitchell Holifield, Chair, 870-972-3062, Fax: 870-680-8130, E-mail: hfield@astate.edu. *Application contact:* Dr. Andrew Sustich, Dean of the Graduate School, 870-972-3029, Fax: 870-972-3857, E-mail: sustich@astate.edu. Web site: http://www.astate.edu/a/education/elcse/.

Armstrong Atlantic State University, School of Graduate Studies, Program in Education, Savannah, GA 31419-1997. Offers adult education (M Ed); curriculum and instruction (M Ed); early childhood education (M Ed); education (M Ed); elementary education (M Ed); middle grades education (M Ed); secondary education (M Ed), including business education, English education, mathematics education, science education, social science education; special education (M Ed), including behavioral disorders, learning disabilities, speech-language pathology. *Accreditation:* NCATE. Part-time and evening/weekend programs available. Postbaccalaureate distance learning degree programs offered (minimal on-campus study). *Faculty:* 33 full-time (23 women), 3 part-time/adjunct (2 women). *Students:* 97 full-time (91 women), 262 part-time (227 women); includes 83 minority (70 Black or African American, non-Hispanic/Latino; 3 Asian, non-Hispanic/Latino; 8 Hispanic/Latino; 2 Two or more races, non-Hispanic/Latino), 5 international. Average age 34. 169 applicants, 69% accepted, 102 enrolled. In 2011, 227 master's awarded. *Degree requirements:* For master's, comprehensive exam, portfolio. *Entrance requirements:* For master's, GRE General Test or MAT, minimum GPA of 2.5, letters of recommendation. Additional exam requirements/recommendations for international students: Required—TOEFL (minimum score 523 paper-based; 193 computer-based). *Application deadline:* For fall admission, 7/1 priority date for domestic students, 5/1 for international students; for spring admission, 11/15 priority date for domestic students, 9/15 for international students. Applications are processed on a rolling basis. Application fee: $30. Electronic applications accepted. *Expenses:* Tuition, state resident: full-time $3402. Tuition, nonresident: full-time $12,636. *Financial support:* In 2011–12, research assistantships with full tuition reimbursements (averaging $5,000 per year) were awarded; career-related internships or fieldwork, Federal Work-Study, scholarships/grants, and unspecified assistantships also available. Support available to part-time students. Financial award applicants required to submit FAFSA. *Unit head:* Dr. Patricia Wachholz, Dean, College of Education, 912-344-2797, E-mail: patricia.wachholz@armstrong.edu. *Application contact:* Jill Bell, Director, Graduate Enrollment Services, 912-344-2798, Fax: 912-344-3488, E-mail: graduate@armstrong.edu. Web site: http://www.armstrong.edu/Education/coe_deans_office/coe_education_welcome.

Asbury University, School of Graduate and Professional Studies, Wilmore, KY 40390-1198. Offers biology: alternative certificate (MA Ed); chemistry: alternative certificate (MA Ed); English (MA Ed); English as a second language (MA Ed); ESL (MA Ed); French (MA Ed); Latin: alternative certificate (MA Ed); mathematics: alternative certificate (MA Ed); reading/writing endorsement (MA Ed); social studies (MA Ed); social work (MSW), including child and family services; Spanish (MA Ed); special education (MA Ed); special education: alternative certificate (MA Ed); teacher as leader endorsement (MA Ed). *Accreditation:* NCATE. Part-time programs available. *Degree requirements:* For master's, action research project, portfolio. *Entrance requirements:* For master's, PRAXIS/NTE, minimum GPA of 2.75, letters of recommendation. Additional exam requirements/recommendations for international students: Required—TOEFL (minimum score 550 paper-based). Electronic applications accepted.

Ashland University, Dwight Schar College of Education, Department of Inclusive Services and Exceptional Learners, Ashland, OH 44805-3702. Offers intervention specialist, mild/moderate (M Ed); intervention specialist, moderate/intensive (M Ed); talented and gifted (M Ed). Part-time and evening/weekend programs available. *Faculty:* 10 full-time (8 women), 36 part-time/adjunct (23 women). *Students:* 74 full-time (57 women), 108 part-time (92 women); includes 12 minority (6 Black or African American, non-Hispanic/Latino; 1 American Indian or Alaska Native, non-Hispanic/Latino; 4 Hispanic/Latino; 1 Two or more races, non-Hispanic/Latino). Average age 33. 31 applicants, 100% accepted, 29 enrolled. In 2011, 74 master's awarded. *Degree requirements:* For master's, thesis or alternative, internship, practicum, inquiry seminar. *Entrance requirements:* Additional exam requirements/recommendations for international students: Required—TOEFL. *Application deadline:* For fall admission, 8/15 for domestic students; for spring admission, 1/15 for domestic students. Applications are processed on a rolling basis. Application fee: $30. Electronic applications accepted. *Expenses: Tuition:* Full-time $5580; part-time $465 per credit hour. *Financial support:* Teaching assistantships with partial tuition reimbursements and scholarships/grants available. Financial award application deadline: 4/15. *Unit head:* Dr. Allison Dickey, Chair, 419-289-5376, Fax: 419-207-4949, E-mail: adickey@ashland.edu. *Application contact:* Dr. Linda Billman, Associate Dean, 419-289-5369, Fax: 419-289-5331, E-mail: lbillman@ashland.edu.

Assumption College, Graduate Studies, Special Education Program, Worcester, MA 01609-1296. Offers positive behavior support (CAGS); special education (MA). Part-time and evening/weekend programs available. *Faculty:* 2 full-time (both women), 2 part-time/adjunct (both women). *Students:* 5 full-time (all women), 19 part-time (15 women); includes 2 minority (1 Black or African American, non-Hispanic/Latino; 1 Two or more races, non-Hispanic/Latino). Average age 29. 48 applicants, 75% accepted, 20 enrolled. In 2011, 15 master's, 10 other advanced degrees awarded. *Degree requirements:* For master's, comprehensive exam, internship, practicum. *Entrance requirements:* For master's and CAGS, 3 letters of recommendation, resume, essay. Additional exam requirements/recommendations for international students: Required—TOEFL (minimum score 540 paper-based; 200 computer-based; 76 iBT), IELTS (minimum score 6). *Application deadline:* For fall admission, 10/1 for domestic and international students; for winter admission, 2/1 for domestic and international students; for spring admission, 4/1 for domestic and international students. Applications are processed on a rolling basis. Application fee: $30. Electronic applications accepted. *Expenses: Tuition:* Full-time $9414; part-time $523 per credit. *Required fees:* $20 per term. Full-time tuition and fees vary according to course load and program. *Financial support:* In 2011–12, 3 students received support. Tuition waivers (partial), unspecified assistantships, and institutional discounts available. Financial award application deadline: 5/1; financial award applicants required to submit FAFSA. *Unit head:* Dr. Nanho Vander Hart, Director, 508-767-7380, Fax: 508-767-7263, E-mail: nvanderh@assumption.edu. *Application contact:* Laura Lawrence, Graduate Programs Operations Manager, 508-767-7387, Fax: 508-767-7030, E-mail: graduate@assumption.edu. Web site: http://graduate.assumption.edu/special-education/ma-special-education.

Auburn University, Graduate School, College of Education, Department of Special Education, Rehabilitation, Counseling and School Psychology, Auburn University, AL 36849. Offers collaborative teacher special education (M Ed, MS); early childhood special education (M Ed, MS); rehabilitation counseling (M Ed, MS, PhD). *Accreditation:* CORE; NCATE. Part-time programs available. *Faculty:* 21 full-time (14 women), 5 part-time/adjunct (3 women). *Students:* 153 full-time (126 women), 101 part-time (78 women); includes 67 minority (60 Black or African American, non-Hispanic/Latino; 2 American Indian or Alaska Native, non-Hispanic/Latino; 2 Asian, non-Hispanic/Latino; 3 Hispanic/Latino), 4 international. Average age 30. 221 applicants, 50% accepted, 89 enrolled. In 2011, 75 master's, 12 doctorates awarded. *Degree requirements:* For master's, thesis (for some programs); for doctorate, thesis/dissertation. *Entrance requirements:* For master's, GRE General Test; for doctorate, GRE General Test, interview. *Application deadline:* For fall admission, 7/7 for domestic students; for spring admission, 11/24 for domestic students. Applications are processed on a rolling basis. Application fee: $50 ($60 for international students). Electronic applications accepted. *Expenses:* Tuition, state resident: full-time $7290; part-time $405 per credit hour. Tuition, nonresident: full-time $21,870; part-time $1215 per credit hour. *International tuition:* $22,000 full-time. *Required fees:* $1402. *Financial support:* Research assistantships, teaching assistantships, and Federal Work-Study available. Support available to part-time students. Financial award application deadline: 3/15; financial award applicants required to submit FAFSA. *Faculty research:* Emotional conflict/behavior disorders, gifted and talented, learning disabilities, mental retardation, multi-handicapped. *Unit head:* Dr. E. Davis Martin, Jr., Head, 334-844-7676. *Application contact:* Dr. George Flowers, Dean of the Graduate School, 334-844-2125.

Auburn University Montgomery, School of Education, Department of Counselor, Leadership, and Special Education, Montgomery, AL 36124-4023. Offers counseling (M Ed, Ed S); education administration (M Ed, Ed S); special education (M Ed, Ed S). *Accreditation:* ACA; NCATE. Part-time and evening/weekend programs available. *Degree requirements:* For master's and Ed S, comprehensive exam. *Entrance requirements:* For master's, GRE General Test or MAT, certification, BS in teaching; for Ed S, GRE General Test or MAT, certification. Electronic applications accepted. *Expenses:* Tuition, state resident: full-time $5076. Tuition, nonresident: full-time $15,228.

Augusta State University, Graduate Studies, College of Education, Program in Special Education, Augusta, GA 30904-2200. Offers M Ed, Ed S. *Accreditation:* NCATE. Part-time and evening/weekend programs available. *Faculty:* 4 full-time (3 women). *Students:* 12 full-time (11 women), 20 part-time (18 women); includes 10 minority (all Black or African American, non-Hispanic/Latino). Average age 36. 4 applicants, 100% accepted, 2 enrolled. In 2011, 20 master's awarded. *Degree requirements:* For master's, thesis, portfolio. *Entrance requirements:* For master's, GRE, MAT, minimum GPA of 2.5; for Ed S, GRE, MAT. *Application deadline:* For fall admission, 8/1 priority date for domestic students. Applications are processed on a rolling basis. Application fee: $20. *Financial support:* Career-related internships or fieldwork, Federal Work-Study, institutionally sponsored loans, and unspecified assistantships available. Support available to part-time students. Financial award application deadline: 4/15; financial award applicants required to submit FAFSA. *Faculty research:* Behavior disorders, gifted programs. *Unit head:* Dr. Charles Jackson, Chair, 706-737-1497, Fax: 706-667-4706, E-mail: cjackson@aug.edu. *Application contact:* Andrea M. Scott, Secretary to the Dean, 706-737-1499, Fax: 706-667-4706, E-mail: ascott1@aug.edu.

Aurora University, College of Education, Aurora, IL 60506-4892. Offers curriculum and instruction (MA, Ed D); early childhood and special education (MA); education (MAT), including elementary certification; education and administration (Ed D); educational leadership (MEL); educational technology (MATL); reading instruction (MA); special education (MA). *Accreditation:* NCATE. Part-time and evening/weekend programs available. *Degree requirements:* For doctorate, comprehensive exam, thesis/dissertation. *Entrance requirements:* For master's, 2 years of teaching experience, valid teaching certificate. Additional exam requirements/recommendations for international students: Required—TOEFL (minimum score 550 paper-based; 213 computer-based). Electronic applications accepted. *Expenses:* Contact institution.

Austin Peay State University, College of Graduate Studies, College of Education, Department of Educational Specialties, Clarksville, TN 37044. Offers administration and supervision (Ed S); curriculum and instruction (MA Ed); education leadership (MA Ed); elementary education (Ed S); secondary education (Ed S); special education (MA Ed). Part-time and evening/weekend programs available. Postbaccalaureate distance learning degree programs offered. *Faculty:* 7 full-time (4 women), 4 part-time/adjunct (3 women). *Students:* 6 full-time (4 women), 86 part-time (66 women); includes 11 minority (6 Black or African American, non-Hispanic/Latino; 1 American Indian or Alaska Native, non-Hispanic/Latino; 4 Hispanic/Latino). Average age 37. 33 applicants, 100% accepted, 23 enrolled. In 2011, 32 master's, 7 Ed Ss awarded. *Degree requirements:* For master's, comprehensive exam, thesis optional. *Entrance requirements:* For master's, GRE General Test, 3 letters of recommendation, minimum undergraduate GPA of 2.75. Additional exam requirements/recommendations for international students: Required—TOEFL (minimum score 500 paper-based; 173 computer-based). *Application deadline:* For fall admission, 8/1 priority date for domestic students. Applications are processed on a rolling basis. Application fee: $25. Electronic applications accepted. *Expenses:* Tuition, state resident: part-time $350 per credit hour. Tuition, nonresident: full-time $20,644; part-time $971 per credit hour. *Required fees:* $1224; $61.20 per credit hour. *Financial support:* Career-related internships or fieldwork, Federal Work-Study, institutionally sponsored loans, scholarships/grants, and unspecified assistantships available. Support available to part-time students. Financial award application deadline: 3/1; financial award applicants required to submit FAFSA. *Unit head:* Dr. Moniqueka Gold, Chair, 931-221-7696, Fax: 931-221-1292, E-mail: goldm@apsu.edu. *Application contact:* Kendra Bryant, Graduate Admissions, 800-844-2778, Fax: 931-221-6188, E-mail: admissionsweb@apsu.edu.

Austin Peay State University, College of Graduate Studies, College of Education, Department of Teaching and Learning, Clarksville, TN 37044. Offers elementary education K-6 (MAT); reading (MA Ed); secondary education 7-12 (MAT); special education K-12 (MAT). Part-time and evening/weekend programs available. Postbaccalaureate distance learning degree programs offered. *Faculty:* 14 full-time (11 women), 3 part-time/adjunct (2 women). *Students:* 84 full-time (67 women), 97 part-time (81 women); includes 27 minority (12 Black or African American, non-Hispanic/Latino; 2 American Indian or Alaska Native, non-Hispanic/Latino; 2 Asian, non-Hispanic/Latino; 4 Hispanic/Latino; 1 Native Hawaiian or other Pacific Islander, non-Hispanic/Latino; 6 Two or more races, non-Hispanic/Latino). Average age 33. 61 applicants, 98% accepted, 51 enrolled. In 2011, 55 master's awarded. *Degree requirements:* For master's, comprehensive exam, thesis optional. *Entrance requirements:* For master's, GRE General Test, 3 letters of recommendation, minimum undergraduate GPA of 2.75. Additional exam requirements/recommendations for international students: Required—TOEFL (minimum score 500 paper-based; 173 computer-based). *Application deadline:* For fall admission, 8/1 priority date for domestic students. Applications are processed on a rolling basis. Application fee: $25. Electronic applications accepted. *Expenses:* Tuition, state resident: part-time $350 per credit hour. Tuition, nonresident: full-time $20,644; part-time $971 per credit hour. *Required fees:* $1224; $61.20 per credit hour. *Financial support:* Career-related internships or fieldwork, Federal Work-Study, institutionally sponsored loans, scholarships/grants, and unspecified assistantships available. Support available to part-time students. Financial award application deadline: 3/1; financial award applicants required to submit FAFSA. *Unit head:* Dr. Rebecca McMahan, Chair, 931-221-7513, Fax: 931-221-1292, E-mail: mcmahanb@apsu.edu. *Application contact:* Kendra Bryant, Graduate Admissions, 800-844-2778, Fax: 931-221-6188, E-mail: admissionsweb@apsu.edu.

Azusa Pacific University, School of Education, Department of Special Education, Program in Special Education, Azusa, CA 91702-7000. Offers MA Ed. *Accreditation:* NCATE. Part-time and evening/weekend programs available. *Degree requirements:* For master's, core exams, oral presentations. *Entrance requirements:* For master's, 12 units of course work in education, minimum GPA of 3.0.

Azusa Pacific University, School of Education, Department of Special Education, Program in Special Education and Educational Technology, Azusa, CA 91702-7000. Offers M Ed.

Baldwin Wallace University, Graduate Programs, Division of Education, Specialization in Mild/Moderate Educational Needs, Berea, OH 44017-2088. Offers MA Ed. *Accreditation:* NCATE. Part-time and evening/weekend programs available. Postbaccalaureate distance learning degree programs offered (no on-campus study). *Faculty:* 4 full-time (3 women), 3 part-time/adjunct (2 women). *Students:* 35 full-time (30 women), 16 part-time (13 women); includes 6 minority (5 Black or African American, non-Hispanic/Latino; 1 Two or more races, non-Hispanic/Latino). Average age 32. 14 applicants, 50% accepted, 4 enrolled. In 2011, 19 master's awarded. *Degree requirements:* For master's, comprehensive exam. *Entrance requirements:* For master's, bachelor's degree in field, MAT or minimum GPA of 2.75. Additional exam requirements/recommendations for international students: Required—TOEFL (minimum score 523 paper-based; 193 computer-based; 70 iBT). *Application deadline:* For fall admission, 8/15 priority date for domestic students; for spring admission, 12/15 priority date for domestic students. Applications are processed on a rolling basis. Application fee: $25. Electronic applications accepted. Application fee is waived when completed online. *Expenses: Tuition:* Full-time $17,016; part-time $727 per credit hour. Tuition and fees vary according to program. *Financial support:* Career-related internships or fieldwork available. Support available to part-time students. Financial award application deadline: 5/1; financial award applicants required to submit FAFSA. *Faculty research:* Adult adjustment of individuals formerly identified as having mild/moderate special education needs, professional development of special educators, teacher beliefs and special education, classroom assessment practices. *Unit head:* Dr. Karen Kaye, Chair, 440-826-2168, Fax: 440-826-3779, E-mail: kkaye@bw.edu. *Application contact:* Winifred W. Gerhardt, Director of Admission for the Evening and Weekend College, 440-826-2222, Fax: 440-826-3830, E-mail: admission@bw.edu. Web site: http://www.bw.edu/academics/mae/needs.

Ball State University, Graduate School, Teachers College, Department of Special Education, Muncie, IN 47306-1099. Offers applied behavior analysis (MA); special education (MA, MAE, Ed D, Ed S). *Accreditation:* NCATE. *Faculty:* 15 full-time (10 women), 13 part-time/adjunct (8 women). *Students:* 193 full-time (167 women), 729 part-time (665 women); includes 52 minority (30 Black or African American, non-Hispanic/Latino; 1 American Indian or Alaska Native, non-Hispanic/Latino; 9 Asian, non-Hispanic/Latino; 7 Hispanic/Latino; 5 Two or more races, non-Hispanic/Latino), 20 international. Average age 33. 427 applicants, 85% accepted, 266 enrolled. In 2011, 81 master's, 4 doctorates awarded. *Degree requirements:* For doctorate, thesis/dissertation; for Ed S, thesis. *Entrance requirements:* For doctorate, GRE General Test, interview, minimum graduate GPA of 3.2; for Ed S, GRE General Test. Application fee: $50. Tuition and fees vary according to program and reciprocity agreements. *Financial support:* In 2011–12, 18 students received support, including 4 research assistantships with full tuition reimbursements available (averaging $10,394 per year), 14 teaching assistantships (averaging $8,374 per year); career-related internships or fieldwork also available. Financial award application deadline: 3/1. *Faculty research:* Language development and utilization in the handicapped (preschool through adult). *Unit head:* John Merbler, Chairperson, 765-285-5700, Fax: 765-285-4280, E-mail: jmerbler@bsu.edu. *Application contact:* Dr. Robert Morris, Associate Provost for Research and Dean of the Graduate School, 765-285-1300, E-mail: rmorris@bsu.edu. Web site: http://www.bsu.edu/teachers/departments/sped/.

Bank Street College of Education, Graduate School, Program in Infant and Family Development and Early Intervention, New York, NY 10025. Offers infant and family development (MS Ed); infant and family early childhood special and general education (MS Ed); infant and family/early childhood special education (Ed M). *Students:* 15 full-time (14 women), 19 part-time (18 women); includes 13 minority (6 Black or African American, non-Hispanic/Latino; 1 Asian, non-Hispanic/Latino; 3 Hispanic/Latino; 3 Two or more races, non-Hispanic/Latino), 1 international. Average age 28. 31 applicants, 74% accepted, 15 enrolled. In 2011, 15 master's awarded. *Degree requirements:* For master's, thesis. *Entrance requirements:* For master's, interview, essays. Additional exam requirements/recommendations for international students: Required—TOEFL (minimum score 600 paper-based; 250 computer-based; 100 iBT), IELTS (minimum score 7). *Application deadline:* For fall admission, 2/15 priority date for domestic students, 2/15 for international students; for spring admission, 11/1 priority date for domestic students, 11/1 for international students. Applications are processed on a rolling basis. Application fee: $65. Electronic applications accepted. *Expenses: Required fees:* $1240 per credit. $100 per term. One-time fee: $250 part-time. *Financial support:* Career-related internships or fieldwork, Federal Work-Study, scholarships/grants, and unspecified assistantships available. Support available to part-time students. Financial award application deadline: 4/15; financial award applicants required to submit FAFSA. *Faculty research:* Early intervention, early attachment practice in infant and toddler childcare, parenting skills in adolescents. *Unit head:* Dr. Virginia Casper, Director, 212-875-4703, Fax: 212-875-4753, E-mail: vcasper@bankstreet.edu. *Application contact:* Ann Morgan, Director of Graduate Admissions, 212-875-4403, Fax: 212-875-4678, E-mail: amorgan@bankstreet.edu. Web site: http://bankstreet.edu/graduate-school/academics/programs/infant-and-family-development-programs-overview/.

Bank Street College of Education, Graduate School, Program in Special Education, New York, NY 10025. Offers early childhood special and general education (MS Ed); early childhood special education (Ed M, MS Ed); elementary/childhood special and general education (MS Ed); elementary/childhood special education (MS Ed); elementary/childhood special education certification (Ed M). *Students:* 109 full-time (95 women), 133 part-time (116 women); includes 44 minority (19 Black or African American, non-Hispanic/Latino; 2 American Indian or Alaska Native, non-Hispanic/Latino; 11 Asian, non-Hispanic/Latino; 7 Hispanic/Latino; 5 Two or more races, non-Hispanic/Latino), 1 international. Average age 29. 139 applicants, 76% accepted, 64 enrolled. In 2011, 79 master's awarded. *Degree requirements:* For master's, thesis. *Entrance requirements:* For master's, interview, essays. Additional exam requirements/recommendations for international students: Required—TOEFL (minimum score 600 paper-based; 250 computer-based; 100 iBT), IELTS (minimum score 7). *Application deadline:* For fall admission, 2/15 priority date for domestic students, 2/15 for international students; for spring admission, 11/1 priority date for domestic students, 11/1 for international students. Applications are processed on a rolling basis. Application fee: $65. Electronic applications accepted. *Expenses: Required fees:* $1240 per credit. $100 per term. One-time fee: $250 part-time. *Financial support:* Career-related internships or fieldwork available. Financial award application deadline: 3/1; financial award applicants required to submit FAFSA. *Faculty research:* Inclusion, observation and assessment; early intervention; neurodevelopmental assessment; teaching students with disabilities. *Unit head:* Dr. Olga Romero, Chairperson, 212-875-4468, Fax: 212-875-4753, E-mail: olgar@bankstreet.edu. *Application contact:* Seena Berg, Associate Director of Graduate Admissions, 212-875-4402, Fax: 212-875-4678, E-mail: sberg@bankstreet.edu. Web site: http://bankstreet.edu/graduate-school/academics/programs/.

Barry University, School of Education, Program in Education for Teachers of Students with Hearing Impairments, Miami Shores, FL 33161-6695. Offers MS.

Barry University, School of Education, Program in Exceptional Student Education, Miami Shores, FL 33161-6695. Offers MS, Ed S. Part-time and evening/weekend programs available. *Degree requirements:* For master's, comprehensive exam; for Ed S, practicum. *Entrance requirements:* For master's, GRE General Test or MAT, minimum GPA of 3.0; for Ed S, GRE General Test, minimum GPA of 3.0. Electronic applications accepted.

Barry University, School of Education, Program in Leadership and Education, Miami Shores, FL 33161-6695. Offers educational technology (PhD); exceptional student education (PhD); higher education administration (PhD); human resource development (PhD); leadership (PhD). Part-time and evening/weekend programs available. *Degree requirements:* For doctorate, thesis/dissertation. *Entrance requirements:* For doctorate, GRE General Test, minimum GPA of 3.25. Electronic applications accepted.

Bayamón Central University, Graduate Programs, Program in Education, Bayamón, PR 00960-1725. Offers administration and supervision (MA Ed); commercial education (MA Ed); elementary education (K–3) (MA Ed); family counseling (Graduate Certificate); guidance and counseling (MA Ed); pre-elementary teacher (MA Ed); rehabilitation counseling (MA Ed); special education (MA Ed), including attention deficit disorder, education of the autistic, learning disabilities. Part-time and evening/weekend programs available. *Degree requirements:* For master's, comprehensive exam. *Entrance requirements:* For master's, EXADEP, bachelor's degree in education or related field.

Baylor University, Graduate School, School of Education, Department of Educational Psychology, Waco, TX 76798-7301. Offers applied behavior analysis (MS Ed); educational psychology (MA); exceptionalities (PhD); gifted (PhD); quantitative (PhD); school psychology (PhD, Ed S). *Accreditation:* NCATE. Part-time programs available. *Faculty:* 7 full-time (4 women), 2 part-time/adjunct (1 woman). *Students:* 42 full-time (34 women), 11 part-time (9 women); includes 15 minority (5 Black or African American, non-Hispanic/Latino; 5 Asian, non-Hispanic/Latino; 3 Hispanic/Latino; 2 Two or more races, non-Hispanic/Latino), 2 international. Average age 28. 31 applicants, 48% accepted, 13 enrolled. In 2011, 3 master's, 5 doctorates, 7 other advanced degrees awarded. *Degree requirements:* For master's, thesis optional; for doctorate, comprehensive exam, thesis/dissertation; for Ed S, comprehensive exam, thesis or alternative. *Entrance requirements:* For master's and Ed S, GRE General Test; for doctorate, GRE General Test, master's degree. Additional exam requirements/recommendations for international students: Required—TOEFL. *Application deadline:* For fall admission, 2/1 priority date for domestic students, 2/1 for international students. Application fee: $50. Electronic applications accepted. *Financial support:* In 2011–12, 20 students received support, including 20 research assistantships with full and partial tuition reimbursements available; career-related internships or fieldwork, Federal Work-Study, institutionally sponsored loans, scholarships/grants, health care benefits, tuition waivers (full and partial), unspecified assistantships, and stipends also available. Financial award application deadline: 2/1. *Faculty research:* Individual differences, quantitative methods, gifted and talented, special education, school psychology, autism, applied behavior analysis. *Unit head:* Dr. Marley W. Watkins, Professor and Chairman, 254-710-4234, Fax: 254-710-3987, E-mail: marley_watkins@baylor.edu. *Application contact:* Lisa Rowe, Administrative Assistant, 254-710-3112, Fax: 254-710-3112, E-mail: lisa_rowe@baylor.edu. Web site: http://www.baylor.edu/soe/EDP/.

Bay Path College, Program in Special Education, Longmeadow, MA 01106-2292. Offers applied behavior analysis (MS Ed); moderate disabilities 5-8 (MS Ed); moderate disabilities PreK-8 (MS Ed); non-licensure (MS Ed); severe disabilities PreK-12 (MS Ed); special education (MS Ed, Ed S). Part-time and evening/weekend programs available. Postbaccalaureate distance learning degree programs offered. *Students:* 47 full-time (42 women), 151 part-time (146 women); includes 17 minority (11 Black or African American, non-Hispanic/Latino; 3 Asian, non-Hispanic/Latino; 3 Hispanic/Latino). Average age 34. 117 applicants, 86% accepted, 80 enrolled. In 2011, 86 master's, 14 Ed Ss awarded. *Application deadline:* Applications are processed on a rolling basis. Application fee: $45. Electronic applications accepted. Application fee is waived when completed online. *Expenses: Tuition:* Part-time $665 per credit. Tuition and fees vary according to program. *Financial support:* Scholarships/grants available. Financial award applicants required to submit FAFSA. *Application contact:* Lisa Adams, Director of Graduate Admissions, 413-565-1317, Fax: 413-565-1250, E-mail: ladams@baypath.edu.

Bellarmine University, Annsley Frazier Thornton School of Education, Louisville, KY 40205-0671. Offers early elementary education (MA Ed, MAT); education and social change (PhD); learning and behavior disorders (MA Ed, MAT); middle school education (MA Ed, MAT); principalship (Ed S); reading and writing endorsement (MA Ed); secondary school education (MAT); teacher leadership, grades P-12 (MA Ed). *Accreditation:* NCATE. Part-time and evening/weekend programs available. *Faculty:* 13 full-time (6 women), 12 part-time/adjunct (10 women). *Students:* 85 full-time (65 women), 186 part-time (144 women); includes 30 minority (22 Black or African American, non-Hispanic/Latino; 1 American Indian or Alaska Native, non-Hispanic/Latino; 6 Asian, non-Hispanic/Latino; 1 Hispanic/Latino). Average age 33. In 2011, 105 master's awarded. *Degree requirements:* For master's, comprehensive exam, thesis (for some programs); for doctorate, comprehensive exam, thesis/dissertation. *Entrance requirements:* For master's, GRE, baccalaureate degree from accredited institution; minimum overall GPA of 2.75, 3.0 in major; letters of recommendation; valid Kentucky provisional or professional certificate; for doctorate, GRE, minimum GPA of 3.5 in all graduate coursework completed at time of application; baccalaureate and master's degrees in education (MA, MS) or fields directly relevant to education; three letters of recommendation; two essays (no more than 1,000 words each); interview. Additional exam requirements/recommendations for international students: Required—TOEFL (minimum score 550 paper-based; 213 computer-based; 80 iBT). *Application deadline:* Applications are processed on a rolling basis. Application fee: $25. *Expenses:* Contact institution. *Financial support:* Scholarships/grants available. Financial award applicants required to submit FAFSA. *Faculty research:* Literacy, service-learning, dispositions, educational technology, special education. *Unit head:* Dr. Robert Cooter, Dean, 502-272-8191, Fax: 502-272-8189, E-mail: rcooter@bellarmine.edu. *Application contact:* Theresa Klapheke, Administrative Director of Graduate Programs, 502-272-8271, Fax: 502-272-8002, E-mail: tklapheke@bellarmine.edu. Web site: http://www.bellarmine.edu/education/graduate.

Belmont University, College of Arts and Sciences, Department of Education, Nashville, TN 37212-3757. Offers education (M Ed); elementary education (MAT), including early childhood education, elementary education, language arts education; English (MAT); history (MAT); mathematics (MAT); middle grade education (MAT); science (MAT); secondary education (MAT); special education (MAT); sports administration (MSA). *Accreditation:* NCATE. Part-time and evening/weekend programs available. *Faculty:* 11 full-time (8 women), 23 part-time/adjunct (12 women). *Students:* 83 full-time (77 women), 205 part-time (162 women); includes 50 minority (36 Black or African American, non-Hispanic/Latino; 1 American Indian or Alaska Native, non-Hispanic/Latino; 1 Asian, non-Hispanic/Latino; 7 Hispanic/Latino; 5 Two or more races, non-Hispanic/Latino), 2 international. Average age 30. 83 applicants, 67% accepted, 35 enrolled. In 2011, 169 master's awarded. *Degree requirements:* For master's, thesis (for some programs). *Entrance requirements:* For master's, MAT or GRE and/or GMAT, minimum GPA of 2.75. Additional exam requirements/recommendations for international students: Required—TOEFL. *Application deadline:* For fall admission, 8/1 priority date for domestic students, 6/1 for international students; for spring admission, 12/1 priority date for domestic students, 10/1 for international students. Applications are processed on a rolling basis. Application fee: $50. *Expenses:* Contact institution. *Financial support:* In 2011–12, 30 students received support. Fellowships with partial tuition reimbursements available, teaching assistantships with partial tuition reimbursements available, institutionally sponsored loans, tuition waivers (partial), and unspecified assistantships available. Financial award application deadline: 4/15; financial award applicants required to submit FAFSA. *Faculty research:* Improving secondary literacy, Montessori, classroom management strategies, teacher residency programs, online professional development, mentoring, leadership, faculty development. *Total annual research expenditures:* $2,500. *Unit head:* Dr. Cynthia R. Watkins, Associate Dean, 615-460-6053, Fax: 615-460-5556, E-mail: cynthia.watkins@belmont.edu. *Application contact:* Andrea McClain, Admission/Licensure Officer, 615-460-5483, Fax: 615-460-5556, E-mail: andrea.mcclain@belmont.edu.

Bemidji State University, School of Graduate Studies, Bemidji, MN 56601-2699. Offers biology (MS); counseling psychology (MS); education (M Ed, MS); English (MA, MS); environmental studies (MS); mathematics (MS); mathematics (elementary and middle level education) (MS); special education (M Sp Ed, MS). Part-time programs available. Postbaccalaureate distance learning degree programs offered (no on-campus study). *Faculty:* 114 full-time (47 women), 22 part-time/adjunct (16 women). *Students:* 68 full-time (45 women), 311 part-time (198 women); includes 21 minority (4 Black or African American, non-Hispanic/Latino; 2 American Indian or Alaska Native, non-Hispanic/Latino; 5 Asian, non-Hispanic/Latino; 5 Hispanic/Latino; 5 Two or more races, non-

Hispanic/Latino), 5 international. Average age 34. 82 applicants, 98% accepted, 37 enrolled. In 2011, 72 master's awarded. *Degree requirements:* For master's, comprehensive exam, thesis (for some programs). *Entrance requirements:* For master's, GRE, letters of recommendation, letters of interest. Additional exam requirements/recommendations for international students: Required—TOEFL (minimum score 550 paper-based; 213 computer-based; 80 iBT). *Application deadline:* Applications are processed on a rolling basis. Application fee: $20. Electronic applications accepted. *Expenses:* Tuition, state resident: full-time $6182; part-time $343.45 per credit. Tuition, nonresident: full-time $6182; part-time $343.45 per credit. *Required fees:* $954. *Financial support:* In 2011–12, 253 students received support, including 36 research assistantships with partial tuition reimbursements available (averaging $7,441 per year), 36 teaching assistantships with partial tuition reimbursements available (averaging $7,441 per year); career-related internships or fieldwork, scholarships/grants, health care benefits, and unspecified assistantships also available. Support available to part-time students. Financial award application deadline: 4/15; financial award applicants required to submit FAFSA. *Unit head:* Dr. Patricia Rogers, Dean of Health Sciences and Human Ecology, 218-755-2027, Fax: 218-755-2258, E-mail: progers@bemidjistate.edu. *Application contact:* Joan Miller, Senior Office and Administrative Specialist, 218-755-2027, Fax: 218-755-2258, E-mail: jmiller@bemidjistate.edu. Web site: http://www.bemidjistate.edu/academics/graduate_studies/.

Benedictine University, Graduate Programs, Program in Education, Lisle, IL 60532-0900. Offers curriculum and instruction and collaborative teaching (M Ed); elementary education (MA Ed); leadership and administration (M Ed); reading and literacy (M Ed); secondary education (MA Ed); special education (MA Ed). Part-time and evening/weekend programs available. *Faculty:* 4 full-time (2 women), 52 part-time/adjunct (30 women). *Students:* 178 full-time (157 women), 239 part-time (211 women); includes 41 minority (29 Black or African American, non-Hispanic/Latino; 4 Asian, non-Hispanic/Latino; 8 Hispanic/Latino), 2 international. Average age 33. 177 applicants, 44% accepted, 68 enrolled. In 2011, 278 master's awarded. *Degree requirements:* For master's, comprehensive exam, thesis (for some programs). *Entrance requirements:* For master's, GRE or MAT. Additional exam requirements/recommendations for international students: Required—TOEFL (minimum score 550 paper-based; 213 computer-based). *Application deadline:* For fall admission, 9/1 for domestic students; for winter admission, 12/1 for domestic students; for spring admission, 2/15 for domestic students. Applications are processed on a rolling basis. Application fee: $40. Electronic applications accepted. *Expenses:* Contact institution. *Financial support:* Career-related internships or fieldwork and health care benefits available. Support available to part-time students. *Unit head:* MeShelda Jackson, Director, 630-829-6282, E-mail: mjackson@ben.edu. *Application contact:* Kari Gibbons, Associate Vice President, Enrollment Center, 630-829-6200, Fax: 630-829-6584, E-mail: kgibbons@ben.edu.

Bethel University, Graduate School, St. Paul, MN 55112-6999. Offers autism spectrum disorders (Certificate); business administration (MBA); communication (MA); counseling psychology (MA); education (M Ed); educational leadership (Ed D); gerontology (MA, Certificate); international baccalaureate education (Certificate); K-12 education (MA); literacy education (MA); nursing (MA); nursing education (Certificate); nursing leadership (Certificate); organizational leadership (MA); postsecondary teaching (Certificate); special education (MA); teaching (MA). Part-time and evening/weekend programs available. Postbaccalaureate distance learning degree programs offered (minimal on-campus study). *Faculty:* 8 full-time (3 women), 98 part-time/adjunct (46 women). *Students:* 651 full-time (419 women), 312 part-time (212 women); includes 79 minority (35 Black or African American, non-Hispanic/Latino; 2 American Indian or Alaska Native, non-Hispanic/Latino; 19 Asian, non-Hispanic/Latino; 17 Hispanic/Latino; 6 Two or more races, non-Hispanic/Latino), 6 international. Average age 36. In 2011, 245 master's, 4 doctorates, 32 other advanced degrees awarded. *Degree requirements:* For master's, comprehensive exam (for some programs), thesis (for some programs); for doctorate, comprehensive exam, thesis/dissertation. *Entrance requirements:* Additional exam requirements/recommendations for international students: Required—TOEFL (minimum score 550 paper-based; 213 computer-based; 80 iBT). *Application deadline:* Applications are processed on a rolling basis. Electronic applications accepted. Tuition and fees vary according to course load, degree level and program. *Financial support:* Applicants required to submit FAFSA. *Unit head:* Dick Crombie, Vice-President/Dean, 651-635-8000, Fax: 651-635-8004, E-mail: gs@bethel.edu. *Application contact:* Paul Ives, Director of Admissions, 651-635-8000, Fax: 651-635-8004, E-mail: gs@bethel.edu. Web site: http://gs.bethel.edu/.

Biola University, School of Education, La Mirada, CA 90639-0001. Offers special education (Certificate). Part-time programs available. Postbaccalaureate distance learning degree programs offered. *Faculty:* 14. *Students:* 40 full-time (35 women), 100 part-time (83 women); includes 34 minority (2 Black or African American, non-Hispanic/Latino; 1 American Indian or Alaska Native, non-Hispanic/Latino; 28 Asian, non-Hispanic/Latino; 3 Two or more races, non-Hispanic/Latino), 2 international. *Entrance requirements:* Additional exam requirements/recommendations for international students: Required—TOEFL (minimum score 100 iBT). *Application deadline:* For fall admission, 7/1 for domestic students, 6/1 for international students; for spring admission, 12/1 for domestic students. Applications are processed on a rolling basis. Application fee: $55. Electronic applications accepted. *Financial support:* Institutionally sponsored loans, scholarships/grants, and unspecified assistantships available. Financial award applicants required to submit FAFSA. *Faculty research:* Early childhood education, elementary education, special education, curriculum development, teacher preparation. *Unit head:* Dr. June Hetzel, Dean, 562-903-4715. *Application contact:* Graduate Admissions Office, 562-903-4752, E-mail: graduate.admissions@biola.edu. Web site: http://education.biola.edu/.

Bloomsburg University of Pennsylvania, School of Graduate Studies, College of Education, Department of Exceptionality Programs, Program in Special Education, Bloomsburg, PA 17815-1301. Offers MS. *Accreditation:* NCATE. *Degree requirements:* For master's, thesis or alternative. *Entrance requirements:* For master's, teaching certificate, minimum QPA of 3.0. Additional exam requirements/recommendations for international students: Required—TOEFL (minimum score 550 paper-based; 213 computer-based; 79 iBT). Electronic applications accepted. *Faculty research:* Exceptionalities, learning disabilities, behavior disorders, gifted, early childhood.

Bob Jones University, Graduate Programs, Greenville, SC 29614. Offers accountancy (MS); Bible (MA); Bible translation (MA); Biblical studies (Certificate); broadcast management (MS); business administration (MBA); church history (MA, PhD); church ministries (MA); church music (MM); cinema and video production (MA); counseling (MS); curriculum and instruction (Ed D); divinity (M Div); dramatic production (MA); educational leadership (MS, Ed D, Ed S); elementary education (M Ed, MAT); English (M Ed, MA, MAT); fine arts (MA); graphic design (MA); history (M Ed, MA); illustration (MA); interpretative speech (MA); mathematics (M Ed, MAT); medical missions (Certificate); ministry (MM, D Min); multi-categorical special education (M Ed, MAT); music (M Ed); New Testament interpretation (PhD); Old Testament interpretation (PhD); orchestral instrument performance (MM); organ performance (MM); pastoral studies (MA); personnel services (MS, Ed S); piano pedagogy (MM); piano performance (MM); platform arts (MA); radio and television broadcasting (MS); rhetoric and public address (MA); secondary education (M Ed); studio art (MA); teaching Bible (MA); theology (MA, PhD); voice performance (MM); youth ministries (MA); M Div/MM.

Boise State University, Graduate College, College of Education, Programs in Teacher Education, Program in Special Education, Boise, ID 83725-0399. Offers M Ed, MA. *Accreditation:* NCATE. *Degree requirements:* For master's, thesis optional. *Entrance requirements:* For master's, minimum GPA of 3.0. Electronic applications accepted.

Boston College, Lynch Graduate School of Education, Program in Special Needs: Moderate Disabilities, Chestnut Hill, MA 02467-3800. Offers M Ed, CAES. *Accreditation:* Teacher Education Accreditation Council. Part-time and evening/weekend programs available. *Students:* 15 full-time (13 women), 12 part-time (9 women); includes 2 minority (both Hispanic/Latino). 54 applicants, 67% accepted, 24 enrolled. In 2011, 26 master's, 1 CAES awarded. *Degree requirements:* For master's and CAES, comprehensive exam. *Entrance requirements:* For master's, GRE General Test or MAT, general licensure at the elementary or secondary level; for CAES, GRE General Test or MAT. Additional exam requirements/recommendations for international students: Required—TOEFL (minimum score 550 paper-based; 213 computer-based; 79 iBT). *Application deadline:* For fall admission, 1/1 priority date for domestic students. Application fee: $65. Electronic applications accepted. *Financial support:* Fellowships with full and partial tuition reimbursements, research assistantships with full and partial tuition reimbursements, teaching assistantships with full and partial tuition reimbursements, career-related internships or fieldwork, Federal Work-Study, scholarships/grants, traineeships, health care benefits, and unspecified assistantships available. Support available to part-time students. Financial award applicants required to submit FAFSA. *Faculty research:* Learning disabilities, emotional behavior difficulties, Universal Design for Learning. *Unit head:* Dr. Maria E. Brisk, Chairperson, 617-552-4214, Fax: 617-552-0398. *Application contact:* Adam Poluzzi, Director, Graduate Admission and Financial Aid, 617-552-4214, Fax: 617-552-0398, E-mail: poluzzi@bc.edu.

Boston College, Lynch Graduate School of Education, Program in Special Needs: Severe Disabilities, Chestnut Hill, MA 02467-3800. Offers M Ed, CAES. *Accreditation:* Teacher Education Accreditation Council. Part-time and evening/weekend programs available. *Students:* 9 full-time (all women), 14 part-time (13 women); includes 2 minority (1 Asian, non-Hispanic/Latino; 1 Hispanic/Latino), 2 international. 29 applicants, 72% accepted, 12 enrolled. In 2011, 18 degrees awarded. *Degree requirements:* For master's, comprehensive exam. *Entrance requirements:* For master's, GRE General Test or MAT. Additional exam requirements/recommendations for international students: Required—TOEFL (minimum score 550 paper-based; 213 computer-based; 79 iBT). *Application deadline:* For fall admission, 1/1 priority date for domestic students. Application fee: $65. Electronic applications accepted. *Financial support:* Fellowships with full and partial tuition reimbursements, research assistantships with full and partial tuition reimbursements, teaching assistantships with full and partial tuition reimbursements, career-related internships or fieldwork, Federal Work-Study, scholarships/grants, traineeships, health care benefits, tuition waivers (full and partial), and unspecified assistantships available. Support available to part-time students. Financial award applicants required to submit FAFSA. *Faculty research:* Communication and language in learners with severe and multiple disabilities, assistive technology. *Unit head:* Dr. Maria E. Brisk, Chairperson, 617-552-4214, Fax: 617-552-0398. *Application contact:* Adam Poluzzi, Director, Graduate Admission and Financial Aid, 617-552-4214, Fax: 617-552-0398, E-mail: poluzzi@bc.edu.

Bowie State University, Graduate Programs, Program in Special Education, Bowie, MD 20715-9465. Offers M Ed. *Accreditation:* NCATE. Part-time and evening/weekend programs available. *Faculty:* 3 full-time (1 woman), 1 part-time/adjunct (0 women). *Students:* 5 full-time (all women), 22 part-time (17 women); includes 19 minority (all Black or African American, non-Hispanic/Latino). Average age 36. 15 applicants, 100% accepted, 15 enrolled. In 2011, 15 master's awarded. *Degree requirements:* For master's, comprehensive exam, thesis optional, research paper. *Entrance requirements:* For master's, teaching experience, 3 professional letters of recommendation. *Application deadline:* For fall admission, 4/1 priority date for domestic students, 4/1 for international students; for spring admission, 11/1 priority date for domestic students, 11/1 for international students. Applications are processed on a rolling basis. Application fee: $40. Electronic applications accepted. *Expenses:* Tuition, state resident: full-time $4140; part-time $3105 per semester. Tuition, nonresident: full-time $7836; part-time $5877 per semester. *Required fees:* $1715; $648 per semester. *Financial support:* Institutionally sponsored loans available. Support available to part-time students. Financial award application deadline: 4/1. *Unit head:* Dr. Thelon Byrd, Coordinator, 301-860-3137, E-mail: tbyrd@bowiestate.edu. *Application contact:* Angela Issac, Information Contact, 301-860-4000.

Bowling Green State University, Graduate College, College of Education and Human Development, School of Education and Intervention Services, Intervention Services Division, Program in Special Education, Bowling Green, OH 43403. Offers assistive technology (M Ed); early childhood intervention (M Ed); gifted education (M Ed); hearing impaired intervention (M Ed); mild/moderate intervention (M Ed); moderate/intensive intervention (M Ed). *Accreditation:* NCATE. Part-time programs available. *Degree requirements:* For master's, thesis or alternative. *Entrance requirements:* For master's, GRE General Test. Additional exam requirements/recommendations for international students: Required—TOEFL. Electronic applications accepted. *Faculty research:* Reading and special populations, deafness, early childhood, gifted and talented, behavior disorders.

Brandman University, School of Education, Irvine, CA 92618. Offers education (MA); educational leadership (MA); school counseling (MA); special education (MA); teaching (MA).

Brandon University, Faculty of Education, Brandon, MB R7A 6A9, Canada. Offers curriculum and instruction (M Ed, Diploma); educational administration (M Ed, Diploma); guidance and counseling (M Ed, Diploma); special education (M Ed, Diploma). *Degree requirements:* For master's, thesis. *Entrance requirements:* For master's, minimum GPA of 3.0, teaching certificate or equivalent. Additional exam requirements/recommendations for international students: Required—TOEFL. *Faculty research:* Comparative education, environmental studies, parent/school council.

Brenau University, Sydney O. Smith Graduate School, School of Education, Gainesville, GA 30501. Offers early childhood (Ed S); early childhood education (M Ed, MAT); middle grades (Ed S); middle grades education (M Ed, MAT); secondary education (MAT); special education (M Ed, MAT). *Accreditation:* NCATE. Part-time and evening/weekend programs available. Postbaccalaureate distance learning degree programs offered (no on-campus study). *Degree requirements:* For master's, thesis optional, comprehensive exam or applied research project, effective portfolio; for Ed S, thesis, applied research project. *Entrance requirements:* For master's, GRE, MAT, interview, minimum GPA of 3.0, 3 references, writing samples; for Ed S, GRE, MAT, master's degree, minimum GPA of 3.0, writing sample, letters of reference. Additional exam requirements/recommendations for international students: Required—TOEFL (minimum score 500 paper-based; 173 computer-based; 61 iBT); Recommended—IELTS (minimum score 5). Electronic applications accepted. *Expenses:* Contact institution.

Bridgewater State University, School of Graduate Studies, School of Education and Allied Studies, Department of Special Education and Communication Disorders, Bridgewater, MA 02325-0001. Offers special education (M Ed). *Accreditation:* NCATE. Part-time and evening/weekend programs available. *Entrance requirements:* For master's, GRE General Test or Massachusetts Test for Educator Licensure.

Brigham Young University, Graduate Studies, David O. McKay School of Education, Department of Counseling Psychology and Special Education, Provo, UT 84602-1001. Offers counseling psychology (PhD); school psychology (Ed S); special education (MS). Part-time programs available. *Faculty:* 11 full-time (6 women), 6 part-time/adjunct (2 women). *Students:* 72 full-time (49 women), 8 part-time (7 women); includes 6 minority (1 Black or African American, non-Hispanic/Latino; 2 American Indian or Alaska Native, non-Hispanic/Latino; 1 Asian, non-Hispanic/Latino; 2 Hispanic/Latino), 5 international. Average age 29. 81 applicants, 33% accepted, 27 enrolled. In 2011, 8 master's, 6 doctorates, 9 other advanced degrees awarded. *Degree requirements:* For master's and Ed S, comprehensive exam, thesis; for doctorate, comprehensive exam, thesis/dissertation. *Entrance requirements:* For master's, doctorate, and Ed S, GRE General Test, minimum GPA of 3.0 in last 60 hours of undergraduate coursework. Additional exam requirements/recommendations for international students: Required—TOEFL (minimum score 580 paper-based; 85 iBT), IELTS (minimum score 7). *Application deadline:* For fall admission, 1/15 for domestic and international students. Application fee: $50. Electronic applications accepted. *Expenses: Tuition:* Full-time $5760; part-time $320 per credit. Tuition and fees vary according to student's religious affiliation. *Financial support:* In 2011–12, 49 students received support, including 51 research assistantships with partial tuition reimbursements available (averaging $6,400 per year), 4 teaching assistantships with partial tuition reimbursements available (averaging $4,662 per year); institutionally sponsored loans and tuition waivers (partial) also available. Financial award application deadline: 3/31. *Faculty research:* Group psychotherapy, career development of Native Americans, multicultural psychology, gender issues in education, crisis management in schools. *Unit head:* Dr. Timothy B. Smith, Professor and Development Chair, 801-422-3857, Fax: 801-422-0198. *Application contact:* Diane E. Hancock, Department Secretary, 801-422-3859, Fax: 801-422-0198, E-mail: diane_hancock@byu.edu. Web site: http://education.byu.edu/cpse/.

Brooklyn College of the City University of New York, Division of Graduate Studies, School of Education, Program in Special Education, Brooklyn, NY 11210-2889. Offers teacher of students with disabilities (MS Ed), including birth-grade 2, grades 1-6, grades 5-9. Part-time programs available. *Entrance requirements:* For master's, LAST, interview; previous course work in education and psychology; minimum GPA of 3.0 in education, 2.8 overall; resume, 2 letters of recommendation; essay. Additional exam requirements/recommendations for international students: Required—TOEFL (minimum score 500 paper-based; 173 computer-based; 61 iBT). Electronic applications accepted. *Faculty research:* School reform, conflict resolution, curriculum for inclusive settings, urban issues in special education.

Buffalo State College, State University of New York, The Graduate School, Faculty of Applied Science and Education, Department of Exceptional Education, Programs in Special Education, Buffalo, NY 14222-1095. Offers special education (MS Ed); special education: adolescents (MS Ed); special education: childhood (MS Ed); special education: early childhood (MS Ed). *Accreditation:* NCATE. Part-time and evening/weekend programs available. *Degree requirements:* For master's, thesis or project. *Entrance requirements:* For master's, minimum GPA of 2.5. Additional exam requirements/recommendations for international students: Required—TOEFL (minimum score 550 paper-based; 213 computer-based).

Butler University, College of Education, Indianapolis, IN 46208-3485. Offers administration (MS); elementary education (MS); reading (MS); school counseling (MS); secondary education (MS); special education (MS). *Accreditation:* ACA; NCATE. Part-time and evening/weekend programs available. *Faculty:* 7 full-time (4 women), 5 part-time/adjunct (all women). *Students:* 9 full-time (6 women), 136 part-time (105 women); includes 21 minority (14 Black or African American, non-Hispanic/Latino; 5 Asian, non-Hispanic/Latino; 1 Hispanic/Latino; 1 Two or more races, non-Hispanic/Latino), 1 international. Average age 31. 69 applicants, 94% accepted, 24 enrolled. In 2011, 66 master's awarded. *Entrance requirements:* For master's, GRE General Test, MAT, interview. *Application deadline:* For fall admission, 8/15 priority date for domestic students. Applications are processed on a rolling basis. Application fee: $35. Electronic applications accepted. *Expenses: Tuition:* Part-time $466 per credit. *Financial support:* Institutionally sponsored loans available. Support available to part-time students. Financial award application deadline: 7/15; financial award applicants required to submit FAFSA. *Faculty research:* Ethics in cybercounseling, history of sports for disabled, effect of fetal alcohol syndrome on perceptual learning, reading recovery's theoretical framework in teacher education. *Unit head:* Dr. Ena Shelley, Dean, 317-940-9752, Fax: 317-940-6481. *Application contact:* Karen Farrell, Department Secretary, 317-940-9220, E-mail: kfarrell@butler.edu.

Caldwell College, Graduate Studies, Division of Education, Caldwell, NJ 07006-6195. Offers curriculum and instruction (MA); educational administration (MA); learning disabilities teacher-consultant (Post-Master's Certificate); literacy instruction (MA); principal (Post-Master's Certificate); reading specialist (Post-Master's Certificate); special education (MA), including special education, teaching of students with disabilities, teaching of students with disabilities and learning disabilities teacher-consultant; superintendent (Post-Master's Certificate); supervisor (Post-Master's Certificate). Part-time and evening/weekend programs available. *Students:* 66 full-time (41 women), 230 part-time (188 women); includes 24 minority (14 Black or African American, non-Hispanic/Latino; 1 Asian, non-Hispanic/Latino; 9 Hispanic/Latino). *Entrance requirements:* Additional exam requirements/recommendations for international students: Required—TOEFL (minimum score 580 paper-based; 237 computer-based). *Application deadline:* Applications are processed on a rolling basis. Application fee: $40. Electronic applications accepted. *Expenses: Tuition:* Full-time $14,400; part-time $800 per credit. *Required fees:* $200; $100 per semester. *Financial support:* Applicants required to submit FAFSA. *Unit head:* Dr. Janice Stewart, Coordinator, 973-618-3626, E-mail: jstewart@caldwell.edu. *Application contact:* Vilma Mueller, Director of Graduate Studies, 973-618-3544, E-mail: graduate@caldwell.edu.

California Baptist University, Program in Education, Riverside, CA 92504-3206. Offers educational leadership for faith-based instruction (MS); educational leadership for public institutions (MS); educational technology (MS); instructional computer applications (MS); international education (MS); reading (MS); school counseling (MS); school psychology (MS); special education (MS); special education in mild/moderate disabilities (MS); special education in moderate/severe disabilities (MS); teaching (MS); teaching and learning with induction program (MS Ed). Part-time and evening/weekend programs available. *Faculty:* 16 full-time (10 women), 1 (woman) part-time/adjunct. *Students:* 380 full-time (323 women); includes 149 minority (28 Black or African American, non-Hispanic/Latino; 2 American Indian or Alaska Native, non-Hispanic/Latino; 13 Asian, non-Hispanic/Latino; 100 Hispanic/Latino; 2 Native Hawaiian or other Pacific Islander, non-Hispanic/Latino; 4 Two or more races, non-Hispanic/Latino). Average age 32. 181 applicants, 70% accepted, 111 enrolled. In 2011, 82 master's awarded. *Degree requirements:* For master's, comprehensive exam or thesis. *Entrance requirements:* For master's, minimum undergraduate GPA of 3.0; 18 semester units of prerequisite course work in education; three recommendations; essay; interview. Additional exam requirements/recommendations for international students: Required—TOEFL (minimum score 575 paper-based; 230 computer-based; 89 iBT). *Application deadline:* For fall admission, 8/1 priority date for domestic students, 7/1 for international students; for spring admission, 12/1 priority date for domestic students, 11/1 for international students. Applications are processed on a rolling basis. Application fee: $45. Electronic applications accepted. *Expenses:* Contact institution. *Financial support:* In 2011–12, 4 students received support. Federal Work-Study and institutionally sponsored loans available. Financial award applicants required to submit FAFSA. *Faculty research:* Special education, neurosciences and education, cultural influences on behavior, faith-based school leadership, social and philosophical contexts of education. *Unit head:* Dr. John Shoup, Dean, School of Education, 951-343-4205, Fax: 951-343-4516, E-mail: jshoup@calbaptist.edu. *Application contact:* Dr. James Heyman, Director, Master of Science Program in Education, 951-343-4243, Fax: 951-343-5095, E-mail: jheyman@calbaptist.edu. Web site: http://www.calbaptist.edu/mastersined/.

California Lutheran University, Graduate Studies, Graduate School of Education, Thousand Oaks, CA 91360-2787. Offers counseling and guidance (MS), including college student personnel, counseling and guidance; educational leadership (MA, Ed D), including educational leadership (K-12) (Ed D), higher education leadership (Ed D); special education (MS); teacher leadership (M Ed); teaching (M Ed). *Accreditation:* NCATE. Part-time and evening/weekend programs available. *Entrance requirements:* For master's, GRE General Test, interview, minimum GPA of 3.0.

California State University, Bakersfield, Division of Graduate Studies, School of Social Sciences and Education, Program in Special Education, Bakersfield, CA 93311. Offers MA. *Accreditation:* NCATE. *Degree requirements:* For master's, thesis or alternative, project or culminating exam. *Entrance requirements:* For master's, 3 letters of recommendation, minimum GPA of 2.67, interview. *Application deadline:* Applications are processed on a rolling basis. Application fee: $55. *Expenses: Required fees:* $1302 per unit. Part-time tuition and fees vary according to course load and program. *Unit head:* Dr. Louis Wildman, Department Chair, 661-654-3047, Fax: 661-654-3029, E-mail: lwildman@csub.edu. Web site: http://www.csub.edu/sse/specialed/.

California State University, Chico, Office of Graduate Studies, College of Communication and Education, School of Education, Teaching English Learners and Special Education Advising Patterns Program, Chico, CA 95929-0722. Offers special education (MA); teaching English learners (MA). Part-time and evening/weekend programs available. *Degree requirements:* For master's, comprehensive exam, thesis or project. *Entrance requirements:* Additional exam requirements/recommendations for international students: Required—TOEFL (minimum score 550 paper-based; 213 computer-based; 80 iBT), IELTS (minimum score 6.5), Pearson Test of English (minimum score 59). *Application deadline:* For fall admission, 3/1 priority date for domestic students, 3/1 for international students; for spring admission, 9/15 priority date for domestic students, 9/15 for international students. Application fee: $55. Electronic applications accepted. Tuition and fees vary according to class time, course load and degree level. *Financial support:* Fellowships, career-related internships or fieldwork, scholarships/grants, and stipends available. *Unit head:* Dr. Deborah Summers, Chair, 530-898-6421, Fax: 530-898-6177, E-mail: educ@csuchico.edu. *Application contact:* Judy I. Rice, Graduate Admissions Coordinator, 530-898-5416, Fax: 530-898-3342, E-mail: jlrice@csuchico.edu. Web site: http://www.csuchico.edu/soe/advanced/education/patterns.shtml.

California State University, Dominguez Hills, College of Professional Studies, School of Education, Division of Teacher Education, Program in Special Education, Carson, CA 90747-0001. Offers early childhood (MA); mild/moderate (MA); moderate/severe (MA). Part-time and evening/weekend programs available. *Faculty:* 8 full-time (all women), 2 part-time/adjunct (both women). *Students:* 118 full-time (89 women), 176 part-time (138 women); includes 175 minority (49 Black or African American, non-Hispanic/Latino; 30 Asian, non-Hispanic/Latino; 91 Hispanic/Latino; 1 Native Hawaiian or other Pacific Islander, non-Hispanic/Latino; 4 Two or more races, non-Hispanic/Latino), 1 international. Average age 36. 88 applicants, 60% accepted, 29 enrolled. In 2011, 39 master's awarded. *Degree requirements:* For master's, comprehensive exam, thesis or alternative. *Entrance requirements:* For master's, minimum GPA of 2.75 in last 60 units, 3 letters of recommendation. *Application deadline:* For fall admission, 6/1 for domestic students. Applications are processed on a rolling basis. Application fee: $55. *Unit head:* Dr. Carrie Blackaller, Coordinator, 310-243-3900, E-mail: cablackaller@csudh.edu. *Application contact:* Admissions Office, 310-243-3530. Web site: http://www.csudh.edu/cps/soe/programsdegrees/special-education.shtml.

California State University, East Bay, Office of Academic Programs and Graduate Studies, College of Education and Allied Studies, Department of Educational Psychology, Special Education Program, Hayward, CA 94542-3000. Offers moderate-severe disabilities (MS). *Accreditation:* NCATE. *Faculty:* 3 full-time (2 women), 5 part-time/adjunct (2 women). *Students:* 49 full-time (42 women), 6 part-time (4 women); includes 12 minority (3 Black or African American, non-Hispanic/Latino; 3 Asian, non-Hispanic/Latino; 4 Hispanic/Latino; 2 Native Hawaiian or other Pacific Islander, non-Hispanic/Latino). Average age 34. 39 applicants, 74% accepted, 4 enrolled. In 2011, 11 master's awarded. *Degree requirements:* For master's, project or thesis. *Entrance requirements:* For master's, GRE or MAT, interview, minimum GPA of 2.5 during previous 2 years of course work. Additional exam requirements/recommendations for international students: Required—TOEFL (minimum score 550 paper-based; 213 computer-based). *Application deadline:* For fall admission, 6/30 for domestic and international students. Application fee: $55. Electronic applications accepted. *Expenses:* Tuition, state resident: full-time $6738; part-time $1302 per quarter. Tuition, nonresident: full-time $12,690; part-time $2294 per quarter. *Required fees:* $449 per quarter. Tuition and fees vary according to degree level, program and reciprocity agreements. *Financial support:* Career-related internships or fieldwork, Federal Work-Study, and institutionally sponsored loans available. Support available to part-time students. Financial award application deadline: 3/2; financial award applicants required to submit FAFSA. *Unit head:* Dr. Jack Davis, Chair, Educational Psychology, 510-885-3011, Fax: 510-885-4642, E-mail: jack.davis@csueastbay.edu. *Application contact:* Prof. Linda Smetana, Graduate Advisor, Special Education, 510-885-4489, Fax: 510-885-4642, E-mail: linda.smetana@csueastbay.edu. Web site: http://www.edschool.csueastbay.edu/departments/epsy.

California State University, Fresno, Division of Graduate Studies, School of Education and Human Development, Department of Counseling and Special Education, Program in Special Education, Fresno, CA 93740-8027. Offers MA. *Accreditation:* NCATE. Part-time and evening/weekend programs available. *Degree requirements:* For master's, thesis or alternative. *Entrance requirements:* For master's, GRE General Test, MAT, minimum GPA of 3.0. Additional exam requirements/recommendations for international students: Required—TOEFL. Electronic applications accepted.

California State University, Fullerton, Graduate Studies, College of Education, Department of Special Education, Fullerton, CA 92834-9480. Offers MS. *Accreditation:* NCATE. Part-time programs available. *Students:* 42 full-time (34 women), 94 part-time (81 women); includes 59 minority (5 Black or African American, non-Hispanic/Latino; 16 Asian, non-Hispanic/Latino; 37 Hispanic/Latino; 1 Two or more races, non-Hispanic/Latino). Average age 34. 64 applicants, 61% accepted, 35 enrolled. In 2011, 51 master's awarded. *Degree requirements:* For master's, comprehensive exam, project or thesis. *Entrance requirements:* For master's, minimum GPA of 2.75. Application fee: $55. *Financial support:* Career-related internships or fieldwork, Federal Work-Study, institutionally sponsored loans, and scholarships/grants available. Support available to part-time students. Financial award application deadline: 3/1; financial award applicants required to submit FAFSA. *Unit head:* Dr. Melinda Pierson, Chair, 657-278-4711. *Application contact:* Admissions/Applications, 657-278-2371.

California State University, Long Beach, Graduate Studies, College of Education, Department of Advanced Studies in Education and Counseling, Master of Science in Special Education Program, Long Beach, CA 90840. Offers MS. *Accreditation:* NCATE. *Students:* 2 full-time (both women), 37 part-time (33 women); includes 19 minority (1 Black or African American, non-Hispanic/Latino; 3 American Indian or Alaska Native, non-Hispanic/Latino; 4 Asian, non-Hispanic/Latino; 8 Hispanic/Latino; 1 Native Hawaiian or other Pacific Islander, non-Hispanic/Latino; 2 Two or more races, non-Hispanic/Latino). Average age 32. 19 applicants, 58% accepted, 9 enrolled. In 2011, 24 master's awarded. *Degree requirements:* For master's, comprehensive exam or thesis. *Entrance requirements:* For master's, GRE General Test, minimum GPA of 2.75. *Application deadline:* For fall admission, 3/1 for domestic students. Applications are processed on a rolling basis. Application fee: $55. Electronic applications accepted. *Financial support:* Federal Work-Study, institutionally sponsored loans, and scholarships/grants available. Financial award application deadline: 3/2. *Unit head:* Dr. Jennifer Coots, Chair, 562-985-8354, Fax: 562-985-4534, E-mail: jcoots@csulb.edu. *Application contact:* Nancy L. McGlothin, Coordinator for Graduate Studies and Research, 562-985-8476, Fax: 562-985-4951, E-mail: nmcgloth@csulb.edu.

California State University, Los Angeles, Graduate Studies, Charter College of Education, Division of Special Education and Counseling, Los Angeles, CA 90032-8530. Offers counseling (MS), including applied behavior analysis, community college counseling, rehabilitation counseling, school counseling and school psychology; special education (MA, PhD). *Accreditation:* ACA. Part-time and evening/weekend programs available. *Faculty:* 20 full-time (14 women), 27 part-time/adjunct (18 women). *Students:* 334 full-time (277 women), 337 part-time (262 women); includes 480 minority (38 Black or African American, non-Hispanic/Latino; 1 American Indian or Alaska Native, non-Hispanic/Latino; 69 Asian, non-Hispanic/Latino; 364 Hispanic/Latino; 8 Two or more races, non-Hispanic/Latino), 24 international. Average age 34. 288 applicants, 38% accepted, 79 enrolled. In 2011, 226 master's awarded. *Entrance requirements:* For master's, minimum GPA of 2.75 in last 90 units of course work, teaching certificate. Additional exam requirements/recommendations for international students: Required—TOEFL (minimum score 500 paper-based; 173 computer-based). *Application deadline:* For fall admission, 5/1 for domestic and international students. Applications are processed on a rolling basis. Application fee: $55. Electronic applications accepted. *Expenses:* Tuition, state resident: full-time $8225. *Financial support:* Career-related internships or fieldwork and Federal Work-Study available. Support available to part-time students. Financial award application deadline: 3/1. *Unit head:* Dr. Andrea Zetlin, Acting Chair, 323-343-4400, Fax: 323-343-5605, E-mail: azetlin@calstatela.edu. *Application contact:* Dr. Karin Brown, Acting Associate Dean of Graduate Studies, 323-343-3820, Fax: 323-343-5653, E-mail: kbrown5@calstatela.edu. Web site: http://www.calstatela.edu/academic/ccoe/index_edsp.htm.

California State University, Northridge, Graduate Studies, College of Education, Department of Special Education, Northridge, CA 91330. Offers early childhood special education (MA); education of the deaf and hard of hearing (MA); educational therapy (MA); mild/moderate disabilities (MA); moderate/severe disabilities (MA). *Accreditation:* NCATE. *Entrance requirements:* For master's, GRE General Test (if cumulative undergraduate GPA less than 3.0). Additional exam requirements/recommendations for international students: Required—TOEFL. *Faculty research:* Teacher training, classroom aide training.

California State University, Sacramento, Office of Graduate Studies, College of Education, Department of Special Education, Rehabilitation, and School Psychology, Sacramento , CA 95819-6079. Offers school psychology (MS); special education (MA); vocational rehabilitation (MS). *Accreditation:* CORE. Part-time programs available. *Faculty:* 17 full-time (11 women), 16 part-time/adjunct (13 women). *Students:* 204 full-time, 93 part-time; includes 81 minority (24 Black or African American, non-Hispanic/Latino; 7 American Indian or Alaska Native, non-Hispanic/Latino; 15 Asian, non-Hispanic/Latino; 24 Hispanic/Latino; 8 Native Hawaiian or other Pacific Islander, non-Hispanic/Latino; 3 Two or more races, non-Hispanic/Latino), 2 international. Average age 36. 210 applicants, 86% accepted, 130 enrolled. In 2011, 86 master's awarded. *Entrance requirements:* For master's, minimum GPA of 2.5. Additional exam requirements/recommendations for international students: Required—TOEFL. *Application deadline:* For fall admission, 3/1 for domestic and international students; for spring admission, 9/15 for domestic students, 9/30 for international students. Applications are processed on a rolling basis. Application fee: $55. Electronic applications accepted. *Financial support:* Career-related internships or fieldwork and Federal Work-Study available. Support available to part-time students. Financial award application deadline: 3/1; financial award applicants required to submit FAFSA. *Faculty research:* Reading and learning disabilities; vocational rehabilitation counseling issues and implementation; school-based crisis intervention; posttraumatic stress disorder; attention-deficit/hyperactivity disorder; school based suicide prevention, intervention, and postvention; autism spectrum disorders; special education technology, strategies and assessment. *Unit head:* Ostertag A. Bruce, Chair, 916-278-6622, Fax: 916-278-3498, E-mail: ostertag@csus.edu. *Application contact:* Jose Martinez, Outreach and Graduate Diversity Coordinator, 916-278-6470, Fax: 916-278-5669, E-mail: martinj@skymail.csus.edu. Web site: http://www.edweb.csus.edu/eds.

California State University, San Bernardino, Graduate Studies, College of Education, Programs in Special Education and Rehabilitation Counseling, San Bernardino, CA 92407-2397. Offers rehabilitation counseling (MA); special education (MA). *Accreditation:* CORE; NCATE. Part-time and evening/weekend programs available. *Students:* 116 full-time (94 women), 64 part-time (50 women); includes 85 minority (18 Black or African American, non-Hispanic/Latino; 11 Asian, non-Hispanic/Latino; 56 Hispanic/Latino), 1 international. Average age 33. 75 applicants, 61% accepted, 36 enrolled. In 2011, 77 master's awarded. *Degree requirements:* For master's, thesis or alternative, advancement to candidacy. *Entrance requirements:* For master's, minimum GPA of 3.0 in education. *Application deadline:* For fall admission, 8/31 priority date for domestic students. Application fee: $55. *Expenses:* Tuition, state resident: full-time $7356. Tuition, nonresident: full-time $7356. *Required fees:* $1077. Tuition and fees vary according to program. *Financial support:* Career-related internships or fieldwork and Federal Work-Study available. Support available to part-time students. *Unit head:* Dr. Joseph Turpin, Coordinator, 909-537-5680, E-mail: jturpin@csusb.edu. *Application contact:* Sandra Kamusikiri, Associate Vice-President/Dean of Graduate Studies, 909-537-5058, E-mail: skamusik@csusb.edu.

California State University, Stanislaus, College of Education, Program in Education (MA), Turlock, CA 95382. Offers curriculum and instruction (MA), including education technology, elementary education, multilingual education, physical education, reading, secondary education, special education; school administration (MA); school counseling (MA). Part-time and evening/weekend programs available. *Degree requirements:* For master's, comprehensive exam (for some programs), thesis (for some programs). *Entrance requirements:* For master's, MAT, GRE, or CBEST (varies by concentration), 3 letters of recommendation, personal statement. Additional exam requirements/recommendations for international students: Required—TOEFL (minimum score 550 paper-based; 213 computer-based). *Application deadline:* For fall admission, 5/1 for domestic students; for spring admission, 1/7 for domestic students. Application fee: $55. Electronic applications accepted. *Expenses: Required fees:* $4616 per year. *Financial support:* Federal Work-Study available. Financial award application deadline: 3/1; financial award applicants required to submit FAFSA. *Faculty research:* Children's perspectives on historical events, method elementary schools dual language education, K-12 reading and CYRM programs. *Unit head:* Dr. Kathy Norman, Dean, College of Education, 209-667-3652, Fax: 209-664-6613, E-mail: coe@csustan.edu. *Application contact:* Graduate School, 209-667-3129, Fax: 209-664-7025, E-mail: graduate_school@csustan.edu. Web site: http://www.csustan.edu/COE/.

California University of Pennsylvania, School of Graduate Studies and Research, College of Education and Human Services, Department of Special Education, California, PA 15419-1394. Offers mentally and/or physically handicapped education (M Ed). *Accreditation:* NCATE. Part-time and evening/weekend programs available. *Degree requirements:* For master's, comprehensive exam, thesis optional. *Entrance requirements:* For master's, MAT, PRAXIS. Additional exam requirements/recommendations for international students: Required—TOEFL (minimum score 550 paper-based; 213 computer-based; 80 iBT). Electronic applications accepted. *Faculty research:* Case-based instruction, electronic performance support tools, students with disabilities, teacher preparation, No Child Left Behind.

Calvin College, Graduate Programs in Education, Grand Rapids, MI 49546-4388. Offers curriculum and instruction (M Ed); educational leadership (M Ed); learning disabilities (M Ed); literacy (M Ed). Part-time programs available. *Degree requirements:* For master's, thesis or seminar. *Entrance requirements:* For master's, teaching certificate. Additional exam requirements/recommendations for international students: Required—TOEFL (minimum score 550 paper-based; 213 computer-based; 80 iBT). Electronic applications accepted. *Faculty research:* Literacy, racialized gender and gendered identity, teacher learning, learning disabilities identification.

Cambridge College, School of Education, Cambridge, MA 02138-5304. Offers autism specialist (M Ed); autism/behavior analyst (M Ed); behavior analyst (Post-Master's Certificate); behavioral management (M Ed); early childhood teacher (M Ed); education specialist in curriculum and instruction (CAGS); educational leadership (Ed D); elementary teacher (M Ed); English as a second language (M Ed, Certificate); general science (M Ed); health education (Post-Master's Certificate); health/family and consumer sciences (M Ed); history (M Ed); individualized (M Ed); information technology literacy (M Ed); instructional technology (M Ed); interdisciplinary studies (M Ed); library teacher (M Ed); literacy education (M Ed); mathematics (M Ed); mathematics specialist (Certificate); middle school mathematics and science (M Ed); school administration (M Ed, CAGS); school guidance counselor (M Ed); school nurse education (M Ed); school social worker/school adjustment counselor (M Ed); special education administrator (CAGS); special education/moderate disabilities (M Ed); teaching skills and methodologies (M Ed). Part-time and evening/weekend programs available. Postbaccalaureate distance learning degree programs offered (minimal on-campus study). *Degree requirements:* For master's, thesis, internship/practicum (licensure program only); for doctorate, thesis/dissertation; for other advanced degree, thesis. *Entrance requirements:* For master's, interview, resume, documentation of licensure, 2 professional references; for doctorate, official transcripts, interview, resume, documentation of licensure (if any), written personal statement/essay, portfolio of scholarly and professional work, qualifying assessment, 2 professional references, health insurance, immunizations form; for other advanced degree, official transcripts, interview, resume, documentation of licensure (if any), written personal statement/essay, 2 professional references, health insurance, immunizations form. Additional exam requirements/recommendations for international students: Required—TOEFL (minimum score 550 paper-based; 213 computer-based; 79 iBT); Recommended—IELTS (minimum score 6). Electronic applications accepted. *Expenses:* Contact institution. *Faculty research:* Adult education, accelerated learning, mathematics education, brain compatible learning, special education and law.

Campbellsville University, School of Education, Campbellsville, KY 42718-2799. Offers curriculum and instruction (MAE); special education (MASE). *Accreditation:* NCATE. Part-time and evening/weekend programs available. Postbaccalaureate distance learning degree programs offered (minimal on-campus study). *Students:* 232 full-time (159 women), 45 part-time (36 women); includes 34 minority (all Black or African American, non-Hispanic/Latino), 8 international. In 2011, 79 master's awarded. *Degree requirements:* For master's, thesis, research paper. *Entrance requirements:* For master's, GRE or PRAXIS, minimum undergraduate GPA of 2.75, teaching certificate, professional growth plan, letters of recommendation, disposition assessment, interview. *Application deadline:* For fall admission, 6/1 priority date for domestic students, 5/1 for international students; for spring admission, 11/1 priority date for domestic students, 10/1 for international students. Applications are processed on a rolling basis. Application fee: $25. Electronic applications accepted. *Expenses: Tuition:* Full-time $6030; part-time $335 per credit hour. *Financial support:* In 2011–12, 250 students received support. Institutionally sponsored loans, scholarships/grants, and unspecified assistantships available. Support available to part-time students. Financial award application deadline: 6/1; financial award applicants required to submit FAFSA. *Faculty research:* Professional development, curriculum development, school governance, assessment, special education. *Unit head:* Dr. Brenda A. Priddy, Dean, 270-789-5344, Fax: 270-789-5206, E-mail: bapriddy@campbellsville.edu. *Application contact:* Monica Bamwine, Assistant Director of Admissions, 270-789-5221, Fax: 270-789-5071, E-mail: redeaton@campbellsville.edu.

Canisius College, Graduate Division, School of Education and Human Services, Department of Graduate Education and Leadership, Buffalo, NY 14208-1098. Offers college student personnel (MS Ed); deaf education (MS Ed); deaf/adolescent education, grades 7-12 (MS Ed); deaf/childhood education, grades 1-6 (MS Ed); differential instruction (MS Ed); education administration (MS Ed); gifted education extention (Certificate); literacy (MS Ed); reading (Certificate); school building leadership (MS Ed, Certificate); school district leadership (Certificate). *Accreditation:* NCATE. Part-time and evening/weekend programs available. Postbaccalaureate distance learning degree programs offered (minimal on-campus study). *Faculty:* 7 full-time (6 women), 36 part-time/adjunct (22 women). *Students:* 149 full-time (114 women), 242 part-time (177 women); includes 42 minority (29 Black or African American, non-Hispanic/Latino; 2 American Indian or Alaska Native, non-Hispanic/Latino; 3 Asian, non-Hispanic/Latino; 6 Hispanic/Latino; 2 Two or more races, non-Hispanic/Latino), 3 international. Average age 30. 250 applicants, 84% accepted, 124 enrolled. In 2011, 135 degrees awarded. *Entrance requirements:* For master's, GRE if cumulative GPA less than 2.7, transcripts, two letters of recommendation. Additional exam requirements/recommendations for international students: Required—TOEFL. *Application deadline:* Applications are processed on a rolling basis. Application fee: $25. Electronic applications accepted. *Financial support:* Career-related internships or fieldwork, Federal Work-Study, scholarships/grants, tuition waivers (partial), and unspecified assistantships available.

Support available to part-time students. Financial award application deadline: 4/30; financial award applicants required to submit FAFSA. *Faculty research:* Asperger's disease, autism, private higher education, reading strategies. *Unit head:* Dr. Rosemary K. Murray, Chair/Associate Professor of Graduate Education and Leadership, 716-888-3723, E-mail: murray1@canisius.edu. *Application contact:* Jim Bagwell, Director of Graduate Recruitment and Admissions, 716-888-2544, Fax: 716-888-3290, E-mail: bagwellj@canisius.edu. Web site: http://www.canisius.edu/education/graduate.asp.

Canisius College, Graduate Division, School of Education and Human Services, Education Department, Buffalo, NY 14208-1098. Offers general education non-matriculated (MS Ed); middle childhood (MS Ed); special education/adolescent (MS Ed); special education/advanced (MS Ed); special education/childhood (MS Ed); special education/childhood education grades 1-6 (MS Ed). Part-time and evening/weekend programs available. Postbaccalaureate distance learning degree programs offered (minimal on-campus study). *Faculty:* 17 full-time (13 women), 23 part-time/adjunct (11 women). *Students:* 139 full-time (103 women), 62 part-time (47 women); includes 10 minority (9 Black or African American, non-Hispanic/Latino; 1 Hispanic/Latino), 67 international. Average age 30. 135 applicants, 70% accepted, 53 enrolled. In 2011, 125 master's awarded. *Degree requirements:* For master's, research project or thesis. *Entrance requirements:* For master's, GRE if cumulative GPA less than 2.7, transcripts, two letters of recommendation. Additional exam requirements/recommendations for international students: Required—TOEFL. *Application deadline:* Applications are processed on a rolling basis. Application fee: $25. Electronic applications accepted. *Financial support:* Career-related internships or fieldwork, Federal Work-Study, scholarships/grants, tuition waivers (partial), and unspecified assistantships available. Support available to part-time students. Financial award application deadline: 4/30; financial award applicants required to submit FAFSA. *Faculty research:* Family as faculty, tutorial experiences in modern math, integrating digital technologies in the classroom. *Unit head:* Dr. Julie Henry, Chair/Professor, 716-888-3729, E-mail: henry1@canisius.edu. *Application contact:* Jim Bagwell, Director of Graduate Recruitment and Admissions, 716-888-2544, Fax: 716-888-3290, E-mail: bagwellj@canisius.edu. Web site: http://www.canisius.edu/education/facultystaff.asp.

Cardinal Stritch University, College of Education, Department of Literacy, Milwaukee, WI 53217-3985. Offers literacy/English as a second language (MA); reading/language arts (MA); reading/learning disability (MA). *Accreditation:* NCATE. Part-time and evening/weekend programs available. *Degree requirements:* For master's, comprehensive exam, thesis, faculty recommendation, research project. *Entrance requirements:* For master's, letters of recommendation (2), minimum GPA of 2.75.

Cardinal Stritch University, College of Education, Department of Special Education, Milwaukee, WI 53217-3985. Offers MA. *Accreditation:* NCATE. Part-time and evening/weekend programs available. *Degree requirements:* For master's, comprehensive exam, thesis, practica. *Entrance requirements:* For master's, letters of recommendation (2), minimum GPA of 2.75.

Caribbean University, Graduate School, Bayamón, PR 00960-0493. Offers administration and supervision (MA Ed); criminal justice (MA); curriculum and instruction (MA Ed, PhD), including elementary education (MA Ed), English education (MA Ed), history education (MA Ed), mathematics education (MA Ed), primary education (MA Ed), science education (MA Ed), Spanish education (MA Ed); educational technology in instructional systems (MA Ed); gerontology (MSN); human resources (MBA); museology, archiving and art history (MA Ed); neonatal pediatrics (MSN); physical education (MA Ed); special education (MA Ed). *Entrance requirements:* For master's, interview, minimum GPA of 2.5.

Carlos Albizu University, Miami Campus, Graduate Programs, Miami, FL 33172-2209. Offers clinical psychology (Psy D); entrepreneurship (MBA); exceptional student education (MS); industrial/organizational psychology (MS); marriage and family therapy (MS); mental health counseling (MS); nonprofit management (MBA); organizational management (MBA); psychology (MS); school counseling (MS); teaching English as a second language (MS). *Accreditation:* APA. Part-time and evening/weekend programs available. *Faculty:* 19 full-time (12 women), 53 part-time/adjunct (27 women). *Students:* 524 full-time (431 women), 216 part-time (169 women); includes 563 minority (50 Black or African American, non-Hispanic/Latino; 1 American Indian or Alaska Native, non-Hispanic/Latino; 4 Asian, non-Hispanic/Latino; 492 Hispanic/Latino; 16 Native Hawaiian or other Pacific Islander, non-Hispanic/Latino), 17 international. Average age 31. 174 applicants, 67% accepted, 116 enrolled. In 2011, 157 master's, 21 doctorates awarded. Terminal master's awarded for partial completion of doctoral program. *Degree requirements:* For master's, one foreign language, comprehensive exam, integrative project (MBA), research project (exceptional student education, teaching English as a second language); for doctorate, one foreign language, comprehensive exam, internship, project. *Entrance requirements:* For master's, 3 letters of recommendation, interview, minimum GPA of 3.0, resume, statement of purpose, official transcripts; for doctorate, 3 letters of recommendation, minimum GPA of 3.0, resume, interview, statement of purpose, official transcripts. Additional exam requirements/recommendations for international students: Required—Michigan Test of English Language Proficiency. *Application deadline:* For fall admission, 4/1 priority date for domestic students, 5/1 for international students; for spring admission, 11/1 priority date for domestic students, 9/1 for international students. Applications are processed on a rolling basis. Application fee: $50. Electronic applications accepted. *Expenses: Tuition:* Full-time $9360; part-time $520 per credit. *Required fees:* $298 per term. Tuition and fees vary according to course load, degree level and program. *Financial support:* In 2011–12, 106 students received support. Federal Work-Study, scholarships/grants, and tuition discounts available. Financial award application deadline: 6/1; financial award applicants required to submit FAFSA. *Faculty research:* Psychotherapy, forensic psychology, neuropsychology, marketing strategy, entrepreneurship, special education. *Unit head:* Dr. Carmen S. Roca, Chancellor, 305-593-1223 Ext. 120, Fax: 305-629-8052, E-mail: croca@albizu.edu. *Application contact:* Vanessa Almendarez, Administrative Assistant, 305-593-1223 Ext. 137, Fax: 305-593-1854, E-mail: valmendarez@albizu.edu.

Carlow University, School of Education, Program in Education, Pittsburgh, PA 15213-3165. Offers art education (M Ed); early childhood education (M Ed); instructional technology specialist (M Ed); middle level education (M Ed); secondary education (M Ed); special education (M Ed). Part-time and evening/weekend programs available. *Students:* 72 full-time (58 women), 16 part-time (13 women); includes 16 minority (15 Black or African American, non-Hispanic/Latino; 1 Hispanic/Latino). Average age 32. 68 applicants, 28% accepted, 11 enrolled. In 2011, 41 master's awarded. *Entrance requirements:* For master's, resume, 3 letters of recommendation, minimum GPA of 3.0, interview. Additional exam requirements/recommendations for international students: Required—TOEFL. *Application deadline:* For fall admission, 6/15 priority date for domestic students, 6/15 for international students; for spring admission, 11/15 priority date for domestic students, 11/15 for international students. Applications are processed on a rolling basis. Application fee: $20. Electronic applications accepted. *Expenses: Tuition:* Full-time $10,290; part-time $686 per credit. Tuition and fees vary according to course load, degree level and program. *Financial support:* Applicants required to submit FAFSA. *Unit head:* Dr. Marilyn J. Llewellyn, Director, 412-578-6011, Fax: 412-578-0816, E-mail: llewellynmj@carlow.edu. *Application contact:* Jo Danhires, Administrative Assistant, Admissions, 412-578-6089, Fax: 412-578-6321, E-mail: gradstudies@carlow.edu. Web site: http://www.carlow.edu.

Castleton State College, Division of Graduate Studies, Department of Education, Program in Special Education, Castleton, VT 05735. Offers MA Ed, CAGS. Part-time and evening/weekend programs available. *Degree requirements:* For master's, thesis or alternative; for CAGS, publishable paper. *Entrance requirements:* For master's, GRE General Test, MAT, interview, minimum undergraduate GPA of 3.0; for CAGS, educational research, master's degree, minimum undergraduate GPA of 3.0.

The Catholic University of America, School of Arts and Sciences, Department of Education, Washington, DC 20064. Offers Catholic educational leadership and policy studies (PhD); Catholic school leadership (MA); education (Certificate); educational psychology (PhD); secondary education (MA); special education (MA). *Accreditation:* NCATE. Part-time programs available. *Faculty:* 10 full-time (8 women), 10 part-time/adjunct (8 women). *Students:* 4 full-time (all women), 44 part-time (34 women); includes 12 minority (6 Black or African American, non-Hispanic/Latino; 4 Hispanic/Latino; 2 Two or more races, non-Hispanic/Latino). Average age 39. 38 applicants, 24% accepted, 2 enrolled. In 2011, 5 master's, 4 doctorates, 3 other advanced degrees awarded. *Degree requirements:* For master's, comprehensive exam, thesis or alternative; for doctorate, comprehensive exam, thesis/dissertation; for Certificate, action research project. *Entrance requirements:* For master's and doctorate, GRE General Test or MAT, statement of purpose, official copies of academic transcripts, three letters of recommendation, interview; for Certificate, PRAXIS I, statement of purpose, official copies of academic transcripts, three letters of recommendation, interview. Additional exam requirements/recommendations for international students: Required—TOEFL (minimum score 580 paper-based; 237 computer-based). *Application deadline:* For fall admission, 8/1 priority date for domestic students, 7/15 for international students; for spring admission, 12/1 priority date for domestic students, 10/15 for international students. Applications are processed on a rolling basis. Application fee: $55. Electronic applications accepted. *Expenses: Tuition:* Full-time $35,260; part-time $1380 per credit. *Required fees:* $80; $40 per semester hour. One-time fee: $425. *Financial support:* Fellowships, research assistantships, teaching assistantships, Federal Work-Study, scholarships/grants, tuition waivers (full and partial), and unspecified assistantships available. Financial award application deadline: 2/1; financial award applicants required to submit FAFSA. *Faculty research:* Special education, early childhood education, educational psychology, Catholic school administration, leadership and policy studies, counseling, curriculum and instruction. *Total annual research expenditures:* $36,210. *Unit head:* Dr. Merylann J. Schuttloffel, Chair, 202-319-5805, Fax: 202-319-5815, E-mail: schuttloffel@cua.edu. *Application contact:* Andrew Woodall, Director of Graduate Admissions, 202-319-5057, Fax: 202-319-6533, E-mail: cua-admissions@cua.edu. Web site: http://education.cua.edu/.

Centenary College, Program in Education, Hackettstown, NJ 07840-2100. Offers educational leadership (MA); instructional leadership (MA); special education (MA). *Accreditation:* Teacher Education Accreditation Council. Part-time and evening/weekend programs available. Postbaccalaureate distance learning degree programs offered (minimal on-campus study). *Degree requirements:* For master's, thesis. *Entrance requirements:* For master's, interview, minimum undergraduate GPA of 2.8.

Central Connecticut State University, School of Graduate Studies, School of Education and Professional Studies, Department of Special Education, New Britain, CT 06050-4010. Offers special education (Certificate); special education for special educators (MS); special education for teachers certified in areas other than education (MS). Part-time and evening/weekend programs available. *Faculty:* 6 full-time (2 women), 8 part-time/adjunct (4 women). *Students:* 33 full-time (29 women), 155 part-time (118 women); includes 15 minority (5 Black or African American, non-Hispanic/Latino; 1 American Indian or Alaska Native, non-Hispanic/Latino; 1 Asian, non-Hispanic/Latino; 4 Hispanic/Latino; 4 Two or more races, non-Hispanic/Latino). Average age 29. 62 applicants, 79% accepted, 33 enrolled. In 2011, 46 master's, 6 other advanced degrees awarded. *Degree requirements:* For master's, comprehensive exam, thesis or alternative; for Certificate, qualifying exam. *Entrance requirements:* For master's, minimum undergraduate GPA of 2.7, teacher certification. Additional exam requirements/recommendations for international students: Required—TOEFL (minimum score 550 paper-based; 213 computer-based). *Application deadline:* For fall admission, 6/1 for domestic students, 5/1 for international students; for spring admission, 11/1 for domestic and international students. Applications are processed on a rolling basis. Application fee: $50. Electronic applications accepted. *Expenses: Tuition, area resident:* Full-time $5137; part-time $482 per credit. Tuition, state resident: full-time $7707; part-time $494 per credit. Tuition, nonresident: full-time $14,311; part-time $494 per credit. *Required fees:* $3865. One-time fee: $62 part-time. *Financial support:* In 2011–12, 3 students received support, including 1 research assistantship; career-related internships or fieldwork, Federal Work-Study, scholarships/grants, and unspecified assistantships also available. Support available to part-time students. Financial award application deadline: 4/15; financial award applicants required to submit FAFSA. *Faculty research:* Learning disabilities/language development, consulting teacher practice, occupational/special education, teaching emotionally disturbed students. *Unit head:* Dr. Mitchell Beck, Chair, 860-832-2400, E-mail: beckm@ccsu.edu. *Application contact:* Patricia Gardner, Associate Director of Graduate Studies, 860-832-2350, Fax: 860-832-2352, E-mail: graduateadmissions@ccsu.edu. Web site: http://finalsite.ccsu.edu/page.cfm?p=1995.

Central Michigan University, College of Graduate Studies, College of Education and Human Services, Department of Counseling and Special Education, Program in Special Education, Mount Pleasant, MI 48859. Offers special education (MA), including the master teacher. *Accreditation:* Teacher Education Accreditation Council. Part-time programs available. *Degree requirements:* For master's, thesis or alternative. *Entrance requirements:* For master's, Michigan elementary or secondary provisional, permanent, or life certificate or special education endorsement. Electronic applications accepted. *Faculty research:* Mainstreaming, learning disabled, attention and organization disorders.

Central Washington University, Graduate Studies and Research, College of Education and Professional Studies, Department of Language, Literacy and Special Education, Program in Special Education, Ellensburg, WA 98926. Offers M Ed. Part-time programs available. *Faculty:* 11 full-time (8 women). *Students:* 1 (woman) full-time, 1 part-time (0 women). 4 applicants, 100% accepted, 2 enrolled. In 2011, 1 master's awarded. *Degree requirements:* For master's, thesis or alternative. *Entrance requirements:* For master's, minimum GPA of 3.0. Additional exam requirements/recommendations for international students: Required—TOEFL (minimum score 550 paper-based; 213 computer-based; 79 iBT), IELTS (minimum score 6.5). *Application deadline:* For fall admission, 2/1 priority date for domestic students; for winter admission, 10/1 for domestic students; for spring admission, 1/1 for domestic students. Applications are processed on a rolling basis. Application fee: $50. *Expenses:* Tuition, state resident: full-time $8112; part-time $270 per credit. Tuition, nonresident: full-time $18,069; part-time $602 per credit. *Required fees:* $924. *Financial support:* Research assistantships with full and partial tuition reimbursements, teaching assistantships with full and partial tuition reimbursements, Federal Work-Study, health care benefits, and unspecified assistantships available. Financial award application deadline: 3/1; financial award applicants required to submit FAFSA. *Unit head:* Dr. Dan Fennerty, Graduate

Coordinator, 509-963-2737, E-mail: fennerty@cwu.edu. *Application contact:* Justine Eason, Admissions Program Coordinator, 509-963-3103, Fax: 509-963-1799, E-mail: masters@cwu.edu. Web site: http://www.cwu.edu/~llse/specedu/spedmaster.html.

Chaminade University of Honolulu, Graduate Services, Program in Education, Honolulu, HI 96816-1578. Offers child development (M Ed); educational leadership (M Ed); elementary education with licensure (MAT); instructional leadership (M Ed); Montessori credential (M Ed); Montessori emphasis (M Ed); secondary education with licensure (MAT), including English, math, science, social studies; special education with licensure (MAT). Part-time and evening/weekend programs available. Postbaccalaureate distance learning degree programs offered (minimal on-campus study). *Faculty:* 2 full-time (both women), 32 part-time/adjunct (25 women). *Students:* 53 full-time (38 women), 88 part-time (67 women); includes 77 minority (6 Black or African American, non-Hispanic/Latino; 1 American Indian or Alaska Native, non-Hispanic/Latino; 44 Asian, non-Hispanic/Latino; 5 Hispanic/Latino; 17 Native Hawaiian or other Pacific Islander, non-Hispanic/Latino; 4 Two or more races, non-Hispanic/Latino), 1 international. Average age 35. 40 applicants, 88% accepted, 30 enrolled. In 2011, 105 master's awarded. *Degree requirements:* For master's, thesis or alternative. *Entrance requirements:* For master's, PRAXIS (for MAT only), minimum GPA of 2.75, 3 letters of recommendation. Additional exam requirements/recommendations for international students: Required—TOEFL (minimum score 550 paper-based). *Application deadline:* For fall admission, 9/1 priority date for domestic students, 9/1 for international students; for winter admission, 12/1 priority date for domestic students, 12/1 for international students; for spring admission, 3/1 priority date for domestic students, 3/1 for international students. Applications are processed on a rolling basis. Application fee: $50. Electronic applications accepted. *Expenses: Required fees:* $600 per credit hour. One-time fee: $93 part-time. *Financial support:* In 2011–12, 172 students received support. Career-related internships or fieldwork, Federal Work-Study, institutionally sponsored loans, scholarships/grants, and tuition waivers (partial) available. Support available to part-time students. Financial award application deadline: 3/1; financial award applicants required to submit FAFSA. *Faculty research:* Peace and curriculum education. *Unit head:* Dr. Joseph Peters, Dean, 808-440-4251, Fax: 808-739-4607, E-mail: joseph.peters@chaminade.edu. *Application contact:* 808-739-4663, Fax: 808-739-8329, E-mail: gradserv@chaminade.edu. Web site: http://www.chaminade.edu/education/grad.php.

Chapman University, College of Educational Studies, Orange, CA 92866. Offers communication sciences and disorders (MS); counseling (MA), including school counseling (MA, Credential); education (MA, PhD), including cultural and curricular studies (PhD), disability studies (PhD), school psychology (PhD, Credential); educational psychology (MA); professional clear (Credential); pupil personnel services (Credential), including school counseling (MA, Credential), school psychology (PhD, Credential); school psychology (Ed S); single subject (Credential); special education (MA); special education (level ii) (Credential), including mild/moderate, moderate/severe; special education (preliminary) (Credential), including mild/moderate, moderate/severe; speech language pathology (Credential); teaching (MA), including elementary education, secondary education. *Accreditation:* Teacher Education Accreditation Council. Part-time and evening/weekend programs available. *Faculty:* 27 full-time (18 women), 35 part-time/adjunct (24 women). *Students:* 220 full-time (188 women), 164 part-time (128 women); includes 140 minority (12 Black or African American, non-Hispanic/Latino; 1 American Indian or Alaska Native, non-Hispanic/Latino; 44 Asian, non-Hispanic/Latino; 73 Hispanic/Latino; 4 Native Hawaiian or other Pacific Islander, non-Hispanic/Latino; 6 Two or more races, non-Hispanic/Latino), 1 international. Average age 29. 436 applicants, 38% accepted, 126 enrolled. In 2011, 130 master's, 5 doctorates awarded. *Entrance requirements:* Additional exam requirements/recommendations for international students: Required—TOEFL (minimum score 550 paper-based; 213 computer-based; 80 iBT). *Application deadline:* Applications are processed on a rolling basis. Application fee: $60. Electronic applications accepted. Tuition and fees vary according to degree level and program. *Financial support:* Fellowships and scholarships/grants available. Financial award application deadline: 6/30; financial award applicants required to submit FAFSA. *Unit head:* Dr. Don Cardinal, Dean, 714-997-6781, E-mail: cardinal@chapman.edu. *Application contact:* Admissions Coordinator, 714-997-6714. Web site: http://www.chapman.edu/CES/.

Chatham University, Program in Education, Pittsburgh, PA 15232-2826. Offers early childhood education (MAT); elementary education (MAT); environmental education (K-12) (MAT); secondary art (MAT); secondary biology education (MAT); secondary chemistry education (MAT); secondary English education (MAT); secondary math education (MAT); secondary physics education (MAT); secondary social studies education (MAT); special education (MAT). *Students:* 52 full-time (42 women), 17 part-time (16 women); includes 2 minority (1 Black or African American, non-Hispanic/Latino; 1 Hispanic/Latino). Average age 29. 39 applicants, 82% accepted, 23 enrolled. In 2011, 37 master's awarded. *Degree requirements:* For master's, thesis, teaching experience. *Entrance requirements:* For master's, minimum GPA of 3.0, sample of written work, recommendation letters. Additional exam requirements/recommendations for international students: Required—TOEFL (minimum score 600 paper-based; 250 computer-based; 100 iBT), IELTS (minimum score 7), TWE. *Application deadline:* For fall admission, 4/1 priority date for domestic students, 4/1 for international students; for spring admission, 11/1 priority date for domestic students, 10/1 for international students. Applications are processed on a rolling basis. Application fee: $45. Electronic applications accepted. Application fee is waived when completed online. *Expenses: Tuition:* Full-time $13,896. Tuition and fees vary according to program. *Financial support:* Career-related internships or fieldwork available. Financial award applicants required to submit FAFSA. *Faculty research:* Gifted education, environmental education, technology in education, writing as learning, class size and achievement. *Unit head:* Dr. Elvira Sanatullova-Allison, Director of Education Programs, 412-365-2773, E-mail: esanatullovaallison@chatham.edu. *Application contact:* Dory Perry, Associate Director of Graduate Admission, 412-365-2758, Fax: 412-365-1609, E-mail: gradadmissions@chatham.edu. Web site: http://www.chatham.edu/mat.

Cheyney University of Pennsylvania, School of Education and Professional Studies, Program in Special Education, Cheyney, PA 19319. Offers M Ed, MS. *Accreditation:* NCATE. Part-time and evening/weekend programs available. *Degree requirements:* For master's, thesis or alternative. *Entrance requirements:* For master's, GRE General Test, MAT, minimum GPA of 2.75. Electronic applications accepted.

Chicago State University, School of Graduate and Professional Studies, College of Education, Department of Special Education, Early Childhood Education and Bilingual Education, Program in Special Education, Chicago, IL 60628. Offers M Ed. *Accreditation:* NCATE. *Degree requirements:* For master's, thesis optional. *Entrance requirements:* For master's, minimum GPA of 2.75. *Faculty research:* Assistive technology, teacher efficiency.

City College of the City University of New York, Graduate School, School of Education, Department of Leadership and Special Education, New York, NY 10031-9198. Offers bilingual special education (MS Ed); educational leadership (MS, AC); teacher of students with disabilities in childhood education (MS Ed); teacher of students with disabilities in middle childhood education (MS Ed). *Degree requirements:* For master's, thesis, research paper. *Entrance requirements:* For master's, Liberal Arts and Sciences Test (LAST), Content Specialty Test (CST), interview; minimum GPA of 3.0 in major, 2.5 overall. Additional exam requirements/recommendations for international students: Required—TOEFL. *Faculty research:* Dynamics of organizational change, impact of laws on educational policy, leadership development in schools.

City College of the City University of New York, Graduate School, School of Education, Program in Teaching Students with Disabilities, New York, NY 10031-9198. Offers MA. *Accreditation:* NCATE. *Degree requirements:* For master's, thesis. *Entrance requirements:* For master's, Liberal Arts and Sciences Test (LAST), Content Specialty Test (CST). Additional exam requirements/recommendations for international students: Required—TOEFL.

City University of Seattle, Graduate Division, Albright School of Education, Bellevue, WA 98005. Offers administrator certification (Certificate); curriculum and instruction (M Ed); educational leadership (Ed D); elementary education (MIT); guidance and counseling (M Ed); higher education leadership (Ed D); leadership (M Ed); leadership and school counseling (M Ed); organizational leadership (Ed D); reading and literacy (M Ed); special education (MIT); superintendent certification (Certificate). Part-time and evening/weekend programs available. Postbaccalaureate distance learning degree programs offered (no on-campus study). *Faculty:* 23 full-time (15 women), 123 part-time/adjunct (82 women). *Students:* 353 full-time (263 women), 75 part-time (50 women); includes 40 minority (12 Black or African American, non-Hispanic/Latino; 5 American Indian or Alaska Native, non-Hispanic/Latino; 7 Asian, non-Hispanic/Latino; 8 Hispanic/Latino; 5 Native Hawaiian or other Pacific Islander, non-Hispanic/Latino; 3 Two or more races, non-Hispanic/Latino). Average age 36. 129 applicants, 98% accepted, 126 enrolled. In 2011, 351 master's, 30 Certificates awarded. *Degree requirements:* For master's, comprehensive exam (for some programs), thesis (for some programs); for doctorate, comprehensive exam, thesis/dissertation. *Entrance requirements:* Additional exam requirements/recommendations for international students: Required—TOEFL (minimum score 567 paper-based; 227 computer-based; 87 iBT); Recommended—IELTS. *Application deadline:* For fall admission, 9/1 for international students; for winter admission, 12/1 for international students; for spring admission, 3/1 for international students. Applications are processed on a rolling basis. Application fee: $50. Electronic applications accepted. *Expenses:* Contact institution. *Financial support:* In 2011–12, 40 students received support. Federal Work-Study and scholarships/grants available. Support available to part-time students. Financial award applicants required to submit FAFSA. *Unit head:* Craig Schieber, Dean, 425-637-101 Ext. 5460, Fax: 425-709-5363, E-mail: schieber@cityu.edu. *Application contact:* Alysa Borelli, 888-422-4898, Fax: 425-709-5363, E-mail: info@cityu.edu. Web site: http://www.cityu.edu/programs/soe/index.aspx.

Claremont Graduate University, Graduate Programs, School of Educational Studies, Claremont, CA 91711-6160. Offers Africana education (Certificate); education and policy (MA, PhD); higher education/student affairs (MA, PhD); human development (MA, PhD); public school administration (MA, PhD); quantitative evaluation (MA, PhD); special education (MA, PhD); teacher education (MA); teaching and learning (MA, PhD); urban leadership (PhD); MBA/PhD. PhD program offered jointly with San Diego State University. Part-time programs available. *Faculty:* 18 full-time (10 women), 2 part-time/adjunct (1 woman). *Students:* 307 full-time (220 women), 134 part-time (96 women); includes 228 minority (59 Black or African American, non-Hispanic/Latino; 3 American Indian or Alaska Native, non-Hispanic/Latino; 37 Asian, non-Hispanic/Latino; 110 Hispanic/Latino; 2 Native Hawaiian or other Pacific Islander, non-Hispanic/Latino; 17 Two or more races, non-Hispanic/Latino), 13 international. Average age 38. In 2011, 93 master's, 23 doctorates, 10 other advanced degrees awarded. Terminal master's awarded for partial completion of doctoral program. *Entrance requirements:* For master's and doctorate, GRE General Test. Additional exam requirements/recommendations for international students: Required—TOEFL (minimum score 550 paper-based; 213 computer-based; 80 iBT). *Application deadline:* For fall admission, 2/1 priority date for domestic students. Applications are processed on a rolling basis. Application fee: $60. Electronic applications accepted. *Expenses: Tuition:* Full-time $36,374; part-time $1581 per unit. *Required fees:* $165 per semester. *Financial support:* Fellowships, research assistantships, Federal Work-Study, institutionally sponsored loans, and scholarships/grants available. Support available to part-time students. Financial award application deadline: 2/15; financial award applicants required to submit FAFSA. *Faculty research:* Education administration, K-12 and higher education, multicultural education, education policy, diversity in higher education, faculty issues. *Unit head:* Margaret Grogan, Dean, 909-621-8075, Fax: 909-621-8734, E-mail: margaret.grogan@cgu.edu. *Application contact:* Julia Evans, Director of Central Recruitment, 909-607-3689, Fax: 909-607-7285, E-mail: admiss@cgu.edu. Web site: http://www.cgu.edu/pages/267.asp.

Clarion University of Pennsylvania, Office of Graduate Programs, Master of Education Program, Clarion, PA 16214. Offers curriculum and instruction (M Ed); early childhood (M Ed, Certificate); English (M Ed); instructional technology specialist (K-12) (Certificate); literacy (M Ed); mathematics education (M Ed); reading specialist (M Ed, Certificate); science education (M Ed); special education (M Ed); technology (M Ed); world language (M Ed). *Accreditation:* NCATE. Part-time programs available. *Students:* 14 full-time (11 women), 207 part-time (163 women); includes 3 minority (1 Black or African American, non-Hispanic/Latino; 2 Hispanic/Latino). Average age 31. In 2011, 96 master's awarded. *Degree requirements:* For master's, thesis or alternative. *Entrance requirements:* For master's, minimum QPA of 3.0. *Application deadline:* Applications are processed on a rolling basis. *Expenses:* Tuition, state resident: part-time $429 per credit. Tuition, nonresident: part-time $644 per credit. *Financial support:* Research assistantships with full and partial tuition reimbursements and career-related internships or fieldwork available. Support available to part-time students. Financial award application deadline: 3/1. *Unit head:* Dr. John Groves, Dean, 814-393-2146, Fax: 514-393-2446. *Application contact:* Dr. Brenda Sanders Dede, Assistant Vice President for Academic Affairs, 814-393-2337, Fax: 814-393-2030, E-mail: bdede@clarion.edu. Web site: http://www.clarion.edu/25887/.

Clark Atlanta University, School of Education, Department of Curriculum, Atlanta, GA 30314. Offers special education general curriculum (MA); teaching math and science (MAT). Part-time programs available. *Faculty:* 4 full-time (all women), 4 part-time/adjunct (3 women). *Students:* 10 full-time (5 women), 9 part-time (7 women); includes 18 minority (all Black or African American, non-Hispanic/Latino). Average age 31. 13 applicants, 100% accepted, 9 enrolled. In 2011, 21 master's awarded. *Degree requirements:* For master's, one foreign language, comprehensive exam. *Entrance requirements:* For master's, GRE General Test, minimum undergraduate GPA of 2.6. Additional exam requirements/recommendations for international students: Required—TOEFL (minimum score 500 paper-based; 173 computer-based; 61 iBT). *Application deadline:* For fall admission, 4/1 for domestic and international students; for spring admission, 11/1 for domestic and international students. Applications are processed on a rolling basis. Application fee: $40 ($55 for international students). *Expenses: Tuition:* Full-time $13,572; part-time $754 per credit hour. *Required fees:* $806; $403 per semester. *Financial support:* Career-related internships or fieldwork, Federal Work-Study, scholarships/grants, and unspecified assistantships available. Support available to part-time students. Financial award application deadline: 4/30; financial award applicants required to submit FAFSA. *Unit head:* Dr. Doris Terrell, Chairperson, 404-

880-6336, E-mail: dterrell@cau.edu. *Application contact:* Michelle Clark-Davis, Graduate Program Admissions, 404-880-6605, E-mail: cauadmissions@cau.edu. Web site: http://www.cau.edu/School_of_Education_curriculum_dept.aspx.

Clarke University, Program in Education, Dubuque, IA 52001-3198. Offers early childhood/special education (MAE); educational administration: elementary and secondary (MAE); educational media: elementary and secondary (MAE); multi-categorical resource k-12 (MAE); multidisciplinary studies (MAE); reading: elementary (MAE); technology in education (MAE). Part-time and evening/weekend programs available. Postbaccalaureate distance learning degree programs offered (minimal on-campus study). *Faculty:* 4 full-time (3 women), 2 part-time/adjunct (1 woman). *Students:* 7 full-time (all women), 43 part-time (40 women). Average age 31. In 2011, 11 master's awarded. *Degree requirements:* For master's, comprehensive exam, thesis optional. *Entrance requirements:* For master's, GRE General Test or MAT, minimum GPA of 2.75. *Application deadline:* Applications are processed on a rolling basis. Application fee: $25. Electronic applications accepted. *Expenses: Tuition:* Part-time $690 per credit hour. *Required fees:* $35 per credit hour. Tuition and fees vary according to program and student level. *Financial support:* Career-related internships or fieldwork available. Financial award applicants required to submit FAFSA. *Unit head:* Dr. Larry Bice, Chair, 319-588-6397, Fax: 319-584-8604. *Application contact:* Joan Coates, Information Contact, 563-588-6354, Fax: 563-588-6789, E-mail: graduate@clarke.edu.

Clemson University, Graduate School, College of Health, Education, and Human Development, Eugene T. Moore School of Education, Program in Special Education, Clemson, SC 29634. Offers M Ed. *Accreditation:* NCATE. Part-time and evening/weekend programs available. *Students:* 6 full-time (all women). Average age 24. 16 applicants, 50% accepted, 5 enrolled. In 2011, 9 master's awarded. *Degree requirements:* For master's, comprehensive exam. *Entrance requirements:* For master's, GRE General Test, minimum GPA of 3.0, teaching certificate. Additional exam requirements/recommendations for international students: Required—TOEFL; Recommended—IELTS. *Application deadline:* Applications are processed on a rolling basis. Application fee: $70 ($80 for international students). Electronic applications accepted. *Expenses:* Contact institution. *Financial support:* In 2011–12, 4 students received support, including 4 teaching assistantships with partial tuition reimbursements available (averaging $6,960 per year); fellowships with full and partial tuition reimbursements available, research assistantships with partial tuition reimbursements available, institutionally sponsored loans, health care benefits, and unspecified assistantships also available. Financial award application deadline: 6/1; financial award applicants required to submit FAFSA. *Faculty research:* Instructional interventions in reading for individuals with learning disabilities, legal and policy issues in special education, Response to Intervention (RTI), behavior management, student progress monitoring. *Unit head:* Dr. Michael J. Padilla, Director/Associate Dean, 864-656-4444, Fax: 864-656-0311, E-mail: padilla@clemson.edu. *Application contact:* Dr. David Fleming, Graduate Coordinator, 864-656-1881, Fax: 864-656-0311, E-mail: dflemin@clemson.edu. Web site: http://www.clemson.edu/hehd/departments/education/index.html.

Cleveland State University, College of Graduate Studies, College of Education and Human Services, Department of Teacher Education, Cleveland, OH 44115. Offers art education (M Ed); early childhood education (M Ed); foreign language education (M Ed); mathematics and science education (M Ed); middle childhood education (M Ed); special education (M Ed), including mild/moderate disabilities, moderate/intensive disabilities; teaching English to speakers of other languages (M Ed). Part-time and evening/weekend programs available. *Faculty:* 20 full-time (12 women), 26 part-time/adjunct (20 women). *Students:* 108 full-time (77 women), 388 part-time (306 women); includes 126 minority (100 Black or African American, non-Hispanic/Latino; 8 Asian, non-Hispanic/Latino; 15 Hispanic/Latino; 1 Native Hawaiian or other Pacific Islander, non-Hispanic/Latino; 2 Two or more races, non-Hispanic/Latino), 25 international. Average age 33. 249 applicants, 73% accepted, 118 enrolled. In 2011, 286 master's awarded. *Degree requirements:* For master's, comprehensive exam (for some programs), thesis or alternative. *Entrance requirements:* For master's, GRE General Test or MAT, minimum GPA of 2.75. Additional exam requirements/recommendations for international students: Required—TOEFL (minimum score 525 paper-based; 197 computer-based), IELTS (minimum score 6). *Application deadline:* For fall admission, 7/15 priority date for domestic students. Applications are processed on a rolling basis. Application fee: $30. *Expenses:* Tuition, state resident: full-time $6416; part-time $494 per credit hour. Tuition, nonresident: full-time $12,074; part-time $929 per credit hour. *Financial support:* In 2011–12, 12 research assistantships with full tuition reimbursements (averaging $3,480 per year) were awarded; tuition waivers (partial) and unspecified assistantships also available. *Faculty research:* Early literacy, professional development in reading, reading recovery, dual language, induction programs. *Total annual research expenditures:* $6.2 million. *Unit head:* Dr. Clifford T. Bennett, Chairperson, 216-523-7105, Fax: 216-687-5379, E-mail: c.t.bennett@csuohio.edu. *Application contact:* Deborah L. Brown, Interim Assistant Director, Graduate Admissions, 216-523-7572, E-mail: d.l.brown@csuohio.edu. Web site: http://www.csuohio.edu/coehs/departments/te.

College of Charleston, Graduate School, School of Education, Health, and Human Performance, Department of Foundations, Secondary, and Special Education, Program in Special Education, Charleston, SC 29424-0001. Offers MAT. Part-time and evening/weekend programs available. *Faculty:* 34 full-time (25 women), 9 part-time/adjunct (all women). *Students:* 22 full-time (16 women), 4 part-time (all women); includes 1 minority (Hispanic/Latino). Average age 30. 17 applicants, 59% accepted, 10 enrolled. In 2011, 11 degrees awarded. *Entrance requirements:* For master's, GRE, minimum GPA of 2.5, 2 letters of recommendation. Additional exam requirements/recommendations for international students: Required—TOEFL (minimum score 81 iBT). *Application deadline:* For fall admission, 4/1 for domestic students; for spring admission, 11/1 for domestic students. Application fee: $45. Electronic applications accepted. *Expenses:* Tuition, state resident: full-time $5455; part-time $455 per credit. Tuition, nonresident: full-time $13,917; part-time $1160 per credit. *Financial support:* Fellowships, scholarships/grants, and unspecified assistantships available. *Unit head:* Dr. Angela Cozart, Director, 843-953-6353, Fax: 843-953-5407, E-mail: cozarta@cofc.edu. *Application contact:* Susan Hallatt, Director of Graduate Admissions, 843-953-5614, Fax: 843-953-1434, E-mail: hallatts@cofc.edu. Web site: http://teachered.cofc.edu/grad-progs/edsp.php.

The College of New Jersey, Graduate Studies, School of Education, Department of Special Education, Language and Literacy, Program in Special Education, Ewing, NJ 08628. Offers M Ed, MAT. *Accreditation:* NCATE. Part-time programs available. *Degree requirements:* For master's, comprehensive exam. *Entrance requirements:* For master's, GRE General Test, minimum GPA of 3.0 in field or 2.75 overall. Additional exam requirements/recommendations for international students: Required—TOEFL. Electronic applications accepted.

The College of New Jersey, Graduate Studies, School of Education, Department of Special Education, Language and Literacy, Program in Special Education with Learning Disabilities, Ewing, NJ 08628. Offers Certificate. *Accreditation:* NCATE. Part-time programs available. *Entrance requirements:* Additional exam requirements/recommendations for international students: Required—TOEFL. Electronic applications accepted.

The College of New Rochelle, Graduate School, Division of Education, Program in Special Education, New Rochelle, NY 10805-2308. Offers MS Ed. Part-time programs available. *Degree requirements:* For master's, practicum. *Entrance requirements:* For master's, interview, minimum GPA of 3.0 in field, 2.7 overall.

College of St. Joseph, Graduate Programs, Division of Education, Program in Special Education, Rutland, VT 05701-3899. Offers M Ed. Part-time and evening/weekend programs available. *Faculty:* 2 full-time (both women), 6 part-time/adjunct (3 women). *Students:* 3 full-time (all women), 11 part-time (9 women). Average age 32. 6 applicants, 83% accepted, 5 enrolled. In 2011, 9 master's awarded. *Degree requirements:* For master's, comprehensive exam. *Entrance requirements:* For master's, PRAXIS I (for initial licensure), official college transcripts; 2 letters of reference; minimum GPA of 3.0 (initial licensure) or 2.7 (nonlicensure); interview. Additional exam requirements/recommendations for international students: Required—TOEFL (minimum score 550 paper-based). *Application deadline:* Applications are processed on a rolling basis. Application fee: $35. Electronic applications accepted. *Expenses: Tuition:* Full-time $15,200; part-time $400 per credit. *Required fees:* $45 per semester. *Financial support:* Career-related internships or fieldwork, Federal Work-Study, and unspecified assistantships available. Support available to part-time students. Financial award application deadline: 3/1. *Faculty research:* Co-teaching, Response to Intervention (RTI). *Unit head:* Dr. Maria Bove, Chair, 802-773-5900 Ext. 3243, Fax: 802-776-5258, E-mail: mbove@csj.edu. *Application contact:* Alan Young, Director of Admissions, 802-773-5900 Ext. 3227, Fax: 802-776-5310, E-mail: alanyoung@csj.edu.

The College of Saint Rose, Graduate Studies, School of Education, Department of Literacy and Special Education, Albany, NY 12203-1419. Offers literacy: birth-grade 6 (MS Ed); literacy: grades 5-12 (MS Ed); reading (Certificate), including literacy: birth - grade 6, literacy: grades 5-12; special education (MS Ed), including adolescent education, childhood education, special education advanced study. Part-time and evening/weekend programs available. *Entrance requirements:* For master's, minimum undergraduate GPA of 3.0. Additional exam requirements/recommendations for international students: Required—TOEFL (minimum score 550 paper-based; 213 computer-based). Electronic applications accepted.

College of Staten Island of the City University of New York, Graduate Programs, Department of Education, Program in Special Education, Staten Island, NY 10314-6600. Offers MS Ed. Part-time and evening/weekend programs available. *Faculty:* 4 full-time (2 women), 10 part-time/adjunct (8 women). *Students:* 13 full-time, 211 part-time. Average age 28. 107 applicants, 80% accepted, 71 enrolled. In 2011, 55 master's awarded. *Degree requirements:* For master's, research project, portfolio. *Entrance requirements:* For master's, minimum GPA of 3.0, 2 letters of recommendation, 2 foreign languages. Additional exam requirements/recommendations for international students: Required—TOEFL (minimum score 550 paper-based; 213 computer-based; 79 iBT), IELTS (minimum score 6.5). *Application deadline:* For fall admission, 4/25 for domestic and international students; for spring admission, 11/15 for domestic and international students. Applications are processed on a rolling basis. Application fee: $125. Electronic applications accepted. *Expenses:* Tuition, state resident: full-time $8210; part-time $345 per credit. Tuition, nonresident: part-time $640 per credit. *Required fees:* $128 per semester. *Financial support:* In 2011–12, 3 students received support. Career-related internships or fieldwork, Federal Work-Study, and scholarships/grants available. Support available to part-time students. Financial award applicants required to submit FAFSA. *Unit head:* Dr. Nelly Tournaki, Associate Professor, 718-982-3728, Fax: 718-982-3743, E-mail: nelly.tournaki@csi.cuny.edu. *Application contact:* Sasha Spence, Assistant Director for Graduate Admissions, 718-982-2699, Fax: 718-982-2500, E-mail: spence@mail.csi.cuny.edu. Web site: http://www.library.csi.cuny.edu/~education/programs.html.

The College of William and Mary, School of Education, Program in Curriculum and Instruction, Williamsburg, VA 23187-8795. Offers elementary education (MA Ed); gifted education (MA Ed); math specialist (MA Ed); reading education (MA Ed); secondary education (MA Ed), including English education, mathematics education, modern foreign languages education, science education, social studies education; special education (MA Ed), including collaborating master educator, general curriculum. *Accreditation:* NCATE. Part-time programs available. *Faculty:* 15 full-time (10 women), 39 part-time/adjunct (32 women). *Students:* 80 full-time (69 women), 13 part-time (11 women); includes 11 minority (3 Black or African American, non-Hispanic/Latino; 1 American Indian or Alaska Native, non-Hispanic/Latino; 2 Hispanic/Latino; 5 Two or more races, non-Hispanic/Latino), 1 international. Average age 25. 220 applicants, 56% accepted, 85 enrolled. In 2011, 78 master's awarded. *Degree requirements:* For master's, project. *Entrance requirements:* For master's, GRE or MAT, minimum GPA of 2.5. Additional exam requirements/recommendations for international students: Required—TOEFL. *Application deadline:* For fall admission, 1/15 for domestic and international students; for spring admission, 10/1 for domestic and international students. Application fee: $50. Electronic applications accepted. *Expenses:* Tuition, state resident: full-time $6400; part-time $365 per credit hour. Tuition, nonresident: full-time $19,720; part-time $985 per credit hour. *Required fees:* $4562. *Financial support:* In 2011–12, 53 students received support, including 10 research assistantships with full and partial tuition reimbursements available (averaging $7,000 per year); career-related internships or fieldwork, Federal Work-Study, institutionally sponsored loans, scholarships/grants, and unspecified assistantships also available. Financial award application deadline: 1/15; financial award applicants required to submit FAFSA. *Faculty research:* National Council of Teachers of Mathematics Standards, counseling, self-concept and self-esteem, special education, curriculum development. *Unit head:* Dr. Margie Mason, Area Coordinator, 757-221-2327, E-mail: mmmaso@wm.edu. *Application contact:* Dorothy Smith Osborne, Assistant Dean for Admission, 757-221-2317, Fax: 757-221-2293, E-mail: dsosbo@wm.edu. Web site: http://education.wm.edu.

Colorado Christian University, Program in Curriculum and Instruction, Lakewood, CO 80226. Offers corporate education (MACI); early childhood educator (MACI); elementary educator (MACI); instructional technology (MACI); master educator (MACI); online course developer (MACI); online teaching and learning (MACI); special education generalist (MACI). Part-time and evening/weekend programs available. *Degree requirements:* For master's, thesis optional, practicum. *Entrance requirements:* For master's, interviews, letters of recommendation. Additional exam requirements/recommendations for international students: Required—TOEFL. Electronic applications accepted. *Expenses:* Contact institution.

Colorado State University–Pueblo, College of Education, Engineering and Professional Studies, Education Program, Pueblo, CO 81001-4901. Offers art education (M Ed); foreign language education (M Ed); health and physical education (M Ed); instructional technology (M Ed); linguistically diverse education (M Ed); music education (M Ed); special education (M Ed). *Accreditation:* Teacher Education Accreditation Council. Part-time programs available. *Degree requirements:* For master's, portfolio. *Entrance requirements:* For master's, 3 recommendations, teaching license. Additional exam requirements/recommendations for international students: Required—TOEFL (minimum score 500 paper-based; 173 computer-based). Electronic applications accepted. *Faculty research:* Portfolio assessment, math education, science education.

Special Education

Columbia International University, Columbia Graduate School, Columbia, SC 29230-3122. Offers Bible teaching (MABT); Christian higher education leadership (Ed D); Christian school educational leadership (Ed D); counseling (MACN); curriculum and instruction (M Ed), including Christian school guidance, English as a second language, learning disabilities, school technology; early childhood and elementary education (MAT); educational administration (M Ed); teaching English as a foreign language (Certificate); teaching English as a foreign language and intercultural studies (MATF). Part-time and evening/weekend programs available. *Degree requirements:* For master's, internships, professional project. *Entrance requirements:* For master's, Minnesota Multiphasic Personality Inventory, MAT, minimum GPA of 2.7. Additional exam requirements/recommendations for international students: Required—TOEFL. Electronic applications accepted.

Columbus State University, Graduate Studies, College of Education and Health Professions, Department of Teacher Education, Columbus, GA 31907-5645. Offers accomplished teaching (M Ed); early childhood education (M Ed, MAT, Ed S); health and physical education (M Ed, MAT); middle grades education (M Ed, MAT, Ed S); school library media (M Ed, MAT); secondary education (M Ed, MAT, Ed S), including English/language arts (M Ed, Ed S), general science (M Ed), mathematics (M Ed), social science (M Ed); special education (M Ed, Ed S), including general curriculum (M Ed). *Accreditation:* NCATE. Part-time and evening/weekend programs available. Postbaccalaureate distance learning degree programs offered (minimal on-campus study). *Degree requirements:* For master's, thesis, exit exam; for Ed S, thesis or alternative. *Entrance requirements:* For master's, GRE General Test, minimum GPA of 2.75; for Ed S, GRE General Test. Additional exam requirements/recommendations for international students: Required—TOEFL (minimum score 550 paper-based; 213 computer-based; 79 iBT). Electronic applications accepted.

Concordia University, St. Paul, College of Education, St. Paul, MN 55104-5494. Offers curriculum and instruction (MA Ed), including K-12 reading endorsement; differentiated instruction (MA Ed); early childhood education (MA Ed); educational leadership (MA Ed); educational technology (MA Ed); family life education (MA); K-12 reading endorsement (Certificate); special education (Certificate); sports management (MA). *Accreditation:* NCATE. Evening/weekend programs available. Postbaccalaureate distance learning degree programs offered (minimal on-campus study). *Faculty:* 7 full-time (3 women), 64 part-time/adjunct (42 women). *Students:* 617 full-time (495 women), 9 part-time (6 women); includes 57 minority (30 Black or African American, non-Hispanic/Latino; 2 American Indian or Alaska Native, non-Hispanic/Latino; 17 Asian, non-Hispanic/Latino; 5 Hispanic/Latino; 1 Native Hawaiian or other Pacific Islander, non-Hispanic/Latino; 2 Two or more races, non-Hispanic/Latino). Average age 36. 302 applicants, 83% accepted, 210 enrolled. In 2011, 320 master's, 68 other advanced degrees awarded. *Application deadline:* Applications are processed on a rolling basis. Application fee: $50. Electronic applications accepted. *Expenses: Tuition:* Full-time $8100; part-time $435 per credit. Tuition and fees vary according to program. *Financial support:* Applicants required to submit FAFSA. *Unit head:* Dr. Donald Helmstetter, Dean, 651-641-8227, Fax: 651-641-8807, E-mail: helmstetter@csp.edu. *Application contact:* Kimberly Craig, Director of Graduate and Cohort Admission, 651-603-6223, Fax: 651-603-6320, E-mail: craig@csp.edu.

Concordia University Wisconsin, Graduate Programs, Department of Education, Mequon, WI 53097-2402. Offers art education (MS Ed); curriculum and instruction (MS Ed); early childhood (MS Ed); educational administration (MS Ed); environmental education (MS Ed); family studies (MS Ed); reading (MS Ed); school counseling (MS Ed); special education (MS Ed). Part-time and evening/weekend programs available. Postbaccalaureate distance learning degree programs offered (minimal on-campus study). *Faculty:* 30. *Students:* 386 full-time (279 women), 808 part-time (598 women); includes 84 minority (42 Black or African American, non-Hispanic/Latino; 4 American Indian or Alaska Native, non-Hispanic/Latino; 9 Asian, non-Hispanic/Latino; 13 Hispanic/Latino; 16 Two or more races, non-Hispanic/Latino), 5 international. Average age 37. In 2011, 51 master's awarded. *Degree requirements:* For master's, comprehensive exam, thesis or alternative. *Entrance requirements:* For master's, minimum GPA of 3.0, teaching license. Additional exam requirements/recommendations for international students: Required—TOEFL. Application fee: $35. *Financial support:* Career-related internships or fieldwork and tuition waivers (partial) available. Financial award application deadline: 8/1. *Faculty research:* Motivation, developmental learning, learning styles. *Unit head:* Dr. James Juergensen, Director, 262-243-4214, E-mail: james.juergensen@cuw.edu. *Application contact:* Graduate Admissions, 262-243-4248, Fax: 262-243-4428.

Converse College, School of Education and Graduate Studies, Program in Special Education, Spartanburg, SC 29302-0006. Offers learning disabilities (MAT); mental disabilities (MAT); special education (M Ed). Part-time programs available. *Degree requirements:* For master's, capstone paper. *Entrance requirements:* For master's, NTE or PRAXIS II (M Ed), minimum GPA of 2.75, 2 recommendations. Electronic applications accepted.

Coppin State University, Division of Graduate Studies, Division of Education, Department of Special Education, Baltimore, MD 21216-3698. Offers M Ed. Part-time and evening/weekend programs available. *Degree requirements:* For master's, exit portfolio. *Entrance requirements:* For master's, PRAXIS I, minimum GPA of 3.0, interview, writing sample, resume, references. *Faculty research:* Survey of colleges and universities in Maryland with programs for the learning disabled.

Creighton University, Graduate School, College of Arts and Sciences, Department of Education, Program in Special Populations in Education, Omaha, NE 68178-0001. Offers MS. Part-time and evening/weekend programs available. *Students:* 3 part-time (all women); includes 1 minority (Hispanic/Latino). Average age 35. In 2011, 1 master's awarded. *Entrance requirements:* For master's, GRE, 3 letters of recommendation, resume. Additional exam requirements/recommendations for international students: Required—TOEFL (minimum score 550 paper-based; 213 computer-based; 80 iBT). *Application deadline:* For fall admission, 7/1 priority date for domestic students, 3/1 for international students; for winter admission, 12/1 priority date for domestic students, 7/1 for international students; for spring admission, 4/1 priority date for domestic students, 10/1 for international students. Applications are processed on a rolling basis. Application fee: $50. Electronic applications accepted. *Expenses: Tuition:* Full-time $12,672; part-time $704 per credit hour. *Required fees:* $1410; $136 per semester. Tuition and fees vary according to campus/location and reciprocity agreements. *Financial support:* Scholarships/grants and tuition waivers (partial) available. Support available to part-time students. Financial award application deadline: 5/1; financial award applicants required to submit FAFSA. *Unit head:* Dr. Sharon Ishii-Jordan, Associate Professor of Education, 402-280-2553, E-mail: sharonishii-jordan@creighton.edu. *Application contact:* Taunya Plater, Senior Program Coordinator, 402-280-2870, Fax: 402-280-2423, E-mail: taunyaplater@creighton.edu.

Curry College, Graduate Studies, Program in Education, Milton, MA 02186-9984. Offers elementary education (M Ed); foundations (non-license) (M Ed); reading (M Ed, Certificate); special education (M Ed). Part-time and evening/weekend programs available. *Degree requirements:* For master's, project or thesis. *Entrance requirements:* For master's, interview, recommendations, resume, written statement. Additional exam requirements/recommendations for international students: Required—TOEFL (minimum score 550 paper-based; 213 computer-based; 80 iBT). *Expenses:* Contact institution. *Faculty research:* Classroom trauma, therapeutic writing, inclusionary practices.

Daemen College, Education Department, Amherst, NY 14226-3592. Offers adolescence education (MS); childhood education (MS); childhood special education (MS); childhood special-alternative certification (MS); early childhood special-alternative certification (MS). Part-time programs available. *Degree requirements:* For master's, thesis optional, research thesis in lieu of comprehensive exam; completion of degree within 5 years. *Entrance requirements:* For master's, 2 letters of recommendation (professional and character), proof of initial certificate of license for professional programs, resume. Additional exam requirements/recommendations for international students: Required—TOEFL (minimum score 500 paper-based; 173 computer-based; 63 iBT), IELTS (minimum score 5.5). Electronic applications accepted. *Faculty research:* Transition for students with disabilities, early childhood special education, traumatic brain injury (TBI), reading assessment.

Defiance College, Program in Education, Defiance, OH 43512-1610. Offers adolescent and young adult licensure (MA); mild and moderate intervention specialist (MA). Part-time programs available. *Faculty:* 7 full-time (4 women), 1 part-time/adjunct (0 women). *Students:* 34 part-time (25 women). *Degree requirements:* For master's, thesis (for some programs). *Entrance requirements:* For master's, teaching certificate. *Application deadline:* For fall admission, 8/1 for domestic students. Applications are processed on a rolling basis. Application fee: $25. *Expenses: Tuition:* Full-time $10,800; part-time $450 per credit hour. *Required fees:* $95; $35 per semester. *Unit head:* Dr. Suzanne McFarland, Coordinator, 419-783-2315, Fax: 419-784-0426, E-mail: smcfarland@defiance.edu. *Application contact:* Sally Bissell, Director of Continuing Education, 419-783-2350, Fax: 419-784-0426, E-mail: sbissell@defiance.edu.

Delaware State University, Graduate Programs, College of Education, Health and Public Policy, Program in Special Education, Dover, DE 19901-2277. Offers MA. Part-time and evening/weekend programs available. *Degree requirements:* For master's, comprehensive exam, thesis optional. *Entrance requirements:* For master's, GRE General Test, minimum GPA of 3.0 in field, 2.75 overall. Additional exam requirements/recommendations for international students: Required—TOEFL (minimum score 550 paper-based). Electronic applications accepted. *Faculty research:* Curriculum and instruction, distributive education.

Delta State University, Graduate Programs, College of Education, Division of Teacher Education, Program in Special Education, Cleveland, MS 38733-0001. Offers M Ed. *Accreditation:* NCATE. Part-time and evening/weekend programs available. *Degree requirements:* For master's, thesis optional, practicum. *Expenses:* Tuition, state resident: full-time $4702; part-time $294 per credit hour. Tuition, nonresident: full-time $12,516; part-time $760 per credit hour. *Required fees:* $586.

DePaul University, College of Education, Chicago, IL 60106. Offers bilingual bicultural education (M Ed, MA); counseling (M Ed, MA), including college student development, community counseling, school counseling; curriculum studies (M Ed, MA, Ed D); early childhood education (M Ed, MA); educational leadership (M Ed, MA, Ed D), including administration and supervision (M Ed, MA), physical education (M Ed, MA); middle school mathematics education (MS); reading specialist (M Ed, MA); social and cultural foundations in education (M Ed, MA), including curriculum studies/development (MA); special education (M Ed, MA); teaching and learning (M Ed, MA), including elementary education, secondary education; world languages education (M Ed, MA). Part-time and evening/weekend programs available. *Faculty:* 49 full-time (28 women), 94 part-time/adjunct (60 women). *Students:* 894 full-time (707 women), 473 part-time (361 women); includes 349 minority (159 Black or African American, non-Hispanic/Latino; 3 American Indian or Alaska Native, non-Hispanic/Latino; 45 Asian, non-Hispanic/Latino; 115 Hispanic/Latino; 2 Native Hawaiian or other Pacific Islander, non-Hispanic/Latino; 25 Two or more races, non-Hispanic/Latino), 21 international. Average age 30. 872 applicants, 64% accepted, 325 enrolled. In 2011, 499 master's, 10 doctorates awarded. *Median time to degree:* Of those who began their doctoral program in fall 2003, 32% received their degree in 8 years or less. *Degree requirements:* For master's, thesis/dissertation (for MA); capstone course or paper (for M Ed); for doctorate, thesis/dissertation. *Entrance requirements:* For master's, interview, minimum GPA of 2.75, 2 letters of recommendation, bachelor's degree conferred by accredited college or university; for doctorate, interview, master's degree, writing sample, 3 letters of recommendation. Additional exam requirements/recommendations for international students: Required—TOEFL (minimum score 550 paper-based; 213 computer-based; 80 iBT). *Application deadline:* For fall admission, 8/15 priority date for domestic students; for winter admission, 12/1 priority date for domestic students; for spring admission, 3/1 priority date for domestic students. Applications are processed on a rolling basis. Application fee: $40. Electronic applications accepted. *Financial support:* In 2011–12, 163 students received support, including 15 research assistantships with full tuition reimbursements available (averaging $6,375 per year); career-related internships or fieldwork, Federal Work-Study, scholarships/grants, and unspecified assistantships also available. Support available to part-time students. Financial award application deadline: 12/31; financial award applicants required to submit FAFSA. *Faculty research:* Reflective teaching, children at risk, loss, ethnicity, urban education. *Total annual research expenditures:* $916,310. *Unit head:* Dr. Paul Zionts, Dean, 773-325-7581, Fax: 773-325-7713, E-mail: pzionts@depaul.edu. *Application contact:* Brandon Washington, Enrollment Management Coordinator, 773-325-1152, Fax: 773-325-2270, E-mail: bwashin3@depaul.edu. Web site: http://education.depaul.edu.

DeSales University, Graduate Division, Program in Education, Center Valley, PA 18034-9568. Offers academic standards and reform (M Ed); academic standards for K-6 (M Ed); English as a second language (M Ed); instructional technology for K-12 (M Ed); special education (M Ed); teaching English to speakers of other languages (M Ed). Part-time and evening/weekend programs available. Postbaccalaureate distance learning degree programs offered (no on-campus study). *Degree requirements:* For master's, thesis project. *Entrance requirements:* Additional exam requirements/recommendations for international students: Required—TOEFL. *Application deadline:* Applications are processed on a rolling basis. Electronic applications accepted. Tuition and fees vary according to degree level. *Financial support:* Application deadline: 5/1. *Unit head:* Dr. Judith Rance-Roney, Interim Director, 610-282-1100 Ext. 1323, E-mail: judith.rance-roney@desales.edu. *Application contact:* Caryn Stopper, Director of Graduate Admissions, 610-282-1100 Ext. 1768, Fax: 610-282-0525, E-mail: caryn.stopper@desales.edu.

Dominican College, Division of Teacher Education, Department of Teacher Education, Orangeburg, NY 10962-1210. Offers childhood education (MS Ed); teacher of students with disabilities (MS Ed); teacher of visually impaired (MS Ed). *Accreditation:* Teacher Education Accreditation Council. Part-time and evening/weekend programs available. Postbaccalaureate distance learning degree programs offered (minimal on-campus study). *Degree requirements:* For master's, practicum, research project. *Entrance requirements:* For master's, interview, 3 letters of recommendation, minimum undergraduate GPA of 3.0. Additional exam requirements/recommendations for international students: Required—TOEFL (minimum score 550 paper-based; 213 computer-based).

Dominican University, School of Education, River Forest, IL 60305-1099. Offers curriculum and instruction (MA Ed); early childhood education (MS); education (MAT); educational administration (MA); elementary (online) (MS); English as a second language (online) (MS); reading (online) (MS); special education (MS). Part-time and evening/weekend programs available. Postbaccalaureate distance learning degree programs offered (no on-campus study). *Faculty:* 19 full-time (13 women), 53 part-time/adjunct (41 women). *Students:* 24 full-time (19 women), 434 part-time (357 women); includes 95 minority (27 Black or African American, non-Hispanic/Latino; 1 American Indian or Alaska Native, non-Hispanic/Latino; 12 Asian, non-Hispanic/Latino; 48 Hispanic/Latino; 7 Two or more races, non-Hispanic/Latino), 1 international. Average age 33. 92 applicants, 99% accepted, 91 enrolled. In 2011, 267 master's awarded. *Entrance requirements:* For master's, Illinois certification test of basic skills. Additional exam requirements/recommendations for international students: Required—TOEFL (minimum score 550 paper-based; 213 computer-based; 79 iBT). *Application deadline:* Applications are processed on a rolling basis. Application fee: $25. *Expenses:* Contact institution. *Financial support:* Career-related internships or fieldwork, scholarships/grants, and tuition waivers (partial) available. Support available to part-time students. Financial award application deadline: 8/15; financial award applicants required to submit FAFSA. *Faculty research:* Governance of private education institutions, reading and language arts, inclusion, organizational planning, leadership and vision. *Unit head:* Dr. Colleen Reardon, Dean, 718-524-6643, Fax: 708-524-6665, E-mail: creardon@dom.edu. *Application contact:* Keven Hansen, Coordinator of Recruitment and Admissions, 708-524-6921, Fax: 708-524-6665, E-mail: educate@dom.edu. Web site: http://www.dom.edu/soe.

Dominican University of California, Graduate Programs, School of Education and Counseling Psychology, Special Education Program, San Rafael, CA 94901-2298. Offers MS, Credential. *Faculty:* 2 full-time (both women), 9 part-time/adjunct (all women). *Students:* 36 full-time (28 women), 18 part-time (15 women); includes 13 minority (2 Black or African American, non-Hispanic/Latino; 2 American Indian or Alaska Native, non-Hispanic/Latino; 3 Asian, non-Hispanic/Latino; 6 Hispanic/Latino). Average age 38. 32 applicants, 56% accepted, 16 enrolled. In 2011, 1 master's, 37 other advanced degrees awarded. *Entrance requirements:* For master's, CBEST and/or CSET. Additional exam requirements/recommendations for international students: Required—TOEFL (minimum score 550 paper-based; 213 computer-based; 80 iBT), IELTS (minimum score 7). *Application deadline:* For fall admission, 6/15 priority date for domestic students, 6/15 for international students; for spring admission, 11/15 priority date for domestic students, 11/15 for international students. Applications are processed on a rolling basis. Application fee: $40. Electronic applications accepted. *Expenses: Tuition:* Full-time $15,660. *Required fees:* $300. Tuition and fees vary according to program. *Financial support:* In 2011–12, 26 students received support. Application deadline: 3/2; applicants required to submit FAFSA. *Unit head:* Dr. Rande Webster, Head, 415-257-1305, E-mail: rwebster@dominican.edu. *Application contact:* Moriah Dunning, Associate Director, 415-485-3246, Fax: 415-485-3214, E-mail: moriah.dunning@dominican.edu. Web site: http://www.dominican.edu/.

Dowling College, Graduate Programs in Education, Oakdale, NY 11769-1999. Offers adolescence education with middle childhood extension (MS); advanced certificate in gifted education (AC); childhood and early childhood education (MS); childhood and gifted education (MS); computers in education (AC); early childhood education (MS); educational administration (Ed D); educational technology leadership (MS); educational technology specialist (AC); literacy education (MS); literary education (AC); school building leader (AC); school district business leader (MBA, AC); school district leader (AC); special education (MS); sports management (MS). *Accreditation:* NCATE. Part-time and evening/weekend programs available. Postbaccalaureate distance learning degree programs offered (minimal on-campus study). *Faculty:* 23 full-time (12 women), 70 part-time/adjunct (44 women). *Students:* 336 full-time (245 women), 631 part-time (485 women); includes 83 minority (29 Black or African American, non-Hispanic/Latino; 2 American Indian or Alaska Native, non-Hispanic/Latino; 7 Asian, non-Hispanic/Latino; 45 Hispanic/Latino). Average age 32. 280 applicants, 85% accepted, 167 enrolled. In 2011, 425 master's, 27 doctorates, 40 other advanced degrees awarded. *Degree requirements:* For master's and AC, comprehensive exam; for doctorate, thesis/dissertation. *Entrance requirements:* For master's, minimum GPA of 3.0; for doctorate, GRE, master's degree; for AC, teaching certificate. Additional exam requirements/recommendations for international students: Required—TOEFL (minimum score 550 paper-based). *Application deadline:* For fall admission, 9/1 priority date for domestic students; for winter admission, 1/1 priority date for domestic students; for spring admission, 2/1 priority date for domestic students. Applications are processed on a rolling basis. Application fee: $50. Electronic applications accepted. *Expenses: Tuition:* Full-time $19,162; part-time $933 per credit. *Required fees:* $1330; $700 per year. Tuition and fees vary according to course load. *Financial support:* Career-related internships or fieldwork and Federal Work-Study available. Support available to part-time students. Financial award application deadline: 6/30; financial award applicants required to submit FAFSA. *Faculty research:* Natural readers, Korean styles and learning strategies, mothers of children with disabilities, computers in instruction, cultural background and organizational roadblocks to problem solving. *Unit head:* Carol Pulsonetti, Director of Operations, School of Education, 631-244-3243, E-mail: pulsonec@dowling.edu. *Application contact:* Ronnie S. Macdonald, Assistant Vice President for Enrollment Services/Dean of Admissions, 631-244-3357, Fax: 631-244-1059, E-mail: macdonar@dowling.edu.

Drexel University, Goodwin College of Professional Studies, School of Education, Program in Special Education, Philadelphia, PA 19104-2875. Offers MS.

Drury University, Graduate Programs in Education, Springfield, MO 65802. Offers elementary education (M Ed); gifted education (M Ed); human services (M Ed); instructional mathematics K-8 (M Ed); instructional technology (M Ed); middle school teaching (M Ed); secondary education (M Ed); special education (M Ed); special reading (M Ed). *Accreditation:* NCATE. Part-time and evening/weekend programs available. *Degree requirements:* For master's, thesis. *Entrance requirements:* For master's, GRE or MAT, minimum GPA of 2.75. Additional exam requirements/recommendations for international students: Required—TOEFL. Electronic applications accepted. *Faculty research:* Cultural enrichment, research skills, parental involvement relating to reading skills, reading strategies for mainstreaming children.

Duquesne University, School of Education, Department of Counseling, Psychology, and Special Education, Program in Special Education, Pittsburgh, PA 15282-0001. Offers cognitive, behavior, physical/health disabilities (MS Ed); community mental health/special education support (MS Ed). Part-time and evening/weekend programs available. *Faculty:* 7 full-time (all women), 1 part-time/adjunct (0 women). *Students:* 28 full-time (26 women), 3 part-time (2 women); includes 1 minority (Black or African American, non-Hispanic/Latino). Average age 25. 15 applicants, 67% accepted, 6 enrolled. In 2011, 21 degrees awarded. *Degree requirements:* For master's, thesis optional. *Entrance requirements:* For master's, bachelor's degree. Additional exam requirements/recommendations for international students: Required—TOEFL (minimum score 550 paper-based; 80 computer-based), IELTS (minimum score 7). *Application deadline:* For fall admission, 9/1 for domestic students; for spring admission, 1/1 for domestic students. Applications are processed on a rolling basis. Application fee: $0. Electronic applications accepted. Application fee is waived when completed online. *Expenses: Tuition:* Full-time $16,596; part-time $922 per credit. *Required fees:* $1584; $88 per credit. Tuition and fees vary according to program. *Financial support:* In 2011–12, 1 research assistantship was awarded. Support available to part-time students. *Unit head:* Dr. Lisa Vernon-Dotson, Assistant Professor, 412-396-1103, Fax: 412-396-1340, E-mail: vernonl@duq.edu. *Application contact:* Michael Dolinger, Director of Student and Academic Services, 412-396-6647, Fax: 412-396-5585, E-mail: dolingerm@duq.edu. Web site: http://www.duq.edu/education.

D'Youville College, Department of Education, Buffalo, NY 14201-1084. Offers elementary education (MS Ed, Teaching Certificate); secondary education (MS Ed, Teaching Certificate); special education (MS Ed). Part-time and evening/weekend programs available. *Faculty:* 29 full-time (18 women), 29 part-time/adjunct (17 women). *Students:* 198 full-time (133 women), 52 part-time (41 women); includes 12 minority (7 Black or African American, non-Hispanic/Latino; 1 American Indian or Alaska Native, non-Hispanic/Latino; 1 Asian, non-Hispanic/Latino; 3 Hispanic/Latino), 161 international. Average age 29. 245 applicants, 46% accepted, 57 enrolled. In 2011, 235 master's awarded. *Degree requirements:* For master's, one foreign language, comprehensive exam, project or thesis. *Entrance requirements:* For master's, GRE (if GPA less than 2.75), minimum GPA of 3.0. Additional exam requirements/recommendations for international students: Required—TOEFL (minimum score 500 paper-based; 173 computer-based). *Application deadline:* For fall admission, 5/1 for international students; for spring admission, 9/1 for international students. Applications are processed on a rolling basis. Application fee: $25. Electronic applications accepted. *Expenses: Tuition:* Full-time $18,960; part-time $790 per credit hour. *Required fees:* $310. Tuition and fees vary according to degree level and program. *Financial support:* In 2011–12, 1 research assistantship with partial tuition reimbursement (averaging $3,000 per year) was awarded; career-related internships or fieldwork, Federal Work-Study, institutionally sponsored loans, scholarships/grants, tuition waivers (full and partial), and unspecified assistantships also available. Support available to part-time students. Financial award application deadline: 3/1; financial award applicants required to submit FAFSA. *Faculty research:* Developmental disabilities, multiculturalism, early childhood education. *Unit head:* Dr. Hilary Lochte, Chair, 716-829-8110, Fax: 716-829-7660. *Application contact:* Linda Fisher, Graduate Admissions Director, 716-829-8400, Fax: 716-829-7900, E-mail: graduateadmissions@dyc.edu.

East Carolina University, Graduate School, College of Education, Department of Business and Information Technologies Education, Greenville, NC 27858-4353. Offers business education (MA Ed); elementary education (MAT); English education (MAT); family and consumer science (MAT); health education (MAT); Hispanic studies (MAT); history education (MAT); marketing education (MA Ed); middle grades education (MAT); music education (MAT); physical education (MAT); science education (MAT); special education (MAT), including general curriculum; vocation education (MS). *Accreditation:* NCATE. Part-time and evening/weekend programs available. Postbaccalaureate distance learning degree programs offered (no on-campus study). *Degree requirements:* For master's, comprehensive exam, thesis optional. *Entrance requirements:* For master's, GRE or MAT, minimum GPA of 2.5, bachelor's degree in related field, teaching license (MA Ed). Additional exam requirements/recommendations for international students: Required—TOEFL. *Application deadline:* For fall admission, 6/1 priority date for domestic students. Applications are processed on a rolling basis. Application fee: $50. *Expenses:* Tuition, state resident: full-time $3557; part-time $444.63 per semester hour. Tuition, nonresident: full-time $14,351; part-time $1793.88 per semester hour. *Required fees:* $2016; $252 per semester hour. Part-time tuition and fees vary according to course load, campus/location and program. *Financial support:* Federal Work-Study available. Support available to part-time students. Financial award application deadline: 6/1. *Unit head:* Dr. Ivan G. Wallace, Chair, 252-328-6983, Fax: 252-328-6835, E-mail: wallacei@ecu.edu. *Application contact:* Dean of Graduate School, 252-328-6012, Fax: 252-328-6071, E-mail: gradschool@ecu.edu. Web site: http://www.ecu.edu/cs-educ/bite/index.cfm.

East Carolina University, Graduate School, College of Education, Department of Curriculum and Instruction, Greenville, NC 27858-4353. Offers assistive technology (Certificate); autism (Certificate); deaf/blindness (Certificate); elementary education (MA Ed); English education (MA Ed); history (MA Ed); middle grade education (MA Ed); reading education (MA Ed); special education (MA Ed); teaching (MAT). Part-time programs available. Postbaccalaureate distance learning degree programs offered. *Degree requirements:* For master's, comprehensive exam, thesis optional. *Entrance requirements:* For master's, GRE General Test or MAT, interview, bachelor's degree in related field, minimum GPA of 2.5, teaching license. Additional exam requirements/recommendations for international students: Required—TOEFL. *Application deadline:* For fall admission, 6/1 priority date for domestic students. Applications are processed on a rolling basis. Application fee: $50. *Expenses:* Tuition, state resident: full-time $3557; part-time $444.63 per semester hour. Tuition, nonresident: full-time $14,351; part-time $1793.88 per semester hour. *Required fees:* $2016; $252 per semester hour. Part-time tuition and fees vary according to course load, campus/location and program. *Financial support:* Research assistantships, teaching assistantships, and Federal Work-Study available. Support available to part-time students. Financial award application deadline: 6/1; financial award applicants required to submit FAFSA. *Unit head:* Carolyn C. Ledford, Interim Chair, 252-328-1100, E-mail: ledfordc@ecu.edu. *Application contact:* Dean of Graduate School, 252-328-6012, Fax: 252-328-6071, E-mail: gradschool@ecu.edu. Web site: http://www.ecu.edu/cs-educ/ci/Graduate.cfm.

Eastern Illinois University, Graduate School, College of Education and Professional Studies, Department of Special Education, Charleston, IL 61920-3099. Offers MS Ed. *Accreditation:* NCATE. Part-time programs available. *Degree requirements:* For master's, comprehensive exam. *Entrance requirements:* For master's, GRE General Test or MAT. *Expenses:* Tuition, state resident: part-time $279 per credit hour. Tuition, nonresident: part-time $670 per credit hour. *Required fees:* $179.07 per credit hour. $1253 per semester.

Eastern Kentucky University, The Graduate School, College of Education, Department of Special Education, Richmond, KY 40475-3102. Offers communication disorders (MA Ed). *Accreditation:* NCATE. Part-time programs available. *Degree requirements:* For master's, comprehensive exam. *Entrance requirements:* For master's, GRE General Test, MAT, minimum GPA of 2.5. *Faculty research:* Personnel needs in communication disorders, education needs of people who stutter, attention of special ed teacher.

Eastern Michigan University, Graduate School, College of Education, Department of Special Education, Program in Autism Spectrum Disorders, Ypsilanti, MI 48197. Offers MA. *Students:* 33 part-time (31 women); includes 2 minority (1 Black or African American, non-Hispanic/Latino; 1 Two or more races, non-Hispanic/Latino). Average age 35. 19 applicants, 74% accepted. In 2011, 6 degrees awarded. Application fee: $35. *Expenses:* Tuition, state resident: full-time $10,367; part-time $432 per credit hour. Tuition, nonresident: full-time $20,435; part-time $851 per credit hour. *Required fees:* $39 per credit hour. $46 per semester. One-time fee: $100. Tuition and fees vary according to course level, degree level and reciprocity agreements. *Unit head:* Dr. Sally Burton-Hoyle, Program Coordinator, 734-487-3300, Fax: 734-487-2473, E-mail:

sburtonh@emich.edu. *Application contact:* Graduate Admissions, 734-487-2400, Fax: 734-487-6559, E-mail: graduate.admissions@emich.edu.

Eastern Michigan University, Graduate School, College of Education, Department of Special Education, Program in Cognitive Impairment, Ypsilanti, MI 48197. Offers cognitive impairment (MA); mentally impaired (MA). *Students:* 22 full-time (13 women), 44 part-time (36 women); includes 8 minority (3 Black or African American, non-Hispanic/Latino; 2 Asian, non-Hispanic/Latino; 3 Hispanic/Latino). Average age 34. 16 applicants, 81% accepted, 11 enrolled. In 2011, 6 degrees awarded. *Expenses:* Tuition, state resident: full-time $10,367; part-time $432 per credit hour. Tuition, nonresident: full-time $20,435; part-time $851 per credit hour. *Required fees:* $39 per credit hour. $46 per semester. One-time fee: $100. Tuition and fees vary according to course level, degree level and reciprocity agreements. *Unit head:* Dr. Derrick Fries, Coordinator, 734-487-3300, Fax: 734-487-2473, E-mail: derrick.fries@emich.edu. *Application contact:* Dr. Kathlyn Parker, Advisor, 734-487-3300, Fax: 734-487-2473, E-mail: kathlyn.parker@emich.edu.

Eastern Michigan University, Graduate School, College of Education, Department of Special Education, Program in Emotional Impairment, Ypsilanti, MI 48197. Offers MA. *Students:* 10 full-time (6 women), 19 part-time (12 women); includes 4 minority (3 Asian, non-Hispanic/Latino; 1 Two or more races, non-Hispanic/Latino). Average age 33. 8 applicants, 50% accepted, 2 enrolled. In 2011, 3 degrees awarded. Application fee: $35. *Expenses:* Tuition, state resident: full-time $10,367; part-time $432 per credit hour. Tuition, nonresident: full-time $20,435; part-time $851 per credit hour. *Required fees:* $39 per credit hour. $46 per semester. One-time fee: $100. Tuition and fees vary according to course level, degree level and reciprocity agreements. *Unit head:* Dr. Gill Stiefel, Coordinator, 734-487-3300, Fax: 734-487-2473, E-mail: gstiefel@emich.edu. *Application contact:* Graduate Admissions, 734-487-2400, Fax: 734-487-6559, E-mail: graduate.admissions@emich.edu.

Eastern Michigan University, Graduate School, College of Education, Department of Special Education, Program in Hearing Impairment, Ypsilanti, MI 48197. Offers MA. *Students:* 1 (woman) full-time; minority (Black or African American, non-Hispanic/Latino). Average age 28. 1 applicant, 0% accepted, 0 enrolled. In 2011, 1 master's awarded. Application fee: $35. *Expenses:* Tuition, state resident: full-time $10,367; part-time $432 per credit hour. Tuition, nonresident: full-time $20,435; part-time $851 per credit hour. *Required fees:* $39 per credit hour. $46 per semester. One-time fee: $100. Tuition and fees vary according to course level, degree level and reciprocity agreements. *Unit head:* Linda Polter, Coordinator, 734-487-3300, Fax: 734-487-2473, E-mail: lpolter1@emich.edu. *Application contact:* Graduate Admissions, 734-487-2400, Fax: 734-487-6559, E-mail: graduate.admissions@emich.edu.

Eastern Michigan University, Graduate School, College of Education, Department of Special Education, Program in Learning Disabilities, Ypsilanti, MI 48197. Offers MA. *Students:* 2 full-time (both women), 21 part-time (18 women); includes 2 minority (1 Black or African American, non-Hispanic/Latino; 1 Hispanic/Latino), 1 international. Average age 35. 11 applicants, 82% accepted, 7 enrolled. In 2011, 9 degrees awarded. Application fee: $35. *Expenses:* Tuition, state resident: full-time $10,367; part-time $432 per credit hour. Tuition, nonresident: full-time $20,435; part-time $851 per credit hour. *Required fees:* $39 per credit hour. $46 per semester. One-time fee: $100. Tuition and fees vary according to course level, degree level and reciprocity agreements. *Unit head:* Dr. Loreena Parks, Coordinator, 734-487-3300, Fax: 734-487-2473, E-mail: lparks1@emich.edu. *Application contact:* Karen Schulte, Advisor, 734-487-3300, Fax: 734-487-2473, E-mail: kschulte@emich.edu.

Eastern Michigan University, Graduate School, College of Education, Department of Special Education, Program in Physical/Other Health Impairment, Ypsilanti, MI 48197. Offers MA. *Students:* 4 part-time (all women). Average age 37. 1 applicant, 0% accepted, 0 enrolled. Application fee: $35. *Expenses:* Tuition, state resident: full-time $10,367; part-time $432 per credit hour. Tuition, nonresident: full-time $20,435; part-time $851 per credit hour. *Required fees:* $39 per credit hour. $46 per semester. One-time fee: $100. Tuition and fees vary according to course level, degree level and reciprocity agreements. *Unit head:* Dr. Jacquelyn McGinnis, Coordinator, 734-487-3300, Fax: 734-487-2473, E-mail: jmcginnis@emich.edu. *Application contact:* Graduate Admissions, 734-487-2400, Fax: 734-487-6559, E-mail: graduate.admissions@emich.edu.

Eastern Michigan University, Graduate School, College of Education, Department of Special Education, Program in Visual Impairment, Ypsilanti, MI 48197. Offers MA. Application fee: $35. *Expenses:* Tuition, state resident: full-time $10,367; part-time $432 per credit hour. Tuition, nonresident: full-time $20,435; part-time $851 per credit hour. *Required fees:* $39 per credit hour. $46 per semester. One-time fee: $100. Tuition and fees vary according to course level, degree level and reciprocity agreements. *Unit head:* Dr. Alicia Li, Coordinator, 734-487-3300, Fax: 734-487-2473, E-mail: tli@emich.edu. *Application contact:* Graduate Admissions, 734-487-2400, Fax: 734-487-6559, E-mail: graduate.admissions@emich.edu.

Eastern Michigan University, Graduate School, College of Education, Department of Special Education, Programs in Special Education, Ypsilanti, MI 48197. Offers special education (MA); special education-administration and supervision (SPA); special education-curriculum development (SPA). *Accreditation:* NCATE. Part-time and evening/weekend programs available. Postbaccalaureate distance learning degree programs offered (minimal on-campus study). *Students:* 14 full-time (11 women), 49 part-time (40 women); includes 13 minority (7 Black or African American, non-Hispanic/Latino; 2 Asian, non-Hispanic/Latino; 4 Hispanic/Latino), 1 international. Average age 38. 23 applicants, 48% accepted, 8 enrolled. In 2011, 3 master's, 3 other advanced degrees awarded. *Entrance requirements:* For master's, GRE General Test. Additional exam requirements/recommendations for international students: Required—TOEFL. *Application deadline:* Applications are processed on a rolling basis. Application fee: $35. *Expenses:* Tuition, state resident: full-time $10,367; part-time $432 per credit hour. Tuition, nonresident: full-time $20,435; part-time $851 per credit hour. *Required fees:* $39 per credit hour. $46 per semester. One-time fee: $100. Tuition and fees vary according to course level, degree level and reciprocity agreements. *Financial support:* Fellowships, research assistantships with full tuition reimbursements, teaching assistantships with full tuition reimbursements, career-related internships or fieldwork, Federal Work-Study, institutionally sponsored loans, scholarships/grants, tuition waivers (partial), and unspecified assistantships available. Support available to part-time students. Financial award applicants required to submit FAFSA. *Unit head:* Dr. Philip Smith, Interim Department Head, 734-487-3300, Fax: 734-487-2473, E-mail: psmith16@emich.edu. *Application contact:* Graduate Admissions, 734-487-2400, Fax: 734-487-6559, E-mail: graduate.admissions@emich.edu.

Eastern Nazarene College, Adult and Graduate Studies, Division of Teacher Education, Quincy, MA 02170. Offers administration (M Ed); early childhood education (M Ed, Certificate); elementary education (M Ed, Certificate); English as a second language (Certificate); instructional enrichment and development (Certificate); middle school education (M Ed, Certificate); moderate special needs education (Certificate); principal (Certificate); program development and supervision (Certificate); secondary education (M Ed, Certificate); special education administrator (Certificate); special needs (M Ed); supervisor (Certificate); teacher of reading (M Ed, Certificate). M Ed also available through weekend program for administration, special needs, and teacher of reading only. Part-time and evening/weekend programs available. *Entrance requirements:* Additional exam requirements/recommendations for international students: Required—TOEFL (minimum score 550 paper-based).

Eastern New Mexico University, Graduate School, College of Education and Technology, Department of Educational Studies, Program in Special Education, Portales, NM 88130. Offers early childhood special education (M Sp Ed); general (M Sp Ed). Part-time programs available. *Degree requirements:* For master's, comprehensive exam, thesis optional. *Entrance requirements:* For master's, minimum GPA of 3.0, letter of recommendation, photocopy of teaching license or confirmation of entrance into alternative licensure program, writing assessment, 2 letters of application, special education license or minimum 30 hours of undergraduate course work. Additional exam requirements/recommendations for international students: Required—TOEFL (minimum score 550 paper-based; 213 computer-based; 79 iBT), IELTS (minimum score 6). Electronic applications accepted.

Eastern Washington University, Graduate Studies, College of Arts, Letters and Education, Program in Special Education, Cheney, WA 99004-2431. Offers M Ed. *Students:* 4 full-time (3 women), 2 part-time (both women); includes 1 minority (Hispanic/Latino). Average age 30. 8 applicants, 0% accepted, 0 enrolled. In 2011, 4 master's awarded. *Degree requirements:* For master's, comprehensive exam, thesis or alternative. *Entrance requirements:* For master's, GRE General Test, minimum GPA of 3.0. *Application deadline:* Applications are processed on a rolling basis. Application fee: $50. *Financial support:* Teaching assistantships with partial tuition reimbursements, career-related internships or fieldwork, Federal Work-Study, institutionally sponsored loans, scholarships/grants, tuition waivers (partial), and unspecified assistantships available. Support available to part-time students. Financial award application deadline: 2/1; financial award applicants required to submit FAFSA. *Unit head:* Ronald C. Martella, Director, 509-359-6196, E-mail: rmartella@mail.ewu.edu. *Application contact:* Julie Marr, Advisor/Recruiter for Graduate Studies, 509-359-6656, E-mail: gradprograms@ewu.edu.

East Stroudsburg University of Pennsylvania, Graduate School, College of Education, Department of Special Education, East Stroudsburg, PA 18301-2999. Offers M Ed. Part-time and evening/weekend programs available. *Degree requirements:* For master's, comprehensive exam. *Entrance requirements:* For master's, PRAXIS/teacher certification, letter of recommendation, Pennsylvania Department of Education requirements. Additional exam requirements/recommendations for international students: Required—TOEFL (minimum score 560 paper-based; 220 computer-based; 83 iBT).

East Tennessee State University, School of Graduate Studies, College of Education, Department of Human Development and Learning, Johnson City, TN 37614. Offers counseling (MA), including community agency counseling, elementary and secondary (school counseling), higher education counseling, marriage and family therapy; early childhood education (MA, PhD), including initial licensure in PreK-3 (MA), master teacher (MA), researcher (MA); special education (MA), including advanced practitioner, early childhood special education, special education. *Accreditation:* ACA; NCATE. Part-time programs available. *Faculty:* 31 full-time (22 women), 5 part-time/adjunct (all women). *Students:* 112 full-time (90 women), 41 part-time (36 women); includes 8 minority (5 Black or African American, non-Hispanic/Latino; 3 Two or more races, non-Hispanic/Latino), 4 international. Average age 32. 145 applicants, 34% accepted, 46 enrolled. In 2011, 34 master's awarded. Terminal master's awarded for partial completion of doctoral program. *Degree requirements:* For master's, comprehensive exam, thesis optional, internship, student teaching, culminating experience; for doctorate, comprehensive exam, thesis/dissertation, research apprenticeship. *Entrance requirements:* For master's, GRE General Test, minimum GPA of 3.0; for doctorate, GRE General Test, professional resume, master's degree in early childhood or related field, interview. Additional exam requirements/recommendations for international students: Required—TOEFL (minimum score 550 paper-based; 213 computer-based; 79 iBT). *Application deadline:* For fall admission, 2/1 for domestic and international students. Application fee: $35 ($45 for international students). Electronic applications accepted. *Expenses:* Tuition, state resident: full-time $7312; part-time $350 per credit hour. Tuition, nonresident: full-time $18,490; part-time $621 per credit hour. *Required fees:* $63 per credit hour. Tuition and fees vary according to course load and program. *Financial support:* In 2011–12, 86 students received support, including 6 fellowships with full tuition reimbursements available (averaging $18,000 per year), 28 research assistantships with full tuition reimbursements available (averaging $6,000 per year), 10 teaching assistantships with full tuition reimbursements available (averaging $6,000 per year); career-related internships or fieldwork, institutionally sponsored loans, scholarships/grants, traineeships, and unspecified assistantships also available. Financial award application deadline: 7/1; financial award applicants required to submit FAFSA. *Faculty research:* Drug and alcohol abuse, marriage and family counseling, severe mental retardation, parenting of children with disabilities. *Total annual research expenditures:* $2,600. *Unit head:* Dr. Pamela Evanshen, Chair, 423-439-7694, Fax: 423-439-7790, E-mail: evanshep@etsu.edu. *Application contact:* Fiona Goodyear, Graduate Specialist, 423-439-6148, Fax: 423-439-5624, E-mail: goodyear@etsu.edu.

Edgewood College, Program in Education, Madison, WI 53711-1997. Offers adult learning (MA Ed); bilingual teaching and learning (MA Ed); director of instruction (Certificate); director of special education and pupil services (Certificate); education (MA Ed); educational administration (MA Ed); educational leadership (Ed D); professional studies (MA Ed); program coordinator (Certificate); reading administration (MA Ed); school business administration (Certificate); school principalship K-12 (Certificate); special education (MA Ed); sustainability leadership (MA Ed); teaching and learning (MA Ed); teaching English to speakers of other languages (TESOL) (MA Ed). *Accreditation:* NCATE (one or more programs are accredited). Part-time and evening/weekend programs available. *Students:* 155 full-time (93 women), 152 part-time (116 women); includes 39 minority (13 Black or African American, non-Hispanic/Latino; 5 Asian, non-Hispanic/Latino; 17 Hispanic/Latino; 4 Two or more races, non-Hispanic/Latino), 9 international. Average age 36. In 2011, 39 master's, 32 doctorates awarded. *Degree requirements:* For master's, practicum, research project; for doctorate, comprehensive exam, thesis/dissertation. *Entrance requirements:* For master's, minimum GPA of 2.75, 2 letters of recommendation, personal statement; for doctorate, resume, letter of intent, 2 letters of recommendation, interview, writing sample. Additional exam requirements/recommendations for international students: Required—TOEFL (minimum score 525 paper-based; 197 computer-based; 72 iBT). *Application deadline:* For fall admission, 8/15 for domestic students, 5/1 for international students; for spring admission, 1/8 for domestic students, 11/1 for international students. Applications are processed on a rolling basis. Application fee: $25. Electronic applications accepted. *Expenses: Tuition:* Part-time $747 per credit. Part-time tuition and fees vary according to program. *Unit head:* Dr. Jane Belmore, Dean, 608-663-8336, Fax: 608-663-3291, E-mail: jbelmore@edgewood.edu. *Application contact:* Joann Eastman, Admissions Counselor, 608-663-3250, Fax: 608-663-2214, E-mail: gps@edgewood.edu. Web site: http://education.edgewood.edu/graduate.html.

Edinboro University of Pennsylvania, School of Education, Department of Early Childhood and Special Education, Edinboro, PA 16444. Offers behavior management

(Certificate); character education (Certificate); online special education (M Ed); special education (M Ed). Part-time and evening/weekend programs available. *Faculty:* 5 full-time (all women). *Students:* 22 full-time (19 women), 154 part-time (129 women); includes 4 minority (3 Black or African American, non-Hispanic/Latino; 1 Two or more races, non-Hispanic/Latino). Average age 31. In 2011, 26 master's, 5 Certificates awarded. *Degree requirements:* For master's, thesis or alternative, competency exam; for Certificate, thesis or alternative. *Entrance requirements:* For master's and Certificate, GRE or MAT, minimum QPA of 2.5. *Application deadline:* Applications are processed on a rolling basis. Application fee: $30. Electronic applications accepted. *Financial support:* In 2011–12, 4 research assistantships with full and partial tuition reimbursements (averaging $4,050 per year) were awarded; career-related internships or fieldwork, Federal Work-Study, scholarships/grants, and unspecified assistantships also available. Support available to part-time students. Financial award application deadline: 2/15; financial award applicants required to submit FAFSA. *Unit head:* Dr. Maureen Walcavich, Program Head, Early Childhood, 814-732-2303, E-mail: mwalcavich@edinboro.edu. *Application contact:* Dr. Mary Jo Melvin, Program Head, Special Education, 814-732-2154, E-mail: mmelvin@edinboro.edu.

Edinboro University of Pennsylvania, School of Education, Department of Professional Studies, Edinboro, PA 16444. Offers counseling (MA), including community counseling, elementary guidance, rehabilitation counseling, secondary guidance, student personnel services; educational leadership (M Ed), including elementary school administration, secondary school administration; educational psychology (M Ed); educational specialist school psychology (MS); elementary principal (Certificate); elementary school guidance counselor (Certificate); K-12 school administration (Certificate); letter of eligibility (Certificate); reading (M Ed); reading specialist (Certificate); school psychology (Certificate); school supervision (Certificate), including music, special education. Part-time and evening/weekend programs available. *Faculty:* 13 full-time (8 women). *Students:* 171 full-time (134 women), 563 part-time (441 women); includes 26 minority (20 Black or African American, non-Hispanic/Latino; 1 American Indian or Alaska Native, non-Hispanic/Latino; 1 Asian, non-Hispanic/Latino; 4 Hispanic/Latino). Average age 31. In 2011, 297 master's, 49 other advanced degrees awarded. *Degree requirements:* For master's, thesis or alternative, competency exam; for Certificate, thesis or alternative. *Entrance requirements:* For master's and Certificate, GRE or MAT, minimum QPA of 2.5. *Application deadline:* Applications are processed on a rolling basis. Application fee: $30. Electronic applications accepted. *Financial support:* In 2011–12, 60 research assistantships with full and partial tuition reimbursements (averaging $4,050 per year) were awarded; career-related internships or fieldwork, Federal Work-Study, scholarships/grants, and unspecified assistantships also available. Support available to part-time students. Financial award application deadline: 2/15; financial award applicants required to submit FAFSA. *Unit head:* Dr. Susan Norton, 814-732-2260, E-mail: scnorton@edinboro.edu. *Application contact:* Dr. Andrew Pushchack, Program Head, Educational Leadership, 814-732-1548, E-mail: apushchack@edinboro.edu.

Elmhurst College, Graduate Programs, Program in Early Childhood Special Education, Elmhurst, IL 60126-3296. Offers M Ed. Part-time and evening/weekend programs available. *Faculty:* 2 full-time (both women), 3 part-time/adjunct (all women). *Students:* 8 full-time (all women), 18 part-time (all women); includes 2 minority (both Two or more races, non-Hispanic/Latino). Average age 30. 26 applicants, 65% accepted, 12 enrolled. In 2011, 10 master's awarded. *Entrance requirements:* For master's, 3 recommendations, resume, statement of purpose. Additional exam requirements/recommendations for international students: Required—TOEFL (minimum score 550 paper-based; 213 computer-based). *Application deadline:* Applications are processed on a rolling basis. Application fee: $0. Electronic applications accepted. *Expenses:* Contact institution. *Financial support:* In 2011–12, 11 students received support. Federal Work-Study and scholarships/grants available. Support available to part-time students. Financial award application deadline: 6/1; financial award applicants required to submit FAFSA. *Unit head:* Elizabeth D. Kuebler, Director of Adult and Graduate Admission, 630-617-3300, Fax: 630-617-5501, E-mail: oaga@elmhurst.edu. *Application contact:* Elizabeth D. Kuebler, Director of Adult and Graduate Admission, 630-617-3300, Fax: 630-617-5501, E-mail: oaga@elmhurst.edu.

Elms College, Division of Education, Chicopee, MA 01013-2839. Offers early childhood education (MAT); education (M Ed, CAGS); elementary education (MAT); English as a second language (MAT); reading (MAT); secondary education (MAT), including biology education, English education, Spanish education; special education (MAT). Part-time and evening/weekend programs available. *Degree requirements:* For master's, thesis (for some programs). *Entrance requirements:* For master's, Massachusetts Educators Certification Test, minimum GPA of 3.0; for CAGS, master's degree in education. Additional exam requirements/recommendations for international students: Required—TOEFL.

Elon University, Program in Education, Elon, NC 27244-2010. Offers elementary education (M Ed); gifted education (M Ed); special education (M Ed). *Accreditation:* NCATE. Part-time programs available. *Faculty:* 19 full-time (15 women). *Students:* 47 part-time (41 women); includes 8 minority (7 Black or African American, non-Hispanic/Latino; 1 Asian, non-Hispanic/Latino). Average age 33. 29 applicants, 86% accepted, 22 enrolled. In 2011, 39 master's awarded. *Entrance requirements:* For master's, GRE, MAT. Additional exam requirements/recommendations for international students: Required—TOEFL (minimum score 550 paper-based; 213 computer-based; 79 iBT). *Application deadline:* For winter admission, 6/1 priority date for domestic students. Applications are processed on a rolling basis. Application fee: $50. Electronic applications accepted. *Expenses:* Contact institution. *Financial support:* In 2011–12, 5 students received support. Federal Work-Study and scholarships/grants available. Support available to part-time students. Financial award application deadline: 6/1; financial award applicants required to submit FAFSA. *Faculty research:* Teaching reading to low-achieving second and third graders, pre- and post-student teaching attitudes , children's writing, whole language methodology, critical creative thinking. *Unit head:* Dr. Angela Owusu-Ansah, Director and Associate Dean of Education, 336-278-5885, Fax: 336-278-5919, E-mail: aansah@elon.edu. *Application contact:* Art Fadde, Director of Graduate Admissions, 800-334-8448 Ext. 3, Fax: 336-278-7699, E-mail: afadde@elon.edu. Web site: http://www.elon.edu/med/.

Emporia State University, Graduate School, Teachers College, Department of Elementary Education, Early Childhood, and Special Education, Program in Early Childhood Education, Emporia, KS 66801-5087. Offers early childhood curriculum (MS); early childhood special education (MS). *Accreditation:* NCATE. Part-time programs available. Postbaccalaureate distance learning degree programs offered. *Students:* 3 full-time (all women), 61 part-time (59 women); includes 9 minority (2 Asian, non-Hispanic/Latino; 6 Hispanic/Latino; 1 Native Hawaiian or other Pacific Islander, non-Hispanic/Latino). 17 applicants, 100% accepted, 15 enrolled. In 2011, 13 master's awarded. *Degree requirements:* For master's, comprehensive exam or thesis, practicum. *Entrance requirements:* For master's, GRE General Test or MAT, graduate essay exam, appropriate bachelor's degree, letters of recommendation. Additional exam requirements/recommendations for international students: Required—TOEFL (minimum score 520 paper-based; 133 computer-based; 68 iBT). *Application deadline:* For fall admission, 8/15 priority date for domestic students. Applications are processed on a rolling basis. Application fee: $30 ($75 for international students). Electronic applications accepted. *Expenses:* Tuition, state resident: full-time $2342; part-time $195 per credit hour. Tuition, nonresident: full-time $7254; part-time $605 per credit hour. *Required fees:* $66 per credit hour. Tuition and fees vary according to campus/location. *Financial support:* Federal Work-Study, institutionally sponsored loans, health care benefits, and unspecified assistantships available. Financial award application deadline: 3/15; financial award applicants required to submit FAFSA. *Unit head:* Dr. Jean Morrow, Chair, 620-341-5766, E-mail: jmorrow@emporia.edu. *Application contact:* Mary Sewell, Admissions Coordinator, 800-950-GRAD, Fax: 620-341-5909, E-mail: msewell@emporia.edu.

Emporia State University, Graduate School, Teachers College, Department of Elementary Education, Early Childhood, and Special Education, Program in Special Education, Emporia, KS 66801-5087. Offers behavior disorders (MS); gifted, talented, and creative (MS); interrelated special education (MS); learning disabilities (MS); mental retardation (MS). *Accreditation:* NCATE. Part-time programs available. *Students:* 7 full-time (6 women), 183 part-time (130 women); includes 12 minority (4 Black or African American, non-Hispanic/Latino; 1 American Indian or Alaska Native, non-Hispanic/Latino; 1 Hispanic/Latino; 2 Native Hawaiian or other Pacific Islander, non-Hispanic/Latino; 4 Two or more races, non-Hispanic/Latino), 1 international. 44 applicants, 84% accepted, 31 enrolled. In 2011, 55 master's awarded. *Degree requirements:* For master's, comprehensive exam or thesis, practicum. *Entrance requirements:* For master's, GRE General Test or MAT, graduate essay exam, appropriate bachelor's degree, teacher certification, letters of recommendation. Additional exam requirements/recommendations for international students: Required—TOEFL (minimum score 520 paper-based; 133 computer-based; 68 iBT). *Application deadline:* For fall admission, 8/15 priority date for domestic students. Applications are processed on a rolling basis. Application fee: $30 ($75 for international students). Electronic applications accepted. *Expenses:* Tuition, state resident: full-time $2342; part-time $195 per credit hour. Tuition, nonresident: full-time $7254; part-time $605 per credit hour. *Required fees:* $66 per credit hour. Tuition and fees vary according to campus/location. *Financial support:* Federal Work-Study, institutionally sponsored loans, health care benefits, and unspecified assistantships available. Financial award application deadline: 3/15; financial award applicants required to submit FAFSA. *Unit head:* Dr. Jean Morrow, Chair, 620-341-5317, E-mail: jmorrow@emporia.edu. *Application contact:* Mary Sewell, Admissions Coordinator, 800-950-GRAD, Fax: 620-341-5909, E-mail: msewell@emporia.edu.

Endicott College, Van Loan School of Graduate and Professional Studies, Program in Autism and Applied Behavior Analysis, Beverly, MA 01915-2096. Offers M Ed. Part-time and evening/weekend programs available. Postbaccalaureate distance learning degree programs offered. *Faculty:* 2 full-time (1 woman). *Students:* 1 full-time, 37 part-time (31 women). 10 applicants, 50% accepted, 5 enrolled. *Degree requirements:* For master's, thesis. *Entrance requirements:* For master's, MAT or GRE. Additional exam requirements/recommendations for international students: Required—TOEFL. *Application deadline:* Applications are processed on a rolling basis. Electronic applications accepted. Tuition and fees vary according to degree level and program. *Financial support:* Applicants required to submit FAFSA. *Unit head:* Dr. Mary Jane Weiss, Director, 978-232-2199, E-mail: mweiss@endicott.edu. Web site: http://www.endicott.edu/GradProf/InstBehavStudiesAutismAppBehavAnalysis.aspx.

Endicott College, Van Loan School of Graduate and Professional Studies, Program in Special Education, Beverly, MA 01915-2096. Offers special needs (M Ed). Part-time and evening/weekend programs available. *Faculty:* 2 full-time (0 women), 30 part-time/adjunct (20 women). *Students:* 39 full-time (33 women), 113 part-time (92 women); includes 4 minority (1 Black or African American, non-Hispanic/Latino; 1 Asian, non-Hispanic/Latino; 2 Hispanic/Latino), 1 international. Average age 32. 80 applicants, 68% accepted, 46 enrolled. In 2011, 28 master's awarded. *Degree requirements:* For master's, comprehensive exam, practicum. *Entrance requirements:* For master's, MAT or GRE, Massachusetts teaching certificate, letters of recommendation. Additional exam requirements/recommendations for international students: Required—TOEFL. *Application deadline:* Applications are processed on a rolling basis. Application fee: $50. Electronic applications accepted. Tuition and fees vary according to degree level and program. *Financial support:* Career-related internships or fieldwork, Federal Work-Study, and institutionally sponsored loans available. Financial award applicants required to submit FAFSA. *Faculty research:* Literacy, parent education, inclusion, school reform, technology in education. *Unit head:* Dr. John D. MacLean, Jr., Director of Licensure Programs, 978-232-2408, E-mail: jmaclean@endicott.edu. *Application contact:* Vice President and Dean of the School of Graduate and Professional Studies.

Fairfield University, Graduate School of Education and Allied Professions, Fairfield, CT 06824-5195. Offers applied psychology (MA); bilingual education (CAS); clinical mental health counseling (MA, CAS); educational technology (MA); elementary education (MA); family studies (MA); marriage and family therapy (MA); school counseling (MA, CAS); school psychology (MA, CAS); special education (MA); teaching (Certificate); teaching and foundations (MA, CAS); TESOL foreign language and bilingual/multicultural education (MA, CAS). *Accreditation:* NCATE. Part-time and evening/weekend programs available. *Faculty:* 24 full-time (19 women). *Students:* 147 full-time (120 women), 391 part-time (321 women); includes 60 minority (13 Black or African American, non-Hispanic/Latino; 8 Asian, non-Hispanic/Latino; 35 Hispanic/Latino; 4 Two or more races, non-Hispanic/Latino), 1 international. Average age 34. 319 applicants, 48% accepted, 80 enrolled. In 2011, 185 master's, 20 other advanced degrees awarded. *Degree requirements:* For master's, comprehensive exam. *Entrance requirements:* For master's, PRAXIS I (for certification programs), minimum QPA of 3.0, 2 recommendations, resume. Additional exam requirements/recommendations for international students: Required—TOEFL (minimum score 550 paper-based; 213 computer-based; 84 iBT) or IELTS (minimum score 7.5). *Application deadline:* For fall admission, 2/15 for international students; for spring admission, 10/1 for international students. Application fee: $60. Electronic applications accepted. *Expenses: Tuition:* Part-time $600 per credit hour. *Required fees:* $25 per term. *Financial support:* In 2011–12, 45 students received support. Career-related internships or fieldwork and unspecified assistantships available. Financial award applicants required to submit FAFSA. *Faculty research:* Literacy, adolescent psychology, special education, early childhood education, teaching development. *Unit head:* Dr. Susan D. Franzosa, Dean, 203-254-4000 Ext. 4250, Fax: 203-254-4241, E-mail: sfranzosa@fairfield.edu. *Application contact:* Marianne Gumpper, Director of Graduate and Continuing Studies Admission, 203-254-4184, Fax: 203-254-4073, E-mail: gradadmis@fairfield.edu. Web site: http://www.fairfield.edu/gseap/gseap_grad_1.html.

Fairleigh Dickinson University, Metropolitan Campus, University College: Arts, Sciences, and Professional Studies, Peter Sammartino School of Education, Program in Learning Disabilities, Teaneck, NJ 07666-1914. Offers MA. *Accreditation:* Teacher Education Accreditation Council.

Fairmont State University, Programs in Education, Fairmont, WV 26554. Offers digital media, new literacies and learning (M Ed); education (MAT); exercise science, fitness and wellness (M Ed); leadership studies (M Ed); online learning (M Ed); professional studies (M Ed); reading (M Ed); special education (M Ed). *Accreditation:* NCATE. Part-time and evening/weekend programs available. Postbaccalaureate distance learning degree programs offered. *Faculty:* 16 part-time/adjunct (10 women). *Students:* 103 full-time (72 women), 142 part-time (103 women); includes 11 minority (2 Black or African American, non-Hispanic/Latino; 1 American Indian or Alaska Native, non-Hispanic/Latino; 6 Hispanic/Latino; 2 Two or more races, non-Hispanic/Latino), 2 international. Average age 33. 71 applicants, 85% accepted. In 2011, 58 master's awarded. *Entrance requirements:* For master's, GRE. *Application deadline:* For fall admission, 5/1 for domestic and international students. Applications are processed on a rolling basis. Application fee: $40. *Expenses:* Tuition, state resident: full-time $5900. Tuition, nonresident: full-time $12,596. *Unit head:* Dr. Van O. Dempsey, III, Dean, School of Education, 304-367-4241, Fax: 304-367-4599, E-mail: vdempsey@fairmontstate.edu. Web site: http://www.fairmontstate.edu/graduatestudies/default.asp.

Ferris State University, College of Education and Human Services, School of Education, Big Rapids, MI 49307. Offers administration (MSCTE); curriculum and instruction (M Ed), including administration, elementary education, experiential education, philanthropic education, reading, secondary education, special education, subject matter option; education technology (MSCTE); instructor (MSCTE); post-secondary administration (MSCTE); training and development (MSCTE). Part-time and evening/weekend programs available. Postbaccalaureate distance learning degree programs offered (minimal on-campus study). *Faculty:* 9 full-time (7 women), 9 part-time/adjunct (6 women). *Students:* 8 full-time (7 women), 132 part-time (75 women); includes 13 minority (11 Black or African American, non-Hispanic/Latino; 1 American Indian or Alaska Native, non-Hispanic/Latino; 1 Hispanic/Latino), 5 international. Average age 36. 20 applicants, 100% accepted, 8 enrolled. In 2011, 51 master's awarded. *Degree requirements:* For master's, thesis, research paper. *Entrance requirements:* For master's, 2 years of work experience for vocational setting, minimum GPA of 2.75. Additional exam requirements/recommendations for international students: Recommended—TOEFL (minimum score 500 paper-based; 173 computer-based; 61 iBT). *Application deadline:* For fall admission, 7/1 priority date for domestic students, 7/1 for international students; for spring admission, 11/1 priority date for domestic students, 11/1 for international students. Applications are processed on a rolling basis. Application fee: $30. Electronic applications accepted. Application fee is waived when completed online. *Financial support:* Career-related internships or fieldwork and scholarships/grants available. Support available to part-time students. Financial award applicants required to submit FAFSA. *Faculty research:* Suicide prevention, reading, women in education, special needs, administration. *Unit head:* Dr. James Powell, Director, 231-591-5362, Fax: 231-591-2043, E-mail: powelj20@ferris.edu. *Application contact:* Kimisue Worrall, Secretary, 231-591-5361, Fax: 231-591-2043. Web site: http://www.ferris.edu/education/education/.

Fitchburg State University, Division of Graduate and Continuing Education, Program in Special Education, Fitchburg, MA 01420-2697. Offers guided studies (M Ed); reading specialist (M Ed); teaching students with moderate disabilities (M Ed); teaching students with severe disabilities (M Ed). *Accreditation:* NCATE. Part-time and evening/weekend programs available. *Students:* 9 full-time (all women), 138 part-time (121 women). Average age 33. 23 applicants, 100% accepted, 19 enrolled. In 2011, 79 master's awarded. *Degree requirements:* For master's, internship. *Entrance requirements:* Additional exam requirements/recommendations for international students: Required—TOEFL (minimum score 550 paper-based; 213 computer-based; 79 iBT). *Application deadline:* For fall admission, 7/15 for international students; for spring admission, 12/1 for international students. Applications are processed on a rolling basis. Application fee: $25 ($50 for international students). Electronic applications accepted. *Expenses:* Tuition, state resident: full-time $2700; part-time $150 per credit. Tuition, nonresident: full-time $2700; part-time $150 per credit. *Required fees:* $2286; $127 per credit. *Financial support:* In 2011–12, research assistantships with partial tuition reimbursements (averaging $5,500 per year) were awarded; Federal Work-Study, scholarships/grants, and unspecified assistantships also available. Support available to part-time students. Financial award application deadline: 3/1; financial award applicants required to submit FAFSA. *Unit head:* Dr. Nancy Kelley, Chair, 978-665-3447, Fax: 978-665-3658, E-mail: gce@fitchburgstate.edu. *Application contact:* Kay Reynolds, Director of Admissions, 978-665-3144, Fax: 978-665-4540, E-mail: admissions@fitchburgstate.edu. Web site: http://www.fitchburgstate.edu/.

Florida Atlantic University, College of Education, Department of Exceptional Student Education, Boca Raton, FL 33431-0991. Offers M Ed, Ed D. *Accreditation:* NCATE. Part-time and evening/weekend programs available. *Faculty:* 13 full-time (7 women), 12 part-time/adjunct (9 women). *Students:* 5 full-time (all women), 33 part-time (30 women); includes 9 minority (2 Black or African American, non-Hispanic/Latino; 6 Hispanic/Latino; 1 Two or more races, non-Hispanic/Latino), 1 international. Average age 33. 30 applicants, 53% accepted, 5 enrolled. In 2011, 3 master's, 1 doctorate awarded. *Degree requirements:* For master's, thesis optional, internship; for doctorate, comprehensive exam, thesis/dissertation, internship. *Entrance requirements:* For master's, GRE General Test, minimum GPA of 3.0 during previous 2 years; for doctorate, GRE General Test, 3 years teaching experience, interview. *Application deadline:* For fall admission, 7/1 for domestic students, 2/15 for international students; for spring admission, 11/1 for domestic students, 7/15 for international students. Applications are processed on a rolling basis. Application fee: $30. Electronic applications accepted. *Expenses: Tuition, area resident:* Part-time $343.02 per credit hour. Tuition, state resident: full-time $8232. Tuition, nonresident: full-time $23,931; part-time $997.14 per credit hour. *Financial support:* Fellowships with tuition reimbursements, research assistantships with tuition reimbursements, teaching assistantships with partial tuition reimbursements, career-related internships or fieldwork, Federal Work-Study, scholarships/grants, tuition waivers (partial), and unspecified assistantships available. Support available to part-time students. Financial award applicants required to submit FAFSA. *Faculty research:* Instructional design, assessment, educational reform, behavioral research, social integration. *Unit head:* Dr. Michael P. Brady, Chairperson, 561-297-3280, Fax: 561-297-2507, E-mail: mbrady@fau.edu. *Application contact:* Dr. Eliah Watlington, Associate Dean, 561-296-8520, Fax: 261-297-2991, E-mail: ewatling@fau.edu. Web site: http://www.coe.fau.edu/academicdepartments/ese/.

Florida Gulf Coast University, College of Education, Program in Special Education, Fort Myers, FL 33965-6565. Offers behavior disorders (MA); mental retardation (MA); specific learning disabilities (MA); varying exceptionalities (MA). Part-time and evening/weekend programs available. *Faculty:* 34 full-time (26 women), 57 part-time/adjunct (40 women). *Students:* 10 full-time (9 women), 2 part-time (both women); includes 1 minority (Black or African American, non-Hispanic/Latino). Average age 35. 7 applicants, 100% accepted, 4 enrolled. In 2011, 13 master's awarded. *Degree requirements:* For master's, thesis or alternative. *Entrance requirements:* For master's, GRE General Test, MAT, minimum GPA of 3.0. Additional exam requirements/recommendations for international students: Required—TOEFL (minimum score 550 paper-based; 213 computer-based). *Application deadline:* For fall admission, 7/1 priority date for domestic students; for spring admission, 10/15 for domestic students. Applications are processed on a rolling basis. Application fee: $30. Electronic applications accepted. *Expenses:* Tuition, state resident: full-time $8289. Tuition, nonresident: full-time $28,895. *Required fees:* $1831. One-time fee: $30 full-time. *Faculty research:* Inclusion, interacting with families, alternative certification. *Unit head:* Dr. Robert Triscari, Department Chair, 239-590-7202, Fax: 239-590-7801, E-mail: rtriscari@fgcu.edu. *Application contact:* Gil Medina, Executive Secretary, 239-590-7776, Fax: 239-590-7801, E-mail: gmedina@fgcu.edu.

Florida International University, College of Education, Department of Curriculum and Instruction, Miami, FL 33199. Offers art education (MAT, MS, Ed D); curriculum and instruction (Ed S); curriculum development (MS); curriculum studies (PhD); early childhood education (MS, Ed D); elementary education (MS, Ed D); English education (MAT, MS, Ed D); foreign language education - teaching English to speakers of other languages (TESOL) (MS, Certificate), including foreign language education (Certificate), teaching English (MS); French education - initial teacher preparation (MAT); international and intercultural development education (Ed D); international and intercultural developmental education (MS); language, literacy and culture (PhD); learning technologies (MS, Ed D, PhD); mathematics education (MAT, MS, Ed D, PhD); modern language education/bilingual education (MS, Ed D); physical education (MS); reading education (MS, Ed D); science education (MAT, MS, Ed D, PhD); social studies education (MAT, MS, Ed D); Spanish education - initial teacher preparation (MAT); special education (MS). Part-time and evening/weekend programs available. *Degree requirements:* For doctorate, comprehensive exam, thesis/dissertation. *Entrance requirements:* For master's, GRE General Test, Florida General Knowledge Test or Florida College Level Academic Skills Test; for doctorate and other advanced degree, GRE General Test. Additional exam requirements/recommendations for international students: Required—TOEFL (minimum score 550 paper-based; 213 computer-based; 80 iBT), IELTS (minimum score 6.3). Electronic applications accepted.

Florida Memorial University, School of Education, Miami-Dade, FL 33054. Offers elementary education (MS); exceptional student education (MS); reading (MS). *Degree requirements:* For master's, comprehensive exam or thesis, field and clinical experiences, exit exam. *Entrance requirements:* For master's, GRE, CLAST, PRAXIS I, baccalaureate or graduate degree with minimum GPA of 3.0 in last 60 hours, 3 recommendations. Additional exam requirements/recommendations for international students: Recommended—TOEFL.

Florida State University, The Graduate School, College of Education, School of Teacher Education, Program in Special Education, Tallahassee, FL 32306. Offers emotional disturbance/learning disabilities (MS); mental retardation (MS); rehabilitation counseling (MS, PhD, Ed S); special education (PhD, Ed S); visual disabilities (MS). *Accreditation:* CORE. *Faculty:* 8 full-time (7 women). *Students:* 55 full-time (49 women), 44 part-time (42 women); includes 20 minority (10 Black or African American, non-Hispanic/Latino; 2 Asian, non-Hispanic/Latino; 8 Hispanic/Latino), 3 international. Average age 32. 57 applicants, 54% accepted, 29 enrolled. In 2011, 47 master's, 1 doctorate awarded. *Degree requirements:* For master's, comprehensive exam, thesis optional; for doctorate, comprehensive exam, thesis/dissertation; for Ed S, comprehensive exam. *Entrance requirements:* For master's, doctorate, and Ed S, GRE General Test, minimum GPA of 3.0. Additional exam requirements/recommendations for international students: Required—TOEFL (minimum score 550 paper-based; 213 computer-based; 80 iBT); Recommended—TWE. *Application deadline:* For fall admission, 7/1 for domestic and international students; for winter admission, 11/1 for domestic and international students; for spring admission, 3/1 for domestic and international students. Applications are processed on a rolling basis. Application fee: $30. Electronic applications accepted. *Expenses:* Tuition, state resident: full-time $9474; part-time $350.88 per credit hour. Tuition, nonresident: full-time $16,236; part-time $601.34 per credit hour. *Required fees:* $630 per semester. One-time fee: $20. Tuition and fees vary according to course load and campus/location. *Financial support:* Fellowships with full and partial tuition reimbursements, research assistantships with full and partial tuition reimbursements, teaching assistantships with full and partial tuition reimbursements, career-related internships or fieldwork, scholarships/grants, health care benefits, and unspecified assistantships available. Financial award applicants required to submit FAFSA. *Unit head:* Dr. Mary Frances Hanline, Chair, 850-644-4880, Fax: 850-644-8715, E-mail: mhanline@fsu.edu. *Application contact:* Harriet Kasper, Program Assistant, 850-644-2122, Fax: 850-644-7736, E-mail: hkasper@fsu.edu. Web site: http://coe.fsu.edu/special-ed.

Fontbonne University, Graduate Programs, Department of Communication Disorders and Deaf Education, Studies in Early Intervention in Deaf Education, St. Louis, MO 63105-3098. Offers MA. *Entrance requirements:* For master's, minimum GPA of 3.0.

Fordham University, Graduate School of Education, Division of Curriculum and Teaching, New York, NY 10023. Offers adult education (MS, MSE); bilingual teacher education (MSE); curriculum and teaching (MSE); early childhood education (MSE); elementary education (MST); language, literacy, and learning (PhD); reading education (MSE, Adv C); secondary education (MAT, MSE); special education (MSE, Adv C); teaching English as a second language (MSE). *Accreditation:* NCATE. *Degree requirements:* For doctorate, thesis/dissertation; for Adv C, thesis. *Entrance requirements:* For doctorate, MAT, GRE General Test. *Expenses: Tuition:* Full-time $30,480; part-time $1270 per credit. *Required fees:* $586; $293 per semester.

Fort Hays State University, Graduate School, College of Education and Technology, Department of Special Education, Hays, KS 67601-4099. Offers MS. *Accreditation:* NCATE. *Degree requirements:* For master's, comprehensive exam, thesis optional. *Entrance requirements:* Additional exam requirements/recommendations for international students: Required—TOEFL (minimum score 550 paper-based; 213 computer-based). Electronic applications accepted. *Faculty research:* Severe behavior disorders, early childhood language, multicultural speech.

Framingham State University, Division of Graduate and Continuing Education, Program in Special Education, Framingham, MA 01701-9101. Offers M Ed. Part-time and evening/weekend programs available. *Entrance requirements:* For master's, MAT, interview.

Francis Marion University, Graduate Programs, School of Education, Florence, SC 29502-0547. Offers early childhood education (M Ed); elementary education (M Ed); learning disabilities (M Ed, MAT); remedial education (M Ed); secondary education (M Ed). *Accreditation:* NCATE. Part-time programs available. *Faculty:* 20 full-time (16 women), 1 (woman) part-time/adjunct. *Students:* 10 full-time (8 women), 115 part-time (88 women); includes 30 minority (26 Black or African American, non-Hispanic/Latino; 3 Asian, non-Hispanic/Latino; 1 Hispanic/Latino), 1 international. Average age 32. 249 applicants, 33% accepted, 77 enrolled. In 2011, 41 master's awarded. *Degree requirements:* For master's, comprehensive exam. *Entrance requirements:* For master's, GRE General Test, MAT, NTE, or PRAXIS II. *Application deadline:* For fall admission, 3/15 priority date for domestic students; for spring admission, 10/15 priority date for domestic students. Applications are processed on a rolling basis. Application fee: $31. *Expenses:* Tuition, state resident: full-time $8467; part-time $443.35 per credit hour. Tuition, nonresident: full-time $16,934; part-time $866.70 per credit hour. *Required fees:* $335; $12.25 per credit hour. $30 per semester. *Financial support:* In 2011–12, 3 research assistantships (averaging $6,000 per year) were awarded; scholarships/grants and unspecified assistantships also available. Support available to part-time students. Financial award application deadline: 3/1; financial award applicants required to submit FAFSA. *Faculty research:* Identification and alternate assessment of at-risk students. *Unit head:* Dr. James R. Faulkenberry, Dean, 843-661-1460, Fax: 843-661-4647. *Application contact:* Rannie Gamble, Administrative Manager, 843-661-1286, Fax: 843-661-4688, E-mail: rgamble@fmarion.edu.

Franklin Pierce University, Graduate Studies, Rindge, NH 03461-0060. Offers curriculum and instruction (M Ed); emerging network technologies (Graduate Certificate); energy and sustainability studies (MBA); health administration (MBA, Graduate Certificate); human resource management (MBA, Graduate Certificate); information technology (MBA); information technology management (MS); leadership (MBA, DA); nursing (MS); physical therapy (DPT); physician assistant studies (MPAS); special education (M Ed); sports management (MBA). *Accreditation:* APTA. Part-time programs available. Postbaccalaureate distance learning degree programs offered (no on-campus study). *Degree requirements:* For master's, concentrated original research projects; student teaching; fieldwork and/or internship; leadership project; PRAXIS I and II (for M Ed); for doctorate, concentrated original research projects, clinical fieldwork and/or internship, leadership project. *Entrance requirements:* For master's, minimum GPA of 2.5, 3 letters of recommendation; competencies in accounting, economics, statistics, and computer skills through life experience or undergraduate coursework (for MBA); certification/e-portfolio, minimum C grade in all education courses (for M Ed); license to practice as RN (for MS in nursing); for doctorate, GRE, BA/BS, 3 letters of recommendation, personal mission statement, interview, writing sample, minimum cumulative GPA of 2.8, master's degree (for DA); 80 hours of observation/work in PT settings, completion of anatomy, chemistry, physics, and statistics, minimum GPA of 3.0 (for DPT). Additional exam requirements/recommendations for international students: Required—TOEFL (minimum score 550 paper-based; 195 computer-based; 61 iBT). Electronic applications accepted. *Faculty research:* Evidence-based practice in sports physical therapy, human resource management in economic crisis, leadership in nursing, innovation in sports facility management, differentiated learning and understanding by design.

Freed-Hardeman University, Program in Education, Henderson, TN 38340-2399. Offers curriculum and instruction (M Ed); school counseling (M Ed), including administration and supervision, special education; school leadership (Ed S). *Accreditation:* NCATE. Part-time and evening/weekend programs available. *Degree requirements:* For master's, comprehensive exam, thesis optional; for Ed S, thesis. *Entrance requirements:* For master's, GRE General Test or NTE; for Ed S, 3 years of teaching experience. Additional exam requirements/recommendations for international students: Required—TOEFL (minimum score 500 paper-based; 173 computer-based).

Fresno Pacific University, Graduate Programs, School of Education, Division of Special Education, Fresno, CA 93702-4709. Offers mild/moderate (MA Ed); moderate/severe (MA Ed); physical and health impairments (MA Ed). Part-time and evening/weekend programs available. *Degree requirements:* For master's, thesis or alternative. *Entrance requirements:* Additional exam requirements/recommendations for international students: Required—TOEFL (minimum score 550 paper-based; 213 computer-based).

Frostburg State University, Graduate School, College of Education, Department of Educational Professions, Program in Special Education, Frostburg, MD 21532-1099. Offers M Ed. *Accreditation:* NCATE. Part-time and evening/weekend programs available. *Degree requirements:* For master's, thesis or alternative, PRAXIS II (special education section). *Entrance requirements:* For master's, teaching certificate. Additional exam requirements/recommendations for international students: Required—TOEFL. Electronic applications accepted.

Furman University, Graduate Division, Department of Education, Greenville, SC 29613. Offers curriculum and instruction (MA); early childhood education (MA); educational leadership (Ed S); English as a second language (MA); literacy (MA); school leadership (MA); special education (MA). *Accreditation:* NCATE. Part-time programs available. Postbaccalaureate distance learning degree programs offered (minimal on-campus study). *Faculty:* 14 full-time (8 women), 6 part-time/adjunct (4 women). *Students:* 237 part-time (188 women); includes 27 minority (22 Black or African American, non-Hispanic/Latino; 1 Asian, non-Hispanic/Latino; 3 Hispanic/Latino; 1 Native Hawaiian or other Pacific Islander, non-Hispanic/Latino). Average age 29. 97 applicants, 100% accepted, 90 enrolled. In 2011, 34 master's awarded. *Degree requirements:* For master's, comprehensive exam (for some programs), thesis or alternative. *Entrance requirements:* For master's, PRAXIS II. *Application deadline:* For fall admission, 8/1 priority date for domestic students, 7/15 for international students; for spring admission, 12/1 priority date for domestic students, 12/1 for international students. Applications are processed on a rolling basis. Application fee: $50. *Financial support:* Scholarships/grants available. Financial award application deadline: 5/15; financial award applicants required to submit FAFSA. *Faculty research:* Literacy, pedagogy and practice, social justice, advanced leadership, achievement in high poverty schools. *Unit head:* Dr. Nelly Hecker, Head, 864-294-3385. *Application contact:* Helen Reynolds, Department Assistant, 864-294-2213, Fax: 864-294-3579, E-mail: helen.reynolds@furman.edu. Web site: http://www.furman.edu/gradstudies/.

Gallaudet University, The Graduate School, Washington, DC 20002-3625. Offers audiology (Au D); clinical psychology (PhD); critical studies in the education of deaf learners (PhD); deaf and hard of hearing infants, toddlers, and their families (Certificate); deaf education (Ed S); deaf education: advanced studies (MA); deaf education: special programs in deaf education (MA); deaf history (Certificate); deaf studies (MA, Certificate); education deaf students with disabilities (Certificate); education: teacher preparation (MA), including deaf education, early childhood education and deaf education, elementary education and deaf education, secondary education and deaf education; hearing, speech and language sciences (MS, PhD); international development (MA); interpretation (MA, PhD); linguistics (MA, PhD); mental health counseling (MA); public administration (MA); school counseling (MA); school psychology (Psy S); sign language teaching (MA); social work (MSW); speech-language pathology (MS). Part-time programs available. *Faculty:* 62 full-time (44 women). *Students:* 300 full-time (246 women), 110 part-time (82 women); includes 80 minority (27 Black or African American, non-Hispanic/Latino; 1 American Indian or Alaska Native, non-Hispanic/Latino; 11 Asian, non-Hispanic/Latino; 25 Hispanic/Latino; 1 Native Hawaiian or other Pacific Islander, non-Hispanic/Latino; 15 Two or more races, non-Hispanic/Latino), 24 international. Average age 30. 498 applicants, 45% accepted, 168 enrolled. In 2011, 129 master's, 24 doctorates, 19 other advanced degrees awarded. Terminal master's awarded for partial completion of doctoral program. *Degree requirements:* For master's, comprehensive exam (for some programs), thesis optional; for doctorate, comprehensive exam, thesis/dissertation. *Entrance requirements:* For master's and doctorate, GRE General Test or MAT, letters of recommendation, interviews, goals statement, ASL proficiency interview, written English competency. Additional exam requirements/recommendations for international students: Required—TOEFL. *Application deadline:* For fall admission, 2/15 for domestic students. Applications are processed on a rolling basis. Application fee: $50. Electronic applications accepted. *Expenses: Tuition:* Full-time $12,770; part-time $710 per credit. *Required fees:* $376. *Financial support:* In 2011–12, 287 students received support. Fellowships, research assistantships, teaching assistantships, career-related internships or fieldwork, Federal Work-Study, scholarships/grants, tuition waivers (partial), and unspecified assistantships available. Support available to part-time students. Financial award applicants required to submit FAFSA. *Faculty research:* Bimodal bilingualism development, audiology, telecommunications access, early childhood education, linguistics, visual language and visual learning, rehabilitation and hearing enhancement. *Unit head:* Dr. Carol J. Erting, Dean, 202-651-5520, Fax: 202-651-5027, E-mail: carol.erting@gallaudet.edu. *Application contact:* Wednesday Luria, Coordinator of Prospective Graduate Student Services, 202-651-5400, Fax: 202-651-5295, E-mail: graduate.school@gallaudet.edu. Web site: http://www.gallaudet.edu/x26696.xml.

Geneva College, Master of Education in Special Education Program, Beaver Falls, PA 15010-3599. Offers M Ed. Part-time and evening/weekend programs available. *Faculty:* 4 full-time (all women). *Students:* 6 part-time (5 women). 2 applicants, 100% accepted, 2 enrolled. In 2011, 3 master's awarded. *Entrance requirements:* For master's, resume, letters of recommendation, proof of certification, transcript. Additional exam requirements/recommendations for international students: Required—TOEFL. *Application deadline:* For fall admission, 3/1 priority date for domestic students; for spring admission, 11/1 priority date for domestic students. Applications are processed on a rolling basis. Application fee: $0. Electronic applications accepted. *Expenses: Tuition:* Part-time $625 per credit hour. Tuition and fees vary according to program. *Financial support:* In 2011–12, 3 students received support. Scholarships/grants available. Financial award applicants required to submit FAFSA. *Unit head:* Dr. Karen Schmalz, Program Head, 724-847-6125, E-mail: kschmalz@geneva.edu. *Application contact:* Lori Hartge, Graduate Student Support Specialist, 724-847-6571, E-mail: speced@geneva.edu. Web site: http://www.geneva.edu/.

George Mason University, College of Education and Human Development, Program in Special Education, Fairfax, VA 22030. Offers M Ed. *Faculty:* 19 full-time (16 women), 112 part-time/adjunct (101 women). *Students:* 95 full-time (83 women), 461 part-time (382 women); includes 97 minority (38 Black or African American, non-Hispanic/Latino; 2 American Indian or Alaska Native, non-Hispanic/Latino; 24 Asian, non-Hispanic/Latino; 21 Hispanic/Latino; 1 Native Hawaiian or other Pacific Islander, non-Hispanic/Latino; 11 Two or more races, non-Hispanic/Latino), 4 international. Average age 33. 264 applicants, 83% accepted, 168 enrolled. In 2011, 236 master's awarded. *Entrance requirements:* For master's, bachelor's degree from regionally-accredited institution with minimum GPA of 3.0, cumulative or in last 60 credits of undergraduate study (or PRAXIS I, SAT, ACT or VCLA); 2 official transcripts; 3 letters of recommendation with recommendation form. Additional exam requirements/recommendations for international students: Required—TOEFL (minimum score 570 paper-based; 230 computer-based; 88 iBT), IELTS, Pearson Test of English. *Application deadline:* For fall admission, 3/1 priority date for domestic students; for spring admission, 11/1 priority date for domestic students. Applications are processed on a rolling basis. Application fee: $65 ($80 for international students). Electronic applications accepted. *Expenses:* Tuition, state resident: full-time $8750; part-time $364.58 per credit. Tuition, nonresident: full-time $24,092; part-time $1003.83 per credit. *Required fees:* $2514; $104.75 per credit. *Financial support:* Career-related internships or fieldwork, Federal Work-Study, and scholarships/grants available. Financial award application deadline: 3/1; financial award applicants required to submit FAFSA. *Unit head:* Michael M. Behrmann, Director, 703-993-2501, Fax: 703-993-3681, E-mail: mbehrman@gmu.edu. *Application contact:* Jancy Templeton, Advisor, 703-993-2387, Fax: 703-993-3681, E-mail: jtemple1@gmu.edu. Web site: http://gse.gmu.edu/programs/sped/.

Georgetown College, Department of Education, Georgetown, KY 40324-1696. Offers reading and writing (MA Ed); special education (MA Ed); teaching (MA Ed). *Accreditation:* NCATE. Part-time programs available. *Degree requirements:* For master's, portfolio. *Entrance requirements:* For master's, teaching certificate, minimum GPA of 2.7 or GRE General Test.

The George Washington University, Graduate School of Education and Human Development, Department of Special Education and Disability Studies, Program in Bilingual Special Education, Washington, DC 20052. Offers MA, Ed D.

The George Washington University, Graduate School of Education and Human Development, Department of Special Education and Disability Studies, Program in Early Childhood Special Education, Washington, DC 20052. Offers MA Ed. *Accreditation:* NCATE. *Degree requirements:* For master's, comprehensive exam. *Entrance requirements:* For master's, GRE General Test or MAT, minimum GPA of 2.75. *Faculty research:* Computer-assisted instruction and learning, disabled learner assessment of preschool, handicapped children.

The George Washington University, Graduate School of Education and Human Development, Department of Special Education and Disability Studies, Program in Secondary Special Education and Transition Services, Washington, DC 20052. Offers M Ed.

The George Washington University, Graduate School of Education and Human Development, Department of Special Education and Disability Studies, Program in Special Education, Washington, DC 20052. Offers Ed D, Ed S. *Accreditation:* NCATE. *Degree requirements:* For doctorate, comprehensive exam, thesis/dissertation; for Ed S, comprehensive exam. *Entrance requirements:* For doctorate and Ed S, GRE General Test or MAT, interview, minimum GPA of 3.3.

The George Washington University, Graduate School of Education and Human Development, Department of Special Education and Disability Studies, Program in Special Education for Children with Emotional and Behavioral Disabilities, Washington, DC 20052. Offers MA Ed. *Accreditation:* NCATE. *Degree requirements:* For master's, comprehensive exam. *Entrance requirements:* For master's, GRE General Test or MAT, interview, minimum GPA of 2.75. *Faculty research:* Action research on the act of teaching emotionally disturbed students, teacher training.

The George Washington University, Graduate School of Education and Human Development, Department of Special Education and Disability Studies, Program in Transition Special Education, Washington, DC 20052. Offers MA Ed, Certificate. *Accreditation:* NCATE. Evening/weekend programs available. *Degree requirements:* For master's, comprehensive exam. *Entrance requirements:* For master's, GRE General Test or MAT, interview, minimum GPA of 2.75. *Faculty research:* Computer applications for transition, transition follow-up research, curriculum-based vocational assessment, traumatic brain injury.

Georgia College & State University, Graduate School, The John H. Lounsbury College of Education, Department of Special Education and Educational Leadership, Program in Special Education, Milledgeville, GA 31061. Offers M Ed, MAT, Ed S. *Accreditation:* NCATE. Part-time and evening/weekend programs available. *Students:* 29 full-time (19 women), 43 part-time (41 women); includes 24 minority (23 Black or African American, non-Hispanic/Latino; 1 Two or more races, non-Hispanic/Latino). Average age 35. 48 applicants, 58% accepted, 25 enrolled. In 2011, 16 master's, 8 other advanced degrees awarded. *Degree requirements:* For master's, comprehensive exam. *Entrance requirements:* For master's, on-site writing exam; for Ed S, on-site writing exam, 2 years of teaching experience, minimum GPA of 3.25. Additional exam requirements/recommendations for international students: Required—TOEFL (minimum score 550 paper-based; 213 computer-based; 79 iBT). *Application deadline:* For fall admission, 7/1 priority date for domestic students; for spring admission, 11/15 priority date for domestic students. Applications are processed on a rolling basis. Application fee: $4. Electronic applications accepted. *Expenses:* Tuition, state resident: full-time $4806; part-time $267 per credit hour. Tuition, nonresident: full-time $17,802; part-time $989 per credit hour. *Required fees:* $936 per semester. Tuition and fees vary according to course load and campus/location. *Financial support:* In 2011–12, 2 research assistantships with full tuition reimbursements were awarded; career-related internships or fieldwork, Federal Work-Study, and unspecified assistantships also available. Support available to part-time students. *Unit head:* Dr. Craig Smith, Chair, 478-445-4577, E-mail: craig.smith@gcsu.edu. *Application contact:* Shanda Brand, Graduate Coordinator, 478-445-1383, E-mail: shanda.brand@gcsu.edu.

Georgia Southern University, Jack N. Averitt College of Graduate Studies, College of Education, Department of Teaching and Learning, Program in Special Education, Statesboro, GA 30460. Offers M Ed, MAT. *Accreditation:* NCATE. Part-time and evening/weekend programs available. *Students:* 6 full-time (4 women), 16 part-time (10 women); includes 9 minority (all Black or African American, non-Hispanic/Latino), 1 international. Average age 30. 9 applicants, 100% accepted, 7 enrolled. In 2011, 3 master's awarded. *Degree requirements:* For master's, portfolio, transition point assessments, exit assessment. *Entrance requirements:* For master's, GRE General Test or MAT; GACE Special Skills and Content Assessments (MAT), minimum cumulative GPA of 2.5. Additional exam requirements/recommendations for international students: Required—TOEFL (minimum score 550 paper-based; 213 computer-based; 80 iBT). *Application deadline:* For fall admission, 3/1 priority date for domestic students, 3/1 for international students; for spring admission, 10/1 priority date for domestic students, 10/1 for international students. Applications are processed on a rolling basis. Application fee: $50. Electronic applications accepted. *Expenses:* Tuition, state resident: full-time $6300; part-time $263 per semester hour. Tuition, nonresident: full-time $25,174; part-time $1049 per semester hour. *Required fees:* $1872. *Financial support:* In 2011–12, 3 students received support, including research assistantships with partial tuition reimbursements available (averaging $7,200 per year), teaching assistantships with partial tuition reimbursements available (averaging $7,200 per year); career-related internships or fieldwork, Federal Work-Study, scholarships/grants, tuition waivers (partial), and unspecified assistantships also available. Support available to part-time students. Financial award application deadline: 4/15; financial award applicants required to submit FAFSA. *Faculty research:* Learning disorders, behavior disorders, education of the mentally retarded. *Unit head:* Dr. Ronnie Sheppard, Department Chair, 912-478-5203, Fax: 912-478-0026, E-mail: sheppard@georgiasouthern.edu. *Application contact:* Amanda Gilliland, Coordinator for Graduate Student Recruitment, 912-478-5384, Fax: 912-478-0740, E-mail: gradadmissions@georgiasouthern.edu.

Georgia Southwestern State University, Graduate Studies, School of Education, Americus, GA 31709-4693. Offers early childhood education (M Ed, Ed S); health and physical education (M Ed); middle grades education (M Ed, Ed S); reading (M Ed); secondary education (M Ed); special education (M Ed). *Accreditation:* NCATE. *Degree requirements:* For master's, comprehensive exam. *Entrance requirements:* For master's, GRE General Test or MAT, minimum GPA of 2.5; for Ed S, GRE General Test or MAT, minimum graduate GPA of 3.25, M Ed from accredited college or university, 3 years teaching experience. Electronic applications accepted.

Georgia State University, College of Education, Department of Educational Psychology and Special Education, Program in Behavior and Learning Disabilities, Atlanta, GA 30302-3083. Offers M Ed. *Accreditation:* NCATE. *Entrance requirements:* For master's, GRE General Test, minimum GPA of 2.5. *Faculty research:* Inclusion, behavior management, basic teaching strategies.

Georgia State University, College of Education, Department of Educational Psychology and Special Education, Program in Communication Disorders, Atlanta, GA 30302-3083. Offers M Ed. *Accreditation:* ASHA; NCATE. *Degree requirements:* For master's, portfolio. *Entrance requirements:* For master's, GRE General Test, minimum GPA of 2.5, 2 letters of recommendation. *Faculty research:* Language development, adult language disorders, voice disorders.

Georgia State University, College of Education, Department of Educational Psychology and Special Education, Program in Education of Students with Exceptionalities, Atlanta, GA 30302-3083. Offers PhD. *Accreditation:* NCATE. *Degree requirements:* For doctorate, comprehensive exam, thesis/dissertation. *Entrance requirements:* For doctorate, GRE General Test, minimum GPA of 3.3. *Faculty research:* Literacy, behavior management, juvenile justice.

Gonzaga University, School of Education, Program in Special Education, Spokane, WA 99258. Offers MES. *Accreditation:* NCATE. *Degree requirements:* For master's, comprehensive exam. *Entrance requirements:* For master's, GRE General Test or MAT, minimum B average in undergraduate course work. Additional exam requirements/recommendations for international students: Required—TOEFL.

Governors State University, College of Education, Program in Multi-Categorical Special Education, University Park, IL 60484. Offers MA. *Accreditation:* NCATE. Part-time and evening/weekend programs available. *Students:* 27 full-time (17 women), 115 part-time (95 women); includes 46 minority (35 Black or African American, non-Hispanic/Latino; 1 Asian, non-Hispanic/Latino; 10 Hispanic/Latino). Average age 33. *Degree requirements:* For master's, comprehensive exam, practicum. *Entrance requirements:* For master's, minimum GPA of 2.75 in last 60 hours of undergraduate course work, 3.0 graduate. *Application deadline:* For fall admission, 7/15 priority date for domestic students; for spring admission, 11/10 for domestic students. Applications are processed on a rolling basis. Application fee: $25. *Financial support:* Career-related internships or fieldwork, Federal Work-Study, institutionally sponsored loans, and tuition waivers (full and partial) available. Support available to part-time students. Financial award application deadline: 5/1. *Unit head:* Dr. Deborah Bordelon, Dean, 708-534-4050.

Graceland University, Gleazer School of Education, Lamoni, IA 50140. Offers collaborative learning and teaching (M Ed); differentiated instruction (M Ed); management in the inclusive classroom (M Ed); mild/moderate special education (M Ed); technology integration (M Ed). *Accreditation:* NCATE. Part-time and evening/weekend programs available. Postbaccalaureate distance learning degree programs offered (no on-campus study). *Faculty:* 12 full-time (11 women), 18 part-time/adjunct (14 women). *Students:* 315 full-time (256 women), 69 part-time (51 women); includes 11 minority (4 Black or African American, non-Hispanic/Latino; 1 American Indian or Alaska Native, non-Hispanic/Latino; 2 Asian, non-Hispanic/Latino; 4 Hispanic/Latino), 8 international. *Degree requirements:* For master's, action research project. *Entrance requirements:* For master's, minimum GPA of 3.0, teaching certificate, current teaching contract. *Application deadline:* For fall admission, 7/15 for domestic students; for winter admission, 10/15 for domestic students; for spring admission, 1/15 priority date for domestic students. Application fee: $50. Electronic applications accepted. *Financial support:* Institutionally sponsored loans and scholarships/grants available. Financial award application deadline: 12/15; financial award applicants required to submit FAFSA. *Unit head:* Dr. Tammy Everett, Dean, 641-784-5000 Ext. 5226, E-mail: teverett@graceland.edu. *Application contact:* Cathy Porter, Program Consultant, 816-833-0524 Ext. 4516, E-mail: cgporter@graceland.edu. Web site: http://www.graceland.edu/education.

Grand Canyon University, College of Education, Phoenix, AZ 85017-1097. Offers curriculum and instruction (M Ed); education administration (M Ed); elementary education (M Ed); secondary education (M Ed); special education (M Ed); teaching (MA). Part-time and evening/weekend programs available. Postbaccalaureate distance learning degree programs offered (no on-campus study). *Degree requirements:* For master's, publishable research paper (M Ed), e-portfolio. *Entrance requirements:* For master's, undergraduate degree from accredited, GCU-approved college, university, or program with minimum GPA 2.8. Additional exam requirements/recommendations for international students: Required—TOEFL (minimum score 550 paper-based; 213 computer-based; 79 iBT), IELTS (minimum score 6). Electronic applications accepted.

Grand Valley State University, College of Education, Program in Special Education, Allendale, MI 49401-9403. Offers cognitive impairment (M Ed); early childhood developmental delay (M Ed); emotional impairment (M Ed); learning disabilities (M Ed); special education endorsements (M Ed). *Accreditation:* NCATE. Part-time and evening/weekend programs available. *Degree requirements:* For master's, thesis. *Entrance requirements:* For master's, GRE General Test or minimum GPA of 3.0. Additional exam requirements/recommendations for international students: Required—TOEFL. Electronic applications accepted. *Faculty research:* Evaluation of special education program effects, adaptive behavior assessment, language development, writing disorders, comparative effects of presentation methods.

Greensboro College, Program in Education, Greensboro, NC 27401-1875. Offers elementary education (M Ed); special education (M Ed). Part-time and evening/weekend programs available. *Degree requirements:* For master's, thesis. *Entrance requirements:* For master's, GRE, teacher license, 2 years of teaching experience, 2 letters of recommendation. Additional exam requirements/recommendations for international students: Required—TOEFL (minimum score 550 paper-based; 213 computer-based). Electronic applications accepted.

Gwynedd-Mercy College, School of Education, Gwynedd Valley, PA 19437-0901. Offers educational administration (MS); master teacher (MS); reading (MS); school counseling (MS); special education (MS). Part-time and evening/weekend programs available. *Faculty:* 8 full-time (5 women), 38 part-time/adjunct (24 women). *Students:* 33 full-time (22 women), 157 part-time (116 women); includes 33 minority (22 Black or African American, non-Hispanic/Latino; 6 Asian, non-Hispanic/Latino; 5 Hispanic/Latino), 1 international. Average age 33. In 2011, 186 master's awarded. *Degree requirements:* For master's, thesis, internship, practicum. *Entrance requirements:* For master's, GRE or MAT; PRAXIS I, minimum GPA of 3.0. *Application deadline:* Applications are processed on a rolling basis. Application fee: $25. *Expenses: Tuition:* Part-time $630 per credit hour. *Financial support:* In 2011–12, 2 research assistantships were awarded; career-related internships or fieldwork, Federal Work-Study, tuition waivers (full and partial), unspecified assistantships, and Federal Stafford loans, Federal work study, alternative loans, graduate assistantships also available. Financial award applicants required to submit FAFSA. *Faculty research:* Learning and the brain, reading literacy, ethics and moral judgment, leadership, teaching and multicultural education. *Unit head:* Dr. Sandra Mangano, Dean, 215-641-5549, Fax: 215-542-4695, E-mail: mangano.s@gmc.edu. *Application contact:* Graduate Program Coordinator. Web site: http://www.gmc.edu/academics/education/.

Hampton University, Graduate College, College of Education and Continuing Studies, Program in Teaching, Hampton, VA 23668. Offers early childhood education (MT); middle school education (MT); music education (MT); secondary education (MT); special education (MT). *Entrance requirements:* For master's, GRE General Test.

Harding University, College of Education, Searcy, AR 72149-0001. Offers advanced studies in teaching and learning (M Ed); art (MSE); behavioral science (MSE); counseling (MS, Ed S); early childhood special education (M Ed, MSE); education (MSE); educational leadership (M Ed, Ed S); elementary education (M Ed); English (MSE); French (MSE); history/social science (MSE); kinesiology (MSE); math (MSE); reading (M Ed); secondary education (M Ed); Spanish (MSE); teaching (MAT); teaching English as a second language (MSE). *Accreditation:* NCATE. Part-time and evening/weekend programs available. *Faculty:* 9 full-time (2 women), 48 part-time/adjunct (26 women). *Students:* 100 full-time (77 women), 333 part-time (239 women); includes 76 minority (59 Black or African American, non-Hispanic/Latino; 1 Asian, non-Hispanic/Latino; 10 Hispanic/Latino; 6 Two or more races, non-Hispanic/Latino), 2 international. Average age 36. 93 applicants, 91% accepted, 83 enrolled. In 2011, 159 master's, 10 other advanced degrees awarded. *Degree requirements:* For master's, comprehensive exam (for some programs), thesis optional, portfolio(s); for Ed S, comprehensive exam, portfolio, project. *Entrance requirements:* For master's, GRE, MAT, PRAXIS; for Ed S, MAT or GRE. Additional exam requirements/recommendations for international students: Required—TOEFL (minimum score 550 paper-based; 79 iBT). *Application deadline:* For fall admission, 8/1 for domestic and international students; for spring admission, 1/1 for domestic and international students. Applications are processed on a rolling basis. Application fee: $35. *Expenses: Tuition:* Full-time $10,512; part-time $584 per credit hour. *Required fees:* $500; $25 per credit hour. Tuition and fees vary according to course load, degree level and program. *Financial support:* In 2011–12, 37 students received support. Unspecified assistantships available. *Faculty research:* Reading, comprehension, school violence, educational technology, behavior, college choice, differentiated instruction, brain-based teaching. *Unit head:* Dr. Clara Carroll, Chair, 501-279-4501, Fax: 501-279-4083, E-mail: ccarroll@harding.edu. *Application contact:* Information Contact, 501-279-4315, E-mail: gradstudiesedu@harding.edu. Web site: http://www.harding.edu/education/grad.html.

Hebrew College, Shoolman Graduate School of Jewish Education, Newton Centre, MA 02459. Offers early childhood Jewish education (Certificate); Jewish day school education (Certificate); Jewish education (MJ Ed); Jewish family education (Certificate); Jewish special education (Certificate); Jewish youth education, informal education and camping (Certificate). Part-time and evening/weekend programs available. Postbaccalaureate distance learning degree programs offered. *Degree requirements:* For master's, one foreign language. *Entrance requirements:* For master's, GRE, interview. Additional exam requirements/recommendations for international students: Required—TOEFL.

Henderson State University, Graduate Studies, Teachers College, Department of Advanced Instructional Studies, Arkadelphia, AR 71999-0001. Offers early childhood (P-4) (MSE); education (MAT); middle school (MSE); reading (MSE); special education (MSE). *Accreditation:* NCATE. Part-time programs available. *Entrance requirements:* For master's, GRE General Test or MAT, minimum GPA of 2.7, teacher certification. Additional exam requirements/recommendations for international students: Required—TOEFL (minimum score 550 paper-based; 213 computer-based); Recommended—IELTS (minimum score 6). Electronic applications accepted.

Heritage University, Graduate Programs in Education, Program in Professional Studies, Toppenish, WA 98948-9599. Offers bilingual education/ESL (M Ed); biology (M Ed); English and literature (M Ed); reading/literacy (M Ed); special education (M Ed). Part-time and evening/weekend programs available. *Degree requirements:* For master's, comprehensive exam (for some programs), thesis (for some programs).

High Point University, Norcross Graduate School, High Point, NC 27262-3598. Offers business administration (MBA); educational leadership (M Ed); elementary education (M Ed); history (MA); nonprofit management (MA); secondary math (M Ed); special education (M Ed); strategic communication (MA); teaching elementary education k-6 (MAT); teaching secondary mathematics 9-12 (MAT). *Accreditation:* ACBSP; NCATE. Part-time and evening/weekend programs available. *Degree requirements:* For master's, comprehensive exam (for some programs), thesis (for some programs).

Entrance requirements: For master's, GMAT (MBA), GRE, MAT, minimum GPA of 3.0. Additional exam requirements/recommendations for international students: Required—TOEFL (minimum score 550 paper-based). Electronic applications accepted.

Hofstra University, School of Education, Health, and Human Services, Department of Literacy Studies, Hempstead, NY 11549. Offers advanced literacy studies (PD), including birth-grade 6 (MA, MS Ed, PD); advanced literary studies (PD), including grades 5-12 (MA, PD); birth-grade 6 (MS Ed, Advanced Certificate); grades 5-12 (Advanced Certificate); literacy studies (Ed D, PhD); special education (MS Ed), including birth-grade 2, birth-grade 6 (MA, MS Ed, PD); special education (MS Ed), including birth-grade 2; teaching of writing (MA), including birth-grade 6 (MA, MS Ed, PD), grades 5-12 (MA, PD). Part-time and evening/weekend programs available. *Students:* 43 full-time (42 women), 70 part-time (63 women); includes 15 minority (7 Black or African American, non-Hispanic/Latino; 1 Asian, non-Hispanic/Latino; 7 Hispanic/Latino). Average age 33. 67 applicants, 81% accepted, 32 enrolled. In 2011, 47 master's, 1 doctorate, 10 other advanced degrees awarded. *Degree requirements:* For master's, comprehensive exam, portfolio, minimum GPA of 3.0; for doctorate, one foreign language, comprehensive exam, thesis/dissertation, qualifying hearing, minimum GPA of 3.0. *Entrance requirements:* For master's, interview, teaching certificate, 2 letters of recommendation; for doctorate, GRE or MAT, interview, resume, essay, master's degree, 3 letters of recommendation, writing sample; for other advanced degree, 2 letters of recommendation, interview, teaching certificate, essay, master's degree. Additional exam requirements/recommendations for international students: Required—TOEFL (minimum score 550 paper-based; 213 computer-based; 80 iBT). *Application deadline:* Applications are processed on a rolling basis. Application fee: $70 ($75 for international students). Electronic applications accepted. *Expenses: Tuition:* Full-time $18,990; part-time $1055 per credit hour. *Required fees:* $970. Tuition and fees vary according to program. *Financial support:* In 2011–12, 78 students received support, including 36 fellowships with full and partial tuition reimbursements available (averaging $3,622 per year); research assistantships with full and partial tuition reimbursements available, career-related internships or fieldwork, Federal Work-Study, institutionally sponsored loans, scholarships/grants, tuition waivers (full and partial), and unspecified assistantships also available. Support available to part-time students. Financial award applicants required to submit FAFSA. *Faculty research:* Research literacy practices of immigrant and urban youth, literature for children and adolescents, eye movement/miscue analysis, literacy strategies for effective instruction, transnational literacies. *Unit head:* Dr. Esther Fusco, Chairperson, 516-463-7704, Fax: 516-463-6196, E-mail: catezf@hofstra.edu. *Application contact:* Carol Drummer, Dean of Graduate Admissions, 516-463-4876, Fax: 516-463-4664, E-mail: gradstudent@hofstra.edu. Web site: http://www.hofstra.edu/education/.

Holy Family University, Graduate School, School of Education, Philadelphia, PA 19114. Offers education (M Ed); education leadership (M Ed); elementary education (M Ed); reading specialist (M Ed); secondary education (M Ed); special education (M Ed). Part-time and evening/weekend programs available. *Degree requirements:* For master's, thesis optional. *Entrance requirements:* For master's, GRE or MAT, interview. Electronic applications accepted. *Faculty research:* Cognition, developmental issues, sociological issues in education.

See Display on page 707 and Close-Up on page 803.

Holy Names University, Graduate Division, Department of Education, Oakland, CA 94619-1699. Offers educational therapy (Certificate); level 1 education specialist mild/moderate disabilities (Credential); level 2 education specialist mild/moderate disabilities (Credential); multiple subject teaching credential (Credential); single subject teaching credential (Credential); teaching English as a second language (TESL) (M Ed); urban education: educational therapy (M Ed); urban education: K-12 education (M Ed); urban education: special education (M Ed). Part-time programs available. *Degree requirements:* For master's, comprehensive exam, research paper, thesis or project. *Entrance requirements:* For master's, minimum undergraduate GPA of 2.6 overall, 3.0 in major. Additional exam requirements/recommendations for international students: Required—TOEFL (minimum score 550 paper-based; 213 computer-based; 80 iBT). *Faculty research:* Cognitive development, language development, learning handicaps.

Hood College, Graduate School, Department of Education, Frederick, MD 21701-8575. Offers curriculum and instruction (MS), including early childhood education, elementary education, elementary school science and mathematics, secondary education, special education; educational leadership (MS, Certificate); reading specialization (MS). Part-time and evening/weekend programs available. *Degree requirements:* For master's, action research project, portfolio (reading). *Entrance requirements:* For master's, minimum GPA of 2.75, teaching certification. Additional exam requirements/recommendations for international students: Required—TOEFL (minimum score 575 paper-based; 231 computer-based; 89 iBT). Electronic applications accepted. *Faculty research:* Leadership, action research, brain research, learning styles.

Howard University, School of Education, Department of Curriculum and Instruction, Program in Special Education, Washington, DC 20059-0002. Offers M Ed. *Accreditation:* NCATE. Part-time programs available. *Faculty:* 3 full-time (1 woman). *Students:* 15 full-time (9 women), 2 part-time (both women); all minorities (all Black or African American, non-Hispanic/Latino). Average age 31. 20 applicants, 80% accepted, 14 enrolled. In 2011, 2 master's awarded. *Degree requirements:* For master's, comprehensive exam, thesis (for some programs), expository writing exam, internships, practicum. *Entrance requirements:* For master's, minimum GPA of 2.7. Additional exam requirements/recommendations for international students: Required—TOEFL (minimum score 550 paper-based). *Application deadline:* For fall admission, 2/15 priority date for domestic students; for spring admission, 11/1 for domestic students. Applications are processed on a rolling basis. Application fee: $45. Electronic applications accepted. *Financial support:* In 2011–12, 1 student received support, including 1 fellowship with full and partial tuition reimbursement available (averaging $16,000 per year); research assistantships, career-related internships or fieldwork, Federal Work-Study, institutionally sponsored loans, scholarships/grants, and unspecified assistantships also available. Financial award application deadline: 3/15; financial award applicants required to submit FAFSA. *Unit head:* Dr. James T. Jackson, Chair, Department of Curriculum and Instruction, 202-806-5300, Fax: 202-806-5297, E-mail: jt_jackson@howard.edu. *Application contact:* June L. Harris, Administrative Assistant, Department of Curriculum and Instruction, 202-806-7343, Fax: 202-806-5297, E-mail: jlharris@howard.edu.

Hunter College of the City University of New York, Graduate School, School of Education, Department of Special Education, New York, NY 10021-5085. Offers blind or visually impaired (MS Ed); deaf or hard of hearing (MS Ed); severe/multiple disabilities (MS Ed); special education (MS Ed). *Accreditation:* NCATE. *Faculty:* 11 full-time (7 women), 63 part-time/adjunct (52 women). *Students:* 96 full-time (84 women), 730 part-time (621 women); includes 221 minority (60 Black or African American, non-Hispanic/Latino; 5 American Indian or Alaska Native, non-Hispanic/Latino; 54 Asian, non-Hispanic/Latino; 102 Hispanic/Latino), 12 international. Average age 28. 560 applicants, 34% accepted, 101 enrolled. In 2011, 281 master's awarded. *Degree requirements:* For master's, comprehensive exam, thesis, student teaching practica, clinical teaching lab courses, New York State Teacher Certification Exams. *Entrance requirements:* For master's, minimum GPA of 2.8. Additional exam requirements/recommendations for international students: Required—TOEFL, TWE. *Application deadline:* For fall admission, 4/1 for domestic students, 2/1 for international students; for spring admission, 11/1 for domestic students, 9/1 for international students. Applications are processed on a rolling basis. Application fee: $50. *Expenses:* Tuition, state resident: full-time $8210; part-time $345 per credit. Tuition, nonresident: full-time $15,360; part-time $640 per credit. *Required fees:* $280 per semester. One-time fee: $125. Tuition and fees vary according to class time, campus/location and program. *Financial support:* Career-related internships or fieldwork, Federal Work-Study, institutionally sponsored loans, and tuition waivers (partial) available. Support available to part-time students. *Faculty research:* Mathematics learning disabilities; street behavior; assessment; bilingual special education; families, diversity, and disabilities. *Unit head:* Dr. Kate Garnett, Chairperson, 212-772-4700, E-mail: kgarnett@hunter.cuny.edu. *Application contact:* William Zlata, Director for Graduate Admissions, 212-772-4482, Fax: 212-650-3336, E-mail: admissions@hunter.cuny.edu. Web site: http://www.hunter.cuny.edu/school-of-education/programs/graduate/special-education.

Idaho State University, Office of Graduate Studies, College of Education, Department of School Psychology, Literacy, and Special Education, Pocatello, ID 83209-8059. Offers deaf education (M Ed); human exceptionality (M Ed); literacy (M Ed); school psychology (Ed S); special education (Ed S). Part-time programs available. *Degree requirements:* For master's, comprehensive exam, thesis (for some programs), oral thesis defense or written comprehensive exam and oral exam; for Ed S, comprehensive exam, thesis (for some programs), oral exam, specialist paper or portfolio. *Entrance requirements:* For master's, GRE or MAT, minimum undergraduate GPA of 3.0, bachelor's degree, professional experience in an educational context; for Ed S, GRE or MAT, master's degree in related field. Additional exam requirements/recommendations for international students: Required—TOEFL (minimum score 550 paper-based; 213 computer-based; 80 iBT). Electronic applications accepted. *Faculty research:* Literacy, school psychology, special education.

Idaho State University, Office of Graduate Studies, Kasiska College of Health Professions, Department of Communication Sciences and Disorders and Education of the Deaf, Pocatello, ID 83209-8116. Offers audiology (MS, Au D); communication sciences and disorders (Postbaccalaureate Certificate); communication sciences and disorders and education of the deaf (Certificate); deaf education (MS); speech language pathology (MS). *Accreditation:* ASHA (one or more programs are accredited). Part-time programs available. *Degree requirements:* For master's, thesis optional, written and oral comprehensive exams; for doctorate, comprehensive exam, thesis/dissertation optional, externship, 1 year full time clinical practicum, 3rd year spent in Boise. *Entrance requirements:* For master's, GRE General Test, minimum GPA of 3.0, 3 letters of recommendation; for doctorate, GRE General Test (at least 2 scores minimum 40th percentile), minimum GPA of 3.0, 3 letters of recommendation, bachelor's degree. Additional exam requirements/recommendations for international students: Required—TOEFL (minimum score 600 paper-based; 250 computer-based; 80 iBT). Electronic applications accepted. *Faculty research:* Neurogenic disorders, central auditory processing disorders, vestibular disorders, cochlear implants, language disorders, professional burnout, swallowing disorders.

Illinois State University, Graduate School, College of Education, Department of Special Education, Normal, IL 61790-2200. Offers MS, MS Ed, Ed D. *Accreditation:* NCATE. *Degree requirements:* For doctorate, thesis/dissertation, 2 terms of residency. *Entrance requirements:* For master's, GRE General Test, minimum GPA of 3.0 in last 60 hours; for doctorate, GRE General Test. *Faculty research:* Center for adult learning leadership, promoting a learning community, autism spectrum professional development and technical assistance project, preparing qualified personnel to provide early intervention for children who are deaf.

Immaculata University, College of Graduate Studies, Program in Educational Leadership and Administration, Immaculata, PA 19345. Offers educational leadership and administration (MA, Ed D); elementary education (Certificate); school principal (Certificate); school superintendent (Certificate); secondary education (Certificate); special education (Certificate). Part-time and evening/weekend programs available. *Degree requirements:* For master's, comprehensive exam, thesis optional; for doctorate, comprehensive exam, thesis/dissertation. *Entrance requirements:* For master's, GRE or MAT, minimum GPA of 3.0; for doctorate, GRE General Test or MAT, minimum GPA of 3.5. Additional exam requirements/recommendations for international students: Required—TOEFL. Electronic applications accepted. *Faculty research:* Cooperative learning, school-based management, whole language, performance assessment.

Indiana University Bloomington, School of Education, Department of Curriculum and Instruction, Bloomington, IN 47405-7000. Offers art education (MS, Ed D, PhD); curriculum studies (Ed D, PhD); elementary education (MS, Ed D, PhD, Ed S); mathematics education (MS, Ed D, PhD); science education (MS, Ed D, PhD); secondary education (MS, Ed D, PhD); social studies education (MS, PhD); special education (PhD, Ed S). *Accreditation:* NCATE. Part-time and evening/weekend programs available. Terminal master's awarded for partial completion of doctoral program. *Degree requirements:* For doctorate, thesis/dissertation; for Ed S, comprehensive exam or project. *Entrance requirements:* For master's, doctorate, and Ed S, GRE General Test. Electronic applications accepted.

Indiana University of Pennsylvania, School of Graduate Studies and Research, College of Education and Educational Technology, Department of Special Education and Clinical Services, Program in Education of Exceptional Persons, Indiana, PA 15705-1087. Offers M Ed. *Accreditation:* NCATE. *Faculty:* 8 full-time (7 women), 3 part-time/adjunct (2 women). *Students:* 6 full-time (5 women), 20 part-time (19 women). Average age 29. 34 applicants, 62% accepted, 17 enrolled. In 2011, 6 master's awarded. *Degree requirements:* For master's, comprehensive exam, thesis optional. *Entrance requirements:* For master's, 2 letters of recommendation. Additional exam requirements/recommendations for international students: Required—TOEFL (minimum score 540 paper-based; 207 computer-based). *Application deadline:* For fall admission, 3/1 priority date for domestic students; for spring admission, 7/1 for domestic students. Applications are processed on a rolling basis. Application fee: $40. Electronic applications accepted. *Expenses:* Tuition, state resident: full-time $7488; part-time $416 per credit. Tuition, nonresident: full-time $11,232; part-time $624 per credit. *Required fees:* $2070; $192.20 per credit. $90 per semester. *Financial support:* In 2011–12, 5 research assistantships with full and partial tuition reimbursements (averaging $3,234 per year) were awarded; career-related internships or fieldwork and Federal Work-Study also available. Support available to part-time students. Financial award application deadline: 4/15; financial award applicants required to submit FAFSA. *Unit head:* Dr. Joann M. Migyanka, Graduate Coordinator, 724-357-5679, E-mail: j.migyanka@iup.edu. *Application contact:* Dr. Edward Nardi, Interim Associate Dean, 724-357-2480, Fax: 724-357-5595, E-mail: ewnardi@iup.edu. Web site: http://www.iup.edu/grad/edex/default.aspx.

Indiana University–Purdue University Fort Wayne, College of Education and Public Policy, Department of Professional Studies, Fort Wayne, IN 46805-1499. Offers counselor education (MS Ed); educational leadership (MS Ed); marriage and family therapy (MS Ed); school counseling (MS Ed); special education (MS Ed, Certificate). Part-time programs available. *Faculty:* 6 full-time (5 women), 1 (woman) part-time/adjunct. *Students:* 2 full-time (1 woman), 158 part-time (124 women); includes 19 minority (11 Black or African American, non-Hispanic/Latino; 6 Hispanic/Latino; 2 Two or more races, non-Hispanic/Latino), 1 international. Average age 33. 59 applicants, 56% accepted, 32 enrolled. In 2011, 56 master's awarded. *Degree requirements:* For master's, comprehensive exam, practicum, internship, portfolio. *Entrance requirements:* For master's, minimum GPA of 2.5, three professional letters of recommendation. Additional exam requirements/recommendations for international students: Required—TOEFL (minimum score 550 paper-based; 213 computer-based; 77 iBT). *Application deadline:* For fall admission, 4/1 priority date for domestic students, 4/1 for international students. Applications are processed on a rolling basis. Application fee: $55. *Financial support:* Research assistantships, teaching assistantships, and scholarships/grants available. Support available to part-time students. Financial award application deadline: 3/1; financial award applicants required to submit FAFSA. *Faculty research:* Improving education with stronger collaborations. *Unit head:* Dr. James Burg, Interim Chair, 260-481-5406, Fax: 260-481-5408, E-mail: burgj@ipfw.edu. *Application contact:* Vicky L. Schmidt, Graduate Recorder, 260-481-6450, Fax: 260-481-5408, E-mail: schmidt@ipfw.edu. Web site: http://www.ipfw.edu/education.

Indiana University–Purdue University Indianapolis, School of Education, Indianapolis, IN 46202-2896. Offers computer education (Certificate); curriculum and instruction (MS); early childhood (MS); educational leadership (MS, Certificate); English as a second language (Certificate); higher education and student affairs (MS); kindergarten (Certificate); language education (MS); reading (Certificate); school counseling (MS); special education (MS, Certificate). Part-time and evening/weekend programs available. *Faculty:* 41 full-time, 80 part-time/adjunct. *Students:* 67 full-time (52 women), 467 part-time (360 women); includes 82 minority (44 Black or African American, non-Hispanic/Latino; 3 American Indian or Alaska Native, non-Hispanic/Latino; 8 Asian, non-Hispanic/Latino; 13 Hispanic/Latino; 14 Two or more races, non-Hispanic/Latino), 10 international. Average age 33. 63 applicants, 57% accepted, 29 enrolled. In 2011, 167 master's awarded. *Degree requirements:* For master's, thesis optional. *Entrance requirements:* For master's, GRE General Test, minimum GPA of 3.0. Additional exam requirements/recommendations for international students: Required—TOEFL. *Application deadline:* For fall admission, 5/1 priority date for domestic students; for spring admission, 11/1 for domestic students. Application fee: $55 ($65 for international students). *Financial support:* Fellowships, research assistantships with partial tuition reimbursements, teaching assistantships, Federal Work-Study, institutionally sponsored loans, scholarships/grants, and tuition waivers (partial) available. Support available to part-time students. *Faculty research:* Teachers in the process of change, learning cycles, children's concepts of science. *Total annual research expenditures:* $614,458. *Unit head:* Dr. Chris Leland, Interim Executive Associate Dean, 317-274-6801, Fax: 317-274-6864. *Application contact:* Sarah Brandenburg, Graduate Advisor, 317-274-6801, Fax: 317-274-6864, E-mail: edugrad@iupui.edu. Web site: http://education.iupui.edu/.

Indiana University South Bend, School of Education, South Bend, IN 46634-7111. Offers counseling and human services (MS Ed); elementary education (MS Ed); secondary education (MS Ed); special education (MS Ed). *Accreditation:* NCATE. Part-time and evening/weekend programs available. *Faculty:* 21 full-time (11 women), 9 part-time/adjunct (3 women). *Students:* 70 full-time (45 women), 262 part-time (206 women); includes 39 minority (15 Black or African American, non-Hispanic/Latino; 3 American Indian or Alaska Native, non-Hispanic/Latino; 5 Asian, non-Hispanic/Latino; 14 Hispanic/Latino; 2 Two or more races, non-Hispanic/Latino), 15 international. Average age 36. 52 applicants, 75% accepted, 28 enrolled. In 2011, 75 master's awarded. *Degree requirements:* For master's, thesis or alternative, exit project. *Entrance requirements:* For master's, letters of recommendation, GRE or minimum GPA of 3.0. Additional exam requirements/recommendations for international students: Required—TOEFL. *Application deadline:* For fall admission, 7/1 for domestic students; for spring admission, 11/1 for domestic students. Applications are processed on a rolling basis. Application fee: $50 ($60 for international students). Electronic applications accepted. *Financial support:* Career-related internships or fieldwork available. Support available to part-time students. Financial award application deadline: 3/1; financial award applicants required to submit FAFSA. *Faculty research:* Professional dispositions, early childhood literacy, online learning, program assessments, problem-based learning. *Unit head:* Dr. Michael Horvath, Professor/Dean, 574-520-4339, Fax: 574-520-4550. *Application contact:* Dr. Todd Norris, Director of Education Student Services, 574-520-4845, E-mail: toanorri@iusb.edu. Web site: http://www.iusb.edu/~edud/.

Inter American University of Puerto Rico, Barranquitas Campus, Program in Education, Barranquitas, PR 00794. Offers curriculum and teaching (M Ed), including biology education, English as a second language, history education, mathematics education, Spanish; educational leadership and management (MA); elementary education (M Ed); information and library service technology (M Ed); special education (MA). *Degree requirements:* For master's, comprehensive exam, thesis optional. *Entrance requirements:* For master's, EXADEP, letter of recommendation. Electronic applications accepted.

Inter American University of Puerto Rico, Metropolitan Campus, Graduate Programs, Program in Special Education, San Juan, PR 00919-1293. Offers MA. *Degree requirements:* For master's, comprehensive exam. *Entrance requirements:* For master's, GRE or EXADEP, interview. Electronic applications accepted.

Inter American University of Puerto Rico, San Germán Campus, Graduate Studies Center, Program in Special Education, San Germán, PR 00683-5008. Offers MA. Part-time and evening/weekend programs available. *Degree requirements:* For master's, comprehensive exam. *Entrance requirements:* For master's, GRE General Test or EXADEP, minimum GPA of 3.0. *Application deadline:* For fall admission, 4/30 priority date for domestic students; for spring admission, 11/15 for domestic students. Applications are processed on a rolling basis. Application fee: $31. *Expenses: Required fees:* $213 per semester. *Financial support:* Teaching assistantships available. *Unit head:* Dr. Elba T. Irizarry, Director of Graduate Studies Center, 787-264-1912 Ext. 7357, Fax: 787-892-6350, E-mail: elbat@sg.inter.edu.

Iona College, School of Arts and Science, Program in Education, New Rochelle, NY 10801-1890. Offers adolescence education: biology (MS Ed, MST); adolescence education: English (MS Ed, MST); adolescence education: Italian (MS Ed, MST); adolescence education: mathematics (MS Ed, MST); adolescence education: social studies (MS Ed, MST); adolescence education: Spanish (MS Ed, MST); adolescence special education 5-12 (MST); adolescence special education/literacy 5-12 (MS Ed); childhood 1-6/special education 1-6 (MST); childhood education (MST); early childhood/childhood (MST); educational leadership (MS Ed); literacy birth-grade 6/special education 1-6 (MS Ed); literacy education: birth-grade 6 (MS Ed). *Accreditation:* NCATE. Part-time and evening/weekend programs available. *Faculty:* 21 full-time (13 women), 13 part-time/adjunct (8 women). *Students:* 59 full-time (45 women), 101 part-time (78 women); includes 11 minority (2 Black or African American, non-Hispanic/Latino; 2 Asian, non-Hispanic/Latino; 7 Hispanic/Latino). Average age 26. 74 applicants, 66% accepted, 35 enrolled. In 2011, 46 master's awarded. *Degree requirements:* For master's, thesis or alternative. *Entrance requirements:* For master's, minimum GPA of 2.5 (MST), New York teaching certificate (MS Ed). Additional exam requirements/recommendations for international students: Required—TOEFL (minimum score 550 paper-based; 213 computer-based). *Application deadline:* Applications are processed on a rolling basis. Application fee: $50. Electronic applications accepted. *Expenses: Tuition:* Part-time $872 per credit. *Required fees:* $225 per term. *Financial support:* Unspecified assistantships available. Support available to part-time students. Financial award application deadline: 4/15; financial award applicants required to submit FAFSA. *Faculty research:* Reading/writing, educational technology, administration, early literacy assessment, literacy development. *Unit head:* Dr. Catherine O'Callaghan, Chair, 914-633-2210, Fax: 914-633-2608, E-mail: cocallaghan@iona.edu. *Application contact:* Dr. Jeanne Zaino, Interim Dean, School of Arts and Science, 914-633-2112, Fax: 914-633-2023, E-mail: jzaino@iona.edu.

Iowa State University of Science and Technology, Department of Curriculum and Instruction, Ames, IA 50011. Offers curriculum and instructional technology (M Ed, MS, PhD); elementary education (M Ed, MS); historical, philosophical, and comparative studies in education (M Ed, MS); special education (M Ed, MS, PhD). *Degree requirements:* For master's, thesis or alternative; for doctorate, thesis/dissertation. *Entrance requirements:* For master's and doctorate, GRE General Test. Additional exam requirements/recommendations for international students: Required—TOEFL (minimum score 560 paper-based; 83 iBT), IELTS (minimum score 6.5). *Application deadline:* For fall admission, 1/1 priority date for domestic students, 1/1 for international students; for spring admission, 9/1 for domestic and international students. Application fee: $40 ($90 for international students). Electronic applications accepted. *Unit head:* Dr. Anne Foegen, Director of Graduate Education, 515-294-7021, Fax: 515-294-6206, E-mail: cigrad@iastate.edu. *Application contact:* Phyllis Kendall, Director of Graduate Education, 515-294-7021, Fax: 515-294-6206, E-mail: cigrad@iastate.edu. Web site: http://www.ci.hs.iastate.edu.

Jackson State University, Graduate School, College of Education and Human Development, Department of Special Education and Rehabilitative Services, Jackson, MS 39217. Offers special education (MS Ed, Ed S). *Accreditation:* NCATE. Evening/weekend programs available. *Degree requirements:* For master's, comprehensive exam, thesis or alternative. *Entrance requirements:* For master's, GRE General Test. Additional exam requirements/recommendations for international students: Required—TOEFL (minimum score 520 paper-based; 195 computer-based; 67 iBT).

Jacksonville State University, College of Graduate Studies and Continuing Education, College of Education and Professional Studies, Program in Special Education, Jacksonville, AL 36265-1602. Offers MS Ed. *Accreditation:* NCATE. *Degree requirements:* For master's, comprehensive exam, thesis (for some programs). *Entrance requirements:* For master's, GRE General Test or MAT. Electronic applications accepted. *Expenses:* Tuition, state resident: part-time $336 per hour. Tuition, nonresident: part-time $672 per hour. Part-time tuition and fees vary according to degree level.

James Madison University, The Graduate School, College of Education, Exceptional Education Department, Program in Exceptional Education, Harrisonburg, VA 22807. Offers M Ed. *Accreditation:* NCATE. Part-time programs available. *Students:* 23 full-time (22 women), 12 part-time (10 women); includes 2 minority (1 Black or African American, non-Hispanic/Latino; 1 Hispanic/Latino). Average age 27. In 2011, 27 master's awarded. *Entrance requirements:* For master's, GRE General Test or PRAXIS, minimum undergraduate GPA of 2.75, resume. Additional exam requirements/recommendations for international students: Required—TOEFL. *Application deadline:* For fall admission, 5/1 priority date for domestic students; for spring admission, 9/1 priority date for domestic students. Applications are processed on a rolling basis. Application fee: $55. Electronic applications accepted. *Expenses:* Tuition, state resident: full-time $8016; part-time $334 per credit hour. Tuition, nonresident: full-time $22,656; part-time $944 per credit hour. *Financial support:* In 2011–12, 5 students received support. Federal Work-Study, unspecified assistantships, and 5 graduate assistantships ($7382) available. Financial award application deadline: 3/1; financial award applicants required to submit FAFSA. *Unit head:* Dr. Laura Desportes, Academic Unit Head, 540-568-6193. *Application contact:* Lynette M. Bible, Director of Graduate Admissions, 540-568-6395, Fax: 540-568-7860, E-mail: biblelm@jmu.edu.

The Johns Hopkins University, School of Education, Department of Special Education, Baltimore, MD 21218. Offers advanced methods for differentiated instruction and inclusive education (Certificate); assistive technology (Certificate); early intervention/preschool special education specialist (Certificate); education of students with autism and other pervasive developmental disorders (Certificate); education of students with severe disabilities (Certificate); special education (MS, Ed D, CAGS), including early childhood special education (MS), general special education studies (MS), mild to moderate disabilities (MS), severe disabilities (MS), technology in special education (MS). *Accreditation:* NCATE. Part-time and evening/weekend programs available. Postbaccalaureate distance learning degree programs offered (minimal on-campus study). *Degree requirements:* For master's, internships, professional portfolio, and PRAXIS II (for licensure); for doctorate, comprehensive exam, thesis/dissertation. *Entrance requirements:* For master's, PRAXIS I, SAT, ACT, or GRE, minimum undergraduate GPA of 3.0, 2 letters of recommendation (for cohort programs); for doctorate, GRE, degree in special education (or related field); minimum GPA of 3.0 in all prior academic work; 3 letters of recommendation; curriculum vitae/resume; professional experience; for other advanced degree, minimum undergraduate GPA of 3.0, master's degree (for CAGS). Additional exam requirements/recommendations for international students: Required—TOEFL (minimum score 600 paper-based; 250 computer-based; 100 iBT). Electronic applications accepted. *Faculty research:* Alternative licensure programs for special educators, collaborative programming, data-based decision-making and knowledge management as keys to school reform, parent training, natural environment teaching (NET).

Johnson & Wales University, The Alan Shawn Feinstein Graduate School, MAT Program in Teacher Education, Providence, RI 02903-3703. Offers business education and secondary special education (MAT); elementary education and elementary special education (MAT); elementary education and elementary/secondary special education (MAT); elementary education and secondary special education (MAT); food service education (MAT). Part-time and evening/weekend programs available. *Entrance requirements:* For master's, MAT, minimum GPA of 2.75. Additional exam requirements/recommendations for international students: Required—TOEFL (minimum score 550 paper-based; 210 computer-based) or IELTS (recommended). *Faculty research:* Secondary education, student teaching, educational reform, evaluation procedures.

Johnson State College, Graduate Program in Education, Program in Applied Behavior Analysis, Johnson, VT 05656. Offers applied behavior analysis (MA Ed); autism (MA Ed); children's mental health (MA Ed). *Degree requirements:* For master's, internships. *Entrance requirements:* Additional exam requirements/recommendations for international students: Required—TOEFL. *Application deadline:* For fall admission, 7/1 priority date for domestic students, 4/15 for international students; for winter admission, 11/1 priority date for domestic students; for spring admission, 4/1 priority date for domestic students, 8/15 for international students. Applications are processed on a rolling basis. Application fee: $35. *Expenses: Tuition, area resident:* Part-time $459 per credit hour. Tuition, nonresident: part-time $990 per credit hour. *Application contact:* Catherine H. Higley, Administrative Assistant, 800-635-2356 Ext. 1244, Fax: 802-635-1248, E-mail: catherine.higley@jsc.edu.

Johnson State College, Graduate Program in Education, Program in Special Education, Johnson, VT 05656. Offers MA Ed. Part-time programs available. *Degree requirements:* For master's, comprehensive exam, thesis or alternative. *Entrance requirements:* For master's, interview. Additional exam requirements/recommendations for international students: Required—TOEFL. *Application deadline:* For fall admission, 7/15 priority date for domestic students, 4/15 for international students; for spring admission, 11/1 priority date for domestic students, 8/15 for international students. Applications are processed on a rolling basis. Application fee: $35. *Expenses: Tuition, area resident:* Part-time $459 per credit hour. Tuition, nonresident: part-time $990 per credit hour. *Financial support:* Career-related internships or fieldwork, Federal Work-Study, and institutionally sponsored loans available. Support available to part-time students. Financial award application deadline: 3/1; financial award applicants required to submit FAFSA. *Unit head:* Dr. Perry LaRoque, Program Coordinator, 800-635-2356, E-mail: perry.laroque@jsc.edu. *Application contact:* Catherine H. Higley, Administrative Assistant, 800-635-2356 Ext. 1244, Fax: 802-635-1248, E-mail: catherine.higley@jsc.edu.

Kansas State University, Graduate School, College of Education, Department of Special Education, Counseling and Student Affairs, Manhattan, KS 66506. Offers academic advising (MS); counseling and student development (MS, Ed D, PhD), including college student development (MS), counselor education and supervision (PhD), school counseling (MS), student affairs in higher education (PhD); special education (MS, Ed D). *Accreditation:* ACA; NCATE. Part-time programs available. *Faculty:* 8 full-time (4 women), 4 part-time/adjunct (1 woman). *Students:* 87 full-time (64 women), 323 part-time (251 women); includes 62 minority (27 Black or African American, non-Hispanic/Latino; 4 American Indian or Alaska Native, non-Hispanic/Latino; 5 Asian, non-Hispanic/Latino; 19 Hispanic/Latino; 2 Native Hawaiian or other Pacific Islander, non-Hispanic/Latino; 5 Two or more races, non-Hispanic/Latino), 4 international. Average age 34. 236 applicants, 70% accepted, 83 enrolled. In 2011, 111 master's, 2 doctorates awarded. *Degree requirements:* For master's, comprehensive exam; for doctorate, comprehensive exam, thesis/dissertation. *Entrance requirements:* For master's, minimum undergraduate GPA of 3.0; for doctorate, GRE General Test, minimum GPA of 3.0 in last 60 hours. Additional exam requirements/recommendations for international students: Required—TOEFL. *Application deadline:* For fall admission, 2/1 priority date for domestic students, 2/1 for international students; for spring admission, 8/1 priority date for domestic students, 8/1 for international students. Applications are processed on a rolling basis. Application fee: $40 ($55 for international students). Electronic applications accepted. *Financial support:* In 2011–12, 3 teaching assistantships (averaging $18,090 per year) were awarded; career-related internships or fieldwork, institutionally sponsored loans, and scholarships/grants also available. Financial award application deadline: 3/1; financial award applicants required to submit FAFSA. *Faculty research:* Counseling supervision, academic advising, career development, student development, universal design for learning, autism, learning disabilities. *Total annual research expenditures:* $2,678. *Unit head:* Kenneth Hughey, Head, 785-532-6445, Fax: 785-532-7304, E-mail: khughey@ksu.edu. *Application contact:* Dona Deam, Application Contact, 785-532-5595, Fax: 785-532-7304, E-mail: ddeam@ksu.edu. Web site: http://coe.ksu.edu/departments/secsa/index.htm.

Kaplan University, Davenport Campus, School of Teacher Education, Davenport, IA 52807-2095. Offers education (M Ed); secondary education (M Ed); teaching and learning (MA); teaching literacy and language: grades 6-12 (MA); teaching literacy and language: grades K-6 (MA); teaching mathematics: grades 6-8 (MA); teaching mathematics: grades 9-12 (MA); teaching mathematics: grades K-5 (MA); teaching science: grades 6-12 (MA); teaching science: grades K-6 (MA); teaching students with special needs (MA); teaching with technology (MA). Part-time and evening/weekend programs available. Postbaccalaureate distance learning degree programs offered (no on-campus study). *Entrance requirements:* Additional exam requirements/recommendations for international students: Required—TOEFL (minimum score 550 paper-based; 218 computer-based; 80 iBT).

Kean University, College of Education, Program in Special Education, Union, NJ 07083. Offers high incidence disabilities (MA); low incidence disabilities (MA). *Accreditation:* NCATE. *Faculty:* 11 full-time (all women). *Students:* 52 full-time (47 women), 273 part-time (234 women); includes 77 minority (30 Black or African American, non-Hispanic/Latino; 1 American Indian or Alaska Native, non-Hispanic/Latino; 7 Asian, non-Hispanic/Latino; 38 Hispanic/Latino; 1 Two or more races, non-Hispanic/Latino), 1 international. Average age 33. 124 applicants, 99% accepted, 98 enrolled. In 2011, 43 master's awarded. *Degree requirements:* For master's, comprehensive exam, thesis, portfolio, two semesters of advanced seminar. *Entrance requirements:* For master's, GRE General Test or MAT, minimum GPA of 3.0, teaching certificate, 2 letters of recommendation, interview, transcripts, writing sample. Additional exam requirements/recommendations for international students: Required—TOEFL (minimum score 79 iBT). *Application deadline:* For fall admission, 6/1 for domestic and international students; for spring admission, 12/1 for domestic and international students. Applications are processed on a rolling basis. Application fee: $75 ($150 for international students). Electronic applications accepted. *Expenses:* Tuition, state resident: full-time $11,302; part-time $550 per credit. Tuition, nonresident: full-time $15,318; part-time $674 per credit. *Required fees:* $2849; $130 per credit. Tuition and fees vary according to degree level. *Financial support:* In 2011–12, 1 research assistantship with full tuition reimbursement (averaging $3,263 per year) was awarded; unspecified assistantships also available. Financial award applicants required to submit FAFSA. *Unit head:* Dr. Beverly Kling, Program Coordinator, 908-737-3845, E-mail: bkling@kean.edu. *Application contact:* Ann-Marie Kay, Assistant Director of Graduate Admissions, 908-737-5922, Fax: 908-737-5925, E-mail: akay@kean.edu. Web site: http://www.kean.edu/KU/Special-Education-High-Incidence-Disabilities.

Keene State College, School of Professional and Graduate Studies, Keene, NH 03435. Offers curriculum and instruction (M Ed); education leadership (PMC); educational leadership (M Ed); safety and occupational health applied science (MS); school counselor (M Ed, PMC); special education (M Ed); teacher certification (Postbaccalaureate Certificate). *Accreditation:* NCATE. Part-time and evening/weekend programs available. *Faculty:* 11 full-time (7 women), 15 part-time/adjunct (8 women). *Students:* 36 full-time (32 women), 69 part-time (54 women); includes 1 minority (American Indian or Alaska Native, non-Hispanic/Latino), 1 international. Average age 33. 48 applicants, 83% accepted, 32 enrolled. In 2011, 39 master's, 12 other advanced degrees awarded. *Entrance requirements:* For master's, PRAXIS I, resume; minimum GPA of 2.5. Additional exam requirements/recommendations for international students: Required—TOEFL (minimum score 550 paper-based; 173 computer-based; 61 iBT). *Application deadline:* For fall admission, 4/1 for domestic students; for spring admission, 12/1 for domestic students. Applications are processed on a rolling basis. Application fee: $50. Electronic applications accepted. *Expenses:* Tuition, state resident: part-time $420 per credit. Tuition, nonresident: part-time $460 per credit. Tuition and fees vary according to course load. *Financial support:* Research assistantships, career-related internships or fieldwork, Federal Work-Study, institutionally sponsored loans, and unspecified assistantships available. Support available to part-time students. Financial award application deadline: 3/1; financial award applicants required to submit FAFSA. *Unit head:* Dr. Melinda Treadwell, Dean, 603-358-2220, E-mail: mtreadwe@keene.edu. *Application contact:* Peggy Richmond, Director of Admissions, 603-358-2276, Fax: 603-358-2767, E-mail: admissions@keene.edu. Web site: http://www.keene.edu/ps/.

Kennesaw State University, Leland and Clarice C. Bagwell College of Education, Program in Graduate Education, Kennesaw, GA 30144-5591. Offers adolescent education (M Ed); educational leadership (M Ed); educational leadership technology (M Ed); elementary and early childhood education (M Ed); special education (M Ed); teaching English to speakers of other languages (M Ed). *Accreditation:* NCATE. Part-time programs available. *Students:* 42 full-time (39 women), 132 part-time (105 women); includes 31 minority (20 Black or African American, non-Hispanic/Latino; 4 Asian, non-Hispanic/Latino; 5 Hispanic/Latino; 2 Two or more races, non-Hispanic/Latino). Average age 34. 48 applicants, 79% accepted, 38 enrolled. In 2011, 117 master's awarded. *Degree requirements:* For master's, thesis or alternative. *Entrance requirements:* For master's, GRE General Test, T-4 state certification, minimum GPA of 2.75. Additional exam requirements/recommendations for international students: Required—TOEFL (minimum score 550 paper-based; 213 computer-based; 80 iBT), IELTS (minimum score 6). *Application deadline:* For fall admission, 7/1 for domestic and international students; for spring admission, 10/1 for domestic and international students. Application fee: $60. Electronic applications accepted. *Expenses:* Tuition, state resident: full-time $3000; part-time $250 per semester hour. Tuition, nonresident: full-time $10,836; part-time $903 per semester hour. *Required fees:* $774 per semester. *Financial support:* Federal Work-Study and unspecified assistantships available. Support available to part-time students. Financial award application deadline: 4/1; financial award applicants required to submit FAFSA. *Unit head:* Dr. Nita Paris, Associate Dean for Graduate Programs, 770-423-6636, E-mail: nparis@kennesaw.edu. *Application contact:* Alisha Bello, Administrative Coordinator, 770-423-6043, Fax: 770-420-4435, E-mail: abello1@kennesaw.edu. Web site: http://www.kennesaw.edu/education/grad/.

Kent State University, Graduate School of Education, Health, and Human Services, School of Lifespan Development and Educational Sciences, Program in Special Education, Kent, OH 44242-0001. Offers deaf education (M Ed); general special education (M Ed); gifted education (M Ed); mild/moderate intervention (M Ed); moderate/intensive intervention (M Ed); special education (PhD, Ed S). *Accreditation:* NCATE. *Faculty:* 24 full-time (18 women), 21 part-time/adjunct (20 women). *Students:* 96 full-time (76 women), 81 part-time (64 women); includes 8 minority (5 Black or African American, non-Hispanic/Latino; 2 Asian, non-Hispanic/Latino; 1 Hispanic/Latino). 66 applicants, 56% accepted. In 2011, 48 master's, 3 doctorates awarded. *Degree requirements:* For doctorate, comprehensive exam, thesis/dissertation. *Entrance requirements:* For master's, minimum undergraduate GPA of 2.75, moral character form, 2 letters of reference, goals statement; for doctorate and Ed S, GRE General Test, goals statement, 2 letter of reference, interview, resume. Additional exam requirements/recommendations for international students: Required—TOEFL (minimum score 550 paper-based; 213 computer-based; 80 iBT). *Application deadline:* Applications are processed on a rolling basis. Application fee: $30 ($60 for international students). Electronic applications accepted. *Expenses:* Tuition, state resident: full-time $8136; part-time $452 per credit hour. Tuition, nonresident: full-time $14,292; part-time $794 per credit hour. *Financial support:* In 2011–12, 1 fellowship with full tuition reimbursement (averaging $12,000 per year), 4 research assistantships with full tuition reimbursements (averaging $9,375 per year) were awarded; teaching assistantships with full tuition reimbursements, career-related internships or fieldwork, Federal Work-Study, institutionally sponsored loans, scholarships/grants, health care benefits, unspecified assistantships, and 5 administrative assistantships (averaging $10,600 per year) also available. Support available to part-time students. Financial award application deadline: 4/1; financial award applicants required to submit FAFSA. *Faculty research:* Social/emotional needs of gifted, inclusion transition services, early intervention/ecobehavioral assessments, applied behavioral analysis. *Unit head:* Lyle Barton, Coordinator, 330-672-0578, E-mail: lbarton@kent.edu. *Application contact:* Nancy Miller, Academic Program Coordinator, Office of Graduate Student Services, 330-672-2576, Fax: 330-672-9162, E-mail: ogs@kent.edu. Web site: http://www.kent.edu/ehhs/sped/.

Kentucky State University, College of Professional Studies, Frankfort, KY 40601. Offers public administration (MPA), including human resource management, international development, management information systems, nonprofit management; special education (MA). Part-time and evening/weekend programs available. Postbaccalaureate distance learning degree programs offered (minimal on-campus study). *Faculty:* 12 full-time (4 women), 2 part-time/adjunct (both women). *Students:* 88 full-time (57 women), 79 part-time (42 women); includes 104 minority (101 Black or African American, non-Hispanic/Latino; 1 Asian, non-Hispanic/Latino; 2 Hispanic/Latino), 2 international. Average age 34. 124 applicants, 62% accepted, 45 enrolled. In 2011, 38 master's awarded. *Degree requirements:* For master's, comprehensive exam, thesis optional. *Entrance requirements:* For master's, GMAT, GRE. Additional exam requirements/recommendations for international students: Required—TOEFL (minimum score 525 paper-based; 173 computer-based). *Application deadline:* Applications are processed on a rolling basis. Application fee: $30 ($100 for international students). Electronic applications accepted. *Expenses:* Tuition, state resident: full-time $6192; part-time $344 per credit hour. Tuition, nonresident: full-time $9522; part-time $529 per credit hour. *Required fees:* $450; $25 per credit hour. Tuition and fees vary according to course load. *Financial support:* In 2011–12, 46 students received support, including 4 research assistantships (averaging $10,975 per year); career-related internships or fieldwork, scholarships/grants, tuition waivers (partial), and unspecified assistantships also available. Financial award application deadline: 4/15; financial award applicants required to submit FAFSA. *Unit head:* Dr. Gashaw Lake, Dean, 502-597-6105, Fax: 502-597-6715, E-mail: gashaw.lake@kysu.edu. *Application contact:* Dr. Titilayo Ufomata, Acting Director of Graduate Studies, 502-597-6443, E-mail: titilayo.ufomata@kysu.edu. Web site: http://www.kysu.edu/academics/collegesAndSchools/collegeofprofessionalstudies/.

Lamar University, College of Graduate Studies, College of Education and Human Development, Department of Counseling and Special Populations, Beaumont, TX 77710. Offers counseling and development (M Ed); school counseling (M Ed); special education (M Ed); student affairs (Certificate). *Faculty:* 7 full-time (5 women). *Students:* 9 full-time (5 women), 654 part-time (619 women); includes 239 minority (140 Black or African American, non-Hispanic/Latino; 8 American Indian or Alaska Native, non-Hispanic/Latino; 8 Asian, non-Hispanic/Latino; 83 Hispanic/Latino). Average age 36. 525 applicants, 96% accepted, 201 enrolled. In 2011, 15 master's awarded. *Application deadline:* For fall admission, 8/1 for domestic students; for spring admission, 12/1 for domestic students. Applications are processed on a rolling basis. Application fee: $25 ($50 for international students). *Expenses:* Tuition, state resident: full-time $5430; part-time $272 per credit hour. Tuition, nonresident: full-time $11,540; part-time $577 per credit hour. *Required fees:* $1916. *Unit head:* Dr. Carl J. Sheperis, Chair, 409-880-8978, Fax: 409-880-2263. *Application contact:* Dr. Lula Henry, Director of Professional Service, 409-880-8218. Web site: http://dept.lamar.edu/counseling/.

Lamar University, College of Graduate Studies, College of Fine Arts and Communication, Department of Deaf Studies and Deaf Education, Beaumont, TX 77710. Offers MS, Ed D. *Accreditation:* ASHA. Part-time and evening/weekend programs available. *Faculty:* 5 full-time (4 women). *Students:* 26 full-time (19 women),

18 part-time (8 women); includes 4 minority (2 Black or African American, non-Hispanic/Latino; 2 Hispanic/Latino), 3 international. Average age 36. 12 applicants, 100% accepted, 8 enrolled. In 2011, 8 master's, 2 doctorates awarded. *Degree requirements:* For master's, thesis optional; for doctorate, thesis/dissertation. *Entrance requirements:* For master's, GRE General Test, performance IQ score of 115 (for deaf students), minimum GPA of 2.5; for doctorate, GRE General Test, performance IQ score of 115 (for deaf students). Additional exam requirements/recommendations for international students: Required—TOEFL. *Application deadline:* For fall admission, 8/1 priority date for domestic students; for spring admission, 12/1 for domestic students. Applications are processed on a rolling basis. Application fee: $25 ($50 for international students). *Expenses:* Tuition, state resident: full-time $5430; part-time $272 per credit hour. Tuition, nonresident: full-time $11,540; part-time $577 per credit hour. *Required fees:* $1916. *Financial support:* In 2011–12, 43 fellowships were awarded; research assistantships also available. Financial award application deadline: 4/1. *Faculty research:* Multicultural and deaf teacher training, central auditory processing, voice sign language. *Unit head:* Dr. Gabriel A. Martin, Chair, 409-880-8175, Fax: 409-880-2265. *Application contact:* Debbie Piper, Coordinator of Graduate Admissions, 409-880-8356, Fax: 409-880-8414, E-mail: gradmissions@hal.lamar.edu.

Lancaster Bible College, Graduate School, Lancaster, PA 17601-5036. Offers adult ministries (MA); Bible (MA); children and family ministry (MA); consulting resource teacher (M Ed); elementary school counseling (M Ed); leadership (PhD); leadership studies (MA); marriage and family counseling (MA); mental health counseling (MA); pastoral studies (MA); secondary school counseling (M Ed); student ministry (MA). Part-time and evening/weekend programs available. *Degree requirements:* For master's, comprehensive exam (for some programs), thesis (for some programs). *Entrance requirements:* For master's, bachelor's degree with a minimum of 30 credits of course work in Bible, minimum undergraduate GPA of 3.0, interview. Additional exam requirements/recommendations for international students: Required—TOEFL.

Lasell College, Graduate and Professional Studies in Education, Newton, MA 02466-2709. Offers elementary education - grades 1-6 (M Ed); special education: moderate disabilities (pre-K-8) (M Ed). Part-time and evening/weekend programs available. Postbaccalaureate distance learning degree programs offered. *Faculty:* 2 full-time (both women). *Students:* 9 part-time (8 women); includes 2 minority (1 Black or African American, non-Hispanic/Latino; 1 Hispanic/Latino). Average age 26. 12 applicants, 42% accepted, 5 enrolled. *Degree requirements:* For master's, 18 credits in licensure requirements for initial licensure; 12 in licensure requirements plus 6 credits selected with advisor and department approval for professional licensure. *Entrance requirements:* For master's, bachelor's degree from an accredited institution. Additional exam requirements/recommendations for international students: Required—TOEFL (minimum score 550 paper-based; 213 computer-based; 79 iBT), IELTS. *Application deadline:* For fall admission, 8/31 priority date for domestic students, 6/30 for international students; for spring admission, 12/31 priority date for domestic students, 10/31 for international students. Applications are processed on a rolling basis. Electronic applications accepted. *Expenses: Tuition:* Part-time $575 per credit. *Required fees:* $70 per semester. *Financial support:* Available to part-time students. Application deadline: 8/31; applicants required to submit FAFSA. *Unit head:* Dr. Joan Dolamore, Dean of Graduate and Professional Studies, 617-243-2485, Fax: 617-243-2450, E-mail: gradinfo@lasell.edu. *Application contact:* Adrienne Franciosi, Director of Graduate Admission, 617-243-2214, Fax: 617-243-2450, E-mail: gradinfo@lasell.edu. Web site: http://www.lasell.edu/Academics/Graduate-and-Professional-Studies/Master-of-Education.html.

Lee University, Program in Education, Cleveland, TN 37320-3450. Offers classroom teaching (M Ed, Ed S); educational leadership (M Ed, Ed S); elementary/secondary education (MAT); secondary education (MAT); special education (M Ed); special education (secondary) (MAT). Part-time programs available. *Faculty:* 14 full-time (6 women), 5 part-time/adjunct (3 women). *Students:* 43 full-time (27 women), 176 part-time (107 women); includes 19 minority (4 Black or African American, non-Hispanic/Latino; 3 American Indian or Alaska Native, non-Hispanic/Latino; 1 Asian, non-Hispanic/Latino; 8 Hispanic/Latino; 3 Two or more races, non-Hispanic/Latino), 4 international. Average age 33. 52 applicants, 100% accepted, 38 enrolled. In 2011, 90 master's, 14 other advanced degrees awarded. *Degree requirements:* For master's, variable foreign language requirement, comprehensive exam, thesis, internship. *Entrance requirements:* For master's, MAT or GRE General Test, minimum GPA of 2.75, 3 letters of recommendation, interview, writing sample. Additional exam requirements/recommendations for international students: Required—TOEFL (minimum score 450 paper-based; 45 computer-based). *Application deadline:* For fall admission, 4/1 priority date for domestic students; for spring admission, 10/1 priority date for domestic students. Applications are processed on a rolling basis. Application fee: $25. *Expenses: Tuition:* Full-time $12,120; part-time $506 per credit hour. *Required fees:* $560; $305 per term. Part-time tuition and fees vary according to course load. *Financial support:* In 2011–12, 18 teaching assistantships (averaging $1,966 per year) were awarded; career-related internships or fieldwork, Federal Work-Study, institutionally sponsored loans, scholarships/grants, and unspecified assistantships also available. Financial award application deadline: 3/1; financial award applicants required to submit FAFSA. *Unit head:* Dr. Gary Riggins, Director, 423-614-8193. *Application contact:* Vicki Glasscock, Graduate Admissions Director, 423-614-8059, E-mail: vglasscock@leeuniversity.edu. Web site: http://www.leeuniversity.edu/academics/graduate/education.

Lehigh University, College of Education, Program in Comparative and International Education, Bethlehem, PA 18015. Offers comparative and international education (MA); globalization and educational change (M Ed); international counseling (Certificate); international development in education (Certificate); special education (Certificate); technology use in schools (Certificate); TESOL (Certificate). Part-time programs available. Postbaccalaureate distance learning degree programs offered (no on-campus study). *Faculty:* 4 full-time (2 women). *Students:* 25 full-time (10 women), 45 part-time (31 women); includes 5 minority (all Asian, non-Hispanic/Latino), 16 international. Average age 34. 45 applicants, 71% accepted, 12 enrolled. In 2011, 21 master's awarded. *Degree requirements:* For master's, thesis (MA). *Entrance requirements:* For master's, 2 letters of recommendation. Additional exam requirements/recommendations for international students: Required—TOEFL (minimum score 600 paper-based; 250 computer-based; 93 iBT). *Application deadline:* For fall and spring admission, 2/1 for domestic and international students. Application fee: $65. Electronic applications accepted. *Financial support:* In 2011–12, 8 students received support, including 3 research assistantships with full and partial tuition reimbursements available (averaging $13,000 per year). Financial award application deadline: 3/15. *Faculty research:* Comparative education, rural education, gender equity in education, post-socialist education transformation, educational borrowing, comparing education systems, education policy an globalization, family-school relationships, China, international testing, social inequities. *Unit head:* Dr. Iveta Silova, Program Director and Associate Professor, 610-758-5750, Fax: 610-758-6223, E-mail: ism207@lehigh.edu. *Application contact:* Donna M. Johnson, Coordinator, 610-758-3231, Fax: 610-758-6223, E-mail: dmj4@lehigh.edu. Web site: http://www.lehigh.edu/education/cie.

Lehigh University, College of Education, Program in Educational Leadership, Bethlehem, PA 18015. Offers educational leadership (M Ed, Ed D); principal certification K-12 (Certificate); pupil services (Certificate); special education (Certificate); superintendent certification (Certificate); supervisor of curriculum and instruction (Certificate); supervisor of pupil services (Certificate); MBA/M Ed. Part-time and evening/weekend programs available. Postbaccalaureate distance learning degree programs offered (minimal on-campus study). *Faculty:* 7 full-time (2 women), 8 part-time/adjunct (6 women). *Students:* 4 full-time (all women), 149 part-time (68 women); includes 6 minority (2 Black or African American, non-Hispanic/Latino; 2 Asian, non-Hispanic/Latino; 2 Hispanic/Latino), 19 international. Average age 38. 61 applicants, 52% accepted, 4 enrolled. In 2011, 36 master's, 5 doctorates awarded. *Degree requirements:* For doctorate, comprehensive exam, thesis/dissertation. *Entrance requirements:* For master's and Certificate, minimum undergraduate GPA of 3.0; for doctorate, GRE General Test or MAT, minimum graduate GPA of 3.6, 2 letters of recommendation, essay, transcript. Additional exam requirements/recommendations for international students: Required—TOEFL (minimum score 600 paper-based; 250 computer-based; 93 iBT). *Application deadline:* For fall admission, 1/15 for domestic and international students; for spring admission, 11/1 for domestic and international students. Applications are processed on a rolling basis. Application fee: $65. Electronic applications accepted. *Expenses:* Contact institution. *Financial support:* In 2011–12, 1 student received support, including 1 research assistantship with full and partial tuition reimbursement available (averaging $13,000 per year); fellowships with full and partial tuition reimbursements available, teaching assistantships with full and partial tuition reimbursements available, career-related internships or fieldwork, Federal Work-Study, institutionally sponsored loans, scholarships/grants, and tuition waivers (full and partial) also available. Financial award application deadline: 1/31. *Faculty research:* School finance and law, supervision of instruction, middle-level education, organizational change, leadership preparation and development, international school leadership, urban school leadership. *Unit head:* Dr. Floyd D. Beachum, Director, 610-758-5955, Fax: 610-758-3227, E-mail: fdb209@lehigh.edu. *Application contact:* Donna M. Johnson, Coordinator, 610-758-3231, Fax: 610-758-6223, E-mail: dmj4@lehigh.edu.

Lehigh University, College of Education, Program in Special Education, Bethlehem, PA 18015. Offers M Ed, PhD, Certificate. Part-time and evening/weekend programs available. *Faculty:* 5 full-time (all women), 5 part-time/adjunct (4 women). *Students:* 15 full-time (11 women), 70 part-time (55 women); includes 7 minority (3 Black or African American, non-Hispanic/Latino; 2 Asian, non-Hispanic/Latino; 2 Hispanic/Latino), 2 international. Average age 29. 51 applicants, 76% accepted, 19 enrolled. In 2011, 19 master's, 2 doctorates awarded. *Degree requirements:* For doctorate, comprehensive exam, thesis/dissertation. *Entrance requirements:* For master's, minimum GPA of 3.0, 2 letters of recommendation (one academic), transcripts; for doctorate, GRE General Test, minimum GPA of 3.0, essay, 2 letters of recommendation (one academic), transcripts. Additional exam requirements/recommendations for international students: Required—TOEFL (minimum score 600 paper-based; 250 computer-based; 93 iBT). *Application deadline:* For fall admission, 2/1 for domestic and international students; for winter admission, 5/15 for domestic and international students. Application fee: $65. Electronic applications accepted. *Financial support:* In 2011–12, 23 students received support, including 7 research assistantships with full and partial tuition reimbursements available (averaging $16,000 per year); fellowships, career-related internships or fieldwork, Federal Work-Study, institutionally sponsored loans, scholarships/grants, tuition waivers (full and partial), unspecified assistantships, and field-based positions also available. Financial award application deadline: 1/31. *Faculty research:* Developmental disabilities, language, literacy, emotional and behavioral disorders. *Unit head:* Dr. Lee Kern, Coordinator, 610-758-3267, Fax: 610-758-6223, E-mail: lek6@lehigh.edu. *Application contact:* Sharon Y. Warden, Coordinator, 610-758-3256, Fax: 610-758-6223, E-mail: sy00@lehigh.edu.

Lehman College of the City University of New York, Division of Education, Department of Specialized Services in Education, Bronx, NY 10468-1589. Offers guidance and counseling (MS Ed); reading teacher (MS Ed); teachers of special education (MS Ed), including bilingual special education, early special education, emotional handicaps, learning disabilities, mental retardation. Part-time and evening/weekend programs available. *Faculty research:* Battered women, whole language classrooms, parent education, mainstreaming.

Lehman College of the City University of New York, Division of Education, Department of Specialized Services in Education, Teachers of Special Education Program, Option in Bilingual Special Education, Bronx, NY 10468-1589. Offers MS Ed. *Accreditation:* NCATE. *Entrance requirements:* For master's, minimum GPA of 3.0.

Lehman College of the City University of New York, Division of Education, Department of Specialized Services in Education, Teachers of Special Education Program, Option in Early Special Education, Bronx, NY 10468-1589. Offers MS Ed. *Accreditation:* NCATE. *Entrance requirements:* For master's, minimum GPA of 3.0.

Lehman College of the City University of New York, Division of Education, Department of Specialized Services in Education, Teachers of Special Education Program, Option in Emotional Handicaps, Bronx, NY 10468-1589. Offers MS Ed. *Accreditation:* NCATE. Part-time and evening/weekend programs available. *Entrance requirements:* For master's, minimum GPA of 2.7. *Faculty research:* Behavioral disorders, self-evaluation, applied behavior analysis.

Lehman College of the City University of New York, Division of Education, Department of Specialized Services in Education, Teachers of Special Education Program, Option in Learning Disabilities, Bronx, NY 10468-1589. Offers MS Ed. *Accreditation:* NCATE. Part-time and evening/weekend programs available. *Entrance requirements:* For master's, interview, minimum GPA of 2.7. *Faculty research:* Emergent literacy, language-based classrooms, primary and secondary social contexts of language and literacy, innovative in-service education models, adult literacy.

Lehman College of the City University of New York, Division of Education, Department of Specialized Services in Education, Teachers of Special Education Program, Option in Mental Retardation, Bronx, NY 10468-1589. Offers MS Ed. *Accreditation:* NCATE. Part-time and evening/weekend programs available. *Entrance requirements:* For master's, minimum GPA of 2.7. *Faculty research:* Conductive education, homeless infants and their families, infant stimulation, hospitalizing infants with AIDS, legislation PL99-457.

Le Moyne College, Department of Education, Syracuse, NY 13214. Offers adolescent education (MS Ed, MST); adolescent education/special education (MS Ed, MST); adolescent English (grades 7-12) (MST); adolescent history (grades 7-12) (MST); childhood education (MS Ed); childhood education/special education (MS Ed); elementary education (MS Ed); general professional education (MS Ed); inclusive childhood education (MST); literacy education (birth to grade 6) (MS Ed); literacy education (grades 5-12) (MS Ed); school building leadership (MS Ed, CAS); school district business leader (MS Ed, CAS); school district leadership (MS Ed, CAS); secondary education (MS Ed); special education (MS Ed); students with disabilities-generalist (grades 7-12) (MS Ed); TESOL (teaching English to speakers of other languages) (MS Ed); urban studies (MS Ed). *Accreditation:* Teacher Education Accreditation Council. Part-time and evening/weekend programs available. *Faculty:* 9 full-time (6 women), 51 part-time/adjunct (28 women). *Students:* 61 full-time (47 women), 311 part-time (222 women); includes 31 minority (19 Black or African

American, non-Hispanic/Latino; 3 American Indian or Alaska Native, non-Hispanic/Latino; 4 Asian, non-Hispanic/Latino; 5 Hispanic/Latino), 2 international. Average age 30. 242 applicants, 90% accepted, 180 enrolled. In 2011, 168 master's, 23 CASs awarded. *Degree requirements:* For master's, thesis. *Entrance requirements:* For master's, GRE General Test, bachelor's degree, 2 letters of recommendation, written statement, transcripts. Additional exam requirements/recommendations for international students: Required—TOEFL (minimum score 550 paper-based; 213 computer-based; 79 iBT). *Application deadline:* For fall admission, 4/1 priority date for domestic students, 4/1 for international students; for spring admission, 10/1 priority date for domestic students, 10/1 for international students. Applications are processed on a rolling basis. Application fee: $50. *Expenses:* Contact institution. *Financial support:* In 2011–12, 32 students received support. Career-related internships or fieldwork and health care benefits available. Support available to part-time students. Financial award applicants required to submit FAFSA. *Faculty research:* Minority teachers, special education, multiculturalism, literacy, technology, video games learning, autism, school district organization, service-learning, higher level problem solving, teacher leadership. *Unit head:* Dr. Suzanne L. Gilmour, Chair, Department of Education and Director of Graduate Education Programs, 315-445-4376, Fax: 315-445-4744, E-mail: gilmous@lemoyne.edu. *Application contact:* Kristen P. Trapasso, Director of Graduate Admission, 315-445-4265, Fax: 315-445-6027, E-mail: trapaskp@lemoyne.edu. Web site: http://www.lemoyne.edu/education.

Lesley University, School of Education, Cambridge, MA 02138-2790. Offers curriculum and instruction (M Ed, CAGS); early childhood education (M Ed); educational studies (PhD); elementary education (M Ed); individually designed (M Ed); middle school education (M Ed); moderate special needs (M Ed); reading (M Ed, CAGS); science in education (M Ed); severe special needs (M Ed); special needs (CAGS); technology in education (M Ed, CAGS). *Accreditation:* Teacher Education Accreditation Council. Part-time and evening/weekend programs available. Postbaccalaureate distance learning degree programs offered (no on-campus study). *Faculty:* 36 full-time (27 women), 170 part-time/adjunct (129 women). *Students:* 552 full-time (437 women), 1,971 part-time (1,697 women); includes 364 minority (189 Black or African American, non-Hispanic/Latino; 19 American Indian or Alaska Native, non-Hispanic/Latino; 45 Asian, non-Hispanic/Latino; 83 Hispanic/Latino; 2 Native Hawaiian or other Pacific Islander, non-Hispanic/Latino; 26 Two or more races, non-Hispanic/Latino), 28 international. Average age 37. In 2011, 1,390 master's, 8 doctorates, 42 other advanced degrees awarded. *Degree requirements:* For master's, practicum; for doctorate, thesis/dissertation. *Entrance requirements:* For doctorate, GRE General Test or MAT, interview, master's degree, resume; for CAGS, interview, master's degree. Additional exam requirements/recommendations for international students: Required—TOEFL (minimum score 550 paper-based; 213 computer-based; 80 iBT). *Application deadline:* Applications are processed on a rolling basis. Application fee: $50. Electronic applications accepted. *Financial support:* In 2011–12, research assistantships (averaging $3,400 per year), teaching assistantships (averaging $3,400 per year) were awarded; career-related internships or fieldwork, Federal Work-Study, scholarships/grants, and unspecified assistantships also available. Support available to part-time students. Financial award application deadline: 4/15; financial award applicants required to submit FAFSA. *Faculty research:* Assessment in literacy, mathematics and science; autism spectrum disorders; instructional technology and online learning; multicultural education and ELL. *Unit head:* Dr. Mario Borunda, Dean, 617-349-8375, Fax: 617-349-8607, E-mail: mborunda@lesley.edu. *Application contact:* Rosie Davis, Senior Assistant Director of Admissions, 617-349-8851, Fax: 617-349-8313, E-mail: rdavis4@lesley.edu. Web site: http://www.lesley.edu/soe.html.

Lewis & Clark College, Graduate School of Education and Counseling, Department of Teacher Education, Program in Special Education, Portland, OR 97219-7899. Offers M Ed. *Accreditation:* NCATE. Part-time and evening/weekend programs available. *Faculty:* 1 (woman) full-time, 2 part-time/adjunct (both women). *Students:* 3 full-time (all women), 21 part-time (17 women); includes 12 minority (1 Black or African American, non-Hispanic/Latino; 3 American Indian or Alaska Native, non-Hispanic/Latino; 4 Asian, non-Hispanic/Latino; 2 Hispanic/Latino; 2 Two or more races, non-Hispanic/Latino), 1 international. Average age 37. 11 applicants, 82% accepted, 8 enrolled. In 2011, 5 master's awarded. *Entrance requirements:* For master's, minimum GPA of 2.75. Additional exam requirements/recommendations for international students: Required—TOEFL (minimum score 575 paper-based; 233 computer-based). *Application deadline:* Applications are processed on a rolling basis. Application fee: $50. Electronic applications accepted. *Expenses: Tuition:* Part-time $738 per semester hour. Tuition and fees vary according to course level and campus/location. *Financial support:* In 2011–12, 1 student received support. Career-related internships or fieldwork, Federal Work-Study, institutionally sponsored loans, scholarships/grants, health care benefits, and tuition waivers (partial) available. Support available to part-time students. Financial award application deadline: 3/1; financial award applicants required to submit FAFSA. *Unit head:* Christine Moore, Program Coordinator, 503-768-6128, E-mail: cmoore@lclark.edu. *Application contact:* Becky Haas, Director of Admissions, 503-768-6200, Fax: 503-768-6205, E-mail: gseadmit@lclark.edu. Web site: http://graduate.lclark.edu/departments/teacher_education/current_teachers/masters_special_education/.

Lewis University, College of Education, Program in Special Education, Romeoville, IL 60446. Offers MA. *Students:* 37 full-time (26 women), 19 part-time (18 women); includes 10 minority (6 Black or African American, non-Hispanic/Latino; 1 Asian, non-Hispanic/Latino; 1 Hispanic/Latino; 2 Two or more races, non-Hispanic/Latino). Average age 32. In 2011, 22 master's awarded. *Entrance requirements:* For master's, departmental qualifying exam, writing exam, minimum GPA of 2.75, 2 letters of recommendation, interview. Additional exam requirements/recommendations for international students: Required—TOEFL (minimum score 550 paper-based; 213 computer-based; 80 iBT). *Application deadline:* For fall admission, 5/1 for international students; for spring admission, 11/15 for international students. Applications are processed on a rolling basis. Application fee: $40. Electronic applications accepted. *Financial support:* Federal Work-Study, scholarships/grants, and unspecified assistantships available. Financial award application deadline: 5/1; financial award applicants required to submit FAFSA. *Unit head:* Dr. Christy Roberts, Director, 815-838-0500 Ext. 5317, E-mail: robertch@lewisu.edu. *Application contact:* Kelly Lofgren, Graduate Admission Counselor, 815-838-5704, E-mail: lofgreke@lewisu.edu.

Liberty University, School of Education, Lynchburg, VA 24502. Offers administration and supervision (M Ed); curriculum and instruction (M Ed); early childhood education (M Ed); educational leadership (Ed D, Ed S); educational technology and online instruction (M Ed); elementary education (M Ed, MAT); gifted education (M Ed); math specialist (M Ed); middle grades (M Ed); outdoor adventure sport (MS); reading specialist (M Ed); school counseling (M Ed); secondary education (M Ed, MAT); special education (M Ed, MAT); sports administration (MS); teaching and learning (Ed D, Ed S). *Accreditation:* NCATE. Part-time programs available. Postbaccalaureate distance learning degree programs offered (minimal on-campus study). *Students:* 2,245 full-time (1,572 women), 3,500 part-time (2,558 women); includes 1,141 minority (888 Black or African American, non-Hispanic/Latino; 19 American Indian or Alaska Native, non-Hispanic/Latino; 21 Asian, non-Hispanic/Latino; 123 Hispanic/Latino; 9 Native Hawaiian or other Pacific Islander, non-Hispanic/Latino; 81 Two or more races, non-Hispanic/Latino), 76 international. Average age 37. In 2011, 760 master's, 48 doctorates, 321 other advanced degrees awarded. *Degree requirements:* For doctorate, comprehensive exam, thesis/dissertation. *Entrance requirements:* For master's, GRE General Test or MAT (if taken in or before 1999), 2 letters of recommendation, minimum undergraduate GPA of 3.0, curriculum vitae; for doctorate, GRE General Test or MAT (if taken before 1999), minimum master's GPA of 3.0, 3 years of teacher experience; for Ed S, GRE General Test or MAT (if taken before 1999), minimum master's GPA of 3.0, 3 years of teaching experience. Additional exam requirements/recommendations for international students: Required—TOEFL (minimum score 600 paper-based; 250 computer-based). *Application deadline:* For fall admission, 6/1 priority date for domestic students; for spring admission, 11/1 for domestic students. Applications are processed on a rolling basis. Application fee: $50. Electronic applications accepted. *Expenses:* Contact institution. *Financial support:* Federal Work-Study and tuition waivers (partial) available. *Faculty research:* Self-determination, character education, bibliotherapy, learning styles, distance education. *Unit head:* Dr. Karen L. Parker, Dean, 434-582-2195, Fax: 434-582-2468, E-mail: kparker@liberty.edu. *Application contact:* Jay Bridge, Director of Graduate Admissions, 800-424-9595, Fax: 800-628-7977, E-mail: gradadmissions@liberty.edu. Web site: http://www.liberty.edu/academics/education/graduate/.

Lincoln University, School of Graduate Studies and Continuing Education, Jefferson City, MO 65102. Offers business administration (MBA), including accounting, entrepreneurship, management, public administration and policy; educational leadership (Ed S), including elementary leadership, secondary leadership, superintendency; guidance and counseling (M Ed), including community/agency counseling, elementary school, secondary school; history (MA); school administration and supervision (M Ed), including elementary school administration, secondary school administration, special education administration; school teaching (M Ed), including elementary school teaching, secondary school teaching; social science (MA), including history, political science, sociology; sociology (MA); sociology/criminal justice (MA). Part-time and evening/weekend programs available. *Degree requirements:* For master's and Ed S, comprehensive exam, thesis optional. *Entrance requirements:* For master's and Ed S, GRE, MAT or GMAT, minimum GPA of 2.75 in major, 2.5 overall; 3 letters of recommendation; minimum C average in English composition; personal statement of purpose. Additional exam requirements/recommendations for international students: Required—TOEFL (minimum score 500 paper-based; 173 computer-based; 61 iBT). *Faculty research:* Suicide prevention.

Lipscomb University, Program in Education, Nashville, TN 37204-3951. Offers educational leadership (M Ed); English language learning (M Ed); instructional practice (M Ed); instructional technology (M Ed); learning organizations and strategic change (Ed D); math specialty (M Ed); special education (M Ed); teaching, learning, and leading (M Ed). *Accreditation:* NCATE. Part-time and evening/weekend programs available. *Faculty:* 18 full-time (10 women), 23 part-time/adjunct (16 women). *Students:* 377 full-time (281 women), 117 part-time (85 women); includes 55 minority (39 Black or African American, non-Hispanic/Latino; 4 American Indian or Alaska Native, non-Hispanic/Latino; 5 Asian, non-Hispanic/Latino; 7 Hispanic/Latino). Average age 32. 300 applicants, 66% accepted, 142 enrolled. In 2011, 190 master's awarded. *Degree requirements:* For master's, comprehensive exam, portfolio, research project and presentation; for doctorate, practical capstone project in experiential setting. *Entrance requirements:* For master's, MAT or GRE General Test, 2 reference letters, goals statement, writing sample, interview; for doctorate, MAT or GRE General Test, 3 reference letters, artifact of demonstrated academic excellence, written personal statements, interview. Additional exam requirements/recommendations for international students: Required—TOEFL (minimum score 570 paper-based; 230 computer-based). *Application deadline:* For fall admission, 8/29 priority date for domestic students; for spring admission, 1/15 priority date for domestic students. Applications are processed on a rolling basis. Application fee: $50 ($75 for international students). *Expenses: Tuition:* Full-time $16,830; part-time $935 per credit hour. Tuition and fees vary according to degree level and program. *Financial support:* In 2011–12, 67 students received support. Scholarships/grants and tuition waivers (partial) available. Financial award applicants required to submit FAFSA. *Faculty research:* Facilitative learning styles, leadership, student assessment, interactive multimedia inclusion, learning organizations and strategic change. *Unit head:* Dr. Deborah Boyd, Director, 615-966-6263, E-mail: deborah.boyd@lipscomb.edu. *Application contact:* Kristin Baese, Assistant Director of Enrollment and Outreach, 615-966-7628 Ext. 6081, Fax: 615-966-5173, E-mail: kristin.baese@lipscomb.edu. Web site: http://graduateeducation.lipscomb.edu/.

Long Island University–Brentwood Campus, School of Education, Brentwood, NY 11717. Offers childhood education (MS); early childhood education (MS); literacy (MS); mental health counseling (MS); school counseling (MS); special education (MS). Part-time and evening/weekend programs available.

Long Island University–Brooklyn Campus, School of Education, Department of Teaching and Learning, Program in Special Education, Brooklyn, NY 11201-8423. Offers MS Ed. Part-time and evening/weekend programs available. *Degree requirements:* For master's, thesis optional. *Entrance requirements:* For master's, 2 letters of recommendation. Additional exam requirements/recommendations for international students: Required—TOEFL (minimum score 500 paper-based; 173 computer-based). Electronic applications accepted.

Long Island University–C. W. Post Campus, School of Education, Department of Special Education and Literacy, Brookville, NY 11548-1300. Offers childhood education/literacy (MS); childhood education/special education (MS); literacy (MS Ed); special education (MS Ed). *Accreditation:* Teacher Education Accreditation Council. Part-time and evening/weekend programs available. *Degree requirements:* For master's, research project, comprehensive exam or thesis. *Entrance requirements:* For master's, interview; minimum GPA of 2.75 in major, 2.5 overall. Electronic applications accepted. *Faculty research:* Autism, mainstreaming, robotics and microcomputers in special education, transition from school to work.

Long Island University–Hudson at Rockland, Graduate School, Programs in Special Education and Literacy, Orangeburg, NY 10962. Offers autism (MS Ed); childhood/literacy (MS Ed); childhood/special education (MS Ed); literacy (MS Ed); special education (MS Ed). Part-time programs available. *Entrance requirements:* For master's, college transcripts, two letters of recommendation, personal statement, resume.

Long Island University–Hudson at Westchester, Programs in Education-Teaching, Program in Special Education and Secondary Education, Purchase, NY 10577. Offers MS Ed, Advanced Certificate. Part-time and evening/weekend programs available.

Long Island University–Riverhead, Education Division, Program in Teaching Students with Disabilities, Riverhead, NY 11901. Offers MS Ed. *Faculty:* 1 full-time (0 women), 11 part-time/adjunct (7 women). *Students:* 4 full-time (all women), 18 part-time (15 women). Average age 31. In 2011, 3 master's awarded. *Degree requirements:* For master's, thesis. *Entrance requirements:* For master's, minimum GPA of 2.75, New York state teacher certification, interview, writing sample. Additional exam requirements/recommendations for international students: Required—TOEFL (minimum score 550 paper-based; 250 computer-based). *Application deadline:* Applications are processed on a rolling basis. Electronic applications accepted. *Expenses: Tuition:* Part-time $1028 per credit. *Financial support:* In 2011–12, 21 students received support, including 1 research assistantship with full tuition reimbursement available. Financial award applicants required to submit FAFSA. *Unit head:* Dr. Sanja Cale, Unit Head, 631-287-8010, Fax: 631-287-8130, E-mail: sanja.cale@liu.edu. *Application contact:* Andrea Borra, Admissions Counselor, 631-287-8010 Ext. 8326, Fax: 631-287-8253, E-mail: andrea.borra@liu.edu.

Longwood University, Office of Graduate Studies, College of Education and Human Services, Farmville, VA 23909. Offers communication sciences and disorders (MS); community and college counseling (MS); curriculum and instruction specialist-elementary (MS), including mild disabilities, modern languages; curriculum and instruction specialist-secondary (MS), including English, mild disabilities, modern languages; educational leadership (MS); guidance and counseling (MS); literacy and culture (MS); school library media (MS). *Accreditation:* NCATE. Part-time and evening/weekend programs available. *Degree requirements:* For master's, comprehensive exam, thesis optional. *Entrance requirements:* For master's, GRE (communication sciences and disorders), minimum GPA of 2.75. Additional exam requirements/recommendations for international students: Required—TOEFL (minimum score 550 paper-based; 213 computer-based).

Loras College, Graduate Division, Program in Education with an Emphasis in Special Education, Dubuque, IA 52004-0178. Offers instructional strategist I K-6 and 7-12 (MA). Part-time and evening/weekend programs available. *Degree requirements:* For master's, comprehensive exam, thesis optional. *Entrance requirements:* For master's, minimum cumulative undergraduate GPA of 3.0.

Louisiana Tech University, Graduate School, College of Education, Department of Behavioral Sciences and Psychology, Ruston, LA 71272. Offers counseling (MA); counseling psychology (PhD); industrial/organizational psychology (MA); special education (MA). *Accreditation:* APA (one or more programs are accredited). Part-time programs available. *Degree requirements:* For master's, thesis or alternative; for doctorate, thesis/dissertation. *Entrance requirements:* For master's and doctorate, GRE General Test.

Loyola Marymount University, School of Education, Department of Educational Support Services, Program in Special Education, Los Angeles, CA 90045. Offers MA. Part-time and evening/weekend programs available. *Faculty:* 10 full-time (5 women), 36 part-time/adjunct (27 women). *Students:* 71 full-time (59 women), 6 part-time (5 women); includes 37 minority (9 Black or African American, non-Hispanic/Latino; 10 Asian, non-Hispanic/Latino; 14 Hispanic/Latino; 4 Two or more races, non-Hispanic/Latino), 1 international. Average age 27. 37 applicants, 89% accepted, 32 enrolled. In 2011, 41 master's awarded. *Degree requirements:* For master's, comprehensive exam. *Entrance requirements:* For master's, CBEST, CSET, RICA, 3 letters of recommendation. Additional exam requirements/recommendations for international students: Required—TOEFL (minimum score 600 paper-based; 250 computer-based; 100 iBT). *Application deadline:* For fall admission, 6/15 for domestic students; for spring admission, 11/15 for domestic students. Application fee: $50. Electronic applications accepted. *Financial support:* In 2011–12, 49 students received support. Scholarships/grants and unspecified assistantships available. Support available to part-time students. Financial award application deadline: 6/15; financial award applicants required to submit FAFSA. *Unit head:* Dr. Victoria Graf, Program Director, 310-338-7305, E-mail: vgraf@lmu.edu. *Application contact:* Chake H. Kouyoumjian, Graduate Admissions Director, 310-338-2721, E-mail: ckouyoum@lmu.edu. Web site: http://soe.lmu.edu/admissions/programs/sped.htm.

Loyola University Chicago, School of Education, Program in Teaching and Learning, Chicago, IL 60660. Offers elementary education (M Ed); English as a second language (Certificate); math education (M Ed); reading specialist (M Ed); reading teacher endorsement (Certificate); school technology (M Ed); science education (M Ed); secondary education (M Ed); special education (M Ed). *Accreditation:* NCATE. *Faculty:* 12 full-time (9 women), 12 part-time/adjunct (6 women). *Students:* 131. Average age 28. 115 applicants, 65% accepted, 30 enrolled. In 2011, 80 master's awarded. *Degree requirements:* For master's, comprehensive exam. *Entrance requirements:* For master's, Illinois Basic Skills Test, 3 letters of recommendation, minimum GPA of 3.0, resume. Additional exam requirements/recommendations for international students: Required—TOEFL (minimum score 550 paper-based; 213 computer-based; 79 iBT). *Application deadline:* For fall admission, 7/1 priority date for domestic students, 7/1 for international students; for spring admission, 11/1 priority date for domestic students, 11/1 for international students. Applications are processed on a rolling basis. Application fee: $50. Electronic applications accepted. Application fee is waived when completed online. *Expenses: Tuition:* Full-time $15,660; part-time $870 per credit hour. *Required fees:* $125 per semester. Tuition and fees vary according to course load and program. *Financial support:* Institutionally sponsored loans, scholarships/grants, and unspecified assistantships available. Support available to part-time students. Financial award application deadline: 2/1; financial award applicants required to submit FAFSA. *Faculty research:* Positive behavior support, school reform, school improvement. *Unit head:* Dr. Dorothy Giroux, Director, 312-915-7027, E-mail: dgiroux@luc.edu. *Application contact:* Marie Rosin-Dittmar, Information Contact, 312-915-6800, E-mail: schleduc@luc.edu.

Loyola University Maryland, Graduate Programs, Department of Education, Program in Special Education, Baltimore, MD 21210-2699. Offers early childhood education (M Ed, CAS); elementary/middle education (M Ed, CAS); secondary education (M Ed, CAS). *Accreditation:* NCATE. Part-time programs available. *Faculty:* 57 full-time (32 women), 21 part-time/adjunct (10 women). *Students:* 6 full-time (5 women), 33 part-time (31 women); includes 3 minority (all Black or African American, non-Hispanic/Latino). Average age 29. In 2011, 11 master's awarded. *Entrance requirements:* For master's and CAS, PRAXIS, SAT, ACT, or GRE. Additional exam requirements/recommendations for international students: Required—TOEFL (minimum score 550 paper-based; 213 computer-based). *Application deadline:* For fall admission, 6/15 priority date for domestic students; for spring admission, 11/1 priority date for domestic students. Application fee: $50. Electronic applications accepted. *Financial support:* Research assistantships and unspecified assistantships available. Financial award application deadline: 4/15; financial award applicants required to submit FAFSA. *Unit head:* Monica J. Phelps, Director, 410-617-2671, E-mail: mphelps@loyola.edu. *Application contact:* Maureen Faux, Executive Director, Graduate Admissions, 410-617-5020, Fax: 410-617-2002, E-mail: graduate@loyola.edu.

Lynchburg College, Graduate Studies, School of Education and Human Development, M Ed Program in Special Education, Lynchburg, VA 24501-3199. Offers M Ed. Part-time and evening/weekend programs available. *Faculty:* 5 full-time (3 women), 1 (woman) part-time/adjunct. *Students:* 13 full-time (10 women), 14 part-time (7 women); includes 1 minority (Hispanic/Latino), 3 international. Average age 36. In 2011, 11 master's awarded. *Degree requirements:* For master's, comprehensive exam. *Entrance requirements:* For master's, GRE, minimum GPA of 3.0 (preferred), official transcripts (bachelor's, others as relevant), three letters of recommendation, career goals statement. Additional exam requirements/recommendations for international students: Required—TOEFL (minimum score 550 paper-based; 213 computer-based; 79 iBT), IELTS (minimum score 6.5). *Application deadline:* For fall admission, 7/31 for domestic students, 6/1 for international students; for spring admission, 11/30 for domestic students, 10/15 for international students. Applications are processed on a rolling basis. Application fee: $30. Electronic applications accepted. Application fee is waived when completed online. *Expenses: Tuition:* Full-time $7740; part-time $430 per credit hour. *Financial support:* Fellowships, research assistantships, Federal Work-Study, scholarships/grants, health care benefits, and unspecified assistantships available. Support available to part-time students. Financial award application deadline: 7/31; financial award applicants required to submit FAFSA. *Unit head:* Dr. Gena Barnhill, Assistant Professor/Director of M Ed in Special Education, 434-544-8771, Fax: 434-544-8483, E-mail: barnhill@lynchburg.edu. *Application contact:* Anne Pingstock, Executive Assistant, Graduate Studies, 434-544-8383, Fax: 434-544-8483, E-mail: gradstudies@lynchburg.edu. Web site: http://www.lynchburg.edu/specialed.xml.

Lyndon State College, Graduate Programs in Education, Department of Education, Lyndonville, VT 05851-0919. Offers curriculum and instruction (M Ed); reading specialist (M Ed); special education (M Ed); teaching and counseling (M Ed). Part-time and evening/weekend programs available. *Degree requirements:* For master's, exam or major field project. *Entrance requirements:* Additional exam requirements/recommendations for international students: Recommended—TOEFL (minimum score 500 paper-based; 173 computer-based).

Lynn University, Donald and Helen Ross College of Education, Boca Raton, FL 33431-5598. Offers educational leadership (M Ed, PhD); exceptional student education (M Ed); teacher preparation (PhD). Part-time and evening/weekend programs available. *Degree requirements:* For master's, thesis (for some programs); for doctorate, thesis/dissertation, qualifying paper. *Entrance requirements:* For master's, GRE, minimum undergraduate GPA of 3.0, resume, 2 letters of recommendation; for doctorate, GRE or GMAT, minimum GPA of 3.25, resume, 2 letters of recommendation. Additional exam requirements/recommendations for international students: Required—TOEFL (minimum score 550 paper-based; 213 computer-based). Electronic applications accepted. *Faculty research:* Non-traditional education, innovative curricula, multicultural education, simulation games.

Madonna University, Programs in Education, Livonia, MI 48150-1173. Offers Catholic school leadership (MSA); educational leadership (MSA); learning disabilities (MAT); literacy education (MAT); teaching and learning (MAT). *Accreditation:* NCATE. Part-time and evening/weekend programs available. *Degree requirements:* For master's, thesis or alternative. Electronic applications accepted.

Malone University, Graduate Program in Education, Canton, OH 44709. Offers curriculum and instruction (MA), including teacher leader endorsement; curriculum, instruction, and professional development (MA); educational leadership (MA), including principal license; intervention specialist (MA); reading (MA). Part-time and evening/weekend programs available. *Faculty:* 9 full-time (5 women), 8 part-time/adjunct (6 women). *Students:* 2 full-time (both women), 43 part-time (33 women); includes 2 minority (both Black or African American, non-Hispanic/Latino). Average age 36. 35 applicants, 91% accepted, 12 enrolled. In 2011, 11 master's awarded. *Degree requirements:* For master's, research project. *Entrance requirements:* For master's, minimum GPA of 3.0, teaching license. Additional exam requirements/recommendations for international students: Required—TOEFL (minimum score 550 paper-based; 213 computer-based; 79 iBT). *Application deadline:* Applications are processed on a rolling basis. *Expenses: Tuition:* Part-time $625 per semester hour. Part-time tuition and fees vary according to program. *Financial support:* Tuition waivers (partial) available. Support available to part-time students. Financial award application deadline: 6/30. *Faculty research:* Educational leadership styles: Jesus as master teacher, assessment accommodations for English language learners, preparing culturally proficient teachers, using naturally occurring text in the classroom to meet the syntactic needs of students with learning disabilities, using iPad instructional technology to meet the needs of students with disabilities. *Unit head:* Dr. Alice E. Christie, Director, 330-478-8541, Fax: 330-471-8563, E-mail: achristie@malone.edu. *Application contact:* Dan DePasquale, Senior Recruiter, 330-471-8381, Fax: 330-471-8343, E-mail: depasquale@malone.edu. Web site: http://www.malone.edu/admissions/graduate/education/.

Manhattan College, Graduate Division, School of Education, Program in Special Education, Riverdale, NY 10471. Offers autism spectrum disorder (Professional Diploma); bilingual special education (Certificate); dual childhood/special education (MS Ed); special education (MS Ed). Part-time and evening/weekend programs available. *Faculty:* 7 full-time (5 women), 22 part-time/adjunct (19 women). *Students:* 29 full-time (27 women), 59 part-time (50 women). Average age 24. 62 applicants, 92% accepted, 57 enrolled. In 2011, 30 master's awarded. *Degree requirements:* For master's, thesis, internship (if not certified). *Entrance requirements:* For master's, LAST, minimum GPA of 3.0. Additional exam requirements/recommendations for international students: Required—TOEFL (minimum score 550 paper-based). *Application deadline:* For fall admission, 8/10 priority date for domestic students; for spring admission, 1/7 priority date for domestic students. Applications are processed on a rolling basis. Application fee: $75. *Expenses:* Contact institution. *Financial support:* Federal Work-Study, scholarships/grants, and unspecified assistantships available. Financial award application deadline: 2/1. *Unit head:* Dr. Elizabeth Mary Kosky, Director of Childhood Special Education Programs, 718-862-7969, Fax: 718-862-7816, E-mail: elizabeth.kosky@manhattan.edu. *Application contact:* William Bisset, Information Contact, 718-862-8000.

Manhattanville College, Graduate Studies, School of Education, Program in Childhood Education, Purchase, NY 10577-2132. Offers childhood and special education (MPS); childhood education (MAT); special education childhood (MPS). Part-time and evening/weekend programs available. *Degree requirements:* For master's, comprehensive exam or research project, field experience. *Entrance requirements:* For master's, minimum undergraduate GPA of 3.0, 2 letters of recommendation. Additional exam requirements/recommendations for international students: Required—TOEFL.

Manhattanville College, Graduate Studies, School of Education, Program in Early Childhood Education, Purchase, NY 10577-2132. Offers childhood and early childhood education (MAT); early childhood education (birth-grade 2) (MAT); literacy (birth-grade 6) (MPS), including reading, writing; literacy (birth-grade 6) and special education (grades 1-6) (MPS); special education (birth-grade 2) (MPS); special education (birth-grade 6) (MPS). Part-time and evening/weekend programs available. *Degree requirements:* For master's, comprehensive exam or research project, field experience. *Entrance requirements:* For master's, minimum undergraduate GPA of 3.0, 2 letters of recommendation. Additional exam requirements/recommendations for international students: Required—TOEFL. Electronic applications accepted.

Manhattanville College, Graduate Studies, School of Education, Program in Middle Childhood/Adolescence Education (Grades 5-12), Purchase, NY 10577-2132. Offers biology (MAT); biology and special education (MPS); chemistry (MAT); chemistry and special education (MPS); English (MAT); English and special education (MPS); literacy (MPS), including reading and writing, writing; literacy and special education (MPS); math (MAT); math and special education (MPS); second language (MAT), including French, Italian, Latin, Spanish; social studies (MAT); social studies and special education (MPS); special education (MPS). Part-time and evening/weekend programs available. *Degree requirements:* For master's, comprehensive exam or research project, field experience. *Entrance requirements:* For master's, minimum undergraduate GPA of 3.0, 2 letters of recommendation. Additional exam requirements/recommendations for international students: Required—TOEFL. Electronic applications accepted.

Mansfield University of Pennsylvania, Graduate Studies, Department of Education and Special Education, Mansfield, PA 16933. Offers elementary education (M Ed); secondary education (MS); special education (M Ed). *Accreditation:* NCATE (one or more programs are accredited). Part-time and evening/weekend programs available. Postbaccalaureate distance learning degree programs offered (no on-campus study). *Degree requirements:* For master's, comprehensive exam, thesis optional. *Entrance requirements:* For master's, minimum GPA of 3.0. Additional exam requirements/ recommendations for international students: Required—TOEFL (minimum score 550 paper-based; 220 computer-based). Electronic applications accepted. *Expenses:* Tuition, state resident: full-time $7488; part-time $416 per credit. Tuition, nonresident: full-time $11,232; part-time $624 per credit.

Marshall University, Academic Affairs Division, Graduate School of Education and Professional Development, Program in Special Education, Huntington, WV 25755. Offers MA. *Accreditation:* NCATE. Part-time and evening/weekend programs available. *Students:* 74 full-time (62 women), 202 part-time (168 women); includes 13 minority (10 Black or African American, non-Hispanic/Latino; 2 Hispanic/Latino; 1 Two or more races, non-Hispanic/Latino), 1 international. Average age 35. In 2011, 55 master's awarded. *Degree requirements:* For master's, thesis optional, comprehensive or oral assessment, research project. *Entrance requirements:* For master's, GRE General Test or MAT, minimum GPA of 3.0. Application fee: $40. *Financial support:* Federal Work-Study, tuition waivers (full), and unspecified assistantships available. Support available to part-time students. Financial award applicants required to submit FAFSA. *Faculty research:* Teaching the severely handicapped, career/vocational education, education of the gifted. *Unit head:* Dr. Mike Sullivan, Director, 304-746-2076, E-mail: msullivan@ marshall.edu. *Application contact:* Information Contact, 304-746-1900, Fax: 304-746-1902, E-mail: services@marshall.edu.

Martin Luther College, Graduate Studies, New Ulm, MN 56073. Offers instruction (MS Ed); leadership (MS Ed); special education (MS Ed). Part-time programs available. Postbaccalaureate distance learning degree programs offered. *Degree requirements:* For master's, capstone project or comprehensive exam. *Entrance requirements:* For master's, undergraduate degree in education from an accredited college or university, minimum undergraduate GPA of 3.0. Electronic applications accepted.

Marymount University, School of Education and Human Services, Program in Education, Arlington, VA 22207-4299. Offers elementary education (M Ed); English as a second language (M Ed); professional studies (M Ed); secondary education (M Ed); special education, general curriculum (M Ed). *Accreditation:* NCATE. Part-time and evening/weekend programs available. *Faculty:* 9 full-time (7 women), 7 part-time/adjunct (5 women). *Students:* 62 full-time (57 women), 103 part-time (86 women); includes 22 minority (3 Black or African American, non-Hispanic/Latino; 4 Asian, non-Hispanic/ Latino; 10 Hispanic/Latino; 5 Two or more races, non-Hispanic/Latino), 13 international. Average age 31. 69 applicants, 100% accepted, 52 enrolled. In 2011, 79 master's awarded. *Degree requirements:* For master's, thesis or alternative. *Entrance requirements:* For master's, GRE or MAT and PRAXIS I or SAT/ACT and VCLA, 2 letters of recommendation, resume, interview. Additional exam requirements/ recommendations for international students: Required—TOEFL (minimum score 600 paper-based; 250 computer-based; 96 iBT), IELTS (minimum score 6.5). *Application deadline:* For fall admission, 7/1 for international students. Applications are processed on a rolling basis. Application fee: $40. Electronic applications accepted. *Expenses: Tuition:* Part-time $770 per credit hour. *Required fees:* $8 per credit hour. One-time fee: $180 full-time. *Financial support:* In 2011–12, 27 students received support. Research assistantships with full tuition reimbursements available, career-related internships or fieldwork, Federal Work-Study, scholarships/grants, and unspecified assistantships available. Support available to part-time students. Financial award applicants required to submit FAFSA. *Unit head:* Dr. Shelly Haser, Chair, 703-526-6855, Fax: 703-284-1631, E-mail: shelly.haser@marymount.edu. *Application contact:* Francesca Reed, Director, Graduate Admissions, 703-284-5901, Fax: 703-527-3815, E-mail: grad.admissions@ marymount.edu. Web site: http://www.marymount.edu/academics/schools/sehs/ grad.aspx.

Marywood University, Academic Affairs, Reap College of Education and Human Development, Department of Education, Program in Special Education, Scranton, PA 18509-1598. Offers MS. *Accreditation:* NCATE. *Entrance requirements:* Additional exam requirements/recommendations for international students: Required—TOEFL (minimum score 550 paper-based; 213 computer-based; 79 iBT). *Application deadline:* For fall admission, 4/1 priority date for domestic students, 3/31 for international students; for spring admission, 11/1 priority date for domestic students, 8/30 for international students. Applications are processed on a rolling basis. Application fee: $35. Electronic applications accepted. *Financial support:* Career-related internships or fieldwork, scholarships/grants, and unspecified assistantships available. Support available to part-time students. Financial award application deadline: 6/30; financial award applicants required to submit FAFSA. *Unit head:* Dr. Patricia S. Arter, Director, 570-348-6211 Ext. 2511, E-mail: psarter@marywood.edu. *Application contact:* Tammy Manka, Associate Director of Graduate Admissions, 570-348-6211 Ext. 2322, E-mail: tmanka@ marywood.edu. Web site: http://www.marywood.edu/education/graduate-programs/ms-special-ed.html.

Marywood University, Academic Affairs, Reap College of Education and Human Development, Department of Education, Program in Special Education Administration and Supervision, Scranton, PA 18509-1598. Offers MS. *Accreditation:* NCATE. *Entrance requirements:* Additional exam requirements/recommendations for international students: Required—TOEFL (minimum score 550 paper-based; 213 computer-based; 79 iBT). *Application deadline:* For fall admission, 4/1 priority date for domestic students, 3/31 for international students; for spring admission, 11/1 priority date for domestic students, 8/31 for international students. Applications are processed on a rolling basis. Application fee: $35. Electronic applications accepted. *Financial support:* Career-related internships or fieldwork, scholarships/grants, and unspecified assistantships available. Support available to part-time students. Financial award application deadline: 6/30; financial award applicants required to submit FAFSA. *Unit head:* Patricia S. Arter, Director, 570-348-6211 Ext. 2511, E-mail: psarter@ marywood.edu. *Application contact:* Tammy Manka, Associate Director of Graduate Admissions, 570-348-6211 Ext. 2322, E-mail: tmanka@marywood.edu. Web site: http:// www.marywood.edu/academics/gradcatalog/.

Massachusetts College of Liberal Arts, Program in Education, North Adams, MA 01247-4100. Offers curriculum (M Ed); educational administration (M Ed); reading (M Ed); special education (M Ed). Part-time and evening/weekend programs available. *Degree requirements:* For master's, thesis. *Entrance requirements:* For master's, writing sample.

McDaniel College, Graduate and Professional Studies, Program in Education of the Deaf, Westminster, MD 21157-4390. Offers MS. *Accreditation:* NCATE. Part-time programs available. *Degree requirements:* For master's, comprehensive exam, thesis optional. *Entrance requirements:* For master's, American Sign Language Proficiency Interview (ASLPI). Additional exam requirements/recommendations for international students: Required—TOEFL (minimum score 213 computer-based), English proficiency essay. *Faculty research:* Mainstreaming of multihandicapped children.

McDaniel College, Graduate and Professional Studies, Program in Human Services Management in Special Education, Westminster, MD 21157-4390. Offers MS. *Accreditation:* NCATE. Evening/weekend programs available. *Degree requirements:* For master's, internship. *Entrance requirements:* For master's, letters of reference (3). Additional exam requirements/recommendations for international students: Required—TOEFL (minimum score 213 computer-based).

McDaniel College, Graduate and Professional Studies, Program in Special Education, Westminster, MD 21157-4390. Offers MS. *Accreditation:* NCATE. Part-time and evening/weekend programs available. *Degree requirements:* For master's, comprehensive exam, thesis optional. *Entrance requirements:* For master's, GRE General Test, MAT, or NTE/PRAXIS I, letters of reference (3). Additional exam requirements/recommendations for international students: Required—TOEFL (minimum score 213 computer-based).

McKendree University, Graduate Programs, Master of Arts in Education Program, Lebanon, IL 62254-1299. Offers certification (MA Ed); educational administration and leadership (MA Ed); educational studies (MA Ed); higher education administrative services (MA Ed); music education (MA Ed); special education (MA Ed); teacher leadership (MA Ed); transition to teaching (MA Ed). *Accreditation:* NCATE. Part-time and evening/weekend programs available. Postbaccalaureate distance learning degree programs offered (no on-campus study). *Entrance requirements:* For master's, official transcripts from institutions attended, minimum GPA of 3.0, resume, references. Additional exam requirements/recommendations for international students: Required—TOEFL. Electronic applications accepted.

McNeese State University, Doré School of Graduate Studies, Burton College of Education, Department of Education Professions, Program in Special Education, Lake Charles, LA 70609. Offers autism (M Ed); educational diagnostician (M Ed); mild moderate (M Ed). *Faculty:* 10 full-time (5 women). *Students:* 10 part-time (8 women); includes 2 minority (both Black or African American, non-Hispanic/Latino). In 2011, 1 master's awarded. *Entrance requirements:* For master's, GRE, teaching certificate. *Application deadline:* For fall admission, 5/15 priority date for domestic students, 5/15 for international students; for spring admission, 10/15 priority date for domestic students, 10/15 for international students. Applications are processed on a rolling basis. Application fee: $20 ($30 for international students). *Expenses:* Tuition, state resident: part-time $519 per credit hour. Tuition and fees vary according to course load. *Financial support:* Application deadline: 5/1. *Unit head:* Dr. Dustin M. Hebert, Director, 337-475-5424, Fax: 337-475-5272, E-mail: dhebert@mcneese.edu. *Application contact:* Dr. George F. Mead, Jr., Interim Dean of Dore' School of Graduate Studies, 337-475-5396, Fax: 337-475-5397, E-mail: admissions@mcneese.edu.

McNeese State University, Doré School of Graduate Studies, Burton College of Education, Department of Education Professions, Program in Teaching, Lake Charles, LA 70609. Offers elementary education grades 1-5 (MAT); secondary education grades 6-12 (MAT); special education (MAT), including mild/moderate grades 1-5. *Faculty:* 10 full-time (5 women). *Students:* 49 full-time (37 women), 89 part-time (69 women); includes 20 minority (16 Black or African American, non-Hispanic/Latino; 4 Hispanic/ Latino), 1 international. In 2011, 61 master's awarded. *Entrance requirements:* For master's, GRE, PRAXIS, 2 letters of recommendation; autobiography. *Application deadline:* For fall admission, 5/15 priority date for domestic students, 5/15 for international students; for spring admission, 10/15 priority date for domestic students, 10/15 for international students. Applications are processed on a rolling basis. Application fee: $20 ($30 for international students). *Expenses:* Tuition, state resident: part-time $519 per credit hour. Tuition and fees vary according to course load. *Financial support:* Application deadline: 5/1. *Unit head:* Dr. Dustin M. Hebert, Director, 337-475-5424, Fax: 337-475-5272, E-mail: dhebert@mcneese.edu. *Application contact:* Dr. George F. Mead, Jr., Interim Dean of Dore' School of Graduate Studies, 337-475-5396, Fax: 337-475-5397, E-mail: admissions@mcneese.edu.

Medaille College, Program in Education, Buffalo, NY 14214-2695. Offers adolescent education (MS Ed); curriculum and instruction (MS Ed); education preparation (MS Ed); literacy (MS Ed); special education (MS). *Accreditation:* Teacher Education Accreditation Council. Part-time and evening/weekend programs available. *Faculty:* 15 full-time (11 women), 31 part-time/adjunct (21 women). *Students:* 371 full-time (281 women), 37 part-time (29 women); includes 75 minority (11 Black or African American, non-Hispanic/Latino; 6 Asian, non-Hispanic/Latino; 3 Hispanic/Latino; 55 Native Hawaiian or other Pacific Islander, non-Hispanic/Latino), 264 international. Average age 29. 354 applicants, 99% accepted, 163 enrolled. In 2011, 457 master's awarded. *Degree requirements:* For master's, comprehensive exam (for some programs), thesis or alternative. *Entrance requirements:* For master's, minimum undergraduate GPA of 2.7. Additional exam requirements/recommendations for international students: Required—TOEFL (minimum score 550 paper-based; 213 computer-based). *Application deadline:* For fall admission, 8/15 priority date for domestic students; for spring admission, 1/15 priority date for domestic students. Applications are processed on a rolling basis. Application fee: $35. Electronic applications accepted. Tuition and fees vary according to program. *Financial support:* Federal Work-Study available. Financial award applicants required to submit FAFSA. *Faculty research:* Curriculum planning, truancy, tracking minority students, curriculum design, mentoring students. *Unit head:* Dr. Robert DiSibio, Director of Graduate Programs, 716-932-2548, Fax: 716-631-1380, E-mail: rdisibio@medaille.edu. *Application contact:* Jacqueline Matheny, Executive Director of Marketing and Enrollment, 716-932-2541, Fax: 716-632-1811, E-mail: jmatheny@medaille.edu. Web site: http://www.medaille.edu.

Mercy College, School of Education, Dobbs Ferry, NY 10522-1189. Offers adolescence education, grades 7-12 (MS); applied behavior analysis (Post Master's Certificate); bilingual education (MS); childhood education, grade 1-6 (MS); early childhood education, birth-grade 2 (MS); early childhood education/students with disabilities (MS); individualized certification plan for teachers (ICPT) (MS); middle childhood education, grades 5-9 (MS); school building leadership (MS, Advanced Certificate); teaching English to speakers of other languages (TESOL) (MS, Advanced Certificate); teaching literacy, birth-6 (MS); teaching literacy/birth-grade 12 (MS); teaching literacy/grades 5-12 (MS); urban education (MS). Postbaccalaureate distance learning degree programs offered (minimal on-campus study). *Degree requirements:* For master's, comprehensive exam, thesis (for some programs). *Entrance requirements:* For master's, interview, resume, minimum undergraduate GPA of 3.0. Additional exam requirements/ recommendations for international students: Required—TOEFL (minimum score 600 paper-based; 250 computer-based; 100 iBT), IELTS (minimum score 8). Electronic applications accepted. *Expenses:* Contact institution. *Faculty research:* Teaching, literacy, educational evaluation.

Mercyhurst College, Graduate Studies, Program in Special Education, Erie, PA 16546. Offers bilingual/bicultural special education (MS); educational leadership (Certificate); special education (MS). Part-time and evening/weekend programs available. *Faculty:* 1 full-time (0 women), 13 part-time/adjunct (8 women). *Students:* 60 full-time (51 women), 19 part-time (14 women); includes 8 minority (3 Black or African American, non-Hispanic/Latino; 1 American Indian or Alaska Native, non-Hispanic/Latino; 1 Asian, non-Hispanic/Latino; 3 Hispanic/Latino), 1 international. Average age 30. 32 applicants, 84% accepted, 18 enrolled. In 2011, 52 master's awarded. *Degree requirements:* For master's, thesis optional. *Entrance requirements:* For master's, GRE or PRAXIS I, interview, resume, essay, three professional references, transcripts. Additional exam requirements/recommendations for international students: Required—TOEFL. *Application deadline:* For fall admission, 8/1 priority date for domestic students, 8/1 for international students; for winter admission, 11/1 for domestic and international students; for spring admission, 2/1 for domestic and international students. Applications are processed on a rolling basis. Application fee: $35. Electronic applications accepted. *Expenses: Tuition:* Part-time $570 per credit. *Required fees:* $90 per term. Tuition and fees vary according to program. *Financial support:* In 2011–12, 25 students received support, including 15 research assistantships with full and partial tuition reimbursements available (averaging $8,000 per year); institutionally sponsored loans and unspecified assistantships also available. Support available to part-time students. Financial award application deadline: 5/15; financial award applicants required to submit FAFSA. *Faculty research:* College-age learning disabled program, teacher preparation/collaboration, applied behavior analysis, special education policy issues. *Total annual research expenditures:* $278,141. *Unit head:* Dr. Phillip J. Belfiore, Coordinator, 814-824-2267, Fax: 814-824-2438, E-mail: belfiore@mercyhurst.edu. *Application contact:* Sarah Murphy, Academic Coordinator, 814-824-2297, Fax: 814-824-2055, E-mail: smurphy@mercyhurst.edu. Web site: http://graduate.mercyhurst.edu/academics/graduate-degrees/special-education/.

Merrimack College, School of Education, North Andover, MA 01845-5800. Offers community engagement (M Ed); early childhood education (M Ed); elementary education (M Ed); elementary education plus moderate disabilities-dual license (M Ed); English as a second language (M Ed); general studies (M Ed); higher education (M Ed); middle (M Ed); moderate disabilities (preK-8) (M Ed); reading (M Ed); secondary (M Ed); teacher leadership (CAGS). Part-time and evening/weekend programs available. *Faculty:* 4 full-time (all women), 9 part-time/adjunct (7 women). *Students:* 70 full-time (60 women), 39 part-time (33 women); includes 2 minority (1 Asian, non-Hispanic/Latino; 1 Hispanic/Latino). Average age 27. In 2011, 26 master's awarded. *Degree requirements:* For master's, portfolio. *Entrance requirements:* Additional exam requirements/recommendations for international students: Required—TOEFL (minimum score 80 iBT). *Application deadline:* For fall admission, 8/1 priority date for domestic students, 7/15 for international students; for winter admission, 12/1 priority date for domestic students, 11/15 for international students; for spring admission, 3/1 priority date for domestic students, 2/15 for international students. Applications are processed on a rolling basis. Electronic applications accepted. *Expenses: Tuition:* Part-time $475 per credit. *Required fees:* $62.50 per semester. *Financial support:* In 2011–12, 50 fellowships were awarded; career-related internships or fieldwork and scholarships/grants also available. Financial award applicants required to submit FAFSA. *Faculty research:* Higher education, community engagement, literacy, leadership. *Unit head:* Dr. Theresa Kirk, Chair, 978-837-5436, E-mail: kirkt@merrimack.edu. *Application contact:* Jessica McCarthy, Program Coordinator, 978-837-5443, E-mail: mccarthyj@merrimack.edu. Web site: http://www.merrimack.edu/academics/education/med/.

Messiah College, Program in Education, Mechanicsburg, PA 17055. Offers special education (M Ed); teaching English to speakers of other languages (M Ed). Part-time programs available. Postbaccalaureate distance learning degree programs offered (no on-campus study). *Faculty:* 5 full-time (3 women). *Students:* 3 full-time (all women), 4 part-time (all women). Average age 30. *Application deadline:* For fall admission, 6/1 priority date for domestic students; for winter admission, 11/1 priority date for domestic students; for spring admission, 11/1 priority date for domestic students. Applications are processed on a rolling basis. Application fee: $30. Electronic applications accepted. *Expenses: Tuition:* Full-time $9648; part-time $536 per credit hour. *Required fees:* $150; $25 per course. *Financial support:* Federal Work-Study available. Financial award applicants required to submit FAFSA. *Faculty research:* Socio-cultural perspectives on education, TESOL, autism, special education. *Unit head:* Dr. Nancy Patric, Faculty Member and Director of the Graduate Program in Education, 717-766-2511 Ext. 7239, E-mail: npatrick@messiah.edu. *Application contact:* Jackie Gehman, Graduate Enrollment Coordinator, 717-796-5061, Fax: 717-691-2386, E-mail: jgehman@messiah.edu. Web site: http://www.messiah.edu/academics/graduate_studies/Education/.

Miami University, School of Education and Allied Professions, Department of Educational Psychology, Oxford, OH 45056. Offers educational psychology (M Ed); instructional design and technology (M Ed, MA); school psychology (MS, Ed S); special education (M Ed). *Accreditation:* NCATE. *Students:* 49 full-time (40 women), 39 part-time (31 women); includes 8 minority (1 Black or African American, non-Hispanic/Latino; 5 Asian, non-Hispanic/Latino; 2 Two or more races, non-Hispanic/Latino), 28 international. Average age 29. In 2011, 50 master's awarded. *Entrance requirements:* For master's, GRE General Test or MAT, minimum undergraduate GPA of 3.0 during previous 2 years or 2.75 overall; for Ed S, GRE General Test or MAT. Additional exam requirements/recommendations for international students: Required—TOEFL. Application fee: $50. *Expenses:* Tuition, state resident: full-time $12,023; part-time $501 per credit hour. Tuition, nonresident: full-time $26,554; part-time $1107 per credit hour. *Required fees:* $528. *Financial support:* Fellowships with full tuition reimbursements, research assistantships with full tuition reimbursements, teaching assistantships with full tuition reimbursements, career-related internships or fieldwork, Federal Work-Study, health care benefits, tuition waivers (full), and unspecified assistantships available. Financial award application deadline: 2/15; financial award applicants required to submit FAFSA. *Unit head:* Dr. Nelda Cambron-McCabe, Chair, 513-529-6836, Fax: 513-529-6621, E-mail: cambron@muohio.edu. *Application contact:* Jennifer Turner, Administrative Assistant, 513-529-6621, Fax: 513-529-3646, E-mail: hillje@muohio.edu. Web site: http://www.units.muohio.edu/eap/departments/edp/edp.htm.

Michigan State University, The Graduate School, College of Education, Department of Counseling, Educational Psychology and Special Education, East Lansing, MI 48824. Offers counseling (MA); educational psychology and educational technology (PhD); educational technology (MA); measurement and quantitative methods (PhD); rehabilitation counseling (MA); rehabilitation counselor education (PhD); school psychology (MA, PhD, Ed S); special education (MA, PhD). *Accreditation:* APA (one or more programs are accredited); CORE (one or more programs are accredited). Part-time programs available. *Entrance requirements:* Additional exam requirements/recommendations for international students: Required—TOEFL. Electronic applications accepted.

MidAmerica Nazarene University, Graduate Studies in Education, Olathe, KS 66062-1899. Offers ESOL (M Ed); professional teaching (M Ed); special education (MA); technology enhanced teaching (M Ed). *Accreditation:* NCATE. Part-time and evening/weekend programs available. Postbaccalaureate distance learning degree programs offered (no on-campus study). *Degree requirements:* For master's, thesis or alternative, creative project, technology leadership practicum. *Entrance requirements:* For master's, minimum undergraduate GPA of 2.8, 2 years of teaching experience. *Expenses:* Contact institution.

Middle Tennessee State University, College of Graduate Studies, College of Education, Department of Elementary and Special Education, Major in Special Education, Murfreesboro, TN 37132. Offers M Ed. *Accreditation:* NCATE. Part-time and evening/weekend programs available. Postbaccalaureate distance learning degree programs offered. *Faculty:* 14 full-time (9 women), 7 part-time/adjunct (all women). *Students:* 1 (woman) full-time, 31 part-time (28 women); includes 7 minority (3 Black or African American, non-Hispanic/Latino; 1 Asian, non-Hispanic/Latino; 1 Hispanic/Latino; 2 Two or more races, non-Hispanic/Latino). 42 applicants, 60% accepted. In 2011, 14 master's awarded. *Degree requirements:* For master's, comprehensive exam. *Entrance requirements:* For master's, GRE, MAT or PRAXIS. Additional exam requirements/recommendations for international students: Required—TOEFL (minimum score 525 paper-based; 195 computer-based; 71 iBT) or IELTS (minimum score 6). *Application deadline:* For fall admission, 6/1 for domestic and international students. Applications are processed on a rolling basis. Application fee: $25 ($30 for international students). Electronic applications accepted. *Expenses:* Tuition, state resident: full-time $10,008. Tuition, nonresident: full-time $25,056. *Financial support:* Institutionally sponsored loans and tuition waivers available. Support available to part-time students. Financial award application deadline: 5/1. *Unit head:* Dr. Kathleen Burris, Interim Chair, 615-898-2680, Fax: 615-898-5309, E-mail: kathleen.burris@mtsu.edu. *Application contact:* Dr. Michael D. Allen, Dean and Vice Provost for Research, 615-898-2840, Fax: 615-904-8020, E-mail: michael.allen@mtsu.edu.

Midwestern State University, Graduate Studies, College of Education, Program in Special Education, Wichita Falls, TX 76308. Offers M Ed. Part-time and evening/weekend programs available. *Degree requirements:* For master's, comprehensive exam. *Entrance requirements:* For master's, GRE General Test, MAT, or GMAT, Texas teacher certificate or equivalent GPA of 3.0 in previous education courses. Additional exam requirements/recommendations for international students: Required—TOEFL (minimum score 550 paper-based; 213 computer-based). Electronic applications accepted. *Faculty research:* Fragile-X syndrome, phenylketonuria and other causes of handicapping conditions, autism, social development of students with disabilities.

Millersville University of Pennsylvania, College of Graduate and Professional Studies, School of Education, Department of Special Education, Millersville, PA 17551-0302. Offers M Ed. *Accreditation:* NCATE. Part-time and evening/weekend programs available. *Faculty:* 7 full-time (5 women), 2 part-time/adjunct (both women). *Students:* 2 full-time (both women), 32 part-time (29 women). Average age 33. 4 applicants, 100% accepted, 4 enrolled. In 2011, 13 master's awarded. *Degree requirements:* For master's, thesis optional. *Entrance requirements:* For master's, GRE or MAT, 3 letters of recommendation. Additional exam requirements/recommendations for international students: Required—TOEFL (minimum score 500 paper-based; 183 computer-based; 65 iBT). *Application deadline:* For fall admission, 1/15 for domestic and international students; for winter admission, 10/1 for domestic and international students; for spring admission, 10/1 for domestic and international students. Application fee: $40 ($50 for international students). Electronic applications accepted. *Expenses:* Tuition, state resident: full-time $3744; part-time $416 per credit. Tuition, nonresident: full-time $5616; part-time $624 per credit. *Required fees:* $1130; $125.50 per credit. Tuition and fees vary according to course load. *Financial support:* In 2011–12, 1 student received support, including 1 research assistantship with full tuition reimbursement available (averaging $4,063 per year); institutionally sponsored loans and unspecified assistantships also available. Support available to part-time students. Financial award application deadline: 3/15; financial award applicants required to submit FAFSA. *Unit head:* Dr. Elba I. Rohena, Chair, 717-872-3671, Fax: 717-871-5754, E-mail: elba.rohena@millersville.edu. *Application contact:* Dr. Victor S. DeSantis, Dean, College of Graduate and Professional Studies, 717-872-3099, Fax: 717-872-3453, E-mail: victor.desantis@millersville.edu. Web site: http://www.millersville.edu/sped/.

Minnesota State University Mankato, College of Graduate Studies, College of Education, Department of Special Education, Mankato, MN 56001. Offers emotional/behavioral disorders (MS, Certificate); learning disabilities (MS, Certificate). *Accreditation:* NCATE. Part-time programs available. Postbaccalaureate distance learning degree programs offered. *Students:* 14 full-time (8 women), 118 part-time (85 women). *Degree requirements:* For master's, comprehensive exam, thesis or alternative. *Entrance requirements:* For master's, Council for Exceptional Children pre-program assessment, minimum GPA of 3.2 during previous 2 years. Additional exam requirements/recommendations for international students: Required—TOEFL. *Application deadline:* For fall admission, 7/1 priority date for domestic students; for spring admission, 11/1 for domestic students. Applications are processed on a rolling basis. Application fee: $40. Electronic applications accepted. *Financial support:* Research assistantships, teaching assistantships with full tuition reimbursements, career-related internships or fieldwork, Federal Work-Study, and institutionally sponsored loans available. Support available to part-time students. Financial award application deadline: 3/15; financial award applicants required to submit FAFSA. *Unit head:* Dr. Gail Zahn, Graduate Coordinator, 507-389-1122. *Application contact:* 507-389-2321, E-mail: grad@mnsu.edu. Web site: http://ed.mnsu.edu/sped/.

Minnesota State University Moorhead, Graduate Studies, College of Education and Human Services, Program in Special Education, Moorhead, MN 56563-0002. Offers MS. *Accreditation:* NCATE. Part-time and evening/weekend programs available. *Degree requirements:* For master's, comprehensive exam, final oral exam, project or thesis. *Entrance requirements:* For master's, MAT, 1 year teaching experience or bachelor's degree in education, minimum GPA of 3.0. Additional exam requirements/recommendations for international students: Required—TOEFL (minimum score 550 paper-based; 213 computer-based). Electronic applications accepted.

Minot State University, Graduate School, Program in Special Education, Minot, ND 58707-0002. Offers education of the deaf (MS); learning disabilities (MS); special education strategist (MS), including early childhood special education, severe multiple handicaps. *Accreditation:* NCATE. *Degree requirements:* For master's, comprehensive exam (for some programs), thesis (for some programs). *Entrance requirements:* For master's, GRE General Test or minimum GPA of 3.0. Additional exam requirements/recommendations for international students: Required—TOEFL. *Faculty research:* Special education team diagnostic unit; individual diagnostic assessments of mentally retarded, learning-disabled, hearing-impaired, and speech-impaired youth; educational programming for the hearing impaired.

Mississippi College, Graduate School, School of Education, Department of Teacher Education and Leadership, Clinton, MS 39058. Offers art (M Ed); biological science (M Ed); business education (M Ed); computer science (M Ed); dyslexia therapy (M Ed); educational leadership (M Ed, Ed D, Ed S); elementary education (M Ed, Ed S); English (M Ed); higher education administration (MS); mathematics (M Ed); secondary education (M Ed); social studies (history) (M Ed); teaching arts (M Ed). Part-time programs available. Postbaccalaureate distance learning degree programs offered (no on-campus study). *Degree requirements:* For master's, comprehensive exam, thesis optional. *Entrance requirements:* For master's, NTE. Additional exam requirements/recommendations for international students: Recommended—TOEFL, IELTS. Electronic applications accepted.

Mississippi State University, College of Education, Department of Curriculum, Instruction and Special Education, Mississippi State, MS 39762. Offers elementary education (MS, PhD, Ed S); middle level education (MAT); secondary education (MAT, MS, Ed S); special education (MS, Ed S). *Accreditation:* NCATE. Part-time and evening/weekend programs available. *Faculty:* 12 full-time (10 women), 2 part-time/adjunct (1 woman). *Students:* 57 full-time (41 women), 104 part-time (81 women); includes 54 minority (52 Black or African American, non-Hispanic/Latino; 1 Hispanic/Latino; 1 Two or more races, non-Hispanic/Latino). Average age 33. 100 applicants, 60% accepted, 48 enrolled. In 2011, 38 master's, 5 doctorates, 5 other advanced degrees awarded. *Degree requirements:* For master's, comprehensive exam; for doctorate, thesis/dissertation; for Ed S, comprehensive exam, thesis or alternative. *Entrance requirements:* For master's, GRE, minimum GPA of 2.75 in junior and senior year, eligibility for initial teacher certification; for doctorate, GRE, minimum graduate GPA of 3.4; for Ed S, GRE, minimum graduate GPA of 3.2. Additional exam requirements/recommendations for international students: Required—TOEFL (minimum score 600 paper-based; 250 computer-based; 100 iBT); Recommended—IELTS (minimum score 7.5). *Application deadline:* For fall admission, 3/1 priority date for domestic students, 5/1 for international students; for spring admission, 9/1 priority date for domestic students, 9/1 for international students. Applications are processed on a rolling basis. Application fee: $40. Electronic applications accepted. *Expenses:* Tuition, state resident: full-time $5805; part-time $322.50 per credit hour. Tuition, nonresident: full-time $14,670; part-time $815 per credit hour. *Financial support:* In 2011–12, 7 research assistantships with full and partial tuition reimbursements (averaging $9,264 per year), 4 teaching assistantships (averaging $8,937 per year) were awarded; Federal Work-Study, institutionally sponsored loans, scholarships/grants, and unspecified assistantships also available. Financial award application deadline: 4/1; financial award applicants required to submit FAFSA. *Faculty research:* Early childhood education, reading, rural schools, multicultural education, use of technology in instruction. *Unit head:* Dr. Devon Brenner, Professor and Interim Head, 662-325-7119, Fax: 662-325-7857, E-mail: devon@ra.msstate.edu. *Application contact:* Dr. C. Susie Burroughs, Professor and Graduate Coordinator, 662-325-3747, Fax: 662-325-7857, E-mail: susie.burroughs@msstate.edu. Web site: http://www.cise.msstate.edu/.

Missouri State University, Graduate College, College of Education, Department of Counseling, Leadership, and Special Education, Program in Special Education, Springfield, MO 65897. Offers mild to moderate disabilities (MS Ed). Part-time and evening/weekend programs available. *Students:* 3 full-time (all women), 83 part-time (69 women); includes 5 minority (1 Black or African American, non-Hispanic/Latino; 2 American Indian or Alaska Native, non-Hispanic/Latino; 1 Asian, non-Hispanic/Latino; 1 Two or more races, non-Hispanic/Latino), 1 international. Average age 35. 29 applicants, 86% accepted, 18 enrolled. In 2011, 29 master's awarded. *Degree requirements:* For master's, comprehensive exam, thesis or alternative. *Entrance requirements:* For master's, GRE or minimum GPA of 3.0, teaching certificate. Additional exam requirements/recommendations for international students: Required—TOEFL (minimum score 550 paper-based; 213 computer-based; 79 iBT). *Application deadline:* For fall admission, 7/20 for domestic students, 5/1 for international students; for spring admission, 12/20 for domestic students, 9/1 for international students. Applications are processed on a rolling basis. Application fee: $35 ($50 for international students). Electronic applications accepted. *Expenses:* Tuition, state resident: full-time $4086; part-time $227 per credit hour. Tuition, nonresident: full-time $8172; part-time $454 per credit hour. *Required fees:* $275 per semester. Tuition and fees vary according to course load, campus/location and program. *Financial support:* Federal Work-Study, institutionally sponsored loans, scholarships/grants, and unspecified assistantships available. Financial award application deadline: 3/31; financial award applicants required to submit FAFSA. *Unit head:* Dr. Tamara Arthaud, Department Head, 417-836-5449, Fax: 417-836-4918, E-mail: clse@missouristate.edu. *Application contact:* Misty Stewart, Coordinator of Graduate Recruitment, 417-836-6079, Fax: 417-836-6200, E-mail: mistystewart@missouristate.edu. Web site: http://education.missouristate.edu/sped/.

Missouri State University, Graduate College, College of Health and Human Services, Department of Communication Sciences and Disorders, Springfield, MO 65897. Offers audiology (Au D); communication sciences and disorders (MS), including education of deaf/hard of hearing, speech-language pathology. *Accreditation:* ASHA (one or more programs are accredited). *Faculty:* 18 full-time (13 women), 5 part-time/adjunct (1 woman). *Students:* 112 full-time (100 women), 1 (woman) part-time; includes 6 minority (1 American Indian or Alaska Native, non-Hispanic/Latino; 2 Asian, non-Hispanic/Latino; 2 Hispanic/Latino; 1 Two or more races, non-Hispanic/Latino), 5 international. Average age 25. 39 applicants, 36% accepted, 14 enrolled. In 2011, 35 master's, 6 doctorates awarded. *Degree requirements:* For master's, comprehensive exam, thesis or alternative; for doctorate, comprehensive exam, thesis/dissertation or alternative, clinical externship. *Entrance requirements:* For master's and doctorate, GRE, minimum GPA of 3.0. Additional exam requirements/recommendations for international students: Required—TOEFL (minimum score 550 paper-based; 213 computer-based; 79 iBT). *Application deadline:* For fall admission, 2/1 for domestic and international students. Application fee: $35 ($50 for international students). Electronic applications accepted. *Expenses:* Tuition, state resident: full-time $4086; part-time $227 per credit hour. Tuition, nonresident: full-time $8172; part-time $454 per credit hour. *Required fees:* $275 per semester. Tuition and fees vary according to course load, campus/location and program. *Financial support:* Career-related internships or fieldwork, Federal Work-Study, scholarships/grants, and unspecified assistantships available. Support available to part-time students. Financial award application deadline: 3/31; financial award applicants required to submit FAFSA. *Faculty research:* Dysphagia, phonological intervention, elderly adult aural rehabilitation, vestibular disorders. *Unit head:* Dr. Neil DiSarno, Head, 417-836-5368, Fax: 417-836-4242, E-mail: neildisarno@missouristate.edu. *Application contact:* Misty Stewart, Coordinator of Graduate Recruitment, 417-836-6079, Fax: 417-836-6200, E-mail: mistystewart@missouristate.edu. Web site: http://www.missouristate.edu/CSD/.

Missouri Western State University, Program in Assessment, St. Joseph, MO 64507-2294. Offers autism spectrum disorders (MAS); learning improvement (MAS); TESOL (MAS); writing (MAS). Part-time programs available. In 2011, 10 degrees awarded. *Application deadline:* Applications are processed on a rolling basis. Application fee: $45 ($50 for international students). Electronic applications accepted. *Expenses:* Tuition, state resident: full-time $4697; part-time $261 per credit hour. Tuition, nonresident: full-time $9355; part-time $520 per credit hour. *Required fees:* $343; $19.10 per credit hour. $30 per semester. Tuition and fees vary according to course load. *Application contact:* Dr. Brian C. Cronk, Dean of the Graduate School, 816-271-4394, E-mail: graduate@missouriwestern.edu.

Monmouth University, The Graduate School, School of Education, West Long Branch, NJ 07764-1898. Offers education (M Ed); initial certification (MAT), including elementary level, K-12, secondary level; learning disabilities-teacher consultant (Certificate); principal (MS Ed); principal/school administrator (MS Ed); reading specialist (MS Ed, Certificate); school counseling (MS Ed); special education (MS Ed), including autism, learning disabilities teacher consultant, teacher of students with disabilities, teaching in inclusive settings; supervisor (Certificate); teacher of the handicapped (Certificate); teaching English to speakers of other languages (TESOL) (Certificate). *Accreditation:* NCATE. Part-time and evening/weekend programs available. *Faculty:* 16 full-time (12 women), 24 part-time/adjunct (17 women). *Students:* 134 full-time (104 women), 293 part-time (246 women); includes 34 minority (11 Black or African American, non-Hispanic/Latino; 2 Asian, non-Hispanic/Latino; 18 Hispanic/Latino; 3 Two or more races, non-Hispanic/Latino), 2 international. Average age 29. 288 applicants, 92% accepted, 182 enrolled. In 2011, 173 master's awarded. *Entrance requirements:* For master's, minimum GPA of 3.0 in major, 2.75 overall; 2 letters of recommendation (for some programs). Additional exam requirements/recommendations for international students: Required—TOEFL (minimum score 550 paper-based; 213 computer-based; 79 iBT), IELTS (minimum score 5), Michigan English Language Assessment Battery (minimum score 77), Cambridge A, B, C. *Application deadline:* For fall admission, 7/15 priority date for domestic students, 7/1 for international students; for spring admission, 11/15 priority date for domestic students, 11/1 for international students. Applications are processed on a rolling basis. Application fee: $50. Electronic applications accepted. *Financial support:* In 2011–12, 274 students received support, including 291 fellowships (averaging $1,783 per year), 21 research assistantships (averaging $8,792 per year); career-related internships or fieldwork, scholarships/grants, and unspecified assistantships also available. Support available to part-time students. Financial award applicants required to submit FAFSA. *Faculty research:* Multicultural literacy, science and mathematics teaching strategies, teacher as reflective practitioner, children with disabilities. *Unit head:* Dr. Jason Barr, Program Director, 732-263-5238, Fax: 732-263-5277, E-mail: jbarr@monmouth.edu. *Application contact:* Kevin Roane, Director, Office of Graduate Admission, 732-571-3452, Fax: 732-263-5123, E-mail: gradadm@monmouth.edu. Web site: http://www.monmouth.edu/academics/schools/education/default.asp.

Montana State University Billings, College of Education, Department of Special Education, Counseling, Reading and Early Childhood, Program in Special Education, Billings, MT 59101-0298. Offers advanced studies (MS Sp Ed); special education generalist (MS Sp Ed). *Accreditation:* NCATE. Part-time programs available. *Degree requirements:* For master's, thesis or professional paper and/or field experience. *Entrance requirements:* For master's, GRE General Test or MAT, minimum GPA of 3.0 (undergraduate), 3.25 (graduate).

Montclair State University, The Graduate School, College of Education and Human Services, Department of Curriculum and Teaching, Doctoral Program in Special Education, Montclair, NJ 07043-1624. Offers M Ed. Part-time and evening/weekend programs available. *Students:* 17 full-time (16 women), 100 part-time (91 women); includes 22 minority (5 Black or African American, non-Hispanic/Latino; 7 Asian, non-Hispanic/Latino; 7 Hispanic/Latino; 3 Two or more races, non-Hispanic/Latino), 1 international. Average age 31. 74 applicants, 69% accepted, 44 enrolled. In 2011, 41 degrees awarded. *Degree requirements:* For master's, comprehensive exam, thesis or alternative. *Entrance requirements:* For master's, GRE General Test, interview, 2 letters of recommendation. Additional exam requirements/recommendations for international students: Required—TOEFL (minimum score 83 iBT), IELTS (minimum score 6.5). *Application deadline:* Applications are processed on a rolling basis. Application fee: $60. Electronic applications accepted. *Financial support:* Federal Work-Study, scholarships/grants, and unspecified assistantships available. Support available to part-time students. Financial award application deadline: 3/1; financial award applicants required to submit FAFSA. *Unit head:* Dr. David Schwarzer, Chairperson, 973-655-5187. *Application contact:* Amy Aiello, Director of Graduate Admissions and Operations, 973-655-5147, Fax: 973-655-7869, E-mail: graduate.school@montclair.edu. Web site: http://cehs.montclair.edu/academic/curriculumteach/programs/masterse.html.

Montclair State University, The Graduate School, College of Education and Human Services, Department of Curriculum and Teaching, Learning Disabilities Teacher-Consultant Post-Master's Certificate Program, Montclair, NJ 07043-1624. Offers Post-Master's Certificate. Part-time and evening/weekend programs available. *Students:* 1 (woman) full-time, 23 part-time (22 women); includes 4 minority (2 Black or African American, non-Hispanic/Latino; 2 Hispanic/Latino). Average age 31. 23 applicants, 57% accepted, 6 enrolled. *Entrance requirements:* Additional exam requirements/recommendations for international students: Required—TOEFL (minimum score 83 iBT), IELTS (minimum score 6.5). *Application deadline:* Applications are processed on a rolling basis. Application fee: $60. Electronic applications accepted. *Financial support:* Federal Work-Study, scholarships/grants, and unspecified assistantships available. Support available to part-time students. Financial award application deadline: 3/1; financial award applicants required to submit FAFSA. *Unit head:* Dr. David Schwarzer, Chairperson, 973-655-5187. *Application contact:* Amy Aiello, Executive Director of The Graduate School, 973-655-5147, Fax: 973-655-7869, E-mail: graduate.school@montclair.edu. Web site: http://cehs.montclair.edu/academic/curriculumteach/programs/pmastercld.html.

Montclair State University, The Graduate School, College of Education and Human Services, Department of Early Childhood, Elementary and Literacy Education, Program in Inclusive Early Childhood Education, Montclair, NJ 07043-1624. Offers M Ed. *Students:* 10 part-time (9 women); includes 2 minority (both Hispanic/Latino). Average age 31. 5 applicants, 60% accepted, 2 enrolled. *Degree requirements:* For master's, comprehensive exam, thesis or alternative. *Entrance requirements:* For master's, GRE General Test, interview, 2 letters of recommendation. Additional exam requirements/recommendations for international students: Required—TOEFL (minimum score 83 iBT), IELTS (minimum score 6.5). *Application deadline:* Applications are processed on a rolling basis. Application fee: $60. Electronic applications accepted. *Unit head:* Dr. Tina Jacobowitz, Chairperson, 973-655-7191. *Application contact:* Amy Aiello, Director of Graduate Admissions and Operations, 973-655-5147, Fax: 973-655-7869, E-mail: graduate.school@montclair.edu. Web site: http://cehs.montclair.edu/academic/ecele/programs/masterspecial.shtml.

Morehead State University, Graduate Programs, College of Education, Department of Curriculum and Instruction, Morehead, KY 40351. Offers curriculum and instruction (Ed S); elementary education (MA Ed), including elementary education, international education, middle school education, reading; secondary education (MA Ed); special education (MA Ed); teaching (MAT). Part-time and evening/weekend programs available. *Degree requirements:* For master's, comprehensive exam, thesis optional; for Ed S, thesis, oral exam. *Entrance requirements:* For master's, GRE General Test, minimum GPA of 2.75, teaching certificate; for Ed S, GRE General Test, interview, master's degree, minimum GPA of 3.5, work experience. Additional exam requirements/recommendations for international students: Required—TOEFL (minimum score 500 paper-based; 173 computer-based). Electronic applications accepted. *Faculty research:* Communicative competence of learning-disabled students, teaching social studies in elementary schools, ungraded primary school organization, study skills.

Morehead State University, Graduate Programs, College of Education, Department of Early Childhood, Elementary and Special Education, Morehead, KY 40351. Offers learning and behavioral disorders P-12 (MAT); moderate and severe disabilities P-12 (MAT). Part-time and evening/weekend programs available. *Degree requirements:* For master's, thesis. *Entrance requirements:* For master's, GRE or PRAXIS II content exam, minimum overall undergraduate GPA of 2.5. Additional exam requirements/recommendations for international students: Required—TOEFL (minimum score 500 paper-based; 173 computer-based). Electronic applications accepted.

Morehead State University, Graduate Programs, College of Education, Department of Foundational and Graduate Studies in Education, Morehead, KY 40351. Offers adult and higher education (MA, Ed S); certified professional counselor (Ed S); counseling P-12 (MA); curriculum and instruction (Ed S); educational technology (MA Ed); instructional leadership (Ed S); school administration (MA); school counseling (Ed S); teacher leader business and marketing content (MA Ed); teacher leader business and marketing technology (MA Ed); teacher leader educational technology (MA Ed); teacher leader English (MA Ed); teacher leader gifted education (MA Ed); teacher leader IECE certification (MA Ed); teacher leader interdisciplinary education P-5 (MA Ed); teacher leader middle grades (MA Ed); teacher leader non IECE certification (MA Ed); teacher leader reading/writing - non-certification (MA Ed); teacher leader reading/writing certification (MA Ed); teacher leader school communication - certification (MA Ed); teacher leader school communication - non-certification (MA Ed); teacher leader social studies (MA Ed); teacher leader special education (MA Ed). *Accreditation:* NCATE. Part-time and evening/weekend programs available. *Degree requirements:* For master's, thesis optional, oral and/or written comprehensive exams; for Ed S, thesis, oral exam. *Entrance requirements:* For master's, GRE General Test, minimum overall undergraduate GPA of 2.5; for Ed S, GRE General Test, interview, master's degree, minimum GPA of 3.5, work experience. Additional exam requirements/recommendations for international students: Required—TOEFL (minimum score 500 paper-based; 173 computer-based). Electronic applications accepted. *Faculty research:* Character education, school accountability, computer applications for school administrators.

Morningside College, Graduate Division, Department of Education, Sioux City, IA 51106. Offers professional educator (MAT); special education: instructional strategist I: mild/moderate elementary (K-6) (MAT); special education: instructional strategist II-mild/moderate secondary (7-12) (MAT); special education: K-12 instructional strategist II-behavior disorders/learning disabilities (MAT); special education: K-12 instructional strategist II-mental disabilities (MAT). Part-time and evening/weekend programs available. *Entrance requirements:* For master's, MAT, writing sample.

Mount Mercy University, Program in Education, Cedar Rapids, IA 52402-4797. Offers reading (MA Ed); special education (MA Ed). *Entrance requirements:* For master's, minimum cumulative GPA of 3.0, 2 letters of recommendation, resume, valid teaching license. Additional exam requirements/recommendations for international students: Required—TOEFL (minimum score 570 paper-based; 88 iBT). Electronic applications accepted.

Mount Saint Mary College, Division of Education, Newburgh, NY 12550-3494. Offers adolescence and special education (MS Ed); adolescence education (MS Ed); childhood and special education (MS Ed); childhood education (MS Ed); literacy (5-12) (Advanced Certificate); literacy (birth-6) (Advanced Certificate); literacy and special education (MS Ed); literacy/childhood (MS Ed); middle school (5-6) (MS Ed); middle school (7-9) (MS Ed); special education (1-6) (MS Ed); special education (7-12) (MS Ed). *Accreditation:* NCATE. Part-time and evening/weekend programs available. *Faculty:* 14 full-time (12 women), 14 part-time/adjunct (8 women). *Students:* 55 full-time (42 women), 158 part-time (125 women); includes 23 minority (4 Black or African American, non-Hispanic/Latino; 1 Asian, non-Hispanic/Latino; 18 Hispanic/Latino). Average age 29. 119 applicants, 45% accepted, 24 enrolled. In 2011, 107 master's awarded. *Application deadline:* Applications are processed on a rolling basis. Application fee: $45. Application fee is waived when completed online. *Expenses: Tuition:* Full-time $13,356; part-time $742 per credit. *Required fees:* $70 per semester. *Financial support:* In 2011–12, 99 students received support. Unspecified assistantships available. Financial award application deadline: 4/15; financial award applicants required to submit FAFSA. *Faculty research:* Learning and teaching styles, computers in special education, language development. *Unit head:* Dr. Theresa Lewis, Coordinator, 845-569-3149, Fax: 845-569-3535, E-mail: tlewis@msmc.edu. *Application contact:* Courtney McDermott, Graduate Recruiter, 845-569-3402, Fax: 845-569-3450, E-mail: courtney.mcdermott@msmc.edu. Web site: http://www.msmc.edu/Academics/Graduate_Programs/Master_of_Science_in_Education.

Mount St. Mary's College, Graduate Division, Department of Education, Specialization in Special Education, Los Angeles, CA 90049-1599. Offers MS, Ed S. Part-time and evening/weekend programs available. *Degree requirements:* For master's, thesis, research project. *Entrance requirements:* For master's, MAT, minimum GPA of 3.0. *Application deadline:* For fall admission, 7/15 priority date for domestic students; for spring admission, 11/15 priority date for domestic students. Application fee: $50 ($75 for international students). *Expenses: Tuition:* Part-time $752 per unit. Part-time tuition and fees vary according to degree level and program. *Financial support:* Institutionally sponsored loans, scholarships/grants, and tuition waivers (partial) available. Support available to part-time students. Financial award application deadline: 3/15; financial award applicants required to submit FAFSA. *Unit head:* Dr. Anne Wilcoxen, Professor, 213-477-2622. *Application contact:* Jessica M. Bibeau, Director of Graduate Admission, 213-477-2800 Ext. 2798, Fax: 213-477-2797, E-mail: jbibeau@msmc.la.edu.

Mount Saint Vincent University, Graduate Programs, Faculty of Education, Program in Educational Psychology, Halifax, NS B3M 2J6, Canada. Offers education of the blind or visually impaired (M Ed, MA Ed); education of the deaf or hard of hearing (M Ed, MA Ed); educational psychology (MA-R); human relations (M Ed, MA Ed). Part-time and evening/weekend programs available. Postbaccalaureate distance learning degree programs offered (minimal on-campus study). *Degree requirements:* For master's, thesis (for some programs). *Entrance requirements:* For master's, bachelor's degree in related field, 1 year of teaching experience. Electronic applications accepted. *Faculty research:* Personality measurement, values reasoning, aggression and sexuality, power and control, quantitative and qualitative research methodologies.

Murray State University, College of Education, Department of Adolescent, Career and Special Education, Program in Special Education, Murray, KY 42071. Offers advanced learning behavior disorders (MA Ed); learning disabilities (MA Ed); moderate/severe disorders (MA Ed). *Accreditation:* NCATE. Part-time and evening/weekend programs available. *Degree requirements:* For master's, thesis optional, portfolio. *Entrance requirements:* For master's, GRE General Test or MAT, teacher certification. Additional exam requirements/recommendations for international students: Required—TOEFL. *Faculty research:* Attention Deficit Hyperactivity Disorder, assistive technology.

National Louis University, National College of Education, Chicago, IL 60603. Offers administration and supervision (M Ed, Ed D, CAS, Ed S); curriculum and instruction (M Ed, MS Ed, CAS); early childhood administration (M Ed, CAS); early childhood education (M Ed, MAT, MS Ed, CAS); education (Ed D); educational psychology/human learning and development (M Ed, MS Ed, CAS, Ed S); elementary education (MAT); interdisciplinary curriculum and instruction (M Ed); mathematics education (M Ed, MS Ed, CAS); reading and language (M Ed, MS Ed, CAS); school psychology (M Ed, Ed S); science education (M Ed, MS Ed, CAS); secondary education (MAT); special education (M Ed, MAT, CAS); technology in education (M Ed, CAS). *Accreditation:* NCATE. Part-time and evening/weekend programs available. *Students:* 224 full-time (162 women), 2,336 part-time (1,767 women); includes 677 minority (366 Black or African American, non-Hispanic/Latino; 8 American Indian or Alaska Native, non-Hispanic/Latino; 68 Asian, non-Hispanic/Latino; 218 Hispanic/Latino; 2 Native Hawaiian or other Pacific Islander, non-Hispanic/Latino; 15 Two or more races, non-Hispanic/Latino), 2 international. Average age 34. In 2011, 1,711 master's, 76 doctorates, 86 other advanced degrees awarded. *Degree requirements:* For doctorate, comprehensive exam, thesis/dissertation. *Entrance requirements:* For master's, MAT or GRE, minimum GPA of 3.0; for doctorate, GRE General Test, minimum GPA of 3.25, interview, resume, writing sample, 4 recommendations. Additional exam requirements/recommendations for international students: Required—TOEFL (minimum score 550 paper-based; 213 computer-based; 79 iBT). *Application deadline:* Applications are processed on a rolling basis. Application fee: $40. *Financial support:* Fellowships, research assistantships, teaching assistantships, career-related internships or fieldwork, Federal Work-Study, institutionally sponsored loans, and scholarships/grants available. Support available to part-time students. Financial award applicants required to submit FAFSA. *Unit head:* Dr. Alison Hilsabeck, Dean, 312-361-3580, Fax: 312-261-2580, E-mail: ahilsabeck@nl.edu. *Application contact:* Ken Kasprzak, Director of Admission, 888-658-8632, Fax: 847-947-5575, E-mail: kkasprzak@nl.edu.

National University, Academic Affairs, School of Education, Department of Special Education, La Jolla, CA 92037-1011. Offers autism (Certificate); deaf and hard-of-hearing education (MS); generalist in special education (MS); juvenile justice special education (MS); special education (MS). Part-time and evening/weekend programs available. Postbaccalaureate distance learning degree programs offered (no on-campus study). *Degree requirements:* For master's, thesis (for some programs). *Entrance requirements:* For master's, interview, minimum GPA of 2.5. Additional exam requirements/recommendations for international students: Required—TOEFL (minimum score 550 paper-based; 213 computer-based; 79 iBT), IELTS (minimum score 6). *Application deadline:* Applications are processed on a rolling basis. Application fee: $60 ($65 for international students). Electronic applications accepted. *Financial support:* Career-related internships or fieldwork, institutionally sponsored loans, scholarships/grants, and tuition waivers (partial) available. Support available to part-time students. Financial award application deadline: 6/30; financial award applicants required to submit FAFSA. *Unit head:* Dr. Denise Hexom, Associate Professor, 858-642-8320, Fax: 858-642-8729, E-mail: dhexom@nu.edu. *Application contact:* Dominick Giovanniello, Associate Regional Dean, 800-NAT-UNIV, Fax: 858-541-779, E-mail: dgiovann@nu.edu. Web site: http://www.nu.edu/OurPrograms/SchoolOfEducation/SpecialEducation.html.

New England College, Program in Education, Henniker, NH 03242-3293. Offers higher education administration (MS, Ed D); K-12 leadership (Ed D); literacy and language arts (M Ed); meeting the needs of all learners/special education (M Ed); teacher leadership/school reform (M Ed). Part-time and evening/weekend programs available.

New Jersey City University, Graduate Studies and Continuing Education, Debra Cannon Partridge Wolfe College of Education, Department of Special Education, Jersey City, NJ 07305-1597. Offers MA. Part-time and evening/weekend programs available. *Students:* 14 full-time (8 women), 101 part-time (71 women); includes 31 minority (17 Black or African American, non-Hispanic/Latino; 1 American Indian or Alaska Native, non-Hispanic/Latino; 2 Asian, non-Hispanic/Latino; 11 Hispanic/Latino), 1 international. Average age 34. In 2011, 79 master's awarded. *Entrance requirements:* Additional exam requirements/recommendations for international students: Required—TOEFL. *Application deadline:* For fall admission, 8/1 priority date for domestic students; for spring admission, 12/1 for domestic students. Applications are processed on a rolling basis. Application fee: $0. *Expenses:* Tuition, state resident: part-time $494 per credit. Tuition, nonresident: part-time $911.30 per credit. *Required fees:* $95.90 per year. *Financial support:* Unspecified assistantships available. *Faculty research:* Mainstreaming the handicapped child and the autistic child. *Unit head:* Dr. Tracy Amerman, Chairperson, 201-200-3023, E-mail: cfleres@njcu.edu. *Application contact:* Dr. William Bajor, Dean of Graduate Studies, 201-200-3409, Fax: 201-200-3411, E-mail: wbajor@njcu.edu.

New Mexico Highlands University, Graduate Studies, School of Education, Las Vegas, NM 87701. Offers curriculum and instruction (MA); education (MA), including counseling, school counseling; educational leadership (MA); exercise and sport sciences (MA), including human performance and sport, sports administration, teacher education; guidance and counseling (MA), including professional counseling, rehabilitation counseling, school counseling; special education (MA), including). Part-time programs available. *Faculty:* 29 full-time (18 women). *Students:* 136 full-time (100 women), 275 part-time (219 women); includes 231 minority (8 Black or African American, non-Hispanic/Latino; 22 American Indian or Alaska Native, non-Hispanic/Latino; 2 Asian, non-Hispanic/Latino; 194 Hispanic/Latino; 1 Native Hawaiian or other Pacific Islander, non-Hispanic/Latino; 4 Two or more races, non-Hispanic/Latino), 14 international. Average age 39. 117 applicants, 82% accepted, 91 enrolled. In 2011, 105 master's awarded. *Degree requirements:* For master's, comprehensive exam, thesis or alternative. *Entrance requirements:* For master's, minimum undergraduate GPA of 3.0. Additional exam requirements/recommendations for international students: Required—TOEFL (minimum score 540 paper-based; 207 computer-based). *Application deadline:* For fall admission, 8/1 priority date for domestic students. Applications are processed on a rolling basis. Application fee: $15. *Expenses:* Tuition, state resident: full-time $2767; part-time $146 per credit hour. Tuition, nonresident: full-time $4879; part-time $234 per credit hour. *International tuition:* $5436 full-time. *Required fees:* $737. *Financial support:* In 2011–12, 12 students received support. Career-related internships or fieldwork, Federal Work-Study, institutionally sponsored loans, scholarships/grants, traineeships, tuition waivers (partial), and unspecified assistantships available. Support available to part-time students. Financial award application deadline: 3/1; financial award applicants required to submit FAFSA. *Faculty research:* Teaching the United States Constitution, middle school curriculum, integrated computer applications for pre-service classroom teachers, adolescent literacy, narrative cognitive modes in NM multicultural setting. *Unit head:* Dr. Michael Anderson, Interim Dean, 505-454-3213, E-mail: mfanderson@nmhu.edu. *Application contact:* Diane Trujillo, Administrative Assistant for Graduate Studies, 505-454-3266, Fax: 505-426-2117, E-mail: dtrujillo@nmhu.edu.

New Mexico State University, Graduate School, College of Education, Department of Special Education and Communication Disorders, Las Cruces, NM 88003-8001. Offers bilingual/multicultural special education (Ed D, PhD); communication disorders (MA); special education (MA, Ed D, PhD). *Accreditation:* ASHA (one or more programs are accredited); NCATE. Part-time and evening/weekend programs available. Postbaccalaureate distance learning degree programs offered. *Faculty:* 13 full-time (11 women), 1 part-time/adjunct (0 women). *Students:* 69 full-time (65 women), 56 part-time (41 women); includes 55 minority (2 American Indian or Alaska Native, non-Hispanic/Latino; 1 Asian, non-Hispanic/Latino; 51 Hispanic/Latino; 1 Two or more races, non-Hispanic/Latino), 4 international. Average age 37. 111 applicants, 32% accepted, 30 enrolled. In 2011, 41 master's, 3 doctorates awarded. *Degree requirements:* For master's, comprehensive exam, thesis optional; for doctorate, comprehensive exam, thesis/dissertation. *Entrance requirements:* For master's, GRE General Test or MAT. Additional exam requirements/recommendations for international students: Required—TOEFL (minimum score 550 paper-based; 79 iBT), IELTS (minimum score 6.5). *Application deadline:* For fall admission, 2/1 priority date for domestic students. Applications are processed on a rolling basis. Application fee: $40 ($50 for international students). Electronic applications accepted. *Expenses:* Tuition, state resident: full-time $5004; part-time $208.50 per credit. Tuition, nonresident: full-time $17,446; part-time $726.90 per credit. *Financial support:* In 2011–12, 1 research assistantship (averaging $1,975 per year), 16 teaching assistantships (averaging $10,248 per year) were awarded; fellowships, career-related internships or fieldwork, Federal Work-Study, and health care benefits also available. Support available to part-time students. Financial award application deadline: 3/1; financial award applicants required to submit FAFSA. *Faculty research:* Multicultural special education, multicultural communication disorders, mild disability, multicultural assessment, deaf education, early childhood, bilingual special education. *Unit head:* Dr. Eric Joseph Lopez, Interim Department Head, 575-

646-2402, Fax: 575-646-7712, E-mail: leric@nmsu.edu. *Application contact:* Coordinator, 575-646-2736, Fax: 575-646-7721, E-mail: gradinfo@nmsu.edu. Web site: http://education.nmsu.edu/spedcd/.

New York University, Steinhardt School of Culture, Education, and Human Development, Department of Teaching and Learning, Program in Early Childhood and Childhood Education, New York, NY 10012-1019. Offers childhood education (MA); childhood education/special education: childhood (MA); early childhood education (MA); positions of leadership: early childhood and elementary education (PhD). *Accreditation:* Teacher Education Accreditation Council. Part-time programs available. *Degree requirements:* For master's, thesis (for some programs); for doctorate, thesis/dissertation. *Entrance requirements:* For doctorate, GRE General Test, interview. Additional exam requirements/recommendations for international students: Required—TOEFL. Electronic applications accepted. *Faculty research:* Teacher evaluation and beliefs about teaching, early literacy development, language arts, child development and education, cultural differences.

New York University, Steinhardt School of Culture, Education, and Human Development, Department of Teaching and Learning, Program in Special Education, New York, NY 10012-1019. Offers childhood (MA); dual certification: childhood education/childhood special education (MA); dual certification: early childhood education/early childhood special education (MA); early childhood (MA). *Accreditation:* Teacher Education Accreditation Council. Part-time programs available. *Degree requirements:* For master's, thesis (for some programs). *Entrance requirements:* Additional exam requirements/recommendations for international students: Required—TOEFL. Electronic applications accepted. *Faculty research:* Special education referrals, attention deficit disorders in children, mainstreaming, curriculum-based assessment and program implementation, special education policy.

Niagara University, Graduate Division of Education, Concentration in Teacher Education, Niagara Falls, Niagara University, NY 14109. Offers early childhood and childhood education (MS Ed); middle and adolescence education (MS Ed); special education (grades 1-12) (MS Ed). *Accreditation:* NCATE. *Faculty:* 4 full-time (1 woman), 6 part-time/adjunct (4 women). *Students:* 249 full-time (162 women), 56 part-time (39 women); includes 11 minority (5 Black or African American, non-Hispanic/Latino; 1 American Indian or Alaska Native, non-Hispanic/Latino; 1 Asian, non-Hispanic/Latino; 2 Hispanic/Latino; 2 Two or more races, non-Hispanic/Latino), 176 international. Average age 24. In 2011, 233 master's, 1 Certificate awarded. *Entrance requirements:* For master's, GRE General Test or MAT. *Application deadline:* For fall admission, 8/1 for domestic students. Applications are processed on a rolling basis. Application fee: $30. *Expenses:* Contact institution. *Financial support:* Career-related internships or fieldwork, Federal Work-Study, and scholarships/grants available. Financial award application deadline: 3/15. *Unit head:* Dr. Chandra Foote, Chair, 716-286-8549. *Application contact:* Dr. Debra A. Colley, Dean of Education, 716-286-8560, Fax: 716-286-8561, E-mail: dcolley@niagara.edu.

Norfolk State University, School of Graduate Studies, School of Education, Department of Special Education, Norfolk, VA 23504. Offers severe disabilities (MA). *Accreditation:* NCATE. Part-time programs available. *Degree requirements:* For master's, thesis or alternative. *Entrance requirements:* For master's, minimum GPA of 3.0 in major, 2.5 overall.

North Carolina Central University, Division of Academic Affairs, School of Education, Special Education Program, Durham, NC 27707-3129. Offers M Ed, MAT. *Accreditation:* NCATE. Part-time and evening/weekend programs available. *Degree requirements:* For master's, comprehensive exam, thesis or alternative. *Entrance requirements:* For master's, GRE, minimum GPA of 3.0 in major, 2.5 overall. Additional exam requirements/recommendations for international students: Required—TOEFL. *Faculty research:* Vocational programs for special needs learners.

North Carolina State University, Graduate School, College of Education, Department of Curriculum and Instruction, Program in Special Education, Raleigh, NC 27695. Offers M Ed, MS. *Accreditation:* NCATE. *Degree requirements:* For master's, thesis optional. *Entrance requirements:* For master's, GRE General Test and MAT, minimum GPA of 3.0 in major. Electronic applications accepted. *Faculty research:* Nature of disabilities, intervention research.

Northeastern Illinois University, Graduate College, College of Education, Department of Special Education, Program in Special Education, Chicago, IL 60625-4699. Offers early childhood special education (MA); educating children with behavior disorders (MA); educating individuals with mental retardation (MA); teaching children with learning disabilities (MA). Part-time and evening/weekend programs available. *Degree requirements:* For master's, thesis optional, project. *Entrance requirements:* For master's, minimum GPA of 2.75; previous course work in history or philosophy of education or teaching certificate. Additional exam requirements/recommendations for international students: Required—TOEFL (minimum score 550 paper-based; 213 computer-based; 79 iBT). Electronic applications accepted. *Faculty research:* Bilingual special education, use of technology in the classroom, teachers' attitudes toward inclusion, standards for special education teachers.

Northern Arizona University, Graduate College, College of Education, Department of Educational Specialties, Flagstaff , AZ 86011. Offers autism spectrum disorders (Certificate); bilingual/multicultural education (M Ed), including bilingual education, ESL education; career and technical education (M Ed, Certificate); curriculum and instruction (Ed D); early childhood special education (M Ed); early intervention (Certificate); educational technology (M Ed, Certificate); special education (M Ed). *Faculty:* 28 full-time (19 women). *Students:* 113 full-time (91 women), 206 part-time (158 women); includes 104 minority (8 Black or African American, non-Hispanic/Latino; 17 American Indian or Alaska Native, non-Hispanic/Latino; 6 Asian, non-Hispanic/Latino; 65 Hispanic/Latino; 2 Native Hawaiian or other Pacific Islander, non-Hispanic/Latino; 6 Two or more races, non-Hispanic/Latino), 3 international. Average age 30. 141 applicants, 75% accepted, 76 enrolled. In 2011, 167 master's, 7 Certificates awarded. *Degree requirements:* For master's, comprehensive exam (for some programs), thesis (for some programs). *Entrance requirements:* For master's, minimum GPA of 3.0. Additional exam requirements/recommendations for international students: Required—TOEFL (minimum score 550 paper-based; 213 computer-based; 80 iBT), IELTS (minimum score 7). *Application deadline:* For fall admission, 3/1 for international students; for spring admission, 9/15 for international students. Applications are processed on a rolling basis. Application fee: $65. Electronic applications accepted. *Expenses:* Tuition, state resident: full-time $7190; part-time $355 per credit hour. Tuition, nonresident: full-time $18,092; part-time $1005 per credit hour. *Required fees:* $818; $328 per semester. *Financial support:* Applicants required to submit FAFSA. *Unit head:* Dr. Jennifer Prior, Chair, 928-523-5064, Fax: 928-523-1929, E-mail: jennifer.prior@nau.edu. *Application contact:* Shirley Robinson, Coordinator, 928-523-4348, Fax: 928-523-8950, E-mail: shirley.robinson@nau.edu. Web site: http://nau.edu/coe/ed-specialties/.

Northern Illinois University, Graduate School, College of Education, Department of Special and Early Education, De Kalb, IL 60115-2854. Offers curriculum and instruction (MS Ed, Ed D), including curriculum leadership (Ed D), elementary education (Ed D), secondary education (Ed D); early childhood education (MS Ed); elementary education (MS Ed); special education (MS Ed). Part-time and evening/weekend programs available. *Faculty:* 22 full-time (14 women), 2 part-time/adjunct (both women). *Students:* 58 full-time (46 women), 241 part-time (189 women); includes 35 minority (17 Black or African American, non-Hispanic/Latino; 7 Asian, non-Hispanic/Latino; 9 Hispanic/Latino; 2 Two or more races, non-Hispanic/Latino), 3 international. Average age 35. 100 applicants, 65% accepted, 45 enrolled. In 2011, 186 master's, 7 doctorates awarded. *Degree requirements:* For master's, comprehensive exam, thesis optional; for doctorate, thesis/dissertation, candidacy exam, dissertation defense. *Entrance requirements:* For master's, GRE General Test or MAT, minimum undergraduate GPA of 2.75; for doctorate, GRE General Test or MAT, minimum undergraduate GPA of 2.75, graduate 3.2. Additional exam requirements/recommendations for international students: Required—TOEFL (minimum score 550 paper-based; 213 computer-based). *Application deadline:* For fall admission, 6/1 for domestic students, 5/1 for international students; for spring admission, 11/1 for domestic students, 10/1 for international students. Applications are processed on a rolling basis. Application fee: $40. Electronic applications accepted. *Financial support:* In 2011–12, 34 research assistantships with full tuition reimbursements were awarded; fellowships with full tuition reimbursements, teaching assistantships with full tuition reimbursements, career-related internships or fieldwork, Federal Work-Study, scholarships/grants, tuition waivers (full), and unspecified assistantships also available. Support available to part-time students. Financial award applicants required to submit FAFSA. *Faculty research:* Teacher certification, stress reduction during student teaching, teaching history, portfolios in student teaching. *Unit head:* Dr. Connie Fox, Interim Chair, 815-753-1619, E-mail: seed@niu.edu. *Application contact:* Gail Myers, 815-753-0381, E-mail: gmyers@niu.edu. Web site: http://www.cedu.niu.edu/seed/.

Northern Kentucky University, Office of Graduate Programs, College of Education and Human Services, Program in Teaching, Highland Heights, KY 41099. Offers rank 1 (Certificate); rank 1 supervisor of instruction (Certificate); school superintendent (Certificate); special education (MA, Certificate); teaching (MA). Part-time programs available. *Students:* 4 full-time (3 women), 50 part-time (28 women); includes 2 minority (both Black or African American, non-Hispanic/Latino). Average age 33. 57 applicants, 40% accepted, 21 enrolled. In 2011, 33 master's, 4 other advanced degrees awarded. *Degree requirements:* For master's, comprehensive exam, thesis optional, portfolio, student teaching or internship. *Entrance requirements:* For master's, GRE, PRAXIS II, minimum GPA of 2.5, criminal background check (state and federal), resume, letter to the reviewer, interview. Additional exam requirements/recommendations for international students: Required—TOEFL (minimum score 550 paper-based; 213 computer-based; 79 iBT); Recommended—IELTS (minimum score 6.5). *Application deadline:* For fall admission, 6/1 for domestic and international students; for spring admission, 10/1 for international students. Application fee: $40. Electronic applications accepted. *Expenses:* Tuition, state resident: full-time $7614; part-time $423 per credit hour. Tuition, nonresident: full-time $13,104; part-time $728 per credit hour. Tuition and fees vary according to degree level and reciprocity agreements. *Financial support:* Unspecified assistantships available. Financial award applicants required to submit FAFSA. *Faculty research:* Middle grades students, secondary students, rural classrooms, urban classrooms, teacher preparation. *Unit head:* Dr. Lenore Kinne, Director, Teacher Education Program, 859-572-1503, E-mail: kinnel1@nku.edu. *Application contact:* Melissa Decker, Alternative Certification Coordinator, 859-572-6330, Fax: 859-572-1384, E-mail: deckerm@nku.edu.

Northern Michigan University, College of Graduate Studies, College of Professional Studies, School of Education, Program in Learning Disabilities, Marquette, MI 49855-5301. Offers MA Ed. Part-time programs available. Postbaccalaureate distance learning degree programs offered. *Degree requirements:* For master's, thesis or alternative. *Entrance requirements:* For master's, GRE General Test, minimum GPA of 3.0. *Faculty research:* Interdisciplinary approaches to learning disabilities, neurological bases for cognitive processing of information.

Northwestern State University of Louisiana, Graduate Studies and Research, College of Education and Human Development, Program in Special Education, Natchitoches, LA 71497. Offers M Ed, MAT. *Students:* 12 full-time (10 women), 78 part-time (70 women); includes 14 minority (5 Black or African American, non-Hispanic/Latino; 1 American Indian or Alaska Native, non-Hispanic/Latino; 3 Asian, non-Hispanic/Latino; 4 Hispanic/Latino; 1 Two or more races, non-Hispanic/Latino). Average age 35. 25 applicants, 100% accepted, 19 enrolled. In 2011, 14 master's awarded. *Degree requirements:* For master's, comprehensive exam, thesis (for some programs). *Entrance requirements:* For master's, GRE General Test. Additional exam requirements/recommendations for international students: Required—TOEFL. *Application deadline:* For fall admission, 3/15 priority date for domestic students; for spring admission, 10/15 priority date for domestic students. Applications are processed on a rolling basis. Application fee: $20 ($30 for international students). Electronic applications accepted. *Expenses:* Tuition, state resident: full-time $3440. Tuition, nonresident: full-time $12,010. *Financial support:* Application deadline: 5/1; applicants required to submit FAFSA. *Unit head:* Dr. Vickie Gentry, Chair, 318-357-6288, Fax: 318-357-6275, E-mail: education@nsula.edu. *Application contact:* Dr. Steven G. Horton, Associate Provost/Dean, Graduate Studies, Research, and Information Systems, 318-357-5851, Fax: 318-357-5019, E-mail: grad_school@nsula.edu.

Northwestern State University of Louisiana, Graduate Studies and Research, College of Education and Human Development, Programs in Educational Leadership and Instruction, Natchitoches, LA 71497. Offers counseling (Ed S); educational leadership (M Ed, Ed S); educational technology (Ed S); elementary teaching (Ed S); reading (Ed S); secondary teaching (Ed S); special education (Ed S). *Accreditation:* NASAD. *Students:* 7 full-time (6 women), 75 part-time (59 women); includes 22 minority (18 Black or African American, non-Hispanic/Latino; 2 American Indian or Alaska Native, non-Hispanic/Latino; 2 Hispanic/Latino). Average age 36. 30 applicants, 97% accepted, 15 enrolled. In 2011, 31 master's, 16 Ed Ss awarded. *Degree requirements:* For master's, comprehensive exam, thesis (for some programs). *Entrance requirements:* For master's and Ed S, GRE General Test. Additional exam requirements/recommendations for international students: Required—TOEFL. *Application deadline:* For fall admission, 3/15 priority date for domestic students; for spring admission, 10/15 priority date for domestic students. Applications are processed on a rolling basis. Application fee: $20 ($30 for international students). Electronic applications accepted. *Expenses:* Tuition, state resident: full-time $3440. Tuition, nonresident: full-time $12,010. *Unit head:* Dr. Vickie Gentry, Chair, 318-357-6288, Fax: 318-357-6275, E-mail: education@nsula.edu. *Application contact:* Dr. Steven G. Horton, Associate Provost/Dean, Graduate Studies, Research, and Information Systems, 318-357-5851, Fax: 318-357-5019, E-mail: grad_school@nsula.edu.

Northwest Missouri State University, Graduate School, College of Education and Human Services, Department of Curriculum and Instruction, Program in Special Education, Maryville, MO 64468-6001. Offers MS Ed. *Faculty:* 11 full-time (all women). *Students:* 2 full-time (both women), 20 part-time (18 women); includes 2 minority (1 Hispanic/Latino; 1 Two or more races, non-Hispanic/Latino). 17 applicants, 100% accepted, 10 enrolled. In 2011, 18 master's awarded. *Entrance requirements:* For master's, GRE General Test, minimum GPA of 2.75, teaching certificate. Additional exam requirements/recommendations for international students: Required—TOEFL (minimum score 550 paper-based; 213 computer-based). *Application deadline:* For fall admission, 7/1 for domestic and international students; for spring admission, 11/15 for domestic and international students. Application fee: $0 ($50 for international students). *Financial support:* Application deadline: 4/1. *Unit head:* Dr. Shirley Steffens, Head, 660-562-1443. *Application contact:* Dr. Gregory Haddock, Dean of Graduate School, 660-562-1145, Fax: 660-562-1096, E-mail: gradsch@nwmissouri.edu.

Northwest Nazarene University, Graduate Studies, Program in Teacher Education, Nampa, ID 83686-5897. Offers curriculum and instruction (M Ed); educational leadership (M Ed, Ed D, Ed S); exceptional child (M Ed); reading education (M Ed). *Accreditation:* ACA (one or more programs are accredited); NCATE. Part-time programs available. Postbaccalaureate distance learning degree programs offered (no on-campus study). *Faculty:* 15 full-time (9 women), 36 part-time/adjunct (21 women). *Students:* 80 full-time (54 women), 119 part-time (98 women); includes 13 minority (1 American Indian or Alaska Native, non-Hispanic/Latino; 10 Hispanic/Latino; 1 Native Hawaiian or other Pacific Islander, non-Hispanic/Latino; 1 Two or more races, non-Hispanic/Latino), 8 international. Average age 36. 60 applicants, 95% accepted, 39 enrolled. In 2011, 43 master's, 24 other advanced degrees awarded. *Degree requirements:* For master's, comprehensive exam (for some programs), action research project. *Entrance requirements:* For master's, minimum undergraduate GPA of 2.8 overall or 3.0 during final 30 semester credits. *Application deadline:* For fall admission, 9/1 for domestic students. Applications are processed on a rolling basis. Application fee: $25. *Faculty research:* Action research, cooperative learning, accountability, institutional accreditation. *Unit head:* Dr. Paula Kellerer, Chair, 208-467-8729, Fax: 208-467-8562. *Application contact:* Jackie Schober, 208-467-8341, Fax: 208-467-8786, E-mail: jsschober@nnu.edu. Web site: http://www.nnu.edu/graded/.

Notre Dame College, Graduate Programs, South Euclid, OH 44121-4293. Offers mild/moderate needs (M Ed); reading (M Ed); security policy studies (MA, Graduate Certificate); technology (M Ed). Part-time and evening/weekend programs available. *Faculty:* 6 full-time (3 women), 19 part-time/adjunct (16 women). *Students:* 344 part-time (253 women). *Degree requirements:* For master's, thesis. *Entrance requirements:* For master's, GRE General Test, MAT, minimum undergraduate GPA of 2.75, valid teaching certificate, bachelor's degree in an education-related field from accredited college or university, official transcripts of most recent college work. *Application deadline:* For fall admission, 8/1 priority date for domestic students; for spring admission, 1/1 for domestic students. Applications are processed on a rolling basis. Application fee: $40. *Expenses: Tuition:* Part-time $528 per credit. *Financial support:* Tuition waivers (full) available. Support available to part-time students. Financial award application deadline: 4/15; financial award applicants required to submit FAFSA. *Faculty research:* Cognitive psychology, teaching critical thinking in the classroom. *Application contact:* Sarah Palace, Assistant Dean of Adult Enrollment, 216-373-5350, Fax: 216-373-6330, E-mail: spalace@ndc.edu.

Notre Dame de Namur University, Division of Academic Affairs, School of Education and Leadership, Program in Special Education, Belmont, CA 94002-1908. Offers preliminary education specialist credential (Certificate); special education (MA). Part-time and evening/weekend programs available. In 2011, 13 master's awarded. *Degree requirements:* For master's, thesis. *Entrance requirements:* For master's, interview, minimum GPA of 2.5. Additional exam requirements/recommendations for international students: Required—TOEFL (minimum score 550 paper-based; 213 computer-based; 79 iBT). *Application deadline:* For fall admission, 8/1 priority date for domestic students; for spring admission, 12/1 priority date for domestic students. Applications are processed on a rolling basis. Application fee: $60. Electronic applications accepted. *Expenses: Tuition:* Full-time $14,220; part-time $790 per credit. *Required fees:* $35 per semester. Tuition and fees vary according to program. *Financial support:* Career-related internships or fieldwork available. Support available to part-time students. Financial award applicants required to submit FAFSA. *Unit head:* Dr. Judith Doktor, Director, 650-508-3627, E-mail: jdoktor@ndnu.edu. *Application contact:* Candace Hallmark, Associate Director of Admissions, 650-508-3600, Fax: 650-508-3426, E-mail: grad.admit@ndnu.edu.

Nyack College, School of Education, Nyack, NY 10960-3698. Offers childhood education (MS); childhood special education (MS). Part-time and evening/weekend programs available. *Students:* 3 full-time (all women), 29 part-time (24 women); includes 16 minority (5 Black or African American, non-Hispanic/Latino; 2 Asian, non-Hispanic/Latino; 8 Hispanic/Latino; 1 Two or more races, non-Hispanic/Latino), 1 international. Average age 29. In 2011, 4 master's awarded. *Degree requirements:* For master's, comprehensive exam, field experience. *Entrance requirements:* For master's, LAST (Liberal Arts and Sciences Test), transcripts, autobiography and statement on reasons for pursuing graduate study in education, recommendations, 6 credits of language, evidence of computer literacy, introductory course in psychology. Additional exam requirements/recommendations for international students: Required—TOEFL (minimum score 550 paper-based), TWE (minimum score 4). *Application deadline:* Applications are processed on a rolling basis. Application fee: $30. Electronic applications accepted. *Expenses:* Contact institution. *Financial support:* Scholarships/grants and state aid (for NY residents) available. Financial award applicants required to submit FAFSA. *Unit head:* Dr. JoAnn Looney, Dean, 845-675-4538, Fax: 845-358-0874. *Application contact:* Traci Piescki, Director of Admissions, 800-541-6891, Fax: 845-348-3912, E-mail: admissions.grad@nyack.edu. Web site: http://www.nyack.edu/education.

Oakland University, Graduate Study and Lifelong Learning, School of Education and Human Services, Department of Human Development and Child Studies, Program in Special Education, Rochester, MI 48309-4401. Offers M Ed, Certificate. *Accreditation:* Teacher Education Accreditation Council. *Entrance requirements:* For master's, minimum GPA of 3.0 for unconditional admission, interview. Additional exam requirements/recommendations for international students: Required—TOEFL (minimum score 550 paper-based; 213 computer-based). Electronic applications accepted.

Ohio University, Graduate College, Gladys W. and David H. Patton College of Education and Human Services, Department of Teacher Education, Athens, OH 45701-2979. Offers adolescent to young adult education (M Ed); curriculum and instruction (M Ed, PhD); early childhood/special education (M Ed); intervention specialist/mild-moderate needs (M Ed); intervention specialist/moderate-intensive needs (M Ed); mathematics education (PhD); middle child education (M Ed); reading education (M Ed); social studies education (PhD). Part-time and evening/weekend programs available. *Students:* 131 full-time (92 women), 82 part-time (62 women); includes 9 minority (4 Black or African American, non-Hispanic/Latino; 2 American Indian or Alaska Native, non-Hispanic/Latino; 1 Asian, non-Hispanic/Latino; 1 Hispanic/Latino; 1 Two or more races, non-Hispanic/Latino), 11 international. 136 applicants, 70% accepted, 65 enrolled. In 2011, 58 master's, 8 doctorates awarded. *Degree requirements:* For master's, thesis or alternative; for doctorate, comprehensive exam, thesis/dissertation. *Entrance requirements:* For master's, GRE General Test or MAT (if GPA is below 2.9); for doctorate, GRE General Test, minimum GPA of 3.4, work experience. Additional exam requirements/recommendations for international students: Required—TOEFL (minimum score 550 paper-based; 80 iBT) or IELTS (minimum score 6.5). *Application deadline:* For fall admission, 5/1 priority date for domestic students, 4/1 for international students; for winter admission, 11/1 priority date for domestic students, 10/1 for international students; for spring admission, 2/15 priority date for domestic students, 1/1 for international students. Applications are processed on a rolling basis. Application fee: $50 ($55 for international students). Electronic applications accepted. *Financial support:* Research assistantships with full tuition reimbursements, teaching assistantships with full tuition reimbursements, Federal Work-Study, institutionally sponsored loans, tuition waivers (partial), and unspecified assistantships available. Financial award application deadline: 3/1. *Faculty research:* Cognition literacy, character education, teacher's education reform, disabilities. *Total annual research expenditures:* $46,933. *Unit head:* Dr. John Henning, Chair, 740-597-1830, Fax: 740-593-0477, E-mail: henningj@ohio.edu. *Application contact:* Floyd J. Doney, Director of Student Affairs, 740-593-4400, Fax: 740-593-9310, E-mail: doney@ohio.edu. Web site: http://www.cehs.ohio.edu/academics/te/index.htm.

Old Dominion University, Darden College of Education, Program in Special Education, Norfolk, VA 23529. Offers MS Ed, PhD. *Accreditation:* NCATE. Part-time and evening/weekend programs available. Postbaccalaureate distance learning degree programs offered (no on-campus study). *Faculty:* 12 full-time (9 women), 8 part-time/adjunct (4 women). *Students:* 30 full-time (28 women), 100 part-time (86 women); includes 18 minority (11 Black or African American, non-Hispanic/Latino; 2 Asian, non-Hispanic/Latino; 2 Hispanic/Latino; 3 Two or more races, non-Hispanic/Latino). Average age 34. 78 applicants, 85% accepted, 61 enrolled. In 2011, 48 master's, 1 doctorate awarded. *Degree requirements:* For master's, comprehensive exam, thesis or alternative; for doctorate, comprehensive exam, thesis/dissertation. *Entrance requirements:* For master's, GRE General Test or MAT, PRAXIS I, minimum GPA of 2.8; for doctorate, GRE. Additional exam requirements/recommendations for international students: Recommended—TOEFL (minimum score 550 paper-based; 213 computer-based). *Application deadline:* For fall admission, 6/1 priority date for domestic students, 6/1 for international students; for winter admission, 11/1 priority date for domestic students, 11/1 for international students; for spring admission, 3/1 priority date for domestic students, 3/1 for international students. Applications are processed on a rolling basis. Application fee: $50. Electronic applications accepted. *Expenses:* Tuition, state resident: full-time $9096; part-time $379 per credit. Tuition, nonresident: full-time $23,064; part-time $961 per credit. *Required fees:* $127 per semester. One-time fee: $50. *Financial support:* In 2011–12, 70 students received support, including 1 fellowship (averaging $15,000 per year), 2 teaching assistantships with tuition reimbursements available (averaging $15,000 per year); research assistantships with tuition reimbursements available, career-related internships or fieldwork, scholarships/grants, tuition waivers (partial), and unspecified assistantships also available. Financial award application deadline: 2/15; financial award applicants required to submit FAFSA. *Faculty research:* Inclusion, autism spectrum disorder, functional behavioral assessment, infant and preschool handicapped, distance learning. *Total annual research expenditures:* $3.6 million. *Unit head:* Dr. Cheryl S. Baker, Graduate Program Director, 757-683-4383, Fax: 757-683-4129, E-mail: csbaker@odu.edu. *Application contact:* William Heffelfinger, Director of Graduate Admissions, 757-683-5554, Fax: 757-683-3255, E-mail: gradadmit@odu.edu. Web site: http://education.odu.edu/esse/academics/sped/speddeg.shtml.

Ottawa University, Graduate Studies-Arizona, Program in Education, Ottawa, KS 66067-3399. Offers community college counseling (MA); curriculum and instruction (MA); early childhood (MA); education intervention (MA); education leadership (MA); education technology (MA); Montessori early childhood education (MA); Montessori elementary education (MA); professional development (MA); school guidance counseling (MA); special education - cross categorical (MA). Programs offered in Mesa, Phoenix, Tempe and West Valley, AZ. *Accreditation:* NCATE. Part-time programs available. *Degree requirements:* For master's, thesis or alternative. *Entrance requirements:* For master's, minimum undergraduate GPA of 3.0, copy of current state certification or teaching license. Additional exam requirements/recommendations for international students: Required—TOEFL (minimum score 550 paper-based; 213 computer-based). Electronic applications accepted. *Expenses:* Contact institution.

Our Lady of the Lake University of San Antonio, School of Professional Studies, Program in Generic Special Education, San Antonio, TX 78207-4689. Offers elementary education (M Ed). Part-time and evening/weekend programs available. *Degree requirements:* For master's, comprehensive exam, thesis optional, examination for the Certification of Education in Texas. *Entrance requirements:* For master's, GRE General Test or MAT, interview. Additional exam requirements/recommendations for international students: Required—TOEFL. Electronic applications accepted.

Pace University, School of Education, New York, NY 10038. Offers adolescent education (MST); childhood education (MST); educational leadership (MS Ed); educational technology studies (MS); literacy (MSE); school business management (Certificate); special education (MS Ed); teaching students with disabilities (MSE). *Accreditation:* NCATE. Part-time and evening/weekend programs available. *Students:* 164 full-time (131 women), 533 part-time (396 women); includes 157 minority (59 Black or African American, non-Hispanic/Latino; 2 American Indian or Alaska Native, non-Hispanic/Latino; 26 Asian, non-Hispanic/Latino; 54 Hispanic/Latino; 1 Native Hawaiian or other Pacific Islander, non-Hispanic/Latino; 15 Two or more races, non-Hispanic/Latino), 10 international. Average age 29. 256 applicants, 79% accepted, 114 enrolled. In 2011, 334 master's, 34 other advanced degrees awarded. *Degree requirements:* For master's, internship. *Entrance requirements:* For master's, interview, teaching certificate. Additional exam requirements/recommendations for international students: Required—TOEFL. *Application deadline:* For fall admission, 7/31 priority date for domestic students; for spring admission, 11/30 for domestic students. Applications are processed on a rolling basis. Application fee: $70. Electronic applications accepted. *Expenses:* Contact institution. *Financial support:* Research assistantships, career-related internships or fieldwork, and Federal Work-Study available. Support available to part-time students. Financial award applicants required to submit FAFSA. *Unit head:* Dr. Andrea M. Spencer, Dean, 212-346-1345, E-mail: aspencer@pace.edu. *Application contact:* Susan Ford-Goldschein, Director of Admissions, 212-346-1660, Fax: 212-346-1585, E-mail: gradnyc@pace.edu. Web site: http://www.pace.edu/.

Pacific University, College of Education, Forest Grove, OR 97116-1797. Offers early childhood education (MAT); education (MAE); elementary education (MAT); high school education (MAT); middle school education (MAT); special education (MAT); visual function in learning (M Ed). *Accreditation:* NCATE. Part-time and evening/weekend programs available. *Degree requirements:* For master's, research project. *Entrance requirements:* For master's, California Basic Educational Skills Test, PRAXIS II, minimum undergraduate GPA of 2.75, 3.0 graduate. Additional exam requirements/recommendations for international students: Required—TOEFL. Electronic applications accepted. *Expenses:* Contact institution. *Faculty research:* Defining a culturally competent classroom, technology in the k-12 classroom, Socratic seminars, social studies education.

Park University, College of Graduate and Professional Studies, Kansas City, MO 54105. Offers adult education (M Ed); at-risk students (M Ed); disaster and emergency management (MPA); educational administration (M Ed); entrepreneurship (MBA); general business (MBA); general education (M Ed); government/business relations (MPA); healthcare/services management (MBA, MPA); international business (MBA); K-12 certification (MAT); management information systems (MBA); management of information systems (MPA); middle school certification (MAT); multi-cultural education (M Ed); nonprofit management (MPA); public management (MPA); school law (M Ed); secondary school certification (MAT); special education (M Ed). Part-time and evening/

weekend programs available. Postbaccalaureate distance learning degree programs offered (no on-campus study). *Degree requirements:* For master's, comprehensive exam, thesis (for some programs). *Entrance requirements:* For master's, GRE, GMAT, teacher certification (M Ed). Additional exam requirements/recommendations for international students: Required—TOEFL (minimum score 550 paper-based). Electronic applications accepted. *Faculty research:* Literacy, leadership, brain based research, multicultural education, diversity.

Penn State Great Valley, Graduate Studies, Education Division, Malvern, PA 19355-1488. Offers education (M Ed); special education (MS). *Unit head:* Dr. Roy Clariana, Division Head, 610-648-3253, Fax: 610-725-5253, E-mail: rbc4@psu.edu. *Application contact:* 610-648-3242, Fax: 610-889-1334. Web site: http://www.sgps.psu.edu/Level3.aspx?id=512.

Penn State University Park, Graduate School, College of Education, Department of Educational Psychology and Special Education, State College, University Park, PA 16802-1503. Offers counselor education (M Ed, MS, PhD); educational psychology (MS, PhD, Certificate); school psychology (M Ed, MS, PhD, Certificate); special education (M Ed, MS, PhD, Certificate). *Unit head:* Dr. David H. Monk, Dean, 814-865-2526, Fax: 814-865-0555, E-mail: dhm6@psu.edu. *Application contact:* Cynthia E. Nicosia, Director, Graduate Enrollment Services, 814-865-1834, E-mail: cey1@psu.edu. Web site: http://www.ed.psu.edu/educ/epcse.

Piedmont College, School of Education, Demorest, GA 30535-0010. Offers early childhood education (MA, MAT); middle grades education (MA); secondary education (MA, MAT); special education (MA, MAT); teacher leadership (Ed S). Part-time and evening/weekend programs available. *Students:* 546 full-time (433 women), 809 part-time (698 women); includes 172 minority (139 Black or African American, non-Hispanic/Latino; 2 American Indian or Alaska Native, non-Hispanic/Latino; 6 Asian, non-Hispanic/Latino; 18 Hispanic/Latino; 7 Two or more races, non-Hispanic/Latino), 17 international. Average age 37. 342 applicants, 83% accepted, 234 enrolled. In 2011, 444 master's, 510 other advanced degrees awarded. *Degree requirements:* For master's, thesis, field experience in the classroom teaching ; for doctorate, thesis/dissertation. *Entrance requirements:* For master's, GRE General Test, MAT, minimum undergraduate GPA of 2.5; for Ed S, minimum graduate GPA of 3.5, valid teaching certificate. Additional exam requirements/recommendations for international students: Required—TOEFL (minimum score 550 paper-based; 213 computer-based). *Application deadline:* For fall admission, 7/15 for domestic students; for spring admission, 12/1 for domestic students. Applications are processed on a rolling basis. Application fee: $0. Electronic applications accepted. *Expenses: Tuition:* Part-time $407 per credit hour. Tuition and fees vary according to program. *Financial support:* Career-related internships or fieldwork, Federal Work-Study, and unspecified assistantships available. Support available to part-time students. Financial award applicants required to submit FAFSA. *Unit head:* Dr. Bob Cummings, Dean, 706-778-3000 Ext. 1201, Fax: 706-776-9608, E-mail: bcummings@piedmont.edu. *Application contact:* Penny Loggins, Director of Graduate Admissions, 706-778-8500 Ext. 1181, Fax: 706-778-0150, E-mail: ploggins@piedmont.edu.

Pittsburg State University, Graduate School, College of Education, Department of Special Services and Leadership Studies, Program in Special Education, Pittsburg, KS 66762. Offers behavioral disorders (MS); learning disabilities (MS); mentally retarded (MS). *Accreditation:* NCATE. *Degree requirements:* For master's, thesis or alternative. *Entrance requirements:* For master's, GRE General Test or MAT.

Plymouth State University, College of Graduate Studies, Graduate Studies in Education, Plymouth, NH 03264-1595. Offers athletic training (M Ed, MS); counselor education (M Ed); education (CAGS); educational leadership (M Ed); elementary education (M Ed); English education (M Ed); health education (M Ed); k-12 education (M Ed); learning, leadership and community (Ed D); mathematics education (M Ed); reading and writing specialist (M Ed); science (MS), including applied meteorology, environmental science and policy, science education; secondary education (M Ed); special education administration (M Ed); special education k-12 (M Ed); teaching (MAT). *Accreditation:* NCATE (one or more programs are accredited). Part-time and evening/weekend programs available. Postbaccalaureate distance learning degree programs offered (minimal on-campus study). *Entrance requirements:* For master's, MAT or other standardized exam, minimum GPA of 3.0. Additional exam requirements/recommendations for international students: Required—TOEFL (minimum score 550 paper-based). *Expenses:* Contact institution. *Faculty research:* Special education, technology, math and science methodology.

Point Park University, School of Arts and Sciences, Department of Education, Pittsburgh, PA 15222-1984. Offers curriculum and instruction (MA); educational administration (MA); special education (M Ed); teaching and leadership (M Ed). Part-time and evening/weekend programs available. *Faculty:* 5 full-time, 9 part-time/adjunct. *Students:* 12 full-time (8 women), 40 part-time (31 women); includes 12 minority (11 Black or African American, non-Hispanic/Latino; 1 Asian, non-Hispanic/Latino), 2 international. Average age 33. 46 applicants, 61% accepted, 18 enrolled. In 2011, 15 master's awarded. *Degree requirements:* For master's, comprehensive exam (for some programs), thesis or alternative. *Entrance requirements:* For master's, minimum GPA of 3.0, resume, 2 letters of recommendation. Additional exam requirements/recommendations for international students: Required—TOEFL. *Application deadline:* Applications are processed on a rolling basis. Application fee: $30. Electronic applications accepted. *Expenses: Tuition:* Full-time $13,050; part-time $725 per credit. *Required fees:* $720; $40 per credit. *Financial support:* In 2011–12, 42 students received support, including 2 teaching assistantships with full tuition reimbursements available (averaging $6,400 per year); scholarships/grants also available. Financial award application deadline: 4/15; financial award applicants required to submit FAFSA. *Unit head:* Dr. Darlene Marnich, Chair, 412-392-3474, Fax: 412-392-3927, E-mail: dmarnich@pointpark.edu. *Application contact:* Lynn C. Ribar, Associate Director, Graduate and Adult Enrollment, 412-392-3908, Fax: 412-392-6164, E-mail: lribar@pointpark.edu.

Portland State University, Graduate Studies, School of Education, Department of Special Education and Counselor Education, Portland, OR 97207-0751. Offers counselor education (MA, MS); special and counselor education (Ed D); special education (MA, MS). *Accreditation:* ACA (one or more programs are accredited). Part-time and evening/weekend programs available. *Degree requirements:* For master's, thesis or alternative. *Entrance requirements:* For master's, California Basic Educational Skills Test, minimum GPA of 3.0 in upper-division course work or 2.75 overall. Additional exam requirements/recommendations for international students: Required—TOEFL (minimum score 550 paper-based; 213 computer-based). *Faculty research:* Transition of students with disabilities, functional curriculum, supported/inclusive education, leisure/recreation, autism.

Prairie View A&M University, College of Education, Department of Curriculum and Instruction, Prairie View, TX 77446-0519. Offers curriculum and instruction (M Ed, MS Ed); special education (M Ed, MS Ed). *Accreditation:* NCATE. Part-time and evening/weekend programs available. *Degree requirements:* For master's, thesis optional. *Entrance requirements:* For master's, GRE, minimum GPA of 2.5, 3 references. Electronic applications accepted. *Faculty research:* Metacognitive strategies, emotionally disturbed, language arts, teachers recruit, diversity, recruitment, retention, school collaboration.

Pratt Institute, School of Art and Design, Programs in Creative Arts Therapy, Brooklyn, NY 11205-3899. Offers art therapy and creativity development (MPS); art therapy-special education (MPS); dance/movement therapy (MS). *Accreditation:* NASAD (one or more programs are accredited). Part-time programs available. *Faculty:* 3 full-time (all women), 19 part-time/adjunct (16 women). *Students:* 120 full-time (111 women), 3 part-time (all women); includes 35 minority (7 Black or African American, non-Hispanic/Latino; 9 Asian, non-Hispanic/Latino; 16 Hispanic/Latino; 3 Two or more races, non-Hispanic/Latino), 7 international. Average age 31. 152 applicants, 47% accepted, 39 enrolled. In 2011, 20 master's awarded. *Degree requirements:* For master's, thesis. *Entrance requirements:* For master's, letters of recommendation, portfolio. Additional exam requirements/recommendations for international students: Required—TOEFL (minimum score 600 paper-based; 250 computer-based; 100 iBT). *Application deadline:* For fall admission, 1/5 for domestic and international students; for spring admission, 10/1 for domestic and international students. Applications are processed on a rolling basis. Application fee: $50 ($90 for international students). Electronic applications accepted. *Expenses: Tuition:* Full-time $24,084; part-time $1338 per credit. *Financial support:* Career-related internships or fieldwork, Federal Work-Study, institutionally sponsored loans, scholarships/grants, health care benefits, tuition waivers (full), and unspecified assistantships available. Support available to part-time students. Financial award application deadline: 2/1; financial award applicants required to submit FAFSA. *Faculty research:* Psychology and aesthetic interaction, art therapy and AIDS, art therapy and autism, art diagnosis. *Unit head:* Jean Davis, Chairperson, 718-636-3428, E-mail: jdavis@pratt.edu. *Application contact:* Young Hah, Director of Graduate Admissions, 718-636-3683, Fax: 718-399-4242, E-mail: yhah@pratt.edu. Web site: http://www.pratt.edu/academics/art_design/art_grad/creative_arts_therapy.

Prescott College, Graduate Programs, Program in Education, Prescott, AZ 86301. Offers early childhood education (MA); early childhood special education (MA); education (MA); elementary education (MA); environmental education leadership and administration (MA); equine-assisted experiential learning (MA); school guidance counseling (MA); secondary education (MA); special education, learning disability (MA); special education, mental retardation (MA); special education, serious emotional disability (MA); student-directed independent study (MA); sustainability education (PhD). Part-time programs available. Postbaccalaureate distance learning degree programs offered (minimal on-campus study). *Faculty:* 2 full-time (both women), 47 part-time/adjunct (31 women). *Students:* 59 full-time (36 women), 48 part-time (30 women); includes 16 minority (3 Black or African American, non-Hispanic/Latino; 1 American Indian or Alaska Native, non-Hispanic/Latino; 1 Asian, non-Hispanic/Latino; 8 Hispanic/Latino; 3 Two or more races, non-Hispanic/Latino), 2 international. Average age 40. 75 applicants, 76% accepted, 36 enrolled. In 2011, 14 master's, 8 doctorates awarded. *Degree requirements:* For master's, thesis, fieldwork or internship, practicum; for doctorate, thesis/dissertation. *Entrance requirements:* For master's, 2 letters of recommendation, resume; for doctorate, 3 letters of recommendation, resume, official transcripts, personal statement, program proposal. Additional exam requirements/recommendations for international students: Required—TOEFL (minimum score 500 paper-based; 173 computer-based). *Application deadline:* For fall admission, 4/15 priority date for domestic students, 4/15 for international students; for spring admission, 9/15 priority date for domestic students, 9/15 for international students. Applications are processed on a rolling basis. Application fee: $40. Electronic applications accepted. *Expenses: Tuition:* Full-time $16,440; part-time $685 per credit. *Required fees:* $150 per semester. One-time fee: $350. *Financial support:* Career-related internships or fieldwork and Federal Work-Study available. Financial award applicants required to submit FAFSA. *Unit head:* Noel Caniglia, Chair, 928-358-3201, Fax: 928-776-5151, E-mail: ncaniglia@prescott.edu. *Application contact:* Kerstin Alicki, Admissions Counselor, 928-350-2100, Fax: 928-776-5242, E-mail: admissions@prescott.edu.

Providence College, Program in Special Education, Providence, RI 02918. Offers elementary special education (M Ed), including elementary, secondary. Part-time and evening/weekend programs available. *Faculty:* 7 part-time/adjunct (5 women). *Students:* 7 full-time (all women), 36 part-time (25 women); includes 2 minority (1 Black or African American, non-Hispanic/Latino; 1 Hispanic/Latino). Average age 31. 21 applicants, 100% accepted, 5 enrolled. In 2011, 33 master's awarded. *Degree requirements:* For master's, comprehensive exam. *Entrance requirements:* For master's, GRE General Test. Additional exam requirements/recommendations for international students: Required—TOEFL (minimum score 550 paper-based; 213 computer-based; 80 iBT). *Application deadline:* For fall admission, 8/1 priority date for domestic students, 8/1 for international students; for spring admission, 12/1 priority date for domestic students, 12/1 for international students. Applications are processed on a rolling basis. Application fee: $55. *Expenses: Tuition:* Part-time $404 per credit. *Required fees:* $404 per credit. *Financial support:* In 2011–12, 1 research assistantship with full tuition reimbursement (averaging $8,400 per year) was awarded; career-related internships or fieldwork and unspecified assistantships also available. Support available to part-time students. Financial award application deadline: 8/1; financial award applicants required to submit FAFSA. *Unit head:* Diane LaMontagne, Director, 401-865-2912, Fax: 401-865-1147, E-mail: dlamonta@providence.edu. *Application contact:* Carol A. Daniels, Coordinator of Graduate Faculty and Administrative Services, 401-865-2247, Fax: 401-865-1147, E-mail: daniels@providence.edu. Web site: http://www.providence.edu/professional-studies/graduate-degrees/Pages/master-education-specialed.aspx.

Purdue University, Graduate School, College of Education, Department of Educational Studies, West Lafayette, IN 47907. Offers administration (MS Ed, PhD, Ed S); counseling and development (MS Ed, PhD); education of the gifted (MS Ed); educational psychology (MS Ed, PhD); foundations of education (MS Ed, PhD); higher education administration (MS Ed, PhD); special education (MS Ed, PhD). *Accreditation:* ACA (one or more programs are accredited); NCATE (one or more programs are accredited). Part-time and evening/weekend programs available. *Faculty:* 23 full-time (17 women), 1 part-time/adjunct (0 women). *Students:* 111 full-time (79 women), 93 part-time (58 women); includes 34 minority (19 Black or African American, non-Hispanic/Latino; 1 American Indian or Alaska Native, non-Hispanic/Latino; 4 Asian, non-Hispanic/Latino; 6 Hispanic/Latino; 4 Two or more races, non-Hispanic/Latino), 30 international. Average age 35. 249 applicants, 37% accepted, 46 enrolled. In 2011, 39 master's, 20 doctorates, 4 other advanced degrees awarded. *Degree requirements:* For master's, thesis optional; for doctorate, thesis/dissertation, oral and written exams; for Ed S, oral presentation, project. *Entrance requirements:* For master's, GRE General Test required for all Educational Studies program areas, except for Special Education if undergraduate GPA is higher than a 3.0, minimum undergraduate GPA of 3.0; for doctorate and Ed S, GRE general test is required, a combined score of 1000 (300 for revised GRE test) or more is expected., minimum undergraduate GPA of 3.0. Additional exam requirements/recommendations for international students: Required—TOEFL (minimum score 550 paper-based; 77 iBT), TWE (minimum score 5). *Application deadline:* Applications are processed on a rolling basis. Application fee: $60 ($75 for international students). Electronic applications accepted. *Financial support:* Fellowships with full tuition reimbursements, research assistantships with full tuition reimbursements, teaching assistantships with full tuition reimbursements, career-related internships or fieldwork, and tuition waivers (full) available. Support available to part-time students. Financial award application deadline: 3/1; financial award applicants required to submit FAFSA. *Faculty research:* Motivation, learning disabilities, school learning, group processes, cognitive development. *Unit head:* Dr. Ala Samrapungavan, Head, 765-494-9170, Fax: 765-496-1228, E-mail: ala@purdue.edu. *Application contact:* Sarah N. Prater, Graduate Contact, 765-494-2345, Fax: 765-494-5832, E-mail: prater0@purdue.edu. Web site: http://www.edst.purdue.edu/.

Purdue University Calumet, Graduate Studies Office, School of Education, Program in Special Education, Hammond, IN 46323-2094. Offers MS Ed.

Queens College of the City University of New York, Division of Graduate Studies, Division of Education, Department of Educational and Community Programs, Program in Special Education, Flushing, NY 11367-1597. Offers MS Ed. Part-time programs available. *Faculty:* 5 full-time (3 women). *Students:* 24 full-time (22 women), 371 part-time (329 women); includes 77 minority (24 Black or African American, non-Hispanic/Latino; 17 Asian, non-Hispanic/Latino; 36 Hispanic/Latino). 255 applicants, 82% accepted, 181 enrolled. In 2011, 164 master's awarded. *Degree requirements:* For master's, research project. *Entrance requirements:* For master's, minimum GPA of 3.0. Additional exam requirements/recommendations for international students: Required—TOEFL. *Application deadline:* For fall admission, 4/1 for domestic students; for spring admission, 11/1 for domestic students. Applications are processed on a rolling basis. Application fee: $125. *Expenses:* Tuition, state resident: part-time $345 per credit. Tuition, nonresident: part-time $640 per credit. *Required fees:* $145.25 per semester. *Financial support:* Career-related internships or fieldwork, Federal Work-Study, institutionally sponsored loans, and tuition waivers (partial) available. Support available to part-time students. Financial award application deadline: 4/1; financial award applicants required to submit FAFSA. *Unit head:* Dr. Craig Michaels, Coordinator/Graduate Adviser, 718-997-5266. *Application contact:* Mario Caruso, Director of Graduate Admissions, 718-997-5200, Fax: 718-997-5193, E-mail: graduate_admissions@qc.edu.

Quincy University, Program in Education, Quincy, IL 62301-2699. Offers alternative certification (MS Ed); curriculum and instruction (MS Ed); leadership (MS Ed); reading education (MS Ed); school administration (MS Ed); special education (MS Ed); teacher leader in reading (MS Ed); teaching certification (MS Ed). Part-time and evening/weekend programs available. Postbaccalaureate distance learning degree programs offered. *Students:* 221 full-time (168 women), 100 part-time (69 women); includes 104 minority (69 Black or African American, non-Hispanic/Latino; 1 American Indian or Alaska Native, non-Hispanic/Latino; 5 Asian, non-Hispanic/Latino; 27 Hispanic/Latino; 2 Two or more races, non-Hispanic/Latino). In 2011, 132 master's awarded. *Degree requirements:* For master's, comprehensive exam (for some programs), thesis or alternative. *Entrance requirements:* For master's, MAT or GRE. Additional exam requirements/recommendations for international students: Required—TOEFL (minimum score 550 paper-based; 79 iBT). *Application deadline:* Applications are processed on a rolling basis. Application fee: $25. Electronic applications accepted. *Expenses: Tuition:* Full-time $9120; part-time $380 per semester hour. *Required fees:* $360; $15 per semester hour. Tuition and fees vary according to course load, campus/location and program. *Financial support:* Applicants required to submit FAFSA. *Unit head:* Kristen Anguiano, Director, 217-228-5432 Ext. 3119, E-mail: anguikr@quincy.edu. *Application contact:* Office of Admissions, 217-228-5210, Fax: 217-228-5479, E-mail: admissions@quincy.edu. Web site: http://www.quincy.edu/academics/graduate-programs/education.

Radford University, College of Graduate and Professional Studies, College of Education and Human Development, School of Teacher Education and Leadership, Program in Special Education, Radford, VA 24142. Offers adapted curriculum (MS); early childhood special education (MS); general curriculum (MS); hearing impairments (MS); visual impairment (MS). *Accreditation:* NCATE. Part-time and evening/weekend programs available. *Faculty:* 9 full-time (8 women), 12 part-time/adjunct (11 women). *Students:* 19 full-time (all women), 39 part-time (31 women); includes 2 minority (both Black or African American, non-Hispanic/Latino). Average age 32. 24 applicants, 92% accepted, 19 enrolled. In 2011, 34 master's awarded. *Degree requirements:* For master's, comprehensive exam. *Entrance requirements:* For master's, GRE, minimum GPA of 2.75, 3 letters of reference, resume, personal essay, official transcripts. Additional exam requirements/recommendations for international students: Required—TOEFL (minimum score 550 paper-based; 213 computer-based; 79 iBT). *Application deadline:* For fall admission, 2/15 for domestic students, 12/1 for international students; for spring admission, 7/1 for international students. Applications are processed on a rolling basis. Application fee: $50. Electronic applications accepted. *Expenses:* Tuition, state resident: full-time $6262; part-time $261 per credit hour. Tuition, nonresident: full-time $14,540; part-time $606 per credit hour. *Required fees:* $2812; $117 per credit hour. Tuition and fees vary according to program. *Financial support:* In 2011–12, 19 students received support, including 5 research assistantships (averaging $7,875 per year); career-related internships or fieldwork, Federal Work-Study, institutionally sponsored loans, scholarships/grants, and unspecified assistantships also available. Financial award application deadline: 3/1; financial award applicants required to submit FAFSA. *Unit head:* Dr. Elizabeth Altieri, Coordinator, 540-831-5590, Fax: 540-831-5059, E-mail: ealtieri@radford.edu. *Application contact:* Rebecca Conner, Graduate Admissions, 540-831-5431, Fax: 540-831-6061, E-mail: gradcollege@radford.edu. Web site: http://www.radford.edu/content/cehd/home/departments/teacher-ed/graduate-programs/special-education.html.

Randolph College, Programs in Education, Lynchburg, VA 24503. Offers curriculum and instruction (MAT); special education-learning disabilities (M Ed, MAT). *Accreditation:* Teacher Education Accreditation Council. *Entrance requirements:* For master's, minimum GPA of 3.0 in prerequisite education coursework, 2.7 in major or field of interest (MAT); teaching license (M Ed); 2 recommendations; interview.

Regent University, Graduate School, School of Education, Virginia Beach, VA 23464-9800. Offers adult education (Ed D); adult/staff development (Ed D, PhD); career switcher with licensure (M Ed), including alternative licensure; character education (Ed D, PhD); Christian education leadership (Ed D, PhD); Christian education specialist (Ed S); Christian school program (M Ed), including ACSI licensure; distance education (Ed D, PhD); education licensure (M Ed), including preK-6th grade; educational leadership (M Ed, PhD); educational leadership - special education (Ed S), including administration and supervision; educational psychology (Ed D, PhD), including learning and development, research and evaluation, special education; higher education (Ed D, PhD), including administration, research and institutional planning, teaching; higher education leadership (Ed D); individualized degree plan (M Ed), including behavior disorders, learning disabilities, mental retardation, reading specialist; K-12 school leadership (Ed D, PhD); leadership in character education (M Ed); master teacher (M Ed), including TESOL; mathematics education (M Ed); special education (PhD); student affairs (M Ed); TESOL (M Ed), including adult education, ESL: preK-12. *Accreditation:* Teacher Education Accreditation Council. Part-time and evening/weekend programs available. Postbaccalaureate distance learning degree programs offered (minimal on-campus study). *Faculty:* 26 full-time (13 women), 54 part-time/adjunct (34 women). *Students:* 140 full-time (109 women), 786 part-time (626 women); includes 218 minority (189 Black or African American, non-Hispanic/Latino; 2 American Indian or Alaska Native, non-Hispanic/Latino; 11 Asian, non-Hispanic/Latino; 16 Hispanic/Latino), 42 international. Average age 39. 673 applicants, 57% accepted, 298 enrolled. In 2011, 178 master's, 15 doctorates awarded. *Degree requirements:* For master's, thesis or alternative; for doctorate, comprehensive exam, thesis/dissertation. *Entrance requirements:* For master's, MAT, minimum undergraduate GPA of 2.75, writing sample, resume, recommendations, interview; for doctorate, GRE, writing sample, 3 years of relevant professional experience, master's-level paper, copies of published work, resume, transcripts, interview, recommendations. Additional exam requirements/recommendations for international students: Required—TOEFL (minimum score 577 paper-based; 233 computer-based). *Application deadline:* For fall admission, 4/1 priority date for domestic students; for spring admission, 10/15 priority date for domestic students. Applications are processed on a rolling basis. Application fee: $50. Electronic applications accepted. *Expenses:* Contact institution. *Financial support:* Fellowships, career-related internships or fieldwork, scholarships/grants, tuition waivers (full and partial), and unspecified assistantships available. Support available to part-time students. Financial award application deadline: 4/1; financial award applicants required to submit FAFSA. *Faculty research:* Character development and discipline for children, education leadership development, diversity in schools, classroom management, technology in education settings. *Unit head:* Dr. Alan A. Arroyo, Dean, 757-352-4261, Fax: 757-352-4318, E-mail: alanarr@regent.edu. *Application contact:* Matthew Chadwick, Director of Enrollment Support Services, 800-373-5504, Fax: 757-352-4381, E-mail: admissions@regent.edu. Web site: http://www.regent.edu/education/.

Regis College, Programs in Education, Weston, MA 02493. Offers elementary teacher (MAT); reading (MAT); special education (MAT). Part-time and evening/weekend programs available. *Degree requirements:* For master's, thesis. *Entrance requirements:* For master's, GRE or MAT. Additional exam requirements/recommendations for international students: Required—TOEFL. Electronic applications accepted. *Faculty research:* Reflective teaching, gender-based education, integrated teaching.

Regis University, College for Professional Studies, School of Education and Counseling, Department of Education, Denver, CO 80221-1099. Offers adult learning, training, and development (M Ed, Certificate); autism (Certificate); curriculum, instruction, and assessment (M Ed); educational leadership (Certificate); educational technology (Certificate); instructional technology (M Ed); literacy (Certificate); professional leadership (M Ed); reading (M Ed); self-designed (M Ed); space studies (M Ed). Program also offered in Henderson and Las Vegas (Summerlin), NV. *Accreditation:* Teacher Education Accreditation Council. Part-time and evening/weekend programs available. Postbaccalaureate distance learning degree programs offered (no on-campus study). *Degree requirements:* For master's, thesis. *Entrance requirements:* For master's, resume, minimum GPA of 2.75, criminal background check. Additional exam requirements/recommendations for international students: Required—TOEFL (minimum score 213 computer-based), TWE (minimum score 5). Electronic applications accepted. *Faculty research:* Issues of equity in the middle school classroom, professional learning communities, school reform, socialinguistic and discursive obstacles to student integration, inclusive language arts curriculum.

Rhode Island College, School of Graduate Studies, Feinstein School of Education and Human Development, Department of Special Education, Providence, RI 02908-1991. Offers autism education (CGS); middle-secondary level special education (CGS); special education (M Ed). *Accreditation:* NCATE. Part-time and evening/weekend programs available. *Faculty:* 6 full-time (4 women), 7 part-time/adjunct (6 women). *Students:* 7 full-time (all women), 49 part-time (46 women); includes 3 minority (2 Black or African American, non-Hispanic/Latino; 1 American Indian or Alaska Native, non-Hispanic/Latino). Average age 31. In 2011, 41 master's awarded. *Degree requirements:* For master's, comprehensive assessment/assignment. *Entrance requirements:* For master's, GRE General Test or MAT, undergraduate transcripts; minimum undergraduate GPA of 3.0; 3 letters of recommendation; for CGS, GRE or MAT, master's degree or equivalent, teaching certificate, 3 letters of recommendation, interview. Additional exam requirements/recommendations for international students: Recommended—TOEFL (minimum score 550 paper-based; 213 computer-based; 79 iBT). *Application deadline:* For fall admission, 3/1 for domestic students; for spring admission, 11/1 for domestic students. Applications are processed on a rolling basis. Application fee: $50. *Expenses:* Tuition, state resident: full-time $8592; part-time $358 per credit hour. Tuition, nonresident: full-time $16,800; part-time $700 per credit hour. *Required fees:* $602; $22 per credit. $72 per term. *Financial support:* Teaching assistantships with full tuition reimbursements, career-related internships or fieldwork, Federal Work-Study, scholarships/grants, health care benefits, and unspecified assistantships available. Support available to part-time students. Financial award application deadline: 5/15; financial award applicants required to submit FAFSA. *Faculty research:* Early detection, handicapped infants. *Unit head:* Dr. Marie Lynch, Chair, 401-456-8763. *Application contact:* Graduate Studies, 401-456-8700. Web site: http://www.ric.edu/specialEducation/.

Rider University, Department of Graduate Education, Leadership and Counseling, Program in Special Education, Lawrenceville, NJ 08648-3001. Offers alternative route in special education (Certificate); special education (MA); teacher of students with disabilities (Certificate); teacher of the handicapped (Certificate). Part-time and evening/weekend programs available. *Degree requirements:* For master's, comprehensive exam. *Entrance requirements:* For master's, letters of reference, resume, NJ teaching license, interview. Additional exam requirements/recommendations for international students: Required—TOEFL (minimum score 550 paper-based; 213 computer-based). Electronic applications accepted. *Expenses: Tuition:* Full-time $32,820; part-time $710 per credit. *Required fees:* $350; $35 per course. Tuition and fees vary according to campus/location and program. *Faculty research:* Collaboration/inclusive, practice, service learning, transition.

Rivier University, School of Graduate Studies, Department of Education, Nashua, NH 03060. Offers curriculum and instruction (M Ed); early childhood education (M Ed); educational administration (M Ed); educational studies (M Ed); elementary education (M Ed); elementary education and general special education (M Ed); emotional and behavioral disorders (M Ed); general social education (M Ed); leadership and learning (Ed D, CAGS); learning disabilities (M Ed); learning disabilities and reading (M Ed); mental health counseling (MA); reading (M Ed); school counseling (M Ed). Part-time and evening/weekend programs available. *Degree requirements:* For master's, comprehensive exam (for some programs), internships. *Entrance requirements:* For master's, GRE General Test or MAT.

Roberts Wesleyan College, Division of Teacher Education, Rochester, NY 14624-1997. Offers adolescence education (M Ed); childhood and special education (M Ed); literacy education (M Ed); urban education (M Ed). Part-time and evening/weekend programs available. *Degree requirements:* For master's, thesis.

Rochester Institute of Technology, Graduate Enrollment Services, National Technical Institute for the Deaf, Department of Research and Teacher Education, Rochester, NY 14623-5603. Offers MS. *Accreditation:* Teacher Education Accreditation Council. *Students:* 54 full-time (38 women), 5 part-time (all women); includes 7 minority (4 Black or African American, non-Hispanic/Latino; 1 Asian, non-Hispanic/Latino; 2 Hispanic/Latino), 1 international. Average age 28. 43 applicants, 60% accepted, 23 enrolled. In 2011, 21 degrees awarded. *Degree requirements:* For master's, thesis or alternative. *Entrance requirements:* For master's, minimum GPA of 3.0. Additional exam requirements/recommendations for international students: Required—TOEFL (minimum score 550 paper-based; 213 computer-based; 88 iBT) or IELTS (minimum score 6.5). *Application deadline:* For fall admission, 2/15 priority date for domestic students, 2/15 for international students. Applications are processed on a rolling basis. Application fee: $50. Electronic applications accepted. *Expenses: Tuition:* Full-time $34,659; part-time $963 per credit hour. *Required fees:* $228; $76 per quarter. *Financial support:* Fellowships with full and partial tuition reimbursements, research assistantships with partial tuition reimbursements, teaching assistantships with partial tuition reimbursements, career-related internships or fieldwork, institutionally sponsored loans, scholarships/grants, and unspecified assistantships available. Support available to part-time students. Financial award applicants required to submit FAFSA. *Faculty research:* Applied research on the effective use of access and support services to enhance learning for deaf and hard-of-hearing students in the mainstreamed classroom, STEM research and instruction. *Unit head:* Gerald Bateman, Director, 585-475-6480, Fax: 585-475-2525, E-mail: gcbnmp@rit.edu. *Application contact:* Diane Ellison, Assistant Vice President, Graduate Enrollment Services, 585-475-2229, Fax: 585-475-7164, E-mail: gradinfo@rit.edu. Web site: http://www.ntid.rit.edu/research/department/.

Rockford College, Graduate Studies, Department of Education, Program in Special Education, Rockford, IL 61108-2393. Offers MAT. Part-time and evening/weekend programs available. *Degree requirements:* For master's, thesis optional. *Entrance requirements:* For master's, GRE General Test, 3 letters of recommendation. Additional exam requirements/recommendations for international students: Required—TOEFL (minimum score 550 paper-based; 213 computer-based; 79 iBT). *Application deadline:* Applications are processed on a rolling basis. Application fee: $50. Electronic applications accepted. *Expenses: Tuition:* Full-time $16,200; part-time $675 per credit. *Required fees:* $80; $40 per semester. Tuition and fees vary according to class time, course level, course load, degree level, campus/location and program. *Financial support:* Scholarships/grants and unspecified assistantships available. Support available to part-time students. Financial award application deadline: 3/1; financial award applicants required to submit FAFSA. *Unit head:* Dr. Michelle McReynolds, MAT Director, 815-226-3390, Fax: 815-394-3706, E-mail: mmcreynolds@rockford.edu. *Application contact:* Michele Mehren, Office Manager for Graduate Studies, 815-226-4041, Fax: 815-394-3706, E-mail: mmehren@rockford.edu. Web site: http://www.rockford.edu/?page=MAT.

Roosevelt University, Graduate Division, College of Education, Department of Teaching and Learning, Program in Special Education, Chicago, IL 60605. Offers MA.

Rowan University, Graduate School, College of Education, Department of Special Educational Services/Instruction, Program in Learning Disabilities, Glassboro, NJ 08028-1701. Offers MA. *Accreditation:* NCATE. Part-time and evening/weekend programs available. *Degree requirements:* For master's, comprehensive exam, thesis. *Entrance requirements:* For master's, GRE General Test, minimum GPA of 2.8, 1 year of teaching experience. Additional exam requirements/recommendations for international students: Required—TOEFL. Electronic applications accepted.

Rowan University, Graduate School, College of Education, Department of Special Educational Services/Instruction, Program in Special Education, Glassboro, NJ 08028-1701. Offers MA. *Accreditation:* NCATE. Part-time and evening/weekend programs available. *Degree requirements:* For master's, comprehensive exam, thesis. *Entrance requirements:* For master's, GRE General Test, minimum GPA of 2.8. Additional exam requirements/recommendations for international students: Required—TOEFL. Electronic applications accepted.

Rutgers, The State University of New Jersey, New Brunswick, Graduate School of Education, Department of Educational Psychology, Program in Special Education, Piscataway, NJ 08854-8097. Offers Ed M, Ed D. Part-time and evening/weekend programs available. *Degree requirements:* For doctorate, thesis/dissertation, residency. *Entrance requirements:* For master's, GRE General Test, 3 letters of recommendation; for doctorate, GRE General Test, 3 letters of recommendation, master's degree. Additional exam requirements/recommendations for international students: Required—TOEFL (minimum score 550 paper-based; 233 computer-based; 83 iBT). Electronic applications accepted. *Faculty research:* Pre- and in-service teacher education, teacher development, inclusion, early identification and intervention of reading disabilities, special education law and social policy.

Sage Graduate School, Esteves School of Education, Program in Childhood Special Education, Troy, NY 12180-4115. Offers MS Ed. *Accreditation:* NCATE. Part-time and evening/weekend programs available. *Faculty:* 10 full-time (6 women), 27 part-time/adjunct (23 women). *Students:* 15 full-time (14 women), 18 part-time (16 women). Average age 27. 12 applicants, 75% accepted, 7 enrolled. In 2011, 4 master's awarded. *Degree requirements:* For master's, thesis optional. *Entrance requirements:* For master's, minimum GPA of 2.75, resume, 2 letters of recommendation, interview, assessment of writing skills. Additional exam requirements/recommendations for international students: Required—TOEFL (minimum score 550 paper-based; 213 computer-based). *Application deadline:* Applications are processed on a rolling basis. Application fee: $40. *Expenses: Tuition:* Full-time $11,880; part-time $660 per credit hour. Tuition and fees vary according to program. *Financial support:* Fellowships, research assistantships, Federal Work-Study, scholarships/grants, and unspecified assistantships available. Support available to part-time students. Financial award application deadline: 3/1; financial award applicants required to submit FAFSA. *Faculty research:* Effective behavioral strategies for classroom instruction. *Unit head:* Dr. Lori Quigley, Dean, Esteves School of Education, 518-244-2326, Fax: 518-244-4571, E-mail: l.quigley@sage.edu. *Application contact:* Mary Grace Luibrand, Director, 518-244-4578, Fax: 518-244-4571, E-mail: luibrm@sage.edu.

Sage Graduate School, Esteves School of Education, Program in Literacy/Childhood Special Education, Troy, NY 12180-4115. Offers MS Ed. *Accreditation:* NCATE. Part-time and evening/weekend programs available. *Faculty:* 10 full-time (6 women). *Students:* 8 full-time (all women), 3 part-time (all women); includes 2 minority (1 Black or African American, non-Hispanic/Latino; 1 Hispanic/Latino). Average age 24. 9 applicants, 67% accepted, 6 enrolled. In 2011, 4 master's awarded. *Entrance requirements:* For master's, assessment of writing skills, minimum GPA of 2.75, resume, 2 letters of recommendation, interview with advisor. Additional exam requirements/recommendations for international students: Required—TOEFL (minimum score 550 paper-based; 213 computer-based). *Application deadline:* Applications are processed on a rolling basis. Application fee: $40. *Expenses: Tuition:* Full-time $11,880; part-time $660 per credit hour. Tuition and fees vary according to program. *Financial support:* Fellowships, research assistantships, Federal Work-Study, scholarships/grants, and unspecified assistantships available. Support available to part-time students. Financial award application deadline: 3/1; financial award applicants required to submit FAFSA. *Faculty research:* Commonalities in the roles of reading specialists and resource/consultant teachers. *Unit head:* Dr. Lori Quigley, Dean, Esteves School of Education, 518-244-2326, Fax: 518-244-4571, E-mail: l.quigley@sage.edu. *Application contact:* Mary Grace Luibrand, Director, 518-244-4578, Fax: 518-244-2334, E-mail: luibrm@sage.edu.

Sage Graduate School, Esteves School of Education, Program in Special Education, Troy, NY 12180-4115. Offers MS Ed. Part-time and evening/weekend programs available. *Faculty:* 10 full-time (6 women). *Students:* 4 full-time (all women), 8 part-time (7 women). Average age 28. 16 applicants, 38% accepted, 4 enrolled. In 2011, 22 master's awarded. *Entrance requirements:* For master's, minimum GPA of 2.75, resume, 2 letters of recommendation. Additional exam requirements/recommendations for international students: Required—TOEFL (minimum score 550 paper-based; 213 computer-based). *Application deadline:* Applications are processed on a rolling basis. Application fee: $40. *Expenses: Tuition:* Full-time $11,880; part-time $660 per credit hour. Tuition and fees vary according to program. *Financial support:* Fellowships, research assistantships, Federal Work-Study, scholarships/grants, tuition waivers (partial), and unspecified assistantships available. Support available to part-time students. Financial award application deadline: 3/1; financial award applicants required to submit FAFSA. *Unit head:* Dr. Lori Quigley, Dean, Esteves School of Education, 518-244-2326, Fax: 518-244-4571, E-mail: l.quigley@sage.edu. *Application contact:* Mary Grace Luibrand, Professional Advisor for Special Education, 518-244-4578, Fax: 518-244/4571, E-mail: luibrm@sage.edu.

Saginaw Valley State University, College of Education, Program in Learning and Behavioral Disorders, University Center, MI 48710. Offers MAT. *Accreditation:* NCATE. *Students:* 4 full-time (1 woman), 19 part-time (15 women). Average age 41. In 2011, 21 master's awarded. *Degree requirements:* For master's, practicum. *Entrance requirements:* For master's, minimum GPA of 3.0, teaching certificate. Additional exam requirements/recommendations for international students: Required—TOEFL (minimum score 525 paper-based; 197 computer-based; 71 iBT). *Application deadline:* Applications are processed on a rolling basis. Application fee: $25. Electronic applications accepted. *Expenses:* Tuition, state resident: full-time $8300; part-time $5333 per year. Tuition, nonresident: full-time $15,613; part-time $10,209 per year. *International tuition:* $15,631 full-time. *Financial support:* Federal Work-Study and scholarships/grants available. Support available to part-time students. Financial award applicants required to submit FAFSA. *Unit head:* Dr. Steve P. Barbus, Jr., Dean, 989-964-6067, Fax: 989-790-4385, E-mail: barbus@svsu.edu. *Application contact:* Kathy Lopez, Certification Officer, 989-964-4661, Fax: 989-964-4385, E-mail: klopez@svsu.edu.

Saginaw Valley State University, College of Education, Program in Special Education, University Center, MI 48710. Offers MAT. Part-time and evening/weekend programs available. *Students:* 17 full-time (16 women), 216 part-time (177 women); includes 6 minority (4 Black or African American, non-Hispanic/Latino; 1 American Indian or Alaska Native, non-Hispanic/Latino; 1 Hispanic/Latino). Average age 34. 35 applicants, 100% accepted, 24 enrolled. In 2011, 80 master's awarded. *Degree requirements:* For master's, capstone course. *Entrance requirements:* For master's, minimum GPA of 3.0. Additional exam requirements/recommendations for international students: Required—TOEFL (minimum score 525 paper-based; 197 computer-based; 71 iBT). *Application deadline:* Applications are processed on a rolling basis. Application fee: $25. Electronic applications accepted. *Expenses:* Tuition, state resident: full-time $8300; part-time $5333 per year. Tuition, nonresident: full-time $15,613; part-time $10,209 per year. *International tuition:* $15,631 full-time. *Financial support:* Federal Work-Study and scholarships/grants available. Support available to part-time students. Financial award applicants required to submit FAFSA. *Unit head:* Dr. Steve P. Barbus, Jr., Dean, 989-964-6067, Fax: 989-790-4385, E-mail: barbus@svsu.edu. *Application contact:* Kathy Lopez, Certification Officer, 989-964-4661, Fax: 989-964-4385, E-mail: klopez@svsu.edu.

St. Ambrose University, College of Education and Health Sciences, Program in Education, Davenport, IA 52803-2898. Offers special education (M Ed); teaching (M Ed). *Accreditation:* Teacher Education Accreditation Council. Part-time and evening/weekend programs available. Postbaccalaureate distance learning degree programs offered (no on-campus study). *Faculty:* 2 full-time (1 woman), 1 part-time/adjunct (0 women). *Students:* 25 part-time (21 women); includes 5 minority (1 Asian, non-Hispanic/Latino; 2 Hispanic/Latino; 2 Two or more races, non-Hispanic/Latino). Average age 31. 9 applicants, 89% accepted, 8 enrolled. In 2011, 10 master's awarded. *Degree requirements:* For master's, comprehensive exam. *Entrance requirements:* For master's, GRE General Test or MAT, minimum GPA of 2.75. Additional exam requirements/recommendations for international students: Required—TOEFL. *Application deadline:* For fall admission, 8/15 priority date for domestic students; for spring admission, 11/1 for domestic students. Applications are processed on a rolling basis. Application fee: $25. Electronic applications accepted. *Expenses: Tuition:* Full-time $13,770; part-time $765 per credit hour. *Required fees:* $60 per semester. Tuition and fees vary according to degree level, program and reciprocity agreements. *Financial support:* In 2011–12, 13 students received support, including 1 research assistantship with partial tuition reimbursement available (averaging $3,600 per year); career-related internships or fieldwork, scholarships/grants, tuition waivers (full and partial), and unspecified assistantships also available. Financial award application deadline: 3/15; financial award applicants required to submit FAFSA. *Faculty research:* Disabilities and postsecondary career avenues, self-determination. *Unit head:* Marguerite K. Woods, Head, 563-388-7653, Fax: 563-388-7662, E-mail: woodsmargueritek@sau.edu. *Application contact:* Penny L. McCulloch, Administrative Assistant, 563-322-1034, Fax: 563-388-7662, E-mail: mccullochpennyl@sau.edu.

St. Bonaventure University, School of Graduate Studies, School of Education, Program in Advanced Inclusive Processes, St. Bonaventure, NY 14778-2284. Offers gifted education (MS Ed); gifted education and students with disabilities (MS Ed). Part-time and evening/weekend programs available. *Faculty:* 3 full-time (all women), 2 part-time/adjunct (both women). *Students:* 29 full-time (27 women), 5 part-time (4 women); includes 2 minority (1 Hispanic/Latino; 1 Two or more races, non-Hispanic/Latino). Average age 25. 22 applicants, 82% accepted, 15 enrolled. In 2011, 19 master's awarded. *Degree requirements:* For master's, comprehensive exam, internship, portfolio. *Entrance requirements:* For master's, teaching certification, interview, references, writing sample, transcripts. Additional exam requirements/recommendations for international students: Required—TOEFL (minimum score 550 paper-based; 213 computer-based; 80 iBT). *Application deadline:* For fall admission, 6/15 priority date for domestic students, 2/1 for international students; for spring admission, 11/15 priority date for domestic students, 7/1 for international students. Applications are processed on a rolling basis. Application fee: $30. Electronic applications accepted. *Expenses: Tuition:* Part-time $670 per credit. *Financial support:* In 2011–12, 3 research assistantships with full and partial tuition reimbursements were awarded; Federal Work-Study, scholarships/grants, health care benefits, tuition waivers (partial), and unspecified assistantships also available. Support available to part-time students. Financial award application deadline: 4/15; financial award applicants required to submit FAFSA. *Unit head:* Dr. Rene Garrison, Director, 716-375-4078, E-mail: rgarriso@sbu.edu. *Application contact:* Bruce Campbell, Director of Graduate Admissions, 716-375-2429, Fax: 716-375-4015, E-mail: gradsch@sbu.edu.

St. Cloud State University, School of Graduate Studies, School of Education, Department of Special Education, St. Cloud, MN 56301-4498. Offers developmental/cognitive disabilities (MS); emotional/behavioral disorders (MS); gifted and talented (MS); learning disabilities (MS); special education (MS). *Accreditation:* NCATE. *Faculty:* 11 full-time (6 women), 5 part-time/adjunct (4 women). *Students:* 48 full-time (43 women), 142 part-time (119 women); includes 9 minority (5 Black or African American, non-Hispanic/Latino; 2 American Indian or Alaska Native, non-Hispanic/Latino; 1 Asian, non-Hispanic/Latino; 1 Hispanic/Latino), 1 international. 13 applicants, 100% accepted. In 2011, 31 master's awarded. *Degree requirements:* For master's, thesis or alternative. *Entrance requirements:* For master's, GRE General Test, minimum GPA of 2.75. Additional exam requirements/recommendations for international students: Required—Michigan English Language Assessment Battery; Recommended—TOEFL (minimum score 550 paper-based; 213 computer-based), IELTS (minimum score 6.5). *Application deadline:* For fall admission, 6/1 priority date for domestic students, 4/1 for international students; for spring admission, 10/1 priority date for domestic students, 8/1 for international students. Applications are processed on a rolling basis. Application fee: $35. Electronic applications accepted. *Financial support:* Federal Work-Study, scholarships/grants, and unspecified assistantships available. Financial award application deadline: 3/1. *Unit head:* Dr. Mary Beth Noll, Chairperson, 320-308-2041, Fax: 320-308-3475, E-mail: mbnoll@stcloudstate.edu. *Application contact:* Linda Lou Krueger, School of Graduate Studies, 320-308-2113, Fax: 320-308-5371, E-mail: lekrueger@stcloudstate.edu.

St. Edward's University, School of Education, Program in Teaching, Austin, TX 78704. Offers curriculum leadership (Certificate); instructional technology (Certificate); mediation (Certificate); mentoring and supervision (Certificate); special education (Certificate); sports management (Certificate); teaching (MA), including conflict resolution, initial teacher certification, liberal arts, special education, sports management, teacher leadership. Part-time and evening/weekend programs available. *Students:* 1 full-time (0 women), 32 part-time (22 women); includes 14 minority (2 Black or African American, non-Hispanic/Latino; 1 Asian, non-Hispanic/Latino; 10 Hispanic/Latino; 1 Two or more races, non-Hispanic/Latino), 1 international. Average age 32. 8 applicants, 75% accepted, 6 enrolled. In 2011, 13 master's awarded. *Degree requirements:* For master's, minimum of 24 resident hours. *Entrance requirements:* For master's, GRE General Test, minimum GPA of 3.0 in last 60 hours or 2.75 overall. Additional exam requirements/recommendations for international students: Required—TOEFL (minimum score 550 paper-based; 213 computer-based; 79 iBT) or IELTS (minimum score 6). *Application deadline:* For fall admission, 7/1 for domestic and international students; for spring admission, 11/1 for domestic and international students. Applications are processed on a rolling basis. Application fee: $45 ($50 for international students). Electronic applications accepted. *Expenses: Tuition:* Full-time $17,550; part-time $975 per credit hour. *Required fees:* $50 per trimester. Full-time tuition and fees vary according to course load and program. *Unit head:* Dr. David Hollier, Director, 512-448-8666, Fax: 512-428-1372, E-mail: davidrh@stedwards.edu. *Application contact:* Sarah Hennes, Graduate Admission Coordinator, 512-448-8600, Fax: 512-428-1032, E-mail: sarahhe@stedwards.edu. Web site: http://www.stedwards.edu.

St. John Fisher College, Ralph C. Wilson Jr. School of Education, Program in Adolescence Education/Special Education, Rochester, NY 14618-3597. Offers adolescence English (MS Ed); adolescence French (MS Ed); adolescence social studies (MS Ed); adolescence Spanish (MS Ed). Part-time and evening/weekend programs available. *Faculty:* 5 full-time (3 women), 2 part-time/adjunct (both women). *Students:* 25 full-time (13 women), 1 (woman) part-time. Average age 22. 19 applicants, 79% accepted, 11 enrolled. In 2011, 18 master's awarded. *Degree requirements:* For master's, field experiences, student teaching, LAST. *Entrance requirements:* For master's, 2 letters of recommendation, personal statement, current resume. Additional exam requirements/recommendations for international students: Required—TOEFL (minimum score 575 paper-based; 233 computer-based; 80 iBT). *Application deadline:* Applications are processed on a rolling basis. Application fee: $30. Electronic applications accepted. *Expenses: Tuition:* Part-time $735 per credit. One-time fee: $50 part-time. Tuition and fees vary according to course load, degree level and program. *Financial support:* In 2011–12, 5 students received support. Scholarships/grants available. Financial award applicants required to submit FAFSA. *Faculty research:* Arts and humanities, urban schools, constructivist learning, at risk students, mentoring. *Unit head:* Dr. Susan Schultz, Program Director, 585-385-7296, E-mail: sschultz@sjfc.edu. *Application contact:* Jose Perales, Director of Graduate Admissions, 585-385-8067, E-mail: jperales@sjfc.edu. Web site: http://www.sjfc.edu/academics/education/departments/ms-special-ed/options/initial-adolescence.dot.

St. John Fisher College, Ralph C. Wilson Jr. School of Education, Program in Childhood Education/Special Education, Rochester, NY 14618-3597. Offers MS. Part-time and evening/weekend programs available. *Faculty:* 5 full-time (3 women), 2 part-time/adjunct (both women). *Students:* 47 full-time (36 women), 4 part-time (all women); includes 9 minority (4 Black or African American, non-Hispanic/Latino; 1 Asian, non-Hispanic/Latino; 4 Hispanic/Latino). Average age 29. 38 applicants, 87% accepted, 16 enrolled. In 2011, 35 master's awarded. *Degree requirements:* For master's, field experience, student teaching, LAST. *Entrance requirements:* For master's, 2 letters of recommendation, personal statement, current resume. Additional exam requirements/recommendations for international students: Required—TOEFL (minimum score 575 paper-based; 233 computer-based; 80 iBT). *Application deadline:* Applications are processed on a rolling basis. Application fee: $30. Electronic applications accepted. *Expenses: Tuition:* Part-time $735 per credit. One-time fee: $50 part-time. Tuition and fees vary according to course load, degree level and program. *Financial support:* In 2011–12, 10 students received support. Scholarships/grants available. Financial award applicants required to submit FAFSA. *Faculty research:* Professional development, science assessment, multi-cultural; educational technology. *Unit head:* Dr. Susan Schultz, Program Director, 585-385-7296, E-mail: sschultz@sjfc.edu. *Application contact:* Jose Perales, Director of Graduate Admissions, 585-385-8067, E-mail: jperales@sjfc.edu. Web site: http://www.sjfc.edu/admissions/graduate/programs/childhood.dot.

St. John Fisher College, Ralph C. Wilson Jr. School of Education, Program in Special Education, Rochester, NY 14618-3597. Offers MS, Certificate. Part-time and evening/weekend programs available. *Faculty:* 5 full-time (3 women), 2 part-time/adjunct (both women). *Students:* 4 full-time (3 women), 31 part-time (23 women); includes 4 minority (1 Black or African American, non-Hispanic/Latino; 1 Asian, non-Hispanic/Latino; 2 Hispanic/Latino). Average age 28. 45 applicants, 91% accepted, 28 enrolled. In 2011, 25 master's awarded. *Degree requirements:* For master's, student teaching, practicum, LAST; for Certificate, practicum. *Entrance requirements:* For master's, teaching certification, 2 letters of recommendation, personal statement, current resume; for Certificate, minimum GPA of 3.0, 2 letters of reference, personal statement, teaching certification. Additional exam requirements/recommendations for international students: Required—TOEFL (minimum score 575 paper-based; 233 computer-based; 80 iBT). *Application deadline:* Applications are processed on a rolling basis. Application fee: $30. Electronic applications accepted. *Expenses: Tuition:* Part-time $735 per credit. One-time fee: $50 part-time. Tuition and fees vary according to course load, degree level and program. *Financial support:* In 2011–12, 10 students received support. Scholarships/grants available. Financial award applicants required to submit FAFSA. *Faculty research:* Inclusion, assistive technology, inquiry-based learning, gifted students, equity in education. *Unit head:* Dr. Susan Schultz, Program Director, 585-385-7296, E-mail: sschultz@sjfc.edu. *Application contact:* Jose Perales, Director of Graduate Admissions, 585-585-8067, E-mail: jperales@sjfc.edu. Web site: http://www.sjfc.edu/academics/education/departments/ms-special-ed/index.dot.

St. John's University, The School of Education, Department of Human Services and Counseling, Program in Teaching Children with Disabilities in Childhood Education, Queens, NY 11439. Offers MS Ed. Part-time and evening/weekend programs available. Postbaccalaureate distance learning degree programs offered. *Students:* 65 full-time (56 women), 107 part-time (93 women); includes 61 minority (23 Black or African American, non-Hispanic/Latino; 9 Asian, non-Hispanic/Latino; 26 Hispanic/Latino; 3 Two or more races, non-Hispanic/Latino), 2 international. Average age 29. 86 applicants, 81% accepted, 44 enrolled. In 2011, 43 master's awarded. *Degree requirements:* For master's, comprehensive exam. *Entrance requirements:* For master's, bachelor's degree from accredited college or university, minimum GPA of 3.0, 2 letters of recommendation. Additional exam requirements/recommendations for international students: Required—TOEFL (minimum score 600 paper-based; 250 computer-based; 100 iBT), IELTS (minimum score 5.5). *Application deadline:* For fall admission, 8/17 for domestic students, 5/1 for international students; for spring admission, 1/5 for domestic students, 11/1 for international students. Applications are processed on a rolling basis. Application fee: $70. Electronic applications accepted. *Expenses: Tuition:* Full-time $18,000; part-time $1000 per credit. *Required fees:* $170 per semester. Tuition and fees vary according to program. *Financial support:* Research assistantships available. *Faculty research:* Demographics in special education, literacy skill development in special populations, effects of distance learning in teacher training programs. *Unit head:* Dr. Francine Guastello, Chair, 718-990-1475, E-mail: guastelf@stjohns.edu. *Application contact:* Dr. Kelly K. Ronayne, Associate Dean for Graduate Admissions, 718-990-2304, Fax: 718-990-2343, E-mail: graded@stjohns.edu.

St. Joseph's College, Long Island Campus, Program in Infant/Toddler Early Childhood Special Education, Patchogue, NY 11772-2399. Offers MA. Part-time and evening/weekend programs available. *Degree requirements:* For master's, thesis, full-time practicum experience. *Entrance requirements:* For master's, 1 course in child development, 2 courses in special education, minimum undergraduate GPA of 3.0, New York state teaching certificate, interview. Additional exam requirements/recommendations for international students: Required—TOEFL (minimum score 550 paper-based; 213 computer-based).

St. Joseph's College, New York, Graduate Programs, Program in Education, Field of Infant/Toddler Early Childhood Special Education, Brooklyn, NY 11205-3688. Offers MA.

St. Joseph's College, New York, Graduate Programs, Program in Education, Field of Special Education, Brooklyn, NY 11205-3688. Offers severe and multiple disabilities (MA).

Saint Joseph's University, College of Arts and Sciences, Department of Education, Philadelphia, PA 19131-1395. Offers curriculum supervisor of instruction (Certificate); educational leadership (MS, Ed D); elementary education (MS, Certificate); elementary/middle years (Certificate); English second language specialist online (Certificate); hearing impaired: N-12th grade (Certificate); instructional technology (MS, Certificate); principal certification (Certificate); professional education (MS); reading specialist (MS, Certificate); reading supervisory (Certificate); secondary education (MS, Certificate); special education (MS, Certificate); superintendent's letter of eligibility (Certificate); supervisor of special education (Certificate); Wilson reading certificate online (Certificate). Part-time and evening/weekend programs available. Postbaccalaureate distance learning degree programs offered (no on-campus study). *Faculty:* 26 full-time (24 women), 83 part-time/adjunct (52 women). *Students:* 112 full-time (92 women), 923 part-time (709 women); includes 147 minority (92 Black or African American, non-Hispanic/Latino; 4 American Indian or Alaska Native, non-Hispanic/Latino; 19 Asian, non-Hispanic/Latino; 28 Hispanic/Latino; 4 Two or more races, non-Hispanic/Latino), 8 international. Average age 31. 285 applicants, 77% accepted, 176 enrolled. In 2011, 276 master's, 13 doctorates, 2 other advanced degrees awarded. *Entrance requirements:* For master's, 2 letters of recommendation, minimum GPA of 3.0, official transcripts, personal statement; for doctorate, GRE, master's degree from accredited institution, minimum graduate GPA of 3.5, computer competence, commitment to participate in cohort, interview with program director. Additional exam requirements/recommendations for international students: Required—TOEFL (minimum score 550 paper-based; 213 computer-based; 79 iBT). *Application deadline:* For fall admission, 7/15 priority date for domestic students, 4/15 for international students; for winter admission, 11/15 for domestic students, 1/15 for international students; for spring admission, 11/15 priority date for domestic students, 10/15 for international students. Applications are processed on a rolling basis. Application fee: $35. Electronic applications accepted. *Expenses:* Contact institution. *Financial support:* Unspecified assistantships available. Financial award applicants required to submit FAFSA. *Faculty research:* Public education professional development, factors predicting early mathematics skills for low income children. *Total annual research expenditures:* $92,975. *Unit head:* Dr. Jeanne Brady, Associate Dean, Education, 610-660-1580, E-mail: jebrady@sju.edu. *Application contact:* Kate McConnell, Director, Graduate College of Arts and Sciences Admissions and Retention, 610-660-3184, Fax: 610-660-3230, E-mail: kate.mcconnell@sju.edu.

Saint Louis University, Graduate Education, College of Education and Public Service, Department of Educational Studies, St. Louis, MO 63103-2097. Offers curriculum and instruction (MA, Ed D, PhD); educational foundations (MA, Ed D, PhD); special education (MA); teaching (MAT). *Accreditation:* NCATE. Part-time programs available. *Degree requirements:* For master's, comprehensive exam; for doctorate, comprehensive exam, thesis/dissertation, preliminary oral and written exams. *Entrance requirements:* For master's, GRE General Test or MAT, letters of recommendation, resume; for doctorate, GRE General Test, letters of recommendation, resumé, goal statement, transcripts. Additional exam requirements/recommendations for international students: Required—TOEFL (minimum score 525 paper-based; 194 computer-based). Electronic applications accepted. *Faculty research:* Teacher preparation, multicultural issues, children with special needs, qualitative research in education, inclusion.

Saint Martin's University, Graduate Programs, College of Education, Lacey, WA 98503. Offers administration (M Ed); English as a second language (M Ed); guidance and counseling (M Ed); reading (M Ed); special education (M Ed); teaching (MIT). *Accreditation:* Teacher Education Accreditation Council. Part-time and evening/weekend programs available. *Faculty:* 12 full-time (8 women), 9 part-time/adjunct (7 women). *Students:* 68 full-time (38 women), 28 part-time (20 women); includes 15 minority (2 Black or African American, non-Hispanic/Latino; 2 American Indian or Alaska Native, non-Hispanic/Latino; 7 Asian, non-Hispanic/Latino; 2 Hispanic/Latino; 2 Two or more races, non-Hispanic/Latino), 4 international. Average age 35. 17 applicants, 94% accepted, 15 enrolled. In 2011, 12 master's awarded. *Degree requirements:* For master's, comprehensive exam (for some programs), thesis or alternative, project or comprehensives. *Entrance requirements:* For master's, GRE General Test or MAT, resume. Additional exam requirements/recommendations for international students: Required—TOEFL (minimum score 560 paper-based; 220 computer-based; 83 iBT). *Application deadline:* For fall admission, 6/1 priority date for domestic students, 6/1 for international students; for spring admission, 10/1 priority date for domestic students, 10/1 for international students. Applications are processed on a rolling basis. Application fee: $35. *Expenses: Tuition:* Part-time $910 per credit hour. Tuition and fees vary according to course level, campus/location and program. *Financial support:* Career-related internships or fieldwork, Federal Work-Study, institutionally sponsored loans, and unspecified assistantships available. Support available to part-time students. Financial award application deadline: 3/1; financial award applicants required to submit FAFSA. *Faculty research:* Reader's theatre and reader/writer workshops, curriculum and assessment integration, gender and equity, classroom evaluations, organizational leadership. *Unit head:* Dr. Joyce Westgard, Dean, College of Education and Professional Psychology, 360-438-4509, Fax: 360-438-4486, E-mail: westgard@stmartin.edu. *Application contact:* Ryan M. Smith, Administrative Assistant, 360-438-4333, Fax: 360-438-4486, E-mail: ryan.smith@stmartin.edu. Web site: http://www.stmartin.edu/CEPP/.

Saint Mary's College of California, Kalmanovitz School of Education, Program in Special Education, Moraga, CA 94556. Offers M Ed, MA. Part-time programs available. *Faculty:* 2 full-time (1 woman), 2 part-time/adjunct (both women). *Students:* 4 full-time (all women), 19 part-time (16 women); includes 5 minority (1 Black or African American, non-Hispanic/Latino; 1 Asian, non-Hispanic/Latino; 2 Hispanic/Latino; 1 Two or more races, non-Hispanic/Latino). Average age 36. In 2011, 2 master's awarded. *Degree requirements:* For master's, thesis or alternative. *Entrance requirements:* For master's, writing proficiency exam, interview, minimum GPA of 3.0, teaching experience. *Application deadline:* Applications are processed on a rolling basis. Application fee: $50. Tuition and fees vary according to course load, degree level and program. *Financial support:* Scholarships/grants and tuition waivers (partial) available. Support available to part-time students. Financial award application deadline: 2/15. *Faculty research:* Consultation model, impact of gifted model on special education. *Unit head:* E. Gail Kirby, Director, 925-631-8177, Fax: 925-376-8379, E-mail: egki@stmarys-ca.edu. *Application contact:* Jane Joyce, Coordinator, Recruitment and Admissions, 925-631-4700, Fax: 925-376-8379, E-mail: soereq@stmarys-ca.edu. Web site: http://www.stmarys-ca.edu/node/3868.

Saint Mary's University of Minnesota, Schools of Graduate and Professional Programs, Graduate School of Education, Educational Administration Program, Winona, MN 55987-1399. Offers educational administration (Certificate, Ed S), including director of special education, K-12 principal, superintendent. *Unit head:* Dr. William Bjorum, Director, 612-728-5126, Fax: 612-728-5121, E-mail: wbjorum@smumn.edu. *Application contact:* Yasin Alsaidi, Director of Admissions for Graduate and Professional Programs, 612-728-5207, Fax: 612-728-5121, E-mail: yalsaidi@smumn.edu. Web site: http://www.smumn.edu/graduate-home/areas-of-study/graduate-school-of-education/eds-in-educational-administration-director-of-special-education-k-12-pr.

Saint Mary's University of Minnesota, Schools of Graduate and Professional Programs, Graduate School of Education, Special Education Program, Winona, MN 55987-1399. Offers behavioral disorders (Certificate); learning disabilities (Certificate); special education (MA). *Unit head:* Troy Gonzales, Director, 612-238-4565, E-mail: tgonzale@smumn.edu. *Application contact:* Yasin Alsaidi, 612-728-5207, E-mail: yalsaidi@smumn.edu. Web site: http://www.smumn.edu/graduate-home/areas-of-study/graduate-school-of-education/ma-in-special-education.

Saint Michael's College, Graduate Programs, Program in Education, Colchester, VT 05439. Offers administration (M Ed, CAGS); arts in education (CAGS); curriculum and instruction (M Ed, CAGS); information technology (CAGS); reading (M Ed); special education (M Ed, CAGS); technology (M Ed). Part-time and evening/weekend programs available. *Degree requirements:* For master's, thesis. *Entrance requirements:* For master's, minimum GPA of 3.0. Electronic applications accepted. *Faculty research:* Integrative curriculum, moral and spiritual dimensions of education, learning styles, multiple intelligences, integrating technology into the curriculum.

Saint Peter's University, Graduate Programs in Education, Program in Special Education, Jersey City, NJ 07306-5997. Offers literacy (MA Ed). Part-time and evening/weekend programs available. *Degree requirements:* For master's, comprehensive exam. *Entrance requirements:* For master's, GRE or MAT. Additional exam requirements/recommendations for international students: Required—TOEFL (minimum score 79 computer-based). Electronic applications accepted.

St. Thomas Aquinas College, Division of Teacher Education, Sparkill, NY 10976. Offers adolescence education (MST); childhood and special education (MST); childhood education (MST); educational leadership (MS Ed); reading (MS Ed, PMC); special education (MS Ed, PMC); teaching (MS Ed), including elementary education, middle school education, secondary education. *Accreditation:* NCATE. Part-time and evening/weekend programs available. *Degree requirements:* For master's, comprehensive exam, comprehensive professional portfolio; for PMC, action research project. *Entrance requirements:* For master's, New York State Qualifying Exam, GRE General Test or minimum GPA of 3.0, teaching certificate; for PMC, GRE General Test or minimum GPA of 3.0. Electronic applications accepted. *Faculty research:* Computer applications in education, adolescent special education students, literacy development, inclusive practices for special education students.

St. Thomas University, School of Leadership Studies, Institute for Education, Miami Gardens, FL 33054-6459. Offers earth/space science (Certificate); educational administration (MS, Certificate); educational leadership (Ed D); elementary education (MS); ESOL (Certificate); gifted education (Certificate); instructional technology (MS, Certificate); professional/studies (Certificate); reading (MS, Certificate); special education (MS). Part-time and evening/weekend programs available. *Degree requirements:* For master's, comprehensive exam; for doctorate, comprehensive exam, thesis/dissertation. *Entrance requirements:* For master's, interview, minimum GPA of 3.0 or GRE; for doctorate, GRE or MAT. Additional exam requirements/recommendations for international students: Required—TOEFL (minimum score 550 paper-based; 213 computer-based; 79 iBT). Electronic applications accepted.

Saint Vincent College, Program in Education, Latrobe, PA 15650-2690. Offers curriculum and instruction (MS); educational media and technology (MS); environmental education (MS); school administration and supervision (MS); special education (MS). Part-time and evening/weekend programs available. *Degree requirements:* For master's, comprehensive exam. *Entrance requirements:* For master's, GRE (if undergraduate GPA less than 3.0). Additional exam requirements/recommendations for international students: Required—TOEFL (minimum score 550 paper-based; 213 computer-based). *Faculty research:* Assessment and instructional technology.

Saint Xavier University, Graduate Studies, School of Education, Chicago, IL 60655-3105. Offers counseling (MA); curriculum and instruction (MA); early childhood education (MA); educational administration (MA); elementary education (MA); individualized studies (MA), including educational technology, English as a second language (ESL), ISTEM (integrative science, technology, engineering, and math), science education; music education (MA); reading (MA); secondary education (MA); Spanish education (MA); special education (MA); teaching and leadership (MA). *Accreditation:* NCATE. Part-time and evening/weekend programs available. *Degree requirements:* For master's, thesis or project. *Entrance requirements:* For master's, minimum GPA of 3.0. *Application deadline:* For fall admission, 8/15 priority date for domestic students. Applications are processed on a rolling basis. Application fee: $35. *Expenses:* Contact institution. *Financial support:* Career-related internships or fieldwork available. Support available to part-time students. Financial award applicants required to submit FAFSA. *Unit head:* Dr. Beverly Gulley, Dean, 773-298-3221, Fax: 773-779-9061, E-mail: gulley@sxu.edu. *Application contact:* Beth Gierach, Managing Director of Admission, 773-298-3053, Fax: 773-298-3076, E-mail: gierach@sxu.edu.

Salem College, Department of Teacher Education, Winston-Salem, NC 27101. Offers art education (MAT); elementary education (M Ed, MAT); language and literacy (M Ed); middle school education (MAT); music education (MAT); school counseling (M Ed); second language studies (MAT); secondary education (MAT); special education (M Ed, MAT). *Accreditation:* NCATE. Part-time and evening/weekend programs available. Postbaccalaureate distance learning degree programs offered (minimal on-campus study). *Degree requirements:* For master's, comprehensive exam, practicum (MAT), project (M Ed), oral and written comprehensive exams. *Entrance requirements:* For master's, GRE, minimum GPA of 2.5. *Faculty research:* Content area reading strategies, literacy development, brain compatible instruction.

Salem State University, School of Graduate Studies, Program in Special Education, Salem, MA 01970-5353. Offers M Ed. *Accreditation:* NCATE. Part-time and evening/weekend programs available. *Entrance requirements:* For master's, GRE, MAT. Additional exam requirements/recommendations for international students: Required—TOEFL (minimum score 550 paper-based; 80 iBT) or IELTS (minimum score 5.5).

Salus University, College of Education and Rehabilitation, Elkins Park, PA 19027-1598. Offers education of children and youth with visual and multiple impairments (M Ed, Certificate); low vision rehabilitation (MS, Certificate); orientation and mobility therapy (MS, Certificate); vision rehabilitation therapy (MS, Certificate); OD/MS. Part-time programs available. Postbaccalaureate distance learning degree programs offered. *Entrance requirements:* For master's, GRE or MAT, letters of reference (3), interviews (2). Additional exam requirements/recommendations for international students: Required—TOEFL, TWE. *Expenses:* Contact institution. *Faculty research:* Knowledge utilization, technology transfer.

Sam Houston State University, College of Education, Department of Language, Literacy, and Special Populations, Huntsville, TX 77341. Offers international literacy (M Ed); reading (M Ed, MA, Ed D); special education (M Ed, MA). Part-time and evening/weekend programs available. *Faculty:* 22 full-time (19 women), 5 part-time/adjunct (4 women). *Students:* 4 full-time (3 women), 151 part-time (146 women); includes 46 minority (19 Black or African American, non-Hispanic/Latino; 6 American Indian or Alaska Native, non-Hispanic/Latino; 2 Asian, non-Hispanic/Latino; 19 Hispanic/Latino), 3 international. Average age 37. 154 applicants, 58% accepted, 45 enrolled. In 2011, 31 master's, 5 doctorates awarded. *Entrance requirements:* For master's, GRE General Test, minimum GPA of 2.5. Additional exam requirements/recommendations for international students: Required—TOEFL (minimum score 550 paper-based; 213 computer-based; 79 iBT). *Application deadline:* For fall admission, 8/1 for domestic students, 6/25 for international students; for spring admission, 12/1 for domestic students, 11/12 for international students. Applications are processed on a rolling basis. Application fee: $45 ($75 for international students). Electronic applications accepted. *Expenses:* Tuition, state resident: full-time $4420; part-time $221 per credit hour. Tuition, nonresident: full-time $10,680; part-time $534 per credit hour. *Required fees:* $329 per credit hour. *Financial support:* Teaching assistantships available. Financial award application deadline: 5/31; financial award applicants required to submit FAFSA. *Unit head:* Dr. Melinda Miller, Chair, 936-294-1122, Fax: 936-294-1131, E-mail: mmiller@shsu.edu. *Application contact:* Molly Doughtie, Advisor, 936-294-1105, E-mail: edu_mxd@shsu.edu. Web site: http://www.shsu.edu/~edu_lls/.

San Diego State University, Graduate and Research Affairs, College of Education, Department of Administration, Rehabilitation and Post-Secondary Education, San Diego, CA 92182. Offers educational leadership in post-secondary education (MA); rehabilitation counseling (MS), including deafness. Evening/weekend programs available. Postbaccalaureate distance learning degree programs offered. *Degree requirements:* For master's, comprehensive exam (for some programs), thesis (for some programs). *Entrance requirements:* For master's, GRE General Test, letters of reference. Additional exam requirements/recommendations for international students: Required—TOEFL. Electronic applications accepted. *Faculty research:* Rehabilitation in cultural diversity, distance learning technology.

San Diego State University, Graduate and Research Affairs, College of Education, Department of Special Education, San Diego, CA 92182. Offers MA. *Accreditation:* NCATE. Evening/weekend programs available. *Entrance requirements:* For master's, GRE General Test, letters of reference. Additional exam requirements/recommendations for international students: Required—TOEFL. Electronic applications accepted.

San Francisco State University, Division of Graduate Studies, College of Education, Department of Special Education, Program in Orientation and Mobility, San Francisco, CA 94132-1722. Offers MA, Credential. *Unit head:* Dr. Sandra Rosen, Program Coordinator, 415-338-1245, E-mail: mobility@sfsu.edu. *Application contact:* Dr. David Hemphill, Associate Dean, 415-338-2689, E-mail: hemphill@sfsu.edu. Web site: http://online.sfsu.edu/~mobility/.

San Jose State University, Graduate Studies and Research, Connie L. Lurie College of Education, Department of Special Education, San Jose, CA 95192-0001. Offers MA. *Accreditation:* NCATE. Evening/weekend programs available. Electronic applications accepted.

Seattle University, College of Education, Program in Special Education, Seattle, WA 98122-1090. Offers M Ed, MA, Certificate. *Students:* 2 full-time (both women), 13 part-time (10 women); includes 2 minority (1 Hispanic/Latino; 1 Two or more races, non-Hispanic/Latino), 1 international. Average age 31. 6 applicants, 67% accepted, 4 enrolled. *Entrance requirements:* For master's, GRE, MAT or minimum GPA of 3.0, 1 year K-12 teaching experience; for Certificate, master's degree, minimum GPA of 3.0, 1 year K-12 teaching experience. *Application deadline:* For fall admission, 8/20 priority date for domestic students; for winter admission, 11/20 priority date for domestic students; for spring admission, 2/20 priority date for domestic students. *Unit head:* Dr. Katherine Schlick Noe, Director, 206-296-5768, E-mail: kschlnoe@seattleu.edu. *Application contact:* Janet Shandley, Associate Dean of Graduate Admissions, 206-296-5900, Fax: 206-298-5656, E-mail: grad_admissions@seattleu.edu.

Seton Hall University, College of Education and Human Services, Department of Educational Studies, South Orange, NJ 07079-2697. Offers Catholic school teaching EPICS (MA); instructional design (MA); professional development (MA); school library media specialist (MA); special education (MA). Part-time and evening/weekend programs available. *Faculty:* 18 full-time (14 women). *Students:* 25 full-time (16 women), 37 part-time (22 women); includes 18 minority (7 Black or African American, non-Hispanic/Latino; 4 Asian, non-Hispanic/Latino; 7 Hispanic/Latino), 2 international. Average age 32. 39 applicants, 90% accepted, 27 enrolled. In 2011, 47 master's awarded. *Entrance requirements:* For master's, GRE or MAT, PRAXIS (for certification candidates), minimum GPA of 2.75. *Application deadline:* For fall admission, 5/1 for domestic students; for spring admission, 10/1 for domestic students. Applications are processed on a rolling basis. Application fee: $50. *Expenses: Tuition:* Part-time $1033 per credit hour. *Required fees:* $85 per semester. *Financial support:* In 2011–12, 2 research assistantships with full tuition reimbursements (averaging $4,000 per year) were awarded; fellowships, career-related internships or fieldwork, institutionally sponsored loans, and unspecified assistantships also available. Financial award application deadline: 2/1. *Unit head:* Dr. Joseph Martinelli, Chair, 973-275-2733, E-mail: joseph.martinelli@shu.edu.

Seton Hill University, Program in Special Education, Greensburg, PA 15601. Offers MA, Certificate. Part-time and evening/weekend programs available. Postbaccalaureate distance learning degree programs offered (minimal on-campus study). *Faculty:* 2 full-time (1 woman), 4 part-time/adjunct (3 women). *Students:* 15 full-time (13 women), 11 part-time (8 women); includes 2 minority (both Black or African American, non-Hispanic/Latino), 1 international. In 2011, 16 degrees awarded. *Entrance requirements:* For master's, 3 letters of recommendation, copy of teacher's certification, transcripts, resume. Additional exam requirements/recommendations for international students: Required—TOEFL (minimum score 600 paper-based; 250 computer-based; 100 iBT), IELTS (minimum score 6.5). *Application deadline:* Applications are processed on a rolling basis. Application fee: $0. Electronic applications accepted. *Expenses: Tuition:* Full-time $13,446; part-time $747 per credit. *Required fees:* $700; $25 per credit. $50 per term. *Financial support:* Tuition discounts available. *Faculty research:* Autism, integrating technology into instruction. *Unit head:* Dr. Sondra Lettrich, Director, 724-830-1010, E-mail: lettrich@setonhill.edu. *Application contact:* Laurel Komarny, Program Counselor, 724-838-4209, E-mail: komarny@setonhill.edu.

Shippensburg University of Pennsylvania, School of Graduate Studies, College of Education and Human Services, Department of Educational Leadership and Special Education, Shippensburg, PA 17257-2299. Offers school administration principal K-12 (M Ed); special education (M Ed), including comprehensive, emotional/behavior disorders, intellectual disabilities and autism, learning disabilities. *Accreditation:* NCATE. Part-time and evening/weekend programs available. *Faculty:* 9 full-time (3 women), 4 part-time/adjunct (2 women). *Students:* 29 full-time (24 women), 118 part-time (78 women); includes 4 minority (2 Black or African American, non-Hispanic/Latino; 1 Asian, non-Hispanic/Latino; 1 Hispanic/Latino), 2 international. Average age 31. 49 applicants, 73% accepted, 31 enrolled. In 2011, 66 master's awarded. *Degree requirements:* For master's, candidacy, thesis, or practicum. *Entrance requirements:* For master's, instructional or educational specialist certificate; 3 letters of reference; 2 years of successful teaching experience; interview and GRE or MAT (if GPA is less than 2.75); statement of purpose; writing sample; personal goals statement. Additional exam requirements/recommendations for international students: Required—TOEFL (minimum score 580 paper-based; 237 computer-based); Recommended—IELTS (minimum score 6). *Application deadline:* For fall admission, 1/6 for domestic students, 4/30 for international students; for spring admission, 1/9 for domestic students, 9/30 for international students. Applications are processed on a rolling basis. Application fee: $30. Electronic applications accepted. *Expenses: Tuition, area resident:* Part-time $416 per credit. Tuition, state resident: part-time $416 per credit. Tuition, nonresident: part-time $624 per credit. *Required fees:* $119 per credit. *Financial support:* In 2011–12, 6 research assistantships with full tuition reimbursements (averaging $5,000 per year) were awarded; career-related internships or fieldwork, scholarships/grants, unspecified assistantships, and resident hall director and student payroll positions also available. Support available to part-time students. Financial award application deadline: 3/1; financial award applicants required to submit FAFSA. *Unit head:* Dr. Christopher L. Schwilk, Chairperson, 717-477-1591, Fax: 717-477-4026, E-mail: clschwi@ship.edu. *Application contact:* Jeremy R. Goshorn, Assistant Dean of Graduate Admissions, 717-477-1231, Fax: 717-477-4016, E-mail: jrgoshorn@ship.edu. Web site: http://www.ship.edu/else/.

Silver Lake College of the Holy Family, Division of Graduate Studies, Program in Special Education, Manitowoc, WI 54220-9319. Offers MASE. Part-time and evening/weekend programs available. *Entrance requirements:* For master's, minimum undergraduate GPA of 3.0, written essay, three letters of recommendation from professional educators. Additional exam requirements/recommendations for international students: Required—TOEFL. Electronic applications accepted.

Simmons College, College of Arts and Sciences Graduate Studies, Boston, MA 02115. Offers applied behavior analysis (PhD); behavior analysis (MS, Ed S); children's literature (MA); education (MS, CAGS, Ed S); educational leadership (PhD, CAGS); English (MA); gender and cultural studies (MA); health professions education (PhD); history (MA); Spanish (MA); special education moderate licensure (Certificate); special needs administration (Ed D); special needs education (Ed S); teaching (MAT); teaching English as a second language (MA, CAGS); urban education (CAGS); writing for children (MFA); MA/MA; MA/MS; MAT/MA. *Unit head:* Renee White, Dean. *Application contact:* Kristen Haack, Director, Graduate Studies Admission, 617-521-2917, Fax: 617-521-3058, E-mail: gsa@simmons.edu. Web site: http://www.simmons.edu/gradstudies/.

Slippery Rock University of Pennsylvania, Graduate Studies (Recruitment), College of Education, Department of Special Education, Slippery Rock, PA 16057-1383. Offers autism (M Ed); birth to grade 8 (M Ed); grade 7 to grade 12 (M Ed); master teacher (M Ed); supervision (M Ed). *Accreditation:* NCATE. Part-time and evening/weekend programs available. Postbaccalaureate distance learning degree programs offered. *Faculty:* 7 full-time (3 women). *Students:* 15 full-time (12 women), 98 part-time (83 women); includes 3 minority (1 Black or African American, non-Hispanic/Latino; 2 Asian, non-Hispanic/Latino). Average age 31. 113 applicants, 70% accepted, 37 enrolled. In 2011, 62 degrees awarded. *Degree requirements:* For master's, thesis optional, portfolio presentation. *Entrance requirements:* For master's, GRE General Test, MAT, minimum GPA of 3.0, official transcripts, teaching certification. Additional exam requirements/recommendations for international students: Required—TOEFL (minimum score 550 paper-based; 213 computer-based; 80 iBT). *Application deadline:* For fall admission, 3/1 priority date for domestic students, 5/1 for international students; for spring admission, 10/1 priority date for domestic students, 9/1 for international students. Applications are processed on a rolling basis. Application fee: $25 ($30 for international students). Electronic applications accepted. *Expenses:* Contact institution. *Financial support:* Career-related internships or fieldwork, institutionally sponsored loans, scholarships/grants, and tuition waivers (partial) available. Support available to part-time students. Financial award application deadline: 5/1; financial award applicants required to submit FAFSA. *Unit head:* Dr. Robert Isherwood, Graduate Coordinator, 724-738-2614, Fax: 724-738-4395, E-mail: robert.isherwood@sru.edu. *Application contact:* Angela Barrett, Director of Graduate Admissions, 724-738-2051, Fax: 724-738-2146, E-mail: graduate.admissions@sru.edu.

Smith College, Graduate and Special Programs, Department of Education and Child Study, Program in the Education of the Deaf, Northampton, MA 01063. Offers MED. Part-time programs available. *Students:* 12 full-time (all women), 1 (woman) part-time. Average age 28. 29 applicants, 48% accepted, 11 enrolled. In 2011, 12 master's awarded. *Entrance requirements:* For master's, GRE General Test or MAT. Additional exam requirements/recommendations for international students: Required—TOEFL (minimum score 590 paper-based; 243 computer-based; 97 iBT). *Application deadline:* For fall admission, 4/1 for domestic students, 1/15 for international students. Applications are processed on a rolling basis. Application fee: $60. *Expenses: Tuition:* Full-time $14,925; part-time $1245 per credit. *Financial support:* In 2011–12, 13 students received support. Career-related internships or fieldwork, institutionally sponsored loans, scholarships/grants, and tuition waivers (full) available. Support available to part-time students. Financial award application deadline: 1/15; financial award applicants required to submit CSS PROFILE or FAFSA. *Unit head:* Danial Salvucci, Interim Director, 413-585-3255, Fax: 413-585-3268, E-mail: dsalvucc@smith.edu. *Application contact:* Ruth Morgan, Administrative Assistant, 413-585-3050, Fax: 413-585-3054, E-mail: gradstdy@smith.edu. Web site: http://www.smith.edu/educ/graduate/clarkeschool.php.

Sonoma State University, School of Education, Rohnert Park, CA 94928-3609. Offers education (MA, Ed D); multiple subject (Credential); single subject (Credential); special education (Credential). *Accreditation:* NCATE. Part-time and evening/weekend programs available. *Faculty:* 12 full-time (9 women), 4 part-time/adjunct (1 woman). *Students:* 226 full-time (175 women), 181 part-time (137 women); includes 70 minority (3 Black or African American, non-Hispanic/Latino; 3 American Indian or Alaska Native, non-Hispanic/Latino; 10 Asian, non-Hispanic/Latino; 28 Hispanic/Latino; 1 Native Hawaiian or other Pacific Islander, non-Hispanic/Latino; 25 Two or more races, non-Hispanic/Latino), 4 international. Average age 31. 336 applicants, 61% accepted, 95 enrolled. In 2011, 54 master's, 478 other advanced degrees awarded. *Degree requirements:* For master's, thesis or alternative. *Entrance requirements:* For master's, minimum GPA of 2.5. Additional exam requirements/recommendations for international students: Required—TOEFL (minimum score 500 paper-based; 173 computer-based). Application fee: $55. *Financial support:* Fellowships, career-related internships or fieldwork, and Federal Work-Study available. Support available to part-time students. Financial award application deadline: 3/2; financial award applicants required to submit FAFSA. *Unit head:* Dr. Carlos Ayala, Dean, 707-664-4412, E-mail: carlos.ayala@sonoma.edu. *Application contact:* Dr. Jennifer Mahdavi, Coordinator of Graduate Studies, 707-664-3311, E-mail: jennifer.mahdavi@sonoma.edu. Web site: http://www.sonoma.edu/education/.

South Carolina State University, School of Graduate Studies, Department of Education, Orangeburg, SC 29117-0001. Offers counseling education (M Ed); early childhood and special education (M Ed); early childhood education (MAT); educational leadership (Ed D, Ed S); elementary education (M Ed, MAT); engineering (MAT); general science (MAT); mathematics (MAT); secondary education (M Ed), including biology education, business education, counselor education, English education, home economics education, industrial education, mathematics education, science education, social studies education; special education (M Ed), including emotionally handicapped, learning disabilities, mentally handicapped. *Accreditation:* NCATE. Part-time and evening/weekend programs available. *Faculty:* 9 full-time (6 women), 6 part-time/adjunct (2 women). *Students:* 34 full-time (29 women), 50 part-time (40 women); includes 74 minority (72 Black or African American, non-Hispanic/Latino; 1 Asian, non-Hispanic/Latino; 1 Hispanic/Latino). Average age 34. 23 applicants, 91% accepted, 14 enrolled. In 2011, 11 master's awarded. *Degree requirements:* For master's, thesis optional, departmental qualifying exam. *Entrance requirements:* For master's, GRE General Test, NTE, interview, teaching certificate. *Application deadline:* For fall admission, 6/15 priority date for domestic students, 6/15 for international students; for spring admission, 11/1 for domestic and international students. Applications are processed on a rolling basis. Application fee: $25. Electronic applications accepted. *Expenses:* Tuition, state resident: full-time $8688; part-time $514 per credit hour. Tuition, nonresident: full-time $17,600; part-time $1009 per credit hour. *Required fees:* $570. *Financial support:* In 2011–12, 3 fellowships (averaging $5,020 per year) were awarded; career-related internships or fieldwork, Federal Work-Study, and institutionally sponsored loans also available. Financial award application deadline: 6/1. *Faculty research:* Critical thinking, child abuse, stress, test-taking skills, conflict resolution, mainstreaming. *Unit head:* Dr. Charlie Spell, Interim Chair, 803-536-7098, Fax: 803-516-4568, E-mail: cspell@scsu.edu. *Application contact:* Annette Hazzard-Jones, Program Coordinator II, 803-536-8809, Fax: 803-536-8812, E-mail: zs_ahazzard@scsu.edu.

South Carolina State University, School of Graduate Studies, Department of Human Services, Orangeburg, SC 29117-0001. Offers counselor education (M Ed); orientation and mobility (Graduate Certificate); rehabilitation counseling (MA). *Accreditation:* CORE. Part-time and evening/weekend programs available. *Faculty:* 9 full-time (6 women), 9 part-time/adjunct (7 women). *Students:* 149 full-time (124 women), 57 part-time (46 women); includes 190 minority (all Black or African American, non-Hispanic/Latino), 2 international. Average age 34. 114 applicants, 98% accepted, 92 enrolled. In 2011, 56 master's awarded. *Degree requirements:* For master's, comprehensive exam (for some programs), departmental qualifying exam, internship. *Entrance requirements:* For master's, GRE, MAT, minimum GPA of 2.7. *Application deadline:* For fall admission, 6/15 priority date for domestic students, 6/15 for international students; for spring admission, 11/1 for domestic and international students. Applications are processed on a rolling basis. Application fee: $25. Electronic applications accepted. *Expenses:* Tuition, state resident: full-time $8688; part-time $514 per credit hour. Tuition, nonresident: full-time $17,600; part-time $1009 per credit hour. *Required fees:* $570. *Financial support:* In 2011–12, 35 students received support, including 14 fellowships (averaging $5,730 per year); career-related internships or fieldwork, institutionally sponsored loans, and unspecified assistantships also available. Financial award application deadline: 6/1. *Faculty research:* Handicap, disability, rehabilitation evaluation, vocation. *Unit head:* Dr. Cassandra Sligh Conway, Chair, 803-536-7075, Fax: 803-533-3636, E-mail: csligh-dewalt@scsu.edu. *Application contact:* Annette Hazzard-Jones, Program Coordinator II, 803-536-8809, Fax: 803-536-8812, E-mail: zs_ahazzard@scsu.edu.

Southeastern Louisiana University, College of Education and Human Development, Department of Teaching and Learning, Hammond, LA 70402. Offers curriculum and instruction (M Ed); elementary education (MAT); special education (M Ed); special education: early interventionist (MAT). *Accreditation:* NCATE. Part-time and evening/weekend programs available. *Faculty:* 13 full-time (11 women). *Students:* 30 full-time (all women), 84 part-time (78 women); includes 15 minority (10 Black or African American, non-Hispanic/Latino; 2 Asian, non-Hispanic/Latino; 3 Hispanic/Latino). Average age 32. 20 applicants, 100% accepted, 14 enrolled. In 2011, 37 degrees awarded. *Degree requirements:* For master's, comprehensive exam (for some programs), thesis (for some programs), action research project, oral defense of research project, portfolio, teaching certificate, minimum cumulative GPA of 3.0. *Entrance requirements:* For master's, GRE (verbal and quantitative), PRAXIS (MAT). Additional exam requirements/recommendations for international students: Required—TOEFL (minimum score 500 paper-based; 173 computer-based; 61 iBT). *Application deadline:* For fall admission, 7/15 priority date for domestic students, 6/1 for international students; for spring admission, 12/1 priority date for domestic students, 10/1 for international students. Applications are processed on a rolling basis. Application fee: $20 ($30 for international students). Electronic applications accepted. *Expenses:* Tuition, state resident: full-time $3977; part-time $283 per semester hour. Tuition, nonresident: full-time $13,482; part-time $811 per semester hour. *Financial support:* Career-related internships or fieldwork, Federal Work-Study, institutionally sponsored loans, scholarships/grants, and unspecified assistantships available. Support available to part-time students. Financial award application deadline: 5/1; financial award applicants required to submit FAFSA. *Faculty research:* ESL, dyslexia, pre-service teachers, inclusion, early childhood education. *Total annual research expenditures:* $356,182. *Unit head:* Dr. Cynthia Elliott, Interim Department Head, 985-549-2221, Fax: 985-549-5009, E-mail: celliott@selu.edu. *Application contact:* Sandra Meyers, Graduate Admissions Analyst, 985-549-5620, Fax: 985-549-5632, E-mail: admissions@selu.edu. Web site: http://www.selu.edu/acad_research/depts/teach_lrn/index.html.

Southeastern Louisiana University, College of Nursing and Health Sciences, Department of Communication Sciences and Disorders, Hammond, LA 70402. Offers MS. *Accreditation:* ASHA; NCATE. *Faculty:* 10 full-time (9 women), 1 (woman) part-time/adjunct. *Students:* 44 full-time (39 women), 17 part-time (15 women); includes 9 minority (3 Black or African American, non-Hispanic/Latino; 1 Asian, non-Hispanic/Latino; 3 Hispanic/Latino; 2 Two or more races, non-Hispanic/Latino), 1 international. Average age 26. 92 applicants, 100% accepted, 18 enrolled. In 2011, 20 degrees awarded. *Degree requirements:* For master's, comprehensive exam, thesis optional, 25 clock hours of clinical observation. *Entrance requirements:* For master's, GRE (verbal and quantitative), minimum GPA of 2.75; undergraduate degree; three letters of reference; favorable criminal background check. Additional exam requirements/recommendations for international students: Required—TOEFL (minimum score 500 paper-based; 173 computer-based; 61 iBT). *Application deadline:* For fall admission, 3/1 priority date for domestic students, 6/1 for international students; for spring admission, 10/1 priority date for domestic students, 10/1 for international students. Applications are processed on a rolling basis. Application fee: $20 ($30 for international students). Electronic applications accepted. *Expenses:* Tuition, state resident: full-time $3977; part-time $283 per semester hour. Tuition, nonresident: full-time $13,482; part-time $811 per semester hour. *Financial support:* Career-related internships or fieldwork, Federal Work-Study, institutionally sponsored loans, scholarships/grants, and unspecified assistantships available. Support available to part-time students. Financial award application deadline: 5/1; financial award applicants required to submit FAFSA. *Faculty research:* Aphasia, autism spectrum disorders, child language and literacy, language and dementia, clinical supervision. *Total annual research expenditures:* $19,424. *Unit head:* Dr. Rebecca Davis, Interim Department Head, 985-549-2214, Fax: 985-549-5030, E-mail: rdavis@selu.edu. *Application contact:* Sandra Meyers, Graduate Admissions Analyst, 985-549-5620, Fax: 985-549-5632, E-mail: admissions@selu.edu. Web site: http://www.selu.edu/acad_research/depts/csd.

Southeastern Oklahoma State University, School of Education, Durant, OK 74701-0609. Offers math specialist (M Ed); reading specialist (M Ed); school administration (M Ed); school counseling (M Ed); special education (M Ed). *Accreditation:* NCATE. Part-time and evening/weekend programs available. *Faculty:* 52 full-time (19 women), 1 (woman) part-time/adjunct. *Students:* 15 full-time (11 women), 54 part-time (40 women); includes 24 minority (2 Black or African American, non-Hispanic/Latino; 16 American Indian or Alaska Native, non-Hispanic/Latino; 6 Hispanic/Latino). Average age 34. 31 applicants, 94% accepted, 29 enrolled. *Degree requirements:* For master's, comprehensive exam, thesis optional, portfolio (M Ed). *Entrance requirements:* For master's, GRE General Test (MBS), minimum GPA of 3.0 in last 60 hours or 2.75 overall. Additional exam requirements/recommendations for international students: Required—TOEFL (minimum score 550 paper-based; 213 computer-based; 79 iBT). *Application deadline:* For fall admission, 8/1 for domestic students, 6/1 for international students; for spring admission, 1/5 for domestic students, 11/1 for international students. Application fee: $20 ($55 for international students). Electronic applications accepted. *Expenses:* Tuition, state resident: full-time $3537; part-time $173.95 per credit hour. Tuition, nonresident: full-time $8673; part-time $459.30 per credit hour. *Required fees:* $22.55 per credit hour. *Financial support:* In 2011–12, 1 teaching assistantship with full tuition reimbursement (averaging $5,000 per year) was awarded; Federal Work-Study, institutionally sponsored loans, and tuition waivers (partial) also available. Support available to part-time students. Financial award application deadline: 6/15; financial award applicants required to submit FAFSA. *Unit head:* Dr. John Love, M Ed Coordinator, 580-745-2226, Fax: 580-745-7508, E-mail: jlove@se.edu. *Application contact:* Carrie Williamson, Graduate Secretary, 580-745-2220, Fax: 580-745-7474, E-mail: cwilliamson@se.edu. Web site: http://www.se.edu/graduate-programs/master-of-education/.

Southeast Missouri State University, School of Graduate Studies, Department of Elementary, Early and Special Education, Program in Exceptional Child Education, Cape Girardeau, MO 63701-4799. Offers MA. *Accreditation:* NCATE. Part-time and evening/weekend programs available. Postbaccalaureate distance learning degree programs offered (no on-campus study). *Faculty:* 3 full-time (all women). *Students:* 4 full-time (3 women), 13 part-time (12 women); includes 1 minority (Black or African American, non-Hispanic/Latino), 1 international. Average age 34. 6 applicants, 100% accepted, 6 enrolled. In 2011, 5 master's awarded. *Degree requirements:* For master's, comprehensive exam, thesis or alternative, minimum GPA of 3.25, 2 years of special education teaching experience, psychology course, completion of Missouri's Administrator's Assessment. *Entrance requirements:* For master's, GRE General Test, MAT, or PRAXIS, minimum undergraduate GPA of 2.75; valid elementary or secondary teaching certificate. Additional exam requirements/recommendations for international students: Required—TOEFL (minimum score 550 paper-based; 213 computer-based; 79 iBT); Recommended—IELTS (minimum score 6). *Application deadline:* For fall admission, 8/1 for domestic students, 7/1 for international students; for spring admission, 11/21 for domestic students, 11/1 for international students. Applications are processed on a rolling basis. Application fee: $30 ($40 for international students). Electronic applications accepted. *Expenses:* Tuition, state resident: full-time $4896; part-time $272 per credit hour. Tuition, nonresident: full-time $8649; part-time $480.50 per credit hour. *Financial support:* In 2011–12, 7 students received support. Career-related internships or fieldwork, Federal Work-Study, scholarships/grants, tuition waivers (full), and unspecified assistantships available. Financial award application deadline: 6/30; financial award applicants required to submit FAFSA. *Unit head:* Dr. Julie Ray, Interim Chairperson and Professor, 573-651-2444, E-mail: jaray@semo.edu. *Application contact:* Alisa Aleen McFerron, Assistant Director of Admissions for Operations, 573-651-5937, Fax: 573-651-5936, E-mail: amcferron@semo.edu. Web site: http://www.semo.edu/eese/.

Southern Connecticut State University, School of Graduate Studies, School of Education, Department of Special Education, New Haven, CT 06515-1355. Offers MS Ed, Diploma. Part-time and evening/weekend programs available. *Faculty:* 13 full-time (8 women), 11 part-time/adjunct (8 women). *Students:* 91 full-time (78 women), 153 part-time (131 women); includes 22 minority (10 Black or African American, non-Hispanic/Latino; 10 Hispanic/Latino; 2 Two or more races, non-Hispanic/Latino). 630 applicants, 17% accepted, 95 enrolled. In 2011, 113 master's, 19 Diplomas awarded. *Degree requirements:* For master's, thesis or alternative. *Entrance requirements:* For master's, interview; for Diploma, 3 years of teaching experience, master's degree, teacher certification, interview. *Application deadline:* For fall admission, 7/15 for domestic students. Applications are processed on a rolling basis. Application fee: $50. Electronic applications accepted. *Expenses:* Tuition, state resident: full-time $5137; part-time $413 per credit. *Required fees:* $4008; $55 per term. *Financial support:* Career-related internships or fieldwork available. Financial award application deadline: 4/15; financial award applicants required to submit FAFSA. *Unit head:* Dr. Deborah Newton, Chairperson, 203-392-5941, Fax: 203-392-5927, E-mail: newtond2@southernct.edu. *Application contact:* Dr. Ruth Eren, Graduate Coordinator, 203-392-5647, Fax: 203-392-5927, E-mail: erenr1@southernct.edu.

Southern Illinois University Carbondale, Graduate School, College of Education and Human Services, Department of Educational Psychology and Special Education, Program in Special Education, Carbondale, IL 62901-4701. Offers MS Ed. *Accreditation:* NCATE. Part-time programs available. *Faculty:* 19 full-time (9 women), 7 part-time/adjunct (2 women). *Students:* 2 full-time (both women), 26 part-time (24 women); includes 5 minority (4 Black or African American, non-Hispanic/Latino; 1 Asian, non-Hispanic/Latino), 2 international. Average age 28. 10 applicants, 40% accepted, 1 enrolled. In 2011, 2 degrees awarded. *Degree requirements:* For master's, thesis. *Entrance requirements:* For master's, GRE General Test, minimum GPA of 2.7. Additional exam requirements/recommendations for international students: Required—TOEFL. *Application deadline:* Applications are processed on a rolling basis. Application fee: $20. *Financial support:* In 2011–12, 3 students received support. Fellowships with full tuition reimbursements available, research assistantships with full tuition reimbursements available, teaching assistantships with full tuition reimbursements available, career-related internships or fieldwork, Federal Work-Study, institutionally sponsored loans, tuition waivers (full), and unspecified assistantships available. Support available to part-time students. *Faculty research:* Applied and action research; scientific methods used to evaluate effectiveness of products and programs for the handicapped; scientific methods used to develop generalizations about instructional, motivational, and learning processes of the handicapped. *Unit head:* Dr. Lyle White, Chairperson, 618-536-7763, E-mail: lwhite@siu.edu. *Application contact:* Cathy Earnhart, Administrative Clerk, 618-453-6932, E-mail: pern@siu.edu.

Southern Illinois University Edwardsville, Graduate School, School of Education, Department of Special Education and Communication Disorders, Program in Special Education, Edwardsville, IL 62026. Offers MS Ed, Post-Master's Certificate. Part-time and evening/weekend programs available. *Students:* 5 full-time (all women), 35 part-time (32 women); includes 6 minority (2 Black or African American, non-Hispanic/Latino; 2 Hispanic/Latino; 2 Two or more races, non-Hispanic/Latino), 1 international. 25 applicants, 60% accepted. In 2011, 13 master's awarded. *Degree requirements:* For master's, thesis or alternative, final project. *Entrance requirements:* Additional exam requirements/recommendations for international students: Required—TOEFL (minimum score 550 paper-based; 213 computer-based; 79 iBT), IELTS (minimum score 6.5). *Application deadline:* For fall admission, 7/22 for domestic students, 6/1 for international students; for spring admission, 12/9 for domestic students, 10/1 for international students. Applications are processed on a rolling basis. Application fee: $30. Electronic applications accepted. Tuition and fees vary according to course load and program. *Financial support:* Fellowships, research assistantships, teaching assistantships, institutionally sponsored loans, scholarships/grants, and unspecified assistantships available. Financial award application deadline: 3/1; financial award applicants required to submit FAFSA. *Unit head:* Dr. Linda Forbringer, Director, 618-650-3488, E-mail: lforbri@siue.edu. *Application contact:* Michelle Robinson, Coordinator of Graduate Recruitment, 618-650-2811, Fax: 618-650-3523, E-mail: michero@siue.edu. Web site: http://www.siue.edu/education/secd/.

Southern New Hampshire University, School of Education, Manchester, NH 03106-1045. Offers business education (MS); child development (M Ed); computer technology education (Certificate); curriculum and instruction (M Ed); education (M Ed, CAS); elementary education (M Ed); general special education (Certificate); school business administrator (Certificate); secondary education (M Ed); training and development (Certificate). Part-time and evening/weekend programs available. Postbaccalaureate distance learning degree programs offered (no on-campus study). *Degree requirements:* For master's, comprehensive exam (for some programs), thesis or alternative. *Entrance requirements:* For master's, PRAXIS I, minimum GPA of 2.75. Additional exam requirements/recommendations for international students: Required—TOEFL (minimum score 550 paper-based; 213 computer-based). Electronic applications accepted. *Expenses:* Contact institution.

Southern Oregon University, Graduate Studies, School of Education, Ashland, OR 97520. Offers elementary education (MA Ed, MS Ed), including classroom teacher, early childhood, handicapped learner, reading, supervision; secondary education (MA Ed, MS Ed), including classroom teacher, handicapped learner, reading, supervision; teaching (MAT). *Faculty:* 18 full-time (10 women), 10 part-time/adjunct (all women). *Students:* 128 full-time (88 women), 145 part-time (103 women); includes 32 minority (1 Black or African American, non-Hispanic/Latino; 3 American Indian or Alaska Native, non-Hispanic/Latino; 5 Asian, non-Hispanic/Latino; 13 Hispanic/Latino; 3 Native Hawaiian or other Pacific Islander, non-Hispanic/Latino; 7 Two or more races, non-Hispanic/Latino), 1 international. Average age 35. 48 applicants, 60% accepted, 23 enrolled. In 2011, 102 degrees awarded. *Degree requirements:* For master's, thesis optional. *Entrance requirements:* For master's, GRE General Test, minimum GPA of 3.0. *Application deadline:* For fall admission, 2/1 for domestic students. Application fee: $50. Electronic applications accepted. *Expenses:* Tuition, state resident: full-time $12,600; part-time $350 per credit. Tuition, nonresident: full-time $16,200; part-time $450 per credit. *Required fees:* $1590. *Financial support:* Research assistantships with partial tuition reimbursements available. *Unit head:* Dr. Geoff Mills, Dean, 541-552-6920, E-mail: mills@sou.edu. *Application contact:* Mark Bottorff, Director of Admissions, 541-552-6411, Fax: 541-552-8403, E-mail: admissions@sou.edu. Web site: http://www.sou.edu/education/.

Southern University and Agricultural and Mechanical College, Graduate School and College of Education, Department of Special Education, Baton Rouge, LA 70813. Offers M Ed, PhD. *Accreditation:* NCATE. Part-time and evening/weekend programs available. *Degree requirements:* For master's, comprehensive exam, thesis optional; for doctorate, thesis/dissertation, comprehensive qualifying exam, oral defense of dissertation. *Entrance requirements:* For master's, GMAT or GRE General Test, PRAXIS; for doctorate, GRE General Test, PRAXIS, letters of recommendation, 2 years experience (individuals with disabilities). Additional exam requirements/recommendations for international students: Required—TOEFL. *Faculty research:* Classroom discipline/management, minority students in gifted/special education, learning styles/brain hemisphericity, school violence and prevention, certifications for special education teachers.

Southwestern College, Education Programs, Winfield, KS 67156-2499. Offers curriculum and instruction (M Ed); education (Ed D); special education (M Ed); teaching (MA). *Accreditation:* NCATE. Part-time and evening/weekend programs available. Postbaccalaureate distance learning degree programs offered (minimal on-campus study). *Faculty:* 6 full-time (3 women), 6 part-time/adjunct (all women). *Students:* 9 full-time (7 women), 94 part-time (73 women); includes 12 minority (4 Black or African American, non-Hispanic/Latino; 2 Asian, non-Hispanic/Latino; 3 Hispanic/Latino; 3 Two or more races, non-Hispanic/Latino), 9 international. Average age 35. 77 applicants, 60% accepted, 34 enrolled. In 2011, 56 master's awarded. *Degree requirements:* For master's, practicum, portfolio. *Entrance requirements:* For master's, baccalaureate degree, minimum GPA of 2.5, valid teaching certificate (for special education). Additional exam requirements/recommendations for international students: Required—TOEFL (minimum score 550 paper-based; 213 computer-based). *Application deadline:* For fall admission, 8/1 for domestic students; for spring admission, 12/1 for domestic students. Applications are processed on a rolling basis. Application fee: $0. Electronic applications accepted. *Expenses:* Contact institution. *Financial support:* In 2011–12, 4 students received support. Federal Work-Study, tuition waivers (partial), and unspecified assistantships available. Financial award application deadline: 4/1; financial award applicants required to submit FAFSA. *Unit head:* Dr. David Hofmeister, Director of Teacher Education, 800-846-1543 Ext. 6115, Fax: 620-229-6341, E-mail:

david.hofmeister@sckans.edu. Web site: http://www.sckans.edu/graduate/education-med/.

Southwestern Oklahoma State University, College of Professional and Graduate Studies, School of Behavioral Sciences and Education, Specialization in Special Education, Weatherford, OK 73096-3098. Offers M Ed. M Ed distance learning degree program offered to Oklahoma residents only. *Accreditation:* NCATE. Part-time and evening/weekend programs available. *Degree requirements:* For master's, exam. *Entrance requirements:* For master's, GRE General Test or minimum undergraduate GPA of 3.0. Additional exam requirements/recommendations for international students: Required—TOEFL.

Southwest Minnesota State University, Department of Education, Marshall, MN 56258. Offers ESL (MS); math (MS); reading (MS); special education (MS), including developmental disabilities, early childhood education, emotional behavioral disorders, learning disabilities; teaching, learning and leadership (MS). Part-time and evening/weekend programs available. Postbaccalaureate distance learning degree programs offered (no on-campus study). *Entrance requirements:* Additional exam requirements/recommendations for international students: Required—TOEFL or IELTS; Recommended—TOEFL (minimum score 550 paper-based; 213 computer-based; 80 iBT), IELTS.

Spalding University, Graduate Studies, College of Education, Programs in Education, Louisville, KY 40203-2188. Offers elementary school education (MAT); general education (MA); high school education (MAT); middle school education (MAT); school administration (MA); special education (learning and behavioral disorders) (MAT); student guidance counselor (MA). MAT programs offered for first teaching certificate/license students. *Accreditation:* NCATE. Part-time and evening/weekend programs available. *Faculty:* 9 full-time (6 women), 32 part-time/adjunct (20 women). *Students:* 142 full-time (100 women), 71 part-time (53 women); includes 75 minority (65 Black or African American, non-Hispanic/Latino; 1 American Indian or Alaska Native, non-Hispanic/Latino; 6 Hispanic/Latino; 3 Two or more races, non-Hispanic/Latino). Average age 36. 96 applicants, 44% accepted, 41 enrolled. In 2011, 69 master's awarded. *Degree requirements:* For master's, portfolio, final project, clinical experience. *Entrance requirements:* For master's, GRE General Test or MAT, interview, recommendations, resume. Additional exam requirements/recommendations for international students: Required—TOEFL (minimum score 535 paper-based; 203 computer-based). *Application deadline:* Applications are processed on a rolling basis. Application fee: $30. Electronic applications accepted. *Expenses: Tuition:* Full-time $12,438. Tuition and fees vary according to course load, degree level and program. *Financial support:* In 2011–12, 72 students received support, including 3 research assistantships with partial tuition reimbursements available (averaging $4,490 per year); scholarships/grants, traineeships, and unspecified assistantships also available. Financial award application deadline: 3/15; financial award applicants required to submit FAFSA. *Faculty research:* Instructional technology, achievement gap, classroom management, assessment. *Unit head:* Dr. Beverly Keepers, Dean, 502-588-7121, Fax: 502-585-7123, E-mail: bkeepers@spalding.edu. *Application contact:* Bonnie Caughron, 502-873-4262, E-mail: bcaughron@spalding.edu.

Spring Arbor University, School of Education, Spring Arbor, MI 49283-9799. Offers education (MAE); reading (MAR); special education (MSE). Part-time and evening/weekend programs available. Postbaccalaureate distance learning degree programs offered (minimal on-campus study). *Faculty:* 6 full-time (5 women), 13 part-time/adjunct (8 women). *Students:* 43 full-time (33 women), 188 part-time (158 women); includes 13 minority (10 Black or African American, non-Hispanic/Latino; 1 Asian, non-Hispanic/Latino; 2 Hispanic/Latino). Average age 36. In 2011, 54 master's awarded. *Degree requirements:* For master's, thesis. *Entrance requirements:* For master's, official transcripts from all institutions attended, including evidence of an earned bachelor's degree from regionally-accredited college or university with minimum cumulative GPA of 3.0 for the last two years of the bachelor's degree; two professional letters of recommendation. Additional exam requirements/recommendations for international students: Required—TOEFL (minimum score 600 paper-based; 220 computer-based). *Application deadline:* For fall admission, 9/1 priority date for domestic students; for winter admission, 2/1 priority date for domestic students; for spring admission, 2/1 priority date for domestic students. Applications are processed on a rolling basis. Application fee: $40. Electronic applications accepted. *Expenses: Tuition:* Full-time $5500; part-time $490 per credit hour. *Required fees:* $240; $120 per term. Tuition and fees vary according to program. *Financial support:* Applicants required to submit FAFSA. *Unit head:* Dr. Linda Sherrill, Dean, 517-750-1200 Ext. 1562, Fax: 517-750-6629, E-mail: lsherril@arbor.edu. *Application contact:* James R. Weidman, Coordinator of Graduate Recruitment, 517-750-6523, Fax: 517-750-6629, E-mail: jimw@arbor.edu. Web site: http://www.arbor.edu/Master-Arts-Education/Graduate/index.aspx.

Springfield College, Graduate Programs, Program in Education, Springfield, MA 01109-3797. Offers counseling and secondary education (M Ed, MS); early childhood education (M Ed, MS); education (M Ed, MS); educational administration (M Ed, MS); educational studies (M Ed, MS); elementary education (M Ed, MS); secondary education (M Ed, MS); special education (M Ed, MS). Part-time and evening/weekend programs available. *Entrance requirements:* Additional exam requirements/recommendations for international students: Required—TOEFL (minimum score 550 paper-based; 213 computer-based). Electronic applications accepted.

State University of New York at Binghamton, Graduate School, School of Education, Program in Special Education, Binghamton, NY 13902-6000. Offers MS Ed. *Accreditation:* Teacher Education Accreditation Council. Part-time and evening/weekend programs available. *Students:* 16 full-time (14 women), 21 part-time (16 women); includes 4 minority (1 Black or African American, non-Hispanic/Latino; 1 American Indian or Alaska Native, non-Hispanic/Latino; 1 Asian, non-Hispanic/Latino; 1 Hispanic/Latino). Average age 27. 44 applicants, 73% accepted, 25 enrolled. In 2011, 34 master's awarded. *Entrance requirements:* For master's, GRE General Test. Additional exam requirements/recommendations for international students: Required—TOEFL (minimum score 550 paper-based; 213 computer-based; 80 iBT). *Application deadline:* For fall admission, 2/1 priority date for domestic students, 2/1 for international students; for spring admission, 10/15 priority date for domestic students, 10/15 for international students. Applications are processed on a rolling basis. Application fee: $60. Electronic applications accepted. *Financial support:* In 2011–12, 3 students received support. Career-related internships or fieldwork, Federal Work-Study, institutionally sponsored loans, and unspecified assistantships available. Support available to part-time students. Financial award application deadline: 2/15; financial award applicants required to submit FAFSA. *Unit head:* Dr. Beverly Rainforth, Coordinator, 607-777-2277, E-mail: bevrain@binghamton.edu. *Application contact:* Catherine Smith, Recruiting and Admissions Coordinator, 607-777-2151, Fax: 607-777-2501, E-mail: cmsmith@binghamton.edu.

State University of New York at New Paltz, Graduate School, School of Education, Department of Educational Studies, Program in Special Education, New Paltz, NY 12561. Offers adolescence (7-12) (MS Ed); adolescence special education and literacy education (MS Ed); childhood (1-6) (MS Ed); childhood special education and literacy education (MS Ed); early childhood (B-2) (MS Ed). *Accreditation:* NCATE. Part-time and evening/weekend programs available. *Faculty:* 6 full-time (4 women), 4 part-time/adjunct (all women). *Students:* 36 full-time (33 women), 54 part-time (44 women); includes 8 minority (5 Black or African American, non-Hispanic/Latino; 2 Asian, non-Hispanic/Latino; 1 Native Hawaiian or other Pacific Islander, non-Hispanic/Latino). Average age 29. 67 applicants, 73% accepted, 40 enrolled. In 2011, 44 master's awarded. *Degree requirements:* For master's, portfolio. *Entrance requirements:* For master's, minimum GPA of 3.0 (3.2 for special education and literacy programs), New York state teaching certificate. Additional exam requirements/recommendations for international students: Required—TOEFL (minimum score 550 paper-based; 213 computer-based; 80 iBT), IELTS (minimum score 6.5). *Application deadline:* For fall admission, 3/15 priority date for domestic students, 3/15 for international students; for spring admission, 11/1 for domestic and international students. Application fee: $50. Electronic applications accepted. *Expenses:* Tuition, state resident: full-time $8870; part-time $370 per credit. Tuition, nonresident: full-time $15,160; part-time $632 per credit. *Required fees:* $1188; $34 per credit. $184 per semester. *Financial support:* In 2011–12, 2 students received support, including 2 fellowships (averaging $3,750 per year); career-related internships or fieldwork, Federal Work-Study, institutionally sponsored loans, and tuition waivers (full) also available. Financial award application deadline: 8/1; financial award applicants required to submit FAFSA. *Unit head:* Dr. Spencer Salend, Coordinator, 845-257-2831, E-mail: salends@newpaltz.edu. *Application contact:* Dr. Catherine Whittaker, Coordinator, 845-257-2831, E-mail: whittakc@newpaltz.edu.

State University of New York at New Paltz, Graduate School, School of Education, Department of Elementary Education, New Paltz, NY 12561. Offers childhood education (1-6) (MS Ed, MST); literacy education (5-12) (MS Ed); literacy education (B-6) (MS Ed); literacy education and adolescence special education (MS Ed); literacy education and childhood education and childhood special education (MS Ed). *Accreditation:* NCATE. Part-time and evening/weekend programs available. *Faculty:* 9 full-time (8 women), 6 part-time/adjunct (5 women). *Students:* 66 full-time (61 women), 129 part-time (115 women); includes 14 minority (3 Black or African American, non-Hispanic/Latino; 1 Asian, non-Hispanic/Latino; 7 Hispanic/Latino; 3 Two or more races, non-Hispanic/Latino). Average age 28. 121 applicants, 64% accepted, 66 enrolled. In 2011, 95 master's awarded. *Degree requirements:* For master's, comprehensive exam (for some programs), portfolio. *Entrance requirements:* For master's, GRE and MAT (MST), minimum GPA of 3.0 (3.2 for literacy and special education), New York state teaching certificate (MS Ed). Additional exam requirements/recommendations for international students: Required—TOEFL (minimum score 550 paper-based; 213 computer-based; 80 iBT), IELTS (minimum score 6.5). *Application deadline:* For fall admission, 4/1 for domestic and international students; for spring admission, 11/15 for domestic and international students. Application fee: $50. Electronic applications accepted. *Expenses:* Tuition, state resident: full-time $8870; part-time $370 per credit. Tuition, nonresident: full-time $15,160; part-time $632 per credit. *Required fees:* $1188; $34 per credit. $184 per semester. *Financial support:* In 2011–12, 1 fellowship (averaging $5,000 per year) was awarded; Federal Work-Study and institutionally sponsored loans also available. Financial award application deadline: 8/1; financial award applicants required to submit FAFSA. *Faculty research:* Multi-sensory teaching methods, volunteer tutoring programs for struggling readers, school readiness and transition, math/science/technology, university-school partnerships. *Unit head:* Dr. Andrea Noel, Chair, 845-257-2860, E-mail: noela@newpaltz.edu. *Application contact:* Caroline Murphy, Graduate Admissions Advisor, 845-257-3285, Fax: 845-257-3284, E-mail: gradschool@newpaltz.edu. Web site: http://www.newpaltz.edu/elementaryed/.

State University of New York at Oswego, Graduate Studies, School of Education, Department of Curriculum and Instruction, Oswego, NY 13126. Offers adolescence education (MST); art education (MAT); childhood education (MST); elementary education (MS Ed); literacy education (MS Ed); secondary education (MS Ed); special education (MS Ed). Part-time and evening/weekend programs available. *Degree requirements:* For master's, comprehensive exam (for some programs), thesis optional. *Entrance requirements:* For master's, GRE General Test, minimum GPA of 2.7, provisional teaching certificate. Additional exam requirements/recommendations for international students: Required—TOEFL (minimum score 560 paper-based; 220 computer-based). *Faculty research:* Classroom applications for microcomputers; classroom questioning, wait-time, and achievement; values clarification and academic achievement.

State University of New York at Plattsburgh, Division of Education, Health, and Human Services, Program in Teacher Education: Special Education, Plattsburgh, NY 12901-2681. Offers birth to grade 2 (MS Ed); grades 1 to 6 (MS Ed); grades 7 to 12 (MS Ed). *Accreditation:* Teacher Education Accreditation Council. Part-time and evening/weekend programs available. *Students:* 33 full-time (28 women), 29 part-time (24 women). Average age 27. *Entrance requirements:* For master's, minimum GPA of 2.75. Additional exam requirements/recommendations for international students: Required—TOEFL. *Application deadline:* For fall admission, 2/15 priority date for domestic students; for spring admission, 10/15 priority date for domestic students. Applications are processed on a rolling basis. Application fee: $75. *Financial support:* Federal Work-Study available. Support available to part-time students. Financial award application deadline: 4/15; financial award applicants required to submit FAFSA. *Faculty research:* Inclusion behavior management technology, applied behavior analysis. *Unit head:* Dr. Heidi Schnackenberg, Coordinator, 518-564-5143, E-mail: schnachl@plattsburgh.edu. *Application contact:* Marguerite Adelman, Assistant Director, Graduate Admissions, 518-564-4723, Fax: 518-564-4722, E-mail: adelmaml@plattsburgh.edu.

State University of New York College at Cortland, Graduate Studies, School of Education, Programs in Teaching Students with Disabilities, Cortland, NY 13045. Offers MS Ed. *Accreditation:* NCATE. Part-time and evening/weekend programs available. *Degree requirements:* For master's, one foreign language, comprehensive exam, thesis (for some programs). *Entrance requirements:* For master's, provisional certification. Additional exam requirements/recommendations for international students: Required—TOEFL.

State University of New York College at Oneonta, Graduate Education, Division of Education, Oneonta, NY 13820-4015. Offers educational psychology and counseling (MS Ed, CAS), including school counselor K-12; educational technology specialist (MS Ed); elementary education and reading (MS Ed), including childhood education, literacy education; secondary education (MS Ed), including adolescence education, family and consumer science education; special education (MS Ed), including adolescence, childhood. *Accreditation:* NCATE. Part-time and evening/weekend programs available. *Entrance requirements:* For master's, GRE General Test.

State University of New York College at Potsdam, School of Education and Professional Studies, Program in Special Education, Potsdam, NY 13676. Offers adolescence (grades 7-12) (MS Ed); childhood (grades 1-6) (MS Ed); early childhood (birth-grade 2) (MS Ed). *Accreditation:* NCATE. Part-time programs available. *Faculty:* 2 full-time (1 woman), 5 part-time/adjunct (4 women). *Students:* 19 full-time (15 women), 3 part-time (all women); includes 4 minority (2 American Indian or Alaska Native, non-Hispanic/Latino; 1 Hispanic/Latino; 1 Two or more races, non-Hispanic/Latino). 27 applicants, 100% accepted, 15 enrolled. In 2011, 18 master's awarded. *Degree requirements:* For master's, culminating experience. *Entrance requirements:* For master's, minimum GPA of 3.0 in last 60 hours of course work. Additional exam requirements/recommendations for international students: Required—TOEFL (minimum score 550 paper-based; 213 computer-based; 80 iBT), IELTS (minimum score 6).

Application deadline: For fall admission, 4/1 for domestic and international students. Applications are processed on a rolling basis. Application fee: $50. *Expenses:* Tuition, state resident: full-time $8870; part-time $370 per credit hour. Tuition, nonresident: full-time $15,160; part-time $632 per credit hour. *Required fees:* $1066; $44.10 per credit hour. One-time fee: $3. *Financial support:* Unspecified assistantships available. Financial award application deadline: 3/1; financial award applicants required to submit FAFSA. *Unit head:* Dr. Dennis Conrad, Chairperson, 315-267-2916, Fax: 315-267-4802, E-mail: conradda@potsdam.edu. *Application contact:* Peter Cutler, Graduate Admissions Counselor, 315-267-2165, Fax: 315-267-4802, E-mail: graduate@potsdam.edu. Web site: http://www.potsdam.edu/academics/SOEPS/SpecialEd/msedspecialed.cfm.

Stephen F. Austin State University, Graduate School, College of Education, Department of Human Services, Nacogdoches, TX 75962. Offers counseling (MA); school psychology (MA); special education (M Ed); speech pathology (MS). *Accreditation:* ACA (one or more programs are accredited); ASHA (one or more programs are accredited); CORE; NCATE. *Degree requirements:* For master's, comprehensive exam, thesis (for some programs). *Entrance requirements:* For master's, GRE General Test, minimum GPA of 2.8. Additional exam requirements/recommendations for international students: Required—TOEFL.

Syracuse University, School of Education, Program in Early Childhood Special Education, Syracuse, NY 13244. Offers MS. Part-time programs available. *Students:* 15 full-time (12 women), 19 part-time (18 women); includes 6 minority (3 Black or African American, non-Hispanic/Latino; 2 American Indian or Alaska Native, non-Hispanic/Latino; 1 Asian, non-Hispanic/Latino). Average age 32. 14 applicants, 86% accepted, 9 enrolled. In 2011, 7 degrees awarded. *Entrance requirements:* For master's, interview. Additional exam requirements/recommendations for international students: Required—TOEFL (minimum score 100 iBT). *Application deadline:* For fall admission, 2/1 for domestic and international students; for spring admission, 10/15 priority date for domestic students, 10/15 for international students. Applications are processed on a rolling basis. Application fee: $75. Electronic applications accepted. *Expenses: Tuition:* Part-time $1206 per credit. *Financial support:* Fellowships with full tuition reimbursements and teaching assistantships with full and partial tuition reimbursements available. Financial award application deadline: 1/1; financial award applicants required to submit FAFSA. *Unit head:* Dr. Gail Ensher, Director, 315-443-9650. *Application contact:* Laurie Deyo, Graduate Recruiter, School of Education, 315-443-2505, E-mail: e-gradrcrt@syr.edu. Web site: http://www.soeweb.syr.edu/.

Syracuse University, School of Education, Program in Inclusive Special Education 7-12 (Generalist), Syracuse, NY 13244. Offers MS. Part-time programs available. *Students:* 4 full-time (all women). Average age 23. 6 applicants, 83% accepted, 4 enrolled. *Degree requirements:* For master's, thesis or alternative. *Entrance requirements:* For master's, certification or eligibility for certification in content area at secondary level (math, social studies science, English or Spanish). Additional exam requirements/recommendations for international students: Required—TOEFL (minimum score 100 iBT). *Application deadline:* For fall admission, 2/1 priority date for domestic students, 2/1 for international students; for spring admission, 10/15 priority date for domestic students, 10/15 for international students. Applications are processed on a rolling basis. Application fee: $75. Electronic applications accepted. *Expenses: Tuition:* Part-time $1206 per credit. *Financial support:* Fellowships with full tuition reimbursements and teaching assistantships with full and partial tuition reimbursements available. Financial award application deadline: 1/1; financial award applicants required to submit FAFSA. *Unit head:* Dr. Beth Ferri, Program Director, 315-443-1465, E-mail: baferri@syr.edu. *Application contact:* Laurie Deyo, Graduate Recruiter, School of Education, 315-443-2505, E-mail: e-gradrcrt@syr.edu. Web site: http://soe.syr.edu/academic/teaching_and_leadership/graduate/masters/inclusive_special_education_grades_7_12/default.aspx.

Syracuse University, School of Education, Program in Inclusive Special Education (grades 1-6), Syracuse, NY 13244. Offers MS. Part-time programs available. *Students:* 3 full-time (all women), 2 part-time (both women); includes 1 minority (Black or African American, non-Hispanic/Latino). Average age 24. 5 applicants, 100% accepted, 4 enrolled. In 2011, 8 degrees awarded. *Degree requirements:* For master's, thesis or alternative. *Entrance requirements:* For master's, provisional/initial certification. Additional exam requirements/recommendations for international students: Required—TOEFL (minimum score 100 iBT). *Application deadline:* For fall admission, 2/1 priority date for domestic students, 2/1 for international students; for spring admission, 10/15 priority date for domestic students, 10/15 for international students. Applications are processed on a rolling basis. Application fee: $75. Electronic applications accepted. *Expenses: Tuition:* Part-time $1206 per credit. *Financial support:* Fellowships with full tuition reimbursements and teaching assistantships with full and partial tuition reimbursements available. Financial award application deadline: 1/1; financial award applicants required to submit FAFSA. *Unit head:* Dr. Corinne Smith, Program Coordinator, 315-443-9321, E-mail: crsmith@syr.edu. *Application contact:* Laurie Deyo, Graduate Recruiter, School of Education, 315-443-2505, E-mail: e-gradrcrt@syr.edu. Web site: http://soeweb.syr.edu/.

Syracuse University, School of Education, Program in Inclusive Special Education: Severe/Multiple Disabilities, Syracuse, NY 13244. Offers MS. Part-time programs available. *Students:* 5 full-time (all women), 4 part-time (3 women). Average age 25. 4 applicants, 50% accepted, 2 enrolled. In 2011, 2 master's awarded. *Entrance requirements:* For master's, New York state initial certification in students with disabilities (Birth-2, 1-6, 5-9, or 7-12). Additional exam requirements/recommendations for international students: Required—TOEFL (minimum score 100 iBT). *Application deadline:* For fall admission, 2/1 priority date for domestic students, 2/1 for international students; for spring admission, 10/15 priority date for domestic students, 10/15 for international students. Applications are processed on a rolling basis. Application fee: $75. Electronic applications accepted. *Expenses: Tuition:* Part-time $1206 per credit. *Financial support:* Fellowships with full tuition reimbursements and teaching assistantships with full and partial tuition reimbursements available. Financial award application deadline: 1/1. *Unit head:* Dr. Gail Ensher, Program Coordinator, 315-443-9650, E-mail: glensher@syr.edu. *Application contact:* Laurie Deyo, Graduate Recruiter, School of Education, 315-443-2505, E-mail: e-gradrcrt@syr.edu. Web site: http://soeweb.syr.edu/.

Syracuse University, School of Education, Program in Special Education, Syracuse, NY 13244. Offers PhD. Part-time and evening/weekend programs available. *Students:* 12 full-time (all women), 6 part-time (all women); includes 3 minority (1 Black or African American, non-Hispanic/Latino; 1 American Indian or Alaska Native, non-Hispanic/Latino; 1 Native Hawaiian or other Pacific Islander, non-Hispanic/Latino), 4 international. Average age 39. 8 applicants, 38% accepted, 3 enrolled. In 2011, 1 degree awarded. *Degree requirements:* For doctorate, thesis/dissertation. *Entrance requirements:* For doctorate, GRE General Test, master's degree, interview, writing sample. Additional exam requirements/recommendations for international students: Required—TOEFL (minimum score 100 iBT). *Application deadline:* For fall admission, 2/1 priority date for domestic students, 2/1 for international students; for spring admission, 10/15 priority date for domestic students, 10/15 for international students. Applications are processed on a rolling basis. Application fee: $75. Electronic applications accepted. *Expenses: Tuition:* Part-time $1206 per credit. *Financial support:* Fellowships with full tuition reimbursements, research assistantships with full and partial tuition reimbursements, teaching assistantships with full and partial tuition reimbursements, and institutionally sponsored loans available. Financial award application deadline: 1/1. *Faculty research:* Aggression, inclusive education, autistic children, validation of social skills, cooperative learning in the heterogeneous classroom. *Unit head:* Dr. Beth Ferri, Program Director, 315-443-1269. *Application contact:* Laurie Deyo, Graduate Recruiter, School of Education, 315-443-2505, E-mail: e-gradrcrt@syr.edu. Web site: http://soeweb.syr.edu/.

Tarleton State University, College of Graduate Studies, College of Education, Department of Psychology and Counseling, Stephenville, TX 76402. Offers counseling and psychology (M Ed), including counseling, counseling psychology, educational psychology; educational administration (M Ed); secondary education (Certificate); special education (Certificate). Part-time and evening/weekend programs available. Postbaccalaureate distance learning degree programs offered (minimal on-campus study). *Faculty:* 8 full-time (5 women), 13 part-time/adjunct (6 women). *Students:* 73 full-time (62 women), 219 part-time (186 women); includes 55 minority (25 Black or African American, non-Hispanic/Latino; 1 American Indian or Alaska Native, non-Hispanic/Latino; 1 Asian, non-Hispanic/Latino; 22 Hispanic/Latino; 1 Native Hawaiian or other Pacific Islander, non-Hispanic/Latino; 5 Two or more races, non-Hispanic/Latino), 1 international. Average age 35. 92 applicants, 91% accepted, 62 enrolled. In 2011, 65 master's awarded. *Degree requirements:* For master's, comprehensive exam, thesis optional. *Entrance requirements:* For master's, GRE General Test, minimum GPA of 3.0. Additional exam requirements/recommendations for international students: Required—TOEFL (minimum score 550 paper-based; 213 computer-based; 80 iBT). *Application deadline:* For fall admission, 8/5 priority date for domestic students; for spring admission, 12/1 for domestic students. Applications are processed on a rolling basis. Application fee: $30 ($130 for international students). Electronic applications accepted. *Expenses:* Tuition, state resident: full-time $3131.46; part-time $174 per credit hour. Tuition, nonresident: full-time $8225; part-time $457 per credit hour. *Required fees:* $1446. Tuition and fees vary according to course load and campus/location. *Financial support:* Research assistantships, teaching assistantships, career-related internships or fieldwork, Federal Work-Study, institutionally sponsored loans, and tuition waivers (partial) available. Support available to part-time students. Financial award application deadline: 5/1; financial award applicants required to submit FAFSA. *Unit head:* Dr. Bob Newby, Interim Department Head, 254-968-9813, Fax: 254-968-1991, E-mail: newby@tarleton.edu. *Application contact:* Information Contact, 254-968-9104, Fax: 254-968-9670, E-mail: gradoffice@tarleton.edu. Web site: http://www.tarleton.edu/~dpc.

Teachers College, Columbia University, Graduate Faculty of Education, Department of Curriculum and Teaching, Program in Dual Certificate Childhood/Disabilities, New York, NY 10027-6696. Offers Certificate. *Students:* 14 full-time (all women), 35 part-time (33 women); includes 9 minority (1 Black or African American, non-Hispanic/Latino; 4 Asian, non-Hispanic/Latino; 3 Hispanic/Latino; 1 Two or more races, non-Hispanic/Latino), 6 international. Average age 30. Application fee: $65. *Unit head:* Prof. Britt Hamre, Chair, 212-678-3695. *Application contact:* Elizabeth Puleio, Assistant Director of Admission, 212-678-3710, Fax: 212-678-4171, E-mail: tcinfo@tc.edu.

Teachers College, Columbia University, Graduate Faculty of Education, Department of Curriculum and Teaching, Program in Early Childhood Special Education, New York, NY 10027-6696. Offers Ed M, MA. *Accreditation:* NCATE. *Faculty:* 4 full-time (all women). *Students:* 59 full-time (48 women), 159 part-time (147 women); includes 69 minority (17 Black or African American, non-Hispanic/Latino; 37 Asian, non-Hispanic/Latino; 15 Hispanic/Latino), 16 international. Average age 26. 337 applicants, 51% accepted, 80 enrolled. In 2011, 91 master's awarded. *Degree requirements:* For master's, culminating project. *Application deadline:* For fall admission, 1/15 priority date for domestic students. Application fee: $65. *Financial support:* Research assistantships, teaching assistantships, career-related internships or fieldwork, Federal Work-Study, institutionally sponsored loans, and tuition waivers (full and partial) available. Support available to part-time students. Financial award application deadline: 2/1; financial award applicants required to submit FAFSA. *Faculty research:* Curriculum development, infants, urban education, visually-impaired infants. *Unit head:* Prof. Susan Recchia, Program Coordinator, 212-678-3860, E-mail: recchia@tc.edu. *Application contact:* Peter Shon, Assistant Director of Admission, 212-678-3305, Fax: 212-678-4171, E-mail: shon@exchange.tc.columbia.edu.

Teachers College, Columbia University, Graduate Faculty of Education, Department of Curriculum and Teaching, Program in Learning Disabilities, New York, NY 10027-6696. Offers Ed M, MA, Ed D. *Accreditation:* NCATE. *Faculty:* 1 (woman) full-time. *Students:* 1 (woman) full-time. Average age 38. In 2011, 1 degree awarded. *Degree requirements:* For doctorate, thesis/dissertation. *Entrance requirements:* For doctorate, GRE General Test or MAT. *Application deadline:* For fall admission, 5/15 for domestic students; for spring admission, 12/1 for domestic students. Application fee: $75. *Financial support:* Fellowships, teaching assistantships, career-related internships or fieldwork, Federal Work-Study, institutionally sponsored loans, and tuition waivers (full and partial) available. Support available to part-time students. Financial award application deadline: 2/1. *Faculty research:* Reading and mathematics disorders in students with learning disabilities, special education curriculum development. *Unit head:* Marjorie Siegel, Chair, 212-678-3765. *Application contact:* Peter Shon, Assistant Director of Admission, 212-678-3305, Fax: 212-678-4171, E-mail: shon@exchange.tc.columbia.edu.

Teachers College, Columbia University, Graduate Faculty of Education, Department of Health and Behavioral Studies, Program in Blind and Visual Impairment, New York, NY 10027-6696. Offers MA, Ed D. *Faculty:* 7 full-time (4 women), 11 part-time/adjunct (10 women). *Students:* 1 (woman) full-time, 4 part-time (all women); includes 2 minority (1 Black or African American, non-Hispanic/Latino; 1 Hispanic/Latino). Average age 33. 1 applicant, 0% accepted, 0 enrolled. In 2011, 2 degrees awarded. *Degree requirements:* For master's, comprehensive exam, integrative project; for doctorate, comprehensive exam, thesis/dissertation. *Entrance requirements:* For doctorate, writing sample. *Application deadline:* For fall admission, 1/15 priority date for domestic students; for spring admission, 11/1 for domestic students. Applications are processed on a rolling basis. Application fee: $65. Electronic applications accepted. *Financial support:* Career-related internships or fieldwork, Federal Work-Study, institutionally sponsored loans, and tuition waivers (full and partial) available. Support available to part-time students. Financial award application deadline: 2/1; financial award applicants required to submit FAFSA. *Faculty research:* Cross-modality transfer, issues in early childhood. *Unit head:* Prof. Peg Cummings, Program Coordinator, 212-678-3880, E-mail: cummins@tc.edu. *Application contact:* Elizabeth Puleio, Assistant Director of Admission, 212-678-3730, E-mail: eap2136@tc.columbia.edu.

Teachers College, Columbia University, Graduate Faculty of Education, Department of Health and Behavioral Studies, Program in Hearing Impairment, New York, NY 10027-6696. Offers MA, Ed D. *Faculty:* 7 full-time (4 women), 11 part-time/adjunct (10 women). *Students:* 12 full-time (11 women), 14 part-time (all women); includes 8 minority (4 Black or African American, non-Hispanic/Latino; 2 Asian, non-Hispanic/Latino; 2 Hispanic/Latino), 1 international. Average age 24. 23 applicants, 78% accepted, 10 enrolled. In 2011, 16 master's awarded. *Degree requirements:* For master's, comprehensive exam (for some programs), project; for doctorate, thesis/dissertation. *Application deadline:* For fall admission, 1/2 priority date for domestic students; for spring admission, 11/1 for domestic students. Applications are processed on a rolling basis. Application fee: $65. Electronic applications accepted. *Financial support:* Fellowships, career-related internships or fieldwork, Federal Work-Study, institutionally sponsored loans, and tuition waivers (full and partial) available. Support available to part-time students. Financial award application deadline: 2/1; financial award applicants required to submit FAFSA. *Faculty research:* Language development, reading/writing, cognitive abilities, text analysis, auditory streaming. *Unit head:* Prof. Robert Kretschmer, Program Coordinator, 212-678-3867, E-mail: kretschmer@tc.edu. *Application contact:* Elizabeth Puleio, Assistant Director of Admission, 212-678-3710, Fax: 212-678-4171, E-mail: tcinfo@tc.edu.

Teachers College, Columbia University, Graduate Faculty of Education, Department of Health and Behavioral Studies, Program in Mental Retardation, New York, NY 10027. Offers MA, Ed D, PhD. Part-time programs available. *Faculty:* 7 full-time (4 women), 11 part-time/adjunct (10 women). *Students:* 1 (woman) full-time, 8 part-time (all women), 1 international. Average age 24. 64 applicants, 56% accepted, 9 enrolled. Terminal master's awarded for partial completion of doctoral program. *Degree requirements:* For master's, comprehensive exam, integrative project, student portfolio; for doctorate, comprehensive exam, thesis/dissertation, certification project. *Entrance requirements:* For master's, minimum GPA of 3.0; for doctorate, 2-3 years of successful teaching experience in special education, writing sample. Additional exam requirements/recommendations for international students: Required—TOEFL (minimum score 600 paper-based). *Application deadline:* For fall admission, 1/2 priority date for domestic students; for spring admission, 11/1 for domestic students. Applications are processed on a rolling basis. Application fee: $65. Electronic applications accepted. *Financial support:* Fellowships, research assistantships, teaching assistantships, career-related internships or fieldwork, Federal Work-Study, institutionally sponsored loans, and tuition waivers (full and partial) available. Support available to part-time students. Financial award application deadline: 2/1. *Faculty research:* Information processing, memory comprehension and problem-solving issues related to mental retardation, transition issues, cognition and comprehension. *Unit head:* Prof. Linda Hickson, Program Coordinator, 212-678-3854, E-mail: hickson@tc.edu. *Application contact:* Peter Shon, Assistant Director of Admission, 212-678-3305, Fax: 212-678-4171, E-mail: shon@exchange.tc.columbia.edu. Web site: http://www.tc.columbia.edu/hbs/SpecialEd/.

Teachers College, Columbia University, Graduate Faculty of Education, Department of Health and Behavioral Studies, Program in Physical Disabilities, New York, NY 10027-6696. Offers Ed D, PhD. Part-time and evening/weekend programs available. *Faculty:* 7 full-time (4 women), 11 part-time/adjunct (10 women). *Students:* 6 part-time (all women); includes 1 minority (Asian, non-Hispanic/Latino). Average age 36. 4 applicants, 25% accepted, 1 enrolled. In 2011, 1 doctorate awarded. *Degree requirements:* For doctorate, comprehensive exam, thesis/dissertation. *Entrance requirements:* For doctorate, GRE General Test or MAT. Additional exam requirements/recommendations for international students: Required—TOEFL. *Application deadline:* For fall admission, 12/15 priority date for domestic students; for spring admission, 11/1 for domestic students. Applications are processed on a rolling basis. Application fee: $65. Electronic applications accepted. *Financial support:* Fellowships, teaching assistantships, career-related internships or fieldwork, Federal Work-Study, institutionally sponsored loans, and tuition waivers (full and partial) available. Support available to part-time students. Financial award application deadline: 2/1; financial award applicants required to submit FAFSA. *Faculty research:* Students with traumatic brain injury, health impairments, learning disabilities. *Unit head:* Prof. Robert Krestchner, Program Coordinator, 212-678-3880. *Application contact:* Elizabeth Puleio, Assistant Director of Admission, 212-678-3710, Fax: 212-678-4171, E-mail: tcinfo@tc.edu.

Teachers College, Columbia University, Graduate Faculty of Education, Department of Health and Behavioral Studies, Program in Severe or Multiple Disabilities, New York, NY 10027-6696. Offers MA. *Faculty:* 7 full-time (4 women), 11 part-time/adjunct (10 women). *Students:* 7 full-time (6 women), 4 part-time (all women); includes 1 minority (Asian, non-Hispanic/Latino). Average age 25. 9 applicants, 100% accepted, 5 enrolled. In 2011, 4 master's awarded. *Degree requirements:* For master's, integrative project. *Entrance requirements:* For master's, minimum GPA of 3.0, evidence of New York State initial teacher certification in one of the required areas. *Application deadline:* For fall admission, 1/15 priority date for domestic students; for spring admission, 11/1 for domestic students. Applications are processed on a rolling basis. Application fee: $65. Electronic applications accepted. *Financial support:* Career-related internships or fieldwork, Federal Work-Study, institutionally sponsored loans, and tuition waivers (partial) available. Support available to part-time students. Financial award application deadline: 2/1; financial award applicants required to submit FAFSA. *Faculty research:* Reading and spelling disorders, workplace literacy, reading and writing among children and adults. *Unit head:* Prof. Linda Hickson, Program Coordinator, 212-678-3854, E-mail: lh76@columbia.edu. *Application contact:* Peter Shon, Assistant Director of Admission, 212-678-3305, Fax: 212-678-4171, E-mail: shon@exchange.tc.columbia.edu. Web site: http://www.tc.edu/hbs/specialed/.

Teachers College, Columbia University, Graduate Faculty of Education, Department of Health and Behavioral Studies, Program in Special Education, New York, NY 10027. Offers Ed M, MA, Ed D. *Accreditation:* NCATE. Part-time and evening/weekend programs available. *Faculty:* 7 full-time (4 women), 11 part-time/adjunct (10 women). *Students:* 3 part-time (all women). Average age 29. 1 applicant, 100% accepted, 0 enrolled. In 2011, 1 degree awarded. Terminal master's awarded for partial completion of doctoral program. *Degree requirements:* For doctorate, thesis/dissertation. *Entrance requirements:* For doctorate, writing sample. *Application deadline:* For fall admission, 1/2 for domestic students. Application fee: $65. Electronic applications accepted. *Financial support:* Career-related internships or fieldwork, Federal Work-Study, institutionally sponsored loans, and tuition waivers (full and partial) available. Support available to part-time students. Financial award application deadline: 2/1; financial award applicants required to submit FAFSA. *Faculty research:* Communication skills, academic skills (reading and math), behavior problems, and cultural differences in individuals with autism as well as transition support services and teacher preparation for these individuals; education of children, adolescents and adults with intellectual disabilities and autism; cognitive, motivational, and emotional aspects of decision-making; prevention of abuse and victimization. *Unit head:* Dr. Douglas Greer, Program Coordinator, 212-678-3880, E-mail: rdg13@columbia.edu. *Application contact:* Peter Shon, Assistant Director of Admission, 212-678-3305, Fax: 212-678-4171, E-mail: shon@exchange.tc.columbia.edu. Web site: http://www.tc.edu/hbs/specialed/.

Teachers College, Columbia University, Graduate Faculty of Education, Department of Health and Behavioral Studies, Program in Teaching of Sign Language, New York, NY 10027-6696. Offers MA. *Accreditation:* NCATE. *Faculty:* 2 full-time (0 women). *Students:* 1 full-time (0 women), 11 part-time (8 women); includes 3 minority (2 Hispanic/Latino; 1 Two or more races, non-Hispanic/Latino). Average age 26. 7 applicants, 100% accepted, 6 enrolled. In 2011, 7 master's awarded. *Degree requirements:* For master's, comprehensive exam, project. *Entrance requirements:* For master's, demonstrated proficiency in American Sign Language. *Application deadline:* For fall admission, 1/15 priority date for domestic students; for spring admission, 11/1 for domestic students. Applications are processed on a rolling basis. Application fee: $65. Electronic applications accepted. *Financial support:* Applicants required to submit FAFSA. *Faculty research:* Teaching of the deaf and hard of hearing; linguistics of English and ASL; literacy development; text structure; school psychology; auditory streaming; sociology, anthropology, and history of deaf community and culture; American Sign Language; second language acquisition, curriculum, and instruction; disability studies. *Unit head:* Prof. Russell S. Rosen, Program Coordinator, 212-678-3813, E-mail: rrosen@tc.edu. *Application contact:* Elizabeth Puleio, Assistant Director of Admission, 212-678-3710, Fax: 212-678-4171, E-mail: eap2136@tc.columbia.edu.

Teachers College, Columbia University, Graduate Faculty of Education, Program in Administration and Supervision in Special Education, New York, NY 10027-6696. Offers Ed M, MA, Ed D, PhD. *Accreditation:* NCATE. *Faculty:* 7 full-time (4 women), 11 part-time/adjunct (10 women). *Students:* 1 part-time (0 women); minority (Asian, non-Hispanic/Latino). Average age 31. In 2011, 2 degrees awarded. *Degree requirements:* For doctorate, thesis/dissertation. *Application deadline:* For fall admission, 5/15 for domestic students. Application fee: $65. *Financial support:* Career-related internships or fieldwork, Federal Work-Study, institutionally sponsored loans, and tuition waivers (full and partial) available. Support available to part-time students. Financial award application deadline: 2/1. *Faculty research:* Cognition and comprehension, disability studies, self-determination, literacy development. *Unit head:* Stephen T. Peverly, Chair, 212-678-3964, Fax: 212-678-8259, E-mail: stp4@columbia.edu. *Application contact:* Thomas P. Rock, Director of Admissions, 212-678-3083, Fax: 212-678-4171, E-mail: rock@tc.edu. Web site: http://www.tc.columbia.edu/hbs/SpecialEd/.

Temple University, College of Education, Department of Curriculum, Instruction, and Technology in Education, Philadelphia, PA 19122-6096. Offers applied behavioral analysis (MS Ed); career and technical education (MS Ed); early childhood education and elementary education (MS Ed); English education (MS Ed); language arts education (Ed D); math/science education (Ed D); mathematics education (MS Ed); science education (MS Ed); second and foreign language education (MS Ed); special education (MS Ed); teaching English as a second language (MS Ed). Part-time and evening/weekend programs available. *Faculty:* 19 full-time (12 women). *Students:* 30 full-time (23 women), 86 part-time (69 women); includes 12 minority (4 Black or African American, non-Hispanic/Latino; 2 Asian, non-Hispanic/Latino; 5 Hispanic/Latino; 1 Two or more races, non-Hispanic/Latino), 5 international. 82 applicants, 71% accepted, 51 enrolled. In 2011, 181 master's, 16 doctorates awarded. Terminal master's awarded for partial completion of doctoral program. *Degree requirements:* For master's, thesis or alternative; for doctorate, thesis/dissertation. *Entrance requirements:* For master's and doctorate, GRE General Test or MAT, minimum GPA of 3.0. Additional exam requirements/recommendations for international students: Required—TOEFL (minimum score 550 paper-based; 213 computer-based; 79 iBT). *Application deadline:* For fall admission, 4/1 for domestic students, 12/15 for international students; for spring admission, 10/1 for domestic students, 8/1 for international students. Application fee: $50. Electronic applications accepted. *Expenses:* Tuition, state resident: full-time $12,366; part-time $687 per credit hour. Tuition, nonresident: full-time $17,298; part-time $961 per credit hour. *Required fees:* $590; $213 per year. *Financial support:* Fellowships, research assistantships with full tuition reimbursements, and teaching assistantships with full tuition reimbursements available. Financial award application deadline: 1/15; financial award applicants required to submit FAFSA. *Faculty research:* School improvement, problem-solving, literacy, language development. *Unit head:* Dr. Michael W. Smith, Chair, 215-204-6387, Fax: 215-204-1414, E-mail: mwsmith@temple.edu. *Application contact:* Dr. Margo Greicar, Director for Graduate Academic and Student Affairs, 215-204-8011, Fax: 215-204-4383, E-mail: margo.greicar@temple.edu. Web site: http://www.temple.edu/education/cite/.

Tennessee State University, The School of Graduate Studies and Research, College of Education, Department of Teaching and Learning, Nashville, TN 37209-1561. Offers curriculum and instruction (M Ed, Ed D); elementary education (M Ed, MA Ed, Ed D); special education (M Ed, MA Ed, Ed D). *Accreditation:* NCATE. *Degree requirements:* For doctorate, thesis/dissertation. *Entrance requirements:* For master's, GRE General Test, GRE Subject Test, or MAT, minimum GPA of 2.5; for doctorate, GRE General Test, GRE Subject Test, or MAT, minimum GPA of 3.25. Electronic applications accepted. *Faculty research:* Multicultural education, teacher education reform, whole language, interactive video teaching, English as a second language.

Tennessee Technological University, Graduate School, College of Education, Department of Curriculum and Instruction, Program in Special Education, Cookeville, TN 38505. Offers MA, Ed S. *Accreditation:* NCATE. Part-time programs available. *Faculty:* 6 full-time (3 women). *Students:* 11 full-time (9 women), 36 part-time (30 women); includes 1 minority (Black or African American, non-Hispanic/Latino). Average age 27. 17 applicants, 82% accepted, 7 enrolled. In 2011, 5 master's, 1 other advanced degree awarded. *Degree requirements:* For master's and Ed S, comprehensive exam, thesis or alternative. *Entrance requirements:* For master's and Ed S, MAT or GRE. Additional exam requirements/recommendations for international students: Required—TOEFL (minimum score 550 paper-based; 79 iBT), IELTS (minimum score 5.5), Pearson Test of English Academic. *Application deadline:* For fall admission, 8/1 for domestic students, 5/1 for international students; for spring admission, 12/1 for domestic students, 10/1 for international students. Application fee: $25 ($30 for international students). Electronic applications accepted. *Expenses:* Tuition, state resident: full-time $8094; part-time $422 per credit hour. Tuition, nonresident: full-time $20,574; part-time $1046 per credit hour. *Financial support:* In 2011–12, fellowships (averaging $8,000 per year), research assistantships (averaging $5,000 per year), 2 teaching assistantships (averaging $4,000 per year) were awarded; career-related internships or fieldwork also available. Financial award application deadline: 4/1. *Unit head:* Dr. Susan Gore, Interim Chairperson, 931-372-3181, Fax: 931-372-6270, E-mail: sgore@tntech.edu. *Application contact:* Shelia K. Kendrick, Coordinator of Graduate Admissions, 931-372-3808, Fax: 931-372-3497, E-mail: skendrick@tntech.edu.

Texas A&M International University, Office of Graduate Studies and Research, College of Education, Department of Professional Programs, Laredo, TX 78041-1900. Offers educational administration (MS Ed); generic special education (MS Ed); school counseling (MS). *Faculty:* 11 full-time (5 women), 1 part-time/adjunct (0 women). *Students:* 11 full-time (8 women), 115 part-time (90 women); includes 125 minority (2 Black or African American, non-Hispanic/Latino; 123 Hispanic/Latino). Average age 34. 33 applicants, 79% accepted, 18 enrolled. In 2011, 42 master's awarded. *Entrance requirements:* Additional exam requirements/recommendations for international students: Required—TOEFL (minimum score 550 paper-based; 213 computer-based; 79 iBT). *Application deadline:* For fall admission, 4/30 priority date for domestic students, 4/30 for international students; for spring admission, 11/30 priority date for domestic students, 10/1 for international students. Application fee: $35 ($50 for international students). *Expenses:* Tuition, state resident: full-time $5063. *Financial support:* In 2011–12, 5 students received support, including 3 fellowships, 2 research assistantships; Federal Work-Study, scholarships/grants, and unspecified assistantships also available. Financial award application deadline: 4/1. *Unit head:* Dr. Randel Brown, Chair, 956-326-2679, E-mail: brown@tamiu.edu. *Application contact:* Suzanne H. Alford, Director of Admissions, 956-326-3023, E-mail: graduateschool@tamiu.edu. Web site: http://www.tamiu.edu/coedu/DOPPPrograms.shtml.

Texas A&M University, College of Education and Human Development, Department of Educational Psychology, College Station, TX 77843. Offers bilingual education (M Ed, PhD); cognition, creativity, instruction and development (MS, PhD); counseling psychology (PhD); educational psychology (PhD); educational technology (PhD); research, measurement and statistics (MS); research, measurement, and statistics (PhD); school psychology (PhD); special education (M Ed, PhD). *Accreditation:* APA (one or more programs are accredited). Part-time and evening/weekend programs available. Postbaccalaureate distance learning degree programs offered (no on-campus study). *Faculty:* 46. *Students:* 151 full-time (124 women), 123 part-time (101 women); includes 97 minority (20 Black or African American, non-Hispanic/Latino; 11 Asian, non-Hispanic/Latino; 59 Hispanic/Latino; 7 Two or more races, non-Hispanic/Latino), 50 international. In 2011, 58 master's, 33 doctorates awarded. *Degree requirements:* For master's, thesis optional; for doctorate, thesis/dissertation. *Entrance requirements:* For master's and doctorate, GRE General Test. Additional exam requirements/recommendations for international students: Required—TOEFL. Application fee: $50 ($75 for international students). Electronic applications accepted. *Expenses:* Tuition, state resident: full-time $5437; part-time $226.55 per credit hour. Tuition, nonresident: full-time $12,949; part-time $539.55 per credit hour. *Required fees:* $2741. *Financial support:* In 2011–12, fellowships (averaging $12,000 per year), research assistantships (averaging $9,000 per year), teaching assistantships (averaging $9,000 per year) were awarded; career-related internships or fieldwork, institutionally sponsored loans, scholarships/grants, and unspecified assistantships also available. Financial award applicants required to submit FAFSA. *Unit head:* Dr. Victor Willson, Head, 979-845-1800. *Application contact:* Carol A. Wagner, Director of Advising, 979-845-1833, Fax: 979-862-1256, E-mail: epsyadvisor@tamu.edu. Web site: http://epsy.tamu.edu.

Texas A&M University–Commerce, Graduate School, College of Education and Human Services, Department of Psychology and Special Education, Commerce, TX 75429-3011. Offers cognition and instruction (PhD); psychology (MA, MS); special education (M Ed, MA, MS). Part-time programs available. Terminal master's awarded for partial completion of doctoral program. *Degree requirements:* For master's, comprehensive exam, thesis (for some programs); for doctorate, thesis/dissertation, departmental qualifying exam. *Entrance requirements:* For master's, GRE General Test; for doctorate, GRE General Test, 3 letters of recommendation. Electronic applications accepted. *Faculty research:* Human learning, study skills, multicultural bilingual, diversity and special education, educationally handicapped.

Texas A&M University–Corpus Christi, Graduate Studies and Research, College of Education, Program in Special Education, Corpus Christi, TX 78412-5503. Offers MS. Part-time and evening/weekend programs available. *Degree requirements:* For master's, comprehensive exam, thesis (for some programs). *Entrance requirements:* For master's, GRE General Test. Additional exam requirements/recommendations for international students: Required—TOEFL. Electronic applications accepted.

Texas A&M University–Kingsville, College of Graduate Studies, College of Education, Department of Education, Program in Special Education, Kingsville, TX 78363. Offers M Ed. Part-time and evening/weekend programs available. *Degree requirements:* For master's, comprehensive exam, mini-thesis. *Entrance requirements:* For master's, GRE General Test, MAT, minimum GPA of 3.0. *Faculty research:* Training for trainers of the disabled.

Texas A&M University–San Antonio, Department of Curriculum and Kinesiology, San Antonio, TX 78224. Offers bilingual education (MA); early childhood education (M Ed); kinesiology (MS); reading (MS); special education (M Ed), including educational diagnostician, instructional specialist. Part-time and evening/weekend programs available. *Students:* 76 full-time (51 women), 240 part-time (180 women). Average age 37. *Degree requirements:* For master's, comprehensive exam, thesis or alternative. *Entrance requirements:* For master's, MAT. Additional exam requirements/recommendations for international students: Required—TOEFL (minimum score 550 paper-based; 213 computer-based; 80 iBT), IELTS (minimum score 6). *Application deadline:* For fall admission, 8/15 priority date for domestic students, 6/1 for international students; for spring admission, 12/15 priority date for domestic students, 10/1 for international students. Applications are processed on a rolling basis. Application fee: $35 ($50 for international students). Electronic applications accepted. *Expenses:* Tuition, state resident: part-time $691.11 per course. Tuition, nonresident: part-time $1621.11 per course. *Financial support:* Application deadline: 3/31; applicants required to submit FAFSA. *Unit head:* Dr. Samuel Garcia, Department Chair, 210-784-2505, E-mail: samuel.garcia@tamusa.tamus.edu. *Application contact:* Jennifer M. Dovalina, Graduate Admissions Specialist, 210-784-1380, E-mail: graduateadmissions@tamusa.tamus.edu. Web site: http://www.tamusa.tamus.edu/education/index.html.

Texas A&M University–Texarkana, Graduate Studies and Research, College of Education and Liberal Arts, Texarkana, TX 75505-5518. Offers adult education (MS); curriculum and instruction (M Ed); education (MS); educational administration (M Ed); English (MA); instructional technology (MS); interdisciplinary studies (MA, MS); special education (MS). Part-time and evening/weekend programs available. *Degree requirements:* For master's, comprehensive exam (for some programs), thesis optional. *Entrance requirements:* For master's, minimum GPA of 2.5 on last 60 hours of bachelor's degree. Additional exam requirements/recommendations for international students: Required—TOEFL. Electronic applications accepted.

Texas Christian University, College of Education, Program in Special Education, Fort Worth, TX 76129-0002. Offers M Ed. Part-time and evening/weekend programs available. *Faculty:* 27 full-time (21 women), 1 part-time/adjunct. *Students:* 2 full-time (both women), 2 part-time (both women). Average age 29. 3 applicants, 100% accepted, 1 enrolled. In 2011, 3 master's awarded. *Degree requirements:* For master's, oral exam. *Entrance requirements:* Additional exam requirements/recommendations for international students: Required—TOEFL (minimum score 550 paper-based; 213 computer-based; 80 iBT). *Application deadline:* For fall admission, 11/15 for domestic and international students; for spring admission, 3/1 for domestic and international students. Application fee: $60. Electronic applications accepted. *Expenses: Tuition:* Full-time $20,250; part-time $1125 per credit hour. Part-time tuition and fees vary according to course load and program. *Financial support:* Teaching assistantships with full tuition reimbursements, career-related internships or fieldwork, scholarships/grants, and unspecified assistantships available. Financial award application deadline: 3/1. *Unit head:* Dr. Jan Lacina, Associate Dean, 817-257-6786, E-mail: j.lacina@tcu.edu. *Application contact:* Patricia Garcia, Academic Program Specialist, 817-257-7661, E-mail: p.m.garcia@tcu.edu. Web site: http://www.coe.tcu.edu/184.asp.

Texas Christian University, College of Education, Program in Special Education (Four-One Option), Fort Worth, TX 76129-0002. Offers M Ed. Part-time and evening/weekend programs available. *Faculty:* 27 full-time (21 women), 1 part-time/adjunct. *Students:* 5 full-time (all women). Average age 22. 4 applicants, 100% accepted, 4 enrolled. In 2011, 5 master's awarded. *Degree requirements:* For master's, oral exam. *Entrance requirements:* Additional exam requirements/recommendations for international students: Required—TOEFL (minimum score 550 paper-based; 213 computer-based; 80 iBT). *Application deadline:* For fall admission, 11/16 for domestic students, 11/15 for international students; for spring admission, 3/1 for domestic and international students. Application fee: $60. Electronic applications accepted. *Expenses: Tuition:* Full-time $20,250; part-time $1125 per credit hour. Part-time tuition and fees vary according to course load and program. *Financial support:* Teaching assistantships with full tuition reimbursements, career-related internships or fieldwork, scholarships/grants, and unspecified assistantships available. Financial award application deadline: 3/1. *Unit head:* Dr. Jan Lacina, Associate Dean, 817-257-6786, E-mail: j.lacina@tcu.edu. *Application contact:* Patricia Garcia, Academic Program Specialist, 817-257-7661, E-mail: p.m.garcia@tcu.edu. Web site: http://www.coe.tcu.edu/186.asp.

Texas State University–San Marcos, Graduate School, College of Education, Department of Curriculum and Instruction, Program in Special Education, San Marcos, TX 78666. Offers M Ed. Part-time programs available. *Faculty:* 7 full-time (5 women), 8 part-time/adjunct (7 women). *Students:* 37 full-time (all women), 54 part-time (49 women); includes 24 minority (4 Black or African American, non-Hispanic/Latino; 1 Asian, non-Hispanic/Latino; 18 Hispanic/Latino; 1 Two or more races, non-Hispanic/Latino). Average age 32. 53 applicants, 51% accepted, 22 enrolled. In 2011, 31 master's awarded. *Degree requirements:* For master's, comprehensive exam. *Entrance requirements:* For master's, GRE General Test, minimum GPA of 2.75 in last 60 hours of course work, teaching experience. Additional exam requirements/recommendations for international students: Required—TOEFL (minimum score 550 paper-based; 213 computer-based; 78 iBT). *Application deadline:* For fall admission, 6/15 priority date for domestic students, 6/1 for international students; for spring admission, 10/15 priority date for domestic students, 10/1 for international students. Applications are processed on a rolling basis. Application fee: $40 ($90 for international students). Electronic applications accepted. *Expenses:* Tuition, state resident: full-time $6408; part-time $3204 per semester. Tuition, nonresident: full-time $14,832; part-time $7416 per semester. *Required fees:* $1824; $912 per semester. Tuition and fees vary according to course load. *Financial support:* In 2011–12, 51 students received support, including 2 research assistantships (averaging $10,152 per year), 1 teaching assistantship (averaging $10,152 per year); fellowships, career-related internships or fieldwork, Federal Work-Study, and institutionally sponsored loans also available. Support available to part-time students. Financial award application deadline: 4/1; financial award applicants required to submit FAFSA. *Faculty research:* Educational diagnostics; generic, severely handicapped, emotionally disturbed, autistic education. *Unit head:* Dr. Larry J. Wheeler, Graduate Adviser, 512-245-2157, Fax: 512-245-7911, E-mail: lw06@txstate.edu. *Application contact:* Dr. J. Michael Willoughby, Dean of Graduate School, 512-245-2581, Fax: 512-245-8365, E-mail: gradcollege@txstate.edu. Web site: http://www.education.txstate.edu/ci/degrees-programs/graduate.html.

Texas Tech University, Graduate School, College of Education, Department of Educational Psychology and Leadership, Lubbock, TX 79409. Offers counselor education (M Ed, PhD); educational leadership (M Ed, Ed D); educational psychology (M Ed, PhD); higher education (M Ed, Ed D); higher education: higher education research (PhD); instructional technology (M Ed, Ed D); instructional technology: distance education (M Ed); special education (M Ed, Ed D). *Accreditation:* ACA; NCATE. Part-time programs available. Postbaccalaureate distance learning degree programs offered (no on-campus study). *Students:* 180 full-time (133 women), 418 part-time (297 women); includes 127 minority (34 Black or African American, non-Hispanic/Latino; 3 American Indian or Alaska Native, non-Hispanic/Latino; 6 Asian, non-Hispanic/Latino; 76 Hispanic/Latino; 8 Two or more races, non-Hispanic/Latino), 41 international. Average age 36. 478 applicants, 42% accepted, 134 enrolled. In 2011, 139 master's, 30 doctorates awarded. *Degree requirements:* For master's, thesis optional; for doctorate, thesis/dissertation. *Entrance requirements:* For master's and doctorate, GRE General Test. Additional exam requirements/recommendations for international students: Required—TOEFL (minimum score 550 paper-based; 213 computer-based; 79 iBT). *Application deadline:* For fall admission, 6/1 priority date for domestic students, 1/15 for international students; for spring admission, 9/1 priority date for domestic students, 6/15 for international students. Applications are processed on a rolling basis. Application fee: $50 ($75 for international students). Electronic applications accepted. *Expenses:* Tuition, state resident: full-time $5899; part-time $245.80 per credit hour. Tuition, nonresident: full-time $13,411; part-time $558.80 per credit hour. *Required fees:* $2680.60; $86.50 per credit hour. $920.30 per semester. *Financial support:* In 2011–12, 142 students received support. Application deadline: 4/15; applicants required to submit FAFSA. *Faculty research:* Psychological processes of teaching and learning, teaching populations with special needs, instructional technology, educational administration in education, theories and practice in counseling and counselor education K-12 and higher. *Total annual research expenditures:* $1.4 million. *Unit head:* Dr. William Lan, Chair, 806-742-1998 Ext. 436, Fax: 806-742-2179, E-mail: william.lan@ttu.edu. *Application contact:* Dr. Hansel Burley, Associate Academic Dean, 806-742-1998 Ext. 447, Fax: 806-742-2179, E-mail: hansel.burley@ttu.edu.

Texas Woman's University, Graduate School, College of Professional Education, Department of Teacher Education, Denton, TX 76201. Offers administration (M Ed, MA); special education (M Ed, MA, PhD), including educational diagnostician (M Ed, MA); teaching, learning, and curriculum (M Ed). Part-time programs available. *Faculty:* 27 full-time (20 women), 2 part-time/adjunct (both women). *Students:* 14 full-time (12 women), 164 part-time (142 women); includes 68 minority (33 Black or African American, non-Hispanic/Latino; 1 American Indian or Alaska Native, non-Hispanic/Latino; 6 Asian, non-Hispanic/Latino; 28 Hispanic/Latino), 1 international. Average age 37. 38 applicants, 74% accepted, 24 enrolled. In 2011, 67 master's, 4 doctorates awarded. Terminal master's awarded for partial completion of doctoral program. *Degree requirements:* For master's, comprehensive exam, thesis, professional paper (M Ed); for doctorate, comprehensive exam, thesis/dissertation. *Entrance requirements:* For master's, minimum GPA of 3.0 on last 60 undergraduate hours, 2 letters of reference, resume, copy of certifications, teacher service record, statement of intent; for doctorate, GRE General Test, minimum GPA of 3.0, 3 letters of reference, resume, copy of certifications, teacher service record, statement of intent. Additional exam requirements/recommendations for international students: Required—TOEFL (minimum score 550 paper-based; 213 computer-based; 79 iBT). *Application deadline:* For fall admission, 7/1 priority date for domestic students, 3/1 for international students; for spring admission, 11/1 priority date for domestic students, 7/1 for international students. Applications are processed on a rolling basis. Application fee: $50 ($75 for international students). Electronic applications accepted. *Expenses:* Tuition, state resident: full-time $3834; part-time $213 per credit hour. Tuition, nonresident: full-time $9468; part-time $526 per credit hour. *Required fees:* $213 per credit hour. Tuition and fees vary according to course load. *Financial support:* In 2011–12, 42 students received support, including 8 research assistantships (averaging $12,942 per year); career-related internships or fieldwork, Federal Work-Study, institutionally sponsored loans, scholarships/grants, traineeships, health care benefits, and unspecified assistantships also available. Support available to part-time students. Financial award application deadline: 3/1; financial award applicants required to submit FAFSA. *Faculty research:* Language and literacy, classroom management, learning disabilities, staff and professional development, leadership preparation practice. *Unit head:* Dr. Jane Pemberton, Chair, 940-898-2271, Fax: 940-898-2270, E-mail: mrule1@twu.edu. *Application contact:* Dr. Samuel Wheeler, Assistant Director of Admissions, 940-898-3188, Fax: 940-898-3081, E-mail: wheelersr@twu.edu. Web site: http://www.twu.edu/teacher-education/.

Touro College, Graduate School of Education, New York, NY 10010. Offers bilingual programs (Advanced Certificate); education and special education (MS); gifted and talented education (Advanced Certificate); instructional technology (MS); mathematics education (MS); school leadership (MS); teaching children with autism and other severe or multiple disabilities (Advanced Certificate); teaching English to speakers of other languages (MS, Advanced Certificate); teaching literacy (MS). Part-time and evening/weekend programs available. Postbaccalaureate distance learning degree programs offered (no on-campus study). *Faculty:* 75 full-time, 131 part-time/adjunct. *Students:* 382 full-time (324 women), 3,790 part-time (3,196 women); includes 1,211 minority (537 Black or African American, non-Hispanic/Latino; 4 American Indian or Alaska Native, non-Hispanic/Latino; 187 Asian, non-Hispanic/Latino; 472 Hispanic/Latino; 3 Native Hawaiian or other Pacific Islander, non-Hispanic/Latino; 8 Two or more races, non-Hispanic/Latino), 1 international. 1,422 applicants, 50% accepted, 675 enrolled. In 2011, 6 master's, 4 other advanced degrees awarded. *Application deadline:* For fall admission, 8/26 for domestic students, 7/15 for international students; for spring admission, 12/31 for domestic students, 12/15 for international students. Applications are processed on a rolling basis. Application fee: $50. *Financial support:* Federal Work-Study available. Financial award applicants required to submit FAFSA. *Faculty research:* Equity assistance, language development, scholar communications, Latin American studies and cultural sensitivity, behavior management techniques and strategies in special education. *Unit head:* Dr. LaMar Miller, Dean, 212-463-0400 Ext. 5561, Fax: 212-462-4889, E-mail: lpmiller@touro.edu. *Application contact:* Natalie Arroyo, Admissions Assistant, 212-463-0400 Ext. 5119, E-mail: natalie.arroyo@touro.edu.

Towson University, Program in Autism Studies, Towson, MD 21252-0001. Offers Graduate Certificate. *Students:* 5 full-time (all women), 19 part-time (18 women); includes 5 minority (3 Black or African American, non-Hispanic/Latino; 1 American Indian or Alaska Native, non-Hispanic/Latino; 1 Two or more races, non-Hispanic/Latino). *Expenses:* Tuition, state resident: part-time $337 per credit. Tuition, nonresident: part-time $709 per credit. *Required fees:* $99 per credit. *Unit head:* Janet DeLany, Dean, 410-704-2371, E-mail: jdelany@towson.edu.

Towson University, Program in Special Education, Towson, MD 21252-0001. Offers special education leadership (M Ed). *Accreditation:* NCATE. Part-time and evening/weekend programs available. *Students:* 5 full-time (4 women), 135 part-time (124 women); includes 9 minority (3 Black or African American, non-Hispanic/Latino; 3 Asian, non-Hispanic/Latino; 1 Hispanic/Latino; 2 Two or more races, non-Hispanic/Latino), 1 international. *Degree requirements:* For master's, thesis optional. *Entrance requirements:* For master's, letter of recommendation, professional teacher certification, minimum GPA of 3.0. Additional exam requirements/recommendations for international students: Required—TOEFL (minimum score 550 paper-based). *Application deadline:* For fall admission, 2/15 priority date for domestic students, 2/15 for international students; for spring admission, 10/15 priority date for domestic students, 10/15 for international students. Applications are processed on a rolling basis. Application fee: $50. Electronic applications accepted. *Expenses:* Tuition, state resident: part-time $337 per credit. Tuition, nonresident: part-time $709 per credit. *Required fees:* $99 per credit. *Unit head:* Lori Jackman, Graduate Program Director, 410-704-3122, Fax: 410-704-2733, E-mail: ljackman@towson.edu.

Trevecca Nazarene University, College of Lifelong Learning, School of Education, Nashville, TN 37210-2877. Offers curriculum, assessment, and instruction K-12 (M Ed); educational leadership (M Ed); English language learners (PreK-12) (M Ed); leadership and professional practice (Ed D); leading instructional improvement for teachers PreK-12 (M Ed); library and information science (MLI Sc); teaching (MAT), including teaching 7-12, teaching K-6; visual impairment special education (M Ed). *Accreditation:* NCATE. Part-time and evening/weekend programs available. Postbaccalaureate distance learning degree programs offered. *Faculty:* 17 full-time (15 women), 22 part-time/adjunct (14 women). *Students:* 379 full-time (283 women), 77 part-time (60 women); includes 87 minority (78 Black or African American, non-Hispanic/Latino; 2 Asian, non-Hispanic/Latino; 3 Hispanic/Latino; 4 Two or more races, non-Hispanic/Latino), 3 international. Average age 36. In 2011, 188 master's, 23 doctorates awarded. *Degree requirements:* For master's, exit assessment; for doctorate, thesis/dissertation, proposal study, symposium presentation. *Entrance requirements:* For master's, GRE General Test, MAT, minimum GPA of 2.7, 2 reference forms; for doctorate, GMAT, GRE, MAT, or NTE, minimum GPA of 3.4, resume, writing sample, interview, reference forms. Additional exam requirements/recommendations for international students: Required—TOEFL (minimum score 550 paper-based; 213 computer-based). *Application deadline:* Applications are processed on a rolling basis. Application fee: $25. *Expenses:* Contact institution. *Financial support:* Applicants required to submit FAFSA. *Unit head:* Dr. Esther Swink, Dean/Director of Graduate Education Programs, 615-248-1201, Fax: 615-248-1597, E-mail: eswink@trevecca.edu. *Application contact:* Melanie Eaton, Admissions, 615-248-1498, E-mail: admissions_ged@trevecca.edu. Web site: http://www.trevecca.edu/academics/schools-colleges/education/.

Trinity Baptist College, Graduate Programs, Jacksonville, FL 32221. Offers educational leadership (M Ed); ministry (MA); special education (M Ed). Postbaccalaureate distance learning degree programs offered. *Entrance requirements:* For master's, GRE (M Ed), 2 letters of recommendation; minimum GPA of 2.5 (M Min) or 3.0 (M Ed); computer proficiency.

Trinity Washington University, School of Education, Washington, DC 20017-1094. Offers counseling (MA); early childhood education (MAT); educating for change (M Ed); educational administration (MSA); elementary education (MAT); school counseling (MA); secondary education (MAT), including English, social studies; special education (MAT); teaching English as a second language (MAT); teaching English to speakers of other languages (M Ed); the teaching of reading (M Ed). *Accreditation:* NCATE. Part-time and evening/weekend programs available. *Degree requirements:* For master's, thesis (for some programs), capstone project(s). *Entrance requirements:* For master's, PRAXIS I, minimum GPA of 2.8. Additional exam requirements/recommendations for international students: Required—TOEFL (minimum score 550 paper-based; 213 computer-based). *Faculty research:* Technology, literacy, special education, organizations, inclusion models.

Union College, Graduate Programs, Department of Education, Program in Special Education, Barbourville, KY 40906-1499. Offers MA. *Degree requirements:* For master's, thesis optional. *Entrance requirements:* For master's, GRE General Test, NTE.

United States University, School of Education, Cypress, CA 90630. Offers administration (MA Ed); early childhood education (MA Ed); general (MA Ed); higher education administration (MA Ed); Spanish language education (MA Ed); special education (MA Ed). *Degree requirements:* For master's, portfolio. *Entrance requirements:* For master's, minimum undergraduate GPA of 2.5. Additional exam requirements/recommendations for international students: Required—TOEFL (minimum score 500 paper-based; 173 computer-based; 61 iBT).

Universidad del Este, Graduate School, Carolina, PR 00984. Offers accounting (MBA); adult education (M Ed); agribusiness (MBA); criminal justice and criminology (MA); curriculum and instruction - early education (M Ed); curriculum and instruction - elementary (M Ed); curriculum and instruction - English (M Ed); curriculum and instruction - Spanish (M Ed); human resources (MBA); information security management (MBA); information technology and Web business development (MBA); management (MBA); public policy (MPA); social work (MA), including clinical social work; special education (M Ed); strategic leadership (MBA).

Universidad del Turabo, Graduate Programs, Programs in Education, Program in Special Education, Gurabo, PR 00778-3030. Offers M Ed. *Faculty:* 3 full-time (1 woman), 13 part-time/adjunct (8 women). *Students:* 29 full-time (26 women), 37 part-time (31 women); includes 57 minority (all Hispanic/Latino). Average age 34. 41 applicants, 98% accepted, 27 enrolled. In 2011, 30 master's awarded. *Entrance requirements:* For master's, GRE, EXADEP, interview. *Application deadline:* For fall admission, 8/5 for domestic students. Application fee: $25. *Financial support:* Institutionally sponsored loans available. *Unit head:* Angela Candelario, Dean, 787-743-7979 Ext. 4126. *Application contact:* Virginia Gonzalez, Admissions Officer, 787-746-3009.

Universidad Iberoamericana, Graduate School, Santo Domingo D.N., Dominican Republic. Offers business administration (MBA, PMBA); constitutional law (LL M); dentistry (DMD); educational management (MA); integrated marketing communication (MA); psychopedagogical intervention (M Ed); real estate law (LL M); strategic management of human talent (MM).

Universidad Metropolitana, School of Education, Program in Special Education, San Juan, PR 00928-1150. Offers M Ed. *Degree requirements:* For master's, thesis or alternative. Electronic applications accepted.

Université de Sherbrooke, Faculty of Education, Program in Special Education, Sherbrooke, QC J1K 2R1, Canada. Offers M Ed, Diploma. Part-time and evening/weekend programs available. *Degree requirements:* For master's, thesis.

University at Albany, State University of New York, School of Education, Department of Educational and Counseling Psychology, Program in Special Education, Albany, NY 12222-0001. Offers MS. *Entrance requirements:* Additional exam requirements/recommendations for international students: Required—TOEFL (minimum score 550 paper-based; 213 computer-based). Electronic applications accepted.

University at Buffalo, the State University of New York, Graduate School, Graduate School of Education, Department of Learning and Instruction, Buffalo, NY 14260. Offers biology education (Ed M, Certificate); chemistry education (Ed M, Certificate); childhood education (Ed M); childhood education with bilingual extension (Ed M); early childhood education (Ed M); early childhood education with bilingual extension (birth-grade 2) (Ed M); earth science education (Ed M, Certificate); educational technology and new literacies (Certificate); educational technology and new literacies (online) (Certificate); elementary education (Ed D, PhD); English education (Ed M, PhD, Certificate); English for speakers of other languages (Ed M); foreign and second language education (PhD); French education (Ed M, Certificate); general education (Ed M); German education (Ed M, Certificate); gifted education (online) (Certificate); Latin education (Ed M, Certificate); literacy teaching and learning (Certificate); literary specialist (Ed M); mathematics education (Ed M, PhD, Certificate); music education (Ed M, Certificate); physics education (Ed M, Certificate); reading education (PhD); science and the public (online) (Ed M); science education (PhD); social studies education (Ed M, Certificate); Spanish education (Ed M, Certificate); special education (PhD); teaching and leading for diversity (Certificate); teaching English to speakers of other languages (Ed M). Part-time and evening/weekend programs available. Postbaccalaureate distance learning degree programs offered (no on-campus study). *Faculty:* 32 full-time (23 women), 54 part-time/adjunct (43 women). *Students:* 294 full-time (222 women), 350 part-time (261 women); includes 75 minority (19 Black or African American, non-Hispanic/Latino; 6 American Indian or Alaska Native, non-Hispanic/Latino; 40 Asian, non-Hispanic/Latino; 10 Hispanic/Latino), 76 international. Average age 29. 548 applicants, 52% accepted, 253 enrolled. In 2011, 225 master's, 17 doctorates, 37 other advanced degrees awarded. *Degree requirements:* For master's, comprehensive exam; for doctorate, thesis/dissertation, research analysis exam, research experience component. *Entrance requirements:* For doctorate, GRE General Test or MAT, interview, writing sample, letters of recommendation. Additional exam requirements/recommendations for international students: Required—TOEFL (minimum score 600 paper-based; 96 iBT). *Application deadline:* For fall admission, 2/1 priority date for domestic students, 2/1 for international students; for spring admission, 11/15 priority date for domestic students, 10/1 for international students. Applications are processed on a rolling basis. Application fee: $50. Electronic applications accepted. *Financial support:* In 2011–12, 40 fellowships (averaging $12,991 per year), 46 research assistantships (averaging $10,986 per year) were awarded; teaching assistantships with full tuition reimbursements, career-related internships or fieldwork, Federal Work-Study, institutionally sponsored loans, scholarships/grants, and unspecified assistantships also available. Financial award application deadline: 2/28; financial award applicants required to submit FAFSA. *Faculty research:* Science assessment, foreign language teaching and learning, early learning, new literacies, gender and education. *Unit head:* Dr. Julie Sarama, Chair, 716-645-2455, Fax: 716-645-3161, E-mail: jcollins@buffalo.edu. *Application contact:* Cathy Dimino, Admissions Assistant, 716-645-2110, Fax: 716-645-7937, E-mail: cadimino@buffalo.edu.

The University of Akron, Graduate School, College of Education, Department of Curricular and Instructional Studies, Program in Special Education, Akron, OH 44325. Offers MA, MS. *Accreditation:* NCATE. *Students:* 55 full-time (40 women), 100 part-time (75 women); includes 23 minority (18 Black or African American, non-Hispanic/Latino; 2 Asian, non-Hispanic/Latino; 3 Two or more races, non-Hispanic/Latino), 3 international. Average age 32. 60 applicants, 65% accepted, 27 enrolled. In 2011, 68 master's awarded. *Degree requirements:* For master's, comprehensive exam. *Entrance requirements:* For master's, minimum GPA of 2.75, valid teaching license. Additional exam requirements/recommendations for international students: Required—TOEFL (minimum score 550 paper-based; 213 computer-based; 79 iBT). *Application deadline:* Applications are processed on a rolling basis. Application fee: $30 ($40 for international students). Electronic applications accepted. *Expenses:* Tuition, state resident: full-time $7038; part-time $391 per credit hour. Tuition, nonresident: full-time $12,051; part-time $670 per credit hour. *Required fees:* $1274; $34 per credit hour. *Unit head:* Dr. Bridgie Ford, Chair, 330-972-6967, E-mail: alexis2@uakron.edu. *Application contact:* Dr. Mark Tausig, Associate Dean, 330-972-6266, Fax: 330-972-6475, E-mail: mtausig@uakron.edu.

The University of Alabama, Graduate School, College of Education, Department of Special Education and Multiple Abilities, Tuscaloosa, AL 35487. Offers collaborative teacher program (M Ed, Ed S); early intervention (M Ed, Ed S); gifted education (M Ed, Ed S); multiple abilities program (M Ed); special education (Ed D, PhD). Part-time and evening/weekend programs available. *Faculty:* 10 full-time (7 women), 1 (woman) part-time/adjunct. *Students:* 26 full-time (21 women), 53 part-time (47 women); includes 10 minority (7 Black or African American, non-Hispanic/Latino; 1 American Indian or Alaska Native, non-Hispanic/Latino; 2 Hispanic/Latino). Average age 32. 32 applicants, 69% accepted, 17 enrolled. In 2011, 14 master's, 7 other advanced degrees awarded. Terminal master's awarded for partial completion of doctoral program. *Degree requirements:* For master's, comprehensive exam, thesis optional; for doctorate, one foreign language, comprehensive exam, thesis/dissertation. *Entrance requirements:* For master's, GRE or MAT, minimum undergraduate GPA of 3.0, teaching certificate, 3 letters of recommendation; for doctorate, GRE or MAT, 3 years of teaching experience, minimum undergraduate GPA of 3.25. Additional exam requirements/recommendations for international students: Required—TOEFL. *Application deadline:* For fall admission, 7/1 for domestic students; for spring admission, 11/1 for domestic students. Applications are processed on a rolling basis. Application fee: $50 ($60 for international students). Electronic applications accepted. *Expenses:* Tuition, state resident: full-time $8600. Tuition, nonresident: full-time $21,900. *Financial support:* In 2011–12, 8 students received support, including 4 research assistantships with tuition reimbursements available (averaging $9,000 per year), 4 teaching assistantships with tuition reimbursements available (averaging $9,000 per year); health care benefits and unspecified assistantships also available. Financial award application deadline: 7/1; financial award applicants required to submit FAFSA. *Faculty research:* Gifted education, mild disabilities, early intervention, severe disabilities. *Unit head:* James A. Siders, Associate Professor and Head, 205-348-5577, Fax: 205-348-6782, E-mail: jsiders@bama.ua.edu. *Application contact:* April Zark, Office Support, 205-348-6093, Fax: 205-348-6782, E-mail: azark@bamaed.ua.edu.

The University of Alabama at Birmingham, College of Arts and Sciences, School of Education, Program in Special Education, Birmingham, AL 35294. Offers MA Ed. *Accreditation:* NCATE. *Degree requirements:* For master's, thesis optional. *Entrance requirements:* For master's, GRE General Test or NTE, minimum GPA of 3.0. *Application deadline:* Applications are processed on a rolling basis. Electronic applications accepted. *Expenses:* Tuition, state resident: full-time $5922; part-time $309 per hour. Tuition, nonresident: full-time $13,428; part-time $726 per hour. Tuition and fees vary according to program. *Unit head:* Dr. Lynn Kirkland, Chair, 205-934-8358. Web site: http://www.uab.edu/ci/special-education.

University of Alaska Anchorage, College of Education, Program in Special Education, Anchorage, AK 99508. Offers early childhood special education (M Ed); special education (M Ed, Certificate). Part-time programs available. *Degree requirements:* For master's, comprehensive exam (for some programs), thesis or alternative. *Entrance requirements:* For master's, GRE or MAT, interview, minimum GPA of 2.75. Additional exam requirements/recommendations for international students: Required—TOEFL (minimum score 550 paper-based; 213 computer-based). *Faculty research:* Mild disabilities, substance abuse issues for educators, partnerships to improve at-risk youth, analysis of planning models for teachers in special education.

University of Alaska Fairbanks, School of Education, Program in Education, Fairbanks, AK 99775. Offers curriculum and instruction (M Ed); education (M Ed, Graduate Certificate); elementary education (M Ed); language and literacy (M Ed); reading (M Ed); secondary education (M Ed); special education (M Ed). *Faculty:* 25 full-time (15 women). *Students:* 30 full-time (23 women), 69 part-time (50 women); includes 17 minority (7 American Indian or Alaska Native, non-Hispanic/Latino; 1 Asian, non-Hispanic/Latino; 2 Hispanic/Latino; 1 Native Hawaiian or other Pacific Islander, non-Hispanic/Latino; 6 Two or more races, non-Hispanic/Latino), 1 international. Average age 33. 68 applicants, 76% accepted, 37 enrolled. In 2011, 26 master's, 22 other advanced degrees awarded. *Degree requirements:* For master's, comprehensive exam, thesis, oral defense. *Entrance requirements:* Additional exam requirements/recommendations for international students: Required—TOEFL (minimum score 550 paper-based; 213 computer-based; 80 iBT). *Application deadline:* For fall admission, 5/1 for domestic students, 3/1 for international students; for spring admission, 10/15 for domestic students, 8/1 for international students. Applications are processed on a rolling basis. Application fee: $60. Electronic applications accepted. *Expenses:* Tuition, state resident: full-time $6696; part-time $372 per credit. Tuition, nonresident: full-time $13,680; part-time $760 per credit. Tuition and fees vary according to course load and reciprocity agreements. *Financial support:* Fellowships with tuition reimbursements, research assistantships with tuition reimbursements, teaching assistantships with tuition reimbursements, career-related internships or fieldwork, Federal Work-Study, scholarships/grants, health care benefits, and unspecified assistantships available. Support available to part-time students. Financial award application deadline: 6/1; financial award applicants required to submit FAFSA. *Unit head:* Allan Morotti, Interim Dean, 907-474-7341, Fax: 907-474-5451, E-mail: uaf-soe-school@alaska.edu. *Application contact:* Mike Earnest, Director of Admissions, 907-474-7500, Fax: 907-474-5379, E-mail: admissions@uaf.edu. Web site: http://www.uaf.edu/educ/graduate/counseling.html.

University of Alberta, Faculty of Graduate Studies and Research, Department of Educational Psychology, Edmonton, AB T6G 2E1, Canada. Offers counseling psychology (M Ed, PhD); educational psychology (M Ed, PhD); instructional technology (M Ed); school counseling (M Ed); school psychology (M Ed, PhD); special education (M Ed, PhD); special education-deafness studies (M Ed); teaching English as a second language (M Ed). Part-time programs available. *Degree requirements:* For master's, thesis optional; for doctorate, comprehensive exam, thesis/dissertation. *Entrance requirements:* For master's and doctorate, minimum GPA of 3.0. Additional exam requirements/recommendations for international students: Required—TOEFL. *Faculty research:* Human learning, development and assessment.

The University of Arizona, College of Education, Department of Disability and Psychoeducational Studies, Tucson, AZ 85721. Offers family studies and human development (M Ed); rehabilitation (MA, PhD); school counseling (M Ed); school psychology (PhD, Ed S); special education (Ed D). *Accreditation:* CORE. Part-time programs available. *Faculty:* 15 full-time (8 women), 1 (woman) part-time/adjunct. *Students:* 155 full-time (120 women), 63 part-time (53 women); includes 53 minority (10 Black or African American, non-Hispanic/Latino; 1 American Indian or Alaska Native, non-Hispanic/Latino; 2 Asian, non-Hispanic/Latino; 24 Hispanic/Latino; 1 Native Hawaiian or other Pacific Islander, non-Hispanic/Latino; 15 Two or more races, non-Hispanic/Latino), 13 international. Average age 36. In 2011, 91 master's, 4 doctorates awarded. Terminal master's awarded for partial completion of doctoral program. *Degree requirements:* For master's, comprehensive exam, thesis optional; for doctorate, comprehensive exam, thesis/dissertation. *Entrance requirements:* For master's, statement of purpose; for doctorate, GRE General Test (minimum score 1100) or MAT, 3 letters of recommendation. Additional exam requirements/recommendations for international students: Required—TOEFL (minimum score 550 paper-based; 213 computer-based; 79 iBT). Application fee: $75. *Expenses:* Tuition, state resident: full-time $10,840. Tuition, nonresident: full-time $25,802. *Financial support:* In 2011–12, 15 research assistantships (averaging $15,552 per year), 1 teaching assistantship (averaging $14,535 per year) were awarded; career-related internships or fieldwork, institutionally sponsored loans, health care benefits, tuition waivers (full), and unspecified assistantships also available. Financial award applicants required to submit FAFSA. *Total annual research expenditures:* $3.6 million. *Unit head:* Dr. Linda R. Shaw, Department Head, 520-621-7822, Fax: 520-621-3821, E-mail: lshaw@email.arizona.edu. *Application contact:* Cecilia Carlon, Coordinator, 520-621-7822, Fax: 520-621-3821, E-mail: ccarlon@email.arizona.edu. Web site: https://www.coe.arizona.edu/dps.

University of Arkansas, Graduate School, College of Education and Health Professions, Department of Curriculum and Instruction, Program in Special Education, Fayetteville, AR 72701-1201. Offers M Ed, MAT. *Accreditation:* NCATE. Part-time and evening/weekend programs available. Postbaccalaureate distance learning degree programs offered (no on-campus study). *Students:* 7 full-time (5 women), 58 part-time (51 women); includes 10 minority (3 Black or African American, non-Hispanic/Latino; 1 American Indian or Alaska Native, non-Hispanic/Latino; 1 Asian, non-Hispanic/Latino; 5 Two or more races, non-Hispanic/Latino), 2 international. In 2011, 13 master's awarded. *Entrance requirements:* For master's, GRE General Test or MAT. *Application deadline:* For fall admission, 4/1 for international students; for spring admission, 10/1 for international students. Applications are processed on a rolling basis. Application fee: $40 ($50 for international students). Electronic applications accepted. *Financial support:* Fellowships, research assistantships, teaching assistantships, career-related internships or fieldwork, and Federal Work-Study available. Support available to part-time students. Financial award application deadline: 4/1; financial award applicants required to submit FAFSA. *Unit head:* Dr. Michael Daugherty, Unit Head, 479-575-4209, E-mail: mkd03@uark.edu. *Application contact:* Dr. Barbara Gartin, Graduate Coordinator, 479-575-7525, Fax: 479-575-6676, E-mail: bgartin@uark.edu. Web site: http://cied.uark.edu/.

University of Arkansas at Little Rock, Graduate School, College of Education, Department of Counseling, Adult and Rehabilitation Education, Little Rock, AR 72204-1099. Offers adult education (M Ed); counselor education (M Ed), including school counseling; orientation and mobility of the blind (Graduate Certificate); rehabilitation counseling (MA, Graduate Certificate); rehabilitation of the blind (MA). *Accreditation:* CORE; NCATE. Part-time programs available. *Entrance requirements:* For master's, interview, minimum GPA of 2.75. *Faculty research:* Low vision, orientation and mobility instruction.

University of Arkansas at Little Rock, Graduate School, College of Education, Department of Teacher Education, Program in Special Education, Little Rock, AR 72204-1099. Offers teaching deaf and hard of hearing (M Ed); teaching the visually impaired (M Ed). *Accreditation:* NCATE. Part-time and evening/weekend programs available. *Degree requirements:* For master's, comprehensive exam, portfolio or thesis. *Entrance requirements:* For master's, interview, minimum GPA of 2.75, GRE General Test or teaching certificate.

The University of British Columbia, Faculty of Education, Department of Educational and Counseling Psychology, and Special Education, Vancouver, BC V6T 1Z1, Canada. Offers counseling psychology (M Ed, MA, PhD); development, learning and culture (PhD); guidance studies (Diploma); human development, learning and culture (M Ed, MA); measurement and evaluation and research methodology (M Ed); measurement, evaluation and research methodology (MA); measurement, evaluation, and research methodology (PhD); school psychology (M Ed, MA, PhD); special education (M Ed, MA, PhD, Diploma). Part-time programs available. *Degree requirements:* For master's, thesis (for some programs); for doctorate, comprehensive exam, thesis/dissertation. *Entrance requirements:* For master's, GRE General Test (counseling psychology MA); for doctorate, GRE General Test. Additional exam requirements/recommendations for international students: Required—TOEFL. Electronic applications accepted. *Faculty research:* Women, family, social problems, career transition, stress and coping problems.

University of Calgary, Faculty of Graduate Studies, Faculty of Education, Division of Applied Psychology, Calgary, AB T2N 1N4, Canada. Offers counseling psychology (M Ed, M Sc, PhD); human development and learning (M Ed, M Sc, PhD); school psychology (M Ed, M Sc, PhD); special education (M Ed, M Sc, PhD). Part-time programs available. *Degree requirements:* For master's, thesis (for some programs), final oral exam; for doctorate, thesis/dissertation, candidacy exam, final oral exam. *Entrance requirements:* For master's, minimum GPA of 3.0, 3 letters of reference; for doctorate, minimum GPA of 3.5, 3 letters of reference. *Faculty research:* Counselor education, family life studies, learning and cognition.

University of California, Berkeley, Graduate Division, School of Education, Program in Special Education, Berkeley, CA 94720-1500. Offers PhD. Applicants must apply to both the University of California, Berkeley and San Francisco State University; Program held jointly with San Francisco State University. *Degree requirements:* For doctorate, thesis/dissertation, oral qualifying exam. *Entrance requirements:* For doctorate, GRE General Test, minimum undergraduate GPA of 3.0 during last 2 years, 3 letters of recommendation. Electronic applications accepted.

University of California, Berkeley, Graduate Division, School of Education, Programs in Education, Berkeley, CA 94720-1500. Offers development in mathematics and science (MA); education in mathematics, science, and technology (MA, PhD); human development and education (MA, PhD); special education (PhD); MA/Credential; PhD/Credential; PhD/MA. Terminal master's awarded for partial completion of doctoral program. *Degree requirements:* For master's, exam or thesis; for doctorate, thesis/dissertation, oral qualifying exam. *Entrance requirements:* For master's and doctorate, GRE General Test, minimum GPA of 3.0 during last 2 years of undergraduate course work. Electronic applications accepted. *Faculty research:* Human development, social and moral educational psychology, developmental teacher preparation.

University of California, Los Angeles, Graduate Division, Graduate School of Education and Information Studies, Program in Special Education, Los Angeles, CA 90095. Offers PhD. Program offered jointly with California State University, Los Angeles. *Degree requirements:* For doctorate, thesis/dissertation, oral and written qualifying exams. *Entrance requirements:* For doctorate, GRE General Test, minimum undergraduate GPA of 3.0. Additional exam requirements/recommendations for international students: Required—TOEFL (minimum score 560 paper-based; 220 computer-based; 87 iBT). Electronic applications accepted.

University of California, Riverside, Graduate Division, Graduate School of Education, Riverside, CA 92521-0102. Offers autism (M Ed); diversity and equity (M Ed); education, society and culture (MA, PhD); educational psychology (MA, PhD); general education (M Ed); higher education administration and policy (M Ed, PhD); reading (M Ed); school psychology (PhD); special education (M Ed, MA, PhD). *Faculty:* 19 full-time (9 women), 9 part-time/adjunct (6 women). *Students:* 181 full-time (128 women); includes 79 minority (8 Black or African American, non-Hispanic/Latino; 1 American Indian or Alaska Native, non-Hispanic/Latino; 26 Asian, non-Hispanic/Latino; 34 Hispanic/Latino; 10 Two or more races, non-Hispanic/Latino), 5 international. Average age 31. 200 applicants, 48% accepted, 76 enrolled. In 2011, 67 master's, 12 doctorates awarded. Terminal master's awarded for partial completion of doctoral program. *Degree requirements:* For master's, thesis optional, comprehensive exams or thesis (MA), case study or analytical report (M Ed); for doctorate, thesis/dissertation, written and oral qualifying exams, college teaching practicum. *Entrance requirements:* For master's, GRE General Test, CBEST, CSET, minimum GPA of 3.2; for doctorate, GRE General Test, master's degree (desirable), minimum GPA of 3.2. Additional exam requirements/recommendations for international students: Required—TOEFL (minimum score 550 paper-based; 213 computer-based; 80 iBT), IELTS (minimum score 7). *Application deadline:* For fall admission, 9/1 for domestic students, 4/1 for international students; for winter admission, 12/1 for domestic students, 7/1 for international students; for spring admission, 3/1 for domestic students, 10/1 for international students. Applications are processed on a rolling basis. Application fee: $80 ($100 for international students). Electronic applications accepted. *Financial support:* In 2011–12, 59 students received support, including 9 fellowships with full and partial tuition reimbursements available (averaging $26,587 per year), 21 research assistantships with full and partial tuition reimbursements available (averaging $14,517 per year), 1 teaching assistantship with full and partial tuition reimbursement available (averaging $17,307 per year); career-related internships or fieldwork, Federal Work-Study, institutionally sponsored loans, scholarships/grants, and unspecified assistantships also available. Financial award application deadline: 1/5. *Faculty research:* Responsiveness to intervention, faculty core, response to intervention of English language learners, advanced modeling techniques, study on social capital, trust, and motivation. *Total annual research expenditures:* $2.8 million. *Unit head:* Prof. Douglas Mitchell, Interim Dean, 951-827-5802, Fax: 951-827-3942, E-mail: douglas.mitchell@ucr.edu. *Application contact:* Prof. Robert Ream, Graduate Advisor for Admission, 951-827-6362, Fax: 951-827-3291, E-mail: edgrad@ucr.edu. Web site: http://www.education.ucr.edu/.

University of California, Santa Barbara, Graduate Division, Gevirtz Graduate School of Education, Santa Barbara, CA 93106-9490. Offers counseling, clinical and school psychology (M Ed, MA, PhD, Credential), including clinical psychology (PhD), counseling psychology (MA, PhD), school psychology (M Ed, PhD), school psychology: pupil personnel services (Credential); education (M Ed, MA, PhD, Credential), including child and adolescent development (MA, PhD), cultural perspectives and comparative education (MA, PhD), educational leadership and organizations (MA, PhD), multiple subject teaching (Credential), research methodology (MA, PhD), single subject teaching (Credential), special education (Credential), special education disabilities and risk studies (MA), special education, disabilities and risk studies (PhD), teaching (M Ed), teaching and learning (MA, PhD); MA/PhD. *Accreditation:* APA (one or more programs are accredited). *Faculty:* 40 full-time (21 women), 2 part-time/adjunct (both women). *Students:* 389 full-time (301 women); includes 131 minority (14 Black or African American, non-Hispanic/Latino; 2 American Indian or Alaska Native, non-Hispanic/Latino; 41 Asian, non-Hispanic/Latino; 69 Hispanic/Latino; 1 Native Hawaiian or other Pacific Islander, non-Hispanic/Latino; 4 Two or more races, non-Hispanic/Latino), 25 international. Average age 28. 691 applicants, 35% accepted, 154 enrolled. In 2011, 145 master's, 45 doctorates, 118 other advanced degrees awarded. Terminal master's awarded for partial completion of doctoral program. *Degree requirements:* For master's, comprehensive exam (for some programs), thesis (for some programs); for doctorate, comprehensive exam (for some programs), thesis/dissertation; for Credential, CA state requirements (varies by credential). *Entrance requirements:* For master's and doctorate, GRE; for Credential, GRE or MAT, CSET and CBEST. Additional exam requirements/recommendations for international students: Required—TOEFL (minimum score 550 paper-based; 80 iBT), IELTS (minimum score 7). Application fee: $80 ($100 for international students). Electronic applications accepted. *Expenses:* Tuition, state resident: full-time $12,192. Tuition, nonresident: full-time $27,294. *Required fees:* $764.13. *Financial support:* In 2011–12, 301 students received support, including 429 fellowships with partial tuition reimbursements available (averaging $5,017 per year), 83 research assistantships with full and partial tuition reimbursements available (averaging $6,262 per year), 55 teaching assistantships with partial tuition reimbursements available (averaging $8,655 per year); career-related internships or fieldwork also available. Financial award applicants required to submit FAFSA. *Faculty research:* Needs of diverse students, school accountability and leadership, school violence, language learning and literacy, science/math education. *Total annual research expenditures:* $3 million. *Unit head:* Arlis Markel, Assistant Dean, 805-893-5492, Fax: 805-893-2588, E-mail: arlis@education.ucsb.edu. *Application contact:* Kathryn Marie Tucciarone, Student Affairs Officer, 805-893-2137, Fax: 805-893-2588, E-mail: katiet@education.ucsb.edu. Web site: http://www.education.ucsb.edu/.

University of Central Arkansas, Graduate School, College of Education, Department of Early Childhood and Special Education, Program in Special Education, Conway, AR 72035-0001. Offers collaborative instructional specialist (ages 0-8) (MSE); collaborative instructional specialist (grades 4-12) (MSE). *Accreditation:* NCATE. *Students:* 2 full-time (both women), 21 part-time (18 women); includes 2 minority (1 American Indian or Alaska Native, non-Hispanic/Latino; 1 Asian, non-Hispanic/Latino), 1 international. Average age 36. 5 applicants, 100% accepted, 3 enrolled. In 2011, 13 master's awarded. *Degree requirements:* For master's, comprehensive exam, thesis optional. *Entrance requirements:* For master's, GRE General Test, minimum GPA of 2.7. Additional exam requirements/recommendations for international students: Required—TOEFL (minimum score 550 paper-based; 213 computer-based). *Application deadline:* For fall admission, 3/1 priority date for domestic students, 3/1 for international students; for spring admission, 10/1 priority date for domestic students, 10/1 for international students. Applications are processed on a rolling basis. Application fee: $25 ($50 for international students). *Expenses:* Tuition, state resident: full-time $4834; part-time $398.35 per credit hour. Tuition, nonresident: full-time $8686. *Financial support:* Federal Work-Study, scholarships/grants, tuition waivers (partial), and unspecified assistantships available. Financial award application deadline: 2/15; financial award applicants required to submit FAFSA. *Unit head:* Dr. Kathleen Atkins, Coordinator, 501-450-3171, Fax: 501-450-5457, E-mail: katkins@uca.edu. *Application contact:* Dr. Sandy Burks, Administrative Specialist, 501-450-3124, Fax: 501-450-5678, E-mail: slburks@uca.edu.

University of Central Florida, College of Education, Department of Child, Family and Community Sciences, Program in Exceptional Student Education, Orlando, FL 32816. Offers autism spectrum disorders (Certificate); exceptional student education (M Ed, MA); severe or profound disabilities (Certificate); special education (Certificate). *Accreditation:* NCATE. Part-time and evening/weekend programs available. *Students:* 29 full-time (25 women), 133 part-time (121 women); includes 42 minority (16 Black or African American, non-Hispanic/Latino; 4 Asian, non-Hispanic/Latino; 21 Hispanic/Latino; 1 Native Hawaiian or other Pacific Islander, non-Hispanic/Latino), 1 international. Average age 33. 75 applicants, 76% accepted, 42 enrolled. In 2011, 78 master's, 98 other advanced degrees awarded. *Degree requirements:* For master's, thesis or alternative, research project. *Entrance requirements:* For master's, GRE General Test. Additional exam requirements/recommendations for international students: Required—TOEFL. *Application deadline:* For fall admission, 7/15 for domestic students; for spring admission, 12/1 for domestic students. Application fee: $30. Electronic applications accepted. *Expenses:* Tuition, state resident: part-time $277.08 per credit hour. Tuition, nonresident: part-time $277.08 per credit hour. Part-time tuition and fees vary according to degree level and program. *Financial support:* In 2011–12, 1 student received support, including 1 research assistantship with partial tuition reimbursement available (averaging $6,900 per year); fellowships with partial tuition reimbursements available, teaching assistantships with partial tuition reimbursements available, career-related internships or fieldwork, Federal Work-Study, institutionally sponsored loans, tuition waivers (partial), and unspecified assistantships also available. Financial award application deadline: 3/1; financial award applicants required to submit FAFSA. *Unit head:* Dr. Mary Little, Program Coordinator, 407-823-3275, E-mail: mary.little@ucf.edu. *Application contact:* Barbara Rodriguez, Director, Admissions and Registration, 407-823-2766, Fax: 407-823-6442, E-mail: gradadmissions@ucf.edu.

University of Central Florida, College of Education, Education Doctoral Programs, Orlando, FL 32816. Offers communication sciences and disorders (PhD); counselor education (PhD); education (Ed D); elementary education (PhD); exceptional education (PhD); exercise physiology (PhD); higher education (PhD); hospitality education (PhD); instructional technology (PhD); mathematics education (PhD); reading education (PhD); science education (PhD); social science education (PhD); TESOL (PhD). *Students:* 135 full-time (87 women), 73 part-time (51 women); includes 49 minority (21 Black or African American, non-Hispanic/Latino; 4 Asian, non-Hispanic/Latino; 20 Hispanic/Latino; 4 Two or more races, non-Hispanic/Latino), 18 international. Average age 39. 125 applicants, 46% accepted, 46 enrolled. In 2011, 43 doctorates awarded. Application fee: $30. Electronic applications accepted. *Expenses:* Tuition, state resident: part-time $277.08 per credit hour. Tuition, nonresident: part-time $277.08 per credit hour. Part-time tuition and fees vary according to degree level and program. *Financial support:* In 2011–12, 85 students received support, including 48 fellowships with partial tuition reimbursements available (averaging $5,900 per year), 36 research assistantships with partial tuition reimbursements available (averaging $6,900 per year), 59 teaching assistantships with partial tuition reimbursements available (averaging $6,900 per year). *Unit head:* Dr. Rex Culp, Associate Dean, 407-823-5391, E-mail: rex.culp@ucf.edu. *Application contact:* Barbara Rodriguez, Associate Director, Admissions and Registration, 407-823-2766, Fax: 407-823-6442, E-mail: gradadmissions@ucf.edu. Web site: http://education.ucf.edu/departments.cfm.

University of Central Missouri, The Graduate School, College of Education, Warrensburg, MO 64093. Offers career and technical education administration (MS); career and technical education industry training (MS); career and technical education leadership/teaching (MS); college student personnel administration (MS); counseling (MS); curriculum and instruction (Ed S); educational leadership (Ed D); educational technology (MS); elementary education/educational foundations and literacy (MSE); elementary school administration (MSE); elementary school principalship (Ed S); human services/learning resources (Ed S); human services/professional counseling (Ed S); human services/special education (Ed S); human services/technology and occupational education (Ed S); K-12 education/educational foundations and literacy (MSE); K-12 special education (MSE); library science and information services (MS); literacy education (MSE); secondary education/educational foundations & literacy (MSE); secondary school administration (MSE); secondary school principalship (Ed S); superintendency (Ed S); teaching (MAT). Ed D offered jointly with University of Missouri. Part-time programs available. Postbaccalaureate distance learning degree programs offered. *Entrance requirements:* Additional exam requirements/recommendations for international students: Required—TOEFL (minimum score 550 paper-based; 79 computer-based). Electronic applications accepted.

University of Central Oklahoma, College of Graduate Studies and Research, College of Education and Professional Studies, Department of Advanced Professional and Special Services, Program in Special Education, Edmond, OK 73034-5209. Offers M Ed. *Accreditation:* NCATE. Part-time programs available. *Faculty:* 16 full-time (11 women), 13 part-time/adjunct (5 women). *Students:* 43 full-time (42 women), 35 part-time (29 women); includes 15 minority (9 Black or African American, non-Hispanic/Latino; 3 Asian, non-Hispanic/Latino; 2 Hispanic/Latino; 1 Two or more races, non-Hispanic/Latino), 4 international. Average age 31. In 2011, 51 master's awarded. *Entrance requirements:* For master's, GRE. Additional exam requirements/recommendations for international students: Required—TOEFL (minimum score 550 paper-based; 213 computer-based). *Application deadline:* Applications are processed on a rolling basis. Application fee: $50. Electronic applications accepted. *Expenses:* Tuition, state resident: full-time $3901; part-time $218.30 per credit hour. Tuition, nonresident: full-time $9198; part-time $511.20 per credit hour. Tuition and fees vary according to program. *Financial support:* Unspecified assistantships available. Financial award application deadline: 3/31; financial award applicants required to submit FAFSA. *Faculty research:* Children's language development, adult motor speech disorders, learning disabilities, mental retardation, emotional disturbance, special education law. *Unit head:* Dr. Scott McLaughlin, Program Coordinator, 405-974-5297, Fax: 405-974-3966, E-mail: smclaughlin@uco.edu. Web site: http://www.uco.edu/ceps/dept/apss/slp/index.asp.

University of Cincinnati, Graduate School, College of Education, Criminal Justice, and Human Services, Division of Teacher Education, Program in Special Education, Cincinnati, OH 45221. Offers M Ed, Ed D. *Accreditation:* NCATE. Part-time programs available. *Degree requirements:* For master's, thesis or alternative; for doctorate, thesis/dissertation. *Entrance requirements:* For master's, GRE General Test; for doctorate, GRE General Test, GRE Subject Test. Additional exam requirements/recommendations for international students: Required—TOEFL (minimum score 550 paper-based; 213 computer-based), TWE (minimum score 4.5), OEPT. Electronic applications accepted.

University of Colorado at Colorado Springs, College of Education, Colorado Springs, CO 80933-7150. Offers counseling and human services (MA); curriculum and instruction (MA); educational administration (MA); educational leadership (MA, PhD); special education (MA). *Accreditation:* ACA; NCATE. Part-time and evening/weekend programs available. Postbaccalaureate distance learning degree programs offered (minimal on-campus study). *Faculty:* 26 full-time (16 women), 9 part-time/adjunct (5 women). *Students:* 307 full-time (203 women), 115 part-time (92 women); includes 82 minority (24 Black or African American, non-Hispanic/Latino; 3 American Indian or Alaska Native, non-Hispanic/Latino; 12 Asian, non-Hispanic/Latino; 36 Hispanic/Latino; 1 Native Hawaiian or other Pacific Islander, non-Hispanic/Latino; 6 Two or more races, non-Hispanic/Latino), 1 international. Average age 36. 99 applicants, 86% accepted, 61 enrolled. In 2011, 165 master's, 6 doctorates awarded. *Degree requirements:* For master's, comprehensive exam, thesis or alternative, microcomputer proficiency; for doctorate, comprehensive exam, thesis/dissertation, research lab. *Entrance requirements:* For master's, GRE General Test. Additional exam requirements/recommendations for international students: Recommended—TOEFL. *Application deadline:* For fall admission, 2/28 priority date for domestic students, 2/28 for international students; for spring admission, 10/15 for domestic and international students. Applications are processed on a rolling basis. Application fee: $60 ($75 for international students). *Expenses:* Tuition, state resident: part-time $660 per credit hour. Tuition, nonresident: part-time $1133 per credit hour. Tuition and fees vary according to degree level, program and student level. *Financial support:* In 2011–12, 57 students received support. Career-related internships or fieldwork, Federal Work-Study, and scholarships/grants available. Support available to part-time students. Financial award application deadline: 3/1; financial award applicants required to submit FAFSA. *Faculty research:* Job training for special populations, materials development for classroom. *Total annual research expenditures:* $1.6 million. *Unit head:* Dr. Mary Snyder, Dean, 719-255-3701, Fax: 719-262-4133, E-mail: msnyder3@uccs.edu. *Application contact:* Juliane Field, Director, 719-255-4526, Fax: 719-255-4110, E-mail: jfield@uccs.edu. Web site: http://www.uccs.edu/coe.

University of Colorado Denver, School of Education and Human Development, Early Childhood Education Program, Denver, CO 80217. Offers early childhood education (MA); special education (MA). *Accreditation:* NCATE. Part-time and evening/weekend programs available. Postbaccalaureate distance learning degree programs offered (no on-campus study). *Students:* 59 full-time (57 women), 38 part-time (all women); includes 11 minority (2 Black or African American, non-Hispanic/Latino; 2 Asian, non-Hispanic/Latino; 7 Hispanic/Latino), 5 international. Average age 32. 21 applicants, 86% accepted, 15 enrolled. In 2011, 42 master's awarded. *Degree requirements:* For master's, comprehensive exam, fieldwork, practica, 40 credit hours. *Entrance requirements:* For master's, GRE or MAT (if GPA is below 2.75), minimum GPA of 2.75, resume, three letters of recommendation. Additional exam requirements/recommendations for international students: Required—TOEFL (minimum score 525 paper-based; 197 computer-based; 71 iBT). *Application deadline:* For fall admission, 4/15 for domestic students, 4/1 for international students; for spring admission, 9/15 for domestic students, 9/1 for international students. Application fee: $50 ($75 for international students). Electronic applications accepted. *Expenses:* Contact institution. *Financial support:* Research assistantships, teaching assistantships, and Federal Work-Study available. Financial award application deadline: 4/1; financial award applicants required to submit FAFSA. *Faculty research:* Early childhood growth and development, faculty development, adult learning, gender and equity issues, research methodology. *Unit head:* William Goodwin, Professor, 303-315-6323, E-mail: bill.goodwin@ucdenver.edu. *Application contact:* Hans Broers, Academic Advisor, 303-315-6351, Fax: 303-315-6311, E-mail: hans.broers@ucdenver.edu. Web site: http://www.ucdenver.edu/academics/colleges/SchoolOfEducation/Academics/MASTERS/ECE/Pages/EarlyChildhoodEducation.aspx.

University of Colorado Denver, School of Education and Human Development, Program in Educational Leadership and Innovation, Denver, CO 80217-3364. Offers educational studies and research (PhD), including administrative leadership and policy, early childhood special education, math education, research, assessment and evaluation, science education, urban ecologies. Part-time and evening/weekend programs available. *Students:* 21 full-time (15 women), 25 part-time (17 women); includes 10 minority (5 Black or African American, non-Hispanic/Latino; 1 American Indian or Alaska Native, non-Hispanic/Latino; 3 Asian, non-Hispanic/Latino; 1 Hispanic/Latino), 1 international. Average age 43. 11 applicants, 45% accepted, 3 enrolled. In 2011, 11 doctorates awarded. *Degree requirements:* For doctorate, comprehensive exam, thesis/dissertation, 75 credit hours (for PhD). *Entrance requirements:* For doctorate, GRE or equivalent, resume or curriculum vitae, written statement, letters of recommendation, master's degree or equivalent, completion of basic or advanced statistics course with minimum B grade. Additional exam requirements/recommendations for international students: Required—TOEFL (minimum score 525 paper-based; 197 computer-based). *Application deadline:* Applications are processed on a rolling basis. Application fee: $50 ($75 for international students). Electronic applications accepted. *Expenses:* Contact institution. *Financial support:* Fellowships, research assistantships, teaching assistantships, scholarships/grants, and unspecified assistantships available. Financial award application deadline: 4/1; financial award applicants required to submit FAFSA. *Faculty research:* Administrative leadership and policy studies, early childhood education, research in diversity, paraprofessionals in education, urban schools lab. *Unit head:* Dr. Deanna Sands, Associate Dean, Research and Professional Development, 303-315-4931, E-mail: deanna.sands@ucdenver.edu. *Application contact:* Student Services Center, 303-315-6300, Fax: 303-315-6311, E-mail: education@ucdenver.edu. Web site: http://www.ucdenver.edu/ACADEMICS/COLLEGES/SCHOOLOFEDUCATION/ACADEMICS/Pages/AcademicPrograms.aspx.

University of Colorado Denver, School of Education and Human Development, Teacher Education Programs, Denver, CO 80217. Offers elementary linguistically diverse education (MA); elementary math and science education (MA); elementary math education (MA); elementary reading and writing (MA); elementary science education (MA); secondary English education (MA); secondary linguistically diverse education (MA); secondary math education (MA); secondary reading and writing (MA); secondary science education (MA); special education (MA). *Accreditation:* NCATE. Part-time and evening/weekend programs available. *Students:* 419 full-time (325 women), 238 part-time (196 women); includes 83 minority (11 Black or African American, non-Hispanic/Latino; 1 American Indian or Alaska Native, non-Hispanic/Latino; 15 Asian, non-Hispanic/Latino; 53 Hispanic/Latino; 3 Two or more races, non-Hispanic/Latino), 9 international. Average age 30. 206 applicants, 88% accepted, 85 enrolled. In 2011, 278 master's awarded. *Degree requirements:* For master's, comprehensive exam. *Entrance requirements:* For master's, GRE or MAT (for those with GPA below 2.75), transcripts, resume, letters of recommendation. Additional exam requirements/recommendations for international students: Required—TOEFL (minimum score 525 paper-based; 197 computer-based). *Application deadline:* For fall admission, 4/15 priority date for domestic students; for spring admission, 9/15 priority date for domestic students. Applications are processed on a rolling basis. Application fee: $50 ($75 for international students). Electronic applications accepted. *Expenses:* Contact institution. *Financial support:* Research assistantships, teaching assistantships, and Federal Work-Study available. Financial award application deadline: 4/1; financial award applicants required to submit FAFSA. *Faculty research:* Linguistically diverse education/ESL, elementary reading and writing, elementary teacher education, secondary teacher education, special education. *Unit head:* Cindy Gutierrez, Director, 303-315-4982, E-mail: cindy.gutierrez@ucdenver.edu. *Application contact:* Lori Sisneros, Student Services Center, 303-315-4979, E-mail: education@ucdenver.edu. Web site: http://www.ucdenver.edu/academics/colleges/SchoolOfEducation/Academics/MASTERS/Pages/default.aspx.

University of Connecticut, Graduate School, Neag School of Education, Department of Educational Psychology, Program in Special Education, Storrs, CT 06269. Offers MA, PhD, Post-Master's Certificate. *Accreditation:* NCATE. Terminal master's awarded for partial completion of doctoral program. *Degree requirements:* For master's, comprehensive exam, thesis or alternative; for doctorate, thesis/dissertation. *Entrance requirements:* For doctorate, GRE General Test. Additional exam requirements/recommendations for international students: Required—TOEFL (minimum score 550 paper-based; 213 computer-based). Electronic applications accepted.

University of Dayton, Department of Teacher Education, Dayton, OH 45469-1300. Offers adolescent/young adult (MS Ed); art education (MS Ed); early childhood education (MS Ed); early childhood leadership advocacy (MS Ed); inclusive early childhood (MS Ed); interdisciplinary education (MS Ed); intervention specialist education, mild/moderate (MS Ed); literacy (MS Ed); middle childhood (MS Ed); multi-age education (MS Ed); music education (MS Ed); teacher as leader (MS Ed); technology in education (MS Ed). Part-time and evening/weekend programs available. Postbaccalaureate distance learning degree programs offered (no on-campus study). *Faculty:* 15 full-time (11 women), 22 part-time/adjunct (20 women). *Students:* 41 full-time (29 women), 95 part-time (87 women); includes 13 minority (9 Black or African American, non-Hispanic/Latino; 1 Asian, non-Hispanic/Latino; 3 Hispanic/Latino), 9 international. Average age 32. 111 applicants, 55% accepted, 38 enrolled. In 2011, 97 degrees awarded. *Degree requirements:* For master's, thesis, capstone research project. *Entrance requirements:* For master's, GRE General Test, minimum GPA of 2.75. Additional exam requirements/recommendations for international students: Required—TOEFL (minimum score 550 paper-based; 213 computer-based; 80 iBT). *Application deadline:* For fall admission, 3/1 priority date for domestic students, 3/1 for international students; for winter admission, 7/1 for international students; for spring admission, 1/1 for international students. Applications are processed on a rolling basis. Application fee: $0 ($50 for international students). Electronic applications accepted. *Expenses:* Contact institution. *Financial support:* In 2011–12, 5 research assistantships with full and partial tuition reimbursements (averaging $8,470 per year) were awarded; career-related internships or fieldwork, institutionally sponsored loans, health care benefits, and unspecified assistantships also available. Financial award applicants required to submit FAFSA. *Faculty research:* Diversity, literacy, art representation by young children, preservice teacher preparation. *Unit head:* Dr. Katie A. Kinnucan-Welsch, Chair, 937-229-3346. *Application contact:* Alexsandar Popovski, Enrollment Management Administrator, 937-229-2357, Fax: 937-229-4729, E-mail: alex.popovski@notes.udayton.edu.

University of Detroit Mercy, College of Liberal Arts and Education, Department of Education, Program in Special Education, Detroit, MI 48221. Offers emotionally impaired (MA); learning disabilities (MA). Part-time programs available. *Degree requirements:* For master's, thesis or alternative, practicum. *Entrance requirements:* For master's, minimum GPA of 2.75. *Faculty research:* Emerging roles of special education, inclusionary education, high potential underachievers in secondary schools.

The University of Findlay, Graduate and Professional Studies, College of Education, Findlay, OH 45840-3653. Offers administration (MA Ed); children's literature (MA Ed); early childhood (MA Ed); human resource development (MA Ed); reading endorsement (MA Ed); science (MA Ed); special education (MA Ed); technology (MA Ed). *Accreditation:* NCATE. Part-time and evening/weekend programs available. Postbaccalaureate distance learning degree programs offered (no on-campus study). *Faculty:* 16 full-time (12 women), 5 part-time/adjunct (2 women). *Students:* 72 full-time (49 women), 198 part-time (119 women); includes 10 minority (7 Black or African American, non-Hispanic/Latino; 1 Asian, non-Hispanic/Latino; 2 Hispanic/Latino), 16 international. Average age 30. 75 applicants, 88% accepted, 36 enrolled. In 2011, 76 master's awarded. *Degree requirements:* For master's, thesis, cumulative project. *Entrance requirements:* For master's, bachelor's degree from accredited institution, minimum undergraduate GPA of 2.75 in last 62 hours of course work. Additional exam requirements/recommendations for international students: Required—TOEFL (minimum score 550 paper-based; 213 computer-based; 80 iBT). *Application deadline:* Applications are processed on a rolling basis. Application fee: $25. Electronic applications accepted. *Expenses:* Contact institution. *Financial support:* In 2011–12, 5 research assistantships with full and partial tuition reimbursements (averaging $4,200 per year) were awarded; Federal Work-Study, health care benefits, and unspecified assistantships also available. Financial award application deadline: 4/1; financial award applicants required to submit FAFSA. *Faculty research:* Children's literature, books and artwork, educational technology, professional development. *Unit head:* Dr. Julie McIntosh, Dean, 419-434-4862, Fax: 419-434-4822. *Application contact:* Heather Riffle, Assistant Director, Graduate and Professional Studies, 419-434-4640, Fax: 419-434-5517, E-mail: riffle@findlay.edu. Web site: http://www.findlay.edu.

University of Florida, Graduate School, College of Education, Department of Special Education, School Psychology and Early Childhood Studies, Gainesville, FL 32611. Offers early childhood education (M Ed, MAE); school psychology (M Ed, MAE, Ed D, PhD, Ed S); special education (M Ed, MAE, Ed D, PhD, Ed S). *Accreditation:* NCATE. Part-time and evening/weekend programs available. Postbaccalaureate distance learning degree programs offered (no on-campus study). *Faculty:* 21 full-time (17 women). *Students:* 151 full-time (134 women), 62 part-time (56 women); includes 61 minority (26 Black or African American, non-Hispanic/Latino; 1 American Indian or Alaska Native, non-Hispanic/Latino; 10 Asian, non-Hispanic/Latino; 24 Hispanic/Latino), 11 international. Average age 31. 189 applicants, 38% accepted, 40 enrolled. In 2011, 60 master's, 10 doctorates, 6 other advanced degrees awarded. *Degree requirements:* For master's, comprehensive exam (for some programs), thesis (MAE); for doctorate, comprehensive exam, thesis/dissertation. *Entrance requirements:* For master's and doctorate, GRE General Test, minimum GPA of 3.0; for Ed S, GRE General Test. Additional exam requirements/recommendations for international students: Required—TOEFL (minimum score 550 paper-based; 213 computer-based; 80 iBT), IELTS (minimum score 6). *Application deadline:* For fall admission, 11/1 priority date for domestic students. Applications are processed on a rolling basis. Application fee: $30. Electronic applications accepted. *Financial support:* Fellowships, research assistantships, teaching assistantships, career-related internships or fieldwork, and unspecified assistantships available. Financial award application deadline: 11/15; financial award applicants required to submit FAFSA. *Faculty research:* Teacher quality/teacher education, early childhood, autism, instructional interventions in reading and mathematics, behavioral interventions. *Unit head:* Dr. Jean Crockett, Chair, 352-273-4292, Fax: 352-392-2655, E-mail: crocketj@ufl.edu. *Application contact:* Dr. Penny R. Cox, Coordinator, 352-273-4280, Fax: 352-392-2655, E-mail: contact-sespecs@coe.ufl.edu. Web site: http://education.ufl.edu/sespecs/.

University of Georgia, College of Education, Department of Communication Sciences and Special Education, Athens, GA 30602. Offers communication science and disorders (M Ed, MA, PhD, Ed S); special education (M Ed, Ed D, PhD, Ed S). *Accreditation:* ASHA (one or more programs are accredited). *Faculty:* 15 full-time (9 women). *Students:* 86 full-time (82 women), 125 part-time (107 women); includes 51 minority (41 Black or African American, non-Hispanic/Latino; 1 American Indian or Alaska Native, non-Hispanic/Latino; 3 Asian, non-Hispanic/Latino; 3 Hispanic/Latino; 3 Two or more races, non-Hispanic/Latino), 1 international. Average age 34. 224 applicants, 30% accepted, 32 enrolled. In 2011, 33 master's, 4 doctorates, 3 other advanced degrees awarded. Terminal master's awarded for partial completion of doctoral program. *Degree requirements:* For master's, comprehensive exam (for some programs), thesis (for some programs); for doctorate, thesis/dissertation. *Entrance requirements:* For master's, doctorate, and Ed S, GRE General Test. Additional exam requirements/recommendations for international students: Required—TOEFL. *Application deadline:* For fall admission, 7/1 priority date for domestic students; for spring admission, 11/15 for domestic students. Application fee: $50. Electronic applications accepted. *Financial support:* Fellowships, research assistantships, teaching assistantships, and unspecified assistantships available. *Unit head:* Dr. Albert De Chicchis, Interim Head, 706-542-4582, Fax: 706-542-5348, E-mail: alde@.uga.edu. *Application contact:* Dr. Rebecca S. Marshall, Interim Graduate Coordinator, 706-542-0737, E-mail: rshisler@.uga.edu. Web site: http://www.coe.uga.edu/csse/.

University of Guam, Office of Graduate Studies, School of Education, Program in Special Education, Mangilao, GU 96923. Offers M Ed. *Degree requirements:* For master's, comprehensive oral and written exams, special project or thesis. *Entrance requirements:* For master's, GRE General Test. Additional exam requirements/recommendations for international students: Required—TOEFL. *Faculty research:* Mainstreaming, multiculturalism.

University of Hawaii at Manoa, Graduate Division, College of Education, Department of Special Education, Honolulu, HI 96822. Offers M Ed. *Accreditation:* NCATE. Part-time programs available. *Degree requirements:* For master's, thesis optional. *Entrance requirements:* For master's, GRE General Test, interview, minimum GPA of 3.0. Additional exam requirements/recommendations for international students: Required—TOEFL (minimum score 580 paper-based; 237 computer-based; 92 iBT), IELTS (minimum score 5). *Faculty research:* Mild/moderate/severe disabilities, early childhood interventions, inclusion, transition.

University of Hawaii at Manoa, Graduate Division, College of Education, PhD in Education Program, Honolulu, HI 96822. Offers curriculum and instruction (PhD); educational administration (PhD); educational foundations (PhD); educational policy studies (PhD); educational technology (PhD); exceptionalities (PhD); kinesiology (PhD). Part-time and evening/weekend programs available. *Degree requirements:* For doctorate, thesis/dissertation. *Entrance requirements:* For doctorate, GRE General Test, sample of written work. Additional exam requirements/recommendations for international students: Required—TOEFL (minimum score 600 paper-based; 250 computer-based; 100 iBT), IELTS (minimum score 7).

University of Houston, College of Education, Department of Educational Psychology, Houston, TX 77204. Offers administration and supervision - higher education (M Ed); counseling (M Ed); counseling psychology (PhD); educational psychology (M Ed); school psychology (PhD); school psychology and individual differences (PhD); special education (M Ed). *Accreditation:* NCATE. Part-time and evening/weekend programs available. Postbaccalaureate distance learning degree programs offered. *Degree requirements:* For master's, comprehensive exam or thesis; for doctorate, comprehensive exam, thesis/dissertation. *Entrance requirements:* For master's, GRE, transcripts, 3 letters of recommendation, curriculum vita, goal statement; for doctorate, GRE, transcripts, 3 letters of recommendation, curriculum vita, goal statement, writing sample, interview. Additional exam requirements/recommendations for international students: Required—TOEFL (minimum score 550 paper-based; 79 iBT), IELTS (minimum score 6.5). Electronic applications accepted. *Faculty research:* Evidence-based assessment and intervention, multicultural issues in psychology, social and cultural context of learning, systemic barriers to college, motivational aspects of self-regulated learning.

University of Houston–Victoria, School of Education and Human Development, Victoria, TX 77901-4450. Offers administration and supervision (M Ed); counseling (M Ed); curriculum and instruction (M Ed); special education (M Ed). Part-time and evening/weekend programs available. Postbaccalaureate distance learning degree programs offered (minimal on-campus study). *Degree requirements:* For master's, comprehensive exam, project or thesis. *Entrance requirements:* For master's, GRE General Test. Additional exam requirements/recommendations for international students: Required—TOEFL. Electronic applications accepted. *Faculty research:* Reading and language arts education, evaluation and diagnosis of special children's abilities.

University of Idaho, College of Graduate Studies, College of Education, Department of Curriculum and Instruction, Program in Special Education, Moscow, ID 83844-2282. Offers M Ed. *Accreditation:* NCATE. *Students:* 9 full-time, 11 part-time. Average age 32. In 2011, 6 master's awarded. *Entrance requirements:* For master's, minimum GPA of 2.8. *Application deadline:* For fall admission, 8/1 for domestic students; for spring admission, 12/15 for domestic students. Applications are processed on a rolling basis. Application fee: $60. Electronic applications accepted. *Expenses:* Tuition, state resident: full-time $3874; part-time $334 per credit hour. Tuition, nonresident: full-time $16,394; part-time $861 per credit hour. *Required fees:* $2808; $99 per credit hour. Tuition and fees vary according to program. *Financial support:* Research assistantships and teaching assistantships available. Financial award applicants required to submit FAFSA. *Unit head:* Dr. Russell A. Joki, Interim Chair, 208-885-4047. *Application contact:* Erick Larson, Director of Graduate Admissions, 208-885-4723, E-mail: gadms@uidaho.edu.

University of Illinois at Chicago, Graduate College, College of Education, Department of Special Education, Chicago, IL 60607-7128. Offers M Ed, PhD. Part-time programs available. Terminal master's awarded for partial completion of doctoral program. *Degree requirements:* For doctorate, thesis/dissertation. *Entrance requirements:* For master's, minimum GPA of 2.75; for doctorate, GRE General Test, minimum GPA of 2.75. Additional exam requirements/recommendations for international students: Required—TOEFL. Electronic applications accepted. *Faculty research:* Teaching and learning for special learners, individual differences.

University of Illinois at Urbana–Champaign, Graduate College, College of Education, Department of Special Education, Champaign, IL 61820. Offers Ed M, MS, Ed D, PhD, CAS. Part-time programs available. Postbaccalaureate distance learning degree programs offered (minimal on-campus study). *Faculty:* 9 full-time (7 women). *Students:* 44 full-time (39 women), 24 part-time (18 women); includes 13 minority (8 Black or African American, non-Hispanic/Latino; 1 Asian, non-Hispanic/Latino; 4 Hispanic/Latino), 4 international. 44 applicants, 39% accepted, 15 enrolled. In 2011, 15 master's, 5 doctorates awarded. *Entrance requirements:* For master's and doctorate, minimum GPA of 3.0. Additional exam requirements/recommendations for international students: Required—TOEFL (minimum score 102 iBT). *Application deadline:* Applications are processed on a rolling basis. Application fee: $75 ($90 for international students). Electronic applications accepted. *Financial support:* In 2011–12, 35 fellowships, 9 research assistantships, 7 teaching assistantships were awarded; tuition waivers (full and partial) also available. *Unit head:* Michaelene Ostrosky, Interim Head, 217-333-0260, Fax: 217-333-6555, E-mail: ostrosky@illinois.edu. *Application contact:* Laura Ketchum, Manager I, 217-333-2155, Fax: 217-333-6555, E-mail: ketchum@illinois.edu. Web site: http://education.illinois.edu/SPED/.

The University of Iowa, Graduate College, College of Education, Department of Teaching and Learning, Program in Special Education, Iowa City, IA 52242-1316. Offers MA, PhD. *Degree requirements:* For master's, thesis optional, exam; for doctorate, comprehensive exam, thesis/dissertation. *Entrance requirements:* For master's and doctorate, GRE General Test, minimum GPA of 3.0. Additional exam requirements/recommendations for international students: Required—TOEFL (minimum score 550 paper-based; 213 computer-based; 81 iBT). Electronic applications accepted.

The University of Kansas, Graduate Studies, School of Education, Department of Special Education, Lawrence, KS 66045. Offers MS Ed, Ed D, PhD. MS Ed offered jointly with Edwards campus in Overland Park. *Accreditation:* NCATE. Part-time programs available. *Faculty:* 19 full-time (9 women). *Students:* 102 full-time (93 women), 129 part-time (112 women); includes 16 minority (4 Black or African American, non-Hispanic/Latino; 3 American Indian or Alaska Native, non-Hispanic/Latino; 5 Asian, non-Hispanic/Latino; 4 Hispanic/Latino), 19 international. Average age 34. 112 applicants, 71% accepted, 64 enrolled. In 2011, 62 master's, 16 doctorates awarded. *Degree requirements:* For master's, project, thesis or capstone; for doctorate, comprehensive exam, thesis/dissertation. *Entrance requirements:* For master's, minimum GPA of 3.0; for doctorate, GRE General Test, master's degree. Additional exam requirements/recommendations for international students: Required—TOEFL (minimum score 57 computer-based; 23 iBT). *Application deadline:* For fall admission, 3/15 for domestic and international students; for spring admission, 10/15 for domestic and international students. Application fee: $55 ($65 for international students). Electronic applications accepted. Tuition and fees vary according to course load, campus/location, program and reciprocity agreements. *Financial support:* Fellowships with full and partial tuition reimbursements, research assistantships with full and partial tuition reimbursements, teaching assistantships with full and partial tuition reimbursements, Federal Work-Study, scholarships/grants, and unspecified assistantships available. Support available to part-time students. Financial award applicants required to submit FAFSA. *Faculty research:* Autism spectrum disorders, learning disabilities research, leadership development, qualitative research and evaluation. *Unit head:* Chriss Walther-Thomas, Chair, 785-864-4954, Fax: 785-864-4149, E-mail: chrisswt@ku.edu. *Application contact:* Sherrie Saathoff, Admissions and Recruitment, 785-864-0556, Fax: 785-864-4149, E-mail: ssaathoff@ku.edu. Web site: http://soe.ku.edu/specialedu.

University of Kentucky, Graduate School, College of Education, Program in Special Education, Lexington, KY 40506-0032. Offers early childhood special education (MS Ed); rehabilitation counseling (MRC); special education (MS Ed); special education leadership personnel preparation (Ed D). *Accreditation:* CORE; NCATE. Terminal master's awarded for partial completion of doctoral program. *Degree requirements:* For master's, comprehensive exam, thesis optional; for doctorate, comprehensive exam, thesis/dissertation. *Entrance requirements:* For master's, GRE General Test, minimum undergraduate GPA of 2.75; for doctorate, GRE General Test, minimum graduate GPA of 3.0. Additional exam requirements/recommendations for international students: Required—TOEFL (minimum score 550 paper-based; 213 computer-based). Electronic applications accepted. *Faculty research:* Applied behavior analysis applications in special education, single subject research design in classroom settings, transition research across life span, rural special education personnel.

University of Louisville, Graduate School, College of Education and Human Development, Department of Teaching and Learning, Louisville, KY 40292-0001. Offers art education (MAT); curriculum and instruction (PhD); early elementary education (MAT); instructional technology (M Ed); interdisciplinary early childhood education (MAT); middle school education (MAT); music education (MAT); reading education (M Ed); secondary education (MAT); special education (M Ed, MAT); teacher leadership (M Ed). Part-time and evening/weekend programs available. *Degree requirements:* For doctorate, comprehensive exam, thesis/dissertation. *Entrance requirements:* For master's, GRE General Test, PRAXIS II (for some programs); for doctorate, GRE General Test. Additional exam requirements/recommendations for international students: Required—TOEFL (minimum score 560 paper-based; 210 computer-based; 83 iBT). Electronic applications accepted. *Expenses:* Tuition, state resident: full-time $9692; part-time $539 per credit hour. Tuition, nonresident: full-time $20,168; part-time $1121 per credit hour. Tuition and fees vary according to program and reciprocity agreements. *Faculty research:* Mathematics teacher education and ongoing professional development in pedagogy and content knowledge; development of literacy, including early literacy in science and mathematics and literacy development for English language learners; immersive visualizations for promoting STEM education from nanoscience to cosmic scales; evidence-based practices for students with disabilities; urban education, including teacher response to intervention systems in schools and cross-cultural competence.

University of Maine, Graduate School, College of Education and Human Development, Program in Special Education, Orono, ME 04469. Offers M Ed, CAS. *Accreditation:* NCATE. Part-time and evening/weekend programs available. *Students:* 31 full-time (all women), 32 part-time (31 women); includes 1 minority (American Indian or Alaska Native, non-Hispanic/Latino). Average age 35. 13 applicants, 54% accepted, 7 enrolled. In 2011, 17 master's, 1 CAS awarded. *Degree requirements:* For master's, thesis or alternative. *Entrance requirements:* For master's, MAT; for CAS, MA, M Ed, or MS. Additional exam requirements/recommendations for international students: Required—TOEFL. *Application deadline:* For fall admission, 2/1 priority date for domestic students. Applications are processed on a rolling basis. Application fee: $65. Electronic applications accepted. *Expenses:* Tuition, state resident: full-time $5016. Tuition, nonresident: full-time $14,424. *Financial support:* Career-related internships or fieldwork and tuition waivers (full and partial) available. Support available to part-time students. Financial award application deadline: 3/1. *Unit head:* Dr. Janet Spector, Coordinator, 207-581-2444, Fax: 207-581-2423. *Application contact:* Scott G. Delcourt, Associate Dean of the Graduate School, 207-581-3291, Fax: 207-581-3232, E-mail: graduate@maine.edu. Web site: http://www2.umaine.edu/graduate/.

University of Manitoba, Faculty of Graduate Studies, Faculty of Education, Department of Educational Administration, Foundations and Psychology, Winnipeg, MB R3T 2N2, Canada. Offers adult and post-secondary education (M Ed); educational administration (M Ed); guidance and counseling (M Ed); inclusive special education (M Ed); social foundations of education (M Ed). *Degree requirements:* For master's, thesis or alternative.

University of Mary, School of Education and Behavioral Sciences, Department of Education, Bismarck, ND 58504-9652. Offers college teaching (M Ed); curriculum, instruction and assessment (M Ed); early childhood education (M Ed); early childhood special education (M Ed); elementary administration (M Ed); emotional disorders (M Ed); learning disabilities (M Ed); reading (M Ed); secondary administration (M Ed); special education strategist (M Ed). Part-time programs available. *Faculty:* 6 full-time (5 women), 12 part-time/adjunct (8 women). *Students:* 5 full-time (4 women), 77 part-time (56 women); includes 9 minority (1 Black or African American, non-Hispanic/Latino; 4 American Indian or Alaska Native, non-Hispanic/Latino; 1 Asian, non-Hispanic/Latino; 3 Hispanic/Latino), 1 international. Average age 30. 58 applicants, 55% accepted, 29 enrolled. In 2011, 16 master's awarded. *Degree requirements:* For master's, portfolio or thesis. *Entrance requirements:* For master's, interview, letters of reference, minimum GPA of 2.5. Additional exam requirements/recommendations for international students: Required—TOEFL (minimum score 500 paper-based; 197 computer-based; 71 iBT). *Application deadline:* Applications are processed on a rolling basis. Application fee: $40. Electronic applications accepted. *Financial support:* In 2011–12, 1 teaching assistantship with full tuition reimbursement was awarded; career-related internships or fieldwork also available. Financial award application deadline: 8/1; financial award applicants required to submit FAFSA. *Faculty research:* Innovative pedagogy in higher education, technology in education, content standards, children of poverty, children with diverse learning needs. *Unit head:* Dr. Rebecca Yunker Salveson, Director, 701-355-8186, E-mail: rysalves@umary.edu. *Application contact:* Leona Friedig, Administrative Secretary, 701-355-8058, E-mail: lfriedig@umary.edu.

University of Maryland, College Park, Academic Affairs, College of Education, Department of Special Education, College Park, MD 20742. Offers M Ed, MA, PhD, CAGS. *Accreditation:* NCATE. Part-time and evening/weekend programs available. *Faculty:* 24 full-time (20 women), 17 part-time/adjunct (14 women). *Students:* 81 full-time (70 women), 54 part-time (43 women); includes 33 minority (14 Black or African American, non-Hispanic/Latino; 10 Asian, non-Hispanic/Latino; 7 Hispanic/Latino; 2 Two or more races, non-Hispanic/Latino), 5 international. 112 applicants, 54% accepted, 43 enrolled. In 2011, 60 master's, 12 doctorates awarded. *Degree requirements:* For master's, thesis (for some programs); for doctorate, thesis/dissertation, 1-year residency. *Entrance requirements:* For master's, GRE General Test or MAT, minimum GPA of 3.0, 3 letters of recommendation; for doctorate, GRE General Test or MAT, minimum undergraduate GPA of 3.0, graduate 3.5; 3 letters of recommendation. *Application deadline:* For fall admission, 3/1 for domestic students, 2/1 for international students; for spring admission, 9/1 for domestic students, 6/1 for international students. Applications are processed on a rolling basis. Application fee: $75. Electronic applications accepted. *Expenses: Tuition, area resident:* Part-time $525 per credit hour. Tuition, state resident: part-time $525 per credit hour. Tuition, nonresident: part-time $1131 per credit hour. *Required fees:* $386.31 per term. Tuition and fees vary according to program. *Financial support:* In 2011–12, 25 fellowships with full tuition reimbursements (averaging $18,980 per year), 3 research assistantships (averaging $15,863 per year), 7 teaching assistantships (averaging $15,633 per year) were awarded; career-related internships or fieldwork, Federal Work-Study, and scholarships/grants also available. Support available to part-time students. Financial award applicants required to submit FAFSA. *Faculty research:* Educational diagnosis and prescription, mental retardation, severely/profoundly handicapped. *Total annual* *research expenditures:* $4.5 million. *Unit head:* Dennis Kivlighan, Chair, 301-405-2858, Fax: 301-314-9158, E-mail: dennisk@umd.edu. *Application contact:* Dr. Charles A. Caramello, Dean of Graduate School, 301-405-0358, Fax: 301-314-9305.

University of Maryland Eastern Shore, Graduate Programs, Department of Education, Program in Special Education, Princess Anne, MD 21853-1299. Offers M Ed. *Accreditation:* NCATE. *Degree requirements:* For master's, comprehensive exam, seminar paper, internship. *Entrance requirements:* For master's, PRAXIS I, interview, minimum GPA of 3.0. Additional exam requirements/recommendations for international students: Required—TOEFL (minimum score 213 computer-based; 80 iBT). Electronic applications accepted.

University of Massachusetts Amherst, Graduate School, School of Education, Program in Education, Amherst, MA 01003. Offers bilingual, English as a second language, and multicultural education (M Ed, CAGS); child study and early education (M Ed); children, families and schools (Ed D, CAGS); early childhood and elementary teacher education (M Ed); educational leadership (M Ed, CAGS); educational policy and leadership (Ed D); higher education (M Ed, CAGS); international education (M Ed); language, literacy and culture (Ed D); learning, media and technology (M Ed, CAGS); mathematics, science, and learning technologies (Ed D); policy studies in education (CAGS); psychometric methods, educational statistics and research methods (Ed D); reading and writing (M Ed); school counselor education (M Ed, CAGS); science education (CAGS); secondary teacher education (M Ed); social justice education (M Ed, Ed D, CAGS); special education (M Ed, Ed D, CAGS). *Accreditation:* NCATE. Part-time programs available. Postbaccalaureate distance learning degree programs offered (minimal on-campus study). *Faculty:* 81 full-time (46 women). *Students:* 341 full-time (240 women), 333 part-time (226 women); includes 113 minority (36 Black or African American, non-Hispanic/Latino; 1 American Indian or Alaska Native, non-Hispanic/Latino; 14 Asian, non-Hispanic/Latino; 51 Hispanic/Latino; 1 Native Hawaiian or other Pacific Islander, non-Hispanic/Latino; 10 Two or more races, non-Hispanic/Latino), 98 international. Average age 36. 721 applicants, 57% accepted, 202 enrolled. In 2011, 166 master's, 33 doctorates, 25 CAGSs awarded. Terminal master's awarded for partial completion of doctoral program. *Degree requirements:* For doctorate, comprehensive exam, thesis/dissertation. *Entrance requirements:* Additional exam requirements/recommendations for international students: Required—TOEFL (minimum score 550 paper-based; 213 computer-based; 80 iBT), IELTS (minimum score 6.5). *Application deadline:* For fall admission, 1/15 for domestic and international students. Applications are processed on a rolling basis. Application fee: $50 ($65 for international students). Electronic applications accepted. Tuition and fees vary according to course load, campus/location and program. *Financial support:* Fellowships with full and partial tuition reimbursements, research assistantships with full and partial tuition reimbursements, teaching assistantships with full and partial tuition reimbursements, career-related internships or fieldwork, Federal Work-Study, scholarships/grants, traineeships, health care benefits, tuition waivers (full and partial), and unspecified assistantships available. Support available to part-time students. Financial award application deadline: 1/15. *Unit head:* Dr. Linda L. Griffin, Graduate Program Director, 413-545-6984, Fax: 413-545-1523. *Application contact:* Lindsay DeSantis, Interim Supervisor of Admissions, 413-545-0722, Fax: 413-577-0010, E-mail: gradadm@grad.umass.edu. Web site: http://www.umass.edu/education/.

University of Massachusetts Boston, Office of Graduate Studies, Graduate College of Education, School Organization, Curriculum and Instruction Department, Program in Special Education, Boston, MA 02125-3393. Offers M Ed. Part-time and evening/weekend programs available. *Degree requirements:* For master's, comprehensive exam, practicum. *Entrance requirements:* For master's, GRE General Test or MAT, minimum GPA of 2.75. *Faculty research:* Inclusionary learning, cross-cultural special needs, special education restructuring.

University of Memphis, Graduate School, College of Education, Department of Instruction and Curriculum Leadership, Memphis, TN 38152. Offers early childhood education (MAT, MS, Ed D); elementary education (MAT); instruction and curriculum (MS, Ed D); instruction design and technology (MS, Ed D); middle grades education (MAT); reading (MS, Ed D); secondary education (MAT); special education (MAT, MS, Ed D). *Accreditation:* NCATE (one or more programs are accredited). Part-time programs available. Terminal master's awarded for partial completion of doctoral program. *Degree requirements:* For master's, comprehensive exam, thesis or alternative; for doctorate, comprehensive exam, thesis/dissertation. *Entrance requirements:* For master's, GRE General Test, minimum GPA of 2.5; for doctorate, GRE General Test, GRE Subject Test, 2 years of teaching experience. Electronic applications accepted. *Faculty research:* Effective urban teachers, preparation and retention of urban teachers, technology utilization in schools, field-based teacher preparation programs, effective use of online instruction.

University of Miami, Graduate School, School of Education and Human Development, Department of Teaching and Learning, Program in Early Childhood Special Education, Coral Gables, FL 33124. Offers MS Ed, Ed S. Part-time and evening/weekend programs available. *Students:* 16 part-time (all women); includes 12 minority (3 Black or African American, non-Hispanic/Latino; 9 Hispanic/Latino). Average age 38. *Degree requirements:* For master's, electronic portfolio. *Entrance requirements:* For master's, GRE General Test. Additional exam requirements/recommendations for international students: Required—TOEFL (minimum score 550 paper-based; 80 iBT); Recommended—IELTS (minimum score 6.5). Application fee: $65. Electronic applications accepted. *Financial support:* Application deadline: 3/1; applicants required to submit FAFSA. *Unit head:* Dr. Elizabeth Harry, Department Chairperson and Program Director, 305-284-4961, Fax: 305-284-6998, E-mail: bharry@miami.edu. *Application contact:* Maria Papazian, Graduate Admissions Coordinator, 305-284-2963, Fax: 305-284-6998, E-mail: m.papazian@miami.edu.

University of Miami, Graduate School, School of Education and Human Development, Department of Teaching and Learning, Program in Teaching and Learning, Coral Gables, FL 33124. Offers language and literacy learning in multilingual settings (PhD); science, technology, engineering and mathematics (PhD); special education (PhD). *Students:* 19 full-time (14 women); includes 10 minority (3 Black or African American, non-Hispanic/Latino; 7 Hispanic/Latino), 1 international. Average age 34. 12 applicants, 17% accepted, 2 enrolled. In 2011, 9 degrees awarded. *Degree requirements:* For doctorate, thesis/dissertation, qualifying exam. *Entrance requirements:* For doctorate, GRE General Test. Additional exam requirements/recommendations for international students: Required—TOEFL (minimum score 550 paper-based; 80 iBT); Recommended—IELTS (minimum score 6.5). *Application deadline:* For fall admission, 2/15 for domestic students, 10/15 for international students. Application fee: $65. Electronic applications accepted. *Financial support:* In 2011–12, 18 students received support, including 5 fellowships with full tuition reimbursements available (averaging $28,800 per year), 9 research assistantships with full and partial tuition reimbursements available (averaging $28,800 per year), 1 teaching assistantship with full and partial tuition reimbursement available (averaging $28,800 per year). Financial award application deadline: 3/1; financial award applicants required to submit FAFSA. *Faculty research:* Teacher education, multicultural education, technology, second language acquisition, math and science education. *Unit head:* Dr. Elizabeth Harry, Department Chairperson and Program Director, 305-284-4961, Fax: 305-284-6998, E-mail: bharry@miami.edu. *Application contact:* Lois Heffernan, Graduate Admission Coordinator, 305-284-2167, Fax: 305-284-9395, E-mail: lheffernan@miami.edu.

University of Michigan–Dearborn, School of Education, Doctoral Program in Education, Dearborn, MI 48126. Offers curriculum and practice (Ed D); educational leadership (Ed D); educational psychology/special education (Ed D); metropolitan education (Ed D). Part-time and evening/weekend programs available. *Faculty:* 8 full-time (6 women), 2 part-time/adjunct (0 women). *Students:* 47 part-time (34 women); includes 12 minority (6 Black or African American, non-Hispanic/Latino; 3 Asian, non-Hispanic/Latino; 1 Hispanic/Latino; 2 Two or more races, non-Hispanic/Latino). Average age 40. 55 applicants, 35% accepted, 17 enrolled. *Degree requirements:* For doctorate, comprehensive exam, thesis/dissertation. *Entrance requirements:* For doctorate, GRE (taken within the last 5 years), master's degree with minimum GPA of 3.3, 3 letters of recommendation (1 from faculty), 3 years' professional and/or teaching experience. Additional exam requirements/recommendations for international students: Required—TOEFL (minimum score 550 paper-based). *Application deadline:* For fall admission, 3/1 for domestic and international students. Application fee: $60 ($75 for international students). *Financial support:* Scholarships/grants available. *Faculty research:* Educational leadership, metropolitan education, curriculum and practice, educational psychology, special education, assessment. *Unit head:* Bonnie Beyer, Coordinator, 313-593-5583, E-mail: beyer@umd.umich.edu. *Application contact:* Catherine Parkins, Customer Service Assistant, 313-583-6349, Fax: 313-593-4748, E-mail: cparkins@umd.umich.edu. Web site: http://www.soe.umd.umich.edu/soe_edd/.

University of Michigan–Dearborn, School of Education, Programs in Special Education, Dearborn, MI 48126. Offers emotional impairments endorsement (M Ed); inclusion specialist (M Ed); learning disabilities endorsement (M Ed). Part-time and evening/weekend programs available. Postbaccalaureate distance learning degree programs offered (minimal on-campus study). *Faculty:* 4 full-time (all women), 5 part-time/adjunct (1 woman). *Students:* 45 full-time (39 women), 130 part-time (111 women); includes 15 minority (8 Black or African American, non-Hispanic/Latino; 1 Asian, non-Hispanic/Latino; 2 Hispanic/Latino; 3 Native Hawaiian or other Pacific Islander, non-Hispanic/Latino; 1 Two or more races, non-Hispanic/Latino). Average age 36. 21 applicants, 100% accepted, 21 enrolled. In 2011, 54 master's awarded. *Entrance requirements:* For master's, minimum GPA of 3.0, Michigan teaching certificate (for learning disabilities and emotional impairments endorsements); statement of purpose; 2 letters of recommendations. Additional exam requirements/recommendations for international students: Required—TOEFL, TWE. *Application deadline:* For fall admission, 9/5 priority date for domestic students, 8/3 for international students; for winter admission, 12/22 for domestic students, 1/4 for international students; for spring admission, 5/5 for domestic students, 3/4 for international students. Applications are processed on a rolling basis. Application fee: $60. *Financial support:* Career-related internships or fieldwork and Federal Work-Study available. Support available to part-time students. Financial award application deadline: 4/1; financial award applicants required to submit FAFSA. *Unit head:* Dr. Belinda Lazarus, Program Coordinator, 313-436-9136, Fax: 313-593-4748, E-mail: blazarus@umd.umich.edu. *Application contact:* Elizabeth M. Morden, Customer Service Assistant, 313-436-9135, Fax: 313-593-4748, E-mail: emorden@umd.umich.edu. Web site: http://medsped.soe.umd.umich.edu/.

University of Michigan–Flint, School of Education and Human Services, Department of Education, Flint, MI 48502-1950. Offers education (MA); elementary education with teaching certification (MA); literacy (K-12) (MA); special education (MA); technology in education (MA). Part-time programs available. *Entrance requirements:* For master's, BS with minimum GPA of 3.0. Additional exam requirements/recommendations for international students: Required—TOEFL (minimum score 560 paper-based; 220 computer-based; 84 iBT), IELTS (minimum score 6.5). *Expenses:* Contact institution.

University of Minnesota, Twin Cities Campus, Graduate School, College of Education and Human Development, Department of Curriculum and Instruction, Program in Teaching, Minneapolis, MN 55455-0213. Offers Chinese (M Ed); earth science (M Ed); elementary special education (M Ed); English (M Ed); English as a second language (M Ed); French (M Ed); German (M Ed); Hebrew (M Ed); Japanese (M Ed); life sciences (M Ed); mathematics (M Ed); middle school science (M Ed); science (M Ed); second languages and cultures (M Ed); social studies (M Ed); Spanish (M Ed). *Students:* 375 full-time (319 women), 72 part-time (56 women); includes 34 minority (8 Black or African American, non-Hispanic/Latino; 16 Asian, non-Hispanic/Latino; 10 Hispanic/Latino), 5 international. Average age 27. 317 applicants, 70% accepted, 215 enrolled. In 2011, 443 master's awarded. Application fee: $55. *Unit head:* Dr. Nina Asher, Chair, 612-624-1357, Fax: 612-624-8277, E-mail: nasher@umn.edu. *Application contact:* Dr. Jennifer Engler, Assistant Dean, 612-626-2887, Fax: 612-626-7496, E-mail: engle009@umn.edu. Web site: http://www.cehd.umn.edu/ci/.

University of Minnesota, Twin Cities Campus, Graduate School, College of Education and Human Development, Department of Educational Psychology, Program in Special Education, Minneapolis, MN 55455-0213. Offers M Ed, MA, PhD, Ed S. *Students:* 114 full-time (101 women), 30 part-time (23 women); includes 15 minority (6 Black or African American, non-Hispanic/Latino; 2 American Indian or Alaska Native, non-Hispanic/Latino; 4 Asian, non-Hispanic/Latino; 3 Hispanic/Latino), 10 international. Average age 30. 146 applicants, 58% accepted, 70 enrolled. In 2011, 38 master's, 6 doctorates, 21 other advanced degrees awarded. Application fee: $55. *Unit head:* Dr. Susan Hupp, Chair, 612-624-1003, Fax: 612-624-8241, E-mail: shupp@umn.edu. *Application contact:* Dr. Jennifer Engler, Assistant Dean, 612-626-2887, Fax: 612-626-7496, E-mail: engle009@umn.edu. Web site: http://www.cehd.umn.edu/EdPsych/specialEd.

University of Missouri, Graduate School, College of Education, Department of Special Education, Columbia, MO 65211. Offers administration and supervision of special education (PhD); behavior disorders (M Ed, PhD); curriculum development of exceptional students (M Ed, PhD); early childhood special education (M Ed, PhD); general special education (M Ed, MA, PhD); learning and instruction (M Ed); learning disabilities (M Ed, PhD); mental retardation (M Ed, PhD). Part-time and evening/weekend programs available. Postbaccalaureate distance learning degree programs offered (no on-campus study). *Faculty:* 11 full-time (8 women), 1 (woman) part-time/adjunct. *Students:* 26 full-time (23 women), 65 part-time (60 women); includes 7 minority (2 Black or African American, non-Hispanic/Latino; 4 Hispanic/Latino; 1 Two or more races, non-Hispanic/Latino). Average age 33. 56 applicants, 64% accepted, 32 enrolled. In 2011, 31 master's, 3 doctorates awarded. *Degree requirements:* For master's, comprehensive exam, thesis or alternative; for doctorate, comprehensive exam, thesis/dissertation. *Entrance requirements:* For master's and doctorate, GRE General Test, letters of recommendation. Additional exam requirements/recommendations for international students: Required—TOEFL (minimum score 500 paper-based; 173 computer-based; 61 iBT). *Application deadline:* For fall admission, 7/1 priority date for domestic students, 7/1 for international students; for winter admission, 11/1 priority date for domestic students, 11/1 for international students; for spring admission, 4/1 priority date for domestic students, 4/1 for international students. Application fee: $55 ($75 for international students). Electronic applications accepted. *Expenses:* Tuition, state resident: full-time $5881. Tuition, nonresident: full-time $15,183. *Required fees:* $952. Tuition and fees vary according to campus/location and program. *Financial support:* Fellowships with full and partial tuition reimbursements, research assistantships with full and partial tuition reimbursements, teaching assistantships with full and partial tuition reimbursements, career-related internships or fieldwork, scholarships/grants, health care benefits, and unspecified assistantships available. *Faculty research:* Positive behavior support, applied behavior analysis, attention deficit disorder, pre-linguistic development, school discipline. *Total annual research expenditures:* $1.4 million. *Unit head:* Dr. Mike Pullis, Department Chair, E-mail: pullism@missouri.edu. *Application contact:* Glenda Rice, 573-882-4421, E-mail: riceg@missouri.edu. Web site: http://education.missouri.edu/SPED/.

University of Missouri–Kansas City, School of Education, Kansas City, MO 64110-2499. Offers administration (Ed D); counseling and guidance (MA, Ed S); counseling psychology (PhD); curriculum and instruction (MA, Ed S); education (PhD); educational administration (MA, Ed S); reading education (MA, Ed S); special education (MA). PhD in education offered through the School of Graduate Studies. *Accreditation:* NCATE. Part-time and evening/weekend programs available. *Faculty:* 59 full-time (47 women), 57 part-time/adjunct (42 women). *Students:* 221 full-time (155 women), 379 part-time (271 women); includes 140 minority (95 Black or African American, non-Hispanic/Latino; 1 American Indian or Alaska Native, non-Hispanic/Latino; 15 Asian, non-Hispanic/Latino; 27 Hispanic/Latino; 2 Two or more races, non-Hispanic/Latino), 16 international. Average age 33. 332 applicants, 51% accepted, 136 enrolled. In 2011, 131 master's, 4 doctorates, 25 other advanced degrees awarded. *Degree requirements:* For doctorate, thesis/dissertation, internship, practicum. *Entrance requirements:* For master's, GRE, minimum GPA of 2.75, 2 letters of reference, written statement of purpose; for doctorate, GRE, minimum GPA of 3.0; for Ed S, minimum GPA of 3.0. Additional exam requirements/recommendations for international students: Required—TOEFL (minimum score 550 paper-based; 213 computer-based; 80 iBT). *Application deadline:* For fall admission, 4/1 priority date for domestic students, 4/1 for international students; for spring admission, 11/1 priority date for domestic students, 11/1 for international students. Applications are processed on a rolling basis. Application fee: $45 ($50 for international students). *Expenses:* Tuition, state resident: full-time $5798; part-time $322.10 per credit hour. Tuition, nonresident: full-time $14,969; part-time $831.60 per credit hour. *Required fees:* $93.51 per credit hour. *Financial support:* In 2011–12, 15 research assistantships with partial tuition reimbursements (averaging $10,720 per year) were awarded; career-related internships or fieldwork, Federal Work-Study, institutionally sponsored loans, and tuition waivers (full and partial) also available. Support available to part-time students. Financial award application deadline: 3/1; financial award applicants required to submit FAFSA. *Faculty research:* Urban education, inquiry-based field study, theories of counseling and psychotherapy, school literacy, educational technology. *Unit head:* Dr. Wanda Blanchett, Dean, 816-235-2234, Fax: 816-235-5270, E-mail: education@umkc.edu. *Application contact:* Erica Hernandez-Scott, Student Recruiter, 816-235-1295, Fax: 816-235-5270, E-mail: hernandeze@umkc.edu. Web site: http://education.umkc.edu.

University of Missouri–St. Louis, College of Education, Division of Teaching and Learning, St. Louis, MO 63121. Offers autism studies (Certificate); elementary education (M Ed), including early childhood, general, reading; secondary education (M Ed), including curriculum and instruction, general, middle level education, reading, teaching English to speakers of other languages (TESOL); secondary school teaching (Certificate); special education (M Ed), including autism and developmental disabilities, early childhood special education, general; teaching English to speakers of other languages (Certificate). Part-time and evening/weekend programs available. *Faculty:* 32 full-time (16 women), 51 part-time/adjunct (36 women). *Students:* 95 full-time (63 women), 703 part-time (541 women); includes 176 minority (125 Black or African American, non-Hispanic/Latino; 1 American Indian or Alaska Native, non-Hispanic/Latino; 16 Asian, non-Hispanic/Latino; 26 Hispanic/Latino; 8 Two or more races, non-Hispanic/Latino), 11 international. Average age 29. 379 applicants, 90% accepted, 263 enrolled. In 2011, 190 master's, 9 Certificates awarded. *Degree requirements:* For master's, comprehensive exam. *Entrance requirements:* Additional exam requirements/recommendations for international students: Recommended—TOEFL (minimum score 550 paper-based; 213 computer-based). *Application deadline:* For fall admission, 7/1 priority date for domestic students, 7/1 for international students; for spring admission, 12/1 priority date for domestic students, 12/1 for international students. Application fee: $35 ($40 for international students). Electronic applications accepted. *Expenses:* Tuition, state resident: full-time $6273; part-time $3866 per year. Tuition, nonresident: full-time $14,969; part-time $9980 per year. *Required fees:* $315 per year. *Financial support:* In 2011–12, 6 research assistantships with full and partial tuition reimbursements (averaging $9,500 per year), 2 teaching assistantships with full and partial tuition reimbursements (averaging $10,500 per year) were awarded. Financial award application deadline: 4/1; financial award applicants required to submit FAFSA. *Unit head:* Dr. Joseph Polman, Chair, 314-516-5791. *Application contact:* 314-516-5458, Fax: 314-516-6996, E-mail: gadadm@umsl.edu. Web site: http://coe.umsl.edu/web/divisions/teach-learn/index.html.

University of Nebraska at Kearney, Graduate Studies, College of Education, Department of Teacher Education, Kearney, NE 68849-0001. Offers curriculum and instruction (MS Ed); instructional technology (MS Ed); reading education (MA Ed); special education (MA Ed). Part-time and evening/weekend programs available. *Degree requirements:* For master's, comprehensive exam, thesis optional. *Entrance requirements:* For master's, portfolio or GRE. Additional exam requirements/recommendations for international students: Required—TOEFL (minimum score 550 paper-based; 213 computer-based). Electronic applications accepted.

University of Nebraska at Omaha, Graduate Studies, College of Education, Department of Special Education and Communication Disorders, Omaha, NE 68182. Offers special education (MS); speech-language pathology (MA, MS). *Accreditation:* ASHA (one or more programs are accredited); NCATE. Part-time and evening/weekend programs available. *Faculty:* 10 full-time (6 women). *Students:* 27 full-time (25 women), 58 part-time (47 women); includes 4 minority (1 American Indian or Alaska Native, non-Hispanic/Latino; 2 Asian, non-Hispanic/Latino; 1 Hispanic/Latino). Average age 29. 108 applicants, 31% accepted, 15 enrolled. In 2011, 45 master's awarded. *Degree requirements:* For master's, comprehensive exam, thesis (for some programs). *Entrance requirements:* For master's, GRE General Test or MAT, minimum GPA of 3.0, statement of purpose, letters of recommendation. Additional exam requirements/recommendations for international students: Required—TOEFL (minimum score 500 paper-based; 173 computer-based; 61 iBT). *Application deadline:* For fall admission, 2/1 for domestic students; for spring admission, 9/1 for domestic students. Applications are processed on a rolling basis. Application fee: $45. Electronic applications accepted. *Financial support:* In 2011–12, 4 students received support, including 2 research assistantships with tuition reimbursements available; fellowships, career-related internships or fieldwork, Federal Work-Study, institutionally sponsored loans, scholarships/grants, tuition waivers (partial), and unspecified assistantships also available. Support available to part-time students. Financial award application deadline: 3/1; financial award applicants required to submit FAFSA. *Unit head:* Dr. Kristine Swain, Chairperson, 402-554-2201. *Application contact:* Dr. Thomas Lorsbach, 402-554-2201.

University of Nebraska–Lincoln, Graduate College, College of Education and Human Sciences, Department of Special Education and Communication Disorders, Program in Special Education, Lincoln, NE 68588. Offers special education (M Ed). *Accreditation:* NCATE; Teacher Education Accreditation Council. *Degree requirements:* For master's, thesis optional. *Entrance requirements:* For master's, GRE. Additional exam requirements/recommendations for international students: Required—TOEFL (minimum score 500 paper-based; 173 computer-based). Electronic applications accepted.

University of Nebraska–Lincoln, Graduate College, College of Education and Human Sciences, Department of Teaching, Learning and Teacher Education, Lincoln, NE 68588. Offers adult and continuing education (MA); educational studies (Ed D, PhD), including special education (Ed D); teaching, learning and teacher education (M Ed, MA, MST, Ed D, PhD); vocational and adult education (M Ed, MA). *Accreditation:* NCATE. *Degree requirements:* For master's, thesis optional. *Entrance requirements:* Additional exam requirements/recommendations for international students: Required—TOEFL (minimum score 550 paper-based; 213 computer-based). Electronic applications accepted. *Faculty research:* Teacher education, instructional leadership, literacy education, technology, improvement of school curriculum.

University of Nevada, Las Vegas, Graduate College, College of Education, Department of Educational and Clinical Studies, Las Vegas, NV 89154-3066. Offers addiction studies (Advanced Certificate); counselor education (M Ed, MS), including clinical mental health counseling (MS), school counseling (M Ed); mental health counseling (Advanced Certificate); rehabilitation counseling (Advanced Certificate); special education (M Ed, MS, PhD), including early childhood education (M Ed), special education (M Ed); PhD/JD. *Faculty:* 21 full-time (13 women), 20 part-time/adjunct (14 women). *Students:* 166 full-time (137 women), 203 part-time (161 women); includes 109 minority (42 Black or African American, non-Hispanic/Latino; 1 American Indian or Alaska Native, non-Hispanic/Latino; 6 Asian, non-Hispanic/Latino; 47 Hispanic/Latino; 1 Native Hawaiian or other Pacific Islander, non-Hispanic/Latino; 12 Two or more races, non-Hispanic/Latino), 7 international. Average age 35. 204 applicants, 71% accepted, 111 enrolled. In 2011, 218 master's, 3 doctorates, 8 other advanced degrees awarded. *Degree requirements:* For master's, comprehensive exam (for some programs), thesis (for some programs); for other advanced degree, thesis (for some programs). *Entrance requirements:* Additional exam requirements/recommendations for international students: Required—TOEFL (minimum score 550 paper-based; 213 computer-based; 80 iBT), IELTS (minimum score 7). *Application deadline:* For fall admission, 3/1 priority date for domestic students, 5/1 for international students; for spring admission, 9/1 for domestic students, 10/1 for international students. Applications are processed on a rolling basis. Application fee: $60 ($95 for international students). Electronic applications accepted. *Financial support:* In 2011–12, 42 students received support, including 1 fellowship with full tuition reimbursement available (averaging $25,000 per year), 17 research assistantships with partial tuition reimbursements available (averaging $8,703 per year), 24 teaching assistantships with partial tuition reimbursements available (averaging $10,686 per year); institutionally sponsored loans, scholarships/grants, health care benefits, and unspecified assistantships also available. Financial award application deadline: 3/1. *Faculty research:* Multicultural issues in counseling, academic interventions for students with disabilities, rough and tumble play in early childhood, inclusive strategies for students with disabilities, addictions. *Total annual research expenditures:* $614,125. *Unit head:* Dr. Thomas Pierce, Interim Chair/Associate Professor, 702-895-1104, Fax: 702-895-5550, E-mail: tom.pierce@unlv.edu. *Application contact:* Graduate College Admissions Evaluator, 702-895-3320, Fax: 702-895-4180, E-mail: gradcollege@unlv.edu. Web site: http://education.unlv.edu/ecs/.

University of Nevada, Reno, Graduate School, College of Education, Department of Curriculum, Teaching and Learning, Reno, NV 89557. Offers curriculum and instruction (PhD); curriculum, teaching and learning (Ed D, PhD); elementary education (M Ed, MA, MS); secondary education (M Ed, MA, MS); special education and disability studies (PhD). *Degree requirements:* For master's, thesis optional; for doctorate, thesis/dissertation. *Entrance requirements:* For master's, GRE General Test, minimum GPA of 2.75; for doctorate, GRE General Test, minimum GPA of 3.0. Additional exam requirements/recommendations for international students: Required—TOEFL (minimum score 500 paper-based; 173 computer-based; 61 iBT), IELTS (minimum score 6). Electronic applications accepted. *Faculty research:* Education, curricula, pedagogy.

University of Nevada, Reno, Graduate School, College of Education, Department of Educational Specialties, Program in Special Education, Reno, NV 89557. Offers M Ed, MA, MS, Ed D, PhD. Terminal master's awarded for partial completion of doctoral program. *Degree requirements:* For master's, thesis optional; for doctorate, thesis/dissertation. *Entrance requirements:* For master's, minimum GPA of 2.75; for doctorate, GRE General Test, minimum GPA of 3.0. Additional exam requirements/recommendations for international students: Required—TOEFL (minimum score 500 paper-based; 173 computer-based; 61 iBT), IELTS (minimum score 6). Electronic applications accepted. *Faculty research:* Learning disabilities, equity and diversity in educational settings.

University of New England, College of Arts and Sciences, Program in Education, Biddeford, ME 04005-9526. Offers advanced educational leadership (CAGS); curriculum and instruction strategies (CAGS); curriculum and instruction strategy (MS Ed); educational leadership (MS Ed, CAGS); general studies (MS Ed); inclusion education (MS Ed); leadership, ethics and change (CAGS); literacy K-12 (MS Ed, CAGS); teaching methodologies (MS Ed). Part-time programs available. Postbaccalaureate distance learning degree programs offered (minimal on-campus study). *Faculty:* 20 part-time/adjunct. *Students:* 514 full-time (417 women), 218 part-time (165 women). In 2011, 307 master's, 86 CAGSs awarded. *Degree requirements:* For master's, collaborative action research project, integrative seminar portfolio. *Entrance requirements:* For master's, teaching certificate, 2 years of teaching experience. Additional exam requirements/recommendations for international students: Required—TOEFL. *Application deadline:* For fall admission, 9/15 for domestic students; for spring admission, 1/15 for domestic students. Applications are processed on a rolling basis. Application fee: $40. Electronic applications accepted. *Expenses:* Contact institution. *Financial support:* Application deadline: 5/1; applicants required to submit FAFSA. *Faculty research:* Distance learning, effective teaching, transition planning, adult learning. *Unit head:* Dr. Doug Lynch, Chair of Education Department, 207-283-0171 Ext. 2888, E-mail: dlynch@une.edu. *Application contact:* Stacy Gato, Assistant Director of Graduate Admissions, 207-221-4225, Fax: 207-221-4898, E-mail: gradadmissions@une.edu.

University of New Hampshire, Graduate School, College of Liberal Arts, Department of Education, Program in Early Childhood Education, Durham, NH 03824. Offers early childhood education (M Ed); special needs (M Ed). Part-time programs available. *Faculty:* 32 full-time. *Students:* 10 full-time (all women), 5 part-time (all women); includes 1 minority (Black or African American, non-Hispanic/Latino). Average age 30. 8 applicants, 38% accepted, 3 enrolled. In 2011, 6 master's awarded. *Degree requirements:* For master's, thesis or alternative. *Entrance requirements:* For master's, GRE General Test. Additional exam requirements/recommendations for international students: Required—TOEFL (minimum score 550 paper-based; 213 computer-based; 80 iBT). *Application deadline:* For fall admission, 2/1 priority date for domestic students, 2/1 for international students; for spring admission, 12/1 for domestic students. Applications are processed on a rolling basis. Application fee: $65. Electronic applications accepted. *Expenses:* Tuition, state resident: full-time $12,360; part-time $687 per credit hour. Tuition, nonresident: full-time $25,680; part-time $1058 per credit hour. *International tuition:* $29,550 full-time. *Required fees:* $1666; $833 per course. $416.50 per semester. Tuition and fees vary according to course load and degree level. *Financial support:* In 2011–12, 14 students received support. Fellowships, research assistantships, teaching assistantships, career-related internships or fieldwork, Federal Work-Study, scholarships/grants, and tuition waivers (full and partial) available. Support available to part-time students. Financial award application deadline: 2/15. *Faculty research:* Young children with special needs. *Unit head:* Dr. Todd Demitchell, Coordinator, 603-862-5043, E-mail: education.department@unh.edu. *Application contact:* Lisa Wilder, Graduate Coordinator, 603-862-2310, E-mail: education.department@unh.edu. Web site: http://www.unh.edu/education.

University of New Hampshire, Graduate School, College of Liberal Arts, Department of Education, Program in Special Education, Durham, NH 03824. Offers M Ed, Postbaccalaureate Certificate. Part-time programs available. *Faculty:* 32 full-time. *Students:* 11 full-time (9 women), 17 part-time (13 women); includes 1 minority (Asian, non-Hispanic/Latino). Average age 38. 15 applicants, 80% accepted, 8 enrolled. In 2011, 5 master's, 5 other advanced degrees awarded. *Degree requirements:* For master's, thesis or alternative. *Entrance requirements:* For master's, GRE General Test. Additional exam requirements/recommendations for international students: Required—TOEFL (minimum score 550 paper-based; 213 computer-based; 80 iBT). *Application deadline:* For fall admission, 6/1 priority date for domestic students, 4/1 for international students; for spring admission, 12/1 for domestic students. Applications are processed on a rolling basis. Application fee: $65. Electronic applications accepted. *Expenses:* Tuition, state resident: full-time $12,360; part-time $687 per credit hour. Tuition, nonresident: full-time $25,680; part-time $1058 per credit hour. *International tuition:* $29,550 full-time. *Required fees:* $1666; $833 per course. $416.50 per semester. Tuition and fees vary according to course load and degree level. *Financial support:* In 2011–12, 2 students received support. Fellowships, research assistantships, teaching assistantships, career-related internships or fieldwork, Federal Work-Study, scholarships/grants, and tuition waivers (full and partial) available. Support available to part-time students. Financial award application deadline: 2/15. *Unit head:* Dr. Georgia Kerns, Coordinator, 603-862-3446, E-mail: education.department@unh.edu. *Application contact:* Lisa Wilder, Graduate Coordinator, 603-862-2310, E-mail: education.department@unh.edu. Web site: http://www.unh.edu/education.

University of New Mexico, Graduate School, College of Education, Department of Educational Specialties, Program in Intensive Social, Language and Behavioral Needs, Albuquerque, NM 87131-2039. Offers Graduate Certificate. Part-time and evening/weekend programs available. *Students:* 5 part-time (all women); includes 3 minority (all Hispanic/Latino), 1 international. Average age 44. 2 applicants, 100% accepted, 2 enrolled. *Entrance requirements:* Additional exam requirements/recommendations for international students: Required—TOEFL (minimum score 550 paper-based; 213 computer-based). *Application deadline:* For fall admission, 3/31 priority date for domestic students, 3/1 for international students; for spring admission, 9/30 priority date for domestic students, 8/1 for international students. Applications are processed on a rolling basis. Application fee: $50. Electronic applications accepted. *Financial support:* In 2011–12, 1 student received support, including 1 fellowship (averaging $3,600 per year). Financial award application deadline: 3/1; financial award applicants required to submit FAFSA. *Unit head:* Ruth Luckasson, Chair, 505-266-6510, Fax: 505-277-6929, E-mail: ruthl@unm.edu. *Application contact:* Jo Sanchez, Information Contact, 505-277-5018, Fax: 505-277-8679, E-mail: jsanchez@unm.edu. Web site: http://coe.unm.edu.

University of New Mexico, Graduate School, College of Education, Department of Educational Specialties, Program in Special Education, Albuquerque, NM 87131. Offers learning and behavioral exceptionalities (MA); mental retardation and severe disabilities (MA); special education (Ed D, PhD, Ed S). *Accreditation:* NCATE. Part-time and evening/weekend programs available. *Students:* 66 full-time (52 women), 104 part-time (82 women); includes 66 minority (8 Black or African American, non-Hispanic/Latino; 6 American Indian or Alaska Native, non-Hispanic/Latino; 2 Asian, non-Hispanic/Latino; 49 Hispanic/Latino; 1 Two or more races, non-Hispanic/Latino), 8 international. Average age 37. 62 applicants, 60% accepted, 29 enrolled. In 2011, 48 master's, 5 doctorates, 1 other advanced degree awarded. *Degree requirements:* For master's, comprehensive exam, thesis optional; for doctorate, comprehensive exam, thesis/dissertation, screening, proposal hearing. *Entrance requirements:* For master's, minimum GPA of 3.2; for doctorate, minimum GPA of 3.2, 2 years of relevant experience; for Ed S, special education degree, 2 years of teaching experience with people with disabilities, writing sample, minimum GPA of 3.2. *Application deadline:* For fall admission, 3/31 priority date for domestic students; for spring admission, 9/30 priority date for domestic students. Applications are processed on a rolling basis. Application fee: $50. Electronic applications accepted. *Financial support:* In 2011–12, 128 students received support, including 4 fellowships (averaging $1,132 per year), 5 research assistantships with tuition reimbursements available (averaging $3,200 per year), 11 teaching assistantships with tuition reimbursements available (averaging $4,168 per year); career-related internships or fieldwork, Federal Work-Study, scholarships/grants, traineeships, health care benefits, unspecified assistantships, and stipends also available. Support available to part-time students. Financial award application deadline: 3/1; financial award applicants required to submit FAFSA. *Faculty research:* Mathematics instruction, bilingual special education, inclusive education, autism, reading instruction for students with cognitive disabilities, alternative assessment, human rights and disability, applied behavior analysis, bilingualism, language and literacy, mathematics, science instruction, special education. *Unit head:* Prof. Ruth Luckasson, Chair, 505-277-6510, Fax: 505-277-6929, E-mail: luckasson@unm.edu. *Application contact:* Della Gallegos, Information Contact, 505-277-5018, Fax: 505-277-8679, E-mail: dgalle06@unm.edu. Web site: http://coe.unm.edu/departments/ed-specialties/special-education.html.

University of New Orleans, Graduate School, College of Education and Human Development, Department of Special Education, New Orleans, LA 70148. Offers M Ed, PhD, GCE. *Accreditation:* NCATE. Evening/weekend programs available. *Degree requirements:* For doctorate, variable foreign language requirement, thesis/dissertation. *Entrance requirements:* For master's, GRE General Test; for doctorate, GRE General Test, GRE Subject Test. Additional exam requirements/recommendations for international students: Required—TOEFL (minimum score 550 paper-based; 213 computer-based; 79 iBT). Electronic applications accepted. *Faculty research:* Inclusion, transition, early childhood, mild/moderate, severe/profound.

University of North Alabama, College of Education, Department of Elementary Education, Collaborative Teacher Special Education Program, Florence, AL 35632-0001. Offers learning disabilities (MA Ed); mentally retarded (MA Ed); mild learning handicapped (MA Ed). *Accreditation:* NCATE. Part-time and evening/weekend programs available. *Faculty:* 3 part-time/adjunct (all women). *Students:* 1 (woman) full-time, 26 part-time (21 women). Average age 32. In 2011, 3 master's awarded. *Degree requirements:* For master's, comprehensive exam. *Entrance requirements:* For master's, GRE, MAT, or NTE, minimum GPA of 2.5, Alabama Class B Certificate or equivalent, teaching experience. *Application deadline:* For fall admission, 7/1 priority date for domestic students; for spring admission, 12/1 for domestic students. Applications are processed on a rolling basis. Application fee: $25. Electronic applications accepted. *Financial support:* Federal Work-Study available. Support available to part-time students. Financial award application deadline: 4/1. *Unit head:* Dr. Linda Armstrong, Chair, 256-765-4251, Fax: 256-765-4664, E-mail: ljarmstrong@una.edu. *Application contact:* Kim Mauldin, Director of Admissions, 256-765-4608, Fax: 256-765-4960, E-mail: komauldin@una.edu.

The University of North Carolina at Charlotte, Graduate School, College of Education, Department of Special Education and Child Development, Charlotte, NC 28223-0001. Offers academically gifted (Graduate Certificate); child and family studies (M Ed); special education (M Ed, PhD), including academically gifted (M Ed), behavioral - emotional handicaps (M Ed), cross-categorical disabilities (M Ed), learning disabilities (M Ed), mental handicaps (M Ed), severe and profound handicaps (M Ed). Part-time programs available. *Faculty:* 25 full-time (18 women), 7 part-time/adjunct (all women). *Students:* 19 full-time (all women), 107 part-time (100 women); includes 20 minority (16 Black or African American, non-Hispanic/Latino; 1 American Indian or Alaska Native, non-Hispanic/Latino; 2 Hispanic/Latino; 1 Native Hawaiian or other Pacific Islander, non-Hispanic/Latino). Average age 34. 26 applicants, 77% accepted, 16 enrolled. In 2011, 29 master's, 4 doctorates awarded. Terminal master's awarded for partial completion of doctoral program. *Degree requirements:* For master's, thesis or alternative; for doctorate, comprehensive exam, thesis/dissertation, portfolio, qualifying exam. *Entrance requirements:* For master's, GRE or MAT; for doctorate, GRE or MAT, 3 letters of reference, resume or curriculum vitae, minimum GPA of 3.5, master's degree in special education or related field, 3 years of teaching experience. Additional exam requirements/recommendations for international students: Required—TOEFL (minimum score 557 paper-based; 220 computer-based; 83 iBT). *Application deadline:* For fall admission, 7/15 for domestic students, 5/1 for international students; for spring admission, 11/15 for domestic students, 10/1 for international students. Application fee: $65 ($75 for international students). *Expenses:* Tuition, state resident: full-time $3689. Tuition, nonresident: full-time $15,226. *Required fees:* $2198. Tuition and fees vary according to course load and program. *Financial support:* In 2011–12, 12 students received support, including 12 research assistantships (averaging $12,144 per year). Financial award application deadline: 4/1; financial award applicants required to submit FAFSA. *Faculty research:* Transition to adulthood and self-determination, teaching reading and other academic skills to students with disabilities, alternate assessment, early intervention, preschool education. *Total annual research expenditures:* $2.7 million. *Unit head:* David Gilmore, Unit Head, 704-687-8186, Fax: 704-687-2916. *Application contact:* Kathy B. Giddings, Director of Graduate Admissions, 704-687-5503, Fax: 704-687-3279, E-mail: gradadm@uncc.edu. Web site: http://education.uncc.edu/spcd/sped/special_ed.htm.

The University of North Carolina at Greensboro, Graduate School, School of Education, Department of Specialized Education Services, Greensboro, NC 27412-5001. Offers cross-categorical special education (M Ed); interdisciplinary studies in special education (M Ed); leadership early care and education (Certificate); special education (M Ed, PhD). *Degree requirements:* For master's, thesis or alternative. *Entrance requirements:* For master's, GRE General Test. Additional exam requirements/recommendations for international students: Required—TOEFL. Electronic applications accepted.

University of North Dakota, Graduate School, College of Education and Human Development, Program in Special Education, Grand Forks, ND 58202. Offers M Ed, MS. *Accreditation:* NCATE. Part-time programs available. Postbaccalaureate distance learning degree programs offered (minimal on-campus study). *Degree requirements:* For master's, comprehensive exam, thesis or alternative. *Entrance requirements:* For master's, minimum GPA of 3.0. Additional exam requirements/recommendations for international students: Required—TOEFL (minimum score 550 paper-based; 213 computer-based; 79 iBT), IELTS (minimum score 6.5). Electronic applications accepted. *Faculty research:* Visual, emotional, and mental disabilities; early childhood.

University of North Dakota, Graduate School, College of Education and Human Development, Teaching and Learning Program, Grand Forks, ND 58202. Offers elementary education (Ed D, PhD); measurement and statistics (Ed D, PhD); secondary education (Ed D, PhD); special education (Ed D, PhD). *Accreditation:* NCATE. Postbaccalaureate distance learning degree programs offered (minimal on-campus study). *Degree requirements:* For doctorate, comprehensive exam, thesis/dissertation, final exam. *Entrance requirements:* For doctorate, minimum GPA of 3.5. Additional exam requirements/recommendations for international students: Required—TOEFL (minimum score 550 paper-based; 213 computer-based; 79 iBT), IELTS (minimum score 6.5). Electronic applications accepted.

University of Northern Colorado, Graduate School, College of Education and Behavioral Sciences, School of Special Education, Program in Special Education, Greeley, CO 80639. Offers MA, Ed D. *Accreditation:* NCATE. Part-time and evening/weekend programs available. Postbaccalaureate distance learning degree programs offered (no on-campus study). *Degree requirements:* For master's, comprehensive exam, thesis or alternative; for doctorate, comprehensive exam, thesis/dissertation. *Entrance requirements:* For master's, letters of recommendation, interview; for doctorate, GRE General Test, resume. Electronic applications accepted.

University of Northern Iowa, Graduate College, College of Education, Department of Special Education, Cedar Falls, IA 50614. Offers special education (MAE, Ed D); teacher of students with visual impairments (MAE). Part-time and evening/weekend programs available. *Students:* 16 full-time (14 women), 32 part-time (31 women); includes 1 minority (Asian, non-Hispanic/Latino), 3 international. 40 applicants, 35% accepted, 11 enrolled. In 2011, 25 master's, 1 doctorate awarded. *Degree requirements:* For master's, comprehensive exam (for some programs), thesis or alternative; for doctorate, thesis/dissertation. *Entrance requirements:* For master's, minimum GPA of 3.0; for doctorate, GRE, minimum GPA of 3.5. Additional exam requirements/recommendations for international students: Required—TOEFL (minimum score 500 paper-based; 180 computer-based; 61 iBT). *Application deadline:* For fall admission, 8/1 priority date for domestic students. Applications are processed on a rolling basis. Application fee: $50 ($70 for international students). Electronic applications accepted. *Expenses:* Tuition, state resident: full-time $7476. Tuition, nonresident: full-time $16,410. *Required fees:* $942. *Financial support:* Career-related internships or fieldwork, Federal Work-Study, scholarships/grants, and tuition waivers (full and partial) available. Support available to part-time students. Financial award application deadline: 2/1. *Unit head:* Dr. Frank Kohler, Interim Head, 319-273-7484, Fax: 319-273-7852, E-mail: frank.kohler@uni.edu. *Application contact:* Laurie S. Russell, Record Analyst, 319-273-2623, Fax: 319-273-2885, E-mail: laurie.russell@uni.edu. Web site: http://www.uni.edu/coe/specialed/.

University of North Florida, College of Education and Human Services, Department of Exceptional Student and Deaf Education, Jacksonville, FL 32224. Offers American sign language/English interpreting (M Ed); applied behavior analysis (M Ed); autism (M Ed); deaf education (M Ed); disability services (M Ed); exceptional student education (M Ed). *Accreditation:* NCATE. Part-time and evening/weekend programs available. *Faculty:* 7 full-time (5 women), 2 part-time/adjunct (both women). *Students:* 51 full-time (48 women), 48 part-time (45 women); includes 20 minority (9 Black or African American, non-Hispanic/Latino; 2 Asian, non-Hispanic/Latino; 7 Hispanic/Latino; 2 Two or more races, non-Hispanic/Latino), 2 international. Average age 31. 53 applicants, 66% accepted, 25 enrolled. In 2011, 34 master's awarded. *Entrance requirements:* For master's, GRE General Test, minimum GPA of 3.0 in last 60 hours, interview, 3 letters of recommendation. Additional exam requirements/recommendations for international students: Required—TOEFL (minimum score 500 paper-based; 173 computer-based). *Application deadline:* For fall admission, 7/1 priority date for domestic students, 5/1 for international students; for spring admission, 11/1 priority date for domestic students, 10/1 for international students. Applications are processed on a rolling basis. Application fee: $30. Electronic applications accepted. *Expenses:* Tuition, state resident: full-time $8793; part-time $366.38 per credit hour. Tuition, nonresident: full-time $23,502; part-time $979.24 per credit hour. *Required fees:* $1384; $57.66 per credit hour. Tuition and fees vary according to course load and program. *Financial support:* In 2011–12, 44 students received support, including 2 research assistantships (averaging $4,800 per year); teaching assistantships, career-related internships or fieldwork, Federal Work-Study, scholarships/grants, tuition waivers (partial), and unspecified assistantships also available. Support available to part-time students. Financial award application deadline: 4/1; financial award applicants required to submit FAFSA. *Faculty research:* Transition, integrating technology into teacher education, written language development, professional school development, learning strategies. *Total annual research expenditures:* $855,653. *Unit head:* Dr. Karen Patterson, Chair, 904-620-2930, Fax: 904-620-3895, E-mail: karen.patterson@unf.edu. *Application contact:* Lillith Richardson, Assistant Director, The Graduate School, 904-620-1360, Fax: 904-620-1362, E-mail: graduateschool@unf.edu. Web site: http://www.unf.edu/coehs/edie/.

University of North Texas, Toulouse Graduate School, College of Education, Department of Educational Psychology, Program in Special Education, Denton, TX 76203. Offers alternative initial certification (Certificate); autism intervention (M Ed); behavioral specialist (Certificate); EC-12 generalist certification (M Ed); emotional/behavioral disorders (M Ed); gifted education (Certificate); special education (M Ed, PhD, Certificate); teaching students with traumatic brain injury (Certificate); transition (M Ed); transition specialist (Certificate); traumatic brain injury (M Ed). *Accreditation:* NCATE. *Degree requirements:* For master's, comprehensive exam (for some programs); for doctorate, one foreign language, comprehensive exam, thesis/dissertation, internship. *Entrance requirements:* For master's, GRE General Test, bachelor's degree; minimum GPA of 2.8, 3.0 in last 60 undergraduate hours; 2 letters of reference; resume or curriculum vitae; personal statement; for doctorate, GRE General Test, admissions exam, master's degree, minimum GPA of 3.0, 3 years teaching experience, 2 letters of reference, resume or curriculum vitae, personal statement, letter of intent; for Certificate, letter of intent. Additional exam requirements/recommendations for international students: Recommended—TOEFL (minimum score 550 paper-based; 213 computer-based). Electronic applications accepted. *Expenses:* Tuition, state resident: part-time $100 per credit hour. Tuition, nonresident: part-time $413 per credit hour. *Faculty research:* Autism, behavior disorders, learning disabilities, transition, teacher preparation, severe disabilities, families of students with disabilities.

University of Oklahoma, Jeannine Rainbolt College of Education, Department of Educational Psychology, Program in Special Education, Norman, OK 73019. Offers M Ed, PhD. *Accreditation:* NCATE. Part-time and evening/weekend programs available. *Students:* 7 full-time (6 women), 26 part-time (22 women); includes 8 minority (5 Black or African American, non-Hispanic/Latino; 2 American Indian or Alaska Native, non-Hispanic/Latino; 1 Asian, non-Hispanic/Latino), 5 international. Average age 38. 8 applicants, 50% accepted, 3 enrolled. In 2011, 8 master's, 3 doctorates awarded. *Degree requirements:* For master's, thesis optional; for doctorate, variable foreign language requirement, thesis/dissertation. *Entrance requirements:* For master's, minimum GPA of 3.0; for doctorate, GRE General Test, master's degree, minimum graduate GPA of 3.0. Additional exam requirements/recommendations for international students: Required—TOEFL (minimum score 550 paper-based; 79 iBT). *Application deadline:* For fall admission, 3/1 for domestic and international students; for spring admission, 10/1 for domestic students, 9/1 for international students. Applications are processed on a rolling basis. Application fee: $40 ($90 for international students). Electronic applications accepted. *Expenses:* Tuition, state resident: full-time $4087; part-time $170.30 per credit hour. Tuition, nonresident: full-time $14,875; part-time $619.80 per credit hour. *Required fees:* $2659; $100.25 per credit hour. Tuition and fees vary according to course load and degree level. *Financial support:* In 2011–12, 21 students received support. Career-related internships or fieldwork, Federal Work-Study, scholarships/grants, health care benefits, and unspecified assistantships available. Support available to part-time students. Financial award applicants required to submit FAFSA. *Faculty research:* Attitudes toward teaching students with disabilities in inclusive settings, influence of ideological beliefs on attitudes toward inclusion, attitudes toward students with cultural and linguistic diversity, evidence-based reading and writing strategies for students with disabilities, technology enhanced curriculum for students with mild/moderate disabilities, early literacy, relationships based interventions, family systems theory, and efficacy of early intervention, personnel preparation. *Unit head:* Dr. Terri K. Debacaker, Chair, 405-325-1068, Fax: 405-325-6655, E-mail: debacker@ou.edu. *Application contact:* Shannon Vazquez, Graduate Programs Officer, 405-325-4525, Fax: 405-325-6655, E-mail: shannonv@ou.edu. Web site: http://education.ou.edu/special_education.

University of Oklahoma Health Sciences Center, Graduate College, College of Allied Health, Department of Communication Sciences and Disorders, Oklahoma City, OK 73190. Offers audiology (MS, Au D, PhD); communication sciences and disorders (Certificate), including reading; speech-language pathology; education of the deaf (MS); speech-language pathology (MS, PhD). *Accreditation:* ASHA (one or more programs are accredited). Part-time programs available. Terminal master's awarded for partial completion of doctoral program. *Degree requirements:* For master's, comprehensive exam, thesis optional; for doctorate, one foreign language, comprehensive exam, thesis/dissertation. *Entrance requirements:* For master's and doctorate, GRE General Test, 3 letters of recommendation. Additional exam requirements/recommendations for international students: Required—TOEFL (minimum score 550 paper-based). *Faculty research:* Event-related potentials, cleft palate, fluency disorders, language disorders, hearing and speech science.

University of Phoenix–Bay Area Campus, College of Education, San Jose, CA 95134-1805. Offers administration and supervision (MA Ed); adult education and training (MA Ed); early childhood education (MA Ed); education (Ed S); educational leadership (Ed D); elementary teacher education (MA Ed); higher education administration (PhD); secondary teacher education (MA Ed); special education (MA Ed); teacher leadership (MA Ed). Evening/weekend programs available. Postbaccalaureate distance learning degree programs offered (no on-campus study). *Degree requirements:* For master's, thesis (for some programs). *Entrance requirements:* For master's, minimum undergraduate GPA of 2.5, 3 years of work experience. Additional exam requirements/recommendations for international students: Required—TOEFL (minimum score 550 paper-based; 213 computer-based; 79 iBT). Electronic applications accepted.

University of Phoenix–Hawaii Campus, College of Education, Honolulu, HI 96813-4317. Offers administration and supervision (MA Ed); curriculum and instruction (MA Ed); elementary education (MA Ed); secondary education (MA Ed); special education (MA Ed); teacher education for elementary licensure (MA Ed). Evening/weekend programs available. *Degree requirements:* For master's, thesis (for some programs). *Entrance requirements:* For master's, minimum undergraduate GPA of 2.5, 3 years of work experience. Additional exam requirements/recommendations for international students: Required—TOEFL (minimum score 550 paper-based; 213 computer-based; 79 iBT). Electronic applications accepted.

University of Phoenix–Metro Detroit Campus, College of Education, Troy, MI 48098-2623. Offers administration and supervision (MA Ed); elementary teacher education (MA Ed); secondary teacher education (MA Ed); special education (MA Ed). Evening/weekend programs available. *Degree requirements:* For master's, thesis (for some programs). *Entrance requirements:* For master's, 3 years of work experience, minimum undergraduate GPA of 2.5. Additional exam requirements/recommendations for international students: Required—TOEFL (minimum score 550 paper-based; 213 computer-based; 79 iBT). Electronic applications accepted.

University of Phoenix–Omaha Campus, College of Education, Omaha, NE 68154-5240. Offers administration and supervision (MA Ed); curriculum and instruction (MA Ed), including adult education, computer education, curriculum and instruction, English and language arts education, English as a second language, mathematics education; elementary teacher education (MA Ed); secondary teacher education (MA Ed); special education (MA Ed).

University of Phoenix–Online Campus, College of Education, Phoenix, AZ 85034-7209. Offers administration and supervision (MAEd, Graduate Certificate); adult education and training (MAEd); curriculum and instruction (MAEd); curriculum and instruction reading (MAEd); curriculum and instruction-computer education (MAEd); curriculum and instruction-language arts (MAEd); curriculum and instruction-mathematics (MAEd); early childhood education (MAEd); educational studies (MAEd); elementary teacher education (MAEd); elementary teacher education-early childhood (MAEd); secondary teacher education (MAEd); special education (MAEd); teacher education - elementary/middle level (MAEd); teacher education middle level generalist (MAEd); teacher education middle level mathematics (MAEd); teacher education middle level science (MAEd); teacher education secondary mathematics (MAEd); teacher education secondary science (MAEd); teacher leadership (MAEd). *Accreditation:* Teacher Education Accreditation Council. Evening/weekend programs available. Postbaccalaureate distance learning degree programs offered. *Students:* 9,180 full-time (7,178 women); includes 2,913 minority (2,069 Black or African American, non-Hispanic/Latino; 50 American Indian or Alaska Native, non-Hispanic/Latino; 100 Asian, non-Hispanic/Latino; 542 Hispanic/Latino; 48 Native Hawaiian or other Pacific Islander, non-Hispanic/Latino; 104 Two or more races, non-Hispanic/Latino), 147 international. Average age 36. *Entrance requirements:* Additional exam requirements/recommendations for international students: Required—TOEFL, TOEIC (Test of English as an International Communication), Berlitz Online English Proficiency Exam, Pearson Test of English, or IELTS. *Application deadline:* Applications are processed on a rolling basis. Application fee: $45. Electronic applications accepted. *Expenses:* Contact institution. *Financial support:* Scholarships/grants available. Financial award applicants required to submit FAFSA. *Application contact:* 866-766-0766. Web site: http://www.phoenix.edu/colleges_divisions/education.html.

University of Phoenix–Phoenix Main Campus, College of Education, Tempe, AZ 85282-2371. Offers administration and supervision (MA Ed); adult education and training (MA Ed); curriculum and instruction reading (MA Ed); curriculum instruction (MA Ed); early childhood education (MA Ed); education studies (MA Ed); elementary teacher education (MA Ed); secondary teacher education (MA Ed); special education (MA Ed); teacher leadership (MA Ed). Evening/weekend programs available. Postbaccalaureate distance learning degree programs offered. *Students:* 297 full-time (203 women); includes 53 minority (19 Black or African American, non-Hispanic/Latino; 1 American Indian or Alaska Native, non-Hispanic/Latino; 6 Asian, non-Hispanic/Latino; 21 Hispanic/Latino; 2 Native Hawaiian or other Pacific Islander, non-Hispanic/Latino; 4 Two or more races, non-Hispanic/Latino), 3 international. Average age 35. *Entrance requirements:* Additional exam requirements/recommendations for international students: Required—TOEFL, TOEIC (Test of English as an International Communication), Berlitz Online English Proficiency Exam, Pearson Test of English, or IELTS. *Application deadline:* Applications are processed on a rolling basis. Application fee: $45. Electronic applications accepted. *Expenses:* Contact institution. *Financial support:* Scholarships/grants available. Financial award applicants required to submit FAFSA. *Application contact:* 866-766-0766. Web site: http://www.phoenix.edu/colleges_divisions/education.html.

University of Phoenix–Southern Arizona Campus, College of Education, Tucson, AZ 85711. Offers administration and supervision (MA Ed); adult education and training (MA Ed); curriculum instruction (MA Ed); educational counseling (MA Ed); elementary teacher education (MA Ed); school counseling (MSC); secondary teacher education (MA Ed); special education (MA Ed, Certificate). Evening/weekend programs available. *Degree requirements:* For master's, thesis (for some programs). *Entrance requirements:* For master's, minimum undergraduate GPA of 2.5, 3 years of work experience. Additional exam requirements/recommendations for international students: Required—TOEFL (minimum score 550 paper-based; 213 computer-based; 79 iBT). Electronic applications accepted.

University of Phoenix–Utah Campus, College of Education, Salt Lake City, UT 84123-4617. Offers administration and supervision (MA Ed); curriculum and instruction (MA Ed); elementary teacher education (MA Ed); school counseling (MSC); secondary teacher education (MA Ed); special education (MA Ed). Evening/weekend programs available. *Degree requirements:* For master's, thesis (for some programs). *Entrance requirements:* For master's, minimum undergraduate GPA of 2.5, 3 years work experience. Additional exam requirements/recommendations for international students: Required—TOEFL (minimum score 550 paper-based; 213 computer-based; 79 iBT). Electronic applications accepted.

University of Phoenix–Washington D.C. Campus, College of Education, Washington, DC 20001. Offers administration and supervision (MA Ed); adult education and training (MA Ed); computer education (MA Ed); curriculum and instruction (MA Ed, Ed D); early childhood education (MA Ed); education (Ed S); educational leadership (Ed D); educational technology (Ed D); elementary teacher education (MA Ed); English and language arts education (MA Ed); English as a second language (MA Ed); higher education administration (PhD); mathematics education (MA Ed); secondary teacher education (MA Ed); special education (MA Ed); teacher leadership (MA Ed).

University of Pittsburgh, School of Education, Department of Instruction and Learning, Program in Special Education, Pittsburgh, PA 15260. Offers combined studies in early childhood and special education (M Ed); early education of disabled students (M Ed); education of students with mental and physical disabilities (M Ed); general special education (M Ed); special education (Ed D, PhD); special education teacher preparation K-8 (M Ed); vision studies (M Ed). Part-time and evening/weekend programs available. *Students:* 65 full-time (57 women), 87 part-time (76 women); includes 9 minority (3 Black or African American, non-Hispanic/Latino; 2 Asian, non-Hispanic/Latino; 2 Hispanic/Latino; 2 Two or more races, non-Hispanic/Latino), 4 international. Average age 32. 58 applicants, 86% accepted, 45 enrolled. In 2011, 62 degrees awarded. *Degree requirements:* For master's, thesis; for doctorate, thesis/dissertation. *Entrance requirements:* For master's, PRAXIS I; for doctorate, GRE General Test. Additional exam requirements/recommendations for international students: Required—TOEFL.

Application deadline: For fall admission, 2/1 priority date for domestic students; for spring admission, 11/1 priority date for domestic students. Applications are processed on a rolling basis. Application fee: $50. *Expenses:* Tuition, state resident: full-time $18,774; part-time $760 per credit. Tuition, nonresident: full-time $30,736; part-time $1258 per credit. *Required fees:* $740; $200 per term. Tuition and fees vary according to program. *Financial support:* Research assistantships, teaching assistantships, career-related internships or fieldwork, Federal Work-Study, and tuition waivers (partial) available. Support available to part-time students. Financial award application deadline: 3/15; financial award applicants required to submit FAFSA. *Unit head:* Dr. Richard Donato, Chairman, 412-624-7248, Fax: 412-648-7081, E-mail: donato@pitt.edu. *Application contact:* Lauren Spadafora, Graduate Enrollment Manager, 412-648-2230, Fax: 412-648-1899, E-mail: soeinfo@pitt.edu. Web site: http://www.education.pitt.edu/AcademicDepartments/InstructionLearning/Programs/GeneralSpecialEducation.aspx.

University of Puerto Rico, Medical Sciences Campus, Graduate School of Public Health, Department of Human Development, Program in Developmental Disabilities-Early Intervention, San Juan, PR 00936-5067. Offers Certificate. Part-time and evening/weekend programs available.

University of Puerto Rico, Río Piedras, College of Education, Program in Special and Differentiated Education, San Juan, PR 00931-3300. Offers M Ed. *Degree requirements:* For master's, thesis. *Entrance requirements:* For master's, GRE or PAEG, interview, minimum GPA of 3.0, letter of recommendation.

University of Rhode Island, Graduate School, College of Human Science and Services, School of Education, Kingston, RI 02881. Offers adult education (MA); education (PhD); elementary education (MA); music education (MM); reading education (MA); secondary education (MA); special education (MA); MS/PhD. *Accreditation:* NCATE. Part-time and evening/weekend programs available. *Faculty:* 21 full-time (13 women), 3 part-time/adjunct (1 woman). *Students:* 54 full-time (48 women), 108 part-time (86 women); includes 14 minority (3 Black or African American, non-Hispanic/Latino; 4 Asian, non-Hispanic/Latino; 7 Hispanic/Latino), 4 international. In 2011, 56 master's, 8 doctorates awarded. *Degree requirements:* For master's, comprehensive exam (for some programs), thesis optional; for doctorate, comprehensive exam, thesis/dissertation. *Entrance requirements:* For master's, 2 letters of recommendation; interview (for special education applicants); for doctorate, GRE, 3 letters of recommendation, resume. Additional exam requirements/recommendations for international students: Required—TOEFL (minimum score 600 paper-based; 250 computer-based; 100 iBT). *Application deadline:* For fall admission, 1/31 for international students. Application fee: $65. Electronic applications accepted. *Expenses:* Tuition, state resident: full-time $10,432; part-time $580 per credit hour. Tuition, nonresident: full-time $23,130; part-time $1285 per credit hour. *Required fees:* $1362; $36 per credit hour. $35 per semester. One-time fee: $130. *Financial support:* In 2011–12, 4 teaching assistantships with full and partial tuition reimbursements (averaging $12,157 per year) were awarded; career-related internships or fieldwork also available. Financial award applicants required to submit FAFSA. *Unit head:* Dr. David Byrd, Director, 401-874-5484, Fax: 401-874-5471, E-mail: dbyrd@uri.edu. *Application contact:* Dr. John Boulmetis, Coordinator of Graduate Studies, 401-874-4159, Fax: 401-874-7610, E-mail: johnb@uri.edu. Web site: http://www.uri.edu/hss/education/.

University of Rio Grande, Graduate School, Rio Grande, OH 45674. Offers classroom teaching (M Ed), including fine arts, learning disabilities, mathematics, reading education. *Accreditation:* NCATE. Part-time and evening/weekend programs available. *Degree requirements:* For master's, final research project, portfolio. *Entrance requirements:* For master's, minimum GPA of 2.7 in major, 2.5 overall. Additional exam requirements/recommendations for international students: Required—TOEFL. *Faculty research:* Interagency collaboration, reading and mathematics, learning styles, college access, literacy.

University of St. Francis, College of Education, Joliet, IL 60435-6169. Offers educational leadership (MS, Ed D); elementary education certification (M Ed); reading (MS); secondary education certification (M Ed), including English education, math education, science education, social studies education, visual arts education; special education (M Ed); teaching and learning (MS). *Accreditation:* NCATE. Part-time and evening/weekend programs available. Postbaccalaureate distance learning degree programs offered (no on-campus study). *Faculty:* 7 full-time (5 women), 21 part-time/adjunct (14 women). *Students:* 32 full-time (21 women), 230 part-time (175 women); includes 23 minority (7 Black or African American, non-Hispanic/Latino; 2 Asian, non-Hispanic/Latino; 13 Hispanic/Latino; 1 Two or more races, non-Hispanic/Latino), 1 international. Average age 32. 147 applicants, 60% accepted, 57 enrolled. In 2011, 156 master's awarded. *Entrance requirements:* For doctorate, master's degree, IL Type 75 or Principal's endorsement, interview. Additional exam requirements/recommendations for international students: Required—TOEFL (minimum score 550 paper-based; 213 computer-based). *Application deadline:* Applications are processed on a rolling basis. Application fee: $30. Electronic applications accepted. *Expenses:* Contact institution. *Financial support:* In 2011–12, 23 students received support. Federal Work-Study, scholarships/grants, tuition waivers (partial), and unspecified assistantships available. Support available to part-time students. Financial award applicants required to submit FAFSA. *Unit head:* Dr. John Gambro, Dean, 815-740-3829, Fax: 815-740-2264, E-mail: jgambro@stfrancis.edu. *Application contact:* Sandra Sloka, Director of Admissions for Graduate and Degree Completion Programs, 800-735-7500, Fax: 815-740-5032, E-mail: ssloka@stfrancis.edu. Web site: http://www.stfrancis.edu/academics/college-of-education/.

University of Saint Francis, Graduate School, Department of Education, Fort Wayne, IN 46808-3994. Offers special education (MS Ed). *Accreditation:* NCATE. Part-time and evening/weekend programs available. Postbaccalaureate distance learning degree programs offered (no on-campus study). *Faculty:* 3 full-time (all women), 4 part-time/adjunct (all women). *Students:* 4 full-time (all women), 15 part-time (12 women); includes 1 minority (Asian, non-Hispanic/Latino). In 2011, 9 master's awarded. *Degree requirements:* For master's, comprehensive exam. *Entrance requirements:* For master's, MAT, PRAXIS, minimum GPA of 2.5. *Application deadline:* For fall admission, 7/1 priority date for domestic students; for spring admission, 11/1 for domestic students. Applications are processed on a rolling basis. Application fee: $20. Application fee is waived when completed online. *Financial support:* Federal Work-Study, scholarships/grants, tuition waivers (full and partial), and unspecified assistantships available. Support available to part-time students. Financial award applicants required to submit FAFSA. *Unit head:* Dr. Jane Swiss, Dean, 260-399-7700 Ext. 8414, Fax: 260-399-8170, E-mail: jswiss@sf.edu. *Application contact:* Kyna Steury-Johnson, Admissions Counselor, 260-399-7700 Ext. 6316, Fax: 260-399-8152, E-mail: ksteury@sf.edu.

University of Saint Joseph, Department of Autism and Applied Behavior Analysis, West Hartford, CT 06117-2700. Offers applied behavior analysis (Postbaccalaureate Certificate); autism and applied behavior analysis (MS); autism spectrum disorders (Postbaccalaureate Certificate). Part-time and evening/weekend programs available. *Students:* 41 part-time (34 women); includes 4 minority (1 Black or African American, non-Hispanic/Latino; 3 Hispanic/Latino). Average age 38. *Application deadline:* Applications are processed on a rolling basis. Application fee: $50. Electronic applications accepted. Application fee is waived when completed online. *Expenses: Tuition:* Part-time $670 per credit. *Required fees:* $40 per credit. Tuition and fees vary according to course load, degree level, campus/location and program. *Financial support:* Career-related internships or fieldwork and unspecified assistantships available. Support available to part-time students. Financial award applicants required to submit FAFSA. *Application contact:* Graduate Admissions Office, 860-231-5261, E-mail: graduate@usj.edu.

University of Saint Joseph, Department of Education, West Hartford, CT 06117-2700. Offers education (MA); special education (MA). Part-time and evening/weekend programs available. *Students:* 61 full-time (53 women), 792 part-time (688 women); includes 68 minority (30 Black or African American, non-Hispanic/Latino; 7 Asian, non-Hispanic/Latino; 28 Hispanic/Latino; 3 Two or more races, non-Hispanic/Latino). Average age 33. *Degree requirements:* For master's, comprehensive exam, thesis or alternative. *Entrance requirements:* For master's, 2 letters of recommendation. *Application deadline:* Applications are processed on a rolling basis. Application fee: $50. Electronic applications accepted. Application fee is waived when completed online. *Expenses: Tuition:* Part-time $670 per credit. *Required fees:* $40 per credit. Tuition and fees vary according to course load, degree level, campus/location and program. *Financial support:* Career-related internships or fieldwork and unspecified assistantships available. Support available to part-time students. Financial award applicants required to submit FAFSA. *Application contact:* Graduate Admissions Office, 860-231-5261, E-mail: graduate@usj.edu.

University of Saint Mary, Graduate Programs, Program in Special Education, Leavenworth, KS 66048-5082. Offers MA. Part-time and evening/weekend programs available.

University of St. Thomas, Graduate Studies, School of Education, Department of Special Education and Gifted Education, St. Paul, MN 55105-1096. Offers autism spectrum disorders (MA, Certificate); developmental disabilities (MA); director of special education (Ed S); early childhood special education (MA); emotional behavioral disorders (MA); gifted, creative, and talented education (MA); learning disabilities (MA); Orton-Gillingham reading (Certificate); special education (MA). *Accreditation:* NCATE. Part-time and evening/weekend programs available. *Faculty:* 7 full-time (5 women), 31 part-time/adjunct (25 women). *Students:* 23 full-time (19 women), 253 part-time (205 women); includes 31 minority (17 Black or African American, non-Hispanic/Latino; 3 Asian, non-Hispanic/Latino; 5 Hispanic/Latino; 2 Native Hawaiian or other Pacific Islander, non-Hispanic/Latino; 4 Two or more races, non-Hispanic/Latino), 2 international. Average age 36. 123 applicants, 88% accepted, 98 enrolled. In 2011, 57 master's, 2 other advanced degrees awarded. *Degree requirements:* For master's, thesis; for other advanced degree, professional portfolio. *Entrance requirements:* For master's, minimum GPA of 3.0 or MAT; for other advanced degree, MAT or minimum GPA of 2.75. Additional exam requirements/recommendations for international students: Required—TOEFL (minimum score 550 paper-based; 213 computer-based; 80 iBT). *Application deadline:* For fall admission, 6/1 priority date for domestic students; for spring admission, 11/1 priority date for domestic students. Applications are processed on a rolling basis. Application fee: $50. *Financial support:* Fellowships, research assistantships, institutionally sponsored loans, and scholarships/grants available. Support available to part-time students. Financial award applicants required to submit FAFSA. *Faculty research:* Reading and math fluency, inclusion curriculum for developmental disorders, parent involvement in positive behavior supports, children's friendships, preschool inclusion. *Unit head:* Dr. Terri L. Vandercook, Chair, 651-962-4389, Fax: 651-962-4169, E-mail: tlvandercook@stthomas.edu. *Application contact:* Patricia L. Thomas, Department Assistant, 651-962-4980, Fax: 651-962-4169, E-mail: thom2319@stthomas.edu. Web site: http://www.stthomas.edu/education.

University of St. Thomas, School of Education, Houston, TX 77006-4696. Offers all level teaching (M Ed); bilingual/dual language (M Ed); Catholic school teaching (M Ed); Catholic/private school leadership (M Ed); counselor education (M Ed); curriculum and instruction (M Ed); educational leadership (M Ed); elementary teaching (M Ed); English as a second language (M Ed); exceptionality/ educational diagnostician (M Ed); exceptionality/special education (M Ed); generalist (M Ed); reading (M Ed); secondary teaching (M Ed). Part-time and evening/weekend programs available. Postbaccalaureate distance learning degree programs offered (no on-campus study). *Faculty:* 30 full-time (17 women), 54 part-time/adjunct (37 women). *Students:* 66 full-time (43 women), 1,178 part-time (1,044 women); includes 777 minority (313 Black or African American, non-Hispanic/Latino; 5 American Indian or Alaska Native, non-Hispanic/Latino; 29 Asian, non-Hispanic/Latino; 395 Hispanic/Latino; 2 Native Hawaiian or other Pacific Islander, non-Hispanic/Latino; 33 Two or more races, non-Hispanic/Latino), 26 international. Average age 36. 551 applicants, 94% accepted, 416 enrolled. In 2011, 72 master's awarded. *Degree requirements:* For master's, thesis, field experience. *Entrance requirements:* For master's, GRE or MAT if GPA is below 3.0, bachelor's degree; minimum GPA of 2.75 in bachelor's degree or last 60 credit hours; official transcripts from all institutions; goal statement of 250-300 words; 1 reference. Additional exam requirements/recommendations for international students: Required—TOEFL. *Application deadline:* Applications are processed on a rolling basis. Application fee: $35. Electronic applications accepted. *Expenses:* Contact institution. *Financial support:* In 2011–12, 9 students received support. Federal Work-Study, scholarships/grants, and state work-study, institutional employment available. Support available to part-time students. Financial award application deadline: 4/15; financial award applicants required to submit FAFSA. *Faculty research:* Leadership, diversity, personality traits, second language acquisition. *Unit head:* Dr. Nora Hutto, Dean, 713-525-3540, Fax: 713-525-3871, E-mail: education@stthom.edu. *Application contact:* Paula C. Hollis, Administrative Assistant, 713-525-3540, Fax: 713-525-3871, E-mail: education@stthom.edu. Web site: http://www.stthom.edu/Schools_Centers_of_Excellence/Schools_of_Study/School_of_Education/Index.aqf.

University of San Diego, School of Leadership and Education Sciences, Department of Learning and Teaching, San Diego, CA 92110-2492. Offers curriculum and instruction (M Ed); special education (M Ed); special education with deaf and hard of hearing (M Ed); teaching (MAT); TESOL, literacy and culture (M Ed). Part-time and evening/weekend programs available. *Faculty:* 11 full-time (8 women), 41 part-time/adjunct (32 women). *Students:* 86 full-time (69 women), 73 part-time (62 women); includes 54 minority (7 Black or African American, non-Hispanic/Latino; 1 American Indian or Alaska Native, non-Hispanic/Latino; 7 Asian, non-Hispanic/Latino; 27 Hispanic/Latino; 1 Native Hawaiian or other Pacific Islander, non-Hispanic/Latino; 11 Two or more races, non-Hispanic/Latino), 12 international. Average age 28. 177 applicants, 60% accepted, 61 enrolled. In 2011, 57 master's awarded. *Degree requirements:* For master's, thesis (for some programs). *Entrance requirements:* For master's, minimum GPA of 3.0. Additional exam requirements/recommendations for international students: Required—TOEFL (minimum score 580 paper-based; 237 computer-based; 83 iBT), TWE. *Application deadline:* For fall admission, 3/1 priority date for domestic students, 3/1 for international students; for spring admission, 10/15 priority date for domestic students, 10/15 for international students. Application fee: $45. Electronic applications accepted. *Expenses: Tuition:* Full-time $22,482; part-time $1249 per unit. *Required fees:* $224. Full-time tuition and fees vary according to course load and degree level. *Financial support:* In 2011–12, 77 students received support. Career-related internships or fieldwork, Federal Work-Study, institutionally sponsored loans, and stipends available. Support available to part-time students. Financial award application deadline: 4/1; financial award applicants required to submit FAFSA. *Faculty research:* Action research methodology, cultural studies, instructional theories and practices, second language acquisition, school reform. *Unit head:* Dr. Heather Lattimer, Director, 619-260-7616, Fax: 619-260-8159, E-mail: hlattimer@sandiego.edu. *Application contact:* Monica Mahon, Associate Director of Graduate Admissions, 619-260-4524, Fax: 619-260-4158, E-mail: grads@sandiego.edu. Web site: http://www.sandiego.edu/soles/programs/learning_and_teaching/.

University of Saskatchewan, College of Graduate Studies and Research, College of Education, Department of Educational Psychology and Special Education, Saskatoon, SK S7N 5A2, Canada. Offers M Ed, PhD, Diploma. *Degree requirements:* For master's, thesis (for some programs); for doctorate, comprehensive exam (for some programs), thesis/dissertation. *Entrance requirements:* Additional exam requirements/recommendations for international students: Required—TOEFL (minimum score 80 iBT); Recommended—IELTS (minimum score 6.5). Electronic applications accepted.

The University of Scranton, College of Graduate and Continuing Education, Department of Education, Program in Special Education, Scranton, PA 18510. Offers MS. Part-time and evening/weekend programs available. *Students:* 11 full-time (10 women), 2 part-time (both women), 1 international. Average age 27. 3 applicants, 67% accepted. In 2011, 7 master's awarded. *Degree requirements:* For master's, comprehensive exam, capstone experience. *Entrance requirements:* For master's, minimum GPA of 2.75. Additional exam requirements/recommendations for international students: Required—TOEFL (minimum score 500 paper-based; 173 computer-based), IELTS (minimum score 5.5). Application fee: $0. *Financial support:* Unspecified assistantships available. *Unit head:* Dr. Art Chambers, Director, 570-941-4668, Fax: 570-941-5515, E-mail: chambersa2@scranton.edu. *Application contact:* Joseph M. Roback, Director of Admissions, 570-941-4385, Fax: 570-941-5928, E-mail: robackj2@scranton.edu.

University of South Alabama, Graduate School, College of Education, Department of Leadership and Teacher Education, Mobile, AL 36688-0002. Offers early childhood education (M Ed); educational administration (Ed S); educational leadership (M Ed); elementary education (M Ed); reading education (M Ed); science education (M Ed); secondary education (M Ed); special education (M Ed, Ed S). *Accreditation:* NCATE. Part-time programs available. *Faculty:* 20 full-time (14 women). *Students:* 135 full-time (106 women), 75 part-time (62 women); includes 50 minority (40 Black or African American, non-Hispanic/Latino; 3 American Indian or Alaska Native, non-Hispanic/Latino; 3 Asian, non-Hispanic/Latino; 3 Hispanic/Latino; 1 Two or more races, non-Hispanic/Latino), 1 international. 89 applicants, 49% accepted, 36 enrolled. In 2011, 88 master's, 13 Ed Ss awarded. *Degree requirements:* For master's, comprehensive exam. *Entrance requirements:* For master's, GRE General Test or MAT, minimum GPA of 3.0. *Application deadline:* For fall admission, 7/15 priority date for domestic students, 6/15 for international students; for spring admission, 12/1 priority date for domestic students, 11/1 for international students. Applications are processed on a rolling basis. Application fee: $35. *Expenses:* Tuition, state resident: full-time $7968; part-time $332 per credit hour. Tuition, nonresident: full-time $15,936; part-time $664 per credit hour. *Financial support:* Research assistantships and career-related internships or fieldwork available. Support available to part-time students. Financial award application deadline: 4/1. *Unit head:* Dr. Harold Dodge, Jr., Chair, 251-380-2894. *Application contact:* Dr. Abigail Baxter, Director of Graduate Studies, 251-460-6310, Fax: 251-461-1513, E-mail: kharriso@usouthal.edu. Web site: http://www.southalabama.edu/coe/lted.

University of South Carolina, The Graduate School, College of Education, Department of Educational Studies, Program in Special Education, Columbia, SC 29208. Offers M Ed, MAT, PhD. *Accreditation:* NCATE. Part-time programs available. *Degree requirements:* For master's, comprehensive exam; for doctorate, one foreign language, comprehensive exam, thesis/dissertation. *Entrance requirements:* For master's, GRE General Test, MAT, interview, sample of written work; for doctorate, GRE General Test or MAT, interview, sample of written work. *Faculty research:* Strategy training, transition, technology, rural special education, behavior management.

University of South Carolina Upstate, Graduate Programs, Spartanburg, SC 29303-4999. Offers early childhood education (M Ed); elementary education (M Ed); special education: visual impairment (M Ed). *Accreditation:* NCATE. Part-time and evening/weekend programs available. *Faculty:* 8 full-time (6 women), 4 part-time/adjunct (2 women). *Students:* 6 full-time (all women), 69 part-time (63 women); includes 16 minority (14 Black or African American, non-Hispanic/Latino; 2 Two or more races, non-Hispanic/Latino), 2 international. Average age 33. In 2011, 8 master's awarded. *Degree requirements:* For master's, professional portfolio. *Entrance requirements:* For master's, GRE General Test or MAT, interview, minimum undergraduate GPA of 2.5, teaching certificate, 2 letters of recommendation. *Application deadline:* Applications are processed on a rolling basis. Application fee: $40. *Expenses:* Tuition, state resident: full-time $10,916; part-time $455 per credit hour. Tuition, nonresident: full-time $23,444; part-time $977 per credit hour. *Required fees:* $450 per semester. Tuition and fees vary according to course load and program. *Financial support:* Institutionally sponsored loans and institutional work-study available. Financial award application deadline: 7/15; financial award applicants required to submit FAFSA. *Faculty research:* Rough and tumble play, social justice education, American Indian literatures and cultures, diversity and multicultural education, science teaching strategy. *Unit head:* Dr. Tina Herzberg, Director of Graduate Programs, 864-503-5572, Fax: 864-503-5573, E-mail: rstevens@uscupstate.edu. *Application contact:* Donette Stewart, Associate Vice Chancellor for Enrollment Services, 864-503-5280, E-mail: dstewart@uscupstate.edu. Web site: http://www.uscupstate.edu/graduate/.

The University of South Dakota, Graduate School, School of Education, Division of Curriculum and Instruction, Program in Special Education, Vermillion, SD 57069-2390. Offers MA. *Accreditation:* NCATE. Part-time programs available. Postbaccalaureate distance learning degree programs offered. *Degree requirements:* For master's, comprehensive exam, thesis or alternative. *Entrance requirements:* For master's, GRE General Test, MAT, minimum GPA of 2.7. Additional exam requirements/recommendations for international students: Required—TOEFL (minimum score 550 paper-based; 213 computer-based; 79 iBT). Electronic applications accepted. *Expenses:* Tuition, state resident: full-time $3118.50; part-time $173.25 per credit hour. Tuition, nonresident: full-time $6601; part-time $366.70 per credit hour. *Required fees:* $2268; $126 per credit hour. Tuition and fees vary according to program.

University of Southern Maine, School of Education and Human Development, Abilities and Disabilities Studies Program, Portland, ME 04104-9300. Offers gifted and talented (MS); self-design in special education (MS); teaching all students (MS); teaching all students (Certificate). *Accreditation:* Teacher Education Accreditation Council. Part-time and evening/weekend programs available. *Degree requirements:* For master's, thesis or alternative, portfolio. *Entrance requirements:* For master's, proof of teacher certification. Additional exam requirements/recommendations for international students: Required—TOEFL (minimum score 550 paper-based; 213 computer-based; 79 iBT). Electronic applications accepted. *Faculty research:* Moderate-to-severe disabilities, gifted and talented.

University of Southern Mississippi, Graduate School, College of Education and Psychology, Department of Curriculum, Instruction, and Special Education, Hattiesburg, MS 39406-0001. Offers alternative secondary teacher education (MAT); early childhood education (M Ed, Ed S); education (Ed D); education of the gifted (M Ed, PhD, Ed S); elementary education (M Ed, PhD, Ed S); reading (M Ed, MS); secondary education (M Ed, MS, PhD); special education (M Ed, PhD, Ed S). Part-time programs available. *Faculty:* 23 full-time (17 women), 3 part-time/adjunct (2 women). *Students:* 39 full-time (34 women), 92 part-time (77 women); includes 36 minority (31 Black or African American, non-Hispanic/Latino; 3 Hispanic/Latino; 2 Two or more races, non-Hispanic/Latino), 3 international. Average age 37. 56 applicants, 55% accepted, 29 enrolled. In 2011, 45 master's, 5 doctorates awarded. *Degree requirements:* For master's and Ed S, comprehensive exam, thesis (for some programs); for doctorate, comprehensive exam, thesis/dissertation. *Entrance requirements:* For master's, GRE General Test, MAT, minimum GPA of 3.0; for doctorate, GRE General Test, minimum GPA of 3.5; for Ed S, GRE General Test, MAT, minimum GPA of 3.25. Additional exam requirements/recommendations for international students: Required—TOEFL, IELTS. *Application deadline:* For fall admission, 3/1 priority date for domestic students, 3/1 for international students; for spring admission, 1/10 priority date for domestic students, 1/10 for international students. Applications are processed on a rolling basis. Application fee: $50. *Financial support:* In 2011–12, 9 research assistantships with tuition reimbursements (averaging $18,316 per year), 2 teaching assistantships with full tuition reimbursements (averaging $8,500 per year) were awarded; Federal Work-Study, institutionally sponsored loans, scholarships/grants, health care benefits, tuition waivers (partial), and unspecified assistantships also available. Financial award application deadline: 3/15; financial award applicants required to submit FAFSA. *Faculty research:* Mathematical problem solving, integrative curriculum, writing process, teacher education models. *Total annual research expenditures:* $100,000. *Unit head:* Dr. David Daves, Chair, 601-266-4547, Fax: 601-266-4175, E-mail: david.daves@usm.edu. *Application contact:* Dr. Marie Crowe, Director of Graduate Studies, 601-266-6005, Fax: 601-266-4548, E-mail: margie.crowe@usm.edu. Web site: http://www.usm.edu/graduateschool/table.php.

University of South Florida, Graduate School, College of Education, Department of Special Education, Tampa, FL 33620-9951. Offers autism spectrum disorders and severe intellectual disabilities (MA); behavior disorders (MA); exceptional student education (MA, MAT); gifted education (MA); mental retardation (MA); special education (PhD); specific learning disabilities (MA). *Accreditation:* NCATE. Part-time and evening/weekend programs available. *Faculty:* 12 full-time (9 women), 2 part-time/adjunct (1 woman). *Students:* 62 full-time (49 women), 104 part-time (94 women); includes 44 minority (22 Black or African American, non-Hispanic/Latino; 2 American Indian or Alaska Native, non-Hispanic/Latino; 4 Asian, non-Hispanic/Latino; 15 Hispanic/Latino; 1 Two or more races, non-Hispanic/Latino), 3 international. Average age 36. 131 applicants, 62% accepted, 60 enrolled. In 2011, 34 master's, 2 doctorates awarded. *Median time to degree:* Of those who began their doctoral program in fall 2003, 14% received their degree in 8 years or less. *Degree requirements:* For master's, comprehensive exam; for doctorate, comprehensive exam, thesis/dissertation, philosophies of inquiry; multiple research methods. *Entrance requirements:* For master's, GRE General Test (if undergraduate GPA less than 3.0), minimum GPA of 3.0 in last 60 hours of course work; for doctorate, GRE General Test, minimum GPA of 3.0 undergraduate, 3.5 graduate; interview. Additional exam requirements/recommendations for international students: Required—TOEFL (minimum score 500 paper-based; 213 computer-based). *Application deadline:* For fall admission, 2/15 for domestic students, 1/2 for international students; for winter admission, 2/15 for domestic students, 1/2 for international students; for spring admission, 10/15 for domestic students, 6/1 for international students. Application fee: $30. Electronic applications accepted. *Financial support:* In 2011–12, 3 fellowships with full tuition reimbursements (averaging $10,000 per year), 4 research assistantships with full tuition reimbursements (averaging $10,000 per year), 7 teaching assistantships with full tuition reimbursements (averaging $10,000 per year) were awarded; scholarships/grants and unspecified assistantships also available. Financial award application deadline: 6/1; financial award applicants required to submit FAFSA. *Faculty research:* Instruction methods for students with learning and behavioral disabilities; teacher preparation, experiential learning, and participatory action research; public policy research; personal preparation for transitional services; case-based instruction, partnerships and mentor development; inclusion and voices of teachers and students with disabilities; narrative ethics and philosophies of research. *Total annual research expenditures:* $2.9 million. *Unit head:* Dr. Daphne Thomas, Chairperson, 813-974-1383, Fax: 813-974-5542, E-mail: dthomas@usf.edu. *Application contact:* Dr. Diane Briscoe, Coordinator of Graduate Studies, 813-974-1804, Fax: 813-974-3391, E-mail: briscoe@usf.edu. Web site: http://www.coedu.usf.edu/main/departments/sped/sped.html.

The University of Tennessee, Graduate School, College of Education, Health and Human Sciences, Program in Education, Knoxville, TN 37996. Offers art education (MS); counseling education (PhD); cultural studies in education (PhD); curriculum (MS, Ed S); curriculum, educational research and evaluation (Ed D, PhD); early childhood education (PhD); early childhood special education (MS); education of deaf and hard of hearing (MS); educational administration and policy studies (Ed D, PhD); educational administration and supervision (Ed S); educational psychology (Ed D, PhD); elementary education (MS, Ed S); elementary teaching (MS); English education (MS, Ed S); exercise science (PhD); foreign language/ESL education (MS, Ed S); instructional technology (MS, Ed D, PhD, Ed S); literacy, language and ESL education (PhD); literacy, language education, and ESL education (Ed D); mathematics education (MS, Ed S); modified and comprehensive special education (MS); reading education (MS, Ed S); school counseling (Ed S); school psychology (PhD, Ed S); science education (MS, Ed S); secondary teaching (MS); social foundations (MS); social science education (MS, Ed S); socio-cultural foundations of sports and education (PhD); special education (Ed S); teacher education (Ed D, PhD). *Accreditation:* NCATE. Part-time and evening/weekend programs available. *Degree requirements:* For master's and Ed S, thesis optional; for doctorate, variable foreign language requirement, thesis/dissertation. *Entrance requirements:* For master's, minimum GPA of 2.7; for doctorate and Ed S, GRE General Test, minimum GPA of 2.7. Additional exam requirements/recommendations for international students: Required—TOEFL. Electronic applications accepted. *Expenses:* Tuition, state resident: full-time $8332; part-time $464 per credit hour. Tuition, nonresident: full-time $25,174; part-time $1400 per credit hour. *Required fees:* $1162; $56 per credit hour. Tuition and fees vary according to program.

The University of Tennessee at Chattanooga, Graduate School, College of Health, Education and Professional Studies, School of Education, Chattanooga, TN 37403-2598. Offers counseling (M Ed), including community counseling, school counseling; education (M Ed, Post-Master's Certificate), including elementary education (M Ed), school leadership, secondary education (M Ed), special education (M Ed); educational specialist (Ed S), including educational technology, school psychology; learning and leadership (Ed D), including educational leadership. *Accreditation:* ACA; NCATE. Part-time and evening/weekend programs available. Postbaccalaureate distance learning degree programs offered (no on-campus study). *Faculty:* 25 full-time (17 women), 10 part-time/adjunct (3 women). *Students:* 145 full-time (104 women), 319 part-time (236 women); includes 63 minority (43 Black or African American, non-Hispanic/Latino; 4 American Indian or Alaska Native, non-Hispanic/Latino; 2 Asian, non-Hispanic/Latino; 6 Hispanic/Latino; 8 Two or more races, non-Hispanic/Latino), 2 international. Average

age 34. 226 applicants, 79% accepted, 111 enrolled. In 2011, 120 master's, 9 doctorates, 17 other advanced degrees awarded. *Degree requirements:* For master's, comprehensive exam, thesis optional, culminating experience; for doctorate, comprehensive exam, thesis/dissertation; for other advanced degree, internship. *Entrance requirements:* For master's, GRE General Test, PPST 1, teaching certificate; for doctorate, GRE General Test, master's degree, two years of practical work experience in organizational environment; for other advanced degree, GRE General Test, letters of reference. Additional exam requirements/recommendations for international students: Required—TOEFL (minimum score 550 paper-based; 213 computer-based; 79 iBT), IELTS (minimum score 6). *Application deadline:* For fall admission, 8/1 for domestic students, 6/1 for international students; for spring admission, 12/1 for domestic students, 10/1 for international students. Applications are processed on a rolling basis. Application fee: $35. Electronic applications accepted. *Expenses:* Tuition, state resident: full-time $6472; part-time $359 per credit hour. Tuition, nonresident: full-time $20,006; part-time $1111 per credit hour. *Required fees:* $1320; $160 per credit hour. *Financial support:* Career-related internships or fieldwork, institutionally sponsored loans, scholarships/grants, and unspecified assistantships available. Support available to part-time students. Financial award applicants required to submit FAFSA. *Faculty research:* School counseling, community counseling, elementary and secondary education, school leadership and administration. *Total annual research expenditures:* $675,479. *Unit head:* Dr. John Freeman, Head, 423-425-4133, Fax: 423-425-5380, E-mail: john-freeman@utc.edu. *Application contact:* Dr. Jerald Ainsworth, Dean of Graduate Studies, 423-425-4478, Fax: 423-425-5223, E-mail: jerald-ainsworth@utc.edu. Web site: http://www.utc.edu/Administration/HealthEducationAndProfessionalStudies/Graduate_Studies/graduate_studies.html.

The University of Texas at Austin, Graduate School, College of Education, Department of Special Education, Austin, TX 78712-1111. Offers autism and developmental disabilities (Ed D, PhD); autism and developmental disability (M Ed, MA); early childhood special education (M Ed, MA, Ed D, PhD); learning disabilities (Ed D, PhD); learning disabilities/behavior disorders (M Ed, MA); multicultural special education (M Ed, MA, Ed D, PhD); rehabilitation counselor (M Ed); rehabilitation counselor education (Ed D, PhD); special education administration (Ed D, PhD). *Accreditation:* CORE. Part-time and evening/weekend programs available. Postbaccalaureate distance learning degree programs offered (no on-campus study). *Degree requirements:* For master's, thesis or alternative; for doctorate, thesis/dissertation. *Entrance requirements:* For master's and doctorate, GRE General Test. *Application deadline:* For fall admission, 2/1 priority date for domestic students; for spring admission, 10/1 priority date for domestic students. Applications are processed on a rolling basis. Application fee: $50 ($75 for international students). *Financial support:* Fellowships with tuition reimbursements, research assistantships with partial tuition reimbursements, teaching assistantships with partial tuition reimbursements, career-related internships or fieldwork, Federal Work-Study, institutionally sponsored loans, scholarships/grants, tuition waivers (full and partial), and unspecified assistantships available. Financial award application deadline: 2/1. *Faculty research:* Anchored instruction, reading disabilities, multicultural/bilingual. *Unit head:* Herbert J. Rieth, Jr., Chairman, 512-475-6552, Fax: 512-471-2471, E-mail: rieth.herb@mail.utexas.edu. *Application contact:* James Schaller, Graduate Adviser, 512-475-6543, E-mail: jschaller@mail.utexas.edu. Web site: http://www.edb.utexas.edu/coe/depts/sped.html.

The University of Texas at Brownsville, Graduate Studies, School of Education, Brownsville, TX 78520-4991. Offers bilingual education (M Ed); counseling and guidance (M Ed); curriculum and instruction (M Ed); early childhood education (M Ed); educational administration (M Ed); educational technology (M Ed); English as a second language (M Ed); reading specialist (M Ed); special education/educational diagnostician (M Ed). Part-time and evening/weekend programs available. Postbaccalaureate distance learning degree programs offered (minimal on-campus study). *Degree requirements:* For master's, thesis optional. *Entrance requirements:* For master's, GRE General Test. Additional exam requirements/recommendations for international students: Required—TOEFL.

The University of Texas at El Paso, Graduate School, College of Education, Department of Educational Psychology and Special Services, El Paso, TX 79968-0001. Offers educational diagnostics (M Ed); guidance and counseling (M Ed); special education (M Ed). Part-time and evening/weekend programs available. *Students:* 289 (250 women); includes 252 minority (9 Black or African American, non-Hispanic/Latino; 1 American Indian or Alaska Native, non-Hispanic/Latino; 2 Asian, non-Hispanic/Latino; 240 Hispanic/Latino), 11 international. Average age 34. 85 applicants, 71% accepted, 53 enrolled. In 2011, 53 master's awarded. *Degree requirements:* For master's, thesis optional. *Entrance requirements:* For master's, minimum GPA of 3.0. Additional exam requirements/recommendations for international students: Required—TOEFL. *Application deadline:* For fall admission, 7/1 priority date for domestic students, 3/1 for international students; for spring admission, 11/1 priority date for domestic students, 9/1 for international students. Applications are processed on a rolling basis. Application fee: $15 ($65 for international students). Electronic applications accepted. *Financial support:* In 2011–12, research assistantships with partial tuition reimbursements (averaging $16,642 per year), teaching assistantships with partial tuition reimbursements (averaging $13,314 per year) were awarded; Federal Work-Study, institutionally sponsored loans, and tuition waivers (partial) also available. Financial award application deadline: 3/15; financial award applicants required to submit FAFSA. *Unit head:* Dr. Don C. Combs, Interim Chair, 915-747-7585, E-mail: dcombs@utep.edu. *Application contact:* Dr. Benjamin Flores, Interim Dean of the Graduate School, 915-747-5491, Fax: 915-747-5788, E-mail: bflores@utep.edu.

The University of Texas at San Antonio, College of Education and Human Development, Department of Interdisciplinary Learning and Teaching, San Antonio, TX 78249-0617. Offers adult learning and teaching (MA); education (MA), including curriculum and instruction, early childhood and elementary education, educational psychology/special education, instructional technology, reading and literacy education; interdisciplinary learning and teaching (PhD). Part-time and evening/weekend programs available. *Faculty:* 26 full-time (21 women), 1 (woman) part-time/adjunct. *Students:* 131 full-time (100 women), 357 part-time (283 women); includes 275 minority (31 Black or African American, non-Hispanic/Latino; 9 Asian, non-Hispanic/Latino; 227 Hispanic/Latino; 8 Two or more races, non-Hispanic/Latino), 31 international. Average age 33. 239 applicants, 75% accepted, 120 enrolled. In 2011, 119 master's awarded. *Degree requirements:* For master's, comprehensive exam, thesis optional, 36 hours of course work without thesis (33 with thesis); for doctorate, comprehensive exam, thesis/dissertation, minimum of 60 semester credit hours. *Entrance requirements:* For master's, GRE General Test, bachelor's degree with minimum GPA of 3.0 in last 60 hours of coursework; resume; two letters of recommendation; statement of purpose; for doctorate, GRE, transcripts from all colleges and universities attended, professional vitae demonstrating experience in work environment where education was primary professional emphasis, 3 letters of recommendation, statement of purpose, master's degree transcript documenting minimum GPA of 3.5. Additional exam requirements/recommendations for international students: Required—TOEFL (minimum score 500 paper-based; 61 iBT), IELTS (minimum score 5). *Application deadline:* For fall admission, 7/1 for domestic students, 4/1 for international students; for spring admission, 11/1 for domestic students, 9/1 for international students. Application fee: $45 ($85 for international students). *Expenses:* Tuition, state resident: full-time $3148; part-time $2176 per semester. Tuition, nonresident: full-time $8782; part-time $5932 per semester. *Required fees:* $719 per semester. *Financial support:* In 2011–12, 9 fellowships with partial tuition reimbursements (averaging $27,000 per year) were awarded; career-related internships or fieldwork, Federal Work-Study, and scholarships/grants also available. Support available to part-time students. *Faculty research:* Explorations of science, learning and teaching, family Involvement in early childhood, culturally-responsive literacy instruction in diverse settings, STEM education, autism spectrum disorders. *Total annual research expenditures:* $5.9 million. *Unit head:* Dr. Maria R. Cortez, Department Chair, 210-458-5969, Fax: 210-458-7281, E-mail: mari.cortez@utsa.edu. *Application contact:* Erin Doran, Student Development Specialist, 210-458-7443, Fax: 210-458-7281, E-mail: erin.doran@utsa.edu.

The University of Texas at Tyler, College of Education and Psychology, School of Education, Tyler, TX 75799-0001. Offers early childhood education (M Ed, MA); reading (M Ed, MA); special education (M Ed, MA). Part-time and evening/weekend programs available. *Degree requirements:* For master's, comprehensive exam, thesis (for some programs), research project. *Entrance requirements:* For master's, GRE General Test. Additional exam requirements/recommendations for international students: Required—TOEFL (minimum score 79 computer-based). Electronic applications accepted. *Faculty research:* Improving quality in childcare settings, play and creativity, teacher interactions, effects of modeling on early childhood teachers, biofeedback, literacy instruction.

The University of Texas of the Permian Basin, Office of Graduate Studies, School of Education, Program in Special Education, Odessa, TX 79762-0001. Offers MA. *Degree requirements:* For master's, comprehensive exam (for some programs), thesis (for some programs). *Entrance requirements:* For master's, GRE General Test. Additional exam requirements/recommendations for international students: Required—TOEFL (minimum score 550 paper-based; 213 computer-based).

The University of Texas–Pan American, College of Education, Department of Educational Psychology, Edinburg, TX 78539. Offers educational diagnostician (M Ed); gifted education (M Ed); guidance and counseling (M Ed); school psychology (MA); special education (M Ed). Part-time and evening/weekend programs available. *Degree requirements:* For master's, comprehensive exam (for some programs), thesis (for some programs). *Entrance requirements:* For master's, GRE General Test, interview. *Application deadline:* For fall admission, 7/17 for domestic students; for spring admission, 11/16 for domestic students. Application fee: $0. Tuition and fees vary according to course load, program and student level. *Financial support:* Research assistantships, career-related internships or fieldwork, Federal Work-Study, and institutionally sponsored loans available. Support available to part-time students. Financial award application deadline: 4/15. *Faculty research:* Reading instruction, assessment practice, behavior interventions consultation, mental retardation. *Unit head:* Dr. Paul Sale, Chair, 956-665-2433, E-mail: psale@utpa.edu. *Application contact:* Dr. Sylvia Ramirez, Associate Dean of Graduate Studies, 956-665-3488, E-mail: ramirezs@utpa.edu. Web site: http://portal.utpa.edu/utpa_main/daa_home/coed_home/edpsy_home.

University of the Cumberlands, Graduate Programs in Education, Williamsburg, KY 40769-1372. Offers all grades (P-12) (M Ed); business and marketing (MA Ed, MAT); director of pupil personnel (Certificate); director of special education (Certificate); educational administration and supervision (Ed S); educational leadership (Ed D); elementary education (MA Ed, MAT); instructional leadership - principalship (MA Ed); instructional leadership - school principal (Certificate); middle school education (MA Ed, MAT); reading and writing (MA Ed); school counseling (MA Ed); school superintendent (Certificate); secondary education (MA Ed, MAT); special education (MAT); supervisor of instruction (Certificate); teacher leader (MA Ed). Part-time and evening/weekend programs available. Postbaccalaureate distance learning degree programs offered. *Degree requirements:* For master's, comprehensive exam. Electronic applications accepted.

University of the District of Columbia, College of Arts and Sciences, Department of Education, Program in Special Education, Washington, DC 20008-1175. Offers MA. *Accreditation:* NCATE. Part-time programs available. *Expenses: Tuition, area resident:* Full-time $7580; part-time $421 per credit hour. Tuition, state resident: full-time $8580; part-time $477 per credit hour. Tuition, nonresident: full-time $14,580; part-time $810 per credit hour. *Required fees:* $620; $30 per credit hour. $310 per semester.

University of the Incarnate Word, School of Graduate Studies and Research, Dreeben School of Education, Programs in Education, San Antonio, TX 78209-6397. Offers adult education (M Ed, MA); cross-cultural education (M Ed, MA); early childhood literacy (M Ed, MA); general education (M Ed, MA); higher education (PhD); instructional technology (M Ed, MA); international education and entrepreneurship (PhD); kinesiology (M Ed, MA); literacy (M Ed, MA); organizational leadership (PhD); organizational learning and learning (M Ed, MA); reading (M Ed, MA); special education (M Ed, MA); teacher leadership (M Ed, MA). Part-time and evening/weekend programs available. *Faculty:* 14 full-time (8 women), 10 part-time/adjunct (9 women). *Students:* 13 full-time (7 women), 197 part-time (129 women); includes 111 minority (23 Black or African American, non-Hispanic/Latino; 2 American Indian or Alaska Native, non-Hispanic/Latino; 1 Asian, non-Hispanic/Latino; 85 Hispanic/Latino), 26 international. Average age 41. 78 applicants, 79% accepted, 34 enrolled. In 2011, 21 master's, 12 doctorates awarded. *Degree requirements:* For master's, capstone; for doctorate, thesis/dissertation, qualifying exam. *Entrance requirements:* For master's, baccalaureate degree; minimum foundation GPA of 2.5; interview; for doctorate, master's degree; interview; supervised writing sample. Additional exam requirements/recommendations for international students: Required—TOEFL (minimum score 560 paper-based; 220 computer-based; 83 iBT). *Application deadline:* Applications are processed on a rolling basis. Application fee: $20. Electronic applications accepted. *Expenses: Tuition:* Part-time $725 per credit hour. Tuition and fees vary according to degree level. *Financial support:* In 2011–12, 5 research assistantships were awarded; Federal Work-Study and scholarships/grants also available. Financial award applicants required to submit FAFSA. *Unit head:* Dr. Denise Staudt, Dean, Dreeben School of Education, 210-829-2762, E-mail: staudt@uiwtx.edu. *Application contact:* Andrea Cyterski-Acosta, Dean of Enrollment, 210-829-6005, Fax: 210-829-3921, E-mail: admis@uiwtx.edu. Web site: http://www.uiw.edu/education/index.htm.

University of the Pacific, School of Education, Department of Curriculum and Instruction, Stockton, CA 95211-0197. Offers curriculum and instruction (M Ed, MA, Ed D); education (M Ed); special education (MA). *Accreditation:* NCATE. *Faculty:* 10 full-time (6 women), 6 part-time/adjunct (4 women). *Students:* 48 full-time (36 women), 112 part-time (93 women); includes 78 minority (4 Black or African American, non-Hispanic/Latino; 59 Asian, non-Hispanic/Latino; 15 Hispanic/Latino), 4 international. Average age 33. 75 applicants, 85% accepted, 43 enrolled. In 2011, 38 master's awarded. *Degree requirements:* For master's, thesis (for some programs). *Entrance requirements:* For master's, GRE General Test. Additional exam requirements/recommendations for international students: Required—TOEFL (minimum score 475 paper-based; 150 computer-based). *Application deadline:* For fall admission, 3/1 priority date for domestic students; for spring admission, 10/1 priority date for domestic students. Applications are processed on a rolling basis. Application fee: $75. *Expenses: Tuition:* Full-time $18,900;

part-time $1181 per unit. *Required fees:* $949. *Financial support:* In 2011–12, 7 teaching assistantships were awarded. Financial award application deadline: 3/1; financial award applicants required to submit FAFSA. *Unit head:* Dr. Marilyn Draheim, Chairperson, 209-946-2685, E-mail: mdraheim@pacific.edu. *Application contact:* Office of Graduate Admissions, 209-946-2344.

University of the Southwest, Graduate Programs, Hobbs, NM 88240-9129. Offers business administration (MBA); curriculum and instruction (MSE); curriculum and instruction: bilingual (MSE); curriculum and instruction: TESOL (MSE); early childhood education (MSE); educational administration (MSE); mental health counseling (MSE); school counseling (MSE); special education (MSE); sports management (MBA). Part-time and evening/weekend programs available. Postbaccalaureate distance learning degree programs offered (no on-campus study). *Faculty:* 13 full-time (6 women), 28 part-time/adjunct (17 women). *Students:* 76 full-time (63 women), 229 part-time (194 women); includes 104 minority (50 Black or African American, non-Hispanic/Latino; 2 American Indian or Alaska Native, non-Hispanic/Latino; 8 Asian, non-Hispanic/Latino; 44 Hispanic/Latino). Average age 38. 173 applicants, 71% accepted, 101 enrolled. In 2011, 75 master's awarded. *Degree requirements:* For master's, comprehensive exam, thesis (for some programs). *Entrance requirements:* Additional exam requirements/recommendations for international students: Recommended—TOEFL. *Application deadline:* Applications are processed on a rolling basis. Application fee: $50. Electronic applications accepted. *Expenses: Tuition:* Full-time $12,288; part-time $512 per credit hour. One-time fee: $50. Tuition and fees vary according to course load. *Financial support:* In 2011–12, 47 students received support. Federal Work-Study available. Financial award application deadline: 4/1; financial award applicants required to submit FAFSA. *Unit head:* Dr. Mary Harris, Dean of Education, 575-492-2162, Fax: 575-392-6006, E-mail: mharris@usw.edu. *Application contact:* Melissa Mitchell, Senior Online Program Advisor, 575-492-2142, Fax: 575-392-6006, E-mail: mmitchell@usw.edu. Web site: http://www.usw.edu/admissions/graduate_admission/graduate_admissions.

The University of Toledo, College of Graduate Studies, Judith Herb College of Education, Health Science and Human Service, Department of Early Childhood, Physical and Special Education, Toledo, OH 43606-3390. Offers early childhood education (ME, PhD); physical education (ME); special education (ME, PhD). Part-time programs available. *Faculty:* 15. *Students:* 29 full-time (20 women), 125 part-time (102 women); includes 15 minority (10 Black or African American, non-Hispanic/Latino; 2 Asian, non-Hispanic/Latino; 3 Hispanic/Latino), 3 international. Average age 32. 61 applicants, 67% accepted, 34 enrolled. In 2011, 55 master's awarded. *Degree requirements:* For master's, thesis. *Entrance requirements:* For master's, minimum cumulative GPA of 2.7 for all previous academic work, letters of recommendation. Additional exam requirements/recommendations for international students: Required—TOEFL (minimum score 550 paper-based; 213 computer-based; 80 iBT), IELTS (minimum score 6.5). *Application deadline:* For fall admission, 1/15 priority date for domestic students, 1/15 for international students. Applications are processed on a rolling basis. Application fee: $45 ($75 for international students). Electronic applications accepted. *Financial support:* In 2011–12, 13 teaching assistantships with full and partial tuition reimbursements (averaging $4,974 per year) were awarded; career-related internships or fieldwork, Federal Work-Study, institutionally sponsored loans, scholarships/grants, tuition waivers (full and partial), and unspecified assistantships also available. Support available to part-time students. *Unit head:* Dr. Richard Welsch, Interim Chair, 419-530-2468, E-mail: richard.welsch@utoledo.edu. *Application contact:* Graduate School Office, 419-530-4723, Fax: 419-530-4724, E-mail: grdsch@utnet.utoledo.edu. Web site: http://www.utoledo.edu/eduhshs/.

University of Utah, Graduate School, College of Education, Department of Special Education, Salt Lake City, UT 84112. Offers early childhood hearing impairments (M Ed, MS); early childhood special education (M Ed, PhD); early childhood vision impairments (M Ed, MS); hearing impairments (M Ed, MS); mild/moderate disabilities (M Ed, MS, PhD); professional practice (M Ed); research in special education (MS); severe disabilities (M Ed, MS, PhD); vision impairments (M Ed). Part-time and evening/weekend programs available. Postbaccalaureate distance learning degree programs offered (no on-campus study). *Faculty:* 16 full-time (11 women). *Students:* 34 full-time (26 women), 25 part-time (22 women); includes 11 minority (1 Black or African American, non-Hispanic/Latino; 3 American Indian or Alaska Native, non-Hispanic/Latino; 4 Hispanic/Latino; 1 Native Hawaiian or other Pacific Islander, non-Hispanic/Latino; 2 Two or more races, non-Hispanic/Latino), 1 international. Average age 35. 37 applicants, 54% accepted, 16 enrolled. In 2011, 26 degrees awarded. Terminal master's awarded for partial completion of doctoral program. *Degree requirements:* For master's, comprehensive exam, thesis (for some programs), qualifying exam; for doctorate, thesis/dissertation, qualifying exam. *Entrance requirements:* For master's, GRE or Analytical/Writing portion of GRE plus PRAXIS I, minimum GPA of 3.0; for doctorate, GRE General Test (minimum scores: Verbal 600; Quantitative 600; Analytical/Writing 4), minimum GPA of 3.0, 3.5 (recommended). Additional exam requirements/recommendations for international students: Required—TOEFL (minimum score 600 paper-based; 250 computer-based; 100 iBT); Recommended—IELTS (minimum score 7). *Application deadline:* For fall admission, 3/1 for domestic and international students; for spring admission, 11/1 for domestic and international students. Applications are processed on a rolling basis. Application fee: $55 ($65 for international students). Electronic applications accepted. *Expenses:* Contact institution. *Financial support:* In 2011–12, 25 students received support, including 25 fellowships with full tuition reimbursements available (averaging $7,124 per year), 3 teaching assistantships with full tuition reimbursements available (averaging $10,750 per year); research assistantships and career-related internships or fieldwork also available. Support available to part-time students. Financial award application deadline: 3/1; financial award applicants required to submit FAFSA. *Faculty research:* Inclusive education, positive behavior support, reading, instruction and intervention strategies. *Total annual research expenditures:* $5,926. *Unit head:* Dr. Robert E. O'Neill, Chair, 801-581-8121, Fax: 801-585-6476, E-mail: rob.oneill@utah.edu. *Application contact:* Patty Davis, Academic Advisor, 801-581-4764, Fax: 801-585-6476, E-mail: patty.davis@utah.edu. Web site: http://www.ed.utah.edu/sped/.

University of Vermont, Graduate College, College of Education and Social Services, Department of Education, Program in Special Education, Burlington, VT 05405. Offers M Ed. *Accreditation:* NCATE. *Students:* 46 (36 women); includes 5 minority (1 Black or African American, non-Hispanic/Latino; 1 American Indian or Alaska Native, non-Hispanic/Latino; 3 Hispanic/Latino). 53 applicants, 79% accepted, 21 enrolled. In 2011, 29 master's awarded. *Degree requirements:* For master's, thesis or alternative. *Entrance requirements:* For master's, must be licensed or eligible for licensure. Additional exam requirements/recommendations for international students: Required—TOEFL (minimum score 550 paper-based; 213 computer-based; 80 iBT). *Application deadline:* For fall admission, 3/15 priority date for domestic students, 3/15 for international students. Applications are processed on a rolling basis. Application fee: $40. Electronic applications accepted. *Financial support:* Research assistantships, teaching assistantships, and career-related internships or fieldwork available. Financial award application deadline: 3/1. *Unit head:* W. Williams, Director, 802-656-2936. *Application contact:* Prof. Wayne Williams, Coordinator, 802-656-2936.

University of Victoria, Faculty of Graduate Studies, Faculty of Education, Department of Educational Psychology and Leadership Studies, Victoria, BC V8W 2Y2, Canada. Offers aboriginal communities counseling (M Ed); counseling (M Ed, MA); educational psychology (M Ed, MA, PhD), including counseling psychology (M Ed, MA), leadership studies (PhD), learning and development (MA, PhD), measurement and evaluation, special education (M Ed, MA); leadership studies (M Ed, MA). Part-time programs available. *Degree requirements:* For master's, thesis (for some programs), comprehensive exam (M Ed); for doctorate, comprehensive exam, thesis/dissertation, candidacy exam. *Entrance requirements:* For master's, 2 years of work experience in a relevant field; for doctorate, GRE, 2 years of work experience in a relevant field, minimum B average. Additional exam requirements/recommendations for international students: Required—TOEFL (minimum score 575 paper-based; 233 computer-based), IELTS (minimum score 7). *Faculty research:* Learning and development (child, adolescent and adult), special education and exceptional children.

University of Virginia, Curry School of Education, Department of Curriculum, Instruction, and Special Education, Program in Special Education, Charlottesville, VA 22903. Offers M Ed, Ed D, Ed S. *Accreditation:* Teacher Education Accreditation Council. *Students:* 2 full-time (both women), 1 (woman) part-time. Average age 27. 17 applicants, 82% accepted, 3 enrolled. In 2011, 14 master's awarded. *Entrance requirements:* For master's, doctorate, and Ed S, GRE General Test, 2 letters of recommendation. Additional exam requirements/recommendations for international students: Required—TOEFL (minimum score 600 paper-based; 250 computer-based; 90 iBT), IELTS (minimum score 7). *Application deadline:* Applications are processed on a rolling basis. Application fee: $60. Electronic applications accepted. *Financial support:* Applicants required to submit FAFSA. *Unit head:* Paige C. Pullen, Program Coordinator. *Application contact:* Karen Dwier, Information Contact, 434-924-0831, E-mail: kgd9g@virginia.edu. Web site: http://curry.virginia.edu/academics/areas-of-study/special-education.

University of Virginia, Curry School of Education, Program in Education, Charlottesville, VA 22903. Offers administration and supervision (PhD); applied developmental science (PhD); counselor education (PhD); curriculum and instruction (PhD); early childhood-developmental risk (MT); education evaluation (PhD); educational psychology (PhD); educational research (PhD); elementary (MT, PhD); English education (MT, PhD); foreign language education (MT); higher education (PhD); instructional technology (PhD); kinesiology (MT, PhD); math education (PhD); reading education (PhD); research statistics and evaluation (PhD); school psychology (PhD); science education (PhD); social studies education (MT, PhD); special education (PhD); world languages education (MT). *Students:* 299 full-time (216 women), 60 part-time (33 women); includes 46 minority (18 Black or African American, non-Hispanic/Latino; 17 Asian, non-Hispanic/Latino; 7 Hispanic/Latino; 4 Two or more races, non-Hispanic/Latino), 23 international. Average age 30. 307 applicants, 42% accepted, 80 enrolled. In 2011, 113 master's, 62 doctorates awarded. *Degree requirements:* For master's, comprehensive exam (for some programs), field project; for doctorate, comprehensive exam, thesis/dissertation. *Entrance requirements:* For doctorate, GRE General Test. Additional exam requirements/recommendations for international students: Required—TOEFL (minimum score 600 paper-based; 250 computer-based; 90 iBT), IELTS (minimum score 7). *Application deadline:* Applications are processed on a rolling basis. Application fee: $60. Electronic applications accepted. *Financial support:* Fellowships, research assistantships, and teaching assistantships available. Financial award application deadline: 1/5; financial award applicants required to submit FAFSA. *Unit head:* Robert C. Pianta, Dean, 434-924-3334. *Application contact:* Joanne McNergney, Assistant Dean for Admissions and Student Services, 434-924-3334, E-mail: curry-admissions@virginia.edu.

University of Washington, Graduate School, College of Education, Program in Special Education, Seattle, WA 98195. Offers early childhood special education (M Ed); emotional and behavioral disabilities (M Ed); learning disabilities (M Ed); low-incidence disabilities (M Ed); severe disabilities (M Ed); special education (Ed D, PhD). *Degree requirements:* For master's, thesis optional; for doctorate, thesis/dissertation. *Entrance requirements:* For master's and doctorate, GRE General Test, minimum GPA of 3.0. Additional exam requirements/recommendations for international students: Required—TOEFL.

University of Washington, Tacoma, Graduate Programs, Program in Education, Tacoma, WA 98402-3100. Offers education (M Ed); educational administration (principal or program administrator certification) (M Ed); elementary education teacher certification (M Ed); elementary education/special education teacher certification (M Ed); secondary science or math teacher certification (M Ed). Part-time and evening/weekend programs available. *Degree requirements:* For master's, culminating project. *Entrance requirements:* For master's, WEST-B, WEST-E (teacher certification programs only), official sealed transcript from every college/university attended, personal goal statement, letters of recommendation, copy of valid teaching certificate. Additional exam requirements/recommendations for international students: Required—TOEFL (minimum score 580 paper-based; 237 computer-based; 92 iBT). Electronic applications accepted. *Faculty research:* Global learning communities for English/Chinese languages, evaluation of mathematics and reading intervention programs, response to intervention, school-wide behavioral and emotional support, mathematics education and culturally responsive mathematics education.

The University of West Alabama, School of Graduate Studies, College of Education, Departments of Instructional Leadership and Support/Curriculum and Instruction, Program in Special Education, Livingston, AL 35470. Offers M Ed. *Accreditation:* NCATE. Part-time programs available. *Faculty:* 29 full-time (13 women). *Students:* 204 (174 women); includes 123 minority (all Black or African American, non-Hispanic/Latino). In 2011, 33 master's awarded. *Degree requirements:* For master's, comprehensive exam. *Entrance requirements:* For master's, GRE General Test, MAT, minimum GPA of 2.75. Additional exam requirements/recommendations for international students: Required—TOEFL (minimum score 61 computer-based). *Application deadline:* For fall admission, 9/10 priority date for domestic students; for spring admission, 3/24 for domestic students. Applications are processed on a rolling basis. Application fee: $25 ($50 for international students). *Expenses:* Tuition, state resident: full-time $5112; part-time $284 per credit hour. Tuition, nonresident: full-time $10,224; part-time $568 per credit hour. *Required fees:* $180; $40 per semester. One-time fee: $65. Tuition and fees vary according to class time, course load, campus/location and program. *Financial support:* Teaching assistantships, career-related internships or fieldwork, Federal Work-Study, scholarships/grants, and unspecified assistantships available. Support available to part-time students. Financial award application deadline: 3/1. *Faculty research:* Learning strategies/reading; imagine, discuss, and decide; transition; at-risk students. *Unit head:* Dr. Esther Howard, Chair of Curriculum and Instruction, 205-652-3428, Fax: 205-652-3706, E-mail: ehoward@uwa.edu. *Application contact:* Dr. Kathy Chandler, Dean of Graduate Studies, 205-652-3421, Fax: 205-652-3706, E-mail: kchandler@uwa.edu. Web site: http://www.uwa.edu/medspecialeducation612.aspx.

The University of Western Ontario, Faculty of Graduate Studies, Social Sciences Division, Faculty of Education, Program in Educational Studies, London, ON N6A 5B8, Canada. Offers curriculum studies (M Ed); educational policy studies (M Ed); educational psychology/special education (M Ed). Part-time programs available. *Faculty* *research:* Reflective practice, gender and schooling, feminist pedagogy, narrative inquiry, second language, multiculturalism in Canada, education and law.

University of West Florida, College of Professional Studies, School of Education, Program in Curriculum and Instruction, Pensacola, FL 32514-5750. Offers curriculum and instruction: special education (M Ed); elementary education (M Ed); primary education (M Ed). Part-time and evening/weekend programs available. *Students:* 10 full-time (all women), 62 part-time (56 women); includes 16 minority (9 Black or African American, non-Hispanic/Latino; 1 American Indian or Alaska Native, non-Hispanic/Latino; 1 Asian, non-Hispanic/Latino; 3 Hispanic/Latino; 1 Native Hawaiian or other Pacific Islander, non-Hispanic/Latino; 1 Two or more races, non-Hispanic/Latino). Average age 35. 67 applicants, 70% accepted, 37 enrolled. In 2011, 62 master's awarded. *Entrance requirements:* For master's, GRE (minimum score 450 verbal) or MAT (minimum score 396) if bachelor's GPA less than 3.0, state teaching certification; letter of intent; two professional references. Additional exam requirements/recommendations for international students: Required—TOEFL (minimum score 550 paper-based; 213 computer-based). *Application deadline:* For fall admission, 6/1 for domestic and international students; for spring admission, 10/1 for domestic and international students. Applications are processed on a rolling basis. Application fee: $30. *Expenses:* Tuition, state resident: full-time $5729; part-time $302 per credit hour. Tuition, nonresident: full-time $20,059; part-time $961 per credit hour. *Required fees:* $1509; $63 per credit hour. *Financial support:* Career-related internships or fieldwork, Federal Work-Study, scholarships/grants, and tuition waivers (partial) available. Support available to part-time students. Financial award application deadline: 4/15; financial award applicants required to submit FAFSA. *Unit head:* Dr. William H. Evans, Acting Director, 850-474-2892, Fax: 850-474-2844, E-mail: wevans@uwf.edu. *Application contact:* Terry McCray, Assistant Director of Graduate Admissions, 850-473-7718, Fax: 850-473-7714, E-mail: gradadmissions@uwf.edu.

University of West Florida, College of Professional Studies, School of Education, Program in Exceptional Student Education, Pensacola, FL 32514-5750. Offers clinical teaching (MA), including emotionally handicapped, learning disabled, mentally handicapped; habilitative science (MA). *Accreditation:* NCATE. Part-time and evening/weekend programs available. Postbaccalaureate distance learning degree programs offered (no on-campus study). *Students:* 10 full-time (8 women), 47 part-time (42 women); includes 8 minority (1 Black or African American, non-Hispanic/Latino; 1 American Indian or Alaska Native, non-Hispanic/Latino; 1 Asian, non-Hispanic/Latino; 4 Hispanic/Latino; 1 Two or more races, non-Hispanic/Latino), 1 international. Average age 34. 39 applicants, 74% accepted, 19 enrolled. In 2011, 13 master's awarded. *Entrance requirements:* For master's, GRE (minimum score 450 verbal) or MAT (minimum score 396) if bachelor's GPA less than 3.0, state teaching certification; letter of intent; two professional references. Additional exam requirements/recommendations for international students: Required—TOEFL (minimum score 550 paper-based; 213 computer-based). *Application deadline:* For fall admission, 6/1 for domestic and international students; for spring admission, 10/1 for domestic and international students. Applications are processed on a rolling basis. Application fee: $30. *Expenses:* Tuition, state resident: full-time $5729; part-time $302 per credit hour. Tuition, nonresident: full-time $20,059; part-time $961 per credit hour. *Required fees:* $1509; $63 per credit hour. *Financial support:* Unspecified assistantships available. Financial award application deadline: 4/15; financial award applicants required to submit FAFSA. *Faculty research:* Memory, semantic structure, remedial programming. *Unit head:* Dr. William H. Evans, Acting Director, 850-474-2892, Fax: 850-474-2844, E-mail: wevans@uwf.edu. *Application contact:* Terry McCray, Assistant Director of Graduate Admissions, 850-473-7718, Fax: 850-473-7714, E-mail: gradadmissions@uwf.edu.

University of West Georgia, College of Education, Department of Collaborative Support and Intervention, Carrollton, GA 30118. Offers English to speakers of other languages (Ed S); guidance and counseling (M Ed, Ed S); professional counseling (M Ed, Ed S); professional counseling and supervision (Ed D, Ed S); reading education (M Ed, Ed S); reading endorsement (Ed S); special education-general (M Ed, Ed S); speech-language pathology (M Ed). Part-time and evening/weekend programs available. *Faculty:* 22 full-time (13 women), 6 part-time/adjunct (4 women). *Students:* 174 full-time (140 women), 253 part-time (228 women); includes 155 minority (127 Black or African American, non-Hispanic/Latino; 3 Asian, non-Hispanic/Latino; 14 Hispanic/Latino; 11 Two or more races, non-Hispanic/Latino), 2 international. Average age 33. 282 applicants, 49% accepted, 50 enrolled. In 2011, 98 master's, 27 other advanced degrees awarded. *Degree requirements:* For master's, comprehensive exam; for Ed S, research project. *Entrance requirements:* For master's, minimum GPA of 2.7; for Ed S, master's degree, minimum graduate GPA of 2.7. Additional exam requirements/recommendations for international students: Required—TOEFL (minimum score 523 paper-based; 193 computer-based; 69 iBT); Recommended—IELTS (minimum score 6). *Application deadline:* For fall admission, 6/3 for domestic students, 6/1 for international students; for spring admission, 10/7 for domestic students, 10/15 for international students. Applications are processed on a rolling basis. Application fee: $30. Electronic applications accepted. *Expenses:* Tuition, state resident: full-time $4336; part-time $181 per credit hour. Tuition, nonresident: full-time $17,362; part-time $724 per credit hour. Tuition and fees vary according to course load, degree level, campus/location and program. *Financial support:* In 2011–12, 5 research assistantships with full tuition reimbursements (averaging $3,000 per year) were awarded; career-related internships or fieldwork and scholarships/grants also available. Support available to part-time students. Financial award applicants required to submit FAFSA. *Unit head:* Dr. Michael Garrett, Chair, 678-839-6567, Fax: 678-839-6162, E-mail: mgarrett@westga.edu. *Application contact:* Deanna Richards, Coordinator, Graduate Studies, 678-839-5946, E-mail: drichard@westga.edu. Web site: http://www.westga.edu/coecsi.

University of Wisconsin–Eau Claire, College of Education and Human Sciences, Program in Special Education, Eau Claire, WI 54702-4004. Offers MSE. Part-time programs available. *Faculty:* 6 full-time (4 women). *Students:* 1 (woman) full-time, 5 part-time (all women); includes 1 minority (Two or more races, non-Hispanic/Latino). Average age 29. 4 applicants, 50% accepted, 0 enrolled. In 2011, 5 master's awarded. *Degree requirements:* For master's, comprehensive exam, thesis, research paper, or written exam; oral exam. *Entrance requirements:* For master's, minimum GPA of 2.75. Additional exam requirements/recommendations for international students: Required—TOEFL (minimum score 550 paper-based; 213 computer-based; 79 iBT); Recommended—IELTS (minimum score 7). *Application deadline:* For fall admission, 7/1 priority date for domestic students, 6/1 for international students; for spring admission, 12/1 priority date for domestic students, 11/1 for international students. Applications are processed on a rolling basis. Application fee: $56. *Expenses:* Tuition, state resident: full-time $7312; part-time $406 per credit. Tuition, nonresident: full-time $16,771; part-time $932 per credit. *Required fees:* $1101; $61 per credit. *Financial support:* In 2011–12, 3 students received support. Federal Work-Study and unspecified assistantships available. Financial award application deadline: 3/1; financial award applicants required to submit FAFSA. *Unit head:* Dr. Rosemary Battalio, Chair, 715-836-5352, Fax: 715-836-3162, E-mail: battalrl@uwec.edu. *Application contact:* Nancy Amdahl, Graduate Dean Assistant, 715-836-2721, Fax: 715-836-2902, E-mail: graduate@uwec.edu. Web site: http://www.uwec.edu/sped/.

University of Wisconsin–La Crosse, Office of University Graduate Studies, College of Liberal Studies, Department of Educational Studies, Program in Special Education, La Crosse, WI 54601-3742. Offers emotional disturbance (MS Ed); learning disabilities (MS Ed). Part-time programs available. *Students:* 10 full-time (8 women), 11 part-time (9 women); includes 2 minority (1 Asian, non-Hispanic/Latino; 1 Hispanic/Latino), 1 international. Average age 32. 9 applicants, 78% accepted, 6 enrolled. In 2011, 3 master's awarded. *Degree requirements:* For master's, thesis optional. *Entrance requirements:* For master's, GRE General Test, minimum undergraduate GPA of 3.0, 3 letters of recommendation. Additional exam requirements/recommendations for international students: Required—TOEFL (minimum score 550 paper-based; 213 computer-based; 79 iBT). *Application deadline:* Applications are processed on a rolling basis. Application fee: $56. Electronic applications accepted. *Expenses:* Tuition, state resident: full-time $8391; part-time $481.17 per credit. Tuition, nonresident: full-time $17,850; part-time $1006.68 per credit. *Required fees:* $2 per credit. $18.25 per semester. Tuition and fees vary according to course load, program, reciprocity agreements and student level. *Financial support:* In 2011–12, 1 research assistantship (averaging $3,340 per year) was awarded; Federal Work-Study, scholarships/grants, health care benefits, and tuition waivers (partial) also available. Support available to part-time students. Financial award application deadline: 3/15; financial award applicants required to submit FAFSA. *Unit head:* Dr. Carol Angell, Director, 608-785-8135, E-mail: angell.caro@uwlax.edu. *Application contact:* Kathryn Kiefer, Director of Admissions, 608-785-8939, E-mail: admissions@uwlax.edu. Web site: http://www.uwlax.edu/des/specialed/.

University of Wisconsin–La Crosse, Office of University Graduate Studies, College of Science and Health, Department of Exercise and Sport Science, La Crosse, WI 54601-3742. Offers clinical exercise physiology (MS); human performance (MS), including applied sport science, strength and conditioning; physical education teaching (MS), including adapted physical education, adventure education; special/adapted physical education (MS). Part-time and evening/weekend programs available. *Faculty:* 10 full-time (1 woman), 3 part-time/adjunct (0 women). *Students:* 53 full-time (25 women), 10 part-time (6 women); includes 6 minority (2 Asian, non-Hispanic/Latino; 3 Hispanic/Latino; 1 Two or more races, non-Hispanic/Latino), 3 international. Average age 25. 51 applicants, 59% accepted, 19 enrolled. In 2011, 38 master's awarded. *Entrance requirements:* Additional exam requirements/recommendations for international students: Required—TOEFL (minimum score 550 paper-based; 213 computer-based; 79 iBT). Application fee: $56. Electronic applications accepted. *Expenses:* Tuition, state resident: full-time $8391; part-time $481.17 per credit. Tuition, nonresident: full-time $17,850; part-time $1006.68 per credit. *Required fees:* $2 per credit. $18.25 per semester. Tuition and fees vary according to course load, program, reciprocity agreements and student level. *Financial support:* In 2011–12, 23 research assistantships with partial tuition reimbursements (averaging $6,682 per year) were awarded; Federal Work-Study, scholarships/grants, health care benefits, and tuition waivers (partial) also available. Support available to part-time students. Financial award application deadline: 3/15; financial award applicants required to submit FAFSA. *Unit head:* Dr. Patrick DiRocco, Chair, 608-785-8173, Fax: 608-785-6520, E-mail: dirocco.patr@uwlax.edu. *Application contact:* Kathryn Kiefer, Director of Admissions, 608-785-8939, E-mail: admissions@uwlax.edu. Web site: http://www.uwlax.edu/sah/ess/index.htm.

University of Wisconsin–Madison, Graduate School, School of Education, Department of Rehabilitation Psychology and Special Education, Program in Special Education, Madison, WI 53706-1380. Offers MA, MS, PhD. *Degree requirements:* For doctorate, thesis/dissertation. *Application deadline:* For fall admission, 3/15 for domestic and international students; for spring admission, 10/15 for domestic and international students. Application fee: $56. Electronic applications accepted. *Expenses:* Tuition, state resident: full-time $10,296; part-time $643.51 per credit. Tuition, nonresident: full-time $24,054; part-time $1503.40 per credit. *Required fees:* $70.06 per credit. Tuition and fees vary according to course load, campus/location, program and reciprocity agreements. *Financial support:* Fellowships with full tuition reimbursements, research assistantships with full tuition reimbursements, teaching assistantships with full tuition reimbursements, and project assistantships available. *Unit head:* Dr. Kimber Wilkerson, Chair, 608-263-5860, E-mail: klwilkerson@wisc.edu. *Application contact:* 608-262-2433, Fax: 608-262-5134, E-mail: gradadmiss@mail.bascom.wisc.edu.

University of Wisconsin–Milwaukee, Graduate School, School of Education, Department of Exceptional Education, Milwaukee, WI 53201-0413. Offers assistive technology and accessible design (Certificate); exceptional education (MS). Part-time programs available. *Faculty:* 11 full-time (9 women). *Students:* 13 full-time (9 women), 30 part-time (28 women); includes 8 minority (5 Black or African American, non-Hispanic/Latino; 2 Hispanic/Latino; 1 Two or more races, non-Hispanic/Latino), 2 international. Average age 34. 10 applicants, 70% accepted, 5 enrolled. In 2011, 28 degrees awarded. *Degree requirements:* For master's, thesis. *Entrance requirements:* Additional exam requirements/recommendations for international students: Required—TOEFL (minimum score 550 paper-based; 79 iBT), IELTS (minimum score 6.5). *Application deadline:* For fall admission, 1/1 priority date for domestic students; for spring admission, 9/1 for domestic students. Applications are processed on a rolling basis. Application fee: $56 ($96 for international students). Electronic applications accepted. One-time fee: $506.10 full-time. Tuition and fees vary according to course load and reciprocity agreements. *Financial support:* Fellowships, research assistantships, teaching assistantships, career-related internships or fieldwork, health care benefits, and unspecified assistantships available. Support available to part-time students. Financial award application deadline: 4/15; financial award applicants required to submit FAFSA. *Faculty research:* Emotional disturbance, hearing impairment, learning disabilities, mental retardation. *Total annual research expenditures:* $49,215. *Unit head:* Elise Frattura, Department Chair, 414-229-3864, E-mail: frattura@uwm.edu. *Application contact:* General Information Contact, 414-229-4982, Fax: 414-229-6967, E-mail: gradschool@uwm.edu. Web site: http://www.uwm.edu/Dept/EXED/.

University of Wisconsin–Oshkosh, Graduate Studies, College of Education and Human Services, Department of Special Education, Oshkosh, WI 54901. Offers cross-categorical (MSE); early childhood: exceptional education needs (MSE); non-licensure (MSE). Part-time and evening/weekend programs available. *Degree requirements:* For master's, comprehensive exam (for some programs), thesis or alternative, field report. *Entrance requirements:* For master's, interview, minimum GPA of 3.0, teaching license, letters of recommendation. Additional exam requirements/recommendations for international students: Required—TOEFL (minimum score 550 paper-based; 213 computer-based; 79 iBT). Electronic applications accepted. *Faculty research:* Private agency contributions to the disabled, graduation requirements for exceptional education needs students, direct instruction in spelling for learning disabled, effects of behavioral parent training, secondary education programming issues.

University of Wisconsin–Stevens Point, College of Professional Studies, School of Education, Program in Education—General/Special, Stevens Point, WI 54481-3897. Offers MSE. Part-time programs available. *Degree requirements:* For master's, comprehensive exam, thesis or alternative. *Entrance requirements:* For master's, minimum undergraduate GPA of 3.0, 2 years teaching experience, letters of recommendation, teacher certification. *Faculty research:* Curriculum and instruction, early childhood special education, standards-based education.

University of Wisconsin–Superior, Graduate Division, Department of Teacher Education, Program in Special Education, Superior, WI 54880-4500. Offers emotional/behavior disabilities (MSE); learning disabilities (MSE). Part-time and evening/weekend programs available. Postbaccalaureate distance learning degree programs offered (minimal on-campus study). *Degree requirements:* For master's, research project. *Entrance requirements:* For master's, minimum GPA of 2.75, teaching certificate.

University of Wisconsin–Whitewater, School of Graduate Studies, College of Education and Professional Studies, Department of Special Education, Whitewater, WI 53190-1790. Offers cross categorical licensure (MSE); professional development (MSE). *Accreditation:* NCATE. Part-time and evening/weekend programs available. Postbaccalaureate distance learning degree programs offered (no on-campus study). *Students:* 13 full-time (8 women), 44 part-time (32 women); includes 5 minority (1 Black or African American, non-Hispanic/Latino; 4 Asian, non-Hispanic/Latino). Average age 32. 16 applicants, 63% accepted, 6 enrolled. In 2011, 30 master's awarded. *Degree requirements:* For master's, thesis or alternative. *Entrance requirements:* Additional exam requirements/recommendations for international students: Required—TOEFL (minimum score 550 paper-based; 213 computer-based; 80 iBT), IELTS (minimum score 6). *Application deadline:* For fall admission, 7/15 priority date for domestic students; for spring admission, 12/1 priority date for domestic students. Applications are processed on a rolling basis. Application fee: $56. Electronic applications accepted. *Expenses:* Tuition, state resident: full-time $4088. Tuition, nonresident: full-time $8817. Tuition and fees vary according to program. *Financial support:* In 2011–12, 5 research assistantships (averaging $5,175 per year) were awarded; Federal Work-Study, unspecified assistantships, and out of state fee waiver also available. Support available to part-time students. Financial award application deadline: 3/15; financial award applicants required to submit FAFSA. *Faculty research:* Language ability, cultural interaction with disability, juvenile corrections, early childhood programming and childcare issues. *Unit head:* Dr. Shannon Stuart, Coordinator, 262-472-4877, Fax: 262-472-2843. *Application contact:* Sally A. Lange, School of Graduate Studies, 262-472-1006, Fax: 262-472-5027, E-mail: gradschl@uww.edu.

University of Wyoming, College of Education, Program in Special Education, Laramie, WY 82070. Offers MA, PhD, Ed S. *Degree requirements:* For master's, comprehensive exam, thesis. *Entrance requirements:* For master's, GRE, 2 years teaching experience, 3 letters of recommendation, writing sample. *Faculty research:* Self-determination; transition; digital learning; severe disabilities; response to intervention.

Ursuline College, School of Graduate Studies, Program in Education, Pepper Pike, OH 44124-4398. Offers art education (MA); early childhood education (MA); language arts education (MA); life science education (MA); math education (MA); middle school education (MA); social studies education (MA); special education (MA). *Accreditation:* NCATE. *Faculty:* 3 full-time (all women), 8 part-time/adjunct (6 women). *Students:* 28 full-time (22 women), 1 (woman) part-time; includes 11 minority (7 Black or African American, non-Hispanic/Latino; 2 Asian, non-Hispanic/Latino; 1 Hispanic/Latino; 1 Native Hawaiian or other Pacific Islander, non-Hispanic/Latino). Average age 32. In 2011, 29 master's awarded. *Degree requirements:* For master's, comprehensive exam. *Entrance requirements:* For master's, minimum undergraduate GPA of 3.0. Additional exam requirements/recommendations for international students: Required—TOEFL (minimum score 500 paper-based; 173 computer-based). *Application deadline:* For fall admission, 8/1 priority date for domestic students. Applications are processed on a rolling basis. Application fee: $25. *Expenses:* Contact institution. *Financial support:* Federal Work-Study available. Financial award application deadline: 3/1. *Unit head:* Dr. Edna West, Director, Master's Apprentice Program, 440-646-6134, Fax: 440-684-6088, E-mail: ewest@ursuline.edu. *Application contact:* Melanie Steele, Graduate Admission Assistant, 440-646-8199, Fax: 440-684-6138, E-mail: graduateadmissions@ursuline.edu.

Utah State University, School of Graduate Studies, Emma Eccles Jones College of Education and Human Services, Department of Special Education and Rehabilitation, Logan, UT 84322. Offers disability disciplines (PhD); rehabilitation counselor education (MRC); special education (M Ed, MS, Ed S). *Accreditation:* NCATE (one or more programs are accredited). Part-time programs available. Postbaccalaureate distance learning degree programs offered (minimal on-campus study). *Degree requirements:* For master's, thesis (for some programs), internships (for some programs); for doctorate, comprehensive exam, thesis/dissertation. *Entrance requirements:* For master's and doctorate, GRE General Test, minimum GPA of 3.0. Additional exam requirements/recommendations for international students: Required—TOEFL (minimum score 550 paper-based; 213 computer-based). Electronic applications accepted. *Faculty research:* Applied behavior analysis, effective instructional practices, early childhood teacher training research, distance education, multicultural rehabilitation.

Valdosta State University, Department of Early Childhood and Special Education, Valdosta, GA 31698. Offers early childhood (M Ed); special education (M Ed, Ed S). *Accreditation:* ASHA (one or more programs are accredited); NCATE. Part-time and evening/weekend programs available. Postbaccalaureate distance learning degree programs offered (no on-campus study). *Faculty:* 17 full-time (14 women). *Students:* 37 full-time (30 women), 110 part-time (78 women); includes 37 minority (33 Black or African American, non-Hispanic/Latino; 2 American Indian or Alaska Native, non-Hispanic/Latino; 2 Asian, non-Hispanic/Latino). Average age 25. 27 applicants, 81% accepted, 22 enrolled. In 2011, 48 master's awarded. *Degree requirements:* For master's, thesis (for some programs), comprehensive written and/or oral exams; for Ed S, thesis. *Entrance requirements:* For master's, GRE General Test or MAT, minimum GPA of 2.5; for Ed S, GRE General Test or MAT, minimum GPA of 3.0. Additional exam requirements/recommendations for international students: Required—TOEFL (minimum score 523 paper-based; 193 computer-based). *Application deadline:* For fall and spring admission, 7/1 for domestic and international students. Applications are processed on a rolling basis. Application fee: $35. Electronic applications accepted. *Expenses:* Tuition, state resident: full-time $7098; part-time $217 per hour. Tuition, nonresident: full-time $20,630; part-time $780 per hour. *Financial support:* In 2011–12, 5 students received support, including 5 research assistantships with full tuition reimbursements available (averaging $3,252 per year); institutionally sponsored loans, scholarships/grants, and unspecified assistantships also available. Support available to part-time students. Financial award application deadline: 7/1; financial award applicants required to submit FAFSA. *Unit head:* Dr. Shirley Andrews, Acting Head, 229-333-5929, E-mail: spandrew@valdosta.edu. *Application contact:* Shantae Lynn, Admissions Specialist, 229-333-5694, Fax: 229-245-3853, E-mail: smlynn@valdosta.edu.

Vanderbilt University, Peabody College, Department of Special Education, Nashville, TN 37240-1001. Offers M Ed. *Accreditation:* NCATE. *Faculty:* 25 full-time (14 women), 6 part-time/adjunct (5 women). *Students:* 81 full-time (75 women), 16 part-time (13 women); includes 7 minority (2 Asian, non-Hispanic/Latino; 3 Hispanic/Latino; 2 Two or more races, non-Hispanic/Latino), 3 international. Average age 26. 102 applicants, 51% accepted, 41 enrolled. In 2011, 34 master's awarded. *Degree requirements:* For master's, comprehensive exam, thesis optional. *Entrance requirements:* For master's, GRE General Test, MAT. Additional exam requirements/recommendations for international students: Required—TOEFL (minimum score 550 paper-based; 213 computer-based). *Application deadline:* For fall admission, 12/31 priority date for domestic students, 12/31 for international students; for spring admission, 11/1 priority date for domestic students, 11/1 for international students. Applications are processed on a rolling basis. Application fee: $0. Electronic applications accepted. *Financial support:* Fellowships with full and partial tuition reimbursements, research assistantships with full and partial tuition reimbursements, teaching assistantships with full and partial tuition reimbursements, Federal Work-Study, institutionally sponsored loans, scholarships/grants, traineeships, health care benefits, tuition waivers (partial), and unspecified assistantships available. Support available to part-time students. Financial award application deadline: 2/1; financial award applicants required to submit CSS PROFILE or FAFSA. *Faculty research:* Evaluation of interventions for children with communication and learning disabilities, behavior disorders, autism, those at risk for disabilities and academic failure. *Unit head:* Dr. Mark Wolery, Chair, 615-322-8150, Fax: 615-343-1570, E-mail: mark.wolery@vanderbilt.edu. *Application contact:* Alfred Brady, Admissions Coordinator, 615-322-8195, Fax: 615-343-1570, E-mail: alfred.l.brady@vanderbilt.edu.

Vanderbilt University, School of Medicine, Department of Hearing and Speech Sciences, Nashville, TN 37240-1001. Offers audiology (Au D, PhD); deaf education (MED); speech-language pathology (MS). *Degree requirements:* For master's, thesis optional; for doctorate, thesis/dissertation, final and qualifying exams. *Entrance requirements:* For master's and doctorate, GRE General Test. Additional exam requirements/recommendations for international students: Required—TOEFL. Electronic applications accepted. *Faculty research:* Child language.

Virginia Commonwealth University, Graduate School, School of Education, Doctoral Program in Education, Special Education and Disability Leadership Track, Richmond, VA 23284-9005. Offers PhD. *Entrance requirements:* For doctorate, GRE. Additional exam requirements/recommendations for international students: Required—TOEFL (minimum score 600 paper-based; 250 computer-based; 100 iBT). Electronic applications accepted. *Expenses:* Tuition, state resident: full-time $9133; part-time $507 per credit. Tuition, nonresident: full-time $18,777; part-time $1043 per credit. *Required fees:* $77 per credit. Tuition and fees vary according to degree level, campus/location, program and student level.

Virginia Commonwealth University, Graduate School, School of Education, Program in Special Education, Richmond, VA 23284-9005. Offers autism spectrum disorders (Certificate); disability leadership (Certificate); early childhood (M Ed); general education (M Ed); severe disabilities (M Ed). *Accreditation:* NCATE. *Degree requirements:* For master's, comprehensive exam. *Entrance requirements:* For master's, GRE General Test or MAT. Additional exam requirements/recommendations for international students: Required—TOEFL (minimum score 600 paper-based; 250 computer-based; 100 iBT). Electronic applications accepted. *Expenses:* Tuition, state resident: full-time $9133; part-time $507 per credit. Tuition, nonresident: full-time $18,777; part-time $1043 per credit. *Required fees:* $77 per credit. Tuition and fees vary according to degree level, campus/location, program and student level.

Walden University, Graduate Programs, Richard W. Riley College of Education and Leadership, Minneapolis, MN 55401. Offers administrator leadership for teaching and learning (Ed D, Ed S); adult education (Ed D, Ed S); adult learning (MS, Postbaccalaureate Certificate), including developmental education (MS), online teaching (MS), teaching adults English as a second language (MS), training and performance management (MS); college teaching and learning (Ed D, Ed S, Postbaccalaureate Certificate); curriculum, instruction and assessment (Ed D, Postbaccalaureate Certificate); curriculum, instruction, and professional development (Ed S); developmental education (Postbaccalaureate Certificate); early childhood administration, management, and leadership (Postbaccalaureate Certificate); early childhood education (birth-grade 3) (MAT); early childhood public policy and advocacy (Postbaccalaureate Certificate); early childhood studies (MS), including administration, management and leadership, early childhood public policy and advocacy, teaching adults in the early childhood field, teaching and diversity; education (MS, PhD), including adolescent literacy and technology (grades 6-12) (MS), adult education leadership (PhD), assessment, evaluation, and accountability (PhD), community college leadership (PhD), curriculum, instruction, and assessment, early childhood education (PhD), educational technology (PhD), elementary reading and literacy (MS), elementary reading and mathematics (MS), general program, global and comparative education (PhD), higher education (PhD), integrating technology in the classroom (MS), K-12 educational leadership (PhD), leadership, policy and change (PhD), learning, instruction and innovation (PhD), literacy and learning in the content areas (MS), mathematics (grades 6-8) (MS), mathematics (grades K-5) (MS), middle level education (grades 5-8) (MS), professional development (MS), science (grades K-8) (MS), self-designed (PhD), special education (PhD), special education (non-licensure) (MS), teacher leadership (grades K-12) (MS), teaching English language learners (grades K-12) (MS); educational leadership and administration (principal preparation) (Ed S); educational technology (Ed S); elementary reading and literacy (Postbaccalaureate Certificate); engaging culturally diverse learners (Postbaccalaureate Certificate); enrollment management and institutional marketing (Postbaccalaureate Certificate); higher education (MS), including college teaching and learning, enrollment management and institutional planning, global higher education, leadership for student success, online and distance learning; higher education leadership (Ed D); instructional design (Postbaccalaureate Certificate); instructional design and technology (MS), including general program (MS, PhD), online learning, training and performance improvement; integrating technology in the classroom (Postbaccalaureate Certificate); online teaching for adult learners (Postbaccalaureate Certificate); professional development (Postbaccalaureate Certificate); reading and literacy leadership (Ed D); science K-8 (Postbaccalaureate Certificate); special education (Ed D, Ed S); special education: emotional/behavioral disorders (K-12) (MAT); special education: learning disabilities (K-12) (MAT); teacher leadership (Ed D, Ed S, Postbaccalaureate Certificate); training and performance management (Postbaccalaureate Certificate). Part-time and evening/weekend programs available. Postbaccalaureate distance learning degree programs offered (minimal on-campus study). *Faculty:* 71 full-time (48 women), 853 part-time/adjunct (585 women). *Students:* 11,326 full-time (9,212 women), 2,148 part-time (1,795 women); includes 5,346 minority (4,403 Black or African American, non-Hispanic/Latino; 76 American Indian or Alaska Native, non-Hispanic/Latino; 140 Asian, non-Hispanic/Latino; 561 Hispanic/Latino; 21 Native Hawaiian or other Pacific Islander, non-Hispanic/Latino; 145 Two or more races, non-Hispanic/Latino), 322 international. Average age 39. In 2011, 3,477 master's, 318 doctorates, 471 other advanced degrees awarded. *Degree requirements:* For doctorate, thesis/dissertation (for some programs), residency; for other advanced degree, residency (for some programs). *Entrance requirements:* For master's, bachelor's degree or equivalent in related field; minimum GPA of 2.5; official transcripts; goal statement; access to computer and Internet; for doctorate, master's degree or equivalent in related field; minimum GPA of 3.0; official transcripts; three years' related professional/academic experience (preferred); access to computer and Internet; for other advanced degree, master's degree or equivalent in related field; minimum GPA of 3.0; 3 years related professional/academic experience (preferred); access to computer and Internet (Ed S). Additional exam requirements/recommendations for international students: Required—TOEFL (minimum score 550 paper-based; 213 computer-based), IELTS (minimum score 6.5), or Michigan English

Language Assessment Battery (minimum score 82). *Application deadline:* Applications are processed on a rolling basis. Application fee: $50. Electronic applications accepted. *Financial support:* Federal Work-Study, scholarships/grants, unspecified assistantships, and family tuition reduction, active duty/veteran tuition reduction, group tuition reduction, interest-free payment plans, employee tuition reduction available. Support available to part-time students. Financial award applicants required to submit FAFSA. *Unit head:* Dr. Kate Steffens, Dean, 800-925-3368. *Application contact:* Jennifer Hall, Vice President of Enrollment Management, 866-4-WALDEN, E-mail: info@waldenu.edu. Web site: http://www.waldenu.edu/Colleges-and-Schools/College-of-Education-and-Leadership.htm.

Walla Walla University, Graduate School, School of Education and Psychology, College Place, WA 99324-1198. Offers counseling psychology (MA); curriculum and instruction (M Ed, MA, MAT); educational leadership (M Ed, MA, MAT); literacy instruction (M Ed, MA, MAT); students at risk (M Ed, MA, MAT); teaching (MAT). Part-time programs available. *Entrance requirements:* For master's, GRE General Test, minimum GPA of 2.75. Additional exam requirements/recommendations for international students: Required—TOEFL (minimum score 550 paper-based; 213 computer-based; 79 iBT). Electronic applications accepted. *Faculty research:* Admissions/retention, instructional psychology, moral development, teaching of reading.

Washburn University, College of Arts and Sciences, Department of Education, Topeka, KS 66621. Offers curriculum and instruction (M Ed); educational leadership (M Ed); reading (M Ed); special education (M Ed). *Accreditation:* NCATE. Part-time programs available. *Faculty:* 6 full-time (3 women), 1 (woman) part-time/adjunct. *Students:* 2 full-time (both women), 26 part-time (16 women). Average age 36. In 2011, 17 master's awarded. *Degree requirements:* For master's, comprehensive exam, thesis or alternative, portfolio, comprehensive paper, or action research project. *Entrance requirements:* For master's, department graduate admissions test, GRE General Test, or MAT, minimum GPA of 3.0 in graduate coursework or last 60 hours of undergraduate coursework. Additional exam requirements/recommendations for international students: Required—TOEFL (minimum score 550 paper-based; 80 iBT). *Application deadline:* For fall admission, 8/1 for domestic and international students; for spring admission, 11/1 for domestic and international students. Applications are processed on a rolling basis. *Expenses:* Tuition, state resident: full-time $5346; part-time $297 per credit hour. Tuition, nonresident: full-time $10,908; part-time $606 per credit hour. *Required fees:* $86; $43 per semester. *Financial support:* Federal Work-Study, institutionally sponsored loans, and scholarships/grants available. Support available to part-time students. Financial award applicants required to submit FAFSA. *Faculty research:* Reading/literature/literacy, foundations, educational administration/leadership, special education, diversity. *Unit head:* Dr. Judith McConnell-Farmer, Interim Chairperson, 785-670-1472, Fax: 785-670-1046, E-mail: judy.mcconnell-farmer@washburn.edu. *Application contact:* Tara Porter, Licensure Officer, 785-670-1434, Fax: 785-670-1046, E-mail: tara.porter@washburn.edu. Web site: http://www.washburn.edu/academics/college-schools/arts-sciences/departments/education/index.html.

Washington University in St. Louis, School of Medicine, Program in Audiology and Communication Sciences, Saint Louis, MO 63110. Offers audiology (Au D); deaf education (MS); speech and hearing sciences (PhD). *Accreditation:* ASHA (one or more programs are accredited). *Faculty:* 22 full-time (12 women), 18 part-time/adjunct (12 women). *Students:* 72 full-time (69 women). Average age 24. 130 applicants, 17% accepted, 22 enrolled. In 2011, 11 master's, 16 doctorates awarded. *Median time to degree:* Of those who began their doctoral program in fall 2003, 100% received their degree in 8 years or less. *Degree requirements:* For master's, comprehensive exam, thesis, independent study project, oral exam; for doctorate, comprehensive exam, thesis/dissertation, capstone project. *Entrance requirements:* For master's, GRE General Test, minimum B average in undergraduate course work; for doctorate, GRE General Test, minimum B average. Additional exam requirements/recommendations for international students: Required—TOEFL (minimum score 600 paper-based; 250 computer-based; 100 iBT). *Application deadline:* For fall admission, 2/15 for domestic and international students. Application fee: $60 ($80 for international students). Electronic applications accepted. *Expenses:* Contact institution. *Financial support:* In 2011–12, 72 students received support, including 72 fellowships with full and partial tuition reimbursements available (averaging $15,000 per year), 5 teaching assistantships with partial tuition reimbursements available (averaging $1,000 per year); career-related internships or fieldwork, Federal Work-Study, institutionally sponsored loans, scholarships/grants, traineeships, health care benefits, tuition waivers (partial), and unspecified assistantships also available. Financial award application deadline: 2/15; financial award applicants required to submit FAFSA. *Faculty research:* Audiology, deaf education, speech and hearing sciences, sensory neuroscience. *Unit head:* Dr. William W. Clark, Program Director, 314-747-0104, Fax: 314-747-0105. *Application contact:* Elizabeth A. Elliott, Manager, Financial Operations and Admissions, 314-747-0104, Fax: 314-747-0105, E-mail: elliottb@wustl.edu. Web site: http://pacs.wustl.edu/.

Wayland Baptist University, Graduate Programs, Program in Education, Plainview, TX 79072-6998. Offers education administration (M Ed); higher education administration (M Ed); instructional leadership (M Ed); instructional technology (M Ed); special education (M Ed). Part-time and evening/weekend programs available. Postbaccalaureate distance learning degree programs offered (no on-campus study). *Degree requirements:* For master's, comprehensive exam, capstone course. *Entrance requirements:* For master's, GRE, GMAT or MAT. Additional exam requirements/recommendations for international students: Required—TOEFL (minimum score 500 paper-based; 173 computer-based; 61 iBT). Electronic applications accepted.

Waynesburg University, Graduate and Professional Studies, Waynesburg, PA 15370-1222. Offers business (MBA), including finance, health systems, human resources, leadership, market development; counseling (MA), including addictions counseling, clinical mental health; education (MAT); nursing (MSN), including administration, education, informatics, palliative care; nursing practice (DNP); special education (M Ed); technology (M Ed); MSN/MBA. *Accreditation:* AACN. Part-time and evening/weekend programs available. *Degree requirements:* For doctorate, thesis/dissertation. *Entrance requirements:* Additional exam requirements/recommendations for international students: Required—TOEFL. Electronic applications accepted.

Wayne State College, School of Education and Counseling, Department of Counseling and Special Education, Program in Special Education, Wayne, NE 68787. Offers MSE. *Accreditation:* NCATE. Part-time and evening/weekend programs available. *Degree requirements:* For master's, comprehensive exam, thesis. *Entrance requirements:* For master's, GRE General Test, minimum GPA of 3.0. Additional exam requirements/recommendations for international students: Required—TOEFL (minimum score 550 paper-based; 213 computer-based). Electronic applications accepted.

Wayne State University, College of Education, Division of Teacher Education, Detroit, MI 48202. Offers art education (M Ed), including art therapy; bilingual/bicultural education (M Ed); career and technical education (M Ed); curriculum and instruction (Ed D, PhD, Ed S), including art education (PhD), bilingual education (Ed D, Ed S), bilingual-bicultural education (PhD), career and technical education (MAT, Ed D, PhD, Ed S), early childhood education (MAT, Ed D, PhD, Ed S), elementary education, English as a second language (MAT, Ed D, Ed S), English education (MAT, Ed D, PhD, Ed S), foreign language education (MAT, PhD), K-12 curriculum, mathematics education (MAT, Ed D, PhD, Ed S), science education (MAT, Ed D, PhD, Ed S), secondary education, social studies education (MAT, Ed S), social studies education: secondary (Ed D, PhD); elementary education (MAT), including special education; elementary education (M Ed, MAT), including children's literature (MAT), early childhood education (MAT, Ed D, PhD, Ed S), general elementary education (MAT); elementary or secondary education (MAT), including bilingual/bicultural education, English as a second language (MAT, Ed D, Ed S), mathematics education (MAT, Ed D, PhD, Ed S), science education (MAT, Ed D, PhD, Ed S), social studies education (MAT, Ed S); English education-secondary (M Ed); foreign language education (M Ed); mathematics education (M Ed); reading (M Ed, Ed S); reading, languages and literature (Ed D); science education (M Ed); secondary education (MAT), including art education (K-12), career and technical education (MAT, Ed D, PhD, Ed S), English education (MAT, Ed D, PhD, Ed S), foreign language education (MAT, PhD), kinesiology; social studies education secondary (M Ed); special education (M Ed, Ed D, PhD, Ed S). *Students:* 216 full-time (154 women), 626 part-time (478 women); includes 289 minority (227 Black or African American, non-Hispanic/Latino; 4 American Indian or Alaska Native, non-Hispanic/Latino; 27 Asian, non-Hispanic/Latino; 21 Hispanic/Latino; 1 Native Hawaiian or other Pacific Islander, non-Hispanic/Latino; 9 Two or more races, non-Hispanic/Latino), 14 international. Average age 37. 347 applicants, 37% accepted, 93 enrolled. In 2011, 226 master's, 12 doctorates, 46 other advanced degrees awarded. *Degree requirements:* For master's, thesis (for some programs), thesis, essay or project (for some M Ed programs), professional field experience (for MAT programs); for doctorate, thesis/dissertation. *Entrance requirements:* For master's, Michigan Basic Skills Test (MA in teaching); for doctorate, minimum undergraduate GPA of 3.0, graduate 3.5; interview, curriculum vitae; references. Additional exam requirements/recommendations for international students: Required—TOEFL (minimum score 550 paper-based; 213 computer-based), TWE (minimum score 5.5). *Application deadline:* For fall admission, 6/1 priority date for domestic students, 5/1 for international students; for winter admission, 10/1 priority date for domestic students, 9/1 for international students; for spring admission, 2/1 priority date for domestic students, 1/1 for international students. Applications are processed on a rolling basis. Application fee: $50. Electronic applications accepted. *Expenses:* Tuition, state resident: part-time $512.85 per credit. Tuition, nonresident: part-time $1132.65 per credit. *Required fees:* $26.60 per credit. $199.65 per semester. Tuition and fees vary according to course load and program. *Financial support:* In 2011–12, 42 students received support. Fellowships, research assistantships with tuition reimbursements available, teaching assistantships, scholarships/grants, and unspecified assistantships available. *Faculty research:* Reading and writing literacy and literature. *Total annual research expenditures:* $264,016. *Unit head:* Dr. Craig Roney, Assistant Dean, 313-577-0902, E-mail: rroney@wayne.edu. Web site: http://coe.wayne.edu/ted/index.php.

Webster University, School of Education, Department of Multidisciplinary Studies, St. Louis, MO 63119-3194. Offers administrative leadership (Ed S); education leadership (Ed S); educational technology (MAT); mathematics (MAT); multidisciplinary studies (MAT); school systems, superintendency and leadership (Ed S); social science (MAT); special education (MAT). Part-time programs available. *Entrance requirements:* For master's, minimum GPA of 2.5. Additional exam requirements/recommendations for international students: Required—TOEFL. *Expenses: Tuition:* Full-time $10,890; part-time $605 per credit hour. Tuition and fees vary according to campus/location and program.

West Chester University of Pennsylvania, College of Education, Department of Special Education, West Chester, PA 19383. Offers autism (Certificate); special education (M Ed, Certificate, Teaching Certificate); special education: distance education (M Ed); universal design for learning and assistive technology (Certificate); universal design for learning and assistive technology: distance education (Certificate). *Accreditation:* NCATE. Part-time and evening/weekend programs available. Postbaccalaureate distance learning degree programs offered (no on-campus study). *Faculty:* 1 full-time (0 women), 5 part-time/adjunct (all women). *Students:* 11 full-time (10 women), 87 part-time (74 women); includes 9 minority (1 Black or African American, non-Hispanic/Latino; 4 Asian, non-Hispanic/Latino; 4 Hispanic/Latino). Average age 29. 56 applicants, 73% accepted, 22 enrolled. In 2011, 12 degrees awarded. *Degree requirements:* For master's, thesis optional, minimum GPA of 3.0. *Entrance requirements:* For master's, GMAT, GRE General Test, or MAT, interview, minimum GPA of 2.8, two letters of recommendation. Additional exam requirements/recommendations for international students: Required—TOEFL (minimum score 550 paper-based; 213 computer-based; 80 iBT). *Application deadline:* For fall admission, 4/15 priority date for domestic students, 3/15 for international students; for spring admission, 10/15 priority date for domestic students, 9/1 for international students. Applications are processed on a rolling basis. Application fee: $45. Electronic applications accepted. *Expenses:* Tuition, state resident: full-time $7488; part-time $416 per credit. Tuition, nonresident: full-time $11,232; part-time $624 per credit. *Required fees:* $1784.64; $67.59 per credit. Tuition and fees vary according to program. *Financial support:* Unspecified assistantships available. Support available to part-time students. Financial award application deadline: 2/15; financial award applicants required to submit FAFSA. *Faculty research:* Developing online instruction for children with disabilities. *Unit head:* Dr. Donna Wandry, Chair, 610-436-3431, Fax: 610-436-3102, E-mail: dwandry@wcupa.edu. *Application contact:* Dr. Vicki McGinley, Graduate Coordinator, 610-436-2867, E-mail: vmcginley@wcupa.edu. Web site: http://www.wcupa.edu/_academics/sch_sed.earlyspecialed/.

Western Connecticut State University, Division of Graduate Studies, School of Professional Studies, Department of Education and Educational Psychology, Special Education Option, Danbury, CT 06810-6885. Offers MS. Part-time programs available. *Faculty:* 2 full-time (1 woman). *Students:* 20 part-time (16 women); includes 1 minority (Two or more races, non-Hispanic/Latino). Average age 29. 11 applicants, 64% accepted, 5 enrolled. In 2011, 20 degrees awarded. *Degree requirements:* For master's, thesis or research project. *Entrance requirements:* For master's, minimum GPA of 2.8, teaching certificate. Additional exam requirements/recommendations for international students: Recommended—TOEFL (minimum score 550 paper-based; 213 computer-based; 79 iBT), IELTS (minimum score 6). *Application deadline:* For fall admission, 8/5 priority date for domestic students; for spring admission, 1/5 priority date for domestic students. Applications are processed on a rolling basis. Application fee: $50. Tuition and fees vary according to course level, course load, degree level and program. *Financial support:* Scholarships/grants available. Financial award application deadline: 5/1; financial award applicants required to submit FAFSA. *Faculty research:* Education and development of exceptional, gifted, talented, and disabled students in a regular (mainstream) classroom. *Unit head:* Dr. Adeline Merrill, Graduate Coordinator, 203-837-3267, Fax: 203-837-8413, E-mail: merrilla@wcsu.edu. *Application contact:* Chris Shankle, Associate Director of Graduate Studies, 203-837-9005, Fax: 203-837-8326, E-mail: shanklec@wcsu.edu.

Western Governors University, Teachers College, Salt Lake City, UT 84107. Offers curriculum and instruction (MS); educational leadership (MS); educational studies (MA); educational studies (5-12) (MA), including mathematics; elementary education (k-8) (Postbaccalaureate Certificate); English language learning (K-12) (MA); instructional design (MAT); learning and technology (M Ed, MA); management and innovation (M Ed); mathematics (5-12) (Postbaccalaureate Certificate); mathematics (5-9) (Postbaccalaureate Certificate); mathematics education (5-12) (MA); mathematics education (5-9) (MA); mathematics education (K-6) (MA); measurement and evaluation (M Ed); science (5-12) (Postbaccalaureate Certificate); science (5-9) (Postbaccalaureate Certificate); science education (5-12) (MA), including biology, chemistry, geology, physics; science education (5-9) (MA); social science (5-12) (MAT); special education (MAT). *Accreditation:* NCATE. Evening/weekend programs available. Postbaccalaureate distance learning degree programs offered (no on-campus study). *Students:* 3,746 full-time (2,811 women); includes 652 minority (332 Black or African American, non-Hispanic/Latino; 37 American Indian or Alaska Native, non-Hispanic/Latino; 74 Asian, non-Hispanic/Latino; 139 Hispanic/Latino; 70 Two or more races, non-Hispanic/Latino), 12 international. Average age 37. In 2011, 1,080 master's, 242 other advanced degrees awarded. *Degree requirements:* For master's, capstone project. *Entrance requirements:* For master's and Postbaccalaureate Certificate, Readiness Assessment, commitment counseling discussion, transcript submissions, completion of orientation. Additional exam requirements/recommendations for international students: Required—TOEFL (minimum score 450 paper-based; 80 iBT). *Application deadline:* Applications are processed on a rolling basis. Application fee: $65. Electronic applications accepted. *Expenses:* Contact institution. *Financial support:* Scholarships/grants and tuition waivers (partial) available. Financial award applicants required to submit FAFSA. *Unit head:* Dr. Philip Schmidt, Dean of the Teachers College, 845-255-4656. *Application contact:* Enrollment Department, 866-225-5948, Fax: 801-274-3306, E-mail: info@wgu.edu.

Western Illinois University, School of Graduate Studies, College of Education and Human Services, Department of Curriculum and Instruction, Department of Special Education, Macomb, IL 61455-1390. Offers MS Ed. *Accreditation:* NCATE. Part-time programs available. *Students:* 5 full-time (all women), 29 part-time (27 women). Average age 34. 4 applicants, 25% accepted. In 2011, 8 master's awarded. *Degree requirements:* For master's, comprehensive exam, thesis or alternative. *Entrance requirements:* For master's, teacher certification. Additional exam requirements/recommendations for international students: Required—TOEFL (minimum score 550 paper-based; 213 computer-based; 80 iBT). *Application deadline:* Applications are processed on a rolling basis. Application fee: $30. Electronic applications accepted. *Expenses:* Tuition, state resident: part-time $281.16 per credit hour. Tuition, nonresident: part-time $562.32 per credit hour. Part-time tuition and fees vary according to campus/location and reciprocity agreements. *Financial support:* Applicants required to submit FAFSA. *Unit head:* Dr. Sharon Maroney, Graduate Committee Chairperson, 309-762-9481. *Application contact:* Dr. Nancy Parsons, Interim Associate Provost and Director of Graduate Studies, 309-298-1806, Fax: 309-298-2345, E-mail: grad-office@wiu.edu. Web site: http://wiu.edu/sped/.

Western Kentucky University, Graduate Studies, College of Education and Behavioral Sciences, School of Teacher Education, Bowling Green, KY 42101. Offers elementary education (MAE, Ed S); exceptional education: learning and behavioral disorders (MAE); exceptional education: moderate and severe disabilities (MAE); instructional design (MS); interdisciplinary early childhood education (MAE); library media education (MS); literacy education (MAE); middle grades education (MAE); secondary education (MAE, Ed S). Part-time and evening/weekend programs available. Postbaccalaureate distance learning degree programs offered (minimal on-campus study). *Degree requirements:* For master's, comprehensive exam. *Entrance requirements:* For master's, GRE General Test. Additional exam requirements/recommendations for international students: Required—TOEFL (minimum score 555 paper-based; 213 computer-based; 79 iBT). *Faculty research:* Teacher preparation in moderate/severe disabilities.

Western Michigan University, Graduate College, College of Education and Human Development, Department of Special Education and Literacy Studies, Kalamazoo, MI 49008. Offers literacy studies (MA); special education (MA, Ed D); teaching children with visual impairments (MA).

Western New Mexico University, Graduate Division, School of Education, Silver City, NM 88062-0680. Offers bilingual education (MAT); counseling (MA); educational leadership (MA); elementary education (MAT); reading (MAT); school psychology (MA); secondary education (MAT); special education (MAT); TESOL (teaching English to speakers of other languages) (MAT). *Accreditation:* NCATE. *Degree requirements:* For master's, comprehensive exam. *Entrance requirements:* For master's, GRE General Test, GRE Subject Test, minimum GPA of 3.2 in last 64 hours of undergraduate study. Additional exam requirements/recommendations for international students: Required—TOEFL (minimum score 550 paper-based; 213 computer-based). Electronic applications accepted.

Western Oregon University, Graduate Programs, College of Education, Division of Special Education, Program in Deaf Education, Monmouth, OR 97361-1394. Offers MS Ed. *Accreditation:* NCATE. Part-time and evening/weekend programs available. *Degree requirements:* For master's, thesis, portfolio. *Entrance requirements:* For master's, California Basic Educational Skills Test or PRAXIS, GRE General Test or MAT, interview, minimum GPA of 3.0, teaching license. Additional exam requirements/recommendations for international students: Required—TOEFL (minimum score 550 paper-based; 213 computer-based; 79 iBT), IELTS (minimum score 6.5). *Faculty research:* Effects of infant massage on the interactions between high-risk infants and their caregivers, work sample methodology.

Western Oregon University, Graduate Programs, College of Education, Division of Special Education, Special Education Program, Monmouth, OR 97361-1394. Offers MS Ed. Part-time and evening/weekend programs available. *Degree requirements:* For master's, comprehensive exam (for some programs), thesis optional, oral exam, portfolio, written exam. *Entrance requirements:* For master's, California Basic Educational Skills Test or PRAXIS, GRE General Test or MAT, interview, minimum GPA of 3.0, teaching license. Additional exam requirements/recommendations for international students: Required—TOEFL (minimum score 550 paper-based; 213 computer-based; 79 iBT), IELTS (minimum score 6.5). *Faculty research:* Interpreter teacher training, hearing disabilities, mental retardation.

Westfield State University, Division of Graduate and Continuing Education, Department of Education, Program in Special Education, Westfield, MA 01086. Offers M Ed. *Accreditation:* NCATE. Part-time and evening/weekend programs available. *Degree requirements:* For master's, comprehensive exam, practicum. *Entrance requirements:* For master's, GRE General Test or MAT, minimum undergraduate GPA of 2.7.

West Texas A&M University, College of Education and Social Sciences, Division of Education, Program in Special Education, Canyon, TX 79016-0001. Offers M Ed. *Degree requirements:* For master's, comprehensive exam, thesis optional. *Entrance requirements:* For master's, GRE, standard classroom teaching certificate. Additional exam requirements/recommendations for international students: Required—TOEFL.

West Virginia University, College of Human Resources and Education, Department of Curriculum and Instruction/Literacy Studies, Morgantown, WV 26506. Offers curriculum and instruction (Ed D); elementary education (MA); reading (MA); secondary education (MA), including higher education curriculum and teaching, secondary education; special education (Ed D), including special education. *Accreditation:* NCATE. Part-time and evening/weekend programs available. *Degree requirements:* For doctorate, comprehensive exam, thesis/dissertation. *Entrance requirements:* For master's, minimum GPA of 2.75; for doctorate, GRE General Test or MAT, 3 letters of recommendation, curriculum vitae. Additional exam requirements/recommendations for international students: Required—TOEFL. *Faculty research:* Teacher education, curriculum development, educational technology, curriculum assessment.

West Virginia University, College of Human Resources and Education, Department of Special Education, Morgantown, WV 26506. Offers autism spectrum disorder (5-adult) (MA); autism spectrum disorder (K-6) (MA); early intervention/early childhood special education (MA); gifted education (1-12) (MA); low vision (PreK-adult) (MA); multicategorical special education (5-adult) (MA); multicategorical special education (K-6) (MA); severe/multiple disabilities (K-adult) (MA); special education (MA, Ed D); vision impairments (PreK-adult) (MA). *Accreditation:* NCATE. Part-time and evening/weekend programs available. Postbaccalaureate distance learning degree programs offered (no on-campus study). *Degree requirements:* For master's, thesis optional; for doctorate, comprehensive exam, thesis/dissertation. *Entrance requirements:* For master's, minimum GPA of 2.75 passing scores on PRAXIS PPST; for doctorate, GRE General Test or MAT. Additional exam requirements/recommendations for international students: Required—TOEFL.

Wheelock College, Graduate Programs, Division of Education, Boston, MA 02215-4176. Offers early childhood education (MS); education leadership (MS); elementary education (MS); language, literacy, and reading (MS); teaching students with moderate disabilities (MS). *Accreditation:* NCATE. Postbaccalaureate distance learning degree programs offered (minimal on-campus study). *Degree requirements:* For master's, comprehensive exam. *Entrance requirements:* Additional exam requirements/recommendations for international students: Required—TOEFL. Electronic applications accepted. *Faculty research:* Symbolic learning, emergent literacy, diversity inclusion, beginning reading language and culture, math education.

Whitworth University, School of Education, Graduate Studies in Education, Program in Special Education, Spokane, WA 99251-0001. Offers MAT. *Accreditation:* NCATE. Part-time and evening/weekend programs available. *Degree requirements:* For master's, comprehensive exam, internship, practicum, research project, or thesis. *Entrance requirements:* For master's, GRE General Test, MAT. Additional exam requirements/recommendations for international students: Required—TOEFL. Tuition and fees vary according to program.

Wichita State University, Graduate School, College of Education, Department of Curriculum and Instruction, Wichita, KS 67260. Offers curriculum and instruction (M Ed); special education (M Ed), including adaptive, early childhood unified (M Ed, MAT), functional, gifted; teaching (MAT), including curriculum and instruction, early childhood unified (M Ed, MAT). *Accreditation:* NCATE. Part-time and evening/weekend programs available. *Entrance requirements:* For master's, MAT, minimum GPA of 2.75. *Expenses:* Tuition, state resident: full-time $4746; part-time $263.65 per credit. Tuition, nonresident: full-time $11,669; part-time $648.30 per credit. *Unit head:* Dr. Janice Ewing, Chairperson, 316-978-3322, E-mail: janice.ewing@wichita.edu. *Application contact:* Dr. Kay Gibson, Graduate Coordinator, 316-978-3322, E-mail: kay.gibson@wichita.edu. Web site: http://www.wichita.edu/.

Widener University, School of Human Service Professions, Center for Education, Chester, PA 19013-5792. Offers adult education (M Ed); counseling in higher education (M Ed); counselor education (M Ed); early childhood education (M Ed); educational foundations (M Ed); educational leadership (M Ed); educational psychology (M Ed); elementary education (M Ed); English and language arts (M Ed); health education (M Ed); higher education leadership (Ed D); home and school visitor (M Ed); human sexuality (M Ed, PhD); mathematics education (M Ed); middle school education (M Ed); principalship (M Ed); reading and language arts (Ed D); reading education (M Ed); school administration (Ed D); science education (M Ed); social studies education (M Ed); special education (M Ed); technology education (M Ed). *Accreditation:* NCATE. Part-time and evening/weekend programs available. Terminal master's awarded for partial completion of doctoral program. *Degree requirements:* For doctorate, thesis/dissertation. *Entrance requirements:* For master's, minimum GPA of 2.5; for doctorate, GRE or MAT, minimum GPA of 2.0 (undergraduate), 3.5 (graduate). Electronic applications accepted. *Expenses:* Contact institution. *Faculty research:* Reading and cognition, adult education, technology education, educational leadership, special education.

Wilkes University, College of Graduate and Professional Studies, School of Education, Wilkes-Barre, PA 18766-0002. Offers art and science of teaching (MS Ed); classroom technology (MS Ed); early childhood literacy (MS Ed); educational computing (MS Ed); educational development and strategies (MS Ed); educational leadership (MS Ed); educational technology (Ed D); higher education administration (Ed D); instructional media (MS Ed); instructional technology (MS Ed); K-12 administration (Ed D); online teaching (MS Ed); reading (MS Ed); school business leadership (MS Ed); secondary education (MS Ed), including biology, chemistry, English, history, mathematics; special education (MS Ed); teaching English as a second language (MS Ed); twenty-first century teaching and learning (MS Ed). Part-time and evening/weekend programs available. Postbaccalaureate distance learning degree programs offered (minimal on-campus study). *Students:* 92 full-time (63 women), 2,005 part-time (1,459 women); includes 89 minority (23 Black or African American, non-Hispanic/Latino; 1 American Indian or Alaska Native, non-Hispanic/Latino; 14 Asian, non-Hispanic/Latino; 33 Hispanic/Latino; 1 Native Hawaiian or other Pacific Islander, non-Hispanic/Latino; 17 Two or more races, non-Hispanic/Latino), 6 international. Average age 33. In 2011, 1,150 master's, 3 doctorates awarded. *Entrance requirements:* Additional exam requirements/recommendations for international students: Required—TOEFL (minimum score 550 paper-based; 213 computer-based; 79 iBT). *Application deadline:* Applications are processed on a rolling basis. Application fee: $45. Electronic applications accepted. *Expenses:* Contact institution. *Financial support:* Federal Work-Study and unspecified assistantships available. Financial award application deadline: 3/1; financial award applicants required to submit FAFSA. *Unit head:* Dr. Michael Speziale, Dean, 570-408-4679, Fax: 570-408-4905, E-mail: michael.speziale@wilkes.edu. *Application contact:* Erin Sutzko, Director of Extended Learning, 570-408-4253, Fax: 570-408-7846, E-mail: erin.sutzko@wilkes.edu. Web site: http://www.wilkes.edu/pages/383.asp.

Willamette University, Graduate School of Education, Salem, OR 97301-3931. Offers environmental literacy (M Ed); reading (M Ed); special education (M Ed); teaching (MAT). *Accreditation:* NCATE. Evening/weekend programs available. *Degree requirements:* For master's, leadership project (action research). *Entrance requirements:* For master's, California Basic Educational Skills Test, Multiple Subject Assessment for Teachers, PRAXIS, minimum GPA of 3.0, classroom experience, 2 letters of reference. Additional exam requirements/recommendations for international students: Recommended—TOEFL. Electronic applications accepted. *Expenses:* Contact institution. *Faculty research:* Educational leadership, multicultural education, middle school education, clinical supervision, educational technology.

William Carey University, School of Education, Hattiesburg, MS 39401-5499. Offers art education (M Ed); art of teaching (M Ed); elementary education (M Ed, Ed S); English education (M Ed); gifted education (M Ed); history and social science (M Ed);

mild/moderate disabilities (M Ed); secondary education (M Ed). Part-time programs available. *Degree requirements:* For master's, comprehensive exam. *Entrance requirements:* For master's, GRE, MAT, minimum GPA of 2.5, Class A teacher's license. Additional exam requirements/recommendations for international students: Required—TOEFL (minimum score 550 paper-based; 213 computer-based).

William Paterson University of New Jersey, College of Education, Department of Special Education and Counseling Services, Wayne, NJ 07470-8420. Offers counseling services (M Ed); special education (M Ed). *Accreditation:* NCATE. *Degree requirements:* For master's, comprehensive exam, thesis. *Entrance requirements:* For master's, GRE General Test, MAT, minimum GPA of 2.75, teaching certificate. Electronic applications accepted.

William Woods University, Graduate and Adult Studies, Fulton, MO 65251-1098. Offers administration (Ed S); agriculture (MBA); athletic/activities administration (M Ed); curriculum and instruction (M Ed); curriculum leadership (Ed S); elementary administration (M Ed); health management (MBA); human resources (MBA); principalship (Ed S); secondary administration (M Ed); special education director (M Ed). Evening/weekend programs available. *Degree requirements:* For master's, capstone course (MBA), action research (M Ed); for Ed S, field experience. *Entrance requirements:* For master's, 2 recommendations, resumé, BA/BS; teaching certification (M Ed); course work in economics and accounting (MBA); for Ed S, M Ed, 2 letters of recommendation, resume, teaching certification. Additional exam requirements/recommendations for international students: Required—TOEFL (minimum score 550 paper-based). Electronic applications accepted.

Wilmington College, Department of Education, Wilmington, OH 45177. Offers reading (M Ed); special education (M Ed). Part-time programs available. *Degree requirements:* For master's, comprehensive exam. *Entrance requirements:* For master's, GRE or MAT, minimum GPA of 3.0, 2 letters of recommendation. Additional exam requirements/recommendations for international students: Required—TOEFL. *Faculty research:* Reading instruction, special education practices, conflict resolution in the schools, models of higher education for teachers.

Wilmington University, College of Education, New Castle, DE 19720-6491. Offers applied technology in education (M Ed); career and technical education (M Ed); educational leadership (Ed D); elementary and secondary school counseling (M Ed); elementary studies (M Ed); ESOL literacy (M Ed); higher education leadership (Ed D); instruction: gifted and talented (M Ed); instruction: teacher of reading (M Ed); instruction: teaching and learning (M Ed); organizational leadership (Ed D); school leadership (M Ed); secondary education (MAT); special education (M Ed). *Accreditation:* NCATE. Part-time and evening/weekend programs available. *Faculty:* 7 full-time (4 women). *Students:* 638 full-time (425 women), 2,014 part-time (1,635 women). Average age 33. *Entrance requirements:* For master's, 2 letters of recommendation, interview. Additional exam requirements/recommendations for international students: Required—TOEFL (minimum score 500 paper-based; 173 computer-based). *Application deadline:* For fall admission, 4/30 for domestic students. Applications are processed on a rolling basis. Application fee: $35. Electronic applications accepted. *Expenses: Tuition:* Part-time $534 per credit hour. *Required fees:* $25 per term. *Financial support:* Applicants required to submit FAFSA. *Unit head:* Dr. John C. Gray, Dean, 302-295-1139. *Application contact:* Chris Ferguson, Director of Admissions, 302-356-4636 Ext. 256, Fax: 302-328-5164, E-mail: inquire@wilmcoll.edu. Web site: http://www.wilmu.edu/education/.

Winona State University, College of Education, Department of Special Education, Winona, MN 55987. Offers special education (MS), including developmental disabilities, learning disabilities. Part-time and evening/weekend programs available. *Students:* 12 full-time (11 women), 3 part-time (2 women). Average age 29. *Degree requirements:* For master's, comprehensive exam, thesis. *Application deadline:* For fall admission, 1/15 priority date for domestic students; for spring admission, 9/1 priority date for domestic students. Application fee: $20. *Financial support:* Teaching assistantships with full tuition reimbursements available. *Unit head:* Dr. Carol Long, Chair, 507-457-5365, Fax: 507-457-2483, E-mail: clong@winona.edu. *Application contact:* Patricia Cichosz, Office Manager, Graduate Studies, 507-457-5038, E-mail: pcichosz@winona.edu.

Winthrop University, College of Education, Program in Special Education, Rock Hill, SC 29733. Offers M Ed. *Accreditation:* NCATE. Part-time programs available. *Entrance requirements:* For master's, PRAXIS, South Carolina Class III Teaching Certificate, sample of written work. Electronic applications accepted.

Worcester State University, Graduate Studies, Department of Education, Program in Moderate Special Needs, Worcester, MA 01602-2597. Offers M Ed, Postbaccalaureate Certificate. Part-time and evening/weekend programs available. *Faculty:* 12 full-time (9 women), 22 part-time/adjunct (10 women). *Students:* 1 (woman) full-time, 31 part-time (22 women); includes 1 minority (Two or more races, non-Hispanic/Latino). Average age 34. 51 applicants, 61% accepted, 11 enrolled. In 2011, 9 master's, 18 other advanced degrees awarded. *Degree requirements:* For master's, comprehensive exam (for some programs), thesis optional. *Entrance requirements:* For master's, GRE General Test or MAT, teaching certificate. Additional exam requirements/recommendations for international students: Required—TOEFL (minimum score 500 paper-based; 61 iBT). *Application deadline:* For fall admission, 6/15 for domestic and international students; for spring admission, 4/1 for domestic and international students. Applications are processed on a rolling basis. Application fee: $40. Electronic applications accepted. *Expenses:* Tuition, state resident: full-time $2700; part-time $150 per credit. Tuition, nonresident: full-time $2700; part-time $150 per credit. *Required fees:* $2016; $112 per credit. *Financial support:* Career-related internships or fieldwork, scholarships/grants, and unspecified assistantships available. Financial award application deadline: 3/1; financial award applicants required to submit FAFSA. *Unit head:* Dr. Sue Fan Foo, Coordinator, 508-929-8071, Fax: 508-929-8164, E-mail: sfoo@worcester.edu. *Application contact:* Sara Grady, Assistant Dean of Graduate and Continuing Education, 508-929-8787, Fax: 508-929-8100, E-mail: sara.grady@worcester.edu.

Wright State University, School of Graduate Studies, College of Education and Human Services, Department of Teacher Education, Programs in Intervention Specialist, Dayton, OH 45435. Offers gifted educational needs (M Ed, MA); mild to moderate educational needs (M Ed, MA); moderate to intensive educational needs (M Ed, MA). *Accreditation:* NCATE. *Degree requirements:* For master's, thesis (for some programs). *Entrance requirements:* For master's, GRE General Test, MAT. Additional exam requirements/recommendations for international students: Required—TOEFL.

Xavier University, College of Social Sciences, Health and Education, School of Education, Department of Secondary and Special Education, Program in Special Education, Cincinnati, OH 45207. Offers M Ed. Part-time programs available. *Faculty:* 3 full-time (all women), 16 part-time/adjunct (12 women). *Students:* 47 full-time (32 women), 97 part-time (75 women); includes 19 minority (17 Black or African American, non-Hispanic/Latino; 1 Asian, non-Hispanic/Latino; 1 Hispanic/Latino), 1 international. Average age 33. 23 applicants, 100% accepted, 15 enrolled. In 2011, 32 master's awarded. *Degree requirements:* For master's, comprehensive exam, presentation of research. *Entrance requirements:* For master's, MAT, GRE. Application fee: $35. *Expenses: Tuition:* Part-time $576 per credit hour. *Financial support:* In 2011–12, 85 students received support. Applicants required to submit FAFSA. *Faculty research:* Autism, collaboration of general education and special education, mental health/special education, training criminal justice personnel in special education, technology and learning. *Unit head:* Dr. Michael Flick, Chair, 513-745-3225, Fax: 513-745-3410, E-mail: flick@xavier.edu. *Application contact:* Dr. Sharon Merrill, Director, 513-745-1078, Fax: 513-745-3410, E-mail: merrill@xavier.edu. Web site: http://www.xavier.edu/education/secondary-special-education/.

Youngstown State University, Graduate School, Beeghly College of Education, Department of Teacher Education, Program in Special Education, Youngstown, OH 44555-0001. Offers gifted and talented education (MS Ed); special education (MS Ed). *Accreditation:* NCATE. Part-time and evening/weekend programs available. *Degree requirements:* For master's, comprehensive exam. *Entrance requirements:* For master's, GRE, MAT, or teaching certificate; interview; minimum GPA of 2.7. Additional exam requirements/recommendations for international students: Required—TOEFL. *Faculty research:* Learning disabilities, learning styles, developing self-esteem and social skills of severe behaviorally handicapped students, inclusion.

Urban Education

Alvernia University, Graduate Studies, Program in Education, Reading, PA 19607-1799. Offers urban education (M Ed). Part-time and evening/weekend programs available. *Degree requirements:* For master's, thesis optional. *Entrance requirements:* For master's, GRE or MAT (alumni excluded). Electronic applications accepted.

Bakke Graduate University, Programs in Pastoral Ministry and Business, Seattle, WA 98104. Offers business (MBA); global urban leadership (MA); social and civic entrepreneurship (MA); transformational leadership for the global city (D Min). Part-time programs available. Postbaccalaureate distance learning degree programs offered (minimal on-campus study). *Degree requirements:* For master's, thesis; for doctorate, thesis/dissertation. *Entrance requirements:* For master's, 2 years of ministry experience, BA in Biblical studies or theology; for doctorate, 3 years of ministry experience, M Div. Additional exam requirements/recommendations for international students: Required—TOEFL (minimum score 60 computer-based). Electronic applications accepted. *Faculty research:* Theological systems, church management, worship.

Brown University, Graduate School, Department of Education, Program in Urban Education Policy, Providence, RI 02912. Offers AM. *Entrance requirements:* For master's, GRE General Test, official transcripts, 3 letters of recommendation, personal statement. Additional exam requirements/recommendations for international students: Required—TOEFL. Electronic applications accepted. *Faculty research:* Mayoral control of school systems.

California State University, East Bay, Office of Academic Programs and Graduate Studies, College of Education and Allied Studies, Department of Educational Leadership, Hayward, CA 94542-3000. Offers educational leadership (MS, Ed D); urban teaching leadership (MS). *Accreditation:* NCATE. Part-time and evening/weekend programs available. Postbaccalaureate distance learning degree programs offered. *Faculty:* 7 full-time (3 women), 10 part-time/adjunct (7 women). *Students:* 77 full-time (42 women), 54 part-time (40 women); includes 61 minority (23 Black or African American, non-Hispanic/Latino; 13 Asian, non-Hispanic/Latino; 20 Hispanic/Latino; 5 Two or more races, non-Hispanic/Latino), 1 international. Average age 40. 87 applicants, 86% accepted, 33 enrolled. In 2011, 46 master's, 7 doctorates awarded. *Degree requirements:* For master's, comprehensive exam, project or thesis; for doctorate, thesis/dissertation. *Entrance requirements:* For master's, CBEST, teaching or services credential and experience; minimum GPA of 3.0; for doctorate, GRE, MA with minimum GPA of 3.0; PK-12 leadership position; portfolio of work samples; employer/district support agreement. Additional exam requirements/recommendations for international students: Required—TOEFL (minimum score 550 paper-based; 213 computer-based). *Application deadline:* For fall admission, 6/30 for domestic and international students. Application fee: $55. Electronic applications accepted. *Expenses:* Tuition, state resident: full-time $6738; part-time $1302 per quarter. Tuition, nonresident: full-time $12,690; part-time $2294 per quarter. *Required fees:* $449 per quarter. Tuition and fees vary according to degree level, program and reciprocity agreements. *Financial support:* Career-related internships or fieldwork, Federal Work-Study, and institutionally sponsored loans available. Support available to part-time students. Financial award application deadline: 3/2; financial award applicants required to submit FAFSA. *Unit head:* Prof. Ray Garcia, Chair, 510-885-4145, Fax: 510-885-4642, E-mail: ray.garcia@csueastbay.edu. *Application contact:* Prof. Gilberto Arriaza, Educational Leadership Graduate Advisor, 510-885-4145, Fax: 510-885-4642, E-mail: gilberto.arriaza@csueastbay.edu. Web site: http://www20.csueastbay.edu/ceas/departments/el/.

Cardinal Stritch University, College of Education, Department of Education, Milwaukee, WI 53217-3985. Offers education (ME); educational leadership (MS); leadership for the advancement of learning and service (Ed D, PhD); teaching (MAT); urban education (MA). *Accreditation:* NCATE. Evening/weekend programs available. *Degree requirements:* For master's, comprehensive exam, thesis (for some programs), research project, faculty recommendation; for doctorate, thesis/dissertation, practica, field experience. *Entrance requirements:* For master's, letters of recommendation (3), minimum GPA of 3.0; for doctorate, minimum GPA of 3.5 in master's coursework, letters of recommendation (3).

Claremont Graduate University, Graduate Programs, School of Educational Studies, Claremont, CA 91711-6160. Offers Africana education (Certificate); education and policy (MA, PhD); higher education/student affairs (MA, PhD); human development (MA, PhD); public school administration (MA, PhD); quantitative evaluation (MA, PhD); special education (MA, PhD); teacher education (MA); teaching and learning (MA, PhD); urban leadership (PhD); MBA/PhD. PhD program offered jointly with San Diego State University. Part-time programs available. *Faculty:* 18 full-time (10 women), 2 part-time/adjunct (1 woman). *Students:* 307 full-time (220 women), 134 part-time (96 women);

includes 228 minority (59 Black or African American, non-Hispanic/Latino; 3 American Indian or Alaska Native, non-Hispanic/Latino; 37 Asian, non-Hispanic/Latino; 110 Hispanic/Latino; 2 Native Hawaiian or other Pacific Islander, non-Hispanic/Latino; 17 Two or more races, non-Hispanic/Latino), 13 international. Average age 38. In 2011, 93 master's, 23 doctorates, 10 other advanced degrees awarded. Terminal master's awarded for partial completion of doctoral program. *Entrance requirements:* For master's and doctorate, GRE General Test. Additional exam requirements/recommendations for international students: Required—TOEFL (minimum score 550 paper-based; 213 computer-based; 80 iBT). *Application deadline:* For fall admission, 2/1 priority date for domestic students. Applications are processed on a rolling basis. Application fee: $60. Electronic applications accepted. *Expenses: Tuition:* Full-time $36,374; part-time $1581 per unit. *Required fees:* $165 per semester. *Financial support:* Fellowships, research assistantships, Federal Work-Study, institutionally sponsored loans, and scholarships/grants available. Support available to part-time students. Financial award application deadline: 2/15; financial award applicants required to submit FAFSA. *Faculty research:* Education administration, K-12 and higher education, multicultural education, education policy, diversity in higher education, faculty issues. *Unit head:* Margaret Grogan, Dean, 909-621-8075, Fax: 909-621-8734, E-mail: margaret.grogan@cgu.edu. *Application contact:* Julia Evans, Director of Central Recruitment, 909-607-3689, Fax: 909-607-7285, E-mail: admiss@cgu.edu. Web site: http://www.cgu.edu/pages/267.asp.

Cleveland State University, College of Graduate Studies, College of Education and Human Services, Program in Urban Education, Cleveland, OH 44115. Offers counseling (PhD); counseling psychology (PhD); leadership and lifelong learning (PhD); learning and development (PhD); policy studies (PhD); school administration (PhD). Part-time programs available. *Faculty:* 16 full-time (8 women), 15 part-time/adjunct (12 women). *Students:* 33 full-time (27 women), 86 part-time (58 women); includes 39 minority (32 Black or African American, non-Hispanic/Latino; 4 Asian, non-Hispanic/Latino; 3 Hispanic/Latino), 8 international. Average age 40. 54 applicants, 44% accepted, 16 enrolled. In 2011, 17 doctorates awarded. *Degree requirements:* For doctorate, one foreign language, comprehensive exam, thesis/dissertation. *Entrance requirements:* For doctorate, GRE General Test, minimum graduate GPA of 3.25. Additional exam requirements/recommendations for international students: Required—TOEFL (minimum score 525 paper-based; 197 computer-based), IELTS (minimum score 6). *Application deadline:* For fall admission, 2/5 for domestic students. Application fee: $30. *Expenses:* Tuition, state resident: full-time $6416; part-time $494 per credit hour. Tuition, nonresident: full-time $12,074; part-time $929 per credit hour. *Financial support:* In 2011–12, 7 students received support, including 4 research assistantships with full and partial tuition reimbursements available (averaging $7,800 per year), 3 teaching assistantships with full and partial tuition reimbursements available (averaging $7,800 per year); tuition waivers (full) and unspecified assistantships also available. Financial award applicants required to submit FAFSA. *Faculty research:* Equity issues (race, ethnicity, and gender), education development consequences for special needs of urban populations, urban education programming, counseling the violent or aggressive adolescent. *Total annual research expenditures:* $5,662. *Unit head:* Dr. Joshua Bagakas, Director, 216-687-4591, Fax: 216-875-9697, E-mail: j.bagakas@csuohio.edu. *Application contact:* Wanda Butler, Administrative Assistant, 216-687-4697, Fax: 216-875-9697, E-mail: w.pruett-butler@csuohio.edu. Web site: http://www.csuohio.edu/coehs/departments/phd/.

Cleveland State University, College of Graduate Studies, School of Nursing, Cleveland, OH 44115. Offers clinical nurse leader (MSN); forensic nursing (MSN); nursing education (MSN); specialized population (MSN); urban education (PhD), including nursing education; MSN/MBA. *Accreditation:* AACN. Part-time programs available. Postbaccalaureate distance learning degree programs offered (no on-campus study). *Faculty:* 4 full-time (all women), 1 (woman) part-time/adjunct. *Students:* 5 full-time (3 women), 50 part-time (47 women); includes 8 minority (7 Black or African American, non-Hispanic/Latino; 1 Hispanic/Latino), 1 international. Average age 43. 41 applicants, 73% accepted, 13 enrolled. In 2011, 7 master's awarded. *Degree requirements:* For master's, thesis or alternative, portfolio, population health project; for doctorate, comprehensive exam, thesis/dissertation. *Entrance requirements:* For master's, RN license, BSN, course work in statistics; for doctorate, GRE (for PhD in urban education). Additional exam requirements/recommendations for international students: Required—TOEFL (minimum score 525 paper-based; 197 computer-based), IELTS (minimum score 6). *Application deadline:* For fall admission, 3/1 priority date for domestic students, 3/1 for international students. Application fee: $55. Electronic applications accepted. *Expenses:* Tuition, state resident: full-time $6416; part-time $494 per credit hour. Tuition, nonresident: full-time $12,074; part-time $929 per credit hour. *Financial support:* In 2011–12, 4 students received support. Tuition waivers (full), unspecified assistantships, and Nurse Faculty Loan Program (NFLP) available. Support available to part-time students. Financial award application deadline: 3/1; financial award applicants required to submit FAFSA. *Faculty research:* Diabetes management, African-American elders medication compliance, risk in home visiting, suffering, COPD and stress, nursing education, disaster health preparedness. *Total annual research expenditures:* $59,000. *Unit head:* Dr. Vida Lock, Dean, 216-523-7237, Fax: 216-687-3556, E-mail: v.lock@csuohio.edu. *Application contact:* Carol Ivan, Recruiter/Advisor, 216-687-5517, Fax: 216-687-3556, E-mail: c.ivan@csuohio.edu. Web site: http://www.csuohio.edu/nursing/.

College of Mount Saint Vincent, School of Professional and Continuing Studies, Department of Teacher Education, Riverdale, NY 10471-1093. Offers instructional technology and global perspectives (Certificate); middle level education (Certificate); multicultural studies (Certificate); urban and multicultural education (MS Ed). *Accreditation:* Teacher Education Accreditation Council. Part-time programs available. *Degree requirements:* For master's, comprehensive exam. *Entrance requirements:* For master's, interview, New York teaching certificate. Additional exam requirements/recommendations for international students: Required—TOEFL.

Columbia College Chicago, Graduate School, Department of Educational Studies, Chicago, IL 60605-1996. Offers elementary education (MAT); English (MAT); interdisciplinary arts (MAT); multicultural education (MA); urban teaching (MA). Part-time and evening/weekend programs available. *Degree requirements:* For master's, thesis, student teaching experience, 100 pre-clinical hours. *Entrance requirements:* For master's, supplemental recommendation form. Additional exam requirements/recommendations for international students: Required—TOEFL (minimum score 550 paper-based; 213 computer-based). Electronic applications accepted.

Florida International University, College of Education, Department of Educational Leadership and Policy Studies, Miami, FL 33199. Offers adult education (MS); adult education in human resource development (Ed D); clinical mental health counseling (MS); conflict resolution and consensus building (Certificate); counselor education (MS); educational administration and supervision (Ed D); educational leadership (MS, Certificate, Ed S); higher education (Ed D); higher education administration (MS); human resource development (MS); instruction in urban settings (MS); international/intercultural education (MS); learning technologies (MS); multicultural-bilingual (MS); multicultural-TESOL (MS); recreation and sport management (MS); recreation therapy (MS); rehabilitation counseling (MS); school counseling (MS); school psychology (Ed S); urban education (MS). Part-time and evening/weekend programs available. *Degree requirements:* For doctorate, thesis/dissertation. *Entrance requirements:* For master's, minimum GPA of 3.0; for doctorate and other advanced degree, GRE General Test. Additional exam requirements/recommendations for international students: Required—TOEFL (minimum score 550 paper-based; 213 computer-based; 80 iBT), IELTS (minimum score 6.3). Electronic applications accepted.

Graduate School and University Center of the City University of New York, Graduate Studies, Program in Urban Education, New York, NY 10016-4039. Offers PhD. *Entrance requirements:* For doctorate, GRE General Test. Additional exam requirements/recommendations for international students: Required—TOEFL. Electronic applications accepted.

Holy Names University, Graduate Division, Department of Education, Oakland, CA 94619-1699. Offers educational therapy (Certificate); level 1 education specialist mild/moderate disabilities (Credential); level 2 education specialist mild/moderate disabilities (Credential); multiple subject teaching credential (Credential); single subject teaching credential (Credential); teaching English as a second language (TESL) (M Ed); urban education: educational therapy (M Ed); urban education: K-12 education (M Ed); urban education: special education (M Ed). Part-time programs available. *Degree requirements:* For master's, comprehensive exam, research paper, thesis or project. *Entrance requirements:* For master's, minimum undergraduate GPA of 2.6 overall, 3.0 in major. Additional exam requirements/recommendations for international students: Required—TOEFL (minimum score 550 paper-based; 213 computer-based; 80 iBT). *Faculty research:* Cognitive development, language development, learning handicaps.

The Johns Hopkins University, School of Education, Department of Interdisciplinary Studies in Education, Baltimore, MD 21218. Offers earth/space science (Certificate); education (MS), including educational studies; health care education (MEHP); mind, brain, and teaching (Certificate); teaching the adult learner (Certificate); urban education (Certificate). Part-time and evening/weekend programs available. Postbaccalaureate distance learning degree programs offered (minimal on-campus study). *Degree requirements:* For master's, capstone course. *Entrance requirements:* For master's and Certificate, minimum undergraduate GPA of 3.0. Additional exam requirements/recommendations for international students: Required—TOEFL (minimum score 600 paper-based; 250 computer-based; 100 iBT). Electronic applications accepted. *Faculty research:* Neuro-education, urban school reform, leadership development, teacher leadership, charter schools, techniques for teaching reading to adolescents with delayed reading skills, school culture.

Kean University, Nathan Weiss Graduate College, Program in Urban Leadership, Union, NJ 07083. Offers Ed D. *Faculty:* 6 full-time (3 women). *Students:* 59 part-time (41 women); includes 43 minority (38 Black or African American, non-Hispanic/Latino; 5 Hispanic/Latino). Average age 44. 20 applicants, 65% accepted, 13 enrolled. *Degree requirements:* For doctorate, comprehensive exam, thesis/dissertation. *Entrance requirements:* For doctorate, GRE General Test, GRE Subject Test in psychology (taken within the last 5 years), master's degree from accredited college, minimum GPA of 3.0 in last degree attained, substantial experience working in education or family support agencies, 2 letters of recommendation, personal interview, transcripts, leadership portfolio, resume. Additional exam requirements/recommendations for international students: Required—TOEFL (minimum score 79 iBT). *Application deadline:* For fall admission, 6/1 for domestic and international students; for spring admission, 12/1 for domestic and international students. Applications are processed on a rolling basis. Application fee: $75 ($150 for international students). Electronic applications accepted. *Expenses:* Contact institution. *Financial support:* In 2011–12, research assistantships (averaging $3,263 per year) were awarded; unspecified assistantships also available. Financial award applicants required to submit FAFSA. *Unit head:* Dr. Effie Christie, Program Director, 908-737-5974, E-mail: echristi@kean.edu. *Application contact:* Reenat Hasan, Admissions Counselor, 908-737-5923, Fax: 908-737-5925, E-mail: hasanr@kean.edu. Web site: http://www.kean.edu/KU/Doctor-of-Education-Ed-D-in-Urban-Leadership.

Langston University, School of Education and Behavioral Sciences, Langston, OK 73050. Offers bilingual/multicultural (M Ed); elementary education (M Ed); English as a second language (M Ed); rehabilitation counseling (M Sc); urban education (M Ed). *Accreditation:* CORE; NCATE (one or more programs are accredited). Part-time programs available. *Degree requirements:* For master's, comprehensive exam, thesis optional. *Entrance requirements:* For master's, GRE, writing skills test, minimum GPA of 2.5, 3 letters of recommendation. Additional exam requirements/recommendations for international students: Required—TOEFL, TWE. *Faculty research:* Bilingual/multicultural education, financing post-secondary education.

Loyola Marymount University, School of Education, Department of Specialized Programs in Urban Education, Program in Urban Education, Los Angeles, CA 90045. Offers MA. *Faculty:* 13 full-time (7 women), 10 part-time/adjunct (6 women). *Students:* 149 full-time (100 women), 1 (woman) part-time; includes 80 minority (16 Black or African American, non-Hispanic/Latino; 18 Asian, non-Hispanic/Latino; 40 Hispanic/Latino; 6 Two or more races, non-Hispanic/Latino). Average age 23. 98 applicants, 99% accepted, 95 enrolled. In 2011, 42 master's awarded. *Entrance requirements:* For master's, CBEST, CSET, letters of recommendation, statement of intent, interview, verification of employment as full-time teacher. Additional exam requirements/recommendations for international students: Required—TOEFL (minimum score 600 paper-based; 250 computer-based; 100 iBT). *Application deadline:* For fall admission, 6/15 for domestic students; for spring admission, 11/15 for domestic students. Application fee: $50. Electronic applications accepted. *Financial support:* In 2011–12, 149 students received support. Scholarships/grants and unspecified assistantships available. Support available to part-time students. Financial award applicants required to submit FAFSA. *Unit head:* Dr. Mary McCullough, Chair, 310-338-7312, E-mail: mmccullo@lmu.edu. *Application contact:* Chake H. Kouyoumjian, Director, Graduate Admissions, 310-338-2721, E-mail: ckouyoum@lmu.edu. Web site: http://bulletin.lmu.edu/specialized-programs-in-urban-education_0.htm.

Marygrove College, Graduate Division, Griot Program, Detroit, MI 48221-2599. Offers M Ed.

Mercy College, School of Education, Program in Urban Education, Dobbs Ferry, NY 10522-1189. Offers MS. Part-time and evening/weekend programs available. *Degree requirements:* For master's, comprehensive exam. *Entrance requirements:* For master's, appropriate New York State Teacher Examinations, including the Liberal Arts and Sciences Test (LAST) and the Content Specialty Test (CST), undergraduate transcript listing conferred bachelor's degree with major in a liberal arts and sciences subject or an interdisciplinary field. Additional exam requirements/recommendations for international students: Required—TOEFL (minimum score 600 paper-based; 250 computer-based; 100 iBT), IELTS (minimum score 8). Electronic applications accepted.

Morgan State University, School of Graduate Studies, School of Education and Urban Studies, Department of Advanced Studies, Leadership and Policy, Baltimore, MD 21251. Offers educational administration and supervision (MS); elementary and middle school education (MS), including elementary education; higher education administration (PhD); higher education-community college leadership (Ed D); mathematics education (MS, Ed D); science education (MS, Ed D); urban educational leadership (Ed D).

Accreditation: NCATE. Part-time and evening/weekend programs available. *Entrance requirements:* Additional exam requirements/recommendations for international students: Required—TOEFL. *Faculty research:* Multicultural education, cooperative learning, psychology of cognition.

New Jersey City University, Graduate Studies and Continuing Education, Debra Cannon Partridge Wolfe College of Education, Department of Educational Leadership, Jersey City, NJ 07305-1597. Offers basics and urban studies (MA); bilingual/bicultural education and English as a second language (MA); educational administration and supervision (MA). Part-time and evening/weekend programs available. *Students:* 16 full-time (12 women), 167 part-time (113 women); includes 72 minority (18 Black or African American, non-Hispanic/Latino; 3 Asian, non-Hispanic/Latino; 51 Hispanic/Latino), 6 international. Average age 34. In 2011, 126 master's awarded. *Entrance requirements:* Additional exam requirements/recommendations for international students: Required—TOEFL. *Application deadline:* For fall admission, 8/1 priority date for domestic students; for spring admission, 12/1 for domestic students. Applications are processed on a rolling basis. Application fee: $0. *Expenses:* Tuition, state resident: part-time $494 per credit. Tuition, nonresident: part-time $911.30 per credit. *Required fees:* $95.90 per year. *Financial support:* Fellowships, teaching assistantships, career-related internships or fieldwork, and unspecified assistantships available. *Unit head:* Dr. Catherine Rogers, Chairperson, 201-200-3012, E-mail: cshevey@njcu.edu. *Application contact:* Dr. William Bajor, Dean of Graduate Studies, 201-200-3409, Fax: 201-200-3411, E-mail: wbajor@njcu.edu.

Norfolk State University, School of Graduate Studies, School of Education, Department of Secondary Education and School Leadership, Program in Urban Education/Administration, Norfolk, VA 23504. Offers teaching (MA). *Accreditation:* NCATE. Part-time programs available. *Entrance requirements:* For master's, GRE General Test, PRAXIS I, minimum GPA of 3.0 in major, 2.5 overall.

Northeastern Illinois University, Graduate College, College of Education, Department of Educational Leadership and Development, Program in Inner City Studies, Chicago, IL 60625-4699. Offers MA. Part-time and evening/weekend programs available. *Degree requirements:* For master's, comprehensive exam, thesis or alternative. *Entrance requirements:* For master's, minimum GPA of 2.75. Additional exam requirements/recommendations for international students: Required—TOEFL (minimum score 550 paper-based; 213 computer-based; 79 iBT). Electronic applications accepted.

Roberts Wesleyan College, Division of Teacher Education, Rochester, NY 14624-1997. Offers adolescence education (M Ed); childhood and special education (M Ed); literacy education (M Ed); urban education (M Ed). Part-time and evening/weekend programs available. *Degree requirements:* For master's, thesis.

Simmons College, College of Arts and Sciences Graduate Studies, Boston, MA 02115. Offers applied behavior analysis (PhD); behavior analysis (MS, Ed S); children's literature (MA); education (MS, CAGS, Ed S); educational leadership (PhD, CAGS); English (MA); gender and cultural studies (MA); health professions education (PhD); history (MA); Spanish (MA); special education moderate licensure (Certificate); special needs administration (Ed D); special needs education (Ed S); teaching (MAT); teaching English as a second language (MA, CAGS); urban education (CAGS); writing for children (MFA); MA/MA; MA/MS; MAT/MA. *Unit head:* Renee White, Dean. *Application contact:* Kristen Haack, Director, Graduate Studies Admission, 617-521-2917, Fax: 617-521-3058, E-mail: gsa@simmons.edu. Web site: http://www.simmons.edu/gradstudies/.

Sojourner-Douglass College, Graduate Program, Baltimore, MD 21205-1814. Offers human services (MASS); public administration (MASS); urban education (reading) (MASS). Part-time and evening/weekend programs available. *Degree requirements:* For master's, comprehensive exam, written proposal oral defense. *Entrance requirements:* For master's, Graduate Examination.

Teachers College, Columbia University, Graduate Faculty of Education, Department of Organization and Leadership, Urban Education Leaders Program, New York, NY 10027. Offers Ed D. *Faculty:* 6 full-time (2 women), 1 part-time/adjunct (0 women). *Entrance requirements:* For doctorate, GRE, master's degree in education leadership, curriculum and teaching, or another relevant field; at least 3 years of teaching experience. *Faculty research:* School leadership, qualitative research methods, and supporting adult development in K-12 schools; ABE/ESOL programs and higher education contexts; school choice reforms. *Unit head:* Dr. Brian Keith Perkins, Director, 212-678-3071, E-mail: bp58@tc.columbia.edu. *Application contact:* Gibran Majdalany, Associate Director, 212-678-3812, E-mail: gm84@tc.columbia.edu. Web site: http://uelp.tc.columbia.edu/.

Temple University, College of Education, Department of Educational Leadership and Policy Studies, Philadelphia, PA 19122-6096. Offers educational administration (Ed M, Ed D); urban education (Ed M, Ed D). Part-time and evening/weekend programs available. *Faculty:* 11 full-time (6 women). *Students:* 69 full-time (43 women), 97 part-time (58 women); includes 46 minority (36 Black or African American, non-Hispanic/Latino; 4 Asian, non-Hispanic/Latino; 2 Hispanic/Latino; 4 Two or more races, non-Hispanic/Latino), 1 international. Average age 34. 107 applicants, 56% accepted, 37 enrolled. In 2011, 29 master's, 11 doctorates awarded. Terminal master's awarded for partial completion of doctoral program. *Degree requirements:* For master's, comprehensive exam, thesis or alternative; for doctorate, thesis/dissertation, preliminary exam. *Entrance requirements:* For master's and doctorate, GRE General Test or MAT, minimum GPA of 3.0. Additional exam requirements/recommendations for international students: Required—TOEFL (minimum score 550 paper-based; 213 computer-based; 79 iBT). *Application deadline:* For fall admission, 12/15 for international students; for spring admission, 8/1 for international students. Application fee: $50. Electronic applications accepted. *Expenses:* Tuition, state resident: full-time $12,366; part-time $687 per credit hour. Tuition, nonresident: full-time $17,298; part-time $961 per credit hour. *Required fees:* $590; $213 per year. *Financial support:* Fellowships, research assistantships with full tuition reimbursements, teaching assistantships with full tuition reimbursements, career-related internships or fieldwork, and Federal Work-Study available. Financial award application deadline: 1/15; financial award applicants required to submit FAFSA. *Faculty research:* Women in education, school effectiveness, financial policy, school improvement in city schools, nongraded schools. *Unit head:* Dr. Corrinne Caldwell, Chair, 215-204-6174, Fax: 215-204-2743, E-mail: corrinne.caldwell@temple.edu. *Application contact:* Dr. Margo Greicar, Director for Graduate Academic and Student Affairs, 215-204-8011, Fax: 215-204-4383, E-mail: margo.greicar@temple.edu. Web site: http://www.temple.edu/education/elps.

Texas A&M University, College of Education and Human Development, Department of Teaching, Learning, and Culture, College Station, TX 77843. Offers culture and curriculum (M Ed, MS); curriculum and instruction (PhD); English as a second language (M Ed, MS, PhD); mathematics education (M Ed, MS, PhD); reading and language arts education (M Ed, MS, PhD); science education (M Ed, MS, PhD); urban education (M Ed, MS, PhD). Part-time programs available. *Faculty:* 30. *Students:* 163 full-time (119 women), 226 part-time (185 women); includes 108 minority (56 Black or African American, non-Hispanic/Latino; 2 American Indian or Alaska Native, non-Hispanic/Latino; 6 Asian, non-Hispanic/Latino; 37 Hispanic/Latino; 7 Two or more races, non-Hispanic/Latino), 62 international. Average age 36. In 2011, 107 master's, 44 doctorates awarded. *Degree requirements:* For master's, comprehensive exam, thesis (for some programs); for doctorate, comprehensive exam, thesis/dissertation. *Entrance requirements:* For master's, GRE General Test, minimum GPA of 3.0; for doctorate, GRE General Test, 3 years of teaching experience. Additional exam requirements/recommendations for international students: Required—TOEFL (minimum score 550 paper-based; 213 computer-based). *Application deadline:* For fall admission, 1/15 priority date for domestic students, 1/15 for international students; for spring admission, 9/15 priority date for domestic students, 9/15 for international students. Applications are processed on a rolling basis. Application fee: $50 ($75 for international students). Electronic applications accepted. *Expenses:* Tuition, state resident: full-time $5437; part-time $226.55 per credit hour. Tuition, nonresident: full-time $12,949; part-time $539.55 per credit hour. *Required fees:* $2741. *Financial support:* In 2011–12, fellowships with partial tuition reimbursements (averaging $3,000 per year), teaching assistantships with partial tuition reimbursements (averaging $7,200 per year) were awarded; research assistantships with partial tuition reimbursements, career-related internships or fieldwork, Federal Work-Study, institutionally sponsored loans, scholarships/grants, tuition waivers (partial), and unspecified assistantships also available. Support available to part-time students. Financial award application deadline: 4/1; financial award applicants required to submit FAFSA. *Unit head:* Dr. Yeping Li, Head, 979-845-8384, Fax: 979-845-9663, E-mail: yepingli@tamu.edu. *Application contact:* Kerri Smith, Senior Academic Advisor II, 979-845-8382, Fax: 979-845-9663, E-mail: krsmith@tamu.edu. Web site: http://tlac.tamu.edu.

University of Central Florida, College of Education, School of Teaching, Learning, and Leadership, Applied Learning and Instruction Program, Orlando, FL 32816. Offers applied learning and instruction (MA); community college education (Certificate); gifted education (Certificate); global and comparative education (Certificate); initial teacher professional preparation (Certificate); urban education (Certificate). *Accreditation:* NCATE. Part-time and evening/weekend programs available. *Students:* 12 full-time (10 women), 79 part-time (65 women); includes 23 minority (6 Black or African American, non-Hispanic/Latino; 1 American Indian or Alaska Native, non-Hispanic/Latino; 3 Asian, non-Hispanic/Latino; 12 Hispanic/Latino; 1 Two or more races, non-Hispanic/Latino), 1 international. Average age 31. 53 applicants, 72% accepted, 24 enrolled. In 2011, 11 master's, 24 other advanced degrees awarded. *Degree requirements:* For Certificate, thesis or alternative, final exam. *Entrance requirements:* For degree, GRE General Test, minimum GPA of 3.0, resume. Additional exam requirements/recommendations for international students: Required—TOEFL. *Application deadline:* For fall admission, 2/20 for domestic students; for spring admission, 9/20 for domestic students. Application fee: $30. Electronic applications accepted. *Expenses:* Tuition, state resident: part-time $277.08 per credit hour. Tuition, nonresident: part-time $277.08 per credit hour. Part-time tuition and fees vary according to degree level and program. *Financial support:* In 2011–12, 3 students received support, including 2 research assistantships with partial tuition reimbursements available (averaging $7,100 per year), 1 teaching assistantship with partial tuition reimbursement available (averaging $6,900 per year); fellowships with partial tuition reimbursements available, career-related internships or fieldwork, Federal Work-Study, institutionally sponsored loans, and unspecified assistantships also available. Financial award application deadline: 3/1; financial award applicants required to submit FAFSA. *Unit head:* Dr. Bobby Hoffman, Program Coordinator, 407-823-1770, E-mail: bobby.hoffman@ucf.edu. *Application contact:* Barbara Rodriguez, Director, Admissions and Registration, 407-823-2766, Fax: 407-823-6442, E-mail: gradadmissions@ucf.edu. Web site: http://education.ucf.edu/departments.cfm.

University of Chicago, Urban Teacher Education Program, Chicago, IL 60637-1513. Offers MAT.

University of Houston–Downtown, College of Public Service, Department of Urban Education, Houston, TX 77002. Offers bilingual education (MAT); curriculum and instruction (MAT); elementary education (MAT); secondary education (MAT). Part-time and evening/weekend programs available. *Faculty:* 12 full-time (8 women). *Students:* 13 full-time (10 women), 25 part-time (22 women); includes 30 minority (15 Black or African American, non-Hispanic/Latino; 3 Asian, non-Hispanic/Latino; 11 Hispanic/Latino; 1 Two or more races, non-Hispanic/Latino). Average age 35. 17 applicants, 100% accepted, 16 enrolled. In 2011, 5 master's awarded. *Degree requirements:* For master's, capstone course with completed project, position paper, grant proposal, empirical study, curriculum development/revision, or advanced technology project presented at annual Graduate Project Exhibition. *Entrance requirements:* For master's, GRE, personal statement, 3 recommendation forms. Additional exam requirements/recommendations for international students: Required—TOEFL (minimum score 550 paper-based; 213 computer-based; 80 iBT). *Application deadline:* For fall admission, 7/15 for domestic and international students; for spring admission, 11/15 for domestic and international students. Applications are processed on a rolling basis. Application fee: $35 ($60 for international students). Electronic applications accepted. *Expenses:* Tuition, state resident: full-time $3420; part-time $2280 per year. Tuition, nonresident: full-time $8424; part-time $5616 per year. *Required fees:* $1018; $840 per year. Tuition and fees vary according to program. *Financial support:* Scholarships/grants available. Financial award applicants required to submit FAFSA. *Unit head:* Dr. Myrna Cohen, Department Chair, 713-221-2759, Fax: 713-226-5294, E-mail: cohenm@uhd.edu. *Application contact:* Traneshia Parker, Associate Director of International Student Services and Graduate Admissions, 713-221-8093, Fax: 713-221-8157, E-mail: parkert@uhd.edu. Web site: http://www.uhd.edu/academic/colleges/publicservice/urbaned/mat.htm.

University of Illinois at Chicago, Graduate College, College of Education, Department of Educational Policy Studies, Chicago, IL 60607-7128. Offers policy studies (M Ed); policy studies in urban education (PhD); urban education leadership (Ed D).

University of Massachusetts Boston, Office of Graduate Studies, Graduate College of Education, School Organization, Curriculum and Instruction Department, Boston, MA 02125-3393. Offers education (M Ed, Ed D), including elementary and secondary education/certification (M Ed), higher education administration (Ed D), teacher certification (M Ed), urban school leadership (Ed D); educational administration (M Ed, CAGS); special education (M Ed). *Degree requirements:* For master's and CAGS, comprehensive exam; for doctorate, comprehensive exam, thesis/dissertation. *Entrance requirements:* For master's, GRE General Test or MAT; for doctorate, GRE General Test or MAT, minimum GPA of 2.75; for CAGS, minimum GPA of 2.75.

University of Massachusetts Boston, Office of Graduate Studies, Graduate College of Education, School Organization, Curriculum and Instruction Department, Program in Education, Track in Urban School Leadership, Boston, MA 02125-3393. Offers Ed D. Part-time and evening/weekend programs available. *Degree requirements:* For doctorate, comprehensive exam, thesis/dissertation. *Entrance requirements:* For doctorate, GRE General Test or MAT, minimum GPA of 2.75. *Faculty research:* School reform, race and culture in schools, race and higher education, language, literacy and writing.

University of Michigan–Dearborn, School of Education, Doctoral Program in Education, Dearborn, MI 48126. Offers curriculum and practice (Ed D); educational leadership (Ed D); educational psychology/special education (Ed D); metropolitan education (Ed D). Part-time and evening/weekend programs available. *Faculty:* 8 full-time (6 women), 2 part-time/adjunct (0 women). *Students:* 47 part-time (34 women); includes 12 minority (6 Black or African American, non-Hispanic/Latino; 3 Asian, non-Hispanic/Latino; 1 Hispanic/Latino; 2 Two or more races, non-Hispanic/Latino). Average

age 40. 55 applicants, 35% accepted, 17 enrolled. *Degree requirements:* For doctorate, comprehensive exam, thesis/dissertation. *Entrance requirements:* For doctorate, GRE (taken within the last 5 years), master's degree with minimum GPA of 3.3, 3 letters of recommendation (1 from faculty), 3 years' professional and/or teaching experience. Additional exam requirements/recommendations for international students: Required—TOEFL (minimum score 550 paper-based). *Application deadline:* For fall admission, 3/1 for domestic and international students. Application fee: $60 ($75 for international students). *Financial support:* Scholarships/grants available. *Faculty research:* Educational leadership, metropolitan education, curriculum and practice, educational psychology, special education, assessment. *Unit head:* Bonnie Beyer, Coordinator, 313-593-5583, E-mail: beyer@umd.umich.edu. *Application contact:* Catherine Parkins, Customer Service Assistant, 313-583-6349, Fax: 313-593-4748, E-mail: cparkins@umd.umich.edu. Web site: http://www.soe.umd.umich.edu/soe_edd/.

University of Nebraska at Omaha, Graduate Studies, College of Education, Department of Teacher Education, Omaha, NE 68182. Offers elementary education (MA, MS); instruction in urban schools (Certificate); instructional technology (Certificate); reading education (MS); secondary education (MA, MS). Part-time and evening/weekend programs available. *Faculty:* 20 full-time (14 women). *Students:* 20 full-time (17 women), 253 part-time (217 women); includes 11 minority (3 Black or African American, non-Hispanic/Latino; 1 American Indian or Alaska Native, non-Hispanic/Latino; 2 Asian, non-Hispanic/Latino; 5 Hispanic/Latino), 1 international. Average age 33. 62 applicants, 77% accepted, 34 enrolled. In 2011, 99 master's, 3 other advanced degrees awarded. *Degree requirements:* For master's, comprehensive exam (for some programs), thesis (for some programs). *Entrance requirements:* For master's, minimum GPA of 3.0. Additional exam requirements/recommendations for international students: Required—TOEFL (minimum score 550 paper-based; 213 computer-based; 80 iBT). *Application deadline:* For fall admission, 8/1 priority date for domestic students; for spring admission, 12/1 priority date for domestic students. Applications are processed on a rolling basis. Application fee: $45. Electronic applications accepted. *Financial support:* In 2011–12, 23 students received support, including 5 research assistantships with tuition reimbursements available; fellowships, teaching assistantships with tuition reimbursements available, Federal Work-Study, institutionally sponsored loans, scholarships/grants, tuition waivers (partial), and unspecified assistantships also available. Support available to part-time students. Financial award application deadline: 3/1; financial award applicants required to submit FAFSA. *Unit head:* Dr. Lana Danielson, Advisor, 402-554-2212. *Application contact:* Dr. Wilma Kuhlman, Student Contact, 402-554-2212.

University of Pennsylvania, Graduate School of Education, Teach for America Program, Philadelphia, PA 19104. Offers MS Ed. Program designed for Teach For America corps members teaching in Philadelphia public and charter schools. *Students:* 225 full-time (150 women), 43 part-time (29 women); includes 83 minority (45 Black or African American, non-Hispanic/Latino; 10 Asian, non-Hispanic/Latino; 19 Hispanic/Latino; 9 Two or more races, non-Hispanic/Latino). 177 applicants, 94% accepted, 138 enrolled. In 2011, 86 degrees awarded. *Expenses: Tuition:* Full-time $26,660; part-time $4944 per course. *Required fees:* $2318; $291 per course. Tuition and fees vary according to course load, degree level and program. *Unit head:* Rona Rosenberg, Interim Director, 215-573-2872, E-mail: ronar@exchange.upenn.edu. *Application contact:* Alyssa D'Alconzo, Associate Director, Admissions, 215-898-6415, Fax: 215-746-6884, E-mail: admissions@gse.upenn.edu. Web site: http://tfa.gse.upenn.edu/.

University of Southern California, Graduate School, Rossier School of Education, Doctor of Education Programs, Los Angeles, CA 90089. Offers educational psychology (Ed D); higher education administration (Ed D); K-12 leadership in urban school settings (Ed D); teacher education in multicultural societies (Ed D). Part-time and evening/weekend programs available. *Degree requirements:* For doctorate, thesis/dissertation. *Entrance requirements:* For doctorate, GRE. Additional exam requirements/recommendations for international students: Required—TOEFL (minimum score 250 computer-based; 100 iBT). Electronic applications accepted. *Faculty research:* Data-driven decision-making in K-12 schools and districts; examination of college and university leadership and management in U. S. and Asia; studies in facilitating student learning; organizational change and the role of leaders; leadership, diversity, learning and accountability.

University of Wisconsin–Milwaukee, Graduate School, School of Education, Department of Curriculum and Instruction, Milwaukee, WI 53201-0413. Offers curriculum planning and instruction improvement (MS); early childhood education (MS); elementary education (MS); junior high/middle school education (MS); reading education (MS); secondary education (MS); teaching in an urban setting (MS). Part-time programs available. *Faculty:* 18 full-time (13 women). *Students:* 29 full-time (23 women), 54 part-time (44 women); includes 21 minority (10 Black or African American, non-Hispanic/Latino; 4 Asian, non-Hispanic/Latino; 3 Hispanic/Latino; 4 Two or more races, non-Hispanic/Latino). Average age 32. 43 applicants, 65% accepted, 13 enrolled. In 2011, 23 degrees awarded. *Degree requirements:* For master's, thesis or alternative. *Entrance requirements:* Additional exam requirements/recommendations for international students: Required—TOEFL (minimum score 550 paper-based; 79 iBT), IELTS (minimum score 6.5). *Application deadline:* For fall admission, 1/1 priority date for domestic students; for spring admission, 9/1 for domestic students. Applications are processed on a rolling basis. Application fee: $56 ($96 for international students). Electronic applications accepted. One-time fee: $506.10 full-time. Tuition and fees vary according to course load and reciprocity agreements. *Financial support:* In 2011–12, 1 fellowship was awarded; research assistantships, teaching assistantships, career-related internships or fieldwork, health care benefits, unspecified assistantships, and project assistantships also available. Support available to part-time students. Financial award application deadline: 4/15; financial award applicants required to submit FAFSA. *Total annual research expenditures:* $21,843. *Unit head:* Hope Longwell-Grice, Department Chair, 414-229-3059, Fax: 414-229-5571, E-mail: hope@uwm.edu. *Application contact:* General Information Contact, 414-229-4982, Fax: 414-229-6967, E-mail: gradschool@uwm.edu. Web site: http://www.uwm.edu/SOE/.

University of Wisconsin–Milwaukee, Graduate School, School of Education, Program in Urban Education, Milwaukee, WI 53201-0413. Offers adult and continuing education (PhD); curriculum and instruction (PhD); educational administration (PhD); educational and media technology (PhD); educational psychology (PhD); multicultural studies (PhD); social foundations of education (PhD). *Students:* 65 full-time (45 women), 37 part-time (25 women); includes 39 minority (18 Black or African American, non-Hispanic/Latino; 1 American Indian or Alaska Native, non-Hispanic/Latino; 6 Asian, non-Hispanic/Latino; 6 Hispanic/Latino; 8 Two or more races, non-Hispanic/Latino), 5 international. Average age 41. 26 applicants, 62% accepted, 2 enrolled. In 2011, 13 degrees awarded. *Degree requirements:* For doctorate, comprehensive exam, thesis/dissertation. *Entrance requirements:* For doctorate, GRE General Test, minimum undergraduate GPA of 2.85, graduate 3.5. Additional exam requirements/recommendations for international students: Required—TOEFL (minimum score 550 paper-based; 79 iBT), IELTS (minimum score 6.5). *Application deadline:* For fall admission, 1/1 priority date for domestic students; for spring admission, 9/1 for domestic students. Applications are processed on a rolling basis. Application fee: $56 ($96 for international students). Electronic applications accepted. One-time fee: $506.10 full-time. Tuition and fees vary according to course load and reciprocity agreements. *Financial support:* In 2011–12, 11 fellowships, 1 teaching assistantship were awarded; research assistantships, career-related internships or fieldwork, health care benefits, unspecified assistantships, and project assistantships also available. Support available to part-time students. Financial award application deadline: 4/15; financial award applicants required to submit FAFSA. *Unit head:* Larry Martin, Representative, 414-229-4729, Fax: 414-229-2920, E-mail: lmartin@uwm.edu. *Application contact:* General Information Contact, 414-229-4982, Fax: 414-229-6967, E-mail: gradschool@uwm.edu. Web site: http://www.uwm.edu/Dept/UrbanEd/.

Vanderbilt University, Peabody College, Department of Teaching and Learning, Nashville, TN 37240-1001. Offers elementary education (M Ed); English language learners (M Ed); learning and instruction (M Ed); learning, diversity, and urban studies (M Ed); reading education (M Ed); secondary education (M Ed). *Accreditation:* NCATE. *Faculty:* 35 full-time (24 women), 19 part-time/adjunct (14 women). *Students:* 123 full-time (96 women), 38 part-time (34 women); includes 26 minority (6 Black or African American, non-Hispanic/Latino; 3 Asian, non-Hispanic/Latino; 7 Hispanic/Latino; 10 Two or more races, non-Hispanic/Latino), 12 international. Average age 26. 251 applicants, 56% accepted, 60 enrolled. In 2011, 80 master's awarded. *Degree requirements:* For master's, comprehensive exam, thesis optional. *Entrance requirements:* For master's, GRE General Test, MAT. Additional exam requirements/recommendations for international students: Required—TOEFL (minimum score 550 paper-based; 213 computer-based). *Application deadline:* For fall admission, 12/31 priority date for domestic students, 12/31 for international students; for spring admission, 11/1 priority date for domestic students, 11/1 for international students. Applications are processed on a rolling basis. Application fee: $0. Electronic applications accepted. *Financial support:* Fellowships with full and partial tuition reimbursements, research assistantships with full and partial tuition reimbursements, teaching assistantships with full and partial tuition reimbursements, Federal Work-Study, institutionally sponsored loans, scholarships/grants, tuition waivers (partial), and unspecified assistantships available. Support available to part-time students. Financial award application deadline: 2/1; financial award applicants required to submit FAFSA. *Faculty research:* Learning environments for mathematics of space and motion, visual programming tools for children's learning of basic science concepts, pathways for elementary and middle school children's learning about measurement and statistics, early reading intervention, professional development for ambitious mathematics teaching. *Unit head:* Dr. David Dickinson, Acting Chair, 615-322-8100, Fax: 615-322-8999, E-mail: david.k.dickinson@vanderbilt.edu. *Application contact:* Angela Saylor, Educational Coordinator, 615-322-8092, Fax: 615-322-8999, E-mail: angela.saylor@vanderbilt.edu.

Virginia Commonwealth University, Graduate School, School of Education, Doctoral Program in Education, Urban Services Leadership Track, Richmond, VA 23284-9005. Offers PhD. *Entrance requirements:* For doctorate, GRE. Additional exam requirements/recommendations for international students: Required—TOEFL (minimum score 600 paper-based; 250 computer-based; 100 iBT). Electronic applications accepted. *Expenses:* Tuition, state resident: full-time $9133; part-time $507 per credit. Tuition, nonresident: full-time $18,777; part-time $1043 per credit. *Required fees:* $77 per credit. Tuition and fees vary according to degree level, campus/location, program and student level.

Wayne State University, School of Library and Information Science, Detroit, MI 48202. Offers archival administration (MLIS, Certificate); arts and museum librarianship (Certificate); general librarianship (MLIS); health sciences librarianship (MLIS); information management for librarians (Certificate); information science (MLIS); law librarianship (MLIS); library and information science (MLIS, Spec), including academic libraries (MLIS); organization of information (MLIS); public libraries (MLIS); public library services to children and young adults (MLIS, Certificate); records and information management (Certificate); records management (MLIS); references services (MLIS); school library media (Spec); school library media specialist endorsement (MLIS); special libraries (MLIS); urban librarianship (Certificate); urban libraries (MLIS); MLIS/MA. *Accreditation:* ALA (one or more programs are accredited). Part-time and evening/weekend programs available. Postbaccalaureate distance learning degree programs offered (no on-campus study). *Faculty:* 13 full-time (8 women), 25 part-time/adjunct (19 women). *Students:* 121 full-time (93 women), 447 part-time (346 women); includes 57 minority (37 Black or African American, non-Hispanic/Latino; 1 American Indian or Alaska Native, non-Hispanic/Latino; 4 Asian, non-Hispanic/Latino; 7 Hispanic/Latino; 8 Two or more races, non-Hispanic/Latino), 4 international. Average age 33. 336 applicants, 62% accepted, 135 enrolled. In 2011, 212 master's, 38 other advanced degrees awarded. *Entrance requirements:* For master's and other advanced degree, GRE or MAT (if undergraduate GPA is between 2.5 and 2.99), minimum undergraduate GPA of 3.0 or graduate degree, personal statement, new student orientation. Additional exam requirements/recommendations for international students: Required—TOEFL (minimum score 550 paper-based; 213 computer-based); Recommended—TWE (minimum score 5.5). *Application deadline:* For fall admission, 7/1 for domestic students, 5/1 for international students; for winter admission, 10/1 for domestic students, 9/1 for international students; for spring admission, 3/15 for domestic students, 1/1 for international students. Applications are processed on a rolling basis. Application fee: $50. Electronic applications accepted. *Expenses:* Tuition, state resident: part-time $512.85 per credit. Tuition, nonresident: part-time $1132.65 per credit. *Required fees:* $26.60 per credit. $199.65 per semester. Tuition and fees vary according to course load and program. *Financial support:* In 2011–12, 1 research assistantship with tuition reimbursement (averaging $12,250 per year) was awarded; fellowships with tuition reimbursements, career-related internships or fieldwork, Federal Work-Study, institutionally sponsored loans, scholarships/grants, and unspecified assistantships also available. Support available to part-time students. Financial award application deadline: 5/15. *Faculty research:* Convergence of academic libraries and other academic services, competitive intelligence and data mining, impact of digitization on libraries, international librarianship, consumer health information, urban library issues, human-computer interaction, universal access to libraries and instructional support services. *Unit head:* Dr. Sandra Yee, Dean, 313-577-4059, Fax: 313-577-7563, E-mail: aj0533@wayne.edu. *Application contact:* Dr. Stephen Fredericks, Associate Dean and Director, 313-577-7563, E-mail: bajjaly@wayne.edu. Web site: http://www.lisp.wayne.edu/.

HAWAI'I PACIFIC UNIVERSITY

Teaching English to Speakers of Other Languages

Programs of Study

Hawai'i Pacific University's (HPU's) Master of Arts in Teaching English to Speakers of Other Languages (M.A.T.E.S.O.L.) focuses on practical, hands-on education that teaches graduates the essential skills they need to become successful educators. By learning about the current theories, methods, and materials, M.A.T.E.S.O.L. graduates are prepared and ready to teach English as a second language in the classroom.

The M.A.T.E.S.O.L. features a solid curriculum in three types of courses. Linguistic theory courses taught from an applied viewpoint help the M.A.T.E.S.O.L. student better understand languages in general and English in particular. The second type is pedagogy courses, which present a range of current approaches, designs, and procedures for teaching language in a wide variety of contexts. In these classes, teaching demonstrations and videotaped peer practice sessions are used extensively. The third type, two practicum courses, allows future teachers to observe master teachers, serve with them in the classroom as assistants, and assume full class responsibility as practice teachers. The capstone activity synthesizes several semesters of classroom study and practicum training. Students have three options for this completion requirement: a portfolio, a comprehensive exam, or an extensive in-service project.

The M.A.T.E.S.O.L. requires a minimum of 37 semester hours of graduate work: 24 semester hours of core courses, 12 semester hours of electives, and 1 semester hour for a capstone activity.

Research Facilities

To support graduate studies, HPU's Meader and Atherton Libraries offer more than 110,000 bound volumes, 350,000 microfiche items, and periodical subscriptions to 1,500 print titles and 30,000 electronic journals. Databases of public and state university libraries, legislative information, and business-oriented statistical data are also available in the library or online. Students can access HPU's library databases, course information, their academic information, and an e-mail account through Pipeline, the university's internal Web site for students. The University's accessible on-campus computer center houses more than 420 computers with specialized software to support graduate academic programs. HPU also provides free Wi-Fi so students can have wireless access to Pipeline resources anywhere on campus using laptops. A significant number of online courses are available.

Students are encouraged to prepare papers for publication in the *TESOL Working Paper Series,* an in-house journal, which displays the best scholarly work from the University's student body.

Financial Aid

The University participates in all federal financial aid programs designated for graduate students. These programs provide aid in the form of subsidized (need-based) and unsubsidized (non-need-based) Federal Stafford Student Loans. Through these loans, funds may be available to cover the student's entire cost of education. To apply for aid, students must submit the Free Application for Federal Student Aid (FAFSA) beginning January 1.

The University also offers several types of institutional graduate scholarships to new full-time, degree-seeking students. U.S. citizens, permanent residents, and international students who have a demonstrated financial need may apply. HPU's graduate scholarships include the Graduate Trustee Scholarship ($6000 for two semesters), the Graduate Dean Scholarship ($4000 for two semesters), and the Graduate Kokua Scholarship ($2000 for two semesters). Factors that may be considered when evaluating requests are previous academic record, community involvement and service, and professional work experience and achievement.

In order to be eligible for the best award package, students should apply by HPU's priority deadline of March 1. Applications received after the priority deadline will be awarded on a funds-available basis. Mailing of student award letters usually begins by the end of March. Applicants will be notified by mail as decisions are made.

Cost of Study

Tuition for graduate students enrolled in fall and spring semesters is determined on a per-credit basis; full-time status for a graduate student is 9 credits. Tuition for the optional winter and summer sessions is also determined on a per-credit basis. For the 2012–13 academic year, full-time tuition is $13,590 for most graduate degree programs, including the M.A.T.E.S.O.L. program. Other expenses, including books, personal expenses, fees, and a student bus pass are estimated at $3285.

Living and Housing Costs

Graduate students live in off-campus housing. The cost of living in off-campus apartments is approximately $12,482 for a double-occupancy room.

Student Group

University enrollment currently stands at more than 8,200. HPU is one of the most culturally diverse universities in America with students from all 50 U.S. states and more than 100 countries.

Location

Hawai'i Pacific combines the excitement of an urban, downtown campus with the serenity of a residential campus. The urban campus is ideally located in downtown Honolulu, the business and financial center of the Pacific. The downtown campus comprises seven buildings in the center of Honolulu's business district and is home to the College of Business Administration and the College of Humanities and Social Sciences.

Eight miles away, situated on 135 acres in Kaneohe, the windward Hawai'i Loa campus is the site of the College of Nursing and Health Sciences and the College of Natural and Computational Sciences. The Hawai'i Loa campus has residence halls, dining commons, the Educational Technology Center, a

Hawai'i Pacific University

student center, and outdoor recreational facilities, including a soccer field, tennis courts, a softball field, and an exercise room.

HPU is affiliated with the Oceanic Institute, an applied aquaculture research facility located on a 56-acre site at Makapu'u Point on the windward coast of Oahu, Hawaii. All three sites are linked by HPU shuttle and easily accessed by public transportation as well.

Notably, the downtown campus location is within walking distance of shopping and dining. Iolani Palace, the only royal palace in the United States, is a few blocks away, as are the State Capitol, City Hall, and the Blaisdell Concert Hall. The Honolulu Academy of Arts, Museum of Contemporary Art, Waikiki Aquarium, Honolulu Zoo, and many other cultural attractions are located nearby.

The University

HPU is a private, nonprofit university with approximately 8,200 students. Founded in 1965, HPU prides itself on maintaining strong academic programs, small class sizes, individual attention to students, and a diverse faculty and student population. HPU is recognized as a Best in the West college by The Princeton Review and a Best Buy by *Barron's* business magazine. HPU offers more than fifty acclaimed undergraduate programs and fourteen distinguished graduate programs. The University has a faculty of more than 500, a student-faculty ratio of 15:1, and an average class size of fewer than 25. A wide range of counseling and other student support services are available. There are more than fifty student organizations on campus, including the Graduate Student Organization. M.A.T.E.S.O.L. students usually join the student club called Intercultural Teachers Organization (ITO), which sponsors many professional and social events throughout the year.

Applying

Students must have a baccalaureate degree from an accredited college or university in the United States or an equivalent degree from another country. Applicants should complete and forward a graduate admissions application, send in the $50 nonrefundable application fee, have official transcripts sent from all colleges or universities previously attended, and forward two letters of recommendation. A personal statement about the applicant's academic and career goals is required; submitting a resume is optional. Applicants who have taken the Graduate Record Examination (GRE) should have their scores sent directly to the Graduate Admissions Office. International students should submit scores of a recognized English proficiency test such as TOEFL. Admissions decisions are made on a rolling basis. Applicants are notified between one and two weeks after all documents have been submitted. Applicants are encouraged to submit their applications online.

Correspondence and Information

Graduate Admissions
Hawai'i Pacific University
1164 Bishop Street, #911
Honolulu, Hawai'i 96813
Phone: 808-544-1135
866-GRAD-HPU (toll-free)
Fax: 808-544-0280
E-mail: graduate@hpu.edu
Web site: http://www.hpu.edu/hpumatesol

THE FACULTY

Kenneth Cook, Professor of Linguistics; Ph.D., California, San Diego.

Barbara Hannum, Assistant Professor of English (ESL); M.A., Hawai'i at Manoa.

Jean Kirschenmann, Assistant Professor of English (ESL); M.A., Hawai'i at Manoa.

Edward F. Klein, Professor of Applied Linguistics; Ph.D., Hawai'i at Manoa.

Candis Lee, Assistant Professor of English (ESL); Ed.D., USC.

Hanh T. Nguyen, Assistant Professor of Applied Linguistics; Ph.D., Wisconsin–Madison.

Catherine Sajna, Assistant Professor of English; M.A., Hawai'i at Manoa.

Section 26
Subject Areas

This section contains a directory of institutions offering graduate work in subject areas. Additional information about programs listed in the directory but not augmented by an in-depth entry may be obtained by writing directly to the dean of a graduate school or chair of a department at the address given in the directory.

For programs offering related work, see also in this book *Administration, Instruction, and Theory; Business Administration and Management; Education; Instructional Levels; Leisure Studies and Recreation; Physical Education and Kinesiology;* and *Special Focus.* In the other guides in this series:

Graduate Programs in the Humanities, Arts & Social Sciences

See *Art and Art History; Family and Consumer Sciences; Language and Literature; Performing Arts; Psychology and Counseling (School Psychology); Public, Regional, and Industrial Affairs (Urban Studies); Religious Studies;* and *Social Sciences*

Graduate Programs in the Biological/Biomedical Sciences & Health-Related Medical Professions

See *Health-Related Professions*

Graduate Programs in the Physical Sciences, Mathematics, Agricultural Sciences, the Environment & Natural Resources

See *Mathematical Sciences*

Graduate Programs in Engineering & Applied Sciences

See *Computer Science and Information Technology*

CONTENTS

Program Directories

Displays and Close-Ups

See:

Agricultural Education

Alcorn State University, School of Graduate Studies, School of Psychology and Education, Alcorn State, MS 39096-7500. Offers agricultural education (MS Ed); elementary education (MS Ed, Ed S); guidance and counseling (MS Ed); industrial education (MS Ed); secondary education (MS Ed), including health and physical education; special education (MS Ed). *Accreditation:* NCATE. *Degree requirements:* For master's, thesis optional.

Arkansas State University, Graduate School, College of Agriculture and Technology, Jonesboro, State University, AR 72467. Offers agricultural education (SCCT); agriculture (MSA); vocational-technical administration (SCCT). Part-time programs available. *Faculty:* 15 full-time (3 women). *Students:* 12 full-time (6 women), 23 part-time (9 women); includes 5 minority (all Black or African American, non-Hispanic/Latino), 7 international. Average age 33. 12 applicants, 83% accepted, 7 enrolled. In 2011, 12 master's awarded. *Degree requirements:* For master's, comprehensive exam, thesis or alternative; for SCCT, comprehensive exam. *Entrance requirements:* For master's, GRE General Test or MAT, appropriate bachelor's degree, official transcripts, immunization records; for SCCT, GRE General Test or MAT, interview, master's degree, official transcript, immunization records. Additional exam requirements/recommendations for international students: Required—TOEFL (minimum score 550 paper-based; 213 computer-based; 79 iBT), IELTS (minimum score 6), Pearson Test of English Academic (minimum score 56). *Application deadline:* For fall admission, 7/1 for domestic and international students; for spring admission, 11/15 for domestic students, 11/14 for international students. Applications are processed on a rolling basis. Application fee: $30 ($40 for international students). Electronic applications accepted. *Expenses:* Tuition, state resident: full-time $4044; part-time $225 per credit hour. Tuition, nonresident: full-time $8087; part-time $449 per credit hour. *Required fees:* $936; $52 per credit hour. $25 per term. One-time fee: $30. Tuition and fees vary according to course load and program. *Financial support:* In 2011–12, 5 students received support. Teaching assistantships, career-related internships or fieldwork, scholarships/grants, and unspecified assistantships available. Financial award application deadline: 7/1; financial award applicants required to submit FAFSA. *Unit head:* Dr. David Beasley, Interim Dean, 870-972-2085, Fax: 870-972-3885, E-mail: dbbeasley@astate.edu. *Application contact:* Dr. Andrew Sustich, Dean of the Graduate School, 870-972-3029, Fax: 870-972-3857, E-mail: sustich@astate.edu. Web site: http://www.astate.edu/agri/.

California Polytechnic State University, San Luis Obispo, College of Agriculture, Food and Environmental Sciences, Department of Agricultural Education and Communication, San Luis Obispo, CA 93407. Offers MAE. Part-time programs available. *Faculty:* 2 full-time (0 women). *Students:* 16 full-time (13 women), 5 part-time (3 women); includes 3 minority (2 Hispanic/Latino; 1 Two or more races, non-Hispanic/Latino). Average age 25. 17 applicants, 76% accepted, 11 enrolled. In 2011, 2 master's awarded. *Degree requirements:* For master's, comprehensive exam. *Entrance requirements:* For master's, minimum GPA of 2.75 in last 90 quarter units of course work. Additional exam requirements/recommendations for international students: Required—TOEFL (minimum score 550 paper-based; 213 computer-based) or IELTS (minimum score 6). *Application deadline:* For fall admission, 4/1 for domestic students, 11/30 for international students; for winter admission, 10/1 for domestic students, 6/30 for international students; for spring admission, 10/1 for domestic students. Applications are processed on a rolling basis. Application fee: $55. Electronic applications accepted. *Expenses:* Tuition, state resident: full-time $6738. Tuition, nonresident: full-time $17,898. *Required fees:* $2449. *Financial support:* Application deadline: 3/2; applicants required to submit FAFSA. *Faculty research:* Agricultural education with emphasis on public school teaching. *Unit head:* Dr. William C. Kellogg, Graduate Coordinator, 805-756-2973, Fax: 805-756-2799, E-mail: bkellogg@calpoly.edu. *Application contact:* Dr. Mark Shelton, Associate Dean/Graduate Coordinator, 805-756-2161, Fax: 805-756-6577, E-mail: mshelton@calpoly.edu. Web site: http://aged.calpoly.edu/.

Clemson University, Graduate School, College of Agriculture, Forestry and Life Sciences, Program in Agricultural Education, Clemson, SC 29634. Offers M Ag Ed. *Accreditation:* NCATE. Part-time programs available. *Students:* 9 full-time (3 women), 5 part-time (3 women). Average age 30. 9 applicants, 78% accepted, 3 enrolled. In 2011, 5 master's awarded. *Entrance requirements:* For master's, GRE General Test. Additional exam requirements/recommendations for international students: Required—TOEFL. *Application deadline:* For fall admission, 3/15 for domestic students; for spring admission, 11/1 for domestic students. Application fee: $70 ($80 for international students). Electronic applications accepted. *Financial support:* In 2011–12, 5 students received support, including 1 research assistantship with partial tuition reimbursement available (averaging $2,271 per year), 3 teaching assistantships with partial tuition reimbursements available (averaging $9,757 per year); career-related internships or fieldwork, institutionally sponsored loans, scholarships/grants, health care benefits, and unspecified assistantships also available. Support available to part-time students. Financial award application deadline: 4/1; financial award applicants required to submit FAFSA. *Faculty research:* Adaptation and change, curriculum assessment and innovation, career development, adult and extension education, technology transfer. *Unit head:* Dr. Young Jo Han, Chair, 864-656-3250, Fax: 864-656-0338, E-mail: yhan@clemson.edu. *Application contact:* Dr. Tom Dobbins, Coordinator, 864-656-3834, Fax: 864-656-5675, E-mail: tdbbns@clemson.edu. Web site: http://www.clemson.edu/cafls/departments/agbioeng/aged/.

Cornell University, Graduate School, Graduate Fields of Agriculture and Life Sciences, Field of Education, Ithaca, NY 14853-0001. Offers agricultural education (MAT); biology (7-12) (MAT); chemistry (7-12) (MAT); curriculum and instruction (MPS, MS, PhD); earth science (7-12) (MAT); extension, and adult education (MPS, MS, PhD); mathematics (7-12) (MAT); physics (7-12) (MAT). *Faculty:* 23 full-time (10 women). *Students:* 32 full-time (18 women); includes 6 minority (4 Asian, non-Hispanic/Latino; 2 Hispanic/Latino), 1 international. Average age 30. 60 applicants, 33% accepted, 12 enrolled. In 2011, 22 master's, 7 doctorates awarded. Terminal master's awarded for partial completion of doctoral program. *Degree requirements:* For master's, thesis (MS); for doctorate, comprehensive exam, thesis/dissertation. *Entrance requirements:* For master's and doctorate, GRE General Test, sample of written work (recommended), 2 letters of recommendation. Additional exam requirements/recommendations for international students: Required—TOEFL (minimum score 550 paper-based; 213 computer-based; 77 iBT). *Application deadline:* For fall admission, 2/15 for domestic students. Application fee: $95. Electronic applications accepted. *Financial support:* In 2011–12, 2 fellowships with full tuition reimbursements, 4 research assistantships with full tuition reimbursements, 12 teaching assistantships with full tuition reimbursements were awarded; institutionally sponsored loans, scholarships/grants, health care benefits, tuition waivers (full and partial), and unspecified assistantships also available. Financial award applicants required to submit FAFSA. *Faculty research:* Moral development and professional ethics, public issues education and community development, socio/political issues in public education, teacher education and curriculum in agricultural science and mathematics, extension research. *Unit head:* Director of Graduate Studies, 607-255-4278, Fax: 607-255-7905. *Application contact:* Graduate Field Assistant, 607-255-4278, Fax: 607-255-7905, E-mail: rh22@cornell.edu. Web site: http://www.gradschool.cornell.edu/fields.php?id-80&a-2.

Eastern Kentucky University, The Graduate School, College of Education, Department of Curriculum and Instruction, Program in Secondary and Higher Education, Richmond, KY 40475-3102. Offers secondary education (MA Ed), including agricultural education, art education, biological sciences education, business education, English education, geography education, history education, home economics education, industrial education, mathematical sciences education, physical education, school health education. *Accreditation:* NCATE. Part-time programs available. *Entrance requirements:* For master's, GRE General Test, minimum GPA of 2.5.

Iowa State University of Science and Technology, Department of Agricultural Education and Studies, Ames, IA 50011-1050. Offers MS, PhD. *Entrance requirements:* For master's and doctorate, resume. Additional exam requirements/recommendations for international students: Required—TOEFL (minimum score 550 paper-based; 79 iBT), IELTS (minimum score 6.5). *Application deadline:* For fall admission, 3/15 priority date for domestic students, 3/15 for international students; for spring admission, 10/15 priority date for domestic students, 10/15 for international students. Applications are processed on a rolling basis. Application fee: $40 ($90 for international students). Electronic applications accepted. *Faculty research:* Agricultural extension education, teaching, learning processes, distance education, international education, adult education. *Unit head:* Dr. Greg Miller, Director of Graduate Education, 515-294-5872, Fax: 515-294-0530, E-mail: agedsinfo@iastate.edu. *Application contact:* Wendy Ortmann, Graduate Secretary, 515-294-5872, Fax: 515-294-0530, E-mail: agedsinfo@iastate.edu. Web site: http://www.ageds.iastate.edu/graduate.html.

Louisiana State University and Agricultural and Mechanical College, Graduate School, College of Agriculture, School of Human Resource Education and Workforce Development, Baton Rouge, LA 70803. Offers agriculture and extension education and youth development (MS, PhD); career and technical education (MS, PhD); comprehensive vocational education (MS, PhD); extension and international education (MS, PhD); human resource and leadership development (MS, PhD); industrial education (MS); vocational agriculture education (MS, PhD); vocational business education (MS); vocational home economics education (MS). *Accreditation:* NCATE. Part-time programs available. *Faculty:* 9 full-time (5 women), 3 part-time/adjunct (0 women). *Students:* 51 full-time (36 women), 85 part-time (59 women); includes 28 minority (23 Black or African American, non-Hispanic/Latino; 1 Asian, non-Hispanic/Latino; 4 Hispanic/Latino), 3 international. Average age 36. 29 applicants, 83% accepted, 20 enrolled. In 2011, 15 master's, 17 doctorates awarded. Terminal master's awarded for partial completion of doctoral program. *Degree requirements:* For master's, thesis (for some programs); for doctorate, thesis/dissertation. *Entrance requirements:* For master's and doctorate, GRE General Test, minimum GPA of 3.0. Additional exam requirements/recommendations for international students: Required—TOEFL (minimum score 550 paper-based; 213 computer-based; 79 iBT) or IELTS (minimum score 6.5). *Application deadline:* For fall admission, 1/25 priority date for domestic students, 5/15 for international students; for spring admission, 10/15 for international students. Applications are processed on a rolling basis. Application fee: $50 ($70 for international students). Electronic applications accepted. *Financial support:* In 2011–12, 84 students received support, including 3 fellowships with full and partial tuition reimbursements available (averaging $14,986 per year), 4 research assistantships with full and partial tuition reimbursements available (averaging $12,000 per year), 11 teaching assistantships with partial tuition reimbursements available (averaging $13,300 per year); career-related internships or fieldwork, Federal Work-Study, institutionally sponsored loans, health care benefits, tuition waivers (full and partial), and unspecified assistantships also available. Financial award application deadline: 3/1; financial award applicants required to submit FAFSA. *Faculty research:* Adult education, history and philosophy of vocational education, curriculum and instruction, career decision-making. *Unit head:* Dr. Michael F. Burnett, Director, 225-578-5748, Fax: 225-578-2526, E-mail: vocbur@lsu.edu. Web site: http://www.lsu.edu/hrleader/.

Mississippi State University, College of Agriculture and Life Sciences, School of Human Sciences, Mississippi State, MS 39762. Offers agricultural sciences (PhD), including agriculture and extension education; agriculture and extension education (MS). *Accreditation:* NCATE (one or more programs are accredited). Part-time programs available. *Faculty:* 14 full-time (7 women). *Students:* 7 full-time (3 women), 48 part-time (34 women); includes 12 minority (all Black or African American, non-Hispanic/Latino), 2 international. Average age 37. 14 applicants, 79% accepted, 10 enrolled. In 2011, 13 master's, 1 doctorate awarded. *Degree requirements:* For master's, thesis optional, comprehensive oral or written exam. *Entrance requirements:* For master's, GRE, minimum GPA of 2.75 in last 4 semesters of course work; for doctorate, minimum GPA of 3.0 on prior graduate work. Additional exam requirements/recommendations for international students: Required—TOEFL (minimum score 475 paper-based; 153 computer-based; 53 iBT); Recommended—IELTS (minimum score 4.5). *Application deadline:* For fall admission, 7/1 for domestic students, 5/1 for international students; for spring admission, 11/1 for domestic students, 9/1 for international students. Applications are processed on a rolling basis. Application fee: $40. Electronic applications accepted. *Expenses:* Tuition, state resident: full-time $5805; part-time $322.50 per credit hour. Tuition, nonresident: full-time $14,670; part-time $815 per credit hour. *Financial support:* In 2011–12, 3 research assistantships (averaging $12,543 per year), 3 teaching assistantships with full tuition reimbursements (averaging $12,536 per year) were awarded; Federal Work-Study, institutionally sponsored loans, and unspecified assistantships also available. Financial award application deadline: 4/1; financial award applicants required to submit FAFSA. *Faculty research:* Animal welfare, agroscience, information technology, learning styles, problem solving. *Unit head:* Dr. Michael Newman, Director and Professor, 662-325-2950, E-mail: mnewman@humansci.msstate.edu. *Application contact:* Dr. Jacquelyn Deeds, Professor and Graduate Coordinator, 662-325-7834, E-mail: jdeeds@ais.msstate.edu. Web site: http://www.humansci.msstate.edu.

Montana State University, College of Graduate Studies, College of Agriculture, Division of Agricultural Education, Bozeman, MT 59717. Offers MS. Part-time programs available. Postbaccalaureate distance learning degree programs offered (no on-campus study). *Degree requirements:* For master's, comprehensive exam. *Entrance requirements:* For master's, GRE General Test. Additional exam requirements/recommendations for international students: Required—TOEFL (minimum score 550 paper-based; 213 computer-based). Electronic applications accepted. *Faculty research:* Extension systems, youth leadership, agricultural, adult and youth education in agriculture, international agricultural education, enzymology of vitamins, coenzymes and metal ions, steroid metabolism, protein structure, impact of wolves on big game hunting demand, prescription drug price dispersion in heterogeneous markets, divorce risk and the labor force participation of women with and without children, the economics of terraces in the Peruvian Andes.

Murray State University, School of Agriculture, Murray, KY 42071. Offers agriculture (MS); agriculture education (MS). Evening/weekend programs available. Postbaccalaureate distance learning degree programs offered (minimal on-campus study). *Degree requirements:* For master's, comprehensive exam, thesis (for some programs). *Entrance requirements:* Additional exam requirements/recommendations for international students: Required—TOEFL. *Faculty research:* Ultrasound in beef, corn and soybean research, tobacco research.

New Mexico State University, Graduate School, College of Agricultural, Consumer and Environmental Sciences, Department of Agricultural and Extension Education, Las Cruces, NM 88003-8001. Offers MA. *Accreditation:* NCATE. Part-time and evening/weekend programs available. Postbaccalaureate distance learning degree programs offered (minimal on-campus study). *Faculty:* 5 full-time (3 women). *Students:* 13 full-time (9 women), 22 part-time (17 women); includes 9 minority (1 American Indian or Alaska Native, non-Hispanic/Latino; 8 Hispanic/Latino). Average age 32. 11 applicants, 82% accepted, 7 enrolled. In 2011, 13 master's awarded. *Degree requirements:* For master's, comprehensive exam, thesis or creative component. *Entrance requirements:* For master's, 3 letters of recommendation. Additional exam requirements/recommendations for international students: Required—TOEFL (minimum score 550 paper-based; 79 iBT), IELTS (minimum score 6.5), Language Proficiency Exam. *Application deadline:* For fall admission, 7/1 priority date for domestic students, 7/1 for international students; for spring admission, 11/1 priority date for domestic students, 11/1 for international students. Applications are processed on a rolling basis. Application fee: $40 ($50 for international students). Electronic applications accepted. *Expenses:* Tuition, state resident: full-time $5004; part-time $208.50 per credit. Tuition, nonresident: full-time $17,446; part-time $726.90 per credit. *Financial support:* In 2011–12, 1 fellowship (averaging $3,754 per year), 2 research assistantships (averaging $11,850 per year), 4 teaching assistantships (averaging $16,886 per year) were awarded; career-related internships or fieldwork, Federal Work-Study, institutionally sponsored loans, scholarships/grants, health care benefits, and unspecified assistantships also available. Financial award application deadline: 3/1. *Faculty research:* Secondary agricultural education programs, teaching and learning, agricultural technology and safety, volunteer programs, youth leadership development, agricultural development. *Unit head:* Dr. Cynda Clary, Head, 575-646-4511, Fax: 575-646-4082, E-mail: cclary@nmsu.edu. *Application contact:* Dr. Brenda S. Seevers, Professor, 575-646-4511, Fax: 575-646-4082, E-mail: bseevers@nmsu.edu. Web site: http://aces.nmsu.edu/academics/axed.

North Carolina Agricultural and Technical State University, School of Graduate Studies, School of Agriculture and Environmental Sciences, Department of Agribusiness, Applied Economics, and Agriscience Education, Greensboro, NC 27411. Offers agricultural economics (MS); agricultural education (MS). *Accreditation:* NCATE. Part-time and evening/weekend programs available. *Degree requirements:* For master's, comprehensive exam, thesis or alternative, qualifying exam. *Entrance requirements:* For master's, GRE General Test, minimum GPA of 3.0. *Faculty research:* Aid for small farmers, agricultural technology resources, labor force mobility, agrology.

North Carolina State University, Graduate School, College of Agriculture and Life Sciences, Department of Agricultural and Extension Education, Program in Agricultural Education, Raleigh, NC 27695. Offers MAE, MS, Certificate. Postbaccalaureate distance learning degree programs offered. *Degree requirements:* For master's, thesis optional. *Entrance requirements:* For master's, GRE or MAT. Electronic applications accepted. *Faculty research:* Instructional methodology, distance education, leadership development, foundations, curriculum development.

North Dakota State University, College of Graduate and Interdisciplinary Studies, College of Human Development and Education, School of Education, Program in Agricultural Education, Fargo, ND 58108. Offers agricultural education (M Ed, MS); agricultural extension education (MS). *Accreditation:* NCATE. Part-time programs available. *Students:* 5 part-time (3 women). Average age 32. In 2011, 1 master's awarded. *Degree requirements:* For master's, comprehensive exam, thesis or alternative. *Entrance requirements:* Additional exam requirements/recommendations for international students: Required—TOEFL (minimum score 525 paper-based; 197 computer-based; 71 iBT). *Application deadline:* Applications are processed on a rolling basis. Application fee: $45 ($60 for international students). *Financial support:* Research assistantships, career-related internships or fieldwork, Federal Work-Study, institutionally sponsored loans, and tuition waivers (full) available. Financial award application deadline: 4/15. *Faculty research:* Vocational and cooperative extension education, rural leadership, rural education, international extension. *Unit head:* Dr. William Martin, Chair, 701-231-7202, Fax: 701-231-7416, E-mail: william.martin@ndsu.edu. *Application contact:* Dr. Brent Young, Assistant Professor, 701-231-7439, Fax: 701-231-9685, E-mail: brent.young@ndsu.edu.

Northwest Missouri State University, Graduate School, Melvin and Valorie Booth College of Business and Professional Studies, Department of Agriculture, Maryville, MO 64468-6001. Offers agricultural economics (MBA); agriculture (MS); teaching agriculture (MS Ed). Part-time programs available. *Faculty:* 7 full-time (2 women). *Students:* 10 full-time (5 women), 4 part-time (1 woman). 10 applicants, 100% accepted, 6 enrolled. In 2011, 6 master's awarded. *Degree requirements:* For master's, comprehensive exam, thesis (for some programs). *Entrance requirements:* For master's, GRE General Test, minimum undergraduate GPA of 2.5, writing sample. Additional exam requirements/recommendations for international students: Required—TOEFL (minimum score 550 paper-based; 213 computer-based). *Application deadline:* For fall admission, 7/1 for domestic and international students; for spring admission, 11/15 for domestic and international students. Applications are processed on a rolling basis. Application fee: $0 ($50 for international students). *Financial support:* In 2011–12, 4 research assistantships with full tuition reimbursements (averaging $6,000 per year), 2 teaching assistantships with full tuition reimbursements (averaging $6,000 per year) were awarded; unspecified assistantships also available. Financial award application deadline: 4/1; financial award applicants required to submit FAFSA. *Unit head:* Dr. Arley Larson, Chairperson, 660-562-1161. *Application contact:* Dr. Gregory Haddock, Dean of Graduate School, 660-562-1145, Fax: 660-562-1096, E-mail: gradsch@nwmissouri.edu.

The Ohio State University, Graduate School, College of Food, Agricultural, and Environmental Sciences, Department of Agricultural Communication, Education and Leadership, Program in Agricultural and Extension Education, Columbus, OH 43210. Offers M Ed, MS, PhD. *Faculty:* 21. *Students:* 14 full-time (11 women), 18 part-time (13 women), 2 international. Average age 36. In 2011, 4 master's, 6 doctorates awarded. *Expenses:* Tuition, state resident: full-time $11,400. Tuition, nonresident: full-time $28,125. Tuition and fees vary according to course load, degree level, campus/location and program. *Unit head:* Ken Martin, Chair, 614-247-8808, E-mail: martin.1540@osu.edu. *Application contact:* Graduate Admissions, 614-292-6031, Fax: 614-292-3656, E-mail: gradadmissions@osu.edu. Web site: http://acel.osu.edu/graduate.

Oklahoma State University, College of Agricultural Science and Natural Resources, Department of Agricultural Education, Communications and Leadership, Stillwater, OK 74078. Offers M Ag, MS, PhD. Postbaccalaureate distance learning degree programs offered. *Faculty:* 12 full-time (5 women), 1 part-time/adjunct (0 women). *Students:* 25 full-time (16 women), 45 part-time (33 women); includes 6 minority (3 American Indian or Alaska Native, non-Hispanic/Latino; 1 Hispanic/Latino; 2 Two or more races, non-Hispanic/Latino), 1 international. Average age 28. 78 applicants, 47% accepted, 22 enrolled. In 2011, 15 master's, 4 doctorates awarded. *Degree requirements:* For master's, thesis (for some programs), thesis or report; for doctorate, comprehensive exam, thesis/dissertation. *Entrance requirements:* For master's and doctorate, GRE or GMAT. Additional exam requirements/recommendations for international students: Required—TOEFL (minimum score 550 paper-based; 79 iBT). *Application deadline:* For fall admission, 3/1 for international students; for spring admission, 8/1 for international students. Applications are processed on a rolling basis. Application fee: $40 ($75 for international students). Electronic applications accepted. *Expenses:* Tuition, state resident: full-time $4044; part-time $168.50 per credit hour. Tuition, nonresident: full-time $16,008; part-time $667 per credit hour. *Required fees:* $2122; $88.45 per credit hour. One-time fee: $50. Tuition and fees vary according to course load and campus/location. *Financial support:* In 2011–12, 6 research assistantships (averaging $8,833 per year), 12 teaching assistantships (averaging $13,164 per year) were awarded; career-related internships or fieldwork, Federal Work-Study, scholarships/grants, health care benefits, tuition waivers (partial), and unspecified assistantships also available. Support available to part-time students. Financial award application deadline: 3/1; financial award applicants required to submit FAFSA. *Faculty research:* Teaching in and learning about agriculture, agriculture teacher evaluation, evaluation of information dissemination delivery methods, agricultural literacy curriculum model development, distance education delivery methods. *Unit head:* Dr. Robert Terry, Head, 405-744-8885, Fax: 405-744-5176. *Application contact:* Dr. Sheryl Tucker, Dean, 405-744-7099, Fax: 405-744-0355, E-mail: grad-i@okstate.edu. Web site: http://aged.okstate.edu/.

Oregon State University, Graduate School, College of Agricultural Sciences, Department of Agricultural Education, Corvallis, OR 97331. Offers M Agr, MAIS, MAT, MS. Part-time programs available. *Degree requirements:* For master's, thesis (for some programs). *Entrance requirements:* For master's, GRE General Test, minimum GPA of 3.0 in last 90 hours of course work. Additional exam requirements/recommendations for international students: Required—TOEFL. *Faculty research:* Curriculum development and vocational education program evaluation, agricultural extension education.

Penn State University Park, Graduate School, College of Agricultural Sciences, Department of Agricultural and Extension Education, State College, University Park, PA 16802-1503. Offers agricultural and extension education (M Ed, MS, PhD, Certificate); applied youth, family and community education (M Ed). *Unit head:* Dr. Bruce A. McPheron, Dean, 814-865-2541, Fax: 814-865-3103, E-mail: bam10@psu.edu. *Application contact:* Cynthia E. Nicosia, Director of Graduate Enrollment Services, 814-865-1834, E-mail: cey1@psu.edu. Web site: http://aee.psu.edu/.

Purdue University, Graduate School, College of Agriculture, Department of Youth Development and Agricultural Education, West Lafayette, IN 47907. Offers MA, PhD. *Faculty:* 8 full-time (2 women), 3 part-time/adjunct (all women). *Students:* 11 full-time (10 women), 5 part-time (4 women), 3 international. Average age 28. 13 applicants, 54% accepted, 5 enrolled. In 2011, 13 master's awarded. *Degree requirements:* For doctorate, comprehensive exam. *Entrance requirements:* For master's and doctorate, GRE general test, must have combined score of 1000, minimum undergraduate GPA of 3.0 or equivalent. Additional exam requirements/recommendations for international students: Required—TOEFL (minimum score 550 paper-based; 77 iBT), TWE recommended for MA, required for Ph D (minimum score 5); Recommended—TWE. *Application deadline:* For fall admission, 3/15 priority date for domestic students, 3/1 for international students; for spring admission, 10/15 priority date for domestic students, 8/1 for international students. Applications are processed on a rolling basis. Application fee: $60 ($75 for international students). Electronic applications accepted. *Unit head:* Roger L Tormoehlen, Head, 765-494-8422, E-mail: torm@purdue.edu. *Application contact:* Neil A. Knobloch, Chair of the Graduate Committee, 765-494-8439, E-mail: nknobloc@purdue.edu.

Purdue University, Graduate School, College of Education, Department of Curriculum and Instruction, West Lafayette, IN 47907. Offers agricultural and extension education (PhD, Ed S); agriculture and extension education (MS, MS Ed); art education (PhD); consumer and family sciences and extension education (MS Ed, PhD, Ed S); curriculum studies (MS Ed, PhD, Ed S); educational technology (MS Ed, PhD, Ed S); elementary education (MS Ed); foreign language education (MS Ed, PhD, Ed S); industrial technology (PhD, Ed S); language arts (MS Ed, PhD, Ed S); literacy (MS Ed, PhD, Ed S); mathematics/science education (MS, MS Ed, PhD, Ed S); social studies (MS Ed, PhD); social studies education (Ed S); vocational/industrial education (MS Ed, PhD, Ed S); vocational/technical education (MS Ed, PhD, Ed S). *Accreditation:* NCATE. Part-time and evening/weekend programs available. *Faculty:* 30 full-time (21 women), 1 (woman) part-time/adjunct. *Students:* 89 full-time (64 women), 134 part-time (84 women); includes 31 minority (12 Black or African American, non-Hispanic/Latino; 3 American Indian or Alaska Native, non-Hispanic/Latino; 7 Asian, non-Hispanic/Latino; 9 Hispanic/Latino), 49 international. Average age 36. 136 applicants, 83% accepted, 72 enrolled. In 2011, 26 master's, 13 doctorates awarded. *Degree requirements:* For master's, thesis optional; for doctorate, thesis/dissertation, oral and written exams; for Ed S, oral presentation, project. *Entrance requirements:* For master's, GRE general test is required if undergraduate GPA is below 3.0, minimum undergraduate GPA of 3.0 or equivalent; for doctorate, GRE General Test, a combined GRE verbal and quantitative score of 1000 (300 for revised GRE Test) or more is expected, minimum undergraduate GPA of 3.0 or equivalent; master's degree with minimum GPA of 3.0 or equivalent; for Ed S, GRE general test, a combined GRE verbal and quantitative score of 1000 (300 for revised GRE Test) or more is expected, minimum undergraduate GPA of 3.0 or equivalent; master's degree. Additional exam requirements/recommendations for international students: Required—TOEFL (minimum score 550 paper-based; 77 iBT). *Application deadline:* For fall admission, 12/15 priority date for domestic students, 3/1 for international students; for spring admission, 9/15 for domestic students, 8/1 for international students. Application fee: $60 ($75 for international students). Electronic applications accepted. *Financial support:* Fellowships with full tuition reimbursements, research assistantships with full tuition reimbursements, teaching assistantships with full tuition reimbursements, career-related internships or fieldwork, and tuition waivers (full) available. Support available to part-time students. Financial award application deadline: 3/1; financial award applicants required to submit FAFSA. *Faculty research:* Literacy acquisition and development, teacher beliefs and knowledge, recruitment and retention of underrepresented students, economic education, literacy discourse. *Unit head:* Dr. Philip J. VanFossen, Head, 765-494-7935, Fax: 765-496-1622, E-mail: vanfoss@purdue.edu. *Application contact:* Sarah N. Prater, Graduate Contact, 765-494-2345, Fax: 765-494-5832, E-mail: prater0@purdue.edu. Web site: http://www.edci.purdue.edu/.

State University of New York at Oswego, Graduate Studies, School of Education, Department of Vocational Teacher Preparation, Oswego, NY 13126. Offers agriculture (MS Ed); business and marketing (MS Ed); family and consumer sciences (MS Ed); health careers (MS Ed); technical education (MS Ed); trade education (MS Ed). *Accreditation:* NCATE. Part-time and evening/weekend programs available. *Degree requirements:* For master's, comprehensive exam, thesis or alternative. *Entrance* *requirements:* Additional exam requirements/recommendations for international students: Required—TOEFL (minimum score 560 paper-based; 220 computer-based).

Stephen F. Austin State University, Graduate School, College of Forestry and Agriculture, Department of Agriculture, Nacogdoches, TX 75962. Offers MS. *Accreditation:* NCATE. *Degree requirements:* For master's, comprehensive exam, thesis (for some programs). *Entrance requirements:* For master's, GRE General Test, minimum GPA of 2.8 in last half of major, 2.5 overall. Additional exam requirements/recommendations for international students: Required—TOEFL (minimum score 550 paper-based; 213 computer-based). *Faculty research:* Asian vegetables, soil fertility, animal breeding, animal nutrition.

Tarleton State University, College of Graduate Studies, College of Agricultural and Environmental Sciences, Department of Agricultural and Consumer Sciences, Stephenville, TX 76402. Offers agriculture education (MS). Part-time and evening/weekend programs available. Postbaccalaureate distance learning degree programs offered (minimal on-campus study). *Faculty:* 4 full-time (1 woman), 3 part-time/adjunct (1 woman). *Students:* 22 full-time (13 women), 11 part-time (4 women); includes 1 minority (Hispanic/Latino), 1 international. Average age 26. 17 applicants, 88% accepted, 12 enrolled. In 2011, 12 master's awarded. *Degree requirements:* For master's, comprehensive exam. *Entrance requirements:* For master's, GRE General Test, minimum GPA of 3.0. Additional exam requirements/recommendations for international students: Required—TOEFL (minimum score 550 paper-based; 213 computer-based; 80 iBT). *Application deadline:* For fall admission, 8/5 priority date for domestic students; for spring admission, 12/1 for domestic students. Applications are processed on a rolling basis. Application fee: $30 ($130 for international students). Electronic applications accepted. *Expenses:* Tuition, state resident: full-time $3131.46; part-time $174 per credit hour. Tuition, nonresident: full-time $8225; part-time $457 per credit hour. *Required fees:* $1446. Tuition and fees vary according to course load and campus/location. *Financial support:* Research assistantships, Federal Work-Study, institutionally sponsored loans, scholarships/grants, and unspecified assistantships available. Financial award application deadline: 5/1; financial award applicants required to submit FAFSA. *Unit head:* Dr. Rudy Tarpley, Head, 254-968-9201, Fax: 254-968-9199, E-mail: tarpley@tarleton.edu. *Application contact:* Information Contact, 254-968-9104, Fax: 254-968-9670, E-mail: gradoffice@tarleton.edu. Web site: http://www.tarleton.edu/~asd.

Texas A&M University, College of Agriculture and Life Sciences, Department of Agricultural Leadership, Education and Communications, College Station, TX 77843. Offers agricultural and life sciences (MS); agricultural development (M Agr); agricultural education (M Ed, Ed D, PhD). Part-time programs available. Postbaccalaureate distance learning degree programs offered (no on-campus study). *Faculty:* 23. *Students:* 75 full-time (51 women), 90 part-time (43 women); includes 21 minority (11 Black or African American, non-Hispanic/Latino; 1 Asian, non-Hispanic/Latino; 8 Hispanic/Latino; 1 Two or more races, non-Hispanic/Latino), 5 international. Average age 27. In 2011, 35 master's, 8 doctorates awarded. Terminal master's awarded for partial completion of doctoral program. *Degree requirements:* For master's, comprehensive exam, thesis (for some programs); for doctorate, comprehensive exam, thesis/dissertation. *Entrance requirements:* For master's, GRE General Test, letters of reference, curriculum vitae; for doctorate, GRE General Test, 3 years of professional experience, letters of reference, curriculum vitae. Additional exam requirements/recommendations for international students: Required—TOEFL. *Application deadline:* For fall admission, 3/15 priority date for domestic students; for spring admission, 10/15 for domestic students. Application fee: $50 ($75 for international students). Electronic applications accepted. *Expenses:* Tuition, state resident: full-time $5437; part-time $226.55 per credit hour. Tuition, nonresident: full-time $12,949; part-time $539.55 per credit hour. *Required fees:* $2741. *Financial support:* In 2011–12, fellowships with partial tuition reimbursements (averaging $12,000 per year), research assistantships with partial tuition reimbursements (averaging $12,000 per year), teaching assistantships with partial tuition reimbursements (averaging $12,000 per year) were awarded; career-related internships or fieldwork, institutionally sponsored loans, scholarships/grants, tuition waivers (partial), and unspecified assistantships also available. Financial award application deadline: 3/15; financial award applicants required to submit FAFSA. *Faculty research:* Planning and needs assessment, instructional design, delivery strategies, evaluation and accountability, distance education. *Unit head:* John Elliot, Head, 979-862-3003, E-mail: jelliot@tamu.edu. *Application contact:* Graduate Admissions, 979-845-1044, E-mail: admissions@tamu.edu. Web site: http://alec.tamu.edu/.

Texas A&M University–Commerce, Graduate School, College of Science, Engineering and Agriculture, Department of Agricultural Sciences, Commerce, TX 75429-3011. Offers agricultural education (M Ed, MS); agricultural sciences (M Ed, MS). Part-time programs available. *Degree requirements:* For master's, comprehensive exam, thesis (for some programs). *Entrance requirements:* For master's, GRE General Test. Electronic applications accepted. *Faculty research:* Soil conservation, retention.

Texas A&M University–Kingsville, College of Graduate Studies, College of Agriculture and Home Economics, Program in Agricultural Education, Kingsville, TX 78363. Offers MS. *Degree requirements:* For master's, comprehensive exam, thesis or alternative. *Entrance requirements:* For master's, GRE General Test, minimum GPA of 3.0. Additional exam requirements/recommendations for international students: Required—TOEFL.

Texas State University–San Marcos, Graduate School, College of Applied Arts, Department of Agriculture, San Marcos, TX 78666. Offers M Ed. Part-time and evening/weekend programs available. *Faculty:* 4 full-time (1 woman), 1 (woman) part-time/adjunct. *Students:* 6 full-time (3 women), 8 part-time (4 women); includes 4 minority (1 Black or African American, non-Hispanic/Latino; 3 Hispanic/Latino), 1 international. Average age 31. 6 applicants, 100% accepted, 6 enrolled. In 2011, 9 master's awarded. *Degree requirements:* For master's, comprehensive exam, thesis (for some programs). *Entrance requirements:* For master's, minimum GPA of 2.75 in last 60 hours of course work, 3 letters of reference (2 from academia). Additional exam requirements/recommendations for international students: Required—TOEFL (minimum score 550 paper-based; 213 computer-based; 78 iBT). *Application deadline:* For fall admission, 6/15 priority date for domestic students, 6/1 for international students; for spring admission, 10/15 priority date for domestic students, 10/1 for international students. Applications are processed on a rolling basis. Application fee: $40 ($90 for international students). Electronic applications accepted. *Expenses:* Tuition, state resident: full-time $6408; part-time $3204 per semester. Tuition, nonresident: full-time $14,832; part-time $7416 per semester. *Required fees:* $1824; $912 per semester. Tuition and fees vary according to course load. *Financial support:* In 2011–12, 7 students received support, including 5 research assistantships (averaging $10,913 per year); teaching assistantships, career-related internships or fieldwork, Federal Work-Study, and institutionally sponsored loans also available. Support available to part-time students. Financial award application deadline: 4/1; financial award applicants required to submit FAFSA. *Faculty research:* ALKA-VITA benefits, FenBendazole Med, diversity of USDA jobs. *Total annual research expenditures:* $22,339. *Unit head:* Dr. C. Reed Richardson, Chair, 512-245-2130, Fax: 512-245-3320, E-mail: cr36@txstate.edu. *Application contact:* Dr. Douglas Morrish, Graduate Adviser, 512-245-2130, Fax: 512-245-3320, E-mail: dm43@txstate.edu. Web site: http://ag.txstate.edu/.

Texas Tech University, Graduate School, College of Agricultural Sciences and Natural Resources, Department of Agricultural Education and Communications, Lubbock, TX 79409. Offers agricultural communication (MS); agricultural communications and education (PhD); agricultural education (MS, Ed D). Part-time and evening/weekend programs available. Postbaccalaureate distance learning degree programs offered (minimal on-campus study). *Faculty:* 10 full-time (3 women). *Students:* 33 full-time (28 women), 36 part-time (18 women); includes 5 minority (1 Black or African American, non-Hispanic/Latino; 1 American Indian or Alaska Native, non-Hispanic/Latino; 2 Hispanic/Latino; 1 Two or more races, non-Hispanic/Latino), 2 international. Average age 29. 51 applicants, 65% accepted, 22 enrolled. In 2011, 22 master's, 9 doctorates awarded. Terminal master's awarded for partial completion of doctoral program. *Degree requirements:* For master's, thesis or alternative; for doctorate, thesis/dissertation. *Entrance requirements:* For master's and doctorate, GRE General Test, formal approval from departmental committee. Additional exam requirements/recommendations for international students: Required—TOEFL (minimum score 550 paper-based; 213 computer-based; 79 iBT). *Application deadline:* For fall admission, 6/1 priority date for domestic students, 1/15 for international students; for spring admission, 9/1 priority date for domestic students, 6/15 for international students. Applications are processed on a rolling basis. Application fee: $50 ($75 for international students). Electronic applications accepted. *Expenses:* Tuition, state resident: full-time $5899; part-time $245.80 per credit hour. Tuition, nonresident: full-time $13,411; part-time $558.80 per credit hour. *Required fees:* $2680.60; $86.50 per credit hour. $920.30 per semester. *Financial support:* In 2011–12, 44 students received support. Application deadline: 4/15; applicants required to submit FAFSA. *Faculty research:* Planning needs assessment, learner-centered instructional design, program delivery, evaluation accountability, research measurement and analysis. *Total annual research expenditures:* $385,688. *Unit head:* Dr. Steve Fraze, Chairman, 806-742-2816, Fax: 806-742-2880, E-mail: steven.fraze@ttu.edu. *Application contact:* Dr. David Doerfert, Graduate Adviser, 806-742-2816, Fax: 806-742-2880, E-mail: david.doerfert@ttu.edu. Web site: http://www.depts.ttu.edu/aged/.

The University of Arizona, College of Agriculture and Life Sciences, Department of Agricultural Education, Tucson, AZ 85721. Offers M Ag Ed, MS. *Faculty:* 3 full-time (0 women). *Students:* 10 full-time (8 women), 7 part-time (5 women); includes 3 minority (1 Hispanic/Latino; 2 Two or more races, non-Hispanic/Latino). Average age 32. 15 applicants, 100% accepted, 11 enrolled. In 2011, 6 master's awarded. *Degree requirements:* For master's, thesis. *Entrance requirements:* For master's, teaching/extension experience or equivalent, minimum GPA of 3.0, 2 letters of recommendation. Additional exam requirements/recommendations for international students: Required—TOEFL. *Application deadline:* For fall admission, 6/1 for domestic students, 2/1 for international students. Applications are processed on a rolling basis. Application fee: $75. Electronic applications accepted. *Expenses:* Tuition, state resident: full-time $10,840. Tuition, nonresident: full-time $25,802. *Financial support:* In 2011–12, 5 students received support, including 4 teaching assistantships with full and partial tuition reimbursements available (averaging $14,982 per year); fellowships, research assistantships, career-related internships or fieldwork, scholarships/grants, health care benefits, tuition waivers (full), and unspecified assistantships also available. *Faculty research:* Career placement, learning styles, noise impact on learning, computer technology, vocational education. *Total annual research expenditures:* $422,646. *Unit head:* Dr. Robert Torres, Head, 520-621-7173, Fax: 520-621-9889, E-mail: rtorres@cals.arizona.edu. *Application contact:* Glen Miller, 520-940-3716, Fax: 520-621-9889, E-mail: vamiller@ag.arizona.edu. Web site: http://ag.arizona.edu/aed/.

University of Arkansas, Graduate School, Dale Bumpers College of Agricultural, Food and Life Sciences, Department of Agricultural and Extension Education, Fayetteville, AR 72701-1201. Offers agricultural and extension education (MS). *Accreditation:* NCATE. *Students:* 12 full-time (6 women), 8 part-time (7 women); includes 4 minority (1 Black or African American, non-Hispanic/Latino; 1 American Indian or Alaska Native, non-Hispanic/Latino; 2 Hispanic/Latino). 11 applicants, 100% accepted. In 2011, 4 master's awarded. *Application deadline:* For fall admission, 4/1 for international students; for spring admission, 10/1 for international students. Applications are processed on a rolling basis. Application fee: $40 ($50 for international students). Electronic applications accepted. *Financial support:* In 2011–12, 3 research assistantships, 4 teaching assistantships were awarded; fellowships, career-related internships or fieldwork, and Federal Work-Study also available. Support available to part-time students. Financial award application deadline: 4/1; financial award applicants required to submit FAFSA. *Unit head:* Dr. George Wardlow, Graduate Coordinator, 479-575-2035, E-mail: wardlow@uark.edu. *Application contact:* Dr. Donna Graham, Graduate Coordinator, 479-575-2039, E-mail: dgraham@uark.edu. Web site: http://aeed.uark.edu/.

University of Connecticut, Graduate School, Neag School of Education, Department of Curriculum and Instruction, Storrs, CT 06269. Offers agriculture (MA), including agriculture education; agriculture education (PhD, Post-Master's Certificate); bilingual and bicultural education (MA, PhD, Post-Master's Certificate); elementary education (MA, PhD, Post-Master's Certificate); English education (MA, PhD, Post-Master's Certificate); history and social sciences education (MA, PhD, Post-Master's Certificate); mathematics education (MA, PhD, Post-Master's Certificate); reading education (MA, PhD, Post-Master's Certificate); science education (MA, PhD); secondary education (MA, PhD, Post-Master's Certificate); world languages education (MA, PhD, Post-Master's Certificate). *Accreditation:* NCATE. Terminal master's awarded for partial completion of doctoral program. *Degree requirements:* For master's, comprehensive exam, thesis or alternative; for doctorate, thesis/dissertation. *Entrance requirements:* For doctorate, GRE General Test. Additional exam requirements/recommendations for international students: Required—TOEFL (minimum score 550 paper-based; 213 computer-based). Electronic applications accepted.

University of Delaware, College of Agriculture and Natural Resources, Department of Food and Resource Economics, Agricultural Education Program, Newark, DE 19716. Offers MA.

University of Florida, Graduate School, College of Agricultural and Life Sciences, Department of Agricultural Education and Communication, Gainesville, FL 32611. Offers M Ag, MS, PhD. Part-time and evening/weekend programs available. *Faculty:* 13 full-time (4 women). *Students:* 28 full-time (19 women), 30 part-time (24 women); includes 6 minority (1 Black or African American, non-Hispanic/Latino; 1 American Indian or Alaska Native, non-Hispanic/Latino; 4 Hispanic/Latino). Average age 33. 35 applicants, 69% accepted, 16 enrolled. In 2011, 31 master's, 4 doctorates awarded. *Degree requirements:* For master's, comprehensive exam (for some programs), thesis (for some programs); for doctorate, comprehensive exam, thesis/dissertation. *Entrance requirements:* For master's and doctorate, GRE General Test (minimum score 1000), minimum GPA of 3.0. Additional exam requirements/recommendations for international students: Required—TOEFL (minimum score 550 paper-based; 213 computer-based; 80 iBT), IELTS (minimum score 6). *Application deadline:* For fall admission, 2/1 priority date for domestic students, 2/1 for international students; for spring admission, 9/1 for domestic and international students. Applications are processed on a rolling basis. Application fee: $30. Electronic applications accepted. *Financial support:* Fellowships, research assistantships, teaching assistantships, and unspecified assistantships available. Financial award application deadline: 1/1; financial award applicants required to submit FAFSA. *Faculty research:* Cooperative extension service, including home economics, agriculture, 4-H, foods, housing, and nutrition. *Unit head:* Dr. Edward W. Osborne, Department Chair, 352-392-0502 Ext. 231, Fax: 352-392-9585, E-mail: ewo@ufl.edu. *Application contact:* Dr. Brian Myers, Graduate Coordinator, 352-392-0502 Ext. 236, E-mail: bmyers@ufl.edu. Web site: http://aec.ifas.ufl.edu/.

University of Georgia, College of Agricultural and Environmental Sciences, Department of Agricultural Leadership, Education, and Communication, Athens, GA 30602. Offers MA Ext, MAL. *Faculty:* 8 full-time (3 women). *Students:* 21 full-time (13 women), 28 part-time (11 women); includes 3 minority (all Black or African American, non-Hispanic/Latino). Average age 32. 41 applicants, 78% accepted, 22 enrolled. In 2011, 24 master's awarded. *Degree requirements:* For master's, comprehensive exam, thesis optional. *Entrance requirements:* For master's, GRE General Test. *Application deadline:* For fall admission, 7/1 priority date for domestic students; for spring admission, 11/15 for domestic students. Application fee: $50. Electronic applications accepted. *Financial support:* In 2011–12, 2 teaching assistantships were awarded; fellowships, research assistantships, and unspecified assistantships also available. *Unit head:* Dr. Dennis Duncan, Interim Head, 706-542-1204, Fax: 706-542-0262, E-mail: dwd@uga.edu. *Application contact:* Dr. Dennis Duncan, Graduate Coordinator, 706-542-1204, E-mail: dwd@uga.edu. Web site: http://www.alec.uga.edu/.

University of Idaho, College of Graduate Studies, College of Agricultural and Life Sciences, Department of Agricultural Education and 4-H Youth Development, Moscow, ID 83844-2040. Offers agricultural education (MS). *Accreditation:* NCATE. *Faculty:* 5 full-time. *Students:* 4 full-time, 4 part-time. Average age 38. In 2011, 2 master's awarded. *Entrance requirements:* For master's, minimum GPA of 2.8. *Application deadline:* For fall admission, 8/1 for domestic students; for spring admission, 12/15 for domestic students. Applications are processed on a rolling basis. Application fee: $60. Electronic applications accepted. *Expenses:* Tuition, state resident: full-time $3874; part-time $334 per credit hour. Tuition, nonresident: full-time $16,394; part-time $861 per credit hour. *Required fees:* $2808; $99 per credit hour. Tuition and fees vary according to program. *Financial support:* Applicants required to submit FAFSA. *Unit head:* Dr. James Joseph Connors, Department Head, 208-885-6358, Fax: 208-885-4039. *Application contact:* Erick Larson, Director of Graduate Admissions, 208-885-4723, E-mail: gadms@uidaho.edu. Web site: http://www.uidaho.edu/cals/ae4hyd.

University of Illinois at Urbana–Champaign, Graduate College, College of Agricultural, Consumer and Environmental Sciences, Department of Human and Community Development, Champaign, IL 61820. Offers agricultural education (MS); human and community development (MS, PhD); MS/MSW. *Faculty:* 17 full-time (10 women), 2 part-time/adjunct (1 woman). *Students:* 36 full-time (28 women), 8 part-time (5 women); includes 10 minority (3 Black or African American, non-Hispanic/Latino; 3 Asian, non-Hispanic/Latino; 2 Hispanic/Latino; 2 Two or more races, non-Hispanic/Latino), 2 international. 38 applicants, 21% accepted, 6 enrolled. In 2011, 7 master's, 2 doctorates awarded. *Entrance requirements:* For master's and doctorate, GRE, minimum GPA of 3.0. Additional exam requirements/recommendations for international students: Required—TOEFL (minimum score 550 paper-based; 213 computer-based; 79 iBT). *Application deadline:* Applications are processed on a rolling basis. Application fee: $75 ($90 for international students). Electronic applications accepted. *Financial support:* In 2011–12, 14 fellowships, 19 research assistantships, 23 teaching assistantships were awarded; tuition waivers (full and partial) also available. *Unit head:* Robert Hughes, Jr., Head, 217-333-3790, Fax: 217-244-7877, E-mail: hughesro@illinois.edu. *Application contact:* Andrea L. Ray, Office Manager, 217-333-3165, Fax: 217-244-7877, E-mail: aray@illinois.edu. Web site: http://www.hcd.illinois.edu/.

University of Minnesota, Twin Cities Campus, Graduate School, College of Education and Human Development, Department of Organizational Leadership, Policy and Development, Program in Agricultural, Food and Environmental Education, Minneapolis, MN 55455-0213. Offers M Ed, MA, Ed D, PhD. *Students:* 4 full-time (all women), 6 part-time (3 women). Average age 30. 4 applicants, 100% accepted, 4 enrolled. In 2011, 2 master's awarded. Application fee: $55. *Unit head:* Dr. Rebecca Ropers-Huilman, Chair, 612-624-1006, Fax: 612-624-3377, E-mail: ropers@umn.edu. *Application contact:* Dr. Jennifer Engler, Assistant Dean, 612-626-2887, Fax: 612-626-7496, E-mail: engle009@umn.edu. Web site: http://www.cehd.umn.edu/WHRE//AFEE.

University of Missouri, Graduate School, College of Agriculture, Food and Natural Resources, Department of Agricultural Education, Columbia, MO 65211. Offers MS, PhD. *Faculty:* 3 full-time (1 woman). *Students:* 15 full-time (9 women), 11 part-time (5 women). Average age 33. 10 applicants, 80% accepted, 5 enrolled. In 2011, 6 master's, 2 doctorates awarded. *Degree requirements:* For doctorate, comprehensive exam, thesis/dissertation. *Entrance requirements:* For master's, minimum GPA of 3.0 for last 60 hours of undergraduate coursework; for doctorate, GRE (preferred minimum score of 1000 verbal and comprehensive), minimum GPA of 3.5 on prior graduate course work; minimum of 3 years full-time appropriate teaching or other professional experience; correspondence with one department faculty member in proposed area of concentration. Additional exam requirements/recommendations for international students: Required—TOEFL (minimum score 550 paper-based; 80 iBT). *Application deadline:* Applications are processed on a rolling basis. Application fee: $55 ($75 for international students). Electronic applications accepted. *Expenses:* Tuition, state resident: full-time $5881. Tuition, nonresident: full-time $15,183. *Required fees:* $952. Tuition and fees vary according to campus/location and program. *Financial support:* Fellowships, research assistantships with tuition reimbursements, and teaching assistantships with tuition reimbursements available. *Faculty research:* Program and professional development, evaluation, teaching and learning theories and practices, educational methods, organization and administration, leadership and communication. *Unit head:* Dr. Anna Ball, Department Chair, 573-882-7451, E-mail: ballan@missouri.edu. *Application contact:* Dr. Tracy Kitchel, Director of Graduate Studies, 573-882-7451, E-mail: kitcheltj@missouri.edu. Web site: http://dass.missouri.edu/aged/grad/.

University of Missouri, Graduate School, College of Education, Department of Learning, Teaching and Curriculum, Columbia, MO 65211. Offers agricultural education (M Ed, PhD, Ed S); art education (M Ed, PhD, Ed S); business and office education (M Ed, PhD, Ed S); early childhood education (M Ed, PhD, Ed S); elementary education (M Ed, PhD, Ed S); English education (M Ed, PhD, Ed S); foreign language education (M Ed, PhD, Ed S); health education and promotion (M Ed, PhD); learning and instruction (M Ed); marketing education (M Ed, PhD, Ed S); mathematics education (M Ed, PhD, Ed S); music education (M Ed, PhD, Ed S); reading education (M Ed, PhD, Ed S); science education (M Ed, PhD, Ed S); social studies education (M Ed, PhD, Ed S); vocational education (M Ed, PhD, Ed S). Part-time programs available. *Faculty:* 26 full-time (16 women), 3 part-time/adjunct (2 women). *Students:* 184 full-time (145 women), 276 part-time (215 women); includes 34 minority (10 Black or African American, non-Hispanic/Latino; 1 American Indian or Alaska Native, non-Hispanic/Latino; 7 Asian, non-Hispanic/Latino; 8 Hispanic/Latino; 8 Two or more races, non-Hispanic/Latino), 39 international. Average age 32. 309 applicants, 76% accepted, 204 enrolled. In 2011, 232 master's, 8 doctorates, 2 other advanced degrees awarded. Terminal master's awarded for partial completion of doctoral program. *Degree requirements:* For doctorate, thesis/dissertation. *Entrance requirements:* For master's and Ed S, GRE General Test or MAT, minimum GPA of 3.0; for doctorate, GRE General Test, minimum GPA of 3.0. Additional exam requirements/recommendations for international students: Required—TOEFL (minimum score 600 paper-based; 250 computer-based; 100 iBT). Application fee: $55 ($75 for international students). Electronic applications accepted. *Expenses:* Tuition, state resident: full-time $5881. Tuition, nonresident: full-time $15,183. *Required fees:* $952. Tuition and fees vary according to campus/location and program. *Financial support:* Fellowships, research assistantships, teaching assistantships, and institutionally sponsored loans available. *Application contact:* Fran Colley, 573-882-6462, E-mail: colleyf@missouri.edu. Web site: http://education.missouri.edu/LTC/.

University of Nebraska–Lincoln, Graduate College, College of Agricultural Sciences and Natural Resources, Department of Agricultural Leadership, Education and Communication, Lincoln, NE 68588. Offers leadership development (MS); leadership education (MS); teaching and extension education (MS). *Accreditation:* Teacher Education Accreditation Council. *Degree requirements:* For master's, thesis optional. *Entrance requirements:* For master's, resume. Additional exam requirements/recommendations for international students: Required—TOEFL (minimum score 550 paper-based; 213 computer-based). Electronic applications accepted. *Faculty research:* Teaching and instruction, extension education, leadership and human resource development, international agricultural education.

University of Puerto Rico, Mayagüez Campus, Graduate Studies, College of Agricultural Sciences, Department of Agricultural Education, Mayagüez, PR 00681-9000. Offers agricultural education (MS); agricultural extension (MS). Part-time programs available. *Students:* 14 full-time (6 women), 3 part-time (1 woman); includes 16 minority (all Hispanic/Latino). 4 applicants, 100% accepted, 4 enrolled. In 2011, 1 master's awarded. *Degree requirements:* For master's, comprehensive exam, thesis. *Entrance requirements:* For master's, BA in home economics; BS in agricultural education, agriculture, home economics, or equivalent. *Application deadline:* For fall admission, 2/15 for domestic and international students; for spring admission, 9/15 for domestic and international students. Applications are processed on a rolling basis. Application fee: $25. Tuition and fees vary according to course level and course load. *Financial support:* In 2011–12, 1 student received support, including 1 teaching assistantship with tuition reimbursement available (averaging $8,500 per year). *Faculty research:* Curricular development and supervision, youth education, rural sociology. *Unit head:* Dr. David Padilla, Director, 787-832-4040 Ext. 3855, Fax: 787-265-3814, E-mail: david.padilla@upr.edu. *Application contact:* Nydia Sanchez, Secretary, 787-832-4040 Ext. 3120, Fax: 787-265-3814, E-mail: nsanchez@uprm.edu. Web site: http://www.uprm.edu/agricultura/edag.

The University of Tennessee, Graduate School, College of Agricultural Sciences and Natural Resources, Department of Agricultural Economics, Knoxville, TN 37996. Offers agricultural education (MS); agricultural extension education (MS). *Accreditation:* NCATE. Part-time programs available. Postbaccalaureate distance learning degree programs offered (minimal on-campus study). *Degree requirements:* For master's, thesis or alternative. *Entrance requirements:* For master's, minimum GPA of 2.7. Additional exam requirements/recommendations for international students: Required—TOEFL. Electronic applications accepted. *Expenses:* Tuition, state resident: full-time $8332; part-time $464 per credit hour. Tuition, nonresident: full-time $25,174; part-time $1400 per credit hour. *Required fees:* $1162; $56 per credit hour. Tuition and fees vary according to program.

University of Wisconsin–River Falls, Outreach and Graduate Studies, College of Agriculture, Food, and Environmental Sciences, Department of Agricultural Education, River Falls, WI 54022. Offers MS. Part-time programs available. *Degree requirements:* For master's, comprehensive exam, thesis (for some programs). *Entrance requirements:* For master's, minimum GPA of 2.75. Additional exam requirements/recommendations for international students: Required—TOEFL (minimum score 500 paper-based; 65 iBT), IELTS (minimum score 5.5). Electronic applications accepted.

Utah State University, School of Graduate Studies, College of Agriculture, Department of Agricultural Systems Technology and Education, Logan, UT 84322. Offers agricultural systems technology (MS), including agricultural extension education, agricultural mechanization, international agricultural extension, secondary and postsecondary agricultural education; family and consumer sciences education (MS). Part-time programs available. Postbaccalaureate distance learning degree programs offered (minimal on-campus study). *Degree requirements:* For master's, comprehensive exam (for some programs), thesis (for some programs). *Entrance requirements:* For master's, GRE General Test, MAT, BS in agricultural education, agricultural extension, or related agricultural or science discipline; minimum GPA of 3.0. Additional exam requirements/recommendations for international students: Required—TOEFL. *Faculty research:* Extension and adult education; structures and environment; low-input agriculture; farm safety, systems, and mechanizations.

Virginia Polytechnic Institute and State University, Graduate School, College of Agriculture and Life Sciences, Department of Agricultural Extension Education, Blacksburg, VA 24061. Offers MS, PhD. *Degree requirements:* For master's, comprehensive exam (for some programs), thesis (for some programs); for doctorate, comprehensive exam (for some programs), thesis/dissertation (for some programs). *Entrance requirements:* For master's and doctorate, GRE. Additional exam requirements/recommendations for international students: Required—TOEFL (minimum score 550 paper-based; 213 computer-based). *Application deadline:* For fall admission, 7/1 for domestic and international students; for spring admission, 12/1 for domestic and international students. Applications are processed on a rolling basis. Application fee: $65. Electronic applications accepted. *Expenses:* Tuition, state resident: full-time $10,048; part-time $558.25 per credit hour. Tuition, nonresident: full-time $19,497; part-time $1083.25 per credit hour. *Required fees:* $405 per semester. Tuition and fees vary according to course load, campus/location and program. *Financial support:* Research assistantships with full tuition reimbursements, teaching assistantships with full tuition reimbursements, career-related internships or fieldwork, Federal Work-Study, scholarships/grants, health care benefits, and unspecified assistantships available. Financial award application deadline: 1/15. *Unit head:* Dr. Rick D. Rudd, Unit Head, 540-231-6836, Fax: 540-231-3824, E-mail: rrudd@vt.edu. Web site: http://www.aee.vt.edu/index.html.

West Virginia University, Davis College of Agriculture, Forestry and Consumer Sciences, Division of Resource Management and Sustainable Development, Program in Agricultural and Extension Education, Morgantown, WV 26506. Offers agricultural and extension education (MS, PhD); teaching vocational-agriculture (MS). *Accreditation:* NCATE. Part-time programs available. *Degree requirements:* For master's, thesis. *Entrance requirements:* For master's, GRE General Test, minimum GPA of 2.75. Additional exam requirements/recommendations for international students: Required—TOEFL. *Faculty research:* Program development in vocational agriculture, agricultural extension, supervised experience programs, leadership development.

Art Education

Academy of Art University, Graduate Program, School of Art Education, San Francisco, CA 94105-3410. Offers MA. Part-time programs available. Postbaccalaureate distance learning degree programs offered (no on-campus study). *Faculty:* 1 (woman) full-time, 7 part-time/adjunct (6 women). *Students:* 19 full-time (16 women), 14 part-time (13 women); includes 5 minority (4 Black or African American, non-Hispanic/Latino; 1 Hispanic/Latino), 16 international. Average age 32. 35 applicants. *Degree requirements:* For master's, final review. *Entrance requirements:* For master's, statement of intent; resume; portfolio/reel; official college transcripts. *Application deadline:* Applications are processed on a rolling basis. Application fee: $100. Electronic applications accepted. *Expenses: Tuition:* Full-time $20,160; part-time $840 per unit. *Required fees:* $90. *Financial support:* Career-related internships or fieldwork and Federal Work-Study available. Support available to part-time students. Financial award application deadline: 8/10; financial award applicants required to submit FAFSA. *Unit head:* 800-544-ARTS, E-mail: info@academyart.edu. *Application contact:* 800-544-ARTS, Fax: 415-263-4130, E-mail: info@academyart.edu. Web site: http://www.academyart.edu/art-education-school/index.html.

Adelphi University, Ruth S. Ammon School of Education, Program in Art Education, Garden City, NY 11530-0701. Offers MA. Part-time programs available. *Students:* 7 full-time (6 women), 12 part-time (10 women); includes 3 minority (1 Black or African American, non-Hispanic/Latino; 1 Asian, non-Hispanic/Latino; 1 Hispanic/Latino), 2 international. Average age 29. In 2011, 12 master's awarded. *Entrance requirements:* For master's, 2 letters of recommendation, visual arts portfolio, essay. Additional exam requirements/recommendations for international students: Required—TOEFL (minimum score 550 paper-based; 213 computer-based; 80 iBT). *Application deadline:* For fall admission, 4/1 for international students; for spring admission, 11/1 for international students. Application fee: $50. Electronic applications accepted. *Expenses: Tuition:* Full-time $29,600; part-time $930 per credit. *Required fees:* $1100. *Financial support:* Fellowships, research assistantships with partial tuition reimbursements, teaching assistantships, career-related internships or fieldwork, Federal Work-Study, institutionally sponsored loans, tuition waivers (full), and unspecified assistantships available. Support available to part-time students. Financial award application deadline: 2/15; financial award applicants required to submit FAFSA. *Unit head:* Courtney Lee Weida, Director, 516-877-4105, E-mail: cweida@adelphi.edu. *Application contact:* Christine Murphy, Director of Admissions, 516-877-3050, Fax: 516-877-3039, E-mail: graduateadmissions@adelphi.edu.

American University of Puerto Rico, Program in Education, Bayamón, PR 00960-2037. Offers art education (M Ed); elementary education 4-6 (M Ed); elementary education K-3 (M Ed); general science education (M Ed); physical education (M Ed); special education (M Ed). *Entrance requirements:* For master's, EXADEP, GRE, or MAT, 2 letters of recommendation, minimum GPA of 2.5. *Application deadline:* For fall admission, 8/1 for domestic students; for winter admission, 10/18 for domestic students; for spring admission, 3/15 for domestic students. Applications are processed on a rolling basis. Application fee: $50. *Expenses: Tuition:* Part-time $190 per credit. *Required fees:* $48.33 per credit. Tuition and fees vary according to course load and program. *Application contact:* Information Contact, 787-620-2040, E-mail: oficnaadmisiones@aupr.edu.

Anna Maria College, Graduate Division, Program in Visual Arts, Paxton, MA 01612. Offers art and visual art (MA); teacher of visual art (M Ed). Part-time and evening/weekend programs available. *Degree requirements:* For master's, thesis. *Entrance requirements:* For master's, minimum GPA of 2.7, undergraduate major in art, portfolio. Additional exam requirements/recommendations for international students: Required—TOEFL (minimum score 500 paper-based). Electronic applications accepted.

Arcadia University, Graduate Studies, Department of Education, Glenside, PA 19038-3295. Offers art education (M Ed); computer education (CAS); curriculum (CAS); curriculum studies (M Ed); early childhood education (M Ed, CAS), including individualized (M Ed), master teacher (M Ed), research in child development (M Ed); educational leadership (M Ed, Ed D, CAS); elementary education (M Ed, CAS); English education (MA Ed); environmental education (MA Ed, CAS); history education (MA Ed); instructional technology (M Ed); language arts (M Ed, CAS); library science (M Ed); mathematics education (M Ed, MA Ed, CAS); music education (MA Ed); psychology (MA Ed); reading (M Ed, CAS); science education (M Ed, CAS); secondary education (M Ed, CAS); special education (M Ed, Ed D, CAS); theater arts (MA Ed); written communication (MA Ed). *Accreditation:* NASAD. Part-time and evening/weekend programs available. Postbaccalaureate distance learning degree programs offered (minimal on-campus study). *Faculty:* 12 full-time (8 women), 38 part-time/adjunct (26 women). *Students:* 66 full-time (48 women), 590 part-time (477 women); includes 65 minority (53 Black or African American, non-Hispanic/Latino; 6 Asian, non-Hispanic/Latino; 3 Hispanic/Latino; 3 Two or more races, non-Hispanic/Latino), 4 international. Average age 36. In 2011, 229 master's, 5 doctorates awarded. *Application deadline:* Applications are processed on a rolling basis. Application fee: $50. Electronic applications accepted. *Expenses:* Contact institution. *Financial support:* Career-related internships or fieldwork, tuition waivers (partial), and unspecified assistantships available. *Unit head:* Dr. Steven P. Gulkus, Associate Professor, 215-572-2120, E-mail: gulkus@arcadia.edu. *Application contact:* 215-572-2925, Fax: 215-572-2126, E-mail: grad@arcadia.edu.

Arizona State University, Herberger Institute for Design and the Arts, School of Art, Tempe, AZ 85287-1505. Offers art (art education) (MA); art (art history) (MA); art (ceramics) (MFA); art (digital technology) (MFA); art (drawing) (MFA); art (fibers) (MFA); art (intermedia) (MFA); art (metals) (MFA); art (painting) (MFA); art (printmaking) (MFA); art (sculpture) (MFA); art (wood) (MFA); design, environment and the arts (history, theory and criticism) (PhD). Terminal master's awarded for partial completion of doctoral program. *Degree requirements:* For master's, thesis/exhibition (MFA, MA in art education); interactive Program of Study (iPOS) submitted before completing 50 percent of required credit hours; for doctorate, comprehensive exam, thesis/dissertation, interactive Program of Study (iPOS) submitted before completing 50 percent of required credit hours. *Entrance requirements:* For master's, GRE or MAT, minimum GPA of 3.0 or equivalent in last 2 years of work leading to bachelor's degree; for doctorate, GRE, master's degree in architecture, graphic design, industrial design, interior design, landscape architecture, or art history or equivalent standing; statement of purpose; 3 letters of recommendation; indication of potential faculty mentor; sample of written work. Additional exam requirements/recommendations for international students: Required—TOEFL, IELTS, or Pearson Test of English. Electronic applications accepted.

Art Academy of Cincinnati, Program in Art Education, Cincinnati, OH 45202. Offers MAAE. Offered during summer only. *Accreditation:* NASAD. Part-time programs available. *Degree requirements:* For master's, thesis, portfolio/exhibit. *Entrance requirements:* For master's, 2 letters of recommendation, portfolio, state teaching license. Additional exam requirements/recommendations for international students: Required—TOEFL (minimum score 550 paper-based; 213 computer-based; 80 iBT). Electronic applications accepted.

Austin College, Program in Education, Sherman, TX 75090-4400. Offers art education (MA); elementary education (MA); middle school education (MA); music education (MA); physical education and coaching (MA); secondary education (MA); theatre education (MA). Part-time programs available. *Faculty:* 5 full-time (4 women). *Students:* 21 full-time (13 women), 2 part-time (both women). Average age 23. In 2011, 24 master's awarded. *Degree requirements:* For master's, one foreign language, thesis or alternative. *Entrance requirements:* For master's, Texas Academic Skills Program Test. *Application deadline:* For fall admission, 5/1 priority date for domestic students; for spring admission, 1/15 priority date for domestic students. Applications are processed on a rolling basis. Application fee: $35. Electronic applications accepted. *Expenses: Tuition:* Full-time $38,445. *Required fees:* $160. *Financial support:* Career-related internships or fieldwork, Federal Work-Study, scholarships/grants, and unspecified assistantships available. Support available to part-time students. Financial award application deadline: 4/1; financial award applicants required to submit FAFSA. *Unit head:* Dr. Barbara Sylvester, Director of Teaching Program, 903-813-2327, E-mail: bsylvester@austincollege.edu. *Application contact:* Dr. Barbara Sylvester, Director of Teaching Program, 903-813-2327, E-mail: bsylvester@austincollege.edu. Web site: http://www.austincollege.edu/.

Boise State University, Graduate College, College of Arts and Sciences, Department of Art, Program in Art Education, Boise, ID 83725-0399. Offers MA. *Accreditation:* NASAD; NCATE. Part-time programs available. *Degree requirements:* For master's, thesis optional. *Entrance requirements:* For master's, minimum GPA of 3.0, portfolio. Additional exam requirements/recommendations for international students: Required—TOEFL (minimum score 587 paper-based; 240 computer-based). Electronic applications accepted.

Boston University, College of Fine Arts, School of Visual Arts, Boston, MA 02215. Offers art education (MA); graphic design (MFA); painting (MFA); sculpture (MFA); studio teaching (MA). *Faculty:* 17 full-time, 4 part-time/adjunct. *Students:* 31 full-time (17 women); includes 6 minority (1 Black or African American, non-Hispanic/Latino; 1 Asian, non-Hispanic/Latino; 4 Hispanic/Latino), 5 international. Average age 28. 257 applicants, 27% accepted, 31 enrolled. In 2011, 27 master's awarded. *Entrance requirements:* For master's, portfolio. Additional exam requirements/recommendations for international students: Required—TOEFL. *Application deadline:* For fall admission, 2/15 for domestic and international students. Applications are processed on a rolling basis. Application fee: $70. *Expenses: Tuition:* Full-time $40,848; part-time $1276 per credit hour. *Required fees:* $572; $286 per semester. *Financial support:* Fellowships and teaching assistantships available. Financial award application deadline: 2/15. *Unit head:* Lynne Allen, Director, 617-353-3371. *Application contact:* Mark Krone, Manager, Graduate Admissions, 617-353-3350, E-mail: arts@bu.edu.

Bowling Green State University, Graduate College, College of Arts and Sciences, School of Art, Bowling Green, OH 43403. Offers 2-D studio art (MA, MFA); 3-D studio art (MA, MFA); art education (MA); art history (MA); computer art (MA); design (MFA); digital arts (MFA); graphics (MFA). *Accreditation:* NASAD. Part-time programs available. *Degree requirements:* For master's, thesis or alternative, final exhibit (MFA). *Entrance requirements:* For master's, GRE General Test (MA), slide portfolio (15-20 slides). Additional exam requirements/recommendations for international students: Required—TOEFL. Electronic applications accepted. *Faculty research:* Computer animation and virtual reality, Spanish still-life painting from 1600 to 1800, art and psychotherapy, Japanese wood-firing techniques in ceramics, non-toxic printmaking technologies.

Bridgewater State University, School of Graduate Studies, School of Arts and Sciences, Department of Art, Bridgewater, MA 02325-0001. Offers MAT. Part-time and evening/weekend programs available. *Degree requirements:* For master's, comprehensive exam. *Entrance requirements:* For master's, GRE General Test.

Brigham Young University, Graduate Studies, College of Fine Arts and Communications, Department of Visual Arts, Provo, UT 84602-6414. Offers art education (MA); art history (MA); studio art (MFA). Art education applications accepted biennially. *Accreditation:* NASAD. *Faculty:* 16 full-time (5 women), 1 (woman) part-time/adjunct. *Students:* 40 full-time (31 women); includes 2 minority (1 Hispanic/Latino; 1 Native Hawaiian or other Pacific Islander, non-Hispanic/Latino). Average age 26. 38 applicants, 58% accepted, 18 enrolled. In 2011, 7 master's awarded. *Degree requirements:* For master's, one foreign language, comprehensive exam, thesis (art history), selected project (MFA), curriculum project (art education). *Entrance requirements:* For master's, GRE (art history), minimum GPA of 3.0 (MFA, MA in art education), 3.5 (MA in art history), portfolio in CD format (MFA), writing samples (MA in art education, art history). Additional exam requirements/recommendations for international students: Required—TOEFL (minimum score 580 paper-based; 85 iBT). *Application deadline:* For fall admission, 2/1 for domestic and international students. Application fee: $50. Electronic applications accepted. *Expenses: Tuition:* Full-time $5760; part-time $320 per credit. Tuition and fees vary according to student's religious affiliation. *Financial support:* In 2011–12, 40 students received support. Research assistantships, teaching assistantships with partial tuition reimbursements available, scholarships/grants, and tuition waivers (partial) available. Financial award application deadline: 2/1. *Faculty research:* Methodology-standards-assessment, medieval architecture, classical/Islamic eighteenth and nineteenth century art, Netherlandish art, contemporary art, modern art, history of photography, exploration of art making processes, new genre. *Unit head:* Prof. Linda A. Reynolds, Chair, 801-422-4429, Fax: 801-422-0695, E-mail: lindareynolds@byu.edu. *Application contact:* Sharon Lyn Heelis, Secretary, 801-422-4429, Fax: 801-422-0695, E-mail: sharon_heelis@byu.edu. Web site: http://visualarts.byu.edu.

Brooklyn College of the City University of New York, Division of Graduate Studies, School of Education, Program in Adolescence Education and Special Subjects, Brooklyn, NY 11210-2889. Offers adolescence science education (MAT); art teacher (MA); biology teacher (MA); chemistry teacher (MA); earth science teacher (MAT); English teacher (MA); French teacher (MA); health and nutrition sciences: health teacher (MS Ed); mathematics teacher (MA); music education (CAS); music teacher (MA); physical education teacher (MS Ed); physics teacher (MA); social studies teacher (MA); Spanish teacher (MA). Part-time and evening/weekend programs available. *Degree requirements:* For master's, comprehensive exam (for some programs), thesis (for some programs). *Entrance requirements:* For master's, LAST, previous course work in education, resume, 2 letters of recommendation, essay. Additional exam requirements/recommendations for international students: Required—TOEFL (minimum score 500 paper-based; 173 computer-based; 61 iBT). Electronic applications accepted.

Faculty research: Interdisciplinary education, semiotics, discourse analysis, autobiography, teacher identity.

Buffalo State College, State University of New York, The Graduate School, Faculty of Arts and Humanities, Department of Art Education, Buffalo, NY 14222-1095. Offers MS Ed. *Accreditation:* NASAD; NCATE. Part-time and evening/weekend programs available. *Degree requirements:* For master's, thesis or alternative, project. *Entrance requirements:* For master's, New York teaching certificate, interview, minimum GPA of 3.0. Additional exam requirements/recommendations for international students: Required—TOEFL (minimum score 550 paper-based; 213 computer-based).

California State University, Long Beach, Graduate Studies, College of the Arts, Department of Art, Long Beach, CA 90840. Offers art education (MA); art history (MA); studio art (MA, MFA). *Accreditation:* NASAD. Part-time programs available. *Faculty:* 25 full-time (14 women), 16 part-time/adjunct (7 women). *Students:* 85 full-time (56 women), 30 part-time (20 women); includes 37 minority (1 Black or African American, non-Hispanic/Latino; 2 American Indian or Alaska Native, non-Hispanic/Latino; 13 Asian, non-Hispanic/Latino; 19 Hispanic/Latino; 2 Two or more races, non-Hispanic/Latino), 9 international. Average age 33. 215 applicants, 26% accepted, 40 enrolled. In 2011, 30 master's awarded. *Degree requirements:* For master's, thesis (for some programs). *Entrance requirements:* For master's, minimum GPA of 3.0 in last 60 hours. *Application deadline:* For fall admission, 7/1 for domestic students; for spring admission, 12/1 for domestic students. Applications are processed on a rolling basis. Application fee: $55. Electronic applications accepted. *Financial support:* Federal Work-Study, institutionally sponsored loans, and scholarships/grants available. Financial award application deadline: 3/2. *Unit head:* Prof. David Hadlock, Chair, 562-985-7908, Fax: 562-985-1650, E-mail: dhadlock@csulb.edu. *Application contact:* Margaret Black, Graduate Advisor, 562-985-7910, Fax: 562-985-1650.

California State University, Los Angeles, Graduate Studies, College of Arts and Letters, Department of Art, Los Angeles, CA 90032-8530. Offers art (MA), including art education, art history, art therapy, ceramics, metals, and textiles, design (MA, MFA), painting, sculpture, and graphic arts, photography; fine arts (MFA), including crafts, design (MA, MFA), studio arts. *Accreditation:* NASAD (one or more programs are accredited). Part-time and evening/weekend programs available. *Faculty:* 9 full-time (3 women), 6 part-time/adjunct (3 women). *Students:* 34 full-time (24 women), 34 part-time (26 women); includes 33 minority (3 Black or African American, non-Hispanic/Latino; 7 Asian, non-Hispanic/Latino; 21 Hispanic/Latino; 2 Two or more races, non-Hispanic/Latino), 8 international. Average age 36. 97 applicants, 29% accepted, 20 enrolled. In 2011, 23 master's awarded. *Degree requirements:* For master's, comprehensive exam, project or thesis. *Entrance requirements:* For master's, portfolio. Additional exam requirements/recommendations for international students: Required—TOEFL (minimum score 500 paper-based; 173 computer-based). *Application deadline:* For fall admission, 5/1 for domestic and international students. Applications are processed on a rolling basis. Application fee: $55. Electronic applications accepted. *Expenses:* Tuition, state resident: full-time $8225. *Financial support:* Federal Work-Study available. Support available to part-time students. Financial award application deadline: 3/1. *Faculty research:* The artist and the book, conceptual art, ceramic processes, computer graphics, architectural graphics. *Unit head:* Dr. Abbas Daneshvari, Chair, 323-343-4010, Fax: 323-343-4045, E-mail: adanesh@calstatela.edu. *Application contact:* Dr. Karin Brown, Acting Associate Dean of Graduate Studies, 323-343-3820, Fax: 323-343-5653, E-mail: kbrown5@calstatela.edu. Web site: http://www.calstatela.edu/academic/art/.

California State University, Northridge, Graduate Studies, College of Arts, Media, and Communication, Department of Art, Northridge, CA 91330. Offers art education (MA); art history (MA); studio art (MA, MFA); visual communications (MA, MFA). *Accreditation:* NASAD.

Carlow University, School of Education, Program in Art Education, Pittsburgh, PA 15213-3165. Offers M Ed. Part-time and evening/weekend programs available. *Students:* 11 full-time (7 women), 6 part-time (all women); includes 2 minority (1 Black or African American, non-Hispanic/Latino; 1 Hispanic/Latino). Average age 28. 26 applicants, 27% accepted, 5 enrolled. In 2011, 5 master's awarded. *Degree requirements:* For master's, thesis or alternative. *Entrance requirements:* Additional exam requirements/recommendations for international students: Required—TOEFL (minimum score 550 paper-based; 213 computer-based). *Application deadline:* For fall admission, 6/15 priority date for domestic students, 6/15 for international students; for spring admission, 11/15 priority date for domestic students, 11/15 for international students. Applications are processed on a rolling basis. Application fee: $20. Electronic applications accepted. *Expenses: Tuition:* Full-time $10,290; part-time $686 per credit. Tuition and fees vary according to course load, degree level and program. *Financial support:* Application deadline: 4/1; applicants required to submit FAFSA. *Unit head:* Susan S. Hamilton, Director, 412-578-6167, Fax: 412-578-8816, E-mail: hamiltonss@carlow.edu. *Application contact:* Jo Danhires, Administrative Assistant, Admissions, 412-578-6059, Fax: 412-578-6321, E-mail: gradstudies@carlow.edu. Web site: http://www.carlow.edu/.

Carlow University, School of Education, Program in Education, Pittsburgh, PA 15213-3165. Offers art education (M Ed); early childhood education (M Ed); instructional technology specialist (M Ed); middle level education (M Ed); secondary education (M Ed); special education (M Ed). Part-time and evening/weekend programs available. *Students:* 72 full-time (58 women), 16 part-time (13 women); includes 16 minority (15 Black or African American, non-Hispanic/Latino; 1 Hispanic/Latino). Average age 32. 68 applicants, 28% accepted, 11 enrolled. In 2011, 41 master's awarded. *Entrance requirements:* For master's, resume, 3 letters of recommendation, minimum GPA of 3.0, interview. Additional exam requirements/recommendations for international students: Required—TOEFL. *Application deadline:* For fall admission, 6/15 priority date for domestic students, 6/15 for international students; for spring admission, 11/15 priority date for domestic students, 11/15 for international students. Applications are processed on a rolling basis. Application fee: $20. Electronic applications accepted. *Expenses: Tuition:* Full-time $10,290; part-time $686 per credit. Tuition and fees vary according to course load, degree level and program. *Financial support:* Applicants required to submit FAFSA. *Unit head:* Dr. Marilyn J. Llewellyn, Director, 412-578-6011, Fax: 412-578-0816, E-mail: llewellynmj@carlow.edu. *Application contact:* Jo Danhires, Administrative Assistant, Admissions, 412-578-6089, Fax: 412-578-6321, E-mail: gradstudies@carlow.edu. Web site: http://www.carlow.edu.

Carthage College, Division of Teacher Education, Kenosha, WI 53140. Offers classroom guidance and counseling (M Ed); creative arts (M Ed); gifted and talented children (M Ed); language arts (M Ed); modern language (M Ed); natural sciences (M Ed); reading (M Ed, Certificate); social sciences (M Ed); teacher leadership (M Ed). Part-time and evening/weekend programs available. *Degree requirements:* For master's, thesis optional. *Entrance requirements:* For master's, MAT, minimum B average, letters of reference.

Case Western Reserve University, School of Graduate Studies, Department of Art History and Art, Program in Art Education, Cleveland, OH 44106. Offers MA. Program offered jointly with The Cleveland Institute of Art. *Accreditation:* Teacher Education Accreditation Council. Part-time programs available. *Faculty:* 10 part-time/adjunct (6 women). *Students:* 5 full-time (all women), 3 part-time (all women), 1 international. Average age 32. 8 applicants, 63% accepted, 5 enrolled. In 2011, 6 degrees awarded. *Degree requirements:* For master's, thesis, art exhibit. *Entrance requirements:* For master's, NTE, interview, portfolio. Additional exam requirements/recommendations for international students: Required—TOEFL (minimum score 600 paper-based; 213 computer-based; 100 iBT). *Application deadline:* For fall admission, 3/1 for domestic students; for spring admission, 11/1 for domestic students. Applications are processed on a rolling basis. Application fee: $50. Electronic applications accepted. *Faculty research:* Visual and aesthetic education, ethnographic arts, multiculturalism. *Unit head:* Tim Shuckerow, Director, 216-368-2714, Fax: 216-368-2715, E-mail: txs10@po.cwru.edu. *Application contact:* Debby Tenenbaum, Assistant, 216-368-4118, Fax: 216-368-4681, E-mail: deborah.tenenbaum@case.edu. Web site: http://www.case.edu/artsci/artedu/.

Central Connecticut State University, School of Graduate Studies, School of Arts and Sciences, Department of Art, New Britain, CT 06050-4010. Offers art education (MS, Certificate). Part-time and evening/weekend programs available. *Faculty:* 13 full-time (5 women), 19 part-time/adjunct (10 women). *Students:* 21 full-time (19 women), 19 part-time (17 women); includes 4 minority (1 Black or African American, non-Hispanic/Latino; 1 Hispanic/Latino; 2 Two or more races, non-Hispanic/Latino). Average age 32. 19 applicants, 68% accepted, 9 enrolled. In 2011, 3 master's, 1 other advanced degree awarded. *Degree requirements:* For master's, thesis or alternative, exhibit or special project; for Certificate, qualifying exam. *Entrance requirements:* For master's, portfolio, essay. Additional exam requirements/recommendations for international students: Required—TOEFL (minimum score 550 paper-based; 213 computer-based). *Application deadline:* For fall admission, 6/1 for domestic students, 5/1 for international students; for spring admission, 11/1 for domestic and international students. Applications are processed on a rolling basis. Application fee: $50. Electronic applications accepted. *Expenses: Tuition, area resident:* Full-time $5137; part-time $482 per credit. Tuition, state resident: full-time $7707; part-time $494 per credit. Tuition, nonresident: full-time $14,311; part-time $494 per credit. *Required fees:* $3865. One-time fee: $62 part-time. *Financial support:* In 2011–12, 4 students received support, including 3 research assistantships; career-related internships or fieldwork, Federal Work-Study, scholarships/grants, and unspecified assistantships also available. Support available to part-time students. Financial award application deadline: 4/15; financial award applicants required to submit FAFSA. *Faculty research:* Visual arts. *Unit head:* Dr. Cora Marshall, Chair, 860-832-2620, E-mail: marshallc@ccsu.edu. *Application contact:* Patricia Gardner, Associate Director of Graduate Studies, 860-832-2350, Fax: 860-832-2352, E-mail: graduateadmissions@ccsu.edu. Web site: http://www.art.ccsu.edu/.

Chatham University, Program in Education, Pittsburgh, PA 15232-2826. Offers early childhood education (MAT); elementary education (MAT); environmental education (K-12) (MAT); secondary art (MAT); secondary biology education (MAT); secondary chemistry education (MAT); secondary English education (MAT); secondary math education (MAT); secondary physics education (MAT); secondary social studies education (MAT); special education (MAT). *Students:* 52 full-time (42 women), 17 part-time (16 women); includes 2 minority (1 Black or African American, non-Hispanic/Latino; 1 Hispanic/Latino). Average age 29. 39 applicants, 82% accepted, 23 enrolled. In 2011, 37 master's awarded. *Degree requirements:* For master's, thesis, teaching experience. *Entrance requirements:* For master's, minimum GPA of 3.0, sample of written work, recommendation letters. Additional exam requirements/recommendations for international students: Required—TOEFL (minimum score 600 paper-based; 250 computer-based; 100 iBT), IELTS (minimum score 7), TWE. *Application deadline:* For fall admission, 4/1 priority date for domestic students, 4/1 for international students; for spring admission, 11/1 priority date for domestic students, 10/1 for international students. Applications are processed on a rolling basis. Application fee: $45. Electronic applications accepted. Application fee is waived when completed online. *Expenses: Tuition:* Full-time $13,896. Tuition and fees vary according to program. *Financial support:* Career-related internships or fieldwork available. Financial award applicants required to submit FAFSA. *Faculty research:* Gifted education, environmental education, technology in education, writing as learning, class size and achievement. *Unit head:* Dr. Elvira Sanatullova-Allison, Director of Education Programs, 412-365-2773, E-mail: esanatullovaallison@chatham.edu. *Application contact:* Dory Perry, Associate Director of Graduate Admission, 412-365-2758, Fax: 412-365-1609, E-mail: gradadmissions@chatham.edu. Web site: http://www.chatham.edu/mat.

Christopher Newport University, Graduate Studies, Department of Teacher Preparation, Newport News, VA 23606-2998. Offers art (PK-12) (MAT); biology (6-12) (MAT); chemistry (6-12) (MAT); computer science (6-12) (MAT); elementary (PK-6) (MAT); English (6-12) (MAT); English as second language (PK-12) (MAT); French (PK-12) (MAT); history and social science (6-12) (MAT); mathematics (6-12) (MAT); music (PK-12) (MAT), including choral, instrumental; physics (6-12) (MAT); Spanish (PK-12) (MAT). Part-time and evening/weekend programs available. *Degree requirements:* For master's, comprehensive exam, thesis or alternative. *Entrance requirements:* For master's, PRAXIS I, minimum GPA of 3.0. Additional exam requirements/recommendations for international students: Required—TOEFL (minimum score 580 paper-based; 237 computer-based; 92 iBT). Electronic applications accepted. *Faculty research:* Early literacy development, instructional innovations, professional teaching standards, multicultural issues, aesthetic education.

Cleveland State University, College of Graduate Studies, College of Education and Human Services, Department of Teacher Education, Cleveland, OH 44115. Offers art education (M Ed); early childhood education (M Ed); foreign language education (M Ed); mathematics and science education (M Ed); middle childhood education (M Ed); special education (M Ed), including mild/moderate disabilities, moderate/intensive disabilities; teaching English to speakers of other languages (M Ed). Part-time and evening/weekend programs available. *Faculty:* 20 full-time (12 women), 26 part-time/adjunct (20 women). *Students:* 108 full-time (77 women), 388 part-time (306 women); includes 126 minority (100 Black or African American, non-Hispanic/Latino; 8 Asian, non-Hispanic/Latino; 15 Hispanic/Latino; 1 Native Hawaiian or other Pacific Islander, non-Hispanic/Latino; 2 Two or more races, non-Hispanic/Latino), 25 international. Average age 33. 249 applicants, 73% accepted, 118 enrolled. In 2011, 286 master's awarded. *Degree requirements:* For master's, comprehensive exam (for some programs), thesis or alternative. *Entrance requirements:* For master's, GRE General Test or MAT, minimum GPA of 2.75. Additional exam requirements/recommendations for international students: Required—TOEFL (minimum score 525 paper-based; 197 computer-based), IELTS (minimum score 6). *Application deadline:* For fall admission, 7/15 priority date for domestic students. Applications are processed on a rolling basis. Application fee: $30. *Expenses:* Tuition, state resident: full-time $6416; part-time $494 per credit hour. Tuition, nonresident: full-time $12,074; part-time $929 per credit hour. *Financial support:* In 2011–12, 12 research assistantships with full tuition reimbursements (averaging $3,480 per year) were awarded; tuition waivers (partial) and unspecified assistantships also available. *Faculty research:* Early literacy, professional development in reading, reading recovery, dual language, induction programs. *Total annual research expenditures:* $6.2 million. *Unit head:* Dr. Clifford T. Bennett, Chairperson, 216-523-7105, Fax: 216-687-5379, E-mail: c.t.bennett@csuohio.edu. *Application contact:* Deborah L. Brown, Interim Assistant Director, Graduate Admissions, 216-523-7572, E-mail: d.l.brown@csuohio.edu.
Web site: http://www.csuohio.edu/coehs/departments/te.

Art Education

Cleveland State University, College of Graduate Studies, College of Liberal Arts and Social Sciences, Department of Art, Cleveland, OH 44115. Offers art education (M Ed); art history (MA). *Faculty:* 3 full-time (2 women). *Students:* 1 (woman) full-time. Average age 32. 1 applicant, 100% accepted, 1 enrolled. *Expenses:* Tuition, state resident: full-time $6416; part-time $494 per credit hour. Tuition, nonresident: full-time $12,074; part-time $929 per credit hour. *Unit head:* Jennifer Visocky-O-Grady, Chair/Associate Professor, 216-523-7546, E-mail: j.visoky@csuohio.edu. *Application contact:* Jan Milic, Administrative Coordinator, 216-687-2065, Fax: 216-687-5400, E-mail: j.milic@csuohio.edu. Web site: http://www.csuohio.edu/art/.

College of Mount St. Joseph, Graduate Education Program, Cincinnati, OH 45233-1670. Offers adolescent young adult education (MA); art (MA); inclusive early childhood education (MA); instructional leadership (MA); middle childhood education (MA); multi-age education (MA); multicultural special education (MA); music (MA); reading (MA). *Accreditation:* Teacher Education Accreditation Council. Part-time and evening/weekend programs available. *Faculty:* 22 full-time (12 women), 11 part-time/adjunct (8 women). *Students:* 51 full-time (40 women), 92 part-time (72 women); includes 17 minority (14 Black or African American, non-Hispanic/Latino; 1 American Indian or Alaska Native, non-Hispanic/Latino; 1 Asian, non-Hispanic/Latino; 1 Hispanic/Latino). Average age 34. 87 applicants, 44% accepted, 29 enrolled. In 2011, 61 master's awarded. *Degree requirements:* For master's, research project, student teaching, clinical and field-based experiences. *Entrance requirements:* For master's, GRE, PRAXIS II in teaching content area (math or science), 2 letters of recommendation, interview, resume. Additional exam requirements/recommendations for international students: Required—TOEFL (minimum score 560 paper-based; 220 computer-based; 83 iBT). *Application deadline:* Applications are processed on a rolling basis. Application fee: $50. Electronic applications accepted. *Expenses: Tuition:* Full-time $24,200; part-time $540 per credit hour. *Required fees:* $112.50 per semester. One-time fee: $200. *Financial support:* In 2011–12, 22 students received support. Scholarships/grants available. Financial award applicants required to submit FAFSA. *Faculty research:* Foreign and second language learning problems/reading disabilities/hyperlexia, multicultural/bilingual special education, alternative educator licensure, science education, pedagogical content knowledge. *Unit head:* Dr. Mary West, Chair, 513-244-3263, Fax: 513-244-4867, E-mail: mary_west@mail.msj.edu. *Application contact:* Marilyn Hoskins, Assistant Director of Graduate Recruitment, 513-244-4723, Fax: 513-244-4629, E-mail: marilyn_hoskins@mail.msj.edu. Web site: http://www.msj.edu/view/academics/graduate-programs/education.aspx.

The College of New Rochelle, Graduate School, Division of Art and Communication Studies, Program in Art Education, New Rochelle, NY 10805-2308. Offers MA. Part-time and evening/weekend programs available. *Degree requirements:* For master's, thesis. *Entrance requirements:* For master's, interview, minimum GPA of 3.0 in field, 2.7 overall, portfolio, 36 credits of course work in studio art. *Faculty research:* Developmental stages in art, assessment and evaluation, curriculum development, multicultural education, art museum education.

The College of Saint Rose, Graduate Studies, School of Arts and Humanities, Center for Art and Design, Albany, NY 12203-1419. Offers art education (MS Ed, Certificate). *Accreditation:* NASAD; NCATE. Part-time and evening/weekend programs available. *Degree requirements:* For master's, final project. *Entrance requirements:* For master's, minimum undergraduate GPA of 3.0, art portfolio, undergraduate art degree; for Certificate, minimum undergraduate GPA of 3.0, slide portfolio. Additional exam requirements/recommendations for international students: Required—TOEFL (minimum score 550 paper-based; 213 computer-based). Electronic applications accepted.

The Colorado College, Education Department, Program in Secondary Education, Colorado Springs, CO 80903-3294. Offers art teaching (K-12) (MAT); English teaching (MAT); foreign language teaching (MAT); mathematics teaching (MAT); music teaching (MAT); science teaching (MAT); social studies teaching (MAT). *Faculty:* 4 full-time (3 women), 6 part-time/adjunct (2 women). *Students:* 11 full-time (7 women); includes 3 minority (1 Asian, non-Hispanic/Latino; 2 Hispanic/Latino). Average age 27. 20 applicants, 85% accepted, 11 enrolled. In 2011, 15 master's awarded. *Degree requirements:* For master's, thesis, internship. *Application deadline:* For fall admission, 12/1 priority date for domestic students, 12/1 for international students. Applications are processed on a rolling basis. Application fee: $50. Electronic applications accepted. *Expenses: Tuition:* Full-time $29,313. *Required fees:* $2000. *Financial support:* In 2011–12, 15 students received support. Career-related internships or fieldwork, institutionally sponsored loans, scholarships/grants, and health care benefits available. Financial award application deadline: 2/15; financial award applicants required to submit FAFSA. *Unit head:* Dr. Mike Taber, Director, 719-389-6026, Fax: 719-389-6473, E-mail: mike.taber@coloradocollege.edu. *Application contact:* Debra Yazulla Mortenson, Education Services Manager, 719-389-6472, Fax: 719-389-6473, E-mail: debra.mortenson@coloradocollege.edu. Web site: http://www.coloradocollege.edu/academics/dept/education/graduate-programs/secondary-mat.dot.

Colorado State University–Pueblo, College of Education, Engineering and Professional Studies, Education Program, Pueblo, CO 81001-4901. Offers art education (M Ed); foreign language education (M Ed); health and physical education (M Ed); instructional technology (M Ed); linguistically diverse education (M Ed); music education (M Ed); special education (M Ed). *Accreditation:* Teacher Education Accreditation Council. Part-time programs available. *Degree requirements:* For master's, portfolio. *Entrance requirements:* For master's, 3 recommendations, teaching license. Additional exam requirements/recommendations for international students: Required—TOEFL (minimum score 500 paper-based; 173 computer-based). Electronic applications accepted. *Faculty research:* Portfolio assessment, math education, science education.

Columbus State University, Graduate Studies, College of the Arts, Program in Art Education, Columbus, GA 31907-5645. Offers M Ed. *Accreditation:* NASAD; NCATE. Part-time and evening/weekend programs available. *Degree requirements:* For master's, exhibit. *Entrance requirements:* For master's, GRE General Test, minimum GPA of 2.75. Additional exam requirements/recommendations for international students: Required—TOEFL (minimum score 550 paper-based; 213 computer-based; 79 iBT). Electronic applications accepted.

Concordia University, School of Graduate Studies, Faculty of Fine Arts, Department of Art Education, Montréal, QC H3G 1M8, Canada. Offers art education (MA, PhD), including art in education (MA). *Degree requirements:* For master's, thesis (for some programs), practicum; for doctorate, comprehensive exam, thesis/dissertation. *Entrance requirements:* For master's, teaching experience; for doctorate, teaching or related professional experience. *Faculty research:* Vernacular culture, museum education, psychotic art, adults and families.

Concordia University Wisconsin, Graduate Programs, Department of Education, Mequon, WI 53097-2402. Offers art education (MS Ed); curriculum and instruction (MS Ed); early childhood (MS Ed); educational administration (MS Ed); environmental education (MS Ed); family studies (MS Ed); reading (MS Ed); school counseling (MS Ed); special education (MS Ed). Part-time and evening/weekend programs available. Postbaccalaureate distance learning degree programs offered (minimal on-campus study). *Faculty:* 30. *Students:* 386 full-time (279 women), 808 part-time (598 women); includes 84 minority (42 Black or African American, non-Hispanic/Latino; 4 American Indian or Alaska Native, non-Hispanic/Latino; 9 Asian, non-Hispanic/Latino; 13 Hispanic/Latino; 16 Two or more races, non-Hispanic/Latino), 5 international. Average age 37. In 2011, 51 master's awarded. *Degree requirements:* For master's, comprehensive exam, thesis or alternative. *Entrance requirements:* For master's, minimum GPA of 3.0, teaching license. Additional exam requirements/recommendations for international students: Required—TOEFL. Application fee: $35. *Financial support:* Career-related internships or fieldwork and tuition waivers (partial) available. Financial award application deadline: 8/1. *Faculty research:* Motivation, developmental learning, learning styles. *Unit head:* Dr. James Juergensen, Director, 262-243-4214, E-mail: james.juergensen@cuw.edu. *Application contact:* Graduate Admissions, 262-243-4248, Fax: 262-243-4428.

Converse College, School of Education and Graduate Studies, Spartanburg, SC 29302-0006. Offers art education (M Ed); early childhood education (MAT); education (Ed S), including administration and supervision, curriculum and instruction, marriage and family therapy; elementary education (M Ed, MAT); gifted education (M Ed); leadership (M Ed); liberal arts (MLA), including English (M Ed, MAT, MLA), history, political science; secondary education (M Ed, MAT), including biology (MAT), chemistry (MAT), English (M Ed, MAT, MLA), mathematics, natural sciences (M Ed), social sciences; special education (M Ed, MAT), including learning disabilities (MAT), mental disabilities (MAT), special education (M Ed). *Accreditation:* NASAD; NCATE. Part-time and evening/weekend programs available. *Entrance requirements:* For master's, PRAXIS II (M Ed), minimum GPA of 2.75; for Ed S, GRE or MAT, minimum GPA of 3.0. Electronic applications accepted. *Faculty research:* Motivation, classroom management, predictors of success in classroom teaching, sex equity in public education, gifted research.

Corcoran College of Art and Design, Graduate Programs, Washington, DC 20006-4804. Offers art education (MAT); history of decorative arts (MA); interior design (MA). *Accreditation:* NASAD. Part-time programs available. *Entrance requirements:* Additional exam requirements/recommendations for international students: Required—TOEFL.

Delaware State University, Graduate Programs, College of Education, Health and Public Policy, Program in Art Education, Dover, DE 19901-2277. Offers MA. *Entrance requirements:* Additional exam requirements/recommendations for international students: Required—TOEFL (minimum score 550 paper-based). Electronic applications accepted.

Eastern Illinois University, Graduate School, College of Arts and Humanities, Department of Art, Charleston, IL 61920-3099. Offers art (MA); art education (MA). *Accreditation:* NASAD. *Faculty:* 8 full-time, 8 part-time/adjunct. In 2011, 7 master's awarded. *Degree requirements:* For master's, thesis or alternative, portfolio. *Application deadline:* For fall admission, 3/31 priority date for domestic students. Applications are processed on a rolling basis. Application fee: $30. *Expenses:* Tuition, state resident: part-time $279 per credit hour. Tuition, nonresident: part-time $670 per credit hour. *Required fees:* $179.07 per credit hour. $1253 per semester. *Financial support:* In 2011–12, research assistantships with tuition reimbursements (averaging $7,650 per year), 6 teaching assistantships with tuition reimbursements (averaging $7,650 per year) were awarded. *Unit head:* Glenn Hild, Chairperson, 217-581-3410. *Application contact:* Chris Kahler, Coordinator, 217-581-6259, E-mail: cbkahler@eiu.edu.

Eastern Kentucky University, The Graduate School, College of Education, Department of Curriculum and Instruction, Program in Secondary and Higher Education, Richmond, KY 40475-3102. Offers secondary education (MA Ed), including agricultural education, art education, biological sciences education, business education, English education, geography education, history education, home economics education, industrial education, mathematical sciences education, physical education, school health education. *Accreditation:* NCATE. Part-time programs available. *Entrance requirements:* For master's, GRE General Test, minimum GPA of 2.5.

Eastern Michigan University, Graduate School, College of Arts and Sciences, Department of Art, Program in Art Education, Ypsilanti, MI 48197. Offers MA. Part-time and evening/weekend programs available. Postbaccalaureate distance learning degree programs offered (minimal on-campus study). *Students:* 3 part-time (all women). Average age 43. In 2011, 4 master's awarded. *Entrance requirements:* Additional exam requirements/recommendations for international students: Required—TOEFL. *Application deadline:* Applications are processed on a rolling basis. *Expenses:* Tuition, state resident: full-time $10,367; part-time $432 per credit hour. Tuition, nonresident: full-time $20,435; part-time $851 per credit hour. *Required fees:* $39 per credit hour. $46 per semester. One-time fee: $100. Tuition and fees vary according to course level, degree level and reciprocity agreements. *Financial support:* Fellowships with tuition reimbursements, research assistantships with full tuition reimbursements, teaching assistantships with full tuition reimbursements, career-related internships or fieldwork, Federal Work-Study, institutionally sponsored loans, scholarships/grants, and unspecified assistantships available. Support available to part-time students. Financial award applicants required to submit FAFSA. *Unit head:* Dr. Colin Blakely, Department Head, 734-487-1268, Fax: 734-487-2324, E-mail: cblakely@emich.edu. *Application contact:* Christopher Bocklage, Graduate Coordinator, 734-487-1268, Fax: 734-487-2324, E-mail: cbocklage@emich.edu.

Endicott College, Van Loan School of Graduate and Professional Studies, Program in Arts and Learning, Beverly, MA 01915-2096. Offers M Ed. Part-time and evening/weekend programs available. Postbaccalaureate distance learning degree programs offered (minimal on-campus study). *Faculty:* 1 (woman) full-time, 3 part-time/adjunct (2 women). *Students:* 2 full-time (both women), 16 part-time (14 women); includes 2 minority (both Hispanic/Latino). Average age 45. 10 applicants, 90% accepted, 7 enrolled. In 2011, 6 master's awarded. *Degree requirements:* For master's, portfolio, written integrative paper, major presentation. *Entrance requirements:* For master's, MAT or GRE, documentation of artistic involvement/skill, two letters of recommendation. Additional exam requirements/recommendations for international students: Required—TOEFL. *Application deadline:* Applications are processed on a rolling basis. Application fee: $50. Electronic applications accepted. *Expenses:* Contact institution. *Financial support:* Available to part-time students. Applicants required to submit FAFSA. *Faculty research:* Linkage of creative processes to effective teaching and learning. *Unit head:* Dr. Enid E. Larsen, Assistant Dean of Academic Programs, 978-232-2198, Fax: 978-232-3000, E-mail: elarsen@endicott.edu. *Application contact:* Enid E. Larsen, Assistant Dean of Academic Programs, 978-232-2198, Fax: 978-232-3000, E-mail: elarsen@endicott.edu. Web site: http://www.endicott.edu/GradProf/GPSGradMEdArtLea.aspx.

Fitchburg State University, Division of Graduate and Continuing Education, Program in Arts Education, Fitchburg, MA 01420-2697. Offers arts education (M Ed); fine arts director (Certificate). *Accreditation:* NCATE. Part-time and evening/weekend programs available. *Students:* 1 full-time (0 women), 9 part-time (6 women). Average age 40. 5 applicants, 100% accepted, 4 enrolled. In 2011, 7 master's awarded. *Entrance requirements:* Additional exam requirements/recommendations for international students: Required—TOEFL (minimum score 550 paper-based; 213 computer-based; 79 iBT). *Application deadline:* For fall admission, 7/15 for international students; for spring admission, 12/1 for international students. Applications are processed on a rolling basis. Application fee: $25 ($50 for international students). Electronic applications accepted. *Expenses:* Tuition, state resident: full-time $2700; part-time $150 per credit.

Tuition, nonresident: full-time $2700; part-time $150 per credit. *Required fees:* $2286; $127 per credit. *Financial support:* In 2011–12, research assistantships with partial tuition reimbursements (averaging $5,500 per year) were awarded; Federal Work-Study, scholarships/grants, and unspecified assistantships also available. Support available to part-time students. Financial award application deadline: 3/1; financial award applicants required to submit FAFSA. *Unit head:* Dr. Harry Semerjian, Chair, 978-665-3279, Fax: 978-665-3658, E-mail: gce@fitchburgstate.edu. *Application contact:* Kay Reynolds, Director of Admissions, 978-665-3144, Fax: 978-665-4540, E-mail: admissions@fitchburgstate.edu. Web site: http://www.fitchburgstate.edu.

Florida Atlantic University, Dorothy F. Schmidt College of Arts and Letters, Department of Visual Arts and Art History, Boca Raton, FL 33431-0991. Offers art education (MAT); ceramics (MFA); computer art (MFA); graphic design (MFA); painting (MFA). *Faculty:* 18 full-time (13 women), 14 part-time/adjunct (9 women). *Students:* 13 full-time (10 women), 5 part-time (3 women); includes 7 minority (1 Asian, non-Hispanic/Latino; 6 Hispanic/Latino). Average age 36. 31 applicants, 26% accepted, 3 enrolled. In 2011, 12 master's awarded. *Degree requirements:* For master's, one foreign language, project. *Entrance requirements:* For master's, GRE General Test, minimum GPA of 3.0 during last 60 hours of course work, slide portfolio. *Application deadline:* For fall admission, 2/21 for domestic and international students; for spring admission, 10/1 for domestic and international students. Application fee: $30. Electronic applications accepted. *Expenses: Tuition, area resident:* Part-time $343.02 per credit hour. Tuition, state resident: full-time $8232. Tuition, nonresident: full-time $23,931; part-time $997.14 per credit hour. *Financial support:* Research assistantships with full tuition reimbursements, teaching assistantships with full tuition reimbursements, career-related internships or fieldwork, Federal Work-Study, and institutionally sponsored loans available. Financial award applicants required to submit FAFSA. *Faculty research:* Painting, ceramics (traditional and non-traditional), installation, video and interactive sculpture. *Unit head:* Dr. Linda Johnson, Chair, 561-297-3870, Fax: 561-297-3078, E-mail: ljohnson@fau.edu. *Application contact:* James A. Novak, Associate Professor/Graduate Coordinator/Advisor, 561-297-2430, Fax: 561-297-3078, E-mail: jnovak@fau.edu. Web site: http://www.fau.edu/VAAH/.

Florida International University, College of Education, Department of Curriculum and Instruction, Miami, FL 33199. Offers art education (MAT, MS, Ed D); curriculum and instruction (Ed S); curriculum development (MS); curriculum studies (PhD); early childhood education (MS, Ed D); elementary education (MS, Ed D); English education (MAT, MS, Ed D); foreign language education - teaching English to speakers of other languages (TESOL) (MS, Certificate), including foreign language education (Certificate), teaching English (MS); French education - initial teacher preparation (MAT); international and intercultural development education (Ed D); international and intercultural developmental education (MS); language, literacy and culture (PhD); learning technologies (MS, Ed D, PhD); mathematics education (MAT, MS, Ed D, PhD); modern language education/bilingual education (MS, Ed D); physical education (MS); reading education (MS, Ed D); science education (MAT, MS, Ed D, PhD); social studies education (MAT, MS, Ed D); Spanish education - initial teacher preparation (MAT); special education (MS). Part-time and evening/weekend programs available. *Degree requirements:* For doctorate, comprehensive exam, thesis/dissertation. *Entrance requirements:* For master's, GRE General Test, Florida General Knowledge Test or Florida College Level Academic Skills Test; for doctorate and other advanced degree, GRE General Test. Additional exam requirements/recommendations for international students: Required—TOEFL (minimum score 550 paper-based; 213 computer-based; 80 iBT), IELTS (minimum score 6.3). Electronic applications accepted.

Florida State University, The Graduate School, College of Visual Arts, Theatre and Dance, Department of Art Education, Tallahassee, FL 32306. Offers MA, MS, Ed D, PhD, Ed S. *Accreditation:* NASAD (one or more programs are accredited). Part-time programs available. *Faculty:* 6 full-time (4 women), 5 part-time/adjunct (all women). *Students:* 66 full-time (60 women), 15 part-time (10 women); includes 27 minority (6 Black or African American, non-Hispanic/Latino; 15 Asian, non-Hispanic/Latino; 6 Hispanic/Latino). Average age 33. 73 applicants, 75% accepted, 32 enrolled. In 2011, 22 master's, 10 doctorates awarded. *Degree requirements:* For master's, thesis (for some programs); for doctorate, thesis/dissertation. *Entrance requirements:* For master's, GRE (minimum score 1000), minimum GPA of 3.0 in last 2 years; for doctorate, GRE (minimum score 1000), minimum GPA of 3.5. Additional exam requirements/recommendations for international students: Required—TOEFL (minimum score 550 paper-based; 213 computer-based; 80 iBT). *Application deadline:* For fall admission, 3/1 priority date for domestic students, 3/1 for international students; for spring admission, 10/15 priority date for domestic students, 10/15 for international students. Applications are processed on a rolling basis. Application fee: $30. Electronic applications accepted. *Expenses:* Tuition, state resident: full-time $9474; part-time $350.88 per credit hour. Tuition, nonresident: full-time $16,236; part-time $601.34 per credit hour. *Required fees:* $630 per semester. One-time fee: $20. Tuition and fees vary according to course load and campus/location. *Financial support:* In 2011–12, 27 students received support, including 20 research assistantships with full tuition reimbursements available (averaging $3,200 per year), 7 teaching assistantships with full tuition reimbursements available (averaging $8,500 per year); fellowships, career-related internships or fieldwork, Federal Work-Study, and scholarships/grants also available. Financial award applicants required to submit FAFSA. *Faculty research:* Teaching and learning in art, museum education, art therapy, arts administration, discipline-based art education. *Total annual research expenditures:* $110,000. *Unit head:* Dr. David E. Gussak, Chairman, 850-645-5663, Fax: 850-644-5067, E-mail: dgussak@fsu.edu. *Application contact:* Susan Messersmith, Academic Support Assistant, 850-644-5473, Fax: 850-644-6067, E-mail: smessersmith@fsu.edu. Web site: http://www.fsu.edu/~are/.

George Mason University, College of Visual and Performing Arts, Program in Art Education, Fairfax, VA 22030. Offers art education (MAT); licensure (Certificate); teaching theatre PK-12 (Certificate). *Expenses:* Tuition, state resident: full-time $8750; part-time $364.58 per credit. Tuition, nonresident: full-time $24,092; part-time $1003.83 per credit. *Required fees:* $2514; $104.75 per credit. *Application contact:* Victoria N. Salmon, Graduate Studies Associate Dean, 703-993-4541, Fax: 703-993-9037, E-mail: vsalmon@gmu.edu.

Georgia Southern University, Jack N. Averitt College of Graduate Studies, College of Education, Department of Teaching and Learning, Program in Art Education, Statesboro, GA 30460. Offers M Ed, MAT. *Accreditation:* NASAD (one or more programs are accredited); NCATE (one or more programs are accredited). Part-time and evening/weekend programs available. In 2011, 2 master's awarded. *Degree requirements:* For master's, transition point assessment. *Entrance requirements:* For master's, GRE General Test or MAT, GACE Basic Skills and Content Assessments, minimum cumulative GPA of 2.5. Additional exam requirements/recommendations for international students: Required—TOEFL (minimum score 550 paper-based; 213 computer-based; 80 iBT). *Application deadline:* For fall admission, 3/1 priority date for domestic students, 3/1 for international students; for spring admission, 10/1 priority date for domestic students, 10/1 for international students. Applications are processed on a rolling basis. Application fee: $50. Electronic applications accepted. *Expenses:* Tuition, state resident: full-time $6300; part-time $263 per semester hour. Tuition, nonresident: full-time $25,174; part-time $1049 per semester hour. *Required fees:* $1872. *Financial support:* In 2011–12, research assistantships with partial tuition reimbursements (averaging $7,200 per year), teaching assistantships with partial tuition reimbursements (averaging $7,200 per year) were awarded; career-related internships or fieldwork, Federal Work-Study, scholarships/grants, tuition waivers (partial), and unspecified assistantships also available. Support available to part-time students. Financial award application deadline: 4/15; financial award applicants required to submit FAFSA. *Unit head:* Ronnie Sheppard, Department Chair, 912-478-0198, Fax: 912-478-0026, E-mail: sheppard@georgiasouthern.edu. *Application contact:* Amanda Gilliland, Coordinator for Graduate Student Recruitment, 912-478-5384, Fax: 912-478-0740, E-mail: gradadmissions@georgiasouthern.edu. Web site: http://coe.georgiasouthern.edu/tandl/.

Georgia State University, College of Arts and Sciences, Ernest G. Welch School of Art and Design, Program in Art Education, Atlanta, GA 30302-3083. Offers MA Ed. *Accreditation:* NASAD. Part-time programs available. *Degree requirements:* For master's, thesis. *Entrance requirements:* For master's, GRE General Test or MAT, portfolio. Additional exam requirements/recommendations for international students: Required—TOEFL (minimum score 550 paper-based; 213 computer-based). Electronic applications accepted. *Faculty research:* Art–maturing adults, computer instruction in art, intercultural thematic art education.

Georgia State University, College of Education, Department of Middle-Secondary Education and Instructional Technology, Programs in Secondary Education, Atlanta, GA 30302-3083. Offers art education (Ed S); English education (M Ed, Ed S); mathematics education (M Ed, PhD, Ed S); music education (PhD); science education (M Ed, PhD, Ed S); social studies education (M Ed, PhD, Ed S). *Accreditation:* NASM (one or more programs are accredited); NCATE. Part-time and evening/weekend programs available. *Degree requirements:* For master's, comprehensive exam; for doctorate, comprehensive exam, thesis/dissertation; for Ed S, project/exam. *Entrance requirements:* For master's, GRE General Test, minimum GPA of 2.5; for doctorate, GRE General Test or MAT, minimum GPA of 3.3; for Ed S, GRE General Test or MAT, minimum graduate GPA of 3.25. *Faculty research:* Women and science, problem solving in mathematics, dialects, economic education.

Harding University, College of Education, Searcy, AR 72149-0001. Offers advanced studies in teaching and learning (M Ed); art (MSE); behavioral science (MSE); counseling (MS, Ed S); early childhood special education (M Ed, MSE); education (MSE); educational leadership (M Ed, Ed S); elementary education (M Ed); English (MSE); French (MSE); history/social science (MSE); kinesiology (MSE); math (MSE); reading (M Ed); secondary education (M Ed); Spanish (MSE); teaching (MAT); teaching English as a second language (MSE). *Accreditation:* NCATE. Part-time and evening/weekend programs available. *Faculty:* 9 full-time (2 women), 48 part-time/adjunct (26 women). *Students:* 100 full-time (77 women), 333 part-time (239 women); includes 76 minority (59 Black or African American, non-Hispanic/Latino; 1 Asian, non-Hispanic/Latino; 10 Hispanic/Latino; 6 Two or more races, non-Hispanic/Latino), 2 international. Average age 36. 93 applicants, 91% accepted, 83 enrolled. In 2011, 159 master's, 10 other advanced degrees awarded. *Degree requirements:* For master's, comprehensive exam (for some programs), thesis optional, portfolio(s); for Ed S, comprehensive exam, portfolio, project. *Entrance requirements:* For master's, GRE, MAT, PRAXIS; for Ed S, MAT or GRE. Additional exam requirements/recommendations for international students: Required—TOEFL (minimum score 550 paper-based; 79 iBT). *Application deadline:* For fall admission, 8/1 for domestic and international students; for spring admission, 1/1 for domestic and international students. Applications are processed on a rolling basis. Application fee: $35. *Expenses: Tuition:* Full-time $10,512; part-time $584 per credit hour. *Required fees:* $500; $25 per credit hour. Tuition and fees vary according to course load, degree level and program. *Financial support:* In 2011–12, 37 students received support. Unspecified assistantships available. *Faculty research:* Reading, comprehension, school violence, educational technology, behavior, college choice, differentiated instruction, brain-based teaching. *Unit head:* Dr. Clara Carroll, Chair, 501-279-4501, Fax: 501-279-4083, E-mail: ccarroll@harding.edu. *Application contact:* Information Contact, 501-279-4315, E-mail: gradstudiesedu@harding.edu. Web site: http://www.harding.edu/education/grad.html.

Harvard University, Harvard Graduate School of Education, Master's Programs in Education, Cambridge, MA 02138. Offers arts in education (Ed M); education policy and management (Ed M); higher education (Ed M); human development and psychology (Ed M); international education policy (Ed M); language and literacy (Ed M); learning and teaching (Ed M); mid-career mathematics and science (teaching certificate) (Ed M); mind brain and education (Ed M); prevention science and practice (Ed M); school leadership (Ed M); special studies (Ed M); teaching and curriculum (teaching certificate) (Ed M); technology innovation and education (Ed M). Part-time programs available. *Faculty:* 83 full-time (44 women), 67 part-time/adjunct (29 women). *Students:* 592 full-time (431 women), 75 part-time (54 women); includes 194 minority (41 Black or African American, non-Hispanic/Latino; 4 American Indian or Alaska Native, non-Hispanic/Latino; 75 Asian, non-Hispanic/Latino; 45 Hispanic/Latino; 2 Native Hawaiian or other Pacific Islander, non-Hispanic/Latino; 27 Two or more races, non-Hispanic/Latino), 95 international. Average age 28. 1,679 applicants, 52% accepted, 627 enrolled. In 2011, 653 master's awarded. *Entrance requirements:* For master's, GRE General Test, statement of purpose, 3 letters of recommendation, resume, official transcripts. Additional exam requirements/recommendations for international students: Required—TOEFL (minimum score 613 paper-based; 104 computer-based; 100 iBT), TWE (minimum score 5). *Application deadline:* For fall admission, 1/4 for domestic and international students. Application fee: $85. Electronic applications accepted. *Expenses:* Contact institution. *Financial support:* In 2011–12, 419 students received support, including 14 fellowships with full and partial tuition reimbursements available (averaging $12,831 per year); career-related internships or fieldwork, Federal Work-Study, institutionally sponsored loans, scholarships/grants, health care benefits, tuition waivers (full and partial), and unspecified assistantships also available. Support available to part-time students. Financial award application deadline: 2/1; financial award applicants required to submit FAFSA. *Faculty research:* Learning and development, educational leadership and organizations, educational policy analysis. *Total annual research expenditures:* $26 million. *Unit head:* Jennifer L. Petrallia, Assistant Dean, 617-495-8445. *Application contact:* Information Contact, 617-495-3414, Fax: 617-496-3577, E-mail: gseadmissions@harvard.edu. Web site: http://www.gse.harvard.edu/.

Hofstra University, School of Education, Health, and Human Services, Programs in Teaching (K-12), Hempstead, NY 11549. Offers bilingual education (MA); bilingual extension (Advanced Certificate), including education/speech language pathology, intensive teacher institute; family and consumer science (MS Ed); fine art and music education (Advanced Certificate); fine arts education (MA, MS Ed); mentoring and coaching for teachers (Advanced Certificate); middle childhood extension (Advanced Certificate), including grades 5-6 or 7-9; music education (MA, MS Ed); teaching languages other than English and TESOL (MS Ed); TESOL (MS Ed, Advanced Certificate), including intensive teacher institute (Advanced Certificate), TESOL (Advanced Certificate); wind conducting (MA). Part-time and evening/weekend programs available. *Students:* 54 full-time (48 women), 60 part-time (53 women); includes 30 minority (10 Black or African American, non-Hispanic/Latino; 9 Asian, non-

Hispanic/Latino; 11 Hispanic/Latino), 8 international. Average age 29. 109 applicants, 76% accepted, 43 enrolled. In 2011, 71 master's, 42 other advanced degrees awarded. *Degree requirements:* For master's, one foreign language, thesis (for some programs), electronic portfolio, Tk20 portfolios, minimum GPA of 3.0. *Entrance requirements:* For master's, 2 letters of recommendation, portfolio, teacher certification (MA), essay; for Advanced Certificate, 2 letters of recommendation, interview, teaching certificate, essay. Additional exam requirements/recommendations for international students: Required—TOEFL (minimum score 550 paper-based; 213 computer-based; 80 iBT). *Application deadline:* Applications are processed on a rolling basis. Application fee: $70 ($75 for international students). Electronic applications accepted. *Expenses: Tuition:* Full-time $18,990; part-time $1055 per credit hour. *Required fees:* $970. Tuition and fees vary according to program. *Financial support:* In 2011–12, 39 students received support, including 13 fellowships with full and partial tuition reimbursements available (averaging $3,347 per year), 2 research assistantships with full and partial tuition reimbursements available (averaging $7,363 per year); career-related internships or fieldwork, Federal Work-Study, institutionally sponsored loans, scholarships/grants, tuition waivers (full and partial), and unspecified assistantships also available. Support available to part-time students. Financial award applicants required to submit FAFSA. *Faculty research:* The teacher/artist, interdisciplinary curriculum, applied linguistics, structural inequalities, creativity. *Unit head:* Dr. Esther Fusco, Chairperson, 516-463-7704, Fax: 516-463-6196, E-mail: catezf@hofstra.edu. *Application contact:* Carol Drummer, Dean of Graduate Admissions, 516-463-4876, Fax: 516-463-4664, E-mail: gradstudent@hofstra.edu. Web site: http://www.hofstra.edu/education/.

Indiana University Bloomington, School of Education, Department of Curriculum and Instruction, Bloomington, IN 47405-7000. Offers art education (MS, Ed D, PhD); curriculum studies (Ed D, PhD); elementary education (MS, Ed D, PhD, Ed S); mathematics education (MS, Ed D, PhD); science education (MS, Ed D, PhD); secondary education (MS, Ed D, PhD); social studies education (MS, PhD); special education (PhD, Ed S). *Accreditation:* NCATE. Part-time and evening/weekend programs available. Terminal master's awarded for partial completion of doctoral program. *Degree requirements:* For doctorate, thesis/dissertation; for Ed S, comprehensive exam or project. *Entrance requirements:* For master's, doctorate, and Ed S, GRE General Test. Electronic applications accepted.

Indiana University–Purdue University Indianapolis, Herron School of Art and Design, Indianapolis, IN 46202-2896. Offers art education (MAE); furniture design (MFA); printmaking (MFA); sculpture (MFA); visual communication (MFA). *Accreditation:* NASAD. Part-time and evening/weekend programs available. *Faculty:* 2 full-time (both women). *Students:* 30 full-time (16 women), 13 part-time (11 women); includes 6 minority (2 Asian, non-Hispanic/Latino; 3 Hispanic/Latino; 1 Two or more races, non-Hispanic/Latino), 4 international. Average age 30. 70 applicants, 46% accepted, 18 enrolled. In 2011, 28 master's awarded. *Entrance requirements:* For master's, portfolio, 44 hours of course work in art history and studio art. *Application deadline:* For fall admission, 5/1 priority date for domestic students, 3/15 for international students; for spring admission, 11/1 priority date for domestic students, 10/15 for international students. Applications are processed on a rolling basis. Application fee: $55 ($65 for international students). Electronic applications accepted. *Financial support:* Career-related internships or fieldwork, Federal Work-Study, institutionally sponsored loans, scholarships/grants, and tuition waivers (partial) available. Support available to part-time students. *Total annual research expenditures:* $6,097. *Unit head:* Valerie Eickmeier, Dean, 317-278-9470, Fax: 317-278-9471, E-mail: herron@iupui.edu. *Application contact:* Herron Student Services Office, 317-378-9400, E-mail: herrart@iupui.edu. Web site: http://www.herron.iupui.edu/.

Indiana University South Bend, School of the Arts, South Bend, IN 46634-7111. Offers music (MM); studio teaching (MM). Part-time programs available. *Faculty:* 1 full-time (0 women). *Students:* 58 full-time (47 women), 4 part-time (all women); includes 9 minority (5 Black or African American, non-Hispanic/Latino; 4 Hispanic/Latino), 45 international. Average age 29. 19 applicants, 74% accepted, 10 enrolled. In 2011, 5 master's awarded. *Entrance requirements:* For master's, performance audition. *Application deadline:* For fall admission, 7/1 priority date for domestic students; for spring admission, 11/1 for domestic students. Applications are processed on a rolling basis. Application fee: $50 ($60 for international students). *Financial support:* In 2011–12, 4 fellowships (averaging $2,855 per year), 1 teaching assistantship (averaging $1,320 per year) were awarded; Federal Work-Study also available. Support available to part-time students. Financial award application deadline: 3/1; financial award applicants required to submit FAFSA. *Faculty research:* Orchestral conducting. *Unit head:* Dr. Thomas Miller, Dean, 574-520-4301, Fax: 574-520-4317, E-mail: messelst@iusb.edu. *Application contact:* Admissions Counselor, 574-520-4839, Fax: 574-520-4834, E-mail: graduate@iusb.edu.

James Madison University, The Graduate School, College of Visual and Performing Arts, School of Art and Art History, Harrisonburg, VA 22807. Offers art education (MA); art history (MA); ceramics (MFA); drawing/painting (MFA); metal/jewelry (MFA); photography (MFA); printmaking (MFA); sculpture (MFA); studio art (MA); weaving/fibers (MFA). *Accreditation:* NASAD. Part-time programs available. *Faculty:* 8 full-time (5 women), 1 (woman) part-time/adjunct. *Students:* 10 full-time (6 women), 5 part-time (all women). Average age 27. In 2011, 3 master's awarded. *Degree requirements:* For master's, thesis (for some programs). *Entrance requirements:* For master's, GRE General Test, language exam in French or German, portfolio, 3 letters of recommendation, research paper. Additional exam requirements/recommendations for international students: Required—TOEFL. *Application deadline:* For fall admission, 2/15 priority date for domestic students, 2/15 for international students; for spring admission, 10/15 priority date for domestic students, 10/15 for international students. Applications are processed on a rolling basis. Application fee: $55. Electronic applications accepted. *Expenses:* Tuition, state resident: full-time $8016; part-time $334 per credit hour. Tuition, nonresident: full-time $22,656; part-time $944 per credit hour. *Financial support:* In 2011–12, 10 students received support, including 3 teaching assistantships with full tuition reimbursements available (averaging $8,664 per year); Federal Work-Study and 7 graduate assistantships ($7382) also available. Financial award application deadline: 3/1; financial award applicants required to submit FAFSA. *Unit head:* Dr. William Wightman, Director, 540-568-6216, E-mail: art-arthistory@jmu.edu. *Application contact:* Lynette M. Bible, Director of Graduate Admissions, 540-568-6395, Fax: 540-568-7860, E-mail: biblelm@jmu.edu.

Kean University, College of Visual and Performing Arts, Program in Fine Arts Education, Union, NJ 07083. Offers certification (MA); studio/research (general) (MA); supervision (MA). *Accreditation:* NASAD. *Faculty:* 11 full-time (4 women). *Students:* 11 full-time (9 women), 31 part-time (23 women); includes 7 minority (3 Black or African American, non-Hispanic/Latino; 2 Asian, non-Hispanic/Latino; 2 Hispanic/Latino), 2 international. Average age 37. 10 applicants, 100% accepted, 8 enrolled. In 2011, 14 master's awarded. *Degree requirements:* For master's, thesis or alternative, exhibition, 3 years teaching experience (supervision), PRAXIS and fieldwork (certification). *Entrance requirements:* For master's, GRE General Test or MAT, studio portfolio, proficiencies in academic writing, dialogic skills, minimum GPA of 3.0, interview, 2 letters of recommendation, official transcripts from all institutions attended. Additional exam requirements/recommendations for international students: Required—TOEFL (minimum score 79 iBT). *Application deadline:* For fall admission, 6/1 for domestic and international students; for spring admission, 12/1 for domestic and international students. Applications are processed on a rolling basis. Application fee: $75 ($150 for international students). Electronic applications accepted. *Expenses:* Tuition, state resident: full-time $11,302; part-time $550 per credit. Tuition, nonresident: full-time $15,318; part-time $674 per credit. *Required fees:* $2849; $130 per credit. Tuition and fees vary according to degree level. *Financial support:* In 2011–12, 4 research assistantships with full tuition reimbursements (averaging $3,263 per year) were awarded; unspecified assistantships also available. Financial award applicants required to submit FAFSA. *Unit head:* Dr. Joseph Amorino, Program Coordinator, 908-737-4403, E-mail: jamorino@kean.edu. *Application contact:* Steven Koch, Admissions Counselor, 908-737-5924, Fax: 908-737-5925, E-mail: skoch@kean.edu. Web site: http://www.kean.edu/KU/Initial-Teaching-Certification.

Kennesaw State University, Leland and Clarice C. Bagwell College of Education, Program in Teaching, Kennesaw, GA 30144-5591. Offers art education (MAT); secondary English or mathematics (MAT); secondary science education (MAT); teaching English to speakers of other languages (MAT). Program offered only in summer. Part-time and evening/weekend programs available. *Students:* 101 full-time (68 women), 20 part-time (15 women); includes 27 minority (14 Black or African American, non-Hispanic/Latino; 6 Asian, non-Hispanic/Latino; 4 Hispanic/Latino; 3 Two or more races, non-Hispanic/Latino), 3 international. Average age 33. 13 applicants, 62% accepted, 7 enrolled. In 2011, 81 master's awarded. *Entrance requirements:* For master's, GRE, GACE I (state certificate exam), minimum GPA of 2.75, 2 recommendations, resume. Additional exam requirements/recommendations for international students: Required—TOEFL (minimum score 550 paper-based; 213 computer-based; 80 iBT), IELTS (minimum score 6). *Application deadline:* For fall admission, 6/1 for domestic and international students; for spring admission, 3/1 for domestic and international students. Application fee: $60. Electronic applications accepted. *Expenses:* Tuition, state resident: full-time $3000; part-time $250 per semester hour. Tuition, nonresident: full-time $10,836; part-time $903 per semester hour. *Required fees:* $774 per semester. *Financial support:* In 2011–12, 2 research assistantships with tuition reimbursements (averaging $4,000 per year) were awarded; unspecified assistantships also available. Financial award application deadline: 4/1; financial award applicants required to submit FAFSA. *Unit head:* Dr. Lynn Stallings, Director, 770-420-4477, E-mail: lstalling@kennesaw.edu. *Application contact:* Alisha Bello, Administrative Coordinator, 770-423-6043, Fax: 770-420-4435, E-mail: abello1@kennesaw.edu. Web site: http://www.kennesaw.edu.

Kent State University, College of the Arts, School of Art, Kent, OH 44242-0001. Offers art education (MA); art history (MA); crafts (MA, MFA), including ceramics (MA), glass, jewelry/metals, textiles/art; fine art (MA, MFA), including drawing/painting, printmaking, sculpture. *Accreditation:* NASAD (one or more programs are accredited). *Degree requirements:* For master's, one foreign language, thesis. *Entrance requirements:* For master's, undergraduate degree in proposed area of study (for fine arts and crafts programs); minimum overall GPA of 2.75 (3.0 for art major); 3 letters of recommendation; portfolio (15-20 slides for MA, 20-25 for MFA). Additional exam requirements/recommendations for international students: Required—TOEFL. Electronic applications accepted. *Expenses:* Tuition, state resident: full-time $8136; part-time $452 per credit hour. Tuition, nonresident: full-time $14,292; part-time $794 per credit hour.

Kutztown University of Pennsylvania, College of Visual and Performing Arts, Program in Art Education, Kutztown, PA 19530-0730. Offers M Ed. *Accreditation:* NASAD; NCATE. Part-time programs available. *Faculty:* 12 full-time (4 women). *Students:* 22 full-time (20 women), 37 part-time (35 women); includes 3 minority (1 Black or African American, non-Hispanic/Latino; 2 Asian, non-Hispanic/Latino). Average age 30. 12 applicants, 100% accepted, 12 enrolled. In 2011, 14 master's awarded. *Degree requirements:* For master's, comprehensive exam, thesis optional. *Entrance requirements:* For master's, GRE, teacher certification. Additional exam requirements/recommendations for international students: Required—TOEFL (minimum score 550 paper-based; 79 iBT). *Application deadline:* For fall admission, 8/1 priority date for domestic students, 8/1 for international students; for spring admission, 12/1 priority date for domestic students, 12/1 for international students. Applications are processed on a rolling basis. Application fee: $35. Electronic applications accepted. *Expenses:* Tuition, state resident: full-time $7488; part-time $416 per credit. Tuition, nonresident: full-time $11,232; part-time $624 per credit. *Financial support:* Career-related internships or fieldwork, Federal Work-Study, scholarships/grants, and unspecified assistantships available. Financial award application deadline: 3/1; financial award applicants required to submit FAFSA. *Faculty research:* Teaching of art history, child development in art, aesthetics and criticism curriculum, multicultural education, assessment in art. *Unit head:* Dr. John White, Chairperson, 610-683-4520, Fax: 610-683-4502, E-mail: white@kutztown.edu. *Application contact:* Kelly D. Burr, Associate Director, Graduate Admissions, 610-683-4200, Fax: 610-683-1393, E-mail: graduate@kutztown.edu.

Lesley University, Graduate School of Arts and Social Sciences, Cambridge, MA 02138-2790. Offers clinical mental health counseling (MA), including expressive therapies counseling, holistic counseling, school and community counseling; counseling psychology (MA, CAGS), including professional counseling (MA), school counseling (MA); creative arts in learning (CAGS); creative writing (MFA); ecological teaching and learning (MS); environmental education (MS); expressive therapies (MA, PhD, CAGS), including art (MA), dance (MA), expressive therapies, music (MA); independent studies (CAGS); independent study (MA); intercultural relations (MA, CAGS); interdisciplinary studies (MA), including individualized studies, integrative holistic health, women's studies; urban environmental leadership (MA); visual arts (MFA). Part-time and evening/weekend programs available. Postbaccalaureate distance learning degree programs offered (minimal on-campus study). *Faculty:* 45 full-time (36 women), 187 part-time/adjunct (139 women). *Students:* 671 full-time (605 women), 404 part-time (364 women); includes 133 minority (32 Black or African American, non-Hispanic/Latino; 4 American Indian or Alaska Native, non-Hispanic/Latino; 17 Asian, non-Hispanic/Latino; 58 Hispanic/Latino; 4 Native Hawaiian or other Pacific Islander, non-Hispanic/Latino; 18 Two or more races, non-Hispanic/Latino), 65 international. Average age 37. In 2011, 473 master's, 6 doctorates, 9 other advanced degrees awarded. *Degree requirements:* For master's, internship, practicum, thesis (expressive therapies); for doctorate, thesis/dissertation, arts apprenticeship, field placement; for CAGS, thesis, internship (counseling psychology, expressive therapies). *Entrance requirements:* For master's, MAT (counseling psychology), interview, writing samples, art portfolio; for doctorate, GRE or MAT; for CAGS, interview, master's degree. Additional exam requirements/recommendations for international students: Required—TOEFL (minimum score 550 paper-based; 213 computer-based; 80 iBT). *Application deadline:* Applications are processed on a rolling basis. Electronic applications accepted. *Financial support:* In 2011–12, research assistantships (averaging $3,400 per year), 1 teaching assistantship (averaging $7,298 per year) was awarded; career-related internships or fieldwork, Federal Work-Study, scholarships/grants, and unspecified assistantships also available. Support available to part-time students. Financial award applicants required to submit FAFSA. *Faculty research:* Psychotherapy and culture; psychotherapy and psychological trauma; women's issues in art, teaching and psychotherapy; community-based art, psycho-spiritual inquiry. *Unit head:* Dr. Julia Halevy, Dean, 617-349-8317, Fax: 617-349-

8366, E-mail: jhalevy@lesley.edu. *Application contact:* Christina Murray, Senior Assistant Director, On-Campus Admissions, 617-349-8827, Fax: 617-349-8313, E-mail: cmurray3@lesley.edu. Web site: http://www.lesley.edu/gsass.html.

Long Island University–C. W. Post Campus, School of Education, Department of Curriculum and Instruction, Brookville, NY 11548-1300. Offers adolescence education (MS); adolescence education: biology (MS); adolescence education: earth science (MS); adolescence education: English (MS); adolescence education: mathematics (MS); adolescence education: social studies (MS); adolescence education: Spanish (MS); art education (MS); bilingual education (MS); childhood education (MS); early childhood education (MS); middle childhood education (MS); music education (MS); teaching English to speakers of other languages (MS). Part-time and evening/weekend programs available. *Degree requirements:* For master's, comprehensive exam or thesis, student teaching. *Entrance requirements:* For master's, minimum GPA of 2.75 in major, 2.5 overall. Electronic applications accepted. *Faculty research:* Ethics and education, teaching strategies.

Long Island University–C. W. Post Campus, School of Visual and Performing Arts, Department of Art, Brookville, NY 11548-1300. Offers art (MA); art education (MS); clinical art therapy (MA); fine art and design (MFA). Part-time and evening/weekend programs available. *Degree requirements:* For master's, thesis. Electronic applications accepted. *Faculty research:* Painting, sculpture, installation, computers, video.

Manhattanville College, Graduate Studies, School of Education, Program in Visual Arts Education, Purchase, NY 10577-2132. Offers MAT. Part-time and evening/weekend programs available. *Entrance requirements:* Additional exam requirements/recommendations for international students: Required—TOEFL. Electronic applications accepted.

Mansfield University of Pennsylvania, Graduate Studies, Department of Art, Mansfield, PA 16933. Offers art education (M Ed). Part-time programs available. *Degree requirements:* For master's, thesis optional. *Entrance requirements:* For master's, minimum GPA of 3.0, portfolio. Additional exam requirements/recommendations for international students: Required—TOEFL (minimum score 550 paper-based; 230 computer-based). Electronic applications accepted. *Expenses:* Tuition, state resident: full-time $7488; part-time $416 per credit. Tuition, nonresident: full-time $11,232; part-time $624 per credit.

Maryland Institute College of Art, Graduate Studies, Program in Art Education, Baltimore, MD 21217. Offers MA, MAT. MA program offered in summer only. *Accreditation:* NASAD. Part-time programs available. *Faculty:* 8 full-time (7 women), 7 part-time/adjunct (3 women). *Students:* 27 full-time (24 women), 7 part-time (6 women); includes 3 minority (1 Black or African American, non-Hispanic/Latino; 1 Asian, non-Hispanic/Latino; 1 Two or more races, non-Hispanic/Latino), 2 international. Average age 26. In 2011, 38 master's awarded. *Degree requirements:* For master's, thesis, seminar. *Entrance requirements:* For master's, portfolio, 40 studio credits, 6 credits in art history. Additional exam requirements/recommendations for international students: Required—TOEFL (minimum score 550 paper-based; 213 computer-based; 80 iBT). *Application deadline:* For fall admission, 1/15 for domestic and international students. Application fee: $75. *Expenses: Tuition:* Full-time $36,170; part-time $1506 per credit. *Required fees:* $1300; $650 per semester. Part-time tuition and fees vary according to program. *Financial support:* In 2011–12, 13 students received support, including 13 fellowships with partial tuition reimbursements available (averaging $5,000 per year); teaching assistantships and scholarships/grants also available. Financial award application deadline: 1/15; financial award applicants required to submit FAFSA. *Unit head:* Dr. Karen Carroll, Dean, 410-225-2297, Fax: 410-225-2257. *Application contact:* Scott G. Kelly, Associate Dean of Graduate Admission, 410-225-2256, Fax: 410-225-2408, E-mail: graduate@mica.edu. Web site: http://www.mica.edu/Programs_of_Study/Graduate_Programs.html.

Maryville University of Saint Louis, School of Education, St. Louis, MO 63141-7299. Offers art education (MA Ed); early childhood education (MA Ed); educational leadership (Ed D); educational leadership: principal certification (MA Ed); elementary education (MA Ed); gifted education (MA Ed); higher education leadership (Ed D); literacy specialist (MA Ed); middle grades education (MA Ed); secondary teaching and inquiry (MA Ed); teacher as leader (MA Ed). *Accreditation:* NCATE. Part-time and evening/weekend programs available. *Faculty:* 10 full-time (6 women), 19 part-time/adjunct (15 women). *Students:* 33 full-time (25 women), 251 part-time (190 women); includes 42 minority (32 Black or African American, non-Hispanic/Latino; 1 American Indian or Alaska Native, non-Hispanic/Latino; 4 Asian, non-Hispanic/Latino; 2 Hispanic/Latino; 3 Two or more races, non-Hispanic/Latino). Average age 38. In 2011, 69 master's, 43 doctorates awarded. *Degree requirements:* For master's, thesis, project. *Entrance requirements:* For master's, minimum cumulative GPA of 3.0, 3 professional recommendations, essays, interview with program faculty; for doctorate, minimum GPA of 3.0, 3 professional recommendations, essay, interview, on-site writing sample. Additional exam requirements/recommendations for international students: Required—TOEFL (minimum score 550 paper-based). *Application deadline:* Applications are processed on a rolling basis. Application fee: $40 ($60 for international students). Electronic applications accepted. *Expenses: Tuition:* Full-time $21,922; part-time $675 per credit hour. *Required fees:* $233.75 per semester. *Financial support:* Career-related internships or fieldwork, Federal Work-Study, tuition waivers (partial), and professional educator discounts available. Financial award application deadline: 3/1; financial award applicants required to submit FAFSA. *Faculty research:* Collaboration with public schools, pre-service program development, mathematics, diversity, literacy. *Unit head:* Dr. Sam Hausfather, Dean, 314-529-9466, Fax: 314-529-9921, E-mail: shausfather@maryville.edu. *Application contact:* Holly Stanwich, Graduate Admissions Coordinator, 314-529-9542, Fax: 314-529-9921, E-mail: teachered@maryville.edu. Web site: http://www.maryville.edu/academics-ed-graduate.

Marywood University, Academic Affairs, Insalaco College of Creative and Performing Arts, Art Department, Program in Art Education, Scranton, PA 18509-1598. Offers MA. *Accreditation:* NASAD; NCATE. *Entrance requirements:* Additional exam requirements/recommendations for international students: Required—TOEFL (minimum score 550 paper-based; 213 computer-based; 79 iBT). *Application deadline:* For fall admission, 4/1 priority date for domestic students, 3/31 for international students; for spring admission, 11/1 priority date for domestic students, 8/31 for international students. Applications are processed on a rolling basis. Application fee: $35. Electronic applications accepted. *Financial support:* Career-related internships or fieldwork, scholarships/grants, and unspecified assistantships available. Support available to part-time students. Financial award application deadline: 6/30; financial award applicants required to submit FAFSA. *Faculty research:* Current trends in art education, color theories, research in Mariology. *Unit head:* Matthew Povse, Chair, 570-348-6211 Ext. 2476, E-mail: povse@marywood.edu. *Application contact:* Tammy Manka, Assistant Director of Graduate Admissions, 570-348-6211 Ext. 2322, E-mail: tmanka@marywood.edu. Web site: http://www.marywood.edu/art/graduate-programs/master-art-education.html.

Massachusetts College of Art and Design, Graduate Programs, Program in Art Education, Boston, MA 02115-5882. Offers MAT, Certificate. *Accreditation:* NASAD. *Faculty:* 5 full-time (2 women), 10 part-time/adjunct (6 women). *Students:* 21 full-time (17 women), 12 part-time (9 women); includes 2 minority (1 Black or African American, non-Hispanic/Latino; 1 Hispanic/Latino), 2 international. 44 applicants, 36% accepted, 9 enrolled. In 2011, 19 master's, 2 other advanced degrees awarded. *Entrance requirements:* For master's and Certificate, portfolio, college transcripts, resume, statement of purpose, letters of reference, interview. Additional exam requirements/recommendations for international students: Required—TOEFL (minimum score 563 paper-based; 223 computer-based; 85 iBT); Recommended—IELTS (minimum score 6.5). *Application deadline:* For fall admission, 1/15 for domestic and international students. Application fee: $75. Electronic applications accepted. *Expenses:* Contact institution. *Financial support:* In 2011–12, 5 research assistantships (averaging $2,000 per year), 4 teaching assistantships (averaging $2,000 per year) were awarded; career-related internships or fieldwork, scholarships/grants, unspecified assistantships, and travel scholarships also available. Support available to part-time students. Financial award application deadline: 3/1; financial award applicants required to submit FAFSA. *Faculty research:* Museum education, history of visual arts education, teaching studio art K-12. *Unit head:* Jenny Gibbs, Assistant Dean of Graduate Programs, 617-879-7181, Fax: 617-879-7171, E-mail: jgibbs@massart.edu. *Application contact:* 617-879-7166, Fax: 617-879-7171, E-mail: gradinfo@massart.edu. Web site: http://www.massart.edu/Admissions/Graduate_Programs.

Memphis College of Art, Graduate Programs, Program in Art Education, Memphis, TN 38104-2764. Offers MA, MAT. Part-time and evening/weekend programs available. *Faculty:* 26 full-time (15 women), 13 part-time/adjunct (8 women). *Students:* 3 full-time (2 women), 32 part-time (24 women); includes 6 minority (5 Black or African American, non-Hispanic/Latino; 1 Asian, non-Hispanic/Latino). Average age 28. 21 applicants, 71% accepted, 13 enrolled. In 2011, 15 master's awarded. *Degree requirements:* For master's, thesis. *Entrance requirements:* For master's, portfolio, resume, interview. Additional exam requirements/recommendations for international students: Required—TOEFL (minimum score 525 paper-based; 195 computer-based). *Application deadline:* For fall admission, 3/1 for domestic and international students; for spring admission, 11/1 for domestic and international students. Applications are processed on a rolling basis. Application fee: $50. Electronic applications accepted. *Expenses: Tuition:* Full-time $27,450; part-time $558 per credit hour. *Financial support:* Application deadline: 8/1; applicants required to submit FAFSA. *Unit head:* Dr. Catherine Wilson, Director of Graduate Education, 901-272-5100, Fax: 901-272-5158, E-mail: cwilson@mca.edu. *Application contact:* Annette Moore, Dean of Admissions, 901-272-5153, Fax: 901-272-5158, E-mail: amoore@mca.edu.

Messiah College, Program in Art Education, Mechanicsburg, PA 17055. Offers MA. *Accreditation:* NASAD. Part-time programs available. *Faculty:* 2 full-time (1 woman), 3 part-time/adjunct (1 woman). *Students:* 9 part-time (7 women). Average age 34. *Degree requirements:* For master's, capstone project (exhibition or thesis). *Application deadline:* For fall admission, 6/15 priority date for domestic students; for winter admission, 11/1 priority date for domestic students; for spring admission, 11/1 priority date for domestic students. Applications are processed on a rolling basis. Application fee: $30. Electronic applications accepted. *Expenses: Tuition:* Full-time $9648; part-time $536 per credit hour. *Required fees:* $150; $25 per course. *Financial support:* Federal Work-Study available. Financial award applicants required to submit FAFSA. *Unit head:* Dr. Gene VanDyke, Program Coordinator, 717-796-1800 Ext. 6726, Fax: 717-691-2386, E-mail: gvandyke@messiah.edu. *Application contact:* Jackie Gehman, Graduate Enrollment Coordinator, 717-796-5061, Fax: 717-691-2386, E-mail: jgehman@messiah.edu. Web site: http://www.messiah.edu/academics/graduate_studies/ArtEd/index.html.

Miami University, School of Fine Arts, Department of Art, Oxford, OH 45056. Offers art education (MA); studio art (MFA). *Accreditation:* NASAD (one or more programs are accredited). *Students:* 14 full-time (5 women); includes 1 minority (Black or African American, non-Hispanic/Latino). Average age 30. In 2011, 4 master's awarded. *Entrance requirements:* For master's, minimum undergraduate GPA of 3.0 during previous 2 years or 2.75 overall. Additional exam requirements/recommendations for international students: Required—TOEFL. *Application deadline:* For fall admission, 2/1 for domestic and international students. Application fee: $50. *Expenses:* Tuition, state resident: full-time $12,023; part-time $501 per credit hour. Tuition, nonresident: full-time $26,554; part-time $1107 per credit hour. *Required fees:* $528. *Financial support:* Fellowships with full tuition reimbursements, research assistantships, teaching assistantships, Federal Work-Study, health care benefits, tuition waivers (full), and unspecified assistantships available. Financial award application deadline: 2/15; financial award applicants required to submit FAFSA. *Unit head:* Dr. Thomas Effler, Chair and Associate Professor, 513-529-2900, E-mail: efflert@muohio.edu. *Application contact:* Ellen Price, Professor/Graduate Director, 513-529-7128, E-mail: priceej@muohio.edu. Web site: http://arts.muohio.edu/art.

Millersville University of Pennsylvania, College of Graduate and Professional Studies, School of Humanities and Social Sciences, Department of Art, Millersville, PA 17551-0302. Offers M Ed. *Accreditation:* NASAD; NCATE. Part-time programs available. *Faculty:* 13 full-time (8 women), 2 part-time/adjunct (both women). *Students:* 3 full-time (2 women), 4 part-time (2 women); includes 1 minority (American Indian or Alaska Native, non-Hispanic/Latino). Average age 29. 3 applicants, 100% accepted, 1 enrolled. In 2011, 5 master's awarded. *Degree requirements:* For master's, comprehensive exam, thesis optional. *Entrance requirements:* For master's, GRE or MAT, 3 letters of recommendation, portfolio. Additional exam requirements/recommendations for international students: Required—TOEFL (minimum score 500 paper-based; 183 computer-based; 65 iBT). *Application deadline:* For fall admission, 1/15 priority date for domestic students, 1/15 for international students; for winter admission, 10/1 priority date for domestic students, 10/1 for international students; for spring admission, 10/1 priority date for domestic students, 10/1 for international students. Applications are processed on a rolling basis. Application fee: $40 ($50 for international students). Electronic applications accepted. *Expenses:* Tuition, state resident: full-time $3744; part-time $416 per credit. Tuition, nonresident: full-time $5616; part-time $624 per credit. *Required fees:* $1130; $125.50 per credit. Tuition and fees vary according to course load. *Financial support:* Research assistantships with full tuition reimbursements, institutionally sponsored loans, and unspecified assistantships available. Support available to part-time students. Financial award application deadline: 3/15; financial award applicants required to submit FAFSA. *Faculty research:* Portraiture; photo theory; pop culture; youth culture; Sumerian lamentations and hymnology; twentieth dynasty in Egypt; experimental ceramic sculpture with Egyptian paste and steel; intersections of science, technology and feminism in contemporary art. *Total annual research expenditures:* $13,500. *Unit head:* Brant D. Schuller, Chair, 717-871-3304, Fax: 717-871-2004, E-mail: brant.schuller@millersville.edu. *Application contact:* Dr. Victor S. DeSantis, Dean, College of Graduate and Professional Studies, 717-872-3099, Fax: 717-872-3453, E-mail: victor.desantis@millersville.edu. Web site: http://www.millersville.edu/art/.

Mills College, Graduate Studies, School of Education, Oakland, CA 94613-1000. Offers child life in hospitals (MA); early childhood education (MA); education (MA), including art education, curriculum and instruction, elementary education, English education, foreign language education, mathematics education, science education, secondary education, social studies education, teaching; educational leadership (MA, Ed D). Part-time and evening/weekend programs available. *Faculty:* 13 full-time (10 women), 14 part-time/adjunct (10 women). *Students:* 149 full-time (133 women), 69 part-time (61 women);

includes 85 minority (32 Black or African American, non-Hispanic/Latino; 1 American Indian or Alaska Native, non-Hispanic/Latino; 16 Asian, non-Hispanic/Latino; 24 Hispanic/Latino; 1 Native Hawaiian or other Pacific Islander, non-Hispanic/Latino; 11 Two or more races, non-Hispanic/Latino), 3 international. Average age 28. 238 applicants, 84% accepted, 106 enrolled. In 2011, 41 master's, 2 doctorates awarded. Terminal master's awarded for partial completion of doctoral program. *Degree requirements:* For master's, comprehensive exam. *Entrance requirements:* For master's, statement of purpose, official transcript, 3 recommendations; for doctorate, GRE General Test. Additional exam requirements/recommendations for international students: Required—TOEFL (minimum score 550 paper-based; 80 iBT) or IELTS (minimum score 6). *Application deadline:* For fall admission, 12/31 priority date for domestic students, 12/15 for international students; for spring admission, 11/1 priority date for domestic students, 10/1 for international students. Applications are processed on a rolling basis. Application fee: $50. Electronic applications accepted. *Expenses: Tuition:* Full-time $28,280; part-time $15,640 per year. *Required fees:* $958. Tuition and fees vary according to program. *Financial support:* In 2011–12, 43 students received support, including 225 fellowships with full and partial tuition reimbursements available (averaging $6,020 per year), 43 teaching assistantships with full and partial tuition reimbursements available (averaging $6,782 per year); career-related internships or fieldwork and scholarships/grants also available. Support available to part-time students. Financial award application deadline: 2/1; financial award applicants required to submit FAFSA. *Faculty research:* Early childhood education, teacher preparation, educational leadership. *Total annual research expenditures:* $2.3 million. *Unit head:* Katherine Schultz, Chairperson, 510-430-3170, Fax: 510-430-3379, E-mail: grad-studies@mills.edu. *Application contact:* Tiana Kozoil, Graduate Admission Specialist, 510-430-3305, Fax: 510-430-2159, E-mail: grad-studies@mills.edu. Web site: http://www.mills.edu/education.

Minnesota State University Mankato, College of Graduate Studies, College of Arts and Humanities, Department of Art, Mankato, MN 56001. Offers studio art (MA); teaching art (MAT). *Accreditation:* NASAD (one or more programs are accredited). Part-time programs available. *Students:* 10 full-time (5 women), 9 part-time (6 women). *Degree requirements:* For master's, one foreign language, comprehensive exam, thesis or alternative. *Entrance requirements:* For master's, minimum GPA of 3.0 during previous 2 years, portfolio (MA). Additional exam requirements/recommendations for international students: Required—TOEFL. *Application deadline:* For fall admission, 7/1 priority date for domestic students, 5/1 for international students; for spring admission, 11/1 for domestic students, 10/1 for international students. Applications are processed on a rolling basis. Application fee: $40. Electronic applications accepted. *Financial support:* Research assistantships, teaching assistantships with full tuition reimbursements, and unspecified assistantships available. Financial award application deadline: 3/15; financial award applicants required to submit FAFSA. *Faculty research:* Photographic documentation. *Unit head:* Brian Frink, Graduate Coordinator, 507-389-6412. *Application contact:* 507-389-2321, E-mail: grad@mnsu.edu. Web site: http://www.mankato.msus.edu/cgi-bin/deptPage?Art/.

Mississippi College, Graduate School, School of Education, Department of Teacher Education and Leadership, Clinton, MS 39058. Offers art (M Ed); biological science (M Ed); business education (M Ed); computer science (M Ed); dyslexia therapy (M Ed); educational leadership (M Ed, Ed D, Ed S); elementary education (M Ed, Ed S); English (M Ed); higher education administration (MS); mathematics (M Ed); secondary education (M Ed); social studies (history) (M Ed); teaching arts (M Ed). Part-time programs available. Postbaccalaureate distance learning degree programs offered (no on-campus study). *Degree requirements:* For master's, comprehensive exam, thesis optional. *Entrance requirements:* For master's, NTE. Additional exam requirements/recommendations for international students: Recommended—TOEFL, IELTS. Electronic applications accepted.

Montclair State University, The Graduate School, College of Education and Human Services, Department of Curriculum and Teaching, Program in Teaching in Content Area, Montclair, NJ 07043-1624. Offers art (MAT); biology (MAT); chemistry (MAT); earth science (MAT); English (MAT); French (MAT); health and physical education (MAT); health education (MAT); mathematics (MAT); music (MAT); physical education (MAT); physical science (MAT); social studies (MAT); Spanish (MAT); teacher of English as a second language (MAT). *Students:* 162 full-time (90 women), 47 part-time (29 women); includes 37 minority (4 Black or African American, non-Hispanic/Latino; 11 Asian, non-Hispanic/Latino; 18 Hispanic/Latino; 4 Two or more races, non-Hispanic/Latino), 5 international. Average age 31. 145 applicants, 41% accepted, 56 enrolled. In 2011, 229 master's awarded. *Degree requirements:* For master's, comprehensive exam, thesis or alternative. *Entrance requirements:* For master's, GRE General Test, interview, 2 letters of recommendation. Additional exam requirements/recommendations for international students: Required—TOEFL (minimum score 83 iBT), IELTS (minimum score 6.5). *Application deadline:* Applications are processed on a rolling basis. Application fee: $60. Electronic applications accepted. *Financial support:* Federal Work-Study, scholarships/grants, and unspecified assistantships available. Support available to part-time students. Financial award application deadline: 3/1; financial award applicants required to submit FAFSA. *Unit head:* Dr. David Schwarzer, Chairperson, 973-655-5187. *Application contact:* Amy Aiello, Executive Director of The Graduate School, 973-655-5147, Fax: 973-655-7869, E-mail: graduate.school@montclair.edu.

Montclair State University, The Graduate School, School of the Arts, Department of Art and Design, Program in Art, Montclair, NJ 07043-1624. Offers MAT. Part-time and evening/weekend programs available. *Students:* 5 full-time (3 women), 1 (woman) part-time; includes 2 minority (1 Asian, non-Hispanic/Latino; 1 Hispanic/Latino). Average age 31. 15 applicants, 47% accepted, 6 enrolled. *Entrance requirements:* For master's, GRE General Test, 2 letters of recommendation, essay. Additional exam requirements/recommendations for international students: Required—TOEFL (minimum score 83 iBT), IELTS (minimum score 6.5). *Application deadline:* Applications are processed on a rolling basis. Application fee: $60. Electronic applications accepted. *Financial support:* Federal Work-Study, scholarships/grants, and unspecified assistantships available. Support available to part-time students. Financial award applicants required to submit FAFSA. *Unit head:* Dr. Scott Gordley, Chairperson, 973-655-7295. *Application contact:* Amy Aiello, Executive Director of The Graduate School, 973-655-5147, E-mail: graduate.school@montclair.edu. Web site: http://www.montclair.edu/arts/academics/programsofstudy/#GR.

Moore College of Art & Design, Program in Art Education, Philadelphia, PA 19103. Offers MA. Part-time programs available. *Degree requirements:* For master's, thesis, field practicum. *Entrance requirements:* For master's, minimum GPA of 3.0, on-site interview, portfolio, 3 letters of recommendation, resume.

Morehead State University, Graduate Programs, Caudill College of Arts, Humanities and Social Sciences, Department of Art and Design, Morehead, KY 40351. Offers art education (MA); graphic design (MA); studio art (MA). Part-time and evening/weekend programs available. *Degree requirements:* For master's, comprehensive exam, thesis (for some programs), oral exam during exhibition. *Entrance requirements:* For master's, GRE General Test, minimum undergraduate GPA of 3.0 in major, 2.5 overall; portfolio; bachelor's degree in art. Additional exam requirements/recommendations for international students: Required—TOEFL (minimum score 500 paper-based; 173 computer-based). Electronic applications accepted. *Faculty research:* Computer art, painting, drawing, ceramics, photography.

Nazareth College of Rochester, Graduate Studies, Department of Art, Program in Art Education, Rochester, NY 14618-3790. Offers MS Ed. *Accreditation:* Teacher Education Accreditation Council. Part-time and evening/weekend programs available. *Entrance requirements:* For master's, minimum GPA of 3.0, portfolio review.

New Jersey City University, Graduate Studies and Continuing Education, William J. Maxwell College of Arts and Sciences, Department of Art, Jersey City, NJ 07305-1597. Offers art (MFA); art education (MA); studio art (MFA). *Accreditation:* NASAD. Part-time and evening/weekend programs available. *Students:* 9 full-time (8 women), 6 part-time (2 women); includes 5 minority (2 Black or African American, non-Hispanic/Latino; 1 American Indian or Alaska Native, non-Hispanic/Latino; 2 Hispanic/Latino), 1 international. Average age 33. In 2011, 2 master's awarded. *Degree requirements:* For master's, thesis or alternative, exhibit. *Entrance requirements:* For master's, portfolio. Additional exam requirements/recommendations for international students: Required—TOEFL. *Application deadline:* For fall admission, 8/1 priority date for domestic students; for spring admission, 12/1 for domestic students. Applications are processed on a rolling basis. Application fee: $0. *Expenses:* Tuition, state resident: part-time $494 per credit. Tuition, nonresident: part-time $911.30 per credit. *Required fees:* $95.90 per year. *Financial support:* Unspecified assistantships available. *Unit head:* Dr. Herbert Rosenberg, Chairperson, 201-200-2367. *Application contact:* Dr. William Bajor, Dean of Graduate Studies, 201-200-3409, Fax: 201-200-3411, E-mail: wbajor@njcu.edu.

New York University, Steinhardt School of Culture, Education, and Human Development, Department of Art and Art Professions, Program in Art Education, New York, NY 10003-5799. Offers MA. *Accreditation:* Teacher Education Accreditation Council. Part-time programs available. *Faculty:* 2 full-time (1 woman). *Students:* 17 full-time (12 women), 10 part-time (8 women); includes 4 minority (1 Black or African American, non-Hispanic/Latino; 1 Asian, non-Hispanic/Latino; 1 Hispanic/Latino; 1 Two or more races, non-Hispanic/Latino), 1 international. Average age 29. 69 applicants, 59% accepted, 21 enrolled. In 2011, 36 master's awarded. *Degree requirements:* For master's, thesis (for some programs). *Entrance requirements:* For master's, portfolio. Additional exam requirements/recommendations for international students: Required—TOEFL. *Application deadline:* For fall admission, 12/1 priority date for domestic students, 12/1 for international students. Applications are processed on a rolling basis. Application fee: $75. Electronic applications accepted. *Financial support:* Career-related internships or fieldwork, Federal Work-Study, institutionally sponsored loans, and tuition waivers (partial) available. Support available to part-time students. Financial award application deadline: 2/1; financial award applicants required to submit FAFSA. *Faculty research:* Multicultural aesthetic inquiry, urban art education, feminism, equity and social justice. *Unit head:* Dr. Dipti Desai, Director, 212-998-9022, Fax: 212-995-4320, E-mail: dd25@nyu.edu. *Application contact:* 212-998-5030, Fax: 212-995-4328, E-mail: steinhardt.gradadmissions@nyu.edu. Web site: http://steinhardt.nyu.edu/art/education.

North Georgia College & State University, School of Education, Dahlonega, GA 30597. Offers art education (MAT); early childhood education (M Ed); English education (MAT); history education (MAT); math education (MAT); middle grades education (M Ed, MAT); physical education (MS); school leadership (Ed S); secondary education (M Ed), including English education, history education, mathematics education, physical education; teacher education (MAT). *Accreditation:* NCATE. Part-time and evening/weekend programs available. Postbaccalaureate distance learning degree programs offered (no on-campus study). *Faculty:* 23 full-time (14 women), 16 part-time/adjunct (11 women). *Students:* 19 full-time (17 women), 199 part-time (147 women); includes 7 minority (3 Black or African American, non-Hispanic/Latino; 1 Asian, non-Hispanic/Latino; 3 Hispanic/Latino), 1 international. Average age 34. 259 applicants, 66% accepted, 112 enrolled. In 2011, 100 master's, 16 other advanced degrees awarded. *Degree requirements:* For master's, comprehensive exam, thesis optional. *Entrance requirements:* For master's, GRE or MAT, GACE, minimum GPA of 2.75; for Ed S, GRE General Test or MAT, 3 years of teaching experience, master's degree, minimum graduate GPA of 3.25, leadership position in the school. Additional exam requirements/recommendations for international students: Required—TOEFL (minimum score 550 paper-based; 213 computer-based; 79 iBT), IELTS (minimum score 6.5). *Application deadline:* For fall admission, 8/1 priority date for domestic students, 7/1 for international students; for spring admission, 12/1 priority date for domestic students, 11/1 for international students. Applications are processed on a rolling basis. Application fee: $40. Electronic applications accepted. *Expenses:* Tuition, state resident: full-time $3528; part-time $196 per credit hour. Tuition, nonresident: full-time $14,094; part-time $783 per credit hour. *Required fees:* $1718; $859 per semester. Tuition and fees vary according to course load, campus/location and program. *Financial support:* Teaching assistantships, career-related internships or fieldwork, scholarships/grants, and unspecified assistantships available. Financial award application deadline: 5/1; financial award applicants required to submit CSS PROFILE or FAFSA. *Faculty research:* Identification of professional development school structures supporting P-12 student achievement, impact of diverse field placement settings in teacher belief development among preservice teachers, use of inquiry methodology in social studies teaching with English language learners, use of instructional differentiation in the middle grades classroom, effects of international school placements on preservice teacher beliefs and attitudes. *Unit head:* Dr. Bob Michael, Dean, School of Education, 706-864-1998, Fax: 706-867-2850, E-mail: bmichael@northgeorgia.edu. *Application contact:* Susan L. Perry, Graduate Admissions Coordinator, 706-864-1543, Fax: 706-867-2795, E-mail: slperry@northgeorgia.edu. Web site: http://www.northgeorgia.edu/soe/.

The Ohio State University, Graduate School, College of Arts and Sciences, Division of Arts and Humanities, Department of Art Education, Columbus, OH 43210. Offers art education (MA, PhD); arts policy and administration (MA). *Accreditation:* NASAD; NCATE. *Faculty:* 12. *Students:* 43 full-time (33 women), 56 part-time (47 women); includes 8 minority (5 Black or African American, non-Hispanic/Latino; 1 American Indian or Alaska Native, non-Hispanic/Latino; 2 Hispanic/Latino), 20 international. Average age 33. In 2011, 25 master's, 13 doctorates awarded. *Degree requirements:* For master's, thesis; for doctorate, thesis/dissertation. *Entrance requirements:* For master's and doctorate, GRE General Test. Additional exam requirements/recommendations for international students: Required—Michigan English Language Assessment Battery (minimum score 82); Recommended—TOEFL (minimum score 550 paper-based; 250 computer-based; 79 iBT). *Application deadline:* For fall admission, 8/15 priority date for domestic students, 7/1 for international students; for winter admission, 12/1 priority date for domestic students, 11/1 for international students; for spring admission, 3/1 priority date for domestic students, 2/1 for international students. Applications are processed on a rolling basis. Application fee: $40 ($50 for international students). Electronic applications accepted. *Expenses:* Tuition, state resident: full-time $11,400. Tuition, nonresident: full-time $28,125. Tuition and fees vary according to course load, degree level, campus/location and program. *Financial support:* Fellowships, research assistantships, teaching assistantships, career-related internships or fieldwork, Federal Work-Study, institutionally sponsored loans, and unspecified assistantships available. Support available to part-time students. Financial award applicants required to submit FAFSA. *Unit head:* Deborah L. Smith-Shank, Interim Chair, 614-688-4346, E-mail: smith-shank.1@osu.edu. *Application* *contact:* Graduate Admissions, 614-292-6031, Fax: 614-292-3656, E-mail: gradadmissions@osu.edu. Web site: http://arted.osu.edu/index.php.

Pittsburg State University, Graduate School, College of Arts and Sciences, Department of Art, Pittsburg, KS 66762. Offers art education (MA); studio art (MA). *Degree requirements:* For master's, thesis or alternative.

Pratt Institute, School of Art and Design, Program in Art and Design Education, Brooklyn, NY 11205-3899. Offers MS, Adv C. *Accreditation:* NASAD. Part-time programs available. *Faculty:* 1 (woman) full-time, 15 part-time/adjunct (13 women). *Students:* 28 full-time (23 women), 2 part-time (both women); includes 9 minority (2 Black or African American, non-Hispanic/Latino; 3 Asian, non-Hispanic/Latino; 2 Hispanic/Latino; 2 Two or more races, non-Hispanic/Latino), 2 international. Average age 30. 37 applicants, 78% accepted, 9 enrolled. In 2011, 12 master's awarded. *Degree requirements:* For master's, thesis. *Entrance requirements:* Additional exam requirements/recommendations for international students: Required—TOEFL (minimum score 600 paper-based; 250 computer-based; 100 iBT). *Application deadline:* For fall admission, 1/5 for domestic and international students; for spring admission, 10/1 for domestic and international students. Application fee: $50 ($90 for international students). *Expenses: Tuition:* Full-time $24,084; part-time $1338 per credit. *Financial support:* Career-related internships or fieldwork, Federal Work-Study, institutionally sponsored loans, scholarships/grants, health care benefits, and unspecified assistantships available. Support available to part-time students. Financial award application deadline: 2/1; financial award applicants required to submit FAFSA. *Unit head:* Amir Parsa, Chairperson, 718-636-3567, E-mail: aparsa@pratt.edu. *Application contact:* Young Hah, Director of Graduate Admissions, 718-636-3683, Fax: 718-399-4242, E-mail: yhah@pratt.edu. Web site: http://www.pratt.edu/academics/art_design/art_grad/art_and_design_education_grad.

Purdue University, Graduate School, College of Education, Department of Curriculum and Instruction, West Lafayette, IN 47907. Offers agricultural and extension education (PhD, Ed S); agriculture and extension education (MS, MS Ed); art education (PhD); consumer and family sciences and extension education (MS Ed, PhD, Ed S); curriculum studies (MS Ed, PhD, Ed S); educational technology (MS Ed, PhD, Ed S); elementary education (MS Ed); foreign language education (MS Ed, PhD, Ed S); industrial technology (PhD, Ed S); language arts (MS Ed, PhD, Ed S); literacy (MS Ed, PhD, Ed S); mathematics/science education (MS, MS Ed, PhD, Ed S); social studies (MS Ed, PhD); social studies education (Ed S); vocational/industrial education (MS Ed, PhD, Ed S); vocational/technical education (MS Ed, PhD, Ed S). *Accreditation:* NCATE. Part-time and evening/weekend programs available. *Faculty:* 30 full-time (21 women), 1 (woman) part-time/adjunct. *Students:* 89 full-time (64 women), 134 part-time (84 women); includes 31 minority (12 Black or African American, non-Hispanic/Latino; 3 American Indian or Alaska Native, non-Hispanic/Latino; 7 Asian, non-Hispanic/Latino; 9 Hispanic/Latino), 49 international. Average age 36. 136 applicants, 83% accepted, 72 enrolled. In 2011, 26 master's, 13 doctorates awarded. *Degree requirements:* For master's, thesis optional; for doctorate, thesis/dissertation, oral and written exams; for Ed S, oral presentation, project. *Entrance requirements:* For master's, GRE general test is required if undergraduate GPA is below 3.0, minimum undergraduate GPA of 3.0 or equivalent; for doctorate, GRE General Test, a combined GRE verbal and quantitative score of 1000 (300 for revised GRE Test) or more is expected, minimum undergraduate GPA of 3.0 or equivalent; master's degree with minimum GPA of 3.0 or equivalent; for Ed S, GRE general test, a combined GRE verbal and quantitative score of 1000 (300 for revised GRE Test) or more is expected, minimum undergraduate GPA of 3.0 or equivalent; master's degree. Additional exam requirements/recommendations for international students: Required—TOEFL (minimum score 550 paper-based; 77 iBT). *Application deadline:* For fall admission, 12/15 priority date for domestic students, 3/1 for international students; for spring admission, 9/15 for domestic students, 8/1 for international students. Application fee: $60 ($75 for international students). Electronic applications accepted. *Financial support:* Fellowships with full tuition reimbursements, research assistantships with full tuition reimbursements, teaching assistantships with full tuition reimbursements, career-related internships or fieldwork, and tuition waivers (full) available. Support available to part-time students. Financial award application deadline: 3/1; financial award applicants required to submit FAFSA. *Faculty research:* Literacy acquisition and development, teacher beliefs and knowledge, recruitment and retention of underrepresented students, economic education, literacy discourse. *Unit head:* Dr. Philip J. VanFossen, Head, 765-494-7935, Fax: 765-496-1622, E-mail: vanfoss@purdue.edu. *Application contact:* Sarah N. Prater, Graduate Contact, 765-494-2345, Fax: 765-494-5832, E-mail: prater0@purdue.edu. Web site: http://www.edci.purdue.edu/.

Queens College of the City University of New York, Division of Graduate Studies, Division of Education, Department of Secondary Education, Flushing, NY 11367-1597. Offers art (MS Ed); biology (MS Ed, AC); chemistry (MS Ed, AC); earth sciences (MS Ed, AC); English (MS Ed, AC); French (MS Ed, AC); Italian (MS Ed, AC); mathematics (MS Ed, AC); music (MS Ed, AC); physics (MS Ed, AC); social studies (MS Ed, AC); Spanish (MS Ed, AC). Part-time and evening/weekend programs available. *Faculty:* 22 full-time (14 women). *Students:* 46 full-time (23 women), 727 part-time (442 women); includes 234 minority (41 Black or African American, non-Hispanic/Latino; 78 Asian, non-Hispanic/Latino; 115 Hispanic/Latino), 5 international. 591 applicants, 60% accepted, 250 enrolled. In 2011, 170 master's awarded. *Degree requirements:* For master's, research project; for AC, thesis optional. *Entrance requirements:* For master's, minimum GPA of 3.0. Additional exam requirements/recommendations for international students: Required—TOEFL. *Application deadline:* For fall admission, 4/1 for domestic students; for spring admission, 11/1 for domestic students. Applications are processed on a rolling basis. Application fee: $125. *Expenses:* Tuition, state resident: part-time $345 per credit. Tuition, nonresident: part-time $640 per credit. *Required fees:* $145.25 per semester. *Financial support:* Career-related internships or fieldwork, Federal Work-Study, institutionally sponsored loans, and tuition waivers (partial) available. Support available to part-time students. Financial award application deadline: 4/1; financial award applicants required to submit FAFSA. *Unit head:* Dr. Eleanor Armour-Thomas, Chairperson, 718-997-5150, E-mail: armourthomas@yahoo.com. *Application contact:* Mario Caruso, Director of Graduate Admissions, 718-997-5200, Fax: 718-997-5193, E-mail: graduate_admissions@qc.edu.

Rhode Island College, School of Graduate Studies, Faculty of Arts and Sciences, Department of Art, Providence, RI 02908-1991. Offers art education (MA, MAT); media studies (MA). *Accreditation:* NASAD (one or more programs are accredited). Part-time and evening/weekend programs available. *Faculty:* 10 full-time (4 women), 1 (woman) part-time/adjunct. *Students:* 2 full-time (1 woman), 19 part-time (14 women), 1 international. Average age 35. In 2011, 9 master's awarded. *Degree requirements:* For master's, thesis. *Entrance requirements:* For master's, GRE General Test, portfolio (MA), 3 letters of recommendation, interview. Additional exam requirements/recommendations for international students: Recommended—TOEFL (minimum score 550 paper-based; 213 computer-based; 79 iBT). *Application deadline:* For fall admission, 3/1 for domestic students. Applications are processed on a rolling basis. Application fee: $50. *Expenses:* Tuition, state resident: full-time $8592; part-time $358 per credit hour. Tuition, nonresident: full-time $16,800; part-time $700 per credit hour. *Required fees:* $602; $22 per credit. $72 per term. *Financial support:* Teaching assistantships with full tuition reimbursements, career-related internships or fieldwork, Federal Work-Study, scholarships/grants, health care benefits, and unspecified assistantships available. Support available to part-time students. Financial award application deadline: 5/15; financial award applicants required to submit FAFSA. *Unit head:* Prof. William Martin, Chair, 401-456-8054. *Application contact:* Graduate Studies, 401-456-8700. Web site: http://www.ric.edu/art/index.php.

Rhode Island School of Design, Graduate Studies, Program in Art Education, Providence, RI 02903-2784. Offers MA, MAT. *Accreditation:* NASAD. *Students:* 16 full-time (14 women); includes 4 minority (2 Hispanic/Latino; 2 Two or more races, non-Hispanic/Latino), 1 international. Average age 27. In 2011, 12 master's awarded. *Degree requirements:* For master's, thesis, exhibit. *Entrance requirements:* For master's, portfolio, statement of purpose, letters of recommendation. Additional exam requirements/recommendations for international students: Required—TOEFL (minimum score 580 paper-based; 93 iBT). *Application deadline:* For fall admission, 1/10 for domestic and international students. Application fee: $60. *Expenses: Tuition:* Full-time $41,022. *Required fees:* $310. *Financial support:* Fellowships, teaching assistantships, career-related internships or fieldwork, Federal Work-Study, and institutionally sponsored loans available. Financial award application deadline: 2/15; financial award applicants required to submit FAFSA. *Unit head:* Paul Sproll, Head, 401-454-6695, Fax: 401-454-6694, E-mail: psproll@risd.edu. *Application contact:* Edward Newhall, Director of Admissions, 401-454-6307, E-mail: enewhall@risd.edu.

Rochester Institute of Technology, Graduate Enrollment Services, College of Imaging Arts and Sciences, School of Art, Program in Visual Art, Rochester, NY 14623-5603. Offers MST. *Accreditation:* NASAD; Teacher Education Accreditation Council. *Students:* 4 full-time (3 women), 1 part-time (0 women). Average age 31. 14 applicants, 71% accepted, 5 enrolled. In 2011, 13 degrees awarded. *Entrance requirements:* For master's, portfolio, minimum GPA of 3.0. Additional exam requirements/recommendations for international students: Required—TOEFL (minimum score 550 paper-based; 230 computer-based; 79 iBT) or IELTS (minimum score 6.5). *Application deadline:* For fall admission, 2/15 priority date for domestic students, 2/15 for international students. Applications are processed on a rolling basis. Application fee: $50. Electronic applications accepted. *Expenses: Tuition:* Full-time $34,659; part-time $963 per credit hour. *Required fees:* $228; $76 per quarter. *Financial support:* Career-related internships or fieldwork, institutionally sponsored loans, and scholarships/grants available. Financial award application deadline: 8/30; financial award applicants required to submit FAFSA. *Unit head:* Carol Woodlock, Graduate Program Director, 585-475-7556, E-mail: cmwfaa@rit.edu. *Application contact:* Diane Ellison, Assistant Vice President, Graduate Enrollment Services, 585-475-2229, Fax: 585-475-7164, E-mail: gradinfo@rit.edu. Web site: http://cias.rit.edu.

Sage Graduate School, Esteves School of Education, Program in Teaching, Troy, NY 12180-4115. Offers art education (MAT); English (MAT); mathematics (MAT); social studies (MAT). *Accreditation:* NASAD. Part-time and evening/weekend programs available. *Faculty:* 10 full-time (6 women), 6 part-time/adjunct (4 women). *Students:* 19 full-time (15 women), 20 part-time (16 women); includes 1 minority (Asian, non-Hispanic/Latino). Average age 27. 44 applicants, 36% accepted, 8 enrolled. In 2011, 37 master's awarded. *Entrance requirements:* For master's, assessment of writing skills, minimum undergraduate GPA of 2.75 overall, 3.0 in content area; current resume; 2 letters of recommendation. Additional exam requirements/recommendations for international students: Required—TOEFL (minimum score 550 paper-based; 213 computer-based). *Application deadline:* For fall admission, 8/1 for domestic students. Applications are processed on a rolling basis. Application fee: $40. *Expenses: Tuition:* Full-time $11,880; part-time $660 per credit hour. Tuition and fees vary according to program. *Financial support:* Fellowships, research assistantships, Federal Work-Study, scholarships/grants, and unspecified assistantships available. Support available to part-time students. Financial award application deadline: 3/1; financial award applicants required to submit FAFSA. *Unit head:* Dr. Lori Quigley, Dean, Esteves School of Education, 518-244-2326, Fax: 518-244-4571, E-mail: l.quigley@sage.edu. *Application contact:* Kelly Jones, Director, 518-244-2433, Fax: 518-244-6880, E-mail: jonesk4@sage.edu.

Saint Michael's College, Graduate Programs, Program in Education, Colchester, VT 05439. Offers administration (M Ed, CAGS); arts in education (CAGS); curriculum and instruction (M Ed, CAGS); information technology (CAGS); reading (M Ed); special education (M Ed, CAGS); technology (M Ed). Part-time and evening/weekend programs available. *Degree requirements:* For master's, thesis. *Entrance requirements:* For master's, minimum GPA of 3.0. Electronic applications accepted. *Faculty research:* Integrative curriculum, moral and spiritual dimensions of education, learning styles, multiple intelligences, integrating technology into the curriculum.

Salem College, Department of Teacher Education, Winston-Salem, NC 27101. Offers art education (MAT); elementary education (M Ed, MAT); language and literacy (M Ed); middle school education (MAT); music education (MAT); school counseling (M Ed); second language studies (MAT); secondary education (MAT); special education (M Ed, MAT). *Accreditation:* NCATE. Part-time and evening/weekend programs available. Postbaccalaureate distance learning degree programs offered (minimal on-campus study). *Degree requirements:* For master's, comprehensive exam, practicum (MAT), project (M Ed), oral and written comprehensive exams. *Entrance requirements:* For master's, GRE, minimum GPA of 2.5. *Faculty research:* Content area reading strategies, literacy development, brain compatible instruction.

Salem State University, School of Graduate Studies, Program in Art, Salem, MA 01970-5353. Offers MAT. *Accreditation:* NASAD. Part-time and evening/weekend programs available. *Entrance requirements:* For master's, GRE or MAT. Additional exam requirements/recommendations for international students: Required—TOEFL (minimum score 550 paper-based; 80 iBT) or IELTS (minimum score 5.5).

School of the Art Institute of Chicago, Graduate Division, Program in Art Education and Art Teaching, Chicago, IL 60603-3103. Offers MAAE, MAT. *Accreditation:* NASAD. *Entrance requirements:* Additional exam requirements/recommendations for international students: Required—TOEFL (minimum score 600 paper-based; 250 computer-based; 100 iBT), IELTS (minimum score 7).

School of the Museum of Fine Arts, Boston, Graduate Programs, Boston, MA 02115. Offers art teacher education (MAT); studio art (MFA). *Accreditation:* NASAD (one or more programs are accredited). Postbaccalaureate distance learning degree programs offered. *Faculty:* 43 full-time (19 women), 54 part-time/adjunct (32 women). *Students:* 143 full-time (102 women), 29 part-time (20 women); includes 23 minority (4 Black or African American, non-Hispanic/Latino; 8 Asian, non-Hispanic/Latino; 3 Hispanic/Latino; 8 Two or more races, non-Hispanic/Latino), 26 international. Average age 30. 367 applicants, 69% accepted, 107 enrolled. In 2011, 39 master's, 26 other advanced degrees awarded. Terminal master's awarded for partial completion of doctoral program. *Degree requirements:* For master's, thesis (for some programs), exhibition thesis. *Entrance requirements:* For master's, BFA, bachelor's degree or equivalent in related area, portfolio; for Postbaccalaureate Certificate, portfolio, BFA or equivalent. Additional exam requirements/recommendations for international students: Required—TOEFL (minimum score 550 paper-based; 213 computer-based). *Application deadline:* For fall admission, 1/1 priority date for domestic students, 2/1 for international students. Applications are processed on a rolling basis. Application fee: $75. Electronic applications accepted. *Expenses: Tuition:* Full-time $37,536. Full-time tuition and fees vary according to program. *Financial support:* In 2011–12, 14 fellowships (averaging $3,000 per year), 30 teaching assistantships (averaging $1,000 per year) were awarded; career-related internships or fieldwork, Federal Work-Study, scholarships/grants, tuition waivers (partial), and unspecified assistantships also available. Support available to part-time students. Financial award application deadline: 2/15; financial award applicants required to submit FAFSA. *Faculty research:* Public art commissions, National Endowment for the Arts grant recipients, international exhibitions. *Unit head:* David L. Brown, Associate Dean of Graduate Programs, 617-369-3870, E-mail: dbrown@smfa.edu. *Application contact:* Admissions Representative, 617-369-3626, Fax: 617-369-4264, E-mail: admissions@smfa.edu. Web site: http://www.smfa.edu/.

School of Visual Arts, Graduate Programs, Art Education Department, New York, NY 10010-3994. Offers MAT. *Entrance requirements:* For master's, portfolio. Additional exam requirements/recommendations for international students: Required—TOEFL (minimum score 550 paper-based; 213 computer-based; 79 iBT). Electronic applications accepted.

School of Visual Arts, Graduate Programs, Program in Art Criticism and Writing, New York, NY 10010-3994. Offers MFA. *Degree requirements:* For master's, thesis. *Entrance requirements:* For master's, writing sample (2,500-3,000 words), three letters of recommendation, official transcripts from each college or university attended, statement of purpose (250-500 words), resume. Additional exam requirements/recommendations for international students: Required—TOEFL (minimum score 550 paper-based; 213 computer-based; 79 iBT). Electronic applications accepted.

Simon Fraser University, Graduate Studies, Faculty of Education, Program in Arts Education, Burnaby, BC V5A 1S6, Canada. Offers M Ed, MA, PhD. *Degree requirements:* For master's, comprehensive exam or thesis; for doctorate, comprehensive exam, thesis/dissertation.

Southern Connecticut State University, School of Graduate Studies, School of Arts and Sciences, Department of Art, New Haven, CT 06515-1355. Offers art education (MS). Part-time and evening/weekend programs available. *Faculty:* 6 full-time (2 women). *Students:* 2 full-time (both women), 22 part-time (16 women); includes 1 minority (Asian, non-Hispanic/Latino). 56 applicants, 5% accepted, 3 enrolled. In 2011, 9 master's awarded. *Degree requirements:* For master's, thesis or alternative. *Entrance requirements:* For master's, interview. *Application deadline:* For fall admission, 5/1 priority date for domestic students; for spring admission, 12/1 priority date for domestic students. Applications are processed on a rolling basis. Application fee: $50. Electronic applications accepted. *Expenses:* Tuition, state resident: full-time $5137; part-time $413 per credit. *Required fees:* $4008; $55 per term. *Financial support:* Application deadline: 4/15; applicants required to submit FAFSA. *Unit head:* Mitchell Bills, Chairperson, 203-392-6649, Fax: 203-392-6658, E-mail: billsm1@southernct.edu. *Application contact:* Dr. Jessie Whitehead, Graduate Coordinator, 203-392-8913, Fax: 203-392-6658, E-mail: whiteheadj3@southernct.edu.

Southern Illinois University Edwardsville, Graduate School, School of Education, Department of Curriculum and Instruction, Program in Secondary Education, Edwardsville, IL 62026. Offers art (MS Ed); biology (MS Ed); chemistry (MS Ed); earth and space sciences (MS Ed); English/language arts (MS Ed); foreign languages (MS Ed); history (MS Ed); mathematics (MS Ed); physics (MS Ed). *Accreditation:* NCATE. Part-time and evening/weekend programs available. *Students:* 1 full-time (0 women), 42 part-time (33 women); includes 2 minority (both Black or African American, non-Hispanic/Latino). 16 applicants, 31% accepted. In 2011, 8 master's awarded. *Degree requirements:* For master's, comprehensive exam (for some programs), final exam/paper. *Entrance requirements:* Additional exam requirements/recommendations for international students: Required—TOEFL (minimum score 550 paper-based; 213 computer-based; 79 iBT), IELTS (minimum score 6.5). *Application deadline:* For fall admission, 7/22 for domestic students, 6/1 for international students; for spring admission, 12/9 for domestic students, 10/1 for international students. Applications are processed on a rolling basis. Application fee: $30. Electronic applications accepted. Tuition and fees vary according to course load and program. *Financial support:* Fellowships, research assistantships, teaching assistantships, institutionally sponsored loans, scholarships/grants, and unspecified assistantships available. Financial award application deadline: 3/1; financial award applicants required to submit FAFSA. *Unit head:* Dr. Susan Breck, Director, 618-650-3444, E-mail: sbreck@siue.edu. *Application contact:* Dr. Michelle Robinson, Coordinator of Graduate Recruitment, 618-650-2811, Fax: 618-650-3523, E-mail: michero@siue.edu. Web site: http://www.siue.edu/education/ci/.

Southwestern Oklahoma State University, College of Arts and Sciences, Department of Art, Weatherford, OK 73096-3098. Offers art education (M Ed). Part-time programs available. *Degree requirements:* For master's, exam. *Entrance requirements:* For master's, GRE General Test or minimum undergraduate GPA of 3.0. Additional exam requirements/recommendations for international students: Required—TOEFL.

Stanford University, School of Education, Program in Curriculum Studies and Teacher Education, Stanford, CA 94305-9991. Offers art education (MA, PhD); dance education (MA); English education (MA, PhD); general curriculum studies (MA, PhD); mathematics education (MA, PhD); science education (MA, PhD); social studies education (PhD); teacher education (MA, PhD). *Degree requirements:* For master's, thesis (for some programs); for doctorate, thesis/dissertation. *Entrance requirements:* For master's and doctorate, GRE General Test. Electronic applications accepted. *Expenses: Tuition:* Full-time $40,050; part-time $890 per credit.

State University of New York at New Paltz, Graduate School, School of Fine and Performing Arts, Department of Art Education, New Paltz, NY 12561. Offers visual arts education (MS Ed). *Accreditation:* NASAD. Part-time and evening/weekend programs available. *Faculty:* 2 full-time (both women). *Students:* 30 part-time (28 women); includes 1 minority (Hispanic/Latino). Average age 32. 24 applicants, 75% accepted, 16 enrolled. In 2011, 13 master's awarded. *Degree requirements:* For master's, thesis, portfolio. *Entrance requirements:* For master's, New York state art education teaching certificate, minimum GPA of 3.0, portfolio. Additional exam requirements/recommendations for international students: Required—TOEFL (minimum score 550 paper-based; 213 computer-based; 80 iBT), IELTS (minimum score 6.5). *Application deadline:* For fall admission, 4/15 for domestic and international students. Application fee: $50. Electronic applications accepted. *Expenses:* Tuition, state resident: full-time $8870; part-time $370 per credit. Tuition, nonresident: full-time $15,160; part-time $632 per credit. *Required fees:* $1188; $34 per credit. $184 per semester. *Financial support:* In 2011–12, 2 students received support, including 1 research assistantship with partial tuition reimbursement available (averaging $5,000 per year); tuition waivers (full) also available. *Unit head:* Prof. Alice Wexler, Director, 845-257-3850, E-mail: wexlera@newpaltz.edu. *Application contact:* Caroline Murphy, Graduate Admissions Advisor, 845-257-3285, E-mail: gradschool@newpaltz.edu.

State University of New York at Oswego, Graduate Studies, School of Education, Department of Curriculum and Instruction, Oswego, NY 13126. Offers adolescence education (MST); art education (MAT); childhood education (MST); elementary education (MS Ed); literacy education (MS Ed); secondary education (MS Ed); special education (MS Ed). Part-time and evening/weekend programs available. *Degree requirements:* For master's, comprehensive exam (for some programs), thesis optional. *Entrance requirements:* For master's, GRE General Test, minimum GPA of 2.7, provisional teaching certificate. Additional exam requirements/recommendations for international students: Required—TOEFL (minimum score 560 paper-based; 220 computer-based). *Faculty research:* Classroom applications for microcomputers; classroom questioning, wait-time, and achievement; values clarification and academic achievement.

Sul Ross State University, School of Arts and Sciences, Department of Fine Arts and Communication, Alpine, TX 79832. Offers art education (M Ed); art history (M Ed); studio art (M Ed), including ceramics, design, drawing, jewelry, painting, printmaking, sculpture, weaving. Part-time programs available. *Degree requirements:* For master's, oral or written exam. *Entrance requirements:* For master's, GRE General Test, minimum GPA of 2.5 in last 60 hours of undergraduate work. *Faculty research:* Ceramic sculpture, watercolor, wood sculpture, rock art.

Syracuse University, School of Education, Program in Art Education, Syracuse, NY 13244. Offers art education (CAS); art education/professional certification (MS); art education: preparation (MS). Part-time and evening/weekend programs available. *Students:* 14 full-time (12 women), 3 part-time (all women); includes 1 minority (Asian, non-Hispanic/Latino). Average age 27. 11 applicants, 91% accepted, 5 enrolled. In 2011, 9 degrees awarded. *Degree requirements:* For master's, thesis or alternative. *Entrance requirements:* For master's, interview. Additional exam requirements/recommendations for international students: Required—TOEFL (minimum score 100 iBT). *Application deadline:* For fall admission, 2/1 priority date for domestic students, 2/1 for international students; for spring admission, 10/15 priority date for domestic students, 10/15 for international students. Applications are processed on a rolling basis. Application fee: $75. Electronic applications accepted. *Expenses: Tuition:* Part-time $1206 per credit. *Financial support:* Fellowships with full tuition reimbursements and teaching assistantships with full and partial tuition reimbursements available. *Unit head:* Dr. James Haywood Rolling, Jr., Director, 315-443-2355, E-mail: jrolling@syr.edu. *Application contact:* Laurie Deyo, Graduate Recruiter, School of Education, 315-443-2505, E-mail: e-gradrcrt@syr.edu. Web site: http://soeweb.syr.edu/future/degree_programs/masters_degrees.aspx.

Teachers College, Columbia University, Graduate Faculty of Education, Department of Arts and Humanities, Program in Art and Art Education, New York, NY 10027. Offers Ed M, MA, Ed D, Ed DCT. *Accreditation:* NCATE. Part-time and evening/weekend programs available. *Faculty:* 3 full-time (2 women), 16 part-time/adjunct (11 women). *Students:* 33 full-time (27 women), 101 part-time (90 women); includes 30 minority (3 Black or African American, non-Hispanic/Latino; 13 Asian, non-Hispanic/Latino; 14 Hispanic/Latino), 19 international. Average age 36. 74 applicants, 69% accepted, 26 enrolled. In 2011, 41 master's, 16 doctorates awarded. *Degree requirements:* For doctorate, variable foreign language requirement, thesis/dissertation. *Entrance requirements:* For master's, portfolio; for doctorate, portfolio, five years of professional experience in arts/museum/studio education. Additional exam requirements/recommendations for international students: Required—TOEFL (minimum score 600 paper-based; 250 computer-based; 100 iBT). *Application deadline:* For fall admission, 1/2 priority date for domestic students; for spring admission, 11/1 for domestic students. Applications are processed on a rolling basis. Application fee: $65. *Financial support:* Research assistantships, teaching assistantships, career-related internships or fieldwork, Federal Work-Study, institutionally sponsored loans, and tuition waivers (full and partial) available. Support available to part-time students. Financial award application deadline: 2/1. *Faculty research:* Learning and transfer of learning in the arts, instructional methods in the arts, role of artists in the education of children, cultural experiences in arts education, twentieth century and contemporary arts practice. *Unit head:* Prof. Judith M. Burton, Program Coordinator, 212-678-3336, E-mail: burton@exchange.tc.columbia.edu. *Application contact:* Thomas P. Rock, Director of Admissions, 212-678-3083, Fax: 212-678-4171, E-mail: rock@tc.edu. Web site: http://www.tc.edu/a%26h/ArtEd/.

Temple University, Tyler School of Art, Department of Art and Art Education, Philadelphia, PA 19122-6096. Offers Ed M. *Faculty:* 5 full-time (2 women). *Students:* 12 full-time (11 women), 7 part-time (6 women); includes 3 minority (1 Black or African American, non-Hispanic/Latino; 2 Asian, non-Hispanic/Latino). Average age 30. 14 applicants, 36% accepted, 4 enrolled. In 2011, 10 master's awarded. *Degree requirements:* For master's, paper, portfolio review. *Entrance requirements:* For master's, GRE or MAT, minimum GPA of 3.0, slide portfolio, 40 credits in studio art, 9 credits in art history. Additional exam requirements/recommendations for international students: Required—TOEFL (minimum score 550 paper-based; 213 computer-based; 79 iBT). *Application deadline:* For fall admission, 4/1 for domestic students, 12/15 for international students; for spring admission, 11/1 for domestic students, 8/1 for international students. Application fee: $50. Electronic applications accepted. *Expenses:* Tuition, state resident: full-time $12,366; part-time $687 per credit hour. Tuition, nonresident: full-time $17,298; part-time $961 per credit hour. *Required fees:* $590; $213 per year. *Financial support:* Research assistantships with full tuition reimbursements, teaching assistantships, and Federal Work-Study available. Support available to part-time students. Financial award application deadline: 1/15; financial award applicants required to submit FAFSA. *Unit head:* Dr. William Yalowitz, Chair, 215-777-9763, E-mail: yalowitz@temple.edu. *Application contact:* Carmina Cianciulli, Assistant Dean for Admissions, 215-782-2875, Fax: 215-782-2711, E-mail: tylerart@temple.edu. Web site: http://www.temple.edu/tyler/arted/.

Texas Tech University, Graduate School, College of Visual and Performing Arts, School of Art, Lubbock, TX 79409. Offers art (MFA); art education (MAE); art history (MA). *Accreditation:* NASAD (one or more programs are accredited). Part-time programs available. *Faculty:* 31 full-time (15 women). *Students:* 32 full-time (12 women), 27 part-time (21 women); includes 11 minority (1 Black or African American, non-Hispanic/Latino; 1 Asian, non-Hispanic/Latino; 8 Hispanic/Latino; 1 Two or more races, non-Hispanic/Latino), 5 international. Average age 34. 52 applicants, 40% accepted, 9 enrolled. In 2011, 21 master's awarded. *Degree requirements:* For master's, thesis (for some programs). *Entrance requirements:* For master's, GRE General Test. Additional exam requirements/recommendations for international students: Required—TOEFL (minimum score 550 paper-based; 213 computer-based; 79 iBT). *Application deadline:* For fall admission, 6/1 priority date for domestic students, 1/15 for international students; for spring admission, 9/1 priority date for domestic students, 6/15 for international students. Applications are processed on a rolling basis. Application fee: $50 ($75 for international students). Electronic applications accepted. *Expenses:* Tuition, state resident: full-time $5899; part-time $245.80 per credit hour. Tuition, nonresident: full-time $13,411; part-time $558.80 per credit hour. *Required fees:* $2680.60; $86.50 per credit hour. $920.30 per semester. *Financial support:* In 2011–12, 34 students received support. Application deadline: 4/15; applicants required to submit FAFSA. *Faculty research:* Studio art, art history, art education. *Unit head:* Prof. Tina Fuentes, Director, 806-742-3825 Ext. 223, Fax: 806-742-1971, E-mail: tina.fuentes@ttu.edu. *Application contact:* Ryan Scheckel, Academic Advisor, 806-742-3825 Ext. 222, Fax: 806-742-1971, E-mail: ryan.scheckel@ttu.edu. Web site: http://www.art.ttu.edu.

Towson University, Arts Integration Institute, Towson, MD 21252-0001. Offers Postbaccalaureate Certificate. Program offered jointly with The Johns Hopkins

University and University of Maryland, College Park. *Students:* 18 part-time (all women); includes 1 minority (Black or African American, non-Hispanic/Latino). *Expenses:* Tuition, state resident: part-time $337 per credit. Tuition, nonresident: part-time $709 per credit. *Required fees:* $99 per credit. *Unit head:* Susan Rotkovitz, Program Director, 410-704-3658, E-mail: srotkovitz@towson.edu.

Towson University, Program in Art Education, Towson, MD 21252-0001. Offers M Ed. *Accreditation:* NCATE. Part-time and evening/weekend programs available. *Students:* 1 full-time (0 women), 36 part-time (33 women); includes 4 minority (3 Black or African American, non-Hispanic/Latino; 1 Asian, non-Hispanic/Latino). *Degree requirements:* For master's, thesis optional, research project. *Entrance requirements:* For master's, bachelor's degree/certification in art education, minimum GPA of 3.0 or certified public school teacher with evidence of undergraduate coursework. *Application deadline:* Applications are processed on a rolling basis. Application fee: $50. Electronic applications accepted. *Expenses:* Tuition, state resident: part-time $337 per credit. Tuition, nonresident: part-time $709 per credit. *Required fees:* $99 per credit. *Financial support:* Federal Work-Study and unspecified assistantships available. Financial award application deadline: 4/1; financial award applicants required to submit FAFSA. *Unit head:* Ray Martens, Graduate Program Director, 410-704-3819, Fax: 410-704-2810, E-mail: rmartens@towson.edu. Web site: http://www.towson.edu/users/jbates/arteducation/.

Troy University, Graduate School, College of Education, Program in Teacher Education-Multiple Levels, Troy, AL 36082. Offers art education (MS); gifted education (MS); instrumental (MS); physical education (MS); reading specialist (MS); vocal/choral (MS). Part-time and evening/weekend programs available. *Faculty:* 6 full-time (4 women). *Students:* 6 full-time (4 women), 20 part-time (10 women); includes 3 minority (all Black or African American, non-Hispanic/Latino). Average age 30. 12 applicants, 83% accepted, 5 enrolled. In 2011, 13 master's awarded. *Degree requirements:* For master's, comprehensive exam, thesis. *Entrance requirements:* For master's, minimum GPA of 2.5. Additional exam requirements/recommendations for international students: Required—TOEFL (minimum score 523 paper-based; 193 computer-based; 70 iBT), IELTS (minimum score 6). *Application deadline:* Applications are processed on a rolling basis. Application fee: $50. Electronic applications accepted. *Expenses:* Tuition, state resident: full-time $6960; part-time $290 per credit hour. Tuition, nonresident: full-time $13,920; part-time $580 per credit hour. *Required fees:* $386 per term. *Financial support:* Available to part-time students. Applicants required to submit FAFSA. *Unit head:* Dr. Charlotte S. Minnick, Director, Teacher Education, 334-670-3544, Fax: 334-670-3548, E-mail: csminnick@troy.edu. *Application contact:* Brenda K. Campbell, Director of Graduate Admissions, 334-670-3178, Fax: 334-670-3733, E-mail: bcamp@troy.edu.

The University of Alabama at Birmingham, College of Arts and Sciences, School of Education, Program in Arts Education, Birmingham, AL 35294. Offers MA Ed. *Accreditation:* NCATE. *Degree requirements:* For master's, thesis optional. *Entrance requirements:* For master's, GRE General Test, MAT, or NTE, minimum GPA of 3.0. *Application deadline:* Applications are processed on a rolling basis. Electronic applications accepted. *Expenses:* Tuition, state resident: full-time $5922; part-time $309 per hour. Tuition, nonresident: full-time $13,428; part-time $726 per hour. Tuition and fees vary according to program. *Unit head:* Dr. Lynn Kirkland, Chair, 205-934-8358. Web site: http://www.uab.edu/ci/art-education-home.

The University of Arizona, College of Fine Arts, School of Art, Program in Art Education, Tucson, AZ 85721. Offers MA. *Accreditation:* NASAD. *Faculty:* 30 full-time (14 women), 3 part-time/adjunct (all women). *Students:* 38 full-time (22 women), 6 part-time (3 women); includes 6 minority (1 American Indian or Alaska Native, non-Hispanic/Latino; 5 Two or more races, non-Hispanic/Latino), 4 international. Average age 34. 21 applicants, 81% accepted, 12 enrolled. In 2011, 13 master's awarded. *Degree requirements:* For master's, thesis. *Entrance requirements:* For master's, portfolio, resume, autobiography, 3 letters of reference, writing sample. Additional exam requirements/recommendations for international students: Required—TOEFL (minimum score 550 paper-based; 213 computer-based; 79 iBT). *Application deadline:* For fall admission, 2/1 for domestic students, 12/1 for international students; for spring admission, 10/1 for domestic students, 9/1 for international students. Applications are processed on a rolling basis. Application fee: $75. Electronic applications accepted. *Expenses:* Tuition, state resident: full-time $10,840. Tuition, nonresident: full-time $25,802. *Financial support:* Career-related internships or fieldwork, Federal Work-Study, institutionally sponsored loans, scholarships/grants, tuition waivers (full and partial), and unspecified assistantships available. Support available to part-time students. Financial award application deadline: 4/1; financial award applicants required to submit FAFSA. *Faculty research:* Artistic styles, visual perception, integration of arts into elementary curricula, aesthetics of the vanishing roadsides of America. *Unit head:* Dr. Lynn Beudert, Chair, 520-626-7639, Fax: 520-621-2955, E-mail: lynng@email.arizona.edu. *Application contact:* Megan Bartel, Graduate Coordinator, 520-621-8518, E-mail: mbartel@email.arizona.edu. Web site: http://www.arts.arizona.edu/arted/grad.html.

University of Arkansas at Little Rock, Graduate School, College of Arts, Humanities, and Social Science, Department of Art, Little Rock, AR 72204-1099. Offers art education (MA); art history (MA); studio art (MA). *Accreditation:* NASAD. Part-time programs available. *Degree requirements:* For master's, 4 foreign languages, oral exam, oral defense of thesis or exhibit. *Entrance requirements:* For master's, portfolio review or term paper evaluation, minimum GPA of 2.7.

The University of British Columbia, Faculty of Education, Department of Curriculum and Pedagogy, Vancouver, BC V6T 1Z4, Canada. Offers art education (M Ed, MA); business education (MA); curriculum studies (M Ed, MA, PhD); home economics education (M Ed, MA); math education (M Ed, MA); music education (M Ed, MA); physical education (M Ed, MA); science education (M Ed, MA); social studies education (M Ed, MA); technology studies education (M Ed, MA). Part-time programs available. *Degree requirements:* For master's, thesis (MA); for doctorate, comprehensive exam, thesis/dissertation. *Entrance requirements:* Additional exam requirements/recommendations for international students: Required—TOEFL (minimum score 580 paper-based; 237 computer-based; 92 iBT). Electronic applications accepted. *Expenses:* Contact institution. *Faculty research:* School subjects, teaching and learning.

University of Central Florida, College of Education, School of Teaching, Learning, and Leadership, Program in Art Education, Orlando, FL 32816. Offers teacher education (MAT); teacher leadership (M Ed). *Accreditation:* NCATE. Part-time and evening/weekend programs available. *Students:* 4 full-time (3 women), 16 part-time (14 women); includes 2 minority (1 Black or African American, non-Hispanic/Latino; 1 Hispanic/Latino). Average age 32. 4 applicants, 75% accepted, 1 enrolled. In 2011, 6 master's awarded. *Degree requirements:* For master's, thesis or alternative, research report, internship (MA). *Entrance requirements:* Additional exam requirements/recommendations for international students: Required—TOEFL. *Application deadline:* For fall admission, 7/15 for domestic students; for spring admission, 12/1 for domestic students. Application fee: $30. Electronic applications accepted. *Expenses:* Tuition, state resident: part-time $277.08 per credit hour. Tuition, nonresident: part-time $277.08 per credit hour. Part-time tuition and fees vary according to degree level and program. *Financial support:* Fellowships with partial tuition reimbursements, research assistantships with tuition reimbursements, teaching assistantships with partial tuition reimbursements, career-related internships or fieldwork, Federal Work-Study, institutionally sponsored loans, tuition waivers (partial), and unspecified assistantships available. Financial award application deadline: 3/1; financial award applicants required to submit FAFSA. *Unit head:* Dr. Janet B. Andreasen, Program Coordinator, 407-823-5430, E-mail: janet.andreasen@ucf.edu. *Application contact:* Barbara Rodriguez, Director, Admissions and Registration, 407-823-2766, Fax: 407-823-6442, E-mail: gradadmissions@ucf.edu. Web site: http://education.ucf.edu/departments.cfm.

University of Cincinnati, Graduate School, College of Design, Architecture, Art, and Planning, School of Art, Program in Art Education, Cincinnati, OH 45221. Offers MA. *Accreditation:* NASAD; NCATE. *Entrance requirements:* For master's, MAT. Electronic applications accepted.

University of Dayton, Department of Teacher Education, Dayton, OH 45469-1300. Offers adolescent/young adult (MS Ed); art education (MS Ed); early childhood education (MS Ed); early childhood leadership advocacy (MS Ed); inclusive early childhood (MS Ed); interdisciplinary education (MS Ed); intervention specialist education, mild/moderate (MS Ed); literacy (MS Ed); middle childhood (MS Ed); multi-age education (MS Ed); music education (MS Ed); teacher as leader (MS Ed); technology in education (MS Ed). Part-time and evening/weekend programs available. Postbaccalaureate distance learning degree programs offered (no on-campus study). *Faculty:* 15 full-time (11 women), 22 part-time/adjunct (20 women). *Students:* 41 full-time (29 women), 95 part-time (87 women); includes 13 minority (9 Black or African American, non-Hispanic/Latino; 1 Asian, non-Hispanic/Latino; 3 Hispanic/Latino), 9 international. Average age 32. 111 applicants, 55% accepted, 38 enrolled. In 2011, 97 degrees awarded. *Degree requirements:* For master's, thesis, capstone research project. *Entrance requirements:* For master's, GRE General Test, minimum GPA of 2.75. Additional exam requirements/recommendations for international students: Required—TOEFL (minimum score 550 paper-based; 213 computer-based; 80 iBT). *Application deadline:* For fall admission, 3/1 priority date for domestic students, 3/1 for international students; for winter admission, 7/1 for international students; for spring admission, 1/1 for international students. Applications are processed on a rolling basis. Application fee: $0 ($50 for international students). Electronic applications accepted. *Expenses:* Contact institution. *Financial support:* In 2011–12, 5 research assistantships with full and partial tuition reimbursements (averaging $8,470 per year) were awarded; career-related internships or fieldwork, institutionally sponsored loans, health care benefits, and unspecified assistantships also available. Financial award applicants required to submit FAFSA. *Faculty research:* Diversity, literacy, art representation by young children, preservice teacher preparation. *Unit head:* Dr. Katie A. Kinnucan-Welsch, Chair, 937-229-3346. *Application contact:* Alexsandar Popovski, Enrollment Management Administrator, 937-229-2357, Fax: 937-229-4729, E-mail: alex.popovski@notes.udayton.edu.

University of Georgia, College of Education, Program in Art Education, Athens, GA 30602. Offers MA Ed, Ed D, PhD, Ed S. *Accreditation:* NASAD; NCATE. *Students:* 13 full-time (12 women), 17 part-time (15 women); includes 2 minority (1 Black or African American, non-Hispanic/Latino; 1 Asian, non-Hispanic/Latino). Average age 31. 14 applicants, 64% accepted, 5 enrolled. In 2011, 6 master's, 1 doctorate awarded. *Degree requirements:* For doctorate, thesis/dissertation. *Entrance requirements:* For master's, GRE General Test, MAT; for doctorate, GRE General Test; for Ed S, GRE General Test or MAT. *Application deadline:* For fall admission, 7/1 priority date for domestic students; for spring admission, 11/15 for domestic students. Application fee: $50. Electronic applications accepted. *Financial support:* Fellowships, research assistantships, teaching assistantships, and unspecified assistantships available. *Unit head:* Prof. Georgia Strange, Department Head, 706-542-1600, E-mail: strange@uga.edu. *Application contact:* Dr. Carole Henry, Graduate Coordinator, 706-542-1624, Fax: 706-542-0226, E-mail: ckhenry@uga.edu. Web site: http://www.art.uga.edu/.

University of Idaho, College of Graduate Studies, College of Art and Architecture, Moscow, ID 83844-2461. Offers architecture (M Arch, MS), including community planning (MS), computing and visualization studies (MS), environment and behavior studies (MS), urban design (MS); art (MFA), including interactive and information design, interface, painting, photography/digital imaging, printmaking, sculpture; landscape architecture (MLA); studio art (MFA), including graphic design; teaching art (MAT). *Accreditation:* NASAD. *Faculty:* 14 full-time, 1 part-time/adjunct. *Students:* 113 full-time, 7 part-time. Average age 27. In 2011, 47 master's awarded. *Application deadline:* For fall admission, 8/1 for domestic students; for spring admission, 12/15 for domestic students. Applications are processed on a rolling basis. Application fee: $60. Electronic applications accepted. *Expenses:* Tuition, state resident: full-time $3874; part-time $334 per credit hour. Tuition, nonresident: full-time $16,394; part-time $861 per credit hour. *Required fees:* $2808; $99 per credit hour. Tuition and fees vary according to program. *Financial support:* Applicants required to submit FAFSA. *Faculty research:* Sustainability in communities, urban research, virtual technology, bioregional planning, environment and behavior interaction. *Unit head:* Dr. Mark Elison Hoversten, Dean, 208-885-5423, E-mail: caa@uidaho.edu. *Application contact:* Erick Larson, Director of Graduate Admissions, 208-885-4723, E-mail: gadms@uidaho.edu. Web site: http://www.uidaho.edu/caa.

University of Illinois at Urbana–Champaign, Graduate College, College of Fine and Applied Arts, School of Art and Design, Program in Art Education, Champaign, IL 61820. Offers Ed M, MA, PhD. *Accreditation:* NASAD. *Students:* 18 full-time (15 women), 5 part-time (1 woman); includes 2 minority (both Asian, non-Hispanic/Latino), 9 international. 25 applicants, 24% accepted, 6 enrolled. In 2011, 7 master's, 1 doctorate awarded. *Entrance requirements:* For master's, minimum GPA of 3.0. Additional exam requirements/recommendations for international students: Required—TOEFL (minimum score 550 paper-based; 213 computer-based; 79 iBT). *Application deadline:* Applications are processed on a rolling basis. Application fee: $75 ($90 for international students). Electronic applications accepted. *Financial support:* Fellowships, research assistantships, teaching assistantships, and tuition waivers (full and partial) available. *Unit head:* Joseph Squier, Chair, 217-333-0855, Fax: 217-244-7688, E-mail: squier@illinois.edu. *Application contact:* Marsha Biddle, Coordinator of Graduate Academic Affairs, 217-333-0642, Fax: 217-244-7688, E-mail: mbiddle@illinois.edu. Web site: http://www.art.illinois.edu.

University of Indianapolis, Graduate Programs, School of Education, Indianapolis, IN 46227-3697. Offers art education (MAT); biology (MAT); chemistry (MAT); curriculum and instruction (MA); earth sciences (MAT); education (MA, MAT); educational leadership (MA); elementary education (MA); English (MAT); French (MAT); math (MAT); physical education (MAT); physics (MAT); secondary education (MA), including art education, education, English education, social studies education; social studies (MAT); Spanish (MAT). *Accreditation:* NCATE. Part-time and evening/weekend programs available. *Faculty:* 3 full-time (2 women), 3 part-time/adjunct (2 women). *Students:* 32 full-time (18 women), 97 part-time (56 women); includes 22 minority (20 Black or African American, non-Hispanic/Latino; 1 Asian, non-Hispanic/Latino; 1 Hispanic/Latino), 3 international. Average age 33. In 2011, 78 master's awarded. *Entrance requirements:* For master's, GRE Subject Test, PRAXIS I, minimum GPA of 2.5, 3 letters of recommendation, interview, writing exercise. Additional exam requirements/recommendations for international students: Required—TOEFL (minimum score 550 paper-based; 213 computer-based). *Application deadline:* Applications are processed on a rolling basis. Application fee: $50. Tuition and fees vary according to degree level and program. *Financial support:* Federal Work-Study available. Financial award application deadline: 5/1; financial award applicants required to submit FAFSA. *Faculty research:* Assessment of teacher education, perceptions of prospective teachers by parents. *Unit head:* Dr. Kathy Moran, Dean, 317-788-3285, Fax: 317-788-3300, E-mail: kmoran@uindy.edu. *Application contact:* Jeni Kirby, 317-788-2113, E-mail: kirbyj@uindy.edu. Web site: http://education.uindy.edu/.

The University of Iowa, Graduate College, College of Education, Department of Teaching and Learning, Program in Secondary Education, Iowa City, IA 52242-1316. Offers art education (PhD); curriculum and supervision (PhD); curriculum supervision (MA); developmental reading (MA); English education (MA, MAT); foreign language education (MA, MAT); foreign language/ESL education (PhD); language, literature and culture (PhD); math education (PhD); mathematics education (MA); social studies (MA, PhD). *Degree requirements:* For master's, thesis optional, exam; for doctorate, comprehensive exam, thesis/dissertation. *Entrance requirements:* For master's and doctorate, GRE General Test, minimum GPA of 3.0. Additional exam requirements/recommendations for international students: Required—TOEFL (minimum score 550 paper-based; 213 computer-based; 81 iBT). Electronic applications accepted.

The University of Kansas, Graduate Studies, College of Liberal Arts and Sciences, Department of Visual Art, Program in Visual Art Education, Lawrence, KS 66045. Offers MA. Part-time programs available. *Faculty:* 3 full-time (2 women). *Students:* 14 full-time (all women), 5 part-time (all women); includes 2 minority (1 Black or African American, non-Hispanic/Latino; 1 Two or more races, non-Hispanic/Latino). Average age 27. 17 applicants, 82% accepted, 12 enrolled. In 2011, 3 master's awarded. *Degree requirements:* For master's, thesis or alternative. *Entrance requirements:* For master's, portfolio, 3 letters of recommendation, minimum GPA of 3.0. Additional exam requirements/recommendations for international students: Required—TOEFL (minimum score 570 paper-based; 230 computer-based) or IELTS (minimum score 6.5). *Application deadline:* For fall admission, 5/1 for domestic and international students; for spring admission, 10/15 for domestic and international students. Application fee: $55 ($65 for international students). Electronic applications accepted. Tuition and fees vary according to course load, campus/location, program and reciprocity agreements. *Financial support:* Teaching assistantships with full tuition reimbursements, Federal Work-Study, scholarships/grants, and unspecified assistantships available. Financial award application deadline: 5/1. *Faculty research:* Museum education, art educator education. *Unit head:* Prof. Mary Anne Jordan, Chairperson, 785-864-4401, E-mail: majordan@ku.edu. *Application contact:* Norman R. Akers, Director, 785-864-2957, Fax: 785-864-4404, E-mail: normanakers2@ku.edu.

University of Kentucky, Graduate School, College of Fine Arts, Program in Art Education, Lexington, KY 40506-0032. Offers MA. *Degree requirements:* For master's, comprehensive exam, thesis optional. *Entrance requirements:* For master's, GRE General Test, minimum undergraduate GPA of 2.75. Additional exam requirements/recommendations for international students: Required—TOEFL (minimum score 550 paper-based; 213 computer-based). Electronic applications accepted. *Faculty research:* Multicultural art education, women's issues in art education, lifelong learning in the arts, the artist-teacher, art teaching as a form of art, place and art, children's home art and creativity as a basis for school art instruction.

University of Louisville, Graduate School, College of Education and Human Development, Department of Teaching and Learning, Louisville, KY 40292-0001. Offers art education (MAT); curriculum and instruction (PhD); early elementary education (MAT); instructional technology (M Ed); interdisciplinary early childhood education (MAT); middle school education (MAT); music education (MAT); reading education (M Ed); secondary education (MAT); special education (M Ed, MAT); teacher leadership (M Ed). Part-time and evening/weekend programs available. *Degree requirements:* For doctorate, comprehensive exam, thesis/dissertation. *Entrance requirements:* For master's, GRE General Test, PRAXIS II (for some programs); for doctorate, GRE General Test. Additional exam requirements/recommendations for international students: Required—TOEFL (minimum score 560 paper-based; 210 computer-based; 83 iBT). Electronic applications accepted. *Expenses:* Tuition, state resident: full-time $9692; part-time $539 per credit hour. Tuition, nonresident: full-time $20,168; part-time $1121 per credit hour. Tuition and fees vary according to program and reciprocity agreements. *Faculty research:* Mathematics teacher education and ongoing professional development in pedagogy and content knowledge; development of literacy, including early literacy in science and mathematics and literacy development for English language learners; immersive visualizations for promoting STEM education from nanoscience to cosmic scales; evidence-based practices for students with disabilities; urban education, including teacher response to intervention systems in schools and cross-cultural competence.

University of Maryland, Baltimore County, Graduate School, College of Arts, Humanities and Social Sciences, Department of Education, Program in Teaching, Baltimore, MD 21250. Offers early childhood education (MAT); elementary education (MAT); secondary education (MAT), including social studies; secondary education (MAT), including art, biology, chemistry, dance, earth/space science, English, foreign language, mathematics, music, physics, theatre. Part-time and evening/weekend programs available. *Faculty:* 24 full-time (18 women), 25 part-time/adjunct (19 women). *Students:* 46 full-time (35 women), 64 part-time (39 women); includes 24 minority (8 Black or African American, non-Hispanic/Latino; 7 Asian, non-Hispanic/Latino; 6 Hispanic/Latino; 1 Native Hawaiian or other Pacific Islander, non-Hispanic/Latino; 2 Two or more races, non-Hispanic/Latino), 4 international. Average age 31. 88 applicants, 57% accepted, 39 enrolled. In 2011, 106 master's awarded. *Degree requirements:* For master's, comprehensive exam (for some programs), thesis (for some programs). *Entrance requirements:* For master's, PRAXIS I or GRE (minimum score of 1000), minimum GPA of 3.0. Additional exam requirements/recommendations for international students: Required—TOEFL. *Application deadline:* For fall admission, 6/1 for domestic students; for spring admission, 11/1 for domestic students. Applications are processed on a rolling basis. Application fee: $50. Electronic applications accepted. *Financial support:* In 2011–12, 6 students received support, including teaching assistantships with full and partial tuition reimbursements available (averaging $12,000 per year); career-related internships or fieldwork, Federal Work-Study, scholarships/grants, tuition waivers, and unspecified assistantships also available. Financial award application deadline: 3/1. *Faculty research:* STEM teacher education, culturally sensitive pedagogy, ESOL/bilingual education, early childhood education, language, literacy and culture. *Unit head:* Dr. Susan M. Blunck, Graduate Program Director, 410-455-2869, Fax: 410-455-3986, E-mail: blunck@umbc.edu. *Application contact:* Cheryl Johnson, 410-455-3388, E-mail: blackwel@umbc.edu. Web site: http://www.umbc.edu/education/.

University of Massachusetts Amherst, Graduate School, College of Humanities and Fine Arts, Department of Art, Programs in Art, Amherst, MA 01003. Offers art education (MA); studio art (MFA). Part-time programs available. *Students:* 17 full-time (10 women), 13 part-time (8 women); includes 4 minority (2 Asian, non-Hispanic/Latino; 2 Hispanic/Latino), 1 international. Average age 34. 77 applicants, 21% accepted, 10 enrolled. In 2011, 12 master's awarded. *Degree requirements:* For master's, comprehensive exam (for some programs), thesis (for some programs). *Entrance requirements:* For master's, portfolio. Additional exam requirements/recommendations for international students: Required—TOEFL (minimum score 530 paper-based; 213 computer-based; 80 iBT), IELTS (minimum score 6.5). *Application deadline:* For fall admission, 2/1 for domestic and international students. Applications are processed on a rolling basis. Application fee: $50 ($65 for international students). Electronic applications accepted. Tuition and fees vary according to course load, campus/location and program. *Financial support:* Fellowships with full and partial tuition reimbursements, research assistantships with full tuition reimbursements, teaching assistantships with full tuition reimbursements, career-related internships or fieldwork, Federal Work-Study, scholarships/grants, traineeships, health care benefits, tuition waivers (full and partial), and unspecified assistantships available. Support available to part-time students. Financial award application deadline: 2/1. *Unit head:* Dr. Young Min Moon, Graduate Program Director, 413-545-1903, Fax: 413-545-3929. *Application contact:* Lindsay DeSantis, Supervisor of Admissions, 413-545-0722, Fax: 413-577-0100, E-mail: gradadm@grad.umass.edu. Web site: http://www.umass.edu/art/studio_arts.html.

University of Massachusetts Dartmouth, Graduate School, College of Visual and Performing Arts, Program in Art Education, North Dartmouth, MA 02747-2300. Offers MAE. *Accreditation:* NASAD. Part-time programs available. *Faculty:* 3 full-time (all women), 2 part-time/adjunct (1 woman). *Students:* 5 full-time (4 women), 23 part-time (19 women); includes 2 minority (1 Asian, non-Hispanic/Latino; 1 Hispanic/Latino), 1 international. Average age 33. 5 applicants, 100% accepted, 4 enrolled. In 2011, 9 degrees awarded. *Degree requirements:* For master's, thesis or alternative. *Entrance requirements:* For master's, Massachusetts Tests for Educator Licensure (MTEL), interview, portfolio, minimum GPA of 2.75, 3 letters of recommendation, statement of intent, resume. Additional exam requirements/recommendations for international students: Required—TOEFL (minimum score 533 paper-based; 200 computer-based; 72 iBT). *Application deadline:* For fall admission, 8/1 priority date for domestic students, 7/1 for international students; for spring admission, 10/15 priority date for domestic students, 9/15 for international students. Applications are processed on a rolling basis. Application fee: $40 ($60 for international students). Electronic applications accepted. *Expenses:* Tuition, state resident: full-time $2071; part-time $86.29 per credit. Tuition, nonresident: full-time $8099; part-time $337.46 per credit. *Required fees:* $438.58 per credit. Part-time tuition and fees vary according to class time, course load, degree level and reciprocity agreements. *Financial support:* In 2011–12, 5 teaching assistantships with partial tuition reimbursements (averaging $2,850 per year) were awarded; research assistantships, Federal Work-Study, and unspecified assistantships also available. Financial award application deadline: 3/1; financial award applicants required to submit FAFSA. *Faculty research:* Creative art, in-service and pre-service teachers, museum partnership in education, authentic visual arts integration . *Total annual research expenditures:* $752. *Unit head:* Dr. Cathy Smilan, Graduate Program Director, 508-910-6594, Fax: 508-999-8901, E-mail: csmilan@umassd.edu. *Application contact:* Elan Turcotte-Shamski, Graduate Admissions Officer, 508-999-8604, Fax: 508-999-8183, E-mail: graduate@umassd.edu. Web site: http://www.umassd.edu/cvpa/graduate/arteducation.

University of Minnesota, Twin Cities Campus, Graduate School, College of Education and Human Development, Department of Curriculum and Instruction, Minneapolis, MN 55455-0213. Offers art education (M Ed, MA, PhD); children's literature (M Ed, MA, PhD); curriculum and instruction (MA, PhD); early childhood education (M Ed, PhD); elementary education (M Ed, MA, PhD); English education (MA, PhD); environmental education (M Ed); family education (M Ed, MA, Ed D, PhD); instructional systems and technology (M Ed, MA, PhD); language arts (MA, PhD); language immersion education (Certificate); literacy education (MA); mathematics education (MA, PhD); reading education (MA, PhD); science education (MA, PhD); second languages and cultures education (MA, PhD); social studies education (MA, PhD); teaching (M Ed), including Chinese, earth science, elementary special education, English, English as a second language, French, German, Hebrew, Japanese, life sciences, mathematics, middle school science, science, second languages and cultures, social studies, Spanish; technology enhanced learning (Certificate); writing education (M Ed, MA, PhD). *Faculty:* 34 full-time (22 women). *Students:* 433 full-time (319 women), 310 part-time (239 women); includes 97 minority (34 Black or African American, non-Hispanic/Latino; 6 American Indian or Alaska Native, non-Hispanic/Latino; 35 Asian, non-Hispanic/Latino; 22 Hispanic/Latino), 47 international. Average age 33. 660 applicants, 68% accepted, 395 enrolled. In 2011, 518 master's, 19 doctorates, 14 other advanced degrees awarded. Application fee: $55. *Financial support:* In 2011–12, 6 fellowships (averaging $9,308 per year), 39 research assistantships with full tuition reimbursements (averaging $8,301 per year), 61 teaching assistantships with full tuition reimbursements (averaging $9,206 per year) were awarded. *Faculty research:* Teaching and learning; quality of education; influence of cultural, linguistic, social, political, technological and economic factors on teaching, learning and educational research; relationship between educational practice and a democratic and just society. *Total annual research expenditures:* $943,365. *Unit head:* Dr. Nina Asher, Chair, 612-624-4772, Fax: 612-624-1357, E-mail: nasher@umn.edu. *Application contact:* Dr. Jennifer Engler, Assistant Dean, 612-626-2887, Fax: 612-626-7496, E-mail: engle009@umn.edu. Web site: http://www.cehd.umn.edu/ci.

University of Mississippi, Graduate School, College of Liberal Arts, Department of Art, Oxford, University, MS 38677. Offers art education (MA); art history (MA); fine arts (MFA). *Accreditation:* NASAD (one or more programs are accredited). Part-time programs available. *Students:* 16 full-time (6 women); includes 5 minority (3 Hispanic/Latino; 2 Two or more races, non-Hispanic/Latino), 1 international. *Degree requirements:* For master's, thesis (for some programs). *Entrance requirements:* For master's, GRE General Test, minimum GPA of 3.0. Additional exam requirements/recommendations for international students: Required—TOEFL. *Application deadline:* For fall admission, 3/1 for domestic students; for spring admission, 10/1 for domestic students. Applications are processed on a rolling basis. Application fee: $40. Electronic applications accepted. *Financial support:* Fellowships, scholarships/grants, and unspecified assistantships available. Financial award application deadline: 3/1; financial award applicants required to submit FAFSA. *Unit head:* Dr. Sheri Fleck Reith, Chair, 662-915-7193, Fax: 662-915-5013, E-mail: art@olemiss.edu. *Application contact:* Dr. Christy M. Wyandt, Associate Dean, 662-915-7474, Fax: 662-915-7577, E-mail: cwyandt@olemiss.edu.

University of Missouri, Graduate School, College of Education, Department of Learning, Teaching and Curriculum, Columbia, MO 65211. Offers agricultural education (M Ed, PhD, Ed S); art education (M Ed, PhD, Ed S); business and office education (M Ed, PhD, Ed S); early childhood education (M Ed, PhD, Ed S); elementary education (M Ed, PhD, Ed S); English education (M Ed, PhD, Ed S); foreign language education (M Ed, PhD, Ed S); health education and promotion (M Ed, PhD); learning and instruction (M Ed); marketing education (M Ed, PhD, Ed S); mathematics education (M Ed, PhD, Ed S); music education (M Ed, PhD, Ed S); reading education (M Ed, PhD, Ed S); science education (M Ed, PhD, Ed S); social studies education (M Ed, PhD, Ed S); vocational education (M Ed, PhD, Ed S). Part-time programs available. *Faculty:* 26 full-time (16 women), 3 part-time/adjunct (2 women). *Students:* 184 full-time (145 women), 276 part-time (215 women); includes 34 minority (10 Black or African American, non-Hispanic/Latino; 1 American Indian or Alaska Native, non-Hispanic/Latino; 7 Asian, non-Hispanic/Latino; 8 Hispanic/Latino; 8 Two or more races, non-

Hispanic/Latino), 39 international. Average age 32. 309 applicants, 76% accepted, 204 enrolled. In 2011, 232 master's, 8 doctorates, 2 other advanced degrees awarded. Terminal master's awarded for partial completion of doctoral program. *Degree requirements:* For doctorate, thesis/dissertation. *Entrance requirements:* For master's and Ed S, GRE General Test or MAT, minimum GPA of 3.0; for doctorate, GRE General Test, minimum GPA of 3.0. Additional exam requirements/recommendations for international students: Required—TOEFL (minimum score 600 paper-based; 250 computer-based; 100 iBT). Application fee: $55 ($75 for international students). Electronic applications accepted. *Expenses:* Tuition, state resident: full-time $5881. Tuition, nonresident: full-time $15,183. *Required fees:* $952. Tuition and fees vary according to campus/location and program. *Financial support:* Fellowships, research assistantships, teaching assistantships, and institutionally sponsored loans available. *Application contact:* Fran Colley, 573-882-6462, E-mail: colleyf@missouri.edu. Web site: http://education.missouri.edu/LTC/.

University of Nebraska at Kearney, Graduate Studies, College of Fine Arts and Humanities, Department of Art, Kearney, NE 68849-0001. Offers art education (MA Ed). *Accreditation:* NCATE. Part-time and evening/weekend programs available. *Degree requirements:* For master's, thesis optional. *Entrance requirements:* For master's, slide portfolio. Additional exam requirements/recommendations for international students: Required—TOEFL (minimum score 550 paper-based; 213 computer-based). Electronic applications accepted. *Faculty research:* Fibers, art education, kiln design construction and low-fire glaze.

University of New Mexico, Graduate School, College of Education, Department of Educational Specialties, Program in Art Education, Albuquerque, NM 87131-2039. Offers MA. *Accreditation:* NCATE. Part-time and evening/weekend programs available. *Students:* 21 full-time (17 women), 18 part-time (13 women); includes 18 minority (1 Black or African American, non-Hispanic/Latino; 2 American Indian or Alaska Native, non-Hispanic/Latino; 3 Asian, non-Hispanic/Latino; 10 Hispanic/Latino; 2 Two or more races, non-Hispanic/Latino), 1 international. Average age 35. 22 applicants, 50% accepted, 10 enrolled. In 2011, 4 degrees awarded. *Degree requirements:* For master's, comprehensive exam, thesis optional, participation in art exhibit. *Entrance requirements:* Additional exam requirements/recommendations for international students: Required—TOEFL. *Application deadline:* For fall admission, 3/30 for domestic students; for spring admission, 10/30 for domestic students. Application fee: $50. Electronic applications accepted. *Financial support:* In 2011–12, 20 students received support, including 1 fellowship (averaging $3,600 per year), 2 research assistantships with full tuition reimbursements available (averaging $12,139 per year); teaching assistantships, Federal Work-Study, institutionally sponsored loans, scholarships/grants, and unspecified assistantships also available. Financial award application deadline: 3/1; financial award applicants required to submit FAFSA. *Faculty research:* Studio in art education, visual culture, curricular issues regarding gender and sexual identity, archetypal thought in art education, teacher preparation. *Unit head:* Prof. Ruth Luckasson, Chair, 505-277-6510, Fax: 505-277-0576, E-mail: luckasson@unm.edu. *Application contact:* Dolores Mendoza, Information Contact, 505-277-4112, Fax: 505-277-0576, E-mail: arted@unm.edu. Web site: http://www.unm.edu/~arted.

The University of North Carolina at Charlotte, Graduate School, College of Education, Department of Middle, Secondary and K-12 Education, Charlotte, NC 28223-0001. Offers art education (MAT); curriculum and instruction (PhD); dance education (MAT); foreign language education (MAT); middle grades education (M Ed, MAT); music education (MAT); secondary education (M Ed, MAT); teaching English as a second language (M Ed); theatre education (MAT). *Faculty:* 18 full-time (9 women), 6 part-time/adjunct (4 women). *Students:* 1 (woman) full-time, 57 part-time (44 women); includes 11 minority (5 Black or African American, non-Hispanic/Latino; 1 American Indian or Alaska Native, non-Hispanic/Latino; 2 Asian, non-Hispanic/Latino; 2 Hispanic/Latino; 1 Two or more races, non-Hispanic/Latino). Average age 33. 19 applicants, 100% accepted, 16 enrolled. In 2011, 12 master's awarded. *Entrance requirements:* For master's, GRE or MAT. Additional exam requirements/recommendations for international students: Required—TOEFL (minimum score 557 paper-based; 220 computer-based; 83 iBT). *Application deadline:* For fall admission, 7/1 for domestic students, 5/1 for international students; for spring admission, 11/1 for domestic students, 10/1 for international students. Applications are processed on a rolling basis. Application fee: $65 ($75 for international students). Electronic applications accepted. *Expenses:* Tuition, state resident: full-time $3689. Tuition, nonresident: full-time $15,226. *Required fees:* $2198. Tuition and fees vary according to course load and program. *Financial support:* In 2011–12, 5 students received support, including 5 research assistantships (averaging $4,290 per year); career-related internships or fieldwork, institutionally sponsored loans, scholarships/grants, and unspecified assistantships also available. Support available to part-time students. Financial award application deadline: 4/1; financial award applicants required to submit FAFSA. *Total annual research expenditures:* $126,589. *Unit head:* Melba Spooner, Chair, 704-687-8704, Fax: 704-687-6430, E-mail: mcspoone@uncc.edu. *Application contact:* Kathy B. Giddings, Director of Graduate Admissions, 704-687-5503, Fax: 704-687-3279, E-mail: gradadm@uncc.edu. Web site: http://education.uncc.edu/mdsk.

The University of North Carolina at Pembroke, Graduate Studies, Department of Art, Pembroke, NC 28372-1510. Offers art education (MA, MAT). Part-time and evening/weekend programs available. *Degree requirements:* For master's, comprehensive exam, capstone show. *Entrance requirements:* For master's, GRE or MAT, minimum GPA of 3.0 in major or 2.5 overall. Additional exam requirements/recommendations for international students: Required—TOEFL. *Expenses:* Contact institution.

University of Northern Iowa, Graduate College, College of Humanities, Arts and Sciences, Department of Art, Cedar Falls, IA 50614. Offers art education (MA). *Accreditation:* NASAD. Part-time and evening/weekend programs available. *Students:* 1 applicant, 0% accepted. In 2011, 1 master's awarded. *Degree requirements:* For master's, comprehensive exam (for some programs), thesis or alternative. *Entrance requirements:* For master's, minimum GPA of 3.0, portfolio. Additional exam requirements/recommendations for international students: Required—TOEFL (minimum score 500 paper-based; 180 computer-based; 61 iBT). *Application deadline:* For fall admission, 8/1 priority date for domestic students. Applications are processed on a rolling basis. Application fee: $50 ($70 for international students). Electronic applications accepted. *Expenses:* Tuition, state resident: full-time $7476. Tuition, nonresident: full-time $16,410. *Required fees:* $942. *Financial support:* Career-related internships or fieldwork, Federal Work-Study, scholarships/grants, and tuition waivers (full and partial) available. Support available to part-time students. Financial award application deadline: 2/1. *Unit head:* Dr. Jeffery Byrd, Head/Professor, 319-273-2077, Fax: 319-273-7333, E-mail: jeffery.byrd@uni.edu. *Application contact:* Laurie S. Russell, Record Analyst, 319-273-2623, Fax: 319-273-2885, E-mail: laurie.russell@uni.edu. Web site: http://www.uni.edu/artdept/.

University of North Texas, Toulouse Graduate School, College of Visual Arts and Design, Department of Art Education and Art History, Denton, TX 76203. Offers art education (MA, PhD); art history (MA); art museum education (Certificate); arts leadership (Certificate). Part-time and evening/weekend programs available. *Degree requirements:* For master's, one foreign language, comprehensive exam (for some programs), thesis (for some programs); for doctorate, comprehensive exam, thesis/dissertation. *Entrance requirements:* For master's, GRE, writing sample, statement of purpose; for doctorate, GRE, master's degree in art education, writing sample, slides, statement of purpose. Additional exam requirements/recommendations for international students: Recommended—TOEFL (minimum score 550 paper-based; 213 computer-based; 79 iBT). *Expenses:* Tuition, state resident: part-time $100 per credit hour. Tuition, nonresident: part-time $413 per credit hour. *Faculty research:* Aesthetics, visual culture, arts leadership, British art, Latin American art, French art, Indian art, contemporary Arab art.

University of Rio Grande, Graduate School, Rio Grande, OH 45674. Offers classroom teaching (M Ed), including fine arts, learning disabilities, mathematics, reading education. *Accreditation:* NCATE. Part-time and evening/weekend programs available. *Degree requirements:* For master's, final research project, portfolio. *Entrance requirements:* For master's, minimum GPA of 2.7 in major, 2.5 overall. Additional exam requirements/recommendations for international students: Required—TOEFL. *Faculty research:* Interagency collaboration, reading and mathematics, learning styles, college access, literacy.

University of St. Francis, College of Education, Joliet, IL 60435-6169. Offers educational leadership (MS, Ed D); elementary education certification (M Ed); reading (MS); secondary education certification (M Ed), including English education, math education, science education, social studies education, visual arts education; special education (M Ed); teaching and learning (MS). *Accreditation:* NCATE. Part-time and evening/weekend programs available. Postbaccalaureate distance learning degree programs offered (no on-campus study). *Faculty:* 7 full-time (5 women), 21 part-time/adjunct (14 women). *Students:* 32 full-time (21 women), 230 part-time (175 women); includes 23 minority (7 Black or African American, non-Hispanic/Latino; 2 Asian, non-Hispanic/Latino; 13 Hispanic/Latino; 1 Two or more races, non-Hispanic/Latino), 1 international. Average age 32. 147 applicants, 60% accepted, 57 enrolled. In 2011, 156 master's awarded. *Entrance requirements:* For doctorate, master's degree, IL Type 75 or Principal's endorsement, interview. Additional exam requirements/recommendations for international students: Required—TOEFL (minimum score 550 paper-based; 213 computer-based). *Application deadline:* Applications are processed on a rolling basis. Application fee: $30. Electronic applications accepted. *Expenses:* Contact institution. *Financial support:* In 2011–12, 23 students received support. Federal Work-Study, scholarships/grants, tuition waivers (partial), and unspecified assistantships available. Support available to part-time students. Financial award applicants required to submit FAFSA. *Unit head:* Dr. John Gambro, Dean, 815-740-3829, Fax: 815-740-2264, E-mail: jgambro@stfrancis.edu. *Application contact:* Sandra Sloka, Director of Admissions for Graduate and Degree Completion Programs, 800-735-7500, Fax: 815-740-5032, E-mail: ssloka@stfrancis.edu. Web site: http://www.stfrancis.edu/academics/college-of-education/.

University of South Carolina, The Graduate School, College of Arts and Sciences, Department of Art, Program in Art Education, Columbia, SC 29208. Offers IMA, MA, MAT. IMA and MAT offered in cooperation with the College of Education. *Accreditation:* NCATE. *Degree requirements:* For master's, comprehensive exam, thesis (for some programs). *Entrance requirements:* For master's, GRE General Test or MAT, portfolio. Additional exam requirements/recommendations for international students: Required—TOEFL. Electronic applications accepted. *Faculty research:* Teaching art at the primary and secondary levels of education.

University of South Carolina, The Graduate School, College of Education, Department of Instruction and Teacher Education, Program in Secondary Education, Columbia, SC 29208. Offers art education (IMA, MAT); business education (IMA, MAT); English (MAT); foreign language (MAT); health education (MAT); mathematics (MAT); science (IMA, MAT); secondary (Ed D); secondary education (MT, PhD); social studies (MAT); theatre and speech (MAT). IMA and MT offered jointly with the subject areas. *Accreditation:* NCATE. *Degree requirements:* For master's, comprehensive exam, thesis (for some programs), foreign language (MA); for doctorate, one foreign language, comprehensive exam, thesis/dissertation. *Entrance requirements:* For master's, GRE General Test or MAT, teaching certificate (IMA, M Ed), interview; for doctorate, GRE General Test or MAT, interview. *Faculty research:* Middle school programs, professional development, school collaboration.

The University of Tennessee, Graduate School, College of Education, Health and Human Sciences, Program in Education, Knoxville, TN 37996. Offers art education (MS); counseling education (PhD); cultural studies in education (PhD); curriculum (MS, Ed S); curriculum, educational research and evaluation (Ed D, PhD); early childhood education (PhD); early childhood special education (MS); education of deaf and hard of hearing (MS); educational administration and policy studies (Ed D, PhD); educational administration and supervision (Ed S); educational psychology (Ed D, PhD); elementary education (MS, Ed S); elementary teaching (MS); English education (MS, Ed S); exercise science (PhD); foreign language/ESL education (MS, Ed S); instructional technology (MS, Ed D, PhD, Ed S); literacy, language and ESL education (PhD); literacy, language education, and ESL education (Ed D); mathematics education (MS, Ed S); modified and comprehensive special education (MS); reading education (MS, Ed S); school counseling (Ed S); school psychology (PhD, Ed S); science education (MS, Ed S); secondary teaching (MS); social foundations (MS); social science education (MS, Ed S); socio-cultural foundations of sports and education (PhD); special education (Ed S); teacher education (Ed D, PhD). *Accreditation:* NCATE. Part-time and evening/weekend programs available. *Degree requirements:* For master's and Ed S, thesis optional; for doctorate, variable foreign language requirement, thesis/dissertation. *Entrance requirements:* For master's, minimum GPA of 2.7; for doctorate and Ed S, GRE General Test, minimum GPA of 2.7. Additional exam requirements/recommendations for international students: Required—TOEFL. Electronic applications accepted. *Expenses:* Tuition, state resident: full-time $8332; part-time $464 per credit hour. Tuition, nonresident: full-time $25,174; part-time $1400 per credit hour. *Required fees:* $1162; $56 per credit hour. Tuition and fees vary according to program.

The University of Texas at Austin, Graduate School, College of Fine Arts, Department of Art and Art History, Program in Art Education, Austin, TX 78712-1111. Offers MA. *Accreditation:* NASAD. Part-time programs available. *Degree requirements:* For master's, thesis, oral and written exam. *Entrance requirements:* For master's, GRE General Test, 2 samples of written work, 10 slides of art work. *Application deadline:* For fall admission, 2/1 for domestic students; for spring admission, 10/1 for domestic students. Application fee: $50 ($75 for international students). Electronic applications accepted. *Financial support:* Teaching assistantships, career-related internships or fieldwork, scholarships/grants, and tuition waivers (partial) available. *Faculty research:* Museum education; community-based, environmental, and multicultural art education; interdisciplinary art education, elementary and secondary art education. *Unit head:* Dr. Paul Bolin, Graduate Advisor/Assistant Chair, 512-471-5343, E-mail: pebolin@mail.utexas.edu. *Application contact:* K. T. Shorb, Graduate Coordinator, 512-471-3377, E-mail: ktshorb@mail.utexas.edu. Web site: http://www.finearts.utexas.edu/aah/visual_art_studies/graduate_program/.

The University of Texas at El Paso, Graduate School, College of Liberal Arts, Department of Art, El Paso, TX 79968-0001. Offers art education (MA); studio art (MA). Part-time and evening/weekend programs available. *Students:* 12 (8 women); includes 9 minority (all Hispanic/Latino), 3 international. Average age 34. 5 applicants, 60%

accepted, 1 enrolled. In 2011, 1 master's awarded. *Degree requirements:* For master's, thesis optional. *Entrance requirements:* For master's, minimum GPA of 3.0, digital portfolio, letters of recommendation. Additional exam requirements/recommendations for international students: Required—TOEFL; Recommended—IELTS. *Application deadline:* For fall admission, 8/1 priority date for domestic students, 3/1 for international students; for spring admission, 11/1 priority date for domestic students, 9/1 for international students. Applications are processed on a rolling basis. Application fee: $45 ($80 for international students). Electronic applications accepted. *Financial support:* In 2011–12, research assistantships with partial tuition reimbursements (averaging $18,625 per year), teaching assistantships with partial tuition reimbursements (averaging $14,900 per year) were awarded; fellowships with partial tuition reimbursements, institutionally sponsored loans, scholarships/grants, health care benefits, tuition waivers (partial), and unspecified assistantships also available. Support available to part-time students. Financial award application deadline: 3/15; financial award applicants required to submit FAFSA. *Unit head:* Dr. J. Quinnan, Chair, 915-747-5181, Fax: 915-747-6749, E-mail: jquinnan@utep.edu. *Application contact:* Dr. Benjamin Flores, Interim Dean of the Graduate School, 915-747-5491, Fax: 915-747-5788, E-mail: bflores@utep.edu.

The University of the Arts, College of Art, Media and Design, Department of Art Education, Philadelphia, PA 19102-4944. Offers art education (MA); visual arts (MAT). *Accreditation:* NASAD (one or more programs are accredited). Part-time programs available. *Degree requirements:* For master's, student teaching (MAT); thesis (MA). *Entrance requirements:* For master's, portfolio, official transcripts from each undergraduate or graduate school attended, three letters of recommendation, one- to two-page statement of professional plans and goals, personal interview, writing sample. Additional exam requirements/recommendations for international students: Required—TOEFL (minimum score 580 paper-based, 92 iBT) or IELTS (minimum score 6.5). *Faculty research:* Using technology and visual arts concepts to develop critical and creative thinking skills.

The University of Toledo, College of Graduate Studies, Judith Herb College of Education, Health Science and Human Service, Department of Curriculum and Instruction, Toledo, OH 43606-3390. Offers art education (ME); career and technical education (ME); curriculum and instruction (ME, PhD, Ed S); education and anthropology (MAE); education and biology (MES); education and chemistry (MES); education and classics (MAE); education and economics (MAE); education and English (MAE); education and French (MAE); education and geography (MAE); education and geology (MES); education and German (MAE); education and history (MAE); education and mathematics (MAE, MES); education and physics (MES); education and political science (MAE); education and sociology (MAE); education and Spanish (MAE); educational media (PhD); educational technology (ME); English as a second language (MAE); gifted and talented (PhD); middle childhood education licensure (ME); music education (MME); secondary education (PhD); secondary education licensure (ME). *Accreditation:* NCATE. Part-time and evening/weekend programs available. *Faculty:* 24. *Students:* 60 full-time (31 women), 211 part-time (161 women); includes 23 minority (21 Black or African American, non-Hispanic/Latino; 2 Hispanic/Latino), 20 international. Average age 35. 115 applicants, 73% accepted, 74 enrolled. In 2011, 105 master's, 3 doctorates, 4 other advanced degrees awarded. *Degree requirements:* For master's, comprehensive exam, thesis or alternative; for doctorate, comprehensive exam, thesis/dissertation; for Ed S, thesis optional. *Entrance requirements:* For master's, doctorate, and Ed S, minimum cumulative GPA of 2.7 for all previous academic work, letters of recommendation. Additional exam requirements/recommendations for international students: Required—TOEFL (minimum score 550 paper-based; 213 computer-based; 80 iBT), IELTS (minimum score 6.5). *Application deadline:* For fall admission, 1/15 priority date for domestic students, 1/15 for international students. Applications are processed on a rolling basis. Application fee: $45 ($75 for international students). Electronic applications accepted. *Financial support:* In 2011–12, 9 research assistantships with full and partial tuition reimbursements (averaging $7,184 per year), 12 teaching assistantships with full and partial tuition reimbursements (averaging $8,425 per year) were awarded; career-related internships or fieldwork, Federal Work-Study, institutionally sponsored loans, scholarships/grants, tuition waivers (full and partial), unspecified assistantships, and administrative assistantships also available. Support available to part-time students. *Unit head:* Dr. Leigh Chiarelott, Chair, 419-530-5371, E-mail: eigh.chiarelott@utoledo.edu. *Application contact:* Graduate School Office, 419-530-4723, Fax: 419-530-4724, E-mail: grdsch@utnet.utoledo.edu. Web site: http://www.utoledo.edu/eduhshs/.

University of Utah, Graduate School, College of Fine Arts, Department of Art and Art History, Salt Lake City, UT 84112-0380. Offers art history (MA); ceramics (MFA); community-based art education (MFA); drawing (MFA); graphic design (MFA); painting (MFA); photography/digital imaging (MFA); printmaking (MFA); sculpture/intermedia (MFA). *Faculty:* 20 full-time (8 women). *Students:* 16 full-time (10 women), 2 part-time (both women); includes 2 minority (both Hispanic/Latino). Average age 30. 58 applicants, 22% accepted, 9 enrolled. In 2011, 7 master's awarded. *Degree requirements:* For master's, variable foreign language requirement, comprehensive exam (for some programs), thesis or alternative, exhibit and final project paper (for MFA). *Entrance requirements:* For master's, CD portfolio (MFA), writing sample (MA), curriculum vitae, letters of recommendation. Additional exam requirements/recommendations for international students: Required—TOEFL (minimum score 575 paper-based; 183 computer-based; 75 iBT). *Application deadline:* For fall admission, 1/2 priority date for domestic students, 1/2 for international students. Application fee: $55 ($65 for international students). Electronic applications accepted. *Financial support:* In 2011–12, 2 fellowships, 6 research assistantships with partial tuition reimbursements, 34 teaching assistantships with partial tuition reimbursements were awarded; Federal Work-Study, institutionally sponsored loans, scholarships/grants, tuition waivers (partial), unspecified assistantships, and stipends also available. Financial award application deadline: 1/2; financial award applicants required to submit FAFSA. *Faculty research:* Studio art, European art history, Asian art history, Latin American art history, twentieth century/contemporary art history. *Total annual research expenditures:* $54,906. *Unit head:* Prof. Brian Snapp, Chair, 801-581-8677, Fax: 801-585-6171, E-mail: b.snapp@utah.edu. *Application contact:* Prof. Paul Stout, Director of Graduate Studies, 801-581-8677, Fax: 801-585-6171, E-mail: pls@utah.edu. Web site: http://www.art.utah.edu/.

University of Victoria, Faculty of Graduate Studies, Faculty of Education, Department of Curriculum and Instruction, Victoria, BC V8W 2Y2, Canada. Offers art education (M Ed, PhD); curriculum studies (M Ed, MA, PhD); early childhood education (M Ed, PhD); educational studies (PhD); language and literacy (M Ed, MA, PhD); mathematics (M Ed, MA, PhD); music education (M Ed, MA, PhD); science (M Ed, MA, PhD); social studies (M Ed, MA); social, cultural and foundational studies (MA, PhD); technology and environmental education (PhD). Part-time programs available. *Degree requirements:* For master's, thesis, project (M Ed); for doctorate, comprehensive exam, thesis/dissertation. *Entrance requirements:* For master's, minimum B average. Additional exam requirements/recommendations for international students: Required—TOEFL (minimum score 575 paper-based; 233 computer-based), IELTS (minimum score 7). Electronic applications accepted. *Faculty research:* Elementary and secondary English, language arts, curriculum theory and practice, educational media and technology, educational administration and leadership, history and philosophy of education.

University of West Georgia, College of Education, Department of Leadership and Applied Instruction, Carrollton, GA 30118. Offers art education (M Ed); art teacher education (Ed S); biology - secondary education (M Ed); biology/secondary education (Ed S); business education (M Ed, Ed S); chemistry/secondary education (Ed S); earth science/secondary education (Ed S); economics/secondary education (Ed S); educational leadership (M Ed, Ed S); English teacher education (M Ed, Ed S); French teacher education (M Ed, Ed S); history teacher education (Ed S); mathematics teacher education (M Ed, Ed S); middle grades education (M Ed, Ed S); physical education and recreation (Ed S); physical education teaching and coaching (M Ed); physics/secondary education (Ed S); science teacher education (M Ed, Ed S); secondary education (M Ed); social science - secondary education (M Ed); social science teacher education (M Ed); Spanish (M Ed); Spanish teacher education (M Ed, Ed S); sports management (M Ed). *Accreditation:* NCATE. Part-time and evening/weekend programs available. *Faculty:* 18 full-time (9 women). *Students:* 75 full-time (49 women), 169 part-time (109 women); includes 90 minority (85 Black or African American, non-Hispanic/Latino; 3 Hispanic/Latino; 2 Two or more races, non-Hispanic/Latino), 1 international. Average age 36. 115 applicants, 67% accepted, 19 enrolled. In 2011, 73 master's, 53 Ed Ss awarded. *Degree requirements:* For master's, internship; for Ed S, research project. *Entrance requirements:* For master's, GRE General Test, minimum GPA of 2.7; for Ed S, GRE General Test, master's degree, minimum graduate GPA of 3.0, district appointment. Additional exam requirements/recommendations for international students: Required—TOEFL (minimum score 523 paper-based; 193 computer-based; 69 iBT); Recommended—IELTS (minimum score 6). *Application deadline:* For fall admission, 7/21 for domestic students, 6/1 for international students; for spring admission, 11/30 for domestic students, 10/15 for international students. Applications are processed on a rolling basis. Application fee: $30. Electronic applications accepted. *Expenses:* Tuition, state resident: full-time $4336; part-time $181 per credit hour. Tuition, nonresident: full-time $17,362; part-time $724 per credit hour. Tuition and fees vary according to course load, degree level, campus/location and program. *Financial support:* In 2011–12, 1 research assistantship with full tuition reimbursement (averaging $7,444 per year) was awarded; career-related internships or fieldwork, scholarships/grants, and unspecified assistantships also available. Support available to part-time students. Financial award application deadline: 7/1; financial award applicants required to submit FAFSA. *Total annual research expenditures:* $5,000. *Unit head:* Dr. Frank Butts, Chair, 678-839-6530, Fax: 678-839-6195, E-mail: fbutts@westga.edu. *Application contact:* Deanna Richards, Coordinator, Graduate Studies, 678-839-5946, E-mail: drichard@westga.edu. Web site: http://www.westga.edu/coelai.

University of Wisconsin–Madison, Graduate School, School of Education, Department of Art and Department of Curriculum and Instruction, Program in Art Education, Madison, WI 53706-1380. Offers MA. *Accreditation:* NASAD. *Application deadline:* For fall admission, 1/10 for domestic students; for spring admission, 11/15 for domestic students. Application fee: $56. *Expenses:* Tuition, state resident: full-time $10,296; part-time $643.51 per credit. Tuition, nonresident: full-time $24,054; part-time $1503.40 per credit. *Required fees:* $70.06 per credit. Tuition and fees vary according to course load, campus/location, program and reciprocity agreements. *Financial support:* Fellowships with full tuition reimbursements, research assistantships with full tuition reimbursements, teaching assistantships with full tuition reimbursements, and project assistantships available. *Unit head:* Dr. Tom Loeser, Chair, 608-262-1662, E-mail: tloeser@facstaff.wisc.edu. *Application contact:* 608-262-2433, Fax: 608-262-5134, E-mail: gradadmiss@mail.bascom.wisc.edu. Web site: http://www.education.wisc.edu/art.

University of Wisconsin–Madison, Graduate School, School of Education, Department of Curriculum and Instruction, Madison, WI 53706-1380. Offers art education (MA); curriculum and instruction (MS, PhD); education and mathematics (MA); French education (MA); German education (MA); music education (MS); science education (MS); Spanish education (MA). *Accreditation:* NASM (one or more programs are accredited). *Degree requirements:* For doctorate, thesis/dissertation. Application fee: $56. *Expenses:* Tuition, state resident: full-time $10,296; part-time $643.51 per credit. Tuition, nonresident: full-time $24,054; part-time $1503.40 per credit. *Required fees:* $70.06 per credit. Tuition and fees vary according to course load, campus/location, program and reciprocity agreements. *Financial support:* Project assistantships available. *Unit head:* Dr. John Rudolph, Chair, 608-263-4600, E-mail: jlrudolp@wisc.edu. *Application contact:* 608-262-2433, Fax: 608-262-5134, E-mail: gradadmiss@mail.bascom.wisc.edu. Web site: http://www.education.wisc.edu/ci.

University of Wisconsin–Milwaukee, Graduate School, Peck School of the Arts, Department of Art, Milwaukee, WI 53201-0413. Offers art (MA, MFA); art education (MA, MFA, MS). Part-time programs available. *Faculty:* 20 full-time (15 women). *Students:* 21 full-time (10 women), 3 part-time (2 women); includes 4 minority (3 Asian, non-Hispanic/Latino; 1 Hispanic/Latino), 2 international. Average age 31. 49 applicants, 33% accepted, 11 enrolled. In 2011, 12 degrees awarded. *Degree requirements:* For master's, comprehensive exam, thesis or alternative. *Entrance requirements:* For master's, portfolio. Additional exam requirements/recommendations for international students: Required—TOEFL (minimum score 550 paper-based; 79 iBT), IELTS (minimum score 6.5). *Application deadline:* For fall admission, 1/1 priority date for domestic students; for spring admission, 9/1 for domestic students. Applications are processed on a rolling basis. Application fee: $56 ($96 for international students). Electronic applications accepted. One-time fee: $506.10 full-time. Tuition and fees vary according to course load and reciprocity agreements. *Financial support:* In 2011–12, 10 teaching assistantships were awarded; career-related internships or fieldwork, health care benefits, unspecified assistantships, and project assistantships also available. Support available to part-time students. Financial award application deadline: 4/15. *Total annual research expenditures:* $24,337. *Unit head:* Lee Ann Garrison, Department Chair, 414-229-4507, E-mail: garrla@uwm.edu. *Application contact:* General Information Contact, 414-229-4982, Fax: 414-229-6967, E-mail: gradschool@uwm.edu. Web site: http://www.uwm.edu/SOA/Art/.

University of Wisconsin–Superior, Graduate Division, Department of Visual Arts, Superior, WI 54880-4500. Offers art education (MA); art history (MA); art therapy (MA); studio arts (MA). Part-time programs available. *Degree requirements:* For master's, comprehensive exam, exhibit. *Entrance requirements:* For master's, minimum GPA of 2.75, portfolio.

Ursuline College, School of Graduate Studies, Program in Education, Pepper Pike, OH 44124-4398. Offers art education (MA); early childhood education (MA); language arts education (MA); life science education (MA); math education (MA); middle school education (MA); social studies education (MA); special education (MA). *Accreditation:* NCATE. *Faculty:* 3 full-time (all women), 8 part-time/adjunct (6 women). *Students:* 28 full-time (22 women), 1 (woman) part-time; includes 11 minority (7 Black or African American, non-Hispanic/Latino; 2 Asian, non-Hispanic/Latino; 1 Hispanic/Latino; 1 Native Hawaiian or other Pacific Islander, non-Hispanic/Latino). Average age 32. In 2011, 29 master's awarded. *Degree requirements:* For master's, comprehensive exam. *Entrance requirements:* For master's, minimum undergraduate GPA of 3.0. Additional exam requirements/recommendations for international students: Required—TOEFL (minimum score 500 paper-based; 173 computer-based). *Application deadline:* For fall admission, 8/1 priority date for domestic students. Applications are processed on a rolling basis. Application fee: $25. *Expenses:* Contact institution. *Financial support:* Federal Work-Study available. Financial award application deadline: 3/1. *Unit head:* Dr. Edna West, Director, Master's Apprentice Program, 440-646-6134, Fax: 440-684-6088, E-mail: ewest@ursuline.edu. *Application contact:* Melanie Steele, Graduate Admission Assistant, 440-646-8199, Fax: 440-684-6138, E-mail: graduateadmissions@ursuline.edu.

Virginia Commonwealth University, Graduate School, School of the Arts, Department of Art Education, Richmond, VA 23284-9005. Offers MAE. *Accreditation:* NASAD. *Degree requirements:* For master's, thesis optional. *Entrance requirements:* For master's, GRE if GPA is below 3.0, portfolio. Additional exam requirements/recommendations for international students: Required—TOEFL (minimum score 600 paper-based; 250 computer-based; 100 iBT). Electronic applications accepted. *Expenses:* Tuition, state resident: full-time $9133; part-time $507 per credit. Tuition, nonresident: full-time $18,777; part-time $1043 per credit. *Required fees:* $77 per credit. Tuition and fees vary according to degree level, campus/location, program and student level. *Faculty research:* Teaching methods.

Wayne State University, College of Education, Division of Teacher Education, Detroit, MI 48202. Offers art education (M Ed), including art therapy; bilingual/bicultural education (M Ed); career and technical education (M Ed); curriculum and instruction (Ed D, PhD, Ed S), including art education (PhD), bilingual education (Ed D, Ed S), bilingual-bicultural education (PhD), career and technical education (MAT, Ed D, PhD, Ed S), early childhood education (MAT, Ed D, PhD, Ed S), elementary education, English as a second language (MAT, Ed D, Ed S), English education (MAT, Ed D, PhD, Ed S), foreign language education (MAT, PhD), K-12 curriculum, mathematics education (MAT, Ed D, PhD, Ed S), science education (MAT, Ed D, PhD, Ed S), secondary education, social studies education (MAT, Ed S), social studies education: secondary (Ed D, PhD); elementary education (MAT), including special education; elementary education (M Ed, MAT), including children's literature (MAT), early childhood education (MAT, Ed D, PhD, Ed S), general elementary education (MAT); elementary or secondary education (MAT), including bilingual/bicultural education, English as a second language (MAT, Ed D, Ed S), mathematics education (MAT, Ed D, PhD, Ed S), science education (MAT, Ed D, PhD, Ed S), social studies education (MAT, Ed S); English education-secondary (M Ed); foreign language education (M Ed); mathematics education (M Ed); reading (M Ed, Ed S); reading, languages and literature (Ed D); science education (M Ed); secondary education (MAT), including art education (K-12), career and technical education (MAT, Ed D, PhD, Ed S), English education (MAT, Ed D, PhD, Ed S), foreign language education (MAT, PhD), kinesiology; social studies education secondary (M Ed); special education (M Ed, Ed D, PhD, Ed S). *Students:* 216 full-time (154 women), 626 part-time (478 women); includes 289 minority (227 Black or African American, non-Hispanic/Latino; 4 American Indian or Alaska Native, non-Hispanic/Latino; 27 Asian, non-Hispanic/Latino; 21 Hispanic/Latino; 1 Native Hawaiian or other Pacific Islander, non-Hispanic/Latino; 9 Two or more races, non-Hispanic/Latino), 14 international. Average age 37. 347 applicants, 37% accepted, 93 enrolled. In 2011, 226 master's, 12 doctorates, 46 other advanced degrees awarded. *Degree requirements:* For master's, thesis (for some programs), thesis, essay or project (for some M Ed programs), professional field experience (for MAT programs); for doctorate, thesis/dissertation. *Entrance requirements:* For master's, Michigan Basic Skills Test (MA in teaching); for doctorate, minimum undergraduate GPA of 3.0, graduate 3.5; interview, curriculum vitae; references. Additional exam requirements/recommendations for international students: Required—TOEFL (minimum score 550 paper-based; 213 computer-based), TWE (minimum score 5.5). *Application deadline:* For fall admission, 6/1 priority date for domestic students, 5/1 for international students; for winter admission, 10/1 priority date for domestic students, 9/1 for international students; for spring admission, 2/1 priority date for domestic students, 1/1 for international students. Applications are processed on a rolling basis. Application fee: $50. Electronic applications accepted. *Expenses:* Tuition, state resident: part-time $512.85 per credit. Tuition, nonresident: part-time $1132.65 per credit. *Required fees:* $26.60 per credit. $199.65 per semester. Tuition and fees vary according to course load and program. *Financial support:* In 2011–12, 42 students received support. Fellowships, research assistantships with tuition reimbursements available, teaching assistantships, scholarships/grants, and unspecified assistantships available. *Faculty research:* Reading and writing literacy and literature. *Total annual research expenditures:* $264,016. *Unit head:* Dr. Craig Roney, Assistant Dean, 313-577-0902, E-mail: rroney@wayne.edu. Web site: http://coe.wayne.edu/ted/index.php.

Western Kentucky University, Graduate Studies, Potter College of Arts and Letters, Department of Art, Bowling Green, KY 42101. Offers art education (MA Ed). *Accreditation:* NASAD; NCATE. Part-time and evening/weekend programs available. *Degree requirements:* For master's, comprehensive exam, final exam. *Entrance requirements:* For master's, GRE General Test, minimum GPA of 2.75. Additional exam requirements/recommendations for international students: Required—TOEFL (minimum score 555 paper-based; 213 computer-based; 79 iBT). *Faculty research:* Nineteenth century Kentucky women artists.

Western Michigan University, Graduate College, College of Fine Arts, Gwen Frostic School of Art, Kalamazoo, MI 49008. Offers art education (MA); studio art (MFA). *Accreditation:* NASAD (one or more programs are accredited). *Degree requirements:* For master's, thesis or alternative.

West Virginia University, College of Creative Arts, Division of Art and Design, Morgantown, WV 26506. Offers art education (MA); art history (MA); ceramics (MFA); graphic design (MFA); painting (MFA); printmaking (MFA); sculpture (MFA); studio art (MA). *Accreditation:* NASAD. *Degree requirements:* For master's, thesis, exhibit. *Entrance requirements:* For master's, minimum GPA of 2.75, portfolio. Additional exam requirements/recommendations for international students: Required—TOEFL. *Expenses:* Contact institution. *Faculty research:* Medieval art history.

William Carey University, School of Education, Hattiesburg, MS 39401-5499. Offers art education (M Ed); art of teaching (M Ed); elementary education (M Ed, Ed S); English education (M Ed); gifted education (M Ed); history and social science (M Ed); mild/moderate disabilities (M Ed); secondary education (M Ed). Part-time programs available. *Degree requirements:* For master's, comprehensive exam. *Entrance requirements:* For master's, GRE, MAT, minimum GPA of 2.5, Class A teacher's license. Additional exam requirements/recommendations for international students: Required—TOEFL (minimum score 550 paper-based; 213 computer-based).

Winthrop University, College of Visual and Performing Arts, Department of Art, Rock Hill, SC 29733. Offers art (MFA); art administration (MA); art education (MA). *Accreditation:* NASAD. Part-time programs available. *Degree requirements:* For master's, thesis, documented exhibit, oral exam. *Entrance requirements:* For master's, GRE General Test or MAT, PRAXIS (MA), minimum GPA of 3.0, resume, slide portfolio, teaching certificate (MA). Electronic applications accepted.

Business Education

Arkansas State University, Graduate School, College of Business, Department of Computer and Information Technology, Jonesboro, State University, AR 72467. Offers business education (SCCT); business technology education (MSE); information systems and e-commerce (MS). Part-time programs available. *Faculty:* 9 full-time (1 woman). *Students:* 4 full-time (2 women), 13 part-time (10 women); includes 5 minority (all Black or African American, non-Hispanic/Latino). Average age 36. 6 applicants, 100% accepted, 5 enrolled. In 2011, 13 master's awarded. *Degree requirements:* For master's, comprehensive exam, thesis or alternative. *Entrance requirements:* For master's, GRE General Test or MAT, appropriate bachelor's degree, official transcript, immunization records. Additional exam requirements/recommendations for international students: Required—TOEFL (minimum score 550 paper-based; 253 computer-based; 79 iBT), IELTS (minimum score 6), Pearson Test of English Academic (minimum score 56). *Application deadline:* For fall admission, 7/1 for domestic and international students; for spring admission, 11/15 for domestic students, 11/14 for international students. Applications are processed on a rolling basis. Application fee: $30 ($40 for international students). Electronic applications accepted. *Expenses:* Contact institution. *Financial support:* Career-related internships or fieldwork, scholarships/grants, and unspecified assistantships available. Financial award application deadline: 7/1; financial award applicants required to submit FAFSA. *Unit head:* Dr. John Robertson, Chair, 870-972-3416, Fax: 870-972-3868, E-mail: jfrobert@astate.edu. *Application contact:* Dr. Andrew Sustich, Dean of the Graduate School, 870-972-3029, Fax: 870-972-3857, E-mail: sustich@astate.edu. Web site: http://www.astate.edu/a/business/departments/computer-information-technology/.

Armstrong Atlantic State University, School of Graduate Studies, Program in Education, Savannah, GA 31419-1997. Offers adult education (M Ed); curriculum and instruction (M Ed); early childhood education (M Ed); education (M Ed); elementary education (M Ed); middle grades education (M Ed); secondary education (M Ed), including business education, English education, mathematics education, science education, social science education; special education (M Ed), including behavioral disorders, learning disabilities, speech-language pathology. *Accreditation:* NCATE. Part-time and evening/weekend programs available. Postbaccalaureate distance learning degree programs offered (minimal on-campus study). *Faculty:* 33 full-time (23 women), 3 part-time/adjunct (2 women). *Students:* 97 full-time (91 women), 262 part-time (227 women); includes 83 minority (70 Black or African American, non-Hispanic/Latino; 3 Asian, non-Hispanic/Latino; 8 Hispanic/Latino; 2 Two or more races, non-Hispanic/Latino), 5 international. Average age 34. 169 applicants, 69% accepted, 102 enrolled. In 2011, 227 master's awarded. *Degree requirements:* For master's, comprehensive exam, portfolio. *Entrance requirements:* For master's, GRE General Test or MAT, minimum GPA of 2.5, letters of recommendation. Additional exam requirements/recommendations for international students: Required—TOEFL (minimum score 523 paper-based; 193 computer-based). *Application deadline:* For fall admission, 7/1 priority date for domestic students, 5/1 for international students; for spring admission, 11/15 priority date for domestic students, 9/15 for international students. Applications are processed on a rolling basis. Application fee: $30. Electronic applications accepted. *Expenses:* Tuition, state resident: full-time $3402. Tuition, nonresident: full-time $12,636. *Financial support:* In 2011–12, research assistantships with full tuition reimbursements (averaging $5,000 per year) were awarded; career-related internships or fieldwork, Federal Work-Study, scholarships/grants, and unspecified assistantships also available. Support available to part-time students. Financial award applicants required to submit FAFSA. *Unit head:* Dr. Patricia Wachholz, Dean, College of Education, 912-344-2797, E-mail: patricia.wachholz@armstrong.edu. *Application contact:* Jill Bell, Director, Graduate Enrollment Services, 912-344-2798, Fax: 912-344-3488, E-mail: graduate@armstrong.edu. Web site: http://www.armstrong.edu/Education/coe_deans_office/coe_education_welcome.

Auburn University, Graduate School, College of Education, Department of Curriculum and Teaching, Auburn University, AL 36849. Offers business education (M Ed, MS, PhD); early childhood education (M Ed, MS, PhD, Ed S); elementary education (M Ed, MS, PhD, Ed S); foreign languages (M Ed, MS); music education (M Ed, MS, PhD, Ed S); postsecondary education (PhD); reading education (PhD, Ed S); secondary education (M Ed, MS, PhD, Ed S), including English language arts, mathematics, science, social studies. *Accreditation:* NASM (one or more programs are accredited); NCATE. Part-time programs available. *Faculty:* 22 full-time (17 women), 3 part-time/adjunct (all women). *Students:* 80 full-time (58 women), 181 part-time (126 women); includes 42 minority (28 Black or African American, non-Hispanic/Latino; 7 Asian, non-Hispanic/Latino; 7 Hispanic/Latino). Average age 34. 184 applicants, 53% accepted, 60 enrolled. In 2011, 77 master's, 10 doctorates, 35 other advanced degrees awarded. *Degree requirements:* For master's, thesis (for some programs); for doctorate, thesis/dissertation; for Ed S, field project. *Entrance requirements:* For master's, doctorate, and Ed S, GRE General Test. *Application deadline:* For fall admission, 7/7 for domestic students; for spring admission, 11/24 for domestic students. Applications are processed on a rolling basis. Application fee: $50 ($60 for international students). Electronic applications accepted. *Expenses:* Tuition, state resident: full-time $7290; part-time $405 per credit hour. Tuition, nonresident: full-time $21,870; part-time $1215 per credit hour. *International tuition:* $22,000 full-time. *Required fees:* $1402. *Financial support:* Fellowships, teaching assistantships, career-related internships or fieldwork, and Federal Work-Study available. Support available to part-time students. Financial award application deadline: 3/15; financial award applicants required to submit FAFSA. *Faculty research:* Emerging literacy, reading attitudes, music for at-risk youth, portfolio assessment. *Unit head:* Dr. Kimberly Walls, Head, 334-844-4434. *Application contact:* Dr. George Flowers, Dean of the Graduate School, 334-844-2125. Web site: http://education.auburn.edu/academic_departments/curr/.

Ball State University, Graduate School, Miller College of Business, Department of Information Systems and Operations Management, Muncie, IN 47306-1099. Offers business education (MAE). *Accreditation:* NCATE. *Faculty:* 13. *Students:* 12 part-time (8 women); includes 1 minority (Black or African American, non-Hispanic/Latino). 6 applicants, 50% accepted, 1 enrolled. In 2011, 3 master's awarded. *Entrance requirements:* For master's, GMAT. Application fee: $50. Tuition and fees vary according to program and reciprocity agreements. *Financial support:* Teaching assistantships with full tuition reimbursements available. Financial award application deadline: 3/1. *Unit head:* Dr. Sushil Sharma, Chair, 765-285-5227, Fax: 765-285-8024. *Application contact:* Jennifer Bott, Graduate Coordinator, 765-285-1931, Fax: 765-285-8818, E-mail: jbott@bsu.edu. Web site: http://www.bsu.edu/business/beoa/.

Bloomsburg University of Pennsylvania, School of Graduate Studies, College of Business, Department of Business Education, Information and Technology Management, and Management Information Systems, Program in Business Education, Bloomsburg, PA 17815-1301. Offers M Ed. *Degree requirements:* For master's, thesis optional. *Entrance requirements:* For master's, GRE General Test, minimum QPA of 3.0, 2 letters of recommendation. Additional exam requirements/recommendations for international students: Required—TOEFL. Electronic applications accepted. *Faculty research:* Records and information management, training and development, ergonomics, office technology, telecommunications.

Bowling Green State University, Graduate College, College of Education and Human Development, School of Education and Intervention Services, Teaching and Learning Division, Department of Business Education, Bowling Green, OH 43403. Offers M Ed. *Accreditation:* NCATE. Part-time programs available. *Degree requirements:* For master's, thesis or alternative. *Entrance requirements:* For master's, GRE General Test. Additional exam requirements/recommendations for international students: Required—TOEFL. Electronic applications accepted. *Faculty research:* School to work, workforce education, marketing education, contextual teaching and learning.

Buffalo State College, State University of New York, The Graduate School, Faculty of Applied Science and Education, Department of Business Studies, Buffalo, NY 14222-1095. Offers business and marketing education (MS Ed). Part-time and evening/weekend programs available. *Degree requirements:* For master's, thesis or alternative, project. *Entrance requirements:* For master's, minimum GPA of 2.5, New York teaching certificate.

Canisius College, Graduate Division, School of Education and Human Services, Department of Adolescence Education, Buffalo, NY 14208-1098. Offers adolescence education (MS Ed); business and marketing education (MS Ed). Part-time and evening/weekend programs available. *Faculty:* 11 full-time (8 women), 26 part-time/adjunct (14 women). *Students:* 73 full-time (37 women), 17 part-time (9 women); includes 4 minority (3 Black or African American, non-Hispanic/Latino; 1 Hispanic/Latino), 27 international. Average age 29. 48 applicants, 71% accepted, 17 enrolled. In 2011, 65 master's awarded. *Degree requirements:* For master's, thesis, project internship. *Entrance requirements:* For master's, GRE if cumulative GPA less than 2.7, transcripts, two letters of recommendation. Additional exam requirements/recommendations for international students: Required—TOEFL. *Application deadline:* Applications are processed on a rolling basis. Application fee: $25. Electronic applications accepted. *Financial support:* Career-related internships or fieldwork, Federal Work-Study, scholarships/grants, tuition waivers (partial), and unspecified assistantships available. Support available to part-time students. Financial award application deadline: 4/30; financial award applicants required to submit FAFSA. *Faculty research:* Culturally congruent pedagogy in physical education, information processing and perceptual styles of athletes, qualities of effective coaches, student perceptions of online courses, teaching effectiveness. *Unit head:* Dr. Barbera A. Burns, Chair of Adolescence Education, 716-888-3291, E-mail: burns1@canisius.edu. *Application contact:* Jim Bagwell, Director of Graduate Recruitment and Admissions, 716-888-2544, Fax: 716-888-3290, E-mail: bagwellj@canisius.edu. Web site: http://www.canisius.edu/catalog/teachcert6.asp.

Chadron State College, School of Professional and Graduate Studies, Department of Education, Chadron, NE 69337. Offers business (MA Ed); community counseling (MA Ed); educational administration (MS Ed, Sp Ed); elementary education (MS Ed); history (MA Ed); language and literature (MA Ed); secondary administration (MS Ed); secondary education (MS Ed). *Accreditation:* NCATE. Part-time and evening/weekend programs available. Postbaccalaureate distance learning degree programs offered. *Degree requirements:* For master's, thesis optional. *Entrance requirements:* For master's, GRE General Test, GRE Writing Test, minimum GPA of 2.75 or 12 graduate hours at CSC with minimum GPA of 3.25. Additional exam requirements/recommendations for international students: Required—TOEFL. Electronic applications accepted. *Faculty research:* Rural education, technology, mental health.

The College of Saint Rose, Graduate Studies, School of Education, Teacher Education Department, Albany, NY 12203-1419. Offers business and marketing (MS Ed); childhood education (MS Ed); curriculum and instruction (MS Ed); early childhood education (MS Ed); elementary education (K-6) (MS Ed); secondary education (MS Ed, Certificate); teacher education (MS Ed, Certificate), including bilingual pupil personnel services (Certificate), teacher education (MS Ed). Part-time and evening/weekend programs available. *Entrance requirements:* For master's, minimum undergraduate GPA of 3.0. Additional exam requirements/recommendations for international students: Required—TOEFL (minimum score 550 paper-based; 213 computer-based). Electronic applications accepted.

Colorado Christian University, Program in Curriculum and Instruction, Lakewood, CO 80226. Offers corporate education (MACI); early childhood educator (MACI); elementary educator (MACI); instructional technology (MACI); master educator (MACI); online course developer (MACI); online teaching and learning (MACI); special education generalist (MACI). Part-time and evening/weekend programs available. *Degree requirements:* For master's, thesis optional, practicum. *Entrance requirements:* For master's, interviews, letters of recommendation. Additional exam requirements/recommendations for international students: Required—TOEFL. Electronic applications accepted. *Expenses:* Contact institution.

East Carolina University, Graduate School, College of Education, Department of Business and Information Technologies Education, Greenville, NC 27858-4353. Offers business education (MA Ed); elementary education (MAT); English education (MAT); family and consumer science (MAT); health education (MAT); Hispanic studies (MAT); history education (MAT); marketing education (MA Ed); middle grades education (MAT); music education (MAT); physical education (MAT); science education (MAT); special education (MAT), including general curriculum; vocation education (MS). *Accreditation:* NCATE. Part-time and evening/weekend programs available. Postbaccalaureate distance learning degree programs offered (no on-campus study). *Degree requirements:* For master's, comprehensive exam, thesis optional. *Entrance requirements:* For master's, GRE or MAT, minimum GPA of 2.5, bachelor's degree in related field, teaching license (MA Ed). Additional exam requirements/recommendations for international students: Required—TOEFL. *Application deadline:* For fall admission, 6/1 priority date for domestic students. Applications are processed on a rolling basis. Application fee: $50. *Expenses:* Tuition, state resident: full-time $3557; part-time $444.63 per semester hour. Tuition, nonresident: full-time $14,351; part-time $1793.88 per semester hour. *Required fees:* $2016; $252 per semester hour. Part-time tuition and fees vary according to course load, campus/location and program. *Financial support:* Federal Work-Study available. Support available to part-time students. Financial award application deadline: 6/1. *Unit head:* Dr. Ivan G. Wallace, Chair, 252-328-6983, Fax: 252-328-6835, E-mail: wallacei@ecu.edu. *Application contact:* Dean of Graduate School, 252-328-6012, Fax: 252-328-6071, E-mail: gradschool@ecu.edu. Web site: http://www.ecu.edu/cs-educ/bite/index.cfm.

Eastern Kentucky University, The Graduate School, College of Education, Department of Curriculum and Instruction, Program in Secondary and Higher Education, Richmond, KY 40475-3102. Offers secondary education (MA Ed), including agricultural education, art education, biological sciences education, business education, English education, geography education, history education, home economics education, industrial education, mathematical sciences education, physical education, school health education. *Accreditation:* NCATE. Part-time programs available. *Entrance requirements:* For master's, GRE General Test, minimum GPA of 2.5.

Emporia State University, Graduate School, School of Business, Department of Business Administration and Education, Program in Business Education, Emporia, KS 66801-5087. Offers MS. Part-time and evening/weekend programs available. Postbaccalaureate distance learning degree programs offered (no on-campus study). *Students:* 3 full-time (1 woman), 9 part-time (5 women); includes 1 minority (Black or African American, non-Hispanic/Latino). 3 applicants, 67% accepted, 1 enrolled. In 2011, 10 master's awarded. *Entrance requirements:* For master's, GRE, 15 undergraduate credits in business; minimum undergraduate GPA of 2.7 over last 60 hours. Additional exam requirements/recommendations for international students: Required—TOEFL (minimum score 520 paper-based; 133 computer-based; 68 iBT). *Application deadline:* For fall admission, 8/15 priority date for domestic students. Applications are processed on a rolling basis. Application fee: $30 ($75 for international students). Electronic applications accepted. *Expenses:* Tuition, state resident: full-time $2342; part-time $195 per credit hour. Tuition, nonresident: full-time $7254; part-time $605 per credit hour. *Required fees:* $66 per credit hour. Tuition and fees vary according to campus/location. *Financial support:* Career-related internships or fieldwork, institutionally sponsored loans, health care benefits, and unspecified assistantships available. Financial award application deadline: 3/15; financial award applicants required to submit FAFSA. *Unit head:* Dr. Jack Sterrett, Chair, 620-341-5345, Fax: 620-341-6345, E-mail: jsterret@emporia.edu. *Application contact:* Dr. Nancy Hite, Information Contact, 620-341-5345, Fax: 620-341-6345, E-mail: nhite@emporia.edu.

Florida Agricultural and Mechanical University, Division of Graduate Studies, Research, and Continuing Education, College of Education, Department of Vocational Education, Tallahassee, FL 32307-3200. Offers business education (MBE); industrial education (M Ed, MS Ed). *Accreditation:* NCATE. *Degree requirements:* For master's, thesis (for some programs). *Entrance requirements:* For master's, GRE General Test, minimum GPA of 3.0. Additional exam requirements/recommendations for international students: Required—TOEFL.

Georgia Southern University, Jack N. Averitt College of Graduate Studies, College of Education, Department of Teaching and Learning, Program in Business Education, Statesboro, GA 30460. Offers M Ed, MAT. *Accreditation:* NCATE. Part-time and evening/weekend programs available. *Students:* 1 full-time (0 women). Average age 29. In 2011, 3 master's awarded. *Degree requirements:* For master's, transition point assessments. *Entrance requirements:* For master's, GRE General Test or MAT, GACE Basic Skills and Content Assessments, minimum cumulative GPA of 2.5. Additional exam requirements/recommendations for international students: Required—TOEFL (minimum score 550 paper-based; 213 computer-based; 80 iBT). *Application deadline:* For fall admission, 3/1 priority date for domestic students, 3/1 for international students; for spring admission, 10/1 priority date for domestic students, 10/1 for international students. Applications are processed on a rolling basis. Application fee: $50. Electronic applications accepted. *Expenses:* Tuition, state resident: full-time $6300; part-time $263 per semester hour. Tuition, nonresident: full-time $25,174; part-time $1049 per semester hour. *Required fees:* $1872. *Financial support:* In 2011–12, research assistantships with partial tuition reimbursements (averaging $7,200 per year), teaching assistantships with partial tuition reimbursements (averaging $7,200 per year) were awarded; Federal Work-Study, scholarships/grants, tuition waivers (partial), and unspecified assistantships also available. Support available to part-time students. Financial award application deadline: 4/15; financial award applicants required to submit FAFSA. *Faculty research:* Technology applications. *Unit head:* Dr. Ronnie Sheppard, Department Chair, 912-478-5203, Fax: 912-478-0026, E-mail: sheppard@georgiasouthern.edu. *Application contact:* Amanda Gilliland, Coordinator for Graduate Student Recruitment, 912-478-5384, Fax: 912-478-0740, E-mail: gradadmissions@georgiasouthern.edu. Web site: http://coe.georgiasouthern.edu/tandl/index.html.

Hofstra University, School of Education, Health, and Human Services, Programs in Teaching - Secondary Education, Hempstead, NY 11549. Offers business education (MS Ed); education technology (Advanced Certificate); English education (MA, MS Ed); foreign language and TESOL (MS Ed); foreign language education (MA, MS Ed), including French, German, Russian, Spanish; mathematics education (MA, MS Ed); science education (MA, MS Ed), including biology, chemistry, earth science, geology, physics; secondary education (Advanced Certificate); social studies education (MA, MS Ed). Part-time and evening/weekend programs available. Postbaccalaureate distance learning degree programs offered (minimal on-campus study). *Students:* 72 full-time (47 women), 51 part-time (30 women); includes 21 minority (9 Black or African American, non-Hispanic/Latino; 7 Asian, non-Hispanic/Latino; 5 Hispanic/Latino). Average age 28. 103 applicants, 91% accepted, 41 enrolled. In 2011, 86 master's, 6 other advanced degrees awarded. *Degree requirements:* For master's, one foreign language, comprehensive exam (for some programs), thesis (for some programs), exit project, electronic portfolio, student teaching, fieldwork, curriculum project, minimum GPA of 3.0; for Advanced Certificate, 3 foreign languages, comprehensive exam (for some programs), thesis project, minimum GPA of 3.0. *Entrance requirements:* For master's, 2 letters of recommendation, teacher certification (MA), essay; for Advanced Certificate, 2 letters of recommendation, essay. Additional exam requirements/recommendations for international students: Required—TOEFL (minimum score 550 paper-based; 213 computer-based; 80 iBT). *Application deadline:* Applications are processed on a rolling basis. Application fee: $70 ($75 for international students). Electronic applications accepted. *Expenses: Tuition:* Full-time $18,990; part-time $1055 per credit hour. *Required fees:* $970. Tuition and fees vary according to program. *Financial support:* In 2011–12, 90 students received support, including 13 fellowships with full and partial tuition reimbursements available (averaging $3,202 per year), 1 research assistantship with full and partial tuition reimbursement available (averaging $11,645 per year); career-related internships or fieldwork, Federal Work-Study, institutionally sponsored loans, scholarships/grants, tuition waivers (full and partial), and unspecified assistantships also available. Support available to part-time students. Financial award applicants required to submit FAFSA. *Faculty research:* Appropriate content and pedagogy in secondary school disciplines, appropriate pedagogy in secondary school disciplines, adolescent development, secondary school organization, alternative secondary school programs. *Unit head:* Dr. Esther Fusco, Chairperson, 516-463-7704, Fax: 516-463-6196, E-mail: catezf@hofstra.edu. *Application contact:* Carol Drummer, Dean of Graduate Admissions, 516-463-4876, Fax: 516-463-4664, E-mail: gradstudent@hofstra.edu. Web site: http://www.hofstra.edu/education/.

Indiana University of Pennsylvania, School of Graduate Studies and Research, Eberly College of Business and Information Technology, Department of Technology Support and Training, Program in Business/Business Specialist, Indiana, PA 15705-

1087. Offers M Ed. *Faculty:* 3 full-time (2 women). *Students:* 7 full-time (4 women), 3 part-time (1 woman); all minorities (all American Indian or Alaska Native, non-Hispanic/Latino). Average age 26. 10 applicants, 40% accepted, 2 enrolled. In 2011, 8 master's awarded. *Entrance requirements:* Additional exam requirements/recommendations for international students: Required—TOEFL (minimum score 540 paper-based; 207 computer-based). *Application deadline:* Applications are processed on a rolling basis. Application fee: $50. Electronic applications accepted. *Expenses:* Tuition, state resident: full-time $7488; part-time $416 per credit. Tuition, nonresident: full-time $11,232; part-time $624 per credit. *Required fees:* $2070; $192.20 per credit. $90 per semester. *Financial support:* In 2011–12, 3 research assistantships (averaging $2,970 per year) were awarded. Financial award application deadline: 4/15; financial award applicants required to submit FAFSA. *Unit head:* Dr. Linda Szul, Chairperson, 724-357-3003, E-mail: lfszul@iup.edu. *Application contact:* Dr. Dawn Woodland, Graduate Coordinator, 724-357-5736, E-mail: woodland@iup.edu. Web site: http://www.iup.edu/upper.aspx?id=49407.

Inter American University of Puerto Rico, Metropolitan Campus, Graduate Programs, Program in Commerical Education, San Juan, PR 00919-1293. Offers MA.

Inter American University of Puerto Rico, San Germán Campus, Graduate Studies Center, Program in Business Education, San Germán, PR 00683-5008. Offers MA. Part-time and evening/weekend programs available. *Degree requirements:* For master's, comprehensive exam. *Entrance requirements:* For master's, GRE General Test or EXADEP, minimum GPA of 3.0. *Application deadline:* For fall admission, 4/30 priority date for domestic students; for spring admission, 11/15 for domestic students. Applications are processed on a rolling basis. Application fee: $31. *Expenses: Required fees:* $213 per semester. *Financial support:* Teaching assistantships, Federal Work-Study, and unspecified assistantships available. *Unit head:* Dr. Elba T. Irizarry, Director of Graduate Studies Center, 787-264-1912 Ext. 7357, Fax: 787-892-6350, E-mail: elbat@sg.inter.edu.

International College of the Cayman Islands, Graduate Program in Management, Newlands, Cayman Islands. Offers business administration (MBA); management (MS), including education, human resources. Part-time and evening/weekend programs available. *Degree requirements:* For master's, comprehensive exam. *Entrance requirements:* Additional exam requirements/recommendations for international students: Recommended—TOEFL. *Faculty research:* International human resources administration.

Johnson & Wales University, The Alan Shawn Feinstein Graduate School, MAT Program in Teacher Education, Providence, RI 02903-3703. Offers business education and secondary special education (MAT); elementary education and elementary special education (MAT); elementary education and elementary/secondary special education (MAT); elementary education and secondary special education (MAT); food service education (MAT). Part-time and evening/weekend programs available. *Entrance requirements:* For master's, MAT, minimum GPA of 2.75. Additional exam requirements/recommendations for international students: Required—TOEFL (minimum score 550 paper-based; 210 computer-based) or IELTS (recommended). *Faculty research:* Secondary education, student teaching, educational reform, evaluation procedures.

Lehman College of the City University of New York, Division of Education, Department of Middle and High School Education, Program in Business Education, Bronx, NY 10468-1589. Offers MS Ed. *Accreditation:* NCATE. Part-time and evening/weekend programs available. *Degree requirements:* For master's, thesis. *Entrance requirements:* For master's, minimum GPA of 2.7.

Louisiana State University and Agricultural and Mechanical College, Graduate School, College of Agriculture, School of Human Resource Education and Workforce Development, Baton Rouge, LA 70803. Offers agriculture and extension education and youth development (MS, PhD); career and technical education (MS, PhD); comprehensive vocational education (MS, PhD); extension and international education (MS, PhD); human resource and leadership development (MS, PhD); industrial education (MS); vocational agriculture education (MS, PhD); vocational business education (MS); vocational home economics education (MS). *Accreditation:* NCATE. Part-time programs available. *Faculty:* 9 full-time (5 women), 3 part-time/adjunct (0 women). *Students:* 51 full-time (36 women), 85 part-time (59 women); includes 28 minority (23 Black or African American, non-Hispanic/Latino; 1 Asian, non-Hispanic/Latino; 4 Hispanic/Latino), 3 international. Average age 36. 29 applicants, 83% accepted, 20 enrolled. In 2011, 15 master's, 17 doctorates awarded. Terminal master's awarded for partial completion of doctoral program. *Degree requirements:* For master's, thesis (for some programs); for doctorate, thesis/dissertation. *Entrance requirements:* For master's and doctorate, GRE General Test, minimum GPA of 3.0. Additional exam requirements/recommendations for international students: Required—TOEFL (minimum score 550 paper-based; 213 computer-based; 79 iBT) or IELTS (minimum score 6.5). *Application deadline:* For fall admission, 1/25 priority date for domestic students, 5/15 for international students; for spring admission, 10/15 for international students. Applications are processed on a rolling basis. Application fee: $50 ($70 for international students). Electronic applications accepted. *Financial support:* In 2011–12, 84 students received support, including 3 fellowships with full and partial tuition reimbursements available (averaging $14,986 per year), 4 research assistantships with full and partial tuition reimbursements available (averaging $12,000 per year), 11 teaching assistantships with partial tuition reimbursements available (averaging $13,300 per year); career-related internships or fieldwork, Federal Work-Study, institutionally sponsored loans, health care benefits, tuition waivers (full and partial), and unspecified assistantships also available. Financial award application deadline: 3/1; financial award applicants required to submit FAFSA. *Faculty research:* Adult education, history and philosophy of vocational education, curriculum and instruction, career decision-making. *Unit head:* Dr. Michael F. Burnett, Director, 225-578-5748, Fax: 225-578-2526, E-mail: vocbur@lsu.edu. Web site: http://www.lsu.edu/hrleader/.

Louisiana Tech University, Graduate School, College of Education, Department of Curriculum, Instruction and Leadership, Ruston, LA 71272. Offers curriculum and instruction (MS, Ed D); educational leadership (Ed D); secondary education (M Ed), including business education, English education, foreign language education, health and physical education, mathematics education, science education, social studies education, speech education. *Accreditation:* NCATE. Part-time programs available. *Degree requirements:* For doctorate, thesis/dissertation. *Entrance requirements:* For master's and doctorate, GRE General Test.

Maryville University of Saint Louis, The John E. Simon School of Business, St. Louis, MO 63141-7299. Offers accounting (MBA, PGC); business studies (PGC); management (MBA, PGC); marketing (MBA, PGC); process and project management (MBA, PGC); sport and entertainment management (MBA, PGC). *Accreditation:* ACBSP. Part-time and evening/weekend programs available. *Faculty:* 8 full-time (3 women), 14 part-time/adjunct (5 women). *Students:* 19 full-time (10 women), 114 part-time (56 women); includes 13 minority (7 Black or African American, non-Hispanic/Latino; 3 Asian, non-Hispanic/Latino; 2 Hispanic/Latino; 1 Two or more races, non-Hispanic/Latino), 3 international. Average age 31. In 2011, 56 master's awarded. *Entrance requirements:* For master's, GMAT (unless applicant possesses undergraduate business degree with minimum cumulative GPA of 3.0, or has completed master's degree from accredited university or one early access course prior to undergraduate degree). Additional exam requirements/recommendations for international students: Required—TOEFL (minimum score 85 iBT). *Application deadline:* Applications are processed on a rolling basis. Application fee: $40 ($60 for international students). Electronic applications accepted. *Expenses: Tuition:* Full-time $21,922; part-time $675 per credit hour. *Required fees:* $233.75 per semester. *Financial support:* Career-related internships or fieldwork, Federal Work-Study, tuition waivers (partial), and campus employment available. Financial award application deadline: 3/1; financial award applicants required to submit FAFSA. *Faculty research:* International business, e-marketing, strategic planning, interpersonal management skills, financial analysis. *Unit head:* Dr. Pamela Horwitz, Dean, 314-529-9418, Fax: 314-529-9975, E-mail: horwitz@maryville.edu. *Application contact:* Kathy Dougherty, Director of MBA Programs, 314-529-9382, Fax: 314-529-9975, E-mail: business@maryville.edu. Web site: http://www.maryville.edu/academics-bu-mba.

Middle Tennessee State University, College of Graduate Studies, Jennings A. Jones College of Business, Department of Business Communication and Entrepreneurship, Murfreesboro, TN 37132. Offers business education (MBE). Part-time and evening/weekend programs available. Postbaccalaureate distance learning degree programs offered. *Faculty:* 8 full-time (5 women). *Students:* 9 full-time (6 women), 31 part-time (18 women); includes 11 minority (10 Black or African American, non-Hispanic/Latino; 1 Hispanic/Latino). Average age 36. 27 applicants, 63% accepted. In 2011, 25 master's awarded. *Degree requirements:* For master's, comprehensive exam. *Entrance requirements:* For master's, GRE or MAT. Additional exam requirements/recommendations for international students: Required—TOEFL (minimum score 525 paper-based; 195 computer-based; 71 iBT) or IELTS (minimum score 6). *Application deadline:* For fall admission, 6/1 for domestic and international students. Applications are processed on a rolling basis. Application fee: $25 ($30 for international students). Electronic applications accepted. *Expenses:* Tuition, state resident: full-time $10,008. Tuition, nonresident: full-time $25,056. *Financial support:* In 2011–12, 10 students received support. Tuition waivers available. Support available to part-time students. Financial award application deadline: 5/1. *Unit head:* Dr. Stephen D. Lewis, Chair, 615-898-2902, Fax: 615-898-5438, E-mail: stephen.lewis@mtsu.edu. *Application contact:* Dr. Michael D. Allen, Dean and Vice Provost for Research, 615-898-2840, Fax: 615-904-8020, E-mail: michael.allen@mtsu.edu.

Mississippi College, Graduate School, School of Business, Clinton, MS 39058. Offers accounting (Certificate); business administration (MBA), including accounting; business education (M Ed); finance (MBA, Certificate); JD/MBA. *Accreditation:* ACBSP. Part-time and evening/weekend programs available. *Degree requirements:* For master's, comprehensive exam, thesis optional. *Entrance requirements:* For master's, GMAT, minimum GPA of 2.5, 24 hours of undergraduate course work in business. Additional exam requirements/recommendations for international students: Recommended—TOEFL, IELTS. Electronic applications accepted.

Mississippi College, Graduate School, School of Education, Department of Teacher Education and Leadership, Clinton, MS 39058. Offers art (M Ed); biological science (M Ed); business education (M Ed); computer science (M Ed); dyslexia therapy (M Ed); educational leadership (M Ed, Ed D, Ed S); elementary education (M Ed, Ed S); English (M Ed); higher education administration (MS); mathematics (M Ed); secondary education (M Ed); social studies (history) (M Ed); teaching arts (M Ed). Part-time programs available. Postbaccalaureate distance learning degree programs offered (no on-campus study). *Degree requirements:* For master's, comprehensive exam, thesis optional. *Entrance requirements:* For master's, NTE. Additional exam requirements/recommendations for international students: Recommended—TOEFL, IELTS. Electronic applications accepted.

Morehead State University, Graduate Programs, College of Education, Department of Foundational and Graduate Studies in Education, Morehead, KY 40351. Offers adult and higher education (MA, Ed S); certified professional counselor (Ed S); counseling P-12 (MA); curriculum and instruction (Ed S); educational technology (MA Ed); instructional leadership (Ed S); school administration (MA); school counseling (Ed S); teacher leader business and marketing content (MA Ed); teacher leader business and marketing technology (MA Ed); teacher leader educational technology (MA Ed); teacher leader English (MA Ed); teacher leader gifted education (MA Ed); teacher leader IECE certification (MA Ed); teacher leader interdisciplinary education P-5 (MA Ed); teacher leader middle grades (MA Ed); teacher leader non IECE certification (MA Ed); teacher leader reading/writing - non-certification (MA Ed); teacher leader reading/writing certification (MA Ed); teacher leader school communication - certification (MA Ed); teacher leader school communication - non-certification (MA Ed); teacher leader social studies (MA Ed); teacher leader special education (MA Ed). *Accreditation:* NCATE. Part-time and evening/weekend programs available. *Degree requirements:* For master's, thesis optional, oral and/or written comprehensive exams; for Ed S, thesis, oral exam. *Entrance requirements:* For master's, GRE General Test, minimum overall undergraduate GPA of 2.5; for Ed S, GRE General Test, interview, master's degree, minimum GPA of 3.5, work experience. Additional exam requirements/recommendations for international students: Required—TOEFL (minimum score 500 paper-based; 173 computer-based). Electronic applications accepted. *Faculty research:* Character education, school accountability, computer applications for school administrators.

Morehead State University, Graduate Programs, College of Education, Department of Middle Grades and Secondary Education, Morehead, KY 40351. Offers business and marketing education (MAT); English/language arts 5-9 (MAT); French (MAT); health P-12 (MAT); mathematics 5-9 (MAT); physical education P-12 (MAT); science 5-9 (MAT); secondary biology (MAT); secondary chemistry (MAT); secondary earth science (MAT); secondary English (MAT); secondary math (MAT); secondary physics (MAT); secondary social studies (MAT); social studies 5-9 (MAT); Spanish (MAT). Part-time and evening/weekend programs available. *Degree requirements:* For master's, portfolio. *Entrance requirements:* For master's, GRE or PRAXIS II content exam, minimum overall undergraduate GPA of 2.5. Additional exam requirements/recommendations for international students: Required—TOEFL (minimum score 500 paper-based; 173 computer-based). Electronic applications accepted.

Nazareth College of Rochester, Graduate Studies, Department of Business, Program in Business Education, Rochester, NY 14618-3790. Offers MS Ed. Part-time and evening/weekend programs available. *Entrance requirements:* For master's, minimum GPA of 3.0.

New York University, Steinhardt School of Culture, Education, and Human Development, Department of Administration, Leadership, and Technology, Program in Business Education, New York, NY 10012-1019. Offers business education (Advanced Certificate); business education in higher education (MA); workplace learning (Advanced Certificate). *Accreditation:* Teacher Education Accreditation Council. Part-time programs available. *Faculty:* 1 (woman) full-time. *Students:* 2 full-time (both women), 20 part-time (17 women); includes 3 minority (2 Black or African American, non-Hispanic/Latino; 1 Asian, non-Hispanic/Latino), 3 international. Average age 32. 20 applicants, 45% accepted, 4 enrolled. In 2011, 8 master's, 1 other advanced degree awarded. *Degree requirements:* For master's, thesis (for some programs). *Entrance requirements:* For degree, master's degree. Additional exam requirements/recommendations for international students: Required—TOEFL. *Application deadline:* For fall admission, 12/1 priority date for domestic students, 12/1 for international students; for spring admission, 11/1 for domestic and international students. Applications are processed on a rolling basis. Application fee: $75. Electronic applications accepted. *Financial support:* Career-related internships or fieldwork, Federal Work-Study, institutionally sponsored loans, scholarships/grants, tuition waivers (partial), and unspecified assistantships available. Support available to part-time students. Financial award application deadline: 2/1; financial award applicants required to submit FAFSA. *Faculty research:* Applications of technology to instruction, workplace and corporate education, adult learning. *Unit head:* Dr. Bridget N. O'Connor, Director, 212-998-5488, Fax: 212-995-4041, E-mail: bridget.oconnor@nyu.edu. *Application contact:* 212-998-5030, Fax: 212-995-4328, E-mail: steinhardt.gradadmissions@nyu.edu. Web site: http://steinhardt.nyu.edu/alt/businessed.

North Carolina State University, Graduate School, College of Education, Department of Curriculum and Instruction, Program in Business and Marketing Education, Raleigh, NC 27695. Offers M Ed, MS. *Entrance requirements:* For master's, MAT or GRE, minimum GPA of 3.0, teaching license, 3 letters of reference.

Old Dominion University, Darden College of Education, Programs in Occupational and Technical Studies, Norfolk, VA 23529. Offers business and industry training (MS); career and technical education (MS, PhD); community college teaching (MS); human resources training (PhD); STEM education (MS); technology education (PhD). *Accreditation:* NCATE (one or more programs are accredited). Part-time and evening/weekend programs available. Postbaccalaureate distance learning degree programs offered (minimal on-campus study). *Faculty:* 7 full-time (1 woman), 8 part-time/adjunct (3 women). *Students:* 14 full-time (10 women), 59 part-time (33 women); includes 28 minority (18 Black or African American, non-Hispanic/Latino; 1 American Indian or Alaska Native, non-Hispanic/Latino; 2 Asian, non-Hispanic/Latino; 6 Hispanic/Latino; 1 Two or more races, non-Hispanic/Latino), 1 international. Average age 42. 44 applicants, 95% accepted, 37 enrolled. In 2011, 27 master's, 5 doctorates awarded. *Degree requirements:* For master's, comprehensive exam, thesis optional, writing exam, candidacy exam; for doctorate, comprehensive exam, thesis/dissertation, writing exam, candidacy exam. *Entrance requirements:* For master's, GRE General Test or MAT, minimum GPA of 2.8, 2 letters of reference; for doctorate, GRE, minimum GPA of 3.0, 3 letters of reference. Additional exam requirements/recommendations for international students: Required—TOEFL. *Application deadline:* For fall admission, 6/1 priority date for domestic students, 6/1 for international students; for winter admission, 11/1 priority date for domestic students, 11/1 for international students; for spring admission, 3/1 priority date for domestic students, 3/1 for international students. Applications are processed on a rolling basis. Application fee: $50. Electronic applications accepted. *Expenses:* Tuition, state resident: full-time $9096; part-time $379 per credit. Tuition, nonresident: full-time $23,064; part-time $961 per credit. *Required fees:* $127 per semester. One-time fee: $50. *Financial support:* In 2011–12, 19 students received support, including 1 fellowship with full tuition reimbursement available (averaging $15,000 per year), 2 research assistantships with partial tuition reimbursements available (averaging $9,000 per year), 4 teaching assistantships with partial tuition reimbursements available (averaging $15,000 per year); career-related internships or fieldwork, scholarships/grants, tuition waivers (partial), and unspecified assistantships also available. Support available to part-time students. Financial award application deadline: 2/15; financial award applicants required to submit FAFSA. *Faculty research:* Training and development, marketing, technology, special populations, STEM education. *Total annual research expenditures:* $799,773. *Unit head:* Dr. John M. Ritz, Graduate Program Director, 757-683-5226, Fax: 757-683-5227, E-mail: jritz@odu.edu. *Application contact:* William Heffelfinger, Director of Graduate Admissions, 757-683-5554, Fax: 757-683-3255, E-mail: gradadmit@odu.edu. Web site: http://education.odu.edu/ots/.

Pontifical Catholic University of Puerto Rico, College of Education, Doctoral Program in Business Teacher Education, Ponce, PR 00717-0777. Offers PhD. *Degree requirements:* For doctorate, thesis/dissertation. *Entrance requirements:* For doctorate, EXADEP, GRE General Test or MAT, 3 letters of recommendation.

Pontifical Catholic University of Puerto Rico, College of Education, Master's Program in Business Teacher Education, Ponce, PR 00717-0777. Offers M Ed. *Degree requirements:* For master's, comprehensive exam, thesis (for some programs). *Entrance requirements:* For master's, GRE, 2 letters of recommendation, interview, minimum GPA of 2.75.

Rider University, Department of Graduate Education, Leadership and Counseling, Teacher Certification Program, Lawrenceville, NJ 08648-3001. Offers business education (Certificate); elementary education (Certificate); English as a second language (Certificate); English education (Certificate); mathematics education (Certificate); preschool to grade 3 (Certificate); science education (Certificate); social studies education (Certificate); world languages (Certificate), including French, German, Spanish. Part-time programs available. *Degree requirements:* For Certificate, internship, professional portfolio. *Entrance requirements:* For degree, PRAXIS, resume. Additional exam requirements/recommendations for international students: Required—TOEFL (minimum score 550 paper-based; 213 computer-based). Electronic applications accepted. *Expenses: Tuition:* Full-time $32,820; part-time $710 per credit. *Required fees:* $350; $35 per course. Tuition and fees vary according to campus/location and program. *Faculty research:* Conceptual foundations for optimal development of creativity; creative theory, cognitive processes in mathematics learning, teacher collaboration.

Robert Morris University, Graduate Studies, School of Education and Social Sciences, Moon Township, PA 15108-1189. Offers business education (MS); education (Postbaccalaureate Certificate); instructional leadership (MS), including education, sport management; instructional management and leadership (PhD). *Accreditation:* Teacher Education Accreditation Council. Part-time and evening/weekend programs available. Postbaccalaureate distance learning degree programs offered (no on-campus study). *Faculty:* 14 full-time (3 women), 11 part-time/adjunct (6 women). *Students:* 326 part-time (217 women); includes 24 minority (21 Black or African American, non-Hispanic/Latino; 1 Asian, non-Hispanic/Latino; 2 Hispanic/Latino), 1 international. *Degree requirements:* For doctorate, thesis/dissertation. *Entrance requirements:* Additional exam requirements/recommendations for international students: Required—TOEFL (minimum score 550 paper-based; 213 computer-based; 79 iBT). *Application deadline:* For fall admission, 7/1 priority date for domestic students, 7/1 for international students; for spring admission, 11/1 priority date for domestic students, 11/1 for international students. Applications are processed on a rolling basis. Application fee: $35. Electronic applications accepted. *Expenses:* Contact institution. *Unit head:* Dr. John E. Graham, Dean, 412-397-6022, Fax: 412-397-2524, E-mail: graham@rmu.edu. *Application contact:* Debra Roach, Assistant Dean, Graduate Admissions, 412-397-5200, Fax: 412-397-2425, E-mail: graduateadmissions@rmu.edu. Web site: http://www.rmu.edu/web/cms/schools/sess/.

Salve Regina University, Program in Management, Newport, RI 02840-4192. Offers business studies (Certificate); holistic leadership and management (Certificate); human resources management (Certificate); law enforcement leadership (MS); leadership and change management (Certificate); management (Certificate); organizational development (Certificate). Part-time and evening/weekend programs available. Postbaccalaureate distance learning degree programs offered (minimal on-campus study). *Faculty:* 2 full-time (1 woman), 15 part-time/adjunct (6 women). *Students:* 9 full-time (6 women), 40 part-time (20 women); includes 2 minority (both Black or African American, non-Hispanic/Latino). *Entrance requirements:* For master's, GMAT, GRE General Test, or MAT. Additional exam requirements/recommendations for international students: Required—TOEFL (minimum score 600 paper-based; 250 computer-based; 100 iBT). *Application deadline:* For fall admission, 3/15 priority date for domestic students, 3/5 for international students; for spring admission, 3/15 priority date for domestic students, 9/15 for international students. Applications are processed on a rolling basis. Application fee: $60. Electronic applications accepted. *Expenses: Tuition:* Full-time $7740; part-time $430 per credit. *Required fees:* $40 per semester. Tuition and fees vary according to program. *Financial support:* Career-related internships or fieldwork and Federal Work-Study available. Support available to part-time students. Financial award application deadline: 3/1; financial award applicants required to submit FAFSA. *Unit head:* Dr. Arlene Nicholas, Director, 401-341-3280, E-mail: arlene.nicholas@salve.edu. *Application contact:* Kelly Alverson, Associate Director of Graduate Admissions, 401-341-2153, Fax: 401-341-2973, E-mail: kelly.alverson@salve.edu. Web site: http://www.salve.edu/graduatestudies/programs/mgt/.

South Carolina State University, School of Graduate Studies, Department of Education, Orangeburg, SC 29117-0001. Offers counseling education (M Ed); early childhood and special education (M Ed); early childhood education (MAT); educational leadership (Ed D, Ed S); elementary education (M Ed, MAT); engineering (MAT); general science (MAT); mathematics (MAT); secondary education (M Ed), including biology education, business education, counselor education, English education, home economics education, industrial education, mathematics education, science education, social studies education; special education (M Ed), including emotionally handicapped, learning disabilities, mentally handicapped. *Accreditation:* NCATE. Part-time and evening/weekend programs available. *Faculty:* 9 full-time (6 women), 6 part-time/adjunct (2 women). *Students:* 34 full-time (29 women), 50 part-time (40 women); includes 74 minority (72 Black or African American, non-Hispanic/Latino; 1 Asian, non-Hispanic/Latino; 1 Hispanic/Latino). Average age 34. 23 applicants, 91% accepted, 14 enrolled. In 2011, 11 master's awarded. *Degree requirements:* For master's, thesis optional, departmental qualifying exam. *Entrance requirements:* For master's, GRE General Test, NTE, interview, teaching certificate. *Application deadline:* For fall admission, 6/15 priority date for domestic students, 6/15 for international students; for spring admission, 11/1 for domestic and international students. Applications are processed on a rolling basis. Application fee: $25. Electronic applications accepted. *Expenses:* Tuition, state resident: full-time $8688; part-time $514 per credit hour. Tuition, nonresident: full-time $17,600; part-time $1009 per credit hour. *Required fees:* $570. *Financial support:* In 2011–12, 3 fellowships (averaging $5,020 per year) were awarded; career-related internships or fieldwork, Federal Work-Study, and institutionally sponsored loans also available. Financial award application deadline: 6/1. *Faculty research:* Critical thinking, child abuse, stress, test-taking skills, conflict resolution, mainstreaming. *Unit head:* Dr. Charlie Spell, Interim Chair, 803-536-7098, Fax: 803-516-4568, E-mail: cspell@scsu.edu. *Application contact:* Annette Hazzard-Jones, Program Coordinator II, 803-536-8809, Fax: 803-536-8812, E-mail: zs_ahazzard@scsu.edu.

Southern New Hampshire University, School of Education, Manchester, NH 03106-1045. Offers business education (MS); child development (M Ed); computer technology education (Certificate); curriculum and instruction (M Ed); education (M Ed, CAS); elementary education (M Ed); general special education (Certificate); school business administrator (Certificate); secondary education (M Ed); training and development (Certificate). Part-time and evening/weekend programs available. Postbaccalaureate distance learning degree programs offered (no on-campus study). *Degree requirements:* For master's, comprehensive exam (for some programs), thesis or alternative. *Entrance requirements:* For master's, PRAXIS I, minimum GPA of 2.75. Additional exam requirements/recommendations for international students: Required—TOEFL (minimum score 550 paper-based; 213 computer-based). Electronic applications accepted. *Expenses:* Contact institution.

State University of New York at Oswego, Graduate Studies, School of Education, Department of Vocational Teacher Preparation, Oswego, NY 13126. Offers agriculture (MS Ed); business and marketing (MS Ed); family and consumer sciences (MS Ed); health careers (MS Ed); technical education (MS Ed); trade education (MS Ed). *Accreditation:* NCATE. Part-time and evening/weekend programs available. *Degree requirements:* For master's, comprehensive exam, thesis or alternative. *Entrance requirements:* Additional exam requirements/recommendations for international students: Required—TOEFL (minimum score 560 paper-based; 220 computer-based).

Thomas College, Graduate School, Programs in Business, Waterville, ME 04901-5097. Offers business (MBA); computer technology education (MS); education (MS); human resource management (MBA). Part-time and evening/weekend programs available. *Entrance requirements:* For master's, GMAT, GRE, MAT or minimum GPA of 3.3 in first 3 graduate-level courses. Additional exam requirements/recommendations for international students: Recommended—TOEFL.

The University of British Columbia, Faculty of Education, Department of Curriculum and Pedagogy, Vancouver, BC V6T 1Z4, Canada. Offers art education (M Ed, MA); business education (MA); curriculum studies (M Ed, MA, PhD); home economics education (M Ed, MA); math education (M Ed, MA); music education (M Ed, MA); physical education (M Ed, MA); science education (M Ed, MA); social studies education (M Ed, MA); technology studies education (M Ed, MA). Part-time programs available. *Degree requirements:* For master's, thesis (MA); for doctorate, comprehensive exam, thesis/dissertation. *Entrance requirements:* Additional exam requirements/recommendations for international students: Required—TOEFL (minimum score 580 paper-based; 237 computer-based; 92 iBT). Electronic applications accepted. *Expenses:* Contact institution. *Faculty research:* School subjects, teaching and learning.

University of Delaware, Alfred Lerner College of Business and Economics, Department of Economics, Newark, DE 19716. Offers economic education (PhD); economics (MA, MS, PhD); economics for entrepreneurship and educators (MA); MA/MBA. Part-time programs available. *Degree requirements:* For master's, comprehensive exam, thesis (for some programs), mathematics review exam, research project; for doctorate, comprehensive exam, thesis/dissertation, field exam. *Entrance requirements:* For master's, GMAT or GRE General Test, minimum GPA of 2.5; for doctorate, GRE General Test, minimum GPA of 3.5 in graduate economics course work. Additional exam requirements/recommendations for international students: Required—TOEFL (minimum score 550 paper-based; 225 computer-based). Electronic applications accepted. *Faculty research:* Applied quantitative economics, industrial organization, resource economics, monetary economics, labor economics.

University of Minnesota, Twin Cities Campus, Graduate School, College of Education and Human Development, Department of Organizational Leadership, Policy and Development, Program in Business and Industry Education, Minneapolis, MN 55455-0213. Offers M Ed, MA, Ed D, PhD. *Students:* 5 full-time (2 women), 9 part-time (2 women). Average age 30. 2 applicants, 100% accepted, 2 enrolled. In 2011, 8 master's awarded. Application fee: $55. *Unit head:* Dr. Rebecca Ropers-Huilman, Chair, 612-624-1006, E-mail: ropers@umn.edu. *Application contact:* Dr. Jennifer Engler,

Assistant Dean, 612-626-2887, Fax: 612-626-7496, E-mail: engle009@umn.edu. Web site: http://www.cehd.umn.edu/WHRE//BIE.

University of Missouri, Graduate School, College of Education, Department of Learning, Teaching and Curriculum, Columbia, MO 65211. Offers agricultural education (M Ed, PhD, Ed S); art education (M Ed, PhD, Ed S); business and office education (M Ed, PhD, Ed S); early childhood education (M Ed, PhD, Ed S); elementary education (M Ed, PhD, Ed S); English education (M Ed, PhD, Ed S); foreign language education (M Ed, PhD, Ed S); health education and promotion (M Ed, PhD); learning and instruction (M Ed); marketing education (M Ed, PhD, Ed S); mathematics education (M Ed, PhD, Ed S); music education (M Ed, PhD, Ed S); reading education (M Ed, PhD, Ed S); science education (M Ed, PhD, Ed S); social studies education (M Ed, PhD, Ed S); vocational education (M Ed, PhD, Ed S). Part-time programs available. *Faculty:* 26 full-time (16 women), 3 part-time/adjunct (2 women). *Students:* 184 full-time (145 women), 276 part-time (215 women); includes 34 minority (10 Black or African American, non-Hispanic/Latino; 1 American Indian or Alaska Native, non-Hispanic/Latino; 7 Asian, non-Hispanic/Latino; 8 Hispanic/Latino; 8 Two or more races, non-Hispanic/Latino), 39 international. Average age 32. 309 applicants, 76% accepted, 204 enrolled. In 2011, 232 master's, 8 doctorates, 2 other advanced degrees awarded. Terminal master's awarded for partial completion of doctoral program. *Degree requirements:* For doctorate, thesis/dissertation. *Entrance requirements:* For master's and Ed S, GRE General Test or MAT, minimum GPA of 3.0; for doctorate, GRE General Test, minimum GPA of 3.0. Additional exam requirements/recommendations for international students: Required—TOEFL (minimum score 600 paper-based; 250 computer-based; 100 iBT). Application fee: $55 ($75 for international students). Electronic applications accepted. *Expenses:* Tuition, state resident: full-time $5881. Tuition, nonresident: full-time $15,183. *Required fees:* $952. Tuition and fees vary according to campus/location and program. *Financial support:* Fellowships, research assistantships, teaching assistantships, and institutionally sponsored loans available. *Application contact:* Fran Colley, 573-882-6462, E-mail: colleyf@missouri.edu. Web site: http://education.missouri.edu/LTC/.

University of St. Francis, College of Business and Health Administration, School of Professional Studies, Joliet, IL 60435-6169. Offers training and development (MS). *Accreditation:* ACBSP. Part-time and evening/weekend programs available. Postbaccalaureate distance learning degree programs offered (no on-campus study). *Faculty:* 2 full-time (1 woman), 4 part-time/adjunct (1 woman). *Students:* 8 full-time (5 women), 38 part-time (35 women); includes 13 minority (10 Black or African American, non-Hispanic/Latino; 1 Asian, non-Hispanic/Latino; 2 Hispanic/Latino), 1 international. Average age 42. 21 applicants, 67% accepted, 13 enrolled. In 2011, 10 degrees awarded. *Entrance requirements:* For master's, minimum GPA of 2.75, 2 letters recommendation, personal essay, computer proficiency. Additional exam requirements/recommendations for international students: Required—TOEFL (minimum score 550 paper-based; 213 computer-based). *Application deadline:* Applications are processed on a rolling basis. Application fee: $30. Electronic applications accepted. *Expenses:* Contact institution. *Financial support:* In 2011–12, 14 students received support. Tuition waivers (partial) and unspecified assistantships available. Support available to part-time students. Financial award applicants required to submit FAFSA. *Unit head:* Dr. Christopher Clott, Dean, 815-740-3395, Fax: 815-774-2920, E-mail: cclott@stfrancis.edu. *Application contact:* Sandra Sloka, Director of Admissions for Graduate and Degree Completion Programs, 800-735-7500, Fax: 815-740-5032, E-mail: ssloka@stfrancis.edu. Web site: http://www.stfrancis.edu/academics/college-of-business-health-administration/school-of-professional-studies/.

University of South Carolina, The Graduate School, College of Education, Department of Instruction and Teacher Education, Program in Secondary Education, Columbia, SC 29208. Offers art education (IMA, MAT); business education (IMA, MAT); English (MAT); foreign language (MAT); health education (MAT); mathematics (MAT); science (IMA, MAT); secondary (Ed D); secondary education (MT, PhD); social studies (MAT); theatre and speech (MAT). IMA and MT offered jointly with the subject areas. *Accreditation:* NCATE. *Degree requirements:* For master's, comprehensive exam, thesis (for some programs), foreign language (MA); for doctorate, one foreign language, comprehensive exam, thesis/dissertation. *Entrance requirements:* For master's, GRE General Test or MAT, teaching certificate (IMA, M Ed), interview; for doctorate, GRE General Test or MAT, interview. *Faculty research:* Middle school programs, professional development, school collaboration.

University of the Cumberlands, Graduate Programs in Education, Williamsburg, KY 40769-1372. Offers all grades (P-12) (M Ed); business and marketing (MA Ed, MAT); director of pupil personnel (Certificate); director of special education (Certificate); educational administration and supervision (Ed S); educational leadership (Ed D); elementary education (MA Ed, MAT); instructional leadership - principalship (MA Ed); instructional leadership - school principal (Certificate); middle school education (MA Ed, MAT); reading and writing (MA Ed); school counseling (MA Ed); school superintendent (Certificate); secondary education (MA Ed, MAT); special education (MAT); supervisor of instruction (Certificate); teacher leader (MA Ed). Part-time and evening/weekend programs available. Postbaccalaureate distance learning degree programs offered. *Degree requirements:* For master's, comprehensive exam. Electronic applications accepted.

The University of Toledo, College of Graduate Studies, Judith Herb College of Education, Health Science and Human Service, Department of Curriculum and Instruction, Toledo, OH 43606-3390. Offers art education (ME); career and technical education (ME); curriculum and instruction (ME, PhD, Ed S); education and anthropology (MAE); education and biology (MES); education and chemistry (MES); education and classics (MAE); education and economics (MAE); education and English (MAE); education and French (MAE); education and geography (MAE); education and geology (MES); education and German (MAE); education and history (MAE); education and mathematics (MAE, MES); education and physics (MES); education and political science (MAE); education and sociology (MAE); education and Spanish (MAE); educational media (PhD); educational technology (ME); English as a second language (MAE); gifted and talented (PhD); middle childhood education licensure (ME); music education (MME); secondary education (PhD); secondary education licensure (ME). *Accreditation:* NCATE. Part-time and evening/weekend programs available. *Faculty:* 24. *Students:* 60 full-time (31 women), 211 part-time (161 women); includes 23 minority (21 Black or African American, non-Hispanic/Latino; 2 Hispanic/Latino), 20 international. Average age 35. 115 applicants, 73% accepted, 74 enrolled. In 2011, 105 master's, 3 doctorates, 4 other advanced degrees awarded. *Degree requirements:* For master's, comprehensive exam, thesis or alternative; for doctorate, comprehensive exam, thesis/dissertation; for Ed S, thesis optional. *Entrance requirements:* For master's, doctorate, and Ed S, minimum cumulative GPA of 2.7 for all previous academic work, letters of recommendation. Additional exam requirements/recommendations for international students: Required—TOEFL (minimum score 550 paper-based; 213 computer-based; 80 iBT), IELTS (minimum score 6.5). *Application deadline:* For fall admission, 1/15 priority date for domestic students, 1/15 for international students. Applications are processed on a rolling basis. Application fee: $45 ($75 for international students). Electronic applications accepted. *Financial support:* In 2011–12, 9 research assistantships with full and partial tuition reimbursements (averaging $7,184 per year), 12 teaching assistantships with full and partial tuition reimbursements (averaging $8,425 per year) were awarded; career-related internships or fieldwork, Federal Work-Study, institutionally sponsored loans, scholarships/grants, tuition waivers (full and partial), unspecified assistantships, and administrative assistantships also available. Support available to part-time students. *Unit head:* Dr. Leigh Chiarelott, Chair, 419-530-5371, E-mail: eigh.chiarelott@utoledo.edu. *Application contact:* Graduate School Office, 419-530-4723, Fax: 419-530-4724, E-mail: grdsch@utnet.utoledo.edu. Web site: http://www.utoledo.edu/eduhshs/.

University of Washington, Graduate School, Michael G. Foster School of Business, Seattle, WA 98195-3233. Offers auditing and assurance (MP Acc); business (PhD); business administration (evening) (MBA); business administration (full-time) (MBA); executive business administration (MBA); global business administration (MBA); global executive business administration (MBA); taxation (MP Acc); technology management (MBA); JD/MBA; MBA/MAIS; MBA/MHA. *Accreditation:* AACSB. Part-time programs available. *Faculty:* 100 full-time (28 women), 55 part-time/adjunct (22 women). *Students:* 385 full-time (116 women), 483 part-time (118 women); includes 183 minority (16 Black or African American, non-Hispanic/Latino; 2 American Indian or Alaska Native, non-Hispanic/Latino; 133 Asian, non-Hispanic/Latino; 25 Hispanic/Latino; 2 Native Hawaiian or other Pacific Islander, non-Hispanic/Latino; 5 Two or more races, non-Hispanic/Latino), 178 international. Average age 32. 1,367 applicants, 76% accepted, 868 enrolled. In 2011, 458 master's, 12 doctorates awarded. Terminal master's awarded for partial completion of doctoral program. *Degree requirements:* For doctorate, comprehensive exam, thesis/dissertation. *Entrance requirements:* For master's, GMAT; for doctorate, GMAT, GRE. Additional exam requirements/recommendations for international students: Required—TOEFL (minimum score 600 paper-based; 250 computer-based; 100 iBT). *Application deadline:* For fall admission, 3/15 for domestic students, 1/20 for international students. Application fee: $75. Electronic applications accepted. *Expenses:* Contact institution. *Financial support:* Fellowships with partial tuition reimbursements, research assistantships with partial tuition reimbursements, teaching assistantships with partial tuition reimbursements, Federal Work-Study, institutionally sponsored loans, and scholarships/grants available. Financial award application deadline: 2/28; financial award applicants required to submit FAFSA. *Faculty research:* Finance, marketing, organizational behavior, information technology, strategy. *Unit head:* Dr. James Jiambalvo, Dean, 206-543-4750. *Application contact:* Erin Ernst, Assistant Director of Admissions, 206-543-4661, Fax: 206-616-7351, E-mail: mba@u.washington.edu. Web site: http://www.foster.washington.edu/mba.

University of West Georgia, College of Education, Department of Leadership and Applied Instruction, Carrollton, GA 30118. Offers art education (M Ed); art teacher education (Ed S); biology - secondary education (M Ed); biology/secondary education (Ed S); business education (M Ed, Ed S); chemistry/secondary education (Ed S); earth science/secondary education (Ed S); economics/secondary education (Ed S); educational leadership (M Ed, Ed S); English teacher education (M Ed, Ed S); French teacher education (M Ed, Ed S); history teacher education (Ed S); mathematics teacher education (M Ed, Ed S); middle grades education (M Ed, Ed S); physical education and recreation (Ed S); physical education teaching and coaching (M Ed); physics/secondary education (Ed S); science teacher education (M Ed, Ed S); secondary education (M Ed); social science - secondary education (M Ed); social science teacher education (M Ed); Spanish (M Ed); Spanish teacher education (M Ed, Ed S); sports management (M Ed). *Accreditation:* NCATE. Part-time and evening/weekend programs available. *Faculty:* 18 full-time (9 women). *Students:* 75 full-time (49 women), 169 part-time (109 women); includes 90 minority (85 Black or African American, non-Hispanic/Latino; 3 Hispanic/Latino; 2 Two or more races, non-Hispanic/Latino), 1 international. Average age 36. 115 applicants, 67% accepted, 19 enrolled. In 2011, 73 master's, 53 Ed Ss awarded. *Degree requirements:* For master's, internship; for Ed S, research project. *Entrance requirements:* For master's, GRE General Test, minimum GPA of 2.7; for Ed S, GRE General Test, master's degree, minimum graduate GPA of 3.0, district appointment. Additional exam requirements/recommendations for international students: Required—TOEFL (minimum score 523 paper-based; 193 computer-based; 69 iBT); Recommended—IELTS (minimum score 6). *Application deadline:* For fall admission, 7/21 for domestic students, 6/1 for international students; for spring admission, 11/30 for domestic students, 10/15 for international students. Applications are processed on a rolling basis. Application fee: $30. Electronic applications accepted. *Expenses:* Tuition, state resident: full-time $4336; part-time $181 per credit hour. Tuition, nonresident: full-time $17,362; part-time $724 per credit hour. Tuition and fees vary according to course load, degree level, campus/location and program. *Financial support:* In 2011–12, 1 research assistantship with full tuition reimbursement (averaging $7,444 per year) was awarded; career-related internships or fieldwork, scholarships/grants, and unspecified assistantships also available. Support available to part-time students. Financial award application deadline: 7/1; financial award applicants required to submit FAFSA. *Total annual research expenditures:* $5,000. *Unit head:* Dr. Frank Butts, Chair, 678-839-6530, Fax: 678-839-6195, E-mail: fbutts@westga.edu. *Application contact:* Deanna Richards, Coordinator, Graduate Studies, 678-839-5946, E-mail: drichard@westga.edu. Web site: http://www.westga.edu/coelai.

University of Wisconsin–Whitewater, School of Graduate Studies, College of Business and Economics, Department of Business Education, Whitewater, WI 53190-1790. Offers business and marketing education (MS), including general, post secondary, secondary. *Accreditation:* NCATE. Part-time and evening/weekend programs available. Postbaccalaureate distance learning degree programs offered (no on-campus study). *Students:* 2 full-time (1 woman), 19 part-time (8 women); includes 1 minority (Hispanic/Latino). Average age 35. 5 applicants, 80% accepted, 2 enrolled. In 2011, 7 master's awarded. *Degree requirements:* For master's, thesis or alternative. *Entrance requirements:* For master's, interview, teaching license. Additional exam requirements/recommendations for international students: Required—TOEFL (minimum score 550 paper-based; 213 computer-based; 80 iBT), IELTS (minimum score 6). *Application deadline:* For fall admission, 7/15 priority date for domestic students, 7/15 for international students; for spring admission, 12/1 priority date for domestic students, 12/1 for international students. Applications are processed on a rolling basis. Application fee: $56. Electronic applications accepted. *Expenses:* Tuition, state resident: full-time $4088. Tuition, nonresident: full-time $8817. Tuition and fees vary according to program. *Financial support:* In 2011–12, 2 research assistantships (averaging $7,245 per year) were awarded; Federal Work-Study, unspecified assistantships, and out of state fee waiver also available. Support available to part-time students. Financial award application deadline: 3/15; financial award applicants required to submit FAFSA. *Faculty research:* Active learning and performance strategies, technology-enhanced formative assessment, computer-supported cooperative work, privacy surveillance. *Unit head:* Dr. Lila Waldman, Coordinator, 262-472-5475. *Application contact:* Sally A. Lange, School of Graduate Studies, 262-472-1006, Fax: 262-472-5027, E-mail: gradschl@uww.edu.

Utah State University, School of Graduate Studies, College of Business, Department of Business Information Systems, Logan, UT 84322. Offers business education (MS); business information systems (MS); business information systems and education (Ed D); education (PhD). Part-time programs available. Terminal master's awarded for partial completion of doctoral program. *Degree requirements:* For master's, thesis optional; for doctorate, thesis/dissertation. *Entrance requirements:* For master's, GMAT, minimum GPA of 3.2; for doctorate, GRE General Test, minimum GPA of 3.0. Additional exam requirements/recommendations for international students: Required—TOEFL. *Faculty research:* Oral and written communication, methods of teaching, CASE tools, object-oriented programming, decision support systems.

Utah State University, School of Graduate Studies, Emma Eccles Jones College of Education and Human Services, Doctoral Program in Education, Logan, UT 84322. Offers business information systems (Ed D, PhD); curriculum and instruction (Ed D, PhD); research and evaluation (PhD). *Degree requirements:* For doctorate, comprehensive exam, thesis/dissertation. *Entrance requirements:* For doctorate, GRE General Test, minimum GPA of 3.0, master's degree. Additional exam requirements/recommendations for international students: Required—TOEFL. Electronic applications accepted. *Faculty research:* Language and literacy development, math and science education, instructional technology, hearing problems/deafness, domestic violence and animal abuse.

Wayne State College, School of Education and Counseling, Department of Educational Foundations and Leadership, Program in Curriculum and Instruction, Wayne, NE 68787. Offers alternative education (MSE); business and information technology education (MSE); communication arts education (MSE); early childhood education (MSE); elementary education (MSE); English as a second language (MSE); English education (MSE); family and consumer sciences education (MSE); industrial technology and vocational education (MSE); learning communities (MSE); mathematics education (MSE); music education (MSE); science education (MSE); social science education (MSE). *Accreditation:* NCATE. Part-time and evening/weekend programs available. *Degree requirements:* For master's, comprehensive exam, thesis optional. *Entrance requirements:* For master's, GRE General Test. Additional exam requirements/recommendations for international students: Required—TOEFL (minimum score 550 paper-based; 213 computer-based).

Wright State University, School of Graduate Studies, College of Education and Human Services, Department of Teacher Education, Programs in Workforce Education, Dayton, OH 45435. Offers career, technology and vocational education (M Ed, MA); computer/technology education (M Ed, MA); library/media (M Ed, MA); vocational education (M Ed, MA). *Accreditation:* NCATE. *Degree requirements:* For master's, thesis (for some programs). *Entrance requirements:* For master's, GRE General Test, MAT. Additional exam requirements/recommendations for international students: Required—TOEFL.

Computer Education

Arcadia University, Graduate Studies, Department of Education, Glenside, PA 19038-3295. Offers art education (M Ed); computer education (CAS); curriculum (CAS); curriculum studies (M Ed); early childhood education (M Ed, CAS), including individualized (M Ed), master teacher (M Ed), research in child development (M Ed); educational leadership (M Ed, Ed D, CAS); elementary education (M Ed, CAS); English education (MA Ed); environmental education (MA Ed, CAS); history education (MA Ed); instructional technology (M Ed); language arts (M Ed, CAS); library science (M Ed); mathematics education (M Ed, MA Ed, CAS); music education (MA Ed); psychology (MA Ed); reading (M Ed, CAS); science education (M Ed, CAS); secondary education (M Ed, CAS); special education (M Ed, Ed D, CAS); theater arts (MA Ed); written communication (MA Ed). *Accreditation:* NASAD. Part-time and evening/weekend programs available. Postbaccalaureate distance learning degree programs offered (minimal on-campus study). *Faculty:* 12 full-time (8 women), 38 part-time/adjunct (26 women). *Students:* 66 full-time (48 women), 590 part-time (477 women); includes 65 minority (53 Black or African American, non-Hispanic/Latino; 6 Asian, non-Hispanic/Latino; 3 Hispanic/Latino; 3 Two or more races, non-Hispanic/Latino), 4 international. Average age 36. In 2011, 229 master's, 5 doctorates awarded. *Application deadline:* Applications are processed on a rolling basis. Application fee: $50. Electronic applications accepted. *Expenses:* Contact institution. *Financial support:* Career-related internships or fieldwork, tuition waivers (partial), and unspecified assistantships available. *Unit head:* Dr. Steven P. Gulkus, Associate Professor, 215-572-2120, E-mail: gulkus@arcadia.edu. *Application contact:* 215-572-2925, Fax: 215-572-2126, E-mail: grad@arcadia.edu.

California State University, Dominguez Hills, College of Professional Studies, School of Education, Division of Graduate Education, Program in Technology-Based Education, Carson, CA 90747-0001. Offers MA, Certificate. Part-time and evening/weekend programs available. *Faculty:* 1 (woman) full-time. *Students:* 7 full-time (4 women), 35 part-time (19 women); includes 30 minority (10 Black or African American, non-Hispanic/Latino; 4 Asian, non-Hispanic/Latino; 14 Hispanic/Latino; 1 Native Hawaiian or other Pacific Islander, non-Hispanic/Latino; 1 Two or more races, non-Hispanic/Latino), 1 international. Average age 38. 23 applicants, 91% accepted, 16 enrolled. In 2011, 27 master's awarded. *Degree requirements:* For master's, comprehensive exam, thesis or alternative. *Entrance requirements:* For master's, minimum GPA of 2.75. *Application deadline:* For fall admission, 6/1 for domestic students. Application fee: $55. *Faculty research:* Media literacy, assistive technology. *Unit head:* Dr. Peter Desberg, Unit Head, 310-243-3908, E-mail: pdesberg@csudh.edu. *Application contact:* Admissions Office, 310-243-3530. Web site: http://www.csudh.edu/cps/soe/programsdegrees/graduate-programs-technology.shtml.

Cardinal Stritch University, College of Education, Department of Educational Computing, Milwaukee, WI 53217-3985. Offers instructional technology (ME, MS). Part-time and evening/weekend programs available. *Degree requirements:* For master's, comprehensive exam, thesis, faculty recommendation. *Entrance requirements:* For master's, letters of recommendation (2), minimum GPA of 2.75.

Christopher Newport University, Graduate Studies, Department of Teacher Preparation, Newport News, VA 23606-2998. Offers art (PK-12) (MAT); biology (6-12) (MAT); chemistry (6-12) (MAT); computer science (6-12) (MAT); elementary (PK-6) (MAT); English (6-12) (MAT); English as second language (PK-12) (MAT); French (PK-12) (MAT); history and social science (6-12) (MAT); mathematics (6-12) (MAT); music (PK-12) (MAT), including choral, instrumental; physics (6-12) (MAT); Spanish (PK-12) (MAT). Part-time and evening/weekend programs available. *Degree requirements:* For master's, comprehensive exam, thesis or alternative. *Entrance requirements:* For master's, PRAXIS I, minimum GPA of 3.0. Additional exam requirements/recommendations for international students: Required—TOEFL (minimum score 580 paper-based; 237 computer-based; 92 iBT). Electronic applications accepted. *Faculty research:* Early literacy development, instructional innovations, professional teaching standards, multicultural issues, aesthetic education.

Duquesne University, School of Education, Department of Instruction and Leadership, Program in Instructional Technology, Pittsburgh, PA 15282-0001. Offers business, computer, and information technology (MS Ed); instructional technology (MS Ed, Ed D, Post-Master's Certificate). Part-time and evening/weekend programs available. Postbaccalaureate distance learning degree programs offered (minimal on-campus study). *Faculty:* 3 full-time (1 woman), 13 part-time/adjunct (10 women). *Students:* 82 full-time (50 women), 14 part-time (9 women); includes 4 minority (2 Black or African American, non-Hispanic/Latino; 2 Hispanic/Latino), 4 international. Average age 32. 23 applicants, 65% accepted, 11 enrolled. In 2011, 30 master's, 1 doctorate awarded. *Degree requirements:* For master's, thesis optional; for doctorate, thesis/dissertation. *Entrance requirements:* For master's, bachelor's degree; for doctorate, GRE, master's degree; for Post-Master's Certificate, bachelor's/master's degree. Additional exam requirements/recommendations for international students: Required—TOEFL (minimum score 550 paper-based; 80 computer-based), IELTS (minimum score 7). *Application deadline:* For fall admission, 9/1 for domestic students; for spring admission, 1/1 for domestic students. Applications are processed on a rolling basis. Application fee: $0. Electronic applications accepted. Application fee is waived when completed online. *Expenses: Tuition:* Full-time $16,596; part-time $922 per credit. *Required fees:* $1584; $88 per credit. Tuition and fees vary according to program. *Financial support:* Available to part-time students. *Unit head:* Dr. David Carbonara, Director, 412-396-4039, Fax: 412-396-1997, E-mail: carbonara@duq.edu. *Application contact:* Michael Dolinger, Director of Student and Academic Services, 412-396-6647, Fax: 412-396-5585, E-mail: dolingerm@duq.edu. Web site: http://www.duq.edu/education.

East Carolina University, Graduate School, College of Education, Department of Mathematics, Science, and Instructional Technology Education, Greenville, NC 27858-4353. Offers computer-based instruction (Certificate); distance learning and administration (Certificate); instructional technology (MA Ed, MS); mathematics (MA Ed); performance improvement (Certificate); science education (MA, MA Ed); special endorsement in computer education (Certificate). Part-time and evening/weekend programs available. *Degree requirements:* For master's, comprehensive exam, thesis optional. *Entrance requirements:* For master's, GRE General Test or MAT, interview, minimum GPA of 2.5, bachelor's degree in related field, teaching license (MA Ed). Additional exam requirements/recommendations for international students: Required—TOEFL. *Application deadline:* For fall admission, 6/1 priority date for domestic students. Applications are processed on a rolling basis. Application fee: $50. *Expenses:* Tuition, state resident: full-time $3557; part-time $444.63 per semester hour. Tuition, nonresident: full-time $14,351; part-time $1793.88 per semester hour. *Required fees:* $2016; $252 per semester hour. Part-time tuition and fees vary according to course load, campus/location and program. *Financial support:* Research assistantships, teaching assistantships, and Federal Work-Study available. Support available to part-time students. Financial award application deadline: 6/1. *Unit head:* Susan Ganter, Chair, 252-328-9353, E-mail: ganters@ecu.edu. *Application contact:* Dean of Graduate School, 252-328-6012, Fax: 252-328-6071, E-mail: gradschool@ecu.edu.

Eastern Washington University, Graduate Studies, College of Science, Health and Engineering, Department of Computer Science, Cheney, WA 99004-2431. Offers computer and technology-supported education (M Ed); computer science (MS). Part-time programs available. *Faculty:* 13 full-time (1 woman). *Students:* 16 full-time (3 women), 9 part-time; includes 2 minority (1 Asian, non-Hispanic/Latino; 1 Hispanic/Latino), 1 international. Average age 31. 38 applicants, 16% accepted, 6 enrolled. In 2011, 7 master's awarded. *Degree requirements:* For master's, comprehensive exam, thesis or alternative. *Entrance requirements:* For master's, minimum GPA of 3.0. *Application deadline:* For fall admission, 4/1 priority date for domestic students; for spring admission, 1/15 for domestic students. Applications are processed on a rolling basis. Application fee: $50. *Financial support:* In 2011–12, 17 teaching assistantships with partial tuition reimbursements (averaging $12,000 per year) were awarded; career-related internships or fieldwork, Federal Work-Study, institutionally sponsored loans, scholarships/grants, health care benefits, tuition waivers (partial), and unspecified assistantships also available. Support available to part-time students. Financial award application deadline: 2/1. *Unit head:* Dr. Ray Hamel, Chair, 509-359-4758, Fax: 509-358-2061. *Application contact:* Dr. Timothy Rolfe, Adviser, 509-359-4276, Fax: 509-359-2215. Web site: http://www.ewu.edu/cshe/programs/computer-science.xml.

Florida Institute of Technology, Graduate Programs, College of Science, Department of Education and Interdisciplinary Studies, Melbourne, FL 32901-6975. Offers computer education (MS); elementary science education (M Ed); environmental education (MS); interdisciplinary science (MS); mathematics education (MS, PhD, Ed S); science education (MS, PhD, Ed S), including informal science education (MS); teaching (MAT). Part-time and evening/weekend programs available. *Faculty:* 4 full-time (1 woman), 3 part-time/adjunct (2 women). *Students:* 22 full-time (16 women), 27 part-time (18 women); includes 8 minority (2 Black or African American, non-Hispanic/Latino; 4 Asian, non-Hispanic/Latino; 2 Hispanic/Latino), 9 international. Average age 34. 57 applicants, 70% accepted, 19 enrolled. In 2011, 5 master's, 1 doctorate awarded. Terminal master's awarded for partial completion of doctoral program. *Median time to degree:* Of those who began their doctoral program in fall 2003, 50% received their degree in 8 years or less. *Degree requirements:* For master's, comprehensive exam (for some programs), thesis optional; for doctorate, comprehensive exam, thesis/dissertation; for Ed S, comprehensive exam. *Entrance requirements:* For master's, minimum GPA of 3.0, resume, 3 letters of recommendation (elementary science education), statement of objectives; for doctorate, minimum GPA of 3.2, resume, 3 letters of recommendation, statement of objectives, 3 years teaching experience (recommended); for Ed S, minimum GPA of 3.0, resume, 3 letters of recommendation, statement of objectives. Additional exam requirements/recommendations for international students: Required—TOEFL (minimum score 550 paper-based; 213 computer-based; 79 iBT). *Application deadline:* For fall admission, 4/1 for international students; for spring admission, 9/30 for international students. Applications are processed on a rolling basis. Electronic applications accepted. *Expenses: Tuition:* Full-time $19,620; part-time $1090 per credit hour. Tuition and fees vary according to campus/location. *Financial support:* In 2011–12, 1 teaching assistantship with full and partial tuition reimbursement (averaging $797 per year) was awarded; research assistantships with full and partial tuition reimbursements, career-related internships or fieldwork, institutionally sponsored loans, tuition waivers (partial), unspecified assistantships, and tuition remissions also available. Support available to part-time students. Financial award application deadline: 3/1; financial award applicants required to submit FAFSA. *Faculty research:* Measurement and evaluation, computers in education, educational technology. *Total annual research expenditures:* $1. *Unit head:* Dr. Lazlo A. Baksay, Department Head, 321-674-7205, Fax: 321-674-7598, E-mail: baksay@fit.edu. *Application contact:* Cheryl A. Brown,

Associate Director of Graduate Admissions, 321-674-7581, Fax: 321-723-9468, E-mail: cbrown@fit.edu. Web site: http://cos.fit.edu/education/.

Fontbonne University, Graduate Programs, Department of Mathematics and Computer Science, St. Louis, MO 63105-3098. Offers computer education (MS). Part-time and evening/weekend programs available. Postbaccalaureate distance learning degree programs offered (no on-campus study). *Degree requirements:* For master's, thesis optional. *Entrance requirements:* For master's, minimum GPA of 3.0.

Indiana University–Purdue University Indianapolis, School of Education, Indianapolis, IN 46202-2896. Offers computer education (Certificate); curriculum and instruction (MS); early childhood (MS); educational leadership (MS, Certificate); English as a second language (Certificate); higher education and student affairs (MS); kindergarten (Certificate); language education (MS); reading (Certificate); school counseling (MS); special education (MS, Certificate). Part-time and evening/weekend programs available. *Faculty:* 41 full-time, 80 part-time/adjunct. *Students:* 67 full-time (52 women), 467 part-time (360 women); includes 82 minority (44 Black or African American, non-Hispanic/Latino; 3 American Indian or Alaska Native, non-Hispanic/Latino; 8 Asian, non-Hispanic/Latino; 13 Hispanic/Latino; 14 Two or more races, non-Hispanic/Latino), 10 international. Average age 33. 63 applicants, 57% accepted, 29 enrolled. In 2011, 167 master's awarded. *Degree requirements:* For master's, thesis optional. *Entrance requirements:* For master's, GRE General Test, minimum GPA of 3.0. Additional exam requirements/recommendations for international students: Required—TOEFL. *Application deadline:* For fall admission, 5/1 priority date for domestic students; for spring admission, 11/1 for domestic students. Application fee: $55 ($65 for international students). *Financial support:* Fellowships, research assistantships with partial tuition reimbursements, teaching assistantships, Federal Work-Study, institutionally sponsored loans, scholarships/grants, and tuition waivers (partial) available. Support available to part-time students. *Faculty research:* Teachers in the process of change, learning cycles, children's concepts of science. *Total annual research expenditures:* $614,458. *Unit head:* Dr. Chris Leland, Interim Executive Associate Dean, 317-274-6801, Fax: 317-274-6864. *Application contact:* Sarah Brandenburg, Graduate Advisor, 317-274-6801, Fax: 317-274-6864, E-mail: edugrad@iupui.edu. Web site: http://education.iupui.edu/.

Kent State University, Graduate School of Education, Health, and Human Services, School of Lifespan Development and Educational Sciences, Program in Instructional Technology, Kent, OH 44242-0001. Offers computer technology (M Ed); general instructional technology (M Ed). *Accreditation:* NCATE. *Faculty:* 12 full-time (4 women), 3 part-time/adjunct (2 women). *Students:* 11 full-time (9 women), 53 part-time (38 women); includes 5 minority (4 Black or African American, non-Hispanic/Latino; 1 Hispanic/Latino). 21 applicants, 71% accepted. In 2011, 29 master's awarded. *Degree requirements:* For master's, thesis (for some programs). *Entrance requirements:* For master's, 2 letters of reference, goals statement, minimum GPA of 2.75. Additional exam requirements/recommendations for international students: Required—TOEFL (minimum score 550 paper-based; 213 computer-based; 80 iBT). *Application deadline:* Applications are processed on a rolling basis. Application fee: $30 ($60 for international students). *Expenses:* Tuition, state resident: full-time $8136; part-time $452 per credit hour. Tuition, nonresident: full-time $14,292; part-time $794 per credit hour. *Financial support:* Fellowships with full tuition reimbursements, research assistantships with full tuition reimbursements, teaching assistantships with full tuition reimbursements, Federal Work-Study, scholarships/grants, unspecified assistantships, and 1 administrative assistantship (averaging $8,500 per year) available. Financial award application deadline: 4/1; financial award applicants required to submit FAFSA. *Faculty research:* Cooperative learning, aesthetics, computers in schools. *Unit head:* Dr. Drew Tiene, Coordinator, 330-672-0607, E-mail: dtiene@kent.edu. *Application contact:* Nancy Miller, Academic Program Coordinator, Office of Graduate Student Services, 330-672-2576, Fax: 330-672-9162, E-mail: ogs@kent.edu. Web site: http://www.kent.edu/ehhs/itec/.

Lesley University, School of Education, Cambridge, MA 02138-2790. Offers curriculum and instruction (M Ed, CAGS); early childhood education (M Ed); educational studies (PhD); elementary education (M Ed); individually designed (M Ed); middle school education (M Ed); moderate special needs (M Ed); reading (M Ed, CAGS); science in education (M Ed); severe special needs (M Ed); special needs (CAGS); technology in education (M Ed, CAGS). *Accreditation:* Teacher Education Accreditation Council. Part-time and evening/weekend programs available. Postbaccalaureate distance learning degree programs offered (no on-campus study). *Faculty:* 36 full-time (27 women), 170 part-time/adjunct (129 women). *Students:* 552 full-time (437 women), 1,971 part-time (1,697 women); includes 364 minority (189 Black or African American, non-Hispanic/Latino; 19 American Indian or Alaska Native, non-Hispanic/Latino; 45 Asian, non-Hispanic/Latino; 83 Hispanic/Latino; 2 Native Hawaiian or other Pacific Islander, non-Hispanic/Latino; 26 Two or more races, non-Hispanic/Latino), 28 international. Average age 37. In 2011, 1,390 master's, 8 doctorates, 42 other advanced degrees awarded. *Degree requirements:* For master's, practicum; for doctorate, thesis/dissertation. *Entrance requirements:* For doctorate, GRE General Test or MAT, interview, master's degree, resume; for CAGS, interview, master's degree. Additional exam requirements/recommendations for international students: Required—TOEFL (minimum score 550 paper-based; 213 computer-based; 80 iBT). *Application deadline:* Applications are processed on a rolling basis. Application fee: $50. Electronic applications accepted. *Financial support:* In 2011–12, research assistantships (averaging $3,400 per year), teaching assistantships (averaging $3,400 per year) were awarded; career-related internships or fieldwork, Federal Work-Study, scholarships/grants, and unspecified assistantships also available. Support available to part-time students. Financial award application deadline: 4/15; financial award applicants required to submit FAFSA. *Faculty research:* Assessment in literacy, mathematics and science; autism spectrum disorders; instructional technology and online learning; multicultural education and ELL. *Unit head:* Dr. Mario Borunda, Dean, 617-349-8375, Fax: 617-349-8607, E-mail: mborunda@lesley.edu. *Application contact:* Rosie Davis, Senior Assistant Director of Admissions, 617-349-8851, Fax: 617-349-8313, E-mail: rdavis4@lesley.edu. Web site: http://www.lesley.edu/soe.html.

Long Island University–C. W. Post Campus, College of Information and Computer Science, Department of Computer Science/Management Engineering, Brookville, NY 11548-1300. Offers information systems (MS); information technology education (MS); management engineering (MS). Part-time and evening/weekend programs available. *Degree requirements:* For master's, comprehensive exam, thesis or alternative. *Entrance requirements:* For master's, bachelor's degree in science, mathematics, or engineering; minimum GPA of 2.5. Additional exam requirements/recommendations for international students: Required—TOEFL (minimum score 500 paper-based; 173 computer-based). Electronic applications accepted. *Faculty research:* Inductive music learning, re-engineering business process, technology and ethics.

Marlboro College, Graduate School, Program in Teaching with Technology, Marlboro, VT 05344. Offers MAT. Part-time and evening/weekend programs available. Postbaccalaureate distance learning degree programs offered (minimal on-campus study). *Degree requirements:* For master's, 30 credits including capstone project. *Entrance requirements:* For master's, letter of intent, 2 letters of recommendation, transcripts. Electronic applications accepted.

Mississippi College, Graduate School, School of Education, Department of Teacher Education and Leadership, Clinton, MS 39058. Offers art (M Ed); biological science (M Ed); business education (M Ed); computer science (M Ed); dyslexia therapy (M Ed); educational leadership (M Ed, Ed D, Ed S); elementary education (M Ed, Ed S); English (M Ed); higher education administration (MS); mathematics (M Ed); secondary education (M Ed); social studies (history) (M Ed); teaching arts (M Ed). Part-time programs available. Postbaccalaureate distance learning degree programs offered (no on-campus study). *Degree requirements:* For master's, comprehensive exam, thesis optional. *Entrance requirements:* For master's, NTE. Additional exam requirements/recommendations for international students: Recommended—TOEFL, IELTS. Electronic applications accepted.

Ohio University, Graduate College, Gladys W. and David H. Patton College of Education and Human Services, Department of Educational Studies, Athens, OH 45701-2979. Offers computer education and technology (M Ed); cultural studies (M Ed); educational administration (M Ed, Ed D); educational research and evaluation (M Ed, PhD); instructional technology (PhD). Part-time and evening/weekend programs available. Postbaccalaureate distance learning degree programs offered (minimal on-campus study). *Students:* 121 full-time (76 women), 94 part-time (57 women); includes 21 minority (15 Black or African American, non-Hispanic/Latino; 1 American Indian or Alaska Native, non-Hispanic/Latino; 2 Hispanic/Latino; 3 Two or more races, non-Hispanic/Latino), 35 international. 73 applicants, 67% accepted, 32 enrolled. In 2011, 52 master's, 13 doctorates awarded. *Degree requirements:* For master's, thesis or alternative; for doctorate, comprehensive exam, thesis/dissertation. *Entrance requirements:* For master's, GRE General Test (if GPA less than 2.9); for doctorate, GRE General Test, GRE Subject Test, minimum GPA of 2.9, work experience, 3 letters of reference, autobiography. Additional exam requirements/recommendations for international students: Required—TOEFL (minimum score 550 paper-based; 80 iBT) or IELTS (minimum score 6.5). *Application deadline:* For fall admission, 3/1 priority date for domestic students, 3/1 for international students; for winter admission, 10/1 priority date for domestic students, 10/1 for international students; for spring admission, 1/30 priority date for domestic students, 1/1 for international students. Applications are processed on a rolling basis. Application fee: $50 ($55 for international students). Electronic applications accepted. *Financial support:* Research assistantships with full tuition reimbursements, teaching assistantships with full tuition reimbursements, Federal Work-Study, institutionally sponsored loans, tuition waivers (partial), and unspecified assistantships available. Financial award application deadline: 3/1. *Faculty research:* Race, class and gender; computer programs; development and organization theory; evaluation/development of instruments, leadership. *Total annual research expenditures:* $158,037. *Unit head:* Dr. David Richard Moore, Chair, 740-597-1322, Fax: 740-593-0477, E-mail: moored3@ohio.edu. *Application contact:* Floyd J. Doney, Director of Student Affairs, 740-593-4400, Fax: 740-593-9310, E-mail: doney@ohio.edu. Web site: http://www.cehs.ohio.edu/academics/es/.

Southern New Hampshire University, School of Education, Manchester, NH 03106-1045. Offers business education (MS); child development (M Ed); computer technology education (Certificate); curriculum and instruction (M Ed); education (M Ed, CAS); elementary education (M Ed); general special education (Certificate); school business administrator (Certificate); secondary education (M Ed); training and development (Certificate). Part-time and evening/weekend programs available. Postbaccalaureate distance learning degree programs offered (no on-campus study). *Degree requirements:* For master's, comprehensive exam (for some programs), thesis or alternative. *Entrance requirements:* For master's, PRAXIS I, minimum GPA of 2.75. Additional exam requirements/recommendations for international students: Required—TOEFL (minimum score 550 paper-based; 213 computer-based). Electronic applications accepted. *Expenses:* Contact institution.

Stanford University, School of Education, Program in Cross-Area Specializations, Stanford, CA 94305-9991. Offers learning, design, and technology (MA, PhD); symbolic systems in education (PhD). *Degree requirements:* For doctorate, thesis/dissertation. Electronic applications accepted. *Expenses: Tuition:* Full-time $40,050; part-time $890 per credit.

Stony Brook University, State University of New York, Graduate School, College of Engineering and Applied Sciences, Department of Technology and Society, Program in Educational Technology, Stony Brook, NY 11794. Offers MS. *Accreditation:* NCATE. Electronic applications accepted.

Teachers College, Columbia University, Graduate Faculty of Education, Department of Math, Science and Technology, Program in Computing in Education, New York, NY 10027-6696. Offers MA. *Accreditation:* NCATE. Part-time and evening/weekend programs available. Postbaccalaureate distance learning degree programs offered (no on-campus study). *Faculty:* 12 full-time (5 women), 13 part-time/adjunct (7 women). *Students:* 2 full-time (both women), 67 part-time (41 women); includes 28 minority (9 Black or African American, non-Hispanic/Latino; 1 American Indian or Alaska Native, non-Hispanic/Latino; 11 Asian, non-Hispanic/Latino; 3 Hispanic/Latino; 4 Two or more races, non-Hispanic/Latino), 8 international. Average age 34. 21 applicants, 81% accepted, 13 enrolled. In 2011, 20 master's awarded. *Degree requirements:* For master's, integrative project. *Application deadline:* For fall admission, 1/15 for domestic students; for spring admission, 11/1 for domestic students. Applications are processed on a rolling basis. Application fee: $65. Electronic applications accepted. *Financial support:* Career-related internships or fieldwork, Federal Work-Study, institutionally sponsored loans, and tuition waivers (full and partial) available. Support available to part-time students. Financial award application deadline: 2/1; financial award applicants required to submit FAFSA. *Faculty research:* Visual and interactive learning, global curriculum, cognition and learning. *Unit head:* Prof. Charles Kinzer, Program Coordinator, 212-678-3344, Fax: 212-678-8227, E-mail: tccte@tc.edu. *Application contact:* Deanna Ghozati, Assistant Director of Admission, 212-678-3710, Fax: 212-678-4171, E-mail: tcinfo@tc.edu.

Thomas College, Graduate School, Programs in Business, Waterville, ME 04901-5097. Offers business (MBA); computer technology education (MS); education (MS); human resource management (MBA). Part-time and evening/weekend programs available. *Entrance requirements:* For master's, GMAT, GRE, MAT or minimum GPA of 3.3 in first 3 graduate-level courses. Additional exam requirements/recommendations for international students: Recommended—TOEFL.

Troy University, Graduate School, College of Education, Program in Secondary Education, Troy, AL 36082. Offers 5th year biology (MS); 5th year computer science (MS); 5th year history (MS); 5th year language arts (MS); 5th year mathematics (MS); 5th year social science (MS); traditional biology (MS); traditional computer science (MS); traditional history (MS); traditional language arts (MS); traditional mathematics (MS); traditional social science (MS). *Accreditation:* NCATE. Part-time and evening/weekend programs available. *Faculty:* 4 full-time (3 women). *Students:* 14 full-time (8 women), 29 part-time (21 women); includes 9 minority (all Black or African American, non-Hispanic/Latino). Average age 28. 11 applicants, 100% accepted, 5 enrolled. In 2011, 16 master's awarded. *Degree requirements:* For master's, comprehensive exam, thesis. *Entrance requirements:* For master's, minimum GPA of 2.5, bachelor's degree. Additional exam requirements/recommendations for international students: Required—TOEFL (minimum score 523 paper-based; 193 computer-based; 70 iBT), IELTS (minimum score 6).

Application deadline: Applications are processed on a rolling basis. Application fee: $50. Electronic applications accepted. *Expenses:* Tuition, state resident: full-time $6960; part-time $290 per credit hour. Tuition, nonresident: full-time $13,920; part-time $580 per credit hour. *Required fees:* $386 per term. *Financial support:* Career-related internships or fieldwork available. Support available to part-time students. Financial award applicants required to submit FAFSA. *Unit head:* Dr. Jan Oliver, Associate Professor, 334-670-3444, Fax: 334-670-3548, E-mail: oliver@troy.edu. *Application contact:* Brenda K. Campbell, Director of Graduate Admissions, 334-670-3178, Fax: 334-670-3733, E-mail: bcamp@troy.edu.

University of Bridgeport, School of Education, Department of Education, Bridgeport, CT 06604. Offers education (MS); educational management (Ed D, Diploma), including intermediate administrator or supervisor (Diploma), leadership (Ed D); elementary education (MS, Diploma), including early childhood education, elementary education; middle school education (MS); music education (MS); remedial reading and language arts (Diploma); secondary education (MS, Diploma), including computer specialist (Diploma), international education (Diploma), reading specialist, secondary education. Part-time and evening/weekend programs available. *Faculty:* 12 full-time (5 women), 108 part-time/adjunct (60 women). *Students:* 232 full-time (161 women), 216 part-time (160 women); includes 61 minority (21 Black or African American, non-Hispanic/Latino; 8 Asian, non-Hispanic/Latino; 22 Hispanic/Latino; 10 Two or more races, non-Hispanic/Latino), 34 international. Average age 30. 412 applicants, 63% accepted, 147 enrolled. In 2011, 216 master's, 7 other advanced degrees awarded. *Degree requirements:* For master's, final exam, final project, or thesis; for doctorate, comprehensive exam, thesis/dissertation; for Diploma, thesis or alternative, final project. *Entrance requirements:* For master's, minimum undergraduate QPA of 2.67; for doctorate, GRE, MAT; for Diploma, GRE General Test or MAT, minimum graduate QPA of 3.0. Additional exam requirements/recommendations for international students: Recommended—TOEFL (minimum score 550 paper-based; 213 computer-based; 80 iBT), IELTS (minimum score 6.5). *Application deadline:* For fall admission, 8/1 priority date for domestic students, 8/1 for international students; for spring admission, 12/1 priority date for domestic students, 12/1 for international students. Applications are processed on a rolling basis. Application fee: $50. Electronic applications accepted. *Expenses: Tuition:* Full-time $22,880; part-time $700 per credit. *Required fees:* $1870; $95 per semester. Tuition and fees vary according to course load and program. *Financial support:* In 2011–12, 120 students received support. Fellowships, research assistantships, teaching assistantships, career-related internships or fieldwork, Federal Work-Study, and institutionally sponsored loans available. Support available to part-time students. Financial award application deadline: 6/1; financial award applicants required to submit FAFSA. *Faculty research:* Self-concept, internship assessment, stress and situational development, follow-up of graduation, trend analysis. *Unit head:* Dr. Allen P. Cook, Dean, 203-576-4192, Fax: 203-576-4200, E-mail: acook@bridgeport.edu. *Application contact:* Karissa Peckham, Dean of Admissions, 203-576-4552, Fax: 203-576-4941, E-mail: admit@bridgeport.edu.

University of Central Oklahoma, College of Graduate Studies and Research, College of Mathematics and Science, Department of Mathematics and Statistics, Edmond, OK 73034-5209. Offers applied mathematical sciences (MS), including computer science, mathematics, mathematics/computer science teaching, statistics. Part-time programs available. *Faculty:* 7 full-time (4 women), 3 part-time/adjunct (0 women). *Students:* 20 full-time (7 women), 11 part-time (8 women); includes 5 minority (3 Black or African American, non-Hispanic/Latino; 2 Two or more races, non-Hispanic/Latino), 11 international. Average age 29. In 2011, 5 master's awarded. *Degree requirements:* For master's, thesis. *Entrance requirements:* Additional exam requirements/recommendations for international students: Required—TOEFL (minimum score 550 paper-based; 213 computer-based). *Application deadline:* Applications are processed on a rolling basis. Application fee: $50. Electronic applications accepted. *Expenses:* Tuition, state resident: full-time $3901; part-time $218.30 per credit hour. Tuition, nonresident: full-time $9198; part-time $511.20 per credit hour. Tuition and fees vary according to program. *Financial support:* Federal Work-Study and unspecified assistantships available. Financial award application deadline: 3/31; financial award applicants required to submit FAFSA. *Faculty research:* Curvature, FAA, math education. *Unit head:* Dr. Michael Fulkerson, 405-974-5575, E-mail: mfulkerson@uco.edu. *Application contact:* Dr. Richard Bernard, Adviser, 405-974-3493, Fax: 405-974-3824, E-mail: jyates@aix1.uco.edu. Web site: http://www.ucok.edu/graduate.applied.htm.

University of Detroit Mercy, College of Engineering and Science, Department of Mathematics and Computer Science, Detroit, MI 48221. Offers computer science (MSCS), including computer systems applications, software engineering; computer science education (MATM); mathematics education (MATM). Evening/weekend programs available. *Entrance requirements:* For master's, minimum GPA of 3.0.

University of North Texas, Toulouse Graduate School, College of Information, Department of Learning Technologies, Program in Computer Education and Cognitive Systems, Denton, TX 76203. Offers MS. *Accreditation:* NCATE. *Entrance requirements:* For master's, GRE General Test. Additional exam requirements/recommendations for international students: Recommended—TOEFL (minimum score 550 paper-based; 213 computer-based). Electronic applications accepted. *Expenses:* Tuition, state resident: part-time $100 per credit hour. Tuition, nonresident: part-time $413 per credit hour.

University of North Texas, Toulouse Graduate School, College of Information, Department of Library and Information Sciences, Denton, TX 76203. Offers information science (MS, PhD); learning technologies (M Ed, Ed D), including applied technology, training and development (M Ed), computer education and cognitive systems, educational computing; library science (MS). *Accreditation:* ALA (one or more programs are accredited). Part-time and evening/weekend programs available. *Degree requirements:* For master's, comprehensive exam; for doctorate, comprehensive exam, thesis/dissertation. *Entrance requirements:* For master's, GRE General Test, MAT; for doctorate, GRE General Test. Additional exam requirements/recommendations for international students: Recommended—TOEFL (minimum score 550 paper-based; 213 computer-based; 79 iBT). Electronic applications accepted. *Expenses:* Tuition, state resident: part-time $100 per credit hour. Tuition, nonresident: part-time $413 per credit hour. *Faculty research:* Information resources and services, information management and retrieval, computer-based information systems, human information behavior.

University of Phoenix–Central Florida Campus, College of Education, Maitland, FL 32751-7057. Offers administration and supervision (MA Ed); curriculum and instruction (MA Ed); curriculum and instruction-computer education (MA Ed); curriculum and instruction-mathematics education (MA Ed); early childhood education (MA Ed); elementary teacher education (MA Ed); secondary teacher education (MA Ed). Evening/weekend programs available. *Degree requirements:* For master's, thesis (for some programs). *Entrance requirements:* For master's, 3 years of work experience, minimum undergraduate GPA of 2.5. Additional exam requirements/recommendations for international students: Required—TOEFL (minimum score 550 paper-based; 213 computer-based; 79 iBT). Electronic applications accepted.

University of Phoenix–Central Valley Campus, College of Education, Fresno, CA 93720-1562. Offers curriculum and instruction (MA Ed); curriculum and instruction-computer education (MA Ed); elementary teacher education (MA Ed); secondary teacher education (MA Ed).

University of Phoenix–North Florida Campus, College of Education, Jacksonville, FL 32216-0959. Offers administration and supervision (MA Ed); curriculum and instruction (MA Ed), including computer education, mathematics education; early childhood education (MA Ed); elementary teacher education (MA Ed); secondary teacher education (MA Ed). Evening/weekend programs available. *Degree requirements:* For master's, thesis (for some programs). *Entrance requirements:* For master's, 3 years of work experience, minimum undergraduate GPA of 2.5. Additional exam requirements/recommendations for international students: Required—TOEFL (minimum score 550 paper-based; 213 computer-based; 49 iBT). Electronic applications accepted.

University of Phoenix–Omaha Campus, College of Education, Omaha, NE 68154-5240. Offers administration and supervision (MA Ed); curriculum and instruction (MA Ed), including adult education, computer education, curriculum and instruction, English and language arts education, English as a second language, mathematics education; elementary teacher education (MA Ed); secondary teacher education (MA Ed); special education (MA Ed).

University of Phoenix–Online Campus, College of Education, Phoenix, AZ 85034-7209. Offers administration and supervision (MAEd, Graduate Certificate); adult education and training (MAEd); curriculum and instruction (MAEd); curriculum and instruction reading (MAEd); curriculum and instruction-computer education (MAEd); curriculum and instruction-language arts (MAEd); curriculum and instruction-mathematics (MAEd); early childhood education (MAEd); educational studies (MAEd); elementary teacher education (MAEd); elementary teacher education-early childhood (MAEd); secondary teacher education (MAEd); special education (MAEd); teacher education - elementary/middle level (MAEd); teacher education middle level generalist (MAEd); teacher education middle level mathematics (MAEd); teacher education middle level science (MAEd); teacher education secondary mathematics (MAEd); teacher education secondary science (MAEd); teacher leadership (MAEd). *Accreditation:* Teacher Education Accreditation Council. Evening/weekend programs available. Postbaccalaureate distance learning degree programs offered. *Students:* 9,180 full-time (7,178 women); includes 2,913 minority (2,069 Black or African American, non-Hispanic/Latino; 50 American Indian or Alaska Native, non-Hispanic/Latino; 100 Asian, non-Hispanic/Latino; 542 Hispanic/Latino; 48 Native Hawaiian or other Pacific Islander, non-Hispanic/Latino; 104 Two or more races, non-Hispanic/Latino), 147 international. Average age 36. *Entrance requirements:* Additional exam requirements/recommendations for international students: Required—TOEFL, TOEIC (Test of English as an International Communication), Berlitz Online English Proficiency Exam, Pearson Test of English, or IELTS. *Application deadline:* Applications are processed on a rolling basis. Application fee: $45. Electronic applications accepted. *Expenses:* Contact institution. *Financial support:* Scholarships/grants available. Financial award applicants required to submit FAFSA. *Application contact:* 866-766-0766. Web site: http://www.phoenix.edu/colleges_divisions/education.html.

University of Phoenix–San Diego Campus, College of Education, San Diego, CA 92123. Offers curriculum and instruction (MA Ed), including computer education, curriculum and instruction, English as a second language; elementary teacher education (MA Ed); secondary teacher education (MA Ed). Evening/weekend programs available. *Degree requirements:* For master's, thesis (for some programs). *Entrance requirements:* For master's, 3 years of work experience, minimum undergraduate GPA of 3.0. Additional exam requirements/recommendations for international students: Required—TOEFL (minimum score 550 paper-based; 213 computer-based; 79 iBT). Electronic applications accepted.

University of Phoenix–South Florida Campus, College of Education, Fort Lauderdale, FL 33309. Offers administration and supervision (MA Ed); curriculum and instruction (MA Ed), including computer education, curriculum and instruction, mathematics education; early childhood education (MA Ed); elementary teacher education (MA Ed); secondary teacher education (MA Ed). Evening/weekend programs available. *Degree requirements:* For master's, thesis (for some programs). *Entrance requirements:* For master's, 3 years of work experience, minimum undergraduate GPA of 2.5. Additional exam requirements/recommendations for international students: Required—TOEFL (minimum score 550 paper-based; 213 computer-based; 79 iBT). Electronic applications accepted.

University of Phoenix–Springfield Campus, College of Education, Springfield, MO 65804-7211. Offers administration and supervision (MA Ed); curriculum and instruction (MA Ed), including computer education, curriculum and instruction, English and language arts education, English as a second language, mathematics education; English and language arts education (MA Ed).

University of Phoenix–Vancouver Campus, The Artemis School, College of Education, Burnaby, BC V5C 6G9, Canada. Offers administration and supervision (MA Ed); curriculum and instruction (MA Ed), including computer education, curriculum and instruction. Evening/weekend programs available. *Degree requirements:* For master's, thesis (for some programs). *Entrance requirements:* For master's, minimum undergraduate GPA of 2.5, 3 years work experience. Additional exam requirements/recommendations for international students: Required—TOEFL (minimum score 550 paper-based; 213 computer-based; 79 iBT). Electronic applications accepted.

University of Phoenix–Washington D.C. Campus, College of Education, Washington, DC 20001. Offers administration and supervision (MA Ed); adult education and training (MA Ed); computer education (MA Ed); curriculum and instruction (MA Ed, Ed D); early childhood education (MA Ed); education (Ed S); educational leadership (Ed D); educational technology (Ed D); elementary teacher education (MA Ed); English and language arts education (MA Ed); English as a second language (MA Ed); higher education administration (PhD); mathematics education (MA Ed); secondary teacher education (MA Ed); special education (MA Ed); teacher leadership (MA Ed).

University of Phoenix–West Florida Campus, College of Education, Temple Terrace, FL 33637. Offers administration and supervision (MA Ed); curriculum and instruction (MA Ed), including computer education, curriculum and instruction, mathematics education; curriculum and technology (MA Ed); early childhood education (MA Ed); elementary teacher education (MA Ed); secondary teacher education (MA Ed). Evening/weekend programs available. *Degree requirements:* For master's, thesis (for some programs). *Entrance requirements:* For master's, 3 years of work experience, minimum undergraduate GPA of 2.5. Additional exam requirements/recommendations for international students: Required—TOEFL (minimum score 550 paper-based; 213 computer-based; 79 iBT).

Wilkes University, College of Graduate and Professional Studies, School of Education, Wilkes-Barre, PA 18766-0002. Offers art and science of teaching (MS Ed); classroom technology (MS Ed); early childhood literacy (MS Ed); educational computing (MS Ed); educational development and strategies (MS Ed); educational leadership (MS Ed); educational technology (Ed D); higher education administration (Ed D); instructional media (MS Ed); instructional technology (MS Ed); K-12 administration (Ed D); online teaching (MS Ed); reading (MS Ed); school business leadership (MS Ed); secondary education (MS Ed), including biology, chemistry, English, history, mathematics; special education (MS Ed); teaching English as a second language (MS Ed); twenty-first century teaching and learning (MS Ed). Part-time and evening/weekend programs available. Postbaccalaureate distance learning degree programs offered (minimal on-campus study). *Students:* 92 full-time (63 women), 2,005 part-time (1,459 women); includes 89 minority (23 Black or African American, non-Hispanic/Latino; 1 American Indian or Alaska Native, non-Hispanic/Latino; 14 Asian, non-Hispanic/Latino; 33 Hispanic/Latino; 1 Native Hawaiian or other Pacific Islander, non-Hispanic/Latino; 17 Two or more races, non-Hispanic/Latino), 6 international. Average age 33. In 2011, 1,150 master's, 3 doctorates awarded. *Entrance requirements:* Additional exam requirements/recommendations for international students: Required—TOEFL (minimum score 550 paper-based; 213 computer-based; 79 iBT). *Application deadline:* Applications are processed on a rolling basis. Application fee: $45. Electronic applications accepted. *Expenses:* Contact institution. *Financial support:* Federal Work-Study and unspecified assistantships available. Financial award application deadline: 3/1; financial award applicants required to submit FAFSA. *Unit head:* Dr. Michael Speziale, Dean, 570-408-4679, Fax: 570-408-4905, E-mail: michael.speziale@wilkes.edu. *Application contact:* Erin Sutzko, Director of Extended Learning, 570-408-4253, Fax: 570-408-7846, E-mail: erin.sutzko@wilkes.edu. Web site: http://www.wilkes.edu/pages/383.asp.

Wright State University, School of Graduate Studies, College of Education and Human Services, Department of Teacher Education, Programs in Workforce Education, Dayton, OH 45435. Offers career, technology and vocational education (M Ed, MA); computer/technology education (M Ed, MA); library/media (M Ed, MA); vocational education (M Ed, MA). *Accreditation:* NCATE. *Degree requirements:* For master's, thesis (for some programs). *Entrance requirements:* For master's, GRE General Test, MAT. Additional exam requirements/recommendations for international students: Required—TOEFL.

Counselor Education

Acadia University, Faculty of Professional Studies, School of Education, Program in Counseling, Wolfville, NS B4P 2R6, Canada. Offers M Ed. Part-time programs available. *Degree requirements:* For master's, thesis optional. *Entrance requirements:* For master's, B Ed, minimum B average in undergraduate course work, 2 years of teaching or related experience. Additional exam requirements/recommendations for international students: Required—TOEFL (minimum score 580 paper-based; 237 computer-based; 93 iBT), IELTS (minimum score 6.5). *Faculty research:* Computer-assisted supervision, rural/remote school counseling, non-custodial fathers, spirituality, counseling relationships.

Adams State University, The Graduate School, Department of Counselor Education, Alamosa, CO 81102. Offers counseling (MA). *Accreditation:* ACA. Part-time programs available. *Degree requirements:* For master's, internship, qualifying exam. *Entrance requirements:* For master's, GRE General Test or MAT, minimum undergraduate GPA of 2.75.

Adler Graduate School, Program in Adlerian Counseling and Psychotherapy, Richfield, MN 55423. Offers art therapy (MA); career development (MA); clinical mental health counseling (MA); marriage and family therapy (MA); non-clinical Adlerian studies (MA); online Adlerian studies (MA); parent coaching (Certificate); personal and professional life coaching (Certificate); school counseling (MA). Part-time and evening/weekend programs available. *Faculty:* 10 full-time (3 women), 44 part-time/adjunct (31 women). *Students:* 359 part-time (291 women). *Degree requirements:* For master's, thesis or alternative, 500-700 hour internship (depending on license choice). *Entrance requirements:* For master's, personal goal statement, three letters of reference, resume or work history, official transcripts. *Application deadline:* Applications are processed on a rolling basis. Application fee: $50. Electronic applications accepted. *Expenses: Tuition:* Full-time $8730; part-time $485 per credit. *Required fees:* $270. Tuition and fees vary according to course load. *Financial support:* Career-related internships or fieldwork and tuition waivers available. Support available to part-time students. Financial award applicants required to submit FAFSA. *Unit head:* Dr. Dan Haugen, President, 612-861-7554 Ext. 107, Fax: 612-861-7559, E-mail: haugen@alfredadler.edu. *Application contact:* Evelyn B. Haas, Director of Student Services and Admissions, 612-861-7554 Ext. 103, Fax: 612-861-7559, E-mail: ev@alfredadler.edu. Web site: http://www.alfredadler.edu/academics/index.htm.

Alabama Agricultural and Mechanical University, School of Graduate Studies, School of Education, Department of Counseling and Special Education, Huntsville, AL 35811. Offers communicative disorders (M Ed, MS); psychology and counseling (MS, Ed S), including clinical psychology (MS), counseling and guidance, counseling psychology (MS), personnel management (MS), psychometry (MS), school psychology (MS); special education (M Ed, MS). *Accreditation:* CORE; NCATE. Part-time and evening/weekend programs available. *Degree requirements:* For master's, comprehensive exam. *Entrance requirements:* For master's, GRE General Test. Additional exam requirements/recommendations for international students: Required—TOEFL (minimum score 500 paper-based; 173 computer-based; 61 iBT). *Faculty research:* Increasing numbers of minorities in special education and speech-language pathology.

Alabama State University, Department of Instructional Support, Program in Guidance and Counseling, Montgomery, AL 36101-0271. Offers general counseling (MS, Ed S); school counseling (M Ed, Ed S). Part-time programs available. *Faculty:* 5 full-time (1 woman), 3 part-time/adjunct (1 woman). *Students:* 7 full-time (5 women), 85 part-time (67 women); includes 90 minority (all Black or African American, non-Hispanic/Latino). Average age 35. In 2011, 2 master's, 1 other advanced degree awarded. *Degree requirements:* For master's, comprehensive exam; for Ed S, comprehensive exam, thesis. *Entrance requirements:* For master's, GRE General Test, MAT, graduate writing competency test; for Ed S, graduate writing competency test, GRE, MAT. Additional exam requirements/recommendations for international students: Required—TOEFL (minimum score 500 paper-based; 173 computer-based). *Application deadline:* For fall admission, 7/15 for domestic students; for spring admission, 12/15 for domestic students. Applications are processed on a rolling basis. Application fee: $10. *Financial support:* In 2011–12, research assistantships (averaging $9,450 per year) were awarded. *Faculty research:* Enhancing self-concept, drug abuse education and training, comparison of group techniques, collaborative counseling. *Unit head:* Dr. Virginia Martin, Coordinator, 334-229-4571, E-mail: vmartin@asunet.alasu.edu. *Application contact:* Dr. Doris Screws, Dean of Graduate Studies, 334-229-4274, Fax: 334-229-4928, E-mail: dscrews@alasu.edu. Web site: http://www.alasu.edu/academics/colleges—departments/college-of-education/instructional-support-programs/counselor-education/index.aspx.

Albany State University, College of Education, Albany, GA 31705-2717. Offers early childhood education (M Ed); education specialist (Ed S); educational leadership and administration (M Ed); health, physical education and recreation (M Ed); middle grades education (M Ed); school counseling (M Ed); special education (M Ed). *Accreditation:* NCATE. Part-time and evening/weekend programs available. Postbaccalaureate distance learning degree programs offered (minimal on-campus study). *Faculty:* 19 full-time (13 women), 7 part-time/adjunct (5 women). *Students:* 90 full-time (69 women), 118 part-time (92 women); includes 152 minority (151 Black or African American, non-Hispanic/Latino; 1 American Indian or Alaska Native, non-Hispanic/Latino), 1 international. Average age 35. 93 applicants, 78% accepted, 38 enrolled. In 2011, 43 master's, 8 Ed Ss awarded. *Degree requirements:* For master's, comprehensive exam, internship, GACE Content Exam. *Entrance requirements:* For master's, GRE or MAT. *Application deadline:* For fall admission, 6/1 for domestic students, 5/1 for international students; for spring admission, 11/1 for domestic students, 10/1 for international students. Applications are processed on a rolling basis. Application fee: $20. Electronic applications accepted. *Expenses:* Tuition, state resident: full-time $3204; part-time $178 per credit hour. Tuition, nonresident: full-time $12,816; part-time $712 per credit hour. *Required fees:* $379 per semester. *Financial support:* Scholarships/grants available. Financial award application deadline: 4/15; financial award applicants required to submit FAFSA. *Faculty research:* GACE preparation, STEM (science, technology, engineering, and mathematics), technology education, special education, professional teacher development, health implications liberation philosophy, NET-Q, learning community, disabled or at-risk students. *Total annual research expenditures:* $252,502. *Unit head:* Dr. Kimberly King-Jupiter, Dean, 229-430-1718, Fax: 229-430-4993, E-mail: kimberly.king-jupiter@asurams.edu. *Application contact:* Jeffrey Pierce, II, Graduate Admissions Counselor, 229-430-4646, Fax: 229-430-4105, E-mail: jeffrey.pierce@asurams.edu. Web site: http://asu-sacs.asurams.edu/ASUCatalog/Graduate/index.html.

Alcorn State University, School of Graduate Studies, School of Psychology and Education, Alcorn State, MS 39096-7500. Offers agricultural education (MS Ed); elementary education (MS Ed, Ed S); guidance and counseling (MS Ed); industrial education (MS Ed); secondary education (MS Ed), including health and physical education; special education (MS Ed). *Accreditation:* NCATE. *Degree requirements:* For master's, thesis optional.

Alfred University, Graduate School, Program in School Psychology, Alfred, NY 14802-1205. Offers school counseling (MS Ed, CAS); school psychology (MA, Psy D, CAS). *Accreditation:* APA. *Degree requirements:* For master's, internship; for doctorate, thesis/dissertation, internship. *Entrance requirements:* For master's and doctorate, GRE General Test. Additional exam requirements/recommendations for international students: Required—TOEFL (minimum score 590 paper-based; 243 computer-based; 90 iBT); Recommended—IELTS (minimum score 6.5). Electronic applications accepted. *Faculty research:* Family processes, alternative assessment approaches, behavior disorders in children, parent involvement, school psychology training issues.

Alliant International University–San Francisco, California School of Professional Psychology, Program in Clinical Counseling, San Francisco, CA 94133-1221. Offers MA. *Faculty:* 2 full-time (both women), 1 part-time/adjunct (0 women). *Students:* 10. Average age 32. *Degree requirements:* For master's, comprehensive exam, project. *Entrance requirements:* For master's, minimum GPA of 3.0, recommendations, essay, interview. Additional exam requirements/recommendations for international students: Required—TOEFL (minimum score 550 paper-based; 213 computer-based; 80 iBT), TWE (minimum score 5). *Application deadline:* For fall admission, 4/1 priority date for domestic students, 4/1 for international students; for spring admission, 11/1 priority date for domestic students, 11/1 for international students. Applications are processed on a rolling basis. Application fee: $55. Electronic applications accepted. *Financial support:* Teaching assistantships, Federal Work-Study, and scholarships/grants available. Financial award application deadline: 2/15; financial award applicants required to submit FAFSA. *Faculty research:* Systems of privilege and oppression, multicultural and social justice advocacy competence, rural issues, LGBTQ affirmative therapy and identity development, college student mental health. *Unit head:* Dr. Janie Pinterits, Program Director, 415-955-2026, Fax: 415-955-, E-mail: admissions@alliant.edu. *Application contact:* Alliant International University Central Contact Center, 866-U-ALLIANT, Fax: 858-635-4555, E-mail: admissions@alliant.edu. Web site: http://www.alliant.edu/cspp/programs-degrees/clinical-counseling/clin-couns-ma-sf.php.

American International College, School of Arts, Education and Sciences, Department of Education, Springfield, MA 01109-3189. Offers early childhood education (M Ed, CAGS); educational leadership and supervision (Ed D); elementary education (M Ed, CAGS); middle/secondary education (M Ed, CAGS); moderate disabilities (M Ed, CAGS); reading (M Ed, CAGS); school adjustment counseling (MA, CAGS); school administration (M Ed, CAGS); school guidance counseling (MA, CAGS); teaching (MA, MS); teaching and learning (Ed D). Part-time and evening/weekend programs available. Terminal master's awarded for partial completion of doctoral program. *Degree requirements:* For master's, comprehensive exam (for some programs), thesis (for some programs), practicum; for doctorate, comprehensive exam (for some programs), thesis/dissertation; for CAGS, practicum. *Entrance requirements:* For master's, minimum B-average in undergraduate course work; for doctorate, GRE General Test, interview. Additional exam requirements/recommendations for international students: Required—TOEFL. Electronic applications accepted.

American Public University System, AMU/APU Graduate Programs, Charles Town, WV 25414. Offers accounting (MBA, MS); administration and supervision (M Ed); criminal justice (MA); emergency and disaster management (MA); entrepreneurship (MBA); environmental policy and management (MS), including environmental planning, environmental sustainability, fish and wildlife management, general (MA, MS), global environmental management; finance (MBA); general (MBA); global business management (MBA); guidance and counseling (M Ed); history (MA), including American history, ancient and classical history, European history, global history, military and diplomatic history, public history; homeland security (MA); homeland security resource allocation (MBA); humanities (MA); information technology (MS), including digital forensics, enterprise software development, information assurance and security, IT project management; information technology management (MBA); intelligence studies (MA), including criminal intelligence, general (MA, MS), homeland security, intelligence analysis, intelligence collection, intelligence operations, terrorism studies; international relations and conflict resolution (MA), including comparative and security issues, conflict resolution, international and transnational security issues, peacekeeping; legal studies (MA); management (MA), including defense management, general (MA, MS), human resource management, organizational leadership, public administration, reverse logistics, strategic consulting; marketing (MBA); military history (MA), including American military history, American revolution, civil war, war since 1946, World War II; military studies (MA), including air warfare, asymmetrical warfare, joint warfare, land warfare, naval warfare, strategic leadership; national security studies (MA), including general (MA, MS), homeland security, regional security studies, security and intelligence analysis, terrorism studies; nonprofit management (MBA); political science (MA), including American politics and government, comparative government and development, public policy; psychology (MA); public administration (MA, MPA), including disaster management (MPA), environmental policy (MA), health policy (MPA), human resources (MPA), national security (MPA), organizational management (MPA), security management (MPA); public health (MA, MPH), including emergency management (MPH), environmental health (MPH), public administration (MA); reverse logistics management (MA); security management (MA); space studies (MS), including aerospace science, planetary science; sports and health sciences (MS); sports management (MS), including coaching theory and strategy, sports administration; teaching (M Ed), including curriculum and instruction for elementary teachers, elementary, elementary reading, English language learners, instructional leadership, online learning, secondary social sciences, special education; transportation and logistics management (MA), including maritime engineering management. Programs offered via distance learning only. Part-time and evening/weekend programs available. Postbaccalaureate distance learning degree programs offered (no on-campus study). *Faculty:* 445 full-time (241 women), 1,360 part-time/adjunct (617 women). *Students:* 688 full-time (338 women), 10,168 part-time (3,706 women); includes 3,130 minority (1,007 Black or African American, non-Hispanic/Latino; 103 American Indian or Alaska Native, non-Hispanic/Latino; 825 Asian, non-Hispanic/Latino; 810 Hispanic/Latino; 51 Native Hawaiian or other Pacific Islander, non-Hispanic/Latino; 334 Two or more races, non-Hispanic/Latino), 134 international. Average age 35. In 2011, 2,386 master's awarded. *Degree requirements:* For master's, comprehensive exam or practicum. *Entrance requirements:* For master's, official transcript showing earned bachelor's degree from institution accredited by recognized accrediting body. Additional exam requirements/recommendations for international students: Required—TOEFL (minimum score 550 paper-based; 213 computer-based), IELTS (minimum score 6.5). *Application deadline:* Applications are processed on a rolling basis. Application fee: $0. Electronic applications accepted. *Expenses: Tuition:* Part-time $325 per credit hour. *Financial support:* Applicants required to submit FAFSA. *Faculty research:* Military history, criminal justice, management performance, national security. *Unit head:* Dr. Karan Powell, Executive Vice President and Provost, 877-468-6268, Fax: 304-724-3780. *Application contact:* Terry Grant, Vice President of Enrollment Management, 877-468-6268, Fax: 304-724-3780, E-mail: info@apus.edu. Web site: http://www.apus.edu.

Amridge University, Graduate and Professional Programs, Montgomery, AL 36117. Offers behavioral leadership and management (MA); Biblical exposition (MA); biblical studies (MA, PhD); family therapy (D Min); historical and theological studies (MA); leadership and management (MS); marriage and family therapy (M Div, MA, PhD); ministerial leadership (M Div, MS); pastoral counseling (M Div, MS); practical ministry (MA); professional counseling (M Div, MA, PhD); theology (M Div, D Min). Part-time and evening/weekend programs available. Postbaccalaureate distance learning degree programs offered (no on-campus study). *Faculty:* 48 full-time (9 women), 27 part-time/adjunct (12 women). *Students:* 161 full-time (79 women), 258 part-time (147 women); includes 160 minority (153 Black or African American, non-Hispanic/Latino; 1 Asian, non-Hispanic/Latino; 6 Hispanic/Latino). Average age 35. *Degree requirements:* For master's, one foreign language, comprehensive exam (for some programs), thesis (for some programs); for doctorate, comprehensive exam (for some programs), thesis/dissertation. *Entrance requirements:* For master's and doctorate, GRE General Test or MAT. Additional exam requirements/recommendations for international students: Required—TOEFL. *Application deadline:* For fall admission, 9/1 priority date for domestic students; for spring admission, 1/1 priority date for domestic students. Applications are processed on a rolling basis. Application fee: $75. Electronic applications accepted. *Expenses: Tuition:* Full-time $10,680; part-time $610 per semester hour. *Required fees:* $600 per semester. *Financial support:* Federal Work-Study and scholarships/grants available. Support available to part-time students. Financial award applicants required to submit FAFSA. *Faculty research:* Homiletics, hermeneutics, ancient Near Eastern history. *Unit head:* Director of Enrollment Management, 800-351-4040 Ext. 7513, Fax: 334-387-3878. *Application contact:* Ora Davis, Admissions Officer, 334-387-3877 Ext. 7524, Fax: 334-387-3878, E-mail: admissions@amridgeuniversity.edu.

Angelo State University, College of Graduate Studies, College of Education, Department of Curriculum and Instruction, Program in Guidance and Counseling, San Angelo, TX 76909. Offers M Ed. Part-time and evening/weekend programs available. *Faculty:* 17 full-time (12 women). *Students:* 21 full-time (20 women), 63 part-time (56 women); includes 18 minority (4 Black or African American, non-Hispanic/Latino; 1 American Indian or Alaska Native, non-Hispanic/Latino; 13 Hispanic/Latino). Average age 36. 28 applicants, 75% accepted, 17 enrolled. In 2011, 20 master's awarded. *Degree requirements:* For master's, comprehensive exam. *Entrance requirements:* Additional exam requirements/recommendations for international students: Required—TOEFL or IELTS. *Application deadline:* For fall admission, 7/15 priority date for domestic students, 6/10 for international students; for spring admission, 12/1 priority date for domestic students, 11/1 for international students. Applications are processed on a rolling basis. Application fee: $40 ($50 for international students). Electronic applications accepted. *Financial support:* In 2011–12, 19 students received support. Career-related internships or fieldwork, Federal Work-Study, scholarships/grants, and unspecified assistantships available. Support available to part-time students. Financial award application deadline: 3/1; financial award applicants required to submit FAFSA. *Unit head:* Dr. Mary McGlamery, Graduate Advisor, 325-942-2052 Ext. 262, Fax: 325-942-2039, E-mail: mary.mcglamery@angelo.edu. *Application contact:* Aly Hunter, Graduate Admissions Assistant, 325-942-2169, Fax: 325-942-2194, E-mail: aly.hunter@angelo.edu. Web site: http://www.angelo.edu/dept/ci.

Appalachian State University, Cratis D. Williams Graduate School, Department of Human Development and Psychological Counseling, Boone, NC 28608. Offers clinical mental health counseling (MA); college student development (MA); marriage and family therapy (MA); school counseling (MA). *Accreditation:* AAMFT/COAMFTE; ACA; NCATE. Part-time programs available. *Faculty:* 13 full-time (8 women), 8 part-time/adjunct (6 women). *Students:* 165 full-time (128 women), 20 part-time (15 women); includes 14 minority (10 Black or African American, non-Hispanic/Latino; 3 Asian, non-Hispanic/Latino; 1 Hispanic/Latino), 1 international. 337 applicants, 33% accepted, 80 enrolled. In 2011, 68 master's awarded. *Degree requirements:* For master's, comprehensive exam (for some programs), thesis optional, internships. *Entrance requirements:* For master's, GRE General Test, 3 letters of recommendation. Additional exam requirements/recommendations for international students: Required—TOEFL (minimum score 570 paper-based; 230 computer-based; 79 iBT), IELTS (minimum score 6.5). *Application deadline:* For fall admission, 2/1 priority date for domestic students, 2/1 for international students; for spring admission, 2/1 for international students. Applications are processed on a rolling basis. Application fee: $55. Electronic applications accepted. *Expenses:* Tuition, state resident: full-time $4040; part-time $180 per semester hour. Tuition, nonresident: full-time $15,900; part-time $760 per semester hour. *Required fees:* $2500; $20 per semester hour. Tuition and fees vary according to campus/location. *Financial support:* In 2011–12, 20 research assistantships (averaging $8,000 per year), 7 teaching assistantships (averaging $8,000 per year) were awarded; fellowships, career-related internships or fieldwork, Federal Work-Study, scholarships/grants, and unspecified assistantships also available. Financial award application deadline: 4/1; financial award applicants required to submit FAFSA. *Faculty research:* Multicultural counseling, addictions counseling, play therapy, expressive arts, child and adolescent therapy, sexual abuse counseling. *Unit head:* Dr. Lee Baruth, Chairman, 828-262-2055, E-mail: baruthlg@appstate.edu. *Application contact:* Sandy Krause, Director of Admissions and Recruiting, 828-262-2130, Fax: 828-262-2709, E-mail: krausesl@appstate.edu. Web site: http://www.ced.appstate.edu/departments/hpc.

Argosy University, Atlanta, College of Psychology and Behavioral Sciences, Atlanta, GA 30328. Offers clinical psychology (MA, Psy D, Postdoctoral Respecialization Certificate), including child and family psychology (Psy D), general adult clinical (Psy D), health psychology (Psy D), neuropsychology/geropsychology (Psy D); community counseling (MA), including marriage and family therapy; counselor education and supervision (Ed D); forensic psychology (MA); industrial organizational psychology (MA); marriage and family therapy (Certificate); sport-exercise psychology (MA). *Accreditation:* APA.

Argosy University, Chicago, College of Psychology and Behavioral Sciences, Program in Counseling Psychology, Chicago, IL 60601. Offers counselor education and supervision (Ed D). Postbaccalaureate distance learning degree programs offered (minimal on-campus study).

Argosy University, Dallas, College of Psychology and Behavioral Sciences, Program in Counselor Education and Supervision, Farmers Branch, TX 75244. Offers Ed D.

Argosy University, Denver, College of Psychology and Behavioral Sciences, Denver, CO 80231. Offers clinical mental health counseling (MA); clinical psychology (MA, Psy D); counseling psychology (Ed D); counselor education and supervision (Ed D); forensic psychology (MA); industrial organizational psychology (MA); marriage and family therapy (MA, DMFT).

Argosy University, Nashville, College of Psychology and Behavioral Sciences, Program in Counselor Education and Supervision, Nashville, TN 37214. Offers Ed D.

Argosy University, Salt Lake City, College of Psychology and Behavioral Sciences, Draper, UT 84020. Offers counseling psychology (Ed D); counselor education and supervision (Ed D); forensic psychology (MA); marriage and family therapy (MA, DMFT); mental health counseling (MA).

Argosy University, Sarasota, College of Education, Sarasota, FL 34235. Offers community college executive leadership (Ed D); educational leadership (MA Ed, Ed D, Ed S), including higher education administration (Ed D), K-12 education (Ed D); school counseling (MA, Ed S); school psychology (MA); teaching and learning (MA Ed, Ed D, Ed S), including education technology (Ed D), higher education (Ed D), K-12 education (Ed D).

See Close-Up on page 789.

Argosy University, Sarasota, College of Psychology and Behavioral Sciences, Sarasota, FL 34235. Offers community counseling (MA); counseling psychology (Ed D); counselor education and supervision (Ed D); forensic psychology (MA); marriage and family therapy (MA); mental health counseling (MA); pastoral community counseling (Ed D).

Argosy University, Schaumburg, College of Psychology and Behavioral Sciences, Schaumburg, IL 60173-5403. Offers clinical health psychology (Post-Graduate Certificate); clinical psychology (MA, Psy D), including child and family psychology (Psy D), clinical health psychology (Psy D), diversity and multicultural psychology (Psy D), forensic psychology (Psy D), neuropsychology (Psy D); community counseling (MA); counseling psychology (Ed D), including counselor education and supervision; counselor education and supervision (Ed D); forensic psychology (Post-Graduate Certificate); industrial organizational psychology (MA). *Accreditation:* ACA; APA.

Argosy University, Tampa, College of Education, Tampa, FL 33607. Offers community college executive leadership (Ed D); educational leadership (MA Ed, Ed D, Ed S), including higher education administration (Ed D), K-12 education (Ed D); school counseling (MA); teaching and learning (MA Ed, Ed D, Ed S), including higher education (Ed D), K-12 education (Ed D).

See Close-Up on page 795.

Argosy University, Tampa, College of Psychology and Behavioral Sciences, Tampa, FL 33607. Offers clinical psychology (MA, Psy D), including clinical psychology; counselor education and supervision (Ed D); industrial organizational psychology (MA); marriage and family therapy (MA); mental health counseling (MA).

Argosy University, Washington DC, College of Psychology and Behavioral Sciences, Arlington, VA 22209. Offers clinical psychology (MA, Psy D), including child and family psychology (Psy D), diversity and multicultural psychology (Psy D), forensic psychology (Psy D), health and neuropsychology (Psy D); community counseling (MA); counseling psychology (Ed D), including counselor education and supervision; counselor education and supervision (Ed D); forensic psychology (MA). *Accreditation:* APA.

Arizona State University, School of Letters and Sciences, Program in Counseling, Tempe, AZ 85287-0811. Offers MC. *Accreditation:* ACA. *Degree requirements:* For master's, comprehensive exam (for some programs), thesis (for some programs), interactive Program of Study (iPOS) submitted before completing 50 percent of required credit hours. *Entrance requirements:* For master's, GRE, minimum GPA of 3.0 or equivalent in last 2 years of work leading to bachelor's degree; 3 letters of recommendation; 3-5 page personal statement with information on significant life experiences, professional experiences and goals. Additional exam requirements/recommendations for international students: Required—TOEFL (minimum score 80 iBT), TOEFL, IELTS, or Pearson Test of English. Electronic applications accepted.

Arkansas State University, Graduate School, College of Education, Department of Psychology and Counseling, Jonesboro, State University, AR 72467. Offers college student personnel services (MS); mental health counseling (Certificate); psychology and counseling (Ed S); rehabilitation counseling (MRC); school counseling (MSE); student affairs (Certificate). *Accreditation:* ACA (one or more programs are accredited); CORE (one or more programs are accredited); NCATE. Part-time programs available. *Faculty:* 15 full-time (9 women). *Students:* 45 full-time (32 women), 91 part-time (73 women); includes 38 minority (all Black or African American, non-Hispanic/Latino), 1 international. Average age 33. 75 applicants, 68% accepted, 40 enrolled. In 2011, 14 master's, 20 other advanced degrees awarded. *Degree requirements:* For master's and other advanced degree, comprehensive exam, thesis or alternative. *Entrance requirements:* For master's, GRE General Test or MAT (MSE), appropriate bachelor's degree, interview, letters of reference, official transcripts, immunization records, written statement, 2-3 page autobiography; for other advanced degree, GRE General Test, interview, master's degree, letters of reference, official transcript, personal statement, immunization records. Additional exam requirements/recommendations for international students: Required—TOEFL (minimum score 550 paper-based; 213 computer-based; 79 iBT), IELTS (minimum score 6), Pearson Test of English Academic (minimum score 56). *Application deadline:* Applications are processed on a rolling basis. Application fee: $30 ($40 for international students). Electronic applications accepted. *Expenses:* Tuition, state resident: full-time $4044; part-time $225 per credit hour. Tuition, nonresident: full-time $8087; part-time $449 per credit hour. *Required fees:* $936; $52 per credit hour. $25 per term. One-time fee: $30. Tuition and fees vary according to course load and program. *Financial support:* In 2011–12, 27 students received support. Teaching assistantships, career-related internships or fieldwork, scholarships/grants, and unspecified assistantships available. Financial award application deadline: 7/1; financial award applicants required to submit FAFSA. *Unit head:* Dr. Loretta McGregor, Chair, 870-972-3064, Fax: 870-972-3962, E-mail: lmcgregor@astate.edu. *Application contact:* Dr. Andrew Sustich, Dean of the Graduate School, 870-972-3029, Fax: 870-972-3857, E-mail: sustich@astate.edu. Web site: http://www.astate.edu/a/education/psychologycounseling/index.dot.

Arkansas Tech University, Center for Leadership and Learning, College of Education, Russellville, AR 72801. Offers college student personnel (MS); educational leadership (Ed S); elementary education (M Ed); instructional improvement (M Ed); instructional technology (M Ed); physical education (M Ed); school counseling and leadership (M Ed); teaching (MAT). *Accreditation:* NCATE. Part-time and evening/weekend programs available. Postbaccalaureate distance learning degree programs offered (no on-campus study). *Students:* 70 full-time (44 women), 247 part-time (189 women); includes 57 minority (38 Black or African American, non-Hispanic/Latino; 1 American Indian or Alaska Native, non-Hispanic/Latino; 8 Asian, non-Hispanic/Latino; 4 Hispanic/Latino; 6 Two or more races, non-Hispanic/Latino), 3 international. Average age 31. In 2011, 58 master's awarded. *Degree requirements:* For master's, comprehensive exam, thesis optional, action research project. *Entrance requirements:* Additional exam requirements/recommendations for international students: Required—TOEFL (minimum score 550 paper-based; 213 computer-based; 79 iBT), IELTS (minimum score 6.5). *Application deadline:* For fall admission, 3/1 priority date for domestic students, 5/1 for international students; for spring admission, 10/1 priority date for domestic students, 10/1 for international students. Applications are processed on a rolling basis. Application fee: $25 ($75 for international students). Electronic applications accepted. *Expenses:* Tuition, state resident: full-time $4968; part-time $207 per credit hour. Tuition, nonresident: full-time $9936; part-time $414 per credit hour. *Required fees:* $375 per semester. Tuition and fees vary according to course load. *Financial support:* In 2011–12, teaching assistantships with full tuition reimbursements (averaging $4,800 per year) were awarded; research assistantships with full tuition reimbursements, career-related internships or fieldwork, Federal Work-Study, scholarships/grants, health care benefits, and unspecified assistantships also available. Support available to part-time students. Financial award application deadline: 4/15; financial award applicants required to submit FAFSA. *Unit head:* Dr. Eldon G. Clary, Jr., Dean, 479-968-0350, Fax: 479-968-0350, E-mail: eclary@atu.edu. *Application contact:* Dr. Mary B. Gunter, Dean of Graduate College, 479-968-0398, Fax: 479-964-0542, E-mail: gradcollege@atu.edu. Web site: http://www.atu.edu/education/.

Ashland Theological Seminary, Graduate Programs, Ashland, OH 44805. Offers Biblical and theological studies (MA), including New Testament, Old Testament; biblical and theological studies (MAR); Christian ministry (MAPT), including Black church studies (M Div, MAPT, D Min), chaplaincy (M Div, MAPT), Christian formation (M Div, MAPT), evangelism/church renewal and missions (M Div, MAPT), general ministry (M Div, MAPT), pastoral counseling and care (M Div, MAPT), specialized ministry, spiritual formation (M Div, MAPT, D Min); Christian studies (Diploma); clinical counseling (MACC); clinical counseling (Detroit) (MAC); historical studies (MA), including church history; ministry (D Min), including Black church studies (M Div, MAPT, D Min), Canadian church studies, formational counseling, independent design, spiritual formation (M Div, MAPT, D Min), transformational leadership, Wesleyan practices; pastoral ministry (M Div), including Biblical studies - Old or New Testament, Black church studies (M Div, MAPT, D Min), chaplaincy (M Div, MAPT), Christian formation (M Div, MAPT), evangelism/church renewal and missions (M Div, MAPT), general Biblical studies, general ministry (M Div, MAPT), pastoral counseling and care (M Div, MAPT), spiritual formation (M Div, MAPT, D Min), theology or history; theological studies (MA), including Anabaptism and Pietism. *Accreditation:* ATS. Part-time programs available. *Faculty:* 24 full-time (6 women), 32 part-time/adjunct (14 women). *Students:* 317 full-time (62 women), 302 part-time (257 women); includes 235 minority (216 Black or African American, non-Hispanic/Latino; 3 American Indian or Alaska Native, non-Hispanic/Latino; 7 Asian, non-Hispanic/Latino; 8 Hispanic/Latino; 1 Two or more races, non-Hispanic/Latino), 8 international. Average age 43. 224 applicants, 67% accepted, 122 enrolled. In 2011, 123 master's, 27 doctorates awarded. *Median time to degree:* Of those who began their doctoral program in fall 2003, 26% received their degree in 8 years or less. *Degree requirements:* For master's, 2 foreign languages, comprehensive exam (for some programs), thesis (for some programs); for doctorate, thesis/dissertation. *Entrance requirements:* For master's, bachelor's degree from accredited institution with a minimum undergraduate GPA of 2.75; for doctorate, M Div, minimum undergraduate GPA of 3.0. Additional exam requirements/recommendations for international students: Required—TOEFL (minimum score 500 paper-based; 173 computer-based; 65 iBT). *Application deadline:* For fall admission, 8/30 for domestic students. Applications are processed on a rolling basis. Application fee: $35. Electronic applications accepted. *Expenses: Tuition:* Full-time $13,500; part-time $375 per credit hour. *Required fees:* $6 per credit. *Financial support:* In 2011–12, 120 students received support, including 46 teaching assistantships; research assistantships, career-related internships or fieldwork, institutionally sponsored loans, scholarships/grants, and unspecified assistantships also available. Support available to part-time students. Financial award application deadline: 5/15; financial award applicants required to submit FAFSA. *Faculty research:* Semitic languages and linguistics, rhetorical and social-scientific criticism, Anabaptist studies, inner spiritual healing, African-American clergy in film and literature. *Unit head:* Dr. John C. Shultz, President, 419-289-5160, Fax: 419-289-5969, E-mail: jshultz@ashland.edu. *Application contact:* Glenn Black, Director of Enrollment Management, 419-289-5151, Fax: 419-289-5969, E-mail: gblack@ashland.edu.

Athabasca University, Graduate Centre for Applied Psychology, Athabasca, AB T9S 3A3, Canada. Offers art therapy (MC); career counseling (MC); counseling (Advanced Certificate); counseling psychology (MC); school counseling (MC).

Auburn University Montgomery, School of Education, Department of Counselor, Leadership, and Special Education, Montgomery, AL 36124-4023. Offers counseling (M Ed, Ed S); education administration (M Ed, Ed S); special education (M Ed, Ed S). *Accreditation:* ACA; NCATE. Part-time and evening/weekend programs available. *Degree requirements:* For master's and Ed S, comprehensive exam. *Entrance requirements:* For master's, GRE General Test or MAT, certification, BS in teaching; for Ed S, GRE General Test or MAT, certification. Electronic applications accepted. *Expenses:* Tuition, state resident: full-time $5076. Tuition, nonresident: full-time $15,228.

Augusta State University, Graduate Studies, College of Education, Program in Counseling/Guidance, Augusta, GA 30904-2200. Offers M Ed. *Accreditation:* ACA; NCATE. Part-time and evening/weekend programs available. *Faculty:* 3 full-time (2 women), 3 part-time/adjunct (2 women). *Students:* 42 full-time (40 women), 32 part-time (29 women); includes 28 minority (25 Black or African American, non-Hispanic/Latino; 1 Asian, non-Hispanic/Latino; 2 Hispanic/Latino). Average age 34. 33 applicants, 73% accepted, 24 enrolled. In 2011, 26 master's awarded. *Degree requirements:* For master's, comprehensive exam, portfolio. *Entrance requirements:* For master's, GRE, MAT, minimum GPA of 2.5. *Application deadline:* For fall admission, 8/1 priority date for domestic students. Applications are processed on a rolling basis. Application fee: $20. *Financial support:* Federal Work-Study, institutionally sponsored loans, and unspecified assistantships available. Support available to part-time students. Financial award application deadline: 4/15; financial award applicants required to submit FAFSA. *Faculty research:* Counseling for AIDS patients, counseling for drug and alcohol abuse. *Unit head:* Dr. Charles Jackson, Chair, 706-737-1497, Fax: 706-667-4706, E-mail: cjackson@aug.edu. *Application contact:* Andrea M. Scott, Secretary to the Dean, 706-737-1499, Fax: 706-667-4706, E-mail: ascott1@aug.edu.

Austin Peay State University, College of Graduate Studies, College of Behavioral and Health Sciences, Department of Psychology, Clarksville, TN 37044. Offers counseling (MS); counseling and guidance (Ed S); psychology (MA). Part-time programs available. Postbaccalaureate distance learning degree programs offered (no on-campus study). *Faculty:* 10 full-time (6 women), 1 (woman) part-time/adjunct. *Students:* 57 full-time (50 women), 31 part-time (24 women); includes 13 minority (8 Black or African American, non-Hispanic/Latino; 2 Asian, non-Hispanic/Latino; 2 Hispanic/Latino; 1 Two or more races, non-Hispanic/Latino), 1 international. Average age 30. 55 applicants, 98% accepted, 32 enrolled. In 2011, 25 master's awarded. *Degree requirements:* For master's, comprehensive exam, thesis (for some programs). *Entrance requirements:* For master's, GRE General Test, minimum undergraduate GPA of 2.5, 3 letters of recommendation, bachelor's degree. Additional exam requirements/recommendations for international students: Required—TOEFL (minimum score 500 paper-based; 173 computer-based). *Application deadline:* For fall admission, 8/1 priority date for domestic students. Applications are processed on a rolling basis. Application fee: $25. Electronic applications accepted. *Expenses:* Tuition, state resident: part-time $350 per credit hour. Tuition, nonresident: full-time $20,644; part-time $971 per credit hour. *Required fees:* $1224; $61.20 per credit hour. *Financial support:* In 2011–12, research assistantships with full tuition reimbursements (averaging $5,184 per year) were awarded; career-related internships or fieldwork, Federal Work-Study, institutionally sponsored loans, scholarships/grants, and unspecified assistantships also available. Support available to part-time students. Financial award application deadline: 3/1; financial award applicants required to submit FAFSA. *Unit head:* Dr. Samuel Fung, Chair, 931-221-7233, Fax: 931-221-6267, E-mail: fungs@apsu.edu. *Application contact:* Kendra Bryant, Graduate Admissions, 800-844-2778, Fax: 931-221-6188, E-mail: admissionsweb@apsu.edu. Web site: http://www.apsu.edu/psychology.

Azusa Pacific University, School of Education, Department of School Counseling and School Psychology, Program in Educational Counseling, Azusa, CA 91702-7000. Offers MA.

Baptist Bible College of Pennsylvania, Graduate School, Clarks Summit, PA 18411-1297. Offers Bible (MA); counseling (MS); education (MS). Part-time and evening/weekend programs available. Postbaccalaureate distance learning degree programs offered (no on-campus study). *Entrance requirements:* Additional exam requirements/recommendations for international students: Required—TOEFL (minimum score 500 paper-based; 173 computer-based).

Barry University, School of Education, Program in Counseling, Miami Shores, FL 33161-6695. Offers MS, PhD, Ed S. *Accreditation:* ACA. Part-time and evening/weekend programs available. *Degree requirements:* For master's, comprehensive exam. *Entrance requirements:* For master's, GRE General Test or MAT, minimum GPA of 3.0; for doctorate, GRE, minimum GPA of 3.25; for Ed S, GRE General Test, minimum GPA of 3.0.

Barry University, School of Education, Program in Mental Health Counseling, Miami Shores, FL 33161-6695. Offers MS, Ed S. *Accreditation:* ACA. Part-time and evening/weekend programs available. *Degree requirements:* For master's, comprehensive exam, scholarly paper; for Ed S, comprehensive exam. *Entrance requirements:* For master's, GRE General Test or MAT, minimum GPA of 3.0; for Ed S, GRE General Test, minimum GPA of 3.0. Electronic applications accepted.

Barry University, School of Education, Program in School Counseling, Miami Shores, FL 33161-6695. Offers MS, Ed S. *Accreditation:* ACA (one or more programs are accredited). Part-time and evening/weekend programs available. *Degree requirements:* For master's, comprehensive exam, scholarly paper; for Ed S, comprehensive exam. *Entrance requirements:* For master's, GRE General Test or MAT, minimum GPA of 3.0; for Ed S, GRE General Test, minimum GPA of 3.0. Electronic applications accepted.

Bayamón Central University, Graduate Programs, Program in Education, Bayamón, PR 00960-1725. Offers administration and supervision (MA Ed); commercial education (MA Ed); elementary education (K–3) (MA Ed); family counseling (Graduate Certificate); guidance and counseling (MA Ed); pre-elementary teacher (MA Ed); rehabilitation counseling (MA Ed); special education (MA Ed), including attention deficit disorder, education of the autistic, learning disabilities. Part-time and evening/weekend programs available. *Degree requirements:* For master's, comprehensive exam. *Entrance requirements:* For master's, EXADEP, bachelor's degree in education or related field.

Bellevue University, Graduate School, College of Arts and Sciences, Bellevue, NE 68005-3098. Offers clinical counseling (MS); healthcare administration (MHA); human services (MA); international security and intelligence studies (MS); managerial communication (MA). Postbaccalaureate distance learning degree programs offered.

Bloomsburg University of Pennsylvania, School of Graduate Studies, College of Education, Department of Educational Studies and Secondary Education, Program in Guidance Counseling and Student Affairs, Bloomsburg, PA 17815-1301. Offers M Ed. *Entrance requirements:* For master's, GRE, 3 letters of recommendation, resume.

Bob Jones University, Graduate Programs, Greenville, SC 29614. Offers accountancy (MS); Bible (MA); Bible translation (MA); Biblical studies (Certificate); broadcast management (MS); business administration (MBA); church history (MA, PhD); church ministries (MA); church music (MM); cinema and video production (MA); counseling (MS); curriculum and instruction (Ed D); divinity (M Div); dramatic production (MA); educational leadership (MS, Ed D, Ed S); elementary education (M Ed, MAT); English (M Ed, MA, MAT); fine arts (MA); graphic design (MA); history (M Ed, MA); illustration (MA); interpretative speech (MA); mathematics (M Ed, MAT); medical missions (Certificate); ministry (MM, D Min); multi-categorical special education (M Ed, MAT); music (M Ed); New Testament interpretation (PhD); Old Testament interpretation (PhD); orchestral instrument performance (MM); organ performance (MM); pastoral studies (MA); personnel services (MS, Ed S); piano pedagogy (MM); piano performance (MM); platform arts (MA); radio and television broadcasting (MS); rhetoric and public address (MA); secondary education (M Ed); studio art (MA); teaching Bible (MA); theology (MA, PhD); voice performance (MM); youth ministries (MA); M Div/MM.

Boise State University, Graduate College, College of Education, Department of Counselor Education, Program in Counseling, Boise, ID 83725-0399. Offers MA.

Counselor Education

Accreditation: ACA; NCATE. *Entrance requirements:* For master's, minimum GPA of 3.0. Electronic applications accepted.

Boston College, Lynch Graduate School of Education, Program in Counseling, Chestnut Hill, MA 02467-3800. Offers counseling psychology (PhD); mental health counseling (MA); school counseling (MA); MA/MA. *Accreditation:* APA (one or more programs are accredited). *Students:* 210 full-time (179 women), 7 part-time (5 women); includes 54 minority (20 Black or African American, non-Hispanic/Latino; 16 Asian, non-Hispanic/Latino; 14 Hispanic/Latino; 4 Two or more races, non-Hispanic/Latino), 14 international. 622 applicants, 39% accepted, 95 enrolled. In 2011, 80 master's, 7 doctorates awarded. Terminal master's awarded for partial completion of doctoral program. *Degree requirements:* For master's, comprehensive exam; for doctorate, comprehensive exam, thesis/dissertation. *Entrance requirements:* For master's and doctorate, GRE General Test. Additional exam requirements/recommendations for international students: Required—TOEFL (minimum score 550 paper-based; 213 computer-based; 79 iBT). Application fee: $65. Electronic applications accepted. *Financial support:* Fellowships with full and partial tuition reimbursements, research assistantships with full and partial tuition reimbursements, teaching assistantships with full and partial tuition reimbursements, career-related internships or fieldwork, Federal Work-Study, scholarships/grants, traineeships, health care benefits, tuition waivers (full and partial), and unspecified assistantships available. Support available to part-time students. Financial award applicants required to submit FAFSA. *Faculty research:* Reducing non-academic barriers to learning; race, gender, culture and social class issues in mental health; domestic violence; career development; community intervention and prevention. *Unit head:* Dr. M. Brinton Lykes, Chairperson, 617-552-4214, Fax: 617-552-0812. *Application contact:* Adam Poluzzi, Director, Graduate Admission and Financial Aid, 617-552-4214, Fax: 617-552-0398, E-mail: poluzzi@bc.edu.

Bowie State University, Graduate Programs, Program in Guidance and Counseling, Bowie, MD 20715-9465. Offers M Ed. Part-time and evening/weekend programs available. *Faculty:* 7 full-time (4 women), 14 part-time/adjunct (9 women). *Students:* 36 full-time (28 women), 111 part-time (97 women); includes 115 minority (110 Black or African American, non-Hispanic/Latino; 1 American Indian or Alaska Native, non-Hispanic/Latino; 2 Asian, non-Hispanic/Latino; 2 Hispanic/Latino), 2 international. Average age 32. 50 applicants, 92% accepted, 37 enrolled. In 2011, 16 master's awarded. *Degree requirements:* For master's, comprehensive exam, thesis optional, research paper. *Entrance requirements:* For master's, teaching experience, minimum GPA of 2.5, 3 recommendations. *Application deadline:* For fall admission, 4/1 priority date for domestic students, 4/1 for international students; for spring admission, 11/1 for domestic and international students. Applications are processed on a rolling basis. Application fee: $40. Electronic applications accepted. *Expenses:* Tuition, state resident: full-time $4140; part-time $3105 per semester. Tuition, nonresident: full-time $7836; part-time $5877 per semester. *Required fees:* $1715; $648 per semester. *Financial support:* Institutionally sponsored loans available. Support available to part-time students. Financial award application deadline: 4/1. *Unit head:* Rhonda Jeter-Tuilley, Chairperson, 301-860-3233, E-mail: rjeter@bowiestate.edu. *Application contact:* Angela Issac, Information Contact, 301-860-4000.

Bowling Green State University, Graduate College, College of Education and Human Development, School of Education and Intervention Services, Intervention Services Division, Program in Counseling, Bowling Green, OH 43403. Offers mental health counseling (MA); school counseling (M Ed). *Accreditation:* ACA; NCATE. Part-time programs available. *Degree requirements:* For master's, thesis or alternative. *Entrance requirements:* For master's, GRE General Test. Additional exam requirements/recommendations for international students: Required—TOEFL. Electronic applications accepted. *Faculty research:* Perfectionism, multicultural counseling, suicide, ethics and legal issues related to counseling, play therapy.

Bradley University, Graduate School, College of Education and Health Sciences, Department of Educational Leadership and Human Development, Peoria, IL 61625-0002. Offers human development counseling (MA), including community and agency counseling, school counseling; leadership in educational administration (MA); leadership in human service administration (MA). *Accreditation:* ACA; NCATE. Part-time and evening/weekend programs available. *Degree requirements:* For master's, comprehensive exam, thesis optional. *Entrance requirements:* For master's, GRE General Test or MAT, interview, 3 letters of recommendation. Additional exam requirements/recommendations for international students: Required—TOEFL (minimum score 550 paper-based; 213 computer-based; 79 iBT).

Brandman University, School of Education, Irvine, CA 92618. Offers education (MA); educational leadership (MA); school counseling (MA); special education (MA); teaching (MA).

Brandon University, Faculty of Education, Brandon, MB R7A 6A9, Canada. Offers curriculum and instruction (M Ed, Diploma); educational administration (M Ed, Diploma); guidance and counseling (M Ed, Diploma); special education (M Ed, Diploma). *Degree requirements:* For master's, thesis. *Entrance requirements:* For master's, minimum GPA of 3.0, teaching certificate or equivalent. Additional exam requirements/recommendations for international students: Required—TOEFL. *Faculty research:* Comparative education, environmental studies, parent/school council.

Bridgewater State University, School of Graduate Studies, School of Education and Allied Studies, Department of Secondary Education and Professional Programs, Program in Counseling, Bridgewater, MA 02325-0001. Offers M Ed, CAGS. *Accreditation:* ACA; NCATE. Part-time and evening/weekend programs available. *Entrance requirements:* For master's, GRE General Test.

Brooklyn College of the City University of New York, Division of Graduate Studies, School of Education, Program in School Counseling, Brooklyn, NY 11210-2889. Offers MS Ed, CAS. *Accreditation:* ACA. Part-time programs available. *Degree requirements:* For master's, comprehensive exam, internship. *Entrance requirements:* For master's, interview, 2 letters of recommendation, resume, essay, supplemental application; for CAS, master's degree. Additional exam requirements/recommendations for international students: Required—TOEFL (minimum score 500 paper-based; 173 computer-based; 61 iBT). Electronic applications accepted. *Faculty research:* Urban school counseling, parent involvement, multicultural competence and counselor training.

Buena Vista University, School of Education, Storm Lake, IA 50588. Offers curriculum and instruction (M Ed), including effective teaching, TESL; school guidance and counseling (MS Ed). Program offered in summer only. Part-time and evening/weekend programs available. Postbaccalaureate distance learning degree programs offered (minimal on-campus study). *Degree requirements:* For master's, thesis, fieldwork/practicum, capstone portfolio. *Entrance requirements:* For master's, Analytical Writing Assessment (in-house), minimum undergraduate GPA of 2.75. Electronic applications accepted. *Faculty research:* Reading, curriculum, educational psychology, special education.

Butler University, College of Education, Indianapolis, IN 46208-3485. Offers administration (MS); elementary education (MS); reading (MS); school counseling (MS); secondary education (MS); special education (MS). *Accreditation:* ACA; NCATE. Part-time and evening/weekend programs available. *Faculty:* 7 full-time (4 women), 5 part-time/adjunct (all women). *Students:* 9 full-time (6 women), 136 part-time (105 women); includes 21 minority (14 Black or African American, non-Hispanic/Latino; 5 Asian, non-Hispanic/Latino; 1 Hispanic/Latino; 1 Two or more races, non-Hispanic/Latino), 1 international. Average age 31. 69 applicants, 94% accepted, 24 enrolled. In 2011, 66 master's awarded. *Entrance requirements:* For master's, GRE General Test, MAT, interview. *Application deadline:* For fall admission, 8/15 priority date for domestic students. Applications are processed on a rolling basis. Application fee: $35. Electronic applications accepted. *Expenses: Tuition:* Part-time $466 per credit. *Financial support:* Institutionally sponsored loans available. Support available to part-time students. Financial award application deadline: 7/15; financial award applicants required to submit FAFSA. *Faculty research:* Ethics in cybercounseling, history of sports for disabled, effect of fetal alcohol syndrome on perceptual learning, reading recovery's theoretical framework in teacher education. *Unit head:* Dr. Ena Shelley, Dean, 317-940-9752, Fax: 317-940-6481. *Application contact:* Karen Farrell, Department Secretary, 317-940-9220, E-mail: kfarrell@butler.edu.

Caldwell College, Graduate Studies, Department of Psychology, Caldwell, NJ 07006-6195. Offers art therapy (MA); counseling (MA), including art therapy, mental health, school counseling; director of school counseling (Post-Master's Certificate); professional counselor (Post-Master's Certificate); school counselor (Post-Master's Certificate). Part-time and evening/weekend programs available. *Students:* 47 full-time (36 women), 84 part-time (71 women); includes 29 minority (11 Black or African American, non-Hispanic/Latino; 4 Asian, non-Hispanic/Latino; 10 Hispanic/Latino; 4 Two or more races, non-Hispanic/Latino), 1 international. *Application deadline:* For fall admission, 7/1 for domestic and international students; for spring admission, 12/1 for domestic and international students. Applications are processed on a rolling basis. Application fee: $40. Electronic applications accepted. *Expenses: Tuition:* Full-time $14,400; part-time $800 per credit. *Required fees:* $200; $100 per semester. *Financial support:* Applicants required to submit FAFSA. *Unit head:* Dr. Stacey Solomon, Program Coordinator, 973-618-3387, E-mail: ssolomon@caldwell.edu. *Application contact:* Vilma Mueller, Director of Graduate Studies, 973-618-3544, E-mail: graduate@caldwell.edu.

California Baptist University, Program in Education, Riverside, CA 92504-3206. Offers educational leadership for faith-based instruction (MS); educational leadership for public institutions (MS); educational technology (MS); instructional computer applications (MS); international education (MS); reading (MS); school counseling (MS); school psychology (MS); special education (MS); special education in mild/moderate disabilities (MS); special education in moderate/severe disabilities (MS); teaching (MS); teaching and learning with induction program (MS Ed). Part-time and evening/weekend programs available. *Faculty:* 16 full-time (10 women), 1 (woman) part-time/adjunct. *Students:* 380 full-time (323 women); includes 149 minority (28 Black or African American, non-Hispanic/Latino; 2 American Indian or Alaska Native, non-Hispanic/Latino; 13 Asian, non-Hispanic/Latino; 100 Hispanic/Latino; 2 Native Hawaiian or other Pacific Islander, non-Hispanic/Latino; 4 Two or more races, non-Hispanic/Latino). Average age 32. 181 applicants, 70% accepted, 111 enrolled. In 2011, 82 master's awarded. *Degree requirements:* For master's, comprehensive exam or thesis. *Entrance requirements:* For master's, minimum undergraduate GPA of 3.0; 18 semester units of prerequisite course work in education; three recommendations; essay; interview. Additional exam requirements/recommendations for international students: Required—TOEFL (minimum score 575 paper-based; 230 computer-based; 89 iBT). *Application deadline:* For fall admission, 8/1 priority date for domestic students, 7/1 for international students; for spring admission, 12/1 priority date for domestic students, 11/1 for international students. Applications are processed on a rolling basis. Application fee: $45. Electronic applications accepted. *Expenses:* Contact institution. *Financial support:* In 2011–12, 4 students received support. Federal Work-Study and institutionally sponsored loans available. Financial award applicants required to submit FAFSA. *Faculty research:* Special education, neurosciences and education, cultural influences on behavior, faith-based school leadership, social and philosophical contexts of education. *Unit head:* Dr. John Shoup, Dean, School of Education, 951-343-4205, Fax: 951-343-4516, E-mail: jshoup@calbaptist.edu. *Application contact:* Dr. James Heyman, Director, Master of Science Program in Education, 951-343-4243, Fax: 951-343-5095, E-mail: jheyman@calbaptist.edu. Web site: http://www.calbaptist.edu/mastersined/.

California Lutheran University, Graduate Studies, Graduate School of Education, Thousand Oaks, CA 91360-2787. Offers counseling and guidance (MS), including college student personnel, counseling and guidance; educational leadership (MA, Ed D), including educational leadership (K-12) (Ed D), higher education leadership (Ed D); special education (MS); teacher leadership (M Ed); teaching (M Ed). *Accreditation:* NCATE. Part-time and evening/weekend programs available. *Entrance requirements:* For master's, GRE General Test, interview, minimum GPA of 3.0.

California State University, Bakersfield, Division of Graduate Studies, School of Social Sciences and Education, Program in Counseling, Bakersfield, CA 93311. Offers school counseling (MS); student affairs (MS). *Accreditation:* NCATE. *Degree requirements:* For master's, thesis or alternative, culminating projects. *Entrance requirements:* For master's, CBEST (school counseling). *Application deadline:* Applications are processed on a rolling basis. Application fee: $55. *Expenses: Required fees:* $1302 per unit. Part-time tuition and fees vary according to course load and program. *Unit head:* Julia Bavier, Evaluator, Advanced Educational Studies, 661-654-3193, Fax: 661-665-6916, E-mail: jbavier@csub.edu. Web site: http://www.csub.edu/sse/advanced_education/counseling_and_personnel_services/.

California State University, Dominguez Hills, College of Professional Studies, School of Education, Division of Graduate Education, Program in Counseling, Carson, CA 90747-0001. Offers MA. Part-time and evening/weekend programs available. *Faculty:* 4 full-time (all women), 2 part-time/adjunct (both women). *Students:* 57 full-time (54 women), 40 part-time (31 women); includes 69 minority (11 Black or African American, non-Hispanic/Latino; 8 Asian, non-Hispanic/Latino; 48 Hispanic/Latino; 2 Two or more races, non-Hispanic/Latino). Average age 33. 57 applicants, 26% accepted, 9 enrolled. In 2011, 59 master's awarded. *Degree requirements:* For master's, comprehensive exam. *Entrance requirements:* For master's, minimum GPA of 3.0. *Application deadline:* For fall admission, 4/1 for domestic students; for spring admission, 10/1 for domestic students. Applications are processed on a rolling basis. Application fee: $55. *Faculty research:* Social development. *Unit head:* Dr. Adriean Mancillas, Associate Professor, 310-243-2680, E-mail: amancillas@csudh.edu. *Application contact:* Admissions Office, 310-243-3530. Web site: http://www.csudh.edu/cps/soe/programsdegrees/graduate-programs-pupil-personnel.shtml.

California State University, East Bay, Office of Academic Programs and Graduate Studies, College of Education and Allied Studies, Department of Educational Psychology, Counseling Program, Hayward, CA 94542-3000. Offers MS. *Accreditation:* NCATE. *Faculty:* 7 full-time (4 women), 8 part-time/adjunct (7 women). *Students:* 104 full-time (85 women); includes 40 minority (5 Black or African American, non-Hispanic/Latino; 15 Asian, non-Hispanic/Latino; 16 Hispanic/Latino; 1 Native Hawaiian or other Pacific Islander, non-Hispanic/Latino; 3 Two or more races, non-Hispanic/Latino). Average age 30. 173 applicants, 29% accepted, 40 enrolled. In 2011, 70 master's awarded. *Degree requirements:* For master's, comprehensive exam, project or thesis. *Entrance requirements:* For master's, GRE or MAT, interview, minimum GPA of 2.5 during previous 2 years of course work. Additional exam requirements/recommendations for international students: Required—TOEFL (minimum score 550 paper-based; 213 computer-based). *Application deadline:* For fall admission, 6/30 for domestic and international students. Application fee: $55. Electronic applications accepted. *Expenses:* Tuition, state resident: full-time $6738; part-time $1302 per quarter. Tuition, nonresident: full-time $12,690; part-time $2294 per quarter. *Required fees:* $449 per quarter. Tuition and fees vary according to degree level, program and reciprocity agreements. *Financial support:* Career-related internships or fieldwork, Federal Work-Study, and institutionally sponsored loans available. Support available to part-time students. Financial award application deadline: 3/2; financial award applicants required to submit FAFSA. *Unit head:* Dr. Jack Davis, Chair, Educational Psychology, 510-885-3011, Fax: 510-885-4642, E-mail: jack.davis@csueastbay.edu. *Application contact:* Prof. Greg Jennings, Counseling Graduate Advisor, 510-885-2296, Fax: 510-885-4642, E-mail: greg.jennings@csueastbay.edu. Web site: http://www20.csueastbay.edu/ceas/departments/epsy/index.html.

California State University, Fresno, Division of Graduate Studies, School of Education and Human Development, Department of Counseling and Special Education, Program in Counseling and Student Services, Fresno, CA 93740-8027. Offers MS. *Accreditation:* NCATE. Part-time and evening/weekend programs available. *Degree requirements:* For master's, thesis or alternative. *Entrance requirements:* For master's, GRE General Test, MAT, minimum GPA of 3.0. Additional exam requirements/recommendations for international students: Required—TOEFL. Electronic applications accepted.

California State University, Fullerton, Graduate Studies, College of Health and Human Development, Department of Counseling, Fullerton, CA 92834-9480. Offers MS. *Accreditation:* ACA; NCATE. Part-time programs available. *Students:* 110 full-time (90 women), 89 part-time (77 women); includes 83 minority (5 Black or African American, non-Hispanic/Latino; 26 Asian, non-Hispanic/Latino; 47 Hispanic/Latino; 5 Two or more races, non-Hispanic/Latino), 4 international. Average age 31. 274 applicants, 23% accepted, 56 enrolled. In 2011, 54 master's awarded. *Degree requirements:* For master's, comprehensive exam, project or thesis. *Entrance requirements:* For master's, minimum GPA of 3.0 in behavioral science and for undergraduate degree. Application fee: $55. *Financial support:* Career-related internships or fieldwork, Federal Work-Study, institutionally sponsored loans, and scholarships/grants available. Support available to part-time students. Financial award application deadline: 3/1; financial award applicants required to submit FAFSA. *Unit head:* Dr. Jeffrey Kottler, Chair, 657-278-7537. *Application contact:* Admissions/Applications, 657-278-2371.

California State University, Long Beach, Graduate Studies, College of Education, Department of Advanced Studies in Education and Counseling, Master of Science in Counseling Program, Long Beach, CA 90840. Offers marriage and family therapy (MS); school counseling (MS); student development in higher education (MS). *Accreditation:* NCATE. *Students:* 150 full-time (114 women), 65 part-time (48 women); includes 153 minority (23 Black or African American, non-Hispanic/Latino; 3 American Indian or Alaska Native, non-Hispanic/Latino; 32 Asian, non-Hispanic/Latino; 86 Hispanic/Latino; 1 Native Hawaiian or other Pacific Islander, non-Hispanic/Latino; 8 Two or more races, non-Hispanic/Latino), 3 international. Average age 28. 488 applicants, 18% accepted, 68 enrolled. In 2011, 59 master's awarded. *Degree requirements:* For master's, comprehensive exam or thesis. *Application deadline:* For fall admission, 3/1 for domestic students. Applications are processed on a rolling basis. Application fee: $55. Electronic applications accepted. *Financial support:* Federal Work-Study, institutionally sponsored loans, and scholarships/grants available. Financial award application deadline: 3/2. *Unit head:* Dr. Jennifer Coots, Chair, 562-985-4517, Fax: 562-985-4534, E-mail: jcoots@csulb.edu. *Application contact:* Dr. Bita Ghafoori, Assistant Chair, 562-985-7864, Fax: 562-985-4534, E-mail: bghafoor@csulb.edu.

California State University, Los Angeles, Graduate Studies, Charter College of Education, Division of Special Education and Counseling, Los Angeles, CA 90032-8530. Offers counseling (MS), including applied behavior analysis, community college counseling, rehabilitation counseling, school counseling and school psychology; special education (MA, PhD). *Accreditation:* ACA. Part-time and evening/weekend programs available. *Faculty:* 20 full-time (14 women), 27 part-time/adjunct (18 women). *Students:* 334 full-time (277 women), 337 part-time (262 women); includes 480 minority (38 Black or African American, non-Hispanic/Latino; 1 American Indian or Alaska Native, non-Hispanic/Latino; 69 Asian, non-Hispanic/Latino; 364 Hispanic/Latino; 8 Two or more races, non-Hispanic/Latino), 24 international. Average age 34. 288 applicants, 38% accepted, 79 enrolled. In 2011, 226 master's awarded. *Entrance requirements:* For master's, minimum GPA of 2.75 in last 90 units of course work, teaching certificate. Additional exam requirements/recommendations for international students: Required—TOEFL (minimum score 500 paper-based; 173 computer-based). *Application deadline:* For fall admission, 5/1 for domestic and international students. Applications are processed on a rolling basis. Application fee: $55. Electronic applications accepted. *Expenses:* Tuition, state resident: full-time $8225. *Financial support:* Career-related internships or fieldwork and Federal Work-Study available. Support available to part-time students. Financial award application deadline: 3/1. *Unit head:* Dr. Andrea Zetlin, Acting Chair, 323-343-4400, Fax: 323-343-5605, E-mail: azetlin@calstatela.edu. *Application contact:* Dr. Karin Brown, Acting Associate Dean of Graduate Studies, 323-343-3820, Fax: 323-343-5653, E-mail: kbrown5@calstatela.edu. Web site: http://www.calstatela.edu/academic/ccoe/index_edsp.htm.

California State University, Northridge, Graduate Studies, College of Education, Department of Educational Psychology and Counseling, Northridge, CA 91330. Offers counseling (MS), including career counseling, college counseling and student services, marriage and family therapy, school counseling, school psychology; educational psychology (MA Ed), including development, learning, and instruction, early childhood education. *Accreditation:* ACA (one or more programs are accredited); NCATE. Part-time and evening/weekend programs available. *Entrance requirements:* For master's, GRE General Test or minimum GPA of 3.0. Additional exam requirements/recommendations for international students: Required—TOEFL.

California State University, Sacramento, Office of Graduate Studies, College of Education, Department of Counselor Education, Sacramento, CA 95819-6079. Offers career counseling (MS); generic counseling (MS); guidance (MA); school counseling (MS). *Accreditation:* ACA. *Faculty:* 9 full-time (6 women), 17 part-time/adjunct (11 women). *Students:* 260 full-time, 79 part-time; includes 136 minority (24 Black or African American, non-Hispanic/Latino; 3 American Indian or Alaska Native, non-Hispanic/Latino; 30 Asian, non-Hispanic/Latino; 61 Hispanic/Latino; 13 Native Hawaiian or other Pacific Islander, non-Hispanic/Latino; 5 Two or more races, non-Hispanic/Latino), 2 international. Average age 31. 238 applicants, 72% accepted, 115 enrolled. In 2011, 78 master's awarded. *Degree requirements:* For master's, thesis or project; writing proficiency exam. *Entrance requirements:* For master's, minimum GPA of 2.5. Additional exam requirements/recommendations for international students: Required—TOEFL. *Application deadline:* For fall admission, 1/14 for domestic students, 3/1 for international students; for spring admission, 9/30 for international students. Applications are processed on a rolling basis. Application fee: $55. Electronic applications accepted. *Financial support:* Career-related internships or fieldwork and Federal Work-Study available. Support available to part-time students. Financial award application deadline: 3/1; financial award applicants required to submit FAFSA. *Unit head:* Rose Borunda, Chair, 916-278-5399, Fax: 916-278-4174, E-mail: rborunda@csus.edu. *Application contact:* Jose Martinez, Outreach and Graduate Diversity Coordinator, 916-278-6470, Fax: 916-278-5669, E-mail: martinj@skymail.csus.edu. Web site: http://www.edweb.csus.edu/edc.

California State University, San Bernardino, Graduate Studies, College of Education, Program in Educational Psychology and Counseling, San Bernardino, CA 92407-2397. Offers correctional and alternative education (MA); counseling and guidance (MS); rehabilitation counseling (MA). *Accreditation:* NCATE. Part-time and evening/weekend programs available. *Students:* 87 full-time (75 women), 17 part-time (14 women); includes 67 minority (14 Black or African American, non-Hispanic/Latino; 1 American Indian or Alaska Native, non-Hispanic/Latino; 9 Asian, non-Hispanic/Latino; 40 Hispanic/Latino; 1 Native Hawaiian or other Pacific Islander, non-Hispanic/Latino; 2 Two or more races, non-Hispanic/Latino). Average age 29. 71 applicants, 68% accepted, 40 enrolled. In 2011, 42 master's awarded. *Degree requirements:* For master's, comprehensive exam, thesis or alternative, counselor preparation comprehensive examination. *Entrance requirements:* For master's, minimum GPA of 3.0 in education. *Application deadline:* For fall admission, 8/31 priority date for domestic students. Application fee: $55. *Expenses:* Tuition, state resident: full-time $7356. Tuition, nonresident: full-time $7356. *Required fees:* $1077. Tuition and fees vary according to program. *Financial support:* Career-related internships or fieldwork and Federal Work-Study available. Support available to part-time students. *Unit head:* Dr. Ruth Ann Sandlin, Chair, 909-537-5641, Fax: 909-537-7040, E-mail: rsandlin@csusb.edu. *Application contact:* Sandra Kamusikiri, Associate Vice-President/Dean of Graduate Studies, 909-537-5058, E-mail: skamusik@csusb.edu.

California State University, Stanislaus, College of Education, Program in Education (MA), Turlock, CA 95382. Offers curriculum and instruction (MA), including education technology, elementary education, multilingual education, physical education, reading, secondary education, special education; school administration (MA); school counseling (MA). Part-time and evening/weekend programs available. *Degree requirements:* For master's, comprehensive exam (for some programs), thesis (for some programs). *Entrance requirements:* For master's, MAT, GRE, or CBEST (varies by concentration), 3 letters of recommendation, personal statement. Additional exam requirements/recommendations for international students: Required—TOEFL (minimum score 550 paper-based; 213 computer-based). *Application deadline:* For fall admission, 5/1 for domestic students; for spring admission, 1/7 for domestic students. Application fee: $55. Electronic applications accepted. *Expenses: Required fees:* $4616 per year. *Financial support:* Federal Work-Study available. Financial award application deadline: 3/1; financial award applicants required to submit FAFSA. *Faculty research:* Children's perspectives on historical events, method elementary schools dual language education, K-12 reading and CYRM programs. *Unit head:* Dr. Kathy Norman, Dean, College of Education, 209-667-3652, Fax: 209-664-6613, E-mail: coe@csustan.edu. *Application contact:* Graduate School, 209-667-3129, Fax: 209-664-7025, E-mail: graduate_school@csustan.edu. Web site: http://www.csustan.edu/COE/.

California University of Pennsylvania, School of Graduate Studies and Research, College of Education and Human Services, Department of Counselor Education, California, PA 15419-1394. Offers community and agency counseling (MS); school counseling (M Ed). *Accreditation:* ACA; NCATE. Part-time and evening/weekend programs available. *Degree requirements:* For master's, comprehensive exam, thesis optional. *Entrance requirements:* For master's, MAT, minimum GPA of 3.0, resume, letters of reference. Additional exam requirements/recommendations for international students: Required—TOEFL (minimum score 550 paper-based; 213 computer-based; 80 iBT). Electronic applications accepted. *Faculty research:* Mind-body theories and practice, grief issues, career development, supervision, sports counseling.

Cambridge College, School of Education, Cambridge, MA 02138-5304. Offers autism specialist (M Ed); autism/behavior analyst (M Ed); behavior analyst (Post-Master's Certificate); behavioral management (M Ed); early childhood teacher (M Ed); education specialist in curriculum and instruction (CAGS); educational leadership (Ed D); elementary teacher (M Ed); English as a second language (M Ed, Certificate); general science (M Ed); health education (Post-Master's Certificate); health/family and consumer sciences (M Ed); history (M Ed); individualized (M Ed); information technology literacy (M Ed); instructional technology (M Ed); interdisciplinary studies (M Ed); library teacher (M Ed); literacy education (M Ed); mathematics (M Ed); mathematics specialist (Certificate); middle school mathematics and science (M Ed); school administration (M Ed, CAGS); school guidance counselor (M Ed); school nurse education (M Ed); school social worker/school adjustment counselor (M Ed); special education administrator (CAGS); special education/moderate disabilities (M Ed); teaching skills and methodologies (M Ed). Part-time and evening/weekend programs available. Postbaccalaureate distance learning degree programs offered (minimal on-campus study). *Degree requirements:* For master's, thesis, internship/practicum (licensure program only); for doctorate, thesis/dissertation; for other advanced degree, thesis. *Entrance requirements:* For master's, interview, resume, documentation of licensure, 2 professional references; for doctorate, official transcripts, interview, resume, documentation of licensure (if any), written personal statement/essay, portfolio of scholarly and professional work, qualifying assessment, 2 professional references, health insurance, immunizations form; for other advanced degree, official transcripts, interview, resume, documentation of licensure (if any), written personal statement/essay, 2 professional references, health insurance, immunizations form. Additional exam requirements/recommendations for international students: Required—TOEFL (minimum score 550 paper-based; 213 computer-based; 79 iBT); Recommended—IELTS (minimum score 6). Electronic applications accepted. *Expenses:* Contact institution. *Faculty research:* Adult education, accelerated learning, mathematics education, brain compatible learning, special education and law.

Cambridge College, School of Psychology and Counseling, Cambridge, MA 02138-5304. Offers addiction counseling (M Ed); alcohol and drug counseling (Certificate); counseling psychology (M Ed, CAGS); counseling psychology: forensic counseling (M Ed); marriage and family therapy (M Ed); mental health and addiction counseling (M Ed); mental health counseling (M Ed); mental health counseling for school guidance counselors (Post Master's Certificate); psychological studies (M Ed); school adjustment and mental health counseling (M Ed); school adjustment, mental health and addiction counseling (M Ed); school guidance counselor (M Ed); trauma studies (Certificate). Part-time and evening/weekend programs available. *Degree requirements:* For master's and other advanced degree, thesis, practicum/internship. *Entrance requirements:* For master's, resume, 2 professional references; for other advanced degree, official transcripts, documents for transfer credit evaluation, resume, written personal statement/essay, 2 professional references, health insurance, immunizations form. Additional exam requirements/recommendations for international students: Required—TOEFL (minimum score 550 paper-based; 213 computer-based; 79 iBT); Recommended—IELTS (minimum score 6). Electronic applications accepted. *Expenses:* Contact institution. *Faculty research:* Trauma, drug and alcohol counseling, cross-cultural issues, school counseling, trauma in schools.

Campbell University, Graduate and Professional Programs, School of Education, Buies Creek, NC 27506. Offers administration (MSA); community counseling (MA); elementary education (M Ed); English education (M Ed); interdisciplinary studies (M Ed); mathematics education (M Ed); middle grades education (M Ed); physical education (M Ed); school counseling (M Ed); secondary education (M Ed); social science education (M Ed). *Accreditation:* NCATE. Part-time and evening/weekend programs available. *Degree requirements:* For master's, comprehensive exam. *Entrance requirements:* For master's, GRE General Test, minimum GPA of 2.7. *Faculty research:* Spiritual values and wellness issues in counseling, stress and professional burnout among counselors, thinking strategies, leadership, adaptive technology.

Canisius College, Graduate Division, School of Education and Human Services, Programs in Counseling and Human Services, Buffalo, NY 14208-1098. Offers community mental health counseling (MS); school agency counseling (MS). *Accreditation:* ACA. Part-time and evening/weekend programs available. *Faculty:* 5 full-time (3 women), 16 part-time/adjunct (12 women). *Students:* 122 full-time (97 women), 70 part-time (54 women); includes 31 minority (21 Black or African American, non-Hispanic/Latino; 1 American Indian or Alaska Native, non-Hispanic/Latino; 3 Asian, non-Hispanic/Latino; 2 Hispanic/Latino; 4 Two or more races, non-Hispanic/Latino), 2 international. Average age 27. 135 applicants, 82% accepted, 50 enrolled. In 2011, 72 master's awarded. *Degree requirements:* For master's, thesis, research project. *Entrance requirements:* For master's, GRE if cumulative GPA less than 2.7, transcripts, two letters of recommendation, interview. Additional exam requirements/recommendations for international students: Required—TOEFL. *Application deadline:* Applications are processed on a rolling basis. Application fee: $25. Electronic applications accepted. *Financial support:* Research assistantships, career-related internships or fieldwork, Federal Work-Study, scholarships/grants, tuition waivers (partial), and unspecified assistantships available. Support available to part-time students. Financial award application deadline: 4/30; financial award applicants required to submit FAFSA. *Faculty research:* Impact of trauma on adults, long term psych-social impact on police officers. *Unit head:* Dr. Christine Moll, Chair, 716-888-3287, E-mail: moll@canisius.edu. *Application contact:* Jim Bagwell, Director of Graduate Recruitment and Admissions, 716-888-2544, E-mail: bagwellj@canisius.edu. Web site: http://www.canisius.edu/counselor_ed/.

Carlow University, School for Social Change, Program in Professional Counseling, Pittsburgh, PA 15213-3165. Offers professional counseling (MS); professional counseling/school counseling (MS). Part-time and evening/weekend programs available. *Students:* 180 full-time (160 women), 17 part-time (15 women); includes 32 minority (26 Black or African American, non-Hispanic/Latino; 1 Asian, non-Hispanic/Latino; 4 Hispanic/Latino; 1 Two or more races, non-Hispanic/Latino). Average age 30. 188 applicants, 47% accepted, 57 enrolled. In 2011, 46 master's awarded. *Entrance requirements:* For master's, personal essay; resume or curriculum vitae; three recommendations; official transcripts; interview; minimum undergraduate GPA of 3.0; undergraduate courses in statistics, abnormal psychology, and personality theory; undergraduate work or work experience in the helping professions. Additional exam requirements/recommendations for international students: Required—TOEFL (minimum score 550 paper-based; 213 computer-based). Application fee: $20. Application fee is waived when completed online. *Expenses: Tuition:* Full-time $10,290; part-time $686 per credit. Tuition and fees vary according to course load, degree level and program. *Unit head:* Dr. Robert A. Reed, Chair, Department of Psychology and Counseling, 412-575-6349, E-mail: reedra@carlow.edu. *Application contact:* Dr. Kathleen A. Chrisman, Associate Director, Graduate Admissions, 412-578-8812, Fax: 412-578-6321, E-mail: kachrisman@carlow.edu. Web site: http://gradstudies.carlow.edu/pro-counsel/index.html.

Carson-Newman College, Graduate Program in Education, Jefferson City, TN 37760. Offers curriculum and instruction (M Ed); educational leadership (M Ed); elementary education (MAT); school counseling (MS); secondary education (MAT); teaching English as a second language (MATESL). *Accreditation:* NCATE. Part-time and evening/weekend programs available. *Faculty:* 5 full-time (2 women), 10 part-time/adjunct (3 women). *Students:* 85 full-time (55 women), 76 part-time (53 women); includes 8 minority (5 Black or African American, non-Hispanic/Latino; 2 Asian, non-Hispanic/Latino; 1 Two or more races, non-Hispanic/Latino), 23 international. Average age 32. 80 applicants, 96% accepted. In 2011, 90 master's awarded. *Degree requirements:* For master's, thesis or alternative. *Entrance requirements:* For master's, NTE, minimum GPA of 3.0 in major, 2.5 overall. *Application deadline:* For fall admission, 7/15 priority date for domestic students. Applications are processed on a rolling basis. Application fee: $25 ($50 for international students). *Expenses: Tuition:* Full-time $6750; part-time $375 per credit hour. *Required fees:* $200. *Financial support:* In 2011–12, 41 students received support. Federal Work-Study and unspecified assistantships available. Financial award application deadline: 4/1; financial award applicants required to submit FAFSA. *Unit head:* Dr. Sharon Teets, Chair, 865-471-3461. *Application contact:* Graduate Admissions and Services Adviser, 865-471-3460, Fax: 865-471-3875.

Carthage College, Division of Teacher Education, Kenosha, WI 53140. Offers classroom guidance and counseling (M Ed); creative arts (M Ed); gifted and talented children (M Ed); language arts (M Ed); modern language (M Ed); natural sciences (M Ed); reading (M Ed, Certificate); social sciences (M Ed); teacher leadership (M Ed). Part-time and evening/weekend programs available. *Degree requirements:* For master's, thesis optional. *Entrance requirements:* For master's, MAT, minimum B average, letters of reference.

Central Connecticut State University, School of Graduate Studies, School of Education and Professional Studies, Department of Counseling and Family Therapy, New Britain, CT 06050-4010. Offers marriage and family therapy (MS); professional counseling (MS, Certificate); school counseling (MS); student development in higher education (MS). *Accreditation:* AAMFT/COAMFTE; ACA. Part-time and evening/weekend programs available. *Faculty:* 8 full-time (4 women), 20 part-time/adjunct (15 women). *Students:* 150 full-time (122 women), 243 part-time (204 women); includes 92 minority (50 Black or African American, non-Hispanic/Latino; 1 American Indian or Alaska Native, non-Hispanic/Latino; 7 Asian, non-Hispanic/Latino; 33 Hispanic/Latino; 1 Two or more races, non-Hispanic/Latino), 2 international. Average age 33. 278 applicants, 48% accepted, 109 enrolled. In 2011, 88 master's awarded. *Degree requirements:* For master's, comprehensive exam, thesis or alternative; for Certificate, qualifying exam. *Entrance requirements:* For master's, minimum undergraduate GPA of 2.7, essay, interview. Additional exam requirements/recommendations for international students: Required—TOEFL (minimum score 550 paper-based; 213 computer-based). *Application deadline:* For fall admission, 4/1 for domestic and international students; for spring admission, 11/1 for domestic and international students. Applications are processed on a rolling basis. Application fee: $50. Electronic applications accepted. *Expenses: Tuition, area resident:* Full-time $5137; part-time $482 per credit. Tuition, state resident: full-time $7707; part-time $494 per credit. Tuition, nonresident: full-time $14,311; part-time $494 per credit. *Required fees:* $3865. One-time fee: $62 part-time. *Financial support:* In 2011–12, 57 students received support, including 16 research assistantships; career-related internships or fieldwork, Federal Work-Study, scholarships/grants, and unspecified assistantships also available. Support available to part-time students. Financial award application deadline: 4/15; financial award applicants required to submit FAFSA. *Faculty research:* Elementary/secondary school counseling, marriage/family therapy, rehabilitation counseling, counseling in higher educational settings. *Unit head:* Dr. Connie Tait, Chair, 860-832-2154, E-mail: taitc@ccsu.edu. *Application contact:* Patricia Gardner, Associate Director of Graduate Studies, 860-832-2350, Fax: 860-832-2352, E-mail: graduateadmissions@ccsu.edu. Web site: http://www.education.ccsu.edu/Departments/Counseling_and_Family_Therapy/.

Central Methodist University, College of Graduate and Extended Studies, Fayette, MO 65248-1198. Offers clinical counseling (MS); clinical nurse leader (MSN); education (M Ed). Part-time and evening/weekend programs available. Postbaccalaureate distance learning degree programs offered (no on-campus study). *Degree requirements:* For master's, thesis. *Entrance requirements:* For master's, GRE General Test, minimum GPA of 2.75. Electronic applications accepted.

Central Michigan University, Central Michigan University Global Campus, Program in Counseling, Mount Pleasant, MI 48859. Offers professional counseling (MA); school counseling (MA). *Accreditation:* Teacher Education Accreditation Council. Part-time and evening/weekend programs available. *Entrance requirements:* For master's, MAT, minimum GPA of 2.7. Additional exam requirements/recommendations for international students: Required—TOEFL. Electronic applications accepted. *Financial support:* Scholarships/grants available. Support available to part-time students. *Unit head:* Dr. Twinet Parmer, Chair, 989-774-3776, E-mail: parme1t@cmich.edu. *Application contact:* 877-268-4636, E-mail: cmuglobal@cmich.edu.

Central Michigan University, College of Graduate Studies, College of Education and Human Services, Department of Counseling and Special Education, Program in Counseling, Mount Pleasant, MI 48859. Offers counseling (MA), including professional counseling, school counseling. *Accreditation:* Teacher Education Accreditation Council. Part-time programs available. *Degree requirements:* For master's, thesis or alternative. *Entrance requirements:* For master's, MAT, Michigan teaching certification. Electronic applications accepted. *Faculty research:* School counseling, professional counseling.

Central Washington University, Graduate Studies and Research, College of the Sciences, Department of Psychology, Program in School Counseling, Ellensburg, WA 98926. Offers M Ed. *Faculty:* 22 full-time (13 women). *Students:* 4 full-time (3 women), 1 (woman) part-time; includes 1 minority (Hispanic/Latino). 10 applicants, 0% accepted, 0 enrolled. In 2011, 4 master's awarded. *Degree requirements:* For master's, thesis or alternative, internship. *Entrance requirements:* For master's, GRE General Test, minimum GPA of 3.0. Additional exam requirements/recommendations for international students: Required—TOEFL (minimum score 550 paper-based; 213 computer-based; 79 iBT). *Application deadline:* For fall admission, 2/1 priority date for domestic students. Applications are processed on a rolling basis. Application fee: $50. Electronic applications accepted. *Expenses:* Tuition, state resident: full-time $8112; part-time $270 per credit. Tuition, nonresident: full-time $18,069; part-time $602 per credit. *Required fees:* $924. *Financial support:* Research assistantships with full and partial tuition reimbursements, career-related internships or fieldwork, Federal Work-Study, health care benefits, and unspecified assistantships available. Financial award application deadline: 3/1. *Unit head:* Dr. Gene Johnson, Chair, 509-963-2381, E-mail: johnsong@cwu.edu. *Application contact:* Justine Eason, Admissions Program Coordinator, 509-963-3103, Fax: 509-963-1799, E-mail: masters@cwu.edu.

Chadron State College, School of Professional and Graduate Studies, Department of Education, Chadron, NE 69337. Offers business (MA Ed); community counseling (MA Ed); educational administration (MS Ed, Sp Ed); elementary education (MS Ed); history (MA Ed); language and literature (MA Ed); secondary administration (MS Ed); secondary education (MS Ed). *Accreditation:* NCATE. Part-time and evening/weekend programs available. Postbaccalaureate distance learning degree programs offered. *Degree requirements:* For master's, thesis optional. *Entrance requirements:* For master's, GRE General Test, GRE Writing Test, minimum GPA of 2.75 or 12 graduate hours at CSC with minimum GPA of 3.25. Additional exam requirements/recommendations for international students: Required—TOEFL. Electronic applications accepted. *Faculty research:* Rural education, technology, mental health.

Chapman University, College of Educational Studies, Orange, CA 92866. Offers communication sciences and disorders (MS); counseling (MA), including school counseling (MA, Credential); education (MA, PhD), including cultural and curricular studies (PhD), disability studies (PhD), school psychology (PhD, Credential); educational psychology (MA); professional clear (Credential); pupil personnel services (Credential), including school counseling (MA, Credential), school psychology (PhD, Credential); school psychology (Ed S); single subject (Credential); special education (MA); special education (level ii) (Credential), including mild/moderate, moderate/severe; special education (preliminary) (Credential), including mild/moderate, moderate/severe; speech language pathology (Credential); teaching (MA), including elementary education, secondary education. *Accreditation:* Teacher Education Accreditation Council. Part-time and evening/weekend programs available. *Faculty:* 27 full-time (18 women), 35 part-time/adjunct (24 women). *Students:* 220 full-time (188 women), 164 part-time (128 women); includes 140 minority (12 Black or African American, non-Hispanic/Latino; 1 American Indian or Alaska Native, non-Hispanic/Latino; 44 Asian, non-Hispanic/Latino; 73 Hispanic/Latino; 4 Native Hawaiian or other Pacific Islander, non-Hispanic/Latino; 6 Two or more races, non-Hispanic/Latino), 1 international. Average age 29. 436 applicants, 38% accepted, 126 enrolled. In 2011, 130 master's, 5 doctorates awarded. *Entrance requirements:* Additional exam requirements/recommendations for international students: Required—TOEFL (minimum score 550 paper-based; 213 computer-based; 80 iBT). *Application deadline:* Applications are processed on a rolling basis. Application fee: $60. Electronic applications accepted. Tuition and fees vary according to degree level and program. *Financial support:* Fellowships and scholarships/grants available. Financial award application deadline: 6/30; financial award applicants required to submit FAFSA. *Unit head:* Dr. Don Cardinal, Dean, 714-997-6781, E-mail: cardinal@chapman.edu. *Application contact:* Admissions Coordinator, 714-997-6714. Web site: http://www.chapman.edu/CES/.

The Chicago School of Professional Psychology, Program in Clinical Psychology, Chicago, IL 60610. Offers applied behavior analysis (MA); clinical psychology (Psy D); counseling (MA). *Accreditation:* APA. *Degree requirements:* For master's, thesis (for some programs); for doctorate, comprehensive exam, thesis/dissertation. *Entrance requirements:* For master's, minimum undergraduate GPA of 3.0, 1 course in psychology, 1 course in either statistics or research methods; for doctorate, GRE, 18 hours of psychology credit (including courses in statistics, normal psychology and human development); minimum GPA of 3.2. Additional exam requirements/recommendations for international students: Required—TOEFL. Electronic applications accepted.

Chicago State University, School of Graduate and Professional Studies, College of Arts and Sciences, Department of Psychology, Chicago, IL 60628. Offers counseling (MA). *Accreditation:* ACA; NCATE. *Degree requirements:* For master's, comprehensive exam, thesis optional. *Entrance requirements:* For master's, minimum GPA of 2.75.

The Citadel, The Military College of South Carolina, Citadel Graduate College, Department of Psychology, Charleston, SC 29409. Offers psychology (MA), including clinical counseling; school psychology (Ed S), including school psychology. Part-time and evening/weekend programs available. *Faculty:* 11 full-time (4 women), 3 part-time/adjunct (2 women). *Students:* 52 full-time (48 women), 67 part-time (58 women); includes 12 minority (6 Black or African American, non-Hispanic/Latino; 3 Asian, non-Hispanic/Latino; 1 Hispanic/Latino; 1 Native Hawaiian or other Pacific Islander, non-Hispanic/Latino; 1 Two or more races, non-Hispanic/Latino), 1 international. Average

age 28. In 2011, 14 master's, 37 other advanced degrees awarded. *Degree requirements:* For master's, comprehensive exam, thesis optional; for Ed S, comprehensive exam, thesis, internship. *Entrance requirements:* For master's, GRE (minimum score 1000) or MAT (minimum score 410), minimum undergraduate GPA of 3.0; 2 letters of reference; for Ed S, GRE (minimum score 1000) or MAT with prior permission (minimum score 410), minimum undergraduate or graduate GPA of 3.0; 2 letters of reference. Additional exam requirements/recommendations for international students: Required—TOEFL (minimum score 550 paper-based; 213 computer-based). *Application deadline:* For fall admission, 3/15 for domestic students. Application fee: $30. Electronic applications accepted. *Expenses: Tuition, area resident:* Part-time $501 per credit hour. Tuition, state resident: part-time $501 per credit hour. Tuition, nonresident: part-time $824 per credit hour. *Required fees:* $40 per term. One-time fee: $30. *Financial support:* Research assistantships, career-related internships or fieldwork, health care benefits, and unspecified assistantships available. Support available to part-time students. Financial award application deadline: 7/1; financial award applicants required to submit FAFSA. *Faculty research:* Ostracism and social exclusion, bullying, social concerns of special-needs children, childhood obesity, phantom limb pain, validation of psychological tests, perfectionism, school-based interventions with at-risk children. *Unit head:* Dr. P. Michael Politano, Department Head, 843-953-5230, Fax: 843-953-6797, E-mail: politanom@citadel.edu. *Application contact:* Dr. William G. Johnson, Program Director, 843-953-6827, Fax: 843-953-6769, E-mail: will.johnson@citadel.edu. Web site: http://www.citadel.edu/root/graduate-program.

The Citadel, The Military College of South Carolina, Citadel Graduate College, School of Education, Program in Guidance and Counseling, Charleston, SC 29409. Offers elementary/secondary school counseling (M Ed); student affairs and college counseling (M Ed). *Accreditation:* ACA; NCATE. Part-time and evening/weekend programs available. *Faculty:* 12 full-time (8 women), 9 part-time/adjunct (4 women). *Students:* 24 full-time (22 women), 36 part-time (31 women); includes 9 minority (8 Black or African American, non-Hispanic/Latino; 1 Hispanic/Latino). Average age 31. In 2011, 22 master's awarded. *Degree requirements:* For master's, comprehensive exam, practicum or internship. *Entrance requirements:* For master's, GRE (minimum score 900) or MAT (minimum score 396), minimum undergraduate GPA of 3.0, 3 letters of reference, group interview. Additional exam requirements/recommendations for international students: Required—TOEFL (minimum score 550 paper-based; 213 computer-based; 79 iBT). *Application deadline:* For fall admission, 6/1 for domestic students; for spring admission, 10/1 for domestic students. Application fee: $30. Electronic applications accepted. *Expenses: Tuition, area resident:* Part-time $501 per credit hour. Tuition, state resident: part-time $501 per credit hour. Tuition, nonresident: part-time $824 per credit hour. *Required fees:* $40 per term. One-time fee: $30. *Financial support:* Career-related internships or fieldwork, health care benefits, and unspecified assistantships available. Support available to part-time students. Financial award application deadline: 7/1; financial award applicants required to submit FAFSA. *Unit head:* Dr. George T. Williams, Director, 843-953-2205, Fax: 843-953-7258, E-mail: williamsg@citadel.edu. *Application contact:* Dr. Steve A. Nida, Associate Provost, The Citadel Graduate College, 843-953-5089, Fax: 843-953-7630, E-mail: cgc@citadel.edu. Web site: http://www.citadel.edu/education/counselor.html.

Clark Atlanta University, School of Education, Department of Counseling and Psychological Studies, Atlanta, GA 30314. Offers MA. Part-time programs available. *Faculty:* 1 (woman) full-time, 5 part-time/adjunct (4 women). *Students:* 19 full-time (15 women), 13 part-time (7 women); includes 30 minority (all Black or African American, non-Hispanic/Latino). Average age 26. 21 applicants, 86% accepted, 8 enrolled. In 2011, 14 master's awarded. *Degree requirements:* For master's, comprehensive exam. *Entrance requirements:* For master's, GRE General Test, minimum undergraduate GPA of 2.6. Additional exam requirements/recommendations for international students: Required—TOEFL (minimum score 500 paper-based; 173 computer-based; 61 iBT). *Application deadline:* For fall admission, 4/1 for domestic and international students; for spring admission, 11/1 for domestic and international students. Applications are processed on a rolling basis. Application fee: $40 ($55 for international students). Electronic applications accepted. *Expenses: Tuition:* Full-time $13,572; part-time $754 per credit hour. *Required fees:* $806; $403 per semester. *Financial support:* Career-related internships or fieldwork, Federal Work-Study, scholarships/grants, and unspecified assistantships available. Support available to part-time students. Financial award application deadline: 4/30; financial award applicants required to submit FAFSA. *Unit head:* Dr. Noran Moffett, Interim Chairperson, 404-880-6330, E-mail: nmoffett@cau.edu. *Application contact:* Michelle Clark-Davis, Graduate Program Admissions, 404-880-6605, E-mail: cauadmissions@cau.edu.

Clemson University, Graduate School, College of Health, Education, and Human Development, Eugene T. Moore School of Education, Program in Counselor Education, Clemson, SC 29634. Offers clinical mental health counseling (M Ed); community mental health (M Ed); school counseling (K-12) (M Ed); student affairs (higher education) (M Ed). *Accreditation:* ACA; NCATE. Part-time and evening/weekend programs available. *Students:* 127 full-time (101 women), 28 part-time (19 women); includes 23 minority (14 Black or African American, non-Hispanic/Latino; 3 Asian, non-Hispanic/Latino; 2 Hispanic/Latino; 1 Native Hawaiian or other Pacific Islander, non-Hispanic/Latino; 3 Two or more races, non-Hispanic/Latino), 1 international. Average age 28. 186 applicants, 58% accepted, 45 enrolled. In 2011, 66 master's awarded. *Degree requirements:* For master's, comprehensive exam. *Entrance requirements:* For master's, GRE General Test. Additional exam requirements/recommendations for international students: Required—TOEFL; Recommended—IELTS. *Application deadline:* For fall admission, 2/1 priority date for domestic students; for spring admission, 10/1 for domestic students. Applications are processed on a rolling basis. Application fee: $70 ($80 for international students). Electronic applications accepted. *Expenses:* Contact institution. *Financial support:* In 2011–12, 74 students received support, including 10 research assistantships with partial tuition reimbursements available (averaging $8,402 per year), 1 teaching assistantship with partial tuition reimbursement available (averaging $12,528 per year); institutionally sponsored loans, health care benefits, and unspecified assistantships also available. Financial award application deadline: 6/1; financial award applicants required to submit FAFSA. *Faculty research:* At-risk youth, ethnic identity development across the life span, postsecondary transitions and college readiness, distance and distributed learning environments, the student veteran experience in college, student development theory. *Unit head:* Dr. Michael J. Padilla, Director/Associate Dean, 864-656-4444, Fax: 864-656-0311, E-mail: padilla@clemson.edu. *Application contact:* Dr. David Fleming, Graduate Coordinator, 864-656-1881, Fax: 864-656-0311, E-mail: dflemin@clemson.edu.

Cleveland State University, College of Graduate Studies, College of Education and Human Services, Department of Counseling, Administration, Supervision and Adult Learning (CASAL), Cleveland, OH 44115. Offers accelerated degree in adult learning and development (M Ed); adult learning and development (M Ed); chemical dependency counseling (Certificate); clinical mental health counseling (M Ed); early childhood mental health counseling (Certificate); educational administration and supervision (M Ed); organizational leadership (M Ed); school administration (Ed S); school counseling (M Ed). *Accreditation:* ACA (one or more programs are accredited). Part-time and evening/weekend programs available. *Faculty:* 15 full-time (8 women), 19 part-time/adjunct (10 women). *Students:* 58 full-time (49 women), 273 part-time (221 women); includes 121 minority (106 Black or African American, non-Hispanic/Latino; 2 Asian, non-Hispanic/Latino; 9 Hispanic/Latino; 4 Two or more races, non-Hispanic/Latino), 1 international. Average age 35. 192 applicants, 86% accepted, 105 enrolled. In 2011, 151 master's, 23 Certificates awarded. *Degree requirements:* For master's, comprehensive exam (for some programs), thesis optional, internship. *Entrance requirements:* For master's, GRE General Test or MAT, letter of recommendation and minimum GPA of 2.75 (for counseling); 2 letters of recommendation and interviews (for organizational leadership). Additional exam requirements/recommendations for international students: Required—TOEFL (minimum score 525 paper-based; 197 computer-based), IELTS (minimum score 6). *Application deadline:* For fall admission, 6/21 for domestic students, 5/15 for international students; for spring admission, 8/31 for domestic students, 11/1 for international students. Application fee: $30. Electronic applications accepted. *Expenses:* Tuition, state resident: full-time $6416; part-time $494 per credit hour. Tuition, nonresident: full-time $12,074; part-time $929 per credit hour. *Financial support:* In 2011–12, 19 students received support, including 10 research assistantships with full and partial tuition reimbursements available (averaging $11,882 per year), 5 teaching assistantships with full and partial tuition reimbursements available (averaging $11,882 per year); scholarships/grants and unspecified assistantships also available. Support available to part-time students. *Faculty research:* Education law, career development, bullying, psychopharmacology, counseling and spirituality. *Total annual research expenditures:* $225,821. *Unit head:* Dr. Ann L. Bauer, Chairperson, 216-687-4582, Fax: 216-687-5378, E-mail: a.l.bauer@csuohio.edu. *Application contact:* Deborah L. Brown, Interim Assistant Director, Graduate Admissions, 216-523-7572, Fax: 216-687-5400, E-mail: d.l.brown@csuohio.edu. Web site: http://www.csuohio.edu/cehs/departments/casal/.

Cleveland State University, College of Graduate Studies, College of Education and Human Services, Program in Urban Education, Cleveland, OH 44115. Offers counseling (PhD); counseling psychology (PhD); leadership and lifelong learning (PhD); learning and development (PhD); policy studies (PhD); school administration (PhD). Part-time programs available. *Faculty:* 16 full-time (8 women), 15 part-time/adjunct (12 women). *Students:* 33 full-time (27 women), 86 part-time (58 women); includes 39 minority (32 Black or African American, non-Hispanic/Latino; 4 Asian, non-Hispanic/Latino; 3 Hispanic/Latino), 8 international. Average age 40. 54 applicants, 44% accepted, 16 enrolled. In 2011, 17 doctorates awarded. *Degree requirements:* For doctorate, one foreign language, comprehensive exam, thesis/dissertation. *Entrance requirements:* For doctorate, GRE General Test, minimum graduate GPA of 3.25. Additional exam requirements/recommendations for international students: Required—TOEFL (minimum score 525 paper-based; 197 computer-based), IELTS (minimum score 6). *Application deadline:* For fall admission, 2/5 for domestic students. Application fee: $30. *Expenses:* Tuition, state resident: full-time $6416; part-time $494 per credit hour. Tuition, nonresident: full-time $12,074; part-time $929 per credit hour. *Financial support:* In 2011–12, 7 students received support, including 4 research assistantships with full and partial tuition reimbursements available (averaging $7,800 per year), 3 teaching assistantships with full and partial tuition reimbursements available (averaging $7,800 per year); tuition waivers (full) and unspecified assistantships also available. Financial award applicants required to submit FAFSA. *Faculty research:* Equity issues (race, ethnicity, and gender), education development consequences for special needs of urban populations, urban education programming, counseling the violent or aggressive adolescent. *Total annual research expenditures:* $5,662. *Unit head:* Dr. Joshua Bagakas, Director, 216-687-4591, Fax: 216-875-9697, E-mail: j.bagakas@csuohio.edu. *Application contact:* Wanda Butler, Administrative Assistant, 216-687-4697, Fax: 216-875-9697, E-mail: w.pruett-butler@csuohio.edu. Web site: http://www.csuohio.edu/coehs/departments/phd/.

The College at Brockport, State University of New York, School of Education and Human Services, Department of Counselor Education, Brockport, NY 14420-2997. Offers college counseling (MS Ed); college counseling, bridge (CAS); mental health counseling (MS); mental health counseling, bridge (CAS); school counseling (MS Ed, CAS); school counseling, bridge (CAS); school counselor supervision (CAS). *Accreditation:* ACA (one or more programs are accredited). Part-time programs available. *Students:* 34 full-time (27 women), 49 part-time (32 women); includes 16 minority (12 Black or African American, non-Hispanic/Latino; 2 Asian, non-Hispanic/Latino; 2 Hispanic/Latino). 98 applicants, 33% accepted, 19 enrolled. In 2011, 16 master's, 2 other advanced degrees awarded. *Degree requirements:* For master's, thesis, internship. *Entrance requirements:* For master's, group interview, letters of recommendation, written objectives; for CAS, master's degree, New York state school counselor certificate. Additional exam requirements/recommendations for international students: Required—TOEFL (minimum score 550 paper-based; 213 computer-based; 79 iBT). *Application deadline:* For fall admission, 2/1 priority date for domestic students, 2/1 for international students; for spring admission, 9/1 priority date for domestic students, 9/1 for international students. Application fee: $80. Electronic applications accepted. *Financial support:* In 2011–12, 1 teaching assistantship with full tuition reimbursement (averaging $6,000 per year) was awarded; Federal Work-Study, scholarships/grants, and unspecified assistantships also available. Support available to part-time students. Financial award application deadline: 3/15; financial award applicants required to submit FAFSA. *Faculty research:* Gender and diversity issues; counseling outcomes; spirituality; school, college and mental health counseling; obesity. *Unit head:* Dr. Thomas J. Hernandez, Chair, 585-395-2258, Fax: 585-395-2366, E-mail: thernandez@brockport.edu. *Application contact:* Dr. Thomas J. Hernandez, Chairperson, 585-395-2258, Fax: 585-395-2366, E-mail: thernandez@brockport.edu. Web site: http://www.brockport.edu/graduate/.

The College of New Jersey, Graduate Studies, School of Education, Department of Counselor Education, Program in Community Counseling: Human Services Specialization, Ewing, NJ 08628. Offers MA. *Accreditation:* ACA. Part-time programs available. *Degree requirements:* For master's, comprehensive exam. *Entrance requirements:* For master's, GRE General Test, minimum GPA of 3.0 in field or 2.75 overall, interview. Additional exam requirements/recommendations for international students: Required—TOEFL. Electronic applications accepted.

The College of New Jersey, Graduate Studies, School of Education, Department of Counselor Education, Program in School Counseling, Ewing, NJ 08628. Offers MA. *Accreditation:* ACA; NCATE. Part-time programs available. *Degree requirements:* For master's, comprehensive exam. *Entrance requirements:* For master's, GRE General Test, minimum GPA of 3.0 in field or 2.75 overall, interview. Additional exam requirements/recommendations for international students: Required—TOEFL. Electronic applications accepted.

College of St. Joseph, Graduate Programs, Division of Psychology and Human Services, Rutland, VT 05701-3899. Offers alcohol and substance abuse counseling (MS); clinical mental health counseling (MS); clinical psychology (MS); community counseling (MS); school guidance counseling (MS). Part-time and evening/weekend programs available. *Faculty:* 3 full-time (0 women), 8 part-time/adjunct (2 women). *Students:* 24 full-time (17 women), 40 part-time (35 women); includes 1 minority (Asian, non-Hispanic/Latino). Average age 36. 24 applicants. In 2011, 15 master's awarded. *Degree requirements:* For master's, comprehensive exam, thesis optional. *Entrance requirements:* For master's, official college transcripts; 2 letters of reference. Additional

Counselor Education

exam requirements/recommendations for international students: Required—TOEFL (minimum score 550 paper-based). *Application deadline:* Applications are processed on a rolling basis. Application fee: $35. Electronic applications accepted. *Expenses: Tuition:* Full-time $15,200; part-time $400 per credit. *Required fees:* $45 per semester. *Financial support:* In 2011–12, 3 students received support, including teaching assistantships with tuition reimbursements available (averaging $3,000 per year); career-related internships or fieldwork, Federal Work-Study, and unspecified assistantships also available. Support available to part-time students. Financial award application deadline: 3/1. *Unit head:* Dr. Craig Knapp, Chair, 802-773-5900 Ext. 3219, Fax: 802-776-5258, E-mail: cknapp@csj.edu. *Application contact:* Alan Young, Dean of Admissions, 802-773-5900 Ext. 3227, Fax: 802-776-5310, E-mail: alanyoung@csj.edu.

The College of Saint Rose, Graduate Studies, School of Education, Department of Counseling and Educational Administration, Program in Counseling, Albany, NY 12203-1419. Offers college student personnel (MS Ed); community counseling (MS Ed); school counseling (MS Ed). *Accreditation:* NCATE. Part-time and evening/weekend programs available. *Degree requirements:* For master's, comprehensive exam or thesis. *Entrance requirements:* For master's, interview, minimum undergraduate GPA of 3.0, 9 hours of psychology coursework. Additional exam requirements/recommendations for international students: Required—TOEFL (minimum score 550 paper-based; 213 computer-based). Electronic applications accepted.

The College of William and Mary, School of Education, Program in Counselor Education, Williamsburg, VA 23187-8795. Offers community and addictions counseling (M Ed); community counseling (M Ed); counselor education (PhD); family counseling (M Ed); school counseling (M Ed). *Accreditation:* ACA; NCATE. Part-time and evening/weekend programs available. *Faculty:* 6 full-time (3 women), 7 part-time/adjunct (5 women). *Students:* 71 full-time (60 women), 6 part-time (3 women); includes 15 minority (4 Black or African American, non-Hispanic/Latino; 1 American Indian or Alaska Native, non-Hispanic/Latino; 1 Asian, non-Hispanic/Latino; 3 Hispanic/Latino; 6 Two or more races, non-Hispanic/Latino), 1 international. Average age 29. 172 applicants, 47% accepted, 36 enrolled. In 2011, 28 master's, 5 doctorates awarded. *Degree requirements:* For doctorate, comprehensive exam, thesis/dissertation. *Entrance requirements:* For master's, GRE, minimum GPA of 3.0; for doctorate, GRE, minimum GPA of 3.5. Additional exam requirements/recommendations for international students: Required—TOEFL. *Application deadline:* For fall admission, 1/15 for domestic and international students. Application fee: $50. Electronic applications accepted. *Expenses:* Tuition, state resident: full-time $6400; part-time $365 per credit hour. Tuition, nonresident: full-time $19,720; part-time $985 per credit hour. *Required fees:* $4562. *Financial support:* In 2011–12, 45 students received support, including 43 research assistantships with full tuition reimbursements available (averaging $13,000 per year); career-related internships or fieldwork, Federal Work-Study, institutionally sponsored loans, scholarships/grants, and unspecified assistantships also available. Financial award application deadline: 1/15; financial award applicants required to submit FAFSA. *Faculty research:* Sexuality, multicultural education, substance abuse, transpersonal psychology. *Unit head:* Dr. Victoria Foster, Area Coordinator, 757-221-2321, E-mail: vafost@wm.edu. *Application contact:* Dorothy Smith Osborne, Assistant Dean for Admission, 757-221-2317, Fax: 757-221-2293, E-mail: dsosbo@wm.edu. Web site: http://education.wm.edu.

Colorado State University, Graduate School, College of Applied Human Sciences, School of Education, Fort Collins, CO 80523-1588. Offers adult education and training (M Ed); community college leadership (PhD); counseling and career development (M Ed); education and human resource studies (M Ed, PhD); educational leadership (M Ed, PhD); interdisciplinary studies (PhD); organizational performance and change (M Ed, PhD); student affairs in higher education (MS). *Accreditation:* ACA; Teacher Education Accreditation Council. Part-time and evening/weekend programs available. *Faculty:* 18 full-time (11 women), 1 part-time/adjunct (0 women). *Students:* 161 full-time (106 women), 491 part-time (291 women); includes 130 minority (28 Black or African American, non-Hispanic/Latino; 5 American Indian or Alaska Native, non-Hispanic/Latino; 12 Asian, non-Hispanic/Latino; 68 Hispanic/Latino; 3 Native Hawaiian or other Pacific Islander, non-Hispanic/Latino; 14 Two or more races, non-Hispanic/Latino), 29 international. Average age 38. 468 applicants, 31% accepted, 112 enrolled. In 2011, 192 master's, 30 doctorates awarded. *Degree requirements:* For master's, comprehensive exam (for some programs), thesis optional; for doctorate, comprehensive exam, thesis/dissertation, minimum of 60 credits. *Entrance requirements:* For master's, GRE, minimum undergraduate GPA of 3.0, 3 letters of recommendation, curriculum vitae/resume; for doctorate, minimum GPA of 3.0, 3 letters of recommendation, curriculum vitae. Additional exam requirements/recommendations for international students: Required—TOEFL (minimum score 550 paper-based; 213 computer-based; 80 iBT). *Application deadline:* For fall admission, 2/15 priority date for domestic students, 2/15 for international students; for spring admission, 9/1 priority date for domestic students, 9/1 for international students. Applications are processed on a rolling basis. Application fee: $50. Electronic applications accepted. *Expenses:* Tuition, state resident: full-time $7992. Tuition, nonresident: full-time $19,592. *Required fees:* $1735; $58 per credit. *Financial support:* In 2011–12, 11 students received support, including 1 fellowship (averaging $37,500 per year), 3 research assistantships with full tuition reimbursements available (averaging $8,911 per year), 7 teaching assistantships with full tuition reimbursements available (averaging $12,691 per year); Federal Work-Study, scholarships/grants, and unspecified assistantships also available. Financial award application deadline: 2/15; financial award applicants required to submit FAFSA. *Faculty research:* Innovative instruction, diverse learners, transition, scientifically-based evaluation methods, leadership and organizational development, research methodology. *Total annual research expenditures:* $455,133. *Unit head:* Dr. Kevin Oltjenbruns, Interim Director, 970-491-6316, Fax: 970-491-1317, E-mail: kevin.oltjenbruns@colostate.edu. *Application contact:* Kathy Lucas, Graduate Contact, 970-491-1963, Fax: 970-491-1317, E-mail: kplucas@cahs.colostate.edu. Web site: http://www.soe.cahs.colostate.edu/.

Columbia International University, Columbia Graduate School, Columbia, SC 29230-3122. Offers Bible teaching (MABT); Christian higher education leadership (Ed D); Christian school educational leadership (Ed D); counseling (MACN); curriculum and instruction (M Ed), including Christian school guidance, English as a second language, learning disabilities, school technology; early childhood and elementary education (MAT); educational administration (M Ed); teaching English as a foreign language (Certificate); teaching English as a foreign language and intercultural studies (MATF). Part-time and evening/weekend programs available. *Degree requirements:* For master's, internships, professional project. *Entrance requirements:* For master's, Minnesota Multiphasic Personality Inventory, MAT, minimum GPA of 2.7. Additional exam requirements/recommendations for international students: Required—TOEFL. Electronic applications accepted.

Columbus State University, Graduate Studies, College of Education and Health Professions, Department of Counseling, Foundations, and Leadership, Columbus, GA 31907-5645. Offers community counseling (MS); curriculum and leadership (Ed D); educational leadership (M Ed, Ed S); higher education (M Ed); school counseling (M Ed, Ed S). *Accreditation:* ACA; NCATE. Part-time and evening/weekend programs available. Postbaccalaureate distance learning degree programs offered (minimal on-campus study). *Degree requirements:* For master's, thesis, exit exam; for Ed S, thesis or alternative. *Entrance requirements:* For master's, GRE General Test, minimum GPA of 2.75; for doctorate, minimum graduate GPA of 3.5, four years of professional service; for Ed S, GRE General Test. Additional exam requirements/recommendations for international students: Required—TOEFL (minimum score 550 paper-based; 213 computer-based; 79 iBT). Electronic applications accepted.

Concordia University, School of Education, Irvine, CA 92612-3299. Offers curriculum and instruction (MA); education and preliminary teaching credential (M Ed); educational administration and preliminary administrative services credential (MA); school counseling with pupil personnel services credential (MA). Part-time and evening/weekend programs available. Postbaccalaureate distance learning degree programs offered (no on-campus study). *Faculty:* 16 full-time (11 women), 68 part-time/adjunct (32 women). *Students:* 556 full-time (434 women), 277 part-time (211 women); includes 278 minority (42 Black or African American, non-Hispanic/Latino; 1 American Indian or Alaska Native, non-Hispanic/Latino; 51 Asian, non-Hispanic/Latino; 172 Hispanic/Latino; 12 Two or more races, non-Hispanic/Latino), 1 international. Average age 39. 296 applicants, 96% accepted, 256 enrolled. In 2011, 378 master's awarded. *Degree requirements:* For master's, action research project. *Entrance requirements:* For master's, California Basic Educational Skills Test, California Subject Examinations for Teachers (M Ed and MA in educational administration and preliminary administrative services credential), official college transcript(s), signed statement of intent, two references, copy of credential. Additional exam requirements/recommendations for international students: Required—TOEFL. *Application deadline:* For fall admission, 7/15 priority date for domestic students, 6/1 for international students; for spring admission, 11/30 priority date for domestic students, 10/1 for international students. Applications are processed on a rolling basis. Application fee: $50 ($125 for international students). Electronic applications accepted. *Expenses:* Contact institution. *Financial support:* In 2011–12, 17 students received support. Scholarships/grants and unspecified assistantships available. Financial award applicants required to submit FAFSA. *Unit head:* Dr. Janice Nelson, Dean, 949-214-3334, E-mail: janice.nelson@cui.edu. *Application contact:* Scott Eskelson, 949-214-3362, Fax: 949-854-6894, E-mail: scott.eskelson@cui.edu.

Concordia University Chicago, College of Graduate and Innovative Programs, Program in School Counseling, River Forest, IL 60305-1499. Offers MA, CAS. *Accreditation:* ACA (one or more programs are accredited); NCATE. Part-time and evening/weekend programs available. *Degree requirements:* For master's, comprehensive exam, thesis optional; for CAS, thesis, final project. *Entrance requirements:* For master's, minimum GPA of 2.9; for CAS, master's degree. Additional exam requirements/recommendations for international students: Required—TOEFL (minimum score 550 paper-based; 195 computer-based). Electronic applications accepted. *Faculty research:* Development of comprehensive school counseling education, training of school counselors for parochial schools.

Concordia University Wisconsin, Graduate Programs, Department of Education, Mequon, WI 53097-2402. Offers art education (MS Ed); curriculum and instruction (MS Ed); early childhood (MS Ed); educational administration (MS Ed); environmental education (MS Ed); family studies (MS Ed); reading (MS Ed); school counseling (MS Ed); special education (MS Ed). Part-time and evening/weekend programs available. Postbaccalaureate distance learning degree programs offered (minimal on-campus study). *Faculty:* 30. *Students:* 386 full-time (279 women), 808 part-time (598 women); includes 84 minority (42 Black or African American, non-Hispanic/Latino; 4 American Indian or Alaska Native, non-Hispanic/Latino; 9 Asian, non-Hispanic/Latino; 13 Hispanic/Latino; 16 Two or more races, non-Hispanic/Latino), 5 international. Average age 37. In 2011, 51 master's awarded. *Degree requirements:* For master's, comprehensive exam, thesis or alternative. *Entrance requirements:* For master's, minimum GPA of 3.0, teaching license. Additional exam requirements/recommendations for international students: Required—TOEFL. Application fee: $35. *Financial support:* Career-related internships or fieldwork and tuition waivers (partial) available. Financial award application deadline: 8/1. *Faculty research:* Motivation, developmental learning, learning styles. *Unit head:* Dr. James Juergensen, Director, 262-243-4214, E-mail: james.juergensen@cuw.edu. *Application contact:* Graduate Admissions, 262-243-4248, Fax: 262-243-4428.

Creighton University, Graduate School, College of Arts and Sciences, Department of Education, Program in Counselor Education, Omaha, NE 68178-0001. Offers college student affairs (MS); community counseling (MS); elementary school guidance (MS); secondary school guidance (MS). Part-time and evening/weekend programs available. *Faculty:* 13 full-time (8 women). *Students:* 2 full-time (1 woman), 28 part-time (22 women); includes 3 minority (1 Black or African American, non-Hispanic/Latino; 1 American Indian or Alaska Native, non-Hispanic/Latino; 1 Hispanic/Latino), 2 international. Average age 33. 12 applicants, 75% accepted, 9 enrolled. In 2011, 8 master's awarded. *Degree requirements:* For master's, comprehensive exam. *Entrance requirements:* For master's, GRE General Test, resume, 3 letters of recommendation, personal statement. Additional exam requirements/recommendations for international students: Required—TOEFL (minimum score 550 paper-based; 213 computer-based; 80 iBT). *Application deadline:* For fall admission, 7/1 for domestic students, 3/1 for international students; for winter admission, 10/1 for domestic students, 7/1 for international students; for spring admission, 3/1 for domestic students, 9/1 for international students. Applications are processed on a rolling basis. Application fee: $50. Electronic applications accepted. *Expenses: Tuition:* Full-time $12,672; part-time $704 per credit hour. *Required fees:* $1410; $136 per semester. Tuition and fees vary according to campus/location and reciprocity agreements. *Financial support:* Scholarships/grants available. Support available to part-time students. Financial award applicants required to submit FAFSA. *Unit head:* Dr. Jeffrey Smith, Associate Professor of Education, 402-280-2413, E-mail: jefsmith@creighton.edu. *Application contact:* Taunya Plater, Senior Program Coordinator, 402-280-2870, Fax: 402-280-2423, E-mail: taunyaplater@creighton.edu.

Dallas Baptist University, Dorothy M. Bush College of Education, Program in School Counseling, Dallas, TX 75211-9299. Offers M Ed, Advanced Certificate. Part-time and evening/weekend programs available. *Entrance requirements:* For master's, GRE General Test, minimum GPA of 3.0. Additional exam requirements/recommendations for international students: Required—TOEFL, IELTS. *Application deadline:* Applications are processed on a rolling basis. Application fee: $25. Electronic applications accepted. *Expenses: Tuition:* Full-time $12,060; part-time $670 per credit hour. *Required fees:* $100; $50 per semester. *Financial support:* Federal Work-Study, institutionally sponsored loans, scholarships/grants, and tuition waivers (full and partial) available. Support available to part-time students. Financial award applicants required to submit FAFSA. *Unit head:* Dr. Bonnie B. Bond, Director, 214-333-5413, Fax: 214-333-5551, E-mail: graduate@dbu.edu. *Application contact:* Kit P. Montgomery, Director of Graduate Programs, 214-333-5242, Fax: 214-333-5579, E-mail: graduate@dbu.edu. Web site: http://www3.dbu.edu/graduate/education_counseling.asp.

Delta State University, Graduate Programs, College of Education, Division of Counselor Education and Psychology, Cleveland, MS 38733-0001. Offers counseling (M Ed). *Accreditation:* ACA; NCATE. Part-time and evening/weekend programs available. *Degree requirements:* For master's, thesis optional, practicum. Electronic applications accepted. *Expenses:* Tuition, state resident: full-time $4702; part-time $294 per credit hour. Tuition, nonresident: full-time $12,516; part-time $760 per credit hour. *Required fees:* $586.

Delta State University, Graduate Programs, College of Education, Thad Cochran Center for Rural School Leadership and Research, Program in Professional Studies, Cleveland, MS 38733-0001. Offers counselor education (Ed D); educational leadership (Ed D); elementary education (Ed D); higher education (Ed D). Part-time and evening/weekend programs available. *Degree requirements:* For doctorate, thesis/dissertation. *Entrance requirements:* For doctorate, GRE General Test. *Expenses:* Tuition, state resident: full-time $4702; part-time $294 per credit hour. Tuition, nonresident: full-time $12,516; part-time $760 per credit hour. *Required fees:* $586.

DePaul University, College of Education, Chicago, IL 60106. Offers bilingual bicultural education (M Ed, MA); counseling (M Ed, MA), including college student development, community counseling, school counseling; curriculum studies (M Ed, MA, Ed D); early childhood education (M Ed, MA); educational leadership (M Ed, MA, Ed D), including administration and supervision (M Ed, MA), physical education (M Ed, MA); middle school mathematics education (MS); reading specialist (M Ed, MA); social and cultural foundations in education (M Ed, MA), including curriculum studies/development (MA); special education (M Ed, MA); teaching and learning (M Ed, MA), including elementary education, secondary education; world languages education (M Ed, MA). Part-time and evening/weekend programs available. *Faculty:* 49 full-time (28 women), 94 part-time/adjunct (60 women). *Students:* 894 full-time (707 women), 473 part-time (361 women); includes 349 minority (159 Black or African American, non-Hispanic/Latino; 3 American Indian or Alaska Native, non-Hispanic/Latino; 45 Asian, non-Hispanic/Latino; 115 Hispanic/Latino; 2 Native Hawaiian or other Pacific Islander, non-Hispanic/Latino; 25 Two or more races, non-Hispanic/Latino), 21 international. Average age 30. 872 applicants, 64% accepted, 325 enrolled. In 2011, 499 master's, 10 doctorates awarded. *Median time to degree:* Of those who began their doctoral program in fall 2003, 32% received their degree in 8 years or less. *Degree requirements:* For master's, thesis/dissertation (for MA); capstone course or paper (for M Ed); for doctorate, thesis/dissertation. *Entrance requirements:* For master's, interview, minimum GPA of 2.75, 2 letters of recommendation, bachelor's degree conferred by accredited college or university; for doctorate, interview, master's degree, writing sample, 3 letters of recommendation. Additional exam requirements/recommendations for international students: Required—TOEFL (minimum score 550 paper-based; 213 computer-based; 80 iBT). *Application deadline:* For fall admission, 8/15 priority date for domestic students; for winter admission, 12/1 priority date for domestic students; for spring admission, 3/1 priority date for domestic students. Applications are processed on a rolling basis. Application fee: $40. Electronic applications accepted. *Financial support:* In 2011–12, 163 students received support, including 15 research assistantships with full tuition reimbursements available (averaging $6,375 per year); career-related internships or fieldwork, Federal Work-Study, scholarships/grants, and unspecified assistantships also available. Support available to part-time students. Financial award application deadline: 12/31; financial award applicants required to submit FAFSA. *Faculty research:* Reflective teaching, children at risk, loss, ethnicity, urban education. *Total annual research expenditures:* $916,310. *Unit head:* Dr. Paul Zionts, Dean, 773-325-7581, Fax: 773-325-7713, E-mail: pzionts@depaul.edu. *Application contact:* Brandon Washington, Enrollment Management Coordinator, 773-325-1152, Fax: 773-325-2270, E-mail: bwashin3@depaul.edu. Web site: http://education.depaul.edu.

Doane College, Program in Counseling, Crete, NE 68333-2430. Offers MAC. Evening/weekend programs available. *Faculty:* 1 full-time (0 women), 11 part-time/adjunct (6 women). *Students:* 129 full-time (102 women), 36 part-time (31 women); includes 16 minority (4 Black or African American, non-Hispanic/Latino; 1 American Indian or Alaska Native, non-Hispanic/Latino; 1 Asian, non-Hispanic/Latino; 9 Hispanic/Latino; 1 Two or more races, non-Hispanic/Latino). Average age 34. In 2011, 45 master's awarded. *Degree requirements:* For master's, thesis. *Entrance requirements:* For master's, minimum GPA of 3.0. Additional exam requirements/recommendations for international students: Required—TOEFL. *Application deadline:* Applications are processed on a rolling basis. Application fee: $25. *Expenses:* Contact institution. *Financial support:* Unspecified assistantships available. Financial award application deadline: 6/1; financial award applicants required to submit FAFSA. *Unit head:* Thomas Gilligan, Dean, 402-466-4774, Fax: 402-466-4228, E-mail: tom.gilligan@doane.edu. *Application contact:* Wilma Daddario, Assistant Dean, 402-466-4774, Fax: 404-466-4228, E-mail: wilma.daddario@doane.edu. Web site: http://www.doane.edu/Admission/Graduate_Admission/MAC/.

Duquesne University, School of Education, Department of Counseling, Psychology, and Special Education, Program in Counselor Education, Pittsburgh, PA 15282-0001. Offers community agency counseling (Post-Master's Certificate); community mental health counseling (MS Ed); counselor education and supervision (Ed D); counselor licensure (Post-Master's Certificate); marriage and family therapy (MS Ed); school counseling (MS Ed). *Accreditation:* ACA (one or more programs are accredited). Part-time and evening/weekend programs available. *Faculty:* 7 full-time (2 women), 4 part-time/adjunct (3 women). *Students:* 182 full-time (139 women), 17 part-time (16 women); includes 38 minority (29 Black or African American, non-Hispanic/Latino; 4 Asian, non-Hispanic/Latino; 3 Hispanic/Latino; 2 Two or more races, non-Hispanic/Latino), 3 international. Average age 31. 175 applicants, 38% accepted, 33 enrolled. In 2011, 30 master's, 5 doctorates awarded. *Degree requirements:* For master's, thesis optional; for doctorate, thesis/dissertation. *Entrance requirements:* For master's, letters of recommendation, essay, interview, bachelor's degree; for doctorate, GRE, letters of recommendation, essay, interview, master's degree; for Post-Master's Certificate, GRE, letters of recommendation, essay, interview, bachelor's/master's degree. Additional exam requirements/recommendations for international students: Required—TOEFL (minimum score 550 paper-based; 80 computer-based), IELTS (minimum score 7). *Application deadline:* For fall admission, 3/1 for domestic students; for spring admission, 9/1 for domestic students. Applications are processed on a rolling basis. Application fee: $0. Electronic applications accepted. Application fee is waived when completed online. *Expenses: Tuition:* Full-time $16,596; part-time $922 per credit. *Required fees:* $1584; $88 per credit. Tuition and fees vary according to program. *Financial support:* Research assistantships, teaching assistantships, and Federal Work-Study available. Support available to part-time students. *Unit head:* Dr. Maura Krushinski, Director, 412-396-4026, Fax: 412-396-1340, E-mail: krushinski@duq.edu. *Application contact:* Michael Dolinger, Director of Student and Academic Services, 412-396-6647, Fax: 412-396-5585, E-mail: dolingerm@duq.edu. Web site: http://www.duq.edu/education.

East Carolina University, Graduate School, College of Education, Department of Higher, Adult, and Counselor Education, Greenville, NC 27858-4353. Offers adult education (MA Ed); counselor education (MS); higher education administration (Ed D). *Accreditation:* NCATE. Part-time and evening/weekend programs available. *Degree requirements:* For master's, comprehensive exam, thesis optional. *Entrance requirements:* For master's, GRE General Test or MAT, interview, minimum GPA of 2.5, bachelor's degree in related field, teaching license (MA Ed). Additional exam requirements/recommendations for international students: Required—TOEFL. *Application deadline:* For fall admission, 5/15 priority date for domestic students. Applications are processed on a rolling basis. Application fee: $50. *Expenses:* Tuition, state resident: full-time $3557; part-time $444.63 per semester hour. Tuition, nonresident: full-time $14,351; part-time $1793.88 per semester hour. *Required fees:* $2016; $252 per semester hour. Part-time tuition and fees vary according to course load, campus/location and program. *Financial support:* Research assistantships with partial tuition reimbursements, teaching assistantships with partial tuition reimbursements, and Federal Work-Study available. Support available to part-time students. Financial award application deadline: 6/1. *Unit head:* Dr. Vivian W. Mott, Chair, 252-328-6177, Fax: 252-328-4368, E-mail: mottv@ecu.edu. *Application contact:* Dean of Graduate School, 252-328-6012, Fax: 252-328-6071, E-mail: gradschool@ecu.edu. Web site: http://www.ecu.edu/cs-educ/hace/index.cfm.

East Central University, School of Graduate Studies, Department of Human Resources, Ada, OK 74820-6899. Offers administration (MSHR); counseling (MSHR); criminal justice (MSHR); rehabilitation counseling (MSHR). *Accreditation:* CORE. Part-time and evening/weekend programs available. *Degree requirements:* For master's, thesis optional. *Entrance requirements:* For master's, GRE General Test, MAT, minimum GPA of 2.5. Electronic applications accepted.

Eastern Illinois University, Graduate School, College of Education and Professional Studies, Department of Counseling and Student Development, Charleston, IL 61920-3099. Offers clinical counseling (MS); college student affairs (MS); school counseling (MS). *Accreditation:* ACA; NCATE. Part-time and evening/weekend programs available. *Degree requirements:* For master's, comprehensive exam. *Entrance requirements:* For master's, GRE General Test or MAT. *Expenses:* Tuition, state resident: part-time $279 per credit hour. Tuition, nonresident: part-time $670 per credit hour. *Required fees:* $179.07 per credit hour. $1253 per semester.

Eastern Kentucky University, The Graduate School, College of Education, Department of Counseling and Educational Leadership, Richmond, KY 40475-3102. Offers human services (MA); instructional leadership (MA Ed); mental health counseling (MA); school counseling (MA Ed). *Accreditation:* ACA (one or more programs are accredited); NCATE. Part-time programs available. Postbaccalaureate distance learning degree programs offered. *Entrance requirements:* For master's, GRE General Test, minimum GPA of 2.5.

Eastern Michigan University, Graduate School, College of Education, Department of Leadership and Counseling, Programs in Counseling, Ypsilanti, MI 48197. Offers college counseling (MA); community counseling (MA); helping interventions in a multicultural society (Graduate Certificate); school counseling (MA); school counselor (MA); school counselor licensure (Post Master's Certificate). Part-time and evening/weekend programs available. *Students:* 25 full-time (23 women), 95 part-time (79 women); includes 28 minority (23 Black or African American, non-Hispanic/Latino; 1 American Indian or Alaska Native, non-Hispanic/Latino; 1 Asian, non-Hispanic/Latino; 1 Hispanic/Latino; 2 Two or more races, non-Hispanic/Latino), 6 international. Average age 31. 85 applicants, 41% accepted, 23 enrolled. In 2011, 33 master's, 2 other advanced degrees awarded. *Degree requirements:* For master's, comprehensive exam, internship. *Entrance requirements:* Additional exam requirements/recommendations for international students: Required—TOEFL. *Application deadline:* For fall admission, 5/1 for domestic and international students; for winter admission, 9/15 for domestic and international students; for spring admission, 2/10 for domestic and international students. Applications are processed on a rolling basis. Application fee: $35. *Expenses:* Tuition, state resident: full-time $10,367; part-time $432 per credit hour. Tuition, nonresident: full-time $20,435; part-time $851 per credit hour. *Required fees:* $39 per credit hour. $46 per semester. One-time fee: $100. Tuition and fees vary according to course level, degree level and reciprocity agreements. *Financial support:* Fellowships, research assistantships with full tuition reimbursements, teaching assistantships with full tuition reimbursements, career-related internships or fieldwork, Federal Work-Study, institutionally sponsored loans, scholarships/grants, tuition waivers (partial), and unspecified assistantships available. Support available to part-time students. Financial award applicants required to submit FAFSA. *Unit head:* Dr. Jaclynn Tracy, Department Head, 734-487-0255, Fax: 734-487-4608, E-mail: jtracy@emich.edu. *Application contact:* Dr. Dibya Choudhuri, Coordinator of Advising, 734-487-0255, Fax: 734-487-4608, E-mail: dchoudhur@emich.edu.

Eastern New Mexico University, Graduate School, College of Education and Technology, Department of Educational Studies, Program in Counseling, Portales, NM 88130. Offers MA. Part-time programs available. *Degree requirements:* For master's, comprehensive exam, thesis optional, counselor preparation comprehensive examination, 48-hour course work including a 600-hour internship in field placement. *Entrance requirements:* For master's, minimum GPA of 3.0, 3 letters of recommendation, interview. Additional exam requirements/recommendations for international students: Required—TOEFL (minimum score 550 paper-based; 213 computer-based; 79 iBT), IELTS (minimum score 6). Electronic applications accepted.

Eastern New Mexico University, Graduate School, College of Education and Technology, Department of Educational Studies, Program in School Counseling, Portales, NM 88130. Offers M Ed. Part-time programs available. *Degree requirements:* For master's, comprehensive exam, thesis optional, 48-hour curriculum, 600-hour internship in field placement. *Entrance requirements:* For master's, minimum GPA of 3.0, three letters of recommendation, interview. Additional exam requirements/recommendations for international students: Required—TOEFL (minimum score 550 paper-based; 213 computer-based; 79 iBT), IELTS (minimum score 6). Electronic applications accepted.

Eastern University, Department of Counseling Psychology, Program in School Counseling, St. Davids, PA 19087-3696. Offers MA, Certificate. *Degree requirements:* For master's, internship. *Entrance requirements:* For master's, minimum GPA of 2.5. Additional exam requirements/recommendations for international students: Required—TOEFL.

Eastern Washington University, Graduate Studies, College of Social and Behavioral Sciences and Social Work, Program in School Counseling, Cheney, WA 99004-2431. Offers applied psychology (MS); school counseling (MS). *Accreditation:* ACA. *Students:* 13 full-time (9 women), 1 international. Average age 28. 72 applicants, 39% accepted, 13 enrolled. In 2011, 19 master's awarded. *Degree requirements:* For master's, comprehensive exam, thesis or alternative. *Entrance requirements:* For master's, GRE General Test, minimum GPA of 3.0. *Application deadline:* For fall admission, 2/1 for domestic students. Applications are processed on a rolling basis. Application fee: $50. *Financial support:* In 2011–12, teaching assistantships with partial tuition reimbursements (averaging $7,000 per year) were awarded; career-related internships or fieldwork, Federal Work-Study, institutionally sponsored loans, scholarships/grants, health care benefits, tuition waivers (partial), and unspecified assistantships also available. Support available to part-time students. Financial award application deadline: 2/1; financial award applicants required to submit FAFSA. *Unit head:* Dr. Marty Slyter, Director, 509-359-6499, E-mail: mslyter@ewu.edu. *Application contact:* Julie Marr, Advisor/Recruiter for Graduate Studies, 509-359-6656, E-mail: gradprograms@ewu.edu. Web site: http://www.ewu.edu/grad/programs/applied-psychology—school-counseling.xml.

East Tennessee State University, School of Graduate Studies, College of Education, Department of Human Development and Learning, Johnson City, TN 37614. Offers counseling (MA), including community agency counseling, elementary and secondary (school counseling), higher education counseling, marriage and family therapy; early childhood education (MA, PhD), including initial licensure in PreK-3 (MA), master teacher (MA), researcher (MA); special education (MA), including advanced practitioner, early childhood special education, special education. *Accreditation:* ACA; NCATE. Part-time programs available. *Faculty:* 31 full-time (22 women), 5 part-time/adjunct (all women). *Students:* 112 full-time (90 women), 41 part-time (36 women); includes 8 minority (5 Black or African American, non-Hispanic/Latino; 3 Two or more races, non-Hispanic/Latino), 4 international. Average age 32. 145 applicants, 34% accepted, 46 enrolled. In 2011, 34 master's awarded. Terminal master's awarded for partial completion of doctoral program. *Degree requirements:* For master's, comprehensive exam, thesis optional, internship, student teaching, culminating experience; for doctorate, comprehensive exam, thesis/dissertation, research apprenticeship. *Entrance requirements:* For master's, GRE General Test, minimum GPA of 3.0; for doctorate, GRE General Test, professional resume, master's degree in early childhood or related field, interview. Additional exam requirements/recommendations for international students: Required—TOEFL (minimum score 550 paper-based; 213 computer-based; 79 iBT). *Application deadline:* For fall admission, 2/1 for domestic and international students. Application fee: $35 ($45 for international students). Electronic applications accepted. *Expenses:* Tuition, state resident: full-time $7312; part-time $350 per credit hour. Tuition, nonresident: full-time $18,490; part-time $621 per credit hour. *Required fees:* $63 per credit hour. Tuition and fees vary according to course load and program. *Financial support:* In 2011–12, 86 students received support, including 6 fellowships with full tuition reimbursements available (averaging $18,000 per year), 28 research assistantships with full tuition reimbursements available (averaging $6,000 per year), 10 teaching assistantships with full tuition reimbursements available (averaging $6,000 per year); career-related internships or fieldwork, institutionally sponsored loans, scholarships/grants, traineeships, and unspecified assistantships also available. Financial award application deadline: 7/1; financial award applicants required to submit FAFSA. *Faculty research:* Drug and alcohol abuse, marriage and family counseling, severe mental retardation, parenting of children with disabilities. *Total annual research expenditures:* $2,600. *Unit head:* Dr. Pamela Evanshen, Chair, 423-439-7694, Fax: 423-439-7790, E-mail: evanshep@etsu.edu. *Application contact:* Fiona Goodyear, Graduate Specialist, 423-439-6148, Fax: 423-439-5624, E-mail: goodyear@etsu.edu.

Edinboro University of Pennsylvania, School of Education, Department of Early Childhood and Special Education, Edinboro, PA 16444. Offers behavior management (Certificate); character education (Certificate); online special education (M Ed); special education (M Ed). Part-time and evening/weekend programs available. *Faculty:* 5 full-time (all women). *Students:* 22 full-time (19 women), 154 part-time (129 women); includes 4 minority (3 Black or African American, non-Hispanic/Latino; 1 Two or more races, non-Hispanic/Latino). Average age 31. In 2011, 26 master's, 5 Certificates awarded. *Degree requirements:* For master's, thesis or alternative, competency exam; for Certificate, thesis or alternative. *Entrance requirements:* For master's and Certificate, GRE or MAT, minimum QPA of 2.5. *Application deadline:* Applications are processed on a rolling basis. Application fee: $30. Electronic applications accepted. *Financial support:* In 2011–12, 4 research assistantships with full and partial tuition reimbursements (averaging $4,050 per year) were awarded; career-related internships or fieldwork, Federal Work-Study, scholarships/grants, and unspecified assistantships also available. Support available to part-time students. Financial award application deadline: 2/15; financial award applicants required to submit FAFSA. *Unit head:* Dr. Maureen Walcavich, Program Head, Early Childhood, 814-732-2303, E-mail: mwalcavich@edinboro.edu. *Application contact:* Dr. Mary Jo Melvin, Program Head, Special Education, 814-732-2154, E-mail: mmelvin@edinboro.edu.

Edinboro University of Pennsylvania, School of Education, Department of Professional Studies, Edinboro, PA 16444. Offers counseling (MA), including community counseling, elementary guidance, rehabilitation counseling, secondary guidance, student personnel services; educational leadership (M Ed), including elementary school administration, secondary school administration; educational psychology (M Ed); educational specialist school psychology (MS); elementary principal (Certificate); elementary school guidance counselor (Certificate); K-12 school administration (Certificate); letter of eligibility (Certificate); reading (M Ed); reading specialist (Certificate); school psychology (Certificate); school supervision (Certificate), including music, special education. Part-time and evening/weekend programs available. *Faculty:* 13 full-time (8 women). *Students:* 171 full-time (134 women), 563 part-time (441 women); includes 26 minority (20 Black or African American, non-Hispanic/Latino; 1 American Indian or Alaska Native, non-Hispanic/Latino; 1 Asian, non-Hispanic/Latino; 4 Hispanic/Latino). Average age 31. In 2011, 297 master's, 49 other advanced degrees awarded. *Degree requirements:* For master's, thesis or alternative, competency exam; for Certificate, thesis or alternative. *Entrance requirements:* For master's and Certificate, GRE or MAT, minimum QPA of 2.5. *Application deadline:* Applications are processed on a rolling basis. Application fee: $30. Electronic applications accepted. *Financial support:* In 2011–12, 60 research assistantships with full and partial tuition reimbursements (averaging $4,050 per year) were awarded; career-related internships or fieldwork, Federal Work-Study, scholarships/grants, and unspecified assistantships also available. Support available to part-time students. Financial award application deadline: 2/15; financial award applicants required to submit FAFSA. *Unit head:* Dr. Susan Norton, 814-732-2260, E-mail: scnorton@edinboro.edu. *Application contact:* Dr. Andrew Pushchack, Program Head, Educational Leadership, 814-732-1548, E-mail: apushchack@edinboro.edu.

Emporia State University, Graduate School, Teachers College, Department of Counselor Education, Program in School Counseling, Emporia, KS 66801-5087. Offers MS. *Accreditation:* ACA; NCATE. Part-time programs available. *Students:* 11 full-time (8 women), 68 part-time (63 women); includes 4 minority (1 Black or African American, non-Hispanic/Latino; 1 Asian, non-Hispanic/Latino; 1 Hispanic/Latino; 1 Native Hawaiian or other Pacific Islander, non-Hispanic/Latino). 14 applicants, 86% accepted, 6 enrolled. In 2011, 25 master's awarded. *Degree requirements:* For master's, comprehensive exam or thesis, practicum. *Entrance requirements:* For master's, GRE or MAT, graduate essay exam, appropriate bachelor's degree, interview, letters of recommendation. *Application deadline:* For fall admission, 8/15 priority date for domestic students. Applications are processed on a rolling basis. Application fee: $30 ($75 for international students). Electronic applications accepted. *Expenses:* Tuition, state resident: full-time $2342; part-time $195 per credit hour. Tuition, nonresident: full-time $7254; part-time $605 per credit hour. *Required fees:* $66 per credit hour. Tuition and fees vary according to campus/location. *Financial support:* Career-related internships or fieldwork, Federal Work-Study, institutionally sponsored loans, health care benefits, and unspecified assistantships available. Financial award application deadline: 3/15; financial award applicants required to submit FAFSA. *Unit head:* Dr. James Costello, Interim Chair, 620-341-5791, E-mail: jcostell@emporia.edu. *Application contact:* Mary Sewell, Admissions Coordinator, 800-950-GRAD, Fax: 620-341-5909, E-mail: msewell@emporia.edu.

Evangel University, School Counseling Program, Springfield, MO 65802. Offers MS. Part-time programs available. *Faculty:* 1 (woman) full-time, 4 part-time/adjunct (2 women). *Students:* 10 full-time (8 women), 65 part-time (54 women). Average age 32. 17 applicants, 94% accepted, 14 enrolled. In 2011, 28 master's awarded. *Degree requirements:* For master's, comprehensive exam (for some programs), thesis or alternative. *Entrance requirements:* For master's, MAT (preferred) or GRE, teaching certificate. Additional exam requirements/recommendations for international students: Required—TOEFL (minimum score 550 paper-based; 213 computer-based). *Application deadline:* For fall admission, 7/15 priority date for domestic students, 7/15 for international students; for spring admission, 11/15 priority date for domestic students, 11/15 for international students. Applications are processed on a rolling basis. Application fee: $25. Electronic applications accepted. *Financial support:* In 2011–12, 2 students received support. Career-related internships or fieldwork, scholarships/grants, and unspecified assistantships available. Support available to part-time students. Financial award application deadline: 3/1; financial award applicants required to submit FAFSA. *Unit head:* Debbie Bicket, Chair, 417-865-2815 Ext. 8567, Fax: 417-575-5484, E-mail: bicketd@evangel.edu. *Application contact:* Micah Hildreth, Admissions Representative, Graduate and Professional Studies, 417-865-2815 Ext. 7227, Fax: 417-575-5484, E-mail: hildrethm@evangel.edu. Web site: http://www.evangel.edu/academics/graduate-studies/graduate-programs/school-counseling/.

Fairfield University, Graduate School of Education and Allied Professions, Fairfield, CT 06824-5195. Offers applied psychology (MA); bilingual education (CAS); clinical mental health counseling (MA, CAS); educational technology (MA); elementary education (MA); family studies (MA); marriage and family therapy (MA); school counseling (MA, CAS); school psychology (MA, CAS); special education (MA); teaching (Certificate); teaching and foundations (MA, CAS); TESOL foreign language and bilingual/multicultural education (MA, CAS). *Accreditation:* NCATE. Part-time and evening/weekend programs available. *Faculty:* 24 full-time (19 women). *Students:* 147 full-time (120 women), 391 part-time (321 women); includes 60 minority (13 Black or African American, non-Hispanic/Latino; 8 Asian, non-Hispanic/Latino; 35 Hispanic/Latino; 4 Two or more races, non-Hispanic/Latino), 1 international. Average age 34. 319 applicants, 48% accepted, 80 enrolled. In 2011, 185 master's, 20 other advanced degrees awarded. *Degree requirements:* For master's, comprehensive exam. *Entrance requirements:* For master's, PRAXIS I (for certification programs), minimum QPA of 3.0, 2 recommendations, resume. Additional exam requirements/recommendations for international students: Required—TOEFL (minimum score 550 paper-based; 213 computer-based; 84 iBT) or IELTS (minimum score 7.5). *Application deadline:* For fall admission, 2/15 for international students; for spring admission, 10/1 for international students. Application fee: $60. Electronic applications accepted. *Expenses: Tuition:* Part-time $600 per credit hour. *Required fees:* $25 per term. *Financial support:* In 2011–12, 45 students received support. Career-related internships or fieldwork and unspecified assistantships available. Financial award applicants required to submit FAFSA. *Faculty research:* Literacy, adolescent psychology, special education, early childhood education, teaching development. *Unit head:* Dr. Susan D. Franzosa, Dean, 203-254-4000 Ext. 4250, Fax: 203-254-4241, E-mail: sfranzosa@fairfield.edu. *Application contact:* Marianne Gumpper, Director of Graduate and Continuing Studies Admission, 203-254-4184, Fax: 203-254-4073, E-mail: gradadmis@fairfield.edu. Web site: http://www.fairfield.edu/gseap/gseap_grad_1.html.

Faulkner University, Alabama Christian College of Arts and Sciences, Department of Social and Behavioral Sciences, Montgomery, AL 36109-3398. Offers counseling (MS). Postbaccalaureate distance learning degree programs offered (no on-campus study).

Fitchburg State University, Division of Graduate and Continuing Education, Programs in Counseling, Fitchburg, MA 01420-2697. Offers elementary school guidance counseling (MS); mental health counseling (MS); secondary school guidance counseling (MS). *Accreditation:* NCATE. Part-time and evening/weekend programs available. *Students:* 18 full-time (16 women), 50 part-time (44 women); includes 6 minority (1 Black or African American, non-Hispanic/Latino; 3 Hispanic/Latino; 2 Two or more races, non-Hispanic/Latino), 1 international. Average age 32. 21 applicants, 90% accepted, 12 enrolled. In 2011, 24 master's awarded. *Entrance requirements:* Additional exam requirements/recommendations for international students: Required—TOEFL (minimum score 550 paper-based; 213 computer-based; 79 iBT). *Application deadline:* For fall admission, 7/15 for international students; for spring admission, 12/1 for international students. Applications are processed on a rolling basis. Application fee: $25 ($50 for international students). Electronic applications accepted. *Expenses:* Tuition, state resident: full-time $2700; part-time $150 per credit. Tuition, nonresident: full-time $2700; part-time $150 per credit. *Required fees:* $2286; $127 per credit. *Financial support:* In 2011–12, research assistantships with partial tuition reimbursements (averaging $5,500 per year) were awarded; Federal Work-Study, scholarships/grants, and unspecified assistantships also available. Support available to part-time students. Financial award application deadline: 3/1; financial award applicants required to submit FAFSA. *Unit head:* Dr. John Hancock, Chair, 978-665-3604, Fax: 978-665-3658, E-mail: gce@fitchburgstate.edu. *Application contact:* Kay Reynolds, Director of Admissions, 978-665-3144, Fax: 978-665-4540, E-mail: admissions@fitchburgstate.edu. Web site: http://www.fitchburgstate.edu.

Florida Agricultural and Mechanical University, Division of Graduate Studies, Research, and Continuing Education, College of Education, Department of Educational Leadership and Human Services, Tallahassee, FL 32307-3200. Offers administration and supervision (M Ed, MS Ed, PhD); adult education (M Ed, MS Ed); educational leadership (PhD); guidance and counseling (M Ed, MS Ed). *Accreditation:* NCATE. *Degree requirements:* For master's, thesis (for some programs); for doctorate, thesis/dissertation. *Entrance requirements:* For master's, GRE General Test, minimum GPA of 3.0. Additional exam requirements/recommendations for international students: Required—TOEFL.

Florida Atlantic University, College of Education, Department of Counselor Education, Boca Raton, FL 33431-0991. Offers counselor education (M Ed, PhD, Ed S); marriage and family therapy (Ed S); mental health counseling (M Ed, Ed S); rehabilitation counseling (M Ed); school counseling (M Ed, Ed S). *Accreditation:* ACA; NCATE. Part-time and evening/weekend programs available. *Faculty:* 9 full-time (4 women), 5 part-time/adjunct (all women). *Students:* 75 full-time (54 women), 92 part-time (80 women); includes 53 minority (26 Black or African American, non-Hispanic/Latino; 5 Asian, non-Hispanic/Latino; 21 Hispanic/Latino; 1 Two or more races, non-Hispanic/Latino), 1 international. Average age 31. 129 applicants, 37% accepted, 21 enrolled. In 2011, 42 degrees awarded. *Degree requirements:* For Ed S, departmental qualifying exam. *Entrance requirements:* For master's, GRE General Test, minimum GPA of 3.0 during previous 2 years; for Ed S, GRE General Test, minimum graduate GPA of 3.25. Additional exam requirements/recommendations for international students: Required—TOEFL. *Application deadline:* For fall admission, 3/1 for domestic students, 2/1 for international students; for spring admission, 9/15 for domestic students, 7/1 for international students. Applications are processed on a rolling basis. Application fee: $30. *Expenses: Tuition, area resident:* Part-time $343.02 per credit hour. Tuition, state resident: full-time $8232. Tuition, nonresident: full-time $23,931; part-time $997.14 per credit hour. *Financial support:* Research assistantships with partial tuition reimbursements, teaching assistantships, career-related internships or fieldwork, scholarships/grants, and unspecified assistantships available. *Faculty research:* Brief therapy, psychological type, marriage and family counseling, international programs, integrated services. *Unit head:* Dr. Irene Johnson, Chair, 561-297-2136, Fax: 561-297-2309. *Application contact:* Darlene Epperson, Office Assistant, 561-297-3601, Fax: 561-297-2309, E-mail: frederic@fau.edu. Web site: http://www.coe.fau.edu/academicdepartments/ce/.

Florida Gulf Coast University, College of Education, Program in Counseling, Fort Myers, FL 33965-6565. Offers MA. *Accreditation:* ACA. Part-time and evening/weekend programs available. *Faculty:* 34 full-time (26 women), 57 part-time/adjunct (40 women). *Students:* 20 full-time (18 women); includes 4 minority (1 Black or African American, non-Hispanic/Latino; 3 Hispanic/Latino). Average age 34. In 2011, 10 master's awarded. *Degree requirements:* For master's, thesis or alternative. *Entrance requirements:* For master's, GRE General Test, MAT, minimum GPA of 3.0. Additional exam requirements/recommendations for international students: Required—TOEFL (minimum score 550 paper-based; 213 computer-based). *Application deadline:* For fall admission, 7/1 priority date for domestic students; for spring admission, 10/15 for domestic students. Applications are processed on a rolling basis. Application fee: $30. Electronic applications accepted. *Expenses:* Tuition, state resident: full-time $8289. Tuition, nonresident: full-time $28,895. *Required fees:* $1831. One-time fee: $30 full-time. *Faculty research:* Sexuality, confidentiality, school counselor roles, distance learning, exceptional students. *Unit head:* Dr. Robert Kenny, Department Chair, 239-590-1147, Fax: 239-590-7801, E-mail: rkenny@fgcu.edu.

Florida International University, College of Education, Department of Educational Leadership and Policy Studies, Miami, FL 33199. Offers adult education (MS); adult education in human resource development (Ed D); clinical mental health counseling (MS); conflict resolution and consensus building (Certificate); counselor education (MS); educational administration and supervision (Ed D); educational leadership (MS, Certificate, Ed S); higher education (Ed D); higher education administration (MS); human resource development (MS); instruction in urban settings (MS); international/intercultural education (MS); learning technologies (MS); multicultural-bilingual (MS); multicultural-TESOL (MS); recreation and sport management (MS); recreation therapy (MS); rehabilitation counseling (MS); school counseling (MS); school psychology (Ed S); urban education (MS). Part-time and evening/weekend programs available. *Degree requirements:* For doctorate, thesis/dissertation. *Entrance requirements:* For master's, minimum GPA of 3.0; for doctorate and other advanced degree, GRE General Test. Additional exam requirements/recommendations for international students: Required—TOEFL (minimum score 550 paper-based; 213 computer-based; 80 iBT), IELTS (minimum score 6.3). Electronic applications accepted.

Florida State University, The Graduate School, College of Education, Department of Educational Psychology and Learning Systems, Tallahassee, FL 32306. Offers counseling/school psychology (PhD); educational psychology (MS, PhD, Ed S), including learning and cognition, sports psychology (MS, PhD); instructional systems (MS, PhD, Ed S), including instructional systems, open and distance learning (MS), performance improvement and human resources (MS); measurement and statistics (MS, PhD, Ed S); mental health counseling (PhD); psychological services (MS, PhD, Ed S); school psychology (MS, Ed S); MS/Ed S. *Faculty:* 25 full-time (16 women), 21 part-time/adjunct (11 women). *Students:* 261 full-time (192 women), 137 part-time (85 women); includes 69 minority (30 Black or African American, non-Hispanic/Latino; 3 American Indian or Alaska Native, non-Hispanic/Latino; 12 Asian, non-Hispanic/Latino; 24 Hispanic/Latino), 95 international. Average age 32. 438 applicants, 41% accepted, 88 enrolled. In 2011, 73 master's, 17 doctorates, 30 other advanced degrees awarded. *Degree requirements:* For master's and Ed S, comprehensive exam, thesis optional; for doctorate, comprehensive exam, thesis/dissertation. *Entrance requirements:* For master's, doctorate, and Ed S, GRE General Test, minimum GPA of 3.0. Additional exam requirements/recommendations for international students: Required—TOEFL (minimum score 550 paper-based; 213 computer-based; 80 iBT); Recommended—TWE. *Application deadline:* For fall admission, 7/1 for domestic and international students; for winter admission, 11/1 for domestic and international students; for spring admission, 3/1 for domestic and international students. Applications are processed on a rolling basis. Application fee: $30. Electronic applications accepted. *Expenses:* Tuition, state resident: full-time $9474; part-time $350.88 per credit hour. Tuition, nonresident: full-time $16,236; part-time $601.34 per credit hour. *Required fees:* $630 per semester. One-time fee: $20. Tuition and fees vary according to course load and campus/location. *Financial support:* In 2011–12, 38 research assistantships with full and partial tuition reimbursements, 42 teaching assistantships with full and partial tuition reimbursements were awarded; fellowships with full tuition reimbursements, career-related internships or fieldwork, scholarships/grants, health care benefits, and unspecified assistantships also available. Financial award application deadline: 1/15; financial award applicants required to submit FAFSA. *Faculty research:* Educational technology, giftedness in children, instructional design, measurement and evaluation. *Total annual research expenditures:* $127,347. *Unit head:* Dr. Betsy Becker, Chair, 850-644-8794, Fax: 850-644-8776, E-mail: bbecker@fsu.edu. *Application contact:* Terri Wehnert, Program Assistant, 850-644-8046, Fax: 850-644-8776, E-mail: tmpowell@fsu.edu. Web site: http://www.coe.fsu.edu/Academic-Programs/Departments/Educational-Psychology-and-Learning-Systems-EPLS.

Fordham University, Graduate School of Education, Division of Psychological and Educational Services, New York, NY 10023. Offers counseling and personnel services (MSE, Adv C); counseling psychology (PhD); educational psychology (MSE, PhD); school psychology (PhD); urban and urban bilingual school psychology (Adv C). *Accreditation:* APA (one or more programs are accredited); NCATE. *Degree requirements:* For doctorate, thesis/dissertation. *Entrance requirements:* For doctorate, GRE General Test. *Expenses: Tuition:* Full-time $30,480; part-time $1270 per credit. *Required fees:* $586; $293 per semester.

Fort Hays State University, Graduate School, College of Education and Technology, Department of Educational Administration and Counseling, Program in Counseling, Hays, KS 67601-4099. Offers MS. *Accreditation:* NCATE. Part-time programs available. *Degree requirements:* For master's, comprehensive exam, thesis or alternative. *Entrance requirements:* For master's, GRE General Test or MAT, minimum undergraduate GPA of 3.0 in last 60 hours. Additional exam requirements/recommendations for international students: Required—TOEFL (minimum score 550 paper-based; 213 computer-based). Electronic applications accepted. *Faculty research:* Career education, evaluation and plans, counseling the disabled, marriage and family parenting, underemployment and work in the family.

Fort Valley State University, College of Graduate Studies and Extended Education, Department of Counseling Psychology, Fort Valley, GA 31030. Offers guidance and counseling (Ed S); mental health counseling (MS); rehabilitation counseling (MS). Part-time programs available. *Degree requirements:* For master's, comprehensive exam (for some programs), thesis optional. *Entrance requirements:* For master's and Ed S, GRE General Test or MAT.

Freed-Hardeman University, Program in Counseling, Henderson, TN 38340-2399. Offers MS. Part-time and evening/weekend programs available. *Degree requirements:* For master's, comprehensive exam, practicum. *Entrance requirements:* For master's, GRE General Test or MAT. Additional exam requirements/recommendations for international students: Required—TOEFL (minimum score 500 paper-based; 173 computer-based).

Freed-Hardeman University, Program in Education, Henderson, TN 38340-2399. Offers curriculum and instruction (M Ed); school counseling (M Ed), including administration and supervision, special education; school leadership (Ed S). *Accreditation:* NCATE. Part-time and evening/weekend programs available. *Degree requirements:* For master's, comprehensive exam, thesis optional; for Ed S, thesis. *Entrance requirements:* For master's, GRE General Test or NTE; for Ed S, 3 years of teaching experience. Additional exam requirements/recommendations for international students: Required—TOEFL (minimum score 500 paper-based; 173 computer-based).

Fresno Pacific University, Graduate Programs, School of Education, Fresno, CA 93702-4709. Offers administration (MA Ed), including administrative services; foundations, curriculum and teaching (MA Ed), including curriculum and teaching, school library and information technology; language, literacy, and culture (MA Ed), including bilingual/cross-cultural education, language development, multilingual contexts, reading; mathematics/science/computer education (MA Ed), including educational technology, integrated mathematics/science education, mathematics education; pupil personnel services (MA Ed), including school counseling, school psychology; special education (MA Ed), including mild/moderate, moderate/severe, physical and health impairments. Part-time and evening/weekend programs available. *Degree requirements:* For master's, thesis (for some programs). *Entrance requirements:* For master's, interview; GMAT, GRE, MAT, or 6 units of course work with a faculty recommendation. Additional exam requirements/recommendations for international students: Required—TOEFL (minimum score 550 paper-based; 213 computer-based). Electronic applications accepted.

Fresno Pacific University, Graduate Programs, School of Education, Division of Pupil Personnel Services, Program in School Counseling, Fresno, CA 93702-4709. Offers MA Ed. Part-time and evening/weekend programs available. *Degree requirements:* For master's, thesis or alternative. *Entrance requirements:* Additional exam requirements/recommendations for international students: Required—TOEFL (minimum score 550 paper-based; 213 computer-based).

Frostburg State University, Graduate School, College of Education, Department of Educational Professions, Program in School Counseling, Frostburg, MD 21532-1099. Offers M Ed. *Accreditation:* NCATE. Part-time and evening/weekend programs available. *Degree requirements:* For master's, comprehensive exam, thesis or alternative. *Entrance requirements:* For master's, GRE General Test or MAT, interview. Additional exam requirements/recommendations for international students: Required—TOEFL. Electronic applications accepted.

Gallaudet University, The Graduate School, Washington, DC 20002-3625. Offers audiology (Au D); clinical psychology (PhD); critical studies in the education of deaf learners (PhD); deaf and hard of hearing infants, toddlers, and their families (Certificate); deaf education (Ed S); deaf education: advanced studies (MA); deaf education: special programs in deaf education (MA); deaf history (Certificate); deaf studies (MA, Certificate); education deaf students with disabilities (Certificate); education: teacher preparation (MA), including deaf education, early childhood education and deaf education, elementary education and deaf education, secondary education and deaf education; hearing, speech and language sciences (MS, PhD); international development (MA); interpretation (MA, PhD); linguistics (MA, PhD); mental health counseling (MA); public administration (MA); school counseling (MA); school psychology (Psy S); sign language teaching (MA); social work (MSW); speech-language pathology (MS). Part-time programs available. *Faculty:* 62 full-time (44 women). *Students:* 300 full-time (246 women), 110 part-time (82 women); includes 80 minority (27 Black or African American, non-Hispanic/Latino; 1 American Indian or Alaska Native, non-Hispanic/Latino; 11 Asian, non-Hispanic/Latino; 25 Hispanic/Latino; 1 Native Hawaiian or other Pacific Islander, non-Hispanic/Latino; 15 Two or more races, non-Hispanic/Latino), 24 international. Average age 30. 498 applicants, 45% accepted, 168 enrolled. In 2011, 129 master's, 24 doctorates, 19 other advanced degrees awarded. Terminal master's awarded for partial completion of doctoral program. *Degree requirements:* For master's, comprehensive exam (for some programs), thesis optional; for doctorate, comprehensive exam, thesis/dissertation. *Entrance requirements:* For master's and doctorate, GRE General Test or MAT, letters of recommendation, interviews, goals statement, ASL proficiency interview, written English competency. Additional exam requirements/recommendations for international students: Required—TOEFL. *Application deadline:* For fall admission, 2/15 for domestic students. Applications are processed on a rolling basis. Application fee: $50. Electronic applications accepted. *Expenses: Tuition:* Full-time $12,770; part-time $710 per credit. *Required fees:* $376. *Financial support:* In 2011–12, 287 students received support. Fellowships, research assistantships, teaching assistantships, career-related internships or fieldwork, Federal Work-Study, scholarships/grants, tuition waivers (partial), and unspecified assistantships available. Support available to part-time students. Financial award applicants required to submit FAFSA. *Faculty research:* Bimodal bilingualism development, audiology, telecommunications access, early childhood education, linguistics, visual language and visual learning, rehabilitation and hearing enhancement. *Unit head:* Dr. Carol J. Erting, Dean, 202-651-5520, Fax: 202-651-5027, E-mail: carol.erting@gallaudet.edu. *Application contact:* Wednesday Luria, Coordinator of Prospective Graduate Student Services, 202-651-5400, Fax: 202-651-5295, E-mail: graduate.school@gallaudet.edu. Web site: http://www.gallaudet.edu/x26696.xml.

Gannon University, School of Graduate Studies, College of Humanities, Education, and Social Sciences, School of Humanities, Program in Advanced Counselor Studies, Erie, PA 16541-0001. Offers Certificate. *Accreditation:* ACA. Part-time and evening/weekend programs available. *Students:* 1 (woman) full-time, 1 (woman) part-time. Average age 35. 2 applicants, 100% accepted, 0 enrolled. *Entrance requirements:* For degree, master's degree in counseling or related field. Additional exam requirements/recommendations for international students: Required—TOEFL (minimum score 79 iBT). *Application deadline:* Applications are processed on a rolling basis. Application fee: $25. Electronic applications accepted. *Financial support:* Scholarships/grants available. Financial award application deadline: 7/1; financial award applicants required to submit FAFSA. *Unit head:* Dr. David Tobin, Director, 814-871-7537, E-mail: tobin001@gannon.edu. *Application contact:* Kara Morgan, Director of Graduate Admissions, 814-871-5831, Fax: 814-871-5827, E-mail: graduate@gannon.edu.

Gannon University, School of Graduate Studies, College of Humanities, Education, and Social Sciences, School of Humanities, Program in Community Counseling, Erie, PA 16541-0001. Offers MS, Certificate. *Accreditation:* ACA. Part-time and evening/weekend programs available. *Students:* 33 full-time (23 women), 14 part-time (10 women); includes 5 minority (4 Black or African American, non-Hispanic/Latino; 1 Asian, non-Hispanic/Latino). Average age 28. 40 applicants, 63% accepted, 0 enrolled. In 2011, 3 master's awarded. *Degree requirements:* For master's, comprehensive exam. *Entrance requirements:* For master's, bachelor's degree, minimum QPA of 3.0, letters of recommendation, essay, interview. Additional exam requirements/recommendations for international students: Required—TOEFL (minimum score 79 iBT). *Application deadline:* Applications are processed on a rolling basis. Application fee: $25. Electronic applications accepted. *Financial support:* Career-related internships or fieldwork, Federal Work-Study, scholarships/grants, and unspecified assistantships available. Financial award application deadline: 7/1; financial award applicants required to submit FAFSA. *Unit head:* Dr. Ken McCurdy, Director, 814-871-7791, E-mail: mccurdy003@gannon.edu. *Application contact:* Kara Morgan, Director of Graduate Admissions, 814-871-5831, Fax: 814-871-5827, E-mail: graduate@gannon.edu.

Gannon University, School of Graduate Studies, College of Humanities, Education, and Social Sciences, School of Humanities, Program in School Counselor Preparation,

Erie, PA 16541-0001. Offers Certificate. *Accreditation:* ACA. Part-time and evening/weekend programs available. *Entrance requirements:* Additional exam requirements/recommendations for international students: Required—TOEFL (minimum score 500 paper-based; 173 computer-based). *Application deadline:* Applications are processed on a rolling basis. Application fee: $25. Electronic applications accepted. *Financial support:* Application deadline: 7/1; applicants required to submit FAFSA. *Unit head:* Dr. David Tobin, Director, 814-871-7537, E-mail: tobin001@gannon.edu. *Application contact:* Kara Morgan, Director of Graduate Admissions, 814-871-5831, Fax: 814-871-5827, E-mail: graduate@gannon.edu.

Geneva College, Master of Arts in Counseling Program, Beaver Falls, PA 15010-3599. Offers clinical mental health counseling (MA); marriage and family counseling (MA); school counseling (MA). *Accreditation:* ACA. Part-time and evening/weekend programs available. *Faculty:* 4 full-time (1 woman), 3 part-time/adjunct (2 women). *Students:* 29 full-time (27 women), 16 part-time (15 women); includes 5 minority (all Black or African American, non-Hispanic/Latino). Average age 30. 27 applicants, 89% accepted, 21 enrolled. In 2011, 23 master's awarded. *Degree requirements:* For master's, 50-60 credits (depending on program); practicum, internship. *Entrance requirements:* For master's, minimum GPA of 3.0 (preferred), 3 letters of recommendation, essay on career goals, resume of educational and professional experiences. Additional exam requirements/recommendations for international students: Required—TOEFL. *Application deadline:* For fall admission, 7/1 priority date for domestic students; for spring admission, 11/1 priority date for domestic students. Applications are processed on a rolling basis. Electronic applications accepted. *Expenses: Tuition:* Part-time $625 per credit hour. Tuition and fees vary according to program. *Financial support:* In 2011–12, 3 students received support, including 3 teaching assistantships (averaging $3,500 per year); career-related internships or fieldwork and unspecified assistantships also available. Financial award application deadline: 8/1; financial award applicants required to submit FAFSA. *Unit head:* Dr. Carol Luce, Program Director, 724-847-6622, Fax: 724-847-6101, E-mail: cbluce@geneva.edu. *Application contact:* Marina Frazier, Graduate Program Manager, 724-847-6697, E-mail: counseling@geneva.edu. Web site: http://www.geneva.edu/.

George Fox University, School of Education, Graduate Department of Counseling, Newberg, OR 97132-2697. Offers clinical mental health counseling (MA); marriage, couple and family counseling (MA, Certificate); mental health trauma (Certificate); school counseling (MA, Certificate); school psychology (Certificate, Ed S). Part-time programs available. *Faculty:* 9 full-time (3 women), 11 part-time/adjunct (9 women). *Students:* 95 full-time (78 women), 139 part-time (110 women); includes 26 minority (5 Black or African American, non-Hispanic/Latino; 3 American Indian or Alaska Native, non-Hispanic/Latino; 6 Asian, non-Hispanic/Latino; 8 Hispanic/Latino; 1 Native Hawaiian or other Pacific Islander, non-Hispanic/Latino; 3 Two or more races, non-Hispanic/Latino). Average age 35. In 2011, 65 master's awarded. *Degree requirements:* For master's, clinical project. *Entrance requirements:* For master's, MAT or GRE, bachelor's degree from regionally-accredited college or university, minimum cumulative GPA of 3.0, 1 professional and 1 academic reference, resume, on-campus interview, official transcripts. Additional exam requirements/recommendations for international students: Required—TOEFL (minimum score 577 paper-based; 233 computer-based; 90 iBT), IELTS (minimum score 7). *Application deadline:* For fall admission, 5/30 for domestic and international students; for winter admission, 11/1 for domestic and international students; for spring admission, 2/28 for domestic and international students. Applications are processed on a rolling basis. Application fee: $40. Electronic applications accepted. *Expenses:* Contact institution. *Financial support:* Career-related internships or fieldwork available. Financial award applicants required to submit FAFSA. *Unit head:* Dr. Richard Shaw, Associate Professor of Marriage and Family Therapy/Chair, 503-554-6142, E-mail: rshaw@georgefox.edu. *Application contact:* Bonnie Nakashimada, Admissions Counselor, 800-493-4937, Fax: 503-554-6111, E-mail: counseling@georgefox.edu. Web site: http://counseling.georgefox.edu/.

George Mason University, College of Education and Human Development, Program in Counseling and Development, Fairfax, VA 22030. Offers M Ed. *Accreditation:* NCATE. *Faculty:* 7 full-time (4 women), 18 part-time/adjunct (14 women). *Students:* 48 full-time (42 women), 104 part-time (89 women); includes 51 minority (21 Black or African American, non-Hispanic/Latino; 9 Asian, non-Hispanic/Latino; 18 Hispanic/Latino; 3 Two or more races, non-Hispanic/Latino), 1 international. Average age 31. 125 applicants, 37% accepted, 21 enrolled. In 2011, 42 degrees awarded. *Degree requirements:* For master's, thesis (for some programs). *Entrance requirements:* For master's, bachelor's degree from regionally-accredited institution with minimum GPA of 3.0 overall or in last 60 credit hours; 2 copies of official transcripts; expanded goals statement; 3 letters of recommendation with recommendation form; 12 credits of undergraduate behavioral sciences; 1,000 hours of counseling or related experience. Additional exam requirements/recommendations for international students: Required—TOEFL (minimum score 570 paper-based; 230 computer-based; 88 iBT), IELTS, Pearson Test of English. *Application deadline:* For fall admission, 2/1 for domestic students; for spring admission, 10/1 for domestic students. Application fee: $65 ($80 for international students). Electronic applications accepted. *Expenses:* Tuition, state resident: full-time $8750; part-time $364.58 per credit. Tuition, nonresident: full-time $24,092; part-time $1003.83 per credit. *Required fees:* $2514; $104.75 per credit. *Financial support:* In 2011–12, 1 student received support, including 1 teaching assistantship with full and partial tuition reimbursement available (averaging $8,000 per year); career-related internships or fieldwork, Federal Work-Study, scholarships/grants, unspecified assistantships, and health care benefits (full-time research or teaching assistantship recipients) also available. Support available to part-time students. Financial award application deadline: 3/1; financial award applicants required to submit FAFSA. *Faculty research:* Leadership, multiculturalism, social justice, and advocacy; global well-being; social psychological, physical, and spiritual health of individuals, families, communities, and organizations. *Unit head:* George McMahon, Associate Professor, 703-993-5342, Fax: 703-993-5577, E-mail: hmcmaho3@gmu.edu. *Application contact:* Deborah Bays, Office Manager, 703-993-2087, Fax: 703-993-5577, E-mail: dbays@gmu.edu. Web site: http://gse.gmu.edu/programs/counseling/.

The George Washington University, Graduate School of Education and Human Development, Department of Counseling and Human Development, Program in Counseling, Washington, DC 20052. Offers PhD, Ed S. *Accreditation:* ACA (one or more programs are accredited); NCATE. Part-time and evening/weekend programs available. *Faculty:* 3 full-time (1 woman). *Students:* 1 full-time (0 women), 6 part-time (all women). Average age 37. 9 applicants, 100% accepted. In 2011, 2 other advanced degrees awarded. *Degree requirements:* For doctorate, comprehensive exam, thesis/dissertation; for Ed S, comprehensive exam. *Entrance requirements:* For doctorate, GRE General Test, interview, minimum GPA of 3.3; for Ed S, GRE General Test or MAT, minimum GPA of 3.3. *Application deadline:* For fall admission, 1/15 priority date for domestic students; for spring admission, 10/1 for domestic students. Applications are processed on a rolling basis. Application fee: $75. *Financial support:* Fellowships, research assistantships, teaching assistantships, career-related internships or fieldwork, Federal Work-Study, and tuition waivers (partial) available. Financial award application deadline: 1/15; financial award applicants required to submit FAFSA. *Faculty research:* Values in counseling, religion and counseling. *Unit head:* Dr. Pat Schwallie-Giddis, Director, 202-994-6856, E-mail: drpat@gwu.edu. *Application contact:* Sarah Lang, Director of Graduate Admissions, 202-994-1447, Fax: 202-994-7207, E-mail: slang@gwu.edu.

The George Washington University, Graduate School of Education and Human Development, Department of Counseling and Human Development, Program in School Counseling, Washington, DC 20052. Offers MA Ed, Graduate Certificate.

The George Washington University, Graduate School of Education and Human Development, Department of Counseling and Human Development, Programs in Counseling: School, Community and Rehabilitation, Washington, DC 20052. Offers community counseling (MA Ed); rehabilitation counseling (MA Ed); school counseling (MA Ed). School counseling program also offered in Alexandria, VA. *Accreditation:* ACA (one or more programs are accredited); CORE (one or more programs are accredited); NCATE. *Students:* 64 full-time (53 women), 54 part-time (47 women); includes 37 minority (24 Black or African American, non-Hispanic/Latino; 1 Asian, non-Hispanic/Latino; 8 Hispanic/Latino; 4 Two or more races, non-Hispanic/Latino), 5 international. Average age 33. 114 applicants, 98% accepted. In 2011, 51 master's awarded. *Degree requirements:* For master's, comprehensive exam. *Entrance requirements:* For master's, GRE General Test or MAT, minimum GPA of 2.75. *Application deadline:* For fall admission, 1/15 priority date for domestic students; for spring admission, 10/1 for domestic students. Applications are processed on a rolling basis. Application fee: $75. *Financial support:* In 2011–12, 27 students received support. Fellowships, research assistantships, teaching assistantships, career-related internships or fieldwork, Federal Work-Study, and tuition waivers (full and partial) available. *Faculty research:* Adjustment to disability, head injury rehabilitation, cross-cultural counseling. *Unit head:* Dr. Pat Schwallie-Giddis, Chair, 202-994-6856, E-mail: drpat@gwu.edu. *Application contact:* Sarah Lang, Director of Graduate Admissions, 202-994-1447, Fax: 202-994-7207, E-mail: slang@gwu.edu.

Georgia Southern University, Jack N. Averitt College of Graduate Studies, College of Education, Department of Leadership, Technology, and Human Development, Program in Counselor Education, Statesboro, GA 30460. Offers M Ed, Ed S. *Accreditation:* ACA; NCATE. Part-time and evening/weekend programs available. *Students:* 40 full-time (31 women), 56 part-time (48 women); includes 38 minority (33 Black or African American, non-Hispanic/Latino; 3 Hispanic/Latino; 2 Two or more races, non-Hispanic/Latino), 1 international. Average age 32. 30 applicants, 97% accepted, 10 enrolled. In 2011, 36 master's, 5 Ed Ss awarded. *Degree requirements:* For master's, comprehensive exam, transition point assessments; for Ed S, comprehensive exam. *Entrance requirements:* For master's, GRE General Test or MAT, minimum GPA of 2.5, letters of recommendation, interview; for Ed S, GRE General Test or MAT, minimum graduate GPA of 3.25, letters of recommendation. Additional exam requirements/recommendations for international students: Required—TOEFL (minimum score 550 paper-based; 213 computer-based; 80 iBT). *Application deadline:* For fall admission, 3/15 for domestic and international students; for spring admission, 10/15 for domestic students, 10/1 for international students. Applications are processed on a rolling basis. Application fee: $50. Electronic applications accepted. *Expenses:* Tuition, state resident: full-time $6300; part-time $263 per semester hour. Tuition, nonresident: full-time $25,174; part-time $1049 per semester hour. *Required fees:* $1872. *Financial support:* In 2011–12, 21 students received support, including research assistantships with partial tuition reimbursements available (averaging $7,200 per year), teaching assistantships with partial tuition reimbursements available (averaging $7,200 per year); career-related internships or fieldwork, Federal Work-Study, scholarships/grants, tuition waivers (partial), and unspecified assistantships also available. Support available to part-time students. Financial award application deadline: 4/15; financial award applicants required to submit FAFSA. *Faculty research:* School counseling, test development, gender equity, career counseling. *Unit head:* Dr. Fayth Parks, Coordinator, 912-478-5738, Fax: 912-478-7104, E-mail: fparks@georgiasouthern.edu. *Application contact:* Amanda Gilliland, Coordinator for Graduate Student Recruitment, 912-478-5384, Fax: 912-478-0740, E-mail: gradadmissions@georgiasouthern.edu. Web site: http://coe.georgiasouthern.edu/hhd/courselored.html.

Georgia State University, College of Education, Department of Counseling and Psychological Services, Program in Professional Counseling, Atlanta, GA 30302-3083. Offers counseling psychology (PhD); counselor education and practice (PhD); professional counseling (MS, Ed S). *Accreditation:* ACA (one or more programs are accredited); APA (one or more programs are accredited). *Degree requirements:* For master's, comprehensive exam; for doctorate, comprehensive exam, thesis/dissertation. *Entrance requirements:* For master's, GRE General Test, minimum GPA of 2.5; for doctorate, GRE General Test, minimum GPA of 3.3; for Ed S, GRE General Test, minimum graduate GPA of 3.25. *Faculty research:* Dropout prevention, school reform, school violence, lifestyle correlates, stress management.

Georgia State University, College of Education, Department of Counseling and Psychological Services, Program in School Counseling, Atlanta, GA 30302-3083. Offers M Ed, Ed S. *Accreditation:* ACA (one or more programs are accredited); NCATE. *Degree requirements:* For master's, comprehensive exam. *Entrance requirements:* For master's, GRE General Test, minimum GPA of 2.5; for Ed S, GRE General Test, minimum graduate GPA of 3.25. *Faculty research:* School reform, play therapy and counseling through play, school violence, school consolation.

Grambling State University, School of Graduate Studies and Research, College of Education, Department of Educational Leadership, Grambling, LA 71245. Offers curriculum and instruction (Ed D); developmental education (MS, Ed D), including curriculum and instruction: reading (Ed D), English (MS), guidance and counseling (MS), higher education administration (Ed D), instructional systems and technology (Ed D), mathematics (MS), reading (MS), science (MS), student development and personnel services (Ed D); educational leadership (MS, Ed D). Part-time and evening/weekend programs available. *Degree requirements:* For master's, comprehensive exam, thesis (for some programs); for doctorate, comprehensive exam, thesis/dissertation. *Entrance requirements:* For master's, GRE, minimum GPA of 2.5 on last degree; for doctorate, GRE (minimum 1000, 500 on Verbal), master's degree, minimum GPA of 3.0 on last degree. Additional exam requirements/recommendations for international students: Required—TOEFL (minimum score 500 paper-based; 173 computer-based; 61 iBT). Electronic applications accepted. *Expenses:* Tuition, state resident: full-time $3546; part-time $192 per credit hour. Tuition, nonresident: full-time $3456; part-time $192 per credit hour. *Required fees:* $1829; $1829 per semester hour.

Grand Canyon University, College of Nursing and Health Sciences, Phoenix, AZ 85017-1097. Offers addiction counseling (MS); health care administration (MS); health care informatics (MS); marriage and family therapy (MS); professional counseling (MS); public health (MS). Part-time and evening/weekend programs available. Postbaccalaureate distance learning degree programs offered (no on-campus study). *Entrance requirements:* For master's, undergraduate degree with minimum GPA of 2.8. Additional exam requirements/recommendations for international students: Required—TOEFL (minimum score 575 paper-based; 233 computer-based; 90 iBT), IELTS (minimum score 7).

Gwynedd-Mercy College, School of Education, Gwynedd Valley, PA 19437-0901. Offers educational administration (MS); master teacher (MS); reading (MS); school counseling (MS); special education (MS). Part-time and evening/weekend programs available. *Faculty:* 8 full-time (5 women), 38 part-time/adjunct (24 women). *Students:* 33 full-time (22 women), 157 part-time (116 women); includes 33 minority (22 Black or African American, non-Hispanic/Latino; 5 Asian, non-Hispanic/Latino; 5 Hispanic/Latino), 1 international. Average age 33. In 2011, 186 master's awarded. *Degree requirements:* For master's, thesis, internship, practicum. *Entrance requirements:* For master's, GRE or MAT; PRAXIS I, minimum GPA of 3.0. *Application deadline:* Applications are processed on a rolling basis. Application fee: $25. *Expenses: Tuition:* Part-time $630 per credit hour. *Financial support:* In 2011–12, 2 research assistantships were awarded; career-related internships or fieldwork, Federal Work-Study, tuition waivers (full and partial), unspecified assistantships, and Federal Stafford loans, Federal work study, alternative loans, graduate assistantships also available. Financial award applicants required to submit FAFSA. *Faculty research:* Learning and the brain, reading literacy, ethics and moral judgment, leadership, teaching and multicultural education. *Unit head:* Dr. Sandra Mangano, Dean, 215-641-5549, Fax: 215-542-4695, E-mail: mangano.s@gmc.edu. *Application contact:* Graduate Program Coordinator. Web site: http://www.gmc.edu/academics/education/.

Hampton University, Graduate College, College of Education and Continuing Studies, Program in Counseling, Hampton, VA 23668. Offers college student development (MA); community agency counseling (MA); pastoral counseling (MA); school counseling (MA). *Accreditation:* NCATE. Part-time and evening/weekend programs available. *Entrance requirements:* For master's, GRE General Test.

Harding University, College of Education, Searcy, AR 72149-0001. Offers advanced studies in teaching and learning (M Ed); art (MSE); behavioral science (MSE); counseling (MS, Ed S); early childhood special education (M Ed, MSE); education (MSE); educational leadership (M Ed, Ed S); elementary education (M Ed); English (MSE); French (MSE); history/social science (MSE); kinesiology (MSE); math (MSE); reading (M Ed); secondary education (M Ed); Spanish (MSE); teaching (MAT); teaching English as a second language (MSE). *Accreditation:* NCATE. Part-time and evening/weekend programs available. *Faculty:* 9 full-time (2 women), 48 part-time/adjunct (26 women). *Students:* 100 full-time (77 women), 333 part-time (239 women); includes 76 minority (59 Black or African American, non-Hispanic/Latino; 1 Asian, non-Hispanic/Latino; 10 Hispanic/Latino; 6 Two or more races, non-Hispanic/Latino), 2 international. Average age 36. 93 applicants, 91% accepted, 83 enrolled. In 2011, 159 master's, 10 other advanced degrees awarded. *Degree requirements:* For master's, comprehensive exam (for some programs), thesis optional, portfolio(s); for Ed S, comprehensive exam, portfolio, project. *Entrance requirements:* For master's, GRE, MAT, PRAXIS; for Ed S, MAT or GRE. Additional exam requirements/recommendations for international students: Required—TOEFL (minimum score 550 paper-based; 79 iBT). *Application deadline:* For fall admission, 8/1 for domestic and international students; for spring admission, 1/1 for domestic and international students. Applications are processed on a rolling basis. Application fee: $35. *Expenses: Tuition:* Full-time $10,512; part-time $584 per credit hour. *Required fees:* $500; $25 per credit hour. Tuition and fees vary according to course load, degree level and program. *Financial support:* In 2011–12, 37 students received support. Unspecified assistantships available. *Faculty research:* Reading, comprehension, school violence, educational technology, behavior, college choice, differentiated instruction, brain-based teaching. *Unit head:* Dr. Clara Carroll, Chair, 501-279-4501, Fax: 501-279-4083, E-mail: ccarroll@harding.edu. *Application contact:* Information Contact, 501-279-4315, E-mail: gradstudiesedu@harding.edu. Web site: http://www.harding.edu/education/grad.html.

Hardin-Simmons University, Graduate School, Irvin School of Education, Department of Counseling and Human Development, Abilene, TX 79698-0001. Offers M Ed. Part-time programs available. *Faculty:* 3 full-time (2 women), 3 part-time/adjunct (2 women). *Students:* 42 full-time (30 women), 19 part-time (15 women); includes 14 minority (7 Black or African American, non-Hispanic/Latino; 1 American Indian or Alaska Native, non-Hispanic/Latino; 6 Hispanic/Latino), 1 international. Average age 31. 22 applicants, 95% accepted, 19 enrolled. In 2011, 25 master's awarded. *Degree requirements:* For master's, comprehensive exam, practicum. *Entrance requirements:* For master's, minimum undergraduate GPA of 3.0 in major, 2.7 overall; interview; 3 letters of recommendation; resume. Additional exam requirements/recommendations for international students: Required—TOEFL (minimum score 550 paper-based; 213 computer-based; 75 iBT). *Application deadline:* For fall admission, 8/15 priority date for domestic students, 4/1 for international students; for spring admission, 1/5 priority date for domestic students, 9/1 for international students. Applications are processed on a rolling basis. Application fee: $50. *Expenses: Tuition:* Full-time $12,870; part-time $715 per credit hour. *Required fees:* $650; $110 per semester. Tuition and fees vary according to degree level. *Financial support:* In 2011–12, 5 fellowships (averaging $1,230 per year) were awarded; career-related internships or fieldwork and scholarships/grants also available. Support available to part-time students. Financial award application deadline: 6/30; financial award applicants required to submit FAFSA. *Unit head:* Dr. Robert Barnes, Head, 325-670-1451, Fax: 325-670-5859, E-mail: rbarnes@hsutx.edu. *Application contact:* Dr. Nancy Kucinski, Dean of Graduate Studies, 325-670-1298, Fax: 325-670-1564, E-mail: gradoff@hsutx.edu. Web site: http://www.hsutx.edu/academics/irvin/graduate/counseling.

Henderson State University, Graduate Studies, Teachers College, Department of Counselor Education, Arkadelphia, AR 71999-0001. Offers clinical mental health counseling (MSE); elementary school counseling (MSE); secondary school counseling (MSE). *Accreditation:* ACA; NCATE. Part-time programs available. *Entrance requirements:* For master's, GRE General Test or MAT, letters of recommendation, minimum GPA of 2.7, teacher certification. Additional exam requirements/recommendations for international students: Required—TOEFL (minimum score 550 paper-based; 213 computer-based); Recommended—IELTS (minimum score 6). Electronic applications accepted.

Heritage University, Graduate Programs in Education, Program in Counseling, Toppenish, WA 98948-9599. Offers M Ed. Part-time programs available. *Degree requirements:* For master's, comprehensive exam. *Entrance requirements:* For master's, interview, letters of recommendation, at least 9 semester-credits of behavioral sciences.

Hofstra University, School of Education, Health, and Human Services, Programs in Counseling, Hempstead, NY 11549. Offers counseling (MS Ed, PD); creative arts therapy (MA); gerontology (MS, Advanced Certificate); interdisciplinary transition specialist (Advanced Certificate); marriage and family therapy (MA); mental health counseling (MA); rehabilitation counseling (MS Ed, Advanced Certificate, PD); rehabilitation counseling in mental health (MS Ed, Advanced Certificate); school counselor-bilingual extension (Advanced Certificate). Part-time and evening/weekend programs available. *Students:* 172 full-time (152 women), 73 part-time (71 women); includes 49 minority (25 Black or African American, non-Hispanic/Latino; 6 Asian, non-Hispanic/Latino; 15 Hispanic/Latino; 1 Native Hawaiian or other Pacific Islander, non-Hispanic/Latino; 2 Two or more races, non-Hispanic/Latino), 11 international. Average age 29. 202 applicants, 70% accepted, 85 enrolled. In 2011, 79 master's, 1 other advanced degree awarded. *Degree requirements:* For master's, comprehensive exam (for some programs), thesis (for some programs), internship, practicum, student teaching, seminars, minimum GPA of 3.0. *Entrance requirements:* For master's, GRE, interview, letters of recommendation, portfolio, essay, professional experience, certification; for other advanced degree, GRE, interview, letters of recommendation, essay, professional experience, resume, master's degree. Additional exam requirements/recommendations for international students: Required—TOEFL (minimum score 550 paper-based; 213 computer-based; 80 iBT). *Application deadline:* Applications are processed on a rolling basis. Application fee: $70 ($75 for international students). Electronic applications accepted. *Expenses: Tuition:* Full-time $18,990; part-time $1055 per credit hour. *Required fees:* $970. Tuition and fees vary according to program. *Financial support:* In 2011–12, 138 students received support, including 39 fellowships with full and partial tuition reimbursements available (averaging $2,751 per year), 8 research assistantships with full and partial tuition reimbursements available (averaging $12,943 per year); career-related internships or fieldwork, Federal Work-Study, institutionally sponsored loans, scholarships/grants, tuition waivers (full and partial), and unspecified assistantships also available. Support available to part-time students. Financial award applicants required to submit FAFSA. *Faculty research:* Bereavement, loss, and trauma counseling; creativity for non-artists. *Unit head:* Dr. Darra Pace, Chairperson, 516-463-6476, Fax: 516-463-6415, E-mail: cprdzp@hofstra.edu. *Application contact:* Carol Drummer, Dean of Graduate Admissions, 516-463-4876, Fax: 516-463-4664, E-mail: gradstudent@hofstra.edu. Web site: http://www.hofstra.edu/education/.

Houston Baptist University, College of Education and Behavioral Sciences, Programs in Education, Houston, TX 77074-3298. Offers bilingual education (M Ed); counselor education (M Ed); curriculum and instruction (M Ed); educational administration (M Ed); educational diagnostician (M Ed); reading education (M Ed). Part-time programs available. *Entrance requirements:* For master's, GRE General Test or MAT. Additional exam requirements/recommendations for international students: Required—TOEFL (minimum score 550 paper-based; 213 computer-based).

Howard University, School of Education, Department of Human Development and Psychoeducational Studies, Program in Counseling and Guidance, Washington, DC 20059-0002. Offers school psychology and counseling services (M Ed). *Accreditation:* NCATE. Part-time programs available. *Faculty:* 2 full-time (1 woman), 1 (woman) part-time/adjunct. *Students:* 8 full-time (all women), 9 part-time (6 women); includes 14 minority (13 Black or African American, non-Hispanic/Latino; 1 Asian, non-Hispanic/Latino). Average age 29. 13 applicants, 77% accepted, 7 enrolled. In 2011, 4 master's awarded. *Entrance requirements:* Additional exam requirements/recommendations for international students: Required—TOEFL (minimum score 550 paper-based). *Application deadline:* For fall admission, 2/15 priority date for domestic students; for spring admission, 11/1 for domestic students. Applications are processed on a rolling basis. Application fee: $45. Electronic applications accepted. *Financial support:* In 2011–12, 2 students received support, including 2 research assistantships (averaging $4,000 per year); fellowships with full and partial tuition reimbursements available, career-related internships or fieldwork, Federal Work-Study, institutionally sponsored loans, scholarships/grants, and unspecified assistantships also available. Financial award application deadline: 3/15. *Faculty research:* Law and forensic evaluation, juvenile justice, ethics, clinical assessment, personality disorders, substance abuse. *Unit head:* Dr. Mercedes Ebanks, Assistant Professor/Coordinator, 202-806-5780, Fax: 202-806-5205, E-mail: mebanks@howard.edu. *Application contact:* Menbere Endale, Administration Assistant, Department of Human Development and Psychoeducational Studies, 202-806-7351, Fax: 202-806-5205, E-mail: mendale@howard.edu.

Howard University, School of Education, Department of Human Development and Psychoeducational Studies, Program in School Psychology, Washington, DC 20059-0002. Offers school psychology (PhD); school psychology and counseling services (M Ed). *Accreditation:* NCATE. *Faculty:* 2 full-time (0 women), 1 part-time/adjunct (0 women). *Students:* 39 full-time (29 women), 10 part-time (7 women); includes 35 minority (32 Black or African American, non-Hispanic/Latino; 2 Hispanic/Latino; 1 Two or more races, non-Hispanic/Latino), 13 international. Average age 32. 35 applicants, 69% accepted, 13 enrolled. In 2011, 7 master's, 1 doctorate awarded. *Degree requirements:* For master's, comprehensive exam, thesis (MA), expository writing exam, practicum; for doctorate, one foreign language, comprehensive exam, thesis/dissertation, expository writing exam, internship. *Entrance requirements:* For master's, GRE General Test, minimum GPA of 2.7; for doctorate, GRE General Test, minimum GPA of 3.4. Additional exam requirements/recommendations for international students: Required—TOEFL (minimum score 550 paper-based). *Application deadline:* For fall admission, 2/15 priority date for domestic students; for spring admission, 11/1 for domestic students. Applications are processed on a rolling basis. Application fee: $45. Electronic applications accepted. *Financial support:* In 2011–12, 5 students received support, including 4 fellowships with full and partial tuition reimbursements available (averaging $16,000 per year), 1 research assistantship (averaging $4,000 per year); career-related internships or fieldwork, Federal Work-Study, institutionally sponsored loans, scholarships/grants, and unspecified assistantships also available. Financial award application deadline: 3/15; financial award applicants required to submit FAFSA. *Faculty research:* Psychopathology, maltreatment abuse and neglect, children exposed to political unrest, family conflict and community violence. *Unit head:* Dr. Salman M. Elbedour, Professor/Coordinator, 202-806-6412, Fax: 202-806-5205, E-mail: selbedour@howard.edu. *Application contact:* Menbere Endale, Administration Assistant, Department of Human Development and Psychoeducational Studies, 202-806-7351, Fax: 202-806-5205, E-mail: mendale@howard.edu.

Hunter College of the City University of New York, Graduate School, School of Education, Department of Educational Foundations and Counseling Programs, Programs in School Counselor, New York, NY 10021-5085. Offers school counseling (MS Ed); school counseling with bilingual extension (MS Ed). *Accreditation:* ACA; NCATE. *Faculty:* 2 full-time (both women), 3 part-time/adjunct (0 women). *Students:* 41 full-time (37 women), 69 part-time (59 women); includes 47 minority (16 Black or African American, non-Hispanic/Latino; 6 Asian, non-Hispanic/Latino; 25 Hispanic/Latino), 2 international. Average age 29. 250 applicants, 15% accepted, 21 enrolled. In 2011, 33 master's awarded. *Degree requirements:* For master's, thesis, internship, practicum, research seminar. *Entrance requirements:* For master's, interview, minimum GPA of 2.7. Additional exam requirements/recommendations for international students: Required—TOEFL, TWE. *Application deadline:* For fall admission, 4/1 for domestic students, 2/1 for international students; for spring admission, 11/1 for domestic students, 9/1 for international students. Applications are processed on a rolling basis. Application fee: $125. *Expenses:* Tuition, state resident: full-time $8210; part-time $345 per credit. Tuition, nonresident: full-time $15,360; part-time $640 per credit. *Required fees:* $280 per semester. One-time fee: $125. Tuition and fees vary according to class time, campus/location and program. *Financial support:* Federal Work-Study and tuition waivers (partial) available. Support available to part-time students. *Unit head:* Dr. Tamara Buckley, Coordinator, 212-772-4758, E-mail: tamara.buckley@hunter.cuny.edu. *Application contact:* William Zlata, Director for Graduate Admissions, 212-772-4482, Fax: 212-650-3336, E-mail: admissions@hunter.cuny.edu. Web site: http://www.hunter.cuny.edu/school-of-education/programs/graduate/counseling/school-counseling.

Husson University, School of Graduate and Professional Studies, Graduate Programs in Counseling and Human Relations, Bangor, ME 04401-2999. Offers clinical mental health counseling (MS); human relations (MS); pastoral counseling (MS); school counseling (MS). Part-time and evening/weekend programs available. *Faculty:* 3 full-time (2 women), 6 part-time/adjunct (3 women). *Students:* 48 full-time (37 women), 24 part-time (14 women); includes 3 minority (2 Black or African American, non-Hispanic/Latino; 1 Two or more races, non-Hispanic/Latino), 1 international. 8 applicants, 88% accepted, 6 enrolled. In 2011, 17 master's awarded. *Degree requirements:* For master's, comprehensive exam (for some programs), thesis optional. *Entrance requirements:* For master's, GRE, BS with minimum GPA of 3.0. Additional exam requirements/recommendations for international students: Required—TOEFL (minimum score 550 paper-based). *Application deadline:* For fall admission, 2/1 for domestic students. Applications are processed on a rolling basis. Application fee: $40. *Expenses: Tuition:* Full-time $4500; part-time $500 per credit hour. One-time fee: $100. Tuition and fees vary according to class time, degree level and program. *Financial support:* Federal Work-Study, scholarships/grants, and unspecified assistantships available. Financial award application deadline: 4/15; financial award applicants required to submit FAFSA. *Unit head:* Dr. Deborah Drew, Dean, Graduate Studies, 207-992-4912, Fax: 207-992-4952, E-mail: drewd@husson.edu. *Application contact:* Kristen M. Card, Director of Graduate Admissions, 207-404-5660, Fax: 207-941-7935, E-mail: cardk@husson.edu. Web site: http://www.husson.edu/human-relations.

Idaho State University, Office of Graduate Studies, Kasiska College of Health Professions, Department of Counseling, Pocatello, ID 83209-8120. Offers counseling (M Coun, Ed S), including marriage and family counseling (M Coun), mental health counseling (M Coun), school counseling (M Coun), student affairs and college counseling (M Coun); counselor education and counseling (PhD). *Accreditation:* ACA (one or more programs are accredited). Part-time programs available. *Degree requirements:* For master's, comprehensive exam, thesis, 4 semesters resident graduate study, practicum/internship; for doctorate, comprehensive exam, thesis/dissertation, 3 semesters internship, 4 consecutive semesters doctoral-level study on campus; for Ed S, comprehensive exam, thesis, case studies, oral exam. *Entrance requirements:* For master's, GRE General Test, MAT, minimum GPA of 3.0, bachelors degree, interview, 3 letters of recommendation; for doctorate, GRE General Test, MAT, minimum graduate GPA of 3.0, resume, interview, counseling license, master's degree; for Ed S, GRE General Test, minimum graduate GPA of 3.0, master's degree in counseling, 3 letters of recommendation, 2 years work experience. Additional exam requirements/recommendations for international students: Required—TOEFL (minimum score 600 paper-based; 213 computer-based; 80 iBT). Electronic applications accepted. *Faculty research:* Group counseling, multicultural counseling, family counseling, child therapy, supervision.

Immaculata University, College of Graduate Studies, Department of Psychology, Immaculata, PA 19345. Offers clinical psychology (Psy D); counseling psychology (MA, Certificate), including school guidance counselor (Certificate), school psychologist (Certificate). *Accreditation:* APA. Part-time and evening/weekend programs available. Terminal master's awarded for partial completion of doctoral program. *Degree requirements:* For master's, comprehensive exam, thesis optional; for doctorate, comprehensive exam, thesis/dissertation. *Entrance requirements:* For master's, GRE General Test or MAT, minimum GPA of 3.0; for doctorate, GRE General Test or MAT, minimum GPA of 3.5. Additional exam requirements/recommendations for international students: Required—TOEFL, IELTS. Electronic applications accepted. *Faculty research:* Supervision ethics, psychology of teaching, gender.

Indiana State University, College of Graduate and Professional Studies, College of Education, Department of Communication Disorders, Counseling and School and Educational Psychology, Terre Haute, IN 47809. Offers counseling psychology (MS, PhD); counselor education (PhD); mental health counseling (MS); school counseling (M Ed); school psychology (PhD, Ed S); MA/MS. *Accreditation:* ACA; NCATE. Part-time and evening/weekend programs available. *Degree requirements:* For master's, thesis optional; for doctorate, thesis/dissertation, research tools proficiency tests. *Entrance requirements:* For master's, GRE General Test or MAT, minimum undergraduate GPA of 2.75; for doctorate, GRE General Test, master's degree, minimum undergraduate GPA of 3.5. Electronic applications accepted. *Faculty research:* Vocational development supervision.

Indiana University Bloomington, School of Education, Department of Counseling and Educational Psychology, Bloomington, IN 47405-1006. Offers counseling (MS, PhD, Ed S); counselor education (MS, Ed S); educational psychology (MS, PhD); inquiry methodology (PhD); learning and developmental sciences (MS, PhD); school psychology (PhD, Ed S). *Accreditation:* ACA (one or more programs are accredited); APA (one or more programs are accredited); NCATE. Terminal master's awarded for partial completion of doctoral program. *Degree requirements:* For master's, thesis optional; for doctorate, thesis/dissertation; for Ed S, comprehensive exam or project. *Entrance requirements:* For master's, doctorate, and Ed S, GRE General Test. Additional exam requirements/recommendations for international students: Required—TOEFL. Electronic applications accepted. *Faculty research:* Counseling psychology, inquiry methodology, school psychology, learning sciences, human development, educational psychology.

Indiana University of Pennsylvania, School of Graduate Studies and Research, College of Education and Educational Technology, Department of Counseling, Program in School Counseling, Indiana, PA 15705-1087. Offers M Ed. Part-time programs available. *Faculty:* 11 full-time (9 women), 6 part-time/adjunct (all women). *Students:* 31 full-time (27 women), 43 part-time (34 women); includes 6 minority (2 Black or African American, non-Hispanic/Latino; 1 Asian, non-Hispanic/Latino; 1 Hispanic/Latino; 2 Two or more races, non-Hispanic/Latino). Average age 27. 81 applicants, 49% accepted, 33 enrolled. In 2011, 25 master's awarded. *Entrance requirements:* Additional exam requirements/recommendations for international students: Required—TOEFL (minimum score 450 paper-based; 207 computer-based). *Application deadline:* Applications are processed on a rolling basis. Application fee: $50. Electronic applications accepted. *Expenses:* Tuition, state resident: full-time $7488; part-time $416 per credit. Tuition, nonresident: full-time $11,232; part-time $624 per credit. *Required fees:* $2070; $192.20 per credit. $90 per semester. *Financial support:* In 2011–12, 8 research assistantships (averaging $4,420 per year) were awarded. *Unit head:* Dr. Claire Dandeneau, Chairperson/Graduate Coordinator, 724-357-2306, E-mail: candean@iup.edu. *Application contact:* Dr. Edward Nardi, Associate Dean, 724-357-2480, Fax: 724-357-5595, E-mail: ewnardi@iup.edu. Web site: http://www.iup.edu/grad/schoolcounseling/.

Indiana University–Purdue University Fort Wayne, College of Education and Public Policy, Department of Professional Studies, Fort Wayne, IN 46805-1499. Offers counselor education (MS Ed); educational leadership (MS Ed); marriage and family therapy (MS Ed); school counseling (MS Ed); special education (MS Ed, Certificate). Part-time programs available. *Faculty:* 6 full-time (5 women), 1 (woman) part-time/adjunct. *Students:* 2 full-time (1 woman), 158 part-time (124 women); includes 19 minority (11 Black or African American, non-Hispanic/Latino; 6 Hispanic/Latino; 2 Two or more races, non-Hispanic/Latino), 1 international. Average age 33. 59 applicants, 56% accepted, 32 enrolled. In 2011, 56 master's awarded. *Degree requirements:* For master's, comprehensive exam, practicum, internship, portfolio. *Entrance requirements:* For master's, minimum GPA of 2.5, three professional letters of recommendation. Additional exam requirements/recommendations for international students: Required—TOEFL (minimum score 550 paper-based; 213 computer-based; 77 iBT). *Application deadline:* For fall admission, 4/1 priority date for domestic students, 4/1 for international students. Applications are processed on a rolling basis. Application fee: $55. *Financial support:* Research assistantships, teaching assistantships, and scholarships/grants available. Support available to part-time students. Financial award application deadline: 3/1; financial award applicants required to submit FAFSA. *Faculty research:* Improving education with stronger collaborations. *Unit head:* Dr. James Burg, Interim Chair, 260-481-5406, Fax: 260-481-5408, E-mail: burgj@ipfw.edu. *Application contact:* Vicky L. Schmidt, Graduate Recorder, 260-481-6450, Fax: 260-481-5408, E-mail: schmidt@ipfw.edu. Web site: http://www.ipfw.edu/education.

Indiana University–Purdue University Indianapolis, School of Education, Indianapolis, IN 46202-2896. Offers computer education (Certificate); curriculum and instruction (MS); early childhood (MS); educational leadership (MS, Certificate); English as a second language (Certificate); higher education and student affairs (MS); kindergarten (Certificate); language education (MS); reading (Certificate); school counseling (MS); special education (MS, Certificate). Part-time and evening/weekend programs available. *Faculty:* 41 full-time, 80 part-time/adjunct. *Students:* 67 full-time (52 women), 467 part-time (360 women); includes 82 minority (44 Black or African American, non-Hispanic/Latino; 3 American Indian or Alaska Native, non-Hispanic/Latino; 8 Asian, non-Hispanic/Latino; 13 Hispanic/Latino; 14 Two or more races, non-Hispanic/Latino), 10 international. Average age 33. 63 applicants, 57% accepted, 29 enrolled. In 2011, 167 master's awarded. *Degree requirements:* For master's, thesis optional. *Entrance requirements:* For master's, GRE General Test, minimum GPA of 3.0. Additional exam requirements/recommendations for international students: Required—TOEFL. *Application deadline:* For fall admission, 5/1 priority date for domestic students; for spring admission, 11/1 for domestic students. Application fee: $55 ($65 for international students). *Financial support:* Fellowships, research assistantships with partial tuition reimbursements, teaching assistantships, Federal Work-Study, institutionally sponsored loans, scholarships/grants, and tuition waivers (partial) available. Support available to part-time students. *Faculty research:* Teachers in the process of change, learning cycles, children's concepts of science. *Total annual research expenditures:* $614,458. *Unit head:* Dr. Chris Leland, Interim Executive Associate Dean, 317-274-6801, Fax: 317-274-6864. *Application contact:* Sarah Brandenburg, Graduate Advisor, 317-274-6801, Fax: 317-274-6864, E-mail: edugrad@iupui.edu. Web site: http://education.iupui.edu/.

Indiana University South Bend, School of Education, South Bend, IN 46634-7111. Offers counseling and human services (MS Ed); elementary education (MS Ed); secondary education (MS Ed); special education (MS Ed). *Accreditation:* NCATE. Part-time and evening/weekend programs available. *Faculty:* 21 full-time (11 women), 9 part-time/adjunct (3 women). *Students:* 70 full-time (45 women), 262 part-time (206 women); includes 39 minority (15 Black or African American, non-Hispanic/Latino; 3 American Indian or Alaska Native, non-Hispanic/Latino; 5 Asian, non-Hispanic/Latino; 14 Hispanic/Latino; 2 Two or more races, non-Hispanic/Latino), 15 international. Average age 36. 52 applicants, 75% accepted, 28 enrolled. In 2011, 75 master's awarded. *Degree requirements:* For master's, thesis or alternative, exit project. *Entrance requirements:* For master's, letters of recommendation, GRE or minimum GPA of 3.0. Additional exam requirements/recommendations for international students: Required—TOEFL. *Application deadline:* For fall admission, 7/1 for domestic students; for spring admission, 11/1 for domestic students. Applications are processed on a rolling basis. Application fee: $50 ($60 for international students). Electronic applications accepted. *Financial support:* Career-related internships or fieldwork available. Support available to part-time students. Financial award application deadline: 3/1; financial award applicants required to submit FAFSA. *Faculty research:* Professional dispositions, early childhood literacy, online learning, program assessments, problem-based learning. *Unit head:* Dr. Michael Horvath, Professor/Dean, 574-520-4339, Fax: 574-520-4550. *Application contact:* Dr. Todd Norris, Director of Education Student Services, 574-520-4845, E-mail: toanorri@iusb.edu. Web site: http://www.iusb.edu/~edud/.

Indiana University Southeast, School of Education, New Albany, IN 47150-6405. Offers counselor education (MS Ed); elementary education (MS Ed); secondary education (MS Ed). *Accreditation:* NCATE. Part-time and evening/weekend programs available. *Students:* 31 full-time (24 women), 622 part-time (497 women); includes 83 minority (63 Black or African American, non-Hispanic/Latino; 2 American Indian or Alaska Native, non-Hispanic/Latino; 5 Asian, non-Hispanic/Latino; 8 Hispanic/Latino; 5 Two or more races, non-Hispanic/Latino). Average age 33. 99 applicants, 93% accepted, 75 enrolled. In 2011, 143 master's awarded. *Entrance requirements:* For master's, minimum undergraduate GPA of 2.5, graduate 3.0. *Application deadline:* Applications are processed on a rolling basis. Application fee: $35. *Financial support:* Career-related internships or fieldwork, Federal Work-Study, and institutionally sponsored loans available. Support available to part-time students. Financial award applicants required to submit FAFSA. *Faculty research:* Learning styles, technology, constructivism, group process, innovative math strategies. *Unit head:* Dr. Gloria Murray, Dean, 812-941-2169, Fax: 812-941-2667, E-mail: soeinfo@ius.edu. *Application contact:* Admissions Counselor, 812-941-2212, Fax: 812-941-2595, E-mail: admissions@ius.edu. Web site: http://www.ius.edu/education/.

Indiana Wesleyan University, Graduate School, College of Arts and Sciences, Marion, IN 46953. Offers addictions counseling (MS); clinical mental health counseling (MS); community counseling (MS); marriage and family therapy (MS); school counseling (MS); student development counseling and administration (MS). *Accreditation:* ACA. Part-time programs available. *Degree requirements:* For master's, thesis or alternative. *Entrance requirements:* For master's, GRE General Test. Additional exam requirements/recommendations for international students: Required—TOEFL. Electronic applications accepted. *Expenses:* Contact institution. *Faculty research:* Community counseling, multicultural counseling, addictions.

Inter American University of Puerto Rico, Arecibo Campus, Programs in Education, Arecibo, PR 00614-4050. Offers administration and educational supervision (MA Ed); counseling and guidance (MA Ed); curriculum and teaching (MA Ed), including biology education, English as a second language, history education, math education, Spanish; elementary education (MA Ed). *Degree requirements:* For master's, comprehensive exam, thesis optional. *Entrance requirements:* For master's, GRE, EXADEP, bachelor's degree in education or teaching license (administration and supervision) or courses in education and psychology (counseling and guidance), minimum GPA of 2.5 in last 60 credits.

Inter American University of Puerto Rico, Metropolitan Campus, Graduate Programs, Program in Education, San Juan, PR 00919-1293. Offers curriculum and instruction (Ed D); educational administration (Ed D); guidance and counseling (MA, Ed D); special education administration (Ed D). *Degree requirements:* For doctorate, comprehensive exam, thesis/dissertation. *Entrance requirements:* For doctorate, GRE, MAT, or EXADEP. Electronic applications accepted.

Inter American University of Puerto Rico, San Germán Campus, Graduate Studies Center, Program in Counseling and Guidance, San Germán, PR 00683-5008. Offers MA. Part-time and evening/weekend programs available. *Degree requirements:* For master's, comprehensive exam. *Entrance requirements:* For master's, GRE General Test or EXADEP, minimum GPA of 3.0. *Application deadline:* For fall admission, 4/30 priority date for domestic students; for spring admission, 11/15 for domestic students.

Applications are processed on a rolling basis. Application fee: $31. *Expenses: Required fees:* $213 per semester. *Financial support:* Teaching assistantships, Federal Work-Study, and unspecified assistantships available. *Unit head:* Dr. Elba T. Irizarry, Director of Graduate Studies Center, 787-264-1912 Ext. 7357, Fax: 787-892-6350, E-mail: elbat@sg.inter.edu.

Iowa State University of Science and Technology, Department of Educational Leadership and Policy Studies, Ames, IA 50011. Offers counselor education (M Ed, MS); educational administration (M Ed, MS); educational leadership (PhD); higher education (M Ed, MS); organizational learning and human resource development (M Ed, MS); research and evaluation (MS); student affairs (MS). *Degree requirements:* For master's, thesis or alternative; for doctorate, thesis/dissertation. *Entrance requirements:* For master's and doctorate, GRE General Test. Additional exam requirements/recommendations for international students: Required—TOEFL (minimum score 560 paper-based; 83 iBT), IELTS (minimum score 6.5). *Application deadline:* For fall admission, 1/1 priority date for domestic students, 1/1 for international students. Application fee: $40 ($90 for international students). Electronic applications accepted. *Unit head:* Dr. Daniel Robinson, Director of Graduate Education, 515-294-1241, Fax: 515-294-4942, E-mail: edldrshp@iastate.edu. *Application contact:* Judy Weiland, Application Contact, 515-294-1241, Fax: 515-294-4942, E-mail: eldrshp@iastate.edu. Web site: http://www.elps.hs.iastate.edu/.

Jackson State University, Graduate School, College of Education and Human Development, Department of School, Community and Rehabilitation Counseling, Jackson, MS 39217. Offers community and agency counseling (MS); guidance and counseling (MS, MS Ed); rehabilitation counseling (MS Ed). *Accreditation:* ACA; CORE (one or more programs are accredited); NCATE. Part-time and evening/weekend programs available. *Degree requirements:* For master's, comprehensive exam, thesis. *Entrance requirements:* For master's, GRE General Test. Additional exam requirements/recommendations for international students: Required—TOEFL (minimum score 520 paper-based; 195 computer-based; 67 iBT).

Jacksonville State University, College of Graduate Studies and Continuing Education, College of Education and Professional Studies, Program in Guidance and Counseling, Jacksonville, AL 36265-1602. Offers MS. *Accreditation:* ACA; NCATE. Part-time and evening/weekend programs available. *Degree requirements:* For master's, comprehensive exam, thesis (for some programs). *Entrance requirements:* For master's, GRE General Test or MAT. Electronic applications accepted. *Expenses:* Tuition, state resident: part-time $336 per hour. Tuition, nonresident: part-time $672 per hour. Part-time tuition and fees vary according to degree level.

John Brown University, Graduate Counseling Programs, Siloam Springs, AR 72761-2121. Offers community counseling (MS); marriage and family therapy (MS); school counseling (MS). *Accreditation:* NCATE. Part-time and evening/weekend programs available. *Faculty:* 7 full-time (1 woman), 5 part-time/adjunct (0 women). *Students:* 82 full-time (59 women), 94 part-time (64 women); includes 31 minority (10 Black or African American, non-Hispanic/Latino; 10 American Indian or Alaska Native, non-Hispanic/Latino; 2 Asian, non-Hispanic/Latino; 5 Hispanic/Latino; 4 Two or more races, non-Hispanic/Latino), 1 international. Average age 32. 57 applicants, 77% accepted. *Degree requirements:* For master's, practica or internships. *Entrance requirements:* For master's, GRE (minimum score of 1000), recommendation forms from three people, 200-word essay describing professional plans and reason for seeking acceptance. Additional exam requirements/recommendations for international students: Required—TOEFL (minimum score 550 paper-based; 213 computer-based; 70 iBT). *Application deadline:* Applications are processed on a rolling basis. Application fee: $35 ($100 for international students). Electronic applications accepted. *Expenses: Tuition:* Part-time $470 per credit hour. *Financial support:* Fellowships, institutionally sponsored loans, and scholarships/grants available. Financial award applicants required to submit FAFSA. *Unit head:* Dr. John V. Carmack, Program Director, 479-524-8630, E-mail: jcarmack@jbu.edu. *Application contact:* Nikki Rader, Graduate Counseling Representative, 479-549-5478, E-mail: nrader@jbu.edu. Web site: http://www.jbu.edu/.

John Carroll University, Graduate School, Department of Education and Allied Studies, Program in School Counseling, University Heights, OH 44118-4581. Offers M Ed, MA. *Accreditation:* ACA; NCATE. Part-time and evening/weekend programs available. *Degree requirements:* For master's, comprehensive exam, research essay or thesis (MA only). *Entrance requirements:* For master's, GRE General Test or MAT, minimum GPA of 2.75, interview. Additional exam requirements/recommendations for international students: Required—TOEFL. Electronic applications accepted.

John Carroll University, Graduate School, Program in Community Counseling, University Heights, OH 44118-4581. Offers clinical counseling (Certificate); community counseling (MA). *Accreditation:* ACA. Part-time and evening/weekend programs available. *Degree requirements:* For master's, comprehensive exam, internship, practicum. *Entrance requirements:* For master's, MAT or GRE, minimum GPA of 2.75, statement of volunteer experience, interview, 12-18 hours social science course work, survey. Additional exam requirements/recommendations for international students: Required—TOEFL. Electronic applications accepted. *Faculty research:* Child and adolescent development, HIV, hypnosis, wellness, women's issues.

The Johns Hopkins University, School of Education, Department of Counseling and Human Services, Baltimore, MD 21218. Offers clinical community counseling (Certificate); clinical supervision (Certificate); counseling (MS, CAGS), including clinical community counseling (MS), school counseling (MS); play therapy (Certificate). Part-time and evening/weekend programs available. *Degree requirements:* For master's, comprehensive exam. *Entrance requirements:* For master's, bachelor's degree, minimum undergraduate GPA of 3.0, 3 letters of recommendation, curriculum vitae/resume, group interview; for other advanced degree, master's degree, minimum undergraduate GPA of 3.0, 3 letters of recommendation, curriculum vitae/resume, interview. Additional exam requirements/recommendations for international students: Required—TOEFL (minimum score 600 paper-based; 250 computer-based; 100 iBT). Electronic applications accepted. *Faculty research:* College access of low-income students and students-of-color; multicultural counseling training; domestic violence, resilience, and traumatic stress; application of behaviorally-based and ethical practices to criminal justice setting and systems.

Johnson State College, Program in Counseling, Johnson, VT 05656. Offers college counseling (MA); school guidance counseling (MA); substance abuse and mental health counseling (MA). Part-time programs available. *Degree requirements:* For master's, comprehensive exam. *Entrance requirements:* For master's, interview. *Application deadline:* For fall admission, 4/1 priority date for domestic students, 4/15 for international students; for spring admission, 11/1 priority date for domestic students, 8/15 for international students. Applications are processed on a rolling basis. Application fee: $35. *Expenses: Tuition, area resident:* Part-time $459 per credit hour. Tuition, nonresident: part-time $990 per credit hour. *Financial support:* Career-related internships or fieldwork, Federal Work-Study, institutionally sponsored loans, and unspecified assistantships available. Support available to part-time students. Financial award application deadline: 3/1; financial award applicants required to submit FAFSA. *Application contact:* Catherine H. Higley, Administrative Assistant, 800-635-2356 Ext. 1244, Fax: 802-635-1248, E-mail: catherine.higley@jsc.edu.

Kansas State University, Graduate School, College of Education, Department of Special Education, Counseling and Student Affairs, Manhattan, KS 66506. Offers academic advising (MS); counseling and student development (MS, Ed D, PhD), including college student development (MS), counselor education and supervision (PhD), school counseling (MS), student affairs in higher education (PhD); special education (MS, Ed D). *Accreditation:* ACA; NCATE. Part-time programs available. *Faculty:* 8 full-time (4 women), 4 part-time/adjunct (1 woman). *Students:* 87 full-time (64 women), 323 part-time (251 women); includes 62 minority (27 Black or African American, non-Hispanic/Latino; 4 American Indian or Alaska Native, non-Hispanic/Latino; 5 Asian, non-Hispanic/Latino; 19 Hispanic/Latino; 2 Native Hawaiian or other Pacific Islander, non-Hispanic/Latino; 5 Two or more races, non-Hispanic/Latino), 4 international. Average age 34. 236 applicants, 70% accepted, 83 enrolled. In 2011, 111 master's, 2 doctorates awarded. *Degree requirements:* For master's, comprehensive exam; for doctorate, comprehensive exam, thesis/dissertation. *Entrance requirements:* For master's, minimum undergraduate GPA of 3.0; for doctorate, GRE General Test, minimum GPA of 3.0 in last 60 hours. Additional exam requirements/recommendations for international students: Required—TOEFL. *Application deadline:* For fall admission, 2/1 priority date for domestic students, 2/1 for international students; for spring admission, 8/1 priority date for domestic students, 8/1 for international students. Applications are processed on a rolling basis. Application fee: $40 ($55 for international students). Electronic applications accepted. *Financial support:* In 2011–12, 3 teaching assistantships (averaging $18,090 per year) were awarded; career-related internships or fieldwork, institutionally sponsored loans, and scholarships/grants also available. Financial award application deadline: 3/1; financial award applicants required to submit FAFSA. *Faculty research:* Counseling supervision, academic advising, career development, student development, universal design for learning, autism, learning disabilities. *Total annual research expenditures:* $2,678. *Unit head:* Kenneth Hughey, Head, 785-532-6445, Fax: 785-532-7304, E-mail: khughey@ksu.edu. *Application contact:* Dona Deam, Application Contact, 785-532-5595, Fax: 785-532-7304, E-mail: ddeam@ksu.edu. Web site: http://coe.ksu.edu/departments/secsa/index.htm.

Kean University, Nathan Weiss Graduate College, Program in Counselor Education, Union, NJ 07083. Offers alcohol and drug abuse counseling (MA); clinical mental heath counseling (MA); school counseling (MA). *Accreditation:* ACA; NCATE. *Faculty:* 7 full-time (5 women). *Students:* 85 full-time (67 women), 200 part-time (174 women); includes 99 minority (49 Black or African American, non-Hispanic/Latino; 6 Asian, non-Hispanic/Latino; 43 Hispanic/Latino; 1 Two or more races, non-Hispanic/Latino), 1 international. Average age 32. 137 applicants, 74% accepted, 65 enrolled. In 2011, 68 master's awarded. *Degree requirements:* For master's, practicum, internship, portfolio. *Entrance requirements:* For master's, GRE General Test or MAT, minimum GPA of 3.0, 2 letters of recommendation, interview, personal statement. Additional exam requirements/recommendations for international students: Required—TOEFL (minimum score 79 iBT). *Application deadline:* For fall admission, 6/1 for domestic and international students; for spring admission, 12/1 for domestic and international students. Applications are processed on a rolling basis. Application fee: $75 ($150 for international students). Electronic applications accepted. *Expenses:* Tuition, state resident: full-time $11,302; part-time $550 per credit. Tuition, nonresident: full-time $15,318; part-time $674 per credit. *Required fees:* $2849; $130 per credit. Tuition and fees vary according to degree level. *Financial support:* In 2011–12, 3 research assistantships with full tuition reimbursements (averaging $3,263 per year) were awarded; unspecified assistantships also available. Financial award applicants required to submit FAFSA. *Unit head:* Dr. J. Barry Mascari, Program Coordinator, 908-737-3863, E-mail: jmascari@kean.edu. *Application contact:* Steven Koch, Admissions Counselor, 908-737-5924, Fax: 908-737-5925, E-mail: skoch@kean.edu. Web site: http://www.kean.edu/KU/Alcohol-and-Drug-Abuse-Counseling.

Keene State College, School of Professional and Graduate Studies, Keene, NH 03435. Offers curriculum and instruction (M Ed); education leadership (PMC); educational leadership (M Ed); safety and occupational health applied science (MS); school counselor (M Ed, PMC); special education (M Ed); teacher certification (Postbaccalaureate Certificate). *Accreditation:* NCATE. Part-time and evening/weekend programs available. *Faculty:* 11 full-time (7 women), 15 part-time/adjunct (8 women). *Students:* 36 full-time (32 women), 69 part-time (54 women); includes 1 minority (American Indian or Alaska Native, non-Hispanic/Latino), 1 international. Average age 33. 48 applicants, 83% accepted, 32 enrolled. In 2011, 39 master's, 12 other advanced degrees awarded. *Entrance requirements:* For master's, PRAXIS I, resume; minimum GPA of 2.5. Additional exam requirements/recommendations for international students: Required—TOEFL (minimum score 550 paper-based; 173 computer-based; 61 iBT). *Application deadline:* For fall admission, 4/1 for domestic students; for spring admission, 12/1 for domestic students. Applications are processed on a rolling basis. Application fee: $50. Electronic applications accepted. *Expenses:* Tuition, state resident: part-time $420 per credit. Tuition, nonresident: part-time $460 per credit. Tuition and fees vary according to course load. *Financial support:* Research assistantships, career-related internships or fieldwork, Federal Work-Study, institutionally sponsored loans, and unspecified assistantships available. Support available to part-time students. Financial award application deadline: 3/1; financial award applicants required to submit FAFSA. *Unit head:* Dr. Melinda Treadwell, Dean, 603-358-2220, E-mail: mtreadwe@keene.edu. *Application contact:* Peggy Richmond, Director of Admissions, 603-358-2276, Fax: 603-358-2767, E-mail: admissions@keene.edu. Web site: http://www.keene.edu/ps/.

Kent State University, Graduate School of Education, Health, and Human Services, School of Lifespan Development and Educational Sciences, Program in Counseling, Kent, OH 44242-0001. Offers Ed S. *Accreditation:* ACA. *Faculty:* 18 full-time (8 women), 28 part-time/adjunct (20 women). *Students:* 8 part-time (all women); includes 1 minority (Black or African American, non-Hispanic/Latino). 7 applicants, 43% accepted. In 2011, 4 Ed Ss awarded. *Entrance requirements:* For degree, 2 letters of reference, goals statement, interview. Additional exam requirements/recommendations for international students: Required—TOEFL (minimum score 550 paper-based; 213 computer-based; 80 iBT). *Application deadline:* Applications are processed on a rolling basis. Application fee: $30 ($60 for international students). Electronic applications accepted. *Expenses:* Tuition, state resident: full-time $8136; part-time $452 per credit hour. Tuition, nonresident: full-time $14,292; part-time $794 per credit hour. *Financial support:* Research assistantships, Federal Work-Study, scholarships/grants, unspecified assistantships, and 1 administrative assistantship (averaging $8,500 per year) available. *Unit head:* Dr. Jason McGlothlin, Coordinator, 330-672-0716, E-mail: jmcgloth@kent.edu. *Application contact:* Nancy Miller, Academic Program Coordinator, Office of Graduate Student Services, 330-672-2576, Fax: 330-672-9162, E-mail: ogs@kent.edu.

Kent State University, Graduate School of Education, Health, and Human Services, School of Lifespan Development and Educational Sciences, Program in Counseling and Human Development Services, Kent, OH 44242-0001. Offers PhD. *Accreditation:* ACA; NCATE. *Faculty:* 18 full-time (8 women), 28 part-time/adjunct (20 women). *Students:* 61 full-time (47 women), 9 part-time (8 women); includes 11 minority (8 Black or African American, non-Hispanic/Latino; 3 Hispanic/Latino). 27 applicants, 59% accepted. In 2011, 5 doctorates awarded. *Degree requirements:* For doctorate, comprehensive exam, thesis/dissertation. *Entrance requirements:* For doctorate, GRE General Test, preliminary written exam, 2 letters of reference, resume, interview. Additional exam requirements/recommendations for international students: Required—TOEFL (minimum score 550 paper-based; 213 computer-based; 80 iBT). *Application deadline:* For fall admission, 2/1 for domestic students. Application fee: $30 ($60 for international students). Electronic applications accepted. *Expenses:* Tuition, state resident: full-time $8136; part-time $452 per credit hour. Tuition, nonresident: full-time $14,292; part-time $794 per credit hour. *Financial support:* In 2011–12, 3 fellowships with full tuition reimbursements (averaging $12,000 per year), 10 research assistantships with full tuition reimbursements (averaging $12,000 per year) were awarded; teaching assistantships with full tuition reimbursements, career-related internships or fieldwork, Federal Work-Study, institutionally sponsored loans, scholarships/grants, health care benefits, and unspecified assistantships also available. Support available to part-time students. Financial award application deadline: 4/1; financial award applicants required to submit FAFSA. *Faculty research:* Family/child therapy, clinical supervision, group work, experiential training methods. *Unit head:* Dr. Jane Cox, Coordinator, 330-672-0698, Fax: 330-672-5396, E-mail: jcox8@kent.edu. *Application contact:* Nancy Miller, Academic Program Coordinator, Office of Graduate Student Services, 330-672-2576, Fax: 330-672-9162, E-mail: ogs@kent.edu. Web site: http://www.kent.edu/ehhs/chds/.

Kent State University, Graduate School of Education, Health, and Human Services, School of Lifespan Development and Educational Sciences, Program in School Counseling, Kent, OH 44242-0001. Offers M Ed. *Accreditation:* ACA; NCATE. *Faculty:* 18 full-time (8 women), 28 part-time/adjunct (20 women). *Students:* 44 full-time (38 women), 67 part-time (59 women); includes 8 minority (7 Black or African American, non-Hispanic/Latino; 1 Native Hawaiian or other Pacific Islander, non-Hispanic/Latino). 59 applicants, 58% accepted. In 2011, 44 master's awarded. *Entrance requirements:* For master's, minimum undergraduate GPA of 2.75, 2 letters of reference, goals statement, moral character statement, interview. Additional exam requirements/recommendations for international students: Required—TOEFL (minimum score 550 paper-based; 213 computer-based; 80 iBT). *Application deadline:* For fall admission, 6/1 for domestic students; for spring admission, 10/1 for domestic students. Application fee: $30 ($60 for international students). Electronic applications accepted. *Expenses:* Tuition, state resident: full-time $8136; part-time $452 per credit hour. Tuition, nonresident: full-time $14,292; part-time $794 per credit hour. *Financial support:* Research assistantships with full tuition reimbursements, Federal Work-Study, scholarships/grants, and unspecified assistantships available. Financial award application deadline: 4/1; financial award applicants required to submit FAFSA. *Faculty research:* Appraisal, diagnosis, group work. *Unit head:* Dr. Jason McGlothlin, Coordinator, 330-672-0716, E-mail: jmcgloth@kent.edu. *Application contact:* Nancy Miller, Academic Program Coordinator, Office of Graduate Student Services, 330-672-2576, Fax: 330-672-9162, E-mail: ogs@kent.edu.

Kutztown University of Pennsylvania, College of Education, Program in Guidance and Counseling, Kutztown, PA 19530-0730. Offers counselor education (M Ed), including elementary counseling, secondary counseling. *Accreditation:* NCATE. Part-time and evening/weekend programs available. *Faculty:* 3 full-time (all women). *Students:* 32 full-time (27 women), 56 part-time (34 women); includes 4 minority (3 Black or African American, non-Hispanic/Latino; 1 Hispanic/Latino). Average age 28. 20 applicants, 95% accepted, 5 enrolled. In 2011, 24 master's awarded. *Degree requirements:* For master's, comprehensive exam, thesis optional. *Entrance requirements:* For master's, GRE General Test, interview. Additional exam requirements/recommendations for international students: Required—TOEFL (minimum score 550 paper-based; 79 iBT). *Application deadline:* For fall admission, 3/1 for domestic and international students; for spring admission, 10/1 for domestic and international students. Application fee: $35. Electronic applications accepted. *Expenses:* Tuition, state resident: full-time $7488; part-time $416 per credit. Tuition, nonresident: full-time $11,232; part-time $624 per credit. *Financial support:* Career-related internships or fieldwork, Federal Work-Study, scholarships/grants, and unspecified assistantships available. Financial award application deadline: 3/1; financial award applicants required to submit FAFSA. *Faculty research:* Family addictions, family roles. *Unit head:* Dr. Deborah Barlieb, Chairperson, 610-683-4204, Fax: 610-683-1585, E-mail: barlieb@kutztown.edu. *Application contact:* Kelly D. Burr, Associate Director, Graduate Admissions, 610-683-4200, Fax: 610-683-1393, E-mail: graduate@kutztown.edu.

Lakeland College, Graduate Studies Division, Program in Counseling, Sheboygan, WI 53082-0359. Offers MA.

Lamar University, College of Graduate Studies, College of Education and Human Development, Department of Counseling and Special Populations, Beaumont, TX 77710. Offers counseling and development (M Ed); school counseling (M Ed); special education (M Ed); student affairs (Certificate). *Faculty:* 7 full-time (5 women). *Students:* 9 full-time (5 women), 654 part-time (619 women); includes 239 minority (140 Black or African American, non-Hispanic/Latino; 8 American Indian or Alaska Native, non-Hispanic/Latino; 8 Asian, non-Hispanic/Latino; 83 Hispanic/Latino). Average age 36. 525 applicants, 96% accepted, 201 enrolled. In 2011, 15 master's awarded. *Application deadline:* For fall admission, 8/1 for domestic students; for spring admission, 12/1 for domestic students. Applications are processed on a rolling basis. Application fee: $25 ($50 for international students). *Expenses:* Tuition, state resident: full-time $5430; part-time $272 per credit hour. Tuition, nonresident: full-time $11,540; part-time $577 per credit hour. *Required fees:* $1916. *Unit head:* Dr. Carl J. Sheperis, Chair, 409-880-8978, Fax: 409-880-2263. *Application contact:* Dr. Lula Henry, Director of Professional Service, 409-880-8218. Web site: http://dept.lamar.edu/counseling/.

Lamar University, College of Graduate Studies, College of Education and Human Development, Department of Educational Leadership, Beaumont, TX 77710. Offers counseling and development (M Ed, Certificate); education administration (M Ed); educational leadership (DE); principal (Certificate); school superintendent (Certificate); supervision (M Ed); technology application (Certificate). Part-time and evening/weekend programs available. *Faculty:* 19 full-time (8 women), 2 part-time/adjunct (1 woman). *Students:* 23 full-time (14 women), 1,716 part-time (1,106 women); includes 476 minority (246 Black or African American, non-Hispanic/Latino; 13 American Indian or Alaska Native, non-Hispanic/Latino; 18 Asian, non-Hispanic/Latino; 198 Hispanic/Latino; 1 Two or more races, non-Hispanic/Latino), 1 international. Average age 37. 956 applicants, 97% accepted, 547 enrolled. In 2011, 1,609 master's, 16 doctorates awarded. Terminal master's awarded for partial completion of doctoral program. *Degree requirements:* For master's, comprehensive exam, thesis optional; for doctorate, thesis/dissertation. *Entrance requirements:* For master's, GRE General Test, minimum GPA of 2.5; for doctorate, GRE. Additional exam requirements/recommendations for international students: Required—TOEFL. *Application deadline:* For fall admission, 8/1 priority date for domestic students; for spring admission, 12/1 priority date for domestic students. Applications are processed on a rolling basis. Application fee: $25 ($50 for international students). *Expenses:* Tuition, state resident: full-time $5430; part-time $272 per credit hour. Tuition, nonresident: full-time $11,540; part-time $577 per credit hour. *Required fees:* $1916. *Financial support:* In 2011–12, 3 fellowships (averaging $20,000 per year), 1 research assistantship with tuition reimbursement (averaging $6,500 per year) were awarded; teaching assistantships with tuition reimbursements, career-related internships or fieldwork, and scholarships/grants also available. Support available to part-time students. Financial award application deadline: 4/1. *Faculty research:* School dropouts, suicide prevention in public school students, school climate and gifted performance, teacher evaluation. *Unit head:* Dr. Carolyn Crawford, Chair, 409-880-8689, Fax: 409-880-8685. *Application contact:* Dr. Lula Henry, Director of Professional Service, 409-880-8218.

Lancaster Bible College, Graduate School, Lancaster, PA 17601-5036. Offers adult ministries (MA); Bible (MA); children and family ministry (MA); consulting resource teacher (M Ed); elementary school counseling (M Ed); leadership (PhD); leadership studies (MA); marriage and family counseling (MA); mental health counseling (MA); pastoral studies (MA); secondary school counseling (M Ed); student ministry (MA). Part-time and evening/weekend programs available. *Degree requirements:* For master's, comprehensive exam (for some programs), thesis (for some programs). *Entrance requirements:* For master's, bachelor's degree with a minimum of 30 credits of course work in Bible, minimum undergraduate GPA of 3.0, interview. Additional exam requirements/recommendations for international students: Required—TOEFL.

La Sierra University, School of Education, Department of School Psychology and Counseling, Riverside, CA 92515. Offers counseling (MA); educational psychology (Ed S); school psychology (Ed S). Part-time and evening/weekend programs available. *Degree requirements:* For master's, thesis optional; for Ed S, practicum (educational psychology). *Entrance requirements:* For master's, California Basic Educational Skills Test, NTE, minimum GPA of 3.0; for Ed S, minimum GPA of 3.3. *Faculty research:* Equivalent score scales, self perception.

Lee University, Graduate Studies in Counseling, Cleveland, TN 37320-3450. Offers college student development (MS); holistic child development (MS); marriage and family therapy (MS); school counseling (MS). Part-time programs available. *Faculty:* 6 full-time (0 women), 7 part-time/adjunct (2 women). *Students:* 66 full-time (53 women), 34 part-time (29 women); includes 6 minority (1 American Indian or Alaska Native, non-Hispanic/Latino; 1 Asian, non-Hispanic/Latino; 3 Hispanic/Latino; 1 Two or more races, non-Hispanic/Latino), 6 international. Average age 27. 57 applicants, 56% accepted, 30 enrolled. In 2011, 44 master's awarded. *Degree requirements:* For master's, variable foreign language requirement, comprehensive exam, thesis, internship. *Entrance requirements:* For master's, GRE General Test or MAT, minimum undergraduate GPA of 3.0, 3 letters of recommendation, interview. Additional exam requirements/recommendations for international students: Required—TOEFL (minimum score 450 paper-based; 45 computer-based). *Application deadline:* For fall admission, 4/1 priority date for domestic students, 4/1 for international students; for spring admission, 10/1 priority date for domestic students, 10/1 for international students. Applications are processed on a rolling basis. Application fee: $25. *Expenses: Tuition:* Full-time $12,120; part-time $506 per credit hour. *Required fees:* $560; $305 per term. Part-time tuition and fees vary according to course load. *Financial support:* In 2011–12, 21 teaching assistantships (averaging $569 per year) were awarded; career-related internships or fieldwork, Federal Work-Study, institutionally sponsored loans, scholarships/grants, and unspecified assistantships also available. Financial award application deadline: 3/1; financial award applicants required to submit FAFSA. *Unit head:* Dr. Trevor Milliron, Director, 423-614-8126, Fax: 423-614-8129, E-mail: tmilliron@leeuniversity.edu. *Application contact:* Vicki Glasscock, Graduate Admissions Director, 423-614-8059, E-mail: vglasscock@leeuniversity.edu. Web site: http://www.leeuniversity.edu/academics/graduate/arts.

Lehigh University, College of Education, Program in Comparative and International Education, Bethlehem, PA 18015. Offers comparative and international education (MA); globalization and educational change (M Ed); international counseling (Certificate); international development in education (Certificate); special education (Certificate); technology use in schools (Certificate); TESOL (Certificate). Part-time programs available. Postbaccalaureate distance learning degree programs offered (no on-campus study). *Faculty:* 4 full-time (2 women). *Students:* 25 full-time (10 women), 45 part-time (31 women); includes 5 minority (all Asian, non-Hispanic/Latino), 16 international. Average age 34. 45 applicants, 71% accepted, 12 enrolled. In 2011, 21 master's awarded. *Degree requirements:* For master's, thesis (MA). *Entrance requirements:* For master's, 2 letters of recommendation. Additional exam requirements/recommendations for international students: Required—TOEFL (minimum score 600 paper-based; 250 computer-based; 93 iBT). *Application deadline:* For fall and spring admission, 2/1 for domestic and international students. Application fee: $65. Electronic applications accepted. *Financial support:* In 2011–12, 8 students received support, including 3 research assistantships with full and partial tuition reimbursements available (averaging $13,000 per year). Financial award application deadline: 3/15. *Faculty research:* Comparative education, rural education, gender equity in education, post-socialist education transformation, educational borrowing, comparing education systems, education policy an globalization, family-school relationships, China, international testing, social inequities. *Unit head:* Dr. Iveta Silova, Program Director and Associate Professor, 610-758-5750, Fax: 610-758-6223, E-mail: ism207@lehigh.edu. *Application contact:* Donna M. Johnson, Coordinator, 610-758-3231, Fax: 610-758-6223, E-mail: dmj4@lehigh.edu. Web site: http://www.lehigh.edu/education/cie.

Lehigh University, College of Education, Program in Counseling Psychology, Bethlehem, PA 18015. Offers counseling and human services (M Ed); counseling psychology (PhD); elementary counseling with certification (M Ed); international counseling (M Ed, Certificate); secondary school counseling with certification (M Ed). *Accreditation:* APA (one or more programs are accredited). Part-time and evening/weekend programs available. Postbaccalaureate distance learning degree programs offered (minimal on-campus study). *Faculty:* 4 full-time (3 women), 9 part-time/adjunct (7 women). *Students:* 52 full-time (49 women), 31 part-time (27 women); includes 8 minority (5 Black or African American, non-Hispanic/Latino; 2 Asian, non-Hispanic/Latino; 1 Hispanic/Latino), 6 international. Average age 28. 193 applicants, 31% accepted, 19 enrolled. In 2011, 26 master's, 9 doctorates awarded. *Degree requirements:* For doctorate, comprehensive exam, thesis/dissertation. *Entrance requirements:* For master's, minimum GPA of 3.0, 2 letters of recommendation, essay, transcript; for doctorate, GRE General Test (Verbal and Quantitative), 2 letters of recommendation, transcript, essay; for Certificate, minimum GPA of 3.0. Additional exam requirements/recommendations for international students: Required—TOEFL (minimum score 600 paper-based; 250 computer-based; 93 iBT). *Application deadline:* For fall admission, 3/1 for domestic students, 11/15 for international students; for winter admission, 2/1 for international students. Application fee: $65. Electronic applications accepted. Application fee is waived when completed online. *Financial support:* In 2011–12, 21 students received support, including 1 research assistantship with full and partial tuition reimbursement available (averaging $16,000 per year); fellowships with full and partial tuition reimbursements available, career-related internships or fieldwork, Federal Work-Study, institutionally sponsored loans, scholarships/grants, tuition waivers (full and partial), and unspecified assistantships also available. Financial award application deadline: 2/15; financial award applicants required to submit FAFSA. *Faculty research:* Supervision, violence prevention, multicultural training and counseling, career development and health interventions, intersection of identities. *Unit head:* Dr. Arpana Inman, Coordinator, 610-758-4443, Fax: 610-758-3227, E-mail: agi2@lehigh.edu. *Application contact:* Donna M. Johnson, Coordinator, 610-758-3231, Fax: 610-758-6223, E-mail: dmj4@lehigh.edu.

Lehman College of the City University of New York, Division of Education, Department of Specialized Services in Education, Program in Guidance and

Counseling, Bronx, NY 10468-1589. Offers MS Ed. *Accreditation:* ACA; NCATE. Part-time and evening/weekend programs available. *Degree requirements:* For master's, thesis. *Entrance requirements:* For master's, minimum GPA of 2.7. *Faculty research:* Crisis intervention, domestic violence, alcohol abuse, gender issues.

Lenoir-Rhyne University, Graduate Programs, School of Counseling and Human Services, Program in School Counseling, Hickory, NC 28601. Offers MA. Part-time and evening/weekend programs available. *Degree requirements:* For master's, comprehensive exam, thesis optional. *Entrance requirements:* For master's, GRE General Test, minimum undergraduate GPA of 2.7, graduate 3.0; writing sample. Additional exam requirements/recommendations for international students: Required—TOEFL (minimum score 600 paper-based). Electronic applications accepted.

Lenoir-Rhyne University, Graduate Programs, School of Counseling and Human Services, Programs in Counseling, Hickory, NC 28601. Offers agency counseling (MA); community counseling (MA). Part-time and evening/weekend programs available. *Degree requirements:* For master's, comprehensive exam, thesis optional. *Entrance requirements:* For master's, GRE General Test, writing sample, minimum undergraduate GPA of 2.7, minimum graduate GPA of 3.0. Additional exam requirements/recommendations for international students: Required—TOEFL (minimum score 600 paper-based). Electronic applications accepted.

Lewis University, College of Arts and Sciences, Program in School Counseling, Romeoville, IL 60446. Offers MA. Part-time and evening/weekend programs available. *Faculty:* 5 full-time (3 women), 10 part-time/adjunct (6 women). *Students:* 72 full-time (58 women), 107 part-time (82 women); includes 50 minority (39 Black or African American, non-Hispanic/Latino; 2 Asian, non-Hispanic/Latino; 8 Hispanic/Latino; 1 Two or more races, non-Hispanic/Latino). Average age 30. In 2011, 73 master's awarded. *Degree requirements:* For master's, comprehensive exam. *Entrance requirements:* For master's, letters of recommendation, interview, minimum GPA of 2.75. Additional exam requirements/recommendations for international students: Required—TOEFL (minimum score 550 paper-based; 213 computer-based; 80 iBT). *Application deadline:* For fall admission, 5/1 for international students; for spring admission, 11/15 for international students. Applications are processed on a rolling basis. Application fee: $40. Electronic applications accepted. *Financial support:* Federal Work-Study, scholarships/grants, tuition waivers (full and partial), and unspecified assistantships available. Financial award application deadline: 5/1; financial award applicants required to submit FAFSA. *Unit head:* Dr. Judith Zito, Director, 815-838-0500 Ext. 5971, E-mail: zitoju@lewisu.edu.

Liberty University, School of Education, Lynchburg, VA 24502. Offers administration and supervision (M Ed); curriculum and instruction (M Ed); early childhood education (M Ed); educational leadership (Ed D, Ed S); educational technology and online instruction (M Ed); elementary education (M Ed, MAT); gifted education (M Ed); math specialist (M Ed); middle grades (M Ed); outdoor adventure sport (MS); reading specialist (M Ed); school counseling (M Ed); secondary education (M Ed, MAT); special education (M Ed, MAT); sports administration (MS); teaching and learning (Ed D, Ed S). *Accreditation:* NCATE. Part-time programs available. Postbaccalaureate distance learning degree programs offered (minimal on-campus study). *Students:* 2,245 full-time (1,572 women), 3,500 part-time (2,558 women); includes 1,141 minority (888 Black or African American, non-Hispanic/Latino; 19 American Indian or Alaska Native, non-Hispanic/Latino; 21 Asian, non-Hispanic/Latino; 123 Hispanic/Latino; 9 Native Hawaiian or other Pacific Islander, non-Hispanic/Latino; 81 Two or more races, non-Hispanic/Latino), 76 international. Average age 37. In 2011, 760 master's, 48 doctorates, 321 other advanced degrees awarded. *Degree requirements:* For doctorate, comprehensive exam, thesis/dissertation. *Entrance requirements:* For master's, GRE General Test or MAT (if taken in or before 1999), 2 letters of recommendation, minimum undergraduate GPA of 3.0, curriculum vitae; for doctorate, GRE General Test or MAT (if taken before 1999), minimum master's GPA of 3.0, 3 years of teacher experience; for Ed S, GRE General Test or MAT (if taken before 1999), minimum master's GPA of 3.0, 3 years of teaching experience. Additional exam requirements/recommendations for international students: Required—TOEFL (minimum score 600 paper-based; 250 computer-based). *Application deadline:* For fall admission, 6/1 priority date for domestic students; for spring admission, 11/1 for domestic students. Applications are processed on a rolling basis. Application fee: $50. Electronic applications accepted. *Expenses:* Contact institution. *Financial support:* Federal Work-Study and tuition waivers (partial) available. *Faculty research:* Self-determination, character education, bibliotherapy, learning styles, distance education. *Unit head:* Dr. Karen L. Parker, Dean, 434-582-2195, Fax: 434-582-2468, E-mail: kparker@liberty.edu. *Application contact:* Jay Bridge, Director of Graduate Admissions, 800-424-9595, Fax: 800-628-7977, E-mail: gradadmissions@liberty.edu. Web site: http://www.liberty.edu/academics/education/graduate/.

Lincoln Memorial University, Carter and Moyers School of Education, Harrogate, TN 37752-1901. Offers administration and supervision (M Ed, Ed S); counseling and guidance (M Ed); curriculum and instruction (M Ed, Ed D, Ed S); English (M Ed); executive leadership (Ed D); higher education administration (Ed D); human resource development (Ed D); leadership and administration (Ed D). Part-time and evening/weekend programs available. Postbaccalaureate distance learning degree programs offered. *Degree requirements:* For master's, comprehensive exam, thesis optional; for Ed S, comprehensive exam. *Entrance requirements:* For master's, PRAXIS, NTE, GRE, MAT, letters of recommendation; for Ed S, graduate transcripts. Additional exam requirements/recommendations for international students: Recommended—TOEFL. *Faculty research:* Brain compatible teaching and learning; poverty in Appalachia; leadership for change; ethics, moral responsibility and social justice; human and organizational learning.

Lincoln University, School of Graduate Studies and Continuing Education, Jefferson City, MO 65102. Offers business administration (MBA), including accounting, entrepreneurship, management, public administration and policy; educational leadership (Ed S), including elementary leadership, secondary leadership, superintendency; guidance and counseling (M Ed), including community/agency counseling, elementary school, secondary school; history (MA); school administration and supervision (M Ed), including elementary school administration, secondary school administration, special education administration; school teaching (M Ed), including elementary school teaching, secondary school teaching; social science (MA), including history, political science, sociology; sociology (MA); sociology/criminal justice (MA). Part-time and evening/weekend programs available. *Degree requirements:* For master's and Ed S, comprehensive exam, thesis optional. *Entrance requirements:* For master's and Ed S, GRE, MAT or GMAT, minimum GPA of 2.75 in major, 2.5 overall; 3 letters of recommendation; minimum C average in English composition; personal statement of purpose. Additional exam requirements/recommendations for international students: Required—TOEFL (minimum score 500 paper-based; 173 computer-based; 61 iBT). *Faculty research:* Suicide prevention.

Loma Linda University, School of Science and Technology, Department of Counseling and Family Science, Loma Linda, CA 92350. Offers MA, MS, DMFT, PhD, Certificate, MA/Certificate. *Degree requirements:* For master's, comprehensive exam, thesis optional; for doctorate, comprehensive exam, thesis/dissertation (for some programs). *Entrance requirements:* For master's, minimum GPA of 3.0; for doctorate, GRE. Additional exam requirements/recommendations for international students: Required—TOEFL (minimum score 550 paper-based; 213 computer-based), MTELP. Electronic applications accepted.

Long Island University–Brentwood Campus, School of Education, Brentwood, NY 11717. Offers childhood education (MS); early childhood education (MS); literacy (MS); mental health counseling (MS); school counseling (MS); special education (MS). Part-time and evening/weekend programs available.

Long Island University–Brooklyn Campus, School of Education, Department of Human Development and Leadership, Program in Counseling and Development, Brooklyn, NY 11201-8423. Offers MS, MS Ed, Certificate. *Degree requirements:* For master's, thesis optional. *Entrance requirements:* For master's, 2 letters of recommendation. Additional exam requirements/recommendations for international students: Required—TOEFL (minimum score 500 paper-based; 173 computer-based).

Long Island University–C. W. Post Campus, School of Education, Department of Counseling and Development, Brookville, NY 11548-1300. Offers mental health counseling (MS); school counseling (MS). *Accreditation:* ACA. Part-time and evening/weekend programs available. *Degree requirements:* For master's, comprehensive exam or thesis, internship. *Entrance requirements:* For master's, interview, minimum GPA of 3.0. Electronic applications accepted. *Faculty research:* Community prevention programs, youth gang violence, community mental health counseling.

Long Island University–Hudson at Rockland, Graduate School, Program in Counseling and Development, Orangeburg, NY 10962. Offers mental health counseling (MS); school counselor (MS Ed). Part-time and evening/weekend programs available. *Entrance requirements:* For master's, transcripts, letters of recommendation, personal statement, interview. Additional exam requirements/recommendations for international students: Required—TOEFL (minimum score 79 iBT).

Long Island University–Hudson at Westchester, Programs in Education-School Counselor and School Psychology, Purchase, NY 10577. Offers school counselor (MS Ed); school psychologist (MS Ed). Part-time and evening/weekend programs available.

Longwood University, Office of Graduate Studies, College of Education and Human Services, Farmville, VA 23909. Offers communication sciences and disorders (MS); community and college counseling (MS); curriculum and instruction specialist-elementary (MS), including mild disabilities, modern languages; curriculum and instruction specialist-secondary (MS), including English, mild disabilities, modern languages; educational leadership (MS); guidance and counseling (MS); literacy and culture (MS); school library media (MS). *Accreditation:* NCATE. Part-time and evening/weekend programs available. *Degree requirements:* For master's, comprehensive exam, thesis optional. *Entrance requirements:* For master's, GRE (communication sciences and disorders), minimum GPA of 2.75. Additional exam requirements/recommendations for international students: Required—TOEFL (minimum score 550 paper-based; 213 computer-based).

Louisiana State University and Agricultural and Mechanical College, Graduate School, College of Education, Department of Educational Theory, Policy and Practice, Baton Rouge, LA 70803. Offers counseling (M Ed, MA, Ed S); educational administration (M Ed, MA, PhD, Ed S); educational technology (MA); elementary education (M Ed, MAT); higher education (PhD); research methodology (PhD); secondary education (M Ed, MAT). PhD programs offered jointly with Louisiana State University in Shreveport. *Accreditation:* ACA (one or more programs are accredited); NCATE. Part-time and evening/weekend programs available. *Faculty:* 17 full-time (all women). *Students:* 188 full-time (145 women), 161 part-time (130 women); includes 104 minority (88 Black or African American, non-Hispanic/Latino; 1 American Indian or Alaska Native, non-Hispanic/Latino; 6 Asian, non-Hispanic/Latino; 5 Hispanic/Latino; 4 Two or more races, non-Hispanic/Latino), 9 international. Average age 31. 151 applicants, 61% accepted, 58 enrolled. In 2011, 129 master's, 17 doctorates, 11 other advanced degrees awarded. Terminal master's awarded for partial completion of doctoral program. *Degree requirements:* For doctorate, thesis/dissertation; for Ed S, thesis optional. *Entrance requirements:* For master's and doctorate, GRE General Test, minimum GPA of 3.0. Additional exam requirements/recommendations for international students: Required—TOEFL (minimum score 550 paper-based; 213 computer-based; 79 iBT) or IELTS (minimum score 6.5). *Application deadline:* For fall admission, 1/25 priority date for domestic students, 5/15 for international students; for spring admission, 10/15 for international students. Applications are processed on a rolling basis. Application fee: $50 ($70 for international students). Electronic applications accepted. *Financial support:* In 2011–12, 230 students received support, including 2 fellowships (averaging $19,353 per year), 24 research assistantships with full and partial tuition reimbursements available (averaging $10,052 per year), 53 teaching assistantships with full and partial tuition reimbursements available (averaging $12,218 per year); career-related internships or fieldwork, Federal Work-Study, institutionally sponsored loans, health care benefits, and unspecified assistantships also available. Support available to part-time students. Financial award applicants required to submit FAFSA. *Faculty research:* Literary, curriculum studies, science education, K-12 leadership, higher education. *Total annual research expenditures:* $774,887. *Unit head:* Dr. Earl Cheek, Jr., Chair, 225-578-6867, Fax: 225-578-9135, E-mail: echeek@lsu.edu. *Application contact:* Dr. Rita Culross, Graduate Coordinator, 225-578-6867, Fax: 225-578-9135, E-mail: acrita@lsu.edu.

Louisiana State University in Shreveport, College of Business, Education, and Human Development, Program in Education, Shreveport, LA 71115-2399. Offers education curriculum and instruction (M Ed); educational leadership (M Ed); school counseling (M Ed). Part-time programs available. *Students:* 6 full-time (all women), 55 part-time (40 women); includes 14 minority (12 Black or African American, non-Hispanic/Latino; 1 Asian, non-Hispanic/Latino; 1 Hispanic/Latino). Average age 35. 34 applicants, 97% accepted, 13 enrolled. In 2011, 14 master's awarded. *Degree requirements:* For master's, orally-presented project, 200-hour internship (educational leadership). *Entrance requirements:* For master's, GRE, minimum GPA of 2.5; teacher certification; recommendations and interview (for educational leadership). Additional exam requirements/recommendations for international students: Required—TOEFL (minimum score 550 paper-based; 213 computer-based; 80 iBT). *Application deadline:* For fall admission, 6/30 for domestic and international students; for spring admission, 11/30 for domestic and international students. Applications are processed on a rolling basis. Application fee: $10 ($20 for international students). *Financial support:* In 2011–12, 5 research assistantships (averaging $2,150 per year) were awarded. *Unit head:* Dr. Julie Bergeron, Coordinator, 318-797-5033, Fax: 318-798-4144, E-mail: julie.bergeron@lsus.edu. *Application contact:* Christianne Wojcik, Director of Academic Services, 318-797-5247, Fax: 318-798-4120, E-mail: christianne.wojcik@lsus.edu.

Louisiana Tech University, Graduate School, College of Education, Department of Behavioral Sciences and Psychology, Ruston, LA 71272. Offers counseling (MA); counseling psychology (PhD); industrial/organizational psychology (MA); special education (MA). *Accreditation:* APA (one or more programs are accredited). Part-time programs available. *Degree requirements:* For master's, thesis or alternative; for doctorate, thesis/dissertation. *Entrance requirements:* For master's and doctorate, GRE General Test.

Counselor Education

Loyola Marymount University, School of Education, Department of Educational Support Services, Program in Counseling, Los Angeles, CA 90045. Offers MA. Part-time programs available. *Faculty:* 10 full-time (5 women), 36 part-time/adjunct (27 women). *Students:* 145 full-time (119 women), 8 part-time (all women); includes 104 minority (24 Black or African American, non-Hispanic/Latino; 12 Asian, non-Hispanic/Latino; 59 Hispanic/Latino; 9 Two or more races, non-Hispanic/Latino). Average age 27. 49 applicants, 94% accepted, 35 enrolled. In 2011, 46 master's awarded. *Degree requirements:* For master's, comprehensive exam. *Entrance requirements:* For master's, CBEST, 2 letters of recommendation, letter of intent. Additional exam requirements/recommendations for international students: Required—TOEFL (minimum score 600 paper-based; 250 computer-based; 100 iBT). *Application deadline:* For fall admission, 6/15 for domestic students; for spring admission, 11/15 for domestic students. Application fee: $50. Electronic applications accepted. *Financial support:* In 2011–12, 68 students received support, including 4 research assistantships (averaging $924 per year); scholarships/grants and unspecified assistantships also available. Support available to part-time students. Financial award application deadline: 6/15; financial award applicants required to submit FAFSA. *Unit head:* Dr. Nick Ladany, Director, 310-258-5591, E-mail: nladany@lmu.edu. *Application contact:* Chake H. Kouyoumjian, Associate Dean of Graduate Studies, 310-338-2721, E-mail: ckouyoum@lmu.edu. Web site: http://soe.lmu.edu/admissions/programs/counseling.htm.

Loyola Marymount University, School of Education, Department of Educational Support Services, Program in Guidance and Counseling, Los Angeles, CA 90045. Offers MA. Part-time programs available. *Faculty:* 10 full-time (5 women), 36 part-time/adjunct (27 women). *Students:* 25 full-time (22 women), 5 part-time (4 women); includes 24 minority (8 Black or African American, non-Hispanic/Latino; 4 Asian, non-Hispanic/Latino; 11 Hispanic/Latino; 1 Two or more races, non-Hispanic/Latino), 1 international. Average age 28. 27 applicants, 85% accepted, 11 enrolled. In 2011, 8 master's awarded. *Degree requirements:* For master's, comprehensive exam. *Entrance requirements:* For master's, CBEST, 2 letters of recommendation, letter of intent. Additional exam requirements/recommendations for international students: Required—TOEFL (minimum score 600 paper-based; 250 computer-based; 100 iBT). *Application deadline:* For fall admission, 6/15 for domestic students; for spring admission, 11/15 for domestic students. Application fee: $50. Electronic applications accepted. *Financial support:* In 2011–12, 13 students received support, including 1 research assistantship (averaging $720 per year); scholarships/grants and unspecified assistantships also available. Support available to part-time students. *Unit head:* Dr. Nicholas Ladany, Program Director, 310-258-5591, E-mail: nladany@lmu.edu. *Application contact:* Chake H. Kouyoumjian, Associate Dean of Graduate Studies, 310-338-2721, E-mail: ckouyoum@lmu.edu. Web site: http://soe.lmu.edu/admissions/programs/counseling.htm.

Loyola University Chicago, School of Education, Program in School Counseling, Chicago, IL 60660. Offers M Ed, Certificate. *Accreditation:* NCATE. *Faculty:* 5 full-time (4 women), 4 part-time/adjunct (2 women). *Students:* 29. Average age 25. 44 applicants, 68% accepted, 7 enrolled. In 2011, 7 master's awarded. *Degree requirements:* For master's, comprehensive exam. *Entrance requirements:* For master's, GRE General Test, minimum GPA of 3.0, letters of recommendation, resume. Additional exam requirements/recommendations for international students: Required—TOEFL (minimum score 550 paper-based; 213 computer-based; 79 iBT). *Application deadline:* For fall admission, 1/1 for domestic and international students. Application fee: $50. Electronic applications accepted. Application fee is waived when completed online. *Expenses: Tuition:* Full-time $15,660; part-time $870 per credit hour. *Required fees:* $125 per semester. Tuition and fees vary according to course load and program. *Financial support:* Career-related internships or fieldwork, institutionally sponsored loans, scholarships/grants, and tuition waivers (partial) available. Support available to part-time students. Financial award application deadline: 2/15; financial award applicants required to submit FAFSA. *Faculty research:* Career development, group counseling, family therapy, child and adolescent development, multicultural counseling. *Unit head:* Dr. Anita Thomas, Director, 312-915-7403, E-mail: athoma9@luc.edu. *Application contact:* Marie Rosin-Dittmar, Information Contact, 312-915-6800, E-mail: schleduc@luc.edu.

Loyola University Maryland, Graduate Programs, Department of Education, Program in School Counseling, Baltimore, MD 21210-2699. Offers M Ed, MA, CAS. *Accreditation:* ACA; NCATE. Part-time programs available. *Faculty:* 57 full-time (32 women), 21 part-time/adjunct (10 women). *Students:* 58 full-time (54 women), 152 part-time (130 women); includes 32 minority (21 Black or African American, non-Hispanic/Latino; 3 Asian, non-Hispanic/Latino; 4 Hispanic/Latino; 4 Two or more races, non-Hispanic/Latino), 1 international. Average age 31. In 2011, 47 master's, 1 other advanced degree awarded. *Degree requirements:* For master's, thesis. *Entrance requirements:* Additional exam requirements/recommendations for international students: Required—TOEFL (minimum score 550 paper-based; 213 computer-based). *Application deadline:* For fall admission, 6/15 priority date for domestic students; for spring admission, 11/1 priority date for domestic students. Application fee: $50. Electronic applications accepted. *Financial support:* Research assistantships and unspecified assistantships available. Financial award application deadline: 4/15; financial award applicants required to submit FAFSA. *Unit head:* Lee Richmond, Director, 410-617-1508, E-mail: lrichmond@loyola.edu. *Application contact:* Maureen Faux, Executive Director, Graduate Admissions, 410-617-5020, Fax: 410-617-2002, E-mail: graduate@loyola.edu.

Loyola University New Orleans, College of Social Sciences, Department of Counseling, Program in Counseling, New Orleans, LA 70118-6195. Offers MS. *Accreditation:* ACA. Part-time and evening/weekend programs available. *Students:* 34 full-time (28 women), 30 part-time (25 women); includes 16 minority (11 Black or African American, non-Hispanic/Latino; 5 Hispanic/Latino), 1 international. Average age 28. 56 applicants, 39% accepted, 14 enrolled. In 2011, 12 master's awarded. *Degree requirements:* For master's, comprehensive exam. *Entrance requirements:* For master's, GRE, MAT (recommended), interview, letters of recommendation, writing sample, resume, work experience. Additional exam requirements/recommendations for international students: Required—TOEFL (minimum score 550 paper-based; 213 computer-based). *Application deadline:* For fall admission, 8/1 priority date for domestic students, 8/1 for international students; for spring admission, 1/5 priority date for domestic students, 1/5 for international students. Applications are processed on a rolling basis. Application fee: $20. Electronic applications accepted. *Expenses:* Contact institution. *Financial support:* Research assistantships, career-related internships or fieldwork, and Federal Work-Study available. Support available to part-time students. Financial award application deadline: 5/1; financial award applicants required to submit FAFSA. *Faculty research:* Counseling theory, spirituality issues, group counseling, multicultural applications. *Unit head:* Le Anne Steen, Chair, 504-864-7855, Fax: 504-864-7844, E-mail: lsteen@loyno.edu. *Application contact:* 800-4LOYOLA, Fax: 504-865-3383, E-mail: admit@loyno.edu. Web site: http://css.loyno.edu/counseling.

Lynchburg College, Graduate Studies, School of Education and Human Development, M Ed Program in School Counseling, Lynchburg, VA 24501-3199. Offers M Ed. Part-time and evening/weekend programs available. *Faculty:* 4 full-time (3 women), 7 part-time/adjunct (6 women). *Students:* 18 full-time (13 women), 13 part-time (10 women); includes 5 minority (all Black or African American, non-Hispanic/Latino). Average age 31. In 2011, 4 master's awarded. *Degree requirements:* For master's, counseling internship. *Entrance requirements:* For master's, GRE, minimum GPA of 3.0 (preferred), official transcripts (bachelor's, others as relevant), three letters of recommendation, career goals statement. Additional exam requirements/recommendations for international students: Required—TOEFL (minimum score 550 paper-based; 213 computer-based; 79 iBT), IELTS (minimum score 6.5). *Application deadline:* For fall admission, 7/31 for domestic students, 6/1 for international students; for spring admission, 11/30 for domestic students, 10/15 for international students. Applications are processed on a rolling basis. Application fee: $30. Electronic applications accepted. Application fee is waived when completed online. *Expenses: Tuition:* Full-time $7740; part-time $430 per credit hour. *Financial support:* Fellowships, research assistantships, Federal Work-Study, scholarships/grants, health care benefits, and unspecified assistantships available. Support available to part-time students. Financial award application deadline: 7/31; financial award applicants required to submit FAFSA. *Unit head:* Dr. Jeanne Booth, Associate Professor/Coordinator of M Ed in School Counseling, 434-544-8551, Fax: 434-544-8483, E-mail: booth@lynchburg.edu. *Application contact:* Anne Pingstock, Executive Assistant, Graduate Studies, 434-544-8383, Fax: 434-544-8483, E-mail: gradstudies@lynchburg.edu. Web site: http://www.lynchburg.edu/schoolcounseling.xml.

Lyndon State College, Graduate Programs in Education, Department of Education, Lyndonville, VT 05851-0919. Offers curriculum and instruction (M Ed); reading specialist (M Ed); special education (M Ed); teaching and counseling (M Ed). Part-time and evening/weekend programs available. *Degree requirements:* For master's, exam or major field project. *Entrance requirements:* Additional exam requirements/recommendations for international students: Recommended—TOEFL (minimum score 500 paper-based; 173 computer-based).

Malone University, Graduate Program in Counseling and Human Development, Canton, OH 44709. Offers classroom-based counseling and advocacy (MA); clinical counseling (MA); school counseling (MA). Part-time and evening/weekend programs available. *Faculty:* 4 full-time (3 women), 11 part-time/adjunct (6 women). *Students:* 29 full-time (26 women), 121 part-time (100 women); includes 33 minority (21 Black or African American, non-Hispanic/Latino; 1 Asian, non-Hispanic/Latino; 8 Hispanic/Latino; 3 Two or more races, non-Hispanic/Latino). Average age 33. 79 applicants, 54% accepted, 37 enrolled. In 2011, 27 master's awarded. *Entrance requirements:* For master's, minimum undergraduate GPA of 3.0. Additional exam requirements/recommendations for international students: Required—TOEFL (minimum score 550 paper-based; 213 computer-based; 79 iBT). *Application deadline:* Applications are processed on a rolling basis. *Expenses: Tuition:* Part-time $625 per semester hour. Part-time tuition and fees vary according to program. *Financial support:* Tuition waivers (partial) available. Support available to part-time students. Financial award application deadline: 6/30. *Faculty research:* Spirituality and clinical counseling supervision, ethical and legal issues in counseling regarding supervision, resilience in adolescent offenders, protective factors for suicidal clients. *Unit head:* Dr. Susan L. Steiner, Director, 330-471-8510, Fax: 330-471-8343, E-mail: ssteiner@malone.edu. *Application contact:* Dan DePasquale, Senior Recruiter, 330-471-8381, Fax: 330-471-8343, E-mail: depasquale@malone.edu. Web site: http://www.malone.edu/admissions/graduate/counseling/.

Manhattan College, Graduate Division, School of Education, Program in Counseling, Riverdale, NY 10471. Offers bilingual pupil personnel services (Advanced Certificate); mental health counseling (MS, Advanced Certificate); school counseling (MA, Diploma). Part-time and evening/weekend programs available. *Faculty:* 4 full-time (2 women), 17 part-time/adjunct (10 women). *Students:* 66 full-time (55 women), 66 part-time (55 women); includes 65 minority (26 Black or African American, non-Hispanic/Latino; 5 Asian, non-Hispanic/Latino; 32 Hispanic/Latino; 2 Two or more races, non-Hispanic/Latino), 4 international. 174 applicants, 95% accepted, 48 enrolled. In 2011, 32 master's, 17 other advanced degrees awarded. *Degree requirements:* For master's, thesis, internship. *Entrance requirements:* For master's, minimum GPA of 3.0. Additional exam requirements/recommendations for international students: Recommended—TOEFL. *Application deadline:* For fall admission, 7/1 priority date for domestic students; for spring admission, 12/20 priority date for domestic students. Applications are processed on a rolling basis. Application fee: $60. *Expenses: Tuition:* Full-time $14,850; part-time $825 per credit. *Required fees:* $390; $150. *Financial support:* In 2011–12, 1 research assistantship with partial tuition reimbursement (averaging $18,000 per year) was awarded; Federal Work-Study, scholarships/grants, health care benefits, and unspecified assistantships also available. Financial award application deadline: 2/1; financial award applicants required to submit FAFSA. *Faculty research:* College advising, cognition, family counseling, group dynamics, cultural attitudes, bullying. *Unit head:* Dr. Corine Fitzpatrick, Director, 718-862-7497, Fax: 718-862-7472, E-mail: corine.fitzpatrick@manhattan.edu. *Application contact:* Dr. Corine Fitzpatrick, Director, 718-862-7497, Fax: 718-862-7472, E-mail: corine.fitzpatrick@manhattan.edu.

Marquette University, Graduate School, College of Education, Department of Counselor Education and Counseling Psychology, Milwaukee, WI 53201-1881. Offers clinical mental health counseling (MS); community counseling (MA); counseling psychology (PhD); school counseling (MA). Part-time programs available. *Faculty:* 8 full-time (4 women). *Students:* 67 full-time (46 women), 35 part-time (25 women); includes 20 minority (6 Black or African American, non-Hispanic/Latino; 3 Asian, non-Hispanic/Latino; 6 Hispanic/Latino; 5 Two or more races, non-Hispanic/Latino), 3 international. Average age 26. 177 applicants, 33% accepted, 32 enrolled. In 2011, 28 master's, 11 doctorates awarded. Terminal master's awarded for partial completion of doctoral program. *Degree requirements:* For master's, comprehensive exam, thesis (for some programs); for doctorate, thesis/dissertation, qualifying exam, supporting minor. *Entrance requirements:* For master's, GRE General Test or MAT, official transcripts from all current and previous colleges/universities except Marquette, three letters of recommendation, statement of purpose; for doctorate, GRE General Test, MAT, sample of written work, official transcripts from all current and previous colleges/universities except Marquette, three letters of recommendation, statement of purpose, resume/curriculum vitae. Additional exam requirements/recommendations for international students: Required—TOEFL (minimum score 530 paper-based; 78 computer-based). *Application deadline:* For fall admission, 1/15 for domestic and international students. Application fee: $50. *Expenses: Tuition:* Full-time $17,010; part-time $945 per credit hour. Tuition and fees vary according to program. *Financial support:* In 2011–12, 25 students received support, including 1 fellowship with partial tuition reimbursement available (averaging $17,500 per year), 6 research assistantships with partial tuition reimbursements available (averaging $13,404 per year); scholarships/grants, health care benefits, tuition waivers (partial), and unspecified assistantships also available. Support available to part-time students. Financial award application deadline: 2/15. *Faculty research:* Ethical and legal issues in education, anxiety disorders, multicultural counseling, child psychopathology, group counseling and dynamics. *Unit head:* Dr. Alan Burkard, Chair, 414-288-3434, E-mail: alan.burkard@marquette.edu. *Application contact:* Craig Pierce, Assistant Dean of the Graduate School, 414-288-5740, Fax: 414-288-1902, E-mail: craig.pierce@marquette.edu.

Marshall University, Academic Affairs Division, Graduate School of Education and Professional Development, Program in Counseling, Huntington, WV 25755. Offers MA, Ed S. *Accreditation:* NCATE. Part-time and evening/weekend programs available.

Students: 111 full-time (89 women), 88 part-time (68 women); includes 14 minority (8 Black or African American, non-Hispanic/Latino; 1 American Indian or Alaska Native, non-Hispanic/Latino; 1 Asian, non-Hispanic/Latino; 4 Hispanic/Latino), 3 international. Average age 32. In 2011, 46 master's awarded. *Degree requirements:* For master's, thesis optional, comprehensive or oral assessment. *Entrance requirements:* For master's, GRE General Test, MAT. Application fee: $40. *Financial support:* Career-related internships or fieldwork, Federal Work-Study, tuition waivers (full), and unspecified assistantships available. Support available to part-time students. Financial award applicants required to submit FAFSA. *Unit head:* Dr. Bob Rubenstein, Director, 304-746-1953, E-mail: brubenstein@marshall.edu. *Application contact:* Information Contact, 304-746-1900, Fax: 304-746-1902, E-mail: services@marshall.edu.

Marymount University, School of Education and Human Services, Program in School Counseling, Arlington, VA 22207-4299. Offers MA. *Accreditation:* ACA. Part-time programs available. *Faculty:* 6 full-time (4 women), 4 part-time/adjunct (all women). *Students:* 20 full-time (all women), 11 part-time (10 women); includes 6 minority (3 Black or African American, non-Hispanic/Latino; 2 Asian, non-Hispanic/Latino; 1 Hispanic/Latino). Average age 28. 25 applicants, 88% accepted, 11 enrolled. In 2011, 16 master's awarded. *Entrance requirements:* For master's, GRE, 2 letters of recommendation, interview, resume, personal statement. Additional exam requirements/recommendations for international students: Required—TOEFL (minimum score 600 paper-based; 250 computer-based; 96 iBT), IELTS (minimum score 6.5). *Application deadline:* For fall admission, 1/16 for domestic students, 1/15 for international students. Application fee: $40. Electronic applications accepted. *Expenses: Tuition:* Part-time $770 per credit hour. *Required fees:* $8 per credit hour. One-time fee: $180 full-time. *Financial support:* In 2011–12, 1 student received support. Research assistantships with full tuition reimbursements available, career-related internships or fieldwork, Federal Work-Study, scholarships/grants, and unspecified assistantships available. Support available to part-time students. Financial award applicants required to submit FAFSA. *Unit head:* Dr. Michele Garofalo, Director, 703-284-3822, Fax: 703-284-5708, E-mail: michele.garofalo@marymount.edu. *Application contact:* Francesca Reed, Director, Graduate Admissions, 703-284-5901, Fax: 703-527-3815, E-mail: grad.admissions@marymount.edu. Web site: http://www.marymount.edu/academics/programs/schoolCounsel.

Marywood University, Academic Affairs, Reap College of Education and Human Development, Department of Psychology and Counseling, Program in Counselor Education–Elementary, Scranton, PA 18509-1598. Offers MS. *Entrance requirements:* Additional exam requirements/recommendations for international students: Required—TOEFL (minimum score 550 paper-based; 213 computer-based; 79 iBT). *Application deadline:* For fall admission, 4/1 priority date for domestic students, 3/31 for international students; for spring admission, 11/1 priority date for domestic students, 8/31 for international students. Applications are processed on a rolling basis. Application fee: $35. Electronic applications accepted. *Financial support:* Career-related internships or fieldwork, scholarships/grants, and unspecified assistantships available. Support available to part-time students. Financial award application deadline: 6/30; financial award applicants required to submit FAFSA. *Unit head:* Dr. John Lemoncelli, Director, 570-348-6211 Ext. 2317, E-mail: lemoncelli@marywood.edu. *Application contact:* Tammy Manka, Associate Director of Graduate Admissions, 570-348-6211 Ext. 2322, E-mail: tmanka@marywood.edu. Web site: http://www.marywood.edu/psych-couns/graduate/counselor-education/.

Marywood University, Academic Affairs, Reap College of Education and Human Development, Department of Psychology and Counseling, Program in Counselor Education–Secondary, Scranton, PA 18509-1598. Offers MS. *Entrance requirements:* Additional exam requirements/recommendations for international students: Required—TOEFL (minimum score 550 paper-based; 213 computer-based; 79 iBT). *Application deadline:* For fall admission, 4/1 priority date for domestic students, 3/31 for international students; for spring admission, 11/1 priority date for domestic students, 8/31 for international students. Applications are processed on a rolling basis. Application fee: $35. Electronic applications accepted. *Financial support:* Career-related internships or fieldwork, scholarships/grants, and unspecified assistantships available. Support available to part-time students. Financial award application deadline: 6/30; financial award applicants required to submit FAFSA. *Unit head:* Dr. John Lemoncelli, Director, 570-348-6211 Ext. 2317, E-mail: lemoncelli@marywood.edu. *Application contact:* Tammy Manka, Associate Director of Graduate Admissions, 570-348-6211 Ext. 2322, E-mail: tmanka@marywood.edu. Web site: http://www.marywood.edu/psych-couns/graduate/counselor-education/.

McDaniel College, Graduate and Professional Studies, Program in Guidance and Counseling, Westminster, MD 21157-4390. Offers MS. Part-time and evening/weekend programs available. *Degree requirements:* For master's, comprehensive exam, thesis optional, internship. *Entrance requirements:* For master's, GRE General Test, MAT, or NTE/PRAXIS I, letters of reference (3). Additional exam requirements/recommendations for international students: Required—TOEFL (minimum score 213 computer-based).

McNeese State University, Doré School of Graduate Studies, Burton College of Education, Department of Education Professions, Program in School Counseling, Lake Charles, LA 70609. Offers M Ed. *Accreditation:* NCATE. Evening/weekend programs available. *Faculty:* 1 (woman) full-time, 1 (woman) part-time/adjunct. *Students:* 12 full-time (11 women), 29 part-time (24 women); includes 14 minority (13 Black or African American, non-Hispanic/Latino; 1 Hispanic/Latino). In 2011, 5 master's awarded. *Entrance requirements:* For master's, GRE, 18 hours in professional education. *Application deadline:* For fall admission, 5/15 priority date for domestic students, 5/15 for international students; for spring admission, 10/15 priority date for domestic students, 10/15 for international students. Applications are processed on a rolling basis. Application fee: $20 ($30 for international students). *Expenses:* Tuition, state resident: part-time $519 per credit hour. Tuition and fees vary according to course load. *Financial support:* Application deadline: 5/1. *Unit head:* Dr. Dustin M. Hebert, Director, 337-475-5424, Fax: 337-475-5272, E-mail: dhebert@mcneese.edu. *Application contact:* Dr. George F. Mead, Jr., Interim Dean of Dore' School of Graduate Studies, 337-475-5396, Fax: 337-475-5397, E-mail: admissions@mcneese.edu.

Mercer University, Graduate Studies, Cecil B. Day Campus, College of Coninuing and Professional Studies, Macon, GA 31207-0003. Offers clinical mental health (MS); counselor education and supervision (PhD); public safety leadership (MS); school counseling (MS). *Application contact:* Tracey M. Wofford, Associate Director of Admissions, 678-547-6422, E-mail: wofford_tm@mercer.edu.

Mercy College, School of Social and Behavioral Sciences, Dobbs Ferry, NY 10522-1189. Offers counseling (MS, Certificate), including alcohol and substance abuse counseling (Certificate), counseling (MS), family counseling (Certificate); health services management (MPA, MS); marriage and family therapy (MS); mental health counseling (MS); psychology (MS); school counseling (Certificate); school counseling and bilingual extension (Certificate); school psychology (MS). Part-time and evening/weekend programs available. Postbaccalaureate distance learning degree programs offered (minimal on-campus study). *Degree requirements:* For master's, comprehensive exam (for some programs), thesis (for some programs). *Entrance requirements:* For master's, 2 letters of recommendation, interview, resume, essay. Additional exam requirements/recommendations for international students: Required—TOEFL (minimum score 600 paper-based; 250 computer-based; 100 iBT), IELTS (minimum score 8). Electronic applications accepted.

Messiah College, Program in Counseling, Mechanicsburg, PA 17055. Offers clinical mental health counseling (MAC); counseling (CAGS); marriage, couple, and family counseling (MAC); school counseling (MAC). Part-time programs available. Postbaccalaureate distance learning degree programs offered (no on-campus study). *Faculty:* 7 full-time (5 women), 15 part-time/adjunct (10 women). *Students:* 93 full-time (78 women), 17 part-time (13 women); includes 8 minority (5 Black or African American, non-Hispanic/Latino; 2 Asian, non-Hispanic/Latino; 1 Hispanic/Latino). Average age 32. *Entrance requirements:* For master's, minimum undergraduate cumulative GPA of 3.0, 2 recommendations, resume or curriculum vitae, interview; for CAGS, bachelor's degree, minimum undergraduate cumulative GPA of 3.0, essay, two recommendations, resume or curriculum vitae, interview. *Application deadline:* For fall admission, 6/1 priority date for domestic students; for winter admission, 11/1 priority date for domestic students; for spring admission, 11/1 priority date for domestic students. Applications are processed on a rolling basis. Application fee: $30. Electronic applications accepted. *Expenses: Tuition:* Full-time $9648; part-time $536 per credit hour. *Required fees:* $150; $25 per course. *Financial support:* Federal Work-Study available. Financial award applicants required to submit FAFSA. *Unit head:* Dr. John Addleman, Director, 717-796-1800 Ext. 2980, Fax: 717-691-2386, E-mail: jaddlemn@messiah.edu. *Application contact:* Jackie Gehman, Graduate Enrollment Coordinator, 717-796-5061, Fax: 717-691-2386, E-mail: jgehman@messiah.edu.

Michigan State University, The Graduate School, College of Education, Department of Counseling, Educational Psychology and Special Education, East Lansing, MI 48824. Offers counseling (MA); educational psychology and educational technology (PhD); educational technology (MA); measurement and quantitative methods (PhD); rehabilitation counseling (MA); rehabilitation counselor education (PhD); school psychology (MA, PhD, Ed S); special education (MA, PhD). *Accreditation:* APA (one or more programs are accredited); CORE (one or more programs are accredited). Part-time programs available. *Entrance requirements:* Additional exam requirements/recommendations for international students: Required—TOEFL. Electronic applications accepted.

Middle Tennessee State University, College of Graduate Studies, College of Education, Department of Educational Leadership, Program in Professional Counseling, Murfreesboro, TN 37132. Offers curriculum and instruction (Ed S), including school psychology; mental health counseling (M Ed); school counseling (M Ed). *Accreditation:* ACA; NCATE. Part-time and evening/weekend programs available. Postbaccalaureate distance learning degree programs offered. *Students:* 1 (woman) full-time, 62 part-time (52 women); includes 5 minority (4 Black or African American, non-Hispanic/Latino; 1 Two or more races, non-Hispanic/Latino). 35 applicants, 69% accepted. In 2011, 20 master's awarded. *Degree requirements:* For master's, comprehensive exam. *Entrance requirements:* For master's, GRE or MAT. Additional exam requirements/recommendations for international students: Required—TOEFL (minimum score 525 paper-based; 195 computer-based; 71 iBT) or IELTS (minimum score 6). *Application deadline:* For fall admission, 6/1 for domestic and international students. Applications are processed on a rolling basis. Application fee: $25 ($30 for international students). Electronic applications accepted. *Expenses:* Tuition, state resident: full-time $10,008. Tuition, nonresident: full-time $25,056. *Financial support:* Application deadline: 5/1. *Unit head:* Dr. James O. Huffman, Chair, 615-898-2855, Fax: 615-898-2859. *Application contact:* Dr. Michael D. Allen, Dean and Vice Provost for Research, 615-898-2840, Fax: 615-904-8020, E-mail: michael.allen@mtsu.edu.

Midwestern State University, Graduate Studies, College of Education, Program in Counseling, Wichita Falls, TX 76308. Offers general counseling (MA); human resource development (MA); school counseling (M Ed); training and development (MA). Part-time and evening/weekend programs available. *Degree requirements:* For master's, comprehensive exam, thesis (for some programs). *Entrance requirements:* For master's, GRE General Test, MAT, or GMAT, valid teaching certificate (M Ed). Additional exam requirements/recommendations for international students: Required—TOEFL (minimum score 550 paper-based; 213 computer-based). Electronic applications accepted. *Faculty research:* Social development of students with disabilities, autism, criminal justice counseling, conflict resolution issues, leadership.

Minnesota State University Mankato, College of Graduate Studies, College of Education, Department of Counseling and Student Personnel, Mankato, MN 56001. Offers college student affairs (MS); counselor education and supervision (Ed D); marriage and family counseling (Certificate); mental health counseling (MS); professional school counseling (MS). *Accreditation:* ACA (one or more programs are accredited); NCATE. *Students:* 174 full-time (61 women), 42 part-time (30 women). *Degree requirements:* For master's, comprehensive exam, thesis or alternative. *Entrance requirements:* For master's, GRE General Test or MAT (if GPA less than 3.0 for last 2 years), minimum GPA of 3.0 during previous 2 years, 3 letters of reference. Additional exam requirements/recommendations for international students: Required—TOEFL. *Application deadline:* For fall admission, 1/15 priority date for domestic students. Applications are processed on a rolling basis. Application fee: $40. Electronic applications accepted. *Financial support:* Research assistantships with full tuition reimbursements, teaching assistantships with full tuition reimbursements, career-related internships or fieldwork, Federal Work-Study, institutionally sponsored loans, and unspecified assistantships available. Support available to part-time students. Financial award application deadline: 3/15; financial award applicants required to submit FAFSA. *Unit head:* Dr. Jacqueline Lewis, Chairperson, 507-389-5658. *Application contact:* 507-389-2321, E-mail: grad@mnsu.edu.

Minnesota State University Moorhead, Graduate Studies, College of Education and Human Services, Program in Counseling and Student Affairs, Moorhead, MN 56563-0002. Offers MS. *Accreditation:* ACA; NCATE. Part-time and evening/weekend programs available. *Degree requirements:* For master's, comprehensive exam, final oral exam, internship, project or thesis. *Entrance requirements:* For master's, GRE or MAT, interview, 3 letters of recommendation, minimum GPA of 3.0. Additional exam requirements/recommendations for international students: Required—TOEFL (minimum score 550 paper-based; 213 computer-based). Electronic applications accepted.

Mississippi College, Graduate School, School of Education, Department of Psychology and Counseling, Clinton, MS 39058. Offers counseling (Ed S); marriage and family counseling (MS); mental health counseling (MS); school counseling (M Ed). Part-time programs available. *Degree requirements:* For master's and Ed S, comprehensive exam, thesis optional. *Entrance requirements:* For master's, GRE or NTE. Additional exam requirements/recommendations for international students: Recommended—TOEFL, IELTS. Electronic applications accepted.

Mississippi State University, College of Education, Department of Counseling and Educational Psychology, Mississippi State, MS 39762. Offers college/postsecondary student counseling and personnel services (PhD); counselor education (MS); education (Ed S), including counselor education, school psychology; educational psychology (MS, PhD). *Accreditation:* ACA (one or more programs are accredited); APA; CORE (one or more programs are accredited); NCATE. Part-time programs available. Postbaccalaureate distance learning degree programs offered (minimal on-campus study). *Faculty:* 18 full-time (13 women), 2 part-time/adjunct (1 woman). *Students:* 167 full-time (133 women), 87 part-time (78 women); includes 81 minority (70 Black or African American, non-Hispanic/Latino; 4 American Indian or Alaska Native, non-Hispanic/Latino; 4 Asian, non-Hispanic/Latino; 1 Native Hawaiian or other Pacific Islander, non-Hispanic/Latino; 2 Two or more races, non-Hispanic/Latino), 7 international. Average age 31. 197 applicants, 55% accepted, 79 enrolled. In 2011, 52 master's, 2 doctorates, 7 other advanced degrees awarded. Terminal master's awarded for partial completion of doctoral program. *Degree requirements:* For master's, comprehensive exam, thesis optional; for doctorate, thesis/dissertation, comprehensive oral and written exam. *Entrance requirements:* For master's, GRE, minimum QPA of 3.0; for doctorate, GRE, interview, minimum GPA of 3.4; for Ed S, GRE, MS in counseling or related field. Additional exam requirements/recommendations for international students: Required—TOEFL (minimum score 475 paper-based; 153 computer-based; 53 iBT); Recommended—IELTS (minimum score 4.5). *Application deadline:* For fall admission, 2/1 priority date for domestic students, 2/1 for international students. Applications are processed on a rolling basis. Application fee: $40. Electronic applications accepted. *Expenses:* Tuition, state resident: full-time $5805; part-time $322.50 per credit hour. Tuition, nonresident: full-time $14,670; part-time $815 per credit hour. *Financial support:* In 2011–12, 7 research assistantships (averaging $10,750 per year), 6 teaching assistantships with full tuition reimbursements (averaging $10,151 per year) were awarded; career-related internships or fieldwork, Federal Work-Study, institutionally sponsored loans, and unspecified assistantships also available. Financial award application deadline: 2/1; financial award applicants required to submit FAFSA. *Faculty research:* HIV-AIDS in college population, substance abuse in youth and college students, ADHD and conduct disorders in youth, assessment and identification of early childhood disabilities, assessment and vocational transition of the disabled. *Unit head:* Dr. Daniel Wong, Professor/Head, 662-325-7928, Fax: 662-325-3263, E-mail: dwong@colled.msstate.edu. *Application contact:* Dr. Tony Doggett, Associate Professor and Graduate Coordinator, 662-325-3312, Fax: 662-325-3263, E-mail: tdoggett@colled.msstate.edu. Web site: http://www.cep.msstate.edu/.

Missouri Baptist University, Graduate Programs, St. Louis, MO 63141-8660. Offers business administration (MBA); Christian ministries (MACM); counseling (MAC); education (MSE); education administration (MEA); educational leadership (MSE, Ed S); teaching (MAT).

Missouri State University, Graduate College, College of Education, Department of Counseling, Leadership, and Special Education, Program in Counseling, Springfield, MO 65897. Offers counseling and assessment (Ed S); secondary school counseling (MS). Part-time and evening/weekend programs available. *Students:* 45 full-time (36 women), 73 part-time (59 women); includes 8 minority (2 Black or African American, non-Hispanic/Latino; 1 American Indian or Alaska Native, non-Hispanic/Latino; 2 Asian, non-Hispanic/Latino; 3 Two or more races, non-Hispanic/Latino). Average age 33. 18 applicants, 94% accepted, 11 enrolled. In 2011, 45 master's awarded. *Degree requirements:* For master's, comprehensive exam, thesis or alternative. *Entrance requirements:* For master's, GRE or MAT, minimum GPA of 2.75. Additional exam requirements/recommendations for international students: Required—TOEFL (minimum score 550 paper-based; 213 computer-based; 79 iBT). *Application deadline:* For fall admission, 2/1 priority date for domestic students, 1/1 for international students; for spring admission, 10/1 priority date for domestic students, 9/1 for international students. Application fee: $35 ($50 for international students). Electronic applications accepted. *Expenses:* Tuition, state resident: full-time $4086; part-time $227 per credit hour. Tuition, nonresident: full-time $8172; part-time $454 per credit hour. *Required fees:* $275 per semester. Tuition and fees vary according to course load, campus/location and program. *Financial support:* Federal Work-Study, institutionally sponsored loans, scholarships/grants, and unspecified assistantships available. Financial award application deadline: 3/31; financial award applicants required to submit FAFSA. *Unit head:* Dr. Joseph Hulgus, Program Coordinator, 417-836-6522, Fax: 417-836-4918, E-mail: clse@missouristate.edu. *Application contact:* Misty Stewart, Coordinator of Admissions and Recruitment, 417-836-6079, Fax: 417-836-6200, E-mail: mistystewart@missouristate.edu. Web site: http://education.missouristate.edu/clse/.

Montana State University Billings, College of Education, Department of Special Education, Counseling, Reading and Early Childhood, Option in School Counseling, Billings, MT 59101-0298. Offers M Ed. *Accreditation:* NCATE. Part-time programs available. *Degree requirements:* For master's, thesis or professional paper and/or field experience. *Entrance requirements:* For master's, GRE General Test or MAT, minimum GPA of 3.0 (undergraduate), 3.25 (graduate).

Montana State University–Northern, Graduate Programs, Option in Counselor Education, Havre, MT 59501-7751. Offers M Ed. Part-time and evening/weekend programs available. *Degree requirements:* For master's, comprehensive exam, thesis optional, oral exams. *Entrance requirements:* For master's, GRE General Test or MAT, minimum GPA of 3.0. Electronic applications accepted.

Montclair State University, The Graduate School, College of Education and Human Services, Department of Counseling and Educational Leadership, Advanced Counseling Certificate Program, Montclair, NJ 07043-1624. Offers Post-Master's Certificate. Part-time and evening/weekend programs available. *Students:* 1 (woman) full-time, 32 part-time (30 women); includes 12 minority (6 Black or African American, non-Hispanic/Latino; 1 Asian, non-Hispanic/Latino; 4 Hispanic/Latino; 1 Native Hawaiian or other Pacific Islander, non-Hispanic/Latino). Average age 31. 24 applicants, 75% accepted, 15 enrolled. In 2011, 15 degrees awarded. *Entrance requirements:* Additional exam requirements/recommendations for international students: Required—TOEFL (minimum score 83 iBT), IELTS (minimum score 6.5). *Application deadline:* For fall admission, 6/1 for international students; for spring admission, 10/1 for international students. Applications are processed on a rolling basis. Application fee: $60. Electronic applications accepted. *Financial support:* Federal Work-Study available. Support available to part-time students. Financial award application deadline: 3/1; financial award applicants required to submit FAFSA. *Unit head:* Dr. Larry Burlew, Chairperson, 973-655-7611. *Application contact:* Amy Aiello, Executive Director of The Graduate School, 973-655-5147, Fax: 973-655-7869, E-mail: graduate.school@montclair.edu. Web site: http://cehs.montclair.edu/academic/counseling/programs/advcouncert.shtml.

Montclair State University, The Graduate School, College of Education and Human Services, Department of Counseling and Educational Leadership, Doctoral Program in Counselor Education, Montclair, NJ 07043-1624. Offers PhD. Part-time and evening/weekend programs available. *Students:* 10 full-time (8 women), 21 part-time (15 women); includes 5 minority (2 Black or African American, non-Hispanic/Latino; 1 Asian, non-Hispanic/Latino; 2 Hispanic/Latino). Average age 31. 24 applicants, 50% accepted, 12 enrolled. *Degree requirements:* For doctorate, comprehensive exam, thesis/dissertation. *Entrance requirements:* For doctorate, GRE General Test, interview, 3 letters of recommendation. Additional exam requirements/recommendations for international students: Required—TOEFL (minimum score 83 iBT), IELTS (minimum score 6.5). *Application deadline:* For fall admission, 2/1 for domestic students. Application fee: $60. Electronic applications accepted. *Financial support:* In 2011–12, 7 research assistantships with full tuition reimbursements (averaging $15,000 per year) were awarded. Financial award application deadline: 3/1. *Unit head:* Dr. Larry Burlew, Chairperson, 973-655-7611. *Application contact:* Amy Aiello, Director of Graduate Admissions and Operations, 973-655-5147, Fax: 973-655-7869, E-mail: graduate.school@montclair.edu. Web site: http://cehs.montclair.edu/academic/counseling/programs/counselorphd.shtml.

Montclair State University, The Graduate School, College of Education and Human Services, Department of Counseling and Educational Leadership, Program in Counseling, Montclair, NJ 07043-1624. Offers MA. Part-time and evening/weekend programs available. *Students:* 123 full-time (95 women), 230 part-time (186 women); includes 80 minority (24 Black or African American, non-Hispanic/Latino; 9 Asian, non-Hispanic/Latino; 46 Hispanic/Latino; 1 Two or more races, non-Hispanic/Latino), 1 international. Average age 31. 249 applicants, 57% accepted, 102 enrolled. In 2011, 92 degrees awarded. *Degree requirements:* For master's, comprehensive exam, thesis or alternative. *Entrance requirements:* For master's, GRE General Test, interview, 2 letters of recommendation. Additional exam requirements/recommendations for international students: Required—TOEFL (minimum score 83 iBT), IELTS (minimum score 6.5). *Application deadline:* For fall admission, 6/1 for international students; for spring admission, 10/1 for international students. Applications are processed on a rolling basis. Application fee: $60. Electronic applications accepted. *Financial support:* In 2011–12, 10 research assistantships with full tuition reimbursements (averaging $7,000 per year) were awarded; Federal Work-Study, scholarships/grants, and unspecified assistantships also available. Support available to part-time students. Financial award application deadline: 3/1; financial award applicants required to submit FAFSA. *Unit head:* Dr. Larry Burlew, Chairperson, 973-655-7611. *Application contact:* Amy Aiello, Director of Graduate Admissions and Operations, 973-655-5147, Fax: 973-655-7869, E-mail: graduate.school@montclair.edu. Web site: http://cehs.montclair.edu/academic/counseling/programs/mastercounseling.shtml.

Morehead State University, Graduate Programs, College of Education, Department of Foundational and Graduate Studies in Education, Morehead, KY 40351. Offers adult and higher education (MA, Ed S); certified professional counselor (Ed S); counseling P-12 (MA); curriculum and instruction (Ed S); educational technology (MA Ed); instructional leadership (Ed S); school administration (MA); school counseling (Ed S); teacher leader business and marketing content (MA Ed); teacher leader business and marketing technology (MA Ed); teacher leader educational technology (MA Ed); teacher leader English (MA Ed); teacher leader gifted education (MA Ed); teacher leader IECE certification (MA Ed); teacher leader interdisciplinary education P-5 (MA Ed); teacher leader middle grades (MA Ed); teacher leader non IECE certification (MA Ed); teacher leader reading/writing - non-certification (MA Ed); teacher leader reading/writing certification (MA Ed); teacher leader school communication - certification (MA Ed); teacher leader school communication - non-certification (MA Ed); teacher leader social studies (MA Ed); teacher leader special education (MA Ed). *Accreditation:* NCATE. Part-time and evening/weekend programs available. *Degree requirements:* For master's, thesis optional, oral and/or written comprehensive exams; for Ed S, thesis, oral exam. *Entrance requirements:* For master's, GRE General Test, minimum overall undergraduate GPA of 2.5; for Ed S, GRE General Test, interview, master's degree, minimum GPA of 3.5, work experience. Additional exam requirements/recommendations for international students: Required—TOEFL (minimum score 500 paper-based; 173 computer-based). Electronic applications accepted. *Faculty research:* Character education, school accountability, computer applications for school administrators.

Mount Mary College, Graduate Programs, Program in Community Counseling, Milwaukee, WI 53222-4597. Offers clinical mental health counseling (MS); community counseling (MS); school counseling (MS). Part-time and evening/weekend programs available. *Faculty:* 2 full-time (both women), 8 part-time/adjunct (4 women). *Students:* 90 full-time (89 women), 26 part-time (24 women); includes 41 minority (30 Black or African American, non-Hispanic/Latino; 1 American Indian or Alaska Native, non-Hispanic/Latino; 1 Asian, non-Hispanic/Latino; 5 Hispanic/Latino; 4 Two or more races, non-Hispanic/Latino). Average age 34. 71 applicants, 55% accepted, 30 enrolled. In 2011, 20 master's awarded. *Degree requirements:* For master's, comprehensive exam, thesis or alternative. *Entrance requirements:* For master's, minimum GPA of 3.0. Additional exam requirements/recommendations for international students: Required—TOEFL (minimum score 500 paper-based; 173 computer-based). *Application deadline:* For fall admission, 8/1 priority date for domestic students, 8/1 for international students; for spring admission, 12/1 priority date for domestic students, 12/1 for international students. Application fee: $45 ($100 for international students). *Financial support:* Career-related internships or fieldwork and Federal Work-Study available. Support available to part-time students. Financial award application deadline: 5/1; financial award applicants required to submit FAFSA. *Faculty research:* Cognitive behavioral interventions for depression, eating disorders and compliance. *Unit head:* Carrie King, Graduate Program Director, 414-258-4810 Ext. 318, E-mail: kingc@mtmary.edu. *Application contact:* Dr. Douglas J. Mickelson, Associate Dean for Graduate and Continuing Education, 414-256-1252, Fax: 414-256-0167, E-mail: mickelsd@mtmary.edu.

Multnomah University, Multnomah Bible College Graduate Degree Programs, Portland, OR 97220-5898. Offers counseling (MA); teaching (MA); TESOL (MA). *Faculty:* 5 full-time (all women), 25 part-time/adjunct (12 women). *Students:* 126 full-time (84 women), 21 part-time (13 women); includes 24 minority (5 Black or African American, non-Hispanic/Latino; 1 American Indian or Alaska Native, non-Hispanic/Latino; 8 Asian, non-Hispanic/Latino; 7 Hispanic/Latino; 3 Two or more races, non-Hispanic/Latino). Average age 35. 73 applicants, 81% accepted, 45 enrolled. In 2011, 13 master's awarded. *Degree requirements:* For master's, variable foreign language requirement, comprehensive exam (for some programs), thesis optional. *Entrance requirements:* For master's, CBEST or WEST-B (for MAT), interview; references (4 for teaching); writing sample (for counseling). Additional exam requirements/recommendations for international students: Required—TOEFL (minimum score 550 paper-based; 213 computer-based). *Application deadline:* For fall admission, 8/1 for domestic students, 12/1 for international students; for spring admission, 12/1 for domestic and international students. Application fee: $40. *Expenses: Tuition:* Part-time $485 per credit hour. *Required fees:* $25 per semester. Tuition and fees vary according to campus/location and program. *Financial support:* Career-related internships or fieldwork and scholarships/grants available. Support available to part-time students. Financial award application deadline: 7/1; financial award applicants required to submit FAFSA. *Unit head:* Dr. Rex Koivisto, Academic Dean, 503-251-6401. *Application contact:* Jennifer Hancock, Assistant Director of Graduate and Seminary Admissions, 503-251-6481, Fax: 503-254-1268, E-mail: admiss@multnomah.edu.

Murray State University, College of Education, Department of Educational Studies, Leadership and Counseling, Program in Community and Agency Counseling, Murray, KY 42071. Offers Ed S. *Accreditation:* NCATE. Part-time programs available. *Degree requirements:* For Ed S, comprehensive exam, thesis. *Entrance requirements:* For degree, GRE General Test. Additional exam requirements/recommendations for international students: Required—TOEFL.

Murray State University, College of Education, Department of Educational Studies, Leadership and Counseling, Programs in School Guidance and Counseling, Murray, KY 42071. Offers MA Ed, Ed S. *Accreditation:* NCATE. Part-time programs available. *Degree requirements:* For master's, comprehensive exam, thesis (for some programs), portfolio; for Ed S, comprehensive exam, portfolio. *Entrance requirements:* For master's, GRE General Test or MAT. Additional exam requirements/recommendations for international students: Required—TOEFL.

Naropa University, Graduate Programs, Program in Transpersonal Counseling Psychology, Concentration in Counseling Psychology, Boulder, CO 80302-6697. Offers MA. *Faculty:* 9 full-time (6 women), 27 part-time/adjunct (16 women). *Students:* 92 full-time (65 women), 45 part-time (34 women); includes 16 minority (1 Black or African American, non-Hispanic/Latino; 2 American Indian or Alaska Native, non-Hispanic/Latino; 2 Asian, non-Hispanic/Latino; 5 Hispanic/Latino; 6 Two or more races, non-Hispanic/Latino), 4 international. Average age 32. 126 applicants, 63% accepted, 52 enrolled. In 2011, 35 master's awarded. *Degree requirements:* For master's, internships. *Entrance requirements:* For master's, in-person interview; course work in psychology, resume, 3 letters of recommendation. Additional exam requirements/recommendations for international students: Required—TOEFL (minimum score 600 paper-based; 250 computer-based). *Application deadline:* For fall admission, 1/15 priority date for domestic students, 1/15 for international students. Applications are processed on a rolling basis. Application fee: $60. Electronic applications accepted. *Expenses: Tuition:* Full-time $20,400; part-time $850 per credit. *Required fees:* $660; $250 per semester. *Financial support:* In 2011–12, 30 students received support, including 10 research assistantships with partial tuition reimbursements available (averaging $2,866 per year), 4 teaching assistantships with partial tuition reimbursements available (averaging $2,866 per year); career-related internships or fieldwork, Federal Work-Study, scholarships/grants, health care benefits, tuition waivers (partial), and unspecified assistantships also available. Support available to part-time students. Financial award application deadline: 3/1; financial award applicants required to submit FAFSA. *Unit head:* MacAndrew Jack, Director, Graduate School of Psychology, 303-245-4752, E-mail: mjack@naropa.edu. *Application contact:* Megan Fredwaldt, Graduate Admissions Counselor, 303-546-3582, Fax: 303-546-3583, E-mail: mfrewaldt@naropa.edu. Web site: http://www.naropa.edu/academics/gsp/grad/somatic-counseling-psychology-ma/index.php.

National Louis University, College of Arts and Sciences, Chicago, IL 60603. Offers adult education (Ed D); counseling and human services (MS); language and academic development (M Ed, Certificate); psychology (MA, PhD, Certificate); public policy (MA); written communication (MS, Certificate). Part-time and evening/weekend programs available. Postbaccalaureate distance learning degree programs offered (minimal on-campus study). *Students:* 33 full-time (25 women), 466 part-time (388 women); includes 233 minority (176 Black or African American, non-Hispanic/Latino; 1 American Indian or Alaska Native, non-Hispanic/Latino; 12 Asian, non-Hispanic/Latino; 41 Hispanic/Latino; 3 Two or more races, non-Hispanic/Latino). Average age 38. In 2011, 196 master's, 7 doctorates, 48 other advanced degrees awarded. *Degree requirements:* For master's and Certificate, comprehensive exam (for some programs), thesis (for some programs); for doctorate, thesis/dissertation. *Entrance requirements:* For master's, MAT or GRE, 3 professional or academic references, interview, minimum GPA of 3.0; for doctorate, GRE General Test, MAT, or Watson-Glaser Critical Thinking Appraisal, three professional or academic references, statement of academic and professional goals, 3 years of experience in field, interview, master's degree, resume, writing sample; for Certificate, GRE, MAT, or Watson-Glaser Critical Thinking Appraisal, three professional or academic references, statement of academic and professional goals, interview, minimum GPA of 3.0. Additional exam requirements/recommendations for international students: Required—Department of Language Studies Assessment or TOEFL (minimum score 550 paper-based; 213 computer-based; 79 iBT). *Application deadline:* Applications are processed on a rolling basis. Application fee: $40. Electronic applications accepted. *Financial support:* Career-related internships or fieldwork, Federal Work-Study, institutionally sponsored loans, scholarships/grants, and tuition waivers available. Support available to part-time students. Financial award applicants required to submit FAFSA. *Unit head:* Dr. Walter Roettger, Interim Dean, 312-261-3073, Fax: 312-261-3073, E-mail: walter.roettger@nl.edu. *Application contact:* Dr. Ken Kasprzak, Director of Admissions, 888-658-8632, Fax: 847-947-5575, E-mail: kkasprzak@nl.edu.

National University, Academic Affairs, School of Education, Department of Educational Administration and School Counseling/Psychology, La Jolla, CA 92037-1011. Offers accomplished collaborative leadership (MA); applied behavior analysis (MS); applied school leadership (MS); educational administration (MS); educational counseling (MS); higher education administration (MS); innovative school leadership (MS); instructional leadership (MS); school psychology (MS). Part-time and evening/weekend programs available. Postbaccalaureate distance learning degree programs offered (no on-campus study). *Degree requirements:* For master's, thesis. *Entrance requirements:* For master's, interview, minimum GPA of 2.5. Additional exam requirements/recommendations for international students: Required—TOEFL (minimum score 550 paper-based; 213 computer-based; 79 iBT), IELTS (minimum score 6). *Application deadline:* Applications are processed on a rolling basis. Application fee: $60 ($65 for international students). Electronic applications accepted. *Financial support:* Career-related internships or fieldwork, institutionally sponsored loans, scholarships/grants, and tuition waivers (partial) available. Support available to part-time students. Financial award application deadline: 6/30; financial award applicants required to submit FAFSA. *Unit head:* Dr. Rollin Nordgren, Chair and Professor, 858-642-8144, Fax: 858-642-8724, E-mail: rnordgren@nu.edu. *Application contact:* Dominick Giovanniello, Associate Regional Dean, 800-NAT-UNIV, Fax: 858-541-7792, E-mail: dgiovann@nu.edu. Web site: http://www.nu.edu/OurPrograms/SchoolOfEducation/EducationalAdministration.html.

New Mexico Highlands University, Graduate Studies, School of Education, Las Vegas, NM 87701. Offers curriculum and instruction (MA); education (MA), including counseling, school counseling; educational leadership (MA); exercise and sport sciences (MA), including human performance and sport, sports administration, teacher education; guidance and counseling (MA), including professional counseling, rehabilitation counseling, school counseling; special education (MA), including). Part-time programs available. *Faculty:* 29 full-time (18 women). *Students:* 136 full-time (100 women), 275 part-time (219 women); includes 231 minority (8 Black or African American, non-Hispanic/Latino; 22 American Indian or Alaska Native, non-Hispanic/Latino; 2 Asian, non-Hispanic/Latino; 194 Hispanic/Latino; 1 Native Hawaiian or other Pacific Islander, non-Hispanic/Latino; 4 Two or more races, non-Hispanic/Latino), 14 international. Average age 39. 117 applicants, 82% accepted, 91 enrolled. In 2011, 105 master's awarded. *Degree requirements:* For master's, comprehensive exam, thesis or alternative. *Entrance requirements:* For master's, minimum undergraduate GPA of 3.0. Additional exam requirements/recommendations for international students: Required—TOEFL (minimum score 540 paper-based; 207 computer-based). *Application deadline:* For fall admission, 8/1 priority date for domestic students. Applications are processed on a rolling basis. Application fee: $15. *Expenses:* Tuition, state resident: full-time $2767; part-time $146 per credit hour. Tuition, nonresident: full-time $4879; part-time $234 per credit hour. *International tuition:* $5436 full-time. *Required fees:* $737. *Financial support:* In 2011–12, 12 students received support. Career-related internships or fieldwork, Federal Work-Study, institutionally sponsored loans, scholarships/grants, traineeships, tuition waivers (partial), and unspecified assistantships available. Support available to part-time students. Financial award application deadline: 3/1; financial award applicants required to submit FAFSA. *Faculty research:* Teaching the United States Constitution, middle school curriculum, integrated computer applications for pre-service classroom teachers, adolescent literacy, narrative cognitive modes in NM multicultural setting. *Unit head:* Dr. Michael Anderson, Interim Dean, 505-454-3213, E-mail: mfanderson@nmhu.edu. *Application contact:* Diane Trujillo, Administrative Assistant for Graduate Studies, 505-454-3266, Fax: 505-426-2117, E-mail: dtrujillo@nmhu.edu.

New Mexico State University, Graduate School, College of Education, Department of Counseling and Educational Psychology, Las Cruces, NM 88003-8001. Offers counseling and guidance (MA); counseling psychology (PhD); school psychology (Ed S). *Accreditation:* ACA; APA (one or more programs are accredited); NCATE. Part-time programs available. *Faculty:* 10 full-time (8 women), 1 part-time/adjunct (0 women). *Students:* 74 full-time (56 women), 19 part-time (all women); includes 53 minority (3 Black or African American, non-Hispanic/Latino; 2 American Indian or Alaska Native, non-Hispanic/Latino; 2 Asian, non-Hispanic/Latino; 44 Hispanic/Latino; 2 Two or more races, non-Hispanic/Latino). Average age 29. 84 applicants, 29% accepted, 23 enrolled. In 2011, 8 master's, 5 doctorates, 11 other advanced degrees awarded. *Degree requirements:* For master's, comprehensive exam, thesis optional, internship; for doctorate, comprehensive exam, thesis/dissertation, internship; for Ed S, thesis or alternative, internship. *Entrance requirements:* For master's, doctorate, and Ed S, GRE General Test, minimum GPA of 3.0. Additional exam requirements/recommendations for international students: Required—IELTS (minimum score 6.5); Recommended—TOEFL (minimum score 550 paper-based; 79 iBT). *Application deadline:* For fall admission, 12/15 for domestic students; for spring admission, 3/1 priority date for domestic students. Application fee: $40 ($50 for international students). Electronic applications accepted. *Expenses:* Tuition, state resident: full-time $5004; part-time $208.50 per credit. Tuition, nonresident: full-time $17,446; part-time $726.90 per credit. *Financial support:* In 2011–12, 30 students received support, including 1 fellowship (averaging $7,000 per year), 9 research assistantships (averaging $20,114 per year), 35 teaching assistantships (averaging $13,778 per year); career-related internships or fieldwork, Federal Work-Study, institutionally sponsored loans, scholarships/grants, traineeships, health care benefits, and unspecified assistantships also available. Support available to part-time students. Financial award application deadline: 4/1; financial award applicants required to submit FAFSA. *Faculty research:* Multicultural counseling, integrative health psychology, group, school counseling, prevention. *Unit head:* Dr. Jonathan Schwartz, Head, 575-646-2121, Fax: 575-646-8035, E-mail: jschwart@nmsu.edu. *Application contact:* Dr. Michael Waldo, Professor, 575-646-2121, Fax: 575-646-8035, E-mail: miwaldo@nmsu.edu. Web site: http://education.nmsu.edu/cep/.

New York Institute of Technology, Graduate Division, School of Education, Program in School Counseling, Old Westbury, NY 11568-8000. Offers MS. *Students:* 2 full-time (1 woman), 80 part-time (65 women); includes 32 minority (10 Black or African American, non-Hispanic/Latino; 5 Asian, non-Hispanic/Latino; 17 Hispanic/Latino), 1 international. Average age 33. In 2011, 19 master's awarded. *Degree requirements:* For master's, internship. *Entrance requirements:* For master's, minimum GPA of 3.0, interview, 3 letters of reference. Additional exam requirements/recommendations for international students: Required—TOEFL (minimum score 550 paper-based; 213 computer-based). *Application deadline:* For fall admission, 7/1 priority date for domestic students; for spring admission, 12/1 priority date for domestic students. Applications are processed on a rolling basis. Application fee: $50. Electronic applications accepted. *Expenses: Tuition:* Part-time $930 per credit hour. *Financial support:* Research assistantships available. *Unit head:* Dr. Carol Dahir, Department Chair, 516-686-7616, Fax: 516-686-7655, E-mail: cdahir@nyit.edu. *Application contact:* Dr. Jacquelyn Nealon, Vice President for Enrollment Services, 516-686-7925, Fax: 516-686-7597, E-mail: jnealon@nyit.edu.

New York University, Steinhardt School of Culture, Education, and Human Development, Department of Applied Psychology, Program in Counseling, New York, NY 10012-1019. Offers counseling and guidance (MA, Advanced Certificate), including bilingual school counseling (MA), school counseling (MA); counseling for mental health and wellness (MA); counseling psychology (PhD). *Accreditation:* APA (one or more programs are accredited). Part-time programs available. *Faculty:* 9 full-time (6 women). *Students:* 157 full-time (120 women), 54 part-time (46 women); includes 88 minority (30 Black or African American, non-Hispanic/Latino; 1 American Indian or Alaska Native, non-Hispanic/Latino; 19 Asian, non-Hispanic/Latino; 33 Hispanic/Latino; 5 Two or more races, non-Hispanic/Latino), 21 international. Average age 26. 891 applicants, 32% accepted, 91 enrolled. In 2011, 76 master's, 5 doctorates awarded. *Degree requirements:* For master's, thesis (for some programs); for doctorate, thesis/dissertation. *Entrance requirements:* For doctorate, GRE General Test, interview. Additional exam requirements/recommendations for international students: Required—TOEFL. *Application deadline:* For fall admission, 12/1 priority date for domestic students, 12/1 for international students. Applications are processed on a rolling basis. Application fee: $75. Electronic applications accepted. *Financial support:* Fellowships with full and partial tuition reimbursements, research assistantships, teaching assistantships with partial tuition reimbursements, career-related internships or fieldwork, Federal Work-Study, institutionally sponsored loans, scholarships/grants, tuition waivers (partial), and unspecified assistantships available. Support available to part-time students. Financial award application deadline: 2/1; financial award applicants required to submit FAFSA. *Faculty research:* Cross-cultural counseling; group dynamics; culture, race and ethnicity; religiosity and psychological development; well-being and mental health. *Unit head:* 212-998-5555, Fax: 212-995-4358. *Application contact:* 212-998-5030, Fax: 212-995-4328, E-mail: steinhardt.gradadmissions@nyu.edu. Web site: http://steinhardt.nyu.edu/appsych/counseling.

Niagara University, Graduate Division of Education, Concentration in Mental Health Counseling, Niagara Falls, Niagara University, NY 14109. Offers MS, Certificate. *Faculty:* 2 full-time (1 woman), 3 part-time/adjunct (all women). *Students:* 21 full-time (20 women), 8 part-time (6 women); includes 4 minority (2 Black or African American, non-Hispanic/Latino; 1 Asian, non-Hispanic/Latino; 1 Two or more races, non-Hispanic/Latino), 6 international. Average age 28. In 2011, 14 master's awarded. *Entrance requirements:* For master's, GRE General Test or MAT. Additional exam requirements/recommendations for international students: Required—TOEFL. *Application deadline:* For fall admission, 8/1 for domestic students. Applications are processed on a rolling basis. Application fee: $30. *Expenses:* Contact institution. *Financial support:* Fellowships, career-related internships or fieldwork, and Federal Work-Study available. Financial award application deadline: 3/15. *Unit head:* Dr. Shannon Hodges, Chair, 716-286-8328. *Application contact:* Dr. Debra A. Colley, Dean of Education, 716-286-8560, Fax: 716-286-8561, E-mail: dcolley@niagara.edu.

Niagara University, Graduate Division of Education, Concentration in School Counseling, Niagara Falls, Niagara University, NY 14109. Offers MS Ed, Certificate. *Accreditation:* NCATE. Part-time and evening/weekend programs available. *Faculty:* 2 full-time (1 woman), 3 part-time/adjunct (all women). *Students:* 22 full-time (14 women), 4 part-time (all women); includes 1 minority (Two or more races, non-Hispanic/Latino). Average age 28. In 2011, 16 master's, 3 Certificates awarded. *Entrance requirements:* For master's, GRE General Test or MAT; for Certificate, GRE General Test, GRE Subject Test or MAT. Additional exam requirements/recommendations for international students: Required—TOEFL. *Application deadline:* For fall admission, 8/1 for domestic students. Applications are processed on a rolling basis. Application fee: $30. *Expenses:* Contact institution. *Financial support:* Career-related internships or fieldwork and Federal Work-Study available. Financial award application deadline: 3/15. *Unit head:* Dr. Kristine Augustyniak, Chair, 716-286-8548, E-mail: kma@niagara.edu. *Application contact:* Dr. Debra A. Colley, Dean of Education, 716-286-8560, Fax: 716-286-8561, E-mail: dcolley@niagara.edu.

Nicholls State University, Graduate Studies, College of Education, Department of Teacher Education, Thibodaux, LA 70310. Offers administration and supervision (M Ed); counselor education (M Ed); curriculum and instruction (M Ed). *Accreditation:* NCATE. Part-time and evening/weekend programs available. *Degree requirements:* For master's, comprehensive exam, portfolio. *Entrance requirements:* For master's, GRE General Test, teaching license. Electronic applications accepted.

North Carolina Agricultural and Technical State University, School of Graduate Studies, School of Education, Department of Human Development and Services, Greensboro, NC 27411. Offers adult education (MS); counseling (MS); school administration (MS). *Accreditation:* ACA. Part-time and evening/weekend programs available. *Degree requirements:* For master's, comprehensive exam, thesis, qualifying exam. *Entrance requirements:* For master's, GRE General Test, minimum GPA of 3.0.

North Carolina Central University, Division of Academic Affairs, School of Education, Department of Counselor Education, Durham, NC 27707-3129. Offers career counseling (MA); community agency counseling (MA); school counseling (MA). *Accreditation:* ACA; NCATE. Part-time and evening/weekend programs available. *Degree requirements:* For master's, comprehensive exam, thesis or alternative. *Entrance requirements:* For master's, GRE, minimum GPA of 3.0 in major, 2.5 overall. Additional exam requirements/recommendations for international students: Required—TOEFL. *Faculty research:* Becoming a leader, skill building in academia.

North Carolina State University, Graduate School, College of Education, Department of Curriculum and Instruction, Program in Counselor Education, Raleigh, NC 27695. Offers M Ed, MS, PhD. *Accreditation:* ACA. *Degree requirements:* For master's, thesis (for some programs). *Entrance requirements:* For master's, GRE or MAT. Electronic applications accepted. *Faculty research:* Career development, retention of at-risk students in higher education, psycho-social development, multicultural issues, cognitive-developmental interventions.

North Dakota State University, College of Graduate and Interdisciplinary Studies, College of Human Development and Education, School of Education, Program in Counseling, Fargo, ND 58108. Offers M Ed, MS, PhD. *Accreditation:* ACA; NCATE. Part-time programs available. Postbaccalaureate distance learning degree programs offered (minimal on-campus study). *Students:* 37 full-time (31 women), 6 part-time (all women); includes 2 minority (1 Black or African American, non-Hispanic/Latino; 1 Two or more races, non-Hispanic/Latino). Average age 35. 41 applicants, 59% accepted, 21 enrolled. In 2011, 18 master's awarded. *Degree requirements:* For master's, comprehensive exam, thesis or alternative; for doctorate, comprehensive exam, thesis/dissertation. *Entrance requirements:* For master's, GRE, MAT, interview. Additional exam requirements/recommendations for international students: Required—TOEFL. *Application deadline:* For fall admission, 2/15 for domestic students. Applications are processed on a rolling basis. Application fee: $35. *Financial support:* Teaching assistantships, career-related internships or fieldwork, Federal Work-Study, institutionally sponsored loans, and tuition waivers (full) available. Financial award application deadline: 4/15. *Faculty research:* Supervision, program assessment, multicultural issues. *Unit head:* Dr. Jill R. Nelson, Coordinator, 701-231-7921, Fax: 701-231-7416, E-mail: jill.r.nelson@ndsu.edu. *Application contact:* Sonya Goergen, Marketing, Recruitment, and Public Relations Coordinator, 701-231-7033, Fax: 701-231-6524.

Northeastern Illinois University, Graduate College, College of Education, Department of Counselor Education, Chicago, IL 60625-4699. Offers guidance and counseling (MA), including career development, community and family counseling, elementary school counseling, rehabilitation counseling, secondary school counseling. *Accreditation:* ACA. Part-time and evening/weekend programs available. *Degree requirements:* For master's, comprehensive exam, thesis or alternative, internship, practicum. *Entrance requirements:* For master's, GRE, minimum GPA of 2.75, workshop. Additional exam requirements/recommendations for international students: Required—TOEFL (minimum score 550 paper-based; 213 computer-based; 79 iBT). Electronic applications accepted. *Faculty research:* Psychological factors of the visually impaired, reclaiming self through art, ego development, multicultural counseling, family therapy.

Northeastern State University, Graduate College, College of Education, Department of Psychology and Counseling, Program in School Counseling, Tahlequah, OK 74464-2399. Offers M Ed. Part-time and evening/weekend programs available. *Students:* 24 full-time (21 women), 29 part-time (25 women); includes 8 minority (2 Black or African American, non-Hispanic/Latino; 6 American Indian or Alaska Native, non-Hispanic/Latino), 1 international. In 2011, 21 master's awarded. *Degree requirements:* For master's, thesis or alternative, innovative project or research paper, written and oral exams. *Entrance requirements:* For master's, MAT or GRE, minimum GPA of 2.5. Additional exam requirements/recommendations for international students: Required—TOEFL (minimum score 213 computer-based). *Application deadline:* For fall admission, 6/1 priority date for domestic students. Applications are processed on a rolling basis. Application fee: $0 ($25 for international students). Electronic applications accepted. *Financial support:* Teaching assistantships and Federal Work-Study available. Financial award application deadline: 3/1. *Unit head:* Dr. Paul Cooper, Associate Professor/Department Chair for Psychology and Counseling, 918-444-3015 Ext. 6533, E-mail: cooperpe@nsuok.edu. *Application contact:* Margie Railey, Administrative Assistant, 918-456-5511 Ext. 2093, Fax: 918-458-2061, E-mail: railey@nsouk.edu.

Northeastern University, Bouvé College of Health Sciences, Department of Counseling and Applied Educational Psychology, Program in College Student Development and Counseling, Boston, MA 02115-5096. Offers MS, CAGS. Part-time and evening/weekend programs available. *Faculty:* 5. *Students:* 45 full-time (35 women), 6 part-time (all women). 53 applicants, 77% accepted, 22 enrolled. In 2011, 25 master's awarded. *Entrance requirements:* For master's, GRE General Test or MAT. Additional exam requirements/recommendations for international students: Required—TOEFL (minimum score 100 iBT). *Application deadline:* For fall admission, 8/1 for domestic students; for spring admission, 12/1 for domestic students. Applications are processed on a rolling basis. Application fee: $50. Electronic applications accepted. *Financial support:* Career-related internships or fieldwork, Federal Work-Study, scholarships/grants, tuition waivers (partial), and unspecified assistantships available. Support available to part-time students. Financial award application deadline: 3/1; financial award applicants required to submit FAFSA. *Unit head:* Prof. Vanessa Johnson, Director, 617-373-4634, E-mail: v.johnson@neu.edu. *Application contact:* Margaret Schnabel, Director of Graduate Admissions, 617-373-2708, E-mail: bouvegrad@neu.edu. Web site: http://www.northeastern.edu/bouve/programs/mstudentdev.html.

Northern Arizona University, Graduate College, College of Education, Department of Educational Psychology, Flagstaff, AZ 86011. Offers counseling (MA); educational psychology (PhD), including counseling psychology, learning and instruction, school psychology; human relations (M Ed); school counseling (M Ed); school psychology (Certificate, Ed S); student affairs (M Ed). Part-time programs available. Postbaccalaureate distance learning degree programs offered. *Faculty:* 18 full-time (8 women). *Students:* 280 full-time (220 women), 241 part-time (198 women); includes 194 minority (29 Black or African American, non-Hispanic/Latino; 37 American Indian or Alaska Native, non-Hispanic/Latino; 8 Asian, non-Hispanic/Latino; 105 Hispanic/Latino; 1 Native Hawaiian or other Pacific Islander, non-Hispanic/Latino; 14 Two or more races, non-Hispanic/Latino), 2 international. 274 applicants, 76% accepted, 141 enrolled. In 2011, 172 master's, 4 doctorates awarded. Terminal master's awarded for partial completion of doctoral program. *Median time to degree:* Of those who began their doctoral program in fall 2003, 75% received their degree in 8 years or less. *Degree requirements:* For master's, internship (for some programs); for doctorate, comprehensive exam, thesis/dissertation, internship. *Entrance requirements:* Additional exam requirements/recommendations for international students: Required—TOEFL (minimum score 550 paper-based; 213 computer-based; 80 iBT), IELTS (minimum score 7). *Application deadline:* For fall admission, 9/15 for domestic students; for spring admission, 1/15 for domestic students. Applications are processed on a rolling basis. Application fee: $65. Electronic applications accepted. *Expenses:* Tuition, state resident: full-time $7190; part-time $355 per credit hour. Tuition, nonresident: full-time $18,092; part-time $1005 per credit hour. *Required fees:* $818; $328 per semester. *Financial support:* In 2011–12, 20 students received support, including 1 research assistantship with partial tuition reimbursement available (averaging $10,222 per year), 14 teaching assistantships with partial tuition reimbursements available (averaging $9,660 per year); career-related internships or fieldwork, Federal Work-Study, scholarships/grants, health care benefits, tuition waivers (full and partial), and unspecified assistantships also available. Financial award applicants required to submit FAFSA. *Unit head:* Dr. Kathy Bohan, Chair, 928-523-0362, Fax: 928-523-9284, E-mail: kathy.bohan@nau.edu. *Application contact:* Hope DeMello, Administrative Assistant, 928-523-7103, Fax: 928-523-9284, E-mail: eps@nau.edu. Web site: http://nau.edu/coe/ed-psych/.

Northern Illinois University, Graduate School, College of Education, Department of Counseling, Adult and Higher Education, De Kalb, IL 60115-2854. Offers adult and higher education (MS Ed, Ed D); counseling (MS Ed, Ed D). *Accreditation:* ACA. Part-time and evening/weekend programs available. *Faculty:* 19 full-time (11 women), 2 part-time/adjunct (1 woman). *Students:* 122 full-time (84 women), 292 part-time (215 women); includes 149 minority (109 Black or African American, non-Hispanic/Latino; 1 American Indian or Alaska Native, non-Hispanic/Latino; 14 Asian, non-Hispanic/Latino; 20 Hispanic/Latino; 5 Two or more races, non-Hispanic/Latino), 14 international. Average age 36. 115 applicants, 55% accepted, 42 enrolled. In 2011, 58 master's, 21 doctorates awarded. Terminal master's awarded for partial completion of doctoral program. *Degree requirements:* For master's, comprehensive exam, thesis optional; for doctorate, thesis/dissertation, candidacy exam, dissertation defense. *Entrance requirements:* For master's, GRE General Test or MAT, minimum undergraduate GPA of 2.75, interview (counseling); for doctorate, GRE General Test, minimum undergraduate GPA of 2.75, 3.2 graduate, interview (counseling). Additional exam requirements/recommendations for international students: Required—TOEFL (minimum score 550 paper-based; 213 computer-based). *Application deadline:* For fall admission, 6/1 for domestic students, 5/1 for international students; for spring admission, 11/1 for domestic students, 10/1 for international students. Applications are processed on a rolling basis. Application fee: $40. Electronic applications accepted. *Financial support:* In 2011–12, 5 research assistantships with full tuition reimbursements, 1 teaching assistantship with full tuition reimbursement were awarded; fellowships with full tuition reimbursements, career-related internships or fieldwork, Federal Work-Study, scholarships/grants, tuition waivers (full), and staff assistantships also available. Support available to part-time students. Financial award applicants required to submit FAFSA. *Unit head:* Dr. Barbara Johnson, Interim Chair, 815-753-1448, E-mail: cahe@niu.edu. *Application contact:* Graduate School Office, 815-753-0395, E-mail: gradsch@niu.edu. Web site: http://www.cedu.niu.edu/cahe/index.html.

Northern Kentucky University, Office of Graduate Programs, College of Education and Human Services, Program in School Counseling, Highland Heights, KY 41099. Offers school counseling (MA); temporary school counseling provision (Certificate). Part-time and evening/weekend programs available. *Faculty:* 12 full-time (7 women), 1 part-time/adjunct (0 women). *Students:* 20 full-time (16 women), 32 part-time (26 women); includes 4 minority (all Black or African American, non-Hispanic/Latino). Average age 30. 31 applicants, 61% accepted, 17 enrolled. In 2011, 11 master's awarded. *Degree requirements:* For master's, portfolio, practicum, internship. *Entrance requirements:* For master's, GRE, interview, 3 letters of recommendation, minimum GPA of 2.75, criminal background check (state and federal). Additional exam requirements/recommendations for international students: Required—TOEFL (minimum score 550 paper-based; 213 computer-based; 79 iBT); Recommended—IELTS (minimum score 6.5). *Application deadline:* For fall admission, 7/1 for domestic students, 6/1 for international students; for spring admission, 11/1 for domestic students, 10/1 for international students. Applications are processed on a rolling basis. Application fee: $40. Electronic applications accepted. *Expenses:* Tuition, state resident: full-time $7614; part-time $423 per credit hour. Tuition, nonresident: full-time $13,104; part-time $728 per credit hour. Tuition and fees vary according to degree level and reciprocity agreements. *Financial support:* Unspecified assistantships available. Financial award applicants required to submit FAFSA. *Faculty research:* Impact of school counseling on achievement, counselor education pedagogy, counselor supervision, equity and social justice issues, instrument development and assessment. *Unit head:* Heidi Waters, CSWL Graduate Coordinator, 859-572-7892, Fax: 859-572-6592, E-mail: watersh2@nku.edu. *Application contact:* Dr. Peg Griffin, Director of Graduate Programs, 859-572-6934, Fax: 859-572-6670, E-mail: griffinp@nku.edu. Web site: http://coehs.nku.edu/departments/counseling/graduate/schooltrack.php.

Northern Michigan University, College of Graduate Studies, College of Professional Studies, School of Education, Program in School Guidance Counseling, Marquette, MI 49855-5301. Offers MA Ed.

Northern State University, Division of Graduate Studies in Education, Counseling Program, Aberdeen, SD 57401-7198. Offers MS Ed. *Accreditation:* NCATE. Part-time and evening/weekend programs available. *Degree requirements:* For master's, thesis optional. *Entrance requirements:* For master's, minimum GPA of 2.75. Additional exam requirements/recommendations for international students: Required—TOEFL (minimum score 550 paper-based; 213 computer-based; 78 iBT), IELTS (minimum score 6). Electronic applications accepted.

Northwest Christian University, School of Education and Counseling, Eugene, OR 97401-3745. Offers community counseling (MA); education (M Ed); school counseling (MA). Part-time and evening/weekend programs available. *Entrance requirements:* For master's, MAT, interview, minimum GPA of 3.0. Electronic applications accepted.

Northwestern Oklahoma State University, School of Professional Studies, Program in School Counseling, Alva, OK 73717-2799. Offers M Ed. *Accreditation:* NCATE. Part-time programs available. *Faculty:* 5 full-time (4 women). *Students:* 13 part-time (all women); includes 3 minority (1 Black or African American, non-Hispanic/Latino; 1 American Indian or Alaska Native, non-Hispanic/Latino; 1 Hispanic/Latino). 5 applicants,

100% accepted, 5 enrolled. In 2011, 7 master's awarded. *Degree requirements:* For master's, thesis optional, portfolio. *Entrance requirements:* For master's, GRE General Test or MAT, minimum GPA of 2.75. *Application deadline:* Applications are processed on a rolling basis. Application fee: $15. *Financial support:* Federal Work-Study available. Support available to part-time students. Financial award application deadline: 5/1; financial award applicants required to submit FAFSA. *Unit head:* Dr. Beverly Warden, Chair, Education Division, 580-327-8451. *Application contact:* Sabrina Watson, Coordinator of Graduate Studies, 580-327-8410, E-mail: sdwatson@nwosu.edu.

Northwestern State University of Louisiana, Graduate Studies and Research, College of Education and Human Development, Program in School Counseling, Natchitoches, LA 71497. Offers MA. *Students:* 18 full-time (15 women), 14 part-time (all women); includes 11 minority (10 Black or African American, non-Hispanic/Latino; 1 Hispanic/Latino). Average age 32. 20 applicants, 100% accepted, 13 enrolled. In 2011, 6 master's awarded. *Degree requirements:* For master's, comprehensive exam, thesis (for some programs). *Entrance requirements:* For master's, GRE General Test. Additional exam requirements/recommendations for international students: Required—TOEFL. *Application deadline:* For fall admission, 3/15 priority date for domestic students; for spring admission, 10/15 priority date for domestic students. Applications are processed on a rolling basis. Application fee: $20 ($30 for international students). Electronic applications accepted. *Expenses:* Tuition, state resident: full-time $3440. Tuition, nonresident: full-time $12,010. *Financial support:* Application deadline: 5/1; applicants required to submit FAFSA. *Unit head:* Dr. Vickie Gentry, Chair, 318-357-6288, Fax: 318-357-6275, E-mail: education@nsula.edu. *Application contact:* Dr. Steven G. Horton, Associate Provost/Dean, Graduate Studies, Research, and Information Systems, 318-357-5851, Fax: 318-357-5019, E-mail: grad_school@nsula.edu.

Northwestern State University of Louisiana, Graduate Studies and Research, College of Education and Human Development, Programs in Educational Leadership and Instruction, Natchitoches, LA 71497. Offers counseling (Ed S); educational leadership (M Ed, Ed S); educational technology (Ed S); elementary teaching (Ed S); reading (Ed S); secondary teaching (Ed S); special education (Ed S). *Accreditation:* NASAD. *Students:* 7 full-time (6 women), 75 part-time (59 women); includes 22 minority (18 Black or African American, non-Hispanic/Latino; 2 American Indian or Alaska Native, non-Hispanic/Latino; 2 Hispanic/Latino). Average age 36. 30 applicants, 97% accepted, 15 enrolled. In 2011, 31 master's, 16 Ed Ss awarded. *Degree requirements:* For master's, comprehensive exam, thesis (for some programs). *Entrance requirements:* For master's and Ed S, GRE General Test. Additional exam requirements/recommendations for international students: Required—TOEFL. *Application deadline:* For fall admission, 3/15 priority date for domestic students; for spring admission, 10/15 priority date for domestic students. Applications are processed on a rolling basis. Application fee: $20 ($30 for international students). Electronic applications accepted. *Expenses:* Tuition, state resident: full-time $3440. Tuition, nonresident: full-time $12,010. *Unit head:* Dr. Vickie Gentry, Chair, 318-357-6288, Fax: 318-357-6275, E-mail: education@nsula.edu. *Application contact:* Dr. Steven G. Horton, Associate Provost/Dean, Graduate Studies, Research, and Information Systems, 318-357-5851, Fax: 318-357-5019, E-mail: grad_school@nsula.edu.

Northwest Missouri State University, Graduate School, College of Education and Human Services, Department of Psychology and Sociology, Program in Guidance and Counseling, Maryville, MO 64468-6001. Offers MS Ed. *Accreditation:* NCATE. *Faculty:* 10 full-time (8 women). *Students:* 11 full-time (all women), 26 part-time (22 women); includes 1 minority (Black or African American, non-Hispanic/Latino). 1 applicant, 100% accepted. In 2011, 18 master's awarded. *Degree requirements:* For master's, comprehensive exam, thesis. *Entrance requirements:* For master's, GRE General Test, teaching certificate; 2 years of experience; minimum undergraduate GPA of 2.5, 3.0 in major; writing sample. Additional exam requirements/recommendations for international students: Required—TOEFL (minimum score 550 paper-based; 213 computer-based). *Application deadline:* For fall admission, 3/1 for domestic and international students. Applications are processed on a rolling basis. Application fee: $0 ($50 for international students). *Financial support:* In 2011–12, 4 research assistantships with full tuition reimbursements (averaging $6,000 per year), 5 teaching assistantships with full tuition reimbursements (averaging $6,000 per year) were awarded. Financial award application deadline: 4/1; financial award applicants required to submit FAFSA. *Unit head:* Dr. Rochelle Hiatt, Program Director, 660-562-1287. *Application contact:* Dr. Gregory Haddock, Dean of Graduate School, 660-562-1145, Fax: 660-562-1096, E-mail: gradsch@nwmissouri.edu.

Northwest Nazarene University, Graduate Studies, Program in Counselor Education, Nampa, ID 83686-5897. Offers clinical counseling (MS); marriage and family counseling (MS); school counseling (MS). Part-time programs available. *Faculty:* 7 full-time (5 women), 9 part-time/adjunct (5 women). *Students:* 101 full-time (75 women), 33 part-time (26 women); includes 11 minority (3 Black or African American, non-Hispanic/Latino; 3 Asian, non-Hispanic/Latino; 5 Hispanic/Latino), 1 international. Average age 34. 32 applicants, 97% accepted, 26 enrolled. In 2011, 29 master's awarded. Application fee: $25. *Unit head:* Dr. Brenda Freeman, Chair, 208-467-8428, Fax: 208-467-8339. *Application contact:* Judy Bassett, Program Assistant, 208-467-8345, Fax: 208-467-8339, E-mail: jbassett@nnu.edu.

Nova Southeastern University, Center for Psychological Studies, Fort Lauderdale, FL 33314-7796. Offers clinical psychology (PhD, Psy D); clinical psychopharmacology (MS); counseling (MS); general psychology (MS); mental health counseling (MS); school counseling (MS); school psychology (Psy D, Psy S). *Accreditation:* APA (one or more programs are accredited). Postbaccalaureate distance learning degree programs offered. *Faculty:* 34 full-time (11 women), 68 part-time/adjunct (32 women). *Students:* 943 full-time (804 women), 787 part-time (703 women); includes 756 minority (265 Black or African American, non-Hispanic/Latino; 2 American Indian or Alaska Native, non-Hispanic/Latino; 39 Asian, non-Hispanic/Latino; 421 Hispanic/Latino; 1 Native Hawaiian or other Pacific Islander, non-Hispanic/Latino; 28 Two or more races, non-Hispanic/Latino), 31 international. Average age 30. 1,433 applicants, 49% accepted, 520 enrolled. In 2011, 339 master's, 102 doctorates, 23 other advanced degrees awarded. Terminal master's awarded for partial completion of doctoral program. *Degree requirements:* For master's, comprehensive exam, 3 practica; for doctorate, thesis/dissertation, clinical internship, competency exam; for Psy S, comprehensive exam, internship. *Entrance requirements:* For doctorate, GRE General Test, GRE Subject Test (recommended), minimum undergraduate GPA of 3.0; for Psy S, GRE General Test. Additional exam requirements/recommendations for international students: Required—TOEFL (minimum score 550 paper-based; 213 computer-based). *Application deadline:* Applications are processed on a rolling basis. Application fee: $50. Electronic applications accepted. *Expenses:* Contact institution. *Financial support:* In 2011–12, 5 research assistantships, 34 teaching assistantships (averaging $1,000 per year) were awarded; career-related internships or fieldwork, Federal Work-Study, institutionally sponsored loans, scholarships/grants, and unspecified assistantships also available. Support available to part-time students. Financial award application deadline: 4/1. *Faculty research:* Clinical and child clinical psychology, geriatrics, interpersonal violence. *Unit head:* Karen Grosby, Dean, 954-262-5701, Fax: 954-262-3859, E-mail: grosby@nova.edu. *Application contact:* Carlos Perez, Enrollment Management, 954-262-5790, Fax: 954-262-3893, E-mail: cpsinfo@cps.nova.edu. Web site: http://www.cps.nova.edu/.

Nyack College, Alliance Graduate School of Counseling, Nyack, NY 10960-3698. Offers marriage and family therapy (MA); mental health counseling (MA). Part-time programs available. *Students:* 58 full-time (47 women), 228 part-time (185 women); includes 206 minority (105 Black or African American, non-Hispanic/Latino; 37 Asian, non-Hispanic/Latino; 55 Hispanic/Latino; 9 Two or more races, non-Hispanic/Latino), 11 international. Average age 40. In 2011, 58 master's awarded. *Degree requirements:* For master's, comprehensive exam, counselor-in-training therapy, internship, CPCE exam. *Entrance requirements:* For master's, Millon Clinical Multiaxial Inventory-III, Minnesota Multiphasic Personality Inventory-2, transcripts, statement of Christian life and experience, statement of support systems. Additional exam requirements/recommendations for international students: Required—TOEFL (minimum score 220 computer-based; 83 iBT). *Application deadline:* For fall admission, 8/1 for domestic students. Applications are processed on a rolling basis. Application fee: $35. Electronic applications accepted. *Expenses:* Contact institution. *Financial support:* Teaching assistantships, career-related internships or fieldwork, and scholarships/grants available. Financial award applicants required to submit FAFSA. *Unit head:* Dr. Carol Robles, Director, 845-770-5730, Fax: 845-348-3923. *Application contact:* Traci Piescki, Director of Admissions, 800-541-6891, Fax: 845-348-3912, E-mail: admissions.grad@nyack.edu. Web site: http://www.nyack.edu/agsc.

Ohio University, Graduate College, Gladys W. and David H. Patton College of Education and Human Services, Department of Counseling and Higher Education, Athens, OH 45701-2979. Offers college student personnel (M Ed); community/agency counseling (M Ed); counselor education (PhD); higher education (PhD); rehabilitation counseling (M Ed); school counseling (M Ed). *Accreditation:* ACA; CORE. Part-time and evening/weekend programs available. *Students:* 174 full-time (133 women), 40 part-time (25 women); includes 38 minority (21 Black or African American, non-Hispanic/Latino; 2 American Indian or Alaska Native, non-Hispanic/Latino; 2 Asian, non-Hispanic/Latino; 7 Hispanic/Latino; 6 Two or more races, non-Hispanic/Latino), 9 international. 130 applicants, 59% accepted, 62 enrolled. In 2011, 45 master's, 7 doctorates awarded. *Degree requirements:* For master's, comprehensive exam (for some programs), thesis or alternative; for doctorate, comprehensive exam, thesis/dissertation. *Entrance requirements:* For master's, GRE General Test or MAT (if GPA less than 2.9), 3 letters of reference; for doctorate, GRE General Test, work experience, minimum GPA of 3.4. Additional exam requirements/recommendations for international students: Required—TOEFL (minimum score 550 paper-based; 80 iBT) or IELTS (minimum score 6.5). *Application deadline:* For fall admission, 1/15 for domestic and international students. Application fee: $50 ($55 for international students). Electronic applications accepted. *Financial support:* Research assistantships with full tuition reimbursements, teaching assistantships with full tuition reimbursements, Federal Work-Study, institutionally sponsored loans, tuition waivers (partial), and unspecified assistantships available. Financial award application deadline: 1/15. *Faculty research:* Youth violence, gender studies, student affairs, chemical dependency, disabilities issues. *Total annual research expenditures:* $527,983. *Unit head:* Dr. Tracy Leinbaugh, Chair, 740-593-0846, Fax: 740-593-0477, E-mail: leinbaug@ohio.edu. *Application contact:* Floyd J. Doney, Director of Student Affairs, 740-593-4400, Fax: 740-593-9310, E-mail: doney@ohio.edu. Web site: http://www.cehs.ohio.edu/academics/che/.

Old Dominion University, Darden College of Education, Counseling Program, Norfolk, VA 23529. Offers MS Ed, PhD, Ed S. *Accreditation:* ACA. Part-time and evening/weekend programs available. Postbaccalaureate distance learning degree programs offered (minimal on-campus study). *Faculty:* 14 full-time (8 women), 10 part-time/adjunct (6 women). *Students:* 135 full-time (114 women), 75 part-time (63 women); includes 73 minority (59 Black or African American, non-Hispanic/Latino; 1 Asian, non-Hispanic/Latino; 6 Hispanic/Latino; 2 Native Hawaiian or other Pacific Islander, non-Hispanic/Latino; 5 Two or more races, non-Hispanic/Latino), 1 international. Average age 30. 175 applicants, 40% accepted, 60 enrolled. In 2011, 50 master's, 14 doctorates, 1 other advanced degree awarded. *Degree requirements:* For master's and Ed S, comprehensive exam; for doctorate, comprehensive exam, thesis/dissertation. *Entrance requirements:* For master's and Ed S, GRE General Test, resume, essay; for doctorate, GRE General Test, resume, interview, essay. Additional exam requirements/recommendations for international students: Required—TOEFL. *Application deadline:* For fall admission, 2/1 for domestic students; for winter admission, 10/1 for domestic students; for spring admission, 10/1 for domestic students. Application fee: $50. Electronic applications accepted. *Expenses:* Tuition, state resident: full-time $9096; part-time $379 per credit. Tuition, nonresident: full-time $23,064; part-time $961 per credit. *Required fees:* $127 per semester. One-time fee: $50. *Financial support:* In 2011–12, 125 students received support, including 2 fellowships with full tuition reimbursements available (averaging $15,000 per year), 20 research assistantships with partial tuition reimbursements available (averaging $10,000 per year), 14 teaching assistantships with full tuition reimbursements available (averaging $15,000 per year); career-related internships or fieldwork, Federal Work-Study, institutionally sponsored loans, scholarships/grants, traineeships, tuition waivers (partial), and unspecified assistantships also available. Support available to part-time students. Financial award applicants required to submit FAFSA. *Faculty research:* Group counseling, counselor education, career counseling, spirituality and counseling, school counseling, GLBT counseling, legal and ethical issues. *Total annual research expenditures:* $75,000. *Unit head:* Dr. Timothy Grothaus, Graduate Program Director, 757-683-3326, Fax: 757-683-5756, E-mail: tgrothau@odu.edu. Web site: http://www.education.odu.edu/chs/academics/counseling.

Oregon State University, Graduate School, College of Education, Program in Counseling, Corvallis, OR 97331. Offers MS, PhD. *Accreditation:* ACA (one or more programs are accredited); NCATE. *Degree requirements:* For master's, thesis or alternative; for doctorate, one foreign language, thesis/dissertation. *Entrance requirements:* For master's, minimum GPA of 3.0 in last 90 hours; for doctorate, GRE or MAT, master's degree, minimum GPA of 3.0 in last 90 hours of course work, 2 years of teaching experience. Additional exam requirements/recommendations for international students: Required—TOEFL. *Faculty research:* Counseling and guidance improvement in social services agencies, elementary and secondary schools.

Ottawa University, Graduate Studies-Arizona, Program in Education, Ottawa, KS 66067-3399. Offers community college counseling (MA); curriculum and instruction (MA); early childhood (MA); education intervention (MA); education leadership (MA); education technology (MA); Montessori early childhood education (MA); Montessori elementary education (MA); professional development (MA); school guidance counseling (MA); special education - cross categorical (MA). Programs offered in Mesa, Phoenix, Tempe and West Valley, AZ. *Accreditation:* NCATE. Part-time programs available. *Degree requirements:* For master's, thesis or alternative. *Entrance requirements:* For master's, minimum undergraduate GPA of 3.0, copy of current state certification or teaching license. Additional exam requirements/recommendations for international students: Required—TOEFL (minimum score 550 paper-based; 213 computer-based). Electronic applications accepted. *Expenses:* Contact institution.

Our Lady of Holy Cross College, Program in Education and Counseling, New Orleans, LA 70131-7399. Offers administration and supervision (M Ed); curriculum and instruction (M Ed); marriage and family counseling (MA); school counseling (M Ed, MA). *Accreditation:* ACA; NCATE. Part-time and evening/weekend programs available. *Degree requirements:* For master's, thesis. *Entrance requirements:* For master's, GRE General Test, minimum GPA of 2.7.

Our Lady of the Lake University of San Antonio, School of Professional Studies, Program in School Counseling, San Antonio, TX 78207-4689. Offers M Ed. Part-time and evening/weekend programs available. *Degree requirements:* For master's, comprehensive exam, thesis optional, practicum. *Entrance requirements:* For master's, GRE General Test or MAT, interview. Additional exam requirements/recommendations for international students: Required—TOEFL. Electronic applications accepted.

Palm Beach Atlantic University, School of Education and Behavioral Studies, West Palm Beach, FL 33416-4708. Offers counseling psychology (MS), including addictions/mental health, marriage and family therapy, mental health counseling, school guidance counseling. Part-time and evening/weekend programs available. *Faculty:* 13 full-time (4 women), 11 part-time/adjunct (6 women). *Students:* 251 full-time (213 women), 53 part-time (46 women); includes 118 minority (65 Black or African American, non-Hispanic/Latino; 4 Asian, non-Hispanic/Latino; 47 Hispanic/Latino; 2 Native Hawaiian or other Pacific Islander, non-Hispanic/Latino), 5 international. Average age 35. 135 applicants, 64% accepted, 72 enrolled. In 2011, 101 master's awarded. *Entrance requirements:* For master's, GRE, minimum GPA of 3.0. Additional exam requirements/recommendations for international students: Required—TOEFL (minimum score 550 paper-based; 213 computer-based; 79 iBT). *Application deadline:* For fall admission, 7/15 priority date for domestic students; for spring admission, 11/15 priority date for domestic students. Applications are processed on a rolling basis. Application fee: $45. Electronic applications accepted. *Expenses: Tuition:* Full-time $11,478; part-time $470 per credit hour. *Required fees:* $99 per semester. Tuition and fees vary according to course load, degree level and campus/location. *Financial support:* Applicants required to submit FAFSA. *Unit head:* Dr. Lisa Stubbs, Program Director, 561-803-2286. *Application contact:* Graduate Admissions, 888-468-6722, E-mail: grad@pba.edu. Web site: http://www.pba.edu/.

Penn State University Park, Graduate School, College of Education, Department of Educational Psychology and Special Education, State College, University Park, PA 16802-1503. Offers counselor education (M Ed, MS, PhD); educational psychology (MS, PhD, Certificate); school psychology (M Ed, MS, PhD, Certificate); special education (M Ed, MS, PhD, Certificate). *Unit head:* Dr. David H. Monk, Dean, 814-865-2526, Fax: 814-865-0555, E-mail: dhm6@psu.edu. *Application contact:* Cynthia E. Nicosia, Director, Graduate Enrollment Services, 814-865-1834, E-mail: cey1@psu.edu. Web site: http://www.ed.psu.edu/educ/epcse.

Phillips Graduate Institute, Programs in Marriage and Family Therapy and School Counseling, Encino, CA 91316-1509. Offers art therapy (MA); marriage and family therapy (MA); school counseling (MA). Evening/weekend programs available. *Degree requirements:* For master's, comprehensive exam, thesis. *Entrance requirements:* For master's, minimum GPA of 2.5. *Application deadline:* For fall admission, 4/16 priority date for domestic students; for spring admission, 11/15 for domestic students. Applications are processed on a rolling basis. Application fee: $75. Electronic applications accepted. *Expenses: Tuition:* Full-time $20,746; part-time $820 per unit. *Required fees:* $300 per semester. *Financial support:* Federal Work-Study and tuition waivers (full and partial) available. Financial award application deadline: 8/15; financial award applicants required to submit FAFSA. *Faculty research:* Integration of interpersonal psychological theory, systems approach, firsthand experiential learning. *Application contact:* Kim Bell, Admissions Advisor, 818-386-5639, Fax: 818-386-5699, E-mail: kbell@pgi.edu.

Pittsburg State University, Graduate School, College of Education, Department of Psychology and Counseling, Program in Counselor Education, Pittsburg, KS 66762. Offers community counseling (MS); school counseling (MS). *Accreditation:* ACA; NCATE. *Degree requirements:* For master's, thesis or alternative. *Entrance requirements:* For master's, GRE General Test, minimum GPA of 2.8.

Plymouth State University, College of Graduate Studies, Graduate Studies in Education, Program in Counselor Education, Plymouth, NH 03264-1595. Offers M Ed. *Accreditation:* ACA; NCATE. Part-time and evening/weekend programs available. *Degree requirements:* For master's, PRAXIS I. *Entrance requirements:* For master's, MAT, minimum GPA of 3.0.

Pontifical Catholic University of Puerto Rico, College of Education, Program in Counselor Education, Ponce, PR 00717-0777. Offers M Ed. *Degree requirements:* For master's, comprehensive exam, thesis (for some programs). *Entrance requirements:* For master's, GRE, 2 letters of recommendation, interview, minimum GPA of 2.75.

Portland State University, Graduate Studies, School of Education, Department of Special Education and Counselor Education, Portland, OR 97207-0751. Offers counselor education (MA, MS); special and counselor education (Ed D); special education (MA, MS). *Accreditation:* ACA (one or more programs are accredited). Part-time and evening/weekend programs available. *Degree requirements:* For master's, thesis or alternative. *Entrance requirements:* For master's, California Basic Educational Skills Test, minimum GPA of 3.0 in upper-division course work or 2.75 overall. Additional exam requirements/recommendations for international students: Required—TOEFL (minimum score 550 paper-based; 213 computer-based). *Faculty research:* Transition of students with disabilities, functional curriculum, supported/inclusive education, leisure/recreation, autism.

Prairie View A&M University, College of Education, Department of Educational Leadership and Counseling, Prairie View, TX 77446-0519. Offers counseling (MA, MS Ed); educational administration (M Ed, MS Ed); educational leadership (PhD). *Accreditation:* NCATE. Part-time and evening/weekend programs available. *Degree requirements:* For master's, thesis optional; for doctorate, comprehensive exam, thesis/dissertation. *Entrance requirements:* For master's, GRE General Test, 3 letters of reference, minimum undergraduate GPA of 2.5; for doctorate, GRE General Test, 3 letters of reference. Additional exam requirements/recommendations for international students: Required—TOEFL (minimum score 550 paper-based). Electronic applications accepted. *Faculty research:* Mentoring, personality assessment, holistic/humanistic education.

Prescott College, Graduate Programs, Program in Education, Prescott, AZ 86301. Offers early childhood education (MA); early childhood special education (MA); education (MA); elementary education (MA); environmental education leadership and administration (MA); equine-assisted experiential learning (MA); school guidance counseling (MA); secondary education (MA); special education, learning disability (MA); special education, mental retardation (MA); special education, serious emotional disability (MA); student-directed independent study (MA); sustainability education (PhD). Part-time programs available. Postbaccalaureate distance learning degree programs offered (minimal on-campus study). *Faculty:* 2 full-time (both women), 47 part-time/adjunct (31 women). *Students:* 59 full-time (36 women), 48 part-time (30 women); includes 16 minority (3 Black or African American, non-Hispanic/Latino; 1 American Indian or Alaska Native, non-Hispanic/Latino; 1 Asian, non-Hispanic/Latino; 8 Hispanic/Latino; 3 Two or more races, non-Hispanic/Latino), 2 international. Average age 40. 75 applicants, 76% accepted, 36 enrolled. In 2011, 14 master's, 8 doctorates awarded. *Degree requirements:* For master's, thesis, fieldwork or internship, practicum; for doctorate, thesis/dissertation. *Entrance requirements:* For master's, 2 letters of recommendation, resume; for doctorate, 3 letters of recommendation, resume, official transcripts, personal statement, program proposal. Additional exam requirements/recommendations for international students: Required—TOEFL (minimum score 500 paper-based; 173 computer-based). *Application deadline:* For fall admission, 4/15 priority date for domestic students, 4/15 for international students; for spring admission, 9/15 priority date for domestic students, 9/15 for international students. Applications are processed on a rolling basis. Application fee: $40. Electronic applications accepted. *Expenses: Tuition:* Full-time $16,440; part-time $685 per credit. *Required fees:* $150 per semester. One-time fee: $350. *Financial support:* Career-related internships or fieldwork and Federal Work-Study available. Financial award applicants required to submit FAFSA. *Unit head:* Noel Caniglia, Chair, 928-358-3201, Fax: 928-776-5151, E-mail: ncaniglia@prescott.edu. *Application contact:* Kerstin Alicki, Admissions Counselor, 928-350-2100, Fax: 928-776-5242, E-mail: admissions@prescott.edu.

Providence College, Program in Counseling, Providence, RI 02918. Offers M Ed. Part-time and evening/weekend programs available. *Faculty:* 14 part-time/adjunct (6 women). *Students:* 33 full-time (26 women), 51 part-time (42 women); includes 5 minority (all Hispanic/Latino). Average age 31. 70 applicants, 83% accepted, 23 enrolled. In 2011, 31 master's awarded. *Degree requirements:* For master's, comprehensive exam. *Entrance requirements:* For master's, GRE General Test. Additional exam requirements/recommendations for international students: Required—TOEFL (minimum score 550 paper-based; 213 computer-based; 80 iBT). *Application deadline:* For fall admission, 8/1 priority date for domestic students, 8/1 for international students; for spring admission, 12/1 priority date for domestic students, 12/1 for international students. Applications are processed on a rolling basis. Application fee: $55. *Expenses: Tuition:* Part-time $404 per credit. *Required fees:* $404 per credit. *Financial support:* In 2011–12, 12 research assistantships with full tuition reimbursements (averaging $8,400 per year) were awarded; career-related internships or fieldwork, institutionally sponsored loans, and unspecified assistantships also available. Support available to part-time students. Financial award application deadline: 8/1; financial award applicants required to submit FAFSA. *Unit head:* Alexander J. Freda, Director, 401-865-2247, Fax: 401-865-1147, E-mail: afreda@providence.edu. *Application contact:* Carol A. Daniels, Coordinator of Graduate Faculty and Administrative Services, 401-865-2247, Fax: 401-865-1147, E-mail: daniels@providence.edu. Web site: http://www.providence.edu/professional-studies/graduate-degrees/Pages/master-education-counseling.aspx.

Purdue University, Graduate School, College of Education, Department of Educational Studies, West Lafayette, IN 47907. Offers administration (MS Ed, PhD, Ed S); counseling and development (MS Ed, PhD); education of the gifted (MS Ed); educational psychology (MS Ed, PhD); foundations of education (MS Ed, PhD); higher education administration (MS Ed, PhD); special education (MS Ed, PhD). *Accreditation:* ACA (one or more programs are accredited); NCATE (one or more programs are accredited). Part-time and evening/weekend programs available. *Faculty:* 23 full-time (17 women), 1 part-time/adjunct (0 women). *Students:* 111 full-time (79 women), 93 part-time (58 women); includes 34 minority (19 Black or African American, non-Hispanic/Latino; 1 American Indian or Alaska Native, non-Hispanic/Latino; 4 Asian, non-Hispanic/Latino; 6 Hispanic/Latino; 4 Two or more races, non-Hispanic/Latino), 30 international. Average age 35. 249 applicants, 37% accepted, 46 enrolled. In 2011, 39 master's, 20 doctorates, 4 other advanced degrees awarded. *Degree requirements:* For master's, thesis optional; for doctorate, thesis/dissertation, oral and written exams; for Ed S, oral presentation, project. *Entrance requirements:* For master's, GRE General Test required for all Educational Studies program areas, except for Special Education if undergraduate GPA is higher than a 3.0, minimum undergraduate GPA of 3.0; for doctorate and Ed S, GRE general test is required, a combined score of 1000 (300 for revised GRE test) or more is expected., minimum undergraduate GPA of 3.0. Additional exam requirements/recommendations for international students: Required—TOEFL (minimum score 550 paper-based; 77 iBT), TWE (minimum score 5). *Application deadline:* Applications are processed on a rolling basis. Application fee: $60 ($75 for international students). Electronic applications accepted. *Financial support:* Fellowships with full tuition reimbursements, research assistantships with full tuition reimbursements, teaching assistantships with full tuition reimbursements, career-related internships or fieldwork, and tuition waivers (full) available. Support available to part-time students. Financial award application deadline: 3/1; financial award applicants required to submit FAFSA. *Faculty research:* Motivation, learning disabilities, school learning, group processes, cognitive development. *Unit head:* Dr. Ala Samrapungavan, Head, 765-494-9170, Fax: 765-496-1228, E-mail: ala@purdue.edu. *Application contact:* Sarah N. Prater, Graduate Contact, 765-494-2345, Fax: 765-494-5832, E-mail: prater0@purdue.edu. Web site: http://www.edst.purdue.edu/.

Purdue University Calumet, Graduate Studies Office, School of Education, Program in Counseling, Hammond, IN 46323-2094. Offers human services (MS Ed); mental health counseling (MS Ed); school counseling (MS Ed). *Entrance requirements:* Additional exam requirements/recommendations for international students: Required—TOEFL.

Queens College of the City University of New York, Division of Graduate Studies, Division of Education, Department of Educational and Community Programs, Program in Counselor Education, Flushing, NY 11367-1597. Offers MS Ed. Part-time programs available. *Faculty:* 3 full-time (1 woman). *Students:* 41 full-time (36 women), 54 part-time (38 women); includes 49 minority (13 Black or African American, non-Hispanic/Latino; 13 Asian, non-Hispanic/Latino; 23 Hispanic/Latino), 2 international. 165 applicants, 26% accepted, 32 enrolled. In 2011, 26 master's awarded. *Degree requirements:* For master's, research project. *Entrance requirements:* For master's, minimum GPA of 3.0. Additional exam requirements/recommendations for international students: Required—TOEFL. *Application deadline:* For fall admission, 4/1 for domestic students; for spring admission, 11/1 for domestic students. Applications are processed on a rolling basis. Application fee: $125. *Expenses:* Tuition, state resident: part-time $345 per credit. Tuition, nonresident: part-time $640 per credit. *Required fees:* $145.25 per semester. *Financial support:* Career-related internships or fieldwork, Federal Work-Study, institutionally sponsored loans, and tuition waivers (partial) available. Support available to part-time students. Financial award application deadline: 4/1; financial award applicants required to submit FAFSA. *Unit head:* Dr. John Pellitteri, Coordinator and Graduate Adviser, 718-997-5246, E-mail: john_pellitteri@qc.edu. *Application contact:* Mario Caruso, Director of Graduate Admissions, 718-997-5200, Fax: 718-997-5193, E-mail: graduate_admissions@qc.edu.

Quincy University, Program in Counseling, Quincy, IL 62301-2699. Offers education (MS Ed), including clinical mental health counseling, school counseling. Part-time and evening/weekend programs available. *Faculty:* 2 full-time (1 woman). *Students:* 6 full-time (5 women), 19 part-time (all women). In 2011, 5 master's awarded. *Degree requirements:* For master's, comprehensive exam, practicum, internship. *Entrance requirements:* For master's, MAT or GRE. Additional exam requirements/recommendations for international students: Required—TOEFL (minimum score 550 paper-based; 79 iBT). *Application deadline:* Applications are processed on a rolling basis. Application fee: $25. Electronic applications accepted. *Expenses: Tuition:* Full-time $9120; part-time $380 per semester hour. *Required fees:* $360; $15 per semester hour. Tuition and fees vary according to course load, campus/location and program.

Financial support: Available to part-time students. Applicants required to submit FAFSA. *Unit head:* Dr. Kenneth Oliver, Director, 217-228-5432 Ext. 3113, E-mail: oliveke@quincy.edu. *Application contact:* Office of Admissions, 217-228-5210, Fax: 217-228-5479, E-mail: admissions@quincy.edu. Web site: http://www.quincy.edu/academics/graduate-programs/counseling.

Radford University, College of Graduate and Professional Studies, College of Education and Human Development, Department of Counselor Education, Radford, VA 24142. Offers clinical mental health counseling (MS); school counseling (MS). *Accreditation:* ACA; NCATE. Part-time and evening/weekend programs available. *Faculty:* 7 full-time (4 women). *Students:* 63 full-time (43 women), 20 part-time (17 women); includes 8 minority (4 Black or African American, non-Hispanic/Latino; 1 American Indian or Alaska Native, non-Hispanic/Latino; 1 Asian, non-Hispanic/Latino; 1 Hispanic/Latino; 1 Two or more races, non-Hispanic/Latino). Average age 28. 68 applicants, 90% accepted, 34 enrolled. In 2011, 52 master's awarded. *Degree requirements:* For master's, comprehensive exam, thesis optional. *Entrance requirements:* For master's, GRE or MAT, minimum GPA of 2.75, 3 letters of reference, personal essay. Additional exam requirements/recommendations for international students: Required—TOEFL (minimum score 550 paper-based; 213 computer-based; 79 iBT). *Application deadline:* For fall admission, 2/15 priority date for domestic students, 12/1 for international students; for spring admission, 7/1 for international students. Applications are processed on a rolling basis. Application fee: $50. Electronic applications accepted. *Expenses:* Tuition, state resident: full-time $6262; part-time $261 per credit hour. Tuition, nonresident: full-time $14,540; part-time $606 per credit hour. *Required fees:* $2812; $117 per credit hour. Tuition and fees vary according to program. *Financial support:* In 2011–12, 26 students received support, including 11 research assistantships (averaging $7,670 per year), 6 teaching assistantships with partial tuition reimbursements available (averaging $8,908 per year); career-related internships or fieldwork, Federal Work-Study, institutionally sponsored loans, scholarships/grants, and unspecified assistantships also available. Financial award application deadline: 3/1; financial award applicants required to submit FAFSA. *Unit head:* Dr. Alan Forrest, Chair, 540-831-5487, Fax: 540-831-6755, E-mail: aforrest@radford.edu. *Application contact:* Rebecca Conner, Graduate Admissions, 540-831-5431, Fax: 540-831-6061, E-mail: gradcollege@radford.edu. Web site: http://www.radford.edu/content/cehd/home/departments/counselor-education.html.

Regent University, Graduate School, School of Psychology and Counseling, Virginia Beach, VA 23464-9800. Offers clinical psychology (MA, Psy D); counseling (MA), including community counseling, school counseling; counseling studies (CAGS); counselor education and supervision (PhD); human services counseling (MA); M Div/MA; M Ed/MA; MBA/MA. PhD program offered online only. *Accreditation:* ACA; APA (one or more programs are accredited). Part-time and evening/weekend programs available. Postbaccalaureate distance learning degree programs offered (minimal on-campus study). *Faculty:* 31 full-time (18 women), 27 part-time/adjunct (17 women). *Students:* 262 full-time (201 women), 212 part-time (167 women); includes 126 minority (104 Black or African American, non-Hispanic/Latino; 1 American Indian or Alaska Native, non-Hispanic/Latino; 9 Asian, non-Hispanic/Latino; 12 Hispanic/Latino), 25 international. Average age 35. 474 applicants, 49% accepted, 161 enrolled. In 2011, 93 master's, 34 doctorates awarded. *Degree requirements:* For master's, thesis or alternative, internship, practicum, written competency exam; for doctorate, thesis/dissertation or alternative. *Entrance requirements:* For master's, GRE General Test including writing exam, minimum undergraduate GPA of 2.75, 3 recommendations, resume, transcripts, writing sample; for doctorate, GRE General Test including writing exam, GRE Subject Test, minimum undergraduate GPA of 3.0, 3.5 (PhD), 10-15 minute VHS tape demonstrating counseling skills, writing sample, 3 recommendations, resume. Additional exam requirements/recommendations for international students: Required—TOEFL (minimum score 577 paper-based; 233 computer-based). *Application deadline:* For fall admission, 4/1 priority date for domestic students; for spring admission, 11/1 priority date for domestic students. Applications are processed on a rolling basis. Application fee: $50. Electronic applications accepted. *Expenses:* Contact institution. *Financial support:* Research assistantships with full and partial tuition reimbursements, teaching assistantships with full and partial tuition reimbursements, career-related internships or fieldwork, scholarships/grants, and tuition waivers (full and partial) available. Support available to part-time students. Financial award application deadline: 9/1; financial award applicants required to submit FAFSA. *Faculty research:* Marriage enrichment, AIDS counseling, troubled youth, faith and learning, trauma. *Unit head:* Dr. William Hathaway, Dean, 757-352-4294, Fax: 757-352-4282, E-mail: willhat@regent.edu. *Application contact:* Matthew Chadwick, Director of Enrollment Support Services, 800-373-5504, Fax: 757-352-4381, E-mail: admissions@regent.edu. Web site: http://www.regent.edu/psychology/.

Rhode Island College, School of Graduate Studies, Feinstein School of Education and Human Development, Department of Counseling, Educational Leadership, and School Psychology, Providence, RI 02908-1991. Offers agency counseling (MA); co-occurring disorders (MA, CGS); educational leadership (M Ed); mental health counseling (CAGS); school counseling (MA); school psychology (CAGS). *Accreditation:* NCATE. Part-time and evening/weekend programs available. *Faculty:* 9 full-time (5 women), 13 part-time/adjunct (8 women). *Students:* 30 full-time (22 women), 147 part-time (111 women); includes 13 minority (4 Black or African American, non-Hispanic/Latino; 1 Asian, non-Hispanic/Latino; 8 Hispanic/Latino). Average age 33. In 2011, 48 master's, 15 other advanced degrees awarded. *Degree requirements:* For master's and other advanced degree, comprehensive exam (for some programs), thesis (for some programs). *Entrance requirements:* For master's, GRE General Test or MAT, undergraduate transcripts; minimum undergraduate GPA of 3.0; for other advanced degree, GRE or MAT (for most programs), undergraduate transcripts; minimum undergraduate GPA of 3.0; 3 letters of recommendation; current resume. Additional exam requirements/recommendations for international students: Recommended—TOEFL (minimum score 550 paper-based; 213 computer-based; 79 iBT). *Application deadline:* For fall admission, 3/1 for domestic students; for spring admission, 11/1 for domestic students. Applications are processed on a rolling basis. Application fee: $50. *Expenses:* Tuition, state resident: full-time $8592; part-time $358 per credit hour. Tuition, nonresident: full-time $16,800; part-time $700 per credit hour. *Required fees:* $602; $22 per credit. $72 per term. *Financial support:* Teaching assistantships with full tuition reimbursements, career-related internships or fieldwork, Federal Work-Study, scholarships/grants, health care benefits, and unspecified assistantships available. Support available to part-time students. Financial award application deadline: 5/15; financial award applicants required to submit FAFSA. *Unit head:* Dr. Monica Darcy, Chair, 401-456-8023. *Application contact:* Graduate Studies, 401-456-8700. Web site: http://www.ric.edu/counselingEducationalLeadershipSchoolPsychology/index.php.

Rider University, Department of Graduate Education, Leadership and Counseling, Program in Counseling Services, Lawrenceville, NJ 08648-3001. Offers counseling services (MA, Ed S); director of school counseling (Certificate); school counseling services (Certificate). *Accreditation:* ACA; NCATE. Part-time and evening/weekend programs available. *Degree requirements:* For master's, comprehensive exam, research project; for other advanced degree, specialty seminar. *Entrance requirements:* For master's, GRE or MAT, interview, resume, 2 letters of recommendation; for other advanced degree, GRE or MAT, interview, professional experience, 2 letters of recommendation. Additional exam requirements/recommendations for international students: Required—TOEFL (minimum score 550 paper-based; 213 computer-based). Electronic applications accepted. *Expenses: Tuition:* Full-time $32,820; part-time $710 per credit. *Required fees:* $350; $35 per course. Tuition and fees vary according to campus/location and program. *Faculty research:* Diversity in counseling.

Rivier University, School of Graduate Studies, Department of Education, Nashua, NH 03060. Offers curriculum and instruction (M Ed); early childhood education (M Ed); educational administration (M Ed); educational studies (M Ed); elementary education (M Ed); elementary education and general special education (M Ed); emotional and behavioral disorders (M Ed); general social education (M Ed); leadership and learning (Ed D, CAGS); learning disabilities (M Ed); learning disabilities and reading (M Ed); mental health counseling (MA); reading (M Ed); school counseling (M Ed). Part-time and evening/weekend programs available. *Degree requirements:* For master's, comprehensive exam (for some programs), internships. *Entrance requirements:* For master's, GRE General Test or MAT.

Roberts Wesleyan College, Division of Social Sciences, Rochester, NY 14624-1997. Offers counseling in ministry (MA); school counseling (MS); school psychology (MS).

Rollins College, Hamilton Holt School, Master of Arts in Counseling Program, Winter Park, FL 32789. Offers mental health counseling (MA). *Accreditation:* ACA. Part-time and evening/weekend programs available. *Faculty:* 5 full-time (2 women), 5 part-time/adjunct (4 women). *Students:* 44 full-time (39 women), 41 part-time (32 women); includes 18 minority (6 Black or African American, non-Hispanic/Latino; 1 Asian, non-Hispanic/Latino; 9 Hispanic/Latino; 2 Two or more races, non-Hispanic/Latino). Average age 30. In 2011, 30 master's awarded. *Degree requirements:* For master's, satisfactory completion of pre-practicum, practicum, and internship (1,000 hours total). *Entrance requirements:* For master's, GRE General Test or MAT, official transcripts, minimum GPA of 3.0, three letters of recommendation, essay, current resume. Additional exam requirements/recommendations for international students: Required—TOEFL (minimum score 550 paper-based; 213 computer-based; 80 iBT). *Application deadline:* For fall admission, 3/15 for domestic students. Application fee: $50. *Expenses:* Contact institution. *Financial support:* In 2011–12, 63 students received support. Federal Work-Study, scholarships/grants, and unspecified assistantships available. Support available to part-time students. Financial award applicants required to submit FAFSA. *Unit head:* Dr. Derrick Paladino, Faculty Director, 407-646-1567, E-mail: dpaladino@rollins.edu. *Application contact:* Rebecca Cordray, Coordinator of Records and Registration, 407-646-1568, Fax: 407-975-6430, E-mail: rcordray@rollins.edu. Web site: http://www.rollins.edu/holt/prospects/mac_programs.

Roosevelt University, Graduate Division, College of Education, Program in Counseling and Human Services, Chicago, IL 60605. Offers MA. *Accreditation:* ACA.

Rosemont College, Schools of Graduate and Professional Studies, Counseling Psychology Program, Rosemont, PA 19010-1699. Offers human services (MA); school counseling (MA). Part-time and evening/weekend programs available. *Faculty:* 2 full-time (both women), 13 part-time/adjunct (6 women). *Students:* 44 full-time (37 women), 85 part-time (70 women); includes 44 minority (38 Black or African American, non-Hispanic/Latino; 4 Asian, non-Hispanic/Latino; 2 Hispanic/Latino), 1 international. Average age 34. 23 applicants, 96% accepted. In 2011, 36 master's awarded. *Degree requirements:* For master's, thesis or alternative, practicum. *Entrance requirements:* For master's, minimum undergraduate GPA of 3.0, 3 letters of recommendation. Additional exam requirements/recommendations for international students: Required—TOEFL. *Application deadline:* Applications are processed on a rolling basis. Application fee: $50. Electronic applications accepted. Application fee is waived when completed online. *Expenses:* Contact institution. *Financial support:* Institutionally sponsored loans and unspecified assistantships available. Financial award applicants required to submit FAFSA. *Faculty research:* Addictions counseling. *Unit head:* Dr. Leslie Smith, Director, 610-527-0200 Ext. 2302, Fax: 610-526-2964, E-mail: leslie.smith@rosemont.edu. *Application contact:* Meghan Mellinger, Graduate Admissions Counselor, 610-527-0200 Ext. 2596, Fax: 610-520-4399, E-mail: gpsadmissions@rosemont.edu. Web site: http://www.rosemont.edu/.

Rowan University, Graduate School, College of Education, Department of Special Educational Services/Instruction, Program in Counseling in Educational Settings, Glassboro, NJ 08028-1701. Offers MA. *Accreditation:* ACA. Part-time and evening/weekend programs available. *Degree requirements:* For master's, thesis. *Entrance requirements:* For master's, GRE General Test, minimum GPA of 2.8, 1 year of teaching experience. Additional exam requirements/recommendations for international students: Required—TOEFL. Electronic applications accepted.

Rutgers, The State University of New Jersey, New Brunswick, Graduate School of Education, Department of Educational Psychology, Programs in School Counseling and Counseling Psychology, Piscataway, NJ 08854-8097. Offers Ed M. Part-time and evening/weekend programs available. *Entrance requirements:* For master's, GRE General Test, 3 letters of recommendation. Additional exam requirements/recommendations for international students: Required—TOEFL (minimum score 550 paper-based; 233 computer-based; 83 iBT). Electronic applications accepted. *Faculty research:* Children and family in cross-cultural context, attachment theory, multicultural counseling, therapy relationship.

Sage Graduate School, Esteves School of Education, Program in Guidance and Counseling, Troy, NY 12180-4115. Offers MS, Post Master's Certificate. *Accreditation:* NCATE. Part-time and evening/weekend programs available. *Faculty:* 10 full-time (6 women), 3 part-time/adjunct (2 women). *Students:* 44 full-time (41 women), 20 part-time (14 women); includes 10 minority (4 Black or African American, non-Hispanic/Latino; 5 Hispanic/Latino; 1 Two or more races, non-Hispanic/Latino). Average age 28. 46 applicants, 72% accepted, 18 enrolled. In 2011, 33 master's, 2 other advanced degrees awarded. *Entrance requirements:* For master's, minimum GPA of 2.75, current resume, essay, official transcripts, 2 letters of recommendation. Additional exam requirements/recommendations for international students: Required—TOEFL (minimum score 550 paper-based; 213 computer-based). *Application deadline:* Applications are processed on a rolling basis. Application fee: $40. *Expenses: Tuition:* Full-time $11,880; part-time $660 per credit hour. Tuition and fees vary according to program. *Financial support:* Fellowships, research assistantships, Federal Work-Study, scholarships/grants, and unspecified assistantships available. Support available to part-time students. Financial award application deadline: 3/1; financial award applicants required to submit FAFSA. *Faculty research:* Roles and responsibilities of guidance personnel, projections of need for guidance counselors. *Unit head:* Dr. Lori Quigley, Dean, Esteves School of Education, 518-244-2326, Fax: 518-244-4571, E-mail: l.quigley@sage.edu. *Application contact:* Mary Grace Luibrand, Director, 518-244-4578, Fax: 518-244-4571, E-mail: luibrm@sage.edu.

St. Bonaventure University, School of Graduate Studies, School of Education, Program in Counselor Education, St. Bonaventure, NY 14778-2284. Offers community mental health counseling (MS Ed); school counseling (MS Ed); school counselor (Adv C). *Accreditation:* ACA. Part-time and evening/weekend programs available. *Faculty:* 6 full-time (2 women), 15 part-time/adjunct (9 women). *Students:* 125 full-time (100 women), 20 part-time (15 women); includes 9 minority (4 Black or African American, non-Hispanic/Latino; 5 Hispanic/Latino), 2 international. Average age 28. 103

applicants, 70% accepted, 46 enrolled. In 2011, 23 master's, 8 Adv Cs awarded. *Degree requirements:* For master's, comprehensive exam, thesis optional, internship, portfolio. *Entrance requirements:* For master's, interview, writing sample, minimum undergraduate GPA of 3.0, references, bachelor's degree. Additional exam requirements/recommendations for international students: Required—TOEFL (minimum score 550 paper-based; 213 computer-based; 79 iBT). *Application deadline:* For fall admission, 8/15 priority date for domestic students, 2/1 for international students; for spring admission, 11/15 priority date for domestic students, 7/1 for international students. Applications are processed on a rolling basis. Application fee: $30. Electronic applications accepted. *Expenses: Tuition:* Part-time $670 per credit. *Financial support:* In 2011–12, 5 research assistantships with full and partial tuition reimbursements were awarded; career-related internships or fieldwork, Federal Work-Study, scholarships/grants, health care benefits, tuition waivers (partial), and unspecified assistantships also available. Support available to part-time students. Financial award application deadline: 4/15; financial award applicants required to submit FAFSA. *Unit head:* Dr. Craig Zuckerman, Director, 716-375-2374, Fax: 716-375-2360, E-mail: czuck@sbu.edu. *Application contact:* Bruce Campbell, Director of Graduate Admissions, 716-375-2429, Fax: 716-375-4015, E-mail: gradsch@sbu.edu. Web site: http://www.sbu.edu/education.aspx?id=3012.

St. Cloud State University, School of Graduate Studies, School of Education, Department of Educational Leadership and Higher Education, Program in College Counseling and Student Development, St. Cloud, MN 56301-4498. Offers MS. *Degree requirements:* For master's, comprehensive exam, thesis or alternative. *Entrance requirements:* For master's, GRE General Test, minimum GPA of 2.75. Additional exam requirements/recommendations for international students: Required—Michigan English Language Assessment Battery; Recommended—TOEFL (minimum score 550 paper-based; 213 computer-based), IELTS (minimum score 6.5). Electronic applications accepted.

St. Cloud State University, School of Graduate Studies, School of Education, Department of Educational Leadership and Higher Education, Program in School Counseling, St. Cloud, MN 56301-4498. Offers MS. *Accreditation:* ACA; NCATE. *Degree requirements:* For master's, comprehensive exam (for some programs), thesis or alternative. *Entrance requirements:* For master's, GRE General Test, minimum GPA of 2.75. Additional exam requirements/recommendations for international students: Required—Michigan English Language Assessment Battery; Recommended—TOEFL (minimum score 550 paper-based; 213 computer-based), IELTS. Electronic applications accepted.

St. John's University, The School of Education, Department of Human Services and Counseling, Program in Mental Health Counseling, Queens, NY 11439. Offers MS Ed. Part-time and evening/weekend programs available. *Students:* 36 full-time (26 women), 39 part-time (32 women); includes 31 minority (7 Black or African American, non-Hispanic/Latino; 5 Asian, non-Hispanic/Latino; 17 Hispanic/Latino; 2 Two or more races, non-Hispanic/Latino), 1 international. Average age 27. 72 applicants, 78% accepted, 26 enrolled. In 2011, 7 master's awarded. *Degree requirements:* For master's, internship, state examination. *Entrance requirements:* For master's, bachelor's degree from an accredited college or university, minimum GPA of 3.0, 2 letters of recommendation, interview, 18 credits in behavioral and social science. Additional exam requirements/recommendations for international students: Required—TOEFL (minimum score 600 paper-based; 250 computer-based; 100 iBT), IELTS (minimum score 5.5). *Application deadline:* For fall admission, 4/1 for domestic and international students; for spring admission, 11/1 for domestic and international students. Applications are processed on a rolling basis. Application fee: $70. Electronic applications accepted. *Expenses: Tuition:* Full-time $18,000; part-time $1000 per credit. *Required fees:* $170 per semester. Tuition and fees vary according to program. *Financial support:* Research assistantships and career-related internships or fieldwork available. Support available to part-time students. Financial award application deadline: 3/1; financial award applicants required to submit FAFSA. *Unit head:* Dr. Francine Guastello, Chair, 718-990-1475, Fax: 718-990-1614, E-mail: guastelf@stjohns.edu. *Application contact:* Dr. Kelly K. Ronayne, Associate Dean for Graduate Admissions, 718-990-2304, Fax: 718-990-2343, E-mail: graded@stjohns.edu.

St. John's University, The School of Education, Department of Human Services and Counseling, Program in School Counseling, Queens, NY 11439. Offers MS Ed, Adv C. *Accreditation:* ACA (one or more programs are accredited). Part-time and evening/weekend programs available. *Students:* 48 full-time (40 women), 38 part-time (31 women); includes 26 minority (13 Black or African American, non-Hispanic/Latino; 3 Asian, non-Hispanic/Latino; 9 Hispanic/Latino; 1 Two or more races, non-Hispanic/Latino), 4 international. Average age 27. 71 applicants, 61% accepted, 16 enrolled. In 2011, 32 master's awarded. *Degree requirements:* For master's, comprehensive exam. *Entrance requirements:* For master's, GRE, bachelor's degree from accredited college or university, minimum GPA of 3.0, 2 letters of recommendation, interview, minimum of 18 credits in behavioral or social science; for Adv C, master's degree in counseling or related field, essay, official transcript showing minimum GPA of 3.0, 2 letters of recommendation, interview. Additional exam requirements/recommendations for international students: Required—TOEFL (minimum score 600 paper-based; 250 computer-based; 100 iBT), IELTS (minimum score 5.5). *Application deadline:* For fall admission, 4/1 for domestic and international students; for spring admission, 11/1 for domestic and international students. Applications are processed on a rolling basis. Application fee: $70. Electronic applications accepted. *Expenses: Tuition:* Full-time $18,000; part-time $1000 per credit. *Required fees:* $170 per semester. Tuition and fees vary according to program. *Financial support:* Research assistantships and career-related internships or fieldwork available. Support available to part-time students. Financial award application deadline: 3/1; financial award applicants required to submit FAFSA. *Faculty research:* Counseling/client engagement; counseling accountability; pipe-line mentoring from grade 4 to college; stress, coping and resilience for children and adults; helping parents deal with aggressive children; effects of bullying and cyber bullying with adolescents; creative connections through the arts. *Unit head:* Dr. Francine Guastello, Chair, 718-990-1475, E-mail: guastelf@stjohns.edu. *Application contact:* Dr. Kelly K. Ronayne, Associate Dean for Graduate Admissions, 718-990-2304, Fax: 718-990-2343, E-mail: graded@stjohns.edu.

St. John's University, The School of Education, Department of Human Services and Counseling, Program in School Counseling with Bilingual Extension, Queens, NY 11439. Offers MS Ed. Part-time and evening/weekend programs available. *Students:* 12 full-time (all women), 7 part-time (all women); includes 15 minority (1 Asian, non-Hispanic/Latino; 14 Hispanic/Latino), 1 international. Average age 27. 8 applicants, 75% accepted, 2 enrolled. In 2011, 4 master's awarded. *Degree requirements:* For master's, comprehensive exam. *Entrance requirements:* For master's, GRE, New York State Bilingual Assessment (BEA), bachelor's degree from an accredited college or university, minimum GPA of 3.0, 2 letters of recommendation, interview, minimum of 18 credits in behavioral or social science. Additional exam requirements/recommendations for international students: Required—TOEFL (minimum score 600 paper-based; 250 computer-based; 100 iBT), IELTS (minimum score 5.5). *Application deadline:* For fall admission, 4/1 for domestic and international students; for spring admission, 11/1 for domestic and international students. Applications are processed on a rolling basis. Application fee: $70. Electronic applications accepted. *Expenses: Tuition:* Full-time $18,000; part-time $1000 per credit. *Required fees:* $170 per semester. Tuition and fees vary according to program. *Financial support:* Research assistantships, career-related internships or fieldwork, and scholarships/grants available. Support available to part-time students. Financial award application deadline: 3/1; financial award applicants required to submit FAFSA. *Faculty research:* Cross-cultural comparisons of predictors of active coping. *Unit head:* Dr. Francine Guastello, Chair, 718-990-1475, E-mail: guastelf@stjohns.edu. *Application contact:* Dr. Kelly K. Ronayne, Associate Dean for Graduate Admissions, 718-990-2304, Fax: 718-990-2343, E-mail: graded@stjohns.edu.

St. Lawrence University, Department of Education, Program in Counseling and Human Development, Canton, NY 13617-1455. Offers mental health counseling (MS); school counseling (M Ed, CAS). Part-time and evening/weekend programs available. *Entrance requirements:* For master's, GRE General Test. *Faculty research:* Defense mechanisms and mediation.

Saint Louis University, Graduate Education, College of Education and Public Service and Graduate Education, Department of Counseling and Family Therapy, St. Louis, MO 63103-2097. Offers counseling and family therapy (PhD); human development counseling (MA); marriage and family therapy (Certificate); school counseling (MA, MA-R). *Accreditation:* AAMFT/COAMFTE; NCATE. Part-time programs available. *Degree requirements:* For master's, comprehensive exam, thesis (for some programs); for doctorate, comprehensive exam, thesis/dissertation, preliminary oral and written exams. *Entrance requirements:* For master's, GRE General Test, letters of recommendation, resume; for doctorate, GRE General Test, letters of recommendation, resumé, transcripts, goal statement. Additional exam requirements/recommendations for international students: Required—TOEFL (minimum score 550 paper-based; 213 computer-based). Electronic applications accepted. *Faculty research:* Medical family therapy/collaborative health care multicultural counseling, mental health needs of diverse, minority, or Immigrant/refugee populations, divorce, aging families.

Saint Martin's University, Graduate Programs, College of Education, Lacey, WA 98503. Offers administration (M Ed); English as a second language (M Ed); guidance and counseling (M Ed); reading (M Ed); special education (M Ed); teaching (MIT). *Accreditation:* Teacher Education Accreditation Council. Part-time and evening/weekend programs available. *Faculty:* 12 full-time (8 women), 9 part-time/adjunct (7 women). *Students:* 68 full-time (38 women), 28 part-time (20 women); includes 15 minority (2 Black or African American, non-Hispanic/Latino; 2 American Indian or Alaska Native, non-Hispanic/Latino; 7 Asian, non-Hispanic/Latino; 2 Hispanic/Latino; 2 Two or more races, non-Hispanic/Latino), 4 international. Average age 35. 17 applicants, 94% accepted, 15 enrolled. In 2011, 12 master's awarded. *Degree requirements:* For master's, comprehensive exam (for some programs), thesis or alternative, project or comprehensives. *Entrance requirements:* For master's, GRE General Test or MAT, resume. Additional exam requirements/recommendations for international students: Required—TOEFL (minimum score 560 paper-based; 220 computer-based; 83 iBT). *Application deadline:* For fall admission, 6/1 priority date for domestic students, 6/1 for international students; for spring admission, 10/1 priority date for domestic students, 10/1 for international students. Applications are processed on a rolling basis. Application fee: $35. *Expenses: Tuition:* Part-time $910 per credit hour. Tuition and fees vary according to course level, campus/location and program. *Financial support:* Career-related internships or fieldwork, Federal Work-Study, institutionally sponsored loans, and unspecified assistantships available. Support available to part-time students. Financial award application deadline: 3/1; financial award applicants required to submit FAFSA. *Faculty research:* Reader's theatre and reader/writer workshops, curriculum and assessment integration, gender and equity, classroom evaluations, organizational leadership. *Unit head:* Dr. Joyce Westgard, Dean, College of Education and Professional Psychology, 360-438-4509, Fax: 360-438-4486, E-mail: westgard@stmartin.edu. *Application contact:* Ryan M. Smith, Administrative Assistant, 360-438-4333, Fax: 360-438-4486, E-mail: ryan.smith@stmartin.edu. Web site: http://www.stmartin.edu/CEPP/.

Saint Mary's College of California, Kalmanovitz School of Education, Program in Counseling, Moraga, CA 94556. Offers general counseling (MA); marital and family therapy (MA); school counseling (MA). Part-time and evening/weekend programs available. *Faculty:* 6 full-time (5 women), 16 part-time/adjunct (13 women). *Students:* 102 full-time (88 women), 115 part-time (92 women); includes 65 minority (21 Black or African American, non-Hispanic/Latino; 2 American Indian or Alaska Native, non-Hispanic/Latino; 13 Asian, non-Hispanic/Latino; 23 Hispanic/Latino; 5 Native Hawaiian or other Pacific Islander, non-Hispanic/Latino; 1 Two or more races, non-Hispanic/Latino), 1 international. Average age 33. In 2011, 69 master's awarded. *Degree requirements:* For master's, thesis or alternative. *Entrance requirements:* For master's, interview, minimum GPA of 3.0. *Application deadline:* Applications are processed on a rolling basis. Application fee: $50. Tuition and fees vary according to course load, degree level and program. *Financial support:* In 2011–12, 5 students received support. Career-related internships or fieldwork and Federal Work-Study available. Support available to part-time students. Financial award application deadline: 2/15; financial award applicants required to submit FAFSA. *Faculty research:* Counselor training effectiveness, multicultural development, empathy, the interface of spirituality and psychotherapy, gender issues. *Unit head:* Dr. Laura Heid, Director, 925-631-4293, Fax: 925-376-8379, E-mail: lheid@stmarys.ca.edu. *Application contact:* Jane Joyce, Coordinator, Recruitment and Admissions, 925-631-4700, Fax: 925-376-8379, E-mail: soereq@stmarys-ca.edu. Web site: http://www.stmarys-ca.edu/graduate-counseling.

St. Mary's University, Graduate School, Department of Counseling and Human Services, Program in Counseling Education and Supervision, San Antonio, TX 78228-8507. Offers PhD. *Accreditation:* ACA. Part-time programs available. *Degree requirements:* For doctorate, comprehensive exam, thesis/dissertation. *Entrance requirements:* For doctorate, GRE, master's degree, work experience, letters of recommendation. Additional exam requirements/recommendations for international students: Required—TOEFL (minimum score 550 paper-based; 213 computer-based; 80 iBT). Electronic applications accepted.

Saint Peter's University, Graduate Programs in Education, Program in School Counseling, Jersey City, NJ 07306-5997. Offers MA, Certificate.

St. Thomas University, Biscayne College, Department of Social Sciences and Counseling, Program in Guidance and Counseling, Miami Gardens, FL 33054-6459. Offers MS, Post-Master's Certificate. Part-time and evening/weekend programs available. *Degree requirements:* For master's, comprehensive exam. *Entrance requirements:* For master's, interview, minimum GPA of 3.0 or GRE. Additional exam requirements/recommendations for international students: Required—TOEFL (minimum score 550 paper-based; 213 computer-based; 79 iBT). Electronic applications accepted.

Saint Xavier University, Graduate Studies, School of Education, Program in Counseling, Chicago, IL 60655-3105. Offers MA. *Degree requirements:* For master's, practicum, internship. *Entrance requirements:* For master's, 3 letters of recommendation, interview. Additional exam requirements/recommendations for international students: Required—TOEFL. Application fee: $35. Electronic applications accepted. *Expenses: Tuition:* Part-time $750 per credit hour. *Required fees:* $135 per semester. Tuition and fees vary according to program. *Financial support:* Research assistantships, teaching assistantships, institutionally sponsored loans, scholarships/grants, and unspecified assistantships available. Financial award applicants required to submit FAFSA. *Application contact:* Office of Graduate Admission, 773-298-3053, Fax: 773-298-3951, E-mail: graduateadmission@sxu.edu.

Salem College, Department of Teacher Education, Winston-Salem, NC 27101. Offers art education (MAT); elementary education (M Ed, MAT); language and literacy (M Ed); middle school education (MAT); music education (MAT); school counseling (M Ed); second language studies (MAT); secondary education (MAT); special education (M Ed, MAT). *Accreditation:* NCATE. Part-time and evening/weekend programs available. Postbaccalaureate distance learning degree programs offered (minimal on-campus study). *Degree requirements:* For master's, comprehensive exam, practicum (MAT), project (M Ed), oral and written comprehensive exams. *Entrance requirements:* For master's, GRE, minimum GPA of 2.5. *Faculty research:* Content area reading strategies, literacy development, brain compatible instruction.

Salem State University, School of Graduate Studies, Program in School Counseling, Salem, MA 01970-5353. Offers M Ed. *Accreditation:* NCATE. Part-time and evening/weekend programs available. *Entrance requirements:* For master's, GRE or MAT. Additional exam requirements/recommendations for international students: Required—TOEFL (minimum score 550 paper-based; 80 iBT) or IELTS (minimum score 5.5).

Sam Houston State University, College of Education, Department of Educational Leadership and Counseling, Huntsville, TX 77341. Offers administration (M Ed); counseling (M Ed, MA); counselor education (PhD); developmental education administration (Ed D); educational leadership (Ed D); higher education administration (MA); instructional leadership (M Ed, MA). Part-time programs available. *Faculty:* 27 full-time (17 women), 27 part-time/adjunct (14 women). *Students:* 98 full-time (78 women), 474 part-time (378 women); includes 182 minority (101 Black or African American, non-Hispanic/Latino; 10 American Indian or Alaska Native, non-Hispanic/Latino; 8 Asian, non-Hispanic/Latino; 63 Hispanic/Latino), 8 international. Average age 37. 407 applicants, 61% accepted, 194 enrolled. In 2011, 166 master's, 25 doctorates awarded. *Entrance requirements:* For master's, GRE General Test. Additional exam requirements/recommendations for international students: Required—TOEFL (minimum score 550 paper-based; 213 computer-based; 79 iBT). *Application deadline:* For fall admission, 8/1 for domestic students, 6/25 for international students; for spring admission, 12/1 for domestic students, 11/12 for international students. Applications are processed on a rolling basis. Application fee: $45 ($75 for international students). Electronic applications accepted. *Expenses:* Tuition, state resident: full-time $4420; part-time $221 per credit hour. Tuition, nonresident: full-time $10,680; part-time $534 per credit hour. *Required fees:* $329 per credit hour. *Financial support:* Career-related internships or fieldwork, Federal Work-Study, and institutionally sponsored loans available. Support available to part-time students. Financial award application deadline: 5/31; financial award applicants required to submit FAFSA. *Unit head:* Dr. Stacey Edmonson, Chair, 936-294-1752, Fax: 936-294-3886, E-mail: edu_sle01@shsu.edu. *Application contact:* Dr. Stacey Edmondson, Advisor, 936-294-1752, E-mail: sedmonson@shsu.edu. Web site: http://www.shsu.edu/~edu_elc/.

San Diego State University, Graduate and Research Affairs, College of Education, Department of Counseling and School Psychology, San Diego, CA 92182. Offers MS. *Accreditation:* NCATE. Evening/weekend programs available. *Degree requirements:* For master's, comprehensive exam (for some programs), thesis (for some programs). *Entrance requirements:* For master's, GRE General Test, interview, letters of reference. Additional exam requirements/recommendations for international students: Required—TOEFL. Electronic applications accepted. *Faculty research:* Multicultural and cross-cultural counseling and training, AIDS counseling.

San Jose State University, Graduate Studies and Research, Connie L. Lurie College of Education, Department of Counselor Education, San Jose, CA 95192-0001. Offers MA. *Accreditation:* NCATE. Evening/weekend programs available. *Degree requirements:* For master's, thesis or alternative. Electronic applications accepted.

Santa Clara University, School of Education and Counseling Psychology, Department of Counseling Psychology, Santa Clara, CA 95053. Offers counseling (MA); counseling psychology (MA). Part-time and evening/weekend programs available. *Students:* 103 full-time (81 women), 158 part-time (138 women); includes 69 minority (5 Black or African American, non-Hispanic/Latino; 31 Asian, non-Hispanic/Latino; 32 Hispanic/Latino; 1 Native Hawaiian or other Pacific Islander, non-Hispanic/Latino), 7 international. Average age 33. 106 applicants, 55% accepted, 35 enrolled. In 2011, 66 degrees awarded. *Degree requirements:* For master's, comprehensive exam. *Entrance requirements:* For master's, GRE or MAT, statement of purpose, letters of recommendation, transcripts. Additional exam requirements/recommendations for international students: Required—TOEFL (minimum score 600 paper-based; 100 computer-based; 100 iBT). *Application deadline:* For fall admission, 6/15 for domestic and international students; for winter admission, 10/15 for domestic and international students; for spring admission, 1/31 for domestic and international students. Applications are processed on a rolling basis. Application fee: $50. Electronic applications accepted. *Expenses:* Contact institution. *Financial support:* Fellowships, Federal Work-Study, institutionally sponsored loans, and scholarships/grants available. Support available to part-time students. Financial award application deadline: 5/15; financial award applicants required to submit FAFSA. *Faculty research:* Making meaning out of adversity, self-concealment and health, Latino mental health, mindfulness, life transitions. *Unit head:* Dr. Atom Yee, Interim Dean, 408-554-4455, Fax: 408-554-5038, E-mail: ayee@scu.edu. *Application contact:* ECP Admissions, 408-554-4355, E-mail: ecpadmissions@scu.edu.

Seattle Pacific University, M Ed/PhD School Counseling Program, Seattle, WA 98119-1997. Offers M Ed, PhD, Certificate. *Accreditation:* NCATE. Part-time programs available. *Degree requirements:* For master's, year long internship. *Entrance requirements:* For master's, GRE General Test or MAT, minimum GPA of 3.0. Electronic applications accepted. *Expenses:* Contact institution.

Seattle University, College of Education, Program in Counseling and School Psychology, Seattle, WA 98122-1090. Offers MA, Certificate, Ed S. *Accreditation:* NCATE. Part-time and evening/weekend programs available. *Students:* 33 full-time (26 women), 128 part-time (104 women); includes 60 minority (9 Black or African American, non-Hispanic/Latino; 1 American Indian or Alaska Native, non-Hispanic/Latino; 19 Asian, non-Hispanic/Latino; 20 Hispanic/Latino; 2 Native Hawaiian or other Pacific Islander, non-Hispanic/Latino; 9 Two or more races, non-Hispanic/Latino). Average age 29. 183 applicants, 38% accepted, 35 enrolled. In 2011, 38 master's, 10 other advanced degrees awarded. *Degree requirements:* For master's, comprehensive exam. *Entrance requirements:* For master's, interview; GRE, MAT, or minimum GPA of 3.0; related work experience. Additional exam requirements/recommendations for international students: Required—TOEFL. *Application deadline:* For fall admission, 7/1 for domestic students; for winter admission, 10/20 for domestic students; for spring admission, 1/20 for domestic students. Application fee: $55. *Unit head:* Hutch Haney, Director, 206-296-5750. *Application contact:* Janet Shandley, Associate Dean of Graduate Admissions, 206-296-5900, Fax: 206-298-5656, E-mail: grad_admissions@seattleu.edu.

Shippensburg University of Pennsylvania, School of Graduate Studies, College of Education and Human Services, Department of Counseling, Shippensburg, PA 17257-2299. Offers clinical mental health counseling (MS); couple and family counseling (Certificate); school counseling (M Ed). *Accreditation:* ACA (one or more programs are accredited); NCATE. Part-time and evening/weekend programs available. *Faculty:* 9 full-time (5 women), 1 part-time/adjunct (0 women). *Students:* 74 full-time (64 women), 74 part-time (60 women); includes 20 minority (10 Black or African American, non-Hispanic/Latino; 1 American Indian or Alaska Native, non-Hispanic/Latino; 3 Asian, non-Hispanic/Latino; 2 Hispanic/Latino; 4 Two or more races, non-Hispanic/Latino), 2 international. Average age 28. 135 applicants, 41% accepted, 34 enrolled. In 2011, 47 master's awarded. *Degree requirements:* For master's, fieldwork, research project, internship, candidacy. *Entrance requirements:* For master's, GRE or MAT (clinical mental health, student personnel, and college counseling applicants if GPA is less than 2.75), minimum GPA of 2.75 (3.0 for M Ed), resume, 3 letters of recommendation, one year of relevant work experience, on-campus interview, and autobiographical statement. Additional exam requirements/recommendations for international students: Required—TOEFL (minimum score 580 paper-based; 237 computer-based); Recommended—IELTS (minimum score 6). *Application deadline:* For fall admission, 4/30 for international students; for spring admission, 9/30 for international students. Applications are processed on a rolling basis. Application fee: $30. Electronic applications accepted. *Expenses: Tuition, area resident:* Part-time $416 per credit. Tuition, state resident: part-time $416 per credit. Tuition, nonresident: part-time $624 per credit. *Required fees:* $119 per credit. *Financial support:* In 2011–12, 48 research assistantships with full tuition reimbursements (averaging $5,000 per year) were awarded; career-related internships or fieldwork, scholarships/grants, unspecified assistantships, and resident hall director and student payroll positions also available. Support available to part-time students. Financial award application deadline: 3/1; financial award applicants required to submit FAFSA. *Unit head:* Dr. Jan Arminio, Chairperson, 717-477-1668, Fax: 717-477-4016, E-mail: jlarmi@ship.edu. *Application contact:* Jeremy R. Goshorn, Assistant Dean of Graduate Admissions, 717-477-1231, Fax: 717-477-4016, E-mail: jrgoshorn@ship.edu. Web site: http://www.ship.edu/counsel/.

Simon Fraser University, Graduate Studies, Faculty of Education, Program in Counseling Psychology, Burnaby, BC V5A 1S6, Canada. Offers M Ed, MA. *Degree requirements:* For master's, project or thesis. *Entrance requirements:* For master's, minimum GPA of 3.0. Additional exam requirements/recommendations for international students: Required—TOEFL or IELTS.

Slippery Rock University of Pennsylvania, Graduate Studies (Recruitment), College of Education, Department of Counseling and Development, Slippery Rock, PA 16057-1383. Offers community counseling (MA), including addiction, adult, aging, child and adolescent; school counseling (M Ed). *Accreditation:* ACA (one or more programs are accredited); NCATE. Part-time and evening/weekend programs available. *Faculty:* 8 full-time (4 women). *Students:* 84 full-time (58 women), 36 part-time (29 women); includes 12 minority (7 Black or African American, non-Hispanic/Latino; 2 American Indian or Alaska Native, non-Hispanic/Latino; 1 Asian, non-Hispanic/Latino; 1 Hispanic/Latino; 1 Two or more races, non-Hispanic/Latino). Average age 28. 145 applicants, 48% accepted, 48 enrolled. In 2011, 38 degrees awarded. *Degree requirements:* For master's, comprehensive exam (for some programs), thesis (for some programs), internship (for some programs). *Entrance requirements:* For master's, GRE General Test, MAT, minimum GPA of 2.75, personal statement, three letters of recommendation, and interview (depending on program). Additional exam requirements/recommendations for international students: Required—TOEFL (minimum score 550 paper-based; 213 computer-based; 80 iBT). *Application deadline:* For fall admission, 3/1 priority date for domestic students, 5/1 for international students. Applications are processed on a rolling basis. Application fee: $25 ($30 for international students). Electronic applications accepted. *Expenses:* Tuition, state resident: full-time $7488; part-time $416 per credit. Tuition, nonresident: full-time $11,232; part-time $624 per credit. *International tuition:* $11,146 full-time. *Required fees:* $2722; $140 per credit. Tuition and fees vary according to degree level and program. *Financial support:* Career-related internships or fieldwork, Federal Work-Study, institutionally sponsored loans, scholarships/grants, tuition waivers (partial), and unspecified assistantships available. Support available to part-time students. Financial award application deadline: 5/1; financial award applicants required to submit FAFSA. *Unit head:* Dr. Donald Strano, Graduate Coordinator, 724-738-2274, Fax: 724-738-4859, E-mail: donald.strano@sru.edu. *Application contact:* Angela Barrett, Director of Graduate Admissions, 724-738-2051, Fax: 724-738-2146, E-mail: graduate.admissions@sru.edu.

Sonoma State University, School of Social Sciences, Department of Counseling, Rohnert Park, CA 94928-3609. Offers counseling (MA); marriage, family, and child counseling (MA); pupil personnel services (MA). *Accreditation:* ACA. Part-time programs available. *Faculty:* 7 full-time (4 women), 5 part-time/adjunct (3 women). *Students:* 57 full-time (48 women), 36 part-time (31 women); includes 23 minority (2 Black or African American, non-Hispanic/Latino; 2 American Indian or Alaska Native, non-Hispanic/Latino; 5 Asian, non-Hispanic/Latino; 11 Hispanic/Latino; 3 Two or more races, non-Hispanic/Latino). Average age 32. 133 applicants, 26% accepted, 19 enrolled. In 2011, 35 master's awarded. *Degree requirements:* For master's, internship. *Entrance requirements:* For master's, minimum GPA of 3.0. Additional exam requirements/recommendations for international students: Required—TOEFL (minimum score 500 paper-based; 173 computer-based). *Application deadline:* For fall admission, 11/30 for domestic students. Application fee: $55. *Financial support:* Career-related internships or fieldwork available. Financial award application deadline: 3/2; financial award applicants required to submit FAFSA. *Unit head:* Dr. Adam Hill, Department Chair, 707-664-2340, E-mail: adam.hill@sonoma.edu. *Application contact:* Dr. Adam Zagelbaum, Program Coordinator, 707-664-4067, Fax: 707-664-2266, E-mail: zagelbau@sonoma.edu. Web site: http://www.sonoma.edu/counseling.

South Carolina State University, School of Graduate Studies, Department of Education, Orangeburg, SC 29117-0001. Offers counseling education (M Ed); early childhood and special education (M Ed); early childhood education (MAT); educational leadership (Ed D, Ed S); elementary education (M Ed, MAT); engineering (MAT); general science (MAT); mathematics (MAT); secondary education (M Ed), including biology education, business education, counselor education, English education, home economics education, industrial education, mathematics education, science education, social studies education; special education (M Ed), including emotionally handicapped, learning disabilities, mentally handicapped. *Accreditation:* NCATE. Part-time and evening/weekend programs available. *Faculty:* 9 full-time (6 women), 6 part-time/adjunct (2 women). *Students:* 34 full-time (29 women), 50 part-time (40 women); includes 74 minority (72 Black or African American, non-Hispanic/Latino; 1 Asian, non-Hispanic/Latino; 1 Hispanic/Latino). Average age 34. 23 applicants, 91% accepted, 14 enrolled. In 2011, 11 master's awarded. *Degree requirements:* For master's, thesis optional, departmental qualifying exam. *Entrance requirements:* For master's, GRE General Test, NTE, interview, teaching certificate. *Application deadline:* For fall admission, 6/15 priority date for domestic students, 6/15 for international students; for spring admission, 11/1 for domestic and international students. Applications are processed on a rolling basis. Application fee: $25. Electronic applications accepted. *Expenses:* Tuition, state resident: full-time $8688; part-time $514 per credit hour. Tuition, nonresident: full-time $17,600; part-time $1009 per credit hour. *Required fees:* $570. *Financial support:* In 2011–12, 3 fellowships (averaging $5,020 per year) were awarded; career-related internships or fieldwork, Federal Work-Study, and institutionally sponsored loans also available. Financial award application deadline: 6/1. *Faculty research:* Critical thinking, child abuse, stress, test-taking skills, conflict resolution, mainstreaming. *Unit head:* Dr. Charlie Spell, Interim Chair, 803-536-7098, Fax: 803-516-4568, E-mail: cspell@scsu.edu. *Application contact:* Annette Hazzard-Jones, Program Coordinator II, 803-536-8809, Fax: 803-536-8812, E-mail: zs_ahazzard@scsu.edu.

South Carolina State University, School of Graduate Studies, Department of Human Services, Orangeburg, SC 29117-0001. Offers counselor education (M Ed); orientation and mobility (Graduate Certificate); rehabilitation counseling (MA). *Accreditation:* CORE. Part-time and evening/weekend programs available. *Faculty:* 9 full-time (6 women), 9 part-time/adjunct (7 women). *Students:* 149 full-time (124 women), 57 part-time (46 women); includes 190 minority (all Black or African American, non-Hispanic/Latino), 2 international. Average age 34. 114 applicants, 98% accepted, 92 enrolled. In 2011, 56 master's awarded. *Degree requirements:* For master's, comprehensive exam (for some programs), departmental qualifying exam, internship. *Entrance requirements:* For master's, GRE, MAT, minimum GPA of 2.7. *Application deadline:* For fall admission, 6/15 priority date for domestic students, 6/15 for international students; for spring admission, 11/1 for domestic and international students. Applications are processed on a rolling basis. Application fee: $25. Electronic applications accepted. *Expenses:* Tuition, state resident: full-time $8688; part-time $514 per credit hour. Tuition, nonresident: full-time $17,600; part-time $1009 per credit hour. *Required fees:* $570. *Financial support:* In 2011–12, 35 students received support, including 14 fellowships (averaging $5,730 per year); career-related internships or fieldwork, institutionally sponsored loans, and unspecified assistantships also available. Financial award application deadline: 6/1. *Faculty research:* Handicap, disability, rehabilitation evaluation, vocation. *Unit head:* Dr. Cassandra Sligh Conway, Chair, 803-536-7075, Fax: 803-533-3636, E-mail: csligh-dewalt@scsu.edu. *Application contact:* Annette Hazzard-Jones, Program Coordinator II, 803-536-8809, Fax: 803-536-8812, E-mail: zs_ahazzard@scsu.edu.

South Dakota State University, Graduate School, College of Education and Human Sciences, Department of Counseling and Human Resource Development, Brookings, SD 57007. Offers MS. *Accreditation:* ACA; NCATE. Part-time and evening/weekend programs available. *Degree requirements:* For master's, comprehensive exam, thesis (for some programs), oral exams. *Entrance requirements:* For master's, minimum GPA of 2.75. Additional exam requirements/recommendations for international students: Required—TOEFL (minimum score 525 paper-based; 197 computer-based; 71 iBT). *Faculty research:* Rural mental health, family issues, character education, student affairs, solution focused therapy.

Southeastern Louisiana University, College of Education and Human Development, Department of Counseling and Human Development, Hammond, LA 70402. Offers counselor education (M Ed), including clinical mental health. *Accreditation:* ACA; NCATE. Part-time programs available. *Faculty:* 7 full-time (5 women), 1 (woman) part-time/adjunct. *Students:* 57 full-time (50 women), 48 part-time (44 women); includes 30 minority (23 Black or African American, non-Hispanic/Latino; 1 Asian, non-Hispanic/Latino; 4 Hispanic/Latino; 2 Two or more races, non-Hispanic/Latino). Average age 29. 34 applicants, 100% accepted, 19 enrolled. In 2011, 32 degrees awarded. *Degree requirements:* For master's, comprehensive exam, thesis optional. *Entrance requirements:* For master's, GRE (verbal and quantitative), nine hours of undergraduate or graduate study in behavioral studies; three hours in statistics; portfolio; letter requesting consideration for program admission; curriculum vitae; three letters of reference; autobiographical narrative; one-day interview. Additional exam requirements/recommendations for international students: Required—TOEFL (minimum score 500 paper-based; 173 computer-based; 61 iBT). *Application deadline:* For fall admission, 7/15 priority date for domestic students, 6/1 for international students; for spring admission, 12/1 priority date for domestic students, 10/1 for international students. Applications are processed on a rolling basis. Application fee: $20 ($30 for international students). Electronic applications accepted. *Expenses:* Tuition, state resident: full-time $3977; part-time $283 per semester hour. Tuition, nonresident: full-time $13,482; part-time $811 per semester hour. *Financial support:* Career-related internships or fieldwork, Federal Work-Study, institutionally sponsored loans, scholarships/grants, and unspecified assistantships available. Support available to part-time students. Financial award application deadline: 5/1; financial award applicants required to submit FAFSA. *Faculty research:* Addiction, cinema therapy, grief, school counseling. *Total annual research expenditures:* $811,668. *Unit head:* Dr. June Williams, Interim Department Head, 985-549-2309, Fax: 985-549-3758, E-mail: jwilliams@selu.edu. *Application contact:* Sandra Meyers, Graduate Admissions Analyst, 985-549-2066, Fax: 985-549-5632, E-mail: admissions@selu.edu. Web site: http://www.selu.edu/acad_research/depts/coun_hd/index.html.

Southeastern Oklahoma State University, School of Behavioral Sciences, Durant, OK 74701-0609. Offers clinical mental health counseling (MS). Part-time and evening/weekend programs available. *Faculty:* 10 full-time (3 women). *Students:* 23 full-time (18 women), 20 part-time (15 women); includes 15 minority (4 Black or African American, non-Hispanic/Latino; 10 American Indian or Alaska Native, non-Hispanic/Latino; 1 Hispanic/Latino), 2 international. Average age 35. 26 applicants, 85% accepted, 22 enrolled. *Degree requirements:* For master's, thesis optional. *Entrance requirements:* For master's, GRE General Test, minimum GPA of 3.0 in last 60 hours or 2.75 overall. Additional exam requirements/recommendations for international students: Required—TOEFL (minimum score 550 paper-based; 213 computer-based; 79 iBT). *Application deadline:* For fall admission, 8/1 for domestic students, 6/1 for international students; for spring admission, 1/5 for domestic students, 11/1 for international students. Application fee: $20 ($55 for international students). Electronic applications accepted. *Expenses:* Tuition, state resident: full-time $3537; part-time $173.95 per credit hour. Tuition, nonresident: full-time $8673; part-time $459.30 per credit hour. *Required fees:* $22.55 per credit hour. *Financial support:* Fellowships, research assistantships, teaching assistantships, and Federal Work-Study available. Support available to part-time students. Financial award application deadline: 6/15. *Unit head:* Dr. Kimberly Donovan, Program Coordinator, 580-745-2312, E-mail: kdonovan@se.edu. *Application contact:* Carrie Williamson, Graduate Secretary, 580-745-2220, Fax: 580-745-7474, E-mail: cwilliamson@se.edu. Web site: http://www.se.edu/graduate-programs/master-of-behavioral-studies/.

Southeastern Oklahoma State University, School of Education, Durant, OK 74701-0609. Offers math specialist (M Ed); reading specialist (M Ed); school administration (M Ed); school counseling (M Ed); special education (M Ed). *Accreditation:* NCATE. Part-time and evening/weekend programs available. *Faculty:* 52 full-time (19 women), 1 (woman) part-time/adjunct. *Students:* 15 full-time (11 women), 54 part-time (40 women); includes 24 minority (2 Black or African American, non-Hispanic/Latino; 16 American Indian or Alaska Native, non-Hispanic/Latino; 6 Hispanic/Latino). Average age 34. 31 applicants, 94% accepted, 29 enrolled. *Degree requirements:* For master's, comprehensive exam, thesis optional, portfolio (M Ed). *Entrance requirements:* For master's, GRE General Test (MBS), minimum GPA of 3.0 in last 60 hours or 2.75 overall. Additional exam requirements/recommendations for international students: Required—TOEFL (minimum score 550 paper-based; 213 computer-based; 79 iBT). *Application deadline:* For fall admission, 8/1 for domestic students, 6/1 for international students; for spring admission, 1/5 for domestic students, 11/1 for international students. Application fee: $20 ($55 for international students). Electronic applications accepted. *Expenses:* Tuition, state resident: full-time $3537; part-time $173.95 per credit hour. Tuition, nonresident: full-time $8673; part-time $459.30 per credit hour. *Required fees:* $22.55 per credit hour. *Financial support:* In 2011–12, 1 teaching assistantship with full tuition reimbursement (averaging $5,000 per year) was awarded; Federal Work-Study, institutionally sponsored loans, and tuition waivers (partial) also available. Support available to part-time students. Financial award application deadline: 6/15; financial award applicants required to submit FAFSA. *Unit head:* Dr. John Love, M Ed Coordinator, 580-745-2226, Fax: 580-745-7508, E-mail: jlove@se.edu. *Application contact:* Carrie Williamson, Graduate Secretary, 580-745-2220, Fax: 580-745-7474, E-mail: cwilliamson@se.edu. Web site: http://www.se.edu/graduate-programs/master-of-education/.

Southeastern University, Department of Behavioral and Social Sciences, Lakeland, FL 33801-6099. Offers human services (MA); professional counseling (MS); school counseling (MS). Evening/weekend programs available.

Southeast Missouri State University, School of Graduate Studies, Department of Educational Leadership and Counseling, Counseling Program, Cape Girardeau, MO 63701-4799. Offers counseling education (Ed S); mental health counseling (MA). *Accreditation:* ACA; NCATE. Part-time and evening/weekend programs available. Postbaccalaureate distance learning degree programs offered (minimal on-campus study). *Faculty:* 12 full-time (7 women). *Students:* 28 full-time (26 women), 58 part-time (51 women); includes 6 minority (4 Black or African American, non-Hispanic/Latino; 2 Hispanic/Latino), 1 international. Average age 33. 20 applicants, 95% accepted, 13 enrolled. In 2011, 15 master's, 13 other advanced degrees awarded. *Degree requirements:* For master's, comprehensive exam, thesis or alternative, minimum GPA of 3.25, practicum/internship, portfolio, oral exam. *Entrance requirements:* For master's, GRE General Test or MAT, minimum undergraduate GPA of 3.0; 3 letters of recommendation; 18 undergraduate hours in social science including statistics (mental health counseling and career counseling); for Ed S, GRE General Test or MAT, minimum graduate GPA of 3.5; master's degree in counseling, education or related field; 4 letters of recommendation. Additional exam requirements/recommendations for international students: Required—TOEFL (minimum score 550 paper-based; 213 computer-based; 79 iBT); Recommended—IELTS (minimum score 6). *Application deadline:* For fall admission, 8/1 for domestic students, 7/1 for international students; for spring admission, 11/21 for domestic students, 11/1 for international students. Applications are processed on a rolling basis. Application fee: $30 ($40 for international students). Electronic applications accepted. *Expenses:* Tuition, state resident: full-time $4896; part-time $272 per credit hour. Tuition, nonresident: full-time $8649; part-time $480.50 per credit hour. *Financial support:* In 2011–12, 10 students received support. Career-related internships or fieldwork, Federal Work-Study, scholarships/grants, tuition waivers (full), and unspecified assistantships available. Financial award application deadline: 6/30; financial award applicants required to submit FAFSA. *Faculty research:* Counselor development, marriage and family counseling, multicultural counseling. *Unit head:* Dr. David Stader, 573-651-2417, E-mail: dstader@semo.edu. *Application contact:* Alisa Aleen McFerron, Assistant Director of Admissions for Operations, 573-651-5937, Fax: 573-651-5936, E-mail: amcferron@semo.edu. Web site: http://www4.semo.edu/counsel/.

Southern Adventist University, School of Education and Psychology, Collegedale, TN 37315-0370. Offers clinical mental health counseling (MS); inclusive education (MS Ed); instructional leadership (MS Ed); literacy education (MS Ed); outdoor teacher education (MS Ed); school counseling (MS). *Accreditation:* NCATE. Part-time and evening/weekend programs available. *Degree requirements:* For master's, comprehensive exam (for some programs), thesis optional, position paper (MS), portfolio (MS Ed in outdoor teacher education). *Entrance requirements:* For master's, interview (MS); 9 semester hours of upper division course work in psychology or related field, including 1 course in psychology research or statistics; 9 semester hours of education (MS Ed). Additional exam requirements/recommendations for international students: Required—TOEFL (minimum score 600 paper-based; 250 computer-based; 100 iBT). Electronic applications accepted.

Southern Arkansas University–Magnolia, Graduate Programs, Magnolia, AR 71754. Offers agriculture (MS); business administration (MBA); computer and information sciences (MS); education (M Ed), including counseling and development, curriculum and instruction, educational administration and supervision, elementary education, middle level, reading, secondary education, TESOL; kinesiology (M Ed); library media and information specialist (M Ed); mental health and clinical counseling (MS); public administration (MPA); school counseling (M Ed); teaching (MAT). *Accreditation:* NCATE. Part-time and evening/weekend programs available. Postbaccalaureate distance learning degree programs offered. *Faculty:* 34 full-time (15 women), 8 part-time/adjunct (5 women). *Students:* 87 full-time (62 women), 320 part-time (224 women); includes 116 minority (111 Black or African American, non-Hispanic/Latino; 2 American Indian or Alaska Native, non-Hispanic/Latino; 2 Asian, non-Hispanic/Latino; 1 Hispanic/Latino), 25 international. Average age 33. 201 applicants, 98% accepted, 156 enrolled. In 2011, 162 master's awarded. *Degree requirements:* For master's, comprehensive exam (for some programs), thesis optional. *Entrance requirements:* For master's, GRE, MAT or GMAT, minimum GPA of 2.5. Additional exam requirements/recommendations for international students: Required—TOEFL (minimum score 173 computer-based). *Application deadline:* For fall admission, 7/15 for domestic and international students; for winter admission, 12/1 for domestic and international students; for spring admission, 12/1 for domestic and international students. Applications are processed on a rolling basis. Application fee: $25 ($35 for international students). Electronic applications accepted. *Expenses:* Tuition, state resident: part-time $232 per credit. Tuition, nonresident: part-time $339 per credit. *Required fees:* $44 per credit. Part-time tuition and fees vary according to course load. *Financial support:* Career-related internships or fieldwork, Federal Work-Study, scholarships/grants, tuition waivers (full), and unspecified assistantships available. Financial award applicants required to submit FAFSA. *Faculty research:* Alternative certification for teachers, supervision of instruction, instructional leadership, counseling. *Unit head:* Dr. Kim Bloss, Dean, School of Graduate Studies, 870-235-4150, Fax: 870-235-5227, E-mail: kkbloss@saumag.edu. *Application contact:* Gaye Calhoun, Admissions Specialist, 870-235-4150, Fax: 870-235-5227, E-mail: glcalhoun@saumag.edu. Web site: http://www.saumag.edu/graduate.

Southern Connecticut State University, School of Graduate Studies, School of Education, Department of Counseling and School Psychology, New Haven, CT 06515-1355. Offers community counseling (MS); counseling (Diploma); school counseling (MS); school psychology (MS, Diploma). *Accreditation:* ACA (one or more programs are accredited); NCATE. *Faculty:* 7 full-time (all women), 7 part-time/adjunct (4 women). *Students:* 94 full-time (74 women), 59 part-time (43 women); includes 21 minority (14 Black or African American, non-Hispanic/Latino; 1 Asian, non-Hispanic/Latino; 5 Hispanic/Latino; 1 Two or more races, non-Hispanic/Latino), 1 international. 405 applicants, 17% accepted, 51 enrolled. In 2011, 43 master's, 15 other advanced degrees awarded. *Degree requirements:* For master's, comprehensive exam. *Entrance requirements:* For master's, interview, previous course work in behavioral sciences, minimum QPA of 2.7. *Application deadline:* For fall admission, 1/15 for domestic students; for spring admission, 10/15 for domestic students. Application fee: $50.

Electronic applications accepted. *Expenses:* Tuition, state resident: full-time $5137; part-time $413 per credit. *Required fees:* $4008; $55 per term. *Financial support:* Teaching assistantships and career-related internships or fieldwork available. Financial award application deadline: 4/15; financial award applicants required to submit FAFSA. *Unit head:* Dr. Patricia DeBarbieri, Chairperson, 203-392-5483, E-mail: debarbierip1@southernct.edu. *Application contact:* Dr. Louisa Foss, Graduate Coordinator, 203-392-5154, E-mail: fossl1@southernct.edu.

Southern Illinois University Carbondale, Graduate School, College of Education and Human Services, Department of Educational Psychology and Special Education, Program in Educational Psychology, Carbondale, IL 62901-4701. Offers counselor education (MS Ed, PhD); educational psychology (PhD); human learning and development (MS Ed); measurement and statistics (PhD). *Accreditation:* NCATE. *Faculty:* 19 full-time (9 women), 7 part-time/adjunct (2 women). *Students:* 47 full-time (33 women), 20 part-time (12 women); includes 12 minority (10 Black or African American, non-Hispanic/Latino; 1 Asian, non-Hispanic/Latino; 1 Hispanic/Latino), 11 international. Average age 36. 29 applicants, 62% accepted, 8 enrolled. In 2011, 21 master's, 3 doctorates awarded. *Degree requirements:* For master's, thesis; for doctorate, thesis/dissertation. *Entrance requirements:* For master's, GRE General Test, minimum GPA of 2.7; for doctorate, minimum GPA of 3.25. Additional exam requirements/recommendations for international students: Required—TOEFL. *Application deadline:* For fall admission, 6/15 priority date for domestic students. Applications are processed on a rolling basis. Application fee: $20. *Financial support:* In 2011–12, 36 students received support, including 2 fellowships with full tuition reimbursements available, 4 research assistantships with full tuition reimbursements available; teaching assistantships with full tuition reimbursements available, career-related internships or fieldwork, Federal Work-Study, institutionally sponsored loans, and tuition waivers (full) also available. Support available to part-time students. Financial award application deadline: 5/1. *Faculty research:* Career development, problem solving, learning and instruction, cognitive development, family assessment. *Total annual research expenditures:* $10,000. *Unit head:* Dr. Lyle White, Chairperson, 618-536-7763, E-mail: lwhite@siu.edu. *Application contact:* Cathy Earnhart, Administrative Clerk, 618-453-6932, E-mail: pern@siu.edu.

Southern Methodist University, Annette Caldwell Simmons School of Education and Human Development, Department of Dispute Resolution and Counseling, Dallas, TX 75275. Offers counseling (MS); dispute resolution (MA, Certificate). Part-time programs available. *Degree requirements:* For master's, practica experience, 2 internships (counseling). *Entrance requirements:* For master's, minimum undergraduate GPA of 2.75 (for dispute resolution), 3.0 (for counseling); 3 letters of recommendation. Additional exam requirements/recommendations for international students: Required—TOEFL. Electronic applications accepted.

Southern University and Agricultural and Mechanical College, Graduate School, College of Education, Department of Behavioral Studies and Educational Leadership, Baton Rouge, LA 70813. Offers administration and supervision (M Ed); counselor education (MA); educational leadership (M Ed); mental health counseling (MA). *Accreditation:* ACA; NCATE. *Degree requirements:* For master's, comprehensive exam, thesis optional. *Entrance requirements:* For master's, GRE General Test. Additional exam requirements/recommendations for international students: Required—TOEFL (minimum score 525 paper-based; 193 computer-based). *Faculty research:* Mental health, computer assisted programs, families relations, head start improvements, careers.

Southwestern Oklahoma State University, College of Professional and Graduate Studies, School of Behavioral Sciences and Education, Specialization in Community Counseling, Weatherford, OK 73096-3098. Offers M Ed. M Ed distance learning degree program offered to Oklahoma residents only. *Accreditation:* NCATE. Part-time and evening/weekend programs available. Postbaccalaureate distance learning degree programs offered (minimal on-campus study). *Degree requirements:* For master's, exam. *Entrance requirements:* For master's, GRE General Test or minimum undergraduate GPA of 3.0. Additional exam requirements/recommendations for international students: Required—TOEFL.

Southwestern Oklahoma State University, College of Professional and Graduate Studies, School of Behavioral Sciences and Education, Specialization in School Counseling, Weatherford, OK 73096-3098. Offers M Ed. M Ed distance learning degree program offered to Oklahoma residents only. *Accreditation:* NCATE. Part-time and evening/weekend programs available. Postbaccalaureate distance learning degree programs offered (minimal on-campus study). *Degree requirements:* For master's, exam. *Entrance requirements:* For master's, GRE General Test or minimum undergraduate GPA of 3.0, portfolio. Additional exam requirements/recommendations for international students: Required—TOEFL.

Spalding University, Graduate Studies, College of Education, Programs in Education, Louisville, KY 40203-2188. Offers elementary school education (MAT); general education (MA); high school education (MAT); middle school education (MAT); school administration (MA); special education (learning and behavioral disorders) (MAT); student guidance counselor (MA). MAT programs offered for first teaching certificate/license students. *Accreditation:* NCATE. Part-time and evening/weekend programs available. *Faculty:* 9 full-time (6 women), 32 part-time/adjunct (20 women). *Students:* 142 full-time (100 women), 71 part-time (53 women); includes 75 minority (65 Black or African American, non-Hispanic/Latino; 1 American Indian or Alaska Native, non-Hispanic/Latino; 6 Hispanic/Latino; 3 Two or more races, non-Hispanic/Latino). Average age 36. 96 applicants, 44% accepted, 41 enrolled. In 2011, 69 master's awarded. *Degree requirements:* For master's, portfolio, final project, clinical experience. *Entrance requirements:* For master's, GRE General Test or MAT, interview, recommendations, resume. Additional exam requirements/recommendations for international students: Required—TOEFL (minimum score 535 paper-based; 203 computer-based). *Application deadline:* Applications are processed on a rolling basis. Application fee: $30. Electronic applications accepted. *Expenses: Tuition:* Full-time $12,438. Tuition and fees vary according to course load, degree level and program. *Financial support:* In 2011–12, 72 students received support, including 3 research assistantships with partial tuition reimbursements available (averaging $4,490 per year); scholarships/grants, traineeships, and unspecified assistantships also available. Financial award application deadline: 3/15; financial award applicants required to submit FAFSA. *Faculty research:* Instructional technology, achievement gap, classroom management, assessment. *Unit head:* Dr. Beverly Keepers, Dean, 502-588-7121, Fax: 502-585-7123, E-mail: bkeepers@spalding.edu. *Application contact:* Bonnie Caughron, 502-873-4262, E-mail: bcaughron@spalding.edu.

Springfield College, Graduate Programs, Program in Education, Springfield, MA 01109-3797. Offers counseling and secondary education (M Ed, MS); early childhood education (M Ed, MS); education (M Ed, MS); educational administration (M Ed, MS); educational studies (M Ed, MS); elementary education (M Ed, MS); secondary education (M Ed, MS); special education (M Ed, MS). Part-time and evening/weekend programs available. *Entrance requirements:* Additional exam requirements/recommendations for international students: Required—TOEFL (minimum score 550 paper-based; 213 computer-based). Electronic applications accepted.

Springfield College, Graduate Programs, Programs in Psychology and Counseling, Springfield, MA 01109-3797. Offers athletic counseling (M Ed, MS, CAGS); industrial/organizational psychology (M Ed, MS, CAGS); marriage and family therapy (M Ed, MS, CAGS); mental health counseling (M Ed, MS, CAGS); school guidance and counseling (M Ed, MS, CAGS); student personnel in higher education (M Ed, MS, CAGS). Part-time programs available. *Degree requirements:* For master's, research project, portfolio. *Entrance requirements:* Additional exam requirements/recommendations for international students: Required—TOEFL (minimum score 550 paper-based; 213 computer-based). Electronic applications accepted.

State University of New York at New Paltz, Graduate School, School of Liberal Arts and Sciences, Department of Psychology, New Paltz, NY 12561. Offers mental health counseling (MS); psychology (MA); school counseling (MS). Part-time and evening/weekend programs available. *Faculty:* 12 full-time (8 women), 1 part-time/adjunct. *Students:* 45 full-time (35 women), 19 part-time (14 women); includes 9 minority (2 Black or African American, non-Hispanic/Latino; 1 Asian, non-Hispanic/Latino; 3 Hispanic/Latino; 3 Two or more races, non-Hispanic/Latino), 1 international. Average age 26. 107 applicants, 42% accepted, 27 enrolled. In 2011, 20 master's awarded. *Degree requirements:* For master's, comprehensive exam, thesis. *Entrance requirements:* For master's, GRE General Test, minimum GPA of 3.0. Additional exam requirements/recommendations for international students: Required—TOEFL (minimum score 550 paper-based; 213 computer-based; 80 iBT), IELTS (minimum score 6.5). *Application deadline:* For fall admission, 1/20 priority date for domestic students, 1/20 for international students; for spring admission, 11/15 for domestic and international students. Application fee: $50. Electronic applications accepted. *Expenses:* Tuition, state resident: full-time $8870; part-time $370 per credit. Tuition, nonresident: full-time $15,160; part-time $632 per credit. *Required fees:* $1188; $34 per credit. $184 per semester. *Financial support:* In 2011–12, 8 students received support, including 5 fellowships with partial tuition reimbursements available (averaging $7,000 per year), 1 research assistantship with partial tuition reimbursement available (averaging $5,000 per year), 6 teaching assistantships with partial tuition reimbursements available (averaging $5,000 per year); career-related internships or fieldwork, Federal Work-Study, institutionally sponsored loans, traineeships, tuition waivers (full), and unspecified assistantships also available. Financial award application deadline: 8/1; financial award applicants required to submit FAFSA. *Faculty research:* Disaster mental health, women's objectification, mate selection, cultural psychology, achievement motivation. *Unit head:* Dr. Glenn Geher, Chair, 845-257-3091, E-mail: geherg@newpaltz.edu. *Application contact:* Dr. Jonathan Raskin, Coordinator, 845-257-3471, E-mail: raskinj@newpaltz.edu. Web site: http://www.newpaltz.edu/psychology/.

State University of New York at Plattsburgh, Division of Education, Health, and Human Services, Department of Counselor Education, Plattsburgh, NY 12901-2681. Offers school counselor (MS Ed, CAS); student affairs counseling (MS), including clinical mental health counseling. *Accreditation:* ACA (one or more programs are accredited); Teacher Education Accreditation Council. Part-time programs available. *Students:* 54 full-time (45 women), 11 part-time (9 women); includes 4 minority (2 Black or African American, non-Hispanic/Latino; 2 Hispanic/Latino), 1 international. Average age 29. *Entrance requirements:* For master's, GRE General Test or MAT, minimum GPA of 2.8. Additional exam requirements/recommendations for international students: Required—TOEFL. *Application deadline:* For fall admission, 2/15 priority date for domestic students; for spring admission, 10/15 priority date for domestic students. Applications are processed on a rolling basis. Application fee: $75. *Financial support:* Research assistantships, teaching assistantships, career-related internships or fieldwork, Federal Work-Study, and administrative assistantships, editorial assistantships available. Support available to part-time students. Financial award application deadline: 4/15; financial award applicants required to submit FAFSA. *Faculty research:* Campus violence, program accreditation, substance abuse, vocational assessment, group counseling, divorce. *Unit head:* Dr. David Stone, Coordinator, 518-564-4170, E-mail: stoneda@plattsburgh.edu. *Application contact:* Marguerite Adelman, Assistant Director, Graduate Admissions, 518-564-4723, Fax: 518-564-4722, E-mail: adelmaml@plattsburgh.edu.

State University of New York College at Oneonta, Graduate Education, Division of Education, Department of Educational Psychology and Counseling, Oneonta, NY 13820-4015. Offers school counselor K-12 (MS Ed, CAS). *Accreditation:* NCATE. Part-time and evening/weekend programs available. *Degree requirements:* For master's, comprehensive exam. *Entrance requirements:* For master's, GRE General Test.

Stephen F. Austin State University, Graduate School, College of Education, Department of Human Services, Nacogdoches, TX 75962. Offers counseling (MA); school psychology (MA); special education (M Ed); speech pathology (MS). *Accreditation:* ACA (one or more programs are accredited); ASHA (one or more programs are accredited); CORE; NCATE. *Degree requirements:* For master's, comprehensive exam, thesis (for some programs). *Entrance requirements:* For master's, GRE General Test, minimum GPA of 2.8. Additional exam requirements/recommendations for international students: Required—TOEFL.

Stephens College, Division of Graduate and Continuing Studies, Programs in Counseling, Columbia, MO 65215-0002. Offers counseling (M Ed), including marriage and family therapy, professional counseling, school counseling. Part-time and evening/weekend programs available. *Faculty:* 1 (woman) full-time, 14 part-time/adjunct (10 women). *Students:* 123 full-time (114 women), 28 part-time (25 women); includes 17 minority (9 Black or African American, non-Hispanic/Latino; 1 American Indian or Alaska Native, non-Hispanic/Latino; 2 Asian, non-Hispanic/Latino; 2 Hispanic/Latino; 3 Two or more races, non-Hispanic/Latino). Average age 34. 33 applicants, 64% accepted, 20 enrolled. In 2011, 40 master's awarded. *Degree requirements:* For master's, thesis. *Entrance requirements:* For master's, minimum GPA of 3.0 in last 60 hours. Additional exam requirements/recommendations for international students: Required—TOEFL (minimum score 213 computer-based). *Application deadline:* For fall admission, 7/25 priority date for domestic students, 7/25 for international students; for winter admission, 12/1 priority date for domestic students, 12/1 for international students; for spring admission, 4/25 priority date for domestic students, 4/25 for international students. Applications are processed on a rolling basis. Application fee: $40. Electronic applications accepted. *Expenses: Tuition:* Full-time $2220; part-time $370 per credit hour. *Required fees:* $228; $38 per credit hour. *Financial support:* In 2011–12, 62 students received support, including 4 fellowships with full tuition reimbursements available (averaging $6,365 per year); scholarships/grants and unspecified assistantships also available. Financial award application deadline: 12/5; financial award applicants required to submit FAFSA. *Unit head:* Dr. Linda Thompson, Program Chair, 800-388-7579. *Application contact:* Jennifer Deaver, Assistant Director of Marketing and Recruitment, 800-388-7579, E-mail: online@stephens.edu.

Stetson University, College of Arts and Sciences, Division of Education, Department of Counselor Education, DeLand, FL 32723. Offers marriage and family therapy (MS); mental health counseling (MS); school guidance and family consultation (MS). *Accreditation:* ACA. Evening/weekend programs available. *Students:* 70 full-time (61 women), 10 part-time (all women); includes 22 minority (9 Black or African American, non-Hispanic/Latino; 1 Asian, non-Hispanic/Latino; 12 Hispanic/Latino), 3 international. Average age 30. In 2011, 20 master's awarded. *Entrance requirements:* For master's,

GRE General Test. *Application deadline:* For fall admission, 3/1 priority date for domestic students; for spring admission, 11/1 for domestic students. Applications are processed on a rolling basis. Application fee: $25. *Unit head:* Dr. Brigid Noonan-Klima, Chair, 386-822-8992. *Application contact:* Diana Belian, Office of Graduate Studies, 386-822-7075, Fax: 386-822-7388, E-mail: dbelian@stetson.edu.

Suffolk University, College of Arts and Sciences, Department of Education and Human Services, Boston, MA 02108-2770. Offers administration of higher education (M Ed, CAGS), including administration of higher education (M Ed), leadership (CAGS); human resource, learning and performance (MS, CAGS, Graduate Certificate), including global human resources (Graduate Certificate), human resources (MS, Graduate Certificate), organizational development (CAGS, Graduate Certificate), organizational learning and development (MS, Graduate Certificate); mental health counseling (MS, CAGS); school counseling (M Ed, CAGS); school teaching (M Ed, CAGS), including foundations of education (M Ed), middle school teaching (M Ed), secondary school teaching (M Ed); MPA/MSMHC; MS/Certificate. Part-time and evening/weekend programs available. *Faculty:* 10 full-time (6 women), 7 part-time/adjunct (3 women). *Students:* 53 full-time (39 women), 131 part-time (112 women); includes 21 minority (7 Black or African American, non-Hispanic/Latino; 2 American Indian or Alaska Native, non-Hispanic/Latino; 5 Asian, non-Hispanic/Latino; 5 Hispanic/Latino; 2 Two or more races, non-Hispanic/Latino), 9 international. Average age 28. 158 applicants, 73% accepted, 60 enrolled. In 2011, 72 master's, 8 other advanced degrees awarded. *Entrance requirements:* For master's, GRE General Test or MAT, 2 letters of recommendation, resume. Additional exam requirements/recommendations for international students: Required—TOEFL (minimum score 550 paper-based; 213 computer-based; 80 iBT). *Application deadline:* For fall admission, 6/15 priority date for domestic students, 6/15 for international students; for spring admission, 11/1 priority date for domestic students, 11/1 for international students. Applications are processed on a rolling basis. Application fee: $50. Electronic applications accepted. *Expenses:* Contact institution. *Financial support:* In 2011–12, 102 students received support, including 30 fellowships with full and partial tuition reimbursements available (averaging $10,664 per year); career-related internships or fieldwork, Federal Work-Study, and institutionally sponsored loans also available. Support available to part-time students. Financial award application deadline: 4/1; financial award applicants required to submit FAFSA. *Faculty research:* Predicting competent Head Start preschools, cultural differences. *Unit head:* Dr. Krisanne Bursik, Associate Dean and Acting Chair, 617-573-8261, Fax: 617-305-1743, E-mail: kbursik@suffolk.edu. *Application contact:* Ellen Driscoll, Director of Graduate Admissions, 617-573-8302, Fax: 617-305-1733, E-mail: grad.admission@suffolk.edu. Web site: http://www.suffolk.edu/college/9785.html.

Sul Ross State University, Rio Grande College of Sul Ross State University, Alpine, TX 79832. Offers business administration (MBA); teacher education (M Ed), including bilingual education, counseling, educational diagnostics, elementary education, general education, reading, school administration, secondary education. Part-time and evening/weekend programs available. Postbaccalaureate distance learning degree programs offered (no on-campus study). *Faculty:* 11 full-time (3 women), 4 part-time/adjunct (3 women). *Students:* 45 full-time (36 women), 255 part-time (168 women); includes 218 minority (2 Black or African American, non-Hispanic/Latino; 1 American Indian or Alaska Native, non-Hispanic/Latino; 215 Hispanic/Latino), 1 international. Average age 36. In 2011, 47 master's awarded. *Degree requirements:* For master's, comprehensive exam, thesis optional, minimum GPA of 3.0. *Entrance requirements:* For master's, GMAT or GRE General Test, minimum GPA of 2.5 in last 60 hours of undergraduate work. Additional exam requirements/recommendations for international students: Required—TOEFL. *Application deadline:* Applications are processed on a rolling basis. Application fee: $0 ($50 for international students). *Financial support:* Career-related internships or fieldwork, Federal Work-Study, and institutionally sponsored loans available. Support available to part-time students. Financial award application deadline: 5/1; financial award applicants required to submit FAFSA. *Unit head:* Dr. Paul Sorrels, Associate Provost/Dean, 512-278-3339, Fax: 512-278-3330. *Application contact:* Claudia R. Wright, Director of Admissions and Records, 915-837-8050, Fax: 915-837-8431, E-mail: rcullins@sulross.edu.

Sul Ross State University, School of Professional Studies, Department of Teacher Education, Program in Counseling, Alpine, TX 79832. Offers M Ed. Part-time and evening/weekend programs available. *Degree requirements:* For master's, thesis optional. *Entrance requirements:* For master's, GMAT or GRE General Test, minimum GPA of 2.5 in last 60 hours of undergraduate work. *Faculty research:* Input variable effects on EXCET for graduate students.

Syracuse University, School of Education, Program in Counseling and Counselor Education, Syracuse, NY 13244. Offers PhD. *Accreditation:* ACA. Part-time programs available. *Students:* 11 full-time (8 women), 4 part-time (3 women); includes 2 minority (both Black or African American, non-Hispanic/Latino), 3 international. Average age 35. 19 applicants, 26% accepted, 4 enrolled. In 2011, 1 degree awarded. *Degree requirements:* For doctorate, thesis/dissertation. *Entrance requirements:* For doctorate, GRE, video of counseling interview, master's degree, interview. Additional exam requirements/recommendations for international students: Required—TOEFL (minimum score 100 iBT). *Application deadline:* For fall admission, 1/1 priority date for domestic students, 1/1 for international students; for spring admission, 10/15 priority date for domestic students, 10/15 for international students. Applications are processed on a rolling basis. Application fee: $75. Electronic applications accepted. *Expenses: Tuition:* Part-time $1206 per credit. *Financial support:* Fellowships with full tuition reimbursements and teaching assistantships with full tuition reimbursements available. Financial award application deadline: 1/1; financial award applicants required to submit FAFSA. *Unit head:* Dr. Janine Bernard, Chair, 315-443-5266, Fax: 315-443-5732, E-mail: bernard@syr.edu. *Application contact:* Laurie Deyo, Graduate Recruiter, School of Education, 315-443-2505, E-mail: e-gradrcrt@syr.edu. Web site: http://soeweb.syr.edu/.

Syracuse University, School of Education, Program in Student Affairs Counseling, Syracuse, NY 13244. Offers MS. Part-time programs available. *Students:* 3 full-time (1 woman), 2 part-time (both women); includes 1 minority (Two or more races, non-Hispanic/Latino). Average age 29. 11 applicants, 45% accepted, 2 enrolled. In 2011, 3 master's awarded. *Entrance requirements:* For master's, GRE General Test or MAT, interview. Additional exam requirements/recommendations for international students: Required—TOEFL (minimum score 100 iBT). *Application deadline:* For fall admission, 2/1 for domestic and international students; for spring admission, 10/15 for domestic and international students. Applications are processed on a rolling basis. Application fee: $75. Electronic applications accepted. *Expenses: Tuition:* Part-time $1206 per credit. *Financial support:* Fellowships with full tuition reimbursements and teaching assistantships with full and partial tuition reimbursements available. Financial award application deadline: 1/1; financial award applicants required to submit FAFSA. *Unit head:* Dr. Dennis Gilbride, Chair, 315-443-2266, E-mail: ddgilbr@syr.edu. *Application contact:* Laurie Deyo, Graduate Recruiter, School of Education, 315-443-2505, E-mail: e-gradrcrt@syr.edu. Web site: http://soeweb.syr.edu/.

Tarleton State University, College of Graduate Studies, College of Education, Department of Psychology and Counseling, Stephenville, TX 76402. Offers counseling and psychology (M Ed), including counseling, counseling psychology, educational psychology; educational administration (M Ed); secondary education (Certificate); special education (Certificate). Part-time and evening/weekend programs available. Postbaccalaureate distance learning degree programs offered (minimal on-campus study). *Faculty:* 8 full-time (5 women), 13 part-time/adjunct (6 women). *Students:* 73 full-time (62 women), 219 part-time (186 women); includes 55 minority (25 Black or African American, non-Hispanic/Latino; 1 American Indian or Alaska Native, non-Hispanic/Latino; 1 Asian, non-Hispanic/Latino; 22 Hispanic/Latino; 1 Native Hawaiian or other Pacific Islander, non-Hispanic/Latino; 5 Two or more races, non-Hispanic/Latino), 1 international. Average age 35. 92 applicants, 91% accepted, 62 enrolled. In 2011, 65 master's awarded. *Degree requirements:* For master's, comprehensive exam, thesis optional. *Entrance requirements:* For master's, GRE General Test, minimum GPA of 3.0. Additional exam requirements/recommendations for international students: Required—TOEFL (minimum score 550 paper-based; 213 computer-based; 80 iBT). *Application deadline:* For fall admission, 8/5 priority date for domestic students; for spring admission, 12/1 for domestic students. Applications are processed on a rolling basis. Application fee: $30 ($130 for international students). Electronic applications accepted. *Expenses:* Tuition, state resident: full-time $3131.46; part-time $174 per credit hour. Tuition, nonresident: full-time $8225; part-time $457 per credit hour. *Required fees:* $1446. Tuition and fees vary according to course load and campus/location. *Financial support:* Research assistantships, teaching assistantships, career-related internships or fieldwork, Federal Work-Study, institutionally sponsored loans, and tuition waivers (partial) available. Support available to part-time students. Financial award application deadline: 5/1; financial award applicants required to submit FAFSA. *Unit head:* Dr. Bob Newby, Interim Department Head, 254-968-9813, Fax: 254-968-1991, E-mail: newby@tarleton.edu. *Application contact:* Information Contact, 254-968-9104, Fax: 254-968-9670, E-mail: gradoffice@tarleton.edu. Web site: http://www.tarleton.edu/~dpc.

Teacher Education University, Graduate Programs, Winter Park, FL 32789. Offers educational leadership (MA); educational technology (MA); elementary education K-6 (MA); instructional strategies (MA Ed); school guidance and counseling (MA).

Teachers College, Columbia University, Graduate Faculty of Education, Department of Health and Behavioral Studies, Program in Guidance and Rehabilitation, New York, NY 10027-6696. Offers MA. *Unit head:* Prof. Linda Hickson, Program Coordinator, 212-678-3880. *Application contact:* Elizabeth Puleio, Admissions Contact, 212-678-3710.

Tennessee State University, The School of Graduate Studies and Research, College of Education, Department of Psychology, Nashville, TN 37209-1561. Offers counseling and guidance (MS), including counseling, elementary school counseling, organizational counseling, secondary school counseling; counseling psychology (PhD); psychology (MS, PhD); school psychology (MS, PhD). *Accreditation:* APA. *Degree requirements:* For doctorate, thesis/dissertation (for some programs). *Entrance requirements:* For master's, GRE General Test or MAT; for doctorate, GRE General Test or MAT, minimum GPA of 3.25, work experience. Electronic applications accepted.

Texas A&M International University, Office of Graduate Studies and Research, College of Education, Department of Professional Programs, Laredo, TX 78041-1900. Offers educational administration (MS Ed); generic special education (MS Ed); school counseling (MS). *Faculty:* 11 full-time (5 women), 1 part-time/adjunct (0 women). *Students:* 11 full-time (8 women), 115 part-time (90 women); includes 125 minority (2 Black or African American, non-Hispanic/Latino; 123 Hispanic/Latino). Average age 34. 33 applicants, 79% accepted, 18 enrolled. In 2011, 42 master's awarded. *Entrance requirements:* Additional exam requirements/recommendations for international students: Required—TOEFL (minimum score 550 paper-based; 213 computer-based; 79 iBT). *Application deadline:* For fall admission, 4/30 priority date for domestic students, 4/30 for international students; for spring admission, 11/30 priority date for domestic students, 10/1 for international students. Application fee: $35 ($50 for international students). *Expenses:* Tuition, state resident: full-time $5063. *Financial support:* In 2011–12, 5 students received support, including 3 fellowships, 2 research assistantships; Federal Work-Study, scholarships/grants, and unspecified assistantships also available. Financial award application deadline: 4/1. *Unit head:* Dr. Randel Brown, Chair, 956-326-2679, E-mail: brown@tamiu.edu. *Application contact:* Suzanne H. Alford, Director of Admissions, 956-326-3023, E-mail: graduateschool@tamiu.edu. Web site: http://www.tamiu.edu/coedu/DOPPPrograms.shtml.

Texas A&M University–Commerce, Graduate School, College of Education and Human Services, Department of Counseling, Commerce, TX 75429-3011. Offers M Ed, MS, PhD. *Accreditation:* ACA (one or more programs are accredited). Part-time programs available. Terminal master's awarded for partial completion of doctoral program. *Degree requirements:* For master's, comprehensive exam, thesis (for some programs); for doctorate, thesis/dissertation, departmental qualifying exam. *Entrance requirements:* For master's and doctorate, GRE General Test. *Faculty research:* Emergency responders, efficacy and effect of web-based instruction, family violence, play therapy.

Texas A&M University–Corpus Christi, Graduate Studies and Research, College of Education, Programs in Counseling, Corpus Christi, TX 78412-5503. Offers counseling (MS); counselor education (PhD). *Accreditation:* ACA. Part-time and evening/weekend programs available. *Degree requirements:* For master's, comprehensive exam, thesis (for some programs). *Entrance requirements:* For master's, GRE General Test. Additional exam requirements/recommendations for international students: Required—TOEFL. Electronic applications accepted.

Texas A&M University–Kingsville, College of Graduate Studies, College of Education, Department of Education, Program in Guidance and Counseling, Kingsville, TX 78363. Offers MA, MS. MS offered jointly with University of North Texas. Part-time and evening/weekend programs available. *Degree requirements:* For master's, comprehensive exam, mini-thesis. *Entrance requirements:* For master's, GRE General Test, MAT, minimum GPA of 3.0. *Faculty research:* Diagnostician requirements for certification, teaching methods for adult learner.

Texas A&M University–San Antonio, Department of Leadership and Counseling, San Antonio, TX 78224. Offers counseling and guidance (MA); educational leadership (MA). Part-time and evening/weekend programs available. *Faculty:* 12 full-time (7 women), 7 part-time/adjunct (5 women). *Students:* 108 full-time (83 women), 157 part-time (131 women). Average age 35. In 2011, 70 master's awarded. *Degree requirements:* For master's, comprehensive exam, thesis or alternative. *Entrance requirements:* For master's, MAT. Additional exam requirements/recommendations for international students: Required—TOEFL (minimum score 550 paper-based; 213 computer-based; 80 iBT), IELTS (minimum score 6). *Application deadline:* For fall admission, 8/15 priority date for domestic students, 6/1 for international students; for spring admission, 12/15 priority date for domestic students, 10/1 for international students. Applications are processed on a rolling basis. Application fee: $35 ($50 for international students). Electronic applications accepted. *Expenses:* Tuition, state resident: part-time $691.11 per course. Tuition, nonresident: part-time $1621.11 per course. *Financial support:* Application deadline: 3/31; applicants required to submit FAFSA. *Unit head:* Dr. Albert Valadez, Department Chair, 210-932-7843, E-mail: albert.valadez@tamusa.tamus.edu. *Application contact:* Jennifer M. Dovalina, Graduate Admissions Specialist, 210-784-1380, E-mail: graduateadmissions@tamusa.tamus.edu. Web site: http://www.tamusa.tamus.edu/leadership-counseling/.

Texas Christian University, College of Education, Program in Counseling, Fort Worth, TX 76129-0002. Offers counseling (M Ed, PhD); LPC (Certificate); school counseling (Certificate). Part-time and evening/weekend programs available. *Faculty:* 27 full-time (21 women), 1 part-time/adjunct. *Students:* 18 full-time (14 women), 29 part-time (25 women); includes 13 minority (4 Black or African American, non-Hispanic/Latino; 9 Hispanic/Latino). Average age 29. 28 applicants, 82% accepted, 21 enrolled. In 2011, 16 master's awarded. *Degree requirements:* For master's, oral exam. *Entrance requirements:* Additional exam requirements/recommendations for international students: Required—TOEFL (minimum score 550 paper-based; 213 computer-based; 80 iBT). *Application deadline:* For fall admission, 11/1 for domestic students, 11/16 for international students; for winter admission, 2/1 for domestic and international students; for spring admission, 3/1 for domestic and international students. Application fee: $50. Electronic applications accepted. *Expenses: Tuition:* Full-time $20,250; part-time $1125 per credit hour. Part-time tuition and fees vary according to course load and program. *Financial support:* Teaching assistantships with full tuition reimbursements, career-related internships or fieldwork, scholarships/grants, and unspecified assistantships available. Financial award application deadline: 3/1. *Unit head:* Dr. Jan Lacina, Associate Dean, 817-257-6786, E-mail: j.lacina@tcu.edu. *Application contact:* Patricia Garcia, Academic Program Specialist, 817-257-7661, E-mail: p.m.garcia@tcu.edu. Web site: http://www.coe.tcu.edu/283.asp.

Texas Southern University, College of Education, Department of Counselor Education, Houston, TX 77004-4584. Offers counseling (M Ed); counselor education (Ed D). Part-time and evening/weekend programs available. *Degree requirements:* For master's, one foreign language, comprehensive exam; for doctorate, comprehensive exam, thesis/dissertation. *Entrance requirements:* For master's, GRE General Test, minimum GPA of 2.5; for doctorate, GRE General Test or MAT, master's degree, minimum B+ average. Additional exam requirements/recommendations for international students: Required—TOEFL. Electronic applications accepted. *Faculty research:* Clinical and urban psychology.

Texas State University–San Marcos, Graduate School, College of Education, Department of Counseling, Leadership, Adult Education, and School Psychology, Program in Professional Counseling, San Marcos, TX 78666. Offers MA. *Accreditation:* ACA. Part-time programs available. *Faculty:* 10 full-time (7 women), 5 part-time/adjunct (2 women). *Students:* 64 full-time (48 women), 98 part-time (81 women); includes 39 minority (7 Black or African American, non-Hispanic/Latino; 1 Asian, non-Hispanic/Latino; 27 Hispanic/Latino; 4 Two or more races, non-Hispanic/Latino). Average age 33. 137 applicants, 27% accepted, 23 enrolled. In 2011, 58 master's awarded. *Degree requirements:* For master's, comprehensive exam, internship. *Entrance requirements:* For master's, GRE General Test, minimum GPA of 3.0 in last 60 hours. Additional exam requirements/recommendations for international students: Required—TOEFL (minimum score 550 paper-based; 213 computer-based; 78 iBT). *Application deadline:* For fall admission, 2/15 for domestic and international students; for spring admission, 10/1 for domestic and international students. Applications are processed on a rolling basis. Application fee: $40 ($90 for international students). Electronic applications accepted. *Expenses:* Tuition, state resident: full-time $6408; part-time $3204 per semester. Tuition, nonresident: full-time $14,832; part-time $7416 per semester. *Required fees:* $1824; $912 per semester. Tuition and fees vary according to course load. *Financial support:* In 2011–12, 97 students received support, including 3 research assistantships (averaging $9,423 per year), 8 teaching assistantships (averaging $6,975 per year); Federal Work-Study and institutionally sponsored loans also available. Support available to part-time students. Financial award application deadline: 4/1; financial award applicants required to submit FAFSA. *Unit head:* Dr. Kevin Fall, Graduate Advisor, 512-245-2575, Fax: 512-245-8872, E-mail: kf22@txstate.edu. *Application contact:* Dr. J. Michael Willoughby, Dean of Graduate School, 512-245-2581, Fax: 512-245-8365, E-mail: gradcollege@txstate.edu. Web site: http://www.txstate.edu/clas/Professional-Counseling/Program-Information.html.

Texas Tech University, Graduate School, College of Education, Department of Educational Psychology and Leadership, Lubbock, TX 79409. Offers counselor education (M Ed, PhD); educational leadership (M Ed, Ed D); educational psychology (M Ed, PhD); higher education (M Ed, Ed D); higher education: higher education research (PhD); instructional technology (M Ed, Ed D); instructional technology: distance education (M Ed); special education (M Ed, Ed D). *Accreditation:* ACA; NCATE. Part-time programs available. Postbaccalaureate distance learning degree programs offered (no on-campus study). *Students:* 180 full-time (133 women), 418 part-time (297 women); includes 127 minority (34 Black or African American, non-Hispanic/Latino; 3 American Indian or Alaska Native, non-Hispanic/Latino; 6 Asian, non-Hispanic/Latino; 76 Hispanic/Latino; 8 Two or more races, non-Hispanic/Latino), 41 international. Average age 36. 478 applicants, 42% accepted, 134 enrolled. In 2011, 139 master's, 30 doctorates awarded. *Degree requirements:* For master's, thesis optional; for doctorate, thesis/dissertation. *Entrance requirements:* For master's and doctorate, GRE General Test. Additional exam requirements/recommendations for international students: Required—TOEFL (minimum score 550 paper-based; 213 computer-based; 79 iBT). *Application deadline:* For fall admission, 6/1 priority date for domestic students, 1/15 for international students; for spring admission, 9/1 priority date for domestic students, 6/15 for international students. Applications are processed on a rolling basis. Application fee: $50 ($75 for international students). Electronic applications accepted. *Expenses:* Tuition, state resident: full-time $5899; part-time $245.80 per credit hour. Tuition, nonresident: full-time $13,411; part-time $558.80 per credit hour. *Required fees:* $2680.60; $86.50 per credit hour. $920.30 per semester. *Financial support:* In 2011–12, 142 students received support. Application deadline: 4/15; applicants required to submit FAFSA. *Faculty research:* Psychological processes of teaching and learning, teaching populations with special needs, instructional technology, educational administration in education, theories and practice in counseling and counselor education K-12 and higher. *Total annual research expenditures:* $1.4 million. *Unit head:* Dr. William Lan, Chair, 806-742-1998 Ext. 436, Fax: 806-742-2179, E-mail: william.lan@ttu.edu. *Application contact:* Dr. Hansel Burley, Associate Academic Dean, 806-742-1998 Ext. 447, Fax: 806-742-2179, E-mail: hansel.burley@ttu.edu.

Texas Wesleyan University, Graduate Programs, Programs in Education, Fort Worth, TX 76105-1536. Offers education (M Ed, Ed D); marriage and family therapy (MSMFT); professional counseling (MA); school counseling (MS). Part-time and evening/weekend programs available. Postbaccalaureate distance learning degree programs offered (no on-campus study). *Faculty:* 11 full-time (7 women), 3 part-time/adjunct (2 women). *Students:* 47 full-time (36 women), 193 part-time (159 women); includes 97 minority (52 Black or African American, non-Hispanic/Latino; 2 American Indian or Alaska Native, non-Hispanic/Latino; 6 Asian, non-Hispanic/Latino; 37 Hispanic/Latino), 4 international. Average age 35. 116 applicants, 72% accepted, 76 enrolled. In 2011, 179 master's awarded. *Entrance requirements:* For master's, GRE General Test, minimum GPA of 3.0 in final 60 hours of undergraduate course work, interview. *Application deadline:* For fall admission, 6/15 priority date for domestic students; for spring admission, 10/15 priority date for domestic students. Applications are processed on a rolling basis. Application fee: $40 ($50 for international students). Tuition and fees vary according to course level, course load, degree level and program. *Financial support:* Career-related internships or fieldwork, Federal Work-Study, scholarships/grants, and tuition waivers (full and partial) available. Support available to part-time students. Financial award application deadline: 3/15; financial award applicants required to submit FAFSA. *Faculty research:* Teacher effectiveness, bilingual education, analytic teaching. *Unit head:* Dr. Carlos Martinez, Dean, School of Education, 817-531-4940, Fax: 817-531-4943. *Application contact:* Beth Hargrove, Coordinator of Graduate Programs, 817-531-4498, Fax: 817-531-4261, E-mail: bhargrove@txwes.edu. Web site: http://www.txwes.edu/academics/education.

Texas Woman's University, Graduate School, College of Professional Education, Department of Family Sciences, Denton, TX 76201. Offers child development (MS); counseling and development (MS); early childhood development and education (PhD); early childhood education (M Ed, MA, MS); family studies (MS, PhD); family therapy (MS, PhD). *Accreditation:* ACA (one or more programs are accredited). Part-time and evening/weekend programs available. *Faculty:* 24 full-time (18 women), 2 part-time/adjunct (both women). *Students:* 135 full-time (129 women), 313 part-time (286 women); includes 185 minority (125 Black or African American, non-Hispanic/Latino; 1 American Indian or Alaska Native, non-Hispanic/Latino; 15 Asian, non-Hispanic/Latino; 44 Hispanic/Latino), 15 international. Average age 36. 220 applicants, 56% accepted, 101 enrolled. In 2011, 77 master's, 26 doctorates awarded. Terminal master's awarded for partial completion of doctoral program. *Degree requirements:* For master's, comprehensive exam (for some programs), thesis (for some programs); for doctorate, comprehensive exam, thesis/dissertation. *Entrance requirements:* Additional exam requirements/recommendations for international students: Required—TOEFL (minimum score 550 paper-based; 213 computer-based; 79 iBT). *Application deadline:* For fall admission, 7/1 priority date for domestic students, 2/15 for international students; for spring admission, 9/15 priority date for domestic students, 7/1 for international students. Applications are processed on a rolling basis. Application fee: $50 ($75 for international students). Electronic applications accepted. *Expenses:* Tuition, state resident: full-time $3834; part-time $213 per credit hour. Tuition, nonresident: full-time $9468; part-time $526 per credit hour. *Required fees:* $213 per credit hour. Tuition and fees vary according to course load. *Financial support:* In 2011–12, 137 students received support, including 15 research assistantships (averaging $12,942 per year), 8 teaching assistantships (averaging $12,942 per year); career-related internships or fieldwork, Federal Work-Study, institutionally sponsored loans, scholarships/grants, traineeships, health care benefits, and unspecified assistantships also available. Support available to part-time students. Financial award application deadline: 3/1; financial award applicants required to submit FAFSA. *Faculty research:* Parenting/parent education, military families, play therapy, family sexuality, diversity, healthy relationships/healthy marriages, childhood obesity, male communication. *Total annual research expenditures:* $24,151. *Unit head:* Dr. Larry LeFlore, Chair, 940-898-2685, Fax: 940-898-2676, E-mail: famsci@twu.edu. *Application contact:* Dr. Samuel Wheeler, Assistant Director of Admissions, 940-898-3188, Fax: 940-898-3081, E-mail: wheelersr@twu.edu. Web site: http://www.twu.edu/family-sciences/.

Touro College, Graduate School of Psychology, School Counseling Program, New York, NY 10010. Offers MS. Postbaccalaureate distance learning degree programs offered. *Entrance requirements:* For master's, baccalaureate degree or its equivalent from accredited academic institution; minimum undergraduate and graduate GPA of 3.0; interview; two letters of reference; personal statement; proof of immunization. *Application deadline:* For fall admission, 8/1 for domestic students; for spring admission, 12/1 for domestic students. Application fee: $50. *Unit head:* Dr. Yair Maman, Chair, 212-242-4668 Ext. 6007, E-mail: yairm@touro.edu. *Application contact:* Jenny Ilina, Administrative Assistant to the Chair, 212-242-4668 Ext. 6007, E-mail: jilina@touro.edu. Web site: http://www.touro.edu/dgsp/schoolcounseling/index_sc.asp.

Trevecca Nazarene University, College of Lifelong Learning, Graduate Counseling Programs, Major in Clinical Counseling, Nashville, TN 37210-2877. Offers PhD. Evening/weekend programs available. *Students:* 48 full-time (30 women), 6 part-time (4 women); includes 19 minority (17 Black or African American, non-Hispanic/Latino; 1 Hispanic/Latino; 1 Two or more races, non-Hispanic/Latino), 1 international. Average age 38. In 2011, 10 doctorates awarded. *Degree requirements:* For doctorate, comprehensive exam, thesis/dissertation. *Entrance requirements:* For doctorate, GRE, minimum GPA of 3.25; 3 recommendation forms; 400-word letter of intent; interview. Additional exam requirements/recommendations for international students: Required—TOEFL (minimum score 550 paper-based; 213 computer-based). *Application deadline:* Applications are processed on a rolling basis. Application fee: $50. *Expenses:* Contact institution. *Financial support:* Applicants required to submit FAFSA. *Unit head:* Dr. Peter Wilson, Director of Graduate Counseling Program, 615-248-1384, Fax: 615-248-1662, E-mail: admissions_gradcouns@trevecca.edu. *Application contact:* Heather Ambrefe, Assistant Director, 615-248-1384, Fax: 615-248-1662, E-mail: admissions_gradcouns@trevecca.edu. Web site: http://www.trevecca.edu/adult-education/graduate-programs/counseling/.

Trevecca Nazarene University, College of Lifelong Learning, Graduate Counseling Programs, Major in Counseling, Nashville, TN 37210-2877. Offers MA. Part-time and evening/weekend programs available. *Students:* 92 full-time (67 women), 12 part-time (9 women); includes 20 minority (12 Black or African American, non-Hispanic/Latino; 2 Hispanic/Latino; 2 Native Hawaiian or other Pacific Islander, non-Hispanic/Latino; 4 Two or more races, non-Hispanic/Latino). In 2011, 36 master's awarded. *Degree requirements:* For master's, comprehensive exam, practicum. *Entrance requirements:* For master's, GRE General Test or MAT, minimum GPA of 2.7, 2 reference assessment forms. Additional exam requirements/recommendations for international students: Required—TOEFL (minimum score 550 paper-based; 213 computer-based). *Application deadline:* Applications are processed on a rolling basis. Application fee: $25. *Expenses:* Contact institution. *Financial support:* Career-related internships or fieldwork available. Financial award applicants required to submit FAFSA. *Unit head:* Dr. Peter Wilson, Director of Graduate Counseling Program, 615-248-1384, Fax: 615-248-1662, E-mail: admissions_gradcouns@trevecca.edu. *Application contact:* Heather Ambrefe, Assistant Director, 615-248-1384, Fax: 615-248-1662, E-mail: admissions_gradcouns@trevecca.edu. Web site: http://www.trevecca.edu/adult-education/graduate-programs/counseling/.

Trinity Washington University, School of Education, Washington, DC 20017-1094. Offers counseling (MA); early childhood education (MAT); educating for change (M Ed); educational administration (MSA); elementary education (MAT); school counseling (MA); secondary education (MAT), including English, social studies; special education (MAT); teaching English as a second language (MAT); teaching English to speakers of other languages (M Ed); the teaching of reading (M Ed). *Accreditation:* NCATE. Part-time and evening/weekend programs available. *Degree requirements:* For master's, thesis (for some programs), capstone project(s). *Entrance requirements:* For master's, PRAXIS I, minimum GPA of 2.8. Additional exam requirements/recommendations for international students: Required—TOEFL (minimum score 550 paper-based; 213 computer-based). *Faculty research:* Technology, literacy, special education, organizations, inclusion models.

Troy University, Graduate School, College of Education, Program in Counseling and Psychology, Troy, AL 36082. Offers agency counseling (Ed S); clinical mental health (MS); community counseling (MS, Ed S); corrections counseling (MS); rehabilitation counseling (MS); school psychology (MS, Ed S); school psychometry (MS); social service counseling (MS); student affairs counseling (MS); substance abuse counseling

(MS). *Accreditation:* ACA; CORE; NCATE. Part-time and evening/weekend programs available. *Faculty:* 38 full-time (21 women), 40 part-time/adjunct (21 women). *Students:* 299 full-time (239 women), 672 part-time (557 women); includes 604 minority (358 Black or African American, non-Hispanic/Latino; 2 American Indian or Alaska Native, non-Hispanic/Latino; 188 Asian, non-Hispanic/Latino; 50 Hispanic/Latino; 1 Native Hawaiian or other Pacific Islander, non-Hispanic/Latino; 5 Two or more races, non-Hispanic/Latino). Average age 34. 384 applicants, 83% accepted, 196 enrolled. In 2011, 242 master's, 1 other advanced degree awarded. *Degree requirements:* For master's, comprehensive exam, thesis. *Entrance requirements:* For master's, MAT, minimum GPA of 2.5. Additional exam requirements/recommendations for international students: Required—TOEFL (minimum score 523 paper-based; 193 computer-based; 70 iBT), IELTS (minimum score 6). *Application deadline:* Applications are processed on a rolling basis. Application fee: $50. Electronic applications accepted. *Expenses:* Tuition, state resident: full-time $6960; part-time $290 per credit hour. Tuition, nonresident: full-time $13,920; part-time $580 per credit hour. *Required fees:* $386 per term. *Unit head:* Dr. Andrew Creamer, Chair, 334-670-3350, Fax: 334-670-32961, E-mail: drcreamer@troy.edu. *Application contact:* Brenda K. Campbell, Director of Graduate Admissions, 334-670-3178, Fax: 334-670-3733, E-mail: bcamp@troy.edu.

Troy University, Graduate School, College of Education, Program in School Counseling, Troy, AL 36082. Offers school counseling (MS, Ed S). *Accreditation:* ACA; CORE; NCATE. Part-time and evening/weekend programs available. *Faculty:* 5 full-time (3 women), 5 part-time/adjunct (4 women). *Students:* 23 full-time (18 women), 91 part-time (76 women); includes 87 minority (82 Black or African American, non-Hispanic/Latino; 2 Asian, non-Hispanic/Latino; 1 Hispanic/Latino; 2 Two or more races, non-Hispanic/Latino). Average age 33. 53 applicants, 72% accepted, 19 enrolled. In 2011, 31 master's, 10 other advanced degrees awarded. *Degree requirements:* For master's, comprehensive exam, thesis. *Entrance requirements:* For master's, minimum GPA of 2.5, teaching certification, 2 years of teaching experience. Additional exam requirements/recommendations for international students: Required—TOEFL (minimum score 523 paper-based; 193 computer-based; 70 iBT), IELTS. *Application deadline:* Applications are processed on a rolling basis. Application fee: $50. Electronic applications accepted. *Expenses:* Tuition, state resident: full-time $6960; part-time $290 per credit hour. Tuition, nonresident: full-time $13,920; part-time $580 per credit hour. *Required fees:* $386 per term. *Unit head:* Dr. Andrew Creamer, Chair, 334-670-3350, Fax: 334-670-32961, E-mail: drcreamer@troy.edu. *Application contact:* Brenda K. Campbell, Director of Graduate Admissions, 334-670-3178, Fax: 334-670-3733, E-mail: bcamp@troy.edu.

Union Institute & University, Education Programs, Cincinnati, OH 45206-1925. Offers adult and higher education (M Ed); curriculum and instruction (M Ed); educational leadership (M Ed, Ed D); guidance and counseling (Ed S); higher education (Ed D); issues in education (M Ed); reading (Ed S). M Ed offered online and in Vermont and Florida, concentrations vary by location; Ed S offered in Florida; Ed D program is a hybrid (online with limited residency) offered in Ohio. Postbaccalaureate distance learning degree programs offered (minimal on-campus study). *Degree requirements:* For master's, comprehensive exam (for some programs), thesis (for some programs), electronic portfolio; for doctorate, comprehensive exam, thesis/dissertation, electronic portfolio.

Union Institute & University, Programs in Psychology and Counseling, Brattleboro, VT 05301. Offers clinical mental health counseling (MA); clinical psychology (Psy D); counseling psychology (MA); counselor education and supervision (CAGS); developmental psychology (MA); educational psychology (MA); human development and wellness (CAGS); organizational psychology (MA); psychology education (CAGS). Psy D offered in Ohio and Vermont. Postbaccalaureate distance learning degree programs offered (minimal on-campus study). *Degree requirements:* For master's, thesis, internship (depending on concentration); for doctorate, thesis/dissertation, internship, practicum. Electronic applications accepted.

Universidad del Turabo, Graduate Programs, Programs in Education, Program in Guidance Counseling, Gurabo, PR 00778-3030. Offers M Ed. *Students:* 4 full-time (all women), 1 (woman) part-time; all minorities (all Hispanic/Latino). Average age 29. 1 applicant, 100% accepted, 1 enrolled. In 2011, 1 master's awarded. *Unit head:* Angela Candelario, Dean, 787-743-7979 Ext. 4126. *Application contact:* Virginia Gonzalez, Admissions Officer, 787-746-3009.

Université de Moncton, Faculty of Education, Graduate Studies in Education, Moncton, NB E1A 3E9, Canada. Offers educational psychology (M Ed, MA Ed); guidance (M Ed, MA Ed); school administration (M Ed, MA Ed); teaching (M Ed, MA Ed). Part-time programs available. *Degree requirements:* For master's, proficiency in English and French. *Entrance requirements:* For master's, minimum GPA of 3.0. *Faculty research:* Guidance, ethnolinguistic vitality, children's rights, ecological education, entrepreneurship.

Université Laval, Faculty of Education, Department of Foundations and Interventions in Education, Programs in Orientation Sciences, Québec, QC G1K 7P4, Canada. Offers MA, PhD. Terminal master's awarded for partial completion of doctoral program. *Degree requirements:* For master's, thesis (for some programs); for doctorate, comprehensive exam, thesis/dissertation. *Entrance requirements:* For master's, English test (comprehension of written English), knowledge of French; for doctorate, oral exam (subject of thesis), knowledge of French and English. Electronic applications accepted. *Faculty research:* Counseling psychology, psychological education, vocational guidance, growth and development.

University at Albany, State University of New York, School of Education, Department of Educational and Counseling Psychology, Albany, NY 12222-0001. Offers counseling psychology (MS, PhD, CAS); educational psychology (Ed D); educational psychology and statistics (MS); measurements and evaluation (Ed D); rehabilitation counseling (MS), including counseling psychology; school counselor (CAS); school psychology (Psy D, CAS); special education (MS); statistics and research design (Ed D). *Accreditation:* APA (one or more programs are accredited). Evening/weekend programs available. *Degree requirements:* For doctorate, thesis/dissertation. *Entrance requirements:* For doctorate, GRE General Test. Additional exam requirements/recommendations for international students: Required—TOEFL (minimum score 550 paper-based; 213 computer-based). Electronic applications accepted.

University at Buffalo, the State University of New York, Graduate School, Graduate School of Education, Department of Counseling, School, and Educational Psychology, Buffalo, NY 14260. Offers counseling/school psychology (PhD); counselor education (PhD); educational psychology (MA, PhD); general education (Ed M); mental health counseling (MS); mental health counseling (online) (Certificate); rehabilitation counseling (MS); school counseling (Ed M, Certificate). *Accreditation:* CORE (one or more programs are accredited). Part-time programs available. Postbaccalaureate distance learning degree programs offered (no on-campus study). *Faculty:* 22 full-time (14 women), 30 part-time/adjunct (26 women). *Students:* 154 full-time (123 women), 116 part-time (92 women); includes 45 minority (24 Black or African American, non-Hispanic/Latino; 3 American Indian or Alaska Native, non-Hispanic/Latino; 9 Asian, non-Hispanic/Latino; 9 Hispanic/Latino), 24 international. Average age 30. 344 applicants, 30% accepted, 98 enrolled. In 2011, 57 master's, 13 doctorates, 19 other advanced degrees awarded. *Degree requirements:* For master's, comprehensive exam (for some programs), thesis (for some programs); for doctorate, comprehensive exam, thesis/dissertation. *Entrance requirements:* For master's and doctorate, GRE General Test, interview, letters of reference. Additional exam requirements/recommendations for international students: Required—TOEFL (minimum score 79 iBT). *Application deadline:* For fall admission, 2/1 priority date for domestic students, 2/1 for international students. Application fee: $50. Electronic applications accepted. *Financial support:* In 2011–12, 25 fellowships (averaging $9,000 per year), 47 research assistantships (averaging $10,074 per year) were awarded; teaching assistantships with tuition reimbursements, career-related internships or fieldwork, Federal Work-Study, institutionally sponsored loans, and unspecified assistantships also available. Financial award application deadline: 2/1; financial award applicants required to submit FAFSA. *Faculty research:* Multicultural counseling, class size effects, good work in counseling, eating disorders, outcome assessment, change agents and therapeutic factors in group counseling. *Unit head:* Dr. Timothy Janikowski, Chair, 716-645-2484, Fax: 716-645-6616, E-mail: tjanikow@buffalo.edu. *Application contact:* Rochelle Cohen, Admissions Assistant, 716-645-2110, Fax: 716-645-7937, E-mail: recohen@buffalo.edu.

The University of Akron, Graduate School, College of Education, Department of Counseling, Program in Community Counseling, Akron, OH 44325. Offers MA, MS. *Accreditation:* ACA; NCATE. *Students:* 49 full-time (36 women), 38 part-time (33 women); includes 12 minority (11 Black or African American, non-Hispanic/Latino; 1 Hispanic/Latino). Average age 31. 70 applicants, 29% accepted, 14 enrolled. In 2011, 17 master's awarded. *Degree requirements:* For master's, comprehensive exam. *Entrance requirements:* For master's, minimum GPA of 2.75, letters of recommendation, interview. Additional exam requirements/recommendations for international students: Required—TOEFL (minimum score 550 paper-based; 213 computer-based; 79 iBT). *Application deadline:* Applications are processed on a rolling basis. Application fee: $30 ($40 for international students). Electronic applications accepted. *Expenses:* Tuition, state resident: full-time $7038; part-time $391 per credit hour. Tuition, nonresident: full-time $12,051; part-time $670 per credit hour. *Required fees:* $1274; $34 per credit hour. *Unit head:* Dr. Robert Schwartz, Coordinator, 330-972-8155, E-mail: rcs@uakron.edu. *Application contact:* Dr. Mark Tausig, Associate Dean, 330-972-6266, Fax: 330-972-6475, E-mail: mtausig@uakron.edu.

The University of Akron, Graduate School, College of Education, Department of Counseling, Program in Counselor Education and Supervision, Akron, OH 44325. Offers PhD. *Accreditation:* ACA. *Students:* 8 full-time (6 women), 23 part-time (18 women); includes 7 minority (6 Black or African American, non-Hispanic/Latino; 1 Native Hawaiian or other Pacific Islander, non-Hispanic/Latino). Average age 39. 21 applicants, 24% accepted, 4 enrolled. In 2011, 2 doctorates awarded. *Degree requirements:* For doctorate, comprehensive exam, thesis/dissertation, written and oral exams. *Entrance requirements:* For doctorate, GRE, minimum GPA of 3.25, three letters of recommendation, professional resume, department supplemental form, interview. Additional exam requirements/recommendations for international students: Required—TOEFL (minimum score 550 paper-based; 213 computer-based; 79 iBT). *Application deadline:* For fall admission, 1/15 for domestic students, 1/5 for international students. Application fee: $30 ($40 for international students). Electronic applications accepted. *Expenses:* Tuition, state resident: full-time $7038; part-time $391 per credit hour. Tuition, nonresident: full-time $12,051; part-time $670 per credit hour. *Required fees:* $1274; $34 per credit hour. *Unit head:* Dr. Sandra Perosa, Program Contact, 330-972-8158, E-mail: sperosa@uakron.edu. *Application contact:* Dr. Mark Tausig, Associate Dean, 330-972-6266, Fax: 330-972-6475, E-mail: mtausig@uakron.edu.

The University of Akron, Graduate School, College of Education, Department of Counseling, Program in School Counseling, Akron, OH 44325. Offers MA, MS. *Accreditation:* ACA; NCATE. *Students:* 25 full-time (23 women), 64 part-time (51 women); includes 8 minority (7 Black or African American, non-Hispanic/Latino; 1 Hispanic/Latino). Average age 30. 38 applicants, 42% accepted, 10 enrolled. In 2011, 24 master's awarded. *Degree requirements:* For master's, comprehensive exam. *Entrance requirements:* For master's, minimum GPA of 2.75, three letters of recommendation, department supplemental forms, Bureau of Criminal Investigation clearance, interview. Additional exam requirements/recommendations for international students: Required—TOEFL (minimum score 550 paper-based; 213 computer-based; 79 iBT). *Application deadline:* For fall admission, 3/15 for domestic and international students; for spring admission, 10/1 for domestic and international students. Application fee: $30 ($40 for international students). Electronic applications accepted. *Expenses:* Tuition, state resident: full-time $7038; part-time $391 per credit hour. Tuition, nonresident: full-time $12,051; part-time $670 per credit hour. *Required fees:* $1274; $34 per credit hour. *Unit head:* Dr. Cynthia Reynolds, Coordinator, 330-972-6748, E-mail: creynol@uakron.edu. *Application contact:* Dr. Mark Tausig, Associate Dean, 330-972-6266, Fax: 330-972-6475, E-mail: mtausig@uakron.edu.

The University of Alabama, Graduate School, College of Education, Department of Educational Studies in Psychology, Research Methodology and Counseling, Tuscaloosa, AL 35487. Offers MA, Ed D, PhD, Ed S. *Accreditation:* ACA (one or more programs are accredited); CORE; NCATE. Part-time programs available. *Faculty:* 20 full-time (9 women), 1 (woman) part-time/adjunct. *Students:* 94 full-time (77 women), 91 part-time (72 women); includes 51 minority (37 Black or African American, non-Hispanic/Latino; 1 American Indian or Alaska Native, non-Hispanic/Latino; 2 Asian, non-Hispanic/Latino; 6 Hispanic/Latino; 5 Two or more races, non-Hispanic/Latino), 9 international. Average age 33. 140 applicants, 62% accepted, 47 enrolled. In 2011, 32 master's, 5 doctorates, 21 other advanced degrees awarded. *Degree requirements:* For master's, comprehensive exam, thesis optional; for doctorate, comprehensive exam, thesis/dissertation; for Ed S, comprehensive exam. *Entrance requirements:* For master's and doctorate, GRE General Test, MAT, or NTE, minimum GPA of 3.0; for Ed S, minimum GPA of 3.0 during previous 2 years. Additional exam requirements/recommendations for international students: Required—TOEFL (minimum score 550 paper-based; 213 computer-based), IELTS (minimum score 6.5). *Application deadline:* For fall admission, 7/1 for domestic students; for spring admission, 11/1 for domestic students. Applications are processed on a rolling basis. Application fee: $50 ($60 for international students). Electronic applications accepted. *Expenses:* Tuition, state resident: full-time $8600. Tuition, nonresident: full-time $21,900. *Financial support:* Research assistantships with tuition reimbursements, teaching assistantships with tuition reimbursements, and career-related internships or fieldwork available. Financial award application deadline: 7/14; financial award applicants required to submit FAFSA. *Faculty research:* Moral development, positive psychology, children's fears, digital storytelling. *Unit head:* Dr. Rick House, Department Head, 205-348-0283. *Application contact:* Marie S. Marshall, Office Associate II, 205-348-8362, Fax: 205-348-0683, E-mail: mmarshal@bamaed.ua.edu. Web site: http://education.ua.edu/departments/esprmc/.

The University of Alabama at Birmingham, College of Arts and Sciences, School of Education, Program in Counseling, Birmingham, AL 35294. Offers MA. *Accreditation:* ACA; CORE; NCATE. *Degree requirements:* For master's, thesis optional. *Entrance requirements:* For master's, GRE General Test, MAT, or NTE, minimum GPA of 3.0. *Application deadline:* Applications are processed on a rolling basis. Application fee: $35 ($60 for international students). Electronic applications accepted. *Expenses:* Tuition, state resident: full-time $5922; part-time $309 per hour. Tuition, nonresident: full-time

$13,428; part-time $726 per hour. Tuition and fees vary according to program. *Financial support:* Career-related internships or fieldwork available. *Unit head:* Dr. Kristi Menear, Chair, 205-975-7409, Fax: 205-975-8040, E-mail: kmenear@uab.edu. Web site: http://www.uab.edu/humanstudies/counseloreducation.

University of Alaska Anchorage, College of Education, Program in Counseling and Guidance, Anchorage, AK 99508. Offers M Ed. Part-time programs available. *Entrance requirements:* For master's, GRE or MAT, interview, resume. Additional exam requirements/recommendations for international students: Required—TOEFL (minimum score 550 paper-based; 213 computer-based).

University of Alaska Fairbanks, School of Education, Program in Counseling, Fairbanks, AK 99775-7520. Offers counseling (M Ed), including community counseling, school counseling. *Students:* 29 full-time (22 women), 47 part-time (37 women); includes 14 minority (6 Black or African American, non-Hispanic/Latino; 3 American Indian or Alaska Native, non-Hispanic/Latino; 2 Hispanic/Latino; 3 Two or more races, non-Hispanic/Latino), 1 international. Average age 34. 50 applicants, 62% accepted, 29 enrolled. In 2011, 7 master's awarded. *Degree requirements:* For master's, comprehensive exam, thesis, oral defense. *Entrance requirements:* For master's, 1 year teaching or administrative experience. *Application deadline:* For fall admission, 6/1 for domestic students, 3/1 for international students; for spring admission, 10/15 for domestic students, 9/1 for international students. Applications are processed on a rolling basis. Application fee: $60. Electronic applications accepted. *Expenses:* Tuition, state resident: full-time $6696; part-time $372 per credit. Tuition, nonresident: full-time $13,680; part-time $760 per credit. Tuition and fees vary according to course load and reciprocity agreements. *Financial support:* In 2011–12, 4 teaching assistantships with tuition reimbursements (averaging $13,330 per year) were awarded; fellowships with tuition reimbursements, career-related internships or fieldwork, Federal Work-Study, scholarships/grants, health care benefits, and unspecified assistantships also available. Support available to part-time students. Financial award application deadline: 7/1; financial award applicants required to submit FAFSA. *Unit head:* Allan Morotti, Interim Dean, 907-474-7341, Fax: 907-474-5451, E-mail: uaf-soe-school@alaska.edu. *Application contact:* Mike Earnest, Director of Admissions, 907-474-7500, Fax: 907-474-5379, E-mail: admissions@uaf.edu. Web site: http://www.uaf.edu/educ/graduate/counseling_med.html.

University of Alberta, Faculty of Graduate Studies and Research, Department of Educational Psychology, Edmonton, AB T6G 2E1, Canada. Offers counseling psychology (M Ed, PhD); educational psychology (M Ed, PhD); instructional technology (M Ed); school counseling (M Ed); school psychology (M Ed, PhD); special education (M Ed, PhD); special education-deafness studies (M Ed); teaching English as a second language (M Ed). Part-time programs available. *Degree requirements:* For master's, thesis optional; for doctorate, comprehensive exam, thesis/dissertation. *Entrance requirements:* For master's and doctorate, minimum GPA of 3.0. Additional exam requirements/recommendations for international students: Required—TOEFL. *Faculty research:* Human learning, development and assessment.

The University of Arizona, College of Education, Department of Disability and Psychoeducational Studies, Progam in School Counseling, Tucson, AZ 85721. Offers M Ed. Part-time programs available. *Faculty:* 13 full-time (6 women), 1 (woman) part-time/adjunct. *Students:* 23 full-time (18 women), 4 part-time (3 women); includes 6 minority (1 Black or African American, non-Hispanic/Latino; 3 Hispanic/Latino; 2 Two or more races, non-Hispanic/Latino). Average age 30. In 2011, 5 master's awarded. *Degree requirements:* For master's, presentation or thesis. *Entrance requirements:* Additional exam requirements/recommendations for international students: Required—TOEFL. *Application deadline:* For fall admission, 3/1 for domestic students, 12/1 for international students. Application fee: $75. *Expenses:* Tuition, state resident: full-time $10,840. Tuition, nonresident: full-time $25,802. *Unit head:* Dr. Linda R. Shaw, Department Head, 520-621-7822, Fax: 520-621-3821, E-mail: lshaw@email.arizona.edu. *Application contact:* Cecilia Carlon, Coordinator, 520-621-7822, Fax: 520-621-3821, E-mail: ccarlon@email.arizona.edu. Web site: http://coe.arizona.edu/dps/med_school_counseling.

University of Arkansas, Graduate School, College of Education and Health Professions, Department of Rehabilitation, Human Resources and Communication Disorders, Program in Counseling, Fayetteville, AR 72701-1201. Offers MS, PhD, Ed S. *Accreditation:* ACA; NCATE. Part-time and evening/weekend programs available. *Students:* 30 full-time (26 women), 18 part-time (14 women); includes 7 minority (5 Black or African American, non-Hispanic/Latino; 2 Hispanic/Latino), 2 international. In 2011, 11 master's, 3 doctorates awarded. *Degree requirements:* For master's, thesis optional; for doctorate, thesis/dissertation. *Entrance requirements:* For master's, GRE General Test or MAT; for doctorate, GRE General Test. *Application deadline:* For fall admission, 3/15 for domestic students, 4/1 for international students; for spring admission, 10/15 for domestic students, 10/1 for international students. Applications are processed on a rolling basis. Application fee: $40 ($50 for international students). Electronic applications accepted. *Financial support:* In 2011–12, 15 research assistantships, 2 teaching assistantships were awarded; fellowships with tuition reimbursements, career-related internships or fieldwork, and Federal Work-Study also available. Support available to part-time students. Financial award application deadline: 4/1; financial award applicants required to submit FAFSA. *Unit head:* Dr. Fran Hagstrom, Unit Head, 479-575-4758, E-mail: fhagstr@uark.edu. *Application contact:* Dr. Brent Williams, Graduate Coordinator, 479-575-4758, E-mail: btwilli@uark.edu. Web site: http://cned.uark.edu.

University of Arkansas at Little Rock, Graduate School, College of Education, Department of Counseling, Adult and Rehabilitation Education, Program in Counselor Education, Little Rock, AR 72204-1099. Offers school counseling (M Ed). Part-time and evening/weekend programs available. *Degree requirements:* For master's, comprehensive exam, portfolio or thesis. *Entrance requirements:* For master's, GRE General Test, minimum GPA of 2.75, teaching certificate.

University of Central Arkansas, Graduate School, College of Education, Department of Leadership Studies, Program in School Counseling, Conway, AR 72035-0001. Offers MS. *Accreditation:* NCATE. Part-time programs available. *Students:* 10 full-time (9 women), 12 part-time (all women); includes 6 minority (5 Black or African American, non-Hispanic/Latino; 1 Two or more races, non-Hispanic/Latino). Average age 36. 9 applicants, 100% accepted, 8 enrolled. In 2011, 17 master's awarded. *Degree requirements:* For master's, comprehensive exam, thesis optional. *Entrance requirements:* For master's, GRE General Test, minimum GPA of 2.7. Additional exam requirements/recommendations for international students: Required—TOEFL (minimum score 550 paper-based; 213 computer-based). *Application deadline:* For fall admission, 3/1 priority date for domestic students, 3/1 for international students; for spring admission, 10/1 priority date for domestic students, 10/1 for international students. Applications are processed on a rolling basis. Application fee: $25 ($50 for international students). *Expenses:* Tuition, state resident: full-time $4834; part-time $398.35 per credit hour. Tuition, nonresident: full-time $8686. *Financial support:* Career-related internships or fieldwork, scholarships/grants, and unspecified assistantships available. Financial award application deadline: 2/15; financial award applicants required to submit FAFSA. *Unit head:* Dr. Abby Hallford, Associate Professor, 501-450-3193, Fax: 501-450-5424, E-mail: ahallford@uca.edu. *Application contact:* Susan Wood, Admissions Assistant, 501-450-3124, Fax: 501-450-5678, E-mail: swood@uca.edu.

University of Central Florida, College of Education, Department of Educational and Human Sciences, Program in Counselor Education, Orlando, FL 32816. Offers mental health counseling (MA); school counseling (M Ed, MA, Ed S). *Accreditation:* ACA. Part-time and evening/weekend programs available. *Students:* 110 full-time (90 women), 55 part-time (47 women); includes 41 minority (15 Black or African American, non-Hispanic/Latino; 4 Asian, non-Hispanic/Latino; 20 Hispanic/Latino; 2 Two or more races, non-Hispanic/Latino), 1 international. Average age 27. 148 applicants, 57% accepted, 51 enrolled. In 2011, 54 master's, 12 other advanced degrees awarded. *Degree requirements:* For master's, comprehensive exam, thesis or alternative. *Entrance requirements:* For master's, GRE General Test, interview, minimum GPA of 3.0. Additional exam requirements/recommendations for international students: Required—TOEFL. *Application deadline:* For fall admission, 2/1 for domestic students; for spring admission, 9/1 for domestic students. Application fee: $30. Electronic applications accepted. *Expenses:* Tuition, state resident: part-time $277.08 per credit hour. Tuition, nonresident: part-time $277.08 per credit hour. Part-time tuition and fees vary according to degree level and program. *Financial support:* In 2011–12, 12 students received support, including 4 fellowships with partial tuition reimbursements available (averaging $1,300 per year), 8 research assistantships with partial tuition reimbursements available (averaging $7,800 per year), 1 teaching assistantship with partial tuition reimbursement available (averaging $6,900 per year); career-related internships or fieldwork, Federal Work-Study, institutionally sponsored loans, tuition waivers (partial), and unspecified assistantships also available. Financial award application deadline: 3/1; financial award applicants required to submit FAFSA. *Unit head:* Dr. W. Bryce Hagedorn, Program Coordinator, 407-823-2999, E-mail: bryce.hagedorn@ucf.edu. *Application contact:* Barbara Rodriguez, Director, Admissions and Registration, 407-823-2766, Fax: 407-823-6442, E-mail: gradadmissions@ucf.edu.

University of Central Florida, College of Education, Education Doctoral Programs, Orlando, FL 32816. Offers communication sciences and disorders (PhD); counselor education (PhD); education (Ed D); elementary education (PhD); exceptional education (PhD); exercise physiology (PhD); higher education (PhD); hospitality education (PhD); instructional technology (PhD); mathematics education (PhD); reading education (PhD); science education (PhD); social science education (PhD); TESOL (PhD). *Students:* 135 full-time (87 women), 73 part-time (51 women); includes 49 minority (21 Black or African American, non-Hispanic/Latino; 4 Asian, non-Hispanic/Latino; 20 Hispanic/Latino; 4 Two or more races, non-Hispanic/Latino), 18 international. Average age 39. 125 applicants, 46% accepted, 46 enrolled. In 2011, 43 doctorates awarded. Application fee: $30. Electronic applications accepted. *Expenses:* Tuition, state resident: part-time $277.08 per credit hour. Tuition, nonresident: part-time $277.08 per credit hour. Part-time tuition and fees vary according to degree level and program. *Financial support:* In 2011–12, 85 students received support, including 48 fellowships with partial tuition reimbursements available (averaging $5,900 per year), 36 research assistantships with partial tuition reimbursements available (averaging $6,900 per year), 59 teaching assistantships with partial tuition reimbursements available (averaging $6,900 per year). *Unit head:* Dr. Rex Culp, Associate Dean, 407-823-5391, E-mail: rex.culp@ucf.edu. *Application contact:* Barbara Rodriguez, Associate Director, Admissions and Registration, 407-823-2766, Fax: 407-823-6442, E-mail: gradadmissions@ucf.edu. Web site: http://education.ucf.edu/departments.cfm.

University of Central Missouri, The Graduate School, College of Education, Warrensburg, MO 64093. Offers career and technical education administration (MS); career and technical education industry training (MS); career and technical education leadership/teaching (MS); college student personnel administration (MS); counseling (MS); curriculum and instruction (Ed S); educational leadership (Ed D); educational technology (MS); elementary education/educational foundations and literacy (MSE); elementary school administration (MSE); elementary school principalship (Ed S); human services/learning resources (Ed S); human services/professional counseling (Ed S); human services/special education (Ed S); human services/technology and occupational education (Ed S); K-12 education/educational foundations and literacy (MSE); K-12 special education (MSE); library science and information services (MS); literacy education (MSE); secondary education/educational foundations & literacy (MSE); secondary school administration (MSE); secondary school principalship (Ed S); superintendency (Ed S); teaching (MAT). Ed D offered jointly with University of Missouri. Part-time programs available. Postbaccalaureate distance learning degree programs offered. *Entrance requirements:* Additional exam requirements/recommendations for international students: Required—TOEFL (minimum score 550 paper-based; 79 computer-based). Electronic applications accepted.

University of Central Oklahoma, College of Graduate Studies and Research, College of Education and Professional Studies, Department of Advanced Professional and Special Services, Program in Guidance and Counseling, Edmond, OK 73034-5209. Offers M Ed. *Accreditation:* NCATE. Part-time programs available. *Entrance requirements:* For master's, GRE General Test. Additional exam requirements/recommendations for international students: Required—TOEFL (minimum score 550 paper-based; 213 computer-based). *Application deadline:* For fall admission, 7/1 for international students; for spring admission, 11/1 for international students. Applications are processed on a rolling basis. Application fee: $25. Electronic applications accepted. *Expenses:* Tuition, state resident: full-time $3901; part-time $218.30 per credit hour. Tuition, nonresident: full-time $9198; part-time $511.20 per credit hour. Tuition and fees vary according to program. *Financial support:* Career-related internships or fieldwork available. Financial award application deadline: 3/31; financial award applicants required to submit FAFSA. *Unit head:* Dr. Pat Couts, Director, 405-974-5888, E-mail: chandler@aix1.uco.edu. *Application contact:* Dr. Richard Bernard, Dean, Jackson College of Graduate Studies, 405-974-3493, Fax: 405-974-3852, E-mail: gradcoll@uco.edu. Web site: http://www.uco.edu/ceps/dept/apss/guidance-and-counseling/index.asp.

University of Cincinnati, Graduate School, College of Education, Criminal Justice, and Human Services, Division of Human Services, Program in Counseling, Cincinnati, OH 45221. Offers counseling (Ed D); counselor education (CAGS); mental health (MA); school counseling (M Ed). *Accreditation:* ACA (one or more programs are accredited); NCATE. Part-time programs available. Terminal master's awarded for partial completion of doctoral program. *Degree requirements:* For master's, comprehensive exam; for doctorate, comprehensive exam, thesis/dissertation. *Entrance requirements:* For master's, GRE General Test, interview; for doctorate, GRE General Test, GRE Subject Test, interview. Additional exam requirements/recommendations for international students: Required—TOEFL (minimum score 620 paper-based), OEPT. Electronic applications accepted. *Faculty research:* Group work, career development, ecology, prevention, multicultural.

University of Colorado at Colorado Springs, College of Education, Colorado Springs, CO 80933-7150. Offers counseling and human services (MA); curriculum and instruction (MA); educational administration (MA); educational leadership (MA, PhD); special education (MA). *Accreditation:* ACA; NCATE. Part-time and evening/weekend programs available. Postbaccalaureate distance learning degree programs offered (minimal on-campus study). *Faculty:* 26 full-time (16 women), 9 part-time/adjunct (5 women). *Students:* 307 full-time (203 women), 115 part-time (92 women); includes 82 minority (24 Black or African American, non-Hispanic/Latino; 3 American Indian or Alaska Native, non-Hispanic/Latino; 12 Asian, non-Hispanic/Latino; 36 Hispanic/Latino; 1 Native

Hawaiian or other Pacific Islander, non-Hispanic/Latino; 6 Two or more races, non-Hispanic/Latino), 1 international. Average age 36. 99 applicants, 86% accepted, 61 enrolled. In 2011, 165 master's, 6 doctorates awarded. *Degree requirements:* For master's, comprehensive exam, thesis or alternative, microcomputer proficiency; for doctorate, comprehensive exam, thesis/dissertation, research lab. *Entrance requirements:* For master's, GRE General Test. Additional exam requirements/recommendations for international students: Recommended—TOEFL. *Application deadline:* For fall admission, 2/28 priority date for domestic students, 2/28 for international students; for spring admission, 10/15 for domestic and international students. Applications are processed on a rolling basis. Application fee: $60 ($75 for international students). *Expenses:* Tuition, state resident: part-time $660 per credit hour. Tuition, nonresident: part-time $1133 per credit hour. Tuition and fees vary according to degree level, program and student level. *Financial support:* In 2011–12, 57 students received support. Career-related internships or fieldwork, Federal Work-Study, and scholarships/grants available. Support available to part-time students. Financial award application deadline: 3/1; financial award applicants required to submit FAFSA. *Faculty research:* Job training for special populations, materials development for classroom. *Total annual research expenditures:* $1.6 million. *Unit head:* Dr. Mary Snyder, Dean, 719-255-3701, Fax: 719-262-4133, E-mail: msnyder3@uccs.edu. *Application contact:* Juliane Field, Director, 719-255-4526, Fax: 719-255-4110, E-mail: jfield@uccs.edu. Web site: http://www.uccs.edu/coe.

University of Colorado Denver, School of Education and Human Development, Program in Counseling Psychology and Counselor Education, Denver, CO 80217-3364. Offers counseling (MA), including clinical mental health counseling, couple and family counseling, multicultural counseling, school counseling; school counseling (MA). *Accreditation:* ACA; NCATE. Part-time and evening/weekend programs available. *Students:* 191 full-time (167 women), 49 part-time (46 women); includes 22 minority (5 Black or African American, non-Hispanic/Latino; 1 American Indian or Alaska Native, non-Hispanic/Latino; 6 Asian, non-Hispanic/Latino; 10 Hispanic/Latino), 2 international. Average age 30. 87 applicants, 47% accepted, 19 enrolled. In 2011, 55 master's awarded. *Degree requirements:* For master's, thesis or alternative, 63-66 hours. *Entrance requirements:* For master's, GRE or MAT, letters of recommendation, interview, resume. Additional exam requirements/recommendations for international students: Required—TOEFL (minimum score 525 paper-based; 197 computer-based; 71 iBT). *Application deadline:* For fall admission, 1/15 for domestic students, 1/1 for international students; for spring admission, 9/15 for domestic students, 9/1 for international students. Application fee: $50 ($75 for international students). Electronic applications accepted. *Expenses:* Contact institution. *Financial support:* Research assistantships, Federal Work-Study, and scholarships/grants available. Financial award application deadline: 4/1; financial award applicants required to submit FAFSA. *Faculty research:* Spiritual issues in counseling, multicultural and diversity issues in counseling, adolescent suicide, career development. *Unit head:* Dr. Marsha Wiggins, Division Coordinator, 303-315-6332, E-mail: marsha.wiggins@ucdenver.edu. *Application contact:* Student Services Coordinator, 303-315-6300, Fax: 303-315-6311, E-mail: education@ucdenver.edu. Web site: http://www.ucdenver.edu/ACADEMICS/COLLEGES/SCHOOLOFEDUCATION/ACADEMICS/Pages/AcademicPrograms.aspx.

University of Connecticut, Graduate School, Neag School of Education, Department of Educational Psychology, Program in Counseling Psychology, Storrs, CT 06269. Offers counseling psychology (PhD); school counseling (MA, Post-Master's Certificate). *Accreditation:* ACA. Terminal master's awarded for partial completion of doctoral program. *Degree requirements:* For master's, comprehensive exam, thesis or alternative; for doctorate, thesis/dissertation. *Entrance requirements:* For doctorate, GRE General Test. Additional exam requirements/recommendations for international students: Required—TOEFL (minimum score 550 paper-based; 213 computer-based). Electronic applications accepted.

University of Dayton, Department of Counselor Education and Human Services, Dayton, OH 45469-1300. Offers college student personnel (MS Ed); community counseling (MS Ed); higher education administration (MS Ed); human services (MS Ed); school counseling (MS Ed); school psychology (MS Ed, Ed S). *Accreditation:* ACA; NCATE. Part-time and evening/weekend programs available. *Faculty:* 12 full-time (9 women), 30 part-time/adjunct (20 women). *Students:* 223 full-time (184 women), 189 part-time (147 women); includes 91 minority (83 Black or African American, non-Hispanic/Latino; 1 American Indian or Alaska Native, non-Hispanic/Latino; 2 Asian, non-Hispanic/Latino; 3 Hispanic/Latino; 2 Two or more races, non-Hispanic/Latino), 5 international. Average age 34. 336 applicants, 40% accepted, 96 enrolled. In 2011, 170 master's, 10 Ed Ss awarded. *Degree requirements:* For master's, comprehensive exam (for some programs), thesis (for some programs), exit exam. *Entrance requirements:* For master's, MAT or GRE (if GPA less than 2.75), interview, writing sample. Additional exam requirements/recommendations for international students: Required—TOEFL (minimum score 550 paper-based; 213 computer-based; 80 iBT). *Application deadline:* For fall admission, 4/10 for domestic students, 3/1 for international students; for winter admission, 9/10 for domestic students, 7/1 for international students; for spring admission, 1/10 for domestic students, 1/1 for international students. Application fee: $0 ($50 for international students). Electronic applications accepted. *Expenses: Tuition:* Full-time $8400; part-time $700 per credit hour. *Required fees:* $25 per semester. Tuition and fees vary according to degree level. *Financial support:* In 2011–12, 7 research assistantships with full and partial tuition reimbursements (averaging $8,550 per year) were awarded; career-related internships or fieldwork, institutionally sponsored loans, health care benefits, and unspecified assistantships also available. Financial award applicants required to submit FAFSA. *Faculty research:* Mindfulness, forgiveness in relationships, positive psychology in couples counseling, traumatic brain injury responses. *Unit head:* Dr. Moly Schaller, Chairperson, 937-229-3644, Fax: 937-229-1055, E-mail: mschaller1@udayton.edu. *Application contact:* Kathleen Brown, 937-229-3644, Fax: 937-229-1055, E-mail: kbrown1@udayton.edu. Web site: http://soeap.udayton.edu/edc.

University of Detroit Mercy, College of Liberal Arts and Education, Department of Counseling and Addiction Studies, Program in Counseling, Detroit, MI 48221. Offers addiction counseling (MA); community counseling (MA); school counseling (MA). *Accreditation:* ACA. Part-time and evening/weekend programs available. *Degree requirements:* For master's, thesis or alternative. *Entrance requirements:* For master's, minimum GPA of 2.75.

University of Florida, Graduate School, College of Education, Department of Counselor Education, Gainesville, FL 32611. Offers marriage and family counseling (M Ed, MAE, Ed D, PhD, Ed S); mental health counseling (M Ed, MAE, Ed D, PhD, Ed S); school counseling and guidance (M Ed, MAE, Ed D, PhD, Ed S). *Accreditation:* ACA (one or more programs are accredited); NCATE. Part-time programs available. Terminal master's awarded for partial completion of doctoral program. *Degree requirements:* For master's, thesis optional; for doctorate, comprehensive exam, thesis/dissertation. *Entrance requirements:* For master's and doctorate, GRE General Test, minimum GPA of 3.0 (undergraduate), 3.5 (graduate); for Ed S, GRE General Test. Additional exam requirements/recommendations for international students: Required—TOEFL (minimum score 550 paper-based; 213 computer-based; 80 iBT), IELTS (minimum score 6). *Application deadline:* Applications are processed on a rolling basis. Application fee: $30. Electronic applications accepted. *Financial support:* Fellowships, research assistantships, teaching assistantships, career-related internships or fieldwork, and unspecified assistantships available. Financial award applicants required to submit FAFSA.

University of Georgia, College of Education, Department of Counseling and Human Development Services, Athens, GA 30602. Offers college student affairs administration (M Ed, PhD); counseling and student personnel (PhD); counseling psychology (PhD); professional counseling (M Ed); professional school counseling (Ed S); recreation and leisure studies (M Ed, MA, PhD). *Accreditation:* ACA (one or more programs are accredited); APA (one or more programs are accredited); NCATE. *Faculty:* 23 full-time (14 women). *Students:* 173 full-time (126 women), 78 part-time (46 women); includes 82 minority (70 Black or African American, non-Hispanic/Latino; 3 Asian, non-Hispanic/Latino; 7 Hispanic/Latino; 1 Native Hawaiian or other Pacific Islander, non-Hispanic/Latino; 1 Two or more races, non-Hispanic/Latino), 1 international. Average age 30. 375 applicants, 26% accepted, 53 enrolled. In 2011, 48 master's, 27 doctorates, 14 other advanced degrees awarded. *Degree requirements:* For master's, thesis (MA); for doctorate, variable foreign language requirement, thesis/dissertation. *Entrance requirements:* For master's, GRE General Test or MAT; for doctorate, GRE General Test. *Application deadline:* For fall admission, 7/1 priority date for domestic students; for spring admission, 11/15 for domestic students. Application fee: $50. Electronic applications accepted. *Financial support:* Fellowships, research assistantships, teaching assistantships, and unspecified assistantships available. *Unit head:* Dr. Rosemary E. Phelps, Head, 706-542-4221, Fax: 706-542-4130, E-mail: rephelps@uga.edu. *Application contact:* Dr. Corey W. Johnson, Graduate Coordinator, 706-542-4335, Fax: 706-542-4130, E-mail: cwjohns@uga.edu. Web site: http://www.coe.uga.edu/chds/.

University of Guam, Office of Graduate Studies, School of Education, Program in Counseling, Mangilao, GU 96923. Offers MA. *Degree requirements:* For master's, comprehensive oral and written exams, special project or thesis. *Entrance requirements:* For master's, GRE General Test. Additional exam requirements/recommendations for international students: Required—TOEFL. *Faculty research:* Drugs in the local schools, standardized teaching procedures in the elementary school, how to address the dropout problems.

University of Hartford, College of Education, Nursing, and Health Professions, Program in Counseling, West Hartford, CT 06117-1599. Offers M Ed, MS, Sixth Year Certificate. *Accreditation:* NCATE. Part-time and evening/weekend programs available. *Degree requirements:* For master's and Sixth Year Certificate, comprehensive exam. *Entrance requirements:* For master's, GRE General Test or MAT, PRAXIS I or waiver, interview, 2 letters of recommendation; for Sixth Year Certificate, GRE General Test or MAT, PRAXIS I or waiver, interview. Additional exam requirements/recommendations for international students: Required—TOEFL (minimum score 550 paper-based; 213 computer-based). Electronic applications accepted.

University of Houston–Clear Lake, School of Education, Program in Foundations and Professional Studies, Houston, TX 77058-1098. Offers counseling (MS); instructional technology (MS); multicultural studies (MS). Part-time and evening/weekend programs available. *Degree requirements:* For master's, thesis optional. *Entrance requirements:* For master's, GRE or minimum GPA of 3.0 in last 60 hours. Additional exam requirements/recommendations for international students: Required—TOEFL (minimum score 550 paper-based; 213 computer-based). Electronic applications accepted.

University of Houston–Victoria, School of Education and Human Development, Victoria, TX 77901-4450. Offers administration and supervision (M Ed); counseling (M Ed); curriculum and instruction (M Ed); special education (M Ed). Part-time and evening/weekend programs available. Postbaccalaureate distance learning degree programs offered (minimal on-campus study). *Degree requirements:* For master's, comprehensive exam, project or thesis. *Entrance requirements:* For master's, GRE General Test. Additional exam requirements/recommendations for international students: Required—TOEFL. Electronic applications accepted. *Faculty research:* Reading and language arts education, evaluation and diagnosis of special children's abilities.

University of Idaho, College of Graduate Studies, College of Education, Department of Leadership and Counseling, Program in Counseling and Human Services, Boise, ID 83702. Offers M Ed, MS. *Accreditation:* ACA (one or more programs are accredited). *Students:* 24 full-time, 10 part-time. Average age 36. In 2011, 10 master's awarded. *Entrance requirements:* For master's, minimum GPA of 2.8. *Application deadline:* Applications are processed on a rolling basis. Application fee: $60. Electronic applications accepted. *Expenses:* Tuition, state resident: full-time $3874; part-time $334 per credit hour. Tuition, nonresident: full-time $16,394; part-time $861 per credit hour. *Required fees:* $2808; $99 per credit hour. Tuition and fees vary according to program. *Financial support:* Teaching assistantships available. Financial award applicants required to submit FAFSA. *Unit head:* Dr. Russell A. Joki, Chair, 208-364-4099, E-mail: rjoki@uidaho.edu. *Application contact:* Erick Larson, Director of Graduate Admissions, 208-885-4723, E-mail: gadms@uidaho.edu. Web site: http://www.uidaho.edu/ed/leadershipcounseling.

University of Illinois at Urbana–Champaign, Graduate College, College of Education, Department of Educational Psychology, Champaign, IL 61820. Offers Ed M, MA, MS, PhD, CAS. *Accreditation:* APA (one or more programs are accredited). Part-time programs available. Postbaccalaureate distance learning degree programs offered. *Faculty:* 16 full-time (8 women). *Students:* 60 full-time (46 women), 35 part-time (30 women); includes 26 minority (9 Black or African American, non-Hispanic/Latino; 2 Asian, non-Hispanic/Latino; 12 Hispanic/Latino; 3 Two or more races, non-Hispanic/Latino), 32 international. 50 applicants, 46% accepted, 13 enrolled. In 2011, 23 master's, 18 doctorates awarded. *Entrance requirements:* For master's, minimum GPA of 3.5; for doctorate, GRE General Test, minimum GPA of 3.5. Additional exam requirements/recommendations for international students: Required—TOEFL (minimum score 610 paper-based; 253 computer-based; 102 iBT). *Application deadline:* Applications are processed on a rolling basis. Application fee: $75 ($90 for international students). Electronic applications accepted. *Financial support:* In 2011–12, 13 fellowships, 37 research assistantships, 39 teaching assistantships were awarded; tuition waivers (full and partial) also available. *Unit head:* Jose Mestre, Chair, 217-333-0098, Fax: 217-244-7620, E-mail: mestre@illinois.edu. *Application contact:* Myranda Lyons, Office Support Specialist, 217-244-3391, Fax: 217-244-7620, E-mail: mjlyons@illinois.edu. Web site: http://education.illinois.edu/EDPSY/.

The University of Iowa, Graduate College, College of Education, Department of Counseling, Rehabilitation, and Student Development, Iowa City, IA 52242-1316. Offers administration and research (PhD); community/rehabilitation counseling (MA); counselor education and supervision (PhD); rehabilitation counselor education (PhD); school counseling (MA); student development (MA, PhD). *Accreditation:* ACA (one or more programs are accredited); CORE (one or more programs are accredited). *Degree requirements:* For master's, thesis optional, exam; for doctorate, comprehensive exam, thesis/dissertation. *Entrance requirements:* For master's and doctorate, GRE General Test, minimum GPA of 3.0. Additional exam requirements/recommendations for international students: Required—TOEFL (minimum score 550 paper-based; 213 computer-based; 81 iBT). Electronic applications accepted.

University of La Verne, College of Education and Organizational Leadership, Program in School Counseling, La Verne, CA 91750-4443. Offers pupil personnel services (Credential); school counseling (MS). Part-time programs available. *Faculty:* 19 full-time (12 women), 28 part-time/adjunct (22 women). *Students:* 16 full-time (all women), 85 part-time (67 women); includes 79 minority (9 Black or African American, non-Hispanic/Latino; 5 Asian, non-Hispanic/Latino; 65 Hispanic/Latino). Average age 32. In 2011, 155 master's awarded. *Degree requirements:* For master's, thesis optional. *Entrance requirements:* For master's, California Basic Educational Skills Test, minimum undergraduate GPA of 2.75, graduate 3.0; interview; 1 year's experience working with children; 3 letters of reference. Additional exam requirements/recommendations for international students: Required—TOEFL (minimum score 550 paper-based; 213 computer-based). *Application deadline:* Applications are processed on a rolling basis. Application fee: $50. *Expenses:* Contact institution. *Financial support:* Institutionally sponsored loans and unspecified assistantships available. Financial award application deadline: 3/2; financial award applicants required to submit FAFSA. *Unit head:* Dr. Laurie Schroeder, Chairperson, 909-593-3511 Ext. 4653, E-mail: lschroeder3@laverne.edu. *Application contact:* Christy Ranells, Admissions Information Specialist, 909-593-3511 Ext. 4644, Fax: 909-392-2761, E-mail: cranells@laverne.edu. Web site: http://laverne.edu/education/.

University of La Verne, Regional Campus Administration, Master's Programs in Education, California Statewide Campus, La Verne, CA 91750-4443. Offers educational management (M Ed), including preliminary administrative services credential; multiple or single subject teaching credential (M Ed); school counseling (MS), including public personnel services credential. *Entrance requirements:* For master's, California Basic Educational Skills Test, 3 letters of recommendation, teaching credential. *Expenses:* Contact institution.

University of Louisiana at Lafayette, Department of Counselor Education, Lafayette, LA 70504. Offers MS. *Entrance requirements:* For master's, GRE General Test, minimum GPA of 2.75. Additional exam requirements/recommendations for international students: Required—TOEFL (minimum score 550 paper-based; 213 computer-based). Electronic applications accepted.

University of Louisiana at Monroe, Graduate School, College of Education and Human Development, Department of Educational Leadership and Counseling, Program in Counseling, Monroe, LA 71209-0001. Offers M Ed. *Accreditation:* ACA; NCATE. Part-time and evening/weekend programs available. *Faculty:* 1 (woman) full-time. *Students:* 23 full-time (19 women), 18 part-time (14 women); includes 20 minority (18 Black or African American, non-Hispanic/Latino; 1 Asian, non-Hispanic/Latino; 1 Two or more races, non-Hispanic/Latino), 1 international. Average age 34. 11 applicants, 73% accepted, 8 enrolled. In 2011, 15 master's awarded. *Degree requirements:* For master's, comprehensive exam, thesis. *Entrance requirements:* For master's, GRE General Test, minimum GPA of 2.8 in last 60 hours. Additional exam requirements/recommendations for international students: Required—TOEFL (minimum score 500 paper-based; 173 computer-based; 61 iBT). *Application deadline:* For fall admission, 8/24 priority date for domestic students, 7/1 for international students; for winter admission, 12/14 priority date for domestic students; for spring admission, 1/19 for domestic students, 11/1 for international students. Applications are processed on a rolling basis. Application fee: $20 ($30 for international students). Electronic applications accepted. *Expenses:* Tuition, state resident: full-time $3436; part-time $240 per credit hour. Tuition, nonresident: full-time $3436; part-time $240 per credit hour. *International tuition:* $10,733 full-time. *Required fees:* $1460.90. *Financial support:* Career-related internships or fieldwork, Federal Work-Study, and unspecified assistantships available. Financial award application deadline: 4/1; financial award applicants required to submit FAFSA. *Unit head:* Dr. Pamela Newman, Department Head, 318-342-1246, E-mail: pnewman@ulm.edu. *Application contact:* Dr. Jack Palmer, Director of Graduate Studies, 318-342-1250, Fax: 318-342-1240, E-mail: palmer@ulm.edu. Web site: http://www.ulm.edu/elc/index.html.

University of Louisville, Graduate School, College of Education and Human Development, Department of Educational and Counseling Psychology, Louisville, KY 40292-0001. Offers counseling and personnel services (M Ed, PhD). *Accreditation:* APA; NCATE. Part-time and evening/weekend programs available. *Degree requirements:* For doctorate, comprehensive exam, thesis/dissertation. *Entrance requirements:* For master's and doctorate, GRE General Test. Additional exam requirements/recommendations for international students: Required—TOEFL (minimum score 560 paper-based; 210 computer-based; 83 iBT). Electronic applications accepted. *Expenses:* Tuition, state resident: full-time $9692; part-time $539 per credit hour. Tuition, nonresident: full-time $20,168; part-time $1121 per credit hour. Tuition and fees vary according to program and reciprocity agreements. *Faculty research:* Classroom processes, school outcomes, adolescent and adult development issues/prevention and treatment, multicultural counseling, spirituality, therapeutic outcomes, college student success, college student affairs administration, career development.

University of Maine, Graduate School, College of Education and Human Development, Program in Counselor Education, Orono, ME 04469. Offers M Ed, MA, MS, Ed D, CAS. *Accreditation:* NCATE. Part-time and evening/weekend programs available. *Students:* 56 full-time (48 women), 32 part-time (30 women); includes 4 minority (2 Black or African American, non-Hispanic/Latino; 2 American Indian or Alaska Native, non-Hispanic/Latino), 1 international. Average age 36. 30 applicants, 70% accepted, 21 enrolled. In 2011, 17 master's, 7 other advanced degrees awarded. *Degree requirements:* For master's, thesis or alternative. *Entrance requirements:* For master's, MAT; for doctorate, GRE General Test, MA, M Ed or MS; for CAS, MA, M Ed, or MS. Additional exam requirements/recommendations for international students: Required—TOEFL. *Application deadline:* For fall admission, 2/1 priority date for domestic students. Applications are processed on a rolling basis. Application fee: $65. Electronic applications accepted. *Expenses:* Tuition, state resident: full-time $5016. Tuition, nonresident: full-time $14,424. *Financial support:* Career-related internships or fieldwork, Federal Work-Study, institutionally sponsored loans, tuition waivers (full and partial), and unspecified assistantships available. Financial award application deadline: 3/1. *Unit head:* Dr. Sandra Caron, Coordinator, 207-581-2444, Fax: 207-581-2423. *Application contact:* Scott G. Delcourt, Associate Dean of the Graduate School, 207-581-3291, Fax: 207-581-3232, E-mail: graduate@maine.edu. Web site: http://www2.umaine.edu/graduate/.

University of Manitoba, Faculty of Graduate Studies, Faculty of Education, Department of Educational Administration, Foundations and Psychology, Winnipeg, MB R3T 2N2, Canada. Offers adult and post-secondary education (M Ed); educational administration (M Ed); guidance and counseling (M Ed); inclusive special education (M Ed); social foundations of education (M Ed). *Degree requirements:* For master's, thesis or alternative.

University of Mary Hardin-Baylor, Graduate Studies in Counseling and Psychology, Belton, TX 76513. Offers clinical mental health counseling (MA); marriage and family Christian counseling (MA); psychology and counseling (MA); school counseling and psychology (MA). Part-time and evening/weekend programs available. *Faculty:* 5 full-time (3 women), 3 part-time/adjunct (1 woman). *Students:* 40 full-time (29 women), 26 part-time (17 women); includes 18 minority (9 Black or African American, non-Hispanic/Latino; 2 Asian, non-Hispanic/Latino; 6 Hispanic/Latino; 1 Two or more races, non-Hispanic/Latino), 3 international. Average age 29. 56 applicants, 45% accepted, 20 enrolled. In 2011, 21 master's awarded. *Degree requirements:* For master's, comprehensive exam. *Entrance requirements:* For master's, GRE General Test (waived if GPA greater than 3.0), minimum GPA of 3.0 in last 60 hours or 2.75 overall. *Application deadline:* For fall admission, 6/1 priority date for domestic students; for spring admission, 11/1 for domestic students. Applications are processed on a rolling basis. Application fee: $35 ($135 for international students). Electronic applications accepted. *Expenses: Tuition:* Full-time $12,780. *Required fees:* $2350. *Financial support:* Research assistantships with full tuition reimbursements, Federal Work-Study, and scholarships (for some active duty military personnel only) available. Support available to part-time students. Financial award applicants required to submit FAFSA. *Unit head:* Dr. Isaac Gusukuma, Interim Director of Counseling and Psychology Graduate Program, 254-295-5017, E-mail: isaac.gusukuma@umhb.edu. *Application contact:* Melissa Ford, Director of Graduate Admissions, 254-295-4020, Fax: 254-295-5301, E-mail: mford@umhb.edu.

University of Maryland, College Park, Academic Affairs, College of Education, Department of Counseling and Personnel Services, College Park, MD 20742. Offers college student personnel (M Ed, MA); college student personnel administration (PhD); community counseling (CAGS); community/career counseling (M Ed, MA); counseling and personnel services (M Ed, MA, PhD), including art therapy (M Ed), college student personnel (M Ed), counseling and personnel services (PhD), counseling psychology (M Ed), mental health counseling (M Ed), school counseling (M Ed); counseling psychology (PhD); counselor education (PhD); rehabilitation counseling (M Ed, MA, AGSC); school counseling (M Ed, MA); school psychology (M Ed, MA, PhD). *Accreditation:* ACA (one or more programs are accredited); APA (one or more programs are accredited); CORE (one or more programs are accredited); NCATE. Part-time and evening/weekend programs available. Postbaccalaureate distance learning degree programs offered (no on-campus study). *Faculty:* 29 full-time (15 women), 6 part-time/adjunct (5 women). *Students:* 114 full-time (88 women), 12 part-time (9 women); includes 45 minority (17 Black or African American, non-Hispanic/Latino; 16 Asian, non-Hispanic/Latino; 10 Hispanic/Latino; 2 Two or more races, non-Hispanic/Latino), 15 international. 266 applicants, 12% accepted, 16 enrolled. In 2011, 30 master's, 15 doctorates awarded. *Median time to degree:* Of those who began their doctoral program in fall 2003, 60% received their degree in 8 years or less. *Degree requirements:* For master's, thesis (for some programs); for doctorate, thesis/dissertation. *Entrance requirements:* For master's, GRE General Test or MAT, minimum GPA of 3.0, 3 letters of recommendation; for doctorate, GRE General Test or MAT, minimum GPA of 3.5, 3 letters of recommendation. Additional exam requirements/recommendations for international students: Required—TOEFL. *Application deadline:* For fall admission, 12/15 for domestic and international students; for spring admission, 6/1 for international students. Applications are processed on a rolling basis. Application fee: $75. Electronic applications accepted. *Expenses: Tuition, area resident:* Part-time $525 per credit hour. Tuition, state resident: part-time $525 per credit hour. Tuition, nonresident: part-time $1131 per credit hour. *Required fees:* $386.31 per term. Tuition and fees vary according to program. *Financial support:* In 2011–12, 8 fellowships with full and partial tuition reimbursements (averaging $11,286 per year), 1 research assistantship (averaging $20,861 per year), 71 teaching assistantships with tuition reimbursements (averaging $16,237 per year) were awarded; career-related internships or fieldwork, Federal Work-Study, and scholarships/grants also available. Support available to part-time students. Financial award applicants required to submit FAFSA. *Faculty research:* Educational psychology, counseling, health. *Total annual research expenditures:* $589,600. *Unit head:* Dr. Dennis Kivlighan, Chair, 301-405-2858, E-mail: dennisk@umd.edu. *Application contact:* Dr. Charles A. Caramello, Dean of Graduate School, 301-405-0358, Fax: 301-314-9305.

University of Maryland Eastern Shore, Graduate Programs, Department of Education, Program in Guidance and Counseling, Princess Anne, MD 21853-1299. Offers M Ed. Evening/weekend programs available. *Degree requirements:* For master's, comprehensive exam, practicum, seminar paper. *Entrance requirements:* For master's, interview, minimum GPA of 3.0. Additional exam requirements/recommendations for international students: Required—TOEFL (minimum score 213 computer-based; 80 iBT). Electronic applications accepted.

University of Massachusetts Amherst, Graduate School, School of Education, Program in Education, Amherst, MA 01003. Offers bilingual, English as a second language, and multicultural education (M Ed, CAGS); child study and early education (M Ed); children, families and schools (Ed D, CAGS); early childhood and elementary teacher education (M Ed); educational leadership (M Ed, CAGS); educational policy and leadership (Ed D); higher education (M Ed, CAGS); international education (M Ed); language, literacy and culture (Ed D); learning, media and technology (M Ed, CAGS); mathematics, science, and learning technologies (Ed D); policy studies in education (CAGS); psychometric methods, educational statistics and research methods (Ed D); reading and writing (M Ed); school counselor education (M Ed, CAGS); science education (CAGS); secondary teacher education (M Ed); social justice education (M Ed, Ed D, CAGS); special education (M Ed, Ed D, CAGS). *Accreditation:* NCATE. Part-time programs available. Postbaccalaureate distance learning degree programs offered (minimal on-campus study). *Faculty:* 81 full-time (46 women). *Students:* 341 full-time (240 women), 333 part-time (226 women); includes 113 minority (36 Black or African American, non-Hispanic/Latino; 1 American Indian or Alaska Native, non-Hispanic/Latino; 14 Asian, non-Hispanic/Latino; 51 Hispanic/Latino; 1 Native Hawaiian or other Pacific Islander, non-Hispanic/Latino; 10 Two or more races, non-Hispanic/Latino), 98 international. Average age 36. 721 applicants, 57% accepted, 202 enrolled. In 2011, 166 master's, 33 doctorates, 25 CAGSs awarded. Terminal master's awarded for partial completion of doctoral program. *Degree requirements:* For doctorate, comprehensive exam, thesis/dissertation. *Entrance requirements:* Additional exam requirements/recommendations for international students: Required—TOEFL (minimum score 550 paper-based; 213 computer-based; 80 iBT), IELTS (minimum score 6.5). *Application deadline:* For fall admission, 1/15 for domestic and international students. Applications are processed on a rolling basis. Application fee: $50 ($65 for international students). Electronic applications accepted. Tuition and fees vary according to course load, campus/location and program. *Financial support:* Fellowships with full and partial tuition reimbursements, research assistantships with full and partial tuition reimbursements, teaching assistantships with full and partial tuition reimbursements, career-related internships or fieldwork, Federal Work-Study, scholarships/grants, traineeships, health care benefits, tuition waivers (full and partial), and unspecified assistantships available. Support available to part-time students. Financial award application deadline: 1/15. *Unit head:* Dr. Linda L. Griffin, Graduate Program Director, 413-545-6984, Fax: 413-545-1523. *Application contact:* Lindsay DeSantis, Interim Supervisor of Admissions, 413-545-0722, Fax: 413-577-0010, E-mail: gradadm@grad.umass.edu. Web site: http://www.umass.edu/education/.

University of Massachusetts Boston, Office of Graduate Studies, Graduate College of Education, Counseling and School Psychology Department, Program in School Guidance Counseling, Boston, MA 02125-3393. Offers M Ed, CAGS.

Counselor Education

University of Memphis, Graduate School, College of Education, Department of Counseling, Educational Psychology and Research, Memphis, TN 38152. Offers counseling (MS, Ed D), including community counseling (MS), rehabilitation counseling (MS), school counseling (MS); counseling psychology (PhD); educational psychology and research (MS, PhD), including educational psychology, educational research. *Accreditation:* ACA (one or more programs are accredited); APA (one or more programs are accredited); CORE (one or more programs are accredited); NCATE. *Degree requirements:* For master's, comprehensive exam, thesis or alternative; for doctorate, comprehensive exam, thesis/dissertation. *Entrance requirements:* For master's, GRE General Test or MAT, minimum GPA of 2.5; for doctorate, GRE General Test. *Faculty research:* Anger management, aging and disability, supervision, multicultural counseling.

University of Miami, Graduate School, School of Education and Human Development, Department of Educational and Psychological Studies, Program in Counseling, Coral Gables, FL 33124. Offers counseling and research (MS Ed); Latino mental health (Certificate); marriage and family therapy (MS Ed); mental health counseling (MS Ed). Part-time and evening/weekend programs available. *Faculty:* 8 full-time (3 women). *Students:* 48 full-time (43 women), 4 part-time (all women); includes 23 minority (5 Black or African American, non-Hispanic/Latino; 2 Asian, non-Hispanic/Latino; 14 Hispanic/Latino; 2 Two or more races, non-Hispanic/Latino), 2 international. Average age 25. 154 applicants, 51% accepted, 21 enrolled. In 2011, 25 master's awarded. *Degree requirements:* For master's, comprehensive exam, personal growth experience. *Entrance requirements:* For master's, GRE General Test. Additional exam requirements/recommendations for international students: Required—TOEFL (minimum score 550 paper-based; 80 iBT); Recommended—IELTS (minimum score 6.5). *Application deadline:* For fall admission, 3/15 for domestic students. Application fee: $65. Electronic applications accepted. *Financial support:* In 2011–12, 21 students received support. Career-related internships or fieldwork and institutionally sponsored loans available. Support available to part-time students. Financial award application deadline: 3/1; financial award applicants required to submit FAFSA. *Faculty research:* Cocaine recidivism, HIV, non-traditional families, health psychology, diversity. *Unit head:* Dr. Anabel Bejarano, Clinical Assistant Professor and Program Director, 305-284-4829, Fax: 305-284-3003, E-mail: bejarano@miami.edu. *Application contact:* Lois Heffernan, Graduate Admissions Coordinator, 305-284-2167, Fax: 305-284-9395, E-mail: lheffernan@miami.edu.

University of Minnesota, Twin Cities Campus, Graduate School, College of Education and Human Development, Department of Educational Psychology, Program in Counseling and Student Personnel Psychology, Minneapolis, MN 55455-0213. Offers MA, PhD, Ed S. *Students:* 97 full-time (60 women), 15 part-time (13 women); includes 18 minority (8 Black or African American, non-Hispanic/Latino; 3 American Indian or Alaska Native, non-Hispanic/Latino; 5 Asian, non-Hispanic/Latino; 2 Hispanic/Latino), 21 international. Average age 28. 197 applicants, 42% accepted, 38 enrolled. In 2011, 38 master's, 7 doctorates, 1 other advanced degree awarded. Application fee: $55. *Unit head:* Dr. Susan Hupp, Chair, 612-624-1003, Fax: 612-624-8241, E-mail: shupp@umn.edu. *Application contact:* Dr. Jennifer Engler, Assistant Dean, 612-626-2887, Fax: 612-626-7496, E-mail: engle009@umn.edu. Web site: http://www.cehd.umn.edu/EdPsych/CSPP.

University of Mississippi, Graduate School, School of Education, Department of Educational Leadership and Counselor Education, Oxford, University, MS 38677. Offers counselor education (M Ed, PhD, Specialist); educational leadership (PhD); educational leadership and counselor education (M Ed, MA, Ed D, Ed S); higher education/student personnel (MA). *Accreditation:* ACA; NCATE. *Students:* 155 full-time (106 women), 177 part-time (110 women); includes 100 minority (91 Black or African American, non-Hispanic/Latino; 1 Asian, non-Hispanic/Latino; 5 Hispanic/Latino; 3 Two or more races, non-Hispanic/Latino), 7 international. In 2011, 82 master's, 13 doctorates, 36 other advanced degrees awarded. *Degree requirements:* For doctorate, thesis/dissertation. *Entrance requirements:* For master's, GRE General Test, minimum GPA of 3.0; for doctorate, GRE General Test. Additional exam requirements/recommendations for international students: Required—TOEFL. *Application deadline:* For fall admission, 4/1 for domestic students; for spring admission, 10/1 for domestic students. Applications are processed on a rolling basis. Application fee: $25. Electronic applications accepted. *Financial support:* Scholarships/grants available. Financial award application deadline: 3/1; financial award applicants required to submit FAFSA. *Unit head:* Dr. Timothy Letzring, Acting Chair, 662-915-7063, Fax: 662-915-7249. *Application contact:* Dr. Christy M. Wyandt, Associate Dean, 662-915-7474, Fax: 662-915-7577, E-mail: cwyandt@olemiss.edu.

University of Missouri–St. Louis, College of Education, Division of Counseling, St. Louis, MO 63121. Offers community counseling (M Ed); elementary school counseling (M Ed); secondary school counseling (M Ed). *Accreditation:* ACA; NCATE. Part-time and evening/weekend programs available. *Faculty:* 6 full-time (3 women), 11 part-time/adjunct (8 women). *Students:* 44 full-time (38 women), 162 part-time (134 women); includes 54 minority (42 Black or African American, non-Hispanic/Latino; 3 Asian, non-Hispanic/Latino; 7 Hispanic/Latino; 2 Two or more races, non-Hispanic/Latino), 2 international. Average age 32. 106 applicants, 48% accepted, 31 enrolled. In 2011, 60 master's awarded. *Degree requirements:* For master's, comprehensive exam. *Entrance requirements:* For master's, 3 letters of recommendation. Additional exam requirements/recommendations for international students: Required—TOEFL (minimum score 550 paper-based; 213 computer-based). *Application deadline:* For fall admission, 6/1 for domestic and international students; for spring admission, 10/1 for domestic and international students. Application fee: $35 ($40 for international students). Electronic applications accepted. *Expenses:* Tuition, state resident: full-time $6273; part-time $3866 per year. Tuition, nonresident: full-time $14,969; part-time $9980 per year. *Required fees:* $315 per year. *Financial support:* In 2011–12, 2 research assistantships with full and partial tuition reimbursements (averaging $12,500 per year), 2 teaching assistantships with full and partial tuition reimbursements (averaging $10,500 per year) were awarded. Financial award application deadline: 4/1; financial award applicants required to submit FAFSA. *Faculty research:* Vocational interests, self-concept, decision-making factors, developmental differences. *Unit head:* Dr. Mark Pope, Chair, 314-516-5782. *Application contact:* 314-516-5458, Fax: 314-516-6996, E-mail: gradadm@umsl.edu.

University of Missouri–St. Louis, College of Education, Interdisciplinary Doctoral Programs, St. Louis, MO 63121. Offers adult and higher education (Ed D); counseling (PhD); counselor education (Ed D); educational administration (Ed D); educational leadership and policy studies (PhD); educational psychology (PhD); teaching-learning processes (Ed D, PhD). *Faculty:* 72 full-time (33 women). *Students:* 44 full-time (29 women), 199 part-time (138 women); includes 65 minority (52 Black or African American, non-Hispanic/Latino; 3 American Indian or Alaska Native, non-Hispanic/Latino; 5 Asian, non-Hispanic/Latino; 5 Hispanic/Latino), 6 international. Average age 43. 47 applicants, 34% accepted, 11 enrolled. In 2011, 27 doctorates awarded. *Degree requirements:* For doctorate, thesis/dissertation. *Entrance requirements:* For doctorate, GRE General Test, 3 letters of recommendation; personal interview. Additional exam requirements/recommendations for international students: Recommended—TOEFL (minimum score 550 paper-based; 230 computer-based). *Application deadline:* For fall admission, 3/1 for domestic and international students; for spring admission, 10/1 for domestic and international students. Application fee: $35 ($40 for international students). Electronic applications accepted. *Expenses:* Tuition, state resident: full-time $6273; part-time $3866 per year. Tuition, nonresident: full-time $14,969; part-time $9980 per year. *Required fees:* $315 per year. *Financial support:* In 2011–12, 15 research assistantships (averaging $12,240 per year), 8 teaching assistantships (averaging $12,240 per year) were awarded. Financial award application deadline: 4/1; financial award applicants required to submit FAFSA. *Faculty research:* Higher education law and policy, gender and higher education, student retention, lifelong learning orientation, school counselor's role in violence prevention. *Unit head:* Dr. Kathleen Haywood, Director of Graduate Studies, 314-516-5483, Fax: 314-516-5227, E-mail: kathleen_haywood@umsl.edu. *Application contact:* 314-516-5458, Fax: 314-516-6996, E-mail: gradadm@umsl.edu.

The University of Montana, Graduate School, Phyllis J. Washington College of Education and Human Sciences, Department of Educational Leadership and Counseling, Program in Counselor Education, Missoula, MT 59812-0002. Offers counselor education (Ed S); counselor education and supervision (Ed D); mental health counseling (MA); school counseling (MA). *Accreditation:* ACA. *Degree requirements:* For doctorate, thesis/dissertation. *Entrance requirements:* For master's, doctorate, and Ed S, GRE General Test. Additional exam requirements/recommendations for international students: Required—TOEFL.

University of Montevallo, College of Education, Program in Counseling, Montevallo, AL 35115. Offers community counseling (M Ed); marriage and family (M Ed); school counseling (M Ed). *Accreditation:* ACA; NCATE. Part-time and evening/weekend programs available. *Students:* 30 full-time (27 women), 47 part-time (32 women); includes 14 minority (12 Black or African American, non-Hispanic/Latino; 1 American Indian or Alaska Native, non-Hispanic/Latino; 1 Two or more races, non-Hispanic/Latino). In 2011, 21 master's awarded. *Entrance requirements:* For master's, GRE General Test or MAT, minimum undergraduate GPA of 2.75 in last 60 hours or 2.5 overall, interview. Additional exam requirements/recommendations for international students: Required—TOEFL (minimum score 550 paper-based). *Application deadline:* For fall admission, 7/15 for domestic students; for spring admission, 11/15 for domestic students. Application fee: $25. *Financial support:* Federal Work-Study, scholarships/grants, and unspecified assistantships available. *Unit head:* Dr. Leland Doebler, Chair, 205-665-6380. *Application contact:* Rebecca Hartley, Assistant Director, 205-665-6350, E-mail: hartleyrs@montevallo.edu. Web site: http://www.montevallo.edu/clf/CounselingProgram/.

University of Nebraska at Kearney, Graduate Studies, College of Education, Department of Counseling and School Psychology, Kearney, NE 68849-0001. Offers counseling (MS Ed, Ed S); school psychology (Ed S). *Accreditation:* ACA; NCATE. Part-time and evening/weekend programs available. *Degree requirements:* For master's, thesis optional; for Ed S, thesis. *Entrance requirements:* For master's and Ed S, interview. Additional exam requirements/recommendations for international students: Required—TOEFL (minimum score 550 paper-based; 213 computer-based). Electronic applications accepted. *Faculty research:* Multicultural counseling and diversity issues, team decision making, adult development, women's issues, brief therapy.

University of Nebraska at Omaha, Graduate Studies, College of Education, Department of Counseling, Omaha, NE 68182. Offers community counseling (MA, MS); counseling gerontology (MA, MS); school counseling (MA, MS); student affairs practice in higher education (MA, MS). *Accreditation:* ACA (one or more programs are accredited); NCATE. Part-time and evening/weekend programs available. *Faculty:* 3 full-time (0 women). *Students:* 44 full-time (38 women), 138 part-time (113 women); includes 10 minority (7 Black or African American, non-Hispanic/Latino; 1 American Indian or Alaska Native, non-Hispanic/Latino; 1 Hispanic/Latino; 1 Two or more races, non-Hispanic/Latino). Average age 31. 47 applicants, 55% accepted, 23 enrolled. In 2011, 40 master's awarded. *Degree requirements:* For master's, comprehensive exam, thesis (for some programs). *Entrance requirements:* For master's, GRE General Test, MAT, department test, interview, minimum GPA of 3.0, 3 letters of recommendation. Additional exam requirements/recommendations for international students: Required—TOEFL (minimum score 550 paper-based; 213 computer-based; 80 iBT). *Application deadline:* For fall admission, 3/1 for domestic students; for spring admission, 10/1 for domestic students. Applications are processed on a rolling basis. Application fee: $45. Electronic applications accepted. *Financial support:* In 2011–12, 24 students received support, including 10 research assistantships with tuition reimbursements available, 3 teaching assistantships with tuition reimbursements available; fellowships, Federal Work-Study, institutionally sponsored loans, scholarships/grants, tuition waivers (partial), and unspecified assistantships also available. Support available to part-time students. Financial award application deadline: 3/1; financial award applicants required to submit FAFSA. *Unit head:* Dr. Paul Barnes, Chairperson, 402-554-2727. *Application contact:* Dr. Paul Barnes, 402-554-2341, Fax: 402-554-3143, E-mail: graduate@unomaha.edu.

University of Nevada, Las Vegas, Graduate College, College of Education, Department of Educational and Clinical Studies, Las Vegas, NV 89154-3066. Offers addiction studies (Advanced Certificate); counselor education (M Ed, MS), including clinical mental health counseling (MS), school counseling (M Ed); mental health counseling (Advanced Certificate); rehabilitation counseling (Advanced Certificate); special education (M Ed, MS, PhD), including early childhood education (M Ed), special education (M Ed); PhD/JD. *Faculty:* 21 full-time (13 women), 20 part-time/adjunct (14 women). *Students:* 166 full-time (137 women), 203 part-time (161 women); includes 109 minority (42 Black or African American, non-Hispanic/Latino; 1 American Indian or Alaska Native, non-Hispanic/Latino; 6 Asian, non-Hispanic/Latino; 47 Hispanic/Latino; 1 Native Hawaiian or other Pacific Islander, non-Hispanic/Latino; 12 Two or more races, non-Hispanic/Latino), 7 international. Average age 35. 204 applicants, 71% accepted, 111 enrolled. In 2011, 218 master's, 3 doctorates, 8 other advanced degrees awarded. *Degree requirements:* For master's, comprehensive exam (for some programs), thesis (for some programs); for other advanced degree, thesis (for some programs). *Entrance requirements:* Additional exam requirements/recommendations for international students: Required—TOEFL (minimum score 550 paper-based; 213 computer-based; 80 iBT), IELTS (minimum score 7). *Application deadline:* For fall admission, 3/1 priority date for domestic students, 5/1 for international students; for spring admission, 9/1 for domestic students, 10/1 for international students. Applications are processed on a rolling basis. Application fee: $60 ($95 for international students). Electronic applications accepted. *Financial support:* In 2011–12, 42 students received support, including 1 fellowship with full tuition reimbursement available (averaging $25,000 per year), 17 research assistantships with partial tuition reimbursements available (averaging $8,703 per year), 24 teaching assistantships with partial tuition reimbursements available (averaging $10,686 per year); institutionally sponsored loans, scholarships/grants, health care benefits, and unspecified assistantships also available. Financial award application deadline: 3/1. *Faculty research:* Multicultural issues in counseling, academic interventions for students with disabilities, rough and tumble play in early childhood, inclusive strategies for students with disabilities, addictions. *Total annual research expenditures:* $614,125. *Unit head:* Dr. Thomas Pierce, Interim Chair/Associate Professor, 702-895-1104, Fax: 702-895-5550, E-mail: tom.pierce@unlv.edu. *Application* *contact:* Graduate College Admissions Evaluator, 702-895-3320, Fax: 702-895-4180, E-mail: gradcollege@unlv.edu. Web site: http://education.unlv.edu/ecs/.

University of Nevada, Reno, Graduate School, College of Education, Department of Counseling and Educational Psychology, Reno, NV 89557. Offers M Ed, MA, MS, Ed D, PhD, Ed S. *Accreditation:* ACA (one or more programs are accredited); NCATE. Terminal master's awarded for partial completion of doctoral program. *Degree requirements:* For master's, comprehensive exam, thesis optional; for doctorate, comprehensive exam, thesis/dissertation, qualifying exam. *Entrance requirements:* For master's, GRE, minimum GPA of 2.75; for doctorate, GRE, minimum GPA of 3.0. Additional exam requirements/recommendations for international students: Required—TOEFL (minimum score 500 paper-based; 173 computer-based; 61 iBT), IELTS (minimum score 6). Electronic applications accepted. *Faculty research:* Marriage and family counseling, substance abuse attitudes of teachers, current supply of counseling educators, HIV-positive services for patients, family counseling for youth at risk.

University of New Hampshire, Graduate School, College of Liberal Arts, Department of Education, Program in Counseling, Durham, NH 03824. Offers M Ed. Part-time programs available. *Faculty:* 32 full-time. *Students:* 17 full-time (13 women), 33 part-time (30 women); includes 3 minority (2 Asian, non-Hispanic/Latino; 1 Hispanic/Latino). Average age 29. 19 applicants, 74% accepted, 6 enrolled. In 2011, 27 master's awarded. *Degree requirements:* For master's, thesis (for some programs). *Entrance requirements:* For master's, GRE General Test. Additional exam requirements/recommendations for international students: Required—TOEFL (minimum score 550 paper-based; 213 computer-based; 80 iBT). *Application deadline:* For fall admission, 2/1 priority date for domestic students, 2/1 for international students; for spring admission, 12/1 for domestic students. Applications are processed on a rolling basis. Application fee: $65. Electronic applications accepted. *Expenses:* Tuition, state resident: full-time $12,360; part-time $687 per credit hour. Tuition, nonresident: full-time $25,680; part-time $1058 per credit hour. *International tuition:* $29,550 full-time. *Required fees:* $1666; $833 per course. $416.50 per semester. Tuition and fees vary according to course load and degree level. *Financial support:* In 2011–12, 8 students received support, including 3 teaching assistantships; fellowships, research assistantships, career-related internships or fieldwork, Federal Work-Study, scholarships/grants, and tuition waivers (full and partial) also available. Support available to part-time students. Financial award application deadline: 2/15. *Faculty research:* Generic approach to counseling. *Unit head:* Dr. Todd Demitchell, Chair, 603-862-3736, E-mail: education.department@unh.edu. *Application contact:* Lisa Wilder, 603-862-2310, E-mail: education.department@unh.edu. Web site: http://www.unh.edu/education.

University of New Hampshire, Graduate School Manchester Campus, Manchester, NH 03101. Offers business administration (MBA); counseling (M Ed); education (M Ed, MAT); educational administration and supervision (M Ed, Ed S); information technology (MS); management of technology (MS); public administration (MPA); public health (MPH, Certificate); social work (MSW); software systems engineering (Certificate). Part-time and evening/weekend programs available. *Students:* 78 full-time (50 women), 130 part-time (65 women); includes 62 minority (2 Black or African American, non-Hispanic/Latino; 56 Asian, non-Hispanic/Latino; 4 Hispanic/Latino), 4 international. Average age 34. 132 applicants, 55% accepted, 57 enrolled. In 2011, 66 master's, 9 other advanced degrees awarded. *Degree requirements:* For master's, thesis or alternative. *Entrance requirements:* Additional exam requirements/recommendations for international students: Required—TOEFL (minimum score 550 paper-based; 213 computer-based; 80 iBT). *Application deadline:* For fall admission, 6/1 for domestic students, 4/1 for international students; for spring admission, 12/1 for domestic students. Applications are processed on a rolling basis. Application fee: $65. Electronic applications accepted. *Expenses:* Tuition, state resident: full-time $12,360; part-time $687 per credit hour. Tuition, nonresident: full-time $25,680; part-time $1058 per credit hour. *International tuition:* $29,550 full-time. *Required fees:* $1666; $833 per course. $416.50 per semester. Tuition and fees vary according to course load and degree level. *Financial support:* In 2011–12, 11 students received support, including 2 teaching assistantships; fellowships, research assistantships, Federal Work-Study, scholarships/grants, health care benefits, and unspecified assistantships also available. Support available to part-time students. Financial award application deadline: 3/1; financial award applicants required to submit FAFSA. *Unit head:* Candice Brown, Director, 603-641-4313, E-mail: unhm.gradcenter@unh.edu. *Application contact:* Graduate Admissions Office, 603-862-3000, Fax: 603-862-0275, E-mail: grad.school@unh.edu. Web site: http://www.gradschool.unh.edu/manchester/.

University of New Mexico, Graduate School, College of Education, Department of Individual, Family and Community Education, Program in Counselor Education, Albuquerque, NM 87131-2039. Offers MA, PhD. *Accreditation:* ACA (one or more programs are accredited); NCATE. Part-time programs available. *Students:* 62 full-time (45 women), 41 part-time (32 women); includes 54 minority (4 Black or African American, non-Hispanic/Latino; 6 American Indian or Alaska Native, non-Hispanic/Latino; 3 Asian, non-Hispanic/Latino; 38 Hispanic/Latino; 1 Native Hawaiian or other Pacific Islander, non-Hispanic/Latino; 2 Two or more races, non-Hispanic/Latino). Average age 36. 96 applicants, 20% accepted, 16 enrolled. In 2011, 26 degrees awarded. *Degree requirements:* For master's, comprehensive exam; for doctorate, comprehensive exam, thesis/dissertation. *Entrance requirements:* For master's, 3 letters of recommendation, personal statement, departmental application; for doctorate, GRE General Test, 3 letters of recommendation, writing sample, personal statement, departmental application. Additional exam requirements/recommendations for international students: Required—TOEFL. *Application deadline:* For fall admission, 2/15 for domestic and international students; for spring admission, 9/15 for domestic and international students. Application fee: $50. Electronic applications accepted. *Financial support:* In 2011–12, 73 students received support, including 1 fellowship (averaging $3,600 per year), 1 research assistantship with full and partial tuition reimbursement available (averaging $7,000 per year), 5 teaching assistantships with full and partial tuition reimbursements available (averaging $7,809 per year); unspecified assistantships also available. Financial award application deadline: 3/1; financial award applicants required to submit FAFSA. *Faculty research:* Crisis and trauma, ethics, supervision, multiculturalism. *Unit head:* Virginia Shipman, Interim Program Coordinator, 505-277-4535, Fax: 505-277-8361, E-mail: vshipman@unm.edu. *Application contact:* Cynthia Salas, Department Administrator, 505-277-4535, Fax: 505-277-8361, E-mail: divbse@unm.edu. Web site: http://coe.unm.edu/index.php/departments/alias-12/counselor-education.html.

University of New Orleans, Graduate School, College of Education and Human Development, Department of Educational Leadership, Counseling, and Foundations, Program in Counselor Education, New Orleans, LA 70148. Offers M Ed, PhD, GCE. *Accreditation:* ACA (one or more programs are accredited); NCATE. Evening/weekend programs available. Terminal master's awarded for partial completion of doctoral program. *Degree requirements:* For master's, thesis (for some programs); for doctorate, variable foreign language requirement, thesis/dissertation. *Entrance requirements:* For master's and doctorate, GRE General Test. Additional exam requirements/recommendations for international students: Required—TOEFL (minimum score 550 paper-based; 213 computer-based; 79 iBT). Electronic applications accepted.

University of North Alabama, College of Education, Department of Counselor Education, Florence, AL 35632-0001. Offers counseling (MA Ed); non-school-based counseling (MA); non-school-based teaching (MA). *Accreditation:* ACA; NCATE. Part-time and evening/weekend programs available. *Faculty:* 3 full-time (2 women), 1 (woman) part-time/adjunct. *Students:* 30 full-time (20 women), 32 part-time (24 women); includes 9 minority (7 Black or African American, non-Hispanic/Latino; 1 American Indian or Alaska Native, non-Hispanic/Latino; 1 Hispanic/Latino), 2 international. Average age 32. In 2011, 17 master's awarded. *Degree requirements:* For master's, comprehensive exam. *Entrance requirements:* For master's, GRE, MAT, or NTE, minimum GPA of 2.5, Alabama Class B Certificate or equivalent, teaching experience. *Application deadline:* For fall admission, 7/1 priority date for domestic students; for spring admission, 12/1 for domestic students. Applications are processed on a rolling basis. Application fee: $25. Electronic applications accepted. *Financial support:* Federal Work-Study available. Support available to part-time students. Financial award application deadline: 4/1. *Unit head:* Dr. Paul Baird, Chair, 256-765-4763, Fax: 256-765-4159, E-mail: jpbaird@una.edu. *Application contact:* Kim Mauldin, Director of Admissions, 256-765-4608, Fax: 256-765-4960, E-mail: komauldin@una.edu. Web site: http://www.una.edu/education/departments/counselor-education.html.

The University of North Carolina at Chapel Hill, Graduate School, School of Education, Program in School Counseling, Chapel Hill, NC 27599. Offers M Ed. *Accreditation:* ACA; NCATE. *Degree requirements:* For master's, comprehensive exam. *Entrance requirements:* For master's, GRE General Test, minimum GPA of 3.0 during last 2 years of undergraduate course work. Additional exam requirements/recommendations for international students: Required—TOEFL (minimum score 550 paper-based; 213 computer-based). Electronic applications accepted. *Faculty research:* Career counseling, development and assessment, multicultural counseling, measurement.

The University of North Carolina at Charlotte, Graduate School, College of Education, Department of Counseling, Charlotte, NC 28223-0001. Offers counseling (MA, PhD); play therapy (Certificate); school counseling (MA); substance abuse counseling (Post-Master's Certificate). *Accreditation:* ACA. Part-time and evening/weekend programs available. Postbaccalaureate distance learning degree programs offered (no on-campus study). *Faculty:* 12 full-time (7 women), 1 (woman) part-time/adjunct. *Students:* 109 full-time (91 women), 98 part-time (89 women); includes 47 minority (39 Black or African American, non-Hispanic/Latino; 2 Asian, non-Hispanic/Latino; 5 Hispanic/Latino; 1 Two or more races, non-Hispanic/Latino), 2 international. Average age 32. 177 applicants, 51% accepted, 71 enrolled. In 2011, 59 master's, 6 doctorates, 24 other advanced degrees awarded. Terminal master's awarded for partial completion of doctoral program. *Degree requirements:* For master's, thesis; for doctorate, thesis/dissertation. *Entrance requirements:* For master's, GRE or MAT. Additional exam requirements/recommendations for international students: Required—TOEFL (minimum score 557 paper-based; 220 computer-based; 83 iBT). *Application deadline:* For fall admission, 7/1 for domestic students, 5/1 for international students; for spring admission, 11/1 for domestic students, 10/1 for international students. Applications are processed on a rolling basis. Application fee: $65 ($75 for international students). Electronic applications accepted. *Expenses:* Tuition, state resident: full-time $3689. Tuition, nonresident: full-time $15,226. *Required fees:* $2198. Tuition and fees vary according to course load and program. *Financial support:* In 2011–12, 12 students received support, including 1 research assistantship (averaging $23,797 per year), 10 teaching assistantships (averaging $6,600 per year); career-related internships or fieldwork, institutionally sponsored loans, scholarships/grants, unspecified assistantships, and administrative assistantships also available. Support available to part-time students. Financial award application deadline: 4/1; financial award applicants required to submit FAFSA. *Total annual research expenditures:* $30,546. *Unit head:* Dr. Susan R. Furr, Chair, 704-687-8967, Fax: 704-687-1013, E-mail: srfurr@uncc.edu. *Application contact:* Kathy B. Giddings, Director of Graduate Admissions, 704-687-5503, Fax: 704-687-3279, E-mail: gradadm@uncc.edu. Web site: http://education.uncc.edu/counseling/.

The University of North Carolina at Greensboro, Graduate School, School of Education, Department of Counseling and Educational Development, Greensboro, NC 27412-5001. Offers advanced school counseling (PMC); counseling and counselor education (PhD); counseling and educational development (MS); couple and family counseling (PMC); school counseling (PMC); MS/Ed S. *Accreditation:* ACA (one or more programs are accredited); NCATE. *Degree requirements:* For master's, comprehensive exam, practicum, internship; for doctorate, comprehensive exam, thesis/dissertation. *Entrance requirements:* For master's, doctorate, and PMC, GRE General Test. Additional exam requirements/recommendations for international students: Required—TOEFL. Electronic applications accepted. *Faculty research:* Gerontology, invitational theory, career development, marriage and family therapy, drug and alcohol abuse prevention.

The University of North Carolina at Pembroke, Graduate Studies, Department of Psychology and Counseling, Program in Service Agency Counseling, Pembroke, NC 28372-1510. Offers MA. Part-time and evening/weekend programs available. *Degree requirements:* For master's, comprehensive exam, thesis optional. *Entrance requirements:* For master's, GRE General Test or MAT, minimum GPA of 3.0 in major, 2.5 overall. Additional exam requirements/recommendations for international students: Required—TOEFL.

The University of North Carolina at Pembroke, Graduate Studies, School of Education, Program in School Counseling, Pembroke, NC 28372-1510. Offers MA Ed. *Accreditation:* NCATE. Part-time and evening/weekend programs available. *Degree requirements:* For master's, comprehensive exam, thesis optional. *Entrance requirements:* For master's, GRE General Test or MAT, minimum GPA of 3.0 in major, 2.5 overall. Additional exam requirements/recommendations for international students: Required—TOEFL.

University of Northern Colorado, Graduate School, College of Education and Behavioral Sciences, Department of Counselor Education and Supervision, Program in Clinical Counseling, Greeley, CO 80639. Offers MA. Part-time programs available. Electronic applications accepted.

University of Northern Colorado, Graduate School, College of Education and Behavioral Sciences, Department of Counselor Education and Supervision, Program in Counselor Education and Supervision, Greeley, CO 80639. Offers PhD. *Accreditation:* ACA. Part-time programs available. *Degree requirements:* For doctorate, comprehensive exam, thesis/dissertation. *Entrance requirements:* For doctorate, GRE General Test, 3 letters of recommendation.

University of Northern Colorado, Graduate School, College of Education and Behavioral Sciences, Department of Counselor Education and Supervision, Program in School Counseling, Greeley, CO 80639. Offers MA. Part-time programs available. Electronic applications accepted.

University of Northern Iowa, Graduate College, College of Social and Behavioral Sciences, School of Applied Human Sciences, Program in Counseling, Cedar Falls, IA 50614. Offers mental health counseling (MA); school counseling (MAE). *Accreditation:* ACA (one or more programs are accredited). Part-time and evening/weekend programs available. *Students:* 44 full-time (35 women), 30 part-time (21 women); includes 5 minority (3 Black or African American, non-Hispanic/Latino; 2 Hispanic/Latino), 1 international. 64 applicants, 30% accepted, 18 enrolled. In 2011, 34 master's awarded. *Degree requirements:* For master's, comprehensive exam, thesis or alternative. *Entrance requirements:* For master's, minimum GPA of 3.0. Additional exam requirements/recommendations for international students: Required—TOEFL (minimum score 500 paper-based; 180 computer-based; 61 iBT). *Application deadline:* For fall admission, 8/1 priority date for domestic students. Applications are processed on a rolling basis. Application fee: $50 ($70 for international students). Electronic applications accepted. *Expenses:* Tuition, state resident: full-time $7476. Tuition, nonresident: full-time $16,410. *Required fees:* $942. *Financial support:* Career-related internships or fieldwork, Federal Work-Study, and tuition waivers (full and partial) available. Support available to part-time students. Financial award application deadline: 2/1. *Unit head:* Dr. Jan Bartlett, Coordinator, 319-273-7979, Fax: 319-273-5175, E-mail: jan.bartlett@uni.edu. *Application contact:* Laurie S. Russell, Record Analyst, 319-273-2623, Fax: 319-273-2885, E-mail: laurie.russell@uni.edu. Web site: http://www.uni.edu/coe/elcpe/.

University of North Florida, College of Education and Human Services, Department of Leadership, School Counseling and Sport Management, Jacksonville, FL 32224. Offers counselor education (M Ed), including school counseling; educational leadership (M Ed, Ed D), including athletic administration (M Ed), educational leadership (Ed D), educational leadership (certification) (M Ed), educational technology (M Ed), instructional leadership (M Ed). Part-time and evening/weekend programs available. *Faculty:* 15 full-time (9 women). *Students:* 48 full-time (35 women), 200 part-time (135 women); includes 67 minority (47 Black or African American, non-Hispanic/Latino; 2 American Indian or Alaska Native, non-Hispanic/Latino; 6 Asian, non-Hispanic/Latino; 10 Hispanic/Latino; 2 Two or more races, non-Hispanic/Latino), 2 international. Average age 36. 97 applicants, 48% accepted, 41 enrolled. In 2011, 84 master's, 6 doctorates awarded. *Degree requirements:* For doctorate, thesis/dissertation. *Entrance requirements:* For master's, GRE General Test, minimum GPA of 3.0 in last 60 hours, interview, 3 letters of recommendation; for doctorate, GRE General Test, master's degree, interview, 3 letters of recommendation, writing sample. Additional exam requirements/recommendations for international students: Required—TOEFL (minimum score 500 paper-based; 173 computer-based). *Application deadline:* For fall admission, 7/1 priority date for domestic students, 5/1 for international students; for spring admission, 11/1 priority date for domestic students, 10/1 for international students. Applications are processed on a rolling basis. Application fee: $30. Electronic applications accepted. *Expenses:* Tuition, state resident: full-time $8793; part-time $366.38 per credit hour. Tuition, nonresident: full-time $23,502; part-time $979.24 per credit hour. *Required fees:* $1384; $57.66 per credit hour. Tuition and fees vary according to course load and program. *Financial support:* In 2011–12, 68 students received support, including 2 research assistantships (averaging $6,200 per year), 2 teaching assistantships (averaging $6,250 per year); career-related internships or fieldwork, Federal Work-Study, scholarships/grants, tuition waivers (partial), and unspecified assistantships also available. Support available to part-time students. Financial award application deadline: 4/1; financial award applicants required to submit FAFSA. *Faculty research:* Counseling: ethics; lesbian, bisexual and transgender issues; educational leadership: school culture and climate; educational assessment and accountability; school safety and student discipline. *Total annual research expenditures:* $137,500. *Unit head:* Dr. Edgar N. Jackson, Jr., Chair, 904-620-1829, E-mail: newton.jackson@unf.edu. *Application contact:* Lillith Richardson, Assistant Director, The Graduate School, 904-620-1360, Fax: 904-620-1362, E-mail: graduateschool@unf.edu. Web site: http://www.unf.edu/coehs/lscsm/.

University of North Texas, Toulouse Graduate School, College of Education, Department of Counseling and Higher Education, Program in Counseling, Denton, TX 76203-5017. Offers adolescent counseling (Certificate); adult counseling (Certificate); child counseling/play therapy (Certificate); college/university counseling (Certificate); community college counseling (MS); community counseling (Certificate); counseling (PhD); couple/family counseling (Certificate); elementary school counseling (M Ed, MS); group counseling (Certificate); secondary school counseling (M Ed); university counseling (M Ed). *Accreditation:* NCATE. Part-time and evening/weekend programs available. *Degree requirements:* For master's, comprehensive exam (for some programs), 600 hour internship; for doctorate, comprehensive exam, thesis/dissertation. *Entrance requirements:* For master's, GRE General Test, 3 recommendations, group interview, writing sample; for doctorate, GRE General Test, admissions exam, 3 recommendations, group interview. Additional exam requirements/recommendations for international students: Recommended—TOEFL (minimum score 550 paper-based; 213 computer-based). Electronic applications accepted. *Expenses:* Tuition, state resident: part-time $100 per credit hour. Tuition, nonresident: part-time $413 per credit hour. *Faculty research:* Play therapy, school counseling, suicide prevention, animal-assisted therapy, transpersonal counseling.

University of Phoenix–Las Vegas Campus, College of Human Services, Las Vegas, NV 89128. Offers marriage, family, and child therapy (MSC); mental health counseling (MSC); school counseling (MSC). Postbaccalaureate distance learning degree programs offered. *Entrance requirements:* For master's, minimum undergraduate GPA of 2.5, 3 years of work experience. Additional exam requirements/recommendations for international students: Required—TOEFL (minimum score 550 paper-based; 213 computer-based; 79 iBT). Electronic applications accepted.

University of Phoenix–New Mexico Campus, College of Education, Albuquerque, NM 87113-1570. Offers administration and supervision (MAEd); curriculum and instruction (MAEd); elementary teacher education (MAEd); school counseling (MSC); secondary teacher education (MAEd). Evening/weekend programs available. *Degree requirements:* For master's, thesis (for some programs). *Entrance requirements:* For master's, minimum undergraduate GPA of 2.5, 3 years of work experience. Additional exam requirements/recommendations for international students: Required—TOEFL (minimum score 550 paper-based; 213 computer-based; 79 iBT). Electronic applications accepted.

University of Phoenix–Phoenix Main Campus, College of Social Sciences, Tempe, AZ 85282-2371. Offers counseling (MS), including community counseling, counseling; psychology (MS). Evening/weekend programs available. Postbaccalaureate distance learning degree programs offered. *Students:* 240 full-time (194 women); includes 37 minority (15 Black or African American, non-Hispanic/Latino; 1 Asian, non-Hispanic/Latino; 18 Hispanic/Latino; 2 Native Hawaiian or other Pacific Islander, non-Hispanic/Latino; 1 Two or more races, non-Hispanic/Latino), 3 international. Average age 35. *Entrance requirements:* Additional exam requirements/recommendations for international students: Required—TOEFL, TOEIC (Test of English as an International Communication), Berlitz Online English Proficiency Exam, Pearson Test of English, or IELTS. *Application deadline:* Applications are processed on a rolling basis. Application fee: $45. Electronic applications accepted. *Expenses:* Contact institution. *Financial support:* Scholarships/grants available. Financial award applicants required to submit FAFSA. *Application contact:* 866-766-0766. Web site: http://www.phoenix.edu/colleges_divisions/social-sciences.html.

University of Phoenix–Southern Arizona Campus, College of Education, Tucson, AZ 85711. Offers administration and supervision (MA Ed); adult education and training (MA Ed); curriculum instruction (MA Ed); educational counseling (MA Ed); elementary teacher education (MA Ed); school counseling (MSC); secondary teacher education (MA Ed); special education (MA Ed, Certificate). Evening/weekend programs available. *Degree requirements:* For master's, thesis (for some programs). *Entrance requirements:* For master's, minimum undergraduate GPA of 2.5, 3 years of work experience. Additional exam requirements/recommendations for international students: Required—TOEFL (minimum score 550 paper-based; 213 computer-based; 79 iBT). Electronic applications accepted.

University of Phoenix–Southern California Campus, College of Social Sciences, Costa Mesa, CA 92626. Offers counseling (MS), including marriage, family and child therapy; psychology (MS). Evening/weekend programs available. Postbaccalaureate distance learning degree programs offered. *Students:* 587 full-time (491 women); includes 288 minority (122 Black or African American, non-Hispanic/Latino; 4 American Indian or Alaska Native, non-Hispanic/Latino; 8 Asian, non-Hispanic/Latino; 146 Hispanic/Latino; 4 Native Hawaiian or other Pacific Islander, non-Hispanic/Latino; 4 Two or more races, non-Hispanic/Latino), 5 international. Average age 37. *Entrance requirements:* Additional exam requirements/recommendations for international students: Required—TOEFL, TOEIC (Test of English as an International Communication), Berlitz Online English Proficiency Exam, Pearson Test of English, or IELTS. *Application deadline:* Applications are processed on a rolling basis. Application fee: $45. Electronic applications accepted. *Expenses:* Contact institution. *Financial support:* Scholarships/grants available. Financial award applicants required to submit FAFSA. *Application contact:* 866-766-0766. Web site: http://www.phoenix.edu/colleges_divisions/social-sciences.html.

University of Puerto Rico, Río Piedras, College of Education, Program in Guidance and Counseling, San Juan, PR 00931-3300. Offers M Ed, Ed D. Part-time programs available. *Degree requirements:* For master's, thesis; for doctorate, thesis/dissertation, internship. *Entrance requirements:* For master's, PAEG or GRE, interview, minimum GPA of 3.0, letter of recommendation; for doctorate, GRE or PAEG, master's degree, minimum GPA of 3.0, letter of recommendation (2), interview.

University of Puget Sound, Graduate Studies, School of Education, Program in Counseling, Tacoma, WA 98416. Offers mental health counseling (M Ed); pastoral counseling (M Ed); school counseling (M Ed). *Accreditation:* NCATE. Part-time programs available. *Faculty:* 2 full-time (both women). *Students:* 3 full-time (2 women), 27 part-time (23 women); includes 4 minority (1 Black or African American, non-Hispanic/Latino; 1 Asian, non-Hispanic/Latino; 2 Two or more races, non-Hispanic/Latino). Average age 30. 33 applicants, 64% accepted, 17 enrolled. In 2011, 12 master's awarded. *Degree requirements:* For master's, capstone course. *Entrance requirements:* For master's, GRE General Test, minimum GPA of 3.0. Additional exam requirements/recommendations for international students: Required—TOEFL (minimum score 550 paper-based; 213 computer-based; 80 iBT). *Application deadline:* For fall admission, 3/1 priority date for domestic students, 3/1 for international students. Applications are processed on a rolling basis. Application fee: $60. Electronic applications accepted. *Expenses:* Contact institution. *Financial support:* Teaching assistantships and career-related internships or fieldwork available. Financial award application deadline: 3/31; financial award applicants required to submit FAFSA. *Faculty research:* Cross-role professional preparation, suicide prevention. *Unit head:* Dr. John Woodward, Dean, 253-879-3375, E-mail: woodward@pugetsound.edu. *Application contact:* Dr. George H. Mills, Jr., Vice President for Enrollment, 253-879-3211, Fax: 253-879-3993, E-mail: admission@pugetsound.edu. Web site: http://www.pugetsound.edu/academics/departments-and-programs/graduate/school-of-education/med/.

University of Rochester, Margaret Warner Graduate School of Education and Human Development, Doctoral Programs in Education, Rochester, NY 14627. Offers counseling (Ed D); educational administration (Ed D); educational policy and theory (PhD); higher education (PhD); human development in educational context (PhD); teaching, curriculum, and change (PhD). *Expenses: Tuition:* Full-time $41,040.

University of Rochester, Margaret Warner Graduate School of Education and Human Development, Master's Program in Counseling, Rochester, NY 14627. Offers school and community counseling (MS); school counseling (MS). *Expenses: Tuition:* Full-time $41,040.

University of Saint Francis, Graduate School, Department of Psychology and Counseling, Fort Wayne, IN 46808-3994. Offers behavioral counseling (MS); clinical mental health counseling (MS); general psychology (MS); pastoral counseling (MS); school counseling (MS Ed). Part-time and evening/weekend programs available. *Faculty:* 4 full-time (1 woman), 3 part-time/adjunct (0 women). *Students:* 28 full-time (23 women), 31 part-time (26 women); includes 9 minority (5 Black or African American, non-Hispanic/Latino; 4 Hispanic/Latino), 1 international. In 2011, 13 master's awarded. *Entrance requirements:* For master's, interview, minimum undergraduate GPA of 3.0. *Application deadline:* For fall admission, 7/1 for domestic students; for spring admission, 11/1 for domestic students. Applications are processed on a rolling basis. Application fee: $20. Application fee is waived when completed online. *Financial support:* Federal Work-Study, scholarships/grants, tuition waivers (full and partial), and unspecified assistantships available. *Unit head:* Dr. Mark Friedmeyer, Dean, 260-399-7700 Ext. 8422, Fax: 260-399-8170, E-mail: mfriedmeyer@sf.edu. *Application contact:* Kyna Steury-Johnson, Admissions Counselor, 260-399-7700 Ext. 6316, Fax: 260-399-8152, E-mail: ksteury@sf.edu.

University of Saint Joseph, Department of Counselor Education, West Hartford, CT 06117-2700. Offers clinical mental health counseling (MA); school counseling (MA). Part-time and evening/weekend programs available. *Students:* 54 full-time (53 women), 99 part-time (89 women); includes 14 minority (4 Black or African American, non-Hispanic/Latino; 9 Hispanic/Latino; 1 Two or more races, non-Hispanic/Latino). Average age 30. *Degree requirements:* For master's, comprehensive exam, thesis optional. *Entrance requirements:* For master's, 2 letters of recommendation. *Application deadline:* Applications are processed on a rolling basis. Application fee: $50. Electronic applications accepted. Application fee is waived when completed online. *Expenses: Tuition:* Part-time $670 per credit. *Required fees:* $40 per credit. Tuition and fees vary according to course load, degree level, campus/location and program. *Financial support:* Career-related internships or fieldwork and unspecified assistantships available. Support available to part-time students. Financial award applicants required to submit FAFSA. *Application contact:* Graduate Admissions Office, 860-231-5261, E-mail: graduate@usj.edu.

University of St. Thomas, School of Education, Houston, TX 77006-4696. Offers all level teaching (M Ed); bilingual/dual language (M Ed); Catholic school teaching (M Ed); Catholic/private school leadership (M Ed); counselor education (M Ed); curriculum and instruction (M Ed); educational leadership (M Ed); elementary teaching (M Ed); English as a second language (M Ed); exceptionality/ educational diagnostician (M Ed); exceptionality/special education (M Ed); generalist (M Ed); reading (M Ed); secondary teaching (M Ed). Part-time and evening/weekend programs available. Postbaccalaureate distance learning degree programs offered (no on-campus study). *Faculty:* 30 full-time (17 women), 54 part-time/adjunct (37 women). *Students:* 66 full-time (43 women), 1,178 part-time (1,044 women); includes 777 minority (313 Black or African American, non-Hispanic/Latino; 5 American Indian or Alaska Native, non-Hispanic/Latino; 29 Asian, non-Hispanic/Latino; 395 Hispanic/Latino; 2 Native Hawaiian or other

Pacific Islander, non-Hispanic/Latino; 33 Two or more races, non-Hispanic/Latino), 26 international. Average age 36. 551 applicants, 94% accepted, 416 enrolled. In 2011, 72 master's awarded. *Degree requirements:* For master's, thesis, field experience. *Entrance requirements:* For master's, GRE or MAT if GPA is below 3.0, bachelor's degree; minimum GPA of 2.75 in bachelor's degree or last 60 credit hours; official transcripts from all institutions; goal statement of 250-300 words; 1 reference. Additional exam requirements/recommendations for international students: Required—TOEFL. *Application deadline:* Applications are processed on a rolling basis. Application fee: $35. Electronic applications accepted. *Expenses:* Contact institution. *Financial support:* In 2011–12, 9 students received support. Federal Work-Study, scholarships/grants, and state work-study, institutional employment available. Support available to part-time students. Financial award application deadline: 4/15; financial award applicants required to submit FAFSA. *Faculty research:* Leadership, diversity, personality traits, second language acquisition. *Unit head:* Dr. Nora Hutto, Dean, 713-525-3540, Fax: 713-525-3871, E-mail: education@stthom.edu. *Application contact:* Paula C. Hollis, Administrative Assistant, 713-525-3540, Fax: 713-525-3871, E-mail: education@stthom.edu. Web site: http://www.stthom.edu/Schools_Centers_of_Excellence/Schools_of_Study/School_of_Education/Index.aqf.

University of San Diego, School of Leadership and Education Sciences, Program in Counseling, San Diego, CA 92110-2492. Offers clinical mental health counseling (MA); school counseling (MA). *Accreditation:* ACA. Part-time and evening/weekend programs available. *Faculty:* 6 full-time (2 women), 5 part-time/adjunct (2 women). *Students:* 56 full-time (48 women), 32 part-time (30 women); includes 37 minority (4 Black or African American, non-Hispanic/Latino; 9 Asian, non-Hispanic/Latino; 15 Hispanic/Latino; 1 Native Hawaiian or other Pacific Islander, non-Hispanic/Latino; 8 Two or more races, non-Hispanic/Latino), 1 international. Average age 27. 191 applicants, 50% accepted, 40 enrolled. In 2011, 30 master's awarded. *Degree requirements:* For master's, comprehensive exam. *Entrance requirements:* For master's, minimum GPA of 3.0, interview with faculty member. Additional exam requirements/recommendations for international students: Required—TOEFL (minimum score 580 paper-based; 237 computer-based; 83 iBT), TWE. *Application deadline:* For fall admission, 2/1 for domestic and international students. Application fee: $45. Electronic applications accepted. *Expenses: Tuition:* Full-time $22,482; part-time $1249 per unit. *Required fees:* $224. Full-time tuition and fees vary according to course load and degree level. *Financial support:* In 2011–12, 76 students received support. Career-related internships or fieldwork, Federal Work-Study, institutionally sponsored loans, unspecified assistantships, and stipends available. Support available to part-time students. Financial award application deadline: 4/1; financial award applicants required to submit FAFSA. *Faculty research:* Action research, forensic psychology, lifespan and career development, multicultural counseling, school counseling. *Unit head:* Dr. Ann Garland, Graduate Program Co-Director, 619-260-4212, Fax: 619-260-8095. *Application contact:* Monica Mahon, Director of Admissions and Enrollment, 619-260-4524, Fax: 619-260-4158, E-mail: grads@sandiego.edu. Web site: http://www.sandiego.edu/soles/programs/counseling/.

University of San Francisco, School of Education, Department of Counseling Psychology, San Francisco, CA 94117-1080. Offers counseling (MA), including educational counseling, life transitions counseling, marital and family therapy; counseling psychology (Ed D). *Faculty:* 7 full-time (3 women), 36 part-time/adjunct (26 women). *Students:* 302 full-time (250 women), 13 part-time (11 women); includes 125 minority (19 Black or African American, non-Hispanic/Latino; 37 Asian, non-Hispanic/Latino; 54 Hispanic/Latino; 15 Two or more races, non-Hispanic/Latino), 4 international. Average age 31. 366 applicants, 55% accepted, 118 enrolled. In 2011, 146 master's awarded. *Degree requirements:* For doctorate, thesis/dissertation. *Entrance requirements:* For doctorate, GRE General Test. Application fee: $55 ($65 for international students). *Expenses: Tuition:* Full-time $20,070; part-time $1115 per unit. Tuition and fees vary according to course load, campus/location and program. *Financial support:* In 2011–12, 20 students received support. Fellowships, research assistantships, and teaching assistantships available. Financial award application deadline: 3/2; financial award applicants required to submit FAFSA. *Unit head:* Dr. Brian Gerrard, Chair, 415-422-6868. *Application contact:* Beth Teague, Associate Director of Graduate Outreach, 415-422-5467, E-mail: schoolofeducation@usfca.edu.

The University of Scranton, College of Graduate and Continuing Education, Department of Counseling and Human Services, Program in School Counseling, Scranton, PA 18510. Offers MS. *Accreditation:* ACA; NCATE. Part-time and evening/weekend programs available. *Students:* 49 full-time (43 women), 10 part-time (7 women), 1 international. Average age 26. 37 applicants, 86% accepted. In 2011, 19 master's awarded. *Degree requirements:* For master's, comprehensive exam, capstone experience. *Entrance requirements:* For master's, minimum GPA of 2.75. Additional exam requirements/recommendations for international students: Required—TOEFL (minimum score 500 paper-based; 173 computer-based), IELTS (minimum score 5.5). *Application deadline:* For fall admission, 3/1 for domestic students. Application fee: $0. *Financial support:* Teaching assistantships, career-related internships or fieldwork, and Federal Work-Study available. Support available to part-time students. Financial award application deadline: 3/1. *Unit head:* Dr. Lee Ann M. Eschbach, Co-Director, 570-941-6299, Fax: 570-941-4201, E-mail: eschbach@scranton.edu. *Application contact:* Joseph M. Roback, Director of Admissions, 570-941-4385, Fax: 570-941-5928, E-mail: robackj2@scranton.edu.

University of South Africa, College of Human Sciences, Pretoria, South Africa. Offers adult education (M Ed); African languages (MA, PhD); African politics (MA, PhD); Afrikaans (MA, PhD); ancient history (MA, PhD); ancient Near Eastern studies (MA, PhD); anthropology (MA, PhD); applied linguistics (MA); Arabic (MA, PhD); archaeology (MA); art history (MA); Biblical archaeology (MA); Biblical studies (M Th, D Th, PhD); Christian spirituality (M Th, D Th); church history (M Th, D Th); classical studies (MA, PhD); clinical psychology (MA); communication (MA, PhD); comparative education (M Ed, Ed D); consulting psychology (D Admin, D Com, PhD); curriculum studies (M Ed, Ed D); development studies (M Admin, MA, D Admin, PhD); didactics (M Ed, Ed D); education (M Tech); education management (M Ed, Ed D); educational psychology (M Ed); English (MA); environmental education (M Ed); French (MA, PhD); German (MA, PhD); Greek (MA); guidance and counseling (M Ed); health studies (MA, PhD), including health sciences education (MA), health services management (MA), medical and surgical nursing science (critical care general) (MA), midwifery and neonatal nursing science (MA), trauma and emergency care (MA); history (MA, PhD); history of education (Ed D); inclusive education (M Ed, Ed D); information and communications technology policy and regulation (MA); information science (MA, MIS, PhD); international politics (MA, PhD); Islamic studies (MA, PhD); Italian (MA, PhD); Judaica (MA, PhD); linguistics (MA, PhD); mathematical education (M Ed); mathematics education (MA); missiology (M Th, D Th); modern Hebrew (MA, PhD); musicology (MA, MMus, D Mus, PhD); natural science education (M Ed); New Testament (M Th, D Th); Old Testament (D Th); pastoral therapy (M Th, D Th); philosophy (MA); philosophy of education (M Ed, Ed D); politics (MA, PhD); Portuguese (MA, PhD); practical theology (M Th, D Th); psychology (MA, MS, PhD); psychology of education (M Ed, Ed D); public health (MA); religious studies (MA, D Th, PhD); Romance languages (MA); Russian (MA, PhD); Semitic languages (MA, PhD); social behavior studies in HIV/AIDS (MA); social science (mental health) (MA); social science in development studies (MA); social science in psychology (MA); social science in social work (MA); social science in sociology (MA); social work (MSW, DSW, PhD); socio-education (M Ed, Ed D); sociolinguistics (MA); sociology (MA, PhD); Spanish (MA, PhD); systematic theology (M Th, D Th); TESOL (teaching English to speakers of other languages) (MA); theological ethics (M Th, D Th); theory of literature (MA, PhD); urban ministries (D Th); urban ministry (M Th).

University of South Alabama, Graduate School, College of Education, Department of Professional Studies, Mobile, AL 36688-0002. Offers community counseling (MS); educational media (M Ed, MS); instructional design and development (MS, PhD); rehabilitation counseling (MS); school counseling (M Ed); school psychometry (M Ed). *Accreditation:* NCATE. Part-time programs available. *Faculty:* 14 full-time (7 women). *Students:* 89 full-time (70 women), 116 part-time (96 women); includes 46 minority (41 Black or African American, non-Hispanic/Latino; 1 American Indian or Alaska Native, non-Hispanic/Latino; 1 Asian, non-Hispanic/Latino; 2 Hispanic/Latino; 1 Two or more races, non-Hispanic/Latino), 5 international. 53 applicants, 49% accepted, 25 enrolled. In 2011, 32 master's, 4 doctorates awarded. *Degree requirements:* For master's, comprehensive exam. *Entrance requirements:* For master's, GRE General Test or MAT, minimum GPA of 3.0. *Application deadline:* For fall admission, 6/15 priority date for domestic students; for spring admission, 11/1 priority date for domestic students. Applications are processed on a rolling basis. Application fee: $35. *Expenses:* Tuition, state resident: full-time $7968; part-time $332 per credit hour. Tuition, nonresident: full-time $15,936; part-time $664 per credit hour. *Financial support:* In 2011–12, 5 research assistantships were awarded; career-related internships or fieldwork also available. Support available to part-time students. Financial award application deadline: 4/1. *Faculty research:* Agency counseling, rehabilitation counseling, school psychometry. *Unit head:* Dr. Charles Guest, Chair, 251-380-2861. *Application contact:* Dr. Abigail Baxter, Director of Graduate Studies, 251-380-6310. Web site: http://www.southalabama.edu/coe/profstudies/.

University of South Carolina, The Graduate School, College of Education, Department of Educational Studies, Program in Counseling Education, Columbia, SC 29208. Offers PhD, Ed S. *Accreditation:* ACA (one or more programs are accredited); NCATE. Part-time programs available. *Degree requirements:* For doctorate, one foreign language, comprehensive exam, thesis/dissertation; for Ed S, comprehensive exam. *Entrance requirements:* For doctorate, GRE General Test or MAT, interview, resume, references; for Ed S, GRE General Test or MAT, interview, resumé, transcripts, letter of intent, references. Electronic applications accepted. *Faculty research:* Multicultural counseling, children's fears, career development, family counseling.

The University of South Dakota, Graduate School, School of Education, Division of Counseling and Psychology in Education, Vermillion, SD 57069-2390. Offers MA, PhD, Ed S. *Accreditation:* ACA (one or more programs are accredited); NCATE. Part-time programs available. *Degree requirements:* For master's and Ed S, comprehensive exam, thesis or alternative; for doctorate, comprehensive exam, thesis/dissertation. *Entrance requirements:* For master's and doctorate, GRE General Test, minimum GPA of 3.0. Additional exam requirements/recommendations for international students: Required—TOEFL (minimum score 550 paper-based; 213 computer-based; 79 iBT). Electronic applications accepted. *Expenses:* Tuition, state resident: full-time $3118.50; part-time $173.25 per credit hour. Tuition, nonresident: full-time $6601; part-time $366.70 per credit hour. *Required fees:* $2268; $126 per credit hour. Tuition and fees vary according to program.

University of Southern California, Graduate School, Rossier School of Education, Master's Programs in Education, Los Angeles, CA 90089-4038. Offers educational counseling (ME); marriage, family and child counseling (MMFT); postsecondary administration and student affairs [PASA] (ME); school counseling (ME); teaching (online) (MAT); teaching and teaching credential (MAT); teaching English to speakers of other languages (MAT). Part-time and evening/weekend programs available. Postbaccalaureate distance learning degree programs offered (no on-campus study). *Degree requirements:* For master's, thesis optional. *Entrance requirements:* For master's, GRE (for all programs except MAT). Additional exam requirements/recommendations for international students: Required—TOEFL (minimum score 250 computer-based; 100 iBT). Electronic applications accepted. *Faculty research:* College access and equity, preparing teachers for culturally diverse populations, sociocultural basis of learning as mediated by instruction with focus on reading and literacy in English learners, social and political aspects of teaching and learning English, school counselor development and training.

University of Southern Maine, School of Education and Human Development, Program in Counselor Education, Portland, ME 04104-9300. Offers clinical mental health (MS); counseling (CAS); mental health rehabilitation technician/community (Certificate); rehabilitation counseling (MS); school counseling (MS). *Accreditation:* ACA (one or more programs are accredited); CORE; Teacher Education Accreditation Council. Part-time and evening/weekend programs available. *Degree requirements:* For master's, comprehensive exam, thesis or alternative; for other advanced degree, thesis or alternative. *Entrance requirements:* For master's, GRE General Test or MAT, interview; for other advanced degree, master's degree. Additional exam requirements/recommendations for international students: Required—TOEFL (minimum score 550 paper-based; 213 computer-based; 79 iBT). Electronic applications accepted. *Faculty research:* Counselor licensure.

University of Southern Mississippi, Graduate School, College of Education and Psychology, Department of Educational Leadership and School Counseling, Hattiesburg, MS 39401. Offers education (Ed D, PhD, Ed S), including educational leadership and school counseling (Ed D, PhD); educational administration (M Ed). Part-time programs available. *Faculty:* 9 full-time (5 women), 3 part-time/adjunct (1 woman). *Students:* 35 full-time (26 women), 266 part-time (184 women); includes 103 minority (93 Black or African American, non-Hispanic/Latino; 5 Hispanic/Latino; 5 Two or more races, non-Hispanic/Latino). Average age 39. 27 applicants, 74% accepted, 18 enrolled. In 2011, 85 master's, 25 doctorates, 18 other advanced degrees awarded. *Degree requirements:* For master's, comprehensive exam, thesis optional, internship; for doctorate, comprehensive exam, thesis/dissertation; for Ed S, comprehensive exam, thesis optional. *Entrance requirements:* For master's, GRE General Test, minimum GPA of 2.75; for doctorate, GRE General Test, minimum GPA of 3.5; for Ed S, GRE General Test, minimum GPA of 3.25. Additional exam requirements/recommendations for international students: Required—TOEFL, IELTS. *Application deadline:* For fall admission, 3/1 priority date for domestic students, 3/1 for international students; for spring admission, 1/10 for domestic and international students. Application fee: $50. *Financial support:* In 2011–12, research assistantships (averaging $9,000 per year), teaching assistantships (averaging $9,000 per year) were awarded; career-related internships or fieldwork, Federal Work-Study, institutionally sponsored loans, scholarships/grants, health care benefits, and unspecified assistantships also available. Financial award application deadline: 3/15; financial award applicants required to submit FAFSA. *Unit head:* Dr. Thelma Roberson, Interim Chair, 601-266-4556, Fax: 601-266-4233, E-mail: thelma.roberson@usm.edu. *Application contact:* Dr. Thelma Roberson, Interim Chair, 601-266-4556, Fax: 601-266-4233, E-mail: thelma.roberson@usm.edu. Web site: http://www.usm.edu/graduateschool/table.php.

University of Southern Mississippi, Graduate School, College of Education and Psychology, Department of Educational Studies and Research, Hattiesburg, MS 39406-

0001. Offers adult education (Graduate Certificate); community college leadership (Graduate Certificate); counseling and personnel services (college) (M Ed); education (PhD, Ed S), including adult education, research, evaluation and statistics (PhD); education (Ed D), including educational administration, educational research; education: educational leadership and research (Ed S), including higher education administration; educational administration and supervision (M Ed); higher education administration (Ed D, PhD); institutional research (Graduate Certificate). *Faculty:* 7 full-time (1 woman), 5 part-time/adjunct (1 woman). *Students:* 33 full-time (25 women), 104 part-time (25 women); includes 46 minority (40 Black or African American, non-Hispanic/Latino; 1 Asian, non-Hispanic/Latino; 3 Hispanic/Latino; 2 Two or more races, non-Hispanic/Latino), 1 international. Average age 36. 27 applicants, 48% accepted, 1 enrolled. In 2011, 27 master's, 13 doctorates, 1 other advanced degree awarded. *Degree requirements:* For master's and other advanced degree, comprehensive exam, thesis (for some programs); for doctorate, comprehensive exam, thesis/dissertation. *Entrance requirements:* For master's, doctorate, and other advanced degree, GRE General Test, minimum GPA of 2.75. Additional exam requirements/recommendations for international students: Required—TOEFL. *Application deadline:* For fall admission, 2/1 for domestic students, 3/1 for international students. Applications are processed on a rolling basis. Application fee: $35. *Financial support:* Career-related internships or fieldwork, Federal Work-Study, and institutionally sponsored loans available. Financial award application deadline: 3/15; financial award applicants required to submit FAFSA. *Total annual research expenditures:* $88,500. *Unit head:* Dr. Thomas V. O'Brien, Chair, 601-266-6093, E-mail: thomas.obrien@usm.edu. *Application contact:* Shonna Breland, Manager of Graduate Admissions, 601-266-6563, Fax: 601-266-5138. Web site: http://www.usm.edu/cep/esr/.

University of South Florida, Graduate School, College of Education, Department of Psychological and Social Foundations, Tampa, FL 33620-9951. Offers college student affairs (M Ed); counselor education (MA, PhD, Ed S); interdisciplinary (PhD, Ed S); school psychology (PhD, Ed S). Part-time and evening/weekend programs available. *Faculty:* 22 full-time (13 women), 6 part-time/adjunct (4 women). *Students:* 172 full-time (135 women), 81 part-time (61 women); includes 59 minority (28 Black or African American, non-Hispanic/Latino; 4 Asian, non-Hispanic/Latino; 22 Hispanic/Latino; 5 Two or more races, non-Hispanic/Latino), 7 international. Average age 30. 243 applicants, 57% accepted, 110 enrolled. In 2011, 70 master's, 15 doctorates, 5 other advanced degrees awarded. *Degree requirements:* For master's, comprehensive exam, thesis (for some programs); for doctorate, comprehensive exam, thesis/dissertation, multiple research methods; philosophies of inquiry (for some programs). *Entrance requirements:* For master's, GRE General Test, minimum GPA of 3.5 in last 60 hours of course work; for doctorate, GRE General Test, MAT, minimum GPA of 3.5 in last 60 hours of course work; for Ed S, GRE General Test. Additional exam requirements/recommendations for international students: Required—TOEFL (minimum score 550 paper-based; 213 computer-based; 79 iBT). *Application deadline:* For fall admission, 1/1 for domestic students, 1/2 for international students. Application fee: $30. Electronic applications accepted. *Financial support:* In 2011–12, 47 students received support, including 6 fellowships with full tuition reimbursements available (averaging $10,000 per year), 6 research assistantships with full tuition reimbursements available (averaging $15,000 per year), 21 teaching assistantships with full tuition reimbursements available (averaging $10,200 per year); career-related internships or fieldwork, scholarships/grants, and unspecified assistantships also available. Financial award application deadline: 1/1; financial award applicants required to submit CSS PROFILE. *Faculty research:* College student affairs, counselor education, educational psychology, school psychology, social foundations. *Total annual research expenditures:* $4.2 million. *Unit head:* Dr. Herbert Exum, Chairperson, 813-974-8395, Fax: 813-974-5814, E-mail: exum@tempest.coedu.usf.edu. *Application contact:* Dr. Kathy Bradley, Program Director, School Psychology, 813-974-9486, Fax: 813-974-5814, E-mail: kbradley@usf.edu. Web site: http://www.coedu.usf.edu/main/departments/psf/psf.html.

University of South Florida–Polytechnic, College of Human and Social Sciences, Lakeland, FL 33803. Offers counselor education (MA), including clinical mental health, professional school counseling; educational leadership (M Ed); reading education (MA).

The University of Tennessee, Graduate School, College of Education, Health and Human Sciences, Department of Educational Psychology and Counseling, Knoxville, TN 37996. Offers adult education (MS); applied educational psychology (MS); collaborative learning (Ed D); college student personnel (MS); mental health counseling (MS); rehabilitation counseling (MS); school counseling (MS). *Accreditation:* ACA (one or more programs are accredited); CORE (one or more programs are accredited); NCATE. Part-time and evening/weekend programs available. *Degree requirements:* For master's, thesis optional. *Entrance requirements:* For master's, GRE General Test, minimum GPA of 2.7. Additional exam requirements/recommendations for international students: Required—TOEFL. Electronic applications accepted. *Expenses:* Tuition, state resident: full-time $8332; part-time $464 per credit hour. Tuition, nonresident: full-time $25,174; part-time $1400 per credit hour. *Required fees:* $1162; $56 per credit hour. Tuition and fees vary according to program.

The University of Tennessee, Graduate School, College of Education, Health and Human Sciences, Program in Education, Knoxville, TN 37996. Offers art education (MS); counseling education (PhD); cultural studies in education (PhD); curriculum (MS, Ed S); curriculum, educational research and evaluation (Ed D, PhD); early childhood education (PhD); early childhood special education (MS); education of deaf and hard of hearing (MS); educational administration and policy studies (Ed D, PhD); educational administration and supervision (Ed S); educational psychology (Ed D, PhD); elementary education (MS, Ed S); elementary teaching (MS); English education (MS, Ed S); exercise science (PhD); foreign language/ESL education (MS, Ed S); instructional technology (MS, Ed D, PhD, Ed S); literacy, language and ESL education (PhD); literacy, language education, and ESL education (Ed D); mathematics education (MS, Ed S); modified and comprehensive special education (MS); reading education (MS, Ed S); school counseling (Ed S); school psychology (PhD, Ed S); science education (MS, Ed S); secondary teaching (MS); social foundations (MS); social science education (MS, Ed S); socio-cultural foundations of sports and education (PhD); special education (Ed S); teacher education (Ed D, PhD). *Accreditation:* NCATE. Part-time and evening/weekend programs available. *Degree requirements:* For master's and Ed S, thesis optional; for doctorate, variable foreign language requirement, thesis/dissertation. *Entrance requirements:* For master's, minimum GPA of 2.7; for doctorate and Ed S, GRE General Test, minimum GPA of 2.7. Additional exam requirements/recommendations for international students: Required—TOEFL. Electronic applications accepted. *Expenses:* Tuition, state resident: full-time $8332; part-time $464 per credit hour. Tuition, nonresident: full-time $25,174; part-time $1400 per credit hour. *Required fees:* $1162; $56 per credit hour. Tuition and fees vary according to program.

The University of Tennessee at Chattanooga, Graduate School, College of Health, Education and Professional Studies, School of Education, Chattanooga, TN 37403-2598. Offers counseling (M Ed), including community counseling, school counseling; education (M Ed, Post-Master's Certificate), including elementary education (M Ed), school leadership, secondary education (M Ed), special education (M Ed); educational specialist (Ed S), including educational technology, school psychology; learning and leadership (Ed D), including educational leadership. *Accreditation:* ACA; NCATE. Part-time and evening/weekend programs available. Postbaccalaureate distance learning degree programs offered (no on-campus study). *Faculty:* 25 full-time (17 women), 10 part-time/adjunct (3 women). *Students:* 145 full-time (104 women), 319 part-time (236 women); includes 63 minority (43 Black or African American, non-Hispanic/Latino; 4 American Indian or Alaska Native, non-Hispanic/Latino; 2 Asian, non-Hispanic/Latino; 6 Hispanic/Latino; 8 Two or more races, non-Hispanic/Latino), 2 international. Average age 34. 226 applicants, 79% accepted, 111 enrolled. In 2011, 120 master's, 9 doctorates, 17 other advanced degrees awarded. *Degree requirements:* For master's, comprehensive exam, thesis optional, culminating experience; for doctorate, comprehensive exam, thesis/dissertation; for other advanced degree, internship. *Entrance requirements:* For master's, GRE General Test, PPST 1, teaching certificate; for doctorate, GRE General Test, master's degree, two years of practical work experience in organizational environment; for other advanced degree, GRE General Test, letters of reference. Additional exam requirements/recommendations for international students: Required—TOEFL (minimum score 550 paper-based; 213 computer-based; 79 iBT), IELTS (minimum score 6). *Application deadline:* For fall admission, 8/1 for domestic students, 6/1 for international students; for spring admission, 12/1 for domestic students, 10/1 for international students. Applications are processed on a rolling basis. Application fee: $35. Electronic applications accepted. *Expenses:* Tuition, state resident: full-time $6472; part-time $359 per credit hour. Tuition, nonresident: full-time $20,006; part-time $1111 per credit hour. *Required fees:* $1320; $160 per credit hour. *Financial support:* Career-related internships or fieldwork, institutionally sponsored loans, scholarships/grants, and unspecified assistantships available. Support available to part-time students. Financial award applicants required to submit FAFSA. *Faculty research:* School counseling, community counseling, elementary and secondary education, school leadership and administration. *Total annual research expenditures:* $675,479. *Unit head:* Dr. John Freeman, Head, 423-425-4133, Fax: 423-425-5380, E-mail: john-freeman@utc.edu. *Application contact:* Dr. Jerald Ainsworth, Dean of Graduate Studies, 423-425-4478, Fax: 423-425-5223, E-mail: jerald-ainsworth@utc.edu. Web site: http://www.utc.edu/Administration/HealthEducationAndProfessionalStudies/Graduate_Studies/graduate_studies.html.

The University of Tennessee at Martin, Graduate Programs, College of Education, Health, and Behavioral Sciences, Program in Counseling, Martin, TN 38238. Offers community counseling (MS Ed); school counseling (MS Ed). *Accreditation:* NCATE. Part-time programs available. Postbaccalaureate distance learning degree programs offered. *Students:* 61 (57 women); includes 8 minority (6 Black or African American, non-Hispanic/Latino; 1 Hispanic/Latino; 1 Two or more races, non-Hispanic/Latino). 37 applicants, 35% accepted, 12 enrolled. In 2011, 11 master's awarded. *Degree requirements:* For master's, comprehensive exam. *Entrance requirements:* For master's, GRE General Test, minimum GPA of 2.5, resume, letters of reference. Additional exam requirements/recommendations for international students: Required—TOEFL (minimum score 525 paper-based; 197 computer-based; 71 iBT). *Application deadline:* For fall admission, 8/1 priority date for domestic students, 7/15 for international students; for spring admission, 12/15 priority date for domestic students, 12/1 for international students. Applications are processed on a rolling basis. Application fee: $30 ($130 for international students). Electronic applications accepted. *Expenses:* Tuition, state resident: full-time $6726; part-time $374 per credit hour. Tuition, nonresident: full-time $19,136; part-time $1064 per credit hour. *Required fees:* $61 per credit hour. *Financial support:* Scholarships/grants and unspecified assistantships available. Support available to part-time students. Financial award application deadline: 2/15; financial award applicants required to submit FAFSA. *Application contact:* Linda S. Arant, Student Services Specialist, 731-881-7012, Fax: 731-881-7499, E-mail: larant@utm.edu.

The University of Texas at Austin, Graduate School, College of Education, Department of Educational Psychology, Austin, TX 78712-1111. Offers academic educational psychology (M Ed, MA); counseling psychology (PhD); counselor education (M Ed); human development, culture and learning sciences (PhD); program evaluation (MA); quantitative methods (M Ed, MA, PhD); school psychology (MA, PhD). *Accreditation:* APA (one or more programs are accredited). *Degree requirements:* For master's, thesis optional; for doctorate, thesis/dissertation. *Entrance requirements:* For master's and doctorate, GRE General Test, 3 letters of recommendation. Additional exam requirements/recommendations for international students: Required—TOEFL. *Application deadline:* For fall admission, 1/15 priority date for domestic students, 1/15 for international students; for spring admission, 10/1 priority date for domestic students, 10/1 for international students. Applications are processed on a rolling basis. Application fee: $50 ($75 for international students). *Financial support:* Fellowships with full and partial tuition reimbursements, research assistantships with partial tuition reimbursements, teaching assistantships with partial tuition reimbursements, career-related internships or fieldwork, Federal Work-Study, institutionally sponsored loans, scholarships/grants, tuition waivers (full and partial), and unspecified assistantships available. Financial award application deadline: 1/15. *Unit head:* Dr. Cindy Carlson, Chair, 512-471-0276, Fax: 512-471-1288, E-mail: ccarlson@austin.utexas.edu. *Application contact:* Diane Schallert, Graduate Adviser, 512-232-4835, E-mail: dschallert@mail.utexas.edu. Web site: http://www.edb.utexas.edu/coe/depts/edp/edp.html.

The University of Texas at Brownsville, Graduate Studies, School of Education, Brownsville, TX 78520-4991. Offers bilingual education (M Ed); counseling and guidance (M Ed); curriculum and instruction (M Ed); early childhood education (M Ed); educational administration (M Ed); educational technology (M Ed); English as a second language (M Ed); reading specialist (M Ed); special education/educational diagnostician (M Ed). Part-time and evening/weekend programs available. Postbaccalaureate distance learning degree programs offered (minimal on-campus study). *Degree requirements:* For master's, thesis optional. *Entrance requirements:* For master's, GRE General Test. Additional exam requirements/recommendations for international students: Required—TOEFL.

The University of Texas at El Paso, Graduate School, College of Education, Department of Educational Psychology and Special Services, El Paso, TX 79968-0001. Offers educational diagnostics (M Ed); guidance and counseling (M Ed); special education (M Ed). Part-time and evening/weekend programs available. *Students:* 289 (250 women); includes 252 minority (9 Black or African American, non-Hispanic/Latino; 1 American Indian or Alaska Native, non-Hispanic/Latino; 2 Asian, non-Hispanic/Latino; 240 Hispanic/Latino), 11 international. Average age 34. 85 applicants, 71% accepted, 53 enrolled. In 2011, 53 master's awarded. *Degree requirements:* For master's, thesis optional. *Entrance requirements:* For master's, minimum GPA of 3.0. Additional exam requirements/recommendations for international students: Required—TOEFL. *Application deadline:* For fall admission, 7/1 priority date for domestic students, 3/1 for international students; for spring admission, 11/1 priority date for domestic students, 9/1 for international students. Applications are processed on a rolling basis. Application fee: $15 ($65 for international students). Electronic applications accepted. *Financial support:* In 2011–12, research assistantships with partial tuition reimbursements (averaging $16,642 per year), teaching assistantships with partial tuition reimbursements (averaging $13,314 per year) were awarded; Federal Work-Study, institutionally sponsored loans, and tuition waivers (partial) also available. Financial award application deadline: 3/15; financial award applicants required to submit FAFSA. *Unit head:* Dr. Don

C. Combs, Interim Chair, 915-747-7585, E-mail: dcombs@utep.edu. *Application contact:* Dr. Benjamin Flores, Interim Dean of the Graduate School, 915-747-5491, Fax: 915-747-5788, E-mail: bflores@utep.edu.

The University of Texas at San Antonio, College of Education and Human Development, Department of Counseling, San Antonio, TX 78249-0617. Offers counseling (MA); counselor education and supervision (PhD). *Accreditation:* ACA. Part-time and evening/weekend programs available. *Faculty:* 18 full-time (9 women), 10 part-time/adjunct (8 women). *Students:* 190 full-time (145 women), 308 part-time (250 women); includes 288 minority (40 Black or African American, non-Hispanic/Latino; 2 American Indian or Alaska Native, non-Hispanic/Latino; 8 Asian, non-Hispanic/Latino; 229 Hispanic/Latino; 1 Native Hawaiian or other Pacific Islander, non-Hispanic/Latino; 8 Two or more races, non-Hispanic/Latino), 10 international. Average age 31. 218 applicants, 81% accepted, 150 enrolled. In 2011, 80 master's, 1 doctorate awarded. *Degree requirements:* For master's, comprehensive exam, thesis optional; for doctorate, comprehensive exam, thesis/dissertation. *Entrance requirements:* For master's, GRE if GPA is below 3.0 on the last 60 hours, minimum of 48 semester credit hours, bachelor's degree with 18 credit hours in field of study or in another appropriate field of study; for doctorate, GRE, minimum GPA of 3.0 in master's-level courses in counseling or in related mental health field; resume; three letters of recommendation; statement of purpose; Counseling Experience Form. Additional exam requirements/recommendations for international students: Required—TOEFL (minimum score 550 paper-based; 79 iBT), IELTS (minimum score 6.5). *Application deadline:* For fall admission, 7/1 for domestic students, 4/1 for international students; for spring admission, 10/1 for domestic students, 9/1 for international students. Applications are processed on a rolling basis. Application fee: $45 ($85 for international students). Electronic applications accepted. *Expenses:* Tuition, state resident: full-time $3148; part-time $2176 per semester. Tuition, nonresident: full-time $8782; part-time $5932 per semester. *Required fees:* $719 per semester. *Financial support:* In 2011–12, 11 students received support, including 11 research assistantships with full tuition reimbursements available (averaging $12,468 per year); scholarships/grants and unspecified assistantships also available. *Faculty research:* Life-threatening behaviors, self-injurious behavior, youth mentoring, relationships/relational competencies and development, addiction counseling. *Unit head:* Dr. Thelma Duffey, Department Chair, 210-458-2600, Fax: 210-458-2605, E-mail: thelma.duffey@utsa.edu. *Application contact:* Dr. Heather Trepal, Graduate Assistant of Record, 210-458-2928, Fax: 210-458-2605, E-mail: heather.trepal@utsa.edu. Web site: http://coehd.utsa.edu/counseling.

The University of Texas of the Permian Basin, Office of Graduate Studies, School of Education, Program in Counseling, Odessa, TX 79762-0001. Offers MA. *Degree requirements:* For master's, comprehensive exam (for some programs), thesis (for some programs). *Entrance requirements:* For master's, GRE General Test. Additional exam requirements/recommendations for international students: Required—TOEFL (minimum score 550 paper-based; 213 computer-based).

The University of Texas–Pan American, College of Education, Department of Educational Psychology, Edinburg, TX 78539. Offers educational diagnostician (M Ed); gifted education (M Ed); guidance and counseling (M Ed); school psychology (MA); special education (M Ed). Part-time and evening/weekend programs available. *Degree requirements:* For master's, comprehensive exam (for some programs), thesis (for some programs). *Entrance requirements:* For master's, GRE General Test, interview. *Application deadline:* For fall admission, 7/17 for domestic students; for spring admission, 11/16 for domestic students. Application fee: $0. Tuition and fees vary according to course load, program and student level. *Financial support:* Research assistantships, career-related internships or fieldwork, Federal Work-Study, and institutionally sponsored loans available. Support available to part-time students. Financial award application deadline: 4/15. *Faculty research:* Reading instruction, assessment practice, behavior interventions consultation, mental retardation. *Unit head:* Dr. Paul Sale, Chair, 956-665-2433, E-mail: psale@utpa.edu. *Application contact:* Dr. Sylvia Ramirez, Associate Dean of Graduate Studies, 956-665-3488, E-mail: ramirezs@utpa.edu. Web site: http://portal.utpa.edu/utpa_main/daa_home/coed_home/edpsy_home.

University of the Cumberlands, Graduate Programs in Education, Williamsburg, KY 40769-1372. Offers all grades (P-12) (M Ed); business and marketing (MA Ed, MAT); director of pupil personnel (Certificate); director of special education (Certificate); educational administration and supervision (Ed S); educational leadership (Ed D); elementary education (MA Ed, MAT); instructional leadership - principalship (MA Ed); instructional leadership - school principal (Certificate); middle school education (MA Ed, MAT); reading and writing (MA Ed); school counseling (MA Ed); school superintendent (Certificate); secondary education (MA Ed, MAT); special education (MAT); supervisor of instruction (Certificate); teacher leader (MA Ed). Part-time and evening/weekend programs available. Postbaccalaureate distance learning degree programs offered. *Degree requirements:* For master's, comprehensive exam. Electronic applications accepted.

University of the District of Columbia, College of Arts and Sciences, Department of Psychology and Counseling, Washington, DC 20008-1175. Offers clinical psychology (MS); counseling (MS). *Degree requirements:* For master's, comprehensive exam, thesis optional, seminar paper. *Entrance requirements:* For master's, GRE General Test, writing proficiency exam. *Expenses: Tuition, area resident:* Full-time $7580; part-time $421 per credit hour. Tuition, state resident: full-time $8580; part-time $477 per credit hour. Tuition, nonresident: full-time $14,580; part-time $810 per credit hour. *Required fees:* $620; $30 per credit hour. $310 per semester.

University of the Southwest, Graduate Programs, Hobbs, NM 88240-9129. Offers business administration (MBA); curriculum and instruction (MSE); curriculum and instruction: bilingual (MSE); curriculum and instruction: TESOL (MSE); early childhood education (MSE); educational administration (MSE); mental health counseling (MSE); school counseling (MSE); special education (MSE); sports management (MBA). Part-time and evening/weekend programs available. Postbaccalaureate distance learning degree programs offered (no on-campus study). *Faculty:* 13 full-time (6 women), 28 part-time/adjunct (17 women). *Students:* 76 full-time (63 women), 229 part-time (194 women); includes 104 minority (50 Black or African American, non-Hispanic/Latino; 2 American Indian or Alaska Native, non-Hispanic/Latino; 8 Asian, non-Hispanic/Latino; 44 Hispanic/Latino). Average age 38. 173 applicants, 71% accepted, 101 enrolled. In 2011, 75 master's awarded. *Degree requirements:* For master's, comprehensive exam, thesis (for some programs). *Entrance requirements:* Additional exam requirements/recommendations for international students: Recommended—TOEFL. *Application deadline:* Applications are processed on a rolling basis. Application fee: $50. Electronic applications accepted. *Expenses: Tuition:* Full-time $12,288; part-time $512 per credit hour. One-time fee: $50. Tuition and fees vary according to course load. *Financial support:* In 2011–12, 47 students received support. Federal Work-Study available. Financial award application deadline: 4/1; financial award applicants required to submit FAFSA. *Unit head:* Dr. Mary Harris, Dean of Education, 575-492-2162, Fax: 575-392-6006, E-mail: mharris@usw.edu. *Application contact:* Melissa Mitchell, Senior Online Program Advisor, 575-492-2142, Fax: 575-392-6006, E-mail: mmitchell@usw.edu. Web site: http://www.usw.edu/admissions/graduate_admission/graduate_admissions.

The University of Toledo, College of Graduate Studies, Judith Herb College of Education, Health Science and Human Service, Department of School Psychology, Legal Specialties and Counselor Education, Toledo, OH 43606-3390. Offers counselor education (MA, PhD); school psychology (MA, Ed S). Part-time programs available. *Faculty:* 17. *Students:* 51 full-time (39 women), 112 part-time (89 women); includes 28 minority (19 Black or African American, non-Hispanic/Latino; 2 Asian, non-Hispanic/Latino; 5 Hispanic/Latino; 2 Two or more races, non-Hispanic/Latino), 5 international. Average age 34. 91 applicants, 54% accepted, 42 enrolled. In 2011, 51 master's, 2 doctorates, 15 other advanced degrees awarded. *Degree requirements:* For master's, comprehensive exam, thesis or alternative; for doctorate, comprehensive exam, thesis/dissertation; for other advanced degree, thesis optional. *Entrance requirements:* For master's, doctorate, and other advanced degree, minimum cumulative GPA of 2.7 for all previous academic work, letters of recommendation. Additional exam requirements/recommendations for international students: Required—TOEFL (minimum score 550 paper-based; 213 computer-based; 80 iBT), IELTS (minimum score 6.5). *Application deadline:* For fall admission, 1/15 priority date for domestic students, 1/15 for international students. Applications are processed on a rolling basis. Application fee: $45 ($75 for international students). Electronic applications accepted. *Financial support:* In 2011–12, 11 teaching assistantships with full and partial tuition reimbursements (averaging $10,682 per year) were awarded; career-related internships or fieldwork, Federal Work-Study, institutionally sponsored loans, scholarships/grants, tuition waivers (full and partial), and unspecified assistantships also available. *Unit head:* Dr. Martin Ritchie, Chair, 419-530-4775, E-mail: martin.ritchie@utoledo.edu. *Application contact:* Graduate School Office, 419-530-4723, Fax: 419-530-4724, E-mail: grdsch@utnet.utoledo.edu. Web site: http://www.utoledo.edu/eduhshs/.

University of Utah, Graduate School, College of Education, Department of Educational Psychology, Salt Lake City, UT 84112. Offers counseling psychology (PhD); educational psychology (MA); elementary education (M Ed); instructional design and educational technology (M Ed); instructional design and technology (M Ed, MS); learning and cognition (MS, PhD); learning sciences (MA); professional counseling (MS); professional psychology (M Ed); reading and literacy (M Ed, PhD); school counseling (M Ed, MS); school psychology (M Ed, MS, PhD); statistics (M Stat). *Accreditation:* APA (one or more programs are accredited). Evening/weekend programs available. Postbaccalaureate distance learning degree programs offered (minimal on-campus study). *Faculty:* 23 full-time (12 women), 9 part-time/adjunct (7 women). *Students:* 104 full-time (85 women), 107 part-time (78 women); includes 26 minority (1 American Indian or Alaska Native, non-Hispanic/Latino; 4 Asian, non-Hispanic/Latino; 17 Hispanic/Latino; 1 Native Hawaiian or other Pacific Islander, non-Hispanic/Latino; 3 Two or more races, non-Hispanic/Latino), 4 international. Average age 32. 213 applicants, 27% accepted, 48 enrolled. In 2011, 39 master's, 9 doctorates awarded. *Median time to degree:* Of those who began their doctoral program in fall 2003, 50% received their degree in 8 years or less. *Degree requirements:* For master's, variable foreign language requirement, comprehensive exam, thesis (for some programs); for doctorate, variable foreign language requirement, thesis/dissertation, oral exam. *Entrance requirements:* For master's and doctorate, GRE General Test, minimum GPA of 3.0. Additional exam requirements/recommendations for international students: Required—TOEFL (minimum score 500 paper-based; 173 computer-based). *Application deadline:* For fall admission, 4/1 for domestic and international students; for spring admission, 11/1 for domestic and international students. Application fee: $55 ($65 for international students). *Expenses:* Contact institution. *Financial support:* In 2011–12, 59 students received support, including 25 fellowships with full and partial tuition reimbursements available (averaging $12,000 per year), 7 research assistantships with full and partial tuition reimbursements available (averaging $12,000 per year), 27 teaching assistantships with full and partial tuition reimbursements available (averaging $12,000 per year); career-related internships or fieldwork, Federal Work-Study, institutionally sponsored loans, scholarships/grants, and unspecified assistantships also available. Financial award application deadline: 2/1; financial award applicants required to submit FAFSA. *Faculty research:* Autism, computer technology and instruction, cognitive behavior, aging, group counseling. *Total annual research expenditures:* $371,256. *Unit head:* Dr. Elaine Clark, Chair, 801-581-7148, Fax: 801-581-5566, E-mail: clark@ed.utah.edu. *Application contact:* Kendra Lee Wiebke, Academic Program Specialist, 801-581-7148, Fax: 801-581-5566, E-mail: kendra.wiebke@utah.edu. Web site: http://www.ed.utah.edu/edps/.

University of Vermont, Graduate College, College of Education and Social Services, Department of Leadership and Developmental Sciences, Counseling Program, Burlington, VT 05405. Offers MS. *Accreditation:* ACA; NCATE. *Faculty:* 3 full-time (2 women), 6 part-time/adjunct (2 women). *Students:* 44 (36 women); includes 1 minority (Hispanic/Latino), 2 international. 62 applicants, 81% accepted, 19 enrolled. In 2011, 13 master's awarded. *Entrance requirements:* For master's, GRE General Test, resume. Additional exam requirements/recommendations for international students: Required—TOEFL (minimum score 550 paper-based; 213 computer-based; 80 iBT). *Application deadline:* For fall admission, 2/1 priority date for domestic students, 2/1 for international students. Applications are processed on a rolling basis. Application fee: $40. Electronic applications accepted. *Financial support:* Fellowships, research assistantships, and teaching assistantships available. Financial award application deadline: 2/1. *Faculty research:* Women and tenure, counseling children and adolescents. *Unit head:* Anne Geroski, Director, 802-656-3888, Fax: 802-656-3173. *Application contact:* Anne Geroski, Coordinator, 802-656-3888. Web site: http://www.uvm.edu/~cslgprog/.

University of Victoria, Faculty of Graduate Studies, Faculty of Education, Department of Educational Psychology and Leadership Studies, Victoria, BC V8W 2Y2, Canada. Offers aboriginal communities counseling (M Ed); counseling (M Ed, MA); educational psychology (M Ed, MA, PhD), including counseling psychology (M Ed, MA), leadership studies (PhD), learning and development (MA, PhD), measurement and evaluation, special education (M Ed, MA); leadership studies (M Ed, MA). Part-time programs available. *Degree requirements:* For master's, thesis (for some programs), comprehensive exam (M Ed); for doctorate, comprehensive exam, thesis/dissertation, candidacy exam. *Entrance requirements:* For master's, 2 years of work experience in a relevant field; for doctorate, GRE, 2 years of work experience in a relevant field, minimum B average. Additional exam requirements/recommendations for international students: Required—TOEFL (minimum score 575 paper-based; 233 computer-based), IELTS (minimum score 7). *Faculty research:* Learning and development (child, adolescent and adult), special education and exceptional children.

University of Virginia, Curry School of Education, Department of Human Services, Program in Counselor Education, Charlottesville, VA 22903. Offers M Ed, Ed S. *Accreditation:* ACA (one or more programs are accredited). *Students:* 16 full-time (14 women); includes 2 minority (1 Asian, non-Hispanic/Latino; 1 Hispanic/Latino). Average age 24. 51 applicants, 55% accepted, 11 enrolled. In 2011, 6 master's awarded. *Entrance requirements:* For master's, GRE General Test, 2 letters of recommendation; for Ed S, GRE General Test. Additional exam requirements/recommendations for international students: Required—TOEFL (minimum score 600 paper-based; 250 computer-based; 90 iBT), IELTS. *Application deadline:* For fall admission, 1/5 for domestic and international students. Applications are processed on a rolling basis. Application fee: $60. Electronic applications accepted. *Financial support:* Applicants required to submit FAFSA. *Unit head:* Sandra I. Lopez-Baez, Program Coordinator, 434-924-0774, E-mail: hlg2n@virginia.edu. *Application contact:* Lynn Renfroe, Information

Contact, 434-924-6254, E-mail: ldr9t@virginia.edu. Web site: http://curry.edschool.virginia.edu/counselor-ed-home-counslered-347?task-view.

University of Virginia, Curry School of Education, Program in Education, Charlottesville, VA 22903. Offers administration and supervision (PhD); applied developmental science (PhD); counselor education (PhD); curriculum and instruction (PhD); early childhood-developmental risk (MT); education evaluation (PhD); educational psychology (PhD); educational research (PhD); elementary (MT, PhD); English education (MT, PhD); foreign language education (MT); higher education (PhD); instructional technology (PhD); kinesiology (MT, PhD); math education (PhD); reading education (PhD); research statistics and evaluation (PhD); school psychology (PhD); science education (PhD); social studies education (MT, PhD); special education (PhD); world languages education (MT). *Students:* 299 full-time (216 women), 60 part-time (33 women); includes 46 minority (18 Black or African American, non-Hispanic/Latino; 17 Asian, non-Hispanic/Latino; 7 Hispanic/Latino; 4 Two or more races, non-Hispanic/Latino), 23 international. Average age 30. 307 applicants, 42% accepted, 80 enrolled. In 2011, 113 master's, 62 doctorates awarded. *Degree requirements:* For master's, comprehensive exam (for some programs), field project; for doctorate, comprehensive exam, thesis/dissertation. *Entrance requirements:* For doctorate, GRE General Test. Additional exam requirements/recommendations for international students: Required—TOEFL (minimum score 600 paper-based; 250 computer-based; 90 iBT), IELTS (minimum score 7). *Application deadline:* Applications are processed on a rolling basis. Application fee: $60. Electronic applications accepted. *Financial support:* Fellowships, research assistantships, and teaching assistantships available. Financial award application deadline: 1/5; financial award applicants required to submit FAFSA. *Unit head:* Robert C. Pianta, Dean, 434-924-3334. *Application contact:* Joanne McNergney, Assistant Dean for Admissions and Student Services, 434-924-3334, E-mail: curry-admissions@virginia.edu.

The University of West Alabama, School of Graduate Studies, College of Education, Departments of Instructional Leadership and Support/Curriculum and Instruction, Program in Guidance and Counseling, Livingston, AL 35470. Offers continuing education (MSCE); guidance and counseling (M Ed). *Accreditation:* NCATE. Part-time and evening/weekend programs available. *Faculty:* 8 full-time (6 women). *Students:* 183 (155 women); includes 136 minority (130 Black or African American, non-Hispanic/Latino; 1 American Indian or Alaska Native, non-Hispanic/Latino; 2 Asian, non-Hispanic/Latino; 3 Hispanic/Latino). In 2011, 116 master's awarded. *Degree requirements:* For master's, comprehensive exam. *Entrance requirements:* For master's, GRE General Test, MAT, minimum GPA of 2.75. Additional exam requirements/recommendations for international students: Required—TOEFL (minimum score 61 computer-based). *Application deadline:* For fall admission, 9/10 priority date for domestic students; for spring admission, 3/21 for domestic students. Applications are processed on a rolling basis. Application fee: $25 ($50 for international students). *Expenses:* Tuition, state resident: full-time $5112; part-time $284 per credit hour. Tuition, nonresident: full-time $10,224; part-time $568 per credit hour. *Required fees:* $180; $40 per semester. One-time fee: $65. Tuition and fees vary according to class time, course load, campus/location and program. *Financial support:* Teaching assistantships, career-related internships or fieldwork, Federal Work-Study, scholarships/grants, and unspecified assistantships available. Support available to part-time students. Financial award application deadline: 3/1. *Unit head:* Dr. Jan Miller, Chair of Instructional Leadership and Support, 205-652-3421, Fax: 205-652-3706, E-mail: jmiller@uwa.edu. *Application contact:* Dr. Kathy Chandler, Dean of Graduate Studies, 205-652-3421, Fax: 205-652-3706, E-mail: kchandler@uwa.edu. Web site: http://www.uwa.edu/msceguidancecounseling.aspx.

University of West Florida, College of Professional Studies, Department of Research and Applied Studies, Pensacola, FL 32514-5750. Offers administration (MSA), including acquisition and contract administration, biomedical/pharmaceutical, criminal justice administration, database administration, education leadership, healthcare administration, human performance technology, leadership, nursing administration, public administration, software engineering and administration; college student personnel administration (M Ed), including college personnel administration, guidance and counseling; curriculum and instruction (M Ed, Ed S); educational leadership (M Ed); middle and secondary level education and ESOL (M Ed). Part-time and evening/weekend programs available. *Faculty:* 2 full-time (both women), 3 part-time/adjunct (2 women). *Students:* 26 full-time (15 women), 13 part-time (9 women); includes 8 minority (4 Black or African American, non-Hispanic/Latino; 2 American Indian or Alaska Native, non-Hispanic/Latino; 1 Hispanic/Latino; 1 Two or more races, non-Hispanic/Latino), 1 international. Average age 26. 51 applicants, 51% accepted, 16 enrolled. In 2011, 17 master's, 49 Ed Ss awarded. *Entrance requirements:* For master's, GRE or MAT, official transcripts; minimum undergraduate GPA of 3.0; letter of intent; three letters of recommendation; resume. Additional exam requirements/recommendations for international students: Required—TOEFL (minimum score 550 paper-based; 213 computer-based). *Application deadline:* For fall admission, 6/1 for domestic and international students; for spring admission, 10/1 for domestic and international students. Applications are processed on a rolling basis. Application fee: $30. *Expenses:* Tuition, state resident: full-time $5729; part-time $302 per credit hour. Tuition, nonresident: full-time $20,059; part-time $961 per credit hour. *Required fees:* $1509; $63 per credit hour. *Financial support:* In 2011–12, 33 fellowships (averaging $860 per year), 10 research assistantships (averaging $3,280 per year), 2 teaching assistantships (averaging $3,760 per year) were awarded; unspecified assistantships also available. Financial award application deadline: 4/15; financial award applicants required to submit FAFSA. *Unit head:* Dr. Joyce Nichols, Chairperson, 850-857-6042, E-mail: jcoleman0@uwf.edu. *Application contact:* Terry McCray, Assistant Director of Graduate Admissions, 850-473-7718, Fax: 850-473-7714, E-mail: gradadmissions@uwf.edu. Web site: http://uwf.edu/pcl/.

University of West Georgia, College of Education, Department of Collaborative Support and Intervention, Carrollton, GA 30118. Offers English to speakers of other languages (Ed S); guidance and counseling (M Ed, Ed S); professional counseling (M Ed, Ed S); professional counseling and supervision (Ed D, Ed S); reading education (M Ed, Ed S); reading endorsement (Ed S); special education-general (M Ed, Ed S); speech-language pathology (M Ed). Part-time and evening/weekend programs available. *Faculty:* 22 full-time (13 women), 6 part-time/adjunct (4 women). *Students:* 174 full-time (140 women), 253 part-time (228 women); includes 155 minority (127 Black or African American, non-Hispanic/Latino; 3 Asian, non-Hispanic/Latino; 14 Hispanic/Latino; 11 Two or more races, non-Hispanic/Latino), 2 international. Average age 33. 282 applicants, 49% accepted, 50 enrolled. In 2011, 98 master's, 27 other advanced degrees awarded. *Degree requirements:* For master's, comprehensive exam; for Ed S, research project. *Entrance requirements:* For master's, minimum GPA of 2.7; for Ed S, master's degree, minimum graduate GPA of 2.7. Additional exam requirements/recommendations for international students: Required—TOEFL (minimum score 523 paper-based; 193 computer-based; 69 iBT); Recommended—IELTS (minimum score 6). *Application deadline:* For fall admission, 6/3 for domestic students, 6/1 for international students; for spring admission, 10/7 for domestic students, 10/15 for international students. Applications are processed on a rolling basis. Application fee: $30. Electronic applications accepted. *Expenses:* Tuition, state resident: full-time $4336; part-time $181 per credit hour. Tuition, nonresident: full-time $17,362; part-time $724 per credit hour. Tuition and fees vary according to course load, degree level, campus/location and program. *Financial support:* In 2011–12, 5 research assistantships with full tuition reimbursements (averaging $3,000 per year) were awarded; career-related internships or fieldwork and scholarships/grants also available. Support available to part-time students. Financial award applicants required to submit FAFSA. *Unit head:* Dr. Michael Garrett, Chair, 678-839-6567, Fax: 678-839-6162, E-mail: mgarrett@westga.edu. *Application contact:* Deanna Richards, Coordinator, Graduate Studies, 678-839-5946, E-mail: drichard@westga.edu. Web site: http://www.westga.edu/coecsi.

University of Wisconsin–Madison, Graduate School, School of Education, Department of Counseling Psychology, Program in Counseling, Madison, WI 53706-1380. Offers MS. *Entrance requirements:* For master's, GRE General Test. *Application deadline:* For fall admission, 12/15 for domestic and international students. Application fee: $56. Electronic applications accepted. *Expenses:* Tuition, state resident: full-time $10,296; part-time $643.51 per credit. Tuition, nonresident: full-time $24,054; part-time $1503.40 per credit. *Required fees:* $70.06 per credit. Tuition and fees vary according to course load, campus/location, program and reciprocity agreements. *Financial support:* Fellowships with full tuition reimbursements, research assistantships with full tuition reimbursements, teaching assistantships with full tuition reimbursements, and project assistantships available. *Unit head:* Dr. Bruce Wampold, Chair, 608-263-9503, E-mail: wampold@education.wisc.edu. *Application contact:* 608-262-2433, Fax: 608-262-5134, E-mail: gradadmiss@mail.bascom.wisc.edu. Web site: http://www.education.wisc.edu/cp.

University of Wisconsin–Milwaukee, Graduate School, School of Education, Department of Educational Psychology, Milwaukee, WI 53201-0413. Offers counseling (school, community) (MS); counseling psychology (PhD); learning and development (MS); research methodology (MS, PhD); school psychology (PhD). *Accreditation:* APA. Part-time programs available. *Faculty:* 15 full-time (9 women), 1 (woman) part-time/adjunct. *Students:* 146 full-time (110 women), 60 part-time (46 women); includes 42 minority (14 Black or African American, non-Hispanic/Latino; 10 Asian, non-Hispanic/Latino; 4 Hispanic/Latino; 14 Two or more races, non-Hispanic/Latino), 11 international. Average age 30. 240 applicants, 52% accepted, 52 enrolled. In 2011, 78 master's, 15 doctorates awarded. *Degree requirements:* For master's, comprehensive exam, thesis; for doctorate, thesis/dissertation. *Entrance requirements:* For master's, minimum GPA of 3.0; for doctorate, GRE General Test, minimum GPA of 3.0. Additional exam requirements/recommendations for international students: Required—TOEFL (minimum score 550 paper-based; 79 iBT), IELTS (minimum score 6.5). *Application deadline:* For fall admission, 1/1 priority date for domestic students; for spring admission, 9/1 for domestic students. Applications are processed on a rolling basis. Application fee: $56 ($96 for international students). Electronic applications accepted. One-time fee: $506.10 full-time. Tuition and fees vary according to course load and reciprocity agreements. *Financial support:* In 2011–12, 14 fellowships, 1 research assistantship, 8 teaching assistantships were awarded; career-related internships or fieldwork, health care benefits, unspecified assistantships, and project assistantships also available. Support available to part-time students. Financial award application deadline: 4/15; financial award applicants required to submit FAFSA. *Total annual research expenditures:* $287,260. *Unit head:* Nadya Fouad, Department Chair, 414-229-6830, Fax: 414-229-4939, E-mail: nadya@uwm.edu. *Application contact:* General Information Contact, 414-229-4982, Fax: 414-229-6967, E-mail: gradschool@uwm.edu. Web site: http://www.uwm.edu/Dept/EdPsych/.

University of Wisconsin–Oshkosh, Graduate Studies, College of Education and Human Services, Department of Professional Counseling, Oshkosh, WI 54901. Offers counseling (MSE). *Accreditation:* ACA. Part-time and evening/weekend programs available. *Degree requirements:* For master's, thesis optional, practicum. *Entrance requirements:* For master's, MAT, interview, minimum GPA of 3.0, letters of recommendation. Additional exam requirements/recommendations for international students: Required—TOEFL (minimum score 550 paper-based; 213 computer-based; 79 iBT). Electronic applications accepted. *Faculty research:* Gender issues, grief and loss, addictions, career development, close relationships.

University of Wisconsin–Platteville, School of Graduate Studies, College of Liberal Arts and Education, Counselor Education Program, Platteville, WI 53818-3099. Offers MSE. *Accreditation:* NCATE. Part-time programs available. *Faculty:* 5 full-time (2 women). *Students:* 45 full-time (37 women), 15 part-time (11 women); includes 5 minority (all Black or African American, non-Hispanic/Latino), 1 international. 11 applicants, 45% accepted. In 2011, 20 master's awarded. *Degree requirements:* For master's, comprehensive exam, thesis or alternative. *Entrance requirements:* Additional exam requirements/recommendations for international students: Required—TOEFL (minimum score 500 paper-based; 61 iBT), IELTS (minimum score 6). *Application deadline:* For fall admission, 7/1 priority date for domestic students; for spring admission, 11/1 for domestic students. Applications are processed on a rolling basis. Application fee: $56. Electronic applications accepted. *Financial support:* Research assistantships with partial tuition reimbursements, career-related internships or fieldwork, Federal Work-Study, institutionally sponsored loans, scholarships/grants, and unspecified assistantships available. Support available to part-time students. Financial award applicants required to submit FAFSA. *Unit head:* Dr. Kimberly Tuescher, Coordinator, 608-342-1252, E-mail: tueschek@uwplatt.edu. *Application contact:* Lisa Popp, School of Graduate Studies, 608-342-1322, Fax: 608-342-1389, E-mail: poppl@uwplatt.edu.

University of Wisconsin–River Falls, Outreach and Graduate Studies, College of Education and Professional Studies, Department of Counseling and School Psychology, River Falls, WI 54022. Offers counseling (MSE); school psychology (MSE, Ed S). Part-time programs available. *Entrance requirements:* For master's, minimum GPA of 2.75, resume, 3 letters of reference, vita. Additional exam requirements/recommendations for international students: Required—TOEFL (minimum score 500 paper-based; 65 iBT), IELTS (minimum score 5.5). Electronic applications accepted.

University of Wisconsin–Stevens Point, College of Professional Studies, School of Education, Program in Guidance and Counseling, Stevens Point, WI 54481-3897. Offers MSE. Program offered jointly with University of Wisconsin–Oshkosh. *Degree requirements:* For master's, comprehensive exam, thesis or alternative.

University of Wisconsin–Superior, Graduate Division, Department of Counseling and Psychological Professions, Superior, WI 54880-4500. Offers community counseling (MSE); human relations (MSE); school counseling (MSE). Part-time and evening/weekend programs available. *Degree requirements:* For master's, position paper, practicum. *Entrance requirements:* For master's, GRE and/or MAT, minimum GPA of 2.75. Electronic applications accepted. *Faculty research:* Women and power, intrafamily dynamics.

University of Wisconsin–Whitewater, School of Graduate Studies, College of Education and Professional Studies, Department of Counselor Education, Whitewater, WI 53190-1790. Offers community counseling (MS Ed); higher education (MS Ed); school (MS Ed). *Accreditation:* ACA; NCATE. Part-time and evening/weekend programs available. *Students:* 86 full-time (72 women), 63 part-time (55 women); includes 17 minority (10 Black or African American, non-Hispanic/Latino; 1 Asian, non-Hispanic/Latino; 6 Hispanic/Latino). Average age 30. 44 applicants, 77% accepted, 16 enrolled. In

2011, 27 master's awarded. *Degree requirements:* For master's, thesis or alternative. *Entrance requirements:* For master's, resume, 2 letters of reference, goal statement, autobiography. Additional exam requirements/recommendations for international students: Required—TOEFL (minimum score 550 paper-based; 213 computer-based; 80 iBT), IELTS (minimum score 6). *Application deadline:* For fall admission, 2/1 for domestic and international students. Application fee: $56. Electronic applications accepted. *Expenses:* Tuition, state resident: full-time $4088. Tuition, nonresident: full-time $8817. Tuition and fees vary according to program. *Financial support:* In 2011–12, 1 research assistantship (averaging $5,175 per year) was awarded; Federal Work-Study, unspecified assistantships, and out of state fee waiver also available. Support available to part-time students. Financial award application deadline: 3/15; financial award applicants required to submit FAFSA. *Faculty research:* Alcohol and other drugs, counseling effectiveness, teacher mentoring. *Unit head:* Dr. Brenda O'Beirne, Coordinator, 262-472-1452, Fax: 262-472-2841, E-mail: obeirneneb@uww.edu. *Application contact:* Sally A. Lange, School of Graduate Studies, 262-472-1006, Fax: 262-472-5027, E-mail: gradschl@uww.edu.

University of Wyoming, College of Education, Programs in Counselor Education, Laramie, WY 82070. Offers community mental health (MS); counselor education and supervision (PhD); school counseling (MS); student affairs (MS). *Accreditation:* ACA (one or more programs are accredited). *Degree requirements:* For master's, comprehensive exam (for some programs), thesis optional; for doctorate, thesis/dissertation, video demonstration. *Entrance requirements:* For master's, interview, background check; for doctorate, video tape session, interview, writing sample, master's degree, background check. Additional exam requirements/recommendations for international students: Required—TOEFL. *Faculty research:* Wyoming SAGE photovoice project; accountable school counseling programs; GLBT issues; addictions; play therapy-early childhood mental health.

Utah State University, School of Graduate Studies, Emma Eccles Jones College of Education and Human Services, Department of Psychology, Logan, UT 84322. Offers clinical/counseling/school psychology (PhD); research and evaluation methodology (PhD); school counseling (MS); school psychology (MS). *Accreditation:* APA (one or more programs are accredited). Part-time and evening/weekend programs available. Postbaccalaureate distance learning degree programs offered (no on-campus study). Terminal master's awarded for partial completion of doctoral program. *Degree requirements:* For master's, thesis (for some programs); for doctorate, thesis/dissertation. *Entrance requirements:* For master's, GRE General Test (school psychology), MAT (school counseling), minimum GPA of 3.5; for doctorate, GRE General Test, minimum GPA of 3.5. Additional exam requirements/recommendations for international students: Required—TOEFL. *Faculty research:* Hearing loss detection in infancy, ADHD, eating disorders, domestic violence, neuropsychology, bilingual/Spanish speaking students/parents.

Valdosta State University, Department of Psychology and Counseling, Valdosta, GA 31698. Offers clinical/counseling psychology (MS); industrial/organizational psychology (MS); school counseling (M Ed, Ed S); school psychology (Ed S). Part-time and evening/weekend programs available. *Faculty:* 17 full-time (6 women). *Students:* 64 full-time (52 women), 60 part-time (48 women); includes 35 minority (25 Black or African American, non-Hispanic/Latino; 1 American Indian or Alaska Native, non-Hispanic/Latino; 3 Asian, non-Hispanic/Latino; 1 Hispanic/Latino; 4 Native Hawaiian or other Pacific Islander, non-Hispanic/Latino; 1 Two or more races, non-Hispanic/Latino). Average age 25. 103 applicants, 52% accepted, 28 enrolled. In 2011, 32 master's awarded. *Degree requirements:* For master's, thesis or alternative, comprehensive written and/or oral exams; for Ed S, thesis. *Entrance requirements:* For master's and Ed S, GRE General Test or MAT. Additional exam requirements/recommendations for international students: Required—TOEFL (minimum score 523 paper-based; 193 computer-based). *Application deadline:* For fall admission, 7/1 for domestic and international students; for spring admission, 11/15 for domestic and international students. Applications are processed on a rolling basis. Application fee: $35. Electronic applications accepted. *Expenses:* Tuition, state resident: full-time $7098; part-time $217 per hour. Tuition, nonresident: full-time $20,630; part-time $780 per hour. *Financial support:* In 2011–12, 6 students received support, including 2 research assistantships with full tuition reimbursements available (averaging $3,652 per year); institutionally sponsored loans and unspecified assistantships also available. Support available to part-time students. Financial award application deadline: 7/1; financial award applicants required to submit FAFSA. *Unit head:* Dr. Robert Bauer, Chair, 229-333-5930, Fax: 229-259-5576, E-mail: bbauer@valdosta.edu. *Application contact:* Jessica DeVane, Coordinator of Graduate Admissions, 229-333-5694, Fax: 229-245-3853, E-mail: jldevane@valdosta.edu.

Valparaiso University, Graduate School, Department of Education, Program in School Counseling, Valparaiso, IN 46383. Offers M Ed/Ed S. *Accreditation:* ACA. Part-time and evening/weekend programs available. *Students:* 5 full-time (4 women). Average age 31. *Entrance requirements:* Additional exam requirements/recommendations for international students: Required—TOEFL (minimum score 550 paper-based; 213 computer-based; 80 iBT). *Application deadline:* For fall admission, 3/1 priority date for domestic students. Applications are processed on a rolling basis. Application fee: $30 ($50 for international students). Electronic applications accepted. *Expenses: Tuition:* Part-time $560 per credit hour. Tuition and fees vary according to course load and program. *Financial support:* Available to part-time students. Applicants required to submit FAFSA. *Unit head:* Dr. David L. Rowland, Dean, Graduate School and Continuing Education/Associate Provost, 219-464-5313, Fax: 219-464-5381, E-mail: david.rowland@valpo.edu. *Application contact:* Dustin Jesch, Coordinator, U.S. Student Engagement, 219-464-5313, Fax: 219-464-5381, E-mail: dustin.jesch@valpo.edu. Web site: http://valpo.edu/grad/psych/masc.php.

Vanderbilt University, Peabody College, Department of Human and Organizational Development, Nashville, TN 37240-1001. Offers community development and action (M Ed); human development counseling (M Ed). *Accreditation:* ACA; NCATE. Part-time programs available. *Faculty:* 26 full-time (15 women), 15 part-time/adjunct (8 women). *Students:* 76 full-time (67 women), 17 part-time (11 women); includes 21 minority (12 Black or African American, non-Hispanic/Latino; 5 Asian, non-Hispanic/Latino; 3 Hispanic/Latino; 1 Two or more races, non-Hispanic/Latino), 2 international. Average age 27. 172 applicants, 53% accepted, 38 enrolled. In 2011, 38 master's awarded. *Degree requirements:* For master's, comprehensive exam, thesis optional. *Entrance requirements:* For master's, GRE General Test, MAT. Additional exam requirements/recommendations for international students: Required—TOEFL (minimum score 550 paper-based; 213 computer-based). *Application deadline:* For fall admission, 12/31 priority date for domestic students, 12/31 for international students; for spring admission, 11/1 priority date for domestic students, 11/1 for international students. Applications are processed on a rolling basis. Application fee: $0. Electronic applications accepted. *Financial support:* Fellowships with full and partial tuition reimbursements, research assistantships with full and partial tuition reimbursements, teaching assistantships with full and partial tuition reimbursements, Federal Work-Study, institutionally sponsored loans, scholarships/grants, tuition waivers (partial), and unspecified assistantships available. Support available to part-time students. Financial award application deadline: 2/1; financial award applicants required to submit FAFSA. *Faculty research:* Community psychology, community development and urban policy, counseling and mental health services, organizational development and institutional change; youth physical and behavioral health in schools and communities. *Unit head:* Dr. Marybeth Shinn, Chair, 615-322-6881, Fax: 615-322-1141, E-mail: marybeth.shinn@vanderbilt.edu. *Application contact:* Sherrie Lane, Educational Coordinator, 615-322-8484, Fax: 615-322-1141, E-mail: sherrie.a.lane@vanderbilt.edu.

Villanova University, Graduate School of Liberal Arts and Sciences, Department of Education and Counseling, Program in Clinical Mental Health Counseling, Villanova, PA 19085-1699. Offers counseling and human relations (MS). Part-time and evening/weekend programs available. *Students:* 30 full-time (19 women), 9 part-time (8 women); includes 1 minority (Black or African American, non-Hispanic/Latino). Average age 28. In 2011, 19 master's awarded. *Degree requirements:* For master's, comprehensive exam. *Entrance requirements:* For master's, GRE or MAT, minimum GPA of 3.0. Additional exam requirements/recommendations for international students: Required—TOEFL. *Application deadline:* For fall admission, 5/1 for international students; for spring admission, 11/15 for international students. Applications are processed on a rolling basis. Application fee: $50. Electronic applications accepted. *Expenses: Tuition:* Part-time $675 per credit. Part-time tuition and fees vary according to degree level and program. *Financial support:* Applicants required to submit FAFSA. *Unit head:* Dr. Edward Fierros, Director, 610-519-4625. *Application contact:* Dean, Graduate School of Liberal Arts and Sciences.

Villanova University, Graduate School of Liberal Arts and Sciences, Department of Education and Counseling, Program in Elementary School Counseling, Villanova, PA 19085-1699. Offers counseling and human relations (MS). Part-time and evening/weekend programs available. *Students:* 9 full-time (8 women), 1 (woman) part-time. Average age 27. In 2011, 11 master's awarded. *Degree requirements:* For master's, comprehensive exam. *Entrance requirements:* For master's, GRE or MAT, minimum GPA of 3.0. Additional exam requirements/recommendations for international students: Required—TOEFL. *Application deadline:* For fall admission, 5/1 for international students; for spring admission, 10/15 for international students. Applications are processed on a rolling basis. Application fee: $50. Electronic applications accepted. *Expenses: Tuition:* Part-time $675 per credit. Part-time tuition and fees vary according to degree level and program. *Financial support:* Career-related internships or fieldwork and Federal Work-Study available. Financial award applicants required to submit FAFSA. *Unit head:* Dr. Edward Fierros, Chair, 610-519-4625. *Application contact:* Dean, Graduate School of Liberal Arts and Sciences.

Villanova University, Graduate School of Liberal Arts and Sciences, Department of Education and Counseling, Program in Secondary School Counseling, Villanova, PA 19085-1699. Offers counseling and human relations (MS). *Students:* 31 full-time (24 women), 3 part-time (2 women); includes 2 minority (1 Hispanic/Latino; 1 Two or more races, non-Hispanic/Latino). Average age 28. In 2011, 23 master's awarded. *Degree requirements:* For master's, comprehensive exam. *Entrance requirements:* For master's, GRE or MAT, minimum GPA of 3.0. *Application deadline:* Applications are processed on a rolling basis. Application fee: $50. Electronic applications accepted. *Expenses: Tuition:* Part-time $675 per credit. Part-time tuition and fees vary according to degree level and program. *Financial support:* Applicants required to submit FAFSA. *Unit head:* Dr. Kenneth M. Davis, Director, 610-519-4634. *Application contact:* Dean, Graduate School of Liberal Arts and Sciences.

Virginia Commonwealth University, Graduate School, School of Education, Program in Counselor Education, Richmond, VA 23284-9005. Offers college student development and counseling (M Ed); school counseling (M Ed). *Accreditation:* ACA; NCATE. *Entrance requirements:* For master's, GRE General Test or MAT. Additional exam requirements/recommendations for international students: Required—TOEFL (minimum score 600 paper-based; 250 computer-based; 100 iBT). Electronic applications accepted. *Expenses:* Tuition, state resident: full-time $9133; part-time $507 per credit. Tuition, nonresident: full-time $18,777; part-time $1043 per credit. *Required fees:* $77 per credit. Tuition and fees vary according to degree level, campus/location, program and student level.

Virginia Polytechnic Institute and State University, Graduate School, College of Liberal Arts and Human Sciences, School of Education, Department of Educational Leadership and Policy Studies, Blacksburg, VA 24061. Offers administration and supervision of special education (Ed D, PhD); counselor education (MA, PhD); educational leadership and policy studies (MA, Ed D, PhD, Ed S); educational research and evaluation (PhD); higher education (MA, PhD). *Accreditation:* ACA; NCATE. *Degree requirements:* For master's, comprehensive exam (for some programs), thesis (for some programs); for doctorate, comprehensive exam (for some programs), thesis/dissertation (for some programs). *Entrance requirements:* For master's and doctorate, GRE. Additional exam requirements/recommendations for international students: Required—TOEFL (minimum score 550 paper-based; 213 computer-based). *Application deadline:* For fall admission, 7/1 for domestic and international students; for spring admission, 12/1 for domestic and international students. Applications are processed on a rolling basis. Application fee: $65. Electronic applications accepted. *Expenses:* Tuition, state resident: full-time $10,048; part-time $558.25 per credit hour. Tuition, nonresident: full-time $19,497; part-time $1083.25 per credit hour. *Required fees:* $405 per semester. Tuition and fees vary according to course load, campus/location and program. *Financial support:* Career-related internships or fieldwork, Federal Work-Study, scholarships/grants, health care benefits, and unspecified assistantships available. Financial award application deadline: 1/15. *Unit head:* Dr. M. David Alexander, Unit Head, 540-231-9723, Fax: 540-231-7845, E-mail: mdavid@vt.edu. *Application contact:* Daisy Stewart, Information Contact, 540-231-8180, Fax: 540-231-7845, E-mail: daisys@vt.edu. Web site: http://www.soe.vt.edu/elps/index.html.

Virginia Polytechnic Institute and State University, Graduate School, College of Liberal Arts and Human Sciences, School of Education, Department of Teaching and Learning, Blacksburg, VA 24061. Offers career and technical education (MS Ed, Ed D, PhD, Ed S); cognition and education (Certificate); counselor education (MA, PhD); curriculum and instruction (MA Ed, Ed D, PhD, Ed S); educational research, evaluation (PhD); higher education administration (Certificate); integrative STEM education (Certificate). *Accreditation:* NCATE. Postbaccalaureate distance learning degree programs offered (no on-campus study). Terminal master's awarded for partial completion of doctoral program. *Degree requirements:* For master's, comprehensive exam (for some programs), thesis (for some programs); for doctorate, comprehensive exam (for some programs), thesis/dissertation (for some programs). *Entrance requirements:* For master's and doctorate, GRE. Additional exam requirements/recommendations for international students: Required—TOEFL (minimum score 550 paper-based; 213 computer-based). *Application deadline:* For fall admission, 7/1 for domestic and international students; for spring admission, 12/1 for domestic and international students. Applications are processed on a rolling basis. Application fee: $65. Electronic applications accepted. *Expenses:* Tuition, state resident: full-time $10,048; part-time $558.25 per credit hour. Tuition, nonresident: full-time $19,497; part-time $1083.25 per credit hour. *Required fees:* $405 per semester. Tuition and fees vary according to course load, campus/location and program. *Financial support:* Career-related internships or fieldwork, Federal Work-Study, scholarships/grants, health care benefits, and unspecified assistantships available. Financial award application deadline:

1/15. *Faculty research:* Instructional technology, teacher evaluation, school change, literacy, teaching strategies. *Unit head:* Dr. Daisy L. Stewart, Unit Head, 540-231-8180, Fax: 540-231-3717, E-mail: daisys@vt.edu. *Application contact:* Daisy Stewart, Contact, 540-231-8180, Fax: 540-231-3717, E-mail: daisys@vt.edu. Web site: http://www.soe.vt.edu/.

Wake Forest University, Graduate School of Arts and Sciences, Counseling Program, Winston-Salem, NC 27109. Offers MA, M Div/MA. *Accreditation:* ACA. *Entrance requirements:* For master's, GRE General Test. Additional exam requirements/recommendations for international students: Required—TOEFL (minimum score 213 computer-based; 79 iBT). Electronic applications accepted.

Walden University, Graduate Programs, School of Counseling and Social Service, Minneapolis, MN 55401. Offers career counseling (MS); counselor education and supervision (PhD), including consultation, counseling and social change, forensic mental health counseling, general program, nonprofit management and leadership, trauma and crisis; human services (PhD), including clinical social work, criminal justice, disaster, crisis and intervention, family studies and intervention strategies, general program, human services administration, public health, social policy analysis and planning; marriage, couple, and family counseling (MS), including forensic counseling, trauma and crisis counseling; mental health counseling (MS), including forensic counseling, trauma and crisis counseling. Part-time and evening/weekend programs available. Postbaccalaureate distance learning degree programs offered (minimal on-campus study). *Faculty:* 26 full-time (19 women), 252 part-time/adjunct (178 women). *Students:* 3,089 full-time (2,614 women), 1,044 part-time (907 women); includes 2,109 minority (1,718 Black or African American, non-Hispanic/Latino; 31 American Indian or Alaska Native, non-Hispanic/Latino; 43 Asian, non-Hispanic/Latino; 236 Hispanic/Latino; 2 Native Hawaiian or other Pacific Islander, non-Hispanic/Latino; 79 Two or more races, non-Hispanic/Latino), 55 international. Average age 39. In 2011, 180 master's, 15 doctorates awarded. *Degree requirements:* For master's, residency (for some programs); for doctorate, thesis/dissertation, residency. *Entrance requirements:* For master's, bachelor's degree or equivalent in related field, minimum GPA of 2.5; for doctorate, master's degree or equivalent in related field; minimum GPA of 3.0; official transcripts; three years' related professional/academic experience (preferred); access to computer and Internet. Additional exam requirements/recommendations for international students: Required—TOEFL (minimum score 550 paper-based; 213 computer-based), IELTS (minimum score 6.5), or Michigan English Language Assessment Battery (minimum score 82). *Application deadline:* Applications are processed on a rolling basis. Application fee: $50. Electronic applications accepted. *Financial support:* Federal Work-Study, scholarships/grants, unspecified assistantships, and family tuition reduction, active duty/veteran tuition reduction, group tuition reduction, interest-free payment plans, employee tuition reduction available. Support available to part-time students. Financial award applicants required to submit FAFSA. *Unit head:* Dr. Savitri Dixon-Saxon, Associate Dean, 800-925-3368. *Application contact:* Jennifer Hall, Vice President of Enrollment Management, 866-4-WALDEN, E-mail: info@waldenu.edu. Web site: http://www.waldenu.edu/Colleges-and-Schools/College-of-Social-and-Behavioral-Sciences/School-of-Counseling-and-Social-Service.htm.

Walsh University, Graduate Studies, Program in Counseling and Human Development, North Canton, OH 44720-3396. Offers clinical mental health counseling (MA); school counseling (MA). *Accreditation:* ACA. Part-time and evening/weekend programs available. *Faculty:* 6 full-time (5 women), 3 part-time/adjunct (2 women). *Students:* 39 full-time (33 women), 40 part-time (26 women); includes 4 minority (2 Black or African American, non-Hispanic/Latino; 1 Hispanic/Latino; 1 Two or more races, non-Hispanic/Latino), 2 international. Average age 29. 39 applicants, 82% accepted, 24 enrolled. In 2011, 21 master's awarded. *Degree requirements:* For master's, comprehensive exam, internship, practicum. *Entrance requirements:* For master's, GRE General Test (minimum score: 900 verbal and quantitative combined) or MAT (400), interview, minimum GPA of 3.0, writing sample, reference forms, moral affidavit. Additional exam requirements/recommendations for international students: Required—TOEFL (minimum score 500 paper-based; 173 computer-based; 61 iBT). *Application deadline:* For fall admission, 7/15 priority date for domestic students. Applications are processed on a rolling basis. Application fee: $25. Electronic applications accepted. *Expenses: Tuition:* Full-time $10,170; part-time $565 per credit hour. *Financial support:* In 2011–12, 40 students received support, including 2 research assistantships with tuition reimbursements available (averaging $5,385 per year), 6 teaching assistantships (averaging $6,215 per year); tuition waivers (partial) and unspecified assistantships also available. Support available to part-time students. Financial award application deadline: 12/31. *Faculty research:* Supervision of clinical mental health counselors, clinical training of clinical mental health counselors, cross-cultural training in counselor education, grief counseling and grief counseling training, refugee mental health and trauma, career counseling for refugees: using ecological and social learning models, social relationships and wellness counseling, outcomes in adventure-based therapies with children, counseling for intimate partner, violence and partner relational issues. *Unit head:* Dr. Linda Barclay, Program Director, 330-490-7264, Fax: 330-490-7323, E-mail: lbarclay@walsh.edu. *Application contact:* Audra Dice, Graduate and Transfer Admissions Counselor, 330-490-7181, Fax: 330-244-4925, E-mail: adice@walsh.edu. Web site: http://www.walsh.edu/counseling-graduate-program.

Washington State University Tri-Cities, Graduate Programs, Program in Education, Richland, WA 99352-1671. Offers counseling (Ed M); educational leadership (Ed M, Ed D); literacy (Ed M); secondary certification (Ed M); teaching (MIT). Part-time programs available. *Faculty:* 24. *Students:* 19 full-time (14 women), 73 part-time (46 women); includes 18 minority (1 Black or African American, non-Hispanic/Latino; 3 Asian, non-Hispanic/Latino; 14 Hispanic/Latino). Average age 34. 26 applicants, 69% accepted, 18 enrolled. In 2011, 31 master's awarded. *Degree requirements:* For master's, comprehensive exam, thesis or alternative; for doctorate, comprehensive exam, thesis/dissertation. *Entrance requirements:* For master's, GRE, minimum GPA of 3.0, Working with Youth form, Character and Fitness form, 3 letters of recommendation. Additional exam requirements/recommendations for international students: Required—TOEFL. *Application deadline:* For fall admission, 1/10 priority date for domestic students, 1/10 for international students; for spring admission, 7/1 priority date for domestic students, 7/1 for international students. Applications are processed on a rolling basis. Application fee: $75. Electronic applications accepted. *Financial support:* In 2011–12, 59 students received support, including research assistantships (averaging $14,634 per year), teaching assistantships (averaging $13,383 per year); Federal Work-Study, scholarships/grants, and unspecified assistantships also available. Financial award application deadline: 2/15. *Faculty research:* Multicultural counseling, socio-cultural influences in schools, diverse learners, teacher education, K-12 educational leadership. *Unit head:* Dr. Elizabeth Nagel, Director, 509-372-7398, E-mail: elizabeth_nagel@tricity.wsu.edu. *Application contact:* Helen Berry, Academic Coordinator, 800-GRADWSU, Fax: 509-372-3796, E-mail: hberry@tricity.wsu.edu. Web site: http://www.tricity.wsu.edu/education/graduate.html.

Wayne State College, School of Education and Counseling, Department of Counseling and Special Education, Program in Guidance and Counseling, Wayne, NE 68787. Offers counseling (MSE); counselor education (MSE); school counseling (MSE). *Accreditation:* NCATE. Part-time and evening/weekend programs available. *Degree requirements:* For master's, comprehensive exam, thesis optional. *Entrance requirements:* For master's, GRE General Test, minimum GPA of 3.0. Additional exam requirements/recommendations for international students: Required—TOEFL (minimum score 550 paper-based; 213 computer-based). Electronic applications accepted.

Wayne State University, College of Education, Division of Theoretical and Behavioral Foundations, Detroit, MI 48202. Offers counseling (M Ed, MA, Ed D, PhD, Ed S); education evaluation and research (M Ed, Ed D, PhD); educational psychology (M Ed, Ed D, PhD, Ed S); educational sociology (M Ed, Ed D, PhD, Ed S); history and philosophy of education (M Ed, Ed D, PhD); rehabilitation counseling and community inclusion (MA, Ed S); school and community psychology (MA, Ed S); school clinical psychology (Ed S). *Accreditation:* ACA (one or more programs are accredited); CORE (one or more programs are accredited). Evening/weekend programs available. *Students:* 199 full-time (156 women), 215 part-time (187 women); includes 162 minority (145 Black or African American, non-Hispanic/Latino; 1 American Indian or Alaska Native, non-Hispanic/Latino; 5 Asian, non-Hispanic/Latino; 5 Hispanic/Latino; 1 Native Hawaiian or other Pacific Islander, non-Hispanic/Latino; 5 Two or more races, non-Hispanic/Latino), 21 international. Average age 35. 278 applicants, 30% accepted, 56 enrolled. In 2011, 94 master's, 15 doctorates, 1 other advanced degree awarded. *Degree requirements:* For master's, thesis (for some programs); for doctorate, thesis/dissertation. *Entrance requirements:* For master's, GRE; for doctorate, GRE, interview, minimum GPA of 3.0, curriculum vitae, references. Additional exam requirements/recommendations for international students: Required—TOEFL (minimum score 550 paper-based; 213 computer-based), TWE (minimum score 5.5). *Application deadline:* For fall admission, 6/1 priority date for domestic students, 5/1 for international students; for winter admission, 10/1 priority date for domestic students, 9/1 for international students; for spring admission, 2/1 priority date for domestic students, 1/1 for international students. Applications are processed on a rolling basis. Application fee: $50. Electronic applications accepted. *Expenses:* Tuition, state resident: part-time $512.85 per credit. Tuition, nonresident: part-time $1132.65 per credit. *Required fees:* $26.60 per credit. $199.65 per semester. Tuition and fees vary according to course load and program. *Financial support:* In 2011–12, 64 students received support, including 3 fellowships with tuition reimbursements available (averaging $16,371 per year), 2 research assistantships with tuition reimbursements available (averaging $15,713 per year), 1 teaching assistantship (averaging $18,000 per year); career-related internships or fieldwork, Federal Work-Study, institutionally sponsored loans, scholarships/grants, health care benefits, and unspecified assistantships also available. *Faculty research:* Adolescents at risk, supervision of counseling. *Total annual research expenditures:* $5,019. *Unit head:* Dr. Alan Hoffman, Assistant Dean, 313-577-5235, E-mail: alanhoffman@wayne.edu. *Application contact:* Janice Green, Assistant Dean, 313-577-1605, E-mail: jwgreen@wayne.edu. Web site: http://coe.wayne.edu/tbf/index.php.

West Chester University of Pennsylvania, College of Education, Department of Counselor Education, West Chester, PA 19383. Offers counseling (Teaching Certificate); elementary school counseling (M Ed); higher education counseling (MS); professional counselor license preparation (Certificate); secondary school counseling (M Ed). *Accreditation:* ACA; NCATE. Part-time and evening/weekend programs available. *Faculty:* 6 full-time (2 women), 18 part-time/adjunct (12 women). *Students:* 115 full-time (101 women), 166 part-time (135 women); includes 31 minority (20 Black or African American, non-Hispanic/Latino; 1 Asian, non-Hispanic/Latino; 7 Hispanic/Latino; 3 Two or more races, non-Hispanic/Latino). Average age 28. 168 applicants, 57% accepted, 80 enrolled. In 2011, 26 master's, 2 other advanced degrees awarded. *Degree requirements:* For master's, comprehensive exam. *Entrance requirements:* For master's, minimum GPA of 3.0, three letters of reference. Additional exam requirements/recommendations for international students: Required—TOEFL (minimum score 550 paper-based; 213 computer-based; 80 iBT). *Application deadline:* For fall admission, 4/15 priority date for domestic students, 3/15 for international students; for spring admission, 10/15 priority date for domestic students, 9/1 for international students. Applications are processed on a rolling basis. Application fee: $45. Electronic applications accepted. *Expenses:* Tuition, state resident: full-time $7488; part-time $416 per credit. Tuition, nonresident: full-time $11,232; part-time $624 per credit. *Required fees:* $1784.64; $67.59 per credit. Tuition and fees vary according to program. *Financial support:* Unspecified assistantships available. Support available to part-time students. Financial award application deadline: 2/15; financial award applicants required to submit FAFSA. *Faculty research:* Teacher and student cognition, adolescent cognitive development, college counseling, motivational interviewing. *Unit head:* Dr. Kathleen Alessandria, Chair, 610-436-2559 Ext. 2550, Fax: 610-425-7432, E-mail: kalessandria@wcupa.edu. *Application contact:* Dr. Matthew Snyder, Graduate Coordinator, 610-436-2559 Ext. 2550, Fax: 610-425-7432, E-mail: msnyder@wcupa.edu. Web site: http://www.wcupa.edu/_academics/sch_sed.counseling&edpsych/.

Western Carolina University, Graduate School, College of Education and Allied Professions, Department of Human Services, Cullowhee, NC 28723. Offers counseling (M Ed, MA Ed, MS), including community counseling (M Ed, MS), school counseling (MA Ed); human resources (MS). *Accreditation:* ACA (one or more programs are accredited). Part-time and evening/weekend programs available. Postbaccalaureate distance learning degree programs offered. *Students:* 114 full-time (87 women), 280 part-time (206 women); includes 44 minority (27 Black or African American, non-Hispanic/Latino; 2 American Indian or Alaska Native, non-Hispanic/Latino; 4 Asian, non-Hispanic/Latino; 8 Hispanic/Latino; 3 Two or more races, non-Hispanic/Latino), 7 international. Average age 35. 224 applicants, 78% accepted, 124 enrolled. In 2011, 125 master's awarded. *Degree requirements:* For master's, comprehensive exam, thesis or alternative. *Entrance requirements:* For master's, GRE General Test, appropriate undergraduate degree with minimum GPA of 3.0, 3 recommendations, writing sample, resume. Additional exam requirements/recommendations for international students: Required—TOEFL (minimum score 550 paper-based; 270 computer-based; 79 iBT). *Application deadline:* For fall admission, 2/1 for domestic students. Applications are processed on a rolling basis. Application fee: $50. *Expenses:* Tuition, state resident: full-time $3348. Tuition, nonresident: full-time $12,933. *Required fees:* $3155. *Financial support:* Fellowships, research assistantships with full and partial tuition reimbursements, teaching assistantships with full and partial tuition reimbursements, career-related internships or fieldwork, institutionally sponsored loans, scholarships/grants, and unspecified assistantships available. Financial award application deadline: 3/31; financial award applicants required to submit FAFSA. *Faculty research:* Marital and family development, spirituality in counseling, home school law, sexuality education, employee recruitment/retention. *Unit head:* Dr. Dale Brotherton, Department Head, 828-227-3284, E-mail: brotherton@email.wcu.edu. *Application contact:* Admissions Specialist for Human Services, 828-227-7398, Fax: 828-227-7480, E-mail: gradsch@email.wcu.edu. Web site: http://www.wcu.edu/3065.asp.

Western Connecticut State University, Division of Graduate Studies, School of Professional Studies, Department of Education and Educational Psychology, Program in School Counseling, Danbury, CT 06810-6885. Offers MS. *Accreditation:* ACA. Part-time programs available. *Faculty:* 5 full-time (2 women). *Students:* 4 full-time (3 women), 32 part-time (29 women); includes 3 minority (1 Asian, non-Hispanic/Latino; 1 Hispanic/Latino; 1 Two or more races, non-Hispanic/Latino). Average age 31. 37 applicants, 19% accepted, 6 enrolled. In 2011, 15 degrees awarded. *Degree requirements:* For master's, practicum, internship, completion of program in 6 years. *Entrance requirements:* For master's, PRAXIS I, minimum GPA of 2.8, 3 letters of reference, essay, 6 hours of psychology. Additional exam requirements/recommendations for international students: Recommended—TOEFL (minimum score 550 paper-based; 213 computer-based; 79 iBT), IELTS (minimum score 6). *Application deadline:* For fall admission, 8/5 priority date for domestic students; for spring admission, 1/5 priority date for domestic students. Applications are processed on a rolling basis. Application fee: $50. Tuition and fees vary according to course level, course load, degree level and program. *Financial support:* Application deadline: 5/1; applicants required to submit FAFSA. *Faculty research:* The effect of affective factors on cognition and learning, statistics and research methods, interviewing, individual and multicultural counseling. *Unit head:* Dr. Kathryn Campbell, Coordinator, 203-837-8513, Fax: 203-837-8413, E-mail: campbellk@wcsu.edu. *Application contact:* Chris Shankle, Associate Director of Graduate Studies, 203-837-9005, Fax: 203-837-8326, E-mail: shanklec@wcsu.edu.

Western Illinois University, School of Graduate Studies, College of Education and Human Services, Department of Counselor Education, Macomb, IL 61455-1390. Offers counseling (MS Ed). *Accreditation:* ACA. Part-time programs available. *Students:* 28 full-time (23 women), 45 part-time (37 women); includes 3 minority (2 Black or African American, non-Hispanic/Latino; 1 Hispanic/Latino). Average age 31. 35 applicants, 17% accepted. In 2011, 37 master's awarded. *Degree requirements:* For master's, thesis or alternative. *Entrance requirements:* For master's, GRE, interview. Additional exam requirements/recommendations for international students: Required—TOEFL (minimum score 550 paper-based; 213 computer-based; 80 iBT). *Application deadline:* Applications are processed on a rolling basis. Application fee: $30. Electronic applications accepted. *Expenses:* Tuition, state resident: part-time $281.16 per credit hour. Tuition, nonresident: part-time $562.32 per credit hour. Part-time tuition and fees vary according to campus/location and reciprocity agreements. *Financial support:* In 2011–12, 8 students received support, including 8 research assistantships with full tuition reimbursements available (averaging $7,360 per year). Financial award applicants required to submit FAFSA. *Unit head:* Dr. Rebecca Newgent, Chairperson, 309-762-1876. *Application contact:* Dr. Nancy Parsons, Assistant Director of Graduate Studies, 309-298-1806, Fax: 309-298-2345, E-mail: grad-office@wiu.edu. Web site: http://wiu.edu/counselored.

Western Kentucky University, Graduate Studies, College of Education and Behavioral Sciences, Department of Counseling and Student Affairs, Bowling Green, KY 42101. Offers counseling (MA Ed), including marriage and family therapy, mental health counseling; school counseling (P-12) (MA Ed); student affairs in higher education (MA Ed). *Accreditation:* ACA; NCATE. Part-time and evening/weekend programs available. *Degree requirements:* For master's, comprehensive exam, thesis optional. *Entrance requirements:* For master's, GRE General Test. Additional exam requirements/recommendations for international students: Required—TOEFL (minimum score 555 paper-based; 213 computer-based; 79 iBT). *Faculty research:* Counselor education, research for residential workers.

Western Michigan University, Graduate College, College of Education and Human Development, Department of Counselor Education and Counseling Psychology, Kalamazoo, MI 49008. Offers counseling psychology (MA, PhD); counselor education (MA, PhD); human resources development (MA). *Accreditation:* ACA (one or more programs are accredited); APA (one or more programs are accredited); CORE; NCATE. *Degree requirements:* For doctorate, thesis/dissertation, oral exams. *Entrance requirements:* For doctorate, GRE General Test.

Western New Mexico University, Graduate Division, School of Education, Silver City, NM 88062-0680. Offers bilingual education (MAT); counseling (MA); educational leadership (MA); elementary education (MAT); reading (MAT); school psychology (MA); secondary education (MAT); special education (MAT); TESOL (teaching English to speakers of other languages) (MAT). *Accreditation:* NCATE. *Degree requirements:* For master's, comprehensive exam. *Entrance requirements:* For master's, GRE General Test, GRE Subject Test, minimum GPA of 3.2 in last 64 hours of undergraduate study. Additional exam requirements/recommendations for international students: Required—TOEFL (minimum score 550 paper-based; 213 computer-based). Electronic applications accepted.

Western Washington University, Graduate School, College of Humanities and Social Sciences, Department of Psychology, Program in School Counseling, Bellingham, WA 98225-5996. Offers M Ed. *Accreditation:* ACA. *Degree requirements:* For master's, comprehensive exam. *Entrance requirements:* For master's, GRE General Test, minimum GPA of 3.0 in last 60 semester hours or last 90 quarter hours. Additional exam requirements/recommendations for international students: Required—TOEFL (minimum score 567 paper-based; 227 computer-based). Electronic applications accepted.

Westfield State University, Division of Graduate and Continuing Education, Department of Psychology, Westfield, MA 01086. Offers applied behavior analysis (MA); mental health counseling (MA); school guidance (MA). Part-time and evening/weekend programs available. *Degree requirements:* For master's, comprehensive exam. *Entrance requirements:* For master's, GRE General Test, MAT, minimum undergraduate GPA of 2.7.

Westminster College, Programs in Education, Program in Guidance and Counseling, New Wilmington, PA 16172-0001. Offers M Ed, Certificate. Part-time and evening/weekend programs available. *Degree requirements:* For master's, comprehensive exam. *Entrance requirements:* For master's, minimum GPA of 3.0.

West Texas A&M University, College of Education and Social Sciences, Division of Education, Program in Counseling Education, Canyon, TX 79016-0001. Offers M Ed. Part-time and evening/weekend programs available. *Degree requirements:* For master's, comprehensive exam, thesis or alternative. *Entrance requirements:* For master's, GRE General Test, interview. Additional exam requirements/recommendations for international students: Required—TOEFL (minimum score 550 paper-based). Electronic applications accepted. *Faculty research:* Reducing the somatoform patient's reliance on primary care through cognitive-relational group therapy, determining effects of premarital sex.

West Texas A&M University, College of Education and Social Sciences, Division of Education, Program in Professional Counseling, Canyon, TX 79016-0001. Offers MA. Part-time programs available. *Degree requirements:* For master's, comprehensive exam. *Entrance requirements:* For master's, GRE General Test, interview, 12 semester hours in education and/or psychology, approval from the Counselor Admissions Committee. Additional exam requirements/recommendations for international students: Required—TOEFL (minimum score 550 paper-based). Electronic applications accepted.

West Virginia University, College of Human Resources and Education, Department of Counseling, Rehabilitation Counseling, and Counseling Psychology, Program in Counseling, Morgantown, WV 26506. Offers MA. *Accreditation:* ACA; APA. *Degree requirements:* For master's, content exams. *Entrance requirements:* For master's, GRE General Test, minimum GPA of 2.8, interview 2.8. Additional exam requirements/recommendations for international students: Required—TOEFL (minimum score 550 paper-based; 213 computer-based; 65 iBT). Electronic applications accepted. *Faculty research:* Career development and placement, family therapy, conflict resolution, interviewing technique, multicultural counseling.

Whitworth University, School of Education, Graduate Studies in Education, Program in Counseling, Spokane, WA 99251-0001. Offers school counselors (M Ed); social agency/church setting (M Ed). *Accreditation:* NCATE. Part-time and evening/weekend programs available. *Degree requirements:* For master's, comprehensive exam, internship, practicum, research project, or thesis. *Entrance requirements:* For master's, GRE General Test, MAT. Tuition and fees vary according to program. *Faculty research:* Church counseling service support.

Wichita State University, Graduate School, College of Education, Department of Counseling, Educational Leadership, Educational and School Psychology, Wichita, KS 67260. Offers counseling (M Ed); educational leadership (M Ed, Ed D); educational psychology (M Ed); school psychology (Ed S). *Accreditation:* NCATE. Part-time and evening/weekend programs available. *Expenses:* Tuition, state resident: full-time $4746; part-time $263.65 per credit. Tuition, nonresident: full-time $11,669; part-time $648.30 per credit. *Unit head:* Dr. Jean Patterson, Chairperson, 316-978-3325, Fax: 316-978-3102, E-mail: jean.patterson@wichita.edu. *Application contact:* Carrie C. Henderson, Admissions Coordinator, 316-978-3095, Fax: 316-978-3253, E-mail: carrie.henderson@wichita.edu. Web site: http://www.wichita.edu/.

Widener University, School of Human Service Professions, Center for Education, Chester, PA 19013-5792. Offers adult education (M Ed); counseling in higher education (M Ed); counselor education (M Ed); early childhood education (M Ed); educational foundations (M Ed); educational leadership (M Ed); educational psychology (M Ed); elementary education (M Ed); English and language arts (M Ed); health education (M Ed); higher education leadership (Ed D); home and school visitor (M Ed); human sexuality (M Ed, PhD); mathematics education (M Ed); middle school education (M Ed); principalship (M Ed); reading and language arts (Ed D); reading education (M Ed); school administration (Ed D); science education (M Ed); social studies education (M Ed); special education (M Ed); technology education (M Ed). *Accreditation:* NCATE. Part-time and evening/weekend programs available. Terminal master's awarded for partial completion of doctoral program. *Degree requirements:* For doctorate, thesis/dissertation. *Entrance requirements:* For master's, minimum GPA of 2.5; for doctorate, GRE or MAT, minimum GPA of 2.0 (undergraduate), 3.5 (graduate). Electronic applications accepted. *Expenses:* Contact institution. *Faculty research:* Reading and cognition, adult education, technology education, educational leadership, special education.

William Paterson University of New Jersey, College of Education, Department of Special Education and Counseling Services, Wayne, NJ 07470-8420. Offers counseling services (M Ed); special education (M Ed). *Accreditation:* NCATE. *Degree requirements:* For master's, comprehensive exam, thesis. *Entrance requirements:* For master's, GRE General Test, MAT, minimum GPA of 2.75, teaching certificate. Electronic applications accepted.

Wilmington University, College of Education, New Castle, DE 19720-6491. Offers applied technology in education (M Ed); career and technical education (M Ed); educational leadership (Ed D); elementary and secondary school counseling (M Ed); elementary studies (M Ed); ESOL literacy (M Ed); higher education leadership (Ed D); instruction: gifted and talented (M Ed); instruction: teacher of reading (M Ed); instruction: teaching and learning (M Ed); organizational leadership (Ed D); school leadership (M Ed); secondary education (MAT); special education (M Ed). *Accreditation:* NCATE. Part-time and evening/weekend programs available. *Faculty:* 7 full-time (4 women). *Students:* 638 full-time (425 women), 2,014 part-time (1,635 women). Average age 33. *Entrance requirements:* For master's, 2 letters of recommendation, interview. Additional exam requirements/recommendations for international students: Required—TOEFL (minimum score 500 paper-based; 173 computer-based). *Application deadline:* For fall admission, 4/30 for domestic students. Applications are processed on a rolling basis. Application fee: $35. Electronic applications accepted. *Expenses: Tuition:* Part-time $534 per credit hour. *Required fees:* $25 per term. *Financial support:* Applicants required to submit FAFSA. *Unit head:* Dr. John C. Gray, Dean, 302-295-1139. *Application contact:* Chris Ferguson, Director of Admissions, 302-356-4636 Ext. 256, Fax: 302-328-5164, E-mail: inquire@wilmcoll.edu. Web site: http://www.wilmu.edu/education/.

Winona State University, College of Education, Counselor Education Department, Winona, MN 55987. Offers community counseling (MS); professional development (MS); school counseling (MS). *Accreditation:* ACA; NCATE. Part-time and evening/weekend programs available. *Students:* 77 full-time (63 women), 26 part-time (23 women); includes 4 minority (2 Black or African American, non-Hispanic/Latino; 1 Asian, non-Hispanic/Latino; 1 Two or more races, non-Hispanic/Latino), 1 international. Average age 30. In 2011, 39 master's awarded. *Degree requirements:* For master's, thesis or alternative. *Entrance requirements:* For master's, letters of reference, interview, group activity, on-site writing. *Application deadline:* For fall admission, 1/15 for domestic students; for spring admission, 9/1 for domestic students. Application fee: $20. Electronic applications accepted. *Financial support:* Fellowships, research assistantships, teaching assistantships, career-related internships or fieldwork, Federal Work-Study, and unspecified assistantships available. Support available to part-time students. Financial award applicants required to submit FAFSA. *Unit head:* Dr. Gayia Borror, Chairperson, 507-285-7137, E-mail: gborror@winona.edu. *Application contact:* Patricia Cichosz, Office Manager, Graduate Studies, 507-457-5038, E-mail: pcichosz@winona.edu. Web site: http://www.winona.edu/counseloreducation.

Winthrop University, College of Education, Program in Counseling and Development, Rock Hill, SC 29733. Offers agency counseling (M Ed); school counseling (M Ed). *Accreditation:* ACA; NCATE. Part-time programs available. *Degree requirements:* For master's, comprehensive exam. *Entrance requirements:* For master's, GRE General Test or MAT, interview. Electronic applications accepted.

Wright State University, School of Graduate Studies, College of Education and Human Services, Department of Human Services, Programs in Counseling, Dayton, OH 45435. Offers counseling (MA, MS), including business and industrial management, community counseling, exceptional children, marriage and family, mental health counseling; pupil personnel services (M Ed, MA), including school counseling. *Accreditation:* ACA (one or more programs are accredited); NCATE. *Degree requirements:* For master's, comprehensive exam, thesis (for some programs). *Entrance requirements:* For master's, GRE General Test, MAT, interview. Additional exam requirements/recommendations for international students: Required—TOEFL.

Xavier University, College of Social Sciences, Health and Education, School of Education, Department of Counseling, Master of Arts in School Counseling Program, Cincinnati, OH 45207. Offers MA. *Accreditation:* ACA. Part-time and evening/weekend programs available. *Faculty:* 5 full-time (2 women), 10 part-time/adjunct (6 women). *Students:* 16 full-time (14 women), 59 part-time (49 women); includes 7 minority (5 Black or African American, non-Hispanic/Latino; 1 American Indian or Alaska Native, non-Hispanic/Latino; 1 Hispanic/Latino). Average age 31. 14 applicants, 79% accepted, 7 enrolled. In 2011, 31 master's awarded. *Degree requirements:* For master's, internship. *Entrance requirements:* For master's, MAT or GRE, minimum GPA of 3.0, letters of recommendation, resume. Additional exam requirements/recommendations for international students: Required—TOEFL (minimum score 550 paper-based; 213 computer-based; 79 iBT). *Application deadline:* For fall admission, 3/1 priority date for domestic students, 3/1 for international students; for winter admission, 4/1 priority date for domestic students, 4/1 for international students; for spring admission, 10/1 priority date for domestic students, 10/1 for international students. Application fee: $35. Electronic applications accepted. *Expenses: Tuition:* Part-time $576 per credit hour. *Financial support:* In 2011–12, 50 students received support. Tuition waivers (partial) and unspecified assistantships available. Financial award applicants required to submit FAFSA. *Faculty research:* Supervision, ethics, consultation, self-injury, bullying. *Unit head:* Dr. Brent Richardson, Chair, 513-745-4294, Fax: 513-745-2920, E-mail: richardb@xavier.edu. *Application contact:* Roger Bosse, Graduate Services Director, 513-745-3357, Fax: 513-745-1048, E-mail: bosse@xavier.edu. Web site: http://www.xavier.edu/school-counseling/.

Xavier University of Louisiana, Graduate School, Programs in Education, New Orleans, LA 70125-1098. Offers curriculum and instruction (MA); education administration and supervision (MA); guidance and counseling (MA). *Accreditation:* NCATE. Part-time and evening/weekend programs available. *Degree requirements:* For master's, comprehensive exam, thesis or alternative. *Entrance requirements:* For master's, GRE General Test, MAT, minimum GPA of 2.5. Additional exam requirements/recommendations for international students: Required—TOEFL.

Youngstown State University, Graduate School, Beeghly College of Education, Department of Counseling, Youngstown, OH 44555-0001. Offers community counseling (MS Ed); school counseling (MS Ed). *Accreditation:* ACA; NCATE. Part-time and evening/weekend programs available. *Degree requirements:* For master's, comprehensive exam. *Entrance requirements:* For master's, MAT, interview, minimum GPA of 2.7. Additional exam requirements/recommendations for international students: Required—TOEFL. *Faculty research:* Suicide, euthanasia, ethical issues, marriage and family.

Developmental Education

Eastern Michigan University, Graduate School, College of Education, Department of Teacher Education, Programs in Educational Psychology and Assessment, Ypsilanti, MI 48197. Offers educational assessment (Graduate Certificate); educational psychology (MA), including development/personality, research and assessment, research and evaluation, the developing learner. *Accreditation:* NCATE. Part-time and evening/weekend programs available. Postbaccalaureate distance learning degree programs offered (minimal on-campus study). *Students:* 2 full-time (both women), 58 part-time (55 women); includes 8 minority (all Black or African American, non-Hispanic/Latino), 3 international. Average age 33. 27 applicants, 74% accepted, 13 enrolled. In 2011, 8 degrees awarded. *Degree requirements:* For master's, thesis or alternative. *Entrance requirements:* For master's, GRE. Additional exam requirements/recommendations for international students: Required—TOEFL. *Application deadline:* Applications are processed on a rolling basis. Application fee: $35. *Expenses:* Tuition, state resident: full-time $10,367; part-time $432 per credit hour. Tuition, nonresident: full-time $20,435; part-time $851 per credit hour. *Required fees:* $39 per credit hour. $46 per semester. One-time fee: $100. Tuition and fees vary according to course level, degree level and reciprocity agreements. *Financial support:* Fellowships, research assistantships with full tuition reimbursements, teaching assistantships with full tuition reimbursements, career-related internships or fieldwork, Federal Work-Study, institutionally sponsored loans, scholarships/grants, tuition waivers (partial), and unspecified assistantships available. Support available to part-time students. Financial award applicants required to submit FAFSA. *Unit head:* Dr. Pat Pokay, Coordinator, 734-487-3260, Fax: 734-487-2101, E-mail: ppokay@emich.edu. *Application contact:* Dr. Anne Bednar, Advisor, 734-487-3260, Fax: 734-487-2101, E-mail: anne.bednar@emich.edu.

Ferris State University, College of Education and Human Services, School of Education, Big Rapids, MI 49307. Offers administration (MSCTE); curriculum and instruction (M Ed), including administration, elementary education, experiential education, philanthropic education, reading, secondary education, special education, subject matter option; education technology (MSCTE); instructor (MSCTE); post-secondary administration (MSCTE); training and development (MSCTE). Part-time and evening/weekend programs available. Postbaccalaureate distance learning degree programs offered (minimal on-campus study). *Faculty:* 9 full-time (7 women), 9 part-time/adjunct (6 women). *Students:* 8 full-time (7 women), 132 part-time (75 women); includes 13 minority (11 Black or African American, non-Hispanic/Latino; 1 American Indian or Alaska Native, non-Hispanic/Latino; 1 Hispanic/Latino), 5 international. Average age 36. 20 applicants, 100% accepted, 8 enrolled. In 2011, 51 master's awarded. *Degree requirements:* For master's, thesis, research paper. *Entrance requirements:* For master's, 2 years of work experience for vocational setting, minimum GPA of 2.75. Additional exam requirements/recommendations for international students: Recommended—TOEFL (minimum score 500 paper-based; 173 computer-based; 61 iBT). *Application deadline:* For fall admission, 7/1 priority date for domestic students, 7/1 for international students; for spring admission, 11/1 priority date for domestic students, 11/1 for international students. Applications are processed on a rolling basis. Application fee: $30. Electronic applications accepted. Application fee is waived when completed online. *Financial support:* Career-related internships or fieldwork and scholarships/grants available. Support available to part-time students. Financial award applicants required to submit FAFSA. *Faculty research:* Suicide prevention, reading, women in education, special needs, administration. *Unit head:* Dr. James Powell, Director, 231-591-5362, Fax: 231-591-2043, E-mail: powelj20@ferris.edu. *Application contact:* Kimisue Worrall, Secretary, 231-591-5361, Fax: 231-591-2043. Web site: http://www.ferris.edu/education/education/.

Grambling State University, School of Graduate Studies and Research, College of Education, Department of Educational Leadership, Grambling, LA 71245. Offers curriculum and instruction (Ed D); developmental education (MS, Ed D), including curriculum and instruction: reading (Ed D), English (MS), guidance and counseling (MS), higher education administration (Ed D), instructional systems and technology (Ed D), mathematics (MS), reading (MS), science (MS), student development and personnel services (Ed D); educational leadership (MS, Ed D). Part-time and evening/weekend programs available. *Degree requirements:* For master's, comprehensive exam, thesis (for some programs); for doctorate, comprehensive exam, thesis/dissertation. *Entrance requirements:* For master's, GRE, minimum GPA of 2.5 on last degree; for doctorate, GRE (minimum 1000, 500 on Verbal), master's degree, minimum GPA of 3.0 on last degree. Additional exam requirements/recommendations for international students: Required—TOEFL (minimum score 500 paper-based; 173 computer-based; 61 iBT). Electronic applications accepted. *Expenses:* Tuition, state resident: full-time $3546; part-time $192 per credit hour. Tuition, nonresident: full-time $3456; part-time $192 per credit hour. *Required fees:* $1829; $1829 per semester hour.

Instituto Tecnológico y de Estudios Superiores de Monterrey, Campus Ciudad Obregón, Programs in Education, Program in Cognitive Development, Ciudad Obregón, Mexico. Offers ME.

National Louis University, College of Arts and Sciences, Chicago, IL 60603. Offers adult education (Ed D); counseling and human services (MS); language and academic development (M Ed, Certificate); psychology (MA, PhD, Certificate); public policy (MA); written communication (MS, Certificate). Part-time and evening/weekend programs available. Postbaccalaureate distance learning degree programs offered (minimal on-campus study). *Students:* 33 full-time (25 women), 466 part-time (388 women); includes 233 minority (176 Black or African American, non-Hispanic/Latino; 1 American Indian or Alaska Native, non-Hispanic/Latino; 12 Asian, non-Hispanic/Latino; 41 Hispanic/Latino; 3 Two or more races, non-Hispanic/Latino). Average age 38. In 2011, 196 master's, 7 doctorates, 48 other advanced degrees awarded. *Degree requirements:* For master's and Certificate, comprehensive exam (for some programs), thesis (for some programs); for doctorate, thesis/dissertation. *Entrance requirements:* For master's, MAT or GRE, 3 professional or academic references, interview, minimum GPA of 3.0; for doctorate, GRE General Test, MAT, or Watson-Glaser Critical Thinking Appraisal, three professional or academic references, statement of academic and professional goals, 3 years of experience in field, interview, master's degree, resume, writing sample; for Certificate, GRE, MAT, or Watson-Glaser Critical Thinking Appraisal, three professional or academic references, statement of academic and professional goals, interview, minimum GPA of 3.0. Additional exam requirements/recommendations for international students: Required—Department of Language Studies Assessment or TOEFL (minimum score 550 paper-based; 213 computer-based; 79 iBT). *Application deadline:* Applications are processed on a rolling basis. Application fee: $40. Electronic applications accepted. *Financial support:* Career-related internships or fieldwork, Federal Work-Study, institutionally sponsored loans, scholarships/grants, and tuition waivers available. Support available to part-time students. Financial award applicants required to submit FAFSA. *Unit head:* Dr. Walter Roettger, Interim Dean, 312-261-3073, Fax: 312-261-3073, E-mail: walter.roettger@nl.edu. *Application contact:* Dr. Ken Kasprzak, Director of Admissions, 888-658-8632, Fax: 847-947-5575, E-mail: kkasprzak@nl.edu.

North Carolina State University, Graduate School, College of Education, Department of Adult and Higher Education, Program in Training and Development, Raleigh, NC 27695. Offers M Ed, Ed D, Certificate. Postbaccalaureate distance learning degree programs offered. *Degree requirements:* For master's, thesis optional. *Entrance requirements:* For master's, GRE General Test or MAT, minimum GPA of 3.0 in major. Electronic applications accepted.

Penn State Harrisburg, Graduate School, School of Behavioral Sciences and Education, Middletown, PA 17057-4898. Offers applied behavior analysis (MA); applied clinical psychology (MA); applied psychological research (MA); community psychology and social change (MA); health education (M Ed); literacy education (M Ed); teaching and curriculum (M Ed); training and development (M Ed). Part-time and evening/weekend programs available. *Financial support:* Career-related internships or fieldwork available. *Unit head:* Dr. Catherine A. Surra, Director, 717-948-6205, Fax: 717-948-6209, E-mail: cas87@psu.edu. *Application contact:* Robert Coffman, Director of Admissions, 717-948-6214, E-mail: rwc11@psu.edu. Web site: http://harrisburg.psu.edu/behavioral-sciences-and-education/.

Rutgers, The State University of New Jersey, New Brunswick, Graduate School of Education, Department of Educational Psychology, Program in Learning, Cognition and Development, Piscataway, NJ 08854-8097. Offers Ed M. Part-time and evening/weekend programs available. *Entrance requirements:* For master's, GRE General Test, 3 letters of recommendation. Additional exam requirements/recommendations for international students: Required—TOEFL (minimum score 550 paper-based; 233 computer-based; 83 iBT). Electronic applications accepted. *Faculty research:* Cognitive development, gender roles, cognition and instruction, peer learning, infancy and early childhood.

Sam Houston State University, College of Education, Department of Educational Leadership and Counseling, Huntsville, TX 77341. Offers administration (M Ed); counseling (M Ed, MA); counselor education (PhD); developmental education administration (Ed D); educational leadership (Ed D); higher education administration (MA); instructional leadership (M Ed, MA). Part-time programs available. *Faculty:* 27 full-time (17 women), 27 part-time/adjunct (14 women). *Students:* 98 full-time (78 women), 474 part-time (378 women); includes 182 minority (101 Black or African American, non-Hispanic/Latino; 10 American Indian or Alaska Native, non-Hispanic/Latino; 8 Asian, non-Hispanic/Latino; 63 Hispanic/Latino), 8 international. Average age 37. 407 applicants, 61% accepted, 194 enrolled. In 2011, 166 master's, 25 doctorates awarded. *Entrance requirements:* For master's, GRE General Test. Additional exam requirements/recommendations for international students: Required—TOEFL (minimum score 550 paper-based; 213 computer-based; 79 iBT). *Application deadline:* For fall admission, 8/1 for domestic students, 6/25 for international students; for spring admission, 12/1 for domestic students, 11/12 for international students. Applications are processed on a rolling basis. Application fee: $45 ($75 for international students). Electronic applications accepted. *Expenses:* Tuition, state resident: full-time $4420; part-time $221 per credit hour. Tuition, nonresident: full-time $10,680; part-time $534 per credit hour. *Required fees:* $329 per credit hour. *Financial support:* Career-related internships or fieldwork, Federal Work-Study, and institutionally sponsored loans available. Support available to part-time students. Financial award application deadline: 5/31; financial award applicants required to submit FAFSA. *Unit head:* Dr. Stacey Edmonson, Chair, 936-294-1752, Fax: 936-294-3886, E-mail: edu_sle01@shsu.edu. *Application contact:* Dr. Stacey Edmondson, Advisor, 936-294-1752, E-mail: sedmonson@shsu.edu. Web site: http://www.shsu.edu/~edu_elc/.

The University of Iowa, Graduate College, College of Education, Department of Teaching and Learning, Program in Elementary Education, Iowa City, IA 52242-1316. Offers curriculum and supervision (MA, PhD); developmental reading (MA); early childhood education and care (MA); elementary education (MA, PhD); language, literature and culture (PhD). *Degree requirements:* For master's, thesis optional, exam; for doctorate, comprehensive exam, thesis/dissertation. *Entrance requirements:* For master's and doctorate, GRE General Test, minimum GPA of 3.0. Additional exam requirements/recommendations for international students: Required—TOEFL (minimum score 550 paper-based; 213 computer-based; 81 iBT). Electronic applications accepted.

The University of Iowa, Graduate College, College of Education, Department of Teaching and Learning, Program in Secondary Education, Iowa City, IA 52242-1316. Offers art education (PhD); curriculum and supervision (PhD); curriculum supervision (MA); developmental reading (MA); English education (MA, MAT); foreign language education (MA, MAT); foreign language/ESL education (PhD); language, literature and culture (PhD); math education (PhD); mathematics education (MA); social studies (MA, PhD). *Degree requirements:* For master's, thesis optional, exam; for doctorate, comprehensive exam, thesis/dissertation. *Entrance requirements:* For master's and doctorate, GRE General Test, minimum GPA of 3.0. Additional exam requirements/recommendations for international students: Required—TOEFL (minimum score 550 paper-based; 213 computer-based; 81 iBT). Electronic applications accepted.

Walden University, Graduate Programs, Richard W. Riley College of Education and Leadership, Minneapolis, MN 55401. Offers administrator leadership for teaching and learning (Ed D, Ed S); adult education (Ed D, Ed S); adult learning (MS, Postbaccalaureate Certificate), including developmental education (MS), online teaching (MS), teaching adults English as a second language (MS), training and performance management (MS); college teaching and learning (Ed D, Ed S, Postbaccalaureate Certificate); curriculum, instruction and assessment (Ed D, Postbaccalaureate Certificate); curriculum, instruction, and professional development (Ed S); developmental education (Postbaccalaureate Certificate); early childhood administration, management, and leadership (Postbaccalaureate Certificate); early childhood education (birth-grade 3) (MAT); early childhood public policy and advocacy (Postbaccalaureate Certificate); early childhood studies (MS), including administration, management and leadership, early childhood public policy and advocacy, teaching adults in the early childhood field, teaching and diversity; education (MS, PhD), including adolescent literacy and technology (grades 6-12) (MS), adult education leadership (PhD), assessment, evaluation, and accountability (PhD), community college leadership (PhD), curriculum, instruction, and assessment, early childhood education (PhD), educational technology (PhD), elementary reading and literacy (MS), elementary reading and mathematics (MS), general program, global and comparative education (PhD), higher education (PhD), integrating technology in the classroom (MS), K-12 educational leadership (PhD), leadership, policy and change (PhD), learning, instruction and innovation (PhD), literacy and learning in the content areas (MS), mathematics (grades 6-8) (MS), mathematics (grades K-5) (MS), middle level education (grades 5-8) (MS), professional development (MS), science (grades K-8) (MS), self-designed (PhD), special education (PhD), special education (non-licensure) (MS), teacher leadership (grades K-12) (MS), teaching English language learners (grades K-12) (MS); educational leadership and administration (principal preparation) (Ed S); educational technology (Ed S); elementary reading and literacy (Postbaccalaureate Certificate); engaging culturally diverse learners (Postbaccalaureate Certificate); enrollment management and institutional marketing (Postbaccalaureate Certificate); higher education (MS), including college teaching and learning, enrollment management and institutional planning, global higher education, leadership for student success, online and distance learning; higher education leadership (Ed D); instructional design (Postbaccalaureate Certificate); instructional design and technology (MS), including general program (MS, PhD), online learning, training and performance improvement; integrating technology in the classroom (Postbaccalaureate Certificate); online teaching for adult learners (Postbaccalaureate Certificate); professional development (Postbaccalaureate Certificate); reading and literacy leadership (Ed D); science K-8 (Postbaccalaureate Certificate); special education (Ed D, Ed S); special education: emotional/behavioral disorders (K-12) (MAT); special education: learning disabilities (K-12) (MAT); teacher leadership (Ed D, Ed S, Postbaccalaureate Certificate); training and performance management (Postbaccalaureate Certificate). Part-time and evening/weekend programs available. Postbaccalaureate distance learning degree programs offered (minimal on-campus study). *Faculty:* 71 full-time (48 women), 853 part-time/adjunct (585 women). *Students:* 11,326 full-time (9,212 women), 2,148 part-time (1,795 women); includes 5,346 minority (4,403 Black or African American, non-Hispanic/Latino; 76 American Indian or Alaska Native, non-Hispanic/Latino; 140 Asian, non-Hispanic/Latino; 561 Hispanic/Latino; 21 Native Hawaiian or other Pacific Islander, non-Hispanic/Latino; 145 Two or more races, non-Hispanic/Latino), 322 international. Average age 39. In 2011, 3,477 master's, 318 doctorates, 471 other advanced degrees awarded. *Degree requirements:* For doctorate, thesis/dissertation (for some programs), residency; for other advanced degree, residency (for some programs). *Entrance requirements:* For master's, bachelor's degree or equivalent in related field; minimum GPA of 2.5; official transcripts; goal statement; access to computer and Internet; for doctorate, master's degree or equivalent in related field; minimum GPA of 3.0; official transcripts; three years' related professional/academic experience (preferred); access to computer and Internet; for other advanced degree, master's degree or equivalent in related field; minimum GPA of 3.0; 3 years related professional/academic experience (preferred); access to computer and Internet (Ed S). Additional exam requirements/recommendations for international students: Required—TOEFL (minimum score 550 paper-based; 213 computer-based), IELTS (minimum score 6.5), or Michigan English Language Assessment Battery (minimum score 82). *Application deadline:* Applications are processed on a rolling basis. Application fee: $50. Electronic applications accepted. *Financial support:* Federal Work-Study, scholarships/grants, unspecified assistantships, and family tuition reduction, active duty/veteran tuition reduction, group tuition reduction, interest-free payment plans, employee tuition reduction available. Support available to part-time students. Financial award applicants required to submit FAFSA. *Unit head:* Dr. Kate Steffens, Dean, 800-925-3368. *Application contact:* Jennifer Hall, Vice President of Enrollment Management, 866-4-WALDEN, E-mail: info@waldenu.edu. Web site: http://www.waldenu.edu/Colleges-and-Schools/College-of-Education-and-Leadership.htm.

English Education

Alabama State University, Department of Curriculum and Instruction, Program in Secondary Education, Montgomery, AL 36101-0271. Offers biology education (M Ed, Ed S); English/language arts (M Ed); history education (M Ed, Ed S); mathematics education (M Ed); secondary education (Ed S); social studies (Ed S). Part-time programs available. *Students:* 16 full-time (12 women), 13 part-time (9 women); includes 26 minority (all Black or African American, non-Hispanic/Latino). Average age 36. 48 applicants, 52% accepted, 5 enrolled. In 2011, 3 master's awarded. *Degree requirements:* For master's, comprehensive exam; for Ed S, comprehensive exam, thesis. *Entrance requirements:* For master's, GRE General Test, MAT, graduate writing competency test; for Ed S, graduate writing competency test, GRE, MAT. Additional exam requirements/recommendations for international students: Required—TOEFL (minimum score 500 paper-based; 173 computer-based). *Application deadline:* For fall admission, 7/15 for domestic students; for spring admission, 12/15 for domestic students. Applications are processed on a rolling basis. Application fee: $10. *Financial support:* In 2011–12, research assistantships (averaging $9,450 per year) were awarded. *Unit head:* Dr. Willa Bing Harris, Acting Chairperson, 334-229-4394, Fax: 334-229-4904, E-mail: wbharris@alasu.edu. *Application contact:* Dr. Doris Screws, Dean of Graduate Studies, 334-229-4274, Fax: 334-229-4928, E-mail: dscrews@alasu.edu. Web site: http://www.alasu.edu/academics/colleges—departments/college-of-education/curriculum—instruction/degree-programs/secondary-education/index.aspx.

Albany State University, College of Arts and Humanities, Albany, GA 31705-2717. Offers English education (M Ed); public administration (MPA), including community and economic development administration, criminal justice administration, general administration, health administration and policy, human resources management, public policy, water resources management; social work (MSW). Part-time programs available. *Faculty:* 13 full-time (6 women). *Students:* 47 full-time (38 women), 38 part-time (22 women); includes 77 minority (all Black or African American, non-Hispanic/Latino), 1 international. Average age 35. 43 applicants, 70% accepted, 23 enrolled. In 2011, 20 master's awarded. *Degree requirements:* For master's, comprehensive exam, professional portfolio (for MPA), internship, capstone report. *Entrance requirements:* For master's, GRE, MAT, minimum GPA of 3.0, official transcript, pre-medical record/certificate of immunization, letters of reference. *Application deadline:* For fall admission, 6/1 for domestic students, 5/1 for international students; for spring admission, 11/1 for domestic students, 10/1 for international students. Applications are processed on a rolling basis. Application fee: $20. Electronic applications accepted. *Expenses:* Tuition, state resident: full-time $3204; part-time $178 per credit hour. Tuition, nonresident: full-time $12,816; part-time $712 per credit hour. *Required fees:* $379 per semester. *Financial support:* Application deadline: 4/15; applicants required to submit FAFSA. *Faculty research:* HIV prevention for minority students . *Total annual research expenditures:* $2,000. *Unit head:* Dr. Leroy Bynum, Dean, 229-430-1877, Fax: 229-430-4296, E-mail: leroy.bynum@asurams.edu. *Application contact:* Jeffrey Pierce, II, Graduate Admissions Counselor, 229-430-4646, Fax: 229-430-4105, E-mail: jeffrey.pierce@asurams.edu. Web site: http://asu-sacs.asurams.edu/ASUCatalog/Graduate/index.html.

Andrews University, School of Graduate Studies, College of Arts and Sciences, Department of English, Berrien Springs, MI 49104. Offers MA, MAT. Part-time programs available. *Faculty:* 10 full-time (4 women), 3 part-time/adjunct (2 women). *Students:* 10 full-time (7 women), 8 part-time (7 women); includes 6 minority (1 Black or African American, non-Hispanic/Latino; 1 Asian, non-Hispanic/Latino; 2 Hispanic/Latino; 1 Native Hawaiian or other Pacific Islander, non-Hispanic/Latino; 1 Two or more races, non-Hispanic/Latino), 6 international. Average age 31. 12 applicants, 83% accepted, 6 enrolled. In 2011, 5 master's awarded. *Degree requirements:* For master's, one foreign language, thesis optional. *Entrance requirements:* For master's, GRE Subject Test. Additional exam requirements/recommendations for international students: Required—TOEFL (minimum score 550 paper-based). *Application deadline:* For fall admission, 8/15 for domestic students. Applications are processed on a rolling basis. Application fee: $40. *Financial support:* Fellowships, research assistantships, teaching assistantships, career-related internships or fieldwork, and Federal Work-Study available. *Faculty research:* Christianity and literature, Victorian literature, social linguistics, rhetoric, American literature. *Unit head:* Dr. Douglas Jones, Chairperson, 269-471-3298. *Application contact:* Carolyn Hurst, Supervisor of Graduate Admission, 800-253-2874, Fax: 269-471-6321, E-mail: graduate@andrews.edu.

Andrews University, School of Graduate Studies, School of Education, Department of Teaching, Learning, and Curriculum, Berrien Springs, MI 49104. Offers curriculum and instruction (MA, Ed D, PhD, Ed S); elementary education (MAT); secondary education (MAT), including biology, education, English, English as a second language, French, history, physics; teacher education (MAT). *Students:* 15 full-time (10 women), 27 part-time (22 women); includes 18 minority (12 Black or African American, non-Hispanic/Latino; 1 Asian, non-Hispanic/Latino; 3 Hispanic/Latino; 1 Native Hawaiian or other Pacific Islander, non-Hispanic/Latino; 1 Two or more races, non-Hispanic/Latino), 10 international. Average age 42. 48 applicants, 48% accepted, 10 enrolled. In 2011, 5 master's, 2 doctorates, 2 other advanced degrees awarded. *Entrance requirements:* For master's, GRE Subject Test. Additional exam requirements/recommendations for international students: Required—TOEFL (minimum score 550 paper-based). *Application deadline:* For fall admission, 8/15 for domestic students. Applications are processed on a rolling basis. Application fee: $40. *Unit head:* Dr. Lee C. Davidson, Chair, 269-471-6364. *Application contact:* Carolyn Hurst, Supervisor of Graduate Admission, 800-253-2874, Fax: 269-471-6321, E-mail: graduate@andrews.edu.

Anna Maria College, Graduate Division, Program in Education, Paxton, MA 01612. Offers early childhood education (M Ed); education (CAGS); elementary education (M Ed); English language arts (M Ed); visual arts (M Ed). Part-time and evening/weekend programs available. *Entrance requirements:* For master's, bachelor's degree in liberal arts or sciences, minimum GPA of 3.0. Additional exam requirements/recommendations for international students: Required—TOEFL (minimum score 500 paper-based). Electronic applications accepted.

Appalachian State University, Cratis D. Williams Graduate School, Department of Curriculum and Instruction, Boone, NC 28608. Offers curriculum specialist (MA); educational media (MA); elementary education (MA); middle grades education (MA), including language arts, mathematics, science, social studies. *Accreditation:* NCATE. Part-time and evening/weekend programs available. Postbaccalaureate distance learning degree programs offered (no on-campus study). *Faculty:* 33 full-time (23 women), 5 part-time/adjunct (2 women). *Students:* 23 full-time (18 women), 110 part-time (90 women); includes 7 minority (4 Black or African American, non-Hispanic/Latino; 1 Asian, non-Hispanic/Latino; 2 Hispanic/Latino). 79 applicants, 94% accepted, 64 enrolled. In 2011, 87 master's awarded. *Degree requirements:* For master's, comprehensive exam, thesis or alternative. *Entrance requirements:* For master's, GRE General Test or MAT, 3 letters of recommendation. Additional exam requirements/recommendations for international students: Required—TOEFL (minimum score 570 paper-based; 230 computer-based; 79 iBT), IELTS (minimum score 6.5). *Application deadline:* For fall admission, 3/14 for domestic students, 2/1 for international students; for spring admission, 11/1 for domestic students, 7/1 for international students. Applications are processed on a rolling basis. Application fee: $55. Electronic applications accepted. *Expenses:* Tuition, state resident: full-time $4040; part-time $180 per semester hour. Tuition, nonresident: full-time $15,900; part-time $760 per semester hour. *Required fees:* $2500; $20 per semester hour. Tuition and fees vary according to campus/location. *Financial support:* In 2011–12, 6 teaching assistantships (averaging $8,000 per year) were awarded; fellowships, research assistantships, career-related internships or fieldwork, Federal Work-Study, scholarships/grants, and unspecified assistantships also available. Financial award application deadline: 4/1; financial award applicants required to submit FAFSA. *Faculty research:* Media literacy, elementary teaching, curriculum development, online learning environments. *Total annual research expenditures:* $480,000. *Unit head:* Dr. Michael Jacobson, Chairperson, 828-262-2224. *Application contact:* Sandy Krause, Director of Admissions and Recruiting, 828-262-2130, Fax: 828-262-2709, E-mail: krausesl@appstate.edu. Web site: http://www.ced.appstate.edu/departments/ci.

Appalachian State University, Cratis D. Williams Graduate School, Department of English, Boone, NC 28608. Offers English (MA); English education (MA). Part-time programs available. Postbaccalaureate distance learning degree programs offered (no on-campus study). *Faculty:* 33 full-time (22 women), 1 part-time/adjunct (0 women). *Students:* 17 full-time (11 women), 4 part-time (3 women); includes 1 minority (Hispanic/Latino). 25 applicants, 68% accepted, 7 enrolled. In 2011, 7 master's awarded. *Degree requirements:* For master's, one foreign language, comprehensive exam, thesis (for some programs). *Entrance requirements:* For master's, GRE General Test, 3 letters of recommendation. Additional exam requirements/recommendations for international students: Required—TOEFL (minimum score 570 paper-based; 230 computer-based; 79 iBT), IELTS (minimum score 6.5). *Application deadline:* For fall admission, 3/15 priority date for domestic students, 2/1 for international students; for spring admission, 11/1 for domestic students, 7/1 for international students. Applications are processed on a rolling basis. Application fee: $55. Electronic applications accepted. *Expenses:* Tuition, state resident: full-time $4040; part-time $180 per semester hour. Tuition, nonresident: full-time $15,900; part-time $760 per semester hour. *Required fees:* $2500; $20 per semester hour. Tuition and fees vary according to campus/location. *Financial support:* In 2011–12, 10 research assistantships (averaging $8,000 per year), 12 teaching assistantships (averaging $8,000 per year) were awarded; fellowships, career-related internships or fieldwork, Federal Work-Study, scholarships/grants, and unspecified assistantships also available. Financial award application deadline: 4/1; financial award applicants required to submit FAFSA. *Faculty research:* Contemporary Irish literature, Romantic psychology, cultural practices of everyday life, Gullah linguistics, Renaissance women's writing. *Total annual research expenditures:* $4,800. *Unit head:* Dr. James Fogelquist, Chair, 828-262-3095, E-mail: fogelquistjd@appstate.edu. *Application contact:* Dr. Susan Staub, Graduate Program Director, 828-262-2335, E-mail: staubsc@appstate.edu. Web site: http://www.english.appstate.edu.

Arcadia University, Graduate Studies, Department of Education, Glenside, PA 19038-3295. Offers art education (M Ed); computer education (CAS); curriculum (CAS); curriculum studies (M Ed); early childhood education (M Ed, CAS), including individualized (M Ed), master teacher (M Ed), research in child development (M Ed); educational leadership (M Ed, Ed D, CAS); elementary education (M Ed, CAS); English education (MA Ed); environmental education (MA Ed, CAS); history education (MA Ed); instructional technology (M Ed); language arts (M Ed, CAS); library science (M Ed); mathematics education (M Ed, MA Ed, CAS); music education (MA Ed); psychology (MA Ed); reading (M Ed, CAS); science education (M Ed, CAS); secondary education (M Ed, CAS); special education (M Ed, Ed D, CAS); theater arts (MA Ed); written communication (MA Ed). *Accreditation:* NASAD. Part-time and evening/weekend programs available. Postbaccalaureate distance learning degree programs offered (minimal on-campus study). *Faculty:* 12 full-time (8 women), 38 part-time/adjunct (26 women). *Students:* 66 full-time (48 women), 590 part-time (477 women); includes 65 minority (53 Black or African American, non-Hispanic/Latino; 6 Asian, non-Hispanic/Latino; 3 Hispanic/Latino; 3 Two or more races, non-Hispanic/Latino), 4 international. Average age 36. In 2011, 229 master's, 5 doctorates awarded. *Application deadline:* Applications are processed on a rolling basis. Application fee: $50. Electronic applications accepted. *Expenses:* Contact institution. *Financial support:* Career-related internships or fieldwork, tuition waivers (partial), and unspecified assistantships available. *Unit head:* Dr. Steven P. Gulkus, Associate Professor, 215-572-2120, E-mail: gulkus@arcadia.edu. *Application contact:* 215-572-2925, Fax: 215-572-2126, E-mail: grad@arcadia.edu.

Arkansas State University, Graduate School, College of Humanities and Social Sciences, Department of English and Philosophy, Jonesboro, State University, AR 72467. Offers English (MA); English education (MSE, SCCT). Part-time programs available. *Faculty:* 19 full-time (6 women). *Students:* 13 full-time (11 women), 22 part-time (16 women); includes 6 minority (5 Black or African American, non-Hispanic/Latino; 1 American Indian or Alaska Native, non-Hispanic/Latino), 4 international. Average age 28. 23 applicants, 70% accepted, 10 enrolled. In 2011, 10 master's awarded. *Degree requirements:* For master's, variable foreign language requirement, comprehensive exam, thesis or alternative, preliminary exam; for SCCT, comprehensive exam. *Entrance requirements:* For master's, GRE General Test or MAT, appropriate bachelor's degree, official transcript, valid teaching certificate (for MSE), immunization records; for SCCT, GRE General Test or MAT, interview, master's degree, official transcript, immunization records. Additional exam requirements/recommendations for international students: Required—TOEFL (minimum score 550 paper-based; 213 computer-based; 79 iBT), IELTS (minimum score 6), Pearson Test of English Academic (minimum score 56). *Application deadline:* Applications are processed on a rolling basis. Application fee: $30 ($40 for international students). Electronic applications accepted. *Expenses:* Tuition, state resident: full-time $4044; part-time $225 per credit hour. Tuition, nonresident: full-time $8087; part-time $449 per credit hour. *Required fees:* $936; $52 per credit hour. $25 per term. One-time fee: $30. Tuition and fees vary according to course load and program. *Financial support:* In 2011–12, 15 students received support. Teaching assistantships, career-related internships or fieldwork, scholarships/grants, and unspecified assistantships available. Financial award application deadline: 7/1; financial award applicants required to submit FAFSA. *Unit head:* Dr. Jerry Ball, Interim Chair, 870-972-3043, Fax: 870-972-3045, E-mail: jball@astate.edu. *Application contact:* Dr. Andrew Sustich, Dean of the Graduate School, 870-972-3029, Fax: 870-972-3857, E-mail: sustich@astate.edu. Web site: http://www.astate.edu/a/chss/departments/ep.dot.

Arkansas Tech University, Center for Leadership and Learning, College of Arts and Humanities, Russellville, AR 72801. Offers English (M Ed, MA); history (MA); liberal arts (MLA); multi-media journalism (MA); psychology (MS); Spanish (MA); teaching English as a second language (MA). Part-time programs available. *Students:* 51 full-time (33 women), 74 part-time (55 women); includes 15 minority (5 Black or African American, non-Hispanic/Latino; 3 American Indian or Alaska Native, non-Hispanic/Latino; 1 Asian, non-Hispanic/Latino; 5 Hispanic/Latino; 1 Two or more races, non-Hispanic/Latino), 22 international. Average age 32. In 2011, 54 master's awarded. *Degree requirements:* For master's, comprehensive exam (for some programs), thesis (for some programs), project. *Entrance requirements:* For master's, GRE General Test or GMAT. Additional exam requirements/recommendations for international students: Required—TOEFL (minimum score 550 paper-based; 213 computer-based; 79 iBT), IELTS (minimum score 6). *Application deadline:* For fall admission, 3/1 priority date for domestic students, 5/1 for international students; for spring admission, 10/1 priority date for domestic students, 10/1 for international students. Applications are processed on a rolling basis. Application fee: $25 ($75 for international students). Electronic applications accepted. *Expenses:* Tuition, state resident: full-time $4968; part-time $207 per credit hour. Tuition, nonresident: full-time $9936; part-time $414 per credit hour. *Required fees:* $375 per semester. Tuition and fees vary according to course load. *Financial support:* In 2011–12, teaching assistantships with full tuition reimbursements (averaging $4,000 per year) were awarded; research assistantships with full tuition reimbursements, career-related internships or fieldwork, Federal Work-Study, scholarships/grants, health care benefits, and unspecified assistantships also available. Support available to part-time students. Financial award application deadline: 4/15; financial award applicants required to submit FAFSA. *Unit head:* Dr. Micheal Tarver, Dean, 479-968-0274, Fax: 479-964-0812, E-mail: mtarver@atu.edu. *Application contact:* Dr. Mary B. Gunter, Dean of Graduate College, 479-968-0398, Fax: 479-964-0542, E-mail: gradcollege@atu.edu. Web site: http://www.atu.edu/lfa/.

Armstrong Atlantic State University, School of Graduate Studies, Program in Education, Savannah, GA 31419-1997. Offers adult education (M Ed); curriculum and instruction (M Ed); early childhood education (M Ed); education (M Ed); elementary education (M Ed); middle grades education (M Ed); secondary education (M Ed), including business education, English education, mathematics education, science education, social science education; special education (M Ed), including behavioral disorders, learning disabilities, speech-language pathology. *Accreditation:* NCATE. Part-time and evening/weekend programs available. Postbaccalaureate distance learning degree programs offered (minimal on-campus study). *Faculty:* 33 full-time (23 women), 3 part-time/adjunct (2 women). *Students:* 97 full-time (91 women), 262 part-time (227 women); includes 83 minority (70 Black or African American, non-Hispanic/Latino; 3 Asian, non-Hispanic/Latino; 8 Hispanic/Latino; 2 Two or more races, non-Hispanic/Latino), 5 international. Average age 34. 169 applicants, 69% accepted, 102 enrolled. In 2011, 227 master's awarded. *Degree requirements:* For master's, comprehensive exam, portfolio. *Entrance requirements:* For master's, GRE General Test or MAT, minimum GPA of 2.5, letters of recommendation. Additional exam requirements/recommendations for international students: Required—TOEFL (minimum score 523 paper-based; 193 computer-based). *Application deadline:* For fall admission, 7/1 priority date for domestic students, 5/1 for international students; for spring admission, 11/15 priority date for domestic students, 9/15 for international students. Applications are processed on a rolling basis. Application fee: $30. Electronic applications accepted. *Expenses:* Tuition, state resident: full-time $3402. Tuition, nonresident: full-time $12,636. *Financial support:* In 2011–12, research assistantships with full tuition reimbursements (averaging $5,000 per year) were awarded; career-related internships or fieldwork, Federal Work-Study, scholarships/grants, and unspecified assistantships also available. Support available to part-time students. Financial award applicants required to submit FAFSA. *Unit head:* Dr. Patricia Wachholz, Dean, College of Education, 912-344-2797, E-mail: patricia.wachholz@armstrong.edu. *Application contact:* Jill Bell, Director, Graduate Enrollment Services, 912-344-2798, Fax: 912-344-3488, E-mail: graduate@armstrong.edu. Web site: http://www.armstrong.edu/Education/coe_deans_office/coe_education_welcome.

Auburn University, Graduate School, College of Education, Department of Curriculum and Teaching, Auburn University, AL 36849. Offers business education (M Ed, MS, PhD); early childhood education (M Ed, MS, PhD, Ed S); elementary education (M Ed, MS, PhD, Ed S); foreign languages (M Ed, MS); music education (M Ed, MS, PhD, Ed S); postsecondary education (PhD); reading education (PhD, Ed S); secondary education (M Ed, MS, PhD, Ed S), including English language arts, mathematics, science, social studies. *Accreditation:* NASM (one or more programs are accredited); NCATE. Part-time programs available. *Faculty:* 22 full-time (17 women), 3 part-time/adjunct (all women). *Students:* 80 full-time (58 women), 181 part-time (126 women); includes 42 minority (28 Black or African American, non-Hispanic/Latino; 7 Asian, non-Hispanic/Latino; 7 Hispanic/Latino). Average age 34. 184 applicants, 53% accepted, 60 enrolled. In 2011, 77 master's, 10 doctorates, 35 other advanced degrees awarded. *Degree requirements:* For master's, thesis (for some programs); for doctorate, thesis/dissertation; for Ed S, field project. *Entrance requirements:* For master's, doctorate, and Ed S, GRE General Test. *Application deadline:* For fall admission, 7/7 for domestic students; for spring admission, 11/24 for domestic students. Applications are processed on a rolling basis. Application fee: $50 ($60 for international students). Electronic applications accepted. *Expenses:* Tuition, state resident: full-time $7290; part-time $405 per credit hour. Tuition, nonresident: full-time $21,870; part-time $1215 per credit hour. *International tuition:* $22,000 full-time. *Required fees:* $1402. *Financial support:* Fellowships, teaching assistantships, career-related internships or fieldwork, and Federal Work-Study available. Support available to part-time students. Financial award application deadline: 3/15; financial award applicants required to submit FAFSA. *Faculty research:* Emerging literacy, reading attitudes, music for at-risk youth, portfolio assessment. *Unit head:* Dr. Kimberly Walls, Head, 334-844-4434. *Application contact:* Dr. George Flowers, Dean of the Graduate School, 334-844-2125. Web site: http://education.auburn.edu/academic_departments/curr/.

Averett University, Master in Education Program, Danville, VA 24541-3692. Offers curriculum and instruction (M Ed); English (M Ed). Program offered at Richmond, VA regional campus location. Part-time and evening/weekend programs available. *Faculty:* 9 full-time (2 women). *Students:* 234 full-time (165 women), 403 part-time (241 women); includes 168 minority (149 Black or African American, non-Hispanic/Latino; 1 American Indian or Alaska Native, non-Hispanic/Latino; 9 Asian, non-Hispanic/Latino; 9 Hispanic/Latino), 1 international. Average age 32. 59 applicants, 59% accepted, 21 enrolled. *Degree requirements:* For master's, 30-credit core curriculum, minimum GPA of 3.0 throughout program, completion of degree requirements within six years from start of program. *Entrance requirements:* For master's, minimum cumulative GPA of 3.0 over the last 60 semester hours of undergraduate study toward a baccalaureate degree. Additional exam requirements/recommendations for international students: Required—TOEFL (minimum score 600 paper-based; 250 computer-based; 100 iBT). *Application deadline:* Applications are processed on a rolling basis. Application fee: $100. *Expenses:* Contact institution. *Financial support:* Career-related internships or fieldwork, Federal Work-Study, and scholarships/grants available. Financial award application deadline: 4/1; financial award applicants required to submit FAFSA. *Unit head:* Dr. Nick Kalafatis, Director of Graduate Education Program, 804-720-4661, E-mail: nkalafat@averett.edu. Web site: http://www.averett.edu/adultprograms/admissions/forms/AVT%20Med_Insert_2-18-11.pdf.

Belmont University, College of Arts and Sciences, Department of Education, Nashville, TN 37212-3757. Offers education (M Ed); elementary education (MAT), including early childhood education, elementary education, language arts education; English (MAT); history (MAT); mathematics (MAT); middle grade education (MAT); science (MAT); secondary education (MAT); special education (MAT); sports administration (MSA). *Accreditation:* NCATE. Part-time and evening/weekend programs available. *Faculty:* 11 full-time (8 women), 23 part-time/adjunct (12 women). *Students:* 83 full-time (77 women), 205 part-time (162 women); includes 50 minority (36 Black or African American, non-Hispanic/Latino; 1 American Indian or Alaska Native, non-Hispanic/Latino; 1 Asian, non-Hispanic/Latino; 7 Hispanic/Latino; 5 Two or more races, non-Hispanic/Latino), 2 international. Average age 30. 83 applicants, 67% accepted, 35 enrolled. In 2011, 169 master's awarded. *Degree requirements:* For master's, thesis (for some programs). *Entrance requirements:* For master's, MAT or GRE and/or GMAT, minimum GPA of 2.75. Additional exam requirements/recommendations for international students: Required—TOEFL. *Application deadline:* For fall admission, 8/1 priority date for domestic students, 6/1 for international students; for spring admission, 12/1 priority date for domestic students, 10/1 for international students. Applications are processed on a rolling basis. Application fee: $50. *Expenses:* Contact institution. *Financial support:* In 2011–12, 30 students received support. Fellowships with partial tuition reimbursements available, teaching assistantships with partial tuition reimbursements available, institutionally sponsored loans, tuition waivers (partial), and unspecified assistantships available. Financial award application deadline: 4/15; financial award applicants required to submit FAFSA. *Faculty research:* Improving secondary literacy, Montessori, classroom management strategies, teacher residency programs, online professional development, mentoring, leadership, faculty development. *Total annual research expenditures:* $2,500. *Unit head:* Dr. Cynthia R. Watkins, Associate Dean, 615-460-6053, Fax: 615-460-5556, E-mail: cynthia.watkins@belmont.edu. *Application contact:* Andrea McClain, Admission/Licensure Officer, 615-460-5483, Fax: 615-460-5556, E-mail: andrea.mcclain@belmont.edu.

Bob Jones University, Graduate Programs, Greenville, SC 29614. Offers accountancy (MS); Bible (MA); Bible translation (MA); Biblical studies (Certificate); broadcast management (MS); business administration (MBA); church history (MA, PhD); church ministries (MA); church music (MM); cinema and video production (MA); counseling (MS); curriculum and instruction (Ed D); divinity (M Div); dramatic production (MA); educational leadership (MS, Ed D, Ed S); elementary education (M Ed, MAT); English (M Ed, MA, MAT); fine arts (MA); graphic design (MA); history (M Ed, MA); illustration (MA); interpretative speech (MA); mathematics (M Ed, MAT); medical missions (Certificate); ministry (MM, D Min); multi-categorical special education (M Ed, MAT); music (M Ed); New Testament interpretation (PhD); Old Testament interpretation (PhD); orchestral instrument performance (MM); organ performance (MM); pastoral studies (MA); personnel services (MS, Ed S); piano pedagogy (MM); piano performance (MM); platform arts (MA); radio and television broadcasting (MS); rhetoric and public address (MA); secondary education (M Ed); studio art (MA); teaching Bible (MA); theology (MA, PhD); voice performance (MM); youth ministries (MA); M Div/MM.

Brooklyn College of the City University of New York, Division of Graduate Studies, School of Education, Program in Adolescence Education and Special Subjects, Brooklyn, NY 11210-2889. Offers adolescence science education (MAT); art teacher (MA); biology teacher (MA); chemistry teacher (MAT); earth science teacher (MAT); English teacher (MA); French teacher (MA); health and nutrition sciences: health teacher (MS Ed); mathematics teacher (MA); music education (CAS); music teacher (MA); physical education teacher (MS Ed); physics teacher (MA); social studies teacher (MA); Spanish teacher (MA). Part-time and evening/weekend programs available. *Degree requirements:* For master's, comprehensive exam (for some programs), thesis (for some programs). *Entrance requirements:* For master's, LAST, previous course work in education, resume, 2 letters of recommendation, essay. Additional exam requirements/recommendations for international students: Required—TOEFL (minimum score 500 paper-based; 173 computer-based; 61 iBT). Electronic applications accepted. *Faculty research:* Interdisciplinary education, semiotics, discourse analysis, autobiography, teacher identity.

Brown University, Graduate School, Department of Education, Program in Teaching, Providence, RI 02912. Offers elementary education (MAT); English (MAT); history/social studies (MAT); science (MAT). *Faculty:* 4 full-time (3 women), 6 part-time/adjunct (all women). *Students:* 36 full-time (30 women); includes 12 minority (3 Black or African American, non-Hispanic/Latino; 2 American Indian or Alaska Native, non-Hispanic/Latino; 4 Asian, non-Hispanic/Latino; 3 Hispanic/Latino). Average age 26. 129 applicants, 60% accepted, 37 enrolled. In 2011, 42 master's awarded. *Degree requirements:* For master's, student teaching, portfolio. *Entrance requirements:* For master's, GRE General Test, transcript, personal statement, 3 letters of recommendation, interview, writing sample (English applicants only). Additional exam requirements/recommendations for international students: Required—TOEFL (minimum score 577 paper-based; 90 computer-based). *Application deadline:* For winter admission, 1/15 for domestic and international students. Application fee: $75. Electronic applications accepted. *Financial support:* In 2011–12, 28 students received support. Federal Work-Study, institutionally sponsored loans, scholarships/grants, and tuition waivers (partial) available. Financial award application deadline: 2/1; financial award applicants required to submit FAFSA. *Faculty research:* Literacy, English language learners, diversity, special education, biodiversity. *Unit head:* Laura Snyder, Director of Graduate Study for the MAT Program, 401-863-2407. *Application contact:* Carin Algava, Assistant Director of Teacher Education, 401-863-3364, Fax: 401-863-1276, E-mail: carin_algava@brown.edu. Web site: http://www.brown.edu/Departments/Education/TE/.

Buffalo State College, State University of New York, The Graduate School, Faculty of Arts and Humanities, Department of English, Buffalo, NY 14222-1095. Offers English (MA); secondary education (MS Ed), including English. Part-time and evening/weekend programs available. *Degree requirements:* For master's, thesis or project, 1 foreign language (MS Ed). *Entrance requirements:* For master's, minimum GPA of 2.75, 36 hours in English, New York teaching certificate (MS Ed). Additional exam requirements/recommendations for international students: Required—TOEFL (minimum score 550 paper-based; 213 computer-based).

California Baptist University, Program in English, Riverside, CA 92504-3206. Offers English pedagogy (MA); literature (MA); teaching English to speakers of other languages (TESOL) (MA). Part-time and evening/weekend programs available. *Faculty:* 8 full-time (5 women). *Students:* 27 full-time (20 women); includes 6 minority (all Hispanic/Latino), 5 international. Average age 30. 15 applicants, 53% accepted, 8 enrolled. In 2011, 6 master's awarded. *Degree requirements:* For master's, comprehensive exam or thesis. *Entrance requirements:* For master's, minimum undergraduate GPA of 3.0; 18 semester hours of course work in English beyond freshman level; three recommendations; essay; demonstration of writing; interview. Additional exam requirements/recommendations for international students: Required—TOEFL (minimum score 575 paper-based; 230 computer-based; 89 iBT). *Application deadline:* For fall admission, 8/1 priority date for domestic students, 7/1 for international students; for spring admission, 12/1 priority date for domestic students, 11/1 for international students. Applications are processed on a rolling basis. Application fee: $45. Electronic applications accepted. *Expenses:* Contact institution. *Financial support:* Federal Work-Study and institutionally sponsored loans available. Financial award applicants required to submit FAFSA. *Faculty research:* Science fiction and fantasy literature, Latin American literature, mythology and folklore, Native American literature, comparative literature. *Unit head:* Dr. James Lu, Chair, Department of Modern Languages and Literature, 951-343-4277, E-mail: jlu@calbaptist.edu. *Application contact:* Dr. Jennifer Newton, Director, Master of Art Program in English, 951-343-4276, Fax: 951-343-4661, E-mail: jnewton@calbaptist.edu. Web site: http://www.calbaptist.edu/maenglish/.

California State University, Northridge, Graduate Studies, College of Education, Department of Secondary Education, Northridge, CA 91330. Offers educational technology (MA); English education (MA); mathematics education (MA); secondary science education (MA); teaching and learning (MA). *Accreditation:* NCATE. Part-time programs available. *Degree requirements:* For master's, thesis optional. *Entrance requirements:* For master's, GRE General Test or minimum GPA of 3.0. Additional exam requirements/recommendations for international students: Required—TOEFL.

California State University, San Bernardino, Graduate Studies, College of Education, San Bernardino, CA 92407-2397. Offers bilingual/cross-cultural education (MA); curriculum and instruction (MA); educational administration (MA); educational leadership and curriculum (Ed D); educational psychology and counseling (MA, MS), including correctional and alternative education (MA), counseling and guidance (MS), rehabilitation counseling (MA); English as a second language (MA); general education (MA); history and English for secondary teachers (MA); instructional technology (MA); reading (MA); secondary education (MA); special education and rehabilitation counseling (MA), including rehabilitation counseling, special education; teaching of science (MA); vocational and career education (MA). *Accreditation:* NCATE. Part-time and evening/weekend programs available. *Students:* 434 full-time (335 women), 188 part-time (139 women); includes 271 minority (54 Black or African American, non-Hispanic/Latino; 2 American Indian or Alaska Native, non-Hispanic/Latino; 29 Asian, non-Hispanic/Latino; 172 Hispanic/Latino; 2 Native Hawaiian or other Pacific Islander, non-Hispanic/Latino; 12 Two or more races, non-Hispanic/Latino), 28 international. Average age 32. 382 applicants, 61% accepted, 186 enrolled. In 2011, 279 master's awarded. *Degree requirements:* For master's, comprehensive exam (for some programs), thesis (for some programs), advancement to candidacy. *Entrance requirements:* For master's, minimum GPA of 3.0 in education. *Application deadline:* For fall admission, 8/31 priority date for domestic students. Application fee: $55. *Expenses:* Tuition, state resident: full-time $7356. Tuition, nonresident: full-time $7356. *Required fees:* $1077. Tuition and fees vary according to program. *Financial support:* Career-related internships or fieldwork and Federal Work-Study available. Support available to part-time students. *Faculty research:* Multicultural education, brain-based learning, science education, social studies/global education. *Unit head:* Dr. Patricia Arlin, Dean, 909-537-5600, Fax: 909-537-7011, E-mail: parlin@csusb.edu. *Application contact:* Olivia Rosas, Director of Admissions, 909-537-7577, Fax: 909-537-7034, E-mail: orosas@csusb.edu.

Campbell University, Graduate and Professional Programs, School of Education, Buies Creek, NC 27506. Offers administration (MSA); community counseling (MA); elementary education (M Ed); English education (M Ed); interdisciplinary studies (M Ed); mathematics education (M Ed); middle grades education (M Ed); physical education (M Ed); school counseling (M Ed); secondary education (M Ed); social science education (M Ed). *Accreditation:* NCATE. Part-time and evening/weekend programs available. *Degree requirements:* For master's, comprehensive exam. *Entrance requirements:* For master's, GRE General Test, minimum GPA of 2.7. *Faculty research:* Spiritual values and wellness issues in counseling, stress and professional burnout among counselors, thinking strategies, leadership, adaptive technology.

Caribbean University, Graduate School, Bayamón, PR 00960-0493. Offers administration and supervision (MA Ed); criminal justice (MA); curriculum and instruction (MA Ed, PhD), including elementary education (MA Ed), English education (MA Ed), history education (MA Ed), mathematics education (MA Ed), primary education (MA Ed), science education (MA Ed), Spanish education (MA Ed); educational technology in instructional systems (MA Ed); gerontology (MSN); human resources (MBA); museology, archiving and art history (MA Ed); neonatal pediatrics (MSN); physical education (MA Ed); special education (MA Ed). *Entrance requirements:* For master's, interview, minimum GPA of 2.5.

Carthage College, Division of Teacher Education, Kenosha, WI 53140. Offers classroom guidance and counseling (M Ed); creative arts (M Ed); gifted and talented children (M Ed); language arts (M Ed); modern language (M Ed); natural sciences (M Ed); reading (M Ed, Certificate); social sciences (M Ed); teacher leadership (M Ed). Part-time and evening/weekend programs available. *Degree requirements:* For master's, thesis optional. *Entrance requirements:* For master's, MAT, minimum B average, letters of reference.

Chadron State College, School of Professional and Graduate Studies, Department of Education, Chadron, NE 69337. Offers business (MA Ed); community counseling (MA Ed); educational administration (MS Ed, Sp Ed); elementary education (MS Ed); history (MA Ed); language and literature (MA Ed); secondary administration (MS Ed); secondary education (MS Ed). *Accreditation:* NCATE. Part-time and evening/weekend programs available. Postbaccalaureate distance learning degree programs offered. *Degree requirements:* For master's, thesis optional. *Entrance requirements:* For master's, GRE General Test, GRE Writing Test, minimum GPA of 2.75 or 12 graduate hours at CSC with minimum GPA of 3.25. Additional exam requirements/recommendations for international students: Required—TOEFL. Electronic applications accepted. *Faculty research:* Rural education, technology, mental health.

Chaminade University of Honolulu, Graduate Services, Program in Education, Honolulu, HI 96816-1578. Offers child development (M Ed); educational leadership (M Ed); elementary education with licensure (MAT); instructional leadership (M Ed); Montessori credential (M Ed); Montessori emphasis (M Ed); secondary education with licensure (MAT), including English, math, science, social studies; special education with licensure (MAT). Part-time and evening/weekend programs available. Postbaccalaureate distance learning degree programs offered (minimal on-campus study). *Faculty:* 2 full-time (both women), 32 part-time/adjunct (25 women). *Students:* 53 full-time (38 women), 88 part-time (67 women); includes 77 minority (6 Black or African American, non-Hispanic/Latino; 1 American Indian or Alaska Native, non-Hispanic/Latino; 44 Asian, non-Hispanic/Latino; 5 Hispanic/Latino; 17 Native Hawaiian or other Pacific Islander, non-Hispanic/Latino; 4 Two or more races, non-Hispanic/Latino), 1 international. Average age 35. 40 applicants, 88% accepted, 30 enrolled. In 2011, 105 master's awarded. *Degree requirements:* For master's, thesis or alternative. *Entrance requirements:* For master's, PRAXIS (for MAT only), minimum GPA of 2.75, 3 letters of recommendation. Additional exam requirements/recommendations for international students: Required—TOEFL (minimum score 550 paper-based). *Application deadline:* For fall admission, 9/1 priority date for domestic students, 9/1 for international students; for winter admission, 12/1 priority date for domestic students, 12/1 for international students; for spring admission, 3/1 priority date for domestic students, 3/1 for international students. Applications are processed on a rolling basis. Application fee: $50. Electronic applications accepted. *Expenses: Required fees:* $600 per credit hour. One-time fee: $93 part-time. *Financial support:* In 2011–12, 172 students received support. Career-related internships or fieldwork, Federal Work-Study, institutionally sponsored loans, scholarships/grants, and tuition waivers (partial) available. Support available to part-time students. Financial award application deadline: 3/1; financial award applicants required to submit FAFSA. *Faculty research:* Peace and curriculum education. *Unit head:* Dr. Joseph Peters, Dean, 808-440-4251, Fax: 808-739-4607, E-mail: joseph.peters@chaminade.edu. *Application contact:* 808-739-4663, Fax: 808-739-8329, E-mail: gradserv@chaminade.edu. Web site: http://www.chaminade.edu/education/grad.php.

Chatham University, Program in Education, Pittsburgh, PA 15232-2826. Offers early childhood education (MAT); elementary education (MAT); environmental education (K-12) (MAT); secondary art (MAT); secondary biology education (MAT); secondary chemistry education (MAT); secondary English education (MAT); secondary math education (MAT); secondary physics education (MAT); secondary social studies education (MAT); special education (MAT). *Students:* 52 full-time (42 women), 17 part-time (16 women); includes 2 minority (1 Black or African American, non-Hispanic/Latino; 1 Hispanic/Latino). Average age 29. 39 applicants, 82% accepted, 23 enrolled. In 2011, 37 master's awarded. *Degree requirements:* For master's, thesis, teaching experience. *Entrance requirements:* For master's, minimum GPA of 3.0, sample of written work, recommendation letters. Additional exam requirements/recommendations for international students: Required—TOEFL (minimum score 600 paper-based; 250 computer-based; 100 iBT), IELTS (minimum score 7), TWE. *Application deadline:* For fall admission, 4/1 priority date for domestic students, 4/1 for international students; for spring admission, 11/1 priority date for domestic students, 10/1 for international students. Applications are processed on a rolling basis. Application fee: $45. Electronic applications accepted. Application fee is waived when completed online. *Expenses: Tuition:* Full-time $13,896. Tuition and fees vary according to program. *Financial support:* Career-related internships or fieldwork available. Financial award applicants required to submit FAFSA. *Faculty research:* Gifted education, environmental education, technology in education, writing as learning, class size and achievement. *Unit head:* Dr. Elvira Sanatullova-Allison, Director of Education Programs, 412-365-2773, E-mail: esanatullovaallison@chatham.edu. *Application contact:* Dory Perry, Associate Director of Graduate Admission, 412-365-2758, Fax: 412-365-1609, E-mail: gradadmissions@chatham.edu. Web site: http://www.chatham.edu/mat.

Christopher Newport University, Graduate Studies, Department of Teacher Preparation, Newport News, VA 23606-2998. Offers art (PK-12) (MAT); biology (6-12) (MAT); chemistry (6-12) (MAT); computer science (6-12) (MAT); elementary (PK-6) (MAT); English (6-12) (MAT); English as second language (PK-12) (MAT); French (PK-12) (MAT); history and social science (6-12) (MAT); mathematics (6-12) (MAT); music (PK-12) (MAT), including choral, instrumental; physics (6-12) (MAT); Spanish (PK-12) (MAT). Part-time and evening/weekend programs available. *Degree requirements:* For master's, comprehensive exam, thesis or alternative. *Entrance requirements:* For master's, PRAXIS I, minimum GPA of 3.0. Additional exam requirements/recommendations for international students: Required—TOEFL (minimum score 580 paper-based; 237 computer-based; 92 iBT). Electronic applications accepted. *Faculty research:* Early literacy development, instructional innovations, professional teaching standards, multicultural issues, aesthetic education.

The Citadel, The Military College of South Carolina, Citadel Graduate College, School of Education, Program in Secondary Education, Charleston, SC 29409. Offers biology (MAT); English language arts (MAT); mathematics (MAT); mathematics education (MAE); physical education (MAT); social studies (MAT). *Accreditation:* NCATE. Part-time and evening/weekend programs available. *Faculty:* 12 full-time (8 women), 9 part-time/adjunct (4 women). *Students:* 21 full-time (11 women), 51 part-time (25 women); includes 10 minority (7 Black or African American, non-Hispanic/Latino; 2 Asian, non-Hispanic/Latino; 1 Hispanic/Latino). Average age 31. In 2011, 34 master's awarded. *Degree requirements:* For master's, comprehensive exam, internship. *Entrance requirements:* For master's, GRE (minimum score 900) or MAT (minimum score 396), minimum undergraduate GPA of 2.5. Additional exam requirements/recommendations for international students: Required—TOEFL (minimum score 550 paper-based; 213 computer-based). *Application deadline:* Applications are processed on a rolling basis. Application fee: $30. Electronic applications accepted. *Expenses: Tuition, area resident:* Part-time $501 per credit hour. Tuition, state resident: part-time $501 per credit hour. Tuition, nonresident: part-time $824 per credit hour. *Required fees:* $40 per term. One-time fee: $30. *Financial support:* Career-related internships or fieldwork, health care benefits, and unspecified assistantships available. Support available to part-time students. Financial award application deadline: 7/1; financial award applicants required to submit FAFSA. *Unit head:* Dr. Kathryn A. Richardson-Jones, Coordinator, 843-953-3163, Fax: 843-953-7258, E-mail: kathryn.jones@citadel.edu. *Application contact:* Dr. Steve A. Nida, Associate Provost, The Citadel Graduate College, 843-953-5089, Fax: 843-953-7630, E-mail: cgc@citadel.edu. Web site: http://www.citadel.edu/education/teacher-education/mat-master-of-arts-in-teaching.html.

City College of the City University of New York, Graduate School, School of Education, Department of Secondary Education, New York, NY 10031-9198. Offers adolescent mathematics education (MA, AC); English education (MA); middle school mathematics education (MS); science education (MA); social studies education (AC). *Accreditation:* NCATE. *Entrance requirements:* For master's, Liberal Arts and Sciences Test (LAST), Content Specialty Test (CST). Additional exam requirements/recommendations for international students: Required—TOEFL.

Clarion University of Pennsylvania, Office of Graduate Programs, Master of Education Program, Clarion, PA 16214. Offers curriculum and instruction (M Ed); early childhood (M Ed, Certificate); English (M Ed); instructional technology specialist (K-12) (Certificate); literacy (M Ed); mathematics education (M Ed); reading specialist (M Ed, Certificate); science education (M Ed); special education (M Ed); technology (M Ed); world language (M Ed). *Accreditation:* NCATE. Part-time programs available. *Students:* 14 full-time (11 women), 207 part-time (163 women); includes 3 minority (1 Black or African American, non-Hispanic/Latino; 2 Hispanic/Latino). Average age 31. In 2011, 96 master's awarded. *Degree requirements:* For master's, thesis or alternative. *Entrance requirements:* For master's, minimum QPA of 3.0. *Application deadline:* Applications are processed on a rolling basis. *Expenses:* Tuition, state resident: part-time $429 per credit. Tuition, nonresident: part-time $644 per credit. *Financial support:* Research assistantships with full and partial tuition reimbursements and career-related internships or fieldwork available. Support available to part-time students. Financial award application deadline: 3/1. *Unit head:* Dr. John Groves, Dean, 814-393-2146, Fax: 514-393-2446. *Application contact:* Dr. Brenda Sanders Dede, Assistant Vice President for Academic Affairs, 814-393-2337, Fax: 814-393-2030, E-mail: bdede@clarion.edu. Web site: http://www.clarion.edu/25887/.

Clayton State University, School of Graduate Studies, Program in Education, Morrow, GA 30260-0285. Offers English (MAT); mathematics (MAT). *Accreditation:* NCATE. *Faculty:* 12 full-time (7 women). *Students:* 11 full-time (8 women), 11 part-time (4 women); includes 10 minority (all Black or African American, non-Hispanic/Latino). Average age 33. 11 applicants, 100% accepted, 8 enrolled. In 2011, 9 master's awarded. *Entrance requirements:* For master's, GRE, GACE, 2 official copies of transcripts, 3 recommendation letters, statement of purpose. Additional exam requirements/recommendations for international students: Required—TOEFL (minimum score 550 paper-based; 213 computer-based). *Application deadline:* For fall admission, 6/15 priority date for domestic students, 5/1 for international students; for spring admission, 10/15 priority date for domestic students. Applications are processed on a rolling basis. Application fee: $75. Electronic applications accepted. *Expenses:* Tuition, state resident: full-time $3528; part-time $196 per credit hour. Tuition, nonresident: full-time $13,176; part-time $732 per credit hour. *Required fees:* $1404; $552 per semester. Tuition and fees vary according to course load and campus/location. *Unit head:* Dr. Mari Ann Roberts, Program Director, Master of Arts in Teaching (Education), 678-466-4720, E-mail: mariroberts@clayton.edu. *Application contact:* Melanie Nolan, Administrative Assistant, Master of Arts in Teaching English, 678-466-4735, Fax: 678-466-4899, E-mail: melanienolan@clayton.edu.

Clemson University, Graduate School, College of Health, Education, and Human Development, Eugene T. Moore School of Education, Program in Teaching and Learning, Clemson, SC 29634. Offers elementary education (M Ed); English education (M Ed); mathematics education (M Ed); science education (M Ed); social studies education (M Ed). *Entrance requirements:* For master's, GRE, baccalaureate degree from regionally-accredited institution, official transcripts, copy of valid teaching certificate, two letters of recommendation. *Application contact:* Dr. David Fleming, Graduate Programs Coordinator, 864-656-1881, Fax: 864-656-0311, E-mail: dflemin@clemson.edu. Web site: http://www.clemson.edu/hehd/departments/education/academics/graduate/MEd-teach-learn.html.

The College at Brockport, State University of New York, School of Education and Human Services, Department of Education and Human Development, Program in Adolescence Education, Brockport, NY 14420-2997. Offers adolescence biology education (MS Ed); adolescence chemistry education (MS Ed); adolescence earth science education (MS Ed); adolescence English education (MS Ed); adolescence mathematics education (MS Ed); adolescence physics education (MS Ed); adolescence social studies education (MS Ed). *Accreditation:* NCATE. Part-time programs available. *Students:* 12 full-time (9 women), 60 part-time (28 women); includes 6 minority (1 American Indian or Alaska Native, non-Hispanic/Latino; 3 Asian, non-Hispanic/Latino; 1 Hispanic/Latino; 1 Native Hawaiian or other Pacific Islander, non-Hispanic/Latino). 26 applicants, 81% accepted, 17 enrolled. In 2011, 47 master's awarded. *Degree requirements:* For master's, thesis or alternative. *Entrance requirements:* For master's, minimum GPA of 3.0, letters of recommendation; statement of objectives, current resume. Additional exam requirements/recommendations for international students: Required—TOEFL (minimum score 550 paper-based; 213 computer-based; 79 iBT). *Application deadline:* For fall admission, 2/15 priority date for domestic students, 2/15 for international students; for spring admission, 9/15 priority date for domestic students, 9/15 for international students. Application fee: $80. Electronic applications accepted. *Financial support:* Federal Work-Study, scholarships/grants, and unspecified assistantships available. Support available to part-time students. Financial award application deadline: 3/15; financial award applicants required to submit FAFSA. *Unit head:* Dr. Don Halquist, Chairperson, 585-395-5550, Fax: 585-395-2172, E-mail: dhalquis@brockport.edu. *Application contact:* Michael Harrison, Coordinator of Certification and Graduate Advisement, 585-395-2326, Fax: 585-395-2172, E-mail: mharriso@brockport.edu. Web site: http://www.brockport.edu/graduate/.

The College at Brockport, State University of New York, School of Education and Human Services, Department of Education and Human Development, Program in Adolescence Inclusive Education, Brockport, NY 14420-2997. Offers English (MS Ed); mathematics (MS Ed); science (MS Ed); social studies (MS Ed). *Students:* 42 full-time (22 women), 21 part-time (10 women); includes 4 minority (2 Black or African American, non-Hispanic/Latino; 2 Hispanic/Latino). 50 applicants, 64% accepted, 19 enrolled. In 2011, 2 master's awarded. *Degree requirements:* For master's, thesis or alternative. *Entrance requirements:* For master's, minimum GPA of 3.0, letters of recommendation, statement of objectives, academic major (or equivalent) in program discipline; current resume. Additional exam requirements/recommendations for international students: Required—TOEFL (minimum score 550 paper-based; 213 computer-based; 79 iBT). *Application deadline:* For fall admission, 2/15 priority date for domestic students, 2/15 for international students; for spring admission, 9/15 priority date for domestic students, 9/15 for international students. Application fee: $80. Electronic applications accepted. *Financial support:* Federal Work-Study, scholarships/grants, and unspecified assistantships available. Support available to part-time students. Financial award application deadline: 3/15; financial award applicants required to submit FAFSA. *Unit head:* Dr. Don Halquist, Chairperson, 585-395-2205, Fax: 585-395-2171, E-mail: dhalquis@brockport.edu. *Application contact:* Michael Harrison, Coordinator of Certification and Graduate Advisement, 585-395-2326, Fax: 585-395-2172, E-mail: mharriso@brockport.edu.

College of St. Joseph, Graduate Programs, Division of Education, Program in Secondary Education, Rutland, VT 05701-3899. Offers English (M Ed); social studies (M Ed). Part-time and evening/weekend programs available. *Faculty:* 2 full-time (both women), 3 part-time/adjunct (1 woman). *Students:* 2 full-time (0 women), 4 part-time (2 women). Average age 29. 3 applicants, 67% accepted, 2 enrolled. *Degree requirements:* For master's, comprehensive exam. *Entrance requirements:* For master's, PRAXIS I, official college transcripts; 2 letters of reference; minimum GPA of 3.0 (initial licensure) or 2.7 (nonlicensure); interview. Additional exam requirements/recommendations for international students: Required—TOEFL (minimum score 550 paper-based). *Application deadline:* Applications are processed on a rolling basis. Application fee: $35. Electronic applications accepted. *Expenses: Tuition:* Full-time $15,200; part-time $400 per credit. *Required fees:* $45 per semester. *Financial support:* Career-related internships or fieldwork, Federal Work-Study, and unspecified assistantships available. Support available to part-time students. Financial award application deadline: 3/1. *Unit head:* Dr. Maria Bove, Chair, 802-773-5900 Ext. 3243, Fax: 802-776-5258, E-mail: mbove@csj.edu. *Application contact:* Alan Young, Director of Admissions, 802-773-5900 Ext. 3227, Fax: 802-776-5310, E-mail: alanyoung@csj.edu.

The College of William and Mary, School of Education, Program in Curriculum and Instruction, Williamsburg, VA 23187-8795. Offers elementary education (MA Ed); gifted education (MA Ed); math specialist (MA Ed); reading education (MA Ed); secondary education (MA Ed), including English education, mathematics education, modern foreign languages education, science education, social studies education; special education (MA Ed), including collaborating master educator, general curriculum. *Accreditation:* NCATE. Part-time programs available. *Faculty:* 15 full-time (10 women), 39 part-time/adjunct (32 women). *Students:* 80 full-time (69 women), 13 part-time (11 women); includes 11 minority (3 Black or African American, non-Hispanic/Latino; 1 American Indian or Alaska Native, non-Hispanic/Latino; 2 Hispanic/Latino; 5 Two or more races, non-Hispanic/Latino), 1 international. Average age 25. 220 applicants, 56% accepted, 85 enrolled. In 2011, 78 master's awarded. *Degree requirements:* For master's, project. *Entrance requirements:* For master's, GRE or MAT, minimum GPA of 2.5. Additional exam requirements/recommendations for international students: Required—TOEFL. *Application deadline:* For fall admission, 1/15 for domestic and international students; for spring admission, 10/1 for domestic and international students. Application fee: $50. Electronic applications accepted. *Expenses:* Tuition, state resident: full-time $6400; part-time $365 per credit hour. Tuition, nonresident: full-time $19,720; part-time $985 per credit hour. *Required fees:* $4562. *Financial support:* In 2011–12, 53 students received support, including 10 research assistantships with full and partial tuition reimbursements available (averaging $7,000 per year); career-related internships or fieldwork, Federal Work-Study, institutionally sponsored loans, scholarships/grants, and unspecified assistantships also available. Financial award application deadline: 1/15; financial award applicants required to submit FAFSA. *Faculty research:* National Council of Teachers of Mathematics Standards, counseling, self-concept and self-esteem, special education, curriculum development. *Unit head:* Dr. Margie Mason, Area Coordinator, 757-221-2327, E-mail: mmmaso@wm.edu. *Application contact:* Dorothy Smith Osborne, Assistant Dean for Admission, 757-221-2317, Fax: 757-221-2293, E-mail: dsosbo@wm.edu. Web site: http://education.wm.edu.

The Colorado College, Education Department, Program in Secondary Education, Colorado Springs, CO 80903-3294. Offers art teaching (K-12) (MAT); English teaching (MAT); foreign language teaching (MAT); mathematics teaching (MAT); music teaching (MAT); science teaching (MAT); social studies teaching (MAT). *Faculty:* 4 full-time (3 women), 6 part-time/adjunct (2 women). *Students:* 11 full-time (7 women); includes 3 minority (1 Asian, non-Hispanic/Latino; 2 Hispanic/Latino). Average age 27. 20 applicants, 85% accepted, 11 enrolled. In 2011, 15 master's awarded. *Degree requirements:* For master's, thesis, internship. *Application deadline:* For fall admission, 12/1 priority date for domestic students, 12/1 for international students. Applications are processed on a rolling basis. Application fee: $50. Electronic applications accepted. *Expenses: Tuition:* Full-time $29,313. *Required fees:* $2000. *Financial support:* In 2011–12, 15 students received support. Career-related internships or fieldwork, institutionally sponsored loans, scholarships/grants, and health care benefits available. Financial award application deadline: 2/15; financial award applicants required to submit FAFSA. *Unit head:* Dr. Mike Taber, Director, 719-389-6026, Fax: 719-389-6473, E-mail: mike.taber@coloradocollege.edu. *Application contact:* Debra Yazulla Mortenson, Education Services Manager, 719-389-6472, Fax: 719-389-6473, E-mail: debra.mortenson@coloradocollege.edu. Web site: http://www.coloradocollege.edu/academics/dept/education/graduate-programs/secondary-mat.dot.

Columbia College Chicago, Graduate School, Department of Educational Studies, Chicago, IL 60605-1996. Offers elementary education (MAT); English (MAT); interdisciplinary arts (MAT); multicultural education (MA); urban teaching (MA). Part-time and evening/weekend programs available. *Degree requirements:* For master's, thesis, student teaching experience, 100 pre-clinical hours. *Entrance requirements:* For master's, supplemental recommendation form. Additional exam requirements/recommendations for international students: Required—TOEFL (minimum score 550 paper-based; 213 computer-based). Electronic applications accepted.

Columbus State University, Graduate Studies, College of Education and Health Professions, Department of Teacher Education, Columbus, GA 31907-5645. Offers accomplished teaching (M Ed); early childhood education (M Ed, MAT, Ed S); health and physical education (M Ed, MAT); middle grades education (M Ed, MAT, Ed S); school library media (M Ed, MAT); secondary education (M Ed, MAT, Ed S), including English/language arts (M Ed, Ed S), general science (M Ed), mathematics (M Ed), social science (M Ed); special education (M Ed, Ed S), including general curriculum (M Ed). *Accreditation:* NCATE. Part-time and evening/weekend programs available. Postbaccalaureate distance learning degree programs offered (minimal on-campus study). *Degree requirements:* For master's, thesis, exit exam; for Ed S, thesis or alternative. *Entrance requirements:* For master's, GRE General Test, minimum GPA of 2.75; for Ed S, GRE General Test. Additional exam requirements/recommendations for international students: Required—TOEFL (minimum score 550 paper-based; 213 computer-based; 79 iBT). Electronic applications accepted.

Converse College, School of Education and Graduate Studies, Program in Secondary Education, Spartanburg, SC 29302-0006. Offers biology (MAT); chemistry (MAT); English (M Ed, MAT); mathematics (M Ed, MAT); natural sciences (M Ed); social sciences (M Ed, MAT). Part-time programs available. *Degree requirements:* For master's, capstone paper. *Entrance requirements:* For master's, NTE or PRAXIS II (M Ed), minimum GPA of 2.75, 2 recommendations. Electronic applications accepted.

Delta State University, Graduate Programs, College of Arts and Sciences, Division of Languages and Literature, Cleveland, MS 38733-0001. Offers secondary education (M Ed), including English. Part-time programs available. *Degree requirements:* For master's, thesis or alternative. *Expenses:* Tuition, state resident: full-time $4702; part-time $294 per credit hour. Tuition, nonresident: full-time $12,516; part-time $760 per credit hour. *Required fees:* $586.

Duquesne University, School of Education, Department of Instruction and Leadership, Pittsburgh, PA 15282-0001. Offers early level (PreK-4) education (MS Ed); English as a second language (MS Ed); instructional technology (MS Ed, Ed D, Post-Master's Certificate), including business, computer, and information technology (MS Ed), instructional technology; middle level (4-8) education (MS Ed); reading and language arts (MS Ed); secondary education (MS Ed), including biology, chemistry, English, Latin education, K-12, mathematics, physics, social studies. Part-time and evening/weekend programs available. Postbaccalaureate distance learning degree programs offered (minimal on-campus study). *Faculty:* 15 full-time (9 women), 28 part-time/adjunct (15 women). *Students:* 213 full-time (145 women), 47 part-time (38 women); includes 19 minority (9 Black or African American, non-Hispanic/Latino; 5 Asian, non-Hispanic/Latino; 4 Hispanic/Latino; 1 Two or more races, non-Hispanic/Latino), 11 international. Average age 26. 160 applicants, 48% accepted, 53 enrolled. In 2011, 111 degrees awarded. *Degree requirements:* For master's, thesis optional; for doctorate, thesis/dissertation. *Entrance requirements:* For master's, letters of recommendation, letter of intent, interview, bachelor's degree; for doctorate, GRE, letters of recommendation, letter of intent, interview, master's degree; for Post-Master's Certificate, letters of recommendation, letter of intent, interview, bachelor's/master's degree. Additional exam requirements/recommendations for international students: Required—TOEFL (minimum score 550 paper-based; 80 computer-based), IELTS (minimum score 7). *Application deadline:* For fall admission, 9/1 priority date for domestic students; for spring admission, 1/1 priority date for domestic students. Applications are processed on a rolling basis. Application fee: $0. Electronic applications accepted. Application fee is waived when completed online. *Expenses: Tuition:* Full-time $16,596; part-time $922 per credit. *Required fees:* $1584; $88 per credit. Tuition and fees vary according to program. *Financial support:* Research assistantships, teaching assistantships with tuition reimbursements, career-related internships or fieldwork, Federal Work-Study, and institutionally sponsored loans available. Support available to part-time students. *Unit head:* Dr. Jason Margolis, Chair, 412-396-6106, Fax: 412-396-5388, E-mail: margolisj@duq.edu. *Application contact:* Michael Dolinger, Director of Student and Academic Services, 412-396-6647, Fax: 412-396-5585, E-mail: dolingerm@duq.edu.

East Carolina University, Graduate School, College of Education, Department of Business and Information Technologies Education, Greenville, NC 27858-4353. Offers business education (MA Ed); elementary education (MAT); English education (MAT); family and consumer science (MAT); health education (MAT); Hispanic studies (MAT); history education (MAT); marketing education (MA Ed); middle grades education (MAT); music education (MAT); physical education (MAT); science education (MAT); special education (MAT), including general curriculum; vocation education (MS). *Accreditation:* NCATE. Part-time and evening/weekend programs available. Postbaccalaureate distance learning degree programs offered (no on-campus study). *Degree requirements:* For master's, comprehensive exam, thesis optional. *Entrance requirements:* For master's, GRE or MAT, minimum GPA of 2.5, bachelor's degree in related field, teaching license (MA Ed). Additional exam requirements/recommendations for international students: Required—TOEFL. *Application deadline:* For fall admission, 6/1 priority date for domestic students. Applications are processed on a rolling basis. Application fee: $50. *Expenses:* Tuition, state resident: full-time $3557; part-time $444.63 per semester hour. Tuition, nonresident: full-time $14,351; part-time $1793.88 per semester hour. *Required fees:* $2016; $252 per semester hour. Part-time tuition and fees vary according to course load, campus/location and program. *Financial support:* Federal Work-Study available. Support available to part-time students. Financial award application deadline: 6/1. *Unit head:* Dr. Ivan G. Wallace, Chair, 252-328-6983, Fax: 252-328-6835, E-mail: wallacei@ecu.edu. *Application contact:* Dean of Graduate School, 252-328-6012, Fax: 252-328-6071, E-mail: gradschool@ecu.edu. Web site: http://www.ecu.edu/cs-educ/bite/index.cfm.

East Carolina University, Graduate School, College of Education, Department of Curriculum and Instruction, Greenville, NC 27858-4353. Offers assistive technology (Certificate); autism (Certificate); deaf/blindness (Certificate); elementary education (MA Ed); English education (MA Ed); history (MA Ed); middle grade education (MA Ed); reading education (MA Ed); special education (MA Ed); teaching (MAT). Part-time programs available. Postbaccalaureate distance learning degree programs offered. *Degree requirements:* For master's, comprehensive exam, thesis optional. *Entrance requirements:* For master's, GRE General Test or MAT, interview, bachelor's degree in related field, minimum GPA of 2.5, teaching license. Additional exam requirements/recommendations for international students: Required—TOEFL. *Application deadline:* For fall admission, 6/1 priority date for domestic students. Applications are processed on a rolling basis. Application fee: $50. *Expenses:* Tuition, state resident: full-time $3557; part-time $444.63 per semester hour. Tuition, nonresident: full-time $14,351; part-time $1793.88 per semester hour. *Required fees:* $2016; $252 per semester hour. Part-time tuition and fees vary according to course load, campus/location and program. *Financial support:* Research assistantships, teaching assistantships, and Federal Work-Study available. Support available to part-time students. Financial award application deadline: 6/1; financial award applicants required to submit FAFSA. *Unit head:* Carolyn C. Ledford, Interim Chair, 252-328-1100, E-mail: ledfordc@ecu.edu. *Application contact:* Dean of Graduate School, 252-328-6012, Fax: 252-328-6071, E-mail: gradschool@ecu.edu. Web site: http://www.ecu.edu/cs-educ/ci/Graduate.cfm.

Eastern Kentucky University, The Graduate School, College of Education, Department of Curriculum and Instruction, Program in Secondary and Higher Education, Richmond, KY 40475-3102. Offers secondary education (MA Ed), including agricultural education, art education, biological sciences education, business education, English education, geography education, history education, home economics education, industrial education, mathematical sciences education, physical education, school health education. *Accreditation:* NCATE. Part-time programs available. *Entrance requirements:* For master's, GRE General Test, minimum GPA of 2.5.

Eastern Michigan University, Graduate School, College of Arts and Sciences, Department of English Language and Literature, Program in English Studies for Teachers, Ypsilanti, MI 48197. Offers MA. Part-time and evening/weekend programs available. *Students:* 12 part-time (8 women); includes 1 minority (Black or African American, non-Hispanic/Latino). Average age 34. 5 applicants, 60% accepted, 2 enrolled. In 2011, 4 degrees awarded. *Entrance requirements:* Additional exam requirements/recommendations for international students: Required—TOEFL. *Expenses:* Tuition, state resident: full-time $10,367; part-time $432 per credit hour. Tuition, nonresident: full-time $20,435; part-time $851 per credit hour. *Required fees:* $39 per credit hour. $46 per semester. One-time fee: $100. Tuition and fees vary according to course level, degree level and reciprocity agreements. *Financial support:* Research assistantships with full tuition reimbursements, teaching assistantships with full tuition reimbursements, career-related internships or fieldwork, Federal Work-Study, institutionally sponsored loans, scholarships/grants, and unspecified assistantships available. Support available to part-time students. *Unit head:* Dr. Joseph Csicsila, Interim Department Head, 734-487-4220, Fax: 734-483-9744, E-mail: jcsicsila@emich.edu. *Application contact:* Prof. Douglas Baker, Program Advisor, 734-487-0150, Fax: 734-487-9744, E-mail: douglas.baker@emich.edu. Web site: http://www.emich.edu/english/english-ed/graduate.php.

Eastern Michigan University, Graduate School, College of Arts and Sciences, Department of English Language and Literature, Program in Teaching of Writing, Ypsilanti, MI 48197. Offers MA, Graduate Certificate. *Students:* 3 part-time (all women); includes 1 minority (Hispanic/Latino). 1 applicant, 100% accepted, 0 enrolled. In 2011, 1 degree awarded. Application fee: $35. *Expenses:* Tuition, state resident: full-time $10,367; part-time $432 per credit hour. Tuition, nonresident: full-time $20,435; part-time $851 per credit hour. *Required fees:* $39 per credit hour. $46 per semester. One-time fee: $100. Tuition and fees vary according to course level, degree level and reciprocity agreements. *Unit head:* Dr. Joseph Csicsila, Interim Department Head, 734-487-4220, Fax: 734-483-9744, E-mail: jcsicsila@emich.edu. *Application contact:* Prof. Steve Krause, Program Advisor, 734-487-3172, Fax: 734-483-9744, E-mail: skrause@emich.edu.

Elms College, Division of Education, Chicopee, MA 01013-2839. Offers early childhood education (MAT); education (M Ed, CAGS); elementary education (MAT); English as a second language (MAT); reading (MAT); secondary education (MAT), including biology education, English education, Spanish education; special education (MAT). Part-time and evening/weekend programs available. *Degree requirements:* For master's, thesis (for some programs). *Entrance requirements:* For master's, Massachusetts Educators Certification Test, minimum GPA of 3.0; for CAGS, master's degree in education. Additional exam requirements/recommendations for international students: Required—TOEFL.

Fitchburg State University, Division of Graduate and Continuing Education, Programs in English and Teaching English (Secondary Level), Fitchburg, MA 01420-2697. Offers MA, MAT, Certificate. *Accreditation:* NCATE. Part-time and evening/weekend programs available. *Students:* 26 part-time (22 women). Average age 32. 9 applicants, 100% accepted, 4 enrolled. In 2011, 8 master's awarded. *Entrance requirements:* Additional exam requirements/recommendations for international students: Required—TOEFL (minimum score 550 paper-based; 213 computer-based; 79 iBT). *Application deadline:* For fall admission, 7/15 for international students; for spring admission, 12/1 for international students. Applications are processed on a rolling basis. Application fee: $25 ($50 for international students). Electronic applications accepted. *Expenses:* Tuition, state resident: full-time $2700; part-time $150 per credit. Tuition, nonresident: full-time $2700; part-time $150 per credit. *Required fees:* $2286; $127 per credit. *Financial support:* In 2011–12, research assistantships with partial tuition reimbursements (averaging $5,500 per year) were awarded; Federal Work-Study, scholarships/grants, and unspecified assistantships also available. Support available to part-time students. Financial award application deadline: 3/1; financial award applicants required to submit FAFSA. *Unit head:* Dr. Chola Chisunka, Chair, 978-665-3445, Fax: 978-665-3658, E-mail: gce@fitchburgstate.edu. *Application contact:* Kay Reynolds, Director of Admissions, 978-665-3144, Fax: 978-665-4540, E-mail: admissions@fitchburgstate.edu. Web site: http://www.fitchburgstate.edu.

Florida Agricultural and Mechanical University, Division of Graduate Studies, Research, and Continuing Education, College of Education, Program in Secondary Education and Foundation, Tallahassee, FL 32307-3200. Offers biology (M Ed); chemistry (MS Ed); English (MS Ed); history (MS Ed); math (MS Ed); physics (MS Ed). *Accreditation:* NCATE. *Degree requirements:* For master's, thesis (for some programs). *Entrance requirements:* For master's, GRE General Test, minimum GPA of 3.0. Additional exam requirements/recommendations for international students: Required—TOEFL.

English Education

Florida Atlantic University, Dorothy F. Schmidt College of Arts and Letters, Department of English, Boca Raton, FL 33431-0991. Offers British and American literature (MA); creative nonfiction (MFA); creative writing (MA); fiction (MFA); multicultural literatures and literacies (MA); poetry (MFA); science fiction and fantasy (MA); teaching English (MAT). Part-time programs available. *Faculty:* 56 full-time (30 women), 7 part-time/adjunct (3 women). *Students:* 58 full-time (36 women), 34 part-time (23 women); includes 22 minority (7 Black or African American, non-Hispanic/Latino; 1 American Indian or Alaska Native, non-Hispanic/Latino; 13 Hispanic/Latino; 1 Two or more races, non-Hispanic/Latino). Average age 32. 98 applicants, 38% accepted, 9 enrolled. In 2011, 26 master's awarded. *Degree requirements:* For master's, one foreign language, thesis. *Entrance requirements:* For master's, GRE General Test, minimum GPA of 3.0, writing samples, 2 letters of recommendation. *Application deadline:* For fall admission, 3/1 for domestic students, 2/15 for international students; for spring admission, 11/1 for domestic students, 7/15 for international students. Applications are processed on a rolling basis. Application fee: $30. Electronic applications accepted. *Expenses: Tuition, area resident:* Part-time $343.02 per credit hour. Tuition, state resident: full-time $8232. Tuition, nonresident: full-time $23,931; part-time $997.14 per credit hour. *Financial support:* Fellowships, teaching assistantships with partial tuition reimbursements, Federal Work-Study, and tuition waivers available. Support available to part-time students. Financial award application deadline: 3/1. *Faculty research:* African-American writers, critical theory, British-American, Asian-American. *Unit head:* Dr. Andy Furman, Chair, 561-297-2065, Fax: 561-297-3807, E-mail: afurman@fau.edu. *Application contact:* Dr. Mark Scroggins, Director of Graduate Studies, 561-297-3561, Fax: 561-297-3807, E-mail: mscroggi@fau.edu. Web site: http://www.fau.edu/english/.

Florida Gulf Coast University, College of Education, Program in Curriculum and Instruction, Fort Myers, FL 33965-6565. Offers curriculum and instruction (Ed D, Ed S); educational technology (M Ed, MA); English education (M Ed). Part-time and evening/weekend programs available. Postbaccalaureate distance learning degree programs offered (minimal on-campus study). *Faculty:* 34 full-time (26 women), 57 part-time/adjunct (40 women). *Students:* 19 full-time (18 women), 8 part-time (all women); includes 2 minority (both Hispanic/Latino). Average age 34. 13 applicants, 85% accepted, 10 enrolled. In 2011, 9 master's awarded. *Degree requirements:* For master's, final project or portfolio. *Entrance requirements:* For master's, GRE General Test, MAT, minimum undergraduate GPA of 3.0 in last 2 years. Additional exam requirements/recommendations for international students: Required—TOEFL (minimum score 550 paper-based; 213 computer-based). *Application deadline:* For fall admission, 7/1 priority date for domestic students; for spring admission, 10/15 for domestic students. Applications are processed on a rolling basis. Application fee: $30. Electronic applications accepted. *Expenses:* Tuition, state resident: full-time $8289. Tuition, nonresident: full-time $28,895. *Required fees:* $1831. One-time fee: $30 full-time. *Faculty research:* Internet in schools, technology in pre-service and in-service teacher training. *Unit head:* Dr. Diane Schmidt, Department Chair, 239-590-7741, Fax: 239-590-7801, E-mail: dschmidt@fgcu.edu. *Application contact:* Keiana Desmore, Adviser/Counselor, 239-590-7759, Fax: 239-590-7801, E-mail: kdesmore@fgcu.edu. Web site: http://edtech.fgcu.edu/.

Florida International University, College of Education, Department of Curriculum and Instruction, Miami, FL 33199. Offers art education (MAT, MS, Ed D); curriculum and instruction (Ed S); curriculum development (MS); curriculum studies (PhD); early childhood education (MS, Ed D); elementary education (MS, Ed D); English education (MAT, MS, Ed D); foreign language education - teaching English to speakers of other languages (TESOL) (MS, Certificate), including foreign language education (Certificate), teaching English (MS); French education - initial teacher preparation (MAT); international and intercultural development education (Ed D); international and intercultural developmental education (MS); language, literacy and culture (PhD); learning technologies (MS, Ed D, PhD); mathematics education (MAT, MS, Ed D, PhD); modern language education/bilingual education (MS, Ed D); physical education (MS); reading education (MS, Ed D); science education (MAT, MS, Ed D, PhD); social studies education (MAT, MS, Ed D); Spanish education - initial teacher preparation (MAT); special education (MS). Part-time and evening/weekend programs available. *Degree requirements:* For doctorate, comprehensive exam, thesis/dissertation. *Entrance requirements:* For master's, GRE General Test, Florida General Knowledge Test or Florida College Level Academic Skills Test; for doctorate and other advanced degree, GRE General Test. Additional exam requirements/recommendations for international students: Required—TOEFL (minimum score 550 paper-based; 213 computer-based; 80 iBT), IELTS (minimum score 6.3). Electronic applications accepted.

Florida State University, The Graduate School, College of Education, School of Teacher Education, Program in English Education, Tallahassee, FL 32306. Offers MS, PhD, Ed S. Part-time programs available. *Faculty:* 5 full-time (all women). *Students:* 10 full-time (all women), 7 part-time (6 women); includes 4 minority (2 Black or African American, non-Hispanic/Latino; 1 American Indian or Alaska Native, non-Hispanic/Latino; 1 Hispanic/Latino), 2 international. Average age 32. 17 applicants, 29% accepted, 2 enrolled. In 2011, 8 master's, 1 other advanced degree awarded. *Degree requirements:* For master's and Ed S, comprehensive exam, thesis optional; for doctorate, comprehensive exam, thesis/dissertation. *Entrance requirements:* For master's, doctorate, and Ed S, GRE General Test, minimum GPA of 3.0. Additional exam requirements/recommendations for international students: Required—TOEFL (minimum score 550 paper-based; 213 computer-based; 80 iBT). *Application deadline:* For fall admission, 7/1 for domestic and international students; for winter admission, 11/1 for domestic and international students; for spring admission, 3/1 for domestic and international students. Applications are processed on a rolling basis. Application fee: $30. Electronic applications accepted. *Expenses:* Tuition, state resident: full-time $9474; part-time $350.88 per credit hour. Tuition, nonresident: full-time $16,236; part-time $601.34 per credit hour. *Required fees:* $630 per semester. One-time fee: $20. Tuition and fees vary according to course load and campus/location. *Financial support:* Fellowships with full and partial tuition reimbursements, research assistantships with full and partial tuition reimbursements, teaching assistantships with full and partial tuition reimbursements, Federal Work-Study, scholarships/grants, health care benefits, and unspecified assistantships available. Financial award applicants required to submit FAFSA. *Faculty research:* Teaching literacies in today's English classroom, technologies for today's student and teacher, young adult literature as art and in the curriculum, adolescent literacy, reading across all subject areas. *Unit head:* Dr. Shelbie Witte, Head, 850-644-6553, Fax: 850-644-1880, E-mail: switte@fsu.edu. *Application contact:* Harriet Kasper, Office Manager, 850-644-2122, Fax: 850-644-7736, E-mail: hkasper@fsu.edu. Web site: http://www.coe.fsu.edu/english-ed.

Framingham State University, Division of Graduate and Continuing Education, Program in English, Framingham, MA 01701-9101. Offers M Ed.

Gardner-Webb University, Graduate School, Department of English, Boiling Springs, NC 28017. Offers English (MA); English education (MA). Part-time and evening/weekend programs available. *Students:* 1 (woman) full-time, 9 part-time (8 women); includes 1 minority (Black or African American, non-Hispanic/Latino). Average age 28. In 2011, 1 master's awarded. *Degree requirements:* For master's, comprehensive exam. *Entrance requirements:* For master's, GRE General Test, MAT, or NTE; PRAXIS, minimum GPA of 2.5. *Application deadline:* For fall admission, 8/1 priority date for domestic students. Applications are processed on a rolling basis. Application fee: $40. Electronic applications accepted. *Expenses: Tuition:* Full-time $6300; part-time $350 per credit hour. *Financial support:* Unspecified assistantships available. *Unit head:* Dr. June Hobbs, Chair, 704-406-4412, Fax: 704-406-3921, E-mail: jhobbs@gardner-webb.edu. *Application contact:* Office of Graduate Admissions, 877-498-4723, Fax: 704-406-3895, E-mail: gradinfo@gardner-webb.edu.

Georgia Southern University, Jack N. Averitt College of Graduate Studies, College of Education, Department of Teaching and Learning, Program in English Education, Statesboro, GA 30460. Offers M Ed, MAT. *Accreditation:* NCATE. Part-time and evening/weekend programs available. *Students:* 14 full-time (10 women). Average age 25. 4 applicants, 100% accepted, 3 enrolled. In 2011, 2 master's awarded. *Degree requirements:* For master's, portfolio, transition point assessments, exit assessment. *Entrance requirements:* For master's, GRE General Test or MAT; GACE Basic Skills and Content Assessments (MAT), minimum cumulative GPA of 2.5. Additional exam requirements/recommendations for international students: Required—TOEFL (minimum score 550 paper-based; 213 computer-based; 80 iBT). *Application deadline:* For fall admission, 3/1 priority date for domestic students, 3/1 for international students; for spring admission, 10/1 priority date for domestic students, 10/1 for international students. Applications are processed on a rolling basis. Application fee: $30 ($50 for international students). Electronic applications accepted. *Expenses:* Tuition, state resident: full-time $6300; part-time $263 per semester hour. Tuition, nonresident: full-time $25,174; part-time $1049 per semester hour. *Required fees:* $1872. *Financial support:* In 2011–12, 3 students received support, including research assistantships with partial tuition reimbursements available (averaging $7,200 per year), teaching assistantships with partial tuition reimbursements available (averaging $7,200 per year); Federal Work-Study, scholarships/grants, tuition waivers (partial), and unspecified assistantships also available. Support available to part-time students. Financial award application deadline: 4/15; financial award applicants required to submit FAFSA. *Faculty research:* Literacy for at-risk students. *Unit head:* Dr. Ronnie Sheppard, Assistant Professor, 912-478-5203, Fax: 912-478-0026, E-mail: sheppard@georgiasouthern.edu. *Application contact:* Amanda Gilliland, Coordinator for Graduate Student Recruitment, 912-478-5384, Fax: 912-478-0740, E-mail: gradadmissions@georgiasouthern.edu. Web site: http://coe.georgiasouthern.edu/tandl/index.html.

Georgia State University, College of Education, Department of Middle-Secondary Education and Instructional Technology, Programs in Secondary Education, Atlanta, GA 30302-3083. Offers art education (Ed S); English education (M Ed, Ed S); mathematics education (M Ed, PhD, Ed S); music education (PhD); science education (M Ed, PhD, Ed S); social studies education (M Ed, PhD, Ed S). *Accreditation:* NASM (one or more programs are accredited); NCATE. Part-time and evening/weekend programs available. *Degree requirements:* For master's, comprehensive exam; for doctorate, comprehensive exam, thesis/dissertation; for Ed S, project/exam. *Entrance requirements:* For master's, GRE General Test, minimum GPA of 2.5; for doctorate, GRE General Test or MAT, minimum GPA of 3.3; for Ed S, GRE General Test or MAT, minimum graduate GPA of 3.25. *Faculty research:* Women and science, problem solving in mathematics, dialects, economic education.

Grand Valley State University, College of Education, Program in Reading and Language Arts, Allendale, MI 49401-9403. Offers M Ed. *Accreditation:* NCATE. Part-time and evening/weekend programs available. *Degree requirements:* For master's, thesis. *Entrance requirements:* For master's, GRE General Test or minimum GPA of 3.0. Additional exam requirements/recommendations for international students: Required—TOEFL. Electronic applications accepted. *Faculty research:* Culture of literacy, literacy acquisition, assessment, content area literacy, writing pedagogy.

Harding University, College of Education, Searcy, AR 72149-0001. Offers advanced studies in teaching and learning (M Ed); art (MSE); behavioral science (MSE); counseling (MS, Ed S); early childhood special education (M Ed, MSE); education (MSE); educational leadership (M Ed, Ed S); elementary education (M Ed); English (MSE); French (MSE); history/social science (MSE); kinesiology (MSE); math (MSE); reading (M Ed); secondary education (M Ed); Spanish (MSE); teaching (MAT); teaching English as a second language (MSE). *Accreditation:* NCATE. Part-time and evening/weekend programs available. *Faculty:* 9 full-time (2 women), 48 part-time/adjunct (26 women). *Students:* 100 full-time (77 women), 333 part-time (239 women); includes 76 minority (59 Black or African American, non-Hispanic/Latino; 1 Asian, non-Hispanic/Latino; 10 Hispanic/Latino; 6 Two or more races, non-Hispanic/Latino), 2 international. Average age 36. 93 applicants, 91% accepted, 83 enrolled. In 2011, 159 master's, 10 other advanced degrees awarded. *Degree requirements:* For master's, comprehensive exam (for some programs), thesis optional, portfolio(s); for Ed S, comprehensive exam, portfolio, project. *Entrance requirements:* For master's, GRE, MAT, PRAXIS; for Ed S, MAT or GRE. Additional exam requirements/recommendations for international students: Required—TOEFL (minimum score 550 paper-based; 79 iBT). *Application deadline:* For fall admission, 8/1 for domestic and international students; for spring admission, 1/1 for domestic and international students. Applications are processed on a rolling basis. Application fee: $35. *Expenses: Tuition:* Full-time $10,512; part-time $584 per credit hour. *Required fees:* $500; $25 per credit hour. Tuition and fees vary according to course load, degree level and program. *Financial support:* In 2011–12, 37 students received support. Unspecified assistantships available. *Faculty research:* Reading, comprehension, school violence, educational technology, behavior, college choice, differentiated instruction, brain-based teaching. *Unit head:* Dr. Clara Carroll, Chair, 501-279-4501, Fax: 501-279-4083, E-mail: ccarroll@harding.edu. *Application contact:* Information Contact, 501-279-4315, E-mail: gradstudiesedu@harding.edu. Web site: http://www.harding.edu/education/grad.html.

Hofstra University, School of Education, Health, and Human Services, Programs in Teaching - Secondary Education, Hempstead, NY 11549. Offers business education (MS Ed); education technology (Advanced Certificate); English education (MA, MS Ed); foreign language and TESOL (MS Ed); foreign language education (MA, MS Ed), including French, German, Russian, Spanish; mathematics education (MA, MS Ed); science education (MA, MS Ed), including biology, chemistry, earth science, geology, physics; secondary education (Advanced Certificate); social studies education (MA, MS Ed). Part-time and evening/weekend programs available. Postbaccalaureate distance learning degree programs offered (minimal on-campus study). *Students:* 72 full-time (47 women), 51 part-time (30 women); includes 21 minority (9 Black or African American, non-Hispanic/Latino; 7 Asian, non-Hispanic/Latino; 5 Hispanic/Latino). Average age 28. 103 applicants, 91% accepted, 41 enrolled. In 2011, 86 master's, 6 other advanced degrees awarded. *Degree requirements:* For master's, one foreign language, comprehensive exam (for some programs), thesis (for some programs), exit project, electronic portfolio, student teaching, fieldwork, curriculum project, minimum GPA of 3.0; for Advanced Certificate, 3 foreign languages, comprehensive exam (for some programs), thesis project, minimum GPA of 3.0. *Entrance requirements:* For master's, 2 letters of recommendation, teacher certification (MA), essay; for Advanced Certificate, 2 letters of recommendation, essay. Additional exam requirements/recommendations for international students: Required—TOEFL (minimum score 550 paper-based; 213 computer-based; 80 iBT). *Application deadline:* Applications are processed on a rolling basis. Application fee: $70 ($75 for international students). Electronic applications accepted. *Expenses: Tuition:* Full-time $18,990; part-time $1055 per credit hour. *Required fees:* $970. Tuition and fees vary according to program. *Financial support:* In 2011–12, 90 students received support, including 13 fellowships with full and partial tuition reimbursements available (averaging $3,202 per year), 1 research assistantship with full and partial tuition reimbursement available (averaging $11,645 per year); career-related internships or fieldwork, Federal Work-Study, institutionally sponsored loans, scholarships/grants, tuition waivers (full and partial), and unspecified assistantships also available. Support available to part-time students. Financial award applicants required to submit FAFSA. *Faculty research:* Appropriate content and pedagogy in secondary school disciplines, appropriate pedagogy in secondary school disciplines, adolescent development, secondary school organization, alternative secondary school programs. *Unit head:* Dr. Esther Fusco, Chairperson, 516-463-7704, Fax: 516-463-6196, E-mail: catezf@hofstra.edu. *Application contact:* Carol Drummer, Dean of Graduate Admissions, 516-463-4876, Fax: 516-463-4664, E-mail: gradstudent@hofstra.edu. Web site: http://www.hofstra.edu/education/.

Humboldt State University, Academic Programs, College of Arts, Humanities, and Social Sciences, Department of English, Arcata, CA 95521-8299. Offers English (MA), including international program, literature, teaching of writing. *Students:* 15 full-time (8 women), 7 part-time (4 women); includes 4 minority (1 American Indian or Alaska Native, non-Hispanic/Latino; 1 Asian, non-Hispanic/Latino; 1 Hispanic/Latino; 1 Two or more races, non-Hispanic/Latino). Average age 31. 23 applicants, 70% accepted, 8 enrolled. In 2011, 9 master's awarded. *Degree requirements:* For master's, variable foreign language requirement, thesis or alternative, qualifying exam. *Entrance requirements:* For master's, GRE, minimum GPA of 3.0, 3 letters of recommendation, sample of writing. Additional exam requirements/recommendations for international students: Required—TOEFL (minimum score 500 paper-based; 173 computer-based). *Application deadline:* For fall admission, 3/1 for domestic students; for spring admission, 11/1 for domestic students. Applications are processed on a rolling basis. Application fee: $55. *Expenses:* Tuition, state resident: full-time $6734. Tuition, nonresident: full-time $15,662; part-time $372 per credit. *Required fees:* $903. Tuition and fees vary according to program. *Financial support:* Teaching assistantships, career-related internships or fieldwork, Federal Work-Study, and institutionally sponsored loans available. Financial award application deadline: 3/1; financial award applicants required to submit FAFSA. *Faculty research:* Teaching of writing, literature. *Unit head:* Dr. MaryAnn Creadon, Chair, 707-826-3758, Fax: 707-826-5939, E-mail: maryann.creadon@humboldt.edu. Web site: http://www.humboldt.edu/english/.

Hunter College of the City University of New York, Graduate School, School of Arts and Sciences, Department of English, New York, NY 10021-5085. Offers British and American literature (MA); creative writing (MFA), including creative writing, fiction, nonfiction, poetry; English education (MA). Part-time and evening/weekend programs available. *Faculty:* 39 full-time (22 women). *Students:* 1 (woman) full-time, 102 part-time (68 women); includes 21 minority (9 Black or African American, non-Hispanic/Latino; 7 Asian, non-Hispanic/Latino; 5 Hispanic/Latino), 6 international. Average age 31. 860 applicants, 6% accepted, 35 enrolled. In 2011, 40 master's awarded. *Entrance requirements:* Additional exam requirements/recommendations for international students: Required—TOEFL. *Application deadline:* For fall admission, 4/1 for domestic students, 2/1 for international students; for spring admission, 11/1 for domestic students, 9/1 for international students. Application fee: $125. *Expenses:* Tuition, state resident: full-time $8210; part-time $345 per credit. Tuition, nonresident: full-time $15,360; part-time $640 per credit. *Required fees:* $280 per semester. One-time fee: $125. Tuition and fees vary according to class time, campus/location and program. *Financial support:* Fellowships, Federal Work-Study, and tuition waivers (partial) available. Support available to part-time students. *Faculty research:* Medieval, early modern, late century, Asian-American, post-colonial literatures. *Unit head:* Dr. Christina Leon-Alfar, Chair, 212-772-5187, Fax: 212-772-5411, E-mail: calfar@hunter.cuny.edu. *Application contact:* Sarah Chinn, Adviser, 212-772-5187, E-mail: gradenghish@hunter.cuny.edu. Web site: http://www.hunter.cuny.edu/.

Hunter College of the City University of New York, Graduate School, School of Education, Programs in Secondary Education, Concentration in English Education, New York, NY 10021-5085. Offers MA. *Accreditation:* NCATE. *Faculty:* 10 full-time (7 women), 21 part-time/adjunct (17 women). *Students:* 2 full-time (1 woman), 62 part-time (50 women); includes 16 minority (7 Black or African American, non-Hispanic/Latino; 3 Asian, non-Hispanic/Latino; 6 Hispanic/Latino), 1 international. Average age 30. 74 applicants, 41% accepted, 11 enrolled. In 2011, 44 master's awarded. *Degree requirements:* For master's, thesis, professional teaching portfolio, New York State Teacher Certification Exam, research project. *Entrance requirements:* For master's, minimum GPA of 2.8, 2 letters of reference, minimum of 21 credits in English. Additional exam requirements/recommendations for international students: Required—TOEFL, TWE. *Application deadline:* For fall admission, 4/1 for domestic students, 2/1 for international students; for spring admission, 11/1 for domestic students, 9/1 for international students. Applications are processed on a rolling basis. Application fee: $125. *Expenses:* Tuition, state resident: full-time $8210; part-time $345 per credit. Tuition, nonresident: full-time $15,360; part-time $640 per credit. *Required fees:* $280 per semester. One-time fee: $125. Tuition and fees vary according to class time, campus/location and program. *Financial support:* Federal Work-Study and tuition waivers (partial) available. Support available to part-time students. *Unit head:* Sema Brainin, Education Adviser, 212-772-4773, E-mail: sbrainin@hunter.cuny.edu. *Application contact:* Marlene Hennessey, English Department Advisor, 212-772-4773, E-mail: mhenness@hunter.cuny.edu. Web site: http://www.hunter.cuny.edu/school-of-education/programs/graduate/adolescent/english.

Indiana State University, College of Graduate and Professional Studies, College of Arts and Sciences, Department of English, Terre Haute, IN 47809. Offers English teaching (MA); history (MA); literature (MA). Part-time and evening/weekend programs available. *Degree requirements:* For master's, one foreign language, thesis optional. *Entrance requirements:* For master's, minimum GPA of 2.75 in all English courses above freshman level. Additional exam requirements/recommendations for international students: Required—TOEFL (minimum score 550 paper-based). Electronic applications accepted.

Indiana University of Pennsylvania, School of Graduate Studies and Research, College of Humanities and Social Sciences, Department of English, Program in Composition and Teaching English to Speakers of Other Languages, Indiana, PA 15705-1087. Offers composition and teaching English to speakers of other languages (PhD); teaching English (MAT); teaching English to speakers of other languages (MA). *Faculty:* 27 full-time (11 women). *Students:* 24 full-time (15 women), 119 part-time (76 women); includes 8 minority (3 Black or African American, non-Hispanic/Latino; 4 Asian, non-Hispanic/Latino; 1 Hispanic/Latino), 38 international. Average age 40. 184 applicants, 24% accepted, 17 enrolled. In 2011, 31 doctorates awarded. *Degree requirements:* For master's, thesis optional; for doctorate, one foreign language, comprehensive exam, thesis/dissertation. *Entrance requirements:* For master's and doctorate, 2 letters of recommendation. Additional exam requirements/recommendations for international students: Required—TOEFL (minimum score 540 paper-based; 207 computer-based). *Application deadline:* Applications are processed on a rolling basis. Application fee: $50. Electronic applications accepted. *Expenses:* Tuition, state resident: full-time $7488; part-time $416 per credit. Tuition, nonresident: full-time $11,232; part-time $624 per credit. *Required fees:* $2070; $192.20 per credit. $90 per semester. *Financial support:* In 2011–12, 19 research assistantships with full and partial tuition reimbursements (averaging $6,699 per year), 10 teaching assistantships with partial tuition reimbursements (averaging $14,558 per year) were awarded; fellowships also available. Financial award application deadline: 4/15; financial award applicants required to submit FAFSA. *Unit head:* Dr. Ben Rafoth, Graduate Coordinator, 724-357-2272. *Application contact:* Paula Stossel, Assistant Dean, 724-357-4511, E-mail: graduate-admissions@iup.edu. Web site: http://www.iup.edu/upper.aspx?id=216.

Indiana University of Pennsylvania, School of Graduate Studies and Research, College of Humanities and Social Sciences, Department of English, Program in Teaching English, Indiana, PA 15705-1087. Offers MA. *Faculty:* 27 full-time (11 women). *Students:* 13 full-time (8 women), 8 part-time (6 women). Average age 27. 18 applicants, 67% accepted, 11 enrolled. In 2011, 7 master's awarded. *Entrance requirements:* Additional exam requirements/recommendations for international students: Required—TOEFL (minimum score 540 paper-based; 207 computer-based). *Application deadline:* Applications are processed on a rolling basis. Application fee: $50. Electronic applications accepted. *Expenses:* Tuition, state resident: full-time $7488; part-time $416 per credit. Tuition, nonresident: full-time $11,232; part-time $624 per credit. *Required fees:* $2070; $192.20 per credit. $90 per semester. *Financial support:* Application deadline: 4/16; applicants required to submit FAFSA. *Unit head:* Dr. Linda Norris, Coordinator, 724-357-2263, E-mail: lnorris@iup.edu. *Application contact:* Paula Stossel, Assistant Dean, 724-357-2222, Fax: 724-357-4862, E-mail: graduate-admissions@iup.edu. Web site: http://www.iup.edu/english/mateachingenglish/.

Indiana University–Purdue University Fort Wayne, College of Arts and Sciences, Department of English and Linguistics, Fort Wayne, IN 46805-1499. Offers English (MA, MAT); TENL (teaching English as a new language) (Certificate). Part-time programs available. *Faculty:* 23 full-time (10 women), 1 (woman) part-time/adjunct. *Students:* 7 full-time (3 women), 26 part-time (19 women); includes 1 minority (Hispanic/Latino). Average age 34. 7 applicants, 71% accepted, 4 enrolled. In 2011, 11 master's, 5 other advanced degrees awarded. *Degree requirements:* For master's, one foreign language, thesis (for some programs), teaching certificate (MAT). *Entrance requirements:* For master's, GRE General Test, minimum GPA of 3.0, major or minor in English, 3 letters of recommendation; for Certificate, bachelor's degree with minimum GPA of 2.5. Additional exam requirements/recommendations for international students: Required—TOEFL (minimum score 600 paper-based; 260 computer-based; 77 iBT). *Application deadline:* For fall admission, 8/1 for domestic students; for spring admission, 10/15 for domestic students. Applications are processed on a rolling basis. Application fee: $50. *Financial support:* In 2011–12, 11 teaching assistantships with partial tuition reimbursements (averaging $12,930 per year) were awarded; career-related internships or fieldwork, scholarships/grants, and unspecified assistantships also available. Support available to part-time students. Financial award application deadline: 3/1; financial award applicants required to submit FAFSA. *Faculty research:* Generosity, basic writers at open-admission universities, three-volume novel. *Total annual research expenditures:* $60,146. *Unit head:* Dr. Hardin Aasand, Chair and Professor, 260-481-6750, Fax: 260-481-6985, E-mail: aasandh@ipfw.edu. *Application contact:* Dr. Lewis Roberts, Graduate Program Director, 260-481-6754, Fax: 260-481-6985, E-mail: robertlc@ipfw.edu. Web site: http://www.ipfw.edu/english.

Indiana University–Purdue University Indianapolis, School of Liberal Arts, Department of English, Indianapolis, IN 46202-2896. Offers English (MA); teaching English (MA); teaching English as a second language (TESOL) (Certificate); teaching writing (Certificate). *Faculty:* 22 full-time (11 women). *Students:* 21 full-time (13 women), 14 part-time (9 women); includes 2 minority (1 Black or African American, non-Hispanic/Latino; 1 Two or more races, non-Hispanic/Latino). Average age 32. 28 applicants, 68% accepted, 14 enrolled. In 2011, 25 master's, 7 other advanced degrees awarded. *Entrance requirements:* For master's, GRE. Additional exam requirements/recommendations for international students: Required—TOEFL. *Application deadline:* For fall admission, 1/15 priority date for domestic students, 1/15 for international students; for spring admission, 10/15 priority date for domestic students, 10/15 for international students. Application fee: $55 ($65 for international students). *Financial support:* In 2011–12, 2 fellowships (averaging $10,000 per year), 4 research assistantships (averaging $9,500 per year), 12 teaching assistantships (averaging $7,103 per year) were awarded; career-related internships or fieldwork also available. *Unit head:* Dr. Thomas Upton, Chair, 317-274-4226, Fax: 317-278-1287, E-mail: tupton@iupuil.edu. *Application contact:* Dr. Robert Rebein, Director of Graduate Studies in English, 317-274-1405, Fax: 317-278-1287, E-mail: rrebein@iupui.edu. Web site: http://liberalarts.iupui.edu/english/.

Iona College, School of Arts and Science, Program in Education, New Rochelle, NY 10801-1890. Offers adolescence education: biology (MS Ed, MST); adolescence education: English (MS Ed, MST); adolescence education: Italian (MS Ed, MST); adolescence education: mathematics (MS Ed, MST); adolescence education: social studies (MS Ed, MST); adolescence education: Spanish (MS Ed, MST); adolescence special education 5-12 (MST); adolescence special education/literacy 5-12 (MS Ed); childhood 1-6/special education 1-6 (MST); childhood education (MST); early childhood/childhood (MST); educational leadership (MS Ed); literacy birth-grade 6/special education 1-6 (MS Ed); literacy education: birth-grade 6 (MS Ed). *Accreditation:* NCATE. Part-time and evening/weekend programs available. *Faculty:* 21 full-time (13 women), 13 part-time/adjunct (8 women). *Students:* 59 full-time (45 women), 101 part-time (78 women); includes 11 minority (2 Black or African American, non-Hispanic/Latino; 2 Asian, non-Hispanic/Latino; 7 Hispanic/Latino). Average age 26. 74 applicants, 66% accepted, 35 enrolled. In 2011, 46 master's awarded. *Degree requirements:* For master's, thesis or alternative. *Entrance requirements:* For master's, minimum GPA of 2.5 (MST), New York teaching certificate (MS Ed). Additional exam requirements/recommendations for international students: Required—TOEFL (minimum score 550 paper-based; 213 computer-based). *Application deadline:* Applications are processed on a rolling basis. Application fee: $50. Electronic applications accepted. *Expenses:* *Tuition:* Part-time $872 per credit. *Required fees:* $225 per term. *Financial support:* Unspecified assistantships available. Support available to part-time students. Financial award application deadline: 4/15; financial award applicants required to submit FAFSA. *Faculty research:* Reading/writing, educational technology, administration, early literacy assessment, literacy development. *Unit head:* Dr. Catherine O'Callaghan, Chair, 914-633-2210, Fax: 914-633-2608, E-mail: cocallaghan@iona.edu. *Application contact:* Dr. Jeanne Zaino, Interim Dean, School of Arts and Science, 914-633-2112, Fax: 914-633-2023, E-mail: jzaino@iona.edu.

Ithaca College, Division of Graduate and Professional Studies, School of Humanities and Sciences, Program in Adolescence Education, Ithaca, NY 14850. Offers biology 7-12 (MAT); chemistry 7-12 (MAT); English 7-12 (MAT); French 7-12 (MAT); math 7-12 (MAT); physics 7-12 (MAT); social studies 7-12 (MAT); Spanish (MAT). Part-time programs available. *Faculty:* 23 full-time (7 women). *Students:* 14 full-time (8 women), 1 part-time (0 women); includes 4 minority (1 Asian, non-Hispanic/Latino; 2 Hispanic/Latino; 1 Two or more races, non-Hispanic/Latino). Average age 27. 33 applicants, 64% accepted, 15 enrolled. In 2011, 15 master's awarded. *Degree requirements:* For master's, thesis or alternative, student teaching. *Entrance requirements:* For master's, minimum GPA of 3.0. Additional exam requirements/recommendations for international students: Required—TOEFL (minimum score 550 paper-based; 213 computer-based; 80 iBT). *Application deadline:* For fall admission, 2/15 priority date for domestic students, 2/15 for international students; for spring admission, 12/1 for domestic and international students. Applications are processed on a rolling basis. Application fee: $40. Electronic applications accepted. *Expenses:* Contact institution. *Financial support:* In 2011–12, 9 students received support, including 9 teaching assistantships (averaging $6,070 per year); career-related internships or fieldwork, Federal Work-Study, scholarships/grants, and unspecified assistantships also available. Support available to part-time students. Financial award application deadline: 2/15; financial award applicants required to submit CSS PROFILE or FAFSA. *Faculty research:* Bilingual education, socio-linguistic perspective on literacy. *Unit head:* Dr. Linda Hanrahan, Chairperson, 607-274-3143, Fax: 607-274-1263, E-mail: gps@ithaca.edu. *Application contact:* Gerard Turbide, Director, Office of Admission, 607-274-3143, Fax: 607-274-1263, E-mail: gps@ithaca.edu. Web site: http://www.ithaca.edu/gps/gradprograms/overview/school/hs/aded.

Jackson State University, Graduate School, College of Liberal Arts, Department of English and Modern Foreign Languages, Jackson, MS 39217. Offers English (MA); teaching English (MAT). Part-time and evening/weekend programs available. *Degree requirements:* For master's, comprehensive exam, thesis or alternative. *Entrance requirements:* For master's, GRE General Test. Additional exam requirements/recommendations for international students: Required—TOEFL (minimum score 520 paper-based; 195 computer-based; 67 iBT).

The Johns Hopkins University, School of Education, Department of Teacher Preparation, Baltimore, MD 21218. Offers early childhood education (MAT); education (MS), including educational studies; elementary education (MAT); English for speakers of other languages (MAT); K-8 mathematics lead-teacher (Certificate); K-8 science lead-teacher (Certificate); secondary education (MAT), including biology, chemistry, earth/space/environmental science, English, French, mathematics, physics, social studies, Spanish. Part-time and evening/weekend programs available. *Degree requirements:* For master's, portfolio, PRAXIS II, internship. *Entrance requirements:* For master's, PRAXIS I, SAT, ACT, or GRE (MAT), minimum undergraduate GPA of 3.0, interview, 1 letter of recommendation, curriculum vitae/resume; for Certificate, bachelor's degree, minimum undergraduate GPA of 3.0, essay/statement of goals, interview. Additional exam requirements/recommendations for international students: Required—TOEFL (minimum score 600 paper-based; 250 computer-based; 100 iBT). Electronic applications accepted. *Faculty research:* Teacher retention, STEM education reform, alternative certification programs, school-university partnerships, urban education, action research/data-informed instruction, family engagement.

Kansas State University, Graduate School, College of Education, Department of Curriculum and Instruction, Manhattan, KS 66506. Offers career and technical education (Ed D, PhD); curriculum studies (Ed D, PhD); digital teaching and learning (MS); educational computing, design and online learning (MS); educational technology (Ed D, PhD); elementary/middle level (MS); English as a second language (MS); language/diversity education (Ed D, PhD); literacy education (Ed D, PhD); mathematics education (Ed D, PhD); middle level/secondary (MS); reading and language arts (MS); reading specialist endorsement (MS); science education (Ed D, PhD); social science education (Ed D, PhD); teacher education (Ed D, PhD); teacher leader/school improvement (MS, Ed D). *Accreditation:* NCATE. Part-time programs available. Postbaccalaureate distance learning degree programs offered (minimal on-campus study). *Faculty:* 15 full-time (12 women), 3 part-time/adjunct (2 women). *Students:* 37 full-time (30 women), 113 part-time (91 women); includes 14 minority (4 Black or African American, non-Hispanic/Latino; 1 American Indian or Alaska Native, non-Hispanic/Latino; 1 Asian, non-Hispanic/Latino; 7 Hispanic/Latino; 1 Two or more races, non-Hispanic/Latino), 15 international. Average age 37. 75 applicants, 51% accepted, 9 enrolled. In 2011, 48 master's, 14 doctorates awarded. *Degree requirements:* For master's, comprehensive exam, portfolio, project, report or thesis; for doctorate, comprehensive exam, thesis/dissertation, preliminary exam. *Entrance requirements:* For master's, minimum GPA of 3.0; for doctorate, GRE, minimum GPA of 3.0. Additional exam requirements/recommendations for international students: Required—TOEFL. *Application deadline:* For fall admission, 2/1 priority date for domestic students, 2/1 for international students; for spring admission, 8/1 priority date for domestic students, 8/1 for international students. Applications are processed on a rolling basis. Application fee: $40 ($55 for international students). Electronic applications accepted. *Financial support:* In 2011–12, 1 research assistantship (averaging $16,900 per year), 8 teaching assistantships (averaging $12,466 per year) were awarded; career-related internships or fieldwork, institutionally sponsored loans, and scholarships/grants also available. Support available to part-time students. Financial award application deadline: 3/1; financial award applicants required to submit FAFSA. *Faculty research:* Literacy and technology, critical race theory and diversity, achievement gaps, school improvement, teacher education. *Total annual research expenditures:* $510,907. *Unit head:* Dr. Gail Shroyer, Chair, 785-532-5550, Fax: 785-532-7304, E-mail: gshroyer@ksu.edu. *Application contact:* Dona Deam, Application Contact, 785-532-5595, Fax: 785-532-7304, E-mail: ddeam@ksu.edu. Web site: http://coe.k-state.edu/departments/currin/curringrad.htm.

Kennesaw State University, Leland and Clarice C. Bagwell College of Education, Program in Teaching, Kennesaw, GA 30144-5591. Offers art education (MAT); secondary English or mathematics (MAT); secondary science education (MAT); teaching English to speakers of other languages (MAT). Program offered only in summer. Part-time and evening/weekend programs available. *Students:* 101 full-time (68 women), 20 part-time (15 women); includes 27 minority (14 Black or African American, non-Hispanic/Latino; 6 Asian, non-Hispanic/Latino; 4 Hispanic/Latino; 3 Two or more races, non-Hispanic/Latino), 3 international. Average age 33. 13 applicants, 62% accepted, 7 enrolled. In 2011, 81 master's awarded. *Entrance requirements:* For master's, GRE, GACE I (state certificate exam), minimum GPA of 2.75, 2 recommendations, resume. Additional exam requirements/recommendations for international students: Required—TOEFL (minimum score 550 paper-based; 213 computer-based; 80 iBT), IELTS (minimum score 6). *Application deadline:* For fall admission, 6/1 for domestic and international students; for spring admission, 3/1 for domestic and international students. Application fee: $60. Electronic applications accepted. *Expenses:* Tuition, state resident: full-time $3000; part-time $250 per semester hour. Tuition, nonresident: full-time $10,836; part-time $903 per semester hour. *Required fees:* $774 per semester. *Financial support:* In 2011–12, 2 research assistantships with tuition reimbursements (averaging $4,000 per year) were awarded; unspecified assistantships also available. Financial award application deadline: 4/1; financial award applicants required to submit FAFSA. *Unit head:* Dr. Lynn Stallings, Director, 770-420-4477, E-mail: lstalling@kennesaw.edu. *Application contact:* Alisha Bello, Administrative Coordinator, 770-423-6043, Fax: 770-420-4435, E-mail: abello1@kennesaw.edu. Web site: http://www.kennesaw.edu.

Kent State University, College of Arts and Sciences, Department of English, Kent, OH 44242-0001. Offers comparative literature (MA); creative writing (MFA); English (PhD); English for teachers (MA); literature and writing (MA); rhetoric and composition (PhD); teaching English as a second language (MA). MFA program offered jointly with Cleveland State University, The University of Akron, and Youngstown State University. Part-time programs available. Terminal master's awarded for partial completion of doctoral program. *Degree requirements:* For master's, one foreign language, thesis optional; for doctorate, one foreign language, thesis/dissertation, qualifying exams. *Entrance requirements:* For master's and doctorate, GRE General Test, writing sample, letters of recommendation. Additional exam requirements/recommendations for international students: Required—TOEFL (minimum score 600 paper-based). Electronic applications accepted. *Expenses:* Tuition, state resident: full-time $8136; part-time $452 per credit hour. Tuition, nonresident: full-time $14,292; part-time $794 per credit hour. *Faculty research:* British and American literature, textual editing, rhetoric and composition, cultural studies, linguistic and critical theories.

Kutztown University of Pennsylvania, College of Education, Program in Secondary Education, Kutztown, PA 19530-0730. Offers biology (M Ed); curriculum and instruction (M Ed); English (M Ed); mathematics (M Ed); social studies (M Ed). *Accreditation:* NCATE. Part-time and evening/weekend programs available. *Faculty:* 7 full-time (2 women). *Students:* 29 full-time (12 women), 73 part-time (43 women); includes 3 minority (1 Black or African American, non-Hispanic/Latino; 1 Asian, non-Hispanic/Latino; 1 Hispanic/Latino). Average age 28. 12 applicants, 100% accepted, 12 enrolled. In 2011, 29 master's awarded. *Degree requirements:* For master's, comprehensive exam, thesis optional. *Entrance requirements:* For master's, GRE General Test. Additional exam requirements/recommendations for international students: Required—TOEFL (minimum score 550 paper-based; 79 iBT). *Application deadline:* For fall admission, 8/1 priority date for domestic students, 8/1 for international students; for spring admission, 12/1 priority date for domestic students, 12/1 for international students. Applications are processed on a rolling basis. Application fee: $35. Electronic applications accepted. *Expenses:* Tuition, state resident: full-time $7488; part-time $416 per credit. Tuition, nonresident: full-time $11,232; part-time $624 per credit. *Financial support:* Career-related internships or fieldwork, Federal Work-Study, scholarships/grants, and unspecified assistantships available. Financial award application deadline: 3/1; financial award applicants required to submit FAFSA. *Unit head:* Dr. Theresa Stahler, Chairperson, 610-683-4259, Fax: 610-683-1338, E-mail: stahler@kutztown.edu. *Application contact:* Kelly D. Burr, Associate Director, Graduate Admissions, 610-683-4200, Fax: 610-683-1393, E-mail: graduate@kutztown.edu.

Lehman College of the City University of New York, Division of Education, Department of Middle and High School Education, Program in English Education, Bronx, NY 10468-1589. Offers MS Ed. *Accreditation:* NCATE. *Entrance requirements:* For master's, minimum GPA of 3.0 in English, 2.8 overall; teaching certificate.

Le Moyne College, Department of Education, Syracuse, NY 13214. Offers adolescent education (MS Ed, MST); adolescent education/special education (MS Ed, MST); adolescent English (grades 7-12) (MST); adolescent history (grades 7-12) (MST); childhood education (MS Ed); childhood education/special education (MS Ed); elementary education (MS Ed); general professional education (MS Ed); inclusive childhood education (MST); literacy education (birth to grade 6) (MS Ed); literacy education (grades 5-12) (MS Ed); school building leadership (MS Ed, CAS); school district business leader (MS Ed, CAS); school district leadership (MS Ed, CAS); secondary education (MS Ed); special education (MS Ed); students with disabilities-generalist (grades 7-12) (MS Ed); TESOL (teaching English to speakers of other languages) (MS Ed); urban studies (MS Ed). *Accreditation:* Teacher Education Accreditation Council. Part-time and evening/weekend programs available. *Faculty:* 9 full-time (6 women), 51 part-time/adjunct (28 women). *Students:* 61 full-time (47 women), 311 part-time (222 women); includes 31 minority (19 Black or African American, non-Hispanic/Latino; 3 American Indian or Alaska Native, non-Hispanic/Latino; 4 Asian, non-Hispanic/Latino; 5 Hispanic/Latino), 2 international. Average age 30. 242 applicants, 90% accepted, 180 enrolled. In 2011, 168 master's, 23 CASs awarded. *Degree requirements:* For master's, thesis. *Entrance requirements:* For master's, GRE General Test, bachelor's degree, 2 letters of recommendation, written statement, transcripts. Additional exam requirements/recommendations for international students: Required—TOEFL (minimum score 550 paper-based; 213 computer-based; 79 iBT). *Application deadline:* For fall admission, 4/1 priority date for domestic students, 4/1 for international students; for spring admission, 10/1 priority date for domestic students, 10/1 for international students. Applications are processed on a rolling basis. Application fee: $50. *Expenses:* Contact institution. *Financial support:* In 2011–12, 32 students received support. Career-related internships or fieldwork and health care benefits available. Support available to part-time students. Financial award applicants required to submit FAFSA. *Faculty research:* Minority teachers, special education, multiculturalism, literacy, technology, video games learning, autism, school district organization, service-learning, higher level problem solving, teacher leadership. *Unit head:* Dr. Suzanne L. Gilmour, Chair, Department of Education and Director of Graduate Education Programs, 315-445-4376, Fax: 315-445-4744, E-mail: gilmous@lemoyne.edu. *Application contact:* Kristen P. Trapasso, Director of Graduate Admission, 315-445-4265, Fax: 315-445-6027, E-mail: trapaskp@lemoyne.edu. Web site: http://www.lemoyne.edu/education.

Lincoln Memorial University, Carter and Moyers School of Education, Harrogate, TN 37752-1901. Offers administration and supervision (M Ed, Ed S); counseling and guidance (M Ed); curriculum and instruction (M Ed, Ed D, Ed S); English (M Ed); executive leadership (Ed D); higher education administration (Ed D); human resource development (Ed D); leadership and administration (Ed D). Part-time and evening/weekend programs available. Postbaccalaureate distance learning degree programs offered. *Degree requirements:* For master's, comprehensive exam, thesis optional; for Ed S, comprehensive exam. *Entrance requirements:* For master's, PRAXIS, NTE, GRE, MAT, letters of recommendation; for Ed S, graduate transcripts. Additional exam requirements/recommendations for international students: Recommended—TOEFL. *Faculty research:* Brain compatible teaching and learning; poverty in Appalachia; leadership for change; ethics, moral responsibility and social justice; human and organizational learning.

Long Island University–Brooklyn Campus, Richard L. Conolly College of Liberal Arts and Sciences, Department of English, Brooklyn, NY 11201-8423. Offers creative writing (MFA); literature (MA); professional writing (MA); writing and rhetoric (MA). Part-time and evening/weekend programs available. *Degree requirements:* For master's, thesis or alternative. *Entrance requirements:* For master's, 2 letters of recommendation (at least 1 from a former professor or teacher). Additional exam requirements/recommendations for international students: Required—TOEFL (minimum score 550 paper-based; 173 computer-based). Electronic applications accepted.

Long Island University–C. W. Post Campus, School of Education, Department of Curriculum and Instruction, Brookville, NY 11548-1300. Offers adolescence education (MS); adolescence education: biology (MS); adolescence education: earth science (MS); adolescence education: English (MS); adolescence education: mathematics (MS); adolescence education: social studies (MS); adolescence education: Spanish (MS); art education (MS); bilingual education (MS); childhood education (MS); early childhood education (MS); middle childhood education (MS); music education (MS); teaching English to speakers of other languages (MS). Part-time and evening/weekend programs available. *Degree requirements:* For master's, comprehensive exam or thesis, student teaching. *Entrance requirements:* For master's, minimum GPA of 2.75 in major, 2.5

overall. Electronic applications accepted. *Faculty research:* Ethics and education, teaching strategies.

Longwood University, Office of Graduate Studies, College of Education and Human Services, Farmville, VA 23909. Offers communication sciences and disorders (MS); community and college counseling (MS); curriculum and instruction specialist-elementary (MS), including mild disabilities, modern languages; curriculum and instruction specialist-secondary (MS), including English, mild disabilities, modern languages; educational leadership (MS); guidance and counseling (MS); literacy and culture (MS); school library media (MS). *Accreditation:* NCATE. Part-time and evening/weekend programs available. *Degree requirements:* For master's, comprehensive exam, thesis optional. *Entrance requirements:* For master's, GRE (communication sciences and disorders), minimum GPA of 2.75. Additional exam requirements/recommendations for international students: Required—TOEFL (minimum score 550 paper-based; 213 computer-based).

Longwood University, Office of Graduate Studies, Department of English and Modern Languages, Farmville, VA 23909. Offers 6-12 initial teaching/licensure (MA); creative writing (MA); English education and writing (MA); literature (MA). Part-time programs available. *Degree requirements:* For master's, comprehensive exam (for some programs), thesis (for some programs). *Entrance requirements:* For master's, minimum GPA of 2.75. Additional exam requirements/recommendations for international students: Required—TOEFL (minimum score 550 paper-based; 213 computer-based).

Louisiana Tech University, Graduate School, College of Education, Department of Curriculum, Instruction and Leadership, Ruston, LA 71272. Offers curriculum and instruction (MS, Ed D); educational leadership (Ed D); secondary education (M Ed), including business education, English education, foreign language education, health and physical education, mathematics education, science education, social studies education, speech education. *Accreditation:* NCATE. Part-time programs available. *Degree requirements:* For doctorate, thesis/dissertation. *Entrance requirements:* For master's and doctorate, GRE General Test.

Loyola University Maryland, Graduate Programs, Department of Education, Program in Teacher Education, Baltimore, MD 21210-2699. Offers elementary/middle education (MAT); secondary education (MAT); secondary education: biology (MAT); secondary education: chemistries (MAT); secondary education: earth science (MAT); secondary education: English (MAT); secondary education: mathematics (MAT); secondary education: physics (MAT). Part-time programs available. *Faculty:* 25 full-time (21 women), 14 part-time/adjunct (11 women). *Students:* 28 full-time (19 women), 58 part-time (45 women); includes 5 minority (1 Black or African American, non-Hispanic/Latino; 2 Asian, non-Hispanic/Latino; 2 Two or more races, non-Hispanic/Latino), 4 international. Average age 28. In 2011, 37 master's awarded. *Entrance requirements:* For master's, PRAXIS, SAT, ACT, or GRE. Additional exam requirements/recommendations for international students: Required—TOEFL (minimum score 550 paper-based; 213 computer-based). *Application deadline:* For fall admission, 6/15 for domestic students; for spring admission, 11/1 for domestic students. Electronic applications accepted. *Financial support:* Research assistantships and unspecified assistantships available. Financial award application deadline: 4/15. *Unit head:* Wendy Smith, Chair, 410-617-2194, E-mail: wmsmith@loyola.edu. *Application contact:* Maureen Faux, Executive Director, Graduate Admissions, 410-617-5020, Fax: 410-617-2002, E-mail: graduate@loyola.edu. Web site: http://www.loyola.edu/academics/theology/.

Manhattanville College, Graduate Studies, School of Education, Program in Middle Childhood/Adolescence Education (Grades 5-12), Purchase, NY 10577-2132. Offers biology (MAT); biology and special education (MPS); chemistry (MAT); chemistry and special education (MPS); English (MAT); English and special education (MPS); literacy (MPS), including reading and writing, writing; literacy and special education (MPS); math (MAT); math and special education (MPS); second language (MAT), including French, Italian, Latin, Spanish; social studies (MAT); social studies and special education (MPS); special education (MPS). Part-time and evening/weekend programs available. *Degree requirements:* For master's, comprehensive exam or research project, field experience. *Entrance requirements:* For master's, minimum undergraduate GPA of 3.0, 2 letters of recommendation. Additional exam requirements/recommendations for international students: Required—TOEFL. Electronic applications accepted.

Millersville University of Pennsylvania, College of Graduate and Professional Studies, School of Humanities and Social Sciences, Department of English, Millersville, PA 17551-0302. Offers English (MA); English education (M Ed). Part-time programs available. *Faculty:* 23 full-time (13 women), 11 part-time/adjunct (7 women). *Students:* 16 full-time (10 women), 24 part-time (18 women); includes 5 minority (2 Black or African American, non-Hispanic/Latino; 2 Asian, non-Hispanic/Latino; 1 Hispanic/Latino). Average age 32. 13 applicants, 100% accepted, 6 enrolled. In 2011, 12 master's awarded. *Degree requirements:* For master's, one foreign language, thesis optional. *Entrance requirements:* For master's, GRE or MAT, 3 letters of recommendation. Additional exam requirements/recommendations for international students: Required—TOEFL (minimum score 500 paper-based; 183 computer-based; 65 iBT). *Application deadline:* For fall admission, 1/15 priority date for domestic students, 1/15 for international students; for winter admission, 10/1 priority date for domestic students, 10/1 for international students; for spring admission, 10/1 priority date for domestic students, 10/1 for international students. Applications are processed on a rolling basis. Application fee: $40 ($50 for international students). Electronic applications accepted. *Expenses:* Tuition, state resident: full-time $3744; part-time $416 per credit. Tuition, nonresident: full-time $5616; part-time $624 per credit. *Required fees:* $1130; $125.50 per credit. Tuition and fees vary according to course load. *Financial support:* In 2011–12, 12 students received support, including 12 research assistantships with full tuition reimbursements available (averaging $3,690 per year); institutionally sponsored loans and unspecified assistantships also available. Support available to part-time students. Financial award application deadline: 3/15; financial award applicants required to submit FAFSA. *Unit head:* Dr. Caleb A. Corkery, Chair, 717-872-3227, Fax: 717-871-2446, E-mail: caleb.corkery@millersville.edu. *Application contact:* Dr. Victor S. DeSantis, Dean, College of Graduate and Professional Studies, 717-872-3099, Fax: 717-872-3453, E-mail: victor.desantis@millersville.edu. Web site: http://www.millersville.edu/english/graduate/index.php.

Mills College, Graduate Studies, School of Education, Oakland, CA 94613-1000. Offers child life in hospitals (MA); early childhood education (MA); education (MA), including art education, curriculum and instruction, elementary education, English education, foreign language education, mathematics education, science education, secondary education, social studies education, teaching; educational leadership (MA, Ed D). Part-time and evening/weekend programs available. *Faculty:* 13 full-time (10 women), 14 part-time/adjunct (10 women). *Students:* 149 full-time (133 women), 69 part-time (61 women); includes 85 minority (32 Black or African American, non-Hispanic/Latino; 1 American Indian or Alaska Native, non-Hispanic/Latino; 16 Asian, non-Hispanic/Latino; 24 Hispanic/Latino; 1 Native Hawaiian or other Pacific Islander, non-Hispanic/Latino; 11 Two or more races, non-Hispanic/Latino), 3 international. Average age 28. 238 applicants, 84% accepted, 106 enrolled. In 2011, 41 master's, 2 doctorates awarded. Terminal master's awarded for partial completion of doctoral program. *Degree requirements:* For master's, comprehensive exam. *Entrance requirements:* For master's, statement of purpose, official transcript, 3 recommendations; for doctorate, GRE General Test. Additional exam requirements/recommendations for international students: Required—TOEFL (minimum score 550 paper-based; 80 iBT) or IELTS (minimum score 6). *Application deadline:* For fall admission, 12/31 priority date for domestic students, 12/15 for international students; for spring admission, 11/1 priority date for domestic students, 10/1 for international students. Applications are processed on a rolling basis. Application fee: $50. Electronic applications accepted. *Expenses: Tuition:* Full-time $28,280; part-time $15,640 per year. *Required fees:* $958. Tuition and fees vary according to program. *Financial support:* In 2011–12, 43 students received support, including 225 fellowships with full and partial tuition reimbursements available (averaging $6,020 per year), 43 teaching assistantships with full and partial tuition reimbursements available (averaging $6,782 per year); career-related internships or fieldwork and scholarships/grants also available. Support available to part-time students. Financial award application deadline: 2/1; financial award applicants required to submit FAFSA. *Faculty research:* Early childhood education, teacher preparation, educational leadership. *Total annual research expenditures:* $2.3 million. *Unit head:* Katherine Schultz, Chairperson, 510-430-3170, Fax: 510-430-3379, E-mail: grad-studies@mills.edu. *Application contact:* Tiana Kozoil, Graduate Admission Specialist, 510-430-3305, Fax: 510-430-2159, E-mail: grad-studies@mills.edu. Web site: http://www.mills.edu/education.

Minnesota State University Mankato, College of Graduate Studies, College of Arts and Humanities, Department of English, Mankato, MN 56001. Offers creative writing (MFA); English (MAT); English studies (MA); teaching English as a second language (MA, Certificate); technical communication (MA, Certificate). Part-time programs available. *Students:* 57 full-time (30 women), 153 part-time (96 women). *Degree requirements:* For master's, one foreign language, comprehensive exam, thesis or alternative. *Entrance requirements:* For master's, minimum GPA of 3.0 during previous 2 years, writing sample (MFA). Additional exam requirements/recommendations for international students: Required—TOEFL (minimum score 500 paper-based; 61 iBT). *Application deadline:* For fall admission, 7/1 for domestic students, 5/1 for international students. Applications are processed on a rolling basis. Application fee: $40. Electronic applications accepted. *Financial support:* Research assistantships with full tuition reimbursements, teaching assistantships with full tuition reimbursements, career-related internships or fieldwork, Federal Work-Study, and unspecified assistantships available. Financial award application deadline: 3/15; financial award applicants required to submit FAFSA. *Faculty research:* Keats and Christianity. *Unit head:* Dr. John Banschbach, Chairperson, 507-389-2117. *Application contact:* 507-389-2321, E-mail: grad@mnsu.edu. Web site: http://english.mnsu.edu/.

Mississippi College, Graduate School, School of Education, Department of Teacher Education and Leadership, Clinton, MS 39058. Offers art (M Ed); biological science (M Ed); business education (M Ed); computer science (M Ed); dyslexia therapy (M Ed); educational leadership (M Ed, Ed D, Ed S); elementary education (M Ed, Ed S); English (M Ed); higher education administration (MS); mathematics (M Ed); secondary education (M Ed); social studies (history) (M Ed); teaching arts (M Ed). Part-time programs available. Postbaccalaureate distance learning degree programs offered (no on-campus study). *Degree requirements:* For master's, comprehensive exam, thesis optional. *Entrance requirements:* For master's, NTE. Additional exam requirements/recommendations for international students: Recommended—TOEFL, IELTS. Electronic applications accepted.

Montclair State University, The Graduate School, College of Education and Human Services, Department of Curriculum and Teaching, Program in Teaching in Content Area, Montclair, NJ 07043-1624. Offers art (MAT); biology (MAT); chemistry (MAT); earth science (MAT); English (MAT); French (MAT); health and physical education (MAT); health education (MAT); mathematics (MAT); music (MAT); physical education (MAT); physical science (MAT); social studies (MAT); Spanish (MAT); teacher of English as a second language (MAT). *Students:* 162 full-time (90 women), 47 part-time (29 women); includes 37 minority (4 Black or African American, non-Hispanic/Latino; 11 Asian, non-Hispanic/Latino; 18 Hispanic/Latino; 4 Two or more races, non-Hispanic/Latino), 5 international. Average age 31. 145 applicants, 41% accepted, 56 enrolled. In 2011, 229 master's awarded. *Degree requirements:* For master's, comprehensive exam, thesis or alternative. *Entrance requirements:* For master's, GRE General Test, interview, 2 letters of recommendation. Additional exam requirements/recommendations for international students: Required—TOEFL (minimum score 83 iBT), IELTS (minimum score 6.5). *Application deadline:* Applications are processed on a rolling basis. Application fee: $60. Electronic applications accepted. *Financial support:* Federal Work-Study, scholarships/grants, and unspecified assistantships available. Support available to part-time students. Financial award application deadline: 3/1; financial award applicants required to submit FAFSA. *Unit head:* Dr. David Schwarzer, Chairperson, 973-655-5187. *Application contact:* Amy Aiello, Executive Director of The Graduate School, 973-655-5147, Fax: 973-655-7869, E-mail: graduate.school@montclair.edu.

Montclair State University, The Graduate School, College of Humanities and Social Sciences, Department of English, Teaching Writing Certificate Program, Montclair, NJ 07043-1624. Offers Certificate. Part-time and evening/weekend programs available. *Students:* 5 part-time (4 women). Average age 31. 8 applicants, 63% accepted, 1 enrolled. In 2011, 7 degrees awarded. *Entrance requirements:* For degree, 2 letters of recommendation, essay. Additional exam requirements/recommendations for international students: Required—TOEFL (minimum score 83 iBT), IELTS (minimum score 6.5). *Application deadline:* Applications are processed on a rolling basis. Application fee: $60. Electronic applications accepted. *Financial support:* Federal Work-Study, scholarships/grants, and unspecified assistantships available. Support available to part-time students. Financial award application deadline: 3/1; financial award applicants required to submit FAFSA. *Faculty research:* Pedagogy in writing. *Unit head:* Dr. Dan Bronson, Chairperson, 973-655-4274. *Application contact:* Amy Aiello, Director of Graduate Admissions and Operations, 973-655-5147, Fax: 973-655-7869, E-mail: graduate.school@montclair.edu. Web site: http://www.montclair.edu/graduate/programs/certificate/twri.php.

Morehead State University, Graduate Programs, College of Education, Department of Foundational and Graduate Studies in Education, Morehead, KY 40351. Offers adult and higher education (MA, Ed S); certified professional counselor (Ed S); counseling P-12 (MA); curriculum and instruction (Ed S); educational technology (MA Ed); instructional leadership (Ed S); school administration (MA); school counseling (Ed S); teacher leader business and marketing content (MA Ed); teacher leader business and marketing technology (MA Ed); teacher leader educational technology (MA Ed); teacher leader English (MA Ed); teacher leader gifted education (MA Ed); teacher leader IECE certification (MA Ed); teacher leader interdisciplinary education P-5 (MA Ed); teacher leader middle grades (MA Ed); teacher leader non IECE certification (MA Ed); teacher leader reading/writing - non-certification (MA Ed); teacher leader reading/writing certification (MA Ed); teacher leader school communication - certification (MA Ed); teacher leader school communication - non-certification (MA Ed); teacher leader social studies (MA Ed); teacher leader special education (MA Ed). *Accreditation:* NCATE. Part-time and evening/weekend programs available. *Degree requirements:* For master's, thesis optional, oral and/or written comprehensive exams; for Ed S, thesis, oral exam. *Entrance requirements:* For master's, GRE General Test, minimum overall undergraduate GPA of 2.5; for Ed S, GRE General Test, interview, master's degree, minimum GPA of 3.5, work experience. Additional exam requirements/ recommendations for international students: Required—TOEFL (minimum score 500 paper-based; 173 computer-based). Electronic applications accepted. *Faculty research:* Character education, school accountability, computer applications for school administrators.

Morehead State University, Graduate Programs, College of Education, Department of Middle Grades and Secondary Education, Morehead, KY 40351. Offers business and marketing education (MAT); English/language arts 5-9 (MAT); French (MAT); health P-12 (MAT); mathematics 5-9 (MAT); physical education P-12 (MAT); science 5-9 (MAT); secondary biology (MAT); secondary chemistry (MAT); secondary earth science (MAT); secondary English (MAT); secondary math (MAT); secondary physics (MAT); secondary social studies (MAT); social studies 5-9 (MAT); Spanish (MAT). Part-time and evening/ weekend programs available. *Degree requirements:* For master's, portfolio. *Entrance requirements:* For master's, GRE or PRAXIS II content exam, minimum overall undergraduate GPA of 2.5. Additional exam requirements/recommendations for international students: Required—TOEFL (minimum score 500 paper-based; 173 computer-based). Electronic applications accepted.

National Louis University, National College of Education, Chicago, IL 60603. Offers administration and supervision (M Ed, Ed D, CAS, Ed S); curriculum and instruction (M Ed, MS Ed, CAS); early childhood administration (M Ed, CAS); early childhood education (M Ed, MAT, MS Ed, CAS); education (Ed D); educational psychology/human learning and development (M Ed, MS Ed, CAS, Ed S); elementary education (MAT); interdisciplinary curriculum and instruction (M Ed); mathematics education (M Ed, MS Ed, CAS); reading and language (M Ed, MS Ed, CAS); school psychology (M Ed, Ed S); science education (M Ed, MS Ed, CAS); secondary education (MAT); special education (M Ed, MAT, CAS); technology in education (M Ed, CAS). *Accreditation:* NCATE. Part-time and evening/weekend programs available. *Students:* 224 full-time (162 women), 2,336 part-time (1,767 women); includes 677 minority (366 Black or African American, non-Hispanic/Latino; 8 American Indian or Alaska Native, non-Hispanic/Latino; 68 Asian, non-Hispanic/Latino; 218 Hispanic/Latino; 2 Native Hawaiian or other Pacific Islander, non-Hispanic/Latino; 15 Two or more races, non-Hispanic/ Latino), 2 international. Average age 34. In 2011, 1,711 master's, 76 doctorates, 86 other advanced degrees awarded. *Degree requirements:* For doctorate, comprehensive exam, thesis/dissertation. *Entrance requirements:* For master's, MAT or GRE, minimum GPA of 3.0; for doctorate, GRE General Test, minimum GPA of 3.25, interview, resume, writing sample, 4 recommendations. Additional exam requirements/recommendations for international students: Required—TOEFL (minimum score 550 paper-based; 213 computer-based; 79 iBT). *Application deadline:* Applications are processed on a rolling basis. Application fee: $40. *Financial support:* Fellowships, research assistantships, teaching assistantships, career-related internships or fieldwork, Federal Work-Study, institutionally sponsored loans, and scholarships/grants available. Support available to part-time students. Financial award applicants required to submit FAFSA. *Unit head:* Dr. Alison Hilsabeck, Dean, 312-361-3580, Fax: 312-261-2580, E-mail: ahilsabeck@nl.edu. *Application contact:* Ken Kasprzak, Director of Admission, 888-658-8632, Fax: 847-947-5575, E-mail: kkasprzak@nl.edu.

New York University, Steinhardt School of Culture, Education, and Human Development, Department of Music and Performing Arts Professions, Program in Educational Theatre, New York, NY 10012-1019. Offers dual certification: educational theatre and English 7-12 (MA); dual certification: educational theatre and social studies (MA); educational theatre (Ed D, PhD, Advanced Certificate); educational theatre for colleges and communities (MA); teaching educational theatre, all grades (MA). Part-time programs available. *Degree requirements:* For master's, thesis (for some programs); for doctorate, thesis/dissertation. *Entrance requirements:* For master's, audition; for doctorate, GRE General Test, interview; for Advanced Certificate, master's degree. Additional exam requirements/recommendations for international students: Required—TOEFL. Electronic applications accepted. *Faculty research:* Theatre for young audiences, drama in education, applied theatre, arts education assessment, reflective praxis.

New York University, Steinhardt School of Culture, Education, and Human Development, Department of Teaching and Learning, Program in English Education, New York, NY 10012-1019. Offers secondary and college (PhD), including applied linguistics, comparative education, curriculum, literature and reading, media education; teachers of English 7-12 (MA); teachers of English language and literature in college (Advanced Certificate). *Accreditation:* Teacher Education Accreditation Council. Part-time programs available. *Degree requirements:* For master's, thesis (for some programs); for doctorate, thesis/dissertation. *Entrance requirements:* For doctorate, GRE General Test, interview; for Advanced Certificate, master's degree. Additional exam requirements/recommendations for international students: Required—TOEFL. Electronic applications accepted. *Faculty research:* Making meaning of literature, teaching of literature, urban adolescent literacy and equity, literacy development and globalization, digital media and literacy .

North Carolina Agricultural and Technical State University, School of Graduate Studies, College of Arts and Sciences, Department of English, Greensboro, NC 27411. Offers English (MA); English and African-American literature (MA); English education (MAT, MS). Part-time and evening/weekend programs available. *Degree requirements:* For master's, comprehensive exam, qualifying exam. *Entrance requirements:* For master's, GRE General Test, minimum GPA of 3.0.

North Carolina State University, Graduate School, College of Education, Department of Curriculum and Instruction, Program in Secondary English Education, Raleigh, NC 27695. Offers M Ed, MS Ed. *Degree requirements:* For master's, thesis optional.

Northeastern Illinois University, Graduate College, College of Education, School of Teacher Education, Program in Instruction, Chicago, IL 60625-4699. Offers language arts (MSI). *Degree requirements:* For master's, 2 research papers, oral exam. *Entrance requirements:* For master's, minimum GPA of 2.75; previous course work in English, linguistics, or speech; teaching certificate. Additional exam requirements/ recommendations for international students: Required—TOEFL (minimum score 550 paper-based; 213 computer-based; 79 iBT). Electronic applications accepted. *Faculty research:* Emergent literacy, literature-based literacy instruction, drama and literature in the classroom, curriculum integration, standards-based assessment, integrating technology.

Northeastern Illinois University, Graduate College, College of Education, School of Teacher Education, Program in Teaching, Chicago, IL 60625-4699. Offers language arts (MAT). *Accreditation:* NCATE. *Degree requirements:* For master's, 2 research papers, oral exam. *Entrance requirements:* For master's, minimum GPA of 2.75; previous course work in English, speech, drama, or linguistics. Additional exam requirements/ recommendations for international students: Required—TOEFL (minimum score 550 paper-based; 213 computer-based; 79 iBT). Electronic applications accepted. *Faculty research:* Emergent literacy, literature-based literacy, drama and literature in the classroom, curriculum integration, standards-based assessment.

Northern Arizona University, Graduate College, College of Arts and Letters, Department of English, Flagstaff, AZ 86011. Offers applied linguistics (PhD); English (MA, MFA), including creative writing (MFA), general English studies (MA), literacy, technology and professional writing (MA), literature (MA), secondary English education (MA); professional writing (Certificate); teaching English as a second language (MA, Certificate). Part-time programs available. *Faculty:* 52 full-time (35 women). *Students:* 107 full-time (70 women), 100 part-time (77 women); includes 41 minority (9 Black or African American, non-Hispanic/Latino; 3 American Indian or Alaska Native, non-Hispanic/Latino; 2 Asian, non-Hispanic/Latino; 20 Hispanic/Latino; 7 Two or more races, non-Hispanic/Latino), 30 international. Average age 31. 209 applicants, 62% accepted, 78 enrolled. In 2011, 115 master's, 5 doctorates, 14 other advanced degrees awarded. *Degree requirements:* For master's, comprehensive exam (for some programs), thesis (for some programs), departmental qualifying exam; for doctorate, comprehensive exam, thesis/dissertation, departmental qualifying exam. *Entrance requirements:* For master's, minimum GPA of 3.0 or GRE; for doctorate, GRE General Test. Additional exam requirements/recommendations for international students: Required—TOEFL (minimum score 550 paper-based; 213 computer-based; 80 iBT), IELTS (minimum score 7), TOEFL (minimum score 600 paper-based; 250 computer-based; 100 iBT) for PhD; TOEFL (minimum score 570 paper-based; 237 computer-based; 89 iBT) for MA. *Application deadline:* For fall admission, 4/15 priority date for domestic students, 2/15 for international students; for spring admission, 11/15 priority date for domestic students, 11/15 for international students. Applications are processed on a rolling basis. Application fee: $65. Electronic applications accepted. *Expenses:* Tuition, state resident: full-time $7190; part-time $355 per credit hour. Tuition, nonresident: full-time $18,092; part-time $1005 per credit hour. *Required fees:* $818; $328 per semester. *Financial support:* In 2011–12, 72 teaching assistantships with partial tuition reimbursements (averaging $11,623 per year) were awarded; Federal Work-Study, scholarships/grants, health care benefits, tuition waivers (full and partial), and unspecified assistantships also available. Financial award applicants required to submit FAFSA. *Unit head:* Dr. John Rothfork, Chair, 928-523-0559, Fax: 928-523-4911, E-mail: john.rothfork@nau.edu. *Application contact:* Yvette Loeffler-Schmelzle, Secretary, 928-523-6842, Fax: 928-523-4911, E-mail: yvette.schmelzle@nau.edu. Web site: http://nau.edu/cal/english/.

North Georgia College & State University, School of Education, Dahlonega, GA 30597. Offers art education (MAT); early childhood education (M Ed); English education (MAT); history education (MAT); math education (MAT); middle grades education (M Ed, MAT); physical education (MS); school leadership (Ed S); secondary education (M Ed), including English education, history education, mathematics education, physical education; teacher education (MAT). *Accreditation:* NCATE. Part-time and evening/ weekend programs available. Postbaccalaureate distance learning degree programs offered (no on-campus study). *Faculty:* 23 full-time (14 women), 16 part-time/adjunct (11 women). *Students:* 19 full-time (17 women), 199 part-time (147 women); includes 7 minority (3 Black or African American, non-Hispanic/Latino; 1 Asian, non-Hispanic/ Latino; 3 Hispanic/Latino), 1 international. Average age 34. 259 applicants, 66% accepted, 112 enrolled. In 2011, 100 master's, 16 other advanced degrees awarded. *Degree requirements:* For master's, comprehensive exam, thesis optional. *Entrance requirements:* For master's, GRE or MAT, GACE, minimum GPA of 2.75; for Ed S, GRE General Test or MAT, 3 years of teaching experience, master's degree, minimum graduate GPA of 3.25, leadership position in the school. Additional exam requirements/ recommendations for international students: Required—TOEFL (minimum score 550 paper-based; 213 computer-based; 79 iBT), IELTS (minimum score 6.5). *Application deadline:* For fall admission, 8/1 priority date for domestic students, 7/1 for international students; for spring admission, 12/1 priority date for domestic students, 11/1 for international students. Applications are processed on a rolling basis. Application fee: $40. Electronic applications accepted. *Expenses:* Tuition, state resident: full-time $3528; part-time $196 per credit hour. Tuition, nonresident: full-time $14,094; part-time $783 per credit hour. *Required fees:* $1718; $859 per semester. Tuition and fees vary according to course load, campus/location and program. *Financial support:* Teaching assistantships, career-related internships or fieldwork, scholarships/grants, and unspecified assistantships available. Financial award application deadline: 5/1; financial award applicants required to submit CSS PROFILE or FAFSA. *Faculty research:* Identification of professional development school structures supporting P-12 student achievement, impact of diverse field placement settings in teacher belief development among preservice teachers, use of inquiry methodology in social studies teaching with English language learners, use of instructional differentiation in the middle grades classroom, effects of international school placements on preservice teacher beliefs and attitudes. *Unit head:* Dr. Bob Michael, Dean, School of Education, 706-864-1998, Fax: 706-867-2850, E-mail: bmichael@northgeorgia.edu. *Application contact:* Susan L. Perry, Graduate Admissions Coordinator, 706-864-1543, Fax: 706-867-2795, E-mail: slperry@northgeorgia.edu. Web site: http://www.northgeorgia.edu/soe/.

Northwest Missouri State University, Graduate School, College of Arts and Sciences, Department of English, Maryville, MO 64468-6001. Offers English (MA); English with speech emphasis (MA); teaching English (option 1) (MS Ed); teaching English with speech emphasis (MS Ed). Part-time programs available. *Faculty:* 11 full-time (4 women). *Students:* 13 full-time (9 women), 3 part-time (2 women); includes 1 minority (Two or more races, non-Hispanic/Latino). 4 applicants, 100% accepted, 3 enrolled. In 2011, 4 master's awarded. *Degree requirements:* For master's, comprehensive exam, thesis optional. *Entrance requirements:* For master's, GRE General Test, minimum undergraduate GPA of 2.5, writing sample. Additional exam requirements/ recommendations for international students: Required—TOEFL (minimum score 550 paper-based; 213 computer-based). *Application deadline:* For fall admission, 7/1 for domestic and international students; for spring admission, 11/15 for domestic and international students. Applications are processed on a rolling basis. Application fee: $0 ($50 for international students). *Financial support:* In 2011–12, 7 teaching assistantships with full tuition reimbursements (averaging $6,000 per year) were awarded. Financial award application deadline: 4/1; financial award applicants required to submit FAFSA. *Unit head:* Dr. Michael Hobbs, Chairperson, 660-562-1285. *Application contact:* Dr. Gregory Haddock, Dean of Graduate School, 660-562-1145, Fax: 660-562-1096, E-mail: gradsch@nwmissouri.edu.

Occidental College, Graduate Studies, Department of Education, Program in Secondary Education, Los Angeles, CA 90041-3314. Offers English and comparative literary studies (MAT); history (MAT); life science (MAT); mathematics (MAT); physical science (MAT); social science (MAT); Spanish (MAT). Part-time programs available. *Degree requirements:* For master's, comprehensive exam, graduate synthesis paper. *Entrance requirements:* For master's, GRE General Test, minimum GPA of 3.0. Additional exam requirements/recommendations for international students: Required—TOEFL (minimum score 625 paper-based; 263 computer-based). *Expenses:* Contact institution.

Our Lady of the Lake University of San Antonio, College of Arts and Sciences, Program in English, San Antonio, TX 78207-4689. Offers communication arts (MA); English and literature (MA); English education (MA); writing (MA). Program offered jointly with University of the Incarnate Word, St. Mary's University. Part-time and evening/weekend programs available. *Degree requirements:* For master's, comprehensive exam, thesis optional. *Entrance requirements:* For master's, GRE General Test or MAT, minimum GPA of 3.0 in last 60 hours, 2.5 overall. Additional exam requirements/recommendations for international students: Required—TOEFL.

Electronic applications accepted. *Faculty research:* Writing theory and research, contemporary Southern literature, popular culture, poetry, literature of the Southwest.

Plymouth State University, College of Graduate Studies, Graduate Studies in Education, Program in English Education, Plymouth, NH 03264-1595. Offers M Ed. Part-time and evening/weekend programs available. *Entrance requirements:* For master's, MAT.

Purdue University, Graduate School, College of Education, Department of Curriculum and Instruction, West Lafayette, IN 47907. Offers agricultural and extension education (PhD, Ed S); agriculture and extension education (MS, MS Ed); art education (PhD); consumer and family sciences and extension education (MS Ed, PhD, Ed S); curriculum studies (MS Ed, PhD, Ed S); educational technology (MS Ed, PhD, Ed S); elementary education (MS Ed); foreign language education (MS Ed, PhD, Ed S); industrial technology (PhD, Ed S); language arts (MS Ed, PhD, Ed S); literacy (MS Ed, PhD, Ed S); mathematics/science education (MS, MS Ed, PhD, Ed S); social studies (MS Ed, PhD); social studies education (Ed S); vocational/industrial education (MS Ed, PhD, Ed S); vocational/technical education (MS Ed, PhD, Ed S). *Accreditation:* NCATE. Part-time and evening/weekend programs available. *Faculty:* 30 full-time (21 women), 1 (woman) part-time/adjunct. *Students:* 89 full-time (64 women), 134 part-time (84 women); includes 31 minority (12 Black or African American, non-Hispanic/Latino; 3 American Indian or Alaska Native, non-Hispanic/Latino; 7 Asian, non-Hispanic/Latino; 9 Hispanic/Latino), 49 international. Average age 36. 136 applicants, 83% accepted, 72 enrolled. In 2011, 26 master's, 13 doctorates awarded. *Degree requirements:* For master's, thesis optional; for doctorate, thesis/dissertation, oral and written exams; for Ed S, oral presentation, project. *Entrance requirements:* For master's, GRE general test is required if undergraduate GPA is below 3.0, minimum undergraduate GPA of 3.0 or equivalent; for doctorate, GRE General Test, a combined GRE verbal and quantitative score of 1000 (300 for revised GRE Test) or more is expected, minimum undergraduate GPA of 3.0 or equivalent; master's degree with minimum GPA of 3.0 or equivalent; for Ed S, GRE general test, a combined GRE verbal and quantitative score of 1000 (300 for revised GRE Test) or more is expected, minimum undergraduate GPA of 3.0 or equivalent; master's degree. Additional exam requirements/recommendations for international students: Required—TOEFL (minimum score 550 paper-based; 77 iBT). *Application deadline:* For fall admission, 12/15 priority date for domestic students, 3/1 for international students; for spring admission, 9/15 for domestic students, 8/1 for international students. Application fee: $60 ($75 for international students). Electronic applications accepted. *Financial support:* Fellowships with full tuition reimbursements, research assistantships with full tuition reimbursements, teaching assistantships with full tuition reimbursements, career-related internships or fieldwork, and tuition waivers (full) available. Support available to part-time students. Financial award application deadline: 3/1; financial award applicants required to submit FAFSA. *Faculty research:* Literacy acquisition and development, teacher beliefs and knowledge, recruitment and retention of underrepresented students, economic education, literacy discourse. *Unit head:* Dr. Philip J. VanFossen, Head, 765-494-7935, Fax: 765-496-1622, E-mail: vanfoss@purdue.edu. *Application contact:* Sarah N. Prater, Graduate Contact, 765-494-2345, Fax: 765-494-5832, E-mail: prater0@purdue.edu. Web site: http://www.edci.purdue.edu/.

Queens College of the City University of New York, Division of Graduate Studies, Division of Education, Department of Secondary Education, Flushing, NY 11367-1597. Offers art (MS Ed); biology (MS Ed, AC); chemistry (MS Ed, AC); earth sciences (MS Ed, AC); English (MS Ed, AC); French (MS Ed, AC); Italian (MS Ed, AC); mathematics (MS Ed, AC); music (MS Ed, AC); physics (MS Ed, AC); social studies (MS Ed, AC); Spanish (MS Ed, AC). Part-time and evening/weekend programs available. *Faculty:* 22 full-time (14 women). *Students:* 46 full-time (23 women), 727 part-time (442 women); includes 234 minority (41 Black or African American, non-Hispanic/Latino; 78 Asian, non-Hispanic/Latino; 115 Hispanic/Latino), 5 international. 591 applicants, 60% accepted, 250 enrolled. In 2011, 170 master's awarded. *Degree requirements:* For master's, research project; for AC, thesis optional. *Entrance requirements:* For master's, minimum GPA of 3.0. Additional exam requirements/recommendations for international students: Required—TOEFL. *Application deadline:* For fall admission, 4/1 for domestic students; for spring admission, 11/1 for domestic students. Applications are processed on a rolling basis. Application fee: $125. *Expenses:* Tuition, state resident: part-time $345 per credit. Tuition, nonresident: part-time $640 per credit. *Required fees:* $145.25 per semester. *Financial support:* Career-related internships or fieldwork, Federal Work-Study, institutionally sponsored loans, and tuition waivers (partial) available. Support available to part-time students. Financial award application deadline: 4/1; financial award applicants required to submit FAFSA. *Unit head:* Dr. Eleanor Armour-Thomas, Chairperson, 718-997-5150, E-mail: armourthomas@yahoo.com. *Application contact:* Mario Caruso, Director of Graduate Admissions, 718-997-5200, Fax: 718-997-5193, E-mail: graduate_admissions@qc.edu.

Quinnipiac University, School of Education, Program in Secondary Education, Hamden, CT 06518-1940. Offers biology (MAT); English (MAT); history/social studies (MAT); mathematics (MAT); Spanish (MAT). *Accreditation:* NCATE. *Faculty:* 7 full-time (5 women), 41 part-time/adjunct (24 women). *Students:* 56 full-time (38 women), 1 (woman) part-time; includes 5 minority (1 Black or African American, non-Hispanic/Latino; 1 Asian, non-Hispanic/Latino; 3 Hispanic/Latino). 51 applicants, 96% accepted, 44 enrolled. In 2011, 49 master's awarded. *Entrance requirements:* For master's, PRAXIS I, minimum GPA of 2.67, interview. *Application deadline:* For fall admission, 3/31 priority date for domestic students. Applications are processed on a rolling basis. Application fee: $45. Electronic applications accepted. *Expenses: Tuition:* Part-time $855 per credit. *Required fees:* $35 per credit. *Financial support:* In 2011–12, 1 student received support. Career-related internships or fieldwork, scholarships/grants, and tuition waivers (full and partial) available. Financial award application deadline: 4/15; financial award applicants required to submit FAFSA. *Faculty research:* Multicultural and urban education/leadership, challenges of teaching diverse learners, scholarship of teaching and learning, technology and teaching, humor and education. *Unit head:* Mordechai Gordon, Program Director, 203-582-8442, Fax: 203-582-3473, E-mail: mordechai.gordon@quinnipiac.edu. *Application contact:* Jennifer Boutin, Associate Director of Graduate Admissions, 800-462-1944, Fax: 203-582-3443, E-mail: jennifer.boutin@quinnipiac.edu. Web site: http://www.quinnipiac.edu/academics/colleges-schools-and-departments/school-of-education/graduate-programs/five-semester-mat-programs/secondary-educat.

Rhode Island College, School of Graduate Studies, Feinstein School of Education and Human Development, Department of Educational Studies, Providence, RI 02908-1991. Offers advanced studies in teaching and learning (M Ed); English (MAT); French (MAT); history (MAT); math (MAT); secondary education (MAT); Spanish (MAT); teaching English as a second language (M Ed). *Accreditation:* NCATE. Part-time and evening/weekend programs available. *Faculty:* 14 full-time (7 women), 4 part-time/adjunct (2 women). *Students:* 10 full-time (all women), 61 part-time (51 women); includes 8 minority (1 Black or African American, non-Hispanic/Latino; 4 Asian, non-Hispanic/Latino; 3 Hispanic/Latino). Average age 33. In 2011, 32 master's awarded. *Degree requirements:* For master's, capstone or comprehensive assessment. *Entrance requirements:* For master's, GRE or MAT (for most programs), minimum undergraduate GPA of 3.0; baccalaureate degree in English, French, history, math or Spanish; evaluation of content area knowledge; 3 letters of recommendation; interview. Additional exam requirements/recommendations for international students: Recommended—TOEFL (minimum score 550 paper-based; 213 computer-based; 79 iBT). *Application deadline:* For fall admission, 3/1 for domestic students; for spring admission, 11/1 for domestic students. Applications are processed on a rolling basis. Application fee: $50. *Expenses:* Tuition, state resident: full-time $8592; part-time $358 per credit hour. Tuition, nonresident: full-time $16,800; part-time $700 per credit hour. *Required fees:* $602; $22 per credit. $72 per term. *Financial support:* Teaching assistantships with full tuition reimbursements, career-related internships or fieldwork, Federal Work-Study, scholarships/grants, health care benefits, and unspecified assistantships available. Support available to part-time students. Financial award application deadline: 5/15; financial award applicants required to submit FAFSA. *Faculty research:* School administration, school/college articulation. *Unit head:* Dr. Ellen Bigler, Chair, 401-456-8170. *Application contact:* Graduate Studies, 401-456-8700. Web site: http://www.ric.edu/educationalStudies/.

Rider University, Department of Graduate Education, Leadership and Counseling, Teacher Certification Program, Lawrenceville, NJ 08648-3001. Offers business education (Certificate); elementary education (Certificate); English as a second language (Certificate); English education (Certificate); mathematics education (Certificate); preschool to grade 3 (Certificate); science education (Certificate); social studies education (Certificate); world languages (Certificate), including French, German, Spanish. Part-time programs available. *Degree requirements:* For Certificate, internship, professional portfolio. *Entrance requirements:* For degree, PRAXIS, resume. Additional exam requirements/recommendations for international students: Required—TOEFL (minimum score 550 paper-based; 213 computer-based). Electronic applications accepted. *Expenses: Tuition:* Full-time $32,820; part-time $710 per credit. *Required fees:* $350; $35 per course. Tuition and fees vary according to campus/location and program. *Faculty research:* Conceptual foundations for optimal development of creativity; creative theory, cognitive processes in mathematics learning, teacher collaboration.

Rutgers, The State University of New Jersey, New Brunswick, Graduate School of Education, Department of Learning and Teaching, Program in English Education, Piscataway, NJ 08854-8097. Offers Ed M. Part-time programs available. *Degree requirements:* For master's, comprehensive exam or paper. *Entrance requirements:* For master's, GRE General Test, minimum GPA of 3.0. Additional exam requirements/recommendations for international students: Required—TOEFL. Electronic applications accepted.

Sage Graduate School, Esteves School of Education, Program in Teaching, Troy, NY 12180-4115. Offers art education (MAT); English (MAT); mathematics (MAT); social studies (MAT). *Accreditation:* NASAD. Part-time and evening/weekend programs available. *Faculty:* 10 full-time (6 women), 6 part-time/adjunct (4 women). *Students:* 19 full-time (15 women), 20 part-time (16 women); includes 1 minority (Asian, non-Hispanic/Latino). Average age 27. 44 applicants, 36% accepted, 8 enrolled. In 2011, 37 master's awarded. *Entrance requirements:* For master's, assessment of writing skills, minimum undergraduate GPA of 2.75 overall, 3.0 in content area; current resume; 2 letters of recommendation. Additional exam requirements/recommendations for international students: Required—TOEFL (minimum score 550 paper-based; 213 computer-based). *Application deadline:* For fall admission, 8/1 for domestic students. Applications are processed on a rolling basis. Application fee: $40. *Expenses: Tuition:* Full-time $11,880; part-time $660 per credit hour. Tuition and fees vary according to program. *Financial support:* Fellowships, research assistantships, Federal Work-Study, scholarships/grants, and unspecified assistantships available. Support available to part-time students. Financial award application deadline: 3/1; financial award applicants required to submit FAFSA. *Unit head:* Dr. Lori Quigley, Dean, Esteves School of Education, 518-244-2326, Fax: 518-244-4571, E-mail: l.quigley@sage.edu. *Application contact:* Kelly Jones, Director, 518-244-2433, Fax: 518-244-6880, E-mail: jonesk4@sage.edu.

St. John Fisher College, Ralph C. Wilson Jr. School of Education, Program in Adolescence Education/Special Education, Rochester, NY 14618-3597. Offers adolescence English (MS Ed); adolescence French (MS Ed); adolescence social studies (MS Ed); adolescence Spanish (MS Ed). Part-time and evening/weekend programs available. *Faculty:* 5 full-time (3 women), 2 part-time/adjunct (both women). *Students:* 25 full-time (13 women), 1 (woman) part-time. Average age 22. 19 applicants, 79% accepted, 11 enrolled. In 2011, 18 master's awarded. *Degree requirements:* For master's, field experiences, student teaching, LAST. *Entrance requirements:* For master's, 2 letters of recommendation, personal statement, current resume. Additional exam requirements/recommendations for international students: Required—TOEFL (minimum score 575 paper-based; 233 computer-based; 80 iBT). *Application deadline:* Applications are processed on a rolling basis. Application fee: $30. Electronic applications accepted. *Expenses: Tuition:* Part-time $735 per credit. One-time fee: $50 part-time. Tuition and fees vary according to course load, degree level and program. *Financial support:* In 2011–12, 5 students received support. Scholarships/grants available. Financial award applicants required to submit FAFSA. *Faculty research:* Arts and humanities, urban schools, constructivist learning, at risk students, mentoring. *Unit head:* Dr. Susan Schultz, Program Director, 585-385-7296, E-mail: sschultz@sjfc.edu. *Application contact:* Jose Perales, Director of Graduate Admissions, 585-385-8067, E-mail: jperales@sjfc.edu. Web site: http://www.sjfc.edu/academics/education/departments/ms-special-ed/options/initial-adolescence.dot.

Salem State University, School of Graduate Studies, Program in English, Salem, MA 01970-5353. Offers English (MA, MAT, MA/MAT); MA/MAT. Part-time and evening/weekend programs available. *Entrance requirements:* For master's, GRE or MAT. Additional exam requirements/recommendations for international students: Required—TOEFL (minimum score 550 paper-based; 80 iBT) or IELTS (minimum score 5.5).

San Francisco State University, Division of Graduate Studies, College of Education, Department of Elementary Education, Program in Language and Literacy Education, San Francisco, CA 94132-1722. Offers MA. *Unit head:* Dr. Debra Luna, Chair, 415-338-1562, E-mail: dluna@sfsu.edu. *Application contact:* Dr. Josephine Arce, Graduate Coordinator, 415-338-2292, E-mail: jarce@sfsu.edu. Web site: http://www.coe.sfsu.edu/eed.

San Francisco State University, Division of Graduate Studies, College of Liberal and Creative Arts, Department of English Language and Literature, San Francisco, CA 94132-1722. Offers composition (MA); immigrant literacies (Certificate); linguistics (MA); literature (MA); teaching English to speakers of other languages (MA); teaching of composition (Certificate); teaching post-secondary reading (Certificate). Part-time programs available. *Application deadline:* Applications are processed on a rolling basis. *Unit head:* Dr. Beverly Voloshin, Chair, 415-338-2264, E-mail: english@sfsu.edu. *Application contact:* Cynthia Losinsky, Administrative Support, Graduate Programs, 415-338-2660, E-mail: english@sfsu.edu. Web site: http://www.sfsu.edu/~english.

Shippensburg University of Pennsylvania, School of Graduate Studies, College of Education and Human Services, Department of Teacher Education, Shippensburg, PA 17257-2299. Offers curriculum and instruction (M Ed), including biology, early childhood education, elementary education, English, geography/earth science, history, mathematics, middle level education, modern languages; reading (M Ed). *Accreditation:*

NCATE. Part-time and evening/weekend programs available. *Faculty:* 14 full-time (11 women), 8 part-time/adjunct (7 women). *Students:* 16 full-time (15 women), 143 part-time (130 women); includes 11 minority (4 Black or African American, non-Hispanic/Latino; 1 Asian, non-Hispanic/Latino; 4 Hispanic/Latino; 2 Two or more races, non-Hispanic/Latino), 1 international. Average age 30. 55 applicants, 55% accepted, 25 enrolled. In 2011, 76 master's awarded. *Degree requirements:* For master's, comprehensive exam (for some programs), thesis optional, practicum or internship; capstone seminar (for some programs). *Entrance requirements:* For master's, MAT (if GPA less than 2.75), interview, 3 letters of reference, questionnaire of teaching background and future goals. Additional exam requirements/recommendations for international students: Required—TOEFL (minimum score 580 paper-based; 237 computer-based); Recommended—IELTS (minimum score 6). *Application deadline:* For fall admission, 6/1 priority date for domestic students, 4/30 for international students; for spring admission, 9/1 priority date for domestic students, 9/30 for international students. Applications are processed on a rolling basis. Application fee: $30. Electronic applications accepted. *Expenses: Tuition, area resident:* Part-time $416 per credit. Tuition, state resident: part-time $416 per credit. Tuition, nonresident: part-time $624 per credit. *Required fees:* $119 per credit. *Financial support:* In 2011–12, 5 research assistantships with full tuition reimbursements (averaging $5,000 per year) were awarded; career-related internships or fieldwork, scholarships/grants, unspecified assistantships, and resident hall director and student payroll positions also available. Support available to part-time students. Financial award application deadline: 3/1; financial award applicants required to submit FAFSA. *Unit head:* Dr. Christine A. Royce, Chairperson, 717-477-1688, Fax: 717-477-4046, E-mail: caroyc@ship.edu. *Application contact:* Jeremy R. Goshorn, Assistant Dean of Graduate Admissions, 717-477-1231, Fax: 717-477-4016, E-mail: jrgoshorn@ship.edu. Web site: http://www.ship.edu/teacher/.

Slippery Rock University of Pennsylvania, Graduate Studies (Recruitment), College of Education, Department of Secondary Education/Foundations of Education, Slippery Rock, PA 16057-1383. Offers educational leadership (M Ed); secondary education in English (M Ed); secondary education in math/science (M Ed); secondary education in social studies (M Ed). *Accreditation:* NCATE. Part-time and evening/weekend programs available. *Faculty:* 9 full-time (4 women), 3 part-time/adjunct (0 women). *Students:* 64 full-time (34 women), 16 part-time (8 women); includes 2 minority (1 Asian, non-Hispanic/Latino; 1 Two or more races, non-Hispanic/Latino). Average age 28. 68 applicants, 76% accepted, 27 enrolled. In 2011, 54 degrees awarded. *Degree requirements:* For master's, comprehensive exam, thesis (for some programs). *Entrance requirements:* For master's, GRE General Test, MAT, minimum GPA of 2.8 (depending on program). Additional exam requirements/recommendations for international students: Required—TOEFL (minimum score 550 paper-based; 213 computer-based; 80 iBT). *Application deadline:* For fall admission, 3/1 priority date for domestic students, 5/1 for international students; for spring admission, 10/1 priority date for domestic students, 9/1 for international students. Applications are processed on a rolling basis. Application fee: $25 ($30 for international students). Electronic applications accepted. *Expenses:* Tuition, state resident: full-time $7488; part-time $416 per credit. Tuition, nonresident: full-time $11,232; part-time $624 per credit. *International tuition:* $11,146 full-time. *Required fees:* $2722; $140 per credit. Tuition and fees vary according to degree level and program. *Financial support:* Career-related internships or fieldwork, Federal Work-Study, institutionally sponsored loans, scholarships/grants, tuition waivers (partial), and unspecified assistantships available. Support available to part-time students. Financial award application deadline: 5/1; financial award applicants required to submit FAFSA. *Unit head:* Dr. Jeffrey Lehman, Graduate Coordinator, 724-738-2311, Fax: 724-738-4987, E-mail: jeffrey.lehman@sru.edu. *Application contact:* Angela Barrett, Interim Director of Graduate Studies, 724-738-2051, Fax: 724-738-2146, E-mail: graduate.admissions@sru.edu.

Smith College, Graduate and Special Programs, Department of Education and Child Study, Program in Secondary Education, Northampton, MA 01063. Offers biological sciences education (MAT); chemistry education (MAT); English education (MAT); French education (MAT); geology education (MAT); government education (MAT); history education (MAT); mathematics education (MAT); physics education (MAT); Spanish education (MAT). Part-time programs available. *Faculty:* 6 full-time (4 women), 3 part-time/adjunct (2 women). *Students:* 11 full-time (8 women), 3 part-time (all women); includes 2 minority (1 Asian, non-Hispanic/Latino; 1 Hispanic/Latino). Average age 26. 21 applicants, 95% accepted, 12 enrolled. In 2011, 2 master's awarded. *Entrance requirements:* For master's, GRE. Additional exam requirements/recommendations for international students: Required—TOEFL (minimum score 590 paper-based; 243 computer-based; 97 iBT). *Application deadline:* For fall admission, 4/1 for domestic students, 1/15 for international students; for spring admission, 12/1 for domestic students. Application fee: $60. *Expenses: Tuition:* Full-time $14,925; part-time $1245 per credit. *Financial support:* In 2011–12, 13 students received support. Career-related internships or fieldwork, institutionally sponsored loans, and scholarships/grants available. Support available to part-time students. Financial award application deadline: 1/15; financial award applicants required to submit CSS PROFILE or FAFSA. *Unit head:* Rosetta Cohen, Graduate Student Advisor, 413-585-3266, E-mail: rcohen@smith.edu. *Application contact:* Ruth Morgan, Administrative Assistant, 413-585-3050, Fax: 413-585-3054, E-mail: gradstdy@smith.edu. Web site: http://www.smith.edu/educ/.

Smith College, Graduate and Special Programs, Department of English Language and Literature, Northampton, MA 01063. Offers MAT. Part-time programs available. *Faculty:* 20 full-time (8 women). *Students:* 2 full-time (both women). Average age 23. 8 applicants, 88% accepted, 2 enrolled. In 2011, 2 master's awarded. *Entrance requirements:* For master's, GRE. Additional exam requirements/recommendations for international students: Required—TOEFL (minimum score 590 paper-based; 243 computer-based; 97 iBT). *Application deadline:* For fall admission, 1/15 for domestic and international students; for spring admission, 12/1 for domestic students. Application fee: $60. *Expenses: Tuition:* Full-time $14,925; part-time $1245 per credit. *Financial support:* In 2011–12, 2 students received support. Career-related internships or fieldwork, institutionally sponsored loans, and scholarships/grants available. Support available to part-time students. Financial award application deadline: 1/15; financial award applicants required to submit CSS PROFILE or FAFSA. *Unit head:* Craig Davis, Graduate Adviser, 413-585-3327, E-mail: cdavis@smith.edu. *Application contact:* Ruth Morgan, Administrative Assistant, 413-585-3050, Fax: 413-585-3054, E-mail: gradstdy@smith.edu. Web site: http://www.smith.edu/english/.

South Carolina State University, School of Graduate Studies, Department of Education, Orangeburg, SC 29117-0001. Offers counseling education (M Ed); early childhood and special education (M Ed); early childhood education (MAT); educational leadership (Ed D, Ed S); elementary education (M Ed, MAT); engineering (MAT); general science (MAT); mathematics (MAT); secondary education (M Ed), including biology education, business education, counselor education, English education, home economics education, industrial education, mathematics education, science education, social studies education; special education (M Ed), including emotionally handicapped, learning disabilities, mentally handicapped. *Accreditation:* NCATE. Part-time and evening/weekend programs available. *Faculty:* 9 full-time (6 women), 6 part-time/adjunct (2 women). *Students:* 34 full-time (29 women), 50 part-time (40 women); includes 74 minority (72 Black or African American, non-Hispanic/Latino; 1 Asian, non-Hispanic/Latino; 1 Hispanic/Latino). Average age 34. 23 applicants, 91% accepted, 14 enrolled. In 2011, 11 master's awarded. *Degree requirements:* For master's, thesis optional, departmental qualifying exam. *Entrance requirements:* For master's, GRE General Test, NTE, interview, teaching certificate. *Application deadline:* For fall admission, 6/15 priority date for domestic students, 6/15 for international students; for spring admission, 11/1 for domestic and international students. Applications are processed on a rolling basis. Application fee: $25. Electronic applications accepted. *Expenses:* Tuition, state resident: full-time $8688; part-time $514 per credit hour. Tuition, nonresident: full-time $17,600; part-time $1009 per credit hour. *Required fees:* $570. *Financial support:* In 2011–12, 3 fellowships (averaging $5,020 per year) were awarded; career-related internships or fieldwork, Federal Work-Study, and institutionally sponsored loans also available. Financial award application deadline: 6/1. *Faculty research:* Critical thinking, child abuse, stress, test-taking skills, conflict resolution, mainstreaming. *Unit head:* Dr. Charlie Spell, Interim Chair, 803-536-7098, Fax: 803-516-4568, E-mail: cspell@scsu.edu. *Application contact:* Annette Hazzard-Jones, Program Coordinator II, 803-536-8809, Fax: 803-536-8812, E-mail: zs_ahazzard@scsu.edu.

Southeastern Louisiana University, College of Arts, Humanities and Social Sciences, Department of English, Hammond, LA 70402. Offers creative writing (MA); language and theory (MA); professional writing (MA). Part-time programs available. *Faculty:* 13 full-time (5 women), 2 part-time/adjunct (1 woman). *Students:* 25 full-time (17 women), 33 part-time (23 women); includes 5 minority (1 Black or African American, non-Hispanic/Latino; 1 Asian, non-Hispanic/Latino; 2 Hispanic/Latino; 1 Two or more races, non-Hispanic/Latino). Average age 31. 20 applicants, 100% accepted, 15 enrolled. In 2011, 5 master's awarded. *Degree requirements:* For master's, comprehensive exam, thesis optional. *Entrance requirements:* For master's, GRE General Test (minimum score of 850), bachelor's degree; minimum undergraduate GPA of 2.5; 24 hours of undergraduate English courses. Additional exam requirements/recommendations for international students: Required—TOEFL (minimum score 500 paper-based; 173 computer-based; 61 iBT). *Application deadline:* For fall admission, 7/15 priority date for domestic students, 6/1 for international students; for spring admission, 12/1 priority date for domestic students, 10/1 for international students. Applications are processed on a rolling basis. Application fee: $20 ($30 for international students). Electronic applications accepted. *Expenses:* Tuition, state resident: full-time $3977; part-time $283 per semester hour. Tuition, nonresident: full-time $13,482; part-time $811 per semester hour. *Financial support:* In 2011–12, 1 fellowship (averaging $10,800 per year), 9 research assistantships (averaging $9,733 per year), 1 teaching assistantship (averaging $9,000 per year) were awarded; career-related internships or fieldwork, Federal Work-Study, institutionally sponsored loans, scholarships/grants, and traineeships also available. Support available to part-time students. Financial award application deadline: 5/1; financial award applicants required to submit FAFSA. *Faculty research:* Creole studies, modernism, digital humanities, library studies, John Donne. *Total annual research expenditures:* $59,686. *Unit head:* Dr. David Hanson, Department Head, 985-549-2100, Fax: 985-549-5021, E-mail: dhanson@selu.edu. *Application contact:* Sandra Meyers, Graduate Admissions Analyst, 985-549-5620, Fax: 985-549-5632, E-mail: admissions@selu.edu. Web site: http://www.selu.edu/acad_research/depts/engl.

Southern Illinois University Edwardsville, Graduate School, College of Arts and Sciences, Department of English Language and Literature, Program in Teaching of Writing, Edwardsville, IL 62026-0001. Offers MA, Postbaccalaureate Certificate. Part-time and evening/weekend programs available. *Students:* 3 full-time (2 women), 21 part-time (13 women); includes 3 minority (2 Black or African American, non-Hispanic/Latino; 1 Hispanic/Latino), 1 international. In 2011, 4 master's, 2 other advanced degrees awarded. *Degree requirements:* For master's, thesis or alternative, final exam. *Entrance requirements:* Additional exam requirements/recommendations for international students: Required—TOEFL (minimum score 550 paper-based; 213 computer-based; 79 iBT), IELTS (minimum score 6.5). *Application deadline:* For fall admission, 7/22 for domestic students, 6/1 for international students; for spring admission, 12/9 for domestic students, 10/1 for international students. Applications are processed on a rolling basis. Application fee: $30. Electronic applications accepted. Tuition and fees vary according to course load and program. *Financial support:* Fellowships with full tuition reimbursements, research assistantships with full tuition reimbursements, teaching assistantships with full tuition reimbursements, institutionally sponsored loans, scholarships/grants, and unspecified assistantships available. Financial award application deadline: 3/1; financial award applicants required to submit FAFSA. *Unit head:* Dr. Joel Hardman, Director, 618-650-5978, E-mail: jhardma@siue.edu. *Application contact:* Dr. Joel Hardman, Director, 618-650-5978, E-mail: jhardma@siue.edu. Web site: http://www.siue.edu/ENGLISH/.

Southern Illinois University Edwardsville, Graduate School, School of Education, Department of Curriculum and Instruction, Program in Secondary Education, Edwardsville, IL 62026. Offers art (MS Ed); biology (MS Ed); chemistry (MS Ed); earth and space sciences (MS Ed); English/language arts (MS Ed); foreign languages (MS Ed); history (MS Ed); mathematics (MS Ed); physics (MS Ed). *Accreditation:* NCATE. Part-time and evening/weekend programs available. *Students:* 1 full-time (0 women), 42 part-time (33 women); includes 2 minority (both Black or African American, non-Hispanic/Latino). 16 applicants, 31% accepted. In 2011, 8 master's awarded. *Degree requirements:* For master's, comprehensive exam (for some programs), final exam/paper. *Entrance requirements:* Additional exam requirements/recommendations for international students: Required—TOEFL (minimum score 550 paper-based; 213 computer-based; 79 iBT), IELTS (minimum score 6.5). *Application deadline:* For fall admission, 7/22 for domestic students, 6/1 for international students; for spring admission, 12/9 for domestic students, 10/1 for international students. Applications are processed on a rolling basis. Application fee: $30. Electronic applications accepted. Tuition and fees vary according to course load and program. *Financial support:* Fellowships, research assistantships, teaching assistantships, institutionally sponsored loans, scholarships/grants, and unspecified assistantships available. Financial award application deadline: 3/1; financial award applicants required to submit FAFSA. *Unit head:* Dr. Susan Breck, Director, 618-650-3444, E-mail: sbreck@siue.edu. *Application contact:* Dr. Michelle Robinson, Coordinator of Graduate Recruitment, 618-650-2811, Fax: 618-650-3523, E-mail: michero@siue.edu. Web site: http://www.siue.edu/education/ci/.

Southwestern Oklahoma State University, College of Arts and Sciences, Specialization in English, Weatherford, OK 73096-3098. Offers M Ed. M Ed distance learning degree program offered to Oklahoma residents only. *Accreditation:* NCATE. Part-time programs available. *Degree requirements:* For master's, exam. *Entrance requirements:* For master's, GRE General Test or minimum undergraduate GPA of 3.0. Additional exam requirements/recommendations for international students: Required—TOEFL.

Stanford University, School of Education, Program in Curriculum Studies and Teacher Education, Stanford, CA 94305-9991. Offers art education (MA, PhD); dance education (MA); English education (MA, PhD); general curriculum studies (MA, PhD); mathematics education (MA, PhD); science education (MA, PhD); social studies education (PhD); teacher education (MA, PhD). *Degree requirements:* For master's, thesis (for some programs); for doctorate, thesis/dissertation. *Entrance requirements:* For master's and doctorate, GRE General Test. Electronic applications accepted. *Expenses: Tuition:* Full-time $40,050; part-time $890 per credit.

Stanford University, School of Education, Teacher Education Program, Stanford, CA 94305-9991. Offers English education (MA); languages education (MA); mathematics education (MA); science education (MA); social studies education (MA). *Degree requirements:* For master's, thesis. *Entrance requirements:* For master's, GRE General Test. Electronic applications accepted. *Expenses: Tuition:* Full-time $40,050; part-time $890 per credit.

State University of New York at Binghamton, Graduate School, School of Education, Program in Adolescence Education, Binghamton, NY 13902-6000. Offers biology education (MAT, MS Ed, MST); earth science education (MAT, MS Ed, MST); English education (MAT, MS Ed, MST); French education (MAT, MST); mathematical sciences education (MAT, MS Ed, MST); physics (MAT, MS Ed, MST); social studies (MAT, MS Ed, MST); Spanish education (MAT, MST). *Accreditation:* Teacher Education Accreditation Council. Part-time and evening/weekend programs available. *Students:* 98 full-time (66 women), 13 part-time (11 women); includes 2 minority (1 Black or African American, non-Hispanic/Latino; 1 Hispanic/Latino). Average age 26. 73 applicants, 70% accepted, 35 enrolled. In 2011, 58 master's awarded. *Entrance requirements:* For master's, GRE General Test. Additional exam requirements/recommendations for international students: Required—TOEFL (minimum score 550 paper-based; 213 computer-based; 80 iBT). *Application deadline:* For fall admission, 2/1 priority date for domestic students, 2/1 for international students; for spring admission, 10/15 priority date for domestic students, 10/15 for international students. Applications are processed on a rolling basis. Application fee: $60. Electronic applications accepted. *Financial support:* In 2011–12, 4 students received support, including 1 fellowship with partial tuition reimbursement available (averaging $12,000 per year); career-related internships or fieldwork, Federal Work-Study, institutionally sponsored loans, scholarships/grants, health care benefits, tuition waivers (full), and unspecified assistantships also available. Financial award application deadline: 2/15; financial award applicants required to submit FAFSA. *Unit head:* Dr. S. G. Grant, Dean of School of Education, 607-777-7329, E-mail: sggrant@binghamton.edu. *Application contact:* Catherine Smith, Recruiting and Admissions Coordinator, 607-777-2151, Fax: 607-777-2501, E-mail: cmsmith@binghamton.edu.

State University of New York at New Paltz, Graduate School, School of Education, Department of Secondary Education, New Paltz, NY 12561. Offers adolescence education: biology (MAT, MS Ed); adolescence education: chemistry (MAT, MS Ed); adolescence education: earth science (MAT, MS Ed); adolescence education: English (MAT, MS Ed); adolescence education: French (MAT, MS Ed); adolescence education: social studies (MAT, MS Ed); adolescence education: Spanish (MAT, MS Ed); second language education (MS Ed). *Accreditation:* NCATE. Part-time and evening/weekend programs available. *Faculty:* 18 full-time (10 women), 2 part-time/adjunct (both women). *Students:* 79 full-time (48 women), 76 part-time (55 women); includes 30 minority (3 Black or African American, non-Hispanic/Latino; 2 Asian, non-Hispanic/Latino; 22 Hispanic/Latino; 3 Two or more races, non-Hispanic/Latino), 1 international. Average age 32. 127 applicants, 69% accepted, 64 enrolled. In 2011, 73 master's awarded. *Degree requirements:* For master's, comprehensive exam (for some programs), portfolio. *Entrance requirements:* For master's, minimum GPA of 3.0, New York state teaching certificate (MS Ed). Additional exam requirements/recommendations for international students: Required—TOEFL (minimum score 550 paper-based; 213 computer-based; 80 iBT), IELTS (minimum score 6.5). *Application deadline:* For fall admission, 3/1 priority date for domestic students, 3/1 for international students; for spring admission, 10/1 priority date for domestic students, 10/1 for international students. Application fee: $50. Electronic applications accepted. *Expenses:* Tuition, state resident: full-time $8870; part-time $370 per credit. Tuition, nonresident: full-time $15,160; part-time $632 per credit. *Required fees:* $1188; $34 per credit. $184 per semester. *Financial support:* In 2011–12, 13 students received support, including 3 fellowships with partial tuition reimbursements available (averaging $7,000 per year); Federal Work-Study, institutionally sponsored loans, and tuition waivers (full) also available. Financial award application deadline: 8/1; financial award applicants required to submit FAFSA. *Unit head:* Dr. Devon Duhaney, Chair, 845-257-2850, E-mail: duhaneyd@newpaltz.edu. *Application contact:* Caroline Murphy, Graduate Admissions Advisor, 845-257-3285, Fax: 845-257-3284, E-mail: gradschool@newpaltz.edu. Web site: http://www.newpaltz.edu/secondaryed/.

State University of New York at Plattsburgh, Division of Education, Health, and Human Services, Program in Teacher Education: Adolescence MST, Plattsburgh, NY 12901-2681. Offers adolescence education (MST); biology 7-12 (MST); chemistry 7-12 (MST); earth science 7-12 (MST); English 7-12 (MST); French 7-12 (MST); mathematics 7-12 (MST); physics 7-12 (MST); social studies 7-12 (MST); Spanish 7-12 (MST). *Accreditation:* Teacher Education Accreditation Council. Part-time and evening/weekend programs available. *Students:* 53 full-time (26 women), 5 part-time (4 women). Average age 29. *Entrance requirements:* For master's, minimum GPA of 2.75. Additional exam requirements/recommendations for international students: Required—TOEFL. *Application deadline:* For fall admission, 2/15 priority date for domestic students. Applications are processed on a rolling basis. Application fee: $75. *Financial support:* Application deadline: 4/15; applicants required to submit FAFSA. *Unit head:* Dr. Robert Ackland, Coordinator, 518-564-5131, E-mail: acklanrt@plattsburgh.edu. *Application contact:* Marguerite Adelman, Assistant Director, Graduate Admissions, 518-564-4723, Fax: 518-564-4722, E-mail: adelmaml@plattsburgh.edu.

State University of New York College at Cortland, Graduate Studies, School of Arts and Sciences, Programs in Adolescence Education, Cortland, NY 13045. Offers biology (MAT, MS Ed); chemistry (MAT, MS Ed); earth science (MAT, MS Ed); English (MS Ed); French (MS Ed); mathematics (MAT, MS Ed); physics (MAT, MS Ed); social studies (MS Ed); Spanish (MS Ed). *Accreditation:* NCATE. Part-time and evening/weekend programs available. *Degree requirements:* For master's, one foreign language, comprehensive exam (for some programs), thesis (for some programs). *Entrance requirements:* For master's, GRE General Test.

Stony Brook University, State University of New York, Graduate School, College of Arts and Sciences, Department of English, Stony Brook, NY 11794. Offers composition studies (Certificate); English (MA, PhD); English education (MAT). MAT offered through the School of Professional Development. Evening/weekend programs available. Terminal master's awarded for partial completion of doctoral program. *Degree requirements:* For doctorate, thesis/dissertation. *Entrance requirements:* For master's and doctorate, GRE General Test. Additional exam requirements/recommendations for international students: Required—TOEFL. *Faculty research:* American literature, British literature, literary critical theory, rhetoric and composition theory, women's studies.

Stony Brook University, State University of New York, School of Professional Development, Stony Brook, NY 11794. Offers biology-grade 7-12 (MAT); chemistry-grade 7-12 (MAT); coaching (Graduate Certificate); coaching online (Graduate Certificate); computer integrated engineering (Graduate Certificate); earth science-grade 7-12 (MAT); educational computing (Graduate Certificate); educational leadership (Advanced Certificate); English-grade 7-12 (MAT); environmental management (Graduate Certificate); environmental/occupational health and safety (Graduate Certificate); French-grade 7-12 (MAT); German-grade 7-12 (MAT); human resource management (Graduate Certificate); human resource management online (Graduate Certificate); information systems management (Graduate Certificate); Italian-grade 7-12 (MAT); liberal studies (MA); liberal studies online (MAT); mathematics-grade 7-12 (MAT); operation research (Graduate Certificate); physics-grade 7-12 (MAT); professional studies online (MPS); school administration and supervision (Graduate Certificate); school building leadership (Graduate Certificate); school district administration (Graduate Certificate); school district business leadership (Advanced Certificate); school district leadership (Graduate Certificate); social science and the professions (MPS), including environmental waste management, human resource management; social studies-grade 7-12 (MAT); Spanish-grade 7-12 (MAT); waste management (Graduate Certificate). Part-time and evening/weekend programs available. Postbaccalaureate distance learning degree programs offered. *Degree requirements:* For master's, one foreign language, thesis or alternative.

Syracuse University, School of Education, Program in English Education: Preparation 7-12, Syracuse, NY 13244. Offers MS. Part-time programs available. *Students:* 7 full-time (5 women). Average age 24. 6 applicants, 67% accepted, 1 enrolled. In 2011, 6 degrees awarded. *Degree requirements:* For master's, thesis or alternative. *Entrance requirements:* For master's, GRE. Additional exam requirements/recommendations for international students: Required—TOEFL (minimum score 100 iBT). *Application deadline:* For fall admission, 2/1 priority date for domestic students, 2/1 for international students; for spring admission, 10/15 priority date for domestic students, 10/15 for international students. Applications are processed on a rolling basis. Application fee: $75. Electronic applications accepted. *Expenses: Tuition:* Part-time $1206 per credit. *Financial support:* Fellowships with full tuition reimbursements and teaching assistantships with full and partial tuition reimbursements available. Financial award application deadline: 1/1. *Unit head:* Dr. Kelly Chandler-Olcott, Director, 315-443-5183, E-mail: kpchandl@syr.edu. *Application contact:* Laurie Deyo, Graduate Recruiter, School of Education, 315-443-2505, E-mail: e-gradrcrt@syr.edu. Web site: http://soeweb.syr.edu/.

Teachers College, Columbia University, Graduate Faculty of Education, Department of Arts and Humanities, Program in Teaching of English and English Education, New York, NY 10027. Offers Ed M, MA, Ed D, PhD. *Accreditation:* NCATE. Part-time and evening/weekend programs available. *Faculty:* 4 full-time (3 women), 23 part-time/adjunct (13 women). *Students:* 64 full-time (52 women), 155 part-time (114 women); includes 46 minority (15 Black or African American, non-Hispanic/Latino; 21 Asian, non-Hispanic/Latino; 10 Hispanic/Latino), 16 international. Average age 31. 158 applicants, 84% accepted, 67 enrolled. In 2011, 167 master's, 9 doctorates awarded. Terminal master's awarded for partial completion of doctoral program. *Degree requirements:* For master's, project; for doctorate, comprehensive exam, thesis/dissertation. *Entrance requirements:* For master's, at least 24 undergraduate and/or graduate credits in English or their equivalent; writing sample and master's degree (for Ed M applicants); for doctorate, at least five years of classroom teaching experience; MA in English, English education or closely-related field; writing sample. *Application deadline:* For fall admission, 1/2 priority date for domestic students; for spring admission, 11/1 for domestic students. Application fee: $65. *Financial support:* Fellowships, research assistantships, teaching assistantships, career-related internships or fieldwork, Federal Work-Study, institutionally sponsored loans, and tuition waivers (full and partial) available. Support available to part-time students. Financial award application deadline: 2/1. *Faculty research:* Teaching of writing and reading, language and curriculum, literacy and health, narrative and action research. *Unit head:* Prof. Ruth Vinz, Program Coordinator, 212-678-3070, E-mail: rav5@tc.columbia.edu. *Application contact:* Thomas P. Rock, Director of Admissions, 212-678-3083, Fax: 212-678-4171, E-mail: rock@tc.edu. Web site: http://www.tc.edu/a%26h/EnglishEd/.

Temple University, College of Education, Department of Curriculum, Instruction, and Technology in Education, Philadelphia, PA 19122-6096. Offers applied behavioral analysis (MS Ed); career and technical education (MS Ed); early childhood education and elementary education (MS Ed); English education (MS Ed); language arts education (Ed D); math/science education (Ed D); mathematics education (MS Ed); science education (MS Ed); second and foreign language education (MS Ed); special education (MS Ed); teaching English as a second language (MS Ed). Part-time and evening/weekend programs available. *Faculty:* 19 full-time (12 women). *Students:* 30 full-time (23 women), 86 part-time (69 women); includes 12 minority (4 Black or African American, non-Hispanic/Latino; 2 Asian, non-Hispanic/Latino; 5 Hispanic/Latino; 1 Two or more races, non-Hispanic/Latino), 5 international. 82 applicants, 71% accepted, 51 enrolled. In 2011, 181 master's, 16 doctorates awarded. Terminal master's awarded for partial completion of doctoral program. *Degree requirements:* For master's, thesis or alternative; for doctorate, thesis/dissertation. *Entrance requirements:* For master's and doctorate, GRE General Test or MAT, minimum GPA of 3.0. Additional exam requirements/recommendations for international students: Required—TOEFL (minimum score 550 paper-based; 213 computer-based; 79 iBT). *Application deadline:* For fall admission, 4/1 for domestic students, 12/15 for international students; for spring admission, 10/1 for domestic students, 8/1 for international students. Application fee: $50. Electronic applications accepted. *Expenses:* Tuition, state resident: full-time $12,366; part-time $687 per credit hour. Tuition, nonresident: full-time $17,298; part-time $961 per credit hour. *Required fees:* $590; $213 per year. *Financial support:* Fellowships, research assistantships with full tuition reimbursements, and teaching assistantships with full tuition reimbursements available. Financial award application deadline: 1/15; financial award applicants required to submit FAFSA. *Faculty research:* School improvement, problem-solving, literacy, language development. *Unit head:* Dr. Michael W. Smith, Chair, 215-204-6387, Fax: 215-204-1414, E-mail: mwsmith@temple.edu. *Application contact:* Dr. Margo Greicar, Director for Graduate Academic and Student Affairs, 215-204-8011, Fax: 215-204-4383, E-mail: margo.greicar@temple.edu. Web site: http://www.temple.edu/education/cite/.

Texas A&M University, College of Education and Human Development, Department of Teaching, Learning, and Culture, College Station, TX 77843. Offers culture and curriculum (M Ed, MS); curriculum and instruction (PhD); English as a second language (M Ed, MS, PhD); mathematics education (M Ed, MS, PhD); reading and language arts education (M Ed, MS, PhD); science education (M Ed, MS, PhD); urban education (M Ed, MS, PhD). Part-time programs available. *Faculty:* 30. *Students:* 163 full-time (119 women), 226 part-time (185 women); includes 108 minority (56 Black or African American, non-Hispanic/Latino; 2 American Indian or Alaska Native, non-Hispanic/Latino; 6 Asian, non-Hispanic/Latino; 37 Hispanic/Latino; 7 Two or more races, non-Hispanic/Latino), 62 international. Average age 36. In 2011, 107 master's, 44 doctorates awarded. *Degree requirements:* For master's, comprehensive exam, thesis (for some programs); for doctorate, comprehensive exam, thesis/dissertation. *Entrance requirements:* For master's, GRE General Test, minimum GPA of 3.0; for doctorate, GRE General Test, 3 years of teaching experience. Additional exam requirements/recommendations for international students: Required—TOEFL (minimum score 550 paper-based; 213 computer-based). *Application deadline:* For fall admission, 1/15 priority date for domestic students, 1/15 for international students; for spring admission, 9/15 priority date for domestic students, 9/15 for international students. Applications are processed on a rolling basis. Application fee: $50 ($75 for international students). Electronic applications accepted. *Expenses:* Tuition, state resident: full-time $5437; part-time $226.55 per credit hour. Tuition, nonresident: full-time $12,949; part-time

$539.55 per credit hour. *Required fees:* $2741. *Financial support:* In 2011–12, fellowships with partial tuition reimbursements (averaging $3,000 per year), teaching assistantships with partial tuition reimbursements (averaging $7,200 per year) were awarded; research assistantships with partial tuition reimbursements, career-related internships or fieldwork, Federal Work-Study, institutionally sponsored loans, scholarships/grants, tuition waivers (partial), and unspecified assistantships also available. Support available to part-time students. Financial award application deadline: 4/1; financial award applicants required to submit FAFSA. *Unit head:* Dr. Yeping Li, Head, 979-845-8384, Fax: 979-845-9663, E-mail: yepingli@tamu.edu. *Application contact:* Kerri Smith, Senior Academic Advisor II, 979-845-8382, Fax: 979-845-9663, E-mail: krsmith@tamu.edu. Web site: http://tlac.tamu.edu.

Texas A&M University–Commerce, Graduate School, College of Humanities, Social Sciences and Arts, Department of Literature and Languages, Commerce, TX 75429-3011. Offers college teaching of English (PhD); English (MA, MS); Spanish (MA). Part-time programs available. Terminal master's awarded for partial completion of doctoral program. *Degree requirements:* For master's, comprehensive exam, thesis (for some programs); for doctorate, one foreign language, thesis/dissertation, departmental qualifying exam. *Entrance requirements:* For master's and doctorate, GRE General Test. Electronic applications accepted. *Faculty research:* Latino literature, American film studies, ethnographic research, Willa Carter.

Trinity Washington University, School of Education, Washington, DC 20017-1094. Offers counseling (MA); early childhood education (MAT); educating for change (M Ed); educational administration (MSA); elementary education (MAT); school counseling (MA); secondary education (MAT), including English, social studies; special education (MAT); teaching English as a second language (MAT); teaching English to speakers of other languages (M Ed); the teaching of reading (M Ed). *Accreditation:* NCATE. Part-time and evening/weekend programs available. *Degree requirements:* For master's, thesis (for some programs), capstone project(s). *Entrance requirements:* For master's, PRAXIS I, minimum GPA of 2.8. Additional exam requirements/recommendations for international students: Required—TOEFL (minimum score 550 paper-based; 213 computer-based). *Faculty research:* Technology, literacy, special education, organizations, inclusion models.

Troy University, Graduate School, College of Education, Program in Postsecondary Education, Troy, AL 36082. Offers adult education (M Ed); biology (M Ed); criminal justice (M Ed); English (M Ed); foundations of education (M Ed); general science (M Ed); higher education administration (M Ed); history (M Ed); instructional technology (M Ed); mathematics (M Ed); music industry (M Ed); physical fitness (M Ed); political science (M Ed); public administration (M Ed); social science (M Ed); teaching English (M Ed). *Accreditation:* NCATE. Part-time and evening/weekend programs available. *Faculty:* 53 full-time (21 women), 22 part-time/adjunct (8 women). *Students:* 74 full-time (51 women), 166 part-time (121 women); includes 148 minority (143 Black or African American, non-Hispanic/Latino; 1 American Indian or Alaska Native, non-Hispanic/Latino; 2 Hispanic/Latino; 2 Two or more races, non-Hispanic/Latino). Average age 34. 174 applicants, 82% accepted, 88 enrolled. In 2011, 221 master's awarded. *Degree requirements:* For master's, comprehensive exam, thesis. *Entrance requirements:* For master's, MAT (minimum score 385), minimum GPA of 2.5. Additional exam requirements/recommendations for international students: Required—TOEFL (minimum score 523 paper-based; 193 computer-based; 70 iBT), IELTS (minimum score 6), or ACT COMPASS ESL (minimum listening, reading, and grammar score 270). *Application deadline:* Applications are processed on a rolling basis. Application fee: $50. Electronic applications accepted. *Expenses:* Tuition, state resident: full-time $6960; part-time $290 per credit hour. Tuition, nonresident: full-time $13,920; part-time $580 per credit hour. *Required fees:* $386 per term. *Financial support:* Available to part-time students. Applicants required to submit FAFSA. *Unit head:* Dr. Jan Oliver, Associate Professor, 334-670-3444, Fax: 334-670-3296, E-mail: oliver@troy.edu. *Application contact:* Brenda K. Campbell, Director of Graduate Admissions, 334-670-3178, Fax: 334-670-3733, E-mail: bcamp@troy.edu.

Union Graduate College, School of Education, Schenectady, NY 12308-3107. Offers biology (MAT, MS); chemistry (MAT); Chinese (MAT); earth science (MAT); English (MAT); French (MAT); general science (MAT); German (MAT); Greek (MAT); languages (MAT); Latin (MAT); mathematics (MAT); mathematics and technology (MS); mentoring and teacher leadership (AC); middle childhood extension (AC); national board certificate and teacher leadership (AC); physical science (MS); physics (MAT); social studies (MAT); Spanish (MAT). *Accreditation:* Teacher Education Accreditation Council. *Faculty:* 3 full-time (1 woman), 51 part-time/adjunct (24 women). *Students:* 37 full-time (26 women), 25 part-time (16 women); includes 4 minority (3 Asian, non-Hispanic/Latino; 1 Hispanic/Latino). Average age 32. 66 applicants, 83% accepted, 41 enrolled. In 2011, 47 master's, 29 other advanced degrees awarded. *Degree requirements:* For master's, thesis or project. *Entrance requirements:* For master's, minimum GPA of 3.0, letters of recommendation. Additional exam requirements/recommendations for international students: Required—TOEFL (minimum score 550 paper-based; 213 computer-based). *Application deadline:* Applications are processed on a rolling basis. Application fee: $60. Electronic applications accepted. *Expenses:* Contact institution. *Financial support:* In 2011–12, 22 students received support. Career-related internships or fieldwork, Federal Work-Study, scholarships/grants, health care benefits, and tuition waivers (partial) available. Support available to part-time students. Financial award applicants required to submit FAFSA. *Faculty research:* Transformative learning, science education, National Board Certification, teacher leadership, teacher quality. *Unit head:* Dr. Patrick Allen, Dean, 518-631-9870, Fax: 518-631-9901. *Application contact:* Christine Angley, Assistant, 518-631-9871, Fax: 518-631-9903, E-mail: angleyc@uniongraduatecollege.edu.

University at Buffalo, the State University of New York, Graduate School, Graduate School of Education, Department of Learning and Instruction, Buffalo, NY 14260. Offers biology education (Ed M, Certificate); chemistry education (Ed M, Certificate); childhood education (Ed M); childhood education with bilingual extension (Ed M); early childhood education (Ed M); early childhood education with bilingual extension (birth-grade 2) (Ed M); earth science education (Ed M, Certificate); educational technology and new literacies (Certificate); educational technology and new literacies (online) (Certificate); elementary education (Ed D, PhD); English education (Ed M, PhD, Certificate); English for speakers of other languages (Ed M); foreign and second language education (PhD); French education (Ed M, Certificate); general education (Ed M); German education (Ed M, Certificate); gifted education (online) (Certificate); Latin education (Ed M, Certificate); literacy teaching and learning (Certificate); literary specialist (Ed M); mathematics education (Ed M, PhD, Certificate); music education (Ed M, Certificate); physics education (Ed M, Certificate); reading education (PhD); science and the public (online) (Ed M); science education (PhD); social studies education (Ed M, Certificate); Spanish education (Ed M, Certificate); special education (PhD); teaching and leading for diversity (Certificate); teaching English to speakers of other languages (Ed M). Part-time and evening/weekend programs available. Postbaccalaureate distance learning degree programs offered (no on-campus study). *Faculty:* 32 full-time (23 women), 54 part-time/adjunct (43 women). *Students:* 294 full-time (222 women), 350 part-time (261 women); includes 75 minority (19 Black or African American, non-Hispanic/Latino; 6 American Indian or Alaska Native, non-Hispanic/Latino; 40 Asian, non-Hispanic/Latino; 10 Hispanic/Latino), 76 international. Average age 29. 548 applicants, 52% accepted, 253 enrolled. In 2011, 225 master's, 17 doctorates, 37 other advanced degrees awarded. *Degree requirements:* For master's, comprehensive exam; for doctorate, thesis/dissertation, research analysis exam, research experience component. *Entrance requirements:* For doctorate, GRE General Test or MAT, interview, writing sample, letters of recommendation. Additional exam requirements/recommendations for international students: Required—TOEFL (minimum score 600 paper-based; 96 iBT). *Application deadline:* For fall admission, 2/1 priority date for domestic students, 2/1 for international students; for spring admission, 11/15 priority date for domestic students, 10/1 for international students. Applications are processed on a rolling basis. Application fee: $50. Electronic applications accepted. *Financial support:* In 2011–12, 40 fellowships (averaging $12,991 per year), 46 research assistantships (averaging $10,986 per year) were awarded; teaching assistantships with full tuition reimbursements, career-related internships or fieldwork, Federal Work-Study, institutionally sponsored loans, scholarships/grants, and unspecified assistantships also available. Financial award application deadline: 2/28; financial award applicants required to submit FAFSA. *Faculty research:* Science assessment, foreign language teaching and learning, early learning, new literacies, gender and education. *Unit head:* Dr. Julie Sarama, Chair, 716-645-2455, Fax: 716-645-3161, E-mail: jcollins@buffalo.edu. *Application contact:* Cathy Dimino, Admissions Assistant, 716-645-2110, Fax: 716-645-7937, E-mail: cadimino@buffalo.edu.

The University of Alabama in Huntsville, School of Graduate Studies, College of Liberal Arts, Department of English, Huntsville, AL 35899. Offers education (MA); English (MA); language arts (MA); reading specialist (MA); technical communications (Certificate). Part-time and evening/weekend programs available. *Faculty:* 11 full-time (5 women), 2 part-time/adjunct (both women). *Students:* 16 full-time (10 women), 37 part-time (26 women); includes 4 minority (2 Black or African American, non-Hispanic/Latino; 2 Hispanic/Latino). Average age 32. 28 applicants, 86% accepted, 17 enrolled. In 2011, 9 master's, 3 other advanced degrees awarded. *Degree requirements:* For master's, one foreign language, comprehensive exam, thesis or alternative, oral and written exams. *Entrance requirements:* For master's and Certificate, GRE General Test, minimum GPA of 3.0. Additional exam requirements/recommendations for international students: Required—TOEFL (minimum score 500 paper-based; 173 computer-based; 62 iBT). *Application deadline:* For fall admission, 7/15 for domestic students, 4/1 for international students; for spring admission, 11/30 for domestic students, 9/1 for international students. Applications are processed on a rolling basis. Application fee: $40 ($50 for international students). Electronic applications accepted. *Expenses:* Tuition, state resident: full-time $7830; part-time $473.50 per credit. Tuition, nonresident: full-time $18,748; part-time $1128.33 per credit. Tuition and fees vary according to course load and program. *Financial support:* In 2011–12, 11 students received support, including 5 teaching assistantships with full tuition reimbursements available (averaging $8,460 per year); career-related internships or fieldwork, Federal Work-Study, institutionally sponsored loans, scholarships/grants, health care benefits, tuition waivers, and unspecified assistantships also available. Support available to part-time students. Financial award application deadline: 4/1; financial award applicants required to submit FAFSA. *Faculty research:* American and British literature, linguistics, technical writing, women's studies, rhetoric. *Unit head:* Dr. Dan Schenker, Chair, 256-824-6320, Fax: 256-824-6949, E-mail: schenkd@uah.edu. *Application contact:* Kim Gray, Graduate Studies Admissions Coordinator, 256-824-6002, Fax: 256-824-6405, E-mail: deangrad@uah.edu. Web site: http://www.uah.edu/colleges/liberal/english/index.php.

University of Alaska Fairbanks, School of Education, Program in Education, Fairbanks, AK 99775. Offers curriculum and instruction (M Ed); education (M Ed, Graduate Certificate); elementary education (M Ed); language and literacy (M Ed); reading (M Ed); secondary education (M Ed); special education (M Ed). *Faculty:* 25 full-time (15 women). *Students:* 30 full-time (23 women), 69 part-time (50 women); includes 17 minority (7 American Indian or Alaska Native, non-Hispanic/Latino; 1 Asian, non-Hispanic/Latino; 2 Hispanic/Latino; 1 Native Hawaiian or other Pacific Islander, non-Hispanic/Latino; 6 Two or more races, non-Hispanic/Latino), 1 international. Average age 33. 68 applicants, 76% accepted, 37 enrolled. In 2011, 26 master's, 22 other advanced degrees awarded. *Degree requirements:* For master's, comprehensive exam, thesis, oral defense. *Entrance requirements:* Additional exam requirements/recommendations for international students: Required—TOEFL (minimum score 550 paper-based; 213 computer-based; 80 iBT). *Application deadline:* For fall admission, 5/1 for domestic students, 3/1 for international students; for spring admission, 10/15 for domestic students, 8/1 for international students. Applications are processed on a rolling basis. Application fee: $60. Electronic applications accepted. *Expenses:* Tuition, state resident: full-time $6696; part-time $372 per credit. Tuition, nonresident: full-time $13,680; part-time $760 per credit. Tuition and fees vary according to course load and reciprocity agreements. *Financial support:* Fellowships with tuition reimbursements, research assistantships with tuition reimbursements, teaching assistantships with tuition reimbursements, career-related internships or fieldwork, Federal Work-Study, scholarships/grants, health care benefits, and unspecified assistantships available. Support available to part-time students. Financial award application deadline: 6/1; financial award applicants required to submit FAFSA. *Unit head:* Allan Morotti, Interim Dean, 907-474-7341, Fax: 907-474-5451, E-mail: uaf-soe-school@alaska.edu. *Application contact:* Mike Earnest, Director of Admissions, 907-474-7500, Fax: 907-474-5379, E-mail: admissions@uaf.edu. Web site: http://www.uaf.edu/educ/graduate/counseling.html.

The University of Arizona, College of Humanities, Department of English, Rhetoric, Composition and the Teaching of English Program, Tucson, AZ 85721. Offers PhD. *Faculty:* 42 full-time (16 women), 2 part-time/adjunct (1 woman). *Students:* 48 full-time (35 women), 3 part-time (2 women); includes 12 minority (4 Asian, non-Hispanic/Latino; 6 Hispanic/Latino; 2 Two or more races, non-Hispanic/Latino). Average age 34. 41 applicants, 15% accepted, 6 enrolled. In 2011, 7 doctorates awarded. *Degree requirements:* For doctorate, one foreign language, comprehensive exam, thesis/dissertation. *Entrance requirements:* For doctorate, GRE General Test, 3 letters of recommendation, writing sample. Additional exam requirements/recommendations for international students: Required—TOEFL (minimum score 550 paper-based; 213 computer-based; 79 iBT). *Application deadline:* Applications are processed on a rolling basis. Application fee: $75. Electronic applications accepted. *Expenses:* Tuition, state resident: full-time $10,840. Tuition, nonresident: full-time $25,802. *Total annual research expenditures:* $252,000. *Unit head:* Larry Evers, Director, 520-621-3287, Fax: 520-621-7397, E-mail: levers@email.arizona.edu. *Application contact:* Alison Miller, Program Assistant, 520-621-7213, Fax: 520-621-7397, E-mail: admiller@u.arizona.edu. Web site: http://grad.arizona.edu/live/programs/description/139.

University of Arkansas at Pine Bluff, School of Education, Pine Bluff, AR 71601-2799. Offers early childhood education (M Ed); secondary education (M Ed), including English education, mathematics education, physical education, science education, social studies education; teaching (MAT). *Accreditation:* NCATE. Part-time and evening/weekend programs available. *Degree requirements:* For master's, comprehensive exam. *Entrance requirements:* For master's, GRE, minimum GPA of 2.75, NTE or Standard Arkansas Teaching Certificate. *Faculty research:* Teacher certification, accreditation, assessment, standards, portfolio development, rehabilitation, technology.

University of Central Florida, College of Education, School of Teaching, Learning, and Leadership, Program in English Language Arts Education, Orlando, FL 32816. Offers teacher education (MAT), including ESOL endorsement; teacher leadership (M Ed). *Accreditation:* NCATE. Part-time and evening/weekend programs available. *Students:* 18 full-time (15 women), 30 part-time (25 women); includes 14 minority (5 Black or African American, non-Hispanic/Latino; 2 Asian, non-Hispanic/Latino; 6 Hispanic/Latino; 1 Two or more races, non-Hispanic/Latino). Average age 29. 14 applicants, 71% accepted, 9 enrolled. In 2011, 14 master's awarded. *Degree requirements:* For master's, thesis or alternative, research project. *Entrance requirements:* For master's, GRE General Test. Additional exam requirements/recommendations for international students: Required—TOEFL. *Application deadline:* For fall admission, 7/15 for domestic students; for spring admission, 12/1 for domestic students. Application fee: $30. Electronic applications accepted. *Expenses:* Tuition, state resident: part-time $277.08 per credit hour. Tuition, nonresident: part-time $277.08 per credit hour. Part-time tuition and fees vary according to degree level and program. *Financial support:* In 2011–12, 1 student received support. Fellowships with partial tuition reimbursements available, research assistantships with partial tuition reimbursements available, teaching assistantships with partial tuition reimbursements available, career-related internships or fieldwork, Federal Work-Study, institutionally sponsored loans, tuition waivers (partial), and unspecified assistantships available. Financial award application deadline: 3/1; financial award applicants required to submit FAFSA. *Unit head:* Dr. Janet B. Andreasen, Program Coordinator, 407-823-5430, E-mail: janet.andreasen@ucf.edu. *Application contact:* Barbara Rodriguez, Director, Admissions and Registration, 407-823-2766, Fax: 407-823-6442, E-mail: gradadmissions@ucf.edu.

University of Colorado Denver, College of Liberal Arts and Sciences, Department of English, Denver, CO 80217. Offers applied linguistics (MA); literature (MA); rhetoric and teaching of writing (MA). Part-time and evening/weekend programs available. *Faculty:* 23 full-time (13 women). *Students:* 37 full-time (23 women), 21 part-time (14 women); includes 6 minority (1 Asian, non-Hispanic/Latino; 5 Hispanic/Latino), 1 international. Average age 30. 26 applicants, 73% accepted, 10 enrolled. In 2011, 16 master's awarded. *Degree requirements:* For master's, variable foreign language requirement, comprehensive exam (for some programs), thesis (for some programs), minimum of 33 credit hours (for literature), 30 (for rhetoric and teaching of writing and applied linguistics). *Entrance requirements:* For master's, GRE General Test, minimum GPA of 3.0, critical writing sample, letters of recommendation, completion of 24 semester hours in English courses (at least 16 at the upper-division), statement of purpose. Additional exam requirements/recommendations for international students: Required—TOEFL (minimum score 525 paper-based; 197 computer-based; 71 iBT). *Application deadline:* For fall admission, 4/1 for domestic and international students; for spring admission, 10/1 for domestic and international students. Application fee: $50 ($75 for international students). Electronic applications accepted. *Financial support:* Fellowships, teaching assistantships, Federal Work-Study, scholarships/grants, and unspecified assistantships available. Financial award application deadline: 4/1; financial award applicants required to submit FAFSA. *Faculty research:* Literature, rhetoric, teaching of writing, applied linguistics. *Unit head:* Prof. Nancy Ciccone, Chair, 303-556-8395, Fax: 303-556-2959, E-mail: nancy.ciccone@ucdenver.edu. *Application contact:* English Department, 303-556-2584, Fax: 303-556-2959. Web site: http://www.ucdenver.edu/academics/colleges/CLAS/Departments/english/Pages/English.aspx.

University of Colorado Denver, School of Education and Human Development, Teacher Education Programs, Denver, CO 80217. Offers elementary linguistically diverse education (MA); elementary math and science education (MA); elementary math education (MA); elementary reading and writing (MA); elementary science education (MA); secondary English education (MA); secondary linguistically diverse education (MA); secondary math education (MA); secondary reading and writing (MA); secondary science education (MA); special education (MA). *Accreditation:* NCATE. Part-time and evening/weekend programs available. *Students:* 419 full-time (325 women), 238 part-time (196 women); includes 83 minority (11 Black or African American, non-Hispanic/Latino; 1 American Indian or Alaska Native, non-Hispanic/Latino; 15 Asian, non-Hispanic/Latino; 53 Hispanic/Latino; 3 Two or more races, non-Hispanic/Latino), 9 international. Average age 30. 206 applicants, 88% accepted, 85 enrolled. In 2011, 278 master's awarded. *Degree requirements:* For master's, comprehensive exam. *Entrance requirements:* For master's, GRE or MAT (for those with GPA below 2.75), transcripts, resume, letters of recommendation. Additional exam requirements/recommendations for international students: Required—TOEFL (minimum score 525 paper-based; 197 computer-based). *Application deadline:* For fall admission, 4/15 priority date for domestic students; for spring admission, 9/15 priority date for domestic students. Applications are processed on a rolling basis. Application fee: $50 ($75 for international students). Electronic applications accepted. *Expenses:* Contact institution. *Financial support:* Research assistantships, teaching assistantships, and Federal Work-Study available. Financial award application deadline: 4/1; financial award applicants required to submit FAFSA. *Faculty research:* Linguistically diverse education/ESL, elementary reading and writing, elementary teacher education, secondary teacher education, special education. *Unit head:* Cindy Gutierrez, Director, 303-315-4982, E-mail: cindy.gutierrez@ucdenver.edu. *Application contact:* Lori Sisneros, Student Services Center, 303-315-4979, E-mail: education@ucdenver.edu. Web site: http://www.ucdenver.edu/academics/colleges/SchoolOfEducation/Academics/MASTERS/Pages/default.aspx.

University of Connecticut, Graduate School, Neag School of Education, Department of Curriculum and Instruction, Program in English Education, Storrs, CT 06269. Offers MA, PhD, Post-Master's Certificate. *Accreditation:* NCATE. Terminal master's awarded for partial completion of doctoral program. *Degree requirements:* For master's, comprehensive exam, thesis or alternative; for doctorate, thesis/dissertation. *Entrance requirements:* For doctorate, GRE General Test. Additional exam requirements/recommendations for international students: Required—TOEFL (minimum score 550 paper-based; 213 computer-based). Electronic applications accepted.

University of Florida, Graduate School, College of Education, School of Teaching and Learning, Gainesville, FL 32611. Offers bilingual/ESOL education (M Ed, MAE, Ed D, PhD, Ed S); curriculum and instruction (M Ed, MAE, Ed D, PhD, Ed S); elementary education (M Ed, MAE); English education (M Ed, MAE); mathematics education (M Ed, MAE); reading education (M Ed, MAE); science education (M Ed, MAE); social foundations of education (M Ed, MAE, Ed D, PhD); social studies education (M Ed, MAE). *Accreditation:* NCATE. Part-time and evening/weekend programs available. Postbaccalaureate distance learning degree programs offered (no on-campus study). *Faculty:* 26 full-time (19 women). *Students:* 247 full-time (201 women), 236 part-time (196 women); includes 100 minority (32 Black or African American, non-Hispanic/Latino; 2 American Indian or Alaska Native, non-Hispanic/Latino; 15 Asian, non-Hispanic/Latino; 51 Hispanic/Latino), 32 international. Average age 33. 290 applicants, 60% accepted, 122 enrolled. In 2011, 284 master's, 19 doctorates, 29 other advanced degrees awarded. Terminal master's awarded for partial completion of doctoral program. *Degree requirements:* For master's, comprehensive exam (for some programs), thesis (for some programs); for doctorate, comprehensive exam (for some programs), thesis/dissertation (for some programs). *Entrance requirements:* For master's and doctorate, GRE General Test, minimum GPA of 3.0; for Ed S, GRE General Test. Additional exam requirements/recommendations for international students: Required—TOEFL (minimum score 550 paper-based; 213 computer-based; 80 iBT), IELTS (minimum score 6). *Application deadline:* For fall admission, 2/15 for domestic students, 12/1 for international students; for spring admission, 9/15 for domestic students, 3/1 for international students. Applications are processed on a rolling basis. Application fee: $30. Electronic applications accepted. *Financial support:* Fellowships, research assistantships, teaching assistantships, career-related internships or fieldwork, and unspecified assistantships available. Financial award applicants required to submit FAFSA. *Faculty research:* Early childhood, child and adolescents, diverse learners, race/ethnicity issues, teacher education, professional development, language and literacy development, policy development. *Unit head:* Dr. Elizabeth Bondy, Chair, 352-273-4242, Fax: 352-392-9193, E-mail: bondy@coe.ufl.edu. *Application contact:* Wevan Terzian, Graduate Coordinator, 352-273-4216, Fax: 352-392-9193, E-mail: sterzian@coe.ufl.edu. Web site: http://education.ufl.edu/school-teaching-learning/.

University of Georgia, College of Education, Department of Language and Literacy Education, Athens, GA 30602. Offers English education (M Ed, Ed S); language and literacy education (PhD); reading education (M Ed, Ed D, Ed S); teaching additional languages (M Ed, Ed S). *Accreditation:* NCATE. *Faculty:* 15 full-time (11 women). *Students:* 100 full-time (81 women), 94 part-time (80 women); includes 21 minority (17 Black or African American, non-Hispanic/Latino; 1 Asian, non-Hispanic/Latino; 2 Hispanic/Latino; 1 Two or more races, non-Hispanic/Latino), 31 international. Average age 33. 185 applicants, 61% accepted, 42 enrolled. In 2011, 43 master's, 15 doctorates, 2 other advanced degrees awarded. *Degree requirements:* For doctorate, variable foreign language requirement. *Entrance requirements:* For master's and Ed S, GRE General Test or MAT; for doctorate, GRE General Test. Additional exam requirements/recommendations for international students: Required—TOEFL (minimum score 550 paper-based; 213 computer-based). *Application deadline:* For fall admission, 7/1 priority date for domestic students; for spring admission, 11/15 for domestic students. Application fee: $50. Electronic applications accepted. *Faculty research:* Comprehension, critical literacy, literacy and technology, vocabulary instruction, content area reading. *Unit head:* Dr. Mark A. Faust, Head, 706-542-4515, Fax: 706-542-4509, E-mail: mfaust@uga.edu. *Application contact:* Dr. Elizabeth St. Pierre, Graduate Coordinator, 706-542-4520, E-mail: stpierre@uga.edu. Web site: http://www.coe.uga.edu/lle/.

University of Illinois at Chicago, Graduate College, College of Liberal Arts and Sciences, Department of English, Chicago, IL 60607-7128. Offers English (MA, PhD), including creative writing (PhD), English education (MA), English studies, writing (MA); linguistics (MA), including teaching English to speakers of other languages/applied linguistics. Part-time and evening/weekend programs available. *Degree requirements:* For doctorate, variable foreign language requirement, thesis/dissertation, written and oral exams. *Entrance requirements:* For master's, GRE General Test, GRE Subject Test; for doctorate, GRE General Test, GRE Subject Test, minimum GPA of 2.0. Additional exam requirements/recommendations for international students: Required—TOEFL. Electronic applications accepted. *Faculty research:* Literary history and theory.

University of Indianapolis, Graduate Programs, School of Education, Indianapolis, IN 46227-3697. Offers art education (MAT); biology (MAT); chemistry (MAT); curriculum and instruction (MA); earth sciences (MAT); education (MA, MAT); educational leadership (MA); elementary education (MA); English (MAT); French (MAT); math (MAT); physical education (MAT); physics (MAT); secondary education (MA), including art education, education, English education, social studies education; social studies (MAT); Spanish (MAT). *Accreditation:* NCATE. Part-time and evening/weekend programs available. *Faculty:* 3 full-time (2 women), 3 part-time/adjunct (2 women). *Students:* 32 full-time (18 women), 97 part-time (56 women); includes 22 minority (20 Black or African American, non-Hispanic/Latino; 1 Asian, non-Hispanic/Latino; 1 Hispanic/Latino), 3 international. Average age 33. In 2011, 78 master's awarded. *Entrance requirements:* For master's, GRE Subject Test, PRAXIS I, minimum GPA of 2.5, 3 letters of recommendation, interview, writing exercise. Additional exam requirements/recommendations for international students: Required—TOEFL (minimum score 550 paper-based; 213 computer-based). *Application deadline:* Applications are processed on a rolling basis. Application fee: $50. Tuition and fees vary according to degree level and program. *Financial support:* Federal Work-Study available. Financial award application deadline: 5/1; financial award applicants required to submit FAFSA. *Faculty research:* Assessment of teacher education, perceptions of prospective teachers by parents. *Unit head:* Dr. Kathy Moran, Dean, 317-788-3285, Fax: 317-788-3300, E-mail: kmoran@uindy.edu. *Application contact:* Jeni Kirby, 317-788-2113, E-mail: kirbyj@uindy.edu. Web site: http://education.uindy.edu/.

The University of Iowa, Graduate College, College of Education, Department of Teaching and Learning, Program in Elementary Education, Iowa City, IA 52242-1316. Offers curriculum and supervision (MA, PhD); developmental reading (MA); early childhood education and care (MA); elementary education (MA, PhD); language, literature and culture (PhD). *Degree requirements:* For master's, thesis optional, exam; for doctorate, comprehensive exam, thesis/dissertation. *Entrance requirements:* For master's and doctorate, GRE General Test, minimum GPA of 3.0. Additional exam requirements/recommendations for international students: Required—TOEFL (minimum score 550 paper-based; 213 computer-based; 81 iBT). Electronic applications accepted.

The University of Iowa, Graduate College, College of Education, Department of Teaching and Learning, Program in Secondary Education, Iowa City, IA 52242-1316. Offers art education (PhD); curriculum and supervision (PhD); curriculum supervision (MA); developmental reading (MA); English education (MA, MAT); foreign language education (MA, MAT); foreign language/ESL education (PhD); language, literature and culture (PhD); math education (PhD); mathematics education (MA); social studies (MA, PhD). *Degree requirements:* For master's, thesis optional, exam; for doctorate, comprehensive exam, thesis/dissertation. *Entrance requirements:* For master's and doctorate, GRE General Test, minimum GPA of 3.0. Additional exam requirements/recommendations for international students: Required—TOEFL (minimum score 550 paper-based; 213 computer-based; 81 iBT). Electronic applications accepted.

University of Maine, Graduate School, College of Liberal Arts and Sciences, Department of English, Orono, ME 04469. Offers composition and pedagogy (MA); creative (MA); gender and literature (MA); poetry and poetics (MA). Part-time and evening/weekend programs available. *Faculty:* 19 full-time (9 women), 29 part-time/adjunct (16 women). *Students:* 24 full-time (10 women), 4 part-time (3 women), 1 international. Average age 28. 34 applicants, 65% accepted, 21 enrolled. In 2011, 13 degrees awarded. *Degree requirements:* For master's, one foreign language, thesis optional. *Entrance requirements:* For master's, GRE General Test, minimum GPA of 3.0. Additional exam requirements/recommendations for international students: Required—TOEFL. *Application deadline:* For fall admission, 2/1 priority date for domestic students. Applications are processed on a rolling basis. Application fee: $65. Electronic applications accepted. *Expenses:* Tuition, state resident: full-time $5016. Tuition, nonresident: full-time $14,424. *Financial support:* In 2011–12, 21 teaching assistantships with full tuition reimbursements (averaging $13,600 per year) were awarded; Federal Work-Study and tuition waivers (full and partial) also available. Financial award application deadline: 3/1. *Faculty research:* Contemporary poetics, contemporary criticism, composition theory and pedagogy, feminist approaches to literature. *Unit head:* Dr. Naomi Jacobs, Chair, 207-581-3822, Fax: 207-581-1604. *Application contact:* Scott G. Delcourt, Associate Dean of the Graduate School, 207-581-3291, Fax: 207-581-3232, E-mail: graduate@maine.edu. Web site: http://www2.umaine.edu/graduate/.

University of Manitoba, Faculty of Graduate Studies, Faculty of Education, Department of Curriculum, Teaching and Learning, Winnipeg, MB R3T 2N2, Canada. Offers language and literacy (M Ed); second language education (M Ed); studies in curriculum, teaching and learning (M Ed). *Degree requirements:* For master's, thesis or alternative.

University of Maryland, Baltimore County, Graduate School, College of Arts, Humanities and Social Sciences, Department of Education, Program in Teaching, Baltimore, MD 21250. Offers early childhood education (MAT); elementary education (MAT); secondary education (MAT), including social studies; secondary education (MAT), including art, biology, chemistry, dance, earth/space science, English, foreign language, mathematics, music, physics, theatre. Part-time and evening/weekend programs available. *Faculty:* 24 full-time (18 women), 25 part-time/adjunct (19 women). *Students:* 46 full-time (35 women), 64 part-time (39 women); includes 24 minority (8 Black or African American, non-Hispanic/Latino; 7 Asian, non-Hispanic/Latino; 6 Hispanic/Latino; 1 Native Hawaiian or other Pacific Islander, non-Hispanic/Latino; 2 Two or more races, non-Hispanic/Latino), 4 international. Average age 31. 88 applicants, 57% accepted, 39 enrolled. In 2011, 106 master's awarded. *Degree requirements:* For master's, comprehensive exam (for some programs), thesis (for some programs). *Entrance requirements:* For master's, PRAXIS I or GRE (minimum score of 1000), minimum GPA of 3.0. Additional exam requirements/recommendations for international students: Required—TOEFL. *Application deadline:* For fall admission, 6/1 for domestic students; for spring admission, 11/1 for domestic students. Applications are processed on a rolling basis. Application fee: $50. Electronic applications accepted. *Financial support:* In 2011–12, 6 students received support, including teaching assistantships with full and partial tuition reimbursements available (averaging $12,000 per year); career-related internships or fieldwork, Federal Work-Study, scholarships/grants, tuition waivers, and unspecified assistantships also available. Financial award application deadline: 3/1. *Faculty research:* STEM teacher education, culturally sensitive pedagogy, ESOL/bilingual education, early childhood education, language, literacy and culture. *Unit head:* Dr. Susan M. Blunck, Graduate Program Director, 410-455-2869, Fax: 410-455-3986, E-mail: blunck@umbc.edu. *Application contact:* Cheryl Johnson, 410-455-3388, E-mail: blackwel@umbc.edu. Web site: http://www.umbc.edu/education/.

University of Michigan, Horace H. Rackham School of Graduate Studies, Joint Ph D Program in English and Education, Ann Arbor, MI 48109-1259. Offers PhD. *Accreditation:* Teacher Education Accreditation Council. *Faculty:* 24 full-time (17 women). *Students:* 24 full-time (17 women); includes 2 minority (both Black or African American, non-Hispanic/Latino). Average age 31. 51 applicants, 18% accepted, 4 enrolled. In 2011, 5 doctorates awarded. *Degree requirements:* For doctorate, one foreign language, comprehensive exam, thesis/dissertation, 3 preliminary exams, oral defense of dissertation. *Entrance requirements:* For doctorate, GRE General Test, master's degree, teaching experience. Additional exam requirements/recommendations for international students: Required—TOEFL. *Application deadline:* For fall admission, 1/5 for domestic and international students. Application fee: $65 ($75 for international students). Electronic applications accepted. *Financial support:* In 2011–12, 24 students received support, including 8 fellowships with full tuition reimbursements available, 6 research assistantships with full tuition reimbursements available, 39 teaching assistantships with full tuition reimbursements available; health care benefits also available. *Faculty research:* Literacy, teacher education, discourse analysis, rhetoric and composition studies. *Unit head:* Dr. Anne Ruggles Gere, Co-Chair, 734-763-6643, Fax: 734-615-6524, E-mail: argere@umich.edu. *Application contact:* Jeanie Mahoney Laubenthal, Graduate Coordinator, 734-763-6643, Fax: 734-615-6524, E-mail: laubenth@umich.edu. Web site: http://www.soe.umich.edu/academics/doctoral_programs/ee/.

University of Minnesota, Twin Cities Campus, Graduate School, College of Education and Human Development, Department of Curriculum and Instruction, Program in Teaching, Minneapolis, MN 55455-0213. Offers Chinese (M Ed); earth science (M Ed); elementary special education (M Ed); English (M Ed); English as a second language (M Ed); French (M Ed); German (M Ed); Hebrew (M Ed); Japanese (M Ed); life sciences (M Ed); mathematics (M Ed); middle school science (M Ed); science (M Ed); second languages and cultures (M Ed); social studies (M Ed); Spanish (M Ed). *Students:* 375 full-time (319 women), 72 part-time (56 women); includes 34 minority (8 Black or African American, non-Hispanic/Latino; 16 Asian, non-Hispanic/Latino; 10 Hispanic/Latino), 5 international. Average age 27. 317 applicants, 70% accepted, 215 enrolled. In 2011, 443 master's awarded. Application fee: $55. *Unit head:* Dr. Nina Asher, Chair, 612-624-1357, Fax: 612-624-8277, E-mail: nasher@umn.edu. *Application contact:* Dr. Jennifer Engler, Assistant Dean, 612-626-2887, Fax: 612-626-7496, E-mail: engle009@umn.edu. Web site: http://www.cehd.umn.edu/ci/.

University of Missouri, Graduate School, College of Education, Department of Learning, Teaching and Curriculum, Columbia, MO 65211. Offers agricultural education (M Ed, PhD, Ed S); art education (M Ed, PhD, Ed S); business and office education (M Ed, PhD, Ed S); early childhood education (M Ed, PhD, Ed S); elementary education (M Ed, PhD, Ed S); English education (M Ed, PhD, Ed S); foreign language education (M Ed, PhD, Ed S); health education and promotion (M Ed, PhD); learning and instruction (M Ed); marketing education (M Ed, PhD, Ed S); mathematics education (M Ed, PhD, Ed S); music education (M Ed, PhD, Ed S); reading education (M Ed, PhD, Ed S); science education (M Ed, PhD, Ed S); social studies education (M Ed, PhD, Ed S); vocational education (M Ed, PhD, Ed S). Part-time programs available. *Faculty:* 26 full-time (16 women), 3 part-time/adjunct (2 women). *Students:* 184 full-time (145 women), 276 part-time (215 women); includes 34 minority (10 Black or African American, non-Hispanic/Latino; 1 American Indian or Alaska Native, non-Hispanic/Latino; 7 Asian, non-Hispanic/Latino; 8 Hispanic/Latino; 8 Two or more races, non-Hispanic/Latino), 39 international. Average age 32. 309 applicants, 76% accepted, 204 enrolled. In 2011, 232 master's, 8 doctorates, 2 other advanced degrees awarded. Terminal master's awarded for partial completion of doctoral program. *Degree requirements:* For doctorate, thesis/dissertation. *Entrance requirements:* For master's and Ed S, GRE General Test or MAT, minimum GPA of 3.0; for doctorate, GRE General Test, minimum GPA of 3.0. Additional exam requirements/recommendations for international students: Required—TOEFL (minimum score 600 paper-based; 250 computer-based; 100 iBT). Application fee: $55 ($75 for international students). Electronic applications accepted. *Expenses:* Tuition, state resident: full-time $5881. Tuition, nonresident: full-time $15,183. *Required fees:* $952. Tuition and fees vary according to campus/location and program. *Financial support:* Fellowships, research assistantships, teaching assistantships, and institutionally sponsored loans available. *Application contact:* Fran Colley, 573-882-6462, E-mail: colleyf@missouri.edu. Web site: http://education.missouri.edu/LTC/.

The University of Montana, Graduate School, College of Arts and Sciences, Department of English, Program in Teaching, Missoula, MT 59812-0002. Offers MA. *Entrance requirements:* For master's, GRE General Test, sample of written work.

University of New Hampshire, Graduate School, College of Liberal Arts, Department of English, Durham, NH 03824. Offers English (MA, PhD); English education (MST); language and linguistics (MA); literature (MA); writing (MFA). Part-time programs available. *Faculty:* 35 full-time (18 women). *Students:* 48 full-time (27 women), 59 part-time (38 women); includes 4 minority (1 Black or African American, non-Hispanic/Latino; 1 Hispanic/Latino; 2 Two or more races, non-Hispanic/Latino), 4 international. Average age 30. 272 applicants, 42% accepted, 34 enrolled. In 2011, 45 master's, 3 doctorates awarded. *Degree requirements:* For master's, one foreign language; for doctorate, 2 foreign languages, thesis/dissertation. *Entrance requirements:* For master's, GRE General Test, sample of written work; for doctorate, GRE General Test, GRE Subject Test, sample of written work. Additional exam requirements/recommendations for international students: Required—TOEFL (minimum score 550 paper-based; 213 computer-based; 80 iBT). *Application deadline:* For fall admission, 6/1 priority date for domestic students, 2/15 for international students; for spring admission, 12/1 for domestic students. Applications are processed on a rolling basis. Application fee: $65. Electronic applications accepted. *Expenses:* Tuition, state resident: full-time $12,360; part-time $687 per credit hour. Tuition, nonresident: full-time $25,680; part-time $1058 per credit hour. *International tuition:* $29,550 full-time. *Required fees:* $1666; $833 per course. $416.50 per semester. Tuition and fees vary according to course load and degree level. *Financial support:* In 2011–12, 58 students received support, including 1 fellowship, 1 research assistantship, 43 teaching assistantships; career-related internships or fieldwork, Federal Work-Study, scholarships/grants, and tuition waivers (full and partial) also available. Support available to part-time students. Financial award application deadline: 2/15. *Unit head:* Dr. Andrew Merton, Chairperson, 603-862-3963. *Application contact:* Jamie Auger, Administrative Assistant, 603-862-3963, E-mail: engl.grad@unh.edu. Web site: http://www.unh.edu/english/.

University of New Mexico, Graduate School, College of Education, Department of Language, Literacy and Sociocultural Studies, Program in Language, Literacy and Sociocultural Studies, Albuquerque, NM 87131. Offers American Indian education (MA); bilingual education (MA, PhD); educational linguistics (PhD); educational thought and sociocultural studies (MA, PhD); literacy/language arts (MA, PhD); social studies (MA); TESOL (MA, PhD). *Faculty:* 19 full-time (12 women), 12 part-time/adjunct (10 women). *Students:* 40 full-time (30 women), 47 part-time (17 women); includes 85 minority (4 Black or African American, non-Hispanic/Latino; 14 American Indian or Alaska Native, non-Hispanic/Latino; 4 Asian, non-Hispanic/Latino; 59 Hispanic/Latino; 4 Two or more races, non-Hispanic/Latino), 14 international. Average age 41. 63 applicants, 57% accepted, 22 enrolled. In 2011, 44 master's, 8 doctorates awarded. *Degree requirements:* For master's, comprehensive exam, thesis optional; for doctorate, comprehensive exam, thesis/dissertation, research skills. *Entrance requirements:* For master's, letter of intent, 3 letters of recommendation, resume, BA/BS, department demographic form, transcripts; for doctorate, writing sample, letter of intent, 3 letters of recommendation, resume, BA/BS, department demographic form, transcripts. Additional exam requirements/recommendations for international students: Required—TOEFL. *Application deadline:* For fall admission, 12/1 for domestic and international students; for spring admission, 9/15 for domestic and international students. Application fee: $50. Electronic applications accepted. *Financial support:* In 2011–12, 7 students received support, including 7 fellowships (averaging $3,170 per year), 1,318 teaching assistantships with tuition reimbursements available (averaging $3,789 per year); research assistantships, career-related internships or fieldwork, institutionally sponsored loans, scholarships/grants, and unspecified assistantships also available. Support available to part-time students. Financial award application deadline: 3/1; financial award applicants required to submit FAFSA. *Faculty research:* School reform, professional development, history of education, Native American education, politics of education, feminism and issues of sexual identity, critical race theory, bilingualism, literacy reading, adolescent literature, second language acquisition, critical theory and schooling, indigenous languages. *Unit head:* Dr. Lois M. Meyer, Chair, 505-277-7244, Fax: 505-277-8362, E-mail: lsmeyer@unm.edu. *Application contact:* Debra Schaffer, Administrative Assistant, 505-277-0437, Fax: 505-277-8362, E-mail: schaffer@unm.edu. Web site: http://coe.unm.edu/departments/department-of-language-literacy-and-sociocultural-studies/llss-program.html.

The University of North Carolina at Chapel Hill, Graduate School, School of Education, Program in Secondary Education, Chapel Hill, NC 27599. Offers English (Grades 9-12) (MAT); English as a second language (MAT); French (Grades K-12) (MAT); German (Grades K-12) (MAT); Japanese (Grades K-12) (MAT); Latin (Grades 9-12) (MAT); mathematics (Grades 9-12) (MAT); music (Grades K-12) (MAT); science (Grades 9-12) (MAT); social studies (Grades 9-12) (MAT); Spanish (Grades K-12) (MAT). *Accreditation:* NCATE. *Degree requirements:* For master's, comprehensive exam. *Entrance requirements:* For master's, GRE General Test, minimum GPA of 3.0 during last 2 years of undergraduate course work. Additional exam requirements/recommendations for international students: Required—TOEFL (minimum score 550 paper-based; 79 computer-based). Electronic applications accepted.

The University of North Carolina at Charlotte, Graduate School, College of Liberal Arts and Sciences, Department of English, Charlotte, NC 28223-0001. Offers English (MA); English education (MA); technical/professional writing (Certificate). Part-time and evening/weekend programs available. *Faculty:* 33 full-time (18 women), 1 part-time/adjunct (0 women). *Students:* 35 full-time (26 women), 76 part-time (54 women); includes 12 minority (10 Black or African American, non-Hispanic/Latino; 1 Asian, non-Hispanic/Latino; 1 Two or more races, non-Hispanic/Latino), 1 international. Average age 30. 47 applicants, 83% accepted, 27 enrolled. In 2011, 31 master's, 2 other advanced degrees awarded. *Degree requirements:* For master's, comprehensive exam, thesis optional. *Entrance requirements:* For master's, GRE General Test, minimum undergraduate GPA of 3.0 in major, 2.75 overall. Additional exam requirements/recommendations for international students: Required—TOEFL (minimum score 557 paper-based; 220 computer-based; 83 iBT). *Application deadline:* For fall admission, 7/15 for domestic students, 5/1 for international students; for spring admission, 11/15 for domestic students, 10/1 for international students. Applications are processed on a rolling basis. Application fee: $65 ($75 for international students). Electronic applications accepted. *Expenses:* Tuition, state resident: full-time $3689. Tuition, nonresident: full-time $15,226. *Required fees:* $2198. Tuition and fees vary according to course load and program. *Financial support:* In 2011–12, 17 teaching assistantships (averaging $7,066 per year) were awarded; career-related internships or fieldwork, institutionally sponsored loans, scholarships/grants, and unspecified assistantships also available. Support available to part-time students. Financial award application deadline: 4/1; financial award applicants required to submit FAFSA. *Faculty research:* English as a second language (ESL), composition theory and pedagogy, children's literature, technical and professional writing, English for specific purposes (ESP). *Total annual research expenditures:* $162,960. *Unit head:* Dr. Malin Pereira, Chair, 704-687-2299, Fax: 704-687-3961, E-mail: mpereira@uncc.edu. *Application contact:* Kathy B. Giddings, Director of Graduate Admissions, 704-687-5503, Fax: 704-687-3279, E-mail: gradadm@uncc.edu. Web site: http://english.uncc.edu/MA-English/graduate-programs.html.

The University of North Carolina at Greensboro, Graduate School, College of Arts and Sciences, Department of English, Program in English, Greensboro, NC 27412-5001. Offers American literature (PhD); English (M Ed, MA); English literature (PhD); rhetoric and composition (PhD). *Degree requirements:* For master's, comprehensive exam, thesis or alternative; for doctorate, variable foreign language requirement, thesis/dissertation, preliminary exam. *Entrance requirements:* For master's, GRE General

Test, GRE Subject Test, minimum GPA of 3.0; for doctorate, GRE General Test, GRE Subject Test, critical writing sample, minimum GPA of 3.0. Additional exam requirements/recommendations for international students: Required—TOEFL. Electronic applications accepted.

The University of North Carolina at Pembroke, Graduate Studies, Department of English, Theater and Languages, Program in English Education, Pembroke, NC 28372-1510. Offers MA, MAT. *Accreditation:* NCATE. Part-time and evening/weekend programs available. *Degree requirements:* For master's, comprehensive exam, thesis optional. *Entrance requirements:* For master's, GRE, MAT, or NTE, minimum GPA of 3.0 in major or 2.5 overall. Additional exam requirements/recommendations for international students: Required—TOEFL.

University of Northern Iowa, Graduate College, College of Humanities, Arts and Sciences, Department of Languages and Literatures, Program in English, Cedar Falls, IA 50614. Offers creative writing (MA); English (MA); literature (MA); teaching English in secondary schools (TESS) (MA), including middle/junior high and senior high; teaching English to speakers of other languages (MA). Part-time and evening/weekend programs available. *Students:* 12 full-time (6 women), 4 part-time (all women); includes 2 minority (1 Black or African American, non-Hispanic/Latino; 1 Hispanic/Latino). 16 applicants, 50% accepted, 5 enrolled. In 2011, 5 master's awarded. *Degree requirements:* For master's, one foreign language, comprehensive exam, thesis or alternative, portfolio. *Entrance requirements:* Additional exam requirements/recommendations for international students: Required—TOEFL (minimum score 600 paper-based; 250 computer-based; 100 iBT). *Application deadline:* For fall admission, 8/1 priority date for domestic students. Applications are processed on a rolling basis. Application fee: $50 ($70 for international students). Electronic applications accepted. *Expenses:* Tuition, state resident: full-time $7476. Tuition, nonresident: full-time $16,410. *Required fees:* $942. *Financial support:* Career-related internships or fieldwork, Federal Work-Study, scholarships/grants, and tuition waivers (full and partial) available. Support available to part-time students. Financial award application deadline: 2/1. *Unit head:* Dr. Julie Husband, Graduate Coordinator, 319-273-3849, Fax: 319-273-5807, E-mail: julie.husband@uni.edu. *Application contact:* Laurie S. Russell, Record Analyst, 319-273-2623, Fax: 319-273-2885, E-mail: laurie.russell@uni.edu. Web site: http://www.uni.edu/langlit/.

University of Oklahoma, Jeannine Rainbolt College of Education, Department of Instructional Leadership and Academic Curriculum, Norman, OK 73072. Offers communication, culture and pedagogy for Hispanic populations in educational settings (Graduate Certificate); instructional leadership and academic curriculum (M Ed, PhD), including bilingual education, early childhood education, elementary education, English education, instructional leadership, mathematics education, reading education, science education, science, technology, engineering and mathematics education (M Ed), secondary education, social studies education, teacher education (M Ed). *Accreditation:* NCATE. Part-time and evening/weekend programs available. *Faculty:* 19 full-time (13 women), 1 (woman) part-time/adjunct. *Students:* 73 full-time (63 women), 114 part-time (87 women); includes 29 minority (5 Black or African American, non-Hispanic/Latino; 12 American Indian or Alaska Native, non-Hispanic/Latino; 5 Asian, non-Hispanic/Latino; 3 Hispanic/Latino; 1 Native Hawaiian or other Pacific Islander, non-Hispanic/Latino; 3 Two or more races, non-Hispanic/Latino), 7 international. Average age 33. 87 applicants, 86% accepted, 68 enrolled. In 2011, 36 master's, 6 doctorates awarded. Terminal master's awarded for partial completion of doctoral program. *Degree requirements:* For doctorate, thesis/dissertation. *Entrance requirements:* For master's, 12 hours of course work in education; for doctorate, GRE General Test, master's degree, minimum graduate GPA of 3.0. Additional exam requirements/recommendations for international students: Required—TOEFL (minimum score 550 paper-based; 79 iBT). *Application deadline:* For fall admission, 6/1 priority date for domestic students, 3/1 for international students; for spring admission, 11/1 for domestic students, 9/1 for international students. Applications are processed on a rolling basis. Application fee: $40 ($90 for international students). Electronic applications accepted. *Expenses:* Tuition, state resident: full-time $4087; part-time $170.30 per credit hour. Tuition, nonresident: full-time $14,875; part-time $619.80 per credit hour. *Required fees:* $2659; $100.25 per credit hour. Tuition and fees vary according to course load and degree level. *Financial support:* In 2011–12, 128 students received support, including 2 research assistantships with partial tuition reimbursements available (averaging $12,431 per year), 12 teaching assistantships with partial tuition reimbursements available (averaging $10,161 per year); institutionally sponsored loans, scholarships/grants, and unspecified assistantships also available. Financial award applicants required to submit FAFSA. *Faculty research:* Engineering in practice for sustainable future, no child left behind (reading), early childhood learning games impact study, Educare randomized control startup, Oklahoma mentoring professional development. *Total annual research expenditures:* $1.1 million. *Unit head:* Lawrence Baines, Chair, 405-325-1498, Fax: 405-325-4061, E-mail: lbaines@ou.edu. *Application contact:* Lynn Crussel, Graduate Programs Officer, 405-325-4843, Fax: 405-325-4061, E-mail: lcrussel@ou.edu. Web site: http://education.ou.edu/departments/ilac.

University of Pennsylvania, Graduate School of Education, Division of Reading, Writing, and Literacy, Program in Reading/Writing/Literacy, Philadelphia, PA 19104. Offers MS Ed, Ed D, PhD. *Students:* 82 full-time (69 women), 37 part-time (31 women); includes 38 minority (22 Black or African American, non-Hispanic/Latino; 10 Asian, non-Hispanic/Latino; 2 Hispanic/Latino; 4 Two or more races, non-Hispanic/Latino), 3 international. 150 applicants, 53% accepted, 49 enrolled. In 2011, 40 master's, 11 doctorates awarded. *Degree requirements:* For master's and doctorate, internship. *Expenses: Tuition:* Full-time $26,660; part-time $4944 per course. *Required fees:* $2318; $291 per course. Tuition and fees vary according to course load, degree level and program. *Unit head:* Dr. Andrew Porter, Dean, 215-898-7014. *Application contact:* Penny Creedon. Web site: http://www.gse.upenn.edu/degrees_programs/rwl.

University of Phoenix–Omaha Campus, College of Education, Omaha, NE 68154-5240. Offers administration and supervision (MA Ed); curriculum and instruction (MA Ed), including adult education, computer education, curriculum and instruction, English and language arts education, English as a second language, mathematics education; elementary teacher education (MA Ed); secondary teacher education (MA Ed); special education (MA Ed).

University of Phoenix–Online Campus, College of Education, Phoenix, AZ 85034-7209. Offers administration and supervision (MAEd, Graduate Certificate); adult education and training (MAEd); curriculum and instruction (MAEd); curriculum and instruction reading (MAEd); curriculum and instruction-computer education (MAEd); curriculum and instruction-language arts (MAEd); curriculum and instruction-mathematics (MAEd); early childhood education (MAEd); educational studies (MAEd); elementary teacher education (MAEd); elementary teacher education-early childhood (MAEd); secondary teacher education (MAEd); special education (MAEd); teacher education - elementary/middle level (MAEd); teacher education middle level generalist (MAEd); teacher education middle level mathematics (MAEd); teacher education middle level science (MAEd); teacher education secondary mathematics (MAEd); teacher education secondary science (MAEd); teacher leadership (MAEd). *Accreditation:* Teacher Education Accreditation Council. Evening/weekend programs available. Postbaccalaureate distance learning degree programs offered. *Students:* 9,180 full-time (7,178 women); includes 2,913 minority (2,069 Black or African American, non-Hispanic/Latino; 50 American Indian or Alaska Native, non-Hispanic/Latino; 100 Asian, non-Hispanic/Latino; 542 Hispanic/Latino; 48 Native Hawaiian or other Pacific Islander, non-Hispanic/Latino; 104 Two or more races, non-Hispanic/Latino), 147 international. Average age 36. *Entrance requirements:* Additional exam requirements/recommendations for international students: Required—TOEFL, TOEIC (Test of English as an International Communication), Berlitz Online English Proficiency Exam, Pearson Test of English, or IELTS. *Application deadline:* Applications are processed on a rolling basis. Application fee: $45. Electronic applications accepted. *Expenses:* Contact institution. *Financial support:* Scholarships/grants available. Financial award applicants required to submit FAFSA. *Application contact:* 866-766-0766. Web site: http://www.phoenix.edu/colleges_divisions/education.html.

University of Phoenix–Springfield Campus, College of Education, Springfield, MO 65804-7211. Offers administration and supervision (MA Ed); curriculum and instruction (MA Ed), including computer education, curriculum and instruction, English and language arts education, English as a second language, mathematics education; English and language arts education (MA Ed).

University of Phoenix–Washington D.C. Campus, College of Education, Washington, DC 20001. Offers administration and supervision (MA Ed); adult education and training (MA Ed); computer education (MA Ed); curriculum and instruction (MA Ed, Ed D); early childhood education (MA Ed); education (Ed S); educational leadership (Ed D); educational technology (Ed D); elementary teacher education (MA Ed); English and language arts education (MA Ed); English as a second language (MA Ed); higher education administration (PhD); mathematics education (MA Ed); secondary teacher education (MA Ed); special education (MA Ed); teacher leadership (MA Ed).

University of Pittsburgh, School of Education, Department of Instruction and Learning, Program in Secondary Education, Pittsburgh, PA 15260. Offers English/communications education (M Ed, MAT); foreign languages education (M Ed, MAT); mathematics education (M Ed, MAT, Ed D); science education (M Ed, MAT, Ed D); social studies education (M Ed, MAT). Part-time and evening/weekend programs available. *Students:* 154 full-time (92 women), 68 part-time (47 women); includes 18 minority (6 Black or African American, non-Hispanic/Latino; 3 Asian, non-Hispanic/Latino; 7 Hispanic/Latino; 2 Two or more races, non-Hispanic/Latino), 6 international. Average age 30. 208 applicants, 48% accepted, 72 enrolled. In 2011, 116 master's, 6 doctorates awarded. *Degree requirements:* For master's, thesis; for doctorate, thesis/dissertation. *Entrance requirements:* For master's, PRAXIS I; for doctorate, GRE General Test. Additional exam requirements/recommendations for international students: Required—TOEFL. *Application deadline:* For fall admission, 2/1 priority date for domestic students; for spring admission, 11/15 priority date for domestic students. Applications are processed on a rolling basis. Application fee: $50. Electronic applications accepted. *Expenses:* Tuition, state resident: full-time $18,774; part-time $760 per credit. Tuition, nonresident: full-time $30,736; part-time $1258 per credit. *Required fees:* $740; $200 per term. Tuition and fees vary according to program. *Financial support:* Fellowships, teaching assistantships, career-related internships or fieldwork, Federal Work-Study, tuition waivers (partial), and unspecified assistantships available. Support available to part-time students. Financial award application deadline: 3/15; financial award applicants required to submit FAFSA. *Unit head:* Dr. Richard Donato, Chairman, 412-624-7248, Fax: 412-648-7081, E-mail: donato@pitt.edu. *Application contact:* Marianne L. Budziszewski, Director of Admissions and Enrollment Services, 412-648-2230, Fax: 412-648-1899, E-mail: soeinfo@pitt.edu. Web site: http://www.education.pitt.edu/.

University of Puerto Rico, Mayagüez Campus, Graduate Studies, College of Arts and Sciences, Department of English, Mayagüez, PR 00681-9000. Offers English education (MA). Part-time programs available. *Students:* 39 full-time (27 women), 5 part-time (2 women); includes 43 minority (all Hispanic/Latino), 1 international. 11 applicants, 73% accepted, 5 enrolled. In 2011, 14 master's awarded. *Degree requirements:* For master's, comprehensive exam, thesis optional. *Entrance requirements:* For master's, course work in linguistics or language, American literature, British literature, and structure/grammar or syntax. Additional exam requirements/recommendations for international students: Required—TOEFL (minimum score 550 paper-based; 213 computer-based). *Application deadline:* For fall admission, 2/15 for domestic and international students; for spring admission, 9/15 for domestic and international students. Applications are processed on a rolling basis. Application fee: $25. Tuition and fees vary according to course level and course load. *Financial support:* In 2011–12, 22 students received support, including 3 research assistantships (averaging $15,000 per year), 19 teaching assistantships (averaging $8,500 per year); Federal Work-Study and institutionally sponsored loans also available. *Faculty research:* Teaching English as a second language, linguistics, American literature, British literature. *Unit head:* Dr. Kevin Carroll, Director, 787-265-3847, Fax: 787-265-3847, E-mail: kevin.carroll@upr.edu. *Application contact:* Dr. Ricia Chansky, Graduate Coordinator, 787-265-3847, E-mail: ricia.chansky@upr.edu. Web site: http://www.uprm.edu./english/.

University of St. Francis, College of Education, Joliet, IL 60435-6169. Offers educational leadership (MS, Ed D); elementary education certification (M Ed); reading (MS); secondary education certification (M Ed), including English education, math education, science education, social studies education, visual arts education; special education (M Ed); teaching and learning (MS). *Accreditation:* NCATE. Part-time and evening/weekend programs available. Postbaccalaureate distance learning degree programs offered (no on-campus study). *Faculty:* 7 full-time (5 women), 21 part-time/adjunct (14 women). *Students:* 32 full-time (21 women), 230 part-time (175 women); includes 23 minority (7 Black or African American, non-Hispanic/Latino; 2 Asian, non-Hispanic/Latino; 13 Hispanic/Latino; 1 Two or more races, non-Hispanic/Latino), 1 international. Average age 32. 147 applicants, 60% accepted, 57 enrolled. In 2011, 156 master's awarded. *Entrance requirements:* For doctorate, master's degree, IL Type 75 or Principal's endorsement, interview. Additional exam requirements/recommendations for international students: Required—TOEFL (minimum score 550 paper-based; 213 computer-based). *Application deadline:* Applications are processed on a rolling basis. Application fee: $30. Electronic applications accepted. *Expenses:* Contact institution. *Financial support:* In 2011–12, 23 students received support. Federal Work-Study, scholarships/grants, tuition waivers (partial), and unspecified assistantships available. Support available to part-time students. Financial award applicants required to submit FAFSA. *Unit head:* Dr. John Gambro, Dean, 815-740-3829, Fax: 815-740-2264, E-mail: jgambro@stfrancis.edu. *Application contact:* Sandra Sloka, Director of Admissions for Graduate and Degree Completion Programs, 800-735-7500, Fax: 815-740-5032, E-mail: ssloka@stfrancis.edu. Web site: http://www.stfrancis.edu/academics/college-of-education/.

University of South Carolina, The Graduate School, College of Arts and Sciences, Department of English Language and Literature, Columbia, SC 29208. Offers creative writing (MFA); English (MA, PhD); English education (MAT); MLIS/MA. MAT offered in cooperation with the College of Education. Part-time programs available. *Degree requirements:* For master's, one foreign language, comprehensive exam, thesis; for doctorate, 2 foreign languages, comprehensive exam, thesis/dissertation. *Entrance requirements:* For master's, GRE General Test (MFA), GRE Subject Test (MA, MAT), sample of written work; for doctorate, GRE General Test, GRE Subject Test, sample of written work. Additional exam requirements/recommendations for international students:

Required—TOEFL. Electronic applications accepted. *Faculty research:* American literature, British literature, composition and rhetoric, linguistics, speech communication.

University of South Carolina, The Graduate School, College of Education, Department of Instruction and Teacher Education, Program in Secondary Education, Columbia, SC 29208. Offers art education (IMA, MAT); business education (IMA, MAT); English (MAT); foreign language (MAT); health education (MAT); mathematics (MAT); science (IMA, MAT); secondary (Ed D); secondary education (MT, PhD); social studies (MAT); theatre and speech (MAT). IMA and MT offered jointly with the subject areas. *Accreditation:* NCATE. *Degree requirements:* For master's, comprehensive exam, thesis (for some programs), foreign language (MA); for doctorate, one foreign language, comprehensive exam, thesis/dissertation. *Entrance requirements:* For master's, GRE General Test or MAT, teaching certificate (IMA, M Ed), interview; for doctorate, GRE General Test or MAT, interview. *Faculty research:* Middle school programs, professional development, school collaboration.

University of South Florida, Graduate School, College of Education, Department of Secondary Education, Tampa, FL 33620-9951. Offers English education (M Ed, MA, MAT, PhD); foreign language education/ESOL (M Ed, MA, MAT); instructional technology (M Ed, PhD, Ed S); mathematics education (M Ed, MA, MAT, PhD, Ed S); science education (M Ed, MA, MAT, PhD); second language acquisition/instructional technology (PhD); secondary education (M Ed, PhD); secondary education/TESOL (M Ed); social science education (M Ed, MA, MAT); teaching and learning in the content area (PhD). *Accreditation:* NCATE. Part-time and evening/weekend programs available. *Faculty:* 28 full-time (17 women), 3 part-time/adjunct (1 woman). *Students:* 174 full-time (116 women), 268 part-time (184 women); includes 103 minority (26 Black or African American, non-Hispanic/Latino; 10 Asian, non-Hispanic/Latino; 58 Hispanic/Latino; 9 Two or more races, non-Hispanic/Latino), 32 international. Average age 37. 229 applicants, 73% accepted, 141 enrolled. In 2011, 115 master's, 16 doctorates, 5 other advanced degrees awarded. *Degree requirements:* For master's, variable foreign language requirement, comprehensive exam, project (for some programs); for doctorate, variable foreign language requirement, comprehensive exam, thesis/dissertation, philosophies of inquiry; multiple research methods. *Entrance requirements:* For master's, GRE General Test or General Knowledge Test, minimum GPA of 3.0; for doctorate, GRE General Test, minimum GPA of 3.5; for Ed S, GRE General Test. Additional exam requirements/recommendations for international students: Required—TOEFL (minimum score 550 paper-based; 213 computer-based; 79 iBT). *Application deadline:* For fall admission, 2/15 for domestic students, 1/2 for international students; for spring admission, 10/15 for domestic students, 6/1 for international students. Application fee: $30. Electronic applications accepted. *Financial support:* In 2011–12, 7 students received support, including 1 research assistantship with full tuition reimbursement available (averaging $10,000 per year), 55 teaching assistantships with full and partial tuition reimbursements available (averaging $7,900 per year); scholarships/grants and unspecified assistantships also available. Financial award application deadline: 4/15; financial award applicants required to submit FAFSA. *Faculty research:* English language learners/multicultural, social science education, mathematics education, science education, instructional technology. *Total annual research expenditures:* $336,023. *Unit head:* Dr. Stephen Thornton, Chairperson, 813-974-3533, Fax: 813-974-3837, E-mail: thornton@usf.edu. *Application contact:* Dr. Diane Briscoe, Coordinator of Graduate Studies, 813-974-1804, Fax: 813-974-3391, E-mail: briscoe@usf.edu. Web site: http://www.coedu.usf.edu/main/departments/seced/seced.html.

University of South Florida–St. Petersburg Campus, College of Education, St. Petersburg, FL 33701. Offers educational leadership development (M Ed); elementary education (MA), including math/science; English education (MA); middle grades STEM education (MS); reading education (MA). Part-time programs available. *Students:* 30 full-time (27 women), 130 part-time (109 women); includes 28 minority (14 Black or African American, non-Hispanic/Latino; 4 Asian, non-Hispanic/Latino; 9 Hispanic/Latino; 1 Two or more races, non-Hispanic/Latino). Average age 34. 63 applicants, 70% accepted, 36 enrolled. In 2011, 74 master's awarded. *Degree requirements:* For master's, comprehensive exam, practicum, internship, comprehensive portfolio. *Entrance requirements:* For master's, State of Florida General Knowledge Test (GKT), Florida Teaching Certificate (for non-initial certification programs), letters of recommendation. Additional exam requirements/recommendations for international students: Required—TOEFL (minimum score 550 paper-based; 79 iBT); Recommended—IELTS. *Application deadline:* For fall admission, 6/1 priority date for domestic students, 6/1 for international students; for spring admission, 10/15 priority date for domestic students, 10/15 for international students. Applications are processed on a rolling basis. Application fee: $30. Electronic applications accepted. *Expenses:* Tuition, state resident: full-time $8847. Tuition, nonresident: full-time $18,423. One-time fee: $35 full-time. Full-time tuition and fees vary according to course load and program. *Financial support:* Applicants required to submit FAFSA. *Unit head:* Dr. Harold W. Heller, Dean, 727-873-4155, Fax: 727-873-4191, E-mail: hheller@usfsp.edu. *Application contact:* Eric Douthirt, Enrollment Management Specialist, 727-873-4450, E-mail: douthirt@usfsp.edu. Web site: http://www1.usfsp.edu/coe/index.asp.

The University of Tennessee, Graduate School, College of Education, Health and Human Sciences, Program in Education, Knoxville, TN 37996. Offers art education (MS); counseling education (PhD); cultural studies in education (PhD); curriculum (MS, Ed S); curriculum, educational research and evaluation (Ed D, PhD); early childhood education (PhD); early childhood special education (MS); education of deaf and hard of hearing (MS); educational administration and policy studies (Ed D, PhD); educational administration and supervision (Ed S); educational psychology (Ed D, PhD); elementary education (MS, Ed S); elementary teaching (MS); English education (MS, Ed S); exercise science (PhD); foreign language/ESL education (MS, Ed S); instructional technology (MS, Ed D, PhD, Ed S); literacy, language and ESL education (PhD); literacy, language education, and ESL education (Ed D); mathematics education (MS, Ed S); modified and comprehensive special education (MS); reading education (MS, Ed S); school counseling (Ed S); school psychology (PhD, Ed S); science education (MS, Ed S); secondary teaching (MS); social foundations (MS); social science education (MS, Ed S); socio-cultural foundations of sports and education (PhD); special education (Ed S); teacher education (Ed D, PhD). *Accreditation:* NCATE. Part-time and evening/weekend programs available. *Degree requirements:* For master's and Ed S, thesis optional; for doctorate, variable foreign language requirement, thesis/dissertation. *Entrance requirements:* For master's, minimum GPA of 2.7; for doctorate and Ed S, GRE General Test, minimum GPA of 2.7. Additional exam requirements/recommendations for international students: Required—TOEFL. Electronic applications accepted. *Expenses:* Tuition, state resident: full-time $8332; part-time $464 per credit hour. Tuition, nonresident: full-time $25,174; part-time $1400 per credit hour. *Required fees:* $1162; $56 per credit hour. Tuition and fees vary according to program.

The University of Texas at El Paso, Graduate School, College of Liberal Arts, Department of English, El Paso, TX 79968-0001. Offers bilingual professional writing (Certificate); English and American literature (MA); rhetoric and composition (PhD); rhetoric and writing studies (MA); teaching English (MAT). Part-time and evening/weekend programs available. *Students:* 115 (78 women); includes 68 minority (2 Black or African American, non-Hispanic/Latino; 1 American Indian or Alaska Native, non-Hispanic/Latino; 3 Asian, non-Hispanic/Latino; 62 Hispanic/Latino), 7 international. Average age 34. 52 applicants, 63% accepted, 31 enrolled. In 2011, 10 master's, 1 doctorate awarded. *Degree requirements:* For master's, thesis optional. *Entrance requirements:* For master's, GRE General Test, minimum GPA of 3.0. Additional exam requirements/recommendations for international students: Required—TOEFL. *Application deadline:* For fall admission, 7/1 priority date for domestic students, 3/1 for international students; for spring admission, 11/1 priority date for domestic students, 9/1 for international students. Applications are processed on a rolling basis. Application fee: $15 ($65 for international students). Electronic applications accepted. *Financial support:* In 2011–12, research assistantships with partial tuition reimbursements (averaging $20,555 per year), teaching assistantships with partial tuition reimbursements (averaging $16,444 per year) were awarded; Federal Work-Study, institutionally sponsored loans, scholarships/grants, and tuition waivers (partial) also available. Financial award application deadline: 3/15; financial award applicants required to submit FAFSA. *Faculty research:* Literature, creative writing, literary theory. *Unit head:* Dr. Evelyn Posey, Chair, 915-747-5731. *Application contact:* Dr. Benjamin Flores, Interim Dean of the Graduate School, 915-747-5491, Fax: 915-747-5788, E-mail: bflores@utep.edu.

University of the Sacred Heart, Graduate Programs, Department of Education, San Juan, PR 00914-0383. Offers early childhood education (M Ed); information technology and multimedia (Certificate); instruction systems and education technology (M Ed), including English, information technology and multimedia, instructional design, mathematics, Spanish. Part-time and evening/weekend programs available. *Degree requirements:* For master's, thesis. *Entrance requirements:* For master's, EXADEP, minimum undergraduate GPA of 2.75, interview.

The University of Toledo, College of Graduate Studies, Judith Herb College of Education, Health Science and Human Service, Department of Curriculum and Instruction, Toledo, OH 43606-3390. Offers art education (ME); career and technical education (ME); curriculum and instruction (ME, PhD, Ed S); education and anthropology (MAE); education and biology (MES); education and chemistry (MES); education and classics (MAE); education and economics (MAE); education and English (MAE); education and French (MAE); education and geography (MAE); education and geology (MES); education and German (MAE); education and history (MAE); education and mathematics (MAE, MES); education and physics (MES); education and political science (MAE); education and sociology (MAE); education and Spanish (MAE); educational media (PhD); educational technology (ME); English as a second language (MAE); gifted and talented (PhD); middle childhood education licensure (ME); music education (MME); secondary education (PhD); secondary education licensure (ME). *Accreditation:* NCATE. Part-time and evening/weekend programs available. *Faculty:* 24. *Students:* 60 full-time (31 women), 211 part-time (161 women); includes 23 minority (21 Black or African American, non-Hispanic/Latino; 2 Hispanic/Latino), 20 international. Average age 35. 115 applicants, 73% accepted, 74 enrolled. In 2011, 105 master's, 3 doctorates, 4 other advanced degrees awarded. *Degree requirements:* For master's, comprehensive exam, thesis or alternative; for doctorate, comprehensive exam, thesis/dissertation; for Ed S, thesis optional. *Entrance requirements:* For master's, doctorate, and Ed S, minimum cumulative GPA of 2.7 for all previous academic work, letters of recommendation. Additional exam requirements/recommendations for international students: Required—TOEFL (minimum score 550 paper-based; 213 computer-based; 80 iBT), IELTS (minimum score 6.5). *Application deadline:* For fall admission, 1/15 priority date for domestic students, 1/15 for international students. Applications are processed on a rolling basis. Application fee: $45 ($75 for international students). Electronic applications accepted. *Financial support:* In 2011–12, 9 research assistantships with full and partial tuition reimbursements (averaging $7,184 per year), 12 teaching assistantships with full and partial tuition reimbursements (averaging $8,425 per year) were awarded; career-related internships or fieldwork, Federal Work-Study, institutionally sponsored loans, scholarships/grants, tuition waivers (full and partial), unspecified assistantships, and administrative assistantships also available. Support available to part-time students. *Unit head:* Dr. Leigh Chiarelott, Chair, 419-530-5371, E-mail: eigh.chiarelott@utoledo.edu. *Application contact:* Graduate School Office, 419-530-4723, Fax: 419-530-4724, E-mail: grdsch@utnet.utoledo.edu. Web site: http://www.utoledo.edu/eduhshs/.

University of Tulsa, Graduate School, College of Arts and Sciences, School of Education, Program in Teaching Arts, Tulsa, OK 74104-3189. Offers art (MTA); biology (MTA); English (MTA); history (MTA); mathematics (MTA); theatre (MTA). Part-time programs available. *Students:* 2 applicants, 0% accepted, 0 enrolled. In 2011, 1 master's awarded. *Entrance requirements:* For master's, GRE General Test. Additional exam requirements/recommendations for international students: Required—TOEFL (minimum score 577 paper-based; 233 computer-based), IELTS (minimum score 6.5). *Application deadline:* Applications are processed on a rolling basis. Application fee: $40. Electronic applications accepted. *Expenses: Tuition:* Full-time $17,748; part-time $986 per hour. *Required fees:* $5 per contact hour. $75 per semester. Tuition and fees vary according to program. *Financial support:* Fellowships with full and partial tuition reimbursements, research assistantships with full and partial tuition reimbursements, teaching assistantships with full and partial tuition reimbursements, career-related internships or fieldwork, Federal Work-Study, scholarships/grants, health care benefits, tuition waivers (full and partial), and unspecified assistantships available. Support available to part-time students. Financial award application deadline: 2/1; financial award applicants required to submit FAFSA. *Unit head:* Dr. David Brown, Advisor, 918-631-2719, Fax: 918-631-2133, E-mail: david-brown@utulsa.edu. *Application contact:* Dr. David Brown, Advisor, 918-631-2719, Fax: 918-631-2133, E-mail: david-brown@utulsa.edu.

University of Victoria, Faculty of Graduate Studies, Faculty of Education, Department of Curriculum and Instruction, Victoria, BC V8W 2Y2, Canada. Offers art education (M Ed, PhD); curriculum studies (M Ed, MA, PhD); early childhood education (M Ed, PhD); educational studies (PhD); language and literacy (M Ed, MA, PhD); mathematics (M Ed, MA, PhD); music education (M Ed, MA, PhD); science (M Ed, MA, PhD); social studies (M Ed, MA); social, cultural and foundational studies (MA, PhD); technology and environmental education (PhD). Part-time programs available. *Degree requirements:* For master's, thesis, project (M Ed); for doctorate, comprehensive exam, thesis/dissertation. *Entrance requirements:* For master's, minimum B average. Additional exam requirements/recommendations for international students: Required—TOEFL (minimum score 575 paper-based; 233 computer-based), IELTS (minimum score 7). Electronic applications accepted. *Faculty research:* Elementary and secondary English, language arts, curriculum theory and practice, educational media and technology, educational administration and leadership, history and philosophy of education.

University of Virginia, Curry School of Education, Department of Curriculum, Instruction, and Special Education, Program in Curriculum and Instruction, Charlottesville, VA 22903. Offers curriculum and instruction (M Ed, Ed S); elementary (M Ed, Ed D); English (M Ed, Ed D); foreign language (M Ed); mathematics (M Ed, Ed D); reading (M Ed, Ed D, Ed S); science (Ed D); social studies (M Ed). *Students:* 22 full-time (17 women), 29 part-time (27 women); includes 4 minority (1 Black or African American, non-Hispanic/Latino; 1 Asian, non-Hispanic/Latino; 2 Two or more races, non-Hispanic/Latino), 1 international. Average age 33. 67 applicants, 75% accepted, 33 enrolled. In 2011, 78 master's, 2 doctorates, 12 other advanced degrees awarded. *Degree requirements:* For master's, comprehensive exam (for some programs); for doctorate, comprehensive exam, thesis/dissertation; for Ed S, comprehensive exam. *Entrance requirements:* For master's, doctorate, and Ed S, GRE General Test, 2 letters of recommendation. Additional exam requirements/recommendations for international students: Required—TOEFL (minimum score 600 paper-based; 250 computer-based; 90 iBT), IELTS (minimum score 7). *Application deadline:* Applications are processed on a rolling basis. Application fee: $60. Electronic applications accepted. *Financial support:* Fellowships with tuition reimbursements, research assistantships with tuition reimbursements, and teaching assistantships with tuition reimbursements available. Financial award application deadline: 1/5; financial award applicants required to submit FAFSA. *Unit head:* Laura Smolkin, Chair, 434-924-0831. *Application contact:* Karen Dwier, Information Contact, 434-924-0831, E-mail: kgd9g@virginia.edu.

University of Virginia, Curry School of Education, Program in Education, Charlottesville, VA 22903. Offers administration and supervision (PhD); applied developmental science (PhD); counselor education (PhD); curriculum and instruction (PhD); early childhood-developmental risk (MT); education evaluation (PhD); educational psychology (PhD); educational research (PhD); elementary (MT, PhD); English education (MT, PhD); foreign language education (MT); higher education (PhD); instructional technology (PhD); kinesiology (MT, PhD); math education (PhD); reading education (PhD); research statistics and evaluation (PhD); school psychology (PhD); science education (PhD); social studies education (MT, PhD); special education (PhD); world languages education (MT). *Students:* 299 full-time (216 women), 60 part-time (33 women); includes 46 minority (18 Black or African American, non-Hispanic/Latino; 17 Asian, non-Hispanic/Latino; 7 Hispanic/Latino; 4 Two or more races, non-Hispanic/Latino), 23 international. Average age 30. 307 applicants, 42% accepted, 80 enrolled. In 2011, 113 master's, 62 doctorates awarded. *Degree requirements:* For master's, comprehensive exam (for some programs), field project; for doctorate, comprehensive exam, thesis/dissertation. *Entrance requirements:* For doctorate, GRE General Test. Additional exam requirements/recommendations for international students: Required—TOEFL (minimum score 600 paper-based; 250 computer-based; 90 iBT), IELTS (minimum score 7). *Application deadline:* Applications are processed on a rolling basis. Application fee: $60. Electronic applications accepted. *Financial support:* Fellowships, research assistantships, and teaching assistantships available. Financial award application deadline: 1/5; financial award applicants required to submit FAFSA. *Unit head:* Robert C. Pianta, Dean, 434-924-3334. *Application contact:* Joanne McNergney, Assistant Dean for Admissions and Student Services, 434-924-3334, E-mail: curry-admissions@virginia.edu.

University of Washington, Graduate School, College of Arts and Sciences, Department of English, Seattle, WA 98195. Offers creative writing (MFA); English as a second language (MAT); English literature and language (MA, MAT, PhD). Part-time programs available. Terminal master's awarded for partial completion of doctoral program. *Degree requirements:* For master's, one foreign language, thesis (for some programs); for doctorate, one foreign language, thesis/dissertation. *Entrance requirements:* For master's, GRE General Test, GRE Subject Test (MA and MAT in English), minimum GPA of 3.0; for doctorate, GRE General Test, GRE Subject Test. Additional exam requirements/recommendations for international students: Required—TOEFL. Electronic applications accepted. *Faculty research:* English and American literature, critical theory, creative writing, language theory.

University of Washington, Graduate School, College of Education, Seattle, WA 98195. Offers curriculum and instruction (M Ed, Ed D, PhD), including educational technology, general curriculum (Ed D, PhD), language, literacy, and culture, mathematics education, multicultural education, reading and language arts education (Ed D), science education, social studies education, teaching and curriculum (M Ed); educational leadership and policy studies (M Ed, Ed D, PhD), including administration (Ed D), educational policy, organization, and leadership (M Ed, PhD), higher education, leadership for learning (Ed D), social and cultural foundations of education (M Ed, PhD); educational psychology (M Ed, PhD), including educational psychology (PhD), human development and cognition (M Ed), learning sciences, measurement, statistics and research design (M Ed), school psychology (M Ed); instructional leadership (M Ed); intercollegiate athletic leadership (M Ed); special education (M Ed, Ed D, PhD), including early childhood special education (M Ed), emotional and behavioral disabilities (M Ed), learning disabilities (M Ed), low-incidence disabilities (M Ed), severe disabilities (M Ed), special education (Ed D, PhD); teacher education (MIT). *Accreditation:* APA. Part-time and evening/weekend programs available. *Degree requirements:* For master's, thesis optional; for doctorate, thesis/dissertation. *Entrance requirements:* For master's and doctorate, GRE General Test, minimum GPA of 3.0. Additional exam requirements/recommendations for international students: Required—TOEFL. Electronic applications accepted. *Faculty research:* School restructuring/effective schools, special education interventions, literacy and writing, technology, school partnerships, teacher preparation.

University of West Georgia, College of Education, Department of Leadership and Applied Instruction, Carrollton, GA 30118. Offers art education (M Ed); art teacher education (Ed S); biology - secondary education (M Ed); biology/secondary education (Ed S); business education (M Ed, Ed S); chemistry/secondary education (Ed S); earth science/secondary education (Ed S); economics/secondary education (Ed S); educational leadership (M Ed, Ed S); English teacher education (M Ed, Ed S); French teacher education (M Ed, Ed S); history teacher education (Ed S); mathematics teacher education (M Ed, Ed S); middle grades education (M Ed, Ed S); physical education and recreation (Ed S); physical education teaching and coaching (M Ed); physics/secondary education (Ed S); science teacher education (M Ed, Ed S); secondary education (M Ed); social science - secondary education (M Ed); social science teacher education (M Ed); Spanish (M Ed); Spanish teacher education (M Ed, Ed S); sports management (M Ed). *Accreditation:* NCATE. Part-time and evening/weekend programs available. *Faculty:* 18 full-time (9 women). *Students:* 75 full-time (49 women), 169 part-time (109 women); includes 90 minority (85 Black or African American, non-Hispanic/Latino; 3 Hispanic/Latino; 2 Two or more races, non-Hispanic/Latino), 1 international. Average age 36. 115 applicants, 67% accepted, 19 enrolled. In 2011, 73 master's, 53 Ed Ss awarded. *Degree requirements:* For master's, internship; for Ed S, research project. *Entrance requirements:* For master's, GRE General Test, minimum GPA of 2.7; for Ed S, GRE General Test, master's degree, minimum graduate GPA of 3.0, district appointment. Additional exam requirements/recommendations for international students: Required—TOEFL (minimum score 523 paper-based; 193 computer-based; 69 iBT); Recommended—IELTS (minimum score 6). *Application deadline:* For fall admission, 7/21 for domestic students, 6/1 for international students; for spring admission, 11/30 for domestic students, 10/15 for international students. Applications are processed on a rolling basis. Application fee: $30. Electronic applications accepted. *Expenses:* Tuition, state resident: full-time $4336; part-time $181 per credit hour. Tuition, nonresident: full-time $17,362; part-time $724 per credit hour. Tuition and fees vary according to course load, degree level, campus/location and program. *Financial support:* In 2011–12, 1 research assistantship with full tuition reimbursement (averaging $7,444 per year) was awarded; career-related internships or fieldwork, scholarships/grants, and unspecified assistantships also available. Support available to part-time students. Financial award application deadline: 7/1; financial award applicants required to submit FAFSA. *Total annual research expenditures:* $5,000. *Unit head:* Dr. Frank Butts, Chair, 678-839-6530, Fax: 678-839-6195, E-mail: fbutts@westga.edu. *Application contact:* Deanna Richards, Coordinator, Graduate Studies, 678-839-5946, E-mail: drichard@westga.edu. Web site: http://www.westga.edu/coelai.

University of Wisconsin–Platteville, School of Graduate Studies, College of Liberal Arts and Education, School of Education, Platteville, WI 53818-3099. Offers adult education (MSE); elementary education (MSE); English education (MSE); middle school education (MSE); secondary education (MSE). *Accreditation:* NCATE. Part-time programs available. *Faculty:* 8 part-time/adjunct (3 women). *Students:* 62 full-time (47 women), 86 part-time (69 women); includes 22 minority (20 Black or African American, non-Hispanic/Latino; 2 Hispanic/Latino), 55 international. 17 applicants, 76% accepted. In 2011, 82 master's awarded. *Degree requirements:* For master's, comprehensive exam, thesis or alternative. *Entrance requirements:* Additional exam requirements/recommendations for international students: Required—TOEFL (minimum score 500 paper-based; 61 iBT), IELTS (minimum score 6). *Application deadline:* For fall admission, 7/1 priority date for domestic students; for spring admission, 11/1 for domestic students. Applications are processed on a rolling basis. Application fee: $56. Electronic applications accepted. *Financial support:* Research assistantships with partial tuition reimbursements, career-related internships or fieldwork, Federal Work-Study, institutionally sponsored loans, scholarships/grants, and unspecified assistantships available. Support available to part-time students. Financial award applicants required to submit FAFSA. *Unit head:* Dr. Karen Stinson, Director, 608-342-1131, Fax: 608-342-1133, E-mail: stinsonk@uwplatt.edu. *Application contact:* Lisa Popp, School of Graduate Studies, 608-342-1322, Fax: 608-342-1389, E-mail: poppl@uwplatt.edu. Web site: http://www.uwplatt.edu/.

Vanderbilt University, Peabody College, Department of Teaching and Learning, Nashville, TN 37240-1001. Offers elementary education (M Ed); English language learners (M Ed); learning and instruction (M Ed); learning, diversity, and urban studies (M Ed); reading education (M Ed); secondary education (M Ed). *Accreditation:* NCATE. *Faculty:* 35 full-time (24 women), 19 part-time/adjunct (14 women). *Students:* 123 full-time (96 women), 38 part-time (34 women); includes 26 minority (6 Black or African American, non-Hispanic/Latino; 3 Asian, non-Hispanic/Latino; 7 Hispanic/Latino; 10 Two or more races, non-Hispanic/Latino), 12 international. Average age 26. 251 applicants, 56% accepted, 60 enrolled. In 2011, 80 master's awarded. *Degree requirements:* For master's, comprehensive exam, thesis optional. *Entrance requirements:* For master's, GRE General Test, MAT. Additional exam requirements/recommendations for international students: Required—TOEFL (minimum score 550 paper-based; 213 computer-based). *Application deadline:* For fall admission, 12/31 priority date for domestic students, 12/31 for international students; for spring admission, 11/1 priority date for domestic students, 11/1 for international students. Applications are processed on a rolling basis. Application fee: $0. Electronic applications accepted. *Financial support:* Fellowships with full and partial tuition reimbursements, research assistantships with full and partial tuition reimbursements, teaching assistantships with full and partial tuition reimbursements, Federal Work-Study, institutionally sponsored loans, scholarships/grants, tuition waivers (partial), and unspecified assistantships available. Support available to part-time students. Financial award application deadline: 2/1; financial award applicants required to submit FAFSA. *Faculty research:* Learning environments for mathematics of space and motion, visual programming tools for children's learning of basic science concepts, pathways for elementary and middle school children's learning about measurement and statistics, early reading intervention, professional development for ambitious mathematics teaching. *Unit head:* Dr. David Dickinson, Acting Chair, 615-322-8100, Fax: 615-322-8999, E-mail: david.k.dickinson@vanderbilt.edu. *Application contact:* Angela Saylor, Educational Coordinator, 615-322-8092, Fax: 615-322-8999, E-mail: angela.saylor@vanderbilt.edu.

Washington State University, Graduate School, College of Liberal Arts, Department of English, Pullman, WA 99164. Offers composition (MA); English (MA, PhD); teaching of English (MA). *Faculty:* 32. *Students:* 49 full-time (28 women), 6 part-time (4 women); includes 10 minority (3 Black or African American, non-Hispanic/Latino; 1 American Indian or Alaska Native, non-Hispanic/Latino; 1 Asian, non-Hispanic/Latino; 1 Hispanic/Latino; 4 Two or more races, non-Hispanic/Latino), 2 international. Average age 29. 99 applicants, 32% accepted, 20 enrolled. In 2011, 8 master's, 6 doctorates awarded. *Degree requirements:* For master's, one foreign language, comprehensive exam (for some programs), thesis (for some programs), oral exam; for doctorate, 2 foreign languages, comprehensive exam, thesis/dissertation, oral exam, written exam. *Entrance requirements:* For master's and doctorate, GRE General Test, GRE Subject Test, official transcripts; writing sample (approximately 10 pages); three letters of recommendation; statement of purpose (approximately 500 words); undergraduate major in English or other appropriate discipline. Additional exam requirements/recommendations for international students: Required—TOEFL, IELTS. *Application deadline:* For fall admission, 1/10 priority date for domestic students, 1/10 for international students. Applications are processed on a rolling basis. Application fee: $75. *Financial support:* In 2011–12, 48 students received support, including 1 fellowship (averaging $2,000 per year), 2 research assistantships with full and partial tuition reimbursements available (averaging $13,917 per year), 44 teaching assistantships with full and partial tuition reimbursements available (averaging $13,056 per year); career-related internships or fieldwork, Federal Work-Study, institutionally sponsored loans, scholarships/grants, health care benefits, and tuition waivers (partial) also available. Financial award application deadline: 2/10; financial award applicants required to submit FAFSA. *Faculty research:* Nationalism and gender in the American West, slavery and exploitation in nineteenth century Britain, photography and the color line, D. H. Lawrence and Mexico, social movement cultures and the arts. *Total annual research expenditures:* $5,000. *Unit head:* Dr. William Hamlin, Director, 509-335-7398, Fax: 509-335-2582, E-mail: whamlin@wsu.edu. *Application contact:* Graduate School Admissions, 800-GRADWSU, Fax: 509-335-1949, E-mail: gradsch@wsu.edu. Web site: http://libarts.wsu.edu/english/.

Wayne State College, School of Education and Counseling, Department of Educational Foundations and Leadership, Program in Curriculum and Instruction, Wayne, NE 68787. Offers alternative education (MSE); business and information technology education (MSE); communication arts education (MSE); early childhood education (MSE); elementary education (MSE); English as a second language (MSE); English education (MSE); family and consumer sciences education (MSE); industrial technology and vocational education (MSE); learning communities (MSE); mathematics education (MSE); music education (MSE); science education (MSE); social science education (MSE). *Accreditation:* NCATE. Part-time and evening/weekend programs available. *Degree requirements:* For master's, comprehensive exam, thesis optional. *Entrance requirements:* For master's, GRE General Test. Additional exam requirements/recommendations for international students: Required—TOEFL (minimum score 550 paper-based; 213 computer-based).

Wayne State University, College of Education, Division of Teacher Education, Detroit, MI 48202. Offers art education (M Ed), including art therapy; bilingual/bicultural education (M Ed); career and technical education (M Ed); curriculum and instruction (Ed D, PhD, Ed S), including art education (PhD), bilingual education (Ed D, Ed S), bilingual-bicultural education (PhD), career and technical education (MAT, Ed D, PhD, Ed S), early childhood education (MAT, Ed D, PhD, Ed S), elementary education,

English Education

English as a second language (MAT, Ed D, Ed S), English education (MAT, Ed D, PhD, Ed S), foreign language education (MAT, PhD), K-12 curriculum, mathematics education (MAT, Ed D, PhD, Ed S), science education (MAT, Ed D, PhD, Ed S), secondary education, social studies education (MAT, Ed S), social studies education: secondary (Ed D, PhD); elementary education (MAT), including special education; elementary education (M Ed, MAT), including children's literature (MAT), early childhood education (MAT, Ed D, PhD, Ed S), general elementary education (MAT); elementary or secondary education (MAT), including bilingual/bicultural education, English as a second language (MAT, Ed D, Ed S), mathematics education (MAT, Ed D, PhD, Ed S), science education (MAT, Ed D, PhD, Ed S), social studies education (MAT, Ed S); English education-secondary (M Ed); foreign language education (M Ed); mathematics education (M Ed); reading (M Ed, Ed S); reading, languages and literature (Ed D); science education (M Ed); secondary education (MAT), including art education (K-12), career and technical education (MAT, Ed D, PhD, Ed S), English education (MAT, Ed D, PhD, Ed S), foreign language education (MAT, PhD), kinesiology; social studies education secondary (M Ed); special education (M Ed, Ed D, PhD, Ed S). *Students:* 216 full-time (154 women), 626 part-time (478 women); includes 289 minority (227 Black or African American, non-Hispanic/Latino; 4 American Indian or Alaska Native, non-Hispanic/Latino; 27 Asian, non-Hispanic/Latino; 21 Hispanic/Latino; 1 Native Hawaiian or other Pacific Islander, non-Hispanic/Latino; 9 Two or more races, non-Hispanic/Latino), 14 international. Average age 37. 347 applicants, 37% accepted, 93 enrolled. In 2011, 226 master's, 12 doctorates, 46 other advanced degrees awarded. *Degree requirements:* For master's, thesis (for some programs), thesis, essay or project (for some M Ed programs), professional field experience (for MAT programs); for doctorate, thesis/dissertation. *Entrance requirements:* For master's, Michigan Basic Skills Test (MA in teaching); for doctorate, minimum undergraduate GPA of 3.0, graduate 3.5; interview, curriculum vitae; references. Additional exam requirements/recommendations for international students: Required—TOEFL (minimum score 550 paper-based; 213 computer-based), TWE (minimum score 5.5). *Application deadline:* For fall admission, 6/1 priority date for domestic students, 5/1 for international students; for winter admission, 10/1 priority date for domestic students, 9/1 for international students; for spring admission, 2/1 priority date for domestic students, 1/1 for international students. Applications are processed on a rolling basis. Application fee: $50. Electronic applications accepted. *Expenses:* Tuition, state resident: part-time $512.85 per credit. Tuition, nonresident: part-time $1132.65 per credit. *Required fees:* $26.60 per credit. $199.65 per semester. Tuition and fees vary according to course load and program. *Financial support:* In 2011–12, 42 students received support. Fellowships, research assistantships with tuition reimbursements available, teaching assistantships, scholarships/grants, and unspecified assistantships available. *Faculty research:* Reading and writing literacy and literature. *Total annual research expenditures:* $264,016. *Unit head:* Dr. Craig Roney, Assistant Dean, 313-577-0902, E-mail: rroney@wayne.edu. Web site: http://coe.wayne.edu/ted/index.php.

Western Connecticut State University, Division of Graduate Studies, School of Professional Studies, Department of Education and Educational Psychology, English Education Option, Danbury, CT 06810-6885. Offers MS. Part-time programs available. *Faculty:* 1 full-time (0 women). *Students:* 1 (woman) full-time, 3 part-time (2 women). Average age 31. *Degree requirements:* For master's, comprehensive exam (for some programs), thesis or comprehensive exam, completion of program in 6 years. *Entrance requirements:* For master's, minimum GPA of 2.8, teaching certificate. Additional exam requirements/recommendations for international students: Recommended—TOEFL (minimum score 550 paper-based; 213 computer-based; 79 iBT), IELTS (minimum score 6). *Application deadline:* For fall admission, 8/5 priority date for domestic students; for spring admission, 1/5 priority date for domestic students. Applications are processed on a rolling basis. Application fee: $50. Tuition and fees vary according to course level, course load, degree level and program. *Financial support:* Applicants required to submit FAFSA. *Faculty research:* Student demonstration of knowledge of: key literary periods and authors; historical, philosophical and social influences; strong writing and critical thinking skills. *Unit head:* Dr. Adeline Merrill, Chairperson, Department of Education and Educational Psychology, 203-837-3267, Fax: 203-837-8413, E-mail: merrilla@wcsu.edu. *Application contact:* Chris Shankle, Associate Director of Graduate Studies, 203-837-9005, Fax: 203-837-8326, E-mail: shanklec@wcsu.edu.

Western Governors University, Teachers College, Salt Lake City, UT 84107. Offers curriculum and instruction (MS); educational leadership (MS); educational studies (MA); educational studies (5-12) (MA), including mathematics; elementary education (k-8) (Postbaccalaureate Certificate); English language learning (K-12) (MA); instructional design (MAT); learning and technology (M Ed, MA); management and innovation (M Ed); mathematics (5-12) (Postbaccalaureate Certificate); mathematics (5-9) (Postbaccalaureate Certificate); mathematics education (5-12) (MA); mathematics education (5-9) (MA); mathematics education (K-6) (MA); measurement and evaluation (M Ed); science (5-12) (Postbaccalaureate Certificate); science (5-9) (Postbaccalaureate Certificate); science education (5-12) (MA), including biology, chemistry, geology, physics; science education (5-9) (MA); social science (5-12) (MAT); special education (MAT). *Accreditation:* NCATE. Evening/weekend programs available. Postbaccalaureate distance learning degree programs offered (no on-campus study). *Students:* 3,746 full-time (2,811 women); includes 652 minority (332 Black or African American, non-Hispanic/Latino; 37 American Indian or Alaska Native, non-Hispanic/Latino; 74 Asian, non-Hispanic/Latino; 139 Hispanic/Latino; 70 Two or more races, non-Hispanic/Latino), 12 international. Average age 37. In 2011, 1,080 master's, 242 other advanced degrees awarded. *Degree requirements:* For master's, capstone project. *Entrance requirements:* For master's and Postbaccalaureate Certificate, Readiness Assessment, commitment counseling discussion, transcript submissions, completion of orientation. Additional exam requirements/recommendations for international students: Required—TOEFL (minimum score 450 paper-based; 80 iBT). *Application deadline:* Applications are processed on a rolling basis. Application fee: $65. Electronic applications accepted. *Expenses:* Contact institution. *Financial support:* Scholarships/grants and tuition waivers (partial) available. Financial award applicants required to submit FAFSA. *Unit head:* Dr. Philip Schmidt, Dean of the Teachers College, 845-255-4656. *Application contact:* Enrollment Department, 866-225-5948, Fax: 801-274-3306, E-mail: info@wgu.edu.

Western Kentucky University, Graduate Studies, Potter College of Arts and Letters, Department of English, Bowling Green, KY 42101. Offers education (MA); English (MA Ed); literature (MA), including American literature, British literature, literary theory, women writers, world literature; teaching English as a second language (MA); writing (MA). Part-time and evening/weekend programs available. *Degree requirements:* For master's, comprehensive exam, thesis optional, final exam. *Entrance requirements:* For master's, GRE General Test, minimum GPA of 2.75. Additional exam requirements/recommendations for international students: Required—TOEFL (minimum score 555 paper-based; 213 computer-based; 79 iBT). *Faculty research:* Improving writing, linking teacher knowledge and performance, Victorian women writers, Kentucky women writers, Kentucky poets.

Western Michigan University, Graduate College, College of Arts and Sciences, Department of English, Kalamazoo, MI 49008. Offers creative writing (MFA, PhD); English (MA, PhD); English education (MA, PhD). *Degree requirements:* For master's, oral exams; for doctorate, one foreign language, thesis/dissertation, oral exam, written exams. *Entrance requirements:* For master's and doctorate, GRE General Test, GRE Subject Test.

Western New England University, College of Arts and Sciences, Program in English for Teachers, Springfield, MA 01119. Offers MAET. Part-time and evening/weekend programs available. *Students:* 27 part-time (15 women); includes 3 minority (2 Black or African American, non-Hispanic/Latino; 1 Asian, non-Hispanic/Latino). In 2011, 14 master's awarded. *Entrance requirements:* For master's, recommendations, personal statement, resume. *Application deadline:* Applications are processed on a rolling basis. Application fee: $30. *Financial support:* Available to part-time students. Application deadline: 4/1; applicants required to submit FAFSA. *Unit head:* Dr. Saeed Ghahramani, Dean, 413-782-1218, Fax: 413-796-2118, E-mail: sghahram@wne.edu. *Application contact:* Matt Fox, Director of Recruiting and Marketing for Adult Learners, 413-782-1249, Fax: 413-782-1779, E-mail: learn@wne.edu. Web site: http://www1.wnec.edu/artsandsciences/index.cfm?selection-doc.859.

Widener University, School of Human Service Professions, Center for Education, Chester, PA 19013-5792. Offers adult education (M Ed); counseling in higher education (M Ed); counselor education (M Ed); early childhood education (M Ed); educational foundations (M Ed); educational leadership (M Ed); educational psychology (M Ed); elementary education (M Ed); English and language arts (M Ed); health education (M Ed); higher education leadership (Ed D); home and school visitor (M Ed); human sexuality (M Ed, PhD); mathematics education (M Ed); middle school education (M Ed); principalship (M Ed); reading and language arts (Ed D); reading education (M Ed); school administration (Ed D); science education (M Ed); social studies education (M Ed); special education (M Ed); technology education (M Ed). *Accreditation:* NCATE. Part-time and evening/weekend programs available. Terminal master's awarded for partial completion of doctoral program. *Degree requirements:* For doctorate, thesis/dissertation. *Entrance requirements:* For master's, minimum GPA of 2.5; for doctorate, GRE or MAT, minimum GPA of 2.0 (undergraduate), 3.5 (graduate). Electronic applications accepted. *Expenses:* Contact institution. *Faculty research:* Reading and cognition, adult education, technology education, educational leadership, special education.

Wilkes University, College of Graduate and Professional Studies, School of Education, Wilkes-Barre, PA 18766-0002. Offers art and science of teaching (MS Ed); classroom technology (MS Ed); early childhood literacy (MS Ed); educational computing (MS Ed); educational development and strategies (MS Ed); educational leadership (MS Ed); educational technology (Ed D); higher education administration (Ed D); instructional media (MS Ed); instructional technology (MS Ed); K-12 administration (Ed D); online teaching (MS Ed); reading (MS Ed); school business leadership (MS Ed); secondary education (MS Ed), including biology, chemistry, English, history, mathematics; special education (MS Ed); teaching English as a second language (MS Ed); twenty-first century teaching and learning (MS Ed). Part-time and evening/weekend programs available. Postbaccalaureate distance learning degree programs offered (minimal on-campus study). *Students:* 92 full-time (63 women), 2,005 part-time (1,459 women); includes 89 minority (23 Black or African American, non-Hispanic/Latino; 1 American Indian or Alaska Native, non-Hispanic/Latino; 14 Asian, non-Hispanic/Latino; 33 Hispanic/Latino; 1 Native Hawaiian or other Pacific Islander, non-Hispanic/Latino; 17 Two or more races, non-Hispanic/Latino), 6 international. Average age 33. In 2011, 1,150 master's, 3 doctorates awarded. *Entrance requirements:* Additional exam requirements/recommendations for international students: Required—TOEFL (minimum score 550 paper-based; 213 computer-based; 79 iBT). *Application deadline:* Applications are processed on a rolling basis. Application fee: $45. Electronic applications accepted. *Expenses:* Contact institution. *Financial support:* Federal Work-Study and unspecified assistantships available. Financial award application deadline: 3/1; financial award applicants required to submit FAFSA. *Unit head:* Dr. Michael Speziale, Dean, 570-408-4679, Fax: 570-408-4905, E-mail: michael.speziale@wilkes.edu. *Application contact:* Erin Sutzko, Director of Extended Learning, 570-408-4253, Fax: 570-408-7846, E-mail: erin.sutzko@wilkes.edu. Web site: http://www.wilkes.edu/pages/383.asp.

William Carey University, School of Education, Hattiesburg, MS 39401-5499. Offers art education (M Ed); art of teaching (M Ed); elementary education (M Ed, Ed S); English education (M Ed); gifted education (M Ed); history and social science (M Ed); mild/moderate disabilities (M Ed); secondary education (M Ed). Part-time programs available. *Degree requirements:* For master's, comprehensive exam. *Entrance requirements:* For master's, GRE, MAT, minimum GPA of 2.5, Class A teacher's license. Additional exam requirements/recommendations for international students: Required—TOEFL (minimum score 550 paper-based; 213 computer-based).

Worcester State University, Graduate Studies, Program in English, Worcester, MA 01602-2597. Offers MA. Part-time programs available. *Faculty:* 1 full-time (0 women), 1 part-time/adjunct (0 women). *Students:* 3 full-time (2 women), 8 part-time (all women). Average age 36. 9 applicants, 78% accepted, 3 enrolled. In 2011, 9 master's awarded. *Degree requirements:* For master's, comprehensive exam (for some programs), thesis optional. *Entrance requirements:* For master's, GRE General Test or MAT, 18 undergraduate credits in English, excluding composition. Additional exam requirements/recommendations for international students: Required—TOEFL (minimum score 500 paper-based; 61 iBT). *Application deadline:* For fall admission, 6/15 for domestic and international students; for spring admission, 4/1 for domestic and international students. Applications are processed on a rolling basis. Application fee: $40. Electronic applications accepted. *Expenses:* Tuition, state resident: full-time $2700; part-time $150 per credit. Tuition, nonresident: full-time $2700; part-time $150 per credit. *Required fees:* $2016; $112 per credit. *Financial support:* In 2011–12, 1 student received support, including 1 research assistantship (averaging $4,800 per year); career-related internships or fieldwork, scholarships/grants, and unspecified assistantships also available. Financial award application deadline: 3/1; financial award applicants required to submit FAFSA. *Unit head:* Dr. Ruth Haber, Coordinator, 508-929-8706, Fax: 508-929-8174, E-mail: rhaber@worcester.edu. *Application contact:* Sara Grady, Assistant Dean of Graduate and Continuing Education, 508-929-8787, Fax: 508-929-8100, E-mail: sara.grady@worcester.edu.

Environmental Education

Alaska Pacific University, Graduate Programs, Environmental Science Department, Program in Outdoor and Environmental Education, Anchorage, AK 99508-4672. Offers MSOEE. Part-time programs available. *Degree requirements:* For master's, thesis. *Entrance requirements:* For master's, MAT or GRE, minimum GPA of 3.0. Additional exam requirements/recommendations for international students: Required—TOEFL (minimum score 550 paper-based; 79 computer-based).

Antioch University New England, Graduate School, Department of Environmental Studies, Program in Environmental Education, Keene, NH 03431-3552. Offers MS. *Degree requirements:* For master's, practicum. *Entrance requirements:* For master's, previous undergraduate course work in biology, chemistry, mathematics (environmental biology); resume; 3 letters of recommendation. Additional exam requirements/recommendations for international students: Required—TOEFL (minimum score 550 paper-based; 213 computer-based). Electronic applications accepted. *Expenses:* Contact institution. *Faculty research:* Sustainability, natural resources inventory.

Arcadia University, Graduate Studies, Department of Education, Glenside, PA 19038-3295. Offers art education (M Ed); computer education (CAS); curriculum (CAS); curriculum studies (M Ed); early childhood education (M Ed, CAS), including individualized (M Ed), master teacher (M Ed), research in child development (M Ed); educational leadership (M Ed, Ed D, CAS); elementary education (M Ed, CAS); English education (MA Ed); environmental education (MA Ed, CAS); history education (MA Ed); instructional technology (M Ed); language arts (M Ed, CAS); library science (M Ed); mathematics education (M Ed, MA Ed, CAS); music education (MA Ed); psychology (MA Ed); reading (M Ed, CAS); science education (M Ed, CAS); secondary education (M Ed, CAS); special education (M Ed, Ed D, CAS); theater arts (MA Ed); written communication (MA Ed). *Accreditation:* NASAD. Part-time and evening/weekend programs available. Postbaccalaureate distance learning degree programs offered (minimal on-campus study). *Faculty:* 12 full-time (8 women), 38 part-time/adjunct (26 women). *Students:* 66 full-time (48 women), 590 part-time (477 women); includes 65 minority (53 Black or African American, non-Hispanic/Latino; 6 Asian, non-Hispanic/Latino; 3 Hispanic/Latino; 3 Two or more races, non-Hispanic/Latino), 4 international. Average age 36. In 2011, 229 master's, 5 doctorates awarded. *Application deadline:* Applications are processed on a rolling basis. Application fee: $50. Electronic applications accepted. *Expenses:* Contact institution. *Financial support:* Career-related internships or fieldwork, tuition waivers (partial), and unspecified assistantships available. *Unit head:* Dr. Steven P. Gulkus, Associate Professor, 215-572-2120, E-mail: gulkus@arcadia.edu. *Application contact:* 215-572-2925, Fax: 215-572-2126, E-mail: grad@arcadia.edu.

Brooklyn College of the City University of New York, Division of Graduate Studies, School of Education, Program in Childhood Education, Brooklyn, NY 11210-2889. Offers bilingual education (MS Ed); liberal arts (MS Ed); mathematics (MS Ed); science/environmental education (MS Ed). Part-time and evening/weekend programs available. *Entrance requirements:* For master's, LAST, interview, previous course work in education, writing sample, resume, 2 letters of recommendation. Additional exam requirements/recommendations for international students: Required—TOEFL (minimum score 500 paper-based; 173 computer-based; 61 iBT). Electronic applications accepted. *Faculty research:* Emotional intelligence, multiculturalism, arts immersion, the Holocaust.

Chatham University, Program in Education, Pittsburgh, PA 15232-2826. Offers early childhood education (MAT); elementary education (MAT); environmental education (K-12) (MAT); secondary art (MAT); secondary biology education (MAT); secondary chemistry education (MAT); secondary English education (MAT); secondary math education (MAT); secondary physics education (MAT); secondary social studies education (MAT); special education (MAT). *Students:* 52 full-time (42 women), 17 part-time (16 women); includes 2 minority (1 Black or African American, non-Hispanic/Latino; 1 Hispanic/Latino). Average age 29. 39 applicants, 82% accepted, 23 enrolled. In 2011, 37 master's awarded. *Degree requirements:* For master's, thesis, teaching experience. *Entrance requirements:* For master's, minimum GPA of 3.0, sample of written work, recommendation letters. Additional exam requirements/recommendations for international students: Required—TOEFL (minimum score 600 paper-based; 250 computer-based; 100 iBT), IELTS (minimum score 7), TWE. *Application deadline:* For fall admission, 4/1 priority date for domestic students, 4/1 for international students; for spring admission, 11/1 priority date for domestic students, 10/1 for international students. Applications are processed on a rolling basis. Application fee: $45. Electronic applications accepted. Application fee is waived when completed online. *Expenses: Tuition:* Full-time $13,896. Tuition and fees vary according to program. *Financial support:* Career-related internships or fieldwork available. Financial award applicants required to submit FAFSA. *Faculty research:* Gifted education, environmental education, technology in education, writing as learning, class size and achievement. *Unit head:* Dr. Elvira Sanatullova-Allison, Director of Education Programs, 412-365-2773, E-mail: esanatullovaallison@chatham.edu. *Application contact:* Dory Perry, Associate Director of Graduate Admission, 412-365-2758, Fax: 412-365-1609, E-mail: gradadmissions@chatham.edu. Web site: http://www.chatham.edu/mat.

Concordia University Wisconsin, Graduate Programs, Department of Education, Mequon, WI 53097-2402. Offers art education (MS Ed); curriculum and instruction (MS Ed); early childhood (MS Ed); educational administration (MS Ed); environmental education (MS Ed); family studies (MS Ed); reading (MS Ed); school counseling (MS Ed); special education (MS Ed). Part-time and evening/weekend programs available. Postbaccalaureate distance learning degree programs offered (minimal on-campus study). *Faculty:* 30. *Students:* 386 full-time (279 women), 808 part-time (598 women); includes 84 minority (42 Black or African American, non-Hispanic/Latino; 4 American Indian or Alaska Native, non-Hispanic/Latino; 9 Asian, non-Hispanic/Latino; 13 Hispanic/Latino; 16 Two or more races, non-Hispanic/Latino), 5 international. Average age 37. In 2011, 51 master's awarded. *Degree requirements:* For master's, comprehensive exam, thesis or alternative. *Entrance requirements:* For master's, minimum GPA of 3.0, teaching license. Additional exam requirements/recommendations for international students: Required—TOEFL. Application fee: $35. *Financial support:* Career-related internships or fieldwork and tuition waivers (partial) available. Financial award application deadline: 8/1. *Faculty research:* Motivation, developmental learning, learning styles. *Unit head:* Dr. James Juergensen, Director, 262-243-4214, E-mail: james.juergensen@cuw.edu. *Application contact:* Graduate Admissions, 262-243-4248, Fax: 262-243-4428.

Florida Atlantic University, College of Education, Department of Teaching and Learning, Boca Raton, FL 33431-0991. Offers curriculum and instruction (M Ed); elementary education (M Ed); environmental education (M Ed); reading education (M Ed); social foundations of education (M Ed). *Accreditation:* NCATE. Part-time and evening/weekend programs available. *Faculty:* 32 full-time (25 women), 90 part-time/adjunct (68 women). *Students:* 34 full-time (30 women), 103 part-time (96 women); includes 29 minority (8 Black or African American, non-Hispanic/Latino; 7 Asian, non-Hispanic/Latino; 11 Hispanic/Latino; 3 Two or more races, non-Hispanic/Latino), 1 international. Average age 32. 96 applicants, 66% accepted, 24 enrolled. In 2011, 71 master's awarded. *Entrance requirements:* For master's, GRE General Test, minimum GPA of 3.0 in last 2 years of undergraduate course work. Additional exam requirements/recommendations for international students: Required—TOEFL. *Application deadline:* For fall admission, 7/1 for domestic students, 2/15 for international students; for spring admission, 11/1 for domestic students, 7/15 for international students. Applications are processed on a rolling basis. Application fee: $30. *Expenses: Tuition, area resident:* Part-time $343.02 per credit hour. Tuition, state resident: full-time $8232. Tuition, nonresident: full-time $23,931; part-time $997.14 per credit hour. *Financial support:* Fellowships with partial tuition reimbursements, research assistantships with partial tuition reimbursements, teaching assistantships with partial tuition reimbursements, career-related internships or fieldwork, scholarships/grants, and unspecified assistantships available. *Faculty research:* Technology, teaching English to speakers of other languages, math teaching, electronic portfolio assessment, global perspectives through social studies. *Unit head:* Dr. Barbara Ridener, Chairperson, 561-297-3588. *Application contact:* Dr. Eliah Watlington, Associate Dean, 561-296-8520, Fax: 261-297-2991, E-mail: ewatling@fau.edu. Web site: http://www.coe.fau.edu/academicdepartments/tl/.

Florida Institute of Technology, Graduate Programs, College of Science, Department of Education and Interdisciplinary Studies, Melbourne, FL 32901-6975. Offers computer education (MS); elementary science education (M Ed); environmental education (MS); interdisciplinary science (MS); mathematics education (MS, PhD, Ed S); science education (MS, PhD, Ed S), including informal science education (MS); teaching (MAT). Part-time and evening/weekend programs available. *Faculty:* 4 full-time (1 woman), 3 part-time/adjunct (2 women). *Students:* 22 full-time (16 women), 27 part-time (18 women); includes 8 minority (2 Black or African American, non-Hispanic/Latino; 4 Asian, non-Hispanic/Latino; 2 Hispanic/Latino), 9 international. Average age 34. 57 applicants, 70% accepted, 19 enrolled. In 2011, 5 master's, 1 doctorate awarded. Terminal master's awarded for partial completion of doctoral program. *Median time to degree:* Of those who began their doctoral program in fall 2003, 50% received their degree in 8 years or less. *Degree requirements:* For master's, comprehensive exam (for some programs), thesis optional; for doctorate, comprehensive exam, thesis/dissertation; for Ed S, comprehensive exam. *Entrance requirements:* For master's, minimum GPA of 3.0, resume, 3 letters of recommendation (elementary science education), statement of objectives; for doctorate, minimum GPA of 3.2, resume, 3 letters of recommendation, statement of objectives, 3 years teaching experience (recommended); for Ed S, minimum GPA of 3.0, resume, 3 letters of recommendation, statement of objectives. Additional exam requirements/recommendations for international students: Required—TOEFL (minimum score 550 paper-based; 213 computer-based; 79 iBT). *Application deadline:* For fall admission, 4/1 for international students; for spring admission, 9/30 for international students. Applications are processed on a rolling basis. Electronic applications accepted. *Expenses: Tuition:* Full-time $19,620; part-time $1090 per credit hour. Tuition and fees vary according to campus/location. *Financial support:* In 2011–12, 1 teaching assistantship with full and partial tuition reimbursement (averaging $797 per year) was awarded; research assistantships with full and partial tuition reimbursements, career-related internships or fieldwork, institutionally sponsored loans, tuition waivers (partial), unspecified assistantships, and tuition remissions also available. Support available to part-time students. Financial award application deadline: 3/1; financial award applicants required to submit FAFSA. *Faculty research:* Measurement and evaluation, computers in education, educational technology. *Total annual research expenditures:* $1. *Unit head:* Dr. Lazlo A. Baksay, Department Head, 321-674-7205, Fax: 321-674-7598, E-mail: baksay@fit.edu. *Application contact:* Cheryl A. Brown, Associate Director of Graduate Admissions, 321-674-7581, Fax: 321-723-9468, E-mail: cbrown@fit.edu. Web site: http://cos.fit.edu/education/.

Gannon University, School of Graduate Studies, College of Engineering and Business, School of Engineering and Computer Science, Program in Natural and Environmental Sciences, Erie, PA 16541-0001. Offers M Ed. Part-time and evening/weekend programs available. *Students:* 1 (woman) full-time, 1 (woman) part-time, 1 international. Average age 34. 3 applicants, 0% accepted, 0 enrolled. *Degree requirements:* For master's, thesis or alternative, research paper. *Entrance requirements:* For master's, GRE or GMAT. Additional exam requirements/recommendations for international students: Required—TOEFL (minimum score 79 iBT). *Application deadline:* Applications are processed on a rolling basis. Application fee: $25. Electronic applications accepted. *Financial support:* Career-related internships or fieldwork, scholarships/grants, and unspecified assistantships available. Financial award application deadline: 7/1; financial award applicants required to submit FAFSA. *Unit head:* Dr. Harry Diz, Chair, 814-871-7633, E-mail: diz001@gannon.edu. *Application contact:* Kara Morgan, Director of Graduate Admissions, 814-871-5831, Fax: 814-871-5827, E-mail: graduate@gannon.edu.

Goshen College, Merry Lea Environmental Learning Center, Goshen, IN 46526-4794. Offers MA. *Accreditation:* NCATE. *Faculty:* 4 full-time (0 women), 3 part-time/adjunct (1 woman). *Students:* 24 full-time (14 women), 1 part-time (0 women); includes 3 minority (all Black or African American, non-Hispanic/Latino), 3 international. In 2011, 3 master's awarded. *Entrance requirements:* Additional exam requirements/recommendations for international students: Required—TOEFL (minimum score 213 computer-based). Application fee: $50. *Expenses: Tuition:* Full-time $26,640. *Required fees:* $555 per credit hour. Tuition and fees vary according to course load and program. *Financial support:* Application deadline: 9/10; applicants required to submit FAFSA. *Unit head:* Dr. Luke Gascho, Executive Director, 260-799-5869, E-mail: lukeag@goshen.edu. *Application contact:* Dr. David Ostergren, Director of the Graduate Program, 260-799-5869, E-mail: daveo@goshen.edu. Web site: http://merrylea.goshen.edu/.

Hamline University, School of Education, St. Paul, MN 55104-1284. Offers education (MA Ed, Ed D); English as a second language (MA); literacy education (MA); natural science and environmental education (MA Ed); teaching (MAT). *Accreditation:* NCATE (one or more programs are accredited). Part-time and evening/weekend programs available. Postbaccalaureate distance learning degree programs offered (no on-campus study). *Faculty:* 33 full-time (24 women), 106 part-time/adjunct (77 women). *Students:* 319 full-time (221 women), 717 part-time (524 women); includes 88 minority (30 Black or African American, non-Hispanic/Latino; 2 American Indian or Alaska Native, non-Hispanic/Latino; 26 Asian, non-Hispanic/Latino; 27 Hispanic/Latino; 3 Two or more races, non-Hispanic/Latino), 21 international. Average age 32. 468 applicants, 76% accepted, 259 enrolled. In 2011, 197 master's, 10 doctorates awarded. *Degree requirements:* For master's, thesis, foreign language (for MA in English as a second language only); for doctorate, comprehensive exam, thesis/dissertation. *Entrance* *requirements:* For master's, written essay, official transcripts, 2 letters of recommendation, minimum GPA of 2.5 from bachelor's work; for doctorate, personal statement, master's degree, 3 years experience, 3 letters of recommendation, writing sample, interview. Additional exam requirements/recommendations for international students: Required—TOEFL (minimum score 625 paper-based; 107 computer-based; 75 iBT) or IELTS. *Application deadline:* Applications are processed on a rolling basis. Application fee: $0 ($100 for international students). Electronic applications accepted. *Expenses: Tuition:* Full-time $3720; part-time $465 per credit. *Required fees:* $28 per year. Tuition and fees vary according to degree level, campus/location and program. *Financial support:* Federal Work-Study and scholarships/grants available. Support available to part-time students. Financial award applicants required to submit FAFSA. *Faculty research:* Adult basic education, service-learning, teacher dispositions, diversity, technology. *Unit head:* Dr. Larry Harris, Interim Dean, 651-523-2600, Fax: 651-523-2489, E-mail: lharris02@gw.hamline.edu. *Application contact:* Michael Hand, Assistant Director, Graduate Admission, 651-523-2900, Fax: 651-523-3058, E-mail: mhand01@gw.hamline.edu. Web site: http://www.hamline.edu/education.

Instituto Tecnologico de Santo Domingo, Graduate School, Area of Basic And Environmental Sciences, Santo Domingo, Dominican Republic. Offers environmental science (M En S), including environmental education, environmental management, marine resources, natural resources management; mathematics (MS, PhD); renewable energy technology (MS, Certificate).

Lesley University, Graduate School of Arts and Social Sciences, Cambridge, MA 02138-2790. Offers clinical mental health counseling (MA), including expressive therapies counseling, holistic counseling, school and community counseling; counseling psychology (MA, CAGS), including professional counseling (MA), school counseling (MA); creative arts in learning (CAGS); creative writing (MFA); ecological teaching and learning (MS); environmental education (MS); expressive therapies (MA, PhD, CAGS), including art (MA), dance (MA), expressive therapies, music (MA); independent studies (CAGS); independent study (MA); intercultural relations (MA, CAGS); interdisciplinary studies (MA), including individualized studies, integrative holistic health, women's studies; urban environmental leadership (MA); visual arts (MFA). Part-time and evening/weekend programs available. Postbaccalaureate distance learning degree programs offered (minimal on-campus study). *Faculty:* 45 full-time (36 women), 187 part-time/adjunct (139 women). *Students:* 671 full-time (605 women), 404 part-time (364 women); includes 133 minority (32 Black or African American, non-Hispanic/Latino; 4 American Indian or Alaska Native, non-Hispanic/Latino; 17 Asian, non-Hispanic/Latino; 58 Hispanic/Latino; 4 Native Hawaiian or other Pacific Islander, non-Hispanic/Latino; 18 Two or more races, non-Hispanic/Latino), 65 international. Average age 37. In 2011, 473 master's, 6 doctorates, 9 other advanced degrees awarded. *Degree requirements:* For master's, internship, practicum, thesis (expressive therapies); for doctorate, thesis/dissertation, arts apprenticeship, field placement; for CAGS, thesis, internship (counseling psychology, expressive therapies). *Entrance requirements:* For master's, MAT (counseling psychology), interview, writing samples, art portfolio; for doctorate, GRE or MAT; for CAGS, interview, master's degree. Additional exam requirements/recommendations for international students: Required—TOEFL (minimum score 550 paper-based; 213 computer-based; 80 iBT). *Application deadline:* Applications are processed on a rolling basis. Electronic applications accepted. *Financial support:* In 2011–12, research assistantships (averaging $3,400 per year), 1 teaching assistantship (averaging $7,298 per year) was awarded; career-related internships or fieldwork, Federal Work-Study, scholarships/grants, and unspecified assistantships also available. Support available to part-time students. Financial award applicants required to submit FAFSA. *Faculty research:* Psychotherapy and culture; psychotherapy and psychological trauma; women's issues in art, teaching and psychotherapy; community-based art, psycho-spiritual inquiry. *Unit head:* Dr. Julia Halevy, Dean, 617-349-8317, Fax: 617-349-8366, E-mail: jhalevy@lesley.edu. *Application contact:* Christina Murray, Senior Assistant Director, On-Campus Admissions, 617-349-8827, Fax: 617-349-8313, E-mail: cmurray3@lesley.edu. Web site: http://www.lesley.edu/gsass.html.

Montclair State University, The Graduate School, College of Science and Mathematics, Department of Earth and Environmental Studies, Program in Environmental Studies, Montclair, NJ 07043-1624. Offers environmental education (MA); environmental management (MA); environmental science (MA). Part-time and evening/weekend programs available. *Students:* 14 full-time (8 women), 21 part-time (12 women); includes 4 minority (1 Asian, non-Hispanic/Latino; 3 Hispanic/Latino), 2 international. Average age 34. 40 applicants, 55% accepted, 12 enrolled. In 2011, 16 master's awarded. *Degree requirements:* For master's, thesis. *Entrance requirements:* For master's, GRE General Test, 2 letters of recommendation, essay. Additional exam requirements/recommendations for international students: Required—TOEFL (minimum score 83 iBT), IELTS (minimum score 6.5). *Application deadline:* Applications are processed on a rolling basis. Application fee: $60. Electronic applications accepted. *Financial support:* In 2011–12, 10 research assistantships with full tuition reimbursements (averaging $7,000 per year) were awarded; Federal Work-Study, scholarships/grants, and unspecified assistantships also available. Support available to part-time students. Financial award application deadline: 3/1; financial award applicants required to submit FAFSA. *Faculty research:* Environmental geochemisty/remediation/forensics, environmental law and policy, regional climate modeling, remote sensing, Cenozoic marine sediment records from polar regions, sustainability science. *Unit head:* Dr. Matthew Goring, Chairperson, 973-655-5409. *Application contact:* Amy Aiello, Executive Director of The Graduate School, 973-655-5147, Fax: 973-655-7869, E-mail: graduate.school@montclair.edu. Web site: http://www.montclair.edu/csam/earth-environment-studies/academic-programs/ma-ms-degrees/ma-concentration-environmental-studies/.

Montreat College, School of Professional and Adult Studies, Montreat, NC 28757-1267. Offers business administration (MBA); clinical mental health counseling (MA); environmental education (MS); management and leadership (MS). Evening/weekend programs available. Postbaccalaureate distance learning degree programs offered (minimal on-campus study). *Faculty:* 12 full-time (3 women), 14 part-time/adjunct (3 women). *Students:* 108 full-time (65 women), 179 part-time (111 women); includes 130 minority (116 Black or African American, non-Hispanic/Latino; 5 American Indian or Alaska Native, non-Hispanic/Latino; 2 Asian, non-Hispanic/Latino; 6 Hispanic/Latino; 1 Two or more races, non-Hispanic/Latino). Average age 34. 145 applicants, 41% accepted, 57 enrolled. In 2011, 142 master's awarded. *Degree requirements:* For master's, business consulting project (for MBA). *Entrance requirements:* For master's, GMAT. Additional exam requirements/recommendations for international students: Required—TOEFL (minimum score 550 paper-based; 213 computer-based; 80 iBT). *Application deadline:* Applications are processed on a rolling basis. *Expenses: Tuition:* Full-time $10,185; part-time $485 per credit. *Financial support:* Available to part-time students. Application deadline: 7/1; applicants required to submit FAFSA. *Unit head:* Jonathan E. Shores, Jr., Vice President for Marketing and Enrollment, 828-669-8012 Ext. 2759, Fax: 828-669-0500, E-mail: jeshores@montreat.edu. *Application contact:* Julia Pacilli, Director of Enrollment, 828-669-8012 Ext. 2756, Fax: 828-669-0500, E-mail: jpacilli@montreat.edu. Web site: http://www.montreat.edu/.

New York University, Steinhardt School of Culture, Education, and Human Development, Department of Teaching and Learning, Program in Environmental Conservation Education, New York, NY 10012-1019. Offers MA. *Accreditation:* Teacher Education Accreditation Council. Part-time programs available. *Faculty:* 2 full-time (1 woman). *Students:* 27 full-time (23 women), 18 part-time (16 women); includes 9 minority (2 Asian, non-Hispanic/Latino; 6 Hispanic/Latino; 1 Two or more races, non-Hispanic/Latino), 2 international. Average age 28. 58 applicants, 79% accepted, 20 enrolled. In 2011, 14 master's awarded. *Degree requirements:* For master's, thesis (for some programs). *Entrance requirements:* Additional exam requirements/recommendations for international students: Required—TOEFL. *Application deadline:* For fall admission, 12/1 priority date for domestic students, 12/1 for international students; for spring admission, 11/1 for domestic and international students. Applications are processed on a rolling basis. Application fee: $75. Electronic applications accepted. *Financial support:* Career-related internships or fieldwork, Federal Work-Study, institutionally sponsored loans, and tuition waivers (partial) available. Support available to part-time students. Financial award application deadline: 2/1; financial award applicants required to submit FAFSA. *Faculty research:* Environmental ethics, values and policy, philosophy and geography. *Unit head:* Dr. Mary Leou, Acting Director, 212-998-5474, Fax: 212-995-4832. *Application contact:* 212-998-5030, Fax: 212-995-4328, E-mail: steinhardt.gradadmissions@nyu.edu. Web site: http://steinhardt.nyu.edu/teachlearn/environmental.

Prescott College, Graduate Programs, Program in Education, Prescott, AZ 86301. Offers early childhood education (MA); early childhood special education (MA); education (MA); elementary education (MA); environmental education leadership and administration (MA); equine-assisted experiential learning (MA); school guidance counseling (MA); secondary education (MA); special education, learning disability (MA); special education, mental retardation (MA); special education, serious emotional disability (MA); student-directed independent study (MA); sustainability education (PhD). Part-time programs available. Postbaccalaureate distance learning degree programs offered (minimal on-campus study). *Faculty:* 2 full-time (both women), 47 part-time/adjunct (31 women). *Students:* 59 full-time (36 women), 48 part-time (30 women); includes 16 minority (3 Black or African American, non-Hispanic/Latino; 1 American Indian or Alaska Native, non-Hispanic/Latino; 1 Asian, non-Hispanic/Latino; 8 Hispanic/Latino; 3 Two or more races, non-Hispanic/Latino), 2 international. Average age 40. 75 applicants, 76% accepted, 36 enrolled. In 2011, 14 master's, 8 doctorates awarded. *Degree requirements:* For master's, thesis, fieldwork or internship, practicum; for doctorate, thesis/dissertation. *Entrance requirements:* For master's, 2 letters of recommendation, resume; for doctorate, 3 letters of recommendation, resume, official transcripts, personal statement, program proposal. Additional exam requirements/recommendations for international students: Required—TOEFL (minimum score 500 paper-based; 173 computer-based). *Application deadline:* For fall admission, 4/15 priority date for domestic students, 4/15 for international students; for spring admission, 9/15 priority date for domestic students, 9/15 for international students. Applications are processed on a rolling basis. Application fee: $40. Electronic applications accepted. *Expenses: Tuition:* Full-time $16,440; part-time $685 per credit. *Required fees:* $150 per semester. One-time fee: $350. *Financial support:* Career-related internships or fieldwork and Federal Work-Study available. Financial award applicants required to submit FAFSA. *Unit head:* Noel Caniglia, Chair, 928-358-3201, Fax: 928-776-5151, E-mail: ncaniglia@prescott.edu. *Application contact:* Kerstin Alicki, Admissions Counselor, 928-350-2100, Fax: 928-776-5242, E-mail: admissions@prescott.edu.

Royal Roads University, Graduate Studies, Environment and Sustainability Program, Victoria, BC V9B 5Y2, Canada. Offers environment and management (M Sc, MA); environmental education and communication (MA, G Dip, Graduate Certificate); MA/MS. Postbaccalaureate distance learning degree programs offered (minimal on-campus study). *Degree requirements:* For master's, thesis. *Entrance requirements:* For master's, 5-7 years of related work experience. Electronic applications accepted. *Faculty research:* Sustainable development, atmospheric processes, sustainable communities, chemical fate and transport of persistent organic pollutants, educational technology.

Saint Vincent College, Program in Education, Latrobe, PA 15650-2690. Offers curriculum and instruction (MS); educational media and technology (MS); environmental education (MS); school administration and supervision (MS); special education (MS). Part-time and evening/weekend programs available. *Degree requirements:* For master's, comprehensive exam. *Entrance requirements:* For master's, GRE (if undergraduate GPA less than 3.0). Additional exam requirements/recommendations for international students: Required—TOEFL (minimum score 550 paper-based; 213 computer-based). *Faculty research:* Assessment and instructional technology.

Slippery Rock University of Pennsylvania, Graduate Studies (Recruitment), College of Health, Environment, and Science, Department of Parks, Recreation, and Environmental Education, Slippery Rock, PA 16057-1383. Offers environmental education (M Ed); park and resource management (MS). Part-time and evening/weekend programs available. Postbaccalaureate distance learning degree programs offered (no on-campus study). *Faculty:* 3 full-time (1 woman), 3 part-time/adjunct (2 women). *Students:* 20 full-time (10 women), 75 part-time (38 women); includes 2 minority (1 Hispanic/Latino; 1 Two or more races, non-Hispanic/Latino), 1 international. Average age 30. 66 applicants, 77% accepted, 32 enrolled. In 2011, 49 degrees awarded. *Degree requirements:* For master's, comprehensive exam (for some programs), thesis (for some programs), internship. *Entrance requirements:* For master's, GRE General Test, MAT, minimum GPA of 2.75. Additional exam requirements/recommendations for international students: Required—TOEFL (minimum score 550 paper-based; 213 computer-based; 80 iBT). *Application deadline:* For fall admission, 3/1 priority date for domestic students, 5/1 for international students; for spring admission, 10/1 priority date for domestic students, 9/1 for international students. Applications are processed on a rolling basis. Application fee: $25 ($30 for international students). Electronic applications accepted. *Expenses:* Contact institution. *Financial support:* Career-related internships or fieldwork, Federal Work-Study, institutionally sponsored loans, scholarships/grants, tuition waivers (partial), and unspecified assistantships available. Support available to part-time students. Financial award application deadline: 5/1; financial award applicants required to submit FAFSA. *Unit head:* Dr. Daniel Dziubek, Graduate Coordinator, 724-738-2958, Fax: 724-738-2938, E-mail: daniel.dziubek@sru.edu. *Application contact:* Angela Barrett, Director of Graduate Admissions, 724-738-2051, Fax: 724-738-2146, E-mail: graduate.admissions@sru.edu.

Southern Connecticut State University, School of Graduate Studies, School of Arts and Sciences, Department of Science Education and Environmental Studies, New Haven, CT 06515-1355. Offers environmental education (MS); science education (MS, Diploma). *Accreditation:* NCATE. Part-time and evening/weekend programs available. *Faculty:* 3 full-time (1 woman), 1 (woman) part-time/adjunct. *Students:* 23 full-time (11 women), 27 part-time (18 women); includes 6 minority (2 Black or African American, non-Hispanic/Latino; 1 Asian, non-Hispanic/Latino; 1 Hispanic/Latino; 2 Two or more races, non-Hispanic/Latino). 54 applicants, 17% accepted, 7 enrolled. In 2011, 18 master's awarded. *Degree requirements:* For master's, thesis or alternative. *Entrance requirements:* For master's, interview; for Diploma, master's degree. *Application deadline:* For fall admission, 7/15 priority date for domestic students. Applications are processed on a rolling basis. Application fee: $50. Electronic applications accepted. *Expenses:* Tuition, state resident: full-time $5137; part-time $413 per credit. *Required fees:* $4008; $55 per term. *Financial support:* Application deadline: 4/15; applicants required to submit FAFSA. *Unit head:* Dr. Susan Cusato, Chairman, 203-392-6610, Fax: 203-392-6614, E-mail: hagemans1@southernct.edu. *Application contact:* Dr. Susan Cusato, Graduate Coordinator, 203-392-6610, Fax: 203-392-6614, E-mail: cusatos1@southernct.edu.

Southern Oregon University, Graduate Studies, Program in Environmental Education, Ashland, OR 97520. Offers MS. Part-time programs available. *Faculty:* 6 full-time (1 woman), 2 part-time/adjunct (1 woman). *Students:* 21 full-time (16 women), 4 part-time (3 women), 1 international. Average age 30. 11 applicants, 18% accepted, 2 enrolled. In 2011, 2 degrees awarded. *Degree requirements:* For master's, thesis (for some programs), comprehensive exam (MA). *Entrance requirements:* For master's, GRE General Test, minimum GPA of 3.0. *Application deadline:* Applications are processed on a rolling basis. Application fee: $50. *Expenses:* Tuition, state resident: full-time $12,600; part-time $350 per credit. Tuition, nonresident: full-time $16,200; part-time $450 per credit. *Required fees:* $1590. *Financial support:* Research assistantships with partial tuition reimbursements, institutionally sponsored loans, and unspecified assistantships available. *Unit head:* Dr. Karen Stone, Chair, 541-552-6749. *Application contact:* Mark Bottorff, Director of Admissions, 541-552-6411, Fax: 541-552-8403. Web site: http://www.sou.edu/ee/.

Université du Québec à Montréal, Graduate Programs, Program in Education, Montréal, QC H3C 3P8, Canada. Offers education (M Ed, MA, PhD); education of the environmental sciences (Diploma). PhD offered jointly with Université du Québec à Chicoutimi, Université du Québec à Rimouski, Université du Québec à Trois-Rivières, Université du Québec en Outaouais, and Université du Québec en Abitibi-Témiscamingue. Part-time programs available. *Degree requirements:* For master's, thesis (for some programs); for doctorate, thesis/dissertation. *Entrance requirements:* For master's and Diploma, appropriate bachelor's degree or equivalent, proficiency in French; for doctorate, appropriate master's degree or equivalent, proficiency in French.

University of Colorado Denver, College of Liberal Arts and Sciences, Department of Geography and Environmental Sciences, Denver, CO 80217. Offers environmental sciences (MS), including air quality, ecosystems, environmental health, environmental science education, geo-spatial analysis, hazardous waste, water quality. Part-time and evening/weekend programs available. *Students:* 42 full-time (25 women), 6 part-time (5 women); includes 6 minority (2 Black or African American, non-Hispanic/Latino; 1 Asian, non-Hispanic/Latino; 2 Hispanic/Latino; 1 Two or more races, non-Hispanic/Latino), 10 international. Average age 29. 31 applicants, 68% accepted, 13 enrolled. In 2011, 24 master's awarded. *Degree requirements:* For master's, thesis or alternative, 30 credits including 21 of core requirements and 9 of environmental science electives. *Entrance requirements:* For master's, GRE General Test, BA in one of the natural/physical sciences or engineering (or equivalent background); prerequisite coursework in calculus and physics (one semester each), general chemistry with lab and general biology with lab (two semesters each), three letters of recommendation. Additional exam requirements/recommendations for international students: Required—TOEFL (minimum score 525 paper-based; 197 computer-based). *Application deadline:* For fall admission, 4/1 for domestic and international students; for spring admission, 10/1 for domestic and international students. Application fee: $50 ($75 for international students). Electronic applications accepted. *Financial support:* Research assistantships, teaching assistantships, and Federal Work-Study available. Financial award application deadline: 4/1; financial award applicants required to submit FAFSA. *Faculty research:* Air quality, environmental health, ecosystems, hazardous waste, water quality, geo-spatial analysis and environmental science education. *Unit head:* Dr. Brian K. Page, Department Chair, 303-556-8332, Fax: 303-556-6197, E-mail: john.wyckoff@cudenver.edu. *Application contact:* Sue Eddleman, Program Assistant, 303-556-6197, E-mail: sue.eddleman@ucdenver.edu. Web site: http://www.ucdenver.edu/academics/colleges/CLAS/Departments/ges/Pages/Geography.aspx.

University of Minnesota, Twin Cities Campus, Graduate School, College of Education and Human Development, Department of Curriculum and Instruction, Minneapolis, MN 55455-0213. Offers art education (M Ed, MA, PhD); children's literature (M Ed, MA, PhD); curriculum and instruction (MA, PhD); early childhood education (M Ed, PhD); elementary education (M Ed, MA, PhD); English education (MA, PhD); environmental education (M Ed); family education (M Ed, MA, Ed D, PhD); instructional systems and technology (M Ed, MA, PhD); language arts (MA, PhD); language immersion education (Certificate); literacy education (MA); mathematics education (MA, PhD); reading education (MA, PhD); science education (MA, PhD); second languages and cultures education (MA, PhD); social studies education (MA, PhD); teaching (M Ed), including Chinese, earth science, elementary special education, English, English as a second language, French, German, Hebrew, Japanese, life sciences, mathematics, middle school science, science, second languages and cultures, social studies, Spanish; technology enhanced learning (Certificate); writing education (M Ed, MA, PhD). *Faculty:* 34 full-time (22 women). *Students:* 433 full-time (319 women), 310 part-time (239 women); includes 97 minority (34 Black or African American, non-Hispanic/Latino; 6 American Indian or Alaska Native, non-Hispanic/Latino; 35 Asian, non-Hispanic/Latino; 22 Hispanic/Latino), 47 international. Average age 33. 660 applicants, 68% accepted, 395 enrolled. In 2011, 518 master's, 19 doctorates, 14 other advanced degrees awarded. Application fee: $55. *Financial support:* In 2011–12, 6 fellowships (averaging $9,308 per year), 39 research assistantships with full tuition reimbursements (averaging $8,301 per year), 61 teaching assistantships with full tuition reimbursements (averaging $9,206 per year) were awarded. *Faculty research:* Teaching and learning; quality of education; influence of cultural, linguistic, social, political, technological and economic factors on teaching, learning and educational research; relationship between educational practice and a democratic and just society. *Total annual research expenditures:* $943,365. *Unit head:* Dr. Nina Asher, Chair, 612-624-4772, Fax: 612-624-1357, E-mail: nasher@umn.edu. *Application contact:* Dr. Jennifer Engler, Assistant Dean, 612-626-2887, Fax: 612-626-7496, E-mail: engle009@umn.edu. Web site: http://www.cehd.umn.edu/ci.

University of New Hampshire, Graduate School, Interdisciplinary Programs, Program in Environmental Education, Durham, NH 03824. Offers MA. Program offered in summer only. Part-time programs available. *Faculty:* 32 full-time. *Students:* 2 full-time (1 woman), 7 part-time (5 women); includes 1 minority (Hispanic/Latino). Average age 30. 1 applicant, 0% accepted, 0 enrolled. In 2011, 9 master's awarded. *Entrance requirements:* Additional exam requirements/recommendations for international students: Required—TOEFL (minimum score 550 paper-based; 213 computer-based; 80 iBT). *Application deadline:* For fall admission, 6/1 for domestic students, 4/1 for international students; for spring admission, 12/1 for domestic students. Applications are processed on a rolling basis. Application fee: $65. Electronic applications accepted. *Expenses:* Tuition, state resident: full-time $12,360; part-time $687 per credit hour. Tuition, nonresident: full-time $25,680; part-time $1058 per credit hour. *International tuition:* $29,550 full-time. *Required fees:* $1666; $833 per course. $416.50 per semester. Tuition and fees vary according to course load and degree level. *Financial support:* Fellowships, research assistantships, and teaching assistantships available. Financial award application deadline: 2/15. *Unit head:* Dr. Eleanor Abrams, Program Coordinator, 603-862-2990, E-mail: education.department@unh.edu. *Application contact:* Lisa Canfield, Administrative Assistant, 603-862-2310, E-mail: education.department@unh.edu. Web site: http://www.learn.unh.edu/maenviron/.

The University of North Carolina Wilmington, College of Arts and Sciences, Department of Environmental Studies, Wilmington, NC 28403-3297. Offers coastal management (MA); environmental education and interpretation (MA); environmental management (MA); individualized study (MA). Part-time programs available. *Degree requirements:* For master's, comprehensive exam, thesis or alternative, final project, practicum. *Entrance requirements:* For master's, GRE, 3 letters of recommendation. Additional exam requirements/recommendations for international students: Required—TOEFL (minimum score 550 paper-based; 217 computer-based; 79 iBT), IELTS (minimum score 6.5). Electronic applications accepted. *Faculty research:* Coastal management, environmental management, environmental education, environmental law, natural resource management.

University of South Africa, College of Human Sciences, Pretoria, South Africa. Offers adult education (M Ed); African languages (MA, PhD); African politics (MA, PhD); Afrikaans (MA, PhD); ancient history (MA, PhD); ancient Near Eastern studies (MA, PhD); anthropology (MA, PhD); applied linguistics (MA); Arabic (MA, PhD); archaeology (MA); art history (MA); Biblical archaeology (MA); Biblical studies (M Th, D Th, PhD); Christian spirituality (M Th, D Th); church history (M Th, D Th); classical studies (MA, PhD); clinical psychology (MA); communication (MA, PhD); comparative education (M Ed, Ed D); consulting psychology (D Admin, D Com, PhD); curriculum studies (M Ed, Ed D); development studies (M Admin, MA, D Admin, PhD); didactics (M Ed, Ed D); education (M Tech); education management (M Ed, Ed D); educational psychology (M Ed); English (MA); environmental education (M Ed); French (MA, PhD); German (MA, PhD); Greek (MA); guidance and counseling (M Ed); health studies (MA, PhD), including health sciences education (MA), health services management (MA), medical and surgical nursing science (critical care general) (MA), midwifery and neonatal nursing science (MA), trauma and emergency care (MA); history (MA, PhD); history of education (Ed D); inclusive education (M Ed, Ed D); information and communications technology policy and regulation (MA); information science (MA, MIS, PhD); international politics (MA, PhD); Islamic studies (MA, PhD); Italian (MA, PhD); Judaica (MA, PhD); linguistics (MA, PhD); mathematical education (M Ed); mathematics education (MA); missiology (M Th, D Th); modern Hebrew (MA, PhD); musicology (MA, MMus, D Mus, PhD); natural science education (M Ed); New Testament (M Th, D Th); Old Testament (D Th); pastoral therapy (M Th, D Th); philosophy (MA); philosophy of education (M Ed, Ed D); politics (MA, PhD); Portuguese (MA, PhD); practical theology (M Th, D Th); psychology (MA, MS, PhD); psychology of education (M Ed, Ed D); public health (MA); religious studies (MA, D Th, PhD); Romance languages (MA); Russian (MA, PhD); Semitic languages (MA, PhD); social behavior studies in HIV/AIDS (MA); social science (mental health) (MA); social science in development studies (MA); social science in psychology (MA); social science in social work (MA); social science in sociology (MA); social work (MSW, DSW, PhD); socio-education (M Ed, Ed D); sociolinguistics (MA); sociology (MA, PhD); Spanish (MA, PhD); systematic theology (M Th, D Th); TESOL (teaching English to speakers of other languages) (MA); theological ethics (M Th, D Th); theory of literature (MA, PhD); urban ministries (D Th); urban ministry (M Th).

University of Victoria, Faculty of Graduate Studies, Faculty of Education, Department of Curriculum and Instruction, Victoria, BC V8W 2Y2, Canada. Offers art education (M Ed, PhD); curriculum studies (M Ed, MA, PhD); early childhood education (M Ed, PhD); educational studies (PhD); language and literacy (M Ed, MA, PhD); mathematics (M Ed, MA, PhD); music education (M Ed, MA, PhD); science (M Ed, MA, PhD); social studies (M Ed, MA); social, cultural and foundational studies (MA, PhD); technology and environmental education (PhD). Part-time programs available. *Degree requirements:* For master's, thesis, project (M Ed); for doctorate, comprehensive exam, thesis/dissertation. *Entrance requirements:* For master's, minimum B average. Additional exam requirements/recommendations for international students: Required—TOEFL (minimum score 575 paper-based; 233 computer-based), IELTS (minimum score 7). Electronic applications accepted. *Faculty research:* Elementary and secondary English, language arts, curriculum theory and practice, educational media and technology, educational administration and leadership, history and philosophy of education.

Western Washington University, Graduate School, Huxley College of the Environment, Department of Environmental Studies, Program in Environmental Education, Bellingham, WA 98225-5996. Offers M Ed. Part-time programs available. *Degree requirements:* For master's, comprehensive exam, thesis optional. *Entrance requirements:* For master's, GRE or MAT, minimum GPA of 3.0 in last 60 semester hours. Additional exam requirements/recommendations for international students: Required—TOEFL (minimum score 567 paper-based; 227 computer-based). Electronic applications accepted. *Faculty research:* Role of wilderness in national park history; history of the conservation movement and sense of place in environmental education; environmental care and responsibility; conservation psychology and environmental education.

West Virginia University, Davis College of Agriculture, Forestry and Consumer Sciences, Division of Resource Management and Sustainable Development, Program in Agricultural and Extension Education, Morgantown, WV 26506. Offers agricultural and extension education (MS, PhD); teaching vocational-agriculture (MS). *Accreditation:* NCATE. Part-time programs available. *Degree requirements:* For master's, thesis. *Entrance requirements:* For master's, GRE General Test, minimum GPA of 2.75. Additional exam requirements/recommendations for international students: Required—TOEFL. *Faculty research:* Program development in vocational agriculture, agricultural extension, supervised experience programs, leadership development.

Foreign Languages Education

The American University in Cairo, School of Humanities and Social Sciences, Arabic Language Institute, Cairo, Egypt. Offers teaching Arabic as a foreign language (MA). *Entrance requirements:* Additional exam requirements/recommendations for international students: Required—English entrance exam and/or TOEFL. *Application deadline:* For fall admission, 3/31 priority date for domestic students; for spring admission, 1/10 priority date for domestic students. Application fee: $45. *Expenses:*

Tuition: Part-time $932 per credit hour. Tuition and fees vary according to course load, degree level and program. *Unit head:* Zeinab Taha, Director, 20-2-2615-1737. *Application contact:* Mary Davidson, Coordinator of Student Affairs, 212-730-8800, Fax: 212-730-1600, E-mail: mdavidson@aucnyo.edu. Web site: http://www.aucegypt.edu/huss/ali/Pages/default.aspx.

Andrews University, School of Graduate Studies, School of Education, Department of Teaching, Learning, and Curriculum, Berrien Springs, MI 49104. Offers curriculum and instruction (MA, Ed D, PhD, Ed S); elementary education (MAT); secondary education (MAT), including biology, education, English, English as a second language, French, history, physics; teacher education (MAT). *Students:* 15 full-time (10 women), 27 part-time (22 women); includes 18 minority (12 Black or African American, non-Hispanic/Latino; 1 Asian, non-Hispanic/Latino; 3 Hispanic/Latino; 1 Native Hawaiian or other Pacific Islander, non-Hispanic/Latino; 1 Two or more races, non-Hispanic/Latino), 10 international. Average age 42. 48 applicants, 48% accepted, 10 enrolled. In 2011, 5 master's, 2 doctorates, 2 other advanced degrees awarded. *Entrance requirements:* For master's, GRE Subject Test. Additional exam requirements/recommendations for international students: Required—TOEFL (minimum score 550 paper-based). *Application deadline:* For fall admission, 8/15 for domestic students. Applications are processed on a rolling basis. Application fee: $40. *Unit head:* Dr. Lee C. Davidson, Chair, 269-471-6364. *Application contact:* Carolyn Hurst, Supervisor of Graduate Admission, 800-253-2874, Fax: 269-471-6321, E-mail: graduate@andrews.edu.

Appalachian State University, Cratis D. Williams Graduate School, Department of Foreign Languages and Literatures, Boone, NC 28608. Offers romance languages (MA), including Spanish or French teaching. Part-time programs available. Postbaccalaureate distance learning degree programs offered (no on-campus study). *Faculty:* 8 full-time (3 women), 2 part-time/adjunct (both women). *Students:* 2 full-time (both women), 13 part-time (12 women). 7 applicants, 100% accepted, 7 enrolled. In 2011, 7 master's awarded. *Degree requirements:* For master's, one foreign language, comprehensive exam, thesis optional. *Entrance requirements:* For master's, GRE General Test, 3 letters of recommendation. Additional exam requirements/recommendations for international students: Required—TOEFL (minimum score 570 paper-based; 230 computer-based; 79 iBT) or IELTS (minimum score 6.5). *Application deadline:* For fall admission, 3/15 priority date for domestic students, 2/1 for international students; for spring admission, 11/1 for domestic students, 7/1 for international students. Applications are processed on a rolling basis. Application fee: $55. Electronic applications accepted. *Expenses:* Tuition, state resident: full-time $4040; part-time $180 per semester hour. Tuition, nonresident: full-time $15,900; part-time $760 per semester hour. *Required fees:* $2500; $20 per semester hour. Tuition and fees vary according to campus/location. *Financial support:* Career-related internships or fieldwork available. Financial award application deadline: 4/1; financial award applicants required to submit FAFSA. *Faculty research:* French and Spanish literature, Latin American culture, teaching foreign languages. *Total annual research expenditures:* $175,000. *Unit head:* Dr. James Fogelquist, Chairperson, 828-262-3096, Fax: 828-262-3095, E-mail: fogelquistjd@appstate.edu. *Application contact:* Dr. Beverly Moser, Graduate Coordinator, 828-262-2929, E-mail: moserba@appstate.edu. Web site: http://fll.appstate.edu.

Arizona State University, College of Liberal Arts and Sciences, School of International Letters and Cultures, Program in Spanish, Tempe, AZ 85287-0202. Offers Spanish (cultural studies) (PhD); Spanish (linguistics) (MA), including second language acquisition/applied linguistics, sociolinguistics; Spanish (literature and culture) (MA); Spanish (literature) (PhD). Part-time programs available. Terminal master's awarded for partial completion of doctoral program. *Degree requirements:* For master's, thesis, oral defense; written comprehensive exam (literature and culture); portfolio review (linguistics); interactive Program of Study (iPOS) submitted before completing 50 percent of required credit hours; for doctorate, comprehensive exam, thesis/dissertation, interactive Program of Study (iPOS) submitted before completing 50 percent of required credit hours. *Entrance requirements:* For master's, GRE (recommended), BA in Spanish or close equivalent from accredited institution with minimum GPA of 3.5, 3 letters of recommendation, personal statement, academic writing sample; for doctorate, GRE (recommended), MA in Spanish or equivalent from accredited institution with minimum GPA of 3.75, 3 letters of recommendation, personal statement, academic writing sample. Additional exam requirements/recommendations for international students: Required—TOEFL (minimum score 550 paper-based; 213 computer-based; 83 iBT), IELTS (minimum score 6.5). Electronic applications accepted.

Auburn University, Graduate School, College of Education, Department of Curriculum and Teaching, Auburn University, AL 36849. Offers business education (M Ed, MS, PhD); early childhood education (M Ed, MS, PhD, Ed S); elementary education (M Ed, MS, PhD, Ed S); foreign languages (M Ed, MS); music education (M Ed, MS, PhD, Ed S); postsecondary education (PhD); reading education (PhD, Ed S); secondary education (M Ed, MS, PhD, Ed S), including English language arts, mathematics, science, social studies. *Accreditation:* NASM (one or more programs are accredited); NCATE. Part-time programs available. *Faculty:* 22 full-time (17 women), 3 part-time/adjunct (all women). *Students:* 80 full-time (58 women), 181 part-time (126 women); includes 42 minority (28 Black or African American, non-Hispanic/Latino; 7 Asian, non-Hispanic/Latino; 7 Hispanic/Latino). Average age 34. 184 applicants, 53% accepted, 60 enrolled. In 2011, 77 master's, 10 doctorates, 35 other advanced degrees awarded. *Degree requirements:* For master's, thesis (for some programs); for doctorate, thesis/dissertation; for Ed S, field project. *Entrance requirements:* For master's, doctorate, and Ed S, GRE General Test. *Application deadline:* For fall admission, 7/7 for domestic students; for spring admission, 11/24 for domestic students. Applications are processed on a rolling basis. Application fee: $50 ($60 for international students). Electronic applications accepted. *Expenses:* Tuition, state resident: full-time $7290; part-time $405 per credit hour. Tuition, nonresident: full-time $21,870; part-time $1215 per credit hour. *International tuition:* $22,000 full-time. *Required fees:* $1402. *Financial support:* Fellowships, teaching assistantships, career-related internships or fieldwork, and Federal Work-Study available. Support available to part-time students. Financial award application deadline: 3/15; financial award applicants required to submit FAFSA. *Faculty research:* Emerging literacy, reading attitudes, music for at-risk youth, portfolio assessment. *Unit head:* Dr. Kimberly Walls, Head, 334-844-4434. *Application contact:* Dr. George Flowers, Dean of the Graduate School, 334-844-2125. Web site: http://education.auburn.edu/academic_departments/curr/.

Bennington College, Graduate Programs, MA in Teaching a Second Language Program, Bennington, VT 05201. Offers education (MATSL); foreign language education (MATSL); French (MATSL); Spanish (MATSL). Part-time programs available. *Faculty:* 2 full-time (both women), 5 part-time/adjunct (3 women). *Students:* 19 part-time (all women); includes 3 minority (1 Black or African American, non-Hispanic/Latino; 2 Hispanic/Latino). Average age 42. 13 applicants, 92% accepted, 9 enrolled. In 2011, 5 master's awarded. *Degree requirements:* For master's, one foreign language, 2 major projects and presentations. *Entrance requirements:* For master's, Oral Proficiency Interview (OPI). Additional exam requirements/recommendations for international students: Required—TOEFL (minimum score 577 paper-based; 233 computer-based; 91 iBT). *Application deadline:* For spring admission, 4/1 priority date for domestic students, 4/1 for international students. Applications are processed on a rolling basis. Application fee: $60. *Expenses:* Contact institution. *Financial support:* In 2011–12, 4 students received support. Scholarships/grants available. Financial award application deadline: 4/1; financial award applicants required to submit FAFSA. *Faculty research:* Acquisition, evaluation, assessment, conceptual teaching and learning, content-driven communication, applied linguistics. *Unit head:* Carol Meyer, Director, 802-440-4375, E-mail: cmeyer@bennington.edu. *Application contact:* Nancy Pearlman, Assistant Director, 802-440-4710, E-mail: matsl@bennington.edu. Web site: http://www.bennington.edu/Academics/GraduateCertificatePrograms/MATSL.aspx.

Bowling Green State University, Graduate College, College of Arts and Sciences, Department of German, Russian, and East Asian Languages, Bowling Green, OH 43403. Offers German (MA, MAT); MA/MA. Part-time programs available. *Degree requirements:* For master's, one foreign language, thesis or alternative. *Entrance requirements:* For master's, GRE General Test. Additional exam requirements/recommendations for international students: Required—TOEFL. Electronic applications accepted.

Bowling Green State University, Graduate College, College of Arts and Sciences, Department of Romance and Classical Studies, Program in French, Bowling Green, OH 43403. Offers French (MA); French education (MAT). Part-time programs available. *Degree requirements:* For master's, one foreign language, thesis or alternative. *Entrance requirements:* For master's, GRE General Test. Additional exam requirements/recommendations for international students: Required—TOEFL. Electronic applications accepted. *Faculty research:* Francophone literature, French cinema, business French, nineteenth and twentieth century literature.

Bowling Green State University, Graduate College, College of Arts and Sciences, Department of Romance and Classical Studies, Program in Spanish, Bowling Green, OH 43403. Offers Spanish (MA); Spanish education (MAT). Part-time programs available. *Degree requirements:* For master's, one foreign language, thesis or alternative. *Entrance requirements:* For master's, GRE General Test. Additional exam requirements/recommendations for international students: Required—TOEFL. Electronic applications accepted. *Faculty research:* U.S. Latino literature and culture, Latin American film and popular culture, applied linguistics, Spanish popular culture.

Brigham Young University, Graduate Studies, College of Humanities, Center for Language Studies, Provo, UT 84602-1001. Offers second language teaching (MA). *Faculty:* 26 full-time (6 women). *Students:* 11 full-time (7 women), 6 part-time (4 women); includes 3 minority (2 Asian, non-Hispanic/Latino; 1 Hispanic/Latino). Average age 28. 12 applicants, 58% accepted, 6 enrolled. In 2011, 8 master's awarded. *Degree requirements:* For master's, one foreign language, thesis. *Entrance requirements:* For master's, GRE General Test (minimum score in 50th percentile on the verbal section and a rating of 4 on the analytical/writing section), demonstrated proficiency in ACTFL OPI rating in the language of specialization, English writing sample, minimum GPA of 3.0, three letters of recommendation, letter of intent, teaching method class. Additional exam requirements/recommendations for international students: Required—TOEFL (minimum score 85 iBT). *Application deadline:* For fall admission, 2/1 for domestic and international students. Application fee: $50. Electronic applications accepted. *Expenses: Tuition:* Full-time $5760; part-time $320 per credit. Tuition and fees vary according to student's religious affiliation. *Financial support:* In 2011–12, 12 students received support, including 24 fellowships with partial tuition reimbursements available (averaging $1,716 per year); career-related internships or fieldwork, scholarships/grants, traineeships, tuition waivers (partial), and unspecified assistantships also available. Support available to part-time students. Financial award application deadline: 2/1. *Faculty research:* Second language vocabulary, applied linguistics, computer-assisted learning and instructing, language comprehension, testing sociolinguists. *Total annual research expenditures:* $1.2 million. *Unit head:* Dr. Ray T. Clifford, Director, 801-422-3263, Fax: 801-422-9741, E-mail: rayc@byu.edu. *Application contact:* Agnes Y. Welch, Program Manager, 801-422-5199, Fax: 801-422-9741, E-mail: agnes_welch@byu.edu. Web site: http://slat.byu.edu.

Brigham Young University, Graduate Studies, College of Humanities, Department of Spanish and Portuguese, Provo, UT 84602. Offers Hispanic literature (MA); Portuguese linguistics (MA); Portuguese literature (MA); Spanish linguistics (MA); Spanish teaching (MA). Part-time programs available. *Faculty:* 27 full-time (5 women). *Students:* 15 full-time (7 women), 20 part-time (12 women); includes 11 minority (10 Hispanic/Latino; 1 Native Hawaiian or other Pacific Islander, non-Hispanic/Latino). Average age 30. 25 applicants, 68% accepted, 13 enrolled. In 2011, 9 master's awarded. *Degree requirements:* For master's, one foreign language, comprehensive exam, thesis, 1 semester of teaching. *Entrance requirements:* For master's, GRE, minimum GPA of 3.5 in Spanish or Portuguese, 3.3 overall. Additional exam requirements/recommendations for international students: Required—TOEFL (minimum score 580 paper-based; 85 iBT). *Application deadline:* For fall admission, 2/1 for domestic and international students. Application fee: $50. Electronic applications accepted. *Expenses: Tuition:* Full-time $5760; part-time $320 per credit. Tuition and fees vary according to student's religious affiliation. *Financial support:* In 2011–12, 25 students received support, including 65 teaching assistantships with partial tuition reimbursements available (averaging $12,500 per year); institutionally sponsored loans, scholarships/grants, tuition waivers (partial), and unspecified assistantships also available. Support available to part-time students. Financial award application deadline: 7/1. *Faculty research:* Mexican prose; Latin American theater, literature, phonetics, and phonology; pedagogy; classical Portuguese literature; Peninsular prose and theater. *Unit head:* Dr. David P. Laraway, Chair, 801-422-3807, Fax: 801-422-0628, E-mail: david_laraway@byu.edu. *Application contact:* Jasmine S. Talbot, Graduate Secretary, 801-422-2196, Fax: 801-422-0628, E-mail: jasmine_talbot@byu.edu. Web site: http://spanport.byu.edu/.

Brooklyn College of the City University of New York, Division of Graduate Studies, School of Education, Program in Adolescence Education and Special Subjects, Brooklyn, NY 11210-2889. Offers adolescence science education (MAT); art teacher (MA); biology teacher (MA); chemistry teacher (MA); earth science teacher (MAT); English teacher (MA); French teacher (MA); health and nutrition sciences: health teacher (MS Ed); mathematics teacher (MA); music education (CAS); music teacher (MA); physical education teacher (MS Ed); physics teacher (MA); social studies teacher (MA); Spanish teacher (MA). Part-time and evening/weekend programs available. *Degree requirements:* For master's, comprehensive exam (for some programs), thesis (for some programs). *Entrance requirements:* For master's, LAST, previous course work in education, resume, 2 letters of recommendation, essay. Additional exam requirements/recommendations for international students: Required—TOEFL (minimum score 500 paper-based; 173 computer-based; 61 iBT). Electronic applications accepted. *Faculty research:* Interdisciplinary education, semiotics, discourse analysis, autobiography, teacher identity.

California State University, Chico, Office of Graduate Studies, College of Communication and Education, School of Education, Program in Teaching International Languages, Chico, CA 95929-0722. Offers MA. Part-time programs available. *Faculty:* 6 full-time (4 women), 1 (woman) part-time/adjunct. *Students:* 25 full-time (17 women), 11 part-time (8 women); includes 6 minority (1 Black or African American, non-Hispanic/Latino; 2 Asian, non-Hispanic/Latino; 3 Hispanic/Latino), 12 international. Average age 33. 33 applicants, 79% accepted, 20 enrolled. *Degree requirements:* For master's, comprehensive exam (for some programs), thesis or project. *Entrance requirements:*

For master's, GRE, faculty mentor, statement of purpose. Additional exam requirements/recommendations for international students: Required—TOEFL (minimum score 550 paper-based; 213 computer-based; 80 iBT), IELTS (minimum score 6.5), Pearson Test of English (minimum score 59). *Application deadline:* For fall admission, 3/1 priority date for domestic students, 3/1 for international students; for spring admission, 9/15 priority date for domestic students, 9/15 for international students. Application fee: $55. Electronic applications accepted. Tuition and fees vary according to class time, course load and degree level. *Financial support:* Career-related internships or fieldwork and scholarships/grants available. Financial award application deadline: 3/1; financial award applicants required to submit FAFSA. *Unit head:* Dr. Deborah I. Summers, Director of School of Education, 530-898-4599, Fax: 530-898-4580, E-mail: educ@csuchico.edu. *Application contact:* Judy L. Rice, Graduate Admissions Coordinator, 530-898-5416, Fax: 530-898-3342, E-mail: jlrice@csuchico.edu. Web site: http://www.csuchico.edu/soe/advanced/international/index.shtml.

California State University, Sacramento, Office of Graduate Studies, College of Arts and Letters, Department of Foreign Languages, Sacrament, CA 95819-6089. Offers MA. Part-time programs available. *Faculty:* 15 full-time (10 women), 10 part-time/adjunct (7 women). *Students:* 5 full-time, 27 part-time; includes 10 minority (all Hispanic/Latino), 1 international. Average age 34. 14 applicants, 57% accepted, 4 enrolled. In 2011, 9 master's awarded. *Entrance requirements:* For master's, interview, minimum GPA of 2.5 during previous 2 years of course work. Additional exam requirements/recommendations for international students: Required—TOEFL. *Application deadline:* For fall admission, 3/1 for domestic and international students; for spring admission, 9/30 for international students. Applications are processed on a rolling basis. Application fee: $55. Electronic applications accepted. *Financial support:* Teaching assistantships, career-related internships or fieldwork, and Federal Work-Study available. Support available to part-time students. Financial award application deadline: 3/1; financial award applicants required to submit FAFSA. *Unit head:* Bernice Bass de Martinez, Chair, 916-278-6333, Fax: 916-278-5502, E-mail: bbdem@csus.edu. *Application contact:* Jose Martinez, Outreach and Graduate Diversity Coordinator, 916-278-6470, Fax: 916-278-5669, E-mail: martinj@skymail.csus.edu. Web site: http://www.csus.edu/fl.

Caribbean University, Graduate School, Bayamón, PR 00960-0493. Offers administration and supervision (MA Ed); criminal justice (MA); curriculum and instruction (MA Ed, PhD), including elementary education (MA Ed), English education (MA Ed), history education (MA Ed), mathematics education (MA Ed), primary education (MA Ed), science education (MA Ed), Spanish education (MA Ed); educational technology in instructional systems (MA Ed); gerontology (MSN); human resources (MBA); museology, archiving and art history (MA Ed); neonatal pediatrics (MSN); physical education (MA Ed); special education (MA Ed). *Entrance requirements:* For master's, interview, minimum GPA of 2.5.

Central Connecticut State University, School of Graduate Studies, School of Arts and Sciences, Department of Modern Languages, New Britain, CT 06050-4010. Offers modern language (MA, Certificate), including French, German (Certificate), Italian (Certificate), modern language (MA), Spanish language and Hispanic culture (MA); Spanish (MS, Certificate). Part-time and evening/weekend programs available. *Faculty:* 12 full-time (8 women), 20 part-time/adjunct (13 women). *Students:* 5 full-time (3 women), 33 part-time (30 women); includes 14 minority (2 Black or African American, non-Hispanic/Latino; 12 Hispanic/Latino). Average age 40. 14 applicants, 57% accepted, 5 enrolled. In 2011, 18 master's awarded. *Degree requirements:* For master's, one foreign language, comprehensive exam, thesis or alternative; for Certificate, qualifying exam. *Entrance requirements:* For master's, minimum undergraduate GPA of 2.7, 24 credits of undergraduate courses in either Italian or Spanish. Additional exam requirements/recommendations for international students: Required—TOEFL (minimum score 550 paper-based; 213 computer-based). *Application deadline:* For fall admission, 6/1 for domestic students, 5/1 for international students; for spring admission, 11/1 for domestic and international students. Applications are processed on a rolling basis. Application fee: $50. Electronic applications accepted. *Expenses: Tuition, area resident:* Full-time $5137; part-time $482 per credit. Tuition, state resident: full-time $7707; part-time $494 per credit. Tuition, nonresident: full-time $14,311; part-time $494 per credit. *Required fees:* $3865. One-time fee: $62 part-time. *Financial support:* In 2011–12, 2 students received support, including 1 research assistantship; career-related internships or fieldwork, Federal Work-Study, scholarships/grants, and unspecified assistantships also available. Support available to part-time students. Financial award application deadline: 4/15; financial award applicants required to submit FAFSA. *Faculty research:* Quebecois literature, Caribbean literature, modern French/Spanish drama, Puerto Rican novel and drama. *Unit head:* Dr. Lilian Uribe, Chair, 860-832-2875, E-mail: uribe@ccsu.edu. *Application contact:* Patricia Gardner, Associate Director of Graduate Studies, 860-832-2350, Fax: 860-832-2352, E-mail: graduateadmissions@ccsu.edu. Web site: http://www.modlang.ccsu.edu/.

Christopher Newport University, Graduate Studies, Department of Teacher Preparation, Newport News, VA 23606-2998. Offers art (PK-12) (MAT); biology (6-12) (MAT); chemistry (6-12) (MAT); computer science (6-12) (MAT); elementary (PK-6) (MAT); English (6-12) (MAT); English as second language (PK-12) (MAT); French (PK-12) (MAT); history and social science (6-12) (MAT); mathematics (6-12) (MAT); music (PK-12) (MAT), including choral, instrumental; physics (6-12) (MAT); Spanish (PK-12) (MAT). Part-time and evening/weekend programs available. *Degree requirements:* For master's, comprehensive exam, thesis or alternative. *Entrance requirements:* For master's, PRAXIS I, minimum GPA of 3.0. Additional exam requirements/recommendations for international students: Required—TOEFL (minimum score 580 paper-based; 237 computer-based; 92 iBT). Electronic applications accepted. *Faculty research:* Early literacy development, instructional innovations, professional teaching standards, multicultural issues, aesthetic education.

Clarion University of Pennsylvania, Office of Graduate Programs, Master of Education Program, Clarion, PA 16214. Offers curriculum and instruction (M Ed); early childhood (M Ed, Certificate); English (M Ed); instructional technology specialist (K-12) (Certificate); literacy (M Ed); mathematics education (M Ed); reading specialist (M Ed, Certificate); science education (M Ed); special education (M Ed); technology (M Ed); world language (M Ed). *Accreditation:* NCATE. Part-time programs available. *Students:* 14 full-time (11 women), 207 part-time (163 women); includes 3 minority (1 Black or African American, non-Hispanic/Latino; 2 Hispanic/Latino). Average age 31. In 2011, 96 master's awarded. *Degree requirements:* For master's, thesis or alternative. *Entrance requirements:* For master's, minimum QPA of 3.0. *Application deadline:* Applications are processed on a rolling basis. *Expenses:* Tuition, state resident: part-time $429 per credit. Tuition, nonresident: part-time $644 per credit. *Financial support:* Research assistantships with full and partial tuition reimbursements and career-related internships or fieldwork available. Support available to part-time students. Financial award application deadline: 3/1. *Unit head:* Dr. John Groves, Dean, 814-393-2146, Fax: 514-393-2446. *Application contact:* Dr. Brenda Sanders Dede, Assistant Vice President for Academic Affairs, 814-393-2337, Fax: 814-393-2030, E-mail: bdede@clarion.edu. Web site: http://www.clarion.edu/25887/.

Cleveland State University, College of Graduate Studies, College of Education and Human Services, Department of Teacher Education, Cleveland, OH 44115. Offers art education (M Ed); early childhood education (M Ed); foreign language education (M Ed); mathematics and science education (M Ed); middle childhood education (M Ed); special education (M Ed), including mild/moderate disabilities, moderate/intensive disabilities; teaching English to speakers of other languages (M Ed). Part-time and evening/weekend programs available. *Faculty:* 20 full-time (12 women), 26 part-time/adjunct (20 women). *Students:* 108 full-time (77 women), 388 part-time (306 women); includes 126 minority (100 Black or African American, non-Hispanic/Latino; 8 Asian, non-Hispanic/Latino; 15 Hispanic/Latino; 1 Native Hawaiian or other Pacific Islander, non-Hispanic/Latino; 2 Two or more races, non-Hispanic/Latino), 25 international. Average age 33. 249 applicants, 73% accepted, 118 enrolled. In 2011, 286 master's awarded. *Degree requirements:* For master's, comprehensive exam (for some programs), thesis or alternative. *Entrance requirements:* For master's, GRE General Test or MAT, minimum GPA of 2.75. Additional exam requirements/recommendations for international students: Required—TOEFL (minimum score 525 paper-based; 197 computer-based), IELTS (minimum score 6). *Application deadline:* For fall admission, 7/15 priority date for domestic students. Applications are processed on a rolling basis. Application fee: $30. *Expenses:* Tuition, state resident: full-time $6416; part-time $494 per credit hour. Tuition, nonresident: full-time $12,074; part-time $929 per credit hour. *Financial support:* In 2011–12, 12 research assistantships with full tuition reimbursements (averaging $3,480 per year) were awarded; tuition waivers (partial) and unspecified assistantships also available. *Faculty research:* Early literacy, professional development in reading, reading recovery, dual language, induction programs. *Total annual research expenditures:* $6.2 million. *Unit head:* Dr. Clifford T. Bennett, Chairperson, 216-523-7105, Fax: 216-687-5379, E-mail: c.t.bennett@csuohio.edu. *Application contact:* Deborah L. Brown, Interim Assistant Director, Graduate Admissions, 216-523-7572, E-mail: d.l.brown@csuohio.edu. Web site: http://www.csuohio.edu/coehs/departments/te.

The College at Brockport, State University of New York, School of Education and Human Services, Department of Education and Human Development, Brockport, NY 14420-2997. Offers adolescence education (MS Ed), including adolescence biology education, adolescence chemistry education, adolescence earth science education, adolescence English education, adolescence mathematics education, adolescence physics education, adolescence social studies education; adolescence inclusive education (MS Ed), including English, mathematics, science, social studies; bilingual education (MS Ed, AGC), including bilingual education, Spanish (AGC); childhood curriculum specialist (MS Ed); childhood literacy (MS Ed). *Accreditation:* NCATE. *Students:* 63 full-time (39 women), 215 part-time (149 women); includes 23 minority (6 Black or African American, non-Hispanic/Latino; 1 American Indian or Alaska Native, non-Hispanic/Latino; 5 Asian, non-Hispanic/Latino; 10 Hispanic/Latino; 1 Native Hawaiian or other Pacific Islander, non-Hispanic/Latino). 133 applicants, 75% accepted, 63 enrolled. In 2011, 97 master's awarded. *Degree requirements:* For master's, thesis or alternative. *Entrance requirements:* For master's, minimum GPA of 3.0, letters of recommendation, interview (for some programs); statement of objectives, current resume. Additional exam requirements/recommendations for international students: Required—TOEFL (minimum score 550 paper-based; 213 computer-based; 79 iBT). *Application deadline:* For fall admission, 2/15 priority date for domestic students, 2/15 for international students; for spring admission, 9/15 priority date for domestic students, 9/15 for international students. Application fee: $80. Electronic applications accepted. *Financial support:* In 2011–12, 2 teaching assistantships with full tuition reimbursements (averaging $6,000 per year) were awarded; Federal Work-Study, scholarships/grants, and unspecified assistantships also available. Support available to part-time students. Financial award application deadline: 3/15; financial award applicants required to submit FAFSA. *Faculty research:* Educational assessment, literacy education, inclusive education, teacher preparation, qualitative methodology. *Unit head:* Dr. Donald Halquist, Chairperson, 585-395-5550, Fax: 585-395-2172, E-mail: snovinge@brockport.edu. *Application contact:* Michael Harrison, Coordinator of Certification and Graduate Advisement, 585-395-2326, Fax: 585-395-2172, E-mail: mharriso@brockport.edu. Web site: http://www.brockport.edu/graduate/.

College of Charleston, Graduate School, School of Education, Health, and Human Performance, Program in Languages, Charleston, SC 29424-0001. Offers M Ed. Part-time and evening/weekend programs available. *Faculty:* 1 (woman) full-time, 10 part-time/adjunct (0 women). *Students:* 6 full-time (3 women), 23 part-time (18 women); includes 10 minority (4 Black or African American, non-Hispanic/Latino; 2 Asian, non-Hispanic/Latino; 3 Hispanic/Latino; 1 Two or more races, non-Hispanic/Latino). Average age 30. 10 applicants, 70% accepted, 6 enrolled. In 2011, 8 degrees awarded. *Degree requirements:* For master's, comprehensive exam or portfolio. *Entrance requirements:* For master's, minimum GPA of 2.5. Additional exam requirements/recommendations for international students: Required—TOEFL (minimum score 81 iBT). *Application deadline:* For fall admission, 4/1 for domestic students; for spring admission, 11/1 for domestic students. Application fee: $45. Electronic applications accepted. *Expenses:* Tuition, state resident: full-time $5455; part-time $455 per credit. Tuition, nonresident: full-time $13,917; part-time $1160 per credit. *Financial support:* Fellowships, research assistantships, scholarships/grants, and unspecified assistantships available. Financial award application deadline: 4/1; financial award applicants required to submit FAFSA. *Unit head:* Dr. Robyn Holman, Director, 843-953-5459. *Application contact:* Susan Hallatt, Director of Graduate Admissions, 843-953-5614, Fax: 843-953-1434, E-mail: hallatts@cofc.edu. Web site: http://www.cofc.edu/~medlang/.

The College of William and Mary, School of Education, Program in Curriculum and Instruction, Williamsburg, VA 23187-8795. Offers elementary education (MA Ed); gifted education (MA Ed); math specialist (MA Ed); reading education (MA Ed); secondary education (MA Ed), including English education, mathematics education, modern foreign languages education, science education, social studies education; special education (MA Ed), including collaborating master educator, general curriculum. *Accreditation:* NCATE. Part-time programs available. *Faculty:* 15 full-time (10 women), 39 part-time/adjunct (32 women). *Students:* 80 full-time (69 women), 13 part-time (11 women); includes 11 minority (3 Black or African American, non-Hispanic/Latino; 1 American Indian or Alaska Native, non-Hispanic/Latino; 2 Hispanic/Latino; 5 Two or more races, non-Hispanic/Latino), 1 international. Average age 25. 220 applicants, 56% accepted, 85 enrolled. In 2011, 78 master's awarded. *Degree requirements:* For master's, project. *Entrance requirements:* For master's, GRE or MAT, minimum GPA of 2.5. Additional exam requirements/recommendations for international students: Required—TOEFL. *Application deadline:* For fall admission, 1/15 for domestic and international students; for spring admission, 10/1 for domestic and international students. Application fee: $50. Electronic applications accepted. *Expenses:* Tuition, state resident: full-time $6400; part-time $365 per credit hour. Tuition, nonresident: full-time $19,720; part-time $985 per credit hour. *Required fees:* $4562. *Financial support:* In 2011–12, 53 students received support, including 10 research assistantships with full and partial tuition reimbursements available (averaging $7,000 per year); career-related internships or fieldwork, Federal Work-Study, institutionally sponsored loans, scholarships/grants, and unspecified assistantships also available. Financial award application deadline: 1/15; financial award applicants required to submit FAFSA. *Faculty research:* National Council of Teachers of Mathematics Standards, counseling, self-concept and self-esteem, special education, curriculum development. *Unit head:* Dr. Margie Mason, Area Coordinator, 757-221-2327, E-mail: mmmaso@wm.edu.

Application contact: Dorothy Smith Osborne, Assistant Dean for Admission, 757-221-2317, Fax: 757-221-2293, E-mail: dsosbo@wm.edu. Web site: http://education.wm.edu.

The Colorado College, Education Department, Program in Secondary Education, Colorado Springs, CO 80903-3294. Offers art teaching (K-12) (MAT); English teaching (MAT); foreign language teaching (MAT); mathematics teaching (MAT); music teaching (MAT); science teaching (MAT); social studies teaching (MAT). *Faculty:* 4 full-time (3 women), 6 part-time/adjunct (2 women). *Students:* 11 full-time (7 women); includes 3 minority (1 Asian, non-Hispanic/Latino; 2 Hispanic/Latino). Average age 27. 20 applicants, 85% accepted, 11 enrolled. In 2011, 15 master's awarded. *Degree requirements:* For master's, thesis, internship. *Application deadline:* For fall admission, 12/1 priority date for domestic students, 12/1 for international students. Applications are processed on a rolling basis. Application fee: $50. Electronic applications accepted. *Expenses: Tuition:* Full-time $29,313. *Required fees:* $2000. *Financial support:* In 2011–12, 15 students received support. Career-related internships or fieldwork, institutionally sponsored loans, scholarships/grants, and health care benefits available. Financial award application deadline: 2/15; financial award applicants required to submit FAFSA. *Unit head:* Dr. Mike Taber, Director, 719-389-6026, Fax: 719-389-6473, E-mail: mike.taber@coloradocollege.edu. *Application contact:* Debra Yazulla Mortenson, Education Services Manager, 719-389-6472, Fax: 719-389-6473, E-mail: debra.mortenson@coloradocollege.edu. Web site: http://www.coloradocollege.edu/academics/dept/education/graduate-programs/secondary-mat.dot.

Colorado State University, Graduate School, College of Liberal Arts, Department of Foreign Languages and Literatures, Fort Collins, CO 80523-1774. Offers MA. Part-time programs available. *Faculty:* 14 full-time (6 women). *Students:* 16 full-time (13 women), 6 part-time (5 women); includes 4 minority (1 Asian, non-Hispanic/Latino; 3 Hispanic/Latino), 3 international. Average age 28. 11 applicants, 73% accepted, 2 enrolled. In 2011, 9 master's awarded. *Degree requirements:* For master's, one foreign language, comprehensive exam (for some programs), thesis or paper, competitive exams. *Entrance requirements:* For master's, minimum GPA of 3.0; undergraduate major/proficiency in foreign languages. Additional exam requirements/recommendations for international students: Required—TOEFL (minimum score 550 paper-based; 213 computer-based; 80 iBT). *Application deadline:* For fall admission, 2/15 priority date for domestic students; for spring admission, 7/15 priority date for domestic students. Applications are processed on a rolling basis. Application fee: $50. Electronic applications accepted. *Expenses:* Tuition, state resident: full-time $7992. Tuition, nonresident: full-time $19,592. *Required fees:* $1735; $58 per credit. *Financial support:* In 2011–12, 12 students received support, including 12 teaching assistantships with full tuition reimbursements available (averaging $11,816 per year); fellowships, career-related internships or fieldwork, scholarships/grants, and unspecified assistantships also available. Financial award application deadline: 3/1; financial award applicants required to submit FAFSA. *Faculty research:* French, German, and Hispanic literatures and cultures; video-assisted language learning; computer-assisted language learners; foreign language teaching methodologies; linguistics. *Total annual research expenditures:* $12,259. *Unit head:* Dr. Paola Malpezzi-Price, Chair, 970-491-3838, Fax: 970-491-2822, E-mail: paola.malpezzi_price@colostate.edu. *Application contact:* Debborah Luntsford, Graduate Contact, 970-491-6296, Fax: 970-491-2822, E-mail: debborah.luntsford@colostate.edu. Web site: http://languages.colostate.edu/.

Colorado State University–Pueblo, College of Education, Engineering and Professional Studies, Education Program, Pueblo, CO 81001-4901. Offers art education (M Ed); foreign language education (M Ed); health and physical education (M Ed); instructional technology (M Ed); linguistically diverse education (M Ed); music education (M Ed); special education (M Ed). *Accreditation:* Teacher Education Accreditation Council. Part-time programs available. *Degree requirements:* For master's, portfolio. *Entrance requirements:* For master's, 3 recommendations, teaching license. Additional exam requirements/recommendations for international students: Required—TOEFL (minimum score 500 paper-based; 173 computer-based). Electronic applications accepted. *Faculty research:* Portfolio assessment, math education, science education.

Concordia College, Program in Education, Moorhead, MN 56562. Offers world language instruction (M Ed). *Degree requirements:* For master's, thesis/seminar. *Entrance requirements:* For master's, 2 professional references, 1 personal reference.

Cornell University, Graduate School, Graduate Fields of Arts and Sciences, Field of Linguistics, Ithaca, NY 14853-0001. Offers applied linguistics (MA, PhD); East Asian linguistics (MA, PhD); English linguistics (MA, PhD); general linguistics (MA, PhD); Germanic linguistics (MA, PhD); Indo-European linguistics (MA, PhD); phonetics (MA, PhD); phonological theory (MA, PhD); Romance linguistics (MA, PhD); second language acquisition (MA, PhD); semantics (MA, PhD); Slavic linguistics (MA, PhD); sociolinguistics (MA, PhD); South Asian linguistics (MA, PhD); Southeast Asian linguistics (MA, PhD); syntactic theory (MA, PhD). *Faculty:* 16 full-time (7 women). *Students:* 27 full-time (18 women); includes 2 minority (1 Asian, non-Hispanic/Latino; 1 Hispanic/Latino), 13 international. Average age 29. 100 applicants, 13% accepted, 3 enrolled. In 2011, 3 master's, 3 doctorates awarded. Terminal master's awarded for partial completion of doctoral program. *Degree requirements:* For master's, one foreign language, thesis; for doctorate, one foreign language, comprehensive exam, thesis/dissertation. *Entrance requirements:* For master's and doctorate, GRE General Test, 2 letters of recommendation. Additional exam requirements/recommendations for international students: Required—TOEFL (minimum score 600 paper-based; 250 computer-based; 77 iBT). *Application deadline:* For fall admission, 1/15 for domestic students. Application fee: $95. Electronic applications accepted. *Financial support:* In 2011–12, 14 fellowships with full tuition reimbursements, 2 research assistantships with full tuition reimbursements, 12 teaching assistantships with full tuition reimbursements were awarded; institutionally sponsored loans, scholarships/grants, health care benefits, tuition waivers (full and partial), and unspecified assistantships also available. Financial award applicants required to submit FAFSA. *Faculty research:* Phonology and phonetics, syntax and semantics, historical linguistics, philosophy of language, language acquisition. *Unit head:* Director of Graduate Studies, 607-255-1105. *Application contact:* Graduate Field Assistant, 607-255-1105, E-mail: lingfield@cornell.edu. Web site: http://www.gradschool.cornell.edu/fields.php?id-90&a-2.

Delaware State University, Graduate Programs, Department of English and Foreign Languages, Dover, DE 19901-2277. Offers French (MA); Spanish (MA). *Entrance requirements:* Additional exam requirements/recommendations for international students: Required—TOEFL (minimum score 550 paper-based). Electronic applications accepted.

DePaul University, College of Education, Chicago, IL 60106. Offers bilingual bicultural education (M Ed, MA); counseling (M Ed, MA), including college student development, community counseling, school counseling; curriculum studies (M Ed, MA, Ed D); early childhood education (M Ed, MA); educational leadership (M Ed, MA, Ed D), including administration and supervision (M Ed, MA), physical education (M Ed, MA); middle school mathematics education (MS); reading specialist (M Ed, MA); social and cultural foundations in education (M Ed, MA), including curriculum studies/development (MA); special education (M Ed, MA); teaching and learning (M Ed, MA), including elementary education, secondary education; world languages education (M Ed, MA). Part-time and evening/weekend programs available. *Faculty:* 49 full-time (28 women), 94 part-time/adjunct (60 women). *Students:* 894 full-time (707 women), 473 part-time (361 women); includes 349 minority (159 Black or African American, non-Hispanic/Latino; 3 American Indian or Alaska Native, non-Hispanic/Latino; 45 Asian, non-Hispanic/Latino; 115 Hispanic/Latino; 2 Native Hawaiian or other Pacific Islander, non-Hispanic/Latino; 25 Two or more races, non-Hispanic/Latino), 21 international. Average age 30. 872 applicants, 64% accepted, 325 enrolled. In 2011, 499 master's, 10 doctorates awarded. *Median time to degree:* Of those who began their doctoral program in fall 2003, 32% received their degree in 8 years or less. *Degree requirements:* For master's, thesis/dissertation (for MA); capstone course or paper (for M Ed); for doctorate, thesis/dissertation. *Entrance requirements:* For master's, interview, minimum GPA of 2.75, 2 letters of recommendation, bachelor's degree conferred by accredited college or university; for doctorate, interview, master's degree, writing sample, 3 letters of recommendation. Additional exam requirements/recommendations for international students: Required—TOEFL (minimum score 550 paper-based; 213 computer-based; 80 iBT). *Application deadline:* For fall admission, 8/15 priority date for domestic students; for winter admission, 12/1 priority date for domestic students; for spring admission, 3/1 priority date for domestic students. Applications are processed on a rolling basis. Application fee: $40. Electronic applications accepted. *Financial support:* In 2011–12, 163 students received support, including 15 research assistantships with full tuition reimbursements available (averaging $6,375 per year); career-related internships or fieldwork, Federal Work-Study, scholarships/grants, and unspecified assistantships also available. Support available to part-time students. Financial award application deadline: 12/31; financial award applicants required to submit FAFSA. *Faculty research:* Reflective teaching, children at risk, loss, ethnicity, urban education. *Total annual research expenditures:* $916,310. *Unit head:* Dr. Paul Zionts, Dean, 773-325-7581, Fax: 773-325-7713, E-mail: pzionts@depaul.edu. *Application contact:* Brandon Washington, Enrollment Management Coordinator, 773-325-1152, Fax: 773-325-2270, E-mail: bwashin3@depaul.edu. Web site: http://education.depaul.edu.

Drew University, Caspersen School of Graduate Studies, Program in Education, Madison, NJ 07940-1493. Offers biology (MAT); chemistry (MAT); English (MAT); French (MAT); Italian (MAT); math (MAT); physics (MAT); social studies (MAT); Spanish (MAT); theatre arts (MAT). Part-time programs available. *Entrance requirements:* For master's, transcripts, personal statement, recommendations. Additional exam requirements/recommendations for international students: Required—TOEFL, TWE. *Expenses:* Contact institution.

Duquesne University, School of Education, Department of Instruction and Leadership, Pittsburgh, PA 15282-0001. Offers early level (PreK-4) education (MS Ed); English as a second language (MS Ed); instructional technology (MS Ed, Ed D, Post-Master's Certificate), including business, computer, and information technology (MS Ed), instructional technology; middle level (4-8) education (MS Ed); reading and language arts (MS Ed); secondary education (MS Ed), including biology, chemistry, English, Latin education, K-12, mathematics, physics, social studies. Part-time and evening/weekend programs available. Postbaccalaureate distance learning degree programs offered (minimal on-campus study). *Faculty:* 15 full-time (9 women), 28 part-time/adjunct (15 women). *Students:* 213 full-time (145 women), 47 part-time (38 women); includes 19 minority (9 Black or African American, non-Hispanic/Latino; 5 Asian, non-Hispanic/Latino; 4 Hispanic/Latino; 1 Two or more races, non-Hispanic/Latino), 11 international. Average age 26. 160 applicants, 48% accepted, 53 enrolled. In 2011, 111 degrees awarded. *Degree requirements:* For master's, thesis optional; for doctorate, thesis/dissertation. *Entrance requirements:* For master's, letters of recommendation, letter of intent, interview, bachelor's degree; for doctorate, GRE, letters of recommendation, letter of intent, interview, master's degree; for Post-Master's Certificate, letters of recommendation, letter of intent, interview, bachelor's/master's degree. Additional exam requirements/recommendations for international students: Required—TOEFL (minimum score 550 paper-based; 80 computer-based), IELTS (minimum score 7). *Application deadline:* For fall admission, 9/1 priority date for domestic students; for spring admission, 1/1 priority date for domestic students. Applications are processed on a rolling basis. Application fee: $0. Electronic applications accepted. Application fee is waived when completed online. *Expenses: Tuition:* Full-time $16,596; part-time $922 per credit. *Required fees:* $1584; $88 per credit. Tuition and fees vary according to program. *Financial support:* Research assistantships, teaching assistantships with tuition reimbursements, career-related internships or fieldwork, Federal Work-Study, and institutionally sponsored loans available. Support available to part-time students. *Unit head:* Dr. Jason Margolis, Chair, 412-396-6106, Fax: 412-396-5388, E-mail: margolisj@duq.edu. *Application contact:* Michael Dolinger, Director of Student and Academic Services, 412-396-6647, Fax: 412-396-5585, E-mail: dolingerm@duq.edu.

Eastern Washington University, Graduate Studies, College of Arts, Letters and Education, Department of Modern Languages and Literatures, Cheney, WA 99004-2431. Offers French education (M Ed). *Faculty:* 2 full-time (1 woman). In 2011, 2 master's awarded. *Degree requirements:* For master's, comprehensive exam. *Entrance requirements:* For master's, minimum GPA of 3.0. *Application deadline:* For fall admission, 4/1 priority date for domestic students. Applications are processed on a rolling basis. Application fee: $50. *Financial support:* In 2011–12, teaching assistantships with partial tuition reimbursements (averaging $7,000 per year) were awarded; career-related internships or fieldwork, Federal Work-Study, institutionally sponsored loans, scholarships/grants, health care benefits, tuition waivers (partial), and unspecified assistantships also available. Support available to part-time students. Financial award application deadline: 2/1; financial award applicants required to submit FAFSA. *Unit head:* Dr. Wayne Kraft, Chair, 509-359-2859, Fax: 509-359-7855. *Application contact:* Dr. Florian Preisig, Adviser, 509-359-6001. Web site: http://www.ewu.edu/CALE/Programs/Modern-Languages.xml.

Elms College, Division of Education, Chicopee, MA 01013-2839. Offers early childhood education (MAT); education (M Ed, CAGS); elementary education (MAT); English as a second language (MAT); reading (MAT); secondary education (MAT), including biology education, English education, Spanish education; special education (MAT). Part-time and evening/weekend programs available. *Degree requirements:* For master's, thesis (for some programs). *Entrance requirements:* For master's, Massachusetts Educators Certification Test, minimum GPA of 3.0; for CAGS, master's degree in education. Additional exam requirements/recommendations for international students: Required—TOEFL.

Florida International University, College of Education, Department of Curriculum and Instruction, Miami, FL 33199. Offers art education (MAT, MS, Ed D); curriculum and instruction (Ed S); curriculum development (MS); curriculum studies (PhD); early childhood education (MS, Ed D); elementary education (MS, Ed D); English education (MAT, MS, Ed D); foreign language education - teaching English to speakers of other languages (TESOL) (MS, Certificate), including foreign language education (Certificate), teaching English (MS); French education - initial teacher preparation (MAT); international and intercultural development education (Ed D); international and intercultural developmental education (MS); language, literacy and culture (PhD); learning technologies (MS, Ed D, PhD); mathematics education (MAT, MS, Ed D, PhD); modern language education/bilingual education (MS, Ed D); physical education (MS); reading education (MS, Ed D); science education (MAT, MS, Ed D, PhD); social studies education (MAT, MS, Ed D); Spanish education - initial teacher preparation (MAT);

special education (MS). Part-time and evening/weekend programs available. *Degree requirements:* For doctorate, comprehensive exam, thesis/dissertation. *Entrance requirements:* For master's, GRE General Test, Florida General Knowledge Test or Florida College Level Academic Skills Test; for doctorate and other advanced degree, GRE General Test. Additional exam requirements/recommendations for international students: Required—TOEFL (minimum score 550 paper-based; 213 computer-based; 80 iBT), IELTS (minimum score 6.3). Electronic applications accepted.

Framingham State University, Division of Graduate and Continuing Education, Program in Spanish, Framingham, MA 01701-9101. Offers M Ed.

George Mason University, College of Humanities and Social Sciences, Department of Modern and Classical Languages, Fairfax, VA 22030. Offers foreign languages (MA). *Faculty:* 26 full-time (16 women), 52 part-time/adjunct (39 women). *Students:* 8 full-time (6 women), 27 part-time (22 women); includes 1 minority (Two or more races, non-Hispanic/Latino). Average age 34. 25 applicants, 48% accepted, 5 enrolled. In 2011, 8 degrees awarded. *Degree requirements:* For master's, comprehensive exam, thesis optional. *Entrance requirements:* For master's, 3 letters of recommendation; official transcripts; expanded goals statement; resume; baccalaureate degree in French or Spanish with minimum GPA of 3.0 (recommended). Additional exam requirements/recommendations for international students: Required—TOEFL (minimum score 570 paper-based; 230 computer-based; 88 iBT), IELTS, Pearson Test of English. *Application deadline:* For fall admission, 4/15 priority date for domestic students; for spring admission, 11/1 priority date for domestic students. Application fee: $65 ($80 for international students). Electronic applications accepted. *Expenses:* Tuition, state resident: full-time $8750; part-time $364.58 per credit. Tuition, nonresident: full-time $24,092; part-time $1003.83 per credit. *Required fees:* $2514; $104.75 per credit. *Financial support:* In 2011–12, 7 students received support, including 7 teaching assistantships with full and partial tuition reimbursements available (averaging $10,448 per year); career-related internships or fieldwork, Federal Work-Study, scholarships/grants, unspecified assistantships, and health care benefits (full-time research or teaching assistantship recipients) also available. Support available to part-time students. Financial award application deadline: 3/1; financial award applicants required to submit FAFSA. *Faculty research:* French Renaissance studies, early Modern (sixteenth-eighteenth centuries) literary and cultural studies, history, literature and philosophy, women's studies. *Total annual research expenditures:* $646. *Unit head:* Julie Christensen, Chair, 703-993-1230, Fax: 703-993-1245, E-mail: jchriste@gmu.edu. *Application contact:* Jen Barnard, Information Contact, 703-993-1230, Fax: 703-993-1245, E-mail: jbarnard@gmu.edu. Web site: http://mcl.gmu.edu/.

Georgia Southern University, Jack N. Averitt College of Graduate Studies, College of Education, Department of Teaching and Learning, Program in Spanish Education, Statesboro, GA 30460. Offers MAT. *Accreditation:* NCATE. Part-time and evening/weekend programs available. *Students:* 1 (woman) full-time, 3 part-time (2 women); includes 2 minority (both Black or African American, non-Hispanic/Latino). Average age 25. 1 applicant, 100% accepted, 1 enrolled. In 2011, 6 master's awarded. *Degree requirements:* For master's, portfolio, transition point assessments, exit assessment. *Entrance requirements:* For master's, GRE General Test or MAT; GACE Basic Skills and Content Assessments, minimum cumulative GPA of 2.5. Additional exam requirements/recommendations for international students: Required—TOEFL (minimum score 550 paper-based; 213 computer-based; 80 iBT). *Application deadline:* For fall admission, 3/1 for domestic and international students; for spring admission, 10/1 priority date for domestic students, 10/1 for international students. Applications are processed on a rolling basis. Application fee: $50. Electronic applications accepted. *Expenses:* Tuition, state resident: full-time $6300; part-time $263 per semester hour. Tuition, nonresident: full-time $25,174; part-time $1049 per semester hour. *Required fees:* $1872. *Financial support:* In 2011–12, research assistantships with partial tuition reimbursements (averaging $7,200 per year), teaching assistantships with partial tuition reimbursements (averaging $7,200 per year) were awarded; Federal Work-Study, scholarships/grants, tuition waivers (partial), and unspecified assistantships also available. Support available to part-time students. Financial award application deadline: 4/15; financial award applicants required to submit FAFSA. *Unit head:* Dr. Ronnie Sheppard, Department Chair, 912-478-5203, Fax: 912-478-0026, E-mail: sheppard@georgiasouthern.edu. *Application contact:* Amanda Gilliland, Coordinator for Graduate Student Recruitment, 912-478-5384, Fax: 912-478-0740, E-mail: gradadmissions@georgiasouthern.edu. Web site: http://coe.georgiasouthern.edu/tandl/index.html.

Georgia Southern University, Jack N. Averitt College of Graduate Studies, College of Liberal Arts and Social Sciences, Department of Foreign Languages, Statesboro, GA 30460. Offers Spanish (MA). Part-time and evening/weekend programs available. *Students:* 12 full-time (7 women), 6 part-time (all women); includes 7 minority (6 Hispanic/Latino; 1 Two or more races, non-Hispanic/Latino). Average age 28. 13 applicants, 100% accepted, 7 enrolled. In 2011, 7 master's awarded. *Degree requirements:* For master's, one foreign language, thesis optional. *Entrance requirements:* For master's, GRE, minimum GPA of 3.0, letters of reference. Additional exam requirements/recommendations for international students: Required—TOEFL (minimum score 550 paper-based; 213 computer-based; 80 iBT). *Application deadline:* For fall admission, 3/1 priority date for domestic students, 3/1 for international students; for spring admission, 10/1 priority date for domestic students, 10/1 for international students. Applications are processed on a rolling basis. Application fee: $50. Electronic applications accepted. *Expenses:* Tuition, state resident: full-time $6300; part-time $263 per semester hour. Tuition, nonresident: full-time $25,174; part-time $1049 per semester hour. *Required fees:* $1872. *Financial support:* In 2011–12, 10 students received support, including research assistantships with partial tuition reimbursements available (averaging $7,200 per year), teaching assistantships with partial tuition reimbursements available (averaging $7,200 per year); career-related internships or fieldwork, Federal Work-Study, scholarships/grants, tuition waivers (partial), and unspecified assistantships also available. Support available to part-time students. Financial award application deadline: 4/15; financial award applicants required to submit FAFSA. *Faculty research:* Lettrism, twentieth century France, Spanish medieval studies, Spanish Renaissance studies, Spanish-American colonial period, Mexican studies, Spanish linguistics, foreign language acquisition and education, drama and cinema of Spain and Latin America. *Unit head:* Dr. Eric Kartchner, Chair, 912-478-5281, Fax: 912-478-0652, E-mail: forlangs@georgiasouthern.edu. *Application contact:* Amanda Gilliland, Coordinator for Graduate Student Recruitment, 912-478-5384, Fax: 912-478-0740, E-mail: gradadmissions@georgiasouthern.edu. Web site: http://class.georgiasouthern.edu/fl.

Harding University, College of Education, Searcy, AR 72149-0001. Offers advanced studies in teaching and learning (M Ed); art (MSE); behavioral science (MSE); counseling (MS, Ed S); early childhood special education (M Ed, MSE); education (MSE); educational leadership (M Ed, Ed S); elementary education (M Ed); English (MSE); French (MSE); history/social science (MSE); kinesiology (MSE); math (MSE); reading (M Ed); secondary education (M Ed); Spanish (MSE); teaching (MAT); teaching English as a second language (MSE). *Accreditation:* NCATE. Part-time and evening/weekend programs available. *Faculty:* 9 full-time (2 women), 48 part-time/adjunct (23 women). *Students:* 100 full-time (77 women), 333 part-time (239 women); includes 76 minority (59 Black or African American, non-Hispanic/Latino; 1 Asian, non-Hispanic/Latino; 10 Hispanic/Latino; 6 Two or more races, non-Hispanic/Latino), 2 international. Average age 36. 93 applicants, 91% accepted, 83 enrolled. In 2011, 159 master's, 10 other advanced degrees awarded. *Degree requirements:* For master's, comprehensive exam (for some programs), thesis optional, portfolio(s); for Ed S, comprehensive exam, portfolio, project. *Entrance requirements:* For master's, GRE, MAT, PRAXIS; for Ed S, MAT or GRE. Additional exam requirements/recommendations for international students: Required—TOEFL (minimum score 550 paper-based; 79 iBT). *Application deadline:* For fall admission, 8/1 for domestic and international students; for spring admission, 1/1 for domestic and international students. Applications are processed on a rolling basis. Application fee: $35. *Expenses: Tuition:* Full-time $10,512; part-time $584 per credit hour. *Required fees:* $500; $25 per credit hour. Tuition and fees vary according to course load, degree level and program. *Financial support:* In 2011–12, 37 students received support. Unspecified assistantships available. *Faculty research:* Reading, comprehension, school violence, educational technology, behavior, college choice, differentiated instruction, brain-based teaching. *Unit head:* Dr. Clara Carroll, Chair, 501-279-4501, Fax: 501-279-4083, E-mail: ccarroll@harding.edu. *Application contact:* Information Contact, 501-279-4315, E-mail: gradstudiesedu@harding.edu. Web site: http://www.harding.edu/education/grad.html.

Hofstra University, School of Education, Health, and Human Services, Programs in Teaching (K-12), Hempstead, NY 11549. Offers bilingual education (MA); bilingual extension (Advanced Certificate), including education/speech language pathology, intensive teacher institute; family and consumer science (MS Ed); fine art and music education (Advanced Certificate); fine arts education (MA, MS Ed); mentoring and coaching for teachers (Advanced Certificate); middle childhood extension (Advanced Certificate), including grades 5-6 or 7-9; music education (MA, MS Ed); teaching languages other than English and TESOL (MS Ed); TESOL (MS Ed, Advanced Certificate), including intensive teacher institute (Advanced Certificate), TESOL (Advanced Certificate); wind conducting (MA). Part-time and evening/weekend programs available. *Students:* 54 full-time (48 women), 60 part-time (53 women); includes 30 minority (10 Black or African American, non-Hispanic/Latino; 9 Asian, non-Hispanic/Latino; 11 Hispanic/Latino), 8 international. Average age 29. 109 applicants, 76% accepted, 43 enrolled. In 2011, 71 master's, 42 other advanced degrees awarded. *Degree requirements:* For master's, one foreign language, thesis (for some programs), electronic portfolio, Tk20 portfolios, minimum GPA of 3.0. *Entrance requirements:* For master's, 2 letters of recommendation, portfolio, teacher certification (MA), essay; for Advanced Certificate, 2 letters of recommendation, interview, teaching certificate, essay. Additional exam requirements/recommendations for international students: Required—TOEFL (minimum score 550 paper-based; 213 computer-based; 80 iBT). *Application deadline:* Applications are processed on a rolling basis. Application fee: $70 ($75 for international students). Electronic applications accepted. *Expenses: Tuition:* Full-time $18,990; part-time $1055 per credit hour. *Required fees:* $970. Tuition and fees vary according to program. *Financial support:* In 2011–12, 39 students received support, including 13 fellowships with full and partial tuition reimbursements available (averaging $3,347 per year), 2 research assistantships with full and partial tuition reimbursements available (averaging $7,363 per year); career-related internships or fieldwork, Federal Work-Study, institutionally sponsored loans, scholarships/grants, tuition waivers (full and partial), and unspecified assistantships also available. Support available to part-time students. Financial award applicants required to submit FAFSA. *Faculty research:* The teacher/artist, interdisciplinary curriculum, applied linguistics, structural inequalities, creativity. *Unit head:* Dr. Esther Fusco, Chairperson, 516-463-7704, Fax: 516-463-6196, E-mail: catezf@hofstra.edu. *Application contact:* Carol Drummer, Dean of Graduate Admissions, 516-463-4876, Fax: 516-463-4664, E-mail: gradstudent@hofstra.edu. Web site: http://www.hofstra.edu/education/.

Hofstra University, School of Education, Health, and Human Services, Programs in Teaching - Secondary Education, Hempstead, NY 11549. Offers business education (MS Ed); education technology (Advanced Certificate); English education (MA, MS Ed); foreign language and TESOL (MS Ed); foreign language education (MA, MS Ed), including French, German, Russian, Spanish; mathematics education (MA, MS Ed); science education (MA, MS Ed), including biology, chemistry, earth science, geology, physics; secondary education (Advanced Certificate); social studies education (MA, MS Ed). Part-time and evening/weekend programs available. Postbaccalaureate distance learning degree programs offered (minimal on-campus study). *Students:* 72 full-time (47 women), 51 part-time (30 women); includes 21 minority (9 Black or African American, non-Hispanic/Latino; 7 Asian, non-Hispanic/Latino; 5 Hispanic/Latino). Average age 28. 103 applicants, 91% accepted, 41 enrolled. In 2011, 86 master's, 6 other advanced degrees awarded. *Degree requirements:* For master's, one foreign language, comprehensive exam (for some programs), thesis (for some programs), exit project, electronic portfolio, student teaching, fieldwork, curriculum project, minimum GPA of 3.0; for Advanced Certificate, 3 foreign languages, comprehensive exam (for some programs), thesis project, minimum GPA of 3.0. *Entrance requirements:* For master's, 2 letters of recommendation, teacher certification (MA), essay; for Advanced Certificate, 2 letters of recommendation, essay. Additional exam requirements/recommendations for international students: Required—TOEFL (minimum score 550 paper-based; 213 computer-based; 80 iBT). *Application deadline:* Applications are processed on a rolling basis. Application fee: $70 ($75 for international students). Electronic applications accepted. *Expenses: Tuition:* Full-time $18,990; part-time $1055 per credit hour. *Required fees:* $970. Tuition and fees vary according to program. *Financial support:* In 2011–12, 90 students received support, including 13 fellowships with full and partial tuition reimbursements available (averaging $3,202 per year), 1 research assistantship with full and partial tuition reimbursement available (averaging $11,645 per year); career-related internships or fieldwork, Federal Work-Study, institutionally sponsored loans, scholarships/grants, tuition waivers (full and partial), and unspecified assistantships also available. Support available to part-time students. Financial award applicants required to submit FAFSA. *Faculty research:* Appropriate content and pedagogy in secondary school disciplines, appropriate pedagogy in secondary school disciplines, adolescent development, secondary school organization, alternative secondary school programs. *Unit head:* Dr. Esther Fusco, Chairperson, 516-463-7704, Fax: 516-463-6196, E-mail: catezf@hofstra.edu. *Application contact:* Carol Drummer, Dean of Graduate Admissions, 516-463-4876, Fax: 516-463-4664, E-mail: gradstudent@hofstra.edu. Web site: http://www.hofstra.edu/education/.

Hunter College of the City University of New York, Graduate School, School of Arts and Sciences, Department of Romance Languages, Program in French, New York, NY 10021-5085. Offers French (MA); French education (MA). Part-time and evening/weekend programs available. *Faculty:* 7 full-time (5 women). *Students:* 1 (woman) full-time, 9 part-time (6 women); includes 5 minority (2 Black or African American, non-Hispanic/Latino; 3 Hispanic/Latino). Average age 29. 7 applicants, 86% accepted, 5 enrolled. In 2011, 2 master's awarded. *Degree requirements:* For master's, 2 foreign languages, comprehensive exam, thesis optional. *Entrance requirements:* For master's, GRE General Test, GRE Subject Test, ability to read, speak, and write French; interview. Additional exam requirements/recommendations for international students: Required—TOEFL. *Application deadline:* For fall admission, 4/1 for domestic students, 2/1 for international students; for spring admission, 11/1 for domestic students, 9/1 for international students. Application fee: $125. *Expenses:* Tuition, state resident: full-time $8210; part-time $345 per credit. Tuition, nonresident: full-time $15,360; part-time $640 per credit. *Required fees:* $280 per semester. One-time fee: $125. Tuition and fees vary according to class time, campus/location and program. *Financial support:* Fellowships, Federal Work-Study, scholarships/grants, and tuition waivers (partial) available. Support available to part-time students. Financial award application deadline: 4/15. *Faculty research:* Contemporary French theater, Villiers-dell Isle-Adam, Voltaire, medieval folklore, fin-de-siécle. *Unit head:* Prof. Marlene Barloum, Graduate Advisor, 212-650-3511, E-mail: mbarloum@hunter.cuny.edu. *Application contact:* William Zlata, Director for Graduate Admissions, 212-772-4482, Fax: 212-650-3336, E-mail: admissions@hunter.cuny.edu. Web site: http://www.hunter.cuny.edu/romancelanguages/graduate/ma-requirements.

Hunter College of the City University of New York, Graduate School, School of Arts and Sciences, Department of Romance Languages, Program in Italian, New York, NY 10021-5085. Offers Italian (MA); Italian education (MA). *Faculty:* 2 full-time (1 woman). *Students:* 5 part-time (3 women), 1 international. Average age 28. 3 applicants, 33% accepted, 0 enrolled. In 2011, 2 master's awarded. *Degree requirements:* For master's, 2 foreign languages, comprehensive exam, thesis optional. *Entrance requirements:* For master's, GRE General Test, GRE Subject Test, ability to read, speak, and write Italian; interview. Additional exam requirements/recommendations for international students: Required—TOEFL. *Application deadline:* For fall admission, 4/1 for domestic students, 2/1 for international students; for spring admission, 11/1 for domestic students, 9/1 for international students. Application fee: $125. *Expenses:* Tuition, state resident: full-time $8210; part-time $345 per credit. Tuition, nonresident: full-time $15,360; part-time $640 per credit. *Required fees:* $280 per semester. One-time fee: $125. Tuition and fees vary according to class time, campus/location and program. *Financial support:* Federal Work-Study, scholarships/grants, and tuition waivers (partial) available. Support available to part-time students. Financial award application deadline: 4/15. *Faculty research:* Dante, Middle Ages, Renaissance, contemporary Italian novel and poetry, late Renaissance and Baroque. *Unit head:* Dr. Paolo Fasoli, Graduate Co-Adviser, 212-772-5129, Fax: 212-772-5094, E-mail: pfasoli@hunter.cuny.edu. *Application contact:* William Zlata, Director for Graduate Admissions, 212-772-4482, Fax: 212-650-3336, E-mail: admissions@hunter.cuny.edu. Web site: http://www.hunter.cuny.edu/romancelanguages/graduate/ma-requirements.

Hunter College of the City University of New York, Graduate School, School of Arts and Sciences, Department of Romance Languages, Program in Spanish, New York, NY 10021-5085. Offers Spanish (MA); Spanish education (MA). Part-time and evening/weekend programs available. *Faculty:* 7 full-time (5 women). *Students:* 19 part-time (15 women); includes 13 minority (all Hispanic/Latino), 3 international. Average age 40. 11 applicants, 64% accepted, 2 enrolled. In 2011, 4 master's awarded. *Degree requirements:* For master's, 2 foreign languages, comprehensive exam, thesis optional. *Entrance requirements:* For master's, GRE General Test, GRE Subject Test, ability to read, speak, and write Spanish; interview. Additional exam requirements/recommendations for international students: Required—TOEFL. *Application deadline:* For fall admission, 4/1 for domestic students, 2/1 for international students; for spring admission, 11/1 for domestic students, 9/1 for international students. Application fee: $125. *Expenses:* Tuition, state resident: full-time $8210; part-time $345 per credit. Tuition, nonresident: full-time $15,360; part-time $640 per credit. *Required fees:* $280 per semester. One-time fee: $125. Tuition and fees vary according to class time, campus/location and program. *Financial support:* Federal Work-Study and tuition waivers (partial) available. Support available to part-time students. Financial award application deadline: 4/15. *Faculty research:* Galician studies, contemporary Spanish poetry, Lope de Vega, comparative Hispanic literatures, contemporary Hispanic poetry. *Unit head:* Dr. James O. Pellier, Graduate Advisor, 212-772-5625, E-mail: jpellice@hunter.cuny.edu. *Application contact:* William Zlata, Director for Graduate Admissions, 212-772-4482, Fax: 212-650-3336, E-mail: admissions@hunter.cuny.edu. Web site: http://www.hunter.cuny.edu/romancelanguages/graduate/ma-requirements.

Hunter College of the City University of New York, Graduate School, School of Education, Programs in Secondary Education, Concentration in French Education, New York, NY 10021-5085. Offers MA. *Accreditation:* NCATE. *Faculty:* 4 full-time (all women), 4 part-time/adjunct (3 women). *Students:* 5 part-time (all women); includes 2 minority (1 Black or African American, non-Hispanic/Latino; 1 Hispanic/Latino). Average age 30. 8 applicants, 25% accepted, 2 enrolled. In 2011, 3 master's awarded. *Degree requirements:* For master's, thesis, professional teaching portfolio, New York State Teacher Certification Exam. *Entrance requirements:* For master's, 24 credits in French; minimum GPA of 3.0 in French, 2.8 overall; 2 letters of reference; interview. Additional exam requirements/recommendations for international students: Required—TOEFL, TWE. *Application deadline:* For fall admission, 4/1 for domestic students, 2/1 for international students; for spring admission, 11/1 for domestic students, 9/1 for international students. Applications are processed on a rolling basis. Application fee: $125. *Expenses:* Tuition, state resident: full-time $8210; part-time $345 per credit. Tuition, nonresident: full-time $15,360; part-time $640 per credit. *Required fees:* $280 per semester. One-time fee: $125. Tuition and fees vary according to class time, campus/location and program. *Financial support:* Federal Work-Study and tuition waivers (partial) available. Support available to part-time students. *Unit head:* Dr. Jenny M. Castillo, Graduate Advisor, 212-772-4614, E-mail: jmcastil@hunter.cuny.edu. *Application contact:* William Zlata, Director for Graduate Admissions, 212-772-4482, Fax: 212-650-3336, E-mail: admissions@hunter.cuny.edu. Web site: http://www.hunter.cuny.edu/school-of-education/programs/graduate/adolescent/foreign-languages/french.

Hunter College of the City University of New York, Graduate School, School of Education, Programs in Secondary Education, Concentration in Italian Education, New York, NY 10021-5085. Offers MA. *Accreditation:* NCATE. *Students:* 6 part-time (4 women), 1 international. Average age 29. 1 applicant, 0% accepted, 0 enrolled. In 2011, 2 master's awarded. *Degree requirements:* For master's, thesis, professional teaching portfolio, New York State Teacher Certification Exam, research project. *Entrance requirements:* For master's, minimum GPA of 3.0 in Italian, 2.8 overall; 24 credits of course work in Italian; 2 letters of reference; interview. Additional exam requirements/recommendations for international students: Required—TOEFL, TWE. *Application deadline:* For fall admission, 4/1 for domestic students, 2/1 for international students; for spring admission, 11/1 for domestic students, 9/1 for international students. Applications are processed on a rolling basis. Application fee: $125. *Expenses:* Tuition, state resident: full-time $8210; part-time $345 per credit. Tuition, nonresident: full-time $15,360; part-time $640 per credit. *Required fees:* $280 per semester. One-time fee: $125. Tuition and fees vary according to class time, campus/location and program. *Financial support:* Federal Work-Study and tuition waivers (partial) available. Support available to part-time students. *Unit head:* Dr. Paolo Fasoli, Chair, 212-772-5129, Fax: 212-772-5094, E-mail: pfasoli@hunter.cuny.edu. *Application contact:* William Zlata, Director for Graduate Admissions, 212-772-4482, Fax: 212-650-3336, E-mail: admissions@hunter.cuny.edu. Web site: http://www.hunter.cuny.edu/school-of-education/programs/graduate/adolescent/foreign-languages/italian.

Hunter College of the City University of New York, Graduate School, School of Education, Programs in Secondary Education, Concentration in Spanish Education, New York, NY 10021-5085. Offers MA. *Accreditation:* NCATE. *Students:* 15 part-time (14 women); includes 12 minority (2 Black or African American, non-Hispanic/Latino; 10 Hispanic/Latino), 1 international. Average age 29. 6 applicants, 33% accepted, 1 enrolled. In 2011, 16 master's awarded. *Degree requirements:* For master's, thesis, professional teaching portfolio, New York State Teacher Certification Exam. *Entrance requirements:* For master's, minimum GPA of 3.0 in Spanish, 2.8 overall; 24 credits of course work in Spanish; 2 letters of reference; interview. Additional exam requirements/recommendations for international students: Required—TOEFL, TWE. *Application deadline:* For fall admission, 4/1 for domestic students, 2/1 for international students; for spring admission, 11/1 for domestic students, 9/1 for international students. Applications are processed on a rolling basis. Application fee: $125. *Expenses:* Tuition, state resident: full-time $8210; part-time $345 per credit. Tuition, nonresident: full-time $15,360; part-time $640 per credit. *Required fees:* $280 per semester. One-time fee: $125. Tuition and fees vary according to class time, campus/location and program. *Financial support:* Federal Work-Study and tuition waivers (partial) available. Support available to part-time students. *Unit head:* Dr. Magdalena Perkowska, Romance Language Advisor (Spanish), 212-772-5132, E-mail: mperkowsk@hunter.cuny.edu. *Application contact:* William Zlata, Director for Graduate Admissions, 212-772-4482, Fax: 212-650-3336, E-mail: admissions@hunter.cuny.edu. Web site: http://www.hunter.cuny.edu/school-of-education/programs/graduate/bilingual.

Indiana University Bloomington, University Graduate School, College of Arts and Sciences, Department of East Asian Languages and Cultures, Bloomington, IN 47408. Offers Chinese (MA, PhD); Chinese - flagship track (MA); Chinese language pedagogy (MA); East Asian studies (MA); Japanese (MA, PhD); Japanese language pedagogy (MA). Part-time programs available. *Faculty:* 18 full-time (9 women), 12 part-time/adjunct (6 women). *Students:* 29 full-time (14 women), 8 part-time (5 women); includes 2 minority (both Black or African American, non-Hispanic/Latino), 7 international. Average age 29. 98 applicants, 31% accepted, 7 enrolled. In 2011, 8 master's, 1 doctorate awarded. *Degree requirements:* For master's, one foreign language, thesis; for doctorate, 2 foreign languages, comprehensive exam, thesis/dissertation. *Entrance requirements:* Additional exam requirements/recommendations for international students: Required—TOEFL (minimum score 93 iBT). *Application deadline:* For fall admission, 1/15 for domestic students, 12/1 for international students. Application fee: $55 ($65 for international students). Electronic applications accepted. *Financial support:* In 2011–12, 21 students received support, including 5 fellowships with full tuition reimbursements available (averaging $15,000 per year), 18 teaching assistantships with full tuition reimbursements available (averaging $13,400 per year). Financial award application deadline: 3/1. *Faculty research:* Postwar/postmodern Japanese fiction, modern Chinese film and literature, classical Chinese literature and philosophy, Chinese and Japanese linguistics and pedagogy, East Asian politics and economics, Chinese and Japanese history, Korean language. *Unit head:* Natsuko Tsujimura, Chair, 812-855-0856, Fax: 812-855-6402, E-mail: tsujimur@indiana.edu. *Application contact:* Scott O'Bryan, Director of Graduate Studies, 812-855-2454, Fax: 812-855-6402, E-mail: spobryan@indiana.edu. Web site: http://www.indiana.edu/~ealc/index.shtml.

Indiana University Bloomington, University Graduate School, College of Arts and Sciences, Department of French and Italian, Bloomington, IN 47405-7000. Offers French (MA, PhD), including French instruction (MA), French linguistics, French literature; Italian (MA, PhD). Part-time programs available. *Faculty:* 23 full-time. *Students:* 79 full-time (51 women); includes 5 minority (3 Black or African American, non-Hispanic/Latino; 2 Hispanic/Latino), 20 international. Average age 30. 46 applicants, 87% accepted, 12 enrolled. In 2011, 7 master's, 4 doctorates awarded. Terminal master's awarded for partial completion of doctoral program. *Degree requirements:* For master's, one foreign language, comprehensive exam, thesis optional; for doctorate, 2 foreign languages, comprehensive exam, thesis/dissertation. *Entrance requirements:* For master's and doctorate, GRE General Test. Additional exam requirements/recommendations for international students: Required—TOEFL (minimum score 550 paper-based; 213 computer-based; 79 iBT). *Application deadline:* For fall admission, 1/15 priority date for domestic students, 12/1 for international students; for spring admission, 9/15 priority date for domestic students, 9/1 for international students. Application fee: $55 ($65 for international students). Electronic applications accepted. *Financial support:* In 2011–12, 2 fellowships with partial tuition reimbursements (averaging $15,000 per year), 5 research assistantships with partial tuition reimbursements (averaging $13,611 per year), 40 teaching assistantships with partial tuition reimbursements (averaging $13,611 per year) were awarded. Financial award application deadline: 1/15. *Faculty research:* All periods of French and Italian literature and various areas of French linguistics, including the novel and political theory, literature and fine arts, literary theory, postcolonialism, French-Creole studies, French literature of Africa and its Diaspora, humanism, medieval folklore and mythology, humor in medieval and Renaissance literature, cinema Old Occitan and Old French, emigration, second language acquisition, syntax, sociolinguistics, phonology, lexicography. *Unit head:* Prof. Andrea Ciccarelli, Chair, 812-855-5458, Fax: 812-855-8877, E-mail: fritchr@indiana.edu. *Application contact:* Valerie Puiatti, Graduate Secretary, 812-855-1088, Fax: 812-855-8877, E-mail: fritgs@indiana.edu. Web site: http://www.indiana.edu/~frithome/.

Indiana University Bloomington, University Graduate School, College of Arts and Sciences, Department of Germanic Studies, Bloomington, IN 47405-7000. Offers German philology and linguistics (PhD); German studies (MA, PhD), including German (MA), German literature and culture (MA), German literature and linguistics (MA); medieval German studies (PhD); teaching German (MAT). *Faculty:* 13 full-time (4 women), 6 part-time/adjunct (2 women). *Students:* 31 full-time (18 women); includes 1 minority (Asian, non-Hispanic/Latino), 9 international. Average age 31. 35 applicants, 34% accepted, 4 enrolled. In 2011, 5 master's, 3 doctorates awarded. Terminal master's awarded for partial completion of doctoral program. *Degree requirements:* For master's, one foreign language, project; for doctorate, one foreign language, comprehensive exam, thesis/dissertation. *Entrance requirements:* For master's, GRE General Test, BA in German or equivalent; for doctorate, GRE General Test, MA in German or equivalent. Additional exam requirements/recommendations for international students: Required—TOEFL. *Application deadline:* For fall admission, 1/15 priority date for domestic students, 12/15 for international students; for spring admission, 9/1 priority date for domestic students, 9/1 for international students. Applications are processed on a rolling basis. Application fee: $55 ($65 for international students). *Financial support:* In 2011–12, fellowships with full and partial tuition reimbursements (averaging $16,000 per year), teaching assistantships with full tuition reimbursements (averaging $13,455 per year) were awarded; research assistantships, Federal Work-Study, institutionally sponsored loans, scholarships/grants, and unspecified assistantships also available. Support available to part-time students. Financial award application deadline: 1/15; financial award applicants required to submit FAFSA. *Faculty research:* German and other European literature: medieval to modern/postmodern, German and culture studies, Germanic philology, literary theory, literature and the other arts. *Unit head:* William Rasch, Department Chairman, 812-855-7947, Fax: 812-855-8292, E-mail: wrasch@indiana.edu. *Application contact:* Michelle Dunbar, Graduate Secretary, 812-855-7947, E-mail: midunbar@indiana.edu. Web site: http://www.indiana.edu/~germanic/.

Indiana University–Purdue University Indianapolis, School of Education, Indianapolis, IN 46202-2896. Offers computer education (Certificate); curriculum and instruction (MS); early childhood (MS); educational leadership (MS, Certificate); English as a second language (Certificate); higher education and student affairs (MS);

kindergarten (Certificate); language education (MS); reading (Certificate); school counseling (MS); special education (MS, Certificate). Part-time and evening/weekend programs available. *Faculty:* 41 full-time, 80 part-time/adjunct. *Students:* 67 full-time (52 women), 467 part-time (360 women); includes 82 minority (44 Black or African American, non-Hispanic/Latino; 3 American Indian or Alaska Native, non-Hispanic/Latino; 8 Asian, non-Hispanic/Latino; 13 Hispanic/Latino; 14 Two or more races, non-Hispanic/Latino), 10 international. Average age 33. 63 applicants, 57% accepted, 29 enrolled. In 2011, 167 master's awarded. *Degree requirements:* For master's, thesis optional. *Entrance requirements:* For master's, GRE General Test, minimum GPA of 3.0. Additional exam requirements/recommendations for international students: Required—TOEFL. *Application deadline:* For fall admission, 5/1 priority date for domestic students; for spring admission, 11/1 for domestic students. Application fee: $55 ($65 for international students). *Financial support:* Fellowships, research assistantships with partial tuition reimbursements, teaching assistantships, Federal Work-Study, institutionally sponsored loans, scholarships/grants, and tuition waivers (partial) available. Support available to part-time students. *Faculty research:* Teachers in the process of change, learning cycles, children's concepts of science. *Total annual research expenditures:* $614,458. *Unit head:* Dr. Chris Leland, Interim Executive Associate Dean, 317-274-6801, Fax: 317-274-6864. *Application contact:* Sarah Brandenburg, Graduate Advisor, 317-274-6801, Fax: 317-274-6864, E-mail: edugrad@iupui.edu. Web site: http://education.iupui.edu/.

Inter American University of Puerto Rico, Arecibo Campus, Programs in Education, Arecibo, PR 00614-4050. Offers administration and educational supervision (MA Ed); counseling and guidance (MA Ed); curriculum and teaching (MA Ed), including biology education, English as a second language, history education, math education, Spanish; elementary education (MA Ed). *Degree requirements:* For master's, comprehensive exam, thesis optional. *Entrance requirements:* For master's, GRE, EXADEP, bachelor's degree in education or teaching license (administration and supervision) or courses in education and psychology (counseling and guidance), minimum GPA of 2.5 in last 60 credits.

Inter American University of Puerto Rico, Barranquitas Campus, Program in Education, Barranquitas, PR 00794. Offers curriculum and teaching (M Ed), including biology education, English as a second language, history education, mathematics education, Spanish; educational leadership and management (MA); elementary education (M Ed); information and library service technology (M Ed); special education (MA). *Degree requirements:* For master's, comprehensive exam, thesis optional. *Entrance requirements:* For master's, EXADEP, letter of recommendation. Electronic applications accepted.

Inter American University of Puerto Rico, Metropolitan Campus, Graduate Programs, Program in Spanish Education, San Juan, PR 00919-1293. Offers MA.

Iona College, School of Arts and Science, Program in Education, New Rochelle, NY 10801-1890. Offers adolescence education: biology (MS Ed, MST); adolescence education: English (MS Ed, MST); adolescence education: Italian (MS Ed, MST); adolescence education: mathematics (MS Ed, MST); adolescence education: social studies (MS Ed, MST); adolescence education: Spanish (MS Ed, MST); adolescence special education 5-12 (MST); adolescence special education/literacy 5-12 (MS Ed); childhood 1-6/special education 1-6 (MST); childhood education (MST); early childhood/childhood (MST); educational leadership (MS Ed); literacy birth-grade 6/special education 1-6 (MS Ed); literacy education: birth-grade 6 (MS Ed). *Accreditation:* NCATE. Part-time and evening/weekend programs available. *Faculty:* 21 full-time (13 women), 13 part-time/adjunct (8 women). *Students:* 59 full-time (45 women), 101 part-time (78 women); includes 11 minority (2 Black or African American, non-Hispanic/Latino; 2 Asian, non-Hispanic/Latino; 7 Hispanic/Latino). Average age 26. 74 applicants, 66% accepted, 35 enrolled. In 2011, 46 master's awarded. *Degree requirements:* For master's, thesis or alternative. *Entrance requirements:* For master's, minimum GPA of 2.5 (MST), New York teaching certificate (MS Ed). Additional exam requirements/recommendations for international students: Required—TOEFL (minimum score 550 paper-based; 213 computer-based). *Application deadline:* Applications are processed on a rolling basis. Application fee: $50. Electronic applications accepted. *Expenses: Tuition:* Part-time $872 per credit. *Required fees:* $225 per term. *Financial support:* Unspecified assistantships available. Support available to part-time students. Financial award application deadline: 4/15; financial award applicants required to submit FAFSA. *Faculty research:* Reading/writing, educational technology, administration, early literacy assessment, literacy development. *Unit head:* Dr. Catherine O'Callaghan, Chair, 914-633-2210, Fax: 914-633-2608, E-mail: cocallaghan@iona.edu. *Application contact:* Dr. Jeanne Zaino, Interim Dean, School of Arts and Science, 914-633-2112, Fax: 914-633-2023, E-mail: jzaino@iona.edu.

Iona College, School of Arts and Science, Program in Foreign Languages, New Rochelle, NY 10801-1890. Offers Italian (MA); Spanish (MA). Part-time and evening/weekend programs available. *Faculty:* 5 full-time (2 women). *Students:* 11 part-time (all women); includes 2 minority (both Hispanic/Latino). Average age 34. In 2011, 2 master's awarded. *Degree requirements:* For master's, thesis or alternative. *Entrance requirements:* For master's, minimum GPA of 3.0. Additional exam requirements/recommendations for international students: Required—TOEFL (minimum score 550 paper-based; 213 computer-based). *Application deadline:* Applications are processed on a rolling basis. Application fee: $50. Electronic applications accepted. *Expenses: Tuition:* Part-time $872 per credit. *Required fees:* $225 per term. *Financial support:* Unspecified assistantships available. Support available to part-time students. Financial award application deadline: 4/15; financial award applicants required to submit FAFSA. *Faculty research:* Contemporary Spanish literature, linguistics, language acquisition, female Hispanic literature, Latina authors. *Unit head:* Dr. Victoria E. Ketz, Chair, 914-637-2738, E-mail: vketz@iona.edu. *Application contact:* Dr. Jeanne Zaino, Interim Dean, School of Arts and Science, 914-633-2112, Fax: 914-633-2023, E-mail: jzaino@iona.edu.

Ithaca College, Division of Graduate and Professional Studies, School of Humanities and Sciences, Program in Adolescence Education, Ithaca, NY 14850. Offers biology 7-12 (MAT); chemistry 7-12 (MAT); English 7-12 (MAT); French 7-12 (MAT); math 7-12 (MAT); physics 7-12 (MAT); social studies 7-12 (MAT); Spanish (MAT). Part-time programs available. *Faculty:* 23 full-time (7 women). *Students:* 14 full-time (8 women), 1 part-time (0 women); includes 4 minority (1 Asian, non-Hispanic/Latino; 2 Hispanic/Latino; 1 Two or more races, non-Hispanic/Latino). Average age 27. 33 applicants, 64% accepted, 15 enrolled. In 2011, 15 master's awarded. *Degree requirements:* For master's, thesis or alternative, student teaching. *Entrance requirements:* For master's, minimum GPA of 3.0. Additional exam requirements/recommendations for international students: Required—TOEFL (minimum score 550 paper-based; 213 computer-based; 80 iBT). *Application deadline:* For fall admission, 2/15 priority date for domestic students, 2/15 for international students; for spring admission, 12/1 for domestic and international students. Applications are processed on a rolling basis. Application fee: $40. Electronic applications accepted. *Expenses:* Contact institution. *Financial support:* In 2011–12, 9 students received support, including 9 teaching assistantships (averaging $6,070 per year); career-related internships or fieldwork, Federal Work-Study, scholarships/grants, and unspecified assistantships also available. Support available to part-time students. Financial award application deadline: 2/15; financial award applicants required to submit CSS PROFILE or FAFSA. *Faculty research:* Bilingual education, socio-linguistic perspective on literacy. *Unit head:* Dr. Linda Hanrahan, Chairperson, 607-274-3143, Fax: 607-274-1263, E-mail: gps@ithaca.edu. *Application contact:* Gerard Turbide, Director, Office of Admission, 607-274-3143, Fax: 607-274-1263, E-mail: gps@ithaca.edu. Web site: http://www.ithaca.edu/gps/gradprograms/overview/school/hs/aded.

The Johns Hopkins University, School of Education, Department of Teacher Preparation, Baltimore, MD 21218. Offers early childhood education (MAT); education (MS), including educational studies; elementary education (MAT); English for speakers of other languages (MAT); K-8 mathematics lead-teacher (Certificate); K-8 science lead-teacher (Certificate); secondary education (MAT), including biology, chemistry, earth/space/environmental science, English, French, mathematics, physics, social studies, Spanish. Part-time and evening/weekend programs available. *Degree requirements:* For master's, portfolio, PRAXIS II, internship. *Entrance requirements:* For master's, PRAXIS I, SAT, ACT, or GRE (MAT), minimum undergraduate GPA of 3.0, interview, 1 letter of recommendation, curriculum vitae/resume; for Certificate, bachelor's degree, minimum undergraduate GPA of 3.0, essay/statement of goals, interview. Additional exam requirements/recommendations for international students: Required—TOEFL (minimum score 600 paper-based; 250 computer-based; 100 iBT). Electronic applications accepted. *Faculty research:* Teacher retention, STEM education reform, alternative certification programs, school-university partnerships, urban education, action research/data-informed instruction, family engagement.

Kean University, College of Education, Program in Instruction and Curriculum, Union, NJ 07083. Offers bilingual (MA); classroom instruction (MA); mathematics/science/computer education (MA); teaching (MA); teaching English as a second language (MA); teaching physics (MA); world languages (Spanish) (MA). *Accreditation:* NCATE. *Faculty:* 22 full-time (12 women). *Students:* 56 full-time (33 women), 139 part-time (103 women); includes 87 minority (27 Black or African American, non-Hispanic/Latino; 8 Asian, non-Hispanic/Latino; 52 Hispanic/Latino), 1 international. Average age 34. 85 applicants, 100% accepted, 72 enrolled. In 2011, 78 master's awarded. *Degree requirements:* For master's, comprehensive exam, two-semester advanced seminar. *Entrance requirements:* For master's, GRE General Test or MAT, PRAXIS, minimum GPA of 3.0, 2 letters of recommendation, interview, teacher certification (for some programs), transcripts, resume. Additional exam requirements/recommendations for international students: Required—TOEFL (minimum score 79 iBT). *Application deadline:* For fall admission, 6/1 for domestic and international students; for spring admission, 12/1 for domestic and international students. Applications are processed on a rolling basis. Application fee: $75 ($150 for international students). Electronic applications accepted. *Expenses:* Tuition, state resident: full-time $11,302; part-time $550 per credit. Tuition, nonresident: full-time $15,318; part-time $674 per credit. *Required fees:* $2849; $130 per credit. Tuition and fees vary according to degree level. *Financial support:* In 2011–12, 3 research assistantships with full tuition reimbursements (averaging $3,263 per year) were awarded; unspecified assistantships also available. Financial award applicants required to submit FAFSA. *Unit head:* Dr. Thomas Walsh, Program Coordinator, 908-737-4003, E-mail: tpwalsh@kean.edu. *Application contact:* Ann-Marie Kay, Assistant Director for Graduate Admissions, 908-737-5922, Fax: 908-737-5925, E-mail: akay@kean.edu. Web site: http://www.kean.edu/KU/Bilingual-Bicultural-Education-Instruction-and-Curriculum.

Kent State University, College of Arts and Sciences, Department of Modern and Classical Language Studies, Kent, OH 44242-0001. Offers French literature (MA); French, Spanish, German and Latin pedagogy (MA); German literature (MA); Spanish literature (MA); translation (MA), including French, German, Japanese, Russian, Spanish; translation studies (PhD). Part-time and evening/weekend programs available. *Degree requirements:* For master's, one foreign language, comprehensive exam (for some programs), thesis (for some programs); for doctorate, comprehensive exam, thesis/dissertation (for some programs). *Entrance requirements:* For master's, minimum GPA of 3.0, writing sample, audio tape or CD; for doctorate, 3 recommendations. Additional exam requirements/recommendations for international students: Required—TOEFL (minimum score 197 computer-based). Electronic applications accepted. *Expenses:* Tuition, state resident: full-time $8136; part-time $452 per credit hour. Tuition, nonresident: full-time $14,292; part-time $794 per credit hour. *Faculty research:* Literature, pedagogy, applied linguistics, translation studies.

Long Island University–C. W. Post Campus, College of Liberal Arts and Sciences, Department of Foreign Languages, Brookville, NY 11548-1300. Offers Spanish (MA); Spanish education (MS). Part-time programs available. *Degree requirements:* For master's, 2 foreign languages, comprehensive exam, thesis or alternative. *Entrance requirements:* For master's, 24 credits of undergraduate course work in Spanish. Electronic applications accepted. *Faculty research:* Making of a superhero, dialogue in the 19th century novel, nicknames, Menendez Pidal and Spanish School of Philology, women writers of Latin America.

Long Island University–C. W. Post Campus, School of Education, Department of Curriculum and Instruction, Brookville, NY 11548-1300. Offers adolescence education (MS); adolescence education: biology (MS); adolescence education: earth science (MS); adolescence education: English (MS); adolescence education: mathematics (MS); adolescence education: social studies (MS); adolescence education: Spanish (MS); art education (MS); bilingual education (MS); childhood education (MS); early childhood education (MS); middle childhood education (MS); music education (MS); teaching English to speakers of other languages (MS). Part-time and evening/weekend programs available. *Degree requirements:* For master's, comprehensive exam or thesis, student teaching. *Entrance requirements:* For master's, minimum GPA of 2.75 in major, 2.5 overall. Electronic applications accepted. *Faculty research:* Ethics and education, teaching strategies.

Louisiana Tech University, Graduate School, College of Education, Department of Curriculum, Instruction and Leadership, Ruston, LA 71272. Offers curriculum and instruction (MS, Ed D); educational leadership (Ed D); secondary education (M Ed); including business education, English education, foreign language education, health and physical education, mathematics education, science education, social studies education, speech education. *Accreditation:* NCATE. Part-time programs available. *Degree requirements:* For doctorate, thesis/dissertation. *Entrance requirements:* For master's and doctorate, GRE General Test.

Manhattanville College, Graduate Studies, School of Education, Program in Middle Childhood/Adolescence Education (Grades 5-12), Purchase, NY 10577-2132. Offers biology (MAT); biology and special education (MPS); chemistry (MAT); chemistry and special education (MPS); English (MAT); English and special education (MPS); literacy (MPS), including reading and writing, writing; literacy and special education (MPS); math (MAT); math and special education (MPS); second language (MAT), including French, Italian, Latin, Spanish; social studies (MAT); social studies and special education (MPS); special education (MPS). Part-time and evening/weekend programs available. *Degree requirements:* For master's, comprehensive exam or research project, field experience. *Entrance requirements:* For master's, minimum undergraduate GPA of 3.0, 2 letters of recommendation. Additional exam requirements/recommendations for international students: Required—TOEFL. Electronic applications accepted.

Foreign Languages Education

Marquette University, Graduate School, College of Arts and Sciences, Department of Foreign Languages and Literatures, Milwaukee, WI 53201-1881. Offers Spanish (MA). Part-time and evening/weekend programs available. *Faculty:* 37 full-time (24 women), 5 part-time/adjunct (4 women). *Students:* 8 full-time (6 women), 4 part-time (all women); includes 4 minority (all Hispanic/Latino), 1 international. Average age 30. 9 applicants, 100% accepted, 2 enrolled. In 2011, 6 master's awarded. *Degree requirements:* For master's, one foreign language, comprehensive exam. *Entrance requirements:* For master's, official transcripts from all current and previous colleges/universities except Marquette, three letters of recommendation, tape recording of foreign speaking voice. Additional exam requirements/recommendations for international students: Required—TOEFL (minimum score 530 paper-based; 78 computer-based). *Application deadline:* For fall admission, 12/15 for domestic and international students. Application fee: $50. Electronic applications accepted. *Expenses: Tuition:* Full-time $17,010; part-time $945 per credit hour. Tuition and fees vary according to program. *Financial support:* In 2011–12, 11 students received support, including 8 teaching assistantships with full tuition reimbursements available (averaging $13,285 per year); fellowships, institutionally sponsored loans, scholarships/grants, health care benefits, tuition waivers (full and partial), and unspecified assistantships also available. Support available to part-time students. Financial award application deadline: 2/15. *Faculty research:* Latin American literature, Afro-Hispanic literature, descriptive Spanish linguistics, inter-American studies, foreign language education. *Total annual research expenditures:* $1,061. *Unit head:* Dr. John Pustejovsky, Chair, 414-288-7063, Fax: 414-288-1578. *Application contact:* Dr. Armando Gonzales-Percz, Director of Graduate Studies, 414-288-7268, Fax: 414-288-1578. Web site: http://www.marquette.edu/fola/grad_director_intro.shtml.

McGill University, Faculty of Graduate and Postdoctoral Studies, Faculty of Education, Department of Integrated Studies in Education, Montréal, QC H3A 2T5, Canada. Offers culture and values in education (MA, PhD); curriculum studies (MA); educational leadership (MA, Certificate); educational studies (PhD); integrated studies in education (M Ed); second language education (MA, PhD).

Michigan State University, The Graduate School, College of Arts and Letters, Program in Second Language Studies, East Lansing, MI 48824. Offers PhD. *Accreditation:* Teacher Education Accreditation Council. *Entrance requirements:* Additional exam requirements/recommendations for international students: Required—TOEFL, Michigan State University ELT (minimum score 85), Michigan English Language Assessment Battery (minimum score 83). Electronic applications accepted.

Middle Tennessee State University, College of Graduate Studies, College of Liberal Arts, Department of Foreign Languages and Literatures, Murfreesboro, TN 37132. Offers English as a second language (M Ed); foreign language (MAT). Part-time and evening/weekend programs available. Postbaccalaureate distance learning degree programs offered. *Faculty:* 16 full-time (12 women). *Students:* 3 full-time (all women), 14 part-time (11 women); includes 3 minority (1 Black or African American, non-Hispanic/Latino; 2 Hispanic/Latino). Average age 29. 15 applicants, 80% accepted. In 2011, 6 master's awarded. *Degree requirements:* For master's, one foreign language, comprehensive exam, thesis optional. *Entrance requirements:* For master's, GRE. Additional exam requirements/recommendations for international students: Required—TOEFL (minimum score 525 paper-based; 195 computer-based; 71 iBT) or IELTS (minimum score 6). *Application deadline:* For fall admission, 6/1 for domestic and international students. Applications are processed on a rolling basis. Application fee: $25 ($30 for international students). Electronic applications accepted. *Expenses:* Tuition, state resident: full-time $10,008. Tuition, nonresident: full-time $25,056. *Financial support:* In 2011–12, 15 students received support. Tuition waivers available. Support available to part-time students. Financial award application deadline: 5/1; financial award applicants required to submit FAFSA. *Faculty research:* Linguistics, holocaust studies, foreign language pedagogy. *Unit head:* Dr. Joan McRae, Chair, 615-898-2981, Fax: 615-898-5735, E-mail: joan.mcrae@mtsu.edu. *Application contact:* Dr. Michael D. Allen, Dean and Vice Provost for Research, 615-898-2840, Fax: 615-904-8020, E-mail: michael.allen@mtsu.edu.

Mills College, Graduate Studies, School of Education, Oakland, CA 94613-1000. Offers child life in hospitals (MA); early childhood education (MA); education (MA), including art education, curriculum and instruction, elementary education, English education, foreign language education, mathematics education, science education, secondary education, social studies education, teaching; educational leadership (MA, Ed D). Part-time and evening/weekend programs available. *Faculty:* 13 full-time (10 women), 14 part-time/adjunct (10 women). *Students:* 149 full-time (133 women), 69 part-time (61 women); includes 85 minority (32 Black or African American, non-Hispanic/Latino; 1 American Indian or Alaska Native, non-Hispanic/Latino; 16 Asian, non-Hispanic/Latino; 24 Hispanic/Latino; 1 Native Hawaiian or other Pacific Islander, non-Hispanic/Latino; 11 Two or more races, non-Hispanic/Latino), 3 international. Average age 28. 238 applicants, 84% accepted, 106 enrolled. In 2011, 41 master's, 2 doctorates awarded. Terminal master's awarded for partial completion of doctoral program. *Degree requirements:* For master's, comprehensive exam. *Entrance requirements:* For master's, statement of purpose, official transcript, 3 recommendations; for doctorate, GRE General Test. Additional exam requirements/recommendations for international students: Required—TOEFL (minimum score 550 paper-based; 80 iBT) or IELTS (minimum score 6). *Application deadline:* For fall admission, 12/31 priority date for domestic students, 12/15 for international students; for spring admission, 11/1 priority date for domestic students, 10/1 for international students. Applications are processed on a rolling basis. Application fee: $50. Electronic applications accepted. *Expenses: Tuition:* Full-time $28,280; part-time $15,640 per year. *Required fees:* $958. Tuition and fees vary according to program. *Financial support:* In 2011–12, 43 students received support, including 225 fellowships with full and partial tuition reimbursements available (averaging $6,020 per year), 43 teaching assistantships with full and partial tuition reimbursements available (averaging $6,782 per year); career-related internships or fieldwork and scholarships/grants also available. Support available to part-time students. Financial award application deadline: 2/1; financial award applicants required to submit FAFSA. *Faculty research:* Early childhood education, teacher preparation, educational leadership. *Total annual research expenditures:* $2.3 million. *Unit head:* Katherine Schultz, Chairperson, 510-430-3170, Fax: 510-430-3379, E-mail: grad-studies@mills.edu. *Application contact:* Tiana Kozoil, Graduate Admission Specialist, 510-430-3305, Fax: 510-430-2159, E-mail: grad-studies@mills.edu. Web site: http://www.mills.edu/education.

Mississippi State University, College of Arts and Sciences, Department of Classical and Modern Languages and Literatures, Mississippi State, MS 39762. Offers foreign language (MA), including French, German, Spanish. Part-time programs available. *Faculty:* 5 full-time (1 woman). *Students:* 12 full-time (10 women), 3 part-time (all women); includes 3 minority (1 Black or African American, non-Hispanic/Latino; 2 Hispanic/Latino), 2 international. Average age 31. 16 applicants, 75% accepted, 7 enrolled. In 2011, 3 master's awarded. *Degree requirements:* For master's, one foreign language, thesis optional, comprehensive oral or written exam. *Entrance requirements:* For master's, minimum GPA of 2.75 on last two years of undergraduate courses. Additional exam requirements/recommendations for international students: Required—TOEFL (minimum score 525 paper-based). *Application deadline:* For fall admission, 7/1 for domestic students, 5/1 for international students; for spring admission, 11/1 for domestic students, 9/1 for international students. Applications are processed on a rolling basis. Application fee: $40. Electronic applications accepted. *Expenses:* Tuition, state resident: full-time $5805; part-time $322.50 per credit hour. Tuition, nonresident: full-time $14,670; part-time $815 per credit hour. *Financial support:* In 2011–12, 9 teaching assistantships with full tuition reimbursements (averaging $8,766 per year) were awarded; Federal Work-Study, institutionally sponsored loans, and unspecified assistantships also available. Financial award application deadline: 4/1; financial award applicants required to submit FAFSA. *Faculty research:* French, German, Spanish literature from medieval era to present; gender and cultural studies in French; Spanish-American literature; foreign language methodology; linguistics. *Unit head:* Dr. Jack Jordan, Professor/Head, 662-325-3480, Fax: 662-325-8209, E-mail: jordan@ra.msstate.edu. *Application contact:* Dr. Edward T. Potter, Assistant Professor/Graduate Coordinator, 662-325-2399, Fax: 662-325-8209, E-mail: ep75@.msstate.edu. Web site: http://www.cmll.msstate.edu/.

Missouri State University, Graduate College, College of Arts and Letters, Department of Modern and Classical Languages, Springfield, MO 65897. Offers secondary education (MS Ed), including Spanish. Part-time programs available. *Faculty:* 5 full-time (2 women). *Students:* 1 (woman) part-time. Average age 35. In 2011, 2 master's awarded. *Entrance requirements:* For master's, grades 9-12 teaching certification. Additional exam requirements/recommendations for international students: Required—TOEFL (minimum score 550 paper-based; 213 computer-based; 79 iBT), IELTS (minimum score 6). *Application deadline:* For fall admission, 7/20 priority date for domestic students, 5/1 for international students; for spring admission, 12/20 priority date for domestic students, 9/1 for international students. Applications are processed on a rolling basis. Application fee: $35 ($50 for international students). Electronic applications accepted. *Expenses:* Tuition, state resident: full-time $4086; part-time $227 per credit hour. Tuition, nonresident: full-time $8172; part-time $454 per credit hour. *Required fees:* $275 per semester. Tuition and fees vary according to course load, campus/location and program. *Financial support:* Federal Work-Study, scholarships/grants, and unspecified assistantships available. Financial award applicants required to submit FAFSA. *Unit head:* Dr. Madeleine Kernen, Head, 417-836-7626, E-mail: mcl@missouristate.edu. *Application contact:* Eric Eckert, Coordinator of Admissions and Recruitment, 417-836-5331, Fax: 417-836-6888, E-mail: ericeckert@missouristate.edu. Web site: http://www.missouristate.edu/MCL/.

Montclair State University, The Graduate School, College of Humanities and Social Sciences, Department of Spanish and Italian, Program in Teaching Spanish, Montclair, NJ 07043-1624. Offers MAT. *Students:* 3 full-time (all women), 1 (woman) part-time; includes 3 minority (all Hispanic/Latino). Average age 33. *Degree requirements:* For master's, comprehensive exam. *Entrance requirements:* For master's, GRE General Test, 2 letters of recommendation, essay, interview. Additional exam requirements/recommendations for international students: Required—TOEFL (minimum score 83 iBT), IELTS (minimum score 6.5). *Application deadline:* Applications are processed on a rolling basis. Application fee: $60. Electronic applications accepted. *Financial support:* Federal Work-Study, scholarships/grants, and unspecified assistantships available. Support available to part-time students. Financial award application deadline: 3/1; financial award applicants required to submit FAFSA. *Faculty research:* Second language acquisition, theory and practice. *Unit head:* Dr. Linda Gould Levine, Chairperson, 973-655-7506. *Application contact:* Amy Aiello, Executive Director of The Graduate School, 973-655-5147, Fax: 973-655-7869, E-mail: graduate.school@montclair.edu.

Monterey Institute of International Studies, Graduate School of Translation, Interpretation and Language Education, Program in Teaching Foreign Language, Monterey, CA 93940-2691. Offers MATFL. *Degree requirements:* For master's, one foreign language, portfolio, oral defense. *Entrance requirements:* For master's, minimum GPA of 3.0, proficiency in foreign language. Additional exam requirements/recommendations for international students: Required—TOEFL (minimum score 600 paper-based; 250 computer-based; 100 iBT). Electronic applications accepted. *Expenses: Tuition:* Full-time $32,800; part-time $1560 per credit. *Required fees:* $28 per semester.

Morehead State University, Graduate Programs, College of Education, Department of Middle Grades and Secondary Education, Morehead, KY 40351. Offers business and marketing education (MAT); English/language arts 5-9 (MAT); French (MAT); health P-12 (MAT); mathematics 5-9 (MAT); physical education P-12 (MAT); science 5-9 (MAT); secondary biology (MAT); secondary chemistry (MAT); secondary earth science (MAT); secondary English (MAT); secondary math (MAT); secondary physics (MAT); secondary social studies (MAT); social studies 5-9 (MAT); Spanish (MAT). Part-time and evening/weekend programs available. *Degree requirements:* For master's, portfolio. *Entrance requirements:* For master's, GRE or PRAXIS II content exam, minimum overall undergraduate GPA of 2.5. Additional exam requirements/recommendations for international students: Required—TOEFL (minimum score 500 paper-based; 173 computer-based). Electronic applications accepted.

New York University, NYU in Paris, Paris, NY 10012-1019, France. Offers teaching French as a foreign language (MA).

New York University, Steinhardt School of Culture, Education, and Human Development, Department of Teaching and Learning, Program in Multilingual/Multicultural Studies, New York, NY 10012-1019. Offers bilingual education (MA, PhD, Advanced Certificate); foreign language education (MA, Advanced Certificate); foreign language education/TESOL (MA); teaching English to speakers of other languages (MA, PhD, Advanced Certificate); teaching French as a foreign language (MA). *Accreditation:* Teacher Education Accreditation Council. Part-time and evening/weekend programs available. *Degree requirements:* For master's, thesis (for some programs); for doctorate, thesis/dissertation. *Entrance requirements:* For doctorate, GRE General Test, interview; for Advanced Certificate, master's degree. Additional exam requirements/recommendations for international students: Required—TOEFL. Electronic applications accepted. *Faculty research:* Second language acquisition, cross-cultural communication, technology-enhanced language learning, language variation, action learning.

Northern Arizona University, Graduate College, College of Arts and Letters, Department of Modern Languages, Flagstaff, AZ 86011. Offers Spanish teaching (MAT); Spanish teaching/Spanish education (MAT). Part-time programs available. *Faculty:* 23 full-time (17 women). *Students:* 13 full-time (9 women), 3 part-time (all women); includes 7 minority (all Hispanic/Latino), 3 international. Average age 30. 5 applicants, 100% accepted, 5 enrolled. In 2011, 7 degrees awarded. *Degree requirements:* For master's, comprehensive exam, thesis optional. *Entrance requirements:* For master's, bachelor's degree in Spanish (coupled with preparation in general or foreign language education courses) or Spanish secondary education, or degree/experience in related field (e.g., bilingual education); minimum GPA of 3.0 or equivalent. Additional exam requirements/recommendations for international students: Required—TOEFL (minimum score 550 paper-based; 213 computer-based; 80 iBT), IELTS (minimum score 7). *Application deadline:* For fall admission, 4/21 priority date for domestic students, 4/21 for international students; for spring admission, 10/21 priority date for domestic students. Applications are processed on a rolling basis. Application fee: $65. Electronic applications accepted. *Expenses:* Tuition, state resident: full-time $7190; part-time $355 per credit hour. Tuition, nonresident: full-time $18,092; part-time $1005 per credit hour. *Required fees:* $818; $328 per semester. *Financial support:* In 2011–12, 13 teaching assistantships with partial tuition reimbursements (averaging $11,300 per year) were awarded; Federal Work-Study, scholarships/grants, health care benefits, tuition waivers (full and partial), and unspecified assistantships also available. Financial award applicants required to submit FAFSA. *Unit head:* Dr. Joseph Collentine, Chair, 928-523-5334, Fax: 928-523-0963, E-mail: j.collentine@nau.edu. *Application contact:* Alexandria McConocha, Administrative Associate, 928-523-2361, Fax: 928-523-0963, E-mail: alexandria.mcconocha@nau.edu. Web site: http://www.cal.nau.edu/languages/.

Occidental College, Graduate Studies, Department of Education, Program in Secondary Education, Los Angeles, CA 90041-3314. Offers English and comparative literary studies (MAT); history (MAT); life science (MAT); mathematics (MAT); physical science (MAT); social science (MAT); Spanish (MAT). Part-time programs available. *Degree requirements:* For master's, comprehensive exam, graduate synthesis paper. *Entrance requirements:* For master's, GRE General Test, minimum GPA of 3.0. Additional exam requirements/recommendations for international students: Required—TOEFL (minimum score 625 paper-based; 263 computer-based). *Expenses:* Contact institution.

Portland State University, Graduate Studies, College of Liberal Arts and Sciences, Department of World Languages and Literatures, Portland, OR 97207-0751. Offers foreign literature and language (MA); French (MA); German (MA); Japanese (MA); Spanish (MA). Part-time programs available. *Degree requirements:* For master's, one foreign language, thesis (for some programs). *Entrance requirements:* Additional exam requirements/recommendations for international students: Required—TOEFL (minimum score 550 paper-based; 213 computer-based). *Faculty research:* Foreign language pedagogy, applied and social linguistics, literary history and criticism.

Purdue University, Graduate School, College of Education, Department of Curriculum and Instruction, West Lafayette, IN 47907. Offers agricultural and extension education (PhD, Ed S); agriculture and extension education (MS, MS Ed); art education (PhD); consumer and family sciences and extension education (MS Ed, PhD, Ed S); curriculum studies (MS Ed, PhD, Ed S); educational technology (MS Ed, PhD, Ed S); elementary education (MS Ed); foreign language education (MS Ed, PhD, Ed S); industrial technology (PhD, Ed S); language arts (MS Ed, PhD, Ed S); literacy (MS Ed, PhD, Ed S); mathematics/science education (MS, MS Ed, PhD, Ed S); social studies (MS Ed, PhD); social studies education (Ed S); vocational/industrial education (MS Ed, PhD, Ed S); vocational/technical education (MS Ed, PhD, Ed S). *Accreditation:* NCATE. Part-time and evening/weekend programs available. *Faculty:* 30 full-time (21 women), 1 (woman) part-time/adjunct. *Students:* 89 full-time (64 women), 134 part-time (84 women); includes 31 minority (12 Black or African American, non-Hispanic/Latino; 3 American Indian or Alaska Native, non-Hispanic/Latino; 7 Asian, non-Hispanic/Latino; 9 Hispanic/Latino), 49 international. Average age 36. 136 applicants, 83% accepted, 72 enrolled. In 2011, 26 master's, 13 doctorates awarded. *Degree requirements:* For master's, thesis optional; for doctorate, thesis/dissertation, oral and written exams; for Ed S, oral presentation, project. *Entrance requirements:* For master's, GRE general test is required if undergraduate GPA is below 3.0, minimum undergraduate GPA of 3.0 or equivalent; for doctorate, GRE General Test, a combined GRE verbal and quantitative score of 1000 (300 for revised GRE Test) or more is expected, minimum undergraduate GPA of 3.0 or equivalent; master's degree with minimum GPA of 3.0 or equivalent; for Ed S, GRE general test, a combined GRE verbal and quantitative score of 1000 (300 for revised GRE Test) or more is expected, minimum undergraduate GPA of 3.0 or equivalent; master's degree. Additional exam requirements/recommendations for international students: Required—TOEFL (minimum score 550 paper-based; 77 iBT). *Application deadline:* For fall admission, 12/15 priority date for domestic students, 3/1 for international students; for spring admission, 9/15 for domestic students, 8/1 for international students. Application fee: $60 ($75 for international students). Electronic applications accepted. *Financial support:* Fellowships with full tuition reimbursements, research assistantships with full tuition reimbursements, teaching assistantships with full tuition reimbursements, career-related internships or fieldwork, and tuition waivers (full) available. Support available to part-time students. Financial award application deadline: 3/1; financial award applicants required to submit FAFSA. *Faculty research:* Literacy acquisition and development, teacher beliefs and knowledge, recruitment and retention of underrepresented students, economic education, literacy discourse. *Unit head:* Dr. Philip J. VanFossen, Head, 765-494-7935, Fax: 765-496-1622, E-mail: vanfoss@purdue.edu. *Application contact:* Sarah N. Prater, Graduate Contact, 765-494-2345, Fax: 765-494-5832, E-mail: prater0@purdue.edu. Web site: http://www.edci.purdue.edu/.

Purdue University, Graduate School, College of Liberal Arts, School of Languages and Cultures, West Lafayette, IN 47907. Offers French (MA, MAT, PhD), including French (MA, PhD), French education (MAT); German (MA, MAT, PhD), including German (MA, PhD), German education (MAT); Japanese pedagogy (MA); Spanish (MA, MAT, PhD), including Spanish (MA, PhD), Spanish education (MAT). *Faculty:* 51 full-time (28 women), 3 part-time/adjunct (2 women). *Students:* 55 full-time (36 women), 30 part-time (16 women); includes 11 minority (3 Asian, non-Hispanic/Latino; 8 Hispanic/Latino), 53 international. Average age 34. 38 applicants, 76% accepted, 12 enrolled. In 2011, 19 master's, 5 doctorates awarded. Terminal master's awarded for partial completion of doctoral program. *Degree requirements:* For master's, one foreign language; for doctorate, 2 foreign languages, thesis/dissertation. *Entrance requirements:* For master's, GRE general test, with minimum score 600 (160 revised GRE test) verbal desirable, two writing samples, one in English, one in language (French, German, Japanese, or Spanish); sample recording of English and language of study; for doctorate, GRE general test, with minimum score 600 (160 revised GRE test) verbal desirable, master's degree with minimum GPA of 3.5 or equivalent; two writing samples, one in English, one in language (French, German, Japanese, or Spanish); sample recording of English and language of study. Additional exam requirements/recommendations for international students: Required—TOEFL (minimum score 550 paper-based; 77 iBT); Recommended—TWE. *Application deadline:* For fall admission, 1/12 for domestic and international students; for spring admission, 10/1 for domestic and international students. Applications are processed on a rolling basis. Application fee: $60 ($75 for international students). Electronic applications accepted. *Financial support:* In 2011–12, fellowships with tuition reimbursements (averaging $15,750 per year), teaching assistantships with tuition reimbursements (averaging $13,463 per year) were awarded. Support available to part-time students. Financial award applicants required to submit FAFSA. *Faculty research:* Linguistics, semiotics, literary criticism, pedagogy. *Unit head:* Dr. Keith M. Dickson, Interim Head, 765-494-3867, E-mail: kdickson@purdue.edu. *Application contact:* Betty L. Lewis, Graduate Contact, 765-494-3841, E-mail: lewisbl@purdue.edu.

Queens College of the City University of New York, Division of Graduate Studies, Division of Education, Department of Secondary Education, Flushing, NY 11367-1597. Offers art (MS Ed); biology (MS Ed, AC); chemistry (MS Ed, AC); earth sciences (MS Ed, AC); English (MS Ed, AC); French (MS Ed, AC); Italian (MS Ed, AC); mathematics (MS Ed, AC); music (MS Ed, AC); physics (MS Ed, AC); social studies (MS Ed, AC); Spanish (MS Ed, AC). Part-time and evening/weekend programs available. *Faculty:* 22 full-time (14 women). *Students:* 46 full-time (23 women), 727 part-time (442 women); includes 234 minority (41 Black or African American, non-Hispanic/Latino; 78 Asian, non-Hispanic/Latino; 115 Hispanic/Latino), 5 international. 591 applicants, 60% accepted, 250 enrolled. In 2011, 170 master's awarded. *Degree requirements:* For master's, research project; for AC, thesis optional. *Entrance requirements:* For master's, minimum GPA of 3.0. Additional exam requirements/recommendations for international students: Required—TOEFL. *Application deadline:* For fall admission, 4/1 for domestic students; for spring admission, 11/1 for domestic students. Applications are processed on a rolling basis. Application fee: $125. *Expenses:* Tuition, state resident: part-time $345 per credit. Tuition, nonresident: part-time $640 per credit. *Required fees:* $145.25 per semester. *Financial support:* Career-related internships or fieldwork, Federal Work-Study, institutionally sponsored loans, and tuition waivers (partial) available. Support available to part-time students. Financial award application deadline: 4/1; financial award applicants required to submit FAFSA. *Unit head:* Dr. Eleanor Armour-Thomas, Chairperson, 718-997-5150, E-mail: armourthomas@yahoo.com. *Application contact:* Mario Caruso, Director of Graduate Admissions, 718-997-5200, Fax: 718-997-5193, E-mail: graduate_admissions@qc.edu.

Quinnipiac University, School of Education, Program in Secondary Education, Hamden, CT 06518-1940. Offers biology (MAT); English (MAT); history/social studies (MAT); mathematics (MAT); Spanish (MAT). *Accreditation:* NCATE. *Faculty:* 7 full-time (5 women), 41 part-time/adjunct (24 women). *Students:* 56 full-time (38 women), 1 (woman) part-time; includes 5 minority (1 Black or African American, non-Hispanic/Latino; 1 Asian, non-Hispanic/Latino; 3 Hispanic/Latino). 51 applicants, 96% accepted, 44 enrolled. In 2011, 49 master's awarded. *Entrance requirements:* For master's, PRAXIS I, minimum GPA of 2.67, interview. *Application deadline:* For fall admission, 3/31 priority date for domestic students. Applications are processed on a rolling basis. Application fee: $45. Electronic applications accepted. *Expenses: Tuition:* Part-time $855 per credit. *Required fees:* $35 per credit. *Financial support:* In 2011–12, 1 student received support. Career-related internships or fieldwork, scholarships/grants, and tuition waivers (full and partial) available. Financial award application deadline: 4/15; financial award applicants required to submit FAFSA. *Faculty research:* Multicultural and urban education/leadership, challenges of teaching diverse learners, scholarship of teaching and learning, technology and teaching, humor and education. *Unit head:* Mordechai Gordon, Program Director, 203-582-8442, Fax: 203-582-3473, E-mail: mordechai.gordon@quinnipiac.edu. *Application contact:* Jennifer Boutin, Associate Director of Graduate Admissions, 800-462-1944, Fax: 203-582-3443, E-mail: jennifer.boutin@quinnipiac.edu. Web site: http://www.quinnipiac.edu/academics/colleges-schools-and-departments/school-of-education/graduate-programs/five-semester-mat-programs/secondary-educat.

Rhode Island College, School of Graduate Studies, Feinstein School of Education and Human Development, Department of Educational Studies, Providence, RI 02908-1991. Offers advanced studies in teaching and learning (M Ed); English (MAT); French (MAT); history (MAT); math (MAT); secondary education (MAT); Spanish (MAT); teaching English as a second language (M Ed). *Accreditation:* NCATE. Part-time and evening/weekend programs available. *Faculty:* 14 full-time (7 women), 4 part-time/adjunct (2 women). *Students:* 10 full-time (all women), 61 part-time (51 women); includes 8 minority (1 Black or African American, non-Hispanic/Latino; 4 Asian, non-Hispanic/Latino; 3 Hispanic/Latino). Average age 33. In 2011, 32 master's awarded. *Degree requirements:* For master's, capstone or comprehensive assessment. *Entrance requirements:* For master's, GRE or MAT (for most programs), minimum undergraduate GPA of 3.0; baccalaureate degree in English, French, history, math or Spanish; evaluation of content area knowledge; 3 letters of recommendation; interview. Additional exam requirements/recommendations for international students: Recommended—TOEFL (minimum score 550 paper-based; 213 computer-based; 79 iBT). *Application deadline:* For fall admission, 3/1 for domestic students; for spring admission, 11/1 for domestic students. Applications are processed on a rolling basis. Application fee: $50. *Expenses:* Tuition, state resident: full-time $8592; part-time $358 per credit hour. Tuition, nonresident: full-time $16,800; part-time $700 per credit hour. *Required fees:* $602; $22 per credit. $72 per term. *Financial support:* Teaching assistantships with full tuition reimbursements, career-related internships or fieldwork, Federal Work-Study, scholarships/grants, health care benefits, and unspecified assistantships available. Support available to part-time students. Financial award application deadline: 5/15; financial award applicants required to submit FAFSA. *Faculty research:* School administration, school/college articulation. *Unit head:* Dr. Ellen Bigler, Chair, 401-456-8170. *Application contact:* Graduate Studies, 401-456-8700. Web site: http://www.ric.edu/educationalStudies/.

Rider University, Department of Graduate Education, Leadership and Counseling, Teacher Certification Program, Lawrenceville, NJ 08648-3001. Offers business education (Certificate); elementary education (Certificate); English as a second language (Certificate); English education (Certificate); mathematics education (Certificate); preschool to grade 3 (Certificate); science education (Certificate); social studies education (Certificate); world languages (Certificate), including French, German, Spanish. Part-time programs available. *Degree requirements:* For Certificate, internship, professional portfolio. *Entrance requirements:* For degree, PRAXIS, resume. Additional exam requirements/recommendations for international students: Required—TOEFL (minimum score 550 paper-based; 213 computer-based). Electronic applications accepted. *Expenses: Tuition:* Full-time $32,820; part-time $710 per credit. *Required fees:* $350; $35 per course. Tuition and fees vary according to campus/location and program. *Faculty research:* Conceptual foundations for optimal development of creativity; creative theory, cognitive processes in mathematics learning, teacher collaboration.

Rivier University, School of Graduate Studies, Department of Modern Languages, Nashua, NH 03060. Offers Spanish (MAT). Part-time and evening/weekend programs available.

Rowan University, Graduate School, College of Education, Department of Teacher Education, Program in Foreign Language Education, Glassboro, NJ 08028-1701. Offers MST. Part-time and evening/weekend programs available. *Entrance requirements:* For master's, GRE General Test, minimum GPA of 2.8, 1 year of teaching experience. Additional exam requirements/recommendations for international students: Required—TOEFL. Electronic applications accepted.

Rutgers, The State University of New Jersey, New Brunswick, Graduate School-New Brunswick, Program in French, Piscataway, NJ 08854-8097. Offers French (MA, PhD); French studies (MAT). Part-time and evening/weekend programs available. Terminal master's awarded for partial completion of doctoral program. *Degree requirements:* For master's, one foreign language, written and oral exams (MA); for doctorate, 3 foreign languages, thesis/dissertation, qualifying exam. *Entrance requirements:* For master's and doctorate, GRE General Test. *Faculty research:* Literatures in French, literary history and theory, rhetoric and poetics.

Rutgers, The State University of New Jersey, New Brunswick, Graduate School-New Brunswick, Program in Italian, Piscataway, NJ 08854-8097. Offers Italian (MA, PhD); Italian literature and literary criticism (MA); language, literature and culture (MAT). Part-time and evening/weekend programs available. Terminal master's awarded for partial completion of doctoral program. *Degree requirements:* For master's, one foreign language, comprehensive exam (for some programs), thesis optional; for doctorate, 2 foreign languages, thesis/dissertation, qualifying exam. *Entrance requirements:* For master's and doctorate, GRE General Test. Additional exam requirements/recommendations for international students: Required—TOEFL. *Faculty research:* Literature.

Rutgers, The State University of New Jersey, New Brunswick, Graduate School-New Brunswick, Program in Spanish, Piscataway, NJ 08854-8097. Offers bilingualism and second language acquisition (MA, PhD); Spanish (MA, MAT, PhD); Spanish literature (MA, PhD); translation (MA). Part-time programs available. *Degree requirements:* For master's, comprehensive exam (for some programs), thesis (for some programs); for doctorate, 2 foreign languages, comprehensive exam, thesis/dissertation. *Entrance requirements:* For master's and doctorate, GRE General Test. Additional exam requirements/recommendations for international students: Required—TOEFL. Electronic applications accepted. *Faculty research:* Hispanic literature, Luso-Brazilian literature, Spanish linguistics, Spanish translation.

Rutgers, The State University of New Jersey, New Brunswick, Graduate School of Education, Department of Learning and Teaching, Program in Language Education, Piscataway, NJ 08854-8097. Offers English as a second language education (Ed M); language education (Ed M, Ed D). Part-time programs available. Terminal master's awarded for partial completion of doctoral program. *Degree requirements:* For master's, comprehensive exam; for doctorate, thesis/dissertation, concept paper, qualifying exam. *Entrance requirements:* For master's, GRE General Test, minimum GPA of 3.0; for doctorate, GRE General Test, minimum GPA of 3.5. Additional exam requirements/recommendations for international students: Required—TOEFL. Electronic applications accepted. *Faculty research:* Linguistics, sociolinguistics, cross-cultural/international communication.

St. John Fisher College, Ralph C. Wilson Jr. School of Education, Program in Adolescence Education/Special Education, Rochester, NY 14618-3597. Offers adolescence English (MS Ed); adolescence French (MS Ed); adolescence social studies (MS Ed); adolescence Spanish (MS Ed). Part-time and evening/weekend programs available. *Faculty:* 5 full-time (3 women), 2 part-time/adjunct (both women). *Students:* 25 full-time (13 women), 1 (woman) part-time. Average age 22. 19 applicants, 79% accepted, 11 enrolled. In 2011, 18 master's awarded. *Degree requirements:* For master's, field experiences, student teaching, LAST. *Entrance requirements:* For master's, 2 letters of recommendation, personal statement, current resume. Additional exam requirements/recommendations for international students: Required—TOEFL (minimum score 575 paper-based; 233 computer-based; 80 iBT). *Application deadline:* Applications are processed on a rolling basis. Application fee: $30. Electronic applications accepted. *Expenses: Tuition:* Part-time $735 per credit. One-time fee: $50 part-time. Tuition and fees vary according to course load, degree level and program. *Financial support:* In 2011–12, 5 students received support. Scholarships/grants available. Financial award applicants required to submit FAFSA. *Faculty research:* Arts and humanities, urban schools, constructivist learning, at risk students, mentoring. *Unit head:* Dr. Susan Schultz, Program Director, 585-385-7296, E-mail: sschultz@sjfc.edu. *Application contact:* Jose Perales, Director of Graduate Admissions, 585-385-8067, E-mail: jperales@sjfc.edu. Web site: http://www.sjfc.edu/academics/education/departments/ms-special-ed/options/initial-adolescence.dot.

Saint Xavier University, Graduate Studies, School of Education, Chicago, IL 60655-3105. Offers counseling (MA); curriculum and instruction (MA); early childhood education (MA); educational administration (MA); elementary education (MA); individualized studies (MA), including educational technology, English as a second language (ESL), ISTEM (integrative science, technology, engineering, and math), science education; music education (MA); reading (MA); secondary education (MA); Spanish education (MA); special education (MA); teaching and leadership (MA). *Accreditation:* NCATE. Part-time and evening/weekend programs available. *Degree requirements:* For master's, thesis or project. *Entrance requirements:* For master's, minimum GPA of 3.0. *Application deadline:* For fall admission, 8/15 priority date for domestic students. Applications are processed on a rolling basis. Application fee: $35. *Expenses:* Contact institution. *Financial support:* Career-related internships or fieldwork available. Support available to part-time students. Financial award applicants required to submit FAFSA. *Unit head:* Dr. Beverly Gulley, Dean, 773-298-3221, Fax: 773-779-9061, E-mail: gulley@sxu.edu. *Application contact:* Beth Gierach, Managing Director of Admission, 773-298-3053, Fax: 773-298-3076, E-mail: gierach@sxu.edu.

Shippensburg University of Pennsylvania, School of Graduate Studies, College of Education and Human Services, Department of Teacher Education, Shippensburg, PA 17257-2299. Offers curriculum and instruction (M Ed), including biology, early childhood education, elementary education, English, geography/earth science, history, mathematics, middle level education, modern languages; reading (M Ed). *Accreditation:* NCATE. Part-time and evening/weekend programs available. *Faculty:* 14 full-time (11 women), 8 part-time/adjunct (7 women). *Students:* 16 full-time (15 women), 143 part-time (130 women); includes 11 minority (4 Black or African American, non-Hispanic/Latino; 1 Asian, non-Hispanic/Latino; 4 Hispanic/Latino; 2 Two or more races, non-Hispanic/Latino), 1 international. Average age 30. 55 applicants, 55% accepted, 25 enrolled. In 2011, 76 master's awarded. *Degree requirements:* For master's, comprehensive exam (for some programs), thesis optional, practicum or internship; capstone seminar (for some programs). *Entrance requirements:* For master's, MAT (if GPA less than 2.75), interview, 3 letters of reference, questionnaire of teaching background and future goals. Additional exam requirements/recommendations for international students: Required—TOEFL (minimum score 580 paper-based; 237 computer-based); Recommended—IELTS (minimum score 6). *Application deadline:* For fall admission, 6/1 priority date for domestic students, 4/30 for international students; for spring admission, 9/1 priority date for domestic students, 9/30 for international students. Applications are processed on a rolling basis. Application fee: $30. Electronic applications accepted. *Expenses: Tuition, area resident:* Part-time $416 per credit. Tuition, state resident: part-time $416 per credit. Tuition, nonresident: part-time $624 per credit. *Required fees:* $119 per credit. *Financial support:* In 2011–12, 5 research assistantships with full tuition reimbursements (averaging $5,000 per year) were awarded; career-related internships or fieldwork, scholarships/grants, unspecified assistantships, and resident hall director and student payroll positions also available. Support available to part-time students. Financial award application deadline: 3/1; financial award applicants required to submit FAFSA. *Unit head:* Dr. Christine A. Royce, Chairperson, 717-477-1688, Fax: 717-477-4046, E-mail: caroyc@ship.edu. *Application contact:* Jeremy R. Goshorn, Assistant Dean of Graduate Admissions, 717-477-1231, Fax: 717-477-4016, E-mail: jrgoshorn@ship.edu. Web site: http://www.ship.edu/teacher/.

Smith College, Graduate and Special Programs, Department of Education and Child Study, Program in Secondary Education, Northampton, MA 01063. Offers biological sciences education (MAT); chemistry education (MAT); English education (MAT); French education (MAT); geology education (MAT); government education (MAT); history education (MAT); mathematics education (MAT); physics education (MAT); Spanish education (MAT). Part-time programs available. *Faculty:* 6 full-time (4 women), 3 part-time/adjunct (2 women). *Students:* 11 full-time (8 women), 3 part-time (all women); includes 2 minority (1 Asian, non-Hispanic/Latino; 1 Hispanic/Latino). Average age 26. 21 applicants, 95% accepted, 12 enrolled. In 2011, 2 master's awarded. *Entrance requirements:* For master's, GRE. Additional exam requirements/recommendations for international students: Required—TOEFL (minimum score 590 paper-based; 243 computer-based; 97 iBT). *Application deadline:* For fall admission, 4/1 for domestic students, 1/15 for international students; for spring admission, 12/1 for domestic students. Application fee: $60. *Expenses: Tuition:* Full-time $14,925; part-time $1245 per credit. *Financial support:* In 2011–12, 13 students received support. Career-related internships or fieldwork, institutionally sponsored loans, and scholarships/grants available. Support available to part-time students. Financial award application deadline: 1/15; financial award applicants required to submit CSS PROFILE or FAFSA. *Unit head:* Rosetta Cohen, Graduate Student Advisor, 413-585-3266, E-mail: rcohen@smith.edu. *Application contact:* Ruth Morgan, Administrative Assistant, 413-585-3050, Fax: 413-585-3054, E-mail: gradstdy@smith.edu. Web site: http://www.smith.edu/educ/.

Smith College, Graduate and Special Programs, Department of Spanish and Portuguese, Northampton, MA 01063. Offers Spanish (MAT). Part-time programs available. *Faculty:* 9 full-time (6 women). *Students:* 3 full-time (all women); includes 1 minority (Hispanic/Latino). Average age 24. 3 applicants, 100% accepted, 3 enrolled. *Entrance requirements:* For master's, GRE. Additional exam requirements/recommendations for international students: Required—TOEFL (minimum score 590 paper-based; 243 computer-based; 97 iBT). *Application deadline:* For fall admission, 4/1 for domestic students, 1/15 for international students; for spring admission, 12/1 for domestic students. Application fee: $60. *Expenses: Tuition:* Full-time $14,925; part-time $1245 per credit. *Financial support:* Career-related internships or fieldwork, institutionally sponsored loans, and scholarships/grants available. Support available to part-time students. Financial award application deadline: 1/15. *Unit head:* Reyes Lazaro, Graduate Adviser, 413-585-3456, E-mail: rlazaro@smith.edu. *Application contact:* Ruth Morgan, Administrative Assistant, 413-585-3050, Fax: 413-585-3054, E-mail: gradstdy@smith.edu. Web site: http://www.smith.edu/spp/.

Soka University of America, Graduate School, Aliso Viejo, CA 92656. Offers teaching Japanese as a foreign language (Certificate). Evening/weekend programs available. *Entrance requirements:* For degree, bachelor's degree with minimum GPA of 3.0, proficiency in Japanese. Additional exam requirements/recommendations for international students: Required—TOEFL (minimum score 600 paper-based; 100 iBT).

Southern Illinois University Edwardsville, Graduate School, School of Education, Department of Curriculum and Instruction, Program in Secondary Education, Edwardsville, IL 62026. Offers art (MS Ed); biology (MS Ed); chemistry (MS Ed); earth and space sciences (MS Ed); English/language arts (MS Ed); foreign languages (MS Ed); history (MS Ed); mathematics (MS Ed); physics (MS Ed). *Accreditation:* NCATE. Part-time and evening/weekend programs available. *Students:* 1 full-time (0 women), 42 part-time (33 women); includes 2 minority (both Black or African American, non-Hispanic/Latino). 16 applicants, 31% accepted. In 2011, 8 master's awarded. *Degree requirements:* For master's, comprehensive exam (for some programs), final exam/paper. *Entrance requirements:* Additional exam requirements/recommendations for international students: Required—TOEFL (minimum score 550 paper-based; 213 computer-based; 79 iBT), IELTS (minimum score 6.5). *Application deadline:* For fall admission, 7/22 for domestic students, 6/1 for international students; for spring admission, 12/9 for domestic students, 10/1 for international students. Applications are processed on a rolling basis. Application fee: $30. Electronic applications accepted. Tuition and fees vary according to course load and program. *Financial support:* Fellowships, research assistantships, teaching assistantships, institutionally sponsored loans, scholarships/grants, and unspecified assistantships available. Financial award application deadline: 3/1; financial award applicants required to submit FAFSA. *Unit head:* Dr. Susan Breck, Director, 618-650-3444, E-mail: sbreck@siue.edu. *Application contact:* Dr. Michelle Robinson, Coordinator of Graduate Recruitment, 618-650-2811, Fax: 618-650-3523, E-mail: michero@siue.edu. Web site: http://www.siue.edu/education/ci/.

Southern Oregon University, Graduate Studies, College of Arts and Sciences, Department of Foreign Languages and Literatures, Ashland, OR 97520. Offers French language teaching (MA); Spanish language teaching (MA). Part-time programs available. *Faculty:* 7 full-time (3 women), 2 part-time/adjunct (both women). *Students:* 19 full-time (14 women), 12 part-time (11 women); includes 10 minority (2 Black or African American, non-Hispanic/Latino; 2 Asian, non-Hispanic/Latino; 6 Hispanic/Latino). Average age 38. 8 applicants, 88% accepted, 7 enrolled. In 2011, 6 degrees awarded. *Entrance requirements:* For master's, GRE General Test, minimum GPA of 3.0. Application fee: $50. *Expenses:* Tuition, state resident: full-time $12,600; part-time $350 per credit. Tuition, nonresident: full-time $16,200; part-time $450 per credit. *Required fees:* $1590. *Financial support:* Research assistantships with partial tuition reimbursements available. *Unit head:* Dr. Diana Maltz, Chair, 541-552-6634. *Application contact:* Mark Bottorff, Director of Admissions, 541-552-6411, Fax: 541-552-8403, E-mail: admissions@sou.edu. Web site: http://www.sou.edu/summerlanguageinstitute/.

Stanford University, School of Education, Teacher Education Program, Stanford, CA 94305-9991. Offers English education (MA); languages education (MA); mathematics education (MA); science education (MA); social studies education (MA). *Degree requirements:* For master's, thesis. *Entrance requirements:* For master's, GRE General Test. Electronic applications accepted. *Expenses: Tuition:* Full-time $40,050; part-time $890 per credit.

State University of New York at Binghamton, Graduate School, School of Education, Program in Adolescence Education, Binghamton, NY 13902-6000. Offers biology education (MAT, MS Ed, MST); earth science education (MAT, MS Ed, MST); English education (MAT, MS Ed, MST); French education (MAT, MST); mathematical sciences education (MAT, MS Ed, MST); physics (MAT, MS Ed, MST); social studies (MAT, MS Ed, MST); Spanish education (MAT, MST). *Accreditation:* Teacher Education Accreditation Council. Part-time and evening/weekend programs available. *Students:* 98 full-time (66 women), 13 part-time (11 women); includes 2 minority (1 Black or African American, non-Hispanic/Latino; 1 Hispanic/Latino). Average age 26. 73 applicants, 70% accepted, 35 enrolled. In 2011, 58 master's awarded. *Entrance requirements:* For master's, GRE General Test. Additional exam requirements/recommendations for international students: Required—TOEFL (minimum score 550 paper-based; 213 computer-based; 80 iBT). *Application deadline:* For fall admission, 2/1 priority date for domestic students, 2/1 for international students; for spring admission, 10/15 priority date for domestic students, 10/15 for international students. Applications are processed on a rolling basis. Application fee: $60. Electronic applications accepted. *Financial support:* In 2011–12, 4 students received support, including 1 fellowship with partial tuition reimbursement available (averaging $12,000 per year); career-related internships or fieldwork, Federal Work-Study, institutionally sponsored loans, scholarships/grants, health care benefits, tuition waivers (full), and unspecified assistantships also available. Financial award application deadline: 2/15; financial award applicants required to submit FAFSA. *Unit head:* Dr. S. G. Grant, Dean of School of Education, 607-777-7329, E-mail: sggrant@binghamton.edu. *Application contact:* Catherine Smith, Recruiting and Admissions Coordinator, 607-777-2151, Fax: 607-777-2501, E-mail: cmsmith@binghamton.edu.

State University of New York at Plattsburgh, Division of Education, Health, and Human Services, Program in Teacher Education: Adolescence MST, Plattsburgh, NY

12901-2681. Offers adolescence education (MST); biology 7-12 (MST); chemistry 7-12 (MST); earth science 7-12 (MST); English 7-12 (MST); French 7-12 (MST); mathematics 7-12 (MST); physics 7-12 (MST); social studies 7-12 (MST); Spanish 7-12 (MST). *Accreditation:* Teacher Education Accreditation Council. Part-time and evening/weekend programs available. *Students:* 53 full-time (26 women), 5 part-time (4 women). Average age 29. *Entrance requirements:* For master's, minimum GPA of 2.75. Additional exam requirements/recommendations for international students: Required—TOEFL. *Application deadline:* For fall admission, 2/15 priority date for domestic students. Applications are processed on a rolling basis. Application fee: $75. *Financial support:* Application deadline: 4/15; applicants required to submit FAFSA. *Unit head:* Dr. Robert Ackland, Coordinator, 518-564-5131, E-mail: acklanrt@plattsburgh.edu. *Application contact:* Marguerite Adelman, Assistant Director, Graduate Admissions, 518-564-4723, Fax: 518-564-4722, E-mail: adelmaml@plattsburgh.edu.

State University of New York College at Cortland, Graduate Studies, School of Arts and Sciences, Programs in Adolescence Education, Cortland, NY 13045. Offers biology (MAT, MS Ed); chemistry (MAT, MS Ed); earth science (MAT, MS Ed); English (MS Ed); French (MS Ed); mathematics (MAT, MS Ed); physics (MAT, MS Ed); social studies (MS Ed); Spanish (MS Ed). *Accreditation:* NCATE. Part-time and evening/weekend programs available. *Degree requirements:* For master's, one foreign language, comprehensive exam (for some programs), thesis (for some programs). *Entrance requirements:* For master's, GRE General Test.

Stony Brook University, State University of New York, School of Professional Development, Stony Brook, NY 11794. Offers biology-grade 7-12 (MAT); chemistry-grade 7-12 (MAT); coaching (Graduate Certificate); coaching online (Graduate Certificate); computer integrated engineering (Graduate Certificate); earth science-grade 7-12 (MAT); educational computing (Graduate Certificate); educational leadership (Advanced Certificate); English-grade 7-12 (MAT); environmental management (Graduate Certificate); environmental/occupational health and safety (Graduate Certificate); French-grade 7-12 (MAT); German-grade 7-12 (MAT); human resource management (Graduate Certificate); human resource management online (Graduate Certificate); information systems management (Graduate Certificate); Italian-grade 7-12 (MAT); liberal studies (MA); liberal studies online (MAT); mathematics-grade 7-12 (MAT); operation research (Graduate Certificate); physics-grade 7-12 (MAT); professional studies online (MPS); school administration and supervision (Graduate Certificate); school building leadership (Graduate Certificate); school district administration (Graduate Certificate); school district business leadership (Advanced Certificate); school district leadership (Graduate Certificate); social science and the professions (MPS), including environmental waste management, human resource management; social studies-grade 7-12 (MAT); Spanish-grade 7-12 (MAT); waste management (Graduate Certificate). Part-time and evening/weekend programs available. Postbaccalaureate distance learning degree programs offered. *Degree requirements:* For master's, one foreign language, thesis or alternative.

Temple University, College of Education, Department of Curriculum, Instruction, and Technology in Education, Philadelphia, PA 19122-6096. Offers applied behavioral analysis (MS Ed); career and technical education (MS Ed); early childhood education and elementary education (MS Ed); English education (MS Ed); language arts education (Ed D); math/science education (Ed D); mathematics education (MS Ed); science education (MS Ed); second and foreign language education (MS Ed); special education (MS Ed); teaching English as a second language (MS Ed). Part-time and evening/weekend programs available. *Faculty:* 19 full-time (12 women). *Students:* 30 full-time (23 women), 86 part-time (69 women); includes 12 minority (4 Black or African American, non-Hispanic/Latino; 2 Asian, non-Hispanic/Latino; 5 Hispanic/Latino; 1 Two or more races, non-Hispanic/Latino), 5 international. 82 applicants, 71% accepted, 51 enrolled. In 2011, 181 master's, 16 doctorates awarded. Terminal master's awarded for partial completion of doctoral program. *Degree requirements:* For master's, thesis or alternative; for doctorate, thesis/dissertation. *Entrance requirements:* For master's and doctorate, GRE General Test or MAT, minimum GPA of 3.0. Additional exam requirements/recommendations for international students: Required—TOEFL (minimum score 550 paper-based; 213 computer-based; 79 iBT). *Application deadline:* For fall admission, 4/1 for domestic students, 12/15 for international students; for spring admission, 10/1 for domestic students, 8/1 for international students. Application fee: $50. Electronic applications accepted. *Expenses:* Tuition, state resident: full-time $12,366; part-time $687 per credit hour. Tuition, nonresident: full-time $17,298; part-time $961 per credit hour. *Required fees:* $590; $213 per year. *Financial support:* Fellowships, research assistantships with full tuition reimbursements, and teaching assistantships with full tuition reimbursements available. Financial award application deadline: 1/15; financial award applicants required to submit FAFSA. *Faculty research:* School improvement, problem-solving, literacy, language development. *Unit head:* Dr. Michael W. Smith, Chair, 215-204-6387, Fax: 215-204-1414, E-mail: mwsmith@temple.edu. *Application contact:* Dr. Margo Greicar, Director for Graduate Academic and Student Affairs, 215-204-8011, Fax: 215-204-4383, E-mail: margo.greicar@temple.edu. Web site: http://www.temple.edu/education/cite/.

Texas A&M International University, Office of Graduate Studies and Research, College of Arts and Sciences, Department of Language and Literature, Laredo, TX 78041-1900. Offers English (MA); Hispanic studies (PhD); Spanish (MA). *Faculty:* 7 full-time (3 women). *Students:* 5 full-time (4 women), 31 part-time (19 women); includes 35 minority (all Hispanic/Latino), 1 international. Average age 33. 23 applicants, 70% accepted, 15 enrolled. In 2011, 8 master's awarded. *Degree requirements:* For master's, comprehensive exam (for some programs), thesis (for some programs). *Entrance requirements:* For master's, GRE General Test. Additional exam requirements/recommendations for international students: Required—TOEFL (minimum score 550 paper-based; 213 computer-based; 79 iBT). *Application deadline:* For fall admission, 4/30 priority date for domestic students, 4/30 for international students; for spring admission, 11/30 for domestic students, 10/1 for international students. Applications are processed on a rolling basis. Application fee: $35 ($50 for international students). *Expenses:* Tuition, state resident: full-time $5063. *Financial support:* Application deadline: 4/1. *Unit head:* Dr. Manuel Broncano, Chair, 956-326-2470, E-mail: manuel.broncano@tamiu.edu. *Application contact:* Suzanne Hansen-Alford, Director of Graduate Recruiting, 956-326-3023, Fax: 956-326-3021, E-mail: enroll@tamiu.edu. Web site: http://www.tamiu.edu/coas/lla/.

Texas A&M University–Kingsville, College of Graduate Studies, College of Arts and Sciences, Department of Language and Literature, Kingsville, TX 78363. Offers English (MA, MS); Spanish (MA). Part-time and evening/weekend programs available. *Degree requirements:* For master's, comprehensive exam, thesis or alternative. *Entrance requirements:* For master's, GRE General Test, minimum GPA of 3.0. Additional exam requirements/recommendations for international students: Required—TOEFL. *Faculty research:* Linguistics, culture, Spanish American literature, Spanish peninsular literature, American literature.

Union Graduate College, School of Education, Schenectady, NY 12308-3107. Offers biology (MAT, MS); chemistry (MAT); Chinese (MAT); earth science (MAT); English (MAT); French (MAT); general science (MAT); German (MAT); Greek (MAT); languages (MAT); Latin (MAT); mathematics (MAT); mathematics and technology (MS); mentoring and teacher leadership (AC); middle childhood extension (AC); national board certificate and teacher leadership (AC); physical science (MS); physics (MAT); social studies (MAT); Spanish (MAT). *Accreditation:* Teacher Education Accreditation Council. *Faculty:* 3 full-time (1 woman), 51 part-time/adjunct (24 women). *Students:* 37 full-time (26 women), 25 part-time (16 women); includes 4 minority (3 Asian, non-Hispanic/Latino; 1 Hispanic/Latino). Average age 32. 66 applicants, 83% accepted, 41 enrolled. In 2011, 47 master's, 29 other advanced degrees awarded. *Degree requirements:* For master's, thesis or project. *Entrance requirements:* For master's, minimum GPA of 3.0, letters of recommendation. Additional exam requirements/recommendations for international students: Required—TOEFL (minimum score 550 paper-based; 213 computer-based). *Application deadline:* Applications are processed on a rolling basis. Application fee: $60. Electronic applications accepted. *Expenses:* Contact institution. *Financial support:* In 2011–12, 22 students received support. Career-related internships or fieldwork, Federal Work-Study, scholarships/grants, health care benefits, and tuition waivers (partial) available. Support available to part-time students. Financial award applicants required to submit FAFSA. *Faculty research:* Transformative learning, science education, National Board Certification, teacher leadership, teacher quality. *Unit head:* Dr. Patrick Allen, Dean, 518-631-9870, Fax: 518-631-9901. *Application contact:* Christine Angley, Assistant, 518-631-9871, Fax: 518-631-9903, E-mail: angleyc@uniongraduatecollege.edu.

United States University, School of Education, Cypress, CA 90630. Offers administration (MA Ed); early childhood education (MA Ed); general (MA Ed); higher education administration (MA Ed); Spanish language education (MA Ed); special education (MA Ed). *Degree requirements:* For master's, portfolio. *Entrance requirements:* For master's, minimum undergraduate GPA of 2.5. Additional exam requirements/recommendations for international students: Required—TOEFL (minimum score 500 paper-based; 173 computer-based; 61 iBT).

Universidad del Este, Graduate School, Carolina, PR 00984. Offers accounting (MBA); adult education (M Ed); agribusiness (MBA); criminal justice and criminology (MA); curriculum and instruction - early education (M Ed); curriculum and instruction - elementary (M Ed); curriculum and instruction - English (M Ed); curriculum and instruction - Spanish (M Ed); human resources (MBA); information security management (MBA); information technology and Web business development (MBA); management (MBA); public policy (MPA); social work (MA), including clinical social work; special education (M Ed); strategic leadership (MBA).

Université du Québec en Outaouais, Graduate Programs, Department of Language Studies, Gatineau, QC J8X 3X7, Canada. Offers localization (DESS); second and foreign language teaching (Diploma). *Students:* 20 part-time. *Application deadline:* For fall admission, 6/1 priority date for domestic students, 3/1 for international students; for winter admission, 11/1 priority date for domestic students, 10/1 for international students. Application fee: $30. *Financial support:* Research assistantships available. *Unit head:* Georges Farid, Director, 819-595-3900 Ext. 4444, Fax: 819-595-4450, E-mail: georges.farid@uqo.ca. *Application contact:* Registrar's Office, 819-773-1850, Fax: 819-773-1835, E-mail: registraire@uqo.ca.

University at Buffalo, the State University of New York, Graduate School, Graduate School of Education, Department of Learning and Instruction, Buffalo, NY 14260. Offers biology education (Ed M, Certificate); chemistry education (Ed M, Certificate); childhood education (Ed M); childhood education with bilingual extension (Ed M); early childhood education (Ed M); early childhood education with bilingual extension (birth-grade 2) (Ed M); earth science education (Ed M, Certificate); educational technology and new literacies (Certificate); educational technology and new literacies (online) (Certificate); elementary education (Ed D, PhD); English education (Ed M, PhD, Certificate); English for speakers of other languages (Ed M); foreign and second language education (PhD); French education (Ed M, Certificate); general education (Ed M); German education (Ed M, Certificate); gifted education (online) (Certificate); Latin education (Ed M, Certificate); literacy teaching and learning (Certificate); literary specialist (Ed M); mathematics education (Ed M, PhD, Certificate); music education (Ed M, Certificate); physics education (Ed M, Certificate); reading education (PhD); science and the public (online) (Ed M); science education (PhD); social studies education (Ed M, Certificate); Spanish education (Ed M, Certificate); special education (PhD); teaching and leading for diversity (Certificate); teaching English to speakers of other languages (Ed M). Part-time and evening/weekend programs available. Postbaccalaureate distance learning degree programs offered (no on-campus study). *Faculty:* 32 full-time (23 women), 54 part-time/adjunct (43 women). *Students:* 294 full-time (222 women), 350 part-time (261 women); includes 75 minority (19 Black or African American, non-Hispanic/Latino; 6 American Indian or Alaska Native, non-Hispanic/Latino; 40 Asian, non-Hispanic/Latino; 10 Hispanic/Latino), 76 international. Average age 29. 548 applicants, 52% accepted, 253 enrolled. In 2011, 225 master's, 17 doctorates, 37 other advanced degrees awarded. *Degree requirements:* For master's, comprehensive exam; for doctorate, thesis/dissertation, research analysis exam, research experience component. *Entrance requirements:* For doctorate, GRE General Test or MAT, interview, writing sample, letters of recommendation. Additional exam requirements/recommendations for international students: Required—TOEFL (minimum score 600 paper-based; 96 iBT). *Application deadline:* For fall admission, 2/1 priority date for domestic students, 2/1 for international students; for spring admission, 11/15 priority date for domestic students, 10/1 for international students. Applications are processed on a rolling basis. Application fee: $50. Electronic applications accepted. *Financial support:* In 2011–12, 40 fellowships (averaging $12,991 per year), 46 research assistantships (averaging $10,986 per year) were awarded; teaching assistantships with full tuition reimbursements, career-related internships or fieldwork, Federal Work-Study, institutionally sponsored loans, scholarships/grants, and unspecified assistantships also available. Financial award application deadline: 2/28; financial award applicants required to submit FAFSA. *Faculty research:* Science assessment, foreign language teaching and learning, early learning, new literacies, gender and education. *Unit head:* Dr. Julie Sarama, Chair, 716-645-2455, Fax: 716-645-3161, E-mail: jcollins@buffalo.edu. *Application contact:* Cathy Dimino, Admissions Assistant, 716-645-2110, Fax: 716-645-7937, E-mail: cadimino@buffalo.edu.

University of Arkansas at Little Rock, Graduate School, College of Arts, Humanities, and Social Science, Department of International and Second Language Studies, Little Rock, AR 72204-1099. Offers second languages (MA).

University of Calgary, Faculty of Graduate Studies, Faculty of Education, Graduate Division of Educational Research, Calgary, AB T2N 1N4, Canada. Offers community rehabilitation and disability studies (M Ed, M Sc, Ed D, PhD, Graduate Certificate, Graduate Diploma); curriculum, teaching and learning (M Ed, M Sc, MA, Ed D, PhD, Graduate Certificate, Graduate Diploma); educational contexts (M Ed, MA, Ed D, PhD, Graduate Certificate, Graduate Diploma); educational leadership (M Ed, MA, Ed D, PhD, Graduate Certificate, Graduate Diploma); educational technology (M Ed, M Sc, MA, Ed D, PhD, Graduate Certificate, Graduate Diploma); gifted education (M Sc, MA, Ed D, PhD, Graduate Certificate, Graduate Diploma); higher education administration (Ed D); interpretive studies in education (M Ed, M Sc, MA, Ed D, PhD, Graduate Certificate, Graduate Diploma); second language teaching (M Ed, Ed D, PhD, Graduate Certificate, Graduate Diploma); teaching English as a second language (M Ed, M Sc, MA, Ed D, PhD, Graduate Certificate, Graduate Diploma); workplace and adult learning (M Ed, MA, Ed D, PhD, Graduate Certificate, Graduate Diploma). Ed D in both higher education administration and educational leadership offered via distance delivery. Part-time and evening/weekend programs available. Postbaccalaureate distance learning degree programs offered (minimal on-campus study). *Degree requirements:* For master's, thesis (for some programs); for doctorate, thesis/dissertation, candidacy exam. *Entrance requirements:* For master's, minimum GPA of 3.0, 3 letters of reference; for doctorate, minimum GPA of 3.5, 3 letters of reference; for other advanced degree, minimum GPA of 3.0. Additional exam requirements/recommendations for international students: Required—TOEFL, IELTS. Electronic applications accepted. *Faculty research:* Curriculum, leadership, technology, contexts, gifted, second language teaching, work place and adult learning.

University of California, Irvine, School of Humanities, Department of Spanish and Portuguese, Irvine, CA 92697. Offers Spanish (MA, MAT, PhD). *Students:* 39 full-time (21 women), 1 (woman) part-time; includes 29 minority (1 Asian, non-Hispanic/Latino; 28 Hispanic/Latino). Average age 34. 25 applicants, 16% accepted, 3 enrolled. In 2011, 7 master's, 4 doctorates awarded. *Degree requirements:* For doctorate, thesis/ dissertation. *Entrance requirements:* For master's and doctorate, GRE General Test, minimum GPA of 3.0. Additional exam requirements/recommendations for international students: Required—TOEFL (minimum score 550 paper-based; 213 computer-based). *Application deadline:* For fall admission, 1/2 priority date for domestic students, 1/2 for international students. Applications are processed on a rolling basis. Application fee: $80 ($100 for international students). Electronic applications accepted. *Financial support:* Fellowships, teaching assistantships, institutionally sponsored loans, traineeships, health care benefits, and unspecified assistantships available. Financial award application deadline: 3/1; financial award applicants required to submit FAFSA. *Faculty research:* Latin American literature, Spanish literature, Spanish linguistics in Creole studies, Hispanic literature in the U. S., Luso-Brazilian literature. *Unit head:* Prof. Horacio Legras, Chair, 949-824-7265, Fax: 949-824-2803, E-mail: hlegras@uci.edu. *Application contact:* June DeTurk, Graduate Program Coordinator, 949-824-8793, Fax: 949-824-2803, E-mail: jdeturk@uci.edu. Web site: http://www.hnet.uci.edu/ spanishandportuguese/.

University of Central Arkansas, Graduate School, College of Liberal Arts, Department of Foreign Languages, Conway, AR 72035-0001. Offers MA. Part-time programs available. *Faculty:* 4 full-time (2 women). *Students:* 6 full-time (3 women), 5 part-time (3 women); includes 5 minority (1 Black or African American, non-Hispanic/Latino; 4 Hispanic/Latino). Average age 34. 3 applicants, 100% accepted, 2 enrolled. In 2011, 3 master's awarded. *Degree requirements:* For master's, one foreign language, comprehensive exam, thesis optional. *Entrance requirements:* For master's, GRE General Test, minimum GPA of 2.7. Additional exam requirements/recommendations for international students: Required—TOEFL (minimum score 550 paper-based; 213 computer-based). *Application deadline:* For fall admission, 3/1 priority date for domestic students, 3/1 for international students; for spring admission, 10/1 priority date for domestic students, 10/1 for international students. Application fee: $25 ($50 for international students). *Expenses:* Tuition, state resident: full-time $4834; part-time $398.35 per credit hour. Tuition, nonresident: full-time $8686. *Financial support:* In 2011–12, 2 teaching assistantships with partial tuition reimbursements (averaging $10,000 per year) were awarded. Financial award application deadline: 2/15; financial award applicants required to submit FAFSA. *Unit head:* Dr. John Parrack, Associate Professor, 501-450-5120, Fax: 501-450-5185, E-mail: johncp@uca.edu. *Application contact:* Susan Wood, Administrative Specialist, 501-450-3124, Fax: 501-450-5678, E-mail: swood@uca.edu.

University of Connecticut, Graduate School, Neag School of Education, Department of Curriculum and Instruction, Program in World Languages Education, Storrs, CT 06269. Offers MA, PhD, Post-Master's Certificate. *Accreditation:* NCATE. Terminal master's awarded for partial completion of doctoral program. *Degree requirements:* For master's, comprehensive exam, thesis or alternative; for doctorate, thesis/dissertation. *Entrance requirements:* For doctorate, GRE General Test. Additional exam requirements/recommendations for international students: Required—TOEFL (minimum score 550 paper-based; 213 computer-based). Electronic applications accepted.

University of Delaware, College of Arts and Sciences, Department of Foreign Languages and Literatures, Newark, DE 19716. Offers foreign languages and literatures (MA), including French, German, Spanish; foreign languages pedagogy (MA), including French, German, Spanish; technical Chinese translation (MA). *Degree requirements:* For master's, one foreign language, comprehensive exam, thesis optional. *Entrance requirements:* For master's, GRE General Test, letters of recommendation, writing sample. Additional exam requirements/recommendations for international students: Required—TOEFL. Electronic applications accepted. *Faculty research:* Medieval to Modern French and Spanish literature, Twentieth Century German, French, Spanish literature by women, computer-assisted instruction.

University of Georgia, College of Education, Department of Language and Literacy Education, Athens, GA 30602. Offers English education (M Ed, Ed S); language and literacy education (PhD); reading education (M Ed, Ed D, Ed S); teaching additional languages (M Ed, Ed S). *Accreditation:* NCATE. *Faculty:* 15 full-time (11 women). *Students:* 100 full-time (81 women), 94 part-time (80 women); includes 21 minority (17 Black or African American, non-Hispanic/Latino; 1 Asian, non-Hispanic/Latino; 2 Hispanic/Latino; 1 Two or more races, non-Hispanic/Latino), 31 international. Average age 33. 185 applicants, 61% accepted, 42 enrolled. In 2011, 43 master's, 15 doctorates, 2 other advanced degrees awarded. *Degree requirements:* For doctorate, variable foreign language requirement. *Entrance requirements:* For master's and Ed S, GRE General Test or MAT; for doctorate, GRE General Test. Additional exam requirements/ recommendations for international students: Required—TOEFL (minimum score 550 paper-based; 213 computer-based). *Application deadline:* For fall admission, 7/1 priority date for domestic students; for spring admission, 11/15 for domestic students. Application fee: $50. Electronic applications accepted. *Faculty research:* Comprehension, critical literacy, literacy and technology, vocabulary instruction, content area reading. *Unit head:* Dr. Mark A. Faust, Head, 706-542-4515, Fax: 706-542-4509, E-mail: mfaust@uga.edu. *Application contact:* Dr. Elizabeth St. Pierre, Graduate Coordinator, 706-542-4520, E-mail: stpierre@uga.edu. Web site: http:// www.coe.uga.edu/lle/.

University of Hawaii at Hilo, Program in Hawaiian and Indigenous Language and Cultural Revitalization, Hilo, HI 96720-4091. Offers PhD.

University of Hawaii at Hilo, Program in Hawaiian Language and Literature, Hilo, HI 96720-4091. Offers MA.

University of Hawaii at Manoa, Graduate Division, College of Languages, Linguistics and Literature, Department of Second Language Studies, Honolulu, HI 96822. Offers English as a second language (MA, Graduate Certificate); second language acquisition (PhD). Part-time programs available. *Degree requirements:* For master's, 2 foreign languages, thesis optional; for doctorate, 2 foreign languages, comprehensive exam, thesis/dissertation. *Entrance requirements:* For master's, GRE General Test, minimum GPA of 3.0; for doctorate, GRE General Test, MA, scholarly publications. Additional exam requirements/recommendations for international students: Required—TOEFL (minimum score 600 paper-based; 250 computer-based; 100 iBT), IELTS (minimum score 7). *Faculty research:* Second language use, second language analysis, second language pedagogy and testing, second language learning, qualitative and quantitative research methods for second languages.

University of Hawaii at Manoa, Graduate Division, Hawai'inuaka School of Hawaiian Knowledge, Program in Hawaiian, Honolulu, HI 96822. Offers MA. Part-time programs available. *Degree requirements:* For master's, thesis optional. *Entrance requirements:* Additional exam requirements/recommendations for international students: Required—TOEFL (minimum score 500 paper-based; 173 computer-based; 61 iBT), IELTS (minimum score 5).

University of Hawaii at Manoa, Graduate Division, Hawai'inuaka School of Hawaiian Knowledge, Program in Hawaiian Studies, Honolulu, HI 96822. Offers MA. Part-time programs available. *Degree requirements:* For master's, thesis optional. *Entrance requirements:* Additional exam requirements/recommendations for international students: Required—TOEFL (minimum score 500 paper-based; 173 computer-based; 61 iBT), IELTS (minimum score 5).

University of Illinois at Urbana–Champaign, Graduate College, College of Liberal Arts and Sciences, School of Literatures, Cultures and Linguistics, Department of Spanish, Italian and Portuguese, Champaign, IL 61820. Offers Italian (MA, PhD); Portuguese (MA, PhD); Spanish (MA, PhD). *Faculty:* 16 full-time (11 women). *Students:* 36 full-time (26 women), 4 part-time (all women); includes 12 minority (all Hispanic/ Latino), 13 international. 57 applicants, 16% accepted, 6 enrolled. In 2011, 8 master's, 8 doctorates awarded. *Entrance requirements:* For master's, GRE General Test, minimum GPA of 3.0; writing sample; for doctorate, GRE, minimum GPA of 3.0; writing sample. Additional exam requirements/recommendations for international students: Required—TOEFL (minimum score 88 iBT). *Application deadline:* Applications are processed on a rolling basis. Application fee: $75 ($90 for international students). Electronic applications accepted. *Financial support:* In 2011–12, 17 fellowships, 2 research assistantships, 33 teaching assistantships were awarded; tuition waivers (full and partial) also available. *Unit head:* Silvina A. Montrul, Head, 217-333-3090, Fax: 217-244-8430, E-mail: montrul@illinois.edu. *Application contact:* Lynn Stanke, Office Support Specialist, 217-333-6269, Fax: 217-244-3050, E-mail: stanke@illinois.edu. Web site: http:// www.sip.illinois.edu/.

University of Illinois at Urbana–Champaign, Graduate College, College of Liberal Arts and Sciences, School of Literatures, Cultures and Linguistics, Department of the Classics, Champaign, IL 61820. Offers classical philology (PhD); classics (MA); teaching of Latin (MA). *Faculty:* 6 full-time (2 women). *Students:* 18 full-time (8 women), 2 part-time (1 woman); includes 5 minority (1 Asian, non-Hispanic/Latino; 3 Hispanic/ Latino; 1 Two or more races, non-Hispanic/Latino), 1 international. 20 applicants, 30% accepted, 5 enrolled. In 2011, 1 master's, 1 doctorate awarded. *Entrance requirements:* For master's, GRE, minimum GPA of 3.0; for doctorate, GRE, writing sample; minimum GPA of 3.0. Additional exam requirements/recommendations for international students: Required—TOEFL (minimum score 79 iBT). *Application deadline:* Applications are processed on a rolling basis. Application fee: $75 ($90 for international students). Electronic applications accepted. *Financial support:* In 2011–12, 6 fellowships, 1 research assistantship, 17 teaching assistantships were awarded; tuition waivers (full and partial) also available. *Faculty research:* Greek and Latin language, papyrology, epigraphy, classical archaeology. *Unit head:* Ariana Traill, Head, 217-333-1008, Fax: 217-244-8430, E-mail: traill@illinois.edu. *Application contact:* Lynn Stanke, Office Support Specialist, 217-333-6269, Fax: 217-244-3050, E-mail: stanke@illinois.edu. Web site: http://www.classics.illinois.edu/.

University of Indianapolis, Graduate Programs, School of Education, Indianapolis, IN 46227-3697. Offers art education (MAT); biology (MAT); chemistry (MAT); curriculum and instruction (MA); earth sciences (MAT); education (MA, MAT); educational leadership (MA); elementary education (MA); English (MAT); French (MAT); math (MAT); physical education (MAT); physics (MAT); secondary education (MA), including art education, education, English education, social studies education; social studies (MAT); Spanish (MAT). *Accreditation:* NCATE. Part-time and evening/weekend programs available. *Faculty:* 3 full-time (2 women), 3 part-time/adjunct (2 women). *Students:* 32 full-time (18 women), 97 part-time (56 women); includes 22 minority (20 Black or African American, non-Hispanic/Latino; 1 Asian, non-Hispanic/Latino; 1 Hispanic/Latino), 3 international. Average age 33. In 2011, 78 master's awarded. *Entrance requirements:* For master's, GRE Subject Test, PRAXIS I, minimum GPA of 2.5, 3 letters of recommendation, interview, writing exercise. Additional exam requirements/recommendations for international students: Required—TOEFL (minimum score 550 paper-based; 213 computer-based). *Application deadline:* Applications are processed on a rolling basis. Application fee: $50. Tuition and fees vary according to degree level and program. *Financial support:* Federal Work-Study available. Financial award application deadline: 5/1; financial award applicants required to submit FAFSA. *Faculty research:* Assessment of teacher education, perceptions of prospective teachers by parents. *Unit head:* Dr. Kathy Moran, Dean, 317-788-3285, Fax: 317-788-3300, E-mail: kmoran@uindy.edu. *Application contact:* Jeni Kirby, 317-788-2113, E-mail: kirbyj@uindy.edu. Web site: http://education.uindy.edu/.

The University of Iowa, Graduate College, College of Education, Department of Teaching and Learning, Program in Secondary Education, Iowa City, IA 52242-1316. Offers art education (PhD); curriculum and supervision (PhD); curriculum supervision (MA); developmental reading (MA); English education (MA, MAT); foreign language education (MA, MAT); foreign language/ESL education (PhD); language, literature and culture (PhD); math education (PhD); mathematics education (MA); social studies (MA, PhD). *Degree requirements:* For master's, thesis optional, exam; for doctorate, comprehensive exam, thesis/dissertation. *Entrance requirements:* For master's and doctorate, GRE General Test, minimum GPA of 3.0. Additional exam requirements/ recommendations for international students: Required—TOEFL (minimum score 550 paper-based; 213 computer-based; 81 iBT). Electronic applications accepted.

The University of Iowa, Graduate College, Program in Second Language Acquisition, Iowa City, IA 52242-1316. Offers PhD. *Degree requirements:* For doctorate, comprehensive exam, thesis/dissertation. *Entrance requirements:* For doctorate, GRE General Test, minimum GPA of 3.0. Additional exam requirements/recommendations for international students: Required—TOEFL (minimum score 600 paper-based; 250 computer-based; 100 iBT). Electronic applications accepted.

University of Kentucky, Graduate School, College of Arts and Sciences and College of Education, Program in Teaching World Languages, Lexington, KY 40506-0032. Offers MA. *Entrance requirements:* For master's, GRE General Test, minimum undergraduate GPA of 2.75. Additional exam requirements/recommendations for international students: Required—TOEFL (minimum score 550 paper-based; 213 computer-based). Electronic applications accepted.

University of Maine, Graduate School, College of Liberal Arts and Sciences, Department of Modern Languages and Classics, Orono, ME 04469. Offers French (MA, MAT); North American French (MA). Part-time programs available. *Faculty:* 7 full-time (5 women), 9 part-time/adjunct (6 women). *Students:* 4 full-time (all women), 4 part-time (3 women). Average age 34. 5 applicants, 60% accepted, 3 enrolled. In 2011, 2 degrees awarded. *Degree requirements:* For master's, one foreign language, thesis (for some programs). *Entrance requirements:* For master's, GRE General Test. Additional exam requirements/recommendations for international students: Required—TOEFL.

Application deadline: For fall admission, 2/1 priority date for domestic students. Applications are processed on a rolling basis. Application fee: $65. Electronic applications accepted. *Expenses:* Tuition, state resident: full-time $5016. Tuition, nonresident: full-time $14,424. *Financial support:* In 2011–12, 3 teaching assistantships with tuition reimbursements (averaging $13,600 per year) were awarded; Federal Work-Study and tuition waivers (full and partial) also available. Financial award application deadline: 3/1. *Faculty research:* Narratology, poetics, Quebec literature, theater, women's studies. *Unit head:* Dr. Raymond Pelletier, Chair, 207-581-2079, Fax: 207-581-1832. *Application contact:* Scott G. Delcourt, Associate Dean of the Graduate School, 207-581-3291, Fax: 207-581-3232, E-mail: graduate@maine.edu. Web site: http://www2.umaine.edu/graduate/.

University of Maryland, Baltimore County, Graduate School, College of Arts, Humanities and Social Sciences, Department of Education, Program in Teaching, Baltimore, MD 21250. Offers early childhood education (MAT); elementary education (MAT); secondary education (MAT), including social studies; secondary education (MAT), including art, biology, chemistry, dance, earth/space science, English, foreign language, mathematics, music, physics, theatre. Part-time and evening/weekend programs available. *Faculty:* 24 full-time (18 women), 25 part-time/adjunct (19 women). *Students:* 46 full-time (35 women), 64 part-time (39 women); includes 24 minority (8 Black or African American, non-Hispanic/Latino; 7 Asian, non-Hispanic/Latino; 6 Hispanic/Latino; 1 Native Hawaiian or other Pacific Islander, non-Hispanic/Latino; 2 Two or more races, non-Hispanic/Latino), 4 international. Average age 31. 88 applicants, 57% accepted, 39 enrolled. In 2011, 106 master's awarded. *Degree requirements:* For master's, comprehensive exam (for some programs), thesis (for some programs). *Entrance requirements:* For master's, PRAXIS I or GRE (minimum score of 1000), minimum GPA of 3.0. Additional exam requirements/recommendations for international students: Required—TOEFL. *Application deadline:* For fall admission, 6/1 for domestic students; for spring admission, 11/1 for domestic students. Applications are processed on a rolling basis. Application fee: $50. Electronic applications accepted. *Financial support:* In 2011–12, 6 students received support, including teaching assistantships with full and partial tuition reimbursements available (averaging $12,000 per year); career-related internships or fieldwork, Federal Work-Study, scholarships/grants, tuition waivers, and unspecified assistantships also available. Financial award application deadline: 3/1. *Faculty research:* STEM teacher education, culturally sensitive pedagogy, ESOL/bilingual education, early childhood education, language, literacy and culture. *Unit head:* Dr. Susan M. Blunck, Graduate Program Director, 410-455-2869, Fax: 410-455-3986, E-mail: blunck@umbc.edu. *Application contact:* Cheryl Johnson, 410-455-3388, E-mail: blackwel@umbc.edu. Web site: http://www.umbc.edu/education/.

University of Maryland, College Park, Academic Affairs, College of Arts and Humanities, School of Languages, Literature, and Cultures, Program in Second Language Acquisition and Application, College Park, MD 20742. Offers second language instruction (PhD); second language learning (PhD); second language measurement and assessment (PhD); second language use (PhD). *Students:* 22 full-time (16 women), 5 part-time (4 women); includes 1 minority (Asian, non-Hispanic/Latino), 11 international. 67 applicants, 15% accepted, 8 enrolled. *Application deadline:* For fall admission, 1/15 for domestic students, 2/1 for international students; for spring admission, 10/15 for domestic students, 6/1 for international students. Applications are processed on a rolling basis. Application fee: $75. Electronic applications accepted. *Expenses: Tuition, area resident:* Part-time $525 per credit hour. Tuition, state resident: part-time $525 per credit hour. Tuition, nonresident: part-time $1131 per credit hour. *Required fees:* $386.31 per term. Tuition and fees vary according to program. *Financial support:* In 2011–12, 5 fellowships with full and partial tuition reimbursements (averaging $15,875 per year), 3 research assistantships (averaging $22,143 per year), 7 teaching assistantships (averaging $21,246 per year) were awarded. *Faculty research:* Second language acquisition, pedagogical perspectives, technological applications, language use in professional contexts. *Unit head:* Robert M. De Keyeser, Director, 301-405-4030, E-mail: rdk@umd.edu. *Application contact:* Dr. Charles A. Caramello, Dean of Graduate School, 301-405-0358, Fax: 301-314-9305.

University of Massachusetts Amherst, Graduate School, College of Humanities and Fine Arts, Department of Languages, Literatures, and Cultures, Program in French and Francophone Studies, Amherst, MA 01003. Offers French (MA, MAT). Part-time programs available. *Faculty:* 10 full-time (5 women). *Students:* 9 full-time (7 women), 2 part-time (1 woman); includes 2 minority (1 Hispanic/Latino; 1 Two or more races, non-Hispanic/Latino). Average age 30. 8 applicants, 100% accepted, 5 enrolled. In 2011, 4 master's awarded. *Degree requirements:* For master's, thesis or alternative. *Entrance requirements:* For master's, GRE General Test. Additional exam requirements/recommendations for international students: Required—TOEFL (minimum score 550 paper-based; 213 computer-based; 80 iBT), IELTS (minimum score 6.5). *Application deadline:* For fall admission, 2/1 for domestic and international students; for spring admission, 10/1 for domestic and international students. Applications are processed on a rolling basis. Application fee: $50 ($65 for international students). Electronic applications accepted. Tuition and fees vary according to course load, campus/location and program. *Financial support:* Fellowships, research assistantships, teaching assistantships with full tuition reimbursements, career-related internships or fieldwork, Federal Work-Study, scholarships/grants, traineeships, health care benefits, tuition waivers (full), and unspecified assistantships available. Support available to part-time students. Financial award application deadline: 2/1. *Unit head:* Dr. Luke P. Bouvier, Graduate Program Director, 413-545-2314, Fax: 412-545-4778. *Application contact:* Lindsay DeSantis, Interim Supervisor of Admissions, 413-545-0722, Fax: 413-577-0100, E-mail: gradadm@grad.umass.edu. Web site: http://www.umass.edu/french/.

University of Massachusetts Boston, Office of Graduate Studies, College of Liberal Arts, Program in Applied Linguistics, Boston, MA 02125-3393. Offers bilingual education (MA); English as a second language (MA); foreign language pedagogy (MA). Part-time and evening/weekend programs available. *Degree requirements:* For master's, one foreign language, comprehensive exam. *Entrance requirements:* For master's, minimum GPA of 2.75. *Faculty research:* Multicultural theory and curriculum development, foreign language pedagogy, language and culture, applied psycholinguistics, bilingual education.

University of Michigan, Horace H. Rackham School of Graduate Studies, College of Literature, Science, and the Arts, Department of Classical Studies, Ann Arbor, MI 48109. Offers classical studies (PhD); teaching Latin (MAT). *Faculty:* 21 full-time (9 women), 6 part-time/adjunct (4 women). *Students:* 29 full-time (19 women); includes 3 minority (2 Asian, non-Hispanic/Latino; 1 Hispanic/Latino), 1 international. Average age 26. 90 applicants, 7% accepted, 4 enrolled. In 2011, 7 master's, 1 doctorate awarded. Terminal master's awarded for partial completion of doctoral program. *Degree requirements:* For master's, one foreign language, comprehensive exam; for doctorate, 4 foreign languages, thesis/dissertation, oral defense of dissertation, preliminary exams. *Entrance requirements:* For master's, GRE General Test; for doctorate, GRE General Test, minimum of 3 years of college-level Latin and 2 years of college-level Greek. Additional exam requirements/recommendations for international students: Required—TOEFL (minimum score 560 paper-based; 220 computer-based). *Application deadline:* For fall admission, 1/5 for domestic and international students. Application fee: $65 ($75 for international students). Electronic applications accepted. *Financial support:* In 2011–12, 26 students received support, including 4 fellowships with full tuition reimbursements available (averaging $18,000 per year), 1 research assistantship, 16 teaching assistantships with full tuition reimbursements available (averaging $16,694 per year); career-related internships or fieldwork, Federal Work-Study, institutionally sponsored loans, scholarships/grants, traineeships, health care benefits, tuition waivers (full), and unspecified assistantships also available. Financial award application deadline: 3/15. *Faculty research:* Greek and Latin literature, ancient history, papyrology, archaeology. *Unit head:* Prof. Ruth Scodel, Chair, 734-764-0360, Fax: 734-763-4959, E-mail: classics@umich.edu. *Application contact:* Michelle M. Biggs, Graduate Coordinator, 734-647-2330, Fax: 734-763-4959, E-mail: mbiggs@umich.edu. Web site: http://www.lsa.umich.edu/classics.

University of Minnesota, Twin Cities Campus, Graduate School, College of Education and Human Development, Department of Curriculum and Instruction, Program in Teaching, Minneapolis, MN 55455-0213. Offers Chinese (M Ed); earth science (M Ed); elementary special education (M Ed); English (M Ed); English as a second language (M Ed); French (M Ed); German (M Ed); Hebrew (M Ed); Japanese (M Ed); life sciences (M Ed); mathematics (M Ed); middle school science (M Ed); science (M Ed); second languages and cultures (M Ed); social studies (M Ed); Spanish (M Ed). *Students:* 375 full-time (319 women), 72 part-time (56 women); includes 34 minority (8 Black or African American, non-Hispanic/Latino; 16 Asian, non-Hispanic/Latino; 10 Hispanic/Latino), 5 international. Average age 27. 317 applicants, 70% accepted, 215 enrolled. In 2011, 443 master's awarded. Application fee: $55. *Unit head:* Dr. Nina Asher, Chair, 612-624-1357, Fax: 612-624-8277, E-mail: nasher@umn.edu. *Application contact:* Dr. Jennifer Engler, Assistant Dean, 612-626-2887, Fax: 612-626-7496, E-mail: engle009@umn.edu. Web site: http://www.cehd.umn.edu/ci/.

University of Missouri, Graduate School, College of Arts and Sciences, Department of Romance Languages and Literature, Columbia, MO 65211. Offers French (MA, PhD); literature (MA); Spanish (MA, PhD); teaching (MA). *Faculty:* 25 full-time (12 women), 1 (woman) part-time/adjunct. *Students:* 27 full-time (16 women), 14 part-time (10 women); includes 13 minority (4 Black or African American, non-Hispanic/Latino; 1 Asian, non-Hispanic/Latino; 7 Hispanic/Latino; 1 Two or more races, non-Hispanic/Latino), 15 international. Average age 34. 23 applicants, 65% accepted, 6 enrolled. In 2011, 13 master's, 2 doctorates awarded. Terminal master's awarded for partial completion of doctoral program. *Degree requirements:* For master's, one foreign language; for doctorate, 4 foreign languages, comprehensive exam, thesis/dissertation. *Entrance requirements:* For master's, GRE General Test, minimum GPA of 3.0 in field of major; bachelor's degree; for doctorate, GRE General Test, minimum GPA of 3.0 in field of major; master's degree. Additional exam requirements/recommendations for international students: Required—TOEFL (minimum score 500 paper-based; 173 computer-based; 61 iBT). *Application deadline:* For fall admission, 2/15 priority date for domestic students; for winter admission, 10/15 for domestic students. Applications are processed on a rolling basis. Application fee: $55 ($75 for international students). Electronic applications accepted. *Expenses:* Tuition, state resident: full-time $5881. Tuition, nonresident: full-time $15,183. *Required fees:* $952. Tuition and fees vary according to campus/location and program. *Financial support:* In 2011–12, 37 teaching assistantships with full tuition reimbursements were awarded; research assistantships, institutionally sponsored loans, health care benefits, and unspecified assistantships also available. *Unit head:* Dr. Flore Zephir, Department Chair, E-mail: zephirf@missouri.edu. *Application contact:* Mary Harriss, Administrative Assistant, 573-882-5039, E-mail: harrisma@missouri.edu. Web site: http://romancelanguages.missouri.edu/grad.shtml.

University of Missouri, Graduate School, College of Education, Department of Learning, Teaching and Curriculum, Columbia, MO 65211. Offers agricultural education (M Ed, PhD, Ed S); art education (M Ed, PhD, Ed S); business and office education (M Ed, PhD, Ed S); early childhood education (M Ed, PhD, Ed S); elementary education (M Ed, PhD, Ed S); English education (M Ed, PhD, Ed S); foreign language education (M Ed, PhD, Ed S); health education and promotion (M Ed, PhD); learning and instruction (M Ed); marketing education (M Ed, PhD, Ed S); mathematics education (M Ed, PhD, Ed S); music education (M Ed, PhD, Ed S); reading education (M Ed, PhD, Ed S); science education (M Ed, PhD, Ed S); social studies education (M Ed, PhD, Ed S); vocational education (M Ed, PhD, Ed S). Part-time programs available. *Faculty:* 26 full-time (16 women), 3 part-time/adjunct (2 women). *Students:* 184 full-time (145 women), 276 part-time (215 women); includes 34 minority (10 Black or African American, non-Hispanic/Latino; 1 American Indian or Alaska Native, non-Hispanic/Latino; 7 Asian, non-Hispanic/Latino; 8 Hispanic/Latino; 8 Two or more races, non-Hispanic/Latino), 39 international. Average age 32. 309 applicants, 76% accepted, 204 enrolled. In 2011, 232 master's, 8 doctorates, 2 other advanced degrees awarded. Terminal master's awarded for partial completion of doctoral program. *Degree requirements:* For doctorate, thesis/dissertation. *Entrance requirements:* For master's and Ed S, GRE General Test or MAT, minimum GPA of 3.0; for doctorate, GRE General Test, minimum GPA of 3.0. Additional exam requirements/recommendations for international students: Required—TOEFL (minimum score 600 paper-based; 250 computer-based; 100 iBT). Application fee: $55 ($75 for international students). Electronic applications accepted. *Expenses:* Tuition, state resident: full-time $5881. Tuition, nonresident: full-time $15,183. *Required fees:* $952. Tuition and fees vary according to campus/location and program. *Financial support:* Fellowships, research assistantships, teaching assistantships, and institutionally sponsored loans available. *Application contact:* Fran Colley, 573-882-6462, E-mail: colleyf@missouri.edu. Web site: http://education.missouri.edu/LTC/.

University of Nebraska at Kearney, Graduate Studies, College of Fine Arts and Humanities, Department of Modern Languages, Kearney, NE 68849-0001. Offers French (MA Ed); German (MA Ed); Spanish (MA Ed). *Accreditation:* NCATE. Part-time and evening/weekend programs available. *Degree requirements:* For master's, thesis optional. *Entrance requirements:* For master's, GRE General Test. Electronic applications accepted. *Faculty research:* Translation theory, Spanish linguistics; Heidegger, Rilke and Nietzsche; symotolistic poetry.

University of Nebraska at Omaha, Graduate Studies, College of Arts and Sciences, Program in Language Teaching, Omaha, NE 68182. Offers MA. Part-time and evening/weekend programs available. *Faculty:* 11 full-time (10 women). *Students:* 2 full-time (both women), 28 part-time (22 women); includes 6 minority (1 Black or African American, non-Hispanic/Latino; 1 Asian, non-Hispanic/Latino; 4 Hispanic/Latino), 1 international. Average age 33. 9 applicants, 33% accepted, 3 enrolled. In 2011, 10 master's awarded. *Degree requirements:* For master's, comprehensive exam, thesis (for some programs). *Entrance requirements:* For master's, 2 letters of recommendation, oral and written language sample. Additional exam requirements/recommendations for international students: Required—TOEFL (minimum score 600 paper-based; 250 computer-based; 100 iBT). *Application deadline:* For fall admission, 4/15 priority date for domestic students; for spring admission, 11/15 priority date for domestic students. Applications are processed on a rolling basis. Application fee: $45. Electronic applications accepted. *Financial support:* In 2011–12, 7 students received support, including 3 teaching assistantships with tuition reimbursements available; tuition waivers (partial) also available. Financial award application deadline: 3/1; financial award applicants required to submit FAFSA. *Unit head:* Dr. Melanie Bloom, Chairperson, 402-554-4841. *Application contact:* Dr. Melanie Bloom, Information Contact, 402-554-4841.

Foreign Languages Education

University of Nevada, Reno, Graduate School, College of Liberal Arts, Department of Foreign Languages and Literatures, Reno, NV 89557. Offers French (MA); German (MA); Spanish (MA). *Degree requirements:* For master's, one foreign language, thesis optional. *Entrance requirements:* For master's, GRE General Test, minimum GPA of 2.75. Additional exam requirements/recommendations for international students: Required—TOEFL (minimum score 500 paper-based; 173 computer-based; 61 iBT), IELTS (minimum score 6). *Faculty research:* Thirteenth century mysticism, contemporary Spanish and Latin American poetry and theater, French interrelation between narration and photography, exile literature and Holocaust.

The University of North Carolina at Chapel Hill, Graduate School, School of Education, Program in Secondary Education, Chapel Hill, NC 27599. Offers English (Grades 9-12) (MAT); English as a second language (MAT); French (Grades K-12) (MAT); German (Grades K-12) (MAT); Japanese (Grades K-12) (MAT); Latin (Grades 9-12) (MAT); mathematics (Grades 9-12) (MAT); music (Grades K-12) (MAT); science (Grades 9-12) (MAT); social studies (Grades 9-12) (MAT); Spanish (Grades K-12) (MAT). *Accreditation:* NCATE. *Degree requirements:* For master's, comprehensive exam. *Entrance requirements:* For master's, GRE General Test, minimum GPA of 3.0 during last 2 years of undergraduate course work. Additional exam requirements/recommendations for international students: Required—TOEFL (minimum score 550 paper-based; 79 computer-based). Electronic applications accepted.

The University of North Carolina at Greensboro, Graduate School, School of Education, Department of Curriculum and Instruction, Greensboro, NC 27412-5001. Offers college teaching and adult learning (Certificate); curriculum and instruction (M Ed), including chemistry education, elementary education, English as a second language, French education, instructional technology, mathematics education, middle grades education, reading education, science education, social studies education, Spanish education; curriculum and teaching (PhD), including higher education, teacher education and development; English as a second language (Certificate); higher education (M Ed); supervision (M Ed). *Accreditation:* NCATE. Part-time programs available. *Degree requirements:* For doctorate, thesis/dissertation. *Entrance requirements:* For master's and doctorate, GRE General Test. Additional exam requirements/recommendations for international students: Required—TOEFL. Electronic applications accepted. *Faculty research:* Community college literacy program, middle school mathematics/computer mathematics.

University of Northern Colorado, Graduate School, College of Humanities and Social Sciences, School of Modern Languages and Cultural Studies, Program in Foreign Languages, Greeley, CO 80639. Offers Spanish/teaching (MA). Part-time programs available. *Degree requirements:* For master's, comprehensive exam, thesis or alternative. *Entrance requirements:* For master's, minimum undergraduate GPA of 3.0, BA in Spanish, 1 year of secondary teaching. Electronic applications accepted.

University of Northern Iowa, Graduate College, College of Humanities, Arts and Sciences, Department of Languages and Literatures, Cedar Falls, IA 50614. Offers English (MA), including creative writing, English, literature, teaching English in secondary schools (TESS), teaching English to speakers of other languages; French (MA), including French, teaching English to speakers of other languages/French; German (MA), including German, teaching English to speakers of other languages/German; Spanish (MA), including Spanish, teaching English to speakers of other languages/Spanish; two languages (MA), including French/German, German/Spanish, Spanish/French. Part-time and evening/weekend programs available. *Students:* 60 full-time (42 women), 52 part-time (44 women); includes 19 minority (3 Black or African American, non-Hispanic/Latino; 1 American Indian or Alaska Native, non-Hispanic/Latino; 6 Asian, non-Hispanic/Latino; 7 Hispanic/Latino; 2 Two or more races, non-Hispanic/Latino), 14 international. 66 applicants, 61% accepted, 23 enrolled. In 2011, 40 master's awarded. *Degree requirements:* For master's, one foreign language, comprehensive exam, thesis or alternative, portfolio. *Entrance requirements:* For master's, minimum GPA of 3.0. Additional exam requirements/recommendations for international students: Required—TOEFL (minimum score 600 paper-based; 250 computer-based; 100 iBT). *Application deadline:* For fall admission, 8/1 priority date for domestic students. Applications are processed on a rolling basis. Application fee: $50 ($70 for international students). Electronic applications accepted. *Expenses:* Tuition, state resident: full-time $7476. Tuition, nonresident: full-time $16,410. *Required fees:* $942. *Financial support:* Career-related internships or fieldwork, Federal Work-Study, scholarships/grants, and tuition waivers (full and partial) available. Support available to part-time students. Financial award application deadline: 2/1. *Unit head:* Dr. Jeffrey S. Copeland, Head, 319-273-3855, Fax: 319-273-5807, E-mail: jeffrey.copeland@uni.edu. *Application contact:* Laurie S. Russell, Record Analyst, 319-273-2623, Fax: 319-273-2885, E-mail: laurie.russell@uni.edu. Web site: http://www.uni.edu/langlit/.

University of Pittsburgh, School of Education, Department of Instruction and Learning, Program in Secondary Education, Pittsburgh, PA 15260. Offers English/communications education (M Ed, MAT); foreign languages education (M Ed, MAT); mathematics education (M Ed, MAT, Ed D); science education (M Ed, MAT, Ed D); social studies education (M Ed, MAT). Part-time and evening/weekend programs available. *Students:* 154 full-time (92 women), 68 part-time (47 women); includes 18 minority (6 Black or African American, non-Hispanic/Latino; 3 Asian, non-Hispanic/Latino; 7 Hispanic/Latino; 2 Two or more races, non-Hispanic/Latino), 6 international. Average age 30. 208 applicants, 48% accepted, 72 enrolled. In 2011, 116 master's, 6 doctorates awarded. *Degree requirements:* For master's, thesis; for doctorate, thesis/dissertation. *Entrance requirements:* For master's, PRAXIS I; for doctorate, GRE General Test. Additional exam requirements/recommendations for international students: Required—TOEFL. *Application deadline:* For fall admission, 2/1 priority date for domestic students; for spring admission, 11/15 priority date for domestic students. Applications are processed on a rolling basis. Application fee: $50. Electronic applications accepted. *Expenses:* Tuition, state resident: full-time $18,774; part-time $760 per credit. Tuition, nonresident: full-time $30,736; part-time $1258 per credit. *Required fees:* $740; $200 per term. Tuition and fees vary according to program. *Financial support:* Fellowships, teaching assistantships, career-related internships or fieldwork, Federal Work-Study, tuition waivers (partial), and unspecified assistantships available. Support available to part-time students. Financial award application deadline: 3/15; financial award applicants required to submit FAFSA. *Unit head:* Dr. Richard Donato, Chairman, 412-624-7248, Fax: 412-648-7081, E-mail: donato@pitt.edu. *Application contact:* Marianne L. Budziszewski, Director of Admissions and Enrollment Services, 412-648-2230, Fax: 412-648-1899, E-mail: soeinfo@pitt.edu. Web site: http://www.education.pitt.edu/.

University of Puerto Rico, Río Piedras, College of Education, Program in Curriculum and Teaching, San Juan, PR 00931-3300. Offers biology education (M Ed); chemistry education (M Ed); curriculum and teaching (Ed D); history education (M Ed); mathematics education (M Ed); physics education (M Ed); Spanish education (M Ed). Part-time programs available. *Degree requirements:* For master's, thesis; for doctorate, thesis/dissertation, internship. *Entrance requirements:* For master's, PAEG or GRE, minimum GPA of 3.0, letter of recommendation; for doctorate, GRE or PAEG, master's degree, minimum GPA of 3.0, letter of recommendation (2), interview. *Faculty research:* Curriculum, math teaching.

University of South Carolina, The Graduate School, College of Arts and Sciences, Department of Languages, Literatures, and Cultures, Columbia, SC 29208. Offers comparative literature (MA, PhD); foreign languages (MAT), including French, German, Spanish; French (MA); German (MA); Spanish (MA). MAT offered in cooperation with the College of Education. Part-time programs available. *Degree requirements:* For master's, one foreign language, comprehensive exam, thesis optional; for doctorate, 2 foreign languages, comprehensive exam, thesis/dissertation. *Entrance requirements:* For master's and doctorate, GRE General Test, writing sample. Additional exam requirements/recommendations for international students: Required—TOEFL (minimum score 230 computer-based; 75 iBT). Electronic applications accepted. *Faculty research:* Modern literature, linguistics, literature and culture, medieval literature, literary theory.

University of South Carolina, The Graduate School, College of Education, Department of Instruction and Teacher Education, Program in Secondary Education, Columbia, SC 29208. Offers art education (IMA, MAT); business education (IMA, MAT); English (MAT); foreign language (MAT); health education (MAT); mathematics (MAT); science (IMA, MAT); secondary (Ed D); secondary education (MT, PhD); social studies (MAT); theatre and speech (MAT). IMA and MT offered jointly with the subject areas. *Accreditation:* NCATE. *Degree requirements:* For master's, comprehensive exam, thesis (for some programs), foreign language (MA); for doctorate, one foreign language, comprehensive exam, thesis/dissertation. *Entrance requirements:* For master's, GRE General Test or MAT, teaching certificate (IMA, M Ed), interview; for doctorate, GRE General Test or MAT, interview. *Faculty research:* Middle school programs, professional development, school collaboration.

University of Southern Mississippi, Graduate School, College of Arts and Letters, Department of Foreign Languages and Literatures, Hattiesburg, MS 39406-0001. Offers French (MATL); Spanish (MATL); teaching English to speakers of other languages (TESOL) (MATL). *Faculty:* 9 full-time (5 women). *Students:* 11 full-time (8 women), 52 part-time (43 women); includes 5 minority (2 Black or African American, non-Hispanic/Latino; 2 Hispanic/Latino; 1 Two or more races, non-Hispanic/Latino), 2 international. Average age 33. 23 applicants, 78% accepted, 14 enrolled. In 2011, 16 master's awarded. *Degree requirements:* For master's, comprehensive exam. *Entrance requirements:* For master's, GRE General Test, minimum GPA of 3.0 in field of study, 2.75 in last 2 years. Additional exam requirements/recommendations for international students: Required—TOEFL, IELTS. *Application deadline:* For fall admission, 3/1 for domestic and international students. Applications are processed on a rolling basis. Application fee: $50. *Financial support:* In 2011–12, 8 teaching assistantships with full tuition reimbursements (averaging $8,350 per year) were awarded; Federal Work-Study, institutionally sponsored loans, scholarships/grants, health care benefits, and unspecified assistantships also available. Financial award application deadline: 3/15; financial award applicants required to submit FAFSA. *Unit head:* Dr. Leah Fonder-Solano, Chair, 601-266-4964, Fax: 601-266-4853. *Application contact:* Dr. Joanne Burnett, Director, Graduate Studies, 601-266-4964, E-mail: graduateschool@usm.edu. Web site: http://www.usm.edu/graduateschool/table.php.

University of South Florida, Graduate School, College of Education, Department of Secondary Education, Tampa, FL 33620-9951. Offers English education (M Ed, MA, MAT, PhD); foreign language education/ESOL (M Ed, MA, MAT); instructional technology (M Ed, PhD, Ed S); mathematics education (M Ed, MA, MAT, PhD, Ed S); science education (M Ed, MA, MAT, PhD); second language acquisition/instructional technology (PhD); secondary education (M Ed, PhD); secondary education/TESOL (M Ed); social science education (M Ed, MA, MAT); teaching and learning in the content area (PhD). *Accreditation:* NCATE. Part-time and evening/weekend programs available. *Faculty:* 28 full-time (17 women), 3 part-time/adjunct (1 woman). *Students:* 174 full-time (116 women), 268 part-time (184 women); includes 103 minority (26 Black or African American, non-Hispanic/Latino; 10 Asian, non-Hispanic/Latino; 58 Hispanic/Latino; 9 Two or more races, non-Hispanic/Latino), 32 international. Average age 37. 229 applicants, 73% accepted, 141 enrolled. In 2011, 115 master's, 16 doctorates, 5 other advanced degrees awarded. *Degree requirements:* For master's, variable foreign language requirement, comprehensive exam, project (for some programs); for doctorate, variable foreign language requirement, comprehensive exam, thesis/dissertation, philosophies of inquiry; multiple research methods. *Entrance requirements:* For master's, GRE General Test or General Knowledge Test, minimum GPA of 3.0; for doctorate, GRE General Test, minimum GPA of 3.5; for Ed S, GRE General Test. Additional exam requirements/recommendations for international students: Required—TOEFL (minimum score 550 paper-based; 213 computer-based; 79 iBT). *Application deadline:* For fall admission, 2/15 for domestic students, 1/2 for international students; for spring admission, 10/15 for domestic students, 6/1 for international students. Application fee: $30. Electronic applications accepted. *Financial support:* In 2011–12, 7 students received support, including 1 research assistantship with full tuition reimbursement available (averaging $10,000 per year), 55 teaching assistantships with full and partial tuition reimbursements available (averaging $7,900 per year); scholarships/grants and unspecified assistantships also available. Financial award application deadline: 4/15; financial award applicants required to submit FAFSA. *Faculty research:* English language learners/multicultural, social science education, mathematics education, science education, instructional technology. *Total annual research expenditures:* $336,023. *Unit head:* Dr. Stephen Thornton, Chairperson, 813-974-3533, Fax: 813-974-3837, E-mail: thornton@usf.edu. *Application contact:* Dr. Diane Briscoe, Coordinator of Graduate Studies, 813-974-1804, Fax: 813-974-3391, E-mail: briscoe@usf.edu. Web site: http://www.coedu.usf.edu/main/departments/seced/seced.html.

The University of Tennessee, Graduate School, College of Education, Health and Human Sciences, Program in Education, Knoxville, TN 37996. Offers art education (MS); counseling education (PhD); cultural studies in education (PhD); curriculum (MS, Ed S); curriculum, educational research and evaluation (Ed D, PhD); early childhood education (PhD); early childhood special education (MS); education of deaf and hard of hearing (MS); educational administration and policy studies (Ed D, PhD); educational administration and supervision (Ed S); educational psychology (Ed D, PhD); elementary education (MS, Ed S); elementary teaching (MS); English education (MS, Ed S); exercise science (PhD); foreign language/ESL education (MS, Ed S); instructional technology (MS, Ed D, PhD, Ed S); literacy, language and ESL education (PhD); literacy, language education, and ESL education (Ed D); mathematics education (MS, Ed S); modified and comprehensive special education (MS); reading education (MS, Ed S); school counseling (Ed S); school psychology (PhD, Ed S); science education (MS, Ed S); secondary teaching (MS); social foundations (MS); social science education (MS, Ed S); socio-cultural foundations of sports and education (PhD); special education (Ed S); teacher education (Ed D, PhD). *Accreditation:* NCATE. Part-time and evening/weekend programs available. *Degree requirements:* For master's and Ed S, thesis optional; for doctorate, variable foreign language requirement, thesis/dissertation. *Entrance requirements:* For master's, minimum GPA of 2.7; for doctorate and Ed S, GRE General Test, minimum GPA of 2.7. Additional exam requirements/recommendations for international students: Required—TOEFL. Electronic applications accepted. *Expenses:* Tuition, state resident: full-time $8332; part-time $464 per credit hour. Tuition, nonresident: full-time $25,174; part-time $1400 per credit hour. *Required fees:* $1162; $56 per credit hour. Tuition and fees vary according to program.

University of the Sacred Heart, Graduate Programs, Department of Education, San Juan, PR 00914-0383. Offers early childhood education (M Ed); information technology and multimedia (Certificate); instruction systems and education technology (M Ed), including English, information technology and multimedia, instructional design, mathematics, Spanish. Part-time and evening/weekend programs available. *Degree requirements:* For master's, thesis. *Entrance requirements:* For master's, EXADEP, minimum undergraduate GPA of 2.75, interview.

The University of Toledo, College of Graduate Studies, Judith Herb College of Education, Health Science and Human Service, Department of Curriculum and Instruction, Toledo, OH 43606-3390. Offers art education (ME); career and technical education (ME); curriculum and instruction (ME, PhD, Ed S); education and anthropology (MAE); education and biology (MES); education and chemistry (MES); education and classics (MAE); education and economics (MAE); education and English (MAE); education and French (MAE); education and geography (MAE); education and geology (MES); education and German (MAE); education and history (MAE); education and mathematics (MAE, MES); education and physics (MES); education and political science (MAE); education and sociology (MAE); education and Spanish (MAE); educational media (PhD); educational technology (ME); English as a second language (MAE); gifted and talented (PhD); middle childhood education licensure (ME); music education (MME); secondary education (PhD); secondary education licensure (ME). *Accreditation:* NCATE. Part-time and evening/weekend programs available. *Faculty:* 24. *Students:* 60 full-time (31 women), 211 part-time (161 women); includes 23 minority (21 Black or African American, non-Hispanic/Latino; 2 Hispanic/Latino), 20 international. Average age 35. 115 applicants, 73% accepted, 74 enrolled. In 2011, 105 master's, 3 doctorates, 4 other advanced degrees awarded. *Degree requirements:* For master's, comprehensive exam, thesis or alternative; for doctorate, comprehensive exam, thesis/dissertation; for Ed S, thesis optional. *Entrance requirements:* For master's, doctorate, and Ed S, minimum cumulative GPA of 2.7 for all previous academic work, letters of recommendation. Additional exam requirements/recommendations for international students: Required—TOEFL (minimum score 550 paper-based; 213 computer-based; 80 iBT), IELTS (minimum score 6.5). *Application deadline:* For fall admission, 1/15 priority date for domestic students, 1/15 for international students. Applications are processed on a rolling basis. Application fee: $45 ($75 for international students). Electronic applications accepted. *Financial support:* In 2011–12, 9 research assistantships with full and partial tuition reimbursements (averaging $7,184 per year), 12 teaching assistantships with full and partial tuition reimbursements (averaging $8,425 per year) were awarded; career-related internships or fieldwork, Federal Work-Study, institutionally sponsored loans, scholarships/grants, tuition waivers (full and partial), unspecified assistantships, and administrative assistantships also available. Support available to part-time students. *Unit head:* Dr. Leigh Chiarelott, Chair, 419-530-5371, E-mail: eigh.chiarelott@utoledo.edu. *Application contact:* Graduate School Office, 419-530-4723, Fax: 419-530-4724, E-mail: grdsch@utnet.utoledo.edu. Web site: http://www.utoledo.edu/eduhshs/.

University of Utah, Graduate School, College of Humanities, Department of Languages and Literature, Salt Lake City, UT 84112. Offers comparative literary and cultural studies (MA, PhD); French (MA, MALP); German (MA, MALP, PhD); Spanish (MA, MALP, PhD); world languages with secondary teaching licensure (MA). *Faculty:* 33 full-time (22 women). *Students:* 39 full-time (27 women), 8 part-time (7 women); includes 6 minority (1 American Indian or Alaska Native, non-Hispanic/Latino; 2 Asian, non-Hispanic/Latino; 3 Hispanic/Latino), 12 international. Average age 33. 42 applicants, 57% accepted, 19 enrolled. In 2011, 10 master's, 1 doctorate awarded. Terminal master's awarded for partial completion of doctoral program. *Median time to degree:* Of those who began their doctoral program in fall 2003, 66% received their degree in 8 years or less. *Degree requirements:* For master's, comprehensive exam (for some programs), thesis (for some programs), standard proficiency in 2 languages other than English; for doctorate, comprehensive exam, thesis/dissertation, standard proficiency in 2 languages other than English and language of study, advanced proficiency in 1 language other than English and language of study. *Entrance requirements:* For master's, GRE, bachelor's degree or strong undergraduate record in target languages, minimum GPA of 3.0; for doctorate, GRE, MA, advanced proficiency in a target language. Additional exam requirements/recommendations for international students: Required—TOEFL (minimum score 500 paper-based; 173 computer-based). *Application deadline:* For fall admission, 1/15 priority date for domestic students, 12/15 for international students. Application fee: $55 ($65 for international students). Electronic applications accepted. *Financial support:* In 2011–12, 24 students received support, including 4 fellowships (averaging $15,000 per year), 23 teaching assistantships with full and partial tuition reimbursements available (averaging $12,000 per year); health care benefits also available. Financial award application deadline: 1/15; financial award applicants required to submit FAFSA. *Faculty research:* Literary study, literary theory, linguistics, cultural studies, comparative studies. *Total annual research expenditures:* $21,521. *Unit head:* Dr. Karin Baumgartner, Director of Graduate Studies, 801-585-3001, Fax: 801-581-7581, E-mail: karin.baumgartner@hum.utah.edu. *Application contact:* Virginia Eaton, Academic Advisor, 801-585-9437, Fax: 801-581-7581, E-mail: v.eaton@utah.edu. Web site: http://www.hum.utah.edu/languages/.

University of Vermont, Graduate College, College of Arts and Sciences, Department of Classics, Burlington, VT 05405. Offers Greek (MA); Greek and Latin (MAT); Latin (MA). *Students:* 8 (5 women); includes 1 minority (Asian, non-Hispanic/Latino). 14 applicants, 86% accepted, 3 enrolled. In 2011, 1 master's awarded. *Degree requirements:* For master's, one foreign language, thesis. *Entrance requirements:* For master's, GRE General Test. Additional exam requirements/recommendations for international students: Required—TOEFL (minimum score 550 paper-based; 213 computer-based; 80 iBT). *Application deadline:* For fall admission, 4/1 priority date for domestic students, 4/1 for international students. Applications are processed on a rolling basis. Application fee: $40. Electronic applications accepted. *Financial support:* Fellowships and teaching assistantships available. Financial award application deadline: 3/1. *Faculty research:* Early Greek literature. *Unit head:* Dr. Mark Usher, Chair, 802-656-3210. *Application contact:* Mark Usher, Coordinator, 802-656-3210.

University of Victoria, Faculty of Graduate Studies, Faculty of Humanities, Department of French, Victoria, BC V8W 2Y2, Canada. Offers literature (MA); teaching emphasis (MA). Part-time and evening/weekend programs available. *Degree requirements:* For master's, 2 foreign languages, thesis optional. *Entrance requirements:* For master's, BA in French. Additional exam requirements/recommendations for international students: Required—TOEFL (minimum score 575 paper-based; 233 computer-based), IELTS (minimum score 7). Electronic applications accepted. *Faculty research:* French-Canadian literature, stylistics, comparative literature, Francophone literature.

University of Virginia, Curry School of Education, Department of Curriculum, Instruction, and Special Education, Program in Curriculum and Instruction, Charlottesville, VA 22903. Offers curriculum and instruction (M Ed, Ed S); elementary (M Ed, Ed D); English (M Ed, Ed D); foreign language (M Ed); mathematics (M Ed, Ed D); reading (M Ed, Ed D, Ed S); science (Ed D); social studies (M Ed). *Students:* 22 full-time (17 women), 29 part-time (27 women); includes 4 minority (1 Black or African American, non-Hispanic/Latino; 1 Asian, non-Hispanic/Latino; 2 Two or more races, non-Hispanic/Latino), 1 international. Average age 33. 67 applicants, 75% accepted, 33 enrolled. In 2011, 78 master's, 2 doctorates, 12 other advanced degrees awarded. *Degree requirements:* For master's, comprehensive exam (for some programs); for doctorate, comprehensive exam, thesis/dissertation; for Ed S, comprehensive exam. *Entrance requirements:* For master's, doctorate, and Ed S, GRE General Test, 2 letters of recommendation. Additional exam requirements/recommendations for international students: Required—TOEFL (minimum score 600 paper-based; 250 computer-based; 90 iBT), IELTS (minimum score 7). *Application deadline:* Applications are processed on a rolling basis. Application fee: $60. Electronic applications accepted. *Financial support:* Fellowships with tuition reimbursements, research assistantships with tuition reimbursements, and teaching assistantships with tuition reimbursements available. Financial award application deadline: 1/5; financial award applicants required to submit FAFSA. *Unit head:* Laura Smolkin, Chair, 434-924-0831. *Application contact:* Karen Dwier, Information Contact, 434-924-0831, E-mail: kgd9g@virginia.edu.

University of Virginia, Curry School of Education, Program in Education, Charlottesville, VA 22903. Offers administration and supervision (PhD); applied developmental science (PhD); counselor education (PhD); curriculum and instruction (PhD); early childhood-developmental risk (MT); education evaluation (PhD); educational psychology (PhD); educational research (PhD); elementary (MT, PhD); English education (MT, PhD); foreign language education (MT); higher education (PhD); instructional technology (PhD); kinesiology (MT, PhD); math education (PhD); reading education (PhD); research statistics and evaluation (PhD); school psychology (PhD); science education (PhD); social studies education (MT, PhD); special education (PhD); world languages education (MT). *Students:* 299 full-time (216 women), 60 part-time (33 women); includes 46 minority (18 Black or African American, non-Hispanic/Latino; 17 Asian, non-Hispanic/Latino; 7 Hispanic/Latino; 4 Two or more races, non-Hispanic/Latino), 23 international. Average age 30. 307 applicants, 42% accepted, 80 enrolled. In 2011, 113 master's, 62 doctorates awarded. *Degree requirements:* For master's, comprehensive exam (for some programs), field project; for doctorate, comprehensive exam, thesis/dissertation. *Entrance requirements:* For doctorate, GRE General Test. Additional exam requirements/recommendations for international students: Required—TOEFL (minimum score 600 paper-based; 250 computer-based; 90 iBT), IELTS (minimum score 7). *Application deadline:* Applications are processed on a rolling basis. Application fee: $60. Electronic applications accepted. *Financial support:* Fellowships, research assistantships, and teaching assistantships available. Financial award application deadline: 1/5; financial award applicants required to submit FAFSA. *Unit head:* Robert C. Pianta, Dean, 434-924-3334. *Application contact:* Joanne McNergney, Assistant Dean for Admissions and Student Services, 434-924-3334, E-mail: curry-admissions@virginia.edu.

University of West Georgia, College of Education, Department of Leadership and Applied Instruction, Carrollton, GA 30118. Offers art education (M Ed); art teacher education (Ed S); biology - secondary education (M Ed); biology/secondary education (Ed S); business education (M Ed, Ed S); chemistry/secondary education (Ed S); earth science/secondary education (Ed S); economics/secondary education (Ed S); educational leadership (M Ed, Ed S); English teacher education (M Ed, Ed S); French teacher education (M Ed, Ed S); history teacher education (Ed S); mathematics teacher education (M Ed, Ed S); middle grades education (M Ed, Ed S); physical education and recreation (Ed S); physical education teaching and coaching (M Ed); physics/secondary education (Ed S); science teacher education (M Ed, Ed S); secondary education (M Ed); social science - secondary education (M Ed); social science teacher education (M Ed); Spanish (M Ed); Spanish teacher education (M Ed, Ed S); sports management (M Ed). *Accreditation:* NCATE. Part-time and evening/weekend programs available. *Faculty:* 18 full-time (9 women). *Students:* 75 full-time (49 women), 169 part-time (109 women); includes 90 minority (85 Black or African American, non-Hispanic/Latino; 3 Hispanic/Latino; 2 Two or more races, non-Hispanic/Latino), 1 international. Average age 36. 115 applicants, 67% accepted, 19 enrolled. In 2011, 73 master's, 53 Ed Ss awarded. *Degree requirements:* For master's, internship; for Ed S, research project. *Entrance requirements:* For master's, GRE General Test, minimum GPA of 2.7; for Ed S, GRE General Test, master's degree, minimum graduate GPA of 3.0, district appointment. Additional exam requirements/recommendations for international students: Required—TOEFL (minimum score 523 paper-based; 193 computer-based; 69 iBT); Recommended—IELTS (minimum score 6). *Application deadline:* For fall admission, 7/21 for domestic students, 6/1 for international students; for spring admission, 11/30 for domestic students, 10/15 for international students. Applications are processed on a rolling basis. Application fee: $30. Electronic applications accepted. *Expenses:* Tuition, state resident: full-time $4336; part-time $181 per credit hour. Tuition, nonresident: full-time $17,362; part-time $724 per credit hour. Tuition and fees vary according to course load, degree level, campus/location and program. *Financial support:* In 2011–12, 1 research assistantship with full tuition reimbursement (averaging $7,444 per year) was awarded; career-related internships or fieldwork, scholarships/grants, and unspecified assistantships also available. Support available to part-time students. Financial award application deadline: 7/1; financial award applicants required to submit FAFSA. *Total annual research expenditures:* $5,000. *Unit head:* Dr. Frank Butts, Chair, 678-839-6530, Fax: 678-839-6195, E-mail: fbutts@westga.edu. *Application contact:* Deanna Richards, Coordinator, Graduate Studies, 678-839-5946, E-mail: drichard@westga.edu. Web site: http://www.westga.edu/coelai.

University of Wisconsin–Madison, Graduate School, School of Education, Department of Curriculum and Instruction, Madison, WI 53706-1380. Offers art education (MA); curriculum and instruction (MS, PhD); education and mathematics (MA); French education (MA); German education (MA); music education (MS); science education (MS); Spanish education (MA). *Accreditation:* NASM (one or more programs are accredited). *Degree requirements:* For doctorate, thesis/dissertation. Application fee: $56. *Expenses:* Tuition, state resident: full-time $10,296; part-time $643.51 per credit. Tuition, nonresident: full-time $24,054; part-time $1503.40 per credit. *Required fees:* $70.06 per credit. Tuition and fees vary according to course load, campus/location, program and reciprocity agreements. *Financial support:* Project assistantships available. *Unit head:* Dr. John Rudolph, Chair, 608-263-4600, E-mail: jlrudolp@wisc.edu. *Application contact:* 608-262-2433, Fax: 608-262-5134, E-mail: gradadmiss@mail.bascom.wisc.edu. Web site: http://www.education.wisc.edu/ci.

Vanderbilt University, Graduate School, Department of French and Italian, Nashville, TN 37240-1001. Offers French (MA, MAT, PhD). *Faculty:* 11 full-time (5 women). *Students:* 10 full-time (8 women), 1 part-time (0 women), 5 international. Average age 31. 47 applicants, 4% accepted, 0 enrolled. In 2011, 2 master's, 1 doctorate awarded. Terminal master's awarded for partial completion of doctoral program. *Degree requirements:* For master's, one foreign language, comprehensive exam; for doctorate, 2 foreign languages, comprehensive exam, thesis/dissertation, final and qualifying exams. *Entrance requirements:* For master's and doctorate, GRE General Test. Additional exam requirements/recommendations for international students: Required—TOEFL (minimum score 570 paper-based; 230 computer-based; 88 iBT). *Application deadline:* For fall admission, 1/15 for domestic and international students. Application fee: $0. Electronic applications accepted. *Financial support:* Fellowships with full and partial tuition reimbursements, teaching assistantships with full and partial tuition reimbursements, career-related internships or fieldwork, Federal Work-Study, institutionally sponsored loans, scholarships/grants, and health care benefits available. Financial award application deadline: 1/15; financial award applicants required to submit CSS PROFILE or FAFSA. *Faculty research:* Baudelaire, Rabelais, voyage literature, postcolonial literature, medieval epic. *Unit head:* Dr. Lynn Ramey, Chair, 615-322-6900,

E-mail: lynn.ramey@vanderbilt.edu. *Application contact:* Dr. Holly Tucker, Director of Graduate Studies, 615-343-6905, Fax: 615-322-6909, E-mail: holly.tucker@vanderbilt.edu. Web site: http://www.vanderbilt.edu/french_ital/graduate/.

Vanderbilt University, Graduate School, Department of Germanic and Slavic Languages, Nashville, TN 37240-1001. Offers German (MA, MAT, PhD). *Faculty:* 7 full-time (2 women). *Students:* 20 full-time (15 women), 1 (woman) part-time; includes 2 minority (1 Asian, non-Hispanic/Latino; 1 Hispanic/Latino), 8 international. Average age 32. 13 applicants, 38% accepted, 3 enrolled. In 2011, 2 master's, 1 doctorate awarded. Terminal master's awarded for partial completion of doctoral program. *Degree requirements:* For master's, one foreign language, comprehensive exam; for doctorate, 2 foreign languages, comprehensive exam, thesis/dissertation, qualifying and final exams. *Entrance requirements:* For master's and doctorate, GRE General Test, sample of written work. Additional exam requirements/recommendations for international students: Required—TOEFL (minimum score 570 paper-based; 230 computer-based; 88 iBT). *Application deadline:* For fall admission, 1/15 for domestic and international students. Application fee: $0. Electronic applications accepted. *Financial support:* Fellowships with full and partial tuition reimbursements, teaching assistantships with full and partial tuition reimbursements, career-related internships or fieldwork, Federal Work-Study, institutionally sponsored loans, scholarships/grants, and health care benefits available. Financial award application deadline: 1/15; financial award applicants required to submit CSS PROFILE or FAFSA. *Faculty research:* 1750 to present, Middle Ages, Baroque, language pedagogy, linguistics. *Unit head:* Dr. Barbara Hahn, Chair, 615-322-2611, Fax: 615-343-7258, E-mail: barbara.hahn@vanderbilt.edu. *Application contact:* Dr. Christoph Zeller, Director of Graduate Studies, 615-322-2611, Fax: 615-343-7258, E-mail: christoph.zeller@vanderbilt.edu. Web site: http://www.vanderbilt.edu/german/graduate/.

Vanderbilt University, Graduate School, Department of Spanish and Portuguese, Nashville, TN 37240-1001. Offers Portuguese (MA); Spanish (MA, MAT, PhD); Spanish and Portuguese (PhD). *Faculty:* 12 full-time (6 women). *Students:* 26 full-time (15 women); includes 5 minority (2 Black or African American, non-Hispanic/Latino; 3 Hispanic/Latino), 10 international. Average age 32. 41 applicants, 17% accepted, 5 enrolled. In 2011, 1 degree awarded. *Degree requirements:* For master's, one foreign language, thesis; for doctorate, 2 foreign languages, thesis/dissertation, final and qualifying exams. *Entrance requirements:* For master's, GRE General Test; for doctorate, GRE General Test, writing sample in Spanish. Additional exam requirements/recommendations for international students: Required—TOEFL (minimum score 570 paper-based; 230 computer-based; 88 iBT). *Application deadline:* For fall admission, 1/15 for domestic and international students. Application fee: $0. Electronic applications accepted. *Financial support:* Fellowships with full and partial tuition reimbursements, teaching assistantships with full tuition reimbursements, Federal Work-Study, institutionally sponsored loans, and health care benefits available. Financial award application deadline: 1/15; financial award applicants required to submit CSS PROFILE or FAFSA. *Faculty research:* Spanish, Portuguese, and Latin American literatures; foreign language pedagogy; Renaissance and Baroque poetry; nineteenth century Spanish novel. *Unit head:* Dr. Cathy L. Jrade, Chair, 615-322-6930, Fax: 615-343-7260, E-mail: cathy.l.jrade@vanderbilt.edu. *Application contact:* Dr. Andres Zamora, Director of Graduate Studies, 615-322-6858, Fax: 615-343-7260, E-mail: andres.zamora@vanderbilt.edu. Web site: http://sitemason.vanderbilt.edu/spanport/graduateprogram/.

Virginia Polytechnic Institute and State University, Graduate School, College of Liberal Arts and Human Sciences, Department of Foreign Languages and Literatures, Blacksburg, VA 24061. Offers MA. *Degree requirements:* For master's, comprehensive exam (for some programs), thesis (for some programs). *Entrance requirements:* For master's, GRE. Additional exam requirements/recommendations for international students: Required—TOEFL (minimum score 550 paper-based; 213 computer-based). *Application deadline:* For fall admission, 7/1 for domestic and international students; for spring admission, 12/1 for domestic and international students. Applications are processed on a rolling basis. Application fee: $65. Electronic applications accepted. *Expenses:* Tuition, state resident: full-time $10,048; part-time $558.25 per credit hour. Tuition, nonresident: full-time $19,497; part-time $1083.25 per credit hour. *Required fees:* $405 per semester. Tuition and fees vary according to course load, campus/location and program. *Financial support:* Teaching assistantships with full tuition reimbursements, career-related internships or fieldwork, Federal Work-Study, scholarships/grants, health care benefits, and unspecified assistantships available. Financial award application deadline: 1/15. *Unit head:* Dr. Richard L. Shryock, Unit Head, 540-231-5361, Fax: 540-231-4812, E-mail: shryock@vt.edu. *Application contact:* Janell Watson, Information Contact, 540-231-9009, Fax: 540-231-4812, E-mail: rjwatson@vt.edu. Web site: http://www.fll.vt.edu/MA/.

Washington State University, Graduate School, College of Liberal Arts, Department of Foreign Languages and Cultures, Pullman, WA 99164. Offers foreign languages with emphasis in Spanish (MA). *Faculty:* 7. *Students:* 11 full-time (7 women), 1 part-time (0 women); includes 2 minority (both Hispanic/Latino), 5 international. Average age 28. 12 applicants, 42% accepted, 5 enrolled. In 2011, 5 master's awarded. *Degree requirements:* For master's, comprehensive exam (for some programs), thesis (for some programs), 4 written exams, oral exam, paper. *Entrance requirements:* For master's, three current letters of recommendation; all original transcripts including an official English translation; two writing samples; letter of application stating qualifications and personal goals; brief (3-5 minute) tape recordings of two informal dialogues between applicant and native speaker. Additional exam requirements/recommendations for international students: Required—TOEFL (minimum score 550 paper-based). *Application deadline:* For fall admission, 1/1 priority date for domestic students, 1/1 for international students; for spring admission, 7/1 priority date for domestic students, 7/1 for international students. Application fee: $75. Electronic applications accepted. *Financial support:* In 2011–12, fellowships (averaging $2,200 per year), teaching assistantships with full and partial tuition reimbursements (averaging $13,056 per year) were awarded; career-related internships or fieldwork, Federal Work-Study, institutionally sponsored loans, scholarships/grants, and health care benefits also available. Financial award application deadline: 2/15; financial award applicants required to submit FAFSA. *Faculty research:* Spanish and Latin American literature, film, and culture; pedagogy; computer-aided instruction. *Total annual research expenditures:* $98,000. *Unit head:* Dr. Eloy Gonzalez, Chair, 509-335-2756, Fax: 509-335-3708, E-mail: eloygonz@wsunix.wsu.edu. *Application contact:* Graduate School Admissions, 800-GRADWSU, Fax: 509-335-1949, E-mail: gradsch@wsu.edu. Web site: http://www.forlang.wsu.edu/.

Wayne State University, College of Education, Division of Teacher Education, Detroit, MI 48202. Offers art education (M Ed), including art therapy; bilingual/bicultural education (M Ed); career and technical education (M Ed); curriculum and instruction (Ed D, PhD, Ed S), including art education (PhD), bilingual education (Ed D, Ed S), bilingual-bicultural education (PhD), career and technical education (MAT, Ed D, PhD, Ed S), early childhood education (MAT, Ed D, PhD, Ed S), elementary education, English as a second language (MAT, Ed D, Ed S), English education (MAT, Ed D, PhD, Ed S), foreign language education (MAT, PhD), K-12 curriculum, mathematics education (MAT, Ed D, PhD, Ed S), science education (MAT, Ed D, PhD, Ed S), social studies education (MAT, Ed S), social studies education: secondary (Ed D, PhD); elementary education (MAT), including special education; elementary education (M Ed, MAT), including children's literature (MAT), early childhood education (MAT, Ed D, PhD, Ed S), general elementary education (MAT); elementary or secondary education (MAT), including bilingual/bicultural education, English as a second language (MAT, Ed D, Ed S), mathematics education (MAT, Ed D, PhD, Ed S), science education (MAT, Ed D, PhD, Ed S), social studies education (MAT, Ed S); English education-secondary (M Ed); foreign language education (M Ed); mathematics education (M Ed); reading (M Ed, Ed S); reading, languages and literature (Ed D); science education (M Ed); secondary education (MAT), including art education (K-12), career and technical education (MAT, Ed D, PhD, Ed S), English education (MAT, Ed D, PhD, Ed S), foreign language education (MAT, PhD), kinesiology; social studies education secondary (M Ed); special education (M Ed, Ed D, PhD, Ed S). *Students:* 216 full-time (154 women), 626 part-time (478 women); includes 289 minority (227 Black or African American, non-Hispanic/Latino; 4 American Indian or Alaska Native, non-Hispanic/Latino; 27 Asian, non-Hispanic/Latino; 21 Hispanic/Latino; 1 Native Hawaiian or other Pacific Islander, non-Hispanic/Latino; 9 Two or more races, non-Hispanic/Latino), 14 international. Average age 37. 347 applicants, 37% accepted, 93 enrolled. In 2011, 226 master's, 12 doctorates, 46 other advanced degrees awarded. *Degree requirements:* For master's, thesis (for some programs), thesis, essay or project (for some M Ed programs), professional field experience (for MAT programs); for doctorate, thesis/dissertation. *Entrance requirements:* For master's, Michigan Basic Skills Test (MA in teaching); for doctorate, minimum undergraduate GPA of 3.0, graduate 3.5; interview, curriculum vitae; references. Additional exam requirements/recommendations for international students: Required—TOEFL (minimum score 550 paper-based; 213 computer-based), TWE (minimum score 5.5). *Application deadline:* For fall admission, 6/1 priority date for domestic students, 5/1 for international students; for winter admission, 10/1 priority date for domestic students, 9/1 for international students; for spring admission, 2/1 priority date for domestic students, 1/1 for international students. Applications are processed on a rolling basis. Application fee: $50. Electronic applications accepted. *Expenses:* Tuition, state resident: part-time $512.85 per credit. Tuition, nonresident: part-time $1132.65 per credit. *Required fees:* $26.60 per credit. $199.65 per semester. Tuition and fees vary according to course load and program. *Financial support:* In 2011–12, 42 students received support. Fellowships, research assistantships with tuition reimbursements available, teaching assistantships, scholarships/grants, and unspecified assistantships available. *Faculty research:* Reading and writing literacy and literature. *Total annual research expenditures:* $264,016. *Unit head:* Dr. Craig Roney, Assistant Dean, 313-577-0902, E-mail: rroney@wayne.edu. Web site: http://coe.wayne.edu/ted/index.php.

Wayne State University, College of Liberal Arts and Sciences, Program in Language Learning, Detroit, MI 48202. Offers MA. *Students:* 1 full-time (0 women), 12 part-time (all women); includes 2 minority (1 Black or African American, non-Hispanic/Latino; 1 Hispanic/Latino), 1 international. Average age 31. 4 applicants, 50% accepted, 2 enrolled. In 2011, 2 master's awarded. *Degree requirements:* For master's, one foreign language, three-credit essay. *Entrance requirements:* For master's, target language proficiency, statement of purpose, three letters of recommendation. Additional exam requirements/recommendations for international students: Required—TOEFL (minimum score 550 paper-based; 213 computer-based); Recommended—TWE (minimum score 5.5). *Application deadline:* For fall admission, 6/1 priority date for domestic students, 5/1 for international students; for winter admission, 10/1 priority date for domestic students, 9/1 for international students; for spring admission, 2/1 priority date for domestic students, 1/1 for international students. Applications are processed on a rolling basis. Application fee: $50. Electronic applications accepted. *Expenses:* Tuition, state resident: part-time $512.85 per credit. Tuition, nonresident: part-time $1132.65 per credit. *Required fees:* $26.60 per credit. $199.65 per semester. Tuition and fees vary according to course load and program. *Financial support:* Teaching assistantships with tuition reimbursements, scholarships/grants, health care benefits, and unspecified assistantships available. *Unit head:* Dr. Catherine Barrette, Associate Professor/Graduate Advisor, 313-577-6263, E-mail: aa1471@wayne.edu. Web site: http://www.clas.wayne.edu/mall/.

West Chester University of Pennsylvania, College of Arts and Sciences, Department of Languages and Cultures, West Chester, PA 19383. Offers French (M Ed, MA, Teaching Certificate); Spanish (M Ed, MA, Teaching Certificate). Part-time and evening/weekend programs available. *Faculty:* 7 part-time/adjunct (6 women). *Students:* 7 full-time (6 women), 12 part-time (11 women); includes 7 minority (1 Black or African American, non-Hispanic/Latino; 6 Hispanic/Latino). Average age 32. 10 applicants, 80% accepted, 6 enrolled. In 2011, 6 degrees awarded. *Degree requirements:* For master's, one foreign language, thesis optional, exit exam, capstone project. *Entrance requirements:* For master's, placement test. Additional exam requirements/recommendations for international students: Required—TOEFL (minimum score 550 paper-based; 213 computer-based; 80 iBT). *Application deadline:* For fall admission, 4/15 priority date for domestic students, 3/15 for international students; for spring admission, 10/15 priority date for domestic students, 9/1 for international students. Applications are processed on a rolling basis. Application fee: $45. Electronic applications accepted. *Expenses:* Tuition, state resident: full-time $7488; part-time $416 per credit. Tuition, nonresident: full-time $11,232; part-time $624 per credit. *Required fees:* $1784.64; $67.59 per credit. Tuition and fees vary according to program. *Financial support:* Unspecified assistantships available. Support available to part-time students. Financial award application deadline: 2/15; financial award applicants required to submit FAFSA. *Faculty research:* Implementation of world languages curriculum framework. *Unit head:* Dr. Jerome Williams, Chair, 610-436-2700, Fax: 610-436-3048, E-mail: jwilliams2@wcupa.edu. *Application contact:* Dr. Rebecca Pauly, Graduate Coordinator, 610-436-2382, Fax: 610-436-3048, E-mail: rpauly@wcupa.edu. Web site: http://www.wcupa.edu/_academics/sch_cas.flg/.

Western Kentucky University, Graduate Studies, Potter College of Arts and Letters, Department of Modern Languages, Bowling Green, KY 42101. Offers French (MA Ed); German (MA Ed); Spanish (MA Ed).

Worcester State University, Graduate Studies, Program in Spanish, Worcester, MA 01602-2597. Offers MA. Part-time programs available. *Faculty:* 2 full-time (both women), 1 part-time/adjunct (0 women). *Students:* 18 part-time (16 women); includes 2 minority (1 Asian, non-Hispanic/Latino; 1 Hispanic/Latino). Average age 32. 13 applicants, 92% accepted, 7 enrolled. In 2011, 13 master's awarded. *Degree requirements:* For master's, comprehensive exam (for some programs), thesis optional. *Entrance requirements:* For master's, GRE, MAT, BA in Spanish or related field and/or interview with faculty member. Additional exam requirements/recommendations for international students: Required—TOEFL (minimum score 500 paper-based; 61 iBT). *Application deadline:* For fall admission, 6/15 for domestic and international students; for spring admission, 4/1 for domestic and international students. Applications are processed on a rolling basis. Application fee: $40. Electronic applications accepted. *Expenses:* Tuition, state resident: full-time $2700; part-time $150 per credit. Tuition, nonresident: full-time $2700; part-time $150 per credit. *Required fees:* $2016; $112 per credit. *Financial support:* Career-related internships or fieldwork, scholarships/grants, and unspecified assistantships available. Financial award application deadline: 3/1; financial award applicants required to submit FAFSA. *Unit head:* Dr. Juan Orbe, Head, 508-929-8704, Fax: 508-929-8174, E-mail: jorbe@worcester.edu. *Application contact:* Sara Grady,

Assistant Dean of Graduate and Continuing Education, 508-929-8787, Fax: 508-929-8100, E-mail: sara.grady@worcester.edu.

Health Education

Adelphi University, Ruth S. Ammon School of Education, Program in Health Studies, Garden City, NY 11530-0701. Offers community health education (MA, Certificate); school health education (MA). Part-time and evening/weekend programs available. *Students:* 11 full-time (9 women), 43 part-time (26 women); includes 6 minority (2 Black or African American, non-Hispanic/Latino; 3 Hispanic/Latino; 1 Two or more races, non-Hispanic/Latino), 3 international. Average age 27. In 2011, 30 master's awarded. *Degree requirements:* For master's, internship. *Entrance requirements:* For master's, 3 letters of recommendation, resume, minimum cumulative GPA of 2.75. Additional exam requirements/recommendations for international students: Required—TOEFL (minimum score 550 paper-based; 213 computer-based; 80 iBT). *Application deadline:* For fall admission, 4/1 for international students; for spring admission, 11/1 for international students. Applications are processed on a rolling basis. Application fee: $50. Electronic applications accepted. *Expenses: Tuition:* Full-time $29,600; part-time $930 per credit. *Required fees:* $1100. *Financial support:* Fellowships, research assistantships with partial tuition reimbursements, teaching assistantships, career-related internships or fieldwork, Federal Work-Study, institutionally sponsored loans, and tuition waivers (full) available. Support available to part-time students. Financial award application deadline: 2/15; financial award applicants required to submit FAFSA. *Faculty research:* Alcohol abuse, tobacco cessation, drug abuse, healthy family lives, healthy personal living. *Unit head:* Dr. Ronald Feingold, Director, 516-877-4764, E-mail: feingold@adelphi.edu. *Application contact:* Christine Murphy, Director of Admissions, 516-877-3050, Fax: 516-877-3039, E-mail: graduateadmissions@adelphi.edu.

Alabama State University, Department of Health, Physical Education, and Recreation, Montgomery, AL 36101-0271. Offers health education (M Ed); physical education (M Ed). Part-time programs available. *Faculty:* 4 full-time (all women), 1 part-time/adjunct (0 women). *Students:* 58 full-time (48 women), 1 (woman) part-time; includes 42 minority (all Black or African American, non-Hispanic/Latino). Average age 27. 166 applicants, 25% accepted, 22 enrolled. In 2011, 1 master's awarded. *Degree requirements:* For master's, comprehensive exam. *Entrance requirements:* For master's, GRE General Test, MAT, graduate writing competency test. Additional exam requirements/recommendations for international students: Required—TOEFL (minimum score 500 paper-based; 173 computer-based). *Application deadline:* For fall admission, 7/15 for domestic students; for spring admission, 12/15 for domestic students. Applications are processed on a rolling basis. Application fee: $10. *Financial support:* In 2011–12, research assistantships (averaging $9,450 per year) were awarded. *Faculty research:* Risk factors for heart disease in the college-age population, cardiovascular reactivity for the Cold Pressor Test. *Unit head:* Dr. Doris Screws, Chair, 334-229-4504, Fax: 334-229-4928. *Application contact:* Dr. Doris Screws, Dean of Graduate Studies, 334-229-4274, Fax: 334-229-4928, E-mail: dscrews@alasu.edu. Web site: http://www.alasu.edu/academics/colleges—departments/college-of-education/health-physical-education—recreation/index.aspx.

Albany State University, College of Education, Albany, GA 31705-2717. Offers early childhood education (M Ed); education specialist (Ed S); educational leadership and administration (M Ed); health, physical education and recreation (M Ed); middle grades education (M Ed); school counseling (M Ed); special education (M Ed). *Accreditation:* NCATE. Part-time and evening/weekend programs available. Postbaccalaureate distance learning degree programs offered (minimal on-campus study). *Faculty:* 19 full-time (13 women), 7 part-time/adjunct (5 women). *Students:* 90 full-time (69 women), 118 part-time (92 women); includes 152 minority (151 Black or African American, non-Hispanic/Latino; 1 American Indian or Alaska Native, non-Hispanic/Latino), 1 international. Average age 35. 93 applicants, 78% accepted, 38 enrolled. In 2011, 43 master's, 8 Ed Ss awarded. *Degree requirements:* For master's, comprehensive exam, internship, GACE Content Exam. *Entrance requirements:* For master's, GRE or MAT. *Application deadline:* For fall admission, 6/1 for domestic students, 5/1 for international students; for spring admission, 11/1 for domestic students, 10/1 for international students. Applications are processed on a rolling basis. Application fee: $20. Electronic applications accepted. *Expenses:* Tuition, state resident: full-time $3204; part-time $178 per credit hour. Tuition, nonresident: full-time $12,816; part-time $712 per credit hour. *Required fees:* $379 per semester. *Financial support:* Scholarships/grants available. Financial award application deadline: 4/15; financial award applicants required to submit FAFSA. *Faculty research:* GACE preparation, STEM (science, technology, engineering, and mathematics), technology education, special education, professional teacher development, health implications liberation philosophy, NET-Q, learning community, disabled or at-risk students. *Total annual research expenditures:* $252,502. *Unit head:* Dr. Kimberly King-Jupiter, Dean, 229-430-1718, Fax: 229-430-4993, E-mail: kimberly.king-jupiter@asurams.edu. *Application contact:* Jeffrey Pierce, II, Graduate Admissions Counselor, 229-430-4646, Fax: 229-430-4105, E-mail: jeffrey.pierce@asurams.edu. Web site: http://asu-sacs.asurams.edu/ASUCatalog/Graduate/index.html.

Alcorn State University, School of Graduate Studies, School of Psychology and Education, Alcorn State, MS 39096-7500. Offers agricultural education (MS Ed); elementary education (MS Ed, Ed S); guidance and counseling (MS Ed); industrial education (MS Ed); secondary education (MS Ed), including health and physical education; special education (MS Ed). *Accreditation:* NCATE. *Degree requirements:* For master's, thesis optional.

Allen College, Program in Nursing, Waterloo, IA 50703. Offers acute care nurse practitioner (MSN, Post-Master's Certificate); adult nurse practitioner (MSN, Post-Master's Certificate); adult psychiatric-mental health nurse practitioner (MSN, Post-Master's Certificate); family nurse practitioner (MSN, Post-Master's Certificate); gerontological nurse practitioner (MSN, Post-Master's Certificate); health education (MSN); leadership in health care delivery (MSN, Post-Master's Certificate); nursing (DNP). *Accreditation:* AACN; NLN. Part-time programs available. *Faculty:* 3 full-time (all women), 16 part-time/adjunct (all women). *Students:* 34 full-time (31 women), 110 part-time (106 women); includes 5 minority (2 Asian, non-Hispanic/Latino; 3 Hispanic/Latino). Average age 36. 156 applicants, 64% accepted, 76 enrolled. In 2011, 61 master's, 1 other advanced degree awarded. *Degree requirements:* For master's, thesis optional. *Entrance requirements:* For master's, minimum GPA of 3.0; for doctorate, minimum GPA of 3.25 in graduate coursework. Additional exam requirements/recommendations for international students: Recommended—TOEFL (minimum score 550 paper-based), IELTS. *Application deadline:* For fall admission, 2/1 priority date for domestic students; for spring admission, 9/1 priority date for domestic students. Applications are processed on a rolling basis. Application fee: $50. Electronic applications accepted. *Expenses: Tuition:* Full-time $13,993; part-time $691 per credit hour. *Required fees:* $832; $69 per credit hour. One-time fee: $100 part-time. Part-time tuition and fees vary according to course load. *Financial support:* In 2011–12, 41 students received support. Institutionally sponsored loans, scholarships/grants, and traineeships available. Support available to part-time students. Financial award application deadline: 8/15; financial award applicants required to submit FAFSA. *Faculty research:* Pain and the aged, congestive heart failure. *Unit head:* Kendra Williams-Perez, Dean, School of Nursing, 319-226-2044, Fax: 319-226-2070, E-mail: williakb@ihs.org. *Application contact:* Michelle Koehn, Admissions Counselor, 319-226-2002, Fax: 319-226-2051, E-mail: koehnml@ihs.org. Web site: http://www.allencollege.edu/.

American University, College of Arts and Sciences, School of Education, Teaching, and Health, Washington, DC 20016-8030. Offers curriculum and instruction (M Ed, Certificate); early childhood education (MAT, Certificate); elementary education (MAT); English for speakers of other languages (MAT, Certificate); health promotion management (MS, Certificate); international training and education (MA, MAT); nutrition education (Certificate); secondary teaching (MAT, Certificate); special education (MA), including special education: learning disabilities; MAT/MA. *Accreditation:* NCATE. Part-time and evening/weekend programs available. *Faculty:* 14 full-time (10 women), 58 part-time/adjunct (41 women). *Students:* 69 full-time (61 women), 257 part-time (188 women); includes 55 minority (35 Black or African American, non-Hispanic/Latino; 2 American Indian or Alaska Native, non-Hispanic/Latino; 5 Asian, non-Hispanic/Latino; 10 Hispanic/Latino; 3 Two or more races, non-Hispanic/Latino), 4 international. Average age 28. 221 applicants, 81% accepted, 96 enrolled. In 2011, 226 master's, 5 other advanced degrees awarded. *Degree requirements:* For master's, comprehensive exam, thesis or alternative, PRAXIS II. *Entrance requirements:* For master's, GRE General Test, two letters of recommendation; for Certificate, bachelor's degree. Additional exam requirements/recommendations for international students: Required—TOEFL. *Application deadline:* For fall admission, 2/1 priority date for domestic students; for spring admission, 10/1 priority date for domestic students. Applications are processed on a rolling basis. Application fee: $80. *Expenses: Tuition:* Full-time $24,264; part-time $1348 per credit hour. *Required fees:* $430. Tuition and fees vary according to course load and program. *Financial support:* Fellowships, research assistantships with full and partial tuition reimbursements, teaching assistantships with full and partial tuition reimbursements, career-related internships or fieldwork, Federal Work-Study, and institutionally sponsored loans available. Support available to part-time students. Financial award application deadline: 2/1; financial award applicants required to submit FAFSA. *Faculty research:* Gender equity, socioeconomic technology, learning disabilities, gifted and talented education. *Unit head:* Dr. Sarah Irvine-Belson, Dean, 202-885-3714, Fax: 202-885-1187, E-mail: educate@american.edu. *Application contact:* Kathleen Clowery, Director, Graduate Admissions, 202-885-3621, Fax: 202-885-1505, E-mail: clowery@american.edu. Web site: http://www.american.edu/cas/seth/.

Arcadia University, Graduate Studies, Department of Medical Science and Community Health, Program in Allied Health, Glenside, PA 19038-3295. Offers MPH, MSHE, MSPH. Part-time and evening/weekend programs available. *Faculty:* 1 (woman) full-time, 9 part-time/adjunct (5 women). *Students:* 30 full-time (26 women), 38 part-time (31 women); includes 9 minority (3 Black or African American, non-Hispanic/Latino; 2 Asian, non-Hispanic/Latino; 4 Two or more races, non-Hispanic/Latino). Average age 30. In 2011, 16 master's awarded. *Entrance requirements:* For master's, GMAT or GRE (MHA). *Application deadline:* Applications are processed on a rolling basis. Application fee: $50. *Expenses: Tuition:* Full-time $25,260; part-time $670 per credit. Full-time tuition and fees vary according to class time, degree level and program. *Financial support:* Tuition waivers (partial) and unspecified assistantships available. *Unit head:* Dr. Andrea Crivelli-Kovach, Director, 215-572-4014, E-mail: crivella@arcadia.edu. *Application contact:* 215-572-2910, Fax: 215-572-4049, E-mail: admiss@arcadia.edu.

Arizona State University, School of Letters and Sciences, Program in Behavioral Health, Phoenix, AZ 85004-2135. Offers DBH. Part-time and evening/weekend programs available. Postbaccalaureate distance learning degree programs offered (minimal on-campus study). *Degree requirements:* For doctorate, thesis/dissertation or alternative, 16 hours/week practicum (400 hours total), applied research paper focused on design, implementation and evaluation of a clinical intervention in primary care or related setting, interactive Program of Study (iPOS) submitted before completing 50 percent of required credit hours. *Entrance requirements:* For doctorate, minimum GPA of 3.0 or equivalent in last 2 years of work leading to bachelor's degree; 3 professional reference letters; copy of current clinical license(s) to practice behavioral health; interview. Additional exam requirements/recommendations for international students: Required—TOEFL (minimum score 80 iBT), TOEFL, IELTS, or Pearson Test of English. Electronic applications accepted. *Expenses:* Contact institution.

Arkansas State University, Graduate School, College of Nursing and Health Professions, School of Nursing, Jonesboro, State University, AR 72467. Offers aging studies (Certificate); disaster preparedness and emergency management (MS, Certificate); health care management (Certificate); health communications (Certificate); health sciences (MS); health sciences education (Certificate); nurse anesthesia (MSN); nursing (MSN). *Accreditation:* AANA/CANAEP (one or more programs are accredited); NLN. Part-time programs available. *Faculty:* 14 full-time (all women). *Students:* 107 full-time (49 women), 118 part-time (110 women); includes 32 minority (27 Black or African American, non-Hispanic/Latino; 3 Asian, non-Hispanic/Latino; 2 Hispanic/Latino). Average age 33. 96 applicants, 25% accepted, 21 enrolled. In 2011, 83 master's awarded. *Degree requirements:* For master's, comprehensive exam, thesis or alternative. *Entrance requirements:* For master's, GRE General Test or MAT, appropriate bachelor's degree, current Arkansas nursing license, CPR certification, physical examination, professional liability insurance, critical care experience, ACLS Certification, PALS Certification, interview, immunization records, personal goal statement, health assessment. Additional exam requirements/recommendations for international students: Required—TOEFL (minimum score 550 paper-based; 213 computer-based; 79 iBT), IELTS (minimum score 6), Pearson Test of English Academic (minimum score 56). *Application deadline:* Applications are processed on a rolling basis. Application fee: $30 ($40 for international students). Electronic applications accepted. *Expenses:* Contact institution. *Financial support:* In 2011–12, 5 students received support. Career-related internships or fieldwork, scholarships/grants, and unspecified assistantships available. Financial award application deadline: 7/1; financial award applicants required to submit FAFSA. *Unit head:* Dr. Sue McLarry, Chair, 870-972-3074, Fax: 870-972-2954, E-mail: smclarry@astate.edu. *Application contact:* Dr. Andrew Sustich, Dean of the Graduate School, 870-972-3029, Fax: 870-972-3857, E-mail: sustich@astate.edu. Web site: http://www.astate.edu/a/conhp/nursing/index.dot.

A.T. Still University of Health Sciences, School of Health Management, Kirksville, MO 63501. Offers dental emphasis (MPH); health administration (MHA); health education (MH Ed, DH Ed); public health (MPH). Part-time and evening/weekend programs available. Postbaccalaureate distance learning degree programs offered (no on-campus study). *Faculty:* 15 full-time (8 women), 52 part-time/adjunct (27 women). *Students:* 50 full-time (36 women), 391 part-time (245 women); includes 125 minority (48 Black or African American, non-Hispanic/Latino; 4 American Indian or Alaska Native, non-Hispanic/Latino; 42 Asian, non-Hispanic/Latino; 26 Hispanic/Latino; 5 Two or more races, non-Hispanic/Latino). Average age 32. 121 applicants, 90% accepted, 89 enrolled. In 2011, 156 master's, 38 doctorates awarded. *Degree requirements:* For master's, thesis, integrated terminal project; for doctorate, thesis/dissertation. *Entrance requirements:* For master's, minimum GPA of 3.0, bachelor's degree or equivalent from U.S. institution; for doctorate, minimum GPA of 3.0, master's or terminal degree. Additional exam requirements/recommendations for international students: Required—TOEFL (minimum score 550 paper-based; 213 computer-based; 80 iBT). *Application deadline:* For fall admission, 7/9 for domestic students, 7/6 for international students; for winter admission, 9/28 for domestic and international students; for spring admission, 1/11 for domestic and international students. Application fee: $60. Electronic applications accepted. *Expenses:* Contact institution. *Financial support:* In 2011–12, 72 students received support. Scholarships/grants available. Financial award application deadline: 5/1; financial award applicants required to submit FAFSA. *Faculty research:* Public health: cultural health disparities, emergency preparedness, infectious disease, maternal and child health, environmental health; health education: overweight and obesity; health administration: leadership, strategic thinking, governance, healthcare reform economics, patient-centered care. *Unit head:* Dr. Kimberly O'Reilly, Interim Dean, 660-626-2820, Fax: 660-626-2826, E-mail: koreilley@atsu.edu. *Application contact:* Sarah Spencer, Associate Director, Admissions, 660-626-2820 Ext. 2669, Fax: 660-626-2826, E-mail: sspencer@atsu.edu. Web site: http://www.atsu.edu/shm.

Auburn University, Graduate School, College of Education, Department of Kinesiology, Auburn University, AL 36849. Offers exercise science (M Ed, MS, PhD); health promotion (M Ed, MS); kinesiology (PhD); physical education/teacher education (M Ed, MS, Ed D, Ed S). *Accreditation:* NCATE. Part-time programs available. *Faculty:* 15 full-time (8 women). *Students:* 60 full-time (30 women), 33 part-time (15 women); includes 17 minority (14 Black or African American, non-Hispanic/Latino; 1 Asian, non-Hispanic/Latino; 2 Hispanic/Latino), 6 international. Average age 27. 116 applicants, 61% accepted, 41 enrolled. In 2011, 48 master's, 4 doctorates awarded. *Degree requirements:* For master's, thesis (for some programs); for doctorate, thesis/dissertation; for Ed S, exam, field project. *Entrance requirements:* For master's, GRE General Test; for doctorate and Ed S, GRE General Test, interview, master's degree. *Application deadline:* For fall admission, 7/7 for domestic students; for spring admission, 11/24 for domestic students. Applications are processed on a rolling basis. Application fee: $50 ($60 for international students). Electronic applications accepted. *Expenses:* Tuition, state resident: full-time $7290; part-time $405 per credit hour. Tuition, nonresident: full-time $21,870; part-time $1215 per credit hour. *International tuition:* $22,000 full-time. *Required fees:* $1402. *Financial support:* Research assistantships, teaching assistantships, and Federal Work-Study available. Support available to part-time students. Financial award application deadline: 3/15; financial award applicants required to submit FAFSA. *Faculty research:* Biomechanics, exercise physiology, motor skill learning, school health, curriculum development. *Unit head:* Dr. Mary E. Rudisill, Head, 334-844-1458. *Application contact:* Dr. George Flowers, Dean of the Graduate School, 334-844-2125.

Augusta State University, Graduate Studies, College of Education, Program in Health and Physical Education, Augusta, GA 30904-2200. Offers M Ed. *Faculty:* 2 full-time (both women). *Students:* 1 full-time (0 women), 6 part-time (3 women); includes 3 minority (all Black or African American, non-Hispanic/Latino). Average age 31. 1 applicant, 100% accepted, 1 enrolled. In 2011, 7 master's awarded. *Entrance requirements:* For master's, GRE, MAT, minimum GPA of 2.5. Application fee: $20. *Financial support:* Career-related internships or fieldwork, Federal Work-Study, institutionally sponsored loans, and unspecified assistantships available. Support available to part-time students. *Unit head:* Dr. Paula J. Dohoney, Chair, 706-731-7922, Fax: 706-667-4140, E-mail: pdohoney@aug.edu. *Application contact:* Andrea M. Scott, Secretary to the Dean, 706-737-1499, Fax: 706-667-4706, E-mail: ascott@aug.edu.

Austin Peay State University, College of Graduate Studies, College of Behavioral and Health Sciences, Department of Health and Human Performance, Clarksville, TN 37044. Offers health leadership (MS). Part-time and evening/weekend programs available. Postbaccalaureate distance learning degree programs offered (no on-campus study). *Faculty:* 6 full-time (3 women). *Students:* 21 full-time (16 women), 45 part-time (32 women); includes 28 minority (19 Black or African American, non-Hispanic/Latino; 6 Hispanic/Latino; 3 Two or more races, non-Hispanic/Latino). Average age 30. 58 applicants, 86% accepted, 38 enrolled. In 2011, 24 master's awarded. *Degree requirements:* For master's, comprehensive exam, thesis optional. *Entrance requirements:* For master's, GRE General Test, 3 letters of recommendation, minimum undergraduate GPA of 2.5. Additional exam requirements/recommendations for international students: Required—TOEFL (minimum score 500 paper-based; 173 computer-based). *Application deadline:* For fall admission, 8/1 priority date for domestic students. Applications are processed on a rolling basis. Application fee: $25. Electronic applications accepted. *Expenses:* Tuition, state resident: part-time $350 per credit hour. Tuition, nonresident: full-time $20,644; part-time $971 per credit hour. *Required fees:* $1224; $61.20 per credit hour. *Financial support:* In 2011–12, research assistantships with full tuition reimbursements (averaging $5,184 per year) were awarded; career-related internships or fieldwork, Federal Work-Study, institutionally sponsored loans, scholarships/grants, and unspecified assistantships also available. Support available to part-time students. Financial award application deadline: 3/1; financial award applicants required to submit FAFSA. *Unit head:* Dr. Marcy Maurer, Chair, 931-221-6105, Fax: 931-221-7040, E-mail: maurerm@apsu.edu. *Application contact:* Kendra Bryant, Graduate Admissions, 800-844-2778, Fax: 931-221-6188, E-mail: admissionsweb@apsu.edu. Web site: http://www.apsu.edu/hhp/.

Baylor University, Graduate School, School of Education, Department of Health, Human Performance and Recreation, Waco, TX 76798. Offers exercise, nutrition and preventive health (PhD); health, human performance and recreation (MS Ed). *Accreditation:* NCATE. Part-time programs available. *Faculty:* 13 full-time (5 women), 3 part-time/adjunct (1 woman). *Students:* 64 full-time (41 women), 28 part-time (10 women); includes 16 minority (5 Black or African American, non-Hispanic/Latino; 1 Asian, non-Hispanic/Latino; 7 Hispanic/Latino; 3 Two or more races, non-Hispanic/Latino), 8 international. 30 applicants, 87% accepted. In 2011, 42 degrees awarded. *Degree requirements:* For master's, thesis optional. *Entrance requirements:* For master's, GRE General Test. *Application deadline:* For fall admission, 4/1 priority date for domestic students; for spring admission, 10/1 for domestic students. Applications are processed on a rolling basis. Application fee: $25. Electronic applications accepted. *Financial support:* In 2011–12, 35 students received support, including 22 teaching assistantships; career-related internships or fieldwork, Federal Work-Study, institutionally sponsored loans, tuition waivers (partial), and recreation supplements also available. *Faculty research:* Behavior change theory, pedagogy, nutrition and enzyme therapy, exercise testing, health planning. *Unit head:* Dr. Glenn Miller, Graduate Program Director, 254-710-4001, Fax: 254-710-3527, E-mail: glenn_miller@baylor.edu. *Application contact:* Eva Berger-Rhodes, Administrative Assistant, 254-710-4945, Fax: 254-710-3870, E-mail: eva_rhodes@baylor.edu. Web site: http://www.baylor.edu/HHPR/.

Benedictine University, Graduate Programs, Program in Public Health, Lisle, IL 60532-0900. Offers administration of health care institutions (MPH); dietetics (MPH); disaster management (MPH); health education (MPH); health information systems (MPH); MBA/MPH; MPH/MS. Part-time and evening/weekend programs available. Postbaccalaureate distance learning degree programs offered. *Faculty:* 2 full-time (0 women), 8 part-time/adjunct (3 women). *Students:* 85 full-time (61 women), 437 part-time (333 women); includes 217 minority (133 Black or African American, non-Hispanic/Latino; 1 American Indian or Alaska Native, non-Hispanic/Latino; 65 Asian, non-Hispanic/Latino; 18 Hispanic/Latino), 28 international. Average age 33. 172 applicants, 80% accepted, 113 enrolled. In 2011, 116 master's awarded. *Entrance requirements:* For master's, MAT, GRE, or GMAT. Additional exam requirements/recommendations for international students: Required—TOEFL (minimum score 550 paper-based; 213 computer-based). *Application deadline:* For fall admission, 9/1 for domestic students; for winter admission, 12/1 for domestic students; for spring admission, 2/15 for domestic students. Application fee: $40. *Financial support:* Career-related internships or fieldwork and health care benefits available. Support available to part-time students. *Unit head:* Dr. Georgeen Polyak, Director, 630-829-6217, E-mail: gpolyak@ben.edu. *Application contact:* Kari Gibbons, Associate Vice President, Enrollment Center, 630-829-6200, Fax: 630-829-6584, E-mail: kgibbons@ben.edu.

Brandeis University, The Heller School for Social Policy and Management, Program in Social Policy, Waltham, MA 02454-9110. Offers assets and inequalities (PhD); children, youth and families (PhD); global health and development (PhD); health and behavioral health (PhD). *Students:* 132 full-time (107 women), 12 part-time (9 women); includes 18 minority (8 Black or African American, non-Hispanic/Latino; 5 Asian, non-Hispanic/Latino; 5 Hispanic/Latino), 18 international. Average age 32. 115 applicants, 47% accepted, 23 enrolled. In 2011, 15 doctorates awarded. *Degree requirements:* For doctorate, comprehensive exam, thesis/dissertation, qualifying paper, 2-year residency. *Entrance requirements:* For doctorate, GRE General Test, 3 letters of recommendation, statement of purpose, writing sample, at least 3-5 years of professional experience. Additional exam requirements/recommendations for international students: Required—TOEFL (minimum score 600 paper-based; 250 computer-based; 100 iBT). *Application deadline:* For fall admission, 1/2 for domestic and international students. Application fee: $55. Electronic applications accepted. *Financial support:* In 2011–12, 15 fellowships with full tuition reimbursements (averaging $20,000 per year) were awarded; scholarships/grants, traineeships, health care benefits, tuition waivers (full and partial), and unspecified assistantships also available. Financial award application deadline: 1/2. *Faculty research:* Health; mental health; substance abuse; children, youth, and families; aging; international and community development; disabilities; work and inequality; hunger and poverty. *Unit head:* Dr. Susan Parish, Program Director, 781-736-3928, E-mail: slp@brandeis.edu. *Application contact:* Elizabeth Cole, Assistant Director for Admissions and Financial Aid, 781-736-2647, E-mail: elcole@brandeis.edu. Web site: http://heller.brandeis.edu/academic/phd.html.

Brigham Young University, Graduate Studies, College of Life Sciences, Department of Health Science, Provo , UT 84602. Offers MPH. *Faculty:* 13 full-time (2 women). *Students:* 23 full-time (16 women); includes 4 minority (1 Asian, non-Hispanic/Latino; 3 Hispanic/Latino). Average age 25. 40 applicants, 33% accepted, 12 enrolled. In 2011, 8 master's awarded. *Degree requirements:* For master's, thesis, oral defense. *Entrance requirements:* For master's, GRE General Test (minimum score of 298), minimum GPA of 3.2 in last 60 hours. Additional exam requirements/recommendations for international students: Required—TOEFL (minimum score 580 paper-based; 237 computer-based; 85 iBT), IELTS (minimum score 7). *Application deadline:* For fall admission, 2/1 for domestic and international students. Application fee: $50. Electronic applications accepted. *Expenses: Tuition:* Full-time $5760; part-time $320 per credit. Tuition and fees vary according to student's religious affiliation. *Financial support:* In 2011–12, 23 students received support, including 23 fellowships with partial tuition reimbursements available (averaging $2,651 per year), 23 research assistantships with partial tuition reimbursements available (averaging $1,069 per year); teaching assistantships, career-related internships or fieldwork, scholarships/grants, and tuition waivers (partial) also available. Financial award application deadline: 3/1. *Faculty research:* Social marketing, health communication, cancer, epidemiology, tobacco prevention and control, maternal and child health. *Total annual research expenditures:* $3,653. *Unit head:* Dr. Michael Dean Barnes, Chair, 801-422-3327, Fax: 801-422-0273, E-mail: michael_barnes@byu.edu. *Application contact:* Dr. Carl Lee Hanson, Graduate Coordinator, 801-422-9103, Fax: 801-422-0273, E-mail: carl_hanson@byu.edu. Web site: http://www.mph.byu.edu.

Brooklyn College of the City University of New York, Division of Graduate Studies, School of Education, Program in Adolescence Education and Special Subjects, Brooklyn, NY 11210-2889. Offers adolescence science education (MAT); art teacher (MA); biology teacher (MA); chemistry teacher (MA); earth science teacher (MAT); English teacher (MA); French teacher (MA); health and nutrition sciences: health teacher (MS Ed); mathematics teacher (MA); music education (CAS); music teacher (MA); physical education teacher (MS Ed); physics teacher (MA); social studies teacher (MA); Spanish teacher (MA). Part-time and evening/weekend programs available. *Degree requirements:* For master's, comprehensive exam (for some programs), thesis (for some programs). *Entrance requirements:* For master's, LAST, previous course work in education, resume, 2 letters of recommendation, essay. Additional exam requirements/recommendations for international students: Required—TOEFL (minimum score 500 paper-based; 173 computer-based; 61 iBT). Electronic applications accepted. *Faculty research:* Interdisciplinary education, semiotics, discourse analysis, autobiography, teacher identity.

California State University, Long Beach, Graduate Studies, College of Health and Human Services, Department of Health Science, Long Beach, CA 90840. Offers MPH, MS, MSN/MPH. *Accreditation:* CEPH; NCATE. Part-time programs available. *Faculty:* 6 full-time (2 women), 1 part-time/adjunct (0 women). *Students:* 40 full-time (32 women), 5 part-time (4 women); includes 23 minority (2 Black or African American, non-Hispanic/Latino; 5 Asian, non-Hispanic/Latino; 15 Hispanic/Latino; 1 Two or more races, non-Hispanic/Latino), 2 international. Average age 26. 91 applicants, 45% accepted, 17 enrolled. In 2011, 24 master's awarded. *Degree requirements:* For master's, thesis optional. *Entrance requirements:* For master's, GRE, minimum GPA of 3.0 in last 60 units. *Application deadline:* For fall admission, 3/1 for domestic students. Applications are processed on a rolling basis. Application fee: $55. Electronic applications accepted. *Financial support:* Federal Work-Study, institutionally sponsored loans, and scholarships/grants available. Financial award application deadline: 3/2. *Unit head:* Dr.

Robert Friis, Chair, 562-985-1537, Fax: 562-985-2384, E-mail: rfriis@csulb.edu. *Application contact:* Dr. Mohammed Forouzesh, Director, Graduate Studies, 562-985-4014, Fax: 562-985-2384, E-mail: mforouze@csulb.edu.

California State University, Los Angeles, Graduate Studies, College of Health and Human Services, School of Nursing, Los Angeles, CA 90032-8530. Offers health science (MA); nursing (MS). *Accreditation:* AACN. Part-time and evening/weekend programs available. *Faculty:* 6 full-time (5 women), 17 part-time/adjunct (16 women). *Students:* 115 full-time (100 women), 101 part-time (82 women); includes 154 minority (18 Black or African American, non-Hispanic/Latino; 90 Asian, non-Hispanic/Latino; 39 Hispanic/Latino; 2 Native Hawaiian or other Pacific Islander, non-Hispanic/Latino; 5 Two or more races, non-Hispanic/Latino), 4 international. Average age 34. 259 applicants, 30% accepted, 41 enrolled. In 2011, 57 master's awarded. *Degree requirements:* For master's, comprehensive exam, project or thesis. *Entrance requirements:* For master's, minimum GPA of 3.0 in nursing, course work in nursing and statistics. Additional exam requirements/recommendations for international students: Required—TOEFL (minimum score 500 paper-based; 173 computer-based). *Application deadline:* For fall admission, 5/1 for domestic and international students. Applications are processed on a rolling basis. Application fee: $55. *Expenses:* Tuition, state resident: full-time $8225. *Financial support:* Federal Work-Study available. Support available to part-time students. Financial award application deadline: 3/1. *Faculty research:* Family stress, geripsychiatric nursing, self-care counseling, holistic nursing, adult health. *Unit head:* Dr. Cynthia Hughes, Director, 323-343-4700, Fax: 323-343-6454, E-mail: chughes2@calstatela.edu. *Application contact:* Dr. Karin Brown, Acting Associate Dean of Graduate Studies, 323-343-3820, Fax: 323-343-5653, E-mail: kbrown5@calstatela.edu. Web site: http://www.calstatela.edu/dept/nursing/index.htm.

California State University, San Bernardino, Graduate Studies, College of Natural Sciences, Program in Health Science, San Bernardino, CA 92407-2397. Offers health science (MS); public health (MPH). *Students:* 14 full-time (13 women), 6 part-time (all women); includes 9 minority (3 Black or African American, non-Hispanic/Latino; 1 Asian, non-Hispanic/Latino; 5 Hispanic/Latino), 2 international. Average age 29. 12 applicants, 42% accepted, 3 enrolled. In 2011, 9 master's awarded. *Expenses:* Tuition, state resident: full-time $7356. Tuition, nonresident: full-time $7356. *Required fees:* $1077. Tuition and fees vary according to program. *Unit head:* Dr. Cynthia Paxton, Assistant Dean, 909-537-5343, Fax: 909-537-7037, E-mail: cpaxton@csusb.edu. *Application contact:* Sandra Kamusikiri, Associate Vice-President/Dean of Graduate Studies, 909-537-5058, E-mail: skamusik@csusb.edu.

Cambridge College, School of Education, Cambridge, MA 02138-5304. Offers autism specialist (M Ed); autism/behavior analyst (M Ed); behavior analyst (Post-Master's Certificate); behavioral management (M Ed); early childhood teacher (M Ed); education specialist in curriculum and instruction (CAGS); educational leadership (Ed D); elementary teacher (M Ed); English as a second language (M Ed, Certificate); general science (M Ed); health education (Post-Master's Certificate); health/family and consumer sciences (M Ed); history (M Ed); individualized (M Ed); information technology literacy (M Ed); instructional technology (M Ed); interdisciplinary studies (M Ed); library teacher (M Ed); literacy education (M Ed); mathematics (M Ed); mathematics specialist (Certificate); middle school mathematics and science (M Ed); school administration (M Ed, CAGS); school guidance counselor (M Ed); school nurse education (M Ed); school social worker/school adjustment counselor (M Ed); special education administrator (CAGS); special education/moderate disabilities (M Ed); teaching skills and methodologies (M Ed). Part-time and evening/weekend programs available. Postbaccalaureate distance learning degree programs offered (minimal on-campus study). *Degree requirements:* For master's, thesis, internship/practicum (licensure program only); for doctorate, thesis/dissertation; for other advanced degree, thesis. *Entrance requirements:* For master's, interview, resume, documentation of licensure, 2 professional references; for doctorate, official transcripts, interview, resume, documentation of licensure (if any), written personal statement/essay, portfolio of scholarly and professional work, qualifying assessment, 2 professional references, health insurance, immunizations form; for other advanced degree, official transcripts, interview, resume, documentation of licensure (if any), written personal statement/essay, 2 professional references, health insurance, immunizations form. Additional exam requirements/recommendations for international students: Required—TOEFL (minimum score 550 paper-based; 213 computer-based; 79 iBT); Recommended—IELTS (minimum score 6). Electronic applications accepted. *Expenses:* Contact institution. *Faculty research:* Adult education, accelerated learning, mathematics education, brain compatible learning, special education and law.

Central Washington University, Graduate Studies and Research, College of Education and Professional Studies, Department of Physical Education, School and Public Health, Ellensburg, WA 98926. Offers athletic administration (MS); health and physical education (MS). Part-time programs available. *Faculty:* 15 full-time (7 women). *Students:* 12 full-time (2 women), 12 part-time (4 women); includes 1 minority (Hispanic/Latino). 4 applicants, 75% accepted, 3 enrolled. In 2011, 12 master's awarded. *Application deadline:* For fall admission, 2/1 priority date for domestic students; for winter admission, 10/1 for domestic students; for spring admission, 1/1 for domestic students. Applications are processed on a rolling basis. Application fee: $50. Electronic applications accepted. *Expenses:* Tuition, state resident: full-time $8112; part-time $270 per credit. Tuition, nonresident: full-time $18,069; part-time $602 per credit. *Required fees:* $924. *Financial support:* In 2011–12, 5 teaching assistantships (averaging $9,234 per year) were awarded; career-related internships or fieldwork, Federal Work-Study, scholarships/grants, health care benefits, and unspecified assistantships also available. Financial award applicants required to submit FAFSA. *Unit head:* Dr. Kirk Mathias, Graduate Coordinator, 509-963-1911. *Application contact:* Justine Eason, Admissions Program Coordinator, 509-963-3103, Fax: 509-963-1799, E-mail: masters@cwu.edu. Web site: http://www.cwu.edu/~pesph/.

The Citadel, The Military College of South Carolina, Citadel Graduate College, Department of Health, Exercise, and Sport Science, Charleston, SC 29409. Offers health, exercise, and sport science (MS); physical education (MAT). *Accreditation:* NCATE. Part-time and evening/weekend programs available. *Faculty:* 7 full-time (2 women). *Students:* 13 full-time (7 women), 42 part-time (18 women); includes 11 minority (8 Black or African American, non-Hispanic/Latino; 2 Hispanic/Latino; 1 Two or more races, non-Hispanic/Latino), 1 international. Average age 26. In 2011, 21 master's awarded. *Degree requirements:* For master's, comprehensive exam, thesis optional. *Entrance requirements:* For master's, GRE (minimum score 900) or MAT (minimum score 396), minimum undergraduate GPA of 2.5, 3 letters of recommendation, resume detailing previous work experience (for MS only). Additional exam requirements/recommendations for international students: Required—TOEFL (minimum score 550 paper-based; 213 computer-based; 79 iBT). *Application deadline:* Applications are processed on a rolling basis. Application fee: $30. Electronic applications accepted. *Expenses: Tuition, area resident:* Part-time $501 per credit hour. Tuition, state resident: part-time $501 per credit hour. Tuition, nonresident: part-time $824 per credit hour. *Required fees:* $40 per term. One-time fee: $30. *Financial support:* Career-related internships or fieldwork, health care benefits, and unspecified assistantships available. Support available to part-time students. Financial award application deadline: 7/1; financial award applicants required to submit FAFSA. *Faculty research:* Risk management in sport and physical activity programs, school-wide physical activity programs, exercise intervention among HIV-infected individuals, factors influencing motor skill in SC physical education programs, effect of mouthpiece use on human performance. *Unit head:* Dr. Dena Garner, Interim Department Head, 843-953-5060, Fax: 843-953-6798, E-mail: dena.garner@citadel.edu. *Application contact:* Dr. Steve A. Nida, Associate Provost, The Citadel Graduate College, 843-953-5089, Fax: 843-953-7630, E-mail: cgc@citadel.edu. Web site: http://www.citadel.edu/hess/index.htm.

Cleveland State University, College of Graduate Studies, College of Education and Human Services, Department of Health, Physical Education, Recreation and Dance, Cleveland, OH 44115. Offers community health education (M Ed); exercise science (M Ed); human performance (M Ed); physical education pedagogy (M Ed); public health (MPH); school health education (M Ed); sport and exercise psychology (M Ed); sports management (M Ed). Part-time programs available. *Faculty:* 7 full-time (4 women), 3 part-time/adjunct (2 women). *Students:* 40 full-time (22 women), 91 part-time (48 women); includes 17 minority (15 Black or African American, non-Hispanic/Latino; 1 Asian, non-Hispanic/Latino; 1 Hispanic/Latino), 17 international. Average age 28. 138 applicants, 80% accepted, 60 enrolled. In 2011, 30 master's awarded. *Degree requirements:* For master's, comprehensive exam, thesis optional. *Entrance requirements:* For master's, GRE General Test or MAT (if undergraduate GPA less than 2.75), minimum undergraduate GPA of 2.75. Additional exam requirements/recommendations for international students: Required—TOEFL (minimum score 525 paper-based; 197 computer-based), IELTS (minimum score 6). *Application deadline:* For fall admission, 7/15 priority date for domestic students; for spring admission, 12/15 priority date for domestic students. Applications are processed on a rolling basis. Application fee: $30. Electronic applications accepted. *Expenses:* Tuition, state resident: full-time $6416; part-time $494 per credit hour. Tuition, nonresident: full-time $12,074; part-time $929 per credit hour. *Financial support:* In 2011–12, 6 research assistantships with full and partial tuition reimbursements (averaging $3,480 per year), 1 teaching assistantship with full and partial tuition reimbursement (averaging $3,480 per year) were awarded; career-related internships or fieldwork, tuition waivers (full), and unspecified assistantships also available. Financial award application deadline: 3/15. *Faculty research:* Bone density, marketing fitness centers, motor development of disabled, online learning and survey research. *Unit head:* Dr. Sheila M. Patterson, Chairperson, 216-687-4870, Fax: 216-687-5410, E-mail: s.m.patterson@csuohio.edu. *Application contact:* Deborah L. Brown, Interim Assistant Director, Graduate Admissions, 216-523-7572, Fax: 216-687-5400, E-mail: d.l.brown@csuohio.edu. Web site: http://www.csuohio.edu/coehs/departments/hperd.

The College at Brockport, State University of New York, School of Health and Human Performance, Department of Health Science, Brockport, NY 14420-2997. Offers health education (MS Ed), including community health education, health education K-12. *Students:* 11 full-time (9 women), 19 part-time (13 women); includes 6 minority (4 Black or African American, non-Hispanic/Latino; 1 American Indian or Alaska Native, non-Hispanic/Latino; 1 Asian, non-Hispanic/Latino). 35 applicants, 43% accepted, 8 enrolled. In 2011, 2 master's awarded. *Degree requirements:* For master's, thesis or alternative. *Entrance requirements:* For master's, minimum GPA of 3.0, letters of recommendation. Additional exam requirements/recommendations for international students: Required—TOEFL (minimum score 550 paper-based; 213 computer-based; 79 iBT). *Application deadline:* For fall admission, 4/1 priority date for domestic students, 4/1 for international students; for spring admission, 11/1 priority date for domestic students, 11/1 for international students. Application fee: $80. Electronic applications accepted. *Financial support:* In 2011–12, 1 teaching assistantship with full tuition reimbursement (averaging $6,000 per year) was awarded; Federal Work-Study, scholarships/grants, and unspecified assistantships also available. Support available to part-time students. Financial award application deadline: 3/15; financial award applicants required to submit FAFSA. *Faculty research:* Nutrition, substance use, HIV/AIDS, bioethics, worksite health. *Unit head:* Dr. Patti Follensbee, Chairperson, 585-395-5483, Fax: 585-395-5246, E-mail: pfallons@brockport.edu. *Application contact:* Dr. Patti Follansbee, Admissions Coordinator, 585-395-5483, Fax: 585-395-5246, E-mail: pfollans@brockport.edu. Web site: http://www.brockport.edu/graduate/.

The College of New Jersey, Graduate Studies, School of Nursing, Health and Exercise Science, Department of Health and Exercise Science, Program in Health Education, Ewing, NJ 08628. Offers health (MAT); physical education (M Ed). *Accreditation:* NCATE. Part-time programs available. *Degree requirements:* For master's, comprehensive exam. *Entrance requirements:* For master's, GRE, minimum GPA of 3.0 in field or 2.75 overall. Additional exam requirements/recommendations for international students: Required—TOEFL. Electronic applications accepted.

College of Saint Mary, Program in Health Professions Education, Omaha, NE 68106. Offers Ed D. Part-time programs available.

Colorado State University–Pueblo, College of Education, Engineering and Professional Studies, Education Program, Pueblo, CO 81001-4901. Offers art education (M Ed); foreign language education (M Ed); health and physical education (M Ed); instructional technology (M Ed); linguistically diverse education (M Ed); music education (M Ed); special education (M Ed). *Accreditation:* Teacher Education Accreditation Council. Part-time programs available. *Degree requirements:* For master's, portfolio. *Entrance requirements:* For master's, 3 recommendations, teaching license. Additional exam requirements/recommendations for international students: Required—TOEFL (minimum score 500 paper-based; 173 computer-based). Electronic applications accepted. *Faculty research:* Portfolio assessment, math education, science education.

Columbus State University, Graduate Studies, College of Education and Health Professions, Department of Teacher Education, Columbus, GA 31907-5645. Offers accomplished teaching (M Ed); early childhood education (M Ed, MAT, Ed S); health and physical education (M Ed, MAT); middle grades education (M Ed, MAT, Ed S); school library media (M Ed, MAT); secondary education (M Ed, MAT, Ed S), including English/language arts (M Ed, Ed S), general science (M Ed), mathematics (M Ed), social science (M Ed); special education (M Ed, Ed S), including general curriculum (M Ed). *Accreditation:* NCATE. Part-time and evening/weekend programs available. Postbaccalaureate distance learning degree programs offered (minimal on-campus study). *Degree requirements:* For master's, thesis, exit exam; for Ed S, thesis or alternative. *Entrance requirements:* For master's, GRE General Test, minimum GPA of 2.75; for Ed S, GRE General Test. Additional exam requirements/recommendations for international students: Required—TOEFL (minimum score 550 paper-based; 213 computer-based; 79 iBT). Electronic applications accepted.

Dalhousie University, Faculty of Health Professions, School of Health and Human Performance, Program in Health Promotion, Halifax, NS B3H 3J5, Canada. Offers MA. Part-time programs available. *Degree requirements:* For master's, thesis. *Entrance requirements:* Additional exam requirements/recommendations for international students: Required—TOEFL, IELTS, CANTEST, CAEL, or Michigan English Language Assessment Battery. Electronic applications accepted. *Faculty research:* AIDS research, health knowledge of adolescents, evaluating health promotion, program evaluation.

Delta State University, Graduate Programs, College of Education, Division of Health, Physical Education, and Recreation, Cleveland, MS 38733-0001. Offers health, physical education, and recreation (M Ed); sport and human performance (MS). Part-time and evening/weekend programs available. *Degree requirements:* For master's, thesis optional. *Entrance requirements:* For master's, GRE General Test or MAT, Class A teaching certificate. *Expenses:* Tuition, state resident: full-time $4702; part-time $294 per credit hour. Tuition, nonresident: full-time $12,516; part-time $760 per credit hour. *Required fees:* $586. *Faculty research:* Blood pressure, body fat, power and reaction time, learning disorders for athletes, effects of walking.

D'Youville College, Doctoral Programs, Buffalo, NY 14201-1084. Offers educational leadership (Ed D); health education (Ed D); health policy (Ed D). Part-time and evening/weekend programs available. *Faculty:* 6 full-time (2 women), 23 part-time/adjunct (13 women). *Students:* 28 full-time (14 women), 32 part-time (25 women); includes 3 minority (2 Black or African American, non-Hispanic/Latino; 1 Hispanic/Latino), 14 international. Average age 44. 38 applicants, 58% accepted, 18 enrolled. In 2011, 13 doctorates awarded. *Degree requirements:* For doctorate, comprehensive exam, thesis/dissertation, fieldwork. *Entrance requirements:* For doctorate, MS/MA; professional experience. *Expenses: Tuition:* Full-time $18,960; part-time $790 per credit hour. *Required fees:* $310. Tuition and fees vary according to degree level and program. *Financial support:* In 2011–12, research assistantships with tuition reimbursements (averaging $3,000 per year) were awarded; scholarships/grants also available. *Faculty research:* Educational assessment, assessment reform, culture and education, market-based reform, men's health, electronic records. *Unit head:* Dr. Mark Garrison, Director, 716-829-8125, E-mail: garrisonm@dyc.edu. *Application contact:* Linda Fisher, Graduate Admissions Director, 716-829-8400, Fax: 716-829-7900, E-mail: graduateadmissions@dyc.edu.

East Carolina University, Graduate School, College of Education, Department of Business and Information Technologies Education, Greenville, NC 27858-4353. Offers business education (MA Ed); elementary education (MAT); English education (MAT); family and consumer science (MAT); health education (MAT); Hispanic studies (MAT); history education (MAT); marketing education (MA Ed); middle grades education (MAT); music education (MAT); physical education (MAT); science education (MAT); special education (MAT), including general curriculum; vocation education (MS). *Accreditation:* NCATE. Part-time and evening/weekend programs available. Postbaccalaureate distance learning degree programs offered (no on-campus study). *Degree requirements:* For master's, comprehensive exam, thesis optional. *Entrance requirements:* For master's, GRE or MAT, minimum GPA of 2.5, bachelor's degree in related field, teaching license (MA Ed). Additional exam requirements/recommendations for international students: Required—TOEFL. *Application deadline:* For fall admission, 6/1 priority date for domestic students. Applications are processed on a rolling basis. Application fee: $50. *Expenses:* Tuition, state resident: full-time $3557; part-time $444.63 per semester hour. Tuition, nonresident: full-time $14,351; part-time $1793.88 per semester hour. *Required fees:* $2016; $252 per semester hour. Part-time tuition and fees vary according to course load, campus/location and program. *Financial support:* Federal Work-Study available. Support available to part-time students. Financial award application deadline: 6/1. *Unit head:* Dr. Ivan G. Wallace, Chair, 252-328-6983, Fax: 252-328-6835, E-mail: wallacei@ecu.edu. *Application contact:* Dean of Graduate School, 252-328-6012, Fax: 252-328-6071, E-mail: gradschool@ecu.edu. Web site: http://www.ecu.edu/cs-educ/bite/index.cfm.

East Carolina University, Graduate School, College of Health and Human Performance, Department of Health Education and Promotion, Greenville, NC 27858-4353. Offers athletic training (MS); environmental health (MS); health education (MA, MA Ed). *Accreditation:* NCATE. *Degree requirements:* For master's, comprehensive exam, thesis optional. *Entrance requirements:* For master's, GRE General Test or MAT. Additional exam requirements/recommendations for international students: Required—TOEFL. *Application deadline:* For fall admission, 6/1 priority date for domestic students. Applications are processed on a rolling basis. Application fee: $50. *Expenses:* Tuition, state resident: full-time $3557; part-time $444.63 per semester hour. Tuition, nonresident: full-time $14,351; part-time $1793.88 per semester hour. *Required fees:* $2016; $252 per semester hour. Part-time tuition and fees vary according to course load, campus/location and program. *Financial support:* Fellowships, research assistantships, teaching assistantships, and career-related internships or fieldwork available. Support available to part-time students. Financial award application deadline: 6/1. *Faculty research:* Community health education, worksite health promotion, school health education, environmental health. *Unit head:* Dr. Tim Kelley, Chair, 252-737-2225, E-mail: kelleyt@ecu.edu. Web site: http://www.ecu.edu/hlth/.

Eastern Kentucky University, The Graduate School, College of Education, Department of Curriculum and Instruction, Program in Secondary and Higher Education, Richmond, KY 40475-3102. Offers secondary education (MA Ed), including agricultural education, art education, biological sciences education, business education, English education, geography education, history education, home economics education, industrial education, mathematical sciences education, physical education, school health education. *Accreditation:* NCATE. Part-time programs available. *Entrance requirements:* For master's, GRE General Test, minimum GPA of 2.5.

Eastern Michigan University, Graduate School, College of Health and Human Services, School of Health Promotion and Human Performance, Program in Health Education, Ypsilanti, MI 48197. Offers MS. Part-time and evening/weekend programs available. *Students:* 1 (woman) full-time, 16 part-time (14 women); includes 7 minority (all Black or African American, non-Hispanic/Latino), 1 international. Average age 29. 12 applicants, 83% accepted, 9 enrolled. In 2011, 5 degrees awarded. *Degree requirements:* For master's, thesis or project. *Entrance requirements:* For master's, teaching credential. Additional exam requirements/recommendations for international students: Required—TOEFL. *Application deadline:* For fall admission, 8/1 for domestic students, 5/1 for international students; for winter admission, 12/1 for domestic students, 10/1 for international students; for spring admission, 4/15 for domestic students, 3/1 for international students. Application fee: $35. *Expenses:* Tuition, state resident: full-time $10,367; part-time $432 per credit hour. Tuition, nonresident: full-time $20,435; part-time $851 per credit hour. *Required fees:* $39 per credit hour. $46 per semester. One-time fee: $100. Tuition and fees vary according to course level, degree level and reciprocity agreements. *Unit head:* Dr. Joan Cowdery, Program Coordinator, 734-487-7120 Ext. 2698, Fax: 734-487-2024, E-mail: jcowdery@emich.edu. *Application contact:* Dr. Brenda Riemer, Chair, Graduate Programs, 734-487-0090 Ext. 2745, Fax: 734-487-2024, E-mail: briemer@emich.edu.

Eastern University, Graduate Education Programs, Program in School Health Services, St. Davids, PA 19087-3696. Offers M Ed. *Entrance requirements:* For master's, minimum GPA of 2.5. Additional exam requirements/recommendations for international students: Required—TOEFL.

East Stroudsburg University of Pennsylvania, Graduate School, College of Health Sciences, Department of Exercise Science, East Stroudsburg, PA 18301-2999. Offers cardiac rehabilitation and exercise science (MS). Part-time and evening/weekend programs available. *Degree requirements:* For master's, comprehensive exam, thesis or alternative, computer literacy. *Entrance requirements:* Additional exam requirements/recommendations for international students: Required—TOEFL (minimum score 560 paper-based; 220 computer-based; 83 iBT).

East Stroudsburg University of Pennsylvania, Graduate School, College of Health Sciences, Department of Health, East Stroudsburg, PA 18301-2999. Offers community health education (MPH); health education (MS). *Accreditation:* CEPH (one or more programs are accredited). Part-time and evening/weekend programs available. *Degree requirements:* For master's, oral comprehensive exam. *Entrance requirements:* For master's, GRE General Test, minimum GPA of 3.0 in major, 2.8 overall; undergraduate prerequisites in anatomy and physiology; 3 verifiable letters of recommendation; professional resume. Additional exam requirements/recommendations for international students: Required—TOEFL (minimum score 560 paper-based; 220 computer-based; 83 iBT) or IELTS (minimum score 6). *Faculty research:* HIV prevention, wellness, international health issues.

East Stroudsburg University of Pennsylvania, Graduate School, College of Health Sciences, Department of Physical Education, East Stroudsburg, PA 18301-2999. Offers health and physical education (M Ed). *Degree requirements:* For master's, computer literacy, portfolio exhibition as exiting research project. *Entrance requirements:* For master's, teacher certification in physical education or health and physical education. Additional exam requirements/recommendations for international students: Required—TOEFL (minimum score 560 paper-based; 220 computer-based; 83 iBT) or IELTS.

Emory University, Rollins School of Public Health, Department of Behavioral Sciences and Health Education, Atlanta, GA 30322-1100. Offers MPH, PhD. *Accreditation:* CEPH. Part-time programs available. *Students:* 75 full-time. Average age 27. 53 applicants, 23% accepted, 6 enrolled. *Degree requirements:* For master's, comprehensive exam (for some programs), thesis, practicum. *Entrance requirements:* For master's, GRE General Test. Additional exam requirements/recommendations for international students: Required—TOEFL (minimum score 550 paper-based; 220 computer-based; 80 iBT). *Application deadline:* For fall admission, 12/1 priority date for domestic students, 12/1 for international students. Application fee: $95. Electronic applications accepted. *Expenses: Tuition:* Full-time $34,800. *Required fees:* $1300. *Financial support:* Fellowships with full and partial tuition reimbursements, career-related internships or fieldwork, Federal Work-Study, institutionally sponsored loans, scholarships/grants, traineeships, health care benefits, and unspecified assistantships available. Support available to part-time students. Financial award application deadline: 1/5; financial award applicants required to submit FAFSA. *Unit head:* Dr. Michael Windle, Chair, 404-727-9868, Fax: 404-712-4299.

Florida Agricultural and Mechanical University, Division of Graduate Studies, Research, and Continuing Education, College of Education, Department of Health, Physical Education, and Recreation, Tallahassee, FL 32307-3200. Offers M Ed, MS Ed. *Accreditation:* NCATE. Part-time and evening/weekend programs available. *Degree requirements:* For master's, thesis optional. *Entrance requirements:* For master's, GRE General Test, minimum GPA of 3.0. Additional exam requirements/recommendations for international students: Required—TOEFL. *Faculty research:* Administration/curriculum, work behavior, psychology.

Florida State University, The Graduate School, College of Human Sciences, Department of Nutrition, Food and Exercise Sciences, Tallahassee, FL 32306-1493. Offers exercise physiology (PhD); nutrition and food science (MS, PhD), including clinical nutrition (MS), food science, human nutrition (PhD), nutrition education and health promotion (MS), nutrition science (MS), sports nutrition (MS); sports sciences (MS). Part-time programs available. *Faculty:* 18 full-time (10 women). *Students:* 88 full-time (56 women), 15 part-time (5 women); includes 24 minority (9 Black or African American, non-Hispanic/Latino; 4 Asian, non-Hispanic/Latino; 10 Hispanic/Latino; 1 Native Hawaiian or other Pacific Islander, non-Hispanic/Latino), 21 international. Average age 26. 172 applicants, 51% accepted, 32 enrolled. In 2011, 38 master's, 7 doctorates awarded. *Degree requirements:* For master's, comprehensive exam (for some programs), thesis optional; for doctorate, thesis/dissertation. *Entrance requirements:* For master's, GRE General Test, minimum upper-division GPA of 3.0; for doctorate, GRE General Test, minimum upper-division GPA of 3.0, MS. Additional exam requirements/recommendations for international students: Required—TOEFL (minimum score 550 paper-based; 80 iBT). *Application deadline:* For fall admission, 7/1 for domestic students, 3/1 for international students; for spring admission, 11/1 for domestic students, 5/1 for international students. Applications are processed on a rolling basis. Application fee: $30. Electronic applications accepted. *Expenses:* Tuition, state resident: full-time $9474; part-time $350.88 per credit hour. Tuition, nonresident: full-time $16,236; part-time $601.34 per credit hour. *Required fees:* $630 per semester. One-time fee: $20. Tuition and fees vary according to course load and campus/location. *Financial support:* In 2011–12, 59 students received support, including fellowships with partial tuition reimbursements available (averaging $10,000 per year), 17 research assistantships with partial tuition reimbursements available (averaging $8,000 per year), 47 teaching assistantships with partial tuition reimbursements available (averaging $8,000 per year); career-related internships or fieldwork, Federal Work-Study, institutionally sponsored loans, scholarships/grants, and unspecified assistantships also available. Financial award application deadline: 1/15; financial award applicants required to submit FAFSA. *Faculty research:* Body composition, functional food, chronic disease and aging response; food safety, food allergy, and safety/quality detection methods; sports nutrition, energy and human performance; strength training, functional performance, cardiovascular physiology, sarcopenia . *Unit head:* Dr. Bahram H. Arjmandi, Professor/Chair, 850-645-1517, Fax: 850-645-5000, E-mail: barjmandi@fsu.edu. *Application contact:* Joseph J. Carroll, Administrative Support Assistant, 850-644-4800, Fax: 850-645-5000, E-mail: jjcarroll@admin.fsu.edu. Web site: http://www.chs.fsu.edu/.

Fort Hays State University, Graduate School, College of Health and Life Sciences, Department of Health and Human Performance, Hays, KS 67601-4099. Offers MS. Part-time programs available. *Degree requirements:* For master's, comprehensive exam, thesis optional. *Entrance requirements:* For master's, GRE General Test or MAT. Additional exam requirements/recommendations for international students: Required—TOEFL (minimum score 550 paper-based; 213 computer-based). Electronic applications accepted. *Faculty research:* Isoproterenol hydrochloride and exercise, dehydrogenase and high-density lipoprotein levels in athletics, venous blood parameters to adipose fat.

Framingham State University, Division of Graduate and Continuing Education, Programs in Food and Nutrition, Program in Human Nutrition: Education and Media Technologies, Framingham, MA 01701-9101. Offers MS.

Georgia College & State University, Graduate School, College of Health Sciences, Department of Kinesiology, Milledgeville, GA 31061. Offers health promotion (M Ed); human performance (M Ed); kinesiology (MAT); outdoor education (M Ed). *Accreditation:* NCATE (one or more programs are accredited). Part-time and evening/weekend programs available. *Students:* 31 full-time (13 women), 11 part-time (7 women); includes 8 minority (6 Black or African American, non-Hispanic/Latino; 2 Hispanic/Latino), 1 international. Average age 27. 32 applicants, 69% accepted, 16 enrolled. In 2011, 12 master's awarded. *Degree requirements:* For master's, comprehensive exam, thesis optional. *Entrance requirements:* For master's, GRE General Test or MAT, minimum GPA of 2.75 in upper-level undergraduate courses, 2 letters of reference. Additional exam requirements/recommendations for international students: Recommended—TOEFL (minimum score 550 paper-based; 213 computer-based; 79 iBT). *Application deadline:* For fall admission, 7/1 priority date for domestic students, 4/1 for international students; for spring admission, 11/15 priority date for domestic students, 9/1 for international students. Applications are processed on a rolling basis. Application fee: $40. Electronic applications accepted. *Expenses:* Tuition, state resident: full-time $4806; part-time $267 per credit hour. Tuition, nonresident: full-time $17,802; part-time $989 per credit hour. *Required fees:* $936 per semester. Tuition and fees vary according to course load and campus/location. *Financial support:* In 2011–12, 25 research assistantships with full tuition reimbursements were awarded; career-related internships or fieldwork and unspecified assistantships also available. Support available to part-time students. Financial award applicants required to submit FAFSA. *Unit head:* Dr. Lisa Griffin, Interim Chair, 478-445-4072, Fax: 478-445-1790, E-mail: lisa.griffin@gcsu.edu. *Application contact:* 800-342-0471, E-mail: grad-admit@gcsu.edu.

Georgia Southern University, Jack N. Averitt College of Graduate Studies, Jiann-Ping Hsu College of Public Health, Program in Public Health, Statesboro, GA 30460. Offers biostatistics (MPH, Dr PH); community health behavior and education (Dr PH); community health education (MPH); environmental health sciences (MPH); epidemiology (MPH); health services policy management (MPH); public health leadership (Dr PH). *Accreditation:* CEPH. Part-time programs available. *Students:* 87 full-time (60 women), 39 part-time (25 women); includes 68 minority (58 Black or African American, non-Hispanic/Latino; 6 Asian, non-Hispanic/Latino; 4 Hispanic/Latino), 20 international. Average age 30. 73 applicants, 84% accepted, 42 enrolled. In 2011, 22 master's, 4 doctorates awarded. *Degree requirements:* For master's, thesis optional, practicum; for doctorate, comprehensive exam, thesis/dissertation, practicum. *Entrance requirements:* For master's, GRE General Test, minimum GPA of 2.75, resume, 3 letters of reference; for doctorate, GRE, GMAT, MCAT, LSAT, 3 letters of reference, statement of purpose, resume or curriculum vitae. Additional exam requirements/recommendations for international students: Required—TOEFL (minimum score 550 paper-based; 213 computer-based; 80 iBT). *Application deadline:* For fall admission, 3/1 priority date for domestic students, 3/1 for international students; for spring admission, 10/1 priority date for domestic students, 10/1 for international students. Applications are processed on a rolling basis. Application fee: $50. Electronic applications accepted. *Expenses:* Contact institution. *Financial support:* In 2011–12, 59 students received support, including research assistantships with partial tuition reimbursements available (averaging $7,200 per year), teaching assistantships with partial tuition reimbursements available (averaging $7,200 per year); career-related internships or fieldwork, Federal Work-Study, scholarships/grants, tuition waivers (partial), and unspecified assistantships also available. Support available to part-time students. Financial award application deadline: 4/15; financial award applicants required to submit FAFSA. *Faculty research:* Rural public health best practices, health disparity elimination, community initiatives to enhance public health, cost effectiveness analysis, epidemiology of rural public health, environmental health issues, health care system assessment, rural health care, health policy and healthcare financing. *Unit head:* Dr. Charles Hardy, Dean, 912-478-2674, Fax: 912-478-5811, E-mail: chardy@georgiasouthern.edu. *Application contact:* Amanda Gilliland, Coordinator for Graduate Student Recruitment, 912-478-5384, Fax: 912-478-0740, E-mail: gradadmissions@georgiasouthern.edu. Web site: http://chhs.georgiasouthern.edu/health/.

Georgia Southwestern State University, Graduate Studies, School of Education, Americus, GA 31709-4693. Offers early childhood education (M Ed, Ed S); health and physical education (M Ed); middle grades education (M Ed, Ed S); reading (M Ed); secondary education (M Ed); special education (M Ed). *Accreditation:* NCATE. *Degree requirements:* For master's, comprehensive exam. *Entrance requirements:* For master's, GRE General Test or MAT, minimum GPA of 2.5; for Ed S, GRE General Test or MAT, minimum graduate GPA of 3.25, M Ed from accredited college or university, 3 years teaching experience. Electronic applications accepted.

Georgia State University, College of Education, Department of Kinesiology and Health, Program in Health and Physical Education, Atlanta, GA 30302-3083. Offers M Ed. Part-time and evening/weekend programs available. *Degree requirements:* For master's, comprehensive exam. *Entrance requirements:* For master's, GRE General Test, minimum GPA of 2.5. *Faculty research:* Exercise science, teacher behavior.

Grand Canyon University, College of Doctoral Studies, Phoenix, AZ 85017-1097. Offers business administration (DBA); general psychology (PhD), including cognition and instruction, industrial and organizational psychology; organizational leadership (Ed D, PhD), including behavioral health (PhD), education and effective schools (PhD), higher education (PhD), instructional leadership (PhD), organizational development (Ed D). *Degree requirements:* For doctorate, comprehensive exam, thesis/dissertation. *Entrance requirements:* For doctorate, minimum GPA of 3.4 on earned advanced degree from regionally-accredited institution; transcripts; goals statement.

Harding University, College of Education, Searcy, AR 72149-0001. Offers advanced studies in teaching and learning (M Ed); art (MSE); behavioral science (MSE); counseling (MS, Ed S); early childhood special education (M Ed, MSE); education (MSE); educational leadership (M Ed, Ed S); elementary education (M Ed); English (MSE); French (MSE); history/social science (MSE); kinesiology (MSE); math (MSE); reading (M Ed); secondary education (M Ed); Spanish (MSE); teaching (MAT); teaching English as a second language (MSE). *Accreditation:* NCATE. Part-time and evening/weekend programs available. *Faculty:* 9 full-time (2 women), 48 part-time/adjunct (26 women). *Students:* 100 full-time (77 women), 333 part-time (239 women); includes 76 minority (59 Black or African American, non-Hispanic/Latino; 1 Asian, non-Hispanic/Latino; 10 Hispanic/Latino; 6 Two or more races, non-Hispanic/Latino), 2 international. Average age 36. 93 applicants, 91% accepted, 83 enrolled. In 2011, 159 master's, 10 other advanced degrees awarded. *Degree requirements:* For master's, comprehensive exam (for some programs), thesis optional, portfolio(s); for Ed S, comprehensive exam, portfolio, project. *Entrance requirements:* For master's, GRE, MAT, PRAXIS; for Ed S, MAT or GRE. Additional exam requirements/recommendations for international students: Required—TOEFL (minimum score 550 paper-based; 79 iBT). *Application deadline:* For fall admission, 8/1 for domestic and international students; for spring admission, 1/1 for domestic and international students. Applications are processed on a rolling basis. Application fee: $35. *Expenses: Tuition:* Full-time $10,512; part-time $584 per credit hour. *Required fees:* $500; $25 per credit hour. Tuition and fees vary according to course load, degree level and program. *Financial support:* In 2011–12, 37 students received support. Unspecified assistantships available. *Faculty research:* Reading, comprehension, school violence, educational technology, behavior, college choice, differentiated instruction, brain-based teaching. *Unit head:* Dr. Clara Carroll, Chair, 501-279-4501, Fax: 501-279-4083, E-mail: ccarroll@harding.edu. *Application contact:* Information Contact, 501-279-4315, E-mail: gradstudiesedu@harding.edu. Web site: http://www.harding.edu/education/grad.html.

Hofstra University, School of Education, Health, and Human Services, Department of Physical Education and Sports Sciences, Hempstead, NY 11549. Offers adventure education (Advanced Certificate); health education (MS), including PK-12 teaching certification; physical education (MA, MS), including adventure education, curriculum (MA), strength and conditioning; sport science (MS), including adventure education (MA, MS), strength and conditioning (MA, MS). Part-time and evening/weekend programs available. *Students:* 81 full-time (34 women), 56 part-time (25 women); includes 12 minority (9 Black or African American, non-Hispanic/Latino; 1 Asian, non-Hispanic/Latino; 2 Hispanic/Latino), 1 international. Average age 27. 52 applicants, 96% accepted, 31 enrolled. In 2011, 80 master's awarded. *Degree requirements:* For master's, one foreign language, electronic portfolio, capstone project, minimum GPA of 3.0. *Entrance requirements:* For master's, interview, 2 letters of recommendation, essay. Additional exam requirements/recommendations for international students: Required—TOEFL (minimum score 550 paper-based; 213 computer-based; 80 iBT). *Application deadline:* Applications are processed on a rolling basis. Application fee: $70 ($75 for international students). Electronic applications accepted. *Expenses: Tuition:* Full-time $18,990; part-time $1055 per credit hour. *Required fees:* $970. Tuition and fees vary according to program. *Financial support:* In 2011–12, 49 students received support, including 19 fellowships with full and partial tuition reimbursements available (averaging $3,216 per year), 3 research assistantships with full and partial tuition reimbursements available (averaging $18,529 per year); Federal Work-Study, institutionally sponsored loans, scholarships/grants, tuition waivers (full and partial), and unspecified assistantships also available. Support available to part-time students. Financial award applicants required to submit FAFSA. *Faculty research:* After school programming, skill development and health behavior, energy expenditures in physical activities, cultural competence and health education, childhood obesity. *Unit head:* Dr. Carol L. Alberts, Chairperson, 516-463-5809, Fax: 516-463-6275, E-mail: hprcla@hofstra.edu. *Application contact:* Carol Drummer, Dean of Graduate Admissions, 516-463-4876, Fax: 516-463-4664, E-mail: gradstudent@hofstra.edu. Web site: http://www.hofstra.edu/education/.

Howard University, Graduate School, Department of Health, Human Performance and Leisure Studies, Washington, DC 20059-0002. Offers exercise physiology (MS); health education (MS); sports studies (MS), including sociology of sports, sports management; urban recreation (MS), including leisure studies. Part-time and evening/weekend programs available. *Degree requirements:* For master's, comprehensive exam, thesis. *Entrance requirements:* For master's, BS in human performance or related field. Additional exam requirements/recommendations for international students: Recommended—TOEFL. Electronic applications accepted. *Faculty research:* Health promotion, cardiovascular hypertension, physical activity, sport and human rights issues.

Idaho State University, Office of Graduate Studies, Kasiska College of Health Professions, Department of Health and Nutrition Sciences, Program in Health Education, Pocatello, ID 83209-8109. Offers MHE. Part-time programs available. *Degree requirements:* For master's, comprehensive exam, thesis or project. *Entrance requirements:* For master's, GRE General Test, previous coursework in statistics, natural sciences, tests and measurements. Additional exam requirements/recommendations for international students: Required—TOEFL (minimum score 600 paper-based; 213 computer-based). Electronic applications accepted. *Faculty research:* Health and wellness.

Illinois State University, Graduate School, College of Applied Science and Technology, School of Kinesiology and Recreation, Normal, IL 61790-2200. Offers health education (MS); physical education (MS). *Degree requirements:* For master's, thesis or alternative. *Entrance requirements:* For master's, GRE General Test, minimum GPA of 2.6 in last 60 hours of course work. *Faculty research:* Influences on positive youth development through sport, country-wide health fitness project, graduate practicum in athletic training, perceived exertion and self-selected intensity during resistance exercise in younger and older.

Indiana State University, College of Graduate and Professional Studies, College of Nursing, Health and Human Services, Department of Health, Safety, and Environmental Health Sciences, Terre Haute, IN 47809. Offers community health promotion (MA, MS); health and safety education (MA, MS); occupational safety management (MA, MS). *Accreditation:* NCATE (one or more programs are accredited). *Degree requirements:* For master's, thesis or alternative. *Entrance requirements:* For master's, GRE General Test. Electronic applications accepted.

Indiana University Bloomington, School of Health, Physical Education and Recreation, Department of Applied Health Science, Bloomington, IN 47405-7000. Offers biostatistics (MPH); environmental health (MPH, PhD); epidemiology (MPH, PhD); health behavior (PhD); health promotion (MS); human development/family studies (MS); nutrition science (MS); public health administration (MPH); safety management (MS); school and college health programs (MS); social, behavioral and community health (MPH). *Accreditation:* CEPH (one or more programs are accredited). *Faculty:* 24 full-time (12 women). *Students:* 169 full-time (126 women), 25 part-time (17 women); includes 56 minority (39 Black or African American, non-Hispanic/Latino; 2 American Indian or Alaska Native, non-Hispanic/Latino; 4 Asian, non-Hispanic/Latino; 9 Hispanic/Latino; 2 Two or more races, non-Hispanic/Latino), 29 international. Average age 30. 170 applicants, 74% accepted, 79 enrolled. In 2011, 52 master's, 9 doctorates awarded. *Degree requirements:* For master's, thesis optional; for doctorate, thesis/dissertation. *Entrance requirements:* For master's, GRE (MS in nutrition science), 3 recommendations; for doctorate, GRE, 3 recommendations. Additional exam requirements/recommendations for international students: Required—TOEFL (minimum score 550 paper-based; 213 computer-based; 79 iBT). *Application deadline:* For fall admission, 4/30 priority date for domestic students, 12/1 for international students; for spring admission, 11/15 priority date for domestic students, 9/1 for international students. Application fee: $55 ($65 for international students). *Financial support:* Fellowships, research assistantships with full and partial tuition reimbursements, teaching assistantships with full and partial tuition reimbursements, career-related internships or fieldwork, Federal Work-Study, institutionally sponsored loans, scholarships/grants, tuition waivers (partial), and fee remissions available. Financial award application deadline: 3/1. *Faculty research:* Cancer education, HIV/AIDS and drug education, public health, parent-child interactions, safety education. *Total annual research expenditures:* $2.8 million. *Unit head:* Dr. David K. Lohrmann, Chair, 812-856-5101, Fax: 812-855-3936, E-mail: dlohrman@indiana.edu. *Application contact:* Dr. Susan Middlestadt, Associate Professor and Graduate Coordinator, 812-856-5768, Fax: 812-855-3936, E-mail: semiddle@indiana.edu. Web site: http://www.indiana.edu/~aphealth/.

Indiana University of Pennsylvania, School of Graduate Studies and Research, College of Health and Human Services, Department of Health and Physical Education, Program in Health and Physical Education, Indiana, PA 15705-1087. Offers M Ed. *Faculty:* 10 full-time (6 women). *Students:* 20 full-time (9 women), 10 part-time (6 women); includes 2 minority (1 Hispanic/Latino; 1 Two or more races, non-Hispanic/Latino). Average age 26. 23 applicants, 61% accepted, 10 enrolled. In 2011, 23 master's awarded. *Entrance requirements:* Additional exam requirements/recommendations for international students: Required—TOEFL (minimum score 540 paper-based; 207 computer-based). *Application deadline:* Applications are processed on a rolling basis. Application fee: $50. Electronic applications accepted. *Expenses:* Tuition, state resident: full-time $7488; part-time $416 per credit. Tuition, nonresident: full-time $11,232; part-time $624 per credit. *Required fees:* $2070; $192.20 per credit. $90 per semester. *Financial support:* In 2011–12, 7 research assistantships with full and partial tuition reimbursements (averaging $5,051 per year) were awarded. Financial award application deadline: 4/15; financial award applicants required to submit FAFSA. *Unit head:* Dr. Elaine Blair, Chairperson, 724-357-2770, E-mail: eblair@iup.edu. *Application* *contact:* Dr. Jacqueline Beck, Associate Dean, 724-357-2560, E-mail: jbeck@iup.edu. Web site: http://www.iup.edu/upper.aspx?id=49407.

Indiana University–Purdue University Indianapolis, Indiana University School of Medicine, Department of Public Health, Indianapolis, IN 46202-2896. Offers behavioral health science (MPH); epidemiology (MPH); health policy and management (MPH). *Accreditation:* CEPH. *Students:* 134 full-time (86 women), 134 part-time (93 women); includes 53 minority (25 Black or African American, non-Hispanic/Latino; 1 American Indian or Alaska Native, non-Hispanic/Latino; 14 Asian, non-Hispanic/Latino; 10 Hispanic/Latino; 3 Two or more races, non-Hispanic/Latino), 13 international. Average age 30. 236 applicants, 58% accepted, 106 enrolled. In 2011, 81 master's awarded. Application fee: $55 ($65 for international students). *Expenses:* Contact institution. *Financial support:* In 2011–12, teaching assistantships (averaging $14,058 per year) were awarded. *Unit head:* Dr. Carole Kacius, Director, 317-274-3126. *Application contact:* Robert M. Stump, Jr., Director of Admissions, 317-274-3772, E-mail: inmedadm@iupui.edu.

Indiana University–Purdue University Indianapolis, School of Health and Rehabilitation Sciences, Indianapolis, IN 46202-2896. Offers health sciences education (MS); nutrition and dietetics (MS); occupational therapy (MS); physical therapy (DPT). Part-time and evening/weekend programs available. *Faculty:* 8 full-time (5 women). *Students:* 197 full-time (162 women), 1 part-time (0 women); includes 13 minority (1 Black or African American, non-Hispanic/Latino; 4 Asian, non-Hispanic/Latino; 2 Hispanic/Latino; 1 Native Hawaiian or other Pacific Islander, non-Hispanic/Latino; 5 Two or more races, non-Hispanic/Latino). Average age 26. 213 applicants, 31% accepted, 62 enrolled. In 2011, 35 master's, 34 doctorates awarded. *Degree requirements:* For master's, thesis (for some programs). *Entrance requirements:* For master's, GRE General Test, minimum GPA of 3.0. Additional exam requirements/recommendations for international students: Required—TOEFL. *Application deadline:* For fall admission, 1/15 priority date for domestic students; for spring admission, 10/15 for domestic students. Application fee: $55 ($65 for international students). *Financial support:* Fellowships, research assistantships, teaching assistantships, Federal Work-Study, institutionally sponsored loans, and scholarships/grants available. Support available to part-time students. Financial award applicants required to submit FAFSA. *Unit head:* Dr. Augustine Agho, Dean, 317-274-4704, E-mail: aagho@iupui.edu. *Application contact:* Dr. Sherry Queener, Director, Graduate Studies and Associate Dean, 317-274-1577, Fax: 317-278-2380. Web site: http://www.shrs.iupui.edu/.

Inter American University of Puerto Rico, Metropolitan Campus, Graduate Programs, Program in Physical Education, San Juan, PR 00919-1293. Offers teaching of physical education (MA); training and sport performance (MA). *Degree requirements:* For master's, comprehensive exam. *Entrance requirements:* For master's, GRE or EXADEP, interview. Electronic applications accepted.

Inter American University of Puerto Rico, San Germán Campus, Graduate Studies Center, Program in Health and Physical Education, San Germán, PR 00683-5008. Offers MA. Part-time and evening/weekend programs available. *Degree requirements:* For master's, comprehensive exam. *Entrance requirements:* For master's, GRE General Test or EXADEP, minimum GPA of 3.0. *Application deadline:* For fall admission, 4/30 priority date for domestic students; for spring admission, 11/15 for domestic students. Applications are processed on a rolling basis. Application fee: $31. *Expenses: Required fees:* $213 per semester. *Financial support:* Teaching assistantships available. *Unit head:* Dr. Elba T. Irizarry, Director of Graduate Studies Center, 787-264-1912 Ext. 7357, Fax: 787-892-6350, E-mail: elbat@sg.inter.edu.

Ithaca College, Division of Graduate and Professional Studies, School of Health Sciences and Human Performance, Program in Health Education, Ithaca, NY 14850. Offers MS. Part-time programs available. *Faculty:* 10 full-time (8 women). *Students:* 14 full-time (11 women); includes 1 minority (Two or more races, non-Hispanic/Latino), 2 international. Average age 23. 22 applicants, 82% accepted, 13 enrolled. In 2011, 15 master's awarded. *Degree requirements:* For master's, thesis optional. *Entrance requirements:* For master's, minimum GPA of 3.0. Additional exam requirements/recommendations for international students: Required—TOEFL (minimum score 550 paper-based; 213 computer-based; 80 iBT). *Application deadline:* For fall admission, 3/1 priority date for domestic students, 3/1 for international students; for spring admission, 12/1 for domestic and international students. Applications are processed on a rolling basis. Application fee: $40. Electronic applications accepted. *Expenses:* Contact institution. *Financial support:* In 2011–12, 14 students received support, including 13 teaching assistantships (averaging $6,163 per year); career-related internships or fieldwork, Federal Work-Study, scholarships/grants, and unspecified assistantships also available. Support available to part-time students. Financial award application deadline: 3/1; financial award applicants required to submit CSS PROFILE or FAFSA. *Faculty research:* Needs assessment evaluation of health education programs, minority health (includes diversity), employee health assessment and program planning, youth at risk/families, multicultural/international health, program planning/health behaviors, sexuality education in the family and school setting, parent-teacher and student-teacher relationships, attitude/interest/motivation, teaching effectiveness, student learning/achievement. *Unit head:* Dr. Srijana Bajacharya, Chairperson, 607-274-3143, Fax: 607-274-1263, E-mail: gps@ithaca.edu. *Application contact:* Gerard Turbide, Director, Office of Admission, 607-274-3143, Fax: 607-274-1263, E-mail: gps@ithaca.edu. Web site: http://www.ithaca.edu/gps/gradprograms/programsites/hppe/programs/healthed.

Jackson State University, Graduate School, College of Education and Human Development, Department of Health, Physical Education and Recreation, Jackson, MS 39217. Offers MS Ed. *Accreditation:* NCATE. Part-time and evening/weekend programs available. *Degree requirements:* For master's, comprehensive exam, thesis or alternative. *Entrance requirements:* For master's, GRE General Test. Additional exam requirements/recommendations for international students: Required—TOEFL (minimum score 520 paper-based; 195 computer-based; 67 iBT).

James Madison University, The Graduate School, College of Integrated Science and Technology, Department of Health Sciences, Program in Health Education, Harrisonburg, VA 22807. Offers MS, MS Ed. Part-time programs available. *Students:* 12 full-time (11 women), 3 part-time (all women); includes 2 minority (1 Black or African American, non-Hispanic/Latino; 1 Hispanic/Latino). Average age 27. In 2011, 4 master's awarded. *Entrance requirements:* For master's, GRE General Test. Additional exam requirements/recommendations for international students: Required—TOEFL. *Application deadline:* For fall admission, 5/1 priority date for domestic students; for spring admission, 9/1 priority date for domestic students. Application fee: $55. *Expenses:* Tuition, state resident: full-time $8016; part-time $334 per credit hour. Tuition, nonresident: full-time $22,656; part-time $944 per credit hour. *Financial support:* In 2011–12, 1 student received support. 1 graduate assistantship ($7382) available. Financial award application deadline: 3/1. *Unit head:* Dr. Maria T. Wessel, Director, 540-568-3955, E-mail: wesselmt@jmu.edu. *Application contact:* Lynette M. Bible, Director of Graduate Admissions, 540-568-6395, Fax: 540-568-7860, E-mail: biblelm@jmu.edu.

John F. Kennedy University, Graduate School of Holistic Studies, Department of Integral Studies, Program in Holistic Health Education, Pleasant Hill, CA 94523-4817. Offers MA. Part-time and evening/weekend programs available. *Degree requirements:* For master's, thesis or alternative. *Entrance requirements:* For master's, interview. Additional exam requirements/recommendations for international students: Required—TOEFL.

The Johns Hopkins University, Bloomberg School of Public Health, Department of Health, Behavior and Society, Baltimore, MD 21218-2699. Offers genetic counseling (Sc M); health education and health communication (MHS); social and behavioral sciences (Dr PH, PhD, Sc D); social factors in health (MHS). *Degree requirements:* For master's, comprehensive exam (for some programs), thesis (for some programs); for doctorate, comprehensive exam, thesis/dissertation. *Entrance requirements:* For master's, GRE, curriculum vitae, 3 letters of recommendation; for doctorate, GRE, transcripts, curriculum vitae, 3 recommendation letters. Additional exam requirements/recommendations for international students: Required—TOEFL (minimum score 600 paper-based; 250 computer-based; 100 iBT). Electronic applications accepted. *Faculty research:* Social determinants of health and structural and community-level inventions to improve health, communication and health education, behavioral and social aspects of genetic counseling.

The Johns Hopkins University, School of Education, Department of Interdisciplinary Studies in Education, Baltimore, MD 21218. Offers earth/space science (Certificate); education (MS), including educational studies; health care education (MEHP); mind, brain, and teaching (Certificate); teaching the adult learner (Certificate); urban education (Certificate). Part-time and evening/weekend programs available. Postbaccalaureate distance learning degree programs offered (minimal on-campus study). *Degree requirements:* For master's, capstone course. *Entrance requirements:* For master's and Certificate, minimum undergraduate GPA of 3.0. Additional exam requirements/recommendations for international students: Required—TOEFL (minimum score 600 paper-based; 250 computer-based; 100 iBT). Electronic applications accepted. *Faculty research:* Neuro-education, urban school reform, leadership development, teacher leadership, charter schools, techniques for teaching reading to adolescents with delayed reading skills, school culture.

Kent State University, Graduate School of Education, Health, and Human Services, School of Health Sciences, Program in Health Education and Promotion, Kent, OH 44242-0001. Offers M Ed, MA, PhD. *Accreditation:* NCATE. *Faculty:* 7 full-time (6 women), 4 part-time/adjunct (all women). *Students:* 22 full-time (19 women), 20 part-time (16 women); includes 8 minority (all Black or African American, non-Hispanic/Latino). 21 applicants, 43% accepted. In 2011, 12 master's, 2 doctorates awarded. *Degree requirements:* For doctorate, comprehensive exam, thesis/dissertation. *Entrance requirements:* For master's, 2 letters of reference, goals statement; for doctorate, GRE General Test, goals statement, resume, interview. Additional exam requirements/recommendations for international students: Required—TOEFL (minimum score 550 paper-based; 213 computer-based; 80 iBT). *Application deadline:* Applications are processed on a rolling basis. Application fee: $30 ($60 for international students). Electronic applications accepted. *Expenses:* Tuition, state resident: full-time $8136; part-time $452 per credit hour. Tuition, nonresident: full-time $14,292; part-time $794 per credit hour. *Financial support:* In 2011–12, 6 fellowships with full tuition reimbursements (averaging $10,250 per year) were awarded; research assistantships with full tuition reimbursements, teaching assistantships with full tuition reimbursements, Federal Work-Study, scholarships/grants, and unspecified assistantships also available. Financial award application deadline: 4/1; financial award applicants required to submit FAFSA. *Faculty research:* Substance use/abuse, sexuality, community health assessment, epidemiology, HIV/AIDS. *Unit head:* Dr. Kele Ding, Coordinator, 330-672-0688, E-mail: kding@kent.edu. *Application contact:* Nancy Miller, Academic Program Coordinator, Office of Graduate Student Services, 330-672-2586, Fax: 330-672-9162, E-mail: ogs@kent.edu. Web site: http://www.kent.edu/ehhs/Schools/hs/programs/hedp/.

Lake Erie College of Osteopathic Medicine, Professional Programs, Erie, PA 16509-1025. Offers biomedical sciences (Postbaccalaureate Certificate); medical education (MS); osteopathic medicine (DO); pharmacy (Pharm D). *Accreditation:* ACPE; AOsA. *Degree requirements:* For doctorate, comprehensive exam, National Osteopathic Medical Licensing Exam, Levels 1 and 2; for Postbaccalaureate Certificate, comprehensive exam, North American Pharmacist Licensure Examination (NAPLEX). *Entrance requirements:* For doctorate, MCAT, minimum GPA of 3.2, letters of recommendation; for Postbaccalaureate Certificate, PCAT, letters of recommendation, minimum GPA of 3.5. Electronic applications accepted. *Faculty research:* Cardiac smooth and skeletal muscle mechanics, chemotherapeutics and vitamins, osteopathic manipulation.

Lehman College of the City University of New York, Division of Natural and Social Sciences, Department of Health Sciences, Program in Health Education and Promotion, Bronx, NY 10468-1589. Offers MA. *Accreditation:* CEPH; NCATE. Part-time and evening/weekend programs available. *Degree requirements:* For master's, thesis or alternative. *Entrance requirements:* For master's, minimum GPA of 2.7.

Lehman College of the City University of New York, Division of Natural and Social Sciences, Department of Health Sciences, Program in Health N–12 Teacher, Bronx, NY 10468-1589. Offers MS Ed. *Accreditation:* NCATE. *Degree requirements:* For master's, thesis or alternative.

Loma Linda University, School of Public Health, Programs in Health Promotion and Education, Loma Linda, CA 92350. Offers MPH, Dr PH. *Accreditation:* CEPH (one or more programs are accredited). *Degree requirements:* For doctorate, thesis/dissertation. *Entrance requirements:* For doctorate, GRE General Test. Additional exam requirements/recommendations for international students: Required—Michigan English Language Assessment Battery or TOEFL.

Long Island University–Brooklyn Campus, School of Health Professions, Division of Sports Sciences, Brooklyn, NY 11201-8423. Offers adapted physical education (MS); athletic training and sports sciences (MS); exercise physiology (MS); health sciences (MS). Part-time and evening/weekend programs available. *Entrance requirements:* For master's, 2 letters of recommendation. Additional exam requirements/recommendations for international students: Required—TOEFL (minimum score 500 paper-based; 173 computer-based). Electronic applications accepted.

Louisiana Tech University, Graduate School, College of Education, Department of Curriculum, Instruction and Leadership, Ruston, LA 71272. Offers curriculum and instruction (MS, Ed D); educational leadership (Ed D); secondary education (M Ed), including business education, English education, foreign language education, health and physical education, mathematics education, science education, social studies education, speech education. *Accreditation:* NCATE. Part-time programs available. *Degree requirements:* For doctorate, thesis/dissertation. *Entrance requirements:* For master's and doctorate, GRE General Test.

Louisiana Tech University, Graduate School, College of Education, Department of Health and Exercise Sciences, Ruston, LA 71272. Offers MS. *Accreditation:* NCATE. Part-time programs available. *Degree requirements:* For master's, thesis or alternative. *Entrance requirements:* For master's, GRE General Test.

Marshall University, Academic Affairs Division, College of Information Technology and Engineering, Division of Applied Science and Technology, Program in Safety, Huntington, WV 25755. Offers MS. *Accreditation:* NCATE. *Students:* 16 full-time (6 women), 20 part-time (3 women); includes 3 minority (1 Black or African American, non-Hispanic/Latino; 2 Hispanic/Latino), 1 international. Average age 36. In 2011, 13 master's awarded. *Degree requirements:* For master's, thesis optional, comprehensive assessment. Application fee: $40. *Unit head:* Dr. D. Allen Stern, 304-696-3069, E-mail: stern@marshall.edu. *Application contact:* Information Contact, 304-746-1900, Fax: 304-746-1902, E-mail: services@marshall.edu. Web site: http://www.marshall.edu/cite/.

Marywood University, Academic Affairs, Reap College of Education and Human Development, Department of Human Development, Emphasis in Health Promotion, Scranton, PA 18509-1598. Offers PhD. *Entrance requirements:* Additional exam requirements/recommendations for international students: Required—TOEFL (minimum score 550 paper-based; 213 computer-based; 79 iBT). *Application deadline:* For fall admission, 1/30 for domestic and international students. Application fee: $35. Electronic applications accepted. *Expenses:* Contact institution. *Financial support:* Career-related internships or fieldwork, scholarships/grants, and unspecified assistantships available. Support available to part-time students. Financial award application deadline: 6/30; financial award applicants required to submit FAFSA. *Unit head:* Dr. Brook Cannon, Director, 570-348-6211 Ext. 2324, E-mail: cannonb@marywood.edu. *Application contact:* Tammy Manka, Assistant Director of Graduate Admissions, 570-348-6211 Ext. 2322, E-mail: tmanka@marywood.edu. Web site: http://www.marywood.edu/phd/specializations.html.

Middle Tennessee State University, College of Graduate Studies, College of Behavioral and Health Sciences, Department of Health and Human Performance, Program in Health, Physical Education and Recreation, Murfreesboro, TN 37132. Offers MS. Part-time and evening/weekend programs available. Postbaccalaureate distance learning degree programs offered. *Faculty:* 24 full-time (9 women), 5 part-time/adjunct (3 women). *Students:* 5 full-time (3 women), 68 part-time (29 women); includes 26 minority (24 Black or African American, non-Hispanic/Latino; 1 Hispanic/Latino; 1 Two or more races, non-Hispanic/Latino). 66 applicants, 83% accepted. In 2011, 31 master's awarded. *Degree requirements:* For master's, comprehensive exam, thesis optional. *Entrance requirements:* For master's, GRE. Additional exam requirements/recommendations for international students: Required—TOEFL (minimum score 525 paper-based; 195 computer-based; 71 iBT) or IELTS (minimum score 6). *Application deadline:* For fall admission, 6/1 for domestic and international students. Applications are processed on a rolling basis. Application fee: $25 ($30 for international students). *Expenses:* Tuition, state resident: full-time $10,008. Tuition, nonresident: full-time $25,056. *Financial support:* In 2011–12, 14 students received support. Tuition waivers available. Support available to part-time students. Financial award application deadline: 5/1. *Faculty research:* Kinesiometrics, leisure behavior, health, lifestyles. *Unit head:* Dr. Harold D. Whiteside, Interim Dean, 615-898-2900, Fax: 615-494-7704, E-mail: harold.whiteside@mtsu.edu. *Application contact:* Dr. Michael D. Allen, Dean and Vice Provost for Research, 615-898-2840, Fax: 615-904-8020, E-mail: michael.allen@mtsu.edu.

Mills College, Graduate Studies, School of Education, Oakland, CA 94613-1000. Offers child life in hospitals (MA); early childhood education (MA); education (MA), including art education, curriculum and instruction, elementary education, English education, foreign language education, mathematics education, science education, secondary education, social studies education, teaching; educational leadership (MA, Ed D). Part-time and evening/weekend programs available. *Faculty:* 13 full-time (10 women), 14 part-time/adjunct (10 women). *Students:* 149 full-time (133 women), 69 part-time (61 women); includes 85 minority (32 Black or African American, non-Hispanic/Latino; 1 American Indian or Alaska Native, non-Hispanic/Latino; 16 Asian, non-Hispanic/Latino; 24 Hispanic/Latino; 1 Native Hawaiian or other Pacific Islander, non-Hispanic/Latino; 11 Two or more races, non-Hispanic/Latino), 3 international. Average age 28. 238 applicants, 84% accepted, 106 enrolled. In 2011, 41 master's, 2 doctorates awarded. Terminal master's awarded for partial completion of doctoral program. *Degree requirements:* For master's, comprehensive exam. *Entrance requirements:* For master's, statement of purpose, official transcript, 3 recommendations; for doctorate, GRE General Test. Additional exam requirements/recommendations for international students: Required—TOEFL (minimum score 550 paper-based; 80 iBT) or IELTS (minimum score 6). *Application deadline:* For fall admission, 12/31 priority date for domestic students, 12/15 for international students; for spring admission, 11/1 priority date for domestic students, 10/1 for international students. Applications are processed on a rolling basis. Application fee: $50. Electronic applications accepted. *Expenses: Tuition:* Full-time $28,280; part-time $15,640 per year. *Required fees:* $958. Tuition and fees vary according to program. *Financial support:* In 2011–12, 43 students received support, including 225 fellowships with full and partial tuition reimbursements available (averaging $6,020 per year), 43 teaching assistantships with full and partial tuition reimbursements available (averaging $6,782 per year); career-related internships or fieldwork and scholarships/grants also available. Support available to part-time students. Financial award application deadline: 2/1; financial award applicants required to submit FAFSA. *Faculty research:* Early childhood education, teacher preparation, educational leadership. *Total annual research expenditures:* $2.3 million. *Unit head:* Katherine Schultz, Chairperson, 510-430-3170, Fax: 510-430-3379, E-mail: grad-studies@mills.edu. *Application contact:* Tiana Kozoil, Graduate Admission Specialist, 510-430-3305, Fax: 510-430-2159, E-mail: grad-studies@mills.edu. Web site: http://www.mills.edu/education.

Minnesota State University Mankato, College of Graduate Studies, College of Allied Health and Nursing, Department of Health Science, Mankato, MN 56001. Offers community health education (MS); school health education (MS, Postbaccalaureate Certificate). Part-time programs available. *Students:* 10 full-time (5 women), 31 part-time (26 women). *Degree requirements:* For master's, comprehensive exam, thesis or alternative. *Entrance requirements:* For master's, minimum GPA of 3.0 during previous 2 years; for Postbaccalaureate Certificate, teaching license. Additional exam requirements/recommendations for international students: Required—TOEFL (minimum score 500 paper-based; 173 computer-based; 61 iBT). *Application deadline:* For fall admission, 7/1 for domestic students, 5/1 for international students; for spring admission, 11/1 for domestic students, 10/1 for international students. Applications are processed on a rolling basis. Application fee: $40. Electronic applications accepted. *Financial support:* Research assistantships with full tuition reimbursements, teaching assistantships with full tuition reimbursements, career-related internships or fieldwork, and Federal Work-Study available. Support available to part-time students. Financial award application deadline: 3/15; financial award applicants required to submit FAFSA. *Faculty research:* Teaching methods, stress prophylaxis and management, effects of alcohol. *Unit head:* Dr. Dawn Larsen, Graduate Coordinator, 507-389-2113. *Application contact:* 507-389-2321, E-mail: grad@mnsu.edu. Web site: http://ahn.mnsu.edu/health/.

Mississippi University for Women, Graduate School, Department of Health and Kinesiology, Columbus, MS 39701-9998. Offers health education (MS). *Degree requirements:* For master's, comprehensive exam.

Montana State University, College of Graduate Studies, College of Education, Health, and Human Development, Department of Health and Human Development, Bozeman, MT 59717. Offers family and consumer sciences (MS). *Accreditation:* ACA. Part-time programs available. Postbaccalaureate distance learning degree programs offered (no on-campus study). *Degree requirements:* For master's, comprehensive exam. *Entrance requirements:* For master's, GRE (minimum scores: verbal 480; quantitative 480). Additional exam requirements/recommendations for international students: Required—TOEFL (minimum score 550 paper-based; 213 computer-based). Electronic applications accepted. *Faculty research:* Community food systems, ethic of care for teachers and coaches, influence of public policy on families and communities, cost effectiveness of early childhood education, exercise metabolism, winter sport performance enhancement, assessment of physical activity.

Montclair State University, The Graduate School, College of Education and Human Services, Department of Curriculum and Teaching, Program in Teaching in Content Area, Montclair, NJ 07043-1624. Offers art (MAT); biology (MAT); chemistry (MAT); earth science (MAT); English (MAT); French (MAT); health and physical education (MAT); health education (MAT); mathematics (MAT); music (MAT); physical education (MAT); physical science (MAT); social studies (MAT); Spanish (MAT); teacher of English as a second language (MAT). *Students:* 162 full-time (90 women), 47 part-time (29 women); includes 37 minority (4 Black or African American, non-Hispanic/Latino; 11 Asian, non-Hispanic/Latino; 18 Hispanic/Latino; 4 Two or more races, non-Hispanic/Latino), 5 international. Average age 31. 145 applicants, 41% accepted, 56 enrolled. In 2011, 229 master's awarded. *Degree requirements:* For master's, comprehensive exam, thesis or alternative. *Entrance requirements:* For master's, GRE General Test, interview, 2 letters of recommendation. Additional exam requirements/recommendations for international students: Required—TOEFL (minimum score 83 iBT), IELTS (minimum score 6.5). *Application deadline:* Applications are processed on a rolling basis. Application fee: $60. Electronic applications accepted. *Financial support:* Federal Work-Study, scholarships/grants, and unspecified assistantships available. Support available to part-time students. Financial award application deadline: 3/1; financial award applicants required to submit FAFSA. *Unit head:* Dr. David Schwarzer, Chairperson, 973-655-5187. *Application contact:* Amy Aiello, Executive Director of The Graduate School, 973-655-5147, Fax: 973-655-7869, E-mail: graduate.school@montclair.edu.

Morehead State University, Graduate Programs, College of Education, Department of Middle Grades and Secondary Education, Morehead, KY 40351. Offers business and marketing education (MAT); English/language arts 5-9 (MAT); French (MAT); health P-12 (MAT); mathematics 5-9 (MAT); physical education P-12 (MAT); science 5-9 (MAT); secondary biology (MAT); secondary chemistry (MAT); secondary earth science (MAT); secondary English (MAT); secondary math (MAT); secondary physics (MAT); secondary social studies (MAT); social studies 5-9 (MAT); Spanish (MAT). Part-time and evening/weekend programs available. *Degree requirements:* For master's, portfolio. *Entrance requirements:* For master's, GRE or PRAXIS II content exam, minimum overall undergraduate GPA of 2.5. Additional exam requirements/recommendations for international students: Required—TOEFL (minimum score 500 paper-based; 173 computer-based). Electronic applications accepted.

Morehead State University, Graduate Programs, College of Science and Technology, Department of Health, Wellness and Human Performance, Morehead, KY 40351. Offers health/physical education (MA). *Accreditation:* NCATE. Part-time and evening/weekend programs available. *Degree requirements:* For master's, comprehensive exam, thesis, oral exam, written core exam. *Entrance requirements:* For master's, GRE General Test or MAT, minimum GPA of 2.5; undergraduate major/minor in health, physical education, or recreation. Additional exam requirements/recommendations for international students: Required—TOEFL (minimum score 500 paper-based; 173 computer-based). Electronic applications accepted. *Faculty research:* Child growth and performance, instructional strategies, outdoor leadership qualities, exercise science, athletic training.

Morehouse School of Medicine, Master of Public Health Program, Atlanta, GA 30310-1495. Offers epidemiology (MPH); health administration, management and policy (MPH); health education/health promotion (MPH); international health (MPH). *Accreditation:* CEPH. Part-time programs available. *Degree requirements:* For master's, thesis, practicum, public health leadership seminar. *Entrance requirements:* For master's, GRE General Test, writing test, public health or human service experience. Additional exam requirements/recommendations for international students: Required—TOEFL (minimum score 550 paper-based; 200 computer-based). Electronic applications accepted. *Expenses:* Contact institution. *Faculty research:* Women's and adolescent health, violence prevention, cancer epidemiology/disparities, substance abuse prevention.

Mount Mary College, Graduate Programs, Program in Dietetics, Milwaukee, WI 53222-4597. Offers administrative dietetics (MS); clinical dietetics (MS); nutrition education (MS). Part-time and evening/weekend programs available. *Faculty:* 1 (woman) full-time, 5 part-time/adjunct (4 women). *Students:* 12 full-time (all women), 21 part-time (all women), 1 international. Average age 28. 102 applicants, 12% accepted, 12 enrolled. In 2011, 1 master's awarded. *Degree requirements:* For master's, thesis. *Entrance requirements:* For master's, minimum GPA of 2.75, completion of ADA and DPD requirements. Additional exam requirements/recommendations for international students: Required—TOEFL (minimum score 500 paper-based; 173 computer-based). *Application deadline:* For fall admission, 2/15 priority date for domestic students. Application fee: $45 ($100 for international students). *Financial support:* In 2011–12, 1 student received support. Career-related internships or fieldwork and Federal Work-Study available. Support available to part-time students. Financial award application deadline: 5/1; financial award applicants required to submit FAFSA. *Unit head:* Lisa Stark, Director, 414-258-4810 Ext. 398, E-mail: starkl@mtmary.edu. *Application contact:* Dr. Douglas J. Mickelson, Associate Dean for Graduate and Continuing Education, 414-256-1252, Fax: 414-256-0167, E-mail: mickelsd@mtmary.edu.

New Jersey City University, Graduate Studies and Continuing Education, College of Professional Studies, Department of Health Sciences, Jersey City, NJ 07305-1597. Offers community health education (MS); health administration (MS); school health education (MS). Part-time and evening/weekend programs available. *Students:* 6 full-time (5 women), 45 part-time (37 women); includes 19 minority (13 Black or African American, non-Hispanic/Latino; 4 Asian, non-Hispanic/Latino; 2 Hispanic/Latino), 2 international. Average age 41. In 2011, 16 master's awarded. *Degree requirements:* For master's, thesis or alternative, internship. *Entrance requirements:* Additional exam requirements/recommendations for international students: Required—TOEFL. *Application deadline:* For fall admission, 8/1 priority date for domestic students; for spring admission, 12/1 for domestic students. Applications are processed on a rolling basis. Application fee: $0. *Expenses:* Tuition, state resident: part-time $494 per credit. Tuition, nonresident: part-time $911.30 per credit. *Required fees:* $95.90 per year. *Financial support:* Career-related internships or fieldwork and unspecified assistantships available. *Unit head:* Dr. Lilliam Rosado, Chairperson, 201-200-3431, E-mail: lrosado@njcu.edu. *Application contact:* Dr. William Bajor, Dean of Graduate Studies, 201-200-3409, Fax: 201-200-3411, E-mail: wbajor@njcu.edu.

New Mexico Highlands University, Graduate Studies, School of Education, Department of Exercise and Sport Sciences, Las Vegas, NM 87701. Offers human performance and sport (MA); sports administration (MA); teacher education (MA). Part-time programs available. *Faculty:* 5 full-time (3 women). *Students:* 20 full-time (4 women), 27 part-time (9 women); includes 25 minority (7 Black or African American, non-Hispanic/Latino; 17 Hispanic/Latino; 1 Native Hawaiian or other Pacific Islander, non-Hispanic/Latino), 1 international. Average age 30. 17 applicants, 94% accepted, 13 enrolled. In 2011, 19 master's awarded. *Degree requirements:* For master's, comprehensive exam, thesis or alternative. *Entrance requirements:* For master's, minimum undergraduate GPA of 3.0. Additional exam requirements/recommendations for international students: Required—TOEFL (minimum score 540 paper-based; 207 computer-based). *Application deadline:* For fall admission, 8/1 priority date for domestic students. Applications are processed on a rolling basis. Application fee: $15. *Expenses:* Tuition, state resident: full-time $2767; part-time $146 per credit hour. Tuition, nonresident: full-time $4879; part-time $234 per credit hour. *International tuition:* $5436 full-time. *Required fees:* $737. *Financial support:* In 2011–12, 6 students received support. Career-related internships or fieldwork, Federal Work-Study, institutionally sponsored loans, scholarships/grants, tuition waivers (partial), and unspecified assistantships available. Support available to part-time students. Financial award application deadline: 3/1; financial award applicants required to submit FAFSA. *Faculty research:* Child obesity and physical inactivity, body composition and fitness assessment, motor development, sport marketing, sport finance. *Unit head:* Yongseek Kim, Department Head, 505-454-3490, E-mail: ykim@nmhu.edu. *Application contact:* Diane Trujillo, Administrative Assistant, Graduate Studies, 505-454-3266, Fax: 505-426-2117, E-mail: dtrujillo@nmhu.edu.

New Mexico State University, Graduate School, College of Health and Social Services, Department of Public Health Sciences, Las Cruces, NM 88003-8001. Offers community health education (MPH). Part-time programs available. Postbaccalaureate distance learning degree programs offered (minimal on-campus study). *Students:* 38 full-time (35 women), 38 part-time (28 women); includes 32 minority (2 Black or African American, non-Hispanic/Latino; 7 American Indian or Alaska Native, non-Hispanic/Latino; 1 Asian, non-Hispanic/Latino; 21 Hispanic/Latino; 1 Two or more races, non-Hispanic/Latino), 7 international. Average age 35. 48 applicants, 58% accepted, 17 enrolled. In 2011, 28 master's awarded. *Degree requirements:* For master's, thesis optional. *Entrance requirements:* For master's, GRE. Additional exam requirements/recommendations for international students: Required—TOEFL (minimum score 550 paper-based; 79 iBT), IELTS (minimum score 6.5). *Application deadline:* For fall admission, 2/15 for domestic and international students. Application fee: $40 ($50 for international students). Electronic applications accepted. *Expenses:* Tuition, state resident: full-time $5004; part-time $208.50 per credit. Tuition, nonresident: full-time $17,446; part-time $726.90 per credit. *Financial support:* In 2011–12, 1 research assistantship (averaging $24,744 per year), 17 teaching assistantships (averaging $15,256 per year) were awarded; fellowships, career-related internships or fieldwork, and health care benefits also available. Financial award application deadline: 4/1. *Faculty research:* Community health education, health issues of U. S.-Mexico border, health policy and management, victims of violence, environmental and occupational health issues. *Unit head:* Dr. Mark J. Kittleson, Head, 575-646-4300, Fax: 575-646-4343, E-mail: kittle@nmsu.edu. *Application contact:* Dr. James Robinson, III, Graduate Coordinator, 575-646-7431, E-mail: jrobin3@nmsu.edu. Web site: http://publichealth.nmsu.edu.

New York Medical College, School of Health Sciences and Practice, Department of Epidemiology and Community Health, Graduate Certificate Program in Health Education, Valhalla, NY 10595-1691. Offers Graduate Certificate. *Faculty:* 2 full-time, 9 part-time/adjunct. *Students:* 15 full-time, 25 part-time. Average age 32. 28 applicants, 75% accepted, 18 enrolled. *Entrance requirements:* Additional exam requirements/recommendations for international students: Required—TOEFL (minimum score 637 paper-based; 110 iBT), IELTS (minimum score 7). *Application deadline:* For fall admission, 8/1 for domestic students; for spring admission, 12/1 for domestic students. Applications are processed on a rolling basis. Application fee: $50 ($100 for international students). Electronic applications accepted. *Unit head:* Dr. Chia-Ching Chen, Director, 914-594-3379, E-mail: chiaching_chen@nymc.edu. *Application contact:* Pamela Suett, Director of Recruitment, 914-594-4510, Fax: 914-594-4292, E-mail: shsp_admissions@nymc.edu.

North Carolina Agricultural and Technical State University, School of Graduate Studies, School of Education, Department of Human Performance and Leisure Studies, Greensboro, NC 27411. Offers physical education (MAT, MS). *Accreditation:* NCATE. Part-time and evening/weekend programs available. *Degree requirements:* For master's, comprehensive exam, thesis or alternative, qualifying exam. *Entrance requirements:* For master's, GRE General Test or MAT.

Northeastern State University, Graduate College, College of Education, Department of Health and Human Performance, Tahlequah, OK 74464-2399. Offers health and kinesiology (MS Ed). Part-time and evening/weekend programs available. *Students:* 6 full-time (2 women), 38 part-time (13 women); includes 14 minority (1 Black or African American, non-Hispanic/Latino; 10 American Indian or Alaska Native, non-Hispanic/Latino; 1 Asian, non-Hispanic/Latino; 2 Hispanic/Latino), 6 international. In 2011, 9 master's awarded. *Entrance requirements:* For master's, MAT or GRE, minimum GPA of 2.5. Additional exam requirements/recommendations for international students: Required—TOEFL (minimum score 213 computer-based). *Application deadline:* For fall admission, 6/1 for domestic students. Application fee: $25. *Unit head:* Dr. Mark Giese, Chair, 918-456-5511 Ext. 3950. *Application contact:* Margie Railey, Administrative Assistant, 918-456-5511 Ext. 2093, Fax: 918-458-2061, E-mail: railey@nsouk.edu.

Northern State University, Division of Graduate Studies in Education, Program in Teaching and Learning, Aberdeen, SD 57401-7198. Offers educational studies (MS Ed); elementary classroom teaching (MS Ed); health, physical education, and coaching (MS Ed); secondary classroom teaching (MS Ed). *Accreditation:* NCATE. Part-time and evening/weekend programs available. *Degree requirements:* For master's, thesis optional. *Entrance requirements:* For master's, minimum GPA of 2.75. Additional exam requirements/recommendations for international students: Required—TOEFL (minimum score 550 paper-based; 213 computer-based; 76 iBT), IELTS (minimum score 6). Electronic applications accepted.

Northwestern State University of Louisiana, Graduate Studies and Research, Department of Health and Human Performance, Natchitoches, LA 71497. Offers MS. *Faculty:* 5 full-time (2 women). *Students:* 37 full-time (12 women), 27 part-time (13 women); includes 16 minority (13 Black or African American, non-Hispanic/Latino; 2 American Indian or Alaska Native, non-Hispanic/Latino; 1 Hispanic/Latino), 2 international. Average age 27. 47 applicants, 87% accepted, 27 enrolled. In 2011, 16 master's awarded. *Degree requirements:* For master's, comprehensive exam, thesis or alternative. *Entrance requirements:* For master's, GRE General Test, minimum undergraduate GPA of 2.5. Additional exam requirements/recommendations for international students: Required—TOEFL. *Application deadline:* For fall admission, 3/15 priority date for domestic students; for spring admission, 10/15 priority date for domestic students. Applications are processed on a rolling basis. Application fee: $20 ($30 for international students). Electronic applications accepted. *Expenses:* Tuition, state resident: full-time $3440. Tuition, nonresident: full-time $12,010. *Financial support:* Career-related internships or fieldwork available. Financial award application deadline: 5/1. *Unit head:* Dr. John Dollar, Department Head, 318-357-5126, E-mail: dollarj@nsula.edu. *Application contact:* Dr. Steven G. Horton, Associate Provost/Dean, Graduate Studies, Research, and Information Systems, 318-357-5851, Fax: 318-357-5019, E-mail: grad_school@nsula.edu. Web site: http://hhp.nsula.edu/.

Northwest Missouri State University, Graduate School, College of Education and Human Services, Department of Health, Physical Education, Recreation and Dance, Maryville, MO 64468-6001. Offers applied health science (MS); health and physical education (MS Ed); recreation (MS). *Accreditation:* NCATE. Part-time programs available. *Faculty:* 10 full-time (4 women). *Students:* 31 full-time (13 women), 10 part-time (4 women); includes 5 minority (2 Black or African American, non-Hispanic/Latino; 2 Hispanic/Latino; 1 Two or more races, non-Hispanic/Latino), 2 international. 25 applicants, 100% accepted, 17 enrolled. In 2011, 22 master's awarded. *Degree requirements:* For master's, comprehensive exam. *Entrance requirements:* For master's, GRE General Test, minimum undergraduate GPA of 2.75, teaching certificate, writing sample. Additional exam requirements/recommendations for international students: Required—TOEFL (minimum score 550 paper-based; 213 computer-based). *Application deadline:* For fall admission, 7/1 for domestic and international students; for spring admission, 11/15 for domestic and international students. Applications are processed on a rolling basis. Application fee: $0 ($50 for international students). *Financial support:* In 2011–12, 35 teaching assistantships with full tuition reimbursements (averaging $6,000 per year) were awarded; unspecified assistantships also available. Financial award application deadline: 4/1; financial award applicants required to submit FAFSA. *Unit head:* Dr. Terry Robertson, Chairperson, 660-562-1781. *Application contact:* Dr. Gregory Haddock, Dean of Graduate School, 660-562-1145, Fax: 660-562-1096, E-mail: gradsch@nwmissouri.edu.

Oklahoma State University, College of Education, School of Applied Health and Educational Psychology, Stillwater, OK 74078. Offers applied behavioral studies (Ed D); applied health and educational psychology (MS, PhD, Ed S). *Accreditation:* APA (one or more programs are accredited). Part-time programs available. *Faculty:* 40 full-time (19 women), 17 part-time/adjunct (9 women). *Students:* 192 full-time (137 women), 150 part-time (102 women); includes 85 minority (22 Black or African American, non-Hispanic/Latino; 18 American Indian or Alaska Native, non-Hispanic/Latino; 8 Asian, non-Hispanic/Latino; 17 Hispanic/Latino; 20 Two or more races, non-Hispanic/Latino), 11 international. Average age 31. 234 applicants, 30% accepted, 55 enrolled. In 2011, 72 master's, 26 doctorates awarded. *Degree requirements:* For master's, thesis (for some programs); for doctorate, comprehensive exam, thesis/dissertation. *Entrance requirements:* For master's and doctorate, GRE or GMAT. Additional exam requirements/recommendations for international students: Required—TOEFL (minimum score 550 paper-based; 79 iBT). *Application deadline:* For fall admission, 3/1 for international students; for spring admission, 8/1 for international students. Applications are processed on a rolling basis. Application fee: $40 ($75 for international students). Electronic applications accepted. *Expenses:* Tuition, state resident: full-time $4044; part-time $168.50 per credit hour. Tuition, nonresident: full-time $16,008; part-time $667 per credit hour. *Required fees:* $2122; $88.45 per credit hour. One-time fee: $50. Tuition and fees vary according to course load and campus/location. *Financial support:* In 2011–12, 17 research assistantships (averaging $9,302 per year), 70 teaching assistantships (averaging $8,447 per year) were awarded; career-related internships or fieldwork, Federal Work-Study, scholarships/grants, health care benefits, tuition waivers (partial), and unspecified assistantships also available. Support available to part-time students. Financial award application deadline: 3/1; financial award applicants required to submit FAFSA. *Unit head:* Dr. John Romans, Head, 405-744-6040, Fax: 405-744-6779. *Application contact:* Dr. Sheryl Tucker, Dean, 405-744-7099, Fax: 405-744-0355, E-mail: grad-i@okstate.edu. Web site: http://education.okstate.edu/index.php/academic-units/school-of-applied-health-a-educational-psychology.

Penn State Harrisburg, Graduate School, School of Behavioral Sciences and Education, Middletown, PA 17057-4898. Offers applied behavior analysis (MA); applied clinical psychology (MA); applied psychological research (MA); community psychology and social change (MA); health education (M Ed); literacy education (M Ed); teaching and curriculum (M Ed); training and development (M Ed). Part-time and evening/weekend programs available. *Financial support:* Career-related internships or fieldwork available. *Unit head:* Dr. Catherine A. Surra, Director, 717-948-6205, Fax: 717-948-6209, E-mail: cas87@psu.edu. *Application contact:* Robert Coffman, Director of Admissions, 717-948-6214, E-mail: rwc11@psu.edu. Web site: http://harrisburg.psu.edu/behavioral-sciences-and-education/.

Plymouth State University, College of Graduate Studies, Graduate Studies in Education, Program in Health Education, Plymouth, NH 03264-1595. Offers M Ed. Part-time and evening/weekend programs available. *Degree requirements:* For master's, PRAXIS. *Entrance requirements:* For master's, MAT, minimum GPA of 3.0.

Portland State University, Graduate Studies, College of Urban and Public Affairs, School of Community Health, Portland, OR 97207-0751. Offers aging (Certificate); health education (MA, MS); health education and health promotion (MPH); health studies (MPA, MPH), including health administration. MPH offered jointly with Oregon State University, Oregon Health and Science University. *Accreditation:* CEPH. Part-time programs available. *Degree requirements:* For master's, oral and written exams. *Entrance requirements:* For master's, GRE General Test, 3 letters of recommendation, minimum GPA of 3.0. Additional exam requirements/recommendations for international students: Required—TOEFL (minimum score 550 paper-based; 213 computer-based).

Prairie View A&M University, College of Education, Department of Health and Human Performance, Prairie View, TX 77446-0519. Offers health education (M Ed, MS); physical education (M Ed, MS). *Accreditation:* NCATE. Part-time and evening/weekend programs available. *Entrance requirements:* For master's, GRE General Test. Additional exam requirements/recommendations for international students: Required—TOEFL.

Purdue University, Graduate School, College of Health and Human Sciences, Department of Health and Kinesiology, West Lafayette, IN 47907. Offers athletic training education administration (MS); exercise, human physiology of movement and sport (PhD); health education (MS, PhD); motor control and development (MS, PhD); physical education pedagogy (MS, PhD); sport and exercise psychology (MS, PhD). Part-time programs available. *Faculty:* 20 full-time (9 women), 14 part-time/adjunct (4 women). *Students:* 53 full-time (27 women), 19 part-time (9 women); includes 9 minority (3 Black or African American, non-Hispanic/Latino; 1 American Indian or Alaska Native, non-Hispanic/Latino; 2 Asian, non-Hispanic/Latino; 1 Hispanic/Latino; 2 Two or more races, non-Hispanic/Latino), 14 international. Average age 30. 108 applicants, 48% accepted, 29 enrolled. In 2011, 17 master's, 6 doctorates awarded. *Degree requirements:* For master's, thesis optional; for doctorate, comprehensive exam, thesis/dissertation, Qualifying Examination, Preliminary Examination. *Entrance requirements:* For master's, GRE General Test, minimum score 1000 combined verbal and quantitative scores, minimum undergraduate GPA of 3.0 or equivalent; for doctorate, GRE General Test, minimum score 1100 combined verbal and quantitative scores, minimum undergraduate GPA of 3.0 or equivalent; master's degree with minimum GPA of 3.25 (recommended). Additional exam requirements/recommendations for international students: Required—TOEFL (minimum score 550 computer-based; 77 iBT); Recommended—TWE. *Application deadline:* For fall admission, 4/30 for domestic and international students; for spring admission, 10/15 for domestic and international students. Applications are processed on a rolling basis. Application fee: $60 ($75 for international students). Electronic applications accepted. *Financial support:* Fellowships with partial tuition reimbursements, research assistantships with partial tuition reimbursements, teaching assistantships with partial tuition reimbursements, and Federal Work-Study available. Support available to part-time students. Financial award applicants required to submit FAFSA. *Faculty research:* Wellness, motivation, teaching effectiveness, learning and development. *Unit head:* Dr. Larry J. Leverenz, Interim Head, 765-494-0865, Fax: 765-494-496-1239, E-mail: llevere@purdue.edu. *Application contact:* Lisa Duncan, Graduate Contact, 765-494-3162, E-mail: llduncan@purdue.edu. Web site: http://www.purdue.edu/hhs/hk/.

Purdue University, Graduate School, College of Health and Human Sciences, Department of Nutrition Science, West Lafayette, IN 47907. Offers animal health (MS, PhD); biochemical and molecular nutrition (MS, PhD); growth and development (MS, PhD); human and clinical nutrition (MS, PhD); public health and education (MS, PhD). *Faculty:* 17 full-time (10 women), 14 part-time/adjunct (12 women). *Students:* 35 full-time (33 women), 2 part-time (both women); includes 3 minority (1 Black or African American, non-Hispanic/Latino; 2 Asian, non-Hispanic/Latino), 17 international. Average age 28. 120 applicants, 18% accepted, 11 enrolled. In 2011, 5 master's, 8 doctorates awarded. *Degree requirements:* For master's, thesis; for doctorate, thesis/dissertation. *Entrance requirements:* For master's and doctorate, GRE General Test, scores in verbal and quantitative areas must be greater than 1000 or 300 if the GRE was taken August 1, 2011 or after, minimum undergraduate GPA of 3.0 or equivalent. Additional exam requirements/recommendations for international students: Required—TOEFL (minimum score 600 paper-based; 77 iBT). *Application deadline:* For fall admission, 1/15 for domestic and international students. Applications are processed on a rolling basis. Application fee: $60 ($75 for international students). Electronic applications accepted. *Financial support:* Fellowships, research assistantships, and teaching assistantships available. Support available to part-time students. Financial award applicants required to submit FAFSA. *Faculty research:* Nutrient requirements, nutrient metabolism, nutrition and disease prevention. *Unit head:* Dr. Connie M. Weaver, Head, 765-494-8237, Fax: 765-494-0674, E-mail: weavercm@purdue.edu. *Application contact:* Marilyn McCammack, Graduate Secretary, 765-476-7492, E-mail: mccammac@purdue.edu. Web site: http://www.cfs.purdue.edu/fn/.

Rhode Island College, School of Graduate Studies, Feinstein School of Education and Human Development, Department of Health and Physical Education, Providence, RI 02908-1991. Offers health education (M Ed); physical education (CGS). *Accreditation:* NCATE. Part-time and evening/weekend programs available. *Faculty:* 2 full-time (1 woman). *Students:* 14 part-time (12 women); includes 1 minority (Hispanic/Latino). Average age 38. In 2011, 10 master's awarded. *Degree requirements:* For master's, comprehensive assessment. *Entrance requirements:* For master's, GRE General Test or MAT, undergraduate transcripts; minimum undergraduate GPA of 3.0; 3 letters of recommendation; for CGS, GRE or MAT (for most programs), undergraduate transcripts; minimum undergraduate GPA of 3.0; 3 letters of recommendation. Additional exam requirements/recommendations for international students: Recommended—TOEFL (minimum score 550 paper-based; 213 computer-based; 79 iBT). *Application deadline:* For fall admission, 3/1 for domestic students; for spring admission, 11/1 for domestic students. Applications are processed on a rolling basis. Application fee: $50. *Expenses:* Tuition, state resident: full-time $8592; part-time $358 per credit hour. Tuition, nonresident: full-time $16,800; part-time $700 per credit hour. *Required fees:* $602; $22 per credit. $72 per term. *Financial support:* Teaching assistantships with full tuition reimbursements, Federal Work-Study, scholarships/grants, health care benefits, and unspecified assistantships available. Support available to part-time students. Financial award application deadline: 5/15; financial award applicants required to submit FAFSA. *Unit head:* Dr. Betty Rauhe, Chair, 401-456-8046. *Application contact:* Graduate Studies, 401-456-8700. Web site: http://www.ric.edu/healthPhysicalEducation/.

Rosalind Franklin University of Medicine and Science, College of Health Professions, Department of Nutrition, North Chicago, IL 60064-3095. Offers clinical nutrition (MS); nutrition education (MS). Part-time and evening/weekend programs available. Postbaccalaureate distance learning degree programs offered (no on-campus study). *Degree requirements:* For master's, thesis optional, portfolio. *Entrance requirements:* For master's, minimum GPA of 2.75, registered dietitian (RD), professional certificate or license. Additional exam requirements/recommendations for international students: Required—TOEFL. *Expenses:* Contact institution. *Faculty research:* Nutrition education, distance learning, computer-based graduate education, childhood obesity, nutrition medical education.

Sage Graduate School, Esteves School of Education, Program in Community Health Education, Troy, NY 12180-4115. Offers MS. Part-time and evening/weekend programs available. *Faculty:* 10 full-time (6 women), 2 part-time/adjunct (both women). *Students:* 2 full-time (both women), 18 part-time (14 women); includes 1 minority (Black or African American, non-Hispanic/Latino). Average age 28. 7 applicants, 43% accepted, 3 enrolled. In 2011, 17 master's awarded. *Degree requirements:* For master's, thesis optional. *Entrance requirements:* For master's, minimum GPA of 2.75, resume, 2 letters of recommendation, interview, assessment of writing skills. Additional exam requirements/recommendations for international students: Required—TOEFL (minimum score 550 paper-based; 213 computer-based). *Application deadline:* Applications are processed on a rolling basis. Application fee: $40. *Expenses: Tuition:* Full-time $11,880; part-time $660 per credit hour. Tuition and fees vary according to program. *Financial support:* Federal Work-Study, scholarships/grants, tuition waivers (partial), and unspecified assistantships available. Support available to part-time students. Financial award application deadline: 3/1; financial award applicants required to submit FAFSA. *Unit head:* Dr. Lori Quigley, Dean, Esteves School of Education, 518-244-2326, Fax: 518-244-4571, E-mail: l.quigley@sage.edu. *Application contact:* Dr. Nancy DeKorp, Director, 518-244-2496, Fax: 518-244-4571, E-mail: dekorn@sage.edu. Web site: http://www.sage.edu/academics/education/programs/commhealth/.

Sage Graduate School, Esteves School of Education, Program in School Health Education, Troy, NY 12180-4115. Offers MS. *Accreditation:* NCATE. Part-time and evening/weekend programs available. *Faculty:* 10 full-time (6 women), 2 part-time/adjunct (both women). *Students:* 15 full-time (10 women), 32 part-time (14 women); includes 3 minority (1 Asian, non-Hispanic/Latino; 2 Hispanic/Latino). Average age 26. 13 applicants, 62% accepted, 7 enrolled. In 2011, 5 master's awarded. *Degree requirements:* For master's, thesis optional. *Entrance requirements:* For master's, minimum GPA of 2.75, resume, 2 letters of recommendation, interview, assessment of writing skills. Additional exam requirements/recommendations for international students: Required—TOEFL (minimum score 550 paper-based; 213 computer-based). *Application deadline:* Applications are processed on a rolling basis. Application fee: $40. *Expenses: Tuition:* Full-time $11,880; part-time $660 per credit hour. Tuition and fees vary according to program. *Financial support:* Fellowships, research assistantships, Federal Work-Study, scholarships/grants, and unspecified assistantships available. Support available to part-time students. Financial award application deadline: 3/1; financial award applicants required to submit FAFSA. *Faculty research:* Policy development in health education and health care. *Unit head:* Dr. Lori Quigley, Dean, Esteves School of Education, 518-244-2326, Fax: 518-244-4571, E-mail: l.quigley@sage.edu. *Application contact:* Dr. John J. Pelizza, Director, 518-244-2051, Fax: 518-244-2334, E-mail: pelizj@sage.edu.

Saint Francis University, Department of Physician Assistant Sciences, Health Science Program, Loretto, PA 15940-0600. Offers MHS. Part-time and evening/weekend programs available. Postbaccalaureate distance learning degree programs offered (no on-campus study). *Faculty:* 2 full-time (both women), 9 part-time/adjunct (4 women). *Students:* 25 part-time (20 women); includes 7 minority (3 Black or African American, non-Hispanic/Latino; 1 Asian, non-Hispanic/Latino; 3 Hispanic/Latino), 1 international. Average age 42. 32 applicants, 75% accepted, 24 enrolled. In 2011, 5 degrees awarded. *Entrance requirements:* For master's, 2 letters of reference, minimum QPA of 2.5, resume. *Application deadline:* For fall admission, 7/21 for domestic students; for spring admission, 11/25 for domestic students. Applications are processed on a rolling basis. Application fee: $50. Electronic applications accepted. *Expenses:* Contact institution. *Financial support:* Available to part-time students. Applicants required to submit FAFSA. *Unit head:* Deborah E. Budash, Director, 814-472-3919, Fax: 814-472-3137, E-mail: dbudash@francis.edu. *Application contact:* Cheryl A. Strittmatter, Office Assistant, 814-472-3357, Fax: 814-472-3137, E-mail: cstrittmatter@francis.edu. Web site: http://www.francis.edu/mhshome.htm.

Saint Joseph's College of Maine, Master of Science in Education Program, Standish, ME 04084. Offers adult education and training (MS Ed); Catholic school leadership (MS Ed); health care educator (MS Ed); school educator (MS Ed). Program available by correspondence. Part-time programs available. Postbaccalaureate distance learning degree programs offered (minimal on-campus study). *Faculty:* 20 part-time/adjunct (13 women). *Students:* 273 part-time (190 women); includes 21 minority (14 Black or African American, non-Hispanic/Latino; 1 American Indian or Alaska Native, non-Hispanic/Latino; 2 Asian, non-Hispanic/Latino; 4 Hispanic/Latino). Average age 43. In 2011, 25 master's awarded. *Application deadline:* Applications are processed on a rolling basis. Application fee: $50. Electronic applications accepted. One-time fee: $50. *Financial support:* Institutionally sponsored loans available. Support available to part-time students. Financial award applicants required to submit FAFSA. *Unit head:* Dr. Thomas Hancock, Director, 207-893-7841, Fax: 207-892-7987, E-mail: thancock@sjcme.edu. *Application contact:* Lynne Robinson, Director of Admissions, 800-752-4723, Fax: 207-892-7480, E-mail: info@sjcme.edu. Web site: http://online.sjcme.edu/master-science-education.php.

Saint Joseph's University, College of Arts and Sciences, Department of Health Services, Philadelphia, PA 19131-1395. Offers health administration (MS, Post-Master's Certificate); health care ethics (Post-Master's Certificate); health education (MS, Post-Master's Certificate); health informatics (Post-Master's Certificate); healthcare ethics (MS); long-term care administration (MS); nurse anesthesia (MS); school nurse certification (MS). Part-time and evening/weekend programs available. *Faculty:* 9 full-time (1 woman), 21 part-time/adjunct (11 women). *Students:* 76 full-time (53 women), 261 part-time (204 women); includes 106 minority (79 Black or African American, non-Hispanic/Latino; 2 American Indian or Alaska Native, non-Hispanic/Latino; 12 Asian, non-Hispanic/Latino; 10 Hispanic/Latino; 1 Native Hawaiian or other Pacific Islander, non-Hispanic/Latino; 2 Two or more races, non-Hispanic/Latino), 17 international. Average age 35. 143 applicants, 69% accepted, 91 enrolled. In 2011, 67 master's awarded. *Entrance requirements:* For master's, GRE (if GPA less than 2.75), 2 letters of recommendation, minimum GPA of 2.75, resume. Additional exam requirements/recommendations for international students: Required—TOEFL (minimum score 550 paper-based; 213 computer-based; 79 iBT). *Application deadline:* For fall admission, 7/15 priority date for domestic students, 4/15 for international students; for winter admission, 1/15 for international students; for spring admission, 11/15 priority date for domestic students, 10/15 for international students. Applications are processed on a rolling basis. Application fee: $35. Electronic applications accepted. *Expenses: Tuition:* Part-time $735 per credit hour. Tuition and fees vary according to degree level and program. *Financial support:* Career-related internships or fieldwork and unspecified assistantships available. Financial award applicants required to submit FAFSA. *Unit head:* Nakia Henderson, Director, 610-660-2952, E-mail: nakia.henderson@sju.edu. *Application contact:* Kate McConnell, Director, Graduate College of Arts and Sciences Admissions and Retention, 610-660-3184, Fax: 610-660-3230, E-mail: kate.mcconnell@sju.edu.

San Francisco State University, Division of Graduate Studies, College of Health and Human Services, Human Sexuality Studies Program, San Francisco, CA 94132-1722. Offers MA. *Unit head:* Dr. Rita Melendez, Chair, 415-405-3572, E-mail: rmelende@sfsu.edu. *Application contact:* Prof. Christopher Carrington, Graduate Advisor, 415-338-1466, E-mail: ccarring@sfsu.edu. Web site: https://sxs.sfsu.edu/.

San Jose State University, Graduate Studies and Research, College of Applied Sciences and Arts, Department of Health Science, San Jose, CA 95192-0001. Offers applied social gerontology (Certificate); community health education (MPH). *Accreditation:* CEPH (one or more programs are accredited). Postbaccalaureate distance learning degree programs offered. *Entrance requirements:* For master's, GRE General Test. Electronic applications accepted. *Faculty research:* Behavioral science in occupational and health care settings, epidemiology in health care settings.

Simmons College, College of Arts and Sciences Graduate Studies, Boston, MA 02115. Offers applied behavior analysis (PhD); behavior analysis (MS, Ed S); children's literature (MA); education (MS, CAGS, Ed S); educational leadership (PhD, CAGS); English (MA); gender and cultural studies (MA); health professions education (PhD); history (MA); Spanish (MA); special education moderate licensure (Certificate); special needs administration (Ed D); special needs education (Ed S); teaching (MAT); teaching English as a second language (MA, CAGS); urban education (CAGS); writing for children (MFA); MA/MA; MA/MS; MAT/MA. *Unit head:* Renee White, Dean. *Application contact:* Kristen Haack, Director, Graduate Studies Admission, 617-521-2917, Fax: 617-521-3058, E-mail: gsa@simmons.edu. Web site: http://www.simmons.edu/gradstudies/.

Simmons College, School of Nursing and Health Sciences, Boston, MA 02115. Offers didactic dietetics (Certificate); health professions education (CAGS); nursing (MS); nursing administration (MS); nursing practice (DNP); nutrition (MS, Certificate); physical therapy (DPT); sports nutrition (Certificate); sports nutrition/didactic dietetics (Certificate); MS/Certificate. *Unit head:* Dr. Judy Beal, Dean, 617-521-2139, Fax: 617-521-3137, E-mail: judy.beal@simmons.edu. *Application contact:* Carmen Fortin, Assistant Dean/Director of Admission, 617-521-2651, Fax: 617-521-3137, E-mail: gshsadm@simmons.edu. Web site: http://www.simmons.edu/snhs/.

South Dakota State University, Graduate School, College of Education and Human Sciences, Department of Health, Physical Education and Recreation, Brookings, SD 57007. Offers MS. Part-time programs available. *Degree requirements:* For master's, thesis, oral and written exams. *Entrance requirements:* Additional exam requirements/recommendations for international students: Required—TOEFL (minimum score 550 paper-based; 213 computer-based; 71 iBT). *Faculty research:* Effective teaching behaviors in physical education, sports nutrition, muscle/bone interaction, hormonal response to exercise.

Southeastern Louisiana University, College of Nursing and Health Sciences, Department of Kinesiology and Health Studies, Hammond, LA 70402. Offers health and kinesiology (MA), including exercise science, health promotion and exercise science, health studies, kinesiology. *Accreditation:* NCATE. Part-time programs available. *Faculty:* 7 full-time (2 women), 1 (woman) part-time/adjunct. *Students:* 40 full-time (26 women), 25 part-time (17 women); includes 15 minority (11 Black or African American, non-Hispanic/Latino; 1 Asian, non-Hispanic/Latino; 1 Hispanic/Latino; 2 Two or more races, non-Hispanic/Latino), 4 international. Average age 27. 27 applicants, 100% accepted, 19 enrolled. In 2011, 24 degrees awarded. *Degree requirements:* For master's, comprehensive exam (for some programs), thesis (for some programs). *Entrance requirements:* For master's, GRE General Test (minimum score 800), undergraduate human anatomy and physiology course. Additional exam requirements/ recommendations for international students: Required—TOEFL (minimum score 500 paper-based; 173 computer-based; 61 iBT). *Application deadline:* For fall admission, 7/15 priority date for domestic students, 6/1 for international students; for spring admission, 12/1 priority date for domestic students, 10/1 for international students. Applications are processed on a rolling basis. Application fee: $20 ($30 for international students). Electronic applications accepted. *Expenses:* Tuition, state resident: full-time $3977; part-time $283 per semester hour. Tuition, nonresident: full-time $13,482; part-time $811 per semester hour. *Financial support:* In 2011–12, 2 fellowships (averaging $10,800 per year), 8 research assistantships (averaging $9,500 per year), 3 teaching assistantships (averaging $9,000 per year) were awarded; career-related internships or fieldwork, Federal Work-Study, institutionally sponsored loans, scholarships/grants, and unspecified assistantships also available. Support available to part-time students. Financial award application deadline: 5/1; financial award applicants required to submit FAFSA. *Faculty research:* Exercise endocrinology, perceptions of exercise intensity and pain, spirituality and health, alternative health practices, use of podcasting and other technology to promote healthy behaviors. *Unit head:* Dr. Edward Hebert, Department Head, 985-549-2129, Fax: 985-549-5119, E-mail: ehebert@selu.edu. *Application contact:* Sandra Meyers, Graduate Admissions Analyst, 985-549-5620, Fax: 985-549-5632, E-mail: admissions@selu.edu. Web site: http://www.selu.edu/acad_research/depts/kin_hs.

Southern Connecticut State University, School of Graduate Studies, School of Education, Department of Exercise Science, Program in School Health Education, New Haven, CT 06515-1355. Offers MS. *Accreditation:* NCATE. Part-time and evening/weekend programs available. *Faculty:* 1 (woman) part-time/adjunct. *Students:* 10 full-time (8 women), 19 part-time (10 women); includes 1 minority (Hispanic/Latino). 45 applicants, 18% accepted, 8 enrolled. In 2011, 18 master's awarded. *Entrance requirements:* For master's, interview. *Application deadline:* For fall admission, 7/15 priority date for domestic students. Applications are processed on a rolling basis. Application fee: $50. Electronic applications accepted. *Expenses:* Tuition, state resident: full-time $5137; part-time $413 per credit. *Required fees:* $4008; $55 per term. *Financial support:* Application deadline: 4/15; applicants required to submit FAFSA. *Unit head:* Dr. Doris Marino, Graduate Coordinator, 203-392-6922, Fax: 203-392-6911, E-mail: marinod1@southernct.edu. *Application contact:* Dr. Robert Axtell, Coordinator, 203-392-6037, Fax: 203-392-6093, E-mail: axtell@southernct.edu.

Southern Illinois University Carbondale, Graduate School, College of Education and Human Services, Department of Health Education and Recreation, Program in Community Health Education, Carbondale, IL 62901-4701. Offers MPH. *Students:* 29 full-time (24 women), 4 part-time (all women); includes 12 minority (8 Black or African American, non-Hispanic/Latino; 1 Asian, non-Hispanic/Latino; 3 Hispanic/Latino), 3 international. 37 applicants, 65% accepted, 16 enrolled. In 2011, 8 master's awarded. *Unit head:* Dr. David Birch, Chair, 618-453-2777, Fax: 618-453-1829, E-mail: dabirch@siu.edu. *Application contact:* Carol Reynolds, Administrative Assistant, 618-453-2415, Fax: 618-453-1829, E-mail: creynolds@siu.edu.

Southern Illinois University Carbondale, Graduate School, College of Education and Human Services, Department of Health Education and Recreation, Program in Health Education, Carbondale, IL 62901-4701. Offers MS Ed, PhD. *Accreditation:* NCATE. Part-time programs available. *Faculty:* 9 full-time (6 women). *Students:* 19 full-time (16 women), 39 part-time (25 women); includes 12 minority (10 Black or African American, non-Hispanic/Latino; 1 American Indian or Alaska Native, non-Hispanic/Latino; 1 Asian, non-Hispanic/Latino), 6 international. Average age 30. 22 applicants, 55% accepted, 6 enrolled. In 2011, 3 master's, 6 doctorates awarded. *Degree requirements:* For master's, thesis; for doctorate, thesis/dissertation. *Entrance requirements:* For master's, MAT, minimum GPA of 2.7; for doctorate, MAT, minimum GPA of 3.25. Additional exam requirements/recommendations for international students: Required—TOEFL. *Application deadline:* For fall admission, 2/15 for domestic students; for spring admission, 9/15 for domestic students. Application fee: $20. *Financial support:* In 2011–12, 33 students received support, including 1 fellowship with full tuition reimbursement available, 10 teaching assistantships with full tuition reimbursements available; research assistantships with full tuition reimbursements available, career-related internships or fieldwork, Federal Work-Study, institutionally sponsored loans, and tuition waivers (full) also available. Support available to part-time students. *Faculty research:* Sexuality education, research design, injury control, program evaluation. *Unit head:* Dr. David Birch, Chair, 618-453-2777, Fax: 618-453-1829, E-mail: dabirch@siu.edu. *Application contact:* Carol Reynolds, Administrative Assistant, 618-453-2415, Fax: 618-453-1829, E-mail: creynolds@siu.edu. Web site: http://web.coehs.siu.edu/Public/her/grad/healthedgraduate.php.

Southern Illinois University Edwardsville, Graduate School, School of Education, Department of Kinesiology and Health Education, Edwardsville, IL 62026. Offers kinesiology (MS Ed), including kinesiology, physical education and sport pedagogy. *Accreditation:* NCATE. Part-time and evening/weekend programs available. *Faculty:* 12 full-time (5 women). *Students:* 31 full-time (16 women), 45 part-time (18 women); includes 17 minority (10 Black or African American, non-Hispanic/Latino; 2 Asian, non-Hispanic/Latino; 5 Hispanic/Latino), 1 international. 70 applicants, 59% accepted. In 2011, 35 master's awarded. *Degree requirements:* For master's, comprehensive exam (for some programs), thesis (for some programs). *Entrance requirements:* Additional exam requirements/recommendations for international students: Required—TOEFL (minimum score 550 paper-based; 213 computer-based; 79 iBT), IELTS (minimum score 6.5). *Application deadline:* For fall admission, 7/22 for domestic students, 6/1 for international students; for spring admission, 12/9 for domestic students, 10/1 for international students. Applications are processed on a rolling basis. Application fee: $30. Electronic applications accepted. Tuition and fees vary according to course load and program. *Financial support:* In 2011–12, 6 teaching assistantships with full tuition reimbursements (averaging $9,927 per year) were awarded; fellowships, research assistantships with full tuition reimbursements, institutionally sponsored loans, scholarships/grants, and unspecified assistantships also available. Financial award application deadline: 3/1; financial award applicants required to submit FAFSA. *Unit head:* Dr. Curt Lox, Director, 618-650-2938, E-mail: clox@siue.edu. *Application contact:* Dr. Erik Kirk, Program Director, 618-650-2718, E-mail: ekirk@siue.edu. Web site: http://www.siue.edu/education/khe.

Springfield College, Graduate Programs, Programs in Physical Education, Springfield, MA 01109-3797. Offers adapted physical education (M Ed, MPE, MS); advanced level coaching (M Ed, MPE, MS); athletic administration (M Ed, MPE, MS); general physical education (PhD, CAGS); health education licensure (MPE, MS); health education licensure program (M Ed); physical education licensure (MPE, MS); physical education licensure program (M Ed); teaching and administration (MS). Part-time programs available. *Degree requirements:* For master's, comprehensive exam, thesis (for some programs). *Entrance requirements:* For master's and doctorate, GRE General Test. Additional exam requirements/recommendations for international students: Required—TOEFL (minimum score 550 paper-based; 213 computer-based). Electronic applications accepted.

State University of New York College at Cortland, Graduate Studies, School of Professional Studies, Department of Health Education, Cortland, NY 13045. Offers MS Ed, MST. *Accreditation:* NCATE. Part-time and evening/weekend programs available. *Entrance requirements:* Additional exam requirements/recommendations for international students: Required—TOEFL.

Suffolk University, College of Arts and Sciences, Program in Women's Health, Boston, MA 02108-2770. Offers MA. *Faculty:* 9 full-time (7 women), 4 part-time/adjunct (all women). *Students:* 19 full-time (all women), 13 part-time (all women); includes 14 minority (12 Black or African American, non-Hispanic/Latino; 1 Hispanic/Latino; 1 Two or more races, non-Hispanic/Latino). Average age 28. 57 applicants, 47% accepted, 17 enrolled. In 2011, 16 master's awarded. *Entrance requirements:* For master's, statement of professional goals, official transcripts, 2 letters of recommendation, resume. Additional exam requirements/recommendations for international students: Required—TOEFL (minimum score 550 paper-based; 213 computer-based; 80 iBT). *Application deadline:* For fall admission, 6/15 priority date for domestic students, 6/15 for international students; for spring admission, 11/1 priority date for domestic students, 11/1 for international students. Applications are processed on a rolling basis. Application fee: $50. Electronic applications accepted. *Expenses:* Contact institution. *Financial support:* In 2011–12, 31 students received support, including 25 fellowships (averaging $5,683 per year). Financial award applicants required to submit FAFSA. *Unit head:* Dr. Amy Agigian, Co-Director, 617-573-8487, Fax: 617-994-4278, E-mail: aagigian@suffolk.edu. *Application contact:* Judith Reynolds, Director of Graduate Admissions, 617-573-8302, Fax: 617-305-1733, E-mail: grad.admission@suffolk.edu. Web site: http://www.suffolk.edu/mawh.

Teachers College, Columbia University, Graduate Faculty of Education, Department of Health and Behavioral Studies, Program in Health Education, New York, NY 10027-6696. Offers MA, MS, Ed D. *Accreditation:* NCATE. Part-time and evening/weekend programs available. *Faculty:* 4 full-time (2 women), 10 part-time/adjunct (6 women). *Students:* 23 full-time (22 women), 76 part-time (66 women); includes 49 minority (22 Black or African American, non-Hispanic/Latino; 8 Asian, non-Hispanic/Latino; 17 Hispanic/Latino; 2 Two or more races, non-Hispanic/Latino), 3 international. Average age 37. 41 applicants, 73% accepted, 15 enrolled. In 2011, 26 master's, 9 doctorates awarded. Terminal master's awarded for partial completion of doctoral program. *Degree requirements:* For master's, thesis optional, integrative project; for doctorate, comprehensive exam, thesis/dissertation. *Entrance requirements:* For doctorate, GRE or MAT. *Application deadline:* For fall admission, 1/2 for domestic students; for spring admission, 11/1 for domestic students. Applications are processed on a rolling basis. Application fee: $65. Electronic applications accepted. *Financial support:* Fellowships and research assistantships available. Financial award application deadline: 2/1; financial award applicants required to submit FAFSA. *Faculty research:* Health behavior, disease self-management, and health outcomes in chronic disease; health education in schools and patient-care settings; behavioral epidemiology. *Unit head:* Prof. Barbara Wallace, Program Coordinator, 212-678-6607, E-mail: bcw3@columbia.edu. *Application contact:* Elizabeth Puleio, Assistant Director of Admission, 212-678-3730, E-mail: eap2136@tc.columbia.edu.

Temple University, Health Sciences Center, College of Health Professions and Social Work, Department of Public Health, Philadelphia, PA 19122-6096. Offers environmental health (MS); epidemiology (MS); public health (MPH, PhD); school health education (Ed M). *Accreditation:* CEPH (one or more programs are accredited). Part-time and evening/weekend programs available. *Faculty:* 15 full-time (8 women). *Students:* 62 full-time (44 women), 28 part-time (25 women); includes 24 minority (14 Black or African American, non-Hispanic/Latino; 5 Asian, non-Hispanic/Latino; 5 Hispanic/Latino), 7 international. Average age 29. 92 applicants, 68% accepted, 29 enrolled. In 2011, 30 master's, 4 doctorates awarded. Terminal master's awarded for partial completion of doctoral program. *Degree requirements:* For doctorate, thesis/dissertation. *Entrance requirements:* For master's and doctorate, minimum undergraduate GPA of 3.0. Additional exam requirements/recommendations for international students: Required—TOEFL (minimum score 550 paper-based; 213 computer-based; 79 iBT). Application fee: $50. Electronic applications accepted. *Expenses:* Tuition, state resident: full-time $12,366; part-time $687 per credit hour. Tuition, nonresident: full-time $17,298; part-time $961 per credit hour. *Required fees:* $590; $213 per year. *Financial support:* Fellowships with tuition reimbursements, research assistantships with tuition reimbursements, teaching assistantships with tuition reimbursements, career-related internships or fieldwork, Federal Work-Study, institutionally sponsored loans, scholarships/grants, and tuition waivers (partial) available. Financial award application deadline: 1/15; financial award applicants required to submit FAFSA. *Faculty research:* Program development and evaluation in HIV prevention, violence prevention, women's health policy, psychosocial aspects of disability. *Unit head:* Dr. Alice J. Hausman, Chair, 215-204-5112, Fax: 215-204-1854, E-mail: publichealth@temple.edu. *Application contact:* Tara Schumacher, Coordinator of Outreach, 215-204-6575, Fax: 215-204-8781, E-mail: tara.schumacher@temple.edu. Web site: http://chpsw.temple.edu/publichealth/.

Tennessee Technological University, Graduate School, College of Education, Department of Exercise Science, Physical Education and Wellness, Cookeville, TN 38505. Offers MA. *Accreditation:* NCATE. Part-time programs available. Postbaccalaureate distance learning degree programs offered (no on-campus study). *Faculty:* 7 full-time (0 women). *Students:* 21 full-time (15 women), 24 part-time (13 women). Average age 27. 32 applicants, 72% accepted, 19 enrolled. In 2011, 21 master's awarded. *Degree requirements:* For master's, comprehensive exam, thesis or alternative. *Entrance requirements:* For master's, MAT or GRE. Additional exam requirements/recommendations for international students: Required—TOEFL (minimum score 527 paper-based; 71 iBT), IELTS (minimum score 5.5), Pearson Test of English Academic. *Application deadline:* For fall admission, 8/1 for domestic students, 5/1 for international students; for spring admission, 12/1 for domestic students, 10/1 for international students. Application fee: $25 ($30 for international students). Electronic applications accepted. *Expenses:* Tuition, state resident: full-time $8094; part-time $422 per credit hour. Tuition, nonresident: full-time $20,574; part-time $1046 per credit hour. *Financial support:* In 2011–12, fellowships (averaging $8,000 per year), 3 research assistantships (averaging $4,000 per year), 4 teaching assistantships (averaging $4,000 per year) were awarded; career-related internships or fieldwork also available. Financial award application deadline: 4/1. *Unit head:* Dr. J. P. Barfield, Interim Chairperson, 931-372-3467, Fax: 931-372-6319, E-mail: jpbarfield@tntech.edu. *Application contact:* Shelia K. Kendrick, Coordinator of Graduate Admissions, 931-372-3808, Fax: 931-372-3497, E-mail: skendrick@tntech.edu.

Texas A&M Health Science Center, Baylor College of Dentistry, Department of Endodontics, Program in Health Professions Education, College Station, TX 77840. Offers MS. Part-time programs available. *Degree requirements:* For master's, thesis. *Entrance requirements:* For master's, GRE General Test, DDS or DMD. Additional exam requirements/recommendations for international students: Required—TOEFL. *Faculty research:* Craniofacial biology, dermatoglyphics, alternative curricula, admissions criteria, competency-based program assessment.

Texas A&M University, College of Education and Human Development, Department of Health and Kinesiology, College Station, TX 77843. Offers health education (MS, PhD);

kinesiology (MS, PhD); physical education (M Ed); sport management (MS). Part-time programs available. *Faculty:* 37. *Students:* 171 full-time (80 women), 38 part-time (22 women); includes 60 minority (21 Black or African American, non-Hispanic/Latino; 8 Asian, non-Hispanic/Latino; 29 Hispanic/Latino; 2 Two or more races, non-Hispanic/ Latino), 35 international. Average age 23. In 2011, 54 master's, 17 doctorates awarded. *Degree requirements:* For master's, thesis (for some programs); for doctorate, comprehensive exam, thesis/dissertation. *Entrance requirements:* For master's and doctorate, GRE General Test. Additional exam requirements/recommendations for international students: Required—TOEFL. *Application deadline:* Applications are processed on a rolling basis. Application fee: $50 ($75 for international students). Electronic applications accepted. *Expenses:* Tuition, state resident: full-time $5437; part-time $226.55 per credit hour. Tuition, nonresident: full-time $12,949; part-time $539.55 per credit hour. *Required fees:* $2741. *Financial support:* Fellowships with partial tuition reimbursements, research assistantships, teaching assistantships, career-related internships or fieldwork, and institutionally sponsored loans available. Financial award application deadline: 2/15; financial award applicants required to submit FAFSA. *Unit head:* Dr. Richard Kreider, Head, 979-845-1333, Fax: 979-847-8987, E-mail: rkreider@hlkn.tamu.edu. *Application contact:* Dr. Becky Carr, Assistant Dean for Administrative Services, 979-862-1342, Fax: 979-845-6129, E-mail: bcarr@tamu.edu. Web site: http://hlknweb.tamu.edu/.

Texas A&M University–Commerce, Graduate School, College of Education and Human Services, Department of Health and Human Performance, Commerce, TX 75429-3011. Offers exercise physiology (MS); health and human performance (M Ed); health promotion (MS); health, kinesiology and sports studies (Ed D); motor performance (MS); sport studies (MS). Part-time programs available. *Degree requirements:* For master's, comprehensive exam, thesis (for some programs). *Entrance requirements:* For master's, GRE General Test. Electronic applications accepted. *Faculty research:* Teaching, physical fitness.

Texas A&M University–Kingsville, College of Graduate Studies, College of Education, Department of Health and Kinesiology, Kingsville, TX 78363. Offers MA, MS. Part-time programs available. *Degree requirements:* For master's, comprehensive exam, thesis or alternative. *Entrance requirements:* For master's, GRE General Test, minimum GPA of 3.0. *Faculty research:* Body composition, electromyography.

Texas Southern University, College of Education, Department of Health and Kinesiology, Houston, TX 77004-4584. Offers health education (MS); human performance (MS). Part-time and evening/weekend programs available. *Degree requirements:* For master's, comprehensive exam, thesis optional. *Entrance requirements:* For master's, GRE General Test, minimum GPA of 2.5. Additional exam requirements/recommendations for international students: Required—TOEFL. Electronic applications accepted.

Texas State University–San Marcos, Graduate School, College of Education, Department of Health and Human Performance, Program in Health Education, San Marcos, TX 78666. Offers M Ed. Part-time and evening/weekend programs available. *Faculty:* 2 full-time (1 woman). *Students:* 18 full-time (16 women), 12 part-time (11 women); includes 12 minority (5 Black or African American, non-Hispanic/Latino; 7 Hispanic/Latino). Average age 28. 23 applicants, 78% accepted, 9 enrolled. In 2011, 3 master's awarded. *Degree requirements:* For master's, comprehensive exam, thesis optional. *Entrance requirements:* For master's, GRE General Test, minimum GPA of 2.75 in last 60 hours of course work, 18 hours of health education background courses. Additional exam requirements/recommendations for international students: Required—TOEFL (minimum score 550 paper-based; 213 computer-based; 78 iBT). *Application deadline:* For fall admission, 6/15 priority date for domestic students, 6/1 for international students; for spring admission, 10/15 priority date for domestic students, 10/1 for international students. Applications are processed on a rolling basis. Application fee: $40 ($90 for international students). Electronic applications accepted. *Expenses:* Tuition, state resident: full-time $6408; part-time $3204 per semester. Tuition, nonresident: full-time $14,832; part-time $7416 per semester. *Required fees:* $1824; $912 per semester. Tuition and fees vary according to course load. *Financial support:* In 2011–12, 12 students received support, including 4 research assistantships (averaging $10,467 per year), 3 teaching assistantships (averaging $10,152 per year); career-related internships or fieldwork, Federal Work-Study, and institutionally sponsored loans also available. Support available to part-time students. Financial award application deadline: 4/1; financial award applicants required to submit FAFSA. *Faculty research:* AIDS education, employee wellness, isometric strength evaluation. *Unit head:* Dr. Kelly Wilson, Chair, 512-245-2561, Fax: 512-245-8678. *Application contact:* Amy Galle, Head, 512-245-2561, Fax: 512-245-8678, E-mail: ag04@txstate.edu. Web site: http://www.hhp.txstate.edu/Degree-Plans/Graduate.html.

Texas Woman's University, Graduate School, College of Health Sciences, Department of Health Studies, Denton, TX 76201. Offers MS, Ed D, PhD. Part-time and evening/ weekend programs available. *Faculty:* 12 full-time (9 women), 1 part-time/adjunct (0 women). *Students:* 10 full-time (all women), 60 part-time (56 women); includes 30 minority (19 Black or African American, non-Hispanic/Latino; 1 American Indian or Alaska Native, non-Hispanic/Latino; 1 Asian, non-Hispanic/Latino; 9 Hispanic/Latino), 4 international. Average age 39. 27 applicants, 74% accepted, 13 enrolled. In 2011, 11 master's, 3 doctorates awarded. *Degree requirements:* For master's, comprehensive exam, thesis or alternative; for doctorate, comprehensive exam, thesis/dissertation, qualifying exam. *Entrance requirements:* For master's, GRE General Test (preferred minimum scores 150 [450 old version] Verbal, 140 [400 old version] Quantitative), 2 letters of recommendation, curriculum vitae, essay; for doctorate, GRE General Test (preferred minimum scores 152 [480 old version] Verbal, 140 [400 old version] Quantitative), minimum GPA of 3.5 on all master's course work, 2 letters of recommendation, curriculum vitae, essay, writing sample. Additional exam requirements/recommendations for international students: Required—TOEFL (minimum score 575 paper-based; 233 computer-based; 90 iBT). *Application deadline:* For fall admission, 4/1 for domestic students, 3/1 for international students; for spring admission, 10/1 for domestic students, 7/1 for international students. Applications are processed on a rolling basis. Application fee: $50 ($75 for international students). Electronic applications accepted. *Expenses:* Tuition, state resident: full-time $3834; part-time $213 per credit hour. Tuition, nonresident: full-time $9468; part-time $526 per credit hour. *Required fees:* $213 per credit hour. Tuition and fees vary according to course load. *Financial support:* In 2011–12, 7 students received support, including 4 research assistantships (averaging $10,764 per year), 1 teaching assistantship (averaging $10,764 per year); career-related internships or fieldwork, Federal Work-Study, institutionally sponsored loans, scholarships/grants, traineeships, health care benefits, tuition waivers (partial), and unspecified assistantships also available. Support available to part-time students. Financial award application deadline: 3/1; financial award applicants required to submit FAFSA. *Faculty research:* Body image and eating disorder prevention, health communication/health literacy, violence prevention, chronic diseases, HIV/AIDS prevention. *Unit head:* Dr. Doug Coyle, Graduate Program Coordinator and Assistant Professor, 940-898-2860, Fax: 940-898-2859, E-mail: tcoyle@twu.edu. *Application contact:* Dr. Samuel Wheeler, Assistant Director of Admissions, 940-898-3188, Fax: 940-898-3081, E-mail: wheelersr@twu.edu. Web site: http://www.twu.edu/health-studies/.

Thomas Jefferson University, Jefferson School of Health Professions, Department of General Studies, Philadelphia, PA 19107. Offers healthcare education (Certificate).

Thomas Jefferson University, Jefferson School of Population Health, Philadelphia, PA 19107. Offers applied health economics and outcomes research (MS, PhD); behavioral health science (PhD); chronic care management (MS, Certificate); health policy (MS, Certificate); healthcare quality and safety (MS, PhD); public health (MPH, Certificate). Part-time and evening/weekend programs available. Postbaccalaureate distance learning degree programs offered (no on-campus study). Terminal master's awarded for partial completion of doctoral program. *Degree requirements:* For master's, thesis; for doctorate, comprehensive exam, thesis/dissertation. *Entrance requirements:* For master's, GRE or other graduate entrance exam (MCAT, LSAT, DAT, etc.), two letters of recommendation, curriculum vitae, transcripts from all undergraduate and graduate institutions; for doctorate, GRE taken within the last 5 years, three letters of recommendation, curriculum vitae, transcripts from all undergraduate and graduate institutions. Additional exam requirements/recommendations for international students: Required—TOEFL. Electronic applications accepted. *Faculty research:* Applied health economics and outcomes research, behavioral and health sciences, chronic disease management, health policy, healthcare quality and patient safety, wellness and prevention.

Trident University International, College of Health Sciences, Program in Health Sciences, Cypress, CA 90630. Offers clinical research administration (MS, Certificate); emergency and disaster management (MS, Certificate); environmental health science (Certificate); health care administration (PhD); health care management (MS), including health informatics; health education (MS, Certificate); health informatics (Certificate); health sciences (PhD); international health (MS); international health: educator or researcher option (PhD); international health: practitioner option (PhD); law and expert witness studies (MS, Certificate); public health (MS); quality assurance (Certificate). Part-time and evening/weekend programs available. Postbaccalaureate distance learning degree programs offered (no on-campus study). *Degree requirements:* For doctorate, comprehensive exam, thesis/dissertation, defense of dissertation. *Entrance requirements:* For master's, minimum GPA of 2.5 (students with GPA 3.0 or greater may transfer up to 30% of graduate level credits); for doctorate, minimum GPA of 3.4, curriculum vitae, course work in research methods or statistics. Additional exam requirements/recommendations for international students: Required—TOEFL. Electronic applications accepted.

Tulane University, School of Public Health and Tropical Medicine, Department of Community Health Sciences, Program in Health Education and Communication, New Orleans, LA 70118-5669. Offers MPH. *Accreditation:* CEPH; Teacher Education Accreditation Council. *Degree requirements:* For master's, comprehensive exam. *Entrance requirements:* For master's, GRE General Test. Additional exam requirements/ recommendations for international students: Required—TOEFL.

Union College, Graduate Programs, Department of Education, Barbourville, KY 40906-1499. Offers elementary education (MA); health and physical education (MA); middle grades (MA); music education (MA); principalship (MA); reading specialist (MA); secondary education (MA); special education (MA). *Degree requirements:* For master's, thesis optional. *Entrance requirements:* For master's, GRE General Test, NTE.

Union College, Graduate Programs, Department of Health and Physical Education, Barbourville, KY 40906-1499. Offers health (MA Ed). *Degree requirements:* For master's, thesis optional. *Entrance requirements:* For master's, GRE General Test, NTE.

United States University, School of Health Science, Cypress, CA 90630. Offers health education (MSHS). *Entrance requirements:* For master's, undergraduate degree from accredited institution, minimum cumulative GPA of 2.5, official transcripts.

Universidad Adventista de las Antillas, EGECED Department, Mayagüez, PR 00681-0118. Offers curriculum and instruction (M Ed); health education (M Ed); medical surgical nursing (MN); pastoral theology (M Div); school administration and supervision (M Ed). *Degree requirements:* For master's, comprehensive exam (for some programs), thesis (for some programs). *Entrance requirements:* For master's, EXADEP or GRE General Test, recommendations. Electronic applications accepted.

The University of Alabama, Graduate School, College of Human Environmental Sciences, Department of Health Science, Tuscaloosa, AL 35487-0311. Offers health education and promotion (PhD); health studies (MA). Part-time programs available. Postbaccalaureate distance learning degree programs offered (no on-campus study). *Faculty:* 8 full-time (5 women). *Students:* 27 full-time (21 women), 86 part-time (71 women); includes 37 minority (28 Black or African American, non-Hispanic/Latino; 1 American Indian or Alaska Native, non-Hispanic/Latino; 4 Asian, non-Hispanic/Latino; 2 Hispanic/Latino; 2 Two or more races, non-Hispanic/Latino). Average age 32. 111 applicants, 76% accepted, 48 enrolled. In 2011, 47 master's, 4 doctorates awarded. *Median time to degree:* Of those who began their doctoral program in fall 2003, 100% received their degree in 8 years or less. *Degree requirements:* For master's, comprehensive exam, thesis optional; for doctorate, one foreign language, comprehensive exam, thesis/dissertation. *Entrance requirements:* For master's, minimum GPA of 3.0; for doctorate, GRE General Test, minimum GPA of 3.0, prerequisites in health education. Additional exam requirements/recommendations for international students: Required—TOEFL. *Application deadline:* For fall admission, 3/15 priority date for domestic students, 3/15 for international students. Applications are processed on a rolling basis. Application fee: $50 ($60 for international students). Electronic applications accepted. *Expenses:* Tuition, state resident: full-time $8600. Tuition, nonresident: full-time $21,900. *Financial support:* In 2011–12, 2 research assistantships with full tuition reimbursements (averaging $10,500 per year), 6 teaching assistantships with full tuition reimbursements (averaging $10,500 per year) were awarded; career-related internships or fieldwork, Federal Work-Study, institutionally sponsored loans, health care benefits, and unspecified assistantships also available. Financial award application deadline: 4/14. *Faculty research:* Program planning, substance abuse prevention, obesity prevention, nutrition, physical activity, athletic training, osteoporosis, health behavior. *Total annual research expenditures:* $106,620. *Unit head:* Dr. Lori W. Turner, Department Head and Professor, 205-348-2956, Fax: 205-348-7568, E-mail: lwturner@ches.ua.edu. *Application contact:* Dr. Stuart Usdan, Associate Professor and Doctoral Program Coordinator, 205-348-8373, Fax: 205-348-7568, E-mail: susdan@ches.ua.edu. Web site: http://ches.ua.edu/.

The University of Alabama at Birmingham, College of Arts and Sciences, School of Education, Program in Health Education, Birmingham, AL 35294. Offers MA Ed. *Accreditation:* NCATE. *Degree requirements:* For master's, thesis optional. *Entrance requirements:* For master's, GRE General Test, MAT, or NTE, minimum GPA of 3.0. *Application deadline:* Applications are processed on a rolling basis. Electronic applications accepted. *Expenses:* Tuition, state resident: full-time $5922; part-time $309 per hour. Tuition, nonresident: full-time $13,428; part-time $726 per hour. Tuition and fees vary according to program. *Unit head:* Dr. Kristi Menear, Chair, 205-975-7409, Fax: 205-975-8040, E-mail: kmenear@uab.edu. Web site: http://www.uab.edu/ humanstudies/healthedmasters.

The University of Alabama at Birmingham, College of Arts and Sciences, School of Education, Program in Health Education and Promotion, Birmingham, AL 35294. Offers

PhD. Program offered jointly with The University of Alabama (Tuscaloosa). *Accreditation:* NCATE. *Degree requirements:* For doctorate, thesis/dissertation. *Entrance requirements:* For doctorate, GRE General Test, MAT, minimum GPA of 3.25. Electronic applications accepted. *Expenses:* Tuition, state resident: full-time $5922; part-time $309 per hour. Tuition, nonresident: full-time $13,428; part-time $726 per hour. Tuition and fees vary according to program. *Unit head:* Dr. Kristi Menear, Chair, 205-975-7409, Fax: 205-975-8040, E-mail: kmenear@uab.edu. Web site: http://www.uab.edu/humanstudies/healthedphd.

The University of Alabama at Birmingham, School of Public Health, Program in Health Education and Promotion, Birmingham, AL 35294. Offers PhD. Program offered jointly with The University of Alabama (Tuscaloosa). *Expenses:* Tuition, state resident: full-time $5922; part-time $309 per hour. Tuition, nonresident: full-time $13,428; part-time $726 per hour. Tuition and fees vary according to program. *Unit head:* Dr. Jalie Tucker, Chair, 205-934-6020, Fax: 205-975-5484.

University of Arkansas, Graduate School, College of Education and Health Professions, Department of Health Science, Kinesiology, Recreation and Dance, Program in Health Science, Fayetteville, AR 72701-1201. Offers MS, PhD. *Accreditation:* NCATE. *Students:* 10 full-time (7 women), 11 part-time (10 women); includes 3 minority (1 Black or African American, non-Hispanic/Latino; 1 Hispanic/Latino; 1 Two or more races, non-Hispanic/Latino), 4 international. In 2011, 9 master's, 1 doctorate awarded. *Degree requirements:* For doctorate, thesis/dissertation. *Entrance requirements:* For doctorate, GRE General Test. *Application deadline:* For fall admission, 4/1 for international students; for spring admission, 10/1 for international students. Applications are processed on a rolling basis. Application fee: $40 ($50 for international students). Electronic applications accepted. *Financial support:* In 2011–12, 3 research assistantships were awarded; fellowships with tuition reimbursements, teaching assistantships, career-related internships or fieldwork, and Federal Work-Study also available. Support available to part-time students. Financial award application deadline: 4/1; financial award applicants required to submit FAFSA. *Unit head:* Dr. Bart Hammig, Department Chairperson, 479-575-2857, Fax: 479-575-5778, E-mail: bhammig@uark.edu. *Application contact:* Dr. Dean Gorman, Coordinator of Graduate Studies, 479-575-2890, E-mail: dgorman@uark.edu. Web site: http://hlsc.uark.edu/.

University of Calgary, Faculty of Medicine and Faculty of Graduate Studies, Department of Medical Science, Calgary, AB T2N 1N4, Canada. Offers cancer biology (M Sc, PhD); immunology (M Sc, PhD); joint injury and arthritis research (M Sc, PhD); medical education (M Sc, PhD); medical science (M Sc, PhD); mountain medicine and high altitude physiology (M Sc). *Degree requirements:* For master's, thesis; for doctorate, thesis/dissertation, candidacy exam. *Entrance requirements:* For master's, minimum undergraduate GPA of 3.2; for doctorate, minimum graduate GPA of 3.2. Additional exam requirements/recommendations for international students: Required—TOEFL (minimum score 600 paper-based; 250 computer-based). Electronic applications accepted. *Faculty research:* Cancer biology, immunology, joint injury and arthritis, medical education, population genomics.

University of Central Arkansas, Graduate School, College of Health and Behavioral Sciences, Department of Health Sciences, Conway, AR 72035-0001. Offers health education (MS); health systems (MS). *Faculty:* 9 full-time (5 women), 1 part-time/adjunct (0 women). *Students:* 17 full-time (14 women), 17 part-time (12 women); includes 18 minority (17 Black or African American, non-Hispanic/Latino; 1 Asian, non-Hispanic/Latino), 1 international. Average age 29. 13 applicants, 92% accepted, 10 enrolled. In 2011, 9 master's awarded. *Degree requirements:* For master's, comprehensive exam, thesis optional. *Entrance requirements:* For master's, GRE General Test, minimum GPA of 2.7. Additional exam requirements/recommendations for international students: Required—TOEFL (minimum score 550 paper-based; 213 computer-based). *Application deadline:* For fall admission, 3/1 priority date for domestic students; for spring admission, 10/1 for domestic students. Applications are processed on a rolling basis. Application fee: $25 ($50 for international students). *Expenses:* Tuition, state resident: full-time $4834; part-time $398.35 per credit hour. Tuition, nonresident: full-time $8686. *Financial support:* In 2011–12, 4 research assistantships (averaging $5,700 per year) were awarded; Federal Work-Study, scholarships/grants, tuition waivers (partial), and unspecified assistantships also available. Financial award application deadline: 2/15; financial award applicants required to submit FAFSA. *Unit head:* Dr. Emogene Fox, Chairperson, 501-450-5508, Fax: 501-450-5515, E-mail: emogenef@uca.edu. *Application contact:* Susan Wood, Administrative Specialist, 501-450-5063, Fax: 501-450-5678, E-mail: swood@uca.edu. Web site: http://www.uca.edu/divisions/academic/healthsci/.

University of Central Oklahoma, College of Graduate Studies and Research, College of Education and Professional Studies, Department of Occupational and Technical Education, Edmond, OK 73034-5209. Offers adult education (M Ed), including community services, gerontology; general education (M Ed); professional health occupations (M Ed). Part-time programs available. *Faculty:* 11 full-time (5 women), 11 part-time/adjunct (6 women). *Students:* 23 full-time (17 women), 76 part-time (59 women); includes 28 minority (15 Black or African American, non-Hispanic/Latino; 4 American Indian or Alaska Native, non-Hispanic/Latino; 6 Hispanic/Latino; 3 Two or more races, non-Hispanic/Latino), 3 international. Average age 40. In 2011, 64 master's awarded. *Entrance requirements:* For master's, GRE General Test. Additional exam requirements/recommendations for international students: Required—TOEFL (minimum score 550 paper-based; 213 computer-based). *Application deadline:* Applications are processed on a rolling basis. Application fee: $50. Electronic applications accepted. *Expenses:* Tuition, state resident: full-time $3901; part-time $218.30 per credit hour. Tuition, nonresident: full-time $9198; part-time $511.20 per credit hour. Tuition and fees vary according to program. *Financial support:* Unspecified assistantships available. Financial award application deadline: 3/31; financial award applicants required to submit FAFSA. *Faculty research:* Violence in the workplace/schools, aging issues, trade and industrial education. *Unit head:* Dr. Candy Sebert, Chairman, 405-974-5780, Fax: 405-974-3822. *Application contact:* Dr. Richard Bernard, Dean, Graduate College, 405-974-3493, Fax: 405-974-3852, E-mail: gradcoll@uco.edu.

University of Cincinnati, Graduate School, College of Education, Criminal Justice, and Human Services, Division of Human Services, Program in Health Promotion/Education, Cincinnati, OH 45221. Offers community health (MS); health education (MS, PhD); health promotion and education (M Ed). *Accreditation:* NCATE. Part-time and evening/weekend programs available. *Degree requirements:* For master's, thesis or alternative. *Entrance requirements:* For master's and doctorate, GRE General Test. Additional exam requirements/recommendations for international students: Required—TOEFL (minimum score 580 paper-based; 237 computer-based), OEPT. Electronic applications accepted.

University of Colorado Denver, College of Liberal Arts and Sciences, Program in Health and Behavioral Sciences, Denver, CO 80217. Offers PhD. Part-time and evening/weekend programs available. *Faculty:* 6 full-time (5 women), 2 part-time/adjunct (both women). *Students:* 23 full-time (19 women), 4 part-time (2 women); includes 4 minority (1 Black or African American, non-Hispanic/Latino; 3 Hispanic/Latino). Average age 36. 18 applicants, 39% accepted, 5 enrolled. In 2011, 3 doctorates awarded. *Degree requirements:* For doctorate, comprehensive exam, thesis/dissertation, minimum of 62 credit hours of course work. *Entrance requirements:* For doctorate, GRE, master's or equivalent graduate degree; prior coursework or experience in social or behavioral sciences (minimum 15 semester hours); human biology or physiology (minimum six semester hours); statistics and epidemiology (minimum three semester hours each); minimum undergraduate GPA of 3.25, graduate 3.5, three letters of recommendation, essay. Additional exam requirements/recommendations for international students: Required—TOEFL (minimum score 525 paper-based; 193 computer-based; 71 iBT). *Application deadline:* For fall admission, 2/15 for domestic and international students. Application fee: $50 ($75 for international students). Electronic applications accepted. *Financial support:* Fellowships with tuition reimbursements, research assistantships with tuition reimbursements, Federal Work-Study, scholarships/grants, and unspecified assistantships available. Financial award application deadline: 4/1; financial award applicants required to submit FAFSA. *Faculty research:* HIV/AIDS prevention, tobacco control, globalization and primary health care, social inequality and health, maternal and child health. *Unit head:* Dr. Debbi Main, Professor/Chair, 303-556-6743, E-mail: debbi.main@ucdenver.edu. *Application contact:* Abby Fitch, Program Assistant, 303-556-4300, Fax: 303-556-8501, E-mail: abby.fitch@ucdenver.edu. Web site: http://www.ucdenver.edu/academics/colleges/CLAS/Departments/hbsc/Programs/PhD/Pages/Overview.aspx.

University of Colorado Denver, Colorado School of Public Health, Program in Public Health, Aurora, CO 80045. Offers community and behavioral health (MPH, Dr PH); environmental and occupational health (MPH); epidemiology (MPH); health systems, management and policy (MPH). *Accreditation:* CEPH. Part-time and evening/weekend programs available. *Students:* 216 full-time (177 women), 47 part-time (38 women); includes 48 minority (10 Black or African American, non-Hispanic/Latino; 5 American Indian or Alaska Native, non-Hispanic/Latino; 14 Asian, non-Hispanic/Latino; 17 Hispanic/Latino; 1 Native Hawaiian or other Pacific Islander, non-Hispanic/Latino; 1 Two or more races, non-Hispanic/Latino), 7 international. Average age 33. 670 applicants, 51% accepted, 160 enrolled. In 2011, 83 degrees awarded. *Degree requirements:* For master's, thesis or alternative, 42 credit hours; for doctorate, comprehensive exam, thesis/dissertation, 67 credit hours. *Entrance requirements:* For master's, GRE, baccalaureate degree or equivalent; minimum GPA of 3.0; transcripts; references; resume; essay; for doctorate, GRE, MPH or master's or higher degree in related field or equivalent; 2 years previous work experience in public health, essay, resume. Additional exam requirements/recommendations for international students: Required—TOEFL (minimum score 550 paper-based; 213 computer-based). *Application deadline:* For fall admission, 2/1 for domestic students. Application fee: $65. Electronic applications accepted. *Expenses:* Contact institution. *Financial support:* Fellowships, research assistantships, Federal Work-Study, scholarships/grants, and unspecified assistantships available. Support available to part-time students. Financial award application deadline: 3/15; financial award applicants required to submit FAFSA. *Faculty research:* Cancer prevention by nutrition, cancer survivorship outcomes, social and cultural factors related to health. *Unit head:* Dr. Jack Barnette, Program Director, 303-724-4472, E-mail: jack.barnette@ucdenver.edu. *Application contact:* Jennifer Pacheco, Admissions Specialist, 303-724-5585, E-mail: jennifer.pacheco@ucdenver.edu. Web site: http://www.ucdenver.edu/academics/colleges/PublicHealth/departments/CommunityBehavioralHealth/Pages/CommunityBehavioralHealth.aspx.

University of Colorado Denver, School of Medicine, Physician Assistant Program, Aurora, CO 80045. Offers child health associate (MPAS), including global health, leadership, education, advocacy, development, and scholarship, rural health, urban/underserved populations. *Accreditation:* ARC-PA. *Students:* 124 full-time (107 women), 2 part-time (both women); includes 12 minority (1 American Indian or Alaska Native, non-Hispanic/Latino; 6 Asian, non-Hispanic/Latino; 5 Hispanic/Latino). Average age 26. 274 applicants, 17% accepted, 44 enrolled. In 2011, 37 master's awarded. *Degree requirements:* For master's, comprehensive exam, successful completion of all coursework and rotations. *Entrance requirements:* For master's, GRE General Test, minimum GPA of 2.8, 3 letters of recommendation, prerequisite courses in chemistry, biology, general genetics, psychology and statistics, interviews for the finalists. Additional exam requirements/recommendations for international students: Required—TOEFL (minimum score 550 paper-based; 213 computer-based). *Application deadline:* For fall admission, 10/1 for domestic students. Application fee: $170. Electronic applications accepted. *Expenses:* Contact institution. *Financial support:* Career-related internships or fieldwork and scholarships/grants available. Financial award application deadline: 3/15; financial award applicants required to submit FAFSA. *Faculty research:* Clinical genetics and genetic counseling, evidence-based medicine, pediatric allergy and asthma, childhood diabetes, standardized patient assessment. *Unit head:* Jonathan Bowser, Interim Program Director, 303-724-1349, E-mail: jonathan.bowser@ucdenver.edu. *Application contact:* Kay Denler, Director of Admissions, 303-724-1340, E-mail: kay.denler@ucdenver.edu. Web site: http://www.ucdenver.edu/academics/colleges/medicalschool/education/degree_programs/PAProgram/Pages/Home.aspx.

University of Florida, Graduate School, College of Health and Human Performance, Department of Health Education and Behavior, Gainesville, FL 32611. Offers health behavior (PhD); health communication (Graduate Certificate); health education and behavior (MS). *Accreditation:* NCATE (one or more programs are accredited). Part-time programs available. Terminal master's awarded for partial completion of doctoral program. *Degree requirements:* For master's, comprehensive exam, thesis (for some programs); for doctorate, comprehensive exam, thesis/dissertation. *Entrance requirements:* For master's and doctorate, GRE General Test, minimum GPA of 3.0. Additional exam requirements/recommendations for international students: Required—TOEFL (minimum score 550 paper-based; 213 computer-based; 80 iBT), IELTS (minimum score 6). Electronic applications accepted. *Faculty research:* Information technology and digital health for health promotion and disease prevention; prevention of high risk drinking among college students; scale development and measurement of youth prescription drug use; evaluation of state, regional, and community-based health education interventions.

University of Georgia, Biomedical and Health Sciences Institute, Athens, GA 30602. Offers neuroscience (PhD). *Students:* 21 full-time (13 women), 2 part-time (both women); includes 3 minority (1 Black or African American, non-Hispanic/Latino; 1 Asian, non-Hispanic/Latino; 1 Hispanic/Latino), 5 international. Average age 30. 42 applicants, 29% accepted, 9 enrolled. In 2011, 1 doctorate awarded. *Entrance requirements:* For doctorate, GRE, official transcripts, 3 letters of recommendation, statement of interest. Additional exam requirements/recommendations for international students: Required—TOEFL. *Financial support:* Unspecified assistantships available. Financial award application deadline: 12/31. *Unit head:* Dr. Harry Dailey, Director, 706-542-5922, Fax: 706-542-5285, E-mail: hdailey@uga.edu. *Application contact:* Joy Peterson, Graduate Coordinator, 706-542-2684, E-mail: biomfg@uga.edu. Web site: http://biomed.uga.edu.

University of Georgia, College of Public Health, Department of Health Promotion and Behavior, Athens, GA 30602. Offers MPH, PhD. *Accreditation:* CEPH; NCATE (one or more programs are accredited). *Faculty:* 8 full-time (6 women). *Students:* 22 full-time (20 women), 8 part-time (6 women); includes 11 minority (8 Black or African American, non-Hispanic/Latino; 2 Asian, non-Hispanic/Latino; 1 Hispanic/Latino), 4 international. Average age 32. 33 applicants, 21% accepted, 3 enrolled. In 2011, 3 doctorates awarded. *Degree requirements:* For master's, thesis (MA); for doctorate, thesis/dissertation. *Entrance requirements:* For master's, GRE General Test or MAT; for doctorate, GRE General Test. *Application deadline:* For fall admission, 7/1 priority date for domestic students; for spring admission, 11/15 for domestic students. Application fee: $50. Electronic applications accepted. *Financial support:* Fellowships, research assistantships, teaching assistantships, and unspecified assistantships available. *Unit head:* Dr. Mark G. Wilson, Head, 706-542-4364, Fax: 706-542-4956, E-mail: mwilson@uga.edu. *Application contact:* Dr. Marsha Davis, Graduate Coordinator, 706-542-4369, Fax: 706-542-4956, E-mail: davism@uga.edu. Web site: http://www.publichealth.uga.edu/hpb/.

University of Houston, College of Liberal Arts and Social Sciences, Department of Health and Human Performance, Houston, TX 77204. Offers exercise science (MS); human nutrition (MS); human space exploration sciences (MS); kinesiology (PhD); physical education (M Ed). *Accreditation:* NCATE (one or more programs are accredited). Part-time and evening/weekend programs available. *Degree requirements:* For master's, comprehensive exam (for some programs), thesis (for some programs); for doctorate, comprehensive exam, thesis/dissertation, qualifying exam, candidacy paper. *Entrance requirements:* For master's, GRE (minimum 35th percentile on each section), minimum cumulative GPA of 3.0; for doctorate, GRE (minimum 35th percentile on each section), minimum cumulative GPA of 3.3. Additional exam requirements/recommendations for international students: Required—TOEFL (minimum score 550 paper-based; 79 iBT). Electronic applications accepted. *Faculty research:* Biomechanics, exercise physiology, obesity, nutrition, space exploration science.

University of Illinois at Chicago, College of Medicine and Graduate College, Graduate Programs in Medicine, Department of Medical Education, Chicago, IL 60607-7128. Offers MHPE. Part-time programs available. *Degree requirements:* For master's, thesis. *Entrance requirements:* For master's, GRE General Test. Additional exam requirements/recommendations for international students: Required—TOEFL. Electronic applications accepted.

The University of Kansas, Graduate Studies, School of Education, Department of Health, Sport, and Exercise Sciences, Lawrence, KS 66045. Offers health and physical education (MS Ed, Ed D, PhD). *Accreditation:* NCATE. Part-time and evening/weekend programs available. *Faculty:* 11 full-time (4 women), 2 part-time/adjunct (0 women). *Students:* 43 full-time (20 women), 20 part-time (10 women); includes 8 minority (2 Asian, non-Hispanic/Latino; 3 Hispanic/Latino; 3 Two or more races, non-Hispanic/Latino), 3 international. Average age 29. 63 applicants, 46% accepted, 22 enrolled. In 2011, 34 master's, 1 doctorate awarded. *Degree requirements:* For master's, comprehensive exam (for some programs), thesis (for some programs); for doctorate, variable foreign language requirement, comprehensive exam, thesis/dissertation. *Entrance requirements:* For master's, GRE General Test (minimum score 1000, 450 verbal, 450 quantitative, 4.0 analytical), minimum GPA of 3.0; for doctorate, GRE General Test (minimum score 1100: verbal 500, quantitative 500, analytical 4.5), minimum graduate GPA of 3.5, undergraduate 3.0. Additional exam requirements/recommendations for international students: Required—TOEFL (minimum score 570 paper-based; 230 computer-based). *Application deadline:* For fall admission, 3/15 priority date for domestic students; for spring admission, 10/15 priority date for domestic students. Applications are processed on a rolling basis. Application fee: $55 ($65 for international students). Electronic applications accepted. Tuition and fees vary according to course load, campus/location, program and reciprocity agreements. *Financial support:* Research assistantships with full and partial tuition reimbursements and teaching assistantships with full and partial tuition reimbursements available. Financial award application deadline: 4/1. *Faculty research:* Exercise and sport psychology, obesity prevention, sexuality health, sport ethics, skeletal muscle cell signaling and performance. *Unit head:* Dr. Andrew Fry, Chair, 785-864-0784, Fax: 785-864-3343, E-mail: acfry@ku.edu. *Application contact:* Dr. Keith D. Tennant, Graduate Coordinator, 785-864-4656, Fax: 785-864-3343, E-mail: ktennant@ku.edu. Web site: http://www.soe.ku.edu/hses/.

The University of Kansas, University of Kansas Medical Center, School of Nursing, Kansas City, KS 66160. Offers adult/gerontological clinical nurse specialist (PMC); adult/gerontological nurse practitioner (PMC); clinical research management (PMC); family nurse practitioner (PMC); health care informatics (PMC); health professions educator (PMC); nurse midwife (PMC); nursing (MS, DNP, PhD); organizational leadership (PMC); psychiatric/mental health nurse practitioner (PMC); public health nursing (PMC). *Accreditation:* AACN; ACNM/ACME. Part-time programs available. Postbaccalaureate distance learning degree programs offered (minimal on-campus study). *Faculty:* 80. *Students:* 79 full-time (71 women), 336 part-time (317 women); includes 63 minority (24 Black or African American, non-Hispanic/Latino; 2 American Indian or Alaska Native, non-Hispanic/Latino; 18 Asian, non-Hispanic/Latino; 15 Hispanic/Latino; 4 Two or more races, non-Hispanic/Latino), 6 international. Average age 37. 155 applicants, 82% accepted, 127 enrolled. In 2011, 79 master's, 15 doctorates, 12 other advanced degrees awarded. Terminal master's awarded for partial completion of doctoral program. *Degree requirements:* For master's, comprehensive exam, thesis optional, general oral exam; for doctorate, variable foreign language requirement, thesis/dissertation, comprehensive oral exam (for DNP); comprehensive written and oral exam (for PhD). *Entrance requirements:* For master's, bachelor's degree in nursing, minimum GPA of 3.0, RN license, 1 year of clinical experience, RN license in KS and MO; for doctorate, GRE General Test, master's degree in nursing, minimum GPA of 3.5, RN license in KS and MO; national certification (for some specialties). Additional exam requirements/recommendations for international students: Required—TOEFL. *Application deadline:* For fall admission, 4/1 for domestic and international students; for spring admission, 9/1 for domestic and international students. Application fee: $60. Electronic applications accepted. Tuition and fees vary according to course load, campus/location, program and reciprocity agreements. *Financial support:* Research assistantships with full and partial tuition reimbursements, teaching assistantships with full and partial tuition reimbursements, and traineeships available. Financial award application deadline: 2/14; financial award applicants required to submit FAFSA. *Faculty research:* Breastfeeding practices of teen mothers, national database of nursing quality indicators, caregiving of families of patients using technology in the home, simulation in nursing education, diaphragm fatigue. *Total annual research expenditures:* $6.1 million. *Unit head:* Dr. Karen L. Miller, Dean, 913-588-1601, Fax: 913-588-1660, E-mail: kmiller@kumc.edu. *Application contact:* Dr. Debra J. Ford, Associate Dean, Student Affairs, 913-588-1619, Fax: 913-588-1615, E-mail: dford@kumc.edu. Web site: http://nursing.kumc.edu.

University of Louisville, Graduate School, College of Education and Human Development, Department of Health and Sport Sciences, Louisville, KY 40292-0001. Offers community health education (M Ed); exercise physiology (MS); health and physical education (MAT); sport administration (MS). Part-time and evening/weekend programs available. *Entrance requirements:* For master's, GRE General Test. Additional exam requirements/recommendations for international students: Required—TOEFL (minimum score 560 paper-based; 210 computer-based; 83 iBT). Electronic applications accepted. *Expenses:* Tuition, state resident: full-time $9692; part-time $539 per credit hour. Tuition, nonresident: full-time $20,168; part-time $1121 per credit hour. Tuition and fees vary according to program and reciprocity agreements. *Faculty research:* Impact of sports and sport marketing on society, factors associated with school and community health, cardiac and pulmonary rehabilitation, impact of participation in activities on student retention and graduation, strength and conditioning.

University of Louisville, Graduate School, School of Nursing, Louisville, KY 40202. Offers adult nurse practitioner (MSN); family nurse practitioner (MSN); health professions education (MSN); neonatal nurse practitioner (MSN); nursing research (PhD); psychiatric mental health nurse practitioner (MSN). *Accreditation:* AACN. Part-time programs available. *Faculty:* 24 full-time (22 women), 4 part-time/adjunct (3 women). *Students:* 82 full-time (74 women), 65 part-time (58 women); includes 20 minority (13 Black or African American, non-Hispanic/Latino; 1 American Indian or Alaska Native, non-Hispanic/Latino; 1 Asian, non-Hispanic/Latino; 1 Hispanic/Latino; 4 Two or more races, non-Hispanic/Latino), 9 international. Average age 34. 41 applicants, 56% accepted, 19 enrolled. In 2011, 42 master's, 2 doctorates awarded. Terminal master's awarded for partial completion of doctoral program. *Degree requirements:* For master's, thesis optional; for doctorate, comprehensive exam, thesis/dissertation. *Entrance requirements:* For master's, GRE General Test, bachelor's degree in nursing, minimum GPA of 3.0, RN license; for doctorate, GRE General Test, BSN or MSN with recommended minimum GPA of 3.0. Additional exam requirements/recommendations for international students: Required—TOEFL. *Application deadline:* For fall admission, 4/1 priority date for domestic students, 4/1 for international students. Applications are processed on a rolling basis. Application fee: $50. Electronic applications accepted. *Expenses:* Tuition, state resident: full-time $9692; part-time $539 per credit hour. Tuition, nonresident: full-time $20,168; part-time $1121 per credit hour. Tuition and fees vary according to program and reciprocity agreements. *Financial support:* In 2011–12, 45 students received support, including 6 research assistantships with full tuition reimbursements available (averaging $20,000 per year), 6 teaching assistantships with full tuition reimbursements available (averaging $19,167 per year); fellowships with full tuition reimbursements available, institutionally sponsored loans, scholarships/grants, traineeships, health care benefits, and unspecified assistantships also available. Support available to part-time students. Financial award application deadline: 4/15; financial award applicants required to submit FAFSA. *Faculty research:* Maternal-child/family stress after pregnancy loss, postpartum depression, access to healthcare (underserved populations), quality of life issues, physical activity (impact on chronic/acute conditions). *Total annual research expenditures:* $795,250. *Unit head:* Dr. Marcia J. Hern, Dean, 502-852-8300, Fax: 502-852-5044, E-mail: m.hern@gwise.louisville.edu. *Application contact:* Dr. Lee Ridner, Interim Associate Dean for Academic Affairs and Director of MSN Programs, 502-852-8518, Fax: 502-852-0704, E-mail: romain01@louisville.edu. Web site: http://www.louisville.edu/nursing/.

University of Maryland, Baltimore County, Graduate School, College of Arts, Humanities and Social Sciences, Department of Emergency Health Services, Baltimore, MD 21250. Offers administration, planning, and policy (MS); education (MS); emergency health services (MS); emergency management (Postbaccalaureate Certificate); preventive medicine and epidemiology (MS). Part-time and evening/weekend programs available. Postbaccalaureate distance learning degree programs offered (no on-campus study). *Faculty:* 2 full-time (0 women), 7 part-time/adjunct (1 woman). *Students:* 20 full-time (8 women), 21 part-time (10 women); includes 2 minority (both Black or African American, non-Hispanic/Latino), 6 international. Average age 32. 13 applicants, 85% accepted, 10 enrolled. In 2011, 13 master's awarded. *Degree requirements:* For master's, comprehensive exam, thesis (for some programs). *Entrance requirements:* For master's, GRE General Test, minimum GPA of 3.0. Additional exam requirements/recommendations for international students: Required—TOEFL (minimum score 85 iBT). *Application deadline:* For fall admission, 7/1 for domestic students, 4/1 for international students. Applications are processed on a rolling basis. Application fee: $45. Electronic applications accepted. *Financial support:* In 2011–12, 2 students received support, including 1 fellowship with tuition reimbursement available (averaging $70,000 per year), 1 research assistantship with tuition reimbursement available (averaging $21,000 per year); career-related internships or fieldwork, Federal Work-Study, health care benefits, and unspecified assistantships also available. Financial award application deadline: 5/30; financial award applicants required to submit FAFSA. *Faculty research:* EMS management, disaster health services, emergency management. *Total annual research expenditures:* $50,000. *Unit head:* Dr. Bruce Walz, Chairman, 410-455-3223. *Application contact:* Dr. Rick Bissell, Program Director, 410-455-3776, Fax: 410-455-3045, E-mail: bissell@umbc.edu. Web site: http://ehs.umbc.edu/.

University of Maryland, College Park, Academic Affairs, School of Public Health, Department of Behavioral and Community Health, College Park, MD 20742. Offers community health education (MPH); public/community health (PhD). *Accreditation:* CEPH. Part-time and evening/weekend programs available. *Faculty:* 30 full-time (19 women), 7 part-time/adjunct (6 women). *Students:* 36 full-time (30 women), 17 part-time (15 women); includes 27 minority (16 Black or African American, non-Hispanic/Latino; 1 American Indian or Alaska Native, non-Hispanic/Latino; 8 Asian, non-Hispanic/Latino; 2 Hispanic/Latino), 5 international. 158 applicants, 34% accepted, 18 enrolled. In 2011, 7 master's, 1 doctorate awarded. *Degree requirements:* For master's, thesis optional; for doctorate, comprehensive exam, thesis/dissertation. *Entrance requirements:* For master's, GRE General Test, minimum GPA of 3.0, 3 letters of recommendation; for doctorate, GRE General Test, minimum GPA of 3.5, 3 letters of recommendation. Additional exam requirements/recommendations for international students: Required—TOEFL. *Application deadline:* For fall admission, 1/15 for domestic and international students. Applications are processed on a rolling basis. Application fee: $75. Electronic applications accepted. *Expenses: Tuition, area resident:* Part-time $525 per credit hour. Tuition, state resident: part-time $525 per credit hour. Tuition, nonresident: part-time $1131 per credit hour. *Required fees:* $386.31 per term. Tuition and fees vary according to program. *Financial support:* In 2011–12, 18 teaching assistantships (averaging $15,913 per year) were awarded; fellowships, research assistantships, career-related internships or fieldwork, Federal Work-Study, and scholarships/grants also available. Support available to part-time students. Financial award applicants required to submit FAFSA. *Faculty research:* Controlling stress and tension, women's health, aging and public policy, adolescent health, long-term care. *Total annual research expenditures:* $3.4 million. *Unit head:* Dr. Elbert Glover, Chair, 301-405-2467, Fax: 301-314-9167, E-mail: eglover1@umd.edu. *Application contact:* Dr. Charles A. Caramello, Dean of Graduate School, 301-405-0358, Fax: 301-314-9305. Web site: http://www.sph.umd.edu/bch/.

University of Massachusetts Amherst, Graduate School, School of Public Health and Health Sciences, Department of Public Health, Amherst, MA 01003. Offers biostatistics (MPH, MS, PhD); community health education (MPH, MS, PhD); environmental health sciences (MPH, MS, PhD); epidemiology (MPH, MS, PhD); health policy and management (MPH, MS, PhD); nutrition (MPH, PhD); public health practice (MPH); MPH/MPPA. *Accreditation:* CEPH (one or more programs are accredited). Part-time and evening/weekend programs available. Postbaccalaureate distance learning degree programs offered (no on-campus study). *Faculty:* 46 full-time (26 women). *Students:* 118 full-time (88 women), 249 part-time (183 women); includes 75 minority (28 Black or African American, non-Hispanic/Latino; 21 Asian, non-Hispanic/Latino; 20 Hispanic/Latino; 6 Two or more races, non-Hispanic/Latino), 55 international. Average age 36. 377 applicants, 67% accepted, 91 enrolled. In 2011, 83 master's, 4 doctorates awarded. Terminal master's awarded for partial completion of doctoral program. *Degree requirements:* For master's, thesis (for some programs); for doctorate, comprehensive exam, thesis/dissertation. *Entrance requirements:* For master's and doctorate, GRE

General Test. Additional exam requirements/recommendations for international students: Required—TOEFL (minimum score 550 paper-based; 213 computer-based; 80 iBT), IELTS (minimum score 6.5). *Application deadline:* For fall admission, 2/1 for domestic and international students. Applications are processed on a rolling basis. Application fee: $40 ($65 for international students). Electronic applications accepted. Tuition and fees vary according to course load, campus/location and program. *Financial support:* Fellowships with full and partial tuition reimbursements, research assistantships with full and partial tuition reimbursements, teaching assistantships with full and partial tuition reimbursements, career-related internships or fieldwork, Federal Work-Study, scholarships/grants, traineeships, health care benefits, tuition waivers (full and partial), and unspecified assistantships available. Support available to part-time students. Financial award application deadline: 2/1. *Unit head:* Dr. Paula Stamps, Graduate Program Director, 413-545-2861, Fax: 413-545-1645. *Application contact:* Lindsay DeSantis, Interim Supervisor of Admissions, 413-545-0722, Fax: 413-577-0010, E-mail: gradadm@grad.umass.edu. Web site: http://www.umass.edu/sphhs/public_health/.

University of Medicine and Dentistry of New Jersey, School of Health Related Professions, Department of Interdisciplinary Studies, Program in Health Sciences, Newark, NJ 07107-1709. Offers cardiopulmonary sciences (PhD); clinical laboratory sciences (PhD); health sciences (MS); interdisciplinary studies (PhD); nutrition (PhD); physical therapy/movement science (PhD). Part-time and evening/weekend programs available. Postbaccalaureate distance learning degree programs offered (no on-campus study). *Faculty:* 4 full-time (all women), 10 part-time/adjunct (7 women). *Students:* 3 full-time, 130 part-time; includes 32 minority (10 Black or African American, non-Hispanic/Latino; 10 Asian, non-Hispanic/Latino; 11 Hispanic/Latino; 1 Native Hawaiian or other Pacific Islander, non-Hispanic/Latino). Average age 41. 132 applicants, 51% accepted, 51 enrolled. In 2011, 17 master's, 4 doctorates awarded. *Degree requirements:* For doctorate, thesis/dissertation. *Entrance requirements:* For master's, BS, 2 reference letters, statement of career goals, curriculum vitae; for doctorate, GRE, interview, writing sample, 3 reference letters, curriculum vitae. Additional exam requirements/recommendations for international students: Required—TOEFL. *Application deadline:* For fall admission, 3/1 for domestic students. Applications are processed on a rolling basis. Application fee: $75. Electronic applications accepted. *Unit head:* Dr. Bob Denmark, Director, 973-972-5410, Fax: 973-972-7403, E-mail: ms-phd-hs@umdnj.edu. *Application contact:* Diane Hanrahan, Manager of Admissions, 973-972-5336, Fax: 973-972-7463, E-mail: shrpadm@umdnj.edu.

University of Medicine and Dentistry of New Jersey, UMDNJ–School of Public Health (UMDNJ, Rutgers, NJIT) Piscataway/New Brunswick Campus, Piscataway, NJ 08854. Offers biostatistics (MPH, MS, Dr PH, PhD); clinical epidemiology (Certificate); environmental and occupational health (MPH, Dr PH, PhD, Certificate); epidemiology (MPH, Dr PH, PhD); general public health (Certificate); health education and behavioral science (MPH, Dr PH, PhD); health systems and policy (MPH, PhD); public health preparedness (Certificate); DO/MPH; JD/MPH; MD/MPH; MPH/MBA; MPH/MSPA; MS/MPH; Psy D/MPH. *Accreditation:* CEPH. Part-time and evening/weekend programs available. *Degree requirements:* For master's, thesis, internship; for doctorate, comprehensive exam, thesis/dissertation. *Entrance requirements:* For master's, GRE General Test; for doctorate, GRE General Test, MPH (Dr PH); MA, MPH, or MS (PhD). Additional exam requirements/recommendations for international students: Required—TOEFL. Electronic applications accepted.

University of Michigan, School of Public Health, Department of Health Behavior and Health Education, Ann Arbor, MI 48109. Offers MPH, PhD, MPH/MSW. PhD offered through the Horace H. Rackham School of Graduate Studies. *Accreditation:* CEPH (one or more programs are accredited). Terminal master's awarded for partial completion of doctoral program. *Degree requirements:* For doctorate, oral defense of dissertation, preliminary exam. *Entrance requirements:* For master's, GRE General Test (preferred); MCAT; for doctorate, GRE General Test. Additional exam requirements/recommendations for international students: Required—TOEFL (minimum score 560 paper-based; 220 computer-based; 100 iBT). Electronic applications accepted. *Faculty research:* Empowerment theory; structure, culture, and health; health disparities; community-based participatory research; health and medical decision-making.

University of Michigan–Flint, School of Health Professions and Studies, Program in Health Education, Flint, MI 48502-1950. Offers MS. Part-time programs available. *Degree requirements:* For master's, thesis or alternative, internship or current employment as health educator. *Entrance requirements:* For master's, minimum GPA of 2.8; course work in anatomy, physiology, statistics, speech, and developmental psychology. Additional exam requirements/recommendations for international students: Required—TOEFL (minimum score 560 paper-based; 220 computer-based; 84 iBT), IELTS (minimum score 6.5). Electronic applications accepted. *Expenses:* Contact institution. *Faculty research:* Minority health, health disparities, cultural competency, HIV/AIDS, women's health.

University of Missouri, Graduate School, College of Education, Department of Learning, Teaching and Curriculum, Columbia, MO 65211. Offers agricultural education (M Ed, PhD, Ed S); art education (M Ed, PhD, Ed S); business and office education (M Ed, PhD, Ed S); early childhood education (M Ed, PhD, Ed S); elementary education (M Ed, PhD, Ed S); English education (M Ed, PhD, Ed S); foreign language education (M Ed, PhD, Ed S); health education and promotion (M Ed, PhD); learning and instruction (M Ed); marketing education (M Ed, PhD, Ed S); mathematics education (M Ed, PhD, Ed S); music education (M Ed, PhD, Ed S); reading education (M Ed, PhD, Ed S); science education (M Ed, PhD, Ed S); social studies education (M Ed, PhD, Ed S); vocational education (M Ed, PhD, Ed S). Part-time programs available. *Faculty:* 26 full-time (16 women), 3 part-time/adjunct (2 women). *Students:* 184 full-time (145 women), 276 part-time (215 women); includes 34 minority (10 Black or African American, non-Hispanic/Latino; 1 American Indian or Alaska Native, non-Hispanic/Latino; 7 Asian, non-Hispanic/Latino; 8 Hispanic/Latino; 8 Two or more races, non-Hispanic/Latino), 39 international. Average age 32. 309 applicants, 76% accepted, 204 enrolled. In 2011, 232 master's, 8 doctorates, 2 other advanced degrees awarded. Terminal master's awarded for partial completion of doctoral program. *Degree requirements:* For doctorate, thesis/dissertation. *Entrance requirements:* For master's and Ed S, GRE General Test or MAT, minimum GPA of 3.0; for doctorate, GRE General Test, minimum GPA of 3.0. Additional exam requirements/recommendations for international students: Required—TOEFL (minimum score 600 paper-based; 250 computer-based; 100 iBT). Application fee: $55 ($75 for international students). Electronic applications accepted. *Expenses:* Tuition, state resident: full-time $5881. Tuition, nonresident: full-time $15,183. *Required fees:* $952. Tuition and fees vary according to campus/location and program. *Financial support:* Fellowships, research assistantships, teaching assistantships, and institutionally sponsored loans available. *Application contact:* Fran Colley, 573-882-6462, E-mail: colleyf@missouri.edu. Web site: http://education.missouri.edu/LTC/.

The University of Montana, Graduate School, Phyllis J. Washington College of Education and Human Sciences, Department of Health and Human Performance, Missoula, MT 59812-0002. Offers exercise science (MS); health and human performance (MS); health promotion (MS). Part-time programs available. *Entrance requirements:* For master's, GRE General Test. Additional exam requirements/recommendations for international students: Required—TOEFL. *Faculty research:* Exercise physiology, performance psychology, nutrition, pre-employment physical screening, program evaluation.

University of Nebraska at Omaha, Graduate Studies, College of Education, School of Health, Physical Education, and Recreation, Omaha, NE 68182. Offers athletic training (MA); health, physical education, and recreation (MA, MS). Part-time and evening/weekend programs available. *Faculty:* 13 full-time (4 women). *Students:* 37 full-time (15 women), 40 part-time (25 women); includes 4 minority (1 Black or African American, non-Hispanic/Latino; 2 Hispanic/Latino; 1 Two or more races, non-Hispanic/Latino), 2 international. Average age 27. 27 applicants, 67% accepted, 15 enrolled. In 2011, 33 master's awarded. *Degree requirements:* For master's, comprehensive exam, thesis (for some programs). *Entrance requirements:* For master's, minimum GPA of 3.0, statement of purpose, letters of recommendation. Additional exam requirements/recommendations for international students: Required—TOEFL (minimum score 550 paper-based; 213 computer-based; 80 iBT). *Application deadline:* For fall admission, 7/1 priority date for domestic students; for spring admission, 12/1 priority date for domestic students. Applications are processed on a rolling basis. Application fee: $45. Electronic applications accepted. *Financial support:* In 2011–12, 40 students received support, including 25 research assistantships with tuition reimbursements available, 10 teaching assistantships with tuition reimbursements available; fellowships, Federal Work-Study, institutionally sponsored loans, scholarships/grants, tuition waivers (full), and unspecified assistantships also available. Support available to part-time students. Financial award application deadline: 3/1; financial award applicants required to submit FAFSA. *Unit head:* Dr. Dan Blanke, Director, 402-554-2670. *Application contact:* Dr. Kris Berg, 402-554-2341, Fax: 402-554-3143, E-mail: graduate@unomaha.edu.

University of New England, College of Osteopathic Medicine, Program in Medical Education Leadership, Biddeford, ME 04005-9526. Offers MS. *Faculty:* 1 full-time, 1 part-time/adjunct. *Students:* 22 full-time (15 women), 4 part-time (2 women). In 2011, 18 master's awarded. *Unit head:* India Broyles, Director, 207-602-2694, Fax: 207-602-5977, E-mail: ibroyles@une.edu. *Application contact:* Stacy Gato, Director of Graduate and Professional Admissions, 207-283-0171, Fax: 207-602-5900, E-mail: gradadmissions@une.edu. Web site: http://www.une.edu/com/mmel/index.cfm.

University of New Mexico, Graduate School, College of Education, Department of Health, Exercise and Sports Sciences, Program in Health Education, Albuquerque, NM 87131-2039. Offers community health education (MS). *Accreditation:* NCATE. Part-time programs available. *Students:* 24 full-time (21 women), 15 part-time (11 women); includes 21 minority (5 Black or African American, non-Hispanic/Latino; 2 American Indian or Alaska Native, non-Hispanic/Latino; 1 Asian, non-Hispanic/Latino; 12 Hispanic/Latino; 1 Two or more races, non-Hispanic/Latino), 3 international. Average age 32. 23 applicants, 87% accepted, 14 enrolled. In 2011, 12 degrees awarded. *Degree requirements:* For master's, comprehensive exam, thesis optional. *Entrance requirements:* For master's, 3 letters of reference, resume, minimum cumulative GPA of 3.0 in last 2 years of bachelor's degree, letter of intent. Additional exam requirements/recommendations for international students: Required—TOEFL (minimum score 550 paper-based; 213 computer-based). *Application deadline:* For fall admission, 6/15 priority date for domestic students; for spring admission, 11/1 priority date for domestic students. Applications are processed on a rolling basis. Application fee: $50. Electronic applications accepted. *Financial support:* In 2011–12, 23 students received support, including 2 fellowships (averaging $2,290 per year), 3 teaching assistantships with full tuition reimbursements available (averaging $11,911 per year); career-related internships or fieldwork, institutionally sponsored loans, scholarships/grants, and health care benefits also available. Financial award application deadline: 3/1; financial award applicants required to submit FAFSA. *Faculty research:* Alcohol and families, health behaviors and sexuality, multicultural health behavior, health promotion policy, school/community-based prevention, health and aging. *Total annual research expenditures:* $91,910. *Unit head:* Dr. Elias Duryea, Coordinator, 505-277-5151, Fax: 505-277-6227, E-mail: duryea@unm.edu. *Application contact:* Carol Catania, Graduate Coordinator, 505-277-5151, Fax: 505-277-6227, E-mail: catania@unm.edu. Web site: http://coe.unm.edu/departments/hess/health-education/health-education-ms.html.

The University of North Carolina at Chapel Hill, Graduate School, School of Public Health, Department of Health Behavior and Health Education, Chapel Hill, NC 27599. Offers MPH, PhD, MPH/MCRP. *Accreditation:* CEPH (one or more programs are accredited). *Degree requirements:* For master's, comprehensive exam, thesis, major paper; for doctorate, comprehensive exam, thesis/dissertation. *Entrance requirements:* For master's, GRE General Test, minimum GPA of 3.0; for doctorate, GRE General Test, minimum GPA of 3.0, master's degree. Additional exam requirements/recommendations for international students: Required—TOEFL. Electronic applications accepted. *Faculty research:* Cancer prevention and control, aging health promotion and disease prevention, adolescent health, nutrition intervention.

University of Northern Colorado, Graduate School, College of Natural and Health Sciences, School of Human Sciences, Program in Public Health, Greeley, CO 80639. Offers public health education (MPH). *Accreditation:* CEPH. *Degree requirements:* For master's, comprehensive exam, thesis or alternative. *Entrance requirements:* For master's, GRE General Test, 2 letters of recommendation. Electronic applications accepted.

University of Northern Iowa, Graduate College, College of Education, School of Health, Physical Education, and Leisure Services, Division of Health Promotion and Education, Cedar Falls, IA 50614. Offers community health education (Ed D); health education (MA). Part-time and evening/weekend programs available. *Students:* 15 full-time (10 women), 14 part-time (13 women); includes 5 minority (4 Black or African American, non-Hispanic/Latino; 1 Hispanic/Latino), 4 international. 27 applicants, 81% accepted, 8 enrolled. In 2011, 9 master's awarded. *Degree requirements:* For master's, comprehensive exam, thesis or alternative; for doctorate, thesis/dissertation. *Entrance requirements:* For master's, minimum GPA of 3.0; for doctorate, GRE, minimum GPA of 3.5. Additional exam requirements/recommendations for international students: Required—TOEFL (minimum score 500 paper-based; 180 computer-based; 61 iBT). *Application deadline:* For fall admission, 8/1 priority date for domestic students. Applications are processed on a rolling basis. Application fee: $50 ($70 for international students). Electronic applications accepted. *Expenses:* Tuition, state resident: full-time $7476. Tuition, nonresident: full-time $16,410. *Required fees:* $942. *Financial support:* Career-related internships or fieldwork, Federal Work-Study, and tuition waivers (full and partial) available. Support available to part-time students. Financial award application deadline: 2/1. *Unit head:* Dr. Diane Depken, Coordinator, 319-273-7287, Fax: 319-273-5958, E-mail: diane.depken@uni.edu. *Application contact:* Laurie S. Russell, Record Analyst, 319-273-2623, Fax: 319-273-2885, E-mail: laurie.russell@uni.edu. Web site: http://www.uni.edu/coe/hpels/HealthPromotion&Ed/.

University of Oklahoma Health Sciences Center, Graduate College, College of Allied Health, Department of Allied Health Sciences, Oklahoma City, OK 73190. Offers PhD. *Degree requirements:* For doctorate, one foreign language, comprehensive exam, thesis/dissertation optional. *Entrance requirements:* For doctorate, GRE General Test, 3 letters of recommendation, master's degree. Additional exam requirements/recommendations for international students: Required—TOEFL (minimum score 550 paper-based).

University of Phoenix–Charlotte Campus, College of Nursing, Charlotte, NC 28273-3409. Offers education (MHA); gerontology (MHA); health administration (MHA); informatics (MHA, MSN); nursing (MSN); nursing/health care education (MSN). Evening/weekend programs available. *Degree requirements:* For master's, thesis (for some programs). *Entrance requirements:* For master's, minimum undergraduate GPA of 2.5, 3 years work experience. Additional exam requirements/recommendations for international students: Required—TOEFL (minimum score 550 paper-based; 213 computer-based; 79 iBT). Electronic applications accepted.

University of Phoenix–Des Moines Campus, College of Nursing, Des Moines, IA 50266. Offers education (MHA); gerontology (MHA); health administration (MHA, DHA); informatics (MHA, MSN); nursing (MSN, PhD); nursing/health care education (MSN).

University of Phoenix–Milwaukee Campus, College of Nursing, Milwaukee, WI 53045. Offers education (MHA); gerontology (MHA); health administration (MHA, DHA); informatics (MHA, MSN); nursing (MSN, PhD); nursing/health care education (MSN); MSN/MBA; MSN/MHA.

University of Phoenix–Online Campus, College of Natural Sciences, Phoenix, AZ 85034-7209. Offers education (MHA); gerontology (MHA, Graduate Certificate); health administration (MHA); health care informatics (Graduate Certificate); health care management (Graduate Certificate), including lifelong learning; informatics (MHA). Evening/weekend programs available. Postbaccalaureate distance learning degree programs offered. *Students:* 2,854 full-time (2,408 women); includes 1,137 minority (855 Black or African American, non-Hispanic/Latino; 24 American Indian or Alaska Native, non-Hispanic/Latino; 73 Asian, non-Hispanic/Latino; 140 Hispanic/Latino; 18 Native Hawaiian or other Pacific Islander, non-Hispanic/Latino; 27 Two or more races, non-Hispanic/Latino), 91 international. Average age 39. *Entrance requirements:* Additional exam requirements/recommendations for international students: Required—TOEFL, TOEIC (Test of English as an International Communication), Berlitz Online English Proficiency Exam, Pearson Test of English, or IELTS. *Application deadline:* Applications are processed on a rolling basis. Application fee: $45. Electronic applications accepted. *Expenses: Tuition:* Full-time $17,160. *Required fees:* $920. One-time fee: $45 full-time. Full-time tuition and fees vary according to course load, degree level, campus/location and program. *Financial support:* Scholarships/grants available. Financial award applicants required to submit FAFSA. *Unit head:* Dr. Hinrich Eylers, Dean/Associate Provost, 866-766-0766. *Application contact:* 866-766-0766. Web site: http://www.phoenix.edu/colleges_divisions/natural-sciences.html.

University of Phoenix–Phoenix Main Campus, College of Natural Science, Tempe, AZ 85282-2371. Offers education (MHA); gerontology (MHA); gerontology health care (Certificate); health administration (MHA); informatics (MHA). Evening/weekend programs available. Postbaccalaureate distance learning degree programs offered. *Students:* 27 full-time (17 women); includes 10 minority (4 Black or African American, non-Hispanic/Latino; 1 American Indian or Alaska Native, non-Hispanic/Latino; 1 Asian, non-Hispanic/Latino; 4 Hispanic/Latino). Average age 42. *Entrance requirements:* Additional exam requirements/recommendations for international students: Required—TOEFL, TOEIC (Test of English as an International Communication), Berlitz Online English Proficiency Exam, Pearson Test of English, or IELTS. *Application deadline:* Applications are processed on a rolling basis. Application fee: $45. Electronic applications accepted. *Expenses:* Contact institution. *Financial support:* Scholarships/grants available. Financial award applicants required to submit FAFSA. *Unit head:* Dr. Hinrich Eylers, Dean/Associate Provost, 866-766-0766. *Application contact:* 866-766-0766. Web site: http://www.phoenix.edu/colleges_divisions/natural-sciences.html.

University of Phoenix–Raleigh Campus, College of Nursing, Raleigh, NC 27606. Offers education (MHA); gerontology (MHA); health administration (MHA, DHA); informatics (MHA, MSN); nursing (MSN, PhD); nursing/health care education (MSN).

University of Phoenix–Southern Colorado Campus, College of Nursing, Colorado Springs, CO 80919-2335. Offers education (MHA); gerontology (MHA); health administration (MHA); nursing (MSN); MSN/MBA. Evening/weekend programs available. *Degree requirements:* For master's, thesis (for some programs). *Entrance requirements:* For master's, minimum undergraduate GPA of 2.5, 3 years of work experience, RN license. Additional exam requirements/recommendations for international students: Required—TOEFL (minimum score 550 paper-based; 213 computer-based; 79 iBT). Electronic applications accepted.

University of Phoenix–Washington D.C. Campus, College of Nursing, Washington, DC 20001. Offers education (MHA); gerontology (MHA); health administration (MHA, DHA); informatics (MHA, MSN); nursing (MSN, PhD); nursing/health care education (MSN); MSN/MBA; MSN/MHA.

University of Pittsburgh, Graduate School of Public Health, Department of Infectious Diseases and Microbiology, Pittsburgh, PA 15260. Offers bioscience of infectious diseases (MPH); community and behavioral intervention of infectious diseases (MPH); infectious diseases and microbiology (MS, PhD); LGBT health and wellness (Certificate). Part-time programs available. *Faculty:* 21 full-time (6 women), 24 part-time/adjunct (7 women). *Students:* 57 full-time (44 women), 13 part-time (9 women); includes 15 minority (4 Black or African American, non-Hispanic/Latino; 9 Asian, non-Hispanic/Latino; 2 Hispanic/Latino), 7 international. Average age 27. 157 applicants, 56% accepted, 29 enrolled. In 2011, 13 master's, 3 doctorates awarded. Terminal master's awarded for partial completion of doctoral program. *Degree requirements:* For master's, one foreign language, comprehensive exam (for some programs), thesis; for doctorate, one foreign language, comprehensive exam, thesis/dissertation. *Entrance requirements:* For master's and doctorate, GRE General Test, MCAT, or DAT. Additional exam requirements/recommendations for international students: Required—TOEFL (minimum score 550 paper-based; 80 iBT) or IELTS (minimum score 6.5). *Application deadline:* For fall admission, 1/4 priority date for domestic students, 1/4 for international students. Applications are processed on a rolling basis. Application fee: $115. Electronic applications accepted. *Expenses:* Tuition, state resident: full-time $18,774; part-time $760 per credit. Tuition, nonresident: full-time $30,736; part-time $1258 per credit. *Required fees:* $740; $200 per term. Tuition and fees vary according to program. *Financial support:* In 2011–12, 31 students received support, including 12 fellowships (averaging $7,248 per year), 19 research assistantships with full and partial tuition reimbursements available (averaging $5,448 per year). Financial award applicants required to submit FAFSA. *Faculty research:* HIV, Epstein-Barr virus, virology, immunology, malaria. *Total annual research expenditures:* $15.6 million. *Unit head:* Dr. Charles R. Rinaldo, Jr., Chairman, 412-624-3928, Fax: 412-624-4953, E-mail: rinaldo@pitt.edu. *Application contact:* Dr. Jeremy Martinson, Assistant Professor, 412-624-5646, Fax: 412-383-8926, E-mail: jmartins@pitt.edu. Web site: http://www.idm.pitt.edu/.

University of Pittsburgh, School of Medicine, Programs in Medical Education, Pittsburgh, PA 15260. Offers medical education (MS, Certificate). Part-time programs available. *Faculty:* 21 full-time (9 women). *Students:* 15 part-time (8 women); includes 3 minority (1 Asian, non-Hispanic/Latino; 1 Hispanic/Latino; 1 Two or more races, non-Hispanic/Latino). Average age 32. 6 applicants, 100% accepted, 6 enrolled. In 2011, 4 master's awarded. *Degree requirements:* For master's, thesis. *Entrance requirements:* For master's, MCAT, GRE, or GMAT. Additional exam requirements/recommendations for international students: Required—TOEFL (minimum score 600 paper-based; 250 computer-based; 100 iBT). *Application deadline:* For fall admission, 10/31 priority date for domestic students, 10/31 for international students; for spring admission, 4/15 priority date for domestic students, 4/15 for international students. Applications are processed on a rolling basis. Application fee: $0. Electronic applications accepted. *Expenses:* Tuition, state resident: full-time $18,774; part-time $760 per credit. Tuition, nonresident: full-time $30,736; part-time $1258 per credit. *Required fees:* $740; $200 per term. Tuition and fees vary according to program. *Financial support:* Tuition waivers (partial) available. *Faculty research:* Medical education. *Unit head:* Dr. Wishwa Kapoor, Program Director, 412-692-2686, Fax: 412-586-9672, E-mail: kapoorwn@upmc.edu. *Application contact:* Jennifer Holliman, Program Coordinator, 412-586-9673, Fax: 412-586-9672, E-mail: hollimanjm@upmc.edu. Web site: http://www.icre.pitt.edu/degrees/degrees.html.

University of Puerto Rico, Medical Sciences Campus, Graduate School of Public Health, Department of Social Sciences, Program in Public Health Education, San Juan, PR 00936-5067. Offers MPHE. Part-time and evening/weekend programs available. *Degree requirements:* For master's, thesis. *Entrance requirements:* For master's, GRE, previous course work in education, social sciences, algebra, and natural sciences.

University of Rhode Island, Graduate School, College of Human Science and Services, Department of Kinesiology, Kingston, RI 02881. Offers cultural studies of sport and physical culture (MS); exercise science (MS); physical education pedagogy (MS); psychosocial/behavioral aspects of physical activity (MS). *Accreditation:* NCATE. Part-time programs available. *Faculty:* 13 full-time (7 women). *Students:* 11 full-time (7 women), 7 part-time (2 women); includes 1 minority (Hispanic/Latino). In 2011, 10 master's awarded. *Degree requirements:* For master's, thesis optional. *Entrance requirements:* For master's, GRE, 2 letters of recommendation. Additional exam requirements/recommendations for international students: Required—TOEFL (minimum score 550 paper-based; 213 computer-based). *Application deadline:* For fall admission, 4/15 for domestic students, 2/1 for international students; for spring admission, 11/15 for domestic students, 7/15 for international students. Application fee: $65. Electronic applications accepted. *Expenses:* Tuition, state resident: full-time $10,432; part-time $580 per credit hour. Tuition, nonresident: full-time $23,130; part-time $1285 per credit hour. *Required fees:* $1362; $36 per credit hour. $35 per semester. One-time fee: $130. *Financial support:* In 2011–12, 5 teaching assistantships with full and partial tuition reimbursements (averaging $8,250 per year) were awarded. Financial award application deadline: 4/15; financial award applicants required to submit FAFSA. *Faculty research:* Strength training and older adults, interventions to promote a healthy lifestyle as well as analysis of the psychosocial outcomes of those interventions, effects of exercise and nutrition on skeletal muscle of aging healthy adults with CVD and other metabolic related diseases, physical activity and fitness of deaf children and youth. *Unit head:* Dr. Deborah Riebe, Chair, 401-874-5444, Fax: 401-874-4215, E-mail: debriebe@uri.edu. *Application contact:* Dr. Lori Ciccomascolo, Director of Graduate Studies, 401-874-5454, Fax: 401-874-4215, E-mail: lecicco@uri.edu. Web site: http://www.uri.edu/hss/physical_education/.

University of South Africa, College of Human Sciences, Pretoria, South Africa. Offers adult education (M Ed); African languages (MA, PhD); African politics (MA, PhD); Afrikaans (MA, PhD); ancient history (MA, PhD); ancient Near Eastern studies (MA, PhD); anthropology (MA, PhD); applied linguistics (MA); Arabic (MA, PhD); archaeology (MA); art history (MA); Biblical archaeology (MA); Biblical studies (M Th, D Th, PhD); Christian spirituality (M Th, D Th); church history (M Th, D Th); classical studies (MA, PhD); clinical psychology (MA); communication (MA, PhD); comparative education (M Ed, Ed D); consulting psychology (D Admin, D Com, PhD); curriculum studies (M Ed, Ed D); development studies (M Admin, MA, D Admin, PhD); didactics (M Ed, Ed D); education (M Tech); education management (M Ed, Ed D); educational psychology (M Ed); English (MA); environmental education (M Ed); French (MA, PhD); German (MA, PhD); Greek (MA); guidance and counseling (M Ed); health studies (MA, PhD), including health sciences education (MA), health services management (MA), medical and surgical nursing science (critical care general) (MA), midwifery and neonatal nursing science (MA), trauma and emergency care (MA); history (MA, PhD); history of education (Ed D); inclusive education (M Ed, Ed D); information and communications technology policy and regulation (MA); information science (MA, MIS, PhD); international politics (MA, PhD); Islamic studies (MA, PhD); Italian (MA, PhD); Judaica (MA, PhD); linguistics (MA, PhD); mathematical education (M Ed); mathematics education (MA); missiology (M Th, D Th); modern Hebrew (MA, PhD); musicology (MA, MMus, D Mus, PhD); natural science education (M Ed); New Testament (M Th, D Th); Old Testament (D Th); pastoral therapy (M Th, D Th); philosophy (MA); philosophy of education (M Ed, Ed D); politics (MA, PhD); Portuguese (MA, PhD); practical theology (M Th, D Th); psychology (MA, MS, PhD); psychology of education (M Ed, Ed D); public health (MA); religious studies (MA, D Th, PhD); Romance languages (MA); Russian (MA, PhD); Semitic languages (MA, PhD); social behavior studies in HIV/AIDS (MA); social science (mental health) (MA); social science in development studies (MA); social science in psychology (MA); social science in social work (MA); social science in sociology (MA); social work (MSW, DSW, PhD); socio-education (M Ed, Ed D); sociolinguistics (MA); sociology (MA, PhD); Spanish (MA, PhD); systematic theology (M Th, D Th); TESOL (teaching English to speakers of other languages) (MA); theological ethics (M Th, D Th); theory of literature (MA, PhD); urban ministries (D Th); urban ministry (M Th).

University of South Alabama, Graduate School, College of Education, Department of Health, Physical Education and Leisure Services, Mobile, AL 36688-0002. Offers exercise science (MS); health education (M Ed); physical education (M Ed); therapeutic recreation (MS). *Accreditation:* NCATE (one or more programs are accredited). Part-time programs available. *Faculty:* 10 full-time (2 women). *Students:* 27 full-time (15 women), 4 part-time (all women); includes 5 minority (4 Black or African American, non-Hispanic/Latino; 1 Asian, non-Hispanic/Latino), 4 international. 29 applicants, 52% accepted, 12 enrolled. In 2011, 17 master's awarded. *Degree requirements:* For master's, comprehensive exam. *Entrance requirements:* For master's, GRE General Test or MAT. *Application deadline:* For fall admission, 7/15 priority date for domestic students, 6/15 for international students; for spring admission, 12/1 priority date for domestic students, 11/1 for international students. Applications are processed on a rolling basis. Application fee: $35. *Expenses:* Tuition, state resident: full-time $7968; part-time $332 per credit hour. Tuition, nonresident: full-time $15,936; part-time $664 per credit hour. *Financial support:* In 2011–12, 10 teaching assistantships were awarded; career-related internships or fieldwork also available. Support available to part-time students. Financial award application deadline: 4/1. *Unit head:* Dr. Frederick M. Scaffidi, Chair, 251-460-7131. *Application contact:* Dr. Abigail Baxter, Director of Graduate Studies, 231-460-7131.

University of South Carolina, The Graduate School, Arnold School of Public Health, Department of Health Promotion, Education, and Behavior, Columbia, SC 29208. Offers health education (MAT); health promotion, education, and behavior (MPH, MS, MSPH, Dr PH, PhD); school health education (Certificate); MSW/MPH. MAT offered in cooperation with the College of Education. *Accreditation:* CEPH (one or more programs are accredited); NCATE (one or more programs are accredited). Part-time programs available. *Degree requirements:* For master's, comprehensive exam, thesis or alternative, practicum (MPH), project (MS); for doctorate, comprehensive exam, thesis/dissertation. *Entrance requirements:* For master's and doctorate, GRE General Test. Additional exam requirements/recommendations for international students: Required—

TOEFL (minimum score 570 paper-based; 230 computer-based; 75 iBT). Electronic applications accepted. *Faculty research:* Health disparities and inequalities in communities, global health and nutrition, cancer and HIV/AIDS prevention, health communication, policy and program design.

University of South Carolina, The Graduate School, College of Education, Department of Instruction and Teacher Education, Program in Secondary Education, Columbia, SC 29208. Offers art education (IMA, MAT); business education (IMA, MAT); English (MAT); foreign language (MAT); health education (MAT); mathematics (MAT); science (IMA, MAT); secondary (Ed D); secondary education (MT, PhD); social studies (MAT); theatre and speech (MAT). IMA and MT offered jointly with the subject areas. *Accreditation:* NCATE. *Degree requirements:* For master's, comprehensive exam, thesis (for some programs), foreign language (MA); for doctorate, one foreign language, comprehensive exam, thesis/dissertation. *Entrance requirements:* For master's, GRE General Test or MAT, teaching certificate (IMA, M Ed), interview; for doctorate, GRE General Test or MAT, interview. *Faculty research:* Middle school programs, professional development, school collaboration.

University of Southern California, Keck School of Medicine and Graduate School, Graduate Programs in Medicine, Department of Preventive Medicine, Master of Public Health Program, Los Angeles, CA 90032-3628. Offers biostatistics/epidemiology (MPH); child and family health (MPH); environmental health (MPH); global health leadership (MPH); health communication (MPH); health education and promotion (MPH); public health policy (MPH). *Accreditation:* CEPH. Part-time programs available. *Faculty:* 22 full-time (12 women), 3 part-time/adjunct (0 women). *Students:* 148 full-time (115 women), 35 part-time (23 women); includes 100 minority (8 Black or African American, non-Hispanic/Latino; 66 Asian, non-Hispanic/Latino; 26 Hispanic/Latino), 26 international. Average age 24. 218 applicants, 73% accepted, 88 enrolled. In 2011, 91 master's awarded. *Degree requirements:* For master's, practicum, final report, oral presentation. *Entrance requirements:* For master's, GRE General Test, MCAT, GMAT, minimum GPA of 3.0. Additional exam requirements/recommendations for international students: Required—TOEFL (minimum score 600 paper-based; 250 computer-based; 100 iBT). *Application deadline:* For fall admission, 6/1 priority date for domestic students, 6/1 for international students; for spring admission, 11/1 priority date for domestic students, 10/1 for international students. Applications are processed on a rolling basis. Application fee: $85. Electronic applications accepted. *Financial support:* In 2011–12, 148 students received support. Career-related internships or fieldwork, Federal Work-Study, institutionally sponsored loans, and scholarships/grants available. Support available to part-time students. Financial award application deadline: 5/4; financial award applicants required to submit CSS PROFILE or FAFSA. *Faculty research:* Substance abuse prevention, cancer and heart disease prevention, mass media and health communication research, health promotion, treatment compliance. *Unit head:* Dr. Louise A. Rohrbach, Director, 323-442-8237, Fax: 323-442-8297, E-mail: rohrbac@usc.edu. *Application contact:* Chrystal Romero, Admissions Counselor, 323-442-7257, Fax: 323-442-8297, E-mail: ccromero@usc.edu. Web site: http://mph.usc.edu/main.php.

University of Southern Mississippi, Graduate School, College of Health, Department of Community Health Sciences, Hattiesburg, MS 39406-0001. Offers epidemiology and biostatistics (MPH); health education (MPH); health policy/administration (MPH); occupational/environmental health (MPH); public health nutrition (MPH). *Accreditation:* CEPH. Part-time and evening/weekend programs available. *Faculty:* 8 full-time (4 women), 1 part-time/adjunct (0 women). *Students:* 81 full-time (66 women), 17 part-time (13 women); includes 49 minority (43 Black or African American, non-Hispanic/Latino; 1 Asian, non-Hispanic/Latino; 2 Hispanic/Latino; 3 Two or more races, non-Hispanic/Latino), 7 international. Average age 32. 70 applicants, 94% accepted, 43 enrolled. In 2011, 45 degrees awarded. *Degree requirements:* For master's, comprehensive exam, thesis (for some programs). *Entrance requirements:* For master's, GRE General Test, minimum GPA of 2.75 in last 60 hours. Additional exam requirements/recommendations for international students: Required—TOEFL, IELTS. *Application deadline:* For fall admission, 3/1 priority date for domestic students, 3/1 for international students; for spring admission, 1/10 priority date for domestic students, 1/10 for international students. Applications are processed on a rolling basis. Application fee: $50. Electronic applications accepted. *Financial support:* In 2011–12, 5 research assistantships with full tuition reimbursements (averaging $7,000 per year), 1 teaching assistantship with full tuition reimbursement (averaging $8,263 per year) were awarded; career-related internships or fieldwork, Federal Work-Study, institutionally sponsored loans, scholarships/grants, health care benefits, and unspecified assistantships also available. Financial award application deadline: 3/15; financial award applicants required to submit FAFSA. *Faculty research:* Rural health care delivery, school health, nutrition of pregnant teens, risk factor reduction, sexually transmitted diseases. *Unit head:* Dr. Emanual Ahua, Interim Chair, 601-266-5437, Fax: 601-266-5043. *Application contact:* Shonna Breland, Manager of Graduate Admissions, 601-266-6563, Fax: 601-266-5138. Web site: http://www.usm.edu/chs.

The University of Tennessee, Graduate School, College of Education, Health and Human Sciences, Program in Health Promotion and Health Education, Knoxville, TN 37996. Offers MS. *Accreditation:* CEPH. Part-time programs available. *Degree requirements:* For master's, thesis optional. *Entrance requirements:* For master's, minimum GPA of 2.7. Additional exam requirements/recommendations for international students: Required—TOEFL. Electronic applications accepted. *Expenses:* Tuition, state resident: full-time $8332; part-time $464 per credit hour. Tuition, nonresident: full-time $25,174; part-time $1400 per credit hour. *Required fees:* $1162; $56 per credit hour. Tuition and fees vary according to program.

The University of Tennessee, Graduate School, College of Education, Health and Human Sciences, Program in Safety, Knoxville, TN 37996. Offers MS. *Accreditation:* NCATE. Part-time programs available. *Degree requirements:* For master's, thesis optional. *Entrance requirements:* For master's, minimum GPA of 2.7. Additional exam requirements/recommendations for international students: Required—TOEFL. Electronic applications accepted. *Expenses:* Tuition, state resident: full-time $8332; part-time $464 per credit hour. Tuition, nonresident: full-time $25,174; part-time $1400 per credit hour. *Required fees:* $1162; $56 per credit hour. Tuition and fees vary according to program.

The University of Texas at Austin, Graduate School, College of Education, Department of Kinesiology and Health Education, Austin, TX 78712-1111. Offers behavioral health (PhD); exercise and sport psychology (M Ed, MA); exercise science (M Ed, MS, PhD); health education (M Ed, MS, Ed D, PhD). Part-time programs available. Terminal master's awarded for partial completion of doctoral program. *Degree requirements:* For master's, thesis (for some programs); for doctorate, thesis/dissertation. *Entrance requirements:* For master's and doctorate, GRE General Test. Additional exam requirements/recommendations for international students: Required—TOEFL. *Application deadline:* For fall admission, 2/1 priority date for domestic students; for spring admission, 10/1 for domestic students. Applications are processed on a rolling basis. Application fee: $50 ($75 for international students). Electronic applications accepted. *Financial support:* Fellowships, research assistantships, teaching assistantships, career-related internships or fieldwork, and Federal Work-Study available. Financial award application deadline: 2/1; financial award applicants required to submit FAFSA. *Faculty research:* Health promotion, human performance and exercise biochemistry, motor behavior and biomechanics, sport management, aging and pediatric development. *Unit head:* Dr. John L. Ivy, Chair, 512-471-1273, Fax: 512-471-8914, E-mail: johnivy@mail.utexas.edu. *Application contact:* Dr. Darla Castelli, Graduate Advisor, 512-232-7636, Fax: 512-232-5334, E-mail: dcastelli@mail.utexas.edu. Web site: http://www.edb.utexas.edu/education/departments/khe/.

The University of Texas at San Antonio, College of Education and Human Development, Department of Health and Kinesiology, San Antonio, TX 78249-0617. Offers MS. Part-time and evening/weekend programs available. *Faculty:* 12 full-time (5 women). *Students:* 62 full-time (33 women), 68 part-time (45 women); includes 83 minority (9 Black or African American, non-Hispanic/Latino; 1 American Indian or Alaska Native, non-Hispanic/Latino; 2 Asian, non-Hispanic/Latino; 69 Hispanic/Latino; 1 Native Hawaiian or other Pacific Islander, non-Hispanic/Latino; 1 Two or more races, non-Hispanic/Latino), 5 international. Average age 29. 70 applicants, 79% accepted, 47 enrolled. In 2011, 40 master's awarded. *Entrance requirements:* For master's, GRE or GMAT, bachelor's degree with minimum GPA of 3.0 in last 60 hours of coursework; resume; statement of purpose; two letters of recommendation. Additional exam requirements/recommendations for international students: Required—TOEFL (minimum score 500 paper-based; 61 iBT), IELTS (minimum score 5). *Application deadline:* For fall admission, 7/1 for domestic students, 4/1 for international students; for spring admission, 11/1 for domestic students, 9/1 for international students. Application fee: $45 ($85 for international students). *Expenses:* Tuition, state resident: full-time $3148; part-time $2176 per semester. Tuition, nonresident: full-time $8782; part-time $5932 per semester. *Required fees:* $719 per semester. *Faculty research:* Motor behavior, motor skills, exercise and nutrition, athlete efficacy, diabetes prevention. *Unit head:* Dr. Wan Xiang Yao, Chair, 210-458-6224, Fax: 210-452-5873, E-mail: wanxiang.yao@utsa.edu. *Application contact:* Dr. Alberto Cordova, Graduate Advisor of Record, 210-458-6226, Fax: 210-458-5873, E-mail: alberto.cordova@utsa.edu. Web site: http://education.utsa.edu/health_and_kinesiology.

The University of Texas at Tyler, College of Nursing and Health Sciences, Department of Health and Kinesiology, Tyler, TX 75799-0001. Offers health and kinesiology (M Ed, MA); health sciences (MS); kinesiology (MS). *Accreditation:* Teacher Education Accreditation Council. Part-time programs available. Postbaccalaureate distance learning degree programs offered. *Degree requirements:* For master's, comprehensive exam (for some programs), thesis (for some programs). *Entrance requirements:* Additional exam requirements/recommendations for international students: Required—TOEFL (minimum score 79 computer-based). Electronic applications accepted. *Faculty research:* Osteoporosis, muscle soreness, economy of locomotion, adoption of rehabilitation programs, effect of inactivity and aging on muscle blood vessels, territoriality.

The University of Toledo, College of Graduate Studies, College of Medicine and Life Sciences, Department of Public Health and Preventative Medicine, Toledo, OH 43606-3390. Offers biostatistics and epidemiology (Certificate); contemporary gerontological practice (Certificate); environmental and occupational health and safety (MPH); epidemiology (MPH, Certificate); global public health (Certificate); health administration (MPH); health promotion (MPH); medical health and science education (Certificate); nutrition (MPH); occupational health (MSOH, Certificate); public health and emergency response (Certificate); MD/MPH. Part-time and evening/weekend programs available. *Faculty:* 6. *Students:* 95 full-time (74 women), 66 part-time (45 women); includes 37 minority (21 Black or African American, non-Hispanic/Latino; 11 Asian, non-Hispanic/Latino; 3 Hispanic/Latino; 2 Two or more races, non-Hispanic/Latino), 6 international. Average age 29. 132 applicants, 75% accepted, 70 enrolled. In 2011, 60 master's, 26 other advanced degrees awarded. *Degree requirements:* For master's, thesis or alternative. *Entrance requirements:* For master's, GRE, minimum undergraduate GPA of 3.0, three letters of recommendation, statement of purpose, transcripts from all prior institutions attended, resume; for Certificate, minimum undergraduate GPA of 3.0, three letters of recommendation, statement of purpose, transcripts from all prior institutions attended, resume. Additional exam requirements/recommendations for international students: Required—TOEFL (minimum score 550 paper-based; 213 computer-based; 80 iBT), IELTS (minimum score 6.5). *Application deadline:* For fall admission, 3/15 for domestic and international students. Applications are processed on a rolling basis. Application fee: $45 ($75 for international students). Electronic applications accepted. *Financial support:* In 2011–12, 15 research assistantships with full tuition reimbursements (averaging $10,000 per year) were awarded; Federal Work-Study, institutionally sponsored loans, scholarships/grants, tuition waivers (full and partial), and unspecified assistantships also available. *Unit head:* Dr. Sheryl A. Milz, Chair, 419-383-3976, Fax: 419-383-6140, E-mail: sheryl.milz@utoledo.edu. *Application contact:* Joan Mulligan, Admissions Analyst, 419-383-4186, Fax: 419-383-6140, E-mail: joan.mulligan@utoledo.edu. Web site: http://nocphmph.org/.

The University of Toledo, College of Graduate Studies, Judith Herb College of Education, Health Science and Human Service, Department of Health and Recreation, Toledo, OH 43606-3390. Offers health education (ME, PhD); health promotions and education (MPH); recreation and leisure studies (MA). Part-time programs available. *Students:* 20 full-time (16 women), 30 part-time (21 women); includes 5 minority (4 Black or African American, non-Hispanic/Latino; 1 Asian, non-Hispanic/Latino), 2 international. Average age 34. 26 applicants, 65% accepted, 12 enrolled. In 2011, 11 master's, 5 doctorates awarded. *Degree requirements:* For master's, comprehensive exam, thesis; for doctorate, thesis/dissertation. *Entrance requirements:* For master's and doctorate, minimum cumulative GPA of 2.7 for all previous academic work, letters of recommendation. Additional exam requirements/recommendations for international students: Required—TOEFL (minimum score 550 paper-based; 213 computer-based; 80 iBT), IELTS (minimum score 6.5). *Application deadline:* For fall admission, 1/15 priority date for domestic students, 1/15 for international students. Applications are processed on a rolling basis. Application fee: $45 ($75 for international students). Electronic applications accepted. *Financial support:* In 2011–12, 11 teaching assistantships with full and partial tuition reimbursements (averaging $9,682 per year) were awarded; career-related internships or fieldwork, Federal Work-Study, institutionally sponsored loans, scholarships/grants, tuition waivers (full and partial), and unspecified assistantships also available. Support available to part-time students. *Unit head:* Joseph Dake, Chair, 419-530-2767, E-mail: joseph.dake@utoledo.edu. *Application contact:* Graduate School Office, 419-530-4723, Fax: 419-530-4724, E-mail: grdsch@utnet.utoledo.edu. Web site: http://www.utoledo.edu/eduhshs/.

University of Utah, Graduate School, College of Health, Department of Health Promotion and Education, Salt Lake City, UT 84112. Offers M Phil, MS, Ed D, PhD. Part-time and evening/weekend programs available. *Faculty:* 6 full-time (3 women), 1 part-time/adjunct (0 women). *Students:* 36 full-time (25 women), 15 part-time (10 women); includes 7 minority (2 Asian, non-Hispanic/Latino; 4 Hispanic/Latino; 1 Two or more races, non-Hispanic/Latino), 5 international. Average age 32. 38 applicants, 58% accepted, 18 enrolled. In 2011, 15 master's, 4 doctorates awarded. Terminal master's awarded for partial completion of doctoral program. *Median time to degree:* Of those who began their doctoral program in fall 2003, 100% received their degree in 8 years or less. *Degree requirements:* For master's, comprehensive exam, thesis or alternative, field experience; for doctorate, comprehensive exam, thesis/dissertation, field experience. *Entrance requirements:* For master's, GRE (for thesis option), minimum

GPA of 3.0; for doctorate, GRE General Test, minimum GPA of 3.2. Additional exam requirements/recommendations for international students: Required—TOEFL (minimum score 500 paper-based; 173 computer-based). *Application deadline:* For fall admission, 10/15 for domestic and international students; for spring admission, 2/15 for domestic and international students. Applications are processed on a rolling basis. Application fee: $55 ($65 for international students). Electronic applications accepted. *Financial support:* In 2011–12, 14 students received support, including 3 research assistantships with full tuition reimbursements available (averaging $12,000 per year), 6 teaching assistantships with full tuition reimbursements available (averaging $12,000 per year); career-related internships or fieldwork, Federal Work-Study, institutionally sponsored loans, and scholarships/grants also available. Financial award application deadline: 2/15; financial award applicants required to submit FAFSA. *Faculty research:* Health behavior and counseling, health service administration, evaluation of health programs. *Total annual research expenditures:* $119,213. *Unit head:* Leslie K. Chatelain, Department Chair, 801-581-4512, Fax: 801-585-3646, E-mail: les.chatelain@utah.edu. *Application contact:* Dr. Glenn E. Richardson, Director of Graduate Studies, 801-581-8039, Fax: 801-585-3646, E-mail: glenn.richardson@health.utah.edu. Web site: http://www.health.utah.edu/healthed/index.htm.

University of Virginia, Curry School of Education, Department of Human Services, Program in Health and Physical Education, Charlottesville, VA 22903. Offers M Ed, Ed D. *Students:* 35 full-time (21 women), 1 (woman) part-time; includes 3 minority (1 Black or African American, non-Hispanic/Latino; 1 Asian, non-Hispanic/Latino; 1 Hispanic/Latino), 3 international. Average age 24. 5 applicants, 100% accepted, 5 enrolled. In 2011, 36 master's awarded. *Entrance requirements:* For master's and doctorate, GRE General Test, 2 letters of recommendation. Additional exam requirements/recommendations for international students: Required—TOEFL (minimum score 600 paper-based; 250 computer-based; 90 iBT), IELTS (minimum score 7). *Application deadline:* Applications are processed on a rolling basis. Application fee: $60. Electronic applications accepted. *Financial support:* Applicants required to submit FAFSA. *Unit head:* Luke E. Kelly, Program Coordinator, 434-924-6207. *Application contact:* Lynn Renfroe, Information Contact, 434-924-6254, E-mail: ldr9t@virginia.edu. Web site: http://curry.virginia.edu/academics/degrees/postgraduate-master-in-teaching/pg-mt-in-health-physical-education.

University of Waterloo, Graduate Studies, Faculty of Applied Health Sciences, School of Public Health and Health Systems, Waterloo, ON N2L 3G1, Canada. Offers health studies and gerontology (M Sc, PhD); public health (MPH). Part-time programs available. *Degree requirements:* For master's, thesis; for doctorate, comprehensive exam, thesis/dissertation. *Entrance requirements:* For master's, honors degree, minimum B average, resume, writing sample; for doctorate, GRE (recommended), master's degree, minimum B average, resumé, writing sample. Additional exam requirements/recommendations for international students: Required—TOEFL, TWE. Electronic applications accepted. *Faculty research:* Population health, health promotion and disease prevention, healthy aging, health policy, planning and evaluation, health information management and health informatics, aging, health and well-being, work and health.

University of West Florida, College of Professional Studies, Department of Health, Leisure, and Exercise Science, Community Health Education Program, Pensacola, FL 32514-5750. Offers aging studies (MS); health promotion and worksite wellness (MS); psychosocial (MS). Part-time and evening/weekend programs available. *Faculty:* 3 full-time (1 woman). *Students:* 10 full-time (9 women), 7 part-time (6 women); includes 4 minority (2 Black or African American, non-Hispanic/Latino; 1 Asian, non-Hispanic/Latino; 1 Hispanic/Latino), 1 international. Average age 28. 7 applicants, 71% accepted, 4 enrolled. In 2011, 9 master's awarded. *Degree requirements:* For master's, thesis or alternative. *Entrance requirements:* For master's, GRE or MAT, official transcripts; minimum GPA of 3.0; letter of intent; three personal references. Additional exam requirements/recommendations for international students: Required—TOEFL (minimum score 550 paper-based; 213 computer-based). *Application deadline:* For fall admission, 6/1 for domestic and international students; for spring admission, 10/1 for domestic and international students. Applications are processed on a rolling basis. Application fee: $30. *Expenses:* Tuition, state resident: full-time $5729; part-time $302 per credit hour. Tuition, nonresident: full-time $20,059; part-time $961 per credit hour. *Required fees:* $1509; $63 per credit hour. *Financial support:* Research assistantships, teaching assistantships, and unspecified assistantships available. *Unit head:* Dr. John Todorovich, Chairperson, 850-473-7248, Fax: 850-474-2106. *Application contact:* Terry McCray, Assistant Director of Graduate Admissions, 850-473-7718, Fax: 850-473-7714, E-mail: gradadmissions@uwf.edu.

University of West Florida, College of Professional Studies, Department of Health, Leisure, and Exercise Science, Program in Health, Leisure, and Exercise Science, Pensacola, FL 32514-5750. Offers exercise science (MS); physical education (MS). Part-time and evening/weekend programs available. *Faculty:* 6 full-time (2 women), 1 (woman) part-time/adjunct. *Students:* 14 full-time (10 women), 16 part-time (7 women); includes 6 minority (2 Black or African American, non-Hispanic/Latino; 1 Asian, non-Hispanic/Latino; 2 Hispanic/Latino; 1 Native Hawaiian or other Pacific Islander, non-Hispanic/Latino), 2 international. Average age 28. 22 applicants, 55% accepted, 7 enrolled. In 2011, 20 master's awarded. *Degree requirements:* For master's, thesis or alternative. *Entrance requirements:* For master's, GRE or MAT, official transcripts; minimum GPA of 3.0; letter of intent; two personal references; work experience. Additional exam requirements/recommendations for international students: Required—TOEFL (minimum score 550 paper-based; 213 computer-based). *Application deadline:* For fall admission, 6/1 for domestic and international students; for spring admission, 10/1 for domestic and international students. Applications are processed on a rolling basis. Application fee: $30. Electronic applications accepted. *Expenses:* Tuition, state resident: full-time $5729; part-time $302 per credit hour. Tuition, nonresident: full-time $20,059; part-time $961 per credit hour. *Required fees:* $1509; $63 per credit hour. *Financial support:* Career-related internships or fieldwork, Federal Work-Study, scholarships/grants, and tuition waivers (partial) available. Support available to part-time students. Financial award application deadline: 4/15; financial award applicants required to submit FAFSA. *Unit head:* Dr. John Todorovich, Chairperson, 850-473-7248, Fax: 850-474-2106. *Application contact:* Terry McCray, Assistant Director of Graduate Admissions, 850-473-7718, Fax: 850-473-7714, E-mail: gradadmissions@uwf.edu.

University of Wisconsin–La Crosse, Office of University Graduate Studies, College of Science and Health, Department of Health Education and Health Promotion, Program in Community Health Education, La Crosse, WI 54601-3742. Offers MPH, MS. *Accreditation:* CEPH. *Faculty:* 7 full-time (4 women), 1 (woman) part-time/adjunct. *Students:* 19 full-time (15 women), 11 part-time (8 women); includes 3 minority (2 Asian, non-Hispanic/Latino; 1 Hispanic/Latino), 5 international. Average age 28. 28 applicants, 71% accepted, 9 enrolled. In 2011, 9 master's awarded. *Degree requirements:* For master's, thesis. *Entrance requirements:* For master's, GRE General Test, GRE Subject Test (MPH), 3 letters of recommendation. Additional exam requirements/recommendations for international students: Required—TOEFL (minimum score 550 paper-based; 213 computer-based; 79 iBT). Application fee: $56. Electronic applications accepted. *Expenses:* Tuition, state resident: full-time $8391; part-time $481.17 per credit. Tuition, nonresident: full-time $17,850; part-time $1006.68 per credit. *Required fees:* $2 per credit. $18.25 per semester. Tuition and fees vary according to course load, program, reciprocity agreements and student level. *Financial support:* In 2011–12, 3 research assistantships with partial tuition reimbursements (averaging $6,682 per year) were awarded; Federal Work-Study, scholarships/grants, health care benefits, and tuition waivers (partial) also available. Support available to part-time students. Financial award applicants required to submit FAFSA. *Unit head:* Dr. Gary Gilmore, Director, 608-785-8163, E-mail: gilmore.gary@uwlax.edu. *Application contact:* Kathryn Kiefer, Director of Admissions, 608-785-8939, E-mail: admissions@uwlax.edu. Web site: http://www.uwlax.edu/sah/hehp/html/grad.htm.

University of Wisconsin–La Crosse, Office of University Graduate Studies, College of Science and Health, Department of Health Education and Health Promotion, Program in School Health Education, La Crosse, WI 54601-3742. Offers MS. *Students:* 3 part-time (2 women). Average age 28. 1 applicant, 100% accepted, 1 enrolled. In 2011, 3 master's awarded. *Entrance requirements:* For master's, GRE General Test, minimum GPA of 2.85. Additional exam requirements/recommendations for international students: Required—TOEFL (minimum score 550 paper-based; 213 computer-based; 79 iBT). *Application deadline:* Applications are processed on a rolling basis. Application fee: $56. Electronic applications accepted. *Expenses:* Tuition, state resident: full-time $8391; part-time $481.17 per credit. Tuition, nonresident: full-time $17,850; part-time $1006.68 per credit. *Required fees:* $2 per credit. $18.25 per semester. Tuition and fees vary according to course load, program, reciprocity agreements and student level. *Financial support:* Federal Work-Study, scholarships/grants, and tuition waivers available. Support available to part-time students. Financial award applicants required to submit FAFSA. *Unit head:* Dr. Tracy Caravella, Director, 608-785-6788, E-mail: caravell.trac@uwlax.edu. *Application contact:* Kathryn Kiefer, Director of Admissions, 608-785-8939, E-mail: admissions@uwlax.edu. Web site: http://www.uwlax.edu/sah/hehp/html/gr_she.htm.

University of Wisconsin–Milwaukee, Graduate School, College of Nursing, Milwaukee, WI 53201-0413. Offers family nursing practitioner (Post Master's Certificate); health professional education (Certificate); nursing (MS, PhD); public health (Certificate). *Accreditation:* AACN. Part-time programs available. *Faculty:* 30 full-time (29 women), 2 part-time/adjunct (both women). *Students:* 125 full-time (114 women), 122 part-time (108 women); includes 34 minority (15 Black or African American, non-Hispanic/Latino; 1 American Indian or Alaska Native, non-Hispanic/Latino; 7 Asian, non-Hispanic/Latino; 1 Hispanic/Latino; 10 Two or more races, non-Hispanic/Latino), 6 international. Average age 39. 128 applicants, 49% accepted, 41 enrolled. In 2011, 52 master's, 16 doctorates awarded. *Degree requirements:* For master's, thesis; for doctorate, thesis/dissertation. *Entrance requirements:* For master's, GRE General Test or MAT, autobiographical sketch; for doctorate, GRE, minimum GPA of 3.2. Additional exam requirements/recommendations for international students: Required—TOEFL (minimum score 550 paper-based; 79 iBT), IELTS (minimum score 6.5). *Application deadline:* For fall admission, 1/1 priority date for domestic students; for spring admission, 9/1 for domestic students. Applications are processed on a rolling basis. Application fee: $56 ($96 for international students). Electronic applications accepted. One-time fee: $506.10 full-time. Tuition and fees vary according to course load and reciprocity agreements. *Financial support:* In 2011–12, 3 fellowships, 1 research assistantship, 9 teaching assistantships were awarded; career-related internships or fieldwork, Federal Work-Study, health care benefits, unspecified assistantships, and project assistantships also available. Support available to part-time students. Financial award application deadline: 4/15; financial award applicants required to submit FAFSA. *Total annual research expenditures:* $3.3 million. *Unit head:* Dr. Sally Lundeen, Dean, 414-229-4189, E-mail: slundeen@uwm.edu. *Application contact:* Kim Litwack, Representative, 414-229-5098. Web site: http://www.uwm.edu/Dept/Nursing/.

University of Wyoming, College of Health Sciences, Division of Kinesiology and Health, Laramie, WY 82070. Offers MS. *Accreditation:* NCATE. Part-time programs available. Postbaccalaureate distance learning degree programs offered (no on-campus study). *Degree requirements:* For master's, comprehensive exam (for some programs), thesis (for some programs). *Entrance requirements:* For master's, GRE General Test, minimum GPA of 3.0. Additional exam requirements/recommendations for international students: Required—TOEFL. Electronic applications accepted. *Faculty research:* Teacher effectiveness, effects of exercising on heart function, physiological responses of overtraining, psychological benefits of physical activity, health behavior.

Utah State University, School of Graduate Studies, Emma Eccles Jones College of Education and Human Services, Department of Health, Physical Education and Recreation, Logan, UT 84322. Offers M Ed, MS. Part-time and evening/weekend programs available. Postbaccalaureate distance learning degree programs offered (minimal on-campus study). *Degree requirements:* For master's, thesis (for some programs). *Entrance requirements:* For master's, GRE General Test or MAT, minimum GPA of 3.0. Additional exam requirements/recommendations for international students: Required—TOEFL. *Faculty research:* Sport psychology intervention, motor learning biomechanics, pedagogy, physiology.

Virginia Commonwealth University, Graduate School, School of Education, Program in Teaching and Learning, Richmond, VA 23284-9005. Offers early and elementary education (MT); health and physical education (MT); secondary 6-12 education (MT); secondary education (Certificate). *Accreditation:* NCATE. Part-time programs available. *Entrance requirements:* For master's, GRE General Test or MAT. Additional exam requirements/recommendations for international students: Required—TOEFL (minimum score 600 paper-based; 250 computer-based; 100 iBT). Electronic applications accepted. *Expenses:* Tuition, state resident: full-time $9133; part-time $507 per credit. Tuition, nonresident: full-time $18,777; part-time $1043 per credit. *Required fees:* $77 per credit. Tuition and fees vary according to degree level, campus/location, program and student level.

Virginia State University, School of Graduate Studies, Research, and Outreach, School of Engineering, Science and Technology, Department of Psychology, Petersburg, VA 23806-0001. Offers behavioral and community health sciences (PhD); clinical health psychology (PhD); clinical psychology (MS); general psychology (MS). *Degree requirements:* For master's, one foreign language, thesis. *Entrance requirements:* For master's, GRE General Test.

Walden University, Graduate Programs, School of Health Sciences, Minneapolis, MN 55401. Offers clinical research administration (MS, Postbaccalaureate Certificate); health informatics (MS); health services (PhD), including community health education and advocacy, general program, healthcare administration, leadership, public health policy, self-designed; healthcare administration (MHA); public health (MPH, PhD), including community health and education (PhD), epidemiology (PhD). Part-time and evening/weekend programs available. Postbaccalaureate distance learning degree programs offered (minimal on-campus study). *Faculty:* 20 full-time (13 women), 175 part-time/adjunct (81 women). *Students:* 2,777 full-time (2,158 women), 1,350 part-time (1,038 women); includes 2,379 minority (1,935 Black or African American, non-Hispanic/Latino; 33 American Indian or Alaska Native, non-Hispanic/Latino; 173 Asian, non-Hispanic/Latino; 180 Hispanic/Latino; 9 Native Hawaiian or other Pacific Islander, non-Hispanic/Latino; 49 Two or more races, non-Hispanic/Latino), 247 international. Average age 40. In 2011, 528 master's, 79 doctorates, 1 other advanced degree awarded. *Degree requirements:* For doctorate, thesis/dissertation, residency. *Entrance* *requirements:* For master's, bachelor's degree or equivalent in related field, minimum GPA of 2.5; for doctorate, master's degree or equivalent in related field; minimum GPA of 3.0; official transcripts; three years of related professional/academic experience (preferred); access to computer and Internet. Additional exam requirements/ recommendations for international students: Required—TOEFL (minimum score 550 paper-based; 213 computer-based), IELTS (minimum score 6.5), or Michigan English Language Assessment Battery (minimum score 82). *Application deadline:* Applications are processed on a rolling basis. Application fee: $50. Electronic applications accepted. *Financial support:* Federal Work-Study, scholarships/grants, unspecified assistantships, and family tuition reduction, active duty/veteran tuition reduction, group tuition reduction, interest-free payment plans, employee tuition reduction available. Support available to part-time students. Financial award applicants required to submit FAFSA. *Unit head:* Dr. Jorg Westermann, Associate Dean, 800-925-3368. *Application contact:* Jennifer Hall, Vice President of Enrollment Management, 866-4-WALDEN, E-mail: info@waldenu.edu. Web site: http://www.waldenu.edu/Colleges-and-Schools/College-of-Health-Sciences/School-of-Health-Sciences.htm.

Wayne State University, College of Education, Division of Kinesiology, Health and Sports Studies, Detroit, MI 48202. Offers exercise and sport science (M Ed); health education (M Ed); kinesiology (M Ed, PhD); physical education (M Ed); sports administration (MA); wellness clinician/research (M Ed). *Students:* 39 full-time (23 women), 68 part-time (31 women); includes 36 minority (31 Black or African American, non-Hispanic/Latino; 1 Asian, non-Hispanic/Latino; 1 Hispanic/Latino; 1 Native Hawaiian or other Pacific Islander, non-Hispanic/Latino; 2 Two or more races, non-Hispanic/ Latino), 3 international. Average age 31. 115 applicants, 39% accepted, 27 enrolled. In 2011, 39 master's, 1 doctorate awarded. *Degree requirements:* For master's, thesis (for some programs). *Entrance requirements:* Additional exam requirements/ recommendations for international students: Required—TOEFL; Recommended—TWE (minimum score 6). *Application deadline:* For fall admission, 6/1 priority date for domestic students, 5/1 for international students; for winter admission, 10/1 priority date for domestic students, 9/1 for international students; for spring admission, 2/1 priority date for domestic students, 1/1 for international students. Applications are processed on a rolling basis. Application fee: $50. Electronic applications accepted. *Expenses:* Tuition, state resident: part-time $512.85 per credit. Tuition, nonresident: part-time $1132.65 per credit. *Required fees:* $26.60 per credit. $199.65 per semester. Tuition and fees vary according to course load and program. *Financial support:* In 2011–12, 6 research assistantships with tuition reimbursements (averaging $16,061 per year) were awarded; teaching assistantships with tuition reimbursements, career-related internships or fieldwork, scholarships/grants, health care benefits, and unspecified assistantships also available. *Faculty research:* Fitness in urban children, motor development of crack babies, effects of caffeine on metabolism/exercise, body composition of elite youth sports participants, systematic observation of teaching. *Unit head:* Dr. Mariane Fahlman, Assistant Dean, 313-577-5066, Fax: 313-577-9301, E-mail: m.fahlman@wayne.edu. *Application contact:* John Wirth, Assistant Professor, 313-993-7972, Fax: 313-577-5999, E-mail: johnwirth@wayne.edu. Web site: http://coe.wayne.edu/kinesiology/index.php.

Wayne State University, School of Medicine, Medical Research Program, Detroit, MI 48202. Offers MS. Program open only to individuals actively participating in post-graduate professional training in Wayne State University affiliated programs. *Students:* 1 (woman) full-time, 1 part-time (0 women); both minorities (1 Black or African American, non-Hispanic/Latino; 1 Asian, non-Hispanic/Latino). Average age 36. 8 applicants, 25% accepted, 2 enrolled. In 2011, 1 master's awarded. *Degree requirements:* For master's, thesis. *Entrance requirements:* For master's, GRE or MCAT, minimum GPA of 3.0, MD or equivalent professional degree in human health care. Additional exam requirements/ recommendations for international students: Required—TOEFL (minimum score 550 paper-based; 213 computer-based; 100 iBT); Recommended—TWE (minimum score 6). *Application deadline:* For fall admission, 6/1 for domestic students, 4/1 for international students; for winter admission, 12/1 for domestic students, 2/1 for international students. Application fee: $50. Electronic applications accepted. *Expenses:* Tuition, state resident: part-time $512.85 per credit. Tuition, nonresident: part-time $1132.65 per credit. *Required fees:* $26.60 per credit. $199.65 per semester. Tuition and fees vary according to course load and program. *Financial support:* Scholarships/ grants available. *Unit head:* Dr. Robert Pauley, Associate Dean, Graduate Program, E-mail: rpauley@med.wayne.edu. *Application contact:* Dr. Thomas Holland, Graduate Program Director, 313-577-1455, E-mail: tholland@med.wayne.edu. Web site: http://gradprograms.med.wayne.edu/program-spotlight.php?id=33.

West Chester University of Pennsylvania, College of Health Sciences, Department of Health, West Chester, PA 19383. Offers emergency preparedness (Certificate); health care management (MPH, Certificate), including health care management (Certificate), integrative (MPH); school health (M Ed). *Accreditation:* CEPH. Part-time and evening/ weekend programs available. *Faculty:* 2 full-time (both women), 15 part-time/adjunct (11 women). *Students:* 112 full-time (85 women), 94 part-time (76 women); includes 82 minority (64 Black or African American, non-Hispanic/Latino; 2 American Indian or Alaska Native, non-Hispanic/Latino; 12 Asian, non-Hispanic/Latino; 3 Hispanic/Latino; 1 Two or more races, non-Hispanic/Latino), 16 international. Average age 29. 149 applicants, 65% accepted, 73 enrolled. In 2011, 34 master's, 3 other advanced degrees awarded. *Degree requirements:* For master's, thesis (for some programs), minimum GPA of 3.0. *Entrance requirements:* For master's, one-page statement of career objectives, two letters of reference. Additional exam requirements/recommendations for international students: Required—TOEFL (minimum score 550 paper-based; 213 computer-based; 80 iBT). *Application deadline:* For fall admission, 4/15 priority date for domestic students, 3/15 for international students; for spring admission, 10/15 priority date for domestic students, 9/1 for international students. Applications are processed on a rolling basis. Application fee: $45. Electronic applications accepted. *Expenses:* Tuition, state resident: full-time $7488; part-time $416 per credit. Tuition, nonresident: full-time $11,232; part-time $624 per credit. *Required fees:* $1784.64; $67.59 per credit. Tuition and fees vary according to program. *Financial support:* Unspecified assistantships available. Support available to part-time students. Financial award application deadline: 2/15; financial award applicants required to submit FAFSA. *Faculty research:* Health school communities, community health issues and evidence-based programs, environment and health, nutrition and health, integrative health. *Unit head:* Dr. Bethann Cinelli, Chair, 610-436-2267, E-mail: bcinelli@wcupa.edu. *Application contact:* Dr. Lynn Carson, Graduate Coordinator, 610-436-2138, E-mail: lcarson@wcupa.edu. Web site: http://www.wcupa.edu/_ACADEMICS/HealthSciences/health/.

Western Illinois University, School of Graduate Studies, College of Education and Human Services, Department of Health Sciences, Macomb, IL 61455-1390. Offers health education (MS); health services administration (Certificate). *Accreditation:* NCATE. Part-time programs available. *Students:* 35 full-time (25 women), 17 part-time (13 women); includes 10 minority (7 Black or African American, non-Hispanic/Latino; 2 Asian, non-Hispanic/Latino; 1 Two or more races, non-Hispanic/Latino), 9 international. Average age 31. 46 applicants, 72% accepted. In 2011, 14 degrees awarded. *Degree requirements:* For master's, comprehensive exam, thesis or alternative. *Entrance requirements:* Additional exam requirements/recommendations for international students: Required—TOEFL (minimum score 550 paper-based; 213 computer-based; 80 iBT). *Application deadline:* Applications are processed on a rolling basis. Application fee: $30. Electronic applications accepted. *Expenses:* Tuition, state resident: part-time $281.16 per credit hour. Tuition, nonresident: part-time $562.32 per credit hour. Part-time tuition and fees vary according to campus/location and reciprocity agreements. *Financial support:* In 2011–12, 11 students received support, including 11 research assistantships with full tuition reimbursements available (averaging $7,360 per year). Financial award applicants required to submit FAFSA. *Unit head:* Dr. R. Mark Kelley, Chairperson, 309-298-1076. *Application contact:* Dr. Nancy Parsons, Interim Associate Provost and Director of Graduate Studies, 309-298-1806, Fax: 309-298-2345, E-mail: grad-office@wiu.edu. Web site: http://wiu.edu/health.

Western Michigan University, Graduate College, College of Health and Human Services, Interdisciplinary Health Sciences Program, Kalamazoo, MI 49008. Offers PhD.

Western Oregon University, Graduate Programs, College of Education, Division of Teacher Education, Program in Secondary Education, Monmouth, OR 97361-1394. Offers bilingual education (MS Ed); health (MS Ed); humanities (MAT, MS Ed); initial licensure (MAT); mathematics (MAT, MS Ed); science (MAT, MS Ed); social science (MAT, MS Ed). *Accreditation:* NCATE. Part-time and evening/weekend programs available. *Degree requirements:* For master's, thesis optional, written exam. *Entrance requirements:* For master's, minimum GPA of 3.0, teaching license. Additional exam requirements/recommendations for international students: Required—TOEFL (minimum score 550 paper-based; 213 computer-based; 79 iBT), IELTS (minimum score 6.5). *Faculty research:* Literacy, science in primary grades, geography education, retention, teacher burnout.

Western University of Health Sciences, College of Allied Health Professions, Program in Health Sciences, Pomona, CA 91766-1854. Offers MS. Part-time and evening/ weekend programs available. *Faculty:* 2 full-time (1 woman), 1 (woman) part-time/ adjunct. *Students:* 23 full-time (16 women), 8 part-time (all women); includes 15 minority (3 Black or African American, non-Hispanic/Latino; 8 Asian, non-Hispanic/Latino; 4 Hispanic/Latino), 2 international. Average age 31. 38 applicants, 50% accepted, 14 enrolled. In 2011, 13 master's awarded. *Degree requirements:* For master's, thesis. *Entrance requirements:* For master's, minimum undergraduate GPA of 2.5, graduate 3.0; letters of recommendation; interview. *Application deadline:* For fall admission, 10/15 priority date for domestic students; for spring admission, 6/15 priority date for domestic students. Applications are processed on a rolling basis. Application fee: $35. Electronic applications accepted. *Expenses:* Contact institution. *Financial support:* Institutionally sponsored loans, scholarships/grants, and veterans educational benefits available. Financial award application deadline: 3/2; financial award applicants required to submit FAFSA. *Unit head:* Tina Meyer, Chair, 909-469-5586, Fax: 909-469-5407. *Application contact:* Susan Hanson, Director of Admissions for the College of Osteopathic Medicine of the Pacific and for Health Professions Education, 909-469-5335, Fax: 909-469-5570, E-mail: admissions@westernu.edu. Web site: http://www.westernu.edu/xp/edu/cahp/mshs_welcome.xml.

West Virginia University, School of Physical Education, Morgantown, WV 26506. Offers athletic coaching education (MS); athletic training (MS); physical education/ teacher education (MS, PhD), including curriculum and instruction (PhD), motor behavior (PhD), physical education supervision (PhD); sport and exercise psychology (PhD); sport management (MS). *Degree requirements:* For doctorate, comprehensive exam, thesis/dissertation, oral exam. *Entrance requirements:* For master's, GRE or MAT, minimum GPA of 3.0; for doctorate, GRE General Test or MAT, minimum GPA of 3.5. Additional exam requirements/recommendations for international students: Required—TOEFL (minimum score 550 paper-based; 213 computer-based). Electronic applications accepted. *Faculty research:* Sport psychosociology, teacher education, exercise psychology, counseling.

Widener University, School of Human Service Professions, Center for Education, Chester, PA 19013-5792. Offers adult education (M Ed); counseling in higher education (M Ed); counselor education (M Ed); early childhood education (M Ed); educational foundations (M Ed); educational leadership (M Ed); educational psychology (M Ed); elementary education (M Ed); English and language arts (M Ed); health education (M Ed); higher education leadership (Ed D); home and school visitor (M Ed); human sexuality (M Ed, PhD); mathematics education (M Ed); middle school education (M Ed); principalship (M Ed); reading and language arts (Ed D); reading education (M Ed); school administration (Ed D); science education (M Ed); social studies education (M Ed); special education (M Ed); technology education (M Ed). *Accreditation:* NCATE. Part-time and evening/weekend programs available. Terminal master's awarded for partial completion of doctoral program. *Degree requirements:* For doctorate, thesis/ dissertation. *Entrance requirements:* For master's, minimum GPA of 2.5; for doctorate, GRE or MAT, minimum GPA of 2.0 (undergraduate), 3.5 (graduate). Electronic applications accepted. *Expenses:* Contact institution. *Faculty research:* Reading and cognition, adult education, technology education, educational leadership, special education.

Wingate University, Thayer School of Education, Wingate, NC 28174-0159. Offers community college leadership (Ed D); educational leadership (MA Ed, Ed D); elementary education (MA Ed, MAT); health and physical education (MA Ed); sport administration (MA Ed). *Accreditation:* NCATE. Part-time and evening/weekend programs available. *Faculty:* 5 full-time (3 women), 10 part-time/adjunct (3 women). *Students:* 7 full-time (4 women), 251 part-time (152 women); includes 68 minority (63 Black or African American, non-Hispanic/Latino; 1 American Indian or Alaska Native, non-Hispanic/Latino; 1 Asian, non-Hispanic/Latino; 3 Hispanic/Latino), 2 international. Average age 35. In 2011, 29 master's awarded. *Degree requirements:* For master's, portfolio. *Entrance requirements:* For master's, GRE General Test or MAT, teaching certificate (MA Ed). *Application deadline:* For fall admission, 8/15 priority date for domestic students; for spring admission, 12/15 for domestic students. Applications are processed on a rolling basis. Application fee: $0. *Expenses: Tuition:* Part-time $455 per credit hour. Part-time tuition and fees vary according to degree level and program. *Financial support:* In 2011–12, 20 students received support. Scholarships/grants available. Support available to part-time students. Financial award applicants required to submit FAFSA. *Unit head:* Dr. Sarah Harrison-Burns, Dean, 704-233-8128, E-mail: shburns@wingate.edu. *Application contact:* Theresa Hopkins, Secretary, 704-321-1470, Fax: 704-233-8273, E-mail: t.hopkins@wingate.edu.

Worcester State University, Graduate Studies, Department of Education, Program in Health Education, Worcester, MA 01602-2597. Offers M Ed. Part-time programs available. *Faculty:* 1 (woman) full-time, 3 part-time/adjunct (2 women). *Students:* 8 part-time (5 women). Average age 30. 8 applicants, 88% accepted, 4 enrolled. In 2011, 6 master's awarded. *Degree requirements:* For master's, comprehensive exam (for some programs), thesis optional. *Entrance requirements:* For master's, GRE General Test or MAT. Additional exam requirements/recommendations for international students: Required—TOEFL (minimum score 500 paper-based; 61 iBT). *Application deadline:* For fall admission, 6/15 for domestic and international students; for spring admission, 4/1 for domestic and international students. Applications are processed on a rolling basis. Application fee: $40. Electronic applications accepted. *Expenses:* Tuition, state resident: full-time $2700; part-time $150 per credit. Tuition, nonresident: full-time $2700; part-time $150 per credit. *Required fees:* $2016; $112 per credit. *Financial support:* In 2011–12, 2 students received support, including 2 research assistantships (averaging $4,800 per year); career-related internships or fieldwork, scholarships/grants, and unspecified assistantships also available. Financial award application deadline: 3/1; financial award applicants required to submit FAFSA. *Unit head:* Dr. Nancy Brewer, Coordinator, 508-929-8838, Fax: 508-929-8164, E-mail: nbrewer@worcester.edu. *Application contact:* Sara Grady, Assistant Dean of Graduate and Continuing Education, 508-929-8787, Fax: 508-929-8100, E-mail: sara.grady@worcester.edu.

Wright State University, School of Graduate Studies, College of Education and Human Services, Department of Health, Physical Education, and Recreation, Dayton, OH 45435. Offers M Ed, MA. *Accreditation:* NCATE. *Degree requirements:* For master's, comprehensive exam, thesis (for some programs). *Entrance requirements:* For master's, GRE General Test, MAT. Additional exam requirements/recommendations for international students: Required—TOEFL. *Faculty research:* Motor learning, motor development, exercise physiology, adapted physical education.

Wright State University, School of Medicine, Program in Public Health, Dayton, OH 45435. Offers health promotion and education (MPH); public health management (MPH); public health nursing (MPH). *Accreditation:* CEPH.

Home Economics Education

Cambridge College, School of Education, Cambridge, MA 02138-5304. Offers autism specialist (M Ed); autism/behavior analyst (M Ed); behavior analyst (Post-Master's Certificate); behavioral management (M Ed); early childhood teacher (M Ed); education specialist in curriculum and instruction (CAGS); educational leadership (Ed D); elementary teacher (M Ed); English as a second language (M Ed, Certificate); general science (M Ed); health education (Post-Master's Certificate); health/family and consumer sciences (M Ed); history (M Ed); individualized (M Ed); information technology literacy (M Ed); instructional technology (M Ed); interdisciplinary studies (M Ed); library teacher (M Ed); literacy education (M Ed); mathematics (M Ed); mathematics specialist (Certificate); middle school mathematics and science (M Ed); school administration (M Ed, CAGS); school guidance counselor (M Ed); school nurse education (M Ed); school social worker/school adjustment counselor (M Ed); special education administrator (CAGS); special education/moderate disabilities (M Ed); teaching skills and methodologies (M Ed). Part-time and evening/weekend programs available. Postbaccalaureate distance learning degree programs offered (minimal on-campus study). *Degree requirements:* For master's, thesis, internship/practicum (licensure program only); for doctorate, thesis/dissertation; for other advanced degree, thesis. *Entrance requirements:* For master's, interview, resume, documentation of licensure, 2 professional references; for doctorate, official transcripts, interview, resume, documentation of licensure (if any), written personal statement/essay, portfolio of scholarly and professional work, qualifying assessment, 2 professional references, health insurance, immunizations form; for other advanced degree, official transcripts, interview, resume, documentation of licensure (if any), written personal statement/essay, 2 professional references, health insurance, immunizations form. Additional exam requirements/recommendations for international students: Required—TOEFL (minimum score 550 paper-based; 213 computer-based; 79 iBT); Recommended—IELTS (minimum score 6). Electronic applications accepted. *Expenses:* Contact institution. *Faculty research:* Adult education, accelerated learning, mathematics education, brain compatible learning, special education and law.

Central Washington University, Graduate Studies and Research, College of Education and Professional Studies, Department of Family and Consumer Sciences, Ellensburg, WA 98926. Offers career and technical education (MS); family and consumer sciences education (MS); family studies (MS). Part-time programs available. *Faculty:* 15 full-time (10 women). *Students:* 14 full-time (10 women), 6 part-time (all women); includes 3 minority (all Hispanic/Latino). 12 applicants, 83% accepted, 8 enrolled. In 2011, 12 master's awarded. *Degree requirements:* For master's, thesis or alternative. *Entrance requirements:* For master's, minimum GPA of 3.0. Additional exam requirements/recommendations for international students: Required—TOEFL (minimum score 550 paper-based; 213 computer-based; 79 iBT). *Application deadline:* For fall admission, 2/1 priority date for domestic students; for winter admission, 10/1 for domestic students; for spring admission, 1/1 for domestic students. Applications are processed on a rolling basis. Application fee: $50. Electronic applications accepted. *Expenses:* Tuition, state resident: full-time $8112; part-time $270 per credit. Tuition, nonresident: full-time $18,069; part-time $602 per credit. *Required fees:* $924. *Financial support:* In 2011–12, research assistantships with full and partial tuition reimbursements (averaging $9,234 per year), 3 teaching assistantships (averaging $9,234 per year) were awarded; Federal Work-Study, health care benefits, and unspecified assistantships also available. Financial award application deadline: 3/1; financial award applicants required to submit FAFSA. *Unit head:* Dr. Robert Perkins, Professor of Leadership and Family and Consumer Sciences Professional Core, 509-963-1292, E-mail: perkinsr@cwu.edu. *Application contact:* Justine Eason, Admissions Program Coordinator, 509-963-3103, Fax: 509-963-1799, E-mail: masters@cwu.edu. Web site: http://www.cwu.edu/~fandcs/.

Eastern Kentucky University, The Graduate School, College of Education, Department of Curriculum and Instruction, Program in Secondary and Higher Education, Richmond, KY 40475-3102. Offers secondary education (MA Ed), including agricultural education, art education, biological sciences education, business education, English education, geography education, history education, home economics education, industrial education, mathematical sciences education, physical education, school health education. *Accreditation:* NCATE. Part-time programs available. *Entrance requirements:* For master's, GRE General Test, minimum GPA of 2.5.

Georgia Southern University, Jack N. Averitt College of Graduate Studies, College of Education, Department of Teaching and Learning, Program in Secondary Education/Family and Consumer Sciences, Statesboro, GA 30460. Offers MAT. *Students:* 1 (woman) full-time; minority (Black or African American, non-Hispanic/Latino). Average age 38. 1 applicant, 100% accepted, 1 enrolled. *Expenses:* Tuition, state resident: full-time $6300; part-time $263 per semester hour. Tuition, nonresident: full-time $25,174; part-time $1049 per semester hour. *Required fees:* $1872. *Unit head:* Dr. Ronnie Sheppard, Chair, 912-478-0198, Fax: 912-478-0026, E-mail: sheppard@georgiasouthern.edu. *Application contact:* Amanda Gilliland, Coordinator for Graduate Student Recruitment, 912-478-5384, Fax: 912-478-0740, E-mail: gradadmissions@georgiasouthern.edu.

Indiana State University, College of Graduate and Professional Studies, College of Arts and Sciences, Department of Family and Consumer Sciences, Terre Haute, IN 47809. Offers dietetics (MS); family and consumer sciences education (MS); inter-area option (MS). *Accreditation:* AND. Part-time programs available. *Degree requirements:* For master's, thesis optional. Electronic applications accepted.

Iowa State University of Science and Technology, Department of Apparel, Education Studies, and Hospitality Management, Ames, IA 50011-1121. Offers family and consumer sciences education and studies (M Ed, MS, PhD); foodservice and lodging management (MFCS, MS, PhD); textiles and clothing (MFCS, MS, PhD). *Degree requirements:* For doctorate, thesis/dissertation. *Entrance requirements:* For master's and doctorate, GRE General Test. Additional exam requirements/recommendations for international students: Required—TOEFL (minimum score 550 paper-based; 79 iBT), IELTS (minimum score 6.5). *Application deadline:* For fall admission, 2/1 priority date for domestic students, 2/1 for international students. Application fee: $40 ($90 for international students). *Unit head:* Dr. Ann Marie Fiore, Director of Graduate Education, 515-294-9303, E-mail: amfiore@iastate.edu. *Application contact:* Ann Marie Fiore, Application Contact, 515-294-9303, E-mail: amfiore@iastate.edu. Web site: http://www.aeshm.hs.iastate.edu/graduate-programs/amd/.

Louisiana State University and Agricultural and Mechanical College, Graduate School, College of Agriculture, School of Human Resource Education and Workforce Development, Baton Rouge, LA 70803. Offers agriculture and extension education and youth development (MS, PhD); career and technical education (MS, PhD); comprehensive vocational education (MS, PhD); extension and international education (MS, PhD); human resource and leadership development (MS, PhD); industrial education (MS); vocational agriculture education (MS, PhD); vocational business education (MS); vocational home economics education (MS). *Accreditation:* NCATE. Part-time programs available. *Faculty:* 9 full-time (5 women), 3 part-time/adjunct (0 women). *Students:* 51 full-time (36 women), 85 part-time (59 women); includes 28 minority (23 Black or African American, non-Hispanic/Latino; 1 Asian, non-Hispanic/Latino; 4 Hispanic/Latino), 3 international. Average age 36. 29 applicants, 83% accepted, 20 enrolled. In 2011, 15 master's, 17 doctorates awarded. Terminal master's awarded for partial completion of doctoral program. *Degree requirements:* For master's, thesis (for some programs); for doctorate, thesis/dissertation. *Entrance requirements:* For master's and doctorate, GRE General Test, minimum GPA of 3.0. Additional exam requirements/recommendations for international students: Required—TOEFL (minimum score 550 paper-based; 213 computer-based; 79 iBT) or IELTS (minimum score 6.5). *Application deadline:* For fall admission, 1/25 priority date for domestic students, 5/15 for international students; for spring admission, 10/15 for international students. Applications are processed on a rolling basis. Application fee: $50 ($70 for international students). Electronic applications accepted. *Financial support:* In 2011–12, 84 students received support, including 3 fellowships with full and partial tuition reimbursements available (averaging $14,986 per year), 4 research assistantships with full and partial tuition reimbursements available (averaging $12,000 per year), 11 teaching assistantships with partial tuition reimbursements available (averaging $13,300 per year); career-related internships or fieldwork, Federal Work-Study, institutionally sponsored loans, health care benefits, tuition waivers (full and partial), and unspecified assistantships also available. Financial award application deadline: 3/1; financial award applicants required to submit FAFSA. *Faculty research:* Adult education, history and philosophy of vocational education, curriculum and instruction, career decision-making. *Unit head:* Dr. Michael F. Burnett, Director, 225-578-5748, Fax: 225-578-2526, E-mail: vocbur@lsu.edu. Web site: http://www.lsu.edu/hrleader/.

Montana State University, College of Graduate Studies, College of Education, Health, and Human Development, Department of Health and Human Development, Bozeman, MT 59717. Offers family and consumer sciences (MS). *Accreditation:* ACA. Part-time programs available. Postbaccalaureate distance learning degree programs offered (no on-campus study). *Degree requirements:* For master's, comprehensive exam. *Entrance requirements:* For master's, GRE (minimum scores: verbal 480; quantitative 480). Additional exam requirements/recommendations for international students: Required—TOEFL (minimum score 550 paper-based; 213 computer-based). Electronic applications accepted. *Faculty research:* Community food systems, ethic of care for teachers and coaches, influence of public policy on families and communities, cost effectiveness of early childhood education, exercise metabolism, winter sport performance enhancement, assessment of physical activity.

Purdue University, Graduate School, College of Education, Department of Curriculum and Instruction, West Lafayette, IN 47907. Offers agricultural and extension education (PhD, Ed S); agriculture and extension education (MS, MS Ed); art education (PhD); consumer and family sciences and extension education (MS Ed, PhD, Ed S); curriculum studies (MS Ed, PhD, Ed S); educational technology (MS Ed, PhD, Ed S); elementary education (MS Ed); foreign language education (MS Ed, PhD, Ed S); industrial technology (PhD, Ed S); language arts (MS Ed, PhD, Ed S); literacy (MS Ed, PhD, Ed S); mathematics/science education (MS, MS Ed, PhD, Ed S); social studies (MS Ed, PhD); social studies education (Ed S); vocational/industrial education (MS Ed, PhD, Ed S); vocational/technical education (MS Ed, PhD, Ed S). *Accreditation:* NCATE. Part-time and evening/weekend programs available. *Faculty:* 30 full-time (21 women), 1 (woman) part-time/adjunct. *Students:* 89 full-time (64 women), 134 part-time (84 women); includes 31 minority (12 Black or African American, non-Hispanic/Latino; 3 American Indian or Alaska Native, non-Hispanic/Latino; 7 Asian, non-Hispanic/Latino; 9 Hispanic/Latino), 49 international. Average age 36. 136 applicants, 83% accepted, 72 enrolled. In 2011, 26 master's, 13 doctorates awarded. *Degree requirements:* For master's, thesis optional; for doctorate, thesis/dissertation, oral and written exams; for Ed S, oral presentation, project. *Entrance requirements:* For master's, GRE general test is required if undergraduate GPA is below 3.0, minimum undergraduate GPA of 3.0 or equivalent; for doctorate, GRE General Test, a combined GRE verbal and quantitative score of 1000 (300 for revised GRE Test) or more is expected, minimum undergraduate GPA of 3.0 or equivalent; master's degree with minimum GPA of 3.0 or equivalent; for Ed S, GRE general test, a combined GRE verbal and quantitative score of 1000 (300 for revised GRE Test) or more is expected, minimum undergraduate GPA of 3.0 or equivalent; master's degree. Additional exam requirements/recommendations for international students: Required—TOEFL (minimum score 550 paper-based; 77 iBT). *Application deadline:* For fall admission, 12/15 priority date for domestic students, 3/1 for international students; for spring admission, 9/15 for domestic students, 8/1 for international students. Application fee: $60 ($75 for international students). Electronic applications accepted. *Financial support:* Fellowships with full tuition reimbursements, research assistantships with full tuition reimbursements, teaching assistantships with full tuition reimbursements, career-related internships or fieldwork, and tuition waivers (full) available. Support available to part-time students. Financial award application deadline: 3/1; financial award applicants required to submit FAFSA. *Faculty research:* Literacy acquisition and development, teacher beliefs and knowledge, recruitment and retention of underrepresented students, economic education, literacy discourse. *Unit head:* Dr.

Philip J. VanFossen, Head, 765-494-7935, Fax: 765-496-1622, E-mail: vanfoss@purdue.edu. *Application contact:* Sarah N. Prater, Graduate Contact, 765-494-2345, Fax: 765-494-5832, E-mail: prater0@purdue.edu. Web site: http://www.edci.purdue.edu/.

Queens College of the City University of New York, Division of Graduate Studies, Mathematics and Natural Sciences Division, Department of Family, Nutrition and Exercise Sciences, Flushing, NY 11367-1597. Offers home economics (MS Ed); physical education and exercise sciences (MS Ed). Part-time and evening/weekend programs available. *Faculty:* 12 full-time (7 women). *Students:* 15 full-time (14 women), 66 part-time (53 women); includes 31 minority (7 Black or African American, non-Hispanic/Latino; 19 Asian, non-Hispanic/Latino; 5 Hispanic/Latino), 4 international. 58 applicants, 78% accepted, 25 enrolled. In 2011, 14 master's awarded. *Degree requirements:* For master's, research project. *Entrance requirements:* For master's, minimum GPA of 3.0. Additional exam requirements/recommendations for international students: Required—TOEFL. *Application deadline:* For fall admission, 4/1 for domestic students; for spring admission, 11/1 for domestic students. Applications are processed on a rolling basis. Application fee: $125. *Expenses:* Tuition, state resident: part-time $345 per credit. Tuition, nonresident: part-time $640 per credit. *Required fees:* $145.25 per semester. *Financial support:* Career-related internships or fieldwork, Federal Work-Study, institutionally sponsored loans, and tuition waivers (partial) available. Support available to part-time students. Financial award application deadline: 4/1; financial award applicants required to submit FAFSA. *Faculty research:* Exercise and environmental physiology, interdisciplinary approaches to school curricula using outdoor education, program development in cardiac rehabilitation and adult fitness, nutrition education. *Unit head:* Dr. Elizabeth Lowe, Chairperson, 718-997-4168. *Application contact:* Mario Caruso, Director of Graduate Admissions, 718-997-5200, Fax: 718-997-5193, E-mail: graduate_admissions@qc.edu.

South Carolina State University, School of Graduate Studies, Department of Education, Orangeburg, SC 29117-0001. Offers counseling education (M Ed); early childhood and special education (M Ed); early childhood education (MAT); educational leadership (Ed D, Ed S); elementary education (M Ed, MAT); engineering (MAT); general science (MAT); mathematics (MAT); secondary education (M Ed), including biology education, business education, counselor education, English education, home economics education, industrial education, mathematics education, science education, social studies education; special education (M Ed), including emotionally handicapped, learning disabilities, mentally handicapped. *Accreditation:* NCATE. Part-time and evening/weekend programs available. *Faculty:* 9 full-time (6 women), 6 part-time/adjunct (2 women). *Students:* 34 full-time (29 women), 50 part-time (40 women); includes 74 minority (72 Black or African American, non-Hispanic/Latino; 1 Asian, non-Hispanic/Latino; 1 Hispanic/Latino). Average age 34. 23 applicants, 91% accepted, 14 enrolled. In 2011, 11 master's awarded. *Degree requirements:* For master's, thesis optional, departmental qualifying exam. *Entrance requirements:* For master's, GRE General Test, NTE, interview, teaching certificate. *Application deadline:* For fall admission, 6/15 priority date for domestic students, 6/15 for international students; for spring admission, 11/1 for domestic and international students. Applications are processed on a rolling basis. Application fee: $25. Electronic applications accepted. *Expenses:* Tuition, state resident: full-time $8688; part-time $514 per credit hour. Tuition, nonresident: full-time $17,600; part-time $1009 per credit hour. *Required fees:* $570. *Financial support:* In 2011–12, 3 fellowships (averaging $5,020 per year) were awarded; career-related internships or fieldwork, Federal Work-Study, and institutionally sponsored loans also available. Financial award application deadline: 6/1. *Faculty research:* Critical thinking, child abuse, stress, test-taking skills, conflict resolution, mainstreaming. *Unit head:* Dr. Charlie Spell, Interim Chair, 803-536-7098, Fax: 803-516-4568, E-mail: cspell@scsu.edu. *Application contact:* Annette Hazzard-Jones, Program Coordinator II, 803-536-8809, Fax: 803-536-8812, E-mail: zs_ahazzard@scsu.edu.

State University of New York College at Oneonta, Graduate Education, Division of Education, Department of Secondary Education, Oneonta, NY 13820-4015. Offers adolescence education (MS Ed); family and consumer science education (MS Ed). *Accreditation:* NCATE. Part-time and evening/weekend programs available. *Entrance requirements:* For master's, GRE General Test.

Texas Tech University, Graduate School, College of Human Sciences, Program in Family and Consumer Sciences Education, Lubbock, TX 79409. Offers MS, PhD. Part-time and evening/weekend programs available. Postbaccalaureate distance learning degree programs offered (no on-campus study). *Students:* 5 full-time (3 women), 24 part-time (17 women); includes 6 minority (2 Black or African American, non-Hispanic/Latino; 4 Hispanic/Latino), 2 international. Average age 43. 6 applicants, 33% accepted, 1 enrolled. In 2011, 4 master's, 2 doctorates awarded. Terminal master's awarded for partial completion of doctoral program. *Degree requirements:* For master's, thesis or alternative; for doctorate, comprehensive exam, thesis/dissertation. *Entrance requirements:* For master's and doctorate, GRE General Test. Additional exam requirements/recommendations for international students: Required—TOEFL (minimum score 500 paper-based; 213 computer-based; 79 iBT). *Application deadline:* For fall admission, 6/1 priority date for domestic students, 1/15 for international students; for spring admission, 9/1 priority date for domestic students, 6/15 for international students. Applications are processed on a rolling basis. Application fee: $50 ($75 for international students). Electronic applications accepted. *Expenses:* Tuition, state resident: full-time $5899; part-time $245.80 per credit hour. Tuition, nonresident: full-time $13,411; part-time $558.80 per credit hour. *Required fees:* $2680.60; $86.50 per credit hour. $920.30 per semester. *Financial support:* Application deadline: 4/15; applicants required to submit FAFSA. *Faculty research:* Teacher professional development, career clusters and pathways, college and career readiness, reading and writing in FCS content, culturally diverse learners in FCS. *Unit head:* Sue Couch, Director, 806-742-5050. *Application contact:* Dr. Karen L. Alexander, Associate Professor, 806-742-3031 Ext. 232, Fax: 806-742-1849, E-mail: karen.alexander@ttu.edu. Web site: http://www.depts.ttu.edu/hs/fcse/.

The University of British Columbia, Faculty of Education, Department of Curriculum and Pedagogy, Vancouver, BC V6T 1Z4, Canada. Offers art education (M Ed, MA); business education (MA); curriculum studies (M Ed, MA, PhD); home economics education (M Ed, MA); math education (M Ed, MA); music education (M Ed, MA); physical education (M Ed, MA); science education (M Ed, MA); social studies education (M Ed, MA); technology studies education (M Ed, MA). Part-time programs available. *Degree requirements:* For master's, thesis (MA); for doctorate, comprehensive exam, thesis/dissertation. *Entrance requirements:* Additional exam requirements/recommendations for international students: Required—TOEFL (minimum score 580 paper-based; 237 computer-based; 92 iBT). Electronic applications accepted. *Expenses:* Contact institution. *Faculty research:* School subjects, teaching and learning.

University of Central Oklahoma, College of Graduate Studies and Research, College of Education and Professional Studies, Department of Human Environmental Sciences, Edmond, OK 73034-5209. Offers family and child studies (MS); family and consumer science education (MS); interior design (MS); nutrition-food management (MS). Part-time programs available. *Faculty:* 8 full-time (7 women), 8 part-time/adjunct (6 women). *Students:* 52 full-time (49 women), 75 part-time (71 women); includes 40 minority (32 Black or African American, non-Hispanic/Latino; 5 Hispanic/Latino; 3 Two or more races, non-Hispanic/Latino), 6 international. Average age 30. In 2011, 45 master's awarded. *Entrance requirements:* Additional exam requirements/recommendations for international students: Required—TOEFL (minimum score 550 paper-based; 213 computer-based). *Application deadline:* Applications are processed on a rolling basis. Application fee: $50. Electronic applications accepted. *Expenses:* Tuition, state resident: full-time $3901; part-time $218.30 per credit hour. Tuition, nonresident: full-time $9198; part-time $511.20 per credit hour. Tuition and fees vary according to program. *Financial support:* Career-related internships or fieldwork and unspecified assistantships available. Financial award application deadline: 3/31; financial award applicants required to submit FAFSA. *Faculty research:* Dietetics and food science. *Unit head:* Dr. Kaye Sears, Chairperson, 405-974-5786, E-mail: ksears@uco.edu. *Application contact:* Dr. Richard Bernard, Dean, Graduate College, 405-974-3493, Fax: 405-974-3852, E-mail: gradcoll@uco.edu.

University of Nebraska–Lincoln, Graduate College, College of Education and Human Sciences, Department of Child, Youth and Family Studies, Lincoln, NE 68588. Offers child development/early childhood education (MS, PhD); child, youth and family studies (MS); family and consumer sciences education (MS, PhD); family financial planning (MS); family science (MS, PhD); gerontology (PhD); human sciences (PhD), including child, youth and family studies, gerontology, medical family therapy; marriage and family therapy (MS); medical family therapy (PhD); youth development (MS). *Accreditation:* AAMFT/COAMFTE (one or more programs are accredited). Postbaccalaureate distance learning degree programs offered. *Degree requirements:* For master's, thesis optional. *Entrance requirements:* For master's, GRE. Additional exam requirements/recommendations for international students: Required—TOEFL (minimum score 550 paper-based; 213 computer-based). Electronic applications accepted. *Faculty research:* Marriage and family therapy, child development/early childhood education, family financial management.

Utah State University, School of Graduate Studies, College of Agriculture, Department of Agricultural Systems Technology and Education, Logan, UT 84322. Offers agricultural systems technology (MS), including agricultural extension education, agricultural mechanization, international agricultural extension, secondary and postsecondary agricultural education; family and consumer sciences education (MS). Part-time programs available. Postbaccalaureate distance learning degree programs offered (minimal on-campus study). *Degree requirements:* For master's, comprehensive exam (for some programs), thesis (for some programs). *Entrance requirements:* For master's, GRE General Test, MAT, BS in agricultural education, agricultural extension, or related agricultural or science discipline; minimum GPA of 3.0. Additional exam requirements/recommendations for international students: Required—TOEFL. *Faculty research:* Extension and adult education; structures and environment; low-input agriculture; farm safety, systems, and mechanizations.

Wayne State College, School of Education and Counseling, Department of Educational Foundations and Leadership, Program in Curriculum and Instruction, Wayne, NE 68787. Offers alternative education (MSE); business and information technology education (MSE); communication arts education (MSE); early childhood education (MSE); elementary education (MSE); English as a second language (MSE); English education (MSE); family and consumer sciences education (MSE); industrial technology and vocational education (MSE); learning communities (MSE); mathematics education (MSE); music education (MSE); science education (MSE); social science education (MSE). *Accreditation:* NCATE. Part-time and evening/weekend programs available. *Degree requirements:* For master's, comprehensive exam, thesis optional. *Entrance requirements:* For master's, GRE General Test. Additional exam requirements/recommendations for international students: Required—TOEFL (minimum score 550 paper-based; 213 computer-based).

Mathematics Education

Acadia University, Faculty of Professional Studies, School of Education, Program in Curriculum Studies, Wolfville, NS B4P 2R6, Canada. Offers cultural and media studies (M Ed); learning and technology (M Ed); science, math and technology (M Ed). Part-time programs available. *Degree requirements:* For master's, thesis optional. *Entrance requirements:* For master's, B Ed or the equivalent, minimum B average in undergraduate course work, 2 years of teaching experience. Additional exam requirements/recommendations for international students: Required—TOEFL (minimum score 580 paper-based; 237 computer-based; 93 iBT), IELTS (minimum score 6.5). *Faculty research:* Literacy development, postmodern philosophy and curriculum theory, historiography, philosophy of education, learning and technology.

Alabama State University, Department of Curriculum and Instruction, Program in Secondary Education, Montgomery, AL 36101-0271. Offers biology education (M Ed, Ed S); English/language arts (M Ed); history education (M Ed, Ed S); mathematics education (M Ed); secondary education (Ed S); social studies (Ed S). Part-time programs available. *Students:* 16 full-time (12 women), 13 part-time (9 women); includes 26 minority (all Black or African American, non-Hispanic/Latino). Average age 36. 48 applicants, 52% accepted, 5 enrolled. In 2011, 3 master's awarded. *Degree requirements:* For master's, comprehensive exam; for Ed S, comprehensive exam, thesis. *Entrance requirements:* For master's, GRE General Test, MAT, graduate writing competency test; for Ed S, graduate writing competency test, GRE, MAT. Additional exam requirements/recommendations for international students: Required—TOEFL (minimum score 500 paper-based; 173 computer-based). *Application deadline:* For fall admission, 7/15 for domestic students; for spring admission, 12/15 for domestic students. Applications are processed on a rolling basis. Application fee: $10. *Financial support:* In 2011–12, research assistantships (averaging $9,450 per year) were awarded. *Unit head:* Dr. Willa Bing Harris, Acting Chairperson, 334-229-4394, Fax: 334-229-4904, E-mail: wbharris@alasu.edu. *Application contact:* Dr. Doris Screws, Dean of Graduate Studies, 334-229-4274, Fax: 334-229-4928, E-mail: dscrews@alasu.edu.

Web site: http://www.alasu.edu/academics/colleges—departments/college-of-education/curriculum—instruction/degree-programs/secondary-education/index.aspx.

Alabama State University, Department of Mathematics and Computer Science, Montgomery, AL 36101-0271. Offers mathematics (M Ed, MS, Ed S). Part-time programs available. *Faculty:* 5 full-time (0 women). *Students:* 1 (woman) full-time; minority (Black or African American, non-Hispanic/Latino). Average age 23. 4 applicants, 25% accepted, 0 enrolled. *Degree requirements:* For Ed S, thesis. *Entrance requirements:* For master's, GRE General Test, GRE Subject Test, graduate writing competence test; for Ed S, GRE General Test, MAT, graduate writing competency test. Additional exam requirements/recommendations for international students: Required—TOEFL (minimum score 500 paper-based; 173 computer-based). *Application deadline:* For fall admission, 7/15 for domestic students; for spring admission, 12/15 for domestic students. Applications are processed on a rolling basis. Application fee: $10. *Financial support:* In 2011–12, 1 research assistantship (averaging $9,450 per year) was awarded. *Faculty research:* Discrete mathematics, symbolic dynamics, mathematical social sciences. *Total annual research expenditures:* $25,000. *Unit head:* Dr. Wallace Maryland, Chair, 334-229-4464, Fax: 334-229-4902, E-mail: wmaryl@asunet.alasu.edu. *Application contact:* Dr. Doris Screws, Dean of Graduate Studies, 334-229-4274, Fax: 334-229-4928, E-mail: dscrews@alasu.edu. Web site: http://www.alasu.edu/academics/colleges—departments/science-mathematics—technology/mathematics—computer-science/index.aspx.

Albany State University, College of Sciences and Health Professions, Albany, GA 31705-2717. Offers criminal justice (MS), including corrections, forensic science, law enforcement, public administration; mathematics education (M Ed); nursing (MSN), including RN to MSN family nurse practitioner, RN to MSN nurse educator; science education (M Ed). *Accreditation:* NLN. Part-time and evening/weekend programs available. Postbaccalaureate distance learning degree programs offered. *Faculty:* 16 full-time (7 women), 7 part-time/adjunct (3 women). *Students:* 34 full-time (26 women), 103 part-time (84 women); includes 94 minority (92 Black or African American, non-Hispanic/Latino; 2 Asian, non-Hispanic/Latino), 2 international. Average age 36. 101 applicants, 48% accepted, 33 enrolled. In 2011, 16 master's awarded. *Degree requirements:* For master's, comprehensive exam, thesis. *Entrance requirements:* For master's, GRE or MAT, official transcript, letters of recommendations, pre-medical/certificate of immunizations. *Application deadline:* For fall admission, 6/15 for domestic students, 5/1 for international students; for spring admission, 11/1 for domestic students, 10/1 for international students. Applications are processed on a rolling basis. Application fee: $20. Electronic applications accepted. *Expenses:* Tuition, state resident: full-time $3204; part-time $178 per credit hour. Tuition, nonresident: full-time $12,816; part-time $712 per credit hour. *Required fees:* $379 per semester. *Financial support:* Scholarships/grants and traineeships available. Financial award application deadline: 4/15; financial award applicants required to submit CSS PROFILE or FAFSA. *Unit head:* Dr. Joyce Johnson, Dean, 229-430-4792, Fax: 229-430-3937, E-mail: joyce.johnson@asurams.edu. *Application contact:* Jeffrey Pierce, II, Graduate Admissions Counselor, 229-430-4646, Fax: 229-430-4105, E-mail: jeffrey.pierce@asurams.edu. Web site: http://asu-sacs.asurams.edu/ASUCatalog/Graduate/index.html.

Alfred University, Graduate School, Division of Education, Alfred, NY 14802-1205. Offers literacy teacher (MS Ed); numeracy (MS). *Accreditation:* Teacher Education Accreditation Council. Part-time programs available. *Entrance requirements:* For master's, LAST, Assessment of Teaching Skills (written), Content Specialty Test. Additional exam requirements/recommendations for international students: Required—TOEFL (minimum score 590 paper-based; 243 computer-based; 90 iBT), IELTS (minimum score 6.5). Electronic applications accepted. *Faculty research:* Whole language, ethics in counseling and psychotherapy.

Appalachian State University, Cratis D. Williams Graduate School, Department of Curriculum and Instruction, Boone, NC 28608. Offers curriculum specialist (MA); educational media (MA); elementary education (MA); middle grades education (MA), including language arts, mathematics, science, social studies. *Accreditation:* NCATE. Part-time and evening/weekend programs available. Postbaccalaureate distance learning degree programs offered (no on-campus study). *Faculty:* 33 full-time (23 women), 5 part-time/adjunct (2 women). *Students:* 23 full-time (18 women), 110 part-time (90 women); includes 7 minority (4 Black or African American, non-Hispanic/Latino; 1 Asian, non-Hispanic/Latino; 2 Hispanic/Latino). 79 applicants, 94% accepted, 64 enrolled. In 2011, 87 master's awarded. *Degree requirements:* For master's, comprehensive exam, thesis or alternative. *Entrance requirements:* For master's, GRE General Test or MAT, 3 letters of recommendation. Additional exam requirements/recommendations for international students: Required—TOEFL (minimum score 570 paper-based; 230 computer-based; 79 iBT), IELTS (minimum score 6.5). *Application deadline:* For fall admission, 3/14 for domestic students, 2/1 for international students; for spring admission, 11/1 for domestic students, 7/1 for international students. Applications are processed on a rolling basis. Application fee: $55. Electronic applications accepted. *Expenses:* Tuition, state resident: full-time $4040; part-time $180 per semester hour. Tuition, nonresident: full-time $15,900; part-time $760 per semester hour. *Required fees:* $2500; $20 per semester hour. Tuition and fees vary according to campus/location. *Financial support:* In 2011–12, 6 teaching assistantships (averaging $8,000 per year) were awarded; fellowships, research assistantships, career-related internships or fieldwork, Federal Work-Study, scholarships/grants, and unspecified assistantships also available. Financial award application deadline: 4/1; financial award applicants required to submit FAFSA. *Faculty research:* Media literacy, elementary teaching, curriculum development, online learning environments. *Total annual research expenditures:* $480,000. *Unit head:* Dr. Michael Jacobson, Chairperson, 828-262-2224. *Application contact:* Sandy Krause, Director of Admissions and Recruiting, 828-262-2130, Fax: 828-262-2709, E-mail: krausesl@appstate.edu. Web site: http://www.ced.appstate.edu/departments/ci.

Appalachian State University, Cratis D. Williams Graduate School, Department of Mathematical Sciences, Boone, NC 28608. Offers mathematics (MA); mathematics education (MA). Part-time programs available. Postbaccalaureate distance learning degree programs offered (no on-campus study). *Faculty:* 24 full-time (9 women), 2 part-time/adjunct (1 woman). *Students:* 12 full-time (5 women), 7 part-time (6 women); includes 1 minority (Hispanic/Latino). 8 applicants, 100% accepted, 5 enrolled. In 2011, 5 master's awarded. *Degree requirements:* For master's, comprehensive exam, thesis optional. *Entrance requirements:* For master's, GRE General Test, 3 letters of recommendation. Additional exam requirements/recommendations for international students: Required—TOEFL (minimum score 570 paper-based; 230 computer-based; 79 iBT), IELTS (minimum score 6.5). *Application deadline:* For fall admission, 3/15 priority date for domestic students, 2/1 for international students; for spring admission, 11/1 for domestic students, 7/1 for international students. Applications are processed on a rolling basis. Application fee: $55. Electronic applications accepted. *Expenses:* Tuition, state resident: full-time $4040; part-time $180 per semester hour. Tuition, nonresident: full-time $15,900; part-time $760 per semester hour. *Required fees:* $2500; $20 per semester hour. Tuition and fees vary according to campus/location. *Financial support:* In 2011–12, 14 teaching assistantships (averaging $9,500 per year) were awarded; fellowships, research assistantships, career-related internships or fieldwork, Federal Work-Study, scholarships/grants, and unspecified assistantships also available. Financial award application deadline: 4/1; financial award applicants required to submit FAFSA. *Faculty research:* Graph theory, differential equations, logic, geometry, complex analysis, topology, algebra, mathematics education. *Total annual research expenditures:* $80,000. *Unit head:* Dr. Mark Ginn, Chair, 828-262-3050, Fax: 828-265-8617, E-mail: ginnmc@appstate.edu. *Application contact:* Dr. Trina Palmer, Graduate Director, 828-262-3050, E-mail: palmerk@appstate.edu. Web site: http://www.mathsci.appstate.edu/.

Arcadia University, Graduate Studies, Department of Education, Glenside, PA 19038-3295. Offers art education (M Ed); computer education (CAS); curriculum (CAS); curriculum studies (M Ed); early childhood education (M Ed, CAS), including individualized (M Ed), master teacher (M Ed), research in child development (M Ed); educational leadership (M Ed, Ed D, CAS); elementary education (M Ed, CAS); English education (MA Ed); environmental education (MA Ed, CAS); history education (MA Ed); instructional technology (M Ed); language arts (M Ed, CAS); library science (M Ed); mathematics education (M Ed, MA Ed, CAS); music education (MA Ed); psychology (MA Ed); reading (M Ed, CAS); science education (M Ed, CAS); secondary education (M Ed, CAS); special education (M Ed, Ed D, CAS); theater arts (MA Ed); written communication (MA Ed). *Accreditation:* NASAD. Part-time and evening/weekend programs available. Postbaccalaureate distance learning degree programs offered (minimal on-campus study). *Faculty:* 12 full-time (8 women), 38 part-time/adjunct (26 women). *Students:* 66 full-time (48 women), 590 part-time (477 women); includes 65 minority (53 Black or African American, non-Hispanic/Latino; 6 Asian, non-Hispanic/Latino; 3 Hispanic/Latino; 3 Two or more races, non-Hispanic/Latino), 4 international. Average age 36. In 2011, 229 master's, 5 doctorates awarded. *Application deadline:* Applications are processed on a rolling basis. Application fee: $50. Electronic applications accepted. *Expenses:* Contact institution. *Financial support:* Career-related internships or fieldwork, tuition waivers (partial), and unspecified assistantships available. *Unit head:* Dr. Steven P. Gulkus, Associate Professor, 215-572-2120, E-mail: gulkus@arcadia.edu. *Application contact:* 215-572-2925, Fax: 215-572-2126, E-mail: grad@arcadia.edu.

Arizona State University, College of Liberal Arts and Sciences, Department of Mathematics and Statistics, Tempe, AZ 85287-1804. Offers applied mathematics (PhD); computational biosciences (PhD); mathematics (MA, MNS, PhD); mathematics education (PhD); statistics (PhD). Part-time programs available. Terminal master's awarded for partial completion of doctoral program. *Degree requirements:* For master's, thesis or alternative, interactive Program of Study (iPOS) submitted before completing 50 percent of required credit hours; for doctorate, comprehensive exam, thesis/dissertation, interactive Program of Study (iPOS) submitted before completing 50 percent of required credit hours. *Entrance requirements:* For master's and doctorate, GRE General Test, minimum GPA of 3.0 or equivalent in last 2 years of work leading to bachelor's degree. Additional exam requirements/recommendations for international students: Required—TOEFL (minimum score 80 iBT), TOEFL, IELTS, or Pearson Test of English. Electronic applications accepted. *Expenses:* Contact institution.

Arkansas State University, Graduate School, College of Sciences and Mathematics, Department of Mathematics and Statistics, Jonesboro, State University, AR 72467. Offers mathematics (MS); mathematics education (MSE). Part-time programs available. *Faculty:* 11 full-time (5 women). *Students:* 12 full-time (7 women), 12 part-time (7 women); includes 2 minority (1 Black or African American, non-Hispanic/Latino; 1 Hispanic/Latino), 4 international. Average age 32. 14 applicants, 93% accepted, 10 enrolled. In 2011, 8 master's awarded. *Degree requirements:* For master's, comprehensive exam, thesis or alternative. *Entrance requirements:* For master's, GRE General Test or MAT, appropriate bachelor's degree, official transcripts, immunization records, valid teaching certificate (for MSE). Additional exam requirements/recommendations for international students: Required—TOEFL (minimum score 550 paper-based; 213 computer-based; 79 iBT), IELTS (minimum score 6), Pearson Test of English Academic (minimum score 56). *Application deadline:* For fall admission, 7/1 for domestic and international students; for spring admission, 11/15 for domestic students, 11/14 for international students. Applications are processed on a rolling basis. Application fee: $30 ($40 for international students). Electronic applications accepted. *Expenses:* Tuition, state resident: full-time $4044; part-time $225 per credit hour. Tuition, nonresident: full-time $8087; part-time $449 per credit hour. *Required fees:* $936; $52 per credit hour. $25 per term. One-time fee: $30. Tuition and fees vary according to course load and program. *Financial support:* In 2011–12, 10 students received support. Teaching assistantships, career-related internships or fieldwork, scholarships/grants, and unspecified assistantships available. Financial award application deadline: 7/1; financial award applicants required to submit FAFSA. *Unit head:* Dr. Debra Ingram, Chair, 870-972-3090, Fax: 870-972-3950, E-mail: dingram@astate.edu. *Application contact:* Dr. Andrew Sustich, Dean of the Graduate School, 870-972-3029, Fax: 870-972-3857, E-mail: sustich@astate.edu. Web site: http://www.mathstat.astate.edu.

Armstrong Atlantic State University, School of Graduate Studies, Program in Education, Savannah, GA 31419-1997. Offers adult education (M Ed); curriculum and instruction (M Ed); early childhood education (M Ed); education (M Ed); elementary education (M Ed); middle grades education (M Ed); secondary education (M Ed), including business education, English education, mathematics education, science education, social science education; special education (M Ed), including behavioral disorders, learning disabilities, speech-language pathology. *Accreditation:* NCATE. Part-time and evening/weekend programs available. Postbaccalaureate distance learning degree programs offered (minimal on-campus study). *Faculty:* 33 full-time (23 women), 3 part-time/adjunct (2 women). *Students:* 97 full-time (91 women), 262 part-time (227 women); includes 83 minority (70 Black or African American, non-Hispanic/Latino; 3 Asian, non-Hispanic/Latino; 8 Hispanic/Latino; 2 Two or more races, non-Hispanic/Latino), 5 international. Average age 34. 169 applicants, 69% accepted, 102 enrolled. In 2011, 227 master's awarded. *Degree requirements:* For master's, comprehensive exam, portfolio. *Entrance requirements:* For master's, GRE General Test or MAT, minimum GPA of 2.5, letters of recommendation. Additional exam requirements/recommendations for international students: Required—TOEFL (minimum score 523 paper-based; 193 computer-based). *Application deadline:* For fall admission, 7/1 priority date for domestic students, 5/1 for international students; for spring admission, 11/15 priority date for domestic students, 9/15 for international students. Applications are processed on a rolling basis. Application fee: $30. Electronic applications accepted. *Expenses:* Tuition, state resident: full-time $3402. Tuition, nonresident: full-time $12,636. *Financial support:* In 2011–12, research assistantships with full tuition reimbursements (averaging $5,000 per year) were awarded; career-related internships or fieldwork, Federal Work-Study, scholarships/grants, and unspecified assistantships also available. Support available to part-time students. Financial award applicants required to submit FAFSA. *Unit head:* Dr. Patricia Wachholz, Dean, College of Education, 912-344-2797, E-mail: patricia.wachholz@armstrong.edu. *Application contact:* Jill Bell, Director, Graduate Enrollment Services, 912-344-2798, Fax: 912-344-3488, E-mail: graduate@armstrong.edu. Web site: http://www.armstrong.edu/Education/coe_deans_office/coe_education_welcome.

Asbury University, School of Graduate and Professional Studies, Wilmore, KY 40390-1198. Offers biology: alternative certificate (MA Ed); chemistry: alternative certificate

(MA Ed); English (MA Ed); English as a second language (MA Ed); ESL (MA Ed); French (MA Ed); Latin: alternative certificate (MA Ed); mathematics: alternative certificate (MA Ed); reading/writing endorsement (MA Ed); social studies (MA Ed); social work (MSW), including child and family services; Spanish (MA Ed); special education (MA Ed); special education: alternative certificate (MA Ed); teacher as leader endorsement (MA Ed). *Accreditation:* NCATE. Part-time programs available. *Degree requirements:* For master's, action research project, portfolio. *Entrance requirements:* For master's, PRAXIS/NTE, minimum GPA of 2.75, letters of recommendation. Additional exam requirements/recommendations for international students: Required—TOEFL (minimum score 550 paper-based). Electronic applications accepted.

Auburn University, Graduate School, College of Education, Department of Curriculum and Teaching, Auburn University, AL 36849. Offers business education (M Ed, MS, PhD); early childhood education (M Ed, MS, PhD, Ed S); elementary education (M Ed, MS, PhD, Ed S); foreign languages (M Ed, MS); music education (M Ed, MS, PhD, Ed S); postsecondary education (PhD); reading education (PhD, Ed S); secondary education (M Ed, MS, PhD, Ed S), including English language arts, mathematics, science, social studies. *Accreditation:* NASM (one or more programs are accredited); NCATE. Part-time programs available. *Faculty:* 22 full-time (17 women), 3 part-time/adjunct (all women). *Students:* 80 full-time (58 women), 181 part-time (126 women); includes 42 minority (28 Black or African American, non-Hispanic/Latino; 7 Asian, non-Hispanic/Latino; 7 Hispanic/Latino). Average age 34. 184 applicants, 53% accepted, 60 enrolled. In 2011, 77 master's, 10 doctorates, 35 other advanced degrees awarded. *Degree requirements:* For master's, thesis (for some programs); for doctorate, thesis/dissertation; for Ed S, field project. *Entrance requirements:* For master's, doctorate, and Ed S, GRE General Test. *Application deadline:* For fall admission, 7/7 for domestic students; for spring admission, 11/24 for domestic students. Applications are processed on a rolling basis. Application fee: $50 ($60 for international students). Electronic applications accepted. *Expenses:* Tuition, state resident: full-time $7290; part-time $405 per credit hour. Tuition, nonresident: full-time $21,870; part-time $1215 per credit hour. *International tuition:* $22,000 full-time. *Required fees:* $1402. *Financial support:* Fellowships, teaching assistantships, career-related internships or fieldwork, and Federal Work-Study available. Support available to part-time students. Financial award application deadline: 3/15; financial award applicants required to submit FAFSA. *Faculty research:* Emerging literacy, reading attitudes, music for at-risk youth, portfolio assessment. *Unit head:* Dr. Kimberly Walls, Head, 334-844-4434. *Application contact:* Dr. George Flowers, Dean of the Graduate School, 334-844-2125. Web site: http://education.auburn.edu/academic_departments/curr/.

Aurora University, College of Arts and Sciences, Aurora, IL 60506-4892. Offers elementary math and science (MATL); life science (MATL); mathematics (MATL, MS). Part-time and evening/weekend programs available. *Entrance requirements:* Additional exam requirements/recommendations for international students: Required—TOEFL (minimum score 550 paper-based; 213 computer-based). Electronic applications accepted. *Expenses:* Contact institution.

Ball State University, Graduate School, College of Sciences and Humanities, Department of Mathematical Sciences, Program in Mathematics, Muncie, IN 47306-1099. Offers mathematics (MA, MS); mathematics education (MA). *Faculty:* 20. *Students:* 6 full-time (3 women), 35 part-time (27 women); includes 2 minority (1 Black or African American, non-Hispanic/Latino; 1 Two or more races, non-Hispanic/Latino), 1 international. Average age 39. 23 applicants, 74% accepted, 11 enrolled. In 2011, 7 master's awarded. Application fee: $50. Tuition and fees vary according to program and reciprocity agreements. *Financial support:* In 2011–12, 5 students received support, including 5 teaching assistantships with tuition reimbursements available (averaging $4,246 per year). Financial award application deadline: 3/1. *Unit head:* Dr. Sheryl Stump, Director, 765-285-8662, Fax: 765-285-1721. *Application contact:* Dr. Hanspeter Fischer, Director, 765-285-8640, Fax: 765-285-1721, E-mail: mali@bsu.edu. Web site: http://cms.bsu.edu/Academics/CollegesandDepartments/Math/AcademicsAdmissions/Programs/Masters/MAorMSinMath.aspx.

Bank Street College of Education, Graduate School, Programs in Educational Leadership, New York, NY 10025. Offers early childhood leadership (MS Ed); educational leadership (MS Ed); leadership for educational change (Ed M, MS Ed); leadership in community-based learning (MS Ed); leadership in mathematics education (MS Ed); leadership in museum education (MS Ed); leadership in the arts: creative writing (MS Ed); leadership in the arts: visual arts (MS Ed). *Students:* 77 full-time (66 women), 130 part-time (108 women); includes 68 minority (33 Black or African American, non-Hispanic/Latino; 8 Asian, non-Hispanic/Latino; 25 Hispanic/Latino; 2 Two or more races, non-Hispanic/Latino), 3 international. Average age 34. 148 applicants, 70% accepted, 92 enrolled. In 2011, 82 master's awarded. *Degree requirements:* For master's, thesis. *Entrance requirements:* For master's, interview, essays, minimum of 2 years experience as a classroom teacher. Additional exam requirements/recommendations for international students: Required—TOEFL (minimum score 600 paper-based; 250 computer-based; 100 iBT), IELTS (minimum score 7). *Application deadline:* For fall admission, 2/15 priority date for domestic students, 2/15 for international students; for spring admission, 11/1 priority date for domestic students, 11/1 for international students. Applications are processed on a rolling basis. Application fee: $65. Electronic applications accepted. *Expenses: Required fees:* $1240 per credit. $100 per term. One-time fee: $250 part-time. *Financial support:* Career-related internships or fieldwork, Federal Work-Study, scholarships/grants, traineeships, and unspecified assistantships available. Support available to part-time students. Financial award application deadline: 4/15; financial award applicants required to submit FAFSA. *Faculty research:* Leadership in small schools, mathematics in elementary schools, professional development in early childhood, leadership in arts education, leadership in special education. *Unit head:* Dr. Rima Shore, Chairperson, 212-875-4478, Fax: 212-875-8753, E-mail: rshore@bankstreet.edu. *Application contact:* Ann Morgan, Director of Graduate Admissions, 212-875-4403, Fax: 212-875-4678, E-mail: amorgan@bankstreet.edu. Web site: http://bankstreet.edu/graduate-school/academics/programs/leadership-programs-overview/.

Belmont University, College of Arts and Sciences, Department of Education, Nashville, TN 37212-3757. Offers education (M Ed); elementary education (MAT), including early childhood education, elementary education, language arts education; English (MAT); history (MAT); mathematics (MAT); middle grade education (MAT); science (MAT); secondary education (MAT); special education (MAT); sports administration (MSA). *Accreditation:* NCATE. Part-time and evening/weekend programs available. *Faculty:* 11 full-time (8 women), 23 part-time/adjunct (12 women). *Students:* 83 full-time (77 women), 205 part-time (162 women); includes 50 minority (36 Black or African American, non-Hispanic/Latino; 1 American Indian or Alaska Native, non-Hispanic/Latino; 1 Asian, non-Hispanic/Latino; 7 Hispanic/Latino; 5 Two or more races, non-Hispanic/Latino), 2 international. Average age 30. 83 applicants, 67% accepted, 35 enrolled. In 2011, 169 master's awarded. *Degree requirements:* For master's, thesis (for some programs). *Entrance requirements:* For master's, MAT or GRE and/or GMAT, minimum GPA of 2.75. Additional exam requirements/recommendations for international students: Required—TOEFL. *Application deadline:* For fall admission, 8/1 priority date for domestic students, 6/1 for international students; for spring admission, 12/1 priority date for domestic students, 10/1 for international students. Applications are processed on a rolling basis. Application fee: $50. *Expenses:* Contact institution. *Financial support:* In 2011–12, 30 students received support. Fellowships with partial tuition reimbursements available, teaching assistantships with partial tuition reimbursements available, institutionally sponsored loans, tuition waivers (partial), and unspecified assistantships available. Financial award application deadline: 4/15; financial award applicants required to submit FAFSA. *Faculty research:* Improving secondary literacy, Montessori, classroom management strategies, teacher residency programs, online professional development, mentoring, leadership, faculty development. *Total annual research expenditures:* $2,500. *Unit head:* Dr. Cynthia R. Watkins, Associate Dean, 615-460-6053, Fax: 615-460-5556, E-mail: cynthia.watkins@belmont.edu. *Application contact:* Andrea McClain, Admission/Licensure Officer, 615-460-5483, Fax: 615-460-5556, E-mail: andrea.mcclain@belmont.edu.

Bemidji State University, School of Graduate Studies, Bemidji, MN 56601-2699. Offers biology (MS); counseling psychology (MS); education (M Ed, MS); English (MA, MS); environmental studies (MS); mathematics (MS); mathematics (elementary and middle level education) (MS); special education (M Sp Ed, MS). Part-time programs available. Postbaccalaureate distance learning degree programs offered (no on-campus study). *Faculty:* 114 full-time (47 women), 22 part-time/adjunct (16 women). *Students:* 68 full-time (45 women), 311 part-time (198 women); includes 21 minority (4 Black or African American, non-Hispanic/Latino; 2 American Indian or Alaska Native, non-Hispanic/Latino; 5 Asian, non-Hispanic/Latino; 5 Hispanic/Latino; 5 Two or more races, non-Hispanic/Latino), 5 international. Average age 34. 82 applicants, 98% accepted, 37 enrolled. In 2011, 72 master's awarded. *Degree requirements:* For master's, comprehensive exam, thesis (for some programs). *Entrance requirements:* For master's, GRE, letters of recommendation, letters of interest. Additional exam requirements/recommendations for international students: Required—TOEFL (minimum score 550 paper-based; 213 computer-based; 80 iBT). *Application deadline:* Applications are processed on a rolling basis. Application fee: $20. Electronic applications accepted. *Expenses:* Tuition, state resident: full-time $6182; part-time $343.45 per credit. Tuition, nonresident: full-time $6182; part-time $343.45 per credit. *Required fees:* $954. *Financial support:* In 2011–12, 253 students received support, including 36 research assistantships with partial tuition reimbursements available (averaging $7,441 per year), 36 teaching assistantships with partial tuition reimbursements available (averaging $7,441 per year); career-related internships or fieldwork, scholarships/grants, health care benefits, and unspecified assistantships also available. Support available to part-time students. Financial award application deadline: 4/15; financial award applicants required to submit FAFSA. *Unit head:* Dr. Patricia Rogers, Dean of Health Sciences and Human Ecology, 218-755-2027, Fax: 218-755-2258, E-mail: progers@bemidjistate.edu. *Application contact:* Joan Miller, Senior Office and Administrative Specialist, 218-755-2027, Fax: 218-755-2258, E-mail: jmiller@bemidjistate.edu. Web site: http://www.bemidjistate.edu/academics/graduate_studies/.

Bob Jones University, Graduate Programs, Greenville, SC 29614. Offers accountancy (MS); Bible (MA); Bible translation (MA); Biblical studies (Certificate); broadcast management (MS); business administration (MBA); church history (MA, PhD); church ministries (MA); church music (MM); cinema and video production (MA); counseling (MS); curriculum and instruction (Ed D); divinity (M Div); dramatic production (MA); educational leadership (MS, Ed D, Ed S); elementary education (M Ed, MAT); English (M Ed, MA, MAT); fine arts (MA); graphic design (MA); history (M Ed, MA); illustration (MA); interpretative speech (MA); mathematics (M Ed, MAT); medical missions (Certificate); ministry (MM, D Min); multi-categorical special education (M Ed, MAT); music (M Ed); New Testament interpretation (PhD); Old Testament interpretation (PhD); orchestral instrument performance (MM); organ performance (MM); pastoral studies (MA); personnel services (MS, Ed S); piano pedagogy (MM); piano performance (MM); platform arts (MA); radio and television broadcasting (MS); rhetoric and public address (MA); secondary education (M Ed); studio art (MA); teaching Bible (MA); theology (MA, PhD); voice performance (MM); youth ministries (MA); M Div/MM.

Bowling Green State University, Graduate College, College of Arts and Sciences, Department of Mathematics and Statistics, Bowling Green, OH 43403. Offers applied statistics (MS); mathematics (MA, MAT, PhD); statistics (PhD). Part-time programs available. *Degree requirements:* For master's, thesis or alternative; for doctorate, comprehensive exam, thesis/dissertation. *Entrance requirements:* For master's and doctorate, GRE General Test. Additional exam requirements/recommendations for international students: Required—TOEFL. Electronic applications accepted. *Faculty research:* Statistics and probability, algebra, analysis.

Bridgewater State University, School of Graduate Studies, School of Arts and Sciences, Department of Mathematics and Computer Science, Bridgewater, MA 02325-0001. Offers computer science (MS); mathematics (MAT). Part-time and evening/weekend programs available. *Entrance requirements:* For master's, GRE General Test.

Brigham Young University, Graduate Studies, College of Physical and Mathematical Sciences, Department of Mathematics Education, Provo, UT 84602-1001. Offers MA. Part-time programs available. *Faculty:* 7 full-time (2 women). *Students:* 12 full-time (8 women), 5 part-time (4 women); includes 2 minority (1 Black or African American, non-Hispanic/Latino; 1 Native Hawaiian or other Pacific Islander, non-Hispanic/Latino). Average age 28. 15 applicants, 53% accepted, 7 enrolled. In 2011, 4 master's awarded. *Degree requirements:* For master's, comprehensive exam, project or thesis. *Entrance requirements:* For master's, GRE General Test, teaching certificate, bachelor's degree in math education or equivalent. Additional exam requirements/recommendations for international students: Required—TOEFL. *Application deadline:* For fall admission, 3/1 priority date for domestic students, 3/1 for international students; for spring admission, 3/1 priority date for domestic students, 3/1 for international students. Application fee: $50. Electronic applications accepted. *Expenses: Tuition:* Full-time $5760; part-time $320 per credit. Tuition and fees vary according to student's religious affiliation. *Financial support:* In 2011–12, 17 students received support, including 4 research assistantships with full tuition reimbursements available (averaging $3,000 per year), 12 teaching assistantships with full tuition reimbursements available (averaging $12,000 per year); institutionally sponsored loans, scholarships/grants, and tuition waivers (partial) also available. Financial award application deadline: 3/1. *Faculty research:* Pre-service mathematics teacher education, teaching and learning with technology, mathematics learning and teaching, communication in mathematics classrooms, mathematical knowledge for teaching. *Unit head:* Steven R. Williams, Chair, 801-422-2887, Fax: 801-422-0511, E-mail: williams@mathed.byu.edu. *Application contact:* Kathy Lee Garrett, Administrative Assistant, 801-422-1840, Fax: 801-422-0511, E-mail: kathylee@mathed.byu.edu. Web site: http://www.mathed.byu.edu/.

Brooklyn College of the City University of New York, Division of Graduate Studies, School of Education, Program in Adolescence Education and Special Subjects, Brooklyn, NY 11210-2889. Offers adolescence science education (MAT); art teacher (MA); biology teacher (MA); chemistry teacher (MA); earth science teacher (MAT); English teacher (MA); French teacher (MA); health and nutrition sciences: health teacher (MS Ed); mathematics teacher (MA); music education (CAS); music teacher (MA); physical education teacher (MS Ed); physics teacher (MA); social studies teacher (MA); Spanish teacher (MA). Part-time and evening/weekend programs available. *Degree requirements:* For master's, comprehensive exam (for some programs), thesis (for some programs). *Entrance requirements:* For master's, LAST, previous course work in education, resume, 2 letters of recommendation, essay. Additional exam requirements/recommendations for international students: Required—TOEFL (minimum score 500 paper-based; 173 computer-based; 61 iBT). Electronic applications accepted. *Faculty research:* Interdisciplinary education, semiotics, discourse analysis, autobiography, teacher identity.

Brooklyn College of the City University of New York, Division of Graduate Studies, School of Education, Program in Childhood Education, Brooklyn, NY 11210-2889. Offers bilingual education (MS Ed); liberal arts (MS Ed); mathematics (MS Ed); science/environmental education (MS Ed). Part-time and evening/weekend programs available. *Entrance requirements:* For master's, LAST, interview, previous course work in education, writing sample, resume, 2 letters of recommendation. Additional exam requirements/recommendations for international students: Required—TOEFL (minimum score 500 paper-based; 173 computer-based; 61 iBT). Electronic applications accepted. *Faculty research:* Emotional intelligence, multiculturalism, arts immersion, the Holocaust.

Brooklyn College of the City University of New York, Division of Graduate Studies, School of Education, Program in Middle Childhood Education (Math), Brooklyn, NY 11210-2889. Offers MS Ed. *Entrance requirements:* For master's, LAST, 2 letters of recommendation, essay, resume. Additional exam requirements/recommendations for international students: Required—TOEFL (minimum score 500 paper-based; 173 computer-based; 61 iBT). Electronic applications accepted.

Buffalo State College, State University of New York, The Graduate School, Faculty of Natural and Social Sciences, Department of Mathematics, Buffalo, NY 14222-1095. Offers mathematics education (MS Ed). *Accreditation:* NCATE. Part-time and evening/weekend programs available. *Degree requirements:* For master's, thesis or alternative. *Entrance requirements:* For master's, 18 undergraduate hours in upper-level mathematics, minimum GPA of 2.5 in undergraduate math courses. Additional exam requirements/recommendations for international students: Required—TOEFL (minimum score 550 paper-based; 213 computer-based).

California State University, Bakersfield, Division of Graduate Studies, School of Natural Sciences, Mathematics, and Engineering, Program in Teaching Mathematics, Bakersfield, CA 93311. Offers MA. *Entrance requirements:* For master's, minimum GPA of 2.5 for last 90 quarter units. *Expenses: Required fees:* $1302 per unit. Part-time tuition and fees vary according to course load and program. *Unit head:* Dr. Joseph Fiedler, Head, 661-654-2058, Fax: 661-664-2039. Web site: http://www.csub.edu/math/GradProgram.shtml.

California State University, Chico, Office of Graduate Studies, College of Natural Sciences, Department of Mathematics and Statistics, Chico, CA 95929-0722. Offers math education (MS). Part-time programs available. *Faculty:* 1 (woman) full-time. *Students:* 1 applicant, 0% accepted. *Degree requirements:* For master's, project or thesis. *Entrance requirements:* For master's, GRE, teaching credential in mathematics, statement of purpose. Additional exam requirements/recommendations for international students: Required—TOEFL (minimum score 550 paper-based; 213 computer-based; 80 iBT), IELTS (minimum score 6.5), Pearson Test of English (minimum score 59). *Application deadline:* For fall admission, 3/1 priority date for domestic students, 3/1 for international students. Application fee: $55. Electronic applications accepted. Tuition and fees vary according to class time, course load and degree level. *Financial support:* Teaching assistantships and scholarships/grants available. Financial award application deadline: 3/1; financial award applicants required to submit FAFSA. *Unit head:* Dr. Terry L. Kiser, Chair, 530-898-3460, Fax: 530-898-6111, E-mail: math@csuchico.edu. *Application contact:* Judy L. Rice, Graduate Admissions Coordinator, 530-898-5416, Fax: 530-898-3342, E-mail: jlrice@csuchico.edu. Web site: http://www.csuchico.edu/math/index.shtml.

California State University, Dominguez Hills, College of Natural and Behavioral Sciences, Program in Teaching of Mathematics, Carson, CA 90747-0001. Offers MA. Part-time and evening/weekend programs available. *Faculty:* 2 full-time (0 women). *Students:* 22 part-time (10 women); includes 21 minority (5 Black or African American, non-Hispanic/Latino; 3 Asian, non-Hispanic/Latino; 11 Hispanic/Latino; 1 Native Hawaiian or other Pacific Islander, non-Hispanic/Latino; 1 Two or more races, non-Hispanic/Latino). Average age 38. 7 applicants, 57% accepted, 3 enrolled. In 2011, 4 master's awarded. *Degree requirements:* For master's, comprehensive exam, thesis. *Entrance requirements:* For master's, 2 years of teaching experience. Additional exam requirements/recommendations for international students: Required—TOEFL. *Application deadline:* For fall admission, 6/1 priority date for domestic students; for spring admission, 11/1 priority date for domestic students. Applications are processed on a rolling basis. Application fee: $55. Electronic applications accepted. *Unit head:* Dr. John Wilkins, Chair, 310-243-3380, E-mail: jwilkins@csudh.edu. *Application contact:* Dr. John Wilkins, Associate Professor, 310-243-3380, E-mail: jwilkins@csudh.edu. Web site: http://www.csudh.edu/math.

California State University, East Bay, Office of Academic Programs and Graduate Studies, College of Science, Department of Mathematics and Computer Science, Mathematics Program, Hayward, CA 94542-3000. Offers applied math (MS); mathematics (MS); mathematics teaching (MS). Part-time and evening/weekend programs available. *Faculty:* 3 full-time (1 woman). *Students:* 22 full-time (9 women), 52 part-time (20 women); includes 22 minority (17 Asian, non-Hispanic/Latino; 3 Hispanic/Latino; 1 Native Hawaiian or other Pacific Islander, non-Hispanic/Latino; 1 Two or more races, non-Hispanic/Latino), 6 international. Average age 38. 37 applicants, 81% accepted, 16 enrolled. In 2011, 19 master's awarded. *Degree requirements:* For master's, comprehensive exam or thesis. *Entrance requirements:* For master's, minimum GPA of 3.0 in field. Additional exam requirements/recommendations for international students: Required—TOEFL (minimum score 550 paper-based; 213 computer-based). *Application deadline:* For fall admission, 6/30 for domestic and international students. Application fee: $55. Electronic applications accepted. *Expenses:* Tuition, state resident: full-time $6738; part-time $1302 per quarter. Tuition, nonresident: full-time $12,690; part-time $2294 per quarter. *Required fees:* $449 per quarter. Tuition and fees vary according to degree level, program and reciprocity agreements. *Financial support:* Fellowships, teaching assistantships, Federal Work-Study, institutionally sponsored loans, and scholarships/grants available. Support available to part-time students. Financial award application deadline: 3/1; financial award applicants required to submit FAFSA. *Unit head:* Prof. Edna Reiter, Chair, 510-885-3414, Fax: 510-885-4169, E-mail: eddie.reiter@csueastbay.edu. *Application contact:* Dr. Donald Wolitzer, Math Graduate Advisor, 510-885-3414, Fax: 510-885-4169, E-mail: donald.wolitzer@csueastbay.edu. Web site: http://www20.csueastbay.edu/csci/departments/math-cs/.

California State University, Fresno, Division of Graduate Studies, College of Science and Mathematics, Department of Mathematics, Fresno, CA 93740-8027. Offers mathematics (MA); teaching (MA). Part-time programs available. *Degree requirements:* For master's, thesis or alternative. *Entrance requirements:* For master's, GRE General Test. Additional exam requirements/recommendations for international students: Required—TOEFL. Electronic applications accepted. *Faculty research:* Diagnostic testing project.

California State University, Fullerton, Graduate Studies, College of Education, Department of Secondary Education, Fullerton, CA 92834-9480. Offers middle school mathematics (MS); secondary education (MS); teacher induction (MS). Part-time programs available. *Students:* 1 (woman) full-time, 39 part-time (34 women); includes 17 minority (1 Black or African American, non-Hispanic/Latino; 6 Asian, non-Hispanic/Latino; 10 Hispanic/Latino). Average age 30. 17 applicants, 65% accepted, 9 enrolled. In 2011, 16 master's awarded. Application fee: $55. *Financial support:* Career-related internships or fieldwork, Federal Work-Study, institutionally sponsored loans, and scholarships/grants available. Support available to part-time students. Financial award application deadline: 3/1; financial award applicants required to submit FAFSA. *Unit head:* Dr. Mark Ellis, Chair, 657-278-2745. *Application contact:* Admissions/Applications, 657-278-2371.

California State University, Fullerton, Graduate Studies, College of Natural Science and Mathematics, Department of Mathematics, Fullerton, CA 92834-9480. Offers applied mathematics (MA); mathematics (MA); mathematics for secondary school teachers (MA). Part-time programs available. *Students:* 17 full-time (7 women), 55 part-time (21 women); includes 33 minority (23 Asian, non-Hispanic/Latino; 9 Hispanic/Latino; 1 Two or more races, non-Hispanic/Latino), 4 international. Average age 31. 83 applicants, 60% accepted, 27 enrolled. In 2011, 25 master's awarded. *Degree requirements:* For master's, comprehensive exam or project. *Entrance requirements:* For master's, minimum GPA of 2.5 in last 60 units of course work, major in mathematics or related field. Application fee: $55. *Financial support:* Research assistantships, teaching assistantships, career-related internships or fieldwork, Federal Work-Study, institutionally sponsored loans, and scholarships/grants available. Support available to part-time students. Financial award application deadline: 3/1; financial award applicants required to submit FAFSA. *Unit head:* Dr. Paul Deland, Chair, 657-278-3631. *Application contact:* Admissions/Applications, 657-278-2371.

California State University, Long Beach, Graduate Studies, College of Natural Sciences and Mathematics, Department of Mathematics and Statistics, Long Beach, CA 90840. Offers mathematics (MS), including applied mathematics, applied statistics, mathematics education for secondary school teachers. Part-time programs available. *Faculty:* 21 full-time (5 women), 1 (woman) part-time/adjunct. *Students:* 67 full-time (31 women), 115 part-time (47 women); includes 95 minority (5 Black or African American, non-Hispanic/Latino; 1 American Indian or Alaska Native, non-Hispanic/Latino; 53 Asian, non-Hispanic/Latino; 29 Hispanic/Latino; 2 Native Hawaiian or other Pacific Islander, non-Hispanic/Latino; 5 Two or more races, non-Hispanic/Latino), 14 international. Average age 31. 162 applicants, 69% accepted, 58 enrolled. In 2011, 41 master's awarded. *Degree requirements:* For master's, comprehensive exam or thesis. *Application deadline:* For fall admission, 7/1 for domestic students; for spring admission, 12/1 for domestic students. Applications are processed on a rolling basis. Application fee: $55. Electronic applications accepted. *Financial support:* Teaching assistantships, Federal Work-Study, institutionally sponsored loans, scholarships/grants, and traineeships available. Financial award application deadline: 3/2. *Faculty research:* Algebra, functional analysis, partial differential equations, operator theory, numerical analysis. *Unit head:* Dr. Robert Mena, Chair, 562-985-4721, Fax: 562-985-8227, E-mail: rmena@csulb.edu. *Application contact:* Dr. Ngo Viet, Graduate Associate Chair, 562-985-4721, Fax: 562-985-8227, E-mail: viet@csulb.edu.

California State University, Northridge, Graduate Studies, College of Education, Department of Secondary Education, Northridge, CA 91330. Offers educational technology (MA); English education (MA); mathematics education (MA); secondary science education (MA); teaching and learning (MA). *Accreditation:* NCATE. Part-time programs available. *Degree requirements:* For master's, thesis optional. *Entrance requirements:* For master's, GRE General Test or minimum GPA of 3.0. Additional exam requirements/recommendations for international students: Required—TOEFL.

California State University, Northridge, Graduate Studies, College of Science and Mathematics, Department of Mathematics, Northridge, CA 91330. Offers applied mathematics (MS); mathematics (MS); mathematics for educational careers (MS). Part-time and evening/weekend programs available. *Degree requirements:* For master's, thesis (for some programs). *Entrance requirements:* For master's, GRE (if cumulative undergraduate GPA less than 3.0). Additional exam requirements/recommendations for international students: Required—TOEFL.

California State University, San Bernardino, Graduate Studies, College of Natural Sciences, Department of Mathematics, San Bernardino, CA 92407-2397. Offers mathematics (MA); teaching mathematics (MAT). Part-time programs available. *Students:* 46 full-time (23 women), 8 part-time (1 woman); includes 26 minority (3 Black or African American, non-Hispanic/Latino; 5 Asian, non-Hispanic/Latino; 16 Hispanic/Latino; 2 Two or more races, non-Hispanic/Latino). Average age 30. 23 applicants, 48% accepted, 10 enrolled. In 2011, 13 master's awarded. *Degree requirements:* For master's, advancement to candidacy. *Entrance requirements:* For master's, writing exam, minimum GPA of 3.0 in math courses. Application fee: $55. *Expenses:* Tuition, state resident: full-time $7356. Tuition, nonresident: full-time $7356. *Required fees:* $1077. Tuition and fees vary according to program. *Financial support:* Teaching assistantships available. *Faculty research:* Mathematics education, technology in education, algebra, combinatorics, real analysis. *Unit head:* Dr. Peter D. Williams, Chair, 909-537-5361, Fax: 909-537-7119, E-mail: pwilliam@csusb.edu. *Application contact:* Sandra Kamusikiri, Associate Vice-President/Dean of Graduate Studies, 909-537-5058, E-mail: skamusik@csusb.edu.

Cambridge College, School of Education, Cambridge, MA 02138-5304. Offers autism specialist (M Ed); autism/behavior analyst (M Ed); behavior analyst (Post-Master's Certificate); behavioral management (M Ed); early childhood teacher (M Ed); education specialist in curriculum and instruction (CAGS); educational leadership (Ed D); elementary teacher (M Ed); English as a second language (M Ed, Certificate); general science (M Ed); health education (Post-Master's Certificate); health/family and consumer sciences (M Ed); history (M Ed); individualized (M Ed); information technology literacy (M Ed); instructional technology (M Ed); interdisciplinary studies (M Ed); library teacher (M Ed); literacy education (M Ed); mathematics (M Ed); mathematics specialist (Certificate); middle school mathematics and science (M Ed); school administration (M Ed, CAGS); school guidance counselor (M Ed); school nurse education (M Ed); school social worker/school adjustment counselor (M Ed); special education administrator (CAGS); special education/moderate disabilities (M Ed); teaching skills and methodologies (M Ed). Part-time and evening/weekend programs available. Postbaccalaureate distance learning degree programs offered (minimal on-campus study). *Degree requirements:* For master's, thesis, internship/practicum (licensure program only); for doctorate, thesis/dissertation; for other advanced degree, thesis. *Entrance requirements:* For master's, interview, resume, documentation of licensure, 2 professional references; for doctorate, official transcripts, interview, resume, documentation of licensure (if any), written personal statement/essay, portfolio of scholarly and professional work, qualifying assessment, 2 professional references, health insurance, immunizations form; for other advanced degree, official transcripts, interview, resume, documentation of licensure (if any), written personal statement/essay, 2 professional references, health insurance, immunizations form. Additional exam requirements/recommendations for international students: Required—TOEFL (minimum score 550 paper-based; 213 computer-based; 79 iBT); Recommended—

IELTS (minimum score 6). Electronic applications accepted. *Expenses:* Contact institution. *Faculty research:* Adult education, accelerated learning, mathematics education, brain compatible learning, special education and law.

Campbell University, Graduate and Professional Programs, School of Education, Buies Creek, NC 27506. Offers administration (MSA); community counseling (MA); elementary education (M Ed); English education (M Ed); interdisciplinary studies (M Ed); mathematics education (M Ed); middle grades education (M Ed); physical education (M Ed); school counseling (M Ed); secondary education (M Ed); social science education (M Ed). *Accreditation:* NCATE. Part-time and evening/weekend programs available. *Degree requirements:* For master's, comprehensive exam. *Entrance requirements:* For master's, GRE General Test, minimum GPA of 2.7. *Faculty research:* Spiritual values and wellness issues in counseling, stress and professional burnout among counselors, thinking strategies, leadership, adaptive technology.

Caribbean University, Graduate School, Bayamón, PR 00960-0493. Offers administration and supervision (MA Ed); criminal justice (MA); curriculum and instruction (MA Ed, PhD), including elementary education (MA Ed), English education (MA Ed), history education (MA Ed), mathematics education (MA Ed), primary education (MA Ed), science education (MA Ed), Spanish education (MA Ed); educational technology in instructional systems (MA Ed); gerontology (MSN); human resources (MBA); museology, archiving and art history (MA Ed); neonatal pediatrics (MSN); physical education (MA Ed); special education (MA Ed). *Entrance requirements:* For master's, interview, minimum GPA of 2.5.

Central Michigan University, College of Graduate Studies, College of Science and Technology, Department of Mathematics, Mount Pleasant, MI 48859. Offers mathematics (MA, PhD), including teaching of college mathematics (PhD). Part-time programs available. *Degree requirements:* For master's, thesis or alternative; for doctorate, thesis/dissertation. *Entrance requirements:* For master's, minimum GPA of 2.7, 20 hours of course work in mathematics; for doctorate, GRE, minimum GPA of 3.0, 20 hours of course work in mathematics. Electronic applications accepted. *Faculty research:* Combinatorics, approximation theory, applied mathematics, statistics, functional analysis and operator theory.

Chaminade University of Honolulu, Graduate Services, Program in Education, Honolulu, HI 96816-1578. Offers child development (M Ed); educational leadership (M Ed); elementary education with licensure (MAT); instructional leadership (M Ed); Montessori credential (M Ed); Montessori emphasis (M Ed); secondary education with licensure (MAT), including English, math, science, social studies; special education with licensure (MAT). Part-time and evening/weekend programs available. Postbaccalaureate distance learning degree programs offered (minimal on-campus study). *Faculty:* 2 full-time (both women), 32 part-time/adjunct (25 women). *Students:* 53 full-time (38 women), 88 part-time (67 women); includes 77 minority (6 Black or African American, non-Hispanic/Latino; 1 American Indian or Alaska Native, non-Hispanic/Latino; 44 Asian, non-Hispanic/Latino; 5 Hispanic/Latino; 17 Native Hawaiian or other Pacific Islander, non-Hispanic/Latino; 4 Two or more races, non-Hispanic/Latino), 1 international. Average age 35. 40 applicants, 88% accepted, 30 enrolled. In 2011, 105 master's awarded. *Degree requirements:* For master's, thesis or alternative. *Entrance requirements:* For master's, PRAXIS (for MAT only), minimum GPA of 2.75, 3 letters of recommendation. Additional exam requirements/recommendations for international students: Required—TOEFL (minimum score 550 paper-based). *Application deadline:* For fall admission, 9/1 priority date for domestic students, 9/1 for international students; for winter admission, 12/1 priority date for domestic students, 12/1 for international students; for spring admission, 3/1 priority date for domestic students, 3/1 for international students. Applications are processed on a rolling basis. Application fee: $50. Electronic applications accepted. *Expenses: Required fees:* $600 per credit hour. One-time fee: $93 part-time. *Financial support:* In 2011–12, 172 students received support. Career-related internships or fieldwork, Federal Work-Study, institutionally sponsored loans, scholarships/grants, and tuition waivers (partial) available. Support available to part-time students. Financial award application deadline: 3/1; financial award applicants required to submit FAFSA. *Faculty research:* Peace and curriculum education. *Unit head:* Dr. Joseph Peters, Dean, 808-440-4251, Fax: 808-739-4607, E-mail: joseph.peters@chaminade.edu. *Application contact:* 808-739-4663, Fax: 808-739-8329, E-mail: gradserv@chaminade.edu. Web site: http://www.chaminade.edu/education/grad.php.

Chatham University, Program in Education, Pittsburgh, PA 15232-2826. Offers early childhood education (MAT); elementary education (MAT); environmental education (K-12) (MAT); secondary art (MAT); secondary biology education (MAT); secondary chemistry education (MAT); secondary English education (MAT); secondary math education (MAT); secondary physics education (MAT); secondary social studies education (MAT); special education (MAT). *Students:* 52 full-time (42 women), 17 part-time (16 women); includes 2 minority (1 Black or African American, non-Hispanic/Latino; 1 Hispanic/Latino). Average age 29. 39 applicants, 82% accepted, 23 enrolled. In 2011, 37 master's awarded. *Degree requirements:* For master's, thesis, teaching experience. *Entrance requirements:* For master's, minimum GPA of 3.0, sample of written work, recommendation letters. Additional exam requirements/recommendations for international students: Required—TOEFL (minimum score 600 paper-based; 250 computer-based; 100 iBT), IELTS (minimum score 7), TWE. *Application deadline:* For fall admission, 4/1 priority date for domestic students, 4/1 for international students; for spring admission, 11/1 priority date for domestic students, 10/1 for international students. Applications are processed on a rolling basis. Application fee: $45. Electronic applications accepted. Application fee is waived when completed online. *Expenses: Tuition:* Full-time $13,896. Tuition and fees vary according to program. *Financial support:* Career-related internships or fieldwork available. Financial award applicants required to submit FAFSA. *Faculty research:* Gifted education, environmental education, technology in education, writing as learning, class size and achievement. *Unit head:* Dr. Elvira Sanatullova-Allison, Director of Education Programs, 412-365-2773, E-mail: esanatullovaallison@chatham.edu. *Application contact:* Dory Perry, Associate Director of Graduate Admission, 412-365-2758, Fax: 412-365-1609, E-mail: gradadmissions@chatham.edu. Web site: http://www.chatham.edu/mat.

Christopher Newport University, Graduate Studies, Department of Teacher Preparation, Newport News, VA 23606-2998. Offers art (PK-12) (MAT); biology (6-12) (MAT); chemistry (6-12) (MAT); computer science (6-12) (MAT); elementary (PK-6) (MAT); English (6-12) (MAT); English as second language (PK-12) (MAT); French (PK-12) (MAT); history and social science (6-12) (MAT); mathematics (6-12) (MAT); music (PK-12) (MAT), including choral, instrumental; physics (6-12) (MAT); Spanish (PK-12) (MAT). Part-time and evening/weekend programs available. *Degree requirements:* For master's, comprehensive exam, thesis or alternative. *Entrance requirements:* For master's, PRAXIS I, minimum GPA of 3.0. Additional exam requirements/recommendations for international students: Required—TOEFL (minimum score 580 paper-based; 237 computer-based; 92 iBT). Electronic applications accepted. *Faculty research:* Early literacy development, instructional innovations, professional teaching standards, multicultural issues, aesthetic education.

The Citadel, The Military College of South Carolina, Citadel Graduate College, Department of Mathematics and Computer Science, Charleston, SC 29409. Offers computer and information science (MS); mathematics education (MAE). *Accreditation:* NCATE (one or more programs are accredited). Part-time and evening/weekend programs available. *Faculty:* 3 full-time (0 women), 1 part-time/adjunct (0 women). *Students:* 1 (woman) full-time, 18 part-time (8 women); includes 1 minority (Asian, non-Hispanic/Latino). Average age 35. In 2011, 3 master's awarded. *Degree requirements:* For master's, comprehensive exam (for some programs), thesis (for some programs). *Entrance requirements:* For master's, GRE (minimum score 1000 for MS; 900 verbal and quantitative for MAT, raw score of 396), minimum undergraduate GPA of 3.0 (MS) or 2.5 (MAT); competency, demonstrated through coursework, approved work experience, or a program-administrated competency exam, in the areas of basic computer architecture, object-oriented programming, discrete mathematics, and data structures (MS); successful completion of 7 courses (MAT). Additional exam requirements/recommendations for international students: Required—TOEFL (minimum score 550 paper-based; 213 computer-based; 79 iBT). *Application deadline:* Applications are processed on a rolling basis. Application fee: $30. Electronic applications accepted. *Expenses: Tuition, area resident:* Part-time $501 per credit hour. Tuition, state resident: part-time $501 per credit hour. Tuition, nonresident: part-time $824 per credit hour. *Required fees:* $40 per term. One-time fee: $30. *Financial support:* Health care benefits and unspecified assistantships available. Support available to part-time students. Financial award application deadline: 7/1; financial award applicants required to submit FAFSA. *Faculty research:* Mathematics: numerical linear algebra, inverse problems, operator algebras, geometric group theory, integral equations; computer science: computer networks, database systems, software engineering, computational systems biology, mobile systems. *Unit head:* Dr. John I. Moore, Jr., Department Head, 843-953-5048, Fax: 843-953-7391, E-mail: john.moore@citadel.edu. *Application contact:* Dr. George L. Rudolph, Computer and Information Science Program Director, 843-953-5032, Fax: 843-953-7391, E-mail: george.rudolph@citadel.edu. Web site: http://www.mathcs.citadel.edu/.

The Citadel, The Military College of South Carolina, Citadel Graduate College, School of Education, Program in Secondary Education, Charleston, SC 29409. Offers biology (MAT); English language arts (MAT); mathematics (MAT); mathematics education (MAE); physical education (MAT); social studies (MAT). *Accreditation:* NCATE. Part-time and evening/weekend programs available. *Faculty:* 12 full-time (8 women), 9 part-time/adjunct (4 women). *Students:* 21 full-time (11 women), 51 part-time (25 women); includes 10 minority (7 Black or African American, non-Hispanic/Latino; 2 Asian, non-Hispanic/Latino; 1 Hispanic/Latino). Average age 31. In 2011, 34 master's awarded. *Degree requirements:* For master's, comprehensive exam, internship. *Entrance requirements:* For master's, GRE (minimum score 900) or MAT (minimum score 396), minimum undergraduate GPA of 2.5. Additional exam requirements/recommendations for international students: Required—TOEFL (minimum score 550 paper-based; 213 computer-based). *Application deadline:* Applications are processed on a rolling basis. Application fee: $30. Electronic applications accepted. *Expenses: Tuition, area resident:* Part-time $501 per credit hour. Tuition, state resident: part-time $501 per credit hour. Tuition, nonresident: part-time $824 per credit hour. *Required fees:* $40 per term. One-time fee: $30. *Financial support:* Career-related internships or fieldwork, health care benefits, and unspecified assistantships available. Support available to part-time students. Financial award application deadline: 7/1; financial award applicants required to submit FAFSA. *Unit head:* Dr. Kathryn A. Richardson-Jones, Coordinator, 843-953-3163, Fax: 843-953-7258, E-mail: kathryn.jones@citadel.edu. *Application contact:* Dr. Steve A. Nida, Associate Provost, The Citadel Graduate College, 843-953-5089, Fax: 843-953-7630, E-mail: cgc@citadel.edu. Web site: http://www.citadel.edu/education/teacher-education/mat-master-of-arts-in-teaching.html.

City College of the City University of New York, Graduate School, School of Education, Department of Secondary Education, New York, NY 10031-9198. Offers adolescent mathematics education (MA, AC); English education (MA); middle school mathematics education (MS); science education (MA); social studies education (AC). *Accreditation:* NCATE. *Entrance requirements:* For master's, Liberal Arts and Sciences Test (LAST), Content Specialty Test (CST). Additional exam requirements/recommendations for international students: Required—TOEFL.

Clarion University of Pennsylvania, Office of Graduate Programs, Master of Education Program, Clarion, PA 16214. Offers curriculum and instruction (M Ed); early childhood (M Ed, Certificate); English (M Ed); instructional technology specialist (K-12) (Certificate); literacy (M Ed); mathematics education (M Ed); reading specialist (M Ed, Certificate); science education (M Ed); special education (M Ed); technology (M Ed); world language (M Ed). *Accreditation:* NCATE. Part-time programs available. *Students:* 14 full-time (11 women), 207 part-time (163 women); includes 3 minority (1 Black or African American, non-Hispanic/Latino; 2 Hispanic/Latino). Average age 31. In 2011, 96 master's awarded. *Degree requirements:* For master's, thesis or alternative. *Entrance requirements:* For master's, minimum QPA of 3.0. *Application deadline:* Applications are processed on a rolling basis. *Expenses:* Tuition, state resident: part-time $429 per credit. Tuition, nonresident: part-time $644 per credit. *Financial support:* Research assistantships with full and partial tuition reimbursements and career-related internships or fieldwork available. Support available to part-time students. Financial award application deadline: 3/1. *Unit head:* Dr. John Groves, Dean, 814-393-2146, Fax: 514-393-2446. *Application contact:* Dr. Brenda Sanders Dede, Assistant Vice President for Academic Affairs, 814-393-2337, Fax: 814-393-2030, E-mail: bdede@clarion.edu. Web site: http://www.clarion.edu/25887/.

Clark Atlanta University, School of Education, Department of Curriculum, Atlanta, GA 30314. Offers special education general curriculum (MA); teaching math and science (MAT). Part-time programs available. *Faculty:* 4 full-time (all women), 4 part-time/adjunct (3 women). *Students:* 10 full-time (5 women), 9 part-time (7 women); includes 18 minority (all Black or African American, non-Hispanic/Latino). Average age 31. 13 applicants, 100% accepted, 9 enrolled. In 2011, 21 master's awarded. *Degree requirements:* For master's, one foreign language, comprehensive exam. *Entrance requirements:* For master's, GRE General Test, minimum undergraduate GPA of 2.6. Additional exam requirements/recommendations for international students: Required—TOEFL (minimum score 500 paper-based; 173 computer-based; 61 iBT). *Application deadline:* For fall admission, 4/1 for domestic and international students; for spring admission, 11/1 for domestic and international students. Applications are processed on a rolling basis. Application fee: $40 ($55 for international students). *Expenses: Tuition:* Full-time $13,572; part-time $754 per credit hour. *Required fees:* $806; $403 per semester. *Financial support:* Career-related internships or fieldwork, Federal Work-Study, scholarships/grants, and unspecified assistantships available. Support available to part-time students. Financial award application deadline: 4/30; financial award applicants required to submit FAFSA. *Unit head:* Dr. Doris Terrell, Chairperson, 404-880-6336, E-mail: dterrell@cau.edu. *Application contact:* Michelle Clark-Davis, Graduate Program Admissions, 404-880-6605, E-mail: cauadmissions@cau.edu. Web site: http://www.cau.edu/School_of_Education_curriculum_dept.aspx.

Clayton State University, School of Graduate Studies, Program in Education, Morrow, GA 30260-0285. Offers English (MAT); mathematics (MAT). *Accreditation:* NCATE. *Faculty:* 12 full-time (7 women). *Students:* 11 full-time (8 women), 11 part-time (4 women); includes 10 minority (all Black or African American, non-Hispanic/Latino). Average age 33. 11 applicants, 100% accepted, 8 enrolled. In 2011, 9 master's awarded. *Entrance requirements:* For master's, GRE, GACE, 2 official copies of transcripts, 3 recommendation letters, statement of purpose. Additional exam requirements/recommendations for international students: Required—TOEFL (minimum score 550 paper-based; 213 computer-based). *Application deadline:* For fall admission, 6/15 priority date for domestic students, 5/1 for international students; for spring admission, 10/15 priority date for domestic students. Applications are processed on a rolling basis. Application fee: $75. Electronic applications accepted. *Expenses:* Tuition, state resident: full-time $3528; part-time $196 per credit hour. Tuition, nonresident: full-time $13,176; part-time $732 per credit hour. *Required fees:* $1404; $552 per semester. Tuition and fees vary according to course load and campus/location. *Unit head:* Dr. Mari Ann Roberts, Program Director, Master of Arts in Teaching (Education), 678-466-4720, E-mail: mariroberts@clayton.edu. *Application contact:* Melanie Nolan, Administrative Assistant, Master of Arts in Teaching English, 678-466-4735, Fax: 678-466-4899, E-mail: melanienolan@clayton.edu.

Clemson University, Graduate School, College of Health, Education, and Human Development, Eugene T. Moore School of Education, Program in Early Childhood Education, Clemson, SC 29634. Offers early childhood education (M Ed); elementary education (M Ed); secondary English (M Ed); secondary math (M Ed); secondary science (M Ed); secondary social studies (M Ed). Part-time and evening/weekend programs available. *Students:* 5 applicants, 0% accepted, 0 enrolled. In 2011, 3 master's awarded. *Degree requirements:* For master's, comprehensive exam. *Entrance requirements:* For master's, GRE, valid teaching certificate. Additional exam requirements/recommendations for international students: Required—TOEFL; Recommended—IELTS. *Application deadline:* Applications are processed on a rolling basis. Application fee: $70 ($80 for international students). Electronic applications accepted. *Expenses:* Contact institution. *Financial support:* Institutionally sponsored loans, health care benefits, and unspecified assistantships available. Financial award application deadline: 3/1; financial award applicants required to submit FAFSA. *Faculty research:* Elementary education, mathematics education, social studies education, English education, science education. *Unit head:* Dr. Michael J. Padilla, Director/Associate Dean, 864-656-4444, Fax: 864-656-0311, E-mail: padilla@clemson.edu. *Application contact:* Dr. David Fleming, Graduate Programs Coordinator, 864-656-1881, Fax: 864-656-0311, E-mail: dflemin@clemson.edu.

Clemson University, Graduate School, College of Health, Education, and Human Development, Eugene T. Moore School of Education, Program in Secondary Education: Math and Science, Clemson, SC 29634. Offers MAT. *Accreditation:* NCATE. *Students:* 9 full-time (6 women), 1 part-time; includes 1 minority (Black or African American, non-Hispanic/Latino). Average age 29. 15 applicants, 93% accepted, 9 enrolled. In 2011, 9 master's awarded. *Degree requirements:* For master's, digital portfolio. *Entrance requirements:* For master's, PRAXIS II. Additional exam requirements/recommendations for international students: Required—TOEFL; Recommended—IELTS. *Application deadline:* For fall admission, 4/1 for domestic students. Applications are processed on a rolling basis. Application fee: $70 ($80 for international students). Electronic applications accepted. *Expenses:* Contact institution. *Financial support:* Institutionally sponsored loans, scholarships/grants, health care benefits, and unspecified assistantships available. Financial award application deadline: 6/1; financial award applicants required to submit FAFSA. *Faculty research:* Science education, math education. *Unit head:* Dr. Michael J. Padilla, Director/Associate Dean, 864-656-4444, Fax: 864-656-0311, E-mail: padilla@clemson.edu. *Application contact:* Dr. David Fleming, Graduate Coordinator, 864-656-1881, Fax: 864-656-0311, E-mail: dflemin@clemson.edu. Web site: http://www.clemson.edu/hehd/departments/education/academics/graduate/MAT/secondary.html.

Clemson University, Graduate School, College of Health, Education, and Human Development, Eugene T. Moore School of Education, Program in Teaching and Learning, Clemson, SC 29634. Offers elementary education (M Ed); English education (M Ed); mathematics education (M Ed); science education (M Ed); social studies education (M Ed). *Entrance requirements:* For master's, GRE, baccalaureate degree from regionally-accredited institution, official transcripts, copy of valid teaching certificate, two letters of recommendation. *Application contact:* Dr. David Fleming, Graduate Programs Coordinator, 864-656-1881, Fax: 864-656-0311, E-mail: dflemin@clemson.edu. Web site: http://www.clemson.edu/hehd/departments/education/academics/graduate/MEd-teach-learn.html.

Cleveland State University, College of Graduate Studies, College of Education and Human Services, Department of Teacher Education, Cleveland, OH 44115. Offers art education (M Ed); early childhood education (M Ed); foreign language education (M Ed); mathematics and science education (M Ed); middle childhood education (M Ed); special education (M Ed), including mild/moderate disabilities, moderate/intensive disabilities; teaching English to speakers of other languages (M Ed). Part-time and evening/weekend programs available. *Faculty:* 20 full-time (12 women), 26 part-time/adjunct (20 women). *Students:* 108 full-time (77 women), 388 part-time (306 women); includes 126 minority (100 Black or African American, non-Hispanic/Latino; 8 Asian, non-Hispanic/Latino; 15 Hispanic/Latino; 1 Native Hawaiian or other Pacific Islander, non-Hispanic/Latino; 2 Two or more races, non-Hispanic/Latino), 25 international. Average age 33. 249 applicants, 73% accepted, 118 enrolled. In 2011, 286 master's awarded. *Degree requirements:* For master's, comprehensive exam (for some programs), thesis or alternative. *Entrance requirements:* For master's, GRE General Test or MAT, minimum GPA of 2.75. Additional exam requirements/recommendations for international students: Required—TOEFL (minimum score 525 paper-based; 197 computer-based), IELTS (minimum score 6). *Application deadline:* For fall admission, 7/15 priority date for domestic students. Applications are processed on a rolling basis. Application fee: $30. *Expenses:* Tuition, state resident: full-time $6416; part-time $494 per credit hour. Tuition, nonresident: full-time $12,074; part-time $929 per credit hour. *Financial support:* In 2011–12, 12 research assistantships with full tuition reimbursements (averaging $3,480 per year) were awarded; tuition waivers (partial) and unspecified assistantships also available. *Faculty research:* Early literacy, professional development in reading, reading recovery, dual language, induction programs. *Total annual research expenditures:* $6.2 million. *Unit head:* Dr. Clifford T. Bennett, Chairperson, 216-523-7105, Fax: 216-687-5379, E-mail: c.t.bennett@csuohio.edu. *Application contact:* Deborah L. Brown, Interim Assistant Director, Graduate Admissions, 216-523-7572, E-mail: d.l.brown@csuohio.edu. Web site: http://www.csuohio.edu/coehs/departments/te.

The College at Brockport, State University of New York, School of Education and Human Services, Department of Education and Human Development, Program in Adolescence Education, Brockport, NY 14420-2997. Offers adolescence biology education (MS Ed); adolescence chemistry education (MS Ed); adolescence earth science education (MS Ed); adolescence English education (MS Ed); adolescence mathematics education (MS Ed); adolescence physics education (MS Ed); adolescence social studies education (MS Ed). *Accreditation:* NCATE. Part-time programs available. *Students:* 12 full-time (9 women), 60 part-time (28 women); includes 6 minority (1 American Indian or Alaska Native, non-Hispanic/Latino; 3 Asian, non-Hispanic/Latino; 1 Hispanic/Latino; 1 Native Hawaiian or other Pacific Islander, non-Hispanic/Latino). 26 applicants, 81% accepted, 17 enrolled. In 2011, 47 master's awarded. *Degree requirements:* For master's, thesis or alternative. *Entrance requirements:* For master's, minimum GPA of 3.0, letters of recommendation; statement of objectives, current resume. Additional exam requirements/recommendations for international students: Required—TOEFL (minimum score 550 paper-based; 213 computer-based; 79 iBT). *Application deadline:* For fall admission, 2/15 priority date for domestic students, 2/15 for international students; for spring admission, 9/15 priority date for domestic students, 9/15 for international students. Application fee: $80. Electronic applications accepted. *Financial support:* Federal Work-Study, scholarships/grants, and unspecified assistantships available. Support available to part-time students. Financial award application deadline: 3/15; financial award applicants required to submit FAFSA. *Unit head:* Dr. Don Halquist, Chairperson, 585-395-5550, Fax: 585-395-2172, E-mail: dhalquis@brockport.edu. *Application contact:* Michael Harrison, Coordinator of Certification and Graduate Advisement, 585-395-2326, Fax: 585-395-2172, E-mail: mharriso@brockport.edu. Web site: http://www.brockport.edu/graduate/.

The College at Brockport, State University of New York, School of Education and Human Services, Department of Education and Human Development, Program in Adolescence Inclusive Education, Brockport, NY 14420-2997. Offers English (MS Ed); mathematics (MS Ed); science (MS Ed); social studies (MS Ed). *Students:* 42 full-time (22 women), 21 part-time (10 women); includes 4 minority (2 Black or African American, non-Hispanic/Latino; 2 Hispanic/Latino). 50 applicants, 64% accepted, 19 enrolled. In 2011, 2 master's awarded. *Degree requirements:* For master's, thesis or alternative. *Entrance requirements:* For master's, minimum GPA of 3.0, letters of recommendation, statement of objectives, academic major (or equivalent) in program discipline; current resume. Additional exam requirements/recommendations for international students: Required—TOEFL (minimum score 550 paper-based; 213 computer-based; 79 iBT). *Application deadline:* For fall admission, 2/15 priority date for domestic students, 2/15 for international students; for spring admission, 9/15 priority date for domestic students, 9/15 for international students. Application fee: $80. Electronic applications accepted. *Financial support:* Federal Work-Study, scholarships/grants, and unspecified assistantships available. Support available to part-time students. Financial award application deadline: 3/15; financial award applicants required to submit FAFSA. *Unit head:* Dr. Don Halquist, Chairperson, 585-395-2205, Fax: 585-395-2171, E-mail: dhalquis@brockport.edu. *Application contact:* Michael Harrison, Coordinator of Certification and Graduate Advisement, 585-395-2326, Fax: 585-395-2172, E-mail: mharriso@brockport.edu.

College of Charleston, Graduate School, School of Education, Health, and Human Performance, Program in Science and Mathematics for Teachers, Charleston, SC 29424-0001. Offers M Ed. *Accreditation:* NCATE. Part-time and evening/weekend programs available. *Faculty:* 4 full-time (2 women). *Students:* 8 full-time (7 women), 17 part-time (14 women); includes 2 minority (1 Black or African American, non-Hispanic/Latino; 1 Two or more races, non-Hispanic/Latino). Average age 31. 18 applicants, 61% accepted, 10 enrolled. In 2011, 7 degrees awarded. *Degree requirements:* For master's, capstone project. *Entrance requirements:* For master's, GRE or PRAXIS, 2 letters of recommendation, copy of teaching certificate. Additional exam requirements/recommendations for international students: Required—TOEFL (minimum score 81 iBT). *Application deadline:* For fall admission, 4/1 for domestic students; for spring admission, 11/1 for domestic students. Application fee: $45. Electronic applications accepted. *Expenses:* Tuition, state resident: full-time $5455; part-time $455 per credit. Tuition, nonresident: full-time $13,917; part-time $1160 per credit. *Financial support:* In 2011–12, research assistantships (averaging $12,400 per year), teaching assistantships (averaging $13,300 per year) were awarded; scholarships/grants and unspecified assistantships also available. Financial award application deadline: 4/1; financial award applicants required to submit FAFSA. *Unit head:* Dr. William Veal, Director, 843-953-8045, E-mail: vealw@cofc.edu. *Application contact:* Susan Hallatt, Director of Graduate Admissions, 843-953-5614, Fax: 843-953-1434, E-mail: hallatts@cofc.edu. Web site: http://www.cofc.edu/~medsm/.

The College of William and Mary, School of Education, Program in Curriculum and Instruction, Williamsburg, VA 23187-8795. Offers elementary education (MA Ed); gifted education (MA Ed); math specialist (MA Ed); reading education (MA Ed); secondary education (MA Ed), including English education, mathematics education, modern foreign languages education, science education, social studies education; special education (MA Ed), including collaborating master educator, general curriculum. *Accreditation:* NCATE. Part-time programs available. *Faculty:* 15 full-time (10 women), 39 part-time/adjunct (32 women). *Students:* 80 full-time (69 women), 13 part-time (11 women); includes 11 minority (3 Black or African American, non-Hispanic/Latino; 1 American Indian or Alaska Native, non-Hispanic/Latino; 2 Hispanic/Latino; 5 Two or more races, non-Hispanic/Latino), 1 international. Average age 25. 220 applicants, 56% accepted, 85 enrolled. In 2011, 78 master's awarded. *Degree requirements:* For master's, project. *Entrance requirements:* For master's, GRE or MAT, minimum GPA of 2.5. Additional exam requirements/recommendations for international students: Required—TOEFL. *Application deadline:* For fall admission, 1/15 for domestic and international students; for spring admission, 10/1 for domestic and international students. Application fee: $50. Electronic applications accepted. *Expenses:* Tuition, state resident: full-time $6400; part-time $365 per credit hour. Tuition, nonresident: full-time $19,720; part-time $985 per credit hour. *Required fees:* $4562. *Financial support:* In 2011–12, 53 students received support, including 10 research assistantships with full and partial tuition reimbursements available (averaging $7,000 per year); career-related internships or fieldwork, Federal Work-Study, institutionally sponsored loans, scholarships/grants, and unspecified assistantships also available. Financial award application deadline: 1/15; financial award applicants required to submit FAFSA. *Faculty research:* National Council of Teachers of Mathematics Standards, counseling, self-concept and self-esteem, special education, curriculum development. *Unit head:* Dr. Margie Mason, Area Coordinator, 757-221-2327, E-mail: mmmaso@wm.edu. *Application contact:* Dorothy Smith Osborne, Assistant Dean for Admission, 757-221-2317, Fax: 757-221-2293, E-mail: dsosbo@wm.edu. Web site: http://education.wm.edu.

The Colorado College, Education Department, Program in Secondary Education, Colorado Springs, CO 80903-3294. Offers art teaching (K-12) (MAT); English teaching (MAT); foreign language teaching (MAT); mathematics teaching (MAT); music teaching (MAT); science teaching (MAT); social studies teaching (MAT). *Faculty:* 4 full-time (3 women), 6 part-time/adjunct (2 women). *Students:* 11 full-time (7 women); includes 3 minority (1 Asian, non-Hispanic/Latino; 2 Hispanic/Latino). Average age 27. 20 applicants, 85% accepted, 11 enrolled. In 2011, 15 master's awarded. *Degree requirements:* For master's, thesis, internship. *Application deadline:* For fall admission, 12/1 priority date for domestic students, 12/1 for international students. Applications are processed on a rolling basis. Application fee: $50. Electronic applications accepted. *Expenses:* *Tuition:* Full-time $29,313. *Required fees:* $2000. *Financial support:* In 2011–12, 15 students received support. Career-related internships or fieldwork, institutionally sponsored loans, scholarships/grants, and health care benefits available. Financial award application deadline: 2/15; financial award applicants required to submit FAFSA. *Unit head:* Dr. Mike Taber, Director, 719-389-6026, Fax: 719-389-6473, E-mail: mike.taber@coloradocollege.edu. *Application contact:* Debra Yazulla Mortenson, Education Services Manager, 719-389-6472, Fax: 719-389-6473, E-mail: debra.mortenson@coloradocollege.edu. Web site: http://www.coloradocollege.edu/academics/dept/education/graduate-programs/secondary-mat.dot.

Mathematics Education

Columbus State University, Graduate Studies, College of Education and Health Professions, Department of Teacher Education, Columbus, GA 31907-5645. Offers accomplished teaching (M Ed); early childhood education (M Ed, MAT, Ed S); health and physical education (M Ed, MAT); middle grades education (M Ed, MAT, Ed S); school library media (M Ed, MAT); secondary education (M Ed, MAT, Ed S), including English/language arts (M Ed, Ed S), general science (M Ed), mathematics (M Ed), social science (M Ed); special education (M Ed, Ed S), including general curriculum (M Ed). *Accreditation:* NCATE. Part-time and evening/weekend programs available. Postbaccalaureate distance learning degree programs offered (minimal on-campus study). *Degree requirements:* For master's, thesis, exit exam; for Ed S, thesis or alternative. *Entrance requirements:* For master's, GRE General Test, minimum GPA of 2.75; for Ed S, GRE General Test. Additional exam requirements/recommendations for international students: Required—TOEFL (minimum score 550 paper-based; 213 computer-based; 79 iBT). Electronic applications accepted.

Concordia University, School of Graduate Studies, Faculty of Arts and Science, Department of Mathematics and Statistics, Montréal, QC H3G 1M8, Canada. Offers mathematics (M Sc, MA, PhD); teaching of mathematics (MTM). *Degree requirements:* For master's, thesis optional; for doctorate, comprehensive exam, thesis/dissertation. *Entrance requirements:* For master's, honors degree in mathematics or equivalent. *Faculty research:* Number theory, computational algebra, mathematical physics, differential geometry, dynamical systems and statistics.

Converse College, School of Education and Graduate Studies, Program in Secondary Education, Spartanburg, SC 29302-0006. Offers biology (MAT); chemistry (MAT); English (M Ed, MAT); mathematics (M Ed, MAT); natural sciences (M Ed); social sciences (M Ed, MAT). Part-time programs available. *Degree requirements:* For master's, capstone paper. *Entrance requirements:* For master's, NTE or PRAXIS II (M Ed), minimum GPA of 2.75, 2 recommendations. Electronic applications accepted.

Cornell University, Graduate School, Graduate Fields of Agriculture and Life Sciences, Field of Education, Ithaca, NY 14853-0001. Offers agricultural education (MAT); biology (7-12) (MAT); chemistry (7-12) (MAT); curriculum and instruction (MPS, MS, PhD); earth science (7-12) (MAT); extension, and adult education (MPS, MS, PhD); mathematics (7-12) (MAT); physics (7-12) (MAT). *Faculty:* 23 full-time (10 women). *Students:* 32 full-time (18 women); includes 6 minority (4 Asian, non-Hispanic/Latino; 2 Hispanic/Latino), 1 international. Average age 30. 60 applicants, 33% accepted, 12 enrolled. In 2011, 22 master's, 7 doctorates awarded. Terminal master's awarded for partial completion of doctoral program. *Degree requirements:* For master's, thesis (MS); for doctorate, comprehensive exam, thesis/dissertation. *Entrance requirements:* For master's and doctorate, GRE General Test, sample of written work (recommended), 2 letters of recommendation. Additional exam requirements/recommendations for international students: Required—TOEFL (minimum score 550 paper-based; 213 computer-based; 77 iBT). *Application deadline:* For fall admission, 2/15 for domestic students. Application fee: $95. Electronic applications accepted. *Financial support:* In 2011–12, 2 fellowships with full tuition reimbursements, 4 research assistantships with full tuition reimbursements, 12 teaching assistantships with full tuition reimbursements were awarded; institutionally sponsored loans, scholarships/grants, health care benefits, tuition waivers (full and partial), and unspecified assistantships also available. Financial award applicants required to submit FAFSA. *Faculty research:* Moral development and professional ethics, public issues education and community development, socio/political issues in public education, teacher education and curriculum in agricultural science and mathematics, extension research. *Unit head:* Director of Graduate Studies, 607-255-4278, Fax: 607-255-7905. *Application contact:* Graduate Field Assistant, 607-255-4278, Fax: 607-255-7905, E-mail: rh22@cornell.edu. Web site: http://www.gradschool.cornell.edu/fields.php?id-80&a-2.

Delaware State University, Graduate Programs, Department of Mathematics, Program in Mathematics Education, Dover, DE 19901-2277. Offers MS. *Entrance requirements:* Additional exam requirements/recommendations for international students: Required—TOEFL (minimum score 550 paper-based). Electronic applications accepted.

DePaul University, College of Science and Health, Department of Mathematical Sciences, Chicago, IL 60614. Offers applied mathematics (MS), including actuarial science or statistics; applied statistics (MS, Certificate); mathematics education (MA). Part-time and evening/weekend programs available. *Faculty:* 23 full-time (6 women), 18 part-time/adjunct (5 women). *Students:* 122 full-time (57 women), 63 part-time (23 women); includes 52 minority (19 Black or African American, non-Hispanic/Latino; 18 Asian, non-Hispanic/Latino; 10 Hispanic/Latino; 1 Native Hawaiian or other Pacific Islander, non-Hispanic/Latino; 4 Two or more races, non-Hispanic/Latino), 15 international. Average age 30. 40 applicants, 100% accepted. In 2011, 30 master's awarded. *Degree requirements:* For master's, comprehensive exam. *Entrance requirements:* Additional exam requirements/recommendations for international students: Required—TOEFL. *Application deadline:* For fall admission, 7/30 for domestic students, 6/30 for international students; for winter admission, 11/30 for domestic students, 10/31 for international students; for spring admission, 2/15 for domestic students. Applications are processed on a rolling basis. Application fee: $25. *Financial support:* In 2011–12, 12 students received support, including research assistantships with partial tuition reimbursements available (averaging $6,000 per year); teaching assistantships and tuition waivers (full) also available. Financial award application deadline: 4/30. *Faculty research:* Verbally prime algebras, enveloping algebras of Lie, superalgebras and related rings, harmonic analysis, estimation theory. *Unit head:* Dr. Ahmed I. Zayed, Chairperson, 773-325-7806, Fax: 773-325-7807, E-mail: azayed@depaul.edu. *Application contact:* Ann Spittle, Director of Graduate Admissions, 312-362-8300, Fax: 312-362-5749, E-mail: admitdpu@depaul.edu. Web site: http://depaul.edu/~math.

Drew University, Caspersen School of Graduate Studies, Program in Education, Madison, NJ 07940-1493. Offers biology (MAT); chemistry (MAT); English (MAT); French (MAT); Italian (MAT); math (MAT); physics (MAT); social studies (MAT); Spanish (MAT); theatre arts (MAT). Part-time programs available. *Entrance requirements:* For master's, transcripts, personal statement, recommendations. Additional exam requirements/recommendations for international students: Required—TOEFL, TWE. *Expenses:* Contact institution.

Drexel University, Goodwin College of Professional Studies, School of Education, Program in Mathematics Learning and Teaching, Philadelphia, PA 19104-2875. Offers MS.

Drury University, Graduate Programs in Education, Springfield, MO 65802. Offers elementary education (M Ed); gifted education (M Ed); human services (M Ed); instructional mathematics K-8 (M Ed); instructional technology (M Ed); middle school teaching (M Ed); secondary education (M Ed); special education (M Ed); special reading (M Ed). *Accreditation:* NCATE. Part-time and evening/weekend programs available. *Degree requirements:* For master's, thesis. *Entrance requirements:* For master's, GRE or MAT, minimum GPA of 2.75. Additional exam requirements/recommendations for international students: Required—TOEFL. Electronic applications accepted. *Faculty research:* Cultural enrichment, research skills, parental involvement relating to reading skills, reading strategies for mainstreaming children.

Duquesne University, School of Education, Department of Instruction and Leadership, Pittsburgh, PA 15282-0001. Offers early level (PreK-4) education (MS Ed); English as a second language (MS Ed); instructional technology (MS Ed, Ed D, Post-Master's Certificate), including business, computer, and information technology (MS Ed), instructional technology; middle level (4-8) education (MS Ed); reading and language arts (MS Ed); secondary education (MS Ed), including biology, chemistry, English, Latin education, K-12, mathematics, physics, social studies. Part-time and evening/weekend programs available. Postbaccalaureate distance learning degree programs offered (minimal on-campus study). *Faculty:* 15 full-time (9 women), 28 part-time/adjunct (15 women). *Students:* 213 full-time (145 women), 47 part-time (38 women); includes 19 minority (9 Black or African American, non-Hispanic/Latino; 5 Asian, non-Hispanic/Latino; 4 Hispanic/Latino; 1 Two or more races, non-Hispanic/Latino), 11 international. Average age 26. 160 applicants, 48% accepted, 53 enrolled. In 2011, 111 degrees awarded. *Degree requirements:* For master's, thesis optional; for doctorate, thesis/dissertation. *Entrance requirements:* For master's, letters of recommendation, letter of intent, interview, bachelor's degree; for doctorate, GRE, letters of recommendation, letter of intent, interview, master's degree; for Post-Master's Certificate, letters of recommendation, letter of intent, interview, bachelor's/master's degree. Additional exam requirements/recommendations for international students: Required—TOEFL (minimum score 550 paper-based; 80 computer-based), IELTS (minimum score 7). *Application deadline:* For fall admission, 9/1 priority date for domestic students; for spring admission, 1/1 priority date for domestic students. Applications are processed on a rolling basis. Application fee: $0. Electronic applications accepted. Application fee is waived when completed online. *Expenses: Tuition:* Full-time $16,596; part-time $922 per credit. *Required fees:* $1584; $88 per credit. Tuition and fees vary according to program. *Financial support:* Research assistantships, teaching assistantships with tuition reimbursements, career-related internships or fieldwork, Federal Work-Study, and institutionally sponsored loans available. Support available to part-time students. *Unit head:* Dr. Jason Margolis, Chair, 412-396-6106, Fax: 412-396-5388, E-mail: margolisj@duq.edu. *Application contact:* Michael Dolinger, Director of Student and Academic Services, 412-396-6647, Fax: 412-396-5585, E-mail: dolingerm@duq.edu.

East Carolina University, Graduate School, College of Education, Department of Mathematics, Science, and Instructional Technology Education, Greenville, NC 27858-4353. Offers computer-based instruction (Certificate); distance learning and administration (Certificate); instructional technology (MA Ed, MS); mathematics (MA Ed); performance improvement (Certificate); science education (MA, MA Ed); special endorsement in computer education (Certificate). Part-time and evening/weekend programs available. *Degree requirements:* For master's, comprehensive exam, thesis optional. *Entrance requirements:* For master's, GRE General Test or MAT, interview, minimum GPA of 2.5, bachelor's degree in related field, teaching license (MA Ed). Additional exam requirements/recommendations for international students: Required—TOEFL. *Application deadline:* For fall admission, 6/1 priority date for domestic students. Applications are processed on a rolling basis. Application fee: $50. *Expenses:* Tuition, state resident: full-time $3557; part-time $444.63 per semester hour. Tuition, nonresident: full-time $14,351; part-time $1793.88 per semester hour. *Required fees:* $2016; $252 per semester hour. Part-time tuition and fees vary according to course load, campus/location and program. *Financial support:* Research assistantships, teaching assistantships, and Federal Work-Study available. Support available to part-time students. Financial award application deadline: 6/1. *Unit head:* Susan Ganter, Chair, 252-328-9353, E-mail: ganters@ecu.edu. *Application contact:* Dean of Graduate School, 252-328-6012, Fax: 252-328-6071, E-mail: gradschool@ecu.edu.

Eastern Illinois University, Graduate School, College of Sciences, Department of Mathematics and Computer Science, Charleston, IL 61920-3099. Offers mathematics (MA); mathematics education (MA). *Entrance requirements:* For master's, GRE General Test. *Expenses:* Tuition, state resident: part-time $279 per credit hour. Tuition, nonresident: part-time $670 per credit hour. *Required fees:* $179.07 per credit hour. $1253 per semester.

Eastern Kentucky University, The Graduate School, College of Education, Department of Curriculum and Instruction, Program in Secondary and Higher Education, Richmond, KY 40475-3102. Offers secondary education (MA Ed), including agricultural education, art education, biological sciences education, business education, English education, geography education, history education, home economics education, industrial education, mathematical sciences education, physical education, school health education. *Accreditation:* NCATE. Part-time programs available. *Entrance requirements:* For master's, GRE General Test, minimum GPA of 2.5.

Eastern Michigan University, Graduate School, College of Arts and Sciences, Department of Mathematics, Ypsilanti, MI 48197. Offers applied statistics (MA); computer science (MA); mathematics (MA); mathematics education (MA). Part-time and evening/weekend programs available. Postbaccalaureate distance learning degree programs offered (minimal on-campus study). *Faculty:* 25 full-time (11 women). *Students:* 16 full-time (9 women), 36 part-time (14 women); includes 9 minority (4 Black or African American, non-Hispanic/Latino; 5 Asian, non-Hispanic/Latino), 6 international. Average age 30. 39 applicants, 82% accepted, 18 enrolled. In 2011, 17 degrees awarded. *Degree requirements:* For master's, thesis optional. *Entrance requirements:* Additional exam requirements/recommendations for international students: Required—TOEFL. *Application deadline:* Applications are processed on a rolling basis. Application fee: $35. *Expenses:* Tuition, state resident: full-time $10,367; part-time $432 per credit hour. Tuition, nonresident: full-time $20,435; part-time $851 per credit hour. *Required fees:* $39 per credit hour. $46 per semester. One-time fee: $100. Tuition and fees vary according to course level, degree level and reciprocity agreements. *Financial support:* Fellowships, research assistantships with full tuition reimbursements, teaching assistantships with full tuition reimbursements, career-related internships or fieldwork, Federal Work-Study, institutionally sponsored loans, scholarships/grants, tuition waivers (partial), and unspecified assistantships available. Support available to part-time students. Financial award applicants required to submit FAFSA. *Unit head:* Dr. Christopher Gardiner, Department Head, 734-487-1444, Fax: 734-487-2489, E-mail: cgardiner@emich.edu. *Application contact:* Dr. Bingwu Wang, Graduate Coordinator, 734-487-5044, Fax: 734-487-2489, E-mail: bwang@emich.edu. Web site: http://www.math.emich.edu.

Eastern Washington University, Graduate Studies, College of Science, Health and Engineering, Department of Mathematics, Cheney, WA 99004-2431. Offers mathematics (MS); teaching mathematics (MA). Part-time programs available. *Faculty:* 11 full-time (4 women). *Students:* 7 full-time (4 women), 12 part-time (6 women); includes 1 minority (Asian, non-Hispanic/Latino). Average age 32. 22 applicants, 45% accepted, 8 enrolled. In 2011, 3 master's awarded. *Degree requirements:* For master's, comprehensive exam, thesis (for some programs). *Entrance requirements:* For master's, GRE General Test, departmental qualifying exam, minimum GPA of 3.0. *Application deadline:* For fall admission, 4/1 priority date for domestic students; for spring admission, 1/15 for domestic students. Applications are processed on a rolling basis. Application fee: $50. *Financial support:* In 2011–12, 12 teaching assistantships with partial tuition reimbursements (averaging $12,000 per year) were awarded; career-related internships or fieldwork, Federal Work-Study, institutionally sponsored loans, scholarships/grants, health care benefits, tuition waivers (partial), and unspecified assistantships also available. Support available to part-time students. Financial award application deadline: 2/1; financial award applicants required to submit FAFSA. *Unit head:* Dr. Christian Hansen, Chair, 509-359-6225, Fax: 509-359-4700. *Application contact:* Dr. Yves Nievergelt, Adviser, 509-359-2219.

Florida Agricultural and Mechanical University, Division of Graduate Studies, Research, and Continuing Education, College of Education, Program in Secondary Education and Foundation, Tallahassee, FL 32307-3200. Offers biology (M Ed); chemistry (MS Ed); English (MS Ed); history (MS Ed); math (MS Ed); physics (MS Ed). *Accreditation:* NCATE. *Degree requirements:* For master's, thesis (for some programs). *Entrance requirements:* For master's, GRE General Test, minimum GPA of 3.0. Additional exam requirements/recommendations for international students: Required—TOEFL.

Florida Institute of Technology, Graduate Programs, College of Science, Department of Education and Interdisciplinary Studies, Melbourne, FL 32901-6975. Offers computer education (MS); elementary science education (M Ed); environmental education (MS); interdisciplinary science (MS); mathematics education (MS, PhD, Ed S); science education (MS, PhD, Ed S), including informal science education (MS); teaching (MAT). Part-time and evening/weekend programs available. *Faculty:* 4 full-time (1 woman), 3 part-time/adjunct (2 women). *Students:* 22 full-time (16 women), 27 part-time (18 women); includes 8 minority (2 Black or African American, non-Hispanic/Latino; 4 Asian, non-Hispanic/Latino; 2 Hispanic/Latino), 9 international. Average age 34. 57 applicants, 70% accepted, 19 enrolled. In 2011, 5 master's, 1 doctorate awarded. Terminal master's awarded for partial completion of doctoral program. *Median time to degree:* Of those who began their doctoral program in fall 2003, 50% received their degree in 8 years or less. *Degree requirements:* For master's, comprehensive exam (for some programs), thesis optional; for doctorate, comprehensive exam, thesis/dissertation; for Ed S, comprehensive exam. *Entrance requirements:* For master's, minimum GPA of 3.0, resume, 3 letters of recommendation (elementary science education), statement of objectives; for doctorate, minimum GPA of 3.2, resume, 3 letters of recommendation, statement of objectives, 3 years teaching experience (recommended); for Ed S, minimum GPA of 3.0, resume, 3 letters of recommendation, statement of objectives. Additional exam requirements/recommendations for international students: Required—TOEFL (minimum score 550 paper-based; 213 computer-based; 79 iBT). *Application deadline:* For fall admission, 4/1 for international students; for spring admission, 9/30 for international students. Applications are processed on a rolling basis. Electronic applications accepted. *Expenses: Tuition:* Full-time $19,620; part-time $1090 per credit hour. Tuition and fees vary according to campus/location. *Financial support:* In 2011–12, 1 teaching assistantship with full and partial tuition reimbursement (averaging $797 per year) was awarded; research assistantships with full and partial tuition reimbursements, career-related internships or fieldwork, institutionally sponsored loans, tuition waivers (partial), unspecified assistantships, and tuition remissions also available. Support available to part-time students. Financial award application deadline: 3/1; financial award applicants required to submit FAFSA. *Faculty research:* Measurement and evaluation, computers in education, educational technology. *Total annual research expenditures:* $1. *Unit head:* Dr. Lazlo A. Baksay, Department Head, 321-674-7205, Fax: 321-674-7598, E-mail: baksay@fit.edu. *Application contact:* Cheryl A. Brown, Associate Director of Graduate Admissions, 321-674-7581, Fax: 321-723-9468, E-mail: cbrown@fit.edu. Web site: http://cos.fit.edu/education/.

Florida International University, College of Education, Department of Curriculum and Instruction, Miami, FL 33199. Offers art education (MAT, MS, Ed D); curriculum and instruction (Ed S); curriculum development (MS); curriculum studies (PhD); early childhood education (MS, Ed D); elementary education (MS, Ed D); English education (MAT, MS, Ed D); foreign language education - teaching English to speakers of other languages (TESOL) (MS, Certificate), including foreign language education (Certificate), teaching English (MS); French education - initial teacher preparation (MAT); international and intercultural development education (Ed D); international and intercultural developmental education (MS); language, literacy and culture (PhD); learning technologies (MS, Ed D, PhD); mathematics education (MAT, MS, Ed D, PhD); modern language education/bilingual education (MS, Ed D); physical education (MS); reading education (MS, Ed D); science education (MAT, MS, Ed D, PhD); social studies education (MAT, MS, Ed D); Spanish education - initial teacher preparation (MAT); special education (MS). Part-time and evening/weekend programs available. *Degree requirements:* For doctorate, comprehensive exam, thesis/dissertation. *Entrance requirements:* For master's, GRE General Test, Florida General Knowledge Test or Florida College Level Academic Skills Test; for doctorate and other advanced degree, GRE General Test. Additional exam requirements/recommendations for international students: Required—TOEFL (minimum score 550 paper-based; 213 computer-based; 80 iBT), IELTS (minimum score 6.3). Electronic applications accepted.

Florida State University, The Graduate School, College of Education, School of Teacher Education, Program in Mathematics Education, Tallahassee, FL 32306. Offers MS, PhD, Ed S. Part-time programs available. Postbaccalaureate distance learning degree programs offered. *Faculty:* 3 full-time (2 women). *Students:* 1 full-time (0 women), 2 part-time (1 woman); includes 1 minority (Black or African American, non-Hispanic/Latino), 1 international. Average age 33. In 2011, 11 master's, 3 doctorates, 2 other advanced degrees awarded. *Degree requirements:* For master's and Ed S, comprehensive exam, thesis optional; for doctorate, comprehensive exam, thesis/dissertation. *Entrance requirements:* For master's, doctorate, and Ed S, GRE General Test, minimum GPA of 3.0. Additional exam requirements/recommendations for international students: Required—TOEFL (minimum score 550 paper-based; 213 computer-based; 80 iBT). *Application deadline:* For fall admission, 7/1 for domestic and international students; for winter admission, 11/1 for domestic and international students; for spring admission, 3/1 for domestic and international students. Applications are processed on a rolling basis. Application fee: $30. Electronic applications accepted. *Expenses:* Tuition, state resident: full-time $9474; part-time $350.88 per credit hour. Tuition, nonresident: full-time $16,236; part-time $601.34 per credit hour. *Required fees:* $630 per semester. One-time fee: $20. Tuition and fees vary according to course load and campus/location. *Financial support:* Fellowships with full and partial tuition reimbursements, research assistantships with full and partial tuition reimbursements, teaching assistantships with full and partial tuition reimbursements, career-related internships or fieldwork, scholarships/grants, health care benefits, and unspecified assistantships available. Financial award applicants required to submit FAFSA. *Faculty research:* History of mathematics, students' ability to develop thinking skills in calculus, development of algebraic thinking, teacher preparation in secondary mathematics. *Unit head:* Dr. Elizabeth M. Jakubowski, Head, 850-644-6553, Fax: 850-644-1880, E-mail: emjakubowski@fsu.edu. *Application contact:* Harriet Kasper, Program Assistant, 850-644-2122, Fax: 850-644-1880, E-mail: hkasper@fsu.edu. Web site: http://fsu-teach.fsu.edu.

Framingham State University, Division of Graduate and Continuing Education, Program in Mathematics, Framingham, MA 01701-9101. Offers M Ed. *Entrance requirements:* For master's, GRE General Test, minimum GPA of 3.0.

Fresno Pacific University, Graduate Programs, School of Education, Fresno, CA 93702-4709. Offers administration (MA Ed), including administrative services; foundations, curriculum and teaching (MA Ed), including curriculum and teaching, school library and information technology; language, literacy, and culture (MA Ed), including bilingual/cross-cultural education, language development, multilingual contexts, reading; mathematics/science/computer education (MA Ed), including educational technology, integrated mathematics/science education, mathematics education; pupil personnel services (MA Ed), including school counseling, school psychology; special education (MA Ed), including mild/moderate, moderate/severe, physical and health impairments. Part-time and evening/weekend programs available. *Degree requirements:* For master's, thesis (for some programs). *Entrance requirements:* For master's, interview; GMAT, GRE, MAT, or 6 units of course work with a faculty recommendation. Additional exam requirements/recommendations for international students: Required—TOEFL (minimum score 550 paper-based; 213 computer-based). Electronic applications accepted.

Fresno Pacific University, Graduate Programs, School of Education, Division of Mathematics/Science/Computer Education, Program in Integrated Mathematics/Science Education, Fresno, CA 93702-4709. Offers MA Ed. Part-time and evening/weekend programs available. *Degree requirements:* For master's, thesis or alternative. *Entrance requirements:* Additional exam requirements/recommendations for international students: Required—TOEFL (minimum score 550 paper-based; 213 computer-based).

Fresno Pacific University, Graduate Programs, School of Education, Division of Mathematics/Science/Computer Education, Program in Mathematics Education, Fresno, CA 93702-4709. Offers elementary and middle school mathematics (MA Ed); secondary school mathematics (MA Ed). Part-time and evening/weekend programs available. *Degree requirements:* For master's, thesis or alternative. *Entrance requirements:* Additional exam requirements/recommendations for international students: Required—TOEFL (minimum score 550 paper-based; 213 computer-based).

Georgia Southern University, Jack N. Averitt College of Graduate Studies, College of Education, Department of Teaching and Learning, Program in Mathematics Education, Statesboro, GA 30460. Offers M Ed, MAT. *Accreditation:* NCATE. Part-time and evening/weekend programs available. *Students:* 7 full-time (5 women); includes 3 minority (1 Black or African American, non-Hispanic/Latino; 1 Hispanic/Latino; 1 Native Hawaiian or other Pacific Islander, non-Hispanic/Latino). Average age 22. 5 applicants, 100% accepted, 5 enrolled. *Degree requirements:* For master's, portfolio, transition point assessments, exit assessment. *Entrance requirements:* For master's, GRE General Test or MAT; GACE Basic Skills and Content Assessments (MAT), minimum cumulative GPA of 2.5. Additional exam requirements/recommendations for international students: Required—TOEFL (minimum score 550 paper-based; 213 computer-based; 80 iBT). *Application deadline:* For fall admission, 3/1 priority date for domestic students, 3/1 for international students; for spring admission, 10/1 priority date for domestic students, 10/1 for international students. Applications are processed on a rolling basis. Application fee: $50. Electronic applications accepted. *Expenses:* Tuition, state resident: full-time $6300; part-time $263 per semester hour. Tuition, nonresident: full-time $25,174; part-time $1049 per semester hour. *Required fees:* $1872. *Financial support:* In 2011–12, 4 students received support, including research assistantships with partial tuition reimbursements available (averaging $7,200 per year), teaching assistantships with partial tuition reimbursements available (averaging $7,200 per year); Federal Work-Study, scholarships/grants, tuition waivers (partial), and unspecified assistantships also available. Support available to part-time students. Financial award application deadline: 4/15; financial award applicants required to submit FAFSA. *Faculty research:* Technology applications. *Unit head:* Dr. Ronnie Sheppard, Department Chair, 912-478-7203, Fax: 912-478-0026, E-mail: sheppard@georgiasouthern.edu. *Application contact:* Amanda Gilliland, Coordinator for Graduate Student Recruitment, 912-478-5384, Fax: 912-478-0740, E-mail: gradadmissions@georgiasouthern.edu. Web site: http://coe.georgiasouthern.edu/tandl/index.html.

Georgia State University, College of Education, Department of Middle-Secondary Education and Instructional Technology, Programs in Secondary Education, Atlanta, GA 30302-3083. Offers art education (Ed S); English education (M Ed, Ed S); mathematics education (M Ed, PhD, Ed S); music education (PhD); science education (M Ed, PhD, Ed S); social studies education (M Ed, PhD, Ed S). *Accreditation:* NASM (one or more programs are accredited); NCATE. Part-time and evening/weekend programs available. *Degree requirements:* For master's, comprehensive exam; for doctorate, comprehensive exam, thesis/dissertation; for Ed S, project/exam. *Entrance requirements:* For master's, GRE General Test, minimum GPA of 2.5; for doctorate, GRE General Test or MAT, minimum GPA of 3.3; for Ed S, GRE General Test or MAT, minimum graduate GPA of 3.25. *Faculty research:* Women and science, problem solving in mathematics, dialects, economic education.

Grambling State University, School of Graduate Studies and Research, College of Education, Department of Educational Leadership, Grambling, LA 71245. Offers curriculum and instruction (Ed D); developmental education (MS, Ed D), including curriculum and instruction: reading (Ed D), English (MS), guidance and counseling (MS), higher education administration (Ed D), instructional systems and technology (Ed D), mathematics (MS), reading (MS), science (MS), student development and personnel services (Ed D); educational leadership (MS, Ed D). Part-time and evening/weekend programs available. *Degree requirements:* For master's, comprehensive exam, thesis (for some programs); for doctorate, comprehensive exam, thesis/dissertation. *Entrance requirements:* For master's, GRE, minimum GPA of 2.5 on last degree; for doctorate, GRE (minimum 1000, 500 on Verbal), master's degree, minimum GPA of 3.0 on last degree. Additional exam requirements/recommendations for international students: Required—TOEFL (minimum score 500 paper-based; 173 computer-based; 61 iBT). Electronic applications accepted. *Expenses:* Tuition, state resident: full-time $3546; part-time $192 per credit hour. Tuition, nonresident: full-time $3456; part-time $192 per credit hour. *Required fees:* $1829; $1829 per semester hour.

Harding University, College of Education, Searcy, AR 72149-0001. Offers advanced studies in teaching and learning (M Ed); art (MSE); behavioral science (MSE); counseling (MS, Ed S); early childhood special education (M Ed, MSE); education (MSE); educational leadership (M Ed, Ed S); elementary education (M Ed); English (MSE); French (MSE); history/social science (MSE); kinesiology (MSE); math (MSE); reading (M Ed); secondary education (M Ed); Spanish (MSE); teaching (MAT); teaching English as a second language (MSE). *Accreditation:* NCATE. Part-time and evening/weekend programs available. *Faculty:* 9 full-time (2 women), 48 part-time/adjunct (26 women). *Students:* 100 full-time (77 women), 333 part-time (239 women); includes 76 minority (59 Black or African American, non-Hispanic/Latino; 1 Asian, non-Hispanic/Latino; 10 Hispanic/Latino; 6 Two or more races, non-Hispanic/Latino), 2 international. Average age 36. 93 applicants, 91% accepted, 83 enrolled. In 2011, 159 master's, 10 other advanced degrees awarded. *Degree requirements:* For master's, comprehensive exam (for some programs), thesis optional, portfolio(s); for Ed S, comprehensive exam, portfolio, project. *Entrance requirements:* For master's, GRE, MAT, PRAXIS; for Ed S, MAT or GRE. Additional exam requirements/recommendations for international students: Required—TOEFL (minimum score 550 paper-based; 79 iBT). *Application deadline:* For fall admission, 8/1 for domestic and international students; for spring admission, 1/1 for domestic and international students. Applications are processed on a rolling basis. Application fee: $35. *Expenses: Tuition:* Full-time $10,512; part-time $584 per credit hour. *Required fees:* $500; $25 per credit hour. Tuition and fees vary according to course load, degree level and program. *Financial support:* In 2011–12, 37 students received support. Unspecified assistantships available. *Faculty research:* Reading, comprehension, school violence, educational technology, behavior, college choice, differentiated instruction, brain-based teaching. *Unit head:* Dr. Clara Carroll, Chair, 501-279-4501, Fax: 501-279-4083, E-mail: ccarroll@harding.edu. *Application contact:* Information Contact, 501-279-4315, E-mail: gradstudiesedu@harding.edu. Web site: http://www.harding.edu/education/grad.html.

Harvard University, Extension School, Cambridge, MA 02138-3722. Offers applied sciences (CAS); biotechnology (ALM); educational technologies (ALM); educational technology (CET); English for graduate and professional studies (DGP); environmental management (ALM, CEM); information technology (ALM); journalism (ALM); liberal arts (ALM); management (ALM, CM); mathematics for teaching (ALM); museum studies (ALM); premedical studies (Diploma); publication and communication (CPC). Part-time and evening/weekend programs available. *Degree requirements:* For master's, thesis. *Entrance requirements:* For master's, 3 completed graduate courses with grade of B or higher. Additional exam requirements/recommendations for international students: Required—TOEFL (minimum score 600 paper-based; 250 computer-based), TWE (minimum score 5). *Expenses:* Contact institution.

Harvard University, Harvard Graduate School of Education, Master's Programs in Education, Cambridge, MA 02138. Offers arts in education (Ed M); education policy and management (Ed M); higher education (Ed M); human development and psychology (Ed M); international education policy (Ed M); language and literacy (Ed M); learning and teaching (Ed M); mid-career mathematics and science (teaching certificate) (Ed M); mind brain and education (Ed M); prevention science and practice (Ed M); school leadership (Ed M); special studies (Ed M); teaching and curriculum (teaching certificate) (Ed M); technology innovation and education (Ed M). Part-time programs available. *Faculty:* 83 full-time (44 women), 67 part-time/adjunct (29 women). *Students:* 592 full-time (431 women), 75 part-time (54 women); includes 194 minority (41 Black or African American, non-Hispanic/Latino; 4 American Indian or Alaska Native, non-Hispanic/Latino; 75 Asian, non-Hispanic/Latino; 45 Hispanic/Latino; 2 Native Hawaiian or other Pacific Islander, non-Hispanic/Latino; 27 Two or more races, non-Hispanic/Latino), 95 international. Average age 28. 1,679 applicants, 52% accepted, 627 enrolled. In 2011, 653 master's awarded. *Entrance requirements:* For master's, GRE General Test, statement of purpose, 3 letters of recommendation, resume, official transcripts. Additional exam requirements/recommendations for international students: Required—TOEFL (minimum score 613 paper-based; 104 computer-based; 100 iBT), TWE (minimum score 5). *Application deadline:* For fall admission, 1/4 for domestic and international students. Application fee: $85. Electronic applications accepted. *Expenses:* Contact institution. *Financial support:* In 2011–12, 419 students received support, including 14 fellowships with full and partial tuition reimbursements available (averaging $12,831 per year); career-related internships or fieldwork, Federal Work-Study, institutionally sponsored loans, scholarships/grants, health care benefits, tuition waivers (full and partial), and unspecified assistantships also available. Support available to part-time students. Financial award application deadline: 2/1; financial award applicants required to submit FAFSA. *Faculty research:* Learning and development, educational leadership and organizations, educational policy analysis. *Total annual research expenditures:* $26 million. *Unit head:* Jennifer L. Petrallia, Assistant Dean, 617-495-8445. *Application contact:* Information Contact, 617-495-3414, Fax: 617-496-3577, E-mail: gseadmissions@harvard.edu. Web site: http://www.gse.harvard.edu/.

High Point University, Norcross Graduate School, High Point, NC 27262-3598. Offers business administration (MBA); educational leadership (M Ed); elementary education (M Ed); history (MA); nonprofit management (MA); secondary math (M Ed); special education (M Ed); strategic communication (MA); teaching elementary education k-6 (MAT); teaching secondary mathematics 9-12 (MAT). *Accreditation:* ACBSP; NCATE. Part-time and evening/weekend programs available. *Degree requirements:* For master's, comprehensive exam (for some programs), thesis (for some programs). *Entrance requirements:* For master's, GMAT (MBA), GRE, MAT, minimum GPA of 3.0. Additional exam requirements/recommendations for international students: Required—TOEFL (minimum score 550 paper-based). Electronic applications accepted.

Hofstra University, School of Education, Health, and Human Services, Program in Elementary Education, Hempstead, NY 11549. Offers early childhood and childhood education (MS Ed); early childhood education (MA, MS Ed); educational technology (MA); elementary education (MS Ed); literacy (MA); math specialist (Advanced Certificate); math, science, technology (MA); multiculturalism (MA). Part-time and evening/weekend programs available. Postbaccalaureate distance learning degree programs offered (minimal on-campus study). *Students:* 54 full-time (48 women), 43 part-time (37 women); includes 17 minority (10 Black or African American, non-Hispanic/Latino; 2 Asian, non-Hispanic/Latino; 5 Hispanic/Latino), 2 international. Average age 29. 65 applicants, 88% accepted, 18 enrolled. In 2011, 58 master's awarded. *Degree requirements:* For master's, comprehensive exam, thesis (for some programs), 35 semester hours (for MA); 38-41 semester hours (for MS Ed), minimum GPA of 3.0. *Entrance requirements:* For master's, 2 letters of recommendation, teacher certification (MA), interview, essay. Additional exam requirements/recommendations for international students: Required—TOEFL (minimum score 550 paper-based; 213 computer-based; 80 iBT). *Application deadline:* Applications are processed on a rolling basis. Application fee: $70 ($75 for international students). Electronic applications accepted. *Expenses: Tuition:* Full-time $18,990; part-time $1055 per credit hour. *Required fees:* $970. Tuition and fees vary according to program. *Financial support:* In 2011–12, 45 students received support, including 22 fellowships with full and partial tuition reimbursements available (averaging $2,560 per year), 2 research assistantships with full and partial tuition reimbursements available (averaging $21,993 per year); career-related internships or fieldwork, Federal Work-Study, institutionally sponsored loans, scholarships/grants, tuition waivers (full and partial), and unspecified assistantships also available. Support available to part-time students. Financial award applicants required to submit FAFSA. *Faculty research:* Dynamic-themes curriculum/complexity theory, joyful learning, teacher education, multicultural education, multiple authentic assessments. *Unit head:* Dr. Esther Fusco, Chairperson, 516-463-7704, Fax: 516-463-6196, E-mail: catezf@hofstra.edu. *Application contact:* Carol Drummer, Dean of Graduate Admissions, 516-463-4876, Fax: 516-463-4664, E-mail: gradstudent@hofstra.edu. Web site: http://www.hofstra.edu/education/.

Hofstra University, School of Education, Health, and Human Services, Programs in Teaching - Secondary Education, Hempstead, NY 11549. Offers business education (MS Ed); education technology (Advanced Certificate); English education (MA, MS Ed); foreign language and TESOL (MS Ed); foreign language education (MA, MS Ed), including French, German, Russian, Spanish; mathematics education (MA, MS Ed); science education (MA, MS Ed), including biology, chemistry, earth science, geology, physics; secondary education (Advanced Certificate); social studies education (MA, MS Ed). Part-time and evening/weekend programs available. Postbaccalaureate distance learning degree programs offered (minimal on-campus study). *Students:* 72 full-time (47 women), 51 part-time (30 women); includes 21 minority (9 Black or African American, non-Hispanic/Latino; 7 Asian, non-Hispanic/Latino; 5 Hispanic/Latino). Average age 28. 103 applicants, 91% accepted, 41 enrolled. In 2011, 86 master's, 6 other advanced degrees awarded. *Degree requirements:* For master's, one foreign language, comprehensive exam (for some programs), thesis (for some programs), exit project, electronic portfolio, student teaching, fieldwork, curriculum project, minimum GPA of 3.0; for Advanced Certificate, 3 foreign languages, comprehensive exam (for some programs), thesis project, minimum GPA of 3.0. *Entrance requirements:* For master's, 2 letters of recommendation, teacher certification (MA), essay; for Advanced Certificate, 2 letters of recommendation, essay. Additional exam requirements/recommendations for international students: Required—TOEFL (minimum score 550 paper-based; 213 computer-based; 80 iBT). *Application deadline:* Applications are processed on a rolling basis. Application fee: $70 ($75 for international students). Electronic applications accepted. *Expenses: Tuition:* Full-time $18,990; part-time $1055 per credit hour. *Required fees:* $970. Tuition and fees vary according to program. *Financial support:* In 2011–12, 90 students received support, including 13 fellowships with full and partial tuition reimbursements available (averaging $3,202 per year), 1 research assistantship with full and partial tuition reimbursement available (averaging $11,645 per year); career-related internships or fieldwork, Federal Work-Study, institutionally sponsored loans, scholarships/grants, tuition waivers (full and partial), and unspecified assistantships also available. Support available to part-time students. Financial award applicants required to submit FAFSA. *Faculty research:* Appropriate content and pedagogy in secondary school disciplines, appropriate pedagogy in secondary school disciplines, adolescent development, secondary school organization, alternative secondary school programs. *Unit head:* Dr. Esther Fusco, Chairperson, 516-463-7704, Fax: 516-463-6196, E-mail: catezf@hofstra.edu. *Application contact:* Carol Drummer, Dean of Graduate Admissions, 516-463-4876, Fax: 516-463-4664, E-mail: gradstudent@hofstra.edu. Web site: http://www.hofstra.edu/education/.

Hood College, Graduate School, Department of Education, Frederick, MD 21701-8575. Offers curriculum and instruction (MS), including early childhood education, elementary education, elementary school science and mathematics, secondary education, special education; educational leadership (MS, Certificate); reading specialization (MS). Part-time and evening/weekend programs available. *Degree requirements:* For master's, action research project, portfolio (reading). *Entrance requirements:* For master's, minimum GPA of 2.75, teaching certification. Additional exam requirements/recommendations for international students: Required—TOEFL (minimum score 575 paper-based; 231 computer-based; 89 iBT). Electronic applications accepted. *Faculty research:* Leadership, action research, brain research, learning styles.

Hood College, Graduate School, Program in Secondary Mathematics Education, Frederick, MD 21701-8575. Offers mathematics education (MS), including high school, middle school; secondary mathematics education (Certificate). Part-time and evening/weekend programs available. *Degree requirements:* For master's, capstone/research project. *Entrance requirements:* For master's, minimum GPA of 2.75. Additional exam requirements/recommendations for international students: Required—TOEFL (minimum score 575 paper-based; 231 computer-based; 89 iBT). Electronic applications accepted.

Hunter College of the City University of New York, Graduate School, School of Arts and Sciences, Department of Mathematics and Statistics, New York, NY 10021-5085. Offers applied mathematics (MA); mathematics for secondary education (MA); pure mathematics (MA). Part-time and evening/weekend programs available. *Faculty:* 8 full-time (1 woman), 2 part-time/adjunct (0 women). *Students:* 9 full-time (7 women), 71 part-time (34 women); includes 25 minority (7 Black or African American, non-Hispanic/Latino; 16 Asian, non-Hispanic/Latino; 2 Hispanic/Latino), 11 international. Average age 28. 54 applicants, 56% accepted, 15 enrolled. In 2011, 30 master's awarded. *Degree requirements:* For master's, one foreign language, comprehensive exam, thesis (for some programs). *Entrance requirements:* For master's, GRE General Test, 24 credits in mathematics. Additional exam requirements/recommendations for international students: Required—TOEFL. *Application deadline:* For fall admission, 4/1 for domestic students, 2/1 for international students; for spring admission, 11/1 for domestic students, 9/1 for international students. Application fee: $125. *Expenses:* Tuition, state resident: full-time $8210; part-time $345 per credit. Tuition, nonresident: full-time $15,360; part-time $640 per credit. *Required fees:* $280 per semester. One-time fee: $125. Tuition and fees vary according to class time, campus/location and program. *Financial support:* Federal Work-Study, institutionally sponsored loans, scholarships/grants, and tuition waivers (partial) available. Support available to part-time students. *Faculty research:* Data analysis, dynamical systems, computer graphics, topology, statistical decision theory. *Unit head:* Ada Peluso, Chairperson, 212-772-5300, Fax: 212-772-4858, E-mail: peluso@math.hunter.cuny.edu. *Application contact:* William Zlata, Director for Graduate Admissions, 212-772-4482, Fax: 212-650-3336, E-mail: admissions@hunter.cuny.edu. Web site: http://math.hunter.cuny.edu/.

Hunter College of the City University of New York, Graduate School, School of Education, Programs in Secondary Education, Concentration in Mathematics Education, New York, NY 10021-5085. Offers MA. *Accreditation:* NCATE. *Faculty:* 8 full-time (1 woman), 1 part-time/adjunct (0 women). *Students:* 3 full-time (0 women), 45 part-time (27 women); includes 16 minority (11 Asian, non-Hispanic/Latino; 5 Hispanic/Latino), 1 international. Average age 29. 35 applicants, 54% accepted, 7 enrolled. In 2011, 32 master's awarded. *Degree requirements:* For master's, thesis, professional teaching portfolio, New York State Teacher Certification Exam, research project. *Entrance requirements:* For master's, minimum GPA of 2.8 overall, 2.7 in mathematics courses; 24 credits of course work in mathematics. Additional exam requirements/recommendations for international students: Required—TOEFL, TWE. *Application deadline:* For fall admission, 4/1 for domestic students, 2/1 for international students; for spring admission, 11/1 for domestic students, 9/1 for international students. Applications are processed on a rolling basis. Application fee: $125. *Expenses:* Tuition, state resident: full-time $8210; part-time $345 per credit. Tuition, nonresident: full-time $15,360; part-time $640 per credit. *Required fees:* $280 per semester. One-time fee: $125. Tuition and fees vary according to class time, campus/location and program. *Financial support:* Federal Work-Study and tuition waivers (partial) available. Support available to part-time students. *Unit head:* Dr. Ptrick Burke, Program Coordinator, 212-396-6043, E-mail: patrick.burke@hunter.cuny.edu. *Application contact:* William Zlata, Director for Graduate Admissions, 212-772-4482, Fax: 212-650-3336, E-mail: admissions@hunter.cuny.edu. Web site: http://www.hunter.cuny.edu/school-of-education/programs/graduate/adolescent/mathematics.

Idaho State University, Office of Graduate Studies, College of Science and Engineering, Department of Mathematics, Pocatello, ID 83209-8085. Offers mathematics (MS, DA); mathematics for secondary teachers (MA). Part-time programs available. *Degree requirements:* For master's, comprehensive exam, thesis (for some programs), oral and written exams; for doctorate, comprehensive exam, thesis/dissertation, teaching internships. *Entrance requirements:* For master's, GRE General Test, GRE Subject Test, course work in modern algebra, differential equations, advanced calculus, introductory analysis; for doctorate, GRE General Test, GRE Subject Test, minimum graduate GPA of 3.5, MS in mathematics, teaching experience, 3 letters of recommendation. Additional exam requirements/recommendations for international students: Required—TOEFL (minimum score 550 paper-based; 213 computer-based; 80 iBT). Electronic applications accepted. *Faculty research:* Algebra, analysis geometry, statistics, applied mathematics.

Illinois Institute of Technology, Graduate College, College of Science and Letters, Department of Mathematics and Science Education, Chicago, IL 60616-3793. Offers collegiate mathematics education (PhD); mathematics education (MME, MS, PhD);

science education (MS, MSE, PhD). *Degree requirements:* For master's, comprehensive exam (for some programs), thesis optional; for doctorate, comprehensive exam, thesis/dissertation. *Entrance requirements:* For master's, GRE General Test, minimum undergraduate GPA of 3.0; for doctorate, GRE General Test, minimum GPA of 3.0, 3 years of teaching experience. Additional exam requirements/recommendations for international students: Required—TOEFL (minimum score 523 paper-based; 70 iBT). Electronic applications accepted. *Faculty research:* Informal science/math education, curriculum development, integration of science/math disciplines and across disciplines, instructional methods, students' and teachers' conceptions of scientific/mathematical inquiry and the nature of science/math.

Illinois State University, Graduate School, College of Arts and Sciences, Department of Mathematics, Program in Mathematics Education, Normal, IL 61790-2200. Offers PhD. *Degree requirements:* For doctorate, variable foreign language requirement, comprehensive exam, thesis/dissertation, 2 terms of residency. *Entrance requirements:* For doctorate, GRE General Test.

Indiana State University, College of Graduate and Professional Studies, College of Arts and Sciences, Department of Mathematics and Computer Science, Terre Haute, IN 47809. Offers math teaching (MA, MS); mathematics and computer science (MA); mathematics and computer sciences (MS). Part-time programs available. *Degree requirements:* For master's, thesis or alternative. *Entrance requirements:* For master's, 24 semester hours of course work in undergraduate mathematics. Electronic applications accepted.

Indiana University Bloomington, School of Education, Department of Curriculum and Instruction, Bloomington, IN 47405-7000. Offers art education (MS, Ed D, PhD); curriculum studies (Ed D, PhD); elementary education (MS, Ed D, PhD, Ed S); mathematics education (MS, Ed D, PhD); science education (MS, Ed D, PhD); secondary education (MS, Ed D, PhD); social studies education (MS, PhD); special education (PhD, Ed S). *Accreditation:* NCATE. Part-time and evening/weekend programs available. Terminal master's awarded for partial completion of doctoral program. *Degree requirements:* For doctorate, thesis/dissertation; for Ed S, comprehensive exam or project. *Entrance requirements:* For master's, doctorate, and Ed S, GRE General Test. Electronic applications accepted.

Indiana University Bloomington, University Graduate School, College of Arts and Sciences, Department of Mathematics, Bloomington, IN 47405-7000. Offers applied mathematics-numerical analysis (MA, PhD); mathematics education (MAT); pure mathematics (MA, PhD). *Faculty:* 49 full-time (3 women). *Students:* 124 full-time (23 women), 1 part-time (0 women); includes 13 minority (2 Black or African American, non-Hispanic/Latino; 10 Asian, non-Hispanic/Latino; 1 Hispanic/Latino), 68 international. Average age 27. 242 applicants, 19% accepted, 17 enrolled. In 2011, 20 master's, 12 doctorates awarded. Terminal master's awarded for partial completion of doctoral program. *Degree requirements:* For doctorate, one foreign language, thesis/dissertation. *Entrance requirements:* For master's and doctorate, GRE General Test, GRE Subject Test. Additional exam requirements/recommendations for international students: Required—TOEFL. *Application deadline:* For fall admission, 1/15 priority date for domestic students, 1/15 for international students. Applications are processed on a rolling basis. Application fee: $55 ($65 for international students). Electronic applications accepted. *Financial support:* In 2011–12, 2 students received support, including 9 fellowships with full tuition reimbursements available (averaging $21,450 per year), 11 research assistantships with full tuition reimbursements available (averaging $16,045 per year), 96 teaching assistantships with full tuition reimbursements available (averaging $15,870 per year); scholarships/grants, health care benefits, and unspecified assistantships also available. Financial award application deadline: 1/15. *Faculty research:* Topology, geometry, algebra, applied, analysis. *Unit head:* Kevin Zumbrun, Chair, 812-855-2200. *Application contact:* Kate Bowman, Graduate Secretary, 812-855-2645, Fax: 812-855-0046, E-mail: gradmath@indiana.edu. Web site: http://www.math.indiana.edu/.

Indiana University of Pennsylvania, School of Graduate Studies and Research, College of Natural Sciences and Mathematics, Department of Mathematics, Program in Elementary and Middle School Mathematics Education, Indiana, PA 15705-1087. Offers M Ed. *Accreditation:* NCATE. *Faculty:* 9 full-time (2 women). *Students:* 3 full-time (all women), 8 part-time (all women); includes 1 minority (Asian, non-Hispanic/Latino). Average age 28. 6 applicants, 67% accepted, 4 enrolled. In 2011, 5 master's awarded. *Degree requirements:* For master's, comprehensive exam (for some programs), thesis optional. *Entrance requirements:* For master's, 2 letters of recommendation. Additional exam requirements/recommendations for international students: Required—TOEFL (minimum score 540 paper-based; 207 computer-based). *Application deadline:* Applications are processed on a rolling basis. Application fee: $50. Electronic applications accepted. *Expenses:* Tuition, state resident: full-time $7488; part-time $416 per credit. Tuition, nonresident: full-time $11,232; part-time $624 per credit. *Required fees:* $2070; $192.20 per credit. $90 per semester. *Financial support:* In 2011–12, 2 research assistantships with full and partial tuition reimbursements (averaging $4,080 per year) were awarded; Federal Work-Study also available. Support available to part-time students. Financial award application deadline: 4/15; financial award applicants required to submit FAFSA. *Unit head:* Dr. Larry Feldman, Graduate Coordinator, 724-357-4764, E-mail: lmfeldmn@iup.edu. *Application contact:* Dr. Jacqueline Gorman, Dean's Associate, 724-357-2609, E-mail: jgorman@iup.edu. Web site: http://www.iup.edu/grad/appliedmath/default.aspx.

Indiana University of Pennsylvania, School of Graduate Studies and Research, College of Natural Sciences and Mathematics, Department of Mathematics, Program in Mathematics Education, Indiana, PA 15705-1087. Offers M Ed. *Accreditation:* NCATE. Part-time programs available. *Faculty:* 9 full-time (2 women). *Students:* 1 (woman) full-time, 2 part-time (both women); includes 1 minority (Asian, non-Hispanic/Latino). Average age 35. 5 applicants, 0% accepted, 0 enrolled. In 2011, 1 master's awarded. *Degree requirements:* For master's, thesis optional. *Entrance requirements:* For master's, 2 letters of recommendation. Additional exam requirements/recommendations for international students: Required—TOEFL (minimum score 540 paper-based; 207 computer-based). *Application deadline:* Applications are processed on a rolling basis. Application fee: $50. Electronic applications accepted. *Expenses:* Tuition, state resident: full-time $7488; part-time $416 per credit. Tuition, nonresident: full-time $11,232; part-time $624 per credit. *Required fees:* $2070; $192.20 per credit. $90 per semester. *Financial support:* Research assistantships, career-related internships or fieldwork, and Federal Work-Study available. Support available to part-time students. Financial award application deadline: 4/15; financial award applicants required to submit FAFSA. *Unit head:* Dr. Margaret Stempien, Graduate Coordinator, 724-357-3791, E-mail: margaret.stempien@iup.edu. *Application contact:* Dr. Jacqueline Gorman, Dean's Associate, 724-357-2609, E-mail: jgorman@iup.edu. Web site: http://www.iup.edu/grad/appliedmath/default.aspx.

Indiana University–Purdue University Fort Wayne, College of Arts and Sciences, Department of Mathematical Sciences, Fort Wayne, IN 46805-1499. Offers applied mathematics (MS); applied statistics (Certificate); mathematics (MS); operations research (MS); teaching (MAT). Part-time and evening/weekend programs available. *Faculty:* 20 full-time (5 women). *Students:* 1 full-time (0 women), 16 part-time (3 women). Average age 32. 6 applicants, 100% accepted, 3 enrolled. In 2011, 8 master's, 2 other advanced degrees awarded. *Entrance requirements:* For master's, minimum GPA of 3.0, major or minor in mathematics, three letters of recommendation. Additional exam requirements/recommendations for international students: Required—TOEFL (minimum score 550 paper-based; 213 computer-based; 77 iBT); Recommended—TWE. *Application deadline:* For fall admission, 8/1 priority date for domestic students, 7/1 for international students; for spring admission, 12/1 for domestic students, 10/1 for international students. Applications are processed on a rolling basis. Application fee: $55 ($60 for international students). Electronic applications accepted. *Financial support:* In 2011–12, 6 teaching assistantships with partial tuition reimbursements (averaging $12,930 per year) were awarded; scholarships/grants and unspecified assistantships also available. Support available to part-time students. Financial award application deadline: 3/1; financial award applicants required to submit FAFSA. *Faculty research:* Brick factory problem, CR singularities, carleman orthogonal polynomials. *Unit head:* Dr. David A. Legg, Chair, 260-481-6222, Fax: 260-481-0155, E-mail: legg@ipfw.edu. *Application contact:* Dr. W. Douglas Weakley, Director of Graduate Studies, 260-481-6233, Fax: 260-481-0155, E-mail: weakley@ipfw.edu. Web site: http://www.ipfw.edu/math/.

Indiana University–Purdue University Indianapolis, School of Science, Department of Mathematical Sciences, Master's Program in Mathematics, Indianapolis, IN 46202-3216. Offers applied mathematics (MS); applied statistics (MS); mathematics (MS); mathematics education (MS). *Students:* 13 full-time (3 women), 30 part-time (12 women); includes 14 minority (1 Black or African American, non-Hispanic/Latino; 9 Asian, non-Hispanic/Latino; 3 Hispanic/Latino; 1 Two or more races, non-Hispanic/Latino), 14 international. Average age 36. 49 applicants, 73% accepted, 15 enrolled. In 2011, 17 master's awarded. *Degree requirements:* For master's, comprehensive exam (for some programs), thesis optional. *Entrance requirements:* Additional exam requirements/recommendations for international students: Required—TOEFL. Application fee: $55 ($65 for international students). *Unit head:* Dr. Evgeny Mukhin, Director of Graduate Programs, 317-274-6918, E-mail: grad-program@math.iupui.edu. *Application contact:* Dr. Sherry Queener, Director, Graduate Studies and Associate Dean, 317-274-1577, Fax: 317-278-2380. Web site: http://www.math.iupui.edu/.

Instituto Tecnológico y de Estudios Superiores de Monterrey, Campus Ciudad Obregón, Programs in Education, Program in Mathematics, Ciudad Obregón, Mexico. Offers ME.

Inter American University of Puerto Rico, Arecibo Campus, Programs in Education, Arecibo, PR 00614-4050. Offers administration and educational supervision (MA Ed); counseling and guidance (MA Ed); curriculum and teaching (MA Ed), including biology education, English as a second language, history education, math education, Spanish; elementary education (MA Ed). *Degree requirements:* For master's, comprehensive exam, thesis optional. *Entrance requirements:* For master's, GRE, EXADEP, bachelor's degree in education or teaching license (administration and supervision) or courses in education and psychology (counseling and guidance), minimum GPA of 2.5 in last 60 credits.

Inter American University of Puerto Rico, Barranquitas Campus, Program in Education, Barranquitas, PR 00794. Offers curriculum and teaching (M Ed), including biology education, English as a second language, history education, mathematics education, Spanish; educational leadership and management (MA); elementary education (M Ed); information and library service technology (M Ed); special education (MA). *Degree requirements:* For master's, comprehensive exam, thesis optional. *Entrance requirements:* For master's, EXADEP, letter of recommendation. Electronic applications accepted.

Inter American University of Puerto Rico, Metropolitan Campus, Graduate Programs, Program in Teaching of Math, San Juan, PR 00919-1293. Offers MA.

Inter American University of Puerto Rico, Ponce Campus, Graduate School, Mercedita, PR 00715-1602. Offers accounting (MBA); biology (M Ed); chemistry (M Ed); criminal justice (MA); elementary education (M Ed); English as a Second Language (M Ed); finance (MBA); history (M Ed); human resources (MBA); marketing (MBA); mathematics (M Ed); Spanish (M Ed). *Entrance requirements:* For master's, minimum GPA of 2.5.

Inter American University of Puerto Rico, San Germán Campus, Graduate Studies Center, Program in Mathematics Education, San Germán, PR 00683-5008. Offers MA. Part-time and evening/weekend programs available. *Degree requirements:* For master's, comprehensive exam. *Entrance requirements:* For master's, EXADEP or GRE General Test, minimum GPA of 3.0. *Application deadline:* For fall admission, 4/30 priority date for domestic students; for spring admission, 11/15 for domestic students. Application fee: $31. *Expenses: Required fees:* $213 per semester. *Financial support:* Teaching assistantships, Federal Work-Study, and unspecified assistantships available. *Unit head:* Dr. Elba T. Irizarry, Director of Graduate Studies Center, 787-264-1912 Ext. 7357, Fax: 787-892-6350, E-mail: elbat@sg.inter.edu.

Iona College, School of Arts and Science, Program in Education, New Rochelle, NY 10801-1890. Offers adolescence education: biology (MS Ed, MST); adolescence education: English (MS Ed, MST); adolescence education: Italian (MS Ed, MST); adolescence education: mathematics (MS Ed, MST); adolescence education: social studies (MS Ed, MST); adolescence education: Spanish (MS Ed, MST); adolescence special education 5-12 (MST); adolescence special education/literacy 5-12 (MS Ed); childhood 1-6/special education 1-6 (MST); childhood education (MST); early childhood/childhood (MST); educational leadership (MS Ed); literacy birth-grade 6/special education 1-6 (MS Ed); literacy education: birth-grade 6 (MS Ed). *Accreditation:* NCATE. Part-time and evening/weekend programs available. *Faculty:* 21 full-time (13 women), 13 part-time/adjunct (8 women). *Students:* 59 full-time (45 women), 101 part-time (78 women); includes 11 minority (2 Black or African American, non-Hispanic/Latino; 2 Asian, non-Hispanic/Latino; 7 Hispanic/Latino). Average age 26. 74 applicants, 66% accepted, 35 enrolled. In 2011, 46 master's awarded. *Degree requirements:* For master's, thesis or alternative. *Entrance requirements:* For master's, minimum GPA of 2.5 (MST), New York teaching certificate (MS Ed). Additional exam requirements/recommendations for international students: Required—TOEFL (minimum score 550 paper-based; 213 computer-based). *Application deadline:* Applications are processed on a rolling basis. Application fee: $50. Electronic applications accepted. *Expenses: Tuition:* Part-time $872 per credit. *Required fees:* $225 per term. *Financial support:* Unspecified assistantships available. Support available to part-time students. Financial award application deadline: 4/15; financial award applicants required to submit FAFSA. *Faculty research:* Reading/writing, educational technology, administration, early literacy assessment, literacy development. *Unit head:* Dr. Catherine O'Callaghan, Chair, 914-633-2210, Fax: 914-633-2608, E-mail: cocallaghan@iona.edu. *Application contact:* Dr. Jeanne Zaino, Interim Dean, School of Arts and Science, 914-633-2112, Fax: 914-633-2023, E-mail: jzaino@iona.edu.

Iowa State University of Science and Technology, Department of Mathematics, Ames, IA 50011. Offers applied mathematics (MS, PhD); mathematics (MS, PhD); school mathematics (MSM). *Degree requirements:* For master's, thesis or alternative; for doctorate, thesis/dissertation. *Entrance requirements:* For master's and doctorate, GRE General Test. Additional exam requirements/recommendations for international students: Required—TOEFL (minimum score 550 paper-based; 79 iBT), IELTS (minimum score 6.5). *Application deadline:* For fall admission, 2/1 priority date for domestic students, 2/1 for international students. Application fee: $40 ($90 for international students). Electronic applications accepted. *Financial support:* Scholarships/grants, health care benefits, and unspecified assistantships available. *Unit head:* Dr. Clifford Bergman, Director of Graduate Education, 515-294-0393, Fax: 515-294-5454, E-mail: gradmath@iastate.edu. *Application contact:* Melanie Erickson, Director of Graduate Education, 515-294-0393, Fax: 515-294-5454, E-mail: gradmath@iastate.edu. Web site: http://http://www.math.iastate.edu/Graduate/Prospective.html.

Iowa State University of Science and Technology, Program in School Mathematics, Ames, IA 50011-2064. Offers MSM. *Entrance requirements:* For master's, official academic transcripts, resume, three letters of recommendation, statement of purpose. Additional exam requirements/recommendations for international students: Required—TOEFL (minimum score 550 paper-based; 79 iBT), IELTS (minimum score 6.5). Electronic applications accepted. *Unit head:* Heather Bolles, Director of Graduate Education, 515-294-0393, Fax: 515-294-5454, E-mail: msm@iastate.edu. *Application contact:* Melanie Erickson, Application Contact, 515-294-0393, Fax: 515-294-5454, E-mail: grad_admissions@iastate.edu. Web site: http://www.math.iastate.edu/MSM/MSMhome.html.

Ithaca College, Division of Graduate and Professional Studies, School of Humanities and Sciences, Program in Adolescence Education, Ithaca, NY 14850. Offers biology 7-12 (MAT); chemistry 7-12 (MAT); English 7-12 (MAT); French 7-12 (MAT); math 7-12 (MAT); physics 7-12 (MAT); social studies 7-12 (MAT); Spanish (MAT). Part-time programs available. *Faculty:* 23 full-time (7 women). *Students:* 14 full-time (8 women), 1 part-time (0 women); includes 4 minority (1 Asian, non-Hispanic/Latino; 2 Hispanic/Latino; 1 Two or more races, non-Hispanic/Latino). Average age 27. 33 applicants, 64% accepted, 15 enrolled. In 2011, 15 master's awarded. *Degree requirements:* For master's, thesis or alternative, student teaching. *Entrance requirements:* For master's, minimum GPA of 3.0. Additional exam requirements/recommendations for international students: Required—TOEFL (minimum score 550 paper-based; 213 computer-based; 80 iBT). *Application deadline:* For fall admission, 2/15 priority date for domestic students, 2/15 for international students; for spring admission, 12/1 for domestic and international students. Applications are processed on a rolling basis. Application fee: $40. Electronic applications accepted. *Expenses:* Contact institution. *Financial support:* In 2011–12, 9 students received support, including 9 teaching assistantships (averaging $6,070 per year); career-related internships or fieldwork, Federal Work-Study, scholarships/grants, and unspecified assistantships also available. Support available to part-time students. Financial award application deadline: 2/15; financial award applicants required to submit CSS PROFILE or FAFSA. *Faculty research:* Bilingual education, socio-linguistic perspective on literacy. *Unit head:* Dr. Linda Hanrahan, Chairperson, 607-274-3143, Fax: 607-274-1263, E-mail: gps@ithaca.edu. *Application contact:* Gerard Turbide, Director, Office of Admission, 607-274-3143, Fax: 607-274-1263, E-mail: gps@ithaca.edu. Web site: http://www.ithaca.edu/gps/gradprograms/overview/school/hs/aded.

Jackson State University, Graduate School, College of Science, Engineering and Technology, Department of Physics, Atmospheric Sciences, and General Science, Jackson, MS 39217. Offers science and mathematics teaching (MST). Part-time and evening/weekend programs available. *Degree requirements:* For master's, comprehensive exam. *Entrance requirements:* For master's, GRE General Test. Additional exam requirements/recommendations for international students: Required—TOEFL (minimum score 520 paper-based; 195 computer-based; 67 iBT).

The Johns Hopkins University, School of Education, Department of Teacher Preparation, Baltimore, MD 21218. Offers early childhood education (MAT); education (MS), including educational studies; elementary education (MAT); English for speakers of other languages (MAT); K-8 mathematics lead-teacher (Certificate); K-8 science lead-teacher (Certificate); secondary education (MAT), including biology, chemistry, earth/space/environmental science, English, French, mathematics, physics, social studies, Spanish. Part-time and evening/weekend programs available. *Degree requirements:* For master's, portfolio, PRAXIS II, internship. *Entrance requirements:* For master's, PRAXIS I, SAT, ACT, or GRE (MAT), minimum undergraduate GPA of 3.0, interview, 1 letter of recommendation, curriculum vitae/resume; for Certificate, bachelor's degree, minimum undergraduate GPA of 3.0, essay/statement of goals, interview. Additional exam requirements/recommendations for international students: Required—TOEFL (minimum score 600 paper-based; 250 computer-based; 100 iBT). Electronic applications accepted. *Faculty research:* Teacher retention, STEM education reform, alternative certification programs, school-university partnerships, urban education, action research/data-informed instruction, family engagement.

Kansas State University, Graduate School, College of Education, Department of Curriculum and Instruction, Manhattan, KS 66506. Offers career and technical education (Ed D, PhD); curriculum studies (Ed D, PhD); digital teaching and learning (MS); educational computing, design and online learning (MS); educational technology (Ed D, PhD); elementary/middle level (MS); English as a second language (MS); language/diversity education (Ed D, PhD); literacy education (Ed D, PhD); mathematics education (Ed D, PhD); middle level/secondary (MS); reading and language arts (MS); reading specialist endorsement (MS); science education (Ed D, PhD); social science education (Ed D, PhD); teacher education (Ed D, PhD); teacher leader/school improvement (MS, Ed D). *Accreditation:* NCATE. Part-time programs available. Postbaccalaureate distance learning degree programs offered (minimal on-campus study). *Faculty:* 15 full-time (12 women), 3 part-time/adjunct (2 women). *Students:* 37 full-time (30 women), 113 part-time (91 women); includes 14 minority (4 Black or African American, non-Hispanic/Latino; 1 American Indian or Alaska Native, non-Hispanic/Latino; 1 Asian, non-Hispanic/Latino; 7 Hispanic/Latino; 1 Two or more races, non-Hispanic/Latino), 15 international. Average age 37. 75 applicants, 51% accepted, 9 enrolled. In 2011, 48 master's, 14 doctorates awarded. *Degree requirements:* For master's, comprehensive exam, portfolio, project, report or thesis; for doctorate, comprehensive exam, thesis/dissertation, preliminary exam. *Entrance requirements:* For master's, minimum GPA of 3.0; for doctorate, GRE, minimum GPA of 3.0. Additional exam requirements/recommendations for international students: Required—TOEFL. *Application deadline:* For fall admission, 2/1 priority date for domestic students, 2/1 for international students; for spring admission, 8/1 priority date for domestic students, 8/1 for international students. Applications are processed on a rolling basis. Application fee: $40 ($55 for international students). Electronic applications accepted. *Financial support:* In 2011–12, 1 research assistantship (averaging $16,900 per year), 8 teaching assistantships (averaging $12,466 per year) were awarded; career-related internships or fieldwork, institutionally sponsored loans, and scholarships/grants also available. Support available to part-time students. Financial award application deadline: 3/1; financial award applicants required to submit FAFSA. *Faculty research:* Literacy and technology, critical race theory and diversity, achievement gaps, school improvement, teacher education. *Total annual research expenditures:* $510,907. *Unit head:* Dr. Gail Shroyer, Chair, 785-532-5550, Fax: 785-532-7304, E-mail: gshroyer@ksu.edu. *Application contact:* Dona Deam, Application Contact, 785-532-5595, Fax: 785-532-7304, E-mail: ddeam@ksu.edu. Web site: http://coe.k-state.edu/departments/currin/curringrad.htm.

Kaplan University, Davenport Campus, School of Teacher Education, Davenport, IA 52807-2095. Offers education (M Ed); secondary education (M Ed); teaching and learning (MA); teaching literacy and language: grades 6-12 (MA); teaching literacy and language: grades K-6 (MA); teaching mathematics: grades 6-8 (MA); teaching mathematics: grades 9-12 (MA); teaching mathematics: grades K-5 (MA); teaching science: grades 6-12 (MA); teaching science: grades K-6 (MA); teaching students with special needs (MA); teaching with technology (MA). Part-time and evening/weekend programs available. Postbaccalaureate distance learning degree programs offered (no on-campus study). *Entrance requirements:* Additional exam requirements/recommendations for international students: Required—TOEFL (minimum score 550 paper-based; 218 computer-based; 80 iBT).

Kean University, College of Education, Program in Instruction and Curriculum, Union, NJ 07083. Offers bilingual (MA); classroom instruction (MA); mathematics/science/computer education (MA); teaching (MA); teaching English as a second language (MA); teaching physics (MA); world languages (Spanish) (MA). *Accreditation:* NCATE. *Faculty:* 22 full-time (12 women). *Students:* 56 full-time (33 women), 139 part-time (103 women); includes 87 minority (27 Black or African American, non-Hispanic/Latino; 8 Asian, non-Hispanic/Latino; 52 Hispanic/Latino), 1 international. Average age 34. 85 applicants, 100% accepted, 72 enrolled. In 2011, 78 master's awarded. *Degree requirements:* For master's, comprehensive exam, two-semester advanced seminar. *Entrance requirements:* For master's, GRE General Test or MAT, PRAXIS, minimum GPA of 3.0, 2 letters of recommendation, interview, teacher certification (for some programs), transcripts, resume. Additional exam requirements/recommendations for international students: Required—TOEFL (minimum score 79 iBT). *Application deadline:* For fall admission, 6/1 for domestic and international students; for spring admission, 12/1 for domestic and international students. Applications are processed on a rolling basis. Application fee: $75 ($150 for international students). Electronic applications accepted. *Expenses:* Tuition, state resident: full-time $11,302; part-time $550 per credit. Tuition, nonresident: full-time $15,318; part-time $674 per credit. *Required fees:* $2849; $130 per credit. Tuition and fees vary according to degree level. *Financial support:* In 2011–12, 3 research assistantships with full tuition reimbursements (averaging $3,263 per year) were awarded; unspecified assistantships also available. Financial award applicants required to submit FAFSA. *Unit head:* Dr. Thomas Walsh, Program Coordinator, 908-737-4003, E-mail: tpwalsh@kean.edu. *Application contact:* Ann-Marie Kay, Assistant Director for Graduate Admissions, 908-737-5922, Fax: 908-737-5925, E-mail: akay@kean.edu. Web site: http://www.kean.edu/KU/Bilingual-Bicultural-Education-Instruction-and-Curriculum.

Kean University, College of Natural, Applied and Health Sciences, Program in Mathematics Education, Union, NJ 07083. Offers supervision of math education (MA); teaching of math (MA). *Faculty:* 15 full-time (4 women). *Students:* 12 part-time (6 women); includes 6 minority (3 Asian, non-Hispanic/Latino; 3 Hispanic/Latino). Average age 32. 8 applicants, 88% accepted, 4 enrolled. In 2011, 4 master's awarded. *Degree requirements:* For master's, research. *Entrance requirements:* For master's, GRE General Test, minimum GPA of 3.0, 2 letters of recommendation, interview, baccalaureate degree with major or strong minor in mathematical science, transcripts, teaching certification, resume, personal statement. Additional exam requirements/recommendations for international students: Required—TOEFL (minimum score 79 iBT). *Application deadline:* For fall admission, 6/1 for domestic and international students; for spring admission, 12/1 for domestic and international students. Applications are processed on a rolling basis. Application fee: $75 ($150 for international students). Electronic applications accepted. *Expenses:* Tuition, state resident: full-time $11,302; part-time $550 per credit. Tuition, nonresident: full-time $15,318; part-time $674 per credit. *Required fees:* $2849; $130 per credit. Tuition and fees vary according to degree level. *Financial support:* In 2011–12, research assistantships with full tuition reimbursements (averaging $3,263 per year) were awarded; unspecified assistantships also available. Financial award applicants required to submit FAFSA. *Unit head:* Dr. Revathi Narasimhan, Program Coordinator, 908-737-3716, E-mail: rnarasim@kean.edu. *Application contact:* Reenat Hasan, Admissions Counselor, 908-737-5923, Fax: 908-737-5925, E-mail: rhasan@exchange.kean.edu. Web site: http://www.kean.edu/KU/Teaching-of-Mathematics.

Kennesaw State University, Leland and Clarice C. Bagwell College of Education, Program in Teaching, Kennesaw, GA 30144-5591. Offers art education (MAT); secondary English or mathematics (MAT); secondary science education (MAT); teaching English to speakers of other languages (MAT). Program offered only in summer. Part-time and evening/weekend programs available. *Students:* 101 full-time (68 women), 20 part-time (15 women); includes 27 minority (14 Black or African American, non-Hispanic/Latino; 6 Asian, non-Hispanic/Latino; 4 Hispanic/Latino; 3 Two or more races, non-Hispanic/Latino), 3 international. Average age 33. 13 applicants, 62% accepted, 7 enrolled. In 2011, 81 master's awarded. *Entrance requirements:* For master's, GRE, GACE I (state certificate exam), minimum GPA of 2.75, 2 recommendations, resume. Additional exam requirements/recommendations for international students: Required—TOEFL (minimum score 550 paper-based; 213 computer-based; 80 iBT), IELTS (minimum score 6). *Application deadline:* For fall admission, 6/1 for domestic and international students; for spring admission, 3/1 for domestic and international students. Application fee: $60. Electronic applications accepted. *Expenses:* Tuition, state resident: full-time $3000; part-time $250 per semester hour. Tuition, nonresident: full-time $10,836; part-time $903 per semester hour. *Required fees:* $774 per semester. *Financial support:* In 2011–12, 2 research assistantships with tuition reimbursements (averaging $4,000 per year) were awarded; unspecified assistantships also available. Financial award application deadline: 4/1; financial award applicants required to submit FAFSA. *Unit head:* Dr. Lynn Stallings, Director, 770-420-4477, E-mail: lstalling@kennesaw.edu. *Application contact:* Alisha Bello, Administrative Coordinator, 770-423-6043, Fax: 770-420-4435, E-mail: abello1@kennesaw.edu. Web site: http://www.kennesaw.edu.

Kutztown University of Pennsylvania, College of Education, Program in Secondary Education, Kutztown, PA 19530-0730. Offers biology (M Ed); curriculum and instruction (M Ed); English (M Ed); mathematics (M Ed); social studies (M Ed). *Accreditation:* NCATE. Part-time and evening/weekend programs available. *Faculty:* 7 full-time (2 women). *Students:* 29 full-time (12 women), 73 part-time (43 women); includes 3 minority (1 Black or African American, non-Hispanic/Latino; 1 Asian, non-Hispanic/Latino; 1 Hispanic/Latino). Average age 28. 12 applicants, 100% accepted, 12 enrolled. In 2011, 29 master's awarded. *Degree requirements:* For master's, comprehensive exam, thesis optional. *Entrance requirements:* For master's, GRE General Test. Additional exam requirements/recommendations for international students: Required—TOEFL (minimum score 550 paper-based; 79 iBT). *Application deadline:* For fall admission, 8/1 priority date for domestic students, 8/1 for international students; for spring admission, 12/1 priority date for domestic students, 12/1 for international students. Applications are processed on a rolling basis. Application fee: $35. Electronic applications accepted. *Expenses:* Tuition, state resident: full-time $7488; part-time $416 per credit. Tuition, nonresident: full-time $11,232; part-time $624 per credit. *Financial support:* Career-related internships or fieldwork, Federal Work-Study, scholarships/grants, and unspecified assistantships available. Financial award application deadline: 3/1; financial award applicants required to submit FAFSA. *Unit head:* Dr. Theresa Stahler, Chairperson, 610-683-4259, Fax: 610-683-1338, E-mail: stahler@kutztown.edu. *Application contact:* Kelly D. Burr, Associate Director, Graduate Admissions, 610-683-4200, Fax: 610-683-1393, E-mail: graduate@kutztown.edu.

Lehman College of the City University of New York, Division of Education, Department of Middle and High School Education, Program in Mathematics 7–12, Bronx, NY 10468-1589. Offers MS Ed. *Accreditation:* NCATE. Part-time and evening/weekend programs available. *Degree requirements:* For master's, comprehensive exam or thesis. *Entrance requirements:* For master's, 18 credits in mathematics, 12 credits in education. *Faculty research:* Mathematical problem solving, Piagetian cognitive theory.

Lewis University, College of Education, Program in Secondary Education, Romeoville, IL 60446. Offers biology (MA); chemistry (MA); English (MA); history (MA); math (MA); physics (MA); psychology and social science (MA). Part-time programs available. *Students:* 17 full-time (11 women), 11 part-time (4 women); includes 4 minority (2 Black or African American, non-Hispanic/Latino; 2 Hispanic/Latino). Average age 30. In 2011, 7 master's awarded. *Entrance requirements:* For master's, departmental qualifying exam, writing exam, minimum GPA of 2.75, 2 letters of recommendation, interview. Additional exam requirements/recommendations for international students: Required—TOEFL (minimum score 550 paper-based; 213 computer-based; 80 iBT). *Application deadline:* For fall admission, 5/1 for international students; for spring admission, 11/15 for international students. Applications are processed on a rolling basis. Application fee: $40. Electronic applications accepted. *Financial support:* Federal Work-Study, scholarships/grants, and unspecified assistantships available. Financial award application deadline: 5/1; financial award applicants required to submit FAFSA. *Unit head:* Dr. Dorene Huvaere, Program Director, 815-838-0500 Ext. 5885, E-mail: huvaersdo@lewisu.edu. *Application contact:* Fran Welsh, Secretary, 815-838-0500 Ext. 5880, E-mail: welshfr@lewisu.edu.

Liberty University, School of Education, Lynchburg, VA 24502. Offers administration and supervision (M Ed); curriculum and instruction (M Ed); early childhood education (M Ed); educational leadership (Ed D, Ed S); educational technology and online instruction (M Ed); elementary education (M Ed, MAT); gifted education (M Ed); math specialist (M Ed); middle grades (M Ed); outdoor adventure sport (MS); reading specialist (M Ed); school counseling (M Ed); secondary education (M Ed, MAT); special education (M Ed, MAT); sports administration (MS); teaching and learning (Ed D, Ed S). *Accreditation:* NCATE. Part-time programs available. Postbaccalaureate distance learning degree programs offered (minimal on-campus study). *Students:* 2,245 full-time (1,572 women), 3,500 part-time (2,558 women); includes 1,141 minority (888 Black or African American, non-Hispanic/Latino; 19 American Indian or Alaska Native, non-Hispanic/Latino; 21 Asian, non-Hispanic/Latino; 123 Hispanic/Latino; 9 Native Hawaiian or other Pacific Islander, non-Hispanic/Latino; 81 Two or more races, non-Hispanic/Latino), 76 international. Average age 37. In 2011, 760 master's, 48 doctorates, 321 other advanced degrees awarded. *Degree requirements:* For doctorate, comprehensive exam, thesis/dissertation. *Entrance requirements:* For master's, GRE General Test or MAT (if taken in or before 1999), 2 letters of recommendation, minimum undergraduate GPA of 3.0, curriculum vitae; for doctorate, GRE General Test or MAT (if taken before 1999), minimum master's GPA of 3.0, 3 years of teacher experience; for Ed S, GRE General Test or MAT (if taken before 1999), minimum master's GPA of 3.0, 3 years of teaching experience. Additional exam requirements/recommendations for international students: Required—TOEFL (minimum score 600 paper-based; 250 computer-based). *Application deadline:* For fall admission, 6/1 priority date for domestic students; for spring admission, 11/1 for domestic students. Applications are processed on a rolling basis. Application fee: $50. Electronic applications accepted. *Expenses:* Contact institution. *Financial support:* Federal Work-Study and tuition waivers (partial) available. *Faculty research:* Self-determination, character education, bibliotherapy, learning styles, distance education. *Unit head:* Dr. Karen L. Parker, Dean, 434-582-2195, Fax: 434-582-2468, E-mail: kparker@liberty.edu. *Application contact:* Jay Bridge, Director of Graduate Admissions, 800-424-9595, Fax: 800-628-7977, E-mail: gradadmissions@liberty.edu. Web site: http://www.liberty.edu/academics/education/graduate/.

Lipscomb University, Program in Education, Nashville, TN 37204-3951. Offers educational leadership (M Ed); English language learning (M Ed); instructional practice (M Ed); instructional technology (M Ed); learning organizations and strategic change (Ed D); math specialty (M Ed); special education (M Ed); teaching, learning, and leading (M Ed). *Accreditation:* NCATE. Part-time and evening/weekend programs available. *Faculty:* 18 full-time (10 women), 23 part-time/adjunct (16 women). *Students:* 377 full-time (281 women), 117 part-time (85 women); includes 55 minority (39 Black or African American, non-Hispanic/Latino; 4 American Indian or Alaska Native, non-Hispanic/Latino; 5 Asian, non-Hispanic/Latino; 7 Hispanic/Latino). Average age 32. 300 applicants, 66% accepted, 142 enrolled. In 2011, 190 master's awarded. *Degree requirements:* For master's, comprehensive exam, portfolio, research project and presentation; for doctorate, practical capstone project in experiential setting. *Entrance requirements:* For master's, MAT or GRE General Test, 2 reference letters, goals statement, writing sample, interview; for doctorate, MAT or GRE General Test, 3 reference letters, artifact of demonstrated academic excellence, written personal statements, interview. Additional exam requirements/recommendations for international students: Required—TOEFL (minimum score 570 paper-based; 230 computer-based). *Application deadline:* For fall admission, 8/29 priority date for domestic students; for spring admission, 1/15 priority date for domestic students. Applications are processed on a rolling basis. Application fee: $50 ($75 for international students). *Expenses: Tuition:* Full-time $16,830; part-time $935 per credit hour. Tuition and fees vary according to degree level and program. *Financial support:* In 2011–12, 67 students received support. Scholarships/grants and tuition waivers (partial) available. Financial award applicants required to submit FAFSA. *Faculty research:* Facilitative learning styles, leadership, student assessment, interactive multimedia inclusion, learning organizations and strategic change. *Unit head:* Dr. Deborah Boyd, Director, 615-966-6263, E-mail: deborah.boyd@lipscomb.edu. *Application contact:* Kristin Baese, Assistant Director of Enrollment and Outreach, 615-966-7628 Ext. 6081, Fax: 615-966-5173, E-mail: kristin.baese@lipscomb.edu. Web site: http://graduateeducation.lipscomb.edu/.

Long Island University–Brooklyn Campus, School of Education, Department of Teaching and Learning, Program in Secondary Education, Brooklyn, NY 11201-8423. Offers mathematics education (MS Ed). Part-time and evening/weekend programs available. *Degree requirements:* For master's, thesis optional. *Entrance requirements:* For master's, 2 letters of recommendation. Additional exam requirements/recommendations for international students: Required—TOEFL (minimum score 500 paper-based; 173 computer-based). Electronic applications accepted.

Long Island University–C. W. Post Campus, College of Liberal Arts and Sciences, Department of Mathematics, Brookville, NY 11548-1300. Offers applied mathematics (MS); mathematics education (MS); mathematics for secondary school teachers (MS). Part-time and evening/weekend programs available. *Degree requirements:* For master's, thesis or alternative, oral presentation. *Entrance requirements:* Additional exam requirements/recommendations for international students: Required—TOEFL. Electronic applications accepted. *Faculty research:* Differential geometry, topological groups, general topology, number theory, analysis and statistics, numerical analysis.

Long Island University–C. W. Post Campus, School of Education, Department of Curriculum and Instruction, Brookville, NY 11548-1300. Offers adolescence education (MS); adolescence education: biology (MS); adolescence education: earth science (MS); adolescence education: English (MS); adolescence education: mathematics (MS); adolescence education: social studies (MS); adolescence education: Spanish (MS); art education (MS); bilingual education (MS); childhood education (MS); early childhood education (MS); middle childhood education (MS); music education (MS); teaching English to speakers of other languages (MS). Part-time and evening/weekend programs available. *Degree requirements:* For master's, comprehensive exam or thesis, student teaching. *Entrance requirements:* For master's, minimum GPA of 2.75 in major, 2.5 overall. Electronic applications accepted. *Faculty research:* Ethics and education, teaching strategies.

Louisiana Tech University, Graduate School, College of Education, Department of Curriculum, Instruction and Leadership, Ruston, LA 71272. Offers curriculum and instruction (MS, Ed D); educational leadership (Ed D); secondary education (M Ed), including business education, English education, foreign language education, health and physical education, mathematics education, science education, social studies education, speech education. *Accreditation:* NCATE. Part-time programs available. *Degree requirements:* For doctorate, thesis/dissertation. *Entrance requirements:* For master's and doctorate, GRE General Test.

Loyola Marymount University, College of Science and Engineering, Department of Mathematics, Program in Teaching in Mathematics, Los Angeles, CA 90045. Offers MAT. Part-time programs available. *Faculty:* 21 full-time (9 women). *Students:* 1 applicant, 0% accepted, 0 enrolled. In 2011, 2 master's awarded. *Entrance requirements:* For master's, 1 letter of recommendation, personal statement. Additional exam requirements/recommendations for international students: Required—TOEFL (minimum score 550 paper-based; 213 computer-based; 80 iBT). *Application deadline:* For fall admission, 6/15 for domestic students; for spring admission, 11/15 for domestic students. Application fee: $50. Electronic applications accepted. *Financial support:* Scholarships/grants and unspecified assistantships available. Financial award application deadline: 6/1; financial award applicants required to submit FAFSA. *Total annual research expenditures:* $106,348. *Unit head:* Dr. Suzanne Larson, Chair, 310-338-5111, E-mail: slarson@lmu.edu. *Application contact:* Chake H. Kouyoumjian, Associate Dean of Graduate Admissions, 310-338-2721, E-mail: ckouyoum@lmu.edu. Web site: http://cse.lmu.edu/departments/math/degrees/mateachingmathematics.htm.

Loyola University Chicago, School of Education, Program in Teaching and Learning, Chicago, IL 60660. Offers elementary education (M Ed); English as a second language (Certificate); math education (M Ed); reading specialist (M Ed); reading teacher endorsement (Certificate); school technology (M Ed); science education (M Ed); secondary education (M Ed); special education (M Ed). *Accreditation:* NCATE. *Faculty:* 12 full-time (9 women), 12 part-time/adjunct (6 women). *Students:* 131. Average age 28. 115 applicants, 65% accepted, 30 enrolled. In 2011, 80 master's awarded. *Degree requirements:* For master's, comprehensive exam. *Entrance requirements:* For master's, Illinois Basic Skills Test, 3 letters of recommendation, minimum GPA of 3.0, resume. Additional exam requirements/recommendations for international students: Required—TOEFL (minimum score 550 paper-based; 213 computer-based; 79 iBT). *Application deadline:* For fall admission, 7/1 priority date for domestic students, 7/1 for international students; for spring admission, 11/1 priority date for domestic students, 11/1 for international students. Applications are processed on a rolling basis. Application fee: $50. Electronic applications accepted. Application fee is waived when completed online. *Expenses: Tuition:* Full-time $15,660; part-time $870 per credit hour. *Required fees:* $125 per semester. Tuition and fees vary according to course load and program. *Financial support:* Institutionally sponsored loans, scholarships/grants, and unspecified assistantships available. Support available to part-time students. Financial award application deadline: 2/1; financial award applicants required to submit FAFSA. *Faculty research:* Positive behavior support, school reform, school improvement. *Unit head:* Dr. Dorothy Giroux, Director, 312-915-7027, E-mail: dgiroux@luc.edu. *Application contact:* Marie Rosin-Dittmar, Information Contact, 312-915-6800, E-mail: schleduc@luc.edu.

Loyola University Maryland, Graduate Programs, Department of Education, Program in Teacher Education, Baltimore, MD 21210-2699. Offers elementary/middle education (MAT); secondary education (MAT); secondary education: biology (MAT); secondary education: chemistries (MAT); secondary education: earth science (MAT); secondary education: English (MAT); secondary education: mathematics (MAT); secondary education: physics (MAT). Part-time programs available. *Faculty:* 25 full-time (21 women), 14 part-time/adjunct (11 women). *Students:* 28 full-time (19 women), 58 part-time (45 women); includes 5 minority (1 Black or African American, non-Hispanic/Latino; 2 Asian, non-Hispanic/Latino; 2 Two or more races, non-Hispanic/Latino), 4 international. Average age 28. In 2011, 37 master's awarded. *Entrance requirements:* For master's, PRAXIS, SAT, ACT, or GRE. Additional exam requirements/recommendations for international students: Required—TOEFL (minimum score 550 paper-based; 213 computer-based). *Application deadline:* For fall admission, 6/15 for domestic students; for spring admission, 11/1 for domestic students. Electronic applications accepted. *Financial support:* Research assistantships and unspecified assistantships available. Financial award application deadline: 4/15. *Unit head:* Wendy Smith, Chair, 410-617-2194, E-mail: wmsmith@loyola.edu. *Application contact:* Maureen Faux, Executive Director, Graduate Admissions, 410-617-5020, Fax: 410-617-2002, E-mail: graduate@loyola.edu. Web site: http://www.loyola.edu/academics/theology/.

Manhattanville College, Graduate Studies, School of Education, Program in Middle Childhood/Adolescence Education (Grades 5-12), Purchase, NY 10577-2132. Offers biology (MAT); biology and special education (MPS); chemistry (MAT); chemistry and special education (MPS); English (MAT); English and special education (MPS); literacy (MPS), including reading and writing, writing; literacy and special education (MPS); math (MAT); math and special education (MPS); second language (MAT), including French, Italian, Latin, Spanish; social studies (MAT); social studies and special education (MPS); special education (MPS). Part-time and evening/weekend programs available. *Degree requirements:* For master's, comprehensive exam or research project, field experience. *Entrance requirements:* For master's, minimum undergraduate GPA of 3.0, 2 letters of recommendation. Additional exam requirements/recommendations for international students: Required—TOEFL. Electronic applications accepted.

Marquette University, Graduate School, College of Arts and Sciences, Department of Mathematics, Statistics, and Computer Science, Milwaukee, WI 53201-1881. Offers bioinformatics (MS); computational sciences (MS, PhD); computing (MS); mathematics education (MS). Part-time and evening/weekend programs available. Postbaccalaureate distance learning degree programs offered (minimal on-campus study). *Faculty:* 28 full-time (9 women), 10 part-time/adjunct (5 women). *Students:* 14 full-time (3 women), 77 part-time (18 women); includes 9 minority (2 Black or African American, non-Hispanic/Latino; 7 Asian, non-Hispanic/Latino), 24 international. Average age 30. 86 applicants, 65% accepted, 24 enrolled. In 2011, 15 master's, 1 doctorate awarded. Terminal master's awarded for partial completion of doctoral program. *Degree requirements:* For master's, thesis (for some programs), essay with oral presentation; for doctorate, comprehensive exam, thesis/dissertation, qualifying examination. *Entrance requirements:* For master's, official transcripts from all current and previous colleges/universities except Marquette, three letters of recommendation; for doctorate, GRE General Test, official transcripts from all current and previous colleges/universities except Marquette, three letters of recommendation. Additional exam requirements/recommendations for international students: Required—TOEFL (minimum score 530 paper-based; 78 computer-based). *Application deadline:* For fall admission, 1/15 for domestic and international students. Applications are processed on a rolling basis. Application fee: $50. Electronic applications accepted. *Expenses: Tuition:* Full-time $17,010; part-time $945 per credit hour. Tuition and fees vary according to program. *Financial support:* In 2011–12, 23 students received support, including 4 fellowships (averaging $1,375 per year), 5 research assistantships with full tuition reimbursements available (averaging $17,000 per year), 15 teaching assistantships with full tuition reimbursements available (averaging $17,000 per year); scholarships/grants, health care benefits, tuition waivers (full and partial), and unspecified assistantships also available. Support available to part-time students. Financial award application deadline: 2/15. *Faculty research:* Models of physiological systems, mathematical immunology, computational group theory, mathematical logic, computational science. *Total annual research expenditures:* $621,359. *Unit head:* Dr. Gary Krenz, Chair, 414-288-7573, Fax: 414-288-1578. *Application contact:* Dr. Francis Pastijn, Director of Graduate Studies, 414-288-5229. Web site: http://www.marquette.edu/mscs/grad.shtml.

Miami University, College of Arts and Science, Department of Mathematics, Oxford, OH 45056. Offers MA, MAT, MS. *Students:* 22 full-time (6 women), 2 part-time (0 women); includes 1 minority (Black or African American, non-Hispanic/Latino), 2 international. Average age 24. In 2011, 13 master's awarded. *Entrance requirements:* For master's, minimum undergraduate GPA of 3.0 during previous 2 years or 2.75 overall. Additional exam requirements/recommendations for international students: Required—TOEFL. *Application deadline:* For fall admission, 2/1 for domestic and international students. Application fee: $50. Electronic applications accepted. *Expenses:* Tuition, state resident: full-time $12,023; part-time $501 per credit hour. Tuition, nonresident: full-time $26,554; part-time $1107 per credit hour. *Required fees:* $528. *Financial support:* Research assistantships, teaching assistantships, health care benefits, and unspecified assistantships available. Financial award application deadline: 2/1; financial award applicants required to submit FAFSA. *Unit head:* Dr. Patrick Dowling, Department Chair, 513-529-5818, E-mail: dowlinpn@muohio.edu. *Application contact:* Dr. Doug Ward, Director of Graduate Studies, 513-529-3534, E-mail: wardde@muohio.edu. Web site: http://unixgen1.mcs.muohio.edu/~mathematics/.

Miami University, School of Education and Allied Professions, Department of Teacher Education, Oxford, OH 45056. Offers elementary education (M Ed, MAT); reading education (M Ed); secondary education (M Ed, MAT), including adolescent education (MAT), elementary mathematics education (M Ed), secondary education. Part-time programs available. *Students:* 32 full-time (19 women), 40 part-time (37 women); includes 6 minority (3 Black or African American, non-Hispanic/Latino; 2 Hispanic/Latino; 1 Two or more races, non-Hispanic/Latino), 3 international. Average age 28. In 2011, 42 master's awarded. *Entrance requirements:* For master's, GRE (for MAT), minimum undergraduate GPA of 3.0 during previous 2 years or 2.75 overall. *Application deadline:* Applications are processed on a rolling basis. Application fee: $50. Electronic applications accepted. *Expenses:* Tuition, state resident: full-time $12,023; part-time $501 per credit hour. Tuition, nonresident: full-time $26,554; part-time $1107 per credit hour. *Required fees:* $528. *Financial support:* Fellowships with full tuition reimbursements, research assistantships, teaching assistantships, career-related internships or fieldwork, Federal Work-Study, scholarships/grants, health care benefits, tuition waivers (full), and unspecified assistantships available. Financial award application deadline: 2/15. *Unit head:* Dr. James Shiveley, Chair, 513-529-6443, Fax: 513-529-4931, E-mail: shiveljm@muohio.edu. *Application contact:* Linda Dennett, Program Associate, 513-529-5708, E-mail: dennetlg@muohio.edu. Web site: http://www.units.muohio.edu/eap/departments/edt/.

Michigan State University, The Graduate School, College of Natural Science, Department of Mathematics, East Lansing, MI 48824. Offers applied mathematics (MS, PhD); industrial mathematics (MS); mathematics (MAT, MS, PhD). *Entrance requirements:* Additional exam requirements/recommendations for international students: Required—TOEFL. Electronic applications accepted.

Michigan State University, The Graduate School, College of Natural Science and College of Education, Division of Science and Mathematics Education, East Lansing, MI 48824. Offers biological, physical and general science for teachers (MAT, MS), including biological science (MS), general science (MAT), physical science (MS); mathematics education (MS, PhD).

Middle Tennessee State University, College of Graduate Studies, College of Basic and Applied Sciences, Department of Mathematical Sciences, Murfreesboro, TN 37132. Offers mathematics (MS, MST, PhD). Part-time and evening/weekend programs available. Postbaccalaureate distance learning degree programs offered. *Faculty:* 26 full-time (12 women). *Students:* 2 full-time (1 woman), 34 part-time (16 women); includes 13 minority (6 Black or African American, non-Hispanic/Latino; 5 Asian, non-Hispanic/Latino; 2 Hispanic/Latino). Average age 32. 47 applicants, 62% accepted. In 2011, 12 master's awarded. *Degree requirements:* For master's, comprehensive exam, thesis optional; for doctorate, comprehensive exam, thesis/dissertation. *Entrance requirements:* For master's, GRE General Test or MAT. Additional exam requirements/recommendations for international students: Required—TOEFL (minimum score 525 paper-based; 195 computer-based; 71 iBT) or IELTS (minimum score 6). *Application deadline:* For fall admission, 6/1 for domestic and international students. Applications are processed on a rolling basis. Application fee: $25 ($30 for international students). Electronic applications accepted. *Expenses:* Tuition, state resident: full-time $10,008. Tuition, nonresident: full-time $25,056. *Financial support:* In 2011–12, 11 students received support. Tuition waivers available. Support available to part-time students. Financial award application deadline: 5/1; financial award applicants required to submit FAFSA. *Faculty research:* Graph theory, computational science. *Unit head:* Dr. Donald A. Nelson, Interim Chair, 615-898-2669, Fax: 615-898-5422, E-mail: donald.nelson@mtsu.edu. *Application contact:* Dr. Michael D. Allen, Dean and Vice Provost for Research, 615-898-2840, Fax: 615-904-8020, E-mail: michael.allen@mtsu.edu.

Millersville University of Pennsylvania, College of Graduate and Professional Studies, School of Science and Mathematics, Department of Mathematics, Millersville, PA 17551-0302. Offers M Ed. *Accreditation:* NCATE. Part-time and evening/weekend programs available. *Faculty:* 19 full-time (7 women), 6 part-time/adjunct (4 women). *Students:* 6 full-time (3 women), 14 part-time (9 women); includes 1 minority (Black or African American, non-Hispanic/Latino). Average age 31. 4 applicants, 100% accepted, 3 enrolled. In 2011, 7 master's awarded. *Degree requirements:* For master's, thesis optional. *Entrance requirements:* For master's, 3 letters of recommendation. Additional exam requirements/recommendations for international students: Required—TOEFL (minimum score 500 paper-based; 183 computer-based; 65 iBT). *Application deadline:* For fall admission, 1/15 priority date for domestic students, 1/15 for international students; for winter admission, 10/1 priority date for domestic students, 10/1 for international students; for spring admission, 10/1 priority date for domestic students, 10/1 for international students. Applications are processed on a rolling basis. Application fee: $40 ($50 for international students). Electronic applications accepted. *Expenses:* Tuition, state resident: full-time $3744; part-time $416 per credit. Tuition, nonresident: full-time $5616; part-time $624 per credit. *Required fees:* $1130; $125.50 per credit. Tuition and fees vary according to course load. *Financial support:* In 2011–12, 3 students received support, including 4 research assistantships with full tuition reimbursements available (averaging $4,125 per year); institutionally sponsored loans and unspecified assistantships also available. Support available to part-time students. Financial award application deadline: 3/15; financial award applicants required to submit FAFSA. *Faculty research:* Training of secondary mathematics teachers, the use of technology in mathematics classes, equity in mathematics, middle school mathematics, questioning techniques of teacher educators. *Unit head:* Dr. Delray J. Schultz, Chair, 717-872-3535, Fax: 717-871-2320, E-mail: delray.schultz@millersville.edu. *Application contact:* Dr. Victor S. DeSantis, Dean, College of Graduate and Professional Studies, 717-872-3099, Fax: 717-872-3453, E-mail: victor.desantis@millersville.edu. Web site: http://www.millersville.edu/math/.

Mills College, Graduate Studies, School of Education, Oakland, CA 94613-1000. Offers child life in hospitals (MA); early childhood education (MA); education (MA), including art education, curriculum and instruction, elementary education, English education, foreign language education, mathematics education, science education, secondary education, social studies education, teaching; educational leadership (MA, Ed D). Part-time and evening/weekend programs available. *Faculty:* 13 full-time (10 women), 14 part-time/adjunct (10 women). *Students:* 149 full-time (133 women), 69 part-time (61 women); includes 85 minority (32 Black or African American, non-Hispanic/Latino; 1 American Indian or Alaska Native, non-Hispanic/Latino; 16 Asian, non-Hispanic/Latino; 24 Hispanic/Latino; 1 Native Hawaiian or other Pacific Islander, non-Hispanic/Latino; 11 Two or more races, non-Hispanic/Latino), 3 international. Average age 28. 238 applicants, 84% accepted, 106 enrolled. In 2011, 41 master's, 2 doctorates awarded. Terminal master's awarded for partial completion of doctoral program. *Degree requirements:* For master's, comprehensive exam. *Entrance requirements:* For master's, statement of purpose, official transcript, 3 recommendations; for doctorate, GRE General Test. Additional exam requirements/recommendations for international students: Required—TOEFL (minimum score 550 paper-based; 80 iBT) or IELTS (minimum score 6). *Application deadline:* For fall admission, 12/31 priority date for domestic students, 12/15 for international students; for spring admission, 11/1 priority date for domestic students, 10/1 for international students. Applications are processed on a rolling basis. Application fee: $50. Electronic applications accepted. *Expenses: Tuition:* Full-time $28,280; part-time $15,640 per year. *Required fees:* $958. Tuition and fees vary according to program. *Financial support:* In 2011–12, 43 students received support, including 225 fellowships with full and partial tuition reimbursements available (averaging $6,020 per year), 43 teaching assistantships with full and partial tuition reimbursements available (averaging $6,782 per year); career-related internships or fieldwork and scholarships/grants also available. Support available to part-time students. Financial award application deadline: 2/1; financial award applicants required to submit FAFSA. *Faculty research:* Early childhood education, teacher preparation, educational leadership. *Total annual research expenditures:* $2.3 million. *Unit head:* Katherine Schultz, Chairperson, 510-430-3170, Fax: 510-430-3379, E-mail: grad-studies@mills.edu. *Application contact:* Tiana Kozoil, Graduate Admission Specialist, 510-430-3305, Fax: 510-430-2159, E-mail: grad-studies@mills.edu. Web site: http://www.mills.edu/education.

Minnesota State University Mankato, College of Graduate Studies, College of Science, Engineering and Technology, Department of Mathematics and Statistics, Mankato, MN 56001. Offers mathematics (MA, MAT, MS); mathematics education (MS); statistics (MS). *Students:* 19 full-time (8 women), 14 part-time (6 women). *Degree requirements:* For master's, one foreign language, comprehensive exam, thesis or alternative. *Entrance requirements:* For master's, GRE General Test (if GPA less than 2.75), minimum GPA of 2.75 during previous 2 years of course work. Additional exam requirements/recommendations for international students: Required—TOEFL. *Application deadline:* For fall admission, 7/1 priority date for domestic students; for spring admission, 11/1 for domestic students. Applications are processed on a rolling basis. Application fee: $40. Electronic applications accepted. *Financial support:* Fellowships with partial tuition reimbursements, research assistantships with full tuition reimbursements, teaching assistantships with full tuition reimbursements, Federal Work-Study, institutionally sponsored loans, and unspecified assistantships available. Support available to part-time students. Financial award application deadline: 3/15; financial award applicants required to submit FAFSA. *Unit head:* Dr. Brian Martensen, Chairperson, 507-389-1453. *Application contact:* 507-389-2321, E-mail: grad@mnsu.edu. Web site: http://cset.mnsu.edu/mathstat/.

Minot State University, Graduate School, Department of Mathematics and Computer Science, Minot, ND 58707-0002. Offers mathematics (MAT). *Degree requirements:* For master's, thesis or alternative. *Entrance requirements:* For master's, minimum GPA of 2.75, undergraduate major in mathematics, teaching certificate. Additional exam requirements/recommendations for international students: Required—TOEFL. *Faculty research:* Mathematics education.

Mississippi College, Graduate School, School of Education, Department of Teacher Education and Leadership, Clinton, MS 39058. Offers art (M Ed); biological science (M Ed); business education (M Ed); computer science (M Ed); dyslexia therapy (M Ed); educational leadership (M Ed, Ed D, Ed S); elementary education (M Ed, Ed S); English (M Ed); higher education administration (MS); mathematics (M Ed); secondary education (M Ed); social studies (history) (M Ed); teaching arts (M Ed). Part-time programs available. Postbaccalaureate distance learning degree programs offered (no on-campus study). *Degree requirements:* For master's, comprehensive exam, thesis optional. *Entrance requirements:* For master's, NTE. Additional exam requirements/recommendations for international students: Recommended—TOEFL, IELTS. Electronic applications accepted.

Missouri University of Science and Technology, Graduate School, Department of Mathematics and Statistics, Rolla, MO 65409. Offers applied mathematics (MS); mathematics (MST, PhD), including mathematics (PhD), mathematics education (MST), statistics (PhD). Terminal master's awarded for partial completion of doctoral program. *Degree requirements:* For master's, thesis or alternative; for doctorate, one foreign language, thesis/dissertation. *Entrance requirements:* For master's and doctorate, GRE General Test, GRE Subject Test. Electronic applications accepted. *Faculty research:* Analysis, differential equations, topology, statistics.

Montana State University, College of Graduate Studies, College of Letters and Science, Department of Mathematical Sciences, Bozeman, MT 59717. Offers mathematics (MS, PhD), including mathematics education option (MS); statistics (MS, PhD). Part-time programs available. Postbaccalaureate distance learning degree programs offered (minimal on-campus study). *Degree requirements:* For master's, comprehensive exam, thesis (for some programs); for doctorate, comprehensive exam, thesis/dissertation. *Entrance requirements:* For master's and doctorate, GRE General Test. Additional exam requirements/recommendations for international students: Required—TOEFL (minimum score 550 paper-based; 213 computer-based). Electronic applications accepted. *Faculty research:* Applied mathematics, dynamical systems, statistics, mathematics education, mathematical and computational biology.

Montclair State University, The Graduate School, College of Education and Human Services, Department of Curriculum and Teaching, Program in Teaching in Content Area, Montclair, NJ 07043-1624. Offers art (MAT); biology (MAT); chemistry (MAT); earth science (MAT); English (MAT); French (MAT); health and physical education (MAT); health education (MAT); mathematics (MAT); music (MAT); physical education (MAT); physical science (MAT); social studies (MAT); Spanish (MAT); teacher of English as a second language (MAT). *Students:* 162 full-time (90 women), 47 part-time (29 women); includes 37 minority (4 Black or African American, non-Hispanic/Latino; 11 Asian, non-Hispanic/Latino; 18 Hispanic/Latino; 4 Two or more races, non-Hispanic/Latino), 5 international. Average age 31. 145 applicants, 41% accepted, 56 enrolled. In 2011, 229 master's awarded. *Degree requirements:* For master's, comprehensive exam, thesis or alternative. *Entrance requirements:* For master's, GRE General Test, interview, 2 letters of recommendation. Additional exam requirements/recommendations for international students: Required—TOEFL (minimum score 83 iBT), IELTS (minimum score 6.5). *Application deadline:* Applications are processed on a rolling basis. Application fee: $60. Electronic applications accepted. *Financial support:* Federal Work-Study, scholarships/grants, and unspecified assistantships available. Support available to part-time students. Financial award application deadline: 3/1; financial award applicants required to submit FAFSA. *Unit head:* Dr. David Schwarzer, Chairperson, 973-655-5187. *Application contact:* Amy Aiello, Executive Director of The Graduate School, 973-655-5147, Fax: 973-655-7869, E-mail: graduate.school@montclair.edu.

Montclair State University, The Graduate School, College of Science and Mathematics, Department of Mathematical Sciences, Program in Mathematics, Montclair, NJ 07043-1624. Offers mathematics education (MS); pure and applied mathematics (MS). Part-time and evening/weekend programs available. *Students:* 17 full-time (4 women), 53 part-time (30 women); includes 14 minority (3 Black or African American, non-Hispanic/Latino; 3 Asian, non-Hispanic/Latino; 6 Hispanic/Latino; 2 Two or more races, non-Hispanic/Latino), 1 international. Average age 34. 38 applicants, 50% accepted, 16 enrolled. In 2011, 11 master's awarded. *Degree requirements:* For master's, comprehensive exam. *Entrance requirements:* For master's, GRE General Test, 2 letters of recommendation, essay. Additional exam requirements/recommendations for international students: Required—TOEFL (minimum score 83 iBT), IELTS (minimum score 6.5). *Application deadline:* Applications are processed on a rolling basis. Application fee: $60. Electronic applications accepted. *Financial support:* In 2011–12, 9 research assistantships with full tuition reimbursements (averaging $7,000 per year) were awarded; Federal Work-Study, scholarships/grants, and unspecified assistantships also available. Support available to part-time students. Financial award application deadline: 3/1; financial award applicants required to submit FAFSA. *Faculty research:* Computation, applied analysis. *Unit head:* Dr. Helen Roberts, Chairperson, 973-655-5132. *Application contact:* Amy Aiello, Director of Graduate Admissions and Operations, 973-655-5147, Fax: 973-655-7869, E-mail: graduate.school@montclair.edu.

Montclair State University, The Graduate School, College of Science and Mathematics, Department of Mathematical Sciences, Program in Mathematics Education, Montclair, NJ 07043-1624. Offers Ed D. *Students:* 3 full-time (0 women), 14 part-time (9 women). Average age 34. 18 applicants, 72% accepted, 7 enrolled. In 2011, 2 doctorates awarded. *Degree requirements:* For doctorate, thesis/dissertation. *Entrance requirements:* For doctorate, GRE General Test, 2 letters of recommendation, essay. Additional exam requirements/recommendations for international students: Required—TOEFL (minimum score 83 iBT), IELTS (minimum score 6.5). *Application deadline:* For fall admission, 2/1 for domestic students. Application fee: $60. Electronic applications accepted. *Financial support:* In 2011–12, 3 research assistantships with full tuition reimbursements (averaging $7,000 per year) were awarded; Federal Work-Study, scholarships/grants, and unspecified assistantships also available. Support available to part-time students. Financial award application deadline: 3/2; financial award applicants required to submit FAFSA. *Faculty research:* Teacher development, student thinking. *Unit head:* Dr. Helen Roberts, Chairperson, 973-655-5132. *Application contact:* Amy Aiello, Executive Director of The Graduate School, 973-655-5147, Fax: 973-655-7869, E-mail: graduate.school@montclair.edu. Web site: http://www.montclair.edu/csam/mathematical-sciences/graduate-programs/math-education/.

Montclair State University, The Graduate School, College of Science and Mathematics, Department of Mathematical Sciences, Program in Teaching Middle Grades Mathematics, Montclair, NJ 07043-1624. Offers MA. Part-time and evening/weekend programs available. *Students:* 23 part-time (18 women); includes 3 minority (1 Asian, non-Hispanic/Latino; 2 Hispanic/Latino). Average age 34. 2 applicants, 100% accepted, 1 enrolled. In 2011, 9 master's awarded. *Degree requirements:* For master's, comprehensive exam, thesis or alternative. *Entrance requirements:* For master's, GRE General Test, 2 letters of recommendation, essay. Additional exam requirements/recommendations for international students: Required—TOEFL (minimum score 83 iBT), IELTS (minimum score 6.5). *Application deadline:* Applications are processed on a rolling basis. Application fee: $60. Electronic applications accepted. *Financial support:* Federal Work-Study, scholarships/grants, and unspecified assistantships available. Support available to part-time students. Financial award application deadline: 3/1; financial award applicants required to submit FAFSA. *Faculty research:* Teacher knowledge, curriculum. *Unit head:* Dr. Helen Roberts, Chairperson, 973-655-5132. *Application contact:* Amy Aiello, Executive Director of The Graduate School, 973-655-5147, Fax: 973-655-7869, E-mail: graduate.school@montclair.edu. Web site: http://www.montclair.edu/catalog/view_requirements.php?CurriculumID=571.

Morehead State University, Graduate Programs, College of Education, Department of Middle Grades and Secondary Education, Morehead, KY 40351. Offers business and marketing education (MAT); English/language arts 5-9 (MAT); French (MAT); health P-12 (MAT); mathematics 5-9 (MAT); physical education P-12 (MAT); science 5-9 (MAT); secondary biology (MAT); secondary chemistry (MAT); secondary earth science (MAT); secondary English (MAT); secondary math (MAT); secondary physics (MAT); secondary social studies (MAT); social studies 5-9 (MAT); Spanish (MAT). Part-time and evening/weekend programs available. *Degree requirements:* For master's, portfolio. *Entrance requirements:* For master's, GRE or PRAXIS II content exam, minimum overall undergraduate GPA of 2.5. Additional exam requirements/recommendations for international students: Required—TOEFL (minimum score 500 paper-based; 173 computer-based). Electronic applications accepted.

Morgan State University, School of Graduate Studies, School of Education and Urban Studies, Department of Advanced Studies, Leadership and Policy, Program in Mathematics Education, Baltimore, MD 21251. Offers MS, Ed D. *Degree requirements:* For doctorate, comprehensive exam, thesis/dissertation. *Entrance requirements:* For doctorate, GRE General Test or MAT. Additional exam requirements/recommendations for international students: Required—TOEFL (minimum score 550 paper-based; 213 computer-based).

National Louis University, National College of Education, Chicago, IL 60603. Offers administration and supervision (M Ed, Ed D, CAS, Ed S); curriculum and instruction (M Ed, MS Ed, CAS); early childhood administration (M Ed, CAS); early childhood education (M Ed, MAT, MS Ed, CAS); education (Ed D); educational psychology/human learning and development (M Ed, MS Ed, CAS, Ed S); elementary education (MAT); interdisciplinary curriculum and instruction (M Ed); mathematics education (M Ed, MS Ed, CAS); reading and language (M Ed, MS Ed, CAS); school psychology (M Ed, Ed S); science education (M Ed, MS Ed, CAS); secondary education (MAT); special education (M Ed, MAT, CAS); technology in education (M Ed, CAS). *Accreditation:* NCATE. Part-time and evening/weekend programs available. *Students:* 224 full-time (162 women), 2,336 part-time (1,767 women); includes 677 minority (366 Black or African American, non-Hispanic/Latino; 8 American Indian or Alaska Native, non-Hispanic/Latino; 68 Asian, non-Hispanic/Latino; 218 Hispanic/Latino; 2 Native Hawaiian or other Pacific Islander, non-Hispanic/Latino; 15 Two or more races, non-Hispanic/Latino), 2 international. Average age 34. In 2011, 1,711 master's, 76 doctorates, 86 other advanced degrees awarded. *Degree requirements:* For doctorate, comprehensive exam, thesis/dissertation. *Entrance requirements:* For master's, MAT or GRE, minimum GPA of 3.0; for doctorate, GRE General Test, minimum GPA of 3.25, interview, resume, writing sample, 4 recommendations. Additional exam requirements/recommendations for international students: Required—TOEFL (minimum score 550 paper-based; 213 computer-based; 79 iBT). *Application deadline:* Applications are processed on a rolling basis. Application fee: $40. *Financial support:* Fellowships, research assistantships, teaching assistantships, career-related internships or fieldwork, Federal Work-Study, institutionally sponsored loans, and scholarships/grants available. Support available to part-time students. Financial award applicants required to submit FAFSA. *Unit head:* Dr. Alison Hilsabeck, Dean, 312-361-3580, Fax: 312-261-2580, E-mail: ahilsabeck@nl.edu. *Application contact:* Ken Kasprzak, Director of Admission, 888-658-8632, Fax: 847-947-5575, E-mail: kkasprzak@nl.edu.

New Jersey City University, Graduate Studies and Continuing Education, William J. Maxwell College of Arts and Sciences, Department of Mathematics, Jersey City, NJ 07305-1597. Offers mathematics education (MA). Part-time and evening/weekend programs available. *Students:* 3 full-time (2 women), 12 part-time (3 women); includes 6 minority (1 Black or African American, non-Hispanic/Latino; 5 Hispanic/Latino). In 2011, 15 master's awarded. *Degree requirements:* For master's, comprehensive exam, thesis optional. *Entrance requirements:* Additional exam requirements/recommendations for international students: Required—TOEFL. *Application deadline:* For fall admission, 8/1 priority date for domestic students; for spring admission, 12/1 for domestic students. Applications are processed on a rolling basis. Application fee: $0. *Expenses:* Tuition, state resident: part-time $494 per credit. Tuition, nonresident: part-time $911.30 per credit. *Required fees:* $95.90 per year. *Financial support:* Unspecified assistantships available. *Unit head:* Dr. Bimnet Teclezghi, Chairperson, 201-200-3202, E-mail: bteclezghi@njcu.edu. *Application contact:* Dr. William Bajor, Dean of Graduate Studies, 201-200-3409, Fax: 201-200-3411, E-mail: wbajor@njcu.edu.

New York University, Steinhardt School of Culture, Education, and Human Development, Department of Teaching and Learning, Program in Mathematics Education, New York, NY 10012-1019. Offers MA. *Accreditation:* Teacher Education Accreditation Council. Part-time and evening/weekend programs available. *Degree requirements:* For master's, thesis (for some programs). *Entrance requirements:* Additional exam requirements/recommendations for international students: Required—TOEFL. Electronic applications accepted. *Faculty research:* Race, gender and mathematics learning; developing mathematical concepts through activity; innovative secondary school mathematics materials.

Nicholls State University, Graduate Studies, College of Arts and Sciences, Department of Mathematics and Computer Science, Thibodaux, LA 70310. Offers community/technical college mathematics (MS). Part-time and evening/weekend programs available. *Degree requirements:* For master's, comprehensive exam. *Entrance requirements:* For master's, GRE General Test. Electronic applications accepted. *Faculty research:* Operations research, statistics, numerical analysis, algebra, topology.

North Carolina Central University, Division of Academic Affairs, College of Science and Technology, Department of Mathematics and Computer Science, Durham, NC 27707-3129. Offers applied mathematics (MS); mathematics education (MS); pure mathematics (MS). Part-time and evening/weekend programs available. *Degree requirements:* For master's, one foreign language, comprehensive exam, thesis. *Entrance requirements:* For master's, minimum GPA of 3.0 in major, 2.5 overall. Additional exam requirements/recommendations for international students: Required—TOEFL. *Faculty research:* Structure theorems for Lie algebra, Kleene monoids and semi-groups, theoretical computer science, mathematics education.

North Carolina State University, Graduate School, College of Education, Department of Mathematics, Science, and Technology Education, Program in Mathematics Education, Raleigh, NC 27695. Offers M Ed, MS, PhD. *Accreditation:* NCATE. Part-time programs available. *Degree requirements:* For master's, thesis (for some programs), oral exam; for doctorate, one foreign language, thesis/dissertation, oral and written exams. *Entrance requirements:* For master's, GRE General Test or MAT, minimum GPA of 3.0; for doctorate, GRE General Test, minimum GPA of 3.0, interview. Electronic applications accepted. *Faculty research:* Teacher education using technology, curriculum development, scientific visualization, problem solving.

North Dakota State University, College of Graduate and Interdisciplinary Studies, College of Human Development and Education, School of Education, Fargo, ND 58108. Offers agricultural education (M Ed, MS), including agricultural education, agricultural extension education (MS); counseling (M Ed, MS, PhD); curriculum and instruction (M Ed, MS), including pedagogy, physical education and athletic administration; education (PhD); educational leadership (M Ed, MS, Ed S); family and consumer sciences education (M Ed, MS); history education (M Ed, MS); institutional analysis (Ed D); mathematics education (M Ed, MS); music education (M Ed, MS); occupational and adult education (Ed D); science education (M Ed, MS). *Accreditation:* NCATE. Part-time and evening/weekend programs available. Postbaccalaureate distance learning degree programs offered (minimal on-campus study). *Faculty:* 24 full-time (10 women), 2 part-time/adjunct (1 woman). *Students:* 91 full-time (64 women), 114 part-time (78 women); includes 13 minority (4 Black or African American, non-Hispanic/Latino; 5 American Indian or Alaska Native, non-Hispanic/Latino; 1 Hispanic/Latino; 3 Two or more races, non-Hispanic/Latino), 8 international. 88 applicants, 67% accepted, 56 enrolled. In 2011, 43 master's, 12 doctorates awarded. *Degree requirements:* For master's, comprehensive exam; for doctorate, thesis/dissertation; for Ed S, thesis. *Entrance requirements:* For degree, GRE General Test, master's degree, minimum GPA of 3.25. Additional exam requirements/recommendations for international students: Required—TOEFL. *Application deadline:* Applications are processed on a rolling basis. Application fee: $45 ($60 for international students). *Financial support:* Research assistantships, teaching assistantships, career-related internships or fieldwork, Federal Work-Study, institutionally sponsored loans, and tuition waivers (full) available. Financial award application deadline: 4/15. *Unit head:* Dr. William Martin, Chair, 701-231-7202, Fax: 701-231-7416, E-mail: william.martin@ndsu.edu. *Application contact:* Sonya Goergen, Marketing, Recruitment, and Public Relations Coordinator, 701-231-7033, Fax: 701-231-6524. Web site: http://www.ndsu.nodak.edu/school_of_education/.

North Dakota State University, College of Graduate and Interdisciplinary Studies, Program in STEM Education, Fargo, ND 58108. Offers PhD. *Students:* 1 (woman) full-time. Application fee: $35. Electronic applications accepted. *Unit head:* Dr. Donald Schwert, Director, 701-231-7496, Fax: 701-231-5924, E-mail: donald.schwert@ndsu.edu. *Application contact:* Sonya Goergen, Marketing, Recruitment, and Public Relations Coordinator, 701-231-7033, Fax: 701-231-6524.

Northeastern Illinois University, Graduate College, College of Arts and Sciences, Department of Mathematics, Programs in Mathematics, Chicago, IL 60625-4699. Offers mathematics (MS); mathematics for elementary school teachers (MA). Part-time and evening/weekend programs available. *Degree requirements:* For master's, comprehensive exam, thesis optional, project. *Entrance requirements:* For master's, minimum GPA of 2.75, 6 undergraduate courses in mathematics. Additional exam requirements/recommendations for international students: Required—TOEFL (minimum score 550 paper-based; 213 computer-based; 79 iBT). Electronic applications accepted. *Faculty research:* Numerical analysis, mathematical biology, operations research, statistics, geometry and mathematics of finance.

Northeastern State University, Graduate College, College of Education, Program in Mathematics Education, Tahlequah, OK 74464-2399. Offers M Ed. *Students:* 3 full-time (2 women), 21 part-time (17 women); includes 5 minority (1 Black or African American, non-Hispanic/Latino; 4 American Indian or Alaska Native, non-Hispanic/Latino). In 2011, 3 master's awarded. *Entrance requirements:* For master's, GRE or MAT, minimum GPA of 2.5. Additional exam requirements/recommendations for international students: Required—TOEFL (minimum score 213 computer-based). *Application deadline:* For fall admission, 6/1 priority date for domestic students. Applications are processed on a rolling basis. Application fee: $25. Electronic applications accepted. *Unit head:* Dr. Martha Parrott, Department Chair of Mathematics, 918-449-6536, E-mail: parrott@nsouk.edu. *Application contact:* Margie Railey, Administrative Assistant, 918-456-5511 Ext. 2093, Fax: 918-458-2061, E-mail: railey@nsouk.edu.

Northern Arizona University, Graduate College, College of Engineering, Forestry and Natural Sciences, Center for Science Teaching and Learning, Flagstaff, AZ 86011. Offers mathematics or science teaching (Certificate); science teaching and learning (M Ed, MAST). Part-time programs available. Postbaccalaureate distance learning degree programs offered (minimal on-campus study). *Faculty:* 7 full-time (5 women). *Students:* 12 full-time (4 women), 10 part-time (7 women); includes 3 minority (1 American Indian or Alaska Native, non-Hispanic/Latino; 1 Hispanic/Latino; 1 Two or more races, non-Hispanic/Latino). In 2011, 7 master's, 3 other advanced degrees awarded. *Entrance requirements:* Additional exam requirements/recommendations for international students: Required—TOEFL (minimum score 550 paper-based; 213 computer-based; 80 iBT), IELTS (minimum score 7). *Application deadline:* For fall admission, 3/1 for international students; for spring admission, 9/15 for international students. Application fee: $65. *Expenses:* Tuition, state resident: full-time $7190; part-time $355 per credit hour. Tuition, nonresident: full-time $18,092; part-time $1005 per credit hour. *Required fees:* $818; $328 per semester. *Financial support:* Career-related internships or fieldwork, Federal Work-Study, and scholarships/grants available. Financial award applicants required to submit FAFSA. *Unit head:* Julie Gess-Newsome, Director, 928-523-9527, E-mail: julie.gess-newsome@nau.edu. *Application contact:* Barbara Molnar, Administrative Associate, 928-523-2114, E-mail: barbara.molnar@nau.edu. Web site: http://nau.edu/cefns/cstl/.

Northern Arizona University, Graduate College, College of Engineering, Forestry and Natural Sciences, Department of Mathematics and Statistics, Flagstaff, AZ 86011. Offers applied statistics (Certificate); mathematics (MAT, MS); statistics (MS). Part-time programs available. *Faculty:* 38 full-time (12 women). *Students:* 23 full-time (9 women), 18 part-time (12 women); includes 11 minority (2 Black or African American, non-Hispanic/Latino; 2 Asian, non-Hispanic/Latino; 7 Hispanic/Latino), 1 international. Average age 28. 25 applicants, 68% accepted, 9 enrolled. In 2011, 15 master's, 7 other advanced degrees awarded. *Degree requirements:* For master's, comprehensive exam (for some programs), thesis (for some programs). *Entrance requirements:* For master's, minimum GPA of 3.0. Additional exam requirements/recommendations for international students: Required—TOEFL (minimum score 550 paper-based; 213 computer-based; 80 iBT), IELTS (minimum score 7). *Application deadline:* For fall admission, 3/15 priority date for domestic students, 3/15 for international students; for spring admission, 10/15 priority date for domestic students, 10/15 for international students. Applications are processed on a rolling basis. Application fee: $65. Electronic applications accepted. *Expenses:* Tuition, state resident: full-time $7190; part-time $355 per credit hour. Tuition, nonresident: full-time $18,092; part-time $1005 per credit hour. *Required fees:* $818; $328 per semester. *Financial support:* In 2011–12, 22 teaching assistantships with partial tuition reimbursements (averaging $14,051 per year) were awarded; Federal Work-Study, scholarships/grants, health care benefits, tuition waivers (full and partial), and unspecified assistantships also available. Financial award applicants required to submit FAFSA. *Faculty research:* Topology, statistics, groups, ring theory, number theory. *Unit head:* Dr. Janet M. McShane, Chair, 928-523-1252, Fax: 928-523-5847, E-mail: janet.mcshane@nau.edu. *Application contact:* Sharon O'Connor, Chair, 928-523-3481, Fax: 928-523-5847, E-mail: math.grad@nau.edu. Web site: http://nau.edu/CEFNS/NatSci/Math/Degrees-Programs/.

North Georgia College & State University, School of Education, Dahlonega, GA 30597. Offers art education (MAT); early childhood education (M Ed); English education (MAT); history education (MAT); math education (MAT); middle grades education (M Ed, MAT); physical education (MS); school leadership (Ed S); secondary education (M Ed), including English education, history education, mathematics education, physical education; teacher education (MAT). *Accreditation:* NCATE. Part-time and evening/weekend programs available. Postbaccalaureate distance learning degree programs offered (no on-campus study). *Faculty:* 23 full-time (14 women), 16 part-time/adjunct (11 women). *Students:* 19 full-time (17 women), 199 part-time (147 women); includes 7 minority (3 Black or African American, non-Hispanic/Latino; 1 Asian, non-Hispanic/Latino; 3 Hispanic/Latino), 1 international. Average age 34. 259 applicants, 66% accepted, 112 enrolled. In 2011, 100 master's, 16 other advanced degrees awarded. *Degree requirements:* For master's, comprehensive exam, thesis optional. *Entrance requirements:* For master's, GRE or MAT, GACE, minimum GPA of 2.75; for Ed S, GRE General Test or MAT, 3 years of teaching experience, master's degree, minimum graduate GPA of 3.25, leadership position in the school. Additional exam requirements/recommendations for international students: Required—TOEFL (minimum score 550 paper-based; 213 computer-based; 79 iBT), IELTS (minimum score 6.5). *Application deadline:* For fall admission, 8/1 priority date for domestic students, 7/1 for international students; for spring admission, 12/1 priority date for domestic students, 11/1 for international students. Applications are processed on a rolling basis. Application fee: $40. Electronic applications accepted. *Expenses:* Tuition, state resident: full-time $3528; part-time $196 per credit hour. Tuition, nonresident: full-time $14,094; part-time $783 per credit hour. *Required fees:* $1718; $859 per semester. Tuition and fees vary according to course load, campus/location and program. *Financial support:* Teaching assistantships, career-related internships or fieldwork, scholarships/grants, and unspecified assistantships available. Financial award application deadline: 5/1; financial award applicants required to submit CSS PROFILE or FAFSA. *Faculty research:* Identification of professional development school structures supporting P-12 student achievement, impact of diverse field placement settings in teacher belief development among preservice teachers, use of inquiry methodology in social studies teaching with English language learners, use of instructional differentiation in the middle grades classroom, effects of international school placements on preservice teacher beliefs and attitudes. *Unit head:* Dr. Bob Michael, Dean, School of Education, 706-864-1998, Fax: 706-867-2850, E-mail: bmichael@northgeorgia.edu. *Application contact:* Susan L. Perry, Graduate Admissions Coordinator, 706-864-1543, Fax: 706-867-2795, E-mail: slperry@northgeorgia.edu. Web site: http://www.northgeorgia.edu/soe/.

Northwest Missouri State University, Graduate School, College of Arts and Sciences, Department of Mathematics and Statistics, Maryville, MO 64468-6001. Offers teaching mathematics (MS Ed). Part-time programs available. *Faculty:* 11 full-time (4 women). *Students:* 1 (woman) full-time, 3 part-time (1 woman). 4 applicants, 100% accepted, 1 enrolled. In 2011, 1 master's awarded. *Degree requirements:* For master's, comprehensive exam. *Entrance requirements:* For master's, GRE General Test, minimum undergraduate GPA of 2.5, writing sample. Additional exam requirements/recommendations for international students: Required—TOEFL (minimum score 550 paper-based; 213 computer-based). *Application deadline:* For fall admission, 7/1 for domestic and international students; for spring admission, 11/15 for domestic and international students. Applications are processed on a rolling basis. Application fee: $0 ($50 for international students). *Financial support:* In 2011–12, 3 teaching assistantships with full tuition reimbursements (averaging $6,000 per year) were awarded. Financial award application deadline: 4/1; financial award applicants required to submit FAFSA. *Unit head:* Dr. Dennis Malm, Chairperson, 660-562-1208. *Application contact:* Dr. Gregory Haddock, Dean of Graduate School, 660-562-1145, Fax: 660-562-1096, E-mail: gradsch@nwmissouri.edu.

Oakland University, Graduate Study and Lifelong Learning, School of Education and Human Services, Department of Human Development and Child Studies, Program in Early Childhood Education, Rochester, MI 48309-4401. Offers early childhood education (M Ed, PhD, Certificate); early mathematics education (Certificate). *Accreditation:* Teacher Education Accreditation Council. *Degree requirements:* For doctorate, thesis/dissertation. *Entrance requirements:* For master's, minimum GPA of 3.0 for unconditional admission; for doctorate, GRE General Test, minimum GPA of 3.0 for unconditional admission. Additional exam requirements/recommendations for international students: Required—TOEFL (minimum score 550 paper-based; 213 computer-based).

Occidental College, Graduate Studies, Department of Education, Program in Secondary Education, Los Angeles, CA 90041-3314. Offers English and comparative literary studies (MAT); history (MAT); life science (MAT); mathematics (MAT); physical science (MAT); social science (MAT); Spanish (MAT). Part-time programs available. *Degree requirements:* For master's, comprehensive exam, graduate synthesis paper. *Entrance requirements:* For master's, GRE General Test, minimum GPA of 3.0. Additional exam requirements/recommendations for international students: Required—TOEFL (minimum score 625 paper-based; 263 computer-based). *Expenses:* Contact institution.

Ohio University, Graduate College, Gladys W. and David H. Patton College of Education and Human Services, Department of Teacher Education, Athens, OH 45701-2979. Offers adolescent to young adult education (M Ed); curriculum and instruction (M Ed, PhD); early childhood/special education (M Ed); intervention specialist/mild-moderate needs (M Ed); intervention specialist/moderate-intensive needs (M Ed); mathematics education (PhD); middle child education (M Ed); reading education (M Ed); social studies education (PhD). Part-time and evening/weekend programs available. *Students:* 131 full-time (92 women), 82 part-time (62 women); includes 9 minority (4 Black or African American, non-Hispanic/Latino; 2 American Indian or Alaska Native, non-Hispanic/Latino; 1 Asian, non-Hispanic/Latino; 1 Hispanic/Latino; 1 Two or more races, non-Hispanic/Latino), 11 international. 136 applicants, 70% accepted, 65 enrolled. In 2011, 58 master's, 8 doctorates awarded. *Degree requirements:* For master's, thesis or alternative; for doctorate, comprehensive exam, thesis/dissertation. *Entrance requirements:* For master's, GRE General Test or MAT (if GPA is below 2.9); for doctorate, GRE General Test, minimum GPA of 3.4, work experience. Additional exam requirements/recommendations for international students: Required—TOEFL (minimum score 550 paper-based; 80 iBT) or IELTS (minimum score 6.5). *Application deadline:* For fall admission, 5/1 priority date for domestic students, 4/1 for international students; for winter admission, 11/1 priority date for domestic students, 10/1 for international students; for spring admission, 2/15 priority date for domestic students, 1/1 for international students. Applications are processed on a rolling basis. Application fee: $50 ($55 for international students). Electronic applications accepted. *Financial support:* Research assistantships with full tuition reimbursements, teaching assistantships with full tuition reimbursements, Federal Work-Study, institutionally sponsored loans, tuition waivers (partial), and unspecified assistantships available. Financial award application deadline: 3/1. *Faculty research:* Cognition literacy, character education, teacher's education reform, disabilities. *Total annual research expenditures:* $46,933. *Unit head:* Dr. John Henning, Chair, 740-597-1830, Fax: 740-593-0477, E-mail: henningj@ohio.edu. *Application contact:* Floyd J. Doney, Director of Student Affairs, 740-593-4400, Fax: 740-593-9310, E-mail: doney@ohio.edu. Web site: http://www.cehs.ohio.edu/academics/te/index.htm.

Oklahoma State University, College of Arts and Sciences, Department of Mathematics, Stillwater, OK 74078. Offers applied mathematics (MS, PhD); mathematics education (MS, PhD); pure mathematics (MS, PhD). *Faculty:* 33 full-time (6 women), 8 part-time/adjunct (5 women). *Students:* 5 full-time (2 women), 27 part-time (8 women); includes 2 minority (1 Asian, non-Hispanic/Latino; 1 Two or more races, non-Hispanic/Latino), 21 international. Average age 31. 66 applicants, 14% accepted, 3 enrolled. In 2011, 2 master's, 1 doctorate awarded. *Degree requirements:* For master's, thesis, creative component, or report; for doctorate, comprehensive exam, thesis/dissertation. *Entrance requirements:* For master's and doctorate, GRE (recommended). Additional exam requirements/recommendations for international students: Required—TOEFL (minimum score 550 paper-based; 79 iBT). *Application deadline:* For fall admission, 3/1 for domestic and international students; for spring admission, 10/15 for domestic and international students. Applications are processed on a rolling basis. Application fee: $40 ($75 for international students). Electronic applications accepted. *Expenses:* Tuition, state resident: full-time $4044; part-time $168.50 per credit hour. Tuition, nonresident: full-time $16,008; part-time $667 per credit hour. *Required fees:* $2122; $88.45 per credit hour. One-time fee: $50. Tuition and fees vary according to course load and campus/location. *Financial support:* In 2011–12, 32 teaching assistantships (averaging $18,748 per year) were awarded; health care benefits and tuition waivers (partial) also available. Financial award application deadline: 3/1; financial award applicants required to submit FAFSA. *Unit head:* Dr. Dale Alspach, Head, 405-744-5688, Fax: 405-744-8275. *Application contact:* Dr. Sheryl Tucker, Dean, 405-744-7099, Fax: 405-744-0355, E-mail: grad-i@okstate.edu. Web site: http://www.math.okstate.edu/.

Oregon State University, Graduate School, College of Science, Department of Science and Mathematics Education, Program in Mathematics Education, Corvallis, OR 97331. Offers MA, MS, PhD. *Accreditation:* NCATE. *Degree requirements:* For master's, variable foreign language requirement; for doctorate, one foreign language, thesis/dissertation. *Entrance requirements:* For master's, minimum GPA of 3.0 in last 90 hours of course work; for doctorate, GRE or MAT, minimum GPA of 3.0 in last 90 hours of course work. Additional exam requirements/recommendations for international students: Required—TOEFL. *Faculty research:* Teacher action when focused on standards, teacher belief, integration of technology.

Our Lady of the Lake University of San Antonio, School of Professional Studies, Program in Curriculum and Instruction, San Antonio, TX 78207-4689. Offers bilingual (M Ed); early childhood education (M Ed); English as a second language (M Ed); integrated math teaching (M Ed); integrated science teaching (M Ed); master reading teacher (M Ed); master technology teacher (M Ed); reading specialist (M Ed).

Our Lady of the Lake University of San Antonio, School of Professional Studies, Program in Intermediate Education, San Antonio, TX 78207-4689. Offers math/science education (M Ed); professional studies (M Ed). Part-time and evening/weekend programs available.

Plymouth State University, College of Graduate Studies, Graduate Studies in Education, Program in Mathematics Education, Plymouth, NH 03264-1595. Offers M Ed. Part-time and evening/weekend programs available. *Degree requirements:* For master's, comprehensive exam, thesis optional. *Entrance requirements:* For master's, MAT, minimum GPA of 3.0.

Portland State University, Graduate Studies, College of Liberal Arts and Sciences, Department of Mathematics and Statistics, Portland, OR 97207-0751. Offers mathematical sciences (PhD); mathematics education (PhD); statistics (MS); MA/MS. *Degree requirements:* For master's, thesis or alternative, exams; for doctorate, 2 foreign languages, thesis/dissertation, exams. *Entrance requirements:* For master's, GRE General Test, GRE Subject Test, minimum GPA of 3.0 in upper-division course work or 2.75 overall; for doctorate, GRE General Test. Additional exam requirements/recommendations for international students: Required—TOEFL (minimum score 550 paper-based; 213 computer-based). *Faculty research:* Algebra, topology, statistical distribution theory, control theory, statistical robustness.

Providence College, Program in Teaching Mathematics, Providence, RI 02918. Offers MA. Part-time and evening/weekend programs available. *Faculty:* 9 full-time (4 women), 1 part-time/adjunct (0 women). *Students:* 2 full-time (0 women), 32 part-time (17 women); includes 1 minority (Black or African American, non-Hispanic/Latino). Average age 34. 10 applicants, 70% accepted, 5 enrolled. In 2011, 9 master's awarded. *Entrance requirements:* Additional exam requirements/recommendations for international students: Required—TOEFL (minimum score 550 paper-based; 213 computer-based; 80 iBT). *Application deadline:* For fall admission, 8/1 priority date for domestic students, 8/1 for international students; for spring admission, 12/1 priority date for domestic students, 12/1 for international students. Applications are processed on a rolling basis. Application fee: $55. *Expenses: Tuition:* Part-time $404 per credit. *Required fees:* $404 per credit. *Financial support:* In 2011–12, 1 research assistantship with full tuition reimbursement (averaging $8,400 per year) was awarded; institutionally sponsored loans and unspecified assistantships also available. Support available to part-time students. Financial award application deadline: 8/1; financial award applicants required to submit FAFSA. *Unit head:* Dr. Wataru Ishizuka, Program Director, 401-865-2784, E-mail: wishizuk@providence.edu. *Application contact:* Carol A. Daniels, Coordinator of Graduate Faculty and Administrative Services, 401-865-2247, Fax: 401-865-1147, E-mail: daniels@providence.edu. Web site: http://www.providence.edu/academics/Pages/master-teaching-math.aspx.

Purdue University, Graduate School, College of Education, Department of Curriculum and Instruction, West Lafayette, IN 47907. Offers agricultural and extension education (PhD, Ed S); agriculture and extension education (MS, MS Ed); art education (PhD); consumer and family sciences and extension education (MS Ed, PhD, Ed S); curriculum studies (MS Ed, PhD, Ed S); educational technology (MS Ed, PhD, Ed S); elementary education (MS Ed); foreign language education (MS Ed, PhD, Ed S); industrial technology (PhD, Ed S); language arts (MS Ed, PhD, Ed S); literacy (MS Ed, PhD, Ed S); mathematics/science education (MS, MS Ed, PhD, Ed S); social studies (MS Ed, PhD); social studies education (Ed S); vocational/industrial education (MS Ed, PhD, Ed S); vocational/technical education (MS Ed, PhD, Ed S). *Accreditation:* NCATE. Part-time and evening/weekend programs available. *Faculty:* 30 full-time (21 women), 1 (woman) part-time/adjunct. *Students:* 89 full-time (64 women), 134 part-time (84 women); includes 31 minority (12 Black or African American, non-Hispanic/Latino; 3 American Indian or Alaska Native, non-Hispanic/Latino; 7 Asian, non-Hispanic/Latino; 9 Hispanic/Latino), 49 international. Average age 36. 136 applicants, 83% accepted, 72 enrolled. In 2011, 26 master's, 13 doctorates awarded. *Degree requirements:* For master's, thesis optional; for doctorate, thesis/dissertation, oral and written exams; for Ed S, oral presentation, project. *Entrance requirements:* For master's, GRE general test is required if undergraduate GPA is below 3.0, minimum undergraduate GPA of 3.0 or equivalent; for doctorate, GRE General Test, a combined GRE verbal and quantitative score of 1000 (300 for revised GRE Test) or more is expected, minimum undergraduate GPA of 3.0 or equivalent; master's degree with minimum GPA of 3.0 or equivalent; for Ed S, GRE general test, a combined GRE verbal and quantitative score of 1000 (300 for revised GRE Test) or more is expected, minimum undergraduate GPA of 3.0 or equivalent; master's degree. Additional exam requirements/recommendations for international students: Required—TOEFL (minimum score 550 paper-based; 77 iBT). *Application deadline:* For fall admission, 12/15 priority date for domestic students, 3/1 for international students; for spring admission, 9/15 for domestic students, 8/1 for international students. Application fee: $60 ($75 for international students). Electronic applications accepted. *Financial support:* Fellowships with full tuition reimbursements, research assistantships with full tuition reimbursements, teaching assistantships with full tuition reimbursements, career-related internships or fieldwork, and tuition waivers (full) available. Support available to part-time students. Financial award application deadline: 3/1; financial award applicants required to submit FAFSA. *Faculty research:* Literacy acquisition and development, teacher beliefs and knowledge, recruitment and retention of underrepresented students, economic education, literacy discourse. *Unit head:* Dr. Philip J. VanFossen, Head, 765-494-7935, Fax: 765-496-1622, E-mail: vanfoss@purdue.edu. *Application contact:* Sarah N. Prater, Graduate Contact, 765-494-2345, Fax: 765-494-5832, E-mail: prater0@purdue.edu. Web site: http://www.edci.purdue.edu/.

Purdue University Calumet, Graduate Studies Office, School of Engineering, Mathematics, and Science, Department of Mathematics, Computer Science, and Statistics, Hammond, IN 46323-2094. Offers computer science (MS); mathematics (MAT, MS). Part-time programs available. *Entrance requirements:* Additional exam requirements/recommendations for international students: Required—TOEFL. *Faculty research:* Topology, analysis, algebra, mathematics education.

Queens College of the City University of New York, Division of Graduate Studies, Division of Education, Department of Secondary Education, Flushing, NY 11367-1597. Offers art (MS Ed); biology (MS Ed, AC); chemistry (MS Ed, AC); earth sciences (MS Ed, AC); English (MS Ed, AC); French (MS Ed, AC); Italian (MS Ed, AC); mathematics (MS Ed, AC); music (MS Ed, AC); physics (MS Ed, AC); social studies (MS Ed, AC); Spanish (MS Ed, AC). Part-time and evening/weekend programs available. *Faculty:* 22 full-time (14 women). *Students:* 46 full-time (23 women), 727 part-time (442 women); includes 234 minority (41 Black or African American, non-Hispanic/Latino; 78 Asian, non-Hispanic/Latino; 115 Hispanic/Latino), 5 international. 591 applicants, 60% accepted, 250 enrolled. In 2011, 170 master's awarded. *Degree requirements:* For master's, research project; for AC, thesis optional. *Entrance requirements:* For master's, minimum GPA of 3.0. Additional exam requirements/recommendations for international students: Required—TOEFL. *Application deadline:* For fall admission, 4/1 for domestic students; for spring admission, 11/1 for domestic students. Applications are processed on a rolling basis. Application fee: $125. *Expenses:* Tuition, state resident: part-time $345 per credit. Tuition, nonresident: part-time $640 per credit. *Required fees:* $145.25 per semester. *Financial support:* Career-related internships or fieldwork, Federal Work-Study, institutionally sponsored loans, and tuition waivers (partial) available. Support available to part-time students. Financial award application deadline: 4/1; financial award applicants required to submit FAFSA. *Unit head:* Dr. Eleanor Armour-Thomas, Chairperson, 718-997-5150, E-mail: armourthomas@yahoo.com. *Application contact:* Mario Caruso, Director of Graduate Admissions, 718-997-5200, Fax: 718-997-5193, E-mail: graduate_admissions@qc.edu.

Quinnipiac University, School of Education, Program in Secondary Education, Hamden, CT 06518-1940. Offers biology (MAT); English (MAT); history/social studies (MAT); mathematics (MAT); Spanish (MAT). *Accreditation:* NCATE. *Faculty:* 7 full-time (5 women), 41 part-time/adjunct (24 women). *Students:* 56 full-time (38 women), 1 (woman) part-time; includes 5 minority (1 Black or African American, non-Hispanic/Latino; 1 Asian, non-Hispanic/Latino; 3 Hispanic/Latino). 51 applicants, 96% accepted, 44 enrolled. In 2011, 49 master's awarded. *Entrance requirements:* For master's, PRAXIS I, minimum GPA of 2.67, interview. *Application deadline:* For fall admission, 3/31 priority date for domestic students. Applications are processed on a rolling basis. Application fee: $45. Electronic applications accepted. *Expenses: Tuition:* Part-time $855 per credit. *Required fees:* $35 per credit. *Financial support:* In 2011–12, 1 student received support. Career-related internships or fieldwork, scholarships/grants, and tuition waivers (full and partial) available. Financial award application deadline: 4/15; financial award applicants required to submit FAFSA. *Faculty research:* Multicultural and urban education/leadership, challenges of teaching diverse learners, scholarship of teaching and learning, technology and teaching, humor and education. *Unit head:* Mordechai Gordon, Program Director, 203-582-8442, Fax: 203-582-3473, E-mail: mordechai.gordon@quinnipiac.edu. *Application contact:* Jennifer Boutin, Associate Director of Graduate Admissions, 800-462-1944, Fax: 203-582-3443, E-mail: jennifer.boutin@quinnipiac.edu. Web site: http://www.quinnipiac.edu/academics/colleges-schools-and-departments/school-of-education/graduate-programs/five-semester-mat-programs/secondary-educat.

Regent University, Graduate School, School of Education, Virginia Beach, VA 23464-9800. Offers adult education (Ed D); adult/staff development (Ed D, PhD); career switcher with licensure (M Ed), including alternative licensure; character education (Ed D, PhD); Christian education leadership (Ed D, PhD); Christian education specialist (Ed S); Christian school program (M Ed), including ACSI licensure; distance education (Ed D, PhD); education licensure (M Ed), including preK-6th grade; educational leadership (M Ed, PhD); educational leadership - special education (Ed S), including administration and supervision; educational psychology (Ed D, PhD), including learning and development, research and evaluation, special education; higher education (Ed D, PhD), including administration, research and institutional planning, teaching; higher education leadership (Ed D); individualized degree plan (M Ed), including behavior disorders, learning disabilities, mental retardation, reading specialist; K-12 school leadership (Ed D, PhD); leadership in character education (M Ed); master teacher (M Ed), including TESOL; mathematics education (M Ed); special education (PhD); student affairs (M Ed); TESOL (M Ed), including adult education, ESL: preK-12. *Accreditation:* Teacher Education Accreditation Council. Part-time and evening/weekend programs available. Postbaccalaureate distance learning degree programs offered (minimal on-campus study). *Faculty:* 26 full-time (13 women), 54 part-time/adjunct (34 women). *Students:* 140 full-time (109 women), 786 part-time (626 women); includes 218 minority (189 Black or African American, non-Hispanic/Latino; 2 American Indian or Alaska Native, non-Hispanic/Latino; 11 Asian, non-Hispanic/Latino; 16 Hispanic/Latino), 42 international. Average age 39. 673 applicants, 57% accepted, 298 enrolled. In 2011, 178 master's, 15 doctorates awarded. *Degree requirements:* For master's, thesis or alternative; for doctorate, comprehensive exam, thesis/dissertation. *Entrance requirements:* For master's, MAT, minimum undergraduate GPA of 2.75, writing sample, resume, recommendations, interview; for doctorate, GRE, writing sample, 3 years of relevant professional experience, master's-level paper, copies of published work, resume, transcripts, interview, recommendations. Additional exam requirements/recommendations for international students: Required—TOEFL (minimum score 577 paper-based; 233 computer-based). *Application deadline:* For fall admission, 4/1 priority date for domestic students; for spring admission, 10/15 priority date for domestic students. Applications are processed on a rolling basis. Application fee: $50. Electronic applications accepted. *Expenses:* Contact institution. *Financial support:* Fellowships, career-related internships or fieldwork, scholarships/grants, tuition waivers (full and partial), and unspecified assistantships available. Support available to part-time students. Financial award application deadline: 4/1; financial award applicants required to submit FAFSA. *Faculty research:* Character development and discipline for children, education leadership development, diversity in schools, classroom management, technology in education settings. *Unit head:* Dr. Alan A. Arroyo, Dean, 757-352-4261, Fax: 757-352-4318, E-mail: alanarr@regent.edu. *Application contact:* Matthew Chadwick, Director of Enrollment Support Services, 800-373-5504, Fax: 757-352-4381, E-mail: admissions@regent.edu. Web site: http://www.regent.edu/education/.

Rhode Island College, School of Graduate Studies, Feinstein School of Education and Human Development, Department of Educational Studies, Providence, RI 02908-1991. Offers advanced studies in teaching and learning (M Ed); English (MAT); French (MAT); history (MAT); math (MAT); secondary education (MAT); Spanish (MAT); teaching English as a second language (M Ed). *Accreditation:* NCATE. Part-time and evening/weekend programs available. *Faculty:* 14 full-time (7 women), 4 part-time/adjunct (2 women). *Students:* 10 full-time (all women), 61 part-time (51 women); includes 8 minority (1 Black or African American, non-Hispanic/Latino; 4 Asian, non-Hispanic/Latino; 3 Hispanic/Latino). Average age 33. In 2011, 32 master's awarded. *Degree requirements:* For master's, capstone or comprehensive assessment. *Entrance requirements:* For master's, GRE or MAT (for most programs), minimum undergraduate GPA of 3.0; baccalaureate degree in English, French, history, math or Spanish; evaluation of content area knowledge; 3 letters of recommendation; interview. Additional exam requirements/recommendations for international students: Recommended—TOEFL (minimum score 550 paper-based; 213 computer-based; 79 iBT). *Application deadline:* For fall admission, 3/1 for domestic students; for spring admission, 11/1 for domestic students. Applications are processed on a rolling basis. Application fee: $50. *Expenses:* Tuition, state resident: full-time $8592; part-time $358 per credit hour. Tuition, nonresident: full-time $16,800; part-time $700 per credit hour. *Required fees:* $602; $22 per credit. $72 per term. *Financial support:* Teaching assistantships with full tuition reimbursements, career-related internships or fieldwork, Federal Work-Study, scholarships/grants, health care benefits, and unspecified assistantships available. Support available to part-time students. Financial award application deadline: 5/15; financial award applicants required to submit FAFSA. *Faculty research:* School administration, school/college articulation. *Unit head:* Dr. Ellen Bigler, Chair, 401-456-8170. *Application contact:* Graduate Studies, 401-456-8700. Web site: http://www.ric.edu/educationalStudies/.

Rider University, Department of Graduate Education, Leadership and Counseling, Teacher Certification Program, Lawrenceville, NJ 08648-3001. Offers business education (Certificate); elementary education (Certificate); English as a second language (Certificate); English education (Certificate); mathematics education (Certificate); preschool to grade 3 (Certificate); science education (Certificate); social studies education (Certificate); world languages (Certificate), including French, German, Spanish. Part-time programs available. *Degree requirements:* For Certificate, internship, professional portfolio. *Entrance requirements:* For degree, PRAXIS, resume. Additional exam requirements/recommendations for international students: Required—TOEFL (minimum score 550 paper-based; 213 computer-based). Electronic applications accepted. *Expenses: Tuition:* Full-time $32,820; part-time $710 per credit. *Required fees:* $350; $35 per course. Tuition and fees vary according to campus/location and program. *Faculty research:* Conceptual foundations for optimal development of creativity; creative theory, cognitive processes in mathematics learning, teacher collaboration.

Rutgers, The State University of New Jersey, Camden, Graduate School of Arts and Sciences, Program in Mathematical Sciences, Camden, NJ 08102. Offers industrial mathematics (MBS); industrial/applied mathematics (MS); mathematical computer science (MS); pure mathematics (MS); teaching in mathematical sciences (MS). Part-time and evening/weekend programs available. *Degree requirements:* For master's, comprehensive exam, thesis optional, survey paper, 30 credits. *Entrance requirements:* For master's, GRE, BS/BA in math or related subject, 2 letters of recommendation. Additional exam requirements/recommendations for international students: Required—TOEFL (minimum score 550 paper-based; 213 computer-based), IELTS. Electronic applications accepted. *Faculty research:* Differential geometry, dynamical systems, vertex operator algebra, automorphic forms, CR-structures.

Rutgers, The State University of New Jersey, New Brunswick, Graduate School of Education, Department of Learning and Teaching, Program in Mathematics Education, Piscataway, NJ 08854-8097. Offers Ed M, Ed D. Part-time programs available. Terminal master's awarded for partial completion of doctoral program. *Degree requirements:* For master's, comprehensive exam (for some programs); for doctorate, thesis/dissertation, qualifying exam. *Entrance requirements:* For master's, GRE General Test, minimum GPA of 3.0; for doctorate, GRE General Test, minimum GPA of 3.5. Additional exam requirements/recommendations for international students: Required—TOEFL. Electronic applications accepted.

Rutgers, The State University of New Jersey, New Brunswick, Graduate School of Education, Doctoral Program in Education, New Brunswick, NJ 08901. Offers educational policy (PhD); educational psychology (PhD); literacy education (PhD); mathematics education (PhD). Part-time programs available. *Degree requirements:* For doctorate, thesis/dissertation, qualifying exam. *Entrance requirements:* For doctorate, GRE General Test, GRE Subject Test (mathematics education). Additional exam requirements/recommendations for international students: Required—TOEFL (minimum score 575 paper-based; 233 computer-based; 83 iBT). Electronic applications accepted. *Faculty research:* Literacy education, math education, educational psychology, educational policy, learning sciences.

Sage Graduate School, Esteves School of Education, Program in Teaching, Troy, NY 12180-4115. Offers art education (MAT); English (MAT); mathematics (MAT); social studies (MAT). *Accreditation:* NASAD. Part-time and evening/weekend programs available. *Faculty:* 10 full-time (6 women), 6 part-time/adjunct (4 women). *Students:* 19 full-time (15 women), 20 part-time (16 women); includes 1 minority (Asian, non-Hispanic/Latino). Average age 27. 44 applicants, 36% accepted, 8 enrolled. In 2011, 37 master's awarded. *Entrance requirements:* For master's, assessment of writing skills, minimum undergraduate GPA of 2.75 overall, 3.0 in content area; current resume; 2 letters of recommendation. Additional exam requirements/recommendations for international students: Required—TOEFL (minimum score 550 paper-based; 213 computer-based). *Application deadline:* For fall admission, 8/1 for domestic students. Applications are processed on a rolling basis. Application fee: $40. *Expenses: Tuition:* Full-time $11,880; part-time $660 per credit hour. Tuition and fees vary according to program. *Financial support:* Fellowships, research assistantships, Federal Work-Study, scholarships/grants, and unspecified assistantships available. Support available to part-time students. Financial award application deadline: 3/1; financial award applicants required to submit FAFSA. *Unit head:* Dr. Lori Quigley, Dean, Esteves School of Education, 518-244-2326, Fax: 518-244-4571, E-mail: l.quigley@sage.edu. *Application contact:* Kelly Jones, Director, 518-244-2433, Fax: 518-244-6880, E-mail: jonesk4@sage.edu.

St. John Fisher College, School of Arts and Sciences, Mathematics/Science/Technology Education Program, Rochester, NY 14618-3597. Offers MS. Part-time and evening/weekend programs available. *Faculty:* 4 full-time (0 women), 5 part-time/adjunct (4 women). *Students:* 6 full-time (4 women), 53 part-time (35 women); includes 7 minority (3 Black or African American, non-Hispanic/Latino; 1 American Indian or Alaska Native, non-Hispanic/Latino; 2 Asian, non-Hispanic/Latino; 1 Two or more races, non-Hispanic/Latino). Average age 29. 29 applicants, 93% accepted, 20 enrolled. In 2011, 12 master's awarded. *Degree requirements:* For master's, thesis, capstone experience. *Entrance requirements:* For master's, 2 letters of recommendation, personal statement, current resume, interview, teaching certification. Additional exam requirements/recommendations for international students: Required—TOEFL (minimum score 575 paper-based; 233 computer-based; 80 iBT). *Application deadline:* Applications are processed on a rolling basis. Application fee: $30. Electronic applications accepted. *Expenses: Tuition:* Part-time $735 per credit. One-time fee: $50 part-time. Tuition and fees vary according to course load, degree level and program. *Financial support:* In 2011–12, 15 students received support. Scholarships/grants available. Financial award applicants required to submit FAFSA. *Faculty research:* Mathematics education, science and technology education. *Unit head:* Dr. Bernard Ricca, Graduate Director, 585-899-3866, E-mail: bricca@sjfc.edu. *Application contact:* Jose Perales, Director of Graduate Admissions, 585-385-8067, E-mail: jperales@sjfc.edu.

Saint Peter's University, Graduate Programs in Education, Jersey City, NJ 07306-5997. Offers director of school counseling services (Certificate); educational leadership (MA Ed, Ed D); middle school mathematics (Certificate); professional/associate counselor (Certificate); reading (MA Ed); school business administrator (Certificate); school counseling (MA, Certificate); special education (MA Ed, Certificate), including applied behavioral analysis (MA Ed), literacy (MA Ed), teacher of students with disabilities (Certificate); teaching (MA Ed, Certificate), including 6-8 middle school education, K-12 secondary education, K-5 elementary education. *Accreditation:* Teacher Education Accreditation Council. Part-time and evening/weekend programs available. *Degree requirements:* For master's, comprehensive exam; for doctorate, comprehensive exam, thesis/dissertation. *Entrance requirements:* For master's and doctorate, GRE or MAT. Additional exam requirements/recommendations for international students: Required—TOEFL (minimum score 79 computer-based). Electronic applications accepted.

Salem State University, School of Graduate Studies, Program in Middle School Education, Salem, MA 01970-5353. Offers humanities (M Ed); math/science (MAT). Part-time and evening/weekend programs available. *Entrance requirements:* For master's, GRE or MAT. Additional exam requirements/recommendations for international students: Required—TOEFL (minimum score 550 paper-based; 80 iBT) or IELTS (minimum score 5.5).

Salem State University, School of Graduate Studies, Program in Middle School Math, Salem, MA 01970-5353. Offers MAT. Part-time and evening/weekend programs available. *Entrance requirements:* For master's, GRE or MAT. Additional exam requirements/recommendations for international students: Required—TOEFL (minimum score 550 paper-based; 80 iBT) or IELTS (minimum score 5.5).

Salisbury University, Graduate Division, Department of Education, Salisbury, MD 21801-6837. Offers education (M Ed); education administration (M Ed); mathematics education (MSME); reading specialist (M Ed); teaching (MAT). *Accreditation:* NCATE. Part-time and evening/weekend programs available. *Faculty:* 23 full-time (13 women), 6 part-time/adjunct (5 women). *Students:* 18 full-time (12 women), 121 part-time (94 women); includes 18 minority (14 Black or African American, non-Hispanic/Latino; 1 Asian, non-Hispanic/Latino; 2 Hispanic/Latino; 1 Two or more races, non-Hispanic/Latino), 5 international. Average age 30. 31 applicants, 81% accepted, 25 enrolled. In 2011, 36 master's awarded. *Degree requirements:* For master's, comprehensive exam (for some programs), thesis optional, advanced seminars, internships, thesis research or practicum courses. *Entrance requirements:* For master's, 2 recommendations, program of study developed and signed by applicant and advisor, copy of teaching certificate (based on program), employment verification (for M Ed in educational leadership), personal statement, minimum GPA of 3.0. Additional exam requirements/recommendations for international students: Required—TOEFL (minimum score 550 paper-based; 79 iBT). *Application deadline:* For fall admission, 3/3 for domestic students; for spring admission, 10/1 for domestic students. Applications are processed on a rolling basis. Application fee: $45. Electronic applications accepted. *Expenses: Tuition, area resident:* Part-time $306 per credit hour. Tuition, state resident: part-time $306 per credit hour. Tuition, nonresident: part-time $595 per credit hour. *Required fees:* $68 per credit hour. *Financial support:* In 2011–12, 22 students received support. Career-related internships or fieldwork, institutionally sponsored loans, scholarships/grants, and unspecified assistantships available. Support available to part-time students. Financial award application deadline: 3/1; financial award applicants required to submit FAFSA. *Faculty research:* Lower Eastern Shore School Leadership Institute Program, using best practices to motivate and engage early childhood teachers to teach in high poverty/high minority schools, TRIOS Student Support Services, SU Elementary STEM Program, design. *Total annual research expenditures:* $167,000. *Unit head:* Dr. Gwen Beegle, Director, 410-543-6393, E-mail: gpbeegle@salisbury.edu. *Application contact:* Debra Clark, Executive Administrative Assistant, 410-543-6335, Fax: 410-548-2593, E-mail: djclark@salisbury.edu. Web site: http://www.salisbury.edu/educationspecialties/med.html.

San Diego State University, Graduate and Research Affairs, College of Sciences, Department of Mathematics and Statistics, San Diego, CA 92182. Offers applied mathematics (MS); mathematics (MA); mathematics and science education (PhD); statistics (MS). PhD offered jointly wtih University of California, San Diego. Part-time programs available. *Degree requirements:* For doctorate, thesis/dissertation. *Entrance requirements:* For master's, GRE General Test; for doctorate, GRE, minimum GPA of 3.25 in last 30 undergraduate semester units, minimum graduate GPA of 3.5, MSE recommendation form, 3 letters of recommendation. Additional exam requirements/recommendations for international students: Required—TOEFL. Electronic applications accepted. *Faculty research:* Teacher education in mathematics.

San Francisco State University, Division of Graduate Studies, College of Education, Department of Elementary Education, Program in Mathematics Education, San Francisco, CA 94132-1722. Offers MA. *Accreditation:* NCATE. *Unit head:* Dr. Debra Luna, Chair, 415-338-1562, E-mail: dluna@sfsu.edu. *Application contact:* Hallie Foster, Graduate Coordinator, 415-338-1562, E-mail: halcyon@sfsu.edu. Web site: http://www.coe.sfsu.edu/eed.

San Jose State University, Graduate Studies and Research, College of Science, Department of Mathematics, San Jose, CA 95192-0001. Offers applied mathematics (MS); mathematics (MA, MS); mathematics education (MA); statistics (MA). Part-time and evening/weekend programs available. *Degree requirements:* For master's, comprehensive exam, thesis (for some programs). *Entrance requirements:* For master's, GRE Subject Test. Electronic applications accepted. *Faculty research:* Artificial intelligence, algorithms, numerical analysis, software database, number theory.

Shippensburg University of Pennsylvania, School of Graduate Studies, College of Education and Human Services, Department of Teacher Education, Shippensburg, PA 17257-2299. Offers curriculum and instruction (M Ed), including biology, early childhood education, elementary education, English, geography/earth science, history, mathematics, middle level education, modern languages; reading (M Ed). *Accreditation:* NCATE. Part-time and evening/weekend programs available. *Faculty:* 14 full-time (11 women), 8 part-time/adjunct (7 women). *Students:* 16 full-time (15 women), 143 part-time (130 women); includes 11 minority (4 Black or African American, non-Hispanic/Latino; 1 Asian, non-Hispanic/Latino; 4 Hispanic/Latino; 2 Two or more races, non-Hispanic/Latino), 1 international. Average age 30. 55 applicants, 55% accepted, 25 enrolled. In 2011, 76 master's awarded. *Degree requirements:* For master's, comprehensive exam (for some programs), thesis optional, practicum or internship; capstone seminar (for some programs). *Entrance requirements:* For master's, MAT (if GPA less than 2.75), interview, 3 letters of reference, questionnaire of teaching background and future goals. Additional exam requirements/recommendations for international students: Required—TOEFL (minimum score 580 paper-based; 237 computer-based); Recommended—IELTS (minimum score 6). *Application deadline:* For fall admission, 6/1 priority date for domestic students, 4/30 for international students; for spring admission, 9/1 priority date for domestic students, 9/30 for international students. Applications are processed on a rolling basis. Application fee: $30. Electronic applications accepted. *Expenses: Tuition, area resident:* Part-time $416 per credit. Tuition, state resident: part-time $416 per credit. Tuition, nonresident: part-time $624 per credit. *Required fees:* $119 per credit. *Financial support:* In 2011–12, 5 research assistantships with full tuition reimbursements (averaging $5,000 per year) were awarded; career-related internships or fieldwork, scholarships/grants, unspecified assistantships, and resident hall director and student payroll positions also available. Support available to part-time students. Financial award application deadline: 3/1; financial award applicants required to submit FAFSA. *Unit head:* Dr. Christine A. Royce, Chairperson, 717-477-1688, Fax: 717-477-4046, E-mail: caroyc@ship.edu. *Application contact:* Jeremy R. Goshorn, Assistant Dean of Graduate Admissions, 717-477-1231, Fax: 717-477-4016, E-mail: jrgoshorn@ship.edu. Web site: http://www.ship.edu/teacher/.

Siena Heights University, Graduate College, Program in Teacher Education, Adrian, MI 49221-1796. Offers early childhood education (MA), including Montessori education; elementary education (MA), including elementary education/reading; mathematics education (MA); middle school education (MA); secondary education (MA), including secondary education/reading. Part-time programs available. *Degree requirements:* For master's, thesis, presentation. *Entrance requirements:* For master's, minimum GPA of 3.0, interview. *Expenses: Tuition:* Full-time $11,400; part-time $475 per credit hour. *Required fees:* $1000; $500 $125 per term. Tuition and fees vary according to degree level. *Faculty research:* Teaching/learning styles, outcomes-based teaching, multiple intelligences, assessment.

Simon Fraser University, Graduate Studies, Faculty of Education, Program in Mathematics Education, Burnaby, BC V5A 1S6, Canada. Offers M Ed, M Sc, PhD. *Degree requirements:* For master's, comprehensive exam or thesis; for doctorate, comprehensive exam, thesis/dissertation.

Slippery Rock University of Pennsylvania, Graduate Studies (Recruitment), College of Education, Department of Elementary Education and Early Childhood, Slippery Rock,

PA 16057-1383. Offers math/science (K-8) (M Ed); reading (M Ed). *Accreditation:* NCATE. Part-time and evening/weekend programs available. Postbaccalaureate distance learning degree programs offered. *Faculty:* 3 full-time (all women). *Students:* 2 full-time (both women), 33 part-time (all women); includes 1 minority (Two or more races, non-Hispanic/Latino). Average age 28. 55 applicants, 69% accepted, 11 enrolled. In 2011, 33 degrees awarded. *Entrance requirements:* For master's, GRE General Test, MAT, minimum GPA of 3.0, resume, teaching certification, letters of recommendation, transcripts (depending on program). Additional exam requirements/recommendations for international students: Required—TOEFL (minimum score 550 paper-based; 213 computer-based; 80 iBT). *Application deadline:* For fall admission, 3/1 priority date for domestic students, 5/1 for international students; for spring admission, 10/1 priority date for domestic students, 9/1 for international students. Applications are processed on a rolling basis. Application fee: $25 ($30 for international students). Electronic applications accepted. *Expenses:* Contact institution. *Financial support:* Career-related internships or fieldwork, Federal Work-Study, institutionally sponsored loans, scholarships/grants, tuition waivers (partial), and unspecified assistantships available. Support available to part-time students. Financial award application deadline: 5/1; financial award applicants required to submit FAFSA. *Unit head:* Dr. Suzanne Rose, Graduate Coordinator, 724-738-2863, Fax: 724-738-4987, E-mail: suzanne.rose@sru.edu. *Application contact:* Angela Barrett, Director of Graduate Admissions, 724-738-2051, Fax: 724-738-2146, E-mail: graduate.admissions@sru.edu.

Slippery Rock University of Pennsylvania, Graduate Studies (Recruitment), College of Education, Department of Secondary Education/Foundations of Education, Slippery Rock, PA 16057-1383. Offers educational leadership (M Ed); secondary education in English (M Ed); secondary education in math/science (M Ed); secondary education in social studies (M Ed). *Accreditation:* NCATE. Part-time and evening/weekend programs available. *Faculty:* 9 full-time (4 women), 3 part-time/adjunct (0 women). *Students:* 64 full-time (34 women), 16 part-time (8 women); includes 2 minority (1 Asian, non-Hispanic/Latino; 1 Two or more races, non-Hispanic/Latino). Average age 28. 68 applicants, 76% accepted, 27 enrolled. In 2011, 54 degrees awarded. *Degree requirements:* For master's, comprehensive exam, thesis (for some programs). *Entrance requirements:* For master's, GRE General Test, MAT, minimum GPA of 2.8 (depending on program). Additional exam requirements/recommendations for international students: Required—TOEFL (minimum score 550 paper-based; 213 computer-based; 80 iBT). *Application deadline:* For fall admission, 3/1 priority date for domestic students, 5/1 for international students; for spring admission, 10/1 priority date for domestic students, 9/1 for international students. Applications are processed on a rolling basis. Application fee: $25 ($30 for international students). Electronic applications accepted. *Expenses:* Tuition, state resident: full-time $7488; part-time $416 per credit. Tuition, nonresident: full-time $11,232; part-time $624 per credit. *International tuition:* $11,146 full-time. *Required fees:* $2722; $140 per credit. Tuition and fees vary according to degree level and program. *Financial support:* Career-related internships or fieldwork, Federal Work-Study, institutionally sponsored loans, scholarships/grants, tuition waivers (partial), and unspecified assistantships available. Support available to part-time students. Financial award application deadline: 5/1; financial award applicants required to submit FAFSA. *Unit head:* Dr. Jeffrey Lehman, Graduate Coordinator, 724-738-2311, Fax: 724-738-4987, E-mail: jeffrey.lehman@sru.edu. *Application contact:* Angela Barrett, Interim Director of Graduate Studies, 724-738-2051, Fax: 724-738-2146, E-mail: graduate.admissions@sru.edu.

Smith College, Graduate and Special Programs, Department of Education and Child Study, Program in Secondary Education, Northampton, MA 01063. Offers biological sciences education (MAT); chemistry education (MAT); English education (MAT); French education (MAT); geology education (MAT); government education (MAT); history education (MAT); mathematics education (MAT); physics education (MAT); Spanish education (MAT). Part-time programs available. *Faculty:* 6 full-time (4 women), 3 part-time/adjunct (2 women). *Students:* 11 full-time (8 women), 3 part-time (all women); includes 2 minority (1 Asian, non-Hispanic/Latino; 1 Hispanic/Latino). Average age 26. 21 applicants, 95% accepted, 12 enrolled. In 2011, 2 master's awarded. *Entrance requirements:* For master's, GRE. Additional exam requirements/recommendations for international students: Required—TOEFL (minimum score 590 paper-based; 243 computer-based; 97 iBT). *Application deadline:* For fall admission, 4/1 for domestic students, 1/15 for international students; for spring admission, 12/1 for domestic students. Application fee: $60. *Expenses: Tuition:* Full-time $14,925; part-time $1245 per credit. *Financial support:* In 2011–12, 13 students received support. Career-related internships or fieldwork, institutionally sponsored loans, and scholarships/grants available. Support available to part-time students. Financial award application deadline: 1/15; financial award applicants required to submit CSS PROFILE or FAFSA. *Unit head:* Rosetta Cohen, Graduate Student Advisor, 413-585-3266, E-mail: rcohen@smith.edu. *Application contact:* Ruth Morgan, Administrative Assistant, 413-585-3050, Fax: 413-585-3054, E-mail: gradstdy@smith.edu. Web site: http://www.smith.edu/educ/.

Smith College, Graduate and Special Programs, Department of Mathematics, Northampton, MA 01063. Offers MAT. Part-time programs available. *Faculty:* 12 full-time (5 women). *Students:* 1 (woman) full-time, 1 (woman) part-time. Average age 29. 2 applicants, 100% accepted, 2 enrolled. *Entrance requirements:* For master's, GRE. Additional exam requirements/recommendations for international students: Required—TOEFL (minimum score 590 paper-based; 243 computer-based; 97 iBT). *Application deadline:* For fall admission, 4/1 for domestic students, 1/5 for international students; for spring admission, 2/1 for domestic students. Application fee: $60. *Expenses: Tuition:* Full-time $14,925; part-time $1245 per credit. *Financial support:* In 2011–12, 2 students received support. Career-related internships or fieldwork, institutionally sponsored loans, and scholarships/grants available. Support available to part-time students. Financial award application deadline: 1/15. *Unit head:* Mary Murphy, Graduate Adviser, 413-585-3876, E-mail: memurphy@smith.edu. *Application contact:* Ruth Morgan, Administrative Assistant, 413-585-3050, Fax: 413-585-3054, E-mail: gradstdy@smith.edu. Web site: http://www.math.smith.edu/.

South Carolina State University, School of Graduate Studies, Department of Education, Orangeburg, SC 29117-0001. Offers counseling education (M Ed); early childhood and special education (M Ed); early childhood education (MAT); educational leadership (Ed D, Ed S); elementary education (M Ed, MAT); engineering (MAT); general science (MAT); mathematics (MAT); secondary education (M Ed), including biology education, business education, counselor education, English education, home economics education, industrial education, mathematics education, science education, social studies education; special education (M Ed), including emotionally handicapped, learning disabilities, mentally handicapped. *Accreditation:* NCATE. Part-time and evening/weekend programs available. *Faculty:* 9 full-time (6 women), 6 part-time/adjunct (2 women). *Students:* 34 full-time (29 women), 50 part-time (40 women); includes 74 minority (72 Black or African American, non-Hispanic/Latino; 1 Asian, non-Hispanic/Latino; 1 Hispanic/Latino). Average age 34. 23 applicants, 91% accepted, 14 enrolled. In 2011, 11 master's awarded. *Degree requirements:* For master's, thesis optional, departmental qualifying exam. *Entrance requirements:* For master's, GRE General Test, NTE, interview, teaching certificate. *Application deadline:* For fall admission, 6/15 priority date for domestic students, 6/15 for international students; for spring admission, 11/1 for domestic and international students. Applications are processed on a rolling basis. Application fee: $25. Electronic applications accepted. *Expenses:* Tuition, state resident: full-time $8688; part-time $514 per credit hour. Tuition, nonresident: full-time $17,600; part-time $1009 per credit hour. *Required fees:* $570. *Financial support:* In 2011–12, 3 fellowships (averaging $5,020 per year) were awarded; career-related internships or fieldwork, Federal Work-Study, and institutionally sponsored loans also available. Financial award application deadline: 6/1. *Faculty research:* Critical thinking, child abuse, stress, test-taking skills, conflict resolution, mainstreaming. *Unit head:* Dr. Charlie Spell, Interim Chair, 803-536-7098, Fax: 803-516-4568, E-mail: cspell@scsu.edu. *Application contact:* Annette Hazzard-Jones, Program Coordinator II, 803-536-8809, Fax: 803-536-8812, E-mail: zs_ahazzard@scsu.edu.

Southeastern Oklahoma State University, School of Education, Durant, OK 74701-0609. Offers math specialist (M Ed); reading specialist (M Ed); school administration (M Ed); school counseling (M Ed); special education (M Ed). *Accreditation:* NCATE. Part-time and evening/weekend programs available. *Faculty:* 52 full-time (19 women), 1 (woman) part-time/adjunct. *Students:* 15 full-time (11 women), 54 part-time (40 women); includes 24 minority (2 Black or African American, non-Hispanic/Latino; 16 American Indian or Alaska Native, non-Hispanic/Latino; 6 Hispanic/Latino). Average age 34. 31 applicants, 94% accepted, 29 enrolled. *Degree requirements:* For master's, comprehensive exam, thesis optional, portfolio (M Ed). *Entrance requirements:* For master's, GRE General Test (MBS), minimum GPA of 3.0 in last 60 hours or 2.75 overall. Additional exam requirements/recommendations for international students: Required—TOEFL (minimum score 550 paper-based; 213 computer-based; 79 iBT). *Application deadline:* For fall admission, 8/1 for domestic students, 6/1 for international students; for spring admission, 1/5 for domestic students, 11/1 for international students. Application fee: $20 ($55 for international students). Electronic applications accepted. *Expenses:* Tuition, state resident: full-time $3537; part-time $173.95 per credit hour. Tuition, nonresident: full-time $8673; part-time $459.30 per credit hour. *Required fees:* $22.55 per credit hour. *Financial support:* In 2011–12, 1 teaching assistantship with full tuition reimbursement (averaging $5,000 per year) was awarded; Federal Work-Study, institutionally sponsored loans, and tuition waivers (partial) also available. Support available to part-time students. Financial award application deadline: 6/15; financial award applicants required to submit FAFSA. *Unit head:* Dr. John Love, M Ed Coordinator, 580-745-2226, Fax: 580-745-7508, E-mail: jlove@se.edu. *Application contact:* Carrie Williamson, Graduate Secretary, 580-745-2220, Fax: 580-745-7474, E-mail: cwilliamson@se.edu. Web site: http://www.se.edu/graduate-programs/master-of-education/.

Southern Illinois University Edwardsville, Graduate School, College of Arts and Sciences, Department of Mathematics and Statistics, Edwardsville, IL 62026. Offers mathematics (MS), including computational mathematics, postsecondary mathematics education, pure math, statistics and operations research. Part-time programs available. *Faculty:* 19 full-time (5 women). *Students:* 13 full-time (2 women), 30 part-time (17 women); includes 2 minority (both Black or African American, non-Hispanic/Latino), 12 international. 34 applicants, 47% accepted. In 2011, 14 master's awarded. *Degree requirements:* For master's, thesis (for some programs), research paper/project. *Entrance requirements:* Additional exam requirements/recommendations for international students: Required—TOEFL (minimum score 550 paper-based; 213 computer-based; 79 iBT), IELTS (minimum score 6.5). *Application deadline:* For fall admission, 7/22 for domestic students, 6/1 for international students; for spring admission, 12/9 for domestic students, 10/1 for international students. Applications are processed on a rolling basis. Application fee: $30. Electronic applications accepted. Tuition and fees vary according to course load and program. *Financial support:* In 2011–12, 3 research assistantships with full tuition reimbursements (averaging $9,927 per year), 22 teaching assistantships with full tuition reimbursements (averaging $9,927 per year) were awarded; fellowships with full tuition reimbursements, institutionally sponsored loans, scholarships/grants, and unspecified assistantships also available. Financial award application deadline: 3/1; financial award applicants required to submit FAFSA. *Unit head:* Dr. Krzysztof Jarosz, Chair, 618-650-2354, E-mail: kjarosz@siue.edu. *Application contact:* Dr. Adam Weyhaupt, Director, 618-650-2220, E-mail: aweyhau@siue.edu. Web site: http://www.siue.edu/artsandsciences/math/.

Southern Illinois University Edwardsville, Graduate School, School of Education, Department of Curriculum and Instruction, Program in Secondary Education, Edwardsville, IL 62026. Offers art (MS Ed); biology (MS Ed); chemistry (MS Ed); earth and space sciences (MS Ed); English/language arts (MS Ed); foreign languages (MS Ed); history (MS Ed); mathematics (MS Ed); physics (MS Ed). *Accreditation:* NCATE. Part-time and evening/weekend programs available. *Students:* 1 full-time (0 women), 42 part-time (33 women); includes 2 minority (both Black or African American, non-Hispanic/Latino). 16 applicants, 31% accepted. In 2011, 8 master's awarded. *Degree requirements:* For master's, comprehensive exam (for some programs), final exam/paper. *Entrance requirements:* Additional exam requirements/recommendations for international students: Required—TOEFL (minimum score 550 paper-based; 213 computer-based; 79 iBT), IELTS (minimum score 6.5). *Application deadline:* For fall admission, 7/22 for domestic students, 6/1 for international students; for spring admission, 12/9 for domestic students, 10/1 for international students. Applications are processed on a rolling basis. Application fee: $30. Electronic applications accepted. Tuition and fees vary according to course load and program. *Financial support:* Fellowships, research assistantships, teaching assistantships, institutionally sponsored loans, scholarships/grants, and unspecified assistantships available. Financial award application deadline: 3/1; financial award applicants required to submit FAFSA. *Unit head:* Dr. Susan Breck, Director, 618-650-3444, E-mail: sbreck@siue.edu. *Application contact:* Dr. Michelle Robinson, Coordinator of Graduate Recruitment, 618-650-2811, Fax: 618-650-3523, E-mail: michero@siue.edu. Web site: http://www.siue.edu/education/ci/.

Southern University and Agricultural and Mechanical College, Graduate School, Department of Science/Mathematics Education, Baton Rouge, LA 70813. Offers PhD. *Accreditation:* NCATE. *Degree requirements:* For doctorate, thesis/dissertation. *Entrance requirements:* For doctorate, GRE General Test. Additional exam requirements/recommendations for international students: Required—TOEFL (minimum score 525 paper-based; 193 computer-based). *Faculty research:* Performance assessment in science/mathematics education, equity in science/mathematics education, technology and distance learning, science/mathematics concept formation, cognitive themes, problem solving in science/mathematics education.

Southwestern Oklahoma State University, College of Arts and Sciences, Department of Mathematics, Weatherford, OK 73096-3098. Offers M Ed. Part-time programs available. *Degree requirements:* For master's, exam. *Entrance requirements:* For master's, GRE General Test or minimum undergraduate GPA of 3.0. Additional exam requirements/recommendations for international students: Required—TOEFL.

Southwest Minnesota State University, Department of Education, Marshall, MN 56258. Offers ESL (MS); math (MS); reading (MS); special education (MS), including developmental disabilities, early childhood education, emotional behavioral disorders, learning disabilities; teaching, learning and leadership (MS). Part-time and evening/weekend programs available. Postbaccalaureate distance learning degree programs offered (no on-campus study). *Entrance requirements:* Additional exam requirements/recommendations for international students: Required—TOEFL or IELTS;

Recommended—TOEFL (minimum score 550 paper-based; 213 computer-based; 80 iBT), IELTS.

Stanford University, School of Education, Program in Curriculum Studies and Teacher Education, Stanford, CA 94305-9991. Offers art education (MA, PhD); dance education (MA); English education (MA, PhD); general curriculum studies (MA, PhD); mathematics education (MA, PhD); science education (MA, PhD); social studies education (PhD); teacher education (MA, PhD). *Degree requirements:* For master's, thesis (for some programs); for doctorate, thesis/dissertation. *Entrance requirements:* For master's and doctorate, GRE General Test. Electronic applications accepted. *Expenses: Tuition:* Full-time $40,050; part-time $890 per credit.

Stanford University, School of Education, Teacher Education Program, Stanford, CA 94305-9991. Offers English education (MA); languages education (MA); mathematics education (MA); science education (MA); social studies education (MA). *Degree requirements:* For master's, thesis. *Entrance requirements:* For master's, GRE General Test. Electronic applications accepted. *Expenses: Tuition:* Full-time $40,050; part-time $890 per credit.

State University of New York at Binghamton, Graduate School, School of Education, Program in Adolescence Education, Binghamton, NY 13902-6000. Offers biology education (MAT, MS Ed, MST); earth science education (MAT, MS Ed, MST); English education (MAT, MS Ed, MST); French education (MAT, MST); mathematical sciences education (MAT, MS Ed, MST); physics (MAT, MS Ed, MST); social studies (MAT, MS Ed, MST); Spanish education (MAT, MST). *Accreditation:* Teacher Education Accreditation Council. Part-time and evening/weekend programs available. *Students:* 98 full-time (66 women), 13 part-time (11 women); includes 2 minority (1 Black or African American, non-Hispanic/Latino; 1 Hispanic/Latino). Average age 26. 73 applicants, 70% accepted, 35 enrolled. In 2011, 58 master's awarded. *Entrance requirements:* For master's, GRE General Test. Additional exam requirements/recommendations for international students: Required—TOEFL (minimum score 550 paper-based; 213 computer-based; 80 iBT). *Application deadline:* For fall admission, 2/1 priority date for domestic students, 2/1 for international students; for spring admission, 10/15 priority date for domestic students, 10/15 for international students. Applications are processed on a rolling basis. Application fee: $60. Electronic applications accepted. *Financial support:* In 2011–12, 4 students received support, including 1 fellowship with partial tuition reimbursement available (averaging $12,000 per year); career-related internships or fieldwork, Federal Work-Study, institutionally sponsored loans, scholarships/grants, health care benefits, tuition waivers (full), and unspecified assistantships also available. Financial award application deadline: 2/15; financial award applicants required to submit FAFSA. *Unit head:* Dr. S. G. Grant, Dean of School of Education, 607-777-7329, E-mail: sggrant@binghamton.edu. *Application contact:* Catherine Smith, Recruiting and Admissions Coordinator, 607-777-2151, Fax: 607-777-2501, E-mail: cmsmith@binghamton.edu.

State University of New York at Plattsburgh, Division of Education, Health, and Human Services, Program in Teacher Education: Adolescence MST, Plattsburgh, NY 12901-2681. Offers adolescence education (MST); biology 7-12 (MST); chemistry 7-12 (MST); earth science 7-12 (MST); English 7-12 (MST); French 7-12 (MST); mathematics 7-12 (MST); physics 7-12 (MST); social studies 7-12 (MST); Spanish 7-12 (MST). *Accreditation:* Teacher Education Accreditation Council. Part-time and evening/weekend programs available. *Students:* 53 full-time (26 women), 5 part-time (4 women). Average age 29. *Entrance requirements:* For master's, minimum GPA of 2.75. Additional exam requirements/recommendations for international students: Required—TOEFL. *Application deadline:* For fall admission, 2/15 priority date for domestic students. Applications are processed on a rolling basis. Application fee: $75. *Financial support:* Application deadline: 4/15; applicants required to submit FAFSA. *Unit head:* Dr. Robert Ackland, Coordinator, 518-564-5131, E-mail: acklanrt@plattsburgh.edu. *Application contact:* Marguerite Adelman, Assistant Director, Graduate Admissions, 518-564-4723, Fax: 518-564-4722, E-mail: adelmaml@plattsburgh.edu.

State University of New York College at Cortland, Graduate Studies, School of Arts and Sciences, Programs in Adolescence Education, Cortland, NY 13045. Offers biology (MAT, MS Ed); chemistry (MAT, MS Ed); earth science (MAT, MS Ed); English (MS Ed); French (MS Ed); mathematics (MAT, MS Ed); physics (MAT, MS Ed); social studies (MS Ed); Spanish (MS Ed). *Accreditation:* NCATE. Part-time and evening/weekend programs available. *Degree requirements:* For master's, one foreign language, comprehensive exam (for some programs), thesis (for some programs). *Entrance requirements:* For master's, GRE General Test.

State University of New York College at Potsdam, School of Education and Professional Studies, Program in Secondary Education, Potsdam, NY 13676. Offers English (MST); mathematics (with grades 5-6 extension) (MST); science (MST), including biology, chemistry, earth science, physics; Social Studies (with grades 5-6 extension) (MST). *Accreditation:* NCATE. *Faculty:* 9 full-time (3 women), 3 part-time/adjunct (2 women). *Students:* 32 full-time (17 women), 1 part-time (0 women); includes 2 minority (1 Black or African American, non-Hispanic/Latino; 1 Asian, non-Hispanic/Latino), 3 international. 43 applicants, 88% accepted, 24 enrolled. In 2011, 43 master's awarded. *Degree requirements:* For master's, culminating experience. *Entrance requirements:* For master's, minimum GPA of 2.75 in last 60 hours of course work (3.0 for English program). Additional exam requirements/recommendations for international students: Required—TOEFL (minimum score 550 paper-based; 213 computer-based; 80 iBT), IELTS (minimum score 6). *Application deadline:* For spring admission, 3/1 for domestic and international students. Applications are processed on a rolling basis. Application fee: $50. *Expenses:* Tuition, state resident: full-time $8870; part-time $370 per credit hour. Tuition, nonresident: full-time $15,160; part-time $632 per credit hour. *Required fees:* $1066; $44.10 per credit hour. One-time fee: $3. *Financial support:* Fellowships, teaching assistantships, career-related internships or fieldwork, Federal Work-Study, scholarships/grants, and unspecified assistantships available. Support available to part-time students. Financial award application deadline: 3/1; financial award applicants required to submit FAFSA. *Unit head:* Donald C. Straight, Chairperson, 315-267-2553, Fax: 315-267-4802, E-mail: straigdc@potsdam.edu. *Application contact:* Peter Cutler, Graduate Admissions Counselor, 315-267-2165, Fax: 315-267-4802, E-mail: graduate@potsdam.edu. Web site: http://www.potsdam.edu/academics/SOEPS/SecondaryEd/index.cfm.

Stephen F. Austin State University, Graduate School, College of Sciences and Mathematics, Department of Mathematics and Statistics, Nacogdoches, TX 75962. Offers mathematics (MS); mathematics education (MS); statistics (MS). *Degree requirements:* For master's, comprehensive exam, thesis optional. *Entrance requirements:* For master's, GRE General Test, minimum GPA of 2.8 in last 60 hours, 2.5 overall. Additional exam requirements/recommendations for international students: Required—TOEFL. *Faculty research:* Kernel type estimators, fractal mappings, spline curve fitting, robust regression continua theory.

Stony Brook University, State University of New York, School of Professional Development, Stony Brook, NY 11794. Offers biology-grade 7-12 (MAT); chemistry-grade 7-12 (MAT); coaching (Graduate Certificate); coaching online (Graduate Certificate); computer integrated engineering (Graduate Certificate); earth science-grade 7-12 (MAT); educational computing (Graduate Certificate); educational leadership (Advanced Certificate); English-grade 7-12 (MAT); environmental management (Graduate Certificate); environmental/occupational health and safety (Graduate Certificate); French-grade 7-12 (MAT); German-grade 7-12 (MAT); human resource management (Graduate Certificate); human resource management online (Graduate Certificate); information systems management (Graduate Certificate); Italian-grade 7-12 (MAT); liberal studies (MA); liberal studies online (MAT); mathematics-grade 7-12 (MAT); operation research (Graduate Certificate); physics-grade 7-12 (MAT); professional studies online (MPS); school administration and supervision (Graduate Certificate); school building leadership (Graduate Certificate); school district administration (Graduate Certificate); school district business leadership (Advanced Certificate); school district leadership (Graduate Certificate); social science and the professions (MPS), including environmental waste management, human resource management; social studies-grade 7-12 (MAT); Spanish-grade 7-12 (MAT); waste management (Graduate Certificate). Part-time and evening/weekend programs available. Postbaccalaureate distance learning degree programs offered. *Degree requirements:* For master's, one foreign language, thesis or alternative.

Syracuse University, School of Education, Program in Mathematics Education, Syracuse, NY 13244. Offers mathematics education (PhD); mathematics education: preparation 7-12 (MS). Part-time programs available. *Students:* 7 full-time (4 women), 3 part-time (all women); includes 1 minority (Hispanic/Latino), 1 international. Average age 34. 12 applicants, 58% accepted, 4 enrolled. In 2011, 7 master's, 1 doctorate awarded. *Degree requirements:* For master's, thesis or alternative; for doctorate, thesis/dissertation. *Entrance requirements:* For master's, GRE (for assistantship applicants); for doctorate, GRE, MS. Additional exam requirements/recommendations for international students: Required—TOEFL (minimum score 100 iBT). *Application deadline:* For fall admission, 2/1 priority date for domestic students, 2/1 for international students; for spring admission, 10/15 for domestic and international students. Applications are processed on a rolling basis. Application fee: $75. Electronic applications accepted. *Expenses: Tuition:* Part-time $1206 per credit. *Financial support:* Fellowships with full tuition reimbursements and teaching assistantships with full and partial tuition reimbursements available. Financial award application deadline: 1/1; financial award applicants required to submit FAFSA. *Unit head:* Dr. Joanna Masingila, Chair, 315-443-1483, E-mail: jomasing@syr.edu. *Application contact:* Laurie Deyo, Graduate Recruiter, School of Education, 315-443-2505, E-mail: e-gradrcrt@syr.edu. Web site: http://soe.syr.edu/.

Teachers College, Columbia University, Graduate Faculty of Education, Department of Math, Science and Technology, Program in Mathematics Education, New York, NY 10027. Offers Ed M, MA, MS, Ed D, Ed DCT, PhD. *Accreditation:* NCATE. *Faculty:* 4 full-time (1 woman), 9 part-time/adjunct (0 women). *Students:* 56 full-time (29 women), 94 part-time (53 women); includes 62 minority (22 Black or African American, non-Hispanic/Latino; 28 Asian, non-Hispanic/Latino; 9 Hispanic/Latino; 3 Two or more races, non-Hispanic/Latino), 25 international. Average age 32. 97 applicants, 78% accepted, 27 enrolled. In 2011, 61 master's, 18 doctorates awarded. *Degree requirements:* For doctorate, thesis/dissertation. *Entrance requirements:* For master's, undergraduate major or minor in mathematics; for doctorate, MA in mathematics or mathematics education. *Application deadline:* For fall admission, 12/15 for domestic students. Applications are processed on a rolling basis. Application fee: $65. Electronic applications accepted. *Financial support:* Career-related internships or fieldwork, Federal Work-Study, institutionally sponsored loans, and tuition waivers (full and partial) available. Support available to part-time students. Financial award applicants required to submit FAFSA. *Faculty research:* Problem solving, curriculum development, international education, history of mathematics. *Unit head:* Prof. Bruce R. Vogeli, Program Coordinator, 212-678-3381, Fax: 212-678-8319, E-mail: tcmath@tc.edu. *Application contact:* Deanna Ghozati, Assistant Director of Admission, 212-678-4018, Fax: 212-678-4171, E-mail: ghozati@tc.edu. Web site: http://www.tc.edu/mst/mathed/.

Temple University, College of Education, Department of Curriculum, Instruction, and Technology in Education, Philadelphia, PA 19122-6096. Offers applied behavioral analysis (MS Ed); career and technical education (MS Ed); early childhood education and elementary education (MS Ed); English education (MS Ed); language arts education (Ed D); math/science education (Ed D); mathematics education (MS Ed); science education (MS Ed); second and foreign language education (MS Ed); special education (MS Ed); teaching English as a second language (MS Ed). Part-time and evening/weekend programs available. *Faculty:* 19 full-time (12 women). *Students:* 30 full-time (23 women), 86 part-time (69 women); includes 12 minority (4 Black or African American, non-Hispanic/Latino; 2 Asian, non-Hispanic/Latino; 5 Hispanic/Latino; 1 Two or more races, non-Hispanic/Latino), 5 international. 82 applicants, 71% accepted, 51 enrolled. In 2011, 181 master's, 16 doctorates awarded. Terminal master's awarded for partial completion of doctoral program. *Degree requirements:* For master's, thesis or alternative; for doctorate, thesis/dissertation. *Entrance requirements:* For master's and doctorate, GRE General Test or MAT, minimum GPA of 3.0. Additional exam requirements/recommendations for international students: Required—TOEFL (minimum score 550 paper-based; 213 computer-based; 79 iBT). *Application deadline:* For fall admission, 4/1 for domestic students, 12/15 for international students; for spring admission, 10/1 for domestic students, 8/1 for international students. Application fee: $50. Electronic applications accepted. *Expenses:* Tuition, state resident: full-time $12,366; part-time $687 per credit hour. Tuition, nonresident: full-time $17,298; part-time $961 per credit hour. *Required fees:* $590; $213 per year. *Financial support:* Fellowships, research assistantships with full tuition reimbursements, and teaching assistantships with full tuition reimbursements available. Financial award application deadline: 1/15; financial award applicants required to submit FAFSA. *Faculty research:* School improvement, problem-solving, literacy, language development. *Unit head:* Dr. Michael W. Smith, Chair, 215-204-6387, Fax: 215-204-1414, E-mail: mwsmith@temple.edu. *Application contact:* Dr. Margo Greicar, Director for Graduate Academic and Student Affairs, 215-204-8011, Fax: 215-204-4383, E-mail: margo.greicar@temple.edu. Web site: http://www.temple.edu/education/cite/.

Texas A&M University, College of Education and Human Development, Department of Teaching, Learning, and Culture, College Station, TX 77843. Offers culture and curriculum (M Ed, MS); curriculum and instruction (PhD); English as a second language (M Ed, MS, PhD); mathematics education (M Ed, MS, PhD); reading and language arts education (M Ed, MS, PhD); science education (M Ed, MS, PhD); urban education (M Ed, MS, PhD). Part-time programs available. *Faculty:* 30. *Students:* 163 full-time (119 women), 226 part-time (185 women); includes 108 minority (56 Black or African American, non-Hispanic/Latino; 2 American Indian or Alaska Native, non-Hispanic/Latino; 6 Asian, non-Hispanic/Latino; 37 Hispanic/Latino; 7 Two or more races, non-Hispanic/Latino), 62 international. Average age 36. In 2011, 107 master's, 44 doctorates awarded. *Degree requirements:* For master's, comprehensive exam, thesis (for some programs); for doctorate, comprehensive exam, thesis/dissertation. *Entrance requirements:* For master's, GRE General Test, minimum GPA of 3.0; for doctorate, GRE General Test, 3 years of teaching experience. Additional exam requirements/recommendations for international students: Required—TOEFL (minimum score 550 paper-based; 213 computer-based). *Application deadline:* For fall admission, 1/15 priority date for domestic students, 1/15 for international students; for spring admission, 9/15 priority date for domestic students, 9/15 for international students. Applications are processed on a rolling basis. Application fee: $50 ($75 for international students).

Electronic applications accepted. *Expenses:* Tuition, state resident: full-time $5437; part-time $226.55 per credit hour. Tuition, nonresident: full-time $12,949; part-time $539.55 per credit hour. *Required fees:* $2741. *Financial support:* In 2011–12, fellowships with partial tuition reimbursements (averaging $3,000 per year), teaching assistantships with partial tuition reimbursements (averaging $7,200 per year) were awarded; research assistantships with partial tuition reimbursements, career-related internships or fieldwork, Federal Work-Study, institutionally sponsored loans, scholarships/grants, tuition waivers (partial), and unspecified assistantships also available. Support available to part-time students. Financial award application deadline: 4/1; financial award applicants required to submit FAFSA. *Unit head:* Dr. Yeping Li, Head, 979-845-8384, Fax: 979-845-9663, E-mail: yepingli@tamu.edu. *Application contact:* Kerri Smith, Senior Academic Advisor II, 979-845-8382, Fax: 979-845-9663, E-mail: krsmith@tamu.edu. Web site: http://tlac.tamu.edu.

Texas A&M University–Corpus Christi, Graduate Studies and Research, College of Science and Technology, Program in Mathematics, Corpus Christi, TX 78412-5503. Offers applied and computational mathematics (MS); curriculum content (MS). Part-time programs available. *Degree requirements:* For master's, thesis (for some programs). *Entrance requirements:* For master's, 2 letters of recommendation.

Texas State University–San Marcos, Graduate School, College of Science and Engineering, Department of Mathematics, Doctoral Program in Mathematics Education, San Marcos, TX 78666. Offers PhD. *Faculty:* 15 full-time (6 women), 1 part-time/adjunct. *Students:* 18 full-time (13 women), 4 part-time (2 women); includes 2 minority (1 Black or African American, non-Hispanic/Latino; 1 Hispanic/Latino), 4 international. Average age 33. 14 applicants, 57% accepted, 4 enrolled. In 2011, 1 doctorate awarded. *Degree requirements:* For doctorate, comprehensive exam, thesis/dissertation. *Entrance requirements:* For doctorate, GRE General Test; GRE Subject Test in mathematics (minimum score in 75th percentile), bachelor's degree or higher in mathematics, mathematics education, or related field; minimum GPA of 3.0 in last 60 hours of undergraduate work. Additional exam requirements/recommendations for international students: Required—TOEFL (minimum score 550 paper-based; 213 computer-based; 78 iBT). *Application deadline:* For fall admission, 6/15 priority date for domestic students, 6/1 for international students; for spring admission, 10/15 priority date for domestic students, 9/1 for international students. Application fee: $40 ($90 for international students). *Expenses:* Tuition, state resident: full-time $6408; part-time $3204 per semester. Tuition, nonresident: full-time $14,832; part-time $7416 per semester. *Required fees:* $1824; $912 per semester. Tuition and fees vary according to course load. *Financial support:* In 2011–12, 4 students received support, including 6 research assistantships (averaging $20,583 per year), 18 teaching assistantships (averaging $25,146 per year); Federal Work-Study, institutionally sponsored loans, scholarships/grants, health care benefits, and unspecified assistantships also available. Support available to part-time students. *Unit head:* Dr. Nathaniel Dean, Graduate Advisor, 512-245-3555, E-mail: nd17@txstate.edu. *Application contact:* Dr. Alex White, Graduate Adviser, 512-245-2551, E-mail: aw22@txstate.edu. Web site: http://www.math.txstate.edu/degrees-programs/phd.html.

Texas State University–San Marcos, Graduate School, College of Science and Engineering, Department of Mathematics, Program in Middle School Mathematics Teaching, San Marcos, TX 78666. Offers M Ed. Part-time programs available. *Faculty:* 3 full-time (2 women). *Students:* 1 (woman) full-time, 8 part-time (7 women); includes 2 minority (both Hispanic/Latino). Average age 38. In 2011, 12 master's awarded. *Degree requirements:* For master's, comprehensive exam. *Entrance requirements:* For master's, GRE, minimum GPA of 2.75 in last 60 hours of undergraduate course work. Additional exam requirements/recommendations for international students: Required—TOEFL (minimum score 550 paper-based; 213 computer-based; 78 iBT). *Application deadline:* For fall admission, 6/15 priority date for domestic students, 6/1 for international students; for spring admission, 10/15 priority date for domestic students, 10/1 for international students. Applications are processed on a rolling basis. Application fee: $40 ($90 for international students). Electronic applications accepted. *Expenses:* Tuition, state resident: full-time $6408; part-time $3204 per semester. Tuition, nonresident: full-time $14,832; part-time $7416 per semester. *Required fees:* $1824; $912 per semester. Tuition and fees vary according to course load. *Financial support:* In 2011–12, 3 students received support, including 1 teaching assistantship (averaging $12,510 per year); Federal Work-Study and institutionally sponsored loans also available. Support available to part-time students. Financial award application deadline: 4/1; financial award applicants required to submit FAFSA. *Unit head:* Dr. Nathaniel Dean, Graduate Advisor, 512-245-3555, Fax: 512-245-3425, E-mail: nd17@txstaate.edu. *Application contact:* Dr. Gregory Passty, Graduate Adviser, 512-245-3446, Fax: 512-245-3425, E-mail: passty@txstate.edu. Web site: http://www.math.txstate.edu/degrees-programs/masters/middle-school.html.

Texas State University–San Marcos, Graduate School, Interdisciplinary Studies Program in Elementary Mathematics, Science, and Technology, San Marcos, TX 78666. Offers MSIS. *Students:* 2 full-time (both women), 2 part-time (both women). Average age 32. 5 applicants, 40% accepted, 2 enrolled. *Degree requirements:* For master's, comprehensive exam, thesis optional. *Entrance requirements:* For master's, minimum GPA of 2.75 in the last 60 hours of undergraduate work. Additional exam requirements/recommendations for international students: Required—TOEFL (minimum score 550 paper-based; 213 computer-based; 78 iBT). *Application deadline:* For fall admission, 6/15 priority date for domestic students, 6/1 for international students; for spring admission, 10/15 priority date for domestic students, 10/1 for international students. Applications are processed on a rolling basis. Application fee: $40 ($90 for international students). Electronic applications accepted. *Expenses:* Tuition, state resident: full-time $6408; part-time $3204 per semester. Tuition, nonresident: full-time $14,832; part-time $7416 per semester. *Required fees:* $1824; $912 per semester. Tuition and fees vary according to course load. *Financial support:* Research assistantships, teaching assistantships, Federal Work-Study, institutionally sponsored loans, scholarships/grants, health care benefits, and unspecified assistantships available. Support available to part-time students. Financial award application deadline: 4/1; financial award applicants required to submit FAFSA. *Unit head:* Dr. Sandra Mody, Acting Dean, 512-245-3360, Fax: 512-245-8095, E-mail: sw04@txstate.edu. *Application contact:* Dr. J. Michael Willoughby, Dean of Graduate School, 512-245-2581, Fax: 512-245-8365, E-mail: gradcollege@txstate.edu.

Texas Woman's University, Graduate School, College of Arts and Sciences, Department of Mathematics and Computer Science, Denton, TX 76201. Offers mathematics (MA, MS); mathematics teaching (MS). Part-time and evening/weekend programs available. *Faculty:* 11 full-time (9 women), 1 part-time/adjunct (0 women). *Students:* 9 full-time (7 women), 37 part-time (30 women); includes 13 minority (1 Black or African American, non-Hispanic/Latino; 4 Asian, non-Hispanic/Latino; 8 Hispanic/Latino), 1 international. Average age 35. 10 applicants, 90% accepted, 8 enrolled. In 2011, 6 master's awarded. *Degree requirements:* For master's, comprehensive exam, thesis. *Entrance requirements:* For master's, 2 letters of reference. Additional exam requirements/recommendations for international students: Required—TOEFL (minimum score 550 paper-based; 213 computer-based; 79 iBT). *Application deadline:* For fall admission, 7/1 priority date for domestic students, 3/1 for international students; for spring admission, 12/1 priority date for domestic students, 7/1 for international students. Applications are processed on a rolling basis. Application fee: $50 ($75 for international students). Electronic applications accepted. *Expenses:* Tuition, state resident: full-time $3834; part-time $213 per credit hour. Tuition, nonresident: full-time $9468; part-time $526 per credit hour. *Required fees:* $213 per credit hour. Tuition and fees vary according to course load. *Financial support:* In 2011–12, 13 students received support, including 4 research assistantships (averaging $13,248 per year), 7 teaching assistantships (averaging $13,248 per year); career-related internships or fieldwork, Federal Work-Study, institutionally sponsored loans, scholarships/grants, traineeships, health care benefits, and unspecified assistantships also available. Support available to part-time students. Financial award application deadline: 3/1; financial award applicants required to submit FAFSA. *Faculty research:* Biopharmaceutical statistics, dynamic systems and control theory, Bayesian inference, math and computer science curriculum innovation, computer modeling of physical phenomenon. *Unit head:* Dr. Don E. Edwards, Chair, 940-898-2166, Fax: 940-898-2179, E-mail: mathcs@twu.edu. *Application contact:* Dr. Samuel Wheeler, Assistant Director of Admissions, 940-898-3188, Fax: 940-898-3081, E-mail: wheelersr@twu.edu. Web site: http://www.twu.edu/math-computer-science/.

Touro College, Graduate School of Education, New York, NY 10010. Offers bilingual programs (Advanced Certificate); education and special education (MS); gifted and talented education (Advanced Certificate); instructional technology (MS); mathematics education (MS); school leadership (MS); teaching children with autism and other severe or multiple disabilities (Advanced Certificate); teaching English to speakers of other languages (MS, Advanced Certificate); teaching literacy (MS). Part-time and evening/weekend programs available. Postbaccalaureate distance learning degree programs offered (no on-campus study). *Faculty:* 75 full-time, 131 part-time/adjunct. *Students:* 382 full-time (324 women), 3,790 part-time (3,196 women); includes 1,211 minority (537 Black or African American, non-Hispanic/Latino; 4 American Indian or Alaska Native, non-Hispanic/Latino; 187 Asian, non-Hispanic/Latino; 472 Hispanic/Latino; 3 Native Hawaiian or other Pacific Islander, non-Hispanic/Latino; 8 Two or more races, non-Hispanic/Latino), 1 international. 1,422 applicants, 50% accepted, 675 enrolled. In 2011, 6 master's, 4 other advanced degrees awarded. *Application deadline:* For fall admission, 8/26 for domestic students, 7/15 for international students; for spring admission, 12/31 for domestic students, 12/15 for international students. Applications are processed on a rolling basis. Application fee: $50. *Financial support:* Federal Work-Study available. Financial award applicants required to submit FAFSA. *Faculty research:* Equity assistance, language development, scholar communications, Latin American studies and cultural sensitivity, behavior management techniques and strategies in special education. *Unit head:* Dr. LaMar Miller, Dean, 212-463-0400 Ext. 5561, Fax: 212-462-4889, E-mail: lpmiller@touro.edu. *Application contact:* Natalie Arroyo, Admissions Assistant, 212-463-0400 Ext. 5119, E-mail: natalie.arroyo@touro.edu.

Towson University, Program in Mathematics Education, Towson, MD 21252-0001. Offers MS. *Accreditation:* NCATE. *Students:* 4 full-time (2 women), 100 part-time (74 women); includes 21 minority (15 Black or African American, non-Hispanic/Latino; 3 Asian, non-Hispanic/Latino; 2 Hispanic/Latino; 1 Two or more races, non-Hispanic/Latino), 2 international. *Entrance requirements:* For master's, current certification for teaching secondary school mathematics, minimum GPA of 3.0. *Application deadline:* Applications are processed on a rolling basis. Application fee: $50. Electronic applications accepted. *Expenses:* Tuition, state resident: part-time $337 per credit. Tuition, nonresident: part-time $709 per credit. *Required fees:* $99 per credit. *Financial support:* Application deadline: 4/1; applicants required to submit FAFSA. *Unit head:* Dr. Maureen Yarnevich, Graduate Program Director, 410-704-2988, Fax: 410-704-4143, E-mail: myarnevich@towson.edu.

Troy University, Graduate School, College of Education, Program in Postsecondary Education, Troy, AL 36082. Offers adult education (M Ed); biology (M Ed); criminal justice (M Ed); English (M Ed); foundations of education (M Ed); general science (M Ed); higher education administration (M Ed); history (M Ed); instructional technology (M Ed); mathematics (M Ed); music industry (M Ed); physical fitness (M Ed); political science (M Ed); public administration (M Ed); social science (M Ed); teaching English (M Ed). *Accreditation:* NCATE. Part-time and evening/weekend programs available. *Faculty:* 53 full-time (21 women), 22 part-time/adjunct (8 women). *Students:* 74 full-time (51 women), 166 part-time (121 women); includes 148 minority (143 Black or African American, non-Hispanic/Latino; 1 American Indian or Alaska Native, non-Hispanic/Latino; 2 Hispanic/Latino; 2 Two or more races, non-Hispanic/Latino). Average age 34. 174 applicants, 82% accepted, 88 enrolled. In 2011, 221 master's awarded. *Degree requirements:* For master's, comprehensive exam, thesis. *Entrance requirements:* For master's, MAT (minimum score 385), minimum GPA of 2.5. Additional exam requirements/recommendations for international students: Required—TOEFL (minimum score 523 paper-based; 193 computer-based; 70 iBT), IELTS (minimum score 6), or ACT COMPASS ESL (minimum listening, reading, and grammar score 270). *Application deadline:* Applications are processed on a rolling basis. Application fee: $50. Electronic applications accepted. *Expenses:* Tuition, state resident: full-time $6960; part-time $290 per credit hour. Tuition, nonresident: full-time $13,920; part-time $580 per credit hour. *Required fees:* $386 per term. *Financial support:* Available to part-time students. Applicants required to submit FAFSA. *Unit head:* Dr. Jan Oliver, Associate Professor, 334-670-3444, Fax: 334-670-3296, E-mail: oliver@troy.edu. *Application contact:* Brenda K. Campbell, Director of Graduate Admissions, 334-670-3178, Fax: 334-670-3733, E-mail: bcamp@troy.edu.

Troy University, Graduate School, College of Education, Program in Secondary Education, Troy, AL 36082. Offers 5th year biology (MS); 5th year computer science (MS); 5th year history (MS); 5th year language arts (MS); 5th year mathematics (MS); 5th year social science (MS); traditional biology (MS); traditional computer science (MS); traditional history (MS); traditional language arts (MS); traditional mathematics (MS); traditional social science (MS). *Accreditation:* NCATE. Part-time and evening/weekend programs available. *Faculty:* 4 full-time (3 women). *Students:* 14 full-time (8 women), 29 part-time (21 women); includes 9 minority (all Black or African American, non-Hispanic/Latino). Average age 28. 11 applicants, 100% accepted, 5 enrolled. In 2011, 16 master's awarded. *Degree requirements:* For master's, comprehensive exam, thesis. *Entrance requirements:* For master's, minimum GPA of 2.5, bachelor's degree. Additional exam requirements/recommendations for international students: Required—TOEFL (minimum score 523 paper-based; 193 computer-based; 70 iBT), IELTS (minimum score 6). *Application deadline:* Applications are processed on a rolling basis. Application fee: $50. Electronic applications accepted. *Expenses:* Tuition, state resident: full-time $6960; part-time $290 per credit hour. Tuition, nonresident: full-time $13,920; part-time $580 per credit hour. *Required fees:* $386 per term. *Financial support:* Career-related internships or fieldwork available. Support available to part-time students. Financial award applicants required to submit FAFSA. *Unit head:* Dr. Jan Oliver, Associate Professor, 334-670-3444, Fax: 334-670-3548, E-mail: oliver@troy.edu. *Application contact:* Brenda K. Campbell, Director of Graduate Admissions, 334-670-3178, Fax: 334-670-3733, E-mail: bcamp@troy.edu.

Union Graduate College, School of Education, Schenectady, NY 12308-3107. Offers biology (MAT, MS); chemistry (MAT); Chinese (MAT); earth science (MAT); English (MAT); French (MAT); general science (MAT); German (MAT); Greek (MAT); languages (MAT); Latin (MAT); mathematics (MAT); mathematics and technology (MS); mentoring and teacher leadership (AC); middle childhood extension (AC); national board certificate and teacher leadership (AC); physical science (MS); physics (MAT); social studies (MAT); Spanish (MAT). *Accreditation:* Teacher Education Accreditation Council. *Faculty:* 3 full-time (1 woman), 51 part-time/adjunct (24 women). *Students:* 37 full-time (26 women), 25 part-time (16 women); includes 4 minority (3 Asian, non-Hispanic/Latino; 1 Hispanic/Latino). Average age 32. 66 applicants, 83% accepted, 41 enrolled. In 2011, 47 master's, 29 other advanced degrees awarded. *Degree requirements:* For master's, thesis or project. *Entrance requirements:* For master's, minimum GPA of 3.0, letters of recommendation. Additional exam requirements/recommendations for international students: Required—TOEFL (minimum score 550 paper-based; 213 computer-based). *Application deadline:* Applications are processed on a rolling basis. Application fee: $60. Electronic applications accepted. *Expenses:* Contact institution. *Financial support:* In 2011–12, 22 students received support. Career-related internships or fieldwork, Federal Work-Study, scholarships/grants, health care benefits, and tuition waivers (partial) available. Support available to part-time students. Financial award applicants required to submit FAFSA. *Faculty research:* Transformative learning, science education, National Board Certification, teacher leadership, teacher quality. *Unit head:* Dr. Patrick Allen, Dean, 518-631-9870, Fax: 518-631-9901. *Application contact:* Christine Angley, Assistant, 518-631-9871, Fax: 518-631-9903, E-mail: angleyc@uniongraduatecollege.edu.

Universidad Autonoma de Guadalajara, Graduate Programs, Guadalajara, Mexico. Offers administrative law and justice (LL M); advertising and corporate communications (MA); architecture (M Arch); business (MBA); computational science (MCC); education (Ed M, Ed D); English-Spanish translation (MA); entrepreneurship and management (MBA); integrated management of digital animation (MA); international business (MIB); international corporate law (LL M); internet technologies (MS); manufacturing systems (MMS); occupational health (MS); philosophy (MA, PhD); power electronics (MS); quality systems (MQS); renewable energy (MS); social evaluation of projects (MBA); strategic market research (MBA); tax law (MA); teaching mathematics (MA).

University at Albany, State University of New York, College of Arts and Sciences, Department of Mathematics and Statistics, Albany, NY 12222-0001. Offers mathematics (PhD); secondary teaching (MA); statistics (MA). *Degree requirements:* For doctorate, one foreign language, thesis/dissertation. *Entrance requirements:* For doctorate, GRE General Test. Additional exam requirements/recommendations for international students: Required—TOEFL (minimum score 550 paper-based; 213 computer-based). Electronic applications accepted.

University at Buffalo, the State University of New York, Graduate School, Graduate School of Education, Department of Learning and Instruction, Buffalo, NY 14260. Offers biology education (Ed M, Certificate); chemistry education (Ed M, Certificate); childhood education (Ed M); childhood education with bilingual extension (Ed M); early childhood education (Ed M); early childhood education with bilingual extension (birth-grade 2) (Ed M); earth science education (Ed M, Certificate); educational technology and new literacies (Certificate); educational technology and new literacies (online) (Certificate); elementary education (Ed D, PhD); English education (Ed M, PhD, Certificate); English for speakers of other languages (Ed M); foreign and second language education (PhD); French education (Ed M, Certificate); general education (Ed M); German education (Ed M, Certificate); gifted education (online) (Certificate); Latin education (Ed M, Certificate); literacy teaching and learning (Certificate); literary specialist (Ed M); mathematics education (Ed M, PhD, Certificate); music education (Ed M, Certificate); physics education (Ed M, Certificate); reading education (PhD); science and the public (online) (Ed M); science education (PhD); social studies education (Ed M, Certificate); Spanish education (Ed M, Certificate); special education (PhD); teaching and leading for diversity (Certificate); teaching English to speakers of other languages (Ed M). Part-time and evening/weekend programs available. Postbaccalaureate distance learning degree programs offered (no on-campus study). *Faculty:* 32 full-time (23 women), 54 part-time/adjunct (43 women). *Students:* 294 full-time (222 women), 350 part-time (261 women); includes 75 minority (19 Black or African American, non-Hispanic/Latino; 6 American Indian or Alaska Native, non-Hispanic/Latino; 40 Asian, non-Hispanic/Latino; 10 Hispanic/Latino), 76 international. Average age 29. 548 applicants, 52% accepted, 253 enrolled. In 2011, 225 master's, 17 doctorates, 37 other advanced degrees awarded. *Degree requirements:* For master's, comprehensive exam; for doctorate, thesis/dissertation, research analysis exam, research experience component. *Entrance requirements:* For doctorate, GRE General Test or MAT, interview, writing sample, letters of recommendation. Additional exam requirements/recommendations for international students: Required—TOEFL (minimum score 600 paper-based; 96 iBT). *Application deadline:* For fall admission, 2/1 priority date for domestic students, 2/1 for international students; for spring admission, 11/15 priority date for domestic students, 10/1 for international students. Applications are processed on a rolling basis. Application fee: $50. Electronic applications accepted. *Financial support:* In 2011–12, 40 fellowships (averaging $12,991 per year), 46 research assistantships (averaging $10,986 per year) were awarded; teaching assistantships with full tuition reimbursements, career-related internships or fieldwork, Federal Work-Study, institutionally sponsored loans, scholarships/grants, and unspecified assistantships also available. Financial award application deadline: 2/28; financial award applicants required to submit FAFSA. *Faculty research:* Science assessment, foreign language teaching and learning, early learning, new literacies, gender and education. *Unit head:* Dr. Julie Sarama, Chair, 716-645-2455, Fax: 716-645-3161, E-mail: jcollins@buffalo.edu. *Application contact:* Cathy Dimino, Admissions Assistant, 716-645-2110, Fax: 716-645-7937, E-mail: cadimino@buffalo.edu.

The University of Alabama in Huntsville, School of Graduate Studies, College of Science, Department of Mathematical Sciences, Huntsville, AL 35899. Offers applied mathematics (PhD); education (MA, MS); mathematics (MA, MS). PhD offered jointly with The University of Alabama (Tuscaloosa) and The University of Alabama at Birmingham. Part-time and evening/weekend programs available. *Faculty:* 15 full-time (1 woman), 1 part-time/adjunct (0 women). *Students:* 17 full-time (8 women), 10 part-time (6 women); includes 5 minority (3 Black or African American, non-Hispanic/Latino; 1 Asian, non-Hispanic/Latino; 1 Hispanic/Latino), 5 international. Average age 28. 21 applicants, 62% accepted, 6 enrolled. In 2011, 5 master's, 1 doctorate awarded. *Degree requirements:* For master's, comprehensive exam, thesis or alternative, oral and written exams; for doctorate, comprehensive exam, thesis/dissertation, oral and written exams. *Entrance requirements:* For master's and doctorate, GRE General Test, minimum GPA of 3.0. Additional exam requirements/recommendations for international students: Required—TOEFL (minimum score 550 paper-based; 213 computer-based; 62 iBT). *Application deadline:* For fall admission, 7/15 for domestic students, 4/1 for international students; for spring admission, 11/30 for domestic students, 9/1 for international students. Applications are processed on a rolling basis. Application fee: $40 ($50 for international students). Electronic applications accepted. *Expenses:* Tuition, state resident: full-time $7830; part-time $473.50 per credit. Tuition, nonresident: full-time $18,748; part-time $1128.33 per credit. Tuition and fees vary according to course load and program. *Financial support:* In 2011–12, 14 students received support, including 1 fellowship with full tuition reimbursement available (averaging $10,000 per year), 1 research assistantship with full tuition reimbursement available (averaging $10,000 per year), 13 teaching assistantships with full tuition reimbursements available (averaging $10,314 per year); career-related internships or fieldwork, Federal Work-Study, institutionally sponsored loans, scholarships/grants, health care benefits, and unspecified assistantships also available. Support available to part-time students. Financial award application deadline: 4/1; financial award applicants required to submit FAFSA. *Faculty research:* Dynamical systems, mathematical biology, stochastic processes, numerical analysis, combinatorics. *Total annual research expenditures:* $222,669. *Unit head:* Dr. Jia Li, Chair, 256-824-6470, Fax: 256-824-6173, E-mail: li@math.uah.edu. *Application contact:* Kim Gray, Graduate Studies Admissions Coordinator, 256-824-6002, Fax: 256-824-6405, E-mail: deangrad@uah.edu. Web site: http://www.math.uah.edu/.

University of Arkansas, Graduate School, J. William Fulbright College of Arts and Sciences, Department of Mathematical Sciences, Program in Secondary Mathematics, Fayetteville, AR 72701-1201. Offers MA. *Accreditation:* NCATE. *Students:* 1 (woman) full-time, 3 part-time (1 woman). *Degree requirements:* For master's, written exam. *Application deadline:* For fall admission, 4/1 for international students; for spring admission, 10/1 for international students. Applications are processed on a rolling basis. Application fee: $40 ($50 for international students). Electronic applications accepted. *Financial support:* In 2011–12, 1 teaching assistantship was awarded; fellowships, research assistantships, career-related internships or fieldwork, and Federal Work-Study also available. Support available to part-time students. Financial award application deadline: 4/1; financial award applicants required to submit FAFSA. *Unit head:* Dr. Chaim Goodman-Strauss, Chair, 479-575-3351, Fax: 479-575-8630, E-mail: strauss@uark.edu. *Application contact:* Dr. John Ryan, Graduate Coordinator, 479-575-3351, Fax: 479-575-8630, E-mail: jryan@uark.edu. Web site: http://math.uark.edu/.

University of Arkansas at Pine Bluff, School of Education, Pine Bluff, AR 71601-2799. Offers early childhood education (M Ed); secondary education (M Ed), including English education, mathematics education, physical education, science education, social studies education; teaching (MAT). *Accreditation:* NCATE. Part-time and evening/weekend programs available. *Degree requirements:* For master's, comprehensive exam. *Entrance requirements:* For master's, GRE, minimum GPA of 2.75, NTE or Standard Arkansas Teaching Certificate. *Faculty research:* Teacher certification, accreditation, assessment, standards, portfolio development, rehabilitation, technology.

The University of British Columbia, Faculty of Education, Department of Curriculum and Pedagogy, Vancouver, BC V6T 1Z4, Canada. Offers art education (M Ed, MA); business education (MA); curriculum studies (M Ed, MA, PhD); home economics education (M Ed, MA); math education (M Ed, MA); music education (M Ed, MA); physical education (M Ed, MA); science education (M Ed, MA); social studies education (M Ed, MA); technology studies education (M Ed, MA). Part-time programs available. *Degree requirements:* For master's, thesis (MA); for doctorate, comprehensive exam, thesis/dissertation. *Entrance requirements:* Additional exam requirements/recommendations for international students: Required—TOEFL (minimum score 580 paper-based; 237 computer-based; 92 iBT). Electronic applications accepted. *Expenses:* Contact institution. *Faculty research:* School subjects, teaching and learning.

University of California, Berkeley, Graduate Division, School of Education, Group in Science and Mathematics Education, Berkeley, CA 94720-1500. Offers PhD, MA/Credential. Electronic applications accepted.

University of California, Berkeley, Graduate Division, School of Education, Programs in Education, Berkeley, CA 94720-1500. Offers development in mathematics and science (MA); education in mathematics, science, and technology (MA, PhD); human development and education (MA, PhD); special education (PhD); MA/Credential; PhD/Credential; PhD/MA. Terminal master's awarded for partial completion of doctoral program. *Degree requirements:* For master's, exam or thesis; for doctorate, thesis/dissertation, oral qualifying exam. *Entrance requirements:* For master's and doctorate, GRE General Test, minimum GPA of 3.0 during last 2 years of undergraduate course work. Electronic applications accepted. *Faculty research:* Human development, social and moral educational psychology, developmental teacher preparation.

University of California, San Diego, Office of Graduate Studies, Program in Mathematics and Science Education, La Jolla, CA 92093. Offers PhD. Program offered jointly with San Diego State University. *Entrance requirements:* For doctorate, GRE General Test. Electronic applications accepted.

University of Central Arkansas, Graduate School, College of Natural Sciences and Math, Department of Mathematics, Conway, AR 72035-0001. Offers applied mathematics (MS); math education (MA). Part-time programs available. *Faculty:* 16 full-time (4 women). *Students:* 13 full-time (7 women), 8 part-time (4 women); includes 2 minority (1 Asian, non-Hispanic/Latino; 1 Two or more races, non-Hispanic/Latino), 3 international. Average age 29. 12 applicants, 92% accepted, 8 enrolled. In 2011, 7 master's awarded. *Degree requirements:* For master's, comprehensive exam, thesis optional. *Entrance requirements:* For master's, GRE General Test, minimum GPA of 2.7. Additional exam requirements/recommendations for international students: Required—TOEFL (minimum score 550 paper-based; 213 computer-based). *Application deadline:* For fall admission, 3/1 priority date for domestic students; for spring admission, 10/1 priority date for domestic students. Applications are processed on a rolling basis. Application fee: $25 ($50 for international students). *Expenses:* Tuition, state resident: full-time $4834; part-time $398.35 per credit hour. Tuition, nonresident: full-time $8686. *Financial support:* In 2011–12, 11 teaching assistantships with partial tuition reimbursements (averaging $8,500 per year) were awarded; Federal Work-Study, scholarships/grants, and unspecified assistantships also available. Financial award application deadline: 2/15; financial award applicants required to submit FAFSA. *Unit head:* Dr. Ramesh Garimella, Chair, 501-450-3147, Fax: 501-450-5662, E-mail: rameshg@uca.edu. *Application contact:* Susan Wood, Admissions Assistant, 501-450-3124, Fax: 501-450-5678, E-mail: swood@uca.edu. Web site: http://uca.edu/math/.

University of Central Florida, College of Education, Education Doctoral Programs, Orlando, FL 32816. Offers communication sciences and disorders (PhD); counselor education (PhD); education (Ed D); elementary education (PhD); exceptional education (PhD); exercise physiology (PhD); higher education (PhD); hospitality education (PhD); instructional technology (PhD); mathematics education (PhD); reading education (PhD); science education (PhD); social science education (PhD); TESOL (PhD). *Students:* 135 full-time (87 women), 73 part-time (51 women); includes 49 minority (21 Black or African American, non-Hispanic/Latino; 4 Asian, non-Hispanic/Latino; 20 Hispanic/Latino; 4 Two or more races, non-Hispanic/Latino), 18 international. Average age 39. 125 applicants, 46% accepted, 46 enrolled. In 2011, 43 doctorates awarded. Application fee: $30. Electronic applications accepted. *Expenses:* Tuition, state resident: part-time $277.08 per credit hour. Tuition, nonresident: part-time $277.08 per credit hour. Part-time tuition and fees vary according to degree level and program. *Financial support:* In 2011–12, 85 students received support, including 48 fellowships with partial tuition reimbursements available (averaging $5,900 per year), 36 research assistantships with partial tuition reimbursements available (averaging $6,900 per year), 59 teaching assistantships with partial tuition reimbursements available (averaging $6,900 per year). *Unit head:* Dr. Rex Culp, Associate Dean, 407-823-5391, E-mail: rex.culp@ucf.edu. *Application contact:* Barbara Rodriguez, Associate Director, Admissions and Registration, 407-823-2766, Fax: 407-823-6442, E-mail: gradadmissions@ucf.edu. Web site: http://education.ucf.edu/departments.cfm.

University of Central Florida, College of Education, School of Teaching, Learning, and Leadership, Program in K-8 Mathematics and Science Education, Orlando, FL 32816. Offers M Ed, Certificate. *Accreditation:* NCATE. *Students:* 21 part-time (17 women); includes 1 minority (Hispanic/Latino). Average age 34. In 2011, 13 master's, 1 Certificate awarded. Application fee: $30. *Expenses:* Tuition, state resident: part-time $277.08 per credit hour. Tuition, nonresident: part-time $277.08 per credit hour. Part-time tuition and fees vary according to degree level and program. *Financial support:* Fellowships available. *Unit head:* Dr. Juli K. Dixon, Program Coordinator, 407-823-4140, E-mail: juli.dixon@ucf.edu. *Application contact:* Barbara Rodriguez, Director, Admissions and Registration, 407-823-2766, Fax: 407-823-6442, E-mail: gradadmissions@ucf.edu.

University of Central Florida, College of Education, School of Teaching, Learning, and Leadership, Program in Mathematics Education, Orlando, FL 32816. Offers teacher education (MAT), including mathematics education, middle school mathematics; teacher leadership (M Ed). *Accreditation:* NCATE. Part-time and evening/weekend programs available. *Students:* 10 full-time (9 women), 32 part-time (23 women); includes 11 minority (4 Black or African American, non-Hispanic/Latino; 3 Asian, non-Hispanic/Latino; 4 Hispanic/Latino). Average age 35. 16 applicants, 63% accepted, 7 enrolled. In 2011, 16 master's awarded. *Entrance requirements:* For master's, GRE General Test. Additional exam requirements/recommendations for international students: Required—TOEFL. *Application deadline:* For fall admission, 7/15 for domestic students; for spring admission, 12/1 for domestic students. Application fee: $30. Electronic applications accepted. *Expenses:* Tuition, state resident: part-time $277.08 per credit hour. Tuition, nonresident: part-time $277.08 per credit hour. Part-time tuition and fees vary according to degree level and program. *Financial support:* In 2011–12, 1 student received support, including 1 research assistantship with partial tuition reimbursement available (averaging $6,900 per year); fellowships with partial tuition reimbursements available, teaching assistantships with partial tuition reimbursements available, career-related internships or fieldwork, Federal Work-Study, institutionally sponsored loans, tuition waivers (partial), and unspecified assistantships also available. Financial award application deadline: 3/1; financial award applicants required to submit FAFSA. *Unit head:* Dr. Janet B. Andreasen, Program Coordinator, 407-823-5430, E-mail: janet.andreasen@ucf.edu. *Application contact:* Barbara Rodriguez, Director, Admissions and Registration, 407-823-2766, Fax: 407-823-6442, E-mail: gradadmissions@ucf.edu.

University of Central Oklahoma, College of Graduate Studies and Research, College of Mathematics and Science, Department of Mathematics and Statistics, Edmond, OK 73034-5209. Offers applied mathematical sciences (MS), including computer science, mathematics, mathematics/computer science teaching, statistics. Part-time programs available. *Faculty:* 7 full-time (4 women), 3 part-time/adjunct (0 women). *Students:* 20 full-time (7 women), 11 part-time (8 women); includes 5 minority (3 Black or African American, non-Hispanic/Latino; 2 Two or more races, non-Hispanic/Latino), 11 international. Average age 29. In 2011, 5 master's awarded. *Degree requirements:* For master's, thesis. *Entrance requirements:* Additional exam requirements/recommendations for international students: Required—TOEFL (minimum score 550 paper-based; 213 computer-based). *Application deadline:* Applications are processed on a rolling basis. Application fee: $50. Electronic applications accepted. *Expenses:* Tuition, state resident: full-time $3901; part-time $218.30 per credit hour. Tuition, nonresident: full-time $9198; part-time $511.20 per credit hour. Tuition and fees vary according to program. *Financial support:* Federal Work-Study and unspecified assistantships available. Financial award application deadline: 3/31; financial award applicants required to submit FAFSA. *Faculty research:* Curvature, FAA, math education. *Unit head:* Dr. Michael Fulkerson, 405-974-5575, E-mail: mfulkerson@uco.edu. *Application contact:* Dr. Richard Bernard, Adviser, 405-974-3493, Fax: 405-974-3824, E-mail: jyates@aix1.uco.edu. Web site: http://www.ucok.edu/graduate.applied.htm.

University of Cincinnati, Graduate School, McMicken College of Arts and Sciences, Department of Mathematical Sciences, Cincinnati, OH 45221. Offers applied mathematics (MS, PhD); mathematics education (MAT); pure mathematics (MS, PhD); statistics (MS, PhD). Part-time programs available. Terminal master's awarded for partial completion of doctoral program. *Degree requirements:* For master's, comprehensive exam, thesis or alternative; for doctorate, one foreign language, comprehensive exam, thesis/dissertation. *Entrance requirements:* For master's, GRE, teacher certification (MAT); for doctorate, GRE. Additional exam requirements/recommendations for international students: Required—TOEFL. Electronic applications accepted. *Faculty research:* Algebra, analysis, differential equations, numerical analysis, statistics.

University of Colorado Denver, College of Liberal Arts and Sciences, Department of Mathematical and Statistical Sciences, Denver, CO 80217. Offers applied mathematics (MS, PhD), including applied mathematics, applied probability (MS), applied statistics (MS), computational biology, computational mathematics (PhD), discrete mathematics, finite geometry (PhD), mathematics education (PhD), mathematics of engineering and science (MS), numerical analysis, operations research (MS), optimization and operations research (PhD), probability (PhD), statistics (PhD). Part-time programs available. *Faculty:* 26 full-time (4 women), 2 part-time/adjunct (1 woman). *Students:* 44 full-time (14 women), 14 part-time (5 women); includes 6 minority (4 Asian, non-Hispanic/Latino; 2 Hispanic/Latino), 10 international. Average age 33. 66 applicants, 79% accepted, 17 enrolled. In 2011, 6 master's, 6 doctorates awarded. *Degree requirements:* For master's, comprehensive exam, thesis optional, 30 hours of course work with minimum GPA of 3.0; for doctorate, comprehensive exam, thesis/dissertation. *Entrance requirements:* For master's and doctorate, GRE General Test; GRE Subject Test in math (recommended), 30 hours of course work in mathematics (24 of which must be upper-division mathematics), minimum GPA of 3.0. Additional exam requirements/recommendations for international students: Required—TOEFL (minimum score 525 paper-based; 192 computer-based; 71 iBT). *Application deadline:* For fall admission, 4/1 for domestic students, 3/1 for international students; for spring admission, 11/1 for domestic students, 10/1 for international students. Application fee: $50 ($75 for international students). Electronic applications accepted. *Financial support:* Fellowships with partial tuition reimbursements, research assistantships with full tuition reimbursements, teaching assistantships with full tuition reimbursements, Federal Work-Study, scholarships/grants, and unspecified assistantships available. Financial award application deadline: 4/1; financial award applicants required to submit FAFSA. *Faculty research:* Computational mathematics, computational biology, discrete mathematics and geometry, probability and statistics, optimization. *Unit head:* Dr. Stephen Billups, Graduate Chair, 303-556-4814, E-mail: stephen.billups@ucdenver.edu. *Application contact:* Lisa Herbert, Graduate Program Assistant, 303-556-2341, E-mail: lisa.herbert@ucdenver.edu. Web site: http://www.ucdenver.edu/academics/colleges/CLAS/Departments/math/Pages/MathStats.aspx.

University of Colorado Denver, School of Education and Human Development, Program in Educational Leadership and Innovation, Denver, CO 80217-3364. Offers educational studies and research (PhD), including administrative leadership and policy, early childhood special education, math education, research, assessment and evaluation, science education, urban ecologies. Part-time and evening/weekend programs available. *Students:* 21 full-time (15 women), 25 part-time (17 women); includes 10 minority (5 Black or African American, non-Hispanic/Latino; 1 American Indian or Alaska Native, non-Hispanic/Latino; 3 Asian, non-Hispanic/Latino; 1 Hispanic/Latino), 1 international. Average age 43. 11 applicants, 45% accepted, 3 enrolled. In 2011, 11 doctorates awarded. *Degree requirements:* For doctorate, comprehensive exam, thesis/dissertation, 75 credit hours (for PhD). *Entrance requirements:* For doctorate, GRE or equivalent, resume or curriculum vitae, written statement, letters of recommendation, master's degree or equivalent, completion of basic or advanced statistics course with minimum B grade. Additional exam requirements/recommendations for international students: Required—TOEFL (minimum score 525 paper-based; 197 computer-based). *Application deadline:* Applications are processed on a rolling basis. Application fee: $50 ($75 for international students). Electronic applications accepted. *Expenses:* Contact institution. *Financial support:* Fellowships, research assistantships, teaching assistantships, scholarships/grants, and unspecified assistantships available. Financial award application deadline: 4/1; financial award applicants required to submit FAFSA. *Faculty research:* Administrative leadership and policy studies, early childhood education, research in diversity, paraprofessionals in education, urban schools lab. *Unit head:* Dr. Deanna Sands, Associate Dean, Research and Professional Development, 303-315-4931, E-mail: deanna.sands@ucdenver.edu. *Application contact:* Student Services Center, 303-315-6300, Fax: 303-315-6311, E-mail: education@ucdenver.edu. Web site: http://www.ucdenver.edu/ACADEMICS/COLLEGES/SCHOOLOFEDUCATION/ACADEMICS/Pages/AcademicPrograms.aspx.

University of Colorado Denver, School of Education and Human Development, Teacher Education Programs, Denver, CO 80217. Offers elementary linguistically diverse education (MA); elementary math and science education (MA); elementary math education (MA); elementary reading and writing (MA); elementary science education (MA); secondary English education (MA); secondary linguistically diverse education (MA); secondary math education (MA); secondary reading and writing (MA); secondary science education (MA); special education (MA). *Accreditation:* NCATE. Part-time and evening/weekend programs available. *Students:* 419 full-time (325 women), 238 part-time (196 women); includes 83 minority (11 Black or African American, non-Hispanic/Latino; 1 American Indian or Alaska Native, non-Hispanic/Latino; 15 Asian, non-Hispanic/Latino; 53 Hispanic/Latino; 3 Two or more races, non-Hispanic/Latino), 9 international. Average age 30. 206 applicants, 88% accepted, 85 enrolled. In 2011, 278 master's awarded. *Degree requirements:* For master's, comprehensive exam. *Entrance requirements:* For master's, GRE or MAT (for those with GPA below 2.75), transcripts, resume, letters of recommendation. Additional exam requirements/recommendations for international students: Required—TOEFL (minimum score 525 paper-based; 197 computer-based). *Application deadline:* For fall admission, 4/15 priority date for domestic students; for spring admission, 9/15 priority date for domestic students. Applications are processed on a rolling basis. Application fee: $50 ($75 for international students). Electronic applications accepted. *Expenses:* Contact institution. *Financial support:* Research assistantships, teaching assistantships, and Federal Work-Study available. Financial award application deadline: 4/1; financial award applicants required to submit FAFSA. *Faculty research:* Linguistically diverse education/ESL, elementary reading and writing, elementary teacher education, secondary teacher education, special education. *Unit head:* Cindy Gutierrez, Director, 303-315-4982, E-mail: cindy.gutierrez@ucdenver.edu. *Application contact:* Lori Sisneros, Student Services Center, 303-315-4979, E-mail: education@ucdenver.edu. Web site: http://www.ucdenver.edu/academics/colleges/SchoolOfEducation/Academics/MASTERS/Pages/default.aspx.

University of Connecticut, Graduate School, Neag School of Education, Department of Curriculum and Instruction, Program in Mathematics Education, Storrs, CT 06269. Offers MA, PhD, Post-Master's Certificate. *Accreditation:* NCATE. Terminal master's awarded for partial completion of doctoral program. *Degree requirements:* For master's, comprehensive exam; for doctorate, thesis/dissertation. *Entrance requirements:* For doctorate, GRE General Test. Additional exam requirements/recommendations for international students: Required—TOEFL (minimum score 550 paper-based; 213 computer-based). Electronic applications accepted.

University of Dayton, Department of Mathematics, Dayton, OH 45469-1300. Offers applied mathematics (MAS); financial mathematics (MFM); mathematics education (MME). Part-time and evening/weekend programs available. *Faculty:* 15 full-time (5 women). *Students:* 37 full-time (20 women), 12 part-time (5 women); includes 4 minority (3 Black or African American, non-Hispanic/Latino; 1 Asian, non-Hispanic/Latino), 31 international. Average age 26. 110 applicants, 62% accepted, 25 enrolled. In 2011, 14 master's awarded. *Entrance requirements:* For master's, minimum undergraduate GPA of 2.8 (MAS), 3.0 (MFM, MME). Additional exam requirements/recommendations for international students: Required—TOEFL (minimum score 550 paper-based; 213 computer-based; 80 iBT). *Application deadline:* For fall admission, 3/1 priority date for domestic students, 7/1 for international students; for winter admission, 7/1 for international students; for spring admission, 1/1 for international students. Application fee: $0 ($50 for international students). Electronic applications accepted. *Expenses: Tuition:* Full-time $8400; part-time $700 per credit hour. *Required fees:* $25 per semester. Tuition and fees vary according to degree level. *Financial support:* In 2011–12, 6 teaching assistantships with full tuition reimbursements (averaging $13,400 per year) were awarded; institutionally sponsored loans, health care benefits, and unspecified assistantships also available. Financial award applicants required to submit FAFSA. *Faculty research:* Differential equations, integral equations, general topology, measure theory, graph theory, financial math, math education, numerical analysis. *Unit head:* Dr. Joe D. Mashburn, Chair, 937-229-2511, Fax: 937-229-2566, E-mail: joe.mashburn@notes.udayton.edu. *Application contact:* Alexander Popovski, Associate Director of Graduate and International Admissions, 937-229-2357, Fax: 937-229-4729, E-mail: alex.popovski@notes.udayton.edu.

University of Detroit Mercy, College of Engineering and Science, Department of Mathematics and Computer Science, Detroit, MI 48221. Offers computer science (MSCS), including computer systems applications, software engineering; computer science education (MATM); mathematics education (MATM). Evening/weekend programs available. *Entrance requirements:* For master's, minimum GPA of 3.0.

University of Florida, Graduate School, College of Education, School of Teaching and Learning, Gainesville, FL 32611. Offers bilingual/ESOL education (M Ed, MAE, Ed D, PhD, Ed S); curriculum and instruction (M Ed, MAE, Ed D, PhD, Ed S); elementary education (M Ed, MAE); English education (M Ed, MAE); mathematics education (M Ed, MAE); reading education (M Ed, MAE); science education (M Ed, MAE); social foundations of education (M Ed, MAE, Ed D, PhD); social studies education (M Ed, MAE). *Accreditation:* NCATE. Part-time and evening/weekend programs available. Postbaccalaureate distance learning degree programs offered (no on-campus study). *Faculty:* 26 full-time (19 women). *Students:* 247 full-time (201 women), 236 part-time (196 women); includes 100 minority (32 Black or African American, non-Hispanic/Latino; 2 American Indian or Alaska Native, non-Hispanic/Latino; 15 Asian, non-Hispanic/Latino; 51 Hispanic/Latino), 32 international. Average age 33. 290 applicants, 60% accepted, 122 enrolled. In 2011, 284 master's, 19 doctorates, 29 other advanced degrees awarded. Terminal master's awarded for partial completion of doctoral program. *Degree requirements:* For master's, comprehensive exam (for some programs), thesis (for some programs); for doctorate, comprehensive exam (for some programs), thesis/dissertation (for some programs). *Entrance requirements:* For master's and doctorate, GRE General Test, minimum GPA of 3.0; for Ed S, GRE General Test. Additional exam requirements/recommendations for international students: Required—TOEFL (minimum score 550 paper-based; 213 computer-based; 80 iBT), IELTS (minimum score 6). *Application deadline:* For fall admission, 2/15 for domestic students, 12/1 for international students; for spring admission, 9/15 for domestic students, 3/1 for international students. Applications are processed on a rolling basis. Application fee: $30. Electronic applications accepted. *Financial support:* Fellowships, research assistantships, teaching assistantships, career-related internships or fieldwork, and unspecified assistantships available. Financial award applicants required to submit FAFSA. *Faculty research:* Early childhood, child and adolescents, diverse learners, race/ethnicity issues, teacher education, professional development, language and literacy development, policy development. *Unit head:* Dr. Elizabeth Bondy, Chair, 352-273-4242, Fax: 352-392-9193, E-mail: bondy@coe.ufl.edu. *Application contact:* Wevan Terzian, Graduate Coordinator, 352-273-4216, Fax: 352-392-9193, E-mail: sterzian@coe.ufl.edu. Web site: http://education.ufl.edu/school-teaching-learning/.

University of Georgia, College of Education, Department of Mathematics and Science Education, Athens, GA 30602. Offers mathematics education (M Ed, Ed D, PhD, Ed S); science education (M Ed, Ed D, PhD, Ed S). *Faculty:* 15 full-time (7 women), 1 (woman) part-time/adjunct. *Students:* 115 full-time (71 women), 87 part-time (60 women); includes 42 minority (29 Black or African American, non-Hispanic/Latino; 6 Asian, non-Hispanic/Latino; 6 Hispanic/Latino; 1 Two or more races, non-Hispanic/Latino), 22 international. Average age 34. 86 applicants, 88% accepted, 38 enrolled. In 2011, 57 master's, 18 doctorates, 13 other advanced degrees awarded. *Application deadline:* For fall admission, 7/1 priority date for domestic students; for spring admission, 11/15 for domestic students. Application fee: $50. *Unit head:* Dr. Denise A. Spangler, Head, 706-542-4548, Fax: 706-542-4551, E-mail: dspangle@uga.edu. *Application contact:* Dr. John Olive, Graduate Coordinator, 706-542-4557, Fax: 706-542-4551, E-mail: jolive@uga.edu. Web site: http://www.coe.uga.edu/mse/.

University of Illinois at Chicago, Graduate College, College of Liberal Arts and Sciences, Department of Mathematics, Statistics, and Computer Science, Program in Teaching of Mathematics, Chicago, IL 60607-7128. Offers elementary (MST); secondary (MST). Part-time programs available. *Degree requirements:* For master's, comprehensive exam. *Entrance requirements:* For master's, GRE General Test, minimum GPA of 2.75. Additional exam requirements/recommendations for international students: Required—TOEFL. Electronic applications accepted.

University of Illinois at Urbana–Champaign, Graduate College, College of Liberal Arts and Sciences, Department of Mathematics, Champaign, IL 61820. Offers applied mathematics (MS); applied mathematics: actuarial science (MS); mathematics (MS, PhD); teaching of mathematics (MS). *Faculty:* 64 full-time (6 women), 9 part-time/adjunct (0 women). *Students:* 166 full-time (52 women), 36 part-time (13 women); includes 16 minority (7 Asian, non-Hispanic/Latino; 5 Hispanic/Latino; 4 Two or more races, non-Hispanic/Latino), 111 international. 455 applicants, 23% accepted, 48 enrolled. In 2011, 32 master's, 26 doctorates awarded. *Entrance requirements:* For master's and doctorate, GRE General Test, GRE Subject Test (math), minimum GPA of 3.0. Additional exam requirements/recommendations for international students: Required—TOEFL (minimum score 550 paper-based; 213 computer-based). *Application deadline:* Applications are processed on a rolling basis. Application fee: $75 ($90 for international students). Electronic applications accepted. *Financial support:* In 2011–12, 26 fellowships, 44 research assistantships, 152 teaching assistantships were awarded; tuition waivers (full and partial) also available. *Unit head:* Matthew Ando, Chair, 217-244-2846, Fax: 217-333-9576, E-mail: mando@illinois.edu. *Application contact:* Marci Blocher, Office Support Specialist, 217-333-5749, Fax: 217-333-9576, E-mail: mblocher@illinois.edu. Web site: http://math.illinois.edu/.

University of Indianapolis, Graduate Programs, School of Education, Indianapolis, IN 46227-3697. Offers art education (MAT); biology (MAT); chemistry (MAT); curriculum and instruction (MA); earth sciences (MAT); education (MA, MAT); educational leadership (MA); elementary education (MA); English (MAT); French (MAT); math (MAT); physical education (MAT); physics (MAT); secondary education (MA), including art education, education, English education, social studies education; social studies (MAT); Spanish (MAT). *Accreditation:* NCATE. Part-time and evening/weekend programs available. *Faculty:* 3 full-time (2 women), 3 part-time/adjunct (2 women). *Students:* 32 full-time (18 women), 97 part-time (56 women); includes 22 minority (20 Black or African American, non-Hispanic/Latino; 1 Asian, non-Hispanic/Latino; 1 Hispanic/Latino), 3 international. Average age 33. In 2011, 78 master's awarded. *Entrance requirements:* For master's, GRE Subject Test, PRAXIS I, minimum GPA of 2.5, 3 letters of recommendation, interview, writing exercise. Additional exam requirements/recommendations for international students: Required—TOEFL (minimum score 550 paper-based; 213 computer-based). *Application deadline:* Applications are processed on a rolling basis. Application fee: $50. Tuition and fees vary according to degree level and program. *Financial support:* Federal Work-Study available. Financial award application deadline: 5/1; financial award applicants required to submit FAFSA. *Faculty research:* Assessment of teacher education, perceptions of prospective teachers by parents. *Unit head:* Dr. Kathy Moran, Dean, 317-788-3285, Fax: 317-788-3300, E-mail: kmoran@uindy.edu. *Application contact:* Jeni Kirby, 317-788-2113, E-mail: kirbyj@uindy.edu. Web site: http://education.uindy.edu/.

The University of Iowa, Graduate College, College of Education, Department of Teaching and Learning, Program in Secondary Education, Iowa City, IA 52242-1316. Offers art education (PhD); curriculum and supervision (PhD); curriculum supervision (MA); developmental reading (MA); English education (MA, MAT); foreign language education (MA, MAT); foreign language/ESL education (PhD); language, literature and culture (PhD); math education (PhD); mathematics education (MA); social studies (MA, PhD). *Degree requirements:* For master's, thesis optional, exam; for doctorate, comprehensive exam, thesis/dissertation. *Entrance requirements:* For master's and doctorate, GRE General Test, minimum GPA of 3.0. Additional exam requirements/recommendations for international students: Required—TOEFL (minimum score 550 paper-based; 213 computer-based; 81 iBT). Electronic applications accepted.

University of Maine, Graduate School, College of Education and Human Development, Interdisciplinary Program in Teaching, Orono, ME 04469. Offers earth sciences (MST); generalist (MST); mathematics (MST); physics and astronomy (MST). *Students:* 8 full-time (6 women), 13 part-time (10 women); includes 1 minority (American Indian or Alaska Native, non-Hispanic/Latino). Average age 40. 2 applicants, 50% accepted, 1 enrolled. In 2011, 6 master's awarded. *Entrance requirements:* For master's, GRE General Test, MAT. Application fee: $65. *Expenses:* Tuition, state resident: full-time $5016. Tuition, nonresident: full-time $14,424. *Unit head:* Dr. Susan McKay, Director, 207-581-1016. *Application contact:* Scott G. Delcourt, Associate Dean of the Graduate School, 207-581-3291, Fax: 207-581-3232, E-mail: graduate@maine.edu. Web site: http://www2.umaine.edu/graduate/.

University of Maryland, Baltimore County, Graduate School, College of Arts, Humanities and Social Sciences, Department of Education, Program in Teaching, Baltimore, MD 21250. Offers early childhood education (MAT); elementary education (MAT); secondary education (MAT), including social studies; secondary education (MAT), including art, biology, chemistry, dance, earth/space science, English, foreign language, mathematics, music, physics, theatre. Part-time and evening/weekend programs available. *Faculty:* 24 full-time (18 women), 25 part-time/adjunct (19 women). *Students:* 46 full-time (35 women), 64 part-time (39 women); includes 24 minority (8 Black or African American, non-Hispanic/Latino; 7 Asian, non-Hispanic/Latino; 6 Hispanic/Latino; 1 Native Hawaiian or other Pacific Islander, non-Hispanic/Latino; 2 Two or more races, non-Hispanic/Latino), 4 international. Average age 31. 88 applicants, 57% accepted, 39 enrolled. In 2011, 106 master's awarded. *Degree requirements:* For master's, comprehensive exam (for some programs), thesis (for some programs). *Entrance requirements:* For master's, PRAXIS I or GRE (minimum score of 1000), minimum GPA of 3.0. Additional exam requirements/recommendations for international students: Required—TOEFL. *Application deadline:* For fall admission, 6/1 for domestic students; for spring admission, 11/1 for domestic students. Applications are processed on a rolling basis. Application fee: $50. Electronic applications accepted. *Financial support:* In 2011–12, 6 students received support, including teaching assistantships with full and partial tuition reimbursements available (averaging $12,000 per year); career-related internships or fieldwork, Federal Work-Study, scholarships/grants, tuition waivers, and unspecified assistantships also available. Financial award application deadline: 3/1. *Faculty research:* STEM teacher education, culturally sensitive pedagogy, ESOL/bilingual education, early childhood education, language, literacy and culture. *Unit head:* Dr. Susan M. Blunck, Graduate Program Director, 410-455-2869, Fax: 410-455-3986, E-mail: blunck@umbc.edu. *Application contact:* Cheryl Johnson, 410-455-3388, E-mail: blackwel@umbc.edu. Web site: http://www.umbc.edu/education/.

University of Massachusetts Dartmouth, Graduate School, School of Education, Public Policy, and Civic Engagement, Department of Science, Technology, Engineering and Mathematics (STEM), North Dartmouth, MA 02747-2300. Offers math education (PhD). Part-time programs available. *Faculty:* 4 full-time (3 women), 1 (woman) part-time/adjunct. *Students:* 9 full-time (3 women), 4 part-time (1 woman); includes 3 minority (2 Hispanic/Latino; 1 Two or more races, non-Hispanic/Latino). Average age 35. 7 applicants, 100% accepted, 6 enrolled. *Entrance requirements:* For doctorate, GRE, 3 letters of recommendation, resume, statement of intent. Additional exam requirements/recommendations for international students: Required—TOEFL (minimum score 533 paper-based; 200 computer-based; 72 iBT). *Application deadline:* For fall admission, 3/31 for domestic students, 2/28 for international students; for spring admission, 11/15 for domestic students, 10/15 for international students. Applications are processed on a rolling basis. Application fee: $40 ($60 for international students). *Expenses:* Tuition, state resident: full-time $2071; part-time $86.29 per credit. Tuition, nonresident: full-time $8099; part-time $337.46 per credit. *Required fees:* $438.58 per credit. Part-time tuition and fees vary according to class time, course load, degree level and reciprocity agreements. *Financial support:* In 2011–12, 4 research assistantships with full tuition reimbursements (averaging $19,810 per year), 3 teaching assistantships with full tuition reimbursements (averaging $12,667 per year) were awarded. Financial award application deadline: 3/1. *Faculty research:* Algebraic thinking in early grades; conceptual and historical development of mathematical concepts, focuses on students understanding of mathematical functions in various representations . *Total annual research expenditures:* $1.5 million. *Unit head:* Dr. Chandra orrill, Graduate Program Director, 774-929-3052, Fax: 508-999-9215, E-mail: corrill@umassd.edu. *Application contact:* Elan Turcotte-Shamski, Graduate Admissions Officer, 508-999-8604, Fax: 508-999-8183, E-mail: graduate@umassd.edu. Web site: http://www.umassd.edu/seppce/stem/.

University of Massachusetts Lowell, Graduate School of Education, Lowell, MA 01854-2881. Offers administration, planning, and policy (CAGS); curriculum and instruction (M Ed, CAGS); educational administration (M Ed); language arts and literacy (Ed D); leadership in schooling (Ed D); math and science education (Ed D); reading and language (M Ed, CAGS). *Accreditation:* NCATE. Part-time and evening/weekend programs available. Postbaccalaureate distance learning degree programs offered (no on-campus study). Terminal master's awarded for partial completion of doctoral program. *Degree requirements:* For doctorate, thesis/dissertation. *Entrance requirements:* For master's, doctorate, and CAGS, GRE General Test. Additional exam requirements/recommendations for international students: Required—TOEFL. Electronic applications accepted.

University of Miami, Graduate School, School of Education and Human Development, Department of Teaching and Learning, Program in Teaching and Learning, Coral Gables, FL 33124. Offers language and literacy learning in multilingual settings (PhD); science, technology, engineering and mathematics (PhD); special education (PhD). *Students:* 19 full-time (14 women); includes 10 minority (3 Black or African American, non-Hispanic/Latino; 7 Hispanic/Latino), 1 international. Average age 34. 12 applicants, 17% accepted, 2 enrolled. In 2011, 9 degrees awarded. *Degree requirements:* For doctorate, thesis/dissertation, qualifying exam. *Entrance requirements:* For doctorate, GRE General Test. Additional exam requirements/recommendations for international students: Required—TOEFL (minimum score 550 paper-based; 80 iBT); Recommended—IELTS (minimum score 6.5). *Application deadline:* For fall admission, 2/15 for domestic students, 10/15 for international students. Application fee: $65. Electronic applications accepted. *Financial support:* In 2011–12, 18 students received support, including 5 fellowships with full tuition reimbursements available (averaging $28,800 per year), 9 research assistantships with full and partial tuition reimbursements available (averaging $28,800 per year), 1 teaching assistantship with full and partial tuition reimbursement available (averaging $28,800 per year). Financial award application deadline: 3/1; financial award applicants required to submit FAFSA. *Faculty research:* Teacher education, multicultural education, technology, second language acquisition, math and science education. *Unit head:* Dr. Elizabeth Harry, Department Chairperson and Program Director, 305-284-4961, Fax: 305-284-6998, E-mail: bharry@miami.edu. *Application contact:* Lois Heffernan, Graduate Admission Coordinator, 305-284-2167, Fax: 305-284-9395, E-mail: lheffernan@miami.edu.

University of Minnesota, Twin Cities Campus, Graduate School, College of Education and Human Development, Department of Curriculum and Instruction, Program in Teaching, Minneapolis, MN 55455-0213. Offers Chinese (M Ed); earth science (M Ed); elementary special education (M Ed); English (M Ed); English as a second language (M Ed); French (M Ed); German (M Ed); Hebrew (M Ed); Japanese (M Ed); life sciences (M Ed); mathematics (M Ed); middle school science (M Ed); science (M Ed); second languages and cultures (M Ed); social studies (M Ed); Spanish (M Ed). *Students:* 375 full-time (319 women), 72 part-time (56 women); includes 34 minority (8 Black or African American, non-Hispanic/Latino; 16 Asian, non-Hispanic/Latino; 10 Hispanic/Latino), 5 international. Average age 27. 317 applicants, 70% accepted, 215 enrolled. In 2011, 443 master's awarded. Application fee: $55. *Unit head:* Dr. Nina Asher, Chair, 612-624-1357, Fax: 612-624-8277, E-mail: nasher@umn.edu. *Application contact:* Dr. Jennifer Engler, Assistant Dean, 612-626-2887, Fax: 612-626-7496, E-mail: engle009@umn.edu. Web site: http://www.cehd.umn.edu/ci/.

University of Missouri, Graduate School, College of Arts and Sciences, Department of Mathematics, Columbia, MO 65211. Offers applied mathematics (MS); mathematics (MA, MST, PhD). *Faculty:* 40 full-time (6 women), 1 (woman) part-time/adjunct. *Students:* 60 full-time (7 women), 12 part-time (2 women); includes 2 minority (1

Hispanic/Latino; 1 Two or more races, non-Hispanic/Latino), 27 international. Average age 28. 119 applicants, 27% accepted, 22 enrolled. In 2011, 14 master's, 10 doctorates awarded. *Degree requirements:* For doctorate, 2 foreign languages, comprehensive exam, thesis/dissertation. *Entrance requirements:* For master's and doctorate, GRE General Test, minimum GPA of 3.0; bachelor's degree from accredited institution. Additional exam requirements/recommendations for international students: Required—TOEFL (minimum score 500 paper-based; 173 computer-based; 61 iBT). *Application deadline:* For fall admission, 1/15 for domestic students. Applications are processed on a rolling basis. Application fee: $55 ($75 for international students). Electronic applications accepted. *Expenses:* Tuition, state resident: full-time $5881. Tuition, nonresident: full-time $15,183. *Required fees:* $952. Tuition and fees vary according to campus/location and program. *Financial support:* In 2011–12, 7 fellowships with full tuition reimbursements, 4 research assistantships with full tuition reimbursements, 64 teaching assistantships with full tuition reimbursements were awarded; institutionally sponsored loans, health care benefits, and unspecified assistantships also available. Financial award applicants required to submit FAFSA. *Faculty research:* Algebraic geometry, analysis (real, complex, functional and harmonic), analytic functions, applied mathematics, financial mathematics and mathematics of insurance, commutative rings, scattering theory, differential equations (ordinary and partial), differential geometry, dynamical systems, general relativity, mathematical physics, number theory, probabilistic analysis and topology. *Unit head:* Dr. Glen Himmelberg, Department Chair, 573-882-6222, E-mail: himmelbergg@missouri.edu. *Application contact:* Amy Crews, Administrative Assistant, 573-882-6222, E-mail: crewsae@missouri.edu. Web site: http://www.math.missouri.edu/.

University of Missouri, Graduate School, College of Education, Department of Learning, Teaching and Curriculum, Columbia, MO 65211. Offers agricultural education (M Ed, PhD, Ed S); art education (M Ed, PhD, Ed S); business and office education (M Ed, PhD, Ed S); early childhood education (M Ed, PhD, Ed S); elementary education (M Ed, PhD, Ed S); English education (M Ed, PhD, Ed S); foreign language education (M Ed, PhD, Ed S); health education and promotion (M Ed, PhD); learning and instruction (M Ed); marketing education (M Ed, PhD, Ed S); mathematics education (M Ed, PhD, Ed S); music education (M Ed, PhD, Ed S); reading education (M Ed, PhD, Ed S); science education (M Ed, PhD, Ed S); social studies education (M Ed, PhD, Ed S); vocational education (M Ed, PhD, Ed S). Part-time programs available. *Faculty:* 26 full-time (16 women), 3 part-time/adjunct (2 women). *Students:* 184 full-time (145 women), 276 part-time (215 women); includes 34 minority (10 Black or African American, non-Hispanic/Latino; 1 American Indian or Alaska Native, non-Hispanic/Latino; 7 Asian, non-Hispanic/Latino; 8 Hispanic/Latino; 8 Two or more races, non-Hispanic/Latino), 39 international. Average age 32. 309 applicants, 76% accepted, 204 enrolled. In 2011, 232 master's, 8 doctorates, 2 other advanced degrees awarded. Terminal master's awarded for partial completion of doctoral program. *Degree requirements:* For doctorate, thesis/dissertation. *Entrance requirements:* For master's and Ed S, GRE General Test or MAT, minimum GPA of 3.0; for doctorate, GRE General Test, minimum GPA of 3.0. Additional exam requirements/recommendations for international students: Required—TOEFL (minimum score 600 paper-based; 250 computer-based; 100 iBT). Application fee: $55 ($75 for international students). Electronic applications accepted. *Expenses:* Tuition, state resident: full-time $5881. Tuition, nonresident: full-time $15,183. *Required fees:* $952. Tuition and fees vary according to campus/location and program. *Financial support:* Fellowships, research assistantships, teaching assistantships, and institutionally sponsored loans available. *Application contact:* Fran Colley, 573-882-6462, E-mail: colleyf@missouri.edu. Web site: http://education.missouri.edu/LTC/.

The University of Montana, Graduate School, College of Arts and Sciences, Department of Mathematical Sciences, Missoula, MT 59812-0002. Offers mathematics (MA, PhD), including college teaching (PhD), traditional mathematics research (PhD); mathematics education (MA). Part-time programs available. Terminal master's awarded for partial completion of doctoral program. *Degree requirements:* For doctorate, thesis/dissertation. *Entrance requirements:* For master's and doctorate, GRE General Test. Additional exam requirements/recommendations for international students: Required—TOEFL (minimum score 525 paper-based; 195 computer-based).

University of Nevada, Reno, Graduate School, College of Science, Department of Mathematics and Statistics, Reno, NV 89557. Offers mathematics (MS); teaching mathematics (MATM). *Degree requirements:* For master's, thesis optional. *Entrance requirements:* For master's, GRE General Test, minimum GPA of 2.75. Additional exam requirements/recommendations for international students: Required—TOEFL (minimum score 500 paper-based; 173 computer-based; 61 iBT), IELTS (minimum score 6). Electronic applications accepted. *Faculty research:* Operator algebra, nonlinear systems, differential equations.

University of New Hampshire, Graduate School, College of Engineering and Physical Sciences, Department of Mathematics and Statistics, Durham, NH 03824. Offers applied mathematics (MS); industrial statistics (Postbaccalaureate Certificate); mathematics (MS, MST, PhD); mathematics education (PhD); statistics (MS). *Faculty:* 21 full-time (5 women). *Students:* 26 full-time (12 women), 30 part-time (12 women); includes 4 minority (1 American Indian or Alaska Native, non-Hispanic/Latino; 2 Asian, non-Hispanic/Latino; 1 Two or more races, non-Hispanic/Latino), 13 international. Average age 29. 86 applicants, 47% accepted, 16 enrolled. In 2011, 1,217 master's, 2 doctorates, 4 other advanced degrees awarded. Terminal master's awarded for partial completion of doctoral program. *Degree requirements:* For doctorate, 2 foreign languages, thesis/dissertation. *Entrance requirements:* Additional exam requirements/recommendations for international students: Required—TOEFL (minimum score 550 paper-based; 213 computer-based; 80 iBT). *Application deadline:* For fall admission, 4/1 priority date for domestic students, 4/1 for international students; for spring admission, 12/1 for domestic students. Applications are processed on a rolling basis. Application fee: $65. Electronic applications accepted. *Expenses:* Tuition, state resident: full-time $12,360; part-time $687 per credit hour. Tuition, nonresident: full-time $25,680; part-time $1058 per credit hour. *International tuition:* $29,550 full-time. *Required fees:* $1666; $833 per course. $416.50 per semester. Tuition and fees vary according to course load and degree level. *Financial support:* In 2011–12, 41 students received support, including 6 research assistantships, 34 teaching assistantships; fellowships, Federal Work-Study, scholarships/grants, and tuition waivers (full and partial) also available. Support available to part-time students. Financial award application deadline: 2/15. *Faculty research:* Operator theory, complex analysis, algebra, nonlinear dynamics, statistics. *Unit head:* Dr. Edward Hinson, Chairperson, 603-862-2688. *Application contact:* Jan Jankowski, Administrative Assistant, 603-862-2320, E-mail: jan.jankowski@unh.edu. Web site: http://www.math.unh.edu/.

The University of North Carolina at Chapel Hill, Graduate School, School of Education, Program in Secondary Education, Chapel Hill, NC 27599. Offers English (Grades 9-12) (MAT); English as a second language (MAT); French (Grades K-12) (MAT); German (Grades K-12) (MAT); Japanese (Grades K-12) (MAT); Latin (Grades 9-12) (MAT); mathematics (Grades 9-12) (MAT); music (Grades K-12) (MAT); science (Grades 9-12) (MAT); social studies (Grades 9-12) (MAT); Spanish (Grades K-12) (MAT). *Accreditation:* NCATE. *Degree requirements:* For master's, comprehensive exam. *Entrance requirements:* For master's, GRE General Test, minimum GPA of 3.0 during last 2 years of undergraduate course work. Additional exam requirements/recommendations for international students: Required—TOEFL (minimum score 550 paper-based; 79 computer-based). Electronic applications accepted.

The University of North Carolina at Charlotte, Graduate School, College of Liberal Arts and Sciences, Department of Mathematics and Statistics, Charlotte, NC 28223-0001. Offers applied mathematics (MS, PhD); mathematics (MS); mathematics education (MA). Part-time and evening/weekend programs available. *Faculty:* 48 full-time (7 women). *Students:* 43 full-time (17 women), 27 part-time (10 women); includes 12 minority (7 Black or African American, non-Hispanic/Latino; 3 Asian, non-Hispanic/Latino; 2 Hispanic/Latino), 33 international. Average age 30. 52 applicants, 98% accepted, 16 enrolled. In 2011, 14 master's, 6 doctorates awarded. *Degree requirements:* For master's, comprehensive exam, thesis or alternative; for doctorate, thesis/dissertation. *Entrance requirements:* For master's, GRE General Test, minimum GPA of 3.0 in undergraduate major, 2.75 overall; for doctorate, GRE General Test, minimum overall GPA of 3.0. Additional exam requirements/recommendations for international students: Required—TOEFL (minimum score 557 paper-based; 220 computer-based; 83 iBT), Michigan English Language Assessment Battery (minimum score 78) or IELTS (minimum score 6.5). *Application deadline:* For fall admission, 7/1 for domestic students, 5/1 for international students; for spring admission, 11/1 for domestic students, 10/1 for international students. Applications are processed on a rolling basis. Application fee: $65 ($75 for international students). Electronic applications accepted. *Expenses:* Tuition, state resident: full-time $3689. Tuition, nonresident: full-time $15,226. *Required fees:* $2198. Tuition and fees vary according to course load and program. *Financial support:* In 2011–12, 37 students received support, including 4 fellowships (averaging $22,321 per year), 4 research assistantships (averaging $19,325 per year), 29 teaching assistantships (averaging $11,988 per year); career-related internships or fieldwork, Federal Work-Study, institutionally sponsored loans, scholarships/grants, and unspecified assistantships also available. Support available to part-time students. Financial award application deadline: 4/1; financial award applicants required to submit FAFSA. *Faculty research:* Numerical analysis, differential equations, probability, algebra, analysis, mathematics education, statistics. *Total annual research expenditures:* $1.2 million. *Unit head:* Dr. Alan S. Dow, Chair, 704-687-4560, Fax: 704-687-6415, E-mail: adow@uncc.edu. *Application contact:* Kathy B. Giddings, Director of Graduate Admissions, 704-687-5503, Fax: 704-687-3279, E-mail: gradadm@uncc.edu. Web site: http://www.math.uncc.edu/.

The University of North Carolina at Greensboro, Graduate School, School of Education, Department of Curriculum and Instruction, Greensboro, NC 27412-5001. Offers college teaching and adult learning (Certificate); curriculum and instruction (M Ed), including chemistry education, elementary education, English as a second language, French education, instructional technology, mathematics education, middle grades education, reading education, science education, social studies education, Spanish education; curriculum and teaching (PhD), including higher education, teacher education and development; English as a second language (Certificate); higher education (M Ed); supervision (M Ed). *Accreditation:* NCATE. Part-time programs available. *Degree requirements:* For doctorate, thesis/dissertation. *Entrance requirements:* For master's and doctorate, GRE General Test. Additional exam requirements/recommendations for international students: Required—TOEFL. Electronic applications accepted. *Faculty research:* Community college literacy program, middle school mathematics/computer mathematics.

The University of North Carolina at Pembroke, Graduate Studies, Department of Mathematics and Computer Science, Program in Mathematics Education, Pembroke, NC 28372-1510. Offers MA, MAT. *Accreditation:* NCATE. Part-time and evening/weekend programs available. *Degree requirements:* For master's, comprehensive exam, thesis optional. *Entrance requirements:* For master's, GRE General Test or MAT, bachelor's degree in mathematics or mathematics education; minimum GPA of 3.0 in major, 2.5 overall. Additional exam requirements/recommendations for international students: Required—TOEFL.

University of Northern Colorado, Graduate School, College of Natural and Health Sciences, School of Mathematical Sciences, Greeley, CO 80639. Offers mathematical teaching (MA); mathematics (MA, PhD); mathematics education (PhD); mathematics: liberal arts (MA). Part-time programs available. *Degree requirements:* For master's, comprehensive exam, thesis or alternative; for doctorate, comprehensive exam, thesis/dissertation. *Entrance requirements:* For master's, GRE General Test (liberal arts), 3 letters of recommendation; for doctorate, GRE General Test, 3 letters of recommendation. Electronic applications accepted.

University of Northern Iowa, Graduate College, College of Humanities, Arts and Sciences, Department of Mathematics, Cedar Falls, IA 50614. Offers industrial mathematics (PSM), including actuarial science, continuous quality improvement, mathematical computing and modeling; mathematics (MA), including mathematics, secondary; mathematics for middle grades 4-8 (MA). Part-time programs available. *Students:* 13 full-time (6 women), 23 part-time (17 women); includes 2 minority (1 Black or African American, non-Hispanic/Latino; 1 Asian, non-Hispanic/Latino), 6 international. 35 applicants, 74% accepted, 11 enrolled. In 2011, 19 master's awarded. *Degree requirements:* For master's, comprehensive exam (for some programs), thesis or alternative. *Entrance requirements:* For master's, minimum GPA of 3.0. Additional exam requirements/recommendations for international students: Required—TOEFL (minimum score 600 paper-based; 250 computer-based; 100 iBT). *Application deadline:* For fall admission, 8/1 priority date for domestic students. Applications are processed on a rolling basis. Application fee: $50 ($70 for international students). Electronic applications accepted. *Expenses:* Tuition, state resident: full-time $7476. Tuition, nonresident: full-time $16,410. *Required fees:* $942. *Financial support:* Career-related internships or fieldwork, Federal Work-Study, scholarships/grants, and tuition waivers (full and partial) available. Support available to part-time students. Financial award application deadline: 2/1. *Unit head:* Dr. Douglas Mupasiri, Interim Head, 319-273-2012, Fax: 319-273-2546, E-mail: douglas.mupasiri@uni.edu. *Application contact:* Laurie S. Russell, Record Analyst, 319-273-2623, Fax: 319-273-2885, E-mail: laurie.russell@uni.edu. Web site: http://www.math.uni.edu/.

University of Oklahoma, Jeannine Rainbolt College of Education, Department of Instructional Leadership and Academic Curriculum, Norman, OK 73072. Offers communication, culture and pedagogy for Hispanic populations in educational settings (Graduate Certificate); instructional leadership and academic curriculum (M Ed, PhD), including bilingual education, early childhood education, elementary education, English education, instructional leadership, mathematics education, reading education, science education, science, technology, engineering and mathematics education (M Ed), secondary education, social studies education, teacher education (M Ed). *Accreditation:* NCATE. Part-time and evening/weekend programs available. *Faculty:* 19 full-time (13 women), 1 (woman) part-time/adjunct. *Students:* 73 full-time (63 women), 114 part-time (87 women); includes 29 minority (5 Black or African American, non-Hispanic/Latino; 12 American Indian or Alaska Native, non-Hispanic/Latino; 5 Asian, non-Hispanic/Latino; 3 Hispanic/Latino; 1 Native Hawaiian or other Pacific Islander, non-Hispanic/Latino; 3 Two or more races, non-Hispanic/Latino), 7 international. Average age 33. 87 applicants, 86% accepted, 68 enrolled. In 2011, 36 master's, 6 doctorates awarded. Terminal master's awarded for partial completion of doctoral program. *Degree requirements:* For doctorate, thesis/dissertation. *Entrance requirements:* For master's, 12 hours of course work in education; for doctorate, GRE General Test, master's degree, minimum graduate GPA of 3.0. Additional exam requirements/recommendations for international students: Required—TOEFL (minimum score 550 paper-based; 79 iBT). *Application deadline:* For fall admission, 6/1 priority date for domestic students, 3/1 for international students; for spring admission, 11/1 for domestic students, 9/1 for international students. Applications are processed on a rolling basis. Application fee: $40 ($90 for international students). Electronic applications accepted. *Expenses:* Tuition, state resident: full-time $4087; part-time $170.30 per credit hour. Tuition, nonresident: full-time $14,875; part-time $619.80 per credit hour. *Required fees:* $2659; $100.25 per credit hour. Tuition and fees vary according to course load and degree level. *Financial support:* In 2011–12, 128 students received support, including 2 research assistantships with partial tuition reimbursements available (averaging $12,431 per year), 12 teaching assistantships with partial tuition reimbursements available (averaging $10,161 per year); institutionally sponsored loans, scholarships/grants, and unspecified assistantships also available. Financial award applicants required to submit FAFSA. *Faculty research:* Engineering in practice for sustainable future, no child left behind (reading), early childhood learning games impact study, Educare randomized control startup, Oklahoma mentoring professional development. *Total annual research expenditures:* $1.1 million. *Unit head:* Lawrence Baines, Chair, 405-325-1498, Fax: 405-325-4061, E-mail: lbaines@ou.edu. *Application contact:* Lynn Crussel, Graduate Programs Officer, 405-325-4843, Fax: 405-325-4061, E-mail: lcrussel@ou.edu. Web site: http://education.ou.edu/departments/ilac.

University of Phoenix–Central Florida Campus, College of Education, Maitland, FL 32751-7057. Offers administration and supervision (MA Ed); curriculum and instruction (MA Ed); curriculum and instruction-computer education (MA Ed); curriculum and instruction-mathematics education (MA Ed); early childhood education (MA Ed); elementary teacher education (MA Ed); secondary teacher education (MA Ed). Evening/weekend programs available. *Degree requirements:* For master's, thesis (for some programs). *Entrance requirements:* For master's, 3 years of work experience, minimum undergraduate GPA of 2.5. Additional exam requirements/recommendations for international students: Required—TOEFL (minimum score 550 paper-based; 213 computer-based; 79 iBT). Electronic applications accepted.

University of Phoenix–North Florida Campus, College of Education, Jacksonville, FL 32216-0959. Offers administration and supervision (MA Ed); curriculum and instruction (MA Ed), including computer education, mathematics education; early childhood education (MA Ed); elementary teacher education (MA Ed); secondary teacher education (MA Ed). Evening/weekend programs available. *Degree requirements:* For master's, thesis (for some programs). *Entrance requirements:* For master's, 3 years of work experience, minimum undergraduate GPA of 2.5. Additional exam requirements/recommendations for international students: Required—TOEFL (minimum score 550 paper-based; 213 computer-based; 49 iBT). Electronic applications accepted.

University of Phoenix–Omaha Campus, College of Education, Omaha, NE 68154-5240. Offers administration and supervision (MA Ed); curriculum and instruction (MA Ed), including adult education, computer education, curriculum and instruction, English and language arts education, English as a second language, mathematics education; elementary teacher education (MA Ed); secondary teacher education (MA Ed); special education (MA Ed).

University of Phoenix–Online Campus, College of Education, Phoenix, AZ 85034-7209. Offers administration and supervision (MAEd, Graduate Certificate); adult education and training (MAEd); curriculum and instruction (MAEd); curriculum and instruction reading (MAEd); curriculum and instruction-computer education (MAEd); curriculum and instruction-language arts (MAEd); curriculum and instruction-mathematics (MAEd); early childhood education (MAEd); educational studies (MAEd); elementary teacher education (MAEd); elementary teacher education-early childhood (MAEd); secondary teacher education (MAEd); special education (MAEd); teacher education - elementary/middle level (MAEd); teacher education middle level generalist (MAEd); teacher education middle level mathematics (MAEd); teacher education middle level science (MAEd); teacher education secondary mathematics (MAEd); teacher education secondary science (MAEd); teacher leadership (MAEd). *Accreditation:* Teacher Education Accreditation Council. Evening/weekend programs available. Postbaccalaureate distance learning degree programs offered. *Students:* 9,180 full-time (7,178 women); includes 2,913 minority (2,069 Black or African American, non-Hispanic/Latino; 50 American Indian or Alaska Native, non-Hispanic/Latino; 100 Asian, non-Hispanic/Latino; 542 Hispanic/Latino; 48 Native Hawaiian or other Pacific Islander, non-Hispanic/Latino; 104 Two or more races, non-Hispanic/Latino), 147 international. Average age 36. *Entrance requirements:* Additional exam requirements/recommendations for international students: Required—TOEFL, TOEIC (Test of English as an International Communication), Berlitz Online English Proficiency Exam, Pearson Test of English, or IELTS. *Application deadline:* Applications are processed on a rolling basis. Application fee: $45. Electronic applications accepted. *Expenses:* Contact institution. *Financial support:* Scholarships/grants available. Financial award applicants required to submit FAFSA. *Application contact:* 866-766-0766. Web site: http://www.phoenix.edu/colleges_divisions/education.html.

University of Phoenix–South Florida Campus, College of Education, Fort Lauderdale, FL 33309. Offers administration and supervision (MA Ed); curriculum and instruction (MA Ed), including computer education, curriculum and instruction, mathematics education; early childhood education (MA Ed); elementary teacher education (MA Ed); secondary teacher education (MA Ed). Evening/weekend programs available. *Degree requirements:* For master's, thesis (for some programs). *Entrance requirements:* For master's, 3 years of work experience, minimum undergraduate GPA of 2.5. Additional exam requirements/recommendations for international students: Required—TOEFL (minimum score 550 paper-based; 213 computer-based; 79 iBT). Electronic applications accepted.

University of Phoenix–Springfield Campus, College of Education, Springfield, MO 65804-7211. Offers administration and supervision (MA Ed); curriculum and instruction (MA Ed), including computer education, curriculum and instruction, English and language arts education, English as a second language, mathematics education; English and language arts education (MA Ed).

University of Phoenix–Washington D.C. Campus, College of Education, Washington, DC 20001. Offers administration and supervision (MA Ed); adult education and training (MA Ed); computer education (MA Ed); curriculum and instruction (MA Ed, Ed D); early childhood education (MA Ed); education (Ed S); educational leadership (Ed D); educational technology (Ed D); elementary teacher education (MA Ed); English and language arts education (MA Ed); English as a second language (MA Ed); higher education administration (PhD); mathematics education (MA Ed); secondary teacher education (MA Ed); special education (MA Ed); teacher leadership (MA Ed).

University of Phoenix–West Florida Campus, College of Education, Temple Terrace, FL 33637. Offers administration and supervision (MA Ed); curriculum and instruction (MA Ed), including computer education, curriculum and instruction, mathematics education; curriculum and technology (MA Ed); early childhood education (MA Ed); elementary teacher education (MA Ed); secondary teacher education (MA Ed). Evening/weekend programs available. *Degree requirements:* For master's, thesis (for some programs). *Entrance requirements:* For master's, 3 years of work experience, minimum undergraduate GPA of 2.5. Additional exam requirements/recommendations for international students: Required—TOEFL (minimum score 550 paper-based; 213 computer-based; 79 iBT).

University of Pittsburgh, School of Education, Department of Instruction and Learning, Program in Secondary Education, Pittsburgh, PA 15260. Offers English/communications education (M Ed, MAT); foreign languages education (M Ed, MAT); mathematics education (M Ed, MAT, Ed D); science education (M Ed, MAT, Ed D); social studies education (M Ed, MAT). Part-time and evening/weekend programs available. *Students:* 154 full-time (92 women), 68 part-time (47 women); includes 18 minority (6 Black or African American, non-Hispanic/Latino; 3 Asian, non-Hispanic/Latino; 7 Hispanic/Latino; 2 Two or more races, non-Hispanic/Latino), 6 international. Average age 30. 208 applicants, 48% accepted, 72 enrolled. In 2011, 116 master's, 6 doctorates awarded. *Degree requirements:* For master's, thesis; for doctorate, thesis/dissertation. *Entrance requirements:* For master's, PRAXIS I; for doctorate, GRE General Test. Additional exam requirements/recommendations for international students: Required—TOEFL. *Application deadline:* For fall admission, 2/1 priority date for domestic students; for spring admission, 11/15 priority date for domestic students. Applications are processed on a rolling basis. Application fee: $50. Electronic applications accepted. *Expenses:* Tuition, state resident: full-time $18,774; part-time $760 per credit. Tuition, nonresident: full-time $30,736; part-time $1258 per credit. *Required fees:* $740; $200 per term. Tuition and fees vary according to program. *Financial support:* Fellowships, teaching assistantships, career-related internships or fieldwork, Federal Work-Study, tuition waivers (partial), and unspecified assistantships available. Support available to part-time students. Financial award application deadline: 3/15; financial award applicants required to submit FAFSA. *Unit head:* Dr. Richard Donato, Chairman, 412-624-7248, Fax: 412-648-7081, E-mail: donato@pitt.edu. *Application contact:* Marianne L. Budziszewski, Director of Admissions and Enrollment Services, 412-648-2230, Fax: 412-648-1899, E-mail: soeinfo@pitt.edu. Web site: http://www.education.pitt.edu/.

University of Puerto Rico, Río Piedras, College of Education, Program in Curriculum and Teaching, San Juan, PR 00931-3300. Offers biology education (M Ed); chemistry education (M Ed); curriculum and teaching (Ed D); history education (M Ed); mathematics education (M Ed); physics education (M Ed); Spanish education (M Ed). Part-time programs available. *Degree requirements:* For master's, thesis; for doctorate, thesis/dissertation, internship. *Entrance requirements:* For master's, PAEG or GRE, minimum GPA of 3.0, letter of recommendation; for doctorate, GRE or PAEG, master's degree, minimum GPA of 3.0, letter of recommendation (2), interview. *Faculty research:* Curriculum, math teaching.

University of Rio Grande, Graduate School, Rio Grande, OH 45674. Offers classroom teaching (M Ed), including fine arts, learning disabilities, mathematics, reading education. *Accreditation:* NCATE. Part-time and evening/weekend programs available. *Degree requirements:* For master's, final research project, portfolio. *Entrance requirements:* For master's, minimum GPA of 2.7 in major, 2.5 overall. Additional exam requirements/recommendations for international students: Required—TOEFL. *Faculty research:* Interagency collaboration, reading and mathematics, learning styles, college access, literacy.

University of St. Francis, College of Education, Joliet, IL 60435-6169. Offers educational leadership (MS, Ed D); elementary education certification (M Ed); reading (MS); secondary education certification (M Ed), including English education, math education, science education, social studies education, visual arts education; special education (M Ed); teaching and learning (MS). *Accreditation:* NCATE. Part-time and evening/weekend programs available. Postbaccalaureate distance learning degree programs offered (no on-campus study). *Faculty:* 7 full-time (5 women), 21 part-time/adjunct (14 women). *Students:* 32 full-time (21 women), 230 part-time (175 women); includes 23 minority (7 Black or African American, non-Hispanic/Latino; 2 Asian, non-Hispanic/Latino; 13 Hispanic/Latino; 1 Two or more races, non-Hispanic/Latino), 1 international. Average age 32. 147 applicants, 60% accepted, 57 enrolled. In 2011, 156 master's awarded. *Entrance requirements:* For doctorate, master's degree, IL Type 75 or Principal's endorsement, interview. Additional exam requirements/recommendations for international students: Required—TOEFL (minimum score 550 paper-based; 213 computer-based). *Application deadline:* Applications are processed on a rolling basis. Application fee: $30. Electronic applications accepted. *Expenses:* Contact institution. *Financial support:* In 2011–12, 23 students received support. Federal Work-Study, scholarships/grants, tuition waivers (partial), and unspecified assistantships available. Support available to part-time students. Financial award applicants required to submit FAFSA. *Unit head:* Dr. John Gambro, Dean, 815-740-3829, Fax: 815-740-2264, E-mail: jgambro@stfrancis.edu. *Application contact:* Sandra Sloka, Director of Admissions for Graduate and Degree Completion Programs, 800-735-7500, Fax: 815-740-5032, E-mail: ssloka@stfrancis.edu. Web site: http://www.stfrancis.edu/academics/college-of-education/.

University of St. Thomas, Graduate Studies, School of Education, Department of Teacher Education, St. Paul, MN 55105-1096. Offers curriculum and instruction (MA), including elementary, individualized, K-12, secondary; elementary (MAT); engineering education (Certificate); English as a second language (MA); math education (Certificate); multicultural education (Certificate); reading (MA, Certificate), including elementary (MA), K-12 (MA). *Accreditation:* NCATE. Part-time and evening/weekend programs available. *Faculty:* 7 full-time (4 women), 26 part-time/adjunct (20 women). *Students:* 19 full-time (14 women), 161 part-time (113 women); includes 28 minority (3 Black or African American, non-Hispanic/Latino; 7 American Indian or Alaska Native, non-Hispanic/Latino; 6 Asian, non-Hispanic/Latino; 9 Hispanic/Latino; 3 Two or more races, non-Hispanic/Latino), 5 international. Average age 35. 150 applicants, 79% accepted, 88 enrolled. In 2011, 83 master's awarded. *Entrance requirements:* For master's, minimum GPA of 3.0 or MAT. Additional exam requirements/recommendations for international students: Required—TOEFL (minimum score 550 paper-based; 210 computer-based; 80 iBT). *Application deadline:* For fall admission, 6/1 for domestic students; for spring admission, 11/1 for domestic students. Applications are processed on a rolling basis. Application fee: $50. *Financial support:* Fellowships, research assistantships, institutionally sponsored loans, and scholarships/grants available. Support available to part-time students. Financial award applicants required to submit FAFSA. *Unit head:* Dr. Jan L. H. Frank, Department Chair, 651-962-4446, Fax: 651-962-4169, E-mail: jlhfrank@stthomas.edu. *Application contact:* Rosemary R. Barreto, Department Assistant, 651-962-4420, Fax: 651-962-4169, E-mail: barr7879@stthomas.edu. Web site: http://www.stthomas.edu/education.

University of South Africa, College of Human Sciences, Pretoria, South Africa. Offers adult education (M Ed); African languages (MA, PhD); African politics (MA, PhD); Afrikaans (MA, PhD); ancient history (MA, PhD); ancient Near Eastern studies (MA, PhD); anthropology (MA, PhD); applied linguistics (MA); Arabic (MA, PhD); archaeology (MA); art history (MA); Biblical archaeology (MA); Biblical studies (M Th, D Th, PhD); Christian spirituality (M Th, D Th); church history (M Th, D Th); classical studies (MA, PhD); clinical psychology (MA); communication (MA, PhD); comparative education (M Ed, Ed D); consulting psychology (D Admin, D Com, PhD); curriculum studies (M Ed, Ed D); development studies (M Admin, MA, D Admin, PhD); didactics (M Ed, Ed D); education (M Tech); education management (M Ed, Ed D); educational psychology

(M Ed); English (MA); environmental education (M Ed); French (MA, PhD); German (MA, PhD); Greek (MA); guidance and counseling (M Ed); health studies (MA, PhD), including health sciences education (MA), health services management (MA), medical and surgical nursing science (critical care general) (MA), midwifery and neonatal nursing science (MA), trauma and emergency care (MA); history (MA, PhD); history of education (Ed D); inclusive education (M Ed, Ed D); information and communications technology policy and regulation (MA); information science (MA, MIS, PhD); international politics (MA, PhD); Islamic studies (MA, PhD); Italian (MA, PhD); Judaica (MA, PhD); linguistics (MA, PhD); mathematical education (M Ed); mathematics education (MA); missiology (M Th, D Th); modern Hebrew (MA, PhD); musicology (MA, MMus, D Mus, PhD); natural science education (M Ed); New Testament (M Th, D Th); Old Testament (D Th); pastoral therapy (M Th, D Th); philosophy (MA); philosophy of education (M Ed, Ed D); politics (MA, PhD); Portuguese (MA, PhD); practical theology (M Th, D Th); psychology (MA, MS, PhD); psychology of education (M Ed, Ed D); public health (MA); religious studies (MA, D Th, PhD); Romance languages (MA); Russian (MA, PhD); Semitic languages (MA, PhD); social behavior studies in HIV/AIDS (MA); social science (mental health) (MA); social science in development studies (MA); social science in psychology (MA); social science in social work (MA); social science in sociology (MA); social work (MSW, DSW, PhD); socio-education (M Ed, Ed D); sociolinguistics (MA); sociology (MA, PhD); Spanish (MA, PhD); systematic theology (M Th, D Th); TESOL (teaching English to speakers of other languages) (MA); theological ethics (M Th, D Th); theory of literature (MA, PhD); urban ministries (D Th); urban ministry (M Th).

University of South Africa, Institute for Science and Technology Education, Pretoria, South Africa. Offers mathematics, science and technology education (M Sc, PhD).

University of South Carolina, The Graduate School, College of Arts and Sciences, Department of Mathematics, Columbia, SC 29208. Offers mathematics (MA, MS, PhD); mathematics education (M Math, MAT). MAT offered in cooperation with the College of Education. Part-time programs available. Terminal master's awarded for partial completion of doctoral program. *Degree requirements:* For master's, comprehensive exam, thesis (for some programs); for doctorate, one foreign language, comprehensive exam, thesis/dissertation, admission to candidacy exam, residency. *Entrance requirements:* For master's and doctorate, GRE General Test. Additional exam requirements/recommendations for international students: Required—TOEFL (minimum score 600 paper-based; 250 computer-based; 100 iBT). Electronic applications accepted. *Faculty research:* Computational mathematics, analysis (classical/modern), discrete mathematics, algebra, number theory.

University of South Carolina, The Graduate School, College of Education, Department of Instruction and Teacher Education, Program in Secondary Education, Columbia, SC 29208. Offers art education (IMA, MAT); business education (IMA, MAT); English (MAT); foreign language (MAT); health education (MAT); mathematics (MAT); science (IMA, MAT); secondary (Ed D); secondary education (MT, PhD); social studies (MAT); theatre and speech (MAT). IMA and MT offered jointly with the subject areas. *Accreditation:* NCATE. *Degree requirements:* For master's, comprehensive exam, thesis (for some programs), foreign language (MA); for doctorate, one foreign language, comprehensive exam, thesis/dissertation. *Entrance requirements:* For master's, GRE General Test or MAT, teaching certificate (IMA, M Ed), interview; for doctorate, GRE General Test or MAT, interview. *Faculty research:* Middle school programs, professional development, school collaboration.

University of Southern Mississippi, Graduate School, College of Science and Technology, Center for Science and Mathematics Education, Hattiesburg, MS 39406-0001. Offers MS, PhD. Part-time programs available. *Faculty:* 1 full-time (0 women), 1 (woman) part-time/adjunct. *Students:* 18 full-time (14 women), 30 part-time (21 women); includes 7 minority (5 Black or African American, non-Hispanic/Latino; 1 Asian, non-Hispanic/Latino; 1 Hispanic/Latino), 7 international. Average age 35. 6 applicants, 83% accepted, 5 enrolled. In 2011, 9 master's, 5 doctorates awarded. *Degree requirements:* For master's, comprehensive exam, thesis or alternative; for doctorate, comprehensive exam, thesis/dissertation. *Entrance requirements:* For master's, GRE General Test, minimum GPA of 2.75 in last 60 hours; for doctorate, GRE General Test, minimum GPA of 3.5. Additional exam requirements/recommendations for international students: Required—TOEFL, IELTS. *Application deadline:* For fall admission, 3/15 priority date for domestic students, 3/15 for international students; for spring admission, 1/10 priority date for domestic students, 1/10 for international students. Applications are processed on a rolling basis. Application fee: $50. *Financial support:* In 2011–12, 1 fellowship with full tuition reimbursement (averaging $21,000 per year), 1 research assistantship with full tuition reimbursement (averaging $14,500 per year), 8 teaching assistantships with full tuition reimbursements (averaging $8,400 per year) were awarded; Federal Work-Study, scholarships/grants, health care benefits, and unspecified assistantships also available. Financial award application deadline: 3/15; financial award applicants required to submit FAFSA. *Unit head:* Dr. Sherry Herron, Director, 601-266-4739, Fax: 601-266-4741. *Application contact:* Sherry Herron, Director, 601-266-4739, Fax: 601-266-4741. Web site: http://www.usm.edu/graduateschool/table.php.

University of South Florida, Graduate School, College of Education, Department of Secondary Education, Tampa, FL 33620-9951. Offers English education (M Ed, MA, MAT, PhD); foreign language education/ESOL (M Ed, MA, MAT); instructional technology (M Ed, PhD, Ed S); mathematics education (M Ed, MA, MAT, PhD, Ed S); science education (M Ed, MA, MAT, PhD); second language acquisition/instructional technology (PhD); secondary education (M Ed, PhD); secondary education/TESOL (M Ed); social science education (M Ed, MA, MAT); teaching and learning in the content area (PhD). *Accreditation:* NCATE. Part-time and evening/weekend programs available. *Faculty:* 28 full-time (17 women), 3 part-time/adjunct (1 woman). *Students:* 174 full-time (116 women), 268 part-time (184 women); includes 103 minority (26 Black or African American, non-Hispanic/Latino; 10 Asian, non-Hispanic/Latino; 58 Hispanic/Latino; 9 Two or more races, non-Hispanic/Latino), 32 international. Average age 37. 229 applicants, 73% accepted, 141 enrolled. In 2011, 115 master's, 16 doctorates, 5 other advanced degrees awarded. *Degree requirements:* For master's, variable foreign language requirement, comprehensive exam, project (for some programs); for doctorate, variable foreign language requirement, comprehensive exam, thesis/dissertation, philosophies of inquiry; multiple research methods. *Entrance requirements:* For master's, GRE General Test or General Knowledge Test, minimum GPA of 3.0; for doctorate, GRE General Test, minimum GPA of 3.5; for Ed S, GRE General Test. Additional exam requirements/recommendations for international students: Required—TOEFL (minimum score 550 paper-based; 213 computer-based; 79 iBT). *Application deadline:* For fall admission, 2/15 for domestic students, 1/2 for international students; for spring admission, 10/15 for domestic students, 6/1 for international students. Application fee: $30. Electronic applications accepted. *Financial support:* In 2011–12, 7 students received support, including 1 research assistantship with full tuition reimbursement available (averaging $10,000 per year), 55 teaching assistantships with full and partial tuition reimbursements available (averaging $7,900 per year); scholarships/grants and unspecified assistantships also available. Financial award application deadline: 4/15; financial award applicants required to submit FAFSA. *Faculty research:* English language learners/multicultural, social science education, mathematics education, science education, instructional technology. *Total annual research expenditures:* $336,023. *Unit head:* Dr. Stephen Thornton, Chairperson, 813-974-3533, Fax: 813-974-3837, E-mail: thornton@usf.edu. *Application contact:* Dr. Diane Briscoe, Coordinator of Graduate Studies, 813-974-1804, Fax: 813-974-3391, E-mail: briscoe@usf.edu. Web site: http://www.coedu.usf.edu/main/departments/seced/seced.html.

University of South Florida–St. Petersburg Campus, College of Education, St. Petersburg, FL 33701. Offers educational leadership development (M Ed); elementary education (MA), including math/science; English education (MA); middle grades STEM education (MS); reading education (MA). Part-time programs available. *Students:* 30 full-time (27 women), 130 part-time (109 women); includes 28 minority (14 Black or African American, non-Hispanic/Latino; 4 Asian, non-Hispanic/Latino; 9 Hispanic/Latino; 1 Two or more races, non-Hispanic/Latino). Average age 34. 63 applicants, 70% accepted, 36 enrolled. In 2011, 74 master's awarded. *Degree requirements:* For master's, comprehensive exam, practicum, internship, comprehensive portfolio. *Entrance requirements:* For master's, State of Florida General Knowledge Test (GKT), Florida Teaching Certificate (for non-initial certification programs), letters of recommendation. Additional exam requirements/recommendations for international students: Required—TOEFL (minimum score 550 paper-based; 79 iBT); Recommended—IELTS. *Application deadline:* For fall admission, 6/1 priority date for domestic students, 6/1 for international students; for spring admission, 10/15 priority date for domestic students, 10/15 for international students. Applications are processed on a rolling basis. Application fee: $30. Electronic applications accepted. *Expenses:* Tuition, state resident: full-time $8847. Tuition, nonresident: full-time $18,423. One-time fee: $35 full-time. Full-time tuition and fees vary according to course load and program. *Financial support:* Applicants required to submit FAFSA. *Unit head:* Dr. Harold W. Heller, Dean, 727-873-4155, Fax: 727-873-4191, E-mail: hheller@usfsp.edu. *Application contact:* Eric Douthirt, Enrollment Management Specialist, 727-873-4450, E-mail: douthirt@usfsp.edu. Web site: http://www1.usfsp.edu/coe/index.asp.

The University of Tennessee, Graduate School, College of Education, Health and Human Sciences, Program in Education, Knoxville, TN 37996. Offers art education (MS); counseling education (PhD); cultural studies in education (PhD); curriculum (MS, Ed S); curriculum, educational research and evaluation (Ed D, PhD); early childhood education (PhD); early childhood special education (MS); education of deaf and hard of hearing (MS); educational administration and policy studies (Ed D, PhD); educational administration and supervision (Ed S); educational psychology (Ed D, PhD); elementary education (MS, Ed S); elementary teaching (MS); English education (MS, Ed S); exercise science (PhD); foreign language/ESL education (MS, Ed S); instructional technology (MS, Ed D, PhD, Ed S); literacy, language and ESL education (PhD); literacy, language education, and ESL education (Ed D); mathematics education (MS, Ed S); modified and comprehensive special education (MS); reading education (MS, Ed S); school counseling (Ed S); school psychology (PhD, Ed S); science education (MS, Ed S); secondary teaching (MS); social foundations (MS); social science education (MS, Ed S); socio-cultural foundations of sports and education (PhD); special education (Ed S); teacher education (Ed D, PhD). *Accreditation:* NCATE. Part-time and evening/weekend programs available. *Degree requirements:* For master's and Ed S, thesis optional; for doctorate, variable foreign language requirement, thesis/dissertation. *Entrance requirements:* For master's, minimum GPA of 2.7; for doctorate and Ed S, GRE General Test, minimum GPA of 2.7. Additional exam requirements/recommendations for international students: Required—TOEFL. Electronic applications accepted. *Expenses:* Tuition, state resident: full-time $8332; part-time $464 per credit hour. Tuition, nonresident: full-time $25,174; part-time $1400 per credit hour. *Required fees:* $1162; $56 per credit hour. Tuition and fees vary according to program.

The University of Texas at Arlington, Graduate School, College of Science, Department of Mathematics, Arlington, TX 76019. Offers applied math (MS); mathematics (PhD); mathematics education (MA). Part-time and evening/weekend programs available. *Faculty:* 24 full-time (8 women), 2 part-time/adjunct (0 women). *Students:* 63 full-time (21 women), 78 part-time (33 women); includes 40 minority (15 Black or African American, non-Hispanic/Latino; 8 Asian, non-Hispanic/Latino; 16 Hispanic/Latino; 1 Two or more races, non-Hispanic/Latino), 36 international. 72 applicants, 92% accepted, 32 enrolled. In 2011, 13 master's, 4 doctorates awarded. *Degree requirements:* For master's, comprehensive exam, thesis or alternative; for doctorate, comprehensive exam, thesis/dissertation, preliminary examinations. *Entrance requirements:* For master's, GRE General Test (minimum score 350 verbal, 650 quantitative); for doctorate, GRE General Test (minimum score 350 verbal, 700 quantitative), 30 hours of graduate course work in mathematics, minimum GPA of 3.0 in last 60 hours of course work. Additional exam requirements/recommendations for international students: Required—TOEFL (minimum score 550 paper-based; 213 computer-based; 79 iBT). *Application deadline:* For fall admission, 6/1 priority date for domestic students, 4/1 for international students; for winter admission, 10/15 priority date for domestic students, 9/15 for international students. Applications are processed on a rolling basis. Application fee: $35 ($50 for international students). Electronic applications accepted. *Financial support:* In 2011–12, 36 students received support, including 17 fellowships with full tuition reimbursements available (averaging $27,500 per year), 2 research assistantships with partial tuition reimbursements available, 23 teaching assistantships with partial tuition reimbursements available (averaging $20,750 per year); Federal Work-Study, institutionally sponsored loans, scholarships/grants, health care benefits, and unspecified assistantships also available. Financial award application deadline: 2/1; financial award applicants required to submit FAFSA. *Faculty research:* Algebra, combinatorics and geometry, applied mathematics and mathematical biology, computational mathematics, mathematics education, probability and statistics. *Unit head:* Dr. Zhu Jiaping, Chair, 817-272-1114, E-mail: jpzhu@uta.edu. *Application contact:* Dr. Jianzhong Su, Graduate Advisor, 817-272-5684, Fax: 817-272-5802, E-mail: su@uta.edu. Web site: http://www.uta.edu/math.

The University of Texas at Dallas, School of Natural Sciences and Mathematics, Department of Science/Mathematics Education, Richardson, TX 75080. Offers mathematics education (MAT); science education (MAT). Part-time and evening/weekend programs available. Postbaccalaureate distance learning degree programs offered (minimal on-campus study). *Faculty:* 6 full-time (2 women). *Students:* 11 full-time (10 women), 55 part-time (36 women); includes 27 minority (6 Black or African American, non-Hispanic/Latino; 7 Asian, non-Hispanic/Latino; 11 Hispanic/Latino; 3 Two or more races, non-Hispanic/Latino), 2 international. Average age 37. 85 applicants, 67% accepted, 45 enrolled. In 2011, 37 master's awarded. *Degree requirements:* For master's, thesis optional. *Entrance requirements:* For master's, GRE General Test, minimum GPA of 3.0 in upper-level coursework in field. Additional exam requirements/recommendations for international students: Required—TOEFL (minimum score 550 paper-based; 215 computer-based). *Application deadline:* For fall admission, 7/15 for domestic students, 5/1 for international students; for spring admission, 11/15 for domestic students, 9/1 for international students. Applications are processed on a rolling basis. Application fee: $50 ($100 for international students). Electronic applications accepted. *Expenses:* Tuition, state resident: full-time $11,170; part-time $620.56 per credit hour. Tuition, nonresident: full-time $20,212; part-time $1122.89 per credit hour. *Financial support:* In 2011–12, 45 students received support, including 2 research assistantships with partial tuition reimbursements available (averaging $20,400 per year), 1 teaching assistantship with partial tuition reimbursement available (averaging $15,300 per year); career-related internships or fieldwork, Federal Work-Study, institutionally sponsored loans, scholarships/grants, and unspecified assistantships also available. Support available to part-time students. Financial award application deadline: 4/30; financial award applicants required to submit FAFSA. *Faculty research:* Innovative science/math education programs. *Unit head:* Dr. Mary L. Urquhart, Department Head, 972-883-2499, Fax: 972-883-6796, E-mail: scimathed@utdallas.edu. *Application contact:* Barbarra Curry, Advisor, 972-883-4008, Fax: 972-883-6796, E-mail: barbc@utdallas.edu. Web site: http://www.utdallas.edu/scimathed/.

The University of Texas at El Paso, Graduate School, College of Science, Department of Mathematical Sciences, El Paso, TX 79968-0001. Offers mathematical sciences (MS); mathematics (teaching) (MAT); statistics (MS). Part-time and evening/weekend programs available. *Students:* 46 (16 women); includes 26 minority (2 Black or African American, non-Hispanic/Latino; 1 Asian, non-Hispanic/Latino; 23 Hispanic/Latino), 16 international. Average age 34. 24 applicants, 83% accepted, 12 enrolled. In 2011, 3 master's awarded. *Degree requirements:* For master's, thesis optional. *Entrance requirements:* For master's, minimum GPA of 3.0, letters of recommendation. Additional exam requirements/recommendations for international students: Required—TOEFL; Recommended—IELTS. *Application deadline:* For fall admission, 8/1 priority date for domestic students, 3/1 for international students; for spring admission, 11/1 priority date for domestic students, 9/1 for international students. Applications are processed on a rolling basis. Application fee: $45 ($80 for international students). Electronic applications accepted. *Financial support:* In 2011–12, research assistantships with partial tuition reimbursements (averaging $21,812 per year), teaching assistantships with partial tuition reimbursements (averaging $17,450 per year) were awarded; fellowships with tuition reimbursements, institutionally sponsored loans, scholarships/grants, health care benefits, tuition waivers (partial), and unspecified assistantships also available. Support available to part-time students. Financial award application deadline: 3/15; financial award applicants required to submit FAFSA. *Unit head:* Dr. Maria C. Mariani, Chair, 915-747-5761, Fax: 915-747-6502, E-mail: mcmariani@utep.edu. *Application contact:* Dr. Benjamin Flores, Interim Dean of the Graduate School, 915-747-5491, Fax: 915-747-5788, E-mail: bflores@utep.edu.

The University of Texas at San Antonio, College of Sciences, Department of Mathematics, San Antonio, TX 78249-0617. Offers applied mathematics (MS), including industrial mathematics; mathematics (MS); mathematics education (MS). Part-time and evening/weekend programs available. *Faculty:* 10 full-time (1 woman), 1 (woman) part-time/adjunct. *Students:* 33 full-time (14 women), 36 part-time (18 women); includes 32 minority (3 Black or African American, non-Hispanic/Latino; 2 Asian, non-Hispanic/Latino; 27 Hispanic/Latino), 10 international. Average age 30. 56 applicants, 80% accepted, 22 enrolled. In 2011, 15 master's awarded. *Degree requirements:* For master's, comprehensive exam (for some programs), thesis or alternative. *Entrance requirements:* For master's, GRE General Test, minimum GPA of 3.0 in last 60 hours. Additional exam requirements/recommendations for international students: Required—TOEFL (minimum score 500 paper-based; 61 iBT), IELTS (minimum score 5). *Application deadline:* For fall admission, 7/1 for domestic students, 4/1 for international students; for spring admission, 11/1 for domestic students, 9/1 for international students. Application fee: $45 ($85 for international students). *Expenses:* Tuition, state resident: full-time $3148; part-time $2176 per semester. Tuition, nonresident: full-time $8782; part-time $5932 per semester. *Required fees:* $719 per semester. *Financial support:* In 2011–12, 15 teaching assistantships (averaging $13,000 per year) were awarded. *Faculty research:* Differential equations, functional analysis, numerical analysis, number theory, logic. *Unit head:* Dr. F. Alexander Norman, Department Chair, 210-458-7254, Fax: 210-458-4439, E-mail: sandy.norman@utsa.edu.

The University of Texas–Pan American, College of Science and Mathematics, Department of Mathematics, Edinburg, TX 78539. Offers mathematical sciences (MS); mathematics teaching (MS). Part-time and evening/weekend programs available. *Degree requirements:* For master's, comprehensive exam. *Entrance requirements:* For master's, GRE General Test, minimum GPA of 3.0. *Application deadline:* For fall admission, 7/12 priority date for domestic students; for spring admission, 11/9 priority date for domestic students. Applications are processed on a rolling basis. Application fee: $0. Tuition and fees vary according to course load, program and student level. *Financial support:* Teaching assistantships, Federal Work-Study, institutionally sponsored loans, scholarships/grants, and tuition waivers (partial) available. Support available to part-time students. Financial award application deadline: 6/1. *Faculty research:* Boundary value problems in differential equations, training of public school teachers in methods of presenting mathematics, harmonic analysis, inverse problems, commulative algebra. *Unit head:* Dr. Andras Balogh, Interim Chair, 956-665-3452, E-mail: abalogh@utpa.edu. *Application contact:* Dr. Monty Taylor, Graduate Program Coordinator, 956-665-3557, E-mail: taylor@utpa.edu. Web site: http://www.math.utpa.edu/gradmath.html.

University of the District of Columbia, College of Arts and Sciences, Department of Mathematics, Washington, DC 20008-1175. Offers applied statistics (MS); teaching mathematics (MST). Part-time and evening/weekend programs available. *Degree requirements:* For master's, comprehensive exam. *Entrance requirements:* For master's, GRE General Test, writing proficiency exam. *Expenses: Tuition, area resident:* Full-time $7580; part-time $421 per credit hour. Tuition, state resident: full-time $8580; part-time $477 per credit hour. Tuition, nonresident: full-time $14,580; part-time $810 per credit hour. *Required fees:* $620; $30 per credit hour. $310 per semester.

University of the Sacred Heart, Graduate Programs, Department of Education, San Juan, PR 00914-0383. Offers early childhood education (M Ed); information technology and multimedia (Certificate); instruction systems and education technology (M Ed), including English, information technology and multimedia, instructional design, mathematics, Spanish. Part-time and evening/weekend programs available. *Degree requirements:* For master's, thesis. *Entrance requirements:* For master's, EXADEP, minimum undergraduate GPA of 2.75, interview.

University of the Virgin Islands, Graduate Programs, Division of Science and Mathematics, Program in Mathematics, Saint Thomas, VI 00802-9990. Offers mathematics for secondary teachers (MA). *Degree requirements:* For master's, action research paper. *Entrance requirements:* For master's, GRE, minimum GPA of 2.5, BA or BS. Additional exam requirements/recommendations for international students: Required—TOEFL (minimum score 550 paper-based; 213 computer-based).

The University of Toledo, College of Graduate Studies, Judith Herb College of Education, Health Science and Human Service, Department of Curriculum and Instruction, Toledo, OH 43606-3390. Offers art education (ME); career and technical education (ME); curriculum and instruction (ME, PhD, Ed S); education and anthropology (MAE); education and biology (MES); education and chemistry (MES); education and classics (MAE); education and economics (MAE); education and English (MAE); education and French (MAE); education and geography (MAE); education and geology (MES); education and German (MAE); education and history (MAE); education and mathematics (MAE, MES); education and physics (MES); education and political science (MAE); education and sociology (MAE); education and Spanish (MAE); educational media (PhD); educational technology (ME); English as a second language (MAE); gifted and talented (PhD); middle childhood education licensure (ME); music education (MME); secondary education (PhD); secondary education licensure (ME). *Accreditation:* NCATE. Part-time and evening/weekend programs available. *Faculty:* 24. *Students:* 60 full-time (31 women), 211 part-time (161 women); includes 23 minority (21 Black or African American, non-Hispanic/Latino; 2 Hispanic/Latino), 20 international. Average age 35. 115 applicants, 73% accepted, 74 enrolled. In 2011, 105 master's, 3 doctorates, 4 other advanced degrees awarded. *Degree requirements:* For master's, comprehensive exam, thesis or alternative; for doctorate, comprehensive exam, thesis/dissertation; for Ed S, thesis optional. *Entrance requirements:* For master's, doctorate, and Ed S, minimum cumulative GPA of 2.7 for all previous academic work, letters of recommendation. Additional exam requirements/recommendations for international students: Required—TOEFL (minimum score 550 paper-based; 213 computer-based; 80 iBT), IELTS (minimum score 6.5). *Application deadline:* For fall admission, 1/15 priority date for domestic students, 1/15 for international students. Applications are processed on a rolling basis. Application fee: $45 ($75 for international students). Electronic applications accepted. *Financial support:* In 2011–12, 9 research assistantships with full and partial tuition reimbursements (averaging $7,184 per year), 12 teaching assistantships with full and partial tuition reimbursements (averaging $8,425 per year) were awarded; career-related internships or fieldwork, Federal Work-Study, institutionally sponsored loans, scholarships/grants, tuition waivers (full and partial), unspecified assistantships, and administrative assistantships also available. Support available to part-time students. *Unit head:* Dr. Leigh Chiarelott, Chair, 419-530-5371, E-mail: eigh.chiarelott@utoledo.edu. *Application contact:* Graduate School Office, 419-530-4723, Fax: 419-530-4724, E-mail: grdsch@utnet.utoledo.edu. Web site: http://www.utoledo.edu/eduhshs/.

University of Tulsa, Graduate School, College of Arts and Sciences, School of Education, Program in Mathematics and Science Education, Tulsa, OK 74104-3189. Offers MSMSE. Part-time programs available. *Students:* 3 full-time (all women), 1 international. Average age 29. 3 applicants, 67% accepted, 2 enrolled. *Entrance requirements:* For master's, GRE General Test. Additional exam requirements/recommendations for international students: Required—TOEFL (minimum score 577 paper-based; 233 computer-based), IELTS (minimum score 6.5). *Application deadline:* Applications are processed on a rolling basis. Application fee: $40. Electronic applications accepted. *Expenses: Tuition:* Full-time $17,748; part-time $986 per hour. *Required fees:* $5 per contact hour. $75 per semester. Tuition and fees vary according to program. *Financial support:* In 2011–12, 3 students received support, including 3 teaching assistantships with full and partial tuition reimbursements available (averaging $9,877 per year); fellowships with full and partial tuition reimbursements available, research assistantships, career-related internships or fieldwork, Federal Work-Study, scholarships/grants, health care benefits, tuition waivers (full and partial), and unspecified assistantships also available. Support available to part-time students. Financial award application deadline: 2/1; financial award applicants required to submit FAFSA. *Unit head:* Dr. David Brown, Advisor, 918-631-2719, Fax: 918-631-2133, E-mail: david-brown@utulsa.edu. *Application contact:* Dr. David Brown, Advisor, 918-631-2719, Fax: 918-631-2133, E-mail: david-brown@utulsa.edu.

University of Vermont, Graduate College, College of Engineering and Mathematics, Department of Mathematics and Statistics, Program in Mathematics, Burlington, VT 05405. Offers mathematics (MS, PhD); mathematics education (MST). *Students:* 23 (6 women), 3 international. 53 applicants, 45% accepted, 5 enrolled. In 2011, 7 degrees awarded. *Degree requirements:* For doctorate, thesis/dissertation. *Entrance requirements:* For master's and doctorate, GRE General Test. Additional exam requirements/recommendations for international students: Required—TOEFL (minimum score 550 paper-based; 213 computer-based; 80 iBT). *Application deadline:* For fall admission, 1/15 priority date for domestic students, 1/15 for international students. Applications are processed on a rolling basis. Application fee: $40. Electronic applications accepted. *Financial support:* Fellowships, research assistantships, and teaching assistantships available. Financial award application deadline: 3/1. *Unit head:* Dr. James Burgmeier, Chair, 802-656-2940. *Application contact:* Prof. Jun Yu, Coordinator, 802-656-2940.

University of Victoria, Faculty of Graduate Studies, Faculty of Education, Department of Curriculum and Instruction, Victoria, BC V8W 2Y2, Canada. Offers art education (M Ed, PhD); curriculum studies (M Ed, MA, PhD); early childhood education (M Ed, PhD); educational studies (PhD); language and literacy (M Ed, MA, PhD); mathematics (M Ed, MA, PhD); music education (M Ed, MA, PhD); science (M Ed, MA, PhD); social studies (M Ed, MA); social, cultural and foundational studies (MA, PhD); technology and environmental education (PhD). Part-time programs available. *Degree requirements:* For master's, thesis, project (M Ed); for doctorate, comprehensive exam, thesis/dissertation. *Entrance requirements:* For master's, minimum B average. Additional exam requirements/recommendations for international students: Required—TOEFL (minimum score 575 paper-based; 233 computer-based), IELTS (minimum score 7). Electronic applications accepted. *Faculty research:* Elementary and secondary English, language arts, curriculum theory and practice, educational media and technology, educational administration and leadership, history and philosophy of education.

University of Virginia, Curry School of Education, Department of Curriculum, Instruction, and Special Education, Program in Curriculum and Instruction, Charlottesville, VA 22903. Offers curriculum and instruction (M Ed, Ed S); elementary (M Ed, Ed D); English (M Ed, Ed D); foreign language (M Ed); mathematics (M Ed, Ed D); reading (M Ed, Ed D, Ed S); science (Ed D); social studies (M Ed). *Students:* 22 full-time (17 women), 29 part-time (27 women); includes 4 minority (1 Black or African American, non-Hispanic/Latino; 1 Asian, non-Hispanic/Latino; 2 Two or more races, non-Hispanic/Latino), 1 international. Average age 33. 67 applicants, 75% accepted, 33 enrolled. In 2011, 78 master's, 2 doctorates, 12 other advanced degrees awarded. *Degree requirements:* For master's, comprehensive exam (for some programs); for doctorate, comprehensive exam, thesis/dissertation; for Ed S, comprehensive exam. *Entrance requirements:* For master's, doctorate, and Ed S, GRE General Test, 2 letters of recommendation. Additional exam requirements/recommendations for international students: Required—TOEFL (minimum score 600 paper-based; 250 computer-based; 90 iBT), IELTS (minimum score 7). *Application deadline:* Applications are processed on a rolling basis. Application fee: $60. Electronic applications accepted. *Financial support:* Fellowships with tuition reimbursements, research assistantships with tuition reimbursements, and teaching assistantships with tuition reimbursements available. Financial award application deadline: 1/5; financial award applicants required to submit FAFSA. *Unit head:* Laura Smolkin, Chair, 434-924-0831. *Application contact:* Karen Dwier, Information Contact, 434-924-0831, E-mail: kgd9g@virginia.edu.

University of Virginia, Curry School of Education, Program in Education, Charlottesville, VA 22903. Offers administration and supervision (PhD); applied developmental science (PhD); counselor education (PhD); curriculum and instruction (PhD); early childhood-developmental risk (MT); education evaluation (PhD); educational psychology (PhD); educational research (PhD); elementary (MT, PhD); English education (MT, PhD); foreign language education (MT); higher education (PhD); instructional technology (PhD); kinesiology (MT, PhD); math education (PhD); reading education (PhD); research statistics and evaluation (PhD); school psychology (PhD); science education (PhD); social studies education (MT, PhD); special education (PhD); world languages education (MT). *Students:* 299 full-time (216 women), 60 part-time (33 women); includes 46 minority (18 Black or African American, non-Hispanic/Latino; 17 Asian, non-Hispanic/Latino; 7 Hispanic/Latino; 4 Two or more races, non-Hispanic/

Latino), 23 international. Average age 30. 307 applicants, 42% accepted, 80 enrolled. In 2011, 113 master's, 62 doctorates awarded. *Degree requirements:* For master's, comprehensive exam (for some programs), field project; for doctorate, comprehensive exam, thesis/dissertation. *Entrance requirements:* For doctorate, GRE General Test. Additional exam requirements/recommendations for international students: Required—TOEFL (minimum score 600 paper-based; 250 computer-based; 90 iBT), IELTS (minimum score 7). *Application deadline:* Applications are processed on a rolling basis. Application fee: $60. Electronic applications accepted. *Financial support:* Fellowships, research assistantships, and teaching assistantships available. Financial award application deadline: 1/5; financial award applicants required to submit FAFSA. *Unit head:* Robert C. Pianta, Dean, 434-924-3334. *Application contact:* Joanne McNergney, Assistant Dean for Admissions and Student Services, 434-924-3334, E-mail: curry-admissions@virginia.edu.

University of Washington, Graduate School, College of Education, Seattle, WA 98195. Offers curriculum and instruction (M Ed, Ed D, PhD), including educational technology, general curriculum (Ed D, PhD), language, literacy, and culture, mathematics education, multicultural education, reading and language arts education (Ed D), science education, social studies education, teaching and curriculum (M Ed); educational leadership and policy studies (M Ed, Ed D, PhD), including administration (Ed D), educational policy, organization, and leadership (M Ed, PhD), higher education, leadership for learning (Ed D), social and cultural foundations of education (M Ed, PhD); educational psychology (M Ed, PhD), including educational psychology (PhD), human development and cognition (M Ed), learning sciences, measurement, statistics and research design (M Ed), school psychology (M Ed); instructional leadership (M Ed); intercollegiate athletic leadership (M Ed); special education (M Ed, Ed D, PhD), including early childhood special education (M Ed), emotional and behavioral disabilities (M Ed), learning disabilities (M Ed), low-incidence disabilities (M Ed), severe disabilities (M Ed), special education (Ed D, PhD); teacher education (MIT). *Accreditation:* APA. Part-time and evening/weekend programs available. *Degree requirements:* For master's, thesis optional; for doctorate, thesis/dissertation. *Entrance requirements:* For master's and doctorate, GRE General Test, minimum GPA of 3.0. Additional exam requirements/recommendations for international students: Required—TOEFL. Electronic applications accepted. *Faculty research:* School restructuring/effective schools, special education interventions, literacy and writing, technology, school partnerships, teacher preparation.

University of Washington, Tacoma, Graduate Programs, Program in Education, Tacoma, WA 98402-3100. Offers education (M Ed); educational administration (principal or program administrator certification) (M Ed); elementary education teacher certification (M Ed); elementary education/special education teacher certification (M Ed); secondary science or math teacher certification (M Ed). Part-time and evening/weekend programs available. *Degree requirements:* For master's, culminating project. *Entrance requirements:* For master's, WEST-B, WEST-E (teacher certification programs only), official sealed transcript from every college/university attended, personal goal statement, letters of recommendation, copy of valid teaching certificate. Additional exam requirements/recommendations for international students: Required—TOEFL (minimum score 580 paper-based; 237 computer-based; 92 iBT). Electronic applications accepted. *Faculty research:* Global learning communities for English/Chinese languages, evaluation of mathematics and reading intervention programs, response to intervention, school-wide behavioral and emotional support, mathematics education and culturally responsive mathematics education.

University of West Georgia, College of Education, Department of Leadership and Applied Instruction, Carrollton, GA 30118. Offers art education (M Ed); art teacher education (Ed S); biology - secondary education (M Ed); biology/secondary education (Ed S); business education (M Ed, Ed S); chemistry/secondary education (Ed S); earth science/secondary education (Ed S); economics/secondary education (Ed S); educational leadership (M Ed, Ed S); English teacher education (M Ed, Ed S); French teacher education (M Ed, Ed S); history teacher education (Ed S); mathematics teacher education (M Ed, Ed S); middle grades education (M Ed, Ed S); physical education and recreation (Ed S); physical education teaching and coaching (M Ed); physics/secondary education (Ed S); science teacher education (M Ed, Ed S); secondary education (M Ed); social science - secondary education (M Ed); social science teacher education (M Ed); Spanish (M Ed); Spanish teacher education (M Ed, Ed S); sports management (M Ed). *Accreditation:* NCATE. Part-time and evening/weekend programs available. *Faculty:* 18 full-time (9 women). *Students:* 75 full-time (49 women), 169 part-time (109 women); includes 90 minority (85 Black or African American, non-Hispanic/Latino; 3 Hispanic/Latino; 2 Two or more races, non-Hispanic/Latino), 1 international. Average age 36. 115 applicants, 67% accepted, 19 enrolled. In 2011, 73 master's, 53 Ed Ss awarded. *Degree requirements:* For master's, internship; for Ed S, research project. *Entrance requirements:* For master's, GRE General Test, minimum GPA of 2.7; for Ed S, GRE General Test, master's degree, minimum graduate GPA of 3.0, district appointment. Additional exam requirements/recommendations for international students: Required—TOEFL (minimum score 523 paper-based; 193 computer-based; 69 iBT); Recommended—IELTS (minimum score 6). *Application deadline:* For fall admission, 7/21 for domestic students, 6/1 for international students; for spring admission, 11/30 for domestic students, 10/15 for international students. Applications are processed on a rolling basis. Application fee: $30. Electronic applications accepted. *Expenses:* Tuition, state resident: full-time $4336; part-time $181 per credit hour. Tuition, nonresident: full-time $17,362; part-time $724 per credit hour. Tuition and fees vary according to course load, degree level, campus/location and program. *Financial support:* In 2011–12, 1 research assistantship with full tuition reimbursement (averaging $7,444 per year) was awarded; career-related internships or fieldwork, scholarships/grants, and unspecified assistantships also available. Support available to part-time students. Financial award application deadline: 7/1; financial award applicants required to submit FAFSA. *Total annual research expenditures:* $5,000. *Unit head:* Dr. Frank Butts, Chair, 678-839-6530, Fax: 678-839-6195, E-mail: fbutts@westga.edu. *Application contact:* Deanna Richards, Coordinator, Graduate Studies, 678-839-5946, E-mail: drichard@westga.edu. Web site: http://www.westga.edu/coelai.

University of West Georgia, College of Science and Mathematics, Department of Mathematics, Carrollton, GA 30118. Offers teaching and applied mathematics (MS). *Faculty:* 15 full-time (3 women). *Students:* 6 full-time (1 woman), 11 part-time (3 women); includes 14 minority (11 Black or African American, non-Hispanic/Latino; 1 Asian, non-Hispanic/Latino; 2 Hispanic/Latino), 5 international. Average age 33. 9 applicants, 56% accepted, 1 enrolled. In 2011, 1 master's awarded. *Degree requirements:* For master's, comprehensive exam, thesis optional, 36 credit hours. *Entrance requirements:* For master's, GRE. Additional exam requirements/recommendations for international students: Required—TOEFL (minimum score 523 paper-based; 193 computer-based; 69 iBT); Recommended—IELTS (minimum score 6). *Application deadline:* For fall admission, 6/1 for domestic and international students; for spring admission, 11/15 for domestic students, 10/15 for international students. Applications are processed on a rolling basis. Application fee: $30. Electronic applications accepted. *Expenses:* Tuition, state resident: full-time $4336; part-time $181 per credit hour. Tuition, nonresident: full-time $17,362; part-time $724 per credit hour. Tuition and fees vary according to course load, degree level, campus/location and program. *Financial support:* In 2011–12, 3 students received support, including 3 teaching assistantships (averaging $6,800 per year); unspecified assistantships also available. Financial award application deadline: 7/1; financial award applicants required to submit FAFSA. *Unit head:* Dr. Minh Nguyen, Interim Chair, 678-839-6489, Fax: 678-839-6490, E-mail: vnguyen@westga.edu. *Application contact:* Alice Wesley, Departmental Assistant, 678-839-5192, E-mail: awesley@westga.edu. Web site: http://www.westga.edu/math/.

University of Wisconsin–Madison, Graduate School, School of Education, Department of Curriculum and Instruction, Madison, WI 53706-1380. Offers art education (MA); curriculum and instruction (MS, PhD); education and mathematics (MA); French education (MA); German education (MA); music education (MS); science education (MS); Spanish education (MA). *Accreditation:* NASM (one or more programs are accredited). *Degree requirements:* For doctorate, thesis/dissertation. Application fee: $56. *Expenses:* Tuition, state resident: full-time $10,296; part-time $643.51 per credit. Tuition, nonresident: full-time $24,054; part-time $1503.40 per credit. *Required fees:* $70.06 per credit. Tuition and fees vary according to course load, campus/location, program and reciprocity agreements. *Financial support:* Project assistantships available. *Unit head:* Dr. John Rudolph, Chair, 608-263-4600, E-mail: jlrudolp@wisc.edu. *Application contact:* 608-262-2433, Fax: 608-262-5134, E-mail: gradadmiss@mail.bascom.wisc.edu. Web site: http://www.education.wisc.edu/ci.

University of Wisconsin–Oshkosh, Graduate Studies, College of Letters and Science, Department of Mathematics, Oshkosh, WI 54901. Offers mathematics education (MS). Part-time programs available. *Degree requirements:* For master's, comprehensive exam, thesis optional. *Entrance requirements:* For master's, 30 undergraduate credits in mathematics. Additional exam requirements/recommendations for international students: Required—TOEFL (minimum score 550 paper-based; 213 computer-based; 79 iBT). Electronic applications accepted. *Faculty research:* Problem solving, number theory, discrete mathematics, statistics.

University of Wisconsin–River Falls, Outreach and Graduate Studies, College of Arts and Science, Program in Mathematics, River Falls, WI 54022. Offers mathematics education (MSE). *Accreditation:* NCATE. Part-time programs available. *Degree requirements:* For master's, thesis (for some programs). *Entrance requirements:* For master's, minimum GPA of 2.75. Additional exam requirements/recommendations for international students: Required—TOEFL (minimum score 500 paper-based; 65 iBT), IELTS (minimum score 5.5). Electronic applications accepted.

University of Wyoming, College of Arts and Sciences, Department of Mathematics, Laramie, WY 82071. Offers mathematics (MA, MAT, MS, MST, PhD); mathematics/computer science (PhD). Part-time programs available. Terminal master's awarded for partial completion of doctoral program. *Degree requirements:* For master's, comprehensive exam, thesis, qualifying exam; for doctorate, comprehensive exam, thesis/dissertation, preliminary exam. *Entrance requirements:* For master's and doctorate, GRE General Test, minimum GPA of 3.0. Additional exam requirements/recommendations for international students: Required—TOEFL (minimum score 540 paper-based; 76 iBT). *Faculty research:* Numerical analysis, classical analysis, mathematical modeling, algebraic combinations.

Ursuline College, School of Graduate Studies, Program in Education, Pepper Pike, OH 44124-4398. Offers art education (MA); early childhood education (MA); language arts education (MA); life science education (MA); math education (MA); middle school education (MA); social studies education (MA); special education (MA). *Accreditation:* NCATE. *Faculty:* 3 full-time (all women), 8 part-time/adjunct (6 women). *Students:* 28 full-time (22 women), 1 (woman) part-time; includes 11 minority (7 Black or African American, non-Hispanic/Latino; 2 Asian, non-Hispanic/Latino; 1 Hispanic/Latino; 1 Native Hawaiian or other Pacific Islander, non-Hispanic/Latino). Average age 32. In 2011, 29 master's awarded. *Degree requirements:* For master's, comprehensive exam. *Entrance requirements:* For master's, minimum undergraduate GPA of 3.0. Additional exam requirements/recommendations for international students: Required—TOEFL (minimum score 500 paper-based; 173 computer-based). *Application deadline:* For fall admission, 8/1 priority date for domestic students. Applications are processed on a rolling basis. Application fee: $25. *Expenses:* Contact institution. *Financial support:* Federal Work-Study available. Financial award application deadline: 3/1. *Unit head:* Dr. Edna West, Director, Master's Apprentice Program, 440-646-6134, Fax: 440-684-6088, E-mail: ewest@ursuline.edu. *Application contact:* Melanie Steele, Graduate Admission Assistant, 440-646-8199, Fax: 440-684-6138, E-mail: graduateadmissions@ursuline.edu.

Virginia Polytechnic Institute and State University, Graduate School, College of Engineering, Department of Engineering Education, Blacksburg, VA 24061. Offers PhD, Certificate. *Degree requirements:* For doctorate, comprehensive exam (for some programs), thesis/dissertation (for some programs). *Entrance requirements:* For doctorate, GRE. Additional exam requirements/recommendations for international students: Required—TOEFL (minimum score 550 paper-based; 213 computer-based). *Application deadline:* For fall admission, 7/1 for domestic and international students; for spring admission, 12/1 for domestic and international students. Applications are processed on a rolling basis. Application fee: $65. Electronic applications accepted. *Expenses:* Tuition, state resident: full-time $10,048; part-time $558.25 per credit hour. Tuition, nonresident: full-time $19,497; part-time $1083.25 per credit hour. *Required fees:* $405 per semester. Tuition and fees vary according to course load, campus/location and program. *Financial support:* Fellowships with full tuition reimbursements, research assistantships with full tuition reimbursements, teaching assistantships with full tuition reimbursements, career-related internships or fieldwork, Federal Work-Study, scholarships/grants, health care benefits, and unspecified assistantships available. Financial award application deadline: 1/15. *Unit head:* Dr. Bev A. Watford, Unit Head, 540-231-7404, Fax: 540-231-6903, E-mail: deuce@vt.edu. *Application contact:* Whitney Hoskins, Graduate Coordinator, 540-231-7359, Fax: 540-231-6903, E-mail: whoskins@vt.edu. Web site: http://www.enge.vt.edu/.

Virginia State University, School of Graduate Studies, Research, and Outreach, School of Engineering, Science and Technology, Department of Mathematics and Computer Science, Petersburg, VA 23806-0001. Offers computer science (MS); mathematics (MS); mathematics education (M Ed). *Degree requirements:* For master's, thesis (for some programs).

Walden University, Graduate Programs, Richard W. Riley College of Education and Leadership, Minneapolis, MN 55401. Offers administrator leadership for teaching and learning (Ed D, Ed S); adult education (Ed D, Ed S); adult learning (MS, Postbaccalaureate Certificate), including developmental education (MS), online teaching (MS), teaching adults English as a second language (MS), training and performance management (MS); college teaching and learning (Ed D, Ed S, Postbaccalaureate Certificate); curriculum, instruction and assessment (Ed D, Postbaccalaureate Certificate); curriculum, instruction, and professional development (Ed S); developmental education (Postbaccalaureate Certificate); early childhood administration, management, and leadership (Postbaccalaureate Certificate); early childhood education (birth-grade 3) (MAT); early childhood public policy and advocacy (Postbaccalaureate Certificate); early childhood studies (MS), including administration, management and leadership, early childhood public policy and advocacy, teaching adults in the early childhood field, teaching and diversity; education (MS, PhD), including adolescent literacy and technology (grades 6-12) (MS), adult education leadership

(PhD), assessment, evaluation, and accountability (PhD), community college leadership (PhD), curriculum, instruction, and assessment, early childhood education (PhD), educational technology (PhD), elementary reading and literacy (MS), elementary reading and mathematics (MS), general program, global and comparative education (PhD), higher education (PhD), integrating technology in the classroom (MS), K-12 educational leadership (PhD), leadership, policy and change (PhD), learning, instruction and innovation (PhD), literacy and learning in the content areas (MS), mathematics (grades 6-8) (MS), mathematics (grades K-5) (MS), middle level education (grades 5-8) (MS), professional development (MS), science (grades K-8) (MS), self-designed (PhD), special education (PhD), special education (non-licensure) (MS), teacher leadership (grades K-12) (MS), teaching English language learners (grades K-12) (MS); educational leadership and administration (principal preparation) (Ed S); educational technology (Ed S); elementary reading and literacy (Postbaccalaureate Certificate); engaging culturally diverse learners (Postbaccalaureate Certificate); enrollment management and institutional marketing (Postbaccalaureate Certificate); higher education (MS), including college teaching and learning, enrollment management and institutional planning, global higher education, leadership for student success, online and distance learning; higher education leadership (Ed D); instructional design (Postbaccalaureate Certificate); instructional design and technology (MS), including general program (MS, PhD), online learning, training and performance improvement; integrating technology in the classroom (Postbaccalaureate Certificate); online teaching for adult learners (Postbaccalaureate Certificate); professional development (Postbaccalaureate Certificate); reading and literacy leadership (Ed D); science K-8 (Postbaccalaureate Certificate); special education (Ed D, Ed S); special education: emotional/behavioral disorders (K-12) (MAT); special education: learning disabilities (K-12) (MAT); teacher leadership (Ed D, Ed S, Postbaccalaureate Certificate); training and performance management (Postbaccalaureate Certificate). Part-time and evening/weekend programs available. Postbaccalaureate distance learning degree programs offered (minimal on-campus study). *Faculty:* 71 full-time (48 women), 853 part-time/adjunct (585 women). *Students:* 11,326 full-time (9,212 women), 2,148 part-time (1,795 women); includes 5,346 minority (4,403 Black or African American, non-Hispanic/Latino; 76 American Indian or Alaska Native, non-Hispanic/Latino; 140 Asian, non-Hispanic/Latino; 561 Hispanic/Latino; 21 Native Hawaiian or other Pacific Islander, non-Hispanic/Latino; 145 Two or more races, non-Hispanic/Latino), 322 international. Average age 39. In 2011, 3,477 master's, 318 doctorates, 471 other advanced degrees awarded. *Degree requirements:* For doctorate, thesis/dissertation (for some programs), residency; for other advanced degree, residency (for some programs). *Entrance requirements:* For master's, bachelor's degree or equivalent in related field; minimum GPA of 2.5; official transcripts; goal statement; access to computer and Internet; for doctorate, master's degree or equivalent in related field; minimum GPA of 3.0; official transcripts; three years' related professional/academic experience (preferred); access to computer and Internet; for other advanced degree, master's degree or equivalent in related field; minimum GPA of 3.0; 3 years related professional/academic experience (preferred); access to computer and Internet (Ed S). Additional exam requirements/recommendations for international students: Required—TOEFL (minimum score 550 paper-based; 213 computer-based), IELTS (minimum score 6.5), or Michigan English Language Assessment Battery (minimum score 82). *Application deadline:* Applications are processed on a rolling basis. Application fee: $50. Electronic applications accepted. *Financial support:* Federal Work-Study, scholarships/grants, unspecified assistantships, and family tuition reduction, active duty/veteran tuition reduction, group tuition reduction, interest-free payment plans, employee tuition reduction available. Support available to part-time students. Financial award applicants required to submit FAFSA. *Unit head:* Dr. Kate Steffens, Dean, 800-925-3368. *Application contact:* Jennifer Hall, Vice President of Enrollment Management, 866-4-WALDEN, E-mail: info@waldenu.edu. Web site: http://www.waldenu.edu/Colleges-and-Schools/College-of-Education-and-Leadership.htm.

Washington State University, Graduate School, College of Education, Department of Teaching and Learning, Pullman, WA 99164. Offers curriculum and instruction (Ed D, PhD); diverse languages (M Ed, MA); elementary education (M Ed, MA, MIT); exercise science (MS); literacy education (M Ed, MA, PhD); math education (PhD); secondary education (M Ed, MA). *Accreditation:* NCATE. *Faculty:* 20. *Students:* 79 full-time (51 women), 40 part-time (31 women); includes 24 minority (3 Black or African American, non-Hispanic/Latino; 5 Asian, non-Hispanic/Latino; 13 Hispanic/Latino; 1 Native Hawaiian or other Pacific Islander, non-Hispanic/Latino; 2 Two or more races, non-Hispanic/Latino), 43 international. Average age 34. 106 applicants, 47% accepted, 43 enrolled. In 2011, 34 master's, 3 doctorates awarded. *Degree requirements:* For master's, comprehensive exam (for some programs), thesis (for some programs), oral or written exam; for doctorate, comprehensive exam, thesis/dissertation, oral and written exam. *Entrance requirements:* For master's and doctorate, GRE General Test, minimum GPA of 3.0, 3 letters of recommendation. Additional exam requirements/recommendations for international students: Required—TOEFL. *Application deadline:* For fall admission, 2/1 for domestic students, 3/1 for international students; for spring admission, 9/1 for domestic students, 7/1 for international students. Applications are processed on a rolling basis. Application fee: $75. *Financial support:* In 2011–12, 130 teaching assistantships with partial tuition reimbursements (averaging $18,204 per year) were awarded; career-related internships or fieldwork, Federal Work-Study, institutionally sponsored loans, tuition waivers (partial), unspecified assistantships, and staff assistantships, teaching associateships also available. Financial award application deadline: 4/1. *Faculty research:* Evolution of middle school education, issues in special education, computer-assisted language learning. *Total annual research expenditures:* $324,000. *Unit head:* Dr. Dawn Shinew, Interim Chair, 509-335-5027, E-mail: dshinew@wsu.edu. *Application contact:* Graduate School Admissions, 800-GRADWSU, Fax: 509-335-1949, E-mail: gradsch@wsu.edu. Web site: http://www.educ.wsu.edu/TL/overview.htm.

Washington State University, Graduate School, College of Sciences, Department of Mathematics, Pullman, WA 99164. Offers applied mathematics (MS, PhD); mathematics teaching (MS, PhD). Part-time programs available. *Faculty:* 26. *Students:* 45 full-time (12 women), 5 part-time (4 women); includes 7 minority (1 Black or African American, non-Hispanic/Latino; 3 Asian, non-Hispanic/Latino; 2 Hispanic/Latino; 1 Two or more races, non-Hispanic/Latino), 14 international. Average age 30. 71 applicants, 54% accepted, 13 enrolled. In 2011, 2 master's, 4 doctorates awarded. *Degree requirements:* For master's, comprehensive exam (for some programs), thesis (for some programs), oral exam, project; for doctorate, 2 foreign languages, comprehensive exam, thesis/dissertation, oral exam, written exam. *Entrance requirements:* For master's and doctorate, minimum GPA of 3.0, 3 letters of recommendation. Additional exam requirements/recommendations for international students: Required—TOEFL (minimum score 600 paper-based; 250 computer-based), IELTS. *Application deadline:* For fall admission, 1/10 for domestic and international students; for spring admission, 7/1 for domestic and international students. Applications are processed on a rolling basis. Application fee: $75. Electronic applications accepted. *Financial support:* In 2011–12, 33 students received support, including 2 fellowships with tuition reimbursements available (averaging $2,500 per year), 3 research assistantships with full and partial tuition reimbursements available (averaging $14,634 per year), 27 teaching assistantships with full and partial tuition reimbursements available (averaging $13,383 per year); career-related internships or fieldwork, Federal Work-Study, institutionally sponsored loans, health care benefits, and tuition waivers (partial) also available. Financial award application deadline: 2/15; financial award applicants required to submit FAFSA. *Faculty research:* Computational mathematics, operations research, modeling in the natural sciences, applied statistics. *Unit head:* Dr. K. A. Ariyawansa, Chair, 509-335-4918, Fax: 509-335-1188, E-mail: ari@wsu.edu. *Application contact:* Graduate School Admissions, 800-GRADWSU, Fax: 509-335-1949, E-mail: gradsch@wsu.edu. Web site: http://www.sci.wsu.edu/math/.

Wayne State College, School of Education and Counseling, Department of Educational Foundations and Leadership, Program in Curriculum and Instruction, Wayne, NE 68787. Offers alternative education (MSE); business and information technology education (MSE); communication arts education (MSE); early childhood education (MSE); elementary education (MSE); English as a second language (MSE); English education (MSE); family and consumer sciences education (MSE); industrial technology and vocational education (MSE); learning communities (MSE); mathematics education (MSE); music education (MSE); science education (MSE); social science education (MSE). *Accreditation:* NCATE. Part-time and evening/weekend programs available. *Degree requirements:* For master's, comprehensive exam, thesis optional. *Entrance requirements:* For master's, GRE General Test. Additional exam requirements/recommendations for international students: Required—TOEFL (minimum score 550 paper-based; 213 computer-based).

Wayne State University, College of Education, Division of Teacher Education, Detroit, MI 48202. Offers art education (M Ed), including art therapy; bilingual/bicultural education (M Ed); career and technical education (M Ed); curriculum and instruction (Ed D, PhD, Ed S), including art education (PhD), bilingual education (Ed D, Ed S), bilingual-bicultural education (PhD), career and technical education (MAT, Ed D, PhD, Ed S), early childhood education (MAT, Ed D, PhD, Ed S), elementary education, English as a second language (MAT, Ed D, Ed S), English education (MAT, Ed D, PhD, Ed S), foreign language education (MAT, PhD), K-12 curriculum, mathematics education (MAT, Ed D, PhD, Ed S), science education (MAT, Ed D, PhD, Ed S), secondary education, social studies education (MAT, Ed S), social studies education: secondary (Ed D, PhD); elementary education (MAT), including special education; elementary education (M Ed, MAT), including children's literature (MAT), early childhood education (MAT, Ed D, PhD, Ed S), general elementary education (MAT); elementary or secondary education (MAT), including bilingual/bicultural education, English as a second language (MAT, Ed D, Ed S), mathematics education (MAT, Ed D, PhD, Ed S), science education (MAT, Ed D, PhD, Ed S), social studies education (MAT, Ed S); English education-secondary (M Ed); foreign language education (M Ed); mathematics education (M Ed); reading (M Ed, Ed S); reading, languages and literature (Ed D); science education (M Ed); secondary education (MAT), including art education (K-12), career and technical education (MAT, Ed D, PhD, Ed S), English education (MAT, Ed D, PhD, Ed S), foreign language education (MAT, PhD), kinesiology; social studies education secondary (M Ed); special education (M Ed, Ed D, PhD, Ed S). *Students:* 216 full-time (154 women), 626 part-time (478 women); includes 289 minority (227 Black or African American, non-Hispanic/Latino; 4 American Indian or Alaska Native, non-Hispanic/Latino; 27 Asian, non-Hispanic/Latino; 21 Hispanic/Latino; 1 Native Hawaiian or other Pacific Islander, non-Hispanic/Latino; 9 Two or more races, non-Hispanic/Latino), 14 international. Average age 37. 347 applicants, 37% accepted, 93 enrolled. In 2011, 226 master's, 12 doctorates, 46 other advanced degrees awarded. *Degree requirements:* For master's, thesis (for some programs), thesis, essay or project (for some M Ed programs), professional field experience (for MAT programs); for doctorate, thesis/dissertation. *Entrance requirements:* For master's, Michigan Basic Skills Test (MA in teaching); for doctorate, minimum undergraduate GPA of 3.0, graduate 3.5; interview, curriculum vitae; references. Additional exam requirements/recommendations for international students: Required—TOEFL (minimum score 550 paper-based; 213 computer-based), TWE (minimum score 5.5). *Application deadline:* For fall admission, 6/1 priority date for domestic students, 5/1 for international students; for winter admission, 10/1 priority date for domestic students, 9/1 for international students; for spring admission, 2/1 priority date for domestic students, 1/1 for international students. Applications are processed on a rolling basis. Application fee: $50. Electronic applications accepted. *Expenses:* Tuition, state resident: part-time $512.85 per credit. Tuition, nonresident: part-time $1132.65 per credit. *Required fees:* $26.60 per credit. $199.65 per semester. Tuition and fees vary according to course load and program. *Financial support:* In 2011–12, 42 students received support. Fellowships, research assistantships with tuition reimbursements available, teaching assistantships, scholarships/grants, and unspecified assistantships available. *Faculty research:* Reading and writing literacy and literature. *Total annual research expenditures:* $264,016. *Unit head:* Dr. Craig Roney, Assistant Dean, 313-577-0902, E-mail: rroney@wayne.edu. Web site: http://coe.wayne.edu/ted/index.php.

Webster University, School of Education, Department of Multidisciplinary Studies, St. Louis, MO 63119-3194. Offers administrative leadership (Ed S); education leadership (Ed S); educational technology (MAT); mathematics (MAT); multidisciplinary studies (MAT); school systems, superintendency and leadership (Ed S); social science (MAT); special education (MAT). Part-time programs available. *Entrance requirements:* For master's, minimum GPA of 2.5. Additional exam requirements/recommendations for international students: Required—TOEFL. *Expenses: Tuition:* Full-time $10,890; part-time $605 per credit hour. Tuition and fees vary according to campus/location and program.

Western Connecticut State University, Division of Graduate Studies, School of Professional Studies, Department of Education and Educational Psychology, Mathematics Education Option, Danbury, CT 06810-6885. Offers MS. Part-time programs available. *Faculty:* 3 full-time (2 women). *Students:* 1 (woman) part-time. Average age 33. 13 applicants, 54% accepted, 1 enrolled. In 2011, 3 degrees awarded. *Degree requirements:* For master's, thesis or alternative, completion of program in 6 years. *Entrance requirements:* For master's, minimum GPA of 2.8, teaching certificate. Additional exam requirements/recommendations for international students: Recommended—TOEFL (minimum score 550 paper-based; 213 computer-based; 79 iBT), IELTS (minimum score 6). *Application deadline:* For fall admission, 8/5 priority date for domestic students; for spring admission, 1/5 priority date for domestic students. Applications are processed on a rolling basis. Application fee: $50. Tuition and fees vary according to course level, course load, degree level and program. *Financial support:* Application deadline: 5/1; applicants required to submit FAFSA. *Faculty research:* Eulerian mathematical principles. *Unit head:* Dr. Adeline Merrill, Chairperson, Department of Education and Educational Psychology, 203-837-3267, Fax: 203-837-8413, E-mail: merrilla@wcsu.edu. *Application contact:* Chris Shankle, Associate Director of Graduate Studies, 203-837-9005, Fax: 203-837-8326, E-mail: shanklec@wcsu.edu.

Western Connecticut State University, Division of Graduate Studies, School of Professional Studies, Department of Education and Educational Psychology, Program in Secondary Education, Danbury, CT 06810-6885. Offers biology (MAT); mathematics (MAT). Part-time programs available. *Faculty:* 4 full-time (all women). *Students:* 10 full-time (4 women), 2 part-time (1 woman); includes 3 minority (all Hispanic/Latino). Average age 36. 27 applicants, 41% accepted, 9 enrolled. In 2011, 14 degrees awarded. *Entrance requirements:* For master's, PRAXIS I Pre-Professional Skills Tests, PRAXIS II subject assessment(s), minimum combined undergraduate GPA of 2.8 or MAT (minimum score in 35th percentile). Additional exam requirements/recommendations for international students: Recommended—TOEFL (minimum score 550 paper-based; 213 computer-based; 79 iBT), IELTS (minimum score 6). *Application deadline:* For fall admission, 8/5 priority date for domestic students; for spring admission, 1/5 priority date for domestic students. Application fee: $50. Tuition and fees vary according to course level, course load, degree level and program. *Financial support:* Application deadline: 5/1; applicants required to submit FAFSA. *Faculty research:* Differentiated instruction, the transition of teacher learning, teacher retention, relationship building through the evaluation process and leadership development, culture development, differentiated instruction, scheduling, transitioning teacher learning and curriculum. *Unit head:* Dr. Bonnie Rabe, Chairperson, Department of Education and Educational Psychology, 203-837-3206. *Application contact:* Chris Shankle, Associate Director of Graduate Studies, 203-837-9005, Fax: 203-837-8326, E-mail: shanklec@wcsu.edu.

Western Governors University, Teachers College, Salt Lake City, UT 84107. Offers curriculum and instruction (MS); educational leadership (MS); educational studies (MA); educational studies (5-12) (MA), including mathematics; elementary education (k-8) (Postbaccalaureate Certificate); English language learning (K-12) (MA); instructional design (MAT); learning and technology (M Ed, MA); management and innovation (M Ed); mathematics (5-12) (Postbaccalaureate Certificate); mathematics (5-9) (Postbaccalaureate Certificate); mathematics education (5-12) (MA); mathematics education (5-9) (MA); mathematics education (K-6) (MA); measurement and evaluation (M Ed); science (5-12) (Postbaccalaureate Certificate); science (5-9) (Postbaccalaureate Certificate); science education (5-12) (MA), including biology, chemistry, geology, physics; science education (5-9) (MA); social science (5-12) (MAT); special education (MAT). *Accreditation:* NCATE. Evening/weekend programs available. Postbaccalaureate distance learning degree programs offered (no on-campus study). *Students:* 3,746 full-time (2,811 women); includes 652 minority (332 Black or African American, non-Hispanic/Latino; 37 American Indian or Alaska Native, non-Hispanic/Latino; 74 Asian, non-Hispanic/Latino; 139 Hispanic/Latino; 70 Two or more races, non-Hispanic/Latino), 12 international. Average age 37. In 2011, 1,080 master's, 242 other advanced degrees awarded. *Degree requirements:* For master's, capstone project. *Entrance requirements:* For master's and Postbaccalaureate Certificate, Readiness Assessment, commitment counseling discussion, transcript submissions, completion of orientation. Additional exam requirements/recommendations for international students: Required—TOEFL (minimum score 450 paper-based; 80 iBT). *Application deadline:* Applications are processed on a rolling basis. Application fee: $65. Electronic applications accepted. *Expenses:* Contact institution. *Financial support:* Scholarships/grants and tuition waivers (partial) available. Financial award applicants required to submit FAFSA. *Unit head:* Dr. Philip Schmidt, Dean of the Teachers College, 845-255-4656. *Application contact:* Enrollment Department, 866-225-5948, Fax: 801-274-3306, E-mail: info@wgu.edu.

Western Michigan University, Graduate College, College of Arts and Sciences, Department of Mathematics, Programs in Mathematics, Kalamazoo, MI 49008. Offers mathematics (MA, PhD); mathematics education (MA, PhD). *Degree requirements:* For master's, oral exams; for doctorate, one foreign language, thesis/dissertation, oral exams, 3 comprehensive exams, internship. *Entrance requirements:* For doctorate, GRE General Test.

Western New England University, College of Arts and Sciences, Program in Mathematics for Teachers, Springfield, MA 01119. Offers MAMT. Part-time and evening/weekend programs available. *Students:* 16 part-time (10 women). In 2011, 17 master's awarded. *Entrance requirements:* For master's, recommendations, resume, personal statement. *Application deadline:* Applications are processed on a rolling basis. Application fee: $30. *Financial support:* Available to part-time students. Application deadline: 4/1; applicants required to submit FAFSA. *Unit head:* Dr. Dennis Luciano, Chair, 413-782-1275, E-mail: dluciano@wne.edu. *Application contact:* Matt Fox, Director of Recruiting and Marketing for Adult Learners, 413-782-1249, Fax: 413-782-1779, E-mail: learn@wne.edu. Web site: http://www1.wnec.edu/continuinged/.

Western Oregon University, Graduate Programs, College of Education, Division of Teacher Education, Program in Secondary Education, Monmouth, OR 97361-1394. Offers bilingual education (MS Ed); health (MS Ed); humanities (MAT, MS Ed); initial licensure (MAT); mathematics (MAT, MS Ed); science (MAT, MS Ed); social science (MAT, MS Ed). *Accreditation:* NCATE. Part-time and evening/weekend programs available. *Degree requirements:* For master's, thesis optional, written exam. *Entrance requirements:* For master's, minimum GPA of 3.0, teaching license. Additional exam requirements/recommendations for international students: Required—TOEFL (minimum score 550 paper-based; 213 computer-based; 79 iBT), IELTS (minimum score 6.5). *Faculty research:* Literacy, science in primary grades, geography education, retention, teacher burnout.

West Virginia University, Eberly College of Arts and Sciences, Department of Mathematics, Morgantown, WV 26506. Offers applied mathematics (MS, PhD); discrete mathematics (PhD); interdisciplinary mathematics (MS); mathematics for secondary education (MS); pure mathematics (MS). Part-time programs available. Terminal master's awarded for partial completion of doctoral program. *Degree requirements:* For master's, comprehensive exam (for some programs), thesis optional; for doctorate, one foreign language, comprehensive exam, thesis/dissertation. *Entrance requirements:* For master's, GRE Subject Test (recommended), minimum GPA of 2.5; for doctorate, GRE Subject Test (recommended), master's degree in mathematics. Additional exam requirements/recommendations for international students: Required—TOEFL (paper-based 550; computer-based 213) or IELTS (paper-based 6). *Faculty research:* Combinatorics and graph theory, differential equations, applied and computational mathematics.

Widener University, School of Human Service Professions, Center for Education, Chester, PA 19013-5792. Offers adult education (M Ed); counseling in higher education (M Ed); counselor education (M Ed); early childhood education (M Ed); educational foundations (M Ed); educational leadership (M Ed); educational psychology (M Ed); elementary education (M Ed); English and language arts (M Ed); health education (M Ed); higher education leadership (Ed D); home and school visitor (M Ed); human sexuality (M Ed, PhD); mathematics education (M Ed); middle school education (M Ed); principalship (M Ed); reading and language arts (Ed D); reading education (M Ed); school administration (Ed D); science education (M Ed); social studies education (M Ed); special education (M Ed); technology education (M Ed). *Accreditation:* NCATE. Part-time and evening/weekend programs available. Terminal master's awarded for partial completion of doctoral program. *Degree requirements:* For doctorate, thesis/dissertation. *Entrance requirements:* For master's, minimum GPA of 2.5; for doctorate, GRE or MAT, minimum GPA of 2.0 (undergraduate), 3.5 (graduate). Electronic applications accepted. *Expenses:* Contact institution. *Faculty research:* Reading and cognition, adult education, technology education, educational leadership, special education.

Wilkes University, College of Graduate and Professional Studies, College of Science and Engineering, Department of Mathematics and Computer Science, Wilkes-Barre, PA 18766-0002. Offers mathematics (MS, MS Ed). Part-time programs available. *Students:* 4 part-time (1 woman). Average age 34. In 2011, 1 master's awarded. *Degree requirements:* For master's, thesis or alternative. *Entrance requirements:* For master's, GRE General Test. Additional exam requirements/recommendations for international students: Required—TOEFL (minimum score 550 paper-based; 213 computer-based; 79 iBT). *Application deadline:* Applications are processed on a rolling basis. Application fee: $45 ($65 for international students). Electronic applications accepted. *Financial support:* Federal Work-Study and unspecified assistantships available. Financial award application deadline: 3/1; financial award applicants required to submit FAFSA. *Unit head:* Dr. Barbara Bracken, Chair, 570-408-4836, Fax: 570-408-7883, E-mail: barbara.bracken@wilkes.edu. *Application contact:* Erin Sutzko, Director of Extended Learning, 570-408-4253, Fax: 570-408-7846, E-mail: erin.sutzko@wilkes.edu. Web site: http://www.wilkes.edu/pages/389.asp.

Wilkes University, College of Graduate and Professional Studies, School of Education, Wilkes-Barre, PA 18766-0002. Offers art and science of teaching (MS Ed); classroom technology (MS Ed); early childhood literacy (MS Ed); educational computing (MS Ed); educational development and strategies (MS Ed); educational leadership (MS Ed); educational technology (Ed D); higher education administration (Ed D); instructional media (MS Ed); instructional technology (MS Ed); K-12 administration (Ed D); online teaching (MS Ed); reading (MS Ed); school business leadership (MS Ed); secondary education (MS Ed), including biology, chemistry, English, history, mathematics; special education (MS Ed); teaching English as a second language (MS Ed); twenty-first century teaching and learning (MS Ed). Part-time and evening/weekend programs available. Postbaccalaureate distance learning degree programs offered (minimal on-campus study). *Students:* 92 full-time (63 women), 2,005 part-time (1,459 women); includes 89 minority (23 Black or African American, non-Hispanic/Latino; 1 American Indian or Alaska Native, non-Hispanic/Latino; 14 Asian, non-Hispanic/Latino; 33 Hispanic/Latino; 1 Native Hawaiian or other Pacific Islander, non-Hispanic/Latino; 17 Two or more races, non-Hispanic/Latino), 6 international. Average age 33. In 2011, 1,150 master's, 3 doctorates awarded. *Entrance requirements:* Additional exam requirements/recommendations for international students: Required—TOEFL (minimum score 550 paper-based; 213 computer-based; 79 iBT). *Application deadline:* Applications are processed on a rolling basis. Application fee: $45. Electronic applications accepted. *Expenses:* Contact institution. *Financial support:* Federal Work-Study and unspecified assistantships available. Financial award application deadline: 3/1; financial award applicants required to submit FAFSA. *Unit head:* Dr. Michael Speziale, Dean, 570-408-4679, Fax: 570-408-4905, E-mail: michael.speziale@wilkes.edu. *Application contact:* Erin Sutzko, Director of Extended Learning, 570-408-4253, Fax: 570-408-7846, E-mail: erin.sutzko@wilkes.edu. Web site: http://www.wilkes.edu/pages/383.asp.

Wright State University, School of Graduate Studies, College of Science and Mathematics, Interdisciplinary Program in Science and Mathematics, Dayton, OH 45435. Offers MST.

Youngstown State University, Graduate School, College of Science, Technology, Engineering and Mathematics, Department of Mathematics and Statistics, Youngstown, OH 44555-0001. Offers applied mathematics (MS); computer science (MS); secondary mathematics (MS); statistics (MS). Part-time programs available. *Degree requirements:* For master's, comprehensive exam, thesis optional. *Entrance requirements:* For master's, minimum GPA of 2.7 in computer science and mathematics. Additional exam requirements/recommendations for international students: Required—TOEFL. *Faculty research:* Regression analysis, numerical analysis, statistics, Markov chain, topology and fuzzy sets.

Museum Education

Bank Street College of Education, Graduate School, Program in Museum Education, New York, NY 10025. Offers museum education (MS Ed); museum education: elementary education certification (MS Ed). *Students:* 30 full-time (29 women), 25 part-time (all women); includes 13 minority (3 Black or African American, non-Hispanic/Latino; 2 Asian, non-Hispanic/Latino; 4 Hispanic/Latino; 4 Two or more races, non-Hispanic/Latino). Average age 28. 41 applicants, 80% accepted, 19 enrolled. In 2011, 21 master's awarded. *Degree requirements:* For master's, thesis. *Entrance requirements:* For master's, interview, essays. Additional exam requirements/recommendations for international students: Required—TOEFL (minimum score 600 paper-based; 250 computer-based; 100 iBT), IELTS (minimum score 7). *Application deadline:* For fall admission, 2/15 priority date for domestic students, 2/15 for international students; for spring admission, 11/1 priority date for domestic students, 11/1 for international students. Applications are processed on a rolling basis. Application fee: $65. Electronic applications accepted. *Expenses: Required fees:* $1240 per credit. $100 per term. One-time fee: $250 part-time. *Financial support:* Federal Work-Study and scholarships/grants available. Support available to part-time students. Financial award application deadline: 4/15; financial award applicants required to submit FAFSA. *Faculty research:* Equitable access and openness to diversity in museum settings, exhibition display and development, museum/school partnerships. *Unit head:* Nina Jensen, Director, 212-875-4491, Fax: 212-875-4753, E-mail: ninajensen@bankstreet.edu. *Application contact:* Seena Berg, Associate Director of Graduate Admissions, 212-875-4402, Fax: 212-875-4678, E-mail: sberg@bankstreet.edu. Web site: http://bankstreet.edu/graduate-school/academics/programs/museum-education-overview/.

Bank Street College of Education, Graduate School, Programs in Educational Leadership, New York, NY 10025. Offers early childhood leadership (MS Ed); educational leadership (MS Ed); leadership for educational change (Ed M, MS Ed); leadership in community-based learning (MS Ed); leadership in mathematics education (MS Ed); leadership in museum education (MS Ed); leadership in the arts: creative writing (MS Ed); leadership in the arts: visual arts (MS Ed). *Students:* 77 full-time (66 women), 130 part-time (108 women); includes 68 minority (33 Black or African American, non-Hispanic/Latino; 8 Asian, non-Hispanic/Latino; 25 Hispanic/Latino; 2 Two or more races, non-Hispanic/Latino), 3 international. Average age 34. 148 applicants, 70% accepted, 92 enrolled. In 2011, 82 master's awarded. *Degree requirements:* For master's, thesis. *Entrance requirements:* For master's, interview, essays, minimum of 2 years experience as a classroom teacher. Additional exam requirements/ recommendations for international students: Required—TOEFL (minimum score 600 paper-based; 250 computer-based; 100 iBT), IELTS (minimum score 7). *Application deadline:* For fall admission, 2/15 priority date for domestic students, 2/15 for international students; for spring admission, 11/1 priority date for domestic students, 11/1 for international students. Applications are processed on a rolling basis. Application fee: $65. Electronic applications accepted. *Expenses: Required fees:* $1240 per credit. $100 per term. One-time fee: $250 part-time. *Financial support:* Career-related internships or fieldwork, Federal Work-Study, scholarships/grants, traineeships, and unspecified assistantships available. Support available to part-time students. Financial award application deadline: 4/15; financial award applicants required to submit FAFSA. *Faculty research:* Leadership in small schools, mathematics in elementary schools, professional development in early childhood, leadership in arts education, leadership in special education. *Unit head:* Dr. Rima Shore, Chairperson, 212-875-4478, Fax: 212-875-8753, E-mail: rshore@bankstreet.edu. *Application contact:* Ann Morgan, Director of Graduate Admissions, 212-875-4403, Fax: 212-875-4678, E-mail: amorgan@bankstreet.edu. Web site: http://bankstreet.edu/graduate-school/academics/programs/leadership-programs-overview/.

The George Washington University, Graduate School of Education and Human Development, Department of Educational Leadership, Program in Museum Education, Washington, DC 20052. Offers MAT. *Students:* 15 full-time (all women); includes 3 minority (2 Black or African American, non-Hispanic/Latino; 1 Asian, non-Hispanic/Latino). Average age 25. 29 applicants, 100% accepted. In 2011, 14 master's awarded. *Degree requirements:* For master's, comprehensive exam. *Entrance requirements:* For master's, GRE General Test or MAT, minimum GPA of 2.75. *Application deadline:* For fall admission, 1/15 priority date for domestic students; for spring admission, 10/1 for domestic students. Applications are processed on a rolling basis. Application fee: $75. *Financial support:* In 2011–12, 7 students received support. Fellowships, career-related internships or fieldwork, Federal Work-Study, and tuition waivers available. Financial award application deadline: 1/15; financial award applicants required to submit FAFSA. *Unit head:* Dr. Carol B. Stapp, Director, 202-994-4960, E-mail: cstapp@gwu.edu. *Application contact:* Sarah Lang, Director of Graduate Admissions, 202-994-1447, Fax: 202-994-7207, E-mail: slang@gwu.edu. Web site: http://gsehd.gwu.edu/MEP.

Seton Hall University, College of Arts and Sciences, Department of Communication and the Arts, South Orange, NJ 07079-2697. Offers corporate and professional communication (MA); museum professions (MA), including exhibition development, museum education, museum management, museum registration; strategic communication (MA); strategic communication and leadership (MA). Part-time and evening/weekend programs available. Postbaccalaureate distance learning degree programs offered (minimal on-campus study). *Degree requirements:* For master's, thesis. *Entrance requirements:* Additional exam requirements/recommendations for international students: Required—TOEFL. Electronic applications accepted. *Expenses: Tuition:* Part-time $1033 per credit hour. *Required fees:* $85 per semester. *Faculty research:* Managerial communication, communication consulting, communication and development.

The University of the Arts, College of Art, Media and Design, Department of Museum Studies, Philadelphia, PA 19102-4944. Offers museum communication (MA); museum education (MA); museum exhibition planning and design (MFA). *Accreditation:* NASAD. *Degree requirements:* For master's, thesis, internship. *Entrance requirements:* For master's, official transcripts, three letters of recommendation, one- to two-page statement, personal interview; academic writing sample and examples of work (for museum communication); two examples of academic and professional writing (for museum education); portfolio and/or writing samples (for museum exhibition planning and design). Additional exam requirements/recommendations for international students: Required—TOEFL (minimum score 580 paper-based, 92 iBT) or IELTS (minimum score 6.5).

Music Education

Alabama Agricultural and Mechanical University, School of Graduate Studies, School of Education, Area in Music Education, Huntsville, AL 35811. Offers music (MS); music education (M Ed). *Accreditation:* NCATE. Part-time and evening/weekend programs available. *Degree requirements:* For master's, comprehensive exam. *Entrance requirements:* For master's, GRE General Test. Additional exam requirements/ recommendations for international students: Required—TOEFL (minimum score 500 paper-based; 173 computer-based; 61 iBT). Electronic applications accepted. *Faculty research:* Jazz and black music, Alabama folk music.

Appalachian State University, Cratis D. Williams Graduate School, School of Music, Boone, NC 28608. Offers music education (MM); music performance (MM); music therapy (MMT). *Accreditation:* NASM. Part-time programs available. *Faculty:* 38 full-time (15 women), 1 part-time/adjunct (0 women). *Students:* 20 full-time (11 women), 1 (woman) part-time, 1 international. 27 applicants, 78% accepted, 9 enrolled. In 2011, 15 master's awarded. *Degree requirements:* For master's, comprehensive exam, thesis or alternative. *Entrance requirements:* For master's, GRE General Test, 3 letters of reference, audition. Additional exam requirements/recommendations for international students: Required—TOEFL (minimum score 550 paper-based; 230 computer-based; 79 iBT), IELTS (minimum score 6.5). *Application deadline:* For fall admission, 3/15 for domestic students, 2/1 for international students; for spring admission, 11/1 for domestic students, 7/1 for international students. Applications are processed on a rolling basis. Application fee: $55. Electronic applications accepted. *Expenses:* Tuition, state resident: full-time $4040; part-time $180 per semester hour. Tuition, nonresident: full-time $15,900; part-time $760 per semester hour. *Required fees:* $2500; $20 per semester hour. Tuition and fees vary according to campus/location. *Financial support:* In 2011–12, 16 research assistantships (averaging $8,000 per year) were awarded; fellowships, teaching assistantships, career-related internships or fieldwork, Federal Work-Study, scholarships/grants, tuition waivers (partial), and unspecified assistantships also available. Financial award application deadline: 4/1; financial award applicants required to submit FAFSA. *Faculty research:* Music of the Holocaust, Celtic folk music, early nineteenth century performance practice, hypermeter and phase rhythm, world music, music and psychoneuroimmunology. *Total annual research expenditures:* $79,000. *Unit head:* Dr. William Pelto, Dean, 828-262-6446, E-mail: peltowl@appstate.edu. *Application contact:* Dr. Jennifer Snodgrass, Graduate Program Director, 828-262-6463, E-mail: snodgrassjs@appstate.edu. Web site: http://www.music.appstate.edu.

Arcadia University, Graduate Studies, Department of Education, Glenside, PA 19038-3295. Offers art education (M Ed); computer education (CAS); curriculum (CAS); curriculum studies (M Ed); early childhood education (M Ed, CAS), including individualized (M Ed), master teacher (M Ed), research in child development (M Ed); educational leadership (M Ed, Ed D, CAS); elementary education (M Ed, CAS); English education (MA Ed); environmental education (MA Ed, CAS); history education (MA Ed); instructional technology (M Ed); language arts (M Ed, CAS); library science (M Ed); mathematics education (M Ed, MA Ed, CAS); music education (MA Ed); psychology (MA Ed); reading (M Ed, CAS); science education (M Ed, CAS); secondary education (M Ed, CAS); special education (M Ed, Ed D, CAS); theater arts (MA Ed); written communication (MA Ed). *Accreditation:* NASAD. Part-time and evening/weekend programs available. Postbaccalaureate distance learning degree programs offered (minimal on-campus study). *Faculty:* 12 full-time (8 women), 38 part-time/adjunct (26 women). *Students:* 66 full-time (48 women), 590 part-time (477 women); includes 65 minority (53 Black or African American, non-Hispanic/Latino; 6 Asian, non-Hispanic/Latino; 3 Hispanic/Latino; 3 Two or more races, non-Hispanic/Latino), 4 international. Average age 36. In 2011, 229 master's, 5 doctorates awarded. *Application deadline:* Applications are processed on a rolling basis. Application fee: $50. Electronic applications accepted. *Expenses:* Contact institution. *Financial support:* Career-related internships or fieldwork, tuition waivers (partial), and unspecified assistantships available. *Unit head:* Dr. Steven P. Gulkus, Associate Professor, 215-572-2120, E-mail: gulkus@arcadia.edu. *Application contact:* 215-572-2925, Fax: 215-572-2126, E-mail: grad@arcadia.edu.

Arizona State University, Herberger Institute for Design and the Arts, School of Music, Tempe, AZ 85287-0405. Offers composition (MM); music (conducting) (DMA); music (ethnomusicology) (MA); music (interdisciplinary digital media/performance) (DMA); music (music history and literature) (MA); music (performance) (DMA); music education (MM, PhD); music therapy (MM); performance (MM). *Accreditation:* NASM. Terminal master's awarded for partial completion of doctoral program. *Degree requirements:* For master's, thesis (for some programs), interactive Program of Study (iPOS) submitted before completing 50 percent of required credit hours; for doctorate, comprehensive exam, thesis/dissertation, interactive Program of Study (iPOS) submitted before completing 50 percent of required credit hours. *Entrance requirements:* For master's, minimum GPA of 3.0 or equivalent in last 2 years of work leading to bachelor's degree, 3 letters of recommendation, resume; for doctorate, GRE or MAT, minimum GPA of 3.0 or equivalent in last 2 years of work leading to bachelor's degree, 3 letters of recommendation, curriculum vitae, statement of intent. Additional exam requirements/ recommendations for international students: Required—TOEFL, IELTS, or Pearson Test of English. Electronic applications accepted.

Arkansas State University, Graduate School, College of Fine Arts, Department of Music, Jonesboro, State University, AR 72467. Offers music education (MME, SCCT); performance (MM). *Accreditation:* NASM (one or more programs are accredited). Part-time programs available. *Faculty:* 16 full-time (2 women). *Students:* 7 full-time (4 women), 10 part-time (6 women), 3 international. Average age 28. 16 applicants, 81% accepted, 9 enrolled. In 2011, 1 master's awarded. *Degree requirements:* For master's, 2 foreign languages, comprehensive exam, thesis or alternative; for SCCT, comprehensive exam. *Entrance requirements:* For master's, GRE General Test or MAT, university entrance exam, appropriate bachelor's degree, audition, letters of recommendation, teaching experience, official transcripts, immunization records, valid teaching certificate; for SCCT, GRE General Test or MAT, interview, master's degree, official transcript, immunization records, letters of recommendation. Additional exam requirements/recommendations for international students: Required—TOEFL (minimum score 550 paper-based; 213 computer-based; 79 iBT), IELTS (minimum score 6), Pearson Test of English Academic (minimum score 56). *Application deadline:* For fall admission, 7/1 for domestic and international students; for spring admission, 11/15 for domestic students, 11/14 for international students. Applications are processed on a rolling basis. Application fee: $30 ($40 for international students). Electronic applications accepted. *Expenses:* Tuition, state resident: full-time $4044; part-time $225 per credit hour. Tuition, nonresident: full-time $8087; part-time $449 per credit hour. *Required fees:* $936; $52 per credit hour. $25 per term. One-time fee: $30. Tuition and fees vary according to course load and program. *Financial support:* In 2011–12, 14 students received support. Teaching assistantships, career-related internships or fieldwork, scholarships/grants, and unspecified assistantships available. Financial award application deadline: 7/1; financial award applicants required to submit FAFSA. *Unit head:* Ken Hatch, Interim Chair, 870-972-2094, Fax: 870-972-3932, E-mail: khatch@astate.edu. *Application contact:* Dr. Andrew Sustich, Dean of the Graduate School, 870-972-3029, Fax: 870-972-3857, E-mail: sustich@astate.edu. Web site: http://www.astate.edu/a/finearts/dept/music/index.dot.

Auburn University, Graduate School, College of Education, Department of Curriculum and Teaching, Auburn University, AL 36849. Offers business education (M Ed, MS, PhD); early childhood education (M Ed, MS, PhD, Ed S); elementary education (M Ed, MS, PhD, Ed S); foreign languages (M Ed, MS); music education (M Ed, MS, PhD, Ed S); postsecondary education (PhD); reading education (PhD, Ed S); secondary education (M Ed, MS, PhD, Ed S), including English language arts, mathematics, science, social studies. *Accreditation:* NASM (one or more programs are accredited); NCATE. Part-time programs available. *Faculty:* 22 full-time (17 women), 3 part-time/adjunct (all women). *Students:* 80 full-time (58 women), 181 part-time (126 women); includes 42 minority (28 Black or African American, non-Hispanic/Latino; 7 Asian, non-Hispanic/Latino; 7 Hispanic/Latino). Average age 34. 184 applicants, 53% accepted, 60 enrolled. In 2011, 77 master's, 10 doctorates, 35 other advanced degrees awarded. *Degree requirements:* For master's, thesis (for some programs); for doctorate, thesis/dissertation; for Ed S, field project. *Entrance requirements:* For master's, doctorate, and Ed S, GRE General Test. *Application deadline:* For fall admission, 7/7 for domestic students; for spring admission, 11/24 for domestic students. Applications are processed on a rolling basis. Application fee: $50 ($60 for international students). Electronic applications accepted. *Expenses:* Tuition, state resident: full-time $7290; part-time $405 per credit hour. Tuition, nonresident: full-time $21,870; part-time $1215 per credit hour. *International tuition:* $22,000 full-time. *Required fees:* $1402. *Financial support:* Fellowships, teaching assistantships, career-related internships or fieldwork, and Federal Work-Study available. Support available to part-time students. Financial award application deadline: 3/15; financial award applicants required to submit FAFSA. *Faculty research:* Emerging literacy, reading attitudes, music for at-risk youth, portfolio assessment. *Unit head:* Dr. Kimberly Walls, Head, 334-844-4434. *Application contact:* Dr. George Flowers, Dean of the Graduate School, 334-844-2125. Web site: http://education.auburn.edu/academic_departments/curr/.

Austin College, Program in Education, Sherman, TX 75090-4400. Offers art education (MA); elementary education (MA); middle school education (MA); music education (MA); physical education and coaching (MA); secondary education (MA); theatre education (MA). Part-time programs available. *Faculty:* 5 full-time (4 women). *Students:* 21 full-time (13 women), 2 part-time (both women). Average age 23. In 2011, 24 master's awarded. *Degree requirements:* For master's, one foreign language, thesis or alternative. *Entrance requirements:* For master's, Texas Academic Skills Program Test. *Application deadline:* For fall admission, 5/1 priority date for domestic students; for spring admission, 1/15 priority date for domestic students. Applications are processed on a rolling basis. Application fee: $35. Electronic applications accepted. *Expenses: Tuition:* Full-time $38,445. *Required fees:* $160. *Financial support:* Career-related internships or fieldwork, Federal Work-Study, scholarships/grants, and unspecified assistantships available. Support available to part-time students. Financial award application deadline: 4/1; financial award applicants required to submit FAFSA. *Unit head:* Dr. Barbara Sylvester, Director of Teaching Program, 903-813-2327, E-mail: bsylvester@austincollege.edu. *Application contact:* Dr. Barbara Sylvester, Director of Teaching Program, 903-813-2327, E-mail: bsylvester@austincollege.edu. Web site: http://www.austincollege.edu/.

Austin Peay State University, College of Graduate Studies, College of Arts and Letters, Department of Music, Clarksville, TN 37044. Offers music education (M Mu); music performance (M Mu). *Accreditation:* NASM. Part-time programs available. *Faculty:* 20 full-time (9 women), 2 part-time/adjunct (1 woman). *Students:* 20 full-time (11 women), 4 part-time (1 woman); includes 4 minority (1 Black or African American, non-Hispanic/Latino; 1 Native Hawaiian or other Pacific Islander, non-Hispanic/Latino; 2 Two or more races, non-Hispanic/Latino). Average age 30. 13 applicants, 100% accepted, 8 enrolled. In 2011, 12 master's awarded. *Degree requirements:* For master's, comprehensive exam, thesis optional. *Entrance requirements:* For master's, GRE General Test, diagnostic exams, audition, bachelor's degree, 3 letters of recommendation. Additional exam requirements/recommendations for international students: Required—TOEFL (minimum score 500 paper-based; 173 computer-based). *Application deadline:* For fall admission, 8/1 priority date for domestic students. Applications are processed on a rolling basis. Application fee: $25. Electronic applications accepted. *Expenses:* Tuition, state resident: part-time $350 per credit hour. Tuition, nonresident: full-time $20,644; part-time $971 per credit hour. *Required fees:* $1224; $61.20 per credit hour. *Financial support:* In 2011–12, research assistantships with full tuition reimbursements (averaging $5,184 per year) were awarded; career-related internships or fieldwork, Federal Work-Study, institutionally sponsored loans, scholarships/grants, and unspecified assistantships also available. Support available to part-time students. Financial award application deadline: 3/1; financial award applicants required to submit FAFSA. *Unit head:* Dr. Douglas Rose, Chair, 931-221-7808, Fax: 931-221-7529, E-mail: rosed@apsu.edu. *Application contact:* Kendra Bryant, Graduate Admissions, 800-844-2778, Fax: 931-221-6188, E-mail: admissionsweb@apsu.edu. Web site: http://www.apsu.edu/music/.

Azusa Pacific University, School of Music, Azusa, CA 91702-7000. Offers education (M Mus); performance (M Mus). *Accreditation:* NASM. Part-time and evening/weekend programs available. *Degree requirements:* For master's, recital. *Entrance requirements:* For master's, interview, audition. Additional exam requirements/recommendations for international students: Required—TOEFL (minimum score 550 paper-based).

Ball State University, Graduate School, College of Fine Arts, School of Music, Muncie, IN 47306-1099. Offers music education (MA, MM, DA). *Accreditation:* NASM; NCATE (one or more programs are accredited). *Faculty:* 50 full-time (17 women), 2 part-time/adjunct (1 woman). *Students:* 51 full-time (26 women), 45 part-time (26 women); includes 6 minority (1 Black or African American, non-Hispanic/Latino; 3 Hispanic/Latino; 2 Two or more races, non-Hispanic/Latino), 21 international. Average age 25. 90 applicants, 56% accepted, 32 enrolled. In 2011, 18 master's, 12 doctorates awarded. *Degree requirements:* For doctorate, thesis/dissertation. *Entrance requirements:* For master's, audition; for doctorate, GRE General Test, audition, minimum graduate GPA of 3.2, writing sample. Application fee: $50. Tuition and fees vary according to program and reciprocity agreements. *Financial support:* In 2011–12, 67 students received support, including 63 teaching assistantships with full tuition reimbursements available (averaging $12,982 per year); research assistantships with full tuition reimbursements available also available. Financial award application deadline: 3/1. *Unit head:* Dr. John Scheib, Unit Head, 765-285-5400, Fax: 765-285-5401. *Application contact:* Dr. Linda Pohly, Coordinator, 765-285-5502, Fax: 765-285-5401, E-mail: lpohly@bsu.edu. Web site: http://www.bsu.edu/music/.

Belmont University, College of Visual and Performing Arts, School of Music, Nashville, TN 37212-3757. Offers church music (MM); commercial music (MM); composition (MM); music education (MM); pedagogy (MM); performance (MM). *Accreditation:* NASM. Part-time programs available. *Faculty:* 30 full-time (9 women), 8 part-time/adjunct (3 women). *Students:* 22 full-time (10 women), 29 part-time (17 women); includes 3 minority (2 Black or African American, non-Hispanic/Latino; 1 Asian, non-Hispanic/Latino). Average age 27. 67 applicants, 48% accepted, 21 enrolled. In 2011, 13 master's awarded. *Degree requirements:* For master's, comprehensive exam, thesis (for some programs). *Entrance requirements:* For master's, placement exam, GRE or MAT, audition, interview, minimum GPA of 2.75. Additional exam requirements/recommendations for international students: Required—TOEFL (minimum score 500 paper-based; 173 computer-based). *Application deadline:* For fall admission, 5/1 priority date for domestic students, 5/1 for international students; for spring admission, 11/1 priority date for domestic students, 11/1 for international students. Applications are processed on a rolling basis. Application fee: $50. Electronic applications accepted. *Expenses: Tuition:* Full-time $28,500; part-time $900 per hour. *Required fees:* $790; $165 per semester. Tuition and fees vary according to course level, degree level and program. *Financial support:* In 2011–12, 26 students received support, including 15 fellowships (averaging $2,000 per year), 7 teaching assistantships (averaging $2,000 per year); career-related internships or fieldwork, scholarships/grants, and unspecified assistantships also available. Financial award application deadline: 3/1; financial award applicants required to submit FAFSA. *Unit head:* Dr. Robert Gregg, Director, 615-460-8111, Fax: 615-386-0239, E-mail: greggr@mail.belmont.edu. *Application contact:* Ben Craine, Graduate Secretary, 615-460-8117, Fax: 615-386-0239, E-mail: ben.craine@belmont.edu.

Bob Jones University, Graduate Programs, Greenville, SC 29614. Offers accountancy (MS); Bible (MA); Bible translation (MA); Biblical studies (Certificate); broadcast management (MS); business administration (MBA); church history (MA, PhD); church ministries (MA); church music (MM); cinema and video production (MA); counseling (MS); curriculum and instruction (Ed D); divinity (M Div); dramatic production (MA); educational leadership (MS, Ed D, Ed S); elementary education (M Ed, MAT); English (M Ed, MA, MAT); fine arts (MA); graphic design (MA); history (M Ed, MA); illustration (MA); interpretative speech (MA); mathematics (M Ed, MAT); medical missions (Certificate); ministry (MM, D Min); multi-categorical special education (M Ed, MAT); music (M Ed); New Testament interpretation (PhD); Old Testament interpretation (PhD); orchestral instrument performance (MM); organ performance (MM); pastoral studies (MA); personnel services (MS, Ed S); piano pedagogy (MM); piano performance (MM); platform arts (MA); radio and television broadcasting (MS); rhetoric and public address (MA); secondary education (M Ed); studio art (MA); teaching Bible (MA); theology (MA, PhD); voice performance (MM); youth ministries (MA); M Div/MM.

Boise State University, Graduate College, College of Arts and Sciences, Department of Music, Program in Music Education, Boise, ID 83725-0399. Offers MM. *Accreditation:* NASM; NCATE. Part-time programs available. *Degree requirements:* For master's, thesis optional. *Entrance requirements:* For master's, minimum GPA of 3.0, performance demonstration. Electronic applications accepted.

Boise State University, Graduate College, College of Arts and Sciences, Department of Music, Program in Pedagogy, Boise, ID 83725-0399. Offers MM. *Accreditation:* NCATE. Part-time programs available. *Degree requirements:* For master's, thesis optional. *Entrance requirements:* For master's, minimum GPA of 3.0, performance demonstration. Electronic applications accepted.

The Boston Conservatory, Graduate Division, Boston, MA 02215. Offers choral conducting (MM); composition (MM); music (MM, ADP, Certificate), including music, music education (MM); music performance (MM, ADP, Certificate); opera (MM, ADP, Certificate); theater (MM). *Accreditation:* NASM (one or more programs are accredited). Part-time programs available. *Degree requirements:* For master's, recital or performance; for other advanced degree, recital. *Entrance requirements:* For master's and other advanced degree, audition. Additional exam requirements/recommendations for international students: Required—TOEFL (minimum score 580 paper-based; 237 computer-based). Electronic applications accepted.

The Boston Conservatory, Graduate Division, Music Division, Department of Music Education, Boston, MA 02215. Offers MM. *Accreditation:* NASM. Part-time programs available. *Degree requirements:* For master's, comprehensive oral exam, thesis or recital. *Entrance requirements:* For master's, audition, interview. Additional exam requirements/recommendations for international students: Required—TOEFL (minimum score 580 paper-based; 237 computer-based). Electronic applications accepted.

Boston University, College of Fine Arts, School of Music, Program in Music Education, Boston, MA 02215. Offers MM, DMA. *Accreditation:* NASM. *Faculty:* 9 full-time (3 women). *Students:* 483 full-time (255 women), 197 part-time (103 women); includes 90 minority (44 Black or African American, non-Hispanic/Latino; 7 American Indian or Alaska Native, non-Hispanic/Latino; 12 Asian, non-Hispanic/Latino; 27 Hispanic/Latino), 28 international. Average age 37. 36 applicants, 56% accepted, 7 enrolled. In 2011, 127 master's, 14 doctorates awarded. *Degree requirements:* For master's, thesis; for doctorate, 2 foreign languages, thesis/dissertation. *Entrance requirements:* For doctorate, GRE or MAT. Additional exam requirements/recommendations for international students: Required—TOEFL (minimum score 100 iBT). *Application deadline:* For fall admission, 1/1 priority date for domestic students, 1/1 for international students. Application fee: $70. Electronic applications accepted. *Expenses: Tuition:* Full-time $40,848; part-time $1276 per credit hour. *Required fees:* $572; $286 per semester. *Financial support:* Fellowships and teaching assistantships available. Financial award application deadline: 1/1. *Unit head:* Robert Dodson, Director, 617-353-8789, Fax: 617-353-7455, E-mail: rdodson@bu.edu. *Application contact:* Mark Krone, Manager, Graduate Admissions, 617-353-3350, E-mail: arts@bu.edu.

Boston University, Graduate School of Arts and Sciences, Department of Music, Boston, MA 02215. Offers composition (MA); music education (MA); music history/theory (PhD); musicology (MA, PhD). *Accreditation:* NASM. *Students:* 4 full-time (3 women), 1 part-time (0 women); includes 2 minority (both Hispanic/Latino). Average age 28. 58 applicants, 16% accepted, 3 enrolled. In 2011, 1 master's awarded. *Degree requirements:* For master's, 2 foreign languages, comprehensive exam, thesis; for doctorate, 2 foreign languages, comprehensive exam, thesis/dissertation. *Entrance requirements:* For master's and doctorate, GRE General Test, musical composition or research paper, 3 letters of recommendation. Additional exam requirements/recommendations for international students: Required—TOEFL (minimum score 550 paper-based; 213 computer-based). *Application deadline:* For fall admission, 1/15 for domestic and international students. Application fee: $70. Electronic applications accepted. *Expenses: Tuition:* Full-time $40,848; part-time $1276 per credit hour. *Required fees:* $572; $286 per semester. *Financial support:* Federal Work-Study, scholarships/grants, and unspecified assistantships available. Support available to part-time students. Financial award application deadline: 1/15; financial award applicants required to submit FAFSA. *Unit head:* Jeremy Yudkin, Director, 617-353-3362, Fax: 617-353-7455, E-mail: yudkinj@bu.edu. *Application contact:* Jessica Smith, Administrative Coordinator, 617-353-6887, Fax: 617-353-7455, E-mail: smithj08@bu.edu.

Bowling Green State University, Graduate College, College of Musical Arts, Bowling Green, OH 43403. Offers composition (MM); contemporary music (DMA), including composition, performance; ethnomusicology (MM); music education (MM), including choral, comprehensive, instrumental; music history (MM); music theory (MM); performance (MM). *Accreditation:* NASM. Part-time programs available. *Degree requirements:* For master's, thesis or alternative, recitals; for doctorate, comprehensive exam, thesis/dissertation. *Entrance requirements:* For master's, GRE General Test, diagnostic placement exams in music history and theory, audition, interview. Additional exam requirements/recommendations for international students: Required—TOEFL. Electronic applications accepted. *Faculty research:* Ethnomusicology.

Brandon University, School of Music, Brandon, MB R7A 6A9, Canada. Offers composition (M Mus); music education (M Mus); performance and literature (M Mus), including clarinet, conducting, jazz, piano, strings. Part-time programs available. *Degree requirements:* For master's, comprehensive exam (for some programs), thesis (for some programs), 2 recitals. *Entrance requirements:* For master's, B Mus. Additional exam requirements/recommendations for international students: Required—TOEFL or IELTS. Electronic applications accepted. *Faculty research:* Composition, evaluation and assessment, performance anxiety, philosophy of music, teacher education.

Brigham Young University, Graduate Studies, College of Fine Arts and Communications, School of Music, Provo, UT 84602-1001. Offers composition (MM); conducting (MM); music education (MA, MM); musicology (MA); performance (MM). *Accreditation:* NASM. *Faculty:* 46 full-time (8 women). *Students:* 55 full-time (39 women), 14 part-time (6 women); includes 8 minority (6 Asian, non-Hispanic/Latino; 2 Hispanic/Latino). Average age 29. 48 applicants, 52% accepted, 19 enrolled. In 2011, 24 master's awarded. *Degree requirements:* For master's, comprehensive exam (for some programs), thesis (for some programs), recital, project or composition (for some programs). *Entrance requirements:* For master's, placement exam, minimum GPA of 3.0 in last 60 hours, BM. Additional exam requirements/recommendations for international students: Required—TOEFL (minimum score 580 paper-based; 237 computer-based; 85 iBT). *Application deadline:* For fall admission, 2/1 priority date for domestic students, 1/15 for international students. Application fee: $50. Electronic applications accepted. *Expenses: Tuition:* Full-time $5760; part-time $320 per credit. Tuition and fees vary according to student's religious affiliation. *Financial support:* In 2011–12, 69 students received support, including 46 teaching assistantships (averaging $5,000 per year); research assistantships, career-related internships or fieldwork, institutionally sponsored loans, scholarships/grants, tuition waivers (partial), and unspecified assistantships also available. Support available to part-time students. Financial award application deadline:

2/1; financial award applicants required to submit FAFSA. *Faculty research:* Louis Armstrong, rock and roll, Balinese gamelan, English hymnody, Christian Wolff biography. *Unit head:* Prof. Kory L. Katseanes, Director, 801-422-6304, Fax: 801-422-0533, E-mail: kory_katseanes@byu.edu. *Application contact:* Dr. Thomas L. Durham, Graduate Coordinator, 801-422-3226, Fax: 801-422-0533, E-mail: thomas_durham@byu.edu. Web site: http://www.music.byu.edu.

Brooklyn College of the City University of New York, Division of Graduate Studies, Conservatory of Music, Brooklyn, NY 11210-2889. Offers composition (MM); music (DMA, PhD); music education (MA); musicology (MA); performance (MM); performance practice (MA). Part-time programs available. *Degree requirements:* For master's, one foreign language, comprehensive exam, thesis. *Entrance requirements:* For master's, placement exam, 36 credits in music, audition, completed composition, writing sample. Additional exam requirements/recommendations for international students: Required—TOEFL (minimum score 550 paper-based; 213 computer-based; 79 iBT). Electronic applications accepted. *Faculty research:* American music, computer music.

Brooklyn College of the City University of New York, Division of Graduate Studies, School of Education, Program in Adolescence Education and Special Subjects, Brooklyn, NY 11210-2889. Offers adolescence science education (MAT); art teacher (MA); biology teacher (MA); chemistry teacher (MA); earth science teacher (MAT); English teacher (MA); French teacher (MA); health and nutrition sciences: health teacher (MS Ed); mathematics teacher (MA); music education (CAS); music teacher (MA); physical education teacher (MS Ed); physics teacher (MA); social studies teacher (MA); Spanish teacher (MA). Part-time and evening/weekend programs available. *Degree requirements:* For master's, comprehensive exam (for some programs), thesis (for some programs). *Entrance requirements:* For master's, LAST, previous course work in education, resume, 2 letters of recommendation, essay. Additional exam requirements/recommendations for international students: Required—TOEFL (minimum score 500 paper-based; 173 computer-based; 61 iBT). Electronic applications accepted. *Faculty research:* Interdisciplinary education, semiotics, discourse analysis, autobiography, teacher identity.

Butler University, Jordan College of Fine Arts, Department of Music, Indianapolis, IN 46208-3485. Offers composition (MM); conducting (MM); music (MM); music education (MM); music history (MM); organ (MM); performance (MM). *Accreditation:* NASM. Part-time and evening/weekend programs available. *Faculty:* 9 full-time (0 women), 3 part-time/adjunct (0 women). *Students:* 19 full-time (10 women), 27 part-time (11 women), 2 international. Average age 26. 18 applicants, 100% accepted, 12 enrolled. In 2011, 13 master's awarded. *Degree requirements:* For master's, thesis (for some programs). *Entrance requirements:* For master's, GRE General Test, GRE Subject Test, audition, interview. *Application deadline:* For fall admission, 8/15 priority date for domestic students. Applications are processed on a rolling basis. Application fee: $35. Electronic applications accepted. *Expenses: Tuition:* Part-time $466 per credit. *Financial support:* In 2011–12, 15 teaching assistantships with full tuition reimbursements (averaging $2,500 per year) were awarded; fellowships, career-related internships or fieldwork, institutionally sponsored loans, and scholarships/grants also available. Support available to part-time students. Financial award application deadline: 7/15; financial award applicants required to submit FAFSA. *Unit head:* Dr. Daniel Bolin, Head, 317-940-9988, Fax: 317-940-9658, E-mail: dbolin@butler.edu. *Application contact:* Kathy Lang, Admission Representative, 317-940-9646, Fax: 317-940-9658, E-mail: klang@butler.edu.

California Baptist University, Program in Music, Riverside, CA 92504-3206. Offers conducting (MM); music education (MM); performance (MM). *Accreditation:* NASM. Part-time and evening/weekend programs available. *Faculty:* 12 full-time (5 women). *Students:* 17 full-time (11 women); includes 3 minority (2 Asian, non-Hispanic/Latino; 1 Hispanic/Latino), 8 international. Average age 27. 13 applicants, 62% accepted, 5 enrolled. In 2011, 9 master's awarded. *Degree requirements:* For master's, comprehensive exam or thesis. *Entrance requirements:* For master's, minimum undergraduate GPA of 3.0; bachelor's degree in music; three recommendations; comprehensive essay; interview/audition. Additional exam requirements/recommendations for international students: Required—TOEFL (minimum score 575 paper-based; 230 computer-based; 89 iBT). *Application deadline:* For fall admission, 8/1 priority date for domestic students, 7/1 for international students; for spring admission, 12/1 priority date for domestic students, 11/1 for international students. Applications are processed on a rolling basis. Application fee: $45. Electronic applications accepted. *Expenses:* Contact institution. *Financial support:* In 2011–12, 13 students received support. Federal Work-Study, institutionally sponsored loans, and scholarships/grants available. Financial award applicants required to submit FAFSA. *Faculty research:* Choral conducting, church music, choir building, hymnology, music technology. *Unit head:* Dr. Judd Bonner, Associate Dean, School of Music, 951-343-4256, Fax: 951-343-4570, E-mail: jbonner@calbaptist.edu. *Application contact:* Gail Ronveaux, Dean of Graduate Enrollment, 951-343-4246, Fax: 951-343-5095, E-mail: graduateadmissions@calbaptist.edu. Web site: http://www.calbaptist.edu/masterofmusic/.

California State University, Fresno, Division of Graduate Studies, College of Arts and Humanities, Department of Music, Fresno, CA 93740-8027. Offers music (MA); music education (MA); performance (MA). *Accreditation:* NASM. Part-time programs available. *Degree requirements:* For master's, thesis or alternative. *Entrance requirements:* For master's, GRE General Test, BA in music, minimum GPA of 3.0. Additional exam requirements/recommendations for international students: Required—TOEFL. Electronic applications accepted. *Faculty research:* Technology transfer, folk art.

California State University, Fullerton, Graduate Studies, College of the Arts, Department of Music, Fullerton, CA 92834-9480. Offers music education (MA); music history and literature (MA); performance (MM); piano pedagogy (MA); theory-composition (MM). *Accreditation:* NASM. Part-time programs available. *Students:* 17 full-time (7 women), 28 part-time (11 women); includes 17 minority (3 Black or African American, non-Hispanic/Latino; 9 Asian, non-Hispanic/Latino; 5 Hispanic/Latino), 3 international. Average age 29. 71 applicants, 37% accepted, 17 enrolled. In 2011, 20 master's awarded. *Degree requirements:* For master's, comprehensive exam, project or thesis. *Entrance requirements:* For master's, audition, major in music or related field, minimum GPA of 2.5 in last 60 units of course work. Application fee: $55. *Financial support:* Career-related internships or fieldwork, Federal Work-Study, institutionally sponsored loans, and scholarships/grants available. Support available to part-time students. Financial award application deadline: 3/1; financial award applicants required to submit FAFSA. *Unit head:* Dr. Marc Dickey, Chair, 657-278-3511. *Application contact:* Admissions/Applications, 657-278-2371.

California State University, Los Angeles, Graduate Studies, College of Arts and Letters, Department of Music, Los Angeles, CA 90032-8530. Offers music composition (MM); music education (MA); musicology (MA); performance (MM). *Accreditation:* NASM. Part-time and evening/weekend programs available. *Faculty:* 9 full-time (1 woman), 8 part-time/adjunct (3 women). *Students:* 24 full-time (7 women), 31 part-time (9 women); includes 27 minority (1 Black or African American, non-Hispanic/Latino; 9 Asian, non-Hispanic/Latino; 17 Hispanic/Latino), 8 international. Average age 36. 52 applicants, 63% accepted, 20 enrolled. In 2011, 38 master's awarded. *Degree requirements:* For master's, comprehensive exam, project or thesis. *Entrance requirements:* For master's, audition. Additional exam requirements/recommendations for international students: Required—TOEFL (minimum score 500 paper-based; 173 computer-based). *Application deadline:* For fall admission, 5/1 for domestic and international students. Applications are processed on a rolling basis. Application fee: $55. Electronic applications accepted. *Expenses:* Tuition, state resident: full-time $8225. *Financial support:* Career-related internships or fieldwork and Federal Work-Study available. Support available to part-time students. Financial award application deadline: 3/1. *Faculty research:* Gregorian semiology, Baroque opera. *Unit head:* Dr. Peter McAllister, Chair, 323-343-4060, Fax: 323-343-4063, E-mail: peter.mcallister2@calstatela.edu. *Application contact:* Dr. Karin Brown, Acting Associate Dean of Graduate Studies, 323-343-3820, Fax: 323-343-5653, E-mail: kbrown5@calstatela.edu. Web site: http://www.calstatela.edu/academic/music/.

California State University, Northridge, Graduate Studies, College of Arts, Media, and Communication, Department of Music, Northridge, CA 91330. Offers composition (MM); conducting (MM); music education (MA); performance (MM). *Accreditation:* NASM. *Degree requirements:* For master's, thesis. *Entrance requirements:* For master's, audition, GRE General Test or minimum GPA of 3.0. Additional exam requirements/recommendations for international students: Required—TOEFL. *Faculty research:* Touring program.

Campbellsville University, School of Music, Campbellsville, KY 42718-2799. Offers church music (MM); music (MA); music education (MM). *Accreditation:* NASM. Part-time programs available. *Students:* 26 full-time (14 women), 5 part-time (1 woman), 19 international. In 2011, 12 master's awarded. *Degree requirements:* For master's, thesis (for some programs), paper or recital. *Entrance requirements:* For master's, GRE General Test or PRAXIS, minimum GPA of 2.75. Additional exam requirements/recommendations for international students: Required—TOEFL (minimum score 550 paper-based). *Application deadline:* For fall admission, 6/1 priority date for domestic students, 5/1 for international students; for spring admission, 11/1 priority date for domestic students, 10/1 for international students. Applications are processed on a rolling basis. Application fee: $25. Electronic applications accepted. *Expenses: Tuition:* Full-time $6030; part-time $335 per credit hour. *Financial support:* In 2011–12, 24 students received support, including 1 fellowship (averaging $4,300 per year); institutionally sponsored loans and scholarships/grants also available. Support available to part-time students. Financial award application deadline: 6/1; financial award applicants required to submit FAFSA. *Unit head:* Dr. J. Robert Gaddis, Dean, 270-789-5269, Fax: 270-789-5524, E-mail: jrgaddis@campbellsville.edu. *Application contact:* Monica Bamwine, Assistant Director of Admissions, 270-789-5221, Fax: 270-789-5071, E-mail: mkbamwine@campbellsville.edu. Web site: http://www.campbellsville.edu/music.

Capital University, Conservatory of Music, Columbus, OH 43209-2394. Offers music education (MM), including instrumental emphasis, Kodály emphasis. Program offered only in summer. *Accreditation:* NASM. Part-time programs available. *Degree requirements:* For master's, comprehensive exam, thesis or alternative, chamber performance exam. *Entrance requirements:* For master's, music theory exam, minimum undergraduate GPA of 3.0. Additional exam requirements/recommendations for international students: Required—TOEFL (minimum score 550 paper-based; 213 computer-based; 80 iBT). Electronic applications accepted. *Expenses:* Contact institution. *Faculty research:* Folk song research, Kodály method, performance, composition.

Carnegie Mellon University, College of Fine Arts, School of Music, Pittsburgh, PA 15213-3891. Offers composition (MM); conducting (MM); instrumental performance (MM); music and technology (MS); music education (MM); vocal performance (MM). *Accreditation:* NASM. Part-time programs available. *Degree requirements:* For master's, comprehensive exam, recital. *Entrance requirements:* For master's, audition. *Faculty research:* Computer music, music history.

Case Western Reserve University, School of Graduate Studies, Department of Music, Program in Music Education, Cleveland, OH 44106. Offers MA, PhD. *Accreditation:* NASM; Teacher Education Accreditation Council. *Faculty:* 5 full-time (2 women). *Students:* 12 full-time (6 women), 6 part-time (1 woman). Average age 31. 11 applicants, 9% accepted, 1 enrolled. In 2011, 2 master's, 1 doctorate awarded. *Degree requirements:* For master's, thesis (for some programs); for doctorate, thesis/dissertation. *Entrance requirements:* For master's, GRE, audition/interview, writing sample, 1 year of teaching; for doctorate, GRE, audition/interview, writing sample. Additional exam requirements/recommendations for international students: Required—TOEFL (minimum score 577 paper-based; 213 computer-based; 90 iBT); Recommended—IELTS (minimum score 7). *Application deadline:* For fall admission, 1/15 priority date for domestic students. Application fee: $50. Electronic applications accepted. *Financial support:* Fellowships, teaching assistantships, career-related internships or fieldwork, tuition waivers (full), and unspecified assistantships available. Financial award application deadline: 1/15; financial award applicants required to submit FAFSA. *Faculty research:* Psychology of music, creative thinking, computer applications, educational psychology. *Unit head:* Ross Duffin, Chair, 216-368-2400, Fax: 216-368-6557, E-mail: info@music.case.edu. *Application contact:* Laura Stauffer, Admissions, 216-368-2400, Fax: 216-368-6557, E-mail: info@music.case.edu. Web site: http://music.case.edu/spotlight/.

Central Connecticut State University, School of Graduate Studies, School of Arts and Sciences, Department of Music, New Britain, CT 06050-4010. Offers music education (MS, Certificate). *Accreditation:* NASM. Part-time and evening/weekend programs available. *Faculty:* 10 full-time (4 women), 32 part-time/adjunct (12 women). *Students:* 7 full-time (2 women), 10 part-time (8 women); includes 2 minority (1 American Indian or Alaska Native, non-Hispanic/Latino; 1 Hispanic/Latino). Average age 30. 10 applicants, 80% accepted, 5 enrolled. In 2011, 3 master's awarded. *Degree requirements:* For master's, comprehensive exam, thesis or alternative; for Certificate, qualifying exam. *Entrance requirements:* For master's, audition, minimum undergraduate GPA of 2.7, essay, portfolio, resume. Additional exam requirements/recommendations for international students: Required—TOEFL (minimum score 550 paper-based; 213 computer-based). *Application deadline:* For fall admission, 6/1 for domestic students, 5/1 for international students; for spring admission, 11/1 for domestic and international students. Applications are processed on a rolling basis. Application fee: $50. Electronic applications accepted. *Expenses: Tuition, area resident:* Full-time $5137; part-time $482 per credit. Tuition, state resident: full-time $7707; part-time $494 per credit. Tuition, nonresident: full-time $14,311; part-time $494 per credit. *Required fees:* $3865. One-time fee: $62 part-time. *Financial support:* In 2011–12, 1 student received support, including 1 research assistantship. Financial award application deadline: 4/15; financial award applicants required to submit FAFSA. *Faculty research:* Applied music. *Unit head:* Dr. Charles Menoche, Chair, 860-832-2912, E-mail: menochec@ccsu.edu. *Application contact:* Patricia Gardner, Associate Director of Graduate Studies, 860-832-2350, Fax: 860-832-2352, E-mail: graduateadmissions@ccsu.edu. Web site: http://www.ccsu.edu/page.cfm?p=10712.

Central Michigan University, College of Graduate Studies, College of Communication and Fine Arts, School of Music, Program in Music Education, Mount Pleasant, MI 48859. Offers MM. *Accreditation:* NASM. Part-time programs available. *Degree requirements:* For master's, thesis or alternative. Electronic applications accepted.

Christopher Newport University, Graduate Studies, Department of Teacher Preparation, Newport News, VA 23606-2998. Offers art (PK-12) (MAT); biology (6-12) (MAT); chemistry (6-12) (MAT); computer science (6-12) (MAT); elementary (PK-6) (MAT); English (6-12) (MAT); English as second language (PK-12) (MAT); French (PK-12) (MAT); history and social science (6-12) (MAT); mathematics (6-12) (MAT); music (PK-12) (MAT), including choral, instrumental; physics (6-12) (MAT); Spanish (PK-12) (MAT). Part-time and evening/weekend programs available. *Degree requirements:* For master's, comprehensive exam, thesis or alternative. *Entrance requirements:* For master's, PRAXIS I, minimum GPA of 3.0. Additional exam requirements/recommendations for international students: Required—TOEFL (minimum score 580 paper-based; 237 computer-based; 92 iBT). Electronic applications accepted. *Faculty research:* Early literacy development, instructional innovations, professional teaching standards, multicultural issues, aesthetic education.

Cleveland State University, College of Graduate Studies, College of Liberal Arts and Social Sciences, Department of Music, Cleveland, OH 44115. Offers composition (MM); music education (MM); performance (MM). *Accreditation:* NASM. Part-time and evening/weekend programs available. *Faculty:* 9 full-time (2 women), 19 part-time/adjunct (6 women). *Students:* 6 full-time (0 women), 22 part-time (12 women); includes 2 minority (1 Black or African American, non-Hispanic/Latino; 1 Asian, non-Hispanic/Latino), 5 international. Average age 27. 36 applicants, 42% accepted, 8 enrolled. In 2011, 18 master's awarded. *Degree requirements:* For master's, comprehensive exam, thesis or recital. *Entrance requirements:* For master's, departmental assessment in music history, minimum undergraduate GPA of 2.75. Additional exam requirements/recommendations for international students: Required—TOEFL (minimum score 525 paper-based; 197 computer-based). *Application deadline:* For fall admission, 7/15 priority date for domestic students. Applications are processed on a rolling basis. Application fee: $30. *Expenses:* Tuition, state resident: full-time $6416; part-time $494 per credit hour. Tuition, nonresident: full-time $12,074; part-time $929 per credit hour. *Financial support:* In 2011–12, 14 students received support, including 14 research assistantships with full tuition reimbursements available (averaging $3,612 per year); tuition waivers (partial) and unspecified assistantships also available. Financial award application deadline: 3/1. *Faculty research:* Ethnomusicology, classical-Romantic music, new performance practices, electronic music, interdisciplinary studies. *Total annual research expenditures:* $162,000. *Unit head:* Dr. Birch P. Browning, Chairperson, 216-687-2301, Fax: 216-687-9279, E-mail: b.browning@csuohio.edu. *Application contact:* Dr. Victor Liva, Coordinator of Graduate Studies and Admission, 216-687-6931, Fax: 216-687-9279, E-mail: v.liva@csuohio.edu. Web site: http://www.csuohio.edu/music/.

College of Charleston, Graduate School, School of Education, Health, and Human Performance, Department of Foundations, Secondary, and Special Education, Program in Performing Arts Education, Charleston, SC 29424-0001. Offers MAT. Part-time and evening/weekend programs available. *Faculty:* 34 full-time (25 women), 9 part-time/adjunct (all women). *Students:* 7 full-time (5 women), 4 part-time (3 women); includes 1 minority (Hispanic/Latino). Average age 27. 3 applicants, 33% accepted, 1 enrolled. In 2011, 1 degree awarded. *Entrance requirements:* For master's, GRE, minimum GPA of 2.5 overall, 3.0 in last 60 hours of undergraduate coursework; 2 letters of recommendation; audition/interview. Additional exam requirements/recommendations for international students: Required—TOEFL (minimum score 81 iBT). *Application deadline:* For fall admission, 7/1 for domestic students; for spring admission, 11/1 for domestic students. Application fee: $45. Electronic applications accepted. *Expenses:* Tuition, state resident: full-time $5455; part-time $455 per credit. Tuition, nonresident: full-time $13,917; part-time $1160 per credit. *Financial support:* Scholarships/grants and unspecified assistantships available. Financial award application deadline: 4/1; financial award applicants required to submit FAFSA. *Unit head:* Dr. Bonnie Springer, Director, 843-953-8048, E-mail: springerb@cofc.edu. *Application contact:* Susan Hallatt, Director of Graduate Admissions, 843-953-5614, Fax: 843-953-1434, E-mail: hallatts@cofc.edu.

College of Mount St. Joseph, Graduate Education Program, Cincinnati, OH 45233-1670. Offers adolescent young adult education (MA); art (MA); inclusive early childhood education (MA); instructional leadership (MA); middle childhood education (MA); multi-age education (MA); multicultural special education (MA); music (MA); reading (MA). *Accreditation:* Teacher Education Accreditation Council. Part-time and evening/weekend programs available. *Faculty:* 22 full-time (12 women), 11 part-time/adjunct (8 women). *Students:* 51 full-time (40 women), 92 part-time (72 women); includes 17 minority (14 Black or African American, non-Hispanic/Latino; 1 American Indian or Alaska Native, non-Hispanic/Latino; 1 Asian, non-Hispanic/Latino; 1 Hispanic/Latino). Average age 34. 87 applicants, 44% accepted, 29 enrolled. In 2011, 61 master's awarded. *Degree requirements:* For master's, research project, student teaching, clinical and field-based experiences. *Entrance requirements:* For master's, GRE, PRAXIS II in teaching content area (math or science), 2 letters of recommendation, interview, resume. Additional exam requirements/recommendations for international students: Required—TOEFL (minimum score 560 paper-based; 220 computer-based; 83 iBT). *Application deadline:* Applications are processed on a rolling basis. Application fee: $50. Electronic applications accepted. *Expenses: Tuition:* Full-time $24,200; part-time $540 per credit hour. *Required fees:* $112.50 per semester. One-time fee: $200. *Financial support:* In 2011–12, 22 students received support. Scholarships/grants available. Financial award applicants required to submit FAFSA. *Faculty research:* Foreign and second language learning problems/reading disabilities/hyperlexia, multicultural/bilingual special education, alternative educator licensure, science education, pedagogical content knowledge. *Unit head:* Dr. Mary West, Chair, 513-244-3263, Fax: 513-244-4867, E-mail: mary_west@mail.msj.edu. *Application contact:* Marilyn Hoskins, Assistant Director of Graduate Recruitment, 513-244-4723, Fax: 513-244-4629, E-mail: marilyn_hoskins@mail.msj.edu. Web site: http://www.msj.edu/view/academics/graduate-programs/education.aspx.

The College of Saint Rose, Graduate Studies, School of Arts and Humanities, Music Department, Program in Music Education, Albany, NY 12203-1419. Offers MS Ed, Certificate. *Accreditation:* NASM; NCATE. *Degree requirements:* For master's, thesis optional, final project. *Entrance requirements:* For master's, audition, minimum undergraduate GPA of 3.0; for Certificate, placement test if undergraduate degree is not in music, audition. Additional exam requirements/recommendations for international students: Required—TOEFL (minimum score 550 paper-based; 213 computer-based). Electronic applications accepted.

The Colorado College, Education Department, Program in Secondary Education, Colorado Springs, CO 80903-3294. Offers art teaching (K-12) (MAT); English teaching (MAT); foreign language teaching (MAT); mathematics teaching (MAT); music teaching (MAT); science teaching (MAT); social studies teaching (MAT). *Faculty:* 4 full-time (3 women), 6 part-time/adjunct (2 women). *Students:* 11 full-time (7 women); includes 3 minority (1 Asian, non-Hispanic/Latino; 2 Hispanic/Latino). Average age 27. 20 applicants, 85% accepted, 11 enrolled. In 2011, 15 master's awarded. *Degree requirements:* For master's, thesis, internship. *Application deadline:* For fall admission, 12/1 priority date for domestic students, 12/1 for international students. Applications are processed on a rolling basis. Application fee: $50. Electronic applications accepted. *Expenses: Tuition:* Full-time $29,313. *Required fees:* $2000. *Financial support:* In 2011–12, 15 students received support. Career-related internships or fieldwork, institutionally sponsored loans, scholarships/grants, and health care benefits available. Financial award application deadline: 2/15; financial award applicants required to submit FAFSA. *Unit head:* Dr. Mike Taber, Director, 719-389-6026, Fax: 719-389-6473, E-mail: mike.taber@coloradocollege.edu. *Application contact:* Debra Yazulla Mortenson, Education Services Manager, 719-389-6472, Fax: 719-389-6473, E-mail: debra.mortenson@coloradocollege.edu. Web site: http://www.coloradocollege.edu/academics/dept/education/graduate-programs/secondary-mat.dot.

Colorado State University–Pueblo, College of Education, Engineering and Professional Studies, Education Program, Pueblo, CO 81001-4901. Offers art education (M Ed); foreign language education (M Ed); health and physical education (M Ed); instructional technology (M Ed); linguistically diverse education (M Ed); music education (M Ed); special education (M Ed). *Accreditation:* Teacher Education Accreditation Council. Part-time programs available. *Degree requirements:* For master's, portfolio. *Entrance requirements:* For master's, 3 recommendations, teaching license. Additional exam requirements/recommendations for international students: Required—TOEFL (minimum score 500 paper-based; 173 computer-based). Electronic applications accepted. *Faculty research:* Portfolio assessment, math education, science education.

Columbus State University, Graduate Studies, College of the Arts, Schwob School of Music, Columbus, GA 31907-5645. Offers artist diploma (Postbaccalaureate Certificate); music education (MM). *Accreditation:* NASM; NCATE (one or more programs are accredited). Part-time and evening/weekend programs available. *Degree requirements:* For master's, exit exam. *Entrance requirements:* For master's, GRE General Test, audition. Additional exam requirements/recommendations for international students: Required—TOEFL (minimum score 550 paper-based; 213 computer-based; 79 iBT). Electronic applications accepted.

Conservatorio de Musica, Program in Music Education, San Juan, PR 00907. Offers MM Ed. *Entrance requirements:* For master's, EXADEP, 3 letters of recommendation, audition, bachelor's degree in music education, interview, minimum GPA of 2.5, performance video, teaching video. Additional exam requirements/recommendations for international students: Required—TOEFL.

Converse College, Petrie School of Music, Spartanburg, SC 29302-0006. Offers instrumental performance (M Mus); music education (M Mus); piano pedagogy (M Mus); vocal performance (M Mus). *Accreditation:* NASM. Part-time and evening/weekend programs available. *Degree requirements:* For master's, variable foreign language requirement, comprehensive exam, thesis (for some programs), recitals. *Entrance requirements:* For master's, NTE (music education), audition, 3 letters of recommendation. Additional exam requirements/recommendations for international students: Required—TOEFL. Electronic applications accepted. *Faculty research:* Chamber music, opera, performance, composition, recording.

DePaul University, School of Music, Chicago, IL 60614. Offers applied music (performance) (MM, Certificate); jazz studies (MM), including composition, performance; music composition (MM); music education (MM). *Accreditation:* NASM (one or more programs are accredited). Part-time and evening/weekend programs available. *Faculty:* 16 full-time (6 women), 50 part-time/adjunct (14 women). *Students:* 85 full-time (36 women), 52 part-time (24 women); includes 14 minority (6 Black or African American, non-Hispanic/Latino; 5 Asian, non-Hispanic/Latino; 2 Hispanic/Latino; 1 Two or more races, non-Hispanic/Latino), 34 international. Average age 26. 464 applicants, 28% accepted, 69 enrolled. In 2011, 42 degrees awarded. *Degree requirements:* For master's, comprehensive exam, terminal project, recital (for performers); for Certificate, recital. *Entrance requirements:* For master's, bachelor's degree in music or related field, minimum GPA of 3.0, auditions (performance), scores (composition); for Certificate, master's degree in performance or related field, auditions (for performance majors). Additional exam requirements/recommendations for international students: Required—TOEFL (minimum score 550 paper-based; 213 computer-based; 80 iBT). *Application deadline:* For fall admission, 1/15 priority date for domestic students, 1/15 for international students. Applications are processed on a rolling basis. Application fee: $40. Electronic applications accepted. *Expenses:* Contact institution. *Financial support:* In 2011–12, 100 students received support, including 4 fellowships with partial tuition reimbursements available; teaching assistantships, career-related internships or fieldwork, Federal Work-Study, scholarships/grants, and tuition waivers also available. Support available to part-time students. Financial award application deadline: 1/15. *Unit head:* Dr. Donald E. Casey, Dean, 773-325-7256, E-mail: dcasey@depaul.edu. *Application contact:* Ross Beacraft, Director of Admissions, 773-325-7444, Fax: 773-325-7429, E-mail: rbeacraf@depaul.edu. Web site: http://Music.depaul.edu.

Duquesne University, Mary Pappert School of Music, Pittsburgh, PA 15282-0001. Offers music composition (MM); music education (MM); music performance (MM, AD); music technology (MM), including digital pedagogy, electronic composition, electronic performance; music theory (MM); sacred music (MM). *Accreditation:* NASM. Part-time programs available. *Faculty:* 24 full-time (8 women), 79 part-time/adjunct (24 women). *Students:* 69 full-time (39 women), 27 part-time (7 women); includes 7 minority (4 Asian, non-Hispanic/Latino; 2 Hispanic/Latino; 1 Two or more races, non-Hispanic/Latino), 21 international. Average age 27. 103 applicants, 57% accepted, 34 enrolled. In 2011, 28 master's awarded. *Degree requirements:* For master's, comprehensive exam, thesis (for some programs), recital (music performance); for AD, recital. *Entrance requirements:* For master's, audition, minimum undergraduate QPA of 3.0 in music, portfolio of original compositions, theoretical papers, or music education experience; for AD, audition. Additional exam requirements/recommendations for international students: Required—TOEFL (minimum score 550 paper-based; 213 computer-based; 79 iBT). *Application deadline:* For fall admission, 7/1 priority date for domestic students, 7/1 for international students; for spring admission, 12/1 priority date for domestic students, 12/1 for international students. Applications are processed on a rolling basis. Application fee: $50. Electronic applications accepted. *Expenses:* Contact institution. *Financial support:* In 2011–12, 55 students received support. Scholarships/grants, tuition waivers (full and partial), and unspecified assistantships available. Financial award application deadline: 4/1. *Faculty research:* Performance; computer-assisted instruction in music at elementary and secondary levels; electronic music; contemporary music, theory, and analysis; development of online graduate music courses. *Total annual research expenditures:* $31,500. *Unit head:* Dr. Edward W. Kocher, Dean, 412-396-6082, Fax: 412-396-1524, E-mail: kocher@duq.edu. *Application contact:* Peggy Eiseman, Administrative Assistant of Admissions, 412-396-5064, Fax: 412-396-5719, E-mail: eiseman@duq.edu. Web site: http://www.duq.edu/music.

East Carolina University, Graduate School, College of Education, Department of Business and Information Technologies Education, Greenville, NC 27858-4353. Offers business education (MA Ed); elementary education (MAT); English education (MAT); family and consumer science (MAT); health education (MAT); Hispanic studies (MAT); history education (MAT); marketing education (MA Ed); middle grades education (MAT); music education (MAT); physical education (MAT); science education (MAT); special education (MAT), including general curriculum; vocation education (MS). *Accreditation:* NCATE. Part-time and evening/weekend programs available. Postbaccalaureate distance learning degree programs offered (no on-campus study). *Degree requirements:* For master's, comprehensive exam, thesis optional. *Entrance requirements:* For master's, GRE or MAT, minimum GPA of 2.5, bachelor's degree in related field, teaching license (MA Ed). Additional exam requirements/recommendations for international students: Required—TOEFL. *Application deadline:* For fall admission, 6/1 priority date for domestic students. Applications are processed on a rolling basis. Application fee: $50. *Expenses:* Tuition, state resident: full-time $3557; part-time $444.63 per semester hour. Tuition, nonresident: full-time $14,351; part-time $1793.88 per semester hour. *Required fees:* $2016; $252 per semester hour. Part-time tuition and fees vary according to course load, campus/location and program. *Financial support:* Federal Work-Study available. Support available to part-time students. Financial award application deadline: 6/1. *Unit head:* Dr. Ivan G. Wallace, Chair, 252-328-6983, Fax: 252-328-6835, E-mail: wallacei@ecu.edu. *Application contact:* Dean of Graduate School, 252-328-6012, Fax: 252-328-6071, E-mail: gradschool@ecu.edu. Web site: http://www.ecu.edu/cs-educ/bite/index.cfm.

East Carolina University, Graduate School, College of Fine Arts and Communication, School of Music, Greenville, NC 27858-4353. Offers advanced performance studies (Certificate); music education (MM); music therapy (MM); performance (MM), including choral conducting, instrumental conducting, jazz, organ, percussion, piano, piano pedagogy, sacred music, sacred music, choral conducting, string (Suzuki) pedagogy, vocal pedagogy, voice, wind instrument, woodwind specialist; theory and composition (MM). *Accreditation:* NASM. Part-time programs available. *Degree requirements:* For master's, comprehensive exam, thesis optional. *Entrance requirements:* For master's, GRE General Test or MAT. Additional exam requirements/recommendations for international students: Required—TOEFL. *Application deadline:* For fall admission, 6/1 priority date for domestic students. Applications are processed on a rolling basis. Application fee: $50. *Expenses:* Tuition, state resident: full-time $3557; part-time $444.63 per semester hour. Tuition, nonresident: full-time $14,351; part-time $1793.88 per semester hour. *Required fees:* $2016; $252 per semester hour. Part-time tuition and fees vary according to course load, campus/location and program. *Financial support:* Fellowships, research assistantships, teaching assistantships, and Federal Work-Study available. Support available to part-time students. Financial award application deadline: 6/1. *Unit head:* Dr. J. Christopher Buddo, Director, 252-328-4270, E-mail: buddoj@ecu.edu. *Application contact:* Dean of Graduate School, 252-328-6012, Fax: 252-328-6071, E-mail: gradschool@ecu.edu. Web site: http://www.music.ecu.edu/.

Eastern Illinois University, Graduate School, College of Arts and Humanities, Department of Music, Charleston, IL 61920-3099. Offers music education (MA). *Accreditation:* NASM. Part-time programs available. *Faculty:* 21 full-time (3 women). *Students:* 14 (7 women). In 2011, 4 master's awarded. *Degree requirements:* For master's, thesis or alternative, recital. *Application deadline:* For fall admission, 3/31 priority date for domestic students. Applications are processed on a rolling basis. Application fee: $30. *Expenses:* Tuition, state resident: part-time $279 per credit hour. Tuition, nonresident: part-time $670 per credit hour. *Required fees:* $179.07 per credit hour. $1253 per semester. *Financial support:* In 2011–12, research assistantships with full tuition reimbursements (averaging $8,100 per year), 8 teaching assistantships with full tuition reimbursements (averaging $8,100 per year) were awarded. *Unit head:* Dr. Jerry Daniels, Chairperson, 217-581-3010, Fax: 217-581-2722, E-mail: wpmelvin@eiu.edu. *Application contact:* Dr. Marilyn Coles, Coordinator, 217-581-3010, E-mail: mjcoles@eiu.edu.

Eastern Kentucky University, The Graduate School, College of Education, Department of Curriculum and Instruction, Richmond, KY 40475-3102. Offers elementary education (MA Ed), including early elementary education, reading; library science (MA Ed); music education (MA Ed); secondary and higher education (MA Ed), including secondary education; teaching (MAT). *Accreditation:* NCATE. Part-time programs available. *Degree requirements:* For master's, portfolio is part of exam. *Entrance requirements:* For master's, GRE General Test, PRAXIS II (KY), minimum GPA of 2.5. *Faculty research:* Technology in education, reading instruction, e-portfolios, induction to teacher education, dispositions of teachers.

Eastern Michigan University, Graduate School, College of Arts and Sciences, Department of Music and Dance, Ypsilanti, MI 48197. Offers music composition (MM); music education (MM); music pedagogy (MM); music performance (MM). *Accreditation:* NASM. Part-time and evening/weekend programs available. Postbaccalaureate distance learning degree programs offered (minimal on-campus study). *Faculty:* 24 full-time (9 women). *Students:* 9 full-time (6 women), 19 part-time (8 women); includes 6 minority (2 Black or African American, non-Hispanic/Latino; 4 Asian, non-Hispanic/Latino), 7 international. Average age 29. 31 applicants, 68% accepted, 10 enrolled. In 2011, 6 degrees awarded. *Entrance requirements:* Additional exam requirements/recommendations for international students: Required—TOEFL. *Application deadline:* Applications are processed on a rolling basis. Application fee: $35. *Expenses:* Tuition, state resident: full-time $10,367; part-time $432 per credit hour. Tuition, nonresident: full-time $20,435; part-time $851 per credit hour. *Required fees:* $39 per credit hour. $46 per semester. One-time fee: $100. Tuition and fees vary according to course level, degree level and reciprocity agreements. *Financial support:* Fellowships, research assistantships with full tuition reimbursements, teaching assistantships with full tuition reimbursements, career-related internships or fieldwork, Federal Work-Study, institutionally sponsored loans, scholarships/grants, tuition waivers (partial), and unspecified assistantships available. Support available to part-time students. Financial award applicants required to submit FAFSA. *Unit head:* Dr. Diane Winder, Department Head, 734-487-4380, Fax: 734-487-6939, E-mail: dwinder@emich.edu. *Application contact:* Dr. David Pierce, Coordinator of Music Advising, 734-487-4380, Fax: 734-487-6939, E-mail: david.pierce@emich.edu. Web site: http://www.emich.edu/musicdance.

Eastern Washington University, Graduate Studies, College of Arts, Letters and Education, Department of Music, Cheney, WA 99004-2431. Offers composition (MA); general (MA); instrumental/vocal performance (MA); jazz pedagogy (MA); music education (MA). *Accreditation:* NASM. Part-time programs available. *Faculty:* 13 full-time (6 women). *Students:* 9 full-time (3 women); includes 1 minority (Native Hawaiian or other Pacific Islander, non-Hispanic/Latino). Average age 33. In 2011, 4 master's awarded. *Degree requirements:* For master's, comprehensive exam, thesis or alternative. *Entrance requirements:* For master's, GRE General Test, minimum GPA of 3.0. *Application deadline:* For fall admission, 4/1 priority date for domestic students; for spring admission, 1/15 for domestic students. Applications are processed on a rolling basis. Application fee: $50. *Financial support:* In 2011–12, 7 teaching assistantships with partial tuition reimbursements (averaging $7,000 per year) were awarded; career-related internships or fieldwork, Federal Work-Study, institutionally sponsored loans, scholarships/grants, health care benefits, tuition waivers (partial), and unspecified assistantships also available. Support available to part-time students. Financial award application deadline: 2/1; financial award applicants required to submit FAFSA. *Unit head:* Dr. Patrick Winters, Chair, 509-359-6129, Fax: 509-359-7028. *Application contact:* Dr. Jane Ellsworth, Assistant Professor, 509-359-7076, E-mail: gradprograms@ewu.edu. Web site: http://www.ewu.edu/cale/programs/music.xml.

Emporia State University, Graduate School, College of Liberal Arts and Sciences, Department of Music, Emporia, KS 66801-5087. Offers music education (MM), including instrumental, vocal; performance (MM). *Accreditation:* NASM. Part-time programs available. *Faculty:* 13 full-time (5 women), 2 part-time/adjunct (both women). *Students:* 9 full-time (6 women), 12 part-time (6 women); includes 2 minority (1 Black or African American, non-Hispanic/Latino; 1 Two or more races, non-Hispanic/Latino), 6 international. 11 applicants, 100% accepted, 6 enrolled. In 2011, 7 master's awarded. *Degree requirements:* For master's, comprehensive exam or thesis. *Entrance requirements:* For master's, music qualifying exam, appropriate undergraduate degree. Additional exam requirements/recommendations for international students: Required—TOEFL (minimum score 520 paper-based; 133 computer-based; 68 iBT). *Application deadline:* For fall admission, 8/15 priority date for domestic students. Applications are processed on a rolling basis. Application fee: $30 ($75 for international students). Electronic applications accepted. *Expenses:* Tuition, state resident: full-time $2342; part-time $195 per credit hour. Tuition, nonresident: full-time $7254; part-time $605 per credit hour. *Required fees:* $66 per credit hour. Tuition and fees vary according to campus/location. *Financial support:* In 2011–12, 4 teaching assistantships with full tuition reimbursements (averaging $6,177 per year) were awarded; research assistantships, Federal Work-Study, institutionally sponsored loans, health care benefits, and unspecified assistantships also available. Financial award application deadline: 3/15; financial award applicants required to submit FAFSA. *Unit head:* Dr. Allan D. Comstock, Chair, 620-341-5431, E-mail: acomstoc@emporia.edu. *Application contact:* Dr. Andrew Houchins, Graduate Coordinator, 620-341-6089, E-mail: ahouchin@emporia.edu. Web site: http://www.emporia.edu/music/.

Five Towns College, Department of Music, Dix Hills, NY 11746-6055. Offers jazz/commercial music (MM); music (DMA); music education (MM). Part-time programs available. *Faculty:* 6 full-time (2 women), 15 part-time/adjunct (4 women). *Students:* 17 full-time (3 women), 29 part-time (7 women); includes 6 minority (2 Black or African American, non-Hispanic/Latino; 1 Asian, non-Hispanic/Latino; 2 Hispanic/Latino; 1 Two or more races, non-Hispanic/Latino), 11 international. Average age 27. 22 applicants, 68% accepted, 5 enrolled. In 2011, 3 master's, 1 doctorate awarded. *Degree requirements:* For master's, thesis, exams, major composition or capstone project, recital; for doctorate, comprehensive exam, thesis/dissertation, final oral exam. *Entrance requirements:* For master's, audition, bachelor's degree in music or music education, minimum GPA of 2.75, 36 hours of course work in performance; for doctorate, master's degree in music, minimum GPA of 3.0, 3 letters of recommendation. Additional exam requirements/recommendations for international students: Required—TOEFL (minimum score 520 paper-based; 213 computer-based; 80 iBT); Recommended—IELTS (minimum score 7). *Application deadline:* For fall admission, 9/1 for domestic and international students; for spring admission, 1/25 for domestic and international students. Applications are processed on a rolling basis. Application fee: $50. *Expenses: Tuition:* Full-time $13,800. *Required fees:* $185; $185 per credit. One-time fee: $85. Tuition and fees vary according to course level, course load, degree level and program. *Financial support:* Fellowships with tuition reimbursements and tuition waivers (partial) available. Financial award applicants required to submit FAFSA. *Faculty research:* Teaching methods, teaching strategies and techniques, analysis of modern music, jazz. *Unit head:* Dr. Jill Miller-Thorn, Dean of Graduate Studies, 631-656-2142, Fax: 631-656-2172, E-mail: jmillerthorn@ftc.edu. *Application contact:* Jerry Cohen, Dean of Enrollment, 631-656-2121, Fax: 631-656-2172, E-mail: jcohen@ftc.edu.

Florida International University, College of Architecture and the Arts, School of Music, Program in Music Education, Miami, FL 33199. Offers MS. *Accreditation:* NASM. Part-time and evening/weekend programs available. *Degree requirements:* For master's, thesis. *Entrance requirements:* For master's, GRE, 2 letters of recommendation; audition, interview and/or writing sample (for some areas). Additional exam requirements/recommendations for international students: Required—TOEFL (minimum score 550 paper-based; 80 iBT). Electronic applications accepted. *Faculty research:* Psychology of music teaching, classroom methodology, biofeedback.

Florida State University, The Graduate School, College of Music, Program in Music Education, Tallahassee, FL 32306. Offers MM Ed, PhD. *Accreditation:* NASM. *Faculty:* 20 full-time. *Students:* 53 full-time (23 women); includes 16 minority (9 Black or African American, non-Hispanic/Latino; 4 Asian, non-Hispanic/Latino; 3 Hispanic/Latino). Average age 25. 69 applicants, 39% accepted, 25 enrolled. In 2011, 23 master's, 6 doctorates awarded. *Degree requirements:* For master's, comprehensive exam (for some programs), thesis optional, departmental qualifying exam; for doctorate, thesis/dissertation, departmental qualifying exam. *Entrance requirements:* For master's and doctorate, minimum GPA of 3.0. Additional exam requirements/recommendations for international students: Required—TOEFL (minimum score 590 paper-based; 97 iBT), IELTS (minimum score 7.5), Michigan English Language Assessment Battery (minimum score 90). *Application deadline:* For fall admission, 7/1 for domestic and international students; for spring admission, 11/1 for domestic and international students. Applications are processed on a rolling basis. Application fee: $30. Electronic applications accepted. *Expenses:* Tuition, state resident: full-time $9474; part-time $350.88 per credit hour. Tuition, nonresident: full-time $16,236; part-time $601.34 per credit hour. *Required fees:* $630 per semester. One-time fee: $20. Tuition and fees vary according to course load and campus/location. *Financial support:* In 2011–12, 31 students received support, including 9 teaching assistantships (averaging $4,000 per year); career-related internships or fieldwork, Federal Work-Study, tuition waivers, and unspecified assistantships also available. Support available to part-time students. Financial award application deadline: 2/28; financial award applicants required to submit FAFSA. *Unit head:* Dr. Don Gibson, Dean, 850-644-4361, Fax: 850-644-2033, E-mail: dgibson@fsu.edu. *Application contact:* Dr. Seth Beckman, Senior Associate Dean for Academic Affairs/Director of Graduate Studies in Music, 850-644-5848, Fax: 850-644-2033, E-mail: sbeckman@admin.fsu.edu. Web site: http://www.music.fsu.edu/.

George Mason University, College of Visual and Performing Arts, School of Music, Fairfax, VA 22030. Offers instrumental performance artist (Certificate); music (MM), including composition; music education (PhD); musical arts (DMA); piano performance artist (Certificate); vocal performance artist (Certificate). *Accreditation:* NASM. *Faculty:* 21 full-time (8 women), 20 part-time/adjunct (10 women). *Students:* 34 full-time (14 women), 44 part-time (23 women); includes 11 minority (3 Black or African American, non-Hispanic/Latino; 2 Asian, non-Hispanic/Latino; 5 Hispanic/Latino; 1 Two or more races, non-Hispanic/Latino), 1 international. Average age 30. 90 applicants, 60% accepted, 35 enrolled. In 2011, 17 degrees awarded. *Degree requirements:* For master's, recital (for all except MM in music education), summer auditions, portfolios, compositions; for doctorate, one foreign language. *Entrance requirements:* For master's, baccalaureate degree in music or another related discipline; audition or portfolio with samples (depending on program); official transcripts; expanded goals statement; 2 letters of recommendation; for doctorate, GRE, master's degree in music; minimum GPA of 3.0 in master's-level coursework, 3.5 in courses related to area of study; 3 letters of recommendations; writing sample; audition or portfolio (depending on program); for Certificate, artist certificate application or current resume; bachelor's degree in music or equivalent; official transcripts; expanded goals statement; 2 letters of recommendation; audition and standard repertory sample on CD. Additional exam requirements/recommendations for international students: Required—TOEFL (minimum score 570 paper-based; 230 computer-based; 88 iBT), IELTS, Pearson Test of English. *Application deadline:* For fall admission, 4/1 priority date for domestic students; for spring admission, 11/1 priority date for domestic students. Application fee: $65 ($80 for international students). Electronic applications accepted. *Expenses:* Contact institution. *Financial support:* In 2011–12, 6 students received support, including 6 teaching assistantships with full and partial tuition reimbursements available (averaging $8,781 per year); career-related internships or fieldwork, Federal Work-Study, scholarships/grants, unspecified assistantships, and health care benefits (full-time research or teaching assistantship recipients) also available. Support available to part-time students. Financial award application deadline: 3/1; financial award applicants required to submit FAFSA. *Faculty research:* Single or multiple instruments, music education, composition, conducting, pedagogy. *Unit head:* Dr. Dennis M. Layendecker, Heritage Chair/Director, 703-993-5082, E-mail: dlayende@gmu.edu. *Application contact:* Dr. Rachel Bergman, Graduate Director, 703-993-1395, E-mail: rbergman@gmu.edu. Web site: http://music.gmu.edu/.

Georgia College & State University, Graduate School, College of Arts and Sciences, Department of Music, Milledgeville, GA 31061. Offers MM Ed. *Accreditation:* NASM. *Faculty:* 10 full-time (5 women). *Students:* 3 full-time (2 women), 4 part-time (1 woman); includes 1 minority (Black or African American, non-Hispanic/Latino). Average age 25. 5 applicants, 60% accepted, 3 enrolled. In 2011, 8 master's awarded. *Degree requirements:* For master's, comprehensive exam, thesis optional. *Entrance requirements:* For master's, GACE II or GRE, bachelor's degree in music education, 3 letters of recommendation, interview. Additional exam requirements/recommendations for international students: Recommended—TOEFL (minimum score 550 paper-based; 213 computer-based; 79 iBT). *Application deadline:* For fall admission, 7/1 priority date for domestic students; for spring admission, 11/15 priority date for domestic students. Application fee: $40. Electronic applications accepted. *Expenses:* Tuition, state resident: full-time $4806; part-time $267 per credit hour. Tuition, nonresident: full-time $17,802; part-time $989 per credit hour. *Required fees:* $936 per semester. Tuition and fees vary according to course load and campus/location. *Financial support:* In 2011–12, 1 research assistantship was awarded. Financial award applicants required to submit FAFSA. *Unit head:* Dr. Jennifer Flory, Graduate Coordinator for Music Education, 478-445-4839, Fax: 478-445-1633, E-mail: jennifer.flory@gcsu.edu. *Application contact:* Kate Marshall, Graduate Admissions Coordinator, 478-445-1184, Fax: 478-445-1336, E-mail: grad-admit@gcsu.edu. Web site: http://www.gcsu.edu/music/graduate.htm.

Georgia State University, College of Education, Department of Middle-Secondary Education and Instructional Technology, Programs in Secondary Education, Atlanta, GA 30302-3083. Offers art education (Ed S); English education (M Ed, Ed S); mathematics education (M Ed, PhD, Ed S); music education (PhD); science education (M Ed, PhD, Ed S); social studies education (M Ed, PhD, Ed S). *Accreditation:* NASM (one or more programs are accredited); NCATE. Part-time and evening/weekend programs available. *Degree requirements:* For master's, comprehensive exam; for doctorate, comprehensive exam, thesis/dissertation; for Ed S, project/exam. *Entrance requirements:* For master's, GRE General Test, minimum GPA of 2.5; for doctorate, GRE General Test or MAT, minimum GPA of 3.3; for Ed S, GRE General Test or MAT, minimum graduate GPA of 3.25. *Faculty research:* Women and science, problem solving in mathematics, dialects, economic education.

Gordon College, Graduate Education, Wenham, MA 01984-1899. Offers education (M Ed, MAT); music education (MME). Part-time and evening/weekend programs available. *Entrance requirements:* For master's, GRE or MAT, references. Additional exam requirements/recommendations for international students: Required—TOEFL (minimum score 550 paper-based; 213 computer-based). *Faculty research:* Reading, early childhood development, ELL (English Language Learners).

Hampton University, Graduate College, College of Education and Continuing Studies, Program in Teaching, Hampton, VA 23668. Offers early childhood education (MT); middle school education (MT); music education (MT); secondary education (MT); special education (MT). *Entrance requirements:* For master's, GRE General Test.

Hardin-Simmons University, Graduate School, School of Music and Fine Arts, Abilene, TX 79698-0001. Offers church music (MM); music education (MM); music performance (MM); theory-composition (MM). *Accreditation:* NASM. Part-time programs available. *Faculty:* 11 full-time (2 women). *Students:* 3 full-time (0 women), 2 part-time (both women). Average age 31. 3 applicants, 100% accepted, 3 enrolled. In 2011, 3 master's awarded. *Degree requirements:* For master's, one foreign language, comprehensive exam, thesis (for some programs). *Entrance requirements:* For master's, minimum undergraduate GPA of 3.0 in major, 2.7 overall; performance; writing sample; demonstrated knowledge in chosen area. Additional exam requirements/recommendations for international students: Required—TOEFL (minimum score 550 paper-based; 213 computer-based; 75 iBT). *Application deadline:* For fall admission, 8/15 priority date for domestic students, 4/1 for international students; for spring admission, 1/5 priority date for domestic students, 9/1 for international students. Applications are processed on a rolling basis. Application fee: $50. *Expenses: Tuition:* Full-time $12,870; part-time $715 per credit hour. *Required fees:* $650; $110 per semester. Tuition and fees vary according to degree level. *Financial support:* In 2011–12, 5 students received support, including 4 fellowships (averaging $2,700 per year); career-related internships or fieldwork and scholarships/grants also available. Support available to part-time students. Financial award application deadline: 6/30; financial award applicants required to submit FAFSA. *Unit head:* Dr. Lynette Chambers, Program Director, 325-670-1430, Fax: 325-670-5873, E-mail: lborman@hsutx.edu. *Application contact:* Dr. Nancy Kucinski, Dean of Graduate Studies, 325-670-1298, Fax: 325-670-1564, E-mail: gradoff@hsutx.edu. Web site: http://www.hsutx.edu/academics/somfa.

Hebrew College, Program in Jewish Studies, Newton Centre, MA 02459. Offers Jewish liturgical music (Certificate); Jewish music education (Certificate); Jewish studies (MA). Part-time and evening/weekend programs available. Postbaccalaureate distance learning degree programs offered (minimal on-campus study). *Degree requirements:* For master's, one foreign language. *Entrance requirements:* For master's, GRE, interview. Additional exam requirements/recommendations for international students: Required—TOEFL.

Heidelberg University, Program in Music Education, Tiffin, OH 44883-2462. Offers MME. Summer program only. *Accreditation:* NASM. Part-time programs available. *Entrance requirements:* For master's, bachelor's degree in music education, minimum cumulative GPA of 2.8, three letters of recommendation, copy of teaching license or certificate. Additional exam requirements/recommendations for international students: Required—TOEFL (minimum score 550 paper-based).

Hofstra University, School of Education, Health, and Human Services, Programs in Teaching (K-12), Hempstead, NY 11549. Offers bilingual education (MA); bilingual extension (Advanced Certificate), including education/speech language pathology, intensive teacher institute; family and consumer science (MS Ed); fine art and music education (Advanced Certificate); fine arts education (MA, MS Ed); mentoring and coaching for teachers (Advanced Certificate); middle childhood extension (Advanced Certificate), including grades 5-6 or 7-9; music education (MA, MS Ed); teaching languages other than English and TESOL (MS Ed); TESOL (MS Ed, Advanced Certificate), including intensive teacher institute (Advanced Certificate), TESOL (Advanced Certificate); wind conducting (MA). Part-time and evening/weekend programs available. *Students:* 54 full-time (48 women), 60 part-time (53 women); includes 30 minority (10 Black or African American, non-Hispanic/Latino; 9 Asian, non-Hispanic/Latino; 11 Hispanic/Latino), 8 international. Average age 29. 109 applicants, 76% accepted, 43 enrolled. In 2011, 71 master's, 42 other advanced degrees awarded. *Degree requirements:* For master's, one foreign language, thesis (for some programs), electronic portfolio, Tk20 portfolios, minimum GPA of 3.0. *Entrance requirements:* For master's, 2 letters of recommendation, portfolio, teacher certification (MA), essay; for Advanced Certificate, 2 letters of recommendation, interview, teaching certificate, essay. Additional exam requirements/recommendations for international students: Required—TOEFL (minimum score 550 paper-based; 213 computer-based; 80 iBT). *Application deadline:* Applications are processed on a rolling basis. Application fee: $70 ($75 for international students). Electronic applications accepted. *Expenses: Tuition:* Full-time $18,990; part-time $1055 per credit hour. *Required fees:* $970. Tuition and fees vary according to program. *Financial support:* In 2011–12, 39 students received support, including 13 fellowships with full and partial tuition reimbursements available (averaging $3,347 per year), 2 research assistantships with full and partial tuition reimbursements available (averaging $7,363 per year); career-related internships or fieldwork, Federal Work-Study, institutionally sponsored loans, scholarships/grants, tuition waivers (full and partial), and unspecified assistantships also available. Support available to part-time students. Financial award applicants required to submit FAFSA. *Faculty research:* The teacher/artist, interdisciplinary curriculum, applied linguistics, structural inequalities, creativity. *Unit head:* Dr. Esther Fusco, Chairperson, 516-463-7704, Fax: 516-463-6196, E-mail: catezf@hofstra.edu. *Application contact:* Carol Drummer, Dean of Graduate Admissions, 516-463-4876, Fax: 516-463-4664, E-mail: gradstudent@hofstra.edu. Web site: http://www.hofstra.edu/education/.

Holy Names University, Graduate Division, Department of Music, Oakland, CA 94619-1699. Offers Kodaly specialist certificate (Certificate); Kodaly summer certificate (Certificate); music education with Kodaly emphasis (MM); piano pedagogy (MM); piano pedagogy with Suzuki emphasis (MM); vocal pedagogy (MM). *Degree requirements:* For master's, comprehensive exam, recital. *Entrance requirements:* For master's, audition, minimum undergraduate GPA of 2.6 overall, 3.0 in major. Additional exam requirements/recommendations for international students: Required—TOEFL (minimum score 550 paper-based; 213 computer-based; 80 iBT). *Faculty research:* Performance practice with special interest in baroque, Romantic, and twentieth-century instrumental and vocal music, choral pedagogy, Hungarian music education.

Howard University, Graduate School, Division of Fine Arts, Department of Music, Washington, DC 20059-0002. Offers applied music (MM); instrument (MM Ed); jazz studies (MM); organ (MM Ed); piano (MM Ed); voice (MM Ed). *Accreditation:* NASM. Part-time programs available. *Degree requirements:* For master's, comprehensive exam, thesis or alternative, departmental qualifying exam, recital. *Entrance requirements:* For master's, minimum GPA of 3.0, bachelor's degree in music or music education. Additional exam requirements/recommendations for international students: Required—TOEFL.

Hunter College of the City University of New York, Graduate School, School of Arts and Sciences, Department of Music, New York, NY 10021-5085. Offers music (MA); music education (MA). Part-time and evening/weekend programs available. *Faculty:* 16 full-time (5 women), 4 part-time/adjunct (2 women). *Students:* 3 full-time (1 woman), 40 part-time (25 women); includes 6 minority (2 Black or African American, non-Hispanic/Latino; 1 Asian, non-Hispanic/Latino; 3 Hispanic/Latino), 5 international. Average age 32. 31 applicants, 48% accepted, 11 enrolled. In 2011, 13 master's awarded. *Degree requirements:* For master's, one foreign language, thesis, composition, essay, or recital; proficiency exam. *Entrance requirements:* For master's, undergraduate major in music (minimum 24 credits) or equivalent, sample of work, research paper. Additional exam requirements/recommendations for international students: Required—TOEFL. *Application deadline:* For fall admission, 4/1 for domestic students, 2/1 for international students; for spring admission, 11/1 for domestic students, 9/1 for international students. Applications are processed on a rolling basis. Application fee: $125. *Expenses:* Tuition, state resident: full-time $8210; part-time $345 per credit. Tuition, nonresident: full-time $15,360; part-time $640 per credit. *Required fees:* $280 per semester. One-time fee: $125. Tuition and fees vary according to class time, campus/location and program. *Financial support:* In 2011–12, 4 fellowships (averaging $1,000 per year) were awarded; Federal Work-Study, tuition waivers (partial), and lesson stipends also available. Support available to part-time students. Financial award application deadline: 4/15. *Faculty research:* African and African-American music, Bach, Renaissance music, early romantic music, theory of tonal music. *Unit head:* Dr. Ruth DeFord, Department Chair, 212-772-5026, Fax: 212-772-5022, E-mail: ruth.deford@hunter.cuny.edu. *Application contact:* L. Pondie Burstein, Graduate Adviser, 212-772-5152, E-mail: huntermust@aol.com. Web site: http://www.hunter.cuny.edu/music/.

Hunter College of the City University of New York, Graduate School, School of Education, Program in Music Education, New York, NY 10021-5085. Offers MA. *Accreditation:* NCATE. *Faculty:* 12 full-time (3 women), 3 part-time/adjunct (2 women). *Students:* 7 full-time (4 women), 27 part-time (15 women); includes 6 minority (1 Black or African American, non-Hispanic/Latino; 5 Asian, non-Hispanic/Latino), 4 international. Average age 29. 21 applicants, 48% accepted, 7 enrolled. In 2011, 12 master's awarded. *Degree requirements:* For master's, one foreign language, comprehensive exam, thesis, professional teaching portfolio, New York State Teacher Certification Exams. *Entrance requirements:* For master's, minimum GPA of 2.8, 2 letters of reference. Additional exam requirements/recommendations for international students: Required—TOEFL, TWE. *Application deadline:* For fall admission, 4/1 for domestic students, 2/1 for international students; for spring admission, 11/1 for domestic students, 9/1 for international students. Applications are processed on a rolling basis. Application fee: $125. *Expenses:* Tuition, state resident: full-time $8210; part-time $345 per credit. Tuition, nonresident: full-time $15,360; part-time $640 per credit. *Required fees:* $280 per semester. One-time fee: $125. Tuition and fees vary according to class time, campus/location and program. *Financial support:* Federal Work-Study and tuition waivers (partial) available. Support available to part-time students. *Unit head:* Dr. Poundie Burstein, Music Department Adviser, 212-772-5154, E-mail: huntermust@aol.com. *Application contact:* Carla Asher, Education Advisor, 212-772-4651, E-mail: carla.asher@hunter.cuny.edu. Web site: http://www.hunter.cuny.edu/school-of-education/programs/graduate/music.

Indiana University of Pennsylvania, School of Graduate Studies and Research, College of Fine Arts, Department of Music and Music Education, Program in Music, Indiana, PA 15705-1087. Offers music education (MA); music history and literature (MA); music theory and composition (MA); performance (MA). *Accreditation:* NASM. Part-time programs available. *Faculty:* 7 full-time (1 woman). *Students:* 4 full-time (1 woman), 1 part-time (0 women), 1 international. Average age 31. 11 applicants, 9% accepted, 1 enrolled. In 2011, 4 master's awarded. *Degree requirements:* For master's, thesis optional. *Entrance requirements:* For master's, 2 letters of recommendation, audition. Additional exam requirements/recommendations for international students: Required—TOEFL (minimum score 540 paper-based; 207 computer-based). *Application deadline:* Applications are processed on a rolling basis. Application fee: $50. Electronic applications accepted. *Expenses:* Tuition, state resident: full-time $7488; part-time $416 per credit. Tuition, nonresident: full-time $11,232; part-time $624 per credit. *Required fees:* $2070; $192.20 per credit. $90 per semester. *Financial support:* In 2011–12, 4 research assistantships with full and partial tuition reimbursements (averaging $5,440 per year) were awarded; fellowships and Federal Work-Study also available. Support available to part-time students. Financial award application deadline: 4/15; financial award applicants required to submit FAFSA. *Unit head:* Dr. Jack Stamp, Chair, 724-357-2390, E-mail: jestamp@iup.edu. *Application contact:* Dr. Kevin Eisensmith, Assistant

Chair, 724-357-2146, E-mail: tstprof@iup.edu. Web site: http://www.iup.edu/upper.aspx?id=89383.

Inter American University of Puerto Rico, Metropolitan Campus, Graduate Programs, Program in Music Education, San Juan, PR 00919-1293. Offers MM.

Inter American University of Puerto Rico, San Germán Campus, Graduate Studies Center, Program in Music Education, San Germán, PR 00683-5008. Offers music (MA); music teacher education (MA). Part-time and evening/weekend programs available. Application fee: $31. *Expenses: Required fees:* $213 per semester. *Financial support:* Federal Work-Study available. *Unit head:* Dr. Elba T. Irizarry, Director of Graduate Studies Center, 787-264-1912 Ext. 7357, Fax: 787-892-6350, E-mail: elbat@sg.inter.edu.

Ithaca College, Division of Graduate and Professional Studies, School of Music, Programs in Music and Music Education, Ithaca, NY 14850. Offers composition (MM); conducting (MM); music education (MM, MS); performance (MM); Suzuki pedagogy (MM). *Accreditation:* NASM. Part-time programs available. *Faculty:* 61 full-time (22 women), 2 part-time/adjunct (1 woman). *Students:* 42 full-time (23 women), 4 part-time (2 women); includes 8 minority (2 Black or African American, non-Hispanic/Latino; 2 Asian, non-Hispanic/Latino; 3 Hispanic/Latino; 1 Two or more races, non-Hispanic/Latino), 6 international. Average age 25. 228 applicants, 37% accepted, 34 enrolled. In 2011, 32 master's awarded. *Degree requirements:* For master's, comprehensive exam (for some programs), thesis (for some programs). *Entrance requirements:* For master's, audition, minimum GPA of 3.0. Additional exam requirements/recommendations for international students: Required—TOEFL (minimum score 550 paper-based; 213 computer-based; 80 iBT). *Application deadline:* For fall admission, 3/1 for domestic and international students; for spring admission, 12/1 for domestic and international students. Applications are processed on a rolling basis. Application fee: $40. Electronic applications accepted. *Expenses: Tuition:* Part-time $663 per credit hour. *Required fees:* $663 per credit hour. *Financial support:* In 2011–12, 39 students received support, including 39 teaching assistantships (averaging $9,092 per year); career-related internships or fieldwork, Federal Work-Study, scholarships/grants, and unspecified assistantships also available. Support available to part-time students. Financial award application deadline: 3/1; financial award applicants required to submit CSS PROFILE or FAFSA. *Faculty research:* Musical performance and performance studies; musical composition; music theory and analysis; music education, teaching and learning; musical direction and conducting. *Unit head:* Dr. Timothy Johnson, Chairperson, Graduate Studies in Music, 607-274-3143, Fax: 607-274-1263, E-mail: gps@ithaca.edu. *Application contact:* Gerard Turbide, Director, Office of Admission, 607-274-3143, Fax: 607-274-1263, E-mail: gps@ithaca.edu. Web site: http://www.ithaca.edu/music/grad.

Jackson State University, Graduate School, College of Liberal Arts, Department of Music, Jackson, MS 39217. Offers music education (MM Ed). *Accreditation:* NASM. Part-time and evening/weekend programs available. *Degree requirements:* For master's, comprehensive exam, thesis or alternative. *Entrance requirements:* For master's, GRE General Test. Additional exam requirements/recommendations for international students: Required—TOEFL (minimum score 520 paper-based; 195 computer-based; 67 iBT).

James Madison University, The Graduate School, College of Visual and Performing Arts, School of Music, Harrisonburg, VA 22807. Offers conducting (MM); music education (MM); musical arts (DMA); performance (MM); theory-composition (MM). *Accreditation:* NASM. Part-time programs available. *Faculty:* 31 full-time (9 women), 5 part-time/adjunct (4 women). *Students:* 17 full-time (8 women), 5 part-time (all women); includes 4 minority (1 Black or African American, non-Hispanic/Latino; 3 Two or more races, non-Hispanic/Latino), 2 international. Average age 27. In 2011, 11 master's awarded. *Degree requirements:* For master's, comprehensive exam. *Entrance requirements:* For master's, GRE General Test, audition, undergraduate degree with major in music and minimum GPA of 3.0. Additional exam requirements/recommendations for international students: Required—TOEFL. *Application deadline:* For fall admission, 4/1 priority date for domestic students, 4/1 for international students; for spring admission, 4/1 priority date for domestic students, 4/1 for international students. Applications are processed on a rolling basis. Application fee: $55. Electronic applications accepted. *Expenses:* Tuition, state resident: full-time $8016; part-time $334 per credit hour. Tuition, nonresident: full-time $22,656; part-time $944 per credit hour. *Financial support:* In 2011–12, 14 students received support, including 2 teaching assistantships with full tuition reimbursements available (averaging $8,664 per year); Federal Work-Study and 12 graduate assistantships ($7382) also available. Financial award application deadline: 3/1; financial award applicants required to submit FAFSA. *Unit head:* Eric Ruple, Interim Academic Unit Head, 540-568-3614, E-mail: rupleek@jmu.edu. *Application contact:* Dr. Mary Jane Speare, Graduate Coordinator, 540-568-3687.

Kansas State University, Graduate School, College of Arts and Sciences, Department of Music, Manhattan, KS 66506. Offers music education (MM); music education/band conducting (MM); music history and literature (MM); performance (MM); performance with pedagogy emphasis (MM); theory and composition (MM). *Accreditation:* NASM. Part-time programs available. *Faculty:* 25 full-time (8 women), 3 part-time/adjunct (1 woman). *Students:* 20 full-time (11 women), 8 part-time (6 women); includes 2 minority (1 Asian, non-Hispanic/Latino; 1 Two or more races, non-Hispanic/Latino), 3 international. Average age 28. 25 applicants, 80% accepted, 8 enrolled. In 2011, 20 master's awarded. *Degree requirements:* For master's, thesis optional. *Entrance requirements:* For master's, GRE, audition (in person or recording), interview (music education). Additional exam requirements/recommendations for international students: Required—TOEFL (minimum score 600 paper-based). *Application deadline:* For fall admission, 2/1 priority date for domestic students, 2/1 for international students; for spring admission, 8/1 priority date for domestic students, 8/1 for international students. Applications are processed on a rolling basis. Application fee: $40 ($55 for international students). Electronic applications accepted. *Financial support:* In 2011–12, 12 teaching assistantships with full tuition reimbursements (averaging $7,500 per year) were awarded; institutionally sponsored loans, scholarships/grants, and tuition waivers (full and partial) also available. Support available to part-time students. Financial award application deadline: 3/1; financial award applicants required to submit FAFSA. *Faculty research:* Music since 1945, music by women composers, American music, opera, current performance practices. *Total annual research expenditures:* $15,670. *Unit head:* Dr. Gary Mortenson, Head, 785-532-3802, Fax: 785-532-5740, E-mail: garym@ksu.edu. *Application contact:* Dr. Fred Burrack, Director, 785-532-3429, Fax: 785-532-5740, E-mail: fburrack@ksu.edu. Web site: http://www.k-state.edu/music/.

Kent State University, College of the Arts, Hugh A. Glauser School of Music, Kent, OH 44242-0001. Offers composition (MA); conducting (MM); ethnomusicology (MA); music education (MM, PhD); musicology (MA); musicology-ethnomusicology (PhD); performance (MM); theory (MA); theory and composition (PhD). *Accreditation:* NASM. *Degree requirements:* For master's, variable foreign language requirement, comprehensive exam, 2 recitals, essay and recital, or thesis; for doctorate, variable foreign language requirement, comprehensive exam, thesis/dissertation. *Entrance requirements:* For master's, diagnostic exams in music history and theory, audition, minimum GPA of 2.75; for doctorate, diagnostic exams in music history and theory, master's thesis or scholarly paper, minimum GPA of 3.0. Additional exam requirements/recommendations for international students: Required—TOEFL. Electronic applications accepted. *Expenses:* Tuition, state resident: full-time $8136; part-time $452 per credit hour. Tuition, nonresident: full-time $14,292; part-time $794 per credit hour. *Faculty research:* Music composition, performance, teaching and history.

Lamar University, College of Graduate Studies, College of Fine Arts and Communication, Mary Morgan Moore Department of Music, Beaumont, TX 77710. Offers music education (MM Ed); music performance (MM). *Accreditation:* NASM (one or more programs are accredited). *Faculty:* 9 full-time (3 women), 2 part-time/adjunct (1 woman). *Students:* 5 full-time (4 women), 2 part-time (1 woman); includes 1 minority (Black or African American, non-Hispanic/Latino). Average age 30. 2 applicants, 50% accepted, 0 enrolled. In 2011, 6 master's awarded. *Degree requirements:* For master's, comprehensive exam, thesis optional. *Entrance requirements:* For master's, GRE General Test, theory placement exams, audition. Additional exam requirements/recommendations for international students: Required—TOEFL. *Application deadline:* For fall admission, 8/1 for domestic students; for spring admission, 12/1 for domestic students. Applications are processed on a rolling basis. Application fee: $25 ($50 for international students). *Expenses:* Tuition, state resident: full-time $5430; part-time $272 per credit hour. Tuition, nonresident: full-time $11,540; part-time $577 per credit hour. *Required fees:* $1916. *Financial support:* In 2011–12, 4 fellowships with tuition reimbursements (averaging $2,000 per year), 2 teaching assistantships were awarded; institutionally sponsored loans and tuition waivers (partial) also available. Support available to part-time students. Financial award application deadline: 4/1. *Faculty research:* Performance: ensembles and personal. *Unit head:* Dr. L. Randolph Babin, Chair, 409-880-8144, Fax: 409-880-8143, E-mail: babinlr@hal.lamar.edu. *Application contact:* Dr. Robert M. Culbertson, Adviser, 409-880-8073, Fax: 409-880-8143, E-mail: culbertsrm@hal.lamar.edu. Web site: http://dept.lamar.edu/cofac/deptmusic/.

Lebanon Valley College, Program in Music Education, Annville, PA 17003-1400. Offers MME. *Accreditation:* NASM. Part-time programs available. *Faculty:* 7 full-time (2 women), 3 part-time/adjunct (1 woman). In 2011, 2 master's awarded. *Degree requirements:* For master's, thesis. *Entrance requirements:* For master's, minimum GPA of 3.0, teaching certificate. *Application deadline:* Applications are processed on a rolling basis. Application fee: $30. Electronic applications accepted. *Expenses: Tuition:* Full-time $35,720; part-time $465 per credit. *Required fees:* $610. Part-time tuition and fees vary according to program. *Financial support:* Application deadline: 5/1; applicants required to submit FAFSA. *Unit head:* Dr. Marian T. Dura, Director, 717-867-6213, E-mail: dura@lvc.edu. *Application contact:* Hope Witmer, Assistant Dean, Graduate Studies and Continuing Education, 717-867-6213, Fax: 717-867-6018, E-mail: witmer@lvc.edu. Web site: http://www.lvc.edu/mme/.

Lee University, Program in Music, Cleveland, TN 37320-3450. Offers church music (MCM); music education (MM); music performance (MM). *Accreditation:* NASM. Part-time programs available. *Faculty:* 22 full-time (5 women), 14 part-time/adjunct (7 women). *Students:* 20 full-time (11 women), 18 part-time (11 women); includes 2 minority (1 Hispanic/Latino; 1 Two or more races, non-Hispanic/Latino), 5 international. Average age 30. 16 applicants, 81% accepted, 11 enrolled. In 2011, 10 master's awarded. *Degree requirements:* For master's, variable foreign language requirement, comprehensive exam, thesis, internship. *Entrance requirements:* For master's, audition, resume, interview, minimum GPA of 2.75. Additional exam requirements/recommendations for international students: Required—TOEFL (minimum score 450 paper-based; 45 computer-based). *Application deadline:* For fall admission, 4/1 for domestic students; for spring admission, 10/1 for domestic students. Applications are processed on a rolling basis. Application fee: $25. *Expenses: Tuition:* Full-time $12,120; part-time $506 per credit hour. *Required fees:* $560; $305 per term. Part-time tuition and fees vary according to course load. *Financial support:* In 2011–12, 18 teaching assistantships (averaging $840 per year) were awarded; career-related internships or fieldwork, Federal Work-Study, institutionally sponsored loans, and scholarships/grants also available. Financial award application deadline: 3/1; financial award applicants required to submit FAFSA. *Unit head:* Dr. Jim W. Burns, Director, 423-614-8240, Fax: 423-614-8242, E-mail: gradmusic@leeuniversity.edu. *Application contact:* Vicki Glasscock, Graduate Admissions Director, 423-614-8059, E-mail: vglasscock@leeuniversity.edu. Web site: http://www.leeuniversity.edu/academics/graduate/music.

Lehman College of the City University of New York, Division of Arts and Humanities, Department of Music, Bronx, NY 10468-1589. Offers MAT. *Accreditation:* NCATE. Part-time and evening/weekend programs available. *Entrance requirements:* For master's, audition. *Faculty research:* Music and music education.

Lehman College of the City University of New York, Division of Education, Department of Middle and High School Education, Program in Music Education, Bronx, NY 10468-1589. Offers MS Ed. Part-time and evening/weekend programs available.

Long Island University–C. W. Post Campus, School of Education, Department of Curriculum and Instruction, Brookville, NY 11548-1300. Offers adolescence education (MS); adolescence education: biology (MS); adolescence education: earth science (MS); adolescence education: English (MS); adolescence education: mathematics (MS); adolescence education: social studies (MS); adolescence education: Spanish (MS); art education (MS); bilingual education (MS); childhood education (MS); early childhood education (MS); middle childhood education (MS); music education (MS); teaching English to speakers of other languages (MS). Part-time and evening/weekend programs available. *Degree requirements:* For master's, comprehensive exam or thesis, student teaching. *Entrance requirements:* For master's, minimum GPA of 2.75 in major, 2.5 overall. Electronic applications accepted. *Faculty research:* Ethics and education, teaching strategies.

Long Island University–C. W. Post Campus, School of Education, Department of Music, Brookville, NY 11548-1300. Offers music education (MS).

Long Island University–C. W. Post Campus, School of Visual and Performing Arts, Department of Music, Brookville, NY 11548-1300. Offers music (MA); music education (MS). Part-time programs available. *Degree requirements:* For master's, thesis. *Entrance requirements:* For master's, GRE General Test (MA), GRE Subject Test in music, minimum undergraduate GPA of 3.0, 2 professional and/or academic letters of recommendation, current resume. Electronic applications accepted. *Faculty research:* Performance, composing, musicology, conducting, computer-based music technology.

Louisiana State University and Agricultural and Mechanical College, Graduate School, College of Music and Dramatic Arts, School of Music, Baton Rouge, LA 70803. Offers music (MM, DMA, PhD); music education (PhD). *Accreditation:* NASM. Part-time programs available. *Faculty:* 49 full-time (15 women). *Students:* 147 full-time (72 women), 38 part-time (16 women); includes 21 minority (9 Black or African American, non-Hispanic/Latino; 1 Asian, non-Hispanic/Latino; 10 Hispanic/Latino; 1 Two or more races, non-Hispanic/Latino), 40 international. Average age 29. 170 applicants, 57% accepted, 56 enrolled. In 2011, 31 master's, 24 doctorates awarded. Terminal master's awarded for partial completion of doctoral program. *Degree requirements:* For doctorate, thesis/dissertation (for some programs). *Entrance requirements:* For master's, minimum GPA of 3.0, audition/interview; for doctorate, GRE General Test, minimum GPA of 3.0, audition/interview. Additional exam requirements/recommendations for international students: Required—TOEFL (minimum score 550 paper-based; 213 computer-based; 79 iBT) or IELTS (minimum score 6.5). *Application deadline:* For fall admission, 3/15 priority date for domestic students, 5/15 for international students; for spring admission, 10/15 for international students. Applications are processed on a rolling basis. Application fee: $50 ($70 for international students). Electronic applications accepted. *Financial support:* In 2011–12, 149 students received support, including 4 fellowships (averaging $15,715 per year), 2 research assistantships with full and partial tuition reimbursements available (averaging $17,000 per year), 81 teaching assistantships with full and partial tuition reimbursements available (averaging $9,972 per year); Federal Work-Study, institutionally sponsored loans, scholarships/grants, health care benefits, tuition waivers (full and partial), and unspecified assistantships also available. Support available to part-time students. Financial award applicants required to submit FAFSA. *Faculty research:* Music education, music literature, formal and harmonic analysis, pedagogy, performance. *Unit head:* Dr. Willis Delony, Interim Dean, 225-578-3261, Fax: 225-578-2562. *Application contact:* Dr. Lori Bade, Director of Graduate Studies, 225-578-3261, Fax: 225-578-2562, E-mail: lbade1@lsu.edu. Web site: http://www.music.lsu.edu/.

Manhattanville College, Graduate Studies, School of Education, Program in Music Education, Purchase, NY 10577-2132. Offers MAT. Part-time and evening/weekend programs available. *Degree requirements:* For master's, comprehensive exam or research project, field experience. *Entrance requirements:* For master's, audition, minimum undergraduate GPA of 3.0, 2 letters of recommendation. Additional exam requirements/recommendations for international students: Required—TOEFL. Electronic applications accepted.

Marywood University, Academic Affairs, Insalaco College of Creative and Performing Arts, Music, Theatre and Dance Department, Program in Music Education, Scranton, PA 18509-1598. Offers MA. *Accreditation:* NASM; NCATE. *Entrance requirements:* Additional exam requirements/recommendations for international students: Required—TOEFL (minimum score 550 paper-based; 213 computer-based; 79 iBT). *Application deadline:* For fall admission, 4/1 priority date for domestic students, 3/31 for international students; for spring admission, 11/1 priority date for domestic students, 8/31 for international students. Applications are processed on a rolling basis. Application fee: $35. Electronic applications accepted. *Financial support:* Career-related internships or fieldwork, scholarships/grants, and unspecified assistantships available. Support available to part-time students. Financial award application deadline: 6/30; financial award applicants required to submit FAFSA. *Unit head:* Sr. Joan McCusker, Chair, 570-348-6268 Ext. 2531, E-mail: mccusker@maryu.marywood.edu. *Application contact:* Tammy Manka, Assistant Director of Graduate Admissions, 570-348-6211 Ext. 2322, E-mail: tmanka@marywood.edu. Web site: http://www.marywood.edu/mtd/grad-programs.html#ma.

McGill University, Faculty of Graduate and Postdoctoral Studies, Schulich School of Music, Montréal, QC H3A 2T5, Canada. Offers composition (M Mus, D Mus, PhD); music education (MA, PhD); music technology (MA, PhD); musicology (MA, PhD); performance (M Mus); performance studies (D Mus); sound recording (M Mus, PhD); theory (MA, PhD).

McKendree University, Graduate Programs, Master of Arts in Education Program, Lebanon, IL 62254-1299. Offers certification (MA Ed); educational administration and leadership (MA Ed); educational studies (MA Ed); higher education administrative services (MA Ed); music education (MA Ed); special education (MA Ed); teacher leadership (MA Ed); transition to teaching (MA Ed). *Accreditation:* NCATE. Part-time and evening/weekend programs available. Postbaccalaureate distance learning degree programs offered (no on-campus study). *Entrance requirements:* For master's, official transcripts from institutions attended, minimum GPA of 3.0, resume, references. Additional exam requirements/recommendations for international students: Required—TOEFL. Electronic applications accepted.

McNeese State University, Doré School of Graduate Studies, College of Liberal Arts, Department of Performing Arts, Program in Music Education, Lake Charles, LA 70609. Offers instrumental (MM Ed); Kodaly studies (Postbaccalaureate Certificate); vocal (MM Ed). *Accreditation:* NASM; NCATE. Evening/weekend programs available. *Faculty:* 6 full-time (2 women). *Students:* 1 part-time (0 women). In 2011, 2 master's awarded. *Entrance requirements:* For master's, GRE, teaching certificate in music education. *Application deadline:* For fall admission, 5/15 priority date for domestic students, 5/15 for international students; for spring admission, 10/15 priority date for domestic students, 10/15 for international students. Applications are processed on a rolling basis. Application fee: $20 ($30 for international students). *Expenses:* Tuition, state resident: part-time $519 per credit hour. Tuition and fees vary according to course load. *Financial support:* Teaching assistantships available. Financial award application deadline: 5/1. *Unit head:* Michele Martin, Head, 337-475-5028, Fax: 337-475-5063, E-mail: mmartin@mcneese.edu. *Application contact:* Dr. George F. Mead, Jr., Interim Dean of Dore' School of Graduate Studies, 337-475-5396, Fax: 337-475-5397, E-mail: admissions@mcneese.edu.

Miami University, School of Fine Arts, Department of Music, Oxford, OH 45056. Offers music education (MM); music performance (MM). *Accreditation:* NASM. *Students:* 21 full-time (7 women), 1 part-time (0 women); includes 4 minority (2 Black or African American, non-Hispanic/Latino; 2 Hispanic/Latino), 3 international. Average age 26. In 2011, 13 master's awarded. *Entrance requirements:* For master's, audition, minimum undergraduate GPA of 3.0 during previous 2 years or overall. Additional exam requirements/recommendations for international students: Required—TOEFL. Application fee: $50. Electronic applications accepted. *Expenses:* Tuition, state resident: full-time $12,023; part-time $501 per credit hour. Tuition, nonresident: full-time $26,554; part-time $1107 per credit hour. *Required fees:* $528. *Financial support:* Fellowships with full tuition reimbursements, research assistantships, teaching assistantships, Federal Work-Study, health care benefits, tuition waivers (full), and unspecified assistantships available. Financial award application deadline: 2/15. *Unit head:* Dr. Judith Delzell, Chair, 513-529-1428. *Application contact:* Dr. Claire Boge, Graduate Advisor, 513-529-1441, E-mail: bogecl@muohio.edu. Web site: http://arts.muohio.edu/music.

Michigan State University, The Graduate School, College of Music, East Lansing, MI 48824. Offers collaborative piano (M Mus); jazz studies (M Mus); music (PhD); music composition (M Mus, DMA); music conducting (M Mus, DMA); music education (M Mus); music performance (M Mus, DMA); music theory (M Mus); music therapy (M Mus); musicology (MA); piano pedagogy (M Mus). *Accreditation:* NASM. *Entrance requirements:* Additional exam requirements/recommendations for international students: Required—TOEFL. Electronic applications accepted.

Minot State University, Graduate School, Division of Music, Minot, ND 58707-0002. Offers music education (MME). Program offered during summer only. *Accreditation:* NASM. *Degree requirements:* For master's, thesis or alternative. *Entrance requirements:* For master's, music exam, minimum GPA of 2.75. Additional exam requirements/recommendations for international students: Required—TOEFL. *Faculty research:* Music education.

Mississippi College, Graduate School, College of Arts and Sciences, School of Christian Studies and the Arts, Department of Music, Clinton, MS 39058. Offers applied music performance (MM); conducting (MM); music education (MM); music performance: organ (MM); vocal pedagogy (MM). *Accreditation:* NASM. Part-time and evening/weekend programs available. *Degree requirements:* For master's, comprehensive exam, recital. *Entrance requirements:* For master's, GRE, minimum GPA of 2.5. Additional exam requirements/recommendations for international students: Recommended—TOEFL, IELTS. Electronic applications accepted.

Missouri State University, Graduate College, College of Arts and Letters, Department of Music, Springfield, MO 65897. Offers music (MM), including conducting, music education, music pedagogy, music theory and composition, performance; secondary education (MS Ed), including music. *Accreditation:* NASM. Part-time programs available. *Faculty:* 25 full-time (10 women). *Students:* 20 full-time (14 women), 19 part-time (10 women); includes 3 minority (2 Asian, non-Hispanic/Latino; 1 Hispanic/Latino), 8 international. Average age 27. 20 applicants, 100% accepted, 17 enrolled. In 2011, 17 master's awarded. *Degree requirements:* For master's, comprehensive exam, thesis or alternative. *Entrance requirements:* For master's, GRE, interview/audition (MM), 9-12 teaching certification (MS Ed). Additional exam requirements/recommendations for international students: Required—TOEFL (minimum score 550 paper-based; 213 computer-based; 79 iBT). *Application deadline:* For fall admission, 7/20 for domestic students, 5/1 for international students; for spring admission, 12/20 for domestic students, 9/1 for international students. Applications are processed on a rolling basis. Application fee: $35 ($50 for international students). Electronic applications accepted. *Expenses:* Tuition, state resident: full-time $4086; part-time $227 per credit hour. Tuition, nonresident: full-time $8172; part-time $454 per credit hour. *Required fees:* $275 per semester. Tuition and fees vary according to course load, campus/location and program. *Financial support:* In 2011–12, 11 teaching assistantships with full tuition reimbursements (averaging $8,000 per year) were awarded; Federal Work-Study, institutionally sponsored loans, scholarships/grants, tuition waivers (partial), and unspecified assistantships also available. Financial award application deadline: 3/31; financial award applicants required to submit FAFSA. *Faculty research:* Bulgarian violin literature, Ozarks fiddle music, carillon, nineteenth century piano. *Unit head:* Dr. Julie Combs, Head, 417-836-5648, Fax: 417-836-7665, E-mail: music@missouristate.edu. *Application contact:* Misty Stewart, Coordinator of Graduate Recruitment, 417-836-6079, Fax: 417-836-6200. Web site: http://www.missouristate.edu/music/.

Montclair State University, The Graduate School, College of Education and Human Services, Department of Curriculum and Teaching, Program in Teaching in Content Area, Montclair, NJ 07043-1624. Offers art (MAT); biology (MAT); chemistry (MAT); earth science (MAT); English (MAT); French (MAT); health and physical education (MAT); health education (MAT); mathematics (MAT); music (MAT); physical education (MAT); physical science (MAT); social studies (MAT); Spanish (MAT); teacher of English as a second language (MAT). *Students:* 162 full-time (90 women), 47 part-time (29 women); includes 37 minority (4 Black or African American, non-Hispanic/Latino; 11 Asian, non-Hispanic/Latino; 18 Hispanic/Latino; 4 Two or more races, non-Hispanic/Latino), 5 international. Average age 31. 145 applicants, 41% accepted, 56 enrolled. In 2011, 229 master's awarded. *Degree requirements:* For master's, comprehensive exam, thesis or alternative. *Entrance requirements:* For master's, GRE General Test, interview, 2 letters of recommendation. Additional exam requirements/recommendations for international students: Required—TOEFL (minimum score 83 iBT), IELTS (minimum score 6.5). *Application deadline:* Applications are processed on a rolling basis. Application fee: $60. Electronic applications accepted. *Financial support:* Federal Work-Study, scholarships/grants, and unspecified assistantships available. Support available to part-time students. Financial award application deadline: 3/1; financial award applicants required to submit FAFSA. *Unit head:* Dr. David Schwarzer, Chairperson, 973-655-5187. *Application contact:* Amy Aiello, Executive Director of The Graduate School, 973-655-5147, Fax: 973-655-7869, E-mail: graduate.school@montclair.edu.

Montclair State University, The Graduate School, School of the Arts, John J. Cali School of Music, Program in Music, Montclair, NJ 07043-1624. Offers music education (MA); music therapy (MA); performance (MA); theory/composition (MA). Part-time and evening/weekend programs available. *Students:* 24 full-time (12 women), 36 part-time (18 women); includes 9 minority (3 Black or African American, non-Hispanic/Latino; 3 Asian, non-Hispanic/Latino; 3 Hispanic/Latino), 5 international. Average age 31. 60 applicants, 45% accepted, 20 enrolled. In 2011, 9 master's awarded. *Degree requirements:* For master's, thesis. *Entrance requirements:* For master's, GRE General Test, 2 letters of recommendation, essay. Additional exam requirements/recommendations for international students: Required—TOEFL (minimum score 83 iBT), IELTS (minimum score 6.5). *Application deadline:* Applications are processed on a rolling basis. Application fee: $60. Electronic applications accepted. *Financial support:* In 2011–12, 3 research assistantships with full tuition reimbursements (averaging $7,000 per year) were awarded; Federal Work-Study, scholarships/grants, and unspecified assistantships also available. Support available to part-time students. Financial award application deadline: 3/1; financial award applicants required to submit FAFSA. *Unit head:* Prof. Robert Aldridge, Chairperson, 973-655-7212. *Application contact:* Amy Aiello, Executive Director of The Graduate School, 973-655-5147, Fax: 973-655-7869, E-mail: graduate.school@montclair.edu. Web site: http://www.montclair.edu/Arts/music/.

Morehead State University, Graduate Programs, Caudill College of Arts, Humanities and Social Sciences, Department of Music, Theatre and Dance, Morehead, KY 40351. Offers music education (MM); music performance (MM). *Accreditation:* NASM. Part-time and evening/weekend programs available. *Degree requirements:* For master's, comprehensive exam, oral and written exams. *Entrance requirements:* For master's, music entrance exam, BA in music with minimum GPA of 3.0, 2.5 overall; audition. Additional exam requirements/recommendations for international students: Required—TOEFL (minimum score 550 paper-based; 173 computer-based). Electronic applications accepted. *Faculty research:* Musical instrument digital interface (MIDI) applications, tonal concepts of euphonium and baritone horn, digital synthesis, computer-assisted instruction in music, musical composition.

Murray State University, College of Humanities and Fine Arts, Program in Music, Murray, KY 42071. Offers music education (MME). *Accreditation:* NASM. Part-time programs available. *Entrance requirements:* For master's, GRE General Test or MAT. Additional exam requirements/recommendations for international students: Required—TOEFL.

Nazareth College of Rochester, Graduate Studies, Department of Music, Program in Music Education, Rochester, NY 14618-3790. Offers MS Ed. *Accreditation:* NASM; Teacher Education Accreditation Council. Part-time and evening/weekend programs available. *Entrance requirements:* For master's, audition, minimum GPA of 3.0.

New Jersey City University, Graduate Studies and Continuing Education, William J. Maxwell College of Arts and Sciences, Department of Music, Dance and Theatre, Jersey City, NJ 07305-1597. Offers music education (MA); performance (MM). *Accreditation:* NASM. Part-time and evening/weekend programs available. *Students:* 16 full-time (6 women), 9 part-time (3 women); includes 10 minority (5 Black or African American, non-Hispanic/Latino; 2 Asian, non-Hispanic/Latino; 3 Hispanic/Latino), 3 international. Average age 33. In 2011, 12 master's awarded. *Degree requirements:* For master's, thesis optional, recital. *Entrance requirements:* Additional exam requirements/recommendations for international students: Required—TOEFL. *Application deadline:* For fall admission, 8/1 priority date for domestic students; for spring admission, 12/1 for domestic students. Applications are processed on a rolling basis. Application fee: $0.

Expenses: Tuition, state resident: part-time $494 per credit. Tuition, nonresident: part-time $911.30 per credit. *Required fees:* $95.90 per year. *Financial support:* Unspecified assistantships available. *Unit head:* Dr. Min Kim, Chairperson, 201-200-3157, E-mail: mkim@njcu.edu. *Application contact:* Dr. William Bajor, Dean of Graduate Studies, 201-200-3409, Fax: 201-200-3411, E-mail: wbajor@njcu.edu.

New Mexico State University, Graduate School, College of Arts and Sciences, Department of Music, Las Cruces, NM 88003-8001. Offers conducting (MM); music education (MM); performance (MM). *Accreditation:* NASM. Part-time programs available. *Faculty:* 8 full-time (3 women), 2 part-time/adjunct (1 woman). *Students:* 14 full-time (7 women), 14 part-time (6 women); includes 8 minority (1 Black or African American, non-Hispanic/Latino; 7 Hispanic/Latino), 9 international. Average age 31. 16 applicants, 88% accepted, 8 enrolled. In 2011, 13 master's awarded. *Degree requirements:* For master's, comprehensive exam (for some programs), thesis (for some programs), recital. *Entrance requirements:* For master's, diagnostic exam, audition, bachelor's degree or equivalent from an accredited institution. Additional exam requirements/recommendations for international students: Required—TOEFL (minimum score 550 paper-based; 79 iBT), IELTS (minimum score 6.5). *Application deadline:* For fall admission, 7/1 priority date for domestic students; for spring admission, 11/1 for domestic students. Applications are processed on a rolling basis. Application fee: $40 ($50 for international students). Electronic applications accepted. *Expenses:* Contact institution. *Financial support:* In 2011–12, 1 fellowship (averaging $394 per year), 1 research assistantship (averaging $7,900 per year), 8 teaching assistantships (averaging $22,503 per year) were awarded; Federal Work-Study and health care benefits also available. Support available to part-time students. Financial award application deadline: 3/1. *Faculty research:* Music education, contemporary wind band literature, performance. *Unit head:* Dr. Lon W. Chaffin, Head, 575-646-2421, Fax: 575-646-8199, E-mail: lchaffin@nmsu.edu. *Application contact:* Dr. James Shearer, Assistant Professor, 575-646-2601, Fax: 575-646-8199, E-mail: jshearer@nmsu.edu. Web site: http://music.nmsu.edu.

New York University, Steinhardt School of Culture, Education, and Human Development, Department of Music and Performing Arts Professions, Program in Music Education, New York, NY 10012-1019. Offers music education (Ed D, PhD, Advanced Certificate); teaching music (MA). *Accreditation:* Teacher Education Accreditation Council. Part-time programs available. *Degree requirements:* For master's, thesis (for some programs); for doctorate, thesis/dissertation. *Entrance requirements:* For master's, audition; for doctorate, GRE General Test, interview; for Advanced Certificate, master's degree. Additional exam requirements/recommendations for international students: Required—TOEFL. Electronic applications accepted. *Faculty research:* Music education philosophy; community music education; integrated curriculum; multiple intelligences; technology in arts education; cognition, emotion, and music.

New York University, Steinhardt School of Culture, Education, and Human Development, Department of Music and Performing Arts Professions, Program in Music Performance and Composition, New York, NY 10012-1019. Offers instrumental performance (MM), including instrumental performance, jazz instrumental performance; music performance and composition (MA, PhD), including composition; music theory and composition (MM, PhD), including music theory and compostition (MM), scoring for film and multimedia (MM); piano performance (MM), including collaborative performance, collaborative piano, solo piano; vocal pedagogy (Advanced Certificate); vocal performance (MM), including classical voice, music theatre performance; vocal performance/vocal pedagogy (MM), including classical voice, music theatre performance; MM/Advanced Certificate. Part-time programs available. *Degree requirements:* For master's, thesis (for some programs); for doctorate, thesis/dissertation. *Entrance requirements:* For master's, audition; for doctorate, GRE General Test, audition, interview. Additional exam requirements/recommendations for international students: Required—TOEFL. Electronic applications accepted. *Faculty research:* Aesthetics, performance analysis, twentieth century music, music methodologies for arts criticism and analysis.

Norfolk State University, School of Graduate Studies, School of Liberal Arts, Department of Music, Norfolk, VA 23504. Offers music (MM); music education (MM); performance (MM); theory and composition (MM). *Accreditation:* NASM. Part-time programs available. *Degree requirements:* For master's, thesis or alternative. *Entrance requirements:* For master's, minimum GPA of 2.7, letters of recommendation. Additional exam requirements/recommendations for international students: Required—TOEFL.

North Dakota State University, College of Graduate and Interdisciplinary Studies, College of Human Development and Education, School of Education, Fargo, ND 58108. Offers agricultural education (M Ed, MS), including agricultural education, agricultural extension education (MS); counseling (M Ed, MS, PhD); curriculum and instruction (M Ed, MS), including pedagogy, physical education and athletic administration; education (PhD); educational leadership (M Ed, MS, Ed S); family and consumer sciences education (M Ed, MS); history education (M Ed, MS); institutional analysis (Ed D); mathematics education (M Ed, MS); music education (M Ed, MS); occupational and adult education (Ed D); science education (M Ed, MS). *Accreditation:* NCATE. Part-time and evening/weekend programs available. Postbaccalaureate distance learning degree programs offered (minimal on-campus study). *Faculty:* 24 full-time (10 women), 2 part-time/adjunct (1 woman). *Students:* 91 full-time (64 women), 114 part-time (78 women); includes 13 minority (4 Black or African American, non-Hispanic/Latino; 5 American Indian or Alaska Native, non-Hispanic/Latino; 1 Hispanic/Latino; 3 Two or more races, non-Hispanic/Latino), 8 international. 88 applicants, 67% accepted, 56 enrolled. In 2011, 43 master's, 12 doctorates awarded. *Degree requirements:* For master's, comprehensive exam; for doctorate, thesis/dissertation; for Ed S, thesis. *Entrance requirements:* For degree, GRE General Test, master's degree, minimum GPA of 3.25. Additional exam requirements/recommendations for international students: Required—TOEFL. *Application deadline:* Applications are processed on a rolling basis. Application fee: $45 ($60 for international students). *Financial support:* Research assistantships, teaching assistantships, career-related internships or fieldwork, Federal Work-Study, institutionally sponsored loans, and tuition waivers (full) available. Financial award application deadline: 4/15. *Unit head:* Dr. William Martin, Chair, 701-231-7202, Fax: 701-231-7416, E-mail: william.martin@ndsu.edu. *Application contact:* Sonya Goergen, Marketing, Recruitment, and Public Relations Coordinator, 701-231-7033, Fax: 701-231-6524. Web site: http://www.ndsu.nodak.edu/school_of_education/.

Northwestern University, Henry and Leigh Bienen School of Music, Department of Music Studies, Evanston, IL 60208. Offers composition (DM); music education (MM, PhD); music theory (MM); music theory and cognition (PhD); musicology (MM, PhD). PhD admissions and degree offered through The Graduate School. *Accreditation:* NASM. *Degree requirements:* For doctorate, comprehensive exam, thesis/dissertation. *Entrance requirements:* For master's, portfolio or research papers; for doctorate, GRE General Test (PhD), portfolio, research papers. Additional exam requirements/recommendations for international students: Required—TOEFL (minimum score 600 paper-based; 250 computer-based; 100 iBT). *Faculty research:* Music cognition, cognitive learning, aesthetic education, computer music, technology in education.

Northwest Missouri State University, Graduate School, College of Arts and Sciences, Department of Music, Maryville, MO 64468-6001. Offers teaching music (MS Ed). *Accreditation:* NASM. Part-time programs available. *Faculty:* 12 full-time (3 women). *Students:* 3 full-time (1 woman); includes 1 minority (Two or more races, non-Hispanic/Latino). In 2011, 4 master's awarded. *Degree requirements:* For master's, comprehensive exam. *Entrance requirements:* For master's, GRE General Test, minimum undergraduate GPA of 2.5, writing sample. Additional exam requirements/recommendations for international students: Required—TOEFL (minimum score 550 paper-based; 213 computer-based). *Application deadline:* For fall admission, 7/1 for domestic and international students; for spring admission, 11/15 for domestic and international students. Applications are processed on a rolling basis. Application fee: $0 ($50 for international students). *Financial support:* In 2011–12, research assistantships with full tuition reimbursements (averaging $6,000 per year), 3 teaching assistantships with full tuition reimbursements (averaging $6,000 per year) were awarded. Financial award application deadline: 4/1; financial award applicants required to submit FAFSA. *Unit head:* Dr. Ernest Woodruff, Chairperson, 660-562-1317. *Application contact:* Dr. Gregory Haddock, Dean of Graduate School, 660-562-1145, Fax: 660-562-1096, E-mail: gradsch@nwmissouri.edu.

Oakland University, Graduate Study and Lifelong Learning, College of Arts and Sciences, Department of Music, Rochester, MI 48309-4401. Offers music (MM); music education (PhD). *Accreditation:* NASM. *Entrance requirements:* For master's, minimum GPA of 3.0 for unconditional admission. Additional exam requirements/recommendations for international students: Required—TOEFL (minimum score 550 paper-based; 213 computer-based). Electronic applications accepted. *Expenses:* Contact institution.

Ohio University, Graduate College, College of Fine Arts, School of Music, Athens, OH 45701-2979. Offers accompanying (MM); composition (MM); conducting (MM); history/literature (MM); music education (MM); music therapy (MM); performance (MM, Certificate); performance/pedagogy (MM); theory (MM). *Accreditation:* NASM. Part-time and evening/weekend programs available. Postbaccalaureate distance learning degree programs offered (minimal on-campus study). *Students:* 40 full-time (19 women), 9 part-time (6 women); includes 6 minority (1 Black or African American, non-Hispanic/Latino; 1 Asian, non-Hispanic/Latino; 2 Hispanic/Latino; 2 Two or more races, non-Hispanic/Latino), 12 international. 67 applicants, 51% accepted, 23 enrolled. In 2011, 25 master's awarded. *Degree requirements:* For master's, comprehensive exam, thesis (for some programs), oral exam. *Entrance requirements:* For master's, audition, interview, portfolio, recordings (varies by program). Additional exam requirements/recommendations for international students: Required—TOEFL (minimum score 550 paper-based; 80 iBT) or IELTS (minimum score 6.5). *Application deadline:* For fall admission, 1/1 priority date for domestic students, 1/1 for international students. Application fee: $50 ($55 for international students). Electronic applications accepted. *Financial support:* In 2011–12, 35 teaching assistantships with full and partial tuition reimbursements (averaging $4,500 per year) were awarded; career-related internships or fieldwork, Federal Work-Study, institutionally sponsored loans, and tuition waivers (full and partial) also available. Financial award application deadline: 1/1. *Unit head:* Dr. W. Michael Parkinson, Director, 740-593-4244, Fax: 740-593-1429, E-mail: parkinsw@ohio.edu. *Application contact:* Dr. Richard Wetzel, Graduate Chair, 740-593-1652, Fax: 740-593-1429, E-mail: wetzel@ohio.edu. Web site: http://www.finearts.ohio.edu/music.

Oklahoma State University, College of Arts and Sciences, Department of Music, Stillwater, OK 74078. Offers pedagogy and performance (MM). *Accreditation:* NASM. *Faculty:* 28 full-time (10 women), 7 part-time/adjunct (3 women). *Students:* 14 full-time (7 women), 3 part-time (1 woman); includes 3 minority (1 Asian, non-Hispanic/Latino; 1 Hispanic/Latino; 1 Two or more races, non-Hispanic/Latino), 2 international. Average age 27. 36 applicants, 36% accepted, 8 enrolled. In 2011, 5 degrees awarded. *Degree requirements:* For master's, final project, oral exam. *Entrance requirements:* For master's, GRE, audition. Additional exam requirements/recommendations for international students: Required—TOEFL (minimum score 550 paper-based; 79 iBT). *Application deadline:* For fall admission, 3/1 for international students; for spring admission, 8/1 for international students. Applications are processed on a rolling basis. Application fee: $40 ($75 for international students). Electronic applications accepted. *Expenses:* Tuition, state resident: full-time $4044; part-time $168.50 per credit hour. Tuition, nonresident: full-time $16,008; part-time $667 per credit hour. *Required fees:* $2122; $88.45 per credit hour. One-time fee: $50. Tuition and fees vary according to course load and campus/location. *Financial support:* In 2011–12, 11 teaching assistantships (averaging $7,594 per year) were awarded; career-related internships or fieldwork, Federal Work-Study, scholarships/grants, health care benefits, tuition waivers (partial), and unspecified assistantships also available. Support available to part-time students. Financial award application deadline: 3/1; financial award applicants required to submit FAFSA. *Faculty research:* Discovery and presentation of music literature of other countries, transportation of ancient music literature to modern notation. *Unit head:* Dr. Brant Adams, Head, 405-744-6133, Fax: 405-744-9324. *Application contact:* Dr. Sheryl Tucker, Dean, 405-744-7099, Fax: 405-744-0355, E-mail: grad-i@okstate.edu. Web site: http://music.okstate.edu/.

Old Dominion University, College of Arts and Letters, Program in Music Education, Norfolk, VA 23529. Offers MME. *Accreditation:* NASM. Part-time and evening/weekend programs available. *Faculty:* 10 full-time (2 women), 4 part-time/adjunct (1 woman). *Students:* 8 full-time (0 women), 10 part-time (8 women); includes 6 minority (2 Black or African American, non-Hispanic/Latino; 1 Asian, non-Hispanic/Latino; 1 Hispanic/Latino; 1 Native Hawaiian or other Pacific Islander, non-Hispanic/Latino; 1 Two or more races, non-Hispanic/Latino). Average age 31. 8 applicants, 88% accepted, 7 enrolled. In 2011, 7 master's awarded. *Degree requirements:* For master's, comprehensive exam, thesis (for some programs), recital. *Entrance requirements:* For master's, music theory exam, diagnostic examination, baccalaureate degree in music theory, history education, or applied music; audition. *Application deadline:* Applications are processed on a rolling basis. Application fee: $40. Electronic applications accepted. *Expenses:* Tuition, state resident: full-time $9096; part-time $379 per credit. Tuition, nonresident: full-time $23,064; part-time $961 per credit. *Required fees:* $127 per semester. One-time fee: $50. *Financial support:* In 2011–12, 1 teaching assistantship with partial tuition reimbursement (averaging $8,000 per year) was awarded; scholarships/grants and unspecified assistantships also available. *Faculty research:* Performance, composition, conducting, music education. *Unit head:* Dr. Nancy K. Klein, Graduate Program Director, 757-683-4061, E-mail: nklein@odu.edu. *Application contact:* Dr. Robert Wojtowicz, Associate Dean, 757-683-6077, Fax: 757-683-5746, E-mail: rwojtowi@odu.edu. Web site: http://al.odu.edu/music/academics/grad.shtml.

Oregon State University, Graduate School, College of Education, Program in Music Education, Corvallis, OR 97331. Offers MAT. *Degree requirements:* For master's, thesis optional. *Entrance requirements:* For master's, minimum GPA of 3.0 in last 90 hours of course work. Additional exam requirements/recommendations for international students: Required—TOEFL. *Faculty research:* Teaching skills and methods, verbal and nonverbal classroom teaching techniques.

Penn State University Park, Graduate School, College of Arts and Architecture, School of Music, State College, University Park, PA 16802-1503. Offers composition-theory (M Mus); conducting (M Mus); music education (MME, PhD, Certificate); music theory (MA); music theory and history (MA); musicology (MA); performance (M Mus); piano pedagogy and performance (M Mus); piano performance (DMA); voice performance and pedagogy (M Mus). *Accreditation:* NASM. *Unit head:* Dr. Barbara O. Korner, Dean, 814-

865-2591, Fax: 814-865-2018, E-mail: bok2@psu.edu. *Application contact:* Cynthia E. Nicosia, Director, Graduate Enrollment Services, 814-865-1834, E-mail: cey1@psu.edu. Web site: http://music.psu.edu/.

Pittsburg State University, Graduate School, College of Arts and Sciences, Department of Music, Pittsburg, KS 66762. Offers instrumental music education (MM); music history/music literature (MM); performance (MM), including orchestral performance, organ, piano, voice; theory and composition (MM); vocal music education (MM). *Accreditation:* NASM. *Degree requirements:* For master's, thesis or alternative.

Portland State University, Graduate Studies, School of Fine and Performing Arts, Department of Music, Portland, OR 97207-0751. Offers conducting (MMC); music education (MAT, MST); performance (MMP). *Accreditation:* NASM. Part-time programs available. *Degree requirements:* For master's, variable foreign language requirement, exit exam. *Entrance requirements:* For master's, GRE General Test, departmental exam, minimum GPA of 3.0 in upper-division course work or 2.75 overall. Additional exam requirements/recommendations for international students: Required—TOEFL (minimum score 550 paper-based; 213 computer-based). *Faculty research:* Composition, music analysis, music history, jazz.

Queens College of the City University of New York, Division of Graduate Studies, Division of Education, Department of Secondary Education, Flushing, NY 11367-1597. Offers art (MS Ed); biology (MS Ed, AC); chemistry (MS Ed, AC); earth sciences (MS Ed, AC); English (MS Ed, AC); French (MS Ed, AC); Italian (MS Ed, AC); mathematics (MS Ed, AC); music (MS Ed, AC); physics (MS Ed, AC); social studies (MS Ed, AC); Spanish (MS Ed, AC). Part-time and evening/weekend programs available. *Faculty:* 22 full-time (14 women). *Students:* 46 full-time (23 women), 727 part-time (442 women); includes 234 minority (41 Black or African American, non-Hispanic/Latino; 78 Asian, non-Hispanic/Latino; 115 Hispanic/Latino), 5 international. 591 applicants, 60% accepted, 250 enrolled. In 2011, 170 master's awarded. *Degree requirements:* For master's, research project; for AC, thesis optional. *Entrance requirements:* For master's, minimum GPA of 3.0. Additional exam requirements/recommendations for international students: Required—TOEFL. *Application deadline:* For fall admission, 4/1 for domestic students; for spring admission, 11/1 for domestic students. Applications are processed on a rolling basis. Application fee: $125. *Expenses:* Tuition, state resident: part-time $345 per credit. Tuition, nonresident: part-time $640 per credit. *Required fees:* $145.25 per semester. *Financial support:* Career-related internships or fieldwork, Federal Work-Study, institutionally sponsored loans, and tuition waivers (partial) available. Support available to part-time students. Financial award application deadline: 4/1; financial award applicants required to submit FAFSA. *Unit head:* Dr. Eleanor Armour-Thomas, Chairperson, 718-997-5150, E-mail: armourthomas@yahoo.com. *Application contact:* Mario Caruso, Director of Graduate Admissions, 718-997-5200, Fax: 718-997-5193, E-mail: graduate_admissions@qc.edu.

Radford University, College of Graduate and Professional Studies, College of Visual and Performing Arts, Department of Music, Radford, VA 24142. Offers music (MA); music education (MS); music therapy (MS). *Accreditation:* NASM. Part-time programs available. *Faculty:* 11 full-time (2 women), 6 part-time/adjunct (4 women). *Students:* 17 full-time (9 women), 4 part-time (2 women); includes 3 minority (1 Black or African American, non-Hispanic/Latino; 2 Asian, non-Hispanic/Latino). Average age 28. 13 applicants, 100% accepted, 9 enrolled. In 2011, 6 master's awarded. *Degree requirements:* For master's, comprehensive exam, thesis or alternative. *Entrance requirements:* For master's, GRE, major field test in music or PRAXIS II (content knowledge), written diagnostics exams in music, minimum GPA of 2.75; 3 letters of reference. Additional exam requirements/recommendations for international students: Required—TOEFL (minimum score 550 paper-based; 213 computer-based; 79 iBT). *Application deadline:* For fall admission, 2/15 priority date for domestic students, 12/1 for international students; for spring admission, 7/1 for international students. Applications are processed on a rolling basis. Application fee: $50. Electronic applications accepted. *Expenses:* Tuition, state resident: full-time $6262; part-time $261 per credit hour. Tuition, nonresident: full-time $14,540; part-time $606 per credit hour. *Required fees:* $2812; $117 per credit hour. Tuition and fees vary according to program. *Financial support:* In 2011–12, 13 students received support, including 5 research assistantships (averaging $5,650 per year), 7 teaching assistantships with partial tuition reimbursements available (averaging $6,014 per year); career-related internships or fieldwork, Federal Work-Study, institutionally sponsored loans, scholarships/grants, and unspecified assistantships also available. Financial award application deadline: 3/1; financial award applicants required to submit FAFSA. *Unit head:* Dr. Allen F. Wojtera, Chair, 540-831-5177, Fax: 540-831-6133, E-mail: awojtera@radford.edu. *Application contact:* Rebecca Conner, Graduate Admissions, 540-831-5431, Fax: 540-831-6061, E-mail: gradcollege@radford.edu. Web site: http://grad-music.asp.radford.edu/.

Reinhardt University, Program in Music, Waleska, GA 30183-2981. Offers conducting (MM); music education (MM); piano pedagogy (MM). *Accreditation:* NASM. Part-time and evening/weekend programs available. Postbaccalaureate distance learning degree programs offered. *Faculty:* 3 full-time (1 woman), 6 part-time/adjunct (2 women). *Entrance requirements:* For master's, GRE, audition (for piano pedagogy and conducting), 2 letters of reference. Additional exam requirements/recommendations for international students: Required—TOEFL. *Application deadline:* For fall admission, 5/7 for domestic and international students. Applications are processed on a rolling basis. Application fee: $25. *Expenses: Tuition:* Full-time $7020; part-time $390 per credit hour. *Required fees:* $70 per semester hour. *Financial support:* Application deadline: 5/1; applicants required to submit FAFSA. *Unit head:* Dr. Paula Thomas-Lee, Coordinator, 770-720-5658, E-mail: ptl@reinhardt.edu. *Application contact:* Ray Schumacher, Admissions Counselor, 770-993-6971, Fax: 770-475-0263, E-mail: res@reinhardt.edu. Web site: http://www.reinhardt.edu/Graduate/Master_Music/.

Rhode Island College, School of Graduate Studies, Faculty of Arts and Sciences, Department of Music, Theatre, and Dance, Providence, RI 02908-1991. Offers music education (MAT, MM Ed). Part-time and evening/weekend programs available. *Faculty:* 10 full-time (5 women), 14 part-time/adjunct (7 women). *Students:* 2 full-time (both women), 4 part-time (1 woman); includes 1 minority (Hispanic/Latino). Average age 30. In 2011, 3 master's awarded. *Degree requirements:* For master's, comprehensive exam, thesis, final project (MFA). *Entrance requirements:* For master's, GRE General Test or MAT; exams in music education, theory, history and literature, audition, 3 letters of recommendation, evidence of musicianship, interview. Additional exam requirements/recommendations for international students: Recommended—TOEFL (minimum score 550 paper-based; 213 computer-based; 79 iBT). *Application deadline:* For fall admission, 3/1 for domestic students; for spring admission, 11/1 for domestic students. Applications are processed on a rolling basis. Application fee: $50. *Expenses:* Tuition, state resident: full-time $8592; part-time $358 per credit hour. Tuition, nonresident: full-time $16,800; part-time $700 per credit hour. *Required fees:* $602; $22 per credit. $72 per term. *Financial support:* Teaching assistantships with full tuition reimbursements, Federal Work-Study, scholarships/grants, health care benefits, and unspecified assistantships available. Support available to part-time students. Financial award application deadline: 5/15; financial award applicants required to submit FAFSA. *Unit head:* Dr. James Taylor, Chair, 401-456-8639. *Application contact:* Graduate Studies, 401-456-8700. Web site: http://www.ric.edu/mtd/index.php.

Rider University, Westminster Choir College, Program in Music Education, Lawrenceville, NJ 08648-3001. Offers MAT, MM, MME. *Accreditation:* NASM. *Entrance requirements:* For master's, audition, interview, repertoire list, 2 letters of reference, resume. Additional exam requirements/recommendations for international students: Required—TOEFL (minimum score 525 paper-based; 195 computer-based). Electronic applications accepted. *Expenses: Tuition:* Full-time $32,820; part-time $710 per credit. *Required fees:* $350; $35 per course. Tuition and fees vary according to campus/location and program.

Rider University, Westminster Choir College, Programs in Music, Lawrenceville, NJ 08648-3001. Offers choral conducting (MM); composition (MM); organ performance (MM); piano accompanying and coaching (MM); piano pedagogy and performance (MM); piano performance (MM); sacred music (MM); vocal pedagogy and performance (MM); vocal training (MVP). Part-time programs available. *Degree requirements:* For master's, variable foreign language requirement, departmental qualifying exam. *Entrance requirements:* For master's, audition, interview, repertoire list, 2 letters of reference, resume. Additional exam requirements/recommendations for international students: Required—TOEFL (minimum score 525 paper-based; 195 computer-based). Electronic applications accepted. *Expenses: Tuition:* Full-time $32,820; part-time $710 per credit. *Required fees:* $350; $35 per course. Tuition and fees vary according to campus/location and program.

Roosevelt University, Graduate Division, Chicago College of Performing Arts, The Music Conservatory, Chicago, IL 60605. Offers music (MM); piano pedagogy (Diploma). *Accreditation:* NASM. Part-time and evening/weekend programs available.

Rutgers, The State University of New Jersey, New Brunswick, Mason Gross School of the Arts, Music Department, New Brunswick, NJ 08901. Offers collaborative piano (MM, DMA); conducting: choral (MM, DMA); conducting: instrumental (MM, DMA); conducting: orchestral (MM, DMA); jazz studies (MM); music (DMA, AD); music education (MM, DMA); music performance (MM). *Accreditation:* NASM. *Degree requirements:* For doctorate, one foreign language. *Entrance requirements:* For master's and doctorate, audition. Additional exam requirements/recommendations for international students: Required—TOEFL (minimum score 550 paper-based; 213 computer-based), IELTS (minimum score 7). Electronic applications accepted. *Faculty research:* Performance, twentieth century music, jazz, music education.

St. Cloud State University, School of Graduate Studies, College of Liberal Arts, Department of Music, St. Cloud, MN 56301-4498. Offers conducting and literature (MM); music education (MM); piano pedagogy (MM). *Accreditation:* NASM. *Faculty:* 16 full-time (7 women), 1 part-time/adjunct (0 women). *Students:* 2 full-time (1 woman), 13 part-time (5 women); includes 1 minority (Asian, non-Hispanic/Latino), 1 international. 4 applicants, 100% accepted. In 2011, 7 master's awarded. *Degree requirements:* For master's, comprehensive exam (for some programs), thesis or alternative. *Entrance requirements:* For master's, GRE General Test, minimum GPA of 2.75. Additional exam requirements/recommendations for international students: Required—Michigan English Language Assessment Battery; Recommended—TOEFL (minimum score 550 paper-based; 213 computer-based), IELTS (minimum score 6.5). *Application deadline:* For fall admission, 6/1 priority date for domestic students, 4/1 for international students; for spring admission, 10/1 priority date for domestic students, 8/1 for international students. Applications are processed on a rolling basis. Application fee: $35. Electronic applications accepted. *Financial support:* Federal Work-Study, scholarships/grants, and unspecified assistantships available. Financial award application deadline: 3/1. *Unit head:* Dr. Mark Springer, Chairperson, 320-308-3223, Fax: 320-308-2902. *Application contact:* Linda Lou Krueger, School of Graduate Studies, 320-308-2113, Fax: 320-308-5371, E-mail: lekrueger@stcloudstate.edu.

Saint Xavier University, Graduate Studies, School of Education, Chicago, IL 60655-3105. Offers counseling (MA); curriculum and instruction (MA); early childhood education (MA); educational administration (MA); elementary education (MA); individualized studies (MA), including educational technology, English as a second language (ESL), ISTEM (integrative science, technology, engineering, and math), science education; music education (MA); reading (MA); secondary education (MA); Spanish education (MA); special education (MA); teaching and leadership (MA). *Accreditation:* NCATE. Part-time and evening/weekend programs available. *Degree requirements:* For master's, thesis or project. *Entrance requirements:* For master's, minimum GPA of 3.0. *Application deadline:* For fall admission, 8/15 priority date for domestic students. Applications are processed on a rolling basis. Application fee: $35. *Expenses:* Contact institution. *Financial support:* Career-related internships or fieldwork available. Support available to part-time students. Financial award applicants required to submit FAFSA. *Unit head:* Dr. Beverly Gulley, Dean, 773-298-3221, Fax: 773-779-9061, E-mail: gulley@sxu.edu. *Application contact:* Beth Gierach, Managing Director of Admission, 773-298-3053, Fax: 773-298-3076, E-mail: gierach@sxu.edu.

Salem College, Department of Teacher Education, Winston-Salem, NC 27101. Offers art education (MAT); elementary education (M Ed, MAT); language and literacy (M Ed); middle school education (MAT); music education (MAT); school counseling (M Ed); second language studies (MAT); secondary education (MAT); special education (M Ed, MAT). *Accreditation:* NCATE. Part-time and evening/weekend programs available. Postbaccalaureate distance learning degree programs offered (minimal on-campus study). *Degree requirements:* For master's, comprehensive exam, practicum (MAT), project (M Ed), oral and written comprehensive exams. *Entrance requirements:* For master's, GRE, minimum GPA of 2.5. *Faculty research:* Content area reading strategies, literacy development, brain compatible instruction.

Samford University, School of the Arts, Birmingham, AL 35229. Offers church music (MM); music (MME), including instrumental, vocal choral; piano pedagogy (MM). *Accreditation:* NASM. Part-time programs available. *Faculty:* 12 full-time (4 women), 4 part-time/adjunct (2 women). *Students:* 11 full-time (7 women), 11 part-time (5 women); includes 2 minority (both Black or African American, non-Hispanic/Latino), 3 international. Average age 28. 11 applicants, 100% accepted, 9 enrolled. In 2011, 5 master's awarded. *Degree requirements:* For master's, oral exams, comprehensive exam (MME). *Entrance requirements:* For master's, GRE General Test or MAT, institutional exam; PRAXIS II (for MME), minimum GPA of 3.0. Additional exam requirements/recommendations for international students: Required—TOEFL (minimum score 550 paper-based; 213 computer-based). *Application deadline:* For fall admission, 5/1 priority date for domestic students; for spring admission, 12/1 priority date for domestic students. Applications are processed on a rolling basis. Application fee: $35. *Expenses: Tuition:* Full-time $29,934; part-time $655 per credit. *Required fees:* $705. *Financial support:* In 2011–12, research assistantships (averaging $4,000 per year) were awarded; Federal Work-Study, scholarships/grants, tuition waivers (partial), and unspecified assistantships also available. Financial award application deadline: 9/1. *Faculty research:* Hymnology, choral techniques, assessment of music learning at elementary and secondary levels, piano pedagogy, special education and inclusion, learning theories. *Unit head:* Dr. Billy J. Strickland, Associate Dean, 205-726-4363, E-mail: bjstrick@samford.edu. *Application contact:* Dr. Moya Nordlund, Director, Graduate Studies, 205-726-2651, Fax: 205-726-2165, E-mail: mlnordlu@samford.edu. Web site: http://www.samford.edu/arts.

Music Education

San Diego State University, Graduate and Research Affairs, College of Professional Studies and Fine Arts, School of Music and Dance, San Diego, CA 92182. Offers composition (acoustic and electronic) (MM); conducting (MM); ethnomusicology (MA); jazz studies (MM); musicology (MA); performance (MM); piano pedagogy (MA); theory (MA). *Degree requirements:* For master's, comprehensive exam (for some programs), thesis (for some programs). *Entrance requirements:* For master's, GRE General Test, bachelor's degree in related field, 2 letters of reference. Additional exam requirements/recommendations for international students: Required—TOEFL. Electronic applications accepted.

San Francisco State University, Division of Graduate Studies, College of Liberal and Creative Arts, School of Music and Dance, San Francisco, CA 94132-1722. Offers chamber music (MM); classical performance (MM); composition (MA); conducting (MM); music education (MA); music history (MA). *Accreditation:* NASM. *Unit head:* Dianthe Spencer, Director, 415-338-1431. *Application contact:* Dr. Cyrus Ginwala, Graduate Coordinator, 415-338-1431, E-mail: cginwala@sfsu.edu. Web site: http://musicdance.sfsu.edu/.

Shenandoah University, Shenandoah Conservatory, Winchester, VA 22601-5195. Offers arts management (MS); church music (MM, Certificate); collaborative piano (MM); composition (MM); conducting (MM); music education (MME); music therapy (MMT, Certificate); pedagogy (MM, DMA); performance (MM, DMA, Artist Diploma). *Accreditation:* NASM. *Faculty:* 35 full-time (13 women), 13 part-time/adjunct (7 women). *Students:* 55 full-time (38 women), 104 part-time (66 women); includes 14 minority (7 Black or African American, non-Hispanic/Latino; 4 Asian, non-Hispanic/Latino; 2 Hispanic/Latino; 1 Two or more races, non-Hispanic/Latino), 25 international. Average age 33. 122 applicants, 74% accepted, 45 enrolled. In 2011, 27 master's, 11 doctorates, 16 other advanced degrees awarded. *Degree requirements:* For master's, comprehensive exam (for some programs), thesis (for some programs), internship (MS), recital (MM), research teaching project or thesis (MME), project (MA); for doctorate, comprehensive exam, thesis/dissertation (for some programs), dissertation or teaching project, recital; for other advanced degree, research project, recital. *Entrance requirements:* For master's, audition, minimum GPA of 2.5, writing sample, resume; for doctorate, audition, minimum GPA of 3.25, 2 letters of recommendation, writing sample, resume; for other advanced degree, bachelor's or master's degree; minimum GPA of 2.5. Additional exam requirements/recommendations for international students: Required—TOEFL (minimum score 550 paper-based; 213 computer-based; 79 iBT), IELTS (minimum score 6.5), Sakae Institute of Study Abroad (minimum score 550). *Application deadline:* Applications are processed on a rolling basis. Application fee: $30. Electronic applications accepted. *Expenses: Tuition:* Full-time $17,952; part-time $748 per credit. *Required fees:* $500 per term. Tuition and fees vary according to course level, course load and program. *Financial support:* In 2011–12, 38 students received support, including 31 teaching assistantships with partial tuition reimbursements available (averaging $6,282 per year); career-related internships or fieldwork, institutionally sponsored loans, scholarships/grants, unspecified assistantships, and federal loans, alternative loans also available. Support available to part-time students. Financial award application deadline: 3/15; financial award applicants required to submit FAFSA. *Unit head:* Dr. Michael J. Stepniak, Dean, 540-665-4600, Fax: 540-665-5402, E-mail: mstepnia@su.edu. *Application contact:* David Anthony, Dean of Admissions, 540-665-4581, Fax: 540-665-4627, E-mail: admit@su.edu. Web site: http://www.su.edu/conservatory.

Silver Lake College of the Holy Family, Division of Graduate Studies, Program in Music Education, Manitowoc, WI 54220-9319. Offers music education-Kodaly emphasis (MM). Program offered jointly with University of Nebraska at Omaha, University of Oklahoma, Webster University. *Accreditation:* NASM. Part-time programs available. Postbaccalaureate distance learning degree programs offered (minimal on-campus study). *Degree requirements:* For master's, comprehensive exam, thesis. *Entrance requirements:* For master's, examination of music theory, music history and literature, and applied music theory and conducting, interview, minimum undergraduate GPA of 3.0, three letters of recommendation. Additional exam requirements/recommendations for international students: Required—TOEFL. Electronic applications accepted. *Faculty research:* Effects of prenatal music on bonding and stimulation, music and the brain, early childhood music, effective use of Smart Music for choral and general music areas.

Southern Illinois University Carbondale, Graduate School, College of Liberal Arts, School of Music, Carbondale, IL 62901-4701. Offers composition and theory (MM); history and literature (MM); music education (MM); opera/music theater (MM); performance (MM); piano pedagogy (MM). *Accreditation:* NASM. Part-time programs available. *Faculty:* 22 full-time (6 women). *Students:* 24 full-time (14 women), 17 part-time (8 women); includes 4 minority (2 Black or African American, non-Hispanic/Latino; 1 Asian, non-Hispanic/Latino; 1 Hispanic/Latino), 6 international. Average age 24. 38 applicants, 63% accepted, 17 enrolled. In 2011, 12 master's awarded. *Degree requirements:* For master's, one foreign language, thesis or alternative. *Entrance requirements:* For master's, audition, minimum GPA of 2.7. Additional exam requirements/recommendations for international students: Required—TOEFL. *Application deadline:* Applications are processed on a rolling basis. Application fee: $0. *Financial support:* In 2011–12, 16 students received support, including 2 fellowships with full tuition reimbursements available, 12 teaching assistantships with full tuition reimbursements available; research assistantships with full tuition reimbursements available, Federal Work-Study, institutionally sponsored loans, and tuition waivers (full) also available. Support available to part-time students. Financial award application deadline: 4/1. *Faculty research:* Performance practices, historical research, operatic development. *Unit head:* Jeanine Wagner, Interim Director, 618-453-2541. *Application contact:* Dr. Frank Stemper, Graduate Coordinator, 618-536-7505, E-mail: gradmus@siu.edu.

Southern Illinois University Edwardsville, Graduate School, College of Arts and Sciences, Department of Music, Program in Music, Edwardsville, IL 62026-0001. Offers music education (MM); music performance (MM). Part-time programs available. *Faculty:* 17 full-time (5 women). *Students:* 6 full-time (5 women), 16 part-time (8 women); includes 4 minority (3 Black or African American, non-Hispanic/Latino; 1 Hispanic/Latino), 1 international. 23 applicants, 52% accepted. In 2011, 11 master's awarded. *Degree requirements:* For master's, one foreign language, thesis (for some programs), recital. *Entrance requirements:* Additional exam requirements/recommendations for international students: Required—TOEFL (minimum score 550 paper-based; 213 computer-based; 79 iBT), IELTS (minimum score 6.5). *Application deadline:* For fall admission, 7/22 for domestic students, 6/1 for international students; for spring admission, 12/9 for domestic students, 10/1 for international students. Applications are processed on a rolling basis. Application fee: $30. Electronic applications accepted. Tuition and fees vary according to course load and program. *Financial support:* In 2011–12, 14 teaching assistantships with full tuition reimbursements (averaging $9,927 per year) were awarded; institutionally sponsored loans, scholarships/grants, and unspecified assistantships also available. Financial award application deadline: 3/1; financial award applicants required to submit FAFSA. *Unit head:* Dr. Audrey Tallant, Chair, 618-650-3900, E-mail: atallan@siue.edu. *Application contact:* Dr. Marc Schapman, Director, 618-650-2034, E-mail: maschap@siue.edu. Web site: http://www.siue.edu/artsandsciences/music/.

Southern Illinois University Edwardsville, Graduate School, College of Arts and Sciences, Department of Music, Program in Piano Pedagogy, Edwardsville, IL 62026. Offers Postbaccalaureate Certificate. Part-time programs available. *Students:* 1 (woman) full-time, 2 part-time (both women), 1 international. 1 applicant, 100% accepted. In 2011, 1 Postbaccalaureate Certificate awarded. *Entrance requirements:* Additional exam requirements/recommendations for international students: Required—TOEFL (minimum score 550 paper-based; 213 computer-based), IELTS. *Application deadline:* For fall admission, 7/22 for domestic students, 6/1 for international students; for spring admission, 12/9 for domestic students, 10/1 for international students. Applications are processed on a rolling basis. Application fee: $30. Electronic applications accepted. Tuition and fees vary according to course load and program. *Financial support:* Fellowships, research assistantships, teaching assistantships, institutionally sponsored loans, scholarships/grants, and unspecified assistantships available. Financial award application deadline: 3/1; financial award applicants required to submit FAFSA. *Unit head:* Dr. Audrey Tallant, Chair, 618-650-3900, E-mail: atallan@siue.edu. *Application contact:* Dr. Linda Perry, Director, 618-650-3593, E-mail: lperry@siue.edu. Web site: http://www.siue.edu/artsandsciences/music/.

Southern Illinois University Edwardsville, Graduate School, College of Arts and Sciences, Department of Music, Program in Vocal Pedagogy, Edwardsville, IL 62026. Offers Postbaccalaureate Certificate. Part-time programs available. *Students:* 2 part-time (1 woman). 2 applicants, 100% accepted. In 2011, 2 Postbaccalaureate Certificates awarded. *Entrance requirements:* Additional exam requirements/recommendations for international students: Required—TOEFL (minimum score 550 paper-based; 213 computer-based; 79 iBT), IELTS (minimum score 6.5). *Application deadline:* For fall admission, 7/22 for domestic students, 6/1 for international students; for spring admission, 12/9 for domestic students, 10/1 for international students. Applications are processed on a rolling basis. Application fee: $30. Electronic applications accepted. Tuition and fees vary according to course load and program. *Financial support:* Fellowships, research assistantships, teaching assistantships, institutionally sponsored loans, scholarships/grants, and unspecified assistantships available. Financial award application deadline: 3/1; financial award applicants required to submit FAFSA. *Unit head:* Dr. Audrey Tallant, Chair, 618-650-3900, E-mail: atallan@siue.edu. *Application contact:* Dr. Emily Truckenbrod, Director, 618-650-5394, E-mail: etrucke@siue.edu. Web site: http://www.siue.edu/artsandsciences/music.

Southern Methodist University, Meadows School of the Arts, Division of Music, Dallas, TX 75275. Offers conducting (MM); music composition (MM); music education (MM); music history (MM); music theory (MM); performance (MM); piano performance and pedagogy (MM); sacred music (MSM). *Accreditation:* NASM. Part-time programs available. *Degree requirements:* For master's, variable foreign language requirement, comprehensive exam, project, recital, or thesis. *Entrance requirements:* For master's, placement exams in music history and theory, audition; bachelor's degree in music or equivalent; minimum GPA of 3.0; research paper in history, theory, education. Additional exam requirements/recommendations for international students: Required—TOEFL (minimum score 550 paper-based; 213 computer-based; 80 iBT). Electronic applications accepted. *Faculty research:* Music perception and cognition, computer-based instruction, music medicine and therapy, theoretical and historical analysis-medieval to contemporary.

Southwestern College, Fifth-Year Graduate Programs, Winfield, KS 67156-2499. Offers leadership (MS); management (MBA); music (MA), including education, performance. Part-time programs available. *Faculty:* 3 full-time (1 woman), 12 part-time/adjunct (4 women). *Students:* 13 full-time (5 women), 8 part-time (4 women); includes 3 minority (2 Black or African American, non-Hispanic/Latino; 1 American Indian or Alaska Native, non-Hispanic/Latino), 5 international. Average age 25. 21 applicants, 90% accepted, 16 enrolled. In 2011, 8 master's awarded. *Entrance requirements:* For master's, baccalaureate degree, minimum GPA of 3.0. Additional exam requirements/recommendations for international students: Required—TOEFL (minimum score 550 paper-based; 213 computer-based). *Application deadline:* For fall admission, 4/1 priority date for domestic students; for spring admission, 12/1 priority date for domestic students. Applications are processed on a rolling basis. Electronic applications accepted. Tuition and fees vary according to program. *Financial support:* In 2011–12, 8 students received support. Federal Work-Study, tuition waivers (partial), and unspecified assistantships available. Financial award application deadline: 4/1; financial award applicants required to submit FAFSA. *Unit head:* Dr. James Sheppard, Vice President for Academic Affairs, 620-229-6227, Fax: 620-229-6224, E-mail: james.sheppard@sckans.edu. *Application contact:* Marla Sexson, Director of Admissions, 800-846-1543 Ext. 6364, Fax: 620-229-6344, E-mail: marla.sexson@sckans.edu. Web site: http://www.sckans.edu/graduate.

Southwestern Oklahoma State University, College of Arts and Sciences, Department of Music, Weatherford, OK 73096-3098. Offers music education (MM); performance (MM). *Accreditation:* NASM. Part-time programs available. *Degree requirements:* For master's, comprehensive exam, recital (music performance). *Entrance requirements:* For master's, minimum GPA of 2.5. Additional exam requirements/recommendations for international students: Required—TOEFL.

State University of New York at Fredonia, Graduate Studies, School of Music, Program in Music Education, Fredonia, NY 14063-1136. Offers MM. *Accreditation:* NASM. Part-time and evening/weekend programs available. *Degree requirements:* For master's, thesis optional. *Expenses:* Tuition, state resident: full-time $6666; part-time $370 per credit hour. Tuition, nonresident: full-time $11,376; part-time $632 per credit hour. *Required fees:* $1059.30; $58.85 per credit hour. Tuition and fees vary according to course load.

State University of New York College at Potsdam, Crane School of Music, Potsdam, NY 13676. Offers music education (MM); music performance (MM). *Accreditation:* NASM. Part-time programs available. *Faculty:* 25 full-time (9 women), 5 part-time/adjunct (1 woman). *Students:* 22 full-time (10 women), 3 part-time (1 woman); includes 3 minority (2 Black or African American, non-Hispanic/Latino; 1 Hispanic/Latino). 52 applicants, 65% accepted, 15 enrolled. In 2011, 18 master's awarded. *Degree requirements:* For master's, variable foreign language requirement, thesis (for some programs). *Entrance requirements:* For master's, audition, minimum GPA of 3.0. Additional exam requirements/recommendations for international students: Required—TOEFL (minimum score 550 paper-based; 213 computer-based; 80 iBT), IELTS (minimum score 6). *Application deadline:* For fall admission, 4/1 for domestic and international students; for winter admission, 10/15 for domestic and international students; for spring admission, 3/1 for domestic and international students. Applications are processed on a rolling basis. Application fee: $50. *Expenses:* Tuition, state resident: full-time $8870; part-time $370 per credit hour. Tuition, nonresident: full-time $15,160; part-time $632 per credit hour. *Required fees:* $1066; $44.10 per credit hour. One-time fee: $3. *Financial support:* In 2011–12, 2 students received support. Teaching assistantships with full tuition reimbursements available, career-related internships or fieldwork, Federal Work-Study, scholarships/grants, and unspecified assistantships available. Support available to part-time students. Financial award application deadline: 3/1; financial award applicants required to submit FAFSA. *Unit head:* Dr. Michael R. Sitton, Dean, 315-267-2415, Fax: 315-267-2413, E-mail: sittonmr@potsdam.edu.

Application contact: Karen Miller, Secretary, 315-267-3418, Fax: 315-267-2413, E-mail: millerkl@potsdam.edu.

Syracuse University, School of Education, Program in Music Education, Syracuse, NY 13244. Offers music education/professional certification (M Mus, MS); music education: teacher preparation (MS). *Accreditation:* NASM. Part-time programs available. *Students:* 10 full-time (7 women), 8 part-time (6 women); includes 1 minority (Hispanic/Latino). Average age 23. 8 applicants, 75% accepted, 4 enrolled. In 2011, 22 degrees awarded. *Degree requirements:* For master's, thesis or alternative. *Entrance requirements:* For master's, New York state teacher certification or eligibility. Additional exam requirements/recommendations for international students: Required—TOEFL (minimum score 100 iBT). *Application deadline:* For fall admission, 2/1 priority date for domestic students, 2/1 for international students; for spring admission, 10/15 for domestic and international students. Applications are processed on a rolling basis. Application fee: $75. Electronic applications accepted. *Expenses: Tuition:* Part-time $1206 per credit. *Financial support:* Fellowships with full tuition reimbursements and teaching assistantships with full and partial tuition reimbursements available. Financial award application deadline: 1/1. *Unit head:* Dr. John Coggiola, Program Coordinator, 315-443-5896, E-mail: jecoggio@syr.edu. *Application contact:* Laurie Deyo, Graduate Recruiter, School of Education, 315-443-2505, E-mail: e-gradrcrt@syr.edu. Web site: http://soe.syr.edu/.

Tarleton State University, College of Graduate Studies, College of Liberal and Fine Arts, Department of Fine Arts, Stephenville, TX 76402. Offers music education (MM). Part-time and evening/weekend programs available. *Faculty:* 1 (woman) full-time. *Degree requirements:* For master's, comprehensive exam, thesis optional. *Entrance requirements:* For master's, GRE, minimum GPA of 3.0. Additional exam requirements/recommendations for international students: Required—TOEFL (minimum score 550 paper-based; 213 computer-based; 80 iBT). *Application deadline:* For fall admission, 8/5 priority date for domestic students; for spring admission, 12/1 for domestic students. Applications are processed on a rolling basis. Application fee: $30 ($130 for international students). Electronic applications accepted. *Expenses:* Tuition, state resident: full-time $3131.46; part-time $174 per credit hour. Tuition, nonresident: full-time $8225; part-time $457 per credit hour. *Required fees:* $1446. Tuition and fees vary according to course load and campus/location. *Financial support:* In 2011–12, 2 research assistantships (averaging $12,019 per year) were awarded; institutionally sponsored loans and scholarships/grants also available. Financial award application deadline: 5/1; financial award applicants required to submit FAFSA. *Unit head:* Teresa Davidian, Head, 254-968-9245, Fax: 254-968-9239, E-mail: davidian@tarleton.edu. *Application contact:* Information Contact, 254-968-9104, Fax: 254-968-9670, E-mail: gradoffice@tarleton.edu. Web site: http://www.tarleton.edu/~finearts/.

Teachers College, Columbia University, Graduate Faculty of Education, Department of Arts and Humanities, Program in Music and Music Education, New York, NY 10027. Offers Ed M, MA, Ed D, Ed DCT. *Accreditation:* NCATE. Part-time programs available. *Faculty:* 4 full-time (2 women), 18 part-time/adjunct (8 women). *Students:* 18 full-time (15 women), 132 part-time (94 women); includes 37 minority (6 Black or African American, non-Hispanic/Latino; 22 Asian, non-Hispanic/Latino; 9 Hispanic/Latino), 26 international. Average age 33. 87 applicants, 69% accepted, 29 enrolled. In 2011, 64 master's, 13 doctorates awarded. Terminal master's awarded for partial completion of doctoral program. *Degree requirements:* For master's, cumulative integrative project, portfolio; for doctorate, comprehensive exam (for some programs), thesis/dissertation. *Entrance requirements:* For master's, initial certification (for MA); master's degree in music (for Ed M); for doctorate, academic writing sample; audition or performance CD/DVD (for Ed DCT). *Application deadline:* For fall admission, 1/2 priority date for domestic students; for spring admission, 11/1 for domestic students. Applications are processed on a rolling basis. Application fee: $65. Electronic applications accepted. *Financial support:* Fellowships, research assistantships, teaching assistantships, career-related internships or fieldwork, Federal Work-Study, institutionally sponsored loans, and tuition waivers (full and partial) available. Support available to part-time students. Financial award application deadline: 2/1. *Faculty research:* Artistry, creativity, and proficiency in production and performance; educational theory and practice; piano pedagogy; research strategies in music pedagogy. *Unit head:* Prof. Lori Custodero, Program Coordinator, 212-678-3285, E-mail: custodero@tc.edu. *Application contact:* Thomas P. Rock, Director of Admissions, 212-678-3083, Fax: 212-678-4171, E-mail: rock@tc.edu. Web site: http://www.tc.edu/a%26h/MusicEd/.

Temple University, Esther Boyer College of Music and Dance, Philadelphia, PA 19122-6096. Offers Ed M, MFA, MM, MMT, DMA, PhD. *Accreditation:* NASM. Part-time and evening/weekend programs available. *Faculty:* 44 full-time (17 women). *Students:* 191 full-time (118 women), 38 part-time (22 women); includes 40 minority (7 Black or African American, non-Hispanic/Latino; 18 Asian, non-Hispanic/Latino; 13 Hispanic/Latino; 2 Two or more races, non-Hispanic/Latino), 54 international. Average age 29. 298 applicants, 53% accepted, 72 enrolled. In 2011, 63 master's, 19 doctorates awarded. *Degree requirements:* For doctorate, thesis/dissertation. *Entrance requirements:* Additional exam requirements/recommendations for international students: Required—TOEFL. *Application deadline:* For fall admission, 12/15 for international students; for spring admission, 8/1 for international students. Applications are processed on a rolling basis. Application fee: $50. Electronic applications accepted. *Expenses:* Tuition, state resident: full-time $12,366; part-time $687 per credit hour. Tuition, nonresident: full-time $17,298; part-time $961 per credit hour. *Required fees:* $590; $213 per year. *Financial support:* Fellowships with full and partial tuition reimbursements, research assistantships with full and partial tuition reimbursements, teaching assistantships with full and partial tuition reimbursements, career-related internships or fieldwork, Federal Work-Study, and scholarships/grants available. Financial award application deadline: 1/15; financial award applicants required to submit FAFSA. *Faculty research:* Music-learning theory, guided imagery in music, computer music synthesis, musical instrument digital interface (MIDI) applications. *Unit head:* Dr. Robert T. Stroker, Dean, 215-204-5527, Fax: 215-204-4957, E-mail: rstroker@temple.edu. *Application contact:* Tara Schumacher, Coordinator of Outreach, 215-204-6575, Fax: 215-204-8781, E-mail: tara.schumacher@temple.edu. Web site: http://www.temple.edu/boyer/.

Tennessee State University, The School of Graduate Studies and Research, College of Arts and Sciences, Department of Music, Nashville, TN 37209-1561. Offers music education (MS). *Accreditation:* NASM. *Degree requirements:* For master's, thesis optional. *Entrance requirements:* For master's, MAT. *Faculty research:* Applications of technology in music education; K-12 Jocal, instrumental and general music pedagogy: historical research in American music education; classical guitar performance practice.

Tennessee Technological University, Graduate School, College of Education, Department of Curriculum and Instruction, Cookeville, TN 38505. Offers advanced studies in teaching and learning (M Ed); curriculum (MA, Ed S); early childhood education (MA, Ed S); elementary education (MA, Ed S); exceptional learning (PhD), including applied behavior and learning, literacy, program planning and evaluation, STEM education; instructional leadership (MA, Ed S); library science (MA); music (MA); reading (MA, Ed S); secondary education (MA, Ed S); special education (MA, Ed S). *Accreditation:* NCATE. Part-time and evening/weekend programs available. *Faculty:* 27 full-time (10 women). *Students:* 117 full-time (84 women), 334 part-time (246 women); includes 22 minority (15 Black or African American, non-Hispanic/Latino; 1 American Indian or Alaska Native, non-Hispanic/Latino; 1 Asian, non-Hispanic/Latino; 5 Hispanic/Latino), 2 international. Average age 27. 177 applicants, 76% accepted, 99 enrolled. In 2011, 163 master's, 7 doctorates, 81 other advanced degrees awarded. *Degree requirements:* For master's and Ed S, comprehensive exam, thesis or alternative; for doctorate, comprehensive exam, thesis/dissertation. *Entrance requirements:* For master's and Ed S, MAT or GRE. Additional exam requirements/recommendations for international students: Required—TOEFL (minimum score 550 paper-based; 71 iBT), IELTS (minimum score 5.5), Pearson Test of English. *Application deadline:* For fall admission, 8/1 for domestic students, 5/1 for international students; for spring admission, 12/1 for domestic students, 10/1 for international students. Application fee: $25 ($30 for international students). Electronic applications accepted. *Expenses:* Tuition, state resident: full-time $8094; part-time $422 per credit hour. Tuition, nonresident: full-time $20,574; part-time $1046 per credit hour. *Financial support:* In 2011–12, 41 fellowships (averaging $8,000 per year), 22 research assistantships (averaging $4,000 per year), 19 teaching assistantships (averaging $4,000 per year) were awarded; career-related internships or fieldwork also available. Financial award application deadline: 4/1. *Faculty research:* Teacher evaluation. *Unit head:* Dr. Susan Gore, Interim Chairperson, 931-372-3181, Fax: 931-372-6270, E-mail: sgore@tntech.edu. *Application contact:* Shelia K. Kendrick, Coordinator of Graduate Admissions, 931-372-3808, Fax: 931-372-3497, E-mail: skendrick@tntech.edu.

Texas A&M University–Commerce, Graduate School, College of Humanities, Social Sciences and Arts, Department of Music, Commerce, TX 75429-3011. Offers music (MA, MS); music composition (MA, MM); music education (MA, MM, MS); music literature (MA); music performance (MA, MM); music theory (MA, MM). *Accreditation:* NASM. Part-time programs available. *Degree requirements:* For master's, comprehensive exam, thesis (for some programs). *Entrance requirements:* For master's, GRE General Test. Electronic applications accepted.

Texas A&M University–Kingsville, College of Graduate Studies, College of Arts and Sciences, Department of Music, Kingsville, TX 78363. Offers music education (MM). *Accreditation:* NASM. *Degree requirements:* For master's, comprehensive exam, thesis or alternative. *Entrance requirements:* For master's, GRE General Test, minimum GPA of 3.0. Additional exam requirements/recommendations for international students: Required—TOEFL.

Texas Christian University, College of Fine Arts, School of Music, Fort Worth, TX 76129-0002. Offers composition (DMA); conducting (M Mus, DMA); music education (MM Ed); musicology (M Mus); organ performance (M Mus); pedagogy (DMA); percussion (Artist Diploma); performance (DMA); piano (Artist Diploma); piano pedagogy (M Mus); piano performance (M Mus); string performance (M Mus); strings (Artist Diploma); theory/composition (M Mus); vocal performance (M Mus); voice (Artist Diploma); voice pedagogy (M Mus); wind and percussion performance (M Mus); winds (Artist Diploma). *Accreditation:* NASM. *Faculty:* 37 full-time (4 women), 3 part-time/adjunct (2 women). *Students:* 21 full-time (11 women), 27 part-time (15 women); includes 10 minority (2 Black or African American, non-Hispanic/Latino; 3 Asian, non-Hispanic/Latino; 4 Hispanic/Latino; 1 Two or more races, non-Hispanic/Latino), 14 international. Average age 26. 58 applicants, 34% accepted, 18 enrolled. In 2011, 19 master's awarded. *Degree requirements:* For master's, comprehensive exam, thesis (for some programs), thesis or recital; for doctorate, comprehensive exam, thesis/dissertation. *Entrance requirements:* For master's, GRE (for musicology, music education, and music theory/composition), audition or composition/theory, letters of recommendation; for doctorate, GRE, audition, interview. Additional exam requirements/recommendations for international students: Required—TOEFL (minimum score 600 paper-based; 250 computer-based; 100 iBT). *Application deadline:* For fall admission, 1/15 for domestic and international students; for spring admission, 12/15 for domestic and international students. Application fee: $60. *Expenses: Tuition:* Full-time $20,250; part-time $1125 per credit hour. Part-time tuition and fees vary according to course load and program. *Financial support:* In 2011–12, 52 research assistantships with full tuition reimbursements (averaging $6,000 per year) were awarded; career-related internships or fieldwork, institutionally sponsored loans, scholarships/grants, tuition waivers, and unspecified assistantships also available. Financial award application deadline: 12/15. *Unit head:* Dr. Richard Gipson, Director, 817-257-7602. *Application contact:* Dr. Joseph Butler, Associate Dean, College of Fine Arts, 817-257-6629, E-mail: j.butler@tcu.edu. Web site: http://www.music.tcu.edu/.

Texas State University–San Marcos, Graduate School, College of Fine Arts and Communication, School of Music, Program in Music Education, San Marcos, TX 78666. Offers MM. *Accreditation:* NASM. Part-time programs available. *Faculty:* 13 full-time (2 women), 2 part-time/adjunct (1 woman). *Students:* 1 full-time (0 women), 7 part-time (6 women). Average age 41. 12 applicants, 33% accepted, 1 enrolled. In 2011, 5 master's awarded. *Degree requirements:* For master's, comprehensive exam. *Entrance requirements:* For master's, minimum GPA of 2.75 in last 60 hours of course work. Additional exam requirements/recommendations for international students: Required—TOEFL (minimum score 550 paper-based; 213 computer-based; 78 iBT). *Application deadline:* For fall admission, 6/15 priority date for domestic students, 6/1 for international students; for spring admission, 10/15 priority date for domestic students, 10/1 for international students. Applications are processed on a rolling basis. Application fee: $40 ($90 for international students). Electronic applications accepted. *Expenses:* Tuition, state resident: full-time $6408; part-time $3204 per semester. Tuition, nonresident: full-time $14,832; part-time $7416 per semester. *Required fees:* $1824; $912 per semester. Tuition and fees vary according to course load. *Financial support:* In 2011–12, 2 teaching assistantships (averaging $7,614 per year) were awarded; career-related internships or fieldwork, Federal Work-Study, institutionally sponsored loans, scholarships/grants, and unspecified assistantships also available. Support available to part-time students. Financial award application deadline: 4/1; financial award applicants required to submit FAFSA. *Unit head:* Dr. Mary Ellen Cavitt, Graduate Advisor, 512-245-8450, Fax: 512-245-8181, E-mail: mc58@txstate.edu. *Application contact:* Dr. J. Michael Willoughby, Dean of Graduate School, 512-245-2581, Fax: 512-245-8365, E-mail: gradcollege@txstate.edu. Web site: http://www.finearts.txstate.edu/music/.

Texas Tech University, Graduate School, College of Visual and Performing Arts, School of Music, Lubbock, TX 79409. Offers music (MM, DMA); music education (MM Ed). *Accreditation:* NASM. Part-time programs available. *Faculty:* 46 full-time (16 women), 1 part-time/adjunct (0 women). *Students:* 87 full-time (47 women), 30 part-time (13 women); includes 12 minority (2 Black or African American, non-Hispanic/Latino; 2 Asian, non-Hispanic/Latino; 6 Hispanic/Latino; 2 Two or more races, non-Hispanic/Latino), 31 international. Average age 30. 131 applicants, 53% accepted, 33 enrolled. In 2011, 29 master's, 16 doctorates awarded. *Degree requirements:* For master's, thesis or alternative; for doctorate, thesis/dissertation. *Entrance requirements:* For master's and doctorate, GRE General Test. Additional exam requirements/recommendations for international students: Required—TOEFL (minimum score 550 paper-based; 213 computer-based; 79 iBT). *Application deadline:* For fall admission, 6/1 priority date for domestic students, 1/15 for international students; for spring admission, 9/1 priority date for domestic students, 6/15 for international students. Applications are processed on a rolling basis. Application fee: $50 ($75 for international students). Electronic applications accepted. *Expenses:* Tuition, state resident: full-time $5899; part-time $245.80 per credit hour. Tuition, nonresident: full-time $13,411; part-time $558.80 per credit hour.

Music Education

Required fees: $2680.60; $86.50 per credit hour. $920.30 per semester. *Financial support:* In 2011–12, 56 students received support. Application deadline: 4/15; applicants required to submit FAFSA. *Faculty research:* Strategies for music pedagogy in grades K-12, performance practice of traditional music, role of the woman piano virtuoso, vernacular music center, voice health and culture. *Unit head:* Prof. William Ballenger, Director, 806-742-2270, Fax: 806-742-2294, E-mail: william.ballenger@ttu.edu. *Application contact:* Carin Wanner, Admissions and Scholarship Coordinator, 806-742-2270 Ext. 225, Fax: 806-742-2294, E-mail: melissacarin.wanner@ttu.edu. Web site: http://www.depts.ttu.edu/music.

Towson University, Program in Music Education, Towson, MD 21252-0001. Offers MS, Postbaccalaureate Certificate. *Accreditation:* NASM; NCATE. Part-time and evening/weekend programs available. *Students:* 11 full-time (3 women), 24 part-time (18 women); includes 5 minority (4 Black or African American, non-Hispanic/Latino; 1 Hispanic/Latino). *Degree requirements:* For master's, thesis optional, exam. *Entrance requirements:* For master's, bachelor's degree in music education or certification as public school music teacher, minimum GPA of 3.0; for Postbaccalaureate Certificate, bachelor's degree in music or certification as public school music teacher. *Application deadline:* Applications are processed on a rolling basis. Application fee: $50. Electronic applications accepted. *Expenses:* Tuition, state resident: part-time $337 per credit. Tuition, nonresident: part-time $709 per credit. *Required fees:* $99 per credit. *Financial support:* Application deadline: 4/1; applicants required to submit FAFSA. *Unit head:* Dr. Dana Rothlisberger, Graduate Program Director, 410-704-2765, Fax: 410-704-3434, E-mail: drothlisberger@towson.edu.

Troy University, Graduate School, College of Education, Program in Postsecondary Education, Troy, AL 36082. Offers adult education (M Ed); biology (M Ed); criminal justice (M Ed); English (M Ed); foundations of education (M Ed); general science (M Ed); higher education administration (M Ed); history (M Ed); instructional technology (M Ed); mathematics (M Ed); music industry (M Ed); physical fitness (M Ed); political science (M Ed); public administration (M Ed); social science (M Ed); teaching English (M Ed). *Accreditation:* NCATE. Part-time and evening/weekend programs available. *Faculty:* 53 full-time (21 women), 22 part-time/adjunct (8 women). *Students:* 74 full-time (51 women), 166 part-time (121 women); includes 148 minority (143 Black or African American, non-Hispanic/Latino; 1 American Indian or Alaska Native, non-Hispanic/Latino; 2 Hispanic/Latino; 2 Two or more races, non-Hispanic/Latino). Average age 34. 174 applicants, 82% accepted, 88 enrolled. In 2011, 221 master's awarded. *Degree requirements:* For master's, comprehensive exam, thesis. *Entrance requirements:* For master's, MAT (minimum score 385), minimum GPA of 2.5. Additional exam requirements/recommendations for international students: Required—TOEFL (minimum score 523 paper-based; 193 computer-based; 70 iBT), IELTS (minimum score 6), or ACT COMPASS ESL (minimum listening, reading, and grammar score 270). *Application deadline:* Applications are processed on a rolling basis. Application fee: $50. Electronic applications accepted. *Expenses:* Tuition, state resident: full-time $6960; part-time $290 per credit hour. Tuition, nonresident: full-time $13,920; part-time $580 per credit hour. *Required fees:* $386 per term. *Financial support:* Available to part-time students. Applicants required to submit FAFSA. *Unit head:* Dr. Jan Oliver, Associate Professor, 334-670-3444, Fax: 334-670-3296, E-mail: oliver@troy.edu. *Application contact:* Brenda K. Campbell, Director of Graduate Admissions, 334-670-3178, Fax: 334-670-3733, E-mail: bcamp@troy.edu.

Troy University, Graduate School, College of Education, Program in Teacher Education-Multiple Levels, Troy, AL 36082. Offers art education (MS); gifted education (MS); instrumental (MS); physical education (MS); reading specialist (MS); vocal/choral (MS). Part-time and evening/weekend programs available. *Faculty:* 6 full-time (4 women). *Students:* 6 full-time (4 women), 20 part-time (10 women); includes 3 minority (all Black or African American, non-Hispanic/Latino). Average age 30. 12 applicants, 83% accepted, 5 enrolled. In 2011, 13 master's awarded. *Degree requirements:* For master's, comprehensive exam, thesis. *Entrance requirements:* For master's, minimum GPA of 2.5. Additional exam requirements/recommendations for international students: Required—TOEFL (minimum score 523 paper-based; 193 computer-based; 70 iBT), IELTS (minimum score 6). *Application deadline:* Applications are processed on a rolling basis. Application fee: $50. Electronic applications accepted. *Expenses:* Tuition, state resident: full-time $6960; part-time $290 per credit hour. Tuition, nonresident: full-time $13,920; part-time $580 per credit hour. *Required fees:* $386 per term. *Financial support:* Available to part-time students. Applicants required to submit FAFSA. *Unit head:* Dr. Charlotte S. Minnick, Director, Teacher Education, 334-670-3544, Fax: 334-670-3548, E-mail: csminnick@troy.edu. *Application contact:* Brenda K. Campbell, Director of Graduate Admissions, 334-670-3178, Fax: 334-670-3733, E-mail: bcamp@troy.edu.

Union College, Graduate Programs, Department of Education, Barbourville, KY 40906-1499. Offers elementary education (MA); health and physical education (MA); middle grades (MA); music education (MA); principalship (MA); reading specialist (MA); secondary education (MA); special education (MA). *Degree requirements:* For master's, thesis optional. *Entrance requirements:* For master's, GRE General Test, NTE.

Université Laval, Faculty of Music, Programs in Music, Québec, QC G1K 7P4, Canada. Offers composition (M Mus); instrumental didactics (M Mus); interpretation (M Mus); music education (M Mus, PhD); musicology (M Mus, PhD). Terminal master's awarded for partial completion of doctoral program. *Degree requirements:* For master's, thesis (for some programs); for doctorate, comprehensive exam, thesis/dissertation. *Entrance requirements:* For master's, English exam, audition, knowledge of French; for doctorate, English exam, knowledge of French, third language. Electronic applications accepted.

University at Buffalo, the State University of New York, Graduate School, Graduate School of Education, Department of Learning and Instruction, Buffalo, NY 14260. Offers biology education (Ed M, Certificate); chemistry education (Ed M, Certificate); childhood education (Ed M); childhood education with bilingual extension (Ed M); early childhood education (Ed M); early childhood education with bilingual extension (birth-grade 2) (Ed M); earth science education (Ed M, Certificate); educational technology and new literacies (Certificate); educational technology and new literacies (online) (Certificate); elementary education (Ed D, PhD); English education (Ed M, PhD, Certificate); English for speakers of other languages (Ed M); foreign and second language education (PhD); French education (Ed M, Certificate); general education (Ed M); German education (Ed M, Certificate); gifted education (online) (Certificate); Latin education (Ed M, Certificate); literacy teaching and learning (Certificate); literary specialist (Ed M); mathematics education (Ed M, PhD, Certificate); music education (Ed M, Certificate); physics education (Ed M, Certificate); reading education (PhD); science and the public (online) (Ed M); science education (PhD); social studies education (Ed M, Certificate); Spanish education (Ed M, Certificate); special education (PhD); teaching and leading for diversity (Certificate); teaching English to speakers of other languages (Ed M). Part-time and evening/weekend programs available. Postbaccalaureate distance learning degree programs offered (no on-campus study). *Faculty:* 32 full-time (23 women), 54 part-time/adjunct (43 women). *Students:* 294 full-time (222 women), 350 part-time (261 women); includes 75 minority (19 Black or African American, non-Hispanic/Latino; 6 American Indian or Alaska Native, non-Hispanic/Latino; 40 Asian, non-Hispanic/Latino; 10 Hispanic/Latino), 76 international. Average age 29. 548 applicants, 52% accepted, 253 enrolled. In 2011, 225 master's, 17 doctorates, 37 other advanced degrees awarded. *Degree requirements:* For master's, comprehensive exam; for doctorate, thesis/dissertation, research analysis exam, research experience component. *Entrance requirements:* For doctorate, GRE General Test or MAT, interview, writing sample, letters of recommendation. Additional exam requirements/recommendations for international students: Required—TOEFL (minimum score 600 paper-based; 96 iBT). *Application deadline:* For fall admission, 2/1 priority date for domestic students, 2/1 for international students; for spring admission, 11/15 priority date for domestic students, 10/1 for international students. Applications are processed on a rolling basis. Application fee: $50. Electronic applications accepted. *Financial support:* In 2011–12, 40 fellowships (averaging $12,991 per year), 46 research assistantships (averaging $10,986 per year) were awarded; teaching assistantships with full tuition reimbursements, career-related internships or fieldwork, Federal Work-Study, institutionally sponsored loans, scholarships/grants, and unspecified assistantships also available. Financial award application deadline: 2/28; financial award applicants required to submit FAFSA. *Faculty research:* Science assessment, foreign language teaching and learning, early learning, new literacies, gender and education. *Unit head:* Dr. Julie Sarama, Chair, 716-645-2455, Fax: 716-645-3161, E-mail: jcollins@buffalo.edu. *Application contact:* Cathy Dimino, Admissions Assistant, 716-645-2110, Fax: 716-645-7937, E-mail: cadimino@buffalo.edu.

The University of Akron, Graduate School, College of Creative and Professional Arts, School of Music, Program in Music Education, Akron, OH 44325. Offers MM. *Accreditation:* NCATE. *Students:* 10 full-time (9 women), 11 part-time (6 women); includes 1 minority (Black or African American, non-Hispanic/Latino). Average age 26. 12 applicants, 75% accepted, 3 enrolled. In 2011, 6 master's awarded. *Degree requirements:* For master's, comprehensive exam, thesis optional. *Entrance requirements:* For master's, minimum GPA of 2.75, interview, three letters of recommendation. Additional exam requirements/recommendations for international students: Required—TOEFL (minimum score 550 paper-based; 213 computer-based; 79 iBT). *Application deadline:* Applications are processed on a rolling basis. Application fee: $30 ($40 for international students). Electronic applications accepted. *Expenses:* Tuition, state resident: full-time $7038; part-time $391 per credit hour. Tuition, nonresident: full-time $12,051; part-time $670 per credit hour. *Required fees:* $1274; $34 per credit hour. *Unit head:* Laurie Lafferty, Program Contact, 330-972-5761, E-mail: laffert@uakron.edu. *Application contact:* Dr. Michele Mills, Graduate Coordinator, 330-972-5762, E-mail: mt4@uakron.edu.

The University of Alabama, Graduate School, College of Arts and Sciences, School of Music, Tuscaloosa, AL 35487. Offers arranging (MM); choral conducting (MM, DMA); composition (MM, DMA); music education (MA, PhD); music history (MM); performance (MM, DMA); theory (MM); wind conducting (MM, DMA). *Accreditation:* NASM. *Faculty:* 36 full-time (13 women), 1 part-time/adjunct (0 women). *Students:* 60 full-time (22 women), 27 part-time (12 women); includes 13 minority (1 Black or African American, non-Hispanic/Latino; 6 Asian, non-Hispanic/Latino; 3 Hispanic/Latino; 3 Two or more races, non-Hispanic/Latino), 12 international. Average age 32. 55 applicants, 58% accepted, 14 enrolled. In 2011, 8 master's, 8 doctorates awarded. *Median time to degree:* Of those who began their doctoral program in fall 2003, 50% received their degree in 8 years or less. *Degree requirements:* For master's, comprehensive exam, thesis, oral and written exams, recital; for doctorate, comprehensive exam, thesis/dissertation, oral and written exams, recital. *Entrance requirements:* For master's and doctorate, audition. Additional exam requirements/recommendations for international students: Required—TOEFL or IELTS. *Application deadline:* For fall admission, 2/1 priority date for domestic students, 2/1 for international students; for winter admission, 2/1 for domestic and international students; for spring admission, 2/1 priority date for domestic students, 2/1 for international students. Applications are processed on a rolling basis. Application fee: $50 ($60 for international students). Electronic applications accepted. *Expenses:* Tuition, state resident: full-time $8600. Tuition, nonresident: full-time $21,900. *Financial support:* In 2011–12, 22 students received support, including 1 fellowship with tuition reimbursement available (averaging $30,000 per year), 40 teaching assistantships with full and partial tuition reimbursements available (averaging $8,181 per year); Federal Work-Study, institutionally sponsored loans, and unspecified assistantships also available. Financial award application deadline: 7/14. *Faculty research:* Performance practice, musicology, theory, composition. *Unit head:* Charles G. Snead, Director, 205-348-7110, Fax: 205-348-1473, E-mail: ssnead@music.ua.edu. *Application contact:* Dr. Marvin Johnson, Director of Graduate Studies, 205-348-6604, Fax: 205-348-1473, E-mail: mjohnson@music.ua.edu. Web site: http://www.music.ua.edu/.

The University of Alabama, Graduate School, College of Education, Department of Music Education, Tuscaloosa, AL 35487-0366. Offers choral music education (MA); instrumental music education (MA); music education (Ed D, PhD, Ed S). *Accreditation:* NASM. Part-time programs available. *Degree requirements:* For master's, comprehensive exam, thesis optional; for doctorate, comprehensive exam, thesis/dissertation, oral exam (PhD). *Entrance requirements:* For master's, GRE or MAT, video of teaching, letters of recommendation; for doctorate, GRE or MAT, interview, writing sample, video of teaching, letters of recommendation; for Ed S, GRE or MAT. Additional exam requirements/recommendations for international students: Required—TOEFL (minimum score 550 paper-based; 213 computer-based). *Application deadline:* For fall admission, 7/1 priority date for domestic students; for spring admission, 11/1 priority date for domestic students. Applications are processed on a rolling basis. Application fee: $50 ($60 for international students). Electronic applications accepted. *Expenses:* Tuition, state resident: full-time $8600. Tuition, nonresident: full-time $21,900. *Financial support:* Research assistantships with full and partial tuition reimbursements and teaching assistantships with full and partial tuition reimbursements available. Financial award application deadline: 3/1. *Faculty research:* Elementary music, music for students with special needs, choral music. *Unit head:* Dr. Carol A. Prickett, Department Head and Professor, 205-348-1432, Fax: 205-348-1675, E-mail: cpricket@bama.ua.edu. *Application contact:* Cathie M. Daniels, Senior Office Associate, 205-348-6054, Fax: 205-348-1675, E-mail: cdaniels@bama.ua.edu. Web site: http://www.musiceducation.ua.edu.

University of Alaska Fairbanks, College of Liberal Arts, Department of Music, Fairbanks, AK 99775-5660. Offers conducting (MA); music education (MA); music history (MA); music theory/composition (MA); performance (MA). *Accreditation:* NASM. Part-time programs available. *Faculty:* 12 full-time (4 women). *Students:* 5 full-time (2 women), 1 part-time (0 women), 1 international. Average age 27. 11 applicants, 45% accepted, 3 enrolled. In 2011, 8 master's awarded. *Degree requirements:* For master's, comprehensive exam, thesis or alternative, oral exam, oral defense. *Entrance requirements:* For master's, evaluative preliminary examination in music theory and history. Additional exam requirements/recommendations for international students: Required—TOEFL (minimum score 550 paper-based; 213 computer-based; 80 iBT). *Application deadline:* For fall admission, 6/1 for domestic students, 3/1 for international students; for spring admission, 10/15 for domestic students, 9/1 for international students. Applications are processed on a rolling basis. Application fee: $60. Electronic applications accepted. *Expenses:* Tuition, state resident: full-time $6696; part-time $372 per credit. Tuition, nonresident: full-time $13,680; part-time $760 per credit. Tuition and fees vary according to course load and reciprocity agreements. *Financial support:* In 2011–12, 4 teaching assistantships with tuition reimbursements (averaging $12,084 per year) were awarded; fellowships with tuition reimbursements, Federal Work-Study, scholarships/grants, health care benefits, and unspecified assistantships also available. Support available to part-time students. Financial award application deadline: 7/1; financial award applicants required to submit FAFSA. *Faculty research:* Symphony, opera, jazz, chamber and solo performance. *Unit head:* Dr. Eduard Zilberkant, Department Chair, 907-474-7555, Fax: 907-474-6420, E-mail: uaf.music@alaska.edu. *Application contact:* Mike Earnest, Director of Admissions, 907-474-7500, Fax: 907-474-5379, E-mail: admissions@uaf.edu. Web site: http://www.uaf.edu/music/.

The University of Arizona, College of Fine Arts, School of Music, Tucson, AZ 85721. Offers composition (MM, A Mus D); conducting (MM, A Mus D); music education (MM, PhD); music theory (MM, PhD); musicology (MM); performance (MM, A Mus D). *Accreditation:* NASD (one or more programs are accredited); NASM (one or more programs are accredited). Part-time programs available. *Faculty:* 37 full-time (12 women), 1 part-time/adjunct (0 women). *Students:* 157 full-time (67 women), 50 part-time (21 women); includes 27 minority (6 Black or African American, non-Hispanic/Latino; 5 Asian, non-Hispanic/Latino; 10 Hispanic/Latino; 6 Two or more races, non-Hispanic/Latino), 48 international. Average age 34. 162 applicants, 48% accepted, 50 enrolled. In 2011, 30 master's, 14 doctorates awarded. *Degree requirements:* For master's, thesis or alternative, orals; for doctorate, comprehensive exam, thesis/dissertation or alternative. *Entrance requirements:* For master's, 3 letters of recommendation; for doctorate, 3 letters of recommendation, statement of purpose. Additional exam requirements/recommendations for international students: Required—TOEFL (minimum score 550 paper-based; 213 computer-based; 79 iBT). *Application deadline:* For fall admission, 6/1 for domestic students, 12/1 for international students; for spring admission, 10/1 for domestic students, 6/1 for international students. Applications are processed on a rolling basis. Application fee: $75. Electronic applications accepted. *Expenses:* Tuition, state resident: full-time $10,840. Tuition, nonresident: full-time $25,802. *Financial support:* In 2011–12, 56 teaching assistantships with full tuition reimbursements (averaging $16,854 per year) were awarded; career-related internships or fieldwork, institutionally sponsored loans, scholarships/grants, health care benefits, tuition waivers (full), and unspecified assistantships also available. Support available to part-time students. Financial award application deadline: 2/15; financial award applicants required to submit FAFSA. *Faculty research:* Music in general education, psychology of music learning, innovation in string music education, Zarzuela, Franz Liszt's work. *Total annual research expenditures:* $5,000. *Unit head:* Dr. Peter A. McAllister, Director, 520-621-7023, Fax: 520-621-1351, E-mail: pmcallis@email.arizona.edu. *Application contact:* Lyneen Elmore, 520-621-5929, Fax: 520-621-8118, E-mail: lyneen@u.arizona.edu. Web site: http://www.atrs.arizona.edu/music.

University of Bridgeport, School of Education, Department of Education, Bridgeport, CT 06604. Offers education (MS); educational management (Ed D, Diploma), including intermediate administrator or supervisor (Diploma), leadership (Ed D); elementary education (MS, Diploma), including early childhood education, elementary education; middle school education (MS); music education (MS); remedial reading and language arts (Diploma); secondary education (MS, Diploma), including computer specialist (Diploma), international education (Diploma), reading specialist, secondary education. Part-time and evening/weekend programs available. *Faculty:* 12 full-time (5 women), 108 part-time/adjunct (60 women). *Students:* 232 full-time (161 women), 216 part-time (160 women); includes 61 minority (21 Black or African American, non-Hispanic/Latino; 8 Asian, non-Hispanic/Latino; 22 Hispanic/Latino; 10 Two or more races, non-Hispanic/Latino), 34 international. Average age 30. 412 applicants, 63% accepted, 147 enrolled. In 2011, 216 master's, 7 other advanced degrees awarded. *Degree requirements:* For master's, final exam, final project, or thesis; for doctorate, comprehensive exam, thesis/dissertation; for Diploma, thesis or alternative, final project. *Entrance requirements:* For master's, minimum undergraduate QPA of 2.67; for doctorate, GRE, MAT; for Diploma, GRE General Test or MAT, minimum graduate QPA of 3.0. Additional exam requirements/recommendations for international students: Recommended—TOEFL (minimum score 550 paper-based; 213 computer-based; 80 iBT), IELTS (minimum score 6.5). *Application deadline:* For fall admission, 8/1 priority date for domestic students, 8/1 for international students; for spring admission, 12/1 priority date for domestic students, 12/1 for international students. Applications are processed on a rolling basis. Application fee: $50. Electronic applications accepted. *Expenses: Tuition:* Full-time $22,880; part-time $700 per credit. *Required fees:* $1870; $95 per semester. Tuition and fees vary according to course load and program. *Financial support:* In 2011–12, 120 students received support. Fellowships, research assistantships, teaching assistantships, career-related internships or fieldwork, Federal Work-Study, and institutionally sponsored loans available. Support available to part-time students. Financial award application deadline: 6/1; financial award applicants required to submit FAFSA. *Faculty research:* Self-concept, internship assessment, stress and situational development, follow-up of graduation, trend analysis. *Unit head:* Dr. Allen P. Cook, Dean, 203-576-4192, Fax: 203-576-4200, E-mail: acook@bridgeport.edu. *Application contact:* Karissa Peckham, Dean of Admissions, 203-576-4552, Fax: 203-576-4941, E-mail: admit@bridgeport.edu.

The University of British Columbia, Faculty of Education, Department of Curriculum and Pedagogy, Vancouver, BC V6T 1Z4, Canada. Offers art education (M Ed, MA); business education (MA); curriculum studies (M Ed, MA, PhD); home economics education (M Ed, MA); math education (M Ed, MA); music education (M Ed, MA); physical education (M Ed, MA); science education (M Ed, MA); social studies education (M Ed, MA); technology studies education (M Ed, MA). Part-time programs available. *Degree requirements:* For master's, thesis (MA); for doctorate, comprehensive exam, thesis/dissertation. *Entrance requirements:* Additional exam requirements/recommendations for international students: Required—TOEFL (minimum score 580 paper-based; 237 computer-based; 92 iBT). Electronic applications accepted. *Expenses:* Contact institution. *Faculty research:* School subjects, teaching and learning.

University of Central Arkansas, Graduate School, College of Fine Arts and Communication, Department of Music, Conway, AR 72035-0001. Offers choral conducting (MM); instrumental conducting (MM); music (PC); music education (MM); music theory (MM); performance (MM). *Accreditation:* NASM. Part-time programs available. *Faculty:* 12 full-time (4 women), 1 part-time/adjunct (0 women). *Students:* 20 full-time (10 women), 6 part-time (4 women); includes 2 minority (1 American Indian or Alaska Native, non-Hispanic/Latino; 1 Native Hawaiian or other Pacific Islander, non-Hispanic/Latino), 8 international. Average age 29. 11 applicants, 100% accepted, 10 enrolled. In 2011, 6 master's awarded. *Degree requirements:* For master's, comprehensive exam, thesis optional. *Entrance requirements:* For master's, GRE General Test, minimum GPA of 2.7. Additional exam requirements/recommendations for international students: Required—TOEFL (minimum score 550 paper-based; 213 computer-based). *Application deadline:* For fall admission, 3/1 priority date for domestic students; for spring admission, 10/1 priority date for domestic students. Applications are processed on a rolling basis. Application fee: $25 ($50 for international students). *Expenses:* Tuition, state resident: full-time $4834; part-time $398.35 per credit hour. Tuition, nonresident: full-time $8686. *Financial support:* Federal Work-Study, scholarships/grants, tuition waivers (partial), and unspecified assistantships available. Financial award application deadline: 2/15; financial award applicants required to submit FAFSA. *Unit head:* Jeffrey Jarvis, Unit Head, 501-450-3163. *Application contact:* Sandy Burks, Admissions Assistant, 501-450-5065, Fax: 501-450-5678, E-mail: slburks@uca.edu.

University of Central Oklahoma, College of Graduate Studies and Research, College of Fine Arts and Design, Department of Music, Edmond, OK 73034-5209. Offers music education (MM); performance (MM). *Accreditation:* NASM. Part-time programs available. *Faculty:* 26 full-time (9 women), 8 part-time/adjunct (3 women). *Students:* 12 full-time (8 women), 15 part-time (11 women); includes 3 minority (2 Black or African American, non-Hispanic/Latino; 1 Two or more races, non-Hispanic/Latino), 11 international. Average age 28. In 2011, 30 master's awarded. *Degree requirements:* For master's, comprehensive exam, recital or project. *Entrance requirements:* Additional exam requirements/recommendations for international students: Required—TOEFL (minimum score 550 paper-based; 213 computer-based). *Application deadline:* Applications are processed on a rolling basis. Application fee: $50. Electronic applications accepted. *Expenses:* Tuition, state resident: full-time $3901; part-time $218.30 per credit hour. Tuition, nonresident: full-time $9198; part-time $511.20 per credit hour. Tuition and fees vary according to program. *Financial support:* Federal Work-Study and unspecified assistantships available. Financial award application deadline: 3/31; financial award applicants required to submit FAFSA. *Faculty research:* Historical performance, history of music education. *Unit head:* Dr. Ted Honea, Head, Graduate Studies, 405-974-3891, E-mail: thonea@uco.edu. *Application contact:* Dr. Richard Bernard, Dean, Graduate College, 405-974-3493, Fax: 405-974-3775, E-mail: gradcoll@ucok.edu. Web site: http://www.uco.edu/cfad/academics/music/graduate-degrees.asp.

University of Cincinnati, Graduate School, College-Conservatory of Music, Division of Music Education, Cincinnati, OH 45221. Offers MM. *Accreditation:* NASM; NCATE. *Degree requirements:* For master's, comprehensive exam, paper or thesis. *Entrance requirements:* For master's, GRE General Test, interview. Additional exam requirements/recommendations for international students: Required—TOEFL (minimum score 520 paper-based; 190 computer-based). Electronic applications accepted. *Faculty research:* Choral, orchestral, and wind conducting; Kodaly; Orff-Schulwerk; jazz studies; string education.

University of Colorado Boulder, Graduate School, College of Music, Boulder, CO 80309. Offers composition (M Mus, D Mus A); conducting (M Mus); instrumental conducting and literature (D Mus A); literature and performance of choral music (D Mus A); music education (M Mus Ed, PhD); musicology (PhD); performance (M Mus, D Mus A); performance/pedagogy (M Mus, D Mus A); theory (M Mus). *Accreditation:* NASM. *Faculty:* 51 full-time (20 women). *Students:* 197 full-time (97 women), 58 part-time (35 women); includes 29 minority (3 Black or African American, non-Hispanic/Latino; 10 Asian, non-Hispanic/Latino; 12 Hispanic/Latino; 4 Two or more races, non-Hispanic/Latino), 29 international. Average age 29. 482 applicants, 32% accepted, 61 enrolled. In 2011, 42 master's, 16 doctorates awarded. Terminal master's awarded for partial completion of doctoral program. *Degree requirements:* For master's, variable foreign language requirement, comprehensive exam, thesis or alternative, recital; for doctorate, variable foreign language requirement, thesis/dissertation. *Entrance requirements:* For master's, GRE General Test, GRE Subject Test (music literature), minimum undergraduate GPA of 2.75; for doctorate, GRE General Test, GRE Subject Test, audition, sample of research. *Application deadline:* For fall admission, 12/1 priority date for domestic students, 12/1 for international students. Applications are processed on a rolling basis. Application fee: $50 ($60 for international students). Electronic applications accepted. *Financial support:* In 2011–12, 342 students received support, including 218 fellowships (averaging $2,874 per year), 101 teaching assistantships with full and partial tuition reimbursements available (averaging $10,859 per year); institutionally sponsored loans, scholarships/grants, health care benefits, and unspecified assistantships also available. Financial award application deadline: 3/1; financial award applicants required to submit FAFSA. *Total annual research expenditures:* $8,116. *Application contact:* E-mail: gradmusc@colorado.edu. Web site: http://www.colorado.edu/music/.

University of Connecticut, Graduate School, School of Fine Arts, Department of Music, Storrs, CT 06269. Offers conducting (M Mus, DMA); historical musicology (MA); music (Performer's Certificate); music education (M Mus, PhD); music theory (MA); music theory and history (PhD); performance (M Mus, DMA). *Accreditation:* NASM. Terminal master's awarded for partial completion of doctoral program. *Degree requirements:* For master's, comprehensive exam; for doctorate, thesis/dissertation. *Entrance requirements:* For master's, GRE General Test, GRE Subject Test, audition; for doctorate, GRE Subject Test, MAT, audition. Additional exam requirements/recommendations for international students: Required—TOEFL (minimum score 550 paper-based; 213 computer-based).

University of Dayton, Department of Teacher Education, Dayton, OH 45469-1300. Offers adolescent/young adult (MS Ed); art education (MS Ed); early childhood education (MS Ed); early childhood leadership advocacy (MS Ed); inclusive early childhood (MS Ed); interdisciplinary education (MS Ed); intervention specialist education, mild/moderate (MS Ed); literacy (MS Ed); middle childhood (MS Ed); multi-age education (MS Ed); music education (MS Ed); teacher as leader (MS Ed); technology in education (MS Ed). Part-time and evening/weekend programs available. Postbaccalaureate distance learning degree programs offered (no on-campus study). *Faculty:* 15 full-time (11 women), 22 part-time/adjunct (20 women). *Students:* 41 full-time (29 women), 95 part-time (87 women); includes 13 minority (9 Black or African American, non-Hispanic/Latino; 1 Asian, non-Hispanic/Latino; 3 Hispanic/Latino), 9 international. Average age 32. 111 applicants, 55% accepted, 38 enrolled. In 2011, 97 degrees awarded. *Degree requirements:* For master's, thesis, capstone research project. *Entrance requirements:* For master's, GRE General Test, minimum GPA of 2.75. Additional exam requirements/recommendations for international students: Required—TOEFL (minimum score 550 paper-based; 213 computer-based; 80 iBT). *Application deadline:* For fall admission, 3/1 priority date for domestic students, 3/1 for international students; for winter admission, 7/1 for international students; for spring admission, 1/1 for international students. Applications are processed on a rolling basis. Application fee: $0 ($50 for international students). Electronic applications accepted. *Expenses:* Contact institution. *Financial support:* In 2011–12, 5 research assistantships with full and partial tuition reimbursements (averaging $8,470 per year) were awarded; career-related internships or fieldwork, institutionally sponsored loans, health care benefits, and unspecified assistantships also available. Financial award applicants required to submit FAFSA. *Faculty research:* Diversity, literacy, art representation by young children, preservice teacher preparation. *Unit head:* Dr. Katie A. Kinnucan-Welsch, Chair, 937-229-3346. *Application contact:* Alexsandar Popovski, Enrollment Management Administrator, 937-229-2357, Fax: 937-229-4729, E-mail: alex.popovski@notes.udayton.edu.

University of Delaware, College of Arts and Sciences, Department of Music, Newark, DE 19716. Offers composition (MM); music education (MM); performance (MM). *Accreditation:* NASM. Part-time programs available. *Entrance requirements:* For master's, audition. Additional exam requirements/recommendations for international students: Required—TOEFL. Electronic applications accepted. *Faculty research:* Teaching of music.

Music Education

University of Denver, Division of Arts, Humanities and Social Sciences, Lamont School of Music, Denver, CO 80208. Offers choral conducting (MM); composition (MM); jazz and commercial music (Certificate); jazz studies (MM); music theory (MA); musicology (MA); orchestral conducting (MM); performance (MM); piano pedagogy (MM); Suzuki pedagogy (MM), including cello, violin; Suzuki teaching (Certificate); wind conducting (MM). *Accreditation:* NASM. Part-time programs available. *Faculty:* 28 full-time (10 women), 42 part-time/adjunct (20 women). *Students:* 33 full-time (21 women), 49 part-time (29 women); includes 9 minority (3 Asian, non-Hispanic/Latino; 3 Hispanic/Latino; 1 Native Hawaiian or other Pacific Islander, non-Hispanic/Latino; 2 Two or more races, non-Hispanic/Latino), 11 international. Average age 27. 121 applicants, 71% accepted, 53 enrolled. In 2011, 19 master's, 7 other advanced degrees awarded. *Degree requirements:* For master's, one foreign language, comprehensive exam, recital or project (for performance), thesis (for musicology, music theory, piano pedagogy). *Entrance requirements:* For master's, GRE General Test (for MA), audition; for Certificate, audition. Additional exam requirements/recommendations for international students: Required—TOEFL (minimum score 550 paper-based; 80 iBT). *Application deadline:* Applications are processed on a rolling basis. Application fee: $60. Electronic applications accepted. *Financial support:* In 2011–12, 69 students received support, including 36 teaching assistantships with full and partial tuition reimbursements available (averaging $6,417 per year); career-related internships or fieldwork, Federal Work-Study, institutionally sponsored loans, scholarships/grants, tuition waivers, and unspecified assistantships also available. Support available to part-time students. Financial award application deadline: 2/15; financial award applicants required to submit FAFSA. *Faculty research:* Performance, jazz studies and commercial music, musicology, music theory, composition, music pedagogy, music recording and production. *Unit head:* Nancy Cochran, School Director, 303-871-6986, Fax: 303-871-3118, E-mail: nancy.cochran@du.edu. *Application contact:* Jerrod Price, Director of Admission, 303-871-6950, Fax: 303-871-3118, E-mail: jerrod.price@du.edu. Web site: http://www.du.edu/lamont/.

University of Florida, Graduate School, College of Fine Arts, Music Department, Gainesville, FL 32611. Offers choral conducting (MM); composition/theory (MM); instrumental conducting (MM); music (MM, PhD); music education (MM, PhD); music history and literature (MM); performance (MM); sacred music (MM). *Accreditation:* NASM. *Faculty:* 32 full-time (9 women), 1 part-time/adjunct (0 women). *Students:* 78 full-time (39 women), 26 part-time (14 women); includes 13 minority (5 Black or African American, non-Hispanic/Latino; 1 American Indian or Alaska Native, non-Hispanic/Latino; 2 Asian, non-Hispanic/Latino; 5 Hispanic/Latino), 22 international. Average age 32. 77 applicants, 68% accepted, 12 enrolled. In 2011, 24 master's, 4 doctorates awarded. *Degree requirements:* For master's, variable foreign language requirement, comprehensive exam, thesis, recital; for doctorate, thesis/dissertation. *Entrance requirements:* For master's and doctorate, GRE General Test, audition, minimum GPA of 3.0. Additional exam requirements/recommendations for international students: Required—TOEFL (minimum score 550 paper-based; 213 computer-based; 80 iBT), IELTS (minimum score 6). *Application deadline:* For fall admission, 1/1 priority date for domestic students, 1/1 for international students; for spring admission, 11/1 for domestic and international students. Applications are processed on a rolling basis. Application fee: $30. Electronic applications accepted. *Financial support:* Fellowships with full tuition reimbursements, research assistantships with tuition reimbursements, teaching assistantships with tuition reimbursements, and unspecified assistantships available. Financial award applicants required to submit FAFSA. *Unit head:* John A. Duff, Program Director, 352-273-3167 Ext. 207, E-mail: jduff@arts.ufl.edu. *Application contact:* Dr. Leslie S. Odom, Graduate Coordinator, 352-273-3172, Fax: 352-352-0461, E-mail: lodom@arts.ufl.edu. Web site: http://www.arts.ufl.edu/welcome/music/.

University of Georgia, College of Education, Program in Music Education, Athens, GA 30602. Offers MM Ed, Ed D, Ed S. *Accreditation:* NASM; NCATE. *Students:* 12 full-time (6 women), 42 part-time (12 women); includes 16 minority (13 Black or African American, non-Hispanic/Latino; 1 Asian, non-Hispanic/Latino; 1 Hispanic/Latino; 1 Two or more races, non-Hispanic/Latino), 2 international. Average age 31. 13 applicants, 77% accepted, 5 enrolled. In 2011, 9 master's, 1 doctorate, 6 other advanced degrees awarded. *Degree requirements:* For doctorate, thesis/dissertation. *Entrance requirements:* For master's, GRE General Test, MAT; for doctorate, GRE General Test; for Ed S, GRE General Test or MAT. *Application deadline:* For fall admission, 7/1 priority date for domestic students; for spring admission, 11/15 for domestic students. Application fee: $50. Electronic applications accepted. *Financial support:* Fellowships, research assistantships, teaching assistantships, and unspecified assistantships available. *Unit head:* Dr. Dale Monson, Director, 706-542-2276, Fax: 706-542-2773, E-mail: dmonson@uga.edu. *Application contact:* Dr. Adrian Childs, Graduate Coordinator, 206-542-2765, E-mail: apchilds@uga.edu. Web site: http://www.music.uga.edu/.

University of Hartford, The Hartt School, West Hartford, CT 06117-1599. Offers choral conducting (MM Ed); composition (MM, DMA, Artist Diploma, Diploma); conducting (MM, DMA, Artist Diploma, Diploma), including choral (MM, Diploma), instrumental (MM, Diploma); early childhood education (MM Ed); instrumental conducting (MM Ed); Kodály (MM Ed); music (CAGS); music education (DMA, PhD); music history (MM); music theory (MM); pedagogy (MM Ed); performance (MM, MM Ed, DMA, Artist Diploma, Diploma); research (MM Ed); technology (MM Ed). *Accreditation:* NASD. Part-time programs available. *Degree requirements:* For master's, variable foreign language requirement, thesis (for some programs), recital; for doctorate, variable foreign language requirement, thesis/dissertation (for some programs), recital; for other advanced degree, recital. *Entrance requirements:* For master's, audition, letters of recommendation; for doctorate, proficiency exam, audition, interview, research paper; for other advanced degree, audition. Additional exam requirements/recommendations for international students: Required—TOEFL. Electronic applications accepted. *Expenses:* Contact institution.

University of Houston, College of Liberal Arts and Social Sciences, Moores School of Music, Houston, TX 77204. Offers accompanying and chamber music (MM); applied music (MM); composition (MM); music education (DMA); music theory (MM); performance (DMA). *Accreditation:* NASM. Part-time programs available. *Degree requirements:* For master's, one foreign language, comprehensive exam, recital; for doctorate, one foreign language, comprehensive exam, thesis/dissertation. *Entrance requirements:* For master's, audition, resume, 3 letters of recommendation; for doctorate, writing sample, audition, statement of purpose, resume. Additional exam requirements/recommendations for international students: Required—TOEFL (minimum score 550 paper-based; 213 computer-based; 79 iBT), IELTS (minimum score 6.5). Electronic applications accepted. *Faculty research:* Twentieth century music, Baroque music, history of music theory, music analysis.

University of Illinois at Urbana–Champaign, Graduate College, College of Fine and Applied Arts, School of Music, Champaign, IL 61820. Offers music (M Mus, AD, DMA); music education (MME, Ed D, PhD); musicology (PhD). *Accreditation:* NASM. *Faculty:* 64 full-time (15 women), 4 part-time/adjunct (2 women). *Students:* 274 full-time (132 women), 77 part-time (44 women); includes 39 minority (8 Black or African American, non-Hispanic/Latino; 1 American Indian or Alaska Native, non-Hispanic/Latino; 9 Asian, non-Hispanic/Latino; 12 Hispanic/Latino; 9 Two or more races, non-Hispanic/Latino), 137 international. 579 applicants, 29% accepted, 94 enrolled. In 2011, 58 master's, 48 doctorates awarded. *Entrance requirements:* For master's and doctorate, minimum GPA of 3.0. Additional exam requirements/recommendations for international students: Required—TOEFL (minimum score 590 paper-based; 243 computer-based). *Application deadline:* Applications are processed on a rolling basis. Application fee: $75 ($90 for international students). Electronic applications accepted. *Financial support:* In 2011–12, 14 fellowships, 18 research assistantships, 115 teaching assistantships were awarded; tuition waivers (full and partial) also available. *Unit head:* Edward Rath, Interim Director, 217-244-2676, Fax: 217-244-4585, E-mail: erath@illinois.edu. *Application contact:* J. Michael Holmes, Enrollment Management Director, 217-244-9879, Fax: 217-244-4585, E-mail: holmes2@illinois.edu. Web site: http://www.music.illinois.edu/.

The University of Kansas, Graduate Studies, School of Music, Program in Music Education, Lawrence, KS 66045. Offers MME, PhD. *Accreditation:* NASM. *Faculty:* 9 full-time, 2 part-time/adjunct. *Students:* 14 full-time (9 women), 17 part-time (11 women); includes 3 minority (1 Asian, non-Hispanic/Latino; 1 Hispanic/Latino; 1 Two or more races, non-Hispanic/Latino), 1 international. Average age 37. 16 applicants, 69% accepted, 8 enrolled. In 2011, 3 master's, 5 doctorates awarded. *Degree requirements:* For master's, comprehensive exam, thesis or alternative; for doctorate, comprehensive exam, thesis/dissertation. *Entrance requirements:* For master's, GRE General Test, minimum undergraduate GPA of 3.0, video, letters of reference, transcripts; for doctorate, GRE General Test, MEMT diagnostic exam, minimum graduate GPA of 3.5, video, reference letters, transcripts, writing sample, proof of professional experience. Additional exam requirements/recommendations for international students: Required—TOEFL (minimum score 570 paper-based; 230 computer-based; 92 iBT) or IELTS (minimum score 6.0). *Application deadline:* For fall admission, 2/15 priority date for domestic students, 2/15 for international students. Applications are processed on a rolling basis. Application fee: $55 ($65 for international students). Electronic applications accepted. Tuition and fees vary according to course load, campus/location, program and reciprocity agreements. *Financial support:* Fellowships with tuition reimbursements, research assistantships, teaching assistantships with full and partial tuition reimbursements, institutionally sponsored loans, scholarships/grants, and unspecified assistantships available. Financial award application deadline: 12/15; financial award applicants required to submit FAFSA. *Faculty research:* Psychology of music, performance, assessment, listener responses, functional music, philosophy of music education, choral pedagogy, choir acoustics, voice science, children's choirs, music in society. *Unit head:* Robert Walzel, Dean, 785-864-3421, Fax: 785-864-5866, E-mail: music@ku.edu. *Application contact:* Dr. James Daugherty, Director of Graduate Studies, 785-864-9637, Fax: 785-864-9640, E-mail: jdaugher@ku.edu. Web site: http://www.memt.ku.edu.

University of Kentucky, Graduate School, College of Fine Arts, Program in Music, Lexington, KY 40506-0032. Offers music (PhD); music composition (MM); music education (MM); music performance (MM); music theory (MA); musical arts (DMA); musicology (MA). *Accreditation:* NASM. Part-time and evening/weekend programs available. *Degree requirements:* For master's, variable foreign language requirement, comprehensive exam, thesis (for some programs); for doctorate, variable foreign language requirement, comprehensive exam, thesis/dissertation. *Entrance requirements:* For master's, GRE General Test, minimum undergraduate GPA of 2.75; for doctorate, GRE General Test, minimum undergraduate GPA of 2.75, graduate 3.0. Additional exam requirements/recommendations for international students: Required—TOEFL (minimum score 550 paper-based; 213 computer-based). Electronic applications accepted. *Faculty research:* Musicology, music theory, jazz, music education, performance and conducting.

University of Louisiana at Lafayette, College of the Arts, School of Music, Lafayette, LA 70504. Offers conducting (MM); pedagogy (MM); vocal and instrumental performance (MM). *Accreditation:* NASM. *Degree requirements:* For master's, thesis or alternative. *Entrance requirements:* For master's, GRE General Test, minimum GPA of 2.75. Additional exam requirements/recommendations for international students: Required—TOEFL (minimum score 550 paper-based; 213 computer-based). Electronic applications accepted. *Faculty research:* Nineteenth century American music, trumpet pedagogy, fifteenth century Renaissance polyphony, Charles Ives.

University of Louisville, Graduate School, College of Education and Human Development, Department of Teaching and Learning, Louisville, KY 40292-0001. Offers art education (MAT); curriculum and instruction (PhD); early elementary education (MAT); instructional technology (M Ed); interdisciplinary early childhood education (MAT); middle school education (MAT); music education (MAT); reading education (M Ed); secondary education (MAT); special education (M Ed, MAT); teacher leadership (M Ed). Part-time and evening/weekend programs available. *Degree requirements:* For doctorate, comprehensive exam, thesis/dissertation. *Entrance requirements:* For master's, GRE General Test, PRAXIS II (for some programs); for doctorate, GRE General Test. Additional exam requirements/recommendations for international students: Required—TOEFL (minimum score 560 paper-based; 210 computer-based; 83 iBT). Electronic applications accepted. *Expenses:* Tuition, state resident: full-time $9692; part-time $539 per credit hour. Tuition, nonresident: full-time $20,168; part-time $1121 per credit hour. Tuition and fees vary according to program and reciprocity agreements. *Faculty research:* Mathematics teacher education and ongoing professional development in pedagogy and content knowledge; development of literacy, including early literacy in science and mathematics and literacy development for English language learners; immersive visualizations for promoting STEM education from nanoscience to cosmic scales; evidence-based practices for students with disabilities; urban education, including teacher response to intervention systems in schools and cross-cultural competence.

University of Louisville, Graduate School, School of Music, Louisville, KY 40292-0001. Offers music composition (MM); music education (MME); music history and literature (MM); music theory (MM); performance (MM). *Accreditation:* NASM. Part-time and evening/weekend programs available. *Degree requirements:* For master's, one foreign language, recital (performance), paper or thesis (music education), major composition (composition). *Entrance requirements:* For master's, GRE General Test, music history and theory entrance exams, jazz entrance exam, audition, portfolio. Additional exam requirements/recommendations for international students: Required—TOEFL (minimum score 550 paper-based; 213 computer-based; 79 iBT). Electronic applications accepted. *Expenses:* Tuition, state resident: full-time $9692; part-time $539 per credit hour. Tuition, nonresident: full-time $20,168; part-time $1121 per credit hour. Tuition and fees vary according to program and reciprocity agreements. *Faculty research:* Performance, composition, music education, music therapy, music history.

University of Maryland, Baltimore County, Graduate School, College of Arts, Humanities and Social Sciences, Department of Education, Program in Teaching, Baltimore, MD 21250. Offers early childhood education (MAT); elementary education (MAT); secondary education (MAT), including social studies; secondary education (MAT), including art, biology, chemistry, dance, earth/space science, English, foreign language, mathematics, music, physics, theatre. Part-time and evening/weekend programs available. *Faculty:* 24 full-time (18 women), 25 part-time/adjunct (19 women). *Students:* 46 full-time (35 women), 64 part-time (39 women); includes 24 minority (8 Black or African American, non-Hispanic/Latino; 7 Asian, non-Hispanic/Latino; 6

Hispanic/Latino; 1 Native Hawaiian or other Pacific Islander, non-Hispanic/Latino; 2 Two or more races, non-Hispanic/Latino), 4 international. Average age 31. 88 applicants, 57% accepted, 39 enrolled. In 2011, 106 master's awarded. *Degree requirements:* For master's, comprehensive exam (for some programs), thesis (for some programs). *Entrance requirements:* For master's, PRAXIS I or GRE (minimum score of 1000), minimum GPA of 3.0. Additional exam requirements/recommendations for international students: Required—TOEFL. *Application deadline:* For fall admission, 6/1 for domestic students; for spring admission, 11/1 for domestic students. Applications are processed on a rolling basis. Application fee: $50. Electronic applications accepted. *Financial support:* In 2011–12, 6 students received support, including teaching assistantships with full and partial tuition reimbursements available (averaging $12,000 per year); career-related internships or fieldwork, Federal Work-Study, scholarships/grants, tuition waivers, and unspecified assistantships also available. Financial award application deadline: 3/1. *Faculty research:* STEM teacher education, culturally sensitive pedagogy, ESOL/bilingual education, early childhood education, language, literacy and culture. *Unit head:* Dr. Susan M. Blunck, Graduate Program Director, 410-455-2869, Fax: 410-455-3986, E-mail: blunck@umbc.edu. *Application contact:* Cheryl Johnson, 410-455-3388, E-mail: blackwel@umbc.edu. Web site: http://www.umbc.edu/education/.

University of Maryland, College Park, Academic Affairs, College of Arts and Humanities, School of Music, Program in Music, College Park, MD 20742. Offers M Ed, MA, MM, DMA, Ed D, PhD. *Students:* 156 full-time (71 women), 52 part-time (29 women); includes 39 minority (9 Black or African American, non-Hispanic/Latino; 21 Asian, non-Hispanic/Latino; 6 Hispanic/Latino; 3 Two or more races, non-Hispanic/Latino), 24 international. 693 applicants, 20% accepted, 64 enrolled. In 2011, 29 master's, 24 doctorates awarded. *Entrance requirements:* Additional exam requirements/recommendations for international students: Required—TOEFL. *Application deadline:* For fall admission, 12/1 for domestic and international students. Application fee: $75. *Expenses: Tuition, area resident:* Part-time $525 per credit hour. Tuition, state resident: part-time $525 per credit hour. Tuition, nonresident: part-time $1131 per credit hour. *Required fees:* $386.31 per term. Tuition and fees vary according to program. *Financial support:* In 2011–12, 2 fellowships with full and partial tuition reimbursements (averaging $17,900 per year), 111 teaching assistantships (averaging $16,136 per year) were awarded. *Unit head:* Dr. Robert Gibson, Director, 301-405-5554, E-mail: rgibson@umd.edu. *Application contact:* Dr. Charles A. Caramello, Dean of Graduate School, 301-405-0358, Fax: 301-314-9305.

University of Massachusetts Amherst, Graduate School, College of Humanities and Fine Arts, Department of Music and Dance, Amherst, MA 01003. Offers collaborative piano (MM); composition (MM); conducting (MM); jazz composition/arranging (MM); music education (MM); music history (MM); music theory (PhD); performance (MM). *Accreditation:* NASM. Part-time programs available. *Faculty:* 17 full-time (4 women). *Students:* 60 full-time (26 women), 31 part-time (11 women); includes 5 minority (1 Black or African American, non-Hispanic/Latino; 1 Asian, non-Hispanic/Latino; 3 Two or more races, non-Hispanic/Latino), 10 international. Average age 28. 104 applicants, 61% accepted, 27 enrolled. In 2011, 26 master's awarded. Terminal master's awarded for partial completion of doctoral program. *Degree requirements:* For master's, thesis or alternative; for doctorate, comprehensive exam, thesis/dissertation. *Entrance requirements:* For master's and doctorate, placement tests, original scores, research, audition or tape. Additional exam requirements/recommendations for international students: Required—TOEFL (minimum score 550 paper-based; 213 computer-based; 80 iBT), IELTS (minimum score 6.5). *Application deadline:* For fall admission, 1/15 for domestic and international students; for spring admission, 10/1 for domestic and international students. Applications are processed on a rolling basis. Application fee: $50 ($65 for international students). Electronic applications accepted. Tuition and fees vary according to course load, campus/location and program. *Financial support:* Fellowships with full and partial tuition reimbursements, research assistantships, teaching assistantships with full and partial tuition reimbursements, career-related internships or fieldwork, Federal Work-Study, scholarships/grants, traineeships, health care benefits, tuition waivers (full and partial), and unspecified assistantships available. Support available to part-time students. Financial award application deadline: 1/15. *Unit head:* Dr. Jeff Cox, Graduate Program Director, 413-545-0311, Fax: 413-545-2092. *Application contact:* Lindsay DeSantis, Interim Supervisor of Admissions, 413-545-0722, Fax: 413-577-0010, E-mail: gradadm@grad.umass.edu. Web site: http://www.umass.edu/music/.

University of Massachusetts Lowell, College of Fine Arts, Humanities and Social Sciences, Department of Music, Lowell, MA 01854-2881. Offers music education (MM); sound recording technology (MM). *Accreditation:* NASM. Part-time programs available. *Degree requirements:* For master's, one foreign language, thesis. *Entrance requirements:* For master's, MAT, audition. Electronic applications accepted.

University of Memphis, Graduate School, College of Communication and Fine Arts, Rudi E. Scheidt School of Music, Memphis, TN 38152. Offers applied music (M Mu, DMA); composition (M Mu, DMA); conducting (M Mu, DMA); historical musicology (PhD); jazz and studio performance (M Mu); music education (M Mu, DMA); musicology (M Mu). *Accreditation:* NASM. Part-time programs available. Terminal master's awarded for partial completion of doctoral program. *Degree requirements:* For master's, comprehensive exam, thesis or alternative; for doctorate, one foreign language, comprehensive exam, thesis/dissertation, exam. *Entrance requirements:* For master's, GRE General Test or MAT, proficiency exam, audition; for doctorate, GRE General Test or MAT, proficiency exam, audition, master's degree. Additional exam requirements/recommendations for international students: Required—TOEFL. *Faculty research:* Spanish Renaissance, twentieth century music, Project OPTIMUS, composition, musical performance, regional music, performance, performance practice, composition.

University of Miami, Graduate School, Frost School of Music, Department of Music Education and Music Therapy, Coral Gables, FL 33124. Offers music education (MM, PhD, Spec M); music therapy (MM). *Accreditation:* NASM. *Degree requirements:* For master's, thesis; for doctorate, thesis/dissertation, 2 research tools; for Spec M, thesis, research project. *Entrance requirements:* For master's and doctorate, GRE General Test. Additional exam requirements/recommendations for international students: Required—TOEFL (minimum score 550 paper-based; 213 computer-based; 59 iBT). Electronic applications accepted. *Faculty research:* Motivation, quantitative research, early childhood, instrumental music, elementary music.

University of Michigan, Horace H. Rackham School of Graduate Studies, School of Music, Theatre, and Dance, Program in Music Education, Ann Arbor, MI 48109-2085. Offers MM, PhD, Spec M. *Accreditation:* NASM; Teacher Education Accreditation Council. *Degree requirements:* For doctorate, thesis/dissertation, oral and preliminary exams. *Entrance requirements:* For doctorate, MAT, writing sample, portfolio. Additional exam requirements/recommendations for international students: Required—TOEFL (minimum score 600 paper-based; 250 computer-based; 100 iBT). Electronic applications accepted.

University of Minnesota, Duluth, Graduate School, School of Fine Arts, Department of Music, Duluth, MN 55812-2496. Offers music education (MM); performance (MM). *Accreditation:* NASM. Part-time programs available. *Degree requirements:* For master's, comprehensive exam, thesis (for some programs), recital (MM in performance). *Entrance requirements:* For master's, audition, minimum GPA of 3.0, sample of written work, interview, bachelor's degree in music, video of teaching. Additional exam requirements/recommendations for international students: Required—TOEFL (minimum score 550 paper-based; 213 computer-based). *Faculty research:* Band composition, music aesthetics, learning theory, value theory, music advocacy.

University of Missouri, Graduate School, College of Education, Department of Learning, Teaching and Curriculum, Columbia, MO 65211. Offers agricultural education (M Ed, PhD, Ed S); art education (M Ed, PhD, Ed S); business and office education (M Ed, PhD, Ed S); early childhood education (M Ed, PhD, Ed S); elementary education (M Ed, PhD, Ed S); English education (M Ed, PhD, Ed S); foreign language education (M Ed, PhD, Ed S); health education and promotion (M Ed, PhD); learning and instruction (M Ed); marketing education (M Ed, PhD, Ed S); mathematics education (M Ed, PhD, Ed S); music education (M Ed, PhD, Ed S); reading education (M Ed, PhD, Ed S); science education (M Ed, PhD, Ed S); social studies education (M Ed, PhD, Ed S); vocational education (M Ed, PhD, Ed S). Part-time programs available. *Faculty:* 26 full-time (16 women), 3 part-time/adjunct (2 women). *Students:* 184 full-time (145 women), 276 part-time (215 women); includes 34 minority (10 Black or African American, non-Hispanic/Latino; 1 American Indian or Alaska Native, non-Hispanic/Latino; 7 Asian, non-Hispanic/Latino; 8 Hispanic/Latino; 8 Two or more races, non-Hispanic/Latino), 39 international. Average age 32. 309 applicants, 76% accepted, 204 enrolled. In 2011, 232 master's, 8 doctorates, 2 other advanced degrees awarded. Terminal master's awarded for partial completion of doctoral program. *Degree requirements:* For doctorate, thesis/dissertation. *Entrance requirements:* For master's and Ed S, GRE General Test or MAT, minimum GPA of 3.0; for doctorate, GRE General Test, minimum GPA of 3.0. Additional exam requirements/recommendations for international students: Required—TOEFL (minimum score 600 paper-based; 250 computer-based; 100 iBT). Application fee: $55 ($75 for international students). Electronic applications accepted. *Expenses:* Tuition, state resident: full-time $5881. Tuition, nonresident: full-time $15,183. *Required fees:* $952. Tuition and fees vary according to campus/location and program. *Financial support:* Fellowships, research assistantships, teaching assistantships, and institutionally sponsored loans available. *Application contact:* Fran Colley, 573-882-6462, E-mail: colleyf@missouri.edu. Web site: http://education.missouri.edu/LTC/.

University of Missouri–Kansas City, Conservatory of Music, Kansas City, MO 64110-2499. Offers composition (MM, DMA); conducting (MM, DMA); music (MA); music education (MME, PhD); music history and literature (MM); music theory (MM); performance (MM, DMA). PhD (interdisciplinary) offered through the School of Graduate Studies. *Accreditation:* NASM. Part-time programs available. *Faculty:* 53 full-time (23 women), 33 part-time/adjunct (13 women). *Students:* 132 full-time (59 women), 94 part-time (45 women); includes 16 minority (8 Black or African American, non-Hispanic/Latino; 4 Asian, non-Hispanic/Latino; 4 Hispanic/Latino), 49 international. Average age 29. 309 applicants, 24% accepted, 68 enrolled. In 2011, 38 master's, 21 doctorates awarded. *Degree requirements:* For master's, variable foreign language requirement, comprehensive exam, thesis (for some programs); for doctorate, variable foreign language requirement, comprehensive exam, thesis/dissertation or alternative. *Entrance requirements:* For master's, minimum GPA of 3.0 in major, auditions (for MM in performance); for doctorate, minimum graduate GPA of 3.5, auditions (for DMA in performance), portfolio of compositions. Additional exam requirements/recommendations for international students: Required—TOEFL (minimum score 550 paper-based; 213 computer-based; 80 iBT). *Application deadline:* For fall admission, 1/15 priority date for domestic students, 1/15 for international students. Application fee: $45 ($50 for international students). *Expenses:* Tuition, state resident: full-time $5798; part-time $322.10 per credit hour. Tuition, nonresident: full-time $14,969; part-time $831.60 per credit hour. *Required fees:* $93.51 per credit hour. *Financial support:* In 2011–12, 62 teaching assistantships with partial tuition reimbursements (averaging $8,716 per year) were awarded; career-related internships or fieldwork, Federal Work-Study, institutionally sponsored loans, scholarships/grants, tuition waivers (partial), and unspecified assistantships also available. Support available to part-time students. Financial award application deadline: 3/1; financial award applicants required to submit FAFSA. *Faculty research:* Electro-acoustic composition, affective music responses, American music theatre, Russian choral music, music therapy and Alzheimer's. *Unit head:* Peter Witte, Dean, 816-235-2731, Fax: 816-235-5265, E-mail: wittep@umkc.edu. *Application contact:* William Everett, Associate Dean, 816-235-2857, Fax: 816-235-5264, E-mail: everettw@umkc.edu. Web site: http://conservatory.umkc.edu/.

University of Missouri–St. Louis, College of Fine Arts and Communication, Program in Music Education, St. Louis, MO 63121. Offers MME. *Accreditation:* NASM. Part-time and evening/weekend programs available. *Faculty:* 15 full-time (4 women), 7 part-time/adjunct (4 women). *Students:* 16 part-time (11 women); includes 3 minority (2 Black or African American, non-Hispanic/Latino; 1 Two or more races, non-Hispanic/Latino). Average age 31. 6 applicants, 50% accepted, 2 enrolled. In 2011, 7 master's awarded. *Entrance requirements:* For master's, 3 letters of recommendation, BA in music education. Additional exam requirements/recommendations for international students: Required—TOEFL (minimum score 550 paper-based; 213 computer-based). *Application deadline:* For fall admission, 7/1 priority date for domestic students, 7/1 for international students; for spring admission, 12/1 for domestic and international students. Applications are processed on a rolling basis. Application fee: $35 ($40 for international students). Electronic applications accepted. *Expenses:* Tuition, state resident: full-time $6273; part-time $3866 per year. Tuition, nonresident: full-time $14,969; part-time $9980 per year. *Required fees:* $315 per year. *Financial support:* In 2011–12, 1 teaching assistantship with full and partial tuition reimbursement (averaging $9,000 per year) was awarded. Financial award applicants required to submit FAFSA. *Faculty research:* Music technology, musicology, music education methods, history of music education, psychology of music. *Unit head:* Dr. Fred Willman, Director of Graduate Studies, 314-516-5980, Fax: 314-516-6593, E-mail: fred_willman@umsl.edu. *Application contact:* 314-516-5458, Fax: 314-516-6996, E-mail: gradadm@umsl.edu. Web site: http://www.umsl.edu/~umslmusic/.

The University of Montana, Graduate School, College of Visual and Performing Arts, School of Music, Missoula, MT 59812-0002. Offers music (MM), including composition/technology, music education, musical theater, performance. *Accreditation:* NASM. *Entrance requirements:* For master's, GRE General Test, GRE Subject Test, portfolio.

University of Nebraska at Kearney, Graduate Studies, College of Fine Arts and Humanities, Department of Music, Kearney, NE 68849-0001. Offers music education (MA Ed). *Accreditation:* NASM; NCATE. Part-time and evening/weekend programs available. *Degree requirements:* For master's, thesis optional. *Entrance requirements:* For master's, interview/audition, portfolio, letters of recommendation. *Faculty research:* Contemporary American music, musical theatre, opera, woodwind performance and pedagogy.

University of Nebraska–Lincoln, Graduate College, College of Fine and Performing Arts, School of Music, Lincoln, NE 68588. Offers composition (MM, DMA); conducting (MM, DMA); music education (MM, PhD); music history (MM); music theory (MM); performance (MM, DMA); piano pedagogy (MM); woodwind specialties (MM). *Accreditation:* NASM. *Degree requirements:* For master's, thesis optional; for doctorate, comprehensive exam, thesis/dissertation. *Entrance requirements:* For master's and doctorate, audition. Additional exam requirements/recommendations for international students: Required—TOEFL. Electronic applications accepted. *Faculty research:* Mozart, Tchaikovsky, Josquin des Prez, practice of J.S. Bach's organ works, instructional strategies in music education.

University of New Hampshire, Graduate School, College of Liberal Arts, Department of Music, Durham, NH 03824. Offers music education (MA); music studies (MA). *Accreditation:* NASM. *Faculty:* 17 full-time (3 women). *Students:* 5 full-time (3 women), 6 part-time (2 women); includes 1 minority (Hispanic/Latino). Average age 30. 15 applicants, 67% accepted, 5 enrolled. In 2011, 5 master's awarded. *Degree requirements:* For master's, one foreign language. *Entrance requirements:* For master's, audition. Additional exam requirements/recommendations for international students: Required—TOEFL (minimum score 550 paper-based; 213 computer-based; 80 iBT). *Application deadline:* For fall admission, 4/1 priority date for domestic students, 4/1 for international students; for spring admission, 12/1 for domestic students. Applications are processed on a rolling basis. Application fee: $65. Electronic applications accepted. *Expenses:* Tuition, state resident: full-time $12,360; part-time $687 per credit hour. Tuition, nonresident: full-time $25,680; part-time $1058 per credit hour. *International tuition:* $29,550 full-time. *Required fees:* $1666; $833 per course. $416.50 per semester. Tuition and fees vary according to course load and degree level. *Financial support:* In 2011–12, 5 students received support, including 4 teaching assistantships; fellowships, research assistantships, career-related internships or fieldwork, Federal Work-Study, scholarships/grants, and tuition waivers (full and partial) also available. Support available to part-time students. Financial award application deadline: 2/15. *Unit head:* Dr. Nicholas Orovich, Chairperson, 603-862-3247. *Application contact:* Susan Adams, Administrative Assistant, 603-862-2404, E-mail: grad.music@unh.edu. Web site: http://www.unh.edu/music/.

University of New Mexico, Graduate School, College of Fine Arts, Department of Music, Albuquerque, NM 87131-0001. Offers collaborative piano (M Mu); conducting (M Mu); music education (M Mu); music history and literature (M Mu); performance (M Mu); theory and composition (M Mu). *Accreditation:* NASM. Part-time programs available. *Faculty:* 48 full-time (16 women), 24 part-time/adjunct (11 women). *Students:* 37 full-time (14 women), 47 part-time (24 women); includes 14 minority (1 Black or African American, non-Hispanic/Latino; 13 Hispanic/Latino), 11 international. Average age 30. 68 applicants, 62% accepted, 22 enrolled. In 2011, 26 degrees awarded. *Degree requirements:* For master's, variable foreign language requirement, comprehensive exam, thesis (for some programs), recital (for some programs). *Entrance requirements:* For master's, placement exams in music history and theory. Additional exam requirements/recommendations for international students: Required—TOEFL (minimum score 550 paper-based; 213 computer-based). *Application deadline:* For fall admission, 7/1 for domestic students, 5/1 for international students; for spring admission, 11/1 for domestic students, 10/1 for international students. Applications are processed on a rolling basis. Application fee: $50. Electronic applications accepted. *Financial support:* In 2011–12, 74 students received support, including 2 research assistantships (averaging $4,062 per year), 10 teaching assistantships with full and partial tuition reimbursements available (averaging $4,761 per year); Federal Work-Study, scholarships/grants, and unspecified assistantships also available. Support available to part-time students. Financial award application deadline: 2/1; financial award applicants required to submit FAFSA. *Faculty research:* Opera, twentieth century and contemporary music, performance, conducting. *Total annual research expenditures:* $16,650. *Unit head:* Dr. Steven Block, Chair, 505-277-2127, Fax: 505-277-4202, E-mail: sblock@unm.edu. *Application contact:* Colleen M. Sheinberg, Graduate Coordinator, 505-277-8401, Fax: 505-277-4202, E-mail: colleens@unm.edu. Web site: http://music.unm.edu/.

The University of North Carolina at Chapel Hill, Graduate School, School of Education, Program in Secondary Education, Chapel Hill, NC 27599. Offers English (Grades 9-12) (MAT); English as a second language (MAT); French (Grades K-12) (MAT); German (Grades K-12) (MAT); Japanese (Grades K-12) (MAT); Latin (Grades 9-12) (MAT); mathematics (Grades 9-12) (MAT); music (Grades K-12) (MAT); science (Grades 9-12) (MAT); social studies (Grades 9-12) (MAT); Spanish (Grades K-12) (MAT). *Accreditation:* NCATE. *Degree requirements:* For master's, comprehensive exam. *Entrance requirements:* For master's, GRE General Test, minimum GPA of 3.0 during last 2 years of undergraduate course work. Additional exam requirements/recommendations for international students: Required—TOEFL (minimum score 550 paper-based; 79 computer-based). Electronic applications accepted.

The University of North Carolina at Charlotte, Graduate School, College of Education, Department of Middle, Secondary and K-12 Education, Charlotte, NC 28223-0001. Offers art education (MAT); curriculum and instruction (PhD); dance education (MAT); foreign language education (MAT); middle grades education (M Ed, MAT); music education (MAT); secondary education (M Ed, MAT); teaching English as a second language (M Ed); theatre education (MAT). *Faculty:* 18 full-time (9 women), 6 part-time/adjunct (4 women). *Students:* 1 (woman) full-time, 57 part-time (44 women); includes 11 minority (5 Black or African American, non-Hispanic/Latino; 1 American Indian or Alaska Native, non-Hispanic/Latino; 2 Asian, non-Hispanic/Latino; 2 Hispanic/Latino; 1 Two or more races, non-Hispanic/Latino). Average age 33. 19 applicants, 100% accepted, 16 enrolled. In 2011, 12 master's awarded. *Entrance requirements:* For master's, GRE or MAT. Additional exam requirements/recommendations for international students: Required—TOEFL (minimum score 557 paper-based; 220 computer-based; 83 iBT). *Application deadline:* For fall admission, 7/1 for domestic students, 5/1 for international students; for spring admission, 11/1 for domestic students, 10/1 for international students. Applications are processed on a rolling basis. Application fee: $65 ($75 for international students). Electronic applications accepted. *Expenses:* Tuition, state resident: full-time $3689. Tuition, nonresident: full-time $15,226. *Required fees:* $2198. Tuition and fees vary according to course load and program. *Financial support:* In 2011–12, 5 students received support, including 5 research assistantships (averaging $4,290 per year); career-related internships or fieldwork, institutionally sponsored loans, scholarships/grants, and unspecified assistantships also available. Support available to part-time students. Financial award application deadline: 4/1; financial award applicants required to submit FAFSA. *Total annual research expenditures:* $126,589. *Unit head:* Melba Spooner, Chair, 704-687-8704, Fax: 704-687-6430, E-mail: mcspoone@uncc.edu. *Application contact:* Kathy B. Giddings, Director of Graduate Admissions, 704-687-5503, Fax: 704-687-3279, E-mail: gradadm@uncc.edu. Web site: http://education.uncc.edu/mdsk.

The University of North Carolina at Greensboro, Graduate School, School of Music, Theatre and Dance, Greensboro, NC 27412-5001. Offers composition (MM); dance (MA, MFA); education (MM); music education (PhD); performance (MM, DMA); theatre (M Ed, MFA), including acting (MFA), design (MFA), directing (MFA), theatre education (M Ed), theatre for youth (MFA); theory (MM). *Accreditation:* NASM. *Degree requirements:* For master's, variable foreign language requirement, thesis (for some programs), recital; for doctorate, comprehensive exam, thesis/dissertation, diagnostic exam, recital. *Entrance requirements:* For master's, GRE General Test, NTE, audition; for doctorate, GRE General Test, GRE Subject Test (music), audition. Additional exam requirements/recommendations for international students: Required—TOEFL. Electronic applications accepted.

The University of North Carolina at Pembroke, Graduate Studies, Program in Music Education, Pembroke, NC 28372-1510. Offers MA, MAT. *Accreditation:* NASM. *Entrance requirements:* For master's, GRE or MAT, minimum GPA of 3.0 in major, 2.5 overall; audition. Additional exam requirements/recommendations for international students: Required—TOEFL.

University of North Dakota, Graduate School, College of Arts and Sciences, Department of Music, Grand Forks, ND 58202. Offers music (M Mus); music education (M Mus, DMEd). *Accreditation:* NASM. Part-time programs available. *Degree requirements:* For master's, comprehensive exam, thesis or alternative. *Entrance requirements:* For master's, minimum GPA of 3.0. Additional exam requirements/recommendations for international students: Required—TOEFL (minimum score 550 paper-based; 213 computer-based; 79 iBT), IELTS (minimum score 6.5). Electronic applications accepted.

University of Northern Colorado, Graduate School, College of Performing and Visual Arts, School of Music, Greeley, CO 80639. Offers collaborative keyboard (MM); conducting (MM); instrumental performance (MM); jazz studies (MM); music conducting (DA); music education (MM, DA); music history and literature (MM, DA); music performance (DA); music theory and composition (MM, DA); vocal performance (MM). *Accreditation:* NASM; NCATE (one or more programs are accredited). Part-time programs available. *Faculty:* 31 full-time (7 women). *Students:* 90 full-time (37 women), 22 part-time (12 women); includes 14 minority (5 Black or African American, non-Hispanic/Latino; 7 Asian, non-Hispanic/Latino; 2 Hispanic/Latino), 9 international. Average age 29. 87 applicants, 68% accepted, 38 enrolled. In 2011, 22 master's, 3 doctorates awarded. *Degree requirements:* For master's, comprehensive exam, thesis or alternative; for doctorate, comprehensive exam, thesis/dissertation. *Entrance requirements:* For master's, audition; for doctorate, GRE General Test, audition, 3 letters of recommendation. *Application deadline:* Applications are processed on a rolling basis. Application fee: $50 ($60 for international students). Electronic applications accepted. *Financial support:* In 2011–12, 45 research assistantships (averaging $4,649 per year), 22 teaching assistantships (averaging $4,219 per year) were awarded; fellowships and unspecified assistantships also available. Financial award application deadline: 3/1; financial award applicants required to submit FAFSA. *Unit head:* David Caffey, Director, 970-351-2679. *Application contact:* Linda Sisson, Graduate Student Admission Coordinator, 970-351-1807, Fax: 970-351-2371, E-mail: linda.sisson@unco.edu. Web site: http://www.arts.unco.edu/.

University of Northern Iowa, Graduate College, College of Humanities, Arts and Sciences, School of Music, Program in Music Education, Cedar Falls, IA 50614. Offers jazz pedagogy (MM); music education (MM); piano performance and pedagogy (MM). *Accreditation:* NASM. Part-time and evening/weekend programs available. *Students:* 9 full-time (5 women), 11 part-time (7 women), 1 international. 12 applicants, 83% accepted, 6 enrolled. *Degree requirements:* For master's, comprehensive exam, thesis or alternative. *Entrance requirements:* For master's, written diagnostic exam in theory, music history, expository writing skills, and in the area of claimed competency, portfolio, tape recordings of compositions, in person auditions, minimum GPA of 3.0. Additional exam requirements/recommendations for international students: Required—TOEFL (minimum score 500 paper-based; 180 computer-based; 61 iBT). *Application deadline:* For fall admission, 8/1 priority date for domestic students. Applications are processed on a rolling basis. Application fee: $50 ($70 for international students). Electronic applications accepted. *Expenses:* Tuition, state resident: full-time $7476. Tuition, nonresident: full-time $16,410. *Required fees:* $942. *Financial support:* Career-related internships or fieldwork, Federal Work-Study, and tuition waivers (full and partial) available. Support available to part-time students. Financial award application deadline: 2/1. *Unit head:* Dr. Julia Bullard, Coordinator, 319-273-3074, Fax: 319-273-7320, E-mail: julia.bullard@uni.edu. *Application contact:* Laurie S. Russell, Record Analyst, 319-273-2623, Fax: 319-273-2885, E-mail: laurie.russell@uni.edu. Web site: http://www.uni.edu/music/.

University of North Texas, Toulouse Graduate School, College of Music, Denton, TX 76203-5017. Offers composition (MM, DMA); jazz studies (MM); music (MA); music education (MM, MME, PhD); music theory (MM, PhD); musicology (MM, PhD); performance (MM, DMA). *Accreditation:* NASM. Terminal master's awarded for partial completion of doctoral program. *Degree requirements:* For master's, one foreign language, comprehensive exam (for some programs), thesis (for some programs); for doctorate, one foreign language, comprehensive exam (for some programs), thesis/dissertation (for some programs). *Entrance requirements:* For master's and doctorate, audition, writing samples. Additional exam requirements/recommendations for international students: Recommended—TOEFL (minimum score 550 paper-based; 213 computer-based). Electronic applications accepted. *Expenses:* Tuition, state resident: part-time $100 per credit hour. Tuition, nonresident: part-time $413 per credit hour. *Faculty research:* Electro-acoustical music, intermedia, music and medicine, music performance.

University of Oklahoma, Weitzenhoffer Family College of Fine Arts, School of Music, Norman, OK 73019. Offers choral conducting (M Mus, M Mus Ed); conducting (DMA); instrumental conducting (M Mus, M Mus Ed); music composition (M Mus, DMA); music education (M Mus Ed, PhD), including choral or wind instrument conducting (PhD), general (PhD), instrumental (primary) (M Mus Ed), instrumental (secondary) (M Mus Ed), Kodaly concepts, piano pedagogy (PhD), voice pedagogy (M Mus Ed); music theory (M Mus); musicology (M Mus); organ (M Mus, DMA), including performance; piano (M Mus, DMA), including performance, performance and pedagogy; piano pedagogy (M Mus Ed); vocal/general (M Mus Ed); voice (M Mus, DMA), including performance, performance and pedagogy; wind/percussion/string (M Mus, DMA), including performance. *Accreditation:* NASM. *Faculty:* 53 full-time (16 women), 1 part-time/adjunct (0 women). *Students:* 103 full-time (54 women), 65 part-time (33 women); includes 18 minority (4 Black or African American, non-Hispanic/Latino; 2 American Indian or Alaska Native, non-Hispanic/Latino; 4 Asian, non-Hispanic/Latino; 4 Hispanic/Latino; 1 Native Hawaiian or other Pacific Islander, non-Hispanic/Latino; 3 Two or more races, non-Hispanic/Latino), 23 international. Average age 30. 120 applicants, 59% accepted, 43 enrolled. In 2011, 35 master's, 16 doctorates awarded. *Degree requirements:* For master's, variable foreign language requirement, thesis (for some programs), departmental qualifying exam, oral and preliminary exams; for doctorate, variable foreign language requirement, thesis/dissertation, departmental qualifying exam, general and oral exams. *Entrance requirements:* For master's, audition, BA in music, minimum GPA of 3.0; for doctorate, audition, minimum GPA of 3.0. Additional exam requirements/recommendations for international students: Required—TOEFL (minimum score 550 paper-based; 79 iBT). *Application deadline:* For fall admission, 6/1 priority date for domestic students, 3/1 for international students; for spring admission, 11/1 for domestic students, 9/1 for international students. Applications are processed on a rolling basis. Application fee: $40 ($90 for international students). Electronic applications accepted. *Expenses:* Tuition, state resident: full-time $4087; part-time $170.30 per credit hour. Tuition, nonresident: full-time $14,875; part-time $619.80 per credit hour. *Required fees:* $2659; $100.25 per credit hour. Tuition and fees vary according to course load and degree level. *Financial support:* In 2011–12, 125 students received support, including 7 fellowships with full tuition reimbursements available (averaging $5,000 per year), 22 research assistantships with partial tuition reimbursements available (averaging $10,999 per year), 67 teaching assistantships with partial tuition reimbursements available (averaging $10,343 per year); Federal Work-Study, scholarships/grants, and unspecified assistantships also available. Financial award applicants required to submit FAFSA. *Faculty research:* Piano pedagogy, performance practice, music education, early music, non-Western music. *Total annual research expenditures:* $25,455. *Unit head:* Dr. Steven Curtis, Director, 405-325-2081, Fax: 405-325-7574, E-mail: scurtis@ou.edu. *Application contact:* Jan Russell, Office Assistant, 405-325-5393, Fax: 405-325-7574, E-mail: jrussell@ou.edu. Web site: http://music.ou.edu.

University of Oregon, Graduate School, School of Music, Program in Music Education, Eugene, OR 97403. Offers M Mus, DMA, PhD. *Accreditation:* NASM. Part-time programs available. Terminal master's awarded for partial completion of doctoral program. *Degree requirements:* For master's, variable foreign language requirement, thesis (for some programs); for doctorate, one foreign language, comprehensive exam, thesis/dissertation. *Entrance requirements:* For master's, minimum GPA of 3.0, videotape or interview; for doctorate, GRE General Test, minimum GPA of 3.0, videotape or interview. Additional exam requirements/recommendations for international students: Required—TOEFL. *Faculty research:* Psalms of DeLasso, stress and muscular tension in stringed instrument performance, piano music of Stravinsky, learning aptitudes in elementary music.

University of Ottawa, Faculty of Graduate and Postdoctoral Studies, Faculty of Arts, Department of Music, Ottawa, ON K1N 6N5, Canada. Offers music (M Mus, MA); orchestral studies (Certificate); piano pedagogy research (Certificate). *Degree requirements:* For master's, thesis optional. *Entrance requirements:* For master's, honors degree or equivalent, minimum B+ average. Electronic applications accepted. *Faculty research:* Performance, theory, musicology.

University of Rhode Island, Graduate School, College of Arts and Sciences, Department of Music, Kingston, RI 02881. Offers music education (MM); music performance (MM). *Accreditation:* NASM. Part-time programs available. *Faculty:* 13 full-time (5 women). *Students:* 12 full-time (3 women), 10 part-time (2 women); includes 1 minority (Two or more races, non-Hispanic/Latino). In 2011, 3 master's awarded. *Entrance requirements:* For master's, 2 letters of recommendation, audition. Additional exam requirements/recommendations for international students: Required—TOEFL (minimum score 550 paper-based; 213 computer-based). *Application deadline:* For fall admission, 7/15 for domestic students, 2/1 for international students; for spring admission, 7/15 for international students. Application fee: $65. Electronic applications accepted. *Expenses:* Tuition, state resident: full-time $10,432; part-time $580 per credit hour. Tuition, nonresident: full-time $23,130; part-time $1285 per credit hour. *Required fees:* $1362; $36 per credit hour. $35 per semester. One-time fee: $130. *Financial support:* In 2011–12, 3 teaching assistantships with full and partial tuition reimbursements (averaging $6,947 per year) were awarded. Financial award application deadline: 3/15; financial award applicants required to submit FAFSA. *Unit head:* Dr. Joe Parillo, Chair, 401-874-2431, Fax: 401-874-2772, E-mail: jparillo@uri.edu. *Application contact:* Dr. Eliane Aberdam, Co-Director of Graduate Studies, 401-874-2794, Fax: 401-874-2772, E-mail: eliane@uri.edu. Web site: http://www.uri.edu/artsci/mus/.

University of Rhode Island, Graduate School, College of Human Science and Services, School of Education, Kingston, RI 02881. Offers adult education (MA); education (PhD); elementary education (MA); music education (MM); reading education (MA); secondary education (MA); special education (MA); MS/PhD. *Accreditation:* NCATE. Part-time and evening/weekend programs available. *Faculty:* 21 full-time (13 women), 3 part-time/adjunct (1 woman). *Students:* 54 full-time (48 women), 108 part-time (86 women); includes 14 minority (3 Black or African American, non-Hispanic/Latino; 4 Asian, non-Hispanic/Latino; 7 Hispanic/Latino), 4 international. In 2011, 56 master's, 8 doctorates awarded. *Degree requirements:* For master's, comprehensive exam (for some programs), thesis optional; for doctorate, comprehensive exam, thesis/dissertation. *Entrance requirements:* For master's, 2 letters of recommendation; interview (for special education applicants); for doctorate, GRE, 3 letters of recommendation, resume. Additional exam requirements/recommendations for international students: Required—TOEFL (minimum score 600 paper-based; 250 computer-based; 100 iBT). *Application deadline:* For fall admission, 1/31 for international students. Application fee: $65. Electronic applications accepted. *Expenses:* Tuition, state resident: full-time $10,432; part-time $580 per credit hour. Tuition, nonresident: full-time $23,130; part-time $1285 per credit hour. *Required fees:* $1362; $36 per credit hour. $35 per semester. One-time fee: $130. *Financial support:* In 2011–12, 4 teaching assistantships with full and partial tuition reimbursements (averaging $12,157 per year) were awarded; career-related internships or fieldwork also available. Financial award applicants required to submit FAFSA. *Unit head:* Dr. David Byrd, Director, 401-874-5484, Fax: 401-874-5471, E-mail: dbyrd@uri.edu. *Application contact:* Dr. John Boulmetis, Coordinator of Graduate Studies, 401-874-4159, Fax: 401-874-7610, E-mail: johnb@uri.edu. Web site: http://www.uri.edu/hss/education/.

University of Rochester, Eastman School of Music, Programs in Music Education, Rochester, NY 14627. Offers MA, MM, DMA, PhD. *Expenses: Tuition:* Full-time $41,040.

University of St. Thomas, Graduate Studies, College of Arts and Sciences, Graduate Programs in Music Education, St. Paul, MN 55105-1096. Offers choral (MA); instrumental (MA); Kodaly (MA); Orff (MA); piano pedagogy (MA). *Accreditation:* NASM; NCATE. Part-time programs available. *Faculty:* 10 full-time (4 women), 25 part-time/adjunct (13 women). *Students:* 35 part-time (29 women); includes 1 minority (Hispanic/Latino), 2 international. Average age 30. 4 applicants, 100% accepted, 3 enrolled. In 2011, 42 master's awarded. *Degree requirements:* For master's, comprehensive exam, thesis, music history theory and diagnostic exam, piano recital (for piano pedagogy students). *Entrance requirements:* For master's, performance assessment hearing, interview. Additional exam requirements/recommendations for international students: Required—TOEFL (minimum score 550 paper-based; 80 iBT). *Application deadline:* For fall admission, 7/1 priority date for domestic students, 7/1 for international students; for winter admission, 12/1 priority date for domestic students, 12/1 for international students; for spring admission, 4/1 priority date for domestic students, 4/1 for international students. Applications are processed on a rolling basis. Application fee: $50. Electronic applications accepted. Application fee is waived when completed online. *Financial support:* In 2011–12, 8 students received support. Fellowships, research assistantships, teaching assistantships, Federal Work-Study, institutionally sponsored loans, scholarships/grants, and tuition waivers (partial) available. Financial award application deadline: 4/1; financial award applicants required to submit FAFSA. *Faculty research:* Kodaly, choral, piano pedagogy, Orff, instrumental. *Unit head:* Dr. Doug C. Orzolek, Director, 800-328-6819 Ext. 25878, Fax: 651-962-5886, E-mail: dcorzolek@stthomas.edu. *Application contact:* Bev Johnson, Program Coordinator, Graduate Programs in Music Education, 800-328-6819 Ext. 25870, Fax: 651-962-5886, E-mail: bhjohnson@stthomas.edu. Web site: http://www.stthomas.edu/music/graduate.

University of South Carolina, The Graduate School, School of Music, Columbia, SC 29208. Offers composition (MM, DMA); conducting (MM, DMA); jazz studies (MM); music education (MM Ed, PhD); music history (MM); music performance (Certificate); music theory (MM); opera theater (MM); performance (MM, DMA); piano pedagogy (MM, DMA). *Accreditation:* NASM (one or more programs are accredited). Part-time programs available. *Degree requirements:* For master's, 5 foreign languages, comprehensive exam, thesis (for some programs); for doctorate, one foreign language, comprehensive exam, thesis/dissertation; for Certificate, recitals. *Entrance requirements:* For master's and doctorate, GRE General Test or MAT, music diagnostic exam. Additional exam requirements/recommendations for international students: Required—TOEFL (minimum score 570 paper-based; 230 computer-based). Electronic applications accepted. *Expenses:* Contact institution. *Faculty research:* Music skills in pre-school children, evaluation of school performing ensembles.

University of Southern California, Graduate School, Thornton School of Music, Los Angeles, CA 90089. Offers brass performance (MM, DMA, Graduate Certificate); choral and sacred music (MM, DMA); classical guitar (MM, DMA, Graduate Certificate); composition (MM, DMA); early music (MA, DMA); harp performance (MM, DMA, Graduate Certificate); historical musicology (PhD); jazz studies (MM, DMA, Graduate Certificate); keyboard collaborative arts (MM, DMA, Graduate Certificate); music education (MM, DMA); organ performance (MM, DMA, Graduate Certificate); percussion performance (MM, DMA, Graduate Certificate); piano performance (MM, DMA, Graduate Certificate); scoring for motion pictures and television (Graduate Certificate); strings performance (MM, DMA, Graduate Certificate); studio jazz guitar (MM, DMA, Graduate Certificate); teaching music (MA); vocal arts (classical voice/opera) (MM, DMA, Graduate Certificate); woodwind performance (MM, DMA, Graduate Certificate). *Accreditation:* NASM. Part-time and evening/weekend programs available. Terminal master's awarded for partial completion of doctoral program. *Degree requirements:* For master's, variable foreign language requirement, comprehensive exam (for some programs), thesis (for some programs); for doctorate, variable foreign language requirement, comprehensive exam, thesis/dissertation (for some programs). *Entrance requirements:* For master's, GRE (for MA in early music and MM in music education); for doctorate, GRE (for DMA). Additional exam requirements/recommendations for international students: Required—TOEFL (minimum score 560 paper-based; 220 computer-based; 83 iBT). Electronic applications accepted. *Expenses:* Contact institution. *Faculty research:* Early Modern musical improvisation and composition, maternal sound stimulation of the premature infant, physiological characteristics of jazz guitarists, the musical experience of the very young child, electronic music.

University of Southern Mississippi, Graduate School, College of Arts and Letters, School of Music, Hattiesburg, MS 39406-0001. Offers conducting (MM); history and literature (MM); music education (MME, PhD); performance (MM); performance and pedagogy (DMA); theory and composition (MM); woodwind performance (MM). *Accreditation:* NASM. *Faculty:* 33 full-time (10 women), 2 part-time/adjunct (0 women). *Students:* 85 full-time (32 women), 47 part-time (22 women); includes 15 minority (9 Black or African American, non-Hispanic/Latino; 3 Hispanic/Latino; 3 Two or more races, non-Hispanic/Latino), 27 international. Average age 32. 68 applicants, 81% accepted, 45 enrolled. In 2011, 34 master's, 3 doctorates awarded. Terminal master's awarded for partial completion of doctoral program. *Degree requirements:* For master's, comprehensive exam, thesis (for some programs); for doctorate, comprehensive exam, thesis/dissertation. *Entrance requirements:* For master's, GRE General Test, minimum GPA of 2.75 in last 60 hours; for doctorate, GRE General Test, minimum GPA of 3.5. Additional exam requirements/recommendations for international students: Required—TOEFL, IELTS. *Application deadline:* For fall admission, 3/1 priority date for domestic students; for spring admission, 12/13 for domestic students. Applications are processed on a rolling basis. Application fee: $50. *Financial support:* In 2011–12, 1 fellowship with full tuition reimbursement (averaging $12,000 per year), 51 teaching assistantships with full tuition reimbursements (averaging $6,000 per year) were awarded; research assistantships, Federal Work-Study, institutionally sponsored loans, scholarships/grants, health care benefits, tuition waivers (partial), and unspecified assistantships also available. Financial award application deadline: 3/15; financial award applicants required to submit FAFSA. *Faculty research:* Music theory, composition, music performance. *Unit head:* Dr. Michael Miles, Director, 601-266-5543, Fax: 601-266-6427, E-mail: michael.a.miles@usm.edu. *Application contact:* Dr. Jennifer Shank, Director, Graduate Studies, 601-266-5369, Fax: 601-266-6427. Web site: http://www.usm.edu/graduateschool/table.php.

University of South Florida, Graduate School, College of The Arts, School of Music, Tampa, FL 33620-9951. Offers music education (MA, PhD); performance (MM); piano pedagogy (MM); theory (MM). *Accreditation:* NASM. Part-time and evening/weekend programs available. *Faculty:* 30 full-time (8 women), 18 part-time/adjunct (4 women). *Students:* 75 full-time (31 women), 46 part-time (18 women); includes 20 minority (10 Black or African American, non-Hispanic/Latino; 2 Asian, non-Hispanic/Latino; 8 Hispanic/Latino), 14 international. Average age 31. 103 applicants, 67% accepted, 45 enrolled. In 2011, 20 master's, 2 doctorates awarded. *Degree requirements:* For master's, comprehensive exam, thesis optional; for doctorate, comprehensive exam, thesis/dissertation. *Entrance requirements:* For master's, diagnostic exam in theory and history, minimum GPA of 3.0, audition, portfolio, resume, 3 letters of recommendation; two years of teaching experience (music education); for doctorate, GRE, minimum GPA of 3.0, master's degree from accredited institution, video recording of applicant teaching music, personal goals statement, writing sample, curriculum vitae, 3 letters of recommendation. Additional exam requirements/recommendations for international students: Required—TOEFL (minimum score 550 paper-based; 213 computer-based; 79 iBT) or IELTS (minimum score 6.5). *Application deadline:* For fall admission, 2/15 priority date for domestic students, 3/15 for international students; for spring admission, 10/15 for domestic students, 6/1 for international students. Application fee: $30. *Financial support:* In 2011–12, 47 students received support, including 1 research assistantship with tuition reimbursement available (averaging $15,724 per year), 46 teaching assistantships with tuition reimbursements available (averaging $10,099 per year); unspecified assistantships also available. Financial award application deadline: 2/15. *Faculty research:* Education, conducting, performance, history, theory. *Total annual research expenditures:* $7,482. *Unit head:* Josef Knott, Director, 813-974-2311, Fax: 813-974-8721, E-mail: jknott1@usf.edu. *Application contact:* William Hayden, Program Director, 813-974-1753, Fax: 813-974-8721, E-mail: wphayden@usf.edu. Web site: http://music.arts.usf.edu/.

The University of Tennessee, Graduate School, College of Arts and Sciences, School of Music, Knoxville, TN 37996. Offers accompanying (MM); choral conducting (MM); composition (MM); instrumental conducting (MM); jazz (MM); music education (MM); music theory (MM); musicology (MM); performance (MM); piano pedagogy and literature (MM). *Accreditation:* NASM. Part-time programs available. *Degree requirements:* For master's, thesis (for some programs). *Entrance requirements:* For master's, audition, minimum GPA of 2.7. Additional exam requirements/recommendations for international students: Required—TOEFL. Electronic applications accepted. *Expenses:* Tuition, state resident: full-time $8332; part-time $464 per credit hour. Tuition, nonresident: full-time $25,174; part-time $1400 per credit hour. *Required fees:* $1162; $56 per credit hour. Tuition and fees vary according to program.

The University of Tennessee at Chattanooga, Graduate School, College of Arts and Sciences, Department of Music, Chattanooga, TN 37403. Offers music education (MM); performance (MM). *Accreditation:* NASM. Part-time programs available. *Faculty:* 14 full-time (4 women), 1 part-time/adjunct (0 women). *Students:* 2 full-time (both women), 9 part-time (6 women); includes 2 minority (both Black or African American, non-Hispanic/

Latino). Average age 32. 4 applicants, 75% accepted, 2 enrolled. In 2011, 10 master's awarded. *Degree requirements:* For master's, comprehensive exam, thesis or alternative, senior recital. *Entrance requirements:* For master's, GRE General Test or MAT, bachelor's degree in music, audition for placement. Additional exam requirements/ recommendations for international students: Required—TOEFL (minimum score 550 paper-based; 213 computer-based; 79 iBT), IELTS (minimum score 6). *Application deadline:* For fall admission, 8/1 priority date for domestic students, 6/1 for international students; for spring admission, 12/1 priority date for domestic students, 10/1 for international students. Applications are processed on a rolling basis. Application fee: $35. Electronic applications accepted. *Expenses:* Tuition, state resident: full-time $6472; part-time $359 per credit hour. Tuition, nonresident: full-time $20,006; part-time $1111 per credit hour. *Required fees:* $1320; $160 per credit hour. *Financial support:* Research assistantships, Federal Work-Study, scholarships/grants, and unspecified assistantships available. Financial award applicants required to submit FAFSA. *Faculty research:* Music education, conducting, opera, vocal instruction, orchestras. *Unit head:* Dr. Lee Harris, Department Head, 423-425-4601, Fax: 423-425-4603, E-mail: lee-harris@utc.edu. *Application contact:* Dr. Jerald Ainsworth, Dean of Graduate Studies, 423-425-4478, Fax: 423-425-5223, E-mail: jerald-ainsworth@utc.edu. Web site: http://www.utc.edu/Academic/Music/.

The University of Texas at Arlington, Graduate School, College of Liberal Arts, Department of Music, Arlington, TX 76019. Offers education (MM); performance (MM). *Accreditation:* NASM. Part-time and evening/weekend programs available. *Faculty:* 24 full-time (9 women), 1 part-time/adjunct (0 women). *Students:* 18 full-time (8 women), 10 part-time (8 women); includes 6 minority (1 Asian, non-Hispanic/Latino; 5 Hispanic/ Latino), 5 international. 17 applicants, 65% accepted, 9 enrolled. In 2011, 14 degrees awarded. *Degree requirements:* For master's, comprehensive exam, thesis optional. *Entrance requirements:* For master's, GRE, 3 letters of recommendation, minimum GPA of 3.0 in last 60 hours of course work. Additional exam requirements/recommendations for international students: Required—TOEFL (minimum score 550 paper-based; 213 computer-based). *Application deadline:* For fall admission, 6/1 priority date for domestic students. Applications are processed on a rolling basis. Application fee: $35 ($50 for international students). Electronic applications accepted. *Financial support:* In 2011–12, 1 fellowship with full tuition reimbursement (averaging $14,400 per year), 7 teaching assistantships with partial tuition reimbursements (averaging $7,500 per year) were awarded; scholarships/grants also available. *Unit head:* Dr. Rick Bogard, Chair, 817-272-3471, Fax: 817-272-3434, E-mail: bogard@uta.edu. *Application contact:* Dr. Clifton Evans, Graduate Advisor, 817-272-5027, Fax: 817-272-3434, E-mail: cevans@uta.edu. Web site: http://www.uta.edu/music/.

The University of Texas at Austin, Graduate School, College of Fine Arts, Sarah and Ernest Butler School of Music, Austin, TX 78712-1111. Offers band and wind conducting (M Music, DMA); brass/woodwind/percussion (MM, DMA); chamber music (MM); choral conducting (MM, DMA); collaborative piano (MM, DMA); composition (MM, DMA), including composition, jazz, jazz (DMA); ethnomusicology (MM, PhD); literature and pedagogy (MM); music and human learning (MM, DMA, PhD), including jazz (MM, DMA); music and human learning (DMA), including piano pedagogy; musicology (MM, PhD); opera performance (MM, DMA); orchestral conducting (MM, DMA); organ (MM), including sacred music; organ performance (MM, DMA); performance (MM), including jazz (MM, DMA); performance (DMA), including jazz (MM, DMA); piano (DMA), including jazz (MM, DMA); piano literature and pedagogy (MM); piano performance (MM, DMA); string performance (MM, DMA); theory (MM, PhD); vocal performance (MM, DMA); voice (DMA), including opera; voice performance pedagogy (DMA); woodwind, brass, percussion performance (MM). *Accreditation:* NASM. Part-time programs available. *Degree requirements:* For master's, one foreign language, comprehensive exam, thesis (for some programs), recital (performance or composition majors); for doctorate, one foreign language, comprehensive exam, thesis/dissertation (for some programs), recital (for performance or composition majors). *Entrance requirements:* For master's and doctorate, GRE General Test (except for performance or composition majors), audition (performance majors). *Application deadline:* For fall admission, 2/1 priority date for domestic students; for spring admission, 10/1 for domestic students. Applications are processed on a rolling basis. Application fee: $50 ($75 for international students). Electronic applications accepted. *Financial support:* Fellowships with partial tuition reimbursements, teaching assistantships with partial tuition reimbursements, scholarships/grants, tuition waivers (partial), unspecified assistantships, and assistant instructorships available. Financial award application deadline: 2/1. *Unit head:* Glenn Richter, Interim Director, 512-232-2093, E-mail: garichterut@mail.utexas.edu. *Application contact:* Dr. John M. Geringer, Graduate Adviser, 512-232-2066, Fax: 512-232-6289, E-mail: gradad@mail.music.utexas.edu. Web site: http://www.utexas.edu/cofa/music/index.html.

The University of Texas at El Paso, Graduate School, College of Liberal Arts, Department of Music, El Paso, TX 79968-0001. Offers music education (MM); music performance (MM). *Accreditation:* NASM. Part-time and evening/weekend programs available. *Students:* 20 (8 women); includes 12 minority (all Hispanic/Latino), 3 international. Average age 34. 14 applicants, 86% accepted, 11 enrolled. In 2011, 1 master's awarded. *Degree requirements:* For master's, thesis optional. *Entrance requirements:* For master's, audition, interview, letters of recommendation. Additional exam requirements/recommendations for international students: Required—TOEFL; Recommended—IELTS. *Application deadline:* For fall admission, 8/1 priority date for domestic students, 3/1 for international students; for spring admission, 11/1 priority date for domestic students, 9/1 for international students. Applications are processed on a rolling basis. Application fee: $45 ($80 for international students). Electronic applications accepted. *Financial support:* In 2011–12, research assistantships (averaging $18,625 per year), teaching assistantships with partial tuition reimbursements (averaging $14,900 per year) were awarded; fellowships with partial tuition reimbursements, institutionally sponsored loans, scholarships/grants, health care benefits, tuition waivers (partial), and unspecified assistantships also available. Support available to part-time students. Financial award application deadline: 3/15; financial award applicants required to submit FAFSA. *Unit head:* Dr. Lowell Graham, Chair, 915-747-5606, Fax: 915-747-5023, E-mail: legraham@utep.edu. *Application contact:* Dr. Benjamin Flores, Interim Dean of the Graduate School, 915-747-5491, Fax: 915-747-5788, E-mail: bflores@utep.edu.

The University of Texas–Pan American, College of Arts and Humanities, Department of Music, Edinburg, TX 78539. Offers ethnomusicology (M Mus); interdisciplinary studies (MAIS); music education (M Mus); performance (M Mus). *Accreditation:* NASM. Part-time programs available. *Degree requirements:* For master's, comprehensive exam, thesis optional, recital (performance). *Entrance requirements:* For master's, audition for performance area, bachelor's degree in music. *Application deadline:* For fall admission, 7/30 priority date for domestic students; for spring admission, 10/31 for domestic students. Applications are processed on a rolling basis. Application fee: $35. Tuition and fees vary according to course load, program and student level. *Faculty research:* Music history, instrumental pedagogy, vocal pedagogy, music education, ethnomusicology. *Unit head:* Dr. Pedro Martinez, Chair, 956-665-5341, E-mail: martinezp@utpa.edu. *Application contact:* Dr. Wendell R. Davis, Associate Professor, 956-381-3473, Fax: 956-381-3472, E-mail: davisw@panam.edu. Web site: http://portal.utpa.edu/utpa_main/daa_home/coah_home/music_home.

The University of the Arts, College of Performing Arts, School of Music, Division of Music Education, Philadelphia, PA 19102-4944. Offers MAT, MM. MM program offered in conjunction with Villanova University's Summer Music Studies program with summer enrollment only and priority application date of January 1. *Accreditation:* NASM. *Degree requirements:* For master's, student teaching (for MAT); thesis/project (for MM). *Entrance requirements:* For master's, official transcripts, three letters of recommendation, one- to two-page statement, personal interview, undergraduate degree with minimum cumulative GPA of 3.0, DVD/CD or link to uploaded film on YouTube or related site (or VHS video tape for MM), live or taped performance audition (for MAT). Additional exam requirements/recommendations for international students: Required—TOEFL (minimum score 580 paper-based, 92 iBT) or IELTS (minimum score 6.5).

University of the Pacific, Conservatory of Music, Stockton, CA 95211-0197. Offers music education (MM); music therapy (MA). *Accreditation:* NASM. *Faculty:* 3 full-time (2 women), 3 part-time/adjunct (2 women). *Students:* 9 full-time (7 women), 14 part-time (8 women); includes 4 minority (1 Black or African American, non-Hispanic/Latino; 3 Asian, non-Hispanic/Latino), 3 international. Average age 30. 33 applicants, 39% accepted, 7 enrolled. In 2011, 3 master's awarded. *Entrance requirements:* For master's, GRE General Test. Additional exam requirements/recommendations for international students: Required—TOEFL (minimum score 475 paper-based; 150 computer-based). *Application deadline:* For fall admission, 3/1 priority date for domestic students; for spring admission, 10/1 priority date for domestic students. Applications are processed on a rolling basis. Application fee: $75. *Expenses: Tuition:* Full-time $18,900; part-time $1181 per unit. *Required fees:* $949. *Financial support:* Teaching assistantships and institutionally sponsored loans available. Support available to part-time students. Financial award application deadline: 3/1; financial award applicants required to submit FAFSA. *Unit head:* Dr. Giulio Ongaro, Dean, 209-946-2417. *Application contact:* Dr. Therese West, Chairperson, 209-946-3194.

The University of Toledo, College of Graduate Studies, Judith Herb College of Education, Health Science and Human Service, Department of Curriculum and Instruction, Toledo, OH 43606-3390. Offers art education (ME); career and technical education (ME); curriculum and instruction (ME, PhD, Ed S); education and anthropology (MAE); education and biology (MES); education and chemistry (MES); education and classics (MAE); education and economics (MAE); education and English (MAE); education and French (MAE); education and geography (MAE); education and geology (MES); education and German (MAE); education and history (MAE); education and mathematics (MAE, MES); education and physics (MES); education and political science (MAE); education and sociology (MAE); education and Spanish (MAE); educational media (PhD); educational technology (ME); English as a second language (MAE); gifted and talented (PhD); middle childhood education licensure (ME); music education (MME); secondary education (PhD); secondary education licensure (ME). *Accreditation:* NCATE. Part-time and evening/weekend programs available. *Faculty:* 24. *Students:* 60 full-time (31 women), 211 part-time (161 women); includes 23 minority (21 Black or African American, non-Hispanic/Latino; 2 Hispanic/Latino), 20 international. Average age 35. 115 applicants, 73% accepted, 74 enrolled. In 2011, 105 master's, 3 doctorates, 4 other advanced degrees awarded. *Degree requirements:* For master's, comprehensive exam, thesis or alternative; for doctorate, comprehensive exam, thesis/ dissertation; for Ed S, thesis optional. *Entrance requirements:* For master's, doctorate, and Ed S, minimum cumulative GPA of 2.7 for all previous academic work, letters of recommendation. Additional exam requirements/recommendations for international students: Required—TOEFL (minimum score 550 paper-based; 213 computer-based; 80 iBT), IELTS (minimum score 6.5). *Application deadline:* For fall admission, 1/15 priority date for domestic students, 1/15 for international students. Applications are processed on a rolling basis. Application fee: $45 ($75 for international students). Electronic applications accepted. *Financial support:* In 2011–12, 9 research assistantships with full and partial tuition reimbursements (averaging $7,184 per year), 12 teaching assistantships with full and partial tuition reimbursements (averaging $8,425 per year) were awarded; career-related internships or fieldwork, Federal Work-Study, institutionally sponsored loans, scholarships/grants, tuition waivers (full and partial), unspecified assistantships, and administrative assistantships also available. Support available to part-time students. *Unit head:* Dr. Leigh Chiarelott, Chair, 419-530-5371, E-mail: eigh.chiarelott@utoledo.edu. *Application contact:* Graduate School Office, 419-530-4723, Fax: 419-530-4724, E-mail: grdsch@utnet.utoledo.edu. Web site: http://www.utoledo.edu/eduhshs/.

University of Toronto, School of Graduate Studies, Faculty of Music, Toronto, ON M5S 1A1, Canada. Offers composition (M Mus, DMA); music education (MA, PhD); musicology/theory (MA, PhD); performance (M Mus, DMA). Part-time programs available. *Degree requirements:* For master's, comprehensive exam (for some programs), oral examination (M Mus in composition), 1 foreign language (MA); for doctorate, recital of original works (DMA), thesis (PhD). *Entrance requirements:* For master's, BM in area of specialization with minimum B average in final 2 years, original compositions (M Mus in composition); for doctorate, master's degree in area of specialization, minimum B+ average, at least 2 extended compositions (DMA). Additional exam requirements/recommendations for international students: Required—TOEFL (minimum score 580 paper-based; 93 iBT), TWE (minimum score 5). Electronic applications accepted.

University of Victoria, Faculty of Graduate Studies, Faculty of Education, Department of Curriculum and Instruction, Victoria, BC V8W 2Y2, Canada. Offers art education (M Ed, PhD); curriculum studies (M Ed, MA, PhD); early childhood education (M Ed, PhD); educational studies (PhD); language and literacy (M Ed, MA, PhD); mathematics (M Ed, MA, PhD); music education (M Ed, MA, PhD); science (M Ed, MA, PhD); social studies (M Ed, MA); social, cultural and foundational studies (MA, PhD); technology and environmental education (PhD). Part-time programs available. *Degree requirements:* For master's, thesis, project (M Ed); for doctorate, comprehensive exam, thesis/ dissertation. *Entrance requirements:* For master's, minimum B average. Additional exam requirements/recommendations for international students: Required—TOEFL (minimum score 575 paper-based; 233 computer-based), IELTS (minimum score 7). Electronic applications accepted. *Faculty research:* Elementary and secondary English, language arts, curriculum theory and practice, educational media and technology, educational administration and leadership, history and philosophy of education.

University of Washington, Graduate School, College of Arts and Sciences, School of Music, Concentration in Music Education, Seattle, WA 98195. Offers MA, PhD. *Accreditation:* NASM. *Degree requirements:* For doctorate, thesis/dissertation. *Entrance requirements:* For master's, GRE General Test, GRE Subject Test, minimum GPA of 3.0; for doctorate, GRE General Test, GRE Subject Test, minimum GPA of 3.0, sample of scholarly writing, videotape of teaching, 1 year of teaching experience. Additional exam requirements/recommendations for international students: Required—TOEFL. Electronic applications accepted. *Faculty research:* Multiethnic issues in music instruction, affective responses to music.

University of West Georgia, College of Arts and Humanities, Department of Music, Carrollton, GA 30118. Offers music education (M Mus); performance (M Mus). *Accreditation:* NASM. Part-time programs available. *Faculty:* 9 full-time (3 women), 5 part-time/adjunct (4 women). *Students:* 4 full-time (all women), 9 part-time (1 woman);

includes 6 minority (5 Black or African American, non-Hispanic/Latino; 1 Asian, non-Hispanic/Latino). Average age 35. 8 applicants, 75% accepted, 4 enrolled. In 2011, 3 master's awarded. *Degree requirements:* For master's, comprehensive exam, thesis optional, recital (MM in performance), departmental qualifying exam. *Entrance requirements:* For master's, qualifying exam, minimum GPA of 2.5, bachelor's degree in music education or teacher certification (music education), performance evaluation. Additional exam requirements/recommendations for international students: Required—TOEFL (minimum score 523 paper-based; 193 computer-based; 69 iBT); Recommended—IELTS (minimum score 6). *Application deadline:* For fall admission, 8/1 for domestic students, 6/1 for international students; for spring admission, 11/15 for domestic students, 10/15 for international students. Applications are processed on a rolling basis. Application fee: $30. Electronic applications accepted. *Expenses:* Tuition, state resident: full-time $4336; part-time $181 per credit hour. Tuition, nonresident: full-time $17,362; part-time $724 per credit hour. Tuition and fees vary according to course load, degree level, campus/location and program. *Financial support:* In 2011–12, 1 student received support, including 1 research assistantship with full tuition reimbursement available (averaging $6,000 per year); career-related internships or fieldwork, tuition waivers (full), and unspecified assistantships also available. Support available to part-time students. Financial award application deadline: 7/1; financial award applicants required to submit FAFSA. *Faculty research:* Musicology, instrumental music/music education, jazz performance, French music. *Unit head:* Dr. Kevin Hibbard, Chair, 678-839-6516, Fax: 678-839-6259, E-mail: khibbard@westga.edu. *Application contact:* Chantrice Copeland, Graduate Studies Associate, 678-839-5453, E-mail: ccopelan@westga.edu. Web site: http://www.westga.edu/music.

University of Wisconsin–Madison, Graduate School, College of Letters and Science, School of Music, Program in Music Education, Madison, WI 53706-1380. Offers curriculum and instruction (MS, PhD); music education (MM). *Accreditation:* NASM. *Degree requirements:* For doctorate, 2 foreign languages, thesis/dissertation. *Entrance requirements:* For doctorate, GRE General Test. *Expenses:* Tuition, state resident: full-time $10,296; part-time $643.51 per credit. Tuition, nonresident: full-time $24,054; part-time $1503.40 per credit. *Required fees:* $70.06 per credit. Tuition and fees vary according to course load, campus/location, program and reciprocity agreements.

University of Wisconsin–Madison, Graduate School, School of Education, Department of Curriculum and Instruction, Madison, WI 53706-1380. Offers art education (MA); curriculum and instruction (MS, PhD); education and mathematics (MA); French education (MA); German education (MA); music education (MS); science education (MS); Spanish education (MA). *Accreditation:* NASM (one or more programs are accredited). *Degree requirements:* For doctorate, thesis/dissertation. Application fee: $56. *Expenses:* Tuition, state resident: full-time $10,296; part-time $643.51 per credit. Tuition, nonresident: full-time $24,054; part-time $1503.40 per credit. *Required fees:* $70.06 per credit. Tuition and fees vary according to course load, campus/location, program and reciprocity agreements. *Financial support:* Project assistantships available. *Unit head:* Dr. John Rudolph, Chair, 608-263-4600, E-mail: jlrudolp@wisc.edu. *Application contact:* 608-262-2433, Fax: 608-262-5134, E-mail: gradadmiss@mail.bascom.wisc.edu. Web site: http://www.education.wisc.edu/ci.

University of Wisconsin–Milwaukee, Graduate School, Peck School of the Arts, Department of Music, Milwaukee, WI 53201-0413. Offers chamber music performance (Certificate); music composition (MM); music education (MM); music history and literature (MM); opera and vocal arts (Certificate); string pedagogy (MM); MLIS/MM. *Accreditation:* NASM. Part-time programs available. *Faculty:* 16 full-time (5 women). *Students:* 51 full-time (30 women), 12 part-time (5 women); includes 8 minority (4 Asian, non-Hispanic/Latino; 4 Two or more races, non-Hispanic/Latino), 8 international. Average age 29. 64 applicants, 64% accepted, 23 enrolled. In 2011, 26 degrees awarded. *Degree requirements:* For master's, variable foreign language requirement, comprehensive exam, thesis or alternative. *Entrance requirements:* For master's, GRE General Test, GRE Subject Test, audition, interview. Additional exam requirements/recommendations for international students: Required—TOEFL (minimum score 550 paper-based; 79 iBT), IELTS (minimum score 6.5). *Application deadline:* For fall admission, 1/1 priority date for domestic students; for spring admission, 9/1 for domestic students. Applications are processed on a rolling basis. Application fee: $56 ($96 for international students). Electronic applications accepted. *Expenses:* Contact institution. *Financial support:* In 2011–12, 14 teaching assistantships were awarded; fellowships, career-related internships or fieldwork, health care benefits, unspecified assistantships, and project assistantships also available. Support available to part-time students. Financial award application deadline: 4/15. *Unit head:* Jon Wellstead, Department Chair, 414-229-5163, E-mail: jonw@uwm.edu. *Application contact:* General Information Contact, 414-229-4982, Fax: 414-229-6967, E-mail: gradschool@uwm.edu. Web site: http://www.uwm.edu/SOA/Music/.

University of Wisconsin–Stevens Point, College of Fine Arts and Communication, Department of Music, Stevens Point, WI 54481-3897. Offers MM Ed. *Accreditation:* NASM. Part-time programs available. *Degree requirements:* For master's, thesis or alternative. *Entrance requirements:* For master's, teaching certificate. *Faculty research:* Music education, music composition, music performance.

University of Wyoming, College of Arts and Sciences, Department of Music, Laramie, WY 82070. Offers music education (MME); performance (MM). *Accreditation:* NASM. *Degree requirements:* For master's, comprehensive exam, thesis or alternative. *Entrance requirements:* For master's, minimum GPA of 3.0. Additional exam requirements/recommendations for international students: Required—TOEFL (minimum score 540 paper-based; 207 computer-based). Electronic applications accepted.

VanderCook College of Music, Master of Music Education Program, Chicago, IL 60616-3731. Offers MM Ed. Offered during summer only. *Accreditation:* NASM. Part-time programs available. *Faculty:* 12 full-time (7 women), 66 part-time/adjunct (21 women). *Students:* 142 full-time (75 women), 49 part-time (28 women); includes 19 minority (14 Black or African American, non-Hispanic/Latino; 4 Hispanic/Latino; 1 Two or more races, non-Hispanic/Latino). Average age 27. 76 applicants, 87% accepted, 64 enrolled. In 2011, 53 master's awarded. *Degree requirements:* For master's, thesis, written comprehensive exam or professional teaching portfolio. *Entrance requirements:* For master's, minimum of one year of teaching experience, or its equivalent, in music; official transcripts; 3 letters of recommendation; minimum undergraduate GPA of 3.0. Additional exam requirements/recommendations for international students: Required—TOEFL (minimum score 500 paper-based; 173 computer-based; 70 iBT). *Application deadline:* For fall admission, 4/1 for domestic and international students; for spring admission, 11/1 for domestic and international students. Applications are processed on a rolling basis. Application fee: $50. *Expenses: Tuition:* Full-time $5520; part-time $460 per semester hour. *Required fees:* $500 per term. *Financial support:* In 2011–12, 26 students received support. Unspecified assistantships available. Financial award application deadline: 5/1; financial award applicants required to submit FAFSA. *Unit head:* Ruth Rhodes, Dean of Graduate Studies, 312-225-6288 Ext. 231, Fax: 312-225-5211, E-mail: rrhodes@vandercook.edu. *Application contact:* Amy Lenting, Director of Admissions, 312-225-6288 Ext. 230, Fax: 312-225-5211, E-mail: admissions@vandercook.edu. Web site: http://www.vandercook.edu/prospective/graduate.asp.

Virginia Commonwealth University, Graduate School, School of the Arts, Department of Music, Richmond, VA 23284-9005. Offers education (MM). *Accreditation:* NASM. *Degree requirements:* For master's, departmental qualifying exam, recital. *Entrance requirements:* For master's, department examination, audition or tapes, portfolio. Additional exam requirements/recommendations for international students: Required—TOEFL (minimum score 600 paper-based; 250 computer-based; 100 iBT). Electronic applications accepted. *Expenses:* Tuition, state resident: full-time $9133; part-time $507 per credit. Tuition, nonresident: full-time $18,777; part-time $1043 per credit. *Required fees:* $77 per credit. Tuition and fees vary according to degree level, campus/location, program and student level. *Faculty research:* Composition, conducting, education, performance.

Washington State University, Graduate School, College of Liberal Arts, School of Music and Theatre Arts, Pullman, WA 99164. Offers composition (MA); jazz (MA); music (MA); music education (MA); performance (MA). *Accreditation:* NASM. *Students:* 16 full-time (9 women), 2 part-time (1 woman); includes 2 minority (1 American Indian or Alaska Native, non-Hispanic/Latino; 1 Hispanic/Latino), 3 international. Average age 27. 20 applicants, 70% accepted, 6 enrolled. In 2011, 3 master's awarded. *Degree requirements:* For master's, comprehensive exam (for some programs), thesis (for some programs), oral exam. *Entrance requirements:* For master's, audition, minimum GPA of 3.0, 3 letters of recommendation, composition portfolio and recording (composition), writing sample and written philosophy (music education), writing sample (music history), in-depth audition (performance). Additional exam requirements/recommendations for international students: Required—TOEFL, IELTS. *Application deadline:* For fall admission, 1/10 priority date for domestic students, 1/10 for international students; for spring admission, 7/1 for domestic and international students. Applications are processed on a rolling basis. Application fee: $75. Electronic applications accepted. *Financial support:* Fellowships, research assistantships, teaching assistantships with full and partial tuition reimbursements, career-related internships or fieldwork, Federal Work-Study, institutionally sponsored loans, and tuition waivers (partial) available. Financial award application deadline: 2/15; financial award applicants required to submit FAFSA. *Unit head:* Dr. Gregory W. Yasinitsky, Director, 509-335-4244, Fax: 509-335-4245, E-mail: yasinits@wsu.edu. *Application contact:* Graduate School Admissions, 800-GRAD-WSU, Fax: 509-335-1949, E-mail: gradsch@wsu.edu. Web site: http://libarts.wsu.edu/musicandtheatre/.

Wayne State College, School of Education and Counseling, Department of Educational Foundations and Leadership, Program in Curriculum and Instruction, Wayne, NE 68787. Offers alternative education (MSE); business and information technology education (MSE); communication arts education (MSE); early childhood education (MSE); elementary education (MSE); English as a second language (MSE); English education (MSE); family and consumer sciences education (MSE); industrial technology and vocational education (MSE); learning communities (MSE); mathematics education (MSE); music education (MSE); science education (MSE); social science education (MSE). *Accreditation:* NCATE. Part-time and evening/weekend programs available. *Degree requirements:* For master's, comprehensive exam, thesis optional. *Entrance requirements:* For master's, GRE General Test. Additional exam requirements/recommendations for international students: Required—TOEFL (minimum score 550 paper-based; 213 computer-based).

Wayne State University, College of Fine, Performing and Communication Arts, Department of Music, Detroit, MI 48202. Offers composition/theory (MM); conducting (MM); jazz performance (MM); music (MA); music education (MM); orchestral studies (Certificate); performance (MM). *Accreditation:* NASM. *Students:* 15 full-time (5 women), 14 part-time (4 women); includes 2 minority (1 Black or African American, non-Hispanic/Latino; 1 American Indian or Alaska Native, non-Hispanic/Latino), 4 international. Average age 33. 28 applicants, 39% accepted, 5 enrolled. In 2011, 5 master's, 1 other advanced degree awarded. *Degree requirements:* For master's, thesis (for some programs), oral examination (for some programs). *Entrance requirements:* For master's, audition, interview; for Certificate, BM with concentration in instrumental performance or its equivalent, audition. Additional exam requirements/recommendations for international students: Required—TOEFL (minimum score 550 paper-based; 213 computer-based); Recommended—TWE (minimum score 5.5). *Application deadline:* For fall admission, 1/1 priority date for domestic students, 1/1 for international students. Applications are processed on a rolling basis. Application fee: $50. Electronic applications accepted. *Expenses:* Tuition, state resident: part-time $512.85 per credit. Tuition, nonresident: part-time $1132.65 per credit. *Required fees:* $26.60 per credit. $199.65 per semester. Tuition and fees vary according to course load and program. *Financial support:* In 2011–12, 18 students received support. Research assistantships with tuition reimbursements available, teaching assistantships with tuition reimbursements available, career-related internships or fieldwork, Federal Work-Study, institutionally sponsored loans, scholarships/grants, and unspecified assistantships available. Support available to part-time students. Financial award application deadline: 2/1. *Faculty research:* Teacher training, pedagogy, musicology, composition/theory, conducting/performance practice. *Unit head:* Dr. John Van Der Weg, Chair, 313-577-1795, E-mail: jdvw@wayne.edu. *Application contact:* Dr. Mary Wischusen, Graduate Officer, 313-577-2612, E-mail: aa2188@wayne.edu. Web site: http://music.wayne.edu/.

Webster University, Leigh Gerdine College of Fine Arts, Department of Music, St. Louis, MO 63119-3194. Offers church music (MM); composition (MM); conducting (MM); jazz studies (MM); music (MA); music education (MM); performance (MM); piano (MM). *Accreditation:* NASM. *Entrance requirements:* Additional exam requirements/recommendations for international students: Required—TOEFL. *Expenses: Tuition:* Full-time $10,890; part-time $605 per credit hour. Tuition and fees vary according to campus/location and program.

West Chester University of Pennsylvania, College of Visual and Performing Arts, Department of Applied Music, West Chester, PA 19383. Offers performance (MM); piano pedagogy (MM, Certificate). Part-time and evening/weekend programs available. *Faculty:* 17 part-time/adjunct (3 women). *Students:* 12 full-time (5 women), 15 part-time (8 women); includes 2 minority (both Asian, non-Hispanic/Latino), 4 international. Average age 29. 17 applicants, 59% accepted, 8 enrolled. In 2011, 1 degree awarded. *Degree requirements:* For master's, comprehensive exam, thesis optional, recital. *Entrance requirements:* For master's and Certificate, GRE General Test, School of Music Graduate Admission Test (GAT), audition, interview. Additional exam requirements/recommendations for international students: Required—TOEFL (minimum score 550 paper-based; 213 computer-based; 80 iBT). *Application deadline:* For fall admission, 4/15 priority date for domestic students, 3/15 for international students; for spring admission, 10/15 priority date for domestic students, 9/1 for international students. Applications are processed on a rolling basis. Application fee: $45. Electronic applications accepted. *Expenses:* Tuition, state resident: full-time $7488; part-time $416 per credit. Tuition, nonresident: full-time $11,232; part-time $624 per credit. *Required fees:* $1784.64; $67.59 per credit. Tuition and fees vary according to program. *Financial support:* Unspecified assistantships available. Support available to part-time students. Financial award application deadline: 2/15; financial award applicants required to submit FAFSA. *Unit head:* Dr. Chris Hanning, Chair, 610-436-4178, Fax: 610-436-2873, E-mail: channing@wcupa.edu. *Application contact:* Dr. J. Bryan Burton, Graduate Coordinator, 610-436-2222, Fax: 610-436-2873, E-mail: jburton@wcupa.edu. Web site: http://www.wcupa.edu/CVPA/som/app_music.html.

Music Education

West Chester University of Pennsylvania, College of Visual and Performing Arts, Department of Music Education, West Chester, PA 19383. Offers Kodaly methodology (Certificate); music education (Teaching Certificate); music technology (Certificate); Orff-Schulwerk (Certificate); performance (MM); research (MM); technology (MM). *Accreditation:* NASM; NCATE. Part-time and evening/weekend programs available. *Faculty:* 2 part-time/adjunct (0 women). *Students:* 3 full-time (2 women), 26 part-time (11 women). Average age 29. 17 applicants, 82% accepted, 4 enrolled. In 2011, 10 master's, 1 Certificate awarded. *Degree requirements:* For master's, comprehensive exam, thesis optional, recital. *Entrance requirements:* For master's and other advanced degree, GRE General Test, School of Music Graduate Admission Test (GAT), audition, interview. Additional exam requirements/recommendations for international students: Required—TOEFL (minimum score 550 paper-based; 213 computer-based; 80 iBT). *Application deadline:* For fall admission, 4/15 priority date for domestic students, 3/15 for international students; for spring admission, 10/15 priority date for domestic students, 9/1 for international students. Applications are processed on a rolling basis. Application fee: $45. Electronic applications accepted. *Expenses:* Tuition, state resident: full-time $7488; part-time $416 per credit. Tuition, nonresident: full-time $11,232; part-time $624 per credit. *Required fees:* $1784.64; $67.59 per credit. Tuition and fees vary according to program. *Financial support:* Unspecified assistantships available. Support available to part-time students. Financial award application deadline: 2/15; financial award applicants required to submit FAFSA. *Faculty research:* Developing music listening skills. *Unit head:* Dr. J. Bryan Burton, Chair and Graduate Coordinator, 610-436-2222, Fax: 610-436-2873, E-mail: jburton@wcupa.edu. Web site: http://www.wcupa.edu/CVPA/som/music_ed.html.

Western Connecticut State University, Division of Graduate Studies, School of Visual and Performing Arts, Music Department, Danbury, CT 06810-6885. Offers music education (MS). *Accreditation:* NASM. Part-time programs available. *Students:* 13 part-time (5 women). Average age 28. In 2011, 10 master's awarded. *Degree requirements:* For master's, thesis or comprehensive exam, completion of program within 6 years. *Entrance requirements:* For master's, minimum GPA of 2.8, teaching certificate. Additional exam requirements/recommendations for international students: Recommended—TOEFL (minimum score 550 paper-based; 213 computer-based; 79 iBT), IELTS (minimum score 6). *Application deadline:* For fall admission, 8/5 priority date for domestic students; for spring admission, 1/5 for domestic students. Applications are processed on a rolling basis. Application fee: $50. Tuition and fees vary according to course level, course load, degree level and program. *Financial support:* Application deadline: 5/1; applicants required to submit FAFSA. *Faculty research:* Ear training. *Unit head:* Dr. Kevin Isaacs, Graduate Coordinator, 203-837-8355, Fax: 203-837-8630, E-mail: isaacsk@wcsu.edu. *Application contact:* Chris Shankle, Associate Director of Graduate Studies, 203-837-9005, Fax: 203-837-8326, E-mail: shanklec@wcsu.edu.

Western Kentucky University, Graduate Studies, Potter College of Arts and Letters, Department of Music, Bowling Green, KY 42101. Offers MA Ed. *Accreditation:* NASM; NCATE. Part-time and evening/weekend programs available. *Degree requirements:* For master's, comprehensive exam, written exam. *Entrance requirements:* For master's, GRE General Test, minimum GPA of 3.0. Additional exam requirements/recommendations for international students: Required—TOEFL (minimum score 555 paper-based; 213 computer-based; 79 iBT). *Faculty research:* Music education, music technology, performance.

Western Michigan University, Graduate College, College of Fine Arts, School of Music, Kalamazoo, MI 49008. Offers composition (MM); conducting (MM); music (MA); music education (MM); music therapy (MM); performance (MM). *Accreditation:* NASM.

West Virginia University, College of Creative Arts, Division of Music, Morgantown, WV 26506. Offers music composition (MM, DMA); music education (MM, PhD); music history (MM); music performance (MM, DMA); music theory (MM). *Accreditation:* NASM. *Degree requirements:* For master's, comprehensive exam, thesis (for some programs), recitals; for doctorate, variable foreign language requirement, comprehensive exam, thesis/dissertation, recitals (DMA). *Entrance requirements:* For master's, GRE General Test (music history), minimum GPA of 3.0, audition; for doctorate, GRE General Test (music education), minimum GPA of 3.0, audition. Additional exam requirements/recommendations for international students: Required—TOEFL. *Faculty research:* Jazz history, seventeenth century French court music, nineteenth century composition theory.

Wichita State University, Graduate School, College of Fine Arts, School of Music, Wichita, KS 67260. Offers music (MM); music education (MME). *Accreditation:* NASM. Part-time programs available. *Expenses:* Tuition, state resident: full-time $4746; part-time $263.65 per credit. Tuition, nonresident: full-time $11,669; part-time $648.30 per credit. *Unit head:* Prof. Russ Widener, Director, 316-978-6435, Fax: 316-978-3625, E-mail: russ.widener@wichita.edu. *Application contact:* Dr. Mark Foley, Graduate Coordinator, 316-978-3103, E-mail: mark.foley@wichita.edu. Web site: http://www.wichita.edu/.

Winthrop University, College of Visual and Performing Arts, Department of Music, Rock Hill, SC 29733. Offers conducting (MM); music education (MME); performance (MM). *Accreditation:* NASM. Part-time programs available. *Degree requirements:* For master's, oral and written exams, recital (MM). *Entrance requirements:* For master's, GRE General Test, audition, minimum GPA of 3.0, 2 recitals. Electronic applications accepted.

Wright State University, School of Graduate Studies, College of Liberal Arts, Department of Music, Dayton, OH 45435. Offers music education (M Mus); performance (M Mus). *Accreditation:* NASM. Part-time programs available. *Degree requirements:* For master's, thesis or alternative, oral exam. *Entrance requirements:* For master's, theory placement test, BA in music. Additional exam requirements/recommendations for international students: Required—TOEFL. *Faculty research:* General music, current needs, role of teacher, expectations in music education.

Youngstown State University, Graduate School, College of Fine and Performing Arts, Dana School of Music, Youngstown, OH 44555-0001. Offers jazz studies (MM); music education (MM); music history and literature (MM); music theory and composition (MM); performance (MM). *Accreditation:* NASM. Part-time and evening/weekend programs available. *Degree requirements:* For master's, one foreign language, thesis optional, final qualifying exam. *Entrance requirements:* For master's, audition; GRE General Test or minimum GPA of 2.7. Additional exam requirements/recommendations for international students: Required—TOEFL. *Faculty research:* Teaching education, use of computers, conducting.

Reading Education

Adelphi University, Ruth S. Ammon School of Education, Program in Literacy, Garden City, NY 11530-0701. Offers birth-grade 12 (MS); birth-grade 6 (MS); grades 5-12 (MS). Part-time and evening/weekend programs available. *Students:* 10 full-time (all women), 46 part-time (45 women); includes 6 minority (2 Black or African American, non-Hispanic/Latino; 1 Asian, non-Hispanic/Latino; 2 Hispanic/Latino; 1 Two or more races, non-Hispanic/Latino). Average age 29. In 2011, 12 master's awarded. *Entrance requirements:* For master's, 2 letters of recommendation, resume, valid New York state teaching certification. Additional exam requirements/recommendations for international students: Required—TOEFL (minimum score 550 paper-based; 213 computer-based; 80 iBT). *Application deadline:* For fall admission, 4/1 priority date for domestic students, 4/1 for international students; for spring admission, 11/1 priority date for domestic students, 11/1 for international students. Applications are processed on a rolling basis. Application fee: $50. Electronic applications accepted. *Expenses: Tuition:* Full-time $29,600; part-time $930 per credit. *Required fees:* $1100. *Financial support:* Fellowships, research assistantships with partial tuition reimbursements, teaching assistantships, career-related internships or fieldwork, Federal Work-Study, institutionally sponsored loans, and tuition waivers (full) available. Support available to part-time students. Financial award application deadline: 2/15; financial award applicants required to submit FAFSA. *Faculty research:* Assessment and intervention, literacy education and development, higher and teacher education, human and adult development, achieving styles and human motivation. *Unit head:* Dr. Lori Wolf, Director, 516-877-4104, E-mail: wolf@adelphi.edu. *Application contact:* Christine Murphy, Director of Admissions, 516-877-3050, Fax: 516-877-3039, E-mail: graduateadmissions@adelphi.edu.

Alfred University, Graduate School, Division of Education, Alfred, NY 14802-1205. Offers literacy teacher (MS Ed); numeracy (MS). *Accreditation:* Teacher Education Accreditation Council. Part-time programs available. *Entrance requirements:* For master's, LAST, Assessment of Teaching Skills (written), Content Specialty Test. Additional exam requirements/recommendations for international students: Required—TOEFL (minimum score 590 paper-based; 243 computer-based; 90 iBT), IELTS (minimum score 6.5). Electronic applications accepted. *Faculty research:* Whole language, ethics in counseling and psychotherapy.

Alverno College, School of Education, Milwaukee, WI 53234-3922. Offers adaptive education (MA); administrative leadership (MA); adult education and organizational development (MA); adult educational and instructional design (MA); adult educational and instructional technology (MA); global connections in the humanities (MA); instructional leadership (MA); instructional technology for K-12 settings (MA); professional development (MA); reading education (MA); reading education with adaptive education (MA); science education (MA); teaching in alternative schools (MA). *Accreditation:* NCATE. Part-time and evening/weekend programs available. *Faculty:* 22 full-time (18 women), 13 part-time/adjunct (all women). *Students:* 63 full-time (58 women), 91 part-time (81 women); includes 36 minority (29 Black or African American, non-Hispanic/Latino; 1 Asian, non-Hispanic/Latino; 4 Hispanic/Latino; 1 Native Hawaiian or other Pacific Islander, non-Hispanic/Latino; 1 Two or more races, non-Hispanic/Latino), 2 international. Average age 38. 151 applicants, 60% accepted, 62 enrolled. In 2011, 52 master's awarded. *Degree requirements:* For master's, presentation/defense of proposal, conference presentation of inquiry projects. *Entrance requirements:* For master's, bachelor's degree in related field, communication samples from work setting, 3 letters of recommendation. Additional exam requirements/recommendations for international students: Required—TOEFL. *Application deadline:* For fall admission, 7/15 priority date for domestic students, 7/15 for international students; for spring admission, 12/15 priority date for domestic students, 12/15 for international students. Applications are processed on a rolling basis. Application fee: $0. Electronic applications accepted. Application fee is waived when completed online. Tuition and fees vary according to program. *Financial support:* In 2011–12, 1 student received support. Federal Work-Study available. Support available to part-time students. Financial award application deadline: 4/15; financial award applicants required to submit FAFSA. *Faculty research:* Student self-assessment, self-reflection, integration of curriculum, identifying needs of students in strategic situations and designing appropriate classroom strategies. *Unit head:* Dr. Desiree Pointer-Mace, Associate Dean, Graduate Program, 414-382-6345, Fax: 414-382-6332, E-mail: desiree.pointer-mace@alverno.edu. *Application contact:* Mary Claire Jones, Graduate Recruiter, 414-382-6106, Fax: 414-382-6354, E-mail: maryclaire.jones@alverno.edu.

American International College, School of Arts, Education and Sciences, Department of Education, Springfield, MA 01109-3189. Offers early childhood education (M Ed, CAGS); educational leadership and supervision (Ed D); elementary education (M Ed, CAGS); middle/secondary education (M Ed, CAGS); moderate disabilities (M Ed, CAGS); reading (M Ed, CAGS); school adjustment counseling (MA, CAGS); school administration (M Ed, CAGS); school guidance counseling (MA, CAGS); teaching (MA, MS); teaching and learning (Ed D). Part-time and evening/weekend programs available. Terminal master's awarded for partial completion of doctoral program. *Degree requirements:* For master's, comprehensive exam (for some programs), thesis (for some programs), practicum; for doctorate, comprehensive exam (for some programs), thesis/dissertation; for CAGS, practicum. *Entrance requirements:* For master's, minimum B-average in undergraduate course work; for doctorate, GRE General Test, interview. Additional exam requirements/recommendations for international students: Required—TOEFL. Electronic applications accepted.

American Public University System, AMU/APU Graduate Programs, Charles Town, WV 25414. Offers accounting (MBA, MS); administration and supervision (M Ed); criminal justice (MA); emergency and disaster management (MA); entrepreneurship (MBA); environmental policy and management (MS), including environmental planning, environmental sustainability, fish and wildlife management, general (MA, MS), global environmental management; finance (MBA); general (MBA); global business management (MBA); guidance and counseling (M Ed); history (MA), including American history, ancient and classical history, European history, global history, military and diplomatic history, public history; homeland security (MA); homeland security resource allocation (MBA); humanities (MA); information technology (MS), including digital forensics, enterprise software development, information assurance and security, IT project management; information technology management (MBA); intelligence studies (MA), including criminal intelligence, general (MA, MS), homeland security, intelligence analysis, intelligence collection, intelligence operations, terrorism studies; international relations and conflict resolution (MA), including comparative and security issues, conflict resolution, international and transnational security issues, peacekeeping; legal studies (MA); management (MA), including defense management, general (MA, MS), human resource management, organizational leadership, public administration, reverse logistics, strategic consulting; marketing (MBA); military history (MA), including American military history, American revolution, civil war, war since 1946, World War II; military studies (MA), including air warfare, asymmetrical warfare, joint warfare, land warfare, naval warfare, strategic leadership; national security studies (MA), including general (MA, MS), homeland security, regional security studies, security and intelligence analysis, terrorism studies; nonprofit management (MBA); political science (MA), including American politics and government, comparative government and development, public policy; psychology (MA); public administration (MA, MPA), including disaster management (MPA), environmental policy (MA), health policy (MPA), human resources (MPA), national security (MPA), organizational management (MPA), security management (MPA); public health (MA, MPH), including emergency management (MPH), environmental health (MPH), public administration (MA); reverse logistics management (MA); security management (MA); space studies (MS), including aerospace science, planetary science; sports and health sciences (MS); sports management (MS), including coaching theory and strategy, sports administration; teaching (M Ed), including curriculum and instruction for elementary teachers, elementary, elementary reading, English language learners, instructional leadership, online learning, secondary social sciences, special education; transportation and logistics management (MA), including maritime engineering management. Programs offered via distance learning only. Part-time and evening/weekend programs available. Postbaccalaureate distance learning degree programs offered (no on-campus study). *Faculty:* 445 full-time (241 women), 1,360 part-time/adjunct (617 women). *Students:* 688 full-time (338 women), 10,168 part-time (3,706 women); includes 3,130 minority (1,007 Black or African American, non-Hispanic/Latino; 103 American Indian or Alaska Native, non-Hispanic/Latino; 825 Asian, non-Hispanic/Latino; 810 Hispanic/Latino; 51 Native Hawaiian or other Pacific Islander, non-Hispanic/Latino; 334 Two or more races, non-Hispanic/Latino), 134 international. Average age 35. In 2011, 2,386 master's awarded. *Degree requirements:* For master's, comprehensive exam or practicum. *Entrance requirements:* For master's, official transcript showing earned bachelor's degree from institution accredited by recognized accrediting body. Additional exam requirements/recommendations for international students: Required—TOEFL (minimum score 550 paper-based; 213 computer-based), IELTS (minimum score 6.5). *Application deadline:* Applications are processed on a rolling basis. Application fee: $0. Electronic applications accepted. *Expenses: Tuition:* Part-time $325 per credit hour. *Financial support:* Applicants required to submit FAFSA. *Faculty research:* Military history, criminal justice, management performance, national security. *Unit head:* Dr. Karan Powell, Executive Vice President and Provost, 877-468-6268, Fax: 304-724-3780. *Application contact:* Terry Grant, Vice President of Enrollment Management, 877-468-6268, Fax: 304-724-3780, E-mail: info@apus.edu. Web site: http://www.apus.edu.

Appalachian State University, Cratis D. Williams Graduate School, Department of Reading Education and Special Education, Boone, NC 28608. Offers reading education (MA); special education (MA). *Accreditation:* ASHA. Part-time and evening/weekend programs available. Postbaccalaureate distance learning degree programs offered (no on-campus study). *Faculty:* 21 full-time (11 women), 3 part-time/adjunct (2 women). *Students:* 11 full-time (all women), 112 part-time (109 women); includes 7 minority (5 Black or African American, non-Hispanic/Latino; 1 American Indian or Alaska Native, non-Hispanic/Latino; 1 Hispanic/Latino). 40 applicants, 83% accepted, 27 enrolled. In 2011, 79 master's awarded. *Degree requirements:* For master's, comprehensive exam, thesis optional. *Entrance requirements:* For master's, GRE General Test or MAT, 3 letters of recommendation. Additional exam requirements/recommendations for international students: Required—TOEFL (minimum score 570 paper-based; 230 computer-based; 79 iBT), IELTS (minimum score 6.5). *Application deadline:* For fall admission, 3/15 priority date for domestic students, 2/1 for international students; for spring admission, 11/1 for domestic students, 7/1 for international students. Applications are processed on a rolling basis. Application fee: $55. Electronic applications accepted. *Expenses:* Tuition, state resident: full-time $4040; part-time $180 per semester hour. Tuition, nonresident: full-time $15,900; part-time $760 per semester hour. *Required fees:* $2500; $20 per semester hour. Tuition and fees vary according to campus/location. *Financial support:* In 2011–12, 4 research assistantships (averaging $8,000 per year) were awarded; Federal Work-Study, scholarships/grants, and unspecified assistantships also available. Financial award application deadline: 4/1; financial award applicants required to submit FAFSA. *Faculty research:* Special education, language arts, reading. *Total annual research expenditures:* $510,000. *Unit head:* Dr. Monica Lambert, Chairperson, 828-262-7173, Fax: 828-262-6767, E-mail: lambertma@appstate.edu. *Application contact:* Eveline Watts, Graduate Student Coordinator, 828-262-2182, E-mail: wattsem@appstate.edu. Web site: http://www.lre.appstate.edu/.

Arcadia University, Graduate Studies, Department of Education, Glenside, PA 19038-3295. Offers art education (M Ed); computer education (CAS); curriculum (CAS); curriculum studies (M Ed); early childhood education (M Ed, CAS), including individualized (M Ed), master teacher (M Ed), research in child development (M Ed); educational leadership (M Ed, Ed D, CAS); elementary education (M Ed, CAS); English education (MA Ed); environmental education (MA Ed, CAS); history education (MA Ed); instructional technology (M Ed); language arts (M Ed, CAS); library science (M Ed); mathematics education (M Ed, MA Ed, CAS); music education (MA Ed); psychology (MA Ed); reading (M Ed, CAS); science education (M Ed, CAS); secondary education (M Ed, CAS); special education (M Ed, Ed D, CAS); theater arts (MA Ed); written communication (MA Ed). *Accreditation:* NASAD. Part-time and evening/weekend programs available. Postbaccalaureate distance learning degree programs offered (minimal on-campus study). *Faculty:* 12 full-time (8 women), 38 part-time/adjunct (26 women). *Students:* 66 full-time (48 women), 590 part-time (477 women); includes 65 minority (53 Black or African American, non-Hispanic/Latino; 6 Asian, non-Hispanic/Latino; 3 Hispanic/Latino; 3 Two or more races, non-Hispanic/Latino), 4 international. Average age 36. In 2011, 229 master's, 5 doctorates awarded. *Application deadline:* Applications are processed on a rolling basis. Application fee: $50. Electronic applications accepted. *Expenses:* Contact institution. *Financial support:* Career-related internships or fieldwork, tuition waivers (partial), and unspecified assistantships available. *Unit head:* Dr. Steven P. Gulkus, Associate Professor, 215-572-2120, E-mail: gulkus@arcadia.edu. *Application contact:* 215-572-2925, Fax: 215-572-2126, E-mail: grad@arcadia.edu.

Arkansas State University, Graduate School, College of Education, Department of Teacher Education, Jonesboro, State University, AR 72467. Offers early childhood education (MAT, MSE); early childhood services (MS); middle level education (MAT, MSE); reading (MSE, Ed S). *Accreditation:* NCATE. Part-time programs available. *Faculty:* 16 full-time (11 women). *Students:* 47 full-time (44 women), 81 part-time (76 women); includes 52 minority (49 Black or African American, non-Hispanic/Latino; 1 Hispanic/Latino; 2 Two or more races, non-Hispanic/Latino), 2 international. Average age 33. 114 applicants, 58% accepted, 57 enrolled. In 2011, 35 master's awarded. *Degree requirements:* For master's, comprehensive exam, thesis or alternative; for Ed S, comprehensive exam. *Entrance requirements:* For master's, GRE General Test or MAT, appropriate bachelor's degree, official transcripts, immunization records; for Ed S, GRE General Test or MAT, interview, master's degree, official transcript, immunization records. Additional exam requirements/recommendations for international students: Required—TOEFL (minimum score 550 paper-based; 213 computer-based; 79 iBT), IELTS (minimum score 6), Pearson Test of English Academic (minimum score 56). *Application deadline:* For fall admission, 7/1 for domestic and international students; for spring admission, 11/15 for domestic students, 11/14 for international students. Applications are processed on a rolling basis. Application fee: $30 ($40 for international students). Electronic applications accepted. *Expenses:* Tuition, state resident: full-time $4044; part-time $225 per credit hour. Tuition, nonresident: full-time $8087; part-time $449 per credit hour. *Required fees:* $936; $52 per credit hour. $25 per term. One-time fee: $30. Tuition and fees vary according to course load and program. *Financial support:* In 2011–12, 5 students received support. Teaching assistantships, career-related internships or fieldwork, scholarships/grants, and unspecified assistantships available. Financial award application deadline: 7/1; financial award applicants required to submit FAFSA. *Unit head:* Dr. Lina Owens, Chair, 870-972-3059, Fax: 870-972-3344, E-mail: llowens@astate.edu. *Application contact:* Dr. Andrew Sustich, Dean of the Graduate School, 870-972-3029, Fax: 870-972-3857, E-mail: sustich@astate.edu. Web site: http://www.astate.edu/a/education/teachered/.

Asbury University, School of Graduate and Professional Studies, Wilmore, KY 40390-1198. Offers biology: alternative certificate (MA Ed); chemistry: alternative certificate (MA Ed); English (MA Ed); English as a second language (MA Ed); ESL (MA Ed); French (MA Ed); Latin: alternative certificate (MA Ed); mathematics: alternative certificate (MA Ed); reading/writing endorsement (MA Ed); social studies (MA Ed); social work (MSW), including child and family services; Spanish (MA Ed); special education (MA Ed); special education: alternative certificate (MA Ed); teacher as leader endorsement (MA Ed). *Accreditation:* NCATE. Part-time programs available. *Degree requirements:* For master's, action research project, portfolio. *Entrance requirements:* For master's, PRAXIS/NTE, minimum GPA of 2.75, letters of recommendation. Additional exam requirements/recommendations for international students: Required—TOEFL (minimum score 550 paper-based). Electronic applications accepted.

Ashland University, Dwight Schar College of Education, Department of Curriculum and Instruction, Ashland, OH 44805-3702. Offers classroom instruction (M Ed); literacy (M Ed); technology facilitator (M Ed). *Accreditation:* NCATE. Part-time and evening/weekend programs available. *Faculty:* 10 full-time (6 women), 39 part-time/adjunct (23 women). *Students:* 75 full-time (62 women), 218 part-time (183 women); includes 17 minority (14 Black or African American, non-Hispanic/Latino; 1 Asian, non-Hispanic/Latino; 2 Hispanic/Latino), 8 international. Average age 36. 72 applicants, 100% accepted, 63 enrolled. In 2011, 256 master's awarded. *Degree requirements:* For master's, thesis or alternative, internship, practicum, inquiry seminar. *Entrance requirements:* For master's, teaching certificate or license, bachelor's degree, minimum cumulative GPA of 2.75. Additional exam requirements/recommendations for international students: Required—TOEFL. *Application deadline:* For fall admission, 8/27 for domestic students; for spring admission, 1/15 for domestic students. Applications are processed on a rolling basis. Application fee: $30. Electronic applications accepted. *Expenses: Tuition:* Full-time $5580; part-time $465 per credit hour. *Financial support:* Institutionally sponsored loans and scholarships/grants available. Financial award application deadline: 4/15. *Faculty research:* Gender equity, postmodern children's and young adult literature, outdoor/experimental education, re-examining literature study in middle grades, morality and giftedness. *Unit head:* Dr. David J. Kommer, Chair, 419-289-5203, Fax: 419-207-4949, E-mail: dkommer@ashland.edu. *Application contact:* Dr. Linda Billman, Associate Dean, 419-289-5369, Fax: 419-289-5331, E-mail: lbillman@ashland.edu.

Auburn University, Graduate School, College of Education, Department of Curriculum and Teaching, Auburn University, AL 36849. Offers business education (M Ed, MS, PhD); early childhood education (M Ed, MS, PhD, Ed S); elementary education (M Ed, MS, PhD, Ed S); foreign languages (M Ed, MS); music education (M Ed, MS, PhD, Ed S); postsecondary education (PhD); reading education (PhD, Ed S); secondary education (M Ed, MS, PhD, Ed S), including English language arts, mathematics, science, social studies. *Accreditation:* NASM (one or more programs are accredited); NCATE. Part-time programs available. *Faculty:* 22 full-time (17 women), 3 part-time/adjunct (all women). *Students:* 80 full-time (58 women), 181 part-time (126 women); includes 42 minority (28 Black or African American, non-Hispanic/Latino; 7 Asian, non-Hispanic/Latino; 7 Hispanic/Latino). Average age 34. 184 applicants, 53% accepted, 60 enrolled. In 2011, 77 master's, 10 doctorates, 35 other advanced degrees awarded. *Degree requirements:* For master's, thesis (for some programs); for doctorate, thesis/dissertation; for Ed S, field project. *Entrance requirements:* For master's, doctorate, and Ed S, GRE General Test. *Application deadline:* For fall admission, 7/7 for domestic students; for spring admission, 11/24 for domestic students. Applications are processed on a rolling basis. Application fee: $50 ($60 for international students). Electronic applications accepted. *Expenses:* Tuition, state resident: full-time $7290; part-time $405 per credit hour. Tuition, nonresident: full-time $21,870; part-time $1215 per credit hour. *International tuition:* $22,000 full-time. *Required fees:* $1402. *Financial support:* Fellowships, teaching assistantships, career-related internships or fieldwork, and Federal Work-Study available. Support available to part-time students. Financial award application deadline: 3/15; financial award applicants required to submit FAFSA. *Faculty research:* Emerging literacy, reading attitudes, music for at-risk youth, portfolio assessment. *Unit head:* Dr. Kimberly Walls, Head, 334-844-4434. *Application contact:* Dr. George Flowers, Dean of the Graduate School, 334-844-2125. Web site: http://education.auburn.edu/academic_departments/curr/.

Auburn University Montgomery, School of Education, Department of Early Childhood, Elementary, and Reading Education, Montgomery, AL 36124-4023. Offers early childhood education (M Ed, Ed S); elementary education (M Ed, Ed S); reading education (M Ed, Ed S). *Accreditation:* NCATE. Part-time and evening/weekend programs available. *Degree requirements:* For master's and Ed S, comprehensive exam. *Entrance requirements:* For master's, GRE General Test or MAT, certification, BS in teaching; for Ed S, GRE General Test or MAT, certification. Electronic applications accepted. *Expenses:* Tuition, state resident: full-time $5076. Tuition, nonresident: full-time $15,228.

Aurora University, College of Education, Aurora, IL 60506-4892. Offers curriculum and instruction (MA, Ed D); early childhood and special education (MA); education (MAT), including elementary certification; education and administration (Ed D); educational leadership (MEL); educational technology (MATL); reading instruction (MA); special education (MA). *Accreditation:* NCATE. Part-time and evening/weekend programs available. *Degree requirements:* For doctorate, comprehensive exam, thesis/dissertation. *Entrance requirements:* For master's, 2 years of teaching experience, valid teaching certificate. Additional exam requirements/recommendations for international students: Required—TOEFL (minimum score 550 paper-based; 213 computer-based). Electronic applications accepted. *Expenses:* Contact institution.

Austin Peay State University, College of Graduate Studies, College of Education, Department of Teaching and Learning, Clarksville, TN 37044. Offers elementary education K-6 (MAT); reading (MA Ed); secondary education 7-12 (MAT); special education K-12 (MAT). Part-time and evening/weekend programs available. Postbaccalaureate distance learning degree programs offered. *Faculty:* 14 full-time (11 women), 3 part-time/adjunct (2 women). *Students:* 84 full-time (67 women), 97 part-time (81 women); includes 27 minority (12 Black or African American, non-Hispanic/Latino; 2 American Indian or Alaska Native, non-Hispanic/Latino; 2 Asian, non-Hispanic/Latino; 4

Reading Education

Hispanic/Latino; 1 Native Hawaiian or other Pacific Islander, non-Hispanic/Latino; 6 Two or more races, non-Hispanic/Latino). Average age 33. 61 applicants, 98% accepted, 51 enrolled. In 2011, 55 master's awarded. *Degree requirements:* For master's, comprehensive exam, thesis optional. *Entrance requirements:* For master's, GRE General Test, 3 letters of recommendation, minimum undergraduate GPA of 2.75. Additional exam requirements/recommendations for international students: Required—TOEFL (minimum score 500 paper-based; 173 computer-based). *Application deadline:* For fall admission, 8/1 priority date for domestic students. Applications are processed on a rolling basis. Application fee: $25. Electronic applications accepted. *Expenses:* Tuition, state resident: part-time $350 per credit hour. Tuition, nonresident: full-time $20,644; part-time $971 per credit hour. *Required fees:* $1224; $61.20 per credit hour. *Financial support:* Career-related internships or fieldwork, Federal Work-Study, institutionally sponsored loans, scholarships/grants, and unspecified assistantships available. Support available to part-time students. Financial award application deadline: 3/1; financial award applicants required to submit FAFSA. *Unit head:* Dr. Rebecca McMahan, Chair, 931-221-7513, Fax: 931-221-1292, E-mail: mcmahanb@apsu.edu. *Application contact:* Kendra Bryant, Graduate Admissions, 800-844-2778, Fax: 931-221-6188, E-mail: admissionsweb@apsu.edu.

Baldwin Wallace University, Graduate Programs, Division of Education, Specialization in Literacy, Berea, OH 44017-2088. Offers MA Ed. *Accreditation:* NCATE. Part-time and evening/weekend programs available. *Faculty:* 3 full-time (all women), 1 (woman) part-time/adjunct. *Students:* 8 full-time (all women), 25 part-time (24 women); includes 3 minority (2 Black or African American, non-Hispanic/Latino; 1 Two or more races, non-Hispanic/Latino). Average age 31. 8 applicants, 100% accepted, 5 enrolled. In 2011, 13 master's awarded. *Degree requirements:* For master's, comprehensive exam. *Entrance requirements:* For master's, bachelor's degree in field, MAT or minimum GPA of 2.75. Additional exam requirements/recommendations for international students: Required—TOEFL (minimum score 523 paper-based; 193 computer-based; 70 iBT). *Application deadline:* For fall admission, 8/15 priority date for domestic students; for spring admission, 12/15 priority date for domestic students. Applications are processed on a rolling basis. Application fee: $25. Electronic applications accepted. Application fee is waived when completed online. *Expenses: Tuition:* Full-time $17,016; part-time $727 per credit hour. Tuition and fees vary according to program. *Financial support:* Career-related internships or fieldwork available. Support available to part-time students. Financial award application deadline: 5/1; financial award applicants required to submit FAFSA. *Faculty research:* Metacognition and the reading process, language acquisition, genres and the reader response theory, cultural responsiveness, content area literacy. *Unit head:* Dr. Karen Kaye, Chair, 440-826-2168, Fax: 440-826-3779, E-mail: kkaye@bw.edu. *Application contact:* Winifred W. Gerhardt, Director of Admission for the Evening and Weekend College, 440-826-2222, Fax: 440-826-3830, E-mail: admission@bw.edu. Web site: http://www.bw.edu/academic/mae/reading/.

Bank Street College of Education, Graduate School, Program in Reading and Literacy, New York, NY 10025. Offers advanced literacy specialization (Ed M); reading and literacy (MS Ed); teaching literacy (MS Ed); teaching literacy and childhood general education (MS Ed). *Students:* 38 full-time (34 women), 56 part-time (52 women); includes 25 minority (10 Black or African American, non-Hispanic/Latino; 4 Asian, non-Hispanic/Latino; 8 Hispanic/Latino; 3 Two or more races, non-Hispanic/Latino), 2 international. Average age 30. 56 applicants, 82% accepted, 32 enrolled. In 2011, 27 master's awarded. *Degree requirements:* For master's, thesis. *Entrance requirements:* For master's, interview, essays. Additional exam requirements/recommendations for international students: Required—TOEFL (minimum score 600 paper-based; 250 computer-based; 100 iBT), IELTS (minimum score 7). *Application deadline:* For fall admission, 2/15 priority date for domestic students, 2/15 for international students; for spring admission, 11/1 priority date for domestic students, 11/1 for international students. Applications are processed on a rolling basis. Application fee: $65. Electronic applications accepted. *Expenses: Required fees:* $1240 per credit. $100 per term. One-time fee: $250 part-time. *Financial support:* Career-related internships or fieldwork, Federal Work-Study, scholarships/grants, and unspecified assistantships available. Support available to part-time students. Financial award application deadline: 4/15; financial award applicants required to submit FAFSA. *Faculty research:* Language development, children's literature, whole language, the reading and writing processes, reading difficulties in multicultural classrooms. *Unit head:* Dr. Susan Goetz-Haver, Director, 212-875-4692, Fax: 212-875-4753, E-mail: sgoetz-haver@bankstreet.edu. *Application contact:* Ann Morgan, Director of Graduate Admissions, 212-875-4403, Fax: 212-875-4678, E-mail: amorgan@bankstreet.edu. Web site: http://bankstreet.edu/graduate-school/academics/programs/reading-and-literacy-program-overview/.

Barry University, School of Education, Program in Curriculum and Instruction, Miami Shores, FL 33161-6695. Offers accomplished teacher (Ed S); culture, language and literacy (TESOL) (PhD); curriculum evaluation and research (PhD); early childhood (Ed S); early childhood education (PhD); elementary (Ed S); elementary education (PhD); ESOL (Ed S); gifted (Ed S); Montessori (Ed S); PKP/elementary (Ed S); reading (Ed S); reading, language and cognition (PhD). *Entrance requirements:* For doctorate, GRE, minimum GPA of 3.25.

Barry University, School of Education, Program in Reading, Miami Shores, FL 33161-6695. Offers MS, Ed S. Part-time and evening/weekend programs available. *Degree requirements:* For master's, comprehensive exam, practicum; for Ed S, practicum. *Entrance requirements:* For master's, GRE General Test or MAT, minimum GPA of 3.0, course work in children's literature; for Ed S, GRE General Test, minimum GPA of 3.0. Electronic applications accepted.

Bellarmine University, Annsley Frazier Thornton School of Education, Louisville, KY 40205-0671. Offers early elementary education (MA Ed, MAT); education and social change (PhD); learning and behavior disorders (MA Ed, MAT); middle school education (MA Ed, MAT); principalship (Ed S); reading and writing endorsement (MA Ed); secondary school education (MAT); teacher leadership, grades P-12 (MA Ed). *Accreditation:* NCATE. Part-time and evening/weekend programs available. *Faculty:* 13 full-time (6 women), 12 part-time/adjunct (10 women). *Students:* 85 full-time (65 women), 186 part-time (144 women); includes 30 minority (22 Black or African American, non-Hispanic/Latino; 1 American Indian or Alaska Native, non-Hispanic/Latino; 6 Asian, non-Hispanic/Latino; 1 Hispanic/Latino). Average age 33. In 2011, 105 master's awarded. *Degree requirements:* For master's, comprehensive exam, thesis (for some programs); for doctorate, comprehensive exam, thesis/dissertation. *Entrance requirements:* For master's, GRE, baccalaureate degree from accredited institution; minimum overall GPA of 2.75, 3.0 in major; letters of recommendation; valid Kentucky provisional or professional certificate; for doctorate, GRE, minimum GPA of 3.5 in all graduate coursework completed at time of application; baccalaureate and master's degrees in education (MA, MS) or fields directly relevant to education; three letters of recommendation; two essays (no more than 1,000 words each); interview. Additional exam requirements/recommendations for international students: Required—TOEFL (minimum score 550 paper-based; 213 computer-based; 80 iBT). *Application deadline:* Applications are processed on a rolling basis. Application fee: $25. *Expenses:* Contact institution. *Financial support:* Scholarships/grants available. Financial award applicants required to submit FAFSA. *Faculty research:* Literacy, service-learning, dispositions, educational technology, special education. *Unit head:* Dr. Robert Cooter, Dean, 502-272-8191, Fax: 502-272-8189, E-mail: rcooter@bellarmine.edu. *Application contact:* Theresa Klapheke, Administrative Director of Graduate Programs, 502-272-8271, Fax: 502-272-8002, E-mail: tklapheke@bellarmine.edu. Web site: http://www.bellarmine.edu/education/graduate.

Benedictine University, Graduate Programs, Program in Education, Lisle, IL 60532-0900. Offers curriculum and instruction and collaborative teaching (M Ed); elementary education (MA Ed); leadership and administration (M Ed); reading and literacy (M Ed); secondary education (MA Ed); special education (MA Ed). Part-time and evening/weekend programs available. *Faculty:* 4 full-time (2 women), 52 part-time/adjunct (30 women). *Students:* 178 full-time (157 women), 239 part-time (211 women); includes 41 minority (29 Black or African American, non-Hispanic/Latino; 4 Asian, non-Hispanic/Latino; 8 Hispanic/Latino), 2 international. Average age 33. 177 applicants, 44% accepted, 68 enrolled. In 2011, 278 master's awarded. *Degree requirements:* For master's, comprehensive exam, thesis (for some programs). *Entrance requirements:* For master's, GRE or MAT. Additional exam requirements/recommendations for international students: Required—TOEFL (minimum score 550 paper-based; 213 computer-based). *Application deadline:* For fall admission, 9/1 for domestic students; for winter admission, 12/1 for domestic students; for spring admission, 2/15 for domestic students. Applications are processed on a rolling basis. Application fee: $40. Electronic applications accepted. *Expenses:* Contact institution. *Financial support:* Career-related internships or fieldwork and health care benefits available. Support available to part-time students. *Unit head:* MeShelda Jackson, Director, 630-829-6282, E-mail: mjackson@ben.edu. *Application contact:* Kari Gibbons, Associate Vice President, Enrollment Center, 630-829-6200, Fax: 630-829-6584, E-mail: kgibbons@ben.edu.

Benedictine University at Springfield, Program in Reading/Literacy, Springfield, IL 62702. Offers M Ed. *Entrance requirements:* For master's, official transcript, minimum cumulative GPA of 3.0, 3 letters of recommendation, statement of goals.

Berry College, Graduate Programs, Graduate Programs in Education, Program in Middle Grades Education and Reading, Mount Berry, GA 30149-0159. Offers middle grades education (MAT); middle grades education and reading (M Ed). *Accreditation:* NCATE. Part-time programs available. *Faculty:* 12 part-time/adjunct (8 women). *Students:* 2 full-time (1 woman), 17 part-time (14 women). Average age 32. In 2011, 7 master's awarded. *Degree requirements:* For master's, thesis optional, oral exams. *Entrance requirements:* For master's, GRE General Test, MAT, or NTE, minimum GPA of 2.5. Additional exam requirements/recommendations for international students: Required—TOEFL (minimum score 550 paper-based; 213 computer-based). *Application deadline:* For fall admission, 5/1 for domestic and international students; for spring admission, 10/1 for domestic and international students. Applications are processed on a rolling basis. Application fee: $25 ($30 for international students). Electronic applications accepted. *Expenses:* Contact institution. *Financial support:* In 2011–12, 5 students received support, including 1 research assistantship with full tuition reimbursement available (averaging $2,440 per year); scholarships/grants, tuition waivers (partial), and unspecified assistantships also available. Support available to part-time students. Financial award application deadline: 3/1; financial award applicants required to submit FAFSA. *Faculty research:* Curriculum development, teacher training, pedagogy, ESOL and immigrant student literacy development. *Unit head:* Dr. Jacqueline McDowell, 706-236-1717, Fax: 706-238-5827, E-mail: jmcdowell@berry.edu. *Application contact:* Brett Kennedy, Director of Admissions, 706-236-2215, Fax: 706-290-2178, E-mail: admissions@berry.edu. Web site: http://www.berry.edu/academics/education/graduate/.

Bethel University, Graduate School, St. Paul, MN 55112-6999. Offers autism spectrum disorders (Certificate); business administration (MBA); communication (MA); counseling psychology (MA); education (M Ed); educational leadership (Ed D); gerontology (MA, Certificate); international baccalaureate education (Certificate); K-12 education (MA); literacy education (MA); nursing (MA); nursing education (Certificate); nursing leadership (Certificate); organizational leadership (MA); postsecondary teaching (Certificate); special education (MA); teaching (MA). Part-time and evening/weekend programs available. Postbaccalaureate distance learning degree programs offered (minimal on-campus study). *Faculty:* 8 full-time (3 women), 98 part-time/adjunct (46 women). *Students:* 651 full-time (419 women), 312 part-time (212 women); includes 79 minority (35 Black or African American, non-Hispanic/Latino; 2 American Indian or Alaska Native, non-Hispanic/Latino; 19 Asian, non-Hispanic/Latino; 17 Hispanic/Latino; 6 Two or more races, non-Hispanic/Latino), 6 international. Average age 36. In 2011, 245 master's, 4 doctorates, 32 other advanced degrees awarded. *Degree requirements:* For master's, comprehensive exam (for some programs), thesis (for some programs); for doctorate, comprehensive exam, thesis/dissertation. *Entrance requirements:* Additional exam requirements/recommendations for international students: Required—TOEFL (minimum score 550 paper-based; 213 computer-based; 80 iBT). *Application deadline:* Applications are processed on a rolling basis. Electronic applications accepted. Tuition and fees vary according to course load, degree level and program. *Financial support:* Applicants required to submit FAFSA. *Unit head:* Dick Crombie, Vice-President/Dean, 651-635-8000, Fax: 651-635-8004, E-mail: gs@bethel.edu. *Application contact:* Paul Ives, Director of Admissions, 651-635-8000, Fax: 651-635-8004, E-mail: gs@bethel.edu. Web site: http://gs.bethel.edu/.

Bloomsburg University of Pennsylvania, School of Graduate Studies, College of Education, Department of Early Childhood and Adolescent Education, Program in Reading, Bloomsburg, PA 17815-1301. Offers M Ed. *Entrance requirements:* For master's, baccalaureate degree, letter of intent, two letters of recommendation, criminal record clearance, interview.

Boise State University, Graduate College, College of Education, Programs in Teacher Education, Program in Reading, Boise, ID 83725-0399. Offers MA. *Accreditation:* NCATE. Part-time programs available. *Degree requirements:* For master's, thesis optional. *Entrance requirements:* For master's, minimum GPA of 3.0. Electronic applications accepted.

Boston College, Lynch Graduate School of Education, Program in Reading and Literacy, Chestnut Hill, MA 02467-3800. Offers M Ed, MAT, CAES. *Accreditation:* Teacher Education Accreditation Council. Part-time and evening/weekend programs available. *Students:* 4 full-time (all women), 4 part-time (3 women); includes 1 minority (Hispanic/Latino). 25 applicants, 28% accepted, 4 enrolled. In 2011, 5 degrees awarded. *Degree requirements:* For master's and CAES, comprehensive exam. *Entrance requirements:* For master's, GRE General Test or MAT, general licensure, one year of teaching experience; for CAES, GRE General Test or MAT. Additional exam requirements/recommendations for international students: Required—TOEFL (minimum score 550 paper-based; 213 computer-based; 79 iBT). *Application deadline:* For fall admission, 1/1 priority date for domestic students. Application fee: $65. Electronic applications accepted. *Financial support:* Fellowships with full and partial tuition reimbursements, research assistantships with full and partial tuition reimbursements, teaching assistantships with full and partial tuition reimbursements, career-related internships or fieldwork, Federal Work-Study, scholarships/grants, traineeships, health care benefits, tuition waivers (full and partial), and unspecified assistantships available. Support available to part-time students. Financial award applicants required to submit FAFSA. *Faculty research:* Creating literacy learning environments, critical literacy and literacy development. *Unit head:* Dr. Maria E. Brisk, Chairperson, 617-552-4214, Fax:

617-552-0398. *Application contact:* Adam Poluzzi, Director, Graduate Admission and Financial Aid, 617-552-4214, Fax: 617-552-0398, E-mail: poluzzi@bc.edu.

Bowie State University, Graduate Programs, Program in Reading Education, Bowie, MD 20715-9465. Offers M Ed. *Accreditation:* NCATE. Part-time and evening/weekend programs available. *Faculty:* 1 (woman) full-time. *Students:* 3 full-time (all women), 24 part-time (22 women); includes 19 minority (17 Black or African American, non-Hispanic/Latino; 2 Asian, non-Hispanic/Latino). Average age 36. In 2011, 17 master's awarded. *Degree requirements:* For master's, comprehensive exam, thesis optional, research paper. *Entrance requirements:* For master's, minimum GPA of 2.5, teaching certificate, teaching experience. *Application deadline:* For fall admission, 4/1 priority date for domestic students, 4/1 for international students; for spring admission, 11/1 for domestic and international students. Applications are processed on a rolling basis. Application fee: $40. *Expenses:* Tuition, state resident: full-time $4140; part-time $3105 per semester. Tuition, nonresident: full-time $7836; part-time $5877 per semester. *Required fees:* $1715; $648 per semester. *Financial support:* Application deadline: 4/1. *Faculty research:* Literacy education, multicultural education. *Unit head:* Dr. Lucille Strain, Coordinator, 301-860-3129, E-mail: lstrain@bowiestate.edu. *Application contact:* Angela Issac, Information Contact, 301-860-4000.

Bowling Green State University, Graduate College, College of Education and Human Development, School of Education and Intervention Services, Teaching and Learning Division, Program in Reading, Bowling Green, OH 43403. Offers M Ed, Ed S. *Accreditation:* NCATE. Part-time programs available. *Degree requirements:* For master's, thesis or alternative; for Ed S, practicum or field experience. *Entrance requirements:* For master's and Ed S, GRE General Test. Additional exam requirements/recommendations for international students: Required—TOEFL. Electronic applications accepted. *Faculty research:* Children's literature, attention deficit disorder (ADD)/reading correlation, content area reading, reading instruction, reading/writing connection.

Bridgewater State University, School of Graduate Studies, School of Education and Allied Studies, Department of Elementary and Early Childhood Education, Program in Reading, Bridgewater, MA 02325-0001. Offers M Ed, CAGS. *Accreditation:* NCATE. Part-time and evening/weekend programs available. *Entrance requirements:* For master's, GRE General Test, 1 year of teaching experience.

Brigham Young University, Graduate Studies, David O. McKay School of Education, Department of Teacher Education, Provo, UT 84602. Offers integrative science-technology-engineering-mathematics (STEM) (MA); literacy education (MA); teacher education (MA). Part-time programs available. *Faculty:* 21 full-time (13 women). *Students:* 14 full-time (10 women). Average age 32. 19 applicants, 100% accepted, 14 enrolled. In 2011, 1 master's awarded. Terminal master's awarded for partial completion of doctoral program. *Degree requirements:* For master's, thesis. *Entrance requirements:* For master's, GRE General Test, minimum 1 year of teaching experience, minimum GPA of 3.25 in last 60 hours of course work, valid teaching credential. Additional exam requirements/recommendations for international students: Recommended—TOEFL. *Application deadline:* For fall admission, 2/1 priority date for domestic students, 2/1 for international students; for winter admission, 2/1 for domestic and international students; for spring admission, 3/15 for domestic students. Application fee: $50. Electronic applications accepted. *Expenses: Tuition:* Full-time $5760; part-time $320 per credit. Tuition and fees vary according to student's religious affiliation. *Financial support:* In 2011–12, 14 students received support. Scholarships/grants and tuition waivers (full and partial) available. *Faculty research:* History pedagogy, early childhood and socio-emotional development, teacher socialization, problem solving in mathematics, technology in teacher education. *Unit head:* Dr. Nancy Wentworth, Chair, 801-422-5617, Fax: 801-422-0652, E-mail: nancy_wentworth@byu.edu. *Application contact:* Dr. Janet Young, Graduate Coordinator, 801-422-4979, Fax: 801-422-0652, E-mail: janet_young@byu.edu. Web site: http://education.byu.edu/ted/.

Buffalo State College, State University of New York, The Graduate School, Faculty of Applied Science and Education, Department of Elementary Education and Reading, Programs in Literacy Specialist, Buffalo, NY 14222-1095. Offers literacy specialist (birth-grade 6) (MS Ed); literacy specialist (grades 5-12) (MPS). *Accreditation:* NCATE. Part-time and evening/weekend programs available. *Degree requirements:* For master's, project. *Entrance requirements:* For master's, minimum GPA of 3.0 in last 60 hours. Additional exam requirements/recommendations for international students: Required—TOEFL (minimum score 550 paper-based; 213 computer-based).

Butler University, College of Education, Indianapolis, IN 46208-3485. Offers administration (MS); elementary education (MS); reading (MS); school counseling (MS); secondary education (MS); special education (MS). *Accreditation:* ACA; NCATE. Part-time and evening/weekend programs available. *Faculty:* 7 full-time (4 women), 5 part-time/adjunct (all women). *Students:* 9 full-time (6 women), 136 part-time (105 women); includes 21 minority (14 Black or African American, non-Hispanic/Latino; 5 Asian, non-Hispanic/Latino; 1 Hispanic/Latino; 1 Two or more races, non-Hispanic/Latino), 1 international. Average age 31. 69 applicants, 94% accepted, 24 enrolled. In 2011, 66 master's awarded. *Entrance requirements:* For master's, GRE General Test, MAT, interview. *Application deadline:* For fall admission, 8/15 priority date for domestic students. Applications are processed on a rolling basis. Application fee: $35. Electronic applications accepted. *Expenses: Tuition:* Part-time $466 per credit. *Financial support:* Institutionally sponsored loans available. Support available to part-time students. Financial award application deadline: 7/15; financial award applicants required to submit FAFSA. *Faculty research:* Ethics in cybercounseling, history of sports for disabled, effect of fetal alcohol syndrome on perceptual learning, reading recovery's theoretical framework in teacher education. *Unit head:* Dr. Ena Shelley, Dean, 317-940-9752, Fax: 317-940-6481. *Application contact:* Karen Farrell, Department Secretary, 317-940-9220, E-mail: kfarrell@butler.edu.

Caldwell College, Graduate Studies, Division of Education, Caldwell, NJ 07006-6195. Offers curriculum and instruction (MA); educational administration (MA); learning disabilities teacher-consultant (Post-Master's Certificate); literacy instruction (MA); principal (Post-Master's Certificate); reading specialist (Post-Master's Certificate); special education (MA), including special education, teaching of students with disabilities, teaching of students with disabilities and learning disabilities teacher-consultant; superintendent (Post-Master's Certificate); supervisor (Post-Master's Certificate). Part-time and evening/weekend programs available. *Students:* 66 full-time (41 women), 230 part-time (188 women); includes 24 minority (14 Black or African American, non-Hispanic/Latino; 1 Asian, non-Hispanic/Latino; 9 Hispanic/Latino). *Entrance requirements:* Additional exam requirements/recommendations for international students: Required—TOEFL (minimum score 580 paper-based; 237 computer-based). *Application deadline:* Applications are processed on a rolling basis. Application fee: $40. Electronic applications accepted. *Expenses: Tuition:* Full-time $14,400; part-time $800 per credit. *Required fees:* $200; $100 per semester. *Financial support:* Applicants required to submit FAFSA. *Unit head:* Dr. Janice Stewart, Coordinator, 973-618-3626, E-mail: jstewart@caldwell.edu. *Application contact:* Vilma Mueller, Director of Graduate Studies, 973-618-3544, E-mail: graduate@caldwell.edu.

California Baptist University, Program in Education, Riverside, CA 92504-3206. Offers educational leadership for faith-based instruction (MS); educational leadership for public institutions (MS); educational technology (MS); instructional computer applications (MS); international education (MS); reading (MS); school counseling (MS); school psychology (MS); special education (MS); special education in mild/moderate disabilities (MS); special education in moderate/severe disabilities (MS); teaching (MS); teaching and learning with induction program (MS Ed). Part-time and evening/weekend programs available. *Faculty:* 16 full-time (10 women), 1 (woman) part-time/adjunct. *Students:* 380 full-time (323 women); includes 149 minority (28 Black or African American, non-Hispanic/Latino; 2 American Indian or Alaska Native, non-Hispanic/Latino; 13 Asian, non-Hispanic/Latino; 100 Hispanic/Latino; 2 Native Hawaiian or other Pacific Islander, non-Hispanic/Latino; 4 Two or more races, non-Hispanic/Latino). Average age 32. 181 applicants, 70% accepted, 111 enrolled. In 2011, 82 master's awarded. *Degree requirements:* For master's, comprehensive exam or thesis. *Entrance requirements:* For master's, minimum undergraduate GPA of 3.0; 18 semester units of prerequisite course work in education; three recommendations; essay; interview. Additional exam requirements/recommendations for international students: Required—TOEFL (minimum score 575 paper-based; 230 computer-based; 89 iBT). *Application deadline:* For fall admission, 8/1 priority date for domestic students, 7/1 for international students; for spring admission, 12/1 priority date for domestic students, 11/1 for international students. Applications are processed on a rolling basis. Application fee: $45. Electronic applications accepted. *Expenses:* Contact institution. *Financial support:* In 2011–12, 4 students received support. Federal Work-Study and institutionally sponsored loans available. Financial award applicants required to submit FAFSA. *Faculty research:* Special education, neurosciences and education, cultural influences on behavior, faith-based school leadership, social and philosophical contexts of education. *Unit head:* Dr. John Shoup, Dean, School of Education, 951-343-4205, Fax: 951-343-4516, E-mail: jshoup@calbaptist.edu. *Application contact:* Dr. James Heyman, Director, Master of Science Program in Education, 951-343-4243, Fax: 951-343-5095, E-mail: jheyman@calbaptist.edu. Web site: http://www.calbaptist.edu/mastersined/.

California State University, East Bay, Office of Academic Programs and Graduate Studies, College of Education and Allied Studies, Department of Teacher Education, Hayward, CA 94542-3000. Offers education (MS), including curriculum, early childhood education, educational technology leadership, online teaching and learning, reading instruction. Postbaccalaureate distance learning degree programs offered. *Faculty:* 5 full-time (4 women), 2 part-time/adjunct (both women). *Students:* 64 full-time (53 women), 55 part-time (39 women); includes 50 minority (14 Black or African American, non-Hispanic/Latino; 17 Asian, non-Hispanic/Latino; 15 Hispanic/Latino; 4 Two or more races, non-Hispanic/Latino), 3 international. Average age 35. 98 applicants, 69% accepted, 30 enrolled. In 2011, 149 master's awarded. *Degree requirements:* For master's, project or thesis. *Entrance requirements:* For master's, minimum GPA of 3.0 in field, 2.5 overall; teaching experience; baccalaureate degree; 3 letters of recommendation. Additional exam requirements/recommendations for international students: Required—TOEFL (minimum score 550 paper-based; 213 computer-based), IELTS. *Application deadline:* For fall admission, 6/30 for domestic and international students. Application fee: $55. Electronic applications accepted. *Expenses:* Tuition, state resident: full-time $6738; part-time $1302 per quarter. Tuition, nonresident: full-time $12,690; part-time $2294 per quarter. *Required fees:* $449 per quarter. Tuition and fees vary according to degree level, program and reciprocity agreements. *Financial support:* Career-related internships or fieldwork, Federal Work-Study, and institutionally sponsored loans available. Support available to part-time students. Financial award application deadline: 3/2; financial award applicants required to submit FAFSA. *Faculty research:* Online, pedagogy, writing, learning, teaching. *Unit head:* Dr. Jeanette Bicais, Chair, 510-885-3027, Fax: 510-885-4632, E-mail: jeanette.bicais@csueastbay.edu. *Application contact:* Prof. Valerie Helgren-Lempesis, Education Graduate Advisor, 510-885-3006, Fax: 510-885-4632, E-mail: valerie.lempesis@csueastbay.edu. Web site: http://www20.csueastbay.edu/ceas/departments/ted/index.html.

California State University, Fresno, Division of Graduate Studies, School of Education and Human Development, Department of Literacy and Early Education, Fresno, CA 93740-8027. Offers education (MA), including early childhood education, reading/language arts. *Accreditation:* NCATE. Part-time and evening/weekend programs available. *Degree requirements:* For master's, thesis or alternative. *Entrance requirements:* For master's, GRE General Test, MAT, minimum GPA of 2.75. Additional exam requirements/recommendations for international students: Required—TOEFL. Electronic applications accepted. *Faculty research:* Reading recovery, monitoring/tutoring programs, character and academics, professional ethics, low-performing partnership schools.

California State University, Fullerton, Graduate Studies, College of Education, Department of Reading, Fullerton, CA 92834-9480. Offers MS. Part-time programs available. *Students:* 11 full-time (all women), 100 part-time (94 women); includes 46 minority (3 Black or African American, non-Hispanic/Latino; 12 Asian, non-Hispanic/Latino; 28 Hispanic/Latino; 3 Two or more races, non-Hispanic/Latino). Average age 35. 40 applicants, 88% accepted, 27 enrolled. In 2011, 53 master's awarded. Application fee: $55. *Financial support:* Career-related internships or fieldwork, Federal Work-Study, institutionally sponsored loans, and scholarships/grants available. Support available to part-time students. Financial award application deadline: 3/1; financial award applicants required to submit FAFSA. *Unit head:* Dr. Ula Manzo, Chair, 657-278-3357. *Application contact:* Admissions/Applications, 657-278-2371.

California State University, Los Angeles, Graduate Studies, Charter College of Education, Division of Curriculum and Instruction, Los Angeles, CA 90032-8530. Offers elementary teaching (MA); reading (MA); secondary teaching (MA). Part-time and evening/weekend programs available. *Faculty:* 12 full-time (7 women), 5 part-time/adjunct (3 women). *Students:* 218 full-time (157 women), 156 part-time (118 women); includes 305 minority (20 Black or African American, non-Hispanic/Latino; 1 American Indian or Alaska Native, non-Hispanic/Latino; 59 Asian, non-Hispanic/Latino; 216 Hispanic/Latino; 9 Two or more races, non-Hispanic/Latino), 5 international. Average age 31. 93 applicants, 59% accepted, 52 enrolled. In 2011, 117 master's awarded. *Entrance requirements:* For master's, minimum GPA of 2.75 in last 90 units of course work, teaching certificate. Additional exam requirements/recommendations for international students: Required—TOEFL (minimum score 500 paper-based; 173 computer-based). *Application deadline:* For fall admission, 5/1 for domestic and international students. Applications are processed on a rolling basis. Application fee: $55. Electronic applications accepted. *Expenses:* Tuition, state resident: full-time $8225. *Financial support:* Federal Work-Study available. Support available to part-time students. Financial award application deadline: 3/1. *Faculty research:* Media, language arts, mathematics, computers, drug-free schools. *Unit head:* Dr. Robert Land, Chair, 323-343-4350, Fax: 323-343-5458, E-mail: rland@calstatela.edu. *Application contact:* Dr. Karin Brown, Acting Associate Dean of Graduate Studies, 323-343-3820 Ext. 3827, Fax: 323-343-5653, E-mail: kbrown5@calstatela.edu. Web site: http://www.calstatela.edu/academic/ccoe/index_edci.htm.

California State University, Northridge, Graduate Studies, College of Education, Department of Elementary Education, Northridge, CA 91330. Offers curriculum and instruction (MA); language and literacy (MA); multilingual/multicultural education (MA); teaching and learning (MA). *Accreditation:* NCATE. Part-time and evening/weekend programs available. *Degree requirements:* For master's, comprehensive exam.

Entrance requirements: For master's, GRE General Test or minimum GPA of 3.0. Additional exam requirements/recommendations for international students: Required—TOEFL.

California State University, Sacramento, Office of Graduate Studies, College of Education, Department of Teacher Education, Sacramento, CA 95819-6079. Offers curriculum and instruction (MA); early childhood education (MA); reading education (MA). Part-time programs available. *Faculty:* 30 full-time (19 women), 23 part-time/adjunct (21 women). *Students:* 116 full-time, 313 part-time; includes 116 minority (7 Black or African American, non-Hispanic/Latino; 4 American Indian or Alaska Native, non-Hispanic/Latino; 28 Asian, non-Hispanic/Latino; 51 Hispanic/Latino; 10 Native Hawaiian or other Pacific Islander, non-Hispanic/Latino; 16 Two or more races, non-Hispanic/Latino). Average age 37. 284 applicants, 96% accepted, 225 enrolled. In 2011, 49 master's awarded. *Entrance requirements:* Additional exam requirements/recommendations for international students: Required—TOEFL. *Application deadline:* For fall admission, 3/1 for domestic and international students; for spring admission, 9/15 for domestic students, 9/30 for international students. Applications are processed on a rolling basis. Application fee: $55. Electronic applications accepted. *Financial support:* Teaching assistantships, career-related internships or fieldwork, and Federal Work-Study available. Support available to part-time students. Financial award application deadline: 3/1; financial award applicants required to submit FAFSA. *Faculty research:* Technology integration and psychological implications for teaching and learning; inquiry-based research and learning in science and technology; uncovering the process of everyday creativity in teachers and other leaders; universal design as a foundation for inclusion; bullying, cyber-bullying and impact on school success; diversity, social justice in adult/vocational education. *Unit head:* Dr. Rita Johnson, Chair, 916-278-6155, Fax: 916-278-6643, E-mail: rjohnson@csus.edu. *Application contact:* Jose Martinez, Outreach and Graduate Diversity Coordinator, 916-278-6470, Fax: 916-278-5669, E-mail: martinj@skymail.csus.edu. Web site: http://www.edweb.csus.edu/edte.

California State University, San Bernardino, Graduate Studies, College of Education, Program in Reading, San Bernardino, CA 92407-2397. Offers MA. *Accreditation:* NCATE. Part-time and evening/weekend programs available. *Students:* 30 full-time (25 women), 14 part-time (all women); includes 11 minority (1 Black or African American, non-Hispanic/Latino; 1 American Indian or Alaska Native, non-Hispanic/Latino; 9 Hispanic/Latino). Average age 34. 24 applicants, 75% accepted, 14 enrolled. In 2011, 23 master's awarded. *Degree requirements:* For master's, comprehensive exam (for some programs), thesis or alternative. *Entrance requirements:* For master's, minimum GPA of 3.0 in education. *Application deadline:* For fall admission, 8/31 priority date for domestic students. Application fee: $55. *Expenses:* Tuition, state resident: full-time $7356. Tuition, nonresident: full-time $7356. *Required fees:* $1077. Tuition and fees vary according to program. *Financial support:* Career-related internships or fieldwork and Federal Work-Study available. Support available to part-time students. *Unit head:* Dr. Maria Balderram, Chair, 909-5477405, Fax: 909-537-5992, E-mail: maria@csusb.edu. *Application contact:* Sandra Kamusikiri, Associate Vice-President/Dean of Graduate Studies, 909-537-5058, E-mail: skamusik@csusb.edu.

California State University, Stanislaus, College of Education, Program in Education (MA), Turlock, CA 95382. Offers curriculum and instruction (MA), including education technology, elementary education, multilingual education, physical education, reading, secondary education, special education; school administration (MA); school counseling (MA). Part-time and evening/weekend programs available. *Degree requirements:* For master's, comprehensive exam (for some programs), thesis (for some programs). *Entrance requirements:* For master's, MAT, GRE, or CBEST (varies by concentration), 3 letters of recommendation, personal statement. Additional exam requirements/recommendations for international students: Required—TOEFL (minimum score 550 paper-based; 213 computer-based). *Application deadline:* For fall admission, 5/1 for domestic students; for spring admission, 1/7 for domestic students. Application fee: $55. Electronic applications accepted. *Expenses: Required fees:* $4616 per year. *Financial support:* Federal Work-Study available. Financial award application deadline: 3/1; financial award applicants required to submit FAFSA. *Faculty research:* Children's perspectives on historical events, method elementary schools dual language education, K-12 reading and CYRM programs. *Unit head:* Dr. Kathy Norman, Dean, College of Education, 209-667-3652, Fax: 209-664-6613, E-mail: coe@csustan.edu. *Application contact:* Graduate School, 209-667-3129, Fax: 209-664-7025, E-mail: graduate_school@csustan.edu. Web site: http://www.csustan.edu/COE/.

California University of Pennsylvania, School of Graduate Studies and Research, College of Education and Human Services, Department of Elementary Education, Program in Reading Specialist, California, PA 15419-1394. Offers M Ed. *Accreditation:* NCATE. Part-time and evening/weekend programs available. *Degree requirements:* For master's, comprehensive exam, thesis optional, practicum. *Entrance requirements:* For master's, MAT, PRAXIS, minimum GPA of 3.0, teaching certificate. Additional exam requirements/recommendations for international students: Required—TOEFL (minimum score 550 paper-based; 213 computer-based; 80 iBT). Electronic applications accepted. *Faculty research:* Online education in reading supervision, phonetics education, remedial reading, injury and reading remediation in brain patients.

Calvin College, Graduate Programs in Education, Grand Rapids, MI 49546-4388. Offers curriculum and instruction (M Ed); educational leadership (M Ed); learning disabilities (M Ed); literacy (M Ed). Part-time programs available. *Degree requirements:* For master's, thesis or seminar. *Entrance requirements:* For master's, teaching certificate. Additional exam requirements/recommendations for international students: Required—TOEFL (minimum score 550 paper-based; 213 computer-based; 80 iBT). Electronic applications accepted. *Faculty research:* Literacy, racialized gender and gendered identity, teacher learning, learning disabilities identification.

Cambridge College, School of Education, Cambridge, MA 02138-5304. Offers autism specialist (M Ed); autism/behavior analyst (M Ed); behavior analyst (Post-Master's Certificate); behavioral management (M Ed); early childhood teacher (M Ed); education specialist in curriculum and instruction (CAGS); educational leadership (Ed D); elementary teacher (M Ed); English as a second language (M Ed, Certificate); general science (M Ed); health education (Post-Master's Certificate); health/family and consumer sciences (M Ed); history (M Ed); individualized (M Ed); information technology literacy (M Ed); instructional technology (M Ed); interdisciplinary studies (M Ed); library teacher (M Ed); literacy education (M Ed); mathematics (M Ed); mathematics specialist (Certificate); middle school mathematics and science (M Ed); school administration (M Ed, CAGS); school guidance counselor (M Ed); school nurse education (M Ed); school social worker/school adjustment counselor (M Ed); special education administrator (CAGS); special education/moderate disabilities (M Ed); teaching skills and methodologies (M Ed). Part-time and evening/weekend programs available. Postbaccalaureate distance learning degree programs offered (minimal on-campus study). *Degree requirements:* For master's, thesis, internship/practicum (licensure program only); for doctorate, thesis/dissertation; for other advanced degree, thesis. *Entrance requirements:* For master's, interview, resume, documentation of licensure, 2 professional references; for doctorate, official transcripts, interview, resume, documentation of licensure (if any), written personal statement/essay, portfolio of scholarly and professional work, qualifying assessment, 2 professional references, health insurance, immunizations form; for other advanced degree, official transcripts, interview, resume, documentation of licensure (if any), written personal statement/essay, 2 professional references, health insurance, immunizations form. Additional exam requirements/recommendations for international students: Required—TOEFL (minimum score 550 paper-based; 213 computer-based; 79 iBT); Recommended—IELTS (minimum score 6). Electronic applications accepted. *Expenses:* Contact institution. *Faculty research:* Adult education, accelerated learning, mathematics education, brain compatible learning, special education and law.

Canisius College, Graduate Division, School of Education and Human Services, Department of Graduate Education and Leadership, Buffalo, NY 14208-1098. Offers college student personnel (MS Ed); deaf education (MS Ed); deaf/adolescent education, grades 7-12 (MS Ed); deaf/childhood education, grades 1-6 (MS Ed); differential instruction (MS Ed); education administration (MS Ed); gifted education extention (Certificate); literacy (MS Ed); reading (Certificate); school building leadership (MS Ed, Certificate); school district leadership (Certificate). *Accreditation:* NCATE. Part-time and evening/weekend programs available. Postbaccalaureate distance learning degree programs offered (minimal on-campus study). *Faculty:* 7 full-time (6 women), 36 part-time/adjunct (22 women). *Students:* 149 full-time (114 women), 242 part-time (177 women); includes 42 minority (29 Black or African American, non-Hispanic/Latino; 2 American Indian or Alaska Native, non-Hispanic/Latino; 3 Asian, non-Hispanic/Latino; 6 Hispanic/Latino; 2 Two or more races, non-Hispanic/Latino), 3 international. Average age 30. 250 applicants, 84% accepted, 124 enrolled. In 2011, 135 degrees awarded. *Entrance requirements:* For master's, GRE if cumulative GPA less than 2.7, transcripts, two letters of recommendation. Additional exam requirements/recommendations for international students: Required—TOEFL. *Application deadline:* Applications are processed on a rolling basis. Application fee: $25. Electronic applications accepted. *Financial support:* Career-related internships or fieldwork, Federal Work-Study, scholarships/grants, tuition waivers (partial), and unspecified assistantships available. Support available to part-time students. Financial award application deadline: 4/30; financial award applicants required to submit FAFSA. *Faculty research:* Asperger's disease, autism, private higher education, reading strategies. *Unit head:* Dr. Rosemary K. Murray, Chair/Associate Professor of Graduate Education and Leadership, 716-888-3723, E-mail: murray1@canisius.edu. *Application contact:* Jim Bagwell, Director of Graduate Recruitment and Admissions, 716-888-2544, Fax: 716-888-3290, E-mail: bagwellj@canisius.edu. Web site: http://www.canisius.edu/education/graduate.asp.

Capella University, School of Education, Minneapolis, MN 55402. Offers college teaching (Certificate); curriculum and instruction (MS, PhD); education (MS); enrollment management (MS); instructional design for online learning (MS, PhD); k-12 studies in education (MS, PhD); leadership for higher education (MS, PhD); leadership in education administration (Certificate); leadership in educational administration (MS, PhD); postsecondary and adult education (MS, PhD); professional studies in education (MS, PhD); reading and literacy (MS); training and performance improvement (MS, PhD). Part-time and evening/weekend programs available. Postbaccalaureate distance learning degree programs offered (minimal on-campus study). Terminal master's awarded for partial completion of doctoral program. *Degree requirements:* For master's, thesis optional, integrative project; for doctorate, comprehensive exam, thesis/dissertation. *Entrance requirements:* Additional exam requirements/recommendations for international students: Required—TOEFL (minimum score 550 paper-based; 213 computer-based), TWE (minimum score 4). Electronic applications accepted. *Faculty research:* Higher education administration, distance learning, adult education, training and curriculum design.

Cardinal Stritch University, College of Education, Department of Literacy, Milwaukee, WI 53217-3985. Offers literacy/English as a second language (MA); reading/language arts (MA); reading/learning disability (MA). *Accreditation:* NCATE. Part-time and evening/weekend programs available. *Degree requirements:* For master's, comprehensive exam, thesis, faculty recommendation, research project. *Entrance requirements:* For master's, letters of recommendation (2), minimum GPA of 2.75.

Carthage College, Division of Teacher Education, Kenosha, WI 53140. Offers classroom guidance and counseling (M Ed); creative arts (M Ed); gifted and talented children (M Ed); language arts (M Ed); modern language (M Ed); natural sciences (M Ed); reading (M Ed, Certificate); social sciences (M Ed); teacher leadership (M Ed). Part-time and evening/weekend programs available. *Degree requirements:* For master's, thesis optional. *Entrance requirements:* For master's, MAT, minimum B average, letters of reference.

Castleton State College, Division of Graduate Studies, Department of Education, Program in Language Arts and Reading, Castleton, VT 05735. Offers MA Ed, CAGS. Part-time and evening/weekend programs available. *Degree requirements:* For master's, thesis or alternative; for CAGS, publishable paper, written exams. *Entrance requirements:* For master's, GRE General Test, MAT, interview, minimum undergraduate GPA of 3.0; for CAGS, educational research, master's degree, minimum undergraduate GPA of 3.0.

Central Connecticut State University, School of Graduate Studies, School of Education and Professional Studies, Department of Reading and Language Arts, New Britain, CT 06050-4010. Offers MS, Sixth Year Certificate. Part-time and evening/weekend programs available. *Faculty:* 8 full-time (6 women), 10 part-time/adjunct (6 women). *Students:* 1 (woman) full-time, 116 part-time (114 women); includes 10 minority (3 Black or African American, non-Hispanic/Latino; 6 Hispanic/Latino; 1 Two or more races, non-Hispanic/Latino). Average age 36. 45 applicants, 56% accepted, 14 enrolled. In 2011, 37 master's, 8 other advanced degrees awarded. *Degree requirements:* For master's, comprehensive exam, thesis or alternative; for Sixth Year Certificate, qualifying exam. *Entrance requirements:* For master's, minimum undergraduate GPA of 2.7, teacher certification, interview, essay; for Sixth Year Certificate, master's degree, essay, teacher certification, interview. Additional exam requirements/recommendations for international students: Required—TOEFL (minimum score 550 paper-based; 213 computer-based). *Application deadline:* For fall admission, 6/1 for domestic students, 5/1 for international students; for spring admission, 11/1 for domestic and international students. Applications are processed on a rolling basis. Application fee: $50. Electronic applications accepted. *Expenses: Tuition, area resident:* Full-time $5137; part-time $482 per credit. Tuition, state resident: full-time $7707; part-time $494 per credit. Tuition, nonresident: full-time $14,311; part-time $494 per credit. *Required fees:* $3865. One-time fee: $62 part-time. *Financial support:* In 2011–12, 2 students received support. Career-related internships or fieldwork, Federal Work-Study, scholarships/grants, and unspecified assistantships available. Support available to part-time students. Financial award application deadline: 4/15; financial award applicants required to submit FAFSA. *Faculty research:* Developmental, clinical, and administrative aspects of reading and language arts instruction. *Unit head:* Dr. Helen Abadiano, Chair, 860-832-2175, E-mail: abadiano@ccsu.edu. *Application contact:* Patricia Gardner, Associate Director of Graduate Studies, 860-832-2350, Fax: 860-832-2352, E-mail: graduateadmissions@ccsu.edu. Web site: http://www.reading.ccsu.edu/.

Central Michigan University, Central Michigan University Global Campus, Program in Education, Mount Pleasant, MI 48859. Offers adult education (MA); college teaching (Graduate Certificate); community college (MA); educational leadership (MA), including charter school leadership; educational technology (MA); guidance and development (MA); instruction (MA); reading and literacy K-12 (MA); school principalship (MA);

teacher leadership (MA). *Accreditation:* Teacher Education Accreditation Council. Part-time and evening/weekend programs available. *Entrance requirements:* For master's, minimum GPA of 2.7 in major. Additional exam requirements/recommendations for international students: Required—TOEFL. *Application deadline:* Applications are processed on a rolling basis. Application fee: $50. Electronic applications accepted. *Financial support:* Scholarships/grants available. Support available to part-time students. *Unit head:* Dr. Peter Ross, Director, 989-774-4456, E-mail: ross1pg@cmich.edu. *Application contact:* 877-268-4636, E-mail: cmuglobal@cmich.edu.

Central Michigan University, College of Graduate Studies, College of Education and Human Services, Department of Teacher Education and Professional Development, Mount Pleasant, MI 48859. Offers educational technology (MA, Graduate Certificate); elementary education (MA), including classroom teaching, early childhood; middle level education (MA); reading and literacy K-12 (MA); secondary education (MA). Part-time and evening/weekend programs available. *Degree requirements:* For master's, thesis or alternative. Electronic applications accepted. *Faculty research:* Integrating literacy across the curriculum, science teaching and aesthetic learning in science, diversity education, educational technology, educational psychology and child development.

Central Washington University, Graduate Studies and Research, College of Education and Professional Studies, Department of Language, Literacy and Special Education, Program in Reading Education, Ellensburg, WA 98926. Offers M Ed. Part-time programs available. *Faculty:* 11 full-time (8 women). *Students:* 2 part-time (both women). 1 applicant, 100% accepted, 1 enrolled. In 2011, 1 master's awarded. *Degree requirements:* For master's, thesis or alternative. *Entrance requirements:* For master's, minimum GPA of 3.0. Additional exam requirements/recommendations for international students: Required—TOEFL (minimum score 550 paper-based; 213 computer-based; 79 iBT), IELTS (minimum score 6.5). *Application deadline:* For fall admission, 2/1 priority date for domestic students; for winter admission, 10/1 for domestic students; for spring admission, 1/1 for domestic students. Applications are processed on a rolling basis. Application fee: $50. Electronic applications accepted. *Expenses:* Tuition, state resident: full-time $8112; part-time $270 per credit. Tuition, nonresident: full-time $18,069; part-time $602 per credit. *Required fees:* $924. *Financial support:* Research assistantships with full and partial tuition reimbursements, teaching assistantships with full and partial tuition reimbursements, Federal Work-Study, health care benefits, and unspecified assistantships available. Financial award application deadline: 3/1; financial award applicants required to submit FAFSA. *Unit head:* Dr. Sharryn Walker, Graduate Coordinator, 509-963-2133, E-mail: swalker@cwu.edu. *Application contact:* Justine Eason, Admissions Program Coordinator, 509-963-3103, Fax: 509-963-1799, E-mail: masters@cwu.edu. Web site: http://www.cwu.edu/~llse/litspec.html.

Chicago State University, School of Graduate and Professional Studies, College of Education, Department of Reading, Elementary Education, Library Information and Media Studies, Program in Reading, Chicago, IL 60628. Offers teaching of reading (MS Ed). *Accreditation:* NCATE. *Entrance requirements:* For master's, minimum GPA of 2.75.

The Citadel, The Military College of South Carolina, Citadel Graduate College, School of Education, Program in Reading, Charleston, SC 29409. Offers literacy education (M Ed). *Accreditation:* NCATE. Part-time and evening/weekend programs available. *Faculty:* 12 full-time (8 women), 9 part-time/adjunct (4 women). *Students:* 34 part-time (all women); includes 3 minority (2 Black or African American, non-Hispanic/Latino; 1 Hispanic/Latino). Average age 30. In 2011, 10 master's awarded. *Degree requirements:* For master's, comprehensive exam. *Entrance requirements:* For master's, GRE (minimum score 900) or MAT (minimum score 396), minimum undergraduate GPA of 2.5, valid teaching certificate. Additional exam requirements/recommendations for international students: Required—TOEFL (minimum score 550 paper-based; 213 computer-based; 79 iBT). *Application deadline:* Applications are processed on a rolling basis. Application fee: $30. Electronic applications accepted. *Expenses: Tuition, area resident:* Part-time $501 per credit hour. Tuition, state resident: part-time $501 per credit hour. Tuition, nonresident: part-time $824 per credit hour. *Required fees:* $40 per term. One-time fee: $30. *Financial support:* Career-related internships or fieldwork, health care benefits, and unspecified assistantships available. Support available to part-time students. Financial award application deadline: 7/1; financial award applicants required to submit FAFSA. *Unit head:* Dr. Jennifer L. Altieri, Coordinator, 843-953-3162, Fax: 843-953-7258, E-mail: jennifer.altieri@citadel.edu. *Application contact:* Dr. Steve A. Nida, Associate Provost, The Citadel Graduate College, 843-953-5089, Fax: 843-953-7630, E-mail: cgc@citadel.edu. Web site: http://www.citadel.edu/education/literacy-education.html.

City College of the City University of New York, Graduate School, College of Liberal Arts and Science, Division of the Humanities and Arts, Department of English, Program in Language and Literacy, New York, NY 10031-9198. Offers MA. *Accreditation:* NCATE. *Entrance requirements:* For master's, 2 writing samples. Additional exam requirements/recommendations for international students: Required—TOEFL (minimum score 600 paper-based; 100 iBT). Electronic applications accepted.

City University of Seattle, Graduate Division, Albright School of Education, Bellevue, WA 98005. Offers administrator certification (Certificate); curriculum and instruction (M Ed); educational leadership (Ed D); elementary education (MIT); guidance and counseling (M Ed); higher education leadership (Ed D); leadership (M Ed); leadership and school counseling (M Ed); organizational leadership (Ed D); reading and literacy (M Ed); special education (MIT); superintendent certification (Certificate). Part-time and evening/weekend programs available. Postbaccalaureate distance learning degree programs offered (no on-campus study). *Faculty:* 23 full-time (15 women), 123 part-time/adjunct (82 women). *Students:* 353 full-time (263 women), 75 part-time (50 women); includes 40 minority (12 Black or African American, non-Hispanic/Latino; 5 American Indian or Alaska Native, non-Hispanic/Latino; 7 Asian, non-Hispanic/Latino; 8 Hispanic/Latino; 5 Native Hawaiian or other Pacific Islander, non-Hispanic/Latino; 3 Two or more races, non-Hispanic/Latino). Average age 36. 129 applicants, 98% accepted, 126 enrolled. In 2011, 351 master's, 30 Certificates awarded. *Degree requirements:* For master's, comprehensive exam (for some programs), thesis (for some programs); for doctorate, comprehensive exam, thesis/dissertation. *Entrance requirements:* Additional exam requirements/recommendations for international students: Required—TOEFL (minimum score 567 paper-based; 227 computer-based; 87 iBT); Recommended—IELTS. *Application deadline:* For fall admission, 9/1 for international students; for winter admission, 12/1 for international students; for spring admission, 3/1 for international students. Applications are processed on a rolling basis. Application fee: $50. Electronic applications accepted. *Expenses:* Contact institution. *Financial support:* In 2011–12, 40 students received support. Federal Work-Study and scholarships/grants available. Support available to part-time students. Financial award applicants required to submit FAFSA. *Unit head:* Craig Schieber, Dean, 425-637-101 Ext. 5460, Fax: 425-709-5363, E-mail: schieber@cityu.edu. *Application contact:* Alysa Borelli, 888-422-4898, Fax: 425-709-5363, E-mail: info@cityu.edu. Web site: http://www.cityu.edu/programs/soe/index.aspx.

Clarion University of Pennsylvania, Office of Graduate Programs, Master of Education Program, Clarion, PA 16214. Offers curriculum and instruction (M Ed); early childhood (M Ed, Certificate); English (M Ed); instructional technology specialist (K-12) (Certificate); literacy (M Ed); mathematics education (M Ed); reading specialist (M Ed, Certificate); science education (M Ed); special education (M Ed); technology (M Ed); world language (M Ed). *Accreditation:* NCATE. Part-time programs available. *Students:* 14 full-time (11 women), 207 part-time (163 women); includes 3 minority (1 Black or African American, non-Hispanic/Latino; 2 Hispanic/Latino). Average age 31. In 2011, 96 master's awarded. *Degree requirements:* For master's, thesis or alternative. *Entrance requirements:* For master's, minimum QPA of 3.0. *Application deadline:* Applications are processed on a rolling basis. *Expenses:* Tuition, state resident: part-time $429 per credit. Tuition, nonresident: part-time $644 per credit. *Financial support:* Research assistantships with full and partial tuition reimbursements and career-related internships or fieldwork available. Support available to part-time students. Financial award application deadline: 3/1. *Unit head:* Dr. John Groves, Dean, 814-393-2146, Fax: 514-393-2446. *Application contact:* Dr. Brenda Sanders Dede, Assistant Vice President for Academic Affairs, 814-393-2337, Fax: 814-393-2030, E-mail: bdede@clarion.edu. Web site: http://www.clarion.edu/25887/.

Clarke University, Program in Education, Dubuque, IA 52001-3198. Offers early childhood/special education (MAE); educational administration: elementary and secondary (MAE); educational media: elementary and secondary (MAE); multi-categorical resource k-12 (MAE); multidisciplinary studies (MAE); reading: elementary (MAE); technology in education (MAE). Part-time and evening/weekend programs available. Postbaccalaureate distance learning degree programs offered (minimal on-campus study). *Faculty:* 4 full-time (3 women), 2 part-time/adjunct (1 woman). *Students:* 7 full-time (all women), 43 part-time (40 women). Average age 31. In 2011, 11 master's awarded. *Degree requirements:* For master's, comprehensive exam, thesis optional. *Entrance requirements:* For master's, GRE General Test or MAT, minimum GPA of 2.75. *Application deadline:* Applications are processed on a rolling basis. Application fee: $25. Electronic applications accepted. *Expenses: Tuition:* Part-time $690 per credit hour. *Required fees:* $35 per credit hour. Tuition and fees vary according to program and student level. *Financial support:* Career-related internships or fieldwork available. Financial award applicants required to submit FAFSA. *Unit head:* Dr. Larry Bice, Chair, 319-588-6397, Fax: 319-584-8604. *Application contact:* Joan Coates, Information Contact, 563-588-6354, Fax: 563-588-6789, E-mail: graduate@clarke.edu.

Clemson University, Graduate School, College of Health, Education, and Human Development, Eugene T. Moore School of Education, Program in Reading Literacy, Clemson, SC 29634. Offers M Ed. *Accreditation:* NCATE. Part-time and evening/weekend programs available. *Students:* 7 full-time (all women), 26 part-time (24 women); includes 2 minority (both Hispanic/Latino). Average age 31. 17 applicants, 94% accepted, 8 enrolled. In 2011, 36 master's awarded. *Degree requirements:* For master's, electronic portfolio. *Entrance requirements:* For master's, GRE General Test, teaching certificate; minimum undergraduate GPA of 3.0. Additional exam requirements/recommendations for international students: Required—TOEFL; Recommended—IELTS. *Application deadline:* For fall admission, 3/1 for domestic and international students; for winter admission, 3/1 for domestic and international students; for spring admission, 10/1 for domestic and international students. Applications are processed on a rolling basis. Application fee: $70 ($80 for international students). Electronic applications accepted. *Expenses:* Contact institution. *Financial support:* In 2011–12, 2 students received support, including 1 research assistantship (averaging $9,083 per year); institutionally sponsored loans, health care benefits, and unspecified assistantships also available. Financial award application deadline: 6/1; financial award applicants required to submit FAFSA. *Faculty research:* Assessment and at-risk readers, use of technology in literacy coaching, strategic reading processes, reading comprehension instruction, African-American children's literature. *Unit head:* Dr. Michael J. Padilla, Director/Associate Dean, 864-656-4444, Fax: 864-656-0311, E-mail: padilla@clemson.edu. *Application contact:* Dr. David Fleming, Graduate Coordinator, 864-656-1881, Fax: 864-656-0311, E-mail: dflemin@clemson.edu. Web site: http://www.clemson.edu/hehd/departments/education/academics/graduate/MEd-RE.html.

The College at Brockport, State University of New York, School of Education and Human Services, Department of Education and Human Development, Program in Childhood Literacy, Brockport, NY 14420-2997. Offers MS Ed. *Accreditation:* NCATE. Part-time programs available. *Students:* 4 full-time (3 women), 98 part-time (86 women); includes 3 minority (2 Black or African American, non-Hispanic/Latino; 1 Asian, non-Hispanic/Latino). 39 applicants, 85% accepted, 22 enrolled. In 2011, 20 master's awarded. *Degree requirements:* For master's, thesis or alternative. *Entrance requirements:* For master's, minimum GPA of 3.0, letters of recommendation, interview. Additional exam requirements/recommendations for international students: Required—TOEFL (minimum score 550 paper-based; 213 computer-based; 79 iBT). *Application deadline:* For fall admission, 2/15 priority date for domestic students, 2/15 for international students. Application fee: $80. Electronic applications accepted. *Financial support:* Federal Work-Study and scholarships/grants available. Support available to part-time students. Financial award application deadline: 3/15; financial award applicants required to submit FAFSA. *Unit head:* Dr. Don Halquist, Chairperson, 585-395-5550, Fax: 585-395-2172, E-mail: dhalquis@brockport.edu. *Application contact:* Michael Harrison, Coordinator of Certification and Graduate Advisement, 585-395-2326, Fax: 585-395-2172, E-mail: mharriso@brockport.edu. Web site: http://www.brockport.edu/graduate/.

College of Mount St. Joseph, Graduate Education Program, Cincinnati, OH 45233-1670. Offers adolescent young adult education (MA); art (MA); inclusive early childhood education (MA); instructional leadership (MA); middle childhood education (MA); multi-age education (MA); multicultural special education (MA); music (MA); reading (MA). *Accreditation:* Teacher Education Accreditation Council. Part-time and evening/weekend programs available. *Faculty:* 22 full-time (12 women), 11 part-time/adjunct (8 women). *Students:* 51 full-time (40 women), 92 part-time (72 women); includes 17 minority (14 Black or African American, non-Hispanic/Latino; 1 American Indian or Alaska Native, non-Hispanic/Latino; 1 Asian, non-Hispanic/Latino; 1 Hispanic/Latino). Average age 34. 87 applicants, 44% accepted, 29 enrolled. In 2011, 61 master's awarded. *Degree requirements:* For master's, research project, student teaching, clinical and field-based experiences. *Entrance requirements:* For master's, GRE, PRAXIS II in teaching content area (math or science), 2 letters of recommendation, interview, resume. Additional exam requirements/recommendations for international students: Required—TOEFL (minimum score 560 paper-based; 220 computer-based; 83 iBT). *Application deadline:* Applications are processed on a rolling basis. Application fee: $50. Electronic applications accepted. *Expenses: Tuition:* Full-time $24,200; part-time $540 per credit hour. *Required fees:* $112.50 per semester. One-time fee: $200. *Financial support:* In 2011–12, 22 students received support. Scholarships/grants available. Financial award applicants required to submit FAFSA. *Faculty research:* Foreign and second language learning problems/reading disabilities/hyperlexia, multicultural/bilingual special education, alternative educator licensure, science education, pedagogical content knowledge. *Unit head:* Dr. Mary West, Chair, 513-244-3263, Fax: 513-244-4867, E-mail: mary_west@mail.msj.edu. *Application contact:* Marilyn Hoskins, Assistant Director of Graduate Recruitment, 513-244-4723, Fax: 513-244-4629, E-mail: marilyn_hoskins@mail.msj.edu. Web site: http://www.msj.edu/view/academics/graduate-programs/education.aspx.

The College of New Jersey, Graduate Studies, School of Education, Department of Special Education, Language and Literacy, Program in Developmental Reading, Ewing,

NJ 08628. Offers M Ed. *Accreditation:* NCATE. Part-time programs available. *Degree requirements:* For master's, comprehensive exam. *Entrance requirements:* For master's, GRE General Test, minimum GPA of 3.0 in field or 2.75 overall. Additional exam requirements/recommendations for international students: Required—TOEFL. Electronic applications accepted.

The College of New Jersey, Graduate Studies, School of Education, Department of Special Education, Language and Literacy, Program in Reading Certification, Ewing, NJ 08628. Offers Certificate. Part-time programs available. *Entrance requirements:* Additional exam requirements/recommendations for international students: Required—TOEFL. Electronic applications accepted.

The College of New Rochelle, Graduate School, Division of Education, Program in Literacy Education, New Rochelle, NY 10805-2308. Offers MS Ed. Part-time and evening/weekend programs available. *Degree requirements:* For master's, practicum. *Entrance requirements:* For master's, interview, minimum GPA of 3.0 in field, 2.7 overall, early elementary teacher certification.

College of St. Joseph, Graduate Programs, Division of Education, Program in Reading, Rutland, VT 05701-3899. Offers M Ed. Part-time and evening/weekend programs available. *Faculty:* 2 full-time (both women), 2 part-time/adjunct (both women). *Students:* 13 part-time (11 women). Average age 27. 4 applicants, 75% accepted, 3 enrolled. In 2011, 12 master's awarded. *Degree requirements:* For master's, comprehensive exam. *Entrance requirements:* For master's, PRAXIS I, official college transcripts; 2 letters of reference; minimum GPA of 3.0 (initial licensure) or 2.7 (nonlicensure); interview. Additional exam requirements/recommendations for international students: Required—TOEFL (minimum score 550 paper-based). *Application deadline:* Applications are processed on a rolling basis. Application fee: $35. Electronic applications accepted. *Expenses: Tuition:* Full-time $15,200; part-time $400 per credit. *Required fees:* $45 per semester. *Financial support:* Career-related internships or fieldwork, Federal Work-Study, and unspecified assistantships available. Support available to part-time students. Financial award application deadline: 3/1. *Unit head:* Dr. Maria Bove, Chair, 802-773-5900 Ext. 3243, Fax: 802-776-5258, E-mail: mbove@csj.edu. *Application contact:* Alan Young, Director of Admissions, 802-773-5900 Ext. 3227, Fax: 802-776-5310, E-mail: alanyoung@csj.edu.

The College of Saint Rose, Graduate Studies, School of Education, Department of Literacy and Special Education, Albany, NY 12203-1419. Offers literacy: birth-grade 6 (MS Ed); literacy: grades 5-12 (MS Ed); reading (Certificate), including literacy: birth - grade 6, literacy: grades 5-12; special education (MS Ed), including adolescent education, childhood education, special education advanced study. Part-time and evening/weekend programs available. *Entrance requirements:* For master's, minimum undergraduate GPA of 3.0. Additional exam requirements/recommendations for international students: Required—TOEFL (minimum score 550 paper-based; 213 computer-based). Electronic applications accepted.

The College of William and Mary, School of Education, Program in Curriculum and Instruction, Williamsburg, VA 23187-8795. Offers elementary education (MA Ed); gifted education (MA Ed); math specialist (MA Ed); reading education (MA Ed); secondary education (MA Ed), including English education, mathematics education, modern foreign languages education, science education, social studies education; special education (MA Ed), including collaborating master educator, general curriculum. *Accreditation:* NCATE. Part-time programs available. *Faculty:* 15 full-time (10 women), 39 part-time/adjunct (32 women). *Students:* 80 full-time (69 women), 13 part-time (11 women); includes 11 minority (3 Black or African American, non-Hispanic/Latino; 1 American Indian or Alaska Native, non-Hispanic/Latino; 2 Hispanic/Latino; 5 Two or more races, non-Hispanic/Latino), 1 international. Average age 25. 220 applicants, 56% accepted, 85 enrolled. In 2011, 78 master's awarded. *Degree requirements:* For master's, project. *Entrance requirements:* For master's, GRE or MAT, minimum GPA of 2.5. Additional exam requirements/recommendations for international students: Required—TOEFL. *Application deadline:* For fall admission, 1/15 for domestic and international students; for spring admission, 10/1 for domestic and international students. Application fee: $50. Electronic applications accepted. *Expenses:* Tuition, state resident: full-time $6400; part-time $365 per credit hour. Tuition, nonresident: full-time $19,720; part-time $985 per credit hour. *Required fees:* $4562. *Financial support:* In 2011–12, 53 students received support, including 10 research assistantships with full and partial tuition reimbursements available (averaging $7,000 per year); career-related internships or fieldwork, Federal Work-Study, institutionally sponsored loans, scholarships/grants, and unspecified assistantships also available. Financial award application deadline: 1/15; financial award applicants required to submit FAFSA. *Faculty research:* National Council of Teachers of Mathematics Standards, counseling, self-concept and self-esteem, special education, curriculum development. *Unit head:* Dr. Margie Mason, Area Coordinator, 757-221-2327, E-mail: mmmaso@wm.edu. *Application contact:* Dorothy Smith Osborne, Assistant Dean for Admission, 757-221-2317, Fax: 757-221-2293, E-mail: dsosbo@wm.edu. Web site: http://education.wm.edu.

Concordia University Chicago, College of Education, Program in Reading Education, River Forest, IL 60305-1499. Offers MA. Part-time and evening/weekend programs available. *Degree requirements:* For master's, comprehensive exam, thesis optional. *Entrance requirements:* For master's, minimum GPA of 2.9. Additional exam requirements/recommendations for international students: Required—TOEFL (minimum score 550 paper-based; 195 computer-based). Electronic applications accepted. *Faculty research:* Early literacy, classroom management and organization in reading, minority students and reading.

Concordia University, Nebraska, Graduate Programs in Education, Program in Reading Education, Seward, NE 68434-1599. Offers M Ed. *Accreditation:* NCATE. Part-time programs available. *Degree requirements:* For master's, thesis or alternative. *Entrance requirements:* For master's, GRE, MAT, or NTE, minimum GPA of 3.0, BS in education or equivalent.

Concordia University, St. Paul, College of Education, St. Paul, MN 55104-5494. Offers curriculum and instruction (MA Ed), including K-12 reading endorsement; differentiated instruction (MA Ed); early childhood education (MA Ed); educational leadership (MA Ed); educational technology (MA Ed); family life education (MA); K-12 reading endorsement (Certificate); special education (Certificate); sports management (MA). *Accreditation:* NCATE. Evening/weekend programs available. Postbaccalaureate distance learning degree programs offered (minimal on-campus study). *Faculty:* 7 full-time (3 women), 64 part-time/adjunct (42 women). *Students:* 617 full-time (495 women), 9 part-time (6 women); includes 57 minority (30 Black or African American, non-Hispanic/Latino; 2 American Indian or Alaska Native, non-Hispanic/Latino; 17 Asian, non-Hispanic/Latino; 5 Hispanic/Latino; 1 Native Hawaiian or other Pacific Islander, non-Hispanic/Latino; 2 Two or more races, non-Hispanic/Latino). Average age 36. 302 applicants, 83% accepted, 210 enrolled. In 2011, 320 master's, 68 other advanced degrees awarded. *Application deadline:* Applications are processed on a rolling basis. Application fee: $50. Electronic applications accepted. *Expenses: Tuition:* Full-time $8100; part-time $435 per credit. Tuition and fees vary according to program. *Financial support:* Applicants required to submit FAFSA. *Unit head:* Dr. Donald Helmstetter, Dean, 651-641-8227, Fax: 651-641-8807, E-mail: helmstetter@csp.edu. *Application contact:* Kimberly Craig, Director of Graduate and Cohort Admission, 651-603-6223, Fax: 651-603-6320, E-mail: craig@csp.edu.

Concordia University Wisconsin, Graduate Programs, Department of Education, Program in Reading, Mequon, WI 53097-2402. Offers MS Ed. Part-time and evening/weekend programs available. Postbaccalaureate distance learning degree programs offered (minimal on-campus study). *Students:* 89 full-time (84 women), 157 part-time (148 women); includes 10 minority (5 Black or African American, non-Hispanic/Latino; 1 American Indian or Alaska Native, non-Hispanic/Latino; 2 Hispanic/Latino; 2 Two or more races, non-Hispanic/Latino). Average age 37. In 2011, 4 master's awarded. *Degree requirements:* For master's, comprehensive exam, thesis or alternative. *Entrance requirements:* For master's, minimum GPA of 3.0. Additional exam requirements/recommendations for international students: Required—TOEFL. Application fee: $35. *Financial support:* Application deadline: 8/1. *Unit head:* Dr. Marsha K. Konz, Dean of Graduate Studies, 262-243-4253, Fax: 262-243-4428, E-mail: marsha.konz@cuw.edu. *Application contact:* Graduate Admissions, 262-243-4248, Fax: 262-243-4428.

Concord University, Graduate Studies, Athens, WV 24712-1000. Offers educational leadership and supervision (M Ed); geography (M Ed); health promotion (M Ed); reading specialist (M Ed). Part-time and evening/weekend programs available. Postbaccalaureate distance learning degree programs offered (no on-campus study). *Entrance requirements:* For master's, GRE or MAT, baccalaureate degree with minimum GPA of 2.5 from regionally-accredited institution; teaching license; 2 letters of recommendation; completed disposition assessment form. Electronic applications accepted.

Coppin State University, Division of Graduate Studies, Division of Education, Baltimore, MD 21216-3698. Offers adult and general education (MS); curriculum and instruction (M Ed, MAT, MS), including curriculum and instruction (M Ed), reading education (MS), teaching (MAT); special education (M Ed). *Accreditation:* NCATE. Part-time and evening/weekend programs available. Postbaccalaureate distance learning degree programs offered. *Degree requirements:* For master's, comprehensive exam (for some programs), thesis (for some programs).

Coppin State University, Division of Graduate Studies, Division of Education, Department of Curriculum and Instruction, Program in Reading Education, Baltimore, MD 21216-3698. Offers MS. Part-time programs available. *Degree requirements:* For master's, 3 hours of capstone experience in urban literacy. *Entrance requirements:* For master's, MAT or GRE, resume, references, teacher certification, 3 years of teaching experience.

Curry College, Graduate Studies, Program in Education, Milton, MA 02186-9984. Offers elementary education (M Ed); foundations (non-license) (M Ed); reading (M Ed, Certificate); special education (M Ed). Part-time and evening/weekend programs available. *Degree requirements:* For master's, project or thesis. *Entrance requirements:* For master's, interview, recommendations, resume, written statement. Additional exam requirements/recommendations for international students: Required—TOEFL (minimum score 550 paper-based; 213 computer-based; 80 iBT). *Expenses:* Contact institution. *Faculty research:* Classroom trauma, therapeutic writing, inclusionary practices.

Dallas Baptist University, Dorothy M. Bush College of Education, Program in Reading and English as a Second Language, Dallas, TX 75211-9299. Offers English as a second language (M Ed); master reading teacher (M Ed); reading specialist (M Ed). Part-time and evening/weekend programs available. *Entrance requirements:* For master's, GRE General Test, minimum GPA of 3.0. Additional exam requirements/recommendations for international students: Required—TOEFL, IELTS. Application fee: $25. *Expenses: Tuition:* Full-time $12,060; part-time $670 per credit hour. *Required fees:* $100; $50 per semester. *Financial support:* Federal Work-Study, institutionally sponsored loans, scholarships/grants, and tuition waivers (full and partial) available. Support available to part-time students. Financial award applicants required to submit FAFSA. *Unit head:* Amie Sarker, Director, 214-333-5200, Fax: 214-333-5551, E-mail: graduate@dbu.edu. *Application contact:* Kit P. Montgomery, Director of Graduate Programs, 214-333-5242, Fax: 214-333-5579, E-mail: graduate@dbu.edu. Web site: http://www3.dbu.edu/graduate/english_reading.asp.

Delaware State University, Graduate Programs, College of Education, Health and Public Policy, Program in Adult Literacy and Basic Education, Dover, DE 19901-2277. Offers MA. *Entrance requirements:* Additional exam requirements/recommendations for international students: Required—TOEFL (minimum score 550 paper-based). Electronic applications accepted.

DePaul University, College of Education, Chicago, IL 60106. Offers bilingual bicultural education (M Ed, MA); counseling (M Ed, MA), including college student development, community counseling, school counseling; curriculum studies (M Ed, MA, Ed D); early childhood education (M Ed, MA); educational leadership (M Ed, MA, Ed D), including administration and supervision (M Ed, MA), physical education (M Ed, MA); middle school mathematics education (MS); reading specialist (M Ed, MA); social and cultural foundations in education (M Ed, MA), including curriculum studies/development (MA); special education (M Ed, MA); teaching and learning (M Ed, MA), including elementary education, secondary education; world languages education (M Ed, MA). Part-time and evening/weekend programs available. *Faculty:* 49 full-time (28 women), 94 part-time/adjunct (60 women). *Students:* 894 full-time (707 women), 473 part-time (361 women); includes 349 minority (159 Black or African American, non-Hispanic/Latino; 3 American Indian or Alaska Native, non-Hispanic/Latino; 45 Asian, non-Hispanic/Latino; 115 Hispanic/Latino; 2 Native Hawaiian or other Pacific Islander, non-Hispanic/Latino; 25 Two or more races, non-Hispanic/Latino), 21 international. Average age 30. 872 applicants, 64% accepted, 325 enrolled. In 2011, 499 master's, 10 doctorates awarded. *Median time to degree:* Of those who began their doctoral program in fall 2003, 32% received their degree in 8 years or less. *Degree requirements:* For master's, thesis/dissertation (for MA); capstone course or paper (for M Ed); for doctorate, thesis/dissertation. *Entrance requirements:* For master's, interview, minimum GPA of 2.75, 2 letters of recommendation, bachelor's degree conferred by accredited college or university; for doctorate, interview, master's degree, writing sample, 3 letters of recommendation. Additional exam requirements/recommendations for international students: Required—TOEFL (minimum score 550 paper-based; 213 computer-based; 80 iBT). *Application deadline:* For fall admission, 8/15 priority date for domestic students; for winter admission, 12/1 priority date for domestic students; for spring admission, 3/1 priority date for domestic students. Applications are processed on a rolling basis. Application fee: $40. Electronic applications accepted. *Financial support:* In 2011–12, 163 students received support, including 15 research assistantships with full tuition reimbursements available (averaging $6,375 per year); career-related internships or fieldwork, Federal Work-Study, scholarships/grants, and unspecified assistantships also available. Support available to part-time students. Financial award application deadline: 12/31; financial award applicants required to submit FAFSA. *Faculty research:* Reflective teaching, children at risk, loss, ethnicity, urban education. *Total annual research expenditures:* $916,310. *Unit head:* Dr. Paul Zionts, Dean, 773-325-7581, Fax: 773-325-7713, E-mail: pzionts@depaul.edu. *Application contact:* Brandon Washington, Enrollment Management Coordinator, 773-325-1152, Fax: 773-325-2270, E-mail: bwashin3@depaul.edu. Web site: http://education.depaul.edu.

Dominican University, School of Education, River Forest, IL 60305-1099. Offers curriculum and instruction (MA Ed); early childhood education (MS); education (MAT); educational administration (MA); elementary (online) (MS); English as a second language (online) (MS); reading (online) (MS); special education (MS). Part-time and evening/weekend programs available. Postbaccalaureate distance learning degree programs offered (no on-campus study). *Faculty:* 19 full-time (13 women), 53 part-time/adjunct (41 women). *Students:* 24 full-time (19 women), 434 part-time (357 women); includes 95 minority (27 Black or African American, non-Hispanic/Latino; 1 American Indian or Alaska Native, non-Hispanic/Latino; 12 Asian, non-Hispanic/Latino; 48 Hispanic/Latino; 7 Two or more races, non-Hispanic/Latino), 1 international. Average age 33. 92 applicants, 99% accepted, 91 enrolled. In 2011, 267 master's awarded. *Entrance requirements:* For master's, Illinois certification test of basic skills. Additional exam requirements/recommendations for international students: Required—TOEFL (minimum score 550 paper-based; 213 computer-based; 79 iBT). *Application deadline:* Applications are processed on a rolling basis. Application fee: $25. *Expenses:* Contact institution. *Financial support:* Career-related internships or fieldwork, scholarships/grants, and tuition waivers (partial) available. Support available to part-time students. Financial award application deadline: 8/15; financial award applicants required to submit FAFSA. *Faculty research:* Governance of private education institutions, reading and language arts, inclusion, organizational planning, leadership and vision. *Unit head:* Dr. Colleen Reardon, Dean, 718-524-6643, Fax: 708-524-6665, E-mail: creardon@dom.edu. *Application contact:* Keven Hansen, Coordinator of Recruitment and Admissions, 708-524-6921, Fax: 708-524-6665, E-mail: educate@dom.edu. Web site: http://www.dom.edu/soe.

Dowling College, Graduate Programs in Education, Oakdale, NY 11769-1999. Offers adolescence education with middle childhood extension (MS); advanced certificate in gifted education (AC); childhood and early childhood education (MS); childhood and gifted education (MS); computers in education (AC); early childhood education (MS); educational administration (Ed D); educational technology leadership (MS); educational technology specialist (AC); literacy education (MS); literary education (AC); school building leader (AC); school district business leader (MBA, AC); school district leader (AC); special education (MS); sports management (MS). *Accreditation:* NCATE. Part-time and evening/weekend programs available. Postbaccalaureate distance learning degree programs offered (minimal on-campus study). *Faculty:* 23 full-time (12 women), 70 part-time/adjunct (44 women). *Students:* 336 full-time (245 women), 631 part-time (485 women); includes 83 minority (29 Black or African American, non-Hispanic/Latino; 2 American Indian or Alaska Native, non-Hispanic/Latino; 7 Asian, non-Hispanic/Latino; 45 Hispanic/Latino). Average age 32. 280 applicants, 85% accepted, 167 enrolled. In 2011, 425 master's, 27 doctorates, 40 other advanced degrees awarded. *Degree requirements:* For master's and AC, comprehensive exam; for doctorate, thesis/dissertation. *Entrance requirements:* For master's, minimum GPA of 3.0; for doctorate, GRE, master's degree; for AC, teaching certificate. Additional exam requirements/recommendations for international students: Required—TOEFL (minimum score 550 paper-based). *Application deadline:* For fall admission, 9/1 priority date for domestic students; for winter admission, 1/1 priority date for domestic students; for spring admission, 2/1 priority date for domestic students. Applications are processed on a rolling basis. Application fee: $50. Electronic applications accepted. *Expenses: Tuition:* Full-time $19,162; part-time $933 per credit. *Required fees:* $1330; $700 per year. Tuition and fees vary according to course load. *Financial support:* Career-related internships or fieldwork and Federal Work-Study available. Support available to part-time students. Financial award application deadline: 6/30; financial award applicants required to submit FAFSA. *Faculty research:* Natural readers, Korean styles and learning strategies, mothers of children with disabilities, computers in instruction, cultural background and organizational roadblocks to problem solving. *Unit head:* Carol Pulsonetti, Director of Operations, School of Education, 631-244-3243, E-mail: pulsonec@dowling.edu. *Application contact:* Ronnie S. Macdonald, Assistant Vice President for Enrollment Services/Dean of Admissions, 631-244-3357, Fax: 631-244-1059, E-mail: macdonar@dowling.edu.

Drury University, Graduate Programs in Education, Springfield, MO 65802. Offers elementary education (M Ed); gifted education (M Ed); human services (M Ed); instructional mathematics K-8 (M Ed); instructional technology (M Ed); middle school teaching (M Ed); secondary education (M Ed); special education (M Ed); special reading (M Ed). *Accreditation:* NCATE. Part-time and evening/weekend programs available. *Degree requirements:* For master's, thesis. *Entrance requirements:* For master's, GRE or MAT, minimum GPA of 2.75. Additional exam requirements/recommendations for international students: Required—TOEFL. Electronic applications accepted. *Faculty research:* Cultural enrichment, research skills, parental involvement relating to reading skills, reading strategies for mainstreaming children.

Duquesne University, School of Education, Department of Instruction and Leadership, Program in Reading and Language Arts, Pittsburgh, PA 15282-0001. Offers MS Ed. Part-time and evening/weekend programs available. *Faculty:* 1 (woman) full-time, 6 part-time/adjunct (2 women). *Students:* 18 full-time (16 women), 16 part-time (all women); includes 4 minority (2 Black or African American, non-Hispanic/Latino; 1 Asian, non-Hispanic/Latino; 1 Hispanic/Latino). Average age 30. 13 applicants, 69% accepted, 7 enrolled. In 2011, 23 master's awarded. *Degree requirements:* For master's, thesis optional. *Entrance requirements:* For master's, bachelor's degree. Additional exam requirements/recommendations for international students: Required—TOEFL (minimum score 550 paper-based; 80 computer-based), IELTS (minimum score 7). *Application deadline:* For fall admission, 9/1 for domestic students; for spring admission, 1/1 for domestic students. Applications are processed on a rolling basis. Application fee: $0. Electronic applications accepted. Application fee is waived when completed online. *Expenses: Tuition:* Full-time $16,596; part-time $922 per credit. *Required fees:* $1584; $88 per credit. Tuition and fees vary according to program. *Financial support:* Research assistantships and Federal Work-Study available. Support available to part-time students. *Unit head:* Dr. Rosemary T. Mautino, Director, 412-396-6089, Fax: 412-396-1759, E-mail: mautino@duq.edu. *Application contact:* Michael Dolinger, Director of Student and Academic Services, 412-396-6647, Fax: 412-396-5585, E-mail: dolingerm@duq.edu. Web site: http://www.duq.edu/education.

East Carolina University, Graduate School, College of Education, Department of Curriculum and Instruction, Greenville, NC 27858-4353. Offers assistive technology (Certificate); autism (Certificate); deaf/blindness (Certificate); elementary education (MA Ed); English education (MA Ed); history (MA Ed); middle grade education (MA Ed); reading education (MA Ed); special education (MA Ed); teaching (MAT). Part-time programs available. Postbaccalaureate distance learning degree programs offered. *Degree requirements:* For master's, comprehensive exam, thesis optional. *Entrance requirements:* For master's, GRE General Test or MAT, interview, bachelor's degree in related field, minimum GPA of 2.5, teaching license. Additional exam requirements/recommendations for international students: Required—TOEFL. *Application deadline:* For fall admission, 6/1 priority date for domestic students. Applications are processed on a rolling basis. Application fee: $50. *Expenses:* Tuition, state resident: full-time $3557; part-time $444.63 per semester hour. Tuition, nonresident: full-time $14,351; part-time $1793.88 per semester hour. *Required fees:* $2016; $252 per semester hour. Part-time tuition and fees vary according to course load, campus/location and program. *Financial support:* Research assistantships, teaching assistantships, and Federal Work-Study available. Support available to part-time students. Financial award application deadline: 6/1; financial award applicants required to submit FAFSA. *Unit head:* Carolyn C. Ledford, Interim Chair, 252-328-1100, E-mail: ledfordc@ecu.edu. *Application contact:* Dean of Graduate School, 252-328-6012, Fax: 252-328-6071, E-mail: gradschool@ecu.edu. Web site: http://www.ecu.edu/cs-educ/ci/Graduate.cfm.

Eastern Connecticut State University, School of Education and Professional Studies/Graduate Division, Program in Reading and Language Arts, Willimantic, CT 06226-2295. Offers MS. *Accreditation:* NCATE. Part-time and evening/weekend programs available. *Degree requirements:* For master's, comprehensive exam or thesis. *Entrance requirements:* For master's, minimum GPA of 2.7, teaching certificate. Additional exam requirements/recommendations for international students: Required—TOEFL (minimum score 550 paper-based; 213 computer-based).

Eastern Michigan University, Graduate School, College of Education, Department of Teacher Education, Program in Reading, Ypsilanti, MI 48197. Offers MA. *Accreditation:* NCATE. Part-time and evening/weekend programs available. Postbaccalaureate distance learning degree programs offered (minimal on-campus study). *Students:* 2 full-time (both women), 78 part-time (74 women); includes 9 minority (3 Black or African American, non-Hispanic/Latino; 1 American Indian or Alaska Native, non-Hispanic/Latino; 3 Asian, non-Hispanic/Latino; 2 Hispanic/Latino). Average age 34. 35 applicants, 97% accepted, 15 enrolled. In 2011, 25 degrees awarded. *Entrance requirements:* For master's, GRE. Additional exam requirements/recommendations for international students: Required—TOEFL. *Application deadline:* Applications are processed on a rolling basis. Application fee: $35. *Expenses:* Tuition, state resident: full-time $10,367; part-time $432 per credit hour. Tuition, nonresident: full-time $20,435; part-time $851 per credit hour. *Required fees:* $39 per credit hour. $46 per semester. One-time fee: $100. Tuition and fees vary according to course level, degree level and reciprocity agreements. *Financial support:* Fellowships, research assistantships with full tuition reimbursements, teaching assistantships with full tuition reimbursements, career-related internships or fieldwork, Federal Work-Study, institutionally sponsored loans, scholarships/grants, tuition waivers (partial), and unspecified assistantships available. Support available to part-time students. Financial award applicants required to submit FAFSA. *Unit head:* Dr. Mary Rearick, Coordinator, 734-487-3260, Fax: 734-487-2101, E-mail: mrearick@emich.edu. *Application contact:* Dr. Anne Bednar, Advisor, 734-487-3260, Fax: 734-487-2101, E-mail: anne.bednar@emich.edu.

Eastern Nazarene College, Adult and Graduate Studies, Division of Teacher Education, Quincy, MA 02170. Offers administration (M Ed); early childhood education (M Ed, Certificate); elementary education (M Ed, Certificate); English as a second language (Certificate); instructional enrichment and development (Certificate); middle school education (M Ed, Certificate); moderate special needs education (Certificate); principal (Certificate); program development and supervision (Certificate); secondary education (M Ed, Certificate); special education administrator (Certificate); special needs (M Ed); supervisor (Certificate); teacher of reading (M Ed, Certificate). M Ed also available through weekend program for administration, special needs, and teacher of reading only. Part-time and evening/weekend programs available. *Entrance requirements:* Additional exam requirements/recommendations for international students: Required—TOEFL (minimum score 550 paper-based).

Eastern New Mexico University, Graduate School, College of Education and Technology, Department of Curriculum and Instruction, Portales, NM 88130. Offers bilingual education (M Ed); educational technology (M Ed); elementary education (M Ed); English as a second language (M Ed); pedagogy and learning (M Ed); professional technical education (M Ed); reading/literacy (M Ed). Part-time programs available. Postbaccalaureate distance learning degree programs offered (minimal on-campus study). *Degree requirements:* For master's, comprehensive exam, thesis optional. *Entrance requirements:* For master's, minimum GPA of 3.0, photocopy of teaching license, writing assessment, letter of recommendation. Additional exam requirements/recommendations for international students: Required—TOEFL (minimum score 550 paper-based; 213 computer-based; 79 iBT), IELTS (minimum score 6). Electronic applications accepted.

Eastern Washington University, Graduate Studies, College of Arts, Letters and Education, Department of Education, Program in Literacy, Cheney, WA 99004-2431. Offers M Ed. *Students:* 3 full-time (all women), 1 (woman) part-time. Average age 33. 2 applicants, 50% accepted, 1 enrolled. In 2011, 7 master's awarded. *Degree requirements:* For master's, comprehensive exam. *Entrance requirements:* For master's, minimum GPA of 3.0. *Application deadline:* For fall admission, 4/1 priority date for domestic students; for spring admission, 1/15 for domestic students. Applications are processed on a rolling basis. Application fee: $50. *Financial support:* In 2011–12, teaching assistantships with partial tuition reimbursements (averaging $7,000 per year) were awarded; career-related internships or fieldwork, Federal Work-Study, institutionally sponsored loans, scholarships/grants, health care benefits, tuition waivers (partial), and unspecified assistantships also available. Support available to part-time students. Financial award application deadline: 2/1; financial award applicants required to submit FAFSA. *Unit head:* Robin Showalter, Program Coordinator, 509-359-6492, E-mail: rshowalter@mail.ewu.edu. *Application contact:* Dr. Kevin Pyatt, Assistant Professor, Science and Technology, 509-359-6091, E-mail: kpyatt@ewu.edu.

East Stroudsburg University of Pennsylvania, Graduate School, College of Education, Department of Reading, East Stroudsburg, PA 18301-2999. Offers M Ed. Part-time and evening/weekend programs available. *Degree requirements:* For master's, comprehensive exam, research paper, electronic program portfolio. *Entrance requirements:* For master's, PRAXIS/teacher certification, letter of recommendation, Pennsylvania Department of Education requirements. Additional exam requirements/recommendations for international students: Required—TOEFL (minimum score 560 paper-based; 220 computer-based; 83 iBT). *Faculty research:* Portfolio assessment, reading assessment.

East Tennessee State University, School of Graduate Studies, College of Education, Department of Curriculum and Instruction, Johnson City, TN 37614. Offers educational media/educational technology (M Ed), including educational communications and technology, school library media; elementary education (M Ed); reading (MA), including reading education, storytelling; school library professional (Post-Master's Certificate); secondary education (M Ed), including classroom technology, secondary education (M Ed, MAT); storytelling (Postbaccalaureate Certificate); teacher education with multiple levels (initial licensure) (MAT), including elementary education, middle grades education, secondary education (M Ed, MAT). *Accreditation:* NCATE. Part-time and evening/weekend programs available. Postbaccalaureate distance learning degree programs offered (no on-campus study). *Faculty:* 20 full-time (13 women), 3 part-time/adjunct (all women). *Students:* 108 full-time (76 women), 107 part-time (97 women); includes 9 minority (4 Black or African American, non-Hispanic/Latino; 1 Asian, non-Hispanic/Latino; 2 Hispanic/Latino; 2 Two or more races, non-Hispanic/Latino), 2 international. Average age 33. 141 applicants, 57% accepted, 79 enrolled. In 2011, 129 master's awarded. *Degree requirements:* For master's, comprehensive exam, thesis optional, student teaching, practicum; for other advanced degree, field work (school library); culminating experience (storytelling). *Entrance requirements:* For master's, GRE, SAT, ACT, PRAXIS, minimum GPA of 3.0; for other advanced degree, master's degree, TN teaching license (school library professional post-master's certificate); three letters of recommendation (storytelling certificate). Additional exam requirements/recommendations for international students: Required—TOEFL (minimum score 550 paper-based; 213 computer-based; 79 iBT). *Application deadline:* For fall admission, 6/1 for domestic students, 4/30 for international students; for spring admission, 11/1 for domestic students, 4/30 for international students. Application fee: $35 ($45 for international students). Electronic applications accepted. *Expenses:* Tuition, state resident: full-time $7312; part-time $350 per credit hour. Tuition, nonresident: full-time $18,490; part-time $621 per credit hour. *Required fees:* $63 per credit hour. Tuition and fees vary according to course load and program. *Financial support:* In 2011–12, 60 students received support, including 7 research assistantships with full tuition reimbursements available (averaging $6,000 per year), 11 teaching assistantships with full tuition reimbursements available (averaging $6,000 per year); career-related internships or fieldwork, institutionally sponsored loans, scholarships/grants, and unspecified assistantships also available. Financial award application deadline: 7/1; financial award applicants required to submit FAFSA. *Faculty research:* Critical thinking; curriculum development in reading, math, and science education; cultural diversity; cognitive processes; effective teaching strategies. *Unit head:* Dr. Rhona Hurwitz, Chair, 423-439-7598, Fax: 423-439-8362, E-mail: hurwitz@etsu.edu. *Application contact:* Fiona Goodyear, Graduate Specialist, 423-439-6148, Fax: 423-439-5624, E-mail: goodyear@etsu.edu.

Edgewood College, Program in Education, Madison, WI 53711-1997. Offers adult learning (MA Ed); bilingual teaching and learning (MA Ed); director of instruction (Certificate); director of special education and pupil services (Certificate); education (MA Ed); educational administration (MA Ed); educational leadership (Ed D); professional studies (MA Ed); program coordinator (Certificate); reading administration (MA Ed); school business administration (Certificate); school principalship K-12 (Certificate); special education (MA Ed); sustainability leadership (MA Ed); teaching and learning (MA Ed); teaching English to speakers of other languages (TESOL) (MA Ed). *Accreditation:* NCATE (one or more programs are accredited). Part-time and evening/weekend programs available. *Students:* 155 full-time (93 women), 152 part-time (116 women); includes 39 minority (13 Black or African American, non-Hispanic/Latino; 5 Asian, non-Hispanic/Latino; 17 Hispanic/Latino; 4 Two or more races, non-Hispanic/Latino), 9 international. Average age 36. In 2011, 39 master's, 32 doctorates awarded. *Degree requirements:* For master's, practicum, research project; for doctorate, comprehensive exam, thesis/dissertation. *Entrance requirements:* For master's, minimum GPA of 2.75, 2 letters of recommendation, personal statement; for doctorate, resume, letter of intent, 2 letters of recommendation, interview, writing sample. Additional exam requirements/recommendations for international students: Required—TOEFL (minimum score 525 paper-based; 197 computer-based; 72 iBT). *Application deadline:* For fall admission, 8/15 for domestic students, 5/1 for international students; for spring admission, 1/8 for domestic students, 11/1 for international students. Applications are processed on a rolling basis. Application fee: $25. Electronic applications accepted. *Expenses: Tuition:* Part-time $747 per credit. Part-time tuition and fees vary according to program. *Unit head:* Dr. Jane Belmore, Dean, 608-663-8336, Fax: 608-663-3291, E-mail: jbelmore@edgewood.edu. *Application contact:* Joann Eastman, Admissions Counselor, 608-663-3250, Fax: 608-663-2214, E-mail: gps@edgewood.edu. Web site: http://education.edgewood.edu/graduate.html.

Edinboro University of Pennsylvania, School of Education, Department of Professional Studies, Edinboro, PA 16444. Offers counseling (MA), including community counseling, elementary guidance, rehabilitation counseling, secondary guidance, student personnel services; educational leadership (M Ed), including elementary school administration, secondary school administration; educational psychology (M Ed); educational specialist school psychology (MS); elementary principal (Certificate); elementary school guidance counselor (Certificate); K-12 school administration (Certificate); letter of eligibility (Certificate); reading (M Ed); reading specialist (Certificate); school psychology (Certificate); school supervision (Certificate), including music, special education. Part-time and evening/weekend programs available. *Faculty:* 13 full-time (8 women). *Students:* 171 full-time (134 women), 563 part-time (441 women); includes 26 minority (20 Black or African American, non-Hispanic/Latino; 1 American Indian or Alaska Native, non-Hispanic/Latino; 1 Asian, non-Hispanic/Latino; 4 Hispanic/Latino). Average age 31. In 2011, 297 master's, 49 other advanced degrees awarded. *Degree requirements:* For master's, thesis or alternative, competency exam; for Certificate, thesis or alternative. *Entrance requirements:* For master's and Certificate, GRE or MAT, minimum QPA of 2.5. *Application deadline:* Applications are processed on a rolling basis. Application fee: $30. Electronic applications accepted. *Financial support:* In 2011–12, 60 research assistantships with full and partial tuition reimbursements (averaging $4,050 per year) were awarded; career-related internships or fieldwork, Federal Work-Study, scholarships/grants, and unspecified assistantships also available. Support available to part-time students. Financial award application deadline: 2/15; financial award applicants required to submit FAFSA. *Unit head:* Dr. Susan Norton, 814-732-2260, E-mail: scnorton@edinboro.edu. *Application contact:* Dr. Andrew Pushchack, Program Head, Educational Leadership, 814-732-1548, E-mail: apushchack@edinboro.edu.

Elms College, Division of Education, Chicopee, MA 01013-2839. Offers early childhood education (MAT); education (M Ed, CAGS); elementary education (MAT); English as a second language (MAT); reading (MAT); secondary education (MAT), including biology education, English education, Spanish education; special education (MAT). Part-time and evening/weekend programs available. *Degree requirements:* For master's, thesis (for some programs). *Entrance requirements:* For master's, Massachusetts Educators Certification Test, minimum GPA of 3.0; for CAGS, master's degree in education. Additional exam requirements/recommendations for international students: Required—TOEFL.

Emory & Henry College, Graduate Programs, Emory, VA 24327-0947. Offers American history (MA Ed); organizational leadership (MCOL); professional studies (M Ed); reading specialist (MA Ed). Part-time and evening/weekend programs available. *Faculty:* 7 full-time (3 women). *Students:* 11 full-time (8 women), 32 part-time (22 women); includes 1 minority (Black or African American, non-Hispanic/Latino). Average age 36. 34 applicants, 85% accepted, 28 enrolled. In 2011, 36 master's awarded. *Entrance requirements:* For master's, GRE or PRAXIS I, recommendations, writing sample. Additional exam requirements/recommendations for international students: Recommended—TOEFL. *Application deadline:* Applications are processed on a rolling basis. Application fee: $30. *Expenses: Tuition:* Full-time $8370; part-time $465 per credit hour. *Financial support:* Applicants required to submit FAFSA. *Unit head:* Dr. Jack Roper, Director of Graduate Studies, 276-944-6188, Fax: 276-944-5223, E-mail: jroper@ehc.edu. *Application contact:* Dr. Jack Roper, Director of Graduate Studies, 276-944-6188, Fax: 276-944-5223, E-mail: jroper@ehc.edu.

Emporia State University, Graduate School, Teachers College, Department of Elementary Education, Early Childhood, and Special Education, Program in Master Teacher, Emporia, KS 66801-5087. Offers elementary subject matter (MS); reading (MS). *Accreditation:* NCATE. Part-time programs available. *Students:* 83 part-time (80 women); includes 6 minority (3 Black or African American, non-Hispanic/Latino; 1 Asian, non-Hispanic/Latino; 2 Hispanic/Latino). 21 applicants, 86% accepted, 15 enrolled. In 2011, 31 master's awarded. *Degree requirements:* For master's, comprehensive exam or thesis, practicum. *Entrance requirements:* For master's, GRE General Test or MAT, graduate essay exam, appropriate bachelor's degree, letters of recommendation. Additional exam requirements/recommendations for international students: Required—TOEFL (minimum score 520 paper-based; 133 computer-based; 68 iBT). *Application deadline:* For fall admission, 8/15 priority date for domestic students. Applications are processed on a rolling basis. Application fee: $30 ($75 for international students). Electronic applications accepted. *Expenses:* Tuition, state resident: full-time $2342; part-time $195 per credit hour. Tuition, nonresident: full-time $7254; part-time $605 per credit hour. *Required fees:* $66 per credit hour. Tuition and fees vary according to campus/location. *Financial support:* Federal Work-Study, institutionally sponsored loans, health care benefits, and unspecified assistantships available. Financial award application deadline: 3/15; financial award applicants required to submit FAFSA. *Unit head:* Dr. Jean Morrow, Chair, 620-341-5766, E-mail: jmorrow@emporia.edu. *Application contact:* Mary Sewell, Admissions Coordinator, 800-950-GRAD, Fax: 620-341-5909, E-mail: msewell@emporia.edu.

Endicott College, Van Loan School of Graduate and Professional Studies, Program in Reading and Literacy, Beverly, MA 01915-2096. Offers initial and professional licensure (M Ed). Part-time and evening/weekend programs available. *Faculty:* 1 full-time (0 women), 3 part-time/adjunct (all women). *Students:* 6 full-time (all women), 31 part-time (29 women); includes 1 minority (Asian, non-Hispanic/Latino). Average age 30. 20 applicants, 85% accepted, 17 enrolled. In 2011, 6 master's awarded. *Degree requirements:* For master's, comprehensive exam, practicum. *Entrance requirements:* For master's, MAT or GRE, Massachusetts teaching certificate, letters of recommendation. Additional exam requirements/recommendations for international students: Required—TOEFL. *Application deadline:* Applications are processed on a rolling basis. Application fee: $50. Electronic applications accepted. *Expenses:* Contact institution. *Financial support:* Career-related internships or fieldwork, Federal Work-Study, and institutionally sponsored loans available. Financial award applicants required to submit FAFSA. *Unit head:* Dr. John D. MacLean, Jr., Director of Licensure Programs, 978-232-2408, E-mail: jmaclean@endicott.edu. *Application contact:* Vice President and Dean of the School of Graduate and Professional Studies. Web site: http://www.endicott.edu/GradProf/GPSGradMEd.aspx.

Evangel University, Department of Education, Springfield, MO 65802. Offers educational leadership (M Ed); reading education (M Ed); secondary teaching (M Ed); teaching (MA). *Accreditation:* NCATE. Part-time and evening/weekend programs available. *Faculty:* 4 full-time (1 woman), 2 part-time/adjunct (1 woman). *Students:* 10 full-time (5 women), 39 part-time (25 women). Average age 33. 14 applicants, 86% accepted, 11 enrolled. In 2011, 21 master's awarded. *Degree requirements:* For master's, comprehensive exam, thesis optional. *Entrance requirements:* For master's, PRAXIS II (preferred) or GRE. Additional exam requirements/recommendations for international students: Required—TOEFL (minimum score 550 paper-based; 213 computer-based). *Application deadline:* For fall admission, 7/15 priority date for domestic students; for spring admission, 11/15 priority date for domestic students. Applications are processed on a rolling basis. Application fee: $25. *Financial support:* In 2011–12, 3 students received support. Career-related internships or fieldwork, institutionally sponsored loans, and scholarships/grants available. Support available to part-time students. Financial award application deadline: 3/1; financial award applicants required to submit FAFSA. *Unit head:* Dr. Matt Stringer, Program Coordinator, 417-865-2815 Ext. 8563, E-mail: stringerm@evangel.edu. *Application contact:* Micah Hildreth, Admissions Representative, Graduate and Professional Studies, 417-865-2811 Ext. 7227, Fax: 417-865-9599, E-mail: hildrethm@evangel.edu. Web site: http://www.evangel.edu/departments/education/about-the-department/.

Fairleigh Dickinson University, College at Florham, University College: Arts, Sciences, and Professional Studies, Peter Sammartino School of Education, Madison, NJ 07940-1099. Offers education for certified teachers (MA, Certificate); educational leadership (MA); instructional technology (Certificate); literacy/reading (Certificate); teaching (MAT).

Fairleigh Dickinson University, Metropolitan Campus, University College: Arts, Sciences, and Professional Studies, Peter Sammartino School of Education, Teaneck, NJ 07666-1914. Offers dyslexia specialist (Certificate); education for certified teachers (MA); educational leadership (MA); instructional technology (Certificate); learning disabilities (MA); literacy/reading (Certificate); multilingual education (MA); teacher of the handicapped (Certificate); teaching (MAT). *Accreditation:* Teacher Education Accreditation Council. Part-time programs available. *Degree requirements:* For master's, research project (MAT).

Fairmont State University, Programs in Education, Fairmont, WV 26554. Offers digital media, new literacies and learning (M Ed); education (MAT); exercise science, fitness and wellness (M Ed); leadership studies (M Ed); online learning (M Ed); professional studies (M Ed); reading (M Ed); special education (M Ed). *Accreditation:* NCATE. Part-time and evening/weekend programs available. Postbaccalaureate distance learning degree programs offered. *Faculty:* 16 part-time/adjunct (10 women). *Students:* 103 full-time (72 women), 142 part-time (103 women); includes 11 minority (2 Black or African American, non-Hispanic/Latino; 1 American Indian or Alaska Native, non-Hispanic/Latino; 6 Hispanic/Latino; 2 Two or more races, non-Hispanic/Latino), 2 international. Average age 33. 71 applicants, 85% accepted. In 2011, 58 master's awarded. *Entrance requirements:* For master's, GRE. *Application deadline:* For fall admission, 5/1 for domestic and international students. Applications are processed on a rolling basis. Application fee: $40. *Expenses:* Tuition, state resident: full-time $5900. Tuition, nonresident: full-time $12,596. *Unit head:* Dr. Van O. Dempsey, III, Dean, School of Education, 304-367-4241, Fax: 304-367-4599, E-mail: vdempsey@fairmontstate.edu. Web site: http://www.fairmontstate.edu/graduatestudies/default.asp.

Fayetteville State University, Graduate School, Program in Middle Grades, Secondary and Special Education, Fayetteville, NC 28301-4298. Offers biology (MA Ed); history (MA Ed); mathematics (MA Ed); middle grades (MA Ed); political science (MA Ed); reading (MA Ed); sociology (MA Ed); special education (MA Ed), including behavioral-emotional handicaps, mentally handicapped, specific training disability. *Accreditation:* NCATE. Part-time and evening/weekend programs available. *Faculty:* 12 full-time (8 women), 4 part-time/adjunct (3 women). *Students:* 37 full-time (31 women), 66 part-time (57 women); includes 75 minority (68 Black or African American, non-Hispanic/Latino; 1 American Indian or Alaska Native, non-Hispanic/Latino; 3 Hispanic/Latino; 3 Two or more races, non-Hispanic/Latino). Average age 35. 18 applicants, 100% accepted, 18 enrolled. In 2011, 35 master's awarded. *Degree requirements:* For master's, comprehensive exam, internship. *Application deadline:* For fall admission, 4/15 for domestic students; for spring admission, 10/15 for domestic students. Applications are processed on a rolling basis. Application fee: $35. Electronic applications accepted. *Faculty research:* Students with disabilities and selected leadership behaviors, new vision for professional development, gifted and talented studentsm emotional and behavioral disabilities, professional development for high school biology teachers. *Unit head:* Dr. Kimberly Smith-Burton, Interim Chair, 910-672-1182, E-mail: cbarringerbrown@uncfsu.edu. *Application contact:* Katrina Hoffman, Graduate Admission Officer, 910-672-1374, Fax: 910-672-1470, E-mail: khoffma1@uncfsu.edu.

Ferris State University, College of Education and Human Services, School of Education, Big Rapids, MI 49307. Offers administration (MSCTE); curriculum and instruction (M Ed), including administration, elementary education, experiential education, philanthropic education, reading, secondary education, special education, subject matter option; education technology (MSCTE); instructor (MSCTE); post-secondary administration (MSCTE); training and development (MSCTE). Part-time and evening/weekend programs available. Postbaccalaureate distance learning degree programs offered (minimal on-campus study). *Faculty:* 9 full-time (7 women), 9 part-time/adjunct (6 women). *Students:* 8 full-time (7 women), 132 part-time (75 women); includes 13 minority (11 Black or African American, non-Hispanic/Latino; 1 American Indian or Alaska Native, non-Hispanic/Latino; 1 Hispanic/Latino), 5 international. Average age 36. 20 applicants, 100% accepted, 8 enrolled. In 2011, 51 master's awarded. *Degree requirements:* For master's, thesis, research paper. *Entrance requirements:* For master's, 2 years of work experience for vocational setting, minimum GPA of 2.75. Additional exam requirements/recommendations for international students: Recommended—TOEFL (minimum score 500 paper-based; 173 computer-based; 61 iBT). *Application deadline:* For fall admission, 7/1 priority date for domestic students, 7/1 for international students; for spring admission, 11/1 priority date for domestic students, 11/1 for international students. Applications are processed on a rolling basis. Application fee: $30. Electronic applications accepted. Application fee is waived when completed online. *Financial support:* Career-related internships or fieldwork and scholarships/grants available. Support available to part-time students. Financial award applicants required to submit FAFSA. *Faculty research:* Suicide prevention, reading, women in education, special needs, administration. *Unit head:* Dr. James Powell, Director, 231-591-5362, Fax: 231-591-2043, E-mail: powelj20@ferris.edu. *Application contact:* Kimisue Worrall, Secretary, 231-591-5361, Fax: 231-591-2043. Web site: http://www.ferris.edu/education/education/.

Florida Atlantic University, College of Education, Department of Teaching and Learning, Boca Raton, FL 33431-0991. Offers curriculum and instruction (M Ed); elementary education (M Ed); environmental education (M Ed); reading education (M Ed); social foundations of education (M Ed). *Accreditation:* NCATE. Part-time and evening/weekend programs available. *Faculty:* 32 full-time (25 women), 90 part-time/adjunct (68 women). *Students:* 34 full-time (30 women), 103 part-time (96 women); includes 29 minority (8 Black or African American, non-Hispanic/Latino; 7 Asian, non-Hispanic/Latino; 11 Hispanic/Latino; 3 Two or more races, non-Hispanic/Latino), 1 international. Average age 32. 96 applicants, 66% accepted, 24 enrolled. In 2011, 71 master's awarded. *Entrance requirements:* For master's, GRE General Test, minimum GPA of 3.0 in last 2 years of undergraduate course work. Additional exam requirements/recommendations for international students: Required—TOEFL. *Application deadline:* For fall admission, 7/1 for domestic students, 2/15 for international students; for spring admission, 11/1 for domestic students, 7/15 for international students. Applications are processed on a rolling basis. Application fee: $30. *Expenses: Tuition, area resident:* Part-time $343.02 per credit hour. Tuition, state resident: full-time $8232. Tuition, nonresident: full-time $23,931; part-time $997.14 per credit hour. *Financial support:* Fellowships with partial tuition reimbursements, research assistantships with partial tuition reimbursements, teaching assistantships with partial tuition reimbursements, career-related internships or fieldwork, scholarships/grants, and unspecified assistantships available. *Faculty research:* Technology, teaching English to speakers of other languages, math teaching, electronic portfolio assessment, global perspectives through social studies. *Unit head:* Dr. Barbara Ridener, Chairperson, 561-297-3588. *Application contact:* Dr. Eliah Watlington, Associate Dean, 561-296-8520, Fax: 261-297-2991, E-mail: ewatling@fau.edu. Web site: http://www.coe.fau.edu/academicdepartments/tl/.

Florida Gulf Coast University, College of Education, Program in Reading Education, Fort Myers, FL 33965-6565. Offers M Ed. Part-time and evening/weekend programs available. *Faculty:* 34 full-time (26 women), 57 part-time/adjunct (40 women). *Students:* 26 full-time (all women), 7 part-time (all women); includes 3 minority (1 Black or African American, non-Hispanic/Latino; 2 Hispanic/Latino), 1 international. Average age 29. 7 applicants, 86% accepted, 4 enrolled. In 2011, 11 master's awarded. *Entrance requirements:* For master's, GRE General Test, MAT, minimum GPA of 3.0. Additional exam requirements/recommendations for international students: Required—TOEFL (minimum score 550 paper-based; 213 computer-based). *Application deadline:* For fall admission, 7/1 priority date for domestic students; for spring admission, 10/15 for domestic students. Applications are processed on a rolling basis. Application fee: $30. Electronic applications accepted. *Expenses:* Tuition, state resident: full-time $8289. Tuition, nonresident: full-time $28,895. *Required fees:* $1831. One-time fee: $30 full-time. *Faculty research:* Struggling readers, reading and writing connection, involving families in reading. *Unit head:* Dr. Patricia Wachholz, Head, 239-590-7808, Fax: 239-590-7801, E-mail: pwachhol@fgcu.edu. *Application contact:* Diane Schmidt, Chair, 239-590-7759, Fax: 239-590-7801, E-mail: dschmidt@fgcu.edu.

Florida International University, College of Education, Department of Curriculum and Instruction, Miami, FL 33199. Offers art education (MAT, MS, Ed D); curriculum and instruction (Ed S); curriculum development (MS); curriculum studies (PhD); early childhood education (MS, Ed D); elementary education (MS, Ed D); English education (MAT, MS, Ed D); foreign language education - teaching English to speakers of other languages (TESOL) (MS, Certificate), including foreign language education (Certificate), teaching English (MS); French education - initial teacher preparation (MAT); international and intercultural development education (Ed D); international and intercultural developmental education (MS); language, literacy and culture (PhD); learning technologies (MS, Ed D, PhD); mathematics education (MAT, MS, Ed D, PhD); modern language education/bilingual education (MS, Ed D); physical education (MS); reading education (MS, Ed D); science education (MAT, MS, Ed D, PhD); social studies education (MAT, MS, Ed D); Spanish education - initial teacher preparation (MAT); special education (MS). Part-time and evening/weekend programs available. *Degree requirements:* For doctorate, comprehensive exam, thesis/dissertation. *Entrance requirements:* For master's, GRE General Test, Florida General Knowledge Test or Florida College Level Academic Skills Test; for doctorate and other advanced degree, GRE General Test. Additional exam requirements/recommendations for international students: Required—TOEFL (minimum score 550 paper-based; 213 computer-based; 80 iBT), IELTS (minimum score 6.3). Electronic applications accepted.

Florida Memorial University, School of Education, Miami-Dade, FL 33054. Offers elementary education (MS); exceptional student education (MS); reading (MS). *Degree requirements:* For master's, comprehensive exam or thesis, field and clinical experiences, exit exam. *Entrance requirements:* For master's, GRE, CLAST, PRAXIS I, baccalaureate or graduate degree with minimum GPA of 3.0 in last 60 hours, 3 recommendations. Additional exam requirements/recommendations for international students: Recommended—TOEFL.

Florida State University, The Graduate School, College of Education, School of Teacher Education, Tallahassee, FL 32306. Offers early childhood education (MS, Ed D, PhD, Ed S); elementary education (MS, Ed D, PhD, Ed S); English education (MS, PhD, Ed S); mathematics education (MS, PhD, Ed S); reading education/language arts (MS, Ed D, PhD, Ed S); science education (MS, PhD, Ed S); social science education (MS, PhD, Ed S); special education (MS, PhD, Ed S), including emotional disturbance/learning disabilities (MS), mental retardation (MS), rehabilitation counseling, special education (PhD, Ed S), visual disabilities (MS). Part-time programs available. *Faculty:* 34 full-time (25 women), 20 part-time/adjunct (17 women). *Students:* 160 full-time (130 women), 116 part-time (98 women); includes 64 minority (36 Black or African American, non-Hispanic/Latino; 4 American Indian or Alaska Native, non-Hispanic/Latino; 6 Asian, non-Hispanic/Latino; 18 Hispanic/Latino), 28 international. Average age 31. 180 applicants, 62% accepted, 53 enrolled. In 2011, 142 master's, 17 doctorates, 8 other advanced degrees awarded. *Degree requirements:* For master's and Ed S, comprehensive exam, thesis optional; for doctorate, comprehensive exam, thesis/dissertation, preliminary exam, prospectus defense. *Entrance requirements:* For master's, doctorate, and Ed S, GRE General Test, minimum GPA of 3.0. Additional exam requirements/recommendations for international students: Required—TOEFL (minimum score 550 paper-based; 213 computer-based; 80 iBT). *Application deadline:* For fall admission, 7/1 for domestic and international students; for winter admission, 10/1 for domestic students, 11/1 for international students; for spring admission, 3/1 for domestic and international students. Applications are processed on a rolling basis. Application fee: $30. Electronic applications accepted. *Expenses:* Tuition, state resident: full-time $9474; part-time $350.88 per credit hour. Tuition, nonresident: full-time $16,236; part-time $601.34 per credit hour. *Required fees:* $630 per semester. One-time fee: $20. Tuition and fees vary according to course load and campus/location. *Financial support:* In 2011–12, 32 research assistantships with full and partial tuition reimbursements, 15 teaching assistantships with full and partial tuition reimbursements were awarded; fellowships with full and partial tuition reimbursements, career-related internships or fieldwork, scholarships/grants, health care benefits, and unspecified assistantships also available. Financial award application deadline: 1/15; financial award applicants required to submit FAFSA. *Faculty research:* Teaching and learning practices and policies, twenty-first century literacies, impact of teacher education programs on student gains. *Total annual research expenditures:* $723,234. *Unit head:* Dr. Lawrence Scharmann, Chair, 850-644-4880, Fax: 850-644-1880, E-mail: lscharmann@fsu.edu. *Application contact:* Harriet Kasper, Program Assistant, 850-644-2122, Fax: 850-644-7736, E-mail: hkasper@fsu.edu. Web site: http://www.coe.fsu.edu/Academic-Programs/Departments/School-of-Teacher-Education-STE.

Fordham University, Graduate School of Education, Division of Curriculum and Teaching, New York, NY 10023. Offers adult education (MS, MSE); bilingual teacher education (MSE); curriculum and teaching (MSE); early childhood education (MSE); elementary education (MST); language, literacy, and learning (PhD); reading education (MSE, Adv C); secondary education (MAT, MSE); special education (MSE, Adv C); teaching English as a second language (MSE). *Accreditation:* NCATE. *Degree requirements:* For doctorate, thesis/dissertation; for Adv C, thesis. *Entrance requirements:* For doctorate, MAT, GRE General Test. *Expenses: Tuition:* Full-time $30,480; part-time $1270 per credit. *Required fees:* $586; $293 per semester.

Framingham State University, Division of Graduate and Continuing Education, Program in Literacy and Language, Framingham, MA 01701-9101. Offers M Ed. Part-time and evening/weekend programs available. *Entrance requirements:* For master's, MAT.

Fresno Pacific University, Graduate Programs, School of Education, Fresno, CA 93702-4709. Offers administration (MA Ed), including administrative services; foundations, curriculum and teaching (MA Ed), including curriculum and teaching, school library and information technology; language, literacy, and culture (MA Ed), including bilingual/cross-cultural education, language development, multilingual contexts, reading; mathematics/science/computer education (MA Ed), including educational technology, integrated mathematics/science education, mathematics education; pupil personnel services (MA Ed), including school counseling, school psychology; special education (MA Ed), including mild/moderate, moderate/severe, physical and health impairments. Part-time and evening/weekend programs available. *Degree requirements:* For master's, thesis (for some programs). *Entrance requirements:* For master's, interview; GMAT, GRE, MAT, or 6 units of course work with a faculty recommendation. Additional exam requirements/recommendations for international students: Required—TOEFL (minimum score 550 paper-based; 213 computer-based). Electronic applications accepted.

Fresno Pacific University, Graduate Programs, School of Education, Division of Language, Literacy, and Culture, Program in Language Development, Fresno, CA 93702-4709. Offers MA Ed. Part-time and evening/weekend programs available. *Degree requirements:* For master's, thesis or alternative. *Entrance requirements:* Additional exam requirements/recommendations for international students: Required—TOEFL (minimum score 550 paper-based; 213 computer-based). Electronic applications accepted.

Fresno Pacific University, Graduate Programs, School of Education, Division of Language, Literacy, and Culture, Program in Literacy in Multilingual Contexts, Fresno, CA 93702-4709. Offers MA Ed. Part-time and evening/weekend programs available. *Degree requirements:* For master's, thesis or alternative. *Entrance requirements:* Additional exam requirements/recommendations for international students: Required—TOEFL (minimum score 550 paper-based; 213 computer-based). Electronic applications accepted.

Fresno Pacific University, Graduate Programs, School of Education, Division of Language, Literacy, and Culture, Program in Reading, Fresno, CA 93702-4709. Offers reading/English as a second language (MA Ed); reading/language arts (MA Ed). Part-time and evening/weekend programs available. *Degree requirements:* For master's, thesis or alternative. *Entrance requirements:* Additional exam requirements/recommendations for international students: Required—TOEFL (minimum score 550 paper-based; 213 computer-based). Electronic applications accepted.

Frostburg State University, Graduate School, College of Education, Department of Educational Professions, Program in Reading, Frostburg, MD 21532-1099. Offers M Ed. *Accreditation:* NCATE. *Degree requirements:* For master's, thesis or alternative, in-service. *Entrance requirements:* For master's, teaching certificate. Additional exam requirements/recommendations for international students: Required—TOEFL. Electronic applications accepted.

Furman University, Graduate Division, Department of Education, Greenville, SC 29613. Offers curriculum and instruction (MA); early childhood education (MA); educational leadership (Ed S); English as a second language (MA); literacy (MA); school leadership (MA); special education (MA). *Accreditation:* NCATE. Part-time programs available. Postbaccalaureate distance learning degree programs offered (minimal on-campus study). *Faculty:* 14 full-time (8 women), 6 part-time/adjunct (4 women). *Students:* 237 part-time (188 women); includes 27 minority (22 Black or African American, non-Hispanic/Latino; 1 Asian, non-Hispanic/Latino; 3 Hispanic/Latino; 1 Native Hawaiian or other Pacific Islander, non-Hispanic/Latino). Average age 29. 97 applicants, 100% accepted, 90 enrolled. In 2011, 34 master's awarded. *Degree requirements:* For master's, comprehensive exam (for some programs), thesis or alternative. *Entrance requirements:* For master's, PRAXIS II. *Application deadline:* For fall admission, 8/1 priority date for domestic students, 7/15 for international students; for spring admission, 12/1 priority date for domestic students, 12/1 for international students. Applications are processed on a rolling basis. Application fee: $50. *Financial support:* Scholarships/grants available. Financial award application deadline: 5/15; financial award applicants required to submit FAFSA. *Faculty research:* Literacy, pedagogy and practice, social justice, advanced leadership, achievement in high poverty schools. *Unit head:* Dr. Nelly Hecker, Head, 864-294-3385. *Application contact:* Helen Reynolds, Department Assistant, 864-294-2213, Fax: 864-294-3579, E-mail: helen.reynolds@furman.edu. Web site: http://www.furman.edu/gradstudies/.

Gannon University, School of Graduate Studies, College of Humanities, Education, and Social Sciences, School of Education, Program in Reading, Erie, PA 16541-0001. Offers M Ed, Certificate. Part-time and evening/weekend programs available. *Students:* 6 full-time (5 women), 12 part-time (all women). Average age 33. 24 applicants, 92% accepted, 7 enrolled. In 2011, 2 master's awarded. *Degree requirements:* For master's, comprehensive exam, thesis; for Certificate, comprehensive exam. *Entrance requirements:* For master's, bachelor's degree, minimum GPA of 3.0, teacher certification, 3 letters of recommendation; for Certificate, bachelor's degree, minimum QPA of 3.0, teacher certification. Additional exam requirements/recommendations for international students: Required—TOEFL (minimum score 79 iBT). *Application deadline:* Applications are processed on a rolling basis. Application fee: $25. Electronic applications accepted. *Expenses:* Contact institution. *Financial support:* Scholarships/grants available. Financial award application deadline: 7/1; financial award applicants required to submit FAFSA. *Unit head:* Dr. Kathleen Kingston, Director, 814-871-5626, E-mail: kingston002@gannon.edu. *Application contact:* Kara Morgan, Director of Graduate Admissions, 814-871-5831, Fax: 814-871-5827, E-mail: graduate@gannon.edu.

Geneva College, Master of Education in Reading Program, Beaver Falls, PA 15010-3599. Offers M Ed. Part-time and evening/weekend programs available. *Faculty:* 4 full-time (all women), 1 (woman) part-time/adjunct. *Students:* 10 part-time (all women). In 2011, 5 master's awarded. *Degree requirements:* For master's, 100 hours of field experience. *Entrance requirements:* For master's, 2 letters of recommendation, resume, copy of current certificate, transcript. Additional exam requirements/recommendations for international students: Required—TOEFL. *Application deadline:* Applications are processed on a rolling basis. Electronic applications accepted. *Expenses: Tuition:* Part-time $625 per credit hour. Tuition and fees vary according to program. *Financial support:* In 2011–12, 4 students received support. Scholarships/grants available. Financial award applicants required to submit FAFSA. *Unit head:* Dr. Adel Aiken, Program Director, 724-847-5002, E-mail: reading@geneva.edu. *Application contact:* Lori Hartge, Graduate Student Support Specialist, 724-846-6571, E-mail: reading@geneva.edu. Web site: http://www.geneva.edu/page/reading.

George Fox University, School of Education, Educational Foundations and Leadership Program, Newberg, OR 97132-2697. Offers continuing administrator license (Certificate); curriculum and instruction (M Ed); educational leadership (M Ed, Ed D); ESOL (Certificate); higher education (M Ed); initial administrator license (Certificate); instructional leadership (Ed S); library media (M Ed, Certificate); literacy (M Ed); reading (M Ed); secondary education (M Ed). *Accreditation:* NCATE. Part-time and evening/weekend programs available. Postbaccalaureate distance learning degree programs offered (minimal on-campus study). *Faculty:* 10 full-time (3 women), 6 part-time/adjunct (3 women). *Students:* 2 full-time (both women), 111 part-time (83 women); includes 16 minority (2 American Indian or Alaska Native, non-Hispanic/Latino; 6 Asian, non-Hispanic/Latino; 7 Hispanic/Latino; 1 Native Hawaiian or other Pacific Islander, non-Hispanic/Latino), 3 international. Average age 39. 44 applicants, 98% accepted, 43 enrolled. In 2011, 34 master's, 7 doctorates, 76 Certificates awarded. *Degree requirements:* For master's, thesis (for some programs); for doctorate, comprehensive exam, thesis/dissertation, project. *Entrance requirements:* For master's, minimum undergraduate GPA of 3.0 during previous 2 years of course work, resume, 3 professional recommendations on university forms, official transcripts; for doctorate, GRE, master's degree with minimum GPA of 3.25, 3 years of relevant professional experience, interview, personal essay, scholarly work, 3 professional recommendations on university forms along with 3 written letters of recommendation, official transcripts. Additional exam requirements/recommendations for international students: Required—TOEFL (minimum score 577 paper-based; 233 computer-based; 90 iBT). *Application deadline:* For fall admission, 7/15 for domestic and international students; for winter admission, 11/1 for domestic and international students; for spring admission, 4/1 for domestic and international students. Applications are processed on a rolling basis. Application fee: $40. Electronic applications accepted. *Expenses:* Contact institution. *Financial support:* Career-related internships or fieldwork available. Financial award applicants required to submit FAFSA. *Unit head:* Dr. Scot Headley, Professor/Chair, 503-554-2836, E-mail: sheadley@georgefox.edu. *Application contact:* Alex Martin, Admissions Counselor, 800-631-0921, Fax: 503-554-3110, E-mail: amartin@georgefox.edu. Web site: http://www.georgefox.edu/education/index.html.

George Fox University, School of Education, Master of Arts in Teaching Program, Newberg, OR 97132-2697. Offers teaching (MAT); teaching plus ESOL (MAT); teaching plus ESOL/bilingual (MAT); teaching plus reading (MAT). Program offered in Oregon and Idaho. Part-time and evening/weekend programs available. *Faculty:* 17 full-time (13 women), 19 part-time/adjunct (16 women). *Students:* 115 full-time (75 women), 55 part-time (36 women); includes 16 minority (1 Black or African American, non-Hispanic/Latino; 11 Asian, non-Hispanic/Latino; 3 Hispanic/Latino; 1 Two or more races, non-Hispanic/Latino). Average age 31. 55 applicants, 76% accepted, 32 enrolled. In 2011, 156 master's awarded. *Entrance requirements:* For master's, CBEST, PRAXIS PPST, or EAS, bachelor's degree with minimum GPA of 3.0 in last two years of course work from regionally-accredited college or university, official transcripts. Additional exam requirements/recommendations for international students: Required—TOEFL (minimum score 577 paper-based; 233 computer-based; 90 iBT), IELTS (minimum score 7). *Application deadline:* For fall admission, 6/1 for domestic and international students; for winter admission, 10/1 for domestic and international students; for spring admission, 2/1 for domestic and international students. Applications are processed on a rolling basis. Application fee: $40. Electronic applications accepted. *Expenses:* Contact institution. *Financial support:* In 2011–12, 20 students received support. Scholarships/grants available. Financial award application deadline: 2/1; financial award applicants required to submit FAFSA. *Unit head:* Carol Brazo, Chair, 503-554-6115, E-mail: cbrazo@georgefox.edu. *Application contact:* Beth Molzahn, Admissions Counselor, 800-631-0921, Fax: 503-554-3110, E-mail: mat@georgefox.edu. Web site: http://www.georgefox.edu/soe/mat/.

Georgetown College, Department of Education, Georgetown, KY 40324-1696. Offers reading and writing (MA Ed); special education (MA Ed); teaching (MA Ed). *Accreditation:* NCATE. Part-time programs available. *Degree requirements:* For master's, portfolio. *Entrance requirements:* For master's, teaching certificate, minimum GPA of 2.7 or GRE General Test.

The George Washington University, Graduate School of Education and Human Development, Department of Curriculum and Pedagogy, Program in Reading and Literacy, Washington, DC 20052. Offers Graduate Certificate. *Entrance requirements:* For degree, GRE or MAT, official transcripts, statement of purpose, two letters of reference, teacher certification.

Georgia Southern University, Jack N. Averitt College of Graduate Studies, College of Education, Department of Curriculum, Foundations, and Reading, Program in Literacy Education, Statesboro, GA 30460. Offers M Ed, Ed D. *Students:* 2 part-time (both women). Average age 28. 1 applicant, 100% accepted, 0 enrolled. *Expenses:* Tuition, state resident: full-time $6300; part-time $263 per semester hour. Tuition, nonresident: full-time $25,174; part-time $1049 per semester hour. *Required fees:* $1872. *Unit head:* Dr. Cordelia Zinskie, Chair, 912-478-5091, Fax: 912-478-5382, E-mail: czinski@georgiasouthern.edu. *Application contact:* Amanda Gilliland, Coordinator for Graduate Student Recruitment, 912-478-5384, Fax: 912-478-0740, E-mail: gradadmissions@georgiasouthern.edu.

Georgia Southern University, Jack N. Averitt College of Graduate Studies, College of Education, Department of Curriculum, Foundations, and Reading, Program in Reading Education, Statesboro, GA 30460. Offers M Ed. *Accreditation:* NCATE. Part-time and evening/weekend programs available. *Students:* 5 full-time (all women), 11 part-time (all women); includes 4 minority (3 Black or African American, non-Hispanic/Latino; 1 Two or more races, non-Hispanic/Latino). Average age 30. 4 applicants, 100% accepted, 3 enrolled. In 2011, 11 master's awarded. *Degree requirements:* For master's, comprehensive exam, transition point assessments. *Entrance requirements:* For master's, GRE General Test or MAT, minimum GPA of 2.5. Additional exam requirements/recommendations for international students: Required—TOEFL (minimum score 550 paper-based; 213 computer-based; 80 iBT). *Application deadline:* For fall admission, 3/1 priority date for domestic students, 3/1 for international students; for spring admission, 10/1 priority date for domestic students, 10/1 for international students. Applications are processed on a rolling basis. Application fee: $50. Electronic applications accepted. *Expenses:* Tuition, state resident: full-time $6300; part-time $263 per semester hour. Tuition, nonresident: full-time $25,174; part-time $1049 per semester hour. *Required fees:* $1872. *Financial support:* In 2011–12, 1 student received support, including research assistantships with partial tuition reimbursements available (averaging $7,200 per year), teaching assistantships with partial tuition reimbursements available (averaging $7,200 per year); career-related internships or fieldwork, Federal Work-Study, scholarships/grants, tuition waivers (partial), and unspecified assistantships also available. Support available to part-time students. Financial award application deadline: 4/15; financial award applicants required to submit FAFSA. *Faculty research:* Emerging literacy, content literacy, literature groups, phonics/whole language, interpreting literacy policy. *Unit head:* Dr. Michael Moore, Coordinator, 912-478-0211, Fax: 912-478-5382, E-mail: mmoore@georgiasouthern.edu. *Application contact:* Amanda Gilliland, Coordinator for Graduate Student Recruitment, 912-478-5384, Fax: 912-478-0740, E-mail: gradadmissions@georgiasouthern.edu. Web site: http://coe.georgiasouthern.edu/reading.

Georgia Southwestern State University, Graduate Studies, School of Education, Americus, GA 31709-4693. Offers early childhood education (M Ed, Ed S); health and physical education (M Ed); middle grades education (M Ed, Ed S); reading (M Ed); secondary education (M Ed); special education (M Ed). *Accreditation:* NCATE. *Degree requirements:* For master's, comprehensive exam. *Entrance requirements:* For master's, GRE General Test or MAT, minimum GPA of 2.5; for Ed S, GRE General Test or MAT, minimum graduate GPA of 3.25, M Ed from accredited college or university, 3 years teaching experience. Electronic applications accepted.

Georgia State University, College of Education, Department of Middle-Secondary Education and Instructional Technology, Program in Reading Instruction, Atlanta, GA 30302-3083. Offers reading, language and literacy (M Ed); reading, language, and literacy (PhD, Ed S); teaching English as a second language (M Ed). *Accreditation:* NCATE. Part-time and evening/weekend programs available. *Degree requirements:* For master's, comprehensive exam; for Ed S, project/exam. *Entrance requirements:* For master's, GRE General Test, minimum GPA of 2.5; for Ed S, GRE General Test or MAT, minimum graduate GPA of 3.25. *Faculty research:* Language development, attribution theory, linguistics.

Gonzaga University, School of Education, Program in Literacy, Spokane, WA 99258. Offers M Ed. *Degree requirements:* For master's, comprehensive exam. *Entrance requirements:* For master's, GRE General Test or MAT, minimum B average in undergraduate course work.

Governors State University, College of Education, Program in Reading, University Park, IL 60484. Offers MA. *Accreditation:* NCATE. *Students:* 3 full-time (all women), 21 part-time (all women); includes 6 minority (5 Black or African American, non-Hispanic/Latino; 1 Hispanic/Latino). Average age 32. Application fee: $25. *Unit head:* Dr. Deborah Bordelon, Dean, 708-534-4050.

Grambling State University, School of Graduate Studies and Research, College of Education, Department of Educational Leadership, Grambling, LA 71245. Offers curriculum and instruction (Ed D); developmental education (MS, Ed D), including curriculum and instruction: reading (Ed D), English (MS), guidance and counseling (MS), higher education administration (Ed D), instructional systems and technology (Ed D), mathematics (MS), reading (MS), science (MS), student development and personnel services (Ed D); educational leadership (MS, Ed D). Part-time and evening/weekend programs available. *Degree requirements:* For master's, comprehensive exam, thesis (for some programs); for doctorate, comprehensive exam, thesis/dissertation. *Entrance requirements:* For master's, GRE, minimum GPA of 2.5 on last degree; for doctorate, GRE (minimum 1000, 500 on Verbal), master's degree, minimum GPA of 3.0 on last degree. Additional exam requirements/recommendations for international students: Required—TOEFL (minimum score 500 paper-based; 173 computer-based; 61 iBT). Electronic applications accepted. *Expenses:* Tuition, state resident: full-time $3546; part-time $192 per credit hour. Tuition, nonresident: full-time $3456; part-time $192 per credit hour. *Required fees:* $1829; $1829 per semester hour.

Grand Valley State University, College of Education, Program in Literacy Studies, Allendale, MI 49401-9403. Offers M Ed.

Grand Valley State University, College of Education, Program in Reading and Language Arts, Allendale, MI 49401-9403. Offers M Ed. *Accreditation:* NCATE. Part-time and evening/weekend programs available. *Degree requirements:* For master's, thesis. *Entrance requirements:* For master's, GRE General Test or minimum GPA of 3.0. Additional exam requirements/recommendations for international students: Required—TOEFL. Electronic applications accepted. *Faculty research:* Culture of literacy, literacy acquisition, assessment, content area literacy, writing pedagogy.

Gwynedd-Mercy College, School of Education, Gwynedd Valley, PA 19437-0901. Offers educational administration (MS); master teacher (MS); reading (MS); school counseling (MS); special education (MS). Part-time and evening/weekend programs available. *Faculty:* 8 full-time (5 women), 38 part-time/adjunct (24 women). *Students:* 33 full-time (22 women), 157 part-time (116 women); includes 33 minority (22 Black or African American, non-Hispanic/Latino; 6 Asian, non-Hispanic/Latino; 5 Hispanic/Latino), 1 international. Average age 33. In 2011, 186 master's awarded. *Degree requirements:* For master's, thesis, internship, practicum. *Entrance requirements:* For master's, GRE or MAT; PRAXIS I, minimum GPA of 3.0. *Application deadline:* Applications are processed on a rolling basis. Application fee: $25. *Expenses: Tuition:* Part-time $630 per credit hour. *Financial support:* In 2011–12, 2 research assistantships were awarded; career-related internships or fieldwork, Federal Work-Study, tuition waivers (full and partial), unspecified assistantships, and Federal Stafford loans, Federal work study, alternative loans, graduate assistantships also available. Financial award applicants required to submit FAFSA. *Faculty research:* Learning and the brain, reading literacy, ethics and moral judgment, leadership, teaching and multicultural education.

Unit head: Dr. Sandra Mangano, Dean, 215-641-5549, Fax: 215-542-4695, E-mail: mangano.s@gmc.edu. *Application contact:* Graduate Program Coordinator. Web site: http://www.gmc.edu/academics/education/.

Hamline University, School of Education, St. Paul, MN 55104-1284. Offers education (MA Ed, Ed D); English as a second language (MA); literacy education (MA); natural science and environmental education (MA Ed); teaching (MAT). *Accreditation:* NCATE (one or more programs are accredited). Part-time and evening/weekend programs available. Postbaccalaureate distance learning degree programs offered (no on-campus study). *Faculty:* 33 full-time (24 women), 106 part-time/adjunct (77 women). *Students:* 319 full-time (221 women), 717 part-time (524 women); includes 88 minority (30 Black or African American, non-Hispanic/Latino; 2 American Indian or Alaska Native, non-Hispanic/Latino; 26 Asian, non-Hispanic/Latino; 27 Hispanic/Latino; 3 Two or more races, non-Hispanic/Latino), 21 international. Average age 32. 468 applicants, 76% accepted, 259 enrolled. In 2011, 197 master's, 10 doctorates awarded. *Degree requirements:* For master's, thesis, foreign language (for MA in English as a second language only); for doctorate, comprehensive exam, thesis/dissertation. *Entrance requirements:* For master's, written essay, official transcripts, 2 letters of recommendation, minimum GPA of 2.5 from bachelor's work; for doctorate, personal statement, master's degree, 3 years experience, 3 letters of recommendation, writing sample, interview. Additional exam requirements/recommendations for international students: Required—TOEFL (minimum score 625 paper-based; 107 computer-based; 75 iBT) or IELTS. *Application deadline:* Applications are processed on a rolling basis. Application fee: $0 ($100 for international students). Electronic applications accepted. *Expenses: Tuition:* Full-time $3720; part-time $465 per credit. *Required fees:* $28 per year. Tuition and fees vary according to degree level, campus/location and program. *Financial support:* Federal Work-Study and scholarships/grants available. Support available to part-time students. Financial award applicants required to submit FAFSA. *Faculty research:* Adult basic education, service-learning, teacher dispositions, diversity, technology. *Unit head:* Dr. Larry Harris, Interim Dean, 651-523-2600, Fax: 651-523-2489, E-mail: lharris02@gw.hamline.edu. *Application contact:* Michael Hand, Assistant Director, Graduate Admission, 651-523-2900, Fax: 651-523-3058, E-mail: mhand01@gw.hamline.edu. Web site: http://www.hamline.edu/education.

Hannibal-LaGrange University, Program in Education, Hannibal, MO 63401-1999. Offers literacy (MS Ed); teaching and learning (MS Ed). Part-time and evening/weekend programs available. *Degree requirements:* For master's, thesis, portfolio, documenting of program outcomes, public sharing of research. *Entrance requirements:* For master's, copy of current teaching certificate; minimum GPA of 2.75. *Faculty research:* Reading assessment, reading remediation, handwriting instruction, early childhood intervention.

Harding University, College of Education, Searcy, AR 72149-0001. Offers advanced studies in teaching and learning (M Ed); art (MSE); behavioral science (MSE); counseling (MS, Ed S); early childhood special education (M Ed, MSE); education (MSE); educational leadership (M Ed, Ed S); elementary education (M Ed); English (MSE); French (MSE); history/social science (MSE); kinesiology (MSE); math (MSE); reading (M Ed); secondary education (M Ed); Spanish (MSE); teaching (MAT); teaching English as a second language (MSE). *Accreditation:* NCATE. Part-time and evening/weekend programs available. *Faculty:* 9 full-time (2 women), 48 part-time/adjunct (26 women). *Students:* 100 full-time (77 women), 333 part-time (239 women); includes 76 minority (59 Black or African American, non-Hispanic/Latino; 1 Asian, non-Hispanic/Latino; 10 Hispanic/Latino; 6 Two or more races, non-Hispanic/Latino), 2 international. Average age 36. 93 applicants, 91% accepted, 83 enrolled. In 2011, 159 master's, 10 other advanced degrees awarded. *Degree requirements:* For master's, comprehensive exam (for some programs), thesis optional, portfolio(s); for Ed S, comprehensive exam, portfolio, project. *Entrance requirements:* For master's, GRE, MAT, PRAXIS; for Ed S, MAT or GRE. Additional exam requirements/recommendations for international students: Required—TOEFL (minimum score 550 paper-based; 79 iBT). *Application deadline:* For fall admission, 8/1 for domestic and international students; for spring admission, 1/1 for domestic and international students. Applications are processed on a rolling basis. Application fee: $35. *Expenses: Tuition:* Full-time $10,512; part-time $584 per credit hour. *Required fees:* $500; $25 per credit hour. Tuition and fees vary according to course load, degree level and program. *Financial support:* In 2011–12, 37 students received support. Unspecified assistantships available. *Faculty research:* Reading, comprehension, school violence, educational technology, behavior, college choice, differentiated instruction, brain-based teaching. *Unit head:* Dr. Clara Carroll, Chair, 501-279-4501, Fax: 501-279-4083, E-mail: ccarroll@harding.edu. *Application contact:* Information Contact, 501-279-4315, E-mail: gradstudiesedu@harding.edu. Web site: http://www.harding.edu/education/grad.html.

Hardin-Simmons University, Graduate School, Irvin School of Education, Department of Educational Studies, Program in Reading Specialist Education, Abilene, TX 79698-0001. Offers M Ed. Part-time programs available. *Faculty:* 2 full-time (both women). *Students:* 2 full-time (both women), 6 part-time (all women); includes 1 minority (Hispanic/Latino), 1 international. Average age 31. 5 applicants, 80% accepted, 3 enrolled. In 2011, 2 master's awarded. *Degree requirements:* For master's, comprehensive exam. *Entrance requirements:* For master's, minimum undergraduate GPA of 3.0 in major, 2.7 overall. Additional exam requirements/recommendations for international students: Required—TOEFL (minimum score 550 paper-based; 213 computer-based; 75 iBT). *Application deadline:* For fall admission, 8/15 priority date for domestic students, 4/1 for international students; for spring admission, 1/5 priority date for domestic students, 9/1 for international students. Applications are processed on a rolling basis. Application fee: $50. *Expenses: Tuition:* Full-time $12,870; part-time $715 per credit hour. *Required fees:* $650; $110 per semester. Tuition and fees vary according to degree level. *Financial support:* In 2011–12, 3 students received support, including 1 fellowship (averaging $900 per year); scholarships/grants also available. Support available to part-time students. Financial award application deadline: 6/30; financial award applicants required to submit FAFSA. *Faculty research:* Social networking as a gatekeeper, reflective process of teachers, growth of reflective practice in pre-service teachers, multicultural children's literature. *Unit head:* Dr. Diana Higgins, Director, 325-670-1354, Fax: 325-670-5859, E-mail: dihigg@hsutx.edu. *Application contact:* Dr. Nancy Kucinski, Dean of Graduate Studies, 325-670-1298, Fax: 325-670-1564, E-mail: gradoff@hsutx.edu. Web site: http://www.hsutx.edu/academics/irvin/graduate/readinged.

Harvard University, Harvard Graduate School of Education, Master's Programs in Education, Cambridge, MA 02138. Offers arts in education (Ed M); education policy and management (Ed M); higher education (Ed M); human development and psychology (Ed M); international education policy (Ed M); language and literacy (Ed M); learning and teaching (Ed M); mid-career mathematics and science (teaching certificate) (Ed M); mind brain and education (Ed M); prevention science and practice (Ed M); school leadership (Ed M); special studies (Ed M); teaching and curriculum (teaching certificate) (Ed M); technology innovation and education (Ed M). Part-time programs available. *Faculty:* 83 full-time (44 women), 67 part-time/adjunct (29 women). *Students:* 592 full-time (431 women), 75 part-time (54 women); includes 194 minority (41 Black or African American, non-Hispanic/Latino; 4 American Indian or Alaska Native, non-Hispanic/Latino; 75 Asian, non-Hispanic/Latino; 45 Hispanic/Latino; 2 Native Hawaiian or other Pacific Islander, non-Hispanic/Latino; 27 Two or more races, non-Hispanic/Latino), 95 international. Average age 28. 1,679 applicants, 52% accepted, 627 enrolled. In 2011, 653 master's awarded. *Entrance requirements:* For master's, GRE General Test, statement of purpose, 3 letters of recommendation, resume, official transcripts. Additional exam requirements/recommendations for international students: Required—TOEFL (minimum score 613 paper-based; 104 computer-based; 100 iBT), TWE (minimum score 5). *Application deadline:* For fall admission, 1/4 for domestic and international students. Application fee: $85. Electronic applications accepted. *Expenses:* Contact institution. *Financial support:* In 2011–12, 419 students received support, including 14 fellowships with full and partial tuition reimbursements available (averaging $12,831 per year); career-related internships or fieldwork, Federal Work-Study, institutionally sponsored loans, scholarships/grants, health care benefits, tuition waivers (full and partial), and unspecified assistantships also available. Support available to part-time students. Financial award application deadline: 2/1; financial award applicants required to submit FAFSA. *Faculty research:* Learning and development, educational leadership and organizations, educational policy analysis. *Total annual research expenditures:* $26 million. *Unit head:* Jennifer L. Petrallia, Assistant Dean, 617-495-8445. *Application contact:* Information Contact, 617-495-3414, Fax: 617-496-3577, E-mail: gseadmissions@harvard.edu. Web site: http://www.gse.harvard.edu/.

Henderson State University, Graduate Studies, Teachers College, Department of Advanced Instructional Studies, Arkadelphia, AR 71999-0001. Offers early childhood (P-4) (MSE); education (MAT); middle school (MSE); reading (MSE); special education (MSE). *Accreditation:* NCATE. Part-time programs available. *Entrance requirements:* For master's, GRE General Test or MAT, minimum GPA of 2.7, teacher certification. Additional exam requirements/recommendations for international students: Required—TOEFL (minimum score 550 paper-based; 213 computer-based); Recommended—IELTS (minimum score 6). Electronic applications accepted.

Heritage University, Graduate Programs in Education, Program in Professional Studies, Toppenish, WA 98948-9599. Offers bilingual education/ESL (M Ed); biology (M Ed); English and literature (M Ed); reading/literacy (M Ed); special education (M Ed). Part-time and evening/weekend programs available. *Degree requirements:* For master's, comprehensive exam (for some programs), thesis (for some programs).

Hofstra University, School of Education, Health, and Human Services, Department of Literacy Studies, Hempstead, NY 11549. Offers advanced literacy studies (PD), including birth-grade 6 (MA, MS Ed, PD); advanced literary studies (PD), including grades 5-12 (MA, PD); birth-grade 6 (MS Ed, Advanced Certificate); grades 5-12 (Advanced Certificate); literacy studies (Ed D, PhD); special education (MS Ed), including birth-grade 2, birth-grade 6 (MA, MS Ed, PD); special education (MS Ed), including birth-grade 2; teaching of writing (MA), including birth-grade 6 (MA, MS Ed, PD), grades 5-12 (MA, PD). Part-time and evening/weekend programs available. *Students:* 43 full-time (42 women), 70 part-time (63 women); includes 15 minority (7 Black or African American, non-Hispanic/Latino; 1 Asian, non-Hispanic/Latino; 7 Hispanic/Latino). Average age 33. 67 applicants, 81% accepted, 32 enrolled. In 2011, 47 master's, 1 doctorate, 10 other advanced degrees awarded. *Degree requirements:* For master's, comprehensive exam, portfolio, minimum GPA of 3.0; for doctorate, one foreign language, comprehensive exam, thesis/dissertation, qualifying hearing, minimum GPA of 3.0. *Entrance requirements:* For master's, interview, teaching certificate, 2 letters of recommendation; for doctorate, GRE or MAT, interview, resume, essay, master's degree, 3 letters of recommendation, writing sample; for other advanced degree, 2 letters of recommendation, interview, teaching certificate, essay, master's degree. Additional exam requirements/recommendations for international students: Required—TOEFL (minimum score 550 paper-based; 213 computer-based; 80 iBT). *Application deadline:* Applications are processed on a rolling basis. Application fee: $70 ($75 for international students). Electronic applications accepted. *Expenses: Tuition:* Full-time $18,990; part-time $1055 per credit hour. *Required fees:* $970. Tuition and fees vary according to program. *Financial support:* In 2011–12, 78 students received support, including 36 fellowships with full and partial tuition reimbursements available (averaging $3,622 per year); research assistantships with full and partial tuition reimbursements available, career-related internships or fieldwork, Federal Work-Study, institutionally sponsored loans, scholarships/grants, tuition waivers (full and partial), and unspecified assistantships also available. Support available to part-time students. Financial award applicants required to submit FAFSA. *Faculty research:* Research literacy practices of immigrant and urban youth, literature for children and adolescents, eye movement/miscue analysis, literacy strategies for effective instruction, transnational literacies. *Unit head:* Dr. Esther Fusco, Chairperson, 516-463-7704, Fax: 516-463-6196, E-mail: catezf@hofstra.edu. *Application contact:* Carol Drummer, Dean of Graduate Admissions, 516-463-4876, Fax: 516-463-4664, E-mail: gradstudent@hofstra.edu. Web site: http://www.hofstra.edu/education/.

Hofstra University, School of Education, Health, and Human Services, Program in Elementary Education, Hempstead, NY 11549. Offers early childhood and childhood education (MS Ed); early childhood education (MA, MS Ed); educational technology (MA); elementary education (MS Ed); literacy (MA); math specialist (Advanced Certificate); math, science, technology (MA); multiculturalism (MA). Part-time and evening/weekend programs available. Postbaccalaureate distance learning degree programs offered (minimal on-campus study). *Students:* 54 full-time (48 women), 43 part-time (37 women); includes 17 minority (10 Black or African American, non-Hispanic/Latino; 2 Asian, non-Hispanic/Latino; 5 Hispanic/Latino), 2 international. Average age 29. 65 applicants, 88% accepted, 18 enrolled. In 2011, 58 master's awarded. *Degree requirements:* For master's, comprehensive exam, thesis (for some programs), 35 semester hours (for MA); 38-41 semester hours (for MS Ed), minimum GPA of 3.0. *Entrance requirements:* For master's, 2 letters of recommendation, teacher certification (MA), interview, essay. Additional exam requirements/recommendations for international students: Required—TOEFL (minimum score 550 paper-based; 213 computer-based; 80 iBT). *Application deadline:* Applications are processed on a rolling basis. Application fee: $70 ($75 for international students). Electronic applications accepted. *Expenses: Tuition:* Full-time $18,990; part-time $1055 per credit hour. *Required fees:* $970. Tuition and fees vary according to program. *Financial support:* In 2011–12, 45 students received support, including 22 fellowships with full and partial tuition reimbursements available (averaging $2,560 per year), 2 research assistantships with full and partial tuition reimbursements available (averaging $21,993 per year); career-related internships or fieldwork, Federal Work-Study, institutionally sponsored loans, scholarships/grants, tuition waivers (full and partial), and unspecified assistantships also available. Support available to part-time students. Financial award applicants required to submit FAFSA. *Faculty research:* Dynamic-themes curriculum/complexity theory, joyful learning, teacher education, multicultural education, multiple authentic assessments. *Unit head:* Dr. Esther Fusco, Chairperson, 516-463-7704, Fax: 516-463-6196, E-mail: catezf@hofstra.edu. *Application contact:* Carol Drummer, Dean of Graduate Admissions, 516-463-4876, Fax: 516-463-4664, E-mail: gradstudent@hofstra.edu. Web site: http://www.hofstra.edu/education/.

Holy Family University, Graduate School, School of Education, Philadelphia, PA 19114. Offers education (M Ed); education leadership (M Ed); elementary education (M Ed); reading specialist (M Ed); secondary education (M Ed); special education (M Ed). Part-time and evening/weekend programs available. *Degree requirements:* For master's, thesis optional. *Entrance requirements:* For master's, GRE or MAT, interview.

Electronic applications accepted. *Faculty research:* Cognition, developmental issues, sociological issues in education.

See Display on page 707 and Close-Up on page 803.

Hood College, Graduate School, Department of Education, Frederick, MD 21701-8575. Offers curriculum and instruction (MS), including early childhood education, elementary education, elementary school science and mathematics, secondary education, special education; educational leadership (MS, Certificate); reading specialization (MS). Part-time and evening/weekend programs available. *Degree requirements:* For master's, action research project, portfolio (reading). *Entrance requirements:* For master's, minimum GPA of 2.75, teaching certification. Additional exam requirements/recommendations for international students: Required—TOEFL (minimum score 575 paper-based; 231 computer-based; 89 iBT). Electronic applications accepted. *Faculty research:* Leadership, action research, brain research, learning styles.

Houston Baptist University, College of Education and Behavioral Sciences, Programs in Education, Houston, TX 77074-3298. Offers bilingual education (M Ed); counselor education (M Ed); curriculum and instruction (M Ed); educational administration (M Ed); educational diagnostician (M Ed); reading education (M Ed). Part-time programs available. *Entrance requirements:* For master's, GRE General Test or MAT. Additional exam requirements/recommendations for international students: Required—TOEFL (minimum score 550 paper-based; 213 computer-based).

Hunter College of the City University of New York, Graduate School, School of Education, Department of Curriculum and Teaching, New York, NY 10021-5085. Offers bilingual education (MS); corrective reading (K-12) (MS Ed); early childhood education (MS); educational supervision and administration (AC); elementary education (MS); literacy education (MS); teaching English as a second language (MA). *Faculty:* 31 full-time (20 women), 103 part-time/adjunct (66 women). *Students:* 96 full-time (77 women), 650 part-time (542 women); includes 316 minority (49 Black or African American, non-Hispanic/Latino; 7 American Indian or Alaska Native, non-Hispanic/Latino; 66 Asian, non-Hispanic/Latino; 194 Hispanic/Latino), 11 international. Average age 31. 506 applicants, 62% accepted, 211 enrolled. In 2011, 311 master's, 39 other advanced degrees awarded. *Degree requirements:* For master's, thesis; for AC, portfolio review. *Entrance requirements:* For degree, minimum B average in graduate course work, teaching certificate, minimum 3 years of full-time teaching experience, interview, 2 letters of support. Additional exam requirements/recommendations for international students: Required—TOEFL, TWE. *Application deadline:* For fall admission, 4/1 for domestic students; for spring admission, 11/1 for domestic students. Applications are processed on a rolling basis. Application fee: $125. *Expenses:* Tuition, state resident: full-time $8210; part-time $345 per credit. Tuition, nonresident: full-time $15,360; part-time $640 per credit. *Required fees:* $280 per semester. One-time fee: $125. Tuition and fees vary according to class time, campus/location and program. *Financial support:* Federal Work-Study, scholarships/grants, and tuition waivers (partial) available. Support available to part-time students. *Faculty research:* Teacher opportunity corps-mentor program for first-year teachers, adult literacy, student literacy corporation. *Unit head:* Dr. Anne M. Ediger, Head, 212-777-4686, E-mail: anne.ediger@hunter.cuny.edu. *Application contact:* Milena Solo, Director for Graduate Admissions, 212-772-4482, Fax: 212-650-3336, E-mail: milena.solo@hunter.cuny.edu. Web site: http://www.hunter.cuny.edu/school-of-education/faculty/curriculum-teaching.

Idaho State University, Office of Graduate Studies, College of Education, Department of Educational Foundations, Pocatello, ID 83209-8059. Offers child and family studies (M Ed); curriculum leadership (M Ed); education (M Ed); educational administration (M Ed); educational foundations (5th Year Certificate); elementary education (M Ed), including K-12 education, literacy, secondary education. Part-time programs available. *Degree requirements:* For master's, comprehensive exam, thesis optional, oral exam, written exam; for 5th Year Certificate, comprehensive exam, thesis (for some programs), oral exam, written exam. *Entrance requirements:* For master's, GRE General Test or MAT, minimum undergraduate GPA of 3.0; for 5th Year Certificate, GRE General Test, minimum undergraduate GPA of 3.0, master's degree. Additional exam requirements/recommendations for international students: Required—TOEFL (minimum score 550 paper-based; 213 computer-based; 80 iBT). Electronic applications accepted. *Faculty research:* Child and families studies; business education; special education; math, science, and technology education.

Idaho State University, Office of Graduate Studies, College of Education, Department of School Psychology, Literacy, and Special Education, Pocatello, ID 83209-8059. Offers deaf education (M Ed); human exceptionality (M Ed); literacy (M Ed); school psychology (Ed S); special education (Ed S). Part-time programs available. *Degree requirements:* For master's, comprehensive exam, thesis (for some programs), oral thesis defense or written comprehensive exam and oral exam; for Ed S, comprehensive exam, thesis (for some programs), oral exam, specialist paper or portfolio. *Entrance requirements:* For master's, GRE or MAT, minimum undergraduate GPA of 3.0, bachelor's degree, professional experience in an educational context; for Ed S, GRE or MAT, master's degree in related field. Additional exam requirements/recommendations for international students: Required—TOEFL (minimum score 550 paper-based; 213 computer-based; 80 iBT). Electronic applications accepted. *Faculty research:* Literacy, school psychology, special education.

Illinois State University, Graduate School, College of Education, Department of Curriculum and Instruction, Program in Reading, Normal, IL 61790-2200. Offers MS Ed. *Accreditation:* NCATE. *Degree requirements:* For master's, practicum. *Entrance requirements:* For master's, GRE General Test, minimum GPA of 3.0 in last 60 hours of course work, course work in reading.

Indiana University Bloomington, School of Education, Department of Literacy, Culture, and Language Education, Bloomington, IN 47405-7000. Offers MS, Ed D, PhD, Ed S. *Accreditation:* NCATE. Part-time and evening/weekend programs available. Postbaccalaureate distance learning degree programs offered (no on-campus study). Terminal master's awarded for partial completion of doctoral program. *Degree requirements:* For doctorate, thesis/dissertation, internship; for Ed S, comprehensive exam or project. *Entrance requirements:* For master's, GRE General Test or minimum GPA of 3.0; for doctorate, GRE General Test, minimum graduate GPA of 3.5; for Ed S, GRE General Test. Additional exam requirements/recommendations for international students: Required—TOEFL. *Faculty research:* Discourse analysis, sociolinguistics, critical literacy, cultural studies.

Indiana University of Pennsylvania, School of Graduate Studies and Research, College of Education and Educational Technology, Department of Professional Studies in Education, Program in Literacy, Indiana, PA 15705-1087. Offers literacy (M Ed); reading (M Ed). *Accreditation:* NCATE. Part-time programs available. *Faculty:* 19 full-time (13 women), 1 (woman) part-time/adjunct. *Students:* 12 full-time (all women), 17 part-time (15 women), 1 international. Average age 27. 24 applicants, 67% accepted, 10 enrolled. In 2011, 23 master's awarded. *Degree requirements:* For master's, thesis optional. *Entrance requirements:* For master's, 2 letters of recommendation. Additional exam requirements/recommendations for international students: Required—TOEFL (minimum score 540 paper-based; 207 computer-based). *Application deadline:* For fall admission, 7/1 priority date for domestic students; for spring admission, 11/1 for domestic students. Applications are processed on a rolling basis. Application fee: $50. Electronic applications accepted. *Expenses:* Tuition, state resident: full-time $7488; part-time $416 per credit. Tuition, nonresident: full-time $11,232; part-time $624 per credit. *Required fees:* $2070; $192.20 per credit. $90 per semester. *Financial support:* In 2011–12, 1 fellowship (averaging $3,220 per year), 7 research assistantships with full and partial tuition reimbursements (averaging $4,877 per year) were awarded; career-related internships or fieldwork and Federal Work-Study also available. Support available to part-time students. Financial award application deadline: 4/15; financial award applicants required to submit FAFSA. *Unit head:* Dr. Anne Creany, Graduate Coordinator, 724-357-2409. *Application contact:* Dr. Edward Nardi, Associate Dean, 724-357-2480, Fax: 724-357-5595, E-mail: ewnardi@iup.edu. Web site: http://www.iup.edu/upper.aspx?id=91232.

Indiana University–Purdue University Indianapolis, School of Education, Indianapolis, IN 46202-2896. Offers computer education (Certificate); curriculum and instruction (MS); early childhood (MS); educational leadership (MS, Certificate); English as a second language (Certificate); higher education and student affairs (MS); kindergarten (Certificate); language education (MS); reading (Certificate); school counseling (MS); special education (MS, Certificate). Part-time and evening/weekend programs available. *Faculty:* 41 full-time, 80 part-time/adjunct. *Students:* 67 full-time (52 women), 467 part-time (360 women); includes 82 minority (44 Black or African American, non-Hispanic/Latino; 3 American Indian or Alaska Native, non-Hispanic/Latino; 8 Asian, non-Hispanic/Latino; 13 Hispanic/Latino; 14 Two or more races, non-Hispanic/Latino), 10 international. Average age 33. 63 applicants, 57% accepted, 29 enrolled. In 2011, 167 master's awarded. *Degree requirements:* For master's, thesis optional. *Entrance requirements:* For master's, GRE General Test, minimum GPA of 3.0. Additional exam requirements/recommendations for international students: Required—TOEFL. *Application deadline:* For fall admission, 5/1 priority date for domestic students; for spring admission, 11/1 for domestic students. Application fee: $55 ($65 for international students). *Financial support:* Fellowships, research assistantships with partial tuition reimbursements, teaching assistantships, Federal Work-Study, institutionally sponsored loans, scholarships/grants, and tuition waivers (partial) available. Support available to part-time students. *Faculty research:* Teachers in the process of change, learning cycles, children's concepts of science. *Total annual research expenditures:* $614,458. *Unit head:* Dr. Chris Leland, Interim Executive Associate Dean, 317-274-6801, Fax: 317-274-6864. *Application contact:* Sarah Brandenburg, Graduate Advisor, 317-274-6801, Fax: 317-274-6864, E-mail: edugrad@iupui.edu. Web site: http://education.iupui.edu/.

Iona College, School of Arts and Science, Program in Education, New Rochelle, NY 10801-1890. Offers adolescence education: biology (MS Ed, MST); adolescence education: English (MS Ed, MST); adolescence education: Italian (MS Ed, MST); adolescence education: mathematics (MS Ed, MST); adolescence education: social studies (MS Ed, MST); adolescence education: Spanish (MS Ed, MST); adolescence special education 5-12 (MST); adolescence special education/literacy 5-12 (MS Ed); childhood 1-6/special education 1-6 (MST); childhood education (MST); early childhood/childhood (MST); educational leadership (MS Ed); literacy birth-grade 6/special education 1-6 (MS Ed); literacy education: birth-grade 6 (MS Ed). *Accreditation:* NCATE. Part-time and evening/weekend programs available. *Faculty:* 21 full-time (13 women), 13 part-time/adjunct (8 women). *Students:* 59 full-time (45 women), 101 part-time (78 women); includes 11 minority (2 Black or African American, non-Hispanic/Latino; 2 Asian, non-Hispanic/Latino; 7 Hispanic/Latino). Average age 26. 74 applicants, 66% accepted, 35 enrolled. In 2011, 46 master's awarded. *Degree requirements:* For master's, thesis or alternative. *Entrance requirements:* For master's, minimum GPA of 2.5 (MST), New York teaching certificate (MS Ed). Additional exam requirements/recommendations for international students: Required—TOEFL (minimum score 550 paper-based; 213 computer-based). *Application deadline:* Applications are processed on a rolling basis. Application fee: $50. Electronic applications accepted. *Expenses: Tuition:* Part-time $872 per credit. *Required fees:* $225 per term. *Financial support:* Unspecified assistantships available. Support available to part-time students. Financial award application deadline: 4/15; financial award applicants required to submit FAFSA. *Faculty research:* Reading/writing, educational technology, administration, early literacy assessment, literacy development. *Unit head:* Dr. Catherine O'Callaghan, Chair, 914-633-2210, Fax: 914-633-2608, E-mail: cocallaghan@iona.edu. *Application contact:* Dr. Jeanne Zaino, Interim Dean, School of Arts and Science, 914-633-2112, Fax: 914-633-2023, E-mail: jzaino@iona.edu.

Jacksonville State University, College of Graduate Studies and Continuing Education, College of Education and Professional Studies, Program in Reading Specialist, Jacksonville, AL 36265-1602. Offers MS Ed. Part-time and evening/weekend programs available. *Degree requirements:* For master's, comprehensive exam, thesis (for some programs). Electronic applications accepted. *Expenses:* Tuition, state resident: part-time $336 per hour. Tuition, nonresident: part-time $672 per hour. Part-time tuition and fees vary according to degree level.

James Madison University, The Graduate School, College of Education, Early, Elementary, and Reading Education Department, Program in Reading Education, Harrisonburg, VA 22807. Offers M Ed. *Accreditation:* NCATE. Part-time programs available. *Students:* Average age 27. *Entrance requirements:* For master's, GRE General Test. Additional exam requirements/recommendations for international students: Required—TOEFL. *Application deadline:* For fall admission, 5/1 priority date for domestic students; for spring admission, 9/1 priority date for domestic students. Applications are processed on a rolling basis. Application fee: $55. Electronic applications accepted. *Expenses:* Tuition, state resident: full-time $8016; part-time $334 per credit hour. Tuition, nonresident: full-time $22,656; part-time $944 per credit hour. *Financial support:* Federal Work-Study and unspecified assistantships available. Financial award application deadline: 3/1; financial award applicants required to submit FAFSA. *Unit head:* Dr. Martha Ross, Academic Unit Head, 540-568-6255. *Application contact:* Lynette M. Bible, Director of Graduate Admissions, 540-568-6395, Fax: 540-568-7860, E-mail: biblelm@jmu.edu.

The Johns Hopkins University, School of Education, Department of Teacher Development and Leadership, Baltimore, MD 21218-2699. Offers adolescent literacy education (Certificate); data-based decision making and organizational improvement (Certificate); education (MS), including reading, school administration and supervision, technology for educators; educational leadership for independent schools (Certificate); effective teaching of reading (Certificate); emergent literacy education (Certificate); English as a second language instruction (Certificate); gifted education (Certificate); leadership for school, family, and community collaboration (Certificate); leadership in technology integration (Certificate); school administration and supervision (Certificate); teacher development and leadership (Ed D); teacher leadership (Certificate). Part-time and evening/weekend programs available. Postbaccalaureate distance learning degree programs offered (minimal on-campus study). *Degree requirements:* For master's and Certificate, portfolio; for doctorate, comprehensive exam (for some programs), thesis/dissertation, portfolio or comprehensive exam. *Entrance requirements:* For master's and Certificate, bachelor's degree; minimum undergraduate GPA of 3.0; essay/statement of goals; for doctorate, GRE, essay/statement of goals; three letters of recommendation; curriculum vitae/resume; K-12 professional experience; interview; writing assessment. Additional exam requirements/recommendations for international students: Required—

TOEFL (minimum score 600 paper-based; 250 computer-based; 100 iBT). Electronic applications accepted. *Faculty research:* Application of psychoanalytic concepts to teaching, schools, and education reform; adolescent literacies; use of emerging technologies for teaching, learning, and school leadership; quantitative analyses of the social contexts of education; school, family, and community collaboration; program evaluation methodologies.

Johnson State College, Graduate Program in Education, Program in Literacy, Johnson, VT 05656. Offers MA Ed. *Degree requirements:* For master's, comprehensive exam, thesis or alternative. *Entrance requirements:* For master's, interview. Additional exam requirements/recommendations for international students: Required—TOEFL. *Application deadline:* For fall admission, 7/15 priority date for domestic students, 4/15 for international students; for spring admission, 11/1 priority date for domestic students, 8/15 for international students. Applications are processed on a rolling basis. Application fee: $35. *Expenses: Tuition, area resident:* Part-time $459 per credit hour. Tuition, nonresident: part-time $990 per credit hour. *Financial support:* Career-related internships or fieldwork, Federal Work-Study, and institutionally sponsored loans available. Support available to part-time students. Financial award application deadline: 3/1; financial award applicants required to submit FAFSA. *Unit head:* Dr. Darlene Witte-Townsend, Program Coordinator, 800-635-2356, E-mail: darlene.witte@jsc.edu. *Application contact:* Catherine H. Higley, Administrative Assistant, 800-635-2356 Ext. 1244, Fax: 802-635-1248, E-mail: catherine.higley@jsc.edu.

Judson University, Graduate Programs, Program in Literacy, Elgin, IL 60123-1498. Offers M Ed. In 2011, 24 master's awarded. *Degree requirements:* For master's, thesis. *Entrance requirements:* For master's, copy of official teaching certificate; bachelor's degree with minimum GPA of 3.0; letters of reference; essay. *Application deadline:* Applications are processed on a rolling basis. Application fee: $40. *Expenses: Tuition:* Full-time $9500. *Required fees:* $350. Tuition and fees vary according to course load and program. *Financial support:* Applicants required to submit FAFSA. *Faculty research:* Affective domain in reading, vocabulary acquisition, children's and adolescent literature, cross-curricular writing, critical thinking, human memory and learning strategies. *Unit head:* Dr. Steven L. Layne, Director, 847-628-1093, E-mail: slayne@judsonu.edu. *Application contact:* Maria Aguirre, Assistant to the Registrar for Graduate Programs, 847-628-1160, E-mail: maguirre@judsonu.edu. Web site: http://www.judsonu.edu/literacymaster/.

Kansas State University, Graduate School, College of Education, Department of Curriculum and Instruction, Manhattan, KS 66506. Offers career and technical education (Ed D, PhD); curriculum studies (Ed D, PhD); digital teaching and learning (MS); educational computing, design and online learning (MS); educational technology (Ed D, PhD); elementary/middle level (MS); English as a second language (MS); language/diversity education (Ed D, PhD); literacy education (Ed D, PhD); mathematics education (Ed D, PhD); middle level/secondary (MS); reading and language arts (MS); reading specialist endorsement (MS); science education (Ed D, PhD); social science education (Ed D, PhD); teacher education (Ed D, PhD); teacher leader/school improvement (MS, Ed D). *Accreditation:* NCATE. Part-time programs available. Postbaccalaureate distance learning degree programs offered (minimal on-campus study). *Faculty:* 15 full-time (12 women), 3 part-time/adjunct (2 women). *Students:* 37 full-time (30 women), 113 part-time (91 women); includes 14 minority (4 Black or African American, non-Hispanic/Latino; 1 American Indian or Alaska Native, non-Hispanic/Latino; 1 Asian, non-Hispanic/Latino; 7 Hispanic/Latino; 1 Two or more races, non-Hispanic/Latino), 15 international. Average age 37. 75 applicants, 51% accepted, 9 enrolled. In 2011, 48 master's, 14 doctorates awarded. *Degree requirements:* For master's, comprehensive exam, portfolio, project, report or thesis; for doctorate, comprehensive exam, thesis/dissertation, preliminary exam. *Entrance requirements:* For master's, minimum GPA of 3.0; for doctorate, GRE, minimum GPA of 3.0. Additional exam requirements/recommendations for international students: Required—TOEFL. *Application deadline:* For fall admission, 2/1 priority date for domestic students, 2/1 for international students; for spring admission, 8/1 priority date for domestic students, 8/1 for international students. Applications are processed on a rolling basis. Application fee: $40 ($55 for international students). Electronic applications accepted. *Financial support:* In 2011–12, 1 research assistantship (averaging $16,900 per year), 8 teaching assistantships (averaging $12,466 per year) were awarded; career-related internships or fieldwork, institutionally sponsored loans, and scholarships/grants also available. Support available to part-time students. Financial award application deadline: 3/1; financial award applicants required to submit FAFSA. *Faculty research:* Literacy and technology, critical race theory and diversity, achievement gaps, school improvement, teacher education. *Total annual research expenditures:* $510,907. *Unit head:* Dr. Gail Shroyer, Chair, 785-532-5550, Fax: 785-532-7304, E-mail: gshroyer@ksu.edu. *Application contact:* Dona Deam, Application Contact, 785-532-5595, Fax: 785-532-7304, E-mail: ddeam@ksu.edu. Web site: http://coe.k-state.edu/departments/currin/curringrad.htm.

Kaplan University, Davenport Campus, School of Teacher Education, Davenport, IA 52807-2095. Offers education (M Ed); secondary education (M Ed); teaching and learning (MA); teaching literacy and language: grades 6-12 (MA); teaching literacy and language: grades K-6 (MA); teaching mathematics: grades 6-8 (MA); teaching mathematics: grades 9-12 (MA); teaching mathematics: grades K-5 (MA); teaching science: grades 6-12 (MA); teaching science: grades K-6 (MA); teaching students with special needs (MA); teaching with technology (MA). Part-time and evening/weekend programs available. Postbaccalaureate distance learning degree programs offered (no on-campus study). *Entrance requirements:* Additional exam requirements/recommendations for international students: Required—TOEFL (minimum score 550 paper-based; 218 computer-based; 80 iBT).

Kean University, College of Education, Program in Reading Specialization, Union, NJ 07083. Offers adult literacy (MA); basic skills (MA); reading specialization (MA). *Faculty:* 11 full-time (all women). *Students:* 1 (woman) full-time, 36 part-time (35 women); includes 1 minority (Black or African American, non-Hispanic/Latino). Average age 29. 4 applicants, 100% accepted, 1 enrolled. In 2011, 20 master's awarded. *Degree requirements:* For master's, thesis, practicum, clinical, research seminar, 2 years of teaching experience by end of program (for certification). *Entrance requirements:* For master's, GRE General Test or MAT, minimum GPA of 3.0, 2 letters of recommendation, interview, teaching certification, transcripts, personal statement. Additional exam requirements/recommendations for international students: Required—TOEFL (minimum score 79 iBT). *Application deadline:* For fall admission, 6/1 for domestic and international students; for spring admission, 12/1 for domestic and international students. Applications are processed on a rolling basis. Application fee: $75 ($150 for international students). Electronic applications accepted. *Expenses:* Tuition, state resident: full-time $11,302; part-time $550 per credit. Tuition, nonresident: full-time $15,318; part-time $674 per credit. *Required fees:* $2849; $130 per credit. Tuition and fees vary according to degree level. *Financial support:* In 2011–12, 1 research assistantship with full tuition reimbursement (averaging $3,263 per year) was awarded; unspecified assistantships also available. Financial award applicants required to submit FAFSA. *Unit head:* Dr. Joan M. Kastner, Program Coordinator, 908-737-3942, E-mail: jkastner@kean.edu. *Application contact:* Reenat Hasan, Admission Counselor, 908-737-5923, Fax: 908-737-5925, E-mail: rhasan@exchange.kean.edu. Web site: http://www.kean.edu/KU/Adult-Literacy.

Kent State University, Graduate School of Education, Health, and Human Services, School of Teaching, Learning and Curriculum Studies, Program in Reading Specialization, Kent, OH 44242-0001. Offers M Ed, MA. *Accreditation:* NCATE. Part-time and evening/weekend programs available. *Faculty:* 5 full-time (all women), 2 part-time/adjunct (1 woman). *Students:* 4 full-time (all women), 36 part-time (35 women); includes 2 minority (1 Black or African American, non-Hispanic/Latino; 1 Asian, non-Hispanic/Latino). 14 applicants, 93% accepted. In 2011, 52 master's awarded. *Degree requirements:* For master's, thesis (for some programs). *Entrance requirements:* For master's, 2 letters of reference, goals statement. Additional exam requirements/recommendations for international students: Required—TOEFL (minimum score 550 paper-based; 213 computer-based; 80 iBT). *Application deadline:* Applications are processed on a rolling basis. Application fee: $30 ($60 for international students). Electronic applications accepted. *Expenses:* Tuition, state resident: full-time $8136; part-time $452 per credit hour. Tuition, nonresident: full-time $14,292; part-time $794 per credit hour. *Financial support:* In 2011–12, 2 research assistantships with full tuition reimbursements (averaging $9,000 per year) were awarded; Federal Work-Study, scholarships/grants, and unspecified assistantships also available. Financial award application deadline: 4/1; financial award applicants required to submit FAFSA. *Faculty research:* Adolescent literacy, adult and family literacy, school change in literacy education, struggling readers. *Unit head:* Dr. Denise Morgan, Coordinator, 330-672-0663, E-mail: dmorgan2@kent.edu. *Application contact:* Nancy Miller, Academic Program Coordinator, Office of Graduate Student Services, 330-672-2576, Fax: 330-672-9162, E-mail: ogs@kent.edu.

King's College, Program in Reading, Wilkes-Barre, PA 18711-0801. Offers M Ed. *Accreditation:* NCATE. Part-time and evening/weekend programs available. *Degree requirements:* For master's, thesis. *Entrance requirements:* Additional exam requirements/recommendations for international students: Required—TOEFL (minimum score 600 paper-based; 250 computer-based).

Kutztown University of Pennsylvania, College of Education, Program in Reading, Kutztown, PA 19530-0730. Offers M Ed. *Accreditation:* NCATE. Part-time and evening/weekend programs available. *Students:* 5 full-time (3 women), 90 part-time (85 women); includes 2 minority (both Hispanic/Latino). Average age 28. 25 applicants, 56% accepted, 13 enrolled. In 2011, 45 master's awarded. *Degree requirements:* For master's, comprehensive project. *Entrance requirements:* For master's, GRE General Test. Additional exam requirements/recommendations for international students: Required—TOEFL (minimum score 550 paper-based; 79 iBT). *Application deadline:* For fall admission, 8/1 priority date for domestic students, 8/1 for international students; for spring admission, 12/1 priority date for domestic students, 12/1 for international students. Applications are processed on a rolling basis. Application fee: $35. Electronic applications accepted. *Expenses:* Tuition, state resident: full-time $7488; part-time $416 per credit. Tuition, nonresident: full-time $11,232; part-time $624 per credit. *Financial support:* Career-related internships or fieldwork, Federal Work-Study, scholarships/grants, and unspecified assistantships available. Financial award application deadline: 3/1; financial award applicants required to submit FAFSA. *Unit head:* Dr. Jeanie Burnett, Chairperson, 610-683-4286, Fax: 610-683-1327, E-mail: burnett@kutztown.edu. *Application contact:* Kelly D. Burr, Associate Director, Graduate Admissions, 610-683-4200, Fax: 610-683-1393, E-mail: graduate@kutztown.edu.

Lake Erie College, School of Professional and Innovative Studies, Painesville, OH 44077-3389. Offers curriculum and instruction (MS Ed); education (MS Ed); educational leadership (MS Ed); reading (MS Ed). Part-time and evening/weekend programs available. *Faculty:* 3 full-time (all women), 1 part-time/adjunct (0 women). *Students:* 20 part-time (15 women); includes 14 minority (all American Indian or Alaska Native, non-Hispanic/Latino). Average age 35. 5 applicants, 100% accepted, 1 enrolled. In 2011, 7 master's awarded. *Degree requirements:* For master's, comprehensive exam (for some programs), thesis optional, applied research project. *Entrance requirements:* For master's, GRE General Test (minimum score of 440 verbal or 500 quantitative) or minimum GPA of 2.75; bachelor's degree from accredited 4-year institution; references; essay. Additional exam requirements/recommendations for international students: Required—TOEFL (minimum score 550 paper-based; 79 computer-based). *Application deadline:* For fall admission, 8/1 priority date for domestic students, 6/1 for international students; for spring admission, 12/15 for domestic students, 10/1 for international students. Applications are processed on a rolling basis. Application fee: $30. Electronic applications accepted. Application fee is waived when completed online. *Expenses:* Contact institution. *Financial support:* Teaching assistantships, tuition waivers, and unspecified assistantships available. Financial award applicants required to submit FAFSA. *Faculty research:* Cooperative learning, portfolio assessment, education systems abroad, Web-based instruction. *Unit head:* Prof. Dale Sheptak, Interim Dean of the School of Professional and Innovative Studies/Assistant Professor, 440-375-7131, E-mail: dsheptak@lec.edu. *Application contact:* Christopher Harris, Dean of Admissions and Financial Aid, 800-916-0904, Fax: 440-375-7000, E-mail: admissions@lec.edu. Web site: http://www.lec.edu/med.

Lehman College of the City University of New York, Division of Education, Department of Specialized Services in Education, Program in Reading Teacher, Bronx, NY 10468-1589. Offers MS Ed. *Accreditation:* NCATE. Evening/weekend programs available. *Entrance requirements:* For master's, interview, minimum GPA of 2.7. *Faculty research:* Emergent literacy, language-based classrooms, primary and secondary social contexts of language and literacy, innovative in-service education models, adult literacy.

Le Moyne College, Department of Education, Syracuse, NY 13214. Offers adolescent education (MS Ed, MST); adolescent education/special education (MS Ed, MST); adolescent English (grades 7-12) (MST); adolescent history (grades 7-12) (MST); childhood education (MS Ed); childhood education/special education (MS Ed); elementary education (MS Ed); general professional education (MS Ed); inclusive childhood education (MST); literacy education (birth to grade 6) (MS Ed); literacy education (grades 5-12) (MS Ed); school building leadership (MS Ed, CAS); school district business leader (MS Ed, CAS); school district leadership (MS Ed, CAS); secondary education (MS Ed); special education (MS Ed); students with disabilities-generalist (grades 7-12) (MS Ed); TESOL (teaching English to speakers of other languages) (MS Ed); urban studies (MS Ed). *Accreditation:* Teacher Education Accreditation Council. Part-time and evening/weekend programs available. *Faculty:* 9 full-time (6 women), 51 part-time/adjunct (28 women). *Students:* 61 full-time (47 women), 311 part-time (222 women); includes 31 minority (19 Black or African American, non-Hispanic/Latino; 3 American Indian or Alaska Native, non-Hispanic/Latino; 4 Asian, non-Hispanic/Latino; 5 Hispanic/Latino), 2 international. Average age 30. 242 applicants, 90% accepted, 180 enrolled. In 2011, 168 master's, 23 CASs awarded. *Degree requirements:* For master's, thesis. *Entrance requirements:* For master's, GRE General Test, bachelor's degree, 2 letters of recommendation, written statement, transcripts. Additional exam requirements/recommendations for international students: Required—TOEFL (minimum score 550 paper-based; 213 computer-based; 79 iBT). *Application deadline:* For fall admission, 4/1 priority date for domestic students, 4/1 for international students; for spring admission, 10/1 priority date for domestic students, 10/1 for international students. Applications are processed on a rolling basis. Application fee: $50. *Expenses:* Contact institution. *Financial support:* In 2011–12, 32 students received support. Career-related internships or fieldwork and health care benefits available. Support available to part-time students. Financial award applicants required to submit FAFSA. *Faculty research:* Minority teachers, special education, multiculturalism, literacy, technology, video games learning, autism, school district organization, service-learning, higher level problem solving, teacher leadership. *Unit head:* Dr. Suzanne L. Gilmour, Chair, Department of Education and Director of Graduate Education Programs, 315-445-4376, Fax: 315-445-4744, E-mail: gilmous@lemoyne.edu. *Application contact:* Kristen P. Trapasso, Director of Graduate Admission, 315-445-4265, Fax: 315-445-6027, E-mail: trapaskp@lemoyne.edu. Web site: http://www.lemoyne.edu/education.

Lesley University, School of Education, Cambridge, MA 02138-2790. Offers curriculum and instruction (M Ed, CAGS); early childhood education (M Ed); educational studies (PhD); elementary education (M Ed); individually designed (M Ed); middle school education (M Ed); moderate special needs (M Ed); reading (M Ed, CAGS); science in education (M Ed); severe special needs (M Ed); special needs (CAGS); technology in education (M Ed, CAGS). *Accreditation:* Teacher Education Accreditation Council. Part-time and evening/weekend programs available. Postbaccalaureate distance learning degree programs offered (no on-campus study). *Faculty:* 36 full-time (27 women), 170 part-time/adjunct (129 women). *Students:* 552 full-time (437 women), 1,971 part-time (1,697 women); includes 364 minority (189 Black or African American, non-Hispanic/Latino; 19 American Indian or Alaska Native, non-Hispanic/Latino; 45 Asian, non-Hispanic/Latino; 83 Hispanic/Latino; 2 Native Hawaiian or other Pacific Islander, non-Hispanic/Latino; 26 Two or more races, non-Hispanic/Latino), 28 international. Average age 37. In 2011, 1,390 master's, 8 doctorates, 42 other advanced degrees awarded. *Degree requirements:* For master's, practicum; for doctorate, thesis/dissertation. *Entrance requirements:* For doctorate, GRE General Test or MAT, interview, master's degree, resume; for CAGS, interview, master's degree. Additional exam requirements/recommendations for international students: Required—TOEFL (minimum score 550 paper-based; 213 computer-based; 80 iBT). *Application deadline:* Applications are processed on a rolling basis. Application fee: $50. Electronic applications accepted. *Financial support:* In 2011–12, research assistantships (averaging $3,400 per year), teaching assistantships (averaging $3,400 per year) were awarded; career-related internships or fieldwork, Federal Work-Study, scholarships/grants, and unspecified assistantships also available. Support available to part-time students. Financial award application deadline: 4/15; financial award applicants required to submit FAFSA. *Faculty research:* Assessment in literacy, mathematics and science; autism spectrum disorders; instructional technology and online learning; multicultural education and ELL. *Unit head:* Dr. Mario Borunda, Dean, 617-349-8375, Fax: 617-349-8607, E-mail: mborunda@lesley.edu. *Application contact:* Rosie Davis, Senior Assistant Director of Admissions, 617-349-8851, Fax: 617-349-8313, E-mail: rdavis4@lesley.edu. Web site: http://www.lesley.edu/soe.html.

Lewis University, College of Education, Programs in Reading and Literacy, Romeoville, IL 60446. Offers M Ed, MA. Part-time and evening/weekend programs available. *Students:* 3 full-time (all women), 44 part-time (38 women); includes 4 minority (3 Black or African American, non-Hispanic/Latino; 1 Hispanic/Latino). Average age 30. In 2011, 8 master's awarded. *Entrance requirements:* For master's, departmental qualifying exam, writing exam, minimum GPA of 2.75, 2 letters of recommendation, interview. Additional exam requirements/recommendations for international students: Required—TOEFL (minimum score 550 paper-based; 213 computer-based; 80 iBT). *Application deadline:* For fall admission, 5/1 for international students; for spring admission, 11/15 for international students. Application fee: $40. *Financial support:* Scholarships/grants and unspecified assistantships available. Support available to part-time students. Financial award application deadline: 5/1; financial award applicants required to submit FAFSA. *Unit head:* Dr. Deborah Augsburger, Program Director, 815-838-0500 Ext. 5883, E-mail: augsbude@lewisu.edu. *Application contact:* Kelly Lofgren, Graduate Admission Counselor, 815-836-5704, Fax: 815-836-5578, E-mail: lofgreke@lewisu.edu.

Liberty University, School of Education, Lynchburg, VA 24502. Offers administration and supervision (M Ed); curriculum and instruction (M Ed); early childhood education (M Ed); educational leadership (Ed D, Ed S); educational technology and online instruction (M Ed); elementary education (M Ed, MAT); gifted education (M Ed); math specialist (M Ed); middle grades (M Ed); outdoor adventure sport (MS); reading specialist (M Ed); school counseling (M Ed); secondary education (M Ed, MAT); special education (M Ed, MAT); sports administration (MS); teaching and learning (Ed D, Ed S). *Accreditation:* NCATE. Part-time programs available. Postbaccalaureate distance learning degree programs offered (minimal on-campus study). *Students:* 2,245 full-time (1,572 women), 3,500 part-time (2,558 women); includes 1,141 minority (888 Black or African American, non-Hispanic/Latino; 19 American Indian or Alaska Native, non-Hispanic/Latino; 21 Asian, non-Hispanic/Latino; 123 Hispanic/Latino; 9 Native Hawaiian or other Pacific Islander, non-Hispanic/Latino; 81 Two or more races, non-Hispanic/Latino), 76 international. Average age 37. In 2011, 760 master's, 48 doctorates, 321 other advanced degrees awarded. *Degree requirements:* For doctorate, comprehensive exam, thesis/dissertation. *Entrance requirements:* For master's, GRE General Test or MAT (if taken in or before 1999), 2 letters of recommendation, minimum undergraduate GPA of 3.0, curriculum vitae; for doctorate, GRE General Test or MAT (if taken before 1999), minimum master's GPA of 3.0, 3 years of teacher experience; for Ed S, GRE General Test or MAT (if taken before 1999), minimum master's GPA of 3.0, 3 years of teaching experience. Additional exam requirements/recommendations for international students: Required—TOEFL (minimum score 600 paper-based; 250 computer-based). *Application deadline:* For fall admission, 6/1 priority date for domestic students; for spring admission, 11/1 for domestic students. Applications are processed on a rolling basis. Application fee: $50. Electronic applications accepted. *Expenses:* Contact institution. *Financial support:* Federal Work-Study and tuition waivers (partial) available. *Faculty research:* Self-determination, character education, bibliotherapy, learning styles, distance education. *Unit head:* Dr. Karen L. Parker, Dean, 434-582-2195, Fax: 434-582-2468, E-mail: kparker@liberty.edu. *Application contact:* Jay Bridge, Director of Graduate Admissions, 800-424-9595, Fax: 800-628-7977, E-mail: gradadmissions@liberty.edu. Web site: http://www.liberty.edu/academics/education/graduate/.

Lincoln University, Graduate Center, Lincoln University, PA 19352. Offers administration (MSA), including finance, human resources management; early childhood education (M Ed); elementary education (M Ed); human services (M Hum Svcs); reading (MSR). Evening/weekend programs available. *Degree requirements:* For master's, thesis. *Entrance requirements:* For master's, 5 years of work experience in human services. *Faculty research:* Gerontology/minority aging, computers in composition instruction.

Long Island University–Brentwood Campus, School of Education, Brentwood, NY 11717. Offers childhood education (MS); early childhood education (MS); literacy (MS); mental health counseling (MS); school counseling (MS); special education (MS). Part-time and evening/weekend programs available.

Long Island University–Brooklyn Campus, School of Education, Department of Teaching and Learning, Program in Reading, Brooklyn, NY 11201-8423. Offers MS Ed. Part-time and evening/weekend programs available. *Degree requirements:* For master's, thesis optional. *Entrance requirements:* For master's, 2 letters of recommendation. Additional exam requirements/recommendations for international students: Required—TOEFL (minimum score 500 paper-based; 173 computer-based). Electronic applications accepted.

Long Island University–C. W. Post Campus, School of Education, Department of Special Education and Literacy, Brookville, NY 11548-1300. Offers childhood education/literacy (MS); childhood education/special education (MS); literacy (MS Ed); special education (MS Ed). *Accreditation:* Teacher Education Accreditation Council. Part-time and evening/weekend programs available. *Degree requirements:* For master's, research project, comprehensive exam or thesis. *Entrance requirements:* For master's, interview; minimum GPA of 2.75 in major, 2.5 overall. Electronic applications accepted. *Faculty research:* Autism, mainstreaming, robotics and microcomputers in special education, transition from school to work.

Long Island University–Hudson at Rockland, Graduate School, Programs in Special Education and Literacy, Orangeburg, NY 10962. Offers autism (MS Ed); childhood/literacy (MS Ed); childhood/special education (MS Ed); literacy (MS Ed); special education (MS Ed). Part-time programs available. *Entrance requirements:* For master's, college transcripts, two letters of recommendation, personal statement, resume.

Long Island University–Hudson at Westchester, Programs in Education-Teaching, Program in Literacy Education, Purchase, NY 10577. Offers MS Ed, Advanced Certificate. Part-time and evening/weekend programs available.

Long Island University–Riverhead, Education Division, Program in Literacy Education, Riverhead, NY 11901. Offers MS Ed. *Accreditation:* Teacher Education Accreditation Council. Part-time programs available. *Faculty:* 4 full-time, 6 part-time/adjunct. *Students:* 2 full-time (both women), 23 part-time (19 women); includes 2 minority (both Black or African American, non-Hispanic/Latino). Average age 30. In 2011, 12 master's awarded. *Degree requirements:* For master's, comprehensive exam. *Entrance requirements:* For master's, minimum undergraduate GPA of 2.75, New York State Provisional or Initial Teacher Certification. Additional exam requirements/recommendations for international students: Required—TOEFL (minimum score 550 paper-based; 250 computer-based). *Application deadline:* Applications are processed on a rolling basis. Electronic applications accepted. *Expenses: Tuition:* Part-time $1028 per credit. *Financial support:* Scholarships/grants and unspecified assistantships available. Support available to part-time students. Financial award applicants required to submit FAFSA. *Unit head:* Dr. Erica Pecorale, Head, 631-287-8010, Fax: 631-287-8253, E-mail: erica.pecorale@liu.edu. *Application contact:* Andrea Borra, Admissions Counselor, 631-287-8010, Fax: 631-287-8253, E-mail: andrea.borra@liu.edu.

Longwood University, Office of Graduate Studies, College of Education and Human Services, Farmville, VA 23909. Offers communication sciences and disorders (MS); community and college counseling (MS); curriculum and instruction specialist-elementary (MS), including mild disabilities, modern languages; curriculum and instruction specialist-secondary (MS), including English, mild disabilities, modern languages; educational leadership (MS); guidance and counseling (MS); literacy and culture (MS); school library media (MS). *Accreditation:* NCATE. Part-time and evening/weekend programs available. *Degree requirements:* For master's, comprehensive exam, thesis optional. *Entrance requirements:* For master's, GRE (communication sciences and disorders), minimum GPA of 2.75. Additional exam requirements/recommendations for international students: Required—TOEFL (minimum score 550 paper-based; 213 computer-based).

Loyola Marymount University, School of Education, Department of Elementary and Secondary Education, Program in Literacy Education, Los Angeles, CA 90045. Offers MA. Part-time and evening/weekend programs available. *Faculty:* 7 full-time (6 women), 17 part-time/adjunct (10 women). *Students:* 6 full-time (all women), 7 part-time (all women); includes 8 minority (2 Asian, non-Hispanic/Latino; 4 Hispanic/Latino; 1 Native Hawaiian or other Pacific Islander, non-Hispanic/Latino; 1 Two or more races, non-Hispanic/Latino). Average age 31. 6 applicants, 83% accepted, 5 enrolled. In 2011, 1 master's awarded. *Degree requirements:* For master's, comprehensive exam. *Entrance requirements:* For master's, CBEST. Additional exam requirements/recommendations for international students: Required—TOEFL (minimum score 600 paper-based; 250 computer-based; 100 iBT). *Application deadline:* For fall admission, 6/15 for domestic students; for spring admission, 11/15 for domestic students. Application fee: $50. Electronic applications accepted. *Financial support:* In 2011–12, 9 students received support. Scholarships/grants and unspecified assistantships available. Support available to part-time students. Financial award application deadline: 6/15; financial award applicants required to submit FAFSA. *Unit head:* Dr. Candace Poindexter, Program Director, 310-338-7314, E-mail: cpoindex@lmu.edu. *Application contact:* Chake H. Kouyoumjian, Director, Graduate Admissions, 310-338-2721, E-mail: ckouyoum@lmu.edu. Web site: http://soe.lmu.edu/admissions/programs/literacy.htm.

Loyola Marymount University, School of Education, Department of Elementary and Secondary Education, Program in Literacy/Language Arts, Los Angeles, CA 90045. Offers MA. Part-time and evening/weekend programs available. *Faculty:* 7 full-time (6 women), 17 part-time/adjunct (10 women). *Students:* 14 full-time (12 women), 3 part-time (all women); includes 7 minority (5 Hispanic/Latino; 2 Two or more races, non-Hispanic/Latino). Average age 30. 9 applicants, 100% accepted, 6 enrolled. In 2011, 15 master's awarded. *Degree requirements:* For master's, comprehensive exam. *Entrance requirements:* For master's, CBEST, CSET, RICA, 3 letters of recommendation. Additional exam requirements/recommendations for international students: Required—TOEFL (minimum score 600 paper-based; 250 computer-based; 100 iBT). *Application deadline:* For fall admission, 6/15 for domestic students; for spring admission, 11/15 for domestic students. Application fee: $50. Electronic applications accepted. *Financial support:* In 2011–12, 4 students received support. Scholarships/grants and unspecified assistantships available. Support available to part-time students. Financial award application deadline: 6/15; financial award applicants required to submit FAFSA. *Unit head:* Dr. Irene Oliver, Chair, 310-338-7302, E-mail: ioliver@lmu.edu. *Application contact:* Chake H. Kouyoumjian, Director, Graduate Admissions, 310-338-2721, E-mail: ckouyoum@lmu.edu. Web site: http://soe.lmu.edu/admissions/programs/tcp.htm.

Loyola Marymount University, School of Education, Department of Elementary and Secondary Education, Program in Reading Instruction, Los Angeles, CA 90045. Offers MA. *Faculty:* 7 full-time (6 women), 17 part-time/adjunct (10 women). *Students:* 18 full-time (17 women), 1 (woman) part-time; includes 18 minority (2 Black or African American, non-Hispanic/Latino; 8 Hispanic/Latino; 8 Two or more races, non-Hispanic/Latino). Average age 25. 6 applicants, 100% accepted, 6 enrolled. *Entrance requirements:* For master's, statement of intent, 2 letters of recommendation, program-specific application. *Application deadline:* For fall admission, 6/15 for domestic students. Application fee: $50. *Financial support:* In 2011–12, 17 students received support. *Unit head:* Dr. Candace Poindexter, Director, 310-338-7314, E-mail: cpoindex@lmu.edu. *Application contact:* Chake H. Kouyoumjian, Graduate Admissions Director, 310-338-2721, E-mail: ckouyoum@lmu.edu. Web site: http://soe.lmu.edu/admissions/programs/onlinereading.htm.

Loyola University Chicago, School of Education, Program in Teaching and Learning, Chicago, IL 60660. Offers elementary education (M Ed); English as a second language (Certificate); math education (M Ed); reading specialist (M Ed); reading teacher endorsement (Certificate); school technology (M Ed); science education (M Ed); secondary education (M Ed); special education (M Ed). *Accreditation:* NCATE. *Faculty:*

12 full-time (9 women), 12 part-time/adjunct (6 women). *Students:* 131. Average age 28. 115 applicants, 65% accepted, 30 enrolled. In 2011, 80 master's awarded. *Degree requirements:* For master's, comprehensive exam. *Entrance requirements:* For master's, Illinois Basic Skills Test, 3 letters of recommendation, minimum GPA of 3.0, resume. Additional exam requirements/recommendations for international students: Required—TOEFL (minimum score 550 paper-based; 213 computer-based; 79 iBT). *Application deadline:* For fall admission, 7/1 priority date for domestic students, 7/1 for international students; for spring admission, 11/1 priority date for domestic students, 11/1 for international students. Applications are processed on a rolling basis. Application fee: $50. Electronic applications accepted. Application fee is waived when completed online. *Expenses: Tuition:* Full-time $15,660; part-time $870 per credit hour. *Required fees:* $125 per semester. Tuition and fees vary according to course load and program. *Financial support:* Institutionally sponsored loans, scholarships/grants, and unspecified assistantships available. Support available to part-time students. Financial award application deadline: 2/1; financial award applicants required to submit FAFSA. *Faculty research:* Positive behavior support, school reform, school improvement. *Unit head:* Dr. Dorothy Giroux, Director, 312-915-7027, E-mail: dgiroux@luc.edu. *Application contact:* Marie Rosin-Dittmar, Information Contact, 312-915-6800, E-mail: schleduc@luc.edu.

Loyola University Maryland, Graduate Programs, Department of Education, Program in Literacy, Baltimore, MD 21210-2699. Offers literacy (CAS); literacy teacher (M Ed); reading specialities (M Ed). *Accreditation:* NCATE. Part-time programs available. *Faculty:* 25 full-time (21 women), 14 part-time/adjunct (11 women). *Students:* 2 full-time (both women), 57 part-time (53 women); includes 12 minority (7 Black or African American, non-Hispanic/Latino; 1 American Indian or Alaska Native, non-Hispanic/Latino; 2 Asian; non-Hispanic/Latino; 1 Hispanic/Latino; 1 Two or more races, non-Hispanic/Latino). Average age 31. In 2011, 16 master's awarded. *Entrance requirements:* Additional exam requirements/recommendations for international students: Required—TOEFL (minimum score 550 paper-based; 213 computer-based). *Application deadline:* For fall admission, 6/15 priority date for domestic students; for spring admission, 11/1 priority date for domestic students. Application fee: $50. Electronic applications accepted. *Financial support:* Research assistantships and unspecified assistantships available. Financial award application deadline: 4/15; financial award applicants required to submit FAFSA. *Unit head:* Wendy Smith, Director, 410-617-2194, E-mail: wmsmith@loyola.edu. *Application contact:* Maureen Faux, Executive Director, Graduate Admissions, 410-617-5020, Fax: 410-617-2002, E-mail: graduate@loyola.edu.

Lynchburg College, Graduate Studies, School of Education and Human Development, M Ed Program in Reading, Lynchburg, VA 24501-3199. Offers reading instruction (M Ed); reading specialist (M Ed). Part-time and evening/weekend programs available. *Faculty:* 3 full-time (all women). *Students:* 1 (woman) full-time, 10 part-time (9 women); includes 2 minority (both Black or African American, non-Hispanic/Latino), 1 international. Average age 30. In 2011, 7 master's awarded. *Degree requirements:* For master's, practicum; portfolio or comprehensive exam. *Entrance requirements:* For master's, GRE, minimum GPA of 3.0 (preferred), three letters of recommendation, official transcripts (bachelor's, others as relevant), career goals statement. Additional exam requirements/recommendations for international students: Required—TOEFL (minimum score 550 paper-based; 213 computer-based; 79 iBT), IELTS (minimum score 6.5). *Application deadline:* For fall admission, 7/31 for domestic students, 6/1 for international students; for spring admission, 11/30 for domestic students, 10/15 for international students. Applications are processed on a rolling basis. Application fee: $30. Electronic applications accepted. Application fee is waived when completed online. *Expenses: Tuition:* Full-time $7740; part-time $430 per credit hour. *Financial support:* Fellowships, research assistantships, Federal Work-Study, scholarships/grants, health care benefits, and unspecified assistantships available. Support available to part-time students. Financial award application deadline: 7/31; financial award applicants required to submit FAFSA. *Unit head:* Dr. Susan Thompson, Associate Professor/Director of M Ed in Reading, 434-544-8510, Fax: 434-544-8483, E-mail: thompson.s@lynchburg.edu. *Application contact:* Anne Pingstock, Executive Assistant, Graduate Studies, 434-544-8383, Fax: 434-544-8483, E-mail: gradstudies@lynchburg.edu. Web site: http://www.lynchburg.edu/reading.xml.

Lyndon State College, Graduate Programs in Education, Department of Education, Lyndonville, VT 05851-0919. Offers curriculum and instruction (M Ed); reading specialist (M Ed); special education (M Ed); teaching and counseling (M Ed). Part-time and evening/weekend programs available. *Degree requirements:* For master's, exam or major field project. *Entrance requirements:* Additional exam requirements/recommendations for international students: Recommended—TOEFL (minimum score 500 paper-based; 173 computer-based).

Madonna University, Programs in Education, Livonia, MI 48150-1173. Offers Catholic school leadership (MSA); educational leadership (MSA); learning disabilities (MAT); literacy education (MAT); teaching and learning (MAT). *Accreditation:* NCATE. Part-time and evening/weekend programs available. *Degree requirements:* For master's, thesis or alternative. Electronic applications accepted.

Malone University, Graduate Program in Education, Canton, OH 44709. Offers curriculum and instruction (MA), including teacher leader endorsement; curriculum, instruction, and professional development (MA); educational leadership (MA), including principal license; intervention specialist (MA); reading (MA). Part-time and evening/weekend programs available. *Faculty:* 9 full-time (5 women), 8 part-time/adjunct (6 women). *Students:* 2 full-time (both women), 43 part-time (33 women); includes 2 minority (both Black or African American, non-Hispanic/Latino). Average age 36. 35 applicants, 91% accepted, 12 enrolled. In 2011, 11 master's awarded. *Degree requirements:* For master's, research project. *Entrance requirements:* For master's, minimum GPA of 3.0, teaching license. Additional exam requirements/recommendations for international students: Required—TOEFL (minimum score 550 paper-based; 213 computer-based; 79 iBT). *Application deadline:* Applications are processed on a rolling basis. *Expenses: Tuition:* Part-time $625 per semester hour. Part-time tuition and fees vary according to program. *Financial support:* Tuition waivers (partial) available. Support available to part-time students. Financial award application deadline: 6/30. *Faculty research:* Educational leadership styles: Jesus as master teacher, assessment accommodations for English language learners, preparing culturally proficient teachers, using naturally occurring text in the classroom to meet the syntactic needs of students with learning disabilities, using iPad instructional technology to meet the needs of students with disabilities. *Unit head:* Dr. Alice E. Christie, Director, 330-478-8541, Fax: 330-471-8563, E-mail: achristie@malone.edu. *Application contact:* Dan DePasquale, Senior Recruiter, 330-471-8381, Fax: 330-471-8343, E-mail: depasquale@malone.edu. Web site: http://www.malone.edu/admissions/graduate/education/.

Manhattanville College, Graduate Studies, School of Education, Program in Early Childhood Education, Purchase, NY 10577-2132. Offers childhood and early childhood education (MAT); early childhood education (birth-grade 2) (MAT); literacy (birth-grade 6) (MPS), including reading, writing; literacy (birth-grade 6) and special education (grades 1-6) (MPS); special education (birth-grade 2) (MPS); special education (birth-grade 6) (MPS). Part-time and evening/weekend programs available. *Degree requirements:* For master's, comprehensive exam or research project, field experience. *Entrance requirements:* For master's, minimum undergraduate GPA of 3.0, 2 letters of recommendation. Additional exam requirements/recommendations for international students: Required—TOEFL. Electronic applications accepted.

Manhattanville College, Graduate Studies, School of Education, Program in Middle Childhood/Adolescence Education (Grades 5-12), Purchase, NY 10577-2132. Offers biology (MAT); biology and special education (MPS); chemistry (MAT); chemistry and special education (MPS); English (MAT); English and special education (MPS); literacy (MPS), including reading and writing, writing; literacy and special education (MPS); math (MAT); math and special education (MPS); second language (MAT), including French, Italian, Latin, Spanish; social studies (MAT); social studies and special education (MPS); special education (MPS). Part-time and evening/weekend programs available. *Degree requirements:* For master's, comprehensive exam or research project, field experience. *Entrance requirements:* For master's, minimum undergraduate GPA of 3.0, 2 letters of recommendation. Additional exam requirements/recommendations for international students: Required—TOEFL. Electronic applications accepted.

Marquette University, Graduate School, College of Education, Department of Educational Policy and Leadership, Milwaukee, WI 53201-1881. Offers college student personnel administration (M Ed); curriculum and instruction (MA); education (MA); educational administration (M Ed); educational policy and foundations (MA); elementary education (Certificate); literacy (MA); principal (Certificate); reading specialist (Certificate); reading teacher (Certificate); secondary education (Certificate); superintendent (Certificate). Part-time and evening/weekend programs available. *Faculty:* 14 full-time (9 women). *Students:* 40 full-time (34 women), 137 part-time (80 women); includes 25 minority (14 Black or African American, non-Hispanic/Latino; 1 American Indian or Alaska Native, non-Hispanic/Latino; 2 Asian, non-Hispanic/Latino; 8 Hispanic/Latino), 2 international. Average age 32. 132 applicants, 73% accepted, 67 enrolled. In 2011, 46 master's, 3 doctorates, 5 other advanced degrees awarded. Terminal master's awarded for partial completion of doctoral program. *Degree requirements:* For master's, comprehensive exam, thesis (for some programs); for doctorate, thesis/dissertation, qualifying exam, supporting minor. *Entrance requirements:* For master's, GRE General Test or MAT, official transcripts from all current and previous colleges/universities except Marquette, three letters of recommendation, statement of purpose; for doctorate, GRE General Test, MAT, sample of written work, official transcripts from all current and previous colleges/universities except Marquette, three letters of recommendation, statement of purpose, resume/curriculum vitae; for Certificate, GRE General Test or MAT, master's degree. Additional exam requirements/recommendations for international students: Required—TOEFL (minimum score 530 paper-based; 78 computer-based). *Application deadline:* For fall admission, 1/15 for domestic and international students. Application fee: $50. *Expenses:* Contact institution. *Financial support:* In 2011–12, 130 students received support, including 1 fellowship with full tuition reimbursement available (averaging $18,780 per year), 5 research assistantships with full tuition reimbursements available (averaging $13,404 per year); health care benefits, tuition waivers (partial), and unspecified assistantships also available. Support available to part-time students. Financial award application deadline: 2/15. *Faculty research:* Leadership; social justice in education; development of lifelong learners; race, class, and schooling in historical perspective; urban teacher education. *Unit head:* Dr. Ellen Eckman, Chair, 414-288-1561, E-mail: ellen.eckman@marquette.edu. *Application contact:* Craig Pierce, Assistant Dean of the Graduate School, 414-288-5740, Fax: 414-288-1902, E-mail: craig.pierce@marquette.edu.

Marshall University, Academic Affairs Division, Graduate School of Education and Professional Development, Program in Reading Education, Huntington, WV 25755. Offers MA, Ed S. *Accreditation:* NCATE. Part-time and evening/weekend programs available. *Students:* 10 full-time (all women), 78 part-time (73 women); includes 2 minority (1 Asian, non-Hispanic/Latino; 1 Hispanic/Latino). Average age 34. In 2011, 52 master's awarded. *Degree requirements:* For master's, thesis optional, comprehensive or oral assessment, final project; for Ed S, thesis optional, research project. *Entrance requirements:* For master's, GRE General Test or MAT; for Ed S, master's degree in reading, minimum GPA of 3.0. Application fee: $40. *Financial support:* Federal Work-Study, tuition waivers (full and partial), and unspecified assistantships available. Support available to part-time students. Financial award applicants required to submit FAFSA. *Unit head:* Dr. Barbara O'Byrne, Program Director, 304-746-1986, E-mail: bobyrne@marshall.edu. *Application contact:* Information Contact, 304-746-1900, Fax: 304-746-1902, E-mail: services@marshall.edu.

Marygrove College, Graduate Division, Program in Reading and Literacy, Detroit, MI 48221-2599. Offers M Ed. Part-time and evening/weekend programs available. *Degree requirements:* For master's, practicum, research project. *Entrance requirements:* For master's, MAT, interview, minimum undergraduate GPA of 3.0, teaching certificate.

Maryville University of Saint Louis, School of Education, St. Louis, MO 63141-7299. Offers art education (MA Ed); early childhood education (MA Ed); educational leadership (Ed D); educational leadership: principal certification (MA Ed); elementary education (MA Ed); gifted education (MA Ed); higher education leadership (Ed D); literacy specialist (MA Ed); middle grades education (MA Ed); secondary teaching and inquiry (MA Ed); teacher as leader (MA Ed). *Accreditation:* NCATE. Part-time and evening/weekend programs available. *Faculty:* 10 full-time (6 women), 19 part-time/adjunct (15 women). *Students:* 33 full-time (25 women), 251 part-time (190 women); includes 42 minority (32 Black or African American, non-Hispanic/Latino; 1 American Indian or Alaska Native, non-Hispanic/Latino; 4 Asian, non-Hispanic/Latino; 2 Hispanic/Latino; 3 Two or more races, non-Hispanic/Latino). Average age 38. In 2011, 69 master's, 43 doctorates awarded. *Degree requirements:* For master's, thesis, project. *Entrance requirements:* For master's, minimum cumulative GPA of 3.0, 3 professional recommendations, essays, interview with program faculty; for doctorate, minimum GPA of 3.0, 3 professional recommendations, essay, interview, on-site writing sample. Additional exam requirements/recommendations for international students: Required—TOEFL (minimum score 550 paper-based). *Application deadline:* Applications are processed on a rolling basis. Application fee: $40 ($60 for international students). Electronic applications accepted. *Expenses: Tuition:* Full-time $21,922; part-time $675 per credit hour. *Required fees:* $233.75 per semester. *Financial support:* Career-related internships or fieldwork, Federal Work-Study, tuition waivers (partial), and professional educator discounts available. Financial award application deadline: 3/1; financial award applicants required to submit FAFSA. *Faculty research:* Collaboration with public schools, pre-service program development, mathematics, diversity, literacy. *Unit head:* Dr. Sam Hausfather, Dean, 314-529-9466, Fax: 314-529-9921, E-mail: shausfather@maryville.edu. *Application contact:* Holly Stanwich, Graduate Admissions Coordinator, 314-529-9542, Fax: 314-529-9921, E-mail: teachered@maryville.edu. Web site: http://www.maryville.edu/academics-ed-graduate.

Marywood University, Academic Affairs, Reap College of Education and Human Development, Department of Education, Program in Reading Education, Scranton, PA 18509-1598. Offers MS. *Accreditation:* NCATE. *Entrance requirements:* Additional exam requirements/recommendations for international students: Required—TOEFL (minimum score 550 paper-based; 213 computer-based; 79 iBT). *Application deadline:* For fall admission, 4/1 priority date for domestic students, 3/31 for international students; for spring admission, 11/1 priority date for domestic students, 8/31 for international students. Applications are processed on a rolling basis. Application fee: $30. Electronic applications accepted. *Financial support:* Career-related internships or fieldwork, scholarships/grants, and unspecified assistantships available. Support available to part-time students. Financial award application deadline: 6/30; financial award applicants required to submit FAFSA. *Faculty research:* Design of school reading programs, whole language. *Unit head:* Patricia S. Arter, Chairperson, 570-348-6211 Ext. 2511, E-mail: psarter@marywood.edu. *Application contact:* Tammy Manka, Assistant Director of Graduate Admissions, 570-348-6211 Ext. 2322, E-mail: tmanka@marywood.edu. Web site: http://www.marywood.edu/education/graduate-programs/m.s.-in-reading-education-.html.

Massachusetts College of Liberal Arts, Program in Education, North Adams, MA 01247-4100. Offers curriculum (M Ed); educational administration (M Ed); reading (M Ed); special education (M Ed). Part-time and evening/weekend programs available. *Degree requirements:* For master's, thesis. *Entrance requirements:* For master's, writing sample.

McDaniel College, Graduate and Professional Studies, Program in Reading Education, Westminster, MD 21157-4390. Offers MS. *Accreditation:* NCATE. Part-time and evening/weekend programs available. *Degree requirements:* For master's, comprehensive exam, thesis optional. *Entrance requirements:* For master's, GRE General Test, MAT, or NTE/PRAXIS I, letters of reference (3). Additional exam requirements/recommendations for international students: Required—TOEFL (minimum score 213 computer-based).

McNeese State University, Doré School of Graduate Studies, Burton College of Education, Department of Education Professions, Program in Curriculum and Instruction, Lake Charles, LA 70609. Offers early childhood education (M Ed); elementary education (M Ed); reading (M Ed); secondary education (M Ed). Evening/weekend programs available. *Faculty:* 10 full-time (5 women). *Students:* 8 full-time (7 women), 11 part-time (all women); includes 6 minority (all Black or African American, non-Hispanic/Latino), 1 international. In 2011, 6 master's awarded. *Entrance requirements:* For master's, GRE, teaching certificate. *Application deadline:* For fall admission, 5/15 priority date for domestic students, 5/15 for international students; for spring admission, 10/15 priority date for domestic students, 10/15 for international students. Applications are processed on a rolling basis. Application fee: $20 ($30 for international students). *Expenses:* Tuition, state resident: part-time $519 per credit hour. Tuition and fees vary according to course load. *Financial support:* Application deadline: 5/1. *Unit head:* Dr. Dustin M. Hebert, Director, 337-475-5424, Fax: 337-475-5272, E-mail: dhebert@mcneese.edu. *Application contact:* Dr. George F. Mead, Jr., Interim Dean of Dore' School of Graduate Studies, 337-475-5396, Fax: 337-475-5397, E-mail: admissions@mcneese.edu.

Medaille College, Program in Education, Buffalo, NY 14214-2695. Offers adolescent education (MS Ed); curriculum and instruction (MS Ed); education preparation (MS Ed); literacy (MS Ed); special education (MS). *Accreditation:* Teacher Education Accreditation Council. Part-time and evening/weekend programs available. *Faculty:* 15 full-time (11 women), 31 part-time/adjunct (21 women). *Students:* 371 full-time (281 women), 37 part-time (29 women); includes 75 minority (11 Black or African American, non-Hispanic/Latino; 6 Asian, non-Hispanic/Latino; 3 Hispanic/Latino; 55 Native Hawaiian or other Pacific Islander, non-Hispanic/Latino), 264 international. Average age 29. 354 applicants, 99% accepted, 163 enrolled. In 2011, 457 master's awarded. *Degree requirements:* For master's, comprehensive exam (for some programs), thesis or alternative. *Entrance requirements:* For master's, minimum undergraduate GPA of 2.7. Additional exam requirements/recommendations for international students: Required—TOEFL (minimum score 550 paper-based; 213 computer-based). *Application deadline:* For fall admission, 8/15 priority date for domestic students; for spring admission, 1/15 priority date for domestic students. Applications are processed on a rolling basis. Application fee: $35. Electronic applications accepted. Tuition and fees vary according to program. *Financial support:* Federal Work-Study available. Financial award applicants required to submit FAFSA. *Faculty research:* Curriculum planning, truancy, tracking minority students, curriculum design, mentoring students. *Unit head:* Dr. Robert DiSibio, Director of Graduate Programs, 716-932-2548, Fax: 716-631-1380, E-mail: rdisibio@medaille.edu. *Application contact:* Jacqueline Matheny, Executive Director of Marketing and Enrollment, 716-932-2541, Fax: 716-632-1811, E-mail: jmatheny@medaille.edu. Web site: http://www.medaille.edu.

Mercer University, Graduate Studies, Cecil B. Day Campus, Tift College of Education (Atlanta), Macon, GA 31207-0003. Offers curriculum and instruction (PhD); early childhood education (M Ed, MAT); educational leadership (PhD, Ed S); higher education leadership (M Ed); middle grades education (M Ed, MAT); reading education (M Ed); school counseling (Ed S); secondary education (M Ed, MAT); teacher leadership (Ed S). *Accreditation:* NCATE. Part-time and evening/weekend programs available. *Faculty:* 31 full-time (17 women), 6 part-time/adjunct (3 women). *Students:* 249 full-time (207 women), 413 part-time (326 women); includes 349 minority (322 Black or African American, non-Hispanic/Latino; 1 American Indian or Alaska Native, non-Hispanic/Latino; 18 Asian, non-Hispanic/Latino; 6 Hispanic/Latino; 2 Two or more races, non-Hispanic/Latino), 6 international. Average age 34. 204 applicants, 76% accepted, 125 enrolled. In 2011, 235 master's, 8 doctorates, 27 other advanced degrees awarded. *Degree requirements:* For master's and Ed S, research project; for doctorate, thesis/dissertation. *Entrance requirements:* For master's, GRE or MAT, minimum undergraduate GPA of 2.75; for doctorate, GRE; for Ed S, GRE or MAT, minimum GPA of 3.25, 3 years of teaching experience. Additional exam requirements/recommendations for international students: Required—TOEFL. *Application deadline:* For fall admission, 8/1 for domestic and international students; for spring admission, 12/1 for domestic and international students. Applications are processed on a rolling basis. Application fee: $25. *Expenses:* Contact institution. *Financial support:* Federal Work-Study available. Support available to part-time students. Financial award application deadline: 5/1. *Faculty research:* Educational technology, multicultural and minority issues in education, educational leadership (P-12 and higher education), school discipline and school bullying, standards-based mathematics education. *Unit head:* Dr. Carl R. Martray, Dean, 478-301-5397, Fax: 478-301-2280, E-mail: martray_cr@mercer.edu. *Application contact:* Dr. Allison Gilmore, Associate Dean for Graduate Teacher Education, 678-547-6333, Fax: 678-547-6055, E-mail: gilmore_a@mercer.edu. Web site: http://www.mercer.edu/education/.

Mercy College, School of Education, Program in Teaching Literacy, Birth-6, Dobbs Ferry, NY 10522. Offers MS. Part-time and evening/weekend programs available. *Degree requirements:* For master's, thesis or alternative, capstone. *Entrance requirements:* For master's, resume, interview by faculty advisor and/or program director. Additional exam requirements/recommendations for international students: Required—TOEFL (minimum score 600 paper-based; 250 computer-based; 100 iBT), IELTS (minimum score 8). Electronic applications accepted. *Faculty research:* Linguistics, literacy.

Mercy College, School of Education, Program in Teaching Literacy/Birth-Grade 12, Dobbs Ferry, NY 10522-1189. Offers MS. Part-time and evening/weekend programs available. Postbaccalaureate distance learning degree programs offered (no on-campus study). *Degree requirements:* For master's, comprehensive exam. *Entrance requirements:* Additional exam requirements/recommendations for international students: Required—TOEFL (minimum score 600 paper-based; 250 computer-based; 100 iBT), IELTS (minimum score 8). Electronic applications accepted. *Faculty research:* Linguistics, literacy.

Mercy College, School of Education, Program in Teaching Literacy/Grades 5-12, Dobbs Ferry, NY 10522-1189. Offers MS. Part-time and evening/weekend programs available. *Entrance requirements:* Additional exam requirements/recommendations for international students: Required—TOEFL (minimum score 600 paper-based; 250 computer-based; 100 iBT). Electronic applications accepted. *Faculty research:* Linguistics, literacy.

Merrimack College, School of Education, North Andover, MA 01845-5800. Offers community engagement (M Ed); early childhood education (M Ed); elementary education (M Ed); elementary education plus moderate disabilities-dual license (M Ed); English as a second language (M Ed); general studies (M Ed); higher education (M Ed); middle (M Ed); moderate disabilities (preK-8) (M Ed); reading (M Ed); secondary (M Ed); teacher leadership (CAGS). Part-time and evening/weekend programs available. *Faculty:* 4 full-time (all women), 9 part-time/adjunct (7 women). *Students:* 70 full-time (60 women), 39 part-time (33 women); includes 2 minority (1 Asian, non-Hispanic/Latino; 1 Hispanic/Latino). Average age 27. In 2011, 26 master's awarded. *Degree requirements:* For master's, portfolio. *Entrance requirements:* Additional exam requirements/recommendations for international students: Required—TOEFL (minimum score 80 iBT). *Application deadline:* For fall admission, 8/1 priority date for domestic students, 7/15 for international students; for winter admission, 12/1 priority date for domestic students, 11/15 for international students; for spring admission, 3/1 priority date for domestic students, 2/15 for international students. Applications are processed on a rolling basis. Electronic applications accepted. *Expenses: Tuition:* Part-time $475 per credit. *Required fees:* $62.50 per semester. *Financial support:* In 2011–12, 50 fellowships were awarded; career-related internships or fieldwork and scholarships/grants also available. Financial award applicants required to submit FAFSA. *Faculty research:* Higher education, community engagement, literacy, leadership. *Unit head:* Dr. Theresa Kirk, Chair, 978-837-5436, E-mail: kirkt@merrimack.edu. *Application contact:* Jessica McCarthy, Program Coordinator, 978-837-5443, E-mail: mccarthyj@merrimack.edu. Web site: http://www.merrimack.edu/academics/education/med/.

MGH Institute of Health Professions, School of Health and Rehabilitation Sciences, Department of Communication Sciences and Disorders, Boston, MA 02129. Offers reading (Certificate); speech-language pathology (MS). *Accreditation:* ASHA (one or more programs are accredited). Part-time programs available. *Faculty:* 12 full-time (9 women), 2 part-time/adjunct (1 woman). *Students:* 111 full-time (104 women), 28 part-time (all women); includes 19 minority (4 Black or African American, non-Hispanic/Latino; 15 Asian, non-Hispanic/Latino). Average age 28. 367 applicants, 31% accepted, 69 enrolled. In 2011, 55 master's, 26 other advanced degrees awarded. *Degree requirements:* For master's, thesis or alternative, research proposal. *Entrance requirements:* For master's, GRE General Test, bachelor's degree from regionally-accredited college or university. Additional exam requirements/recommendations for international students: Required—TOEFL (minimum score 550 paper-based; 213 computer-based; 80 iBT). *Application deadline:* For fall admission, 1/15 for domestic and international students. Application fee: $65. Electronic applications accepted. *Expenses: Tuition:* Full-time $12,720; part-time $1060 per credit. *Required fees:* $1725; $430 per semester. One-time fee: $350. *Financial support:* In 2011–12, 45 students received support, including 8 research assistantships (averaging $1,200 per year), 4 teaching assistantships (averaging $1,200 per year); career-related internships or fieldwork, scholarships/grants, and unspecified assistantships also available. Support available to part-time students. Financial award application deadline: 4/1; financial award applicants required to submit FAFSA. *Faculty research:* Children's language disorders, reading, speech disorders, voice disorders, augmentative communication, autism. *Unit head:* Dr. Gregory L. Lof, Department Chair, 617-724-6313, E-mail: glot@mghihp.edu. *Application contact:* Maureen Rika Judd, Director of Admissions, 617-726-6069, Fax: 617-726-8010, E-mail: admissions@mghihp.edu. Web site: http://www.mghihp.edu/academics/communication-sciences-and-disorders/.

Miami University, School of Education and Allied Professions, Department of Teacher Education, Oxford, OH 45056. Offers elementary education (M Ed, MAT); reading education (M Ed); secondary education (M Ed, MAT), including adolescent education (MAT), elementary mathematics education (M Ed), secondary education. Part-time programs available. *Students:* 32 full-time (19 women), 40 part-time (37 women); includes 6 minority (3 Black or African American, non-Hispanic/Latino; 2 Hispanic/Latino; 1 Two or more races, non-Hispanic/Latino), 3 international. Average age 28. In 2011, 42 master's awarded. *Entrance requirements:* For master's, GRE (for MAT), minimum undergraduate GPA of 3.0 during previous 2 years or 2.75 overall. *Application deadline:* Applications are processed on a rolling basis. Application fee: $50. Electronic applications accepted. *Expenses:* Tuition, state resident: full-time $12,023; part-time $501 per credit hour. Tuition, nonresident: full-time $26,554; part-time $1107 per credit hour. *Required fees:* $528. *Financial support:* Fellowships with full tuition reimbursements, research assistantships, teaching assistantships, career-related internships or fieldwork, Federal Work-Study, scholarships/grants, health care benefits, tuition waivers (full), and unspecified assistantships available. Financial award application deadline: 2/15. *Unit head:* Dr. James Shiveley, Chair, 513-529-6443, Fax: 513-529-4931, E-mail: shiveljm@muohio.edu. *Application contact:* Linda Dennett, Program Associate, 513-529-5708, E-mail: dennetlg@muohio.edu. Web site: http://www.units.muohio.edu/eap/departments/edt/.

Michigan State University, The Graduate School, College of Education, Program in Literacy Instruction, East Lansing, MI 48824. Offers MA. *Accreditation:* Teacher Education Accreditation Council. Part-time programs available. *Degree requirements:* For master's, comprehensive exam (for some programs), final exam or portfolio. *Entrance requirements:* Additional exam requirements/recommendations for international students: Required—TOEFL, Michigan State University ELT (minimum score 85), Michigan English Language Assessment Battery (minimum score 83). Electronic applications accepted.

Middle Tennessee State University, College of Graduate Studies, College of Education, Department of Elementary and Special Education, Major in Reading, Murfreesboro, TN 37132. Offers M Ed. *Accreditation:* NCATE. Part-time and evening/weekend programs available. Postbaccalaureate distance learning degree programs offered. *Faculty:* 14 full-time (9 women), 7 part-time/adjunct (all women). *Students:* 1 (woman) part-time. In 2011, 2 master's awarded. *Degree requirements:* For master's, comprehensive exam. *Entrance requirements:* For master's, GRE, MAT or PRAXIS. Additional exam requirements/recommendations for international students: Required—TOEFL (minimum score 525 paper-based; 195 computer-based; 71 iBT) or IELTS (minimum score 6). *Application deadline:* For fall admission, 6/1 for domestic and international students. Applications are processed on a rolling basis. Application fee: $25 ($30 for international students). Electronic applications accepted. *Expenses:* Tuition, state resident: full-time $10,008. Tuition, nonresident: full-time $25,056. *Financial support:* Tuition waivers available. Support available to part-time students. Financial award application deadline: 5/1. *Unit head:* Dr. Kathleen Burris, Interim Chair, 615-898-2680, Fax: 615-898-5309, E-mail: kathleen.burris@mtsu.edu. *Application contact:* Dr. Michael D. Allen, Dean and Vice Provost for Research, 615-898-2840, Fax: 615-904-8020, E-mail: michael.allen@mtsu.edu.

Middle Tennessee State University, College of Graduate Studies, College of Education, PhD in Literacy Studies Program, Murfreesboro, TN 37132. Offers PhD. Part-time and evening/weekend programs available. Postbaccalaureate distance learning degree programs offered. *Faculty:* 14 full-time (9 women), 7 part-time/adjunct (all women). *Students:* 23 part-time (21 women); includes 4 minority (2 Black or African American, non-Hispanic/Latino; 2 Asian, non-Hispanic/Latino). Average age 38. 8 applicants, 88% accepted. *Degree requirements:* For doctorate, comprehensive exam, thesis/dissertation. *Entrance requirements:* For doctorate, GRE. Additional exam requirements/recommendations for international students: Required—TOEFL (minimum score 525 paper-based; 195 computer-based; 71 iBT) or IELTS (minimum score 6). *Application deadline:* For fall admission, 6/1 for domestic and international students. Applications are processed on a rolling basis. Application fee: $25 ($30 for international students). *Expenses:* Tuition, state resident: full-time $10,008. Tuition, nonresident: full-time $25,056. *Financial support:* Institutionally sponsored loans and tuition waivers available. Support available to part-time students. Financial award application deadline: 5/1. *Unit head:* Dr. Lana Seivers, Dean, 615-898-2874, Fax: 615-898-2530, E-mail: lana.seivers@mtsu.edu. *Application contact:* Dr. Michael D. Allen, Dean and Vice Provost for Research, 615-898-2840, Fax: 615-904-8020, E-mail: michael.allen@mtsu.edu.

Midwestern State University, Graduate Studies, College of Education, Program in Reading Education, Wichita Falls, TX 76308. Offers M Ed. Part-time and evening/weekend programs available. *Degree requirements:* For master's, comprehensive exam. *Entrance requirements:* For master's, GRE General Test, MAT or GMAT. Additional exam requirements/recommendations for international students: Required—TOEFL (minimum score 550 paper-based; 213 computer-based). Electronic applications accepted. *Faculty research:* Collective learning, school culture, early literacy development, family literacy, brain-based learning.

Millersville University of Pennsylvania, College of Graduate and Professional Studies, School of Education, Department of Elementary and Early Childhood Education, Program in Language and Literacy Education, Millersville, PA 17551-0302. Offers M Ed. *Accreditation:* NCATE. Part-time and evening/weekend programs available. *Faculty:* 16 full-time (12 women), 8 part-time/adjunct (5 women). *Students:* 6 full-time (all women), 83 part-time (78 women); includes 3 minority (1 Black or African American, non-Hispanic/Latino; 1 Asian, non-Hispanic/Latino; 1 Hispanic/Latino). Average age 28. 19 applicants, 95% accepted, 16 enrolled. In 2011, 52 master's awarded. *Degree requirements:* For master's, thesis optional. *Entrance requirements:* For master's, GRE or MAT, 3 letters of recommendation, copy of teaching certificate. Additional exam requirements/recommendations for international students: Required—TOEFL (minimum score 500 paper-based; 183 computer-based; 65 iBT). *Application deadline:* For fall admission, 1/15 priority date for domestic students, 1/15 for international students; for winter admission, 10/1 priority date for domestic students, 10/1 for international students; for spring admission, 10/1 priority date for domestic students, 10/1 for international students. Applications are processed on a rolling basis. Application fee: $40 ($50 for international students). Electronic applications accepted. *Expenses:* Tuition, state resident: full-time $3744; part-time $416 per credit. Tuition, nonresident: full-time $5616; part-time $624 per credit. *Required fees:* $1130; $125.50 per credit. Tuition and fees vary according to course load. *Financial support:* In 2011–12, 7 students received support, including 8 research assistantships with full tuition reimbursements available (averaging $2,659 per year); institutionally sponsored loans and unspecified assistantships also available. Support available to part-time students. Financial award application deadline: 3/15; financial award applicants required to submit FAFSA. *Faculty research:* Integration of technology and literacy, ethnographic teacher research, literacy coaching, content area literacy, emergent/early literacy. *Unit head:* Dr. William J. Himmele, Coordinator, 717-872-3125, Fax: 717-871-5462, E-mail: william.himmele@millersville.edu. *Application contact:* Dr. Victor S. DeSantis, Dean, College of Graduate and Professional Studies, 717-872-3099, Fax: 717-872-3453, E-mail: victor.desantis@millersville.edu. Web site: http://www.millersville.edu/academics/educ/eled/graduate.php.

Minnesota State University Moorhead, Graduate Studies, College of Education and Human Services, Program in Reading, Moorhead, MN 56563-0002. Offers MS. *Accreditation:* NCATE. Part-time and evening/weekend programs available. *Degree requirements:* For master's, comprehensive exam, final oral exam, project or thesis. *Entrance requirements:* For master's, MAT, minimum GPA of 2.75, 2 years of teaching experience. Additional exam requirements/recommendations for international students: Required—TOEFL (minimum score 550 paper-based; 213 computer-based). Electronic applications accepted.

Mississippi University for Women, Graduate School, College of Education and Human Sciences, Columbus, MS 39701-9998. Offers differentiated instruction (M Ed); educational leadership (M Ed); gifted studies (M Ed); reading/literacy (M Ed); teaching (MAT). *Accreditation:* ASHA; NCATE. Part-time programs available. *Degree requirements:* For master's, comprehensive exam, thesis optional. *Entrance requirements:* For master's, GRE General Test or NTE (M Ed in gifted education or MS in speech/language pathology), MAT (M Ed in instructional management), minimum QPA of 3.0.

Missouri State University, Graduate College, College of Education, Department of Reading, Foundations, and Technology, Program in Literacy, Springfield, MO 65897. Offers MS Ed. Part-time programs available. *Students:* 2 full-time (both women), 35 part-time (34 women). Average age 30. 4 applicants, 100% accepted, 2 enrolled. In 2011, 18 master's awarded. *Degree requirements:* For master's, comprehensive exam, thesis or alternative. *Entrance requirements:* For master's, GRE or minimum GPA of 3.0, teaching certificate. Additional exam requirements/recommendations for international students: Required—TOEFL (minimum score 550 paper-based; 213 computer-based; 79 iBT). *Application deadline:* For fall admission, 7/20 priority date for domestic students, 5/1 for international students; for spring admission, 12/20 for domestic students, 9/1 for international students. Applications are processed on a rolling basis. Application fee: $35 ($50 for international students). Electronic applications accepted. *Expenses:* Tuition, state resident: full-time $4086; part-time $227 per credit hour. Tuition, nonresident: full-time $8172; part-time $454 per credit hour. *Required fees:* $275 per semester. Tuition and fees vary according to course load, campus/location and program. *Financial support:* Federal Work-Study, institutionally sponsored loans, scholarships/grants, and unspecified assistantships available. Financial award application deadline: 3/31; financial award applicants required to submit FAFSA. *Unit head:* Dr. Deanne Camp, Program Director, 417-836-6983, E-mail: deannecamp@missouristate.edu. *Application contact:* Misty Stewart, Coordinator of Graduate Recruitment, 417-836-6079, Fax: 417-836-6200, E-mail: ericeckert@missouristate.edu. Web site: http://education.missouristate.edu/rft/.

Monmouth University, The Graduate School, School of Education, West Long Branch, NJ 07764-1898. Offers education (M Ed); initial certification (MAT), including elementary level, K-12, secondary level; learning disabilities-teacher consultant (Certificate); principal (MS Ed); principal/school administrator (MS Ed); reading specialist (MS Ed, Certificate); school counseling (MS Ed); special education (MS Ed), including autism, learning disabilities teacher consultant, teacher of students with disabilities, teaching in inclusive settings; supervisor (Certificate); teacher of the handicapped (Certificate); teaching English to speakers of other languages (TESOL) (Certificate). *Accreditation:* NCATE. Part-time and evening/weekend programs available. *Faculty:* 16 full-time (12 women), 24 part-time/adjunct (17 women). *Students:* 134 full-time (104 women), 293 part-time (246 women); includes 34 minority (11 Black or African American, non-Hispanic/Latino; 2 Asian, non-Hispanic/Latino; 18 Hispanic/Latino; 3 Two or more races, non-Hispanic/Latino), 2 international. Average age 29. 288 applicants, 92% accepted, 182 enrolled. In 2011, 173 master's awarded. *Entrance requirements:* For master's, minimum GPA of 3.0 in major, 2.75 overall; 2 letters of recommendation (for some programs). Additional exam requirements/recommendations for international students: Required—TOEFL (minimum score 550 paper-based; 213 computer-based; 79 iBT), IELTS (minimum score 5), Michigan English Language Assessment Battery (minimum score 77), Cambridge A, B, C. *Application deadline:* For fall admission, 7/15 priority date for domestic students, 7/1 for international students; for spring admission, 11/15 priority date for domestic students, 11/1 for international students. Applications are processed on a rolling basis. Application fee: $50. Electronic applications accepted. *Financial support:* In 2011–12, 274 students received support, including 291 fellowships (averaging $1,783 per year), 21 research assistantships (averaging $8,792 per year); career-related internships or fieldwork, scholarships/grants, and unspecified assistantships also available. Support available to part-time students. Financial award applicants required to submit FAFSA. *Faculty research:* Multicultural literacy, science and mathematics teaching strategies, teacher as reflective practitioner, children with disabilities. *Unit head:* Dr. Jason Barr, Program Director, 732-263-5238, Fax: 732-263-5277, E-mail: jbarr@monmouth.edu. *Application contact:* Kevin Roane, Director, Office of Graduate Admission, 732-571-3452, Fax: 732-263-5123, E-mail: gradadm@monmouth.edu. Web site: http://www.monmouth.edu/academics/schools/education/default.asp.

Montana State University Billings, College of Education, Department of Special Education, Counseling, Reading and Early Childhood, Option in Reading, Billings, MT 59101-0298. Offers M Ed. *Accreditation:* NCATE. Part-time programs available. *Degree requirements:* For master's, thesis or professional paper and/or field experience. *Entrance requirements:* For master's, GRE General Test or MAT, minimum GPA of 3.0 (undergraduate), 3.25 (graduate).

Montclair State University, The Graduate School, College of Education and Human Services, Department of Early Childhood, Elementary and Literacy Education, Program in Reading, Montclair, NJ 07043-1624. Offers MA. Part-time and evening/weekend programs available. *Students:* 94 part-time (89 women); includes 13 minority (5 Black or African American, non-Hispanic/Latino; 8 Hispanic/Latino). Average age 31. 39 applicants, 92% accepted, 33 enrolled. In 2011, 27 master's awarded. *Entrance requirements:* For master's, GRE General Test, interview, essay, 2 letters of recommendation. Additional exam requirements/recommendations for international students: Required—TOEFL (minimum score 83 iBT), IELTS (minimum score 6.5). *Application deadline:* Applications are processed on a rolling basis. Application fee: $30. Electronic applications accepted. *Financial support:* Federal Work-Study, scholarships/grants, and unspecified assistantships available. Support available to part-time students. Financial award application deadline: 3/1; financial award applicants required to submit FAFSA. *Unit head:* Dr. Tina Jacobowitz, Chairperson, 973-655-7191. *Application contact:* Amy Aiello, Executive Director of The Graduate School, 973-655-5147, Fax: 973-655-7869, E-mail: graduate.school@montclair.edu. Web site: http://cehs.montclair.edu/academic/ecele/programs/masterreading.shtml.

Montclair State University, The Graduate School, College of Humanities and Social Sciences, Department of English, Montclair, NJ 07043-1624. Offers elementary language arts/literacy (grades 5-8) (Certificate); English (MA); teaching writing (Certificate). Part-time and evening/weekend programs available. *Faculty:* 45 full-time (30 women), 65 part-time/adjunct (50 women). *Students:* 16 full-time (11 women), 51 part-time (38 women); includes 3 minority (all Hispanic/Latino), 2 international. Average age 34. 50 applicants, 12% accepted, 2 enrolled. In 2011, 17 master's, 7 other advanced degrees awarded. *Degree requirements:* For master's, thesis. *Entrance requirements:* For master's, GRE General Test, 2 letters of recommendation, essay. Additional exam requirements/recommendations for international students: Required—TOEFL (minimum score 83 iBT) or IELTS (minimum score 6.5). *Application deadline:* For fall admission, 6/1 for international students; for spring admission, 10/1 for international students. Applications are processed on a rolling basis. Application fee: $60. Electronic applications accepted. *Financial support:* In 2011–12, 10 research assistantships with full tuition reimbursements (averaging $7,000 per year) were awarded; Federal Work-Study, scholarships/grants, and unspecified assistantships also available. Support available to part-time students. Financial award application deadline: 3/1; financial award applicants required to submit FAFSA. *Faculty research:* Modernism, Shakespeare, Victorian poetry, contemporary European film, nineteenth century American literature. *Unit head:* Dr. Dan Bronson, Chairperson, 973-655-4274. *Application contact:* Amy Aiello, Director of Graduate Admissions and Operations, 973-655-5147, Fax: 973-655-7869, E-mail: graduate.school@montclair.edu. Web site: http://chss.montclair.edu/english/.

Morehead State University, Graduate Programs, College of Education, Department of Curriculum and Instruction, Morehead, KY 40351. Offers curriculum and instruction (Ed S); elementary education (MA Ed), including elementary education, international education, middle school education, reading; secondary education (MA Ed); special education (MA Ed); teaching (MAT). Part-time and evening/weekend programs available. *Degree requirements:* For master's, comprehensive exam, thesis optional; for Ed S, thesis, oral exam. *Entrance requirements:* For master's, GRE General Test, minimum GPA of 2.75, teaching certificate; for Ed S, GRE General Test, interview, master's degree, minimum GPA of 3.5, work experience. Additional exam requirements/recommendations for international students: Required—TOEFL (minimum score 500 paper-based; 173 computer-based). Electronic applications accepted. *Faculty research:* Communicative competence of learning-disabled students, teaching social studies in elementary schools, ungraded primary school organization, study skills.

Morehead State University, Graduate Programs, College of Education, Department of Foundational and Graduate Studies in Education, Morehead, KY 40351. Offers adult and higher education (MA, Ed S); certified professional counselor (Ed S); counseling P-12 (MA); curriculum and instruction (Ed S); educational technology (MA Ed); instructional leadership (Ed S); school administration (MA); school counseling (Ed S); teacher leader business and marketing content (MA Ed); teacher leader business and marketing technology (MA Ed); teacher leader educational technology (MA Ed); teacher leader English (MA Ed); teacher leader gifted education (MA Ed); teacher leader IECE certification (MA Ed); teacher leader interdisciplinary education P-5 (MA Ed); teacher leader middle grades (MA Ed); teacher leader non IECE certification (MA Ed); teacher leader reading/writing - non-certification (MA Ed); teacher leader reading/writing certification (MA Ed); teacher leader school communication - certification (MA Ed); teacher leader school communication - non-certification (MA Ed); teacher leader social studies (MA Ed); teacher leader special education (MA Ed). *Accreditation:* NCATE. Part-time and evening/weekend programs available. *Degree requirements:* For master's, thesis optional, oral and/or written comprehensive exams; for Ed S, thesis, oral exam. *Entrance requirements:* For master's, GRE General Test, minimum overall undergraduate GPA of 2.5; for Ed S, GRE General Test, interview, master's degree, minimum GPA of 3.5, work experience. Additional exam requirements/ recommendations for international students: Required—TOEFL (minimum score 500 paper-based; 173 computer-based). Electronic applications accepted. *Faculty research:* Character education, school accountability, computer applications for school administrators.

Mount Mercy University, Program in Education, Cedar Rapids, IA 52402-4797. Offers reading (MA Ed); special education (MA Ed). *Entrance requirements:* For master's, minimum cumulative GPA of 3.0, 2 letters of recommendation, resume, valid teaching license. Additional exam requirements/recommendations for international students: Required—TOEFL (minimum score 570 paper-based; 88 iBT). Electronic applications accepted.

Mount Saint Mary College, Division of Education, Newburgh, NY 12550-3494. Offers adolescence and special education (MS Ed); adolescence education (MS Ed); childhood and special education (MS Ed); childhood education (MS Ed); literacy (5-12) (Advanced Certificate); literacy (birth-6) (Advanced Certificate); literacy and special education (MS Ed); literacy/childhood (MS Ed); middle school (5-6) (MS Ed); middle school (7-9) (MS Ed); special education (1-6) (MS Ed); special education (7-12) (MS Ed). *Accreditation:* NCATE. Part-time and evening/weekend programs available. *Faculty:* 14 full-time (12 women), 14 part-time/adjunct (8 women). *Students:* 55 full-time (42 women), 158 part-time (125 women); includes 23 minority (4 Black or African American, non-Hispanic/Latino; 1 Asian, non-Hispanic/Latino; 18 Hispanic/Latino). Average age 29. 119 applicants, 45% accepted, 24 enrolled. In 2011, 107 master's awarded. *Application deadline:* Applications are processed on a rolling basis. Application fee: $45. Application fee is waived when completed online. *Expenses: Tuition:* Full-time $13,356; part-time $742 per credit. *Required fees:* $70 per semester. *Financial support:* In 2011–12, 99 students received support. Unspecified assistantships available. Financial award application deadline: 4/15; financial award applicants required to submit FAFSA. *Faculty research:* Learning and teaching styles, computers in special education, language development. *Unit head:* Dr. Theresa Lewis, Coordinator, 845-569-3149, Fax: 845-569-3535, E-mail: tlewis@msmc.edu. *Application contact:* Courtney McDermott, Graduate Recruiter, 845-569-3402, Fax: 845-569-3450, E-mail: courtney.mcdermott@msmc.edu. Web site: http://www.msmc.edu/Academics/Graduate_Programs/Master_of_Science_in_Education.

Mount Saint Vincent University, Graduate Programs, Faculty of Education, Program in Literacy Education, Halifax, NS B3M 2J6, Canada. Offers M Ed, MA Ed, MA-R. Part-time and evening/weekend programs available. Postbaccalaureate distance learning degree programs offered (no on-campus study). *Degree requirements:* For master's, thesis (for some programs). *Entrance requirements:* For master's, minimum B average, 1 year of teaching experience, bachelor's degree in related field. Electronic applications accepted. *Faculty research:* Writing processes and instruction, assessment and evaluation of literacy education, critical literacy, early literacy development, gender and literacy.

Murray State University, College of Education, Department of Early Childhood and Elementary Education, Programs in Elementary Education/Reading and Writing, Murray, KY 42071. Offers elementary education (MA Ed, Ed S); reading and writing (MA Ed). *Accreditation:* NCATE. Part-time programs available. *Degree requirements:* For master's, comprehensive exam, thesis optional; for Ed S, comprehensive exam. *Entrance requirements:* For master's, minimum GPA of 2.5 for conditional admittance, 3.0 for unconditional; for Ed S, GRE General Test or MAT. Additional exam requirements/recommendations for international students: Required—TOEFL.

National Louis University, National College of Education, Chicago, IL 60603. Offers administration and supervision (M Ed, Ed D, CAS, Ed S); curriculum and instruction (M Ed, MS Ed, CAS); early childhood administration (M Ed, CAS); early childhood education (M Ed, MAT, MS Ed, CAS); education (Ed D); educational psychology/human learning and development (M Ed, MS Ed, CAS, Ed S); elementary education (MAT); interdisciplinary curriculum and instruction (M Ed); mathematics education (M Ed, MS Ed, CAS); reading and language (M Ed, MS Ed, CAS); school psychology (M Ed, Ed S); science education (M Ed, MS Ed, CAS); secondary education (MAT); special education (M Ed, MAT, CAS); technology in education (M Ed, CAS). *Accreditation:* NCATE. Part-time and evening/weekend programs available. *Students:* 224 full-time (162 women), 2,336 part-time (1,767 women); includes 677 minority (366 Black or African American, non-Hispanic/Latino; 8 American Indian or Alaska Native, non-Hispanic/Latino; 68 Asian, non-Hispanic/Latino; 218 Hispanic/Latino; 2 Native Hawaiian or other Pacific Islander, non-Hispanic/Latino; 15 Two or more races, non-Hispanic/Latino), 2 international. Average age 34. In 2011, 1,711 master's, 76 doctorates, 86 other advanced degrees awarded. *Degree requirements:* For doctorate, comprehensive exam, thesis/dissertation. *Entrance requirements:* For master's, MAT or GRE, minimum GPA of 3.0; for doctorate, GRE General Test, minimum GPA of 3.25, interview, resume, writing sample, 4 recommendations. Additional exam requirements/recommendations for international students: Required—TOEFL (minimum score 550 paper-based; 213 computer-based; 79 iBT). *Application deadline:* Applications are processed on a rolling basis. Application fee: $40. *Financial support:* Fellowships, research assistantships, teaching assistantships, career-related internships or fieldwork, Federal Work-Study, institutionally sponsored loans, and scholarships/grants available. Support available to part-time students. Financial award applicants required to submit FAFSA. *Unit head:* Dr. Alison Hilsabeck, Dean, 312-361-3580, Fax: 312-261-2580, E-mail: ahilsabeck@nl.edu. *Application contact:* Ken Kasprzak, Director of Admission, 888-658-8632, Fax: 847-947-5575, E-mail: kkasprzak@nl.edu.

Nazareth College of Rochester, Graduate Studies, Department of Education, Program in Literacy Education, Rochester, NY 14618-3790. Offers MS Ed. *Accreditation:* Teacher Education Accreditation Council. Part-time and evening/weekend programs available. *Entrance requirements:* For master's, minimum GPA of 3.0.

New Jersey City University, Graduate Studies and Continuing Education, Debra Cannon Partridge Wolfe College of Education, Department of Literacy Education, Jersey City, NJ 07305-1597. Offers elementary school reading (MA); reading specialist (MA); secondary school reading (MA). Part-time and evening/weekend programs available. *Students:* 3 full-time (2 women), 34 part-time (33 women); includes 10 minority (4 Black or African American, non-Hispanic/Latino; 2 Asian, non-Hispanic/Latino; 4 Hispanic/Latino). Average age 31. In 2011, 20 master's awarded. *Degree requirements:* For master's, comprehensive exam. *Entrance requirements:* Additional exam requirements/recommendations for international students: Required—TOEFL. *Application deadline:* For fall admission, 8/1 priority date for domestic students; for spring admission, 12/1 for domestic students. Applications are processed on a rolling basis. Application fee: $0. *Expenses:* Tuition, state resident: part-time $494 per credit. Tuition, nonresident: part-time $911.30 per credit. *Required fees:* $95.90 per year. *Financial support:* Research assistantships and unspecified assistantships available. *Faculty research:* Reading clinic. *Unit head:* Dr. Mary McCullough, Chairperson, 201-200-3521, E-mail: mmccullough@njcu.edu. *Application contact:* Dr. William Bajor, Dean of Graduate Studies, 201-200-3409, Fax: 201-200-3411, E-mail: wbajor@njcu.edu.

Newman University, Master of Education Program, Wichita, KS 67213-2097. Offers building leadership (MS Ed); curriculum and instruction (MS Ed), including accountability, English as a second language, reading specialist. *Accreditation:* NCATE. Part-time and evening/weekend programs available. Postbaccalaureate distance learning degree programs offered (no on-campus study). *Faculty:* 4 full-time (2 women), 38 part-time/adjunct (all women). *Students:* 47 full-time (40 women), 414 part-time (318 women); includes 62 minority (20 Black or African American, non-Hispanic/Latino; 8 Asian, non-Hispanic/Latino; 30 Hispanic/Latino; 3 Native Hawaiian or other Pacific Islander, non-Hispanic/Latino; 1 Two or more races, non-Hispanic/Latino), 3 international. Average age 35. 42 applicants, 76% accepted, 27 enrolled. In 2011, 46 master's awarded. *Degree requirements:* For master's, thesis optional. *Entrance requirements:* For master's, interview, minimum GPA of 3.0, writing sample, 2 letters of recommendation, evidence of teaching certification. Additional exam requirements/recommendations for international students: Required—TOEFL (minimum score 600 paper-based; 250 computer-based; 100 iBT). *Application deadline:* For fall admission, 8/15 priority date for domestic students, 7/15 for international students; for spring admission, 1/10 priority date for domestic students, 11/15 for international students. Applications are processed on a rolling basis. Application fee: $25 ($40 for international students). Electronic applications accepted. *Expenses:* Contact institution. *Financial support:* In 2011–12, 18 students received support. Federal Work-Study available. Financial award application deadline: 8/15; financial award applicants required to submit FAFSA. *Unit head:* Dr. Guy Glidden, Director, Graduate Education, 316-942-4291 Ext. 2331, Fax: 316-942-4483, E-mail: gliddeng@newmanu.edu. *Application contact:* Linda Kay Sabala, Director of Graduate Admissions, 316-942-4291 Ext. 2230, Fax: 316-942-4483, E-mail: sabalal@newmanu.edu.

New York University, Steinhardt School of Culture, Education, and Human Development, Department of Teaching and Learning, Program in Literacy Education, New York, NY 10012-1019. Offers literacy education (MA), including literacy education: birth-grade 6, literacy education: grades 5-12. *Accreditation:* Teacher Education Accreditation Council. Part-time programs available. *Faculty:* 1 (woman) full-time. *Students:* 11 full-time (all women), 6 part-time (all women); includes 3 minority (1 Black or African American, non-Hispanic/Latino; 2 Hispanic/Latino), 1 international. Average age 25. 69 applicants, 94% accepted, 14 enrolled. In 2011, 21 master's awarded. *Degree requirements:* For master's, thesis (for some programs), Fieldwork. *Entrance requirements:* For master's, teacher certification. Additional exam requirements/recommendations for international students: Required—TOEFL. *Application deadline:* For fall admission, 2/1 priority date for domestic students, 2/1 for international students. Applications are processed on a rolling basis. Application fee: $75. Electronic applications accepted. *Financial support:* Career-related internships or fieldwork, Federal Work-Study, institutionally sponsored loans, scholarships/grants, and tuition waivers (partial) available. Support available to part-time students. Financial award application deadline: 2/1; financial award applicants required to submit FAFSA. *Faculty research:* Early literacy intervention and development, psycho and sociolinguistics, multicultural education, literacy assessment and instruction. *Unit head:* Dr. Kay Stahl, Director, 212-998-5402, Fax: 212-995-4049, E-mail: kay.stahl@nyu.edu. *Application contact:* Office of Graduate Admissions, 212-998-5030, Fax: 212-995-4328, E-mail: steinhardt.gradadmissions@nyu.edu. Web site: http://steinhardt.nyu.edu/teachlearn/literacy.

Niagara University, Graduate Division of Education, Concentration in Literacy Instruction, Niagara Falls, Niagara University, NY 14109. Offers MS Ed. *Students:* 36 full-time (31 women), 43 part-time (37 women); includes 2 minority (both Hispanic/Latino), 1 international. Average age 26. In 2011, 44 master's awarded. *Entrance requirements:* Additional exam requirements/recommendations for international students: Required—TOEFL. *Expenses: Tuition:* Full-time $13,626; part-time $757 per credit hour. *Required fees:* $50. *Unit head:* Dr. Chandra Foote, Chair, 716-286-8549. *Application contact:* Carlos Tejada, Associate Dean for Graduate Recruitment, 716-286-8769, Fax: 716-286-8170.

North Carolina Agricultural and Technical State University, School of Graduate Studies, School of Education, Department of Curriculum and Instruction, Program in Reading Education, Greensboro, NC 27411. Offers MA Ed. *Accreditation:* NCATE. Part-time and evening/weekend programs available. *Degree requirements:* For master's, comprehensive exam, comprehensive portfolio. *Entrance requirements:* For master's, GRE General Test, minimum GPA of 3.0.

Northeastern Illinois University, Graduate College, College of Education, School of Teacher Education, Program in Reading, Chicago, IL 60625-4699. Offers MA. Part-time and evening/weekend programs available. *Degree requirements:* For master's, comprehensive exam, thesis optional. *Entrance requirements:* For master's, previous course work in psychology or tests and measurements, minimum GPA of 2.75. Additional exam requirements/recommendations for international students: Required—TOEFL (minimum score 550 paper-based; 213 computer-based; 79 iBT). Electronic applications accepted. *Faculty research:* Early literacy, reading disabilities, cognitive processes, multicultural and linguistic diversity, use of literature in the classroom.

Northeastern State University, Graduate College, College of Education, Department of Curriculum and Instruction, Program in Reading, Tahlequah, OK 74464-2399. Offers M Ed. Part-time and evening/weekend programs available. *Students:* 5 full-time (4 women), 132 part-time (131 women); includes 23 minority (3 Black or African American, non-Hispanic/Latino; 18 American Indian or Alaska Native, non-Hispanic/Latino; 2 Hispanic/Latino). In 2011, 72 master's awarded. *Degree requirements:* For master's, thesis. *Entrance requirements:* For master's, MAT or GRE, minimum GPA of 2.5. Additional exam requirements/recommendations for international students: Required—TOEFL (minimum score 213 computer-based). *Application deadline:* For fall admission, 6/1 priority date for domestic students. Applications are processed on a rolling basis. Application fee: $25. Electronic applications accepted. *Financial support:* Teaching assistantships and Federal Work-Study available. Financial award application deadline: 3/1. *Unit head:* Dr. Steve Sargent, Coordinator, 918-449-6000 Ext. 6587, Fax: 918-458-2351, E-mail: sargents@nsuok.edu. *Application contact:* Margie Railey, Administrative Assistant, 918-456-5511 Ext. 2093, Fax: 918-458-2061, E-mail: railey@nsuok.edu.

Northern Illinois University, Graduate School, College of Education, Department of Literacy Education, De Kalb, IL 60115-2854. Offers curriculum and instruction (Ed D), including reading; literacy education (MS Ed). Part-time and evening/weekend programs available. *Faculty:* 12 full-time (10 women), 1 part-time/adjunct (0 women). *Students:* 5 full-time (4 women), 114 part-time (111 women); includes 18 minority (2 Black or African American, non-Hispanic/Latino; 5 Asian, non-Hispanic/Latino; 11 Hispanic/Latino), 4 international. Average age 33. 24 applicants, 67% accepted, 2 enrolled. In 2011, 105 master's, 4 doctorates awarded. *Degree requirements:* For master's, comprehensive exam, thesis optional; for doctorate, thesis/dissertation, candidacy exam, dissertation defense. *Entrance requirements:* For master's, GRE General Test or MAT, minimum undergraduate GPA of 2.75; for doctorate, GRE General Test, minimum GPA of 2.75 (undergraduate), 3.2 (graduate). Additional exam requirements/recommendations for international students: Required—TOEFL (minimum score 550 paper-based; 213 computer-based). *Application deadline:* For fall admission, 3/1 priority date for domestic students, 5/1 for international students; for spring admission, 11/1 for domestic students, 10/1 for international students. Applications are processed on a rolling basis. Application fee: $40. Electronic applications accepted. *Financial support:* In 2011–12, 2 research assistantships with full tuition reimbursements, 15 teaching assistantships with full tuition reimbursements were awarded; fellowships with full tuition reimbursements, career-related internships or fieldwork, Federal Work-Study, scholarships/grants, tuition waivers (full), and staff assistantships also available. Support available to part-time students. Financial award applicants required to submit FAFSA. *Faculty research:* Early reading development, literacy for bilingual students, family literacy, expository writing, fluency. *Unit head:* Dr. Laurie Elish-Piper, Interim Chair, 815-753-8556, E-mail: ltcy@niu.edu. *Application contact:* Graduate School Office, 815-753-0395, E-mail: gradsch@niu.edu. Web site: http://www.cedu.niu.edu/ltcy/.

Northern Michigan University, College of Graduate Studies, College of Professional Studies, School of Education, Programs in Reading Education, Marquette, MI 49855-5301. Offers literacy leadership (Ed S); reading (MA Ed); reading specialist (MA Ed). Postbaccalaureate distance learning degree programs offered.

Northwestern Oklahoma State University, School of Professional Studies, Reading Specialist Program, Alva, OK 73717-2799. Offers M Ed. *Accreditation:* NCATE. Part-time programs available. *Faculty:* 10 full-time (7 women). *Students:* 3 part-time (all women); includes 1 minority (Black or African American, non-Hispanic/Latino). 3 applicants, 100% accepted, 2 enrolled. In 2011, 4 master's awarded. *Degree requirements:* For master's, thesis optional, portfolio. *Entrance requirements:* For master's, GRE General Test or MAT, minimum GPA of 2.75. *Application deadline:* Applications are processed on a rolling basis. Application fee: $15. *Financial support:* Application deadline: 5/1; applicants required to submit FAFSA. *Unit head:* Dr. Martie Young, Director, 580-213-3195. *Application contact:* Sabrina Watson, Coordinator of Graduate Studies, 580-327-8410, E-mail: sdwatson@nwosu.edu.

Northwestern State University of Louisiana, Graduate Studies and Research, College of Education and Human Development, Programs in Educational Leadership and Instruction, Natchitoches, LA 71497. Offers counseling (Ed S); educational leadership (M Ed, Ed S); educational technology (Ed S); elementary teaching (Ed S); reading (Ed S); secondary teaching (Ed S); special education (Ed S). *Accreditation:* NASAD. *Students:* 7 full-time (6 women), 75 part-time (59 women); includes 22 minority (18 Black or African American, non-Hispanic/Latino; 2 American Indian or Alaska Native, non-Hispanic/Latino; 2 Hispanic/Latino). Average age 36. 30 applicants, 97% accepted, 15 enrolled. In 2011, 31 master's, 16 Ed Ss awarded. *Degree requirements:* For master's, comprehensive exam, thesis (for some programs). *Entrance requirements:* For master's and Ed S, GRE General Test. Additional exam requirements/recommendations for international students: Required—TOEFL. *Application deadline:* For fall admission, 3/15 priority date for domestic students; for spring admission, 10/15 priority date for domestic students. Applications are processed on a rolling basis. Application fee: $20 ($30 for international students). Electronic applications accepted. *Expenses:* Tuition, state resident: full-time $3440. Tuition, nonresident: full-time $12,010. *Unit head:* Dr. Vickie Gentry, Chair, 318-357-6288, Fax: 318-357-6275, E-mail: education@nsula.edu. *Application contact:* Dr. Steven G. Horton, Associate Provost/Dean, Graduate Studies, Research, and Information Systems, 318-357-5851, Fax: 318-357-5019, E-mail: grad_school@nsula.edu.

Northwest Missouri State University, Graduate School, College of Education and Human Services, Department of Curriculum and Instruction, Program in Reading, Maryville, MO 64468-6001. Offers MS Ed. *Accreditation:* NCATE. Part-time programs available. *Faculty:* 11 full-time (all women). *Students:* 5 full-time (all women), 34 part-time (32 women). 9 applicants, 100% accepted, 5 enrolled. In 2011, 9 master's awarded. *Degree requirements:* For master's, comprehensive exam. *Entrance requirements:* For master's, GRE General Test, minimum undergraduate GPA of 2.75, teaching certificate, writing sample. Additional exam requirements/recommendations for international students: Required—TOEFL (minimum score 550 paper-based; 213 computer-based). *Application deadline:* For fall admission, 7/1 for domestic and international students; for spring admission, 11/15 for domestic and international students. Applications are processed on a rolling basis. Application fee: $0 ($50 for international students). *Financial support:* In 2011–12, 3 teaching assistantships with full tuition reimbursements (averaging $6,000 per year) were awarded. Financial award application deadline: 3/1; financial award applicants required to submit FAFSA. *Unit head:* Dr. Margaret Drew, Director, 660-562-1668, E-mail: mdrew@mail.nwmissouri.edu. *Application contact:* Dr. Gregory Haddock, Dean of Graduate School, 660-562-1145, Fax: 660-562-1096, E-mail: gradsch@nwmissouri.edu.

Northwest Nazarene University, Graduate Studies, Program in Teacher Education, Nampa, ID 83686-5897. Offers curriculum and instruction (M Ed); educational leadership (M Ed, Ed D, Ed S); exceptional child (M Ed); reading education (M Ed). *Accreditation:* ACA (one or more programs are accredited); NCATE. Part-time programs available. Postbaccalaureate distance learning degree programs offered (no on-campus study). *Faculty:* 15 full-time (9 women), 36 part-time/adjunct (21 women). *Students:* 80 full-time (54 women), 119 part-time (98 women); includes 13 minority (1 American Indian or Alaska Native, non-Hispanic/Latino; 10 Hispanic/Latino; 1 Native Hawaiian or other Pacific Islander, non-Hispanic/Latino; 1 Two or more races, non-Hispanic/Latino), 8 international. Average age 36. 60 applicants, 95% accepted, 39 enrolled. In 2011, 43 master's, 24 other advanced degrees awarded. *Degree requirements:* For master's, comprehensive exam (for some programs), action research project. *Entrance requirements:* For master's, minimum undergraduate GPA of 2.8 overall or 3.0 during final 30 semester credits. *Application deadline:* For fall admission, 9/1 for domestic students. Applications are processed on a rolling basis. Application fee: $25. *Faculty research:* Action research, cooperative learning, accountability, institutional accreditation. *Unit head:* Dr. Paula Kellerer, Chair, 208-467-8729, Fax: 208-467-8562. *Application contact:* Jackie Schober, 208-467-8341, Fax: 208-467-8786, E-mail: jsschober@nnu.edu. Web site: http://www.nnu.edu/graded/.

Notre Dame College, Graduate Programs, South Euclid, OH 44121-4293. Offers mild/moderate needs (M Ed); reading (M Ed); security policy studies (MA, Graduate Certificate); technology (M Ed). Part-time and evening/weekend programs available. *Faculty:* 6 full-time (3 women), 19 part-time/adjunct (16 women). *Students:* 344 part-time (253 women). *Degree requirements:* For master's, thesis. *Entrance requirements:* For master's, GRE General Test, MAT, minimum undergraduate GPA of 2.75, valid teaching certificate, bachelor's degree in an education-related field from accredited college or university, official transcripts of most recent college work. *Application deadline:* For fall admission, 8/1 priority date for domestic students; for spring admission, 1/1 for domestic students. Applications are processed on a rolling basis. Application fee: $40. *Expenses: Tuition:* Part-time $528 per credit. *Financial support:* Tuition waivers (full) available. Support available to part-time students. Financial award application deadline: 4/15; financial award applicants required to submit FAFSA. *Faculty research:* Cognitive psychology, teaching critical thinking in the classroom. *Application contact:* Sarah Palace, Assistant Dean of Adult Enrollment, 216-373-5350, Fax: 216-373-6330, E-mail: spalace@ndc.edu.

Oakland University, Graduate Study and Lifelong Learning, School of Education and Human Services, Program in Reading and Language Arts, Rochester, MI 48309-4401. Offers reading (Certificate); reading and language arts (MAT); reading education (PhD); reading, language arts and literature (Certificate). *Accreditation:* Teacher Education Accreditation Council. *Degree requirements:* For doctorate, thesis/dissertation. *Entrance requirements:* For master's, minimum GPA of 3.0 for unconditional admission; for doctorate, MAT, minimum GPA of 3.0 for unconditional admission. Electronic applications accepted.

Ohio University, Graduate College, Gladys W. and David H. Patton College of Education and Human Services, Department of Teacher Education, Athens, OH 45701-2979. Offers adolescent to young adult education (M Ed); curriculum and instruction (M Ed, PhD); early childhood/special education (M Ed); intervention specialist/mild-moderate needs (M Ed); intervention specialist/moderate-intensive needs (M Ed); mathematics education (PhD); middle child education (M Ed); reading education (M Ed); social studies education (PhD). Part-time and evening/weekend programs available. *Students:* 131 full-time (92 women), 82 part-time (62 women); includes 9 minority (4 Black or African American, non-Hispanic/Latino; 2 American Indian or Alaska Native, non-Hispanic/Latino; 1 Asian, non-Hispanic/Latino; 1 Hispanic/Latino; 1 Two or more races, non-Hispanic/Latino), 11 international. 136 applicants, 70% accepted, 65 enrolled. In 2011, 58 master's, 8 doctorates awarded. *Degree requirements:* For master's, thesis or alternative; for doctorate, comprehensive exam, thesis/dissertation. *Entrance requirements:* For master's, GRE General Test or MAT (if GPA is below 2.9); for doctorate, GRE General Test, minimum GPA of 3.4, work experience. Additional exam requirements/recommendations for international students: Required—TOEFL (minimum score 550 paper-based; 80 iBT) or IELTS (minimum score 6.5). *Application deadline:* For fall admission, 5/1 priority date for domestic students, 4/1 for international students; for winter admission, 11/1 priority date for domestic students, 10/1 for international students; for spring admission, 2/15 priority date for domestic students, 1/1 for international students. Applications are processed on a rolling basis. Application fee: $50 ($55 for international students). Electronic applications accepted. *Financial support:* Research assistantships with full tuition reimbursements, teaching assistantships with full tuition reimbursements, Federal Work-Study, institutionally sponsored loans, tuition waivers (partial), and unspecified assistantships available. Financial award application deadline: 3/1. *Faculty research:* Cognition literacy, character education, teacher's education reform, disabilities. *Total annual research expenditures:* $46,933. *Unit head:* Dr. John Henning, Chair, 740-597-1830, Fax: 740-593-0477, E-mail: henningj@ohio.edu. *Application contact:* Floyd J. Doney, Director of Student Affairs, 740-593-4400, Fax: 740-593-9310, E-mail: doney@ohio.edu. Web site: http://www.cehs.ohio.edu/academics/te/index.htm.

Old Dominion University, Darden College of Education, Program in Literacy Leadership, Norfolk, VA 23529. Offers PhD. Part-time and evening/weekend programs available. *Faculty:* 4 full-time (all women). *Students:* 4 full-time (all women), 7 part-time (all women); includes 2 minority (both Black or African American, non-Hispanic/Latino). Average age 43. 4 applicants, 50% accepted, 2 enrolled. In 2011, 1 doctorate awarded. *Degree requirements:* For doctorate, comprehensive exam, thesis/dissertation. *Entrance requirements:* For doctorate, GRE, minimum GPA of 3.0, MS in reading or related degree, letters of recommendation. Additional exam requirements/recommendations for international students: Required—TOEFL (minimum score 600 paper-based; 250 computer-based). *Application deadline:* For fall admission, 3/15 for domestic and international students; for spring admission, 11/15 for domestic and international students. Applications are processed on a rolling basis. Application fee: $50. Electronic applications accepted. *Expenses:* Tuition, state resident: full-time $9096; part-time $379 per credit. Tuition, nonresident: full-time $23,064; part-time $961 per credit. *Required fees:* $127 per semester. One-time fee: $50. *Financial support:* Career-related internships or fieldwork, scholarships/grants, and unspecified assistantships available. *Faculty research:* Literacy for students with special needs, children's Reading First instruction, reading in the content area. *Total annual research expenditures:* $600,000. *Unit head:* Dr. Charlene Fleener, Graduate Program Director, 757-683-4387, E-mail: cfleener@odu.edu. *Application contact:* William Heffelfinger, Director of Graduate Admissions, 757-683-5554, Fax: 757-683-3255, E-mail: gradadmit@odu.edu. Web site: http://education.odu.edu/eci/litphd/.

Old Dominion University, Darden College of Education, Program in Reading Education, Norfolk, VA 23529. Offers reading specialist (MS Ed). *Accreditation:* NCATE. Part-time and evening/weekend programs available. Postbaccalaureate distance learning degree programs offered (no on-campus study). *Faculty:* 6 full-time (all women), 11 part-time/adjunct (9 women). *Students:* 2 full-time (both women), 61 part-time (60 women); includes 24 minority (22 Black or African American, non-Hispanic/Latino; 1 Hispanic/Latino; 1 Native Hawaiian or other Pacific Islander, non-Hispanic/Latino). Average age 38. 33 applicants, 55% accepted, 18 enrolled. In 2011, 19 master's awarded. *Degree requirements:* For master's, thesis optional. *Entrance requirements:* For master's, GRE General Test or MAT, minimum GPA of 3.0 in major, 2.8 overall; teaching certificate. Additional exam requirements/recommendations for international students: Required—TOEFL. *Application deadline:* For fall admission, 6/1 for domestic students, 4/15 for international students; for spring admission, 11/1 for domestic students, 10/1 for international students. Applications are processed on a rolling basis. Application fee: $50. Electronic applications accepted. *Expenses:* Tuition, state resident: full-time $9096; part-time $379 per credit. Tuition, nonresident: full-time $23,064; part-time $961 per credit. *Required fees:* $127 per semester. One-time fee: $50. *Financial support:* In 2011–12, 7 students received support. Career-related internships or fieldwork, Federal Work-Study, institutionally sponsored loans, scholarships/grants, and unspecified assistantships available. Support available to part-time students. Financial award application deadline: 2/15; financial award applicants required to submit FAFSA. *Faculty research:* Metacognition and reading, strategies for improving comprehension in reading science, reading in content areas, vocabulary instruction for adolescents, literacy with special needs children, Reading First instruction, reading in the content area, vocabulary, diversity and literacy. *Total annual research expenditures:* $150,000. *Unit head:* Dr. Charlene Fleener, Graduate Program Director, 757-683-3284, Fax: 757-683-3284, E-mail: cfleener@odu.edu. *Application contact:* William Heffelfinger, Director of Graduate Admissions, 757-683-5554, Fax: 757-683-3255, E-mail: gradadmit@odu.edu. Web site: http://education.odu.edu/eci/reading/masters.shtml.

Olivet Nazarene University, Graduate School, Division of Education, Program in Reading Specialist, Bourbonnais, IL 60914. Offers MAE.

Our Lady of the Lake University of San Antonio, School of Professional Studies, Program in Curriculum and Instruction, San Antonio, TX 78207-4689. Offers bilingual (M Ed); early childhood education (M Ed); English as a second language (M Ed); integrated math teaching (M Ed); integrated science teaching (M Ed); master reading teacher (M Ed); master technology teacher (M Ed); reading specialist (M Ed).

Pace University, School of Education, New York, NY 10038. Offers adolescent education (MST); childhood education (MST); educational leadership (MS Ed); educational technology studies (MS); literacy (MSE); school business management (Certificate); special education (MS Ed); teaching students with disabilities (MSE). *Accreditation:* NCATE. Part-time and evening/weekend programs available. *Students:* 164 full-time (131 women), 533 part-time (396 women); includes 157 minority (59 Black or African American, non-Hispanic/Latino; 2 American Indian or Alaska Native, non-Hispanic/Latino; 26 Asian, non-Hispanic/Latino; 54 Hispanic/Latino; 1 Native Hawaiian or other Pacific Islander, non-Hispanic/Latino; 15 Two or more races, non-Hispanic/Latino), 10 international. Average age 29. 256 applicants, 79% accepted, 114 enrolled. In 2011, 334 master's, 34 other advanced degrees awarded. *Degree requirements:* For master's, internship. *Entrance requirements:* For master's, interview, teaching certificate. Additional exam requirements/recommendations for international students:

Required—TOEFL. *Application deadline:* For fall admission, 7/31 priority date for domestic students; for spring admission, 11/30 for domestic students. Applications are processed on a rolling basis. Application fee: $70. Electronic applications accepted. *Expenses:* Contact institution. *Financial support:* Research assistantships, career-related internships or fieldwork, and Federal Work-Study available. Support available to part-time students. Financial award applicants required to submit FAFSA. *Unit head:* Dr. Andrea M. Spencer, Dean, 212-346-1345, E-mail: aspencer@pace.edu. *Application contact:* Susan Ford-Goldschein, Director of Admissions, 212-346-1660, Fax: 212-346-1585, E-mail: gradnyc@pace.edu. Web site: http://www.pace.edu/.

Penn State Harrisburg, Graduate School, School of Behavioral Sciences and Education, Middletown, PA 17057-4898. Offers applied behavior analysis (MA); applied clinical psychology (MA); applied psychological research (MA); community psychology and social change (MA); health education (M Ed); literacy education (M Ed); teaching and curriculum (M Ed); training and development (M Ed). Part-time and evening/weekend programs available. *Financial support:* Career-related internships or fieldwork available. *Unit head:* Dr. Catherine A. Surra, Director, 717-948-6205, Fax: 717-948-6209, E-mail: cas87@psu.edu. *Application contact:* Robert Coffman, Director of Admissions, 717-948-6214, E-mail: rwc11@psu.edu. Web site: http://harrisburg.psu.edu/behavioral-sciences-and-education/.

Pittsburg State University, Graduate School, College of Education, Department of Curriculum and Instruction, Pittsburg, KS 66762. Offers classroom reading teacher (MS); early childhood education (MS); elementary education (MS); reading (MS); reading specialist (MS); secondary education (MS); teaching (MAT). *Accreditation:* NCATE. *Degree requirements:* For master's, thesis or alternative. *Entrance requirements:* For master's, GRE or MAT.

Plymouth State University, College of Graduate Studies, Graduate Studies in Education, Program in Reading and Writing Specialist, Plymouth, NH 03264-1595. Offers M Ed. Part-time and evening/weekend programs available. *Degree requirements:* For master's, PRAXIS. *Entrance requirements:* For master's, GRE General Test or MAT, minimum GPA of 3.0.

Portland State University, Graduate Studies, School of Education, Department of Curriculum and Instruction, Portland, OR 97207-0751. Offers early childhood education (MA, MS); education (M Ed, MA, MS); educational leadership: curriculum and instruction (Ed D); educational media/school librarianship (MA, MS); elementary education (M Ed, MAT, MST); reading (MA, MS); secondary education (M Ed, MAT, MST). *Accreditation:* NCATE. Part-time programs available. *Degree requirements:* For master's, comprehensive exam, thesis or alternative; for doctorate, thesis/dissertation. *Entrance requirements:* For master's, California Basic Educational Skills Test, minimum GPA of 3.0 in upper-division course work or 2.75 overall. Additional exam requirements/recommendations for international students: Required—TOEFL (minimum score 550 paper-based; 213 computer-based). *Faculty research:* Early literacy, characteristics of successful teachers of at-risk students, participation of women/minorities in technology courses, selection of cooperating teachers.

Providence College, Program in Literacy, Providence, RI 02918. Offers M Ed. Part-time and evening/weekend programs available. *Faculty:* 9 part-time/adjunct (8 women). *Students:* 2 full-time (both women), 43 part-time (42 women). Average age 31. 18 applicants, 100% accepted, 15 enrolled. In 2011, 19 master's awarded. *Degree requirements:* For master's, comprehensive exam. *Entrance requirements:* For master's, GRE General Test. Additional exam requirements/recommendations for international students: Required—TOEFL (minimum score 550 paper-based; 213 computer-based; 80 iBT). *Application deadline:* For fall admission, 8/1 priority date for domestic students, 8/1 for international students; for spring admission, 12/1 priority date for domestic students, 12/1 for international students. Applications are processed on a rolling basis. Application fee: $55. *Expenses: Tuition:* Part-time $404 per credit. *Required fees:* $404 per credit. *Financial support:* In 2011–12, 1 research assistantship with full tuition reimbursement (averaging $8,400 per year) was awarded; career-related internships or fieldwork, institutionally sponsored loans, and unspecified assistantships also available. Support available to part-time students. Financial award application deadline: 8/1; financial award applicants required to submit FAFSA. *Unit head:* Dr. Beverly Paesano, Director, 401-865-1987, Fax: 401-865-1147, E-mail: bpaesano@providence.edu. *Application contact:* Carol A. Daniels, Coordinator of Graduate Faculty and Administrative Services, 401-865-2247, Fax: 401-865-1147, E-mail: daniels@providence.edu. Web site: http://www.providence.edu/professional-studies/graduate-degrees/Pages/master-education-literacy.aspx.

Purdue University, Graduate School, College of Education, Department of Curriculum and Instruction, West Lafayette, IN 47907. Offers agricultural and extension education (PhD, Ed S); agriculture and extension education (MS, MS Ed); art education (PhD); consumer and family sciences and extension education (MS Ed, PhD, Ed S); curriculum studies (MS Ed, PhD, Ed S); educational technology (MS Ed, PhD, Ed S); elementary education (MS Ed); foreign language education (MS Ed, PhD, Ed S); industrial technology (PhD, Ed S); language arts (MS Ed, PhD, Ed S); literacy (MS Ed, PhD, Ed S); mathematics/science education (MS, MS Ed, PhD, Ed S); social studies (MS Ed, PhD); social studies education (Ed S); vocational/industrial education (MS Ed, PhD, Ed S); vocational/technical education (MS Ed, PhD, Ed S). *Accreditation:* NCATE. Part-time and evening/weekend programs available. *Faculty:* 30 full-time (21 women), 1 (woman) part-time/adjunct. *Students:* 89 full-time (64 women), 134 part-time (84 women); includes 31 minority (12 Black or African American, non-Hispanic/Latino; 3 American Indian or Alaska Native, non-Hispanic/Latino; 7 Asian, non-Hispanic/Latino; 9 Hispanic/Latino), 49 international. Average age 36. 136 applicants, 83% accepted, 72 enrolled. In 2011, 26 master's, 13 doctorates awarded. *Degree requirements:* For master's, thesis optional; for doctorate, thesis/dissertation, oral and written exams; for Ed S, oral presentation, project. *Entrance requirements:* For master's, GRE general test is required if undergraduate GPA is below 3.0, minimum undergraduate GPA of 3.0 or equivalent; for doctorate, GRE General Test, a combined GRE verbal and quantitative score of 1000 (300 for revised GRE Test) or more is expected, minimum undergraduate GPA of 3.0 or equivalent; master's degree with minimum GPA of 3.0 or equivalent; for Ed S, GRE general test, a combined GRE verbal and quantitative score of 1000 (300 for revised GRE Test) or more is expected, minimum undergraduate GPA of 3.0 or equivalent; master's degree. Additional exam requirements/recommendations for international students: Required—TOEFL (minimum score 550 paper-based; 77 iBT). *Application deadline:* For fall admission, 12/15 priority date for domestic students, 3/1 for international students; for spring admission, 9/15 for domestic students, 8/1 for international students. Application fee: $60 ($75 for international students). Electronic applications accepted. *Financial support:* Fellowships with full tuition reimbursements, research assistantships with full tuition reimbursements, teaching assistantships with full tuition reimbursements, career-related internships or fieldwork, and tuition waivers (full) available. Support available to part-time students. Financial award application deadline: 3/1; financial award applicants required to submit FAFSA. *Faculty research:* Literacy acquisition and development, teacher beliefs and knowledge, recruitment and retention of underrepresented students, economic education, literacy discourse. *Unit head:* Dr. Philip J. VanFossen, Head, 765-494-7935, Fax: 765-496-1622, E-mail: vanfoss@purdue.edu. *Application contact:* Sarah N. Prater, Graduate Contact, 765-494-2345, Fax: 765-494-5832, E-mail: prater0@purdue.edu. Web site: http://www.edci.purdue.edu/.

Queens College of the City University of New York, Division of Graduate Studies, Division of Education, Department of Elementary and Early Childhood Education, Program in Literacy, Flushing, NY 11367-1597. Offers MS Ed. Part-time programs available. *Faculty:* 8 full-time (6 women). *Students:* 1 (woman) full-time, 194 part-time (180 women); includes 45 minority (17 Black or African American, non-Hispanic/Latino; 2 Asian, non-Hispanic/Latino; 26 Hispanic/Latino). 74 applicants, 92% accepted, 54 enrolled. In 2011, 68 master's awarded. *Degree requirements:* For master's, research project. *Entrance requirements:* For master's, minimum GPA of 3.0. Additional exam requirements/recommendations for international students: Required—TOEFL. *Application deadline:* For fall admission, 4/1 for domestic students; for spring admission, 11/1 for domestic students. Applications are processed on a rolling basis. Application fee: $125. *Expenses:* Tuition, state resident: part-time $345 per credit. Tuition, nonresident: part-time $640 per credit. *Required fees:* $145.25 per semester. *Financial support:* Career-related internships or fieldwork, Federal Work-Study, institutionally sponsored loans, and tuition waivers (partial) available. Support available to part-time students. Financial award application deadline: 4/1; financial award applicants required to submit FAFSA. *Unit head:* Dr. Marcia Braghban, Coordinator, 718-997-5339. *Application contact:* Mario Caruso, Director of Graduate Admissions, 718-997-5200, Fax: 718-997-5193, E-mail: graduate_admissions@qc.edu.

Queens University of Charlotte, Wayland H. Cato, Jr. School of Education, Charlotte, NC 28274-0002. Offers education in literacy (M Ed); elementary education (MAT); school administration (MSA). *Accreditation:* NCATE. Part-time and evening/weekend programs available. *Degree requirements:* For master's, comprehensive exam. *Entrance requirements:* For master's, GRE General Test. *Expenses:* Contact institution.

Quincy University, Program in Education, Quincy, IL 62301-2699. Offers alternative certification (MS Ed); curriculum and instruction (MS Ed); leadership (MS Ed); reading education (MS Ed); school administration (MS Ed); special education (MS Ed); teacher leader in reading (MS Ed); teaching certification (MS Ed). Part-time and evening/weekend programs available. Postbaccalaureate distance learning degree programs offered. *Students:* 221 full-time (168 women), 100 part-time (69 women); includes 104 minority (69 Black or African American, non-Hispanic/Latino; 1 American Indian or Alaska Native, non-Hispanic/Latino; 5 Asian, non-Hispanic/Latino; 27 Hispanic/Latino; 2 Two or more races, non-Hispanic/Latino). In 2011, 132 master's awarded. *Degree requirements:* For master's, comprehensive exam (for some programs), thesis or alternative. *Entrance requirements:* For master's, MAT or GRE. Additional exam requirements/recommendations for international students: Required—TOEFL (minimum score 550 paper-based; 79 iBT). *Application deadline:* Applications are processed on a rolling basis. Application fee: $25. Electronic applications accepted. *Expenses: Tuition:* Full-time $9120; part-time $380 per semester hour. *Required fees:* $360; $15 per semester hour. Tuition and fees vary according to course load, campus/location and program. *Financial support:* Applicants required to submit FAFSA. *Unit head:* Kristen Anguiano, Director, 217-228-5432 Ext. 3119, E-mail: anguikr@quincy.edu. *Application contact:* Office of Admissions, 217-228-5210, Fax: 217-228-5479, E-mail: admissions@quincy.edu. Web site: http://www.quincy.edu/academics/graduate-programs/education.

Radford University, College of Graduate and Professional Studies, College of Education and Human Development, School of Teacher Education and Leadership, Program in Literacy Education, Radford, VA 24142. Offers MS. *Accreditation:* NCATE. Part-time and evening/weekend programs available. *Faculty:* 4 full-time (3 women), 2 part-time/adjunct (both women). *Students:* 27 part-time (all women). Average age 35. 12 applicants, 100% accepted, 10 enrolled. In 2011, 11 master's awarded. *Degree requirements:* For master's, comprehensive exam. *Entrance requirements:* For master's, minimum GPA of 2.75; copy of teaching license; 2 letters of reference; personal essay; resume; official transcripts. Additional exam requirements/recommendations for international students: Required—TOEFL (minimum score 550 paper-based; 213 computer-based; 79 iBT). *Application deadline:* For fall admission, 2/15 priority date for domestic students, 12/1 for international students; for spring admission, 7/1 for international students. Applications are processed on a rolling basis. Application fee: $50. Electronic applications accepted. *Expenses:* Tuition, state resident: full-time $6262; part-time $261 per credit hour. Tuition, nonresident: full-time $14,540; part-time $606 per credit hour. *Required fees:* $2812; $117 per credit hour. Tuition and fees vary according to program. *Financial support:* Career-related internships or fieldwork, Federal Work-Study, institutionally sponsored loans, scholarships/grants, and unspecified assistantships available. Financial award application deadline: 3/1; financial award applicants required to submit FAFSA. *Unit head:* Dr. Donald B. Langrehr, Coordinator, 540-831-6580, Fax: 540-831-5059, E-mail: dlangreh@radford.edu. *Application contact:* Rebecca Conner, Graduate Admissions, 540-831-5431, Fax: 540-831-6061, E-mail: gradcollege@radford.edu. Web site: https://php.radford.edu/~stel/index.php?option-com_content&view-article&id-12temid-18.

Regent University, Graduate School, School of Education, Virginia Beach, VA 23464-9800. Offers adult education (Ed D); adult/staff development (Ed D, PhD); career switcher with licensure (M Ed), including alternative licensure; character education (Ed D, PhD); Christian education leadership (Ed D, PhD); Christian education specialist (Ed S); Christian school program (M Ed), including ACSI licensure; distance education (Ed D, PhD); education licensure (M Ed), including preK-6th grade; educational leadership (M Ed, PhD); educational leadership - special education (Ed S), including administration and supervision; educational psychology (Ed D, PhD), including learning and development, research and evaluation, special education; higher education (Ed D, PhD), including administration, research and institutional planning, teaching; higher education leadership (Ed D); individualized degree plan (M Ed), including behavior disorders, learning disabilities, mental retardation, reading specialist; K-12 school leadership (Ed D, PhD); leadership in character education (M Ed); master teacher (M Ed), including TESOL; mathematics education (M Ed); special education (PhD); student affairs (M Ed); TESOL (M Ed), including adult education, ESL: preK-12. *Accreditation:* Teacher Education Accreditation Council. Part-time and evening/weekend programs available. Postbaccalaureate distance learning degree programs offered (minimal on-campus study). *Faculty:* 26 full-time (13 women), 54 part-time/adjunct (34 women). *Students:* 140 full-time (109 women), 786 part-time (626 women); includes 218 minority (189 Black or African American, non-Hispanic/Latino; 2 American Indian or Alaska Native, non-Hispanic/Latino; 11 Asian, non-Hispanic/Latino; 16 Hispanic/Latino), 42 international. Average age 39. 673 applicants, 57% accepted, 298 enrolled. In 2011, 178 master's, 15 doctorates awarded. *Degree requirements:* For master's, thesis or alternative; for doctorate, comprehensive exam, thesis/dissertation. *Entrance requirements:* For master's, MAT, minimum undergraduate GPA of 2.75, writing sample, resume, recommendations, interview; for doctorate, GRE, writing sample, 3 years of relevant professional experience, master's-level paper, copies of published work, resume, transcripts, interview, recommendations. Additional exam requirements/recommendations for international students: Required—TOEFL (minimum score 577 paper-based; 233 computer-based). *Application deadline:* For fall admission, 4/1 priority date for domestic students; for spring admission, 10/15 priority date for domestic students. Applications are processed on a rolling basis. Application fee: $50. Electronic applications accepted. *Expenses:* Contact institution. *Financial support:* Fellowships, career-related internships or fieldwork, scholarships/grants, tuition waivers (full and partial), and unspecified assistantships available. Support available to part-time students. Financial award application deadline: 4/1; financial award applicants required to submit FAFSA. *Faculty research:* Character development and discipline for children, education leadership development, diversity in schools, classroom management, technology in education settings. *Unit head:* Dr. Alan A. Arroyo, Dean, 757-352-4261, Fax: 757-352-4318, E-mail: alanarr@regent.edu. *Application contact:* Matthew Chadwick, Director of Enrollment Support Services, 800-373-5504, Fax: 757-352-4381, E-mail: admissions@regent.edu. Web site: http://www.regent.edu/education/.

Regis College, Programs in Education, Weston, MA 02493. Offers elementary teacher (MAT); reading (MAT); special education (MAT). Part-time and evening/weekend programs available. *Degree requirements:* For master's, thesis. *Entrance requirements:* For master's, GRE or MAT. Additional exam requirements/recommendations for international students: Required—TOEFL. Electronic applications accepted. *Faculty research:* Reflective teaching, gender-based education, integrated teaching.

Regis University, College for Professional Studies, School of Education and Counseling, Department of Education, Denver, CO 80221-1099. Offers adult learning, training, and development (M Ed, Certificate); autism (Certificate); curriculum, instruction, and assessment (M Ed); educational leadership (Certificate); educational technology (Certificate); instructional technology (M Ed); literacy (Certificate); professional leadership (M Ed); reading (M Ed); self-designed (M Ed); space studies (M Ed). Program also offered in Henderson and Las Vegas (Summerlin), NV. *Accreditation:* Teacher Education Accreditation Council. Part-time and evening/weekend programs available. Postbaccalaureate distance learning degree programs offered (no on-campus study). *Degree requirements:* For master's, thesis. *Entrance requirements:* For master's, resume, minimum GPA of 2.75, criminal background check. Additional exam requirements/recommendations for international students: Required—TOEFL (minimum score 213 computer-based), TWE (minimum score 5). Electronic applications accepted. *Faculty research:* Issues of equity in the middle school classroom, professional learning communities, school reform, socialinguistic and discursive obstacles to student integration, inclusive language arts curriculum.

Rhode Island College, School of Graduate Studies, Feinstein School of Education and Human Development, Department of Elementary Education, Providence, RI 02908-1991. Offers early childhood education (M Ed); elementary education (M Ed, MAT); reading (M Ed). *Accreditation:* NCATE. Part-time and evening/weekend programs available. *Faculty:* 11 full-time (7 women), 2 part-time/adjunct (both women). *Students:* 23 full-time (20 women), 37 part-time (36 women); includes 3 minority (1 Black or African American, non-Hispanic/Latino; 1 Asian, non-Hispanic/Latino; 1 Hispanic/Latino). Average age 31. In 2011, 30 master's awarded. *Degree requirements:* For master's, comprehensive exam (for some programs), comprehensive assessment. *Entrance requirements:* For master's, GRE General Test or MAT, PRAXIS II (elementary content knowledge), undergraduate transcripts; minimum undergraduate GPA of 3.0; 3 letters of recommendation. Additional exam requirements/recommendations for international students: Recommended—TOEFL (minimum score 550 paper-based; 213 computer-based; 79 iBT). *Application deadline:* For fall admission, 3/1 for domestic students; for spring admission, 11/1 for domestic students. Applications are processed on a rolling basis. Application fee: $50. *Expenses:* Tuition, state resident: full-time $8592; part-time $358 per credit hour. Tuition, nonresident: full-time $16,800; part-time $700 per credit hour. *Required fees:* $602; $22 per credit. $72 per term. *Financial support:* Teaching assistantships with full tuition reimbursements, Federal Work-Study, scholarships/grants, and health care benefits available. Support available to part-time students. Financial award application deadline: 5/15; financial award applicants required to submit FAFSA. *Unit head:* Dr. Patricia Cordeiro, Chair, 401-456-8016. *Application contact:* Graduate Studies, 401-456-8700. Web site: http://www.ric.edu/elementaryEducation/.

Rider University, Department of Graduate Education, Leadership and Counseling, Program in Reading/Language Arts, Lawrenceville, NJ 08648-3001. Offers reading specialist (Certificate); reading/language arts (MA). *Accreditation:* NCATE. Part-time and evening/weekend programs available. *Degree requirements:* For master's, comprehensive exam, research project. *Entrance requirements:* For master's, interview, resume. Additional exam requirements/recommendations for international students: Required—TOEFL (minimum score 550 paper-based; 213 computer-based). Electronic applications accepted. *Expenses: Tuition:* Full-time $32,820; part-time $710 per credit. *Required fees:* $350; $35 per course. Tuition and fees vary according to campus/location and program. *Faculty research:* Ethnography in the reading/language arts process.

Rivier University, School of Graduate Studies, Department of Education, Nashua, NH 03060. Offers curriculum and instruction (M Ed); early childhood education (M Ed); educational administration (M Ed); educational studies (M Ed); elementary education (M Ed); elementary education and general special education (M Ed); emotional and behavioral disorders (M Ed); general social education (M Ed); leadership and learning (Ed D, CAGS); learning disabilities (M Ed); learning disabilities and reading (M Ed); mental health counseling (MA); reading (M Ed); school counseling (M Ed). Part-time and evening/weekend programs available. *Degree requirements:* For master's, comprehensive exam (for some programs), internships. *Entrance requirements:* For master's, GRE General Test or MAT.

Roberts Wesleyan College, Division of Teacher Education, Rochester, NY 14624-1997. Offers adolescence education (M Ed); childhood and special education (M Ed); literacy education (M Ed); urban education (M Ed). Part-time and evening/weekend programs available. *Degree requirements:* For master's, thesis.

Rockford College, Graduate Studies, Department of Education, Program in Reading, Rockford, IL 61108-2393. Offers MAT. Part-time and evening/weekend programs available. *Degree requirements:* For master's, thesis optional. *Entrance requirements:* For master's, GRE General Test, 3 letters of recommendation. Additional exam requirements/recommendations for international students: Required—TOEFL (minimum score 550 paper-based; 213 computer-based; 79 iBT). *Application deadline:* Applications are processed on a rolling basis. Application fee: $50. Electronic applications accepted. *Expenses: Tuition:* Full-time $16,200; part-time $675 per credit. *Required fees:* $80; $40 per semester. Tuition and fees vary according to class time, course level, course load, degree level, campus/location and program. *Financial support:* Scholarships/grants and unspecified assistantships available. Support available to part-time students. Financial award application deadline: 3/1; financial award applicants required to submit FAFSA. *Unit head:* Dr. Michelle McReynolds, MAT Director, 815-226-3390, Fax: 815-394-3706, E-mail: mmcreynolds@rockford.edu. *Application contact:* Michele Mehren, Office Manager for Graduate Studies, 815-226-4041, Fax: 815-394-3706, E-mail: mmehren@rockford.edu.

Roger Williams University, School of Education, Program in Literacy Education, Bristol, RI 02809. Offers literacy (MA). Part-time and evening/weekend programs available. *Degree requirements:* For master's, state-mandated exams. *Entrance requirements:* For master's, interview; teacher's certification, 2 recommendation letters, curriculum vitae/resume. Additional exam requirements/recommendations for international students: Recommended—TOEFL, IELTS. Electronic applications accepted. *Expenses:* Contact institution. *Faculty research:* Assessment of reading difficulties, action research in reading, comprehension and writing, student mediation techniques.

Roosevelt University, Graduate Division, College of Education, Program in Language and Literacy, Chicago, IL 60605. Offers reading teacher education (MA).

Rowan University, Graduate School, College of Education, Department of Reading Education, Glassboro, NJ 08028-1701. Offers MA. *Accreditation:* NCATE. Part-time and evening/weekend programs available. *Degree requirements:* For master's, comprehensive exam, thesis. *Entrance requirements:* For master's, GRE General Test, GRE Subject Test, interview, minimum GPA of 2.8. Additional exam requirements/recommendations for international students: Required—TOEFL. Electronic applications accepted.

Rutgers, The State University of New Jersey, New Brunswick, Graduate School of Education, Department of Learning and Teaching, Program in Literacy Education, Piscataway, NJ 08854-8097. Offers Ed M, Ed D. Part-time programs available. Terminal master's awarded for partial completion of doctoral program. *Degree requirements:* For master's, comprehensive exam; for doctorate, thesis/dissertation, qualifying exam. *Entrance requirements:* For master's, GRE General Test, minimum undergraduate GPA of 3.0; for doctorate, GRE General Test, 2 years of teaching experience, certification, minimum graduate GPA of 3.5. Additional exam requirements/recommendations for international students: Required—TOEFL. Electronic applications accepted. *Faculty research:* Early childhood literacy development, discourse analysis-adult literacy.

Rutgers, The State University of New Jersey, New Brunswick, Graduate School of Education, Department of Learning and Teaching, Program in Reading Education, Piscataway, NJ 08854-8097. Offers Ed M. Part-time programs available. *Degree requirements:* For master's, comprehensive exam or paper. *Entrance requirements:* For master's, GRE General Test. Electronic applications accepted.

Rutgers, The State University of New Jersey, New Brunswick, Graduate School of Education, Doctoral Program in Education, New Brunswick, NJ 08901. Offers educational policy (PhD); educational psychology (PhD); literacy education (PhD); mathematics education (PhD). Part-time programs available. *Degree requirements:* For doctorate, thesis/dissertation, qualifying exam. *Entrance requirements:* For doctorate, GRE General Test, GRE Subject Test (mathematics education). Additional exam requirements/recommendations for international students: Required—TOEFL (minimum score 575 paper-based; 233 computer-based; 83 iBT). Electronic applications accepted. *Faculty research:* Literacy education, math education, educational psychology, educational policy, learning sciences.

Sacred Heart University, Graduate Programs, Isabelle Farrington College of Education, Fairfield, CT 06825-1000. Offers administration (CAS); educational technology (MAT); elementary education (MAT); reading (CAS); secondary education (MAT); teaching (CAS). Part-time and evening/weekend programs available. Postbaccalaureate distance learning degree programs offered (minimal on-campus study). *Degree requirements:* For master's, thesis or alternative. *Entrance requirements:* For master's, PRAXIS (teacher certification/MAT); for CAS, PRAXIS I. Additional exam requirements/recommendations for international students: Required—TOEFL (minimum score 550 paper-based; 213 computer-based). Electronic applications accepted. *Expenses:* Contact institution. *Faculty research:* Reading education, learning theory, teacher preparation, education of underachievers.

Sage Graduate School, Esteves School of Education, Program in Childhood Education/Literacy, Troy, NY 12180-4115. Offers MS. Part-time and evening/weekend programs available. *Faculty:* 10 full-time (6 women), 27 part-time/adjunct (23 women). *Students:* 5 full-time (all women), 13 part-time (all women); includes 1 minority (Asian, non-Hispanic/Latino). Average age 28. 12 applicants, 33% accepted, 4 enrolled. In 2011, 7 master's awarded. *Degree requirements:* For master's, thesis optional. *Entrance requirements:* For master's, minimum GPA of 2.75, resume, 2 letters of recommendation, interview, assessment of writing skills. Additional exam requirements/recommendations for international students: Required—TOEFL (minimum score 550 paper-based; 213 computer-based). *Application deadline:* Applications are processed on a rolling basis. Application fee: $40. *Expenses: Tuition:* Full-time $11,880; part-time $660 per credit hour. Tuition and fees vary according to program. *Financial support:* Fellowships, research assistantships, Federal Work-Study, scholarships/grants, and unspecified assistantships available. Support available to part-time students. Financial award application deadline: 3/1. *Unit head:* Dr. Lori Quigley, Dean, Esteves School of Education, 518-244-2326, Fax: 518-244-4571, E-mail: l.quigley@sage.edu. *Application contact:* Mary Grace Luibrand, Director, 518-244-4578, Fax: 518-244-4571, E-mail: luibrm@sage.edu.

Sage Graduate School, Esteves School of Education, Program in Literacy, Troy, NY 12180-4115. Offers MS Ed. *Accreditation:* NCATE. Part-time and evening/weekend programs available. *Faculty:* 10 full-time (6 women), 2 part-time/adjunct (both women). *Students:* 4 full-time (all women), 29 part-time (27 women). Average age 26. 28 applicants, 68% accepted, 8 enrolled. In 2011, 22 master's awarded. *Entrance requirements:* For master's, minimum GPA of 2.75, resume, 2 letters of recommendation. Additional exam requirements/recommendations for international students: Required—TOEFL (minimum score 550 paper-based; 213 computer-based). *Application deadline:* Applications are processed on a rolling basis. Application fee: $40. *Expenses: Tuition:* Full-time $11,880; part-time $660 per credit hour. Tuition and fees vary according to program. *Financial support:* Fellowships, research assistantships, Federal Work-Study, scholarships/grants, and unspecified assistantships available. Support available to part-time students. Financial award application deadline: 3/1; financial award applicants required to submit FAFSA. *Faculty research:* Literacy development in at-risk children. *Unit head:* Dr. Lori Quigley, Dean, Esteves School of Education, 518-244-2326, Fax: 518-244-4571, E-mail: l.quigley@sage.edu. *Application contact:* Dr. Ellen Adams, Department Chair, 518-244-2054, Fax: 518-244-2334, E-mail: adamse@sage.edu.

Sage Graduate School, Esteves School of Education, Program in Literacy/Childhood Special Education, Troy, NY 12180-4115. Offers MS Ed. *Accreditation:* NCATE. Part-time and evening/weekend programs available. *Faculty:* 10 full-time (6 women). *Students:* 8 full-time (all women), 3 part-time (all women); includes 2 minority (1 Black or African American, non-Hispanic/Latino; 1 Hispanic/Latino). Average age 24. 9 applicants, 67% accepted, 6 enrolled. In 2011, 4 master's awarded. *Entrance requirements:* For master's, assessment of writing skills, minimum GPA of 2.75, resume, 2 letters of recommendation, interview with advisor. Additional exam requirements/recommendations for international students: Required—TOEFL (minimum score 550 paper-based; 213 computer-based). *Application deadline:* Applications are processed on a rolling basis. Application fee: $40. *Expenses: Tuition:* Full-time $11,880; part-time $660 per credit hour. Tuition and fees vary according to program. *Financial support:* Fellowships, research assistantships, Federal Work-Study, scholarships/grants, and unspecified assistantships available. Support available to part-time students. Financial award application deadline: 3/1; financial award applicants required to submit FAFSA. *Faculty research:* Commonalities in the roles of reading specialists and resource/consultant teachers. *Unit head:* Dr. Lori Quigley, Dean, Esteves School of Education, 518-244-2326, Fax: 518-244-4571, E-mail: l.quigley@sage.edu. *Application contact:*

Mary Grace Luibrand, Director, 518-244-4578, Fax: 518-244-2334, E-mail: luibrm@sage.edu.

Saginaw Valley State University, College of Education, Program in Reading Education, University Center, MI 48710. Offers MAT. *Accreditation:* NCATE. Part-time and evening/weekend programs available. *Students:* 50 part-time (47 women); includes 1 minority (Hispanic/Latino). Average age 33. 18 applicants, 100% accepted, 13 enrolled. In 2011, 32 master's awarded. *Degree requirements:* For master's, capstone course, practicum. *Entrance requirements:* For master's, minimum GPA of 3.0, teaching certificate. Additional exam requirements/recommendations for international students: Required—TOEFL (minimum score 525 paper-based; 197 computer-based; 71 iBT). *Application deadline:* Applications are processed on a rolling basis. Application fee: $25. Electronic applications accepted. *Expenses:* Tuition, state resident: full-time $8300; part-time $5333 per year. Tuition, nonresident: full-time $15,613; part-time $10,209 per year. *International tuition:* $15,631 full-time. *Financial support:* Federal Work-Study and scholarships/grants available. Support available to part-time students. Financial award applicants required to submit FAFSA. *Faculty research:* Pre-service, middle school, secondary teacher, literacy education. *Unit head:* Dr. Steve P. Barbus, Jr., Dean, 989-964-6067, Fax: 989-790-4385, E-mail: barbus@svsu.edu. *Application contact:* Kathy Lopez, Certification Officer, 989-964-4661, Fax: 989-964-4385, E-mail: klopez@svsu.edu.

St. Bonaventure University, School of Graduate Studies, School of Education, Literacy Programs, St. Bonaventure, NY 14778-2284. Offers adolescent literacy 5-12 (MS Ed); childhood literacy B-6 (MS Ed). *Accreditation:* NCATE. Part-time and evening/weekend programs available. *Faculty:* 2 full-time (both women). *Students:* 18 full-time (16 women), 33 part-time (32 women). Average age 24. 33 applicants, 67% accepted, 15 enrolled. In 2011, 50 master's awarded. *Degree requirements:* For master's, comprehensive exam, thesis optional, literacy coaching internship, portfolio. *Entrance requirements:* For master's, interview, writing sample, minimum undergraduate GPA of 3.0, references, teaching certificate in matching area. Additional exam requirements/recommendations for international students: Required—TOEFL (minimum score 550 paper-based; 213 computer-based; 80 iBT). *Application deadline:* For fall admission, 6/15 priority date for domestic students, 2/1 for international students; for spring admission, 11/15 priority date for domestic students, 7/1 for international students. Applications are processed on a rolling basis. Application fee: $30. Electronic applications accepted. *Expenses: Tuition:* Part-time $670 per credit. *Financial support:* In 2011–12, 4 research assistantships with full and partial tuition reimbursements were awarded; Federal Work-Study, scholarships/grants, health care benefits, and unspecified assistantships also available. Support available to part-time students. Financial award application deadline: 4/15; financial award applicants required to submit FAFSA. *Unit head:* Dr. Pamela Sharp Crawford, Director, 716-375-2387, E-mail: pcrawfor@sbu.edu. *Application contact:* Bruce Campbell, 716-375-2429, Fax: 716-375-4015, E-mail: gradsch@sbu.edu. Web site: http://www.sbu.edu/education.aspx?id-2994.

Saint Francis University, Graduate Education Program, Loretto, PA 15940-0600. Offers education (M Ed); leadership (M Ed); reading (M Ed). Part-time and evening/weekend programs available. *Faculty:* 22 part-time/adjunct (9 women). *Students:* 130 part-time (95 women); includes 1 minority (Hispanic/Latino). Average age 30. 30 applicants, 100% accepted, 30 enrolled. In 2011, 53 master's awarded. *Degree requirements:* For master's, comprehensive exam, thesis optional. *Entrance requirements:* For master's, GRE or MAT (if undergraduate GPA less than 2.8), minimum undergraduate QPA of 2.5. *Application deadline:* Applications are processed on a rolling basis. Application fee: $30. *Expenses:* Contact institution. *Financial support:* Applicants required to submit FAFSA. *Unit head:* Dr. Janette D. Kelly, Director, 814-472-3068, Fax: 814-472-3864, E-mail: jkelly@francis.edu. *Application contact:* Sherri L. Toth, Coordinator, 814-472-3058, Fax: 814-472-3864, E-mail: stoth@francis.edu. Web site: http://www.francis.edu/medhome.htm.

St. John Fisher College, Ralph C. Wilson Jr. School of Education, Program in Literacy Education, Rochester, NY 14618-3597. Offers literacy birth to grade 6 (MS); literacy grades 5 to 12 (MS). Part-time and evening/weekend programs available. *Faculty:* 4 full-time (all women), 3 part-time/adjunct (all women). *Students:* 14 full-time (all women), 72 part-time (65 women); includes 3 minority (2 Black or African American, non-Hispanic/Latino; 1 Asian, non-Hispanic/Latino). Average age 26. 49 applicants, 90% accepted, 26 enrolled. In 2011, 41 master's awarded. *Degree requirements:* For master's, capstone project, practicum. *Entrance requirements:* For master's, teacher certification, 2 letters of recommendation, personal statement, current resume. Additional exam requirements/recommendations for international students: Required—TOEFL (minimum score 575 paper-based; 233 computer-based; 80 iBT). *Application deadline:* Applications are processed on a rolling basis. Application fee: $30. Electronic applications accepted. *Expenses: Tuition:* Part-time $735 per credit. One-time fee: $50 part-time. Tuition and fees vary according to course load, degree level and program. *Financial support:* In 2011–12, 19 students received support. Scholarships/grants available. Financial award applicants required to submit FAFSA. *Faculty research:* Adolescent use of new literacies (instant messaging), referral practices, at risk early literacy, new literacies (Internet, technology), equity in education. *Unit head:* Dr. Kathleen Broikou, Program Director, 585-385-8112, E-mail: kbroikou@sjfc.edu. *Application contact:* Jose Perales, Director of Graduate Admissions, 585-385-8067, E-mail: jperales@sjfc.edu. Web site: http://www.sjfc.edu/academics/education/departments/literacy/.

St. John's University, The School of Education, Department of Human Services and Counseling, Literacy Program, Queens, NY 11439. Offers literacy (PhD); literacy B-6 or 5-12 (Adv C); teaching literacy 5-12 (MS Ed); teaching literacy B-12 (MS Ed); teaching literacy B-6 (MS Ed). Part-time and evening/weekend programs available. *Students:* 28 full-time (27 women), 90 part-time (86 women); includes 23 minority (8 Black or African American, non-Hispanic/Latino; 3 Asian, non-Hispanic/Latino; 12 Hispanic/Latino). Average age 29. 67 applicants, 91% accepted, 35 enrolled. In 2011, 24 master's, 1 other advanced degree awarded. *Degree requirements:* For master's, comprehensive exam; for doctorate, thesis/dissertation, residency; for Adv C, 50 hour practicum, content specialty test in literacy. *Entrance requirements:* For master's, minimum GPA of 3.0; for doctorate, MAT, GRE General Test (analytical), statement of goals, official transcripts showing conferral of degree, minimum GPA of 3.2, 2 letters of recommendation, resume, evidence of teaching experience; for Adv C, master's degree, initial teaching certification, minimum GPA of 3.0. Additional exam requirements/recommendations for international students: Required—TOEFL (minimum score 600 paper-based; 250 computer-based; 100 iBT), IELTS (minimum score 5.5). *Application deadline:* For fall admission, 4/1 for domestic and international students; for spring admission, 11/1 for international students. Applications are processed on a rolling basis. Application fee: $70. Electronic applications accepted. *Expenses: Tuition:* Full-time $18,000; part-time $1000 per credit. *Required fees:* $170 per semester. Tuition and fees vary according to program. *Financial support:* Research assistantships, career-related internships or fieldwork, and scholarships/grants available. Support available to part-time students. Financial award application deadline: 3/1; financial award applicants required to submit FAFSA. *Faculty research:* Higher order reading comprehension development and instruction, children's literature theory and children's reading interests, critical comprehension development, early writing development at the primary level, self-efficacy with textbook formats, out of school time program effects for at-risk students, teacher training effects for low performing parochial school students. *Unit head:* Dr. Francine Guastello, Chair, 718-990-1475, E-mail: guastelf@stjohns.edu. *Application contact:* Dr. Kelly K. Ronayne, Associate Dean of Graduate Admissions, 718-990-2304, Fax: 718-990-2343, E-mail: graded@stjohns.edu.

St. Joseph's College, Long Island Campus, Program in Literacy and Cognition, Patchogue, NY 11772-2399. Offers MA.

St. Joseph's College, New York, Graduate Programs, Program in Education, Field of Literacy and Cognition, Brooklyn, NY 11205-3688. Offers MA.

Saint Joseph's University, College of Arts and Sciences, Department of Education, Philadelphia, PA 19131-1395. Offers curriculum supervisor of instruction (Certificate); educational leadership (MS, Ed D); elementary education (MS, Certificate); elementary/middle years (Certificate); English second language specialist online (Certificate); hearing impaired: N-12th grade (Certificate); instructional technology (MS, Certificate); principal certification (Certificate); professional education (MS); reading specialist (MS, Certificate); reading supervisory (Certificate); secondary education (MS, Certificate); special education (MS, Certificate); superintendent's letter of eligibility (Certificate); supervisor of special education (Certificate); Wilson reading certificate online (Certificate). Part-time and evening/weekend programs available. Postbaccalaureate distance learning degree programs offered (no on-campus study). *Faculty:* 26 full-time (24 women), 83 part-time/adjunct (52 women). *Students:* 112 full-time (92 women), 923 part-time (709 women); includes 147 minority (92 Black or African American, non-Hispanic/Latino; 4 American Indian or Alaska Native, non-Hispanic/Latino; 19 Asian, non-Hispanic/Latino; 28 Hispanic/Latino; 4 Two or more races, non-Hispanic/Latino), 8 international. Average age 31. 285 applicants, 77% accepted, 176 enrolled. In 2011, 276 master's, 13 doctorates, 2 other advanced degrees awarded. *Entrance requirements:* For master's, 2 letters of recommendation, minimum GPA of 3.0, official transcripts, personal statement; for doctorate, GRE, master's degree from accredited institution, minimum graduate GPA of 3.5, computer competence, commitment to participate in cohort, interview with program director. Additional exam requirements/recommendations for international students: Required—TOEFL (minimum score 550 paper-based; 213 computer-based; 79 iBT). *Application deadline:* For fall admission, 7/15 priority date for domestic students, 4/15 for international students; for winter admission, 11/15 for domestic students, 1/15 for international students; for spring admission, 11/15 priority date for domestic students, 10/15 for international students. Applications are processed on a rolling basis. Application fee: $35. Electronic applications accepted. *Expenses:* Contact institution. *Financial support:* Unspecified assistantships available. Financial award applicants required to submit FAFSA. *Faculty research:* Public education professional development, factors predicting early mathematics skills for low income children. *Total annual research expenditures:* $92,975. *Unit head:* Dr. Jeanne Brady, Associate Dean, Education, 610-660-1580, E-mail: jebrady@sju.edu. *Application contact:* Kate McConnell, Director, Graduate College of Arts and Sciences Admissions and Retention, 610-660-3184, Fax: 610-660-3230, E-mail: kate.mcconnell@sju.edu.

Saint Leo University, Graduate Studies in Education, Saint Leo, FL 33574-6665. Offers educational leadership (M Ed); exceptional student education (M Ed); higher education leadership (Ed S); instructional design (MS); instructional leadership (M Ed); reading (M Ed); school leadership (Ed S). Part-time and evening/weekend programs available. Postbaccalaureate distance learning degree programs offered (minimal on-campus study). *Faculty:* 14 full-time (10 women), 21 part-time/adjunct (16 women). *Students:* 523 full-time (427 women), 20 part-time (17 women); includes 65 minority (43 Black or African American, non-Hispanic/Latino; 2 Asian, non-Hispanic/Latino; 16 Hispanic/Latino; 4 Two or more races, non-Hispanic/Latino), 3 international. Average age 37. In 2011, 153 master's, 18 other advanced degrees awarded. *Degree requirements:* For master's, comprehensive exam, appropriate State of Florida certification tests. *Entrance requirements:* For master's, GRE (minimum score of 1000) or MAT (minimum score of 410) if undergraduate GPA for last 60 hours of coursework was below 3.0 (for M Ed), bachelor's degree with minimum GPA of 3.0 for last 60 hours of coursework from regionally-accredited college or university, 2 recommendations, resume, statement of professional goals, copy of valid teaching certificate (for M Ed); for Ed S, GRE (minimum score 1000) or MAT (minimum score 410) if undergraduate GPA for last 60 hours of coursework less than 3.0, bachelor's degree with minimum GPA of 3.0 for last 60 hours of coursework from regionally-accredited college or university, 2 recommendations, resume, valid teaching certificate. Additional exam requirements/recommendations for international students: Required—TOEFL (minimum score 550 paper-based; 213 computer-based; 80 iBT). *Application deadline:* For fall admission, 7/1 priority date for domestic students, 7/1 for international students; for winter admission, 7/1 for international students; for spring admission, 11/1 priority date for domestic students. Applications are processed on a rolling basis. Application fee: $80. Electronic applications accepted. *Expenses:* Contact institution. *Financial support:* In 2011–12, 20 students received support. Career-related internships or fieldwork, Federal Work-Study, scholarships/grants, and health care benefits available. Financial award application deadline: 3/1; financial award applicants required to submit FAFSA. *Faculty research:* The role of the school leader in data analysis of student achievement, teacher recruitment, teacher effectiveness. *Unit head:* Dr. Sharyn Disabato, Director, 352-588-8309, Fax: 352-588-8861, E-mail: med@saintleo.edu. *Application contact:* Jared Welling, Director of Graduate Admission, 800-707-8846, Fax: 352-588-7873, E-mail: grad.admissions@saintleo.edu. Web site: http://www.saintleo.edu/Academics/School-of-Education-Social-Services/Graduate-Degree-Programs.

Saint Martin's University, Graduate Programs, College of Education, Lacey, WA 98503. Offers administration (M Ed); English as a second language (M Ed); guidance and counseling (M Ed); reading (M Ed); special education (M Ed); teaching (MIT). *Accreditation:* Teacher Education Accreditation Council. Part-time and evening/weekend programs available. *Faculty:* 12 full-time (8 women), 9 part-time/adjunct (7 women). *Students:* 68 full-time (38 women), 28 part-time (20 women); includes 15 minority (2 Black or African American, non-Hispanic/Latino; 2 American Indian or Alaska Native, non-Hispanic/Latino; 7 Asian, non-Hispanic/Latino; 2 Hispanic/Latino; 2 Two or more races, non-Hispanic/Latino), 4 international. Average age 35. 17 applicants, 94% accepted, 15 enrolled. In 2011, 12 master's awarded. *Degree requirements:* For master's, comprehensive exam (for some programs), thesis or alternative, project or comprehensives. *Entrance requirements:* For master's, GRE General Test or MAT, resume. Additional exam requirements/recommendations for international students: Required—TOEFL (minimum score 560 paper-based; 220 computer-based; 83 iBT). *Application deadline:* For fall admission, 6/1 priority date for domestic students, 6/1 for international students; for spring admission, 10/1 priority date for domestic students, 10/1 for international students. Applications are processed on a rolling basis. Application fee: $35. *Expenses: Tuition:* Part-time $910 per credit hour. Tuition and fees vary according to course level, campus/location and program. *Financial support:* Career-related internships or fieldwork, Federal Work-Study, institutionally sponsored loans, and unspecified assistantships available. Support available to part-time students. Financial award application deadline: 3/1; financial award applicants required to submit FAFSA. *Faculty research:* Reader's theatre and reader/writer workshops, curriculum and assessment integration, gender and equity, classroom evaluations, organizational leadership. *Unit head:* Dr. Joyce Westgard, Dean, College of Education and

Professional Psychology, 360-438-4509, Fax: 360-438-4486, E-mail: westgard@stmartin.edu. *Application contact:* Ryan M. Smith, Administrative Assistant, 360-438-4333, Fax: 360-438-4486, E-mail: ryan.smith@stmartin.edu. Web site: http://www.stmartin.edu/CEPP/.

Saint Mary's College of California, Kalmanovitz School of Education, Program in Montessori Education, Moraga, CA 94556. Offers reading and language arts (M Ed, MA). *Students:* 56 part-time (51 women); includes 23 minority (2 Black or African American, non-Hispanic/Latino; 1 American Indian or Alaska Native, non-Hispanic/Latino; 11 Asian, non-Hispanic/Latino; 9 Hispanic/Latino), 1 international. Average age 34. Tuition and fees vary according to course load, degree level and program. *Unit head:* Dr. Phyllis Metcalf-Turner, Dean, 925-631-4309, Fax: 925-376-8379. *Application contact:* Jane Joyce, Coordinator, Recruitment and Admissions, 925-631-4700, Fax: 925-376-8379, E-mail: soereq@stmarys-ca.edu. Web site: http://www.stmarys-ca.edu/montessori-education.

Saint Mary's College of California, Kalmanovitz School of Education, Program in Reading Leadership, Moraga, CA 94556. Offers reading and language arts (M Ed, MA). Part-time and evening/weekend programs available. *Students:* 6 full-time (all women), 57 part-time (55 women); includes 8 minority (2 Black or African American, non-Hispanic/Latino; 6 American Indian or Alaska Native, non-Hispanic/Latino). Average age 41. In 2011, 2 master's awarded. *Degree requirements:* For master's, thesis or alternative. *Entrance requirements:* For master's, interview, minimum GPA of 3.0. *Application deadline:* Applications are processed on a rolling basis. Application fee: $50. Tuition and fees vary according to course load, degree level and program. *Financial support:* Career-related internships or fieldwork available. Support available to part-time students. Financial award application deadline: 2/15. *Unit head:* Dr. Mary Kay Moskal, Director, 925-631-4726, Fax: 925-376-8379, E-mail: mmoskal@stmarys-ca.edu. *Application contact:* Jane Joyce, Coordinator of Recruitment and Admissions, 925-631-4700, Fax: 925-376-8379, E-mail: soereq@stmarys-ca.edu. Web site: http://www.stmarys-ca.edu/node/3893.

St. Mary's University, Graduate School, Department of Teacher Education, Program in Reading, San Antonio, TX 78228-8507. Offers MA. Part-time programs available. Postbaccalaureate distance learning degree programs offered (no on-campus study). *Degree requirements:* For master's, comprehensive exam. *Entrance requirements:* For master's, GRE. Additional exam requirements/recommendations for international students: Required—TOEFL (minimum score 550 paper-based; 213 computer-based; 80 iBT). Electronic applications accepted.

Saint Mary's University of Minnesota, Schools of Graduate and Professional Programs, Graduate School of Education, Literacy Education Program, Winona, MN 55987-1399. Offers K-12 reading teacher (Certificate); literacy education (MA). *Unit head:* Cory Hanson, Director, 507-457-6607, E-mail: cxhans05@smumn.edu. *Application contact:* Denise Cichosz, Director of Admissions for Graduate and Professional Programs, 507-457-6629, E-mail: dcichosz@smumn.edu. Web site: http://www.smumn.edu/graduate-home/areas-of-study/graduate-school-of-education/ma-in-literacy-education.

Saint Michael's College, Graduate Programs, Program in Education, Colchester, VT 05439. Offers administration (M Ed, CAGS); arts in education (CAGS); curriculum and instruction (M Ed, CAGS); information technology (CAGS); reading (M Ed); special education (M Ed, CAGS); technology (M Ed). Part-time and evening/weekend programs available. *Degree requirements:* For master's, thesis. *Entrance requirements:* For master's, minimum GPA of 3.0. Electronic applications accepted. *Faculty research:* Integrative curriculum, moral and spiritual dimensions of education, learning styles, multiple intelligences, integrating technology into the curriculum.

Saint Peter's University, Graduate Programs in Education, Program in Special Education, Jersey City, NJ 07306-5997. Offers literacy (MA Ed). Part-time and evening/weekend programs available. *Degree requirements:* For master's, comprehensive exam. *Entrance requirements:* For master's, GRE or MAT. Additional exam requirements/recommendations for international students: Required—TOEFL (minimum score 79 computer-based). Electronic applications accepted.

Saint Peter's University, Graduate Programs in Education, Reading Program, Jersey City, NJ 07306-5997. Offers MA Ed. *Accreditation:* Teacher Education Accreditation Council. Part-time and evening/weekend programs available. *Degree requirements:* For master's, comprehensive exam. *Entrance requirements:* For master's, GRE or MAT. Additional exam requirements/recommendations for international students: Required—TOEFL (minimum score 79 computer-based). Electronic applications accepted.

St. Thomas Aquinas College, Division of Teacher Education, Sparkill, NY 10976. Offers adolescence education (MST); childhood and special education (MST); childhood education (MST); educational leadership (MS Ed); reading (MS Ed, PMC); special education (MS Ed, PMC); teaching (MS Ed), including elementary education, middle school education, secondary education. *Accreditation:* NCATE. Part-time and evening/weekend programs available. *Degree requirements:* For master's, comprehensive exam, comprehensive professional portfolio; for PMC, action research project. *Entrance requirements:* For master's, New York State Qualifying Exam, GRE General Test or minimum GPA of 3.0, teaching certificate; for PMC, GRE General Test or minimum GPA of 3.0. Electronic applications accepted. *Faculty research:* Computer applications in education, adolescent special education students, literacy development, inclusive practices for special education students.

St. Thomas University, School of Leadership Studies, Institute for Education, Miami Gardens, FL 33054-6459. Offers earth/space science (Certificate); educational administration (MS, Certificate); educational leadership (Ed D); elementary education (MS); ESOL (Certificate); gifted education (Certificate); instructional technology (MS, Certificate); professional/studies (Certificate); reading (MS, Certificate); special education (MS). Part-time and evening/weekend programs available. *Degree requirements:* For master's, comprehensive exam; for doctorate, comprehensive exam, thesis/dissertation. *Entrance requirements:* For master's, interview, minimum GPA of 3.0 or GRE; for doctorate, GRE or MAT. Additional exam requirements/recommendations for international students: Required—TOEFL (minimum score 550 paper-based; 213 computer-based; 79 iBT). Electronic applications accepted.

Saint Xavier University, Graduate Studies, School of Education, Chicago, IL 60655-3105. Offers counseling (MA); curriculum and instruction (MA); early childhood education (MA); educational administration (MA); elementary education (MA); individualized studies (MA), including educational technology, English as a second language (ESL), ISTEM (integrative science, technology, engineering, and math), science education; music education (MA); reading (MA); secondary education (MA); Spanish education (MA); special education (MA); teaching and leadership (MA). *Accreditation:* NCATE. Part-time and evening/weekend programs available. *Degree requirements:* For master's, thesis or project. *Entrance requirements:* For master's, minimum GPA of 3.0. *Application deadline:* For fall admission, 8/15 priority date for domestic students. Applications are processed on a rolling basis. Application fee: $35. *Expenses:* Contact institution. *Financial support:* Career-related internships or fieldwork available. Support available to part-time students. Financial award applicants required to submit FAFSA. *Unit head:* Dr. Beverly Gulley, Dean, 773-298-3221, Fax: 773-779-9061, E-mail: gulley@sxu.edu. *Application contact:* Beth Gierach, Managing Director of Admission, 773-298-3053, Fax: 773-298-3076, E-mail: gierach@sxu.edu.

Salem College, Department of Teacher Education, Winston-Salem, NC 27101. Offers art education (MAT); elementary education (M Ed, MAT); language and literacy (M Ed); middle school education (MAT); music education (MAT); school counseling (M Ed); second language studies (MAT); secondary education (MAT); special education (M Ed, MAT). *Accreditation:* NCATE. Part-time and evening/weekend programs available. Postbaccalaureate distance learning degree programs offered (minimal on-campus study). *Degree requirements:* For master's, comprehensive exam, practicum (MAT), project (M Ed), oral and written comprehensive exams. *Entrance requirements:* For master's, GRE, minimum GPA of 2.5. *Faculty research:* Content area reading strategies, literacy development, brain compatible instruction.

Salem State University, School of Graduate Studies, Program in Reading, Salem, MA 01970-5353. Offers M Ed. *Accreditation:* NCATE. Part-time and evening/weekend programs available. *Entrance requirements:* For master's, GRE or MAT. Additional exam requirements/recommendations for international students: Required—TOEFL (minimum score 550 paper-based; 80 iBT) or IELTS (minimum score 5.5).

Salisbury University, Graduate Division, Department of Education, Salisbury, MD 21801-6837. Offers education (M Ed); education administration (M Ed); mathematics education (MSME); reading specialist (M Ed); teaching (MAT). *Accreditation:* NCATE. Part-time and evening/weekend programs available. *Faculty:* 23 full-time (13 women), 6 part-time/adjunct (5 women). *Students:* 18 full-time (12 women), 121 part-time (94 women); includes 18 minority (14 Black or African American, non-Hispanic/Latino; 1 Asian, non-Hispanic/Latino; 2 Hispanic/Latino; 1 Two or more races, non-Hispanic/Latino), 5 international. Average age 30. 31 applicants, 81% accepted, 25 enrolled. In 2011, 36 master's awarded. *Degree requirements:* For master's, comprehensive exam (for some programs), thesis optional, advanced seminars, internships, thesis research or practicum courses. *Entrance requirements:* For master's, 2 recommendations, program of study developed and signed by applicant and advisor, copy of teaching certificate (based on program), employment verification (for M Ed in educational leadership), personal statement, minimum GPA of 3.0. Additional exam requirements/recommendations for international students: Required—TOEFL (minimum score 550 paper-based; 79 iBT). *Application deadline:* For fall admission, 3/3 for domestic students; for spring admission, 10/1 for domestic students. Applications are processed on a rolling basis. Application fee: $45. Electronic applications accepted. *Expenses: Tuition, area resident:* Part-time $306 per credit hour. Tuition, state resident: part-time $306 per credit hour. Tuition, nonresident: part-time $595 per credit hour. *Required fees:* $68 per credit hour. *Financial support:* In 2011–12, 22 students received support. Career-related internships or fieldwork, institutionally sponsored loans, scholarships/grants, and unspecified assistantships available. Support available to part-time students. Financial award application deadline: 3/1; financial award applicants required to submit FAFSA. *Faculty research:* Lower Eastern Shore School Leadership Institute Program, using best practices to motivate and engage early childhood teachers to teach in high poverty/high minority schools, TRIOS Student Support Services, SU Elementary STEM Program, design. *Total annual research expenditures:* $167,000. *Unit head:* Dr. Gwen Beegle, Director, 410-543-6393, E-mail: gpbeegle@salisbury.edu. *Application contact:* Debra Clark, Executive Administrative Assistant, 410-543-6335, Fax: 410-548-2593, E-mail: djclark@salisbury.edu. Web site: http://www.salisbury.edu/educationspecialties/med.html.

Sam Houston State University, College of Education, Department of Language, Literacy, and Special Populations, Huntsville, TX 77341. Offers international literacy (M Ed); reading (M Ed, MA, Ed D); special education (M Ed, MA). Part-time and evening/weekend programs available. *Faculty:* 22 full-time (19 women), 5 part-time/adjunct (4 women). *Students:* 4 full-time (3 women), 151 part-time (146 women); includes 46 minority (19 Black or African American, non-Hispanic/Latino; 6 American Indian or Alaska Native, non-Hispanic/Latino; 2 Asian, non-Hispanic/Latino; 19 Hispanic/Latino), 3 international. Average age 37. 154 applicants, 58% accepted, 45 enrolled. In 2011, 31 master's, 5 doctorates awarded. *Entrance requirements:* For master's, GRE General Test, minimum GPA of 2.5. Additional exam requirements/recommendations for international students: Required—TOEFL (minimum score 550 paper-based; 213 computer-based; 79 iBT). *Application deadline:* For fall admission, 8/1 for domestic students, 6/25 for international students; for spring admission, 12/1 for domestic students, 11/12 for international students. Applications are processed on a rolling basis. Application fee: $45 ($75 for international students). Electronic applications accepted. *Expenses:* Tuition, state resident: full-time $4420; part-time $221 per credit hour. Tuition, nonresident: full-time $10,680; part-time $534 per credit hour. *Required fees:* $329 per credit hour. *Financial support:* Teaching assistantships available. Financial award application deadline: 5/31; financial award applicants required to submit FAFSA. *Unit head:* Dr. Melinda Miller, Chair, 936-294-1122, Fax: 936-294-1131, E-mail: mmiller@shsu.edu. *Application contact:* Molly Doughtie, Advisor, 936-294-1105, E-mail: edu_mxd@shsu.edu. Web site: http://www.shsu.edu/~edu_lls/.

San Diego State University, Graduate and Research Affairs, College of Education, School of Teacher Education, Program in Reading Education, San Diego, CA 92182. Offers MA. *Accreditation:* NCATE. Part-time programs available. *Entrance requirements:* For master's, GRE General Test, letters of reference. Additional exam requirements/recommendations for international students: Required—TOEFL. Electronic applications accepted. *Faculty research:* Literacy, writing, reading/writing connection, class size reduction in reading, book clubs, evaluation instruments in reading/language arts.

San Francisco State University, Division of Graduate Studies, College of Education, Department of Elementary Education, Program in Language and Literacy Education, San Francisco, CA 94132-1722. Offers MA. *Unit head:* Dr. Debra Luna, Chair, 415-338-1562, E-mail: dluna@sfsu.edu. *Application contact:* Dr. Josephine Arce, Graduate Coordinator, 415-338-2292, E-mail: jarce@sfsu.edu. Web site: http://www.coe.sfsu.edu/eed.

San Francisco State University, Division of Graduate Studies, College of Liberal and Creative Arts, Department of English Language and Literature, San Francisco, CA 94132-1722. Offers composition (MA); immigrant literacies (Certificate); linguistics (MA); literature (MA); teaching English to speakers of other languages (MA); teaching of composition (Certificate); teaching post-secondary reading (Certificate). Part-time programs available. *Application deadline:* Applications are processed on a rolling basis. *Unit head:* Dr. Beverly Voloshin, Chair, 415-338-2264, E-mail: english@sfsu.edu. *Application contact:* Cynthia Losinsky, Administrative Support, Graduate Programs, 415-338-2660, E-mail: english@sfsu.edu. Web site: http://www.sfsu.edu/~english.

San Jose State University, Graduate Studies and Research, Connie L. Lurie College of Education, Department of Elementary Education, San Jose, CA 95192-0001. Offers curriculum and instruction (MA); reading (Certificate). *Accreditation:* NCATE. *Degree requirements:* For master's, thesis or alternative. Electronic applications accepted.

Seattle Pacific University, M Ed in Curriculum and Instruction Program, Seattle, WA 98119-1997. Offers reading/language arts education (M Ed). *Accreditation:* NCATE. Part-time and evening/weekend programs available. *Degree requirements:* For master's, comprehensive exam. *Entrance requirements:* For master's, GRE General

Test or MAT, minimum GPA of 3.0. Additional exam requirements/recommendations for international students: Required—TOEFL (minimum score 550 paper-based). Electronic applications accepted. *Expenses:* Contact institution. *Faculty research:* Educational technology, classroom environments, character education.

Seattle Pacific University, M Ed in Literacy Program, Seattle, WA 98119-1997. Offers M Ed. Part-time programs available. *Degree requirements:* For master's, comprehensive exam. *Entrance requirements:* For master's, MAT or GRE (unless minimum undergraduate GPA of 3.4 or master's degree from accredited university). Electronic applications accepted.

Seattle University, College of Education, Program in Literacy, Seattle, WA 98122-1090. Offers M Ed, Post-Master's Certificate. *Students:* 10 part-time (all women); includes 2 minority (1 Asian, non-Hispanic/Latino; 1 Hispanic/Latino). Average age 35. *Entrance requirements:* For master's, GRE, MAT or minimum GPA of 3.0, 1 year of K-12 work experience; for Post-Master's Certificate, GRE, MAT or minimum GPA of 3.0, master's degree, WA state teaching certification. Additional exam requirements/recommendations for international students: Required—TOEFL. *Application deadline:* For fall admission, 8/20 priority date for domestic students; for winter admission, 11/20 priority date for domestic students; for spring admission, 2/20 priority date for domestic students. Application fee: $55. *Unit head:* Dr. Katherine Schlick Noe, Director, 206-296-5768, E-mail: kschlnoe@seattleu.edu. *Application contact:* Janet Shandley, Associate Dean of Graduate Admissions, 206-296-5900, Fax: 206-298-5656, E-mail: grad_admissions@seattleu.edu.

Shippensburg University of Pennsylvania, School of Graduate Studies, College of Education and Human Services, Department of Teacher Education, Shippensburg, PA 17257-2299. Offers curriculum and instruction (M Ed), including biology, early childhood education, elementary education, English, geography/earth science, history, mathematics, middle level education, modern languages; reading (M Ed). *Accreditation:* NCATE. Part-time and evening/weekend programs available. *Faculty:* 14 full-time (11 women), 8 part-time/adjunct (7 women). *Students:* 16 full-time (15 women), 143 part-time (130 women); includes 11 minority (4 Black or African American, non-Hispanic/Latino; 1 Asian, non-Hispanic/Latino; 4 Hispanic/Latino; 2 Two or more races, non-Hispanic/Latino), 1 international. Average age 30. 55 applicants, 55% accepted, 25 enrolled. In 2011, 76 master's awarded. *Degree requirements:* For master's, comprehensive exam (for some programs), thesis optional, practicum or internship; capstone seminar (for some programs). *Entrance requirements:* For master's, MAT (if GPA less than 2.75), interview, 3 letters of reference, questionnaire of teaching background and future goals. Additional exam requirements/recommendations for international students: Required—TOEFL (minimum score 580 paper-based; 237 computer-based); Recommended—IELTS (minimum score 6). *Application deadline:* For fall admission, 6/1 priority date for domestic students, 4/30 for international students; for spring admission, 9/1 priority date for domestic students, 9/30 for international students. Applications are processed on a rolling basis. Application fee: $30. Electronic applications accepted. *Expenses: Tuition, area resident:* Part-time $416 per credit. Tuition, state resident: part-time $416 per credit. Tuition, nonresident: part-time $624 per credit. *Required fees:* $119 per credit. *Financial support:* In 2011–12, 5 research assistantships with full tuition reimbursements (averaging $5,000 per year) were awarded; career-related internships or fieldwork, scholarships/grants, unspecified assistantships, and resident hall director and student payroll positions also available. Support available to part-time students. Financial award application deadline: 3/1; financial award applicants required to submit FAFSA. *Unit head:* Dr. Christine A. Royce, Chairperson, 717-477-1688, Fax: 717-477-4046, E-mail: caroyc@ship.edu. *Application contact:* Jeremy R. Goshorn, Assistant Dean of Graduate Admissions, 717-477-1231, Fax: 717-477-4016, E-mail: jrgoshorn@ship.edu. Web site: http://www.ship.edu/teacher/.

Siena Heights University, Graduate College, Program in Teacher Education, Concentration in Elementary Education, Adrian, MI 49221-1796. Offers elementary education/reading (MA). Part-time programs available. *Degree requirements:* For master's, thesis, presentation. *Entrance requirements:* For master's, interview, minimum GPA of 3.0. *Expenses: Tuition:* Full-time $11,400; part-time $475 per credit hour. *Required fees:* $1000; $500 $125 per term. Tuition and fees vary according to degree level.

Siena Heights University, Graduate College, Program in Teacher Education, Concentration in Secondary Education, Adrian, MI 49221-1796. Offers secondary education/reading (MA). Part-time programs available. *Degree requirements:* For master's, thesis, presentation. *Entrance requirements:* For master's, minimum GPA of 3.0, interview. *Expenses: Tuition:* Full-time $11,400; part-time $475 per credit hour. *Required fees:* $1000; $500 $125 per term. Tuition and fees vary according to degree level.

Simmons College, College of Arts and Sciences Graduate Studies, Boston, MA 02115. Offers applied behavior analysis (PhD); behavior analysis (MS, Ed S); children's literature (MA); education (MS, CAGS, Ed S); educational leadership (PhD, CAGS); English (MA); gender and cultural studies (MA); health professions education (PhD); history (MA); Spanish (MA); special education moderate licensure (Certificate); special needs administration (Ed D); special needs education (Ed S); teaching (MAT); teaching English as a second language (MA, CAGS); urban education (CAGS); writing for children (MFA); MA/MA; MA/MS; MAT/MA. *Unit head:* Renee White, Dean. *Application contact:* Kristen Haack, Director, Graduate Studies Admission, 617-521-2917, Fax: 617-521-3058, E-mail: gsa@simmons.edu. Web site: http://www.simmons.edu/gradstudies/.

Slippery Rock University of Pennsylvania, Graduate Studies (Recruitment), College of Education, Department of Elementary Education and Early Childhood, Slippery Rock, PA 16057-1383. Offers math/science (K-8) (M Ed); reading (M Ed). *Accreditation:* NCATE. Part-time and evening/weekend programs available. Postbaccalaureate distance learning degree programs offered. *Faculty:* 3 full-time (all women). *Students:* 2 full-time (both women), 33 part-time (all women); includes 1 minority (Two or more races, non-Hispanic/Latino). Average age 28. 55 applicants, 69% accepted, 11 enrolled. In 2011, 33 degrees awarded. *Entrance requirements:* For master's, GRE General Test, MAT, minimum GPA of 3.0, resume, teaching certification, letters of recommendation, transcripts (depending on program). Additional exam requirements/recommendations for international students: Required—TOEFL (minimum score 550 paper-based; 213 computer-based; 80 iBT). *Application deadline:* For fall admission, 3/1 priority date for domestic students, 5/1 for international students; for spring admission, 10/1 priority date for domestic students, 9/1 for international students. Applications are processed on a rolling basis. Application fee: $25 ($30 for international students). Electronic applications accepted. *Expenses:* Contact institution. *Financial support:* Career-related internships or fieldwork, Federal Work-Study, institutionally sponsored loans, scholarships/grants, tuition waivers (partial), and unspecified assistantships available. Support available to part-time students. Financial award application deadline: 5/1; financial award applicants required to submit FAFSA. *Unit head:* Dr. Suzanne Rose, Graduate Coordinator, 724-738-2863, Fax: 724-738-4987, E-mail: suzanne.rose@sru.edu. *Application contact:* Angela Barrett, Director of Graduate Admissions, 724-738-2051, Fax: 724-738-2146, E-mail: graduate.admissions@sru.edu.

Sojourner-Douglass College, Graduate Program, Baltimore, MD 21205-1814. Offers human services (MASS); public administration (MASS); urban education (reading) (MASS). Part-time and evening/weekend programs available. *Degree requirements:* For master's, comprehensive exam, written proposal oral defense. *Entrance requirements:* For master's, Graduate Examination.

Southeastern Louisiana University, College of Arts, Humanities and Social Sciences, Department of English, Hammond, LA 70402. Offers creative writing (MA); language and theory (MA); professional writing (MA). Part-time programs available. *Faculty:* 13 full-time (5 women), 2 part-time/adjunct (1 woman). *Students:* 25 full-time (17 women), 33 part-time (23 women); includes 5 minority (1 Black or African American, non-Hispanic/Latino; 1 Asian, non-Hispanic/Latino; 2 Hispanic/Latino; 1 Two or more races, non-Hispanic/Latino). Average age 31. 20 applicants, 100% accepted, 15 enrolled. In 2011, 5 master's awarded. *Degree requirements:* For master's, comprehensive exam, thesis optional. *Entrance requirements:* For master's, GRE General Test (minimum score of 850), bachelor's degree; minimum undergraduate GPA of 2.5; 24 hours of undergraduate English courses. Additional exam requirements/recommendations for international students: Required—TOEFL (minimum score 500 paper-based; 173 computer-based; 61 iBT). *Application deadline:* For fall admission, 7/15 priority date for domestic students, 6/1 for international students; for spring admission, 12/1 priority date for domestic students, 10/1 for international students. Applications are processed on a rolling basis. Application fee: $20 ($30 for international students). Electronic applications accepted. *Expenses:* Tuition, state resident: full-time $3977; part-time $283 per semester hour. Tuition, nonresident: full-time $13,482; part-time $811 per semester hour. *Financial support:* In 2011–12, 1 fellowship (averaging $10,800 per year), 9 research assistantships (averaging $9,733 per year), 1 teaching assistantship (averaging $9,000 per year) were awarded; career-related internships or fieldwork, Federal Work-Study, institutionally sponsored loans, scholarships/grants, and traineeships also available. Support available to part-time students. Financial award application deadline: 5/1; financial award applicants required to submit FAFSA. *Faculty research:* Creole studies, modernism, digital humanities, library studies, John Donne. *Total annual research expenditures:* $59,686. *Unit head:* Dr. David Hanson, Department Head, 985-549-2100, Fax: 985-549-5021, E-mail: dhanson@selu.edu. *Application contact:* Sandra Meyers, Graduate Admissions Analyst, 985-549-5620, Fax: 985-549-5632, E-mail: admissions@selu.edu. Web site: http://www.selu.edu/acad_research/depts/engl.

Southeastern Oklahoma State University, School of Education, Durant, OK 74701-0609. Offers math specialist (M Ed); reading specialist (M Ed); school administration (M Ed); school counseling (M Ed); special education (M Ed). *Accreditation:* NCATE. Part-time and evening/weekend programs available. *Faculty:* 52 full-time (19 women), 1 (woman) part-time/adjunct. *Students:* 15 full-time (11 women), 54 part-time (40 women); includes 24 minority (2 Black or African American, non-Hispanic/Latino; 16 American Indian or Alaska Native, non-Hispanic/Latino; 6 Hispanic/Latino). Average age 34. 31 applicants, 94% accepted, 29 enrolled. *Degree requirements:* For master's, comprehensive exam, thesis optional, portfolio (M Ed). *Entrance requirements:* For master's, GRE General Test (MBS), minimum GPA of 3.0 in last 60 hours or 2.75 overall. Additional exam requirements/recommendations for international students: Required—TOEFL (minimum score 550 paper-based; 213 computer-based; 79 iBT). *Application deadline:* For fall admission, 8/1 for domestic students, 6/1 for international students; for spring admission, 1/5 for domestic students, 11/1 for international students. Application fee: $20 ($55 for international students). Electronic applications accepted. *Expenses:* Tuition, state resident: full-time $3537; part-time $173.95 per credit hour. Tuition, nonresident: full-time $8673; part-time $459.30 per credit hour. *Required fees:* $22.55 per credit hour. *Financial support:* In 2011–12, 1 teaching assistantship with full tuition reimbursement (averaging $5,000 per year) was awarded; Federal Work-Study, institutionally sponsored loans, and tuition waivers (partial) also available. Support available to part-time students. Financial award application deadline: 6/15; financial award applicants required to submit FAFSA. *Unit head:* Dr. John Love, M Ed Coordinator, 580-745-2226, Fax: 580-745-7508, E-mail: jlove@se.edu. *Application contact:* Carrie Williamson, Graduate Secretary, 580-745-2220, Fax: 580-745-7474, E-mail: cwilliamson@se.edu. Web site: http://www.se.edu/graduate-programs/master-of-education/.

Southern Adventist University, School of Education and Psychology, Collegedale, TN 37315-0370. Offers clinical mental health counseling (MS); inclusive education (MS Ed); instructional leadership (MS Ed); literacy education (MS Ed); outdoor teacher education (MS Ed); school counseling (MS). *Accreditation:* NCATE. Part-time and evening/weekend programs available. *Degree requirements:* For master's, comprehensive exam (for some programs), thesis optional, position paper (MS), portfolio (MS Ed in outdoor teacher education). *Entrance requirements:* For master's, interview (MS); 9 semester hours of upper division course work in psychology or related field, including 1 course in psychology research or statistics; 9 semester hours of education (MS Ed). Additional exam requirements/recommendations for international students: Required—TOEFL (minimum score 600 paper-based; 250 computer-based; 100 iBT). Electronic applications accepted.

Southern Arkansas University–Magnolia, Graduate Programs, Magnolia, AR 71754. Offers agriculture (MS); business administration (MBA); computer and information sciences (MS); education (M Ed), including counseling and development, curriculum and instruction, educational administration and supervision, elementary education, middle level, reading, secondary education, TESOL; kinesiology (M Ed); library media and information specialist (M Ed); mental health and clinical counseling (MS); public administration (MPA); school counseling (M Ed); teaching (MAT). *Accreditation:* NCATE. Part-time and evening/weekend programs available. Postbaccalaureate distance learning degree programs offered. *Faculty:* 34 full-time (15 women), 8 part-time/adjunct (5 women). *Students:* 87 full-time (62 women), 320 part-time (224 women); includes 116 minority (111 Black or African American, non-Hispanic/Latino; 2 American Indian or Alaska Native, non-Hispanic/Latino; 2 Asian, non-Hispanic/Latino; 1 Hispanic/Latino), 25 international. Average age 33. 201 applicants, 98% accepted, 156 enrolled. In 2011, 162 master's awarded. *Degree requirements:* For master's, comprehensive exam (for some programs), thesis optional. *Entrance requirements:* For master's, GRE, MAT or GMAT, minimum GPA of 2.5. Additional exam requirements/recommendations for international students: Required—TOEFL (minimum score 173 computer-based). *Application deadline:* For fall admission, 7/15 for domestic and international students; for winter admission, 12/1 for domestic and international students; for spring admission, 12/1 for domestic and international students. Applications are processed on a rolling basis. Application fee: $25 ($35 for international students). Electronic applications accepted. *Expenses:* Tuition, state resident: part-time $232 per credit. Tuition, nonresident: part-time $339 per credit. *Required fees:* $44 per credit. Part-time tuition and fees vary according to course load. *Financial support:* Career-related internships or fieldwork, Federal Work-Study, scholarships/grants, tuition waivers (full), and unspecified assistantships available. Financial award applicants required to submit FAFSA. *Faculty research:* Alternative certification for teachers, supervision of instruction, instructional leadership, counseling. *Unit head:* Dr. Kim Bloss, Dean, School of Graduate Studies, 870-235-4150, Fax: 870-235-5227, E-mail: kkbloss@saumag.edu. *Application contact:* Gaye Calhoun, Admissions Specialist, 870-235-4150, Fax: 870-235-5227, E-mail: glcalhoun@saumag.edu. Web site: http://www.saumag.edu/graduate.

Southern Connecticut State University, School of Graduate Studies, School of Education, Program in Reading, New Haven, CT 06515-1355. Offers MS, Diploma. Part-time and evening/weekend programs available. *Faculty:* 2 full-time (both women), 1 (woman) part-time/adjunct. *Students:* 20 full-time (19 women), 103 part-time (96 women); includes 5 minority (3 Asian, non-Hispanic/Latino; 2 Hispanic/Latino). 160 applicants, 21% accepted, 29 enrolled. In 2011, 23 master's, 15 other advanced degrees awarded. *Degree requirements:* For master's, thesis or alternative. *Entrance requirements:* For master's, interview, teaching certificate; for Diploma, master's degree. *Application deadline:* For fall admission, 7/15 priority date for domestic students. Applications are processed on a rolling basis. Application fee: $50. Electronic applications accepted. *Expenses:* Tuition, state resident: full-time $5137; part-time $413 per credit. *Required fees:* $4008; $55 per term. *Financial support:* Application deadline: 4/15; applicants required to submit FAFSA. *Unit head:* Dr. Deborah Newton, Chairperson, 203-392-5941, Fax: 203-392-5927, E-mail: newtond2@southernct.edu. *Application contact:* Dr. Nancy Boyles, Graduate Coordinator, 203-392-5946, E-mail: boylesn1@southernct.edu.

Southern Illinois University Edwardsville, Graduate School, School of Education, Department of Curriculum and Instruction, Program in Literacy Education, Edwardsville, IL 62026-0001. Offers MS Ed. Part-time programs available. *Students:* 52 part-time (50 women); includes 3 minority (2 Black or African American, non-Hispanic/Latino; 1 Hispanic/Latino). 14 applicants, 64% accepted. In 2011, 5 master's awarded. *Degree requirements:* For master's, comprehensive exam, research paper. *Entrance requirements:* Additional exam requirements/recommendations for international students: Required—TOEFL (minimum score 550 paper-based; 213 computer-based; 79 iBT), IELTS (minimum score 6.5). *Application deadline:* For fall admission, 7/22 for domestic students, 6/1 for international students; for spring admission, 12/9 for domestic students, 10/1 for international students. Applications are processed on a rolling basis. Application fee: $30. Electronic applications accepted. Tuition and fees vary according to course load and program. *Financial support:* Fellowships, research assistantships, teaching assistantships, institutionally sponsored loans, scholarships/grants, and unspecified assistantships available. Support available to part-time students. Financial award application deadline: 3/1; financial award applicants required to submit FAFSA. *Unit head:* Dr. Stephanie McAndrews, Director, 618-650-3426, E-mail: smcandr@siue.edu. *Application contact:* Dr. Michelle Robinson, Coordinator of Graduate Recruitment, 618-650-2811, Fax: 618-650-3523, E-mail: michero@siue.edu. Web site: http://www.siue.edu/education/ci/.

Southern Illinois University Edwardsville, Graduate School, School of Education, Department of Curriculum and Instruction, Program in Literacy Specialist, Edwardsville, IL 62026. Offers Post-Master's Certificate. Part-time programs available. *Students:* 5 part-time (all women). 1 applicant, 100% accepted. In 2011, 1 Post-Master's Certificate awarded. *Entrance requirements:* Additional exam requirements/recommendations for international students: Required—TOEFL (minimum score 550 paper-based; 213 computer-based; 79 iBT), IELTS (minimum score 6.5). *Application deadline:* For fall admission, 7/22 for domestic students, 6/1 for international students; for spring admission, 12/9 for domestic students, 10/1 for international students. Applications are processed on a rolling basis. Application fee: $30. Electronic applications accepted. Tuition and fees vary according to course load and program. *Financial support:* Fellowships with full tuition reimbursements, research assistantships with full tuition reimbursements, teaching assistantships with full tuition reimbursements, institutionally sponsored loans, scholarships/grants, and unspecified assistantships available. Financial award application deadline: 3/1; financial award applicants required to submit FAFSA. *Unit head:* Dr. Stephanie McAndrews, Director, 618-650-3426, E-mail: smcandr@siue.edu. *Application contact:* Dr. Michelle Robinson, Coordinator of Graduate Recruitment, 618-650-2811, Fax: 618-650-3523, E-mail: michero@siue.edu. Web site: http://www.siue.edu/education/ci/.

Southern Oregon University, Graduate Studies, School of Education, Ashland, OR 97520. Offers elementary education (MA Ed, MS Ed), including classroom teacher, early childhood, handicapped learner, reading, supervision; secondary education (MA Ed, MS Ed), including classroom teacher, handicapped learner, reading, supervision; teaching (MAT). *Faculty:* 18 full-time (10 women), 10 part-time/adjunct (all women). *Students:* 128 full-time (88 women), 145 part-time (103 women); includes 32 minority (1 Black or African American, non-Hispanic/Latino; 3 American Indian or Alaska Native, non-Hispanic/Latino; 5 Asian, non-Hispanic/Latino; 13 Hispanic/Latino; 3 Native Hawaiian or other Pacific Islander, non-Hispanic/Latino; 7 Two or more races, non-Hispanic/Latino), 1 international. Average age 35. 48 applicants, 60% accepted, 23 enrolled. In 2011, 102 degrees awarded. *Degree requirements:* For master's, thesis optional. *Entrance requirements:* For master's, GRE General Test, minimum GPA of 3.0. *Application deadline:* For fall admission, 2/1 for domestic students. Application fee: $50. Electronic applications accepted. *Expenses:* Tuition, state resident: full-time $12,600; part-time $350 per credit. Tuition, nonresident: full-time $16,200; part-time $450 per credit. *Required fees:* $1590. *Financial support:* Research assistantships with partial tuition reimbursements available. *Unit head:* Dr. Geoff Mills, Dean, 541-552-6920, E-mail: mills@sou.edu. *Application contact:* Mark Bottorff, Director of Admissions, 541-552-6411, Fax: 541-552-8403, E-mail: admissions@sou.edu. Web site: http://www.sou.edu/education/.

Southwestern Adventist University, Education Department, Keene, TX 76059. Offers curriculum and instruction with reading emphasis (M Ed); educational leadership (M Ed). Part-time and evening/weekend programs available. *Degree requirements:* For master's, thesis or alternative, professional paper. *Entrance requirements:* For master's, GRE General Test.

Southwest Minnesota State University, Department of Education, Marshall, MN 56258. Offers ESL (MS); math (MS); reading (MS); special education (MS), including developmental disabilities, early childhood education, emotional behavioral disorders, learning disabilities; teaching, learning and leadership (MS). Part-time and evening/weekend programs available. Postbaccalaureate distance learning degree programs offered (no on-campus study). *Entrance requirements:* Additional exam requirements/recommendations for international students: Required—TOEFL or IELTS; Recommended—TOEFL (minimum score 550 paper-based; 213 computer-based; 80 iBT), IELTS.

Spring Arbor University, School of Education, Spring Arbor, MI 49283-9799. Offers education (MAE); reading (MAR); special education (MSE). Part-time and evening/weekend programs available. Postbaccalaureate distance learning degree programs offered (minimal on-campus study). *Faculty:* 6 full-time (5 women), 13 part-time/adjunct (8 women). *Students:* 43 full-time (33 women), 188 part-time (158 women); includes 13 minority (10 Black or African American, non-Hispanic/Latino; 1 Asian, non-Hispanic/Latino; 2 Hispanic/Latino). Average age 36. In 2011, 54 master's awarded. *Degree requirements:* For master's, thesis. *Entrance requirements:* For master's, official transcripts from all institutions attended, including evidence of an earned bachelor's degree from regionally-accredited college or university with minimum cumulative GPA of 3.0 for the last two years of the bachelor's degree; two professional letters of recommendation. Additional exam requirements/recommendations for international students: Required—TOEFL (minimum score 600 paper-based; 220 computer-based). *Application deadline:* For fall admission, 9/1 priority date for domestic students; for winter admission, 2/1 priority date for domestic students; for spring admission, 2/1 priority date for domestic students. Applications are processed on a rolling basis. Application fee: $40. Electronic applications accepted. *Expenses:* *Tuition:* Full-time $5500; part-time $490 per credit hour. *Required fees:* $240; $120 per term. Tuition and fees vary according to program. *Financial support:* Applicants required to submit FAFSA. *Unit head:* Dr. Linda Sherrill, Dean, 517-750-1200 Ext. 1562, Fax: 517-750-6629, E-mail: lsherril@arbor.edu. *Application contact:* James R. Weidman, Coordinator of Graduate Recruitment, 517-750-6523, Fax: 517-750-6629, E-mail: jimw@arbor.edu. Web site: http://www.arbor.edu/Master-Arts-Education/Graduate/index.aspx.

State University of New York at Binghamton, Graduate School, School of Education, Program in Literacy Education, Binghamton, NY 13902-6000. Offers MS Ed. *Accreditation:* Teacher Education Accreditation Council. Part-time and evening/weekend programs available. *Students:* 20 full-time (all women), 33 part-time (30 women). Average age 27. 32 applicants, 88% accepted, 19 enrolled. In 2011, 30 master's awarded. *Entrance requirements:* For master's, GRE General Test. Additional exam requirements/recommendations for international students: Required—TOEFL (minimum score 550 paper-based; 213 computer-based; 80 iBT). *Application deadline:* For fall admission, 2/1 priority date for domestic students, 2/1 for international students; for spring admission, 10/15 priority date for domestic students, 10/15 for international students. Applications are processed on a rolling basis. Application fee: $60. Electronic applications accepted. *Financial support:* In 2011–12, 6 students received support, including 1 fellowship with full tuition reimbursement available (averaging $5,000 per year); research assistantships, career-related internships or fieldwork, Federal Work-Study, institutionally sponsored loans, scholarships/grants, health care benefits, tuition waivers, and unspecified assistantships also available. Financial award application deadline: 2/15; financial award applicants required to submit FAFSA. *Unit head:* Dr. S. G. Grant, Dean of School of Education, 607-777-7329, E-mail: sggrant@binghamton.edu. *Application contact:* Catherine Smith, Recruiting and Admissions Coordinator, 607-777-2151, Fax: 607-777-2501, E-mail: cmsmith@binghamton.edu.

State University of New York at Fredonia, Graduate Studies, College of Education, Program in Literacy, Fredonia, NY 14063-1136. Offers MS Ed. *Accreditation:* NCATE. Part-time and evening/weekend programs available. *Degree requirements:* For master's, thesis optional. *Expenses:* Tuition, state resident: full-time $6666; part-time $370 per credit hour. Tuition, nonresident: full-time $11,376; part-time $632 per credit hour. *Required fees:* $1059.30; $58.85 per credit hour. Tuition and fees vary according to course load.

State University of New York at New Paltz, Graduate School, School of Education, Department of Educational Studies, Program in Special Education, New Paltz, NY 12561. Offers adolescence (7-12) (MS Ed); adolescence special education and literacy education (MS Ed); childhood (1-6) (MS Ed); childhood special education and literacy education (MS Ed); early childhood (B-2) (MS Ed). *Accreditation:* NCATE. Part-time and evening/weekend programs available. *Faculty:* 6 full-time (4 women), 4 part-time/adjunct (all women). *Students:* 36 full-time (33 women), 54 part-time (44 women); includes 8 minority (5 Black or African American, non-Hispanic/Latino; 2 Asian, non-Hispanic/Latino; 1 Native Hawaiian or other Pacific Islander, non-Hispanic/Latino). Average age 29. 67 applicants, 73% accepted, 40 enrolled. In 2011, 44 master's awarded. *Degree requirements:* For master's, portfolio. *Entrance requirements:* For master's, minimum GPA of 3.0 (3.2 for special education and literacy programs), New York state teaching certificate. Additional exam requirements/recommendations for international students: Required—TOEFL (minimum score 550 paper-based; 213 computer-based; 80 iBT), IELTS (minimum score 6.5). *Application deadline:* For fall admission, 3/15 priority date for domestic students, 3/15 for international students; for spring admission, 11/1 for domestic and international students. Application fee: $50. Electronic applications accepted. *Expenses:* Tuition, state resident: full-time $8870; part-time $370 per credit. Tuition, nonresident: full-time $15,160; part-time $632 per credit. *Required fees:* $1188; $34 per credit. $184 per semester. *Financial support:* In 2011–12, 2 students received support, including 2 fellowships (averaging $3,750 per year); career-related internships or fieldwork, Federal Work-Study, institutionally sponsored loans, and tuition waivers (full) also available. Financial award application deadline: 8/1; financial award applicants required to submit FAFSA. *Unit head:* Dr. Spencer Salend, Coordinator, 845-257-2831, E-mail: salends@newpaltz.edu. *Application contact:* Dr. Catherine Whittaker, Coordinator, 845-257-2831, E-mail: whittakc@newpaltz.edu.

State University of New York at New Paltz, Graduate School, School of Education, Department of Elementary Education, New Paltz, NY 12561. Offers childhood education (1-6) (MS Ed, MST); literacy education (5-12) (MS Ed); literacy education (B-6) (MS Ed); literacy education and adolescence special education (MS Ed); literacy education and childhood education and childhood special education (MS Ed). *Accreditation:* NCATE. Part-time and evening/weekend programs available. *Faculty:* 9 full-time (8 women), 6 part-time/adjunct (5 women). *Students:* 66 full-time (61 women), 129 part-time (115 women); includes 14 minority (3 Black or African American, non-Hispanic/Latino; 1 Asian, non-Hispanic/Latino; 7 Hispanic/Latino; 3 Two or more races, non-Hispanic/Latino). Average age 28. 121 applicants, 64% accepted, 66 enrolled. In 2011, 95 master's awarded. *Degree requirements:* For master's, comprehensive exam (for some programs), portfolio. *Entrance requirements:* For master's, GRE and MAT (MST), minimum GPA of 3.0 (3.2 for literacy and special education), New York state teaching certificate (MS Ed). Additional exam requirements/recommendations for international students: Required—TOEFL (minimum score 550 paper-based; 213 computer-based; 80 iBT), IELTS (minimum score 6.5). *Application deadline:* For fall admission, 4/1 for domestic and international students; for spring admission, 11/15 for domestic and international students. Application fee: $50. Electronic applications accepted. *Expenses:* Tuition, state resident: full-time $8870; part-time $370 per credit. Tuition, nonresident: full-time $15,160; part-time $632 per credit. *Required fees:* $1188; $34 per credit. $184 per semester. *Financial support:* In 2011–12, 1 fellowship (averaging $5,000 per year) was awarded; Federal Work-Study and institutionally sponsored loans also available. Financial award application deadline: 8/1; financial award applicants required to submit FAFSA. *Faculty research:* Multi-sensory teaching methods, volunteer tutoring programs for struggling readers, school readiness and transition, math/science/technology, university-school partnerships. *Unit head:* Dr. Andrea Noel, Chair, 845-257-2860, E-mail: noela@newpaltz.edu. *Application contact:* Caroline Murphy, Graduate Admissions Advisor, 845-257-3285, Fax: 845-257-3284, E-mail: gradschool@newpaltz.edu. Web site: http://www.newpaltz.edu/elementaryed/.

State University of New York at Oswego, Graduate Studies, School of Education, Department of Curriculum and Instruction, Oswego, NY 13126. Offers adolescence education (MST); art education (MAT); childhood education (MST); elementary education (MS Ed); literacy education (MS Ed); secondary education (MS Ed); special education (MS Ed). Part-time and evening/weekend programs available. *Degree requirements:* For master's, comprehensive exam (for some programs), thesis optional. *Entrance requirements:* For master's, GRE General Test, minimum GPA of 2.7, provisional teaching certificate. Additional exam requirements/recommendations for international students: Required—TOEFL (minimum score 560 paper-based; 220 computer-based). *Faculty research:* Classroom applications for microcomputers; classroom questioning, wait-time, and achievement; values clarification and academic achievement.

Reading Education

State University of New York at Plattsburgh, Division of Education, Health, and Human Services, Program in Teacher Education: Literacy Education, Plattsburgh, NY 12901-2681. Offers birth-grade 6 (MS Ed); grades 5-12 (MS Ed). *Accreditation:* Teacher Education Accreditation Council. Part-time and evening/weekend programs available. *Students:* 15 full-time (14 women), 1 (woman) part-time. Average age 25. *Entrance requirements:* For master's, minimum GPA of 2.75. Additional exam requirements/recommendations for international students: Required—TOEFL. *Application deadline:* For fall admission, 2/15 priority date for domestic students; for spring admission, 10/15 priority date for domestic students. Applications are processed on a rolling basis. Application fee: $75. *Financial support:* Federal Work-Study available. Support available to part-time students. Financial award application deadline: 4/15; financial award applicants required to submit FAFSA. *Faculty research:* Reading pedagogy, early childhood literacy, children's literature, integrated language arts. *Unit head:* Dr. Heidi Schnackenberg, Coordinator, 518-564-5143, E-mail: schnachl@plattsburgh.edu. *Application contact:* Marguerite Adelman, Assistant Director, Graduate Admissions, 518-564-4723, Fax: 518-564-4722, E-mail: adelmaml@plattsburgh.edu.

State University of New York College at Cortland, Graduate Studies, School of Education, Program in Literacy, Cortland, NY 13045. Offers MS Ed. *Accreditation:* NCATE. Part-time and evening/weekend programs available. *Degree requirements:* For master's, one foreign language, comprehensive exam, thesis (for some programs). *Entrance requirements:* Additional exam requirements/recommendations for international students: Required—TOEFL.

State University of New York College at Geneseo, Graduate Studies, School of Education, Program in Reading, Geneseo, NY 14454-1401. Offers MS Ed. Part-time and evening/weekend programs available. *Degree requirements:* For master's, reading clinics, action research project.

State University of New York College at Oneonta, Graduate Education, Division of Education, Department of Elementary Education and Reading, Oneonta, NY 13820-4015. Offers childhood education (MS Ed); literacy education (MS Ed). *Accreditation:* NCATE. Part-time and evening/weekend programs available. *Entrance requirements:* For master's, GRE General Test.

State University of New York College at Potsdam, School of Education and Professional Studies, Program in Literacy, Potsdam, NY 13676. Offers literacy educator (MS Ed); literacy specialist (MS Ed), including birth-grade 6, grades 5-12. *Accreditation:* NCATE. Part-time programs available. Postbaccalaureate distance learning degree programs offered (minimal on-campus study). *Faculty:* 5 full-time (3 women), 9 part-time/adjunct (all women). *Students:* 56 full-time (55 women), 23 part-time (17 women); includes 2 minority (1 American Indian or Alaska Native, non-Hispanic/Latino; 1 Hispanic/Latino), 1 international. 49 applicants, 100% accepted, 45 enrolled. In 2011, 71 master's awarded. *Entrance requirements:* For master's, minimum GPA of 2.75 in last 60 hours of course work. Additional exam requirements/recommendations for international students: Required—TOEFL (minimum score 550 paper-based; 213 computer-based; 80 iBT), IELTS (minimum score 6). *Application deadline:* For fall admission, 4/1 for domestic and international students; for winter admission, 10/15 for domestic and international students; for spring admission, 3/1 for domestic and international students. Applications are processed on a rolling basis. Application fee: $50. *Expenses:* Tuition, state resident: full-time $8870; part-time $370 per credit hour. Tuition, nonresident: full-time $15,160; part-time $632 per credit hour. *Required fees:* $1066; $44.10 per credit hour. One-time fee: $3. *Financial support:* In 2011–12, 2 students received support. Fellowships, teaching assistantships with full tuition reimbursements available, career-related internships or fieldwork, Federal Work-Study, scholarships/grants, and unspecified assistantships available. Support available to part-time students. Financial award application deadline: 3/1; financial award applicants required to submit FAFSA. *Unit head:* Kathryn Jeror, Chairperson, 315-267-2535, Fax: 315-267-4802, E-mail: jerorkm@potsdam.edu. *Application contact:* Peter Cutler, Graduate Admissions Counselor, 315-267-2165, Fax: 315-267-4802, E-mail: graduate@potsdam.edu. Web site: http://www.potsdam.edu/academics/SOEPS/Literacy/index.cfm.

Stetson University, College of Arts and Sciences, Division of Education, Department of Teacher Education, Program in Reading Education, DeLand, FL 32723. Offers M Ed. *Students:* 25 full-time (23 women), 3 part-time (all women); includes 4 minority (2 Black or African American, non-Hispanic/Latino; 2 Hispanic/Latino). Average age 38. In 2011, 32 master's awarded. *Unit head:* Dr. Gail Choice, Coordinator, 386-822-7075. *Application contact:* Diana Belian, Office of Graduate Studies, 386-822-7075, Fax: 386-822-7388, E-mail: dbelian@stetson.edu.

Sul Ross State University, Rio Grande College of Sul Ross State University, Alpine, TX 79832. Offers business administration (MBA); teacher education (M Ed), including bilingual education, counseling, educational diagnostics, elementary education, general education, reading, school administration, secondary education. Part-time and evening/weekend programs available. Postbaccalaureate distance learning degree programs offered (no on-campus study). *Faculty:* 11 full-time (3 women), 4 part-time/adjunct (3 women). *Students:* 45 full-time (36 women), 255 part-time (168 women); includes 218 minority (2 Black or African American, non-Hispanic/Latino; 1 American Indian or Alaska Native, non-Hispanic/Latino; 215 Hispanic/Latino), 1 international. Average age 36. In 2011, 47 master's awarded. *Degree requirements:* For master's, comprehensive exam, thesis optional, minimum GPA of 3.0. *Entrance requirements:* For master's, GMAT or GRE General Test, minimum GPA of 2.5 in last 60 hours of undergraduate work. Additional exam requirements/recommendations for international students: Required—TOEFL. *Application deadline:* Applications are processed on a rolling basis. Application fee: $0 ($50 for international students). *Financial support:* Career-related internships or fieldwork, Federal Work-Study, and institutionally sponsored loans available. Support available to part-time students. Financial award application deadline: 5/1; financial award applicants required to submit FAFSA. *Unit head:* Dr. Paul Sorrels, Associate Provost/Dean, 512-278-3339, Fax: 512-278-3330. *Application contact:* Claudia R. Wright, Director of Admissions and Records, 915-837-8050, Fax: 915-837-8431, E-mail: rcullins@sulross.edu.

Sul Ross State University, School of Professional Studies, Department of Teacher Education, Program in Reading Specialist, Alpine, TX 79832. Offers M Ed. Part-time and evening/weekend programs available. *Degree requirements:* For master's, thesis optional. *Entrance requirements:* For master's, GMAT or GRE General Test, minimum GPA of 2.5 in last 60 hours of undergraduate work.

Syracuse University, School of Education, Program in Literacy Education, Syracuse, NY 13244. Offers PhD. Part-time programs available. *Students:* 3 full-time (all women), 7 part-time (all women). Average age 40. 2 applicants, 100% accepted, 1 enrolled. In 2011, 1 degree awarded. *Degree requirements:* For doctorate, thesis/dissertation. *Entrance requirements:* For doctorate, GRE, master's degree. Additional exam requirements/recommendations for international students: Required—TOEFL (minimum score 100 iBT). *Application deadline:* For fall admission, 2/1 priority date for domestic students, 2/1 for international students; for spring admission, 10/15 priority date for domestic students, 10/15 for international students. Applications are processed on a rolling basis. Application fee: $75. Electronic applications accepted. *Expenses: Tuition:* Part-time $1206 per credit. *Financial support:* Fellowships with full tuition reimbursements, research assistantships with full and partial tuition reimbursements, and teaching assistantships with full and partial tuition reimbursements available. Financial award application deadline: 1/1. *Unit head:* Dr. Kathleen Hinchman, Graduate Chair, 315-443-4757, E-mail: kahinchm@syr.edu. *Application contact:* Laurie Deyo, Graduate Recruiter, School of Education, 315-443-2505, E-mail: e-gradrcrt@syr.edu. Web site: http://soeweb.syr.edu/.

Syracuse University, School of Education, Program in Literacy Education: Birth-Grade 6, Syracuse, NY 13244. Offers MS. Part-time programs available. *Students:* 6 full-time (all women), 1 (woman) part-time. Average age 22. 15 applicants, 87% accepted, 4 enrolled. In 2011, 13 degrees awarded. *Degree requirements:* For master's, thesis or alternative. *Entrance requirements:* For master's, New York state teacher certification or eligibility for certification. Additional exam requirements/recommendations for international students: Required—TOEFL (minimum score 100 iBT). *Application deadline:* For fall admission, 2/1 priority date for domestic students, 2/1 for international students; for spring admission, 10/15 for domestic and international students. Applications are processed on a rolling basis. Application fee: $75. Electronic applications accepted. *Expenses: Tuition:* Part-time $1206 per credit. *Financial support:* Fellowships with full tuition reimbursements and teaching assistantships with full and partial tuition reimbursements available. Financial award application deadline: 1/1; financial award applicants required to submit FAFSA. *Faculty research:* Literacy, knowledge modeling, assessment, teaching of literature, writing. *Unit head:* Dr. Rachel Brown, Program Coordinator, 315-443-4755, E-mail: rfbrown@syr.edu. *Application contact:* Laurie Deyo, Graduate Recruiter, School of Education, 315-443-2505, E-mail: e-gradrcrt@syr.edu. Web site: http://soeweb.syr.edu/.

Syracuse University, School of Education, Program in Literacy Education: Grades 5-12, Syracuse, NY 13244. Offers MS. Part-time programs available. *Students:* 7 full-time (6 women), 5 part-time (4 women); includes 2 minority (1 Black or African American, non-Hispanic/Latino; 1 Native Hawaiian or other Pacific Islander, non-Hispanic/Latino). Average age 25. 8 applicants, 100% accepted, 6 enrolled. In 2011, 6 degrees awarded. *Entrance requirements:* For master's, New York state teacher certification or eligibility. Additional exam requirements/recommendations for international students: Required—TOEFL (minimum score 100 iBT). *Application deadline:* For fall admission, 2/1 priority date for domestic students, 2/1 for international students. Application fee: $75. Electronic applications accepted. *Expenses: Tuition:* Part-time $1206 per credit. *Financial support:* Fellowships with full tuition reimbursements and teaching assistantships with full and partial tuition reimbursements available. Financial award application deadline: 1/1. *Unit head:* Dr. Rachel Brown, Program Coordinator, 315-443-4755, E-mail: rfbrown@syr.edu. *Application contact:* Laurie Deyo, Graduate Recruiter, School of Education, 315-443-2505, E-mail: e-gradrcrt@syr.edu. Web site: http://soeweb.syr.edu/academic/reading_language_arts/graduate/masters/literacy_ed_5_12/default.aspx.

Teachers College, Columbia University, Graduate Faculty of Education, Department of Curriculum and Teaching, Program in Literacy Specialist, New York, NY 10027-6696. Offers MA. *Faculty:* 2 full-time (both women), 2 part-time/adjunct (both women). *Students:* 30 full-time (27 women), 55 part-time (51 women); includes 22 minority (3 Black or African American, non-Hispanic/Latino; 11 Asian, non-Hispanic/Latino; 8 Hispanic/Latino), 2 international. Average age 27. 71 applicants, 83% accepted, 15 enrolled. In 2011, 49 master's awarded. *Application deadline:* For fall admission, 1/15 priority date for domestic students; for spring admission, 11/1 for domestic students. Application fee: $65. Electronic applications accepted. *Financial support:* Applicants required to submit FAFSA. *Faculty research:* Teaching of reading and writing, staff development and school reform, reading in mathematics classrooms, cultural and critical perspectives on literacy education, literacy and the arts. *Unit head:* Prof. Lucy Calkins, Program Coordinator, 212-678-3931. *Application contact:* Elizabeth Puleio, Assistant Director of Admission, 212-678-3730, E-mail: eap2136@tc.columbia.edu.

Teachers College, Columbia University, Graduate Faculty of Education, Department of Health and Behavioral Studies, Program in Reading Specialist, New York, NY 10027. Offers MA. *Faculty:* 1 (woman) full-time, 5 part-time/adjunct (all women). *Students:* 2 full-time (both women), 62 part-time (61 women); includes 10 minority (1 Black or African American, non-Hispanic/Latino; 4 Asian, non-Hispanic/Latino; 3 Hispanic/Latino; 2 Two or more races, non-Hispanic/Latino), 1 international. Average age 30. 28 applicants, 96% accepted, 19 enrolled. In 2011, 23 master's awarded. *Degree requirements:* For master's, integrative project. *Application deadline:* For fall admission, 1/15 priority date for domestic students; for spring admission, 11/1 for domestic students. Application fee: $65. Electronic applications accepted. *Financial support:* Application deadline: 2/1; applicants required to submit FAFSA. *Faculty research:* Reading and writing processes in children and adults, adult education and workplace literacy, early childhood education and mental health, learning disabilities. *Unit head:* Prof. Dolores Perin, Program Coordinator, 212-678-3942, E-mail: perin@tc.edu. *Application contact:* Peter Shon, Assistant Director of Admission, 212-678-3305, Fax: 212-678-4171, E-mail: shon@exchange.tc.columbia.edu. Web site: http://www.tc.edu/hbs/reading-specialist/.

Temple University, College of Education, Department of Curriculum, Instruction, and Technology in Education, Philadelphia, PA 19122-6096. Offers applied behavioral analysis (MS Ed); career and technical education (MS Ed); early childhood education and elementary education (MS Ed); English education (MS Ed); language arts education (Ed D); math/science education (Ed D); mathematics education (MS Ed); science education (MS Ed); second and foreign language education (MS Ed); special education (MS Ed); teaching English as a second language (MS Ed). Part-time and evening/weekend programs available. *Faculty:* 19 full-time (12 women). *Students:* 30 full-time (23 women), 86 part-time (69 women); includes 12 minority (4 Black or African American, non-Hispanic/Latino; 2 Asian, non-Hispanic/Latino; 5 Hispanic/Latino; 1 Two or more races, non-Hispanic/Latino), 5 international. 82 applicants, 71% accepted, 51 enrolled. In 2011, 181 master's, 16 doctorates awarded. Terminal master's awarded for partial completion of doctoral program. *Degree requirements:* For master's, thesis or alternative; for doctorate, thesis/dissertation. *Entrance requirements:* For master's and doctorate, GRE General Test or MAT, minimum GPA of 3.0. Additional exam requirements/recommendations for international students: Required—TOEFL (minimum score 550 paper-based; 213 computer-based; 79 iBT). *Application deadline:* For fall admission, 4/1 for domestic students, 12/15 for international students; for spring admission, 10/1 for domestic students, 8/1 for international students. Application fee: $50. Electronic applications accepted. *Expenses:* Tuition, state resident: full-time $12,366; part-time $687 per credit hour. Tuition, nonresident: full-time $17,298; part-time $961 per credit hour. *Required fees:* $590; $213 per year. *Financial support:* Fellowships, research assistantships with full tuition reimbursements, and teaching assistantships with full tuition reimbursements available. Financial award application deadline: 1/15; financial award applicants required to submit FAFSA. *Faculty research:* School improvement, problem-solving, literacy, language development. *Unit head:* Dr. Michael W. Smith, Chair, 215-204-6387, Fax: 215-204-1414, E-mail: mwsmith@temple.edu. *Application contact:* Dr. Margo Greicar, Director for Graduate Academic and Student Affairs, 215-204-8011, Fax: 215-204-4383, E-mail: margo.greicar@temple.edu. Web site: http://www.temple.edu/education/cite/.

Tennessee Technological University, Graduate School, College of Education, Department of Curriculum and Instruction, Program in Exceptional Learning, Cookeville,

TN 38505. Offers applied behavior and learning (PhD); literacy (PhD); program planning and evaluation (PhD); STEM education (PhD). Part-time and evening/weekend programs available. *Students:* 11 full-time (7 women), 12 part-time (9 women); includes 2 minority (both Black or African American, non-Hispanic/Latino), 1 international. 18 applicants, 50% accepted, 8 enrolled. In 2011, 7 doctorates awarded. *Degree requirements:* For doctorate, comprehensive exam, thesis/dissertation. *Entrance requirements:* For doctorate, GRE, minimum GPA of 3.0. Additional exam requirements/recommendations for international students: Required—TOEFL (minimum score 550 paper-based; 71 iBT), IELTS (minimum score 5.5), Pearson Test of English Academic. *Application deadline:* For fall admission, 8/1 for domestic students, 5/1 for international students; for spring admission, 12/1 for domestic students, 10/1 for international students. Application fee: $25 ($30 for international students). Electronic applications accepted. *Expenses:* Tuition, state resident: full-time $8094; part-time $422 per credit hour. Tuition, nonresident: full-time $20,574; part-time $1046 per credit hour. *Financial support:* In 2011–12, 4 fellowships (averaging $8,000 per year), 10 research assistantships (averaging $12,000 per year), 1 teaching assistantship (averaging $12,000 per year) were awarded. Financial award application deadline: 4/1. *Unit head:* Dr. Lisa Zagumny, Director, 931-372-3078, Fax: 931-372-3517, E-mail: lzagumny@tntech.edu. *Application contact:* Shelia K. Kendrick, Coordinator of Graduate Admissions, 931-372-3808, Fax: 931-372-3497, E-mail: skendrick@tntech.edu.

Tennessee Technological University, Graduate School, College of Education, Department of Curriculum and Instruction, Program in Reading, Cookeville, TN 38505. Offers MA, Ed S. *Accreditation:* NCATE. Part-time and evening/weekend programs available. *Faculty:* 2 full-time (both women). *Students:* 11 full-time (all women), 34 part-time (32 women); includes 1 minority (American Indian or Alaska Native, non-Hispanic/Latino). Average age 27. 8 applicants, 88% accepted, 7 enrolled. In 2011, 11 master's, 1 other advanced degree awarded. *Degree requirements:* For master's and Ed S, comprehensive exam, thesis or alternative. *Entrance requirements:* For master's and Ed S, MAT or GRE. Additional exam requirements/recommendations for international students: Required—TOEFL (minimum score 550 paper-based; 71 iBT), IELTS (minimum score 5.5), Pearson Test of English Academic. *Application deadline:* For fall admission, 8/1 for domestic students, 5/1 for international students; for spring admission, 12/1 for domestic students, 10/1 for international students. Application fee: $25 ($30 for international students). Electronic applications accepted. *Expenses:* Tuition, state resident: full-time $8094; part-time $422 per credit hour. Tuition, nonresident: full-time $20,574; part-time $1046 per credit hour. *Financial support:* In 2011–12, fellowships (averaging $8,000 per year), 4 teaching assistantships (averaging $4,000 per year) were awarded; research assistantships and career-related internships or fieldwork also available. Financial award application deadline: 4/1. *Unit head:* Dr. Susan Gore, Interim Chairperson, 931-372-3181, Fax: 931-372-6270, E-mail: sgore@tntech.edu. *Application contact:* Shelia K. Kendrick, Coordinator of Graduate Admissions, 931-372-3808, Fax: 931-372-3497, E-mail: skendrick@tntech.edu.

Texas A&M University, College of Education and Human Development, Department of Teaching, Learning, and Culture, College Station, TX 77843. Offers culture and curriculum (M Ed, MS); curriculum and instruction (PhD); English as a second language (M Ed, MS, PhD); mathematics education (M Ed, MS, PhD); reading and language arts education (M Ed, MS, PhD); science education (M Ed, MS, PhD); urban education (M Ed, MS, PhD). Part-time programs available. *Faculty:* 30. *Students:* 163 full-time (119 women), 226 part-time (185 women); includes 108 minority (56 Black or African American, non-Hispanic/Latino; 2 American Indian or Alaska Native, non-Hispanic/Latino; 6 Asian, non-Hispanic/Latino; 37 Hispanic/Latino; 7 Two or more races, non-Hispanic/Latino), 62 international. Average age 36. In 2011, 107 master's, 44 doctorates awarded. *Degree requirements:* For master's, comprehensive exam, thesis (for some programs); for doctorate, comprehensive exam, thesis/dissertation. *Entrance requirements:* For master's, GRE General Test, minimum GPA of 3.0; for doctorate, GRE General Test, 3 years of teaching experience. Additional exam requirements/recommendations for international students: Required—TOEFL (minimum score 550 paper-based; 213 computer-based). *Application deadline:* For fall admission, 1/15 priority date for domestic students, 1/15 for international students; for spring admission, 9/15 priority date for domestic students, 9/15 for international students. Applications are processed on a rolling basis. Application fee: $50 ($75 for international students). Electronic applications accepted. *Expenses:* Tuition, state resident: full-time $5437; part-time $226.55 per credit hour. Tuition, nonresident: full-time $12,949; part-time $539.55 per credit hour. *Required fees:* $2741. *Financial support:* In 2011–12, fellowships with partial tuition reimbursements (averaging $3,000 per year), teaching assistantships with partial tuition reimbursements (averaging $7,200 per year) were awarded; research assistantships with partial tuition reimbursements, career-related internships or fieldwork, Federal Work-Study, institutionally sponsored loans, scholarships/grants, tuition waivers (partial), and unspecified assistantships also available. Support available to part-time students. Financial award application deadline: 4/1; financial award applicants required to submit FAFSA. *Unit head:* Dr. Yeping Li, Head, 979-845-8384, Fax: 979-845-9663, E-mail: yepingli@tamu.edu. *Application contact:* Kerri Smith, Senior Academic Advisor II, 979-845-8382, Fax: 979-845-9663, E-mail: krsmith@tamu.edu. Web site: http://tlac.tamu.edu.

Texas A&M University–Commerce, Graduate School, College of Education and Human Services, Department of Curriculum and Instruction, Commerce, TX 75429-3011. Offers bilingual/ESL education (M Ed, MS); early childhood education (M Ed, MS); elementary education (M Ed, MS); reading (M Ed, MS); secondary education (M Ed, MS); supervision, curriculum and instruction: elementary education (Ed D). MS and M Ed programs in early childhood education offered jointly with Texas Woman's University and University of North Texas. Part-time programs available. Terminal master's awarded for partial completion of doctoral program. *Degree requirements:* For master's, comprehensive exam, thesis (for some programs); for doctorate, 2 foreign languages, thesis/dissertation, departmental qualifying exam. *Entrance requirements:* For master's and doctorate, GRE General Test. Electronic applications accepted. *Faculty research:* Literacy and learning, early childhood, preservice teacher education, technology.

Texas A&M University–Corpus Christi, Graduate Studies and Research, College of Education, Corpus Christi, TX 78412-5503. Offers counseling (MS, PhD), including counseling (MS), counselor education (PhD); curriculum and instruction (MS, Ed D); early childhood education (MS); educational administration (MS); educational leadership (Ed D); educational technology (MS); elementary education (MS); kinesiology (MS); reading (MS); secondary education (MS); special education (MS). Part-time and evening/weekend programs available. *Degree requirements:* For master's, comprehensive exam, thesis (for some programs); for doctorate, comprehensive exam, thesis/dissertation. *Entrance requirements:* For master's, GRE General Test. Additional exam requirements/recommendations for international students: Required—TOEFL. Electronic applications accepted.

Texas A&M University–Kingsville, College of Graduate Studies, College of Education, Department of Education, Program in Reading Specialization, Kingsville, TX 78363. Offers MS. Part-time and evening/weekend programs available. *Degree requirements:* For master's, comprehensive exam, mini-thesis. *Entrance requirements:* For master's, GRE General Test, MAT, minimum GPA of 3.0. *Faculty research:* Reading programs for preparing the handicapped, reading methods in elementary education, literature-based reading instruction.

Texas A&M University–San Antonio, Department of Curriculum and Kinesiology, San Antonio, TX 78224. Offers bilingual education (MA); early childhood education (M Ed); kinesiology (MS); reading (MS); special education (M Ed), including educational diagnostician, instructional specialist. Part-time and evening/weekend programs available. *Students:* 76 full-time (51 women), 240 part-time (180 women). Average age 37. *Degree requirements:* For master's, comprehensive exam, thesis or alternative. *Entrance requirements:* For master's, MAT. Additional exam requirements/recommendations for international students: Required—TOEFL (minimum score 550 paper-based; 213 computer-based; 80 iBT), IELTS (minimum score 6). *Application deadline:* For fall admission, 8/15 priority date for domestic students, 6/1 for international students; for spring admission, 12/15 priority date for domestic students, 10/1 for international students. Applications are processed on a rolling basis. Application fee: $35 ($50 for international students). Electronic applications accepted. *Expenses:* Tuition, state resident: part-time $691.11 per course. Tuition, nonresident: part-time $1621.11 per course. *Financial support:* Application deadline: 3/31; applicants required to submit FAFSA. *Unit head:* Dr. Samuel Garcia, Department Chair, 210-784-2505, E-mail: samuel.garcia@tamusa.tamus.edu. *Application contact:* Jennifer M. Dovalina, Graduate Admissions Specialist, 210-784-1380, E-mail: graduateadmissions@tamusa.tamus.edu. Web site: http://www.tamusa.tamus.edu/education/index.html.

Texas State University–San Marcos, Graduate School, College of Education, Department of Curriculum and Instruction, Program in Reading Education, San Marcos, TX 78666. Offers M Ed. Part-time and evening/weekend programs available. *Faculty:* 8 full-time (all women), 1 (woman) part-time/adjunct. *Students:* 2 full-time (both women), 32 part-time (all women); includes 8 minority (2 Black or African American, non-Hispanic/Latino; 1 American Indian or Alaska Native, non-Hispanic/Latino; 5 Hispanic/Latino). Average age 36. 11 applicants, 100% accepted, 11 enrolled. In 2011, 7 master's awarded. *Degree requirements:* For master's, comprehensive exam, thesis optional. *Entrance requirements:* For master's, minimum GPA of 2.75 in last 60 hours of course work, teaching experience. Additional exam requirements/recommendations for international students: Required—TOEFL (minimum score 550 paper-based; 213 computer-based; 78 iBT). *Application deadline:* For fall admission, 6/15 priority date for domestic students, 6/1 for international students; for spring admission, 10/15 priority date for domestic students, 10/1 for international students. Applications are processed on a rolling basis. Application fee: $40 ($90 for international students). Electronic applications accepted. *Expenses:* Tuition, state resident: full-time $6408; part-time $3204 per semester. Tuition, nonresident: full-time $14,832; part-time $7416 per semester. *Required fees:* $1824; $912 per semester. Tuition and fees vary according to course load. *Financial support:* In 2011–12, 12 students received support. Research assistantships, teaching assistantships, career-related internships or fieldwork, Federal Work-Study, and institutionally sponsored loans available. Support available to part-time students. Financial award application deadline: 4/1; financial award applicants required to submit FAFSA. *Faculty research:* Reading comprehension, computer-assisted instruction. *Unit head:* Dr. Gwynne Ash, Graduate Advisor, 512-245-8068, Fax: 512-245-8365, E-mail: ga13@txstate.edu. *Application contact:* Dr. J. Michael Willoughby, Dean of Graduate School, 512-245-2581, Fax: 512-245-8365, E-mail: gradcollege@txstate.edu. Web site: http://www.education.txstate.edu/ci/degrees-programs/graduate/elementary-education.html.

Texas Tech University, Graduate School, College of Education, Department of Curriculum and Instruction, Lubbock, TX 79409. Offers bilingual education (M Ed); curriculum and instruction (M Ed, PhD); elementary education (M Ed); language/literacy education (M Ed); secondary education (M Ed). *Accreditation:* NCATE. Part-time programs available. *Students:* 69 full-time (50 women), 115 part-time (91 women); includes 62 minority (9 Black or African American, non-Hispanic/Latino; 3 Asian, non-Hispanic/Latino; 47 Hispanic/Latino; 3 Two or more races, non-Hispanic/Latino), 18 international. Average age 34. 95 applicants, 41% accepted, 26 enrolled. In 2011, 62 master's, 9 doctorates awarded. *Degree requirements:* For master's, comprehensive written exam with 36 hours of course credit or thesis (6 hours) with 30 hours of course credit; for doctorate, thesis/dissertation. *Entrance requirements:* For doctorate, GRE General Test. Additional exam requirements/recommendations for international students: Required—TOEFL (minimum score 550 paper-based; 213 computer-based; 79 iBT). *Application deadline:* For fall admission, 6/1 priority date for domestic students, 1/15 for international students; for spring admission, 9/1 priority date for domestic students, 6/15 for international students. Applications are processed on a rolling basis. Application fee: $50 ($75 for international students). Electronic applications accepted. *Expenses:* Tuition, state resident: full-time $5899; part-time $245.80 per credit hour. Tuition, nonresident: full-time $13,411; part-time $558.80 per credit hour. *Required fees:* $2680.60; $86.50 per credit hour. $920.30 per semester. *Financial support:* In 2011–12, 58 students received support. Application deadline: 4/15; applicants required to submit FAFSA. *Faculty research:* Multicultural foundations of education, teacher education, instruction and pedagogy in subject areas, curriculum theory, language and literary. *Total annual research expenditures:* $948,943. *Unit head:* Dr. Margaret A. Price, Interim Chair, 806-742-1997 Ext. 318, Fax: 806-742-2179, E-mail: peggie.price@ttu.edu. *Application contact:* Stephenie Allyn McDaniel, Administrative Assistant, 806-742-1988 Ext. 434, Fax: 806-742-2179, E-mail: stephenie.mcdaniel@ttu.edu.

Texas Woman's University, Graduate School, College of Professional Education, Department of Reading, Denton, TX 76201. Offers reading education (M Ed, MA, MS, Ed D, PhD). Part-time and evening/weekend programs available. *Faculty:* 8 full-time (all women). *Students:* 1 (woman) full-time, 68 part-time (65 women); includes 19 minority (8 Black or African American, non-Hispanic/Latino; 2 Asian, non-Hispanic/Latino; 9 Hispanic/Latino). Average age 40. 17 applicants, 100% accepted, 16 enrolled. In 2011, 24 master's, 1 doctorate awarded. Terminal master's awarded for partial completion of doctoral program. *Degree requirements:* For master's, comprehensive exam, thesis (for some programs); for doctorate, comprehensive exam, thesis/dissertation. *Entrance requirements:* For master's, GRE General Test (preferred minimum score 143 [350 old version] Verbal, 138 [350 old version] Quantitative); for doctorate, GRE General Test (preferred minimum score 153 [500 old version] Verbal, 144 [500 old version] Quantitative), master's degree, minimum GPA of 3.5, on-site writing sample, interview, 3 letters of reference, curriculum vitae/resume, 1-2 page statement of professional experience and goals, 3 years teaching experience. Additional exam requirements/recommendations for international students: Required—TOEFL (minimum score 550 paper-based; 213 computer-based; 79 iBT). *Application deadline:* For fall admission, 7/1 priority date for domestic students, 3/1 for international students; for spring admission, 12/1 priority date for domestic students, 7/1 for international students. Applications are processed on a rolling basis. Application fee: $50 ($75 for international students). Electronic applications accepted. *Expenses:* Tuition, state resident: full-time $3834; part-time $213 per credit hour. Tuition, nonresident: full-time $9468; part-time $526 per credit hour. *Required fees:* $213 per credit hour. Tuition and fees vary according to course load. *Financial support:* In 2011–12, 16 students received support, including 1 research assistantship (averaging $10,746 per year); career-related internships or fieldwork, Federal Work-Study, institutionally sponsored loans, scholarships/grants, traineeships, health care benefits, and unspecified assistantships also available. Support available to part-time students. Financial award application deadline: 3/1;

financial award applicants required to submit FAFSA. *Faculty research:* Teacher change, home/school partnerships, literacy (middle grades), early literacy, language acquisitions, new literacies, multicultural education, children's literature, literacy leadership and coaching. *Total annual research expenditures:* $230,601. *Unit head:* Dr. Margaret Compton, Chair, 940-898-2230, Fax: 940-898-2224, E-mail: reading@twu.edu. *Application contact:* Dr. Samuel Wheeler, Assistant Director of Admissions, 940-898-3188, Fax: 940-898-3081, E-mail: wheelersr@twu.edu. Web site: http://www.twu.edu/reading/.

Touro College, Graduate School of Education, New York, NY 10010. Offers bilingual programs (Advanced Certificate); education and special education (MS); gifted and talented education (Advanced Certificate); instructional technology (MS); mathematics education (MS); school leadership (MS); teaching children with autism and other severe or multiple disabilities (Advanced Certificate); teaching English to speakers of other languages (MS, Advanced Certificate); teaching literacy (MS). Part-time and evening/weekend programs available. Postbaccalaureate distance learning degree programs offered (no on-campus study). *Faculty:* 75 full-time, 131 part-time/adjunct. *Students:* 382 full-time (324 women), 3,790 part-time (3,196 women); includes 1,211 minority (537 Black or African American, non-Hispanic/Latino; 4 American Indian or Alaska Native, non-Hispanic/Latino; 187 Asian, non-Hispanic/Latino; 472 Hispanic/Latino; 3 Native Hawaiian or other Pacific Islander, non-Hispanic/Latino; 8 Two or more races, non-Hispanic/Latino), 1 international. 1,422 applicants, 50% accepted, 675 enrolled. In 2011, 6 master's, 4 other advanced degrees awarded. *Application deadline:* For fall admission, 8/26 for domestic students, 7/15 for international students; for spring admission, 12/31 for domestic students, 12/15 for international students. Applications are processed on a rolling basis. Application fee: $50. *Financial support:* Federal Work-Study available. Financial award applicants required to submit FAFSA. *Faculty research:* Equity assistance, language development, scholar communications, Latin American studies and cultural sensitivity, behavior management techniques and strategies in special education. *Unit head:* Dr. LaMar Miller, Dean, 212-463-0400 Ext. 5561, Fax: 212-462-4889, E-mail: lpmiller@touro.edu. *Application contact:* Natalie Arroyo, Admissions Assistant, 212-463-0400 Ext. 5119, E-mail: natalie.arroyo@touro.edu.

Towson University, Program in Reading, Towson, MD 21252-0001. Offers reading (M Ed); reading education (CAS). *Accreditation:* NCATE. Part-time and evening/weekend programs available. Postbaccalaureate distance learning degree programs offered (minimal on-campus study). *Students:* 3 full-time (all women), 229 part-time (215 women); includes 30 minority (20 Black or African American, non-Hispanic/Latino; 2 American Indian or Alaska Native, non-Hispanic/Latino; 4 Asian, non-Hispanic/Latino; 3 Hispanic/Latino; 1 Two or more races, non-Hispanic/Latino), 1 international. *Degree requirements:* For master's, exam. *Entrance requirements:* For master's, minimum GPA of 3.0; for CAS, letters of reference, portfolio, master's degree in reading or related field. *Application deadline:* Applications are processed on a rolling basis. Application fee: $50. Electronic applications accepted. *Expenses:* Tuition, state resident: part-time $337 per credit. Tuition, nonresident: part-time $709 per credit. *Required fees:* $99 per credit. *Financial support:* In 2011–12, 4 students received support. Application deadline: 4/1; applicants required to submit FAFSA. *Unit head:* Dr. Barbara Laster, Graduate Program Co-Director, 410-704-2556, Fax: 410-704-3434, E-mail: reed@towson.edu. *Application contact:* Steve Mogge, Graduate Program Co-Director, 410-704-5771, Fax: 410-704-3434, E-mail: reed@towson.edu.

Trident University International, College of Education, Program in Education, Cypress, CA 90630. Offers adult education (MA Ed); aviation education (MA Ed); children's literacy development (MA Ed); e-learning (MA Ed); early childhood education (MA Ed); enrollment management (MA Ed); higher education (MA Ed); teaching and instruction (MA Ed); training and development (MA Ed). Part-time and evening/weekend programs available. Postbaccalaureate distance learning degree programs offered (no on-campus study). *Degree requirements:* For master's, capstone project with integrative paper. *Entrance requirements:* For master's, minimum GPA of 2.5 (students with GPA 3.0 or greater may transfer up to 30% of graduate level credits). Additional exam requirements/recommendations for international students: Required—TOEFL (minimum score 525 paper-based). Electronic applications accepted.

Trinity Washington University, School of Education, Washington, DC 20017-1094. Offers counseling (MA); early childhood education (MAT); educating for change (M Ed); educational administration (MSA); elementary education (MAT); school counseling (MA); secondary education (MAT), including English, social studies; special education (MAT); teaching English as a second language (MAT); teaching English to speakers of other languages (M Ed); the teaching of reading (M Ed). *Accreditation:* NCATE. Part-time and evening/weekend programs available. *Degree requirements:* For master's, thesis (for some programs), capstone project(s). *Entrance requirements:* For master's, PRAXIS I, minimum GPA of 2.8. Additional exam requirements/recommendations for international students: Required—TOEFL (minimum score 550 paper-based; 213 computer-based). *Faculty research:* Technology, literacy, special education, organizations, inclusion models.

Troy University, Graduate School, College of Education, Program in Secondary Education, Troy, AL 36082. Offers 5th year biology (MS); 5th year computer science (MS); 5th year history (MS); 5th year language arts (MS); 5th year mathematics (MS); 5th year social science (MS); traditional biology (MS); traditional computer science (MS); traditional history (MS); traditional language arts (MS); traditional mathematics (MS); traditional social science (MS). *Accreditation:* NCATE. Part-time and evening/weekend programs available. *Faculty:* 4 full-time (3 women). *Students:* 14 full-time (8 women), 29 part-time (21 women); includes 9 minority (all Black or African American, non-Hispanic/Latino). Average age 28. 11 applicants, 100% accepted, 5 enrolled. In 2011, 16 master's awarded. *Degree requirements:* For master's, comprehensive exam, thesis. *Entrance requirements:* For master's, minimum GPA of 2.5, bachelor's degree. Additional exam requirements/recommendations for international students: Required—TOEFL (minimum score 523 paper-based; 193 computer-based; 70 iBT), IELTS (minimum score 6). *Application deadline:* Applications are processed on a rolling basis. Application fee: $50. Electronic applications accepted. *Expenses:* Tuition, state resident: full-time $6960; part-time $290 per credit hour. Tuition, nonresident: full-time $13,920; part-time $580 per credit hour. *Required fees:* $386 per term. *Financial support:* Career-related internships or fieldwork available. Support available to part-time students. Financial award applicants required to submit FAFSA. *Unit head:* Dr. Jan Oliver, Associate Professor, 334-670-3444, Fax: 334-670-3548, E-mail: oliver@troy.edu. *Application contact:* Brenda K. Campbell, Director of Graduate Admissions, 334-670-3178, Fax: 334-670-3733, E-mail: bcamp@troy.edu.

Troy University, Graduate School, College of Education, Program in Teacher Education-Multiple Levels, Troy, AL 36082. Offers art education (MS); gifted education (MS); instrumental (MS); physical education (MS); reading specialist (MS); vocal/choral (MS). Part-time and evening/weekend programs available. *Faculty:* 6 full-time (4 women). *Students:* 6 full-time (4 women), 20 part-time (10 women); includes 3 minority (all Black or African American, non-Hispanic/Latino). Average age 30. 12 applicants, 83% accepted, 5 enrolled. In 2011, 13 master's awarded. *Degree requirements:* For master's, comprehensive exam, thesis. *Entrance requirements:* For master's, minimum GPA of 2.5. Additional exam requirements/recommendations for international students: Required—TOEFL (minimum score 523 paper-based; 193 computer-based; 70 iBT), IELTS (minimum score 6). *Application deadline:* Applications are processed on a rolling basis. Application fee: $50. Electronic applications accepted. *Expenses:* Tuition, state resident: full-time $6960; part-time $290 per credit hour. Tuition, nonresident: full-time $13,920; part-time $580 per credit hour. *Required fees:* $386 per term. *Financial support:* Available to part-time students. Applicants required to submit FAFSA. *Unit head:* Dr. Charlotte S. Minnick, Director, Teacher Education, 334-670-3544, Fax: 334-670-3548, E-mail: csminnick@troy.edu. *Application contact:* Brenda K. Campbell, Director of Graduate Admissions, 334-670-3178, Fax: 334-670-3733, E-mail: bcamp@troy.edu.

Union College, Graduate Programs, Department of Education, Barbourville, KY 40906-1499. Offers elementary education (MA); health and physical education (MA); middle grades (MA); music education (MA); principalship (MA); reading specialist (MA); secondary education (MA); special education (MA). *Degree requirements:* For master's, thesis optional. *Entrance requirements:* For master's, GRE General Test, NTE.

Union Institute & University, Education Programs, Cincinnati, OH 45206-1925. Offers adult and higher education (M Ed); curriculum and instruction (M Ed); educational leadership (M Ed, Ed D); guidance and counseling (Ed S); higher education (Ed D); issues in education (M Ed); reading (Ed S). M Ed offered online and in Vermont and Florida, concentrations vary by location; Ed S offered in Florida; Ed D program is a hybrid (online with limited residency) offered in Ohio. Postbaccalaureate distance learning degree programs offered (minimal on-campus study). *Degree requirements:* For master's, comprehensive exam (for some programs), thesis (for some programs), electronic portfolio; for doctorate, comprehensive exam, thesis/dissertation, electronic portfolio.

University at Albany, State University of New York, School of Education, Department of Reading, Albany, NY 12222-0001. Offers MS, Ed D, CAS. Evening/weekend programs available. *Degree requirements:* For doctorate, one foreign language, thesis/dissertation. *Entrance requirements:* For doctorate, GRE General Test. Additional exam requirements/recommendations for international students: Required—TOEFL (minimum score 550 paper-based; 213 computer-based). Electronic applications accepted.

University at Buffalo, the State University of New York, Graduate School, Graduate School of Education, Department of Learning and Instruction, Buffalo, NY 14260. Offers biology education (Ed M, Certificate); chemistry education (Ed M, Certificate); childhood education (Ed M); childhood education with bilingual extension (Ed M); early childhood education (Ed M); early childhood education with bilingual extension (birth-grade 2) (Ed M); earth science education (Ed M, Certificate); educational technology and new literacies (Certificate); educational technology and new literacies (online) (Certificate); elementary education (Ed D, PhD); English education (Ed M, PhD, Certificate); English for speakers of other languages (Ed M); foreign and second language education (PhD); French education (Ed M, Certificate); general education (Ed M); German education (Ed M, Certificate); gifted education (online) (Certificate); Latin education (Ed M, Certificate); literacy teaching and learning (Certificate); literary specialist (Ed M); mathematics education (Ed M, PhD, Certificate); music education (Ed M, Certificate); physics education (Ed M, Certificate); reading education (PhD); science and the public (online) (Ed M); science education (PhD); social studies education (Ed M, Certificate); Spanish education (Ed M, Certificate); special education (PhD); teaching and leading for diversity (Certificate); teaching English to speakers of other languages (Ed M). Part-time and evening/weekend programs available. Postbaccalaureate distance learning degree programs offered (no on-campus study). *Faculty:* 32 full-time (23 women), 54 part-time/adjunct (43 women). *Students:* 294 full-time (222 women), 350 part-time (261 women); includes 75 minority (19 Black or African American, non-Hispanic/Latino; 6 American Indian or Alaska Native, non-Hispanic/Latino; 40 Asian, non-Hispanic/Latino; 10 Hispanic/Latino), 76 international. Average age 29. 548 applicants, 52% accepted, 253 enrolled. In 2011, 225 master's, 17 doctorates, 37 other advanced degrees awarded. *Degree requirements:* For master's, comprehensive exam; for doctorate, thesis/dissertation, research analysis exam, research experience component. *Entrance requirements:* For doctorate, GRE General Test or MAT, interview, writing sample, letters of recommendation. Additional exam requirements/recommendations for international students: Required—TOEFL (minimum score 600 paper-based; 96 iBT). *Application deadline:* For fall admission, 2/1 priority date for domestic students, 2/1 for international students; for spring admission, 11/15 priority date for domestic students, 10/1 for international students. Applications are processed on a rolling basis. Application fee: $50. Electronic applications accepted. *Financial support:* In 2011–12, 40 fellowships (averaging $12,991 per year), 46 research assistantships (averaging $10,986 per year) were awarded; teaching assistantships with full tuition reimbursements, career-related internships or fieldwork, Federal Work-Study, institutionally sponsored loans, scholarships/grants, and unspecified assistantships also available. Financial award application deadline: 2/28; financial award applicants required to submit FAFSA. *Faculty research:* Science assessment, foreign language teaching and learning, early learning, new literacies, gender and education. *Unit head:* Dr. Julie Sarama, Chair, 716-645-2455, Fax: 716-645-3161, E-mail: jcollins@buffalo.edu. *Application contact:* Cathy Dimino, Admissions Assistant, 716-645-2110, Fax: 716-645-7937, E-mail: cadimino@buffalo.edu.

The University of Alabama in Huntsville, School of Graduate Studies, College of Liberal Arts, Department of English, Huntsville, AL 35899. Offers education (MA); English (MA); language arts (MA); reading specialist (MA); technical communications (Certificate). Part-time and evening/weekend programs available. *Faculty:* 11 full-time (5 women), 2 part-time/adjunct (both women). *Students:* 16 full-time (10 women), 37 part-time (26 women); includes 4 minority (2 Black or African American, non-Hispanic/Latino; 2 Hispanic/Latino). Average age 32. 28 applicants, 86% accepted, 17 enrolled. In 2011, 9 master's, 3 other advanced degrees awarded. *Degree requirements:* For master's, one foreign language, comprehensive exam, thesis or alternative, oral and written exams. *Entrance requirements:* For master's and Certificate, GRE General Test, minimum GPA of 3.0. Additional exam requirements/recommendations for international students: Required—TOEFL (minimum score 500 paper-based; 173 computer-based; 62 iBT). *Application deadline:* For fall admission, 7/15 for domestic students, 4/1 for international students; for spring admission, 11/30 for domestic students, 9/1 for international students. Applications are processed on a rolling basis. Application fee: $40 ($50 for international students). Electronic applications accepted. *Expenses:* Tuition, state resident: full-time $7830; part-time $473.50 per credit. Tuition, nonresident: full-time $18,748; part-time $1128.33 per credit. Tuition and fees vary according to course load and program. *Financial support:* In 2011–12, 11 students received support, including 5 teaching assistantships with full tuition reimbursements available (averaging $8,460 per year); career-related internships or fieldwork, Federal Work-Study, institutionally sponsored loans, scholarships/grants, health care benefits, tuition waivers, and unspecified assistantships also available. Support available to part-time students. Financial award application deadline: 4/1; financial award applicants required to submit FAFSA. *Faculty research:* American and British literature, linguistics, technical writing, women's studies, rhetoric. *Unit head:* Dr. Dan Schenker, Chair, 256-824-6320, Fax: 256-824-6949, E-mail: schenkd@uah.edu. *Application contact:* Kim Gray, Graduate Studies Admissions Coordinator, 256-824-6002, Fax: 256-824-6405, E-mail: deangrad@uah.edu. Web site: http://www.uah.edu/colleges/liberal/english/index.php.

University of Alaska Fairbanks, School of Education, Program in Education, Fairbanks, AK 99775. Offers curriculum and instruction (M Ed); education (M Ed, Graduate Certificate); elementary education (M Ed); language and literacy (M Ed); reading (M Ed); secondary education (M Ed); special education (M Ed). *Faculty:* 25 full-time (15 women). *Students:* 30 full-time (23 women), 69 part-time (50 women); includes 17 minority (7 American Indian or Alaska Native, non-Hispanic/Latino; 1 Asian, non-Hispanic/Latino; 2 Hispanic/Latino; 1 Native Hawaiian or other Pacific Islander, non-Hispanic/Latino; 6 Two or more races, non-Hispanic/Latino), 1 international. Average age 33. 68 applicants, 76% accepted, 37 enrolled. In 2011, 26 master's, 22 other advanced degrees awarded. *Degree requirements:* For master's, comprehensive exam, thesis, oral defense. *Entrance requirements:* Additional exam requirements/recommendations for international students: Required—TOEFL (minimum score 550 paper-based; 213 computer-based; 80 iBT). *Application deadline:* For fall admission, 5/1 for domestic students, 3/1 for international students; for spring admission, 10/15 for domestic students, 8/1 for international students. Applications are processed on a rolling basis. Application fee: $60. Electronic applications accepted. *Expenses:* Tuition, state resident: full-time $6696; part-time $372 per credit. Tuition, nonresident: full-time $13,680; part-time $760 per credit. Tuition and fees vary according to course load and reciprocity agreements. *Financial support:* Fellowships with tuition reimbursements, research assistantships with tuition reimbursements, teaching assistantships with tuition reimbursements, career-related internships or fieldwork, Federal Work-Study, scholarships/grants, health care benefits, and unspecified assistantships available. Support available to part-time students. Financial award application deadline: 6/1; financial award applicants required to submit FAFSA. *Unit head:* Allan Morotti, Interim Dean, 907-474-7341, Fax: 907-474-5451, E-mail: uaf-soe-school@alaska.edu. *Application contact:* Mike Earnest, Director of Admissions, 907-474-7500, Fax: 907-474-5379, E-mail: admissions@uaf.edu. Web site: http://www.uaf.edu/educ/graduate/counseling.html.

The University of Arizona, College of Education, Department of Teaching, Learning and Sociocultural Studies, Tucson, AZ 85721. Offers bilingual education (M Ed); bilingual/multicultural education (MA); language, reading and culture (MA, Ed D, PhD, Ed S). Part-time programs available. *Faculty:* 23 full-time (18 women). *Students:* 162 full-time (108 women), 80 part-time (65 women); includes 71 minority (8 Black or African American, non-Hispanic/Latino; 3 American Indian or Alaska Native, non-Hispanic/Latino; 3 Asian, non-Hispanic/Latino; 38 Hispanic/Latino; 19 Two or more races, non-Hispanic/Latino), 23 international. Average age 37. 63 applicants, 71% accepted, 30 enrolled. In 2011, 89 master's, 19 doctorates awarded. Terminal master's awarded for partial completion of doctoral program. *Degree requirements:* For master's, thesis optional, thesis (MA); for doctorate, comprehensive exam, thesis/dissertation; for Ed S, thesis optional. *Entrance requirements:* For master's, 2 letters of recommendation, resume; for doctorate, GRE or MAT, 2 letters of recommendation, resume; for Ed S, GRE, MAT. Additional exam requirements/recommendations for international students: Required—TOEFL (minimum score 550 paper-based; 213 computer-based; 79 iBT). *Application deadline:* For fall admission, 2/1 for domestic and international students. Application fee: $75. Electronic applications accepted. *Expenses:* Tuition, state resident: full-time $10,840. Tuition, nonresident: full-time $25,802. *Financial support:* In 2011–12, 21 research assistantships with full tuition reimbursements (averaging $17,252 per year), 24 teaching assistantships with full tuition reimbursements (averaging $16,472 per year) were awarded; career-related internships or fieldwork, scholarships/grants, health care benefits, tuition waivers (full and partial), and unspecified assistantships also available. Financial award application deadline: 3/7; financial award applicants required to submit FAFSA. *Faculty research:* Reading, Native American education, language policy, children's literature, bilingual/bicultural literacy. *Total annual research expenditures:* $3.8 million. *Unit head:* Dr. Norma E. Gonzalez, Department Head, 520-621-1311, Fax: 520-621-1853, E-mail: ngonzale@email.arizona.edu. *Application contact:* Information Contact, 520-621-1311, Fax: 520-621-1853, E-mail: lrcinfo@email.arizona.edu. Web site: https://www.coe.arizona.edu/tls.

University of Arkansas at Little Rock, Graduate School, College of Education, Department of Teacher Education, Program in Reading Education, Little Rock, AR 72204-1099. Offers literacy coach (Graduate Certificate); reading (M Ed, Ed S).

University of Bridgeport, School of Education, Department of Education, Bridgeport, CT 06604. Offers education (MS); educational management (Ed D, Diploma), including intermediate administrator or supervisor (Diploma), leadership (Ed D); elementary education (MS, Diploma), including early childhood education, elementary education; middle school education (MS); music education (MS); remedial reading and language arts (Diploma); secondary education (MS, Diploma), including computer specialist (Diploma), international education (Diploma), reading specialist, secondary education. Part-time and evening/weekend programs available. *Faculty:* 12 full-time (5 women), 108 part-time/adjunct (60 women). *Students:* 232 full-time (161 women), 216 part-time (160 women); includes 61 minority (21 Black or African American, non-Hispanic/Latino; 8 Asian, non-Hispanic/Latino; 22 Hispanic/Latino; 10 Two or more races, non-Hispanic/Latino), 34 international. Average age 30. 412 applicants, 63% accepted, 147 enrolled. In 2011, 216 master's, 7 other advanced degrees awarded. *Degree requirements:* For master's, final exam, final project, or thesis; for doctorate, comprehensive exam, thesis/dissertation; for Diploma, thesis or alternative, final project. *Entrance requirements:* For master's, minimum undergraduate QPA of 2.67; for doctorate, GRE, MAT; for Diploma, GRE General Test or MAT, minimum graduate QPA of 3.0. Additional exam requirements/recommendations for international students: Recommended—TOEFL (minimum score 550 paper-based; 213 computer-based; 80 iBT), IELTS (minimum score 6.5). *Application deadline:* For fall admission, 8/1 priority date for domestic students, 8/1 for international students; for spring admission, 12/1 priority date for domestic students, 12/1 for international students. Applications are processed on a rolling basis. Application fee: $50. Electronic applications accepted. *Expenses: Tuition:* Full-time $22,880; part-time $700 per credit. *Required fees:* $1870; $95 per semester. Tuition and fees vary according to course load and program. *Financial support:* In 2011–12, 120 students received support. Fellowships, research assistantships, teaching assistantships, career-related internships or fieldwork, Federal Work-Study, and institutionally sponsored loans available. Support available to part-time students. Financial award application deadline: 6/1; financial award applicants required to submit FAFSA. *Faculty research:* Self-concept, internship assessment, stress and situational development, follow-up of graduation, trend analysis. *Unit head:* Dr. Allen P. Cook, Dean, 203-576-4192, Fax: 203-576-4200, E-mail: acook@bridgeport.edu. *Application contact:* Karissa Peckham, Dean of Admissions, 203-576-4552, Fax: 203-576-4941, E-mail: admit@bridgeport.edu.

The University of British Columbia, Faculty of Education, Program in Language and Literacy Education, Vancouver, BC V6T 1Z1, Canada. Offers library education (M Ed); literacy education (M Ed, MA, PhD); modern language education (M Ed, MA, PhD); teaching English as a second language (M Ed, MA, PhD). Part-time and evening/weekend programs available. *Degree requirements:* For master's, thesis (MA); for doctorate, thesis/dissertation. *Entrance requirements:* For master's and doctorate, minimum B+ average in last 2 years with minimum 2 courses at A standing. Additional exam requirements/recommendations for international students: Required—TOEFL (minimum score 580 paper-based; 237 computer-based; 92 iBT), TWE (minimum score 5). Electronic applications accepted. *Faculty research:* Language and literacy development, second language acquisition, Asia Pacific language curriculum, children's literature, whole language instruction.

University of California, Riverside, Graduate Division, Graduate School of Education, Riverside, CA 92521-0102. Offers autism (M Ed); diversity and equity (M Ed); education, society and culture (MA, PhD); educational psychology (MA, PhD); general education (M Ed); higher education administration and policy (M Ed, PhD); reading (M Ed); school psychology (PhD); special education (M Ed, MA, PhD). *Faculty:* 19 full-time (9 women), 9 part-time/adjunct (6 women). *Students:* 181 full-time (128 women); includes 79 minority (8 Black or African American, non-Hispanic/Latino; 1 American Indian or Alaska Native, non-Hispanic/Latino; 26 Asian, non-Hispanic/Latino; 34 Hispanic/Latino; 10 Two or more races, non-Hispanic/Latino), 5 international. Average age 31. 200 applicants, 48% accepted, 76 enrolled. In 2011, 67 master's, 12 doctorates awarded. Terminal master's awarded for partial completion of doctoral program. *Degree requirements:* For master's, thesis optional, comprehensive exams or thesis (MA), case study or analytical report (M Ed); for doctorate, thesis/dissertation, written and oral qualifying exams, college teaching practicum. *Entrance requirements:* For master's, GRE General Test, CBEST, CSET, minimum GPA of 3.2; for doctorate, GRE General Test, master's degree (desirable), minimum GPA of 3.2. Additional exam requirements/recommendations for international students: Required—TOEFL (minimum score 550 paper-based; 213 computer-based; 80 iBT), IELTS (minimum score 7). *Application deadline:* For fall admission, 9/1 for domestic students, 4/1 for international students; for winter admission, 12/1 for domestic students, 7/1 for international students; for spring admission, 3/1 for domestic students, 10/1 for international students. Applications are processed on a rolling basis. Application fee: $80 ($100 for international students). Electronic applications accepted. *Financial support:* In 2011–12, 59 students received support, including 9 fellowships with full and partial tuition reimbursements available (averaging $26,587 per year), 21 research assistantships with full and partial tuition reimbursements available (averaging $14,517 per year), 1 teaching assistantship with full and partial tuition reimbursement available (averaging $17,307 per year); career-related internships or fieldwork, Federal Work-Study, institutionally sponsored loans, scholarships/grants, and unspecified assistantships also available. Financial award application deadline: 1/5. *Faculty research:* Responsiveness to intervention, faculty core, response to intervention of English language learners, advanced modeling techniques, study on social capital, trust, and motivation. *Total annual research expenditures:* $2.8 million. *Unit head:* Prof. Douglas Mitchell, Interim Dean, 951-827-5802, Fax: 951-827-3942, E-mail: douglas.mitchell@ucr.edu. *Application contact:* Prof. Robert Ream, Graduate Advisor for Admission, 951-827-6362, Fax: 951-827-3291, E-mail: edgrad@ucr.edu. Web site: http://www.education.ucr.edu/.

University of Central Arkansas, Graduate School, College of Education, Department of Early Childhood and Special Education, Program in Reading Education, Conway, AR 72035-0001. Offers MSE. *Accreditation:* NCATE. Part-time programs available. *Faculty:* 2 full-time (1 woman). *Students:* 12 part-time (all women); includes 1 minority (Two or more races, non-Hispanic/Latino). Average age 29. 8 applicants, 100% accepted, 6 enrolled. In 2011, 14 master's awarded. *Degree requirements:* For master's, comprehensive exam, thesis optional. *Entrance requirements:* For master's, GRE General Test, minimum GPA of 2.7. Additional exam requirements/recommendations for international students: Required—TOEFL (minimum score 550 paper-based; 213 computer-based). *Application deadline:* For fall admission, 3/1 priority date for domestic students, 3/1 for international students; for spring admission, 10/1 priority date for domestic students, 10/1 for international students. Applications are processed on a rolling basis. Application fee: $25 ($50 for international students). *Expenses:* Tuition, state resident: full-time $4834; part-time $398.35 per credit hour. Tuition, nonresident: full-time $8686. *Financial support:* Federal Work-Study, scholarships/grants, tuition waivers (partial), and unspecified assistantships available. Support available to part-time students. Financial award application deadline: 2/15; financial award applicants required to submit FAFSA. *Unit head:* Dr. Kathleen Atkins, Associate Professor, 501-450-5429, Fax: 501-450-5358, E-mail: katkins@uca.edu. *Application contact:* Sandy Burks, Administrative Specialist, 501-450-3124, Fax: 501-450-5678, E-mail: slburks@uca.edu.

University of Central Florida, College of Education, Education Doctoral Programs, Orlando, FL 32816. Offers communication sciences and disorders (PhD); counselor education (PhD); education (Ed D); elementary education (PhD); exceptional education (PhD); exercise physiology (PhD); higher education (PhD); hospitality education (PhD); instructional technology (PhD); mathematics education (PhD); reading education (PhD); science education (PhD); social science education (PhD); TESOL (PhD). *Students:* 135 full-time (87 women), 73 part-time (51 women); includes 49 minority (21 Black or African American, non-Hispanic/Latino; 4 Asian, non-Hispanic/Latino; 20 Hispanic/Latino; 4 Two or more races, non-Hispanic/Latino), 18 international. Average age 39. 125 applicants, 46% accepted, 46 enrolled. In 2011, 43 doctorates awarded. Application fee: $30. Electronic applications accepted. *Expenses:* Tuition, state resident: part-time $277.08 per credit hour. Tuition, nonresident: part-time $277.08 per credit hour. Part-time tuition and fees vary according to degree level and program. *Financial support:* In 2011–12, 85 students received support, including 48 fellowships with partial tuition reimbursements available (averaging $5,900 per year), 36 research assistantships with partial tuition reimbursements available (averaging $6,900 per year), 59 teaching assistantships with partial tuition reimbursements available (averaging $6,900 per year). *Unit head:* Dr. Rex Culp, Associate Dean, 407-823-5391, E-mail: rex.culp@ucf.edu. *Application contact:* Barbara Rodriguez, Associate Director, Admissions and Registration, 407-823-2766, Fax: 407-823-6442, E-mail: gradadmissions@ucf.edu. Web site: http://education.ucf.edu/departments.cfm.

University of Central Florida, College of Education, School of Teaching, Learning, and Leadership, Program in Reading Education, Orlando, FL 32816. Offers M Ed, Certificate. *Accreditation:* NCATE. Part-time and evening/weekend programs available. *Students:* 16 full-time (15 women), 72 part-time (69 women); includes 21 minority (8 Black or African American, non-Hispanic/Latino; 1 Asian, non-Hispanic/Latino; 11 Hispanic/Latino; 1 Two or more races, non-Hispanic/Latino). Average age 31. 42 applicants, 93% accepted, 25 enrolled. In 2011, 44 master's, 8 Certificates awarded. *Degree requirements:* For master's, thesis or alternative. *Entrance requirements:* For master's, GRE General Test. Additional exam requirements/recommendations for international students: Required—TOEFL. *Application deadline:* For fall admission, 7/15 for domestic students; for spring admission, 12/1 for domestic students. Application fee: $30. Electronic applications accepted. *Expenses:* Tuition, state resident: part-time $277.08 per credit hour. Tuition, nonresident: part-time $277.08 per credit hour. Part-time tuition and fees vary according to degree level and program. *Financial support:* In 2011–12, 1 student received support, including 1 research assistantship with partial tuition reimbursement available (averaging $7,100 per year); fellowships with partial tuition reimbursements available, teaching assistantships with partial tuition reimbursements available, career-related internships or fieldwork, Federal Work-Study, institutionally sponsored loans, tuition waivers (full), and unspecified assistantships also available. Financial award application deadline: 3/1; financial award applicants required to submit FAFSA. *Unit head:* Dr. Karri J. Williams, Program Coordinator, 321-433-7922, E-mail: karri.williams@ucf.edu. *Application contact:* Barbara Rodriguez, Director, Admissions and Registration, 407-823-2766, Fax: 407-823-6442, E-mail: gradadmissions@ucf.edu.

Reading Education

University of Central Missouri, The Graduate School, College of Education, Warrensburg, MO 64093. Offers career and technical education administration (MS); career and technical education industry training (MS); career and technical education leadership/teaching (MS); college student personnel administration (MS); counseling (MS); curriculum and instruction (Ed S); educational leadership (Ed D); educational technology (MS); elementary education/educational foundations and literacy (MSE); elementary school administration (MSE); elementary school principalship (Ed S); human services/learning resources (Ed S); human services/professional counseling (Ed S); human services/special education (Ed S); human services/technology and occupational education (Ed S); K-12 education/educational foundations and literacy (MSE); K-12 special education (MSE); library science and information services (MS); literacy education (MSE); secondary education/educational foundations & literacy (MSE); secondary school administration (MSE); secondary school principalship (Ed S); superintendency (Ed S); teaching (MAT). Ed D offered jointly with University of Missouri. Part-time programs available. Postbaccalaureate distance learning degree programs offered. *Entrance requirements:* Additional exam requirements/recommendations for international students: Required—TOEFL (minimum score 550 paper-based; 79 computer-based). Electronic applications accepted.

University of Central Oklahoma, College of Graduate Studies and Research, College of Education and Professional Studies, Department of Advanced Professional and Special Services, Program in Reading, Edmond, OK 73034-5209. Offers M Ed. *Accreditation:* NCATE. Part-time programs available. *Entrance requirements:* For master's, GRE General Test. Additional exam requirements/recommendations for international students: Required—TOEFL (minimum score 550 paper-based; 213 computer-based). *Application deadline:* For fall admission, 7/1 for international students; for spring admission, 11/1 for international students. Applications are processed on a rolling basis. Application fee: $25. Electronic applications accepted. *Expenses:* Tuition, state resident: full-time $3901; part-time $218.30 per credit hour. Tuition, nonresident: full-time $9198; part-time $511.20 per credit hour. Tuition and fees vary according to program. *Financial support:* Unspecified assistantships available. Financial award application deadline: 3/31; financial award applicants required to submit FAFSA. *Unit head:* Dr. Barbara Green, Director, 405-974-5283, Fax: 405-974-3822, E-mail: mmonfort@aix1.uco.edu. *Application contact:* Dr. Richard Bernard, Dean, Jackson College of Graduate Studies, 405-974-3493, Fax: 405-974-3852, E-mail: gradcoll@uco.edu. Web site: http://www.uco.edu/ceps/dept/apss/reading/index.asp.

University of Cincinnati, Graduate School, College of Education, Criminal Justice, and Human Services, Division of Teacher Education, Program in Reading/Literacy, Cincinnati, OH 45221. Offers M Ed, Ed D. *Accreditation:* NCATE. Part-time programs available. *Degree requirements:* For master's, thesis or alternative; for doctorate, thesis/dissertation. *Entrance requirements:* For master's, GRE General Test. Additional exam requirements/recommendations for international students: Required—TOEFL (minimum score 550 paper-based; 213 computer-based), TWE (minimum score 4.5), OEPT. Electronic applications accepted.

University of Colorado Denver, School of Education and Human Development, Teacher Education Programs, Denver, CO 80217. Offers elementary linguistically diverse education (MA); elementary math and science education (MA); elementary math education (MA); elementary reading and writing (MA); elementary science education (MA); secondary English education (MA); secondary linguistically diverse education (MA); secondary math education (MA); secondary reading and writing (MA); secondary science education (MA); special education (MA). *Accreditation:* NCATE. Part-time and evening/weekend programs available. *Students:* 419 full-time (325 women), 238 part-time (196 women); includes 83 minority (11 Black or African American, non-Hispanic/Latino; 1 American Indian or Alaska Native, non-Hispanic/Latino; 15 Asian, non-Hispanic/Latino; 53 Hispanic/Latino; 3 Two or more races, non-Hispanic/Latino), 9 international. Average age 30. 206 applicants, 88% accepted, 85 enrolled. In 2011, 278 master's awarded. *Degree requirements:* For master's, comprehensive exam. *Entrance requirements:* For master's, GRE or MAT (for those with GPA below 2.75), transcripts, resume, letters of recommendation. Additional exam requirements/recommendations for international students: Required—TOEFL (minimum score 525 paper-based; 197 computer-based). *Application deadline:* For fall admission, 4/15 priority date for domestic students; for spring admission, 9/15 priority date for domestic students. Applications are processed on a rolling basis. Application fee: $50 ($75 for international students). Electronic applications accepted. *Expenses:* Contact institution. *Financial support:* Research assistantships, teaching assistantships, and Federal Work-Study available. Financial award application deadline: 4/1; financial award applicants required to submit FAFSA. *Faculty research:* Linguistically diverse education/ESL, elementary reading and writing, elementary teacher education, secondary teacher education, special education. *Unit head:* Cindy Gutierrez, Director, 303-315-4982, E-mail: cindy.gutierrez@ucdenver.edu. *Application contact:* Lori Sisneros, Student Services Center, 303-315-4979, E-mail: education@ucdenver.edu. Web site: http://www.ucdenver.edu/academics/colleges/SchoolOfEducation/Academics/MASTERS/Pages/default.aspx.

University of Connecticut, Graduate School, Neag School of Education, Department of Curriculum and Instruction, Program in Reading Education, Storrs, CT 06269. Offers MA, PhD, Post-Master's Certificate. *Accreditation:* NCATE. Terminal master's awarded for partial completion of doctoral program. *Degree requirements:* For master's, comprehensive exam, thesis or alternative; for doctorate, thesis/dissertation. *Entrance requirements:* For doctorate, GRE General Test. Additional exam requirements/recommendations for international students: Required—TOEFL (minimum score 550 paper-based; 213 computer-based). Electronic applications accepted.

University of Dayton, Department of Teacher Education, Dayton, OH 45469-1300. Offers adolescent/young adult (MS Ed); art education (MS Ed); early childhood education (MS Ed); early childhood leadership advocacy (MS Ed); inclusive early childhood (MS Ed); interdisciplinary education (MS Ed); intervention specialist education, mild/moderate (MS Ed); literacy (MS Ed); middle childhood (MS Ed); multi-age education (MS Ed); music education (MS Ed); teacher as leader (MS Ed); technology in education (MS Ed). Part-time and evening/weekend programs available. Postbaccalaureate distance learning degree programs offered (no on-campus study). *Faculty:* 15 full-time (11 women), 22 part-time/adjunct (20 women). *Students:* 41 full-time (29 women), 95 part-time (87 women); includes 13 minority (9 Black or African American, non-Hispanic/Latino; 1 Asian, non-Hispanic/Latino; 3 Hispanic/Latino), 9 international. Average age 32. 111 applicants, 55% accepted, 38 enrolled. In 2011, 97 degrees awarded. *Degree requirements:* For master's, thesis, capstone research project. *Entrance requirements:* For master's, GRE General Test, minimum GPA of 2.75. Additional exam requirements/recommendations for international students: Required—TOEFL (minimum score 550 paper-based; 213 computer-based; 80 iBT). *Application deadline:* For fall admission, 3/1 priority date for domestic students, 3/1 for international students; for winter admission, 7/1 for international students; for spring admission, 1/1 for international students. Applications are processed on a rolling basis. Application fee: $0 ($50 for international students). Electronic applications accepted. *Expenses:* Contact institution. *Financial support:* In 2011–12, 5 research assistantships with full and partial tuition reimbursements (averaging $8,470 per year) were awarded; career-related internships or fieldwork, institutionally sponsored loans, health care benefits, and unspecified assistantships also available. Financial award applicants required to submit FAFSA. *Faculty research:* Diversity, literacy, art representation by young children, preservice teacher preparation. *Unit head:* Dr. Katie A. Kinnucan-Welsch, Chair, 937-229-3346. *Application contact:* Alexsandar Popovski, Enrollment Management Administrator, 937-229-2357, Fax: 937-229-4729, E-mail: alex.popovski@notes.udayton.edu.

The University of Findlay, Graduate and Professional Studies, College of Education, Findlay, OH 45840-3653. Offers administration (MA Ed); children's literature (MA Ed); early childhood (MA Ed); human resource development (MA Ed); reading endorsement (MA Ed); science (MA Ed); special education (MA Ed); technology (MA Ed). *Accreditation:* NCATE. Part-time and evening/weekend programs available. Postbaccalaureate distance learning degree programs offered (no on-campus study). *Faculty:* 16 full-time (12 women), 5 part-time/adjunct (2 women). *Students:* 72 full-time (49 women), 198 part-time (119 women); includes 10 minority (7 Black or African American, non-Hispanic/Latino; 1 Asian, non-Hispanic/Latino; 2 Hispanic/Latino), 16 international. Average age 30. 75 applicants, 88% accepted, 36 enrolled. In 2011, 76 master's awarded. *Degree requirements:* For master's, thesis, cumulative project. *Entrance requirements:* For master's, bachelor's degree from accredited institution, minimum undergraduate GPA of 2.75 in last 62 hours of course work. Additional exam requirements/recommendations for international students: Required—TOEFL (minimum score 550 paper-based; 213 computer-based; 80 iBT). *Application deadline:* Applications are processed on a rolling basis. Application fee: $25. Electronic applications accepted. *Expenses:* Contact institution. *Financial support:* In 2011–12, 5 research assistantships with full and partial tuition reimbursements (averaging $4,200 per year) were awarded; Federal Work-Study, health care benefits, and unspecified assistantships also available. Financial award application deadline: 4/1; financial award applicants required to submit FAFSA. *Faculty research:* Children's literature, books and artwork, educational technology, professional development. *Unit head:* Dr. Julie McIntosh, Dean, 419-434-4862, Fax: 419-434-4822. *Application contact:* Heather Riffle, Assistant Director, Graduate and Professional Studies, 419-434-4640, Fax: 419-434-5517, E-mail: riffle@findlay.edu. Web site: http://www.findlay.edu.

University of Florida, Graduate School, College of Education, School of Teaching and Learning, Gainesville, FL 32611. Offers bilingual/ESOL education (M Ed, MAE, Ed D, PhD, Ed S); curriculum and instruction (M Ed, MAE, Ed D, PhD, Ed S); elementary education (M Ed, MAE); English education (M Ed, MAE); mathematics education (M Ed, MAE); reading education (M Ed, MAE); science education (M Ed, MAE); social foundations of education (M Ed, MAE, Ed D, PhD); social studies education (M Ed, MAE). *Accreditation:* NCATE. Part-time and evening/weekend programs available. Postbaccalaureate distance learning degree programs offered (no on-campus study). *Faculty:* 26 full-time (19 women). *Students:* 247 full-time (201 women), 236 part-time (196 women); includes 100 minority (32 Black or African American, non-Hispanic/Latino; 2 American Indian or Alaska Native, non-Hispanic/Latino; 15 Asian, non-Hispanic/Latino; 51 Hispanic/Latino), 32 international. Average age 33. 290 applicants, 60% accepted, 122 enrolled. In 2011, 284 master's, 19 doctorates, 29 other advanced degrees awarded. Terminal master's awarded for partial completion of doctoral program. *Degree requirements:* For master's, comprehensive exam (for some programs), thesis (for some programs); for doctorate, comprehensive exam (for some programs), thesis/dissertation (for some programs). *Entrance requirements:* For master's and doctorate, GRE General Test, minimum GPA of 3.0; for Ed S, GRE General Test. Additional exam requirements/recommendations for international students: Required—TOEFL (minimum score 550 paper-based; 213 computer-based; 80 iBT), IELTS (minimum score 6). *Application deadline:* For fall admission, 2/15 for domestic students, 12/1 for international students; for spring admission, 9/15 for domestic students, 3/1 for international students. Applications are processed on a rolling basis. Application fee: $30. Electronic applications accepted. *Financial support:* Fellowships, research assistantships, teaching assistantships, career-related internships or fieldwork, and unspecified assistantships available. Financial award applicants required to submit FAFSA. *Faculty research:* Early childhood, child and adolescents, diverse learners, race/ethnicity issues, teacher education, professional development, language and literacy development, policy development. *Unit head:* Dr. Elizabeth Bondy, Chair, 352-273-4242, Fax: 352-392-9193, E-mail: bondy@coe.ufl.edu. *Application contact:* Wevan Terzian, Graduate Coordinator, 352-273-4216, Fax: 352-392-9193, E-mail: sterzian@coe.ufl.edu. Web site: http://education.ufl.edu/school-teaching-learning/.

University of Georgia, College of Education, Department of Language and Literacy Education, Athens, GA 30602. Offers English education (M Ed, Ed S); language and literacy education (PhD); reading education (M Ed, Ed D, Ed S); teaching additional languages (M Ed, Ed S). *Accreditation:* NCATE. *Faculty:* 15 full-time (11 women). *Students:* 100 full-time (81 women), 94 part-time (80 women); includes 21 minority (17 Black or African American, non-Hispanic/Latino; 1 Asian, non-Hispanic/Latino; 2 Hispanic/Latino; 1 Two or more races, non-Hispanic/Latino), 31 international. Average age 33. 185 applicants, 61% accepted, 42 enrolled. In 2011, 43 master's, 15 doctorates, 2 other advanced degrees awarded. *Degree requirements:* For doctorate, variable foreign language requirement. *Entrance requirements:* For master's and Ed S, GRE General Test or MAT; for doctorate, GRE General Test. Additional exam requirements/recommendations for international students: Required—TOEFL (minimum score 550 paper-based; 213 computer-based). *Application deadline:* For fall admission, 7/1 priority date for domestic students; for spring admission, 11/15 for domestic students. Application fee: $50. Electronic applications accepted. *Faculty research:* Comprehension, critical literacy, literacy and technology, vocabulary instruction, content area reading. *Unit head:* Dr. Mark A. Faust, Head, 706-542-4515, Fax: 706-542-4509, E-mail: mfaust@uga.edu. *Application contact:* Dr. Elizabeth St. Pierre, Graduate Coordinator, 706-542-4520, E-mail: stpierre@uga.edu. Web site: http://www.coe.uga.edu/lle/.

University of Guam, Office of Graduate Studies, School of Education, Program in Language and Literacy, Mangilao, GU 96923. Offers M Ed. Part-time programs available. *Degree requirements:* For master's, comprehensive oral and written exams, special project or thesis. *Entrance requirements:* For master's, GRE General Test. Additional exam requirements/recommendations for international students: Required—TOEFL.

University of Houston–Clear Lake, School of Education, Program in Curriculum and Instruction, Houston, TX 77058-1098. Offers curriculum and instruction (MS); early childhood education (MS); reading (MS); school library and information science (MS). Part-time and evening/weekend programs available. *Degree requirements:* For master's, thesis (for some programs). *Entrance requirements:* For master's, GRE or minimum GPA of 3.0 in last 60 hours. Additional exam requirements/recommendations for international students: Required—TOEFL (minimum score 550 paper-based; 213 computer-based). Electronic applications accepted.

University of Illinois at Chicago, Graduate College, College of Education, Department of Curriculum and Instruction, Chicago, IL 60607-7128. Offers curriculum studies (PhD); educational studies (M Ed); elementary education (M Ed); literacy, language and culture (M Ed, PhD); secondary education (M Ed). Part-time and evening/weekend programs available. *Degree requirements:* For doctorate, thesis/dissertation. *Entrance* *requirements:* For master's, minimum GPA of 2.75; for doctorate, GRE General Test, minimum GPA of 2.75. Additional exam requirements/recommendations for international students: Required—TOEFL. Electronic applications accepted. *Faculty research:* Curriculum theory, curriculum development, research on teaching, curriculum and context, reading/literacy.

University of La Verne, College of Education and Organizational Leadership, Program in Reading, La Verne, CA 91750-4443. Offers reading (M Ed, Certificate); reading and language arts specialist (Credential). *Faculty:* 19 full-time (12 women), 28 part-time/adjunct (22 women). *Students:* 2 full-time (both women), 35 part-time (all women); includes 22 minority (2 Black or African American, non-Hispanic/Latino; 3 Asian, non-Hispanic/Latino; 17 Hispanic/Latino). Average age 38. In 2011, 19 master's awarded. *Degree requirements:* For master's, thesis optional. *Entrance requirements:* For master's, MAT, California Basic Educational Skills Test, minimum GPA of 3.0, basic teaching credential, interview, 3 letters of reference. *Application deadline:* Applications are processed on a rolling basis. Application fee: $50. *Expenses:* Contact institution. *Financial support:* Institutionally sponsored loans, scholarships/grants, and unspecified assistantships available. Financial award application deadline: 3/2; financial award applicants required to submit FAFSA. *Unit head:* Dr. Janice Pilgreen, Chairperson, 909-593-3511 Ext. 4624, E-mail: jpilgreen@laverne.edu. *Application contact:* Christy Ranells, Program and Admission Specialist, 909-593-3511 Ext. 4644, Fax: 909-392-2761, E-mail: cranells@laverne.edu. Web site: http://laverne.edu/education/.

University of Louisiana at Monroe, Graduate School, College of Education and Human Development, Department of Curriculum and Instruction, Program in Curriculum and Instruction, Monroe, LA 71209-0001. Offers curriculum and instruction (Ed D); elementary education (1-5) (M Ed); reading education (K-12) (M Ed); SPED-academically gifted education (K-12) (M Ed); SPED-early intervention education (birth-3) (M Ed); SPED-educational diagnostics education (PreK-12) (M Ed). *Accreditation:* NCATE. *Students:* 42 full-time (37 women), 54 part-time (47 women); includes 20 minority (18 Black or African American, non-Hispanic/Latino; 1 Asian, non-Hispanic/Latino; 1 Hispanic/Latino), 12 international. Average age 36. 55 applicants, 95% accepted, 38 enrolled. In 2011, 27 master's, 1 doctorate awarded. *Degree requirements:* For master's, comprehensive exam (for some programs), thesis; for doctorate, thesis/dissertation, internships. *Entrance requirements:* For master's, GRE General Test; for doctorate, GRE General Test, minimum undergraduate GPA of 2.75, graduate 3.25. Additional exam requirements/recommendations for international students: Required—TOEFL (minimum score 500 paper-based; 173 computer-based; 61 iBT). *Application deadline:* For fall admission, 8/24 priority date for domestic students, 7/1 for international students; for winter admission, 12/14 priority date for domestic students; for spring admission, 1/19 for domestic students, 11/1 for international students. Applications are processed on a rolling basis. Application fee: $20 ($30 for international students). Electronic applications accepted. *Expenses:* Tuition, state resident: full-time $3436; part-time $240 per credit hour. Tuition, nonresident: full-time $3436; part-time $240 per credit hour. *International tuition:* $10,733 full-time. *Required fees:* $1460.90. *Financial support:* In 2011–12, 12 research assistantships with full tuition reimbursements (averaging $2,500 per year) were awarded; career-related internships or fieldwork, Federal Work-Study, and unspecified assistantships also available. Financial award application deadline: 4/1; financial award applicants required to submit FAFSA. *Unit head:* Dr. Dorothy Schween, Coordinator, 318-342-1269, Fax: 318-342-3131, E-mail: schween@ulm.edu. *Application contact:* Whitney Sutherland, Administrative Assistant to the Department Head, 318-342-1266, Fax: 318-342-3131, E-mail: sutherland@ulm.edu. Web site: http://www.ulm.edu/ci/.

University of Louisville, Graduate School, College of Education and Human Development, Department of Teaching and Learning, Louisville, KY 40292-0001. Offers art education (MAT); curriculum and instruction (PhD); early elementary education (MAT); instructional technology (M Ed); interdisciplinary early childhood education (MAT); middle school education (MAT); music education (MAT); reading education (M Ed); secondary education (MAT); special education (M Ed, MAT); teacher leadership (M Ed). Part-time and evening/weekend programs available. *Degree requirements:* For doctorate, comprehensive exam, thesis/dissertation. *Entrance requirements:* For master's, GRE General Test, PRAXIS II (for some programs); for doctorate, GRE General Test. Additional exam requirements/recommendations for international students: Required—TOEFL (minimum score 560 paper-based; 210 computer-based; 83 iBT). Electronic applications accepted. *Expenses:* Tuition, state resident: full-time $9692; part-time $539 per credit hour. Tuition, nonresident: full-time $20,168; part-time $1121 per credit hour. Tuition and fees vary according to program and reciprocity agreements. *Faculty research:* Mathematics teacher education and ongoing professional development in pedagogy and content knowledge; development of literacy, including early literacy in science and mathematics and literacy development for English language learners; immersive visualizations for promoting STEM education from nanoscience to cosmic scales; evidence-based practices for students with disabilities; urban education, including teacher response to intervention systems in schools and cross-cultural competence.

University of Maine, Graduate School, College of Education and Human Development, Program in Literacy Education, Orono, ME 04469. Offers M Ed, MA, MS, Ed D, CAS. *Accreditation:* NCATE. Part-time and evening/weekend programs available. *Students:* 23 full-time (21 women), 58 part-time (51 women); includes 2 minority (1 Asian, non-Hispanic/Latino; 1 Hispanic/Latino). Average age 42. 30 applicants, 73% accepted, 21 enrolled. In 2011, 16 master's, 1 doctorate, 9 other advanced degrees awarded. *Degree requirements:* For master's, thesis or alternative; for doctorate, thesis/dissertation. *Entrance requirements:* For master's, MAT; for doctorate, GRE General Test, MA, M Ed, or MS; for CAS, MAT, MA, M Ed, or MS. Additional exam requirements/recommendations for international students: Required—TOEFL. *Application deadline:* For fall admission, 2/1 priority date for domestic students. Applications are processed on a rolling basis. Application fee: $65. Electronic applications accepted. *Expenses:* Tuition, state resident: full-time $5016. Tuition, nonresident: full-time $14,424. *Financial support:* Career-related internships or fieldwork, Federal Work-Study, institutionally sponsored loans, tuition waivers (full and partial), and unspecified assistantships available. Support available to part-time students. Financial award application deadline: 3/1. *Unit head:* Dr. Janet Spector, Coordinator, 207-581-2444, Fax: 207-581-2423. *Application contact:* Scott G. Delcourt, Associate Dean of the Graduate School, 207-581-3291, Fax: 207-581-3232, E-mail: graduate@maine.edu. Web site: http://www2.umaine.edu/graduate/.

University of Mary, School of Education and Behavioral Sciences, Department of Education, Bismarck, ND 58504-9652. Offers college teaching (M Ed); curriculum, instruction and assessment (M Ed); early childhood education (M Ed); early childhood special education (M Ed); elementary administration (M Ed); emotional disorders (M Ed); learning disabilities (M Ed); reading (M Ed); secondary administration (M Ed); special education strategist (M Ed). Part-time programs available. *Faculty:* 6 full-time (5 women), 12 part-time/adjunct (8 women). *Students:* 5 full-time (4 women), 77 part-time (56 women); includes 9 minority (1 Black or African American, non-Hispanic/Latino; 4 American Indian or Alaska Native, non-Hispanic/Latino; 1 Asian, non-Hispanic/Latino; 3 Hispanic/Latino), 1 international. Average age 30. 58 applicants, 55% accepted, 29 enrolled. In 2011, 16 master's awarded. *Degree requirements:* For master's, portfolio or thesis. *Entrance requirements:* For master's, interview, letters of reference, minimum GPA of 2.5. Additional exam requirements/recommendations for international students: Required—TOEFL (minimum score 500 paper-based; 197 computer-based; 71 iBT). *Application deadline:* Applications are processed on a rolling basis. Application fee: $40. Electronic applications accepted. *Financial support:* In 2011–12, 1 teaching assistantship with full tuition reimbursement was awarded; career-related internships or fieldwork also available. Financial award application deadline: 8/1; financial award applicants required to submit FAFSA. *Faculty research:* Innovative pedagogy in higher education, technology in education, content standards, children of poverty, children with diverse learning needs. *Unit head:* Dr. Rebecca Yunker Salveson, Director, 701-355-8186, E-mail: rysalves@umary.edu. *Application contact:* Leona Friedig, Administrative Secretary, 701-355-8058, E-mail: lfriedig@umary.edu.

University of Maryland, College Park, Academic Affairs, College of Education, Department of Curriculum and Instruction, College Park, MD 20742. Offers reading (M Ed, MA, PhD, CAGS); secondary education (M Ed, MA, Ed D, PhD, CAGS); teaching English to speakers of other languages (M Ed). *Accreditation:* NCATE. Part-time and evening/weekend programs available. Postbaccalaureate distance learning degree programs offered (no on-campus study). *Faculty:* 51 full-time (38 women), 23 part-time/adjunct (18 women). *Students:* 252 full-time (177 women), 178 part-time (134 women); includes 121 minority (51 Black or African American, non-Hispanic/Latino; 37 Asian, non-Hispanic/Latino; 24 Hispanic/Latino; 9 Two or more races, non-Hispanic/Latino), 41 international. 264 applicants, 48% accepted, 80 enrolled. In 2011, 176 master's, 17 doctorates awarded. *Degree requirements:* For master's, comprehensive exam, seminar paper; for doctorate, comprehensive exam, thesis/dissertation, published paper, oral exam. *Entrance requirements:* For master's, GRE General Test or MAT, minimum GPA of 3.0, 3 letters of recommendation; for doctorate, GRE General Test or MAT, minimum undergraduate GPA of 3.0, graduate 3.5; 3 letters of recommendation. *Application deadline:* For fall admission, 11/15 priority date for domestic students, 11/15 for international students. Applications are processed on a rolling basis. Application fee: $75. Electronic applications accepted. *Expenses: Tuition, area resident:* Part-time $525 per credit hour. Tuition, state resident: part-time $525 per credit hour. Tuition, nonresident: part-time $1131 per credit hour. *Required fees:* $386.31 per term. Tuition and fees vary according to program. *Financial support:* In 2011–12, 11 research assistantships (averaging $17,535 per year), 79 teaching assistantships (averaging $17,270 per year) were awarded; Federal Work-Study and scholarships/grants also available. Support available to part-time students. Financial award applicants required to submit FAFSA. *Faculty research:* Teacher preparation, curriculum study, in-service education. *Total annual research expenditures:* $3.6 million. *Unit head:* Francine Hultgren, Interim Chair, 301-405-3117, E-mail: fh@umd.edu. *Application contact:* Dr. Charles A. Caramello, Dean of Graduate School, 301-405-0358, Fax: 301-314-9305.

University of Massachusetts Amherst, Graduate School, School of Education, Program in Education, Amherst, MA 01003. Offers bilingual, English as a second language, and multicultural education (M Ed, CAGS); child study and early education (M Ed); children, families and schools (Ed D, CAGS); early childhood and elementary teacher education (M Ed); educational leadership (M Ed, CAGS); educational policy and leadership (Ed D); higher education (M Ed, CAGS); international education (M Ed); language, literacy and culture (Ed D); learning, media and technology (M Ed, CAGS); mathematics, science, and learning technologies (Ed D); policy studies in education (CAGS); psychometric methods, educational statistics and research methods (Ed D); reading and writing (M Ed); school counselor education (M Ed, CAGS); science education (CAGS); secondary teacher education (M Ed); social justice education (M Ed, Ed D, CAGS); special education (M Ed, Ed D, CAGS). *Accreditation:* NCATE. Part-time programs available. Postbaccalaureate distance learning degree programs offered (minimal on-campus study). *Faculty:* 81 full-time (46 women). *Students:* 341 full-time (240 women), 333 part-time (226 women); includes 113 minority (36 Black or African American, non-Hispanic/Latino; 1 American Indian or Alaska Native, non-Hispanic/Latino; 14 Asian, non-Hispanic/Latino; 51 Hispanic/Latino; 1 Native Hawaiian or other Pacific Islander, non-Hispanic/Latino; 10 Two or more races, non-Hispanic/Latino), 98 international. Average age 36. 721 applicants, 57% accepted, 202 enrolled. In 2011, 166 master's, 33 doctorates, 25 CAGSs awarded. Terminal master's awarded for partial completion of doctoral program. *Degree requirements:* For doctorate, comprehensive exam, thesis/dissertation. *Entrance requirements:* Additional exam requirements/recommendations for international students: Required—TOEFL (minimum score 550 paper-based; 213 computer-based; 80 iBT), IELTS (minimum score 6.5). *Application deadline:* For fall admission, 1/15 for domestic and international students. Applications are processed on a rolling basis. Application fee: $50 ($65 for international students). Electronic applications accepted. Tuition and fees vary according to course load, campus/location and program. *Financial support:* Fellowships with full and partial tuition reimbursements, research assistantships with full and partial tuition reimbursements, teaching assistantships with full and partial tuition reimbursements, career-related internships or fieldwork, Federal Work-Study, scholarships/grants, traineeships, health care benefits, tuition waivers (full and partial), and unspecified assistantships available. Support available to part-time students. Financial award application deadline: 1/15. *Unit head:* Dr. Linda L. Griffin, Graduate Program Director, 413-545-6984, Fax: 413-545-1523. *Application contact:* Lindsay DeSantis, Interim Supervisor of Admissions, 413-545-0722, Fax: 413-577-0010, E-mail: gradadm@grad.umass.edu. Web site: http://www.umass.edu/education/.

University of Massachusetts Lowell, Graduate School of Education, Lowell, MA 01854-2881. Offers administration, planning, and policy (CAGS); curriculum and instruction (M Ed, CAGS); educational administration (M Ed); language arts and literacy (Ed D); leadership in schooling (Ed D); math and science education (Ed D); reading and language (M Ed, CAGS). *Accreditation:* NCATE. Part-time and evening/weekend programs available. Postbaccalaureate distance learning degree programs offered (no on-campus study). Terminal master's awarded for partial completion of doctoral program. *Degree requirements:* For doctorate, thesis/dissertation. *Entrance requirements:* For master's, doctorate, and CAGS, GRE General Test. Additional exam requirements/recommendations for international students: Required—TOEFL. Electronic applications accepted.

University of Memphis, Graduate School, College of Education, Department of Instruction and Curriculum Leadership, Memphis, TN 38152. Offers early childhood education (MAT, MS, Ed D); elementary education (MAT); instruction and curriculum (MS, Ed D); instruction design and technology (MS, Ed D); middle grades education (MAT); reading (MS, Ed D); secondary education (MAT); special education (MAT, MS, Ed D). *Accreditation:* NCATE (one or more programs are accredited). Part-time programs available. Terminal master's awarded for partial completion of doctoral program. *Degree requirements:* For master's, comprehensive exam, thesis or alternative; for doctorate, comprehensive exam, thesis/dissertation. *Entrance requirements:* For master's, GRE General Test, minimum GPA of 2.5; for doctorate, GRE General Test, GRE Subject Test, 2 years of teaching experience. Electronic applications accepted. *Faculty research:* Effective urban teachers, preparation and retention of urban teachers, technology utilization in schools, field-based teacher preparation programs, effective use of online instruction.

Reading Education

University of Miami, Graduate School, School of Education and Human Development, Department of Teaching and Learning, Program in Teaching and Learning, Coral Gables, FL 33124. Offers language and literacy learning in multilingual settings (PhD); science, technology, engineering and mathematics (PhD); special education (PhD). *Students:* 19 full-time (14 women); includes 10 minority (3 Black or African American, non-Hispanic/Latino; 7 Hispanic/Latino), 1 international. Average age 34. 12 applicants, 17% accepted, 2 enrolled. In 2011, 9 degrees awarded. *Degree requirements:* For doctorate, thesis/dissertation, qualifying exam. *Entrance requirements:* For doctorate, GRE General Test. Additional exam requirements/recommendations for international students: Required—TOEFL (minimum score 550 paper-based; 80 iBT); Recommended—IELTS (minimum score 6.5). *Application deadline:* For fall admission, 2/15 for domestic students, 10/15 for international students. Application fee: $65. Electronic applications accepted. *Financial support:* In 2011–12, 18 students received support, including 5 fellowships with full tuition reimbursements available (averaging $28,800 per year), 9 research assistantships with full and partial tuition reimbursements available (averaging $28,800 per year), 1 teaching assistantship with full and partial tuition reimbursement available (averaging $28,800 per year). Financial award application deadline: 3/1; financial award applicants required to submit FAFSA. *Faculty research:* Teacher education, multicultural education, technology, second language acquisition, math and science education. *Unit head:* Dr. Elizabeth Harry, Department Chairperson and Program Director, 305-284-4961, Fax: 305-284-6998, E-mail: bharry@miami.edu. *Application contact:* Lois Heffernan, Graduate Admission Coordinator, 305-284-2167, Fax: 305-284-9395, E-mail: lheffernan@miami.edu.

University of Michigan–Flint, School of Education and Human Services, Department of Education, Flint, MI 48502-1950. Offers education (MA); elementary education with teaching certification (MA); literacy (K-12) (MA); special education (MA); technology in education (MA). Part-time programs available. *Entrance requirements:* For master's, BS with minimum GPA of 3.0. Additional exam requirements/recommendations for international students: Required—TOEFL (minimum score 560 paper-based; 220 computer-based; 84 iBT), IELTS (minimum score 6.5). *Expenses:* Contact institution.

University of Minnesota, Twin Cities Campus, Graduate School, College of Education and Human Development, Department of Curriculum and Instruction, Minneapolis, MN 55455-0213. Offers art education (M Ed, MA, PhD); children's literature (M Ed, MA, PhD); curriculum and instruction (MA, PhD); early childhood education (M Ed, PhD); elementary education (M Ed, MA, PhD); English education (MA, PhD); environmental education (M Ed); family education (M Ed, MA, Ed D, PhD); instructional systems and technology (M Ed, MA, PhD); language arts (MA, PhD); language immersion education (Certificate); literacy education (MA); mathematics education (MA, PhD); reading education (MA, PhD); science education (MA, PhD); second languages and cultures education (MA, PhD); social studies education (MA, PhD); teaching (M Ed), including Chinese, earth science, elementary special education, English, English as a second language, French, German, Hebrew, Japanese, life sciences, mathematics, middle school science, science, second languages and cultures, social studies, Spanish; technology enhanced learning (Certificate); writing education (M Ed, MA, PhD). *Faculty:* 34 full-time (22 women). *Students:* 433 full-time (319 women), 310 part-time (239 women); includes 97 minority (34 Black or African American, non-Hispanic/Latino; 6 American Indian or Alaska Native, non-Hispanic/Latino; 35 Asian, non-Hispanic/Latino; 22 Hispanic/Latino), 47 international. Average age 33. 660 applicants, 68% accepted, 395 enrolled. In 2011, 518 master's, 19 doctorates, 14 other advanced degrees awarded. Application fee: $55. *Financial support:* In 2011–12, 6 fellowships (averaging $9,308 per year), 39 research assistantships with full tuition reimbursements (averaging $8,301 per year), 61 teaching assistantships with full tuition reimbursements (averaging $9,206 per year) were awarded. *Faculty research:* Teaching and learning; quality of education; influence of cultural, linguistic, social, political, technological and economic factors on teaching, learning and educational research; relationship between educational practice and a democratic and just society. *Total annual research expenditures:* $943,365. *Unit head:* Dr. Nina Asher, Chair, 612-624-4772, Fax: 612-624-1357, E-mail: nasher@umn.edu. *Application contact:* Dr. Jennifer Engler, Assistant Dean, 612-626-2887, Fax: 612-626-7496, E-mail: engle009@umn.edu. Web site: http://www.cehd.umn.edu/ci.

University of Missouri, Graduate School, College of Education, Department of Learning, Teaching and Curriculum, Columbia, MO 65211. Offers agricultural education (M Ed, PhD, Ed S); art education (M Ed, PhD, Ed S); business and office education (M Ed, PhD, Ed S); early childhood education (M Ed, PhD, Ed S); elementary education (M Ed, PhD, Ed S); English education (M Ed, PhD, Ed S); foreign language education (M Ed, PhD, Ed S); health education and promotion (M Ed, PhD); learning and instruction (M Ed); marketing education (M Ed, PhD, Ed S); mathematics education (M Ed, PhD, Ed S); music education (M Ed, PhD, Ed S); reading education (M Ed, PhD, Ed S); science education (M Ed, PhD, Ed S); social studies education (M Ed, PhD, Ed S); vocational education (M Ed, PhD, Ed S). Part-time programs available. *Faculty:* 26 full-time (16 women), 3 part-time/adjunct (2 women). *Students:* 184 full-time (145 women), 276 part-time (215 women); includes 34 minority (10 Black or African American, non-Hispanic/Latino; 1 American Indian or Alaska Native, non-Hispanic/Latino; 7 Asian, non-Hispanic/Latino; 8 Hispanic/Latino; 8 Two or more races, non-Hispanic/Latino), 39 international. Average age 32. 309 applicants, 76% accepted, 204 enrolled. In 2011, 232 master's, 8 doctorates, 2 other advanced degrees awarded. Terminal master's awarded for partial completion of doctoral program. *Degree requirements:* For doctorate, thesis/dissertation. *Entrance requirements:* For master's and Ed S, GRE General Test or MAT, minimum GPA of 3.0; for doctorate, GRE General Test, minimum GPA of 3.0. Additional exam requirements/recommendations for international students: Required—TOEFL (minimum score 600 paper-based; 250 computer-based; 100 iBT). Application fee: $55 ($75 for international students). Electronic applications accepted. *Expenses:* Tuition, state resident: full-time $5881. Tuition, nonresident: full-time $15,183. *Required fees:* $952. Tuition and fees vary according to campus/location and program. *Financial support:* Fellowships, research assistantships, teaching assistantships, and institutionally sponsored loans available. *Application contact:* Fran Colley, 573-882-6462, E-mail: colleyf@missouri.edu. Web site: http://education.missouri.edu/LTC/.

University of Missouri–Kansas City, School of Education, Kansas City, MO 64110-2499. Offers administration (Ed D); counseling and guidance (MA, Ed S); counseling psychology (PhD); curriculum and instruction (MA, Ed S); education (PhD); educational administration (MA, Ed S); reading education (MA, Ed S); special education (MA). PhD in education offered through the School of Graduate Studies. *Accreditation:* NCATE. Part-time and evening/weekend programs available. *Faculty:* 59 full-time (47 women), 57 part-time/adjunct (42 women). *Students:* 221 full-time (155 women), 379 part-time (271 women); includes 140 minority (95 Black or African American, non-Hispanic/Latino; 1 American Indian or Alaska Native, non-Hispanic/Latino; 15 Asian, non-Hispanic/Latino; 27 Hispanic/Latino; 2 Two or more races, non-Hispanic/Latino), 16 international. Average age 33. 332 applicants, 51% accepted, 136 enrolled. In 2011, 131 master's, 4 doctorates, 25 other advanced degrees awarded. *Degree requirements:* For doctorate, thesis/dissertation, internship, practicum. *Entrance requirements:* For master's, GRE, minimum GPA of 2.75, 2 letters of reference, written statement of purpose; for doctorate, GRE, minimum GPA of 3.0; for Ed S, minimum GPA of 3.0. Additional exam requirements/recommendations for international students: Required—TOEFL (minimum score 550 paper-based; 213 computer-based; 80 iBT). *Application deadline:* For fall admission, 4/1 priority date for domestic students, 4/1 for international students; for spring admission, 11/1 priority date for domestic students, 11/1 for international students. Applications are processed on a rolling basis. Application fee: $45 ($50 for international students). *Expenses:* Tuition, state resident: full-time $5798; part-time $322.10 per credit hour. Tuition, nonresident: full-time $14,969; part-time $831.60 per credit hour. *Required fees:* $93.51 per credit hour. *Financial support:* In 2011–12, 15 research assistantships with partial tuition reimbursements (averaging $10,720 per year) were awarded; career-related internships or fieldwork, Federal Work-Study, institutionally sponsored loans, and tuition waivers (full and partial) also available. Support available to part-time students. Financial award application deadline: 3/1; financial award applicants required to submit FAFSA. *Faculty research:* Urban education, inquiry-based field study, theories of counseling and psychotherapy, school literacy, educational technology. *Unit head:* Dr. Wanda Blanchett, Dean, 816-235-2234, Fax: 816-235-5270, E-mail: education@umkc.edu. *Application contact:* Erica Hernandez-Scott, Student Recruiter, 816-235-1295, Fax: 816-235-5270, E-mail: hernandeze@umkc.edu. Web site: http://education.umkc.edu.

University of Missouri–St. Louis, College of Education, Division of Teaching and Learning, St. Louis, MO 63121. Offers autism studies (Certificate); elementary education (M Ed), including early childhood, general, reading; secondary education (M Ed), including curriculum and instruction, general, middle level education, reading, teaching English to speakers of other languages (TESOL); secondary school teaching (Certificate); special education (M Ed), including autism and developmental disabilities, early childhood special education, general; teaching English to speakers of other languages (Certificate). Part-time and evening/weekend programs available. *Faculty:* 32 full-time (16 women), 51 part-time/adjunct (36 women). *Students:* 95 full-time (63 women), 703 part-time (541 women); includes 176 minority (125 Black or African American, non-Hispanic/Latino; 1 American Indian or Alaska Native, non-Hispanic/Latino; 16 Asian, non-Hispanic/Latino; 26 Hispanic/Latino; 8 Two or more races, non-Hispanic/Latino), 11 international. Average age 29. 379 applicants, 90% accepted, 263 enrolled. In 2011, 190 master's, 9 Certificates awarded. *Degree requirements:* For master's, comprehensive exam. *Entrance requirements:* Additional exam requirements/recommendations for international students: Recommended—TOEFL (minimum score 550 paper-based; 213 computer-based). *Application deadline:* For fall admission, 7/1 priority date for domestic students, 7/1 for international students; for spring admission, 12/1 priority date for domestic students, 12/1 for international students. Application fee: $35 ($40 for international students). Electronic applications accepted. *Expenses:* Tuition, state resident: full-time $6273; part-time $3866 per year. Tuition, nonresident: full-time $14,969; part-time $9980 per year. *Required fees:* $315 per year. *Financial support:* In 2011–12, 6 research assistantships with full and partial tuition reimbursements (averaging $9,500 per year), 2 teaching assistantships with full and partial tuition reimbursements (averaging $10,500 per year) were awarded. Financial award application deadline: 4/1; financial award applicants required to submit FAFSA. *Unit head:* Dr. Joseph Polman, Chair, 314-516-5791. *Application contact:* 314-516-5458, Fax: 314-516-6996, E-mail: gadadm@umsl.edu. Web site: http://coe.umsl.edu/web/divisions/teach-learn/index.html.

University of Nebraska at Kearney, Graduate Studies, College of Education, Department of Teacher Education, Kearney, NE 68849-0001. Offers curriculum and instruction (MS Ed); instructional technology (MS Ed); reading education (MA Ed); special education (MA Ed). Part-time and evening/weekend programs available. *Degree requirements:* For master's, comprehensive exam, thesis optional. *Entrance requirements:* For master's, portfolio or GRE. Additional exam requirements/recommendations for international students: Required—TOEFL (minimum score 550 paper-based; 213 computer-based). Electronic applications accepted.

University of Nebraska at Omaha, Graduate Studies, College of Education, Department of Teacher Education, Program in Reading Education, Omaha, NE 68182. Offers MS. *Accreditation:* NCATE. Part-time and evening/weekend programs available. *Faculty:* 4 full-time (3 women). *Students:* 51 part-time (all women). Average age 35. 12 applicants, 83% accepted, 6 enrolled. In 2011, 13 master's awarded. *Degree requirements:* For master's, comprehensive exam, thesis (for some programs). *Entrance requirements:* For master's, minimum GPA of 3.0. Additional exam requirements/recommendations for international students: Required—TOEFL (minimum score 550 paper-based; 213 computer-based; 80 iBT). *Application deadline:* For fall admission, 8/1 priority date for domestic students; for spring admission, 12/1 priority date for domestic students. Applications are processed on a rolling basis. Application fee: $45. Electronic applications accepted. *Financial support:* In 2011–12, 23 students received support, including 1 research assistantship with tuition reimbursement available; fellowships, teaching assistantships with tuition reimbursements available, Federal Work-Study, institutionally sponsored loans, scholarships/grants, tuition waivers (full), and unspecified assistantships also available. Support available to part-time students. Financial award application deadline: 3/1. *Unit head:* Dr. Lana Danielson, Advisor, 402-554-2212. *Application contact:* Dr. Wilma Kuhlman, Student Contact, 402-554-2212.

University of Nevada, Reno, Graduate School, College of Education, Department of Educational Specialties, Program in Literacy Studies, Reno, NV 89557. Offers M Ed, MA, Ed D, PhD. Terminal master's awarded for partial completion of doctoral program. *Degree requirements:* For master's, thesis optional; for doctorate, thesis/dissertation. *Entrance requirements:* For master's, minimum GPA of 2.75; for doctorate, GRE General Test, minimum GPA of 3.0. Additional exam requirements/recommendations for international students: Required—TOEFL (minimum score 500 paper-based; 173 computer-based; 61 iBT), IELTS (minimum score 6). Electronic applications accepted. *Faculty research:* Cognitive language process, literacy.

University of New England, College of Arts and Sciences, Program in Education, Biddeford, ME 04005-9526. Offers advanced educational leadership (CAGS); curriculum and instruction strategies (CAGS); curriculum and instruction strategy (MS Ed); educational leadership (MS Ed, CAGS); general studies (MS Ed); inclusion education (MS Ed); leadership, ethics and change (CAGS); literacy K-12 (MS Ed, CAGS); teaching methodologies (MS Ed). Part-time programs available. Postbaccalaureate distance learning degree programs offered (minimal on-campus study). *Faculty:* 20 part-time/adjunct. *Students:* 514 full-time (417 women), 218 part-time (165 women). In 2011, 307 master's, 86 CAGSs awarded. *Degree requirements:* For master's, collaborative action research project, integrative seminar portfolio. *Entrance requirements:* For master's, teaching certificate, 2 years of teaching experience. Additional exam requirements/recommendations for international students: Required—TOEFL. *Application deadline:* For fall admission, 9/15 for domestic students; for spring admission, 1/15 for domestic students. Applications are processed on a rolling basis. Application fee: $40. Electronic applications accepted. *Expenses:* Contact institution. *Financial support:* Application deadline: 5/1; applicants required to submit FAFSA. *Faculty research:* Distance learning, effective teaching, transition planning, adult learning. *Unit head:* Dr. Doug Lynch, Chair of Education Department, 207-283-0171 Ext. 2888, E-mail: dlynch@une.edu. *Application contact:* Stacy Gato, Assistant Director of Graduate Admissions, 207-221-4225, Fax: 207-221-4898, E-mail: gradadmissions@une.edu.

University of New Mexico, Graduate School, College of Education, Department of Language, Literacy and Sociocultural Studies, Program in Language, Literacy and Sociocultural Studies, Albuquerque, NM 87131. Offers American Indian education (MA); bilingual education (MA, PhD); educational linguistics (PhD); educational thought and sociocultural studies (MA, PhD); literacy/language arts (MA, PhD); social studies (MA); TESOL (MA, PhD). *Faculty:* 19 full-time (12 women), 12 part-time/adjunct (10 women). *Students:* 40 full-time (30 women), 47 part-time (17 women); includes 85 minority (4 Black or African American, non-Hispanic/Latino; 14 American Indian or Alaska Native, non-Hispanic/Latino; 4 Asian, non-Hispanic/Latino; 59 Hispanic/Latino; 4 Two or more races, non-Hispanic/Latino), 14 international. Average age 41. 63 applicants, 57% accepted, 22 enrolled. In 2011, 44 master's, 8 doctorates awarded. *Degree requirements:* For master's, comprehensive exam, thesis optional; for doctorate, comprehensive exam, thesis/dissertation, research skills. *Entrance requirements:* For master's, letter of intent, 3 letters of recommendation, resume, BA/BS, department demographic form, transcripts; for doctorate, writing sample, letter of intent, 3 letters of recommendation, resume, BA/BS, department demographic form, transcripts. Additional exam requirements/recommendations for international students: Required—TOEFL. *Application deadline:* For fall admission, 12/1 for domestic and international students; for spring admission, 9/15 for domestic and international students. Application fee: $50. Electronic applications accepted. *Financial support:* In 2011–12, 7 students received support, including 7 fellowships (averaging $3,170 per year), 1,318 teaching assistantships with tuition reimbursements available (averaging $3,789 per year); research assistantships, career-related internships or fieldwork, institutionally sponsored loans, scholarships/grants, and unspecified assistantships also available. Support available to part-time students. Financial award application deadline: 3/1; financial award applicants required to submit FAFSA. *Faculty research:* School reform, professional development, history of education, Native American education, politics of education, feminism and issues of sexual identity, critical race theory, bilingualism, literacy reading, adolescent literature, second language acquisition, critical theory and schooling, indigenous languages. *Unit head:* Dr. Lois M. Meyer, Chair, 505-277-7244, Fax: 505-277-8362, E-mail: lsmeyer@unm.edu. *Application contact:* Debra Schaffer, Administrative Assistant, 505-277-0437, Fax: 505-277-8362, E-mail: schaffer@unm.edu. Web site: http://coe.unm.edu/departments/department-of-language-literacy-and-sociocultural-studies/llss-program.html.

The University of North Carolina at Chapel Hill, Graduate School, School of Education, Program in Education, Chapel Hill, NC 27599. Offers culture, curriculum and change (MA, PhD); early childhood, intervention and literacy (MA, PhD); educational psychology, measurement and evaluation (MA, PhD). *Accreditation:* NCATE. *Degree requirements:* For master's, thesis; for doctorate, comprehensive exam, thesis/dissertation. *Entrance requirements:* For master's, GRE General Test, minimum GPA of 3.0 during last 2 years of undergraduates course work; for doctorate, GRE General Test, minimum GPA of 3.0 during last 2 years of undergraduate course work. Additional exam requirements/recommendations for international students: Required—TOEFL (minimum score 550 paper-based; 213 computer-based). Electronic applications accepted.

The University of North Carolina at Charlotte, Graduate School, College of Education, Department of Reading and Elementary Education, Charlotte, NC 28223-0001. Offers elementary education (M Ed); reading, language and literacy (M Ed). Part-time and evening/weekend programs available. Postbaccalaureate distance learning degree programs offered (no on-campus study). *Faculty:* 26 full-time (13 women), 6 part-time/adjunct (5 women). *Students:* 5 full-time (4 women), 58 part-time (all women); includes 3 minority (2 Hispanic/Latino; 1 Two or more races, non-Hispanic/Latino). Average age 30. 45 applicants, 98% accepted, 35 enrolled. In 2011, 63 master's awarded. *Degree requirements:* For master's, thesis or alternative. *Entrance requirements:* For master's, GRE or MAT. Additional exam requirements/recommendations for international students: Required—TOEFL (minimum score 557 paper-based; 220 computer-based; 83 iBT). *Application deadline:* For fall admission, 7/1 for domestic students, 5/1 for international students; for spring admission, 11/1 for domestic students, 10/1 for international students. Applications are processed on a rolling basis. Application fee: $65 ($75 for international students). Electronic applications accepted. *Expenses:* Tuition, state resident: full-time $3689. Tuition, nonresident: full-time $15,226. *Required fees:* $2198. Tuition and fees vary according to course load and program. *Financial support:* In 2011–12, 2 students received support, including 1 research assistantship (averaging $13,500 per year); career-related internships or fieldwork, institutionally sponsored loans, scholarships/grants, unspecified assistantships, and administrative assistantship also available. Support available to part-time students. Financial award application deadline: 4/1; financial award applicants required to submit FAFSA. *Total annual research expenditures:* $8,327. *Unit head:* Dr. Robert J. Rickelman, Chair, 704-687-8890, Fax: 704-687-3749, E-mail: rjrickel@uncc.edu. *Application contact:* Kathy B. Giddings, Director of Graduate Admissions, 704-687-5503, Fax: 704-687-3279, E-mail: gradadm@uncc.edu. Web site: http://education.uncc.edu/reel.

The University of North Carolina at Greensboro, Graduate School, School of Education, Department of Curriculum and Instruction, Greensboro, NC 27412-5001. Offers college teaching and adult learning (Certificate); curriculum and instruction (M Ed), including chemistry education, elementary education, English as a second language, French education, instructional technology, mathematics education, middle grades education, reading education, science education, social studies education, Spanish education; curriculum and teaching (PhD), including higher education, teacher education and development; English as a second language (Certificate); higher education (M Ed); supervision (M Ed). *Accreditation:* NCATE. Part-time programs available. *Degree requirements:* For doctorate, thesis/dissertation. *Entrance requirements:* For master's and doctorate, GRE General Test. Additional exam requirements/recommendations for international students: Required—TOEFL. Electronic applications accepted. *Faculty research:* Community college literacy program, middle school mathematics/computer mathematics.

The University of North Carolina at Pembroke, Graduate Studies, School of Education, Program in Reading Education, Pembroke, NC 28372-1510. Offers MA Ed. *Accreditation:* NCATE. Part-time and evening/weekend programs available. *Degree requirements:* For master's, comprehensive exam, thesis optional. *Entrance requirements:* For master's, GRE General Test or MAT, minimum GPA of 3.0 in major, 2.5 overall; teaching license. Additional exam requirements/recommendations for international students: Required—TOEFL.

The University of North Carolina Wilmington, Watson School of Education, Department of Elementary, Middle Level and Literacy Education, Program in Language and Literacy Education, Wilmington, NC 28403-3297. Offers M Ed. *Accreditation:* NCATE. Part-time and evening/weekend programs available. *Degree requirements:* For master's, comprehensive exam. *Entrance requirements:* For master's, GRE General Test, MAT, minimum B average in upper-division undergraduate course work.

University of North Dakota, Graduate School, College of Education and Human Development, Program in Reading Education, Grand Forks, ND 58202. Offers M Ed, MS. *Accreditation:* NCATE. Part-time programs available. Postbaccalaureate distance learning degree programs offered (minimal on-campus study). *Degree requirements:* For master's, comprehensive exam, thesis or alternative. *Entrance requirements:* For master's, minimum GPA of 3.0. Additional exam requirements/recommendations for international students: Required—TOEFL (minimum score 550 paper-based; 213 computer-based; 79 iBT), IELTS (minimum score 6.5). Electronic applications accepted. *Faculty research:* Whole language, multicultural education, child-focused learning, experiential science, cooperative learning.

University of Northern Colorado, Graduate School, College of Education and Behavioral Sciences, School of Teacher Education, Program in Reading, Greeley, CO 80639. Offers MA. *Accreditation:* NCATE. Part-time and evening/weekend programs available. Postbaccalaureate distance learning degree programs offered (no on-campus study). *Degree requirements:* For master's, comprehensive exam, thesis or alternative. *Entrance requirements:* For master's, GRE General Test (if undergraduate GPA less than 3.0), resume, letters of reference. Electronic applications accepted.

University of Northern Iowa, Graduate College, College of Education, Department of Curriculum and Instruction, Program in Reading, Cedar Falls, IA 50614. Offers curriculum and instruction: literacy education (MAE). Part-time and evening/weekend programs available. *Students:* 13 part-time (all women); includes 1 minority (Black or African American, non-Hispanic/Latino). 4 applicants, 0% accepted, 0 enrolled. In 2011, 5 master's awarded. *Degree requirements:* For master's, comprehensive exam, thesis or alternative. *Entrance requirements:* For master's, writing exam, minimum GPA of 3.0, two recommendations from professional educators. Additional exam requirements/recommendations for international students: Required—TOEFL (minimum score 500 paper-based; 180 computer-based; 61 iBT). *Application deadline:* For fall admission, 8/1 priority date for domestic students. Applications are processed on a rolling basis. Application fee: $50 ($70 for international students). Electronic applications accepted. *Expenses:* Tuition, state resident: full-time $7476. Tuition, nonresident: full-time $16,410. *Required fees:* $942. *Financial support:* Career-related internships or fieldwork, Federal Work-Study, and tuition waivers (full and partial) available. Support available to part-time students. Financial award application deadline: 2/1. *Unit head:* Dr. Deborah Tidwell, Coordinator, 319-273-2167, Fax: 319-273-5886, E-mail: deborah.tidwell@uni.edu. *Application contact:* Laurie S. Russell, Record Analyst, 319-273-2623, Fax: 319-273-2885, E-mail: laurie.russell@uni.edu. Web site: http://www.uni.edu/coe/ci/literacy/index.shtml.

University of North Florida, College of Education and Human Services, Department of Childhood Education, Jacksonville, FL 32224. Offers literacy K-12 (M Ed); professional education - elementary education (M Ed); TESOL K-12 (M Ed). *Accreditation:* NCATE. Part-time and evening/weekend programs available. *Faculty:* 11 full-time (9 women). *Students:* 16 full-time (15 women), 38 part-time (37 women); includes 9 minority (3 Black or African American, non-Hispanic/Latino; 1 American Indian or Alaska Native, non-Hispanic/Latino; 1 Asian, non-Hispanic/Latino; 4 Hispanic/Latino), 3 international. Average age 29. 24 applicants, 67% accepted, 12 enrolled. In 2011, 17 master's awarded. *Entrance requirements:* For master's, GRE General Test, minimum GPA of 3.0 in last 60 hours, 3 letters of recommendation, interview. Additional exam requirements/recommendations for international students: Required—TOEFL (minimum score 500 paper-based; 173 computer-based). *Application deadline:* For fall admission, 7/1 priority date for domestic students, 5/1 for international students; for spring admission, 11/1 priority date for domestic students, 10/1 for international students. Applications are processed on a rolling basis. Application fee: $30. Electronic applications accepted. *Expenses:* Tuition, state resident: full-time $8793; part-time $366.38 per credit hour. Tuition, nonresident: full-time $23,502; part-time $979.24 per credit hour. *Required fees:* $1384; $57.66 per credit hour. Tuition and fees vary according to course load and program. *Financial support:* In 2011–12, 16 students received support, including 1 research assistantship (averaging $5,700 per year); Federal Work-Study, tuition waivers (partial), and unspecified assistantships also available. Support available to part-time students. Financial award application deadline: 4/1; financial award applicants required to submit FAFSA. *Faculty research:* The social context of and processes in learning, inter-disciplinary instruction, cross-cultural conflict resolution, the Vygotskian perspective on literacy diagnosis and instruction, performance poetry and teaching the language arts through drama. *Total annual research expenditures:* $118,609. *Unit head:* Dr. Ronghua Ouyang, Chair, 904-620-2611, Fax: 904-620-1025, E-mail: ronghua.ouyang@unf.edu. *Application contact:* Lillith Richardson, Assistant Director, The Graduate School, 904-620-1360, Fax: 904-620-1362, E-mail: graduateschool@unf.edu. Web site: http://www.unf.edu/coehs/childhood/.

University of North Texas, Toulouse Graduate School, College of Education, Department of Teacher Education and Administration, Program in Reading Education, Denton, TX 76203. Offers M Ed, MS, Ed D, PhD. *Accreditation:* NCATE. Part-time and evening/weekend programs available. *Degree requirements:* For master's, portfolio development and presentation; for doctorate, comprehensive exam, thesis/dissertation. *Entrance requirements:* For master's, GRE General Test, goals statement, writing sample, curriculum vitae/resume; for doctorate, GRE General Test, curriculum vitae/resume, writing sample, 3 letters of recommendation, screening interview. Additional exam requirements/recommendations for international students: Recommended—TOEFL (minimum score 550 paper-based; 213 computer-based; 79 iBT). Electronic applications accepted. *Expenses:* Tuition, state resident: part-time $100 per credit hour. Tuition, nonresident: part-time $413 per credit hour. *Faculty research:* Writing instruction for adolescent ELL, literacy development in Thailand, language acquisition literacy development in emergent readers, current children's/adolescent literature relating to global issues, policy issues in bilingual/ESL education.

University of Oklahoma, Jeannine Rainbolt College of Education, Department of Instructional Leadership and Academic Curriculum, Norman, OK 73072. Offers communication, culture and pedagogy for Hispanic populations in educational settings (Graduate Certificate); instructional leadership and academic curriculum (M Ed, PhD), including bilingual education, early childhood education, elementary education, English education, instructional leadership, mathematics education, reading education, science education, science, technology, engineering and mathematics education (M Ed), secondary education, social studies education, teacher education (M Ed). *Accreditation:* NCATE. Part-time and evening/weekend programs available. *Faculty:* 19 full-time (13 women), 1 (woman) part-time/adjunct. *Students:* 73 full-time (63 women), 114 part-time (87 women); includes 29 minority (5 Black or African American, non-Hispanic/Latino; 12 American Indian or Alaska Native, non-Hispanic/Latino; 5 Asian, non-Hispanic/Latino; 3 Hispanic/Latino; 1 Native Hawaiian or other Pacific Islander, non-Hispanic/Latino; 3 Two or more races, non-Hispanic/Latino), 7 international. Average age 33. 87 applicants, 86% accepted, 68 enrolled. In 2011, 36 master's, 6 doctorates awarded. Terminal master's awarded for partial completion of doctoral program. *Degree requirements:* For doctorate, thesis/dissertation. *Entrance requirements:* For master's, 12 hours of course work in education; for doctorate, GRE General Test, master's degree, minimum graduate GPA of 3.0. Additional exam requirements/recommendations for international students: Required—TOEFL (minimum score 550 paper-based; 79 iBT). *Application deadline:* For fall admission, 6/1 priority date for domestic students, 3/1 for international students; for spring admission, 11/1 for domestic students, 9/1 for international students. Applications are processed on a rolling basis. Application fee: $40 ($90 for international students). Electronic applications accepted. *Expenses:* Tuition, state resident: full-time $4087; part-time $170.30 per credit hour. Tuition, nonresident: full-time $14,875; part-time $619.80 per credit hour. *Required fees:* $2659; $100.25 per credit hour. Tuition and fees vary according to course load and degree level. *Financial support:* In 2011–12, 128 students received support, including 2 research assistantships with partial tuition reimbursements available (averaging $12,431 per year), 12 teaching assistantships with partial tuition reimbursements available (averaging $10,161 per year); institutionally sponsored loans, scholarships/grants, and unspecified assistantships also available. Financial award applicants required to submit FAFSA. *Faculty research:* Engineering in practice for sustainable future, no child left behind (reading), early childhood learning games impact study, Educare randomized control startup, Oklahoma mentoring professional development. *Total annual research expenditures:* $1.1 million. *Unit head:* Lawrence Baines, Chair, 405-325-1498, Fax: 405-325-4061, E-mail: lbaines@ou.edu. *Application contact:* Lynn Crussel, Graduate Programs Officer, 405-325-4843, Fax: 405-325-4061, E-mail: lcrussel@ou.edu. Web site: http://education.ou.edu/departments/ilac.

University of Oklahoma Health Sciences Center, Graduate College, College of Allied Health, Department of Communication Sciences and Disorders, Oklahoma City, OK 73190. Offers audiology (MS, Au D, PhD); communication sciences and disorders (Certificate), including reading, speech-language pathology; education of the deaf (MS); speech-language pathology (MS, PhD). *Accreditation:* ASHA (one or more programs are accredited). Part-time programs available. Terminal master's awarded for partial completion of doctoral program. *Degree requirements:* For master's, comprehensive exam, thesis optional; for doctorate, one foreign language, comprehensive exam, thesis/dissertation. *Entrance requirements:* For master's and doctorate, GRE General Test, 3 letters of recommendation. Additional exam requirements/recommendations for international students: Required—TOEFL (minimum score 550 paper-based). *Faculty research:* Event-related potentials, cleft palate, fluency disorders, language disorders, hearing and speech science.

University of Pennsylvania, Graduate School of Education, Division of Reading, Writing, and Literacy, Program in Language and Literacy, Philadelphia, PA 19104. Offers MS Ed. *Students:* 6 full-time (4 women), 1 (woman) part-time; includes 3 minority (1 Asian, non-Hispanic/Latino; 1 Hispanic/Latino; 1 Two or more races, non-Hispanic/Latino), 1 international. 15 applicants, 60% accepted, 5 enrolled. In 2011, 1 degree awarded. *Expenses: Tuition:* Full-time $26,660; part-time $4944 per course. *Required fees:* $2318; $291 per course. Tuition and fees vary according to course load, degree level and program. *Unit head:* Dr. Andrew Porter, Dean, 215-898-7014. *Application contact:* Penny Creedon. Web site: http://www.gse.upenn.edu/degrees_programs/lang_lit.

University of Phoenix–Online Campus, College of Education, Phoenix, AZ 85034-7209. Offers administration and supervision (MAEd, Graduate Certificate); adult education and training (MAEd); curriculum and instruction (MAEd); curriculum and instruction reading (MAEd); curriculum and instruction-computer education (MAEd); curriculum and instruction-language arts (MAEd); curriculum and instruction-mathematics (MAEd); early childhood education (MAEd); educational studies (MAEd); elementary teacher education (MAEd); elementary teacher education-early childhood (MAEd); secondary teacher education (MAEd); special education (MAEd); teacher education - elementary/middle level (MAEd); teacher education middle level generalist (MAEd); teacher education middle level mathematics (MAEd); teacher education middle level science (MAEd); teacher education secondary mathematics (MAEd); teacher education secondary science (MAEd); teacher leadership (MAEd). *Accreditation:* Teacher Education Accreditation Council. Evening/weekend programs available. Postbaccalaureate distance learning degree programs offered. *Students:* 9,180 full-time (7,178 women); includes 2,913 minority (2,069 Black or African American, non-Hispanic/Latino; 50 American Indian or Alaska Native, non-Hispanic/Latino; 100 Asian, non-Hispanic/Latino; 542 Hispanic/Latino; 48 Native Hawaiian or other Pacific Islander, non-Hispanic/Latino; 104 Two or more races, non-Hispanic/Latino), 147 international. Average age 36. *Entrance requirements:* Additional exam requirements/recommendations for international students: Required—TOEFL, TOEIC (Test of English as an International Communication), Berlitz Online English Proficiency Exam, Pearson Test of English, or IELTS. *Application deadline:* Applications are processed on a rolling basis. Application fee: $45. Electronic applications accepted. *Expenses:* Contact institution. *Financial support:* Scholarships/grants available. Financial award applicants required to submit FAFSA. *Application contact:* 866-766-0766. Web site: http://www.phoenix.edu/colleges_divisions/education.html.

University of Phoenix–Phoenix Main Campus, College of Education, Tempe, AZ 85282-2371. Offers administration and supervision (MA Ed); adult education and training (MA Ed); curriculum and instruction reading (MA Ed); curriculum instruction (MA Ed); early childhood education (MA Ed); education studies (MA Ed); elementary teacher education (MA Ed); secondary teacher education (MA Ed); special education (MA Ed); teacher leadership (MA Ed). Evening/weekend programs available. Postbaccalaureate distance learning degree programs offered. *Students:* 297 full-time (203 women); includes 53 minority (19 Black or African American, non-Hispanic/Latino; 1 American Indian or Alaska Native, non-Hispanic/Latino; 6 Asian, non-Hispanic/Latino; 21 Hispanic/Latino; 2 Native Hawaiian or other Pacific Islander, non-Hispanic/Latino; 4 Two or more races, non-Hispanic/Latino), 3 international. Average age 35. *Entrance requirements:* Additional exam requirements/recommendations for international students: Required—TOEFL, TOEIC (Test of English as an International Communication), Berlitz Online English Proficiency Exam, Pearson Test of English, or IELTS. *Application deadline:* Applications are processed on a rolling basis. Application fee: $45. Electronic applications accepted. *Expenses:* Contact institution. *Financial support:* Scholarships/grants available. Financial award applicants required to submit FAFSA. *Application contact:* 866-766-0766. Web site: http://www.phoenix.edu/colleges_divisions/education.html.

University of Pittsburgh, School of Education, Department of Instruction and Learning, Program in Reading Education, Pittsburgh, PA 15260. Offers M Ed, Ed D, PhD. *Students:* 9 full-time (8 women), 53 part-time (49 women); includes 5 minority (4 Black or African American, non-Hispanic/Latino; 1 Hispanic/Latino). Average age 31. 51 applicants, 78% accepted, 32 enrolled. In 2011, 25 master's, 2 doctorates awarded. *Degree requirements:* For master's, thesis; for doctorate, thesis/dissertation. *Entrance requirements:* For master's, PRAXIS I; for doctorate, GRE General Test. Additional exam requirements/recommendations for international students: Required—TOEFL. *Application deadline:* For fall admission, 2/15 for domestic students. Application fee: $50. *Expenses:* Tuition, state resident: full-time $18,774; part-time $760 per credit. Tuition, nonresident: full-time $30,736; part-time $1258 per credit. *Required fees:* $740; $200 per term. Tuition and fees vary according to program. *Financial support:* Application deadline: 3/15; applicants required to submit FAFSA. *Unit head:* Dr. Richard Donato, Chairman, 412-624-7248, Fax: 412-648-7081, E-mail: donato@pitt.edu. *Application contact:* Dr. Marjie Schermer, Graduate Enrollment Manager, 412-648-2230, Fax: 412-648-1899, E-mail: soeinfo@pitt.edu.

University of Rhode Island, Graduate School, College of Human Science and Services, School of Education, Kingston, RI 02881. Offers adult education (MA); education (PhD); elementary education (MA); music education (MM); reading education (MA); secondary education (MA); special education (MA); MS/PhD. *Accreditation:* NCATE. Part-time and evening/weekend programs available. *Faculty:* 21 full-time (13 women), 3 part-time/adjunct (1 woman). *Students:* 54 full-time (48 women), 108 part-time (86 women); includes 14 minority (3 Black or African American, non-Hispanic/Latino; 4 Asian, non-Hispanic/Latino; 7 Hispanic/Latino), 4 international. In 2011, 56 master's, 8 doctorates awarded. *Degree requirements:* For master's, comprehensive exam (for some programs), thesis optional; for doctorate, comprehensive exam, thesis/dissertation. *Entrance requirements:* For master's, 2 letters of recommendation; interview (for special education applicants); for doctorate, GRE, 3 letters of recommendation, resume. Additional exam requirements/recommendations for international students: Required—TOEFL (minimum score 600 paper-based; 250 computer-based; 100 iBT). *Application deadline:* For fall admission, 1/31 for international students. Application fee: $65. Electronic applications accepted. *Expenses:* Tuition, state resident: full-time $10,432; part-time $580 per credit hour. Tuition, nonresident: full-time $23,130; part-time $1285 per credit hour. *Required fees:* $1362; $36 per credit hour. $35 per semester. One-time fee: $130. *Financial support:* In 2011–12, 4 teaching assistantships with full and partial tuition reimbursements (averaging $12,157 per year) were awarded; career-related internships or fieldwork also available. Financial award applicants required to submit FAFSA. *Unit head:* Dr. David Byrd, Director, 401-874-5484, Fax: 401-874-5471, E-mail: dbyrd@uri.edu. *Application contact:* Dr. John Boulmetis, Coordinator of Graduate Studies, 401-874-4159, Fax: 401-874-7610, E-mail: johnb@uri.edu. Web site: http://www.uri.edu/hss/education/.

University of Rio Grande, Graduate School, Rio Grande, OH 45674. Offers classroom teaching (M Ed), including fine arts, learning disabilities, mathematics, reading education. *Accreditation:* NCATE. Part-time and evening/weekend programs available. *Degree requirements:* For master's, final research project, portfolio. *Entrance requirements:* For master's, minimum GPA of 2.7 in major, 2.5 overall. Additional exam requirements/recommendations for international students: Required—TOEFL. *Faculty research:* Interagency collaboration, reading and mathematics, learning styles, college access, literacy.

University of St. Francis, College of Education, Joliet, IL 60435-6169. Offers educational leadership (MS, Ed D); elementary education certification (M Ed); reading (MS); secondary education certification (M Ed), including English education, math education, science education, social studies education, visual arts education; special education (M Ed); teaching and learning (MS). *Accreditation:* NCATE. Part-time and evening/weekend programs available. Postbaccalaureate distance learning degree programs offered (no on-campus study). *Faculty:* 7 full-time (5 women), 21 part-time/adjunct (14 women). *Students:* 32 full-time (21 women), 230 part-time (175 women); includes 23 minority (7 Black or African American, non-Hispanic/Latino; 2 Asian, non-Hispanic/Latino; 13 Hispanic/Latino; 1 Two or more races, non-Hispanic/Latino), 1 international. Average age 32. 147 applicants, 60% accepted, 57 enrolled. In 2011, 156 master's awarded. *Entrance requirements:* For doctorate, master's degree, IL Type 75 or Principal's endorsement, interview. Additional exam requirements/recommendations for international students: Required—TOEFL (minimum score 550 paper-based; 213 computer-based). *Application deadline:* Applications are processed on a rolling basis. Application fee: $30. Electronic applications accepted. *Expenses:* Contact institution. *Financial support:* In 2011–12, 23 students received support. Federal Work-Study, scholarships/grants, tuition waivers (partial), and unspecified assistantships available. Support available to part-time students. Financial award applicants required to submit FAFSA. *Unit head:* Dr. John Gambro, Dean, 815-740-3829, Fax: 815-740-2264, E-mail: jgambro@stfrancis.edu. *Application contact:* Sandra Sloka, Director of Admissions for Graduate and Degree Completion Programs, 800-735-7500, Fax: 815-740-5032, E-mail: ssloka@stfrancis.edu. Web site: http://www.stfrancis.edu/academics/college-of-education/.

University of St. Thomas, Graduate Studies, School of Education, Department of Teacher Education, St. Paul, MN 55105-1096. Offers curriculum and instruction (MA), including elementary, individualized, K-12, secondary; elementary (MAT); engineering education (Certificate); English as a second language (MA); math education (Certificate); multicultural education (Certificate); reading (MA, Certificate), including elementary (MA), K-12 (MA). *Accreditation:* NCATE. Part-time and evening/weekend programs available. *Faculty:* 7 full-time (4 women), 26 part-time/adjunct (20 women). *Students:* 19 full-time (14 women), 161 part-time (113 women); includes 28 minority (3 Black or African American, non-Hispanic/Latino; 7 American Indian or Alaska Native, non-Hispanic/Latino; 6 Asian, non-Hispanic/Latino; 9 Hispanic/Latino; 3 Two or more races, non-Hispanic/Latino), 5 international. Average age 35. 150 applicants, 79% accepted, 88 enrolled. In 2011, 83 master's awarded. *Entrance requirements:* For master's, minimum GPA of 3.0 or MAT. Additional exam requirements/recommendations for international students: Required—TOEFL (minimum score 550 paper-based; 210 computer-based; 80 iBT). *Application deadline:* For fall admission, 6/1 for domestic students; for spring admission, 11/1 for domestic students. Applications are processed on a rolling basis. Application fee: $50. *Financial support:* Fellowships, research assistantships, institutionally sponsored loans, and scholarships/grants available. Support available to part-time students. Financial award applicants required to submit FAFSA. *Unit head:* Dr. Jan L. H. Frank, Department Chair, 651-962-4446, Fax: 651-962-4169, E-mail: jlhfrank@stthomas.edu. *Application contact:* Rosemary R. Barreto, Department Assistant, 651-962-4420, Fax: 651-962-4169, E-mail: barr7879@stthomas.edu. Web site: http://www.stthomas.edu/education.

University of St. Thomas, School of Education, Houston, TX 77006-4696. Offers all level teaching (M Ed); bilingual/dual language (M Ed); Catholic school teaching (M Ed); Catholic/private school leadership (M Ed); counselor education (M Ed); curriculum and instruction (M Ed); educational leadership (M Ed); elementary teaching (M Ed); English as a second language (M Ed); exceptionality/ educational diagnostician (M Ed); exceptionality/special education (M Ed); generalist (M Ed); reading (M Ed); secondary teaching (M Ed). Part-time and evening/weekend programs available. Postbaccalaureate distance learning degree programs offered (no on-campus study). *Faculty:* 30 full-time (17 women), 54 part-time/adjunct (37 women). *Students:* 66 full-time (43 women), 1,178 part-time (1,044 women); includes 777 minority (313 Black or African American, non-Hispanic/Latino; 5 American Indian or Alaska Native, non-Hispanic/Latino; 29 Asian, non-Hispanic/Latino; 395 Hispanic/Latino; 2 Native Hawaiian or other Pacific Islander, non-Hispanic/Latino; 33 Two or more races, non-Hispanic/Latino), 26 international. Average age 36. 551 applicants, 94% accepted, 416 enrolled. In 2011, 72 master's awarded. *Degree requirements:* For master's, thesis, field experience. *Entrance requirements:* For master's, GRE or MAT if GPA is below 3.0, bachelor's degree; minimum GPA of 2.75 in bachelor's degree or last 60 credit hours; official transcripts from all institutions; goal statement of 250-300 words; 1 reference. Additional exam requirements/recommendations for international students: Required—TOEFL. *Application deadline:* Applications are processed on a rolling basis. Application fee: $35. Electronic applications accepted. *Expenses:* Contact institution. *Financial support:* In 2011–12, 9 students received support. Federal Work-Study, scholarships/grants, and state work-study, institutional employment available. Support available to part-time students. Financial award application deadline: 4/15; financial award applicants required to submit FAFSA. *Faculty research:* Leadership, diversity, personality traits, second language acquisition. *Unit head:* Dr. Nora Hutto, Dean, 713-525-3540, Fax: 713-525-3871, E-mail: education@stthom.edu. *Application contact:* Paula C. Hollis, Administrative Assistant, 713-525-3540, Fax: 713-525-3871, E-mail: education@stthom.edu. Web site: http://www.stthom.edu/Schools_Centers_of_Excellence/Schools_of_Study/School_of_Education/Index.aqf.

University of San Diego, School of Leadership and Education Sciences, Department of Learning and Teaching, San Diego, CA 92110-2492. Offers curriculum and instruction (M Ed); special education (M Ed); special education with deaf and hard of hearing (M Ed); teaching (MAT); TESOL, literacy and culture (M Ed). Part-time and evening/weekend programs available. *Faculty:* 11 full-time (8 women), 41 part-time/adjunct (32 women). *Students:* 86 full-time (69 women), 73 part-time (62 women); includes 54 minority (7 Black or African American, non-Hispanic/Latino; 1 American Indian or Alaska Native, non-Hispanic/Latino; 7 Asian, non-Hispanic/Latino; 27 Hispanic/Latino; 1 Native Hawaiian or other Pacific Islander, non-Hispanic/Latino; 11 Two or more races, non-Hispanic/Latino), 12 international. Average age 28. 177 applicants, 60% accepted, 61 enrolled. In 2011, 57 master's awarded. *Degree requirements:* For master's, thesis (for some programs). *Entrance requirements:* For master's, minimum GPA of 3.0. Additional exam requirements/recommendations for international students: Required—TOEFL (minimum score 580 paper-based; 237 computer-based; 83 iBT), TWE. *Application deadline:* For fall admission, 3/1 priority date for domestic students, 3/1 for international students; for spring admission, 10/15 priority date for domestic students, 10/15 for international students. Application fee: $45. Electronic applications accepted. *Expenses: Tuition:* Full-time $22,482; part-time $1249 per unit. *Required fees:* $224. Full-time tuition and fees vary according to course load and degree level. *Financial support:* In 2011–12, 77 students received support. Career-related internships or fieldwork, Federal Work-Study, institutionally sponsored loans, and stipends available. Support available to part-time students. Financial award application deadline: 4/1; financial award applicants required to submit FAFSA. *Faculty research:* Action research methodology, cultural studies, instructional theories and practices, second language acquisition, school reform. *Unit head:* Dr. Heather Lattimer, Director, 619-260-7616, Fax: 619-260-8159, E-mail: hlattimer@sandiego.edu. *Application contact:* Monica Mahon, Associate Director of Graduate Admissions, 619-260-4524, Fax: 619-260-4158, E-mail: grads@sandiego.edu. Web site: http://www.sandiego.edu/soles/programs/learning_and_teaching/.

University of San Francisco, School of Education, Department of Learning and Instruction, San Francisco, CA 94117-1080. Offers digital media and learning (MA); learning and instruction (MA, Ed D); teaching (MA); teaching reading (MA). *Faculty:* 10 full-time (6 women), 1 part-time/adjunct (0 women). *Students:* 275 full-time (201 women), 67 part-time (42 women); includes 97 minority (7 Black or African American, non-Hispanic/Latino; 3 American Indian or Alaska Native, non-Hispanic/Latino; 32 Asian, non-Hispanic/Latino; 34 Hispanic/Latino; 1 Native Hawaiian or other Pacific Islander, non-Hispanic/Latino; 20 Two or more races, non-Hispanic/Latino), 4 international. Average age 32. 310 applicants, 72% accepted, 135 enrolled. In 2011, 118 master's, 10 doctorates awarded. *Degree requirements:* For doctorate, thesis/dissertation. Application fee: $55 ($65 for international students). *Expenses: Tuition:* Full-time $20,070; part-time $1115 per unit. Tuition and fees vary according to course load, campus/location and program. *Financial support:* In 2011–12, 54 students received support. Fellowships, research assistantships, and teaching assistantships available. Financial award application deadline: 3/2; financial award applicants required to submit FAFSA. *Unit head:* Dr. Robert Burns, Chair, 415-422-6289. *Application contact:* Beth Teague, Associate Director of Graduate Outreach, 415-422-5467, E-mail: schoolofeducation@usfca.edu.

The University of Scranton, College of Graduate and Continuing Education, Department of Education, Program in Reading Education, Scranton, PA 18510. Offers MS. *Accreditation:* NCATE. Part-time and evening/weekend programs available. *Students:* 9 full-time (all women), 3 part-time (all women). Average age 25. 5 applicants, 100% accepted. In 2011, 13 master's awarded. *Degree requirements:* For master's, comprehensive exam, thesis (for some programs), capstone experience. *Entrance requirements:* For master's, minimum GPA of 2.75. Additional exam requirements/recommendations for international students: Required—TOEFL (minimum score 500 paper-based; 173 computer-based), IELTS (minimum score 5.5). *Application deadline:* Applications are processed on a rolling basis. Application fee: $0. *Financial support:* Fellowships, teaching assistantships, career-related internships or fieldwork, Federal Work-Study, and unspecified assistantships available. Support available to part-time students. Financial award application deadline: 3/1. *Unit head:* Dr. Art Chambers, Director, 570-941-4668, Fax: 570-941-5515, E-mail: chambersa2@scranton.edu. *Application contact:* Joseph M. Roback, Director of Admissions, 570-941-4385, Fax: 570-941-5928, E-mail: robackj2@scranton.edu.

University of Sioux Falls, Fredrikson School of Education, Sioux Falls, SD 57105-1699. Offers educational administration (Ed S), including principal leadership, superintendent and district leadership; leadership in reading (M Ed); leadership in schools (M Ed); leadership in technology (M Ed); teaching (M Ed). Admission in summer only. *Accreditation:* NCATE. Part-time and evening/weekend programs available. *Faculty:* 9 full-time (8 women), 10 part-time/adjunct (7 women). *Students:* 196 part-time (144 women); includes 2 minority (1 Black or African American, non-Hispanic/Latino; 1 American Indian or Alaska Native, non-Hispanic/Latino). 55 applicants, 100% accepted, 47 enrolled. *Degree requirements:* For master's, comprehensive exam (for some programs), research application project; for Ed S, comprehensive exam, portfolio. *Entrance requirements:* For master's, minimum GPA of 3.0, 1 year of teaching experience; for Ed S, minimum 3 years of teaching experience, minimum cumulative GPA of 3.5, 1 year of administrative experience. Additional exam requirements/recommendations for international students: Required—TOEFL. *Application deadline:* Applications are processed on a rolling basis. Application fee: $25. *Expenses: Tuition:* Part-time $345 per semester hour. *Required fees:* $35 per term. Part-time tuition and fees vary according to degree level and program. *Financial support:* Available to part-time students. Applicants required to submit FAFSA. *Faculty research:* Reading, literacy, leadership. *Unit head:* Dawn Olson, Director of Graduate Programs in Education, 605-575-2083, Fax: 605-575-2079, E-mail: dawn.olson@usiouxfalls.edu. *Application contact:* Student Contact, 605-331-5000.

University of South Alabama, Graduate School, College of Education, Department of Leadership and Teacher Education, Mobile, AL 36688-0002. Offers early childhood education (M Ed); educational administration (Ed S); educational leadership (M Ed); elementary education (M Ed); reading education (M Ed); science education (M Ed); secondary education (M Ed); special education (M Ed, Ed S). *Accreditation:* NCATE. Part-time programs available. *Faculty:* 20 full-time (14 women). *Students:* 135 full-time (106 women), 75 part-time (62 women); includes 50 minority (40 Black or African American, non-Hispanic/Latino; 3 American Indian or Alaska Native, non-Hispanic/Latino; 3 Asian, non-Hispanic/Latino; 3 Hispanic/Latino; 1 Two or more races, non-Hispanic/Latino), 1 international. 89 applicants, 49% accepted, 36 enrolled. In 2011, 88 master's, 13 Ed Ss awarded. *Degree requirements:* For master's, comprehensive exam. *Entrance requirements:* For master's, GRE General Test or MAT, minimum GPA of 3.0. *Application deadline:* For fall admission, 7/15 priority date for domestic students, 6/15 for international students; for spring admission, 12/1 priority date for domestic students, 11/1 for international students. Applications are processed on a rolling basis. Application fee: $35. *Expenses:* Tuition, state resident: full-time $7968; part-time $332 per credit hour. Tuition, nonresident: full-time $15,936; part-time $664 per credit hour. *Financial support:* Research assistantships and career-related internships or fieldwork available. Support available to part-time students. Financial award application deadline: 4/1. *Unit head:* Dr. Harold Dodge, Jr., Chair, 251-380-2894. *Application contact:* Dr. Abigail Baxter, Director of Graduate Studies, 251-460-6310, Fax: 251-461-1513, E-mail: kharriso@usouthal.edu. Web site: http://www.southalabama.edu/coe/lted.

University of South Carolina, The Graduate School, College of Education, Department of Instruction and Teacher Education, Program in Language and Literacy, Columbia, SC 29208. Offers M Ed, PhD. *Accreditation:* NCATE. *Degree requirements:* For master's, comprehensive exam; for doctorate, one foreign language, comprehensive exam, thesis/dissertation. *Entrance requirements:* For master's, GRE General Test, Miller Analogies Test, teaching certificate, resume, letters of reference, letter of intent; for doctorate, GRE General Test, Miller Analogies Test, resumé, letters of reference, letter of intent, interview. *Faculty research:* Remedial and compensatory education, metacognition and learning, literacy, learning, teacher change.

University of Southern Maine, School of Education and Human Development, Program in Literacy Education, Portland, ME 04104-9300. Offers applied literacy (MS Ed); early language and literacy (Certificate); English as a second language (MS Ed, CAS); literacy education (MS Ed, CAS, Certificate). *Accreditation:* Teacher Education Accreditation Council. Part-time and evening/weekend programs available. *Degree requirements:* For master's, comprehensive exam, thesis or alternative; for other advanced degree, thesis or alternative. *Entrance requirements:* For master's, teacher certification; for other advanced degree, master's degree. Additional exam requirements/recommendations for international students: Required—TOEFL (minimum score 550 paper-based; 213 computer-based; 79 iBT). Electronic applications accepted.

University of Southern Mississippi, Graduate School, College of Education and Psychology, Department of Curriculum, Instruction, and Special Education, Hattiesburg, MS 39406-0001. Offers alternative secondary teacher education (MAT); early childhood education (M Ed, Ed S); education (Ed D); education of the gifted (M Ed, PhD, Ed S); elementary education (M Ed, PhD, Ed S); reading (M Ed, MS); secondary education (M Ed, MS, PhD); special education (M Ed, PhD, Ed S). Part-time programs available. *Faculty:* 23 full-time (17 women), 3 part-time/adjunct (2 women). *Students:* 39 full-time (34 women), 92 part-time (77 women); includes 36 minority (31 Black or African American, non-Hispanic/Latino; 3 Hispanic/Latino; 2 Two or more races, non-Hispanic/Latino), 3 international. Average age 37. 56 applicants, 55% accepted, 29 enrolled. In 2011, 45 master's, 5 doctorates awarded. *Degree requirements:* For master's and Ed S, comprehensive exam, thesis (for some programs); for doctorate, comprehensive exam, thesis/dissertation. *Entrance requirements:* For master's, GRE General Test, MAT, minimum GPA of 3.0; for doctorate, GRE General Test, minimum GPA of 3.5; for Ed S, GRE General Test, MAT, minimum GPA of 3.25. Additional exam requirements/recommendations for international students: Required—TOEFL, IELTS. *Application deadline:* For fall admission, 3/1 priority date for domestic students, 3/1 for international students; for spring admission, 1/10 priority date for domestic students, 1/10 for international students. Applications are processed on a rolling basis. Application fee: $50. *Financial support:* In 2011–12, 9 research assistantships with tuition reimbursements (averaging $18,316 per year), 2 teaching assistantships with full tuition reimbursements (averaging $8,500 per year) were awarded; Federal Work-Study, institutionally sponsored loans, scholarships/grants, health care benefits, tuition waivers (partial), and unspecified assistantships also available. Financial award application deadline: 3/15; financial award applicants required to submit FAFSA. *Faculty research:* Mathematical problem solving, integrative curriculum, writing process, teacher education models. *Total annual research expenditures:* $100,000. *Unit head:* Dr. David Daves, Chair, 601-266-4547, Fax: 601-266-4175, E-mail: david.daves@usm.edu. *Application contact:* Dr. Marie Crowe, Director of Graduate Studies, 601-266-6005, Fax: 601-266-4548, E-mail: margie.crowe@usm.edu. Web site: http://www.usm.edu/graduateschool/table.php.

University of South Florida, Graduate School, College of Education, Department of Childhood Education, Tampa, FL 33620-9951. Offers early childhood education (M Ed, MA, PhD); elementary education (MA, MAT, PhD); reading/language arts (MA, PhD, Ed S). *Accreditation:* NCATE. Part-time and evening/weekend programs available. *Faculty:* 24 full-time (21 women), 2 part-time/adjunct (both women). *Students:* 88 full-time (81 women), 116 part-time (110 women); includes 48 minority (21 Black or African American, non-Hispanic/Latino; 6 Asian, non-Hispanic/Latino; 19 Hispanic/Latino; 2 Two or more races, non-Hispanic/Latino), 7 international. Average age 33. 200 applicants, 67% accepted, 76 enrolled. In 2011, 87 master's, 8 doctorates, 1 other advanced degree awarded. *Degree requirements:* For master's, comprehensive exam; for doctorate, comprehensive exam, thesis/dissertation, philosophies of inquiry; multiple research methods. *Entrance requirements:* For master's, GRE (if GPA less than 3.0), minimum GPA of 3.0 in last 60 hours of course work; for doctorate, GRE General Test, minimum GPA of 3.0 undergraduate, 3.5 graduate; interview; for Ed S, GRE General Test, interview. Additional exam requirements/recommendations for international students: Required—TOEFL (minimum score 550 paper-based; 213 computer-based). *Application deadline:* For fall admission, 2/15 for domestic students, 1/2 for international students; for winter admission, 2/15 for domestic students, 1/2 for international students; for spring admission, 10/15 for domestic students, 6/1 for international students. Application fee: $30. Electronic applications accepted. *Financial support:* In 2011–12, 7 teaching assistantships with full tuition reimbursements (averaging $10,300 per year) were awarded; institutionally sponsored loans, scholarships/grants, and unspecified assistantships also available. Financial award applicants required to submit FAFSA. *Faculty research:* Evaluating interventions for struggling readers, prevention and intervention services for young children at risk for behavioral and mental health challenges, preservice teacher education and young adolescent middle school experience, art and inquiry-based approaches to teaching and learning, study of children's writing development. *Total annual research expenditures:* $381,048. *Unit head:* Dr. Diane Yendol-Hoppey, Chairperson, 813-974-3460, Fax: 813-974-0938. *Application contact:* Dr. Diane Briscoe, Coordinator of Graduate Studies, 813-974-1804, Fax: 813-974-3391, E-mail: briscoe@usf.edu. Web site: http://www.coedu.usf.edu/main/departments/ce/ce.html.

University of South Florida–Polytechnic, College of Human and Social Sciences, Lakeland, FL 33803. Offers counselor education (MA), including clinical mental health, professional school counseling; educational leadership (M Ed); reading education (MA).

University of South Florida–St. Petersburg Campus, College of Education, St. Petersburg, FL 33701. Offers educational leadership development (M Ed); elementary education (MA), including math/science; English education (MA); middle grades STEM education (MS); reading education (MA). Part-time programs available. *Students:* 30 full-time (27 women), 130 part-time (109 women); includes 28 minority (14 Black or African American, non-Hispanic/Latino; 4 Asian, non-Hispanic/Latino; 9 Hispanic/Latino; 1 Two or more races, non-Hispanic/Latino). Average age 34. 63 applicants, 70% accepted, 36 enrolled. In 2011, 74 master's awarded. *Degree requirements:* For master's, comprehensive exam, practicum, internship, comprehensive portfolio. *Entrance requirements:* For master's, State of Florida General Knowledge Test (GKT), Florida Teaching Certificate (for non-initial certification programs), letters of recommendation. Additional exam requirements/recommendations for international students: Required—TOEFL (minimum score 550 paper-based; 79 iBT); Recommended—IELTS. *Application deadline:* For fall admission, 6/1 priority date for domestic students, 6/1 for international students; for spring admission, 10/15 priority date for domestic students, 10/15 for international students. Applications are processed on a rolling basis. Application fee: $30. Electronic applications accepted. *Expenses:* Tuition, state resident: full-time $8847. Tuition, nonresident: full-time $18,423. One-time fee: $35 full-time. Full-time tuition and fees vary according to course load and program. *Financial support:* Applicants required to submit FAFSA. *Unit head:* Dr. Harold W. Heller, Dean, 727-873-4155, Fax: 727-873-4191, E-mail: hheller@usfsp.edu. *Application contact:* Eric Douthirt, Enrollment Management Specialist, 727-873-4450, E-mail: douthirt@usfsp.edu. Web site: http://www1.usfsp.edu/coe/index.asp.

University of South Florida Sarasota-Manatee, College of Education, Sarasota, FL 34243. Offers educational leadership (M Ed), including curriculum leadership, K-12, non-public/charter school leadership; elementary education K-6 (MA); K-6 with ESOL endorsement (MAT); reading education K-12 (MA); MAT/MA. Part-time and evening/weekend programs available. *Faculty:* 12 full-time (8 women), 4 part-time/adjunct (3 women). *Students:* 19 full-time (17 women), 64 part-time (50 women); includes 7 minority (1 Black or African American, non-Hispanic/Latino; 1 Asian, non-Hispanic/Latino; 4 Hispanic/Latino; 1 Two or more races, non-Hispanic/Latino). Average age 33. 50 applicants, 62% accepted, 21 enrolled. In 2011, 41 master's awarded. *Degree requirements:* For master's, comprehensive exam (for some programs). *Entrance requirements:* For master's, GRE. Additional exam requirements/recommendations for international students: Required—TOEFL (minimum score 213 computer-based; 79 iBT) or IELTS. *Application deadline:* For fall admission, 2/15 for domestic students, 1/2 for international students; for spring admission, 10/15 for domestic students, 6/1 for international students. Applications are processed on a rolling basis. Application fee: $30. Electronic applications accepted. *Expenses:* Tuition, state resident: full-time $9301; part-time $387.55 per credit hour. Tuition, nonresident: full-time $19,412; part-time $808.85 per credit hour. *Required fees:* $15; $5 per semester. One-time fee: $30. *Financial support:* Federal Work-Study, scholarships/grants, health care benefits, and unspecified assistantships available. Support available to part-time students. Financial award application deadline: 3/1; financial award applicants required to submit FAFSA. *Faculty research:* Child development, student achievement, intergenerational studies. *Unit head:* Dr. Terry A. Osborn, Dean, 941-359-4531, E-mail: terryosborn@sar.usf.edu. *Application contact:* Jo Lynn Raudebaugh, Graduate Admissions Advisor, 941-359-4587, E-mail: jraudeba@sar.usf.edu. Web site: http://www.sarasota.usf.edu/Academics/COE/.

The University of Tennessee, Graduate School, College of Education, Health and Human Sciences, Program in Education, Knoxville, TN 37996. Offers art education (MS); counseling education (PhD); cultural studies in education (PhD); curriculum (MS, Ed S); curriculum, educational research and evaluation (Ed D, PhD); early childhood education (PhD); early childhood special education (MS); education of deaf and hard of hearing (MS); educational administration and policy studies (Ed D, PhD); educational administration and supervision (Ed S); educational psychology (Ed D, PhD); elementary education (MS, Ed S); elementary teaching (MS); English education (MS, Ed S); exercise science (PhD); foreign language/ESL education (MS, Ed S); instructional technology (MS, Ed D, PhD, Ed S); literacy, language and ESL education (PhD); literacy, language education, and ESL education (Ed D); mathematics education (MS, Ed S); modified and comprehensive special education (MS); reading education (MS, Ed S); school counseling (Ed S); school psychology (PhD, Ed S); science education (MS, Ed S); secondary teaching (MS); social foundations (MS); social science education (MS, Ed S); socio-cultural foundations of sports and education (PhD); special education (Ed S); teacher education (Ed D, PhD). *Accreditation:* NCATE. Part-time and evening/weekend programs available. *Degree requirements:* For master's and Ed S, thesis optional; for doctorate, variable foreign language requirement, thesis/dissertation. *Entrance requirements:* For master's, minimum GPA of 2.7; for doctorate and Ed S, GRE General Test, minimum GPA of 2.7. Additional exam requirements/recommendations for international students: Required—TOEFL. Electronic applications accepted. *Expenses:* Tuition, state resident: full-time $8332; part-time $464 per credit hour. Tuition, nonresident: full-time $25,174; part-time $1400 per credit hour. *Required fees:* $1162; $56 per credit hour. Tuition and fees vary according to program.

The University of Texas at Austin, Graduate School, College of Education, Department of Curriculum and Instruction, Austin, TX 78712-1111. Offers bilingual/bicultural education (M Ed, MA, PhD); cultural studies in education (M Ed, MA, PhD); early childhood education (M Ed, MA, PhD); language and literacy studies (M Ed, PhD); learning technologies (M Ed, MA, PhD); physical education (M Ed, MA, PhD). Terminal master's awarded for partial completion of doctoral program. *Degree requirements:* For doctorate, thesis/dissertation. *Entrance requirements:* For master's and doctorate, GRE General Test. *Application deadline:* For fall admission, 3/1 for domestic students; for spring admission, 10/1 for domestic students. Applications are processed on a rolling basis. Application fee: $50 ($75 for international students). Electronic applications accepted. *Financial support:* Fellowships and teaching assistantships with partial tuition reimbursements available. Financial award application deadline: 2/1. *Unit head:* Betty Maloch, Chair, 512-232-4262, E-mail: bmaloch@austin.utexas.edu. *Application contact:* Stephen Flynn, Graduate Coordinator, 512-471-3747, E-mail: sflynn@austin.utexas.edu. Web site: http://www.edb.utexas.edu/coe/depts/ci/cti.html.

The University of Texas at Brownsville, Graduate Studies, School of Education, Brownsville, TX 78520-4991. Offers bilingual education (M Ed); counseling and guidance (M Ed); curriculum and instruction (M Ed); early childhood education (M Ed); educational administration (M Ed); educational technology (M Ed); English as a second language (M Ed); reading specialist (M Ed); special education/educational diagnostician (M Ed). Part-time and evening/weekend programs available. Postbaccalaureate distance learning degree programs offered (minimal on-campus study). *Degree requirements:* For master's, thesis optional. *Entrance requirements:* For master's, GRE General Test. Additional exam requirements/recommendations for international students: Required—TOEFL.

The University of Texas at El Paso, Graduate School, College of Education, Department of Teacher Education, El Paso, TX 79968-0001. Offers education (MA); instruction (M Ed); reading education (M Ed); teaching, learning, and culture (PhD). Part-time and evening/weekend programs available. *Students:* 595 (433 women); includes 473 minority (16 Black or African American, non-Hispanic/Latino; 2 American Indian or Alaska Native, non-Hispanic/Latino; 13 Asian, non-Hispanic/Latino; 439 Hispanic/Latino; 2 Native Hawaiian or other Pacific Islander, non-Hispanic/Latino; 1 Two or more races, non-Hispanic/Latino), 22 international. Average age 34. 168 applicants, 79% accepted, 108 enrolled. In 2011, 79 master's awarded. *Degree requirements:* For master's, thesis optional. *Entrance requirements:* For master's, GRE General Test, minimum GPA of 3.0. Additional exam requirements/recommendations for international students: Required—TOEFL. *Application deadline:* For fall admission, 7/1 priority date for domestic students, 3/1 for international students; for spring admission, 11/1 priority date for domestic students, 9/1 for international students. Applications are processed on a rolling basis. Application fee: $15 ($65 for international students). Electronic applications accepted. *Financial support:* In 2011–12, research assistantships with partial tuition reimbursements (averaging $16,642 per year), teaching assistantships with partial tuition reimbursements (averaging $13,134 per year) were awarded; Federal Work-Study, institutionally sponsored loans, scholarships/grants, and tuition waivers (partial) also available. Financial award application deadline: 3/15; financial award applicants required to submit FAFSA. *Unit head:* Dr. Elaine Hampton, Chair, 915-747-5426, E-mail: ehampton@utep.edu. *Application contact:* Dr. Benjamin Flores, Interim Dean of the Graduate School, 915-747-5491, Fax: 915-747-5788, E-mail: bflores@utep.edu.

The University of Texas at San Antonio, College of Education and Human Development, Department of Bicultural and Bilingual Studies, San Antonio, TX 78249-0617. Offers bicultural studies (MA); bicultural/bilingual education (MA); culture, literacy, and language (PhD); teaching English as a second language (MA). Part-time and evening/weekend programs available. *Faculty:* 13 full-time (8 women). *Students:* 61 full-time (51 women), 113 part-time (91 women); includes 107 minority (8 Asian, non-Hispanic/Latino; 96 Hispanic/Latino; 1 Native Hawaiian or other Pacific Islander, non-Hispanic/Latino; 2 Two or more races, non-Hispanic/Latino), 29 international. Average age 35. 93 applicants, 78% accepted, 46 enrolled. In 2011, 38 master's, 4 doctorates awarded. *Degree requirements:* For master's, one foreign language, comprehensive exam, thesis optional; for doctorate, one foreign language, comprehensive exam, thesis/dissertation. *Entrance requirements:* For master's, GRE General Test if GPA is less than 3.0 for last 60 hours, bachelor's degree with 18 credit hours in field of study or in another appropriate field of study; for doctorate, GRE General Test, resume or curriculum vitae, 3 letters of recommendation, statement of purpose. Additional exam requirements/recommendations for international students: Required—TOEFL (minimum score 500 paper-based; 61 iBT), IELTS (minimum score 5). *Application deadline:* For fall admission, 7/1 for domestic students, 4/1 for international students; for spring admission, 11/1 for domestic students, 9/1 for international students. Applications are processed on a rolling basis. Application fee: $45 ($85 for international students). Electronic applications accepted. *Expenses:* Tuition, state resident: full-time $3148; part-time $2176 per semester. Tuition, nonresident: full-time $8782; part-time $5932 per semester. *Required fees:* $719 per semester. *Financial support:* In 2011–12, 28 students received support, including 14 fellowships with full tuition reimbursements available (averaging $25,385 per year), 2 research assistantships with full tuition reimbursements available (averaging $12,468 per year), 12 teaching assistantships with full tuition reimbursements available (averaging $11,000 per year). *Faculty research:* Bilingualism and biliteracy development, second language teaching and learning, language minority education, Mexican American studies, transnationalism and immigration. *Unit head:* Dr. Robert Milk, Chair, 210-458-4426, Fax: 210-458-5962, E-mail: robert.milk@utsa.edu. *Application contact:* Armando Trujillo, Assistant Dean of the Graduate School, 210-458-5576, Fax: 210-458-5576, E-mail: armando.trujillo@utsa.edu. Web site: http://coehd.utsa.edu/bicultural-bilingual_studies.

The University of Texas at San Antonio, College of Education and Human Development, Department of Interdisciplinary Learning and Teaching, San Antonio, TX 78249-0617. Offers adult learning and teaching (MA); education (MA), including curriculum and instruction, early childhood and elementary education, educational psychology/special education, instructional technology, reading and literacy education; interdisciplinary learning and teaching (PhD). Part-time and evening/weekend programs available. *Faculty:* 26 full-time (21 women), 1 (woman) part-time/adjunct. *Students:* 131 full-time (100 women), 357 part-time (283 women); includes 275 minority (31 Black or African American, non-Hispanic/Latino; 9 Asian, non-Hispanic/Latino; 227 Hispanic/Latino; 8 Two or more races, non-Hispanic/Latino), 31 international. Average age 33. 239 applicants, 75% accepted, 120 enrolled. In 2011, 119 master's awarded. *Degree requirements:* For master's, comprehensive exam, thesis optional, 36 hours of course work without thesis (33 with thesis); for doctorate, comprehensive exam, thesis/dissertation, minimum of 60 semester credit hours. *Entrance requirements:* For master's, GRE General Test, bachelor's degree with minimum GPA of 3.0 in last 60 hours of coursework; resume; two letters of recommendation; statement of purpose; for doctorate, GRE, transcripts from all colleges and universities attended, professional vitae demonstrating experience in work environment where education was primary professional emphasis, 3 letters of recommendation, statement of purpose, master's degree transcript documenting minimum GPA of 3.5. Additional exam requirements/recommendations for international students: Required—TOEFL (minimum score 500 paper-based; 61 iBT), IELTS (minimum score 5). *Application deadline:* For fall admission, 7/1 for domestic students, 4/1 for international students; for spring admission, 11/1 for domestic students, 9/1 for international students. Application fee: $45 ($85 for international students). *Expenses:* Tuition, state resident: full-time $3148; part-time $2176 per semester. Tuition, nonresident: full-time $8782; part-time $5932 per semester. *Required fees:* $719 per semester. *Financial support:* In 2011–12, 9 fellowships with partial tuition reimbursements (averaging $27,000 per year) were awarded; career-related internships or fieldwork, Federal Work-Study, and scholarships/grants also available. Support available to part-time students. *Faculty research:* Explorations of science, learning and teaching, family Involvement in early childhood, culturally-responsive literacy instruction in diverse settings, STEM education, autism spectrum disorders. *Total annual research expenditures:* $5.9 million. *Unit head:* Dr. Maria R. Cortez, Department Chair, 210-458-5969, Fax: 210-458-7281, E-mail: mari.cortez@utsa.edu. *Application contact:* Erin Doran, Student Development Specialist, 210-458-7443, Fax: 210-458-7281, E-mail: erin.doran@utsa.edu.

The University of Texas at Tyler, College of Education and Psychology, School of Education, Tyler, TX 75799-0001. Offers early childhood education (M Ed, MA); reading (M Ed, MA); special education (M Ed, MA). Part-time and evening/weekend programs available. *Degree requirements:* For master's, comprehensive exam, thesis (for some programs), research project. *Entrance requirements:* For master's, GRE General Test. Additional exam requirements/recommendations for international students: Required—TOEFL (minimum score 79 computer-based). Electronic applications accepted. *Faculty research:* Improving quality in childcare settings, play and creativity, teacher interactions, effects of modeling on early childhood teachers, biofeedback, literacy instruction.

The University of Texas of the Permian Basin, Office of Graduate Studies, School of Education, Program in Reading, Odessa, TX 79762-0001. Offers MA. *Degree requirements:* For master's, comprehensive exam (for some programs), thesis (for some programs). *Entrance requirements:* For master's, GRE General Test. Additional exam requirements/recommendations for international students: Required—TOEFL (minimum score 550 paper-based; 213 computer-based).

The University of Texas–Pan American, College of Education, Department of Curriculum and Instruction: Elementary and Secondary, Edinburg, TX 78539. Offers bilingual education (M Ed); early childhood education (M Ed); elementary education (M Ed); reading (M Ed); secondary education (M Ed). Part-time programs available. *Degree requirements:* For master's, comprehensive exam, thesis optional. *Entrance requirements:* For master's, GRE. Additional exam requirements/recommendations for international students: Required—TOEFL, IELTS. *Application deadline:* For fall admission, 7/17 for domestic and international students; for spring admission, 11/16 for domestic and international students. Application fee: $0. Tuition and fees vary according to course load, program and student level. *Financial support:* Research assistantships with tuition reimbursements, Federal Work-Study, institutionally sponsored loans, scholarships/grants, and unspecified assistantships available. Financial award application deadline: 4/15. *Faculty research:* Dual language instruction, literacy and technology, teacher education in diverse populations, mathematics and science education. *Unit head:* Dr. Veronica L. Estrada, Chair, 956-665-2431, Fax: 956-665-

2434, E-mail: vlestradaa@utpa.edu. Web site: http://www.utpa.edu/dept/curr_ins/graduat.html.

University of the Cumberlands, Graduate Programs in Education, Williamsburg, KY 40769-1372. Offers all grades (P-12) (M Ed); business and marketing (MA Ed, MAT); director of pupil personnel (Certificate); director of special education (Certificate); educational administration and supervision (Ed S); educational leadership (Ed D); elementary education (MA Ed, MAT); instructional leadership - principalship (MA Ed); instructional leadership - school principal (Certificate); middle school education (MA Ed, MAT); reading and writing (MA Ed); school counseling (MA Ed); school superintendent (Certificate); secondary education (MA Ed, MAT); special education (MAT); supervisor of instruction (Certificate); teacher leader (MA Ed). Part-time and evening/weekend programs available. Postbaccalaureate distance learning degree programs offered. *Degree requirements:* For master's, comprehensive exam. Electronic applications accepted.

University of the Incarnate Word, School of Graduate Studies and Research, Dreeben School of Education, Programs in Education, San Antonio, TX 78209-6397. Offers adult education (M Ed, MA); cross-cultural education (M Ed, MA); early childhood literacy (M Ed, MA); general education (M Ed, MA); higher education (PhD); instructional technology (M Ed, MA); international education and entrepreneurship (PhD); kinesiology (M Ed, MA); literacy (M Ed, MA); organizational leadership (PhD); organizational learning and learning (M Ed, MA); reading (M Ed, MA); special education (M Ed, MA); teacher leadership (M Ed, MA). Part-time and evening/weekend programs available. *Faculty:* 14 full-time (8 women), 10 part-time/adjunct (9 women). *Students:* 13 full-time (7 women), 197 part-time (129 women); includes 111 minority (23 Black or African American, non-Hispanic/Latino; 2 American Indian or Alaska Native, non-Hispanic/Latino; 1 Asian, non-Hispanic/Latino; 85 Hispanic/Latino), 26 international. Average age 41. 78 applicants, 79% accepted, 34 enrolled. In 2011, 21 master's, 12 doctorates awarded. *Degree requirements:* For master's, capstone; for doctorate, thesis/dissertation, qualifying exam. *Entrance requirements:* For master's, baccalaureate degree; minimum foundation GPA of 2.5; interview; for doctorate, master's degree; interview; supervised writing sample. Additional exam requirements/recommendations for international students: Required—TOEFL (minimum score 560 paper-based; 220 computer-based; 83 iBT). *Application deadline:* Applications are processed on a rolling basis. Application fee: $20. Electronic applications accepted. *Expenses: Tuition:* Part-time $725 per credit hour. Tuition and fees vary according to degree level. *Financial support:* In 2011–12, 5 research assistantships were awarded; Federal Work-Study and scholarships/grants also available. Financial award applicants required to submit FAFSA. *Unit head:* Dr. Denise Staudt, Dean, Dreeben School of Education, 210-829-2762, E-mail: staudt@uiwtx.edu. *Application contact:* Andrea Cyterski-Acosta, Dean of Enrollment, 210-829-6005, Fax: 210-829-3921, E-mail: admis@uiwtx.edu. Web site: http://www.uiw.edu/education/index.htm.

University of Utah, Graduate School, College of Education, Department of Educational Psychology, Salt Lake City, UT 84112. Offers counseling psychology (PhD); educational psychology (MA); elementary education (M Ed); instructional design and educational technology (M Ed); instructional design and technology (M Ed, MS); learning and cognition (MS, PhD); learning sciences (MA); professional counseling (MS); professional psychology (M Ed); reading and literacy (M Ed, PhD); school counseling (M Ed, MS); school psychology (M Ed, MS, PhD); statistics (M Stat). *Accreditation:* APA (one or more programs are accredited). Evening/weekend programs available. Postbaccalaureate distance learning degree programs offered (minimal on-campus study). *Faculty:* 23 full-time (12 women), 9 part-time/adjunct (7 women). *Students:* 104 full-time (85 women), 107 part-time (78 women); includes 26 minority (1 American Indian or Alaska Native, non-Hispanic/Latino; 4 Asian, non-Hispanic/Latino; 17 Hispanic/Latino; 1 Native Hawaiian or other Pacific Islander, non-Hispanic/Latino; 3 Two or more races, non-Hispanic/Latino), 4 international. Average age 32. 213 applicants, 27% accepted, 48 enrolled. In 2011, 39 master's, 9 doctorates awarded. *Median time to degree:* Of those who began their doctoral program in fall 2003, 50% received their degree in 8 years or less. *Degree requirements:* For master's, variable foreign language requirement, comprehensive exam, thesis (for some programs); for doctorate, variable foreign language requirement, thesis/dissertation, oral exam. *Entrance requirements:* For master's and doctorate, GRE General Test, minimum GPA of 3.0. Additional exam requirements/recommendations for international students: Required—TOEFL (minimum score 500 paper-based; 173 computer-based). *Application deadline:* For fall admission, 4/1 for domestic and international students; for spring admission, 11/1 for domestic and international students. Application fee: $55 ($65 for international students). *Expenses:* Contact institution. *Financial support:* In 2011–12, 59 students received support, including 25 fellowships with full and partial tuition reimbursements available (averaging $12,000 per year), 7 research assistantships with full and partial tuition reimbursements available (averaging $12,000 per year), 27 teaching assistantships with full and partial tuition reimbursements available (averaging $12,000 per year); career-related internships or fieldwork, Federal Work-Study, institutionally sponsored loans, scholarships/grants, and unspecified assistantships also available. Financial award application deadline: 2/1; financial award applicants required to submit FAFSA. *Faculty research:* Autism, computer technology and instruction, cognitive behavior, aging, group counseling. *Total annual research expenditures:* $371,256. *Unit head:* Dr. Elaine Clark, Chair, 801-581-7148, Fax: 801-581-5566, E-mail: clark@ed.utah.edu. *Application contact:* Kendra Lee Wiebke, Academic Program Specialist, 801-581-7148, Fax: 801-581-5566, E-mail: kendra.wiebke@utah.edu. Web site: http://www.ed.utah.edu/edps/.

University of Vermont, Graduate College, College of Education and Social Services, Department of Education, Program in Reading and Language Arts, Burlington, VT 05405. Offers M Ed. *Accreditation:* NCATE. *Students:* 1 woman (international). 2 applicants, 0% accepted, 0 enrolled. In 2011, 2 master's awarded. *Degree requirements:* For master's, thesis or alternative. *Entrance requirements:* Additional exam requirements/recommendations for international students: Required—TOEFL (minimum score 550 paper-based; 213 computer-based; 80 iBT). *Application deadline:* Applications are processed on a rolling basis. Application fee: $40. Electronic applications accepted. *Financial support:* Teaching assistantships and career-related internships or fieldwork available. Financial award application deadline: 3/1.

University of Victoria, Faculty of Graduate Studies, Faculty of Education, Department of Curriculum and Instruction, Victoria, BC V8W 2Y2, Canada. Offers art education (M Ed, PhD); curriculum studies (M Ed, MA, PhD); early childhood education (M Ed, PhD); educational studies (PhD); language and literacy (M Ed, MA, PhD); mathematics (M Ed, MA, PhD); music education (M Ed, MA, PhD); science (M Ed, MA, PhD); social studies (M Ed, MA); social, cultural and foundational studies (MA, PhD); technology and environmental education (PhD). Part-time programs available. *Degree requirements:* For master's, thesis, project (M Ed); for doctorate, comprehensive exam, thesis/dissertation. *Entrance requirements:* For master's, minimum B average. Additional exam requirements/recommendations for international students: Required—TOEFL (minimum score 575 paper-based; 233 computer-based), IELTS (minimum score 7). Electronic applications accepted. *Faculty research:* Elementary and secondary English, language arts, curriculum theory and practice, educational media and technology, educational administration and leadership, history and philosophy of education.

University of Virginia, Curry School of Education, Department of Curriculum, Instruction, and Special Education, Program in Curriculum and Instruction, Charlottesville, VA 22903. Offers curriculum and instruction (M Ed, Ed S); elementary (M Ed, Ed D); English (M Ed, Ed D); foreign language (M Ed); mathematics (M Ed, Ed D); reading (M Ed, Ed D, Ed S); science (Ed D); social studies (M Ed). *Students:* 22 full-time (17 women), 29 part-time (27 women); includes 4 minority (1 Black or African American, non-Hispanic/Latino; 1 Asian, non-Hispanic/Latino; 2 Two or more races, non-Hispanic/Latino), 1 international. Average age 33. 67 applicants, 75% accepted, 33 enrolled. In 2011, 78 master's, 2 doctorates, 12 other advanced degrees awarded. *Degree requirements:* For master's, comprehensive exam (for some programs); for doctorate, comprehensive exam, thesis/dissertation; for Ed S, comprehensive exam. *Entrance requirements:* For master's, doctorate, and Ed S, GRE General Test, 2 letters of recommendation. Additional exam requirements/recommendations for international students: Required—TOEFL (minimum score 600 paper-based; 250 computer-based; 90 iBT), IELTS (minimum score 7). *Application deadline:* Applications are processed on a rolling basis. Application fee: $60. Electronic applications accepted. *Financial support:* Fellowships with tuition reimbursements, research assistantships with tuition reimbursements, and teaching assistantships with tuition reimbursements available. Financial award application deadline: 1/5; financial award applicants required to submit FAFSA. *Unit head:* Laura Smolkin, Chair, 434-924-0831. *Application contact:* Karen Dwier, Information Contact, 434-924-0831, E-mail: kgd9g@virginia.edu.

University of Virginia, Curry School of Education, Program in Education, Charlottesville, VA 22903. Offers administration and supervision (PhD); applied developmental science (PhD); counselor education (PhD); curriculum and instruction (PhD); early childhood-developmental risk (MT); education evaluation (PhD); educational psychology (PhD); educational research (PhD); elementary (MT, PhD); English education (MT, PhD); foreign language education (MT); higher education (PhD); instructional technology (PhD); kinesiology (MT, PhD); math education (PhD); reading education (PhD); research statistics and evaluation (PhD); school psychology (PhD); science education (PhD); social studies education (MT, PhD); special education (PhD); world languages education (MT). *Students:* 299 full-time (216 women), 60 part-time (33 women); includes 46 minority (18 Black or African American, non-Hispanic/Latino; 17 Asian, non-Hispanic/Latino; 7 Hispanic/Latino; 4 Two or more races, non-Hispanic/Latino), 23 international. Average age 30. 307 applicants, 42% accepted, 80 enrolled. In 2011, 113 master's, 62 doctorates awarded. *Degree requirements:* For master's, comprehensive exam (for some programs), field project; for doctorate, comprehensive exam, thesis/dissertation. *Entrance requirements:* For doctorate, GRE General Test. Additional exam requirements/recommendations for international students: Required—TOEFL (minimum score 600 paper-based; 250 computer-based; 90 iBT), IELTS (minimum score 7). *Application deadline:* Applications are processed on a rolling basis. Application fee: $60. Electronic applications accepted. *Financial support:* Fellowships, research assistantships, and teaching assistantships available. Financial award application deadline: 1/5; financial award applicants required to submit FAFSA. *Unit head:* Robert C. Pianta, Dean, 434-924-3334. *Application contact:* Joanne McNergney, Assistant Dean for Admissions and Student Services, 434-924-3334, E-mail: curry-admissions@virginia.edu.

University of Washington, Graduate School, College of Education, Seattle, WA 98195. Offers curriculum and instruction (M Ed, Ed D, PhD), including educational technology, general curriculum (Ed D, PhD), language, literacy, and culture, mathematics education, multicultural education, reading and language arts education (Ed D), science education, social studies education, teaching and curriculum (M Ed); educational leadership and policy studies (M Ed, Ed D, PhD), including administration (Ed D), educational policy, organization, and leadership (M Ed, PhD), higher education, leadership for learning (Ed D), social and cultural foundations of education (M Ed, PhD); educational psychology (M Ed, PhD), including educational psychology (PhD), human development and cognition (M Ed), learning sciences, measurement, statistics and research design (M Ed), school psychology (M Ed); instructional leadership (M Ed); intercollegiate athletic leadership (M Ed); special education (M Ed, Ed D, PhD), including early childhood special education (M Ed), emotional and behavioral disabilities (M Ed), learning disabilities (M Ed), low-incidence disabilities (M Ed), severe disabilities (M Ed), special education (Ed D, PhD); teacher education (MIT). *Accreditation:* APA. Part-time and evening/weekend programs available. *Degree requirements:* For master's, thesis optional; for doctorate, thesis/dissertation. *Entrance requirements:* For master's and doctorate, GRE General Test, minimum GPA of 3.0. Additional exam requirements/recommendations for international students: Required—TOEFL. Electronic applications accepted. *Faculty research:* School restructuring/effective schools, special education interventions, literacy and writing, technology, school partnerships, teacher preparation.

University of West Florida, College of Professional Studies, School of Education, Program in Reading Education, Pensacola, FL 32514-5750. Offers M Ed. Part-time and evening/weekend programs available. *Students:* 18 part-time (all women); includes 2 minority (1 Black or African American, non-Hispanic/Latino; 1 Hispanic/Latino). Average age 32. 19 applicants, 74% accepted, 10 enrolled. In 2011, 13 master's awarded. *Degree requirements:* For master's, portfolio, teacher certification exams (general knowledge, professional, reading subject area). *Entrance requirements:* For master's, GRE (minimum score 450 verbal) or MAT (minimum score 396) if bachelor's GPA less than 3.0, state teaching certification; letter of intent; two professional references. Additional exam requirements/recommendations for international students: Required—TOEFL (minimum score 550 paper-based; 213 computer-based). *Application deadline:* For fall admission, 6/1 for domestic and international students; for spring admission, 10/1 for domestic and international students. Applications are processed on a rolling basis. Application fee: $30. *Expenses:* Tuition, state resident: full-time $5729; part-time $302 per credit hour. Tuition, nonresident: full-time $20,059; part-time $961 per credit hour. *Required fees:* $1509; $63 per credit hour. *Financial support:* Fellowships, teaching assistantships, career-related internships or fieldwork, Federal Work-Study, scholarships/grants, and unspecified assistantships available. Financial award application deadline: 4/15; financial award applicants required to submit FAFSA. *Unit head:* Dr. William H. Evans, Acting Director, 850-474-2892, Fax: 850-474-2844, E-mail: wevans@uwf.edu. *Application contact:* Terry McCray, Assistant Director of Graduate Admissions, 850-473-7718, Fax: 850-473-7714, E-mail: gradadmissions@uwf.edu.

University of West Georgia, College of Education, Department of Collaborative Support and Intervention, Carrollton, GA 30118. Offers English to speakers of other languages (Ed S); guidance and counseling (M Ed, Ed S); professional counseling (M Ed, Ed S); professional counseling and supervision (Ed D, Ed S); reading education (M Ed, Ed S); reading endorsement (Ed S); special education-general (M Ed, Ed S); speech-language pathology (M Ed). Part-time and evening/weekend programs available. *Faculty:* 22 full-time (13 women), 6 part-time/adjunct (4 women). *Students:* 174 full-time (140 women), 253 part-time (228 women); includes 155 minority (127 Black or African American, non-Hispanic/Latino; 3 Asian, non-Hispanic/Latino; 14 Hispanic/Latino; 11 Two or more races, non-Hispanic/Latino), 2 international. Average age 33. 282 applicants, 49% accepted, 50 enrolled. In 2011, 98 master's, 27 other advanced degrees awarded. *Degree requirements:* For master's, comprehensive exam; for Ed S, research project. *Entrance requirements:* For master's, minimum GPA of 2.7; for Ed S, master's degree, minimum graduate GPA of 2.7. Additional exam requirements/recommendations for international students: Required—TOEFL (minimum score 523 paper-based; 193 computer-based; 69 iBT); Recommended—IELTS (minimum score 6). *Application deadline:* For fall admission, 6/3 for domestic students, 6/1 for international students; for spring admission, 10/7 for domestic students, 10/15 for international students. Applications are processed on a rolling basis. Application fee: $30. Electronic applications accepted. *Expenses:* Tuition, state resident: full-time $4336; part-time $181 per credit hour. Tuition, nonresident: full-time $17,362; part-time $724 per credit hour. Tuition and fees vary according to course load, degree level, campus/location and program. *Financial support:* In 2011–12, 5 research assistantships with full tuition reimbursements (averaging $3,000 per year) were awarded; career-related internships or fieldwork and scholarships/grants also available. Support available to part-time students. Financial award applicants required to submit FAFSA. *Unit head:* Dr. Michael Garrett, Chair, 678-839-6567, Fax: 678-839-6162, E-mail: mgarrett@westga.edu. *Application contact:* Deanna Richards, Coordinator, Graduate Studies, 678-839-5946, E-mail: drichard@westga.edu. Web site: http://www.westga.edu/coecsi.

University of Wisconsin–Eau Claire, College of Education and Human Sciences, Program in Reading, Eau Claire, WI 54702-4004. Offers MST. Part-time programs available. *Faculty:* 13 full-time (9 women). *Students:* 8 part-time (7 women). Average age 32. 2 applicants, 100% accepted, 2 enrolled. In 2011, 9 master's awarded. *Degree requirements:* For master's, comprehensive exam, portfolio with an oral examination. *Entrance requirements:* For master's, certification to teach. Additional exam requirements/recommendations for international students: Required—TOEFL (minimum score 550 paper-based; 213 computer-based; 79 iBT); Recommended—IELTS (minimum score 7). *Application deadline:* For fall admission, 7/1 priority date for domestic students, 6/1 for international students; for spring admission, 12/1 priority date for domestic students, 11/1 for international students. Applications are processed on a rolling basis. Application fee: $56. *Expenses:* Tuition, state resident: full-time $7312; part-time $406 per credit. Tuition, nonresident: full-time $16,771; part-time $932 per credit. *Required fees:* $1101; $61 per credit. *Financial support:* Federal Work-Study and unspecified assistantships available. Financial award application deadline: 3/1; financial award applicants required to submit FAFSA. *Unit head:* Dr. Jill Pastrana, Chair, 715-836-2013, Fax: 715-836-4868, E-mail: pastrajp@uwec.edu. *Application contact:* Dr. Sherry Macaul, Coordinator, 715-836-5735, E-mail: macaulsl@uwec.edu. Web site: http://www.uwec.edu/ES/programs/readinglicensure.htm.

University of Wisconsin–Milwaukee, Graduate School, School of Education, Department of Curriculum and Instruction, Milwaukee, WI 53201-0413. Offers curriculum planning and instruction improvement (MS); early childhood education (MS); elementary education (MS); junior high/middle school education (MS); reading education (MS); secondary education (MS); teaching in an urban setting (MS). Part-time programs available. *Faculty:* 18 full-time (13 women). *Students:* 29 full-time (23 women), 54 part-time (44 women); includes 21 minority (10 Black or African American, non-Hispanic/Latino; 4 Asian, non-Hispanic/Latino; 3 Hispanic/Latino; 4 Two or more races, non-Hispanic/Latino). Average age 32. 43 applicants, 65% accepted, 13 enrolled. In 2011, 23 degrees awarded. *Degree requirements:* For master's, thesis or alternative. *Entrance requirements:* Additional exam requirements/recommendations for international students: Required—TOEFL (minimum score 550 paper-based; 79 iBT), IELTS (minimum score 6.5). *Application deadline:* For fall admission, 1/1 priority date for domestic students; for spring admission, 9/1 for domestic students. Applications are processed on a rolling basis. Application fee: $56 ($96 for international students). Electronic applications accepted. One-time fee: $506.10 full-time. Tuition and fees vary according to course load and reciprocity agreements. *Financial support:* In 2011–12, 1 fellowship was awarded; research assistantships, teaching assistantships, career-related internships or fieldwork, health care benefits, unspecified assistantships, and project assistantships also available. Support available to part-time students. Financial award application deadline: 4/15; financial award applicants required to submit FAFSA. *Total annual research expenditures:* $21,843. *Unit head:* Hope Longwell-Grice, Department Chair, 414-229-3059, Fax: 414-229-5571, E-mail: hope@uwm.edu. *Application contact:* General Information Contact, 414-229-4982, Fax: 414-229-6967, E-mail: gradschool@uwm.edu. Web site: http://www.uwm.edu/SOE/.

University of Wisconsin–Oshkosh, Graduate Studies, College of Education and Human Services, Department of Reading Education, Oshkosh, WI 54901. Offers MSE. Program offered jointly with University of Wisconsin–Green Bay. Part-time programs available. *Degree requirements:* For master's, thesis or alternative, reflective journey course. *Entrance requirements:* For master's, interview, teaching certificate, undergraduate degree in teacher education, letters of recommendation. Additional exam requirements/recommendations for international students: Required—TOEFL (minimum score 550 paper-based; 213 computer-based; 79 iBT). Electronic applications accepted. *Faculty research:* Writing and reading, assessment, learner-centered instruction, multicultural literature, family literacy.

University of Wisconsin–River Falls, Outreach and Graduate Studies, College of Education and Professional Studies, Department of Teacher Education, River Falls, WI 54022. Offers elementary education (MSE); professional development shared inquiry communities (MSE); reading (MSE). Part-time programs available. *Degree requirements:* For master's, comprehensive exam, thesis or alternative. *Entrance requirements:* For master's, minimum GPA of 2.75. Additional exam requirements/recommendations for international students: Required—TOEFL (minimum score 500 paper-based; 65 iBT), IELTS (minimum score 5.5). Electronic applications accepted.

University of Wisconsin–Stevens Point, College of Professional Studies, School of Education, Program in Education—General/Reading, Stevens Point, WI 54481-3897. Offers MSE. Part-time programs available. *Degree requirements:* For master's, comprehensive exam, thesis or alternative. *Entrance requirements:* For master's, minimum undergraduate GPA of 3.0, teacher certification, 2 years teaching experience, letters of recommendation. Additional exam requirements/recommendations for international students: Required—TOEFL (minimum score 523 paper-based; 193 computer-based). *Faculty research:* Reading strategies in the content areas, gifted education, curriculum and instruction, standards-based education.

University of Wisconsin–Superior, Graduate Division, Department of Teacher Education, Program in Teaching Reading, Superior, WI 54880-4500. Offers MSE. Part-time and evening/weekend programs available. *Degree requirements:* For master's, comprehensive exam, thesis or alternative, research project. *Entrance requirements:* For master's, minimum GPA of 2.75, teaching certificate.

University of Wisconsin–Whitewater, School of Graduate Studies, College of Education and Professional Studies, Department of Curriculum and Instruction, Whitewater, WI 53190-1790. Offers professional development (MS), including bilingual education, challenging advanced learners, curriculum and instruction, educational leadership, health, human performance and recreation, health, physical education and coaching, information technologies and libraries, reading. *Accreditation:* NCATE. Part-time and evening/weekend programs available. Postbaccalaureate distance learning degree programs offered. *Students:* 25 full-time (12 women), 68 part-time (51 women); includes 26 minority (15 Black or African American, non-Hispanic/Latino; 3 Asian, non-Hispanic/Latino; 8 Hispanic/Latino). Average age 33. 29 applicants, 86% accepted, 16 enrolled. In 2011, 44 master's awarded. *Degree requirements:* For master's, thesis or integrated project. *Entrance requirements:* Additional exam requirements/recommendations for international students: Required—TOEFL (minimum score 550 paper-based; 213 computer-based; 80 iBT), IELTS (minimum score 6). *Application deadline:* For fall admission, 7/15 priority date for domestic students, 7/15 for international students; for spring admission, 12/1 priority date for domestic students, 12/1 for international students. Applications are processed on a rolling basis. Application fee: $56. Electronic applications accepted. *Expenses:* Tuition, state resident: full-time $4088. Tuition, nonresident: full-time $8817. Tuition and fees vary according to program. *Financial support:* Research assistantships, Federal Work-Study, unspecified assistantships, and out-of-state fee waivers available. Support available to part-time students. Financial award application deadline: 3/15; financial award applicants required to submit FAFSA. *Faculty research:* Hybrid of exercise physiology and psychology; gender equity; education, pedagogy, and technology; comprehensive school health education. *Unit head:* Dr. John Zbikowski, Coordinator, 262-472-4860, Fax: 262-472-1988, E-mail: zbikowskij@uww.edu. *Application contact:* Sally A. Lange, School of Graduate Studies, 262-472-1006, Fax: 262-472-5027, E-mail: gradschl@uww.edu.

Ursuline College, School of Graduate Studies, Program in Education, Pepper Pike, OH 44124-4398. Offers art education (MA); early childhood education (MA); language arts education (MA); life science education (MA); math education (MA); middle school education (MA); social studies education (MA); special education (MA). *Accreditation:* NCATE. *Faculty:* 3 full-time (all women), 8 part-time/adjunct (6 women). *Students:* 28 full-time (22 women), 1 (woman) part-time; includes 11 minority (7 Black or African American, non-Hispanic/Latino; 2 Asian, non-Hispanic/Latino; 1 Hispanic/Latino; 1 Native Hawaiian or other Pacific Islander, non-Hispanic/Latino). Average age 32. In 2011, 29 master's awarded. *Degree requirements:* For master's, comprehensive exam. *Entrance requirements:* For master's, minimum undergraduate GPA of 3.0. Additional exam requirements/recommendations for international students: Required—TOEFL (minimum score 500 paper-based; 173 computer-based). *Application deadline:* For fall admission, 8/1 priority date for domestic students. Applications are processed on a rolling basis. Application fee: $25. *Expenses:* Contact institution. *Financial support:* Federal Work-Study available. Financial award application deadline: 3/1. *Unit head:* Dr. Edna West, Director, Master's Apprentice Program, 440-646-6134, Fax: 440-684-6088, E-mail: ewest@ursuline.edu. *Application contact:* Melanie Steele, Graduate Admission Assistant, 440-646-8199, Fax: 440-684-6138, E-mail: graduateadmissions@ursuline.edu.

Vanderbilt University, Peabody College, Department of Teaching and Learning, Nashville, TN 37240-1001. Offers elementary education (M Ed); English language learners (M Ed); learning and instruction (M Ed); learning, diversity, and urban studies (M Ed); reading education (M Ed); secondary education (M Ed). *Accreditation:* NCATE. *Faculty:* 35 full-time (24 women), 19 part-time/adjunct (14 women). *Students:* 123 full-time (96 women), 38 part-time (34 women); includes 26 minority (6 Black or African American, non-Hispanic/Latino; 3 Asian, non-Hispanic/Latino; 7 Hispanic/Latino; 10 Two or more races, non-Hispanic/Latino), 12 international. Average age 26. 251 applicants, 56% accepted, 60 enrolled. In 2011, 80 master's awarded. *Degree requirements:* For master's, comprehensive exam, thesis optional. *Entrance requirements:* For master's, GRE General Test, MAT. Additional exam requirements/recommendations for international students: Required—TOEFL (minimum score 550 paper-based; 213 computer-based). *Application deadline:* For fall admission, 12/31 priority date for domestic students, 12/31 for international students; for spring admission, 11/1 priority date for domestic students, 11/1 for international students. Applications are processed on a rolling basis. Application fee: $0. Electronic applications accepted. *Financial support:* Fellowships with full and partial tuition reimbursements, research assistantships with full and partial tuition reimbursements, teaching assistantships with full and partial tuition reimbursements, Federal Work-Study, institutionally sponsored loans, scholarships/grants, tuition waivers (partial), and unspecified assistantships available. Support available to part-time students. Financial award application deadline: 2/1; financial award applicants required to submit FAFSA. *Faculty research:* Learning environments for mathematics of space and motion, visual programming tools for children's learning of basic science concepts, pathways for elementary and middle school children's learning about measurement and statistics, early reading intervention, professional development for ambitious mathematics teaching. *Unit head:* Dr. David Dickinson, Acting Chair, 615-322-8100, Fax: 615-322-8999, E-mail: david.k.dickinson@vanderbilt.edu. *Application contact:* Angela Saylor, Educational Coordinator, 615-322-8092, Fax: 615-322-8999, E-mail: angela.saylor@vanderbilt.edu.

Virginia Commonwealth University, Graduate School, School of Education, Program in Adult Learning, Richmond, VA 23284-9005. Offers adult literacy (M Ed); human resource development (M Ed); teaching and learning with technology (M Ed). *Accreditation:* NCATE. Part-time programs available. *Entrance requirements:* For master's, GRE General Test or MAT. Additional exam requirements/recommendations for international students: Required—TOEFL (minimum score 600 paper-based; 250 computer-based; 100 iBT). Electronic applications accepted. *Expenses:* Tuition, state resident: full-time $9133; part-time $507 per credit. Tuition, nonresident: full-time $18,777; part-time $1043 per credit. *Required fees:* $77 per credit. Tuition and fees vary according to degree level, campus/location, program and student level. *Faculty research:* Adult development and learning, program planning and evaluation.

Virginia Commonwealth University, Graduate School, School of Education, Program in Reading, Richmond, VA 23284-9005. Offers reading (M Ed); reading specialist (Certificate). *Accreditation:* NCATE. *Degree requirements:* For master's, comprehensive exam. *Entrance requirements:* For master's, GRE General Test or MAT. Additional exam requirements/recommendations for international students: Required—TOEFL (minimum score 600 paper-based; 250 computer-based; 100 iBT). Electronic applications accepted. *Expenses:* Tuition, state resident: full-time $9133; part-time $507 per credit. Tuition, nonresident: full-time $18,777; part-time $1043 per credit. *Required fees:* $77 per credit. Tuition and fees vary according to degree level, campus/location, program and student level.

Wagner College, Division of Graduate Studies, Department of Education, Program in Literacy (B-6), Staten Island, NY 10301-4495. Offers MS Ed. Part-time programs available. *Faculty:* 3 full-time (2 women), 2 part-time/adjunct (both women). *Students:* 12 full-time (11 women), 12 part-time (all women); includes 1 minority (Hispanic/Latino). Average age 24. 12 applicants, 100% accepted, 12 enrolled. In 2011, 10 master's awarded. *Degree requirements:* For master's, thesis. *Entrance requirements:* For master's, minimum GPA of 2.75. Additional exam requirements/recommendations for international students: Required—TOEFL (minimum score 550 paper-based; 217 computer-based; 79 iBT). *Application deadline:* For fall admission, 4/1 priority date for domestic students, 3/1 for international students; for spring admission, 11/1 priority date for domestic students, 10/1 for international students. Applications are processed on a rolling basis. Application fee: $50 ($85 for international students). *Expenses:* Tuition: Full-time $16,200; part-time $890 per credit. *Financial support:* Fellowships, unspecified assistantships, and alumni fellowship grant available. Financial award applicants required to submit FAFSA. *Unit head:* Dr. Stephen Preskill, Graduate Coordinator, 718-420-4070, Fax: 718-390-3456, E-mail: stephen.preskill@wagner.edu. *Application contact:* Patricia Clancy, Administrative Assistant, Admissions, 718-420-4464, Fax: 718-390-3105, E-mail: patricia.clancy@wagner.edu.

Walden University, Graduate Programs, Richard W. Riley College of Education and Leadership, Minneapolis, MN 55401. Offers administrator leadership for teaching and

learning (Ed D, Ed S); adult education (Ed D, Ed S); adult learning (MS, Postbaccalaureate Certificate), including developmental education (MS), online teaching (MS), teaching adults English as a second language (MS), training and performance management (MS); college teaching and learning (Ed D, Ed S, Postbaccalaureate Certificate); curriculum, instruction and assessment (Ed D, Postbaccalaureate Certificate); curriculum, instruction, and professional development (Ed S); developmental education (Postbaccalaureate Certificate); early childhood administration, management, and leadership (Postbaccalaureate Certificate); early childhood education (birth-grade 3) (MAT); early childhood public policy and advocacy (Postbaccalaureate Certificate); early childhood studies (MS), including administration, management and leadership, early childhood public policy and advocacy, teaching adults in the early childhood field, teaching and diversity; education (MS, PhD), including adolescent literacy and technology (grades 6-12) (MS), adult education leadership (PhD), assessment, evaluation, and accountability (PhD), community college leadership (PhD), curriculum, instruction, and assessment, early childhood education (PhD), educational technology (PhD), elementary reading and literacy (MS), elementary reading and mathematics (MS), general program, global and comparative education (PhD), higher education (PhD), integrating technology in the classroom (MS), K-12 educational leadership (PhD), leadership, policy and change (PhD), learning, instruction and innovation (PhD), literacy and learning in the content areas (MS), mathematics (grades 6-8) (MS), mathematics (grades K-5) (MS), middle level education (grades 5-8) (MS), professional development (MS), science (grades K-8) (MS), self-designed (PhD), special education (PhD), special education (non-licensure) (MS), teacher leadership (grades K-12) (MS), teaching English language learners (grades K-12) (MS); educational leadership and administration (principal preparation) (Ed S); educational technology (Ed S); elementary reading and literacy (Postbaccalaureate Certificate); engaging culturally diverse learners (Postbaccalaureate Certificate); enrollment management and institutional marketing (Postbaccalaureate Certificate); higher education (MS), including college teaching and learning, enrollment management and institutional planning, global higher education, leadership for student success, online and distance learning; higher education leadership (Ed D); instructional design (Postbaccalaureate Certificate); instructional design and technology (MS), including general program (MS, PhD), online learning, training and performance improvement; integrating technology in the classroom (Postbaccalaureate Certificate); online teaching for adult learners (Postbaccalaureate Certificate); professional development (Postbaccalaureate Certificate); reading and literacy leadership (Ed D); science K-8 (Postbaccalaureate Certificate); special education (Ed D, Ed S); special education: emotional/behavioral disorders (K-12) (MAT); special education: learning disabilities (K-12) (MAT); teacher leadership (Ed D, Ed S, Postbaccalaureate Certificate); training and performance management (Postbaccalaureate Certificate). Part-time and evening/weekend programs available. Postbaccalaureate distance learning degree programs offered (minimal on-campus study). *Faculty:* 71 full-time (48 women), 853 part-time/adjunct (585 women). *Students:* 11,326 full-time (9,212 women), 2,148 part-time (1,795 women); includes 5,346 minority (4,403 Black or African American, non-Hispanic/Latino; 76 American Indian or Alaska Native, non-Hispanic/Latino; 140 Asian, non-Hispanic/Latino; 561 Hispanic/Latino; 21 Native Hawaiian or other Pacific Islander, non-Hispanic/Latino; 145 Two or more races, non-Hispanic/Latino), 322 international. Average age 39. In 2011, 3,477 master's, 318 doctorates, 471 other advanced degrees awarded. *Degree requirements:* For doctorate, thesis/dissertation (for some programs), residency; for other advanced degree, residency (for some programs). *Entrance requirements:* For master's, bachelor's degree or equivalent in related field; minimum GPA of 2.5; official transcripts; goal statement; access to computer and Internet; for doctorate, master's degree or equivalent in related field; minimum GPA of 3.0; official transcripts; three years' related professional/academic experience (preferred); access to computer and Internet; for other advanced degree, master's degree or equivalent in related field; minimum GPA of 3.0; 3 years related professional/academic experience (preferred); access to computer and Internet (Ed S). Additional exam requirements/recommendations for international students: Required—TOEFL (minimum score 550 paper-based; 213 computer-based), IELTS (minimum score 6.5), or Michigan English Language Assessment Battery (minimum score 82). *Application deadline:* Applications are processed on a rolling basis. Application fee: $50. Electronic applications accepted. *Financial support:* Federal Work-Study, scholarships/grants, unspecified assistantships, and family tuition reduction, active duty/veteran tuition reduction, group tuition reduction, interest-free payment plans, employee tuition reduction available. Support available to part-time students. Financial award applicants required to submit FAFSA. *Unit head:* Dr. Kate Steffens, Dean, 800-925-3368. *Application contact:* Jennifer Hall, Vice President of Enrollment Management, 866-4-WALDEN, E-mail: info@waldenu.edu. Web site: http://www.waldenu.edu/Colleges-and-Schools/College-of-Education-and-Leadership.htm.

Walla Walla University, Graduate School, School of Education and Psychology, College Place, WA 99324-1198. Offers counseling psychology (MA); curriculum and instruction (M Ed, MA, MAT); educational leadership (M Ed, MA, MAT); literacy instruction (M Ed, MA, MAT); students at risk (M Ed, MA, MAT); teaching (MAT). Part-time programs available. *Entrance requirements:* For master's, GRE General Test, minimum GPA of 2.75. Additional exam requirements/recommendations for international students: Required—TOEFL (minimum score 550 paper-based; 213 computer-based; 79 iBT). Electronic applications accepted. *Faculty research:* Admissions/retention, instructional psychology, moral development, teaching of reading.

Washburn University, College of Arts and Sciences, Department of Education, Topeka, KS 66621. Offers curriculum and instruction (M Ed); educational leadership (M Ed); reading (M Ed); special education (M Ed). *Accreditation:* NCATE. Part-time programs available. *Faculty:* 6 full-time (3 women), 1 (woman) part-time/adjunct. *Students:* 2 full-time (both women), 26 part-time (16 women). Average age 36. In 2011, 17 master's awarded. *Degree requirements:* For master's, comprehensive exam, thesis or alternative, portfolio, comprehensive paper, or action research project. *Entrance requirements:* For master's, department graduate admissions test, GRE General Test, or MAT, minimum GPA of 3.0 in graduate coursework or last 60 hours of undergraduate coursework. Additional exam requirements/recommendations for international students: Required—TOEFL (minimum score 550 paper-based; 80 iBT). *Application deadline:* For fall admission, 8/1 for domestic and international students; for spring admission, 11/1 for domestic and international students. Applications are processed on a rolling basis. *Expenses:* Tuition, state resident: full-time $5346; part-time $297 per credit hour. Tuition, nonresident: full-time $10,908; part-time $606 per credit hour. *Required fees:* $86; $43 per semester. *Financial support:* Federal Work-Study, institutionally sponsored loans, and scholarships/grants available. Support available to part-time students. Financial award applicants required to submit FAFSA. *Faculty research:* Reading/literature/literacy, foundations, educational administration/leadership, special education, diversity. *Unit head:* Dr. Judith McConnell-Farmer, Interim Chairperson, 785-670-1472, Fax: 785-670-1046, E-mail: judy.mcconnell-farmer@washburn.edu. *Application contact:* Tara Porter, Licensure Officer, 785-670-1434, Fax: 785-670-1046, E-mail: tara.porter@washburn.edu. Web site: http://www.washburn.edu/academics/college-schools/arts-sciences/departments/education/index.html.

Washington State University, Graduate School, College of Education, Department of Teaching and Learning, Pullman, WA 99164. Offers curriculum and instruction (Ed D, PhD); diverse languages (M Ed, MA); elementary education (M Ed, MA, MIT); exercise science (MS); literacy education (M Ed, MA, PhD); math education (PhD); secondary education (M Ed, MA). *Accreditation:* NCATE. *Faculty:* 20. *Students:* 79 full-time (51 women), 40 part-time (31 women); includes 24 minority (3 Black or African American, non-Hispanic/Latino; 5 Asian, non-Hispanic/Latino; 13 Hispanic/Latino; 1 Native Hawaiian or other Pacific Islander, non-Hispanic/Latino; 2 Two or more races, non-Hispanic/Latino), 43 international. Average age 34. 106 applicants, 47% accepted, 43 enrolled. In 2011, 34 master's, 3 doctorates awarded. *Degree requirements:* For master's, comprehensive exam (for some programs), thesis (for some programs), oral or written exam; for doctorate, comprehensive exam, thesis/dissertation, oral and written exam. *Entrance requirements:* For master's and doctorate, GRE General Test, minimum GPA of 3.0, 3 letters of recommendation. Additional exam requirements/recommendations for international students: Required—TOEFL. *Application deadline:* For fall admission, 2/1 for domestic students, 3/1 for international students; for spring admission, 9/1 for domestic students, 7/1 for international students. Applications are processed on a rolling basis. Application fee: $75. *Financial support:* In 2011–12, 130 teaching assistantships with partial tuition reimbursements (averaging $18,204 per year) were awarded; career-related internships or fieldwork, Federal Work-Study, institutionally sponsored loans, tuition waivers (partial), unspecified assistantships, and staff assistantships, teaching associateships also available. Financial award application deadline: 4/1. *Faculty research:* Evolution of middle school education, issues in special education, computer-assisted language learning. *Total annual research expenditures:* $324,000. *Unit head:* Dr. Dawn Shinew, Interim Chair, 509-335-5027, E-mail: dshinew@wsu.edu. *Application contact:* Graduate School Admissions, 800-GRADWSU, Fax: 509-335-1949, E-mail: gradsch@wsu.edu. Web site: http://www.educ.wsu.edu/TL/overview.htm.

Washington State University Tri-Cities, Graduate Programs, Program in Education, Richland, WA 99352-1671. Offers counseling (Ed M); educational leadership (Ed M, Ed D); literacy (Ed M); secondary certification (Ed M); teaching (MIT). Part-time programs available. *Faculty:* 24. *Students:* 19 full-time (14 women), 73 part-time (46 women); includes 18 minority (1 Black or African American, non-Hispanic/Latino; 3 Asian, non-Hispanic/Latino; 14 Hispanic/Latino). Average age 34. 26 applicants, 69% accepted, 18 enrolled. In 2011, 31 master's awarded. *Degree requirements:* For master's, comprehensive exam, thesis or alternative; for doctorate, comprehensive exam, thesis/dissertation. *Entrance requirements:* For master's, GRE, minimum GPA of 3.0, Working with Youth form, Character and Fitness form, 3 letters of recommendation. Additional exam requirements/recommendations for international students: Required—TOEFL. *Application deadline:* For fall admission, 1/10 priority date for domestic students, 1/10 for international students; for spring admission, 7/1 priority date for domestic students, 7/1 for international students. Applications are processed on a rolling basis. Application fee: $75. Electronic applications accepted. *Financial support:* In 2011–12, 59 students received support, including research assistantships (averaging $14,634 per year), teaching assistantships (averaging $13,383 per year); Federal Work-Study, scholarships/grants, and unspecified assistantships also available. Financial award application deadline: 2/15. *Faculty research:* Multicultural counseling, socio-cultural influences in schools, diverse learners, teacher education, K-12 educational leadership. *Unit head:* Dr. Elizabeth Nagel, Director, 509-372-7398, E-mail: elizabeth_nagel@tricity.wsu.edu. *Application contact:* Helen Berry, Academic Coordinator, 800-GRADWSU, Fax: 509-372-3796, E-mail: hberry@tricity.wsu.edu. Web site: http://www.tricity.wsu.edu/education/graduate.html.

Wayne State University, College of Education, Division of Teacher Education, Detroit, MI 48202. Offers art education (M Ed), including art therapy; bilingual/bicultural education (M Ed); career and technical education (M Ed); curriculum and instruction (Ed D, PhD, Ed S), including art education (PhD), bilingual education (Ed D, Ed S), bilingual-bicultural education (PhD), career and technical education (MAT, Ed D, PhD, Ed S), early childhood education (MAT, Ed D, PhD, Ed S), elementary education, English as a second language (MAT, Ed D, Ed S), English education (MAT, Ed D, PhD, Ed S), foreign language education (MAT, PhD), K-12 curriculum, mathematics education (MAT, Ed D, PhD, Ed S), science education (MAT, Ed D, PhD, Ed S), secondary education, social studies education (MAT, Ed S), social studies education: secondary (Ed D, PhD); elementary education (MAT), including special education; elementary education (M Ed, MAT), including children's literature (MAT), early childhood education (MAT, Ed D, PhD, Ed S), general elementary education (MAT); elementary or secondary education (MAT), including bilingual/bicultural education, English as a second language (MAT, Ed D, Ed S), mathematics education (MAT, Ed D, PhD, Ed S), science education (MAT, Ed D, PhD, Ed S), social studies education (MAT, Ed S); English education-secondary (M Ed); foreign language education (M Ed); mathematics education (M Ed); reading (M Ed, Ed S); reading, languages and literature (Ed D); science education (M Ed); secondary education (MAT), including art education (K-12), career and technical education (MAT, Ed D, PhD, Ed S), English education (MAT, Ed D, PhD, Ed S), foreign language education (MAT, PhD), kinesiology; social studies education secondary (M Ed); special education (M Ed, Ed D, PhD, Ed S). *Students:* 216 full-time (154 women), 626 part-time (478 women); includes 289 minority (227 Black or African American, non-Hispanic/Latino; 4 American Indian or Alaska Native, non-Hispanic/Latino; 27 Asian, non-Hispanic/Latino; 21 Hispanic/Latino; 1 Native Hawaiian or other Pacific Islander, non-Hispanic/Latino; 9 Two or more races, non-Hispanic/Latino), 14 international. Average age 37. 347 applicants, 37% accepted, 93 enrolled. In 2011, 226 master's, 12 doctorates, 46 other advanced degrees awarded. *Degree requirements:* For master's, thesis (for some programs), thesis, essay or project (for some M Ed programs), professional field experience (for MAT programs); for doctorate, thesis/dissertation. *Entrance requirements:* For master's, Michigan Basic Skills Test (MA in teaching); for doctorate, minimum undergraduate GPA of 3.0, graduate 3.5; interview, curriculum vitae; references. Additional exam requirements/recommendations for international students: Required—TOEFL (minimum score 550 paper-based; 213 computer-based), TWE (minimum score 5.5). *Application deadline:* For fall admission, 6/1 priority date for domestic students, 5/1 for international students; for winter admission, 10/1 priority date for domestic students, 9/1 for international students; for spring admission, 2/1 priority date for domestic students, 1/1 for international students. Applications are processed on a rolling basis. Application fee: $50. Electronic applications accepted. *Expenses:* Tuition, state resident: part-time $512.85 per credit. Tuition, nonresident: part-time $1132.65 per credit. *Required fees:* $26.60 per credit. $199.65 per semester. Tuition and fees vary according to course load and program. *Financial support:* In 2011–12, 42 students received support. Fellowships, research assistantships with tuition reimbursements available, teaching assistantships, scholarships/grants, and unspecified assistantships available. *Faculty research:* Reading and writing literacy and literature. *Total annual research expenditures:* $264,016. *Unit head:* Dr. Craig Roney, Assistant Dean, 313-577-0902, E-mail: rroney@wayne.edu. Web site: http://coe.wayne.edu/ted/index.php.

West Chester University of Pennsylvania, College of Education, Department of Literacy, West Chester, PA 19383. Offers literacy (Certificate); literacy coaching (Certificate); reading (M Ed, Teaching Certificate). Part-time programs available. *Faculty:* 11 part-time/adjunct (8 women). *Students:* 17 full-time (all women), 136 part-time (132 women); includes 6 minority (2 Black or African American, non-Hispanic/Latino; 1 Asian, non-Hispanic/Latino; 2 Hispanic/Latino; 1 Two or more races, non-Hispanic/Latino). Average age 28. 47 applicants, 87% accepted, 30 enrolled. In 2011,

29 degrees awarded. *Degree requirements:* For master's, comprehensive exam, minimum GPA of 3.0; for other advanced degree, comprehensive exam. *Entrance requirements:* For master's, GRE or MAT if GPA is below 3.0, minimum GPA of 3.0, teaching certificate, two letters of reference. Additional exam requirements/recommendations for international students: Required—TOEFL (minimum score 550 paper-based; 213 computer-based; 80 iBT). *Application deadline:* For fall admission, 4/15 priority date for domestic students, 3/15 for international students; for spring admission, 10/15 priority date for domestic students, 9/1 for international students. Applications are processed on a rolling basis. Application fee: $45. Electronic applications accepted. *Expenses:* Tuition, state resident: full-time $7488; part-time $416 per credit. Tuition, nonresident: full-time $11,232; part-time $624 per credit. *Required fees:* $1784.64; $67.59 per credit. Tuition and fees vary according to program. *Financial support:* Unspecified assistantships available. Support available to part-time students. Financial award application deadline: 2/15; financial award applicants required to submit FAFSA. *Faculty research:* Teaching and mentoring pre-service and in-service teachers to teach reading in urban settings. *Unit head:* Dr. Sunita Mayor, Chair, 610-436-2282, Fax: 610-436-3102, E-mail: smayor@wcupa.edu. *Application contact:* Dr. Kevin Flanigan, Graduate Coordinator, 610-430-5642, Fax: 610-436-3102, E-mail: kflanigan@wcupa.edu. Web site: http://www.wcupa.edu/_academics/sch_sed.literacy/.

Western Connecticut State University, Division of Graduate Studies, School of Professional Studies, Department of Education and Educational Psychology, Reading Option, Danbury, CT 06810-6885. Offers MS. Part-time programs available. *Faculty:* 2 full-time (both women). *Students:* 24 part-time (21 women). Average age 32. 12 applicants, 83% accepted, 5 enrolled. In 2011, 7 degrees awarded. *Degree requirements:* For master's, thesis or research project, completion of program in 6 years. *Entrance requirements:* For master's, minimum GPA of 2.8, teaching certificate in elementary education. Additional exam requirements/recommendations for international students: Recommended—TOEFL (minimum score 550 paper-based; 213 computer-based; 79 iBT), IELTS (minimum score 6). *Application deadline:* For fall admission, 8/5 priority date for domestic students; for spring admission, 1/5 priority date for domestic students. Applications are processed on a rolling basis. Application fee: $50. Tuition and fees vary according to course level, course load, degree level and program. *Financial support:* In 2011–12, 1 student received support. Scholarships/grants available. Financial award application deadline: 5/1; financial award applicants required to submit FAFSA. *Faculty research:* Training guides for educators. *Unit head:* Dr. Adeline Merrill, Graduate Coordinator, 203-837-3267, Fax: 203-837-8413, E-mail: merrilla@wcsu.edu. *Application contact:* Chris Shankle, Associate Director of Graduate Studies, 203-837-9005, Fax: 203-837-8326, E-mail: shanklec@wcsu.edu.

Western Illinois University, School of Graduate Studies, College of Education and Human Services, Department of Curriculum and Instruction, Program in Reading, Macomb, IL 61455-1390. Offers MS Ed. *Accreditation:* NCATE. Part-time programs available. *Students:* 3 full-time (2 women), 117 part-time (115 women); includes 7 minority (4 Black or African American, non-Hispanic/Latino; 1 Asian, non-Hispanic/Latino; 2 Hispanic/Latino). Average age 34. 11 applicants, 73% accepted. In 2011, 33 master's awarded. *Degree requirements:* For master's, thesis or alternative. *Entrance requirements:* For master's, teacher certification. Additional exam requirements/recommendations for international students: Required—TOEFL (minimum score 550 paper-based; 213 computer-based; 80 iBT). *Application deadline:* Applications are processed on a rolling basis. Application fee: $30. Electronic applications accepted. *Expenses:* Tuition, state resident: part-time $281.16 per credit hour. Tuition, nonresident: part-time $562.32 per credit hour. Part-time tuition and fees vary according to campus/location and reciprocity agreements. *Financial support:* In 2011–12, 2 students received support, including 2 research assistantships with full tuition reimbursements available (averaging $7,360 per year). Financial award applicants required to submit FAFSA. *Unit head:* Dr. Laurel Borgia, Graduate Committee Chairperson, 309-298-1961. *Application contact:* Dr. Nancy Parsons, Assistant Director of Graduate Studies, 309-298-1806, Fax: 309-298-2345, E-mail: grad-office@wiu.edu. Web site: http://wiu.edu/curriculum.

Western Kentucky University, Graduate Studies, College of Education and Behavioral Sciences, School of Teacher Education, Bowling Green, KY 42101. Offers elementary education (MAE, Ed S); exceptional education: learning and behavioral disorders (MAE); exceptional education: moderate and severe disabilities (MAE); instructional design (MS); interdisciplinary early childhood education (MAE); library media education (MS); literacy education (MAE); middle grades education (MAE); secondary education (MAE, Ed S). Part-time and evening/weekend programs available. Postbaccalaureate distance learning degree programs offered (minimal on-campus study). *Degree requirements:* For master's, comprehensive exam. *Entrance requirements:* For master's, GRE General Test. Additional exam requirements/recommendations for international students: Required—TOEFL (minimum score 555 paper-based; 213 computer-based; 79 iBT). *Faculty research:* Teacher preparation in moderate/severe disabilities.

Western Michigan University, Graduate College, College of Education and Human Development, Department of Special Education and Literacy Studies, Kalamazoo, MI 49008. Offers literacy studies (MA); special education (MA, Ed D); teaching children with visual impairments (MA).

Western New Mexico University, Graduate Division, School of Education, Silver City, NM 88062-0680. Offers bilingual education (MAT); counseling (MA); educational leadership (MA); elementary education (MAT); reading (MAT); school psychology (MA); secondary education (MAT); special education (MAT); TESOL (teaching English to speakers of other languages) (MAT). *Accreditation:* NCATE. *Degree requirements:* For master's, comprehensive exam. *Entrance requirements:* For master's, GRE General Test, GRE Subject Test, minimum GPA of 3.2 in last 64 hours of undergraduate study. Additional exam requirements/recommendations for international students: Required—TOEFL (minimum score 550 paper-based; 213 computer-based). Electronic applications accepted.

Western State College of Colorado, Graduate Programs in Education, Gunnison, CO 81231. Offers education administrator leadership (MA); reading leadership (MA); teacher leadership (MA). Postbaccalaureate distance learning degree programs offered (minimal on-campus study). *Degree requirements:* For master's, capstone.

Westfield State University, Division of Graduate and Continuing Education, Department of Education, Program in Reading, Westfield, MA 01086. Offers M Ed. *Accreditation:* NCATE. Part-time and evening/weekend programs available. *Degree requirements:* For master's, comprehensive exam, practicum. *Entrance requirements:* For master's, GRE General Test or MAT, minimum undergraduate GPA of 2.7.

Westminster College, Programs in Education, Program in Reading, New Wilmington, PA 16172-0001. Offers M Ed, Certificate. Part-time and evening/weekend programs available. *Degree requirements:* For master's, comprehensive exam, portfolio. *Entrance requirements:* For master's, minimum GPA of 3.0.

West Texas A&M University, College of Education and Social Sciences, Division of Education, Program in Reading, Canyon, TX 79016-0001. Offers M Ed. Part-time and evening/weekend programs available. *Degree requirements:* For master's, comprehensive exam. *Entrance requirements:* For master's, GRE General Test, interview with master's committee chairperson, state certification as a reading specialist with 3 years of teaching experience. Electronic applications accepted. *Faculty research:* Multicultural child and adolescent literature, bilingual, dual language, monolingual classrooms.

West Virginia University, College of Human Resources and Education, Department of Curriculum and Instruction/Literacy Studies, Program in Reading, Morgantown, WV 26506. Offers MA. *Accreditation:* NCATE. Part-time programs available. *Degree requirements:* For master's, thesis optional, content exams. *Entrance requirements:* For master's, minimum GPA of 2.75. Additional exam requirements/recommendations for international students: Required—TOEFL. Electronic applications accepted. *Faculty research:* Teacher education, current practices, protocol research, metacognitive studies.

Wheelock College, Graduate Programs, Division of Education, Boston, MA 02215-4176. Offers early childhood education (MS); education leadership (MS); elementary education (MS); language, literacy, and reading (MS); teaching students with moderate disabilities (MS). *Accreditation:* NCATE. Postbaccalaureate distance learning degree programs offered (minimal on-campus study). *Degree requirements:* For master's, comprehensive exam. *Entrance requirements:* Additional exam requirements/recommendations for international students: Required—TOEFL. Electronic applications accepted. *Faculty research:* Symbolic learning, emergent literacy, diversity inclusion, beginning reading language and culture, math education.

Widener University, School of Human Service Professions, Center for Education, Chester, PA 19013-5792. Offers adult education (M Ed); counseling in higher education (M Ed); counselor education (M Ed); early childhood education (M Ed); educational foundations (M Ed); educational leadership (M Ed); educational psychology (M Ed); elementary education (M Ed); English and language arts (M Ed); health education (M Ed); higher education leadership (Ed D); home and school visitor (M Ed); human sexuality (M Ed, PhD); mathematics education (M Ed); middle school education (M Ed); principalship (M Ed); reading and language arts (Ed D); reading education (M Ed); school administration (Ed D); science education (M Ed); social studies education (M Ed); special education (M Ed); technology education (M Ed). *Accreditation:* NCATE. Part-time and evening/weekend programs available. Terminal master's awarded for partial completion of doctoral program. *Degree requirements:* For doctorate, thesis/dissertation. *Entrance requirements:* For master's, minimum GPA of 2.5; for doctorate, GRE or MAT, minimum GPA of 2.0 (undergraduate), 3.5 (graduate). Electronic applications accepted. *Expenses:* Contact institution. *Faculty research:* Reading and cognition, adult education, technology education, educational leadership, special education.

Wilkes University, College of Graduate and Professional Studies, School of Education, Wilkes-Barre, PA 18766-0002. Offers art and science of teaching (MS Ed); classroom technology (MS Ed); early childhood literacy (MS Ed); educational computing (MS Ed); educational development and strategies (MS Ed); educational leadership (MS Ed); educational technology (Ed D); higher education administration (Ed D); instructional media (MS Ed); instructional technology (MS Ed); K-12 administration (Ed D); online teaching (MS Ed); reading (MS Ed); school business leadership (MS Ed); secondary education (MS Ed), including biology, chemistry, English, history, mathematics; special education (MS Ed); teaching English as a second language (MS Ed); twenty-first century teaching and learning (MS Ed). Part-time and evening/weekend programs available. Postbaccalaureate distance learning degree programs offered (minimal on-campus study). *Students:* 92 full-time (63 women), 2,005 part-time (1,459 women); includes 89 minority (23 Black or African American, non-Hispanic/Latino; 1 American Indian or Alaska Native, non-Hispanic/Latino; 14 Asian, non-Hispanic/Latino; 33 Hispanic/Latino; 1 Native Hawaiian or other Pacific Islander, non-Hispanic/Latino; 17 Two or more races, non-Hispanic/Latino), 6 international. Average age 33. In 2011, 1,150 master's, 3 doctorates awarded. *Entrance requirements:* Additional exam requirements/recommendations for international students: Required—TOEFL (minimum score 550 paper-based; 213 computer-based; 79 iBT). *Application deadline:* Applications are processed on a rolling basis. Application fee: $45. Electronic applications accepted. *Expenses:* Contact institution. *Financial support:* Federal Work-Study and unspecified assistantships available. Financial award application deadline: 3/1; financial award applicants required to submit FAFSA. *Unit head:* Dr. Michael Speziale, Dean, 570-408-4679, Fax: 570-408-4905, E-mail: michael.speziale@wilkes.edu. *Application contact:* Erin Sutzko, Director of Extended Learning, 570-408-4253, Fax: 570-408-7846, E-mail: erin.sutzko@wilkes.edu. Web site: http://www.wilkes.edu/pages/383.asp.

Willamette University, Graduate School of Education, Salem, OR 97301-3931. Offers environmental literacy (M Ed); reading (M Ed); special education (M Ed); teaching (MAT). *Accreditation:* NCATE. Evening/weekend programs available. *Degree requirements:* For master's, leadership project (action research). *Entrance requirements:* For master's, California Basic Educational Skills Test, Multiple Subject Assessment for Teachers, PRAXIS, minimum GPA of 3.0, classroom experience, 2 letters of reference. Additional exam requirements/recommendations for international students: Recommended—TOEFL. Electronic applications accepted. *Expenses:* Contact institution. *Faculty research:* Educational leadership, multicultural education, middle school education, clinical supervision, educational technology.

William Paterson University of New Jersey, College of Education, Wayne, NJ 07470-8420. Offers curriculum and learning (M Ed); educational leadership (M Ed); reading (M Ed); special education and counseling services (M Ed), including counseling services, special education; teaching (MAT). *Accreditation:* NCATE. Part-time and evening/weekend programs available. *Degree requirements:* For master's, comprehensive exam. *Entrance requirements:* For master's, GRE General Test, MAT, minimum GPA of 2.75, teaching certificate. Electronic applications accepted. *Faculty research:* Urban community service.

Wilmington College, Department of Education, Wilmington, OH 45177. Offers reading (M Ed); special education (M Ed). Part-time programs available. *Degree requirements:* For master's, comprehensive exam. *Entrance requirements:* For master's, GRE or MAT, minimum GPA of 3.0, 2 letters of recommendation. Additional exam requirements/recommendations for international students: Required—TOEFL. *Faculty research:* Reading instruction, special education practices, conflict resolution in the schools, models of higher education for teachers.

Wilmington University, College of Education, New Castle, DE 19720-6491. Offers applied technology in education (M Ed); career and technical education (M Ed); educational leadership (Ed D); elementary and secondary school counseling (M Ed); elementary studies (M Ed); ESOL literacy (M Ed); higher education leadership (Ed D); instruction: gifted and talented (M Ed); instruction: teacher of reading (M Ed); instruction: teaching and learning (M Ed); organizational leadership (Ed D); school leadership (M Ed); secondary education (MAT); special education (M Ed). *Accreditation:* NCATE. Part-time and evening/weekend programs available. *Faculty:* 7 full-time (4 women). *Students:* 638 full-time (425 women), 2,014 part-time (1,635 women). Average age 33. *Entrance requirements:* For master's, 2 letters of recommendation, interview. Additional exam requirements/recommendations for international students: Required—TOEFL (minimum score 500 paper-based; 173 computer-based). *Application deadline:* For fall admission, 4/30 for domestic students. Applications are processed on a rolling basis. Application fee: $35. Electronic applications accepted. *Expenses: Tuition:* Part-time $534 per credit hour. *Required fees:* $25 per term. *Financial support:* Applicants required to submit FAFSA. *Unit head:* Dr. John C. Gray, Dean, 302-295-1139. *Application contact:* Chris Ferguson, Director of Admissions, 302-356-4636 Ext. 256, Fax: 302-328-5164, E-mail: inquire@wilmcoll.edu. Web site: http://www.wilmu.edu/education/.

Winthrop University, College of Education, Program in Reading Education, Rock Hill, SC 29733. Offers M Ed. *Accreditation:* NCATE. Part-time programs available. *Entrance requirements:* For master's, PRAXIS, South Carolina Class III Teaching Certificate, 1 year of teaching experience. Electronic applications accepted.

Worcester State University, Graduate Studies, Department of Education, Program in Reading, Worcester, MA 01602-2597. Offers M Ed, CAGS. Part-time and evening/weekend programs available. *Faculty:* 12 full-time (9 women), 22 part-time/adjunct (10 women). *Students:* 1 (woman) full-time, 13 part-time (12 women). Average age 36. 4 applicants, 100% accepted, 1 enrolled. In 2011, 2 master's, 2 CAGSs awarded. *Degree requirements:* For master's, comprehensive exam (for some programs), thesis optional. *Entrance requirements:* For master's, GRE General Test or MAT, teaching certificate. Additional exam requirements/recommendations for international students: Required—TOEFL (minimum score 500 paper-based; 61 iBT). *Application deadline:* For fall admission, 6/15 for domestic and international students; for spring admission, 4/1 for domestic and international students. Applications are processed on a rolling basis. Application fee: $40. Electronic applications accepted. *Expenses:* Tuition, state resident: full-time $2700; part-time $150 per credit. Tuition, nonresident: full-time $2700; part-time $150 per credit. *Required fees:* $2016; $112 per credit. *Financial support:* Career-related internships or fieldwork, scholarships/grants, and unspecified assistantships available. Financial award application deadline: 3/1; financial award applicants required to submit FAFSA. *Unit head:* Dr. Margaret Pray-Bouchard, Coordinator, 508-929-8840, Fax: 508-929-8164, E-mail: mbouchard@worcester.edu. *Application contact:* Sara Grady, Assistant Dean of Graduate and Continuing Education, 508-929-8787, Fax: 508-929-8100, E-mail: sara.grady@worcester.edu.

Xavier University, College of Social Sciences, Health and Education, School of Education, Department of Childhood Education and Literacy, Program in Reading, Cincinnati, OH 45207. Offers M Ed. Part-time programs available. *Faculty:* 2 full-time (both women), 4 part-time/adjunct (2 women). *Students:* 4 full-time (3 women), 34 part-time (32 women). Average age 32. 4 applicants, 100% accepted, 1 enrolled. In 2011, 31 master's awarded. *Degree requirements:* For master's, comprehensive exam, research project or thesis. *Entrance requirements:* For master's, GRE or MAT. Additional exam requirements/recommendations for international students: Required—TOEFL (minimum score 550 paper-based; 213 computer-based; 79 iBT). *Application deadline:* Applications are processed on a rolling basis. Application fee: $35. Electronic applications accepted. *Expenses: Tuition:* Part-time $576 per credit hour. *Financial support:* In 2011–12, 18 students received support. Unspecified assistantships available. Financial award applicants required to submit FAFSA. *Faculty research:* First-year teacher retention, teaching efficacy of science educators, adolescents' literacy practices, family resiliency, preparing culturally responsive teachers. *Unit head:* Dr. Cynthia Hayes Geer, Chair, 513-745-3262, Fax: 513-745-3504, E-mail: geer@xavier.edu. *Application contact:* Roger Bosse, Graduate Services Director, 513-745-3357, Fax: 513-745-1048, E-mail: bosse@xavier.edu. Web site: http://www.xavier.edu/reading/.

York College of Pennsylvania, Department of Education, York, PA 17405-7199. Offers educational leadership (M Ed); reading specialist (M Ed). Part-time and evening/weekend programs available. *Faculty:* 3 full-time (2 women), 4 part-time/adjunct (2 women). *Students:* 82 part-time (65 women). 10 applicants, 60% accepted, 5 enrolled. In 2011, 17 master's awarded. *Degree requirements:* For master's, comprehensive exam, thesis optional, portfolio. *Entrance requirements:* For master's, GRE, MAT or PRAXIS, letters of recommendation, portfolio. *Application deadline:* For fall admission, 7/15 priority date for domestic students; for spring admission, 11/15 priority date for domestic students. Applications are processed on a rolling basis. Application fee: $50. Electronic applications accepted. *Expenses: Tuition:* Full-time $12,060; part-time $670 per credit hour. *Required fees:* $340 per semester. Tuition and fees vary according to degree level. *Faculty research:* Mentoring, principal development, principal retention. *Unit head:* Dr. Philip Monteith, Director, 717-815-6406, E-mail: med@ycp.edu. *Application contact:* Irene Z. Altland, Administrative Assistant, 717-815-6406, Fax: 717-849-1629, E-mail: med@ycp.edu. Web site: http://www.ycp.edu/academics/academic-departments/education/.

Youngstown State University, Graduate School, Beeghly College of Education, Department of Teacher Education, Youngstown, OH 44555-0001. Offers adolescent/young adult education (MS Ed); content area concentration (MS Ed); early childhood education (MS Ed); educational technology (MS Ed); literacy (MS Ed); middle childhood education (MS Ed); special education (MS Ed), including gifted and talented education, special education. *Accreditation:* NCATE. Part-time and evening/weekend programs available. *Degree requirements:* For master's, comprehensive exam. *Entrance requirements:* For master's, GRE, MAT, or teaching certificate; minimum GPA of 2.7. Additional exam requirements/recommendations for international students: Required—TOEFL. *Faculty research:* Multicultural literacy, hands-on mathematics teaching, integrated instruction, reading comprehension, emergent curriculum.

Religious Education

Andover Newton Theological School, Graduate and Professional Programs, Newton Centre, MA 02459-2243. Offers divinity (M Div); religious education (MA); theological research (MA); theological studies (MA); theology (D Min). *Accreditation:* ACIPE; ATS. Part-time programs available. *Degree requirements:* For master's, comprehensive exam (for some programs), thesis (for some programs); for doctorate, comprehensive exam, thesis/dissertation. *Entrance requirements:* For doctorate, M Div or equivalent. Additional exam requirements/recommendations for international students: Required—TOEFL (minimum score 550 paper-based; 213 computer-based). Electronic applications accepted.

Andrews University, School of Graduate Studies, Seventh-day Adventist Theological Seminary, Program in Religious Education, Berrien Springs, MI 49104. Offers MA, Ed D, PhD, Ed S. Part-time programs available. *Students:* 12 full-time (9 women), 18 part-time (11 women); includes 6 minority (4 Black or African American, non-Hispanic/Latino; 1 Hispanic/Latino; 1 Two or more races, non-Hispanic/Latino), 18 international. Average age 40. 19 applicants, 53% accepted, 9 enrolled. In 2011, 5 master's, 1 doctorate, 1 other advanced degree awarded. Terminal master's awarded for partial completion of doctoral program. *Degree requirements:* For doctorate, thesis/dissertation. *Entrance requirements:* For master's, GRE Subject Test. Additional exam requirements/recommendations for international students: Required—TOEFL (minimum score 550 paper-based). *Application deadline:* For fall admission, 8/31 for domestic students. Applications are processed on a rolling basis. Application fee: $40. *Financial support:* Fellowships, research assistantships, teaching assistantships, and career-related internships or fieldwork available. Financial award application deadline: 6/1. *Faculty research:* Marriage and family, spiritual gifts and temperament. *Unit head:* Coordinator, 269-471-8618. *Application contact:* Carolyn Hurst, Supervisor of Graduate Admission, 800-253-2874, Fax: 269-471-6321, E-mail: graduate@andrews.edu.

Asbury Theological Seminary, Graduate and Professional Programs, Wilmore, KY 40390-1199. Offers MA, MACE, MACL, MACM, MAMFC, MAMHC, MAPC, MAYM, Th M, PhD, Certificate. *Accreditation:* ATS. Part-time programs available. Postbaccalaureate distance learning degree programs offered (minimal on-campus study). *Faculty:* 64 full-time (12 women), 136 part-time/adjunct (21 women). *Students:* 692 full-time (237 women), 837 part-time (283 women); includes 227 minority (103 Black or African American, non-Hispanic/Latino; 7 American Indian or Alaska Native, non-Hispanic/Latino; 48 Asian, non-Hispanic/Latino; 54 Hispanic/Latino; 1 Native Hawaiian or other Pacific Islander, non-Hispanic/Latino; 14 Two or more races, non-Hispanic/Latino), 127 international. Average age 38. 603 applicants, 59% accepted, 244 enrolled. In 2011, 258 master's, 38 doctorates, 3 other advanced degrees awarded. Terminal master's awarded for partial completion of doctoral program. *Degree requirements:* For master's, thesis (for some programs); for doctorate, thesis/dissertation, qualifying exam. *Entrance requirements:* For master's, minimum GPA of 2.75; for doctorate, minimum GPA of 3.0. Additional exam requirements/recommendations for international students: Required—TOEFL, IELTS. *Application deadline:* Applications are processed on a rolling basis. Application fee: $50. Electronic applications accepted. *Expenses: Tuition:* Part-time $520 per credit hour. One-time fee: $100 part-time. *Financial support:* In 2011–12, 1,317 students received support. Career-related internships or fieldwork, Federal Work-Study, institutionally sponsored loans, and scholarships/grants available. Support available to part-time students. Financial award applicants required to submit FAFSA. *Unit head:* Dr. Leslie A. Andrews, Provost, 859-858-2206, Fax: 859-858-2025, E-mail: leslie.andrews@asburyseminary.edu. *Application contact:* Kevin Bish, Vice President of Enrollment Management, 859-858-2211, Fax: 859-858-2287, E-mail: admissions.office@asburyseminary.edu. Web site: http://www.asburyseminary.edu.

Azusa Pacific University, Haggard Graduate School of Theology, Program in Pastoral Studies, Concentration in Christian Education in Youth Ministry, Azusa, CA 91702-7000. Offers MA. *Accreditation:* NCATE.

Baptist Bible College of Pennsylvania, Baptist Bible Seminary, Clarks Summit, PA 18411-1297. Offers biblical studies (PhD); church planting (M Div); global missions (M Div); military chaplaincy (M Div); ministry (M Min, D Min); pastor of church education (M Div); pastor of outreach (M Div); pastoral counseling (M Div); pastoral leadership (M Div); theology (M Div, Th M); youth pastor (M Div). Part-time and evening/weekend programs available. Postbaccalaureate distance learning degree programs offered (minimal on-campus study). Terminal master's awarded for partial completion of doctoral program. *Degree requirements:* For master's, 2 foreign languages, thesis, oral exam (for M Div); for doctorate, 2 foreign languages, comprehensive exam (for some programs), thesis/dissertation, oral exam. *Entrance requirements:* For doctorate, Greek and Hebrew entrance exams (PhD). Electronic applications accepted.

Baptist Bible College of Pennsylvania, Graduate School, Clarks Summit, PA 18411-1297. Offers Bible (MA); counseling (MS); education (MS). Part-time and evening/weekend programs available. Postbaccalaureate distance learning degree programs offered (no on-campus study). *Entrance requirements:* Additional exam requirements/recommendations for international students: Required—TOEFL (minimum score 500 paper-based; 173 computer-based).

Baptist Theological Seminary at Richmond, Graduate and Professional Programs, Richmond, VA 23227. Offers biblical interpretation (M Div); Christian education (M Div); justice and peacebuilding (M Div); theological studies (MATS); theology (D Min); youth and student ministries (M Div); M Div/MS; M Div/MSW. *Accreditation:* ATS. Part-time programs available. Postbaccalaureate distance learning degree programs offered (minimal on-campus study). *Faculty:* 8 full-time (2 women), 10 part-time/adjunct (4 women). *Students:* 77 full-time (33 women), 33 part-time (19 women); includes 10 minority (9 Black or African American, non-Hispanic/Latino; 1 Hispanic/Latino), 3 international. Average age 46. 40 applicants, 88% accepted, 30 enrolled. In 2011, 4 doctorates awarded. *Degree requirements:* For doctorate, one foreign language, comprehensive exam, thesis/dissertation, field study, independent study. *Entrance requirements:* For doctorate, MAT, M Div, 3 years of full-time ministry experience. Additional exam requirements/recommendations for international students: Required—TOEFL (minimum score 550 paper-based; 213 computer-based). *Application deadline:* For fall admission, 12/1 priority date for domestic students, 5/1 for international students; for winter admission, 12/15 for domestic students, 9/1 for international students; for spring admission, 1/15 for domestic students, 10/1 for international students. Applications are processed on a rolling basis. Application fee: $35. *Expenses: Tuition:* Full-time $10,000; part-time $4000 per year. *Required fees:* $485; $180 per term. *Financial support:* In 2011–12, 12 teaching assistantships (averaging $1,650 per year) were awarded; scholarships/grants and tuition waivers (partial) also available. Financial award application deadline: 2/1. *Faculty research:* Biblical studies, pastoral care, church history, theology, ministry. *Unit head:* Dr. Ronald W. Crawford, President, 804-204-1201, Fax: 804-355-8182, E-mail: rcrawford@btsr.edu. *Application contact:* Tiffany Kellogg Pittman, Director of Admissions and Recruitment, 804-204-1208, Fax: 804-355-8182, E-mail: admissions@btsr.edu.

Bethel Seminary, Graduate and Professional Programs, St. Paul, MN 55112-6998. Offers Anglican studies (Certificate); applied ministry (MA, Certificate); biblical studies (Certificate); children's and family ministry (MACFM); Christian education (MACE); Christian thought (MACT); community ministry leadership (MA, Certificate); global and contextual studies (MA); Greek and Hebrew language (M Div); Greek language (M Div); Hebrew language (M Div); lay ministry (Certificate); marriage and family therapy (MAMFT, Certificate); men's ministry leadership (Certificate); ministry (D Min); ministry leadership (Certificate); spiritual formation (Certificate); theological studies (MATS, Certificate); transformational leadership (MATL, Certificate); young life youth ministry (Certificate). *Accreditation:* ACIPE; ATS (one or more programs are accredited). Part-time and evening/weekend programs available. Postbaccalaureate distance learning degree programs offered (minimal on-campus study). *Faculty:* 24 full-time (2 women), 92 part-time/adjunct (34 women). *Students:* 668 full-time (247 women), 241 part-time (118 women); includes 155 minority (65 Black or African American, non-Hispanic/Latino; 2 American Indian or Alaska Native, non-Hispanic/Latino; 50 Asian, non-Hispanic/Latino; 26 Hispanic/Latino; 2 Native Hawaiian or other Pacific Islander, non-Hispanic/Latino; 10 Two or more races, non-Hispanic/Latino), 14 international. Average age 38. 459 applicants, 75% accepted, 252 enrolled. In 2011, 151 master's, 12 doctorates, 13 other advanced degrees awarded. *Degree requirements:* For master's, variable foreign language requirement, thesis (for some programs); for doctorate, thesis/dissertation. *Entrance requirements:* For master's, letters of reference, transcripts, personal statement; for doctorate, M Div, letters of reference, organizational support. Additional exam requirements/recommendations for international students: Required—TOEFL (minimum score 550 paper-based; 213 computer-based; 87 iBT). *Application deadline:* For fall admission, 8/1 priority date for domestic students, 2/1 for international students; for winter admission, 12/1 priority date for domestic students; for spring admission, 3/1 priority date for domestic students. Applications are processed on a rolling basis. Application fee: $20. Electronic applications accepted. Application fee is waived when completed online. *Financial support:* In 2011–12, 647 students received support, including 15 teaching assistantships; career-related internships or fieldwork, Federal Work-Study, scholarships/grants, and Tuition waivers for employees and their spouses also available. Financial award applicants required to submit FAFSA. *Faculty research:* Nature of theology, ethics, Biblical commentaries, nature of God, science and theology. *Unit head:* Dr. David Clark, Provost, 651-638-6370. *Application contact:* Joseph V. Dworak, Director of Admissions, 651-638-6288, Fax: 651-638-6002, E-mail: j-dworak@bethel.edu.

Biola University, Talbot School of Theology, La Mirada, CA 90639-0001. Offers adult/family ministry (MACE); Bible exposition (MA, Th M); Biblical and theological studies (MA); Biblical studies (Certificate); children's ministry (MACE); Christian education (M Div); Christian ministry and leadership (MA), including pastoral care and counseling, women's ministry; cross-cultural education ministry (MACE); educational studies (Ed D, PhD); evangelism and discipleship (M Div); general Christian education (MACE); Messianic Jewish studies (M Div, Certificate); missions and intercultural studies (M Div, Th M); New Testament (MA, Th M); Old Testament (MA); Old Testament and semitics (Th M); pastoral and general ministry (M Div); pastoral care and counseling (M Div); philosophy (MA); spiritual formation (M Div); spiritual formation and soul care (MA); theology (Th M, D Min); youth ministry (MACE). *Accreditation:* ATS. Part-time programs available. *Faculty:* 79. *Students:* 610 full-time (119 women), 605 part-time (157 women); includes 406 minority (49 Black or African American, non-Hispanic/Latino; 2 American Indian or Alaska Native, non-Hispanic/Latino; 317 Asian, non-Hispanic/Latino; 5 Native Hawaiian or other Pacific Islander, non-Hispanic/Latino; 33 Two or more races, non-Hispanic/Latino), 162 international. In 2011, 191 master's, 28 doctorates awarded. *Entrance requirements:* For master's, minimum GPA of 3.0, bachelor's degree from accredited college or university; for doctorate, M Div. Additional exam requirements/recommendations for international students: Required—TOEFL (minimum score 600 paper-based; 250 computer-based; 100 iBT). *Application deadline:* For fall admission, 7/1 for domestic students, 6/1 for international students; for spring admission, 12/1 for domestic students. Applications are processed on a rolling basis. Application fee: $55. Electronic applications accepted. *Financial support:* Federal Work-Study, institutionally sponsored loans, scholarships/grants, and unspecified assistantships available. *Faculty research:* New Testament, Old Testament, spiritual formation, Christian education, theological studies. *Unit head:* Dr. Clint Arnold, Dean, 562-903-4816, Fax: 562-903-4748. *Application contact:* Graduate Admissions Office, 562-903-4752, E-mail: graduate.admissions@biola.edu. Web site: http://www.talbot.edu/.

Boston College, Lynch Graduate School of Education, Program in Religious Education, Chestnut Hill, MA 02467-3800. Offers M Ed, CAES. *Accreditation:* Teacher Education Accreditation Council. Part-time and evening/weekend programs available. *Students:* 12 full-time (5 women), 10 part-time (9 women); includes 1 minority (Hispanic/Latino), 4 international. In 2011, 11 master's, 2 CAESs awarded. *Degree requirements:* For master's and CAES, comprehensive exam. *Entrance requirements:* For master's, GRE General Test or MAT. Additional exam requirements/recommendations for international students: Required—TOEFL. Application fee: $65. Electronic applications accepted. *Financial support:* Fellowships with full and partial tuition reimbursements, research assistantships with full and partial tuition reimbursements, teaching assistantships with full and partial tuition reimbursements, career-related internships or fieldwork, Federal Work-Study, scholarships/grants, traineeships, health care benefits, tuition waivers (full and partial), and unspecified assistantships available. Support available to part-time students. Financial award applicants required to submit FAFSA. *Faculty research:* Curriculum development, inter-religious dialogue, ethical and value issues and pedagogy. *Unit head:* Adam Poluzzi, Director, Graduate Admission and Financial Aid, 617-552-4214, Fax: 617-552-0398, E-mail: poluzzi@bc.edu. *Application contact:* Adam Poluzzi, Director, Graduate Admission and Financial Aid, 617-552-4214, Fax: 617-552-0398, E-mail: poluzzi@bc.edu.

Boston College, School of Theology and Ministry, Chestnut Hill, MA 02467-3800. Offers church leadership (MA); divinity (M Div); pastoral ministry (MA), including Hispanic ministry, liturgy and worship, pastoral care and counseling, spirituality; religious education (MA, PhD); sacred theology (STD, STL); social justice/social ministry (MA); spiritual direction (MA); theological studies (MTS); theology (Th M, PhD); youth ministry (MA); MA/MA; MS/MA; MSW/MA. *Accreditation:* Teacher Education Accreditation Council. Part-time programs available. *Degree requirements:* For doctorate, one foreign language, thesis/dissertation. *Entrance requirements:* For doctorate, GRE. Additional exam requirements/recommendations for international students: Required—TOEFL (minimum score 550 paper-based; 213 computer-based). Electronic applications accepted. *Faculty research:* Philosophy and practice of religious education, pastoral psychology, liturgical and spiritual theology, spiritual formation for the practice of ministry.

Brandeis University, Graduate School of Arts and Sciences, Teaching Program, Waltham, MA 02454-9110. Offers elementary education (public) (MAT); Jewish day school (MAT); secondary education (MAT), including Bible, biology, chemistry, Chinese, English, history, math, physics. *Faculty:* 5 full-time (3 women), 9 part-time/adjunct (6 women). *Students:* 31 full-time (23 women); includes 3 minority (2 Asian, non-Hispanic/Latino; 1 Hispanic/Latino), 3 international. 76 applicants, 67% accepted, 31 enrolled. In 2011, 23 master's awarded. *Degree requirements:* For master's, internship; research project. *Entrance requirements:* For master's, GRE General Test or Miller Analogies Test, official transcript(s), 3 letters of recommendation, resume, statement of purpose. Additional exam requirements/recommendations for international students: Required—TOEFL (minimum score 600 paper-based; 250 computer-based; 100 iBT); Recommended—IELTS (minimum score 7). *Application deadline:* Applications are processed on a rolling basis. Application fee: $75. Electronic applications accepted. *Expenses:* Contact institution. *Financial support:* Scholarships/grants and tuition waivers (partial) available. Financial award applicants required to submit FAFSA. *Faculty research:* Teacher education, education, teaching, elementary education, secondary education, Jewish education, English, history, biology, chemistry, physics, math, Chinese, Bible/Tanakh. *Unit head:* Prof. Marya Levenson, Director, 781-736-2020, Fax: 781-736-5020, E-mail: mlevenso@brandeis.edu. *Application contact:* Manuel Tuan, Department Administrator, 781-736-2633, Fax: 781-736-5020, E-mail: tuan@brandeis.edu. Web site: http://www.brandeis.edu/programs/mat.

Brigham Young University, Graduate Studies, College of Religious Education, Provo, UT 84602-1001. Offers MA. *Faculty:* 56 full-time (4 women). *Students:* 15 full-time (0 women), 8 part-time (1 woman). Average age 32. In 2011, 3 master's awarded. *Degree requirements:* For master's, thesis. *Entrance requirements:* For master's, GRE, minimum GPA of 3.0 in last 60 hours, letter of recommendation. *Application deadline:* For fall admission, 12/1 for domestic and international students. Application fee: $50. Electronic applications accepted. *Expenses: Tuition:* Full-time $5760; part-time $320 per credit. Tuition and fees vary according to student's religious affiliation. *Financial support:* Scholarships/grants available. *Unit head:* Dr. Terry B. Ball, Dean, 801-422-2736, Fax: 801-422-0616, E-mail: terry_ball@byu.edu. *Application contact:* Dr. Ray L. Huntington, Professor of Ancient Scripture, 801-422-3125, Fax: 801-422-0616, E-mail: ray_huntington@byu.edu.

Calvin Theological Seminary, Graduate and Professional Programs, Grand Rapids, MI 49546-4387. Offers Bible and theology (MA); divinity (M Div), including ancient near eastern languages and literature, contextual ministry, evangelism and teaching, history of Christianity, new church development, New Testament, Old Testament, pastoral care and leadership, preaching and worship, theological studies, youth and family ministries; educational ministry (MA); historical theology (PhD); missions and evangelism (MA); pastoral care (MA); philosophical and moral theology (PhD); systematic theology (PhD); theological studies (MTS); theology (Th M); worship (MA); youth and family ministries (MA). *Accreditation:* ACIPE; ATS. Part-time programs available. *Degree requirements:* For master's, variable foreign language requirement, thesis (for some programs); for doctorate, 4 foreign languages, comprehensive exam, thesis/dissertation. *Entrance requirements:* For doctorate, GRE General Test, Hebrew, Greek, and a modern foreign language. Additional exam requirements/recommendations for international students: Required—TOEFL (minimum score 550 paper-based; 213 computer-based), TWE (minimum score 4). Electronic applications accepted. *Faculty research:* Recent Trinity theory, Christian anthropology, Proverbs, reformed confessions, Paul's view of law.

Campbell University, Graduate and Professional Programs, Divinity School, Buies Creek, NC 27506. Offers Christian education (MA); divinity (M Div); ministry (D Min); M Div/MA; M Div/MBA. *Accreditation:* ATS. *Degree requirements:* For doctorate, final project. *Entrance requirements:* For master's, minimum GPA of 2.5; for doctorate, MAT, M Div, minimum graduate GPA of 3.0. Additional exam requirements/recommendations for international students: Required—TOEFL (minimum score 580 paper-based; 237 computer-based). *Expenses:* Contact institution. *Faculty research:* New Testament, theology, spiritual formation, Old Testament, Christian leadership.

Claremont School of Theology, Graduate and Professional Programs, Program in Religion, Claremont, CA 91711-3199. Offers practical theology (PhD), including religious education, spiritual care and counseling; religion (PhD), including Hebrew Bible, New Testament and Christian origins, process studies, religion, ethics, and society; religion and theology (MA); religious education (MARE). *Accreditation:* ACIPE; ATS. Terminal master's awarded for partial completion of doctoral program. *Degree requirements:* For master's, thesis; for doctorate, 2 foreign languages, thesis/dissertation. *Entrance requirements:* For doctorate, GRE General Test. Additional exam requirements/recommendations for international students: Required—TOEFL (minimum score 250 computer-based). Electronic applications accepted.

College of Mount St. Joseph, Graduate Program in Religious Studies, Cincinnati, OH 45233-1670. Offers religious education (Certificate); spiritual and pastoral care (MA, Certificate); spiritual direction (Certificate). Part-time and evening/weekend programs available. *Faculty:* 3 full-time (all women). *Students:* 1 (woman) full-time, 16 part-time (11 women); includes 1 minority (Black or African American, non-Hispanic/Latino). Average age 48. 9 applicants, 67% accepted, 6 enrolled. In 2011, 6 master's awarded. *Degree requirements:* For master's, integrating project, field experience. *Entrance requirements:* For master's, 3 letters of recommendation, interview, minimum GPA of 3.0, academic transcripts, essay. Additional exam requirements/recommendations for international students: Required—TOEFL (minimum score 560 paper-based; 220 computer-based; 83 iBT). *Application deadline:* Applications are processed on a rolling basis. Application fee: $50. Electronic applications accepted. *Expenses: Tuition:* Full-time $24,200; part-time $540 per credit hour. *Required fees:* $112.50 per semester. One-time fee: $200. *Financial support:* In 2011–12, 17 students received support. Scholarships/grants available. Financial award application deadline: 3/1; financial award applicants required to submit FAFSA. *Faculty research:* Contextual/cultural/systematic theology, historical/spiritual theology, business/economics ethics, social justice, Biblical/cultural/pastoral theology. *Unit head:* Dr. John Trokan, Chair of Religious/Pastoral Studies, 513-244-4272, Fax: 513-244-4222, E-mail: john_trokan@mail.msj.edu. *Application contact:* Marilyn Hoskins, Assistant Director of Graduate Recruitment, 513-244-4723, Fax: 513-244-4629, E-mail: marilyn_hoskins@mail.msj.edu. Web site: http://www.msj.edu/view/academics/graduate-programs/religious-studies_2.aspx.

Columbia International University, Columbia Graduate School, Columbia, SC 29230-3122. Offers Bible teaching (MABT); Christian higher education leadership (Ed D); Christian school educational leadership (Ed D); counseling (MACN); curriculum and instruction (M Ed), including Christian school guidance, English as a second language, learning disabilities, school technology; early childhood and elementary education (MAT); educational administration (M Ed); teaching English as a foreign language (Certificate); teaching English as a foreign language and intercultural studies (MATF). Part-time and evening/weekend programs available. *Degree requirements:* For master's, internships, professional project. *Entrance requirements:* For master's, Minnesota Multiphasic Personality Inventory, MAT, minimum GPA of 2.7. Additional exam requirements/recommendations for international students: Required—TOEFL. Electronic applications accepted.

Columbia International University, Seminary and School of Ministry, Columbia, SC 29230-3122. Offers academic ministries (M Div); bible exposition (M Div, MABE); biblical studies (Certificate); counseling ministries (Certificate); divinity (M Div); educational ministries (M Div, MAEM, Certificate); intercultural studies (M Div, MAIS, Certificate); leadership (D Min); member care (D Min); ministry (Certificate); missions (D Min); pastoral counseling and spiritual formation (M Div); preaching (D Min); theology (MA). *Accreditation:* ATS (one or more programs are accredited). Part-time and evening/weekend programs available. *Degree requirements:* For doctorate, comprehensive exam, thesis/dissertation. *Entrance requirements:* For doctorate, 3 years of ministerial experience, M Div. Additional exam requirements/recommendations for international students: Required—TOEFL. Electronic applications accepted.

Concordia University Chicago, College of Education, Program in Christian Education, River Forest, IL 60305-1499. Offers MA. *Entrance requirements:* Additional exam requirements/recommendations for international students: Required—TOEFL (minimum score 550 paper-based; 195 computer-based). Electronic applications accepted.

Concordia University, Nebraska, Graduate Programs in Education, Program in Parish Education, Seward, NE 68434-1599. Offers MPE. *Accreditation:* NCATE. Part-time and evening/weekend programs available. *Degree requirements:* For master's, thesis or alternative. *Entrance requirements:* For master's, GRE, MAT, or NTE, minimum GPA of 3.0, BS in education or equivalent.

Concordia University, St. Paul, College of Vocation and Ministry, St. Paul, MN 55104-5494. Offers Christian education (Certificate); Christian outreach (MA, Certificate). Evening/weekend programs available. Postbaccalaureate distance learning degree programs offered (minimal on-campus study). *Faculty:* 1 full-time (0 women), 4 part-time/adjunct (0 women). *Students:* 13 full-time (7 women), 3 part-time (2 women); includes 1 minority (Asian, non-Hispanic/Latino). Average age 38. In 2011, 1 master's, 6 other advanced degrees awarded. *Application deadline:* Applications are processed on a rolling basis. Application fee: $50. Electronic applications accepted. *Expenses: Tuition:* Full-time $8100; part-time $435 per credit. Tuition and fees vary according to program. *Financial support:* Applicants required to submit FAFSA. *Unit head:* Dr. David Lumpp, Dean, 651-641-8217, E-mail: lumpp@csp.edu. *Application contact:* Kimberly Craig, Director of Graduate and Cohort Admission, 651-603-6223, Fax: 651-603-6320, E-mail: craig@csp.edu.

Dallas Baptist University, Gary Cook School of Leadership, Program in Christian Education and Business Administration, Dallas, TX 75211-9299. Offers MA/MBA. Part-time and evening/weekend programs available. *Students:* 15 applicants, 80% accepted, 6 enrolled. *Entrance requirements:* Additional exam requirements/recommendations for international students: Required—TOEFL, IELTS. Application fee: $25. *Expenses: Tuition:* Full-time $12,060; part-time $670 per credit hour. *Required fees:* $100; $50 per semester. *Financial support:* Federal Work-Study, institutionally sponsored loans, scholarships/grants, and tuition waivers available. Support available to part-time students. Financial award applicants required to submit FAFSA. *Unit head:* Dr. Judy Morris, Co-Director, 214-333-5246, Fax: 214-333-5115, E-mail: graduate@dbu.edu. *Application contact:* Kit P. Montgomery, Director of Graduate Programs, 214-333-5242, Fax: 214-333-5579, E-mail: graduate@dbu.edu. Web site: http://www3.dbu.edu/leadership/dual_degrees/mace_mba.asp.

Dallas Baptist University, Gary Cook School of Leadership, Program in Christian Education: Childhood Ministry, Dallas, TX 75211-9299. Offers MA, MA/MA. Part-time and evening/weekend programs available. *Entrance requirements:* For master's, minimum GPA of 3.0. Additional exam requirements/recommendations for international students: Required—TOEFL, IELTS. Application fee: $25. *Expenses: Tuition:* Full-time $12,060; part-time $670 per credit hour. *Required fees:* $100; $50 per semester. *Financial support:* Federal Work-Study, institutionally sponsored loans, scholarships/grants, and tuition waivers (full and partial) available. Support available to part-time students. Financial award applicants required to submit FAFSA. *Unit head:* Tommy Sanders, Director, 214-333-6851, Fax: 214-333-6853, E-mail: graduate@dbu.edu. *Application contact:* Kit P. Montgomery, Director of Graduate Programs, 214-333-5242, Fax: 214-333-5579, E-mail: graduate@dbu.edu. Web site: http://www3.dbu.edu/leadership/childhoodministry.asp.

Dallas Baptist University, Gary Cook School of Leadership, Program in Christian Education: Student Ministry, Dallas, TX 75211-9299. Offers MA, MA/MA. Part-time and evening/weekend programs available. *Entrance requirements:* For master's, minimum GPA of 3.0. Additional exam requirements/recommendations for international students: Required—TOEFL, IELTS. Application fee: $25. *Expenses: Tuition:* Full-time $12,060; part-time $670 per credit hour. *Required fees:* $100; $50 per semester. *Financial support:* Federal Work-Study, institutionally sponsored loans, scholarships/grants, and tuition waivers (full and partial) available. Support available to part-time students. Financial award applicants required to submit FAFSA. *Unit head:* Dr. Dwayne Ulmer, Director, 214-333-5246, Fax: 214-333-5115, E-mail: graduate@dbu.edu. *Application contact:* Kit P. Montgomery, Director of Graduate Programs, 214-333-5242, Fax: 214-333-5579, E-mail: graduate@dbu.edu. Web site: http://www3.dbu.edu/leadership/mace/macestudentministry.asp.

Dallas Theological Seminary, Graduate Programs, Dallas, TX 75204-6499. Offers adult education (Th M); apologetics (Th M); Bible backgrounds (Th M); Bible translation (Th M); Biblical and theological studies (Certificate); biblical counseling (MA); biblical exegesis and linguistics (MA); biblical exposition (PhD); biblical studies (MA); Biblical theology (Th M); children's education (Th M); Christian education (MA, D Min); Christian leadership (MA); cross-cultural ministries (MA); educational administration (Th M); educational leadership (Th M); evangelism and discipleship (Th M); exposition of Biblical books (Th M); family life education (Th M); general studies (Th M); Hebrew and cognate studies (Th M); hermeneutics (Th M); historical theology (Th M); homiletics (Th M); intercultural ministries (Th M); Jesus studies (Th M); leadership studies (Th M); media and communication (MA); media arts (Th M); ministry (D Min); ministry with women (Th M); New Testament studies (Th M, PhD); Old Testament studies (Th M, PhD); parachurch ministries (Th M); pastoral care and counseling (Th M); pastoral theology and practice (Th M); philosophy (Th M); sacred theology (STM); spiritual formation (Th M); systematic theology (Th M); teaching in Christian institutions (Th M); theological studies (PhD); urban ministries (Th M); worship studies (Th M); youth education (Th M). *Accreditation:* ATS (one or more programs are accredited). Part-time programs available. Postbaccalaureate distance learning degree programs offered (minimal on-campus study). *Faculty:* 68 full-time (3 women), 35 part-time/adjunct (8 women). *Students:* 809 full-time (181 women), 1,215 part-time (450 women); includes 487 minority (208 Black or African American, non-Hispanic/Latino; 6 American Indian or Alaska Native, non-Hispanic/Latino; 141 Asian, non-Hispanic/Latino; 96 Hispanic/Latino; 5 Native Hawaiian or other Pacific Islander, non-Hispanic/Latino; 31 Two or more races, non-Hispanic/Latino), 223 international. Average age 36. 891 applicants, 70% accepted, 372 enrolled. In 2011, 336 master's, 27 doctorates, 46 other advanced degrees awarded. *Degree requirements:* For master's, variable foreign language requirement, thesis (for some programs); for doctorate, 2 foreign languages, thesis/dissertation. *Entrance requirements:* For master's, GRE or MAT if minimum undergraduate cumulative GPA is below 2.5 or undergraduate degree is unaccredited. Additional exam requirements/recommendations for international students: Required—TOEFL (minimum score 575 paper-based; 233 computer-based; 85 iBT), TWE (minimum score 4.5). *Application deadline:* For fall admission, 7/1 for domestic students, 1/1 for international students; for winter admission, 11/1 for domestic students; for spring admission, 11/1 for domestic students. *Expenses: Tuition:* Full-time $12,450; part-time $440 per credit hour. *Required fees:* $380; $190 per semester. *Financial support:* In 2011–12, 1,030 students received support. Career-related internships or fieldwork, scholarships/grants, and tuition waivers (full and partial) available. Financial award application deadline: 2/28. *Unit head:* Dr. Mark L. Bailey, President, 214-841-3676, Fax: 214-841-3565. *Application contact:* Josh Bleeker, Director of Admissions and Student Advising, 214-841-3661, Fax: 214-841-3664, E-mail: admissions@dts.edu.

Emmanuel Christian Seminary, Graduate and Professional Programs, Johnson City, TN 37601-9438. Offers Christian care and counseling (M Div); Christian doctrine (MAR); Christian doctrine/theology (M Div); Christian education (M Div); Christian ministries (MCM); Christian ministry (M Div); church history (MAR); church history/historical theology (M Div); general studies (M Div); ministry (D Min); New Testament (M Div, MAR); Old Testament (M Div, MAR); urban ministry (M Div); world missions (M Div). *Accreditation:* ACIPE; ATS. Part-time programs available. Postbaccalaureate distance learning degree programs offered (minimal on-campus study). *Faculty:* 9 full-time (2 women), 12 part-time/adjunct (2 women). *Students:* 84 full-time (19 women), 30 part-time (10 women); includes 4 minority (1 Black or African American, non-Hispanic/Latino; 1 American Indian or Alaska Native, non-Hispanic/Latino; 2 Hispanic/Latino), 17 international. Average age 27. 34 applicants, 88% accepted, 20 enrolled. In 2011, 34 master's, 2 doctorates awarded. *Degree requirements:* For master's, 2 foreign languages, thesis or alternative, portfolio; for doctorate, thesis/dissertation. *Entrance requirements:* For master's, bachelor's degree from accredited undergraduate institution; for doctorate, M Div or equivalent. Additional exam requirements/recommendations for international students: Required—TOEFL (minimum score 80 computer-based). *Application deadline:* For fall admission, 8/1 for domestic and international students; for spring admission, 1/20 for domestic and international students. Applications are processed on a rolling basis. Application fee: $25. Electronic applications accepted. *Expenses: Tuition:* Full-time $9840; part-time $410 per credit hour. Tuition and fees vary according to course load and reciprocity agreements. *Financial support:* In 2011–12, 102 students received support, including 10 teaching assistantships with partial tuition reimbursements available (averaging $3,000 per year); career-related internships or fieldwork and scholarships/grants also available. Support available to part-time students. Financial award application deadline: 3/1; financial award applicants required to submit FAFSA. *Faculty research:* Theology of Old Testament prophets, spiritual formation for Christian leaders, history of African churches and religions, social world of early Christianity, lay pastoral counseling, ANE epigraphy. *Total annual research expenditures:* $12,000. *Unit head:* Dr. Jack Holland, Dean and Professor of Christian Care and Counseling, 423-461-1524, Fax: 423-926-6198, E-mail: jholland@ecs.edu. *Application contact:* Erin Layton, Director of Admissions, 423-461-1535, Fax: 423-926-6198, E-mail: elayton@ecs.edu.

Felician College, Program in Religious Education, Lodi, NJ 07644-2117. Offers MA, Certificate. *Accreditation:* Teacher Education Accreditation Council. Part-time and evening/weekend programs available. Postbaccalaureate distance learning degree programs offered (no on-campus study). *Students:* 52 part-time (34 women); includes 6 minority (1 Black or African American, non-Hispanic/Latino; 2 Asian, non-Hispanic/Latino; 3 Hispanic/Latino). Average age 48. 24 applicants, 79% accepted, 18 enrolled. *Degree requirements:* For master's, thesis. *Entrance requirements:* For master's, minimum GPA of 3.0, 1 letter of recommendation. Additional exam requirements/recommendations for international students: Recommended—TOEFL (minimum score 550 paper-based; 213 computer-based). *Application deadline:* Applications are processed on a rolling basis. Application fee: $40. *Expenses: Tuition:* Part-time $925 per credit. *Required fees:* $262.50 per semester. Part-time tuition and fees vary according to class time and student level. *Financial support:* Scholarships/grants and tuition waivers (partial) available. *Faculty research:* Spirituality, race and ethnicity in religious settings. *Unit head:* Dr. Dolores M. Henchy, Director, 201-559-6053, Fax: 973-472-8936, E-mail: henchyd@felician.edu. *Application contact:* Michael Szarek, Assistant Vice-President for Graduate and International Enrollment Services, 201-559-6047, Fax: 201-559-6047, E-mail: adultandgraduate@felician.edu.

Fordham University, Graduate School of Religion and Religious Education, New York, NY 10458. Offers pastoral counseling and spiritual care (MA); pastoral ministry/spirituality/pastoral counseling (D Min); religion and religious education (MA); religious education (MS, PhD, PD); spiritual direction (Certificate). Part-time programs available. Terminal master's awarded for partial completion of doctoral program. *Degree requirements:* For master's, research paper; for doctorate, comprehensive exam, thesis/dissertation. *Entrance requirements:* For doctorate, MAT. Electronic applications accepted. *Expenses:* Contact institution. *Faculty research:* Spirituality and spiritual direction, pastoral care and counseling, adult family and community, growth and young adult.

Gardner-Webb University, School of Divinity, Boiling Springs, NC 28017. Offers biblical studies (M Div); Christian education and formation (M Div); intercultural studies (M Div); ministry (D Min); missiology (M Div); pastoral care and counseling (M Div); pastoral care and counseling/member care for missionaries (D Min); pastoral studies (M Div); M Div/MA; M Div/MBA. *Accreditation:* ACIPE; ATS. Part-time programs available. *Students:* 130 full-time (64 women), 79 part-time (27 women); includes 86 minority (80 Black or African American, non-Hispanic/Latino; 6 Hispanic/Latino). Average age 41. 170 applicants, 46% accepted, 46 enrolled. *Entrance requirements:* For master's, minimum GPA of 2.6; for doctorate, minimum GPA of 2.75. Additional exam requirements/recommendations for international students: Required—TOEFL (minimum score 500 paper-based; 173 computer-based; 61 iBT). *Application deadline:* Applications are processed on a rolling basis. Application fee: $40. Electronic applications accepted. *Expenses:* Contact institution. *Financial support:* Fellowships, institutionally sponsored loans, and unspecified assistantships available. Support available to part-time students. Financial award application deadline: 5/15. *Faculty research:* Jewish-Christian dialogue, Islam. *Unit head:* Dr. Robert W. Canoy, Sr., Dean, 704-406-4400, Fax: 704-406-3935, E-mail: rcanoy@gardner-webb.edu. *Application contact:* Kheresa Harmon, Director of Admissions, 704-406-3205, Fax: 704-406-3895, E-mail: kharmon@gardner-webb.edu. Web site: http://www.gardner-webb.edu/divinity.

Garrett-Evangelical Theological Seminary, Graduate and Professional Programs, Evanston, IL 60201-3298. Offers Bible and culture (PhD); Christian education (MA); Christian education and congregational studies (PhD); contemporary theology and culture (PhD); divinity (M Div); ethics, church, and society (MA); liturgical studies (PhD); ministry (D Min); music ministry (MA); pastoral care and counseling (MA); pastoral theology, personality, and culture (PhD); spiritual formation and evangelism (MA); theological studies (MTS); M Div/MSW. M Div/MSW offered jointly with Loyola University Chicago. *Accreditation:* ACIPE; ATS (one or more programs are accredited). Part-time programs available. *Degree requirements:* For master's, thesis (for some programs); for doctorate, thesis/dissertation. *Entrance requirements:* For doctorate, GRE (PhD). Additional exam requirements/recommendations for international students: Required—TOEFL (minimum score 560 paper-based; 230 computer-based). Electronic applications accepted.

George Fox University, George Fox Evangelical Seminary, Newberg, OR 97132-2697. Offers Biblical studies (M Div); Christian earthkeeping (M Div); Christian history and theology (M Div); clinical pastoral education and hospital chaplaincy (M Div); leadership and spiritual formation (D Min), including global missional leadership, semiotics and future studies; military chaplaincy (M Div); ministry leadership (MA); pastoral studies (M Div); spiritual formation (MA, Certificate); spiritual formation and discipleship (M Div); theological studies (MA). *Accreditation:* ACIPE; ATS. Part-time and evening/weekend programs available. Postbaccalaureate distance learning degree programs offered (minimal on-campus study). *Faculty:* 8 full-time (2 women), 26 part-time/adjunct (10 women). *Students:* 43 full-time (9 women), 289 part-time (111 women); includes 20 minority (7 Black or African American, non-Hispanic/Latino; 1 American Indian or Alaska Native, non-Hispanic/Latino; 8 Asian, non-Hispanic/Latino; 3 Hispanic/Latino; 1 Two or more races, non-Hispanic/Latino), 12 international. Average age 40. 171 applicants, 78% accepted, 86 enrolled. In 2011, 52 master's, 28 doctorates, 3 other advanced degrees awarded. *Degree requirements:* For master's, thesis optional, internship; for doctorate, comprehensive exam (for some programs), thesis/dissertation, internship. *Entrance requirements:* For master's, resume, three references (one pastoral, one academic or professional, one personal), one official transcript from each college or university attended; for doctorate, resume, 3 references (1 professional, 1 academic, 1 personal), one official transcript from each college or university attended. Additional exam requirements/recommendations for international students: Required—TOEFL (minimum score 577 paper-based; 233 computer-based; 90 iBT). *Application deadline:* For fall admission, 7/1 for domestic and international students; for winter admission, 11/1 for domestic and international students; for spring admission, 4/1 for domestic and international students. Applications are processed on a rolling basis. Application fee: $40. Electronic applications accepted. *Expenses:* Contact institution. *Financial support:* Career-related internships or fieldwork and scholarships/grants available. Financial award application deadline: 5/1; financial award applicants required to submit FAFSA. *Unit head:* Dr. Chuck Conniry, Professor of Theology/Vice President and Dean, 503-554-6152, E-mail: cconniry@georgefox.edu. *Application contact:* Sheila Bartlett, Admissions Counselor, 800-631-0921, Fax: 503-554-6122, E-mail: seminary@georgefox.edu. Web site: http://www.seminary.georgefox.edu/.

Georgian Court University, School of Arts and Sciences, Lakewood, NJ 08701-2697. Offers biology (MA); Catholic school leadership (Certificate); clinical mental health counseling (MA); holistic health studies (MA); mathematics (MA); pastoral ministry (Certificate); religious education (Certificate); school psychology (Certificate); theology (MA, Certificate). Part-time and evening/weekend programs available. *Faculty:* 21 full-time (10 women), 6 part-time/adjunct (5 women). *Students:* 88 full-time (84 women), 126 part-time (107 women); includes 29 minority (11 Black or African American, non-Hispanic/Latino; 5 Asian, non-Hispanic/Latino; 12 Hispanic/Latino; 1 Two or more races, non-Hispanic/Latino), 1 international. Average age 39. 210 applicants, 54% accepted, 79 enrolled. In 2011, 5 master's awarded. *Degree requirements:* For master's, comprehensive exam (for some programs), thesis (for some programs). *Entrance requirements:* For master's, GRE, MAT, or NTE/PRAXIS, 3 letters of recommendation. Additional exam requirements/recommendations for international students: Required—TOEFL (minimum score 550 paper-based; 213 computer-based). *Application deadline:* For fall admission, 8/1 priority date for domestic students, 4/1 for international students; for spring admission, 1/1 priority date for domestic students, 7/1 for international students. Applications are processed on a rolling basis. Application fee: $40. Electronic applications accepted. *Expenses: Tuition:* Full-time $13,410; part-time $745 per credit. *Required fees:* $450 per year. Tuition and fees vary according to campus/location and program. *Financial support:* Scholarships/grants, health care benefits, and unspecified assistantships available. Financial award application deadline: 4/15; financial award applicants required to submit FAFSA. *Unit head:* Dr. Rita Kipp, Dean, 732-987-2493, Fax: 732-987-2007. *Application contact:* Patrick Givens, Assistant Director of Graduate Admissions, 732-987-2736, Fax: 732-987-2084, E-mail: graduateadmissions@georgian.edu. Web site: http://www.georgian.edu/arts_sciences/index.htm.

Global University, Graduate School of Theology, Springfield, MO 65804. Offers biblical studies (MA); divinity (M Div); ministerial studies (MA), including education, leadership, missions, New Testament, Old Testament. Part-time and evening/weekend programs available. Postbaccalaureate distance learning degree programs offered (no on-campus study). *Degree requirements:* For master's, thesis (for some programs). *Entrance requirements:* For master's, minimum undergraduate GPA of 3.0. Electronic applications accepted. *Faculty research:* Higher education, cross-cultural missions.

Grand Rapids Theological Seminary of Cornerstone University, Graduate Programs, Grand Rapids, MI 49525-5897. Offers biblical counseling (MA); Biblical counseling (M Div); chaplaincy (M Div); Christian education (M Div, MA); intercultural studies (M Div, MA); New Testament (MA, Th M); Old Testament (MA, Th M); pastoral studies (M Div); systematic theology (MA); theology (Th M). *Accreditation:* ATS. Part-time programs available. Postbaccalaureate distance learning degree programs offered (minimal on-campus study). *Entrance requirements:* Additional exam requirements/recommendations for international students: Required—TOEFL (minimum score 577 paper-based; 233 computer-based; 90 iBT). Electronic applications accepted.

Gratz College, Graduate Programs, Program in Jewish Education, Melrose Park, PA 19027. Offers MA, Ed D, Certificate, MA/MA. Part-time and evening/weekend programs available. Postbaccalaureate distance learning degree programs offered. *Faculty:* 8 full-time (4 women), 11 part-time/adjunct (7 women). *Students:* 9 full-time, 47 part-time. In 2011, 2 master's, 1 other advanced degree awarded. *Degree requirements:* For master's, one foreign language, internship. *Entrance requirements:* For master's, interview. *Application deadline:* Applications are processed on a rolling basis. Application fee: $50. *Financial support:* Fellowships, career-related internships or fieldwork, Federal Work-Study, and unspecified assistantships available. Support available to part-time students. Financial award application deadline: 4/15; financial award applicants required to submit FAFSA. *Unit head:* Dr. Saul Wachs, Coordinator, 215-635-7300 Ext. 139, Fax: 215-635-7320. *Application contact:* Joanna Boeing Bratton, Director of Admissions, 215-635-7300 Ext. 140, Fax: 215-635-7399, E-mail: admissions@gratz.edu.

Hebrew College, Shoolman Graduate School of Jewish Education, Newton Centre, MA 02459. Offers early childhood Jewish education (Certificate); Jewish day school education (Certificate); Jewish education (MJ Ed); Jewish family education (Certificate); Jewish special education (Certificate); Jewish youth education, informal education and camping (Certificate). Part-time and evening/weekend programs available. Postbaccalaureate distance learning degree programs offered. *Degree requirements:* For master's, one foreign language. *Entrance requirements:* For master's, GRE, interview. Additional exam requirements/recommendations for international students: Required—TOEFL.

Hebrew Union College–Jewish Institute of Religion, School of Education, New York, NY 10012-1186. Offers MARE. Part-time programs available. *Degree requirements:* For master's, one foreign language, thesis. *Entrance requirements:* For master's, GRE, minimum 2 years of college-level Hebrew.

Inter American University of Puerto Rico, Metropolitan Campus, Graduate Programs, Program in Christian Education, San Juan, PR 00919-1293. Offers PhD.

The Jewish Theological Seminary, William Davidson Graduate School of Jewish Education, New York, NY 10027-4649. Offers MA, Ed D. Offered in conjunction with Rabbinical School; H. L. Miller Cantorial School and College of Jewish Music; Teacher's College, Columbia University; and Union Theological Seminary. Part-time programs available. Postbaccalaureate distance learning degree programs offered (minimal on-campus study). *Degree requirements:* For master's, one foreign language, thesis optional; for doctorate, one foreign language, comprehensive exam, thesis/dissertation. *Entrance requirements:* For master's, GRE or MAT, 3 letters of recommendation; for doctorate, GRE or MAT, writing sample, 3 letters of recommendation. Additional exam requirements/recommendations for international students: Recommended—TOEFL.

Jewish University of America, Graduate School, Program in Jewish Education, Skokie, IL 60077-3248. Offers MJ Ed, DJ Ed. *Degree requirements:* For master's, thesis optional; for doctorate, one foreign language, thesis/dissertation. *Entrance requirements:* For master's and doctorate, interview.

Lancaster Theological Seminary, Graduate and Professional Programs, Lancaster, PA 17603-2812. Offers biblical studies (MAR); Christian education (MAR); Christianity and the arts (MAR); church history (MAR); congregational life (MAR); lay leadership (Certificate); theological studies (M Div); theology (D Min); theology and ethics (MAR). *Accreditation:* ACIPE; ATS. *Degree requirements:* For doctorate, thesis/dissertation.

La Sierra University, School of Religion, Riverside, CA 92515. Offers pastoral ministry (M Div); religion (MA); religious education (MA); religious studies (MA). Part-time programs available. *Degree requirements:* For master's, one foreign language, thesis or alternative. *Entrance requirements:* For master's, GRE General Test, minimum GPA of 3.0.

Laura and Alvin Siegal College of Judaic Studies, Graduate Programs, Program in Religious Education, Beachwood, OH 44122-7116. Offers Jewish education (MAJS); Judaic studies (MAJS). Part-time and evening/weekend programs available. Postbaccalaureate distance learning degree programs offered (minimal on-campus study). *Degree requirements:* For master's, one foreign language, thesis. *Entrance requirements:* For master's, interview.

Lincoln Christian Seminary, Graduate and Professional Programs, Lincoln, IL 62656-2167. Offers Bible and theology (MA); Christian ministries (MA); counseling (MA); divinity (M Div); leadership ministry (D Min); religious education (MRE). *Accreditation:* ACIPE; ATS. Part-time programs available. *Degree requirements:* For master's, 2 foreign languages, thesis; for doctorate, thesis/dissertation. *Entrance requirements:* For master's, minimum GPA of 2.5; for doctorate, M Div or equivalent. Additional exam requirements/recommendations for international students: Required—TOEFL (minimum score 550 paper-based; 213 computer-based). Electronic applications accepted.

Loyola Marymount University, School of Education, Department of Educational Support Services, Program in Catholic Inclusive Education, Los Angeles, CA 90045. Offers MA. Part-time programs available. *Faculty:* 10 full-time (5 women), 36 part-time/adjunct (27 women). In 2011, 3 master's awarded. *Degree requirements:* For master's, comprehensive exam. *Entrance requirements:* For master's, CBEST, CSET, full-time employment in Archdiocese of Los Angeles, 2 letters of recommendation, letter of intent. Additional exam requirements/recommendations for international students: Required—TOEFL (minimum score 600 paper-based; 250 computer-based; 100 iBT). *Application deadline:* For fall admission, 6/15 for domestic students; for spring admission, 11/15 for domestic students. Application fee: $50. Electronic applications accepted. *Financial support:* Scholarships/grants and unspecified assistantships available. Support available to part-time students. Financial award application deadline: 5/15; financial award applicants required to submit FAFSA. *Unit head:* Dr. Brian P. Leung, Chair, 310-338-7313, E-mail: bleung@lmu.edu. *Application contact:* Chake H. Kouyoumjian, Associate Dean of Graduate Studies, 310-338-2721, E-mail: ckouyoum@lmu.edu. Web site: http://soe.lmu.edu/admissions/programs/sped/inclusive.htm.

Loyola University Chicago, Institute of Pastoral Studies, Master of Arts in Religious Education Program, Chicago, IL 60660. Offers MA, Certificate. Part-time programs available. Postbaccalaureate distance learning degree programs offered (no on-campus study). *Students:* 3 full-time (1 woman), 8 part-time (all women); includes 1 minority (Hispanic/Latino), 2 international. Average age 40. 9 applicants, 67% accepted, 4 enrolled. In 2011, 5 master's awarded. *Entrance requirements:* Additional exam requirements/recommendations for international students: Required—TOEFL. *Application deadline:* Applications are processed on a rolling basis. Application fee: $50. *Expenses: Tuition:* Full-time $15,660; part-time $870 per credit hour. *Required fees:* $125 per semester. Tuition and fees vary according to course load and program. *Financial support:* Application deadline: 3/1. *Unit head:* Dr. Eileen Daily, Graduate Program Director, 312-915-7477, Fax: 312-915-7410, E-mail: edaily@luc.edu. *Application contact:* Rachel D. Gibbons, Assistant Director, 312-915-7450, Fax: 312-915-7410, E-mail: rgibbon@luc.edu. Web site: http://www.luc.edu/ips/academics/mare/.

Luther Rice University, Graduate Programs, Lithonia, GA 30038-2454. Offers Bible/theology (M Div); Christian education (M Div); Christian studies (MA); church ministry (D Min); counseling (M Div); discipleship counseling (MA); ministry (M Div, MA); missions/evangelism (M Div). Part-time programs available. Postbaccalaureate distance learning degree programs offered (no on-campus study). *Degree requirements:* For doctorate, thesis/dissertation. *Entrance requirements:* Additional exam requirements/recommendations for international students: Required—TOEFL (minimum score 500 paper-based; 173 computer-based).

Maple Springs Baptist Bible College and Seminary, Graduate and Professional Programs, Capitol Heights, MD 20743. Offers biblical studies (MA, Certificate); Christian counseling (MA); church administration (MA); divinity (M Div); ministry (D Min); religious education (MRE).

Midwestern Baptist Theological Seminary, Graduate and Professional Programs, Kansas City, MO 64118-4697. Offers Christian education (MACE); Christian foundations); church music (MCM); counseling (MA); ministry (D Ed Min, D Min); theology (M Div). *Accreditation:* ATS. Part-time programs available. Postbaccalaureate distance learning degree programs offered (minimal on-campus study). *Faculty:* 18 full-time (1 woman), 12 part-time/adjunct (1 woman). *Students:* 440 full-time (72 women), 383 part-time (55 women); includes 65 minority (33 Black or African American, non-Hispanic/Latino; 8 American Indian or Alaska Native, non-Hispanic/Latino; 16 Asian, non-Hispanic/Latino; 8 Hispanic/Latino), 25 international. 75 applicants, 80% accepted. *Degree requirements:* For doctorate, thesis/dissertation. *Entrance requirements:* For doctorate, MAT. *Application deadline:* For fall admission, 7/20 priority date for domestic students; for winter admission, 1/7 priority date for domestic students; for spring admission, 1/28 priority date for domestic students. Applications are processed on a rolling basis. Application fee: $25. Electronic applications accepted. *Financial support:* Career-related internships or fieldwork, institutionally sponsored loans, and scholarships/grants available. Financial award application deadline: 3/31; financial award applicants required to submit FAFSA. *Faculty research:* Ministerial studies, Biblical and theological studies, missions, counseling. *Unit head:* Jerry Sutton, Vice President of Academic Development/Dean, 816-414-3745, E-mail: jsutton@mbts.edu. *Application contact:* Rhonda Nichols, Admissions Office, 800-944-6287, E-mail: admissions@mbts.edu. Web site: http://www.mbts.edu/.

Moody Theological SeminaryMichigan, Graduate Programs, Plymouth, MI 48170. Offers Bible (Graduate Certificate); Christian education (MA); counseling psychology (MA); divinity (M Div); theological studies (MA). Part-time and evening/weekend programs available. *Degree requirements:* For master's, one foreign language, thesis. *Faculty research:* Judaism, cults, world religions.

Newman Theological College, Religious Education Programs, Edmonton, AB T6V 1H3, Canada. Offers catholic school administration (CCSA); religious education (MRE, GDRE). Part-time programs available. Postbaccalaureate distance learning degree programs offered (no on-campus study). *Faculty:* 15 part-time/adjunct (6 women). *Students:* 2 full-time (1 woman), 64 part-time (37 women). Average age 39. 30 applicants, 100% accepted, 30 enrolled. In 2011, 6 master's, 22 other advanced degrees awarded. *Degree requirements:* For master's, thesis or alternative. *Entrance requirements:* For master's, 2 years of successful teaching experience, graduate diploma in religious education; for other advanced degree, bachelor's degree in education, teaching certificate. Additional exam requirements/recommendations for international students: Required—TOEFL (minimum score 560 paper-based; 220 computer-based; 86 iBT). *Application deadline:* For fall admission, 8/6 priority date for domestic students; for winter admission, 1/3 priority date for domestic students; for spring admission, 5/7 priority date for domestic students. Applications are processed on a rolling basis. Application fee: $45 ($250 for international students). Tuition and fees charges are reported in Canadian dollars. *Expenses: Tuition:* Full-time $5880 Canadian dollars; part-time $588 Canadian dollars per course. *Required fees:* $230 Canadian dollars; $70 Canadian dollars per semester. *Financial support:* Tuition bursaries available. Support available to part-time students. Financial award application deadline: 5/31. *Unit head:* Sandra Talarico, Director, 780-392-2450 Ext. 5239, Fax: 780-462-4013, E-mail: sandra.talarico@newman.edu. *Application contact:* Maria Saulnier, Registrar, 780-392-2451, Fax: 780-462-4013, E-mail: registrar@newman.edu. Web site: http://www.newman.edu/.

New Orleans Baptist Theological Seminary, Graduate and Professional Programs, Division of Christian Education Ministries, New Orleans, LA 70126-4858. Offers Christian education (M Div, MACE, D Min, DEM, PhD). Evening/weekend programs available. Postbaccalaureate distance learning degree programs offered. *Degree requirements:* For master's, 2 foreign languages; for doctorate, 3 foreign languages, comprehensive exam, thesis/dissertation. *Entrance requirements:* For doctorate, GRE General Test.

The Nigerian Baptist Theological Seminary, Graduate Studies, Ogbomoso, Nigeria. Offers church music (M Div, M Th, Diploma); divinity (M Div); ministry (D Min); religious education (M Div, M Th, PhD); theological studies (MATS); theology (M Th, PhD). Part-time programs available. *Degree requirements:* For master's, thesis, 2 Nigerian languages; for Diploma, thesis or alternative.

Northwest Nazarene University, Graduate Studies, Program in Religion, Nampa, ID 83686-5897. Offers Christian education (M Div, MA); missional leadership (M Div, MA); pastoral ministry (MA); spiritual formation (M Div, MA); youth, church and culture (M Div, MA). Part-time and evening/weekend programs available. Postbaccalaureate distance learning degree programs offered (no on-campus study). *Faculty:* 11 full-time (2 women), 23 part-time/adjunct (5 women). *Students:* 110 full-time (26 women), 16 part-time (3 women); includes 7 minority (3 Black or African American, non-Hispanic/Latino; 1 American Indian or Alaska Native, non-Hispanic/Latino; 1 Asian, non-Hispanic/Latino; 2 Hispanic/Latino), 4 international. Average age 38. 51 applicants, 86% accepted, 38 enrolled. In 2011, 42 master's awarded. *Application deadline:* Applications are processed on a rolling basis. Application fee: $50. Electronic applications accepted. *Unit head:* Dr. Jay Akkerman, Director, Graduate Studies, 208-467-8437, Fax: 208-467-8252. *Application contact:* Jill Jones, Program Assistant, 208-467-8368, Fax: 208-467-8252, E-mail: jdjones@nnu.edu. Web site: http://www.nnu.edu/online/.

Oral Roberts University, School of Theology and Missions, Tulsa, OK 74171. Offers biblical literature (MA), including advanced languages, Judaic-Christian studies; Christian counseling (MA), including marriage and family therapy; divinity (M Div); missions (MA); practical theology (MA); theological/historical studies (MA); theology (D Min). Part-time programs available. Postbaccalaureate distance learning degree programs offered (minimal on-campus study). *Degree requirements:* For master's, thesis (for some programs), practicum/internship; for doctorate, thesis/dissertation, applied research project. *Entrance requirements:* For master's, GRE General Test or MAT, minimum GPA of 2.5; for doctorate, M Div, minimum GPA of 3.0, 3 years of full-time ministry experience. Additional exam requirements/recommendations for international students: Required—TOEFL (minimum score 550 paper-based; 213 computer-based; 79 iBT). Electronic applications accepted.

Pfeiffer University, Program in Practical Theology, Misenheimer, NC 28109-0960. Offers MA. Part-time and evening/weekend programs available. *Entrance requirements:* For master's, minimum GPA of 2.75.

Phillips Theological Seminary, Programs in Theology, Tulsa, OK 74116. Offers administration of church agencies (M Div); campus ministry (M Div); church-related social work (M Div); college and seminary teaching (M Div); global mission work (M Div); institutional chaplaincy (M Div); ministerial vocations in Christian education (M Div); ministry (D Min), including parish ministry, pastoral counseling, practices of ministry; ministry and culture (MAMC), including Christian education, congregational leadership, history and practice of Christian spirituality, theology, ethics, and culture; ministry of music (M Div); pastoral care and counseling (M Div); pastoral ministry (M Div); theological studies (MTS). *Accreditation:* ATS. Part-time programs available. Postbaccalaureate distance learning degree programs offered (minimal on-campus study). *Degree requirements:* For master's, thesis (for some programs); for doctorate, thesis/dissertation. *Entrance requirements:* For master's, minimum GPA of 2.5; for doctorate, M Div, minimum GPA of 3.0. *Faculty research:* Biblical studies, historical studies, theology and culture, practical theology, theology and film.

Pontifical Catholic University of Puerto Rico, College of Education, Program in Religious Education, Ponce, PR 00717-0777. Offers MRE.

Providence College and Theological Seminary, Theological Seminary, Otterburne, MB R0A 1G0, Canada. Offers children's ministry (Certificate); Christian studies (MA, Certificate); counseling (MA); cross-cultural discipleship (Certificate); divinity (M Div); educational studies (MA), including counseling psychology, educational ministries, student development, teaching English to speakers of other languages, training teachers of English to speakers of other languages; global studies (MA); lay counseling (Diploma); ministry (D Min); teaching English to speakers of other languages (Certificate); theological studies (MA); training teacher of English to speakers of other languages (Certificate); youth ministry (Certificate). *Accreditation:* ATS. Part-time programs available. *Degree requirements:* For master's, variable foreign language requirement, thesis (for some programs); for doctorate, thesis/dissertation. *Entrance requirements:* Additional exam requirements/recommendations for international students: Recommended—TOEFL (minimum score 550 paper-based; 213 computer-based). *Faculty research:* Studies in Isaiah, theology of sin.

Reformed Theological Seminary–Jackson Campus, Graduate and Professional Programs, Jackson, MS 39209-3099. Offers Bible, theology, and missions (Certificate); biblical studies (MA); Christian education (M Div, MA); counseling (M Div); divinity (M Div, Diploma); marriage and family therapy (MA); ministry (D Min); missions (M Div, MA, D Min); New Testament (Th M); Old Testament (Th M); theological studies (MA); theology (Th M); M Div/MA. *Accreditation:* AAMFT/COAMFTE (one or more programs are accredited); ATS (one or more programs are accredited). *Degree requirements:* For master's, thesis (for some programs), fieldwork; for doctorate, 2 foreign languages, thesis/dissertation. *Entrance requirements:* For master's, minimum GPA of 2.6; for doctorate, minimum GPA of 3.0. Additional exam requirements/recommendations for international students: Required—TOEFL.

Regent University, Graduate School, School of Divinity, Virginia Beach, VA 23464-9800. Offers Biblical studies (MA), including Biblical interpretation, Christian doctrine and history, English Bible, New Testament, Old Testament; leadership and renewal (D Min), including Christian leadership and renewal, clinical pastoral education, community transformation, military ministry, ministry leadership coaching; missiology (M Div, MA), including Biblical languages (M Div), Biblical studies (M Div), church and ministry, interdisciplinary studies, TESOL, worship and renewal; practical theology (M Div, MA), including Biblical studies (M Div), church and ministry, interdisciplinary studies, military chaplaincy (MA), worship and renewal; renewal studies (PhD), including history, theology. *Accreditation:* ACIPE; ATS. Part-time programs available. Postbaccalaureate distance learning degree programs offered (minimal on-campus study). *Faculty:* 20 full-time (4 women), 16 part-time/adjunct (4 women). *Students:* 124 full-time (64 women), 529 part-time (209 women); includes 298 minority (260 Black or African American, non-Hispanic/Latino; 5 American Indian or Alaska Native, non-Hispanic/Latino; 13 Asian, non-Hispanic/Latino; 20 Hispanic/Latino), 41 international. Average age 41. 506 applicants, 60% accepted, 179 enrolled. In 2011, 94 master's, 14 doctorates awarded. *Degree requirements:* For master's, comprehensive exam, thesis or alternative, internship; for doctorate, thesis/dissertation or alternative. *Entrance requirements:* For master's, GRE General Test or MAT, minimum undergraduate GPA of 2.75, writing sample, clergy recommendation; for doctorate, M Div or theological master's degree; minimum graduate GPA of 3.5 (PhD), 3.0 (D Min); recommendations; writing sample; transcripts. Additional exam requirements/recommendations for international students: Required—TOEFL (minimum score 577 paper-based; 233 computer-based). *Application deadline:* For fall admission, 5/1 priority date for domestic students. Applications are processed on a rolling basis. Application fee: $50. Electronic applications accepted. *Expenses:* Contact institution. *Financial support:* Fellowships with full and partial tuition reimbursements, career-related internships or fieldwork, scholarships/grants, tuition waivers (full and partial), and unspecified assistantships available. Support available to part-time students. Financial award application deadline: 9/1; financial award applicants required to submit FAFSA. *Faculty research:* Greek and Hebrew, theology, spiritual formation, global missions and world Christianity, women's studies. *Unit head:* Dr. Michael Palmer, Dean, 757-352-4406, Fax: 757-352-4597, E-mail: mpalmer@regent.edu. *Application contact:* Matthew Chadwick, Director of Enrollment Support Services, 800-373-5504, Fax: 757-352-4381, E-mail: admissions@regent.edu. Web site: http://www.regent.edu/acad/schdiv/home.shtml?r=home.cfm.

Regent University, Graduate School, School of Education, Virginia Beach, VA 23464-9800. Offers adult education (Ed D); adult/staff development (Ed D, PhD); career switcher with licensure (M Ed), including alternative licensure; character education (Ed D, PhD); Christian education leadership (Ed D, PhD); Christian education specialist (Ed S); Christian school program (M Ed), including ACSI licensure; distance education (Ed D, PhD); education licensure (M Ed), including preK-6th grade; educational leadership (M Ed, PhD); educational leadership - special education (Ed S), including administration and supervision; educational psychology (Ed D, PhD), including learning and development, research and evaluation, special education; higher education (Ed D, PhD), including administration, research and institutional planning, teaching; higher education leadership (Ed D); individualized degree plan (M Ed), including behavior disorders, learning disabilities, mental retardation, reading specialist; K-12 school leadership (Ed D, PhD); leadership in character education (M Ed); master teacher (M Ed), including TESOL; mathematics education (M Ed); special education (PhD); student affairs (M Ed); TESOL (M Ed), including adult education, ESL: preK-12. *Accreditation:* Teacher Education Accreditation Council. Part-time and evening/weekend programs available. Postbaccalaureate distance learning degree programs offered (minimal on-campus study). *Faculty:* 26 full-time (13 women), 54 part-time/adjunct (34 women). *Students:* 140 full-time (109 women), 786 part-time (626 women); includes 218 minority (189 Black or African American, non-Hispanic/Latino; 2 American Indian or Alaska Native, non-Hispanic/Latino; 11 Asian, non-Hispanic/Latino; 16 Hispanic/Latino), 42 international. Average age 39. 673 applicants, 57% accepted, 298 enrolled. In 2011, 178 master's, 15 doctorates awarded. *Degree requirements:* For master's, thesis or alternative; for doctorate, comprehensive exam, thesis/dissertation. *Entrance requirements:* For master's, MAT, minimum undergraduate GPA of 2.75, writing sample, resume, recommendations, interview; for doctorate, GRE, writing sample, 3 years of relevant professional experience, master's-level paper, copies of published work, resume, transcripts, interview, recommendations. Additional exam requirements/recommendations for international students: Required—TOEFL (minimum score 577 paper-based; 233 computer-based). *Application deadline:* For fall admission, 4/1 priority date for domestic students; for spring admission, 10/15 priority date for domestic students. Applications are processed on a rolling basis. Application fee: $50. Electronic applications accepted. *Expenses:* Contact institution. *Financial support:* Fellowships, career-related internships or fieldwork, scholarships/grants, tuition waivers (full and partial), and unspecified assistantships available. Support available to part-time students. Financial award application deadline: 4/1; financial award applicants required to submit FAFSA. *Faculty research:* Character development and discipline for children, education leadership development, diversity in schools, classroom management, technology in education settings. *Unit head:* Dr. Alan A. Arroyo, Dean, 757-352-4261, Fax: 757-352-4318, E-mail: alanarr@regent.edu. *Application contact:* Matthew Chadwick, Director of Enrollment Support Services, 800-373-5504, Fax: 757-352-4381, E-mail: admissions@regent.edu. Web site: http://www.regent.edu/education/.

Rochester College, Center for Missional Leadership, Rochester Hills, MI 48307-2764. Offers MRE.

St. Augustine's Seminary of Toronto, Graduate and Professional Programs, Scarborough, ON M1M 1M3, Canada. Offers divinity (M Div); lay ministry (Diploma); religious education (MRE); theological studies (MTS, Diploma). *Accreditation:* ATS. Part-time and evening/weekend programs available. *Entrance requirements:* Additional exam requirements/recommendations for international students: Required—TOEFL (minimum score 580 paper-based; 237 computer-based), TWE (minimum score 5).

Saint Mary's University of Minnesota, Schools of Graduate and Professional Programs, Graduate School of Education, Institute for LaSallian Studies, Winona, MN 55987-1399. Offers LaSallian leadership (MA); LaSallian studies (MA). *Unit head:* Dr. Roxanne Eubank, Director, 612-728-5217, E-mail: reubank@smumn.edu. *Application contact:* Yasin Alsaidi, Director of Admissions for Graduate and Professional Programs, 612-728-5207, Fax: 612-728-5121, E-mail: yalsaidi@smumn.edu. Web site: http://www.smumn.edu/graduate-home/areas-of-study/graduate-school-of-education/ma-in-lasallian-studies.

Saints Cyril and Methodius Seminary, Graduate and Professional Programs, Orchard Lake, MI 48324. Offers pastoral ministry (MAPM); religious education (MARE); theology (M Div, MA). *Accreditation:* ATS. Part-time programs available.

St. Vladimir's Orthodox Theological Seminary, Graduate School of Theology, Crestwood, NY 10707-1699. Offers general theological studies (MA); liturgical music (MA); religious education (MA); theology (M Div, M Th, D Min); M Div/MA. MA in general theological studies, M Div offered jointly with St. Nersess Seminary. *Accreditation:* ATS. Part-time programs available. *Degree requirements:* For master's, one foreign language, thesis, fieldwork; for doctorate, thesis/dissertation, fieldwork. *Entrance requirements:* For doctorate, M Div, minimum GPA of 3.0. Additional exam requirements/recommendations for international students: Required—TOEFL (minimum score 250 computer-based).

Shasta Bible College, Program in Biblical Counseling, Redding, CA 96002. Offers biblical counseling and Christian family life education (MA). Part-time programs available. *Degree requirements:* For master's, comprehensive exam (for some programs), thesis or alternative. *Entrance requirements:* For master's, minimum GPA of 2.5. Additional exam requirements/recommendations for international students: Required—TOEFL (minimum score 550 paper-based; 213 computer-based).

Southeastern Baptist Theological Seminary, Graduate and Professional Programs, Wake Forest, NC 27588-1889. Offers advanced biblical studies (M Div); Christian education (M Div, MACE); Christian ethics (PhD); Christian ministry (M Div); Christian planting (M Div); church music (MACM); counseling (MACO); evangelism (PhD); language (M Div); ministry (D Min); New Testament (PhD); Old Testament (PhD); philosophy (PhD); theology (Th M, PhD); women's studies (M Div). *Accreditation:* ACIPE; ATS (one or more programs are accredited). *Degree requirements:* For master's, thesis (for some programs), oral exam; for doctorate, thesis/dissertation, fieldwork. *Entrance requirements:* For master's, Cooperative English Test, minimum GPA of 2.0, M Div or equivalent (Th M); for doctorate, GRE General Test or MAT, Cooperative English Test, M Div or equivalent, 3 years of professional experience.

Southern Adventist University, School of Religion, Collegedale, TN 37315-0370. Offers Biblical and theological studies (MA); church leadership and management (M Min); church ministry and homiletics (M Min); evangelism and world mission (M Min); religious studies (MA). Part-time programs available. *Degree requirements:* For master's, comprehensive exam, thesis (for some programs). *Entrance requirements:* For master's, GRE. Additional exam requirements/recommendations for international students: Required—TOEFL (minimum score 600 paper-based; 250 computer-based). *Faculty research:* Biblical archaeology.

Southern Baptist Theological Seminary, School of Church Ministries, Louisville, KY 40280-0004. Offers Biblical counseling (M Div, MA); children's and family ministry (M Div, MA); Christian education (MA); Christian worship (PhD); church ministries (M Div); church music (MCM); college ministry (M Div, MA); discipleship and family ministry (M Div, MA); education (Ed D); family ministry (D Min, PhD); higher education (PhD); leadership (M Div, MA, D Min, PhD); ministry (D Ed Min); missions and ethnodoxology (M Div); women's leadership (M Div, MA); worship leadership (M Div, MA); worship leadership and church ministry (MA); youth and family ministry (M Div, MA). Part-time programs available. Postbaccalaureate distance learning degree programs offered (minimal on-campus study). *Faculty:* 10 full-time (2 women), 5 part-time/adjunct (2 women). *Students:* 393. *Degree requirements:* For doctorate, thesis/dissertation. *Entrance requirements:* For doctorate, GRE General Test, interview, M Div or MACE. Additional exam requirements/recommendations for international students: Required—TWE. *Application deadline:* For fall admission, 7/15 priority date for domestic students; for spring admission, 12/1 for domestic students. Applications are processed on a rolling basis. Application fee: $35. *Financial support:* Research assistantships, teaching assistantships, career-related internships or fieldwork, institutionally sponsored loans, and tuition waivers (partial) available. Financial award application deadline: 4/1. *Faculty research:* Gerontology, creative teaching methods, faith development in children, faith development in youth, transformational learning. *Unit head:* Dr. Randy Stinson, Dean, 800-626-5525, E-mail: rstinson@sbts.edu. *Application contact:* John Powell, Director of Admissions and Recruiting, 800-626-5525 Ext. 4617. Web site: http://www.sbts.edu/church-ministries/.

Southern Evangelical Seminary, Graduate Programs, Matthews, NC 28105. Offers apologetics (MA, Certificate); Christian education (MA); church ministry (MA, Certificate); divinity (Certificate), including apologetics (M Div, Certificate); Islamic studies (MA, Certificate); Jewish studies (MA); philosophy (MA); religion (MA); theology (M Div), including apologetics (M Div, Certificate), Biblical studies; youth ministry (MA). Part-time and evening/weekend programs available. Postbaccalaureate distance learning degree programs offered. *Degree requirements:* For master's, thesis (for some programs); for doctorate, 2 foreign languages, comprehensive exam (for some programs), thesis/dissertation. *Entrance requirements:* Additional exam requirements/recommendations for international students: Required—TOEFL (minimum score 600 paper-based; 250 computer-based).

Southwestern Assemblies of God University, Thomas F. Harrison School of Graduate Studies, Program in Education, Waxahachie, TX 75165-5735. Offers Christian school administration (MS); curriculum development (MS); early education administration (M Ed); middle and secondary education (M Ed). *Degree requirements:* For master's, comprehensive written and oral exams. *Entrance requirements:* For master's, GRE General Test, minimum GPA of 2.5. Electronic applications accepted.

Southwestern Baptist Theological Seminary, School of Educational Ministries, Fort Worth, TX 76122-0000. Offers MA Comm, MACC, MACCM, MACE, MACSE, MAMFC, DEM, PhD, SPEM. Part-time and evening/weekend programs available. Terminal master's awarded for partial completion of doctoral program. *Degree requirements:* For master's, thesis; for doctorate, thesis/dissertation, statistics comprehensive exam. *Entrance requirements:* For doctorate, GRE or MAT, MACE or equivalent, minimum GPA of 3.0; for SPEM, 3 years of ministry experience after master's degree, MACE or equivalent. Additional exam requirements/recommendations for international students: Required—TOEFL, TWE. Electronic applications accepted.

Spertus Institute of Jewish Studies, Graduate Programs, Program in Jewish Education, Chicago, IL 60605-1901. Offers MAJ Ed. Part-time and evening/weekend programs available. *Faculty:* 9 part-time/adjunct (1 woman). *Students:* 2 part-time (both women). *Degree requirements:* For master's, one foreign language, thesis. *Entrance requirements:* For master's, bachelor of arts in Jewish studies. *Application deadline:* Applications are processed on a rolling basis. Application fee: $50. *Expenses: Tuition:* Full-time $18,750; part-time $350 per credit. *Financial support:* Scholarships/grants available. Financial award applicants required to submit FAFSA. *Unit head:* Dr. Dean Phillip Bell, Dean, 312-322-1791, Fax: 312-994-5360, E-mail: dbell@spertus.edu.

Temple Baptist Seminary, Program in Theology, Chattanooga, TN 37404-3530. Offers biblical languages (M Div); Biblical studies (MABS); Christian education (MACE); English Bible language tools (M Div); theology (MM, D Min). Part-time and evening/weekend programs available. Postbaccalaureate distance learning degree programs offered (minimal on-campus study). *Degree requirements:* For doctorate, thesis/dissertation. *Entrance requirements:* For doctorate, minimum GPA of 3.0, M Div.

Towson University, Baltimore Hebrew Institute, Towson, MD 21252-0001. Offers Jewish communal service (MAJCS); Jewish education (MAJE, Postbaccalaureate Certificate); Jewish studies (MAJS). *Students:* 9 full-time (4 women), 25 part-time (16 women); includes 4 minority (all Black or African American, non-Hispanic/Latino). *Expenses:* Tuition, state resident: part-time $337 per credit. Tuition, nonresident: part-time $709 per credit. *Required fees:* $99 per credit. *Unit head:* Hana Bor, Director, 410-704-5026, E-mail: hbor@towson.edu. Web site: http://www.towson.edu/bhi/.

Trinity International University, Trinity Evangelical Divinity School, Deerfield, IL 60015-1284. Offers Biblical and Near Eastern archaeology and languages (MA); Christian studies (MA, Certificate); Christian thought (MA); church history (MA, Th M); congregational ministry: pastor-teacher (M Div); congregational ministry: team ministry (M Div); counseling ministries (MA); counseling psychology (MA); cross-cultural ministry (M Div); educational studies (PhD); evangelism (MA); history of Christianity in America (MA); intercultural studies (MA, PhD); leadership and ministry management (D Min); military chaplaincy (D Min); ministry (MA); mission and evangelism (Th M); missions and evangelism (D Min); New Testament (MA, Th M); Old Testament (Th M); Old Testament and Semitic languages (MA); pastoral care (M Div); pastoral care and counseling (D Min); pastoral counseling and psychology (Th M); pastoral theology (Th M); philosophy of religion (MA); preaching (D Min); religion (MA); research ministry (M Div); systematic theology (Th M); theological studies (PhD); urban ministry (MA). *Accreditation:* ATS (one or more programs are accredited). Part-time programs available. Postbaccalaureate distance learning degree programs offered (minimal on-campus study). *Degree requirements:* For master's, comprehensive exam, thesis, fieldwork; for doctorate, comprehensive exam (for some programs), thesis/dissertation; for Certificate, comprehensive exam, integrative papers. *Entrance requirements:* For master's, GRE, MAT, minimum cumulative undergraduate GPA of 3.0; for doctorate, GRE, minimum cumulative graduate GPA of 3.2; for Certificate, GRE, MAT, minimum undergraduate GPA of 2.5. Additional exam requirements/recommendations for international students: Required—TOEFL (minimum score 580 paper-based; 237 computer-based), TWE (minimum score 4). Electronic applications accepted.

Trinity Lutheran Seminary, Graduate and Professional Programs, Columbus, OH 43209-2334. Offers African American studies (MTS); Biblical studies (MTS); Christian education (MA); Christian spirituality (STM); church in the world (MTS); church music (MA); divinity (M Div), including Bible in mission and ministry, Christian spirituality, church in diverse world, leadership for missional church, youth and family ministry; general theological studies (MTS); mission and evangelism (STM); pastoral leadership/practice (STM); sacred theology in Biblical studies (STM); theological studies (STM); theology and ethics (MTS); youth and family ministry (MA); MSN/MTS; MTS/JD. *Accreditation:* ACIPE; ATS. Part-time programs available. *Faculty:* 11 full-time (5 women), 4 part-time/adjunct (3 women). *Students:* 75 full-time (31 women), 61 part-time (28 women); includes 23 minority (19 Black or African American, non-Hispanic/Latino; 3 Asian, non-Hispanic/Latino; 1 Two or more races, non-Hispanic/Latino), 2 international. Average age 35. 77 applicants, 71% accepted, 35 enrolled. In 2011, 39 master's awarded. *Degree requirements:* For master's, variable foreign language requirement, comprehensive exam (for some programs), thesis (for some programs), field experience (for some programs). *Entrance requirements:* For master's, BA or equivalent (MA, M Div, MTS); M Div, MTS, or equivalent (STM); audition (MACM). Additional exam requirements/recommendations for international students: Required—TOEFL (minimum score 500 paper-based; 173 computer-based; 61 iBT). *Application deadline:* For fall admission, 7/15 priority date for domestic students, 7/15 for international students. Applications are processed on a rolling basis. Application fee: $25. *Expenses: Tuition:* Full-time $13,680; part-time $456 per semester hour. *Required fees:* $115 per semester. One-time fee: $100. Part-time tuition and fees vary according to course level. *Financial support:* In 2011–12, 78 students received support. Career-related internships or fieldwork, Federal Work-Study, and scholarships/grants available. Support available to part-time students. Financial award application deadline: 5/1; financial award applicants required to submit FAFSA. *Unit head:* Dr. Brad A. Binau, Academic Dean, 614-235-4136 Ext. 4674, Fax: 614-384-4635, E-mail: bbinau@TLSohio.edu. *Application contact:* Rev. Shari L. Ayers, Director of Admissions, 614-235-4136 Ext. 4614, Fax: 866-610-8572, E-mail: sayers@tls.edu. Web site: http://www.tlsohio.edu.

Unification Theological Seminary, Graduate Program, Main Campus, Barrytown, NY 12507. Offers divinity (M Div); ministry (D Min); religious education (MRE); religious studies (MA). Part-time and evening/weekend programs available. *Faculty:* 2 full-time (1 woman), 5 part-time/adjunct (0 women). *Students:* 33 full-time (7 women); includes 21 minority (16 Black or African American, non-Hispanic/Latino; 1 American Indian or Alaska Native, non-Hispanic/Latino; 3 Asian, non-Hispanic/Latino; 1 Hispanic/Latino). Average age 45. In 2011, 20 master's, 5 doctorates awarded. *Degree requirements:* For master's, one foreign language, thesis or alternative; for doctorate, thesis/dissertation. *Entrance requirements:* For master's, bachelor's degree; for doctorate, M Div or equivalency. Additional exam requirements/recommendations for international students: Required—TOEFL (minimum score 450 paper-based; 133 computer-based; 45 iBT). *Application deadline:* For fall admission, 8/15 priority date for domestic students; for spring admission, 1/15 priority date for domestic students. Applications are processed on a rolling basis. Application fee: $30. *Expenses: Tuition:* Full-time $11,040; part-time $460 per credit. *Required fees:* $125 per semester. *Financial support:* Career-related internships or fieldwork, institutionally sponsored loans, scholarships/grants, and tuition waivers (partial) available. Support available to part-time students. Financial award applicants required to submit FAFSA. *Faculty research:* Church leadership, church history, world religions, ecumenism, interfaith peace building, service-learning. *Unit head:* Dr. Kathy Winings, Academic Dean, 845-752-3000 Ext. 228, Fax: 845-752-3014, E-mail: academics@uts.edu. *Application contact:* Davetta Ogunlola, Director of Admissions, 212-563-6647 Ext. 105, Fax: 212-563-6431, E-mail: d.ogunlola@uts.edu.

Unification Theological Seminary, Graduate Program, New York Extension, New York, NY 10036. Offers divinity (M Div); religious education (MRE); religious studies (MA). Part-time and evening/weekend programs available. *Faculty:* 3 full-time (0 women), 9 part-time/adjunct (3 women). *Students:* 37 full-time (15 women), 56 part-time (17 women); includes 32 minority (26 Black or African American, non-Hispanic/Latino; 4 Asian, non-Hispanic/Latino; 2 Hispanic/Latino), 56 international. Average age 38. *Degree requirements:* For master's, thesis or alternative. *Entrance requirements:* For master's, bachelor's degree. Additional exam requirements/recommendations for international students: Required—TOEFL (minimum score 450 paper-based; 133 computer-based). *Application deadline:* For fall admission, 8/15 priority date for domestic students; for spring admission, 1/15 priority date for domestic students. Applications are processed on a rolling basis. Application fee: $30. *Expenses: Tuition:* Full-time $11,040; part-time $460 per credit. *Required fees:* $125 per semester. *Financial support:* In 2011–12, 93 students received support. Career-related internships or fieldwork, institutionally sponsored loans, scholarships/grants, and tuition waivers (partial) available. Support available to part-time students. Financial award applicants required to submit FAFSA. *Faculty research:* Church history, world religions, ecumenism, interfaith peace building, service-learning. *Unit head:* Dr. Kathy Winings, Academic Dean, 212-563-6647 Ext. 101, Fax: 212-563-6431, E-mail: academics@uts.edu. *Application contact:* Paul G. Rajan, Director of Recruitment, 212-563-6647 Ext. 113, Fax: 212-563-6431, E-mail: p.rajan@uts.edu.

Union Presbyterian Seminary, Graduate and Professional Programs, Richmond, VA 23227-4597. Offers M Div, MACE, Th M, PhD, M Div/MACE. Part-time and evening/weekend programs available. Postbaccalaureate distance learning degree programs offered (minimal on-campus study). *Faculty:* 28 full-time (10 women), 14 part-time/adjunct (5 women). *Students:* 121 full-time (60 women), 100 part-time (68 women). *Degree requirements:* For master's, oral and written exams. *Entrance requirements:* For master's, three references, transcripts, background check; for doctorate, GRE General Test, three references, transcripts, background check, statement of goals. essay. Additional exam requirements/recommendations for international students: Required—TOEFL (minimum score 550 paper-based; 213 computer-based), TWE (minimum score 4). *Application deadline:* For fall admission, 3/15 for domestic students; for winter admission, 9/1 for domestic students; for spring admission, 3/1 for domestic students. Applications are processed on a rolling basis. Application fee: $65. Electronic applications accepted. *Expenses: Tuition:* Full-time $12,320; part-time $1232 per credit. *Required fees:* $200; $13 per term. Tuition and fees vary according to degree level. *Financial support:* Fellowships, teaching assistantships, career-related internships or fieldwork, and institutionally sponsored loans available. Financial award application deadline: 5/15; financial award applicants required to submit FAFSA. *Unit head:* Dean, 804-254-8047, Fax: 804-355-3919. *Application contact:* Katherine Fiedler Boswell, Director of Admissions, 804-355-0671 Ext. 222, Fax: 804-355-3919, E-mail: kboswell@upsem.edu. Web site: http://www.upsem.edu/.

University of St. Michael's College, Faculty of Theology, Toronto, ON M5S 1J4, Canada. Offers Catholic leadership (MA); eastern Christian studies (Diploma); religious education (Diploma); theological studies (Diploma); theology (M Div, MA, MRE, MTS, D Min, PhD, Th D); theology and Jewish studies (MA). Th D offered jointly with University of Toronto. *Accreditation:* ATS (one or more programs are accredited). Part-time programs available. *Degree requirements:* For master's, thesis (for some programs), 1 foreign language (MA), 2 foreign languages (Th M); for doctorate, 3 foreign languages, comprehensive exam, thesis/dissertation; for other advanced degree, thesis optional. *Entrance requirements:* For master's, M Div or BA, course work in an ancient or modern language, minimum GPA of 3.3; for doctorate, MA in theology, Th M, or M Div with thesis, minimum GPA of 3.7; for other advanced degree, minimum GPA of 2.7. Additional exam requirements/recommendations for international students: Required—TOEFL (minimum score 600 paper-based; 250 computer-based). Electronic applications accepted. *Expenses:* Contact institution. *Faculty research:* Patristics, eastern Christianity, ecology and theology, ecumenism, Jewish Christian studies.

University of St. Thomas, Graduate Studies, The Saint Paul Seminary School of Divinity, Saint Paul, MN 55105. Offers M Div, MA, MARE. *Accreditation:* ACIPE; ATS. Part-time and evening/weekend programs available. *Faculty:* 13 full-time (5 women), 5 part-time/adjunct (2 women). *Students:* 107 full-time (3 women), 28 part-time (12 women); includes 4 minority (2 Asian, non-Hispanic/Latino; 2 Hispanic/Latino), 12 international. Average age 28. 32 applicants, 100% accepted, 30 enrolled. In 2011, 23 master's awarded. *Degree requirements:* For master's, one foreign language, comprehensive exam (for some programs), thesis (for some programs). *Entrance requirements:* For master's, GRE, 3 letters of recommendation, interview. Additional exam requirements/recommendations for international students: Required—TOEFL (minimum score 550 paper-based; 213 computer-based). *Application deadline:* For fall admission, 6/1 priority date for domestic students. Applications are processed on a rolling basis. Application fee: $40. Electronic applications accepted. *Expenses:* Contact institution. *Financial support:* In 2011–12, 52 students received support. Fellowships, research assistantships, institutionally sponsored loans, and scholarships/grants available. Support available to part-time students. Financial award application deadline: 4/1; financial award applicants required to submit FAFSA. *Faculty research:* Theological education. *Unit head:* Rev. Msgr. Aloysius R. Callaghan, Rector, 651-962-5052, Fax: 651-962-5790, E-mail: arcallaghan@stthomas.edu. *Application contact:* Rev. Peter A. Laird, Vice Rector and Admissions Chair, 651-962-5070, Fax: 651-962-5790, E-mail: palaird@stthomas.edu. Web site: http://www.stthomas.edu/sod/.

University of St. Thomas, School of Education, Houston, TX 77006-4696. Offers all level teaching (M Ed); bilingual/dual language (M Ed); Catholic school teaching (M Ed); Catholic/private school leadership (M Ed); counselor education (M Ed); curriculum and instruction (M Ed); educational leadership (M Ed); elementary teaching (M Ed); English as a second language (M Ed); exceptionality/ educational diagnostician (M Ed); exceptionality/special education (M Ed); generalist (M Ed); reading (M Ed); secondary teaching (M Ed). Part-time and evening/weekend programs available. Postbaccalaureate distance learning degree programs offered (no on-campus study). *Faculty:* 30 full-time (17 women), 54 part-time/adjunct (37 women). *Students:* 66 full-time (43 women), 1,178 part-time (1,044 women); includes 777 minority (313 Black or African American, non-Hispanic/Latino; 5 American Indian or Alaska Native, non-Hispanic/Latino; 29 Asian, non-Hispanic/Latino; 395 Hispanic/Latino; 2 Native Hawaiian or other Pacific Islander, non-Hispanic/Latino; 33 Two or more races, non-Hispanic/Latino), 26 international. Average age 36. 551 applicants, 94% accepted, 416 enrolled. In 2011, 72 master's awarded. *Degree requirements:* For master's, thesis, field experience. *Entrance requirements:* For master's, GRE or MAT if GPA is below 3.0, bachelor's degree; minimum GPA of 2.75 in bachelor's degree or last 60 credit hours; official transcripts from all institutions; goal statement of 250-300 words; 1 reference. Additional exam requirements/recommendations for international students: Required—TOEFL. *Application deadline:* Applications are processed on a rolling basis. Application fee: $35. Electronic applications accepted. *Expenses:* Contact institution. *Financial support:* In 2011–12, 9 students received support. Federal Work-Study, scholarships/grants, and state work-study, institutional employment available. Support available to part-time students. Financial award application deadline: 4/15; financial award applicants required to submit FAFSA. *Faculty research:* Leadership, diversity, personality traits, second language acquisition. *Unit head:* Dr. Nora Hutto, Dean, 713-525-3540, Fax: 713-525-3871, E-mail: education@stthom.edu. *Application contact:* Paula C. Hollis, Administrative Assistant, 713-525-3540, Fax: 713-525-3871, E-mail: education@stthom.edu. Web site: http://www.stthom.edu/Schools_Centers_of_Excellence/Schools_of_Study/School_of_Education/Index.aqf.

University of San Francisco, School of Education, Catholic Educational Leadership Program, San Francisco, CA 94117-1080. Offers Catholic school leadership (MA, Ed D); Catholic school teaching (MA). *Faculty:* 2 full-time (1 woman), 2 part-time/adjunct (both women). *Students:* 9 full-time (4 women), 25 part-time (11 women); includes 6 minority (1 Black or African American, non-Hispanic/Latino; 2 Asian, non-Hispanic/Latino; 3 Hispanic/Latino), 3 international. Average age 41. 24 applicants, 71% accepted, 8 enrolled. In 2011, 2 master's, 6 doctorates awarded. *Degree requirements:* For doctorate, thesis/dissertation. Application fee: $55 ($65 for international students). *Expenses: Tuition:* Full-time $20,070; part-time $1115 per unit. Tuition and fees vary according to course load, campus/location and program. *Financial support:* In 2011–12, 1 student received support. Fellowships, research assistantships, and teaching assistantships available. Financial award application deadline: 3/2; financial award applicants required to submit FAFSA. *Unit head:* Dr. Christopher Thomas, Chair, 415-422-2204. *Application contact:* Beth Teague, Associate Director of Graduate Outreach, 415-422-5467, E-mail: schoolofeducation@usfca.edu. Web site: http://www.soe.usfca.edu/departments/leadership/cel_index.html.

Walsh University, Graduate Studies, Program in Theology, North Canton, OH 44720-3396. Offers parish administration (MA); pastoral ministry (MA); religious education (MA). Part-time and evening/weekend programs available. *Faculty:* 2 full-time (0 women), 2 part-time/adjunct (0 women). *Students:* 1 full-time (0 women), 2 part-time (1 woman). Average age 40. 6 applicants, 83% accepted, 3 enrolled. In 2011, 1 master's awarded. *Degree requirements:* For master's, thesis or alternative. *Entrance requirements:* For master's, MAT or GRE, minimum GPA of 3.0. Additional exam requirements/recommendations for international students: Required—TOEFL. *Application deadline:* For fall admission, 7/15 priority date for domestic students. Applications are processed on a rolling basis. Application fee: $25. Electronic applications accepted. *Expenses: Tuition:* Full-time $10,170; part-time $565 per credit hour. *Financial support:* In 2011–12, 3 students received support. Research assistantships and unspecified assistantships available. Financial award application deadline: 12/31; financial award applicants required to submit FAFSA. *Faculty research:* Historical theology, patristics, twentieth century Catholic theologians, theological anthropology, peace studies. *Unit head:* Dr. Patrick Manning, Chair, 330-244-4922, Fax: 330-244-4955, E-mail: pmanning@walsh.edu. *Application contact:* Vanessa Freiman, Graduate and Transfer Admissions Counselor, 330-490-7177, Fax: 330-244-4925, E-mail: vfreiman@walsh.edu.

Wesley Biblical Seminary, Graduate Programs, Jackson, MS 39206. Offers apologetics (MA); Biblical languages (M Div); Biblical literature (MA); Christian studies (MA); context and mission (M Div); honors research (M Div); interpretation (M Div); ministry (M Div); spiritual formation (M Div); teaching (M Div); theology (MA). *Accreditation:* ATS. Part-time programs available. *Faculty:* 11 full-time (2 women), 5 part-time/adjunct (0 women). *Students:* 42 full-time (7 women), 67 part-time (15 women). *Degree requirements:* For master's, thesis. *Entrance requirements:* Additional exam requirements/recommendations for international students: Required—TOEFL. *Application deadline:* For fall admission, 7/1 priority date for domestic students; for spring admission, 12/1 priority date for domestic students. Applications are processed on a rolling basis. Application fee: $40. Electronic applications accepted. *Financial support:* Scholarships/grants available. Support available to part-time students. *Faculty research:* Patristics, missiology, culture, hermeneutics. *Unit head:* Dr. Daniel Burnett, Vice President for Academic Affairs, 601-366-8880 Ext. 112, Fax: 601-366-8832. *Application contact:* Laura McMillan, Assistant to the Vice President for Business and Student Development, 601-366-8880 Ext. 110, Fax: 601-366-8832, E-mail: admissions@wbs.edu. Web site: http://www.wbs.edu.

Wheaton College, Graduate School, Department of Christian Formation and Ministry, Wheaton, IL 60187-5593. Offers MA. Part-time programs available. *Students:* 24 full-time (11 women), 31 part-time (13 women); includes 6 minority (1 Black or African American, non-Hispanic/Latino; 1 Asian, non-Hispanic/Latino; 4 Hispanic/Latino), 7 international. Average age 30. 31 applicants, 97% accepted, 20 enrolled. In 2011, 13 master's awarded. *Degree requirements:* For master's, thesis or alternative. *Entrance requirements:* For master's, GRE General Test or MAT. Additional exam requirements/recommendations for international students: Required—TOEFL (minimum score 550 paper-based; 80 iBT), IELTS (minimum score 6.5). *Application deadline:* For fall admission, 5/1 for domestic students, 1/1 for international students; for spring admission, 11/1 for domestic students. Applications are processed on a rolling basis. Application fee: $30. Electronic applications accepted. *Expenses: Tuition:* Full-time $16,440; part-time $685 per credit hour. Tuition and fees vary according to degree level and program. *Financial support:* Career-related internships or fieldwork, scholarships/grants, and unspecified assistantships available. Financial award application deadline: 3/1; financial award applicants required to submit FAFSA. *Unit head:* Dr. Barrett McRay, Coordinator, 630-752-5198. *Application contact:* Julie A. Huebner, Director of Graduate Admissions, 630-752-5195, Fax: 630-752-5935, E-mail: gradadm@wheaton.edu. Web site: http://www.wheaton.edu/Academics/Departments/CFM/MA-in-CFM.

Xavier University, College of Arts and Sciences, Department of Theology, Cincinnati, OH 45207. Offers health care mission integration (MA); theology (MA), including religious education, social and pastoral ministry, theology. Part-time and evening/weekend programs available. *Faculty:* 5 full-time (2 women), 1 part-time/adjunct (0 women). *Students:* 1 (woman) full-time, 16 part-time (7 women); includes 1 minority (Black or African American, non-Hispanic/Latino). Average age 43. 6 applicants, 67% accepted, 4 enrolled. In 2011, 8 master's awarded. *Degree requirements:* For master's, thesis optional, final paper (or thesis) and defense. *Entrance requirements:* For master's, MAT or GRE, letters of recommendation; statement of reasons and goals for enrolling in program (1,000-2,000 words). Additional exam requirements/recommendations for international students: Required—TOEFL (minimum score 550 paper-based; 213 computer-based). *Application deadline:* Applications are processed on a rolling basis. Application fee: $35. Electronic applications accepted. *Expenses: Tuition:* Part-time $576 per credit hour. *Financial support:* Scholarships/grants and unspecified assistantships available. Financial award applicants required to submit FAFSA. *Faculty research:* Scripture, ethics, constructive theology, historical theology. *Unit head:* Dr. Sarah Melcher, Chair, 513-745-2043, Fax: 513-745-3215, E-mail: melcher@xavier.edu. *Application contact:* Roger Bosse, Graduate Services Director, 513-745-3357, Fax: 513-745-1048, E-mail: bosse@xavier.edu. Web site: http://www.xavier.edu/theology/.

Yeshiva University, Azrieli Graduate School of Jewish Education and Administration, New York, NY 10033-4391. Offers MS, Ed D, Specialist. Part-time and evening/weekend programs available. Terminal master's awarded for partial completion of doctoral program. *Degree requirements:* For master's, one foreign language, student teaching experience, comprehensive exam or thesis; for doctorate, one foreign language, comprehensive exam, thesis/dissertation, certifying exams, internship; for Specialist, one foreign language, comprehensive exam, certifying exams, internship. *Entrance requirements:* For master's, GRE General Test, BA in Jewish studies or equivalent; for doctorate and Specialist, GRE General Test, master's degree in Jewish education, 2 years of teaching experience. *Expenses:* Contact institution. *Faculty research:* Social patterns of American and Israeli Jewish population, special education, adult education, technology in education, return to religious values.

Science Education

Acadia University, Faculty of Professional Studies, School of Education, Program in Curriculum Studies, Wolfville, NS B4P 2R6, Canada. Offers cultural and media studies (M Ed); learning and technology (M Ed); science, math and technology (M Ed). Part-time programs available. *Degree requirements:* For master's, thesis optional. *Entrance requirements:* For master's, B Ed or the equivalent, minimum B average in undergraduate course work, 2 years of teaching experience. Additional exam requirements/recommendations for international students: Required—TOEFL (minimum score 580 paper-based; 237 computer-based; 93 iBT), IELTS (minimum score 6.5). *Faculty research:* Literacy development, postmodern philosophy and curriculum theory, historiography, philosophy of education, learning and technology.

Alabama State University, Department of Curriculum and Instruction, Program in Secondary Education, Montgomery, AL 36101-0271. Offers biology education (M Ed, Ed S); English/language arts (M Ed); history education (M Ed, Ed S); mathematics education (M Ed); secondary education (Ed S); social studies (Ed S). Part-time programs available. *Students:* 16 full-time (12 women), 13 part-time (9 women); includes 26 minority (all Black or African American, non-Hispanic/Latino). Average age 36. 48

applicants, 52% accepted, 5 enrolled. In 2011, 3 master's awarded. *Degree requirements:* For master's, comprehensive exam; for Ed S, comprehensive exam, thesis. *Entrance requirements:* For master's, GRE General Test, MAT, graduate writing competency test; for Ed S, graduate writing competency test, GRE, MAT. Additional exam requirements/recommendations for international students: Required—TOEFL (minimum score 500 paper-based; 173 computer-based). *Application deadline:* For fall admission, 7/15 for domestic students; for spring admission, 12/15 for domestic students. Applications are processed on a rolling basis. Application fee: $10. *Financial support:* In 2011–12, research assistantships (averaging $9,450 per year) were awarded. *Unit head:* Dr. Willa Bing Harris, Acting Chairperson, 334-229-4394, Fax: 334-229-4904, E-mail: wbharris@alasu.edu. *Application contact:* Dr. Doris Screws, Dean of Graduate Studies, 334-229-4274, Fax: 334-229-4928, E-mail: dscrews@alasu.edu. Web site: http://www.alasu.edu/academics/colleges—departments/college-of-education/curriculum—instruction/degree-programs/secondary-education/index.aspx.

Albany State University, College of Sciences and Health Professions, Albany, GA 31705-2717. Offers criminal justice (MS), including corrections, forensic science, law enforcement, public administration; mathematics education (M Ed); nursing (MSN), including RN to MSN family nurse practitioner, RN to MSN nurse educator; science education (M Ed). *Accreditation:* NLN. Part-time and evening/weekend programs available. Postbaccalaureate distance learning degree programs offered. *Faculty:* 16 full-time (7 women), 7 part-time/adjunct (3 women). *Students:* 34 full-time (26 women), 103 part-time (84 women); includes 94 minority (92 Black or African American, non-Hispanic/Latino; 2 Asian, non-Hispanic/Latino), 2 international. Average age 36. 101 applicants, 48% accepted, 33 enrolled. In 2011, 16 master's awarded. *Degree requirements:* For master's, comprehensive exam, thesis. *Entrance requirements:* For master's, GRE or MAT, official transcript, letters of recommendations, pre-medical/certificate of immunizations. *Application deadline:* For fall admission, 6/15 for domestic students, 5/1 for international students; for spring admission, 11/1 for domestic students, 10/1 for international students. Applications are processed on a rolling basis. Application fee: $20. Electronic applications accepted. *Expenses:* Tuition, state resident: full-time $3204; part-time $178 per credit hour. Tuition, nonresident: full-time $12,816; part-time $712 per credit hour. *Required fees:* $379 per semester. *Financial support:* Scholarships/grants and traineeships available. Financial award application deadline: 4/15; financial award applicants required to submit CSS PROFILE or FAFSA. *Unit head:* Dr. Joyce Johnson, Dean, 229-430-4792, Fax: 229-430-3937, E-mail: joyce.johnson@asurams.edu. *Application contact:* Jeffrey Pierce, II, Graduate Admissions Counselor, 229-430-4646, Fax: 229-430-4105, E-mail: jeffrey.pierce@asurams.edu. Web site: http://asu-sacs.asurams.edu/ASUCatalog/Graduate/index.html.

Alverno College, School of Education, Milwaukee, WI 53234-3922. Offers adaptive education (MA); administrative leadership (MA); adult education and organizational development (MA); adult educational and instructional design (MA); adult educational and instructional technology (MA); global connections in the humanities (MA); instructional leadership (MA); instructional technology for K-12 settings (MA); professional development (MA); reading education (MA); reading education with adaptive education (MA); science education (MA); teaching in alternative schools (MA). *Accreditation:* NCATE. Part-time and evening/weekend programs available. *Faculty:* 22 full-time (18 women), 13 part-time/adjunct (all women). *Students:* 63 full-time (58 women), 91 part-time (81 women); includes 36 minority (29 Black or African American, non-Hispanic/Latino; 1 Asian, non-Hispanic/Latino; 4 Hispanic/Latino; 1 Native Hawaiian or other Pacific Islander, non-Hispanic/Latino; 1 Two or more races, non-Hispanic/Latino), 2 international. Average age 38. 151 applicants, 60% accepted, 62 enrolled. In 2011, 52 master's awarded. *Degree requirements:* For master's, presentation/defense of proposal, conference presentation of inquiry projects. *Entrance requirements:* For master's, bachelor's degree in related field, communication samples from work setting, 3 letters of recommendation. Additional exam requirements/recommendations for international students: Required—TOEFL. *Application deadline:* For fall admission, 7/15 priority date for domestic students, 7/15 for international students; for spring admission, 12/15 priority date for domestic students, 12/15 for international students. Applications are processed on a rolling basis. Application fee: $0. Electronic applications accepted. Application fee is waived when completed online. Tuition and fees vary according to program. *Financial support:* In 2011–12, 1 student received support. Federal Work-Study available. Support available to part-time students. Financial award application deadline: 4/15; financial award applicants required to submit FAFSA. *Faculty research:* Student self-assessment, self-reflection, integration of curriculum, identifying needs of students in strategic situations and designing appropriate classroom strategies. *Unit head:* Dr. Desiree Pointer-Mace, Associate Dean, Graduate Program, 414-382-6345, Fax: 414-382-6332, E-mail: desiree.pointer-mace@alverno.edu. *Application contact:* Mary Claire Jones, Graduate Recruiter, 414-382-6106, Fax: 414-382-6354, E-mail: maryclaire.jones@alverno.edu.

American University of Puerto Rico, Program in Education, Bayamón, PR 00960-2037. Offers art education (M Ed); elementary education 4-6 (M Ed); elementary education K-3 (M Ed); general science education (M Ed); physical education (M Ed); special education (M Ed). *Entrance requirements:* For master's, EXADEP, GRE, or MAT, 2 letters of recommendation, minimum GPA of 2.5. *Application deadline:* For fall admission, 8/1 for domestic students; for winter admission, 10/18 for domestic students; for spring admission, 3/15 for domestic students. Applications are processed on a rolling basis. Application fee: $50. *Expenses: Tuition:* Part-time $190 per credit. *Required fees:* $48.33 per credit. Tuition and fees vary according to course load and program. *Application contact:* Information Contact, 787-620-2040, E-mail: oficnaadmisiones@aupr.edu.

Andrews University, School of Graduate Studies, College of Arts and Sciences, Department of Biology, Berrien Springs, MI 49104. Offers MAT, MS. *Faculty:* 7 full-time (0 women). *Students:* 3 full-time (1 woman), 4 part-time (all women), 1 international. Average age 26. 8 applicants, 25% accepted, 1 enrolled. In 2011, 1 master's awarded. *Degree requirements:* For master's, comprehensive exam, thesis. *Entrance requirements:* For master's, GRE Subject Test. Additional exam requirements/recommendations for international students: Required—TOEFL (minimum score 550 paper-based). *Application deadline:* Applications are processed on a rolling basis. Application fee: $40. *Financial support:* Fellowships, research assistantships, teaching assistantships, career-related internships or fieldwork, Federal Work-Study, and institutionally sponsored loans available. Financial award application deadline: 3/15. *Unit head:* Dr. David A. Steen, Chairman, 269-471-3243. *Application contact:* Carolyn Hurst, Supervisor of Graduate Admission, 800-253-2874, Fax: 269-471-6321, E-mail: graduate@andrews.edu.

Andrews University, School of Graduate Studies, School of Education, Department of Teaching, Learning, and Curriculum, Berrien Springs, MI 49104. Offers curriculum and instruction (MA, Ed D, PhD, Ed S); elementary education (MAT); secondary education (MAT), including biology, education, English, English as a second language, French, history, physics; teacher education (MAT). *Students:* 15 full-time (10 women), 27 part-time (22 women); includes 18 minority (12 Black or African American, non-Hispanic/Latino; 1 Asian, non-Hispanic/Latino; 3 Hispanic/Latino; 1 Native Hawaiian or other Pacific Islander, non-Hispanic/Latino; 1 Two or more races, non-Hispanic/Latino), 10 international. Average age 42. 48 applicants, 48% accepted, 10 enrolled. In 2011, 5 master's, 2 doctorates, 2 other advanced degrees awarded. *Entrance requirements:* For master's, GRE Subject Test. Additional exam requirements/recommendations for international students: Required—TOEFL (minimum score 550 paper-based). *Application deadline:* For fall admission, 8/15 for domestic students. Applications are processed on a rolling basis. Application fee: $40. *Unit head:* Dr. Lee C. Davidson, Chair, 269-471-6364. *Application contact:* Carolyn Hurst, Supervisor of Graduate Admission, 800-253-2874, Fax: 269-471-6321, E-mail: graduate@andrews.edu.

Antioch University New England, Graduate School, Department of Environmental Studies, Science Teacher Certification Program, Keene, NH 03431-3552. Offers MS. *Degree requirements:* For master's, practicum, seminar, student teaching.

Appalachian State University, Cratis D. Williams Graduate School, Department of Curriculum and Instruction, Boone, NC 28608. Offers curriculum specialist (MA); educational media (MA); elementary education (MA); middle grades education (MA), including language arts, mathematics, science, social studies. *Accreditation:* NCATE. Part-time and evening/weekend programs available. Postbaccalaureate distance learning degree programs offered (no on-campus study). *Faculty:* 33 full-time (23 women), 5 part-time/adjunct (2 women). *Students:* 23 full-time (18 women), 110 part-time (90 women); includes 7 minority (4 Black or African American, non-Hispanic/Latino; 1 Asian, non-Hispanic/Latino; 2 Hispanic/Latino). 79 applicants, 94% accepted, 64 enrolled. In 2011, 87 master's awarded. *Degree requirements:* For master's, comprehensive exam, thesis or alternative. *Entrance requirements:* For master's, GRE General Test or MAT, 3 letters of recommendation. Additional exam requirements/recommendations for international students: Required—TOEFL (minimum score 570 paper-based; 230 computer-based; 79 iBT), IELTS (minimum score 6.5). *Application deadline:* For fall admission, 3/14 for domestic students, 2/1 for international students; for spring admission, 11/1 for domestic students, 7/1 for international students. Applications are processed on a rolling basis. Application fee: $55. Electronic applications accepted. *Expenses:* Tuition, state resident: full-time $4040; part-time $180 per semester hour. Tuition, nonresident: full-time $15,900; part-time $760 per semester hour. *Required fees:* $2500; $20 per semester hour. Tuition and fees vary according to campus/location. *Financial support:* In 2011–12, 6 teaching assistantships (averaging $8,000 per year) were awarded; fellowships, research assistantships, career-related internships or fieldwork, Federal Work-Study, scholarships/grants, and unspecified assistantships also available. Financial award application deadline: 4/1; financial award applicants required to submit FAFSA. *Faculty research:* Media literacy, elementary teaching, curriculum development, online learning environments. *Total annual research expenditures:* $480,000. *Unit head:* Dr. Michael Jacobson, Chairperson, 828-262-2224. *Application contact:* Sandy Krause, Director of Admissions and Recruiting, 828-262-2130, Fax: 828-262-2709, E-mail: krausesl@appstate.edu. Web site: http://www.ced.appstate.edu/departments/ci.

Arcadia University, Graduate Studies, Department of Education, Glenside, PA 19038-3295. Offers art education (M Ed); computer education (CAS); curriculum (CAS); curriculum studies (M Ed); early childhood education (M Ed, CAS), including individualized (M Ed), master teacher (M Ed), research in child development (M Ed); educational leadership (M Ed, Ed D, CAS); elementary education (M Ed, CAS); English education (MA Ed); environmental education (MA Ed, CAS); history education (MA Ed); instructional technology (M Ed); language arts (M Ed, CAS); library science (M Ed); mathematics education (M Ed, MA Ed, CAS); music education (MA Ed); psychology (MA Ed); reading (M Ed, CAS); science education (M Ed, CAS); secondary education (M Ed, CAS); special education (M Ed, Ed D, CAS); theater arts (MA Ed); written communication (MA Ed). *Accreditation:* NASAD. Part-time and evening/weekend programs available. Postbaccalaureate distance learning degree programs offered (minimal on-campus study). *Faculty:* 12 full-time (8 women), 38 part-time/adjunct (26 women). *Students:* 66 full-time (48 women), 590 part-time (477 women); includes 65 minority (53 Black or African American, non-Hispanic/Latino; 6 Asian, non-Hispanic/Latino; 3 Hispanic/Latino; 3 Two or more races, non-Hispanic/Latino), 4 international. Average age 36. In 2011, 229 master's, 5 doctorates awarded. *Application deadline:* Applications are processed on a rolling basis. Application fee: $50. Electronic applications accepted. *Expenses:* Contact institution. *Financial support:* Career-related internships or fieldwork, tuition waivers (partial), and unspecified assistantships available. *Unit head:* Dr. Steven P. Gulkus, Associate Professor, 215-572-2120, E-mail: gulkus@arcadia.edu. *Application contact:* 215-572-2925, Fax: 215-572-2126, E-mail: grad@arcadia.edu.

Arkansas State University, Graduate School, College of Sciences and Mathematics, Department of Biological Sciences, Jonesboro, State University, AR 72467. Offers biological sciences (MA); biology (MS); biology education (MSE, SCCT); biotechnology (PSM). Part-time programs available. *Faculty:* 22 full-time (7 women). *Students:* 13 full-time (8 women), 22 part-time (14 women); includes 2 minority (1 Black or African American, non-Hispanic/Latino; 1 American Indian or Alaska Native, non-Hispanic/Latino), 9 international. Average age 27. 31 applicants, 71% accepted, 13 enrolled. In 2011, 14 master's awarded. *Degree requirements:* For master's, comprehensive exam, thesis (for some programs); for SCCT, comprehensive exam. *Entrance requirements:* For master's, GRE General Test, appropriate bachelor's degree, letters of reference, interview, official transcripts, immunization records, statement of educational objectives and career goals, teaching certificate (MSE); for SCCT, GRE General Test or MAT, interview, master's degree, letters of reference, official transcript, personal statement, immunization records. Additional exam requirements/recommendations for international students: Required—TOEFL (minimum score 550 paper-based; 213 computer-based; 79 iBT), IELTS (minimum score 6), Pearson Test of English Academic (minimum score 56). *Application deadline:* For fall admission, 7/1 for domestic and international students; for spring admission, 11/15 for domestic students, 11/14 for international students. Applications are processed on a rolling basis. Application fee: $30 ($40 for international students). Electronic applications accepted. *Expenses:* Tuition, state resident: full-time $4044; part-time $225 per credit hour. Tuition, nonresident: full-time $8087; part-time $449 per credit hour. *Required fees:* $936; $52 per credit hour. $25 per term. One-time fee: $30. Tuition and fees vary according to course load and program. *Financial support:* In 2011–12, 17 students received support. Research assistantships, career-related internships or fieldwork, scholarships/grants, and unspecified assistantships available. Financial award application deadline: 7/1; financial award applicants required to submit FAFSA. *Unit head:* Dr. Thomas Risch, Chair, 870-972-3082, Fax: 870-972-2638, E-mail: trisch@astate.edu. *Application contact:* Dr. Andrew Sustich, Dean of the Graduate School, 870-972-3029, Fax: 870-972-3857, E-mail: sustich@astate.edu. Web site: http://www.astate.edu/a/scimath/biology/.

Arkansas State University, Graduate School, College of Sciences and Mathematics, Department of Chemistry and Physics, Jonesboro, State University, AR 72467. Offers chemistry (MS); chemistry education (MSE, SCCT). Part-time programs available. *Faculty:* 12 full-time (1 woman). *Students:* 2 full-time (1 woman), 12 part-time (5 women); includes 2 minority (both Black or African American, non-Hispanic/Latino), 6 international. Average age 27. 13 applicants, 85% accepted, 3 enrolled. In 2011, 10 master's awarded. *Degree requirements:* For master's, comprehensive exam, thesis or alternative; for SCCT, comprehensive exam. *Entrance requirements:* For master's, GRE General Test or MAT, appropriate bachelor's degree, official transcript, immunization records, valid teaching certificate (for MSE); for SCCT, GRE General Test or MAT, interview, master's degree, official transcript, immunization records. Additional exam requirements/recommendations for international students: Required—TOEFL (minimum score 550 paper-based; 213 computer-based; 79 iBT), IELTS (minimum score 6), Pearson Test of English Academic (minimum score 56). *Application deadline:* For fall admission, 7/1 for domestic and international students; for spring admission, 11/15 for domestic students, 11/14 for international students. Applications are processed on a rolling basis. Application fee: $30 ($40 for international students). Electronic applications accepted. *Expenses:* Tuition, state resident: full-time $4044; part-time $225 per credit hour. Tuition, nonresident: full-time $8087; part-time $449 per credit hour. *Required fees:* $936; $52 per credit hour. $25 per term. One-time fee: $30. Tuition and fees vary according to course load and program. *Financial support:* In 2011–12, 6 students received support. Teaching assistantships, career-related internships or fieldwork, scholarships/grants, and unspecified assistantships available. Financial award application deadline: 7/1; financial award applicants required to submit FAFSA. *Unit head:* Dr. William Burns, Interim Chair, 870-972-3086, Fax: 870-972-3089, E-mail: wburns@astate.edu. *Application contact:* Dr. Andrew Sustich, Dean of the Graduate School, 870-972-3029, Fax: 870-972-3857, E-mail: sustich@astate.edu. Web site: http://www.astate.edu/a/scimath/chemistryphysics/.

Armstrong Atlantic State University, School of Graduate Studies, Program in Education, Savannah, GA 31419-1997. Offers adult education (M Ed); curriculum and instruction (M Ed); early childhood education (M Ed); education (M Ed); elementary education (M Ed); middle grades education (M Ed); secondary education (M Ed), including business education, English education, mathematics education, science education, social science education; special education (M Ed), including behavioral disorders, learning disabilities, speech-language pathology. *Accreditation:* NCATE. Part-time and evening/weekend programs available. Postbaccalaureate distance learning degree programs offered (minimal on-campus study). *Faculty:* 33 full-time (23 women), 3 part-time/adjunct (2 women). *Students:* 97 full-time (91 women), 262 part-time (227 women); includes 83 minority (70 Black or African American, non-Hispanic/Latino; 3 Asian, non-Hispanic/Latino; 8 Hispanic/Latino; 2 Two or more races, non-Hispanic/Latino), 5 international. Average age 34. 169 applicants, 69% accepted, 102 enrolled. In 2011, 227 master's awarded. *Degree requirements:* For master's, comprehensive exam, portfolio. *Entrance requirements:* For master's, GRE General Test or MAT, minimum GPA of 2.5, letters of recommendation. Additional exam requirements/recommendations for international students: Required—TOEFL (minimum score 523 paper-based; 193 computer-based). *Application deadline:* For fall admission, 7/1 priority date for domestic students, 5/1 for international students; for spring admission, 11/15 priority date for domestic students, 9/15 for international students. Applications are processed on a rolling basis. Application fee: $30. Electronic applications accepted. *Expenses:* Tuition, state resident: full-time $3402. Tuition, nonresident: full-time $12,636. *Financial support:* In 2011–12, research assistantships with full tuition reimbursements (averaging $5,000 per year) were awarded; career-related internships or fieldwork, Federal Work-Study, scholarships/grants, and unspecified assistantships also available. Support available to part-time students. Financial award applicants required to submit FAFSA. *Unit head:* Dr. Patricia Wachholz, Dean, College of Education, 912-344-2797, E-mail: patricia.wachholz@armstrong.edu. *Application contact:* Jill Bell, Director, Graduate Enrollment Services, 912-344-2798, Fax: 912-344-3488, E-mail: graduate@armstrong.edu. Web site: http://www.armstrong.edu/Education/coe_deans_office/coe_education_welcome.

Asbury University, School of Graduate and Professional Studies, Wilmore, KY 40390-1198. Offers biology: alternative certificate (MA Ed); chemistry: alternative certificate (MA Ed); English (MA Ed); English as a second language (MA Ed); ESL (MA Ed); French (MA Ed); Latin: alternative certificate (MA Ed); mathematics: alternative certificate (MA Ed); reading/writing endorsement (MA Ed); social studies (MA Ed); social work (MSW), including child and family services; Spanish (MA Ed); special education (MA Ed); special education: alternative certificate (MA Ed); teacher as leader endorsement (MA Ed). *Accreditation:* NCATE. Part-time programs available. *Degree requirements:* For master's, action research project, portfolio. *Entrance requirements:* For master's, PRAXIS/NTE, minimum GPA of 2.75, letters of recommendation. Additional exam requirements/recommendations for international students: Required—TOEFL (minimum score 550 paper-based). Electronic applications accepted.

Auburn University, Graduate School, College of Education, Department of Curriculum and Teaching, Auburn University, AL 36849. Offers business education (M Ed, MS, PhD); early childhood education (M Ed, MS, PhD, Ed S); elementary education (M Ed, MS, PhD, Ed S); foreign languages (M Ed, MS); music education (M Ed, MS, PhD, Ed S); postsecondary education (PhD); reading education (PhD, Ed S); secondary education (M Ed, MS, PhD, Ed S), including English language arts, mathematics, science, social studies. *Accreditation:* NASM (one or more programs are accredited); NCATE. Part-time programs available. *Faculty:* 22 full-time (17 women), 3 part-time/adjunct (all women). *Students:* 80 full-time (58 women), 181 part-time (126 women); includes 42 minority (28 Black or African American, non-Hispanic/Latino; 7 Asian, non-Hispanic/Latino; 7 Hispanic/Latino). Average age 34. 184 applicants, 53% accepted, 60 enrolled. In 2011, 77 master's, 10 doctorates, 35 other advanced degrees awarded. *Degree requirements:* For master's, thesis (for some programs); for doctorate, thesis/dissertation; for Ed S, field project. *Entrance requirements:* For master's, doctorate, and Ed S, GRE General Test. *Application deadline:* For fall admission, 7/7 for domestic students; for spring admission, 11/24 for domestic students. Applications are processed on a rolling basis. Application fee: $50 ($60 for international students). Electronic applications accepted. *Expenses:* Tuition, state resident: full-time $7290; part-time $405 per credit hour. Tuition, nonresident: full-time $21,870; part-time $1215 per credit hour. *International tuition:* $22,000 full-time. *Required fees:* $1402. *Financial support:* Fellowships, teaching assistantships, career-related internships or fieldwork, and Federal Work-Study available. Support available to part-time students. Financial award application deadline: 3/15; financial award applicants required to submit FAFSA. *Faculty research:* Emerging literacy, reading attitudes, music for at-risk youth, portfolio assessment. *Unit head:* Dr. Kimberly Walls, Head, 334-844-4434. *Application contact:* Dr. George Flowers, Dean of the Graduate School, 334-844-2125. Web site: http://education.auburn.edu/academic_departments/curr/.

Aurora University, College of Arts and Sciences, Aurora, IL 60506-4892. Offers elementary math and science (MATL); life science (MATL); mathematics (MATL, MS). Part-time and evening/weekend programs available. *Entrance requirements:* Additional exam requirements/recommendations for international students: Required—TOEFL (minimum score 550 paper-based; 213 computer-based). Electronic applications accepted. *Expenses:* Contact institution.

Ball State University, Graduate School, College of Sciences and Humanities, Department of Biology, Muncie, IN 47306-1099. Offers biology (MA, MAE, MS); biology education (Ed D). *Faculty:* 22 full-time (8 women). *Students:* 26 full-time (8 women), 26 part-time (14 women); includes 3 minority (2 Asian, non-Hispanic/Latino; 1 Two or more races, non-Hispanic/Latino), 3 international. Average age 24. 47 applicants, 68% accepted, 21 enrolled. In 2011, 17 master's awarded. *Degree requirements:* For doctorate, thesis/dissertation. *Entrance requirements:* For master's, GRE General Test; for doctorate, GRE General Test, minimum graduate GPA of 3.2. Application fee: $50. Tuition and fees vary according to program and reciprocity agreements. *Financial support:* In 2011–12, 36 students received support, including 35 teaching assistantships with full and partial tuition reimbursements available (averaging $7,672 per year); research assistantships with full tuition reimbursements available and career-related internships or fieldwork also available. Financial award application deadline: 3/1. *Faculty research:* Aquatics and fisheries, tumors, water and air pollution, developmental biology and genetics. *Unit head:* Dr. Kemuel Badger, Chairman, 765-285-8820, Fax: 765-285-8804. *Application contact:* Dr. Robert Morris, Associate Provost for Research and Dean of the Graduate School, 765-285-1300, E-mail: rmorris@bsu.edu. Web site: http://cms.bsu.edu/Academics/CollegesandDepartments/Biology.aspx.

Belmont University, College of Arts and Sciences, Department of Education, Nashville, TN 37212-3757. Offers education (M Ed); elementary education (MAT), including early childhood education, elementary education, language arts education; English (MAT); history (MAT); mathematics (MAT); middle grade education (MAT); science (MAT); secondary education (MAT); special education (MAT); sports administration (MSA). *Accreditation:* NCATE. Part-time and evening/weekend programs available. *Faculty:* 11 full-time (8 women), 23 part-time/adjunct (12 women). *Students:* 83 full-time (77 women), 205 part-time (162 women); includes 50 minority (36 Black or African American, non-Hispanic/Latino; 1 American Indian or Alaska Native, non-Hispanic/Latino; 1 Asian, non-Hispanic/Latino; 7 Hispanic/Latino; 5 Two or more races, non-Hispanic/Latino), 2 international. Average age 30. 83 applicants, 67% accepted, 35 enrolled. In 2011, 169 master's awarded. *Degree requirements:* For master's, thesis (for some programs). *Entrance requirements:* For master's, MAT or GRE and/or GMAT, minimum GPA of 2.75. Additional exam requirements/recommendations for international students: Required—TOEFL. *Application deadline:* For fall admission, 8/1 priority date for domestic students, 6/1 for international students; for spring admission, 12/1 priority date for domestic students, 10/1 for international students. Applications are processed on a rolling basis. Application fee: $50. *Expenses:* Contact institution. *Financial support:* In 2011–12, 30 students received support. Fellowships with partial tuition reimbursements available, teaching assistantships with partial tuition reimbursements available, institutionally sponsored loans, tuition waivers (partial), and unspecified assistantships available. Financial award application deadline: 4/15; financial award applicants required to submit FAFSA. *Faculty research:* Improving secondary literacy, Montessori, classroom management strategies, teacher residency programs, online professional development, mentoring, leadership, faculty development. *Total annual research expenditures:* $2,500. *Unit head:* Dr. Cynthia R. Watkins, Associate Dean, 615-460-6053, Fax: 615-460-5556, E-mail: cynthia.watkins@belmont.edu. *Application contact:* Andrea McClain, Admission/Licensure Officer, 615-460-5483, Fax: 615-460-5556, E-mail: andrea.mcclain@belmont.edu.

Benedictine University, Graduate Programs, Program in Science Content and Process, Lisle, IL 60532-0900. Offers MSSCP. In 2011, 6 master's awarded. *Application deadline:* For fall admission, 9/1 for domestic students; for winter admission, 12/1 for domestic students; for spring admission, 2/15 for domestic students. Application fee: $40. *Unit head:* Dr. Allison Wilson, Director, 630-829-6520, E-mail: awilson@ben.edu. *Application contact:* Kari Gibbons, Associate Vice President, Enrollment Center, 630-829-6200, Fax: 630-829-6584, E-mail: kgibbons@ben.edu.

Biola University, School of Arts and Sciences, La Mirada, CA 90639-0001. Offers Christian apologetics (MA); science and religion (MA). Part-time and evening/weekend programs available. Postbaccalaureate distance learning degree programs offered (minimal on-campus study). *Faculty:* 16. *Students:* 24 full-time (3 women), 204 part-time (46 women); includes 30 minority (9 Black or African American, non-Hispanic/Latino; 19 Asian, non-Hispanic/Latino; 2 Two or more races, non-Hispanic/Latino), 9 international. In 2011, 36 master's awarded. *Entrance requirements:* For master's, minimum GPA of 3.0, bachelor's degree from accredited college or university (in science-related field for science and religion program). Additional exam requirements/recommendations for international students: Required—TOEFL (minimum score 550 paper-based; 213 computer-based). *Application deadline:* For fall admission, 7/1 for domestic students, 6/1 for international students; for spring admission, 12/1 for domestic students. Applications are processed on a rolling basis. Application fee: $55. Electronic applications accepted. *Financial support:* Institutionally sponsored loans, scholarships/grants, and unspecified assistantships available. Financial award applicants required to submit FAFSA. *Faculty research:* Apologetics, science and religion, intelligent design. *Application contact:* Graduate Admissions Office, 562-903-4752, E-mail: graduate.admissions@biola.edu. Web site: http://www.biola.edu/academics/sas/.

Bloomsburg University of Pennsylvania, School of Graduate Studies, College of Science and Technology, Department of Biological and Allied Health Sciences, Program in Biology Education, Bloomsburg, PA 17815-1301. Offers M Ed. *Accreditation:* NCATE. *Degree requirements:* For master's, thesis or alternative. *Entrance requirements:* For master's, teaching certificate, minimum QPA of 3.0. Additional exam requirements/recommendations for international students: Required—TOEFL (minimum score 550 paper-based; 213 computer-based; 79 iBT). Electronic applications accepted.

Boise State University, Graduate College, College of Arts and Sciences, Department of Geosciences, Boise, ID 83725-0399. Offers earth science (MS); geology (MS, PhD); geophysics (MS, PhD). Part-time programs available. *Degree requirements:* For master's, thesis. *Entrance requirements:* For master's, GRE General Test, BS in related field, minimum GPA of 3.0; for doctorate, GRE General Test. Electronic applications accepted. *Faculty research:* Seismology, geothermal aquifers, sedimentation, tectonics, seismo-acoustic propagation.

Boston College, Graduate School of Arts and Sciences, Department of Chemistry, Chestnut Hill, MA 02467-3800. Offers biochemistry (PhD); inorganic chemistry (PhD); organic chemistry (PhD); physical chemistry (PhD); science education (MST). *Degree requirements:* For doctorate, thesis/dissertation, qualifying exam. *Entrance requirements:* For doctorate, GRE General Test, GRE Subject Test. Additional exam requirements/recommendations for international students: Required—TOEFL (minimum score 600 paper-based; 250 computer-based; 100 iBT). Electronic applications accepted.

Bowling Green State University, Graduate College, College of Arts and Sciences, Department of Physics and Astronomy, Bowling Green, OH 43403. Offers geophysics (MS); physics (MAT, MS). *Degree requirements:* For master's, thesis or alternative. *Entrance requirements:* For master's, GRE General Test. Additional exam requirements/recommendations for international students: Required—TOEFL. Electronic applications accepted. *Faculty research:* Computational physics, solid-state physics, materials science, theoretical physics.

Bridgewater State University, School of Graduate Studies, School of Arts and Sciences, Department of Biological Sciences, Bridgewater, MA 02325-0001. Offers MAT. Part-time and evening/weekend programs available. *Entrance requirements:* For master's, GRE General Test.

Bridgewater State University, School of Graduate Studies, School of Arts and Sciences, Department of Physics, Bridgewater, MA 02325-0001. Offers MAT. *Accreditation:* NCATE. Part-time and evening/weekend programs available. *Entrance requirements:* For master's, GRE General Test.

Bridgewater State University, School of Graduate Studies, School of Arts and Sciences, Program in Physical Sciences, Bridgewater, MA 02325-0001. Offers MAT.

Science Education

Accreditation: NCATE. Part-time and evening/weekend programs available. *Entrance requirements:* For master's, GRE General Test.

Brigham Young University, Graduate Studies, College of Life Sciences, Department of Biology, Provo, UT 84602. Offers biological science education (MS); biology (MS, PhD). *Faculty:* 19 full-time (2 women). *Students:* 35 full-time (12 women); includes 7 minority (2 Asian, non-Hispanic/Latino; 5 Hispanic/Latino). Average age 31. 20 applicants, 75% accepted, 11 enrolled. In 2011, 2 master's, 3 doctorates awarded. *Degree requirements:* For master's, comprehensive exam, thesis, prospectus, defense of research, defense of thesis; for doctorate, comprehensive exam, thesis/dissertation, prospectus, defense of research, defense of dissertation. *Entrance requirements:* For master's and doctorate, GRE General Test, GRE Subject Test (biology), minimum GPA of 3.0 for last 60 credit hours of course work. Additional exam requirements/recommendations for international students: Required—TOEFL (minimum score 580 paper-based; 85 iBT). *Application deadline:* For fall admission, 1/15 for domestic and international students. Application fee: $50. Electronic applications accepted. *Expenses: Tuition:* Full-time $5760; part-time $320 per credit. Tuition and fees vary according to student's religious affiliation. *Financial support:* In 2011–12, 5 fellowships with full and partial tuition reimbursements (averaging $15,000 per year) were awarded; research assistantships with full and partial tuition reimbursements, teaching assistantships with full and partial tuition reimbursements, career-related internships or fieldwork, institutionally sponsored loans, scholarships/grants, health care benefits, tuition waivers (full and partial), and unspecified assistantships also available. Financial award application deadline: 2/1; financial award applicants required to submit FAFSA. *Faculty research:* Systematics, bioinformatics, ecology, evolution. *Total annual research expenditures:* $1.1 million. *Unit head:* Dr. Keith A. Crandall, Chair, 801-422-3495, Fax: 801-422-0090, E-mail: keith_crandall@byu.edu. *Application contact:* Sarah Willardson, Graduate Secretary, 801-422-7137, Fax: 801-422-0090, E-mail: biogradsec@byu.edu. Web site: http://biology.byu.edu/.

Brooklyn College of the City University of New York, Division of Graduate Studies, School of Education, Program in Adolescence Education and Special Subjects, Brooklyn, NY 11210-2889. Offers adolescence science education (MAT); art teacher (MA); biology teacher (MA); chemistry teacher (MA); earth science teacher (MAT); English teacher (MA); French teacher (MA); health and nutrition sciences: health teacher (MS Ed); mathematics teacher (MA); music education (CAS); music teacher (MA); physical education teacher (MS Ed); physics teacher (MA); social studies teacher (MA); Spanish teacher (MA). Part-time and evening/weekend programs available. *Degree requirements:* For master's, comprehensive exam (for some programs), thesis (for some programs). *Entrance requirements:* For master's, LAST, previous course work in education, resume, 2 letters of recommendation, essay. Additional exam requirements/recommendations for international students: Required—TOEFL (minimum score 500 paper-based; 173 computer-based; 61 iBT). Electronic applications accepted. *Faculty research:* Interdisciplinary education, semiotics, discourse analysis, autobiography, teacher identity.

Brooklyn College of the City University of New York, Division of Graduate Studies, School of Education, Program in Childhood Education, Brooklyn, NY 11210-2889. Offers bilingual education (MS Ed); liberal arts (MS Ed); mathematics (MS Ed); science/environmental education (MS Ed). Part-time and evening/weekend programs available. *Entrance requirements:* For master's, LAST, interview, previous course work in education, writing sample, resume, 2 letters of recommendation. Additional exam requirements/recommendations for international students: Required—TOEFL (minimum score 500 paper-based; 173 computer-based; 61 iBT). Electronic applications accepted. *Faculty research:* Emotional intelligence, multiculturalism, arts immersion, the Holocaust.

Brooklyn College of the City University of New York, Division of Graduate Studies, School of Education, Program in Middle Childhood Education (Science), Brooklyn, NY 11210-2889. Offers biology (MA); chemistry (MA); earth science (MA); general science (MA); physics (MA). Part-time and evening/weekend programs available. *Entrance requirements:* For master's, LAST, interview, previous course work in education and mathematics, resume, 2 letters of recommendation, essay. Additional exam requirements/recommendations for international students: Required—TOEFL (minimum score 500 paper-based; 173 computer-based; 61 iBT). Electronic applications accepted. *Faculty research:* Geometric thinking, mastery of basic facts, problem-solving strategies, history of mathematics.

Brown University, Graduate School, Department of Education, Program in Teaching, Providence, RI 02912. Offers elementary education (MAT); English (MAT); history/social studies (MAT); science (MAT). *Faculty:* 4 full-time (3 women), 6 part-time/adjunct (all women). *Students:* 36 full-time (30 women); includes 12 minority (3 Black or African American, non-Hispanic/Latino; 2 American Indian or Alaska Native, non-Hispanic/Latino; 4 Asian, non-Hispanic/Latino; 3 Hispanic/Latino). Average age 26. 129 applicants, 60% accepted, 37 enrolled. In 2011, 42 master's awarded. *Degree requirements:* For master's, student teaching, portfolio. *Entrance requirements:* For master's, GRE General Test, transcript, personal statement, 3 letters of recommendation, interview, writing sample (English applicants only). Additional exam requirements/recommendations for international students: Required—TOEFL (minimum score 577 paper-based; 90 computer-based). *Application deadline:* For winter admission, 1/15 for domestic and international students. Application fee: $75. Electronic applications accepted. *Financial support:* In 2011–12, 28 students received support. Federal Work-Study, institutionally sponsored loans, scholarships/grants, and tuition waivers (partial) available. Financial award application deadline: 2/1; financial award applicants required to submit FAFSA. *Faculty research:* Literacy, English language learners, diversity, special education, biodiversity. *Unit head:* Laura Snyder, Director of Graduate Study for the MAT Program, 401-863-2407. *Application contact:* Carin Algava, Assistant Director of Teacher Education, 401-863-3364, Fax: 401-863-1276, E-mail: carin_algava@brown.edu. Web site: http://www.brown.edu/Departments/Education/TE/.

Buffalo State College, State University of New York, The Graduate School, Faculty of Natural and Social Sciences, Department of Biology, Buffalo, NY 14222-1095. Offers biology (MA); secondary education (MS Ed), including biology. Evening/weekend programs available. *Degree requirements:* For master's, thesis (for some programs), project. *Entrance requirements:* For master's, minimum GPA of 2.75. Additional exam requirements/recommendations for international students: Required—TOEFL (minimum score 550 paper-based; 213 computer-based).

Buffalo State College, State University of New York, The Graduate School, Faculty of Natural and Social Sciences, Department of Chemistry, Buffalo, NY 14222-1095. Offers chemistry (MA); secondary education (MS Ed), including chemistry. Part-time and evening/weekend programs available. *Degree requirements:* For master's, thesis (for some programs), project. *Entrance requirements:* For master's, minimum GPA of 2.6, New York teaching certificate (MS Ed). Additional exam requirements/recommendations for international students: Required—TOEFL (minimum score 550 paper-based; 213 computer-based).

Buffalo State College, State University of New York, The Graduate School, Faculty of Natural and Social Sciences, Department of Earth Science and Science Education, Buffalo, NY 14222-1095. Offers secondary education (MS Ed), including geoscience, science. *Accreditation:* NCATE. Part-time and evening/weekend programs available. *Degree requirements:* For master's, thesis or alternative, project. *Entrance requirements:* For master's, 36 undergraduate hours in mathematics and science. Additional exam requirements/recommendations for international students: Required—TOEFL (minimum score 550 paper-based; 213 computer-based).

Buffalo State College, State University of New York, The Graduate School, Faculty of Natural and Social Sciences, Department of Physics, Buffalo, NY 14222-1095. Offers secondary education physics (MS Ed). *Degree requirements:* For master's, project. *Entrance requirements:* For master's, minimum GPA of 2.5, New York State teaching certification. Additional exam requirements/recommendations for international students: Required—TOEFL (minimum score 550 paper-based; 213 computer-based).

California State University, Dominguez Hills, College of Professional Studies, School of Education, Division of Graduate Education, Program in Curriculum and Instruction: Science Education, Carson, CA 90747-0001. Offers MA. Part-time and evening/weekend programs available. *Students:* 1 full-time (0 women), 1 (woman) part-time; both minorities (1 Asian, non-Hispanic/Latino; 1 Hispanic/Latino). Average age 39. 6 applicants, 67% accepted, 1 enrolled. *Degree requirements:* For master's, comprehensive exam. *Entrance requirements:* For master's, minimum GPA of 2.75. Additional exam requirements/recommendations for international students: Required—TOEFL. *Application deadline:* For fall admission, 6/1 for domestic students. Applications are processed on a rolling basis. Application fee: $55. *Unit head:* Dr. James L. Cooper, Professor, 310-243-3961, E-mail: jcooper@csudh.edu. *Application contact:* Admissions Office, 310-243-3530. Web site: http://www.csudh.edu/cps/soe/programsdegrees/graduate-programs-curriculum.shtml.

California State University, Fullerton, Graduate Studies, College of Natural Science and Mathematics, Program in Science Education, Fullerton, CA 92834-9480. Offers teaching science (MAT). Part-time programs available. *Students:* 5 part-time (4 women); includes 2 minority (1 Asian, non-Hispanic/Latino; 1 Hispanic/Latino). Average age 33. 3 applicants, 33% accepted, 1 enrolled. In 2011, 2 master's awarded. *Degree requirements:* For master's, project or thesis. *Entrance requirements:* For master's, diagnostic exam, minimum GPA of 2.5 in last 60 units of course work, teaching credential, bachelor's degree in science. Application fee: $55. *Financial support:* Teaching assistantships, career-related internships or fieldwork, Federal Work-Study, institutionally sponsored loans, and scholarships/grants available. Support available to part-time students. Financial award application deadline: 3/1; financial award applicants required to submit FAFSA. *Faculty research:* Earth and space science education. *Unit head:* Dr. Victoria Costa, Director, 657-278-2307. *Application contact:* Admissions/Applications, 657-278-2731.

California State University, Long Beach, Graduate Studies, College of Natural Sciences and Mathematics, Department of Science Education, Long Beach, CA 90840. Offers MS. *Faculty:* 6 full-time (2 women), 1 (woman) part-time/adjunct. *Students:* 31 part-time (22 women); includes 13 minority (2 Black or African American, non-Hispanic/Latino; 1 American Indian or Alaska Native, non-Hispanic/Latino; 3 Asian, non-Hispanic/Latino; 6 Hispanic/Latino; 1 Native Hawaiian or other Pacific Islander, non-Hispanic/Latino). Average age 38. 7 applicants, 86% accepted, 5 enrolled. In 2011, 1 master's awarded. *Unit head:* Laura Henriques, Chair, 562-985-4801, E-mail: lhenriqu@csulb.edu. *Application contact:* Dr. Henry Fung, Associate Dean for Curriculum and Instruction, 562-985-7898, Fax: 562-985-2315, E-mail: hcfung@csulb.edu. Web site: http://www.cnsm.csulb.edu/depts/scied/.

California State University, Northridge, Graduate Studies, College of Education, Department of Secondary Education, Northridge, CA 91330. Offers educational technology (MA); English education (MA); mathematics education (MA); secondary science education (MA); teaching and learning (MA). *Accreditation:* NCATE. Part-time programs available. *Degree requirements:* For master's, thesis optional. *Entrance requirements:* For master's, GRE General Test or minimum GPA of 3.0. Additional exam requirements/recommendations for international students: Required—TOEFL.

California State University, San Bernardino, Graduate Studies, College of Education, Program in Teaching of Science, San Bernardino, CA 92407-2397. Offers MA. *Accreditation:* NCATE. *Students:* 2 full-time (both women). Average age 51. *Entrance requirements:* For master's, minimum GPA of 3.0. Application fee: $55. *Expenses:* Tuition, state resident: full-time $7356. Tuition, nonresident: full-time $7356. *Required fees:* $1077. Tuition and fees vary according to program. *Unit head:* Dr. Herbert Brunkhorst, Coordinator, 909-537-5613, Fax: 909-537-7119, E-mail: hkbrunkh@csusb.edu. *Application contact:* Sandra Kamusikiri, Associate Vice-President/Dean of Graduate Studies, 909-537-5058, E-mail: skamusik@csusb.edu.

Cambridge College, School of Education, Cambridge, MA 02138-5304. Offers autism specialist (M Ed); autism/behavior analyst (M Ed); behavior analyst (Post-Master's Certificate); behavioral management (M Ed); early childhood teacher (M Ed); education specialist in curriculum and instruction (CAGS); educational leadership (Ed D); elementary teacher (M Ed); English as a second language (M Ed, Certificate); general science (M Ed); health education (Post-Master's Certificate); health/family and consumer sciences (M Ed); history (M Ed); individualized (M Ed); information technology literacy (M Ed); instructional technology (M Ed); interdisciplinary studies (M Ed); library teacher (M Ed); literacy education (M Ed); mathematics (M Ed); mathematics specialist (Certificate); middle school mathematics and science (M Ed); school administration (M Ed, CAGS); school guidance counselor (M Ed); school nurse education (M Ed); school social worker/school adjustment counselor (M Ed); special education administrator (CAGS); special education/moderate disabilities (M Ed); teaching skills and methodologies (M Ed). Part-time and evening/weekend programs available. Postbaccalaureate distance learning degree programs offered (minimal on-campus study). *Degree requirements:* For master's, thesis, internship/practicum (licensure program only); for doctorate, thesis/dissertation; for other advanced degree, thesis. *Entrance requirements:* For master's, interview, resume, documentation of licensure, 2 professional references; for doctorate, official transcripts, interview, resume, documentation of licensure (if any), written personal statement/essay, portfolio of scholarly and professional work, qualifying assessment, 2 professional references, health insurance, immunizations form; for other advanced degree, official transcripts, interview, resume, documentation of licensure (if any), written personal statement/essay, 2 professional references, health insurance, immunizations form. Additional exam requirements/recommendations for international students: Required—TOEFL (minimum score 550 paper-based; 213 computer-based; 79 iBT); Recommended—IELTS (minimum score 6). Electronic applications accepted. *Expenses:* Contact institution. *Faculty research:* Adult education, accelerated learning, mathematics education, brain compatible learning, special education and law.

Caribbean University, Graduate School, Bayamón, PR 00960-0493. Offers administration and supervision (MA Ed); criminal justice (MA); curriculum and instruction (MA Ed, PhD), including elementary education (MA Ed), English education (MA Ed), history education (MA Ed), mathematics education (MA Ed), primary education (MA Ed), science education (MA Ed), Spanish education (MA Ed); educational technology in instructional systems (MA Ed); gerontology (MSN); human resources (MBA); museology, archiving and art history (MA Ed); neonatal pediatrics (MSN); physical education (MA Ed); special education (MA Ed). *Entrance requirements:* For master's, interview, minimum GPA of 2.5.

Carthage College, Division of Teacher Education, Kenosha, WI 53140. Offers classroom guidance and counseling (M Ed); creative arts (M Ed); gifted and talented children (M Ed); language arts (M Ed); modern language (M Ed); natural sciences (M Ed); reading (M Ed, Certificate); social sciences (M Ed); teacher leadership (M Ed). Part-time and evening/weekend programs available. *Degree requirements:* For master's, thesis optional. *Entrance requirements:* For master's, MAT, minimum B average, letters of reference.

Central Connecticut State University, School of Graduate Studies, School of Arts and Sciences, Department of Biology, New Britain, CT 06050-4010. Offers biological sciences (MA, MS), including anesthesia (MS), ecology and environmental sciences (MA), general biology (MA), health sciences specialization (MS), professional education program (MS); biology (Certificate). Part-time and evening/weekend programs available. *Faculty:* 13 full-time (5 women), 6 part-time/adjunct (5 women). *Students:* 133 full-time (74 women), 40 part-time (27 women); includes 35 minority (9 Black or African American, non-Hispanic/Latino; 1 American Indian or Alaska Native, non-Hispanic/Latino; 11 Asian, non-Hispanic/Latino; 11 Hispanic/Latino; 3 Two or more races, non-Hispanic/Latino). Average age 31. 25 applicants, 60% accepted, 8 enrolled. In 2011, 40 master's, 4 other advanced degrees awarded. *Degree requirements:* For master's, comprehensive exam, thesis or alternative; for Certificate, qualifying exam. *Entrance requirements:* For master's, minimum undergraduate GPA of 2.7, essay. Additional exam requirements/recommendations for international students: Required—TOEFL (minimum score 550 paper-based; 213 computer-based). *Application deadline:* For fall admission, 6/1 for domestic students, 5/1 for international students; for spring admission, 11/1 for domestic and international students. Applications are processed on a rolling basis. Application fee: $50. Electronic applications accepted. *Expenses: Tuition, area resident:* Full-time $5137; part-time $482 per credit. Tuition, state resident: full-time $7707; part-time $494 per credit. Tuition, nonresident: full-time $14,311; part-time $494 per credit. *Required fees:* $3865. One-time fee: $62 part-time. *Financial support:* In 2011–12, 6 students received support, including 3 research assistantships; career-related internships or fieldwork, Federal Work-Study, scholarships/grants, and unspecified assistantships also available. Support available to part-time students. Financial award application deadline: 4/15; financial award applicants required to submit FAFSA. *Faculty research:* Environmental science, anesthesia, health sciences, zoology, animal behavior. *Unit head:* Dr. Jeremiah Jarrett, Chair, 860-832-2645, E-mail: jarrettj@ccsu.edu. *Application contact:* Patricia Gardner, Associate Director of Graduate Studies, 860-832-2350, Fax: 860-832-2352, E-mail: graduateadmissions@ccsu.edu. Web site: http://www.biology.ccsu.edu/.

Central Connecticut State University, School of Graduate Studies, School of Arts and Sciences, Department of Physics and Earth Science, New Britain, CT 06050-4010. Offers natural sciences (MS); science education (Certificate). Part-time and evening/weekend programs available. *Faculty:* 11 full-time (4 women), 17 part-time/adjunct (3 women). *Students:* 1 full-time (0 women), 9 part-time (6 women); includes 1 minority (Asian, non-Hispanic/Latino). Average age 38. 5 applicants, 80% accepted, 2 enrolled. In 2011, 7 master's awarded. *Degree requirements:* For master's, comprehensive exam, thesis or alternative; for Certificate, qualifying exam. *Entrance requirements:* For master's, minimum undergraduate GPA of 2.7. Additional exam requirements/recommendations for international students: Required—TOEFL (minimum score 550 paper-based; 213 computer-based). *Application deadline:* For fall admission, 6/1 for domestic students, 5/1 for international students; for spring admission, 11/1 for domestic and international students. Applications are processed on a rolling basis. Application fee: $50. Electronic applications accepted. *Expenses: Tuition, area resident:* Full-time $5137; part-time $482 per credit. Tuition, state resident: full-time $7707; part-time $494 per credit. Tuition, nonresident: full-time $14,311; part-time $494 per credit. *Required fees:* $3865. One-time fee: $62 part-time. *Financial support:* In 2011–12, 1 student received support. Career-related internships or fieldwork, Federal Work-Study, scholarships/grants, and unspecified assistantships available. Support available to part-time students. Financial award application deadline: 4/15; financial award applicants required to submit FAFSA. *Faculty research:* Elementary/secondary science education, particle and solid states, weather patterns, planetary studies. *Unit head:* Dr. Steven Newman, Chair, 860-832-2930, E-mail: newman@ccsu.edu. *Application contact:* Patricia Gardner, Associate Director of Graduate Studies, 860-832-2350, Fax: 860-832-2352, E-mail: graduateadmissions@ccsu.edu. Web site: http://www.physics.ccsu.edu/.

Central Michigan University, College of Graduate Studies, College of Science and Technology, Department of Chemistry, Mount Pleasant, MI 48859. Offers chemistry (MS); teaching chemistry (MA), including teaching college chemistry, teaching high school chemistry. Part-time programs available. *Degree requirements:* For master's, comprehensive exam, thesis or alternative. *Entrance requirements:* For master's, GRE. Electronic applications accepted. *Faculty research:* Analytical and organic-inorganic chemistry, biochemistry, catalysis, dendrimer and polymer studies, nanotechnology.

Chaminade University of Honolulu, Graduate Services, Program in Education, Honolulu, HI 96816-1578. Offers child development (M Ed); educational leadership (M Ed); elementary education with licensure (MAT); instructional leadership (M Ed); Montessori credential (M Ed); Montessori emphasis (M Ed); secondary education with licensure (MAT), including English, math, science, social studies; special education with licensure (MAT). Part-time and evening/weekend programs available. Postbaccalaureate distance learning degree programs offered (minimal on-campus study). *Faculty:* 2 full-time (both women), 32 part-time/adjunct (25 women). *Students:* 53 full-time (38 women), 88 part-time (67 women); includes 77 minority (6 Black or African American, non-Hispanic/Latino; 1 American Indian or Alaska Native, non-Hispanic/Latino; 44 Asian, non-Hispanic/Latino; 5 Hispanic/Latino; 17 Native Hawaiian or other Pacific Islander, non-Hispanic/Latino; 4 Two or more races, non-Hispanic/Latino), 1 international. Average age 35. 40 applicants, 88% accepted, 30 enrolled. In 2011, 105 master's awarded. *Degree requirements:* For master's, thesis or alternative. *Entrance requirements:* For master's, PRAXIS (for MAT only), minimum GPA of 2.75, 3 letters of recommendation. Additional exam requirements/recommendations for international students: Required—TOEFL (minimum score 550 paper-based). *Application deadline:* For fall admission, 9/1 priority date for domestic students, 9/1 for international students; for winter admission, 12/1 priority date for domestic students, 12/1 for international students; for spring admission, 3/1 priority date for domestic students, 3/1 for international students. Applications are processed on a rolling basis. Application fee: $50. Electronic applications accepted. *Expenses: Required fees:* $600 per credit hour. One-time fee: $93 part-time. *Financial support:* In 2011–12, 172 students received support. Career-related internships or fieldwork, Federal Work-Study, institutionally sponsored loans, scholarships/grants, and tuition waivers (partial) available. Support available to part-time students. Financial award application deadline: 3/1; financial award applicants required to submit FAFSA. *Faculty research:* Peace and curriculum education. *Unit head:* Dr. Joseph Peters, Dean, 808-440-4251, Fax: 808-739-4607, E-mail: joseph.peters@chaminade.edu. *Application contact:* 808-739-4663, Fax: 808-739-8329, E-mail: gradserv@chaminade.edu. Web site: http://www.chaminade.edu/education/grad.php.

Chatham University, Program in Education, Pittsburgh, PA 15232-2826. Offers early childhood education (MAT); elementary education (MAT); environmental education (K-12) (MAT); secondary art (MAT); secondary biology education (MAT); secondary chemistry education (MAT); secondary English education (MAT); secondary math education (MAT); secondary physics education (MAT); secondary social studies education (MAT); special education (MAT). *Students:* 52 full-time (42 women), 17 part-time (16 women); includes 2 minority (1 Black or African American, non-Hispanic/Latino; 1 Hispanic/Latino). Average age 29. 39 applicants, 82% accepted, 23 enrolled. In 2011, 37 master's awarded. *Degree requirements:* For master's, thesis, teaching experience. *Entrance requirements:* For master's, minimum GPA of 3.0, sample of written work, recommendation letters. Additional exam requirements/recommendations for international students: Required—TOEFL (minimum score 600 paper-based; 250 computer-based; 100 iBT), IELTS (minimum score 7), TWE. *Application deadline:* For fall admission, 4/1 priority date for domestic students, 4/1 for international students; for spring admission, 11/1 priority date for domestic students, 10/1 for international students. Applications are processed on a rolling basis. Application fee: $45. Electronic applications accepted. Application fee is waived when completed online. *Expenses: Tuition:* Full-time $13,896. Tuition and fees vary according to program. *Financial support:* Career-related internships or fieldwork available. Financial award applicants required to submit FAFSA. *Faculty research:* Gifted education, environmental education, technology in education, writing as learning, class size and achievement. *Unit head:* Dr. Elvira Sanatullova-Allison, Director of Education Programs, 412-365-2773, E-mail: esanatullovaallison@chatham.edu. *Application contact:* Dory Perry, Associate Director of Graduate Admission, 412-365-2758, Fax: 412-365-1609, E-mail: gradadmissions@chatham.edu. Web site: http://www.chatham.edu/mat.

Christopher Newport University, Graduate Studies, Department of Teacher Preparation, Newport News, VA 23606-2998. Offers art (PK-12) (MAT); biology (6-12) (MAT); chemistry (6-12) (MAT); computer science (6-12) (MAT); elementary (PK-6) (MAT); English (6-12) (MAT); English as second language (PK-12) (MAT); French (PK-12) (MAT); history and social science (6-12) (MAT); mathematics (6-12) (MAT); music (PK-12) (MAT), including choral, instrumental; physics (6-12) (MAT); Spanish (PK-12) (MAT). Part-time and evening/weekend programs available. *Degree requirements:* For master's, comprehensive exam, thesis or alternative. *Entrance requirements:* For master's, PRAXIS I, minimum GPA of 3.0. Additional exam requirements/recommendations for international students: Required—TOEFL (minimum score 580 paper-based; 237 computer-based; 92 iBT). Electronic applications accepted. *Faculty research:* Early literacy development, instructional innovations, professional teaching standards, multicultural issues, aesthetic education.

The Citadel, The Military College of South Carolina, Citadel Graduate College, School of Education, Program in Secondary Education, Charleston, SC 29409. Offers biology (MAT); English language arts (MAT); mathematics (MAT); mathematics education (MAE); physical education (MAT); social studies (MAT). *Accreditation:* NCATE. Part-time and evening/weekend programs available. *Faculty:* 12 full-time (8 women), 9 part-time/adjunct (4 women). *Students:* 21 full-time (11 women), 51 part-time (25 women); includes 10 minority (7 Black or African American, non-Hispanic/Latino; 2 Asian, non-Hispanic/Latino; 1 Hispanic/Latino). Average age 31. In 2011, 34 master's awarded. *Degree requirements:* For master's, comprehensive exam, internship. *Entrance requirements:* For master's, GRE (minimum score 900) or MAT (minimum score 396), minimum undergraduate GPA of 2.5. Additional exam requirements/recommendations for international students: Required—TOEFL (minimum score 550 paper-based; 213 computer-based). *Application deadline:* Applications are processed on a rolling basis. Application fee: $30. Electronic applications accepted. *Expenses: Tuition, area resident:* Part-time $501 per credit hour. Tuition, state resident: part-time $501 per credit hour. Tuition, nonresident: part-time $824 per credit hour. *Required fees:* $40 per term. One-time fee: $30. *Financial support:* Career-related internships or fieldwork, health care benefits, and unspecified assistantships available. Support available to part-time students. Financial award application deadline: 7/1; financial award applicants required to submit FAFSA. *Unit head:* Dr. Kathryn A. Richardson-Jones, Coordinator, 843-953-3163, Fax: 843-953-7258, E-mail: kathryn.jones@citadel.edu. *Application contact:* Dr. Steve A. Nida, Associate Provost, The Citadel Graduate College, 843-953-5089, Fax: 843-953-7630, E-mail: cgc@citadel.edu. Web site: http://www.citadel.edu/education/teacher-education/mat-master-of-arts-in-teaching.html.

City College of the City University of New York, Graduate School, School of Education, Department of Secondary Education, Program in Science Education, New York, NY 10031-9198. Offers MA. *Accreditation:* NCATE. *Entrance requirements:* For master's, Liberal Arts and Sciences Test (LAST), Content Specialty Test (CST). Additional exam requirements/recommendations for international students: Required—TOEFL.

Clarion University of Pennsylvania, Office of Graduate Programs, Master of Education Program, Clarion, PA 16214. Offers curriculum and instruction (M Ed); early childhood (M Ed, Certificate); English (M Ed); instructional technology specialist (K-12) (Certificate); literacy (M Ed); mathematics education (M Ed); reading specialist (M Ed, Certificate); science education (M Ed); special education (M Ed); technology (M Ed); world language (M Ed). *Accreditation:* NCATE. Part-time programs available. *Students:* 14 full-time (11 women), 207 part-time (163 women); includes 3 minority (1 Black or African American, non-Hispanic/Latino; 2 Hispanic/Latino). Average age 31. In 2011, 96 master's awarded. *Degree requirements:* For master's, thesis or alternative. *Entrance requirements:* For master's, minimum QPA of 3.0. *Application deadline:* Applications are processed on a rolling basis. *Expenses:* Tuition, state resident: part-time $429 per credit. Tuition, nonresident: part-time $644 per credit. *Financial support:* Research assistantships with full and partial tuition reimbursements and career-related internships or fieldwork available. Support available to part-time students. Financial award application deadline: 3/1. *Unit head:* Dr. John Groves, Dean, 814-393-2146, Fax: 514-393-2446. *Application contact:* Dr. Brenda Sanders Dede, Assistant Vice President for Academic Affairs, 814-393-2337, Fax: 814-393-2030, E-mail: bdede@clarion.edu. Web site: http://www.clarion.edu/25887/.

Clark Atlanta University, School of Education, Department of Curriculum, Atlanta, GA 30314. Offers special education general curriculum (MA); teaching math and science (MAT). Part-time programs available. *Faculty:* 4 full-time (all women), 4 part-time/adjunct (3 women). *Students:* 10 full-time (5 women), 9 part-time (7 women); includes 18 minority (all Black or African American, non-Hispanic/Latino). Average age 31. 13 applicants, 100% accepted, 9 enrolled. In 2011, 21 master's awarded. *Degree requirements:* For master's, one foreign language, comprehensive exam. *Entrance requirements:* For master's, GRE General Test, minimum undergraduate GPA of 2.6. Additional exam requirements/recommendations for international students: Required—TOEFL (minimum score 500 paper-based; 173 computer-based; 61 iBT). *Application deadline:* For fall admission, 4/1 for domestic and international students; for spring admission, 11/1 for domestic and international students. Applications are processed on a rolling basis. Application fee: $40 ($55 for international students). *Expenses: Tuition:* Full-time $13,572; part-time $754 per credit hour. *Required fees:* $806; $403 per semester. *Financial support:* Career-related internships or fieldwork, Federal Work-Study, scholarships/grants, and unspecified assistantships available. Support available to part-time students. Financial award application deadline: 4/30; financial award applicants required to submit FAFSA. *Unit head:* Dr. Doris Terrell, Chairperson, 404-880-6336, E-mail: dterrell@cau.edu. *Application contact:* Michelle Clark-Davis, Graduate Program Admissions, 404-880-6605, E-mail: cauadmissions@cau.edu. Web site: http://www.cau.edu/School_of_Education_curriculum_dept.aspx.

Clemson University, Graduate School, College of Health, Education, and Human Development, Eugene T. Moore School of Education, Program in Early Childhood Education, Clemson, SC 29634. Offers early childhood education (M Ed); elementary education (M Ed); secondary English (M Ed); secondary math (M Ed); secondary science (M Ed); secondary social studies (M Ed). Part-time and evening/weekend programs available. *Students:* 5 applicants, 0% accepted, 0 enrolled. In 2011, 3 master's awarded. *Degree requirements:* For master's, comprehensive exam. *Entrance requirements:* For master's, GRE, valid teaching certificate. Additional exam requirements/recommendations for international students: Required—TOEFL; Recommended—IELTS. *Application deadline:* Applications are processed on a rolling basis. Application fee: $70 ($80 for international students). Electronic applications accepted. *Expenses:* Contact institution. *Financial support:* Institutionally sponsored loans, health care benefits, and unspecified assistantships available. Financial award application deadline: 3/1; financial award applicants required to submit FAFSA. *Faculty research:* Elementary education, mathematics education, social studies education, English education, science education. *Unit head:* Dr. Michael J. Padilla, Director/Associate Dean, 864-656-4444, Fax: 864-656-0311, E-mail: padilla@clemson.edu. *Application contact:* Dr. David Fleming, Graduate Programs Coordinator, 864-656-1881, Fax: 864-656-0311, E-mail: dflemin@clemson.edu.

Clemson University, Graduate School, College of Health, Education, and Human Development, Eugene T. Moore School of Education, Program in Secondary Education: Math and Science, Clemson, SC 29634. Offers MAT. *Accreditation:* NCATE. *Students:* 9 full-time (6 women), 1 part-time; includes 1 minority (Black or African American, non-Hispanic/Latino). Average age 29. 15 applicants, 93% accepted, 9 enrolled. In 2011, 9 master's awarded. *Degree requirements:* For master's, digital portfolio. *Entrance requirements:* For master's, PRAXIS II. Additional exam requirements/recommendations for international students: Required—TOEFL; Recommended—IELTS. *Application deadline:* For fall admission, 4/1 for domestic students. Applications are processed on a rolling basis. Application fee: $70 ($80 for international students). Electronic applications accepted. *Expenses:* Contact institution. *Financial support:* Institutionally sponsored loans, scholarships/grants, health care benefits, and unspecified assistantships available. Financial award application deadline: 6/1; financial award applicants required to submit FAFSA. *Faculty research:* Science education, math education. *Unit head:* Dr. Michael J. Padilla, Director/Associate Dean, 864-656-4444, Fax: 864-656-0311, E-mail: padilla@clemson.edu. *Application contact:* Dr. David Fleming, Graduate Coordinator, 864-656-1881, Fax: 864-656-0311, E-mail: dflemin@clemson.edu. Web site: http://www.clemson.edu/hehd/departments/education/academics/graduate/MAT/secondary.html.

Clemson University, Graduate School, College of Health, Education, and Human Development, Eugene T. Moore School of Education, Program in Teaching and Learning, Clemson, SC 29634. Offers elementary education (M Ed); English education (M Ed); mathematics education (M Ed); science education (M Ed); social studies education (M Ed). *Entrance requirements:* For master's, GRE, baccalaureate degree from regionally-accredited institution, official transcripts, copy of valid teaching certificate, two letters of recommendation. *Application contact:* Dr. David Fleming, Graduate Programs Coordinator, 864-656-1881, Fax: 864-656-0311, E-mail: dflemin@clemson.edu. Web site: http://www.clemson.edu/hehd/departments/education/academics/graduate/MEd-teach-learn.html.

Cleveland State University, College of Graduate Studies, College of Education and Human Services, Department of Teacher Education, Cleveland, OH 44115. Offers art education (M Ed); early childhood education (M Ed); foreign language education (M Ed); mathematics and science education (M Ed); middle childhood education (M Ed); special education (M Ed), including mild/moderate disabilities, moderate/intensive disabilities; teaching English to speakers of other languages (M Ed). Part-time and evening/weekend programs available. *Faculty:* 20 full-time (12 women), 26 part-time/adjunct (20 women). *Students:* 108 full-time (77 women), 388 part-time (306 women); includes 126 minority (100 Black or African American, non-Hispanic/Latino; 8 Asian, non-Hispanic/Latino; 15 Hispanic/Latino; 1 Native Hawaiian or other Pacific Islander, non-Hispanic/Latino; 2 Two or more races, non-Hispanic/Latino), 25 international. Average age 33. 249 applicants, 73% accepted, 118 enrolled. In 2011, 286 master's awarded. *Degree requirements:* For master's, comprehensive exam (for some programs), thesis or alternative. *Entrance requirements:* For master's, GRE General Test or MAT, minimum GPA of 2.75. Additional exam requirements/recommendations for international students: Required—TOEFL (minimum score 525 paper-based; 197 computer-based), IELTS (minimum score 6). *Application deadline:* For fall admission, 7/15 priority date for domestic students. Applications are processed on a rolling basis. Application fee: $30. *Expenses:* Tuition, state resident: full-time $6416; part-time $494 per credit hour. Tuition, nonresident: full-time $12,074; part-time $929 per credit hour. *Financial support:* In 2011–12, 12 research assistantships with full tuition reimbursements (averaging $3,480 per year) were awarded; tuition waivers (partial) and unspecified assistantships also available. *Faculty research:* Early literacy, professional development in reading, reading recovery, dual language, induction programs. *Total annual research expenditures:* $6.2 million. *Unit head:* Dr. Clifford T. Bennett, Chairperson, 216-523-7105, Fax: 216-687-5379, E-mail: c.t.bennett@csuohio.edu. *Application contact:* Deborah L. Brown, Interim Assistant Director, Graduate Admissions, 216-523-7572, E-mail: d.l.brown@csuohio.edu. Web site: http://www.csuohio.edu/coehs/departments/te.

The College at Brockport, State University of New York, School of Education and Human Services, Department of Education and Human Development, Program in Adolescence Education, Brockport, NY 14420-2997. Offers adolescence biology education (MS Ed); adolescence chemistry education (MS Ed); adolescence earth science education (MS Ed); adolescence English education (MS Ed); adolescence mathematics education (MS Ed); adolescence physics education (MS Ed); adolescence social studies education (MS Ed). *Accreditation:* NCATE. Part-time programs available. *Students:* 12 full-time (9 women), 60 part-time (28 women); includes 6 minority (1 American Indian or Alaska Native, non-Hispanic/Latino; 3 Asian, non-Hispanic/Latino; 1 Hispanic/Latino; 1 Native Hawaiian or other Pacific Islander, non-Hispanic/Latino). 26 applicants, 81% accepted, 17 enrolled. In 2011, 47 master's awarded. *Degree requirements:* For master's, thesis or alternative. *Entrance requirements:* For master's, minimum GPA of 3.0, letters of recommendation; statement of objectives, current resume. Additional exam requirements/recommendations for international students: Required—TOEFL (minimum score 550 paper-based; 213 computer-based; 79 iBT). *Application deadline:* For fall admission, 2/15 priority date for domestic students, 2/15 for international students; for spring admission, 9/15 priority date for domestic students, 9/15 for international students. Application fee: $80. Electronic applications accepted. *Financial support:* Federal Work-Study, scholarships/grants, and unspecified assistantships available. Support available to part-time students. Financial award application deadline: 3/15; financial award applicants required to submit FAFSA. *Unit head:* Dr. Don Halquist, Chairperson, 585-395-5550, Fax: 585-395-2172, E-mail: dhalquis@brockport.edu. *Application contact:* Michael Harrison, Coordinator of Certification and Graduate Advisement, 585-395-2326, Fax: 585-395-2172, E-mail: mharriso@brockport.edu. Web site: http://www.brockport.edu/graduate/.

The College at Brockport, State University of New York, School of Education and Human Services, Department of Education and Human Development, Program in Adolescence Inclusive Education, Brockport, NY 14420-2997. Offers English (MS Ed); mathematics (MS Ed); science (MS Ed); social studies (MS Ed). *Students:* 42 full-time (22 women), 21 part-time (10 women); includes 4 minority (2 Black or African American, non-Hispanic/Latino; 2 Hispanic/Latino). 50 applicants, 64% accepted, 19 enrolled. In 2011, 2 master's awarded. *Degree requirements:* For master's, thesis or alternative. *Entrance requirements:* For master's, minimum GPA of 3.0, letters of recommendation, statement of objectives, academic major (or equivalent) in program discipline; current resume. Additional exam requirements/recommendations for international students: Required—TOEFL (minimum score 550 paper-based; 213 computer-based; 79 iBT). *Application deadline:* For fall admission, 2/15 priority date for domestic students, 2/15 for international students; for spring admission, 9/15 priority date for domestic students, 9/15 for international students. Application fee: $80. Electronic applications accepted. *Financial support:* Federal Work-Study, scholarships/grants, and unspecified assistantships available. Support available to part-time students. Financial award application deadline: 3/15; financial award applicants required to submit FAFSA. *Unit head:* Dr. Don Halquist, Chairperson, 585-395-2205, Fax: 585-395-2171, E-mail: dhalquis@brockport.edu. *Application contact:* Michael Harrison, Coordinator of Certification and Graduate Advisement, 585-395-2326, Fax: 585-395-2172, E-mail: mharriso@brockport.edu.

College of Charleston, Graduate School, School of Education, Health, and Human Performance, Program in Science and Mathematics for Teachers, Charleston, SC 29424-0001. Offers M Ed. *Accreditation:* NCATE. Part-time and evening/weekend programs available. *Faculty:* 4 full-time (2 women). *Students:* 8 full-time (7 women), 17 part-time (14 women); includes 2 minority (1 Black or African American, non-Hispanic/Latino; 1 Two or more races, non-Hispanic/Latino). Average age 31. 18 applicants, 61% accepted, 10 enrolled. In 2011, 7 degrees awarded. *Degree requirements:* For master's, capstone project. *Entrance requirements:* For master's, GRE or PRAXIS, 2 letters of recommendation, copy of teaching certificate. Additional exam requirements/recommendations for international students: Required—TOEFL (minimum score 81 iBT). *Application deadline:* For fall admission, 4/1 for domestic students; for spring admission, 11/1 for domestic students. Application fee: $45. Electronic applications accepted. *Expenses:* Tuition, state resident: full-time $5455; part-time $455 per credit. Tuition, nonresident: full-time $13,917; part-time $1160 per credit. *Financial support:* In 2011–12, research assistantships (averaging $12,400 per year), teaching assistantships (averaging $13,300 per year) were awarded; scholarships/grants and unspecified assistantships also available. Financial award application deadline: 4/1; financial award applicants required to submit FAFSA. *Unit head:* Dr. William Veal, Director, 843-953-8045, E-mail: vealw@cofc.edu. *Application contact:* Susan Hallatt, Director of Graduate Admissions, 843-953-5614, Fax: 843-953-1434, E-mail: hallatts@cofc.edu. Web site: http://www.cofc.edu/~medsm/.

The College of William and Mary, School of Education, Program in Curriculum and Instruction, Williamsburg, VA 23187-8795. Offers elementary education (MA Ed); gifted education (MA Ed); math specialist (MA Ed); reading education (MA Ed); secondary education (MA Ed), including English education, mathematics education, modern foreign languages education, science education, social studies education; special education (MA Ed), including collaborating master educator, general curriculum. *Accreditation:* NCATE. Part-time programs available. *Faculty:* 15 full-time (10 women), 39 part-time/adjunct (32 women). *Students:* 80 full-time (69 women), 13 part-time (11 women); includes 11 minority (3 Black or African American, non-Hispanic/Latino; 1 American Indian or Alaska Native, non-Hispanic/Latino; 2 Hispanic/Latino; 5 Two or more races, non-Hispanic/Latino), 1 international. Average age 25. 220 applicants, 56% accepted, 85 enrolled. In 2011, 78 master's awarded. *Degree requirements:* For master's, project. *Entrance requirements:* For master's, GRE or MAT, minimum GPA of 2.5. Additional exam requirements/recommendations for international students: Required—TOEFL. *Application deadline:* For fall admission, 1/15 for domestic and international students; for spring admission, 10/1 for domestic and international students. Application fee: $50. Electronic applications accepted. *Expenses:* Tuition, state resident: full-time $6400; part-time $365 per credit hour. Tuition, nonresident: full-time $19,720; part-time $985 per credit hour. *Required fees:* $4562. *Financial support:* In 2011–12, 53 students received support, including 10 research assistantships with full and partial tuition reimbursements available (averaging $7,000 per year); career-related internships or fieldwork, Federal Work-Study, institutionally sponsored loans, scholarships/grants, and unspecified assistantships also available. Financial award application deadline: 1/15; financial award applicants required to submit FAFSA. *Faculty research:* National Council of Teachers of Mathematics Standards, counseling, self-concept and self-esteem, special education, curriculum development. *Unit head:* Dr. Margie Mason, Area Coordinator, 757-221-2327, E-mail: mmmaso@wm.edu. *Application contact:* Dorothy Smith Osborne, Assistant Dean for Admission, 757-221-2317, Fax: 757-221-2293, E-mail: dsosbo@wm.edu. Web site: http://education.wm.edu.

The Colorado College, Education Department, Experienced Teacher Program, Colorado Springs, CO 80903-3294. Offers arts and humanities (MAT); integrated natural sciences (MAT); liberal arts (MAT); Southwest studies (MAT). Programs offered during summer only. Part-time programs available. *Students:* 1 applicant, 100% accepted, 0 enrolled. *Degree requirements:* For master's, thesis, oral exam, 50-page paper. *Application deadline:* Applications are processed on a rolling basis. Application fee: $50. *Expenses:* Contact institution. *Financial support:* Institutionally sponsored loans and half-tuition scholarships to teachers with a contract available. *Unit head:* Paul Kuerbis, Chair, 719-389-6726, Fax: 719-389-6473, E-mail: pkuerbis@coloradocollege.edu. *Application contact:* Debra Yazulla Mortenson, Education Services Manager, 719-389-6472, Fax: 719-389-6473, E-mail: debra.mortenson@coloradocollege.edu. Web site: http://www.coloradocollege.edu/academics/dept/education/graduate-programs/mat-for-experienced-teachers.dot.

The Colorado College, Education Department, Program in Secondary Education, Colorado Springs, CO 80903-3294. Offers art teaching (K-12) (MAT); English teaching (MAT); foreign language teaching (MAT); mathematics teaching (MAT); music teaching (MAT); science teaching (MAT); social studies teaching (MAT). *Faculty:* 4 full-time (3 women), 6 part-time/adjunct (2 women). *Students:* 11 full-time (7 women); includes 3 minority (1 Asian, non-Hispanic/Latino; 2 Hispanic/Latino). Average age 27. 20 applicants, 85% accepted, 11 enrolled. In 2011, 15 master's awarded. *Degree requirements:* For master's, thesis, internship. *Application deadline:* For fall admission, 12/1 priority date for domestic students, 12/1 for international students. Applications are processed on a rolling basis. Application fee: $50. Electronic applications accepted. *Expenses: Tuition:* Full-time $29,313. *Required fees:* $2000. *Financial support:* In 2011–12, 15 students received support. Career-related internships or fieldwork, institutionally sponsored loans, scholarships/grants, and health care benefits available. Financial award application deadline: 2/15; financial award applicants required to submit

FAFSA. *Unit head:* Dr. Mike Taber, Director, 719-389-6026, Fax: 719-389-6473, E-mail: mike.taber@coloradocollege.edu. *Application contact:* Debra Yazulla Mortenson, Education Services Manager, 719-389-6472, Fax: 719-389-6473, E-mail: debra.mortenson@coloradocollege.edu. Web site: http://www.coloradocollege.edu/academics/dept/education/graduate-programs/secondary-mat.dot.

Columbia University, College of Dental Medicine and Graduate School of Arts and Sciences, Programs in Dental Specialties, New York, NY 10027. Offers advanced education in general dentistry (Certificate); biomedical informatics (MA, PhD); endodontics (Certificate); orthodontics (MS, Certificate); periodontics (MS, Certificate); prosthodontics (MS, Certificate); science education (MA). *Degree requirements:* For master's, thesis, presentation of seminar. *Entrance requirements:* For master's, GRE General Test, DDS or equivalent. *Expenses:* Contact institution. *Faculty research:* Analysis of growth/form, pulpal microcirculation, implants, microbiology of oral environment, calcified tissues.

Columbus State University, Graduate Studies, College of Education and Health Professions, Department of Teacher Education, Columbus, GA 31907-5645. Offers accomplished teaching (M Ed); early childhood education (M Ed, MAT, Ed S); health and physical education (M Ed, MAT); middle grades education (M Ed, MAT, Ed S); school library media (M Ed, MAT); secondary education (M Ed, MAT, Ed S), including English/language arts (M Ed, Ed S), general science (M Ed), mathematics (M Ed), social science (M Ed); special education (M Ed, Ed S), including general curriculum (M Ed). *Accreditation:* NCATE. Part-time and evening/weekend programs available. Postbaccalaureate distance learning degree programs offered (minimal on-campus study). *Degree requirements:* For master's, thesis, exit exam; for Ed S, thesis or alternative. *Entrance requirements:* For master's, GRE General Test, minimum GPA of 2.75; for Ed S, GRE General Test. Additional exam requirements/recommendations for international students: Required—TOEFL (minimum score 550 paper-based; 213 computer-based; 79 iBT). Electronic applications accepted.

Converse College, School of Education and Graduate Studies, Program in Secondary Education, Spartanburg, SC 29302-0006. Offers biology (MAT); chemistry (MAT); English (M Ed, MAT); mathematics (M Ed, MAT); natural sciences (M Ed); social sciences (M Ed, MAT). Part-time programs available. *Degree requirements:* For master's, capstone paper. *Entrance requirements:* For master's, NTE or PRAXIS II (M Ed), minimum GPA of 2.75, 2 recommendations. Electronic applications accepted.

Cornell University, Graduate School, Graduate Fields of Agriculture and Life Sciences, Field of Education, Ithaca, NY 14853-0001. Offers agricultural education (MAT); biology (7-12) (MAT); chemistry (7-12) (MAT); curriculum and instruction (MPS, MS, PhD); earth science (7-12) (MAT); extension, and adult education (MPS, MS, PhD); mathematics (7-12) (MAT); physics (7-12) (MAT). *Faculty:* 23 full-time (10 women). *Students:* 32 full-time (18 women); includes 6 minority (4 Asian, non-Hispanic/Latino; 2 Hispanic/Latino), 1 international. Average age 30. 60 applicants, 33% accepted, 12 enrolled. In 2011, 22 master's, 7 doctorates awarded. Terminal master's awarded for partial completion of doctoral program. *Degree requirements:* For master's, thesis (MS); for doctorate, comprehensive exam, thesis/dissertation. *Entrance requirements:* For master's and doctorate, GRE General Test, sample of written work (recommended), 2 letters of recommendation. Additional exam requirements/recommendations for international students: Required—TOEFL (minimum score 550 paper-based; 213 computer-based; 77 iBT). *Application deadline:* For fall admission, 2/15 for domestic students. Application fee: $95. Electronic applications accepted. *Financial support:* In 2011–12, 2 fellowships with full tuition reimbursements, 4 research assistantships with full tuition reimbursements, 12 teaching assistantships with full tuition reimbursements were awarded; institutionally sponsored loans, scholarships/grants, health care benefits, tuition waivers (full and partial), and unspecified assistantships also available. Financial award applicants required to submit FAFSA. *Faculty research:* Moral development and professional ethics, public issues education and community development, socio/political issues in public education, teacher education and curriculum in agricultural science and mathematics, extension research. *Unit head:* Director of Graduate Studies, 607-255-4278, Fax: 607-255-7905. *Application contact:* Graduate Field Assistant, 607-255-4278, Fax: 607-255-7905, E-mail: rh22@cornell.edu. Web site: http://www.gradschool.cornell.edu/fields.php?id-80&a-2.

Delaware State University, Graduate Programs, College of Education, Health and Public Policy, Program in Science Education, Dover, DE 19901-2277. Offers MA. Part-time and evening/weekend programs available. *Degree requirements:* For master's, comprehensive exam, thesis optional. *Entrance requirements:* For master's, GRE General Test, minimum GPA of 3.0 in major, 2.75 overall. Electronic applications accepted. *Faculty research:* Science reform in schools, inquiry science.

Delaware State University, Graduate Programs, Department of Biological Sciences, Program in Biology Education, Dover, DE 19901-2277. Offers MS. *Entrance requirements:* Additional exam requirements/recommendations for international students: Required—TOEFL (minimum score 550 paper-based).

Delaware State University, Graduate Programs, Department of Physics, Dover, DE 19901-2277. Offers applied optics (MS); optics (PhD); physics (MS); physics teaching (MS). Part-time and evening/weekend programs available. *Entrance requirements:* For master's, minimum GPA of 3.0 in major, 2.75 overall. Additional exam requirements/recommendations for international students: Required—TOEFL. Electronic applications accepted. *Faculty research:* Thermal properties of solids, nuclear physics, radiation damage in solids.

Drew University, Caspersen School of Graduate Studies, Program in Education, Madison, NJ 07940-1493. Offers biology (MAT); chemistry (MAT); English (MAT); French (MAT); Italian (MAT); math (MAT); physics (MAT); social studies (MAT); Spanish (MAT); theatre arts (MAT). Part-time programs available. *Entrance requirements:* For master's, transcripts, personal statement, recommendations. Additional exam requirements/recommendations for international students: Required—TOEFL, TWE. *Expenses:* Contact institution.

Duquesne University, School of Education, Department of Instruction and Leadership, Program in Secondary Education, Pittsburgh, PA 15282-0001. Offers biology (MS Ed). Part-time and evening/weekend programs available. *Faculty:* 4 full-time (3 women), 2 part-time/adjunct (0 women). *Students:* 50 full-time (28 women), 8 part-time (5 women); includes 2 minority (1 Asian, non-Hispanic/Latino; 1 Hispanic/Latino). Average age 26. 62 applicants, 34% accepted, 17 enrolled. In 2011, 32 master's awarded. *Degree requirements:* For master's, thesis optional. *Entrance requirements:* For master's, letters of recommendation, letter of intent, interview, bachelor's degree. Additional exam requirements/recommendations for international students: Required—TOEFL (minimum score 550 paper-based; 80 computer-based), IELTS (minimum score 7). *Application deadline:* For fall admission, 9/1 for domestic students; for spring admission, 1/1 for domestic students. Applications are processed on a rolling basis. Application fee: $0. Electronic applications accepted. Application fee is waived when completed online. *Expenses: Tuition:* Full-time $16,596; part-time $922 per credit. *Required fees:* $1584; $88 per credit. Tuition and fees vary according to program. *Financial support:* Research assistantships and Federal Work-Study available. Support available to part-time students. *Unit head:* Dr. Melissa Boston, Assistant Professor, 412-396-6109, E-mail: bostonm@duq.edu. *Application contact:* Michael Dolinger, Director of Student and Academic Services, 412-396-6647, Fax: 412-396-5585, E-mail: dolingerm@duq.edu. Web site: http://www.duq.edu/education.

East Carolina University, Graduate School, College of Education, Department of Business and Information Technologies Education, Greenville, NC 27858-4353. Offers business education (MA Ed); elementary education (MAT); English education (MAT); family and consumer science (MAT); health education (MAT); Hispanic studies (MAT); history education (MAT); marketing education (MA Ed); middle grades education (MAT); music education (MAT); physical education (MAT); science education (MAT); special education (MAT), including general curriculum; vocation education (MS). *Accreditation:* NCATE. Part-time and evening/weekend programs available. Postbaccalaureate distance learning degree programs offered (no on-campus study). *Degree requirements:* For master's, comprehensive exam, thesis optional. *Entrance requirements:* For master's, GRE or MAT, minimum GPA of 2.5, bachelor's degree in related field, teaching license (MA Ed). Additional exam requirements/recommendations for international students: Required—TOEFL. *Application deadline:* For fall admission, 6/1 priority date for domestic students. Applications are processed on a rolling basis. Application fee: $50. *Expenses:* Tuition, state resident: full-time $3557; part-time $444.63 per semester hour. Tuition, nonresident: full-time $14,351; part-time $1793.88 per semester hour. *Required fees:* $2016; $252 per semester hour. Part-time tuition and fees vary according to course load, campus/location and program. *Financial support:* Federal Work-Study available. Support available to part-time students. Financial award application deadline: 6/1. *Unit head:* Dr. Ivan G. Wallace, Chair, 252-328-6983, Fax: 252-328-6835, E-mail: wallacei@ecu.edu. *Application contact:* Dean of Graduate School, 252-328-6012, Fax: 252-328-6071, E-mail: gradschool@ecu.edu. Web site: http://www.ecu.edu/cs-educ/bite/index.cfm.

East Carolina University, Graduate School, College of Education, Department of Mathematics, Science, and Instructional Technology Education, Greenville, NC 27858-4353. Offers computer-based instruction (Certificate); distance learning and administration (Certificate); instructional technology (MA Ed, MS); mathematics (MA Ed); performance improvement (Certificate); science education (MA, MA Ed); special endorsement in computer education (Certificate). Part-time and evening/weekend programs available. *Degree requirements:* For master's, comprehensive exam, thesis optional. *Entrance requirements:* For master's, GRE General Test or MAT, interview, minimum GPA of 2.5, bachelor's degree in related field, teaching license (MA Ed). Additional exam requirements/recommendations for international students: Required—TOEFL. *Application deadline:* For fall admission, 6/1 priority date for domestic students. Applications are processed on a rolling basis. Application fee: $50. *Expenses:* Tuition, state resident: full-time $3557; part-time $444.63 per semester hour. Tuition, nonresident: full-time $14,351; part-time $1793.88 per semester hour. *Required fees:* $2016; $252 per semester hour. Part-time tuition and fees vary according to course load, campus/location and program. *Financial support:* Research assistantships, teaching assistantships, and Federal Work-Study available. Support available to part-time students. Financial award application deadline: 6/1. *Unit head:* Susan Ganter, Chair, 252-328-9353, E-mail: ganters@ecu.edu. *Application contact:* Dean of Graduate School, 252-328-6012, Fax: 252-328-6071, E-mail: gradschool@ecu.edu.

Eastern Connecticut State University, School of Education and Professional Studies/Graduate Division, Program in Science Education, Willimantic, CT 06226-2295. Offers MS. *Accreditation:* NCATE. Part-time and evening/weekend programs available. *Degree requirements:* For master's, comprehensive exam or thesis. *Entrance requirements:* For master's, minimum GPA of 2.7, teaching certificate. Additional exam requirements/recommendations for international students: Required—TOEFL (minimum score 550 paper-based; 213 computer-based).

Eastern Kentucky University, The Graduate School, College of Education, Department of Curriculum and Instruction, Program in Secondary and Higher Education, Richmond, KY 40475-3102. Offers secondary education (MA Ed), including agricultural education, art education, biological sciences education, business education, English education, geography education, history education, home economics education, industrial education, mathematical sciences education, physical education, school health education. *Accreditation:* NCATE. Part-time programs available. *Entrance requirements:* For master's, GRE General Test, minimum GPA of 2.5.

Eastern Michigan University, Graduate School, College of Arts and Sciences, Department of Biology, Ypsilanti, MI 48197. Offers cell and molecular biology (MS); community college biology teaching (MS); ecology and organismal biology (MS); general biology (MS); water resources (MS). Part-time and evening/weekend programs available. Postbaccalaureate distance learning degree programs offered (minimal on-campus study). *Faculty:* 20 full-time (4 women). *Students:* 12 full-time (7 women), 40 part-time (21 women); includes 3 minority (1 Black or African American, non-Hispanic/Latino; 1 Asian, non-Hispanic/Latino; 1 Two or more races, non-Hispanic/Latino), 12 international. Average age 27. 70 applicants, 43% accepted, 12 enrolled. In 2011, 19 degrees awarded. *Entrance requirements:* For master's, GRE General Test, GRE Subject Test. Additional exam requirements/recommendations for international students: Required—TOEFL. *Application deadline:* Applications are processed on a rolling basis. Application fee: $35. *Expenses:* Tuition, state resident: full-time $10,367; part-time $432 per credit hour. Tuition, nonresident: full-time $20,435; part-time $851 per credit hour. *Required fees:* $39 per credit hour. $46 per semester. One-time fee: $100. Tuition and fees vary according to course level, degree level and reciprocity agreements. *Financial support:* Fellowships, research assistantships with full tuition reimbursements, teaching assistantships with full tuition reimbursements, career-related internships or fieldwork, Federal Work-Study, institutionally sponsored loans, scholarships/grants, tuition waivers (partial), and unspecified assistantships available. Support available to part-time students. Financial award applicants required to submit FAFSA. *Unit head:* Dr. Marianne Laporte, Department Head, 734-487-4242, Fax: 734-487-9235, E-mail: mlaporte@emich.edu. *Application contact:* Graduate Admissions, 734-487-2400, Fax: 734-487-6559, E-mail: graduate.admissions@emich.edu. Web site: http://www.emich.edu/biology.

Eastern Michigan University, Graduate School, College of Arts and Sciences, Department of Geography and Geology, Program in Earth Science Education, Ypsilanti, MI 48197. Offers MS. *Students:* 2 full-time (both women), 11 part-time (7 women). Average age 34. 6 applicants, 67% accepted, 4 enrolled. In 2011, 3 degrees awarded. Application fee: $35. *Expenses:* Tuition, state resident: full-time $10,367; part-time $432 per credit hour. Tuition, nonresident: full-time $20,435; part-time $851 per credit hour. *Required fees:* $39 per credit hour. $46 per semester. One-time fee: $100. Tuition and fees vary according to course level, degree level and reciprocity agreements. *Unit head:* Dr. Richard Sambrook, Department Head, 734-487-0218, Fax: 734-487-6979, E-mail: rsambroo@emich.edu. *Application contact:* Dr. Sandra Rutherford, Program Advisor, 734-487-8588, Fax: 734-487-6979, E-mail: srutherf@emich.edu.

Eastern Michigan University, Graduate School, College of Arts and Sciences, Department of Physics and Astronomy, Ypsilanti, MI 48197. Offers general science (MS); physics (MS); physics education (MS). Part-time and evening/weekend programs available. Postbaccalaureate distance learning degree programs offered (minimal on-campus study). *Faculty:* 10 full-time (3 women). *Students:* 3 full-time (0 women), 12 part-time (3 women); includes 1 minority (Black or African American, non-Hispanic/Latino), 1 international. Average age 27. 19 applicants, 74% accepted, 7 enrolled. In 2011, 4 master's awarded. *Entrance requirements:* Additional exam requirements/ recommendations for international students: Required—TOEFL. *Application deadline:* Applications are processed on a rolling basis. Application fee: $35. *Expenses:* Tuition, state resident: full-time $10,367; part-time $432 per credit hour. Tuition, nonresident: full-time $20,435; part-time $851 per credit hour. *Required fees:* $39 per credit hour. $46 per semester. One-time fee: $100. Tuition and fees vary according to course level, degree level and reciprocity agreements. *Financial support:* Fellowships, research assistantships with full tuition reimbursements, teaching assistantships with full tuition reimbursements, career-related internships or fieldwork, Federal Work-Study, institutionally sponsored loans, scholarships/grants, tuition waivers, and unspecified assistantships available. Support available to part-time students. Financial award applicants required to submit FAFSA. *Unit head:* Dr. Alexandria Oakes, Interim Department Head, 734-487-4144, Fax: 734-487-0989, E-mail: aoakes@emich.edu. *Application contact:* Graduate Admissions, 734-487-2400, Fax: 734-487-6559, E-mail: graduate.admissions@emich.edu. Web site: http://www.emich.edu/physics/.

Eastern New Mexico University, Graduate School, College of Liberal Arts and Sciences, Department of Biology, Portales, NM 88130. Offers applied ecology (MS); cell, molecular biology and biotechnology (MS); education (non-thesis) (MS); microbiology (MS); plant biology (MS); zoology (MS). Part-time programs available. *Faculty:* 7 full-time (0 women). *Students:* 2 full-time (1 woman), 15 part-time (9 women); includes 7 minority (5 Hispanic/Latino; 2 Two or more races, non-Hispanic/Latino), 2 international. Average age 26. 17 applicants, 82% accepted, 3 enrolled. In 2011, 4 master's awarded. *Degree requirements:* For master's, comprehensive exam, thesis optional. *Entrance requirements:* For master's, GRE, minimum GPA of 3.0, 2 letters of recommendation, statement of research interest, bachelor's degree related to field of study or proof of common knowledge. Additional exam requirements/recommendations for international students: Required—TOEFL (minimum score 550 paper-based; 213 computer-based; 79 iBT), IELTS (minimum score 6). *Application deadline:* For fall admission, 7/20 priority date for domestic students, 6/20 for international students; for spring admission, 12/15 priority date for domestic students, 11/15 for international students. Applications are processed on a rolling basis. Application fee: $10. Electronic applications accepted. *Financial support:* In 2011–12, 8 teaching assistantships with partial tuition reimbursements (averaging $8,500 per year) were awarded; scholarships/ grants and unspecified assistantships also available. Support available to part-time students. Financial award applicants required to submit FAFSA. *Unit head:* Dr. Zach Jones, Graduate Coordinator, 575-562-2723, Fax: 575-562-2192, E-mail: zach.jones@ enmu.edu. *Application contact:* Sharon Potter, Department Secretary, Biology and Physical Sciences, 575-562-2174, Fax: 575-562-2192, E-mail: sharon.potter@ enmu.edu. Web site: http://liberal-arts.enmu.edu/biology/graduate.shtml.

East Stroudsburg University of Pennsylvania, Graduate School, College of Arts and Sciences, Department of Biology, East Stroudsburg, PA 18301-2999. Offers M Ed, MS. Part-time and evening/weekend programs available. *Degree requirements:* For master's, comprehensive exam, thesis or alternative. *Entrance requirements:* For master's, GRE, resume, undergraduate major in life science (or equivalent), completion of organic chemistry (minimum two semesters), 3 letters of recommendation, letter of intent. Additional exam requirements/recommendations for international students: Required—TOEFL (minimum score 560 paper-based; 220 computer-based; 83 iBT) or IELTS.

Elms College, Division of Education, Chicopee, MA 01013-2839. Offers early childhood education (MAT); education (M Ed, CAGS); elementary education (MAT); English as a second language (MAT); reading (MAT); secondary education (MAT), including biology education, English education, Spanish education; special education (MAT). Part-time and evening/weekend programs available. *Degree requirements:* For master's, thesis (for some programs). *Entrance requirements:* For master's, Massachusetts Educators Certification Test, minimum GPA of 3.0; for CAGS, master's degree in education. Additional exam requirements/recommendations for international students: Required—TOEFL.

Fairleigh Dickinson University, Metropolitan Campus, University College: Arts, Sciences, and Professional Studies, School of Natural Sciences, Program in Science, Teaneck, NJ 07666-1914. Offers MA. *Accreditation:* Teacher Education Accreditation Council.

Fitchburg State University, Division of Graduate and Continuing Education, Program in Science Education, Fitchburg, MA 01420-2697. Offers M Ed. *Accreditation:* NCATE. Part-time and evening/weekend programs available. *Students:* 3 part-time (2 women). Average age 38. In 2011, 1 master's awarded. *Entrance requirements:* Additional exam requirements/recommendations for international students: Required—TOEFL (minimum score 550 paper-based; 213 computer-based; 79 iBT). *Application deadline:* For fall admission, 7/15 for international students; for spring admission, 12/1 for international students. Applications are processed on a rolling basis. Application fee: $25 ($50 for international students). Electronic applications accepted. *Expenses:* Tuition, state resident: full-time $2700; part-time $150 per credit. Tuition, nonresident: full-time $2700; part-time $150 per credit. *Required fees:* $2286; $127 per credit. *Financial support:* In 2011–12, research assistantships with partial tuition reimbursements (averaging $5,500 per year) were awarded; Federal Work-Study, scholarships/grants, and unspecified assistantships also available. Support available to part-time students. Financial award application deadline: 3/1; financial award applicants required to submit FAFSA. *Unit head:* Dr. George Babich, Chair, 978-665-3245, Fax: 978-665-3658, E-mail: gce@ fitchburgstate.edu. *Application contact:* Director of Admissions, 978-665-3144, Fax: 978-665-4540, E-mail: admissions@fitchburgstate.edu. Web site: http:// www.fitchburgstate.edu.

Fitchburg State University, Division of Graduate and Continuing Education, Programs in Biology and Teaching Biology (Secondary Level), Fitchburg, MA 01420-2697. Offers MA, MAT, Certificate. *Accreditation:* NCATE. Part-time and evening/weekend programs available. *Students:* 2 full-time (both women), 9 part-time (4 women); includes 1 minority (Hispanic/Latino). Average age 37. 5 applicants, 100% accepted, 5 enrolled. In 2011, 1 master's awarded. *Entrance requirements:* Additional exam requirements/ recommendations for international students: Required—TOEFL (minimum score 550 paper-based; 213 computer-based; 79 iBT). *Application deadline:* For fall admission, 7/ 15 for international students; for spring admission, 12/1 for international students. Applications are processed on a rolling basis. Application fee: $25 ($50 for international students). Electronic applications accepted. *Expenses:* Tuition, state resident: full-time $2700; part-time $150 per credit. Tuition, nonresident: full-time $2700; part-time $150 per credit. *Required fees:* $2286; $127 per credit. *Financial support:* In 2011–12, research assistantships with partial tuition reimbursements (averaging $5,500 per year) were awarded; Federal Work-Study, scholarships/grants, and unspecified assistantships also available. Support available to part-time students. Financial award application deadline: 3/1; financial award applicants required to submit FAFSA. *Unit head:* Dr. George Babich, Chair, 978-665-3245, Fax: 978-665-3658, E-mail: gce@ fitchburgstate.edu. *Application contact:* Director of Admissions, 978-665-3144, Fax: 978-665-4540, E-mail: admissions@fitchburgstate.edu. Web site: http:// www.fitchburgstate.edu.

Florida Agricultural and Mechanical University, Division of Graduate Studies, Research, and Continuing Education, College of Education, Program in Secondary Education and Foundation, Tallahassee, FL 32307-3200. Offers biology (M Ed); chemistry (MS Ed); English (MS Ed); history (MS Ed); math (MS Ed); physics (MS Ed). *Accreditation:* NCATE. *Degree requirements:* For master's, thesis (for some programs). *Entrance requirements:* For master's, GRE General Test, minimum GPA of 3.0. Additional exam requirements/recommendations for international students: Required—TOEFL.

Florida Institute of Technology, Graduate Programs, College of Science, Department of Education and Interdisciplinary Studies, Melbourne, FL 32901-6975. Offers computer education (MS); elementary science education (M Ed); environmental education (MS); interdisciplinary science (MS); mathematics education (MS, PhD, Ed S); science education (MS, PhD, Ed S), including informal science education (MS); teaching (MAT). Part-time and evening/weekend programs available. *Faculty:* 4 full-time (1 woman), 3 part-time/adjunct (2 women). *Students:* 22 full-time (16 women), 27 part-time (18 women); includes 8 minority (2 Black or African American, non-Hispanic/Latino; 4 Asian, non-Hispanic/Latino; 2 Hispanic/Latino), 9 international. Average age 34. 57 applicants, 70% accepted, 19 enrolled. In 2011, 5 master's, 1 doctorate awarded. Terminal master's awarded for partial completion of doctoral program. *Median time to degree:* Of those who began their doctoral program in fall 2003, 50% received their degree in 8 years or less. *Degree requirements:* For master's, comprehensive exam (for some programs), thesis optional; for doctorate, comprehensive exam, thesis/dissertation; for Ed S, comprehensive exam. *Entrance requirements:* For master's, minimum GPA of 3.0, resume, 3 letters of recommendation (elementary science education), statement of objectives; for doctorate, minimum GPA of 3.2, resume, 3 letters of recommendation, statement of objectives, 3 years teaching experience (recommended); for Ed S, minimum GPA of 3.0, resume, 3 letters of recommendation, statement of objectives. Additional exam requirements/recommendations for international students: Required—TOEFL (minimum score 550 paper-based; 213 computer-based; 79 iBT). *Application deadline:* For fall admission, 4/1 for international students; for spring admission, 9/30 for international students. Applications are processed on a rolling basis. Electronic applications accepted. *Expenses: Tuition:* Full-time $19,620; part-time $1090 per credit hour. Tuition and fees vary according to campus/location. *Financial support:* In 2011–12, 1 teaching assistantship with full and partial tuition reimbursement (averaging $797 per year) was awarded; research assistantships with full and partial tuition reimbursements, career-related internships or fieldwork, institutionally sponsored loans, tuition waivers (partial), unspecified assistantships, and tuition remissions also available. Support available to part-time students. Financial award application deadline: 3/1; financial award applicants required to submit FAFSA. *Faculty research:* Measurement and evaluation, computers in education, educational technology. *Total annual research expenditures:* $1. *Unit head:* Dr. Lazlo A. Baksay, Department Head, 321-674-7205, Fax: 321-674-7598, E-mail: baksay@fit.edu. *Application contact:* Cheryl A. Brown, Associate Director of Graduate Admissions, 321-674-7581, Fax: 321-723-9468, E-mail: cbrown@fit.edu. Web site: http://cos.fit.edu/education/.

Florida International University, College of Education, Department of Curriculum and Instruction, Miami, FL 33199. Offers art education (MAT, MS, Ed D); curriculum and instruction (Ed S); curriculum development (MS); curriculum studies (PhD); early childhood education (MS, Ed D); elementary education (MS, Ed D); English education (MAT, MS, Ed D); foreign language education - teaching English to speakers of other languages (TESOL) (MS, Certificate), including foreign language education (Certificate), teaching English (MS); French education - initial teacher preparation (MAT); international and intercultural development education (Ed D); international and intercultural developmental education (MS); language, literacy and culture (PhD); learning technologies (MS, Ed D, PhD); mathematics education (MAT, MS, Ed D, PhD); modern language education/bilingual education (MS, Ed D); physical education (MS); reading education (MS, Ed D); science education (MAT, MS, Ed D, PhD); social studies education (MAT, MS, Ed D); Spanish education - initial teacher preparation (MAT); special education (MS). Part-time and evening/weekend programs available. *Degree requirements:* For doctorate, comprehensive exam, thesis/dissertation. *Entrance requirements:* For master's, GRE General Test, Florida General Knowledge Test or Florida College Level Academic Skills Test; for doctorate and other advanced degree, GRE General Test. Additional exam requirements/recommendations for international students: Required—TOEFL (minimum score 550 paper-based; 213 computer-based; 80 iBT), IELTS (minimum score 6.3). Electronic applications accepted.

Florida State University, The Graduate School, College of Arts and Sciences, Department of Biological Science, Master of Science Teaching Program, Tallahassee, FL 32306. Offers MST. *Faculty:* 2 full-time (1 woman). *Students:* 5 full-time (2 women); includes 1 minority (Native Hawaiian or other Pacific Islander, non-Hispanic/Latino). Average age 23. 1 applicant, 100% accepted, 1 enrolled. In 2011, 2 master's awarded. *Degree requirements:* For master's, teacher work sample (action research). *Entrance requirements:* For master's, GRE. *Application deadline:* For fall admission, 6/1 for domestic students. Application fee: $30. Electronic applications accepted. *Expenses:* Tuition, state resident: full-time $9474; part-time $350.88 per credit hour. Tuition, nonresident: full-time $16,236; part-time $601.34 per credit hour. *Required fees:* $630 per semester. One-time fee: $20. Tuition and fees vary according to course load and campus/location. *Faculty research:* Science and mathematics education, science and mathematics teacher preparation. *Total annual research expenditures:* $300,000. *Unit head:* Dr. George W. Bates, Professor and Associate Chairman, 850-644-5749, Fax: 850-644-9829, E-mail: bates@bio.fsu.edu. *Application contact:* Dr. Randall Ketola, Assistant Director, Office of Science Teaching Activities, 850-644-1142, Fax: 850-644-0643, E-mail: rketola@fsu.edu.

Florida State University, The Graduate School, College of Education, School of Teacher Education, Tallahassee, FL 32306. Offers early childhood education (MS, Ed D, PhD, Ed S); elementary education (MS, Ed D, PhD, Ed S); English education (MS, PhD, Ed S); mathematics education (MS, PhD, Ed S); reading education/language arts (MS, Ed D, PhD, Ed S); science education (MS, PhD, Ed S); social science education (MS, PhD, Ed S); special education (MS, PhD, Ed S), including emotional disturbance/learning disabilities (MS), mental retardation (MS), rehabilitation counseling, special education (PhD, Ed S), visual disabilities (MS). Part-time programs available. *Faculty:* 34 full-time (25 women), 20 part-time/adjunct (17 women). *Students:* 160 full-time (130 women), 116 part-time (98 women); includes 64 minority (36 Black or African American, non-Hispanic/Latino; 4 American Indian or Alaska Native, non-Hispanic/ Latino; 6 Asian, non-Hispanic/Latino; 18 Hispanic/Latino), 28 international. Average age 31. 180 applicants, 62% accepted, 53 enrolled. In 2011, 142 master's, 17 doctorates, 8 other advanced degrees awarded. *Degree requirements:* For master's and Ed S, comprehensive exam, thesis optional; for doctorate, comprehensive exam, thesis/ dissertation, preliminary exam, prospectus defense. *Entrance requirements:* For master's, doctorate, and Ed S, GRE General Test, minimum GPA of 3.0. Additional exam requirements/recommendations for international students: Required—TOEFL (minimum score 550 paper-based; 213 computer-based; 80 iBT). *Application deadline:* For fall admission, 7/1 for domestic and international students; for winter admission, 10/ 1 for domestic students, 11/1 for international students; for spring admission, 3/1 for domestic and international students. Applications are processed on a rolling basis. Application fee: $30. Electronic applications accepted. *Expenses:* Tuition, state resident: full-time $9474; part-time $350.88 per credit hour. Tuition, nonresident: full-time $16,236; part-time $601.34 per credit hour. *Required fees:* $630 per semester.

One-time fee: $20. Tuition and fees vary according to course load and campus/location. *Financial support:* In 2011–12, 32 research assistantships with full and partial tuition reimbursements, 15 teaching assistantships with full and partial tuition reimbursements were awarded; fellowships with full and partial tuition reimbursements, career-related internships or fieldwork, scholarships/grants, health care benefits, and unspecified assistantships also available. Financial award application deadline: 1/15; financial award applicants required to submit FAFSA. *Faculty research:* Teaching and learning practices and policies, twenty-first century literacies, impact of teacher education programs on student gains. *Total annual research expenditures:* $723,234. *Unit head:* Dr. Lawrence Scharmann, Chair, 850-644-4880, Fax: 850-644-1880, E-mail: lscharmann@fsu.edu. *Application contact:* Harriet Kasper, Program Assistant, 850-644-2122, Fax: 850-644-7736, E-mail: hkasper@fsu.edu. Web site: http://www.coe.fsu.edu/Academic-Programs/Departments/School-of-Teacher-Education-STE.

Fresno Pacific University, Graduate Programs, School of Education, Fresno, CA 93702-4709. Offers administration (MA Ed), including administrative services; foundations, curriculum and teaching (MA Ed), including curriculum and teaching, school library and information technology; language, literacy, and culture (MA Ed), including bilingual/cross-cultural education, language development, multilingual contexts, reading; mathematics/science/computer education (MA Ed), including educational technology, integrated mathematics/science education, mathematics education; pupil personnel services (MA Ed), including school counseling, school psychology; special education (MA Ed), including mild/moderate, moderate/severe, physical and health impairments. Part-time and evening/weekend programs available. *Degree requirements:* For master's, thesis (for some programs). *Entrance requirements:* For master's, interview; GMAT, GRE, MAT, or 6 units of course work with a faculty recommendation. Additional exam requirements/recommendations for international students: Required—TOEFL (minimum score 550 paper-based; 213 computer-based). Electronic applications accepted.

Fresno Pacific University, Graduate Programs, School of Education, Division of Mathematics/Science/Computer Education, Program in Integrated Mathematics/Science Education, Fresno, CA 93702-4709. Offers MA Ed. Part-time and evening/weekend programs available. *Degree requirements:* For master's, thesis or alternative. *Entrance requirements:* Additional exam requirements/recommendations for international students: Required—TOEFL (minimum score 550 paper-based; 213 computer-based).

Gannon University, School of Graduate Studies, College of Engineering and Business, School of Engineering and Computer Science, Program in Natural and Environmental Sciences, Erie, PA 16541-0001. Offers M Ed. Part-time and evening/weekend programs available. *Students:* 1 (woman) full-time, 1 (woman) part-time, 1 international. Average age 34. 3 applicants, 0% accepted, 0 enrolled. *Degree requirements:* For master's, thesis or alternative, research paper. *Entrance requirements:* For master's, GRE or GMAT. Additional exam requirements/recommendations for international students: Required—TOEFL (minimum score 79 iBT). *Application deadline:* Applications are processed on a rolling basis. Application fee: $25. Electronic applications accepted. *Financial support:* Career-related internships or fieldwork, scholarships/grants, and unspecified assistantships available. Financial award application deadline: 7/1; financial award applicants required to submit FAFSA. *Unit head:* Dr. Harry Diz, Chair, 814-871-7633, E-mail: diz001@gannon.edu. *Application contact:* Kara Morgan, Director of Graduate Admissions, 814-871-5831, Fax: 814-871-5827, E-mail: graduate@gannon.edu.

Georgia Southern University, Jack N. Averitt College of Graduate Studies, College of Education, Department of Teaching and Learning, Program in Science Education, Statesboro, GA 30460. Offers M Ed, MAT. *Accreditation:* NCATE. Part-time and evening/weekend programs available. *Students:* 9 full-time (7 women), 1 (woman) part-time; includes 2 minority (both Black or African American, non-Hispanic/Latino). Average age 24. 5 applicants, 100% accepted, 4 enrolled. In 2011, 5 master's awarded. *Degree requirements:* For master's, portfolio, transition point assessments, exit assessment. *Entrance requirements:* For master's, GRE General Test or MAT; GACE Basic Skills and Content Assessments (MAT), minimum GPA of 2.5. Additional exam requirements/recommendations for international students: Required—TOEFL (minimum score 550 paper-based; 213 computer-based; 80 iBT). *Application deadline:* For fall admission, 3/1 priority date for domestic students, 3/1 for international students; for spring admission, 10/1 priority date for domestic students, 10/1 for international students. Applications are processed on a rolling basis. Application fee: $50. Electronic applications accepted. *Expenses:* Tuition, state resident: full-time $6300; part-time $263 per semester hour. Tuition, nonresident: full-time $25,174; part-time $1049 per semester hour. *Required fees:* $1872. *Financial support:* In 2011–12, 4 students received support, including research assistantships with partial tuition reimbursements available (averaging $7,200 per year), teaching assistantships with partial tuition reimbursements available (averaging $7,200 per year); Federal Work-Study, scholarships/grants, tuition waivers (partial), and unspecified assistantships also available. Support available to part-time students. Financial award application deadline: 4/15; financial award applicants required to submit FAFSA. *Faculty research:* Gender. *Unit head:* Dr. Ronnie Sheppard, Department Chair, 912-478-5203, Fax: 912-478-0026, E-mail: sheppard@georgiasouthern.edu. *Application contact:* Amanda Gilliland, Coordinator for Graduate Student Recruitment, 912-478-5384, Fax: 912-478-0740, E-mail: gradadmissions@georgiasouthern.edu. Web site: http://coe.georgiasouthern.edu/tandl/index.html.

Georgia State University, College of Education, Department of Middle-Secondary Education and Instructional Technology, Programs in Secondary Education, Atlanta, GA 30302-3083. Offers art education (Ed S); English education (M Ed, Ed S); mathematics education (M Ed, PhD, Ed S); music education (PhD); science education (M Ed, PhD, Ed S); social studies education (M Ed, PhD, Ed S). *Accreditation:* NASM (one or more programs are accredited); NCATE. Part-time and evening/weekend programs available. *Degree requirements:* For master's, comprehensive exam; for doctorate, comprehensive exam, thesis/dissertation; for Ed S, project/exam. *Entrance requirements:* For master's, GRE General Test, minimum GPA of 2.5; for doctorate, GRE General Test or MAT, minimum GPA of 3.3; for Ed S, GRE General Test or MAT, minimum graduate GPA of 3.25. *Faculty research:* Women and science, problem solving in mathematics, dialects, economic education.

Grambling State University, School of Graduate Studies and Research, College of Education, Department of Educational Leadership, Grambling, LA 71245. Offers curriculum and instruction (Ed D); developmental education (MS, Ed D), including curriculum and instruction: reading (Ed D), English (MS), guidance and counseling (MS), higher education administration (Ed D), instructional systems and technology (Ed D), mathematics (MS), reading (MS), science (MS), student development and personnel services (Ed D); educational leadership (MS, Ed D). Part-time and evening/weekend programs available. *Degree requirements:* For master's, comprehensive exam, thesis (for some programs); for doctorate, comprehensive exam, thesis/dissertation. *Entrance requirements:* For master's, GRE, minimum GPA of 2.5 on last degree; for doctorate, GRE (minimum 1000, 500 on Verbal), master's degree, minimum GPA of 3.0 on last degree. Additional exam requirements/recommendations for international students: Required—TOEFL (minimum score 500 paper-based; 173 computer-based; 61 iBT). Electronic applications accepted. *Expenses:* Tuition, state resident: full-time $3546; part-time $192 per credit hour. Tuition, nonresident: full-time $3456; part-time $192 per credit hour. *Required fees:* $1829; $1829 per semester hour.

Hamline University, School of Education, St. Paul, MN 55104-1284. Offers education (MA Ed, Ed D); English as a second language (MA); literacy education (MA); natural science and environmental education (MA Ed); teaching (MAT). *Accreditation:* NCATE (one or more programs are accredited). Part-time and evening/weekend programs available. Postbaccalaureate distance learning degree programs offered (no on-campus study). *Faculty:* 33 full-time (24 women), 106 part-time/adjunct (77 women). *Students:* 319 full-time (221 women), 717 part-time (524 women); includes 88 minority (30 Black or African American, non-Hispanic/Latino; 2 American Indian or Alaska Native, non-Hispanic/Latino; 26 Asian, non-Hispanic/Latino; 27 Hispanic/Latino; 3 Two or more races, non-Hispanic/Latino), 21 international. Average age 32. 468 applicants, 76% accepted, 259 enrolled. In 2011, 197 master's, 10 doctorates awarded. *Degree requirements:* For master's, thesis, foreign language (for MA in English as a second language only); for doctorate, comprehensive exam, thesis/dissertation. *Entrance requirements:* For master's, written essay, official transcripts, 2 letters of recommendation, minimum GPA of 2.5 from bachelor's work; for doctorate, personal statement, master's degree, 3 years experience, 3 letters of recommendation, writing sample, interview. Additional exam requirements/recommendations for international students: Required—TOEFL (minimum score 625 paper-based; 107 computer-based; 75 iBT) or IELTS. *Application deadline:* Applications are processed on a rolling basis. Application fee: $0 ($100 for international students). Electronic applications accepted. *Expenses: Tuition:* Full-time $3720; part-time $465 per credit. *Required fees:* $28 per year. Tuition and fees vary according to degree level, campus/location and program. *Financial support:* Federal Work-Study and scholarships/grants available. Support available to part-time students. Financial award applicants required to submit FAFSA. *Faculty research:* Adult basic education, service-learning, teacher dispositions, diversity, technology. *Unit head:* Dr. Larry Harris, Interim Dean, 651-523-2600, Fax: 651-523-2489, E-mail: lharris02@gw.hamline.edu. *Application contact:* Michael Hand, Assistant Director, Graduate Admission, 651-523-2900, Fax: 651-523-3058, E-mail: mhand01@gw.hamline.edu. Web site: http://www.hamline.edu/education.

Hardin-Simmons University, Graduate School, Holland School of Sciences and Mathematics, Abilene, TX 79698-0001. Offers MS, DPT. Part-time programs available. *Faculty:* 5 full-time (0 women). *Students:* 4 full-time (2 women), 1 part-time (0 women). Average age 25. 4 applicants, 100% accepted, 4 enrolled. In 2011, 8 master's awarded. *Degree requirements:* For master's, comprehensive exam, thesis or alternative, internship; for doctorate, comprehensive exam, thesis/dissertation or alternative. *Entrance requirements:* For master's, minimum undergraduate GPA of 3.0 in major, 2.7 overall; 2 semesters of course work each in biology, chemistry and geology; interview; writing sample; occupational experience; for doctorate, letters of recommendation, interview, writing sample. Additional exam requirements/recommendations for international students: Required—TOEFL (minimum score 550 paper-based; 213 computer-based; 75 iBT). *Application deadline:* For fall admission, 8/15 priority date for domestic students, 4/1 for international students; for spring admission, 1/5 priority date for domestic students, 9/1 for international students. Applications are processed on a rolling basis. Application fee: $50. *Expenses: Tuition:* Full-time $12,870; part-time $715 per credit hour. *Required fees:* $650; $110 per semester. Tuition and fees vary according to degree level. *Financial support:* In 2011–12, 1 fellowship (averaging $300 per year) was awarded; career-related internships or fieldwork and scholarships/grants also available. Support available to part-time students. Financial award application deadline: 6/30; financial award applicants required to submit FAFSA. *Unit head:* Dr. Christopher McNair, Dean, 325-670-1401, Fax: 325-670-1385, E-mail: cmcnair@hsutx.edu. *Application contact:* Dr. Nancy Kucinski, Dean of Graduate Studies, 325-670-1298, Fax: 325-670-1564, E-mail: gradoff@hsutx.edu. Web site: http://www.hsutx.edu/academics/holland.

Harrison Middleton University, Graduate Program, Tempe, AZ 85282. Offers education (MA, Ed D); humanities (MA); imaginative literature (MA); interdisciplinary studies (DA); jurisprudence (MA); natural science (MA); philosophy and religion (MA); social science (MA). Part-time and evening/weekend programs available. Postbaccalaureate distance learning degree programs offered (no on-campus study). *Faculty:* 18 full-time (7 women), 14 part-time/adjunct (6 women). *Students:* 53 full-time (20 women). 4 applicants, 100% accepted, 4 enrolled. In 2011, 4 master's awarded. *Degree requirements:* For master's and doctorate, capstone project. *Entrance requirements:* For doctorate, 2 academic letters of reference, interview. Additional exam requirements/recommendations for international students: Required—TOEFL (minimum score 550 paper-based; 80 iBT). *Application deadline:* Applications are processed on a rolling basis. Application fee: $50. Electronic applications accepted. One-time fee: $400 full-time. Full-time tuition and fees vary according to course load and degree level. *Faculty research:* Japanese animation, educational leadership, war art, John Muir's wilderness. *Unit head:* Susan Chiaramonte, Director of Accreditation and Licensure, 877-248-6724, Fax: 800-762-1622, E-mail: schiaramonte@hmu.edu. *Application contact:* Dr. Deborah Deacon, Dean of Graduate Studies, 877-248-6724, Fax: 800-762-1622, E-mail: ddeacon@hmu.edu. Web site: http://www.hmu.edu.

Harvard University, Harvard Graduate School of Education, Master's Programs in Education, Cambridge, MA 02138. Offers arts in education (Ed M); education policy and management (Ed M); higher education (Ed M); human development and psychology (Ed M); international education policy (Ed M); language and literacy (Ed M); learning and teaching (Ed M); mid-career mathematics and science (teaching certificate) (Ed M); mind brain and education (Ed M); prevention science and practice (Ed M); school leadership (Ed M); special studies (Ed M); teaching and curriculum (teaching certificate) (Ed M); technology innovation and education (Ed M). Part-time programs available. *Faculty:* 83 full-time (44 women), 67 part-time/adjunct (29 women). *Students:* 592 full-time (431 women), 75 part-time (54 women); includes 194 minority (41 Black or African American, non-Hispanic/Latino; 4 American Indian or Alaska Native, non-Hispanic/Latino; 75 Asian, non-Hispanic/Latino; 45 Hispanic/Latino; 2 Native Hawaiian or other Pacific Islander, non-Hispanic/Latino; 27 Two or more races, non-Hispanic/Latino), 95 international. Average age 28. 1,679 applicants, 52% accepted, 627 enrolled. In 2011, 653 master's awarded. *Entrance requirements:* For master's, GRE General Test, statement of purpose, 3 letters of recommendation, resume, official transcripts. Additional exam requirements/recommendations for international students: Required—TOEFL (minimum score 613 paper-based; 104 computer-based; 100 iBT), TWE (minimum score 5). *Application deadline:* For fall admission, 1/4 for domestic and international students. Application fee: $85. Electronic applications accepted. *Expenses:* Contact institution. *Financial support:* In 2011–12, 419 students received support, including 14 fellowships with full and partial tuition reimbursements available (averaging $12,831 per year); career-related internships or fieldwork, Federal Work-Study, institutionally sponsored loans, scholarships/grants, health care benefits, tuition waivers (full and partial), and unspecified assistantships also available. Support available to part-time students. Financial award application deadline: 2/1; financial award applicants required to submit FAFSA. *Faculty research:* Learning and development, educational leadership and organizations, educational policy analysis. *Total annual research expenditures:* $26 million. *Unit head:* Jennifer L. Petrallia, Assistant Dean, 617-495-8445. *Application contact:* Information Contact, 617-495-3414, Fax: 617-496-3577, E-mail: gseadmissions@harvard.edu. Web site: http://www.gse.harvard.edu/.

Science Education

Heritage University, Graduate Programs in Education, Toppenish, WA 98948-9599. Offers counseling (M Ed); educational administration (M Ed); professional studies (M Ed), including bilingual education/ESL, biology, English and literature, reading/literacy, special education; teaching (MIT). Part-time and evening/weekend programs available. *Degree requirements:* For master's, comprehensive exam, thesis (for some programs). *Entrance requirements:* For master's, interview, letters of recommendation, teaching certificate. Additional exam requirements/recommendations for international students: Recommended—TOEFL (minimum score 550 paper-based; 213 computer-based).

Hofstra University, School of Education, Health, and Human Services, Program in Elementary Education, Hempstead, NY 11549. Offers early childhood and childhood education (MS Ed); early childhood education (MA, MS Ed); educational technology (MA); elementary education (MS Ed); literacy (MA); math specialist (Advanced Certificate); math, science, technology (MA); multiculturalism (MA). Part-time and evening/weekend programs available. Postbaccalaureate distance learning degree programs offered (minimal on-campus study). *Students:* 54 full-time (48 women), 43 part-time (37 women); includes 17 minority (10 Black or African American, non-Hispanic/Latino; 2 Asian, non-Hispanic/Latino; 5 Hispanic/Latino), 2 international. Average age 29. 65 applicants, 88% accepted, 18 enrolled. In 2011, 58 master's awarded. *Degree requirements:* For master's, comprehensive exam, thesis (for some programs), 35 semester hours (for MA); 38-41 semester hours (for MS Ed), minimum GPA of 3.0. *Entrance requirements:* For master's, 2 letters of recommendation, teacher certification (MA), interview, essay. Additional exam requirements/recommendations for international students: Required—TOEFL (minimum score 550 paper-based; 213 computer-based; 80 iBT). *Application deadline:* Applications are processed on a rolling basis. Application fee: $70 ($75 for international students). Electronic applications accepted. *Expenses: Tuition:* Full-time $18,990; part-time $1055 per credit hour. *Required fees:* $970. Tuition and fees vary according to program. *Financial support:* In 2011–12, 45 students received support, including 22 fellowships with full and partial tuition reimbursements available (averaging $2,560 per year), 2 research assistantships with full and partial tuition reimbursements available (averaging $21,993 per year); career-related internships or fieldwork, Federal Work-Study, institutionally sponsored loans, scholarships/grants, tuition waivers (full and partial), and unspecified assistantships also available. Support available to part-time students. Financial award applicants required to submit FAFSA. *Faculty research:* Dynamic-themes curriculum/complexity theory, joyful learning, teacher education, multicultural education, multiple authentic assessments. *Unit head:* Dr. Esther Fusco, Chairperson, 516-463-7704, Fax: 516-463-6196, E-mail: catezf@hofstra.edu. *Application contact:* Carol Drummer, Dean of Graduate Admissions, 516-463-4876, Fax: 516-463-4664, E-mail: gradstudent@hofstra.edu. Web site: http://www.hofstra.edu/education/.

Hofstra University, School of Education, Health, and Human Services, Programs in Teaching - Secondary Education, Hempstead, NY 11549. Offers business education (MS Ed); education technology (Advanced Certificate); English education (MA, MS Ed); foreign language and TESOL (MS Ed); foreign language education (MA, MS Ed), including French, German, Russian, Spanish; mathematics education (MA, MS Ed); science education (MA, MS Ed), including biology, chemistry, earth science, geology, physics; secondary education (Advanced Certificate); social studies education (MA, MS Ed). Part-time and evening/weekend programs available. Postbaccalaureate distance learning degree programs offered (minimal on-campus study). *Students:* 72 full-time (47 women), 51 part-time (30 women); includes 21 minority (9 Black or African American, non-Hispanic/Latino; 7 Asian, non-Hispanic/Latino; 5 Hispanic/Latino). Average age 28. 103 applicants, 91% accepted, 41 enrolled. In 2011, 86 master's, 6 other advanced degrees awarded. *Degree requirements:* For master's, one foreign language, comprehensive exam (for some programs), thesis (for some programs), exit project, electronic portfolio, student teaching, fieldwork, curriculum project, minimum GPA of 3.0; for Advanced Certificate, 3 foreign languages, comprehensive exam (for some programs), thesis project, minimum GPA of 3.0. *Entrance requirements:* For master's, 2 letters of recommendation, teacher certification (MA), essay; for Advanced Certificate, 2 letters of recommendation, essay. Additional exam requirements/recommendations for international students: Required—TOEFL (minimum score 550 paper-based; 213 computer-based; 80 iBT). *Application deadline:* Applications are processed on a rolling basis. Application fee: $70 ($75 for international students). Electronic applications accepted. *Expenses: Tuition:* Full-time $18,990; part-time $1055 per credit hour. *Required fees:* $970. Tuition and fees vary according to program. *Financial support:* In 2011–12, 90 students received support, including 13 fellowships with full and partial tuition reimbursements available (averaging $3,202 per year), 1 research assistantship with full and partial tuition reimbursement available (averaging $11,645 per year); career-related internships or fieldwork, Federal Work-Study, institutionally sponsored loans, scholarships/grants, tuition waivers (full and partial), and unspecified assistantships also available. Support available to part-time students. Financial award applicants required to submit FAFSA. *Faculty research:* Appropriate content and pedagogy in secondary school disciplines, appropriate pedagogy in secondary school disciplines, adolescent development, secondary school organization, alternative secondary school programs. *Unit head:* Dr. Esther Fusco, Chairperson, 516-463-7704, Fax: 516-463-6196, E-mail: catezf@hofstra.edu. *Application contact:* Carol Drummer, Dean of Graduate Admissions, 516-463-4876, Fax: 516-463-4664, E-mail: gradstudent@hofstra.edu. Web site: http://www.hofstra.edu/education/.

Hood College, Graduate School, Department of Education, Frederick, MD 21701-8575. Offers curriculum and instruction (MS), including early childhood education, elementary education, elementary school science and mathematics, secondary education, special education; educational leadership (MS, Certificate); reading specialization (MS). Part-time and evening/weekend programs available. *Degree requirements:* For master's, action research project, portfolio (reading). *Entrance requirements:* For master's, minimum GPA of 2.75, teaching certification. Additional exam requirements/recommendations for international students: Required—TOEFL (minimum score 575 paper-based; 231 computer-based; 89 iBT). Electronic applications accepted. *Faculty research:* Leadership, action research, brain research, learning styles.

Hunter College of the City University of New York, Graduate School, School of Arts and Sciences, Department of Geography, New York, NY 10021-5085. Offers analytical geography (MA); earth system science (MA); environmental and social issues (MA); geographic information science (Certificate); geographic information systems (MA); teaching earth science (MA). Part-time and evening/weekend programs available. *Faculty:* 7 full-time (3 women), 8 part-time/adjunct (1 woman). *Students:* 2 full-time (1 woman), 49 part-time (24 women); includes 11 minority (4 Black or African American, non-Hispanic/Latino; 4 Asian, non-Hispanic/Latino; 3 Hispanic/Latino), 1 international. Average age 35. 27 applicants, 74% accepted, 13 enrolled. In 2011, 12 master's, 3 other advanced degrees awarded. *Degree requirements:* For master's, comprehensive exam or thesis. *Entrance requirements:* For master's, GRE General Test, minimum B average in major, B- overall; 18 credits of course work in geography; 2 letters of recommendation; for Certificate, minimum B average in major, B- overall. Additional exam requirements/recommendations for international students: Required—TOEFL. *Application deadline:* For fall admission, 4/1 for domestic students; for spring admission, 11/1 for domestic students. Applications are processed on a rolling basis. Application fee: $125. *Expenses:* Tuition, state resident: full-time $8210; part-time $345 per credit. Tuition, nonresident: full-time $15,360; part-time $640 per credit. *Required fees:* $280 per semester. One-time fee: $125. Tuition and fees vary according to class time, campus/location and program. *Financial support:* In 2011–12, 1 fellowship (averaging $3,000 per year), 2 research assistantships (averaging $10,000 per year), 10 teaching assistantships (averaging $6,000 per year) were awarded; career-related internships or fieldwork, Federal Work-Study, institutionally sponsored loans, and unspecified assistantships also available. Financial award application deadline: 3/1. *Faculty research:* Urban geography, economic geography, geographic information science, demographic methods, climate change. *Unit head:* Prof. William Solecki, Chair, 212-772-4536, Fax: 212-772-5268, E-mail: wsolecki@hunter.cuny.edu. *Application contact:* Prof. Marianna Pavlovskaya, Graduate Adviser, 212-772-5320, Fax: 212-772-5268, E-mail: mpavlov@geo.hunter.cuny.edu. Web site: http://www.geo.hunter.cuny.edu/.

Hunter College of the City University of New York, Graduate School, School of Education, Programs in Secondary Education, Concentration in Biology Education, New York, NY 10021-5085. Offers MA. *Accreditation:* NCATE. *Faculty:* 10 full-time (7 women), 21 part-time/adjunct (17 women). *Students:* 3 full-time (1 woman), 14 part-time (8 women); includes 6 minority (2 Black or African American, non-Hispanic/Latino; 4 Asian, non-Hispanic/Latino). Average age 25. 24 applicants, 46% accepted, 6 enrolled. In 2011, 5 master's awarded. *Degree requirements:* For master's, thesis, professional teaching portfolio, New York State Teacher Certification Exams, research project. *Entrance requirements:* For master's, minimum GPA of 2.8, 2 letters of reference, 21 credits of course work in biology. Additional exam requirements/recommendations for international students: Required—TOEFL, TWE. *Application deadline:* For fall admission, 4/1 for domestic students, 2/1 for international students; for spring admission, 11/1 for domestic students, 9/1 for international students. Application fee: $125. *Expenses:* Tuition, state resident: full-time $8210; part-time $345 per credit. Tuition, nonresident: full-time $15,360; part-time $640 per credit. *Required fees:* $280 per semester. One-time fee: $125. Tuition and fees vary according to class time, campus/location and program. *Financial support:* Federal Work-Study and tuition waivers (partial) available. Support available to part-time students. *Unit head:* Dr. Steve Demeo, Program Advisor, 212-772-4776, E-mail: sdemeo@hunter.cuny.edu. *Application contact:* William Zlata, Director for Graduate Admissions, 212-772-4482, Fax: 212-650-3336, E-mail: admissions@hunter.cuny.edu. Web site: http://www.hunter.cuny.edu/school-of-education/programs/graduate/adolescent/science/biology.

Hunter College of the City University of New York, Graduate School, School of Education, Programs in Secondary Education, Concentration in Chemistry Education, New York, NY 10021-5085. Offers MA. *Accreditation:* NCATE. *Faculty:* 10 full-time (7 women), 21 part-time/adjunct (17 women). *Students:* 7 part-time (5 women); includes 5 minority (all Asian, non-Hispanic/Latino). Average age 26. 9 applicants, 67% accepted, 2 enrolled. In 2011, 4 master's awarded. *Degree requirements:* For master's, thesis, professional teaching portfolio, New York State Teacher Certification Exam. *Entrance requirements:* For master's, minimum GPA of 2.8, 2 letters of reference, minimum of 29 credits in science and mathematics. *Application deadline:* For fall admission, 4/1 for domestic students, 2/1 for international students; for spring admission, 11/1 for domestic students, 9/1 for international students. Application fee: $125. *Expenses:* Tuition, state resident: full-time $8210; part-time $345 per credit. Tuition, nonresident: full-time $15,360; part-time $640 per credit. *Required fees:* $280 per semester. One-time fee: $125. Tuition and fees vary according to class time, campus/location and program. *Financial support:* Federal Work-Study and tuition waivers (partial) available. Support available to part-time students. *Unit head:* Dr. Stephen DeMeo, Education Advisor, 212-772-4776, E-mail: sdemeo@patsy.hunter.cuny.edu. *Application contact:* Pamela Mills, Chemistry Department Advisor, 212-772-5331, E-mail: pam.mills@hunter.cuny.edu. Web site: http://www.hunter.cuny.edu/school-of-education/programs/graduate/adolescent/science/chemistry.

ICR Graduate School, Graduate Programs, Santee, CA 92071. Offers astro/geophysics (MS); biology (MS); geology (MS); science education (MS). Part-time programs available. *Degree requirements:* For master's, comprehensive exam (for some programs), thesis (for some programs). *Entrance requirements:* For master's, minimum undergraduate GPA of 3.0, bachelor's degree in science or science education. *Faculty research:* Age of the earth, limits of variation, catastrophe, optimum methods for teaching.

Illinois Institute of Technology, Graduate College, College of Science and Letters, Department of Mathematics and Science Education, Chicago, IL 60616-3793. Offers collegiate mathematics education (PhD); mathematics education (MME, MS, PhD); science education (MS, MSE, PhD). *Degree requirements:* For master's, comprehensive exam (for some programs), thesis optional; for doctorate, comprehensive exam, thesis/dissertation. *Entrance requirements:* For master's, GRE General Test, minimum undergraduate GPA of 3.0; for doctorate, GRE General Test, minimum GPA of 3.0, 3 years of teaching experience. Additional exam requirements/recommendations for international students: Required—TOEFL (minimum score 523 paper-based; 70 iBT). Electronic applications accepted. *Faculty research:* Informal science/math education, curriculum development, integration of science/math disciplines and across disciplines, instructional methods, students' and teachers' conceptions of scientific/mathematical inquiry and the nature of science/math.

Indiana State University, College of Graduate and Professional Studies, College of Arts and Sciences, Department of Biology, Terre Haute, IN 47809. Offers ecology (PhD); life sciences (MS); microbiology (PhD); physiology (PhD); science education (MS). *Degree requirements:* For master's, thesis (for some programs); for doctorate, comprehensive exam, thesis/dissertation. *Entrance requirements:* For master's and doctorate, GRE General Test. Electronic applications accepted.

Indiana State University, College of Graduate and Professional Studies, College of Arts and Sciences, Department of Science Education, Terre Haute, IN 47809. Offers MS. *Accreditation:* NCATE. *Degree requirements:* For master's, thesis optional. Electronic applications accepted.

Indiana Tech, Program in Science, Fort Wayne, IN 46803-1297. Offers MSE. Part-time and evening/weekend programs available. *Entrance requirements:* For master's, undergraduate transcript from accredited university with minimum GPA of 2.5, 3 letters of recommendation. Electronic applications accepted.

Indiana University Bloomington, School of Education, Department of Curriculum and Instruction, Bloomington, IN 47405-7000. Offers art education (MS, Ed D, PhD); curriculum studies (Ed D, PhD); elementary education (MS, Ed D, PhD, Ed S); mathematics education (MS, Ed D, PhD); science education (MS, Ed D, PhD); secondary education (MS, Ed D, PhD); social studies education (MS, PhD); special education (PhD, Ed S). *Accreditation:* NCATE. Part-time and evening/weekend programs available. Terminal master's awarded for partial completion of doctoral program. *Degree requirements:* For doctorate, thesis/dissertation; for Ed S, comprehensive exam or project. *Entrance requirements:* For master's, doctorate, and Ed S, GRE General Test. Electronic applications accepted.

Indiana University Bloomington, University Graduate School, College of Arts and Sciences, Department of Biology, Bloomington, IN 47405. Offers biology teaching (MAT); biotechnology (MA); evolution, ecology, and behavior (MA, PhD); genetics

(PhD); microbiology (MA, PhD); molecular, cellular, and developmental biology (PhD); plant sciences (MA, PhD); zoology (MA, PhD). *Faculty:* 58 full-time (15 women), 21 part-time/adjunct (6 women). *Students:* 175 full-time (100 women), 3 part-time (all women); includes 20 minority (5 Black or African American, non-Hispanic/Latino; 8 Asian, non-Hispanic/Latino; 7 Hispanic/Latino), 55 international. Average age 27. 316 applicants, 22% accepted, 31 enrolled. In 2011, 8 master's, 20 doctorates awarded. Terminal master's awarded for partial completion of doctoral program. *Degree requirements:* For master's, thesis, oral defense; for doctorate, thesis/dissertation, oral defense. *Entrance requirements:* For master's and doctorate, GRE General Test. Additional exam requirements/recommendations for international students: Required—TOEFL (minimum score 100 iBT). *Application deadline:* For fall admission, 1/5 priority date for domestic students, 12/1 for international students. Application fee: $55 ($65 for international students). Electronic applications accepted. *Financial support:* In 2011–12, fellowships with tuition reimbursements (averaging $19,484 per year), research assistantships with tuition reimbursements (averaging $20,300 per year), teaching assistantships with tuition reimbursements (averaging $20,521 per year) were awarded; scholarships/grants, traineeships, health care benefits, and unspecified assistantships also available. Financial award application deadline: 1/5. *Faculty research:* Evolution, ecology and behavior; microbiology; molecular biology and genetics; plant biology. *Unit head:* Dr. Roger Innes, Chair, 812-855-2219, Fax: 812-855-6082, E-mail: rinnes@indiana.edu. *Application contact:* Tracey D. Stohr, Graduate Student Recruitment Coordinator, 812-856-6303, Fax: 812-855-6082, E-mail: gradbio@indiana.edu. Web site: http://www.bio.indiana.edu/.

Indiana University Bloomington, University Graduate School, College of Arts and Sciences, Department of Chemistry, Bloomington, IN 47405. Offers analytical chemistry (PhD); chemical biology chemistry (PhD); chemistry (MAT); inorganic chemistry (PhD); materials chemistry (PhD); organic chemistry (PhD); physical chemistry (PhD). *Faculty:* 42 full-time (4 women). *Students:* 200 full-time (82 women), 3 part-time (0 women); includes 18 minority (7 Black or African American, non-Hispanic/Latino; 8 Asian, non-Hispanic/Latino; 1 Hispanic/Latino; 1 Native Hawaiian or other Pacific Islander, non-Hispanic/Latino; 1 Two or more races, non-Hispanic/Latino), 63 international. Average age 27. 290 applicants, 49% accepted, 46 enrolled. In 2011, 11 master's, 20 doctorates awarded. Terminal master's awarded for partial completion of doctoral program. *Median time to degree:* Of those who began their doctoral program in fall 2003, 49% received their degree in 8 years or less. *Degree requirements:* For master's, thesis; for doctorate, thesis/dissertation. *Entrance requirements:* For master's and doctorate, GRE General Test, GRE Subject Test. Additional exam requirements/recommendations for international students: Required—TOEFL. *Application deadline:* For fall admission, 1/15 priority date for domestic students, 12/15 for international students. Applications are processed on a rolling basis. Application fee: $55 ($65 for international students). *Financial support:* In 2011–12, 200 students received support, including 10 fellowships with full tuition reimbursements available, 76 research assistantships with full tuition reimbursements available, 111 teaching assistantships with full tuition reimbursements available; Federal Work-Study and institutionally sponsored loans also available. *Faculty research:* Synthesis of complex natural products, organic reaction mechanisms, organic electrochemistry, transitive-metal chemistry, solid-state and surface chemistry. *Total annual research expenditures:* $7.7 million. *Unit head:* David Giedroc, Chairperson, 812-855-6239, E-mail: chemchair@indiana.edu. *Application contact:* Daniel Mindiola, Director of Graduate Admissions, 812-855-2069, Fax: 812-855-8385, E-mail: mindiola@indiana.edu. Web site: http://www.chem.indiana.edu/.

Instituto Tecnológico y de Estudios Superiores de Monterrey, Campus Monterrey, Graduate and Research Division, Program in Natural and Social Sciences, Monterrey, Mexico. Offers biotechnology (MS); chemistry (MS, PhD); communications (MS); education (MA). Part-time programs available. *Degree requirements:* For master's, one foreign language, thesis; for doctorate, one foreign language, thesis/dissertation. *Entrance requirements:* For master's, EXADEP; for doctorate, EXADEP, master's degree in related field. Additional exam requirements/recommendations for international students: Required—TOEFL. *Faculty research:* Cultural industries, mineral substances, bioremediation, food processing, CQ in industrial chemical processing.

Inter American University of Puerto Rico, Arecibo Campus, Programs in Education, Arecibo, PR 00614-4050. Offers administration and educational supervision (MA Ed); counseling and guidance (MA Ed); curriculum and teaching (MA Ed), including biology education, English as a second language, history education, math education, Spanish; elementary education (MA Ed). *Degree requirements:* For master's, comprehensive exam, thesis optional. *Entrance requirements:* For master's, GRE, EXADEP, bachelor's degree in education or teaching license (administration and supervision) or courses in education and psychology (counseling and guidance), minimum GPA of 2.5 in last 60 credits.

Inter American University of Puerto Rico, Barranquitas Campus, Program in Education, Barranquitas, PR 00794. Offers curriculum and teaching (M Ed), including biology education, English as a second language, history education, mathematics education, Spanish; educational leadership and management (MA); elementary education (M Ed); information and library service technology (M Ed); special education (MA). *Degree requirements:* For master's, comprehensive exam, thesis optional. *Entrance requirements:* For master's, EXADEP, letter of recommendation. Electronic applications accepted.

Inter American University of Puerto Rico, Metropolitan Campus, Graduate Programs, Program in Teaching of Science, San Juan, PR 00919-1293. Offers MA. *Degree requirements:* For master's, comprehensive exam. *Entrance requirements:* For master's, GRE or EXADEP, interview. Electronic applications accepted.

Inter American University of Puerto Rico, Ponce Campus, Graduate School, Mercedita, PR 00715-1602. Offers accounting (MBA); biology (M Ed); chemistry (M Ed); criminal justice (MA); elementary education (M Ed); English as a Second Language (M Ed); finance (MBA); history (M Ed); human resources (MBA); marketing (MBA); mathematics (M Ed); Spanish (M Ed). *Entrance requirements:* For master's, minimum GPA of 2.5.

Inter American University of Puerto Rico, San Germán Campus, Graduate Studies Center, Program in Science Education, San Germán, PR 00683-5008. Offers MA. Part-time and evening/weekend programs available. *Degree requirements:* For master's, comprehensive exam. *Entrance requirements:* For master's, GRE General Test or EXADEP, minimum GPA of 3.0. *Application deadline:* For fall admission, 4/30 priority date for domestic students; for spring admission, 11/15 for domestic students. Applications are processed on a rolling basis. Application fee: $31. *Expenses: Required fees:* $213 per semester. *Financial support:* Teaching assistantships and unspecified assistantships available. *Unit head:* Dr. Elba T. Irizarry, Director of Graduate Studies Center, 787-264-1912 Ext. 7357, Fax: 787-892-6350, E-mail: elbat@sg.inter.edu.

Iona College, School of Arts and Science, Program in Education, New Rochelle, NY 10801-1890. Offers adolescence education: biology (MS Ed, MST); adolescence education: English (MS Ed, MST); adolescence education: Italian (MS Ed, MST); adolescence education: mathematics (MS Ed, MST); adolescence education: social studies (MS Ed, MST); adolescence education: Spanish (MS Ed, MST); adolescence special education 5-12 (MST); adolescence special education/literacy 5-12 (MS Ed); childhood 1-6/special education 1-6 (MST); childhood education (MST); early childhood/childhood (MST); educational leadership (MS Ed); literacy birth-grade 6/special education 1-6 (MS Ed); literacy education: birth-grade 6 (MS Ed). *Accreditation:* NCATE. Part-time and evening/weekend programs available. *Faculty:* 21 full-time (13 women), 13 part-time/adjunct (8 women). *Students:* 59 full-time (45 women), 101 part-time (78 women); includes 11 minority (2 Black or African American, non-Hispanic/Latino; 2 Asian, non-Hispanic/Latino; 7 Hispanic/Latino). Average age 26. 74 applicants, 66% accepted, 35 enrolled. In 2011, 46 master's awarded. *Degree requirements:* For master's, thesis or alternative. *Entrance requirements:* For master's, minimum GPA of 2.5 (MST), New York teaching certificate (MS Ed). Additional exam requirements/recommendations for international students: Required—TOEFL (minimum score 550 paper-based; 213 computer-based). *Application deadline:* Applications are processed on a rolling basis. Application fee: $50. Electronic applications accepted. *Expenses: Tuition:* Part-time $872 per credit. *Required fees:* $225 per term. *Financial support:* Unspecified assistantships available. Support available to part-time students. Financial award application deadline: 4/15; financial award applicants required to submit FAFSA. *Faculty research:* Reading/writing, educational technology, administration, early literacy assessment, literacy development. *Unit head:* Dr. Catherine O'Callaghan, Chair, 914-633-2210, Fax: 914-633-2608, E-mail: cocallaghan@iona.edu. *Application contact:* Dr. Jeanne Zaino, Interim Dean, School of Arts and Science, 914-633-2112, Fax: 914-633-2023, E-mail: jzaino@iona.edu.

Iowa State University of Science and Technology, Program in Science Education, Ames, IA 50011. Offers MAT. *Entrance requirements:* For master's, GRE, three letters of recommendation, undergraduate degree in sciences (preferred). Additional exam requirements/recommendations for international students: Required—TOEFL (minimum score 560 paper-based; 83 iBT), IELTS (minimum score 6.5). *Application deadline:* For fall admission, 2/1 for domestic students. Electronic applications accepted. *Unit head:* Anne Foegen, Director of Graduate Education, 515-294-7021, Fax: 515-294-6206, E-mail: cigrad@iastate.edu. *Application contact:* Phyllis Kendall, Application Contact, 515-294-7021, Fax: 515-294-6206, E-mail: grad_admissions@iastate.edu. Web site: http://www.admissions.iastate.edu/apply/index.php.

Ithaca College, Division of Graduate and Professional Studies, School of Humanities and Sciences, Program in Adolescence Education, Ithaca, NY 14850. Offers biology 7-12 (MAT); chemistry 7-12 (MAT); English 7-12 (MAT); French 7-12 (MAT); math 7-12 (MAT); physics 7-12 (MAT); social studies 7-12 (MAT); Spanish (MAT). Part-time programs available. *Faculty:* 23 full-time (7 women). *Students:* 14 full-time (8 women), 1 part-time (0 women); includes 4 minority (1 Asian, non-Hispanic/Latino; 2 Hispanic/Latino; 1 Two or more races, non-Hispanic/Latino). Average age 27. 33 applicants, 64% accepted, 15 enrolled. In 2011, 15 master's awarded. *Degree requirements:* For master's, thesis or alternative, student teaching. *Entrance requirements:* For master's, minimum GPA of 3.0. Additional exam requirements/recommendations for international students: Required—TOEFL (minimum score 550 paper-based; 213 computer-based; 80 iBT). *Application deadline:* For fall admission, 2/15 priority date for domestic students, 2/15 for international students; for spring admission, 12/1 for domestic and international students. Applications are processed on a rolling basis. Application fee: $40. Electronic applications accepted. *Expenses:* Contact institution. *Financial support:* In 2011–12, 9 students received support, including 9 teaching assistantships (averaging $6,070 per year); career-related internships or fieldwork, Federal Work-Study, scholarships/grants, and unspecified assistantships also available. Support available to part-time students. Financial award application deadline: 2/15; financial award applicants required to submit CSS PROFILE or FAFSA. *Faculty research:* Bilingual education, socio-linguistic perspective on literacy. *Unit head:* Dr. Linda Hanrahan, Chairperson, 607-274-3143, Fax: 607-274-1263, E-mail: gps@ithaca.edu. *Application contact:* Gerard Turbide, Director, Office of Admission, 607-274-3143, Fax: 607-274-1263, E-mail: gps@ithaca.edu. Web site: http://www.ithaca.edu/gps/gradprograms/overview/school/hs/aded.

Jackson State University, Graduate School, College of Science, Engineering and Technology, Department of Physics, Atmospheric Sciences, and General Science, Jackson, MS 39217. Offers science and mathematics teaching (MST). Part-time and evening/weekend programs available. *Degree requirements:* For master's, comprehensive exam. *Entrance requirements:* For master's, GRE General Test. Additional exam requirements/recommendations for international students: Required—TOEFL (minimum score 520 paper-based; 195 computer-based; 67 iBT).

John Carroll University, Graduate School, Program in Integrated Science, University Heights, OH 44118-4581. Offers MA. Part-time programs available. *Degree requirements:* For master's, thesis optional. *Entrance requirements:* For master's, minimum GPA of 2.5, teachers license. Electronic applications accepted.

The Johns Hopkins University, School of Education, Department of Interdisciplinary Studies in Education, Baltimore, MD 21218. Offers earth/space science (Certificate); education (MS), including educational studies; health care education (MEHP); mind, brain, and teaching (Certificate); teaching the adult learner (Certificate); urban education (Certificate). Part-time and evening/weekend programs available. Postbaccalaureate distance learning degree programs offered (minimal on-campus study). *Degree requirements:* For master's, capstone course. *Entrance requirements:* For master's and Certificate, minimum undergraduate GPA of 3.0. Additional exam requirements/recommendations for international students: Required—TOEFL (minimum score 600 paper-based; 250 computer-based; 100 iBT). Electronic applications accepted. *Faculty research:* Neuro-education, urban school reform, leadership development, teacher leadership, charter schools, techniques for teaching reading to adolescents with delayed reading skills, school culture.

The Johns Hopkins University, School of Education, Department of Teacher Preparation, Baltimore, MD 21218. Offers early childhood education (MAT); education (MS), including educational studies; elementary education (MAT); English for speakers of other languages (MAT); K-8 mathematics lead-teacher (Certificate); K-8 science lead-teacher (Certificate); secondary education (MAT), including biology, chemistry, earth/space/environmental science, English, French, mathematics, physics, social studies, Spanish. Part-time and evening/weekend programs available. *Degree requirements:* For master's, portfolio, PRAXIS II, internship. *Entrance requirements:* For master's, PRAXIS I, SAT, ACT, or GRE (MAT), minimum undergraduate GPA of 3.0, interview, 1 letter of recommendation, curriculum vitae/resume; for Certificate, bachelor's degree, minimum undergraduate GPA of 3.0, essay/statement of goals, interview. Additional exam requirements/recommendations for international students: Required—TOEFL (minimum score 600 paper-based; 250 computer-based; 100 iBT). Electronic applications accepted. *Faculty research:* Teacher retention, STEM education reform, alternative certification programs, school-university partnerships, urban education, action research/data-informed instruction, family engagement.

Johnson State College, Graduate Program in Education, Program in Science Education, Johnson, VT 05656. Offers MA Ed. *Expenses: Tuition, area resident:* Part-time $459 per credit hour. Tuition, nonresident: part-time $990 per credit hour. *Financial support:* Federal Work-Study and unspecified assistantships available. Support available to part-time students. Financial award application deadline: 3/1; financial award applicants required to submit FAFSA. *Unit head:* Dr. Elizabeth Dolci, Chair, 802-635-1482, E-mail: elizabeth.dolci@jsc.edu. *Application contact:* Catherine H. Higley,

Administrative Assistant, 800-635-2356 Ext. 1244, Fax: 802-635-1248, E-mail: catherine.higley@jsc.edu.

Kansas State University, Graduate School, College of Education, Department of Curriculum and Instruction, Manhattan, KS 66506. Offers career and technical education (Ed D, PhD); curriculum studies (Ed D, PhD); digital teaching and learning (MS); educational computing, design and online learning (MS); educational technology (Ed D, PhD); elementary/middle level (MS); English as a second language (MS); language/ diversity education (Ed D, PhD); literacy education (Ed D, PhD); mathematics education (Ed D, PhD); middle level/secondary (MS); reading and language arts (MS); reading specialist endorsement (MS); science education (Ed D, PhD); social science education (Ed D, PhD); teacher education (Ed D, PhD); teacher leader/school improvement (MS, Ed D). *Accreditation:* NCATE. Part-time programs available. Postbaccalaureate distance learning degree programs offered (minimal on-campus study). *Faculty:* 15 full-time (12 women), 3 part-time/adjunct (2 women). *Students:* 37 full-time (30 women), 113 part-time (91 women); includes 14 minority (4 Black or African American, non-Hispanic/ Latino; 1 American Indian or Alaska Native, non-Hispanic/Latino; 1 Asian, non-Hispanic/ Latino; 7 Hispanic/Latino; 1 Two or more races, non-Hispanic/Latino), 15 international. Average age 37. 75 applicants, 51% accepted, 9 enrolled. In 2011, 48 master's, 14 doctorates awarded. *Degree requirements:* For master's, comprehensive exam, portfolio, project, report or thesis; for doctorate, comprehensive exam, thesis/ dissertation, preliminary exam. *Entrance requirements:* For master's, minimum GPA of 3.0; for doctorate, GRE, minimum GPA of 3.0. Additional exam requirements/ recommendations for international students: Required—TOEFL. *Application deadline:* For fall admission, 2/1 priority date for domestic students, 2/1 for international students; for spring admission, 8/1 priority date for domestic students, 8/1 for international students. Applications are processed on a rolling basis. Application fee: $40 ($55 for international students). Electronic applications accepted. *Financial support:* In 2011–12, 1 research assistantship (averaging $16,900 per year), 8 teaching assistantships (averaging $12,466 per year) were awarded; career-related internships or fieldwork, institutionally sponsored loans, and scholarships/grants also available. Support available to part-time students. Financial award application deadline: 3/1; financial award applicants required to submit FAFSA. *Faculty research:* Literacy and technology, critical race theory and diversity, achievement gaps, school improvement, teacher education. *Total annual research expenditures:* $510,907. *Unit head:* Dr. Gail Shroyer, Chair, 785-532-5550, Fax: 785-532-7304, E-mail: gshroyer@ksu.edu. *Application contact:* Dona Deam, Application Contact, 785-532-5595, Fax: 785-532-7304, E-mail: ddeam@ksu.edu. Web site: http://coe.k-state.edu/departments/currin/curringrad.htm.

Kaplan University, Davenport Campus, School of Teacher Education, Davenport, IA 52807-2095. Offers education (M Ed); secondary education (M Ed); teaching and learning (MA); teaching literacy and language: grades 6-12 (MA); teaching literacy and language: grades K-6 (MA); teaching mathematics: grades 6-8 (MA); teaching mathematics: grades 9-12 (MA); teaching mathematics: grades K-5 (MA); teaching science: grades 6-12 (MA); teaching science: grades K-6 (MA); teaching students with special needs (MA); teaching with technology (MA). Part-time and evening/weekend programs available. Postbaccalaureate distance learning degree programs offered (no on-campus study). *Entrance requirements:* Additional exam requirements/ recommendations for international students: Required—TOEFL (minimum score 550 paper-based; 218 computer-based; 80 iBT).

Kean University, College of Education, Program in Instruction and Curriculum, Union, NJ 07083. Offers bilingual (MA); classroom instruction (MA); mathematics/science/ computer education (MA); teaching (MA); teaching English as a second language (MA); teaching physics (MA); world languages (Spanish) (MA). *Accreditation:* NCATE. *Faculty:* 22 full-time (12 women). *Students:* 56 full-time (33 women), 139 part-time (103 women); includes 87 minority (27 Black or African American, non-Hispanic/Latino; 8 Asian, non-Hispanic/Latino; 52 Hispanic/Latino), 1 international. Average age 34. 85 applicants, 100% accepted, 72 enrolled. In 2011, 78 master's awarded. *Degree requirements:* For master's, comprehensive exam, two-semester advanced seminar. *Entrance requirements:* For master's, GRE General Test or MAT, PRAXIS, minimum GPA of 3.0, 2 letters of recommendation, interview, teacher certification (for some programs), transcripts, resume. Additional exam requirements/recommendations for international students: Required—TOEFL (minimum score 79 iBT). *Application deadline:* For fall admission, 6/1 for domestic and international students; for spring admission, 12/1 for domestic and international students. Applications are processed on a rolling basis. Application fee: $75 ($150 for international students). Electronic applications accepted. *Expenses:* Tuition, state resident: full-time $11,302; part-time $550 per credit. Tuition, nonresident: full-time $15,318; part-time $674 per credit. *Required fees:* $2849; $130 per credit. Tuition and fees vary according to degree level. *Financial support:* In 2011–12, 3 research assistantships with full tuition reimbursements (averaging $3,263 per year) were awarded; unspecified assistantships also available. Financial award applicants required to submit FAFSA. *Unit head:* Dr. Thomas Walsh, Program Coordinator, 908-737-4003, E-mail: tpwalsh@kean.edu. *Application contact:* Ann-Marie Kay, Assistant Director for Graduate Admissions, 908-737-5922, Fax: 908-737-5925, E-mail: akay@kean.edu. Web site: http://www.kean.edu/KU/Bilingual-Bicultural-Education-Instruction-and-Curriculum.

Kennesaw State University, Leland and Clarice C. Bagwell College of Education, Program in Teaching, Kennesaw, GA 30144-5591. Offers art education (MAT); secondary English or mathematics (MAT); secondary science education (MAT); teaching English to speakers of other languages (MAT). Program offered only in summer. Part-time and evening/weekend programs available. *Students:* 101 full-time (68 women), 20 part-time (15 women); includes 27 minority (14 Black or African American, non-Hispanic/Latino; 6 Asian, non-Hispanic/Latino; 4 Hispanic/Latino; 3 Two or more races, non-Hispanic/Latino), 3 international. Average age 33. 13 applicants, 62% accepted, 7 enrolled. In 2011, 81 master's awarded. *Entrance requirements:* For master's, GRE, GACE I (state certificate exam), minimum GPA of 2.75, 2 recommendations, resume. Additional exam requirements/recommendations for international students: Required—TOEFL (minimum score 550 paper-based; 213 computer-based; 80 iBT), IELTS (minimum score 6). *Application deadline:* For fall admission, 6/1 for domestic and international students; for spring admission, 3/1 for domestic and international students. Application fee: $60. Electronic applications accepted. *Expenses:* Tuition, state resident: full-time $3000; part-time $250 per semester hour. Tuition, nonresident: full-time $10,836; part-time $903 per semester hour. *Required fees:* $774 per semester. *Financial support:* In 2011–12, 2 research assistantships with tuition reimbursements (averaging $4,000 per year) were awarded; unspecified assistantships also available. Financial award application deadline: 4/1; financial award applicants required to submit FAFSA. *Unit head:* Dr. Lynn Stallings, Director, 770-420-4477, E-mail: lstalling@kennesaw.edu. *Application contact:* Alisha Bello, Administrative Coordinator, 770-423-6043, Fax: 770-420-4435, E-mail: abello1@ kennesaw.edu. Web site: http://www.kennesaw.edu.

Kutztown University of Pennsylvania, College of Education, Program in Secondary Education, Kutztown, PA 19530-0730. Offers biology (M Ed); curriculum and instruction (M Ed); English (M Ed); mathematics (M Ed); social studies (M Ed). *Accreditation:* NCATE. Part-time and evening/weekend programs available. *Faculty:* 7 full-time (2 women). *Students:* 29 full-time (12 women), 73 part-time (43 women); includes 3 minority (1 Black or African American, non-Hispanic/Latino; 1 Asian, non-Hispanic/ Latino; 1 Hispanic/Latino). Average age 28. 12 applicants, 100% accepted, 12 enrolled. In 2011, 29 master's awarded. *Degree requirements:* For master's, comprehensive exam, thesis optional. *Entrance requirements:* For master's, GRE General Test. Additional exam requirements/recommendations for international students: Required—TOEFL (minimum score 550 paper-based; 79 iBT). *Application deadline:* For fall admission, 8/1 priority date for domestic students, 8/1 for international students; for spring admission, 12/1 priority date for domestic students, 12/1 for international students. Applications are processed on a rolling basis. Application fee: $35. Electronic applications accepted. *Expenses:* Tuition, state resident: full-time $7488; part-time $416 per credit. Tuition, nonresident: full-time $11,232; part-time $624 per credit. *Financial support:* Career-related internships or fieldwork, Federal Work-Study, scholarships/ grants, and unspecified assistantships available. Financial award application deadline: 3/1; financial award applicants required to submit FAFSA. *Unit head:* Dr. Theresa Stahler, Chairperson, 610-683-4259, Fax: 610-683-1338, E-mail: stahler@ kutztown.edu. *Application contact:* Kelly D. Burr, Associate Director, Graduate Admissions, 610-683-4200, Fax: 610-683-1393, E-mail: graduate@kutztown.edu.

Laurentian University, School of Graduate Studies and Research, Programme in Science Communication, Sudbury, ON P3E 2C6, Canada. Offers G Dip.

Lawrence Technological University, College of Arts and Sciences, Southfield, MI 48075-1058. Offers computer science (MS); educational technology (MS); educational technology - training and performance (MA); integrated science (MSE); science education (MSE); technical and professional communication (MS). Part-time and evening/weekend programs available. *Faculty:* 9 full-time (5 women), 16 part-time/ adjunct (8 women). *Students:* 5 full-time (1 woman), 79 part-time (48 women); includes 30 minority (18 Black or African American, non-Hispanic/Latino; 8 Asian, non-Hispanic/ Latino; 1 Hispanic/Latino; 3 Two or more races, non-Hispanic/Latino), 6 international. Average age 37. 382 applicants, 66% accepted, 17 enrolled. In 2011, 32 master's awarded. *Degree requirements:* For master's, thesis (for some programs). *Entrance requirements:* For master's, GRE. Additional exam requirements/recommendations for international students: Required—TOEFL (minimum score 550 paper-based; 213 computer-based; 79 iBT). *Application deadline:* For fall admission, 6/27 priority date for domestic students, 5/23 for international students; for spring admission, 11/15 priority date for domestic students, 11/15 for international students. Applications are processed on a rolling basis. Application fee: $50. Electronic applications accepted. *Financial support:* In 2011–12, 25 students received support, including 3 research assistantships (averaging $18,480 per year); Federal Work-Study also available. Financial award application deadline: 4/1; financial award applicants required to submit FAFSA. *Unit head:* Dr. Hsiao-Ping Moore, Dean, 248-204-3500, Fax: 248-204-3518, E-mail: scidean@ltu.edu. *Application contact:* Jane Rohrback, Director of Admissions, 248-204-3160, Fax: 248-204-2228, E-mail: admissions@ltu.edu. Web site: http://www.ltu.edu/ arts_sciences/graduate.asp.

Lebanon Valley College, Program in Science Education, Annville, PA 17003-1400. Offers MSE. Part-time and evening/weekend programs available. *Faculty:* 2 full-time (0 women), 15 part-time/adjunct (6 women). *Students:* 34 part-time (23 women). Average age 36. In 2011, 15 master's awarded. *Degree requirements:* For master's, thesis. *Entrance requirements:* For master's, minimum GPA of 3.0, teacher certification. *Application deadline:* Applications are processed on a rolling basis. Application fee: $30. *Expenses: Tuition:* Full-time $35,720; part-time $465 per credit. *Required fees:* $610. Part-time tuition and fees vary according to program. *Financial support:* Application deadline: 5/1; applicants required to submit FAFSA. *Unit head:* Patricia Woods, Coordinator, 717-867-6190, Fax: 717-867-6018, E-mail: woods@lvc.edu. *Application contact:* Hope Witmer, Assistant Dean, Graduate Studies and Continuing Education, 717-867-6213, Fax: 717-867-6018, E-mail: witmer@lvc.edu. Web site: http:// www.lvc.edu/mse/.

Lehman College of the City University of New York, Division of Education, Department of Middle and High School Education, Program in Science Education, Bronx, NY 10468-1589. Offers MS Ed. *Accreditation:* NCATE.

Lesley University, School of Education, Cambridge, MA 02138-2790. Offers curriculum and instruction (M Ed, CAGS); early childhood education (M Ed); educational studies (PhD); elementary education (M Ed); individually designed (M Ed); middle school education (M Ed); moderate special needs (M Ed); reading (M Ed, CAGS); science in education (M Ed); severe special needs (M Ed); special needs (CAGS); technology in education (M Ed, CAGS). *Accreditation:* Teacher Education Accreditation Council. Part-time and evening/weekend programs available. Postbaccalaureate distance learning degree programs offered (no on-campus study). *Faculty:* 36 full-time (27 women), 170 part-time/adjunct (129 women). *Students:* 552 full-time (437 women), 1,971 part-time (1,697 women); includes 364 minority (189 Black or African American, non-Hispanic/ Latino; 19 American Indian or Alaska Native, non-Hispanic/Latino; 45 Asian, non-Hispanic/Latino; 83 Hispanic/Latino; 2 Native Hawaiian or other Pacific Islander, non-Hispanic/Latino; 26 Two or more races, non-Hispanic/Latino), 28 international. Average age 37. In 2011, 1,390 master's, 8 doctorates, 42 other advanced degrees awarded. *Degree requirements:* For master's, practicum; for doctorate, thesis/dissertation. *Entrance requirements:* For doctorate, GRE General Test or MAT, interview, master's degree, resume; for CAGS, interview, master's degree. Additional exam requirements/ recommendations for international students: Required—TOEFL (minimum score 550 paper-based; 213 computer-based; 80 iBT). *Application deadline:* Applications are processed on a rolling basis. Application fee: $50. Electronic applications accepted. *Financial support:* In 2011–12, research assistantships (averaging $3,400 per year), teaching assistantships (averaging $3,400 per year) were awarded; career-related internships or fieldwork, Federal Work-Study, scholarships/grants, and unspecified assistantships also available. Support available to part-time students. Financial award application deadline: 4/15; financial award applicants required to submit FAFSA. *Faculty research:* Assessment in literacy, mathematics and science; autism spectrum disorders; instructional technology and online learning; multicultural education and ELL. *Unit head:* Dr. Mario Borunda, Dean, 617-349-8375, Fax: 617-349-8607, E-mail: mborunda@ lesley.edu. *Application contact:* Rosie Davis, Senior Assistant Director of Admissions, 617-349-8851, Fax: 617-349-8313, E-mail: rdavis4@lesley.edu. Web site: http:// www.lesley.edu/soe.html.

Lewis University, College of Education, Program in Secondary Education, Romeoville, IL 60446. Offers biology (MA); chemistry (MA); English (MA); history (MA); math (MA); physics (MA); psychology and social science (MA). Part-time programs available. *Students:* 17 full-time (11 women), 11 part-time (4 women); includes 4 minority (2 Black or African American, non-Hispanic/Latino; 2 Hispanic/Latino). Average age 30. In 2011, 7 master's awarded. *Entrance requirements:* For master's, departmental qualifying exam, writing exam, minimum GPA of 2.75, 2 letters of recommendation, interview. Additional exam requirements/recommendations for international students: Required—TOEFL (minimum score 550 paper-based; 213 computer-based; 80 iBT). *Application deadline:* For fall admission, 5/1 for international students; for spring admission, 11/15 for international students. Applications are processed on a rolling basis. Application fee: $40. Electronic applications accepted. *Financial support:* Federal Work-Study, scholarships/grants, and unspecified assistantships available. Financial award application deadline: 5/1; financial award applicants required to submit FAFSA. *Unit* *head:* Dr. Dorene Huvaere, Program Director, 815-838-0500 Ext. 5885, E-mail: huvaersdo@lewisu.edu. *Application contact:* Fran Welsh, Secretary, 815-838-0500 Ext. 5880, E-mail: welshfr@lewisu.edu.

Long Island University–C. W. Post Campus, College of Liberal Arts and Sciences, Department of Biology, Brookville, NY 11548-1300. Offers biology (MS); biology education (MS); genetic counseling (MS). Part-time and evening/weekend programs available. *Degree requirements:* For master's, thesis optional. *Entrance requirements:* For master's, GRE General Test, minimum GPA of 2.75 in major. Electronic applications accepted. *Faculty research:* Immunology, molecular biology, systematics, behavioral ecology, microbiology.

Long Island University–C. W. Post Campus, College of Liberal Arts and Sciences, Department of Earth and Environmental Science, Brookville, NY 11548-1300. Offers earth science (MS); earth science education (MS); environmental studies (MS).

Long Island University–C. W. Post Campus, School of Education, Department of Curriculum and Instruction, Brookville, NY 11548-1300. Offers adolescence education (MS); adolescence education: biology (MS); adolescence education: earth science (MS); adolescence education: English (MS); adolescence education: mathematics (MS); adolescence education: social studies (MS); adolescence education: Spanish (MS); art education (MS); bilingual education (MS); childhood education (MS); early childhood education (MS); middle childhood education (MS); music education (MS); teaching English to speakers of other languages (MS). Part-time and evening/weekend programs available. *Degree requirements:* For master's, comprehensive exam or thesis, student teaching. *Entrance requirements:* For master's, minimum GPA of 2.75 in major, 2.5 overall. Electronic applications accepted. *Faculty research:* Ethics and education, teaching strategies.

Louisiana Tech University, Graduate School, College of Education, Department of Curriculum, Instruction and Leadership, Ruston, LA 71272. Offers curriculum and instruction (MS, Ed D); educational leadership (Ed D); secondary education (M Ed), including business education, English education, foreign language education, health and physical education, mathematics education, science education, social studies education, speech education. *Accreditation:* NCATE. Part-time programs available. *Degree requirements:* For doctorate, thesis/dissertation. *Entrance requirements:* For master's and doctorate, GRE General Test.

Loyola University Chicago, School of Education, Program in Teaching and Learning, Chicago, IL 60660. Offers elementary education (M Ed); English as a second language (Certificate); math education (M Ed); reading specialist (M Ed); reading teacher endorsement (Certificate); school technology (M Ed); science education (M Ed); secondary education (M Ed); special education (M Ed). *Accreditation:* NCATE. *Faculty:* 12 full-time (9 women), 12 part-time/adjunct (6 women). *Students:* 131. Average age 28. 115 applicants, 65% accepted, 30 enrolled. In 2011, 80 master's awarded. *Degree requirements:* For master's, comprehensive exam. *Entrance requirements:* For master's, Illinois Basic Skills Test, 3 letters of recommendation, minimum GPA of 3.0, resume. Additional exam requirements/recommendations for international students: Required—TOEFL (minimum score 550 paper-based; 213 computer-based; 79 iBT). *Application deadline:* For fall admission, 7/1 priority date for domestic students, 7/1 for international students; for spring admission, 11/1 priority date for domestic students, 11/1 for international students. Applications are processed on a rolling basis. Application fee: $50. Electronic applications accepted. Application fee is waived when completed online. *Expenses: Tuition:* Full-time $15,660; part-time $870 per credit hour. *Required fees:* $125 per semester. Tuition and fees vary according to course load and program. *Financial support:* Institutionally sponsored loans, scholarships/grants, and unspecified assistantships available. Support available to part-time students. Financial award application deadline: 2/1; financial award applicants required to submit FAFSA. *Faculty research:* Positive behavior support, school reform, school improvement. *Unit head:* Dr. Dorothy Giroux, Director, 312-915-7027, E-mail: dgiroux@luc.edu. *Application contact:* Marie Rosin-Dittmar, Information Contact, 312-915-6800, E-mail: schleduc@luc.edu.

Loyola University Maryland, Graduate Programs, Department of Education, Program in Teacher Education, Baltimore, MD 21210-2699. Offers elementary/middle education (MAT); secondary education (MAT); secondary education: biology (MAT); secondary education: chemistries (MAT); secondary education: earth science (MAT); secondary education: English (MAT); secondary education: mathematics (MAT); secondary education: physics (MAT). Part-time programs available. *Faculty:* 25 full-time (21 women), 14 part-time/adjunct (11 women). *Students:* 28 full-time (19 women), 58 part-time (45 women); includes 5 minority (1 Black or African American, non-Hispanic/Latino; 2 Asian, non-Hispanic/Latino; 2 Two or more races, non-Hispanic/Latino), 4 international. Average age 28. In 2011, 37 master's awarded. *Entrance requirements:* For master's, PRAXIS, SAT, ACT, or GRE. Additional exam requirements/recommendations for international students: Required—TOEFL (minimum score 550 paper-based; 213 computer-based). *Application deadline:* For fall admission, 6/15 for domestic students; for spring admission, 11/1 for domestic students. Electronic applications accepted. *Financial support:* Research assistantships and unspecified assistantships available. Financial award application deadline: 4/15. *Unit head:* Wendy Smith, Chair, 410-617-2194, E-mail: wmsmith@loyola.edu. *Application contact:* Maureen Faux, Executive Director, Graduate Admissions, 410-617-5020, Fax: 410-617-2002, E-mail: graduate@loyola.edu. Web site: http://www.loyola.edu/academics/theology/.

Lynchburg College, Graduate Studies, School of Education and Human Development, M Ed Program in Science Education, Lynchburg, VA 24501-3199. Offers M Ed. Part-time and evening/weekend programs available. *Faculty:* 9 full-time (3 women), 1 part-time/adjunct (0 women). *Students:* 2 full-time (both women), 7 part-time (4 women); includes 1 minority (Two or more races, non-Hispanic/Latino). Average age 33. In 2011, 5 master's awarded. *Degree requirements:* For master's, comprehensive exam. *Entrance requirements:* For master's, GRE, minimum GPA of 3.0 (preferred), official transcripts (bachelor's, others as relevant), three letters of recommendation, career goals statement. Additional exam requirements/recommendations for international students: Required—TOEFL (minimum score 550 paper-based; 213 computer-based; 79 iBT), IELTS (minimum score 6.5). *Application deadline:* For fall admission, 7/31 for domestic students, 6/1 for international students; for spring admission, 11/30 for domestic students, 10/15 for international students. Applications are processed on a rolling basis. Application fee: $30. Electronic applications accepted. Application fee is waived when completed online. *Expenses: Tuition:* Full-time $7740; part-time $430 per credit hour. *Financial support:* Fellowships, research assistantships, Federal Work-Study, scholarships/grants, health care benefits, and unspecified assistantships available. Support available to part-time students. Financial award application deadline: 7/31; financial award applicants required to submit FAFSA. *Unit head:* Dr. Woody McKenzie, Associate Professor/Director of M Ed in Science Education, 434-544-8480, Fax: 434-544-8483, E-mail: mckenzie@lynchburg.edu. *Application contact:* Anne Pingstock, Executive Assistant, Graduate Studies, 434-544-8383, Fax: 544-8483, E-mail: gradstudies@lynchburg.edu. Web site: http://www.lynchburg.edu/scienceed.xml.

Lyndon State College, Graduate Programs in Education, Department of Natural Sciences, Lyndonville, VT 05851-0919. Offers science education (MST). Part-time programs available. *Degree requirements:* For master's, exam or major field project. *Entrance requirements:* Additional exam requirements/recommendations for international students: Recommended—TOEFL (minimum score 500 paper-based; 173 computer-based). *Faculty research:* Fern genetics, comparative butterfly research.

Manhattanville College, Graduate Studies, School of Education, Program in Middle Childhood/Adolescence Education (Grades 5-12), Purchase, NY 10577-2132. Offers biology (MAT); biology and special education (MPS); chemistry (MAT); chemistry and special education (MPS); English (MAT); English and special education (MPS); literacy (MPS), including reading and writing, writing; literacy and special education (MPS); math (MAT); math and special education (MPS); second language (MAT), including French, Italian, Latin, Spanish; social studies (MAT); social studies and special education (MPS); special education (MPS). Part-time and evening/weekend programs available. *Degree requirements:* For master's, comprehensive exam or research project, field experience. *Entrance requirements:* For master's, minimum undergraduate GPA of 3.0, 2 letters of recommendation. Additional exam requirements/recommendations for international students: Required—TOEFL. Electronic applications accepted.

McNeese State University, Doré School of Graduate Studies, College of Science, Department of Chemistry, Program in Environmental and Chemical Sciences, Lake Charles, LA 70609. Offers chemistry (MS); chemistry/environmental science education (MS). Evening/weekend programs available. *Faculty:* 4 full-time (0 women). *Students:* 15 full-time (6 women), 2 part-time (1 woman); includes 4 minority (3 Black or African American, non-Hispanic/Latino; 1 Asian, non-Hispanic/Latino), 11 international. In 2011, 6 master's awarded. *Degree requirements:* For master's, comprehensive exam, thesis or alternative. *Entrance requirements:* For master's, GRE. *Application deadline:* For fall admission, 5/15 priority date for domestic students, 5/15 for international students; for spring admission, 10/15 priority date for domestic students, 10/15 for international students. Applications are processed on a rolling basis. Application fee: $20 ($30 for international students). *Expenses:* Tuition, state resident: part-time $519 per credit hour. Tuition and fees vary according to course load. *Financial support:* Application deadline: 5/1. *Unit head:* Dr. Bruce C. Wyman, Coordinator, 337-475-5669, Fax: 337-475-5677, E-mail: wyman@mcneese.edu. *Application contact:* Dr. Bruce C. Wyman, Coordinator, 337-475-5669, Fax: 337-475-5677, E-mail: wyman@mcneese.edu.

Michigan State University, The Graduate School, College of Natural Science and College of Education, Division of Science and Mathematics Education, East Lansing, MI 48824. Offers biological, physical and general science for teachers (MAT, MS), including biological science (MS), general science (MAT), physical science (MS); mathematics education (MS, PhD).

Michigan Technological University, Graduate School, College of Sciences and Arts, Department of Cognitive and Learning Sciences, Houghton, MI 49931. Offers applied cognitive science and human factors (PhD); applied science education (MS). *Faculty:* 12 full-time (4 women), 3 part-time/adjunct (0 women). *Students:* 12 full-time (7 women), 21 part-time (13 women); includes 4 minority (2 American Indian or Alaska Native, non-Hispanic/Latino; 1 Asian, non-Hispanic/Latino; 1 Hispanic/Latino), 3 international. Average age 38. 26 applicants, 31% accepted, 6 enrolled. In 2011, 3 master's awarded. *Degree requirements:* For master's, comprehensive exam (for some programs), thesis (for some programs); for doctorate, comprehensive exam, thesis/dissertation. *Entrance requirements:* For master's and doctorate, GRE (recommended minimum score of 310 [1200 old version]), statement of purpose, official transcripts, 3 letters of recommendation, bachelor's/master's degree in a field related to cognitive science, human factors, or ergonomics, minimum GPA of 3.5 (recommended), resume/curriculum vitae, writing sample (preferably related to the field of interest). Additional exam requirements/recommendations for international students: Required—TOEFL (minimum score 79 iBT) or IELTS. *Application deadline:* For fall admission, 2/15 for domestic and international students. Applications are processed on a rolling basis. Electronic applications accepted. *Expenses:* Tuition, state resident: full-time $12,636; part-time $702 per credit. Tuition, nonresident: full-time $12,636; part-time $702 per credit. *Required fees:* $226; $226 per year. *Financial support:* In 2011–12, 15 students received support, including 1 fellowship with full tuition reimbursement available (averaging $6,065 per year), 4 research assistantships with full tuition reimbursements available (averaging $6,065 per year), teaching assistantships (averaging $6,065 per year). Financial award applicants required to submit FAFSA. *Faculty research:* Cognitive engineering and decision-making, human-centered design, individual differences in human performance. *Total annual research expenditures:* $167,794. *Unit head:* Dr. Bradley H. Baltensperger, Chair, 906-487-2460, Fax: 906-487-2468, E-mail: brad@mtu.edu. *Application contact:* Carol T. Wingerson, Senior Staff Assistant, 906-487-2327, Fax: 906-487-2463, E-mail: gradadms@mtu.edu. Web site: http://cls.mtu.edu/.

Middle Tennessee State University, College of Graduate Studies, College of Basic and Applied Sciences, Department of Aerospace, Murfreesboro, TN 37132. Offers aerospace education (M Ed); aviation administration (MS). Part-time and evening/weekend programs available. Postbaccalaureate distance learning degree programs offered. *Faculty:* 4 full-time (1 woman). *Students:* 10 full-time (2 women), 24 part-time (4 women); includes 6 minority (5 Black or African American, non-Hispanic/Latino; 1 Hispanic/Latino). Average age 30. 34 applicants, 71% accepted. In 2011, 12 master's awarded. *Degree requirements:* For master's, comprehensive exam, thesis optional. *Entrance requirements:* For master's, GRE General Test or MAT. Additional exam requirements/recommendations for international students: Required—TOEFL (minimum score 525 paper-based; 195 computer-based; 71 iBT) or IELTS (minimum score 6). *Application deadline:* For fall admission, 6/1 for domestic and international students. Applications are processed on a rolling basis. Application fee: $25 ($30 for international students). Electronic applications accepted. *Expenses:* Tuition, state resident: full-time $10,008. Tuition, nonresident: full-time $25,056. *Financial support:* In 2011–12, 4 students received support. Tuition waivers available. Support available to part-time students. Financial award application deadline: 5/1. *Faculty research:* Unmanned vehicles, air traffic control. *Unit head:* Dr. Ron Ferrara, Interim Chair, 615-898-2788, Fax: 615-904-8273, E-mail: ron.ferrara@mtsu.edu. *Application contact:* Dr. Michael D. Allen, Dean and Vice Provost for Research, 615-898-2840, Fax: 615-904-8020, E-mail: michael.allen@mtsu.edu.

Mills College, Graduate Studies, School of Education, Oakland, CA 94613-1000. Offers child life in hospitals (MA); early childhood education (MA); education (MA), including art education, curriculum and instruction, elementary education, English education, foreign language education, mathematics education, science education, secondary education, social studies education, teaching; educational leadership (MA, Ed D). Part-time and evening/weekend programs available. *Faculty:* 13 full-time (10 women), 14 part-time/adjunct (10 women). *Students:* 149 full-time (133 women), 69 part-time (61 women); includes 85 minority (32 Black or African American, non-Hispanic/Latino; 1 American Indian or Alaska Native, non-Hispanic/Latino; 16 Asian, non-Hispanic/Latino; 24 Hispanic/Latino; 1 Native Hawaiian or other Pacific Islander, non-Hispanic/Latino; 11 Two or more races, non-Hispanic/Latino), 3 international. Average age 28. 238 applicants, 84% accepted, 106 enrolled. In 2011, 41 master's, 2 doctorates awarded. Terminal master's awarded for partial completion of doctoral program. *Degree requirements:* For master's, comprehensive exam. *Entrance requirements:* For master's, statement of purpose, official transcript, 3 recommendations; for doctorate, GRE General Test. Additional exam requirements/recommendations for international students: Required—TOEFL (minimum score 550 paper-based; 80 iBT) or IELTS (minimum score 6). *Application deadline:* For fall admission, 12/31 priority date for domestic students, 12/15 for international students; for spring admission, 11/1 priority date for domestic students, 10/1 for international students. Applications are processed on a rolling basis. Application fee: $50. Electronic applications accepted. *Expenses: Tuition:* Full-time $28,280; part-time $15,640 per year. *Required fees:* $958. Tuition and fees vary according to program. *Financial support:* In 2011–12, 43 students received support, including 225 fellowships with full and partial tuition reimbursements available (averaging $6,020 per year), 43 teaching assistantships with full and partial tuition reimbursements available (averaging $6,782 per year); career-related internships or fieldwork and scholarships/grants also available. Support available to part-time students. Financial award application deadline: 2/1; financial award applicants required to submit FAFSA. *Faculty research:* Early childhood education, teacher preparation, educational leadership. *Total annual research expenditures:* $2.3 million. *Unit head:* Katherine Schultz, Chairperson, 510-430-3170, Fax: 510-430-3379, E-mail: grad-studies@mills.edu. *Application contact:* Tiana Kozoil, Graduate Admission Specialist, 510-430-3305, Fax: 510-430-2159, E-mail: grad-studies@mills.edu. Web site: http://www.mills.edu/education.

Minnesota State University Mankato, College of Graduate Studies, College of Science, Engineering and Technology, Department of Biological Sciences, Mankato, MN 56001. Offers biology (MS); biology education (MS); environmental sciences (MS). Part-time programs available. *Students:* 14 full-time (5 women), 17 part-time (9 women). *Degree requirements:* For master's, one foreign language, comprehensive exam, thesis or alternative. *Entrance requirements:* For master's, minimum GPA of 3.0 during previous 2 years of course work. Additional exam requirements/recommendations for international students: Required—TOEFL. *Application deadline:* For fall admission, 7/1 priority date for domestic students; for spring admission, 11/1 for domestic students. Applications are processed on a rolling basis. Application fee: $40. Electronic applications accepted. *Financial support:* Fellowships, research assistantships with full tuition reimbursements, teaching assistantships with full tuition reimbursements, career-related internships or fieldwork, Federal Work-Study, institutionally sponsored loans, and unspecified assistantships available. Support available to part-time students. Financial award application deadline: 3/15; financial award applicants required to submit FAFSA. *Faculty research:* Limnology, enzyme analysis, membrane engineering, converters. *Unit head:* Dr. Penny Knoblich, Graduate Coordinator, 507-389-5736. *Application contact:* 507-389-2321, E-mail: grad@mnsu.edu.

Minot State University, Graduate School, Program in Biological and Agricultural Sciences, Minot, ND 58707-0002. Offers science (MAT). *Degree requirements:* For master's, thesis. *Entrance requirements:* For master's, minimum GPA of 3.0 or GRE General Test, secondary teaching certificate. Additional exam requirements/recommendations for international students: Required—TOEFL.

Mississippi College, Graduate School, School of Education, Department of Teacher Education and Leadership, Clinton, MS 39058. Offers art (M Ed); biological science (M Ed); business education (M Ed); computer science (M Ed); dyslexia therapy (M Ed); educational leadership (M Ed, Ed D, Ed S); elementary education (M Ed, Ed S); English (M Ed); higher education administration (MS); mathematics (M Ed); secondary education (M Ed); social studies (history) (M Ed); teaching arts (M Ed). Part-time programs available. Postbaccalaureate distance learning degree programs offered (no on-campus study). *Degree requirements:* For master's, comprehensive exam, thesis optional. *Entrance requirements:* For master's, NTE. Additional exam requirements/recommendations for international students: Recommended—TOEFL, IELTS. Electronic applications accepted.

Mississippi State University, College of Arts and Sciences, Department of Geosciences, Mississippi State, MS 39762. Offers applied meteorology (MS); broadcast meteorology (MS); earth and atmospheric science (PhD); environmental geoscience (MS); geography (MS); geology (MS); geospatial sciences (MS); professional meteorology/climatology (MS); teachers in geoscience (MS). Postbaccalaureate distance learning degree programs offered (no on-campus study). *Faculty:* 19 full-time (3 women), 2 part-time/adjunct (0 women). *Students:* 72 full-time (27 women), 279 part-time (127 women); includes 40 minority (12 Black or African American, non-Hispanic/Latino; 4 American Indian or Alaska Native, non-Hispanic/Latino; 6 Asian, non-Hispanic/Latino; 14 Hispanic/Latino; 4 Two or more races, non-Hispanic/Latino), 10 international. Average age 35. 228 applicants, 77% accepted, 144 enrolled. In 2011, 89 degrees awarded. *Degree requirements:* For master's, thesis (for some programs), comprehensive oral or written exam. *Entrance requirements:* For master's, GRE (for on-campus applicants), minimum undergraduate GPA of 2.75. Additional exam requirements/recommendations for international students: Required—TOEFL (minimum score 475 paper-based; 153 computer-based; 53 iBT); Recommended—IELTS (minimum score 4.5). *Application deadline:* For fall admission, 7/1 for domestic students, 5/1 for international students; for spring admission, 11/1 for domestic students, 9/1 for international students. Applications are processed on a rolling basis. Application fee: $40. Electronic applications accepted. *Expenses:* Tuition, state resident: full-time $5805; part-time $322.50 per credit hour. Tuition, nonresident: full-time $14,670; part-time $815 per credit hour. *Financial support:* In 2011–12, 13 research assistantships with full tuition reimbursements (averaging $20,746 per year), 31 teaching assistantships with full tuition reimbursements (averaging $14,151 per year) were awarded; Federal Work-Study, institutionally sponsored loans, scholarships/grants, tuition waivers (partial), and unspecified assistantships also available. Financial award application deadline: 4/1; financial award applicants required to submit FAFSA. *Faculty research:* Climatology, hydrogeology, sedimentology, meteorology. *Total annual research expenditures:* $6.2 million. *Unit head:* Dr. Darrel Schmitz, Professor and Head, 662-325-3915, Fax: 662-325-9423, E-mail: schmitz@geosci.msstate.edu. *Application contact:* Dr. Christopher P. Dewey, Associate Professor/Graduate Coordinator, 662-325-2909, Fax: 662-325-9423, E-mail: cpd4@msstate.edu. Web site: http://www.msstate.edu/dept/geosciences/.

Missouri State University, Graduate College, College of Natural and Applied Sciences, Department of Physics, Astronomy, and Materials Science, Springfield, MO 65897. Offers materials science (MS); physics, astronomy, and materials science (MNAS); secondary education (MS Ed), including physics. Part-time programs available. *Faculty:* 13 full-time (0 women). *Students:* 9 full-time (1 woman), 4 part-time (1 woman); includes 2 minority (1 Black or African American, non-Hispanic/Latino; 1 Hispanic/Latino), 8 international. Average age 29. 7 applicants, 100% accepted, 6 enrolled. In 2011, 6 master's awarded. *Degree requirements:* For master's, comprehensive exam, thesis. *Entrance requirements:* For master's, GRE (MS, MNAS), minimum undergraduate GPA of 3.0 (MS and MNAS), 9-12 teaching certification (MS Ed). Additional exam requirements/recommendations for international students: Required—TOEFL (minimum score 550 paper-based; 213 computer-based; 79 iBT). *Application deadline:* For fall admission, 7/20 priority date for domestic students, 5/1 for international students; for spring admission, 12/20 priority date for domestic students, 9/1 for international students. Applications are processed on a rolling basis. Application fee: $35 ($50 for international students). Electronic applications accepted. *Expenses:* Tuition, state resident: full-time $4086; part-time $227 per credit hour. Tuition, nonresident: full-time $8172; part-time $454 per credit hour. *Required fees:* $275 per semester. Tuition and fees vary according to course load, campus/location and program. *Financial support:* In 2011–12, 3 teaching assistantships with full tuition reimbursements (averaging $9,730 per year) were awarded; Federal Work-Study, institutionally sponsored loans, scholarships/grants, and unspecified assistantships also available. Financial award application deadline: 3/31; financial award applicants required to submit FAFSA. *Faculty research:* Nanocomposites, ferroelectricity, infrared focal plane array sensors, biosensors, pulsating stars. *Unit head:* Dr. David Cornelison, Head, 417-836-5131, Fax: 417-836-6226, E-mail: physics@missouristate.edu. *Application contact:* Misty Stewart, Coordinator of Admissions and Recruitment, 417-836-6079, Fax: 417-836-6200, E-mail: mistystewart@missouristate.edu. Web site: http://physics.missouristate.edu/.

Montclair State University, The Graduate School, College of Education and Human Services, Department of Curriculum and Teaching, Program in Teaching in Content Area, Montclair, NJ 07043-1624. Offers art (MAT); biology (MAT); chemistry (MAT); earth science (MAT); English (MAT); French (MAT); health and physical education (MAT); health education (MAT); mathematics (MAT); music (MAT); physical education (MAT); physical science (MAT); social studies (MAT); Spanish (MAT); teacher of English as a second language (MAT). *Students:* 162 full-time (90 women), 47 part-time (29 women); includes 37 minority (4 Black or African American, non-Hispanic/Latino; 11 Asian, non-Hispanic/Latino; 18 Hispanic/Latino; 4 Two or more races, non-Hispanic/Latino), 5 international. Average age 31. 145 applicants, 41% accepted, 56 enrolled. In 2011, 229 master's awarded. *Degree requirements:* For master's, comprehensive exam, thesis or alternative. *Entrance requirements:* For master's, GRE General Test, interview, 2 letters of recommendation. Additional exam requirements/recommendations for international students: Required—TOEFL (minimum score 83 iBT), IELTS (minimum score 6.5). *Application deadline:* Applications are processed on a rolling basis. Application fee: $60. Electronic applications accepted. *Financial support:* Federal Work-Study, scholarships/grants, and unspecified assistantships available. Support available to part-time students. Financial award application deadline: 3/1; financial award applicants required to submit FAFSA. *Unit head:* Dr. David Schwarzer, Chairperson, 973-655-5187. *Application contact:* Amy Aiello, Executive Director of The Graduate School, 973-655-5147, Fax: 973-655-7869, E-mail: graduate.school@montclair.edu.

Montclair State University, The Graduate School, College of Science and Mathematics, Department of Biology and Molecular Biology, Montclair, NJ 07043-1624. Offers biology (MS), including biological science education, biology, ecology and evolution, physiology; molecular biology (MS, Certificate). Part-time and evening/weekend programs available. *Students:* 15 full-time (10 women), 33 part-time (23 women); includes 3 minority (all Hispanic/Latino), 1 international. Average age 28. 53 applicants, 47% accepted, 14 enrolled. In 2011, 14 degrees awarded. *Degree requirements:* For master's, comprehensive exam, thesis or alternative. *Entrance requirements:* For master's, GRE General Test, 24 credits of course work in undergraduate biology, 2 letters of recommendation, teaching certificate (biology sciences education concentration); for Certificate, 2 letters of recommendation, essay. Additional exam requirements/recommendations for international students: Required—TOEFL (minimum score 83 iBT) or IELTS. *Application deadline:* For fall admission, 6/1 for international students; for spring admission, 10/1 for international students. Applications are processed on a rolling basis. Application fee: $60. Electronic applications accepted. *Financial support:* In 2011–12, 16 research assistantships with full tuition reimbursements (averaging $7,000 per year), 3 teaching assistantships (averaging $7,000 per year) were awarded; Federal Work-Study, scholarships/grants, and unspecified assistantships also available. Support available to part-time students. Financial award application deadline: 3/1; financial award applicants required to submit FAFSA. *Faculty research:* Ecosystem biology, molecular biology, signal transduction, neuroscience, aquatic and coastal biology. *Total annual research expenditures:* $1.3 million. *Unit head:* Dr. Quinn Vega, Chairperson, 973-655-7178. *Application contact:* Amy Aiello, Director of Graduate Admissions and Operations, 973-655-5147, Fax: 973-655-7869, E-mail: graduate.school@montclair.edu. Web site: http://www.montclair.edu/csam/biology/.

Montclair State University, The Graduate School, College of Science and Mathematics, Department of Mathematical Sciences, Program in Physical Science, Montclair, NJ 07043-1624. Offers MAT. *Degree requirements:* For master's, comprehensive exam. *Entrance requirements:* For master's, GRE General Test, interview, 2 letters of recommendation, essay. Additional exam requirements/recommendations for international students: Required—TOEFL (minimum score 83 iBT), IELTS (minimum score 6.5). *Application deadline:* Applications are processed on a rolling basis. Application fee: $60. Electronic applications accepted. *Financial support:* Federal Work-Study, scholarships/grants, and unspecified assistantships available. Support available to part-time students. Financial award application deadline: 3/1; financial award applicants required to submit FAFSA. *Faculty research:* Teaching physics. *Unit head:* Dr. Helen Roberts, Chairperson, 973-655-5132. *Application contact:* Amy Aiello, Director of Graduate Admissions and Operations, 973-655-5147, Fax: 973-655-7869, E-mail: graduate.school@montclair.edu. Web site: http://www.montclair.edu/cehs/academics/programs/ma-exercise-sci-physed/.

Morehead State University, Graduate Programs, College of Education, Department of Middle Grades and Secondary Education, Morehead, KY 40351. Offers business and marketing education (MAT); English/language arts 5-9 (MAT); French (MAT); health P-12 (MAT); mathematics 5-9 (MAT); physical education P-12 (MAT); science 5-9 (MAT); secondary biology (MAT); secondary chemistry (MAT); secondary earth science (MAT); secondary English (MAT); secondary math (MAT); secondary physics (MAT); secondary social studies (MAT); social studies 5-9 (MAT); Spanish (MAT). Part-time and evening/weekend programs available. *Degree requirements:* For master's, portfolio. *Entrance requirements:* For master's, GRE or PRAXIS II content exam, minimum overall undergraduate GPA of 2.5. Additional exam requirements/recommendations for international students: Required—TOEFL (minimum score 500 paper-based; 173 computer-based). Electronic applications accepted.

Morgan State University, School of Graduate Studies, School of Education and Urban Studies, Department of Advanced Studies, Leadership and Policy, Program in Science Education, Baltimore, MD 21251. Offers MS, Ed D. *Entrance requirements:* Additional exam requirements/recommendations for international students: Required—TOEFL (minimum score 550 paper-based; 213 computer-based).

National Louis University, National College of Education, Chicago, IL 60603. Offers administration and supervision (M Ed, Ed D, CAS, Ed S); curriculum and instruction (M Ed, MS Ed, CAS); early childhood administration (M Ed, CAS); early childhood education (M Ed, MAT, MS Ed, CAS); education (Ed D); educational psychology/human learning and development (M Ed, MS Ed, CAS, Ed S); elementary education (MAT); interdisciplinary curriculum and instruction (M Ed); mathematics education (M Ed, MS Ed, CAS); reading and language (M Ed, MS Ed, CAS); school psychology (M Ed, Ed S); science education (M Ed, MS Ed, CAS); secondary education (MAT); special education (M Ed, MAT, CAS); technology in education (M Ed, CAS). *Accreditation:* NCATE. Part-time and evening/weekend programs available. *Students:* 224 full-time (162 women), 2,336 part-time (1,767 women); includes 677 minority (366 Black or African American, non-Hispanic/Latino; 8 American Indian or Alaska Native, non-Hispanic/Latino; 68 Asian, non-Hispanic/Latino; 218 Hispanic/Latino; 2 Native Hawaiian or other Pacific Islander, non-Hispanic/Latino; 15 Two or more races, non-Hispanic/

Latino), 2 international. Average age 34. In 2011, 1,711 master's, 76 doctorates, 86 other advanced degrees awarded. *Degree requirements:* For doctorate, comprehensive exam, thesis/dissertation. *Entrance requirements:* For master's, MAT or GRE, minimum GPA of 3.0; for doctorate, GRE General Test, minimum GPA of 3.25, interview, resume, writing sample, 4 recommendations. Additional exam requirements/recommendations for international students: Required—TOEFL (minimum score 550 paper-based; 213 computer-based; 79 iBT). *Application deadline:* Applications are processed on a rolling basis. Application fee: $40. *Financial support:* Fellowships, research assistantships, teaching assistantships, career-related internships or fieldwork, Federal Work-Study, institutionally sponsored loans, and scholarships/grants available. Support available to part-time students. Financial award applicants required to submit FAFSA. *Unit head:* Dr. Alison Hilsabeck, Dean, 312-361-3580, Fax: 312-261-2580, E-mail: ahilsabeck@nl.edu. *Application contact:* Ken Kasprzak, Director of Admission, 888-658-8632, Fax: 847-947-5575, E-mail: kkasprzak@nl.edu.

New Mexico Institute of Mining and Technology, Graduate Studies, Master of Science for Teachers Interdepartmental Program, Socorro, NM 87801. Offers MST. *Faculty:* 1 (woman) full-time, 7 part-time/adjunct (1 woman). *Students:* 1 (woman) full-time, 62 part-time (39 women); includes 12 minority (1 Black or African American, non-Hispanic/Latino; 10 Hispanic/Latino; 1 Two or more races, non-Hispanic/Latino). Average age 42. 16 applicants, 25% accepted, 4 enrolled. In 2011, 20 master's awarded. *Degree requirements:* For master's, thesis optional. *Entrance requirements:* For master's, GRE General Test. Additional exam requirements/recommendations for international students: Required—TOEFL (minimum score 540 paper-based; 207 computer-based). *Application deadline:* For fall admission, 3/1 priority date for domestic students; for spring admission, 6/1 for domestic students. Applications are processed on a rolling basis. Application fee: $16. Electronic applications accepted. *Expenses:* Tuition, state resident: full-time $4849; part-time $269.41 per credit hour. Tuition, nonresident: full-time $16,041; part-time $891.15 per credit hour. *Required fees:* $622; $65 per credit hour. $20 per semester. Part-time tuition and fees vary according to course load. *Financial support:* In 2011–12, 1 research assistantship (averaging $20,218 per year) was awarded; fellowships, teaching assistantships, Federal Work-Study, and institutionally sponsored loans also available. Financial award application deadline: 3/1; financial award applicants required to submit CSS PROFILE or FAFSA. *Faculty research:* Teaching secondary school science and/or mathematics. *Unit head:* Dr. Peter Gerity, Vice President for Academic Affairs, 575-835-5227, Fax: 575-835-5678, E-mail: science@nmt.edu. *Application contact:* Dr. Lorie Liebrock, Dean of Graduate Studies, 575-835-5513, Fax: 575-835-5476, E-mail: graduate@nmt.edu.

New York University, Steinhardt School of Culture, Education, and Human Development, Department of Teaching and Learning, Program in Science Education, New York, NY 10012-1019. Offers biology grades 7-12 (MA); chemistry grades 7-12 (MA); physics grades 7-12 (MA). Part-time and evening/weekend programs available. *Degree requirements:* For master's, thesis (for some programs). *Entrance requirements:* Additional exam requirements/recommendations for international students: Required—TOEFL. Electronic applications accepted. *Faculty research:* Science curriculum development, gender and ethnicity, technology use, history and philosophy of school science, science in urban schools.

North Carolina Agricultural and Technical State University, School of Graduate Studies, College of Arts and Sciences, Department of Biology, Greensboro, NC 27411. Offers biology (MS); biology education (MAT). Part-time and evening/weekend programs available. *Degree requirements:* For master's, comprehensive exam, thesis (for some programs), qualifying exam. *Entrance requirements:* For master's, GRE General Test, personal statement. *Faculty research:* Physical ecology, cytochemistry, botany, parasitology, microbiology.

North Carolina State University, Graduate School, College of Education, Department of Mathematics, Science, and Technology Education, Program in Science Education, Raleigh, NC 27695. Offers M Ed, MS, PhD. *Accreditation:* NCATE. Part-time programs available. *Degree requirements:* For master's, thesis (for some programs), oral exam; for doctorate, one foreign language, thesis/dissertation, oral and written exams. *Entrance requirements:* For master's, GRE General Test or MAT, minimum GPA of 3.0; for doctorate, GRE General Test, minimum GPA of 3.0, interview. Electronic applications accepted. *Faculty research:* Teacher development, sociocultural issues in learning, student science misconceptions, technical applications to science teaching.

North Dakota State University, College of Graduate and Interdisciplinary Studies, College of Human Development and Education, School of Education, Fargo, ND 58108. Offers agricultural education (M Ed, MS), including agricultural education, agricultural extension education (MS); counseling (M Ed, MS, PhD); curriculum and instruction (M Ed, MS), including pedagogy, physical education and athletic administration; education (PhD); educational leadership (M Ed, MS, Ed S); family and consumer sciences education (M Ed, MS); history education (M Ed, MS); institutional analysis (Ed D); mathematics education (M Ed, MS); music education (M Ed, MS); occupational and adult education (Ed D); science education (M Ed, MS). *Accreditation:* NCATE. Part-time and evening/weekend programs available. Postbaccalaureate distance learning degree programs offered (minimal on-campus study). *Faculty:* 24 full-time (10 women), 2 part-time/adjunct (1 woman). *Students:* 91 full-time (64 women), 114 part-time (78 women); includes 13 minority (4 Black or African American, non-Hispanic/Latino; 5 American Indian or Alaska Native, non-Hispanic/Latino; 1 Hispanic/Latino; 3 Two or more races, non-Hispanic/Latino), 8 international. 88 applicants, 67% accepted, 56 enrolled. In 2011, 43 master's, 12 doctorates awarded. *Degree requirements:* For master's, comprehensive exam; for doctorate, thesis/dissertation; for Ed S, thesis. *Entrance requirements:* For degree, GRE General Test, master's degree, minimum GPA of 3.25. Additional exam requirements/recommendations for international students: Required—TOEFL. *Application deadline:* Applications are processed on a rolling basis. Application fee: $45 ($60 for international students). *Financial support:* Research assistantships, teaching assistantships, career-related internships or fieldwork, Federal Work-Study, institutionally sponsored loans, and tuition waivers (full) available. Financial award application deadline: 4/15. *Unit head:* Dr. William Martin, Chair, 701-231-7202, Fax: 701-231-7416, E-mail: william.martin@ndsu.edu. *Application contact:* Sonya Goergen, Marketing, Recruitment, and Public Relations Coordinator, 701-231-7033, Fax: 701-231-6524. Web site: http://www.ndsu.nodak.edu/school_of_education/.

North Dakota State University, College of Graduate and Interdisciplinary Studies, Program in STEM Education, Fargo, ND 58108. Offers PhD. *Students:* 1 (woman) full-time. Application fee: $35. Electronic applications accepted. *Unit head:* Dr. Donald Schwert, Director, 701-231-7496, Fax: 701-231-5924, E-mail: donald.schwert@ndsu.edu. *Application contact:* Sonya Goergen, Marketing, Recruitment, and Public Relations Coordinator, 701-231-7033, Fax: 701-231-6524.

Northeastern State University, Graduate College, College of Science and Health Professions, Program in Science Education, Tahlequah, OK 74464-2399. Offers M Ed. Part-time and evening/weekend programs available. *Students:* 3 full-time (all women), 14 part-time (10 women); includes 5 minority (4 American Indian or Alaska Native, non-Hispanic/Latino; 1 Hispanic/Latino). In 2011, 3 master's awarded. *Entrance requirements:* For master's, MAT or GRE, minimum GPA of 2.5. *Application deadline:* For fall admission, 6/1 for domestic students. Application fee: $25. *Unit head:* Dr. April Adams, Chair, 918-456-5511 Ext. 3819. *Application contact:* Margie Railey, Administrative Assistant, 918-456-5511 Ext. 2093, Fax: 918-458-2061, E-mail: railey@nsouk.edu.

Northern Arizona University, Graduate College, College of Engineering, Forestry and Natural Sciences, Center for Science Teaching and Learning, Flagstaff, AZ 86011. Offers mathematics or science teaching (Certificate); science teaching and learning (M Ed, MAST). Part-time programs available. Postbaccalaureate distance learning degree programs offered (minimal on-campus study). *Faculty:* 7 full-time (5 women). *Students:* 12 full-time (4 women), 10 part-time (7 women); includes 3 minority (1 American Indian or Alaska Native, non-Hispanic/Latino; 1 Hispanic/Latino; 1 Two or more races, non-Hispanic/Latino). In 2011, 7 master's, 3 other advanced degrees awarded. *Entrance requirements:* Additional exam requirements/recommendations for international students: Required—TOEFL (minimum score 550 paper-based; 213 computer-based; 80 iBT), IELTS (minimum score 7). *Application deadline:* For fall admission, 3/1 for international students; for spring admission, 9/15 for international students. Application fee: $65. *Expenses:* Tuition, state resident: full-time $7190; part-time $355 per credit hour. Tuition, nonresident: full-time $18,092; part-time $1005 per credit hour. *Required fees:* $818; $328 per semester. *Financial support:* Career-related internships or fieldwork, Federal Work-Study, and scholarships/grants available. Financial award applicants required to submit FAFSA. *Unit head:* Julie Gess-Newsome, Director, 928-523-9527, E-mail: julie.gess-newsome@nau.edu. *Application contact:* Barbara Molnar, Administrative Associate, 928-523-2114, E-mail: barbara.molnar@nau.edu. Web site: http://nau.edu/cefns/cstl/.

Northern Michigan University, College of Graduate Studies, College of Professional Studies, School of Education, Program in Science Education, Marquette, MI 49855-5301. Offers MS. Postbaccalaureate distance learning degree programs offered.

Northwest Missouri State University, Graduate School, College of Arts and Sciences, Program in Teaching: Science, Maryville, MO 64468-6001. Offers MS Ed. *Accreditation:* NCATE. Part-time programs available. *Faculty:* 11 full-time (2 women). *Students:* 1 full-time (0 women), 1 (woman) part-time. 1 applicant, 100% accepted, 1 enrolled. In 2011, 4 master's awarded. *Degree requirements:* For master's, comprehensive exam, thesis optional. *Entrance requirements:* For master's, GRE General Test, minimum GPA of 2.75 in major, 2.5 overall; teaching certificate; writing sample. Additional exam requirements/recommendations for international students: Required—TOEFL (minimum score 550 paper-based; 213 computer-based). *Application deadline:* For fall admission, 7/1 for domestic and international students; for spring admission, 11/15 for domestic and international students. Applications are processed on a rolling basis. Application fee: $0 ($50 for international students). *Financial support:* In 2011–12, research assistantships with full tuition reimbursements (averaging $6,000 per year) were awarded. Financial award application deadline: 4/1; financial award applicants required to submit FAFSA. *Unit head:* Dr. Rafiq Islam, Chairperson, 660-562-1210. *Application contact:* Dr. Gregory Haddock, Dean of Graduate School, 660-562-1145, Fax: 660-562-1096, E-mail: gradsch@nwmissouri.edu.

Norwich University, College of Graduate and Continuing Studies, Master of Arts in Military History Program, Northfield, VT 05663. Offers U. S. military history (MA). Evening/weekend programs available. *Faculty:* 14 part-time/adjunct (3 women). *Students:* 99 full-time (10 women); includes 2 minority (1 American Indian or Alaska Native, non-Hispanic/Latino; 1 Hispanic/Latino). Average age 38. 152 applicants, 38% accepted, 56 enrolled. In 2011, 121 master's awarded. *Entrance requirements:* For master's, minimum undergraduate GPA of 2.75. Additional exam requirements/recommendations for international students: Required—TOEFL (minimum score 550 paper-based; 212 computer-based; 83 iBT). *Application deadline:* For fall admission, 8/10 for domestic and international students; for winter admission, 11/7 for domestic and international students; for spring admission, 2/6 for domestic and international students. Applications are processed on a rolling basis. Application fee: $50. Electronic applications accepted. *Expenses: Tuition:* Full-time $16,174. *Required fees:* $2130. Full-time tuition and fees vary according to program. *Financial support:* In 2011–12, 11 students received support. Scholarships/grants available. Financial award applicants required to submit FAFSA. *Unit head:* Dr. James Ehrman, Program Director, 802-485-2567, Fax: 802-485-2533. *Application contact:* Lars Nielsen, Administrative Director, 802-485-2853, Fax: 802-485-2533, E-mail: lnielsen@norwich.edu. Web site: http://militaryhistory.norwich.edu/.

Occidental College, Graduate Studies, Department of Education, Program in Secondary Education, Los Angeles, CA 90041-3314. Offers English and comparative literary studies (MAT); history (MAT); life science (MAT); mathematics (MAT); physical science (MAT); social science (MAT); Spanish (MAT). Part-time programs available. *Degree requirements:* For master's, comprehensive exam, graduate synthesis paper. *Entrance requirements:* For master's, GRE General Test, minimum GPA of 3.0. Additional exam requirements/recommendations for international students: Required—TOEFL (minimum score 625 paper-based; 263 computer-based). *Expenses:* Contact institution.

Ohio University, Graduate College, College of Arts and Sciences, Department of Geological Sciences, Athens, OH 45701-2979. Offers environmental geochemistry (MS); environmental geology (MS); environmental/hydrology (MS); geology (MS); geology education (MS); geomorphology/surficial processes (MS); geophysics (MS); hydrogeology (MS); sedimentology (MS); structure/tectonics (MS). Part-time programs available. *Students:* 19 full-time (10 women). 14 applicants, 64% accepted, 9 enrolled. In 2011, 8 master's awarded. *Degree requirements:* For master's, thesis. *Entrance requirements:* Additional exam requirements/recommendations for international students: Required—TOEFL (minimum score 550 paper-based; 80 iBT) or IELTS (minimum score 6.5). *Application deadline:* For fall admission, 2/1 priority date for domestic students, 2/1 for international students. Application fee: $50 ($55 for international students). Electronic applications accepted. *Financial support:* Research assistantships with full tuition reimbursements, teaching assistantships with full tuition reimbursements, Federal Work-Study, institutionally sponsored loans, scholarships/grants, tuition waivers (partial), and unspecified assistantships available. Financial award application deadline: 2/1. *Faculty research:* Geoscience education, tectonics, fluvial geomorphology, invertebrate paleontology, mine/hydrology. *Total annual research expenditures:* $649,020. *Unit head:* Dr. Gregory Nadon, Chair, 740-593-4212, Fax: 740-593-0486, E-mail: nadon@ohio.edu. *Application contact:* Dr. Keith Milam, Graduate Chair, 740-593-1106, Fax: 740-593-0486, E-mail: milamk@ohio.edu. Web site: http://www.ohiou.edu/geology/.

Old Dominion University, Darden College of Education, Programs in Secondary Education, Norfolk, VA 23529. Offers biology (MS Ed); chemistry (MS Ed); English (MS Ed); instructional technology (MS Ed); library science (MS Ed); secondary education (MS Ed). *Accreditation:* NCATE. Part-time and evening/weekend programs available. Postbaccalaureate distance learning degree programs offered (minimal on-campus study). *Faculty:* 20 full-time (16 women). *Students:* 82 full-time (49 women), 95 part-time (63 women); includes 37 minority (21 Black or African American, non-Hispanic/Latino; 3 Asian, non-Hispanic/Latino; 8 Hispanic/Latino; 5 Two or more races, non-Hispanic/Latino), 1 international. Average age 32. 67 applicants, 79% accepted, 53 enrolled. In 2011, 84 degrees awarded. *Degree requirements:* For master's, comprehensive exam, thesis. *Entrance requirements:* For master's, GRE General Test or MAT, PRAXIS I (for licensure), minimum GPA of 2.8, teaching certificate. Additional exam requirements/recommendations for international students: Required—TOEFL. *Application deadline:* For fall admission, 6/1 for domestic and international students; for winter admission, 11/1 for domestic and international students; for spring admission, 3/1 for domestic and international students. Applications are processed on a rolling basis. Application fee: $50. Electronic applications accepted. *Expenses:* Tuition, state resident: full-time $9096; part-time $379 per credit. Tuition, nonresident: full-time $23,064; part-time $961 per credit. *Required fees:* $127 per semester. One-time fee: $50. *Financial support:* In 2011–12, 56 students received support, including fellowships (averaging $15,000 per year), 2 research assistantships with tuition reimbursements available (averaging $9,000 per year), 3 teaching assistantships with tuition reimbursements available (averaging $12,500 per year); career-related internships or fieldwork, Federal Work-Study, institutionally sponsored loans, scholarships/grants, and tuition waivers (partial) also available. Support available to part-time students. Financial award application deadline: 2/15; financial award applicants required to submit FAFSA. *Faculty research:* Use of technology, writing project for teachers, geography teaching, reading. *Unit head:* Dr. Robert Lucking, Graduate Program Director, 757-683-5545, Fax: 757-683-5862, E-mail: rlucking@odu.edu. *Application contact:* William Heffelfinger, Director of Graduate Admissions, 757-683-5554, Fax: 757-683-3255, E-mail: gradadmit@odu.edu. Web site: http://education.odu.edu/eci/secondary/.

Oregon State University, Graduate School, College of Science, Department of Science and Mathematics Education, Program in Science Education, Corvallis, OR 97331. Offers MA, MS, PhD. *Accreditation:* NCATE. *Degree requirements:* For doctorate, thesis/dissertation. *Entrance requirements:* For master's, minimum GPA of 3.0 in last 90 hours; for doctorate, GRE or MAT, minimum GPA of 3.0 in last 90 hours. Additional exam requirements/recommendations for international students: Required—TOEFL. *Faculty research:* Teacher thought processes, pedagogical content knowledge and teacher preparation.

Our Lady of the Lake University of San Antonio, School of Professional Studies, Program in Curriculum and Instruction, San Antonio, TX 78207-4689. Offers bilingual (M Ed); early childhood education (M Ed); English as a second language (M Ed); integrated math teaching (M Ed); integrated science teaching (M Ed); master reading teacher (M Ed); master technology teacher (M Ed); reading specialist (M Ed).

Our Lady of the Lake University of San Antonio, School of Professional Studies, Program in Intermediate Education, San Antonio, TX 78207-4689. Offers math/science education (M Ed); professional studies (M Ed). Part-time and evening/weekend programs available.

Plymouth State University, College of Graduate Studies, Graduate Studies in Education, Program in Science, Plymouth, NH 03264-1595. Offers applied meteorology (MS); environmental science and policy (MS); science education (MS).

Portland State University, Graduate Studies, College of Liberal Arts and Sciences, Department of Geology, Portland, OR 97207-0751. Offers environmental sciences and resources (PhD); geology (MA, MS); science/geology (MAT, MST). Part-time programs available. *Degree requirements:* For master's, comprehensive exam, thesis, field comprehensive; for doctorate, thesis/dissertation, 2 years of residency. *Entrance requirements:* For master's, GRE General Test, GRE Subject Test, BA/BS in geology, minimum GPA of 3.0 in upper-division course work or 2.75 overall. Additional exam requirements/recommendations for international students: Required—TOEFL (minimum score 550 paper-based; 213 computer-based). *Faculty research:* Sediment transport, volcanic environmental geology, coastal and fluvial processes.

Portland State University, Graduate Studies, College of Liberal Arts and Sciences, Interdisciplinary Programs in General Science, General Social Science, and General Arts and Letters, Portland, OR 97207-0751. Offers general arts and letters education (MAT, MST); general science education (MAT, MST); general social science education (MAT, MST). Part-time and evening/weekend programs available. *Degree requirements:* For master's, variable foreign language requirement, written exam. *Entrance requirements:* For master's, minimum GPA of 3.0 in upper-division course work or 2.75 overall. Additional exam requirements/recommendations for international students: Required—TOEFL (minimum score 550 paper-based; 213 computer-based).

Portland State University, Graduate Studies, College of Liberal Arts and Sciences, Program in Environmental Sciences and Management, Portland, OR 97207-0751. Offers environmental management (MEM); environmental sciences/biology (PhD); environmental sciences/chemistry (PhD); environmental sciences/civil engineering (PhD); environmental sciences/geography (PhD); environmental sciences/geology (PhD); environmental sciences/physics (PhD); environmental studies (MS); science/environmental science (MST). Part-time programs available. *Degree requirements:* For master's, thesis or alternative; for doctorate, variable foreign language requirement, comprehensive exam, thesis/dissertation, oral and qualifying exams. *Entrance requirements:* For master's, GRE General Test, 3 letters of recommendation; for doctorate, minimum GPA of 3.0 in upper-division course work or 2.75 overall. Additional exam requirements/recommendations for international students: Required—TOEFL (minimum score 550 paper-based; 213 computer-based). *Faculty research:* Environmental aspects of biology, chemistry, civil engineering, geology, physics.

Purdue University, Graduate School, College of Education, Department of Curriculum and Instruction, West Lafayette, IN 47907. Offers agricultural and extension education (PhD, Ed S); agriculture and extension education (MS, MS Ed); art education (PhD); consumer and family sciences and extension education (MS Ed, PhD, Ed S); curriculum studies (MS Ed, PhD, Ed S); educational technology (MS Ed, PhD, Ed S); elementary education (MS Ed); foreign language education (MS Ed, PhD, Ed S); industrial technology (PhD, Ed S); language arts (MS Ed, PhD, Ed S); literacy (MS Ed, PhD, Ed S); mathematics/science education (MS, MS Ed, PhD, Ed S); social studies (MS Ed, PhD); social studies education (Ed S); vocational/industrial education (MS Ed, PhD, Ed S); vocational/technical education (MS Ed, PhD, Ed S). *Accreditation:* NCATE. Part-time and evening/weekend programs available. *Faculty:* 30 full-time (21 women), 1 (woman) part-time/adjunct. *Students:* 89 full-time (64 women), 134 part-time (84 women); includes 31 minority (12 Black or African American, non-Hispanic/Latino; 3 American Indian or Alaska Native, non-Hispanic/Latino; 7 Asian, non-Hispanic/Latino; 9 Hispanic/Latino), 49 international. Average age 36. 136 applicants, 83% accepted, 72 enrolled. In 2011, 26 master's, 13 doctorates awarded. *Degree requirements:* For master's, thesis optional; for doctorate, thesis/dissertation, oral and written exams; for Ed S, oral presentation, project. *Entrance requirements:* For master's, GRE general test is required if undergraduate GPA is below 3.0, minimum undergraduate GPA of 3.0 or equivalent; for doctorate, GRE General Test, a combined GRE verbal and quantitative score of 1000 (300 for revised GRE Test) or more is expected, minimum undergraduate GPA of 3.0 or equivalent; master's degree with minimum GPA of 3.0 or equivalent; for Ed S, GRE general test, a combined GRE verbal and quantitative score of 1000 (300 for revised GRE Test) or more is expected, minimum undergraduate GPA of 3.0 or equivalent; master's degree. Additional exam requirements/recommendations for international students: Required—TOEFL (minimum score 550 paper-based; 77 iBT). *Application deadline:* For fall admission, 12/15 priority date for domestic students, 3/1 for international students; for spring admission, 9/15 for domestic students, 8/1 for international students. Application fee: $60 ($75 for international students). Electronic applications accepted. *Financial support:* Fellowships with full tuition reimbursements, research assistantships with full tuition reimbursements, teaching assistantships with full tuition reimbursements, career-related internships or fieldwork, and tuition waivers (full) available. Support available to part-time students. Financial award application deadline: 3/1; financial award applicants required to submit FAFSA. *Faculty research:* Literacy acquisition and development, teacher beliefs and knowledge, recruitment and retention of underrepresented students, economic education, literacy discourse. *Unit head:* Dr. Philip J. VanFossen, Head, 765-494-7935, Fax: 765-496-1622, E-mail: vanfoss@purdue.edu. *Application contact:* Sarah N. Prater, Graduate Contact, 765-494-2345, Fax: 765-494-5832, E-mail: prater0@purdue.edu. Web site: http://www.edci.purdue.edu/.

Purdue University, Graduate School, College of Science, Department of Chemistry, West Lafayette, IN 47907. Offers analytical chemistry (MS, PhD); biochemistry (MS, PhD); chemical education (MS, PhD); inorganic chemistry (MS, PhD); organic chemistry (MS, PhD); physical chemistry (MS, PhD). *Faculty:* 47 full-time (16 women), 6 part-time/adjunct (0 women). *Students:* 275 full-time (103 women), 33 part-time (10 women); includes 38 minority (19 Black or African American, non-Hispanic/Latino; 6 Asian, non-Hispanic/Latino; 12 Hispanic/Latino; 1 Two or more races, non-Hispanic/Latino), 94 international. Average age 27. 777 applicants, 26% accepted, 62 enrolled. In 2011, 4 master's, 67 doctorates awarded. Terminal master's awarded for partial completion of doctoral program. *Degree requirements:* For master's, thesis; for doctorate, comprehensive exam, thesis/dissertation. *Entrance requirements:* For master's and doctorate, minimum undergraduate GPA of 3.0. Additional exam requirements/recommendations for international students: Required—TOEFL (minimum score 550 computer-based; 77 iBT); Recommended—TWE. *Application deadline:* For fall admission, 2/15 priority date for domestic students, 1/1 for international students. Applications are processed on a rolling basis. Application fee: $60 ($75 for international students). Electronic applications accepted. *Financial support:* In 2011–12, 2 fellowships with partial tuition reimbursements (averaging $18,000 per year), 55 teaching assistantships with partial tuition reimbursements (averaging $18,000 per year) were awarded; research assistantships with partial tuition reimbursements and tuition waivers (partial) also available. Support available to part-time students. Financial award applicants required to submit FAFSA. *Unit head:* Dr. Paul B. Shepson, Head, 765-494-5203, E-mail: pshepson@purdue.edu. *Application contact:* Betty L.. Hatfield, Director of Graduate Admissions, 765-494-5208, E-mail: bettyh@purdue.edu.

Purdue University Calumet, Graduate Studies Office, School of Engineering, Mathematics, and Science, Department of Biological Sciences, Hammond, IN 46323-2094. Offers biology (MS); biology teaching (MS); biotechnology (MS). *Entrance requirements:* For master's, GRE. Additional exam requirements/recommendations for international students: Required—TOEFL. Electronic applications accepted. *Faculty research:* Cell biology, molecular biology, genetics, microbiology, neurophysiology.

Queens College of the City University of New York, Division of Graduate Studies, Division of Education, Department of Secondary Education, Flushing, NY 11367-1597. Offers art (MS Ed); biology (MS Ed, AC); chemistry (MS Ed, AC); earth sciences (MS Ed, AC); English (MS Ed, AC); French (MS Ed, AC); Italian (MS Ed, AC); mathematics (MS Ed, AC); music (MS Ed, AC); physics (MS Ed, AC); social studies (MS Ed, AC); Spanish (MS Ed, AC). Part-time and evening/weekend programs available. *Faculty:* 22 full-time (14 women). *Students:* 46 full-time (23 women), 727 part-time (442 women); includes 234 minority (41 Black or African American, non-Hispanic/Latino; 78 Asian, non-Hispanic/Latino; 115 Hispanic/Latino), 5 international. 591 applicants, 60% accepted, 250 enrolled. In 2011, 170 master's awarded. *Degree requirements:* For master's, research project; for AC, thesis optional. *Entrance requirements:* For master's, minimum GPA of 3.0. Additional exam requirements/recommendations for international students: Required—TOEFL. *Application deadline:* For fall admission, 4/1 for domestic students; for spring admission, 11/1 for domestic students. Applications are processed on a rolling basis. Application fee: $125. *Expenses:* Tuition, state resident: part-time $345 per credit. Tuition, nonresident: part-time $640 per credit. *Required fees:* $145.25 per semester. *Financial support:* Career-related internships or fieldwork, Federal Work-Study, institutionally sponsored loans, and tuition waivers (partial) available. Support available to part-time students. Financial award application deadline: 4/1; financial award applicants required to submit FAFSA. *Unit head:* Dr. Eleanor Armour-Thomas, Chairperson, 718-997-5150, E-mail: armourthomas@yahoo.com. *Application contact:* Mario Caruso, Director of Graduate Admissions, 718-997-5200, Fax: 718-997-5193, E-mail: graduate_admissions@qc.edu.

Quinnipiac University, School of Education, Program in Secondary Education, Hamden, CT 06518-1940. Offers biology (MAT); English (MAT); history/social studies (MAT); mathematics (MAT); Spanish (MAT). *Accreditation:* NCATE. *Faculty:* 7 full-time (5 women), 41 part-time/adjunct (24 women). *Students:* 56 full-time (38 women), 1 (woman) part-time; includes 5 minority (1 Black or African American, non-Hispanic/Latino; 1 Asian, non-Hispanic/Latino; 3 Hispanic/Latino). 51 applicants, 96% accepted, 44 enrolled. In 2011, 49 master's awarded. *Entrance requirements:* For master's, PRAXIS I, minimum GPA of 2.67, interview. *Application deadline:* For fall admission, 3/31 priority date for domestic students. Applications are processed on a rolling basis. Application fee: $45. Electronic applications accepted. *Expenses: Tuition:* Part-time $855 per credit. *Required fees:* $35 per credit. *Financial support:* In 2011–12, 1 student received support. Career-related internships or fieldwork, scholarships/grants, and tuition waivers (full and partial) available. Financial award application deadline: 4/15; financial award applicants required to submit FAFSA. *Faculty research:* Multicultural and urban education/leadership, challenges of teaching diverse learners, scholarship of teaching and learning, technology and teaching, humor and education. *Unit head:* Mordechai Gordon, Program Director, 203-582-8442, Fax: 203-582-3473, E-mail: mordechai.gordon@quinnipiac.edu. *Application contact:* Jennifer Boutin, Associate Director of Graduate Admissions, 800-462-1944, Fax: 203-582-3443, E-mail: jennifer.boutin@quinnipiac.edu. Web site: http://www.quinnipiac.edu/academics/colleges-schools-and-departments/school-of-education/graduate-programs/five-semester-mat-programs/secondary-educat.

Regis University, College for Professional Studies, School of Education and Counseling, Department of Education, Denver, CO 80221-1099. Offers adult learning, training, and development (M Ed, Certificate); autism (Certificate); curriculum, instruction, and assessment (M Ed); educational leadership (Certificate); educational technology (Certificate); instructional technology (M Ed); literacy (Certificate); professional leadership (M Ed); reading (M Ed); self-designed (M Ed); space studies (M Ed). Program also offered in Henderson and Las Vegas (Summerlin), NV. *Accreditation:* Teacher Education Accreditation Council. Part-time and evening/weekend programs available. Postbaccalaureate distance learning degree programs offered (no on-campus study). *Degree requirements:* For master's, thesis. *Entrance requirements:* For master's, resume, minimum GPA of 2.75, criminal background check. Additional exam requirements/recommendations for international students: Required—TOEFL (minimum score 213 computer-based), TWE (minimum score 5). Electronic applications accepted. *Faculty research:* Issues of equity in the middle school classroom, professional learning communities, school reform, socialinguistic and discursive obstacles to student integration, inclusive language arts curriculum.

Rice University, Graduate Programs, Wiess School of Natural Sciences, Department of Physics and Astronomy, Houston, TX 77251-1892. Offers nanoscale physics (MS);

physics and astronomy (PhD); science teaching (MST). Part-time programs available. *Degree requirements:* For master's, thesis (for some programs); for doctorate, thesis/dissertation, minimum B average. *Entrance requirements:* For master's, GRE General Test; for doctorate, GRE General Test, GRE Subject Test. Additional exam requirements/recommendations for international students: Required—TOEFL (minimum score 600 paper-based; 250 computer-based; 90 iBT). Electronic applications accepted. *Faculty research:* Optical physics; ultra cold atoms; membrane electr-statics, peptides, proteins and lipids; solar astrophysics; stellar activity; magnetic fields; young stars.

Rider University, Department of Graduate Education, Leadership and Counseling, Teacher Certification Program, Lawrenceville, NJ 08648-3001. Offers business education (Certificate); elementary education (Certificate); English as a second language (Certificate); English education (Certificate); mathematics education (Certificate); preschool to grade 3 (Certificate); science education (Certificate); social studies education (Certificate); world languages (Certificate), including French, German, Spanish. Part-time programs available. *Degree requirements:* For Certificate, internship, professional portfolio. *Entrance requirements:* For degree, PRAXIS, resume. Additional exam requirements/recommendations for international students: Required—TOEFL (minimum score 550 paper-based; 213 computer-based). Electronic applications accepted. *Expenses: Tuition:* Full-time $32,820; part-time $710 per credit. *Required fees:* $350; $35 per course. Tuition and fees vary according to campus/location and program. *Faculty research:* Conceptual foundations for optimal development of creativity; creative theory, cognitive processes in mathematics learning, teacher collaboration.

Rutgers, The State University of New Jersey, New Brunswick, Graduate School of Education, Department of Learning and Teaching, Program in Science Education, Piscataway, NJ 08854-8097. Offers Ed M, Ed D. Part-time programs available. Terminal master's awarded for partial completion of doctoral program. *Degree requirements:* For master's, comprehensive exam (for some programs); for doctorate, thesis/dissertation, qualifying exam. *Entrance requirements:* For master's, GRE General Test, minimum GPA of 3.0; for doctorate, GRE General Test, minimum GPA of 3.5. Additional exam requirements/recommendations for international students: Required—TOEFL. Electronic applications accepted.

Saginaw Valley State University, College of Education, Program in Natural Science Teaching, University Center, MI 48710. Offers elementary (MAT); middle school (MAT); secondary school (MAT). *Accreditation:* NCATE. Part-time and evening/weekend programs available. *Students:* 9 part-time (7 women); includes 1 minority (Black or African American, non-Hispanic/Latino). Average age 35. 1 applicant, 100% accepted, 0 enrolled. In 2011, 14 master's awarded. *Degree requirements:* For master's, capstone course. *Entrance requirements:* For master's, minimum GPA of 3.0, teaching certificate. Additional exam requirements/recommendations for international students: Required—TOEFL (minimum score 525 paper-based; 197 computer-based; 71 iBT). *Application deadline:* Applications are processed on a rolling basis. Application fee: $25. Electronic applications accepted. *Expenses:* Tuition, state resident: full-time $8300; part-time $5333 per year. Tuition, nonresident: full-time $15,613; part-time $10,209 per year. *International tuition:* $15,631 full-time. *Financial support:* Federal Work-Study and scholarships/grants available. Support available to part-time students. Financial award applicants required to submit FAFSA. *Unit head:* Dr. Steve P. Barbus, Jr., Dean, 989-964-6067, Fax: 989-790-4385, E-mail: barbus@svsu.edu. *Application contact:* Kathy Lopez, Certification Officer, 989-964-4661, Fax: 989-964-4385, E-mail: klopez@svsu.edu.

St. John Fisher College, School of Arts and Sciences, Mathematics/Science/Technology Education Program, Rochester, NY 14618-3597. Offers MS. Part-time and evening/weekend programs available. *Faculty:* 4 full-time (0 women), 5 part-time/adjunct (4 women). *Students:* 6 full-time (4 women), 53 part-time (35 women); includes 7 minority (3 Black or African American, non-Hispanic/Latino; 1 American Indian or Alaska Native, non-Hispanic/Latino; 2 Asian, non-Hispanic/Latino; 1 Two or more races, non-Hispanic/Latino). Average age 29. 29 applicants, 93% accepted, 20 enrolled. In 2011, 12 master's awarded. *Degree requirements:* For master's, thesis, capstone experience. *Entrance requirements:* For master's, 2 letters of recommendation, personal statement, current resume, interview, teaching certification. Additional exam requirements/recommendations for international students: Required—TOEFL (minimum score 575 paper-based; 233 computer-based; 80 iBT). *Application deadline:* Applications are processed on a rolling basis. Application fee: $30. Electronic applications accepted. *Expenses: Tuition:* Part-time $735 per credit. One-time fee: $50 part-time. Tuition and fees vary according to course load, degree level and program. *Financial support:* In 2011–12, 15 students received support. Scholarships/grants available. Financial award applicants required to submit FAFSA. *Faculty research:* Mathematics education, science and technology education. *Unit head:* Dr. Bernard Ricca, Graduate Director, 585-899-3866, E-mail: bricca@sjfc.edu. *Application contact:* Jose Perales, Director of Graduate Admissions, 585-385-8067, E-mail: jperales@sjfc.edu.

Saint Xavier University, Graduate Studies, School of Education, Chicago, IL 60655-3105. Offers counseling (MA); curriculum and instruction (MA); early childhood education (MA); educational administration (MA); elementary education (MA); individualized studies (MA), including educational technology, English as a second language (ESL), ISTEM (integrative science, technology, engineering, and math), science education; music education (MA); reading (MA); secondary education (MA); Spanish education (MA); special education (MA); teaching and leadership (MA). *Accreditation:* NCATE. Part-time and evening/weekend programs available. *Degree requirements:* For master's, thesis or project. *Entrance requirements:* For master's, minimum GPA of 3.0. *Application deadline:* For fall admission, 8/15 priority date for domestic students. Applications are processed on a rolling basis. Application fee: $35. *Expenses:* Contact institution. *Financial support:* Career-related internships or fieldwork available. Support available to part-time students. Financial award applicants required to submit FAFSA. *Unit head:* Dr. Beverly Gulley, Dean, 773-298-3221, Fax: 773-779-9061, E-mail: gulley@sxu.edu. *Application contact:* Beth Gierach, Managing Director of Admission, 773-298-3053, Fax: 773-298-3076, E-mail: gierach@sxu.edu.

Salem State University, School of Graduate Studies, Program in Biology, Salem, MA 01970-5353. Offers MAT. Part-time and evening/weekend programs available. *Entrance requirements:* For master's, GRE or MAT. Additional exam requirements/recommendations for international students: Required—TOEFL (minimum score 550 paper-based; 80 iBT) or IELTS (minimum score 5.5).

Salem State University, School of Graduate Studies, Program in Chemistry, Salem, MA 01970-5353. Offers MAT. Part-time and evening/weekend programs available. *Entrance requirements:* For master's, GRE or MAT. Additional exam requirements/recommendations for international students: Required—TOEFL (minimum score 550 paper-based; 80 iBT) or IELTS (minimum score 5.5).

Salem State University, School of Graduate Studies, Program in Middle School General Science, Salem, MA 01970-5353. Offers MAT. Part-time and evening/weekend programs available. *Entrance requirements:* For master's, GRE or MAT. Additional exam requirements/recommendations for international students: Required—TOEFL (minimum score 550 paper-based; 80 iBT) or IELTS (minimum score 5.5).

San Diego State University, Graduate and Research Affairs, College of Sciences, Department of Mathematics and Statistics, San Diego, CA 92182. Offers applied mathematics (MS); mathematics (MA); mathematics and science education (PhD); statistics (MS). PhD offered jointly wtih University of California, San Diego. Part-time programs available. *Degree requirements:* For doctorate, thesis/dissertation. *Entrance requirements:* For master's, GRE General Test; for doctorate, GRE, minimum GPA of 3.25 in last 30 undergraduate semester units, minimum graduate GPA of 3.5, MSE recommendation form, 3 letters of recommendation. Additional exam requirements/recommendations for international students: Required—TOEFL. Electronic applications accepted. *Faculty research:* Teacher education in mathematics.

San Jose State University, Graduate Studies and Research, College of Science, Program in Science Education, San Jose, CA 95192-0001. Offers natural science (MA). *Degree requirements:* For master's, project or thesis.

Shippensburg University of Pennsylvania, School of Graduate Studies, College of Education and Human Services, Department of Teacher Education, Shippensburg, PA 17257-2299. Offers curriculum and instruction (M Ed), including biology, early childhood education, elementary education, English, geography/earth science, history, mathematics, middle level education, modern languages; reading (M Ed). *Accreditation:* NCATE. Part-time and evening/weekend programs available. *Faculty:* 14 full-time (11 women), 8 part-time/adjunct (7 women). *Students:* 16 full-time (15 women), 143 part-time (130 women); includes 11 minority (4 Black or African American, non-Hispanic/Latino; 1 Asian, non-Hispanic/Latino; 4 Hispanic/Latino; 2 Two or more races, non-Hispanic/Latino), 1 international. Average age 30. 55 applicants, 55% accepted, 25 enrolled. In 2011, 76 master's awarded. *Degree requirements:* For master's, comprehensive exam (for some programs), thesis optional, practicum or internship; capstone seminar (for some programs). *Entrance requirements:* For master's, MAT (if GPA less than 2.75), interview, 3 letters of reference, questionnaire of teaching background and future goals. Additional exam requirements/recommendations for international students: Required—TOEFL (minimum score 580 paper-based; 237 computer-based); Recommended—IELTS (minimum score 6). *Application deadline:* For fall admission, 6/1 priority date for domestic students, 4/30 for international students; for spring admission, 9/1 priority date for domestic students, 9/30 for international students. Applications are processed on a rolling basis. Application fee: $30. Electronic applications accepted. *Expenses: Tuition, area resident:* Part-time $416 per credit. Tuition, state resident: part-time $416 per credit. Tuition, nonresident: part-time $624 per credit. *Required fees:* $119 per credit. *Financial support:* In 2011–12, 5 research assistantships with full tuition reimbursements (averaging $5,000 per year) were awarded; career-related internships or fieldwork, scholarships/grants, unspecified assistantships, and resident hall director and student payroll positions also available. Support available to part-time students. Financial award application deadline: 3/1; financial award applicants required to submit FAFSA. *Unit head:* Dr. Christine A. Royce, Chairperson, 717-477-1688, Fax: 717-477-4046, E-mail: caroyc@ship.edu. *Application contact:* Jeremy R. Goshorn, Assistant Dean of Graduate Admissions, 717-477-1231, Fax: 717-477-4016, E-mail: jrgoshorn@ship.edu. Web site: http://www.ship.edu/teacher/.

Slippery Rock University of Pennsylvania, Graduate Studies (Recruitment), College of Education, Department of Elementary Education and Early Childhood, Slippery Rock, PA 16057-1383. Offers math/science (K-8) (M Ed); reading (M Ed). *Accreditation:* NCATE. Part-time and evening/weekend programs available. Postbaccalaureate distance learning degree programs offered. *Faculty:* 3 full-time (all women). *Students:* 2 full-time (both women), 33 part-time (all women); includes 1 minority (Two or more races, non-Hispanic/Latino). Average age 28. 55 applicants, 69% accepted, 11 enrolled. In 2011, 33 degrees awarded. *Entrance requirements:* For master's, GRE General Test, MAT, minimum GPA of 3.0, resume, teaching certification, letters of recommendation, transcripts (depending on program). Additional exam requirements/recommendations for international students: Required—TOEFL (minimum score 550 paper-based; 213 computer-based; 80 iBT). *Application deadline:* For fall admission, 3/1 priority date for domestic students, 5/1 for international students; for spring admission, 10/1 priority date for domestic students, 9/1 for international students. Applications are processed on a rolling basis. Application fee: $25 ($30 for international students). Electronic applications accepted. *Expenses:* Contact institution. *Financial support:* Career-related internships or fieldwork, Federal Work-Study, institutionally sponsored loans, scholarships/grants, tuition waivers (partial), and unspecified assistantships available. Support available to part-time students. Financial award application deadline: 5/1; financial award applicants required to submit FAFSA. *Unit head:* Dr. Suzanne Rose, Graduate Coordinator, 724-738-2863, Fax: 724-738-4987, E-mail: suzanne.rose@sru.edu. *Application contact:* Angela Barrett, Director of Graduate Admissions, 724-738-2051, Fax: 724-738-2146, E-mail: graduate.admissions@sru.edu.

Slippery Rock University of Pennsylvania, Graduate Studies (Recruitment), College of Education, Department of Secondary Education/Foundations of Education, Slippery Rock, PA 16057-1383. Offers educational leadership (M Ed); secondary education in English (M Ed); secondary education in math/science (M Ed); secondary education in social studies (M Ed). *Accreditation:* NCATE. Part-time and evening/weekend programs available. *Faculty:* 9 full-time (4 women), 3 part-time/adjunct (0 women). *Students:* 64 full-time (34 women), 16 part-time (8 women); includes 2 minority (1 Asian, non-Hispanic/Latino; 1 Two or more races, non-Hispanic/Latino). Average age 28. 68 applicants, 76% accepted, 27 enrolled. In 2011, 54 degrees awarded. *Degree requirements:* For master's, comprehensive exam, thesis (for some programs). *Entrance requirements:* For master's, GRE General Test, MAT, minimum GPA of 2.8 (depending on program). Additional exam requirements/recommendations for international students: Required—TOEFL (minimum score 550 paper-based; 213 computer-based; 80 iBT). *Application deadline:* For fall admission, 3/1 priority date for domestic students, 5/1 for international students; for spring admission, 10/1 priority date for domestic students, 9/1 for international students. Applications are processed on a rolling basis. Application fee: $25 ($30 for international students). Electronic applications accepted. *Expenses:* Tuition, state resident: full-time $7488; part-time $416 per credit. Tuition, nonresident: full-time $11,232; part-time $624 per credit. *International tuition:* $11,146 full-time. *Required fees:* $2722; $140 per credit. Tuition and fees vary according to degree level and program. *Financial support:* Career-related internships or fieldwork, Federal Work-Study, institutionally sponsored loans, scholarships/grants, tuition waivers (partial), and unspecified assistantships available. Support available to part-time students. Financial award application deadline: 5/1; financial award applicants required to submit FAFSA. *Unit head:* Dr. Jeffrey Lehman, Graduate Coordinator, 724-738-2311, Fax: 724-738-4987, E-mail: jeffrey.lehman@sru.edu. *Application contact:* Angela Barrett, Interim Director of Graduate Studies, 724-738-2051, Fax: 724-738-2146, E-mail: graduate.admissions@sru.edu.

Smith College, Graduate and Special Programs, Department of Education and Child Study, Program in Secondary Education, Northampton, MA 01063. Offers biological sciences education (MAT); chemistry education (MAT); English education (MAT); French education (MAT); geology education (MAT); government education (MAT); history education (MAT); mathematics education (MAT); physics education (MAT); Spanish education (MAT). Part-time programs available. *Faculty:* 6 full-time (4 women), 3 part-time/adjunct (2 women). *Students:* 11 full-time (8 women), 3 part-time (all women); includes 2 minority (1 Asian, non-Hispanic/Latino; 1 Hispanic/Latino). Average age 26. 21 applicants, 95% accepted, 12 enrolled. In 2011, 2 master's awarded. *Entrance requirements:* For master's, GRE. Additional exam requirements/recommendations for international students: Required—TOEFL (minimum score 590 paper-based; 243 computer-based; 97 iBT). *Application deadline:* For fall admission, 4/1 for domestic students, 1/15 for international students; for spring admission, 12/1 for domestic students. Application fee: $60. *Expenses: Tuition:* Full-time $14,925; part-time $1245 per credit. *Financial support:* In 2011–12, 13 students received support. Career-related internships or fieldwork, institutionally sponsored loans, and scholarships/grants available. Support available to part-time students. Financial award application deadline: 1/15; financial award applicants required to submit CSS PROFILE or FAFSA. *Unit head:* Rosetta Cohen, Graduate Student Advisor, 413-585-3266, E-mail: rcohen@smith.edu. *Application contact:* Ruth Morgan, Administrative Assistant, 413-585-3050, Fax: 413-585-3054, E-mail: gradstdy@smith.edu. Web site: http://www.smith.edu/educ/.

South Carolina State University, School of Graduate Studies, Department of Education, Orangeburg, SC 29117-0001. Offers counseling education (M Ed); early childhood and special education (M Ed); early childhood education (MAT); educational leadership (Ed D, Ed S); elementary education (M Ed, MAT); engineering (MAT); general science (MAT); mathematics (MAT); secondary education (M Ed), including biology education, business education, counselor education, English education, home economics education, industrial education, mathematics education, science education, social studies education; special education (M Ed), including emotionally handicapped, learning disabilities, mentally handicapped. *Accreditation:* NCATE. Part-time and evening/weekend programs available. *Faculty:* 9 full-time (6 women), 6 part-time/adjunct (2 women). *Students:* 34 full-time (29 women), 50 part-time (40 women); includes 74 minority (72 Black or African American, non-Hispanic/Latino; 1 Asian, non-Hispanic/Latino; 1 Hispanic/Latino). Average age 34. 23 applicants, 91% accepted, 14 enrolled. In 2011, 11 master's awarded. *Degree requirements:* For master's, thesis optional, departmental qualifying exam. *Entrance requirements:* For master's, GRE General Test, NTE, interview, teaching certificate. *Application deadline:* For fall admission, 6/15 priority date for domestic students, 6/15 for international students; for spring admission, 11/1 for domestic and international students. Applications are processed on a rolling basis. Application fee: $25. Electronic applications accepted. *Expenses:* Tuition, state resident: full-time $8688; part-time $514 per credit hour. Tuition, nonresident: full-time $17,600; part-time $1009 per credit hour. *Required fees:* $570. *Financial support:* In 2011–12, 3 fellowships (averaging $5,020 per year) were awarded; career-related internships or fieldwork, Federal Work-Study, and institutionally sponsored loans also available. Financial award application deadline: 6/1. *Faculty research:* Critical thinking, child abuse, stress, test-taking skills, conflict resolution, mainstreaming. *Unit head:* Dr. Charlie Spell, Interim Chair, 803-536-7098, Fax: 803-516-4568, E-mail: cspell@scsu.edu. *Application contact:* Annette Hazzard-Jones, Program Coordinator II, 803-536-8809, Fax: 803-536-8812, E-mail: zs_ahazzard@scsu.edu.

Southeast Missouri State University, School of Graduate Studies, College of Science and Mathematics, Cape Girardeau, MO 63701-4799. Offers science education (MNS). Part-time programs available. *Faculty:* 3 full-time (all women). *Students:* 7 part-time (6 women). Average age 37. 2 applicants, 100% accepted, 2 enrolled. In 2011, 1 master's awarded. *Degree requirements:* For master's, comprehensive exam, research paper. *Entrance requirements:* For master's, minimum undergraduate GPA of 2.5, 2.75 in last 30 hours of undergraduate course work in science and math; 2 letters of recommendation. Additional exam requirements/recommendations for international students: Required—TOEFL (minimum score 550 paper-based; 213 computer-based; 79 iBT); Recommended—IELTS (minimum score 6). *Application deadline:* For fall admission, 8/1 for domestic students, 7/1 for international students; for spring admission, 11/21 for domestic students, 11/1 for international students. Applications are processed on a rolling basis. Application fee: $30 ($40 for international students). Electronic applications accepted. *Expenses:* Tuition, state resident: full-time $4896; part-time $272 per credit hour. Tuition, nonresident: full-time $8649; part-time $480.50 per credit hour. *Financial support:* In 2011–12, 6 students received support. Career-related internships or fieldwork, Federal Work-Study, scholarships/grants, tuition waivers (full), and unspecified assistantships available. Financial award application deadline: 6/30; financial award applicants required to submit FAFSA. *Faculty research:* Investigative case-based learning (PBL) with computer simulations, tools, models; inquiry chemistry laboratory; pre-K-G science education emphasizing constructivist, engaged learning; science outreach. *Total annual research expenditures:* $548,000. *Unit head:* Dr. Rachel Morgan Theall, Director of Graduate Program in Science Education, 573-651-2372, Fax: 573-986-6792, E-mail: rmtheall@semo.edu. *Application contact:* Alisa Aleen McFerron, Assistant Director of Admissions for Operations, 573-651-5937, Fax: 573-651-5936, E-mail: amcferron@semo.edu. Web site: http://www.semo.edu/costa/.

Southern Connecticut State University, School of Graduate Studies, School of Arts and Sciences, Department of Science Education and Environmental Studies, New Haven, CT 06515-1355. Offers environmental education (MS); science education (MS, Diploma). *Accreditation:* NCATE. Part-time and evening/weekend programs available. *Faculty:* 3 full-time (1 woman), 1 (woman) part-time/adjunct. *Students:* 23 full-time (11 women), 27 part-time (18 women); includes 6 minority (2 Black or African American, non-Hispanic/Latino; 1 Asian, non-Hispanic/Latino; 1 Hispanic/Latino; 2 Two or more races, non-Hispanic/Latino). 54 applicants, 17% accepted, 7 enrolled. In 2011, 18 master's awarded. *Degree requirements:* For master's, thesis or alternative. *Entrance requirements:* For master's, interview; for Diploma, master's degree. *Application deadline:* For fall admission, 7/15 priority date for domestic students. Applications are processed on a rolling basis. Application fee: $50. Electronic applications accepted. *Expenses:* Tuition, state resident: full-time $5137; part-time $413 per credit. *Required fees:* $4008; $55 per term. *Financial support:* Application deadline: 4/15; applicants required to submit FAFSA. *Unit head:* Dr. Susan Cusato, Chairman, 203-392-6610, Fax: 203-392-6614, E-mail: hagemans1@southernct.edu. *Application contact:* Dr. Susan Cusato, Graduate Coordinator, 203-392-6610, Fax: 203-392-6614, E-mail: cusatos1@southernct.edu.

Southern Illinois University Edwardsville, Graduate School, School of Education, Department of Curriculum and Instruction, Program in Secondary Education, Edwardsville, IL 62026. Offers art (MS Ed); biology (MS Ed); chemistry (MS Ed); earth and space sciences (MS Ed); English/language arts (MS Ed); foreign languages (MS Ed); history (MS Ed); mathematics (MS Ed); physics (MS Ed). *Accreditation:* NCATE. Part-time and evening/weekend programs available. *Students:* 1 full-time (0 women), 42 part-time (33 women); includes 2 minority (both Black or African American, non-Hispanic/Latino). 16 applicants, 31% accepted. In 2011, 8 master's awarded. *Degree requirements:* For master's, comprehensive exam (for some programs), final exam/paper. *Entrance requirements:* Additional exam requirements/recommendations for international students: Required—TOEFL (minimum score 550 paper-based; 213 computer-based; 79 iBT), IELTS (minimum score 6.5). *Application deadline:* For fall admission, 7/22 for domestic students, 6/1 for international students; for spring admission, 12/9 for domestic students, 10/1 for international students. Applications are processed on a rolling basis. Application fee: $30. Electronic applications accepted. Tuition and fees vary according to course load and program. *Financial support:* Fellowships, research assistantships, teaching assistantships, institutionally sponsored loans, scholarships/grants, and unspecified assistantships available. Financial award application deadline: 3/1; financial award applicants required to submit FAFSA. *Unit head:* Dr. Susan Breck, Director, 618-650-3444, E-mail: sbreck@siue.edu. *Application contact:* Dr. Michelle Robinson, Coordinator of Graduate Recruitment, 618-650-2811, Fax: 618-650-3523, E-mail: michero@siue.edu. Web site: http://www.siue.edu/education/ci/.

Southern University and Agricultural and Mechanical College, Graduate School, Department of Science/Mathematics Education, Baton Rouge, LA 70813. Offers PhD. *Accreditation:* NCATE. *Degree requirements:* For doctorate, thesis/dissertation. *Entrance requirements:* For doctorate, GRE General Test. Additional exam requirements/recommendations for international students: Required—TOEFL (minimum score 525 paper-based; 193 computer-based). *Faculty research:* Performance assessment in science/mathematics education, equity in science/mathematics education, technology and distance learning, science/mathematics concept formation, cognitive themes, problem solving in science/mathematics education.

Southwestern Oklahoma State University, College of Arts and Sciences, Specialization in Natural Sciences, Weatherford, OK 73096-3098. Offers M Ed. Part-time programs available. *Degree requirements:* For master's, exam. *Entrance requirements:* For master's, GRE General Test or minimum undergraduate GPA of 3.0. Additional exam requirements/recommendations for international students: Required—TOEFL.

Stanford University, School of Education, Program in Curriculum Studies and Teacher Education, Stanford, CA 94305-9991. Offers art education (MA, PhD); dance education (MA); English education (MA, PhD); general curriculum studies (MA, PhD); mathematics education (MA, PhD); science education (MA, PhD); social studies education (PhD); teacher education (MA, PhD). *Degree requirements:* For master's, thesis (for some programs); for doctorate, thesis/dissertation. *Entrance requirements:* For master's and doctorate, GRE General Test. Electronic applications accepted. *Expenses: Tuition:* Full-time $40,050; part-time $890 per credit.

Stanford University, School of Education, Teacher Education Program, Stanford, CA 94305-9991. Offers English education (MA); languages education (MA); mathematics education (MA); science education (MA); social studies education (MA). *Degree requirements:* For master's, thesis. *Entrance requirements:* For master's, GRE General Test. Electronic applications accepted. *Expenses: Tuition:* Full-time $40,050; part-time $890 per credit.

State University of New York at Binghamton, Graduate School, School of Education, Program in Adolescence Education, Binghamton, NY 13902-6000. Offers biology education (MAT, MS Ed, MST); earth science education (MAT, MS Ed, MST); English education (MAT, MS Ed, MST); French education (MAT, MST); mathematical sciences education (MAT, MS Ed, MST); physics (MAT, MS Ed, MST); social studies (MAT, MS Ed, MST); Spanish education (MAT, MST). *Accreditation:* Teacher Education Accreditation Council. Part-time and evening/weekend programs available. *Students:* 98 full-time (66 women), 13 part-time (11 women); includes 2 minority (1 Black or African American, non-Hispanic/Latino; 1 Hispanic/Latino). Average age 26. 73 applicants, 70% accepted, 35 enrolled. In 2011, 58 master's awarded. *Entrance requirements:* For master's, GRE General Test. Additional exam requirements/recommendations for international students: Required—TOEFL (minimum score 550 paper-based; 213 computer-based; 80 iBT). *Application deadline:* For fall admission, 2/1 priority date for domestic students, 2/1 for international students; for spring admission, 10/15 priority date for domestic students, 10/15 for international students. Applications are processed on a rolling basis. Application fee: $60. Electronic applications accepted. *Financial support:* In 2011–12, 4 students received support, including 1 fellowship with partial tuition reimbursement available (averaging $12,000 per year); career-related internships or fieldwork, Federal Work-Study, institutionally sponsored loans, scholarships/grants, health care benefits, tuition waivers (full), and unspecified assistantships also available. Financial award application deadline: 2/15; financial award applicants required to submit FAFSA. *Unit head:* Dr. S. G. Grant, Dean of School of Education, 607-777-7329, E-mail: sggrant@binghamton.edu. *Application contact:* Catherine Smith, Recruiting and Admissions Coordinator, 607-777-2151, Fax: 607-777-2501, E-mail: cmsmith@binghamton.edu.

State University of New York at Fredonia, Graduate Studies, Department of Chemistry and Biochemistry, Fredonia, NY 14063-1136. Offers chemistry (MS); curriculum and instruction science education (MS Ed). Part-time and evening/weekend programs available. *Degree requirements:* For master's, thesis optional. *Expenses:* Tuition, state resident: full-time $6666; part-time $370 per credit hour. Tuition, nonresident: full-time $11,376; part-time $632 per credit hour. *Required fees:* $1059.30; $58.85 per credit hour. Tuition and fees vary according to course load.

State University of New York at New Paltz, Graduate School, School of Education, Department of Secondary Education, New Paltz, NY 12561. Offers adolescence education: biology (MAT, MS Ed); adolescence education: chemistry (MAT, MS Ed); adolescence education: earth science (MAT, MS Ed); adolescence education: English (MAT, MS Ed); adolescence education: French (MAT, MS Ed); adolescence education: social studies (MAT, MS Ed); adolescence education: Spanish (MAT, MS Ed); second language education (MS Ed). *Accreditation:* NCATE. Part-time and evening/weekend programs available. *Faculty:* 18 full-time (10 women), 2 part-time/adjunct (both women). *Students:* 79 full-time (48 women), 76 part-time (55 women); includes 30 minority (3 Black or African American, non-Hispanic/Latino; 2 Asian, non-Hispanic/Latino; 22 Hispanic/Latino; 3 Two or more races, non-Hispanic/Latino), 1 international. Average age 32. 127 applicants, 69% accepted, 64 enrolled. In 2011, 73 master's awarded. *Degree requirements:* For master's, comprehensive exam (for some programs), portfolio. *Entrance requirements:* For master's, minimum GPA of 3.0, New York state teaching certificate (MS Ed). Additional exam requirements/recommendations for international students: Required—TOEFL (minimum score 550 paper-based; 213 computer-based; 80 iBT), IELTS (minimum score 6.5). *Application deadline:* For fall admission, 3/1 priority date for domestic students, 3/1 for international students; for spring admission, 10/1 priority date for domestic students, 10/1 for international students. Application fee: $50. Electronic applications accepted. *Expenses:* Tuition, state resident: full-time $8870; part-time $370 per credit. Tuition, nonresident: full-time $15,160; part-time $632 per credit. *Required fees:* $1188; $34 per credit. $184 per semester. *Financial support:* In 2011–12, 13 students received support, including 3 fellowships with partial tuition reimbursements available (averaging $7,000 per year); Federal Work-Study, institutionally sponsored loans, and tuition waivers (full) also available. Financial award application deadline: 8/1; financial award applicants required to submit FAFSA. *Unit head:* Dr. Devon Duhaney, Chair, 845-257-2850, E-mail: duhaneyd@newpaltz.edu. *Application contact:* Caroline Murphy, Graduate Admissions Advisor, 845-257-3285, Fax: 845-257-3284, E-mail: gradschool@newpaltz.edu. Web site: http://www.newpaltz.edu/secondaryed/.

State University of New York at Plattsburgh, Division of Education, Health, and Human Services, Program in Teacher Education: Adolescence MST, Plattsburgh, NY 12901-2681. Offers adolescence education (MST); biology 7-12 (MST); chemistry 7-12 (MST); earth science 7-12 (MST); English 7-12 (MST); French 7-12 (MST); mathematics 7-12 (MST); physics 7-12 (MST); social studies 7-12 (MST); Spanish 7-12 (MST).

Accreditation: Teacher Education Accreditation Council. Part-time and evening/weekend programs available. *Students:* 53 full-time (26 women), 5 part-time (4 women). Average age 29. *Entrance requirements:* For master's, minimum GPA of 2.75. Additional exam requirements/recommendations for international students: Required—TOEFL. *Application deadline:* For fall admission, 2/15 priority date for domestic students. Applications are processed on a rolling basis. Application fee: $75. *Financial support:* Application deadline: 4/15; applicants required to submit FAFSA. *Unit head:* Dr. Robert Ackland, Coordinator, 518-564-5131, E-mail: acklanrt@plattsburgh.edu. *Application contact:* Marguerite Adelman, Assistant Director, Graduate Admissions, 518-564-4723, Fax: 518-564-4722, E-mail: adelmaml@plattsburgh.edu.

State University of New York at Plattsburgh, Faculty of Arts and Science, Program in Natural Science, Plattsburgh, NY 12901-2681. Offers MS, PSM. *Accreditation:* Teacher Education Accreditation Council. Part-time programs available. *Students:* 3 full-time (0 women), 2 part-time (1 woman). Average age 27. *Entrance requirements:* For master's, GRE General Test (minimum score of 1200), bachelor's degree in science discipline, minimum GPA of 3.0. Additional exam requirements/recommendations for international students: Required—TOEFL. *Application deadline:* For fall admission, 2/15 priority date for domestic students; for spring admission, 10/15 priority date for domestic students. Applications are processed on a rolling basis. Application fee: $75. *Financial support:* Federal Work-Study available. Support available to part-time students. Financial award application deadline: 4/15; financial award applicants required to submit FAFSA. *Unit head:* Dr. Timothy B. Mihuc, Program Coordinator, 518-564-3039, Fax: 518-564-3036, E-mail: timothy.mihuc@plattsburgh.edu. *Application contact:* Marguerite Adelman, Assistant Director, Graduate Admissions, 518-564-4723, Fax: 518-564-4722, E-mail: adelmaml@plattsburgh.edu.

State University of New York College at Cortland, Graduate Studies, School of Arts and Sciences, Programs in Adolescence Education, Cortland, NY 13045. Offers biology (MAT, MS Ed); chemistry (MAT, MS Ed); earth science (MAT, MS Ed); English (MS Ed); French (MS Ed); mathematics (MAT, MS Ed); physics (MAT, MS Ed); social studies (MS Ed); Spanish (MS Ed). *Accreditation:* NCATE. Part-time and evening/weekend programs available. *Degree requirements:* For master's, one foreign language, comprehensive exam (for some programs), thesis (for some programs). *Entrance requirements:* For master's, GRE General Test.

State University of New York College at Potsdam, School of Education and Professional Studies, Program in Secondary Education, Potsdam, NY 13676. Offers English (MST); mathematics (with grades 5-6 extension) (MST); science (MST), including biology, chemistry, earth science, physics; Social Studies (with grades 5-6 extension) (MST). *Accreditation:* NCATE. *Faculty:* 9 full-time (3 women), 3 part-time/adjunct (2 women). *Students:* 32 full-time (17 women), 1 part-time (0 women); includes 2 minority (1 Black or African American, non-Hispanic/Latino; 1 Asian, non-Hispanic/Latino), 3 international. 43 applicants, 88% accepted, 24 enrolled. In 2011, 43 master's awarded. *Degree requirements:* For master's, culminating experience. *Entrance requirements:* For master's, minimum GPA of 2.75 in last 60 hours of course work (3.0 for English program). Additional exam requirements/recommendations for international students: Required—TOEFL (minimum score 550 paper-based; 213 computer-based; 80 iBT), IELTS (minimum score 6). *Application deadline:* For spring admission, 3/1 for domestic and international students. Applications are processed on a rolling basis. Application fee: $50. *Expenses:* Tuition, state resident: full-time $8870; part-time $370 per credit hour. Tuition, nonresident: full-time $15,160; part-time $632 per credit hour. *Required fees:* $1066; $44.10 per credit hour. One-time fee: $3. *Financial support:* Fellowships, teaching assistantships, career-related internships or fieldwork, Federal Work-Study, scholarships/grants, and unspecified assistantships available. Support available to part-time students. Financial award application deadline: 3/1; financial award applicants required to submit FAFSA. *Unit head:* Donald C. Straight, Chairperson, 315-267-2553, Fax: 315-267-4802, E-mail: straigdc@potsdam.edu. *Application contact:* Peter Cutler, Graduate Admissions Counselor, 315-267-2165, Fax: 315-267-4802, E-mail: graduate@potsdam.edu. Web site: http://www.potsdam.edu/academics/SOEPS/SecondaryEd/index.cfm.

Stony Brook University, State University of New York, Graduate School, College of Arts and Sciences, Department of Physics and Astronomy, Program in Physics, Stony Brook, NY 11794. Offers modern research instrumentation (MS); physics (MA, PhD); physics education (MAT). *Degree requirements:* For doctorate, one foreign language, thesis/dissertation. *Entrance requirements:* For master's and doctorate, GRE General Test. Additional exam requirements/recommendations for international students: Required—TOEFL.

Stony Brook University, State University of New York, Graduate School, College of Arts and Sciences, Program in Science Education, Stony Brook, NY 11794. Offers PhD. *Degree requirements:* For doctorate, comprehensive exam, thesis/dissertation. *Entrance requirements:* For doctorate, GRE. Additional exam requirements/recommendations for international students: Required—TOEFL (minimum score 550 paper-based; 213 computer-based; 90 iBT), IELTS (minimum score 6.5).

Stony Brook University, State University of New York, School of Professional Development, Stony Brook, NY 11794. Offers biology-grade 7-12 (MAT); chemistry-grade 7-12 (MAT); coaching (Graduate Certificate); coaching online (Graduate Certificate); computer integrated engineering (Graduate Certificate); earth science-grade 7-12 (MAT); educational computing (Graduate Certificate); educational leadership (Advanced Certificate); English-grade 7-12 (MAT); environmental management (Graduate Certificate); environmental/occupational health and safety (Graduate Certificate); French-grade 7-12 (MAT); German-grade 7-12 (MAT); human resource management (Graduate Certificate); human resource management online (Graduate Certificate); information systems management (Graduate Certificate); Italian-grade 7-12 (MAT); liberal studies (MA); liberal studies online (MAT); mathematics-grade 7-12 (MAT); operation research (Graduate Certificate); physics-grade 7-12 (MAT); professional studies online (MPS); school administration and supervision (Graduate Certificate); school building leadership (Graduate Certificate); school district administration (Graduate Certificate); school district business leadership (Advanced Certificate); school district leadership (Graduate Certificate); social science and the professions (MPS), including environmental waste management, human resource management; social studies-grade 7-12 (MAT); Spanish-grade 7-12 (MAT); waste management (Graduate Certificate). Part-time and evening/weekend programs available. Postbaccalaureate distance learning degree programs offered. *Degree requirements:* For master's, one foreign language, thesis or alternative.

Syracuse University, College of Arts and Sciences, Program in College Science Teaching, Syracuse, NY 13244. Offers PhD. Part-time programs available. *Students:* 5 full-time (3 women), 3 part-time (2 women). Average age 39. 2 applicants, 100% accepted, 1 enrolled. In 2011, 1 degree awarded. *Entrance requirements:* For doctorate, GRE General Test, GRE Subject Test. Additional exam requirements/recommendations for international students: Required—TOEFL (minimum score 100 iBT). *Application deadline:* For fall admission, 2/1 for international students. Applications are processed on a rolling basis. Application fee: $75. Electronic applications accepted. *Expenses: Tuition:* Part-time $1206 per credit. *Financial support:* Fellowships with full tuition reimbursements and teaching assistantships with full and partial tuition reimbursements available. Financial award application deadline: 1/1; financial award applicants required to submit FAFSA. *Unit head:* Dr. Joanna Masingila, Chair, 315-443-1483, E-mail: jomasing@syr.edu. *Application contact:* Cynthia Daley, Information Contact, 315-443-2586, E-mail: cyndaley@syr.edu. Web site: http://sciteach.syr.edu/.

Syracuse University, School of Education, Emphasis in Biology Education, Syracuse, NY 13244. Offers MS. Part-time programs available. *Students:* 7 full-time (4 women), 1 (woman) part-time; includes 1 minority (Asian, non-Hispanic/Latino). Average age 27. 5 applicants, 100% accepted, 2 enrolled. In 2011, 8 master's awarded. *Entrance requirements:* Additional exam requirements/recommendations for international students: Required—TOEFL (minimum score 100 iBT). *Application deadline:* For fall admission, 2/1 priority date for domestic students, 2/1 for international students. Applications are processed on a rolling basis. Application fee: $75. Electronic applications accepted. *Expenses: Tuition:* Part-time $1206 per credit. *Financial support:* Fellowships with full tuition reimbursements, teaching assistantships, scholarships/grants, and tuition waivers (partial) available. Financial award application deadline: 1/1; financial award applicants required to submit FAFSA. *Unit head:* Dr. John Tillotson, Program Director, 315-443-9137, E-mail: jwtillot@syr.edu. *Application contact:* Laurie Deyo, Graduate Recruiter, School of Education, 315-443-2505, E-mail: e-gradrcrt@syr.edu. Web site: http://soeweb.syr.edu/academic/teaching_and_leadership/graduate/masters/science_education/biology/default.aspx.

Syracuse University, School of Education, Emphasis in Chemistry Education, Syracuse, NY 13244. Offers MS. Part-time programs available. *Students:* 1 full-time (0 women). Average age 22. 3 applicants, 100% accepted, 1 enrolled. *Entrance requirements:* For master's, GRE. Additional exam requirements/recommendations for international students: Required—TOEFL (minimum score 100 iBT). *Application deadline:* For fall admission, 2/1 priority date for domestic students, 2/1 for international students. Applications are processed on a rolling basis. Application fee: $75. Electronic applications accepted. *Expenses: Tuition:* Part-time $1206 per credit. *Financial support:* Fellowships with full tuition reimbursements, teaching assistantships with full and partial tuition reimbursements, scholarships/grants, and tuition waivers (partial) available. Financial award application deadline: 1/1; financial award applicants required to submit FAFSA. *Unit head:* Dr. John Tillotson, Program Director, 315-443-9137, E-mail: jwtillot@syr.edu. *Application contact:* Laurie Deyo, Graduate Recruiter, School of Education, 315-443-2505, E-mail: e-gradrcrt@syr.edu. Web site: http://soeweb.syr.edu/academic/teaching_and_leadership/graduate/masters/science_education/chemistry/default.aspx.

Syracuse University, School of Education, Emphasis in Earth Science Education, Syracuse, NY 13244. Offers MS. Part-time programs available. *Students:* 4 applicants, 75% accepted, 0 enrolled. *Entrance requirements:* For master's, GRE. Additional exam requirements/recommendations for international students: Required—TOEFL (minimum score 100 iBT). *Application deadline:* For fall admission, 2/1 priority date for domestic students, 2/1 for international students. Applications are processed on a rolling basis. Electronic applications accepted. *Expenses: Tuition:* Part-time $1206 per credit. *Financial support:* Fellowships with full tuition reimbursements, teaching assistantships with full and partial tuition reimbursements, scholarships/grants, and tuition waivers (full and partial) available. Financial award application deadline: 1/1; financial award applicants required to submit FAFSA. *Unit head:* Dr. John Tillotson, Program Director, 315-443-9137, E-mail: jwtillot@syr.edu. *Application contact:* Laurie Deyo, Graduate Recruiter, School of Education, 315-443-2505, E-mail: e-gradrcrt@syr.edu. Web site: http://soeweb.syr.edu/academic/teaching_and_leadership/graduate/masters/science_education/earth_science/default.aspx.

Syracuse University, School of Education, Emphasis in Physics Education, Syracuse, NY 13244. Offers MS. Part-time programs available. *Students:* 1 applicant, 0% accepted, 0 enrolled. In 2011, 1 degree awarded. *Entrance requirements:* For master's, GRE. Additional exam requirements/recommendations for international students: Required—TOEFL (minimum score 100 iBT). *Application deadline:* For fall admission, 2/1 priority date for domestic students, 2/1 for international students. Applications are processed on a rolling basis. Application fee: $75. Electronic applications accepted. *Expenses: Tuition:* Part-time $1206 per credit. *Financial support:* Fellowships with full tuition reimbursements, teaching assistantships with full and partial tuition reimbursements, scholarships/grants, and tuition waivers (partial) available. Financial award application deadline: 1/1; financial award applicants required to submit FAFSA. *Unit head:* Dr. John Tillotson, Program Director, 315-443-9137, E-mail: jwtillot@syr.edu. *Application contact:* Laurie Deyo, Graduate Recruiter, School of Education, 315-443-2505, E-mail: e-gradrcrt@syr.edu. Web site: http://soeweb.syr.edu/academic/teaching_and_leadership/graduate/masters/science_education/physics/default.aspx.

Syracuse University, School of Education, Program in Science Education, Syracuse, NY 13244. Offers PhD. Part-time programs available. *Students:* 17 full-time (8 women), 9 part-time (6 women); includes 3 minority (1 Black or African American, non-Hispanic/Latino; 1 Asian, non-Hispanic/Latino; 1 Native Hawaiian or other Pacific Islander, non-Hispanic/Latino), 3 international. Average age 35. 5 applicants, 100% accepted, 3 enrolled. *Degree requirements:* For doctorate, thesis/dissertation. *Entrance requirements:* For doctorate, GRE, interview, master's degree. Additional exam requirements/recommendations for international students: Required—TOEFL (minimum score 100 iBT). *Application deadline:* For fall admission, 2/1 priority date for domestic students, 2/1 for international students; for spring admission, 10/15 priority date for domestic students, 10/15 for international students. Applications are processed on a rolling basis. Application fee: $75. Electronic applications accepted. *Expenses: Tuition:* Part-time $1206 per credit. *Financial support:* Fellowships with full tuition reimbursements, research assistantships with full and partial tuition reimbursements, and teaching assistantships with full and partial tuition reimbursements available. Financial award application deadline: 1/1. *Unit head:* Dr. John Tillotson, Coordinator, 315-443-9137, E-mail: jwtillot@syr.edu. *Application contact:* Laurie Deyo, Graduate Recruiter, School of Education, 315-443-2505, E-mail: e-gradrcrt@syr.edu. Web site: http://soeweb.syr.edu/.

Teachers College, Columbia University, Graduate Faculty of Education, Department of Math, Science and Technology, Programs in Science Education, New York, NY 10027. Offers Ed M, MA, MS, Ed D, Ed DCT, PhD. *Accreditation:* NCATE. Part-time and evening/weekend programs available. *Faculty:* 6 full-time (4 women), 9 part-time/adjunct (5 women). *Students:* 32 full-time (21 women), 67 part-time (43 women); includes 21 minority (9 Black or African American, non-Hispanic/Latino; 7 Asian, non-Hispanic/Latino; 5 Hispanic/Latino), 4 international. Average age 32. 70 applicants, 86% accepted, 27 enrolled. In 2011, 22 master's, 3 doctorates awarded. Terminal master's awarded for partial completion of doctoral program. *Degree requirements:* For master's, culminating paper; for doctorate, comprehensive exam, thesis/dissertation. *Entrance requirements:* For master's, bachelor's degree in one of the sciences or its equivalent with preferred minimum B+ average in courses within science; for doctorate, bachelor's degree in one of the sciences or its equivalent. *Application deadline:* For fall admission, 12/15 for domestic students. Application fee: $65. *Financial support:* Fellowships, career-related internships or fieldwork, Federal Work-Study, institutionally sponsored loans, and tuition waivers (full and partial) available. Support available to part-time students. Financial award applicants required to submit FAFSA. *Faculty research:* Cell biology and physiological ecology of protozoa, teaching and learning of pre-college and college sciences, homelessness. *Total annual research expenditures:* $100,000. *Unit head:* Prof. Felicia Moore Mensah, Program Coordinator, 212-678-8174, Fax: 212-678-

8145, E-mail: tcscience@tc.edu. *Application contact:* Deanna Ghozati, Assistant Director of Admission, 212-678-4018, Fax: 212-678-4171, E-mail: ghozati@tc.edu. Web site: http://www.tc.edu/mst/scienceed/.

Temple University, College of Education, Department of Curriculum, Instruction, and Technology in Education, Philadelphia, PA 19122-6096. Offers applied behavioral analysis (MS Ed); career and technical education (MS Ed); early childhood education and elementary education (MS Ed); English education (MS Ed); language arts education (Ed D); math/science education (Ed D); mathematics education (MS Ed); science education (MS Ed); second and foreign language education (MS Ed); special education (MS Ed); teaching English as a second language (MS Ed). Part-time and evening/weekend programs available. *Faculty:* 19 full-time (12 women). *Students:* 30 full-time (23 women), 86 part-time (69 women); includes 12 minority (4 Black or African American, non-Hispanic/Latino; 2 Asian, non-Hispanic/Latino; 5 Hispanic/Latino; 1 Two or more races, non-Hispanic/Latino), 5 international. 82 applicants, 71% accepted, 51 enrolled. In 2011, 181 master's, 16 doctorates awarded. Terminal master's awarded for partial completion of doctoral program. *Degree requirements:* For master's, thesis or alternative; for doctorate, thesis/dissertation. *Entrance requirements:* For master's and doctorate, GRE General Test or MAT, minimum GPA of 3.0. Additional exam requirements/recommendations for international students: Required—TOEFL (minimum score 550 paper-based; 213 computer-based; 79 iBT). *Application deadline:* For fall admission, 4/1 for domestic students, 12/15 for international students; for spring admission, 10/1 for domestic students, 8/1 for international students. Application fee: $50. Electronic applications accepted. *Expenses:* Tuition, state resident: full-time $12,366; part-time $687 per credit hour. Tuition, nonresident: full-time $17,298; part-time $961 per credit hour. *Required fees:* $590; $213 per year. *Financial support:* Fellowships, research assistantships with full tuition reimbursements, and teaching assistantships with full tuition reimbursements available. Financial award application deadline: 1/15; financial award applicants required to submit FAFSA. *Faculty research:* School improvement, problem-solving, literacy, language development. *Unit head:* Dr. Michael W. Smith, Chair, 215-204-6387, Fax: 215-204-1414, E-mail: mwsmith@temple.edu. *Application contact:* Dr. Margo Greicar, Director for Graduate Academic and Student Affairs, 215-204-8011, Fax: 215-204-4383, E-mail: margo.greicar@temple.edu. Web site: http://www.temple.edu/education/cite/.

Texas A&M University, College of Education and Human Development, Department of Teaching, Learning, and Culture, College Station, TX 77843. Offers culture and curriculum (M Ed, MS); curriculum and instruction (PhD); English as a second language (M Ed, MS, PhD); mathematics education (M Ed, MS, PhD); reading and language arts education (M Ed, MS, PhD); science education (M Ed, MS, PhD); urban education (M Ed, MS, PhD). Part-time programs available. *Faculty:* 30. *Students:* 163 full-time (119 women), 226 part-time (185 women); includes 108 minority (56 Black or African American, non-Hispanic/Latino; 2 American Indian or Alaska Native, non-Hispanic/Latino; 6 Asian, non-Hispanic/Latino; 37 Hispanic/Latino; 7 Two or more races, non-Hispanic/Latino), 62 international. Average age 36. In 2011, 107 master's, 44 doctorates awarded. *Degree requirements:* For master's, comprehensive exam, thesis (for some programs); for doctorate, comprehensive exam, thesis/dissertation. *Entrance requirements:* For master's, GRE General Test, minimum GPA of 3.0; for doctorate, GRE General Test, 3 years of teaching experience. Additional exam requirements/recommendations for international students: Required—TOEFL (minimum score 550 paper-based; 213 computer-based). *Application deadline:* For fall admission, 1/15 priority date for domestic students, 1/15 for international students; for spring admission, 9/15 priority date for domestic students, 9/15 for international students. Applications are processed on a rolling basis. Application fee: $50 ($75 for international students). Electronic applications accepted. *Expenses:* Tuition, state resident: full-time $5437; part-time $226.55 per credit hour. Tuition, nonresident: full-time $12,949; part-time $539.55 per credit hour. *Required fees:* $2741. *Financial support:* In 2011–12, fellowships with partial tuition reimbursements (averaging $3,000 per year), teaching assistantships with partial tuition reimbursements (averaging $7,200 per year) were awarded; research assistantships with partial tuition reimbursements, career-related internships or fieldwork, Federal Work-Study, institutionally sponsored loans, scholarships/grants, tuition waivers (partial), and unspecified assistantships also available. Support available to part-time students. Financial award application deadline: 4/1; financial award applicants required to submit FAFSA. *Unit head:* Dr. Yeping Li, Head, 979-845-8384, Fax: 979-845-9663, E-mail: yepingli@tamu.edu. *Application contact:* Kerri Smith, Senior Academic Advisor II, 979-845-8382, Fax: 979-845-9663, E-mail: krsmith@tamu.edu. Web site: http://tlac.tamu.edu.

Texas Christian University, College of Education, Program in Science Education, Fort Worth, TX 76129-0002. Offers M Ed, PhD. Part-time and evening/weekend programs available. *Faculty:* 27 full-time (21 women), 1 part-time/adjunct. *Students:* 7 full-time (all women), 13 part-time (12 women); includes 2 minority (1 Black or African American, non-Hispanic/Latino; 1 Asian, non-Hispanic/Latino), 2 international. Average age 35. 8 applicants, 88% accepted, 4 enrolled. In 2011, 2 master's, 2 doctorates awarded. *Degree requirements:* For master's, comprehensive exam, thesis; for doctorate, comprehensive exam, thesis/dissertation. *Entrance requirements:* For master's, essay, letters of recommendation, interview; for doctorate, GRE or MAT. Additional exam requirements/recommendations for international students: Required—TOEFL (minimum score 550 paper-based; 213 computer-based; 80 iBT). *Application deadline:* For fall admission, 11/15 for domestic and international students; for winter admission, 2/1 for domestic and international students; for spring admission, 3/1 for domestic and international students. Application fee: $60. Electronic applications accepted. *Expenses: Tuition:* Full-time $20,250; part-time $1125 per credit hour. Part-time tuition and fees vary according to course load and program. *Financial support:* Teaching assistantships with full tuition reimbursements, career-related internships or fieldwork, scholarships/grants, tuition waivers (partial), and unspecified assistantships available. Financial award application deadline: 3/1. *Unit head:* Dr. Jan Lacina, Associate Dean, 817-257-6786, E-mail: j.lacina@tcu.edu. *Application contact:* Patricia Garcia, Academic Program Specialist, 817-257-7661, E-mail: p.m.garcia@tcu.edu. Web site: http://www.coe.tcu.edu/185.asp.

Texas State University–San Marcos, Graduate School, Interdisciplinary Studies Program in Elementary Mathematics, Science, and Technology, San Marcos, TX 78666. Offers MSIS. *Students:* 2 full-time (both women), 2 part-time (both women). Average age 32. 5 applicants, 40% accepted, 2 enrolled. *Degree requirements:* For master's, comprehensive exam, thesis optional. *Entrance requirements:* For master's, minimum GPA of 2.75 in the last 60 hours of undergraduate work. Additional exam requirements/recommendations for international students: Required—TOEFL (minimum score 550 paper-based; 213 computer-based; 78 iBT). *Application deadline:* For fall admission, 6/15 priority date for domestic students, 6/1 for international students; for spring admission, 10/15 priority date for domestic students, 10/1 for international students. Applications are processed on a rolling basis. Application fee: $40 ($90 for international students). Electronic applications accepted. *Expenses:* Tuition, state resident: full-time $6408; part-time $3204 per semester. Tuition, nonresident: full-time $14,832; part-time $7416 per semester. *Required fees:* $1824; $912 per semester. Tuition and fees vary according to course load. *Financial support:* Research assistantships, teaching assistantships, Federal Work-Study, institutionally sponsored loans, scholarships/grants, health care benefits, and unspecified assistantships available. Support available to part-time students. Financial award application deadline: 4/1; financial award applicants required to submit FAFSA. *Unit head:* Dr. Sandra Mody, Acting Dean, 512-245-3360, Fax: 512-245-8095, E-mail: sw04@txstate.edu. *Application contact:* Dr. J. Michael Willoughby, Dean of Graduate School, 512-245-2581, Fax: 512-245-8365, E-mail: gradcollege@txstate.edu.

Troy University, Graduate School, College of Education, Program in Postsecondary Education, Troy, AL 36082. Offers adult education (M Ed); biology (M Ed); criminal justice (M Ed); English (M Ed); foundations of education (M Ed); general science (M Ed); higher education administration (M Ed); history (M Ed); instructional technology (M Ed); mathematics (M Ed); music industry (M Ed); physical fitness (M Ed); political science (M Ed); public administration (M Ed); social science (M Ed); teaching English (M Ed). *Accreditation:* NCATE. Part-time and evening/weekend programs available. *Faculty:* 53 full-time (21 women), 22 part-time/adjunct (8 women). *Students:* 74 full-time (51 women), 166 part-time (121 women); includes 148 minority (143 Black or African American, non-Hispanic/Latino; 1 American Indian or Alaska Native, non-Hispanic/Latino; 2 Hispanic/Latino; 2 Two or more races, non-Hispanic/Latino). Average age 34. 174 applicants, 82% accepted, 88 enrolled. In 2011, 221 master's awarded. *Degree requirements:* For master's, comprehensive exam, thesis. *Entrance requirements:* For master's, MAT (minimum score 385), minimum GPA of 2.5. Additional exam requirements/recommendations for international students: Required—TOEFL (minimum score 523 paper-based; 193 computer-based; 70 iBT), IELTS (minimum score 6), or ACT COMPASS ESL (minimum listening, reading, and grammar score 270). *Application deadline:* Applications are processed on a rolling basis. Application fee: $50. Electronic applications accepted. *Expenses:* Tuition, state resident: full-time $6960; part-time $290 per credit hour. Tuition, nonresident: full-time $13,920; part-time $580 per credit hour. *Required fees:* $386 per term. *Financial support:* Available to part-time students. Applicants required to submit FAFSA. *Unit head:* Dr. Jan Oliver, Associate Professor, 334-670-3444, Fax: 334-670-3296, E-mail: oliver@troy.edu. *Application contact:* Brenda K. Campbell, Director of Graduate Admissions, 334-670-3178, Fax: 334-670-3733, E-mail: bcamp@troy.edu.

Troy University, Graduate School, College of Education, Program in Secondary Education, Troy, AL 36082. Offers 5th year biology (MS); 5th year computer science (MS); 5th year history (MS); 5th year language arts (MS); 5th year mathematics (MS); 5th year social science (MS); traditional biology (MS); traditional computer science (MS); traditional history (MS); traditional language arts (MS); traditional mathematics (MS); traditional social science (MS). *Accreditation:* NCATE. Part-time and evening/weekend programs available. *Faculty:* 4 full-time (3 women). *Students:* 14 full-time (8 women), 29 part-time (21 women); includes 9 minority (all Black or African American, non-Hispanic/Latino). Average age 28. 11 applicants, 100% accepted, 5 enrolled. In 2011, 16 master's awarded. *Degree requirements:* For master's, comprehensive exam, thesis. *Entrance requirements:* For master's, minimum GPA of 2.5, bachelor's degree. Additional exam requirements/recommendations for international students: Required—TOEFL (minimum score 523 paper-based; 193 computer-based; 70 iBT), IELTS (minimum score 6). *Application deadline:* Applications are processed on a rolling basis. Application fee: $50. Electronic applications accepted. *Expenses:* Tuition, state resident: full-time $6960; part-time $290 per credit hour. Tuition, nonresident: full-time $13,920; part-time $580 per credit hour. *Required fees:* $386 per term. *Financial support:* Career-related internships or fieldwork available. Support available to part-time students. Financial award applicants required to submit FAFSA. *Unit head:* Dr. Jan Oliver, Associate Professor, 334-670-3444, Fax: 334-670-3548, E-mail: oliver@troy.edu. *Application contact:* Brenda K. Campbell, Director of Graduate Admissions, 334-670-3178, Fax: 334-670-3733, E-mail: bcamp@troy.edu.

Union Graduate College, School of Education, Schenectady, NY 12308-3107. Offers biology (MAT, MS); chemistry (MAT); Chinese (MAT); earth science (MAT); English (MAT); French (MAT); general science (MAT); German (MAT); Greek (MAT); languages (MAT); Latin (MAT); mathematics (MAT); mathematics and technology (MS); mentoring and teacher leadership (AC); middle childhood extension (AC); national board certificate and teacher leadership (AC); physical science (MS); physics (MAT); social studies (MAT); Spanish (MAT). *Accreditation:* Teacher Education Accreditation Council. *Faculty:* 3 full-time (1 woman), 51 part-time/adjunct (24 women). *Students:* 37 full-time (26 women), 25 part-time (16 women); includes 4 minority (3 Asian, non-Hispanic/Latino; 1 Hispanic/Latino). Average age 32. 66 applicants, 83% accepted, 41 enrolled. In 2011, 47 master's, 29 other advanced degrees awarded. *Degree requirements:* For master's, thesis or project. *Entrance requirements:* For master's, minimum GPA of 3.0, letters of recommendation. Additional exam requirements/recommendations for international students: Required—TOEFL (minimum score 550 paper-based; 213 computer-based). *Application deadline:* Applications are processed on a rolling basis. Application fee: $60. Electronic applications accepted. *Expenses:* Contact institution. *Financial support:* In 2011–12, 22 students received support. Career-related internships or fieldwork, Federal Work-Study, scholarships/grants, health care benefits, and tuition waivers (partial) available. Support available to part-time students. Financial award applicants required to submit FAFSA. *Faculty research:* Transformative learning, science education, National Board Certification, teacher leadership, teacher quality. *Unit head:* Dr. Patrick Allen, Dean, 518-631-9870, Fax: 518-631-9901. *Application contact:* Christine Angley, Assistant, 518-631-9871, Fax: 518-631-9903, E-mail: angleyc@uniongraduatecollege.edu.

Universidad Nacional Pedro Henriquez Urena, Graduate School, Santo Domingo, Dominican Republic. Offers agricultural diversity (MS), including horticultural/fruit production, tropical animal production; conservation of monuments and cultural assets (M Arch); ecology and environment (MS); environmental engineering (MEE); international relations (MA); natural resource management (MS); political science (MA); project optimization (MPM); project feasibility (MPM); project management (MPM); sanitation engineering (ME); science for teachers (MS); tropical Caribbean architecture (M Arch).

University at Albany, State University of New York, College of Arts and Sciences, Department of Mathematics and Statistics, Albany, NY 12222-0001. Offers mathematics (PhD); secondary teaching (MA); statistics (MA). *Degree requirements:* For doctorate, one foreign language, thesis/dissertation. *Entrance requirements:* For doctorate, GRE General Test. Additional exam requirements/recommendations for international students: Required—TOEFL (minimum score 550 paper-based; 213 computer-based). Electronic applications accepted.

University at Buffalo, the State University of New York, Graduate School, Graduate School of Education, Department of Learning and Instruction, Buffalo, NY 14260. Offers biology education (Ed M, Certificate); chemistry education (Ed M, Certificate); childhood education (Ed M); childhood education with bilingual extension (Ed M); early childhood education (Ed M); early childhood education with bilingual extension (birth-grade 2) (Ed M); earth science education (Ed M, Certificate); educational technology and new literacies (Certificate); educational technology and new literacies (online) (Certificate); elementary education (Ed D, PhD); English education (Ed M, PhD, Certificate); English for speakers of other languages (Ed M); foreign and second language education (PhD); French education (Ed M, Certificate); general education (Ed M); German education (Ed M, Certificate); gifted education (online) (Certificate); Latin education (Ed M, Certificate); literacy teaching and learning (Certificate); literary specialist (Ed M);

mathematics education (Ed M, PhD, Certificate); music education (Ed M, Certificate); physics education (Ed M, Certificate); reading education (PhD); science and the public (online) (Ed M); science education (PhD); social studies education (Ed M, Certificate); Spanish education (Ed M, Certificate); special education (PhD); teaching and leading for diversity (Certificate); teaching English to speakers of other languages (Ed M). Part-time and evening/weekend programs available. Postbaccalaureate distance learning degree programs offered (no on-campus study). *Faculty:* 32 full-time (23 women), 54 part-time/adjunct (43 women). *Students:* 294 full-time (222 women), 350 part-time (261 women); includes 75 minority (19 Black or African American, non-Hispanic/Latino; 6 American Indian or Alaska Native, non-Hispanic/Latino; 40 Asian, non-Hispanic/Latino; 10 Hispanic/Latino), 76 international. Average age 29. 548 applicants, 52% accepted, 253 enrolled. In 2011, 225 master's, 17 doctorates, 37 other advanced degrees awarded. *Degree requirements:* For master's, comprehensive exam; for doctorate, thesis/dissertation, research analysis exam, research experience component. *Entrance requirements:* For doctorate, GRE General Test or MAT, interview, writing sample, letters of recommendation. Additional exam requirements/recommendations for international students: Required—TOEFL (minimum score 600 paper-based; 96 iBT). *Application deadline:* For fall admission, 2/1 priority date for domestic students, 2/1 for international students; for spring admission, 11/15 priority date for domestic students, 10/1 for international students. Applications are processed on a rolling basis. Application fee: $50. Electronic applications accepted. *Financial support:* In 2011–12, 40 fellowships (averaging $12,991 per year), 46 research assistantships (averaging $10,986 per year) were awarded; teaching assistantships with full tuition reimbursements, career-related internships or fieldwork, Federal Work-Study, institutionally sponsored loans, scholarships/grants, and unspecified assistantships also available. Financial award application deadline: 2/28; financial award applicants required to submit FAFSA. *Faculty research:* Science assessment, foreign language teaching and learning, early learning, new literacies, gender and education. *Unit head:* Dr. Julie Sarama, Chair, 716-645-2455, Fax: 716-645-3161, E-mail: jcollins@buffalo.edu. *Application contact:* Cathy Dimino, Admissions Assistant, 716-645-2110, Fax: 716-645-7937, E-mail: cadimino@buffalo.edu.

The University of Alabama in Huntsville, School of Graduate Studies, College of Science, Department of Biological Sciences, Huntsville, AL 35899. Offers biology (MS); education (MS). Part-time and evening/weekend programs available. *Faculty:* 9 full-time (2 women), 4 part-time/adjunct (1 woman). *Students:* 16 full-time (9 women), 15 part-time (11 women); includes 10 minority (4 Black or African American, non-Hispanic/Latino; 2 American Indian or Alaska Native, non-Hispanic/Latino; 3 Asian, non-Hispanic/Latino; 1 Hispanic/Latino), 5 international. Average age 31. 38 applicants, 55% accepted, 14 enrolled. In 2011, 10 master's awarded. *Degree requirements:* For master's, comprehensive exam, thesis or alternative, oral and written exams. *Entrance requirements:* For master's, GRE General Test, previous course work in biochemistry and organic chemistry, minimum GPA of 3.0. Additional exam requirements/recommendations for international students: Required—TOEFL (minimum score 550 paper-based; 213 computer-based; 62 iBT). *Application deadline:* For fall admission, 7/15 for domestic students, 4/1 for international students; for spring admission, 11/30 for domestic students, 9/1 for international students. Applications are processed on a rolling basis. Application fee: $40 ($50 for international students). Electronic applications accepted. *Expenses:* Tuition, state resident: full-time $7830; part-time $473.50 per credit. Tuition, nonresident: full-time $18,748; part-time $1128.33 per credit. Tuition and fees vary according to course load and program. *Financial support:* In 2011–12, 16 students received support, including 2 fellowships with full tuition reimbursements available (averaging $12,000 per year), 14 teaching assistantships with full and partial tuition reimbursements available (averaging $8,278 per year); career-related internships or fieldwork, Federal Work-Study, institutionally sponsored loans, scholarships/grants, health care benefits, and unspecified assistantships also available. Support available to part-time students. Financial award application deadline: 4/1; financial award applicants required to submit FAFSA. *Faculty research:* Physiology and developmental biology, functional genomics, biotechnology, proteomics, microbiology. *Total annual research expenditures:* $898,355. *Unit head:* Dr. Debra M. Moriarity, Interim Chair, 256-824-6045, Fax: 256-824-6305, E-mail: moriard@uah.edu. *Application contact:* Kim Gray, Graduate Studies Admissions Manager, 256-824-6002, Fax: 256-824-6405, E-mail: deangrad@uah.edu. Web site: http://www.uah.edu/colleges/science/biology/.

The University of Alabama in Huntsville, School of Graduate Studies, College of Science, Department of Chemistry, Huntsville, AL 35899. Offers chemistry (MS); education (MS). Part-time and evening/weekend programs available. *Faculty:* 11 full-time (1 woman). *Students:* 13 full-time (9 women), 5 part-time (3 women); includes 7 minority (4 Black or African American, non-Hispanic/Latino; 1 American Indian or Alaska Native, non-Hispanic/Latino; 1 Asian, non-Hispanic/Latino; 1 Two or more races, non-Hispanic/Latino), 2 international. Average age 28. 10 applicants, 60% accepted, 5 enrolled. In 2011, 4 master's awarded. *Degree requirements:* For master's, comprehensive exam, thesis or alternative, oral and written exams. *Entrance requirements:* For master's, GRE General Test, minimum GPA of 3.0. Additional exam requirements/recommendations for international students: Required—TOEFL (minimum score 550 paper-based; 213 computer-based; 62 iBT). *Application deadline:* For fall admission, 7/15 for domestic students, 4/1 for international students; for spring admission, 11/30 for domestic students, 9/1 for international students. Applications are processed on a rolling basis. Application fee: $40 ($50 for international students). Electronic applications accepted. *Expenses:* Tuition, state resident: full-time $7830; part-time $473.50 per credit. Tuition, nonresident: full-time $18,748; part-time $1128.33 per credit. Tuition and fees vary according to course load and program. *Financial support:* In 2011–12, 12 students received support, including 12 teaching assistantships with full tuition reimbursements available (averaging $11,121 per year); career-related internships or fieldwork, Federal Work-Study, institutionally sponsored loans, scholarships/grants, health care benefits, tuition waivers, and unspecified assistantships also available. Support available to part-time students. Financial award application deadline: 4/1; financial award applicants required to submit FAFSA. *Faculty research:* Kinetics and bonding, organic nonlinear optical materials, x-ray crystallography, crystal growth in space, polymers, Raman spectroscopy. *Total annual research expenditures:* $1.5 million. *Unit head:* Dr. William Setzer, Chair, 256-824-6153, Fax: 256-824-6349, E-mail: setzerw@uah.edu. *Application contact:* Kim Gray, Graduate Studies Admissions Coordinator, 256-824-6002, Fax: 256-824-6405, E-mail: deangrad@uah.edu. Web site: http://chemistry.uah.edu.

The University of Alabama in Huntsville, School of Graduate Studies, College of Science, Department of Physics, Huntsville, AL 35899. Offers education (MS); optics and photonics technology (MS); physics (MS, PhD). Part-time and evening/weekend programs available. *Faculty:* 18 full-time (0 women), 4 part-time/adjunct (1 woman). *Students:* 34 full-time (7 women), 22 part-time (9 women); includes 2 minority (both Asian, non-Hispanic/Latino), 12 international. Average age 29. 48 applicants, 60% accepted, 15 enrolled. In 2011, 10 master's, 3 doctorates awarded. *Degree requirements:* For master's, comprehensive exam, thesis or alternative, oral and written exams; for doctorate, comprehensive exam, thesis/dissertation, oral and written exams. *Entrance requirements:* For master's and doctorate, GRE General Test, minimum GPA of 3.0. Additional exam requirements/recommendations for international students: Required—TOEFL (minimum score 550 paper-based; 213 computer-based; 62 iBT). *Application deadline:* For fall admission, 7/15 for domestic students, 4/1 for international students; for spring admission, 11/30 for domestic students, 9/1 for international students. Applications are processed on a rolling basis. Application fee: $40 ($50 for international students). Electronic applications accepted. *Expenses:* Tuition, state resident: full-time $7830; part-time $473.50 per credit. Tuition, nonresident: full-time $18,748; part-time $1128.33 per credit. Tuition and fees vary according to course load and program. *Financial support:* In 2011–12, 30 students received support, including 18 research assistantships with full and partial tuition reimbursements available (averaging $15,553 per year), 12 teaching assistantships with full and partial tuition reimbursements available (averaging $16,500 per year); career-related internships or fieldwork, Federal Work-Study, institutionally sponsored loans, scholarships/grants, health care benefits, and unspecified assistantships also available. Support available to part-time students. Financial award application deadline: 4/1; financial award applicants required to submit FAFSA. *Faculty research:* Space physics, cosmology/general relativity, optics/quantum optics, astrophysics/gamma-ray astronomy, strophysical instrumentation. *Total annual research expenditures:* $6.2 million. *Unit head:* Dr. Gary Zank, Chair, 256-824-2481, Fax: 256-824-6873, E-mail: gary.zank@uah.edu. *Application contact:* Kim Gray, Graduate Studies Admissions Coordinator, 256-824-6002, Fax: 256-824-6405, E-mail: deangrad@uah.edu. Web site: http://physics.uah.edu/.

The University of Alabama in Huntsville, School of Graduate Studies, Interdisciplinary Studies, Interdisciplinary Program in Integrated Science, Technology, Engineering and Mathematics, Huntsville, AL 35899. Offers general science (MS). Part-time and evening/weekend programs available. *Entrance requirements:* For master's, GRE General Test, minimum GPA of 3.0. Additional exam requirements/recommendations for international students: Required—TOEFL (minimum score 500 paper-based; 173 computer-based; 62 iBT). *Application deadline:* For fall admission, 7/15 for domestic students, 4/1 for international students; for spring admission, 11/30 for domestic students, 9/1 for international students. Applications are processed on a rolling basis. Application fee: $40 ($50 for international students). Electronic applications accepted. *Expenses:* Tuition, state resident: full-time $7830; part-time $473.50 per credit. Tuition, nonresident: full-time $18,748; part-time $1128.33 per credit. Tuition and fees vary according to course load and program. *Financial support:* Application deadline: 4/1; applicants required to submit FAFSA. *Unit head:* Dr. Rhonda Kay Gaede, Dean of Graduate Studies, 256-824-6002, Fax: 256-824-6405, E-mail: rhonda.gaede@uah.edu. *Application contact:* Kim Gray, Graduate Studies Admissions Coordinator, 256-824-6002, Fax: 256-824-6405, E-mail: deangrad@uah.edu.

University of Arkansas at Pine Bluff, School of Education, Pine Bluff, AR 71601-2799. Offers early childhood education (M Ed); secondary education (M Ed), including English education, mathematics education, physical education, science education, social studies education; teaching (MAT). *Accreditation:* NCATE. Part-time and evening/weekend programs available. *Degree requirements:* For master's, comprehensive exam. *Entrance requirements:* For master's, GRE, minimum GPA of 2.75, NTE or Standard Arkansas Teaching Certificate. *Faculty research:* Teacher certification, accreditation, assessment, standards, portfolio development, rehabilitation, technology.

The University of British Columbia, Faculty of Education, Department of Curriculum and Pedagogy, Vancouver, BC V6T 1Z4, Canada. Offers art education (M Ed, MA); business education (MA); curriculum studies (M Ed, MA, PhD); home economics education (M Ed, MA); math education (M Ed, MA); music education (M Ed, MA); physical education (M Ed, MA); science education (M Ed, MA); social studies education (M Ed, MA); technology studies education (M Ed, MA). Part-time programs available. *Degree requirements:* For master's, thesis (MA); for doctorate, comprehensive exam, thesis/dissertation. *Entrance requirements:* Additional exam requirements/recommendations for international students: Required—TOEFL (minimum score 580 paper-based; 237 computer-based; 92 iBT). Electronic applications accepted. *Expenses:* Contact institution. *Faculty research:* School subjects, teaching and learning.

University of California, Berkeley, Graduate Division, School of Education, Group in Science and Mathematics Education, Berkeley, CA 94720-1500. Offers PhD, MA/Credential. Electronic applications accepted.

University of California, Berkeley, Graduate Division, School of Education, Programs in Education, Berkeley, CA 94720-1500. Offers development in mathematics and science (MA); education in mathematics, science, and technology (MA, PhD); human development and education (MA, PhD); special education (PhD); MA/Credential; PhD/Credential; PhD/MA. Terminal master's awarded for partial completion of doctoral program. *Degree requirements:* For master's, exam or thesis; for doctorate, thesis/dissertation, oral qualifying exam. *Entrance requirements:* For master's and doctorate, GRE General Test, minimum GPA of 3.0 during last 2 years of undergraduate course work. Electronic applications accepted. *Faculty research:* Human development, social and moral educational psychology, developmental teacher preparation.

University of California, San Diego, Office of Graduate Studies, Program in Mathematics and Science Education, La Jolla, CA 92093. Offers PhD. Program offered jointly with San Diego State University. *Entrance requirements:* For doctorate, GRE General Test. Electronic applications accepted.

University of Central Florida, College of Education, Education Doctoral Programs, Orlando, FL 32816. Offers communication sciences and disorders (PhD); counselor education (PhD); education (Ed D); elementary education (PhD); exceptional education (PhD); exercise physiology (PhD); higher education (PhD); hospitality education (PhD); instructional technology (PhD); mathematics education (PhD); reading education (PhD); science education (PhD); social science education (PhD); TESOL (PhD). *Students:* 135 full-time (87 women), 73 part-time (51 women); includes 49 minority (21 Black or African American, non-Hispanic/Latino; 4 Asian, non-Hispanic/Latino; 20 Hispanic/Latino; 4 Two or more races, non-Hispanic/Latino), 18 international. Average age 39. 125 applicants, 46% accepted, 46 enrolled. In 2011, 43 doctorates awarded. Application fee: $30. Electronic applications accepted. *Expenses:* Tuition, state resident: part-time $277.08 per credit hour. Tuition, nonresident: part-time $277.08 per credit hour. Part-time tuition and fees vary according to degree level and program. *Financial support:* In 2011–12, 85 students received support, including 48 fellowships with partial tuition reimbursements available (averaging $5,900 per year), 36 research assistantships with partial tuition reimbursements available (averaging $6,900 per year), 59 teaching assistantships with partial tuition reimbursements available (averaging $6,900 per year). *Unit head:* Dr. Rex Culp, Associate Dean, 407-823-5391, E-mail: rex.culp@ucf.edu. *Application contact:* Barbara Rodriguez, Associate Director, Admissions and Registration, 407-823-2766, Fax: 407-823-6442, E-mail: gradadmissions@ucf.edu. Web site: http://education.ucf.edu/departments.cfm.

University of Central Florida, College of Education, School of Teaching, Learning, and Leadership, Program in K-8 Mathematics and Science Education, Orlando, FL 32816. Offers M Ed, Certificate. *Accreditation:* NCATE. *Students:* 21 part-time (17 women); includes 1 minority (Hispanic/Latino). Average age 34. In 2011, 13 master's, 1 Certificate awarded. Application fee: $30. *Expenses:* Tuition, state resident: part-time $277.08 per credit hour. Tuition, nonresident: part-time $277.08 per credit hour. Part-time tuition and fees vary according to degree level and program. *Financial support:* Fellowships available. *Unit head:* Dr. Juli K. Dixon, Program Coordinator, 407-823-4140, E-mail: juli.dixon@ucf.edu. *Application contact:* Barbara Rodriguez, Director,

Admissions and Registration, 407-823-2766, Fax: 407-823-6442, E-mail: gradadmissions@ucf.edu.

University of Central Florida, College of Education, School of Teaching, Learning, and Leadership, Program in Science Education, Orlando, FL 32816. Offers teacher education (MAT), including biology, middle school science, physics; teacher leadership (M Ed), including science education. *Accreditation:* NCATE. Part-time and evening/weekend programs available. *Students:* 9 full-time (6 women), 19 part-time (12 women); includes 5 minority (1 Asian, non-Hispanic/Latino; 3 Hispanic/Latino; 1 Two or more races, non-Hispanic/Latino). Average age 33. 19 applicants, 58% accepted, 7 enrolled. In 2011, 21 master's awarded. *Entrance requirements:* For master's, GRE General Test. Additional exam requirements/recommendations for international students: Required—TOEFL. *Application deadline:* For fall admission, 7/15 for domestic students; for spring admission, 12/1 for domestic students. Application fee: $30. Electronic applications accepted. *Expenses:* Tuition, state resident: part-time $277.08 per credit hour. Tuition, nonresident: part-time $277.08 per credit hour. Part-time tuition and fees vary according to degree level and program. *Financial support:* Career-related internships or fieldwork, Federal Work-Study, institutionally sponsored loans, tuition waivers (partial), and unspecified assistantships available. Financial award application deadline: 3/1; financial award applicants required to submit FAFSA. *Unit head:* Dr. Janet B. Andreasen, Program Coordinator, 407-823-5430, E-mail: janet.andreasen@ucf.edu. *Application contact:* Barbara Rodriguez, Director, Admissions and Registration, 407-823-2766, Fax: 407-823-6442, E-mail: gradadmissions@ucf.edu.

University of Chicago, Division of Social Sciences, Committee on Conceptual and Historical Studies of Science, Chicago, IL 60637-1513. Offers PhD. *Degree requirements:* For doctorate, thesis/dissertation. *Entrance requirements:* For doctorate, GRE General Test, GRE Subject Test. Additional exam requirements/recommendations for international students: Required—TOEFL, IELTS (minimum score 7). Electronic applications accepted.

University of Cincinnati, Graduate School, College of Education, Criminal Justice, and Human Services, Division of Teacher Education, Cincinnati, OH 45221. Offers curriculum and instruction (M Ed, Ed D); deaf studies (Certificate); early childhood education (M Ed); middle childhood education (M Ed); postsecondary literacy instruction (Certificate); reading/literacy (M Ed, Ed D); secondary education (M Ed); special education (M Ed, Ed D); teaching English as a second language (M Ed, Ed D, Certificate); teaching science (MS). Part-time programs available. *Degree requirements:* For doctorate, thesis/dissertation. *Entrance requirements:* For master's, GRE General Test. Additional exam requirements/recommendations for international students: Required—TOEFL (minimum score 550 paper-based). Electronic applications accepted.

University of Colorado Denver, School of Education and Human Development, Program in Educational Leadership and Innovation, Denver, CO 80217-3364. Offers educational studies and research (PhD), including administrative leadership and policy, early childhood special education, math education, research, assessment and evaluation, science education, urban ecologies. Part-time and evening/weekend programs available. *Students:* 21 full-time (15 women), 25 part-time (17 women); includes 10 minority (5 Black or African American, non-Hispanic/Latino; 1 American Indian or Alaska Native, non-Hispanic/Latino; 3 Asian, non-Hispanic/Latino; 1 Hispanic/Latino), 1 international. Average age 43. 11 applicants, 45% accepted, 3 enrolled. In 2011, 11 doctorates awarded. *Degree requirements:* For doctorate, comprehensive exam, thesis/dissertation, 75 credit hours (for PhD). *Entrance requirements:* For doctorate, GRE or equivalent, resume or curriculum vitae, written statement, letters of recommendation, master's degree or equivalent, completion of basic or advanced statistics course with minimum B grade. Additional exam requirements/recommendations for international students: Required—TOEFL (minimum score 525 paper-based; 197 computer-based). *Application deadline:* Applications are processed on a rolling basis. Application fee: $50 ($75 for international students). Electronic applications accepted. *Expenses:* Contact institution. *Financial support:* Fellowships, research assistantships, teaching assistantships, scholarships/grants, and unspecified assistantships available. Financial award application deadline: 4/1; financial award applicants required to submit FAFSA. *Faculty research:* Administrative leadership and policy studies, early childhood education, research in diversity, paraprofessionals in education, urban schools lab. *Unit head:* Dr. Deanna Sands, Associate Dean, Research and Professional Development, 303-315-4931, E-mail: deanna.sands@ucdenver.edu. *Application contact:* Student Services Center, 303-315-6300, Fax: 303-315-6311, E-mail: education@ucdenver.edu. Web site: http://www.ucdenver.edu/ACADEMICS/COLLEGES/SCHOOLOFEDUCATION/ACADEMICS/Pages/AcademicPrograms.aspx.

University of Colorado Denver, School of Education and Human Development, Teacher Education Programs, Denver, CO 80217. Offers elementary linguistically diverse education (MA); elementary math and science education (MA); elementary math education (MA); elementary reading and writing (MA); elementary science education (MA); secondary English education (MA); secondary linguistically diverse education (MA); secondary math education (MA); secondary reading and writing (MA); secondary science education (MA); special education (MA). *Accreditation:* NCATE. Part-time and evening/weekend programs available. *Students:* 419 full-time (325 women), 238 part-time (196 women); includes 83 minority (11 Black or African American, non-Hispanic/Latino; 1 American Indian or Alaska Native, non-Hispanic/Latino; 15 Asian, non-Hispanic/Latino; 53 Hispanic/Latino; 3 Two or more races, non-Hispanic/Latino), 9 international. Average age 30. 206 applicants, 88% accepted, 85 enrolled. In 2011, 278 master's awarded. *Degree requirements:* For master's, comprehensive exam. *Entrance requirements:* For master's, GRE or MAT (for those with GPA below 2.75), transcripts, resume, letters of recommendation. Additional exam requirements/recommendations for international students: Required—TOEFL (minimum score 525 paper-based; 197 computer-based). *Application deadline:* For fall admission, 4/15 priority date for domestic students; for spring admission, 9/15 priority date for domestic students. Applications are processed on a rolling basis. Application fee: $50 ($75 for international students). Electronic applications accepted. *Expenses:* Contact institution. *Financial support:* Research assistantships, teaching assistantships, and Federal Work-Study available. Financial award application deadline: 4/1; financial award applicants required to submit FAFSA. *Faculty research:* Linguistically diverse education/ESL, elementary reading and writing, elementary teacher education, secondary teacher education, special education. *Unit head:* Cindy Gutierrez, Director, 303-315-4982, E-mail: cindy.gutierrez@ucdenver.edu. *Application contact:* Lori Sisneros, Student Services Center, 303-315-4979, E-mail: education@ucdenver.edu. Web site: http://www.ucdenver.edu/academics/colleges/SchoolOfEducation/Academics/MASTERS/Pages/default.aspx.

University of Connecticut, Graduate School, Neag School of Education, Department of Curriculum and Instruction, Program in Science Education, Storrs, CT 06269. Offers MA, PhD. *Accreditation:* NCATE. Terminal master's awarded for partial completion of doctoral program. *Degree requirements:* For master's, comprehensive exam, thesis or alternative; for doctorate, thesis/dissertation. *Entrance requirements:* For doctorate, GRE General Test. Additional exam requirements/recommendations for international students: Required—TOEFL (minimum score 550 paper-based; 213 computer-based). Electronic applications accepted.

The University of Findlay, Graduate and Professional Studies, College of Education, Findlay, OH 45840-3653. Offers administration (MA Ed); children's literature (MA Ed); early childhood (MA Ed); human resource development (MA Ed); reading endorsement (MA Ed); science (MA Ed); special education (MA Ed); technology (MA Ed). *Accreditation:* NCATE. Part-time and evening/weekend programs available. Postbaccalaureate distance learning degree programs offered (no on-campus study). *Faculty:* 16 full-time (12 women), 5 part-time/adjunct (2 women). *Students:* 72 full-time (49 women), 198 part-time (119 women); includes 10 minority (7 Black or African American, non-Hispanic/Latino; 1 Asian, non-Hispanic/Latino; 2 Hispanic/Latino), 16 international. Average age 30. 75 applicants, 88% accepted, 36 enrolled. In 2011, 76 master's awarded. *Degree requirements:* For master's, thesis, cumulative project. *Entrance requirements:* For master's, bachelor's degree from accredited institution, minimum undergraduate GPA of 2.75 in last 62 hours of course work. Additional exam requirements/recommendations for international students: Required—TOEFL (minimum score 550 paper-based; 213 computer-based; 80 iBT). *Application deadline:* Applications are processed on a rolling basis. Application fee: $25. Electronic applications accepted. *Expenses:* Contact institution. *Financial support:* In 2011–12, 5 research assistantships with full and partial tuition reimbursements (averaging $4,200 per year) were awarded; Federal Work-Study, health care benefits, and unspecified assistantships also available. Financial award application deadline: 4/1; financial award applicants required to submit FAFSA. *Faculty research:* Children's literature, books and artwork, educational technology, professional development. *Unit head:* Dr. Julie McIntosh, Dean, 419-434-4862, Fax: 419-434-4822. *Application contact:* Heather Riffle, Assistant Director, Graduate and Professional Studies, 419-434-4640, Fax: 419-434-5517, E-mail: riffle@findlay.edu. Web site: http://www.findlay.edu.

University of Florida, Graduate School, College of Education, School of Teaching and Learning, Gainesville, FL 32611. Offers bilingual/ESOL education (M Ed, MAE, Ed D, PhD, Ed S); curriculum and instruction (M Ed, MAE, Ed D, PhD, Ed S); elementary education (M Ed, MAE); English education (M Ed, MAE); mathematics education (M Ed, MAE); reading education (M Ed, MAE); science education (M Ed, MAE); social foundations of education (M Ed, MAE, Ed D, PhD); social studies education (M Ed, MAE). *Accreditation:* NCATE. Part-time and evening/weekend programs available. Postbaccalaureate distance learning degree programs offered (no on-campus study). *Faculty:* 26 full-time (19 women). *Students:* 247 full-time (201 women), 236 part-time (196 women); includes 100 minority (32 Black or African American, non-Hispanic/Latino; 2 American Indian or Alaska Native, non-Hispanic/Latino; 15 Asian, non-Hispanic/Latino; 51 Hispanic/Latino), 32 international. Average age 33. 290 applicants, 60% accepted, 122 enrolled. In 2011, 284 master's, 19 doctorates, 29 other advanced degrees awarded. Terminal master's awarded for partial completion of doctoral program. *Degree requirements:* For master's, comprehensive exam (for some programs), thesis (for some programs); for doctorate, comprehensive exam (for some programs), thesis/dissertation (for some programs). *Entrance requirements:* For master's and doctorate, GRE General Test, minimum GPA of 3.0; for Ed S, GRE General Test. Additional exam requirements/recommendations for international students: Required—TOEFL (minimum score 550 paper-based; 213 computer-based; 80 iBT), IELTS (minimum score 6). *Application deadline:* For fall admission, 2/15 for domestic students, 12/1 for international students; for spring admission, 9/15 for domestic students, 3/1 for international students. Applications are processed on a rolling basis. Application fee: $30. Electronic applications accepted. *Financial support:* Fellowships, research assistantships, teaching assistantships, career-related internships or fieldwork, and unspecified assistantships available. Financial award applicants required to submit FAFSA. *Faculty research:* Early childhood, child and adolescents, diverse learners, race/ethnicity issues, teacher education, professional development, language and literacy development, policy development. *Unit head:* Dr. Elizabeth Bondy, Chair, 352-273-4242, Fax: 352-392-9193, E-mail: bondy@coe.ufl.edu. *Application contact:* Wevan Terzian, Graduate Coordinator, 352-273-4216, Fax: 352-392-9193, E-mail: sterzian@coe.ufl.edu. Web site: http://education.ufl.edu/school-teaching-learning/.

University of Georgia, College of Education, Department of Mathematics and Science Education, Athens, GA 30602. Offers mathematics education (M Ed, Ed D, PhD, Ed S); science education (M Ed, Ed D, PhD, Ed S). *Faculty:* 15 full-time (7 women), 1 (woman) part-time/adjunct. *Students:* 115 full-time (71 women), 87 part-time (60 women); includes 42 minority (29 Black or African American, non-Hispanic/Latino; 6 Asian, non-Hispanic/Latino; 6 Hispanic/Latino; 1 Two or more races, non-Hispanic/Latino), 22 international. Average age 34. 86 applicants, 88% accepted, 38 enrolled. In 2011, 57 master's, 18 doctorates, 13 other advanced degrees awarded. *Application deadline:* For fall admission, 7/1 priority date for domestic students; for spring admission, 11/15 for domestic students. Application fee: $50. *Unit head:* Dr. Denise A. Spangler, Head, 706-542-4548, Fax: 706-542-4551, E-mail: dspangle@uga.edu. *Application contact:* Dr. John Olive, Graduate Coordinator, 706-542-4557, Fax: 706-542-4551, E-mail: jolive@uga.edu. Web site: http://www.coe.uga.edu/mse/.

University of Illinois at Urbana–Champaign, Graduate College, College of Engineering, Department of Physics, Champaign, IL 61820. Offers physics (MS, PhD); teaching of physics (MS). *Faculty:* 49 full-time (6 women), 2 part-time/adjunct (0 women). *Students:* 183 full-time (28 women), 86 part-time (11 women); includes 22 minority (1 Black or African American, non-Hispanic/Latino; 17 Asian, non-Hispanic/Latino; 3 Hispanic/Latino; 1 Two or more races, non-Hispanic/Latino), 133 international. 445 applicants, 12% accepted, 52 enrolled. In 2011, 11 master's, 39 doctorates awarded. *Entrance requirements:* For master's, GRE, minimum GPA of 3.0; for doctorate, GRE, minimum GPA of 3.5. Additional exam requirements/recommendations for international students: Required—TOEFL (minimum score 550 paper-based; 213 computer-based; 79 iBT) or IELTS (minimum score 6.5). *Application deadline:* Applications are processed on a rolling basis. Application fee: $75 ($90 for international students). Electronic applications accepted. *Financial support:* In 2011–12, 17 fellowships, 173 research assistantships, 131 teaching assistantships were awarded; tuition waivers (full and partial) also available. *Unit head:* Dale J. VanHarlingen, Head, 217-333-3760, Fax: 217-244-4293, E-mail: dvh@illinois.edu. *Application contact:* Melodee Jo Schweighart, Office Manager, 217-333-3645, Fax: 217-244-5073, E-mail: mschweig@illinois.edu. Web site: http://www.physics.illinois.edu/.

University of Illinois at Urbana–Champaign, Graduate College, College of Liberal Arts and Sciences, School of Chemical Sciences, Department of Chemistry, Champaign, IL 61820. Offers astrochemistry (PhD); chemical physics (PhD); chemistry (MA, MS, PhD); teaching of chemistry (MS); MS/JD; MS/MBA. *Faculty:* 29 full-time (5 women), 1 part-time/adjunct (0 women). *Students:* 279 full-time (95 women), 5 part-time (1 woman); includes 39 minority (4 Black or African American, non-Hispanic/Latino; 1 American Indian or Alaska Native, non-Hispanic/Latino; 19 Asian, non-Hispanic/Latino; 7 Hispanic/Latino; 8 Two or more races, non-Hispanic/Latino), 73 international. 476 applicants, 15% accepted, 71 enrolled. In 2011, 14 master's, 56 doctorates awarded. *Entrance requirements:* For master's and doctorate, GRE General Test, GRE Subject Test, minimum GPA of 3.0. Additional exam requirements/recommendations for international students: Required—TOEFL (minimum score 580 paper-based; 237 computer-based). *Application deadline:* Applications are processed on a rolling basis. Application fee: $75 ($90 for international students). Electronic applications accepted. *Financial support:* In 2011–12, 114 fellowships, 162 research assistantships, 167 teaching assistantships were awarded; tuition waivers (full and partial) also available. *Unit head:* Steven C. Zimmerman, Head, 217-333-6655, Fax: 217-244-5943, E-mail: sczimmer@illinois.edu. *Application contact:* Krista Smith, Program Coordinator, 217-244-4844, Fax: 217-244-5943, E-mail: kristasm@illinois.edu. Web site: http://chemistry.illinois.edu/.

University of Illinois at Urbana–Champaign, Graduate College, College of Liberal Arts and Sciences, School of Earth, Society and Environment, Department of Geology, Champaign, IL 61820. Offers geology (MS, PhD); teaching of earth sciences (MS). *Faculty:* 12 full-time (3 women). *Students:* 21 full-time (10 women), 4 part-time (all women); includes 1 minority (Asian, non-Hispanic/Latino), 10 international. 53 applicants, 17% accepted, 5 enrolled. In 2011, 6 master's, 1 doctorate awarded. Terminal master's awarded for partial completion of doctoral program. *Entrance requirements:* For master's and doctorate, GRE General Test, minimum GPA of 3.0. Additional exam requirements/recommendations for international students: Required—TOEFL. *Application deadline:* Applications are processed on a rolling basis. Application fee: $75 ($90 for international students). Electronic applications accepted. *Financial support:* In 2011–12, 4 fellowships, 17 research assistantships, 12 teaching assistantships were awarded; Federal Work-Study and tuition waivers (full and partial) also available. *Faculty research:* Hydrogeology, structure/tectonics, mineral science. *Unit head:* Thomas M. Johnson, Head, 217-244-2002, Fax: 217-244-4996, E-mail: tmjohnsn@illinois.edu. *Application contact:* Marilyn K. Whalen, Office Administrator, 217-333-3542, Fax: 217-244-4996, E-mail: mkt@illinois.edu. Web site: http://www.geology.illinois.edu/.

University of Indianapolis, Graduate Programs, School of Education, Indianapolis, IN 46227-3697. Offers art education (MAT); biology (MAT); chemistry (MAT); curriculum and instruction (MA); earth sciences (MAT); education (MA, MAT); educational leadership (MA); elementary education (MA); English (MAT); French (MAT); math (MAT); physical education (MAT); physics (MAT); secondary education (MA), including art education, education, English education, social studies education; social studies (MAT); Spanish (MAT). *Accreditation:* NCATE. Part-time and evening/weekend programs available. *Faculty:* 3 full-time (2 women), 3 part-time/adjunct (2 women). *Students:* 32 full-time (18 women), 97 part-time (56 women); includes 22 minority (20 Black or African American, non-Hispanic/Latino; 1 Asian, non-Hispanic/Latino; 1 Hispanic/Latino), 3 international. Average age 33. In 2011, 78 master's awarded. *Entrance requirements:* For master's, GRE Subject Test, PRAXIS I, minimum GPA of 2.5, 3 letters of recommendation, interview, writing exercise. Additional exam requirements/recommendations for international students: Required—TOEFL (minimum score 550 paper-based; 213 computer-based). *Application deadline:* Applications are processed on a rolling basis. Application fee: $50. Tuition and fees vary according to degree level and program. *Financial support:* Federal Work-Study available. Financial award application deadline: 5/1; financial award applicants required to submit FAFSA. *Faculty research:* Assessment of teacher education, perceptions of prospective teachers by parents. *Unit head:* Dr. Kathy Moran, Dean, 317-788-3285, Fax: 317-788-3300, E-mail: kmoran@uindy.edu. *Application contact:* Jeni Kirby, 317-788-2113, E-mail: kirbyj@uindy.edu. Web site: http://education.uindy.edu/.

The University of Iowa, Graduate College, College of Liberal Arts and Sciences, Program in Science Education, Iowa City, IA 52242-1316. Offers MS, PhD. *Degree requirements:* For master's, thesis, exam; for doctorate, comprehensive exam, thesis/dissertation. *Entrance requirements:* For master's and doctorate, GRE General Test, minimum GPA of 3.0. Additional exam requirements/recommendations for international students: Required—TOEFL (minimum score 550 paper-based; 213 computer-based; 81 iBT). Electronic applications accepted.

University of Maine, Graduate School, College of Education and Human Development, Interdisciplinary Program in Teaching, Orono, ME 04469. Offers earth sciences (MST); generalist (MST); mathematics (MST); physics and astronomy (MST). *Students:* 8 full-time (6 women), 13 part-time (10 women); includes 1 minority (American Indian or Alaska Native, non-Hispanic/Latino). Average age 40. 2 applicants, 50% accepted, 1 enrolled. In 2011, 6 master's awarded. *Entrance requirements:* For master's, GRE General Test, MAT. Application fee: $65. *Expenses:* Tuition, state resident: full-time $5016. Tuition, nonresident: full-time $14,424. *Unit head:* Dr. Susan McKay, Director, 207-581-1016. *Application contact:* Scott G. Delcourt, Associate Dean of the Graduate School, 207-581-3291, Fax: 207-581-3232, E-mail: graduate@maine.edu. Web site: http://www2.umaine.edu/graduate/.

University of Maine, Graduate School, College of Education and Human Development, Program in Science Education, Orono, ME 04469. Offers M Ed, MS, CAS. *Accreditation:* NCATE. Part-time and evening/weekend programs available. *Students:* 3 full-time (all women), 1 part-time (0 women), 1 international. Average age 29. 4 applicants, 75% accepted, 3 enrolled. In 2011, 3 degrees awarded. *Degree requirements:* For master's, thesis or alternative. *Entrance requirements:* For master's, MAT; for CAS, MA, M Ed, or MS. Additional exam requirements/recommendations for international students: Required—TOEFL. *Application deadline:* For fall admission, 2/1 priority date for domestic students. Applications are processed on a rolling basis. Application fee: $65. Electronic applications accepted. *Expenses:* Tuition, state resident: full-time $5016. Tuition, nonresident: full-time $14,424. *Financial support:* Federal Work-Study, institutionally sponsored loans, and tuition waivers (full and partial) available. Financial award application deadline: 3/1. *Unit head:* Dr. Janet Spector, Coordinator, 207-581-2444, Fax: 207-581-2423. *Application contact:* Scott G. Delcourt, Associate Dean of the Graduate School, 207-581-3291, Fax: 207-581-3232, E-mail: graduate@maine.edu. Web site: http://www2.umaine.edu/graduate/.

University of Maryland, Baltimore County, Graduate School, College of Arts, Humanities and Social Sciences, Department of Education, Program in Teaching, Baltimore, MD 21250. Offers early childhood education (MAT); elementary education (MAT); secondary education (MAT), including social studies; secondary education (MAT), including art, biology, chemistry, dance, earth/space science, English, foreign language, mathematics, music, physics, theatre. Part-time and evening/weekend programs available. *Faculty:* 24 full-time (18 women), 25 part-time/adjunct (19 women). *Students:* 46 full-time (35 women), 64 part-time (39 women); includes 24 minority (8 Black or African American, non-Hispanic/Latino; 7 Asian, non-Hispanic/Latino; 6 Hispanic/Latino; 1 Native Hawaiian or other Pacific Islander, non-Hispanic/Latino; 2 Two or more races, non-Hispanic/Latino), 4 international. Average age 31. 88 applicants, 57% accepted, 39 enrolled. In 2011, 106 master's awarded. *Degree requirements:* For master's, comprehensive exam (for some programs), thesis (for some programs). *Entrance requirements:* For master's, PRAXIS I or GRE (minimum score of 1000), minimum GPA of 3.0. Additional exam requirements/recommendations for international students: Required—TOEFL. *Application deadline:* For fall admission, 6/1 for domestic students; for spring admission, 11/1 for domestic students. Applications are processed on a rolling basis. Application fee: $50. Electronic applications accepted. *Financial support:* In 2011–12, 6 students received support, including teaching assistantships with full and partial tuition reimbursements available (averaging $12,000 per year); career-related internships or fieldwork, Federal Work-Study, scholarships/grants, tuition waivers, and unspecified assistantships also available. Financial award application deadline: 3/1. *Faculty research:* STEM teacher education, culturally sensitive pedagogy, ESOL/bilingual education, early childhood education, language, literacy and culture. *Unit head:* Dr. Susan M. Blunck, Graduate Program Director, 410-455-2869, Fax: 410-455-3986, E-mail: blunck@umbc.edu. *Application contact:* Cheryl Johnson, 410-455-3388, E-mail: blackwel@umbc.edu. Web site: http://www.umbc.edu/education/.

University of Massachusetts Amherst, Graduate School, School of Education, Program in Education, Amherst, MA 01003. Offers bilingual, English as a second language, and multicultural education (M Ed, CAGS); child study and early education (M Ed); children, families and schools (Ed D, CAGS); early childhood and elementary teacher education (M Ed); educational leadership (M Ed, CAGS); educational policy and leadership (Ed D); higher education (M Ed, CAGS); international education (M Ed); language, literacy and culture (Ed D); learning, media and technology (M Ed, CAGS); mathematics, science, and learning technologies (Ed D); policy studies in education (CAGS); psychometric methods, educational statistics and research methods (Ed D); reading and writing (M Ed); school counselor education (M Ed, CAGS); science education (CAGS); secondary teacher education (M Ed); social justice education (M Ed, Ed D, CAGS); special education (M Ed, Ed D, CAGS). *Accreditation:* NCATE. Part-time programs available. Postbaccalaureate distance learning degree programs offered (minimal on-campus study). *Faculty:* 81 full-time (46 women). *Students:* 341 full-time (240 women), 333 part-time (226 women); includes 113 minority (36 Black or African American, non-Hispanic/Latino; 1 American Indian or Alaska Native, non-Hispanic/Latino; 14 Asian, non-Hispanic/Latino; 51 Hispanic/Latino; 1 Native Hawaiian or other Pacific Islander, non-Hispanic/Latino; 10 Two or more races, non-Hispanic/Latino), 98 international. Average age 36. 721 applicants, 57% accepted, 202 enrolled. In 2011, 166 master's, 33 doctorates, 25 CAGSs awarded. Terminal master's awarded for partial completion of doctoral program. *Degree requirements:* For doctorate, comprehensive exam, thesis/dissertation. *Entrance requirements:* Additional exam requirements/recommendations for international students: Required—TOEFL (minimum score 550 paper-based; 213 computer-based; 80 iBT), IELTS (minimum score 6.5). *Application deadline:* For fall admission, 1/15 for domestic and international students. Applications are processed on a rolling basis. Application fee: $50 ($65 for international students). Electronic applications accepted. Tuition and fees vary according to course load, campus/location and program. *Financial support:* Fellowships with full and partial tuition reimbursements, research assistantships with full and partial tuition reimbursements, teaching assistantships with full and partial tuition reimbursements, career-related internships or fieldwork, Federal Work-Study, scholarships/grants, traineeships, health care benefits, tuition waivers (full and partial), and unspecified assistantships available. Support available to part-time students. Financial award application deadline: 1/15. *Unit head:* Dr. Linda L. Griffin, Graduate Program Director, 413-545-6984, Fax: 413-545-1523. *Application contact:* Lindsay DeSantis, Interim Supervisor of Admissions, 413-545-0722, Fax: 413-577-0010, E-mail: gradadm@grad.umass.edu. Web site: http://www.umass.edu/education/.

University of Massachusetts Lowell, Graduate School of Education, Lowell, MA 01854-2881. Offers administration, planning, and policy (CAGS); curriculum and instruction (M Ed, CAGS); educational administration (M Ed); language arts and literacy (Ed D); leadership in schooling (Ed D); math and science education (Ed D); reading and language (M Ed, CAGS). *Accreditation:* NCATE. Part-time and evening/weekend programs available. Postbaccalaureate distance learning degree programs offered (no on-campus study). Terminal master's awarded for partial completion of doctoral program. *Degree requirements:* For doctorate, thesis/dissertation. *Entrance requirements:* For master's, doctorate, and CAGS, GRE General Test. Additional exam requirements/recommendations for international students: Required—TOEFL. Electronic applications accepted.

University of Miami, Graduate School, School of Education and Human Development, Department of Teaching and Learning, Program in Teaching and Learning, Coral Gables, FL 33124. Offers language and literacy learning in multilingual settings (PhD); science, technology, engineering and mathematics (PhD); special education (PhD). *Students:* 19 full-time (14 women); includes 10 minority (3 Black or African American, non-Hispanic/Latino; 7 Hispanic/Latino), 1 international. Average age 34. 12 applicants, 17% accepted, 2 enrolled. In 2011, 9 degrees awarded. *Degree requirements:* For doctorate, thesis/dissertation, qualifying exam. *Entrance requirements:* For doctorate, GRE General Test. Additional exam requirements/recommendations for international students: Required—TOEFL (minimum score 550 paper-based; 80 iBT); Recommended—IELTS (minimum score 6.5). *Application deadline:* For fall admission, 2/15 for domestic students, 10/15 for international students. Application fee: $65. Electronic applications accepted. *Financial support:* In 2011–12, 18 students received support, including 5 fellowships with full tuition reimbursements available (averaging $28,800 per year), 9 research assistantships with full and partial tuition reimbursements available (averaging $28,800 per year), 1 teaching assistantship with full and partial tuition reimbursement available (averaging $28,800 per year). Financial award application deadline: 3/1; financial award applicants required to submit FAFSA. *Faculty research:* Teacher education, multicultural education, technology, second language acquisition, math and science education. *Unit head:* Dr. Elizabeth Harry, Department Chairperson and Program Director, 305-284-4961, Fax: 305-284-6998, E-mail: bharry@miami.edu. *Application contact:* Lois Heffernan, Graduate Admission Coordinator, 305-284-2167, Fax: 305-284-9395, E-mail: lheffernan@miami.edu.

University of Michigan–Dearborn, School of Education, Program in Science Education, Dearborn, MI 48126. Offers MS. Part-time and evening/weekend programs available. Postbaccalaureate distance learning degree programs offered (minimal on-campus study). *Faculty:* 11 full-time (7 women), 1 part-time/adjunct (0 women). *Students:* 22 part-time (17 women). Average age 36. 2 applicants, 100% accepted, 2 enrolled. In 2011, 12 master's awarded. *Entrance requirements:* For master's, minimum GPA of 3.0, 2 letters of recommendation from supervisors or university faculty, proof of baccalaureate degree, valid teaching certificate, one-page statement of philosophy of teaching science, one-page statement of educational/career goals. Additional exam requirements/recommendations for international students: Required—TOEFL (minimum score 560 paper-based; 220 computer-based; 84 iBT), TWE. *Application deadline:* For fall admission, 9/5 priority date for domestic students, 9/5 for international students; for winter admission, 12/22 for domestic and international students; for spring admission, 5/5 for domestic and international students. Applications are processed on a rolling basis. Application fee: $60. Electronic applications accepted. *Financial support:* Available to part-time students. Applicants required to submit FAFSA. *Faculty research:* Inquiry pedagogy. *Unit head:* Dr. Susan A. Everett, Program Coordinator, 313-593-5133, Fax: 313-593-4748, E-mail: everetts@umd.umich.edu. *Application contact:* Elizabeth M. Morden, Customer Service Assistant, 313-583-6333, Fax: 313-593-4748, E-mail: emorden@umd.umich.edu. Web site: http://www.soe.umd.umich.edu/soe_msse/.

University of Minnesota, Twin Cities Campus, Graduate School, College of Education and Human Development, Department of Curriculum and Instruction, Program in Teaching, Minneapolis, MN 55455-0213. Offers Chinese (M Ed); earth science (M Ed); elementary special education (M Ed); English (M Ed); English as a second language (M Ed); French (M Ed); German (M Ed); Hebrew (M Ed); Japanese (M Ed); life sciences (M Ed); mathematics (M Ed); middle school science (M Ed); science (M Ed); second languages and cultures (M Ed); social studies (M Ed); Spanish (M Ed). *Students:* 375 full-time (319 women), 72 part-time (56 women); includes 34 minority (8 Black or African American, non-Hispanic/Latino; 16 Asian, non-Hispanic/

Latino; 10 Hispanic/Latino), 5 international. Average age 27. 317 applicants, 70% accepted, 215 enrolled. In 2011, 443 master's awarded. Application fee: $55. *Unit head:* Dr. Nina Asher, Chair, 612-624-1357, Fax: 612-624-8277, E-mail: nasher@umn.edu. *Application contact:* Dr. Jennifer Engler, Assistant Dean, 612-626-2887, Fax: 612-626-7496, E-mail: engle009@umn.edu. Web site: http://www.cehd.umn.edu/ci/.

University of Missouri, Graduate School, College of Education, Department of Learning, Teaching and Curriculum, Columbia, MO 65211. Offers agricultural education (M Ed, PhD, Ed S); art education (M Ed, PhD, Ed S); business and office education (M Ed, PhD, Ed S); early childhood education (M Ed, PhD, Ed S); elementary education (M Ed, PhD, Ed S); English education (M Ed, PhD, Ed S); foreign language education (M Ed, PhD, Ed S); health education and promotion (M Ed, PhD); learning and instruction (M Ed); marketing education (M Ed, PhD, Ed S); mathematics education (M Ed, PhD, Ed S); music education (M Ed, PhD, Ed S); reading education (M Ed, PhD, Ed S); science education (M Ed, PhD, Ed S); social studies education (M Ed, PhD, Ed S); vocational education (M Ed, PhD, Ed S). Part-time programs available. *Faculty:* 26 full-time (16 women), 3 part-time/adjunct (2 women). *Students:* 184 full-time (145 women), 276 part-time (215 women); includes 34 minority (10 Black or African American, non-Hispanic/Latino; 1 American Indian or Alaska Native, non-Hispanic/Latino; 7 Asian, non-Hispanic/Latino; 8 Hispanic/Latino; 8 Two or more races, non-Hispanic/Latino), 39 international. Average age 32. 309 applicants, 76% accepted, 204 enrolled. In 2011, 232 master's, 8 doctorates, 2 other advanced degrees awarded. Terminal master's awarded for partial completion of doctoral program. *Degree requirements:* For doctorate, thesis/dissertation. *Entrance requirements:* For master's and Ed S, GRE General Test or MAT, minimum GPA of 3.0; for doctorate, GRE General Test, minimum GPA of 3.0. Additional exam requirements/recommendations for international students: Required—TOEFL (minimum score 600 paper-based; 250 computer-based; 100 iBT). Application fee: $55 ($75 for international students). Electronic applications accepted. *Expenses:* Tuition, state resident: full-time $5881. Tuition, nonresident: full-time $15,183. *Required fees:* $952. Tuition and fees vary according to campus/location and program. *Financial support:* Fellowships, research assistantships, teaching assistantships, and institutionally sponsored loans available. *Application contact:* Fran Colley, 573-882-6462, E-mail: colleyf@missouri.edu. Web site: http://education.missouri.edu/LTC/.

University of Nebraska at Kearney, Graduate Studies, College of Natural and Social Sciences, Department of Biology, Kearney, NE 68849-0001. Offers biology (MS); science education (MS Ed). Part-time and evening/weekend programs available. *Degree requirements:* For master's, thesis optional. *Entrance requirements:* For master's, GRE General Test. Additional exam requirements/recommendations for international students: Required—TOEFL (minimum score 550 paper-based; 213 computer-based). Electronic applications accepted. *Faculty research:* Pollution injury, molecular biology-viral gene expression, prairie range condition modeling, evolution of symbiotic nitrogen fixation.

University of New Hampshire, Graduate School, College of Engineering and Physical Sciences, Department of Chemistry, Durham, NH 03824. Offers chemistry (MS, MST, PhD); chemistry education (PhD). *Faculty:* 28 full-time (17 women). *Students:* 40 full-time (18 women), 10 part-time (4 women); includes 3 minority (2 Hispanic/Latino; 1 Two or more races, non-Hispanic/Latino), 18 international. Average age 28. 68 applicants, 44% accepted, 12 enrolled. In 2011, 5 master's, 3 doctorates awarded. Terminal master's awarded for partial completion of doctoral program. *Degree requirements:* For master's, thesis; for doctorate, one foreign language, thesis/dissertation. *Entrance requirements:* Additional exam requirements/recommendations for international students: Required—TOEFL (minimum score 550 paper-based; 213 computer-based; 80 iBT). *Application deadline:* For fall admission, 4/1 priority date for domestic students, 4/1 for international students; for spring admission, 12/1 for domestic students. Applications are processed on a rolling basis. Application fee: $65. *Expenses:* Tuition, state resident: full-time $12,360; part-time $687 per credit hour. Tuition, nonresident: full-time $25,680; part-time $1058 per credit hour. *International tuition:* $29,550 full-time. *Required fees:* $1666; $833 per course. $416.50 per semester. Tuition and fees vary according to course load and degree level. *Financial support:* In 2011–12, 48 students received support, including 2 fellowships, 8 research assistantships, 35 teaching assistantships; Federal Work-Study, scholarships/grants, and tuition waivers (full and partial) also available. Support available to part-time students. Financial award application deadline: 2/15. *Faculty research:* Analytical, physical, organic, and inorganic chemistry. *Unit head:* Dr. Chuck Zercher, Chairperson, 603-862-1550. *Application contact:* Cindi Rohwer, Coordinator, 603-862-1550, E-mail: chem.dept@unh.edu. Web site: http://www.unh.edu/chemistry/.

University of New Mexico, Health Sciences Center Graduate Programs, Program in Biomedical Sciences, Program in University Science Teaching, Albuquerque, NM 87131-2039. Offers Certificate. In 2011, 3 Certificates awarded. *Unit head:* Dr. Sherry Rogers, Program Director, 505-272-0007, E-mail: srogers@salud.unm.edu. *Application contact:* Dr. Angela Wandinger-Ness, Coordinator, 505-272-1459, Fax: 505-272-8738, E-mail: awandinger@salud.unm.edu.

The University of North Carolina at Chapel Hill, Graduate School, School of Education, Program in Secondary Education, Chapel Hill, NC 27599. Offers English (Grades 9-12) (MAT); English as a second language (MAT); French (Grades K-12) (MAT); German (Grades K-12) (MAT); Japanese (Grades K-12) (MAT); Latin (Grades 9-12) (MAT); mathematics (Grades 9-12) (MAT); music (Grades K-12) (MAT); science (Grades 9-12) (MAT); social studies (Grades 9-12) (MAT); Spanish (Grades K-12) (MAT). *Accreditation:* NCATE. *Degree requirements:* For master's, comprehensive exam. *Entrance requirements:* For master's, GRE General Test, minimum GPA of 3.0 during last 2 years of undergraduate course work. Additional exam requirements/recommendations for international students: Required—TOEFL (minimum score 550 paper-based; 79 computer-based). Electronic applications accepted.

The University of North Carolina at Greensboro, Graduate School, School of Education, Department of Curriculum and Instruction, Greensboro, NC 27412-5001. Offers college teaching and adult learning (Certificate); curriculum and instruction (M Ed), including chemistry education, elementary education, English as a second language, French education, instructional technology, mathematics education, middle grades education, reading education, science education, social studies education, Spanish education; curriculum and teaching (PhD), including higher education, teacher education and development; English as a second language (Certificate); higher education (M Ed); supervision (M Ed). *Accreditation:* NCATE. Part-time programs available. *Degree requirements:* For doctorate, thesis/dissertation. *Entrance requirements:* For master's and doctorate, GRE General Test. Additional exam requirements/recommendations for international students: Required—TOEFL. Electronic applications accepted. *Faculty research:* Community college literacy program, middle school mathematics/computer mathematics.

The University of North Carolina at Pembroke, Graduate Studies, Department of Biology, Pembroke, NC 28372-1510. Offers science education (MA). Part-time and evening/weekend programs available. *Degree requirements:* For master's, thesis. *Entrance requirements:* For master's, GRE or MAT, minimum GPA of 3.0 in major or 2.5 overall.

University of Northern Colorado, Graduate School, College of Natural and Health Sciences, Department of Chemistry and Biochemistry, Greeley, CO 80639. Offers chemical education (MS, PhD); chemistry (MS). Part-time programs available. *Degree requirements:* For master's, comprehensive exam, thesis or alternative; for doctorate, comprehensive exam, thesis/dissertation. *Entrance requirements:* For master's, 3 letters of reference; for doctorate, GRE General Test, 3 letters of reference. Electronic applications accepted.

University of Northern Colorado, Graduate School, College of Natural and Health Sciences, School of Biological Sciences, Program in Biological Education, Greeley, CO 80639. Offers PhD. Part-time programs available. *Degree requirements:* For doctorate, comprehensive exam, thesis/dissertation. *Entrance requirements:* For doctorate, GRE General Test, 3 letters of recommendation. Electronic applications accepted.

University of Northern Iowa, Graduate College, College of Humanities, Arts and Sciences, Program in Science Education, Cedar Falls, IA 50614. Offers earth science education (MA); physics education (MA); science education (MA). *Students:* 4 full-time (3 women), 27 part-time (19 women); includes 1 minority (Two or more races, non-Hispanic/Latino). 4 applicants, 50% accepted, 2 enrolled. In 2011, 7 master's awarded. *Degree requirements:* For master's, comprehensive exam (for some programs), thesis or alternative. *Entrance requirements:* For master's, minimum GPA of 3.0. Additional exam requirements/recommendations for international students: Required—TOEFL (minimum score 500 paper-based; 180 computer-based; 61 iBT). *Application deadline:* For fall admission, 8/1 priority date for domestic students. Applications are processed on a rolling basis. Application fee: $50 ($70 for international students). Electronic applications accepted. *Expenses:* Tuition, state resident: full-time $7476. Tuition, nonresident: full-time $16,410. *Required fees:* $942. *Financial support:* Application deadline: 2/1. *Unit head:* Dr. Cherin A. Lee, Director, 319-273-7357, Fax: 319-273-3051, E-mail: cherin.lee@uni.edu. *Application contact:* Laurie S. Russell, Record Analyst, 319-273-2623, Fax: 319-273-2885, E-mail: laurie.russell@uni.edu. Web site: http://www.science-ed.uni.edu/.

University of North Texas Health Science Center at Fort Worth, Graduate School of Biomedical Sciences, Fort Worth, TX 76107-2699. Offers anatomy and cell biology (MS, PhD); biochemistry and molecular biology (MS, PhD); biomedical sciences (MS, PhD); biotechnology (MS); forensic genetics (MS); integrative physiology (MS, PhD); medical science (MS); microbiology and immunology (MS, PhD); pharmacology (MS, PhD); science education (MS); DO/MS; DO/PhD. Terminal master's awarded for partial completion of doctoral program. *Degree requirements:* For master's, thesis; for doctorate, thesis/dissertation. *Entrance requirements:* For master's and doctorate, GRE General Test. Additional exam requirements/recommendations for international students: Required—TOEFL. *Expenses:* Contact institution. *Faculty research:* Alzheimer's disease, aging, eye diseases, cancer, cardiovascular disease.

University of Oklahoma, Jeannine Rainbolt College of Education, Department of Instructional Leadership and Academic Curriculum, Norman, OK 73072. Offers communication, culture and pedagogy for Hispanic populations in educational settings (Graduate Certificate); instructional leadership and academic curriculum (M Ed, PhD), including bilingual education, early childhood education, elementary education, English education, instructional leadership, mathematics education, reading education, science education, science, technology, engineering and mathematics education (M Ed), secondary education, social studies education, teacher education (M Ed). *Accreditation:* NCATE. Part-time and evening/weekend programs available. *Faculty:* 19 full-time (13 women), 1 (woman) part-time/adjunct. *Students:* 73 full-time (63 women), 114 part-time (87 women); includes 29 minority (5 Black or African American, non-Hispanic/Latino; 12 American Indian or Alaska Native, non-Hispanic/Latino; 5 Asian, non-Hispanic/Latino; 3 Hispanic/Latino; 1 Native Hawaiian or other Pacific Islander, non-Hispanic/Latino; 3 Two or more races, non-Hispanic/Latino), 7 international. Average age 33. 87 applicants, 86% accepted, 68 enrolled. In 2011, 36 master's, 6 doctorates awarded. Terminal master's awarded for partial completion of doctoral program. *Degree requirements:* For doctorate, thesis/dissertation. *Entrance requirements:* For master's, 12 hours of course work in education; for doctorate, GRE General Test, master's degree, minimum graduate GPA of 3.0. Additional exam requirements/recommendations for international students: Required—TOEFL (minimum score 550 paper-based; 79 iBT). *Application deadline:* For fall admission, 6/1 priority date for domestic students, 3/1 for international students; for spring admission, 11/1 for domestic students, 9/1 for international students. Applications are processed on a rolling basis. Application fee: $40 ($90 for international students). Electronic applications accepted. *Expenses:* Tuition, state resident: full-time $4087; part-time $170.30 per credit hour. Tuition, nonresident: full-time $14,875; part-time $619.80 per credit hour. *Required fees:* $2659; $100.25 per credit hour. Tuition and fees vary according to course load and degree level. *Financial support:* In 2011–12, 128 students received support, including 2 research assistantships with partial tuition reimbursements available (averaging $12,431 per year), 12 teaching assistantships with partial tuition reimbursements available (averaging $10,161 per year); institutionally sponsored loans, scholarships/grants, and unspecified assistantships also available. Financial award applicants required to submit FAFSA. *Faculty research:* Engineering in practice for sustainable future, no child left behind (reading), early childhood learning games impact study, Educare randomized control startup, Oklahoma mentoring professional development. *Total annual research expenditures:* $1.1 million. *Unit head:* Lawrence Baines, Chair, 405-325-1498, Fax: 405-325-4061, E-mail: lbaines@ou.edu. *Application contact:* Lynn Crussel, Graduate Programs Officer, 405-325-4843, Fax: 405-325-4061, E-mail: lcrussel@ou.edu. Web site: http://education.ou.edu/departments/ilac.

University of Phoenix–Online Campus, College of Education, Phoenix, AZ 85034-7209. Offers administration and supervision (MAEd, Graduate Certificate); adult education and training (MAEd); curriculum and instruction (MAEd); curriculum and instruction reading (MAEd); curriculum and instruction-computer education (MAEd); curriculum and instruction-language arts (MAEd); curriculum and instruction-mathematics (MAEd); early childhood education (MAEd); educational studies (MAEd); elementary teacher education (MAEd); elementary teacher education-early childhood (MAEd); secondary teacher education (MAEd); special education (MAEd); teacher education - elementary/middle level (MAEd); teacher education middle level generalist (MAEd); teacher education middle level mathematics (MAEd); teacher education middle level science (MAEd); teacher education secondary mathematics (MAEd); teacher education secondary science (MAEd); teacher leadership (MAEd). *Accreditation:* Teacher Education Accreditation Council. Evening/weekend programs available. Postbaccalaureate distance learning degree programs offered. *Students:* 9,180 full-time (7,178 women); includes 2,913 minority (2,069 Black or African American, non-Hispanic/Latino; 50 American Indian or Alaska Native, non-Hispanic/Latino; 100 Asian, non-Hispanic/Latino; 542 Hispanic/Latino; 48 Native Hawaiian or other Pacific Islander, non-Hispanic/Latino; 104 Two or more races, non-Hispanic/Latino), 147 international. Average age 36. *Entrance requirements:* Additional exam requirements/recommendations for international students: Required—TOEFL, TOEIC (Test of English as an International Communication), Berlitz Online English Proficiency Exam, Pearson Test of English, or IELTS. *Application deadline:* Applications are processed on a rolling basis. Application fee: $45. Electronic applications accepted. *Expenses:* Contact institution. *Financial support:* Scholarships/grants available. Financial award applicants required to submit FAFSA. *Application contact:* 866-766-0766. Web site: http://www.phoenix.edu/colleges_divisions/education.html.

University of Pittsburgh, School of Education, Department of Instruction and Learning, Program in Secondary Education, Pittsburgh, PA 15260. Offers English/communications education (M Ed, MAT); foreign languages education (M Ed, MAT); mathematics education (M Ed, MAT, Ed D); science education (M Ed, MAT, Ed D); social studies education (M Ed, MAT). Part-time and evening/weekend programs available. *Students:* 154 full-time (92 women), 68 part-time (47 women); includes 18 minority (6 Black or African American, non-Hispanic/Latino; 3 Asian, non-Hispanic/Latino; 7 Hispanic/Latino; 2 Two or more races, non-Hispanic/Latino), 6 international. Average age 30. 208 applicants, 48% accepted, 72 enrolled. In 2011, 116 master's, 6 doctorates awarded. *Degree requirements:* For master's, thesis; for doctorate, thesis/dissertation. *Entrance requirements:* For master's, PRAXIS I; for doctorate, GRE General Test. Additional exam requirements/recommendations for international students: Required—TOEFL. *Application deadline:* For fall admission, 2/1 priority date for domestic students; for spring admission, 11/15 priority date for domestic students. Applications are processed on a rolling basis. Application fee: $50. Electronic applications accepted. *Expenses:* Tuition, state resident: full-time $18,774; part-time $760 per credit. Tuition, nonresident: full-time $30,736; part-time $1258 per credit. *Required fees:* $740; $200 per term. Tuition and fees vary according to program. *Financial support:* Fellowships, teaching assistantships, career-related internships or fieldwork, Federal Work-Study, tuition waivers (partial), and unspecified assistantships available. Support available to part-time students. Financial award application deadline: 3/15; financial award applicants required to submit FAFSA. *Unit head:* Dr. Richard Donato, Chairman, 412-624-7248, Fax: 412-648-7081, E-mail: donato@pitt.edu. *Application contact:* Marianne L. Budziszewski, Director of Admissions and Enrollment Services, 412-648-2230, Fax: 412-648-1899, E-mail: soeinfo@pitt.edu. Web site: http://www.education.pitt.edu/.

University of Puerto Rico, Río Piedras, College of Education, Program in Curriculum and Teaching, San Juan, PR 00931-3300. Offers biology education (M Ed); chemistry education (M Ed); curriculum and teaching (Ed D); history education (M Ed); mathematics education (M Ed); physics education (M Ed); Spanish education (M Ed). Part-time programs available. *Degree requirements:* For master's, thesis; for doctorate, thesis/dissertation, internship. *Entrance requirements:* For master's, PAEG or GRE, minimum GPA of 3.0, letter of recommendation; for doctorate, GRE or PAEG, master's degree, minimum GPA of 3.0, letter of recommendation (2), interview. *Faculty research:* Curriculum, math teaching.

University of St. Francis, College of Education, Joliet, IL 60435-6169. Offers educational leadership (MS, Ed D); elementary education certification (M Ed); reading (MS); secondary education certification (M Ed), including English education, math education, science education, social studies education, visual arts education; special education (M Ed); teaching and learning (MS). *Accreditation:* NCATE. Part-time and evening/weekend programs available. Postbaccalaureate distance learning degree programs offered (no on-campus study). *Faculty:* 7 full-time (5 women), 21 part-time/adjunct (14 women). *Students:* 32 full-time (21 women), 230 part-time (175 women); includes 23 minority (7 Black or African American, non-Hispanic/Latino; 2 Asian, non-Hispanic/Latino; 13 Hispanic/Latino; 1 Two or more races, non-Hispanic/Latino), 1 international. Average age 32. 147 applicants, 60% accepted, 57 enrolled. In 2011, 156 master's awarded. *Entrance requirements:* For doctorate, master's degree, IL Type 75 or Principal's endorsement, interview. Additional exam requirements/recommendations for international students: Required—TOEFL (minimum score 550 paper-based; 213 computer-based). *Application deadline:* Applications are processed on a rolling basis. Application fee: $30. Electronic applications accepted. *Expenses:* Contact institution. *Financial support:* In 2011–12, 23 students received support. Federal Work-Study, scholarships/grants, tuition waivers (partial), and unspecified assistantships available. Support available to part-time students. Financial award applicants required to submit FAFSA. *Unit head:* Dr. John Gambro, Dean, 815-740-3829, Fax: 815-740-2264, E-mail: jgambro@stfrancis.edu. *Application contact:* Sandra Sloka, Director of Admissions for Graduate and Degree Completion Programs, 800-735-7500, Fax: 815-740-5032, E-mail: ssloka@stfrancis.edu. Web site: http://www.stfrancis.edu/academics/college-of-education/.

University of South Africa, College of Human Sciences, Pretoria, South Africa. Offers adult education (M Ed); African languages (MA, PhD); African politics (MA, PhD); Afrikaans (MA, PhD); ancient history (MA, PhD); ancient Near Eastern studies (MA, PhD); anthropology (MA, PhD); applied linguistics (MA); Arabic (MA, PhD); archaeology (MA); art history (MA); Biblical archaeology (MA); Biblical studies (M Th, D Th, PhD); Christian spirituality (M Th, D Th); church history (M Th, D Th); classical studies (MA, PhD); clinical psychology (MA); communication (MA, PhD); comparative education (M Ed, Ed D); consulting psychology (D Admin, D Com, PhD); curriculum studies (M Ed, Ed D); development studies (M Admin, MA, D Admin, PhD); didactics (M Ed, Ed D); education (M Tech); education management (M Ed, Ed D); educational psychology (M Ed); English (MA); environmental education (M Ed); French (MA, PhD); German (MA, PhD); Greek (MA); guidance and counseling (M Ed); health studies (MA, PhD), including health sciences education (MA), health services management (MA), medical and surgical nursing science (critical care general) (MA), midwifery and neonatal nursing science (MA), trauma and emergency care (MA); history (MA, PhD); history of education (Ed D); inclusive education (M Ed, Ed D); information and communications technology policy and regulation (MA); information science (MA, MIS, PhD); international politics (MA, PhD); Islamic studies (MA, PhD); Italian (MA, PhD); Judaica (MA, PhD); linguistics (MA, PhD); mathematical education (M Ed); mathematics education (MA); missiology (M Th, D Th); modern Hebrew (MA, PhD); musicology (MA, MMus, D Mus, PhD); natural science education (M Ed); New Testament (M Th, D Th); Old Testament (D Th); pastoral therapy (M Th, D Th); philosophy (MA); philosophy of education (M Ed, Ed D); politics (MA, PhD); Portuguese (MA, PhD); practical theology (M Th, D Th); psychology (MA, MS, PhD); psychology of education (M Ed, Ed D); public health (MA); religious studies (MA, D Th, PhD); Romance languages (MA); Russian (MA, PhD); Semitic languages (MA, PhD); social behavior studies in HIV/AIDS (MA); social science (mental health) (MA); social science in development studies (MA); social science in psychology (MA); social science in social work (MA); social science in sociology (MA); social work (MSW, DSW, PhD); socio-education (M Ed, Ed D); sociolinguistics (MA); sociology (MA, PhD); Spanish (MA, PhD); systematic theology (M Th, D Th); TESOL (teaching English to speakers of other languages) (MA); theological ethics (M Th, D Th); theory of literature (MA, PhD); urban ministries (D Th); urban ministry (M Th).

University of South Africa, Institute for Science and Technology Education, Pretoria, South Africa. Offers mathematics, science and technology education (M Sc, PhD).

University of South Alabama, Graduate School, College of Education, Department of Leadership and Teacher Education, Mobile, AL 36688-0002. Offers early childhood education (M Ed); educational administration (Ed S); educational leadership (M Ed); elementary education (M Ed); reading education (M Ed); science education (M Ed); secondary education (M Ed); special education (M Ed, Ed S). *Accreditation:* NCATE. Part-time programs available. *Faculty:* 20 full-time (14 women). *Students:* 135 full-time (106 women), 75 part-time (62 women); includes 50 minority (40 Black or African American, non-Hispanic/Latino; 3 American Indian or Alaska Native, non-Hispanic/Latino; 3 Asian, non-Hispanic/Latino; 3 Hispanic/Latino; 1 Two or more races, non-Hispanic/Latino), 1 international. 89 applicants, 49% accepted, 36 enrolled. In 2011, 88 master's, 13 Ed Ss awarded. *Degree requirements:* For master's, comprehensive exam. *Entrance requirements:* For master's, GRE General Test or MAT, minimum GPA of 3.0. *Application deadline:* For fall admission, 7/15 priority date for domestic students, 6/15 for international students; for spring admission, 12/1 priority date for domestic students, 11/1 for international students. Applications are processed on a rolling basis. Application fee: $35. *Expenses:* Tuition, state resident: full-time $7968; part-time $332 per credit hour. Tuition, nonresident: full-time $15,936; part-time $664 per credit hour. *Financial support:* Research assistantships and career-related internships or fieldwork available. Support available to part-time students. Financial award application deadline: 4/1. *Unit head:* Dr. Harold Dodge, Jr., Chair, 251-380-2894. *Application contact:* Dr. Abigail Baxter, Director of Graduate Studies, 251-460-6310, Fax: 251-461-1513, E-mail: kharriso@usouthal.edu. Web site: http://www.southalabama.edu/coe/lted.

University of South Carolina, The Graduate School, College of Arts and Sciences, Department of Biological Sciences, Columbia, SC 29208. Offers biology (MS, PhD); biology education (IMA, MAT); ecology, evolution and organismal biology (MS, PhD); molecular, cellular, and developmental biology (MS, PhD). IMA and MAT offered in cooperation with the College of Education. Terminal master's awarded for partial completion of doctoral program. *Degree requirements:* For master's, one foreign language, thesis (for some programs); for doctorate, one foreign language, thesis/dissertation. *Entrance requirements:* For master's and doctorate, GRE General Test, minimum GPA of 3.0 in science. Electronic applications accepted. *Faculty research:* Marine ecology, population and evolutionary biology, molecular biology and genetics, development.

University of South Carolina, The Graduate School, College of Arts and Sciences, Department of Geography, Columbia, SC 29208. Offers geography (MA, MS, PhD); geography education (IMA). IMA and MAT offered in cooperation with the College of Education. Part-time programs available. *Degree requirements:* For master's, comprehensive exam, thesis (for some programs); for doctorate, comprehensive exam, thesis/dissertation. *Entrance requirements:* For master's, GRE General Test; for doctorate, GRE General Test, master's degree. Electronic applications accepted. *Faculty research:* Geographic information processing; economic, cultural, physical, and environmental geography.

University of South Carolina, The Graduate School, College of Education, Department of Instruction and Teacher Education, Program in Secondary Education, Columbia, SC 29208. Offers art education (IMA, MAT); business education (IMA, MAT); English (MAT); foreign language (MAT); health education (MAT); mathematics (MAT); science (IMA, MAT); secondary (Ed D); secondary education (MT, PhD); social studies (MAT); theatre and speech (MAT). IMA and MT offered jointly with the subject areas. *Accreditation:* NCATE. *Degree requirements:* For master's, comprehensive exam, thesis (for some programs), foreign language (MA); for doctorate, one foreign language, comprehensive exam, thesis/dissertation. *Entrance requirements:* For master's, GRE General Test or MAT, teaching certificate (IMA, M Ed), interview; for doctorate, GRE General Test or MAT, interview. *Faculty research:* Middle school programs, professional development, school collaboration.

University of Southern Mississippi, Graduate School, College of Science and Technology, Center for Science and Mathematics Education, Hattiesburg, MS 39406-0001. Offers MS, PhD. Part-time programs available. *Faculty:* 1 full-time (0 women), 1 (woman) part-time/adjunct. *Students:* 18 full-time (14 women), 30 part-time (21 women); includes 7 minority (5 Black or African American, non-Hispanic/Latino; 1 Asian, non-Hispanic/Latino; 1 Hispanic/Latino), 7 international. Average age 35. 6 applicants, 83% accepted, 5 enrolled. In 2011, 9 master's, 5 doctorates awarded. *Degree requirements:* For master's, comprehensive exam, thesis or alternative; for doctorate, comprehensive exam, thesis/dissertation. *Entrance requirements:* For master's, GRE General Test, minimum GPA of 2.75 in last 60 hours; for doctorate, GRE General Test, minimum GPA of 3.5. Additional exam requirements/recommendations for international students: Required—TOEFL, IELTS. *Application deadline:* For fall admission, 3/15 priority date for domestic students, 3/15 for international students; for spring admission, 1/10 priority date for domestic students, 1/10 for international students. Applications are processed on a rolling basis. Application fee: $50. *Financial support:* In 2011–12, 1 fellowship with full tuition reimbursement (averaging $21,000 per year), 1 research assistantship with full tuition reimbursement (averaging $14,500 per year), 8 teaching assistantships with full tuition reimbursements (averaging $8,400 per year) were awarded; Federal Work-Study, scholarships/grants, health care benefits, and unspecified assistantships also available. Financial award application deadline: 3/15; financial award applicants required to submit FAFSA. *Unit head:* Dr. Sherry Herron, Director, 601-266-4739, Fax: 601-266-4741. *Application contact:* Sherry Herron, Director, 601-266-4739, Fax: 601-266-4741. Web site: http://www.usm.edu/graduateschool/table.php.

University of South Florida, Graduate School, College of Education, Department of Secondary Education, Tampa, FL 33620-9951. Offers English education (M Ed, MA, MAT, PhD); foreign language education/ESOL (M Ed, MA, MAT); instructional technology (M Ed, PhD, Ed S); mathematics education (M Ed, MA, MAT, PhD, Ed S); science education (M Ed, MA, MAT, PhD); second language acquisition/instructional technology (PhD); secondary education (M Ed, PhD); secondary education/TESOL (M Ed); social science education (M Ed, MA, MAT); teaching and learning in the content area (PhD). *Accreditation:* NCATE. Part-time and evening/weekend programs available. *Faculty:* 28 full-time (17 women), 3 part-time/adjunct (1 woman). *Students:* 174 full-time (116 women), 268 part-time (184 women); includes 103 minority (26 Black or African American, non-Hispanic/Latino; 10 Asian, non-Hispanic/Latino; 58 Hispanic/Latino; 9 Two or more races, non-Hispanic/Latino), 32 international. Average age 37. 229 applicants, 73% accepted, 141 enrolled. In 2011, 115 master's, 16 doctorates, 5 other advanced degrees awarded. *Degree requirements:* For master's, variable foreign language requirement, comprehensive exam, project (for some programs); for doctorate, variable foreign language requirement, comprehensive exam, thesis/dissertation, philosophies of inquiry; multiple research methods. *Entrance requirements:* For master's, GRE General Test or General Knowledge Test, minimum GPA of 3.0; for doctorate, GRE General Test, minimum GPA of 3.5; for Ed S, GRE General Test. Additional exam requirements/recommendations for international students: Required—TOEFL (minimum score 550 paper-based; 213 computer-based; 79 iBT). *Application deadline:* For fall admission, 2/15 for domestic students, 1/2 for international students; for spring admission, 10/15 for domestic students, 6/1 for international students. Application fee: $30. Electronic applications accepted. *Financial support:* In 2011–12, 7 students received support, including 1 research assistantship with full tuition reimbursement available (averaging $10,000 per year), 55 teaching assistantships with full and partial tuition reimbursements available (averaging $7,900 per year); scholarships/grants and unspecified assistantships also available. Financial award application deadline: 4/15; financial award applicants required to submit FAFSA. *Faculty research:* English language learners/multicultural, social science education, mathematics education, science education, instructional technology. *Total annual research expenditures:* $336,023. *Unit head:* Dr. Stephen Thornton, Chairperson, 813-974-3533, Fax: 813-974-3837, E-mail: thornton@usf.edu. *Application contact:* Dr. Diane Briscoe, Coordinator of Graduate Studies, 813-974-1804, Fax: 813-974-3391, E-mail:

briscoe@usf.edu. Web site: http://www.coedu.usf.edu/main/departments/seced/seced.html.

University of South Florida–St. Petersburg Campus, College of Education, St. Petersburg, FL 33701. Offers educational leadership development (M Ed); elementary education (MA), including math/science; English education (MA); middle grades STEM education (MS); reading education (MA). Part-time programs available. *Students:* 30 full-time (27 women), 130 part-time (109 women); includes 28 minority (14 Black or African American, non-Hispanic/Latino; 4 Asian, non-Hispanic/Latino; 9 Hispanic/Latino; 1 Two or more races, non-Hispanic/Latino). Average age 34. 63 applicants, 70% accepted, 36 enrolled. In 2011, 74 master's awarded. *Degree requirements:* For master's, comprehensive exam, practicum, internship, comprehensive portfolio. *Entrance requirements:* For master's, State of Florida General Knowledge Test (GKT), Florida Teaching Certificate (for non-initial certification programs), letters of recommendation. Additional exam requirements/recommendations for international students: Required—TOEFL (minimum score 550 paper-based; 79 iBT); Recommended—IELTS. *Application deadline:* For fall admission, 6/1 priority date for domestic students, 6/1 for international students; for spring admission, 10/15 priority date for domestic students, 10/15 for international students. Applications are processed on a rolling basis. Application fee: $30. Electronic applications accepted. *Expenses:* Tuition, state resident: full-time $8847. Tuition, nonresident: full-time $18,423. One-time fee: $35 full-time. Full-time tuition and fees vary according to course load and program. *Financial support:* Applicants required to submit FAFSA. *Unit head:* Dr. Harold W. Heller, Dean, 727-873-4155, Fax: 727-873-4191, E-mail: hheller@usfsp.edu. *Application contact:* Eric Douthirt, Enrollment Management Specialist, 727-873-4450, E-mail: douthirt@usfsp.edu. Web site: http://www1.usfsp.edu/coe/index.asp.

The University of Tennessee, Graduate School, College of Education, Health and Human Sciences, Program in Education, Knoxville, TN 37996. Offers art education (MS); counseling education (PhD); cultural studies in education (PhD); curriculum (MS, Ed S); curriculum, educational research and evaluation (Ed D, PhD); early childhood education (PhD); early childhood special education (MS); education of deaf and hard of hearing (MS); educational administration and policy studies (Ed D, PhD); educational administration and supervision (Ed S); educational psychology (Ed D, PhD); elementary education (MS, Ed S); elementary teaching (MS); English education (MS, Ed S); exercise science (PhD); foreign language/ESL education (MS, Ed S); instructional technology (MS, Ed D, PhD, Ed S); literacy, language and ESL education (PhD); literacy, language education, and ESL education (Ed D); mathematics education (MS, Ed S); modified and comprehensive special education (MS); reading education (MS, Ed S); school counseling (Ed S); school psychology (PhD, Ed S); science education (MS, Ed S); secondary teaching (MS); social foundations (MS); social science education (MS, Ed S); socio-cultural foundations of sports and education (PhD); special education (Ed S); teacher education (Ed D, PhD). *Accreditation:* NCATE. Part-time and evening/weekend programs available. *Degree requirements:* For master's and Ed S, thesis optional; for doctorate, variable foreign language requirement, thesis/dissertation. *Entrance requirements:* For master's, minimum GPA of 2.7; for doctorate and Ed S, GRE General Test, minimum GPA of 2.7. Additional exam requirements/recommendations for international students: Required—TOEFL. Electronic applications accepted. *Expenses:* Tuition, state resident: full-time $8332; part-time $464 per credit hour. Tuition, nonresident: full-time $25,174; part-time $1400 per credit hour. *Required fees:* $1162; $56 per credit hour. Tuition and fees vary according to program.

The University of Texas at Dallas, School of Natural Sciences and Mathematics, Department of Science/Mathematics Education, Richardson, TX 75080. Offers mathematics education (MAT); science education (MAT). Part-time and evening/weekend programs available. Postbaccalaureate distance learning degree programs offered (minimal on-campus study). *Faculty:* 6 full-time (2 women). *Students:* 11 full-time (10 women), 55 part-time (36 women); includes 27 minority (6 Black or African American, non-Hispanic/Latino; 7 Asian, non-Hispanic/Latino; 11 Hispanic/Latino; 3 Two or more races, non-Hispanic/Latino), 2 international. Average age 37. 85 applicants, 67% accepted, 45 enrolled. In 2011, 37 master's awarded. *Degree requirements:* For master's, thesis optional. *Entrance requirements:* For master's, GRE General Test, minimum GPA of 3.0 in upper-level coursework in field. Additional exam requirements/recommendations for international students: Required—TOEFL (minimum score 550 paper-based; 215 computer-based). *Application deadline:* For fall admission, 7/15 for domestic students, 5/1 for international students; for spring admission, 11/15 for domestic students, 9/1 for international students. Applications are processed on a rolling basis. Application fee: $50 ($100 for international students). Electronic applications accepted. *Expenses:* Tuition, state resident: full-time $11,170; part-time $620.56 per credit hour. Tuition, nonresident: full-time $20,212; part-time $1122.89 per credit hour. *Financial support:* In 2011–12, 45 students received support, including 2 research assistantships with partial tuition reimbursements available (averaging $20,400 per year), 1 teaching assistantship with partial tuition reimbursement available (averaging $15,300 per year); career-related internships or fieldwork, Federal Work-Study, institutionally sponsored loans, scholarships/grants, and unspecified assistantships also available. Support available to part-time students. Financial award application deadline: 4/30; financial award applicants required to submit FAFSA. *Faculty research:* Innovative science/math education programs. *Unit head:* Dr. Mary L. Urquhart, Department Head, 972-883-2499, Fax: 972-883-6796, E-mail: scimathed@utdallas.edu. *Application contact:* Barbarra Curry, Advisor, 972-883-4008, Fax: 972-883-6796, E-mail: barbc@utdallas.edu. Web site: http://www.utdallas.edu/scimathed/.

The University of Texas at El Paso, Graduate School, College of Science, Teaching Science Program, El Paso, TX 79968-0001. Offers MAT. Part-time and evening/weekend programs available. *Students:* 48 (35 women); includes 39 minority (1 Black or African American, non-Hispanic/Latino; 38 Hispanic/Latino), 3 international. In 2011, 4 master's awarded. *Degree requirements:* For master's, thesis optional. *Entrance requirements:* For master's, minimum GPA of 3.0. Additional exam requirements/recommendations for international students: Required—TOEFL; Recommended—IELTS. *Application deadline:* For fall admission, 8/1 for domestic students, 3/1 for international students; for spring admission, 11/1 for domestic students, 9/3 for international students. Applications are processed on a rolling basis. Application fee: $45 ($80 for international students). Electronic applications accepted. *Financial support:* Fellowships with tuition reimbursements, research assistantships with tuition reimbursements, teaching assistantships with tuition reimbursements, institutionally sponsored loans, scholarships/grants, health care benefits, tuition waivers (partial), and unspecified assistantships available. Support available to part-time students. Financial award application deadline: 3/15; financial award applicants required to submit FAFSA. *Unit head:* Dr. Laura Serpa, Coordinator, 915-747-6085, Fax: 915-747-6807, E-mail: lfserpa@utep.edu. *Application contact:* Dr. Benjamin Flores, Interim Dean of the Graduate School, 915-747-5491, Fax: 915-747-5788, E-mail: bflores@utep.edu. Web site: http://www.math.utep.edu/mat/science/.

University of the Incarnate Word, School of Graduate Studies and Research, School of Mathematics, Science, and Engineering, Program in Mathematics, San Antonio, TX 78209-6397. Offers mathematics teaching (MA); research statistics (MS). Part-time and evening/weekend programs available. *Faculty:* 1 full-time (0 women), 1 (woman) part-time/adjunct. *Students:* 1 (woman) full-time, 1 (woman) part-time; includes 1 minority (Hispanic/Latino). Average age 23. 4 applicants, 100% accepted, 1 enrolled. *Degree requirements:* For master's, capstone or prerequisite knowledge (for research statistics). *Entrance requirements:* For master's, GRE (minimum score 800 verbal and quantitative), 18 hours of undergraduate mathematics with minimum GPA of 3.0; letter of recommendation by a professional in the field, writing sample, teaching experience at the precollege level. Additional exam requirements/recommendations for international students: Required—TOEFL (minimum score 560 paper-based; 220 computer-based; 83 iBT). *Application deadline:* Applications are processed on a rolling basis. Application fee: $20. Electronic applications accepted. *Expenses: Tuition:* Part-time $725 per credit hour. Tuition and fees vary according to degree level. *Financial support:* Federal Work-Study and scholarships/grants available. Financial award applicants required to submit FAFSA. *Faculty research:* Scholarship and career development for undergraduate mathematics majors. *Total annual research expenditures:* $140,844. *Unit head:* Dr. Paul Messina, Mathematics Graduate Program Coordinator, 210-832-5665, Fax: 210-829-3153, E-mail: messina@uiwtx.edu. *Application contact:* Andrea Cyterski-Acosta, Dean of Enrollment, 210-829-6005, Fax: 210-829-3921, E-mail: admis@uiwtx.edu. Web site: http://www.uiw.edu/math/mathprogramsgrad.html and.

The University of Toledo, College of Graduate Studies, Judith Herb College of Education, Health Science and Human Service, Department of Curriculum and Instruction, Toledo, OH 43606-3390. Offers art education (ME); career and technical education (ME); curriculum and instruction (ME, PhD, Ed S); education and anthropology (MAE); education and biology (MES); education and chemistry (MES); education and classics (MAE); education and economics (MAE); education and English (MAE); education and French (MAE); education and geography (MAE); education and geology (MES); education and German (MAE); education and history (MAE); education and mathematics (MAE, MES); education and physics (MES); education and political science (MAE); education and sociology (MAE); education and Spanish (MAE); educational media (PhD); educational technology (ME); English as a second language (MAE); gifted and talented (PhD); middle childhood education licensure (ME); music education (MME); secondary education (PhD); secondary education licensure (ME). *Accreditation:* NCATE. Part-time and evening/weekend programs available. *Faculty:* 24. *Students:* 60 full-time (31 women), 211 part-time (161 women); includes 23 minority (21 Black or African American, non-Hispanic/Latino; 2 Hispanic/Latino), 20 international. Average age 35. 115 applicants, 73% accepted, 74 enrolled. In 2011, 105 master's, 3 doctorates, 4 other advanced degrees awarded. *Degree requirements:* For master's, comprehensive exam, thesis or alternative; for doctorate, comprehensive exam, thesis/dissertation; for Ed S, thesis optional. *Entrance requirements:* For master's, doctorate, and Ed S, minimum cumulative GPA of 2.7 for all previous academic work, letters of recommendation. Additional exam requirements/recommendations for international students: Required—TOEFL (minimum score 550 paper-based; 213 computer-based; 80 iBT), IELTS (minimum score 6.5). *Application deadline:* For fall admission, 1/15 priority date for domestic students, 1/15 for international students. Applications are processed on a rolling basis. Application fee: $45 ($75 for international students). Electronic applications accepted. *Financial support:* In 2011–12, 9 research assistantships with full and partial tuition reimbursements (averaging $7,184 per year), 12 teaching assistantships with full and partial tuition reimbursements (averaging $8,425 per year) were awarded; career-related internships or fieldwork, Federal Work-Study, institutionally sponsored loans, scholarships/grants, tuition waivers (full and partial), unspecified assistantships, and administrative assistantships also available. Support available to part-time students. *Unit head:* Dr. Leigh Chiarelott, Chair, 419-530-5371, E-mail: eigh.chiarelott@utoledo.edu. *Application contact:* Graduate School Office, 419-530-4723, Fax: 419-530-4724, E-mail: grdsch@utnet.utoledo.edu. Web site: http://www.utoledo.edu/eduhshs/.

University of Tulsa, Graduate School, College of Arts and Sciences, School of Education, Program in Mathematics and Science Education, Tulsa, OK 74104-3189. Offers MSMSE. Part-time programs available. *Students:* 3 full-time (all women), 1 international. Average age 29. 3 applicants, 67% accepted, 2 enrolled. *Entrance requirements:* For master's, GRE General Test. Additional exam requirements/recommendations for international students: Required—TOEFL (minimum score 577 paper-based; 233 computer-based), IELTS (minimum score 6.5). *Application deadline:* Applications are processed on a rolling basis. Application fee: $40. Electronic applications accepted. *Expenses: Tuition:* Full-time $17,748; part-time $986 per hour. *Required fees:* $5 per contact hour. $75 per semester. Tuition and fees vary according to program. *Financial support:* In 2011–12, 3 students received support, including 3 teaching assistantships with full and partial tuition reimbursements available (averaging $9,877 per year); fellowships with full and partial tuition reimbursements available, research assistantships, career-related internships or fieldwork, Federal Work-Study, scholarships/grants, health care benefits, tuition waivers (full and partial), and unspecified assistantships also available. Support available to part-time students. Financial award application deadline: 2/1; financial award applicants required to submit FAFSA. *Unit head:* Dr. David Brown, Advisor, 918-631-2719, Fax: 918-631-2133, E-mail: david-brown@utulsa.edu. *Application contact:* Dr. David Brown, Advisor, 918-631-2719, Fax: 918-631-2133, E-mail: david-brown@utulsa.edu.

University of Utah, Graduate School, College of Science, Department of Chemistry, Salt Lake City, UT 84112-0850. Offers chemical physics (PhD); chemistry (M Phil, MA, MS, PhD); science teacher education (MS). Part-time programs available. Postbaccalaureate distance learning degree programs offered. *Faculty:* 35 full-time (7 women). *Students:* 144 full-time (43 women), 40 part-time (15 women); includes 6 minority (1 Black or African American, non-Hispanic/Latino; 3 Asian, non-Hispanic/Latino; 1 Hispanic/Latino; 1 Two or more races, non-Hispanic/Latino), 54 international. Average age 28. 311 applicants, 28% accepted, 35 enrolled. In 2011, 10 master's, 21 doctorates awarded. Terminal master's awarded for partial completion of doctoral program. *Median time to degree:* Of those who began their doctoral program in fall 2003, 100% received their degree in 8 years or less. *Degree requirements:* For master's, thesis optional, 20 hours course work, 10 hours research; for doctorate, thesis/dissertation, 18 hours course work, 14 hours research. *Entrance requirements:* For master's and doctorate, GRE General Test, minimum GPA of 3.0. Additional exam requirements/recommendations for international students: Required—TOEFL (minimum score 620 paper-based; 260 computer-based; 105 iBT). *Application deadline:* For fall admission, 4/1 for domestic students, 2/1 for international students; for spring admission, 11/1 for domestic and international students. Application fee: $55 ($65 for international students). Electronic applications accepted. *Financial support:* In 2011–12, 1 fellowship with tuition reimbursement (averaging $22,000 per year), 128 research assistantships with tuition reimbursements (averaging $22,500 per year), 55 teaching assistantships with tuition reimbursements (averaging $22,000 per year) were awarded; scholarships/grants and tuition waivers (full) also available. Financial award application deadline: 4/1; financial award applicants required to submit FAFSA. *Faculty research:* Biological, theoretical, inorganic, organic, and physical-analytical chemistry. *Total annual research expenditures:* $13.3 million. *Unit head:* Dr. Henry S. White, Chair, 801-585-6256, Fax: 801-581-8433, E-mail: chair@chemistry.utah.edu. *Application contact:* Jo Hoovey, Graduate Coordinator, 801-581-4393, Fax: 801-581-5408, E-mail: jhoovey@chem.utah.edu. Web site: http://www.chem.utah.edu/.

University of Utah, Graduate School, College of Science, Department of Physics and Astronomy, Salt Lake City, UT 84112. Offers chemical physics (PhD); medical physics

(MS, PhD); physics (MA, MS, PhD); physics teaching (PhD). Part-time programs available. *Faculty:* 38 full-time (3 women), 1 part-time/adjunct (0 women). *Students:* 77 full-time (22 women), 17 part-time (4 women); includes 3 minority (1 Asian, non-Hispanic/Latino; 2 Hispanic/Latino), 50 international. Average age 29. 68 applicants, 72% accepted, 24 enrolled. In 2011, 7 master's, 9 doctorates awarded. Terminal master's awarded for partial completion of doctoral program. *Median time to degree:* Of those who began their doctoral program in fall 2003, 44% received their degree in 8 years or less. *Degree requirements:* For master's, comprehensive exam (for some programs), thesis or alternative, teaching experience, departmental exam; for doctorate, comprehensive exam, thesis/dissertation, departmental qualifying exam. *Entrance requirements:* For master's and doctorate, GRE General Test, GRE Subject Test, minimum GPA of 3.0. Additional exam requirements/recommendations for international students: Required—TOEFL (minimum score 500 paper-based; 173 computer-based; 69 iBT). *Application deadline:* For fall admission, 4/1 priority date for domestic students, 4/1 for international students. Applications are processed on a rolling basis. Application fee: $55 ($65 for international students). Electronic applications accepted. *Financial support:* In 2011–12, 61 teaching assistantships with full and partial tuition reimbursements (averaging $14,626 per year) were awarded; Federal Work-Study, institutionally sponsored loans, and scholarships/grants also available. Financial award application deadline: 2/15; financial award applicants required to submit FAFSA. *Faculty research:* High-energy, cosmic-ray, astrophysics, medical physics, condensed matter, relativity applied physics, biophysics, astronomy. *Total annual research expenditures:* $6.8 million. *Unit head:* Dr. David Kieda, Chair, 801-581-6901, Fax: 801-581-4801, E-mail: kieda@physics.utah.edu. *Application contact:* Jackie Hadley, Graduate Secretary, 801-581-6861, Fax: 801-581-4801, E-mail: jackie@physics.utah.edu. Web site: http://www.physics.utah.edu/.

University of Vermont, Graduate College, College of Arts and Sciences, Department of Biology, Burlington, VT 05405. Offers biology (MS, PhD); biology education (MST). *Faculty:* 17. *Students:* 32 (14 women); includes 5 minority (1 Black or African American, non-Hispanic/Latino; 4 Hispanic/Latino), 11 international. 43 applicants, 33% accepted, 5 enrolled. In 2011, 2 master's, 3 doctorates awarded. *Degree requirements:* For master's, thesis; for doctorate, thesis/dissertation. *Entrance requirements:* For master's and doctorate, GRE General Test. Additional exam requirements/recommendations for international students: Required—TOEFL (minimum score 550 paper-based; 213 computer-based; 80 iBT). *Application deadline:* For fall admission, 1/15 priority date for domestic students, 1/15 for international students. Applications are processed on a rolling basis. Application fee: $40. Electronic applications accepted. *Financial support:* Fellowships, research assistantships, and teaching assistantships available. Financial award application deadline: 3/1. *Unit head:* Dr. Jim Vigoreaux, Chairperson, 802-656-2922. *Application contact:* Dr. Judith Van Houten, Coordinator, 802-656-2922.

University of Victoria, Faculty of Graduate Studies, Faculty of Education, Department of Curriculum and Instruction, Victoria, BC V8W 2Y2, Canada. Offers art education (M Ed, PhD); curriculum studies (M Ed, MA, PhD); early childhood education (M Ed, PhD); educational studies (PhD); language and literacy (M Ed, MA, PhD); mathematics (M Ed, MA, PhD); music education (M Ed, MA, PhD); science (M Ed, MA, PhD); social studies (M Ed, MA); social, cultural and foundational studies (MA, PhD); technology and environmental education (PhD). Part-time programs available. *Degree requirements:* For master's, thesis, project (M Ed); for doctorate, comprehensive exam, thesis/dissertation. *Entrance requirements:* For master's, minimum B average. Additional exam requirements/recommendations for international students: Required—TOEFL (minimum score 575 paper-based; 233 computer-based), IELTS (minimum score 7). Electronic applications accepted. *Faculty research:* Elementary and secondary English, language arts, curriculum theory and practice, educational media and technology, educational administration and leadership, history and philosophy of education.

University of Virginia, College and Graduate School of Arts and Sciences, Department of Physics, Charlottesville, VA 22903. Offers physics (MA, MS, PhD); physics education (MA). *Faculty:* 32 full-time (4 women). *Students:* 82 full-time (20 women); includes 3 minority (2 Asian, non-Hispanic/Latino; 1 Hispanic/Latino), 59 international. Average age 26. 192 applicants, 31% accepted, 15 enrolled. In 2011, 19 master's, 18 doctorates awarded. *Degree requirements:* For master's, thesis (for some programs); for doctorate, comprehensive exam, thesis/dissertation. *Entrance requirements:* For master's and doctorate, GRE General Test, GRE Subject Test, 2 or more letters of recommendation. Additional exam requirements/recommendations for international students: Required—TOEFL (minimum score 600 paper-based; 250 computer-based; 90 iBT), IELTS. *Application deadline:* For fall admission, 1/7 for domestic and international students. Applications are processed on a rolling basis. Application fee: $60. Electronic applications accepted. *Financial support:* Fellowships, research assistantships, and teaching assistantships available. Financial award applicants required to submit FAFSA. *Unit head:* Joe Poon, Chair, 434-924-3781, Fax: 434-924-4576, E-mail: phys-chair@physics.virginia.edu. *Application contact:* Despina Louca, Associate Chair for Graduate Studies, 434-924-3781, Fax: 434-924-4576, E-mail: grad-info-request@physics.virginia.edu. Web site: http://www.phys.virginia.edu/.

University of Virginia, Curry School of Education, Department of Curriculum, Instruction, and Special Education, Program in Curriculum and Instruction, Charlottesville, VA 22903. Offers curriculum and instruction (M Ed, Ed S); elementary (M Ed, Ed D); English (M Ed, Ed D); foreign language (M Ed); mathematics (M Ed, Ed D); reading (M Ed, Ed D, Ed S); science (Ed D); social studies (M Ed). *Students:* 22 full-time (17 women), 29 part-time (27 women); includes 4 minority (1 Black or African American, non-Hispanic/Latino; 1 Asian, non-Hispanic/Latino; 2 Two or more races, non-Hispanic/Latino), 1 international. Average age 33. 67 applicants, 75% accepted, 33 enrolled. In 2011, 78 master's, 2 doctorates, 12 other advanced degrees awarded. *Degree requirements:* For master's, comprehensive exam (for some programs); for doctorate, comprehensive exam, thesis/dissertation; for Ed S, comprehensive exam. *Entrance requirements:* For master's, doctorate, and Ed S, GRE General Test, 2 letters of recommendation. Additional exam requirements/recommendations for international students: Required—TOEFL (minimum score 600 paper-based; 250 computer-based; 90 iBT), IELTS (minimum score 7). *Application deadline:* Applications are processed on a rolling basis. Application fee: $60. Electronic applications accepted. *Financial support:* Fellowships with tuition reimbursements, research assistantships with tuition reimbursements, and teaching assistantships with tuition reimbursements available. Financial award application deadline: 1/5; financial award applicants required to submit FAFSA. *Unit head:* Laura Smolkin, Chair, 434-924-0831. *Application contact:* Karen Dwier, Information Contact, 434-924-0831, E-mail: kgd9g@virginia.edu.

University of Virginia, Curry School of Education, Program in Education, Charlottesville, VA 22903. Offers administration and supervision (PhD); applied developmental science (PhD); counselor education (PhD); curriculum and instruction (PhD); early childhood-developmental risk (MT); education evaluation (PhD); educational psychology (PhD); educational research (PhD); elementary (MT, PhD); English education (MT, PhD); foreign language education (MT); higher education (PhD); instructional technology (PhD); kinesiology (MT, PhD); math education (PhD); reading education (PhD); research statistics and evaluation (PhD); school psychology (PhD); science education (PhD); social studies education (MT, PhD); special education (PhD); world languages education (MT). *Students:* 299 full-time (216 women), 60 part-time (33 women); includes 46 minority (18 Black or African American, non-Hispanic/Latino; 17 Asian, non-Hispanic/Latino; 7 Hispanic/Latino; 4 Two or more races, non-Hispanic/Latino), 23 international. Average age 30. 307 applicants, 42% accepted, 80 enrolled. In 2011, 113 master's, 62 doctorates awarded. *Degree requirements:* For master's, comprehensive exam (for some programs), field project; for doctorate, comprehensive exam, thesis/dissertation. *Entrance requirements:* For doctorate, GRE General Test. Additional exam requirements/recommendations for international students: Required—TOEFL (minimum score 600 paper-based; 250 computer-based; 90 iBT), IELTS (minimum score 7). *Application deadline:* Applications are processed on a rolling basis. Application fee: $60. Electronic applications accepted. *Financial support:* Fellowships, research assistantships, and teaching assistantships available. Financial award application deadline: 1/5; financial award applicants required to submit FAFSA. *Unit head:* Robert C. Pianta, Dean, 434-924-3334. *Application contact:* Joanne McNergney, Assistant Dean for Admissions and Student Services, 434-924-3334, E-mail: curry-admissions@virginia.edu.

University of Washington, Graduate School, College of Education, Seattle, WA 98195. Offers curriculum and instruction (M Ed, Ed D, PhD), including educational technology, general curriculum (Ed D, PhD), language, literacy, and culture, mathematics education, multicultural education, reading and language arts education (Ed D), science education, social studies education, teaching and curriculum (M Ed); educational leadership and policy studies (M Ed, Ed D, PhD), including administration (Ed D), educational policy, organization, and leadership (M Ed, PhD), higher education, leadership for learning (Ed D), social and cultural foundations of education (M Ed, PhD); educational psychology (M Ed, PhD), including educational psychology (PhD), human development and cognition (M Ed), learning sciences, measurement, statistics and research design (M Ed), school psychology (M Ed); instructional leadership (M Ed); intercollegiate athletic leadership (M Ed); special education (M Ed, Ed D, PhD), including early childhood special education (M Ed), emotional and behavioral disabilities (M Ed), learning disabilities (M Ed), low-incidence disabilities (M Ed), severe disabilities (M Ed), special education (Ed D, PhD); teacher education (MIT). *Accreditation:* APA. Part-time and evening/weekend programs available. *Degree requirements:* For master's, thesis optional; for doctorate, thesis/dissertation. *Entrance requirements:* For master's and doctorate, GRE General Test, minimum GPA of 3.0. Additional exam requirements/recommendations for international students: Required—TOEFL. Electronic applications accepted. *Faculty research:* School restructuring/effective schools, special education interventions, literacy and writing, technology, school partnerships, teacher preparation.

University of Washington, Graduate School, Interdisciplinary Program in Biology for Teachers, Seattle, WA 98195. Offers MS. Part-time programs available. *Degree requirements:* For master's, research project and oral exam. *Entrance requirements:* For master's, GRE General Test, minimum GPA of 3.0, teaching certificate or professional teaching experience. Electronic applications accepted.

University of Washington, Tacoma, Graduate Programs, Program in Education, Tacoma, WA 98402-3100. Offers education (M Ed); educational administration (principal or program administrator certification) (M Ed); elementary education teacher certification (M Ed); elementary education/special education teacher certification (M Ed); secondary science or math teacher certification (M Ed). Part-time and evening/weekend programs available. *Degree requirements:* For master's, culminating project. *Entrance requirements:* For master's, WEST-B, WEST-E (teacher certification programs only), official sealed transcript from every college/university attended, personal goal statement, letters of recommendation, copy of valid teaching certificate. Additional exam requirements/recommendations for international students: Required—TOEFL (minimum score 580 paper-based; 237 computer-based; 92 iBT). Electronic applications accepted. *Faculty research:* Global learning communities for English/Chinese languages, evaluation of mathematics and reading intervention programs, response to intervention, school-wide behavioral and emotional support, mathematics education and culturally responsive mathematics education.

University of West Florida, College of Arts and Sciences: Sciences, School of Allied Health and Life Sciences, Department of Biology, Pensacola, FL 32514-5750. Offers biological chemistry (MS); biology (MS); biology education (MST); biotechnology (MS); coastal zone studies (MS); environmental biology (MS). *Faculty:* 12 full-time (3 women), 1 part-time/adjunct (0 women). *Students:* 9 full-time (7 women), 30 part-time (16 women); includes 2 minority (both Hispanic/Latino), 3 international. Average age 29. 21 applicants, 48% accepted, 5 enrolled. In 2011, 4 master's awarded. *Degree requirements:* For master's, thesis. *Entrance requirements:* For master's, GRE (minimum score: verbal 450, quantitative 550), official transcripts; BS in biology or related field; letter of interest; relevant past experience; three letters of recommendation from individuals who can evaluate applicant's academic ability. Additional exam requirements/recommendations for international students: Required—TOEFL (minimum score 550 paper-based; 213 computer-based). *Application deadline:* For fall admission, 6/1 for domestic and international students; for spring admission, 10/1 for domestic and international students. Applications are processed on a rolling basis. Application fee: $30. *Expenses:* Tuition, state resident: full-time $5729; part-time $302 per credit hour. Tuition, nonresident: full-time $20,059; part-time $961 per credit hour. *Required fees:* $1509; $63 per credit hour. *Financial support:* In 2011–12, 18 fellowships with partial tuition reimbursements (averaging $126 per year), 14 research assistantships with partial tuition reimbursements (averaging $5,980 per year), 4 teaching assistantships with partial tuition reimbursements (averaging $7,858 per year) were awarded; unspecified assistantships also available. Financial award application deadline: 4/15; financial award applicants required to submit FAFSA. *Unit head:* Dr. George L. Stewart, Chairperson, 850-474-2748. *Application contact:* Terry McCray, Assistant Director of Graduate Admissions, 850-473-7718, Fax: 850-473-7714, E-mail: gradadmissions@uwf.edu.

University of West Florida, College of Professional Studies, Ed D Programs, Specialization in Curriculum and Instruction: Science and Social Sciences, Pensacola, FL 32514-5750. Offers Ed D. Part-time and evening/weekend programs available. *Students:* 2 full-time (1 woman), 24 part-time (11 women); includes 4 minority (1 Black or African American, non-Hispanic/Latino; 1 Asian, non-Hispanic/Latino; 2 Hispanic/Latino). Average age 41. 9 applicants, 67% accepted, 6 enrolled. *Degree requirements:* For doctorate, comprehensive exam, thesis/dissertation. *Entrance requirements:* For doctorate, GRE, MAT, or GMAT, letter of intent; writing sample; three letters of recommendation; two completed disposition assessment forms; written statement of goals; interview with admissions committee. Additional exam requirements/recommendations for international students: Required—TOEFL (minimum score 550 paper-based; 213 computer-based). *Application deadline:* For fall admission, 6/1 for domestic and international students; for spring admission, 10/1 for domestic students. Applications are processed on a rolling basis. Application fee: $30. *Expenses:* Tuition, state resident: full-time $5729; part-time $302 per credit hour. Tuition, nonresident: full-time $20,059; part-time $961 per credit hour. *Required fees:* $1509; $63 per credit hour. *Unit head:* Dr. Pam Northrup, Interim Dean, 850-474-2769, Fax: 850-474-3205. *Application contact:* Terry McCray, Assistant Director of Graduate Admissions, 850-473-7718, Fax: 850-473-7714, E-mail: gradadmissions@uwf.edu. Web site: http://uwf.edu/edd/science_socialscience.cfm.

Science Education

University of West Georgia, College of Education, Department of Leadership and Applied Instruction, Carrollton, GA 30118. Offers art education (M Ed); art teacher education (Ed S); biology - secondary education (M Ed); biology/secondary education (Ed S); business education (M Ed, Ed S); chemistry/secondary education (Ed S); earth science/secondary education (Ed S); economics/secondary education (Ed S); educational leadership (M Ed, Ed S); English teacher education (M Ed, Ed S); French teacher education (M Ed, Ed S); history teacher education (Ed S); mathematics teacher education (M Ed, Ed S); middle grades education (M Ed, Ed S); physical education and recreation (Ed S); physical education teaching and coaching (M Ed); physics/secondary education (Ed S); science teacher education (M Ed, Ed S); secondary education (M Ed); social science - secondary education (M Ed); social science teacher education (M Ed); Spanish (M Ed); Spanish teacher education (M Ed, Ed S); sports management (M Ed). *Accreditation:* NCATE. Part-time and evening/weekend programs available. *Faculty:* 18 full-time (9 women). *Students:* 75 full-time (49 women), 169 part-time (109 women); includes 90 minority (85 Black or African American, non-Hispanic/Latino; 3 Hispanic/Latino; 2 Two or more races, non-Hispanic/Latino), 1 international. Average age 36. 115 applicants, 67% accepted, 19 enrolled. In 2011, 73 master's, 53 Ed Ss awarded. *Degree requirements:* For master's, internship; for Ed S, research project. *Entrance requirements:* For master's, GRE General Test, minimum GPA of 2.7; for Ed S, GRE General Test, master's degree, minimum graduate GPA of 3.0, district appointment. Additional exam requirements/recommendations for international students: Required—TOEFL (minimum score 523 paper-based; 193 computer-based; 69 iBT); Recommended—IELTS (minimum score 6). *Application deadline:* For fall admission, 7/21 for domestic students, 6/1 for international students; for spring admission, 11/30 for domestic students, 10/15 for international students. Applications are processed on a rolling basis. Application fee: $30. Electronic applications accepted. *Expenses:* Tuition, state resident: full-time $4336; part-time $181 per credit hour. Tuition, nonresident: full-time $17,362; part-time $724 per credit hour. Tuition and fees vary according to course load, degree level, campus/location and program. *Financial support:* In 2011–12, 1 research assistantship with full tuition reimbursement (averaging $7,444 per year) was awarded; career-related internships or fieldwork, scholarships/grants, and unspecified assistantships also available. Support available to part-time students. Financial award application deadline: 7/1; financial award applicants required to submit FAFSA. *Total annual research expenditures:* $5,000. *Unit head:* Dr. Frank Butts, Chair, 678-839-6530, Fax: 678-839-6195, E-mail: fbutts@westga.edu. *Application contact:* Deanna Richards, Coordinator, Graduate Studies, 678-839-5946, E-mail: drichard@westga.edu. Web site: http://www.westga.edu/coelai.

University of Wisconsin–Madison, Graduate School, School of Education, Department of Curriculum and Instruction, Madison, WI 53706-1380. Offers art education (MA); curriculum and instruction (MS, PhD); education and mathematics (MA); French education (MA); German education (MA); music education (MS); science education (MS); Spanish education (MA). *Accreditation:* NASM (one or more programs are accredited). *Degree requirements:* For doctorate, thesis/dissertation. Application fee: $56. *Expenses:* Tuition, state resident: full-time $10,296; part-time $643.51 per credit. Tuition, nonresident: full-time $24,054; part-time $1503.40 per credit. *Required fees:* $70.06 per credit. Tuition and fees vary according to course load, campus/location, program and reciprocity agreements. *Financial support:* Project assistantships available. *Unit head:* Dr. John Rudolph, Chair, 608-263-4600, E-mail: jlrudolp@wisc.edu. *Application contact:* 608-262-2433, Fax: 608-262-5134, E-mail: gradadmiss@mail.bascom.wisc.edu. Web site: http://www.education.wisc.edu/ci.

University of Wisconsin–River Falls, Outreach and Graduate Studies, College of Arts and Science, Program in Science, River Falls, WI 54022. Offers science education (MSE). Part-time programs available. *Degree requirements:* For master's, comprehensive exam, thesis or alternative. *Entrance requirements:* For master's, minimum GPA of 2.75. Additional exam requirements/recommendations for international students: Required—TOEFL (minimum score 500 paper-based; 65 iBT), IELTS (minimum score 5.5). Electronic applications accepted.

University of Wisconsin–Stevens Point, College of Letters and Science, Department of Biology, Stevens Point, WI 54481-3897. Offers MST. *Degree requirements:* For master's, thesis or alternative. *Entrance requirements:* For master's, minimum overall undergraduate GPA of 2.75, bachelor's degree in biology with minimum GPA of 3.0, teacher's license.

University of Wyoming, College of Education, Science and Mathematics Teaching Center, Laramie, WY 82070. Offers MS, MST. *Degree requirements:* For master's, thesis. *Entrance requirements:* For master's, GRE General Test, minimum GPA of 3.0, writing sample, 3 letters of recommendation. Electronic applications accepted.

Ursuline College, School of Graduate Studies, Program in Education, Pepper Pike, OH 44124-4398. Offers art education (MA); early childhood education (MA); language arts education (MA); life science education (MA); math education (MA); middle school education (MA); social studies education (MA); special education (MA). *Accreditation:* NCATE. *Faculty:* 3 full-time (all women), 8 part-time/adjunct (6 women). *Students:* 28 full-time (22 women), 1 (woman) part-time; includes 11 minority (7 Black or African American, non-Hispanic/Latino; 2 Asian, non-Hispanic/Latino; 1 Hispanic/Latino; 1 Native Hawaiian or other Pacific Islander, non-Hispanic/Latino). Average age 32. In 2011, 29 master's awarded. *Degree requirements:* For master's, comprehensive exam. *Entrance requirements:* For master's, minimum undergraduate GPA of 3.0. Additional exam requirements/recommendations for international students: Required—TOEFL (minimum score 500 paper-based; 173 computer-based). *Application deadline:* For fall admission, 8/1 priority date for domestic students. Applications are processed on a rolling basis. Application fee: $25. *Expenses:* Contact institution. *Financial support:* Federal Work-Study available. Financial award application deadline: 3/1. *Unit head:* Dr. Edna West, Director, Master's Apprentice Program, 440-646-6134, Fax: 440-684-6088, E-mail: ewest@ursuline.edu. *Application contact:* Melanie Steele, Graduate Admission Assistant, 440-646-8199, Fax: 440-684-6138, E-mail: graduateadmissions@ursuline.edu.

Vanderbilt University, Graduate School, Department of Physics and Astronomy, Nashville, TN 37240-1001. Offers astronomy (MS); physics (MA, MAT, MS, PhD). *Faculty:* 34 full-time (4 women), 2 part-time/adjunct (0 women). *Students:* 78 full-time (20 women), 3 part-time (0 women); includes 13 minority (6 Black or African American, non-Hispanic/Latino; 1 Asian, non-Hispanic/Latino; 4 Hispanic/Latino; 2 Two or more races, non-Hispanic/Latino), 22 international. Average age 28. 171 applicants, 25% accepted, 15 enrolled. In 2011, 8 master's, 4 doctorates awarded. *Degree requirements:* For master's, thesis; for doctorate, comprehensive exam, thesis/dissertation, final and qualifying exams. *Entrance requirements:* For master's, GRE General Test; for doctorate, GRE General Test, GRE Subject Test. Additional exam requirements/recommendations for international students: Required—TOEFL (minimum score 570 paper-based; 230 computer-based; 88 iBT). *Application deadline:* For fall admission, 1/15 for domestic and international students. Application fee: $0. Electronic applications accepted. *Financial support:* Fellowships with full and partial tuition reimbursements, research assistantships with full tuition reimbursements, teaching assistantships with full tuition reimbursements, career-related internships or fieldwork, Federal Work-Study, and institutionally sponsored loans available. Financial award application deadline: 1/15; financial award applicants required to submit CSS PROFILE or FAFSA. *Faculty research:* Experimental and theoretical physics, free electron laser, living-state physics, heavy-ion physics, nuclear structure. *Unit head:* Dr. Robert J. Scherrer, Chair, 615-322-2828, Fax: 615-343-7263, E-mail: robert.scherrer@vanderbilt.edu. *Application contact:* Dr. Julia Velkovska, Director of Graduate Studies, 615-322-0656, Fax: 615-343-7263, E-mail: julia.velkovska@vanderbilt.edu. Web site: http://www.vanderbilt.edu/physics/.

Walden University, Graduate Programs, Richard W. Riley College of Education and Leadership, Minneapolis, MN 55401. Offers administrator leadership for teaching and learning (Ed D, Ed S); adult education (Ed D, Ed S); adult learning (MS, Postbaccalaureate Certificate), including developmental education (MS), online teaching (MS), teaching adults English as a second language (MS), training and performance management (MS); college teaching and learning (Ed D, Ed S, Postbaccalaureate Certificate); curriculum, instruction and assessment (Ed D, Postbaccalaureate Certificate); curriculum, instruction, and professional development (Ed S); developmental education (Postbaccalaureate Certificate); early childhood administration, management, and leadership (Postbaccalaureate Certificate); early childhood education (birth-grade 3) (MAT); early childhood public policy and advocacy (Postbaccalaureate Certificate); early childhood studies (MS), including administration, management and leadership, early childhood public policy and advocacy, teaching adults in the early childhood field, teaching and diversity; education (MS, PhD), including adolescent literacy and technology (grades 6-12) (MS), adult education leadership (PhD), assessment, evaluation, and accountability (PhD), community college leadership (PhD), curriculum, instruction, and assessment, early childhood education (PhD), educational technology (PhD), elementary reading and literacy (MS), elementary reading and mathematics (MS), general program, global and comparative education (PhD), higher education (PhD), integrating technology in the classroom (MS), K-12 educational leadership (PhD), leadership, policy and change (PhD), learning, instruction and innovation (PhD), literacy and learning in the content areas (MS), mathematics (grades 6-8) (MS), mathematics (grades K-5) (MS), middle level education (grades 5-8) (MS), professional development (MS), science (grades K-8) (MS), self-designed (PhD), special education (PhD), special education (non-licensure) (MS), teacher leadership (grades K-12) (MS), teaching English language learners (grades K-12) (MS); educational leadership and administration (principal preparation) (Ed S); educational technology (Ed S); elementary reading and literacy (Postbaccalaureate Certificate); engaging culturally diverse learners (Postbaccalaureate Certificate); enrollment management and institutional marketing (Postbaccalaureate Certificate); higher education (MS), including college teaching and learning, enrollment management and institutional planning, global higher education, leadership for student success, online and distance learning; higher education leadership (Ed D); instructional design (Postbaccalaureate Certificate); instructional design and technology (MS), including general program (MS, PhD), online learning, training and performance improvement; integrating technology in the classroom (Postbaccalaureate Certificate); online teaching for adult learners (Postbaccalaureate Certificate); professional development (Postbaccalaureate Certificate); reading and literacy leadership (Ed D); science K-8 (Postbaccalaureate Certificate); special education (Ed D, Ed S); special education: emotional/behavioral disorders (K-12) (MAT); special education: learning disabilities (K-12) (MAT); teacher leadership (Ed D, Ed S, Postbaccalaureate Certificate); training and performance management (Postbaccalaureate Certificate). Part-time and evening/weekend programs available. Postbaccalaureate distance learning degree programs offered (minimal on-campus study). *Faculty:* 71 full-time (48 women), 853 part-time/adjunct (585 women). *Students:* 11,326 full-time (9,212 women), 2,148 part-time (1,795 women); includes 5,346 minority (4,403 Black or African American, non-Hispanic/Latino; 76 American Indian or Alaska Native, non-Hispanic/Latino; 140 Asian, non-Hispanic/Latino; 561 Hispanic/Latino; 21 Native Hawaiian or other Pacific Islander, non-Hispanic/Latino; 145 Two or more races, non-Hispanic/Latino), 322 international. Average age 39. In 2011, 3,477 master's, 318 doctorates, 471 other advanced degrees awarded. *Degree requirements:* For doctorate, thesis/dissertation (for some programs), residency; for other advanced degree, residency (for some programs). *Entrance requirements:* For master's, bachelor's degree or equivalent in related field; minimum GPA of 2.5; official transcripts; goal statement; access to computer and Internet; for doctorate, master's degree or equivalent in related field; minimum GPA of 3.0; official transcripts; three years' related professional/academic experience (preferred); access to computer and Internet; for other advanced degree, master's degree or equivalent in related field; minimum GPA of 3.0; 3 years related professional/academic experience (preferred); access to computer and Internet (Ed S). Additional exam requirements/recommendations for international students: Required—TOEFL (minimum score 550 paper-based; 213 computer-based), IELTS (minimum score 6.5), or Michigan English Language Assessment Battery (minimum score 82). *Application deadline:* Applications are processed on a rolling basis. Application fee: $50. Electronic applications accepted. *Financial support:* Federal Work-Study, scholarships/grants, unspecified assistantships, and family tuition reduction, active duty/veteran tuition reduction, group tuition reduction, interest-free payment plans, employee tuition reduction available. Support available to part-time students. Financial award applicants required to submit FAFSA. *Unit head:* Dr. Kate Steffens, Dean, 800-925-3368. *Application contact:* Jennifer Hall, Vice President of Enrollment Management, 866-4-WALDEN, E-mail: info@waldenu.edu. Web site: http://www.waldenu.edu/Colleges-and-Schools/College-of-Education-and-Leadership.htm.

Wayne State College, School of Education and Counseling, Department of Educational Foundations and Leadership, Program in Curriculum and Instruction, Wayne, NE 68787. Offers alternative education (MSE); business and information technology education (MSE); communication arts education (MSE); early childhood education (MSE); elementary education (MSE); English as a second language (MSE); English education (MSE); family and consumer sciences education (MSE); industrial technology and vocational education (MSE); learning communities (MSE); mathematics education (MSE); music education (MSE); science education (MSE); social science education (MSE). *Accreditation:* NCATE. Part-time and evening/weekend programs available. *Degree requirements:* For master's, comprehensive exam, thesis optional. *Entrance requirements:* For master's, GRE General Test. Additional exam requirements/recommendations for international students: Required—TOEFL (minimum score 550 paper-based; 213 computer-based).

Wayne State University, College of Education, Division of Teacher Education, Detroit, MI 48202. Offers art education (M Ed), including art therapy; bilingual/bicultural education (M Ed); career and technical education (M Ed); curriculum and instruction (Ed D, PhD, Ed S), including art education (PhD), bilingual education (Ed D, Ed S), bilingual-bicultural education (PhD), career and technical education (MAT, Ed D, PhD, Ed S), early childhood education (MAT, Ed D, PhD, Ed S), elementary education, English as a second language (MAT, Ed D, Ed S), English education (MAT, Ed D, PhD, Ed S), foreign language education (MAT, PhD), K-12 curriculum, mathematics education (MAT, Ed D, PhD, Ed S), science education (MAT, Ed D, PhD, Ed S), secondary education, social studies education (MAT, Ed S), social studies education: secondary (Ed D, PhD); elementary education (MAT), including special education; elementary education (M Ed, MAT), including children's literature (MAT), early childhood education (MAT, Ed D, PhD, Ed S), general elementary education (MAT); elementary or secondary education (MAT), including bilingual/bicultural education, English as a second language (MAT, Ed D, Ed S), mathematics education (MAT, Ed D, PhD, Ed S), science education (MAT, Ed D, PhD, Ed S), social studies education (MAT, Ed S);

English education-secondary (M Ed); foreign language education (M Ed); mathematics education (M Ed); reading (M Ed, Ed S); reading, languages and literature (Ed D); science education (M Ed); secondary education (MAT), including art education (K-12), career and technical education (MAT, Ed D, PhD, Ed S), English education (MAT, Ed D, PhD, Ed S), foreign language education (MAT, PhD), kinesiology; social studies education secondary (M Ed); special education (M Ed, Ed D, PhD, Ed S). *Students:* 216 full-time (154 women), 626 part-time (478 women); includes 289 minority (227 Black or African American, non-Hispanic/Latino; 4 American Indian or Alaska Native, non-Hispanic/Latino; 27 Asian, non-Hispanic/Latino; 21 Hispanic/Latino; 1 Native Hawaiian or other Pacific Islander, non-Hispanic/Latino; 9 Two or more races, non-Hispanic/ Latino), 14 international. Average age 37. 347 applicants, 37% accepted, 93 enrolled. In 2011, 226 master's, 12 doctorates, 46 other advanced degrees awarded. *Degree requirements:* For master's, thesis (for some programs), thesis, essay or project (for some M Ed programs), professional field experience (for MAT programs); for doctorate, thesis/dissertation. *Entrance requirements:* For master's, Michigan Basic Skills Test (MA in teaching); for doctorate, minimum undergraduate GPA of 3.0, graduate 3.5; interview, curriculum vitae; references. Additional exam requirements/recommendations for international students: Required—TOEFL (minimum score 550 paper-based; 213 computer-based), TWE (minimum score 5.5). *Application deadline:* For fall admission, 6/ 1 priority date for domestic students, 5/1 for international students; for winter admission, 10/1 priority date for domestic students, 9/1 for international students; for spring admission, 2/1 priority date for domestic students, 1/1 for international students. Applications are processed on a rolling basis. Application fee: $50. Electronic applications accepted. *Expenses:* Tuition, state resident: part-time $512.85 per credit. Tuition, nonresident: part-time $1132.65 per credit. *Required fees:* $26.60 per credit. $199.65 per semester. Tuition and fees vary according to course load and program. *Financial support:* In 2011–12, 42 students received support. Fellowships, research assistantships with tuition reimbursements available, teaching assistantships, scholarships/grants, and unspecified assistantships available. *Faculty research:* Reading and writing literacy and literature. *Total annual research expenditures:* $264,016. *Unit head:* Dr. Craig Roney, Assistant Dean, 313-577-0902, E-mail: rroney@ wayne.edu. Web site: http://coe.wayne.edu/ted/index.php.

Wayne State University, College of Liberal Arts and Sciences, Program in Multidisciplinary Science, Detroit, MI 48202. Offers MA. *Faculty:* 9 full-time (5 women), 1 part-time/adjunct (0 women). *Students:* 1 (woman) full-time, 5 part-time (3 women), 1 international. Average age 31. In 2011, 2 master's awarded. *Expenses:* Tuition, state resident: part-time $512.85 per credit. Tuition, nonresident: part-time $1132.65 per credit. *Required fees:* $26.60 per credit. $199.65 per semester. Tuition and fees vary according to course load and program. *Unit head:* Prof. Karur Padmanabhan, Director, 313-577-3005, E-mail: ad2639@wayne.edu. *Application contact:* Janet Hankin, Professor, 313-577-0841, E-mail: janet.hankin@wayne.edu. Web site: http:// www.clas.wayne.edu/mams/.

West Chester University of Pennsylvania, College of Arts and Sciences, Department of Biology, West Chester, PA 19383. Offers biology (Teaching Certificate); biology - non-thesis (MS); biology - thesis (MS). Part-time and evening/weekend programs available. *Faculty:* 7 part-time/adjunct (0 women). *Students:* 22 full-time (12 women), 21 part-time (11 women); includes 7 minority (1 Black or African American, non-Hispanic/Latino; 2 Asian, non-Hispanic/Latino; 4 Hispanic/Latino). Average age 29. 29 applicants, 24% accepted, 7 enrolled. In 2011, 5 degrees awarded. *Degree requirements:* For master's, comprehensive exam, thesis (for some programs). *Entrance requirements:* For master's, two letters of reference. Additional exam requirements/recommendations for international students: Required—TOEFL (minimum score 550 paper-based; 213 computer-based; 80 iBT). *Application deadline:* For fall admission, 4/15 priority date for domestic students, 3/15 for international students; for spring admission, 10/15 priority date for domestic students, 9/1 for international students. Applications are processed on a rolling basis. Application fee: $45. Electronic applications accepted. *Expenses:* Tuition, state resident: full-time $7488; part-time $416 per credit. Tuition, nonresident: full-time $11,232; part-time $624 per credit. *Required fees:* $1784.64; $67.59 per credit. Tuition and fees vary according to program. *Financial support:* Unspecified assistantships available. Support available to part-time students. Financial award application deadline: 2/15; financial award applicants required to submit FAFSA. *Faculty research:* Medical microbiology, molecular genetics and physiology of living systems, mammalian biomechanics, invertebrate and vertebrate animal systems, aquatic and terrestrial ecology. *Unit head:* Dr. Jack Waber, Chair, 610-436-2319, E-mail: jwaber@ wcupa.edu. *Application contact:* Dr. Xin Fan, Graduate Coordinator, 610-436-2281, E-mail: xfan@wcupa.edu. Web site: http://bio.wcupa.edu/biology/index.php.

West Chester University of Pennsylvania, College of Arts and Sciences, Department of Physics, West Chester, PA 19383. Offers Teaching Certificate. *Students:* 2 full-time (0 women). Average age 31. *Entrance requirements:* For degree, bachelor's degree or higher, minimum GPA of 3.0. Additional exam requirements/recommendations for international students: Required—TOEFL (minimum score 550 paper-based; 213 computer-based; 80 iBT). *Application deadline:* For fall admission, 4/15 priority date for domestic students, 3/5 for international students; for spring admission, 10/15 priority date for domestic students, 9/1 for international students. Applications are processed on a rolling basis. Application fee: $45. Electronic applications accepted. *Expenses:* Tuition, state resident: full-time $7488; part-time $416 per credit. Tuition, nonresident: full-time $11,232; part-time $624 per credit. *Required fees:* $1784.64; $67.59 per credit. Tuition and fees vary according to program. *Financial support:* Unspecified assistantships available. Support available to part-time students. Financial award application deadline: 2/15; financial award applicants required to submit FAFSA. *Unit head:* Dr. Anthony J. Nicastro, Chairperson, 610-436-2497, Fax: 610-436-3013. *Application contact:* Dr. Jeffrey J. Sudol, Graduate Coordinator, 610-436-2592, Fax: 610-436-3013, E-mail: jsudol@wcupa.edu. Web site: http://www.wcupa.edu/ _ACADEMICS/SCH_CAS.PHY/.

Western Connecticut State University, Division of Graduate Studies, School of Professional Studies, Department of Education and Educational Psychology, Program in Secondary Education, Danbury, CT 06810-6885. Offers biology (MAT); mathematics (MAT). Part-time programs available. *Faculty:* 4 full-time (all women). *Students:* 10 full-time (4 women), 2 part-time (1 woman); includes 3 minority (all Hispanic/Latino). Average age 36. 27 applicants, 41% accepted, 9 enrolled. In 2011, 14 degrees awarded. *Entrance requirements:* For master's, PRAXIS I Pre-Professional Skills Tests, PRAXIS II subject assessment(s), minimum combined undergraduate GPA of 2.8 or MAT (minimum score in 35th percentile). Additional exam requirements/recommendations for international students: Recommended—TOEFL (minimum score 550 paper-based; 213 computer-based; 79 iBT), IELTS (minimum score 6). *Application deadline:* For fall admission, 8/5 priority date for domestic students; for spring admission, 1/5 priority date for domestic students. Application fee: $50. Tuition and fees vary according to course level, course load, degree level and program. *Financial support:* Application deadline: 5/ 1; applicants required to submit FAFSA. *Faculty research:* Differentiated instruction, the transition of teacher learning, teacher retention, relationship building through the evaluation process and leadership development, culture development, differentiated instruction, scheduling, transitioning teacher learning and curriculum. *Unit head:* Dr. Bonnie Rabe, Chairperson, Department of Education and Educational Psychology, 203-837-3206. *Application contact:* Chris Shankle, Associate Director of Graduate Studies, 203-837-9005, Fax: 203-837-8326, E-mail: shanklec@wcsu.edu.

Western Governors University, Teachers College, Salt Lake City, UT 84107. Offers curriculum and instruction (MS); educational leadership (MS); educational studies (MA); educational studies (5-12) (MA), including mathematics; elementary education (k-8) (Postbaccalaureate Certificate); English language learning (K-12) (MA); instructional design (MAT); learning and technology (M Ed, MA); management and innovation (M Ed); mathematics (5-12) (Postbaccalaureate Certificate); mathematics (5-9) (Postbaccalaureate Certificate); mathematics education (5-12) (MA); mathematics education (5-9) (MA); mathematics education (K-6) (MA); measurement and evaluation (M Ed); science (5-12) (Postbaccalaureate Certificate); science (5-9) (Postbaccalaureate Certificate); science education (5-12) (MA), including biology, chemistry, geology, physics; science education (5-9) (MA); social science (5-12) (MAT); special education (MAT). *Accreditation:* NCATE. Evening/weekend programs available. Postbaccalaureate distance learning degree programs offered (no on-campus study). *Students:* 3,746 full-time (2,811 women); includes 652 minority (332 Black or African American, non-Hispanic/Latino; 37 American Indian or Alaska Native, non-Hispanic/ Latino; 74 Asian, non-Hispanic/Latino; 139 Hispanic/Latino; 70 Two or more races, non-Hispanic/Latino), 12 international. Average age 37. In 2011, 1,080 master's, 242 other advanced degrees awarded. *Degree requirements:* For master's, capstone project. *Entrance requirements:* For master's and Postbaccalaureate Certificate, Readiness Assessment, commitment counseling discussion, transcript submissions, completion of orientation. Additional exam requirements/recommendations for international students: Required—TOEFL (minimum score 450 paper-based; 80 iBT). *Application deadline:* Applications are processed on a rolling basis. Application fee: $65. Electronic applications accepted. *Expenses:* Contact institution. *Financial support:* Scholarships/ grants and tuition waivers (partial) available. Financial award applicants required to submit FAFSA. *Unit head:* Dr. Philip Schmidt, Dean of the Teachers College, 845-255-4656. *Application contact:* Enrollment Department, 866-225-5948, Fax: 801-274-3306, E-mail: info@wgu.edu.

Western Michigan University, Graduate College, College of Arts and Sciences, Mallinson Institute for Science Education, Kalamazoo, MI 49008. Offers science education (MA, PhD); science education: biological sciences (PhD); science education: chemistry (PhD); science education: geosciences (PhD); science education: physical geography (PhD); science education: physics (PhD). *Degree requirements:* For doctorate, thesis/dissertation, oral and written exams. *Entrance requirements:* For master's, undergraduate degree in a science or science education, teacher certification (or appropriate education courses); for doctorate, GRE General Test, master's degree in a science or science education. Additional exam requirements/recommendations for international students: Recommended—TOEFL. Electronic applications accepted. *Faculty research:* History and philosophy of science, curriculum and instruction, science content learning, college science teaching and learning, social and cultural factors in science education.

Western Oregon University, Graduate Programs, College of Education, Division of Teacher Education, Program in Secondary Education, Monmouth, OR 97361-1394. Offers bilingual education (MS Ed); health (MS Ed); humanities (MAT, MS Ed); initial licensure (MAT); mathematics (MAT, MS Ed); science (MAT, MS Ed); social science (MAT, MS Ed). *Accreditation:* NCATE. Part-time and evening/weekend programs available. *Degree requirements:* For master's, thesis optional, written exam. *Entrance requirements:* For master's, minimum GPA of 3.0, teaching license. Additional exam requirements/recommendations for international students: Required—TOEFL (minimum score 550 paper-based; 213 computer-based; 79 iBT), IELTS (minimum score 6.5). *Faculty research:* Literacy, science in primary grades, geography education, retention, teacher burnout.

Western Washington University, Graduate School, College of Sciences and Technology, Program in Natural Science/Science Education, Bellingham, WA 98225-5996. Offers M Ed. Electronic applications accepted. *Faculty research:* Science education reform.

Widener University, School of Human Service Professions, Center for Education, Chester, PA 19013-5792. Offers adult education (M Ed); counseling in higher education (M Ed); counselor education (M Ed); early childhood education (M Ed); educational foundations (M Ed); educational leadership (M Ed); educational psychology (M Ed); elementary education (M Ed); English and language arts (M Ed); health education (M Ed); higher education leadership (Ed D); home and school visitor (M Ed); human sexuality (M Ed, PhD); mathematics education (M Ed); middle school education (M Ed); principalship (M Ed); reading and language arts (Ed D); reading education (M Ed); school administration (Ed D); science education (M Ed); social studies education (M Ed); special education (M Ed); technology education (M Ed). *Accreditation:* NCATE. Part-time and evening/weekend programs available. Terminal master's awarded for partial completion of doctoral program. *Degree requirements:* For doctorate, thesis/ dissertation. *Entrance requirements:* For master's, minimum GPA of 2.5; for doctorate, GRE or MAT, minimum GPA of 2.0 (undergraduate), 3.5 (graduate). Electronic applications accepted. *Expenses:* Contact institution. *Faculty research:* Reading and cognition, adult education, technology education, educational leadership, special education.

Wilkes University, College of Graduate and Professional Studies, School of Education, Wilkes-Barre, PA 18766-0002. Offers art and science of teaching (MS Ed); classroom technology (MS Ed); early childhood literacy (MS Ed); educational computing (MS Ed); educational development and strategies (MS Ed); educational leadership (MS Ed); educational technology (Ed D); higher education administration (Ed D); instructional media (MS Ed); instructional technology (MS Ed); K-12 administration (Ed D); online teaching (MS Ed); reading (MS Ed); school business leadership (MS Ed); secondary education (MS Ed), including biology, chemistry, English, history, mathematics; special education (MS Ed); teaching English as a second language (MS Ed); twenty-first century teaching and learning (MS Ed). Part-time and evening/weekend programs available. Postbaccalaureate distance learning degree programs offered (minimal on-campus study). *Students:* 92 full-time (63 women), 2,005 part-time (1,459 women); includes 89 minority (23 Black or African American, non-Hispanic/Latino; 1 American Indian or Alaska Native, non-Hispanic/Latino; 14 Asian, non-Hispanic/Latino; 33 Hispanic/Latino; 1 Native Hawaiian or other Pacific Islander, non-Hispanic/Latino; 17 Two or more races, non-Hispanic/Latino), 6 international. Average age 33. In 2011, 1,150 master's, 3 doctorates awarded. *Entrance requirements:* Additional exam requirements/recommendations for international students: Required—TOEFL (minimum score 550 paper-based; 213 computer-based; 79 iBT). *Application deadline:* Applications are processed on a rolling basis. Application fee: $45. Electronic applications accepted. *Expenses:* Contact institution. *Financial support:* Federal Work-Study and unspecified assistantships available. Financial award application deadline: 3/ 1; financial award applicants required to submit FAFSA. *Unit head:* Dr. Michael Speziale, Dean, 570-408-4679, Fax: 570-408-4905, E-mail: michael.speziale@ wilkes.edu. *Application contact:* Erin Sutzko, Director of Extended Learning, 570-408-4253, Fax: 570-408-7846, E-mail: erin.sutzko@wilkes.edu. Web site: http:// www.wilkes.edu/pages/383.asp.

Science Education

Wright State University, School of Graduate Studies, College of Science and Mathematics, Department of Earth and Environmental Sciences, Program in Earth Science Education, Dayton, OH 45435. Offers MST. *Entrance requirements:* For master's, GRE General Test. Additional exam requirements/recommendations for international students: Required—TOEFL. *Faculty research:* Pedagogy.

Wright State University, School of Graduate Studies, College of Science and Mathematics, Department of Physics, Program in Physics Education, Dayton, OH 45435. Offers MST. Part-time and evening/weekend programs available. *Entrance requirements:* Additional exam requirements/recommendations for international students: Required—TOEFL. *Faculty research:* Pedagogy.

Wright State University, School of Graduate Studies, College of Science and Mathematics, Interdisciplinary Program in Science and Mathematics, Dayton, OH 45435. Offers MST.

Youngstown State University, Graduate School, College of Science, Technology, Engineering and Mathematics, Department of Chemistry, Youngstown, OH 44555-0001. Offers analytical chemistry (MS); biochemistry (MS); chemistry education (MS); inorganic chemistry (MS); organic chemistry (MS); physical chemistry (MS). Part-time programs available. *Degree requirements:* For master's, thesis. *Entrance requirements:* For master's, bachelor's degree in chemistry, minimum GPA of 2.7. Additional exam requirements/recommendations for international students: Required—TOEFL. *Faculty research:* Analysis of antioxidants, chromatography, defects and disorder in crystalline oxides, hydrogen bonding, novel organic and organometallic materials.

Social Sciences Education

Acadia University, Faculty of Professional Studies, School of Education, Program in Curriculum Studies, Wolfville, NS B4P 2R6, Canada. Offers cultural and media studies (M Ed); learning and technology (M Ed); science, math and technology (M Ed). Part-time programs available. *Degree requirements:* For master's, thesis optional. *Entrance requirements:* For master's, B Ed or the equivalent, minimum B average in undergraduate course work, 2 years of teaching experience. Additional exam requirements/recommendations for international students: Required—TOEFL (minimum score 580 paper-based; 237 computer-based; 93 iBT), IELTS (minimum score 6.5). *Faculty research:* Literacy development, postmodern philosophy and curriculum theory, historiography, philosophy of education, learning and technology.

Alabama State University, Department of Curriculum and Instruction, Program in Secondary Education, Montgomery, AL 36101-0271. Offers biology education (M Ed, Ed S); English/language arts (M Ed); history education (M Ed, Ed S); mathematics education (M Ed); secondary education (Ed S); social studies (Ed S). Part-time programs available. *Students:* 16 full-time (12 women), 13 part-time (9 women); includes 26 minority (all Black or African American, non-Hispanic/Latino). Average age 36. 48 applicants, 52% accepted, 5 enrolled. In 2011, 3 master's awarded. *Degree requirements:* For master's, comprehensive exam; for Ed S, comprehensive exam, thesis. *Entrance requirements:* For master's, GRE General Test, MAT, graduate writing competency test; for Ed S, graduate writing competency test, GRE, MAT. Additional exam requirements/recommendations for international students: Required—TOEFL (minimum score 500 paper-based; 173 computer-based). *Application deadline:* For fall admission, 7/15 for domestic students; for spring admission, 12/15 for domestic students. Applications are processed on a rolling basis. Application fee: $10. *Financial support:* In 2011–12, research assistantships (averaging $9,450 per year) were awarded. *Unit head:* Dr. Willa Bing Harris, Acting Chairperson, 334-229-4394, Fax: 334-229-4904, E-mail: wbharris@alasu.edu. *Application contact:* Dr. Doris Screws, Dean of Graduate Studies, 334-229-4274, Fax: 334-229-4928, E-mail: dscrews@alasu.edu. Web site: http://www.alasu.edu/academics/colleges—departments/college-of-education/curriculum—instruction/degree-programs/secondary-education/index.aspx.

American Public University System, AMU/APU Graduate Programs, Charles Town, WV 25414. Offers accounting (MBA, MS); administration and supervision (M Ed); criminal justice (MA); emergency and disaster management (MA); entrepreneurship (MBA); environmental policy and management (MS), including environmental planning, environmental sustainability, fish and wildlife management, general (MA, MS), global environmental management; finance (MBA); general (MBA); global business management (MBA); guidance and counseling (M Ed); history (MA), including American history, ancient and classical history, European history, global history, military and diplomatic history, public history; homeland security (MA); homeland security resource allocation (MBA); humanities (MA); information technology (MS), including digital forensics, enterprise software development, information assurance and security, IT project management; information technology management (MBA); intelligence studies (MA), including criminal intelligence, general (MA, MS), homeland security, intelligence analysis, intelligence collection, intelligence operations, terrorism studies; international relations and conflict resolution (MA), including comparative and security issues, conflict resolution, international and transnational security issues, peacekeeping; legal studies (MA); management (MA), including defense management, general (MA, MS), human resource management, organizational leadership, public administration, reverse logistics, strategic consulting; marketing (MBA); military history (MA), including American military history, American revolution, civil war, war since 1946, World War II; military studies (MA), including air warfare, asymmetrical warfare, joint warfare, land warfare, naval warfare, strategic leadership; national security studies (MA), including general (MA, MS), homeland security, regional security studies, security and intelligence analysis, terrorism studies; nonprofit management (MBA); political science (MA), including American politics and government, comparative government and development, public policy; psychology (MA); public administration (MA, MPA), including disaster management (MPA), environmental policy (MA), health policy (MPA), human resources (MPA), national security (MPA), organizational management (MPA), security management (MPA); public health (MA, MPH), including emergency management (MPH), environmental health (MPH), public administration (MA); reverse logistics management (MA); security management (MA); space studies (MS), including aerospace science, planetary science; sports and health sciences (MS); sports management (MS), including coaching theory and strategy, sports administration; teaching (M Ed), including curriculum and instruction for elementary teachers, elementary, elementary reading, English language learners, instructional leadership, online learning, secondary social sciences, special education; transportation and logistics management (MA), including maritime engineering management. Programs offered via distance learning only. Part-time and evening/weekend programs available. Postbaccalaureate distance learning degree programs offered (no on-campus study). *Faculty:* 445 full-time (241 women), 1,360 part-time/adjunct (617 women). *Students:* 688 full-time (338 women), 10,168 part-time (3,706 women); includes 3,130 minority (1,007 Black or African American, non-Hispanic/Latino; 103 American Indian or Alaska Native, non-Hispanic/Latino; 825 Asian, non-Hispanic/Latino; 810 Hispanic/Latino; 51 Native Hawaiian or other Pacific Islander, non-Hispanic/Latino; 334 Two or more races, non-Hispanic/Latino), 134 international. Average age 35. In 2011, 2,386 master's awarded. *Degree requirements:* For master's, comprehensive exam or practicum. *Entrance requirements:* For master's, official transcript showing earned bachelor's degree from institution accredited by recognized accrediting body. Additional exam requirements/recommendations for international students: Required—TOEFL (minimum score 550 paper-based; 213 computer-based), IELTS (minimum score 6.5). *Application deadline:* Applications are processed on a rolling basis. Application fee: $0. Electronic applications accepted. *Expenses: Tuition:* Part-time $325 per credit hour. *Financial support:* Applicants required to submit FAFSA. *Faculty research:* Military history, criminal justice, management performance, national security. *Unit head:* Dr. Karan Powell, Executive Vice President and Provost, 877-468-6268, Fax: 304-724-3780. *Application contact:* Terry Grant, Vice President of Enrollment Management, 877-468-6268, Fax: 304-724-3780, E-mail: info@apus.edu. Web site: http://www.apus.edu.

Andrews University, School of Graduate Studies, School of Education, Department of Teaching, Learning, and Curriculum, Berrien Springs, MI 49104. Offers curriculum and instruction (MA, Ed D, PhD, Ed S); elementary education (MAT); secondary education (MAT), including biology, education, English, English as a second language, French, history, physics; teacher education (MAT). *Students:* 15 full-time (10 women), 27 part-time (22 women); includes 18 minority (12 Black or African American, non-Hispanic/Latino; 1 Asian, non-Hispanic/Latino; 3 Hispanic/Latino; 1 Native Hawaiian or other Pacific Islander, non-Hispanic/Latino; 1 Two or more races, non-Hispanic/Latino), 10 international. Average age 42. 48 applicants, 48% accepted, 10 enrolled. In 2011, 5 master's, 2 doctorates, 2 other advanced degrees awarded. *Entrance requirements:* For master's, GRE Subject Test. Additional exam requirements/recommendations for international students: Required—TOEFL (minimum score 550 paper-based). *Application deadline:* For fall admission, 8/15 for domestic students. Applications are processed on a rolling basis. Application fee: $40. *Unit head:* Dr. Lee C. Davidson, Chair, 269-471-6364. *Application contact:* Carolyn Hurst, Supervisor of Graduate Admission, 800-253-2874, Fax: 269-471-6321, E-mail: graduate@andrews.edu.

Appalachian State University, Cratis D. Williams Graduate School, Department of Curriculum and Instruction, Boone, NC 28608. Offers curriculum specialist (MA); educational media (MA); elementary education (MA); middle grades education (MA), including language arts, mathematics, science, social studies. *Accreditation:* NCATE. Part-time and evening/weekend programs available. Postbaccalaureate distance learning degree programs offered (no on-campus study). *Faculty:* 33 full-time (23 women), 5 part-time/adjunct (2 women). *Students:* 23 full-time (18 women), 110 part-time (90 women); includes 7 minority (4 Black or African American, non-Hispanic/Latino; 1 Asian, non-Hispanic/Latino; 2 Hispanic/Latino). 79 applicants, 94% accepted, 64 enrolled. In 2011, 87 master's awarded. *Degree requirements:* For master's, comprehensive exam, thesis or alternative. *Entrance requirements:* For master's, GRE General Test or MAT, 3 letters of recommendation. Additional exam requirements/recommendations for international students: Required—TOEFL (minimum score 570 paper-based; 230 computer-based; 79 iBT), IELTS (minimum score 6.5). *Application deadline:* For fall admission, 3/14 for domestic students, 2/1 for international students; for spring admission, 11/1 for domestic students, 7/1 for international students. Applications are processed on a rolling basis. Application fee: $55. Electronic applications accepted. *Expenses:* Tuition, state resident: full-time $4040; part-time $180 per semester hour. Tuition, nonresident: full-time $15,900; part-time $760 per semester hour. *Required fees:* $2500; $20 per semester hour. Tuition and fees vary according to campus/location. *Financial support:* In 2011–12, 6 teaching assistantships (averaging $8,000 per year) were awarded; fellowships, research assistantships, career-related internships or fieldwork, Federal Work-Study, scholarships/grants, and unspecified assistantships also available. Financial award application deadline: 4/1; financial award applicants required to submit FAFSA. *Faculty research:* Media literacy, elementary teaching, curriculum development, online learning environments. *Total annual research expenditures:* $480,000. *Unit head:* Dr. Michael Jacobson, Chairperson, 828-262-2224. *Application contact:* Sandy Krause, Director of Admissions and Recruiting, 828-262-2130, Fax: 828-262-2709, E-mail: krausesl@appstate.edu. Web site: http://www.ced.appstate.edu/departments/ci.

Arcadia University, Graduate Studies, Department of Education, Glenside, PA 19038-3295. Offers art education (M Ed); computer education (CAS); curriculum (CAS); curriculum studies (M Ed); early childhood education (M Ed, CAS), including individualized (M Ed), master teacher (M Ed), research in child development (M Ed); educational leadership (M Ed, Ed D, CAS); elementary education (M Ed, CAS); English education (MA Ed); environmental education (MA Ed, CAS); history education (MA Ed); instructional technology (M Ed); language arts (M Ed, CAS); library science (M Ed); mathematics education (M Ed, MA Ed, CAS); music education (MA Ed); psychology (MA Ed); reading (M Ed, CAS); science education (M Ed, CAS); secondary education (M Ed, CAS); special education (M Ed, Ed D, CAS); theater arts (MA Ed); written communication (MA Ed). *Accreditation:* NASAD. Part-time and evening/weekend programs available. Postbaccalaureate distance learning degree programs offered (minimal on-campus study). *Faculty:* 12 full-time (8 women), 38 part-time/adjunct (26 women). *Students:* 66 full-time (48 women), 590 part-time (477 women); includes 65 minority (53 Black or African American, non-Hispanic/Latino; 6 Asian, non-Hispanic/Latino; 3 Hispanic/Latino; 3 Two or more races, non-Hispanic/Latino), 4 international. Average age 36. In 2011, 229 master's, 5 doctorates awarded. *Application deadline:* Applications are processed on a rolling basis. Application fee: $50. Electronic applications accepted. *Expenses:* Contact institution. *Financial support:* Career-related internships or fieldwork, tuition waivers (partial), and unspecified assistantships available. *Unit head:* Dr. Steven P. Gulkus, Associate Professor, 215-572-2120, E-mail: gulkus@arcadia.edu. *Application contact:* 215-572-2925, Fax: 215-572-2126, E-mail: grad@arcadia.edu.

Arkansas State University, Graduate School, College of Humanities and Social Sciences, Department of Criminology, Sociology, and Geography, Jonesboro, State University, AR 72467. Offers criminal justice (MA); sociology (MA); sociology education (SCCT). Part-time programs available. *Faculty:* 9 full-time (5 women). *Students:* 12 full-time (9 women), 29 part-time (22 women); includes 19 minority (all Black or African American, non-Hispanic/Latino). Average age 34. 27 applicants, 37% accepted, 7 enrolled. In 2011, 16 master's awarded. *Degree requirements:* For master's, one foreign language, comprehensive exam, thesis or alternative; for SCCT, comprehensive exam. *Entrance requirements:* For master's, GRE General Test or MAT, appropriate bachelor's degree, letters of recommendation, official transcripts, immunization records; for SCCT, GRE General Test or MAT, interview, master's degree, official transcript, immunization records. Additional exam requirements/recommendations for international students: Required—TOEFL (minimum score 550 paper-based; 213 computer-based; 79 iBT), IELTS (minimum score 6), Pearson Test of English Academic (minimum score 56). *Application deadline:* For fall admission, 7/1 for domestic and international students; for spring admission, 11/15 for domestic students, 11/14 for international students. Applications are processed on a rolling basis. Application fee: $30 ($40 for international students). Electronic applications accepted. *Expenses:* Tuition, state resident: full-time $4044; part-time $225 per credit hour. Tuition, nonresident: full-time $8087; part-time $449 per credit hour. *Required fees:* $936; $52 per credit hour. $25 per term. One-time fee: $30. Tuition and fees vary according to course load and program. *Financial support:* In 2011–12, 8 students received support. Career-related internships or fieldwork, scholarships/grants, and unspecified assistantships available. Financial award application deadline: 7/1; financial award applicants required to submit FAFSA. *Unit head:* Dr. Gretchen Hill, Interim Chair, 870-972-3705, Fax: 870-972-3694, E-mail: ghill@astate.edu. *Application contact:* Dr. Andrew Sustich, Dean of the Graduate School, 870-972-3029, Fax: 870-972-3857, E-mail: sustich@astate.edu. Web site: http://www.astate.edu/a/chss/departments/csg.dot.

Arkansas State University, Graduate School, College of Humanities and Social Sciences, Department of History, Jonesboro, State University, AR 72467. Offers history (MA); history education (MSE, SCCT); social science education (MSE). Part-time programs available. *Faculty:* 13 full-time (7 women). *Students:* 6 full-time (1 woman), 17 part-time (10 women); includes 1 minority (Hispanic/Latino). Average age 34. 20 applicants, 50% accepted, 7 enrolled. In 2011, 20 master's awarded. *Degree requirements:* For master's, comprehensive exam, thesis or alternative; for SCCT, comprehensive exam. *Entrance requirements:* For master's, GRE General Test or MAT, GMAT, appropriate bachelor's degree, letters of reference, official transcript, valid teaching certificate (for MSE), immunization records; for SCCT, GRE General Test or MAT, interview, master's degree, letters of reference, official transcript, immunization records. Additional exam requirements/recommendations for international students: Required—TOEFL (minimum score 550 paper-based; 213 computer-based; 79 iBT), IELTS (minimum score 6), Pearson Test of English Academic (minimum score 56). *Application deadline:* For fall admission, 7/1 for domestic and international students; for spring admission, 11/15 for domestic students, 11/14 for international students. Applications are processed on a rolling basis. Application fee: $30 ($40 for international students). Electronic applications accepted. *Expenses:* Tuition, state resident: full-time $4044; part-time $225 per credit hour. Tuition, nonresident: full-time $8087; part-time $449 per credit hour. *Required fees:* $936; $52 per credit hour. $25 per term. One-time fee: $30. Tuition and fees vary according to course load and program. *Financial support:* In 2011–12, 7 students received support. Career-related internships or fieldwork, scholarships/grants, and unspecified assistantships available. Financial award application deadline: 7/1; financial award applicants required to submit FAFSA. *Unit head:* Dr. Gina Hogue, Chair, 870-972-3046, Fax: 870-972-2880, E-mail: ghogue@astate.edu. *Application contact:* Dr. Andrew Sustich, Dean of the Graduate School, 870-972-3029, Fax: 870-972-3857, E-mail: sustich@astate.edu. Web site: http://www.astate.edu/a/chss/departments/history/index.dot.

Arkansas State University, Graduate School, College of Humanities and Social Sciences, Department of Political Science, Jonesboro, State University, AR 72467. Offers political science (MA); political science education (SCCT); public administration (MPA). *Accreditation:* NASPAA (one or more programs are accredited). Part-time programs available. *Faculty:* 7 full-time (2 women). *Students:* 31 full-time (13 women), 20 part-time (9 women); includes 18 minority (15 Black or African American, non-Hispanic/Latino; 1 American Indian or Alaska Native, non-Hispanic/Latino; 2 Hispanic/Latino), 12 international. Average age 30. 45 applicants, 56% accepted, 17 enrolled. In 2011, 20 master's awarded. *Degree requirements:* For master's, comprehensive exam, thesis or alternative; for SCCT, comprehensive exam. *Entrance requirements:* For master's, GRE General Test or MAT, GMAT, appropriate bachelor's degree, letters of recommendation, official transcripts, immunization records, statement of purpose; for SCCT, GRE General Test or MAT, GMAT, interview, master's degree, official transcript, letters of recommendation, immunization records. Additional exam requirements/recommendations for international students: Required—TOEFL (minimum score 550 paper-based; 213 computer-based; 79 iBT), IELTS (minimum score 6), Pearson Test of English Academic (minimum score 56). *Application deadline:* For fall admission, 7/1 for domestic and international students; for spring admission, 11/15 for domestic students, 11/14 for international students. Applications are processed on a rolling basis. Application fee: $30 ($40 for international students). Electronic applications accepted. *Expenses:* Tuition, state resident: full-time $4044; part-time $225 per credit hour. Tuition, nonresident: full-time $8087; part-time $449 per credit hour. *Required fees:* $936; $52 per credit hour. $25 per term. One-time fee: $30. Tuition and fees vary according to course load and program. *Financial support:* In 2011–12, 9 students received support. Teaching assistantships, career-related internships or fieldwork, scholarships/grants, and unspecified assistantships available. Financial award application deadline: 7/1; financial award applicants required to submit FAFSA. *Unit head:* Dr. William McLean, Chair, 870-972-3048, Fax: 870-972-2720, E-mail: wmclean@astate.edu. *Application contact:* Dr. Andrew Sustich, Dean of the Graduate School, 870-972-3029, Fax: 870-972-3857, E-mail: sustich@astate.edu. Web site: http://www.astate.edu/a/chss/departments/political-sciences/index.dot.

Armstrong Atlantic State University, School of Graduate Studies, Program in Education, Savannah, GA 31419-1997. Offers adult education (M Ed); curriculum and instruction (M Ed); early childhood education (M Ed); education (M Ed); elementary education (M Ed); middle grades education (M Ed); secondary education (M Ed), including business education, English education, mathematics education, science education, social science education; special education (M Ed), including behavioral disorders, learning disabilities, speech-language pathology. *Accreditation:* NCATE. Part-time and evening/weekend programs available. Postbaccalaureate distance learning degree programs offered (minimal on-campus study). *Faculty:* 33 full-time (23 women), 3 part-time/adjunct (2 women). *Students:* 97 full-time (91 women), 262 part-time (227 women); includes 83 minority (70 Black or African American, non-Hispanic/Latino; 3 Asian, non-Hispanic/Latino; 8 Hispanic/Latino; 2 Two or more races, non-Hispanic/Latino), 5 international. Average age 34. 169 applicants, 69% accepted, 102 enrolled. In 2011, 227 master's awarded. *Degree requirements:* For master's, comprehensive exam, portfolio. *Entrance requirements:* For master's, GRE General Test or MAT, minimum GPA of 2.5, letters of recommendation. Additional exam requirements/recommendations for international students: Required—TOEFL (minimum score 523 paper-based; 193 computer-based). *Application deadline:* For fall admission, 7/1 priority date for domestic students, 5/1 for international students; for spring admission, 11/15 priority date for domestic students, 9/15 for international students. Applications are processed on a rolling basis. Application fee: $30. Electronic applications accepted. *Expenses:* Tuition, state resident: full-time $3402. Tuition, nonresident: full-time $12,636. *Financial support:* In 2011–12, research assistantships with full tuition reimbursements (averaging $5,000 per year) were awarded; career-related internships or fieldwork, Federal Work-Study, scholarships/grants, and unspecified assistantships also available. Support available to part-time students. Financial award applicants required to submit FAFSA. *Unit head:* Dr. Patricia Wachholz, Dean, College of Education, 912-344-2797, E-mail: patricia.wachholz@armstrong.edu. *Application contact:* Jill Bell, Director, Graduate Enrollment Services, 912-344-2798, Fax: 912-344-3488, E-mail: graduate@armstrong.edu. Web site: http://www.armstrong.edu/Education/coe_deans_office/coe_education_welcome.

Asbury University, School of Graduate and Professional Studies, Wilmore, KY 40390-1198. Offers biology: alternative certificate (MA Ed); chemistry: alternative certificate (MA Ed); English (MA Ed); English as a second language (MA Ed); ESL (MA Ed); French (MA Ed); Latin: alternative certificate (MA Ed); mathematics: alternative certificate (MA Ed); reading/writing endorsement (MA Ed); social studies (MA Ed); social work (MSW), including child and family services; Spanish (MA Ed); special education (MA Ed); special education: alternative certificate (MA Ed); teacher as leader endorsement (MA Ed). *Accreditation:* NCATE. Part-time programs available. *Degree requirements:* For master's, action research project, portfolio. *Entrance requirements:* For master's, PRAXIS/NTE, minimum GPA of 2.75, letters of recommendation. Additional exam requirements/recommendations for international students: Required—TOEFL (minimum score 550 paper-based). Electronic applications accepted.

Auburn University, Graduate School, College of Education, Department of Curriculum and Teaching, Auburn University, AL 36849. Offers business education (M Ed, MS, PhD); early childhood education (M Ed, MS, PhD, Ed S); elementary education (M Ed, MS, PhD, Ed S); foreign languages (M Ed, MS); music education (M Ed, MS, PhD, Ed S); postsecondary education (PhD); reading education (PhD, Ed S); secondary education (M Ed, MS, PhD, Ed S), including English language arts, mathematics, science, social studies. *Accreditation:* NASM (one or more programs are accredited); NCATE. Part-time programs available. *Faculty:* 22 full-time (17 women), 3 part-time/adjunct (all women). *Students:* 80 full-time (58 women), 181 part-time (126 women); includes 42 minority (28 Black or African American, non-Hispanic/Latino; 7 Asian, non-Hispanic/Latino; 7 Hispanic/Latino). Average age 34. 184 applicants, 53% accepted, 60 enrolled. In 2011, 77 master's, 10 doctorates, 35 other advanced degrees awarded. *Degree requirements:* For master's, thesis (for some programs); for doctorate, thesis/dissertation; for Ed S, field project. *Entrance requirements:* For master's, doctorate, and Ed S, GRE General Test. *Application deadline:* For fall admission, 7/7 for domestic students; for spring admission, 11/24 for domestic students. Applications are processed on a rolling basis. Application fee: $50 ($60 for international students). Electronic applications accepted. *Expenses:* Tuition, state resident: full-time $7290; part-time $405 per credit hour. Tuition, nonresident: full-time $21,870; part-time $1215 per credit hour. *International tuition:* $22,000 full-time. *Required fees:* $1402. *Financial support:* Fellowships, teaching assistantships, career-related internships or fieldwork, and Federal Work-Study available. Support available to part-time students. Financial award application deadline: 3/15; financial award applicants required to submit FAFSA. *Faculty research:* Emerging literacy, reading attitudes, music for at-risk youth, portfolio assessment. *Unit head:* Dr. Kimberly Walls, Head, 334-844-4434. *Application contact:* Dr. George Flowers, Dean of the Graduate School, 334-844-2125. Web site: http://education.auburn.edu/academic_departments/curr/.

Belmont University, College of Arts and Sciences, Department of Education, Nashville, TN 37212-3757. Offers education (M Ed); elementary education (MAT), including early childhood education, elementary education, language arts education; English (MAT); history (MAT); mathematics (MAT); middle grade education (MAT); science (MAT); secondary education (MAT); special education (MAT); sports administration (MSA). *Accreditation:* NCATE. Part-time and evening/weekend programs available. *Faculty:* 11 full-time (8 women), 23 part-time/adjunct (12 women). *Students:* 83 full-time (77 women), 205 part-time (162 women); includes 50 minority (36 Black or African American, non-Hispanic/Latino; 1 American Indian or Alaska Native, non-Hispanic/Latino; 1 Asian, non-Hispanic/Latino; 7 Hispanic/Latino; 5 Two or more races, non-Hispanic/Latino), 2 international. Average age 30. 83 applicants, 67% accepted, 35 enrolled. In 2011, 169 master's awarded. *Degree requirements:* For master's, thesis (for some programs). *Entrance requirements:* For master's, MAT or GRE and/or GMAT, minimum GPA of 2.75. Additional exam requirements/recommendations for international students: Required—TOEFL. *Application deadline:* For fall admission, 8/1 priority date for domestic students, 6/1 for international students; for spring admission, 12/1 priority date for domestic students, 10/1 for international students. Applications are processed on a rolling basis. Application fee: $50. *Expenses:* Contact institution. *Financial support:* In 2011–12, 30 students received support. Fellowships with partial tuition reimbursements available, teaching assistantships with partial tuition reimbursements available, institutionally sponsored loans, tuition waivers (partial), and unspecified assistantships available. Financial award application deadline: 4/15; financial award applicants required to submit FAFSA. *Faculty research:* Improving secondary literacy, Montessori, classroom management strategies, teacher residency programs, online professional development, mentoring, leadership, faculty development. *Total annual research expenditures:* $2,500. *Unit head:* Dr. Cynthia R. Watkins, Associate Dean, 615-460-6053, Fax: 615-460-5556, E-mail: cynthia.watkins@belmont.edu. *Application contact:* Andrea McClain, Admission/Licensure Officer, 615-460-5483, Fax: 615-460-5556, E-mail: andrea.mcclain@belmont.edu.

Bob Jones University, Graduate Programs, Greenville, SC 29614. Offers accountancy (MS); Bible (MA); Bible translation (MA); Biblical studies (Certificate); broadcast management (MS); business administration (MBA); church history (MA, PhD); church ministries (MA); church music (MM); cinema and video production (MA); counseling (MS); curriculum and instruction (Ed D); divinity (M Div); dramatic production (MA); educational leadership (MS, Ed D, Ed S); elementary education (M Ed, MAT); English (M Ed, MA, MAT); fine arts (MA); graphic design (MA); history (M Ed, MA); illustration (MA); interpretative speech (MA); mathematics (M Ed, MAT); medical missions (Certificate); ministry (MM, D Min); multi-categorical special education (M Ed, MAT); music (M Ed); New Testament interpretation (PhD); Old Testament interpretation (PhD); orchestral instrument performance (MM); organ performance (MM); pastoral studies (MA); personnel services (MS, Ed S); piano pedagogy (MM); piano performance (MM); platform arts (MA); radio and television broadcasting (MS); rhetoric and public address (MA); secondary education (M Ed); studio art (MA); teaching Bible (MA); theology (MA, PhD); voice performance (MM); youth ministries (MA); M Div/MM.

Bridgewater State University, School of Graduate Studies, School of Arts and Sciences, Department of History, Bridgewater, MA 02325-0001. Offers MAT. Part-time and evening/weekend programs available. *Entrance requirements:* For master's, GRE General Test.

Brooklyn College of the City University of New York, Division of Graduate Studies, School of Education, Program in Adolescence Education and Special Subjects, Brooklyn, NY 11210-2889. Offers adolescence science education (MAT); art teacher (MA); biology teacher (MA); chemistry teacher (MA); earth science teacher (MAT); English teacher (MA); French teacher (MA); health and nutrition sciences: health teacher (MS Ed); mathematics teacher (MA); music education (CAS); music teacher (MA); physical education teacher (MS Ed); physics teacher (MA); social studies teacher (MA); Spanish teacher (MA). Part-time and evening/weekend programs available. *Degree requirements:* For master's, comprehensive exam (for some programs), thesis (for some programs). *Entrance requirements:* For master's, LAST, previous course work in education, resume, 2 letters of recommendation, essay. Additional exam requirements/recommendations for international students: Required—TOEFL (minimum score 500 paper-based; 173 computer-based; 61 iBT). Electronic applications accepted. *Faculty research:* Interdisciplinary education, semiotics, discourse analysis, autobiography, teacher identity.

Brown University, Graduate School, Department of Education, Program in Teaching, Providence, RI 02912. Offers elementary education (MAT); English (MAT); history/social studies (MAT); science (MAT). *Faculty:* 4 full-time (3 women), 6 part-time/adjunct (all women). *Students:* 36 full-time (30 women); includes 12 minority (3 Black or African American, non-Hispanic/Latino; 2 American Indian or Alaska Native, non-Hispanic/Latino; 4 Asian, non-Hispanic/Latino; 3 Hispanic/Latino). Average age 26. 129 applicants, 60% accepted, 37 enrolled. In 2011, 42 master's awarded. *Degree requirements:* For master's, student teaching, portfolio. *Entrance requirements:* For master's, GRE General Test, transcript, personal statement, 3 letters of recommendation, interview, writing sample (English applicants only). Additional exam requirements/recommendations for international students: Required—TOEFL (minimum score 577 paper-based; 90 computer-based). *Application deadline:* For winter admission, 1/15 for domestic and international students. Application fee: $75. Electronic applications accepted. *Financial support:* In 2011–12, 28 students received support. Federal Work-Study, institutionally sponsored loans, scholarships/grants, and tuition waivers (partial) available. Financial award application deadline: 2/1; financial award applicants required to submit FAFSA. *Faculty research:* Literacy, English language learners, diversity, special education, biodiversity. *Unit head:* Laura Snyder, Director of Graduate Study for the MAT Program, 401-863-2407. *Application contact:* Carin Algava, Assistant Director of Teacher Education, 401-863-3364, Fax: 401-863-1276, E-mail: carin_algava@brown.edu. Web site: http://www.brown.edu/Departments/Education/TE/.

Buffalo State College, State University of New York, The Graduate School, Faculty of Natural and Social Sciences, Department of History and Social Studies, Buffalo, NY 14222-1095. Offers history (MA); secondary education (MS Ed), including social studies. Part-time and evening/weekend programs available. *Degree requirements:* For master's, one foreign language, thesis (for some programs), project (MS Ed). *Entrance requirements:* For master's, minimum GPA of 2.75, 30 hours in history (MA), 36 hours in history or social sciences (MS Ed). Additional exam requirements/recommendations for international students: Required—TOEFL (minimum score 550 paper-based; 213 computer-based).

California State University, Chico, Office of Graduate Studies, College of Behavioral and Social Sciences, Social Science Program, Chico, CA 95929-0722. Offers social science (MA); social science education (MA). *Faculty:* 1 (woman) part-time/adjunct. *Students:* 10 full-time (7 women), 3 part-time (2 women); includes 3 minority (1 Asian, non-Hispanic/Latino; 2 Hispanic/Latino), 1 international. Average age 38. *Degree requirements:* For master's, thesis or project. *Entrance requirements:* For master's, GRE General Test or MAT, two letters of recommendation, statement of purpose. Additional exam requirements/recommendations for international students: Required—TOEFL (minimum score 550 paper-based; 213 computer-based; 80 iBT), IELTS (minimum score 6.5), Pearson Test of English (minimum score 59). *Application deadline:* For fall admission, 3/1 priority date for domestic students, 3/1 for international students; for spring admission, 9/15 priority date for domestic students, 9/15 for international students. Application fee: $55. Electronic applications accepted. Tuition and fees vary according to class time, course load and degree level. *Financial support:* Fellowships, teaching assistantships, career-related internships or fieldwork, institutionally sponsored loans, traineeships, and unspecified assistantships available. Financial award application deadline: 3/1; financial award applicants required to submit FAFSA. *Unit head:* Dr. Gayle E. Hutchinson, Dean, 530-895-6171, Fax: 530-898-5986, E-mail: bss@csuchico.edu. *Application contact:* Judy L. Rice, Graduate Admissions Counselor, 530-898-5416, Fax: 530-898-3342, E-mail: jlrice@csuchico.edu. Web site: http://www.csuchico.edu/sosc.

California State University, East Bay, Office of Academic Programs and Graduate Studies, College of Letters, Arts, and Social Sciences, Department of History, Hayward, CA 94542-3000. Offers examination option (MA); public history option (MA); teaching option (MA); thesis option (MA). Part-time and evening/weekend programs available. *Faculty:* 2 full-time (1 woman). *Students:* 10 full-time (7 women), 23 part-time (9 women); includes 6 minority (1 Asian, non-Hispanic/Latino; 2 Hispanic/Latino; 2 Native Hawaiian or other Pacific Islander, non-Hispanic/Latino; 1 Two or more races, non-Hispanic/Latino). Average age 36. 37 applicants, 59% accepted, 13 enrolled. In 2011, 11 master's awarded. *Degree requirements:* For master's, one foreign language, comprehensive exam, thesis optional, project, thesis, or exam. *Entrance requirements:* For master's, GRE (strongly recommended), minimum GPA of 3.0 in field, 3.3 in history; 2 letters of recommendation; writing sample. Additional exam requirements/recommendations for international students: Required—TOEFL (minimum score 550 paper-based; 213 computer-based). *Application deadline:* For fall admission, 5/16 for domestic and international students. Applications are processed on a rolling basis. Application fee: $55. Electronic applications accepted. *Expenses:* Tuition, state resident: full-time $6738; part-time $1302 per quarter. Tuition, nonresident: full-time $12,690; part-time $2294 per quarter. *Required fees:* $449 per quarter. Tuition and fees vary according to degree level, program and reciprocity agreements. *Financial support:* Fellowships, teaching assistantships, career-related internships or fieldwork, Federal Work-Study, institutionally sponsored loans, and scholarships/grants available. Support available to part-time students. Financial award application deadline: 3/2; financial award applicants required to submit FAFSA. *Faculty research:* Digital history, American women, early America, Native Americans, medieval colonial India. *Unit head:* Dr. Nancy Thompson, Chair, 510-885-3207, Fax: 510-885-4791, E-mail: nancy.thompson@csueastbay.edu. *Application contact:* Prof. Khal Schneider, Graduate Advisor for History, 510-885-3237, Fax: 510-885-4791, E-mail: khal.schneider@csueastbay.edu. Web site: http://class.csueastbay.edu/history/Home_Page.php.

California State University, Fresno, Division of Graduate Studies, College of Social Sciences, Department of History, Fresno, CA 93740-8027. Offers history-teaching option (MA); history-traditional track (MA). Part-time and evening/weekend programs available. *Degree requirements:* For master's, thesis or alternative. *Entrance requirements:* For master's, GRE General Test, minimum GPA of 3.0. Additional exam requirements/recommendations for international students: Required—TOEFL. Electronic applications accepted. *Faculty research:* International education, classical art history, improving teacher quality.

California State University, San Bernardino, Graduate Studies, College of Education, San Bernardino, CA 92407-2397. Offers bilingual/cross-cultural education (MA); curriculum and instruction (MA); educational administration (MA); educational leadership and curriculum (Ed D); educational psychology and counseling (MA, MS), including correctional and alternative education (MA), counseling and guidance (MS), rehabilitation counseling (MA); English as a second language (MA); general education (MA); history and English for secondary teachers (MA); instructional technology (MA); reading (MA); secondary education (MA); special education and rehabilitation counseling (MA), including rehabilitation counseling, special education; teaching of science (MA); vocational and career education (MA). *Accreditation:* NCATE. Part-time and evening/weekend programs available. *Students:* 434 full-time (335 women), 188 part-time (139 women); includes 271 minority (54 Black or African American, non-Hispanic/Latino; 2 American Indian or Alaska Native, non-Hispanic/Latino; 29 Asian, non-Hispanic/Latino; 172 Hispanic/Latino; 2 Native Hawaiian or other Pacific Islander, non-Hispanic/Latino; 12 Two or more races, non-Hispanic/Latino), 28 international. Average age 32. 382 applicants, 61% accepted, 186 enrolled. In 2011, 279 master's awarded. *Degree requirements:* For master's, comprehensive exam (for some programs), thesis (for some programs), advancement to candidacy. *Entrance requirements:* For master's, minimum GPA of 3.0 in education. *Application deadline:* For fall admission, 8/31 priority date for domestic students. Application fee: $55. *Expenses:* Tuition, state resident: full-time $7356. Tuition, nonresident: full-time $7356. *Required fees:* $1077. Tuition and fees vary according to program. *Financial support:* Career-related internships or fieldwork and Federal Work-Study available. Support available to part-time students. *Faculty research:* Multicultural education, brain-based learning, science education, social studies/global education. *Unit head:* Dr. Patricia Arlin, Dean, 909-537-5600, Fax: 909-537-7011, E-mail: parlin@csusb.edu. *Application contact:* Olivia Rosas, Director of Admissions, 909-537-7577, Fax: 909-537-7034, E-mail: orosas@csusb.edu.

Cambridge College, School of Education, Cambridge, MA 02138-5304. Offers autism specialist (M Ed); autism/behavior analyst (M Ed); behavior analyst (Post-Master's Certificate); behavioral management (M Ed); early childhood teacher (M Ed); education specialist in curriculum and instruction (CAGS); educational leadership (Ed D); elementary teacher (M Ed); English as a second language (M Ed, Certificate); general science (M Ed); health education (Post-Master's Certificate); health/family and consumer sciences (M Ed); history (M Ed); individualized (M Ed); information technology literacy (M Ed); instructional technology (M Ed); interdisciplinary studies (M Ed); library teacher (M Ed); literacy education (M Ed); mathematics (M Ed); mathematics specialist (Certificate); middle school mathematics and science (M Ed); school administration (M Ed, CAGS); school guidance counselor (M Ed); school nurse education (M Ed); school social worker/school adjustment counselor (M Ed); special education administrator (CAGS); special education/moderate disabilities (M Ed); teaching skills and methodologies (M Ed). Part-time and evening/weekend programs available. Postbaccalaureate distance learning degree programs offered (minimal on-campus study). *Degree requirements:* For master's, thesis, internship/practicum (licensure program only); for doctorate, thesis/dissertation; for other advanced degree, thesis. *Entrance requirements:* For master's, interview, resume, documentation of licensure, 2 professional references; for doctorate, official transcripts, interview, resume, documentation of licensure (if any), written personal statement/essay, portfolio of scholarly and professional work, qualifying assessment, 2 professional references, health insurance, immunizations form; for other advanced degree, official transcripts, interview, resume, documentation of licensure (if any), written personal statement/essay, 2 professional references, health insurance, immunizations form. Additional exam requirements/recommendations for international students: Required—TOEFL (minimum score 550 paper-based; 213 computer-based; 79 iBT); Recommended—IELTS (minimum score 6). Electronic applications accepted. *Expenses:* Contact institution. *Faculty research:* Adult education, accelerated learning, mathematics education, brain compatible learning, special education and law.

Campbell University, Graduate and Professional Programs, School of Education, Buies Creek, NC 27506. Offers administration (MSA); community counseling (MA); elementary education (M Ed); English education (M Ed); interdisciplinary studies (M Ed); mathematics education (M Ed); middle grades education (M Ed); physical education (M Ed); school counseling (M Ed); secondary education (M Ed); social science education (M Ed). *Accreditation:* NCATE. Part-time and evening/weekend programs available. *Degree requirements:* For master's, comprehensive exam. *Entrance requirements:* For master's, GRE General Test, minimum GPA of 2.7. *Faculty research:* Spiritual values and wellness issues in counseling, stress and professional burnout among counselors, thinking strategies, leadership, adaptive technology.

Caribbean University, Graduate School, Bayamón, PR 00960-0493. Offers administration and supervision (MA Ed); criminal justice (MA); curriculum and instruction (MA Ed, PhD), including elementary education (MA Ed), English education (MA Ed), history education (MA Ed), mathematics education (MA Ed), primary education (MA Ed), science education (MA Ed), Spanish education (MA Ed); educational technology in instructional systems (MA Ed); gerontology (MSN); human resources (MBA); museology, archiving and art history (MA Ed); neonatal pediatrics (MSN); physical education (MA Ed); special education (MA Ed). *Entrance requirements:* For master's, interview, minimum GPA of 2.5.

Carthage College, Division of Teacher Education, Kenosha, WI 53140. Offers classroom guidance and counseling (M Ed); creative arts (M Ed); gifted and talented children (M Ed); language arts (M Ed); modern language (M Ed); natural sciences (M Ed); reading (M Ed, Certificate); social sciences (M Ed); teacher leadership (M Ed). Part-time and evening/weekend programs available. *Degree requirements:* For master's, thesis optional. *Entrance requirements:* For master's, MAT, minimum B average, letters of reference.

Chadron State College, School of Professional and Graduate Studies, Department of Education, Chadron, NE 69337. Offers business (MA Ed); community counseling (MA Ed); educational administration (MS Ed, Sp Ed); elementary education (MS Ed); history (MA Ed); language and literature (MA Ed); secondary administration (MS Ed); secondary education (MS Ed). *Accreditation:* NCATE. Part-time and evening/weekend programs available. Postbaccalaureate distance learning degree programs offered. *Degree requirements:* For master's, thesis optional. *Entrance requirements:* For master's, GRE General Test, GRE Writing Test, minimum GPA of 2.75 or 12 graduate hours at CSC with minimum GPA of 3.25. Additional exam requirements/recommendations for international students: Required—TOEFL. Electronic applications accepted. *Faculty research:* Rural education, technology, mental health.

Chaminade University of Honolulu, Graduate Services, Program in Education, Honolulu, HI 96816-1578. Offers child development (M Ed); educational leadership (M Ed); elementary education with licensure (MAT); instructional leadership (M Ed); Montessori credential (M Ed); Montessori emphasis (M Ed); secondary education with licensure (MAT), including English, math, science, social studies; special education with licensure (MAT). Part-time and evening/weekend programs available. Postbaccalaureate distance learning degree programs offered (minimal on-campus study). *Faculty:* 2 full-time (both women), 32 part-time/adjunct (25 women). *Students:* 53 full-time (38 women), 88 part-time (67 women); includes 77 minority (6 Black or African American, non-Hispanic/Latino; 1 American Indian or Alaska Native, non-Hispanic/Latino; 44 Asian, non-Hispanic/Latino; 5 Hispanic/Latino; 17 Native Hawaiian or other Pacific Islander, non-Hispanic/Latino; 4 Two or more races, non-Hispanic/Latino), 1 international. Average age 35. 40 applicants, 88% accepted, 30 enrolled. In 2011, 105 master's awarded. *Degree requirements:* For master's, thesis or alternative. *Entrance requirements:* For master's, PRAXIS (for MAT only), minimum GPA of 2.75, 3 letters of recommendation. Additional exam requirements/recommendations for international students: Required—TOEFL (minimum score 550 paper-based). *Application deadline:* For fall admission, 9/1 priority date for domestic students, 9/1 for international students;

for winter admission, 12/1 priority date for domestic students, 12/1 for international students; for spring admission, 3/1 priority date for domestic students, 3/1 for international students. Applications are processed on a rolling basis. Application fee: $50. Electronic applications accepted. *Expenses: Required fees:* $600 per credit hour. One-time fee: $93 part-time. *Financial support:* In 2011–12, 172 students received support. Career-related internships or fieldwork, Federal Work-Study, institutionally sponsored loans, scholarships/grants, and tuition waivers (partial) available. Support available to part-time students. Financial award application deadline: 3/1; financial award applicants required to submit FAFSA. *Faculty research:* Peace and curriculum education. *Unit head:* Dr. Joseph Peters, Dean, 808-440-4251, Fax: 808-739-4607, E-mail: joseph.peters@chaminade.edu. *Application contact:* 808-739-4663, Fax: 808-739-8329, E-mail: gradserv@chaminade.edu. Web site: http://www.chaminade.edu/education/grad.php.

Chatham University, Program in Education, Pittsburgh, PA 15232-2826. Offers early childhood education (MAT); elementary education (MAT); environmental education (K-12) (MAT); secondary art (MAT); secondary biology education (MAT); secondary chemistry education (MAT); secondary English education (MAT); secondary math education (MAT); secondary physics education (MAT); secondary social studies education (MAT); special education (MAT). *Students:* 52 full-time (42 women), 17 part-time (16 women); includes 2 minority (1 Black or African American, non-Hispanic/Latino; 1 Hispanic/Latino). Average age 29. 39 applicants, 82% accepted, 23 enrolled. In 2011, 37 master's awarded. *Degree requirements:* For master's, thesis, teaching experience. *Entrance requirements:* For master's, minimum GPA of 3.0, sample of written work, recommendation letters. Additional exam requirements/recommendations for international students: Required—TOEFL (minimum score 600 paper-based; 250 computer-based; 100 iBT), IELTS (minimum score 7), TWE. *Application deadline:* For fall admission, 4/1 priority date for domestic students, 4/1 for international students; for spring admission, 11/1 priority date for domestic students, 10/1 for international students. Applications are processed on a rolling basis. Application fee: $45. Electronic applications accepted. Application fee is waived when completed online. *Expenses: Tuition:* Full-time $13,896. Tuition and fees vary according to program. *Financial support:* Career-related internships or fieldwork available. Financial award applicants required to submit FAFSA. *Faculty research:* Gifted education, environmental education, technology in education, writing as learning, class size and achievement. *Unit head:* Dr. Elvira Sanatullova-Allison, Director of Education Programs, 412-365-2773, E-mail: esanatullovaallison@chatham.edu. *Application contact:* Dory Perry, Associate Director of Graduate Admission, 412-365-2758, Fax: 412-365-1609, E-mail: gradadmissions@chatham.edu. Web site: http://www.chatham.edu/mat.

Christopher Newport University, Graduate Studies, Department of Teacher Preparation, Newport News, VA 23606-2998. Offers art (PK-12) (MAT); biology (6-12) (MAT); chemistry (6-12) (MAT); computer science (6-12) (MAT); elementary (PK-6) (MAT); English (6-12) (MAT); English as second language (PK-12) (MAT); French (PK-12) (MAT); history and social science (6-12) (MAT); mathematics (6-12) (MAT); music (PK-12) (MAT), including choral, instrumental; physics (6-12) (MAT); Spanish (PK-12) (MAT). Part-time and evening/weekend programs available. *Degree requirements:* For master's, comprehensive exam, thesis or alternative. *Entrance requirements:* For master's, PRAXIS I, minimum GPA of 3.0. Additional exam requirements/recommendations for international students: Required—TOEFL (minimum score 580 paper-based; 237 computer-based; 92 iBT). Electronic applications accepted. *Faculty research:* Early literacy development, instructional innovations, professional teaching standards, multicultural issues, aesthetic education.

The Citadel, The Military College of South Carolina, Citadel Graduate College, School of Education, Program in Secondary Education, Charleston, SC 29409. Offers biology (MAT); English language arts (MAT); mathematics (MAT); mathematics education (MAE); physical education (MAT); social studies (MAT). *Accreditation:* NCATE. Part-time and evening/weekend programs available. *Faculty:* 12 full-time (8 women), 9 part-time/adjunct (4 women). *Students:* 21 full-time (11 women), 51 part-time (25 women); includes 10 minority (7 Black or African American, non-Hispanic/Latino; 2 Asian, non-Hispanic/Latino; 1 Hispanic/Latino). Average age 31. In 2011, 34 master's awarded. *Degree requirements:* For master's, comprehensive exam, internship. *Entrance requirements:* For master's, GRE (minimum score 900) or MAT (minimum score 396), minimum undergraduate GPA of 2.5. Additional exam requirements/recommendations for international students: Required—TOEFL (minimum score 550 paper-based; 213 computer-based). *Application deadline:* Applications are processed on a rolling basis. Application fee: $30. Electronic applications accepted. *Expenses: Tuition, area resident:* Part-time $501 per credit hour. Tuition, state resident: part-time $501 per credit hour. Tuition, nonresident: part-time $824 per credit hour. *Required fees:* $40 per term. One-time fee: $30. *Financial support:* Career-related internships or fieldwork, health care benefits, and unspecified assistantships available. Support available to part-time students. Financial award application deadline: 7/1; financial award applicants required to submit FAFSA. *Unit head:* Dr. Kathryn A. Richardson-Jones, Coordinator, 843-953-3163, Fax: 843-953-7258, E-mail: kathryn.jones@citadel.edu. *Application contact:* Dr. Steve A. Nida, Associate Provost, The Citadel Graduate College, 843-953-5089, Fax: 843-953-7630, E-mail: cgc@citadel.edu. Web site: http://www.citadel.edu/education/teacher-education/mat-master-of-arts-in-teaching.html.

City College of the City University of New York, Graduate School, School of Education, Department of Secondary Education, New York, NY 10031-9198. Offers adolescent mathematics education (MA, AC); English education (MA); middle school mathematics education (MS); science education (MA); social studies education (AC). *Accreditation:* NCATE. *Entrance requirements:* For master's, Liberal Arts and Sciences Test (LAST), Content Specialty Test (CST). Additional exam requirements/recommendations for international students: Required—TOEFL.

Clemson University, Graduate School, College of Health, Education, and Human Development, Eugene T. Moore School of Education, Program in Early Childhood Education, Clemson, SC 29634. Offers early childhood education (M Ed); elementary education (M Ed); secondary English (M Ed); secondary math (M Ed); secondary science (M Ed); secondary social studies (M Ed). Part-time and evening/weekend programs available. *Students:* 5 applicants, 0% accepted, 0 enrolled. In 2011, 3 master's awarded. *Degree requirements:* For master's, comprehensive exam. *Entrance requirements:* For master's, GRE, valid teaching certificate. Additional exam requirements/recommendations for international students: Required—TOEFL; Recommended—IELTS. *Application deadline:* Applications are processed on a rolling basis. Application fee: $70 ($80 for international students). Electronic applications accepted. *Expenses:* Contact institution. *Financial support:* Institutionally sponsored loans, health care benefits, and unspecified assistantships available. Financial award application deadline: 3/1; financial award applicants required to submit FAFSA. *Faculty research:* Elementary education, mathematics education, social studies education, English education, science education. *Unit head:* Dr. Michael J. Padilla, Director/Associate Dean, 864-656-4444, Fax: 864-656-0311, E-mail: padilla@clemson.edu. *Application contact:* Dr. David Fleming, Graduate Programs Coordinator, 864-656-1881, Fax: 864-656-0311, E-mail: dflemin@clemson.edu.

Clemson University, Graduate School, College of Health, Education, and Human Development, Eugene T. Moore School of Education, Program in Teaching and Learning, Clemson, SC 29634. Offers elementary education (M Ed); English education (M Ed); mathematics education (M Ed); science education (M Ed); social studies education (M Ed). *Entrance requirements:* For master's, GRE, baccalaureate degree from regionally-accredited institution, official transcripts, copy of valid teaching certificate, two letters of recommendation. *Application contact:* Dr. David Fleming, Graduate Programs Coordinator, 864-656-1881, Fax: 864-656-0311, E-mail: dflemin@clemson.edu. Web site: http://www.clemson.edu/hehd/departments/education/academics/graduate/MEd-teach-learn.html.

The College at Brockport, State University of New York, School of Education and Human Services, Department of Education and Human Development, Program in Adolescence Education, Brockport, NY 14420-2997. Offers adolescence biology education (MS Ed); adolescence chemistry education (MS Ed); adolescence earth science education (MS Ed); adolescence English education (MS Ed); adolescence mathematics education (MS Ed); adolescence physics education (MS Ed); adolescence social studies education (MS Ed). *Accreditation:* NCATE. Part-time programs available. *Students:* 12 full-time (9 women), 60 part-time (28 women); includes 6 minority (1 American Indian or Alaska Native, non-Hispanic/Latino; 3 Asian, non-Hispanic/Latino; 1 Hispanic/Latino; 1 Native Hawaiian or other Pacific Islander, non-Hispanic/Latino). 26 applicants, 81% accepted, 17 enrolled. In 2011, 47 master's awarded. *Degree requirements:* For master's, thesis or alternative. *Entrance requirements:* For master's, minimum GPA of 3.0, letters of recommendation; statement of objectives, current resume. Additional exam requirements/recommendations for international students: Required—TOEFL (minimum score 550 paper-based; 213 computer-based; 79 iBT). *Application deadline:* For fall admission, 2/15 priority date for domestic students, 2/15 for international students; for spring admission, 9/15 priority date for domestic students, 9/15 for international students. Application fee: $80. Electronic applications accepted. *Financial support:* Federal Work-Study, scholarships/grants, and unspecified assistantships available. Support available to part-time students. Financial award application deadline: 3/15; financial award applicants required to submit FAFSA. *Unit head:* Dr. Don Halquist, Chairperson, 585-395-5550, Fax: 585-395-2172, E-mail: dhalquis@brockport.edu. *Application contact:* Michael Harrison, Coordinator of Certification and Graduate Advisement, 585-395-2326, Fax: 585-395-2172, E-mail: mharriso@brockport.edu. Web site: http://www.brockport.edu/graduate/.

The College at Brockport, State University of New York, School of Education and Human Services, Department of Education and Human Development, Program in Adolescence Inclusive Education, Brockport, NY 14420-2997. Offers English (MS Ed); mathematics (MS Ed); science (MS Ed); social studies (MS Ed). *Students:* 42 full-time (22 women), 21 part-time (10 women); includes 4 minority (2 Black or African American, non-Hispanic/Latino; 2 Hispanic/Latino). 50 applicants, 64% accepted, 19 enrolled. In 2011, 2 master's awarded. *Degree requirements:* For master's, thesis or alternative. *Entrance requirements:* For master's, minimum GPA of 3.0, letters of recommendation, statement of objectives, academic major (or equivalent) in program discipline; current resume. Additional exam requirements/recommendations for international students: Required—TOEFL (minimum score 550 paper-based; 213 computer-based; 79 iBT). *Application deadline:* For fall admission, 2/15 priority date for domestic students, 2/15 for international students; for spring admission, 9/15 priority date for domestic students, 9/15 for international students. Application fee: $80. Electronic applications accepted. *Financial support:* Federal Work-Study, scholarships/grants, and unspecified assistantships available. Support available to part-time students. Financial award application deadline: 3/15; financial award applicants required to submit FAFSA. *Unit head:* Dr. Don Halquist, Chairperson, 585-395-2205, Fax: 585-395-2171, E-mail: dhalquis@brockport.edu. *Application contact:* Michael Harrison, Coordinator of Certification and Graduate Advisement, 585-395-2326, Fax: 585-395-2172, E-mail: mharriso@brockport.edu.

College of St. Joseph, Graduate Programs, Division of Education, Program in Secondary Education, Rutland, VT 05701-3899. Offers English (M Ed); social studies (M Ed). Part-time and evening/weekend programs available. *Faculty:* 2 full-time (both women), 3 part-time/adjunct (1 woman). *Students:* 2 full-time (0 women), 4 part-time (2 women). Average age 29. 3 applicants, 67% accepted, 2 enrolled. *Degree requirements:* For master's, comprehensive exam. *Entrance requirements:* For master's, PRAXIS I, official college transcripts; 2 letters of reference; minimum GPA of 3.0 (initial licensure) or 2.7 (nonlicensure); interview. Additional exam requirements/recommendations for international students: Required—TOEFL (minimum score 550 paper-based). *Application deadline:* Applications are processed on a rolling basis. Application fee: $35. Electronic applications accepted. *Expenses: Tuition:* Full-time $15,200; part-time $400 per credit. *Required fees:* $45 per semester. *Financial support:* Career-related internships or fieldwork, Federal Work-Study, and unspecified assistantships available. Support available to part-time students. Financial award application deadline: 3/1. *Unit head:* Dr. Maria Bove, Chair, 802-773-5900 Ext. 3243, Fax: 802-776-5258, E-mail: mbove@csj.edu. *Application contact:* Alan Young, Director of Admissions, 802-773-5900 Ext. 3227, Fax: 802-776-5310, E-mail: alanyoung@csj.edu.

The College of William and Mary, School of Education, Program in Curriculum and Instruction, Williamsburg, VA 23187-8795. Offers elementary education (MA Ed); gifted education (MA Ed); math specialist (MA Ed); reading education (MA Ed); secondary education (MA Ed), including English education, mathematics education, modern foreign languages education, science education, social studies education; special education (MA Ed), including collaborating master educator, general curriculum. *Accreditation:* NCATE. Part-time programs available. *Faculty:* 15 full-time (10 women), 39 part-time/adjunct (32 women). *Students:* 80 full-time (69 women), 13 part-time (11 women); includes 11 minority (3 Black or African American, non-Hispanic/Latino; 1 American Indian or Alaska Native, non-Hispanic/Latino; 2 Hispanic/Latino; 5 Two or more races, non-Hispanic/Latino), 1 international. Average age 25. 220 applicants, 56% accepted, 85 enrolled. In 2011, 78 master's awarded. *Degree requirements:* For master's, project. *Entrance requirements:* For master's, GRE or MAT, minimum GPA of 2.5. Additional exam requirements/recommendations for international students: Required—TOEFL. *Application deadline:* For fall admission, 1/15 for domestic and international students; for spring admission, 10/1 for domestic and international students. Application fee: $50. Electronic applications accepted. *Expenses:* Tuition, state resident: full-time $6400; part-time $365 per credit hour. Tuition, nonresident: full-time $19,720; part-time $985 per credit hour. *Required fees:* $4562. *Financial support:* In 2011–12, 53 students received support, including 10 research assistantships with full and partial tuition reimbursements available (averaging $7,000 per year); career-related internships or fieldwork, Federal Work-Study, institutionally sponsored loans, scholarships/grants, and unspecified assistantships also available. Financial award application deadline: 1/15; financial award applicants required to submit FAFSA. *Faculty research:* National Council of Teachers of Mathematics Standards, counseling, self-concept and self-esteem, special education, curriculum development. *Unit head:* Dr. Margie Mason, Area Coordinator, 757-221-2327, E-mail: mmmaso@wm.edu. *Application contact:* Dorothy Smith Osborne, Assistant Dean for Admission, 757-221-2317, Fax: 757-221-2293, E-mail: dsosbo@wm.edu. Web site: http://education.wm.edu.

Social Sciences Education

The Colorado College, Education Department, Program in Secondary Education, Colorado Springs, CO 80903-3294. Offers art teaching (K-12) (MAT); English teaching (MAT); foreign language teaching (MAT); mathematics teaching (MAT); music teaching (MAT); science teaching (MAT); social studies teaching (MAT). *Faculty:* 4 full-time (3 women), 6 part-time/adjunct (2 women). *Students:* 11 full-time (7 women); includes 3 minority (1 Asian, non-Hispanic/Latino; 2 Hispanic/Latino). Average age 27. 20 applicants, 85% accepted, 11 enrolled. In 2011, 15 master's awarded. *Degree requirements:* For master's, thesis, internship. *Application deadline:* For fall admission, 12/1 priority date for domestic students, 12/1 for international students. Applications are processed on a rolling basis. Application fee: $50. Electronic applications accepted. *Expenses: Tuition:* Full-time $29,313. *Required fees:* $2000. *Financial support:* In 2011–12, 15 students received support. Career-related internships or fieldwork, institutionally sponsored loans, scholarships/grants, and health care benefits available. Financial award application deadline: 2/15; financial award applicants required to submit FAFSA. *Unit head:* Dr. Mike Taber, Director, 719-389-6026, Fax: 719-389-6473, E-mail: mike.taber@coloradocollege.edu. *Application contact:* Debra Yazulla Mortenson, Education Services Manager, 719-389-6472, Fax: 719-389-6473, E-mail: debra.mortenson@coloradocollege.edu. Web site: http://www.coloradocollege.edu/academics/dept/education/graduate-programs/secondary-mat.dot.

Columbus State University, Graduate Studies, College of Education and Health Professions, Department of Teacher Education, Columbus, GA 31907-5645. Offers accomplished teaching (M Ed); early childhood education (M Ed, MAT, Ed S); health and physical education (M Ed, MAT); middle grades education (M Ed, MAT, Ed S); school library media (M Ed, MAT); secondary education (M Ed, MAT, Ed S), including English/language arts (M Ed, Ed S), general science (M Ed), mathematics (M Ed), social science (M Ed); special education (M Ed, Ed S), including general curriculum (M Ed). *Accreditation:* NCATE. Part-time and evening/weekend programs available. Postbaccalaureate distance learning degree programs offered (minimal on-campus study). *Degree requirements:* For master's, thesis, exit exam; for Ed S, thesis or alternative. *Entrance requirements:* For master's, GRE General Test, minimum GPA of 2.75; for Ed S, GRE General Test. Additional exam requirements/recommendations for international students: Required—TOEFL (minimum score 550 paper-based; 213 computer-based; 79 iBT). Electronic applications accepted.

Concord University, Graduate Studies, Athens, WV 24712-1000. Offers educational leadership and supervision (M Ed); geography (M Ed); health promotion (M Ed); reading specialist (M Ed). Part-time and evening/weekend programs available. Postbaccalaureate distance learning degree programs offered (no on-campus study). *Entrance requirements:* For master's, GRE or MAT, baccalaureate degree with minimum GPA of 2.5 from regionally-accredited institution; teaching license; 2 letters of recommendation; completed disposition assessment form. Electronic applications accepted.

Converse College, School of Education and Graduate Studies, Program in Secondary Education, Spartanburg, SC 29302-0006. Offers biology (MAT); chemistry (MAT); English (M Ed, MAT); mathematics (M Ed, MAT); natural sciences (M Ed); social sciences (M Ed, MAT). Part-time programs available. *Degree requirements:* For master's, capstone paper. *Entrance requirements:* For master's, NTE or PRAXIS II (M Ed), minimum GPA of 2.75, 2 recommendations. Electronic applications accepted.

Delta State University, Graduate Programs, College of Arts and Sciences, Department of History, Cleveland, MS 38733-0001. Offers secondary education (M Ed), including history. Part-time programs available. *Degree requirements:* For master's, thesis or alternative. *Entrance requirements:* For master's, GRE General Test or MAT. *Expenses:* Tuition, state resident: full-time $4702; part-time $294 per credit hour. Tuition, nonresident: full-time $12,516; part-time $760 per credit hour. *Required fees:* $586.

Delta State University, Graduate Programs, College of Arts and Sciences, Division of Social Sciences and History, Program in Social Science Secondary Education, Cleveland, MS 38733-0001. Offers secondary education (M Ed), including social science. Part-time programs available. *Degree requirements:* For master's, thesis or alternative. *Expenses:* Tuition, state resident: full-time $4702; part-time $294 per credit hour. Tuition, nonresident: full-time $12,516; part-time $760 per credit hour. *Required fees:* $586.

Drew University, Caspersen School of Graduate Studies, Program in Education, Madison, NJ 07940-1493. Offers biology (MAT); chemistry (MAT); English (MAT); French (MAT); Italian (MAT); math (MAT); physics (MAT); social studies (MAT); Spanish (MAT); theatre arts (MAT). Part-time programs available. *Entrance requirements:* For master's, transcripts, personal statement, recommendations. Additional exam requirements/recommendations for international students: Required—TOEFL, TWE. *Expenses:* Contact institution.

Duquesne University, School of Education, Department of Instruction and Leadership, Pittsburgh, PA 15282-0001. Offers early level (PreK-4) education (MS Ed); English as a second language (MS Ed); instructional technology (MS Ed, Ed D, Post-Master's Certificate), including business, computer, and information technology (MS Ed), instructional technology; middle level (4-8) education (MS Ed); reading and language arts (MS Ed); secondary education (MS Ed), including biology, chemistry, English, Latin education, K-12, mathematics, physics, social studies. Part-time and evening/weekend programs available. Postbaccalaureate distance learning degree programs offered (minimal on-campus study). *Faculty:* 15 full-time (9 women), 28 part-time/adjunct (15 women). *Students:* 213 full-time (145 women), 47 part-time (38 women); includes 19 minority (9 Black or African American, non-Hispanic/Latino; 5 Asian, non-Hispanic/Latino; 4 Hispanic/Latino; 1 Two or more races, non-Hispanic/Latino), 11 international. Average age 26. 160 applicants, 48% accepted, 53 enrolled. In 2011, 111 degrees awarded. *Degree requirements:* For master's, thesis optional; for doctorate, thesis/dissertation. *Entrance requirements:* For master's, letters of recommendation, letter of intent, interview, bachelor's degree; for doctorate, GRE, letters of recommendation, letter of intent, interview, master's degree; for Post-Master's Certificate, letters of recommendation, letter of intent, interview, bachelor's/master's degree. Additional exam requirements/recommendations for international students: Required—TOEFL (minimum score 550 paper-based; 80 computer-based), IELTS (minimum score 7). *Application deadline:* For fall admission, 9/1 priority date for domestic students; for spring admission, 1/1 priority date for domestic students. Applications are processed on a rolling basis. Application fee: $0. Electronic applications accepted. Application fee is waived when completed online. *Expenses: Tuition:* Full-time $16,596; part-time $922 per credit. *Required fees:* $1584; $88 per credit. Tuition and fees vary according to program. *Financial support:* Research assistantships, teaching assistantships with tuition reimbursements, career-related internships or fieldwork, Federal Work-Study, and institutionally sponsored loans available. Support available to part-time students. *Unit head:* Dr. Jason Margolis, Chair, 412-396-6106, Fax: 412-396-5388, E-mail: margolisj@duq.edu. *Application contact:* Michael Dolinger, Director of Student and Academic Services, 412-396-6647, Fax: 412-396-5585, E-mail: dolingerm@duq.edu.

East Carolina University, Graduate School, College of Education, Department of Business and Information Technologies Education, Greenville, NC 27858-4353. Offers business education (MA Ed); elementary education (MAT); English education (MAT); family and consumer science (MAT); health education (MAT); Hispanic studies (MAT); history education (MAT); marketing education (MA Ed); middle grades education (MAT); music education (MAT); physical education (MAT); science education (MAT); special education (MAT), including general curriculum; vocation education (MS). *Accreditation:* NCATE. Part-time and evening/weekend programs available. Postbaccalaureate distance learning degree programs offered (no on-campus study). *Degree requirements:* For master's, comprehensive exam, thesis optional. *Entrance requirements:* For master's, GRE or MAT, minimum GPA of 2.5, bachelor's degree in related field, teaching license (MA Ed). Additional exam requirements/recommendations for international students: Required—TOEFL. *Application deadline:* For fall admission, 6/1 priority date for domestic students. Applications are processed on a rolling basis. Application fee: $50. *Expenses:* Tuition, state resident: full-time $3557; part-time $444.63 per semester hour. Tuition, nonresident: full-time $14,351; part-time $1793.88 per semester hour. *Required fees:* $2016; $252 per semester hour. Part-time tuition and fees vary according to course load, campus/location and program. *Financial support:* Federal Work-Study available. Support available to part-time students. Financial award application deadline: 6/1. *Unit head:* Dr. Ivan G. Wallace, Chair, 252-328-6983, Fax: 252-328-6835, E-mail: wallacei@ecu.edu. *Application contact:* Dean of Graduate School, 252-328-6012, Fax: 252-328-6071, E-mail: gradschool@ecu.edu. Web site: http://www.ecu.edu/cs-educ/bite/index.cfm.

Eastern Kentucky University, The Graduate School, College of Education, Department of Curriculum and Instruction, Program in Secondary and Higher Education, Richmond, KY 40475-3102. Offers secondary education (MA Ed), including agricultural education, art education, biological sciences education, business education, English education, geography education, history education, home economics education, industrial education, mathematical sciences education, physical education, school health education. *Accreditation:* NCATE. Part-time programs available. *Entrance requirements:* For master's, GRE General Test, minimum GPA of 2.5.

East Stroudsburg University of Pennsylvania, Graduate School, College of Arts and Sciences, Department of History, East Stroudsburg, PA 18301-2999. Offers M Ed, MA. Part-time and evening/weekend programs available. *Degree requirements:* For master's, comprehensive exam, thesis, thesis defense. *Entrance requirements:* For master's, Commonwealth of Pennsylvania Department of Education Certification Requirements (M Ed). Additional exam requirements/recommendations for international students: Required—TOEFL (minimum score 560 paper-based; 220 computer-based; 83 iBT).

East Stroudsburg University of Pennsylvania, Graduate School, College of Arts and Sciences, Department of Political Science, East Stroudsburg, PA 18301-2999. Offers M Ed, MA. Part-time and evening/weekend programs available. *Degree requirements:* For master's, variable foreign language requirement, comprehensive exam, thesis or alternative. *Entrance requirements:* Additional exam requirements/recommendations for international students: Required—TOEFL (minimum score 560 paper-based; 220 computer-based; 83 iBT).

Emporia State University, Graduate School, College of Liberal Arts and Sciences, Department of Social Sciences, Program in Social Sciences, Emporia, KS 66801-5087. Offers American history (MAT); anthropology (MAT); economics (MAT); geography (MAT); political science (MAT); social studies education (MAT); sociology (MAT); world history (MAT). *Accreditation:* NCATE. Part-time programs available. *Students:* 4 part-time (1 woman); includes 1 minority (Asian, non-Hispanic/Latino). In 2011, 4 master's awarded. *Degree requirements:* For master's, comprehensive exam or thesis. *Entrance requirements:* For master's, appropriate bachelor's degree, teacher certification. Additional exam requirements/recommendations for international students: Required—TOEFL (minimum score 520 paper-based; 133 computer-based; 68 iBT). *Application deadline:* For fall admission, 8/15 priority date for domestic students. Applications are processed on a rolling basis. Application fee: $30 ($75 for international students). Electronic applications accepted. *Expenses:* Tuition, state resident: full-time $2342; part-time $195 per credit hour. Tuition, nonresident: full-time $7254; part-time $605 per credit hour. *Required fees:* $66 per credit hour. Tuition and fees vary according to campus/location. *Financial support:* Federal Work-Study, institutionally sponsored loans, health care benefits, and unspecified assistantships available. Financial award application deadline: 3/15; financial award applicants required to submit FAFSA. *Unit head:* Dr. Ellen Hansen, Chair, 620-341-5461, E-mail: ehansen@emporia.edu. *Application contact:* Dr. Christopher Lovett, Associate Professor, 620-341-5577, E-mail: clovett@emporia.edu.

Fayetteville State University, Graduate School, Program in Middle Grades, Secondary and Special Education, Fayetteville, NC 28301-4298. Offers biology (MA Ed); history (MA Ed); mathematics (MA Ed); middle grades (MA Ed); political science (MA Ed); reading (MA Ed); sociology (MA Ed); special education (MA Ed), including behavioral-emotional handicaps, mentally handicapped, specific training disability. *Accreditation:* NCATE. Part-time and evening/weekend programs available. *Faculty:* 12 full-time (8 women), 4 part-time/adjunct (3 women). *Students:* 37 full-time (31 women), 66 part-time (57 women); includes 75 minority (68 Black or African American, non-Hispanic/Latino; 1 American Indian or Alaska Native, non-Hispanic/Latino; 3 Hispanic/Latino; 3 Two or more races, non-Hispanic/Latino). Average age 35. 18 applicants, 100% accepted, 18 enrolled. In 2011, 35 master's awarded. *Degree requirements:* For master's, comprehensive exam, internship. *Application deadline:* For fall admission, 4/15 for domestic students; for spring admission, 10/15 for domestic students. Applications are processed on a rolling basis. Application fee: $35. Electronic applications accepted. *Faculty research:* Students with disabilities and selected leadership behaviors, new vision for professional development, gifted and talented studentsm emotional and behavioral disabilities, professional development for high school biology teachers. *Unit head:* Dr. Kimberly Smith-Burton, Interim Chair, 910-672-1182, E-mail: cbarringerbrown@uncfsu.edu. *Application contact:* Katrina Hoffman, Graduate Admission Officer, 910-672-1374, Fax: 910-672-1470, E-mail: khoffma1@uncfsu.edu.

Fitchburg State University, Division of Graduate and Continuing Education, Programs in History and Teaching History (Secondary Level), Fitchburg, MA 01420-2697. Offers MA, MAT, Certificate. *Accreditation:* NCATE. Part-time and evening/weekend programs available. *Students:* 3 full-time (all women), 25 part-time (13 women); includes 1 minority (Hispanic/Latino). Average age 35. 3 applicants, 100% accepted, 2 enrolled. In 2011, 9 master's awarded. *Entrance requirements:* Additional exam requirements/recommendations for international students: Required—TOEFL (minimum score 550 paper-based; 213 computer-based; 79 iBT). *Application deadline:* For fall admission, 7/15 for international students; for spring admission, 12/1 for international students. Applications are processed on a rolling basis. Application fee: $25 ($50 for international students). Electronic applications accepted. *Expenses:* Tuition, state resident: full-time $2700; part-time $150 per credit. Tuition, nonresident: full-time $2700; part-time $150 per credit. *Required fees:* $2286; $127 per credit. *Financial support:* In 2011–12, research assistantships with partial tuition reimbursements (averaging $5,500 per year) were awarded; Federal Work-Study, scholarships/grants, and unspecified assistantships also available. Support available to part-time students. Financial award application deadline: 3/1; financial award applicants required to submit FAFSA. *Unit head:* Dr. Laura Baker, Chair, 978-665-3379, Fax: 978-665-3658, E-mail: gce@fitchburgstate.edu. *Application contact:* Kay Reynolds, Director of Admissions, 978-665-3144, Fax: 978-

665-4540, E-mail: admissions@fitchburgstate.edu. Web site: http://www.fitchburgstate.edu.

Florida Agricultural and Mechanical University, Division of Graduate Studies, Research, and Continuing Education, College of Education, Program in Secondary Education and Foundation, Tallahassee, FL 32307-3200. Offers biology (M Ed); chemistry (MS Ed); English (MS Ed); history (MS Ed); math (MS Ed); physics (MS Ed). *Accreditation:* NCATE. *Degree requirements:* For master's, thesis (for some programs). *Entrance requirements:* For master's, GRE General Test, minimum GPA of 3.0. Additional exam requirements/recommendations for international students: Required—TOEFL.

Florida International University, College of Education, Department of Curriculum and Instruction, Miami, FL 33199. Offers art education (MAT, MS, Ed D); curriculum and instruction (Ed S); curriculum development (MS); curriculum studies (PhD); early childhood education (MS, Ed D); elementary education (MS, Ed D); English education (MAT, MS, Ed D); foreign language education - teaching English to speakers of other languages (TESOL) (MS, Certificate), including foreign language education (Certificate), teaching English (MS); French education - initial teacher preparation (MAT); international and intercultural development education (Ed D); international and intercultural developmental education (MS); language, literacy and culture (PhD); learning technologies (MS, Ed D, PhD); mathematics education (MAT, MS, Ed D, PhD); modern language education/bilingual education (MS, Ed D); physical education (MS); reading education (MS, Ed D); science education (MAT, MS, Ed D, PhD); social studies education (MAT, MS, Ed D); Spanish education - initial teacher preparation (MAT); special education (MS). Part-time and evening/weekend programs available. *Degree requirements:* For doctorate, comprehensive exam, thesis/dissertation. *Entrance requirements:* For master's, GRE General Test, Florida General Knowledge Test or Florida College Level Academic Skills Test; for doctorate and other advanced degree, GRE General Test. Additional exam requirements/recommendations for international students: Required—TOEFL (minimum score 550 paper-based; 213 computer-based; 80 iBT), IELTS (minimum score 6.3). Electronic applications accepted.

Florida State University, The Graduate School, College of Education, School of Teacher Education, Program in Social Science Education, Tallahassee, FL 32306. Offers MS. Part-time programs available. *Faculty:* 3 full-time (1 woman). *Students:* 10 full-time (6 women), 4 part-time (all women); includes 2 minority (1 Black or African American, non-Hispanic/Latino; 1 Hispanic/Latino), 2 international. Average age 29. 15 applicants, 73% accepted, 7 enrolled. In 2011, 12 master's awarded. *Degree requirements:* For master's, comprehensive exam, thesis optional. *Entrance requirements:* For master's, GRE General Test, minimum GPA of 3.0. Additional exam requirements/recommendations for international students: Required—TOEFL (minimum score 550 paper-based; 213 computer-based; 80 iBT). *Application deadline:* For fall admission, 7/1 for domestic and international students; for winter admission, 11/1 for domestic students, 10/1 for international students; for spring admission, 3/1 for domestic and international students. Applications are processed on a rolling basis. Application fee: $30. Electronic applications accepted. *Expenses:* Tuition, state resident: full-time $9474; part-time $350.88 per credit hour. Tuition, nonresident: full-time $16,236; part-time $601.34 per credit hour. *Required fees:* $630 per semester. One-time fee: $20. Tuition and fees vary according to course load and campus/location. *Financial support:* Fellowships with full and partial tuition reimbursements, research assistantships with full and partial tuition reimbursements, teaching assistantships with full and partial tuition reimbursements, career-related internships or fieldwork, scholarships/grants, health care benefits, and unspecified assistantships available. Financial award applicants required to submit FAFSA. *Faculty research:* Globalization, desegregation and Civil Rights in the Deep South. *Unit head:* Dr. Helge Swanson, Head, 850-644-6553, Fax: 850-644-1880, E-mail: hswanson@fsu.edu. *Application contact:* Harriet Kasper, Program Assistant, 850-644-2122, Fax: 850-644-7736, E-mail: hkasper@fsu.edu.

Framingham State University, Division of Graduate and Continuing Education, Program in History, Framingham, MA 01701-9101. Offers M Ed.

Georgia Southern University, Jack N. Averitt College of Graduate Studies, College of Education, Department of Teaching and Learning, Program in Social Science Education, Statesboro, GA 30460. Offers M Ed, MAT. *Accreditation:* NCATE. Part-time and evening/weekend programs available. *Students:* 9 full-time (4 women), 2 part-time (0 women); includes 1 minority (Hispanic/Latino). Average age 27. 6 applicants, 100% accepted, 3 enrolled. In 2011, 6 master's awarded. *Degree requirements:* For master's, portfolio, transition point assessments, exit assessment. *Entrance requirements:* For master's, GRE General Test or MAT; GACE Basic Skills and Content Assessments (MAT), minimum cumulative GPA of 2.5. Additional exam requirements/recommendations for international students: Required—TOEFL (minimum score 550 paper-based; 213 computer-based; 80 iBT). *Application deadline:* For fall admission, 3/1 priority date for domestic students, 3/1 for international students; for spring admission, 10/1 priority date for domestic students, 10/1 for international students. Applications are processed on a rolling basis. Application fee: $50. Electronic applications accepted. *Expenses:* Tuition, state resident: full-time $6300; part-time $263 per semester hour. Tuition, nonresident: full-time $25,174; part-time $1049 per semester hour. *Required fees:* $1872. *Financial support:* In 2011–12, 1 research assistantship with partial tuition reimbursement (averaging $7,200 per year), teaching assistantships with partial tuition reimbursements (averaging $7,200 per year) were awarded; Federal Work-Study, scholarships/grants, tuition waivers (partial), and unspecified assistantships also available. Support available to part-time students. Financial award application deadline: 4/15; financial award applicants required to submit FAFSA. *Faculty research:* Environmental issues. *Unit head:* Dr. Ronnie Sheppard, Department Chair, 912-478-5203, Fax: 912-478-0026, E-mail: sheppard@georgiasouthern.edu. *Application contact:* Amanda Gilliland, Coordinator for Graduate Student Recruitment, 912-478-5384, Fax: 912-478-0740, E-mail: gradadmissions@georgiasouthern.edu. Web site: http://coe.georgiasouthern.edu/tandl/index.html.

Georgia State University, College of Education, Department of Middle-Secondary Education and Instructional Technology, Programs in Secondary Education, Atlanta, GA 30302-3083. Offers art education (Ed S); English education (M Ed, Ed S); mathematics education (M Ed, PhD, Ed S); music education (PhD); science education (M Ed, PhD, Ed S); social studies education (M Ed, PhD, Ed S). *Accreditation:* NASM (one or more programs are accredited); NCATE. Part-time and evening/weekend programs available. *Degree requirements:* For master's, comprehensive exam; for doctorate, comprehensive exam, thesis/dissertation; for Ed S, project/exam. *Entrance requirements:* For master's, GRE General Test, minimum GPA of 2.5; for doctorate, GRE General Test or MAT, minimum GPA of 3.3; for Ed S, GRE General Test or MAT, minimum graduate GPA of 3.25. *Faculty research:* Women and science, problem solving in mathematics, dialects, economic education.

Grambling State University, School of Graduate Studies and Research, College of Arts and Sciences, Program in Social Sciences, Grambling, LA 71245. Offers MAT. Part-time programs available. *Degree requirements:* For master's, comprehensive exam (for some programs), thesis optional. *Entrance requirements:* For master's, GRE, minimum GPA of 3.0 on last degree. Additional exam requirements/recommendations for international students: Required—TOEFL (minimum score 500 paper-based; 173 computer-based; 61 iBT). Electronic applications accepted. *Expenses:* Tuition, state resident: full-time $3546; part-time $192 per credit hour. Tuition, nonresident: full-time $3456; part-time $192 per credit hour. *Required fees:* $1829; $1829 per semester hour.

Harding University, College of Education, Searcy, AR 72149-0001. Offers advanced studies in teaching and learning (M Ed); art (MSE); behavioral science (MSE); counseling (MS, Ed S); early childhood special education (M Ed, MSE); education (MSE); educational leadership (M Ed, Ed S); elementary education (M Ed); English (MSE); French (MSE); history/social science (MSE); kinesiology (MSE); math (MSE); reading (M Ed); secondary education (M Ed); Spanish (MSE); teaching (MAT); teaching English as a second language (MSE). *Accreditation:* NCATE. Part-time and evening/weekend programs available. *Faculty:* 9 full-time (2 women), 48 part-time/adjunct (26 women). *Students:* 100 full-time (77 women), 333 part-time (239 women); includes 76 minority (59 Black or African American, non-Hispanic/Latino; 1 Asian, non-Hispanic/Latino; 10 Hispanic/Latino; 6 Two or more races, non-Hispanic/Latino), 2 international. Average age 36. 93 applicants, 91% accepted, 83 enrolled. In 2011, 159 master's, 10 other advanced degrees awarded. *Degree requirements:* For master's, comprehensive exam (for some programs), thesis optional, portfolio(s); for Ed S, comprehensive exam, portfolio, project. *Entrance requirements:* For master's, GRE, MAT, PRAXIS; for Ed S, MAT or GRE. Additional exam requirements/recommendations for international students: Required—TOEFL (minimum score 550 paper-based; 79 iBT). *Application deadline:* For fall admission, 8/1 for domestic and international students; for spring admission, 1/1 for domestic and international students. Applications are processed on a rolling basis. Application fee: $35. *Expenses: Tuition:* Full-time $10,512; part-time $584 per credit hour. *Required fees:* $500; $25 per credit hour. Tuition and fees vary according to course load, degree level and program. *Financial support:* In 2011–12, 37 students received support. Unspecified assistantships available. *Faculty research:* Reading, comprehension, school violence, educational technology, behavior, college choice, differentiated instruction, brain-based teaching. *Unit head:* Dr. Clara Carroll, Chair, 501-279-4501, Fax: 501-279-4083, E-mail: ccarroll@harding.edu. *Application contact:* Information Contact, 501-279-4315, E-mail: gradstudiesedu@harding.edu. Web site: http://www.harding.edu/education/grad.html.

Hofstra University, School of Education, Health, and Human Services, Programs in Learning and Teaching, Hempstead, NY 11549. Offers social studies education (Ed D). Part-time and evening/weekend programs available. *Students:* 4 full-time (all women), 33 part-time (28 women); includes 5 minority (3 Black or African American, non-Hispanic/Latino; 1 American Indian or Alaska Native, non-Hispanic/Latino; 1 Hispanic/Latino), 1 international. Average age 37. 25 applicants, 56% accepted, 11 enrolled. In 2011, 1 doctorate awarded. *Degree requirements:* For doctorate, comprehensive exam, thesis/dissertation, minimum GPA of 3.0. *Entrance requirements:* For doctorate, GRE, 3 letters of recommendation, essay, interview, 2 years full-time teaching. Additional exam requirements/recommendations for international students: Required—TOEFL (minimum score 550 paper-based; 213 computer-based; 80 iBT). *Application deadline:* Applications are processed on a rolling basis. Application fee: $70 ($75 for international students). Electronic applications accepted. *Expenses: Tuition:* Full-time $18,990; part-time $1055 per credit hour. *Required fees:* $970. Tuition and fees vary according to program. *Financial support:* In 2011–12, 27 students received support, including 21 fellowships with full and partial tuition reimbursements available (averaging $7,778 per year); research assistantships with full and partial tuition reimbursements available, Federal Work-Study, institutionally sponsored loans, scholarships/grants, and tuition waivers (full and partial) also available. Support available to part-time students. Financial award applicants required to submit FAFSA. *Faculty research:* Critical thinking, professional development, teacher quality, quantitative research. *Unit head:* Dr. Esther Fusco, Chairperson, 516-463-7704, Fax: 516-463-6196, E-mail: catezf@hofstra.edu. *Application contact:* Carol Drummer, Dean of Graduate Admissions, 516-463-4876, Fax: 516-463-4664, E-mail: gradstudent@hofstra.edu. Web site: http://www.hofstra.edu/education/.

Hofstra University, School of Education, Health, and Human Services, Programs in Teaching - Secondary Education, Hempstead, NY 11549. Offers business education (MS Ed); education technology (Advanced Certificate); English education (MA, MS Ed); foreign language and TESOL (MS Ed); foreign language education (MA, MS Ed), including French, German, Russian, Spanish; mathematics education (MA, MS Ed); science education (MA, MS Ed), including biology, chemistry, earth science, geology, physics; secondary education (Advanced Certificate); social studies education (MA, MS Ed). Part-time and evening/weekend programs available. Postbaccalaureate distance learning degree programs offered (minimal on-campus study). *Students:* 72 full-time (47 women), 51 part-time (30 women); includes 21 minority (9 Black or African American, non-Hispanic/Latino; 7 Asian, non-Hispanic/Latino; 5 Hispanic/Latino). Average age 28. 103 applicants, 91% accepted, 41 enrolled. In 2011, 86 master's, 6 other advanced degrees awarded. *Degree requirements:* For master's, one foreign language, comprehensive exam (for some programs), thesis (for some programs), exit project, electronic portfolio, student teaching, fieldwork, curriculum project, minimum GPA of 3.0; for Advanced Certificate, 3 foreign languages, comprehensive exam (for some programs), thesis project, minimum GPA of 3.0. *Entrance requirements:* For master's, 2 letters of recommendation, teacher certification (MA), essay; for Advanced Certificate, 2 letters of recommendation, essay. Additional exam requirements/recommendations for international students: Required—TOEFL (minimum score 550 paper-based; 213 computer-based; 80 iBT). *Application deadline:* Applications are processed on a rolling basis. Application fee: $70 ($75 for international students). Electronic applications accepted. *Expenses: Tuition:* Full-time $18,990; part-time $1055 per credit hour. *Required fees:* $970. Tuition and fees vary according to program. *Financial support:* In 2011–12, 90 students received support, including 13 fellowships with full and partial tuition reimbursements available (averaging $3,202 per year), 1 research assistantship with full and partial tuition reimbursement available (averaging $11,645 per year); career-related internships or fieldwork, Federal Work-Study, institutionally sponsored loans, scholarships/grants, tuition waivers (full and partial), and unspecified assistantships also available. Support available to part-time students. Financial award applicants required to submit FAFSA. *Faculty research:* Appropriate content and pedagogy in secondary school disciplines, appropriate pedagogy in secondary school disciplines, adolescent development, secondary school organization, alternative secondary school programs. *Unit head:* Dr. Esther Fusco, Chairperson, 516-463-7704, Fax: 516-463-6196, E-mail: catezf@hofstra.edu. *Application contact:* Carol Drummer, Dean of Graduate Admissions, 516-463-4876, Fax: 516-463-4664, E-mail: gradstudent@hofstra.edu. Web site: http://www.hofstra.edu/education/.

Hunter College of the City University of New York, Graduate School, School of Education, Programs in Secondary Education, Concentration in Social Studies Education, New York, NY 10021-5085. Offers MA. *Accreditation:* NCATE. *Faculty:* 8 full-time (6 women), 2 part-time/adjunct (1 woman). *Students:* 7 full-time (5 women), 50 part-time (27 women); includes 11 minority (3 Black or African American, non-Hispanic/Latino; 1 American Indian or Alaska Native, non-Hispanic/Latino; 5 Asian, non-Hispanic/Latino; 2 Hispanic/Latino). Average age 28. 80 applicants, 43% accepted, 15 enrolled. In 2011, 24 master's awarded. *Degree requirements:* For master's, thesis, professional teaching portfolio, New York State Teacher Certification Exam, research project. *Entrance requirements:* For master's, minimum GPA of 3.0 in history, 2.8 overall; 2 letters of reference; minimum of 30 credits in social studies areas. Additional exam requirements/recommendations for international students: Required—TOEFL, TWE.

Social Sciences Education

Application deadline: For fall admission, 4/1 for domestic students, 2/1 for international students; for spring admission, 11/1 for domestic students, 9/1 for international students. Applications are processed on a rolling basis. Application fee: $125. *Expenses:* Tuition, state resident: full-time $8210; part-time $345 per credit. Tuition, nonresident: full-time $15,360; part-time $640 per credit. *Required fees:* $280 per semester. One-time fee: $125. Tuition and fees vary according to class time, campus/location and program. *Financial support:* Federal Work-Study and tuition waivers (partial) available. Support available to part-time students. *Unit head:* Dr. Barbara Welter, Graduate Advisor, 212-772-5487, E-mail: bwelter@shiva.hunter.cuny.edu. *Application contact:* William Zlata, Director for Graduate Admissions, 212-772-4482, Fax: 212-650-3336, E-mail: admissions@hunter.cuny.edu. Web site: http://www.hunter.cuny.edu/school-of-education/programs/graduate/adolescent/social-studies.

Indiana University Bloomington, School of Education, Department of Curriculum and Instruction, Bloomington, IN 47405-7000. Offers art education (MS, Ed D, PhD); curriculum studies (Ed D, PhD); elementary education (MS, Ed D, PhD, Ed S); mathematics education (MS, Ed D, PhD); science education (MS, Ed D, PhD); secondary education (MS, Ed D, PhD); social studies education (MS, PhD); special education (PhD, Ed S). *Accreditation:* NCATE. Part-time and evening/weekend programs available. Terminal master's awarded for partial completion of doctoral program. *Degree requirements:* For doctorate, thesis/dissertation; for Ed S, comprehensive exam or project. *Entrance requirements:* For master's, doctorate, and Ed S, GRE General Test. Electronic applications accepted.

Instituto Tecnologico de Santo Domingo, Graduate School, Area of Humanities and Social Sciences, Santo Domingo, Dominican Republic. Offers accounting (Certificate); adult education (Certificate); applied linguistics (MA); economics (MA); education (M Ed); educational psychology (MA, Certificate); gender and development (MA, Certificate); humanistic studies (MA); international marketing management (Certificate); international relations in the Caribbean basin (Certificate); intervention systems in family therapy (MA); linguistic and literary communication (Certificate); pedagogical support (MA); social science education (M Ed); sustainable human development (MA); terminal illness and death psychology (Certificate); youth and adult education (M Ed).

Inter American University of Puerto Rico, Arecibo Campus, Programs in Education, Arecibo, PR 00614-4050. Offers administration and educational supervision (MA Ed); counseling and guidance (MA Ed); curriculum and teaching (MA Ed), including biology education, English as a second language, history education, math education, Spanish; elementary education (MA Ed). *Degree requirements:* For master's, comprehensive exam, thesis optional. *Entrance requirements:* For master's, GRE, EXADEP, bachelor's degree in education or teaching license (administration and supervision) or courses in education and psychology (counseling and guidance), minimum GPA of 2.5 in last 60 credits.

Inter American University of Puerto Rico, Barranquitas Campus, Program in Education, Barranquitas, PR 00794. Offers curriculum and teaching (M Ed), including biology education, English as a second language, history education, mathematics education, Spanish; educational leadership and management (MA); elementary education (M Ed); information and library service technology (M Ed); special education (MA). *Degree requirements:* For master's, comprehensive exam, thesis optional. *Entrance requirements:* For master's, EXADEP, letter of recommendation. Electronic applications accepted.

Inter American University of Puerto Rico, Metropolitan Campus, Graduate Programs, Program in History Education, San Juan, PR 00919-1293. Offers MA.

Inter American University of Puerto Rico, Ponce Campus, Graduate School, Mercedita, PR 00715-1602. Offers accounting (MBA); biology (M Ed); chemistry (M Ed); criminal justice (MA); elementary education (M Ed); English as a Second Language (M Ed); finance (MBA); history (M Ed); human resources (MBA); marketing (MBA); mathematics (M Ed); Spanish (M Ed). *Entrance requirements:* For master's, minimum GPA of 2.5.

Iona College, School of Arts and Science, Program in Education, New Rochelle, NY 10801-1890. Offers adolescence education: biology (MS Ed, MST); adolescence education: English (MS Ed, MST); adolescence education: Italian (MS Ed, MST); adolescence education: mathematics (MS Ed, MST); adolescence education: social studies (MS Ed, MST); adolescence education: Spanish (MS Ed, MST); adolescence special education 5-12 (MST); adolescence special education/literacy 5-12 (MS Ed); childhood 1-6/special education 1-6 (MST); childhood education (MST); early childhood/childhood (MST); educational leadership (MS Ed); literacy birth-grade 6/special education 1-6 (MS Ed); literacy education: birth-grade 6 (MS Ed). *Accreditation:* NCATE. Part-time and evening/weekend programs available. *Faculty:* 21 full-time (13 women), 13 part-time/adjunct (8 women). *Students:* 59 full-time (45 women), 101 part-time (78 women); includes 11 minority (2 Black or African American, non-Hispanic/Latino; 2 Asian, non-Hispanic/Latino; 7 Hispanic/Latino). Average age 26. 74 applicants, 66% accepted, 35 enrolled. In 2011, 46 master's awarded. *Degree requirements:* For master's, thesis or alternative. *Entrance requirements:* For master's, minimum GPA of 2.5 (MST), New York teaching certificate (MS Ed). Additional exam requirements/recommendations for international students: Required—TOEFL (minimum score 550 paper-based; 213 computer-based). *Application deadline:* Applications are processed on a rolling basis. Application fee: $50. Electronic applications accepted. *Expenses: Tuition:* Part-time $872 per credit. *Required fees:* $225 per term. *Financial support:* Unspecified assistantships available. Support available to part-time students. Financial award application deadline: 4/15; financial award applicants required to submit FAFSA. *Faculty research:* Reading/writing, educational technology, administration, early literacy assessment, literacy development. *Unit head:* Dr. Catherine O'Callaghan, Chair, 914-633-2210, Fax: 914-633-2608, E-mail: cocallaghan@iona.edu. *Application contact:* Dr. Jeanne Zaino, Interim Dean, School of Arts and Science, 914-633-2112, Fax: 914-633-2023, E-mail: jzaino@iona.edu.

Ithaca College, Division of Graduate and Professional Studies, School of Humanities and Sciences, Program in Adolescence Education, Ithaca, NY 14850. Offers biology 7-12 (MAT); chemistry 7-12 (MAT); English 7-12 (MAT); French 7-12 (MAT); math 7-12 (MAT); physics 7-12 (MAT); social studies 7-12 (MAT); Spanish (MAT). Part-time programs available. *Faculty:* 23 full-time (7 women). *Students:* 14 full-time (8 women), 1 part-time (0 women); includes 4 minority (1 Asian, non-Hispanic/Latino; 2 Hispanic/Latino; 1 Two or more races, non-Hispanic/Latino). Average age 27. 33 applicants, 64% accepted, 15 enrolled. In 2011, 15 master's awarded. *Degree requirements:* For master's, thesis or alternative, student teaching. *Entrance requirements:* For master's, minimum GPA of 3.0. Additional exam requirements/recommendations for international students: Required—TOEFL (minimum score 550 paper-based; 213 computer-based; 80 iBT). *Application deadline:* For fall admission, 2/15 priority date for domestic students, 2/15 for international students; for spring admission, 12/1 for domestic and international students. Applications are processed on a rolling basis. Application fee: $40. Electronic applications accepted. *Expenses:* Contact institution. *Financial support:* In 2011–12, 9 students received support, including 9 teaching assistantships (averaging $6,070 per year); career-related internships or fieldwork, Federal Work-Study, scholarships/grants, and unspecified assistantships also available. Support available to part-time students. Financial award application deadline: 2/15; financial award applicants required to submit CSS PROFILE or FAFSA. *Faculty research:* Bilingual education, socio-linguistic perspective on literacy. *Unit head:* Dr. Linda Hanrahan, Chairperson, 607-274-3143, Fax: 607-274-1263, E-mail: gps@ithaca.edu. *Application contact:* Gerard Turbide, Director, Office of Admission, 607-274-3143, Fax: 607-274-1263, E-mail: gps@ithaca.edu. Web site: http://www.ithaca.edu/gps/gradprograms/overview/school/hs/aded.

The Johns Hopkins University, School of Education, Department of Teacher Preparation, Baltimore, MD 21218. Offers early childhood education (MAT); education (MS), including educational studies; elementary education (MAT); English for speakers of other languages (MAT); K-8 mathematics lead-teacher (Certificate); K-8 science lead-teacher (Certificate); secondary education (MAT), including biology, chemistry, earth/space/environmental science, English, French, mathematics, physics, social studies, Spanish. Part-time and evening/weekend programs available. *Degree requirements:* For master's, portfolio, PRAXIS II, internship. *Entrance requirements:* For master's, PRAXIS I, SAT, ACT, or GRE (MAT), minimum undergraduate GPA of 3.0, interview, 1 letter of recommendation, curriculum vitae/resume; for Certificate, bachelor's degree, minimum undergraduate GPA of 3.0, essay/statement of goals, interview. Additional exam requirements/recommendations for international students: Required—TOEFL (minimum score 600 paper-based; 250 computer-based; 100 iBT). Electronic applications accepted. *Faculty research:* Teacher retention, STEM education reform, alternative certification programs, school-university partnerships, urban education, action research/data-informed instruction, family engagement.

Kansas State University, Graduate School, College of Education, Department of Curriculum and Instruction, Manhattan, KS 66506. Offers career and technical education (Ed D, PhD); curriculum studies (Ed D, PhD); digital teaching and learning (MS); educational computing, design and online learning (MS); educational technology (Ed D, PhD); elementary/middle level (MS); English as a second language (MS); language/diversity education (Ed D, PhD); literacy education (Ed D, PhD); mathematics education (Ed D, PhD); middle level/secondary (MS); reading and language arts (MS); reading specialist endorsement (MS); science education (Ed D, PhD); social science education (Ed D, PhD); teacher education (Ed D, PhD); teacher leader/school improvement (MS, Ed D). *Accreditation:* NCATE. Part-time programs available. Postbaccalaureate distance learning degree programs offered (minimal on-campus study). *Faculty:* 15 full-time (12 women), 3 part-time/adjunct (2 women). *Students:* 37 full-time (30 women), 113 part-time (91 women); includes 14 minority (4 Black or African American, non-Hispanic/Latino; 1 American Indian or Alaska Native, non-Hispanic/Latino; 1 Asian, non-Hispanic/Latino; 7 Hispanic/Latino; 1 Two or more races, non-Hispanic/Latino), 15 international. Average age 37. 75 applicants, 51% accepted, 9 enrolled. In 2011, 48 master's, 14 doctorates awarded. *Degree requirements:* For master's, comprehensive exam, portfolio, project, report or thesis; for doctorate, comprehensive exam, thesis/dissertation, preliminary exam. *Entrance requirements:* For master's, minimum GPA of 3.0; for doctorate, GRE, minimum GPA of 3.0. Additional exam requirements/recommendations for international students: Required—TOEFL. *Application deadline:* For fall admission, 2/1 priority date for domestic students, 2/1 for international students; for spring admission, 8/1 priority date for domestic students, 8/1 for international students. Applications are processed on a rolling basis. Application fee: $40 ($55 for international students). Electronic applications accepted. *Financial support:* In 2011–12, 1 research assistantship (averaging $16,900 per year), 8 teaching assistantships (averaging $12,466 per year) were awarded; career-related internships or fieldwork, institutionally sponsored loans, and scholarships/grants also available. Support available to part-time students. Financial award application deadline: 3/1; financial award applicants required to submit FAFSA. *Faculty research:* Literacy and technology, critical race theory and diversity, achievement gaps, school improvement, teacher education. *Total annual research expenditures:* $510,907. *Unit head:* Dr. Gail Shroyer, Chair, 785-532-5550, Fax: 785-532-7304, E-mail: gshroyer@ksu.edu. *Application contact:* Dona Deam, Application Contact, 785-532-5595, Fax: 785-532-7304, E-mail: ddeam@ksu.edu. Web site: http://coe.k-state.edu/departments/currin/curringrad.htm.

Kutztown University of Pennsylvania, College of Education, Program in Secondary Education, Kutztown, PA 19530-0730. Offers biology (M Ed); curriculum and instruction (M Ed); English (M Ed); mathematics (M Ed); social studies (M Ed). *Accreditation:* NCATE. Part-time and evening/weekend programs available. *Faculty:* 7 full-time (2 women). *Students:* 29 full-time (12 women), 73 part-time (43 women); includes 3 minority (1 Black or African American, non-Hispanic/Latino; 1 Asian, non-Hispanic/Latino; 1 Hispanic/Latino). Average age 28. 12 applicants, 100% accepted, 12 enrolled. In 2011, 29 master's awarded. *Degree requirements:* For master's, comprehensive exam, thesis optional. *Entrance requirements:* For master's, GRE General Test. Additional exam requirements/recommendations for international students: Required—TOEFL (minimum score 550 paper-based; 79 iBT). *Application deadline:* For fall admission, 8/1 priority date for domestic students, 8/1 for international students; for spring admission, 12/1 priority date for domestic students, 12/1 for international students. Applications are processed on a rolling basis. Application fee: $35. Electronic applications accepted. *Expenses:* Tuition, state resident: full-time $7488; part-time $416 per credit. Tuition, nonresident: full-time $11,232; part-time $624 per credit. *Financial support:* Career-related internships or fieldwork, Federal Work-Study, scholarships/grants, and unspecified assistantships available. Financial award application deadline: 3/1; financial award applicants required to submit FAFSA. *Unit head:* Dr. Theresa Stahler, Chairperson, 610-683-4259, Fax: 610-683-1338, E-mail: stahler@kutztown.edu. *Application contact:* Kelly D. Burr, Associate Director, Graduate Admissions, 610-683-4200, Fax: 610-683-1393, E-mail: graduate@kutztown.edu.

Lehman College of the City University of New York, Division of Education, Department of Middle and High School Education, Program in Social Studies 7–12, Bronx, NY 10468-1589. Offers MA. *Accreditation:* NCATE. *Entrance requirements:* For master's, minimum GPA of 3.0 in social sciences, 2.7 overall.

Le Moyne College, Department of Education, Syracuse, NY 13214. Offers adolescent education (MS Ed, MST); adolescent education/special education (MS Ed, MST); adolescent English (grades 7-12) (MST); adolescent history (grades 7-12) (MST); childhood education (MS Ed); childhood education/special education (MS Ed); elementary education (MS Ed); general professional education (MS Ed); inclusive childhood education (MST); literacy education (birth to grade 6) (MS Ed); literacy education (grades 5-12) (MS Ed); school building leadership (MS Ed, CAS); school district business leader (MS Ed, CAS); school district leadership (MS Ed, CAS); secondary education (MS Ed); special education (MS Ed); students with disabilities-generalist (grades 7-12) (MS Ed); TESOL (teaching English to speakers of other languages) (MS Ed); urban studies (MS Ed). *Accreditation:* Teacher Education Accreditation Council. Part-time and evening/weekend programs available. *Faculty:* 9 full-time (6 women), 51 part-time/adjunct (28 women). *Students:* 61 full-time (47 women), 311 part-time (222 women); includes 31 minority (19 Black or African American, non-Hispanic/Latino; 3 American Indian or Alaska Native, non-Hispanic/Latino; 4 Asian, non-Hispanic/Latino; 5 Hispanic/Latino), 2 international. Average age 30. 242 applicants, 90% accepted, 180 enrolled. In 2011, 168 master's, 23 CASs awarded. *Degree requirements:* For master's, thesis. *Entrance requirements:* For master's, GRE General Test, bachelor's degree, 2 letters of recommendation, written statement, transcripts. Additional exam requirements/recommendations for international students: Required—TOEFL (minimum score 550 paper-based; 213 computer-based; 79 iBT). *Application deadline:* For fall admission, 4/1 priority date for domestic students, 4/1 for international students; for spring admission, 10/1 priority date for domestic students, 10/1 for international students. Applications are processed on a rolling basis. Application fee: $50. *Expenses:* Contact institution. *Financial support:* In 2011–12, 32 students received support. Career-related internships or fieldwork and health care benefits available. Support available to part-time students. Financial award applicants required to submit FAFSA. *Faculty research:* Minority teachers, special education, multiculturalism, literacy, technology, video games learning, autism, school district organization, service-learning, higher level problem solving, teacher leadership. *Unit head:* Dr. Suzanne L. Gilmour, Chair, Department of Education and Director of Graduate Education Programs, 315-445-4376, Fax: 315-445-4744, E-mail: gilmous@lemoyne.edu. *Application contact:* Kristen P. Trapasso, Director of Graduate Admission, 315-445-4265, Fax: 315-445-6027, E-mail: trapaskp@lemoyne.edu. Web site: http://www.lemoyne.edu/education.

Lewis University, College of Education, Program in Secondary Education, Romeoville, IL 60446. Offers biology (MA); chemistry (MA); English (MA); history (MA); math (MA); physics (MA); psychology and social science (MA). Part-time programs available. *Students:* 17 full-time (11 women), 11 part-time (4 women); includes 4 minority (2 Black or African American, non-Hispanic/Latino; 2 Hispanic/Latino). Average age 30. In 2011, 7 master's awarded. *Entrance requirements:* For master's, departmental qualifying exam, writing exam, minimum GPA of 2.75, 2 letters of recommendation, interview. Additional exam requirements/recommendations for international students: Required—TOEFL (minimum score 550 paper-based; 213 computer-based; 80 iBT). *Application deadline:* For fall admission, 5/1 for international students; for spring admission, 11/15 for international students. Applications are processed on a rolling basis. Application fee: $40. Electronic applications accepted. *Financial support:* Federal Work-Study, scholarships/grants, and unspecified assistantships available. Financial award application deadline: 5/1; financial award applicants required to submit FAFSA. *Unit head:* Dr. Dorene Huvaere, Program Director, 815-838-0500 Ext. 5885, E-mail: huvaersdo@lewisu.edu. *Application contact:* Fran Welsh, Secretary, 815-838-0500 Ext. 5880, E-mail: welshfr@lewisu.edu.

Louisiana Tech University, Graduate School, College of Education, Department of Curriculum, Instruction and Leadership, Ruston, LA 71272. Offers curriculum and instruction (MS, Ed D); educational leadership (Ed D); secondary education (M Ed), including business education, English education, foreign language education, health and physical education, mathematics education, science education, social studies education, speech education. *Accreditation:* NCATE. Part-time programs available. *Degree requirements:* For doctorate, thesis/dissertation. *Entrance requirements:* For master's and doctorate, GRE General Test.

Manhattanville College, Graduate Studies, School of Education, Program in Middle Childhood/Adolescence Education (Grades 5-12), Purchase, NY 10577-2132. Offers biology (MAT); biology and special education (MPS); chemistry (MAT); chemistry and special education (MPS); English (MAT); English and special education (MPS); literacy (MPS), including reading and writing, writing; literacy and special education (MPS); math (MAT); math and special education (MPS); second language (MAT), including French, Italian, Latin, Spanish; social studies (MAT); social studies and special education (MPS); special education (MPS). Part-time and evening/weekend programs available. *Degree requirements:* For master's, comprehensive exam or research project, field experience. *Entrance requirements:* For master's, minimum undergraduate GPA of 3.0, 2 letters of recommendation. Additional exam requirements/recommendations for international students: Required—TOEFL. Electronic applications accepted.

Michigan State University, The Graduate School, College of Social Science, Department of History, East Lansing, MI 48824. Offers history (MA, PhD); history-secondary school teaching (MA). *Entrance requirements:* Additional exam requirements/recommendations for international students: Required—TOEFL. Electronic applications accepted.

Mills College, Graduate Studies, School of Education, Oakland, CA 94613-1000. Offers child life in hospitals (MA); early childhood education (MA); education (MA), including art education, curriculum and instruction, elementary education, English education, foreign language education, mathematics education, science education, secondary education, social studies education, teaching; educational leadership (MA, Ed D). Part-time and evening/weekend programs available. *Faculty:* 13 full-time (10 women), 14 part-time/adjunct (10 women). *Students:* 149 full-time (133 women), 69 part-time (61 women); includes 85 minority (32 Black or African American, non-Hispanic/Latino; 1 American Indian or Alaska Native, non-Hispanic/Latino; 16 Asian, non-Hispanic/Latino; 24 Hispanic/Latino; 1 Native Hawaiian or other Pacific Islander, non-Hispanic/Latino; 11 Two or more races, non-Hispanic/Latino), 3 international. Average age 28. 238 applicants, 84% accepted, 106 enrolled. In 2011, 41 master's, 2 doctorates awarded. Terminal master's awarded for partial completion of doctoral program. *Degree requirements:* For master's, comprehensive exam. *Entrance requirements:* For master's, statement of purpose, official transcript, 3 recommendations; for doctorate, GRE General Test. Additional exam requirements/recommendations for international students: Required—TOEFL (minimum score 550 paper-based; 80 iBT) or IELTS (minimum score 6). *Application deadline:* For fall admission, 12/31 priority date for domestic students, 12/15 for international students; for spring admission, 11/1 priority date for domestic students, 10/1 for international students. Applications are processed on a rolling basis. Application fee: $50. Electronic applications accepted. *Expenses: Tuition:* Full-time $28,280; part-time $15,640 per year. *Required fees:* $958. Tuition and fees vary according to program. *Financial support:* In 2011–12, 43 students received support, including 225 fellowships with full and partial tuition reimbursements available (averaging $6,020 per year), 43 teaching assistantships with full and partial tuition reimbursements available (averaging $6,782 per year); career-related internships or fieldwork and scholarships/grants also available. Support available to part-time students. Financial award application deadline: 2/1; financial award applicants required to submit FAFSA. *Faculty research:* Early childhood education, teacher preparation, educational leadership. *Total annual research expenditures:* $2.3 million. *Unit head:* Katherine Schultz, Chairperson, 510-430-3170, Fax: 510-430-3379, E-mail: grad-studies@mills.edu. *Application contact:* Tiana Kozoil, Graduate Admission Specialist, 510-430-3305, Fax: 510-430-2159, E-mail: grad-studies@mills.edu. Web site: http://www.mills.edu/education.

Minnesota State University Mankato, College of Graduate Studies, College of Social and Behavioral Sciences, Department of History, Mankato, MN 56001. Offers history (MA, MS); social studies (MAT). *Students:* 8 part-time (3 women). *Degree requirements:* For master's, one foreign language, comprehensive exam, thesis or alternative. *Entrance requirements:* For master's, minimum GPA of 3.0 during previous 2 years. Additional exam requirements/recommendations for international students: Required—TOEFL. *Application deadline:* For fall admission, 7/1 priority date for domestic students; for spring admission, 11/1 for domestic students. Applications are processed on a rolling basis. Application fee: $40. Electronic applications accepted. *Financial support:* Research assistantships, teaching assistantships with full tuition reimbursements, career-related internships or fieldwork, Federal Work-Study, institutionally sponsored loans, and unspecified assistantships available. Support available to part-time students. Financial award application deadline: 3/15. *Faculty research:* Charivaris, Lindbergh in the U. S., Dutch trade to South America in the seventeenth and eighteenth centuries. *Unit head:* Dr. Kathleen Gorman, Graduate Coordinator, 507-389-2720. *Application contact:* 507-389-2321, E-mail: grad@mnsu.edu. Web site: http://sbs.mnsu.edu/history/.

Mississippi College, Graduate School, School of Education, Department of Teacher Education and Leadership, Clinton, MS 39058. Offers art (M Ed); biological science (M Ed); business education (M Ed); computer science (M Ed); dyslexia therapy (M Ed); educational leadership (M Ed, Ed D, Ed S); elementary education (M Ed, Ed S); English (M Ed); higher education administration (MS); mathematics (M Ed); secondary education (M Ed); social studies (history) (M Ed); teaching arts (M Ed). Part-time programs available. Postbaccalaureate distance learning degree programs offered (no on-campus study). *Degree requirements:* For master's, comprehensive exam, thesis optional. *Entrance requirements:* For master's, NTE. Additional exam requirements/recommendations for international students: Recommended—TOEFL, IELTS. Electronic applications accepted.

Missouri State University, Graduate College, College of Humanities and Public Affairs, Department of History, Springfield, MO 65897. Offers history (MA); secondary education (MS Ed), including history, social science. Part-time programs available. *Faculty:* 18 full-time (5 women). *Students:* 19 full-time (8 women), 46 part-time (14 women); includes 3 minority (2 American Indian or Alaska Native, non-Hispanic/Latino; 1 Two or more races, non-Hispanic/Latino). Average age 31. 23 applicants, 87% accepted, 18 enrolled. In 2011, 17 master's awarded. *Degree requirements:* For master's, comprehensive exam, thesis or alternative. *Entrance requirements:* For master's, minimum GPA of 2.75, 24 hours of undergraduate course work in history (MA), 9-12 teaching certification (MS Ed). Additional exam requirements/recommendations for international students: Required—TOEFL (minimum score 550 paper-based; 213 computer-based; 79 iBT). *Application deadline:* For fall admission, 7/20 priority date for domestic students, 5/1 for international students; for spring admission, 12/20 priority date for domestic students, 9/1 for international students. Applications are processed on a rolling basis. Application fee: $35 ($50 for international students). Electronic applications accepted. *Expenses:* Tuition, state resident: full-time $4086; part-time $227 per credit hour. Tuition, nonresident: full-time $8172; part-time $454 per credit hour. *Required fees:* $275 per semester. Tuition and fees vary according to course load, campus/location and program. *Financial support:* In 2011–12, 1 teaching assistantship with full tuition reimbursement (averaging $8,000 per year) was awarded; Federal Work-Study, scholarships/grants, and unspecified assistantships also available. Support available to part-time students. Financial award application deadline: 3/31; financial award applicants required to submit FAFSA. *Faculty research:* U. S. history, Native American history, Latin American history, women's history, ancient Near East. *Unit head:* Dr. Kathleen Kennedy, Head, 417-836-5511, Fax: 417-836-5523, E-mail: history@missouristate.edu. *Application contact:* Misty Stewart, Coordinator of Graduate Recruitment, 417-836-6079, Fax: 417-836-6200, E-mail: mistystewart@missouristate.edu. Web site: http://history.missouristate.edu/.

Morehead State University, Graduate Programs, College of Education, Department of Foundational and Graduate Studies in Education, Morehead, KY 40351. Offers adult and higher education (MA, Ed S); certified professional counselor (Ed S); counseling P-12 (MA); curriculum and instruction (Ed S); educational technology (MA Ed); instructional leadership (Ed S); school administration (MA); school counseling (Ed S); teacher leader business and marketing content (MA Ed); teacher leader business and marketing technology (MA Ed); teacher leader educational technology (MA Ed); teacher leader English (MA Ed); teacher leader gifted education (MA Ed); teacher leader IECE certification (MA Ed); teacher leader interdisciplinary education P-5 (MA Ed); teacher leader middle grades (MA Ed); teacher leader non IECE certification (MA Ed); teacher leader reading/writing - non-certification (MA Ed); teacher leader reading/writing certification (MA Ed); teacher leader school communication - certification (MA Ed); teacher leader school communication - non-certification (MA Ed); teacher leader social studies (MA Ed); teacher leader special education (MA Ed). *Accreditation:* NCATE. Part-time and evening/weekend programs available. *Degree requirements:* For master's, thesis optional, oral and/or written comprehensive exams; for Ed S, thesis, oral exam. *Entrance requirements:* For master's, GRE General Test, minimum overall undergraduate GPA of 2.5; for Ed S, GRE General Test, interview, master's degree, minimum GPA of 3.5, work experience. Additional exam requirements/recommendations for international students: Required—TOEFL (minimum score 500 paper-based; 173 computer-based). Electronic applications accepted. *Faculty research:* Character education, school accountability, computer applications for school administrators.

Morehead State University, Graduate Programs, College of Education, Department of Middle Grades and Secondary Education, Morehead, KY 40351. Offers business and marketing education (MAT); English/language arts 5-9 (MAT); French (MAT); health P-12 (MAT); mathematics 5-9 (MAT); physical education P-12 (MAT); science 5-9 (MAT); secondary biology (MAT); secondary chemistry (MAT); secondary earth science (MAT); secondary English (MAT); secondary math (MAT); secondary physics (MAT); secondary social studies (MAT); social studies 5-9 (MAT); Spanish (MAT). Part-time and evening/weekend programs available. *Degree requirements:* For master's, portfolio. *Entrance requirements:* For master's, GRE or PRAXIS II content exam, minimum overall undergraduate GPA of 2.5. Additional exam requirements/recommendations for international students: Required—TOEFL (minimum score 500 paper-based; 173 computer-based). Electronic applications accepted.

New York University, Steinhardt School of Culture, Education, and Human Development, Department of Music and Performing Arts Professions, Program in Educational Theatre, New York, NY 10012-1019. Offers dual certification: educational theatre and English 7-12 (MA); dual certification: educational theatre and social studies (MA); educational theatre (Ed D, PhD, Advanced Certificate); educational theatre for colleges and communities (MA); teaching educational theatre, all grades (MA). Part-time programs available. *Degree requirements:* For master's, thesis (for some programs); for doctorate, thesis/dissertation. *Entrance requirements:* For master's, audition; for doctorate, GRE General Test, interview; for Advanced Certificate, master's degree. Additional exam requirements/recommendations for international students: Required—TOEFL. Electronic applications accepted. *Faculty research:* Theatre for young audiences, drama in education, applied theatre, arts education assessment, reflective praxis.

New York University, Steinhardt School of Culture, Education, and Human Development, Department of Teaching and Learning, Program in Social Studies Education, New York, NY 10012-1019. Offers MA. *Accreditation:* Teacher Education Accreditation Council. Part-time and evening/weekend programs available. *Degree requirements:* For master's, thesis (for some programs). *Entrance requirements:* Additional exam requirements/recommendations for international students: Required—TOEFL. Electronic applications accepted. *Faculty research:* Social studies education reform, ethnography and oral history, civic education, labor history and social studies curriculum, material culture.

North Carolina State University, Graduate School, College of Education, Department of Curriculum and Instruction, Program in Social Studies Education, Raleigh, NC 27695.

Social Sciences Education

Offers M Ed. *Entrance requirements:* For master's, GRE or MAT, 3 letters of reference, interview, minimum GPA of 3.0.

North Dakota State University, College of Graduate and Interdisciplinary Studies, College of Human Development and Education, School of Education, Fargo, ND 58108. Offers agricultural education (M Ed, MS), including agricultural education, agricultural extension education (MS); counseling (M Ed, MS, PhD); curriculum and instruction (M Ed, MS), including pedagogy, physical education and athletic administration; education (PhD); educational leadership (M Ed, MS, Ed S); family and consumer sciences education (M Ed, MS); history education (M Ed, MS); institutional analysis (Ed D); mathematics education (M Ed, MS); music education (M Ed, MS); occupational and adult education (Ed D); science education (M Ed, MS). *Accreditation:* NCATE. Part-time and evening/weekend programs available. Postbaccalaureate distance learning degree programs offered (minimal on-campus study). *Faculty:* 24 full-time (10 women), 2 part-time/adjunct (1 woman). *Students:* 91 full-time (64 women), 114 part-time (78 women); includes 13 minority (4 Black or African American, non-Hispanic/Latino; 5 American Indian or Alaska Native, non-Hispanic/Latino; 1 Hispanic/Latino; 3 Two or more races, non-Hispanic/Latino), 8 international. 88 applicants, 67% accepted, 56 enrolled. In 2011, 43 master's, 12 doctorates awarded. *Degree requirements:* For master's, comprehensive exam; for doctorate, thesis/dissertation; for Ed S, thesis. *Entrance requirements:* For degree, GRE General Test, master's degree, minimum GPA of 3.25. Additional exam requirements/recommendations for international students: Required—TOEFL. *Application deadline:* Applications are processed on a rolling basis. Application fee: $45 ($60 for international students). *Financial support:* Research assistantships, teaching assistantships, career-related internships or fieldwork, Federal Work-Study, institutionally sponsored loans, and tuition waivers (full) available. Financial award application deadline: 4/15. *Unit head:* Dr. William Martin, Chair, 701-231-7202, Fax: 701-231-7416, E-mail: william.martin@ndsu.edu. *Application contact:* Sonya Goergen, Marketing, Recruitment, and Public Relations Coordinator, 701-231-7033, Fax: 701-231-6524. Web site: http://www.ndsu.nodak.edu/school_of_education/.

North Georgia College & State University, School of Education, Dahlonega, GA 30597. Offers art education (MAT); early childhood education (M Ed); English education (MAT); history education (MAT); math education (MAT); middle grades education (M Ed, MAT); physical education (MS); school leadership (Ed S); secondary education (M Ed), including English education, history education, mathematics education, physical education; teacher education (MAT). *Accreditation:* NCATE. Part-time and evening/weekend programs available. Postbaccalaureate distance learning degree programs offered (no on-campus study). *Faculty:* 23 full-time (14 women), 16 part-time/adjunct (11 women). *Students:* 19 full-time (17 women), 199 part-time (147 women); includes 7 minority (3 Black or African American, non-Hispanic/Latino; 1 Asian, non-Hispanic/Latino; 3 Hispanic/Latino), 1 international. Average age 34. 259 applicants, 66% accepted, 112 enrolled. In 2011, 100 master's, 16 other advanced degrees awarded. *Degree requirements:* For master's, comprehensive exam, thesis optional. *Entrance requirements:* For master's, GRE or MAT, GACE, minimum GPA of 2.75; for Ed S, GRE General Test or MAT, 3 years of teaching experience, master's degree, minimum graduate GPA of 3.25, leadership position in the school. Additional exam requirements/recommendations for international students: Required—TOEFL (minimum score 550 paper-based; 213 computer-based; 79 iBT), IELTS (minimum score 6.5). *Application deadline:* For fall admission, 8/1 priority date for domestic students, 7/1 for international students; for spring admission, 12/1 priority date for domestic students, 11/1 for international students. Applications are processed on a rolling basis. Application fee: $40. Electronic applications accepted. *Expenses:* Tuition, state resident: full-time $3528; part-time $196 per credit hour. Tuition, nonresident: full-time $14,094; part-time $783 per credit hour. *Required fees:* $1718; $859 per semester. Tuition and fees vary according to course load, campus/location and program. *Financial support:* Teaching assistantships, career-related internships or fieldwork, scholarships/grants, and unspecified assistantships available. Financial award application deadline: 5/1; financial award applicants required to submit CSS PROFILE or FAFSA. *Faculty research:* Identification of professional development school structures supporting P-12 student achievement, impact of diverse field placement settings in teacher belief development among preservice teachers, use of inquiry methodology in social studies teaching with English language learners, use of instructional differentiation in the middle grades classroom, effects of international school placements on preservice teacher beliefs and attitudes. *Unit head:* Dr. Bob Michael, Dean, School of Education, 706-864-1998, Fax: 706-867-2850, E-mail: bmichael@northgeorgia.edu. *Application contact:* Susan L. Perry, Graduate Admissions Coordinator, 706-864-1543, Fax: 706-867-2795, E-mail: slperry@northgeorgia.edu. Web site: http://www.northgeorgia.edu/soe/.

Northwest Missouri State University, Graduate School, College of Arts and Sciences, Department of History, Humanities, and Political Science, Maryville, MO 64468-6001. Offers history (MA); teaching history (MS Ed). Part-time programs available. *Faculty:* 11 full-time (2 women). *Students:* 11 full-time (5 women), 5 part-time (3 women); includes 1 minority (Two or more races, non-Hispanic/Latino), 1 international. 9 applicants, 100% accepted, 3 enrolled. In 2011, 2 master's awarded. *Degree requirements:* For master's, comprehensive exam, thesis. *Entrance requirements:* For master's, GRE General Test, undergraduate major/minor in social studies/humanities, minimum undergraduate GPA of 2.5, writing sample. Additional exam requirements/recommendations for international students: Required—TOEFL (minimum score 550 paper-based; 213 computer-based). *Application deadline:* For fall admission, 7/1 for domestic and international students; for spring admission, 11/15 for domestic and international students. Applications are processed on a rolling basis. Application fee: $0 ($50 for international students). *Financial support:* In 2011–12, research assistantships with full tuition reimbursements (averaging $6,000 per year), 1 teaching assistantship with full tuition reimbursement (averaging $600 per year) was awarded. Financial award application deadline: 4/1; financial award applicants required to submit FAFSA. *Unit head:* Dr. Michael Steiner, Chairperson, 660-562-1288. *Application contact:* Dr. Gregory Haddock, Dean of Graduate School, 660-562-1145, Fax: 660-562-1096, E-mail: gradsch@nwmissouri.edu.

Occidental College, Graduate Studies, Department of Education, Program in Secondary Education, Los Angeles, CA 90041-3314. Offers English and comparative literary studies (MAT); history (MAT); life science (MAT); mathematics (MAT); physical science (MAT); social science (MAT); Spanish (MAT). Part-time programs available. *Degree requirements:* For master's, comprehensive exam, graduate synthesis paper. *Entrance requirements:* For master's, GRE General Test, minimum GPA of 3.0. Additional exam requirements/recommendations for international students: Required—TOEFL (minimum score 625 paper-based; 263 computer-based). *Expenses:* Contact institution.

Ohio University, Graduate College, Gladys W. and David H. Patton College of Education and Human Services, Department of Teacher Education, Athens, OH 45701-2979. Offers adolescent to young adult education (M Ed); curriculum and instruction (M Ed, PhD); early childhood/special education (M Ed); intervention specialist/mild-moderate needs (M Ed); intervention specialist/moderate-intensive needs (M Ed); mathematics education (PhD); middle child education (M Ed); reading education (M Ed); social studies education (PhD). Part-time and evening/weekend programs available. *Students:* 131 full-time (92 women), 82 part-time (62 women); includes 9 minority (4 Black or African American, non-Hispanic/Latino; 2 American Indian or Alaska Native, non-Hispanic/Latino; 1 Asian, non-Hispanic/Latino; 1 Hispanic/Latino; 1 Two or more races, non-Hispanic/Latino), 11 international. 136 applicants, 70% accepted, 65 enrolled. In 2011, 58 master's, 8 doctorates awarded. *Degree requirements:* For master's, thesis or alternative; for doctorate, comprehensive exam, thesis/dissertation. *Entrance requirements:* For master's, GRE General Test or MAT (if GPA is below 2.9); for doctorate, GRE General Test, minimum GPA of 3.4, work experience. Additional exam requirements/recommendations for international students: Required—TOEFL (minimum score 550 paper-based; 80 iBT) or IELTS (minimum score 6.5). *Application deadline:* For fall admission, 5/1 priority date for domestic students, 4/1 for international students; for winter admission, 11/1 priority date for domestic students, 10/1 for international students; for spring admission, 2/15 priority date for domestic students, 1/1 for international students. Applications are processed on a rolling basis. Application fee: $50 ($55 for international students). Electronic applications accepted. *Financial support:* Research assistantships with full tuition reimbursements, teaching assistantships with full tuition reimbursements, Federal Work-Study, institutionally sponsored loans, tuition waivers (partial), and unspecified assistantships available. Financial award application deadline: 3/1. *Faculty research:* Cognition literacy, character education, teacher's education reform, disabilities. *Total annual research expenditures:* $46,933. *Unit head:* Dr. John Henning, Chair, 740-597-1830, Fax: 740-593-0477, E-mail: henningj@ohio.edu. *Application contact:* Floyd J. Doney, Director of Student Affairs, 740-593-4400, Fax: 740-593-9310, E-mail: doney@ohio.edu. Web site: http://www.cehs.ohio.edu/academics/te/index.htm.

Portland State University, Graduate Studies, College of Liberal Arts and Sciences, Interdisciplinary Programs in General Science, General Social Science, and General Arts and Letters, Portland, OR 97207-0751. Offers general arts and letters education (MAT, MST); general science education (MAT, MST); general social science education (MAT, MST). Part-time and evening/weekend programs available. *Degree requirements:* For master's, variable foreign language requirement, written exam. *Entrance requirements:* For master's, minimum GPA of 3.0 in upper-division course work or 2.75 overall. Additional exam requirements/recommendations for international students: Required—TOEFL (minimum score 550 paper-based; 213 computer-based).

Purdue University, Graduate School, College of Education, Department of Curriculum and Instruction, West Lafayette, IN 47907. Offers agricultural and extension education (PhD, Ed S); agriculture and extension education (MS, MS Ed); art education (PhD); consumer and family sciences and extension education (MS Ed, PhD, Ed S); curriculum studies (MS Ed, PhD, Ed S); educational technology (MS Ed, PhD, Ed S); elementary education (MS Ed); foreign language education (MS Ed, PhD, Ed S); industrial technology (PhD, Ed S); language arts (MS Ed, PhD, Ed S); literacy (MS Ed, PhD, Ed S); mathematics/science education (MS, MS Ed, PhD, Ed S); social studies (MS Ed, PhD); social studies education (Ed S); vocational/industrial education (MS Ed, PhD, Ed S); vocational/technical education (MS Ed, PhD, Ed S). *Accreditation:* NCATE. Part-time and evening/weekend programs available. *Faculty:* 30 full-time (21 women), 1 (woman) part-time/adjunct. *Students:* 89 full-time (64 women), 134 part-time (84 women); includes 31 minority (12 Black or African American, non-Hispanic/Latino; 3 American Indian or Alaska Native, non-Hispanic/Latino; 7 Asian, non-Hispanic/Latino; 9 Hispanic/Latino), 49 international. Average age 36. 136 applicants, 83% accepted, 72 enrolled. In 2011, 26 master's, 13 doctorates awarded. *Degree requirements:* For master's, thesis optional; for doctorate, thesis/dissertation, oral and written exams; for Ed S, oral presentation, project. *Entrance requirements:* For master's, GRE general test is required if undergraduate GPA is below 3.0, minimum undergraduate GPA of 3.0 or equivalent; for doctorate, GRE General Test, a combined GRE verbal and quantitative score of 1000 (300 for revised GRE Test) or more is expected, minimum undergraduate GPA of 3.0 or equivalent; master's degree with minimum GPA of 3.0 or equivalent; for Ed S, GRE general test, a combined GRE verbal and quantitative score of 1000 (300 for revised GRE Test) or more is expected, minimum undergraduate GPA of 3.0 or equivalent; master's degree. Additional exam requirements/recommendations for international students: Required—TOEFL (minimum score 550 paper-based; 77 iBT). *Application deadline:* For fall admission, 12/15 priority date for domestic students, 3/1 for international students; for spring admission, 9/15 for domestic students, 8/1 for international students. Application fee: $60 ($75 for international students). Electronic applications accepted. *Financial support:* Fellowships with full tuition reimbursements, research assistantships with full tuition reimbursements, teaching assistantships with full tuition reimbursements, career-related internships or fieldwork, and tuition waivers (full) available. Support available to part-time students. Financial award application deadline: 3/1; financial award applicants required to submit FAFSA. *Faculty research:* Literacy acquisition and development, teacher beliefs and knowledge, recruitment and retention of underrepresented students, economic education, literacy discourse. *Unit head:* Dr. Philip J. VanFossen, Head, 765-494-7935, Fax: 765-496-1622, E-mail: vanfoss@purdue.edu. *Application contact:* Sarah N. Prater, Graduate Contact, 765-494-2345, Fax: 765-494-5832, E-mail: prater0@purdue.edu. Web site: http://www.edci.purdue.edu/.

Queens College of the City University of New York, Division of Graduate Studies, Division of Education, Department of Secondary Education, Flushing, NY 11367-1597. Offers art (MS Ed); biology (MS Ed, AC); chemistry (MS Ed, AC); earth sciences (MS Ed, AC); English (MS Ed, AC); French (MS Ed, AC); Italian (MS Ed, AC); mathematics (MS Ed, AC); music (MS Ed, AC); physics (MS Ed, AC); social studies (MS Ed, AC); Spanish (MS Ed, AC). Part-time and evening/weekend programs available. *Faculty:* 22 full-time (14 women). *Students:* 46 full-time (23 women), 727 part-time (442 women); includes 234 minority (41 Black or African American, non-Hispanic/Latino; 78 Asian, non-Hispanic/Latino; 115 Hispanic/Latino), 5 international. 591 applicants, 60% accepted, 250 enrolled. In 2011, 170 master's awarded. *Degree requirements:* For master's, research project; for AC, thesis optional. *Entrance requirements:* For master's, minimum GPA of 3.0. Additional exam requirements/recommendations for international students: Required—TOEFL. *Application deadline:* For fall admission, 4/1 for domestic students; for spring admission, 11/1 for domestic students. Applications are processed on a rolling basis. Application fee: $125. *Expenses:* Tuition, state resident: part-time $345 per credit. Tuition, nonresident: part-time $640 per credit. *Required fees:* $145.25 per semester. *Financial support:* Career-related internships or fieldwork, Federal Work-Study, institutionally sponsored loans, and tuition waivers (partial) available. Support available to part-time students. Financial award application deadline: 4/1; financial award applicants required to submit FAFSA. *Unit head:* Dr. Eleanor Armour-Thomas, Chairperson, 718-997-5150, E-mail: armourthomas@yahoo.com. *Application contact:* Mario Caruso, Director of Graduate Admissions, 718-997-5200, Fax: 718-997-5193, E-mail: graduate_admissions@qc.edu.

Quinnipiac University, School of Education, Program in Secondary Education, Hamden, CT 06518-1940. Offers biology (MAT); English (MAT); history/social studies (MAT); mathematics (MAT); Spanish (MAT). *Accreditation:* NCATE. *Faculty:* 7 full-time (5 women), 41 part-time/adjunct (24 women). *Students:* 56 full-time (38 women), 1 (woman) part-time; includes 5 minority (1 Black or African American, non-Hispanic/Latino; 1 Asian, non-Hispanic/Latino; 3 Hispanic/Latino). 51 applicants, 96% accepted, 44 enrolled. In 2011, 49 master's awarded. *Entrance requirements:* For master's, PRAXIS I, minimum GPA of 2.67, interview. *Application deadline:* For fall admission, 3/31 priority date for domestic students. Applications are processed on a rolling basis.

Application fee: $45. Electronic applications accepted. *Expenses: Tuition:* Part-time $855 per credit. *Required fees:* $35 per credit. *Financial support:* In 2011–12, 1 student received support. Career-related internships or fieldwork, scholarships/grants, and tuition waivers (full and partial) available. Financial award application deadline: 4/15; financial award applicants required to submit FAFSA. *Faculty research:* Multicultural and urban education/leadership, challenges of teaching diverse learners, scholarship of teaching and learning, technology and teaching, humor and education. *Unit head:* Mordechai Gordon, Program Director, 203-582-8442, Fax: 203-582-3473, E-mail: mordechai.gordon@quinnipiac.edu. *Application contact:* Jennifer Boutin, Associate Director of Graduate Admissions, 800-462-1944, Fax: 203-582-3443, E-mail: jennifer.boutin@quinnipiac.edu. Web site: http://www.quinnipiac.edu/academics/colleges-schools-and-departments/school-of-education/graduate-programs/five-semester-mat-programs/secondary-educat.

Rhode Island College, School of Graduate Studies, Feinstein School of Education and Human Development, Department of Educational Studies, Providence, RI 02908-1991. Offers advanced studies in teaching and learning (M Ed); English (MAT); French (MAT); history (MAT); math (MAT); secondary education (MAT); Spanish (MAT); teaching English as a second language (M Ed). *Accreditation:* NCATE. Part-time and evening/weekend programs available. *Faculty:* 14 full-time (7 women), 4 part-time/adjunct (2 women). *Students:* 10 full-time (all women), 61 part-time (51 women); includes 8 minority (1 Black or African American, non-Hispanic/Latino; 4 Asian, non-Hispanic/Latino; 3 Hispanic/Latino). Average age 33. In 2011, 32 master's awarded. *Degree requirements:* For master's, capstone or comprehensive assessment. *Entrance requirements:* For master's, GRE or MAT (for most programs), minimum undergraduate GPA of 3.0; baccalaureate degree in English, French, history, math or Spanish; evaluation of content area knowledge; 3 letters of recommendation; interview. Additional exam requirements/recommendations for international students: Recommended—TOEFL (minimum score 550 paper-based; 213 computer-based; 79 iBT). *Application deadline:* For fall admission, 3/1 for domestic students; for spring admission, 11/1 for domestic students. Applications are processed on a rolling basis. Application fee: $50. *Expenses:* Tuition, state resident: full-time $8592; part-time $358 per credit hour. Tuition, nonresident: full-time $16,800; part-time $700 per credit hour. *Required fees:* $602; $22 per credit. $72 per term. *Financial support:* Teaching assistantships with full tuition reimbursements, career-related internships or fieldwork, Federal Work-Study, scholarships/grants, health care benefits, and unspecified assistantships available. Support available to part-time students. Financial award application deadline: 5/15; financial award applicants required to submit FAFSA. *Faculty research:* School administration, school/college articulation. *Unit head:* Dr. Ellen Bigler, Chair, 401-456-8170. *Application contact:* Graduate Studies, 401-456-8700. Web site: http://www.ric.edu/educationalStudies/.

Rider University, Department of Graduate Education, Leadership and Counseling, Teacher Certification Program, Lawrenceville, NJ 08648-3001. Offers business education (Certificate); elementary education (Certificate); English as a second language (Certificate); English education (Certificate); mathematics education (Certificate); preschool to grade 3 (Certificate); science education (Certificate); social studies education (Certificate); world languages (Certificate), including French, German, Spanish. Part-time programs available. *Degree requirements:* For Certificate, internship, professional portfolio. *Entrance requirements:* For degree, PRAXIS, resume. Additional exam requirements/recommendations for international students: Required—TOEFL (minimum score 550 paper-based; 213 computer-based). Electronic applications accepted. *Expenses: Tuition:* Full-time $32,820; part-time $710 per credit. *Required fees:* $350; $35 per course. Tuition and fees vary according to campus/location and program. *Faculty research:* Conceptual foundations for optimal development of creativity; creative theory, cognitive processes in mathematics learning, teacher collaboration.

Rivier University, School of Graduate Studies, Department of History, Law and Government, Nashua, NH 03060. Offers social studies education (MAT).

Rutgers, The State University of New Jersey, New Brunswick, Graduate School of Education, Department of Educational Theory, Policy and Administration, Program in Social Studies Education, Piscataway, NJ 08854-8097. Offers Ed M, Ed D. Part-time and evening/weekend programs available. Terminal master's awarded for partial completion of doctoral program. *Degree requirements:* For master's, comprehensive exam; for doctorate, thesis/dissertation, qualifying exam. *Entrance requirements:* For master's and doctorate, GRE General Test. Additional exam requirements/recommendations for international students: Required—TOEFL. Electronic applications accepted. *Faculty research:* Academic freedom, equal educational opportunity, social studies curricula.

Sage Graduate School, Esteves School of Education, Program in Teaching, Troy, NY 12180-4115. Offers art education (MAT); English (MAT); mathematics (MAT); social studies (MAT). *Accreditation:* NASAD. Part-time and evening/weekend programs available. *Faculty:* 10 full-time (6 women), 6 part-time/adjunct (4 women). *Students:* 19 full-time (15 women), 20 part-time (16 women); includes 1 minority (Asian, non-Hispanic/Latino). Average age 27. 44 applicants, 36% accepted, 8 enrolled. In 2011, 37 master's awarded. *Entrance requirements:* For master's, assessment of writing skills, minimum undergraduate GPA of 2.75 overall, 3.0 in content area; current resume; 2 letters of recommendation. Additional exam requirements/recommendations for international students: Required—TOEFL (minimum score 550 paper-based; 213 computer-based). *Application deadline:* For fall admission, 8/1 for domestic students. Applications are processed on a rolling basis. Application fee: $40. *Expenses: Tuition:* Full-time $11,880; part-time $660 per credit hour. Tuition and fees vary according to program. *Financial support:* Fellowships, research assistantships, Federal Work-Study, scholarships/grants, and unspecified assistantships available. Support available to part-time students. Financial award application deadline: 3/1; financial award applicants required to submit FAFSA. *Unit head:* Dr. Lori Quigley, Dean, Esteves School of Education, 518-244-2326, Fax: 518-244-4571, E-mail: l.quigley@sage.edu. *Application contact:* Kelly Jones, Director, 518-244-2433, Fax: 518-244-6880, E-mail: jonesk4@sage.edu.

St. John Fisher College, Ralph C. Wilson Jr. School of Education, Program in Adolescence Education/Special Education, Rochester, NY 14618-3597. Offers adolescence English (MS Ed); adolescence French (MS Ed); adolescence social studies (MS Ed); adolescence Spanish (MS Ed). Part-time and evening/weekend programs available. *Faculty:* 5 full-time (3 women), 2 part-time/adjunct (both women). *Students:* 25 full-time (13 women), 1 (woman) part-time. Average age 22. 19 applicants, 79% accepted, 11 enrolled. In 2011, 18 master's awarded. *Degree requirements:* For master's, field experiences, student teaching, LAST. *Entrance requirements:* For master's, 2 letters of recommendation, personal statement, current resume. Additional exam requirements/recommendations for international students: Required—TOEFL (minimum score 575 paper-based; 233 computer-based; 80 iBT). *Application deadline:* Applications are processed on a rolling basis. Application fee: $30. Electronic applications accepted. *Expenses: Tuition:* Part-time $735 per credit. One-time fee: $50 part-time. Tuition and fees vary according to course load, degree level and program. *Financial support:* In 2011–12, 5 students received support. Scholarships/grants available. Financial award applicants required to submit FAFSA. *Faculty research:* Arts and humanities, urban schools, constructivist learning, at risk students, mentoring. *Unit head:* Dr. Susan Schultz, Program Director, 585-385-7296, E-mail: sschultz@sjfc.edu. *Application contact:* Jose Perales, Director of Graduate Admissions, 585-385-8067, E-mail: jperales@sjfc.edu. Web site: http://www.sjfc.edu/academics/education/departments/ms-special-ed/options/initial-adolescence.dot.

Slippery Rock University of Pennsylvania, Graduate Studies (Recruitment), College of Education, Department of Secondary Education/Foundations of Education, Slippery Rock, PA 16057-1383. Offers educational leadership (M Ed); secondary education in English (M Ed); secondary education in math/science (M Ed); secondary education in social studies (M Ed). *Accreditation:* NCATE. Part-time and evening/weekend programs available. *Faculty:* 9 full-time (4 women), 3 part-time/adjunct (0 women). *Students:* 64 full-time (34 women), 16 part-time (8 women); includes 2 minority (1 Asian, non-Hispanic/Latino; 1 Two or more races, non-Hispanic/Latino). Average age 28. 68 applicants, 76% accepted, 27 enrolled. In 2011, 54 degrees awarded. *Degree requirements:* For master's, comprehensive exam, thesis (for some programs). *Entrance requirements:* For master's, GRE General Test, MAT, minimum GPA of 2.8 (depending on program). Additional exam requirements/recommendations for international students: Required—TOEFL (minimum score 550 paper-based; 213 computer-based; 80 iBT). *Application deadline:* For fall admission, 3/1 priority date for domestic students, 5/1 for international students; for spring admission, 10/1 priority date for domestic students, 9/1 for international students. Applications are processed on a rolling basis. Application fee: $25 ($30 for international students). Electronic applications accepted. *Expenses:* Tuition, state resident: full-time $7488; part-time $416 per credit. Tuition, nonresident: full-time $11,232; part-time $624 per credit. *International tuition:* $11,146 full-time. *Required fees:* $2722; $140 per credit. Tuition and fees vary according to degree level and program. *Financial support:* Career-related internships or fieldwork, Federal Work-Study, institutionally sponsored loans, scholarships/grants, tuition waivers (partial), and unspecified assistantships available. Support available to part-time students. Financial award application deadline: 5/1; financial award applicants required to submit FAFSA. *Unit head:* Dr. Jeffrey Lehman, Graduate Coordinator, 724-738-2311, Fax: 724-738-4987, E-mail: jeffrey.lehman@sru.edu. *Application contact:* Angela Barrett, Interim Director of Graduate Studies, 724-738-2051, Fax: 724-738-2146, E-mail: graduate.admissions@sru.edu.

Smith College, Graduate and Special Programs, Department of Education and Child Study, Program in Secondary Education, Northampton, MA 01063. Offers biological sciences education (MAT); chemistry education (MAT); English education (MAT); French education (MAT); geology education (MAT); government education (MAT); history education (MAT); mathematics education (MAT); physics education (MAT); Spanish education (MAT). Part-time programs available. *Faculty:* 6 full-time (4 women), 3 part-time/adjunct (2 women). *Students:* 11 full-time (8 women), 3 part-time (all women); includes 2 minority (1 Asian, non-Hispanic/Latino; 1 Hispanic/Latino). Average age 26. 21 applicants, 95% accepted, 12 enrolled. In 2011, 2 master's awarded. *Entrance requirements:* For master's, GRE. Additional exam requirements/recommendations for international students: Required—TOEFL (minimum score 590 paper-based; 243 computer-based; 97 iBT). *Application deadline:* For fall admission, 4/1 for domestic students, 1/15 for international students; for spring admission, 12/1 for domestic students. Application fee: $60. *Expenses: Tuition:* Full-time $14,925; part-time $1245 per credit. *Financial support:* In 2011–12, 13 students received support. Career-related internships or fieldwork, institutionally sponsored loans, and scholarships/grants available. Support available to part-time students. Financial award application deadline: 1/15; financial award applicants required to submit CSS PROFILE or FAFSA. *Unit head:* Rosetta Cohen, Graduate Student Advisor, 413-585-3266, E-mail: rcohen@smith.edu. *Application contact:* Ruth Morgan, Administrative Assistant, 413-585-3050, Fax: 413-585-3054, E-mail: gradstdy@smith.edu. Web site: http://www.smith.edu/educ/.

South Carolina State University, School of Graduate Studies, Department of Education, Orangeburg, SC 29117-0001. Offers counseling education (M Ed); early childhood and special education (M Ed); early childhood education (MAT); educational leadership (Ed D, Ed S); elementary education (M Ed, MAT); engineering (MAT); general science (MAT); mathematics (MAT); secondary education (M Ed), including biology education, business education, counselor education, English education, home economics education, industrial education, mathematics education, science education, social studies education; special education (M Ed), including emotionally handicapped, learning disabilities, mentally handicapped. *Accreditation:* NCATE. Part-time and evening/weekend programs available. *Faculty:* 9 full-time (6 women), 6 part-time/adjunct (2 women). *Students:* 34 full-time (29 women), 50 part-time (40 women); includes 74 minority (72 Black or African American, non-Hispanic/Latino; 1 Asian, non-Hispanic/Latino; 1 Hispanic/Latino). Average age 34. 23 applicants, 91% accepted, 14 enrolled. In 2011, 11 master's awarded. *Degree requirements:* For master's, thesis optional, departmental qualifying exam. *Entrance requirements:* For master's, GRE General Test, NTE, interview, teaching certificate. *Application deadline:* For fall admission, 6/15 priority date for domestic students, 6/15 for international students; for spring admission, 11/1 for domestic and international students. Applications are processed on a rolling basis. Application fee: $25. Electronic applications accepted. *Expenses:* Tuition, state resident: full-time $8688; part-time $514 per credit hour. Tuition, nonresident: full-time $17,600; part-time $1009 per credit hour. *Required fees:* $570. *Financial support:* In 2011–12, 3 fellowships (averaging $5,020 per year) were awarded; career-related internships or fieldwork, Federal Work-Study, and institutionally sponsored loans also available. Financial award application deadline: 6/1. *Faculty research:* Critical thinking, child abuse, stress, test-taking skills, conflict resolution, mainstreaming. *Unit head:* Dr. Charlie Spell, Interim Chair, 803-536-7098, Fax: 803-516-4568, E-mail: cspell@scsu.edu. *Application contact:* Annette Hazzard-Jones, Program Coordinator II, 803-536-8809, Fax: 803-536-8812, E-mail: zs_ahazzard@scsu.edu.

Southern Illinois University Edwardsville, Graduate School, School of Education, Department of Curriculum and Instruction, Program in Secondary Education, Edwardsville, IL 62026. Offers art (MS Ed); biology (MS Ed); chemistry (MS Ed); earth and space sciences (MS Ed); English/language arts (MS Ed); foreign languages (MS Ed); history (MS Ed); mathematics (MS Ed); physics (MS Ed). *Accreditation:* NCATE. Part-time and evening/weekend programs available. *Students:* 1 full-time (0 women), 42 part-time (33 women); includes 2 minority (both Black or African American, non-Hispanic/Latino). 16 applicants, 31% accepted. In 2011, 8 master's awarded. *Degree requirements:* For master's, comprehensive exam (for some programs), final exam/paper. *Entrance requirements:* Additional exam requirements/recommendations for international students: Required—TOEFL (minimum score 550 paper-based; 213 computer-based; 79 iBT), IELTS (minimum score 6.5). *Application deadline:* For fall admission, 7/22 for domestic students, 6/1 for international students; for spring admission, 12/9 for domestic students, 10/1 for international students. Applications are processed on a rolling basis. Application fee: $30. Electronic applications accepted. Tuition and fees vary according to course load and program. *Financial support:* Fellowships, research assistantships, teaching assistantships, institutionally sponsored loans, scholarships/grants, and unspecified assistantships available. Financial award application deadline: 3/1; financial award applicants required to submit FAFSA. *Unit head:* Dr. Susan Breck, Director, 618-650-3444, E-mail: sbreck@siue.edu. *Application contact:* Dr. Michelle Robinson, Coordinator of Graduate Recruitment, 618-650-2811, Fax: 618-650-3523, E-mail: michero@siue.edu. Web site: http://www.siue.edu/education/ci/.

Social Sciences Education

Southwestern Oklahoma State University, College of Arts and Sciences, Department of Social Sciences, Weatherford, OK 73096-3098. Offers M Ed. *Degree requirements:* For master's, exam. *Entrance requirements:* For master's, GRE General Test or minimum undergraduate GPA of 3.0. Additional exam requirements/recommendations for international students: Required—TOEFL.

Spring Hill College, Graduate Programs, Program in Liberal Arts, Mobile, AL 36608-1791. Offers fine arts (MLA); history and social science (MLA); leadership and ethics (MLA, Postbaccalaureate Certificate); literature (MLA); studio art (Postbaccalaureate Certificate). Part-time and evening/weekend programs available. *Faculty:* 1 full-time (0 women), 4 part-time/adjunct (2 women). *Students:* 3 full-time (1 woman), 37 part-time (24 women); includes 9 minority (7 Black or African American, non-Hispanic/Latino; 1 American Indian or Alaska Native, non-Hispanic/Latino; 1 Native Hawaiian or other Pacific Islander, non-Hispanic/Latino). Average age 35. In 2011, 20 master's, 7 other advanced degrees awarded. *Degree requirements:* For master's, capstone course, completion of program within 6 years of initial admittance. *Entrance requirements:* For master's, bachelor's degree with minimum undergraduate GPA of 3.0 or graduate/professional degree. Additional exam requirements/recommendations for international students: Required—TOEFL (minimum score 550 paper-based; 213 computer-based; 80 iBT), IELTS (minimum score 6.5), CPE or CAE (minimum score C), Michigan English Language Assessment Battery (minimum score 90). *Application deadline:* For fall admission, 8/1 priority date for domestic students, 8/1 for international students; for spring admission, 12/1 priority date for domestic students, 12/1 for international students. Applications are processed on a rolling basis. Application fee: $25 ($35 for international students). Electronic applications accepted. *Expenses:* Contact institution. *Financial support:* Applicants required to submit FAFSA. *Unit head:* Dr. Alexander R. Landi, Director, 251-380-3056, Fax: 251-460-2115, E-mail: landi@shc.edu. *Application contact:* Donna B. Tarasavage, Director of Admissions, Graduate and Continuing Studies, 251-380-3067, Fax: 251-460-2190, E-mail: dtarasavage@shc.edu. Web site: http://www.shc.edu/grad/academics/liberal-arts.

Stanford University, School of Education, Program in Curriculum Studies and Teacher Education, Stanford, CA 94305-9991. Offers art education (MA, PhD); dance education (MA); English education (MA, PhD); general curriculum studies (MA, PhD); mathematics education (MA, PhD); science education (MA, PhD); social studies education (PhD); teacher education (MA, PhD). *Degree requirements:* For master's, thesis (for some programs); for doctorate, thesis/dissertation. *Entrance requirements:* For master's and doctorate, GRE General Test. Electronic applications accepted. *Expenses: Tuition:* Full-time $40,050; part-time $890 per credit.

Stanford University, School of Education, Teacher Education Program, Stanford, CA 94305-9991. Offers English education (MA); languages education (MA); mathematics education (MA); science education (MA); social studies education (MA). *Degree requirements:* For master's, thesis. *Entrance requirements:* For master's, GRE General Test. Electronic applications accepted. *Expenses: Tuition:* Full-time $40,050; part-time $890 per credit.

State University of New York at Binghamton, Graduate School, School of Education, Program in Adolescence Education, Binghamton, NY 13902-6000. Offers biology education (MAT, MS Ed, MST); earth science education (MAT, MS Ed, MST); English education (MAT, MS Ed, MST); French education (MAT, MST); mathematical sciences education (MAT, MS Ed, MST); physics (MAT, MS Ed, MST); social studies (MAT, MS Ed, MST); Spanish education (MAT, MST). *Accreditation:* Teacher Education Accreditation Council. Part-time and evening/weekend programs available. *Students:* 98 full-time (66 women), 13 part-time (11 women); includes 2 minority (1 Black or African American, non-Hispanic/Latino; 1 Hispanic/Latino). Average age 26. 73 applicants, 70% accepted, 35 enrolled. In 2011, 58 master's awarded. *Entrance requirements:* For master's, GRE General Test. Additional exam requirements/recommendations for international students: Required—TOEFL (minimum score 550 paper-based; 213 computer-based; 80 iBT). *Application deadline:* For fall admission, 2/1 priority date for domestic students, 2/1 for international students; for spring admission, 10/15 priority date for domestic students, 10/15 for international students. Applications are processed on a rolling basis. Application fee: $60. Electronic applications accepted. *Financial support:* In 2011–12, 4 students received support, including 1 fellowship with partial tuition reimbursement available (averaging $12,000 per year); career-related internships or fieldwork, Federal Work-Study, institutionally sponsored loans, scholarships/grants, health care benefits, tuition waivers (full), and unspecified assistantships also available. Financial award application deadline: 2/15; financial award applicants required to submit FAFSA. *Unit head:* Dr. S. G. Grant, Dean of School of Education, 607-777-7329, E-mail: sggrant@binghamton.edu. *Application contact:* Catherine Smith, Recruiting and Admissions Coordinator, 607-777-2151, Fax: 607-777-2501, E-mail: cmsmith@binghamton.edu.

State University of New York at New Paltz, Graduate School, School of Education, Department of Secondary Education, New Paltz, NY 12561. Offers adolescence education: biology (MAT, MS Ed); adolescence education: chemistry (MAT, MS Ed); adolescence education: earth science (MAT, MS Ed); adolescence education: English (MAT, MS Ed); adolescence education: French (MAT, MS Ed); adolescence education: social studies (MAT, MS Ed); adolescence education: Spanish (MAT, MS Ed); second language education (MS Ed). *Accreditation:* NCATE. Part-time and evening/weekend programs available. *Faculty:* 18 full-time (10 women), 2 part-time/adjunct (both women). *Students:* 79 full-time (48 women), 76 part-time (55 women); includes 30 minority (3 Black or African American, non-Hispanic/Latino; 2 Asian, non-Hispanic/Latino; 22 Hispanic/Latino; 3 Two or more races, non-Hispanic/Latino), 1 international. Average age 32. 127 applicants, 69% accepted, 64 enrolled. In 2011, 73 master's awarded. *Degree requirements:* For master's, comprehensive exam (for some programs), portfolio. *Entrance requirements:* For master's, minimum GPA of 3.0, New York state teaching certificate (MS Ed). Additional exam requirements/recommendations for international students: Required—TOEFL (minimum score 550 paper-based; 213 computer-based; 80 iBT), IELTS (minimum score 6.5). *Application deadline:* For fall admission, 3/1 priority date for domestic students, 3/1 for international students; for spring admission, 10/1 priority date for domestic students, 10/1 for international students. Application fee: $50. Electronic applications accepted. *Expenses:* Tuition, state resident: full-time $8870; part-time $370 per credit. Tuition, nonresident: full-time $15,160; part-time $632 per credit. *Required fees:* $1188; $34 per credit. $184 per semester. *Financial support:* In 2011–12, 13 students received support, including 3 fellowships with partial tuition reimbursements available (averaging $7,000 per year); Federal Work-Study, institutionally sponsored loans, and tuition waivers (full) also available. Financial award application deadline: 8/1; financial award applicants required to submit FAFSA. *Unit head:* Dr. Devon Duhaney, Chair, 845-257-2850, E-mail: duhaneyd@newpaltz.edu. *Application contact:* Caroline Murphy, Graduate Admissions Advisor, 845-257-3285, Fax: 845-257-3284, E-mail: gradschool@newpaltz.edu. Web site: http://www.newpaltz.edu/secondaryed/.

State University of New York at Plattsburgh, Division of Education, Health, and Human Services, Program in Teacher Education: Adolescence MST, Plattsburgh, NY 12901-2681. Offers adolescence education (MST); biology 7-12 (MST); chemistry 7-12 (MST); earth science 7-12 (MST); English 7-12 (MST); French 7-12 (MST); mathematics 7-12 (MST); physics 7-12 (MST); social studies 7-12 (MST); Spanish 7-12 (MST). *Accreditation:* Teacher Education Accreditation Council. Part-time and evening/weekend programs available. *Students:* 53 full-time (26 women), 5 part-time (4 women). Average age 29. *Entrance requirements:* For master's, minimum GPA of 2.75. Additional exam requirements/recommendations for international students: Required—TOEFL. *Application deadline:* For fall admission, 2/15 priority date for domestic students. Applications are processed on a rolling basis. Application fee: $75. *Financial support:* Application deadline: 4/15; applicants required to submit FAFSA. *Unit head:* Dr. Robert Ackland, Coordinator, 518-564-5131, E-mail: acklanrt@plattsburgh.edu. *Application contact:* Marguerite Adelman, Assistant Director, Graduate Admissions, 518-564-4723, Fax: 518-564-4722, E-mail: adelmaml@plattsburgh.edu.

State University of New York College at Cortland, Graduate Studies, School of Arts and Sciences, Programs in Adolescence Education, Cortland, NY 13045. Offers biology (MAT, MS Ed); chemistry (MAT, MS Ed); earth science (MAT, MS Ed); English (MS Ed); French (MS Ed); mathematics (MAT, MS Ed); physics (MAT, MS Ed); social studies (MS Ed); Spanish (MS Ed). *Accreditation:* NCATE. Part-time and evening/weekend programs available. *Degree requirements:* For master's, one foreign language, comprehensive exam (for some programs), thesis (for some programs). *Entrance requirements:* For master's, GRE General Test.

State University of New York College at Potsdam, School of Education and Professional Studies, Program in Secondary Education, Potsdam, NY 13676. Offers English (MST); mathematics (with grades 5-6 extension) (MST); science (MST), including biology, chemistry, earth science, physics; Social Studies (with grades 5-6 extension) (MST). *Accreditation:* NCATE. *Faculty:* 9 full-time (3 women), 3 part-time/adjunct (2 women). *Students:* 32 full-time (17 women), 1 part-time (0 women); includes 2 minority (1 Black or African American, non-Hispanic/Latino; 1 Asian, non-Hispanic/Latino), 3 international. 43 applicants, 88% accepted, 24 enrolled. In 2011, 43 master's awarded. *Degree requirements:* For master's, culminating experience. *Entrance requirements:* For master's, minimum GPA of 2.75 in last 60 hours of course work (3.0 for English program). Additional exam requirements/recommendations for international students: Required—TOEFL (minimum score 550 paper-based; 213 computer-based; 80 iBT), IELTS (minimum score 6). *Application deadline:* For spring admission, 3/1 for domestic and international students. Applications are processed on a rolling basis. Application fee: $50. *Expenses:* Tuition, state resident: full-time $8870; part-time $370 per credit hour. Tuition, nonresident: full-time $15,160; part-time $632 per credit hour. *Required fees:* $1066; $44.10 per credit hour. One-time fee: $3. *Financial support:* Fellowships, teaching assistantships, career-related internships or fieldwork, Federal Work-Study, scholarships/grants, and unspecified assistantships available. Support available to part-time students. Financial award application deadline: 3/1; financial award applicants required to submit FAFSA. *Unit head:* Donald C. Straight, Chairperson, 315-267-2553, Fax: 315-267-4802, E-mail: straigdc@potsdam.edu. *Application contact:* Peter Cutler, Graduate Admissions Counselor, 315-267-2165, Fax: 315-267-4802, E-mail: graduate@potsdam.edu. Web site: http://www.potsdam.edu/academics/SOEPS/SecondaryEd/index.cfm.

Stony Brook University, State University of New York, School of Professional Development, Stony Brook, NY 11794. Offers biology-grade 7-12 (MAT); chemistry-grade 7-12 (MAT); coaching (Graduate Certificate); coaching online (Graduate Certificate); computer integrated engineering (Graduate Certificate); earth science-grade 7-12 (MAT); educational computing (Graduate Certificate); educational leadership (Advanced Certificate); English-grade 7-12 (MAT); environmental management (Graduate Certificate); environmental/occupational health and safety (Graduate Certificate); French-grade 7-12 (MAT); German-grade 7-12 (MAT); human resource management (Graduate Certificate); human resource management online (Graduate Certificate); information systems management (Graduate Certificate); Italian-grade 7-12 (MAT); liberal studies (MA); liberal studies online (MAT); mathematics-grade 7-12 (MAT); operation research (Graduate Certificate); physics-grade 7-12 (MAT); professional studies online (MPS); school administration and supervision (Graduate Certificate); school building leadership (Graduate Certificate); school district administration (Graduate Certificate); school district business leadership (Advanced Certificate); school district leadership (Graduate Certificate); social science and the professions (MPS), including environmental waste management, human resource management; social studies-grade 7-12 (MAT); Spanish-grade 7-12 (MAT); waste management (Graduate Certificate). Part-time and evening/weekend programs available. Postbaccalaureate distance learning degree programs offered. *Degree requirements:* For master's, one foreign language, thesis or alternative.

Syracuse University, School of Education, Program in Social Studies Education: Preparation 7-12, Syracuse, NY 13244. Offers MS. Part-time programs available. *Students:* 9 full-time (7 women), 1 part-time (0 women); includes 4 minority (2 Black or African American, non-Hispanic/Latino; 1 Hispanic/Latino; 1 Two or more races, non-Hispanic/Latino). Average age 24. 8 applicants, 100% accepted, 5 enrolled. In 2011, 4 degrees awarded. *Degree requirements:* For master's, thesis or alternative. *Entrance requirements:* Additional exam requirements/recommendations for international students: Required—TOEFL (minimum score 100 iBT). *Application deadline:* For fall admission, 2/1 priority date for domestic students, 2/1 for international students; for spring admission, 10/15 priority date for domestic students, 10/15 for international students. Applications are processed on a rolling basis. Application fee: $75. Electronic applications accepted. *Expenses: Tuition:* Part-time $1206 per credit. *Financial support:* Fellowships with full tuition reimbursements and teaching assistantships with full and partial tuition reimbursements available. Financial award application deadline: 1/1; financial award applicants required to submit FAFSA. *Unit head:* Dr. Jeffery Mangram, Program Coordinator, 315-443-9077, E-mail: jamangra@syr.edu. *Application contact:* Laurie Deyo, Graduate Recruiter, School of Education, 315-443-2505, E-mail: e-gradrcrt@syr.edu. Web site: http://soeweb.syr.edu/.

Teachers College, Columbia University, Graduate Faculty of Education, Department of Arts and Humanities, Program in Social Studies Education, New York, NY 10027. Offers MA, Ed D, PhD. *Accreditation:* NCATE. Part-time and evening/weekend programs available. *Faculty:* 3 full-time (1 woman), 11 part-time/adjunct (5 women). *Students:* 49 full-time (29 women), 68 part-time (32 women); includes 19 minority (5 Black or African American, non-Hispanic/Latino; 1 American Indian or Alaska Native, non-Hispanic/Latino; 9 Asian, non-Hispanic/Latino; 4 Hispanic/Latino), 4 international. Average age 28. 103 applicants, 75% accepted, 36 enrolled. In 2011, 56 master's, 2 doctorates awarded. Terminal master's awarded for partial completion of doctoral program. *Degree requirements:* For master's, one foreign language, integrative project; New York State certification standards for study of language other than English; for doctorate, one foreign language, thesis/dissertation. *Entrance requirements:* For master's, GRE if GPA below 3.5 (recommended), minimum of 12 credits in history; for doctorate, GRE if GPA below 3.5 (recommended), at least 1-2 years of teaching experience, MA in social studies education or related content field. *Application deadline:* For fall admission, 12/15 priority date for domestic students. Applications are processed on a rolling basis. Application fee: $65. Electronic applications accepted. *Financial support:* Fellowships, research assistantships, teaching assistantships, career-related internships or fieldwork, Federal Work-Study, institutionally sponsored loans, and tuition waivers (full and partial) available. Support available to part-time students. Financial award application deadline: 2/1. *Faculty research:* History of social studies education, social studies curriculum and teaching, women's history, gender and diversity issues in the classroom. *Unit head:* Prof. Margaret Smith Crocco, Program Coordinator, 212-678-4083, E-mail: crocco@tc.edu. *Application contact:* Thomas P. Rock, Director of Admissions, 212-678-3083, Fax: 212-678-4171, E-mail: rock@tc.edu. Web site: http://www.tc.columbia.edu/a%26h/socialstudies/.

Texas A&M University–Commerce, Graduate School, College of Humanities, Social Sciences and Arts, Department of History, Commerce, TX 75429-3011. Offers history (MA, MS); social sciences (M Ed, MS). Part-time programs available. *Degree requirements:* For master's, comprehensive exam, thesis (for some programs). *Entrance requirements:* For master's, GRE General Test. Electronic applications accepted. *Faculty research:* American foreign policy, colonial America, Texas politics, Medieval England.

Texas State University–San Marcos, Graduate School, College of Liberal Arts, Department of Geography, Program in Environmental Geography, Geography Education, and Geography Information Science, San Marcos, TX 78666. Offers environmental geography (PhD); geography education (PhD); information science (PhD). Part-time programs available. *Faculty:* 24 full-time (4 women), 4 part-time/adjunct (0 women). *Students:* 38 full-time (18 women), 28 part-time (15 women); includes 7 minority (6 Hispanic/Latino; 1 Two or more races, non-Hispanic/Latino), 13 international. Average age 39. 19 applicants, 37% accepted, 5 enrolled. In 2011, 11 doctorates awarded. *Degree requirements:* For doctorate, thesis/dissertation. *Entrance requirements:* For doctorate, GRE General Test, minimum GPA of 3.5, master's degree in geography, demonstrated scholarly research. Additional exam requirements/recommendations for international students: Required—TOEFL (minimum score 550 paper-based; 213 computer-based; 78 iBT). *Application deadline:* For fall admission, 6/15 priority date for domestic students, 6/1 for international students; for spring admission, 10/15 priority date for domestic students, 10/1 for international students. Applications are processed on a rolling basis. Application fee: $40 ($90 for international students). Electronic applications accepted. *Expenses:* Tuition, state resident: full-time $6408; part-time $3204 per semester. Tuition, nonresident: full-time $14,832; part-time $7416 per semester. *Required fees:* $1824; $912 per semester. Tuition and fees vary according to course load. *Financial support:* In 2011–12, 29 students received support, including 8 research assistantships (averaging $22,788 per year), 29 teaching assistantships (averaging $21,024 per year); career-related internships or fieldwork, Federal Work-Study, and institutionally sponsored loans also available. Support available to part-time students. Financial award application deadline: 4/1; financial award applicants required to submit FAFSA. *Unit head:* Dr. David Butler, Graduate Adviser, 512-245-2170, Fax: 512-245-8353, E-mail: db25@txstate.edu. *Application contact:* Dr. J. Michael Willoughby, Dean of Graduate School, 512-245-2581, Fax: 512-245-8365, E-mail: gradcollege@txstate.edu. Web site: http://www.geo.txstate.edu/.

Trinity Washington University, School of Education, Washington, DC 20017-1094. Offers counseling (MA); early childhood education (MAT); educating for change (M Ed); educational administration (MSA); elementary education (MAT); school counseling (MA); secondary education (MAT), including English, social studies; special education (MAT); teaching English as a second language (MAT); teaching English to speakers of other languages (M Ed); the teaching of reading (M Ed). *Accreditation:* NCATE. Part-time and evening/weekend programs available. *Degree requirements:* For master's, thesis (for some programs), capstone project(s). *Entrance requirements:* For master's, PRAXIS I, minimum GPA of 2.8. Additional exam requirements/recommendations for international students: Required—TOEFL (minimum score 550 paper-based; 213 computer-based). *Faculty research:* Technology, literacy, special education, organizations, inclusion models.

Troy University, Graduate School, College of Education, Program in Postsecondary Education, Troy, AL 36082. Offers adult education (M Ed); biology (M Ed); criminal justice (M Ed); English (M Ed); foundations of education (M Ed); general science (M Ed); higher education administration (M Ed); history (M Ed); instructional technology (M Ed); mathematics (M Ed); music industry (M Ed); physical fitness (M Ed); political science (M Ed); public administration (M Ed); social science (M Ed); teaching English (M Ed). *Accreditation:* NCATE. Part-time and evening/weekend programs available. *Faculty:* 53 full-time (21 women), 22 part-time/adjunct (8 women). *Students:* 74 full-time (51 women), 166 part-time (121 women); includes 148 minority (143 Black or African American, non-Hispanic/Latino; 1 American Indian or Alaska Native, non-Hispanic/Latino; 2 Hispanic/Latino; 2 Two or more races, non-Hispanic/Latino). Average age 34. 174 applicants, 82% accepted, 88 enrolled. In 2011, 221 master's awarded. *Degree requirements:* For master's, comprehensive exam, thesis. *Entrance requirements:* For master's, MAT (minimum score 385), minimum GPA of 2.5. Additional exam requirements/recommendations for international students: Required—TOEFL (minimum score 523 paper-based; 193 computer-based; 70 iBT), IELTS (minimum score 6), or ACT COMPASS ESL (minimum listening, reading, and grammar score 270). *Application deadline:* Applications are processed on a rolling basis. Application fee: $50. Electronic applications accepted. *Expenses:* Tuition, state resident: full-time $6960; part-time $290 per credit hour. Tuition, nonresident: full-time $13,920; part-time $580 per credit hour. *Required fees:* $386 per term. *Financial support:* Available to part-time students. Applicants required to submit FAFSA. *Unit head:* Dr. Jan Oliver, Associate Professor, 334-670-3444, Fax: 334-670-3296, E-mail: oliver@troy.edu. *Application contact:* Brenda K. Campbell, Director of Graduate Admissions, 334-670-3178, Fax: 334-670-3733, E-mail: bcamp@troy.edu.

Troy University, Graduate School, College of Education, Program in Secondary Education, Troy, AL 36082. Offers 5th year biology (MS); 5th year computer science (MS); 5th year history (MS); 5th year language arts (MS); 5th year mathematics (MS); 5th year social science (MS); traditional biology (MS); traditional computer science (MS); traditional history (MS); traditional language arts (MS); traditional mathematics (MS); traditional social science (MS). *Accreditation:* NCATE. Part-time and evening/weekend programs available. *Faculty:* 4 full-time (3 women). *Students:* 14 full-time (8 women), 29 part-time (21 women); includes 9 minority (all Black or African American, non-Hispanic/Latino). Average age 28. 11 applicants, 100% accepted, 5 enrolled. In 2011, 16 master's awarded. *Degree requirements:* For master's, comprehensive exam, thesis. *Entrance requirements:* For master's, minimum GPA of 2.5, bachelor's degree. Additional exam requirements/recommendations for international students: Required—TOEFL (minimum score 523 paper-based; 193 computer-based; 70 iBT), IELTS (minimum score 6). *Application deadline:* Applications are processed on a rolling basis. Application fee: $50. Electronic applications accepted. *Expenses:* Tuition, state resident: full-time $6960; part-time $290 per credit hour. Tuition, nonresident: full-time $13,920; part-time $580 per credit hour. *Required fees:* $386 per term. *Financial support:* Career-related internships or fieldwork available. Support available to part-time students. Financial award applicants required to submit FAFSA. *Unit head:* Dr. Jan Oliver, Associate Professor, 334-670-3444, Fax: 334-670-3548, E-mail: oliver@troy.edu. *Application contact:* Brenda K. Campbell, Director of Graduate Admissions, 334-670-3178, Fax: 334-670-3733, E-mail: bcamp@troy.edu.

Union Graduate College, School of Education, Schenectady, NY 12308-3107. Offers biology (MAT, MS); chemistry (MAT); Chinese (MAT); earth science (MAT); English (MAT); French (MAT); general science (MAT); German (MAT); Greek (MAT); languages (MAT); Latin (MAT); mathematics (MAT); mathematics and technology (MS); mentoring and teacher leadership (AC); middle childhood extension (AC); national board certificate and teacher leadership (AC); physical science (MS); physics (MAT); social studies (MAT); Spanish (MAT). *Accreditation:* Teacher Education Accreditation Council. *Faculty:* 3 full-time (1 woman), 51 part-time/adjunct (24 women). *Students:* 37 full-time (26 women), 25 part-time (16 women); includes 4 minority (3 Asian, non-Hispanic/Latino; 1 Hispanic/Latino). Average age 32. 66 applicants, 83% accepted, 41 enrolled. In 2011, 47 master's, 29 other advanced degrees awarded. *Degree requirements:* For master's, thesis or project. *Entrance requirements:* For master's, minimum GPA of 3.0, letters of recommendation. Additional exam requirements/recommendations for international students: Required—TOEFL (minimum score 550 paper-based; 213 computer-based). *Application deadline:* Applications are processed on a rolling basis. Application fee: $60. Electronic applications accepted. *Expenses:* Contact institution. *Financial support:* In 2011–12, 22 students received support. Career-related internships or fieldwork, Federal Work-Study, scholarships/grants, health care benefits, and tuition waivers (partial) available. Support available to part-time students. Financial award applicants required to submit FAFSA. *Faculty research:* Transformative learning, science education, National Board Certification, teacher leadership, teacher quality. *Unit head:* Dr. Patrick Allen, Dean, 518-631-9870, Fax: 518-631-9901. *Application contact:* Christine Angley, Assistant, 518-631-9871, Fax: 518-631-9903, E-mail: angleyc@uniongraduatecollege.edu.

University at Buffalo, the State University of New York, Graduate School, Graduate School of Education, Department of Learning and Instruction, Buffalo, NY 14260. Offers biology education (Ed M, Certificate); chemistry education (Ed M, Certificate); childhood education (Ed M); childhood education with bilingual extension (Ed M); early childhood education (Ed M); early childhood education with bilingual extension (birth-grade 2) (Ed M); earth science education (Ed M, Certificate); educational technology and new literacies (Certificate); educational technology and new literacies (online) (Certificate); elementary education (Ed D, PhD); English education (Ed M, PhD, Certificate); English for speakers of other languages (Ed M); foreign and second language education (PhD); French education (Ed M, Certificate); general education (Ed M); German education (Ed M, Certificate); gifted education (online) (Certificate); Latin education (Ed M, Certificate); literacy teaching and learning (Certificate); literary specialist (Ed M); mathematics education (Ed M, PhD, Certificate); music education (Ed M, Certificate); physics education (Ed M, Certificate); reading education (PhD); science and the public (online) (Ed M); science education (PhD); social studies education (Ed M, Certificate); Spanish education (Ed M, Certificate); special education (PhD); teaching and leading for diversity (Certificate); teaching English to speakers of other languages (Ed M). Part-time and evening/weekend programs available. Postbaccalaureate distance learning degree programs offered (no on-campus study). *Faculty:* 32 full-time (23 women), 54 part-time/adjunct (43 women). *Students:* 294 full-time (222 women), 350 part-time (261 women); includes 75 minority (19 Black or African American, non-Hispanic/Latino; 6 American Indian or Alaska Native, non-Hispanic/Latino; 40 Asian, non-Hispanic/Latino; 10 Hispanic/Latino), 76 international. Average age 29. 548 applicants, 52% accepted, 253 enrolled. In 2011, 225 master's, 17 doctorates, 37 other advanced degrees awarded. *Degree requirements:* For master's, comprehensive exam; for doctorate, thesis/dissertation, research analysis exam, research experience component. *Entrance requirements:* For doctorate, GRE General Test or MAT, interview, writing sample, letters of recommendation. Additional exam requirements/recommendations for international students: Required—TOEFL (minimum score 600 paper-based; 96 iBT). *Application deadline:* For fall admission, 2/1 priority date for domestic students, 2/1 for international students; for spring admission, 11/15 priority date for domestic students, 10/1 for international students. Applications are processed on a rolling basis. Application fee: $50. Electronic applications accepted. *Financial support:* In 2011–12, 40 fellowships (averaging $12,991 per year), 46 research assistantships (averaging $10,986 per year) were awarded; teaching assistantships with full tuition reimbursements, career-related internships or fieldwork, Federal Work-Study, institutionally sponsored loans, scholarships/grants, and unspecified assistantships also available. Financial award application deadline: 2/28; financial award applicants required to submit FAFSA. *Faculty research:* Science assessment, foreign language teaching and learning, early learning, new literacies, gender and education. *Unit head:* Dr. Julie Sarama, Chair, 716-645-2455, Fax: 716-645-3161, E-mail: jcollins@buffalo.edu. *Application contact:* Cathy Dimino, Admissions Assistant, 716-645-2110, Fax: 716-645-7937, E-mail: cadimino@buffalo.edu.

The University of Alabama in Huntsville, School of Graduate Studies, College of Liberal Arts, Department of History, Huntsville, AL 35899. Offers education (MA); history (MA); social science (MA). Part-time and evening/weekend programs available. *Faculty:* 7 full-time (2 women). *Students:* 6 full-time (3 women), 13 part-time (7 women); includes 2 minority (1 Black or African American, non-Hispanic/Latino; 1 American Indian or Alaska Native, non-Hispanic/Latino). Average age 32. 16 applicants, 81% accepted, 10 enrolled. In 2011, 2 master's awarded. *Degree requirements:* For master's, one foreign language, comprehensive exam, thesis or alternative, oral and written exams. *Entrance requirements:* For master's, GRE General Test, minimum GPA of 3.0, bachelor's degree in history or related area. Additional exam requirements/recommendations for international students: Required—TOEFL (minimum score 500 paper-based; 173 computer-based; 62 iBT). *Application deadline:* For fall admission, 7/15 for domestic students, 4/1 for international students; for spring admission, 11/30 for domestic students, 9/1 for international students. Applications are processed on a rolling basis. Application fee: $40 ($50 for international students). Electronic applications accepted. *Expenses:* Tuition, state resident: full-time $7830; part-time $473.50 per credit. Tuition, nonresident: full-time $18,748; part-time $1128.33 per credit. Tuition and fees vary according to course load and program. *Financial support:* In 2011–12, 1 student received support, including 1 research assistantship with full tuition reimbursement available (averaging $8,460 per year); career-related internships or fieldwork, Federal Work-Study, institutionally sponsored loans, scholarships/grants, health care benefits, and unspecified assistantships also available. Support available to part-time students. Financial award application deadline: 4/1; financial award applicants required to submit FAFSA. *Faculty research:* American and European history, U. S. diplomatic history, Old South, ancient and medieval history, Latin American history. *Unit head:* Dr. Andrew Dunar, Chair, 256-824-6312, Fax: 256-824-6477, E-mail: dunara@uah.edu. *Application contact:* Kim Gray, Graduate Studies Admissions Coordinator, 256-824-6002, Fax: 256-824-6405, E-mail: deangrad@uah.edu. Web site: http://www.uah.edu/colleges/liberal/history/.

University of Arkansas at Pine Bluff, School of Education, Pine Bluff, AR 71601-2799. Offers early childhood education (M Ed); secondary education (M Ed), including English education, mathematics education, physical education, science education, social studies education; teaching (MAT). *Accreditation:* NCATE. Part-time and evening/weekend programs available. *Degree requirements:* For master's, comprehensive exam. *Entrance requirements:* For master's, GRE, minimum GPA of 2.75, NTE or Standard Arkansas Teaching Certificate. *Faculty research:* Teacher certification, accreditation, assessment, standards, portfolio development, rehabilitation, technology.

The University of British Columbia, Faculty of Education, Department of Curriculum and Pedagogy, Vancouver, BC V6T 1Z4, Canada. Offers art education (M Ed, MA); business education (MA); curriculum studies (M Ed, MA, PhD); home economics education (M Ed, MA); math education (M Ed, MA); music education (M Ed, MA);

physical education (M Ed, MA); science education (M Ed, MA); social studies education (M Ed, MA); technology studies education (M Ed, MA). Part-time programs available. *Degree requirements:* For master's, thesis (MA); for doctorate, comprehensive exam, thesis/dissertation. *Entrance requirements:* Additional exam requirements/ recommendations for international students: Required—TOEFL (minimum score 580 paper-based; 237 computer-based; 92 iBT). Electronic applications accepted. *Expenses:* Contact institution. *Faculty research:* School subjects, teaching and learning.

University of California, Santa Cruz, Division of Graduate Studies, Division of Social Sciences, Program in Social Documentation, Santa Cruz, CA 95064. Offers MA. *Entrance requirements:* For master's, resume or curriculum vitae, sample of documentary production work. Additional exam requirements/recommendations for international students: Required—TOEFL (minimum score 550 paper-based; 220 computer-based; 83 iBT); Recommended—IELTS (minimum score 8). Electronic applications accepted. *Faculty research:* Documentation of underrepresented areas of community life.

University of Central Florida, College of Education, Education Doctoral Programs, Orlando, FL 32816. Offers communication sciences and disorders (PhD); counselor education (PhD); education (Ed D); elementary education (PhD); exceptional education (PhD); exercise physiology (PhD); higher education (PhD); hospitality education (PhD); instructional technology (PhD); mathematics education (PhD); reading education (PhD); science education (PhD); social science education (PhD); TESOL (PhD). *Students:* 135 full-time (87 women), 73 part-time (51 women); includes 49 minority (21 Black or African American, non-Hispanic/Latino; 4 Asian, non-Hispanic/Latino; 20 Hispanic/Latino; 4 Two or more races, non-Hispanic/Latino), 18 international. Average age 39. 125 applicants, 46% accepted, 46 enrolled. In 2011, 43 doctorates awarded. Application fee: $30. Electronic applications accepted. *Expenses:* Tuition, state resident: part-time $277.08 per credit hour. Tuition, nonresident: part-time $277.08 per credit hour. Part-time tuition and fees vary according to degree level and program. *Financial support:* In 2011–12, 85 students received support, including 48 fellowships with partial tuition reimbursements available (averaging $5,900 per year), 36 research assistantships with partial tuition reimbursements available (averaging $6,900 per year), 59 teaching assistantships with partial tuition reimbursements available (averaging $6,900 per year). *Unit head:* Dr. Rex Culp, Associate Dean, 407-823-5391, E-mail: rex.culp@ucf.edu. *Application contact:* Barbara Rodriguez, Associate Director, Admissions and Registration, 407-823-2766, Fax: 407-823-6442, E-mail: gradadmissions@ucf.edu. Web site: http://education.ucf.edu/departments.cfm.

University of Central Florida, College of Education, School of Teaching, Learning, and Leadership, Program in Social Science Education, Orlando, FL 32816. Offers teacher education (MAT); teacher leadership (M Ed). *Accreditation:* NCATE. Part-time and evening/weekend programs available. *Students:* 14 full-time (6 women), 47 part-time (27 women); includes 5 minority (3 Black or African American, non-Hispanic/Latino; 2 Hispanic/Latino). Average age 31. 22 applicants, 68% accepted, 14 enrolled. In 2011, 28 master's awarded. *Entrance requirements:* For master's, GRE General Test. Additional exam requirements/recommendations for international students: Required—TOEFL. *Application deadline:* For fall admission, 7/15 for domestic students; for spring admission, 12/1 for domestic students. Application fee: $12. Electronic applications accepted. *Expenses:* Tuition, state resident: part-time $277.08 per credit hour. Tuition, nonresident: part-time $277.08 per credit hour. Part-time tuition and fees vary according to degree level and program. *Financial support:* In 2011–12, 2 students received support, including 2 research assistantships (averaging $4,100 per year), 1 teaching assistantship (averaging $4,900 per year); career-related internships or fieldwork, Federal Work-Study, institutionally sponsored loans, tuition waivers (partial), and unspecified assistantships also available. Financial award application deadline: 3/1; financial award applicants required to submit FAFSA. *Unit head:* Dr. Janet B. Andreasen, Program Coordinator, 407-823-5430, E-mail: janet.andreasen@ucf.edu. *Application contact:* Barbara Rodriguez, Director, Admissions and Registration, 407-823-2766, Fax: 407-823-6442, E-mail: gradadmissions@ucf.edu.

University of Cincinnati, Graduate School, College of Education, Criminal Justice, and Human Services, Division of Teacher Education, Cincinnati, OH 45221. Offers curriculum and instruction (M Ed, Ed D); deaf studies (Certificate); early childhood education (M Ed); middle childhood education (M Ed); postsecondary literacy instruction (Certificate); reading/literacy (M Ed, Ed D); secondary education (M Ed); special education (M Ed, Ed D); teaching English as a second language (M Ed, Ed D, Certificate); teaching science (MS). Part-time programs available. *Degree requirements:* For doctorate, thesis/dissertation. *Entrance requirements:* For master's, GRE General Test. Additional exam requirements/recommendations for international students: Required—TOEFL (minimum score 550 paper-based). Electronic applications accepted.

University of Connecticut, Graduate School, Neag School of Education, Department of Curriculum and Instruction, Program in History and Social Sciences Education, Storrs, CT 06269. Offers MA, PhD, Post-Master's Certificate. *Accreditation:* NCATE. Terminal master's awarded for partial completion of doctoral program. *Degree requirements:* For master's, comprehensive exam, thesis or alternative; for doctorate, thesis/dissertation. *Entrance requirements:* For doctorate, GRE General Test. Additional exam requirements/recommendations for international students: Required—TOEFL (minimum score 550 paper-based; 213 computer-based). Electronic applications accepted.

University of Florida, Graduate School, College of Education, School of Teaching and Learning, Gainesville, FL 32611. Offers bilingual/ESOL education (M Ed, MAE, Ed D, PhD, Ed S); curriculum and instruction (M Ed, MAE, Ed D, PhD, Ed S); elementary education (M Ed, MAE); English education (M Ed, MAE); mathematics education (M Ed, MAE); reading education (M Ed, MAE); science education (M Ed, MAE); social foundations of education (M Ed, MAE, Ed D, PhD); social studies education (M Ed, MAE). *Accreditation:* NCATE. Part-time and evening/weekend programs available. Postbaccalaureate distance learning degree programs offered (no on-campus study). *Faculty:* 26 full-time (19 women). *Students:* 247 full-time (201 women), 236 part-time (196 women); includes 100 minority (32 Black or African American, non-Hispanic/Latino; 2 American Indian or Alaska Native, non-Hispanic/Latino; 15 Asian, non-Hispanic/ Latino; 51 Hispanic/Latino), 32 international. Average age 33. 290 applicants, 60% accepted, 122 enrolled. In 2011, 284 master's, 19 doctorates, 29 other advanced degrees awarded. Terminal master's awarded for partial completion of doctoral program. *Degree requirements:* For master's, comprehensive exam (for some programs), thesis (for some programs); for doctorate, comprehensive exam (for some programs), thesis/dissertation (for some programs). *Entrance requirements:* For master's and doctorate, GRE General Test, minimum GPA of 3.0; for Ed S, GRE General Test. Additional exam requirements/recommendations for international students: Required—TOEFL (minimum score 550 paper-based; 213 computer-based; 80 iBT), IELTS (minimum score 6). *Application deadline:* For fall admission, 2/15 for domestic students, 12/1 for international students; for spring admission, 9/15 for domestic students, 3/1 for international students. Applications are processed on a rolling basis. Application fee: $30. Electronic applications accepted. *Financial support:* Fellowships, research assistantships, teaching assistantships, career-related internships or fieldwork, and unspecified assistantships available. Financial award applicants required to submit FAFSA. *Faculty research:* Early childhood, child and adolescents, diverse learners, race/ethnicity issues, teacher education, professional development, language and literacy development, policy development. *Unit head:* Dr. Elizabeth Bondy, Chair, 352-273-4242, Fax: 352-392-9193, E-mail: bondy@coe.ufl.edu. *Application contact:* Wevan Terzian, Graduate Coordinator, 352-273-4216, Fax: 352-392-9193, E-mail: sterzian@coe.ufl.edu. Web site: http://education.ufl.edu/school-teaching-learning/.

University of Georgia, College of Education, Department of Elementary and Social Studies Education, Athens, GA 30602. Offers early childhood education (M Ed, MAT, PhD, Ed S), including child and family development (MAT); elementary education (PhD); middle school education (M Ed, PhD, Ed S); social studies education (M Ed, Ed D, PhD, Ed S). *Faculty:* 17 full-time (10 women). *Students:* 119 full-time (96 women), 110 part-time (96 women); includes 42 minority (22 Black or African American, non-Hispanic/ Latino; 1 American Indian or Alaska Native, non-Hispanic/Latino; 11 Asian, non-Hispanic/Latino; 6 Hispanic/Latino; 2 Two or more races, non-Hispanic/Latino), 12 international. Average age 30. 68 applicants, 72% accepted, 22 enrolled. In 2011, 92 master's, 12 doctorates, 2 other advanced degrees awarded. *Entrance requirements:* For master's and Ed S, GRE General Test or MAT; for doctorate, GRE General Test. *Application deadline:* For fall admission, 7/1 priority date for domestic students; for spring admission, 11/15 for domestic students. Application fee: $50. Electronic applications accepted. *Financial support:* Fellowships, research assistantships, teaching assistantships, and unspecified assistantships available. *Unit head:* Dr. Ronald Butchart, Interim Head, 706-542-6490, E-mail: butchart@uga.edu. *Application contact:* Dr. Stephanie R. Jones, Graduate Coordinator, 706-542-4283, Fax: 706-542-8996, E-mail: essegrad@uga.edu. Web site: http://www.coe.uga.edu/esse/.

University of Indianapolis, Graduate Programs, School of Education, Indianapolis, IN 46227-3697. Offers art education (MAT); biology (MAT); chemistry (MAT); curriculum and instruction (MA); earth sciences (MAT); education (MA, MAT); educational leadership (MA); elementary education (MA); English (MAT); French (MAT); math (MAT); physical education (MAT); physics (MAT); secondary education (MA), including art education, education, English education, social studies education; social studies (MAT); Spanish (MAT). *Accreditation:* NCATE. Part-time and evening/weekend programs available. *Faculty:* 3 full-time (2 women), 3 part-time/adjunct (2 women). *Students:* 32 full-time (18 women), 97 part-time (56 women); includes 22 minority (20 Black or African American, non-Hispanic/Latino; 1 Asian, non-Hispanic/Latino; 1 Hispanic/Latino), 3 international. Average age 33. In 2011, 78 master's awarded. *Entrance requirements:* For master's, GRE Subject Test, PRAXIS I, minimum GPA of 2.5, 3 letters of recommendation, interview, writing exercise. Additional exam requirements/recommendations for international students: Required—TOEFL (minimum score 550 paper-based; 213 computer-based). *Application deadline:* Applications are processed on a rolling basis. Application fee: $50. Tuition and fees vary according to degree level and program. *Financial support:* Federal Work-Study available. Financial award application deadline: 5/1; financial award applicants required to submit FAFSA. *Faculty research:* Assessment of teacher education, perceptions of prospective teachers by parents. *Unit head:* Dr. Kathy Moran, Dean, 317-788-3285, Fax: 317-788-3300, E-mail: kmoran@uindy.edu. *Application contact:* Jeni Kirby, 317-788-2113, E-mail: kirbyj@uindy.edu. Web site: http://education.uindy.edu/.

The University of Iowa, Graduate College, College of Education, Department of Teaching and Learning, Program in Secondary Education, Iowa City, IA 52242-1316. Offers art education (PhD); curriculum and supervision (PhD); curriculum supervision (MA); developmental reading (MA); English education (MA, MAT); foreign language education (MA, MAT); foreign language/ESL education (PhD); language, literature and culture (PhD); math education (PhD); mathematics education (MA); social studies (MA, PhD). *Degree requirements:* For master's, thesis optional, exam; for doctorate, comprehensive exam, thesis/dissertation. *Entrance requirements:* For master's and doctorate, GRE General Test, minimum GPA of 3.0. Additional exam requirements/ recommendations for international students: Required—TOEFL (minimum score 550 paper-based; 213 computer-based; 81 iBT). Electronic applications accepted.

University of Maine, Graduate School, College of Education and Human Development, Program in Social Studies Education, Orono, ME 04469. Offers M Ed, MA, MS, CAS. *Accreditation:* NCATE. Part-time and evening/weekend programs available. *Students:* 1 (woman) full-time. Average age 59. In 2011, 1 degree awarded. *Degree requirements:* For master's, thesis or alternative. *Entrance requirements:* For master's, MAT; for CAS, MA, M Ed, or MS. Additional exam requirements/recommendations for international students: Required—TOEFL. *Application deadline:* For fall admission, 2/1 priority date for domestic students. Applications are processed on a rolling basis. Application fee: $65. Electronic applications accepted. *Expenses:* Tuition, state resident: full-time $5016. Tuition, nonresident: full-time $14,424. *Financial support:* Tuition waivers (full and partial) available. Financial award application deadline: 3/1. *Unit head:* Dr. Janet Spector, Coordinator, 207-581-2444, Fax: 207-581-2423. *Application contact:* Scott G. Delcourt, Associate Dean of the Graduate School, 207-581-3291, Fax: 207-581-3232, E-mail: graduate@maine.edu. Web site: http://www2.umaine.edu/graduate/.

University of Maryland, Baltimore County, Graduate School, College of Arts, Humanities and Social Sciences, Department of Education, Program in Teaching, Baltimore, MD 21250. Offers early childhood education (MAT); elementary education (MAT); secondary education (MAT), including social studies; secondary education (MAT), including art, biology, chemistry, dance, earth/space science, English, foreign language, mathematics, music, physics, theatre. Part-time and evening/weekend programs available. *Faculty:* 24 full-time (18 women), 25 part-time/adjunct (19 women). *Students:* 46 full-time (35 women), 64 part-time (39 women); includes 24 minority (8 Black or African American, non-Hispanic/Latino; 7 Asian, non-Hispanic/Latino; 6 Hispanic/Latino; 1 Native Hawaiian or other Pacific Islander, non-Hispanic/Latino; 2 Two or more races, non-Hispanic/Latino), 4 international. Average age 31. 88 applicants, 57% accepted, 39 enrolled. In 2011, 106 master's awarded. *Degree requirements:* For master's, comprehensive exam (for some programs), thesis (for some programs). *Entrance requirements:* For master's, PRAXIS I or GRE (minimum score of 1000), minimum GPA of 3.0. Additional exam requirements/recommendations for international students: Required—TOEFL. *Application deadline:* For fall admission, 6/1 for domestic students; for spring admission, 11/1 for domestic students. Applications are processed on a rolling basis. Application fee: $50. Electronic applications accepted. *Financial support:* In 2011–12, 6 students received support, including teaching assistantships with full and partial tuition reimbursements available (averaging $12,000 per year); career-related internships or fieldwork, Federal Work-Study, scholarships/grants, tuition waivers, and unspecified assistantships also available. Financial award application deadline: 3/1. *Faculty research:* STEM teacher education, culturally sensitive pedagogy, ESOL/bilingual education, early childhood education, language, literacy and culture. *Unit head:* Dr. Susan M. Blunck, Graduate Program Director, 410-455-2869, Fax: 410-455-3986, E-mail: blunck@umbc.edu. *Application contact:* Cheryl Johnson, 410-455-3388, E-mail: blackwel@umbc.edu. Web site: http://www.umbc.edu/education/.

University of Minnesota, Twin Cities Campus, Graduate School, College of Education and Human Development, Department of Curriculum and Instruction, Program in Teaching, Minneapolis, MN 55455-0213. Offers Chinese (M Ed); earth science (M Ed); elementary special education (M Ed); English (M Ed); English as a second language (M Ed); French (M Ed); German (M Ed); Hebrew (M Ed); Japanese (M Ed); life sciences (M Ed); mathematics (M Ed); middle school science (M Ed);

science (M Ed); second languages and cultures (M Ed); social studies (M Ed); Spanish (M Ed). *Students:* 375 full-time (319 women), 72 part-time (56 women); includes 34 minority (8 Black or African American, non-Hispanic/Latino; 16 Asian, non-Hispanic/Latino; 10 Hispanic/Latino), 5 international. Average age 27. 317 applicants, 70% accepted, 215 enrolled. In 2011, 443 master's awarded. Application fee: $55. *Unit head:* Dr. Nina Asher, Chair, 612-624-1357, Fax: 612-624-8277, E-mail: nasher@umn.edu. *Application contact:* Dr. Jennifer Engler, Assistant Dean, 612-626-2887, Fax: 612-626-7496, E-mail: engle009@umn.edu. Web site: http://www.cehd.umn.edu/ci/.

University of Missouri, Graduate School, College of Education, Department of Learning, Teaching and Curriculum, Columbia, MO 65211. Offers agricultural education (M Ed, PhD, Ed S); art education (M Ed, PhD, Ed S); business and office education (M Ed, PhD, Ed S); early childhood education (M Ed, PhD, Ed S); elementary education (M Ed, PhD, Ed S); English education (M Ed, PhD, Ed S); foreign language education (M Ed, PhD, Ed S); health education and promotion (M Ed, PhD); learning and instruction (M Ed); marketing education (M Ed, PhD, Ed S); mathematics education (M Ed, PhD, Ed S); music education (M Ed, PhD, Ed S); reading education (M Ed, PhD, Ed S); science education (M Ed, PhD, Ed S); social studies education (M Ed, PhD, Ed S); vocational education (M Ed, PhD, Ed S). Part-time programs available. *Faculty:* 26 full-time (16 women), 3 part-time/adjunct (2 women). *Students:* 184 full-time (145 women), 276 part-time (215 women); includes 34 minority (10 Black or African American, non-Hispanic/Latino; 1 American Indian or Alaska Native, non-Hispanic/Latino; 7 Asian, non-Hispanic/Latino; 8 Hispanic/Latino; 8 Two or more races, non-Hispanic/Latino), 39 international. Average age 32. 309 applicants, 76% accepted, 204 enrolled. In 2011, 232 master's, 8 doctorates, 2 other advanced degrees awarded. Terminal master's awarded for partial completion of doctoral program. *Degree requirements:* For doctorate, thesis/dissertation. *Entrance requirements:* For master's and Ed S, GRE General Test or MAT, minimum GPA of 3.0; for doctorate, GRE General Test, minimum GPA of 3.0. Additional exam requirements/recommendations for international students: Required—TOEFL (minimum score 600 paper-based; 250 computer-based; 100 iBT). Application fee: $55 ($75 for international students). Electronic applications accepted. *Expenses:* Tuition, state resident: full-time $5881. Tuition, nonresident: full-time $15,183. *Required fees:* $952. Tuition and fees vary according to campus/location and program. *Financial support:* Fellowships, research assistantships, teaching assistantships, and institutionally sponsored loans available. *Application contact:* Fran Colley, 573-882-6462, E-mail: colleyf@missouri.edu. Web site: http://education.missouri.edu/LTC/.

The University of North Carolina at Chapel Hill, Graduate School, School of Education, Program in Secondary Education, Chapel Hill, NC 27599. Offers English (Grades 9-12) (MAT); English as a second language (MAT); French (Grades K-12) (MAT); German (Grades K-12) (MAT); Japanese (Grades K-12) (MAT); Latin (Grades 9-12) (MAT); mathematics (Grades 9-12) (MAT); music (Grades K-12) (MAT); science (Grades 9-12) (MAT); social studies (Grades 9-12) (MAT); Spanish (Grades K-12) (MAT). *Accreditation:* NCATE. *Degree requirements:* For master's, comprehensive exam. *Entrance requirements:* For master's, GRE General Test, minimum GPA of 3.0 during last 2 years of undergraduate course work. Additional exam requirements/recommendations for international students: Required—TOEFL (minimum score 550 paper-based; 79 computer-based). Electronic applications accepted.

The University of North Carolina at Charlotte, Graduate School, College of Liberal Arts and Sciences, Department of Sociology, Charlotte, NC 28223-0001. Offers health research (MA); mathematical sociology and quantitative methods (MA); organizations, occupations, and work (MA); political sociology (MA); race and gender (MA); social psychology (MA); social theory (MA); sociology of education (MA); stratification (MA). Part-time and evening/weekend programs available. *Faculty:* 17 full-time (10 women). *Students:* 14 full-time (8 women), 12 part-time (5 women); includes 5 minority (2 Black or African American, non-Hispanic/Latino; 3 Asian, non-Hispanic/Latino). Average age 30. 13 applicants, 85% accepted, 8 enrolled. In 2011, 4 master's awarded. *Degree requirements:* For master's, thesis or comprehensive exam. *Entrance requirements:* For master's, GRE or MAT, minimum GPA of 3.0 in last 2 years, 2.75 overall. Additional exam requirements/recommendations for international students: Required—TOEFL (minimum score 557 paper-based; 220 computer-based; 83 iBT). *Application deadline:* For fall admission, 7/1 for domestic students, 5/1 for international students; for spring admission, 11/1 for domestic students, 10/1 for international students. Applications are processed on a rolling basis. Application fee: $65 ($75 for international students). Electronic applications accepted. *Expenses:* Tuition, state resident: full-time $3689. Tuition, nonresident: full-time $15,226. *Required fees:* $2198. Tuition and fees vary according to course load and program. *Financial support:* In 2011–12, 11 students received support, including 6 research assistantships (averaging $13,125 per year), 5 teaching assistantships (averaging $10,800 per year); career-related internships or fieldwork, institutionally sponsored loans, scholarships/grants, and unspecified assistantships also available. Support available to part-time students. Financial award application deadline: 4/1; financial award applicants required to submit FAFSA. *Faculty research:* Social psychology, sociology of education, social gerontology, quantitative methodology, medical sociology. *Total annual research expenditures:* $448,481. *Unit head:* Dr. Lisa Rachotte, Chair, 704-687-2288, Fax: 704-687-3091, E-mail: lrashott@uncc.edu. *Application contact:* Kathy B. Giddings, Director of Graduate Admissions, 704-687-5503, Fax: 704-687-3279, E-mail: gradadm@uncc.edu. Web site: http://sociology.uncc.edu/.

The University of North Carolina at Greensboro, Graduate School, School of Education, Department of Curriculum and Instruction, Greensboro, NC 27412-5001. Offers college teaching and adult learning (Certificate); curriculum and instruction (M Ed), including chemistry education, elementary education, English as a second language, French education, instructional technology, mathematics education, middle grades education, reading education, science education, social studies education, Spanish education; curriculum and teaching (PhD), including higher education, teacher education and development; English as a second language (Certificate); higher education (M Ed); supervision (M Ed). *Accreditation:* NCATE. Part-time programs available. *Degree requirements:* For doctorate, thesis/dissertation. *Entrance requirements:* For master's and doctorate, GRE General Test. Additional exam requirements/recommendations for international students: Required—TOEFL. Electronic applications accepted. *Faculty research:* Community college literacy program, middle school mathematics/computer mathematics.

The University of North Carolina at Pembroke, Graduate Studies, Department of History, Program in Social Studies Education, Pembroke, NC 28372-1510. Offers MA, MAT. Part-time and evening/weekend programs available. *Degree requirements:* For master's, thesis optional. *Entrance requirements:* For master's, GRE or MAT, minimum GPA of 3.0 in major, 2.5 overall. Additional exam requirements/recommendations for international students: Required—TOEFL.

University of Oklahoma, Jeannine Rainbolt College of Education, Department of Instructional Leadership and Academic Curriculum, Norman, OK 73072. Offers communication, culture and pedagogy for Hispanic populations in educational settings (Graduate Certificate); instructional leadership and academic curriculum (M Ed, PhD), including bilingual education, early childhood education, elementary education, English education, instructional leadership, mathematics education, reading education, science education, science, technology, engineering and mathematics education (M Ed), secondary education, social studies education, teacher education (M Ed). *Accreditation:* NCATE. Part-time and evening/weekend programs available. *Faculty:* 19 full-time (13 women), 1 (woman) part-time/adjunct. *Students:* 73 full-time (63 women), 114 part-time (87 women); includes 29 minority (5 Black or African American, non-Hispanic/Latino; 12 American Indian or Alaska Native, non-Hispanic/Latino; 5 Asian, non-Hispanic/Latino; 3 Hispanic/Latino; 1 Native Hawaiian or other Pacific Islander, non-Hispanic/Latino; 3 Two or more races, non-Hispanic/Latino), 7 international. Average age 33. 87 applicants, 86% accepted, 68 enrolled. In 2011, 36 master's, 6 doctorates awarded. Terminal master's awarded for partial completion of doctoral program. *Degree requirements:* For doctorate, thesis/dissertation. *Entrance requirements:* For master's, 12 hours of course work in education; for doctorate, GRE General Test, master's degree, minimum graduate GPA of 3.0. Additional exam requirements/recommendations for international students: Required—TOEFL (minimum score 550 paper-based; 79 iBT). *Application deadline:* For fall admission, 6/1 priority date for domestic students, 3/1 for international students; for spring admission, 11/1 for domestic students, 9/1 for international students. Applications are processed on a rolling basis. Application fee: $40 ($90 for international students). Electronic applications accepted. *Expenses:* Tuition, state resident: full-time $4087; part-time $170.30 per credit hour. Tuition, nonresident: full-time $14,875; part-time $619.80 per credit hour. *Required fees:* $2659; $100.25 per credit hour. Tuition and fees vary according to course load and degree level. *Financial support:* In 2011–12, 128 students received support, including 2 research assistantships with partial tuition reimbursements available (averaging $12,431 per year), 12 teaching assistantships with partial tuition reimbursements available (averaging $10,161 per year); institutionally sponsored loans, scholarships/grants, and unspecified assistantships also available. Financial award applicants required to submit FAFSA. *Faculty research:* Engineering in practice for sustainable future, no child left behind (reading), early childhood learning games impact study, Educare randomized control startup, Oklahoma mentoring professional development. *Total annual research expenditures:* $1.1 million. *Unit head:* Lawrence Baines, Chair, 405-325-1498, Fax: 405-325-4061, E-mail: lbaines@ou.edu. *Application contact:* Lynn Crussel, Graduate Programs Officer, 405-325-4843, Fax: 405-325-4061, E-mail: lcrussel@ou.edu. Web site: http://education.ou.edu/departments/ilac.

University of Pittsburgh, School of Education, Department of Instruction and Learning, Program in Secondary Education, Pittsburgh, PA 15260. Offers English/communications education (M Ed, MAT); foreign languages education (M Ed, MAT); mathematics education (M Ed, MAT, Ed D); science education (M Ed, MAT, Ed D); social studies education (M Ed, MAT). Part-time and evening/weekend programs available. *Students:* 154 full-time (92 women), 68 part-time (47 women); includes 18 minority (6 Black or African American, non-Hispanic/Latino; 3 Asian, non-Hispanic/Latino; 7 Hispanic/Latino; 2 Two or more races, non-Hispanic/Latino), 6 international. Average age 30. 208 applicants, 48% accepted, 72 enrolled. In 2011, 116 master's, 6 doctorates awarded. *Degree requirements:* For master's, thesis; for doctorate, thesis/dissertation. *Entrance requirements:* For master's, PRAXIS I; for doctorate, GRE General Test. Additional exam requirements/recommendations for international students: Required—TOEFL. *Application deadline:* For fall admission, 2/1 priority date for domestic students; for spring admission, 11/15 priority date for domestic students. Applications are processed on a rolling basis. Application fee: $50. Electronic applications accepted. *Expenses:* Tuition, state resident: full-time $18,774; part-time $760 per credit. Tuition, nonresident: full-time $30,736; part-time $1258 per credit. *Required fees:* $740; $200 per term. Tuition and fees vary according to program. *Financial support:* Fellowships, teaching assistantships, career-related internships or fieldwork, Federal Work-Study, tuition waivers (partial), and unspecified assistantships available. Support available to part-time students. Financial award application deadline: 3/15; financial award applicants required to submit FAFSA. *Unit head:* Dr. Richard Donato, Chairman, 412-624-7248, Fax: 412-648-7081, E-mail: donato@pitt.edu. *Application contact:* Marianne L. Budziszewski, Director of Admissions and Enrollment Services, 412-648-2230, Fax: 412-648-1899, E-mail: soeinfo@pitt.edu. Web site: http://www.education.pitt.edu/.

University of Puerto Rico, Río Piedras, College of Education, Program in Curriculum and Teaching, San Juan, PR 00931-3300. Offers biology education (M Ed); chemistry education (M Ed); curriculum and teaching (Ed D); history education (M Ed); mathematics education (M Ed); physics education (M Ed); Spanish education (M Ed). Part-time programs available. *Degree requirements:* For master's, thesis; for doctorate, thesis/dissertation, internship. *Entrance requirements:* For master's, PAEG or GRE, minimum GPA of 3.0, letter of recommendation; for doctorate, GRE or PAEG, master's degree, minimum GPA of 3.0, letter of recommendation (2), interview. *Faculty research:* Curriculum, math teaching.

University of St. Francis, College of Education, Joliet, IL 60435-6169. Offers educational leadership (MS, Ed D); elementary education certification (M Ed); reading (MS); secondary education certification (M Ed), including English education, math education, science education, social studies education, visual arts education; special education (M Ed); teaching and learning (MS). *Accreditation:* NCATE. Part-time and evening/weekend programs available. Postbaccalaureate distance learning degree programs offered (no on-campus study). *Faculty:* 7 full-time (5 women), 21 part-time/adjunct (14 women). *Students:* 32 full-time (21 women), 230 part-time (175 women); includes 23 minority (7 Black or African American, non-Hispanic/Latino; 2 Asian, non-Hispanic/Latino; 13 Hispanic/Latino; 1 Two or more races, non-Hispanic/Latino), 1 international. Average age 32. 147 applicants, 60% accepted, 57 enrolled. In 2011, 156 master's awarded. *Entrance requirements:* For doctorate, master's degree, IL Type 75 or Principal's endorsement, interview. Additional exam requirements/recommendations for international students: Required—TOEFL (minimum score 550 paper-based; 213 computer-based). *Application deadline:* Applications are processed on a rolling basis. Application fee: $30. Electronic applications accepted. *Expenses:* Contact institution. *Financial support:* In 2011–12, 23 students received support. Federal Work-Study, scholarships/grants, tuition waivers (partial), and unspecified assistantships available. Support available to part-time students. Financial award applicants required to submit FAFSA. *Unit head:* Dr. John Gambro, Dean, 815-740-3829, Fax: 815-740-2264, E-mail: jgambro@stfrancis.edu. *Application contact:* Sandra Sloka, Director of Admissions for Graduate and Degree Completion Programs, 800-735-7500, Fax: 815-740-5032, E-mail: ssloka@stfrancis.edu. Web site: http://www.stfrancis.edu/academics/college-of-education/.

University of South Carolina, The Graduate School, College of Education, Department of Instruction and Teacher Education, Program in Secondary Education, Columbia, SC 29208. Offers art education (IMA, MAT); business education (IMA, MAT); English (MAT); foreign language (MAT); health education (MAT); mathematics (MAT); science (IMA, MAT); secondary (Ed D); secondary education (MT, PhD); social studies (MAT); theatre and speech (MAT). IMA and MT offered jointly with the subject areas. *Accreditation:* NCATE. *Degree requirements:* For master's, comprehensive exam, thesis (for some programs), foreign language (MA); for doctorate, one foreign language, comprehensive exam, thesis/dissertation. *Entrance requirements:* For master's, GRE General Test or MAT, teaching certificate (IMA, M Ed), interview; for doctorate, GRE General Test or MAT, interview. *Faculty research:* Middle school programs, professional development, school collaboration.

Social Sciences Education

University of Southern Mississippi, Graduate School, College of Education and Psychology, Department of Curriculum, Instruction, and Special Education, Hattiesburg, MS 39406-0001. Offers alternative secondary teacher education (MAT); early childhood education (M Ed, Ed S); education (Ed D); education of the gifted (M Ed, PhD, Ed S); elementary education (M Ed, PhD, Ed S); reading (M Ed, MS); secondary education (M Ed, MS, PhD); special education (M Ed, PhD, Ed S). Part-time programs available. *Faculty:* 23 full-time (17 women), 3 part-time/adjunct (2 women). *Students:* 39 full-time (34 women), 92 part-time (77 women); includes 36 minority (31 Black or African American, non-Hispanic/Latino; 3 Hispanic/Latino; 2 Two or more races, non-Hispanic/Latino), 3 international. Average age 37. 56 applicants, 55% accepted, 29 enrolled. In 2011, 45 master's, 5 doctorates awarded. *Degree requirements:* For master's and Ed S, comprehensive exam, thesis (for some programs); for doctorate, comprehensive exam, thesis/dissertation. *Entrance requirements:* For master's, GRE General Test, MAT, minimum GPA of 3.0; for doctorate, GRE General Test, minimum GPA of 3.5; for Ed S, GRE General Test, MAT, minimum GPA of 3.25. Additional exam requirements/recommendations for international students: Required—TOEFL, IELTS. *Application deadline:* For fall admission, 3/1 priority date for domestic students, 3/1 for international students; for spring admission, 1/10 priority date for domestic students, 1/10 for international students. Applications are processed on a rolling basis. Application fee: $50. *Financial support:* In 2011–12, 9 research assistantships with tuition reimbursements (averaging $18,316 per year), 2 teaching assistantships with full tuition reimbursements (averaging $8,500 per year) were awarded; Federal Work-Study, institutionally sponsored loans, scholarships/grants, health care benefits, tuition waivers (partial), and unspecified assistantships also available. Financial award application deadline: 3/15; financial award applicants required to submit FAFSA. *Faculty research:* Mathematical problem solving, integrative curriculum, writing process, teacher education models. *Total annual research expenditures:* $100,000. *Unit head:* Dr. David Daves, Chair, 601-266-4547, Fax: 601-266-4175, E-mail: david.daves@usm.edu. *Application contact:* Dr. Marie Crowe, Director of Graduate Studies, 601-266-6005, Fax: 601-266-4548, E-mail: margie.crowe@usm.edu. Web site: http://www.usm.edu/graduateschool/table.php.

University of South Florida, Graduate School, College of Education, Department of Secondary Education, Tampa, FL 33620-9951. Offers English education (M Ed, MA, MAT, PhD); foreign language education/ESOL (M Ed, MA, MAT); instructional technology (M Ed, PhD, Ed S); mathematics education (M Ed, MA, MAT, PhD, Ed S); science education (M Ed, MA, MAT, PhD); second language acquisition/instructional technology (PhD); secondary education (M Ed, PhD); secondary education/TESOL (M Ed); social science education (M Ed, MA, MAT); teaching and learning in the content area (PhD). *Accreditation:* NCATE. Part-time and evening/weekend programs available. *Faculty:* 28 full-time (17 women), 3 part-time/adjunct (1 woman). *Students:* 174 full-time (116 women), 268 part-time (184 women); includes 103 minority (26 Black or African American, non-Hispanic/Latino; 10 Asian, non-Hispanic/Latino; 58 Hispanic/Latino; 9 Two or more races, non-Hispanic/Latino), 32 international. Average age 37. 229 applicants, 73% accepted, 141 enrolled. In 2011, 115 master's, 16 doctorates, 5 other advanced degrees awarded. *Degree requirements:* For master's, variable foreign language requirement, comprehensive exam, project (for some programs); for doctorate, variable foreign language requirement, comprehensive exam, thesis/dissertation, philosophies of inquiry; multiple research methods. *Entrance requirements:* For master's, GRE General Test or General Knowledge Test, minimum GPA of 3.0; for doctorate, GRE General Test, minimum GPA of 3.5; for Ed S, GRE General Test. Additional exam requirements/recommendations for international students: Required—TOEFL (minimum score 550 paper-based; 213 computer-based; 79 iBT). *Application deadline:* For fall admission, 2/15 for domestic students, 1/2 for international students; for spring admission, 10/15 for domestic students, 6/1 for international students. Application fee: $30. Electronic applications accepted. *Financial support:* In 2011–12, 7 students received support, including 1 research assistantship with full tuition reimbursement available (averaging $10,000 per year), 55 teaching assistantships with full and partial tuition reimbursements available (averaging $7,900 per year); scholarships/grants and unspecified assistantships also available. Financial award application deadline: 4/15; financial award applicants required to submit FAFSA. *Faculty research:* English language learners/multicultural, social science education, mathematics education, science education, instructional technology. *Total annual research expenditures:* $336,023. *Unit head:* Dr. Stephen Thornton, Chairperson, 813-974-3533, Fax: 813-974-3837, E-mail: thornton@usf.edu. *Application contact:* Dr. Diane Briscoe, Coordinator of Graduate Studies, 813-974-1804, Fax: 813-974-3391, E-mail: briscoe@usf.edu. Web site: http://www.coedu.usf.edu/main/departments/seced/seced.html.

The University of Tennessee, Graduate School, College of Education, Health and Human Sciences, Program in Education, Knoxville, TN 37996. Offers art education (MS); counseling education (PhD); cultural studies in education (PhD); curriculum (MS, Ed S); curriculum, educational research and evaluation (Ed D, PhD); early childhood education (PhD); early childhood special education (MS); education of deaf and hard of hearing (MS); educational administration and policy studies (Ed D, PhD); educational administration and supervision (Ed S); educational psychology (Ed D, PhD); elementary education (MS, Ed S); elementary teaching (MS); English education (MS, Ed S); exercise science (PhD); foreign language/ESL education (MS, Ed S); instructional technology (MS, Ed D, PhD, Ed S); literacy, language and ESL education (PhD); literacy, language education, and ESL education (Ed D); mathematics education (MS, Ed S); modified and comprehensive special education (MS); reading education (MS, Ed S); school counseling (Ed S); school psychology (PhD, Ed S); science education (MS, Ed S); secondary teaching (MS); social foundations (MS); social science education (MS, Ed S); socio-cultural foundations of sports and education (PhD); special education (Ed S); teacher education (Ed D, PhD). *Accreditation:* NCATE. Part-time and evening/weekend programs available. *Degree requirements:* For master's and Ed S, thesis optional; for doctorate, variable foreign language requirement, thesis/dissertation. *Entrance requirements:* For master's, minimum GPA of 2.7; for doctorate and Ed S, GRE General Test, minimum GPA of 2.7. Additional exam requirements/recommendations for international students: Required—TOEFL. Electronic applications accepted. *Expenses:* Tuition, state resident: full-time $8332; part-time $464 per credit hour. Tuition, nonresident: full-time $25,174; part-time $1400 per credit hour. *Required fees:* $1162; $56 per credit hour. Tuition and fees vary according to program.

The University of Toledo, College of Graduate Studies, Judith Herb College of Education, Health Science and Human Service, Department of Curriculum and Instruction, Toledo, OH 43606-3390. Offers art education (ME); career and technical education (ME); curriculum and instruction (ME, PhD, Ed S); education and anthropology (MAE); education and biology (MES); education and chemistry (MES); education and classics (MAE); education and economics (MAE); education and English (MAE); education and French (MAE); education and geography (MAE); education and geology (MES); education and German (MAE); education and history (MAE); education and mathematics (MAE, MES); education and physics (MES); education and political science (MAE); education and sociology (MAE); education and Spanish (MAE); educational media (PhD); educational technology (ME); English as a second language (MAE); gifted and talented (PhD); middle childhood education licensure (ME); music education (MME); secondary education (PhD); secondary education licensure (ME). *Accreditation:* NCATE. Part-time and evening/weekend programs available. *Faculty:* 24. *Students:* 60 full-time (31 women), 211 part-time (161 women); includes 23 minority (21 Black or African American, non-Hispanic/Latino; 2 Hispanic/Latino), 20 international. Average age 35. 115 applicants, 73% accepted, 74 enrolled. In 2011, 105 master's, 3 doctorates, 4 other advanced degrees awarded. *Degree requirements:* For master's, comprehensive exam, thesis or alternative; for doctorate, comprehensive exam, thesis/dissertation; for Ed S, thesis optional. *Entrance requirements:* For master's, doctorate, and Ed S, minimum cumulative GPA of 2.7 for all previous academic work, letters of recommendation. Additional exam requirements/recommendations for international students: Required—TOEFL (minimum score 550 paper-based; 213 computer-based; 80 iBT), IELTS (minimum score 6.5). *Application deadline:* For fall admission, 1/15 priority date for domestic students, 1/15 for international students. Applications are processed on a rolling basis. Application fee: $45 ($75 for international students). Electronic applications accepted. *Financial support:* In 2011–12, 9 research assistantships with full and partial tuition reimbursements (averaging $7,184 per year), 12 teaching assistantships with full and partial tuition reimbursements (averaging $8,425 per year) were awarded; career-related internships or fieldwork, Federal Work-Study, institutionally sponsored loans, scholarships/grants, tuition waivers (full and partial), unspecified assistantships, and administrative assistantships also available. Support available to part-time students. *Unit head:* Dr. Leigh Chiarelott, Chair, 419-530-5371, E-mail: eigh.chiarelott@utoledo.edu. *Application contact:* Graduate School Office, 419-530-4723, Fax: 419-530-4724, E-mail: grdsch@utnet.utoledo.edu. Web site: http://www.utoledo.edu/eduhshs/.

University of Victoria, Faculty of Graduate Studies, Faculty of Education, Department of Curriculum and Instruction, Victoria, BC V8W 2Y2, Canada. Offers art education (M Ed, PhD); curriculum studies (M Ed, MA, PhD); early childhood education (M Ed, PhD); educational studies (PhD); language and literacy (M Ed, MA, PhD); mathematics (M Ed, MA, PhD); music education (M Ed, MA, PhD); science (M Ed, MA, PhD); social studies (M Ed, MA); social, cultural and foundational studies (MA, PhD); technology and environmental education (PhD). Part-time programs available. *Degree requirements:* For master's, thesis, project (M Ed); for doctorate, comprehensive exam, thesis/dissertation. *Entrance requirements:* For master's, minimum B average. Additional exam requirements/recommendations for international students: Required—TOEFL (minimum score 575 paper-based; 233 computer-based), IELTS (minimum score 7). Electronic applications accepted. *Faculty research:* Elementary and secondary English, language arts, curriculum theory and practice, educational media and technology, educational administration and leadership, history and philosophy of education.

University of Virginia, Curry School of Education, Department of Curriculum, Instruction, and Special Education, Program in Curriculum and Instruction, Charlottesville, VA 22903. Offers curriculum and instruction (M Ed, Ed S); elementary (M Ed, Ed D); English (M Ed, Ed D); foreign language (M Ed); mathematics (M Ed, Ed D); reading (M Ed, Ed D, Ed S); science (Ed D); social studies (M Ed). *Students:* 22 full-time (17 women), 29 part-time (27 women); includes 4 minority (1 Black or African American, non-Hispanic/Latino; 1 Asian, non-Hispanic/Latino; 2 Two or more races, non-Hispanic/Latino), 1 international. Average age 33. 67 applicants, 75% accepted, 33 enrolled. In 2011, 78 master's, 2 doctorates, 12 other advanced degrees awarded. *Degree requirements:* For master's, comprehensive exam (for some programs); for doctorate, comprehensive exam, thesis/dissertation; for Ed S, comprehensive exam. *Entrance requirements:* For master's, doctorate, and Ed S, GRE General Test, 2 letters of recommendation. Additional exam requirements/recommendations for international students: Required—TOEFL (minimum score 600 paper-based; 250 computer-based; 90 iBT), IELTS (minimum score 7). *Application deadline:* Applications are processed on a rolling basis. Application fee: $60. Electronic applications accepted. *Financial support:* Fellowships with tuition reimbursements, research assistantships with tuition reimbursements, and teaching assistantships with tuition reimbursements available. Financial award application deadline: 1/5; financial award applicants required to submit FAFSA. *Unit head:* Laura Smolkin, Chair, 434-924-0831. *Application contact:* Karen Dwier, Information Contact, 434-924-0831, E-mail: kgd9g@virginia.edu.

University of Virginia, Curry School of Education, Program in Education, Charlottesville, VA 22903. Offers administration and supervision (PhD); applied developmental science (PhD); counselor education (PhD); curriculum and instruction (PhD); early childhood-developmental risk (MT); education evaluation (PhD); educational psychology (PhD); educational research (PhD); elementary (MT, PhD); English education (MT, PhD); foreign language education (MT); higher education (PhD); instructional technology (PhD); kinesiology (MT, PhD); math education (PhD); reading education (PhD); research statistics and evaluation (PhD); school psychology (PhD); science education (PhD); social studies education (MT, PhD); special education (PhD); world languages education (MT). *Students:* 299 full-time (216 women), 60 part-time (33 women); includes 46 minority (18 Black or African American, non-Hispanic/Latino; 17 Asian, non-Hispanic/Latino; 7 Hispanic/Latino; 4 Two or more races, non-Hispanic/Latino), 23 international. Average age 30. 307 applicants, 42% accepted, 80 enrolled. In 2011, 113 master's, 62 doctorates awarded. *Degree requirements:* For master's, comprehensive exam (for some programs), field project; for doctorate, comprehensive exam, thesis/dissertation. *Entrance requirements:* For doctorate, GRE General Test. Additional exam requirements/recommendations for international students: Required—TOEFL (minimum score 600 paper-based; 250 computer-based; 90 iBT), IELTS (minimum score 7). *Application deadline:* Applications are processed on a rolling basis. Application fee: $60. Electronic applications accepted. *Financial support:* Fellowships, research assistantships, and teaching assistantships available. Financial award application deadline: 1/5; financial award applicants required to submit FAFSA. *Unit head:* Robert C. Pianta, Dean, 434-924-3334. *Application contact:* Joanne McNergney, Assistant Dean for Admissions and Student Services, 434-924-3334, E-mail: curry-admissions@virginia.edu.

University of Washington, Graduate School, College of Education, Seattle, WA 98195. Offers curriculum and instruction (M Ed, Ed D, PhD), including educational technology, general curriculum (Ed D, PhD), language, literacy, and culture, mathematics education, multicultural education, reading and language arts education (Ed D), science education, social studies education, teaching and curriculum (M Ed); educational leadership and policy studies (M Ed, Ed D, PhD), including administration (Ed D), educational policy, organization, and leadership (M Ed, PhD), higher education, leadership for learning (Ed D), social and cultural foundations of education (M Ed, PhD); educational psychology (M Ed, PhD), including educational psychology (PhD), human development and cognition (M Ed), learning sciences, measurement, statistics and research design (M Ed), school psychology (M Ed); instructional leadership (M Ed); intercollegiate athletic leadership (M Ed); special education (M Ed, Ed D, PhD), including early childhood special education (M Ed), emotional and behavioral disabilities (M Ed), learning disabilities (M Ed), low-incidence disabilities (M Ed), severe disabilities (M Ed), special education (Ed D, PhD); teacher education (MIT). *Accreditation:* APA. Part-time and evening/weekend programs available. *Degree requirements:* For master's, thesis optional; for doctorate, thesis/dissertation. *Entrance requirements:* For master's and doctorate, GRE General Test, minimum GPA of 3.0. Additional exam requirements/recommendations for international students: Required—TOEFL. Electronic applications accepted. *Faculty research:* School restructuring/effective schools, special education interventions, literacy and writing, technology, school partnerships, teacher preparation.

University of West Florida, College of Professional Studies, Ed D Programs, Specialization in Curriculum and Instruction: Science and Social Sciences, Pensacola, FL 32514-5750. Offers Ed D. Part-time and evening/weekend programs available. *Students:* 2 full-time (1 woman), 24 part-time (11 women); includes 4 minority (1 Black or African American, non-Hispanic/Latino; 1 Asian, non-Hispanic/Latino; 2 Hispanic/Latino). Average age 41. 9 applicants, 67% accepted, 6 enrolled. *Degree requirements:* For doctorate, comprehensive exam, thesis/dissertation. *Entrance requirements:* For doctorate, GRE, MAT, or GMAT, letter of intent; writing sample; three letters of recommendation; two completed disposition assessment forms; written statement of goals; interview with admissions committee. Additional exam requirements/recommendations for international students: Required—TOEFL (minimum score 550 paper-based; 213 computer-based). *Application deadline:* For fall admission, 6/1 for domestic and international students; for spring admission, 10/1 for domestic students. Applications are processed on a rolling basis. Application fee: $30. *Expenses:* Tuition, state resident: full-time $5729; part-time $302 per credit hour. Tuition, nonresident: full-time $20,059; part-time $961 per credit hour. *Required fees:* $1509; $63 per credit hour. *Unit head:* Dr. Pam Northrup, Interim Dean, 850-474-2769, Fax: 850-474-3205. *Application contact:* Terry McCray, Assistant Director of Graduate Admissions, 850-473-7718, Fax: 850-473-7714, E-mail: gradadmissions@uwf.edu. Web site: http://uwf.edu/edd/science_socialscience.cfm.

University of West Georgia, College of Education, Department of Leadership and Applied Instruction, Carrollton, GA 30118. Offers art education (M Ed); art teacher education (Ed S); biology - secondary education (M Ed); biology/secondary education (Ed S); business education (M Ed, Ed S); chemistry/secondary education (Ed S); earth science/secondary education (Ed S); economics/secondary education (Ed S); educational leadership (M Ed, Ed S); English teacher education (M Ed, Ed S); French teacher education (M Ed, Ed S); history teacher education (Ed S); mathematics teacher education (M Ed, Ed S); middle grades education (M Ed, Ed S); physical education and recreation (Ed S); physical education teaching and coaching (M Ed); physics/secondary education (Ed S); science teacher education (M Ed, Ed S); secondary education (M Ed); social science - secondary education (M Ed); social science teacher education (M Ed); Spanish (M Ed); Spanish teacher education (M Ed, Ed S); sports management (M Ed). *Accreditation:* NCATE. Part-time and evening/weekend programs available. *Faculty:* 18 full-time (9 women). *Students:* 75 full-time (49 women), 169 part-time (109 women); includes 90 minority (85 Black or African American, non-Hispanic/Latino; 3 Hispanic/Latino; 2 Two or more races, non-Hispanic/Latino), 1 international. Average age 36. 115 applicants, 67% accepted, 19 enrolled. In 2011, 73 master's, 53 Ed Ss awarded. *Degree requirements:* For master's, internship; for Ed S, research project. *Entrance requirements:* For master's, GRE General Test, minimum GPA of 2.7; for Ed S, GRE General Test, master's degree, minimum graduate GPA of 3.0, district appointment. Additional exam requirements/recommendations for international students: Required—TOEFL (minimum score 523 paper-based; 193 computer-based; 69 iBT); Recommended—IELTS (minimum score 6). *Application deadline:* For fall admission, 7/21 for domestic students, 6/1 for international students; for spring admission, 11/30 for domestic students, 10/15 for international students. Applications are processed on a rolling basis. Application fee: $30. Electronic applications accepted. *Expenses:* Tuition, state resident: full-time $4336; part-time $181 per credit hour. Tuition, nonresident: full-time $17,362; part-time $724 per credit hour. Tuition and fees vary according to course load, degree level, campus/location and program. *Financial support:* In 2011–12, 1 research assistantship with full tuition reimbursement (averaging $7,444 per year) was awarded; career-related internships or fieldwork, scholarships/grants, and unspecified assistantships also available. Support available to part-time students. Financial award application deadline: 7/1; financial award applicants required to submit FAFSA. *Total annual research expenditures:* $5,000. *Unit head:* Dr. Frank Butts, Chair, 678-839-6530, Fax: 678-839-6195, E-mail: fbutts@westga.edu. *Application contact:* Deanna Richards, Coordinator, Graduate Studies, 678-839-5946, E-mail: drichard@westga.edu. Web site: http://www.westga.edu/coelai.

University of Wisconsin–River Falls, Outreach and Graduate Studies, College of Arts and Science, Department of History and Philosophy, River Falls, WI 54022. Offers social science education (MSE). Part-time programs available. *Degree requirements:* For master's, thesis (for some programs). *Entrance requirements:* For master's, minimum GPA of 2.75. Additional exam requirements/recommendations for international students: Required—TOEFL (minimum score 500 paper-based; 65 iBT), IELTS (minimum score 5.5). Electronic applications accepted. *Faculty research:* WW II, Hitler, modern China, women's history, immigration history.

Ursuline College, School of Graduate Studies, Program in Education, Pepper Pike, OH 44124-4398. Offers art education (MA); early childhood education (MA); language arts education (MA); life science education (MA); math education (MA); middle school education (MA); social studies education (MA); special education (MA). *Accreditation:* NCATE. *Faculty:* 3 full-time (all women), 8 part-time/adjunct (6 women). *Students:* 28 full-time (22 women), 1 (woman) part-time; includes 11 minority (7 Black or African American, non-Hispanic/Latino; 2 Asian, non-Hispanic/Latino; 1 Hispanic/Latino; 1 Native Hawaiian or other Pacific Islander, non-Hispanic/Latino). Average age 32. In 2011, 29 master's awarded. *Degree requirements:* For master's, comprehensive exam. *Entrance requirements:* For master's, minimum undergraduate GPA of 3.0. Additional exam requirements/recommendations for international students: Required—TOEFL (minimum score 500 paper-based; 173 computer-based). *Application deadline:* For fall admission, 8/1 priority date for domestic students. Applications are processed on a rolling basis. Application fee: $25. *Expenses:* Contact institution. *Financial support:* Federal Work-Study available. Financial award application deadline: 3/1. *Unit head:* Dr. Edna West, Director, Master's Apprentice Program, 440-646-6134, Fax: 440-684-6088, E-mail: ewest@ursuline.edu. *Application contact:* Melanie Steele, Graduate Admission Assistant, 440-646-8199, Fax: 440-684-6138, E-mail: graduateadmissions@ursuline.edu.

Virginia Polytechnic Institute and State University, Graduate School, College of Liberal Arts and Human Sciences, Alliance for Social, Political, Ethical, and Cultural Thought, Blacksburg, VA 24061. Offers PhD, Certificate. *Expenses:* Tuition, state resident: full-time $10,048; part-time $558.25 per credit hour. Tuition, nonresident: full-time $19,497; part-time $1083.25 per credit hour. *Required fees:* $405 per semester. Tuition and fees vary according to course load, campus/location and program. *Unit head:* Sue Ott Rowlands, Dean, 540-231-6779, Fax: 540-231-7157, E-mail: sottrowlands@vt.edu. Web site: http://www.aspect.vt.edu/.

Wayne State College, School of Education and Counseling, Department of Educational Foundations and Leadership, Program in Curriculum and Instruction, Wayne, NE 68787. Offers alternative education (MSE); business and information technology education (MSE); communication arts education (MSE); early childhood education (MSE); elementary education (MSE); English as a second language (MSE); English education (MSE); family and consumer sciences education (MSE); industrial technology and vocational education (MSE); learning communities (MSE); mathematics education (MSE); music education (MSE); science education (MSE); social science education (MSE). *Accreditation:* NCATE. Part-time and evening/weekend programs available. *Degree requirements:* For master's, comprehensive exam, thesis optional. *Entrance requirements:* For master's, GRE General Test. Additional exam requirements/recommendations for international students: Required—TOEFL (minimum score 550 paper-based; 213 computer-based).

Wayne State University, College of Education, Division of Teacher Education, Detroit, MI 48202. Offers art education (M Ed), including art therapy; bilingual/bicultural education (M Ed); career and technical education (M Ed); curriculum and instruction (Ed D, PhD, Ed S), including art education (PhD), bilingual education (Ed D, Ed S), bilingual-bicultural education (PhD), career and technical education (MAT, Ed D, PhD, Ed S), early childhood education (MAT, Ed D, PhD, Ed S), elementary education, English as a second language (MAT, Ed D, Ed S), English education (MAT, Ed D, PhD, Ed S), foreign language education (MAT, PhD), K-12 curriculum, mathematics education (MAT, Ed D, PhD, Ed S), science education (MAT, Ed D, PhD, Ed S), secondary education, social studies education (MAT, Ed S), social studies education: secondary (Ed D, PhD); elementary education (MAT), including special education; elementary education (M Ed, MAT), including children's literature (MAT), early childhood education (MAT, Ed D, PhD, Ed S), general elementary education (MAT); elementary or secondary education (MAT), including bilingual/bicultural education, English as a second language (MAT, Ed D, Ed S), mathematics education (MAT, Ed D, PhD, Ed S), science education (MAT, Ed D, PhD, Ed S), social studies education (MAT, Ed S); English education-secondary (M Ed); foreign language education (M Ed); mathematics education (M Ed); reading (M Ed, Ed S); reading, languages and literature (Ed D); science education (M Ed); secondary education (MAT), including art education (K-12), career and technical education (MAT, Ed D, PhD, Ed S), English education (MAT, Ed D, PhD, Ed S), foreign language education (MAT, PhD), kinesiology; social studies education secondary (M Ed); special education (M Ed, Ed D, PhD, Ed S). *Students:* 216 full-time (154 women), 626 part-time (478 women); includes 289 minority (227 Black or African American, non-Hispanic/Latino; 4 American Indian or Alaska Native, non-Hispanic/Latino; 27 Asian, non-Hispanic/Latino; 21 Hispanic/Latino; 1 Native Hawaiian or other Pacific Islander, non-Hispanic/Latino; 9 Two or more races, non-Hispanic/Latino), 14 international. Average age 37. 347 applicants, 37% accepted, 93 enrolled. In 2011, 226 master's, 12 doctorates, 46 other advanced degrees awarded. *Degree requirements:* For master's, thesis (for some programs), thesis, essay or project (for some M Ed programs), professional field experience (for MAT programs); for doctorate, thesis/dissertation. *Entrance requirements:* For master's, Michigan Basic Skills Test (MA in teaching); for doctorate, minimum undergraduate GPA of 3.0, graduate 3.5; interview, curriculum vitae; references. Additional exam requirements/recommendations for international students: Required—TOEFL (minimum score 550 paper-based; 213 computer-based), TWE (minimum score 5.5). *Application deadline:* For fall admission, 6/1 priority date for domestic students, 5/1 for international students; for winter admission, 10/1 priority date for domestic students, 9/1 for international students; for spring admission, 2/1 priority date for domestic students, 1/1 for international students. Applications are processed on a rolling basis. Application fee: $50. Electronic applications accepted. *Expenses:* Tuition, state resident: part-time $512.85 per credit. Tuition, nonresident: part-time $1132.65 per credit. *Required fees:* $26.60 per credit. $199.65 per semester. Tuition and fees vary according to course load and program. *Financial support:* In 2011–12, 42 students received support. Fellowships, research assistantships with tuition reimbursements available, teaching assistantships, scholarships/grants, and unspecified assistantships available. *Faculty research:* Reading and writing literacy and literature. *Total annual research expenditures:* $264,016. *Unit head:* Dr. Craig Roney, Assistant Dean, 313-577-0902, E-mail: rroney@wayne.edu. Web site: http://coe.wayne.edu/ted/index.php.

Wayne State University, College of Education, Division of Theoretical and Behavioral Foundations, Detroit, MI 48202. Offers counseling (M Ed, MA, Ed D, PhD, Ed S); education evaluation and research (M Ed, Ed D, PhD); educational psychology (M Ed, Ed D, PhD, Ed S); educational sociology (M Ed, Ed D, PhD, Ed S); history and philosophy of education (M Ed, Ed D, PhD); rehabilitation counseling and community inclusion (MA, Ed S); school and community psychology (MA, Ed S); school clinical psychology (Ed S). *Accreditation:* ACA (one or more programs are accredited); CORE (one or more programs are accredited). Evening/weekend programs available. *Students:* 199 full-time (156 women), 215 part-time (187 women); includes 162 minority (145 Black or African American, non-Hispanic/Latino; 1 American Indian or Alaska Native, non-Hispanic/Latino; 5 Asian, non-Hispanic/Latino; 5 Hispanic/Latino; 1 Native Hawaiian or other Pacific Islander, non-Hispanic/Latino; 5 Two or more races, non-Hispanic/Latino), 21 international. Average age 35. 278 applicants, 30% accepted, 56 enrolled. In 2011, 94 master's, 15 doctorates, 1 other advanced degree awarded. *Degree requirements:* For master's, thesis (for some programs); for doctorate, thesis/dissertation. *Entrance requirements:* For master's, GRE; for doctorate, GRE, interview, minimum GPA of 3.0, curriculum vitae, references. Additional exam requirements/recommendations for international students: Required—TOEFL (minimum score 550 paper-based; 213 computer-based), TWE (minimum score 5.5). *Application deadline:* For fall admission, 6/1 priority date for domestic students, 5/1 for international students; for winter admission, 10/1 priority date for domestic students, 9/1 for international students; for spring admission, 2/1 priority date for domestic students, 1/1 for international students. Applications are processed on a rolling basis. Application fee: $50. Electronic applications accepted. *Expenses:* Tuition, state resident: part-time $512.85 per credit. Tuition, nonresident: part-time $1132.65 per credit. *Required fees:* $26.60 per credit. $199.65 per semester. Tuition and fees vary according to course load and program. *Financial support:* In 2011–12, 64 students received support, including 3 fellowships with tuition reimbursements available (averaging $16,371 per year), 2 research assistantships with tuition reimbursements available (averaging $15,713 per year), 1 teaching assistantship (averaging $18,000 per year); career-related internships or fieldwork, Federal Work-Study, institutionally sponsored loans, scholarships/grants, health care benefits, and unspecified assistantships also available. *Faculty research:* Adolescents at risk, supervision of counseling. *Total annual research expenditures:* $5,019. *Unit head:* Dr. Alan Hoffman, Assistant Dean, 313-577-5235, E-mail: alanhoffman@wayne.edu. *Application contact:* Janice Green, Assistant Dean, 313-577-1605, E-mail: jwgreen@wayne.edu. Web site: http://coe.wayne.edu/tbf/index.php.

Webster University, School of Education, Department of Multidisciplinary Studies, St. Louis, MO 63119-3194. Offers administrative leadership (Ed S); education leadership (Ed S); educational technology (MAT); mathematics (MAT); multidisciplinary studies (MAT); school systems, superintendency and leadership (Ed S); social science (MAT); special education (MAT). Part-time programs available. *Entrance requirements:* For master's, minimum GPA of 2.5. Additional exam requirements/recommendations for international students: Required—TOEFL. *Expenses: Tuition:* Full-time $10,890; part-time $605 per credit hour. Tuition and fees vary according to campus/location and program.

Western Governors University, Teachers College, Salt Lake City, UT 84107. Offers curriculum and instruction (MS); educational leadership (MS); educational studies (MA); educational studies (5-12) (MA), including mathematics; elementary education (k-8) (Postbaccalaureate Certificate); English language learning (K-12) (MA); instructional design (MAT); learning and technology (M Ed, MA); management and innovation (M Ed); mathematics (5-12) (Postbaccalaureate Certificate); mathematics (5-9) (Postbaccalaureate Certificate); mathematics education (5-12) (MA); mathematics education (5-9) (MA); mathematics education (K-6) (MA); measurement and evaluation (M Ed); science (5-12) (Postbaccalaureate Certificate); science (5-9)

(Postbaccalaureate Certificate); science education (5-12) (MA), including biology, chemistry, geology, physics; science education (5-9) (MA); social science (5-12) (MAT); special education (MAT). *Accreditation:* NCATE. Evening/weekend programs available. Postbaccalaureate distance learning degree programs offered (no on-campus study). *Students:* 3,746 full-time (2,811 women); includes 652 minority (332 Black or African American, non-Hispanic/Latino; 37 American Indian or Alaska Native, non-Hispanic/Latino; 74 Asian, non-Hispanic/Latino; 139 Hispanic/Latino; 70 Two or more races, non-Hispanic/Latino), 12 international. Average age 37. In 2011, 1,080 master's, 242 other advanced degrees awarded. *Degree requirements:* For master's, capstone project. *Entrance requirements:* For master's and Postbaccalaureate Certificate, Readiness Assessment, commitment counseling discussion, transcript submissions, completion of orientation. Additional exam requirements/recommendations for international students: Required—TOEFL (minimum score 450 paper-based; 80 iBT). *Application deadline:* Applications are processed on a rolling basis. Application fee: $65. Electronic applications accepted. *Expenses:* Contact institution. *Financial support:* Scholarships/grants and tuition waivers (partial) available. Financial award applicants required to submit FAFSA. *Unit head:* Dr. Philip Schmidt, Dean of the Teachers College, 845-255-4656. *Application contact:* Enrollment Department, 866-225-5948, Fax: 801-274-3306, E-mail: info@wgu.edu.

Western Oregon University, Graduate Programs, College of Education, Division of Teacher Education, Program in Secondary Education, Monmouth, OR 97361-1394. Offers bilingual education (MS Ed); health (MS Ed); humanities (MAT, MS Ed); initial licensure (MAT); mathematics (MAT, MS Ed); science (MAT, MS Ed); social science (MAT, MS Ed). *Accreditation:* NCATE. Part-time and evening/weekend programs available. *Degree requirements:* For master's, thesis optional, written exam. *Entrance requirements:* For master's, minimum GPA of 3.0, teaching license. Additional exam requirements/recommendations for international students: Required—TOEFL (minimum score 550 paper-based; 213 computer-based; 79 iBT), IELTS (minimum score 6.5). *Faculty research:* Literacy, science in primary grades, geography education, retention, teacher burnout.

Widener University, School of Human Service Professions, Center for Education, Chester, PA 19013-5792. Offers adult education (M Ed); counseling in higher education (M Ed); counselor education (M Ed); early childhood education (M Ed); educational foundations (M Ed); educational leadership (M Ed); educational psychology (M Ed); elementary education (M Ed); English and language arts (M Ed); health education (M Ed); higher education leadership (Ed D); home and school visitor (M Ed); human sexuality (M Ed, PhD); mathematics education (M Ed); middle school education (M Ed); principalship (M Ed); reading and language arts (Ed D); reading education (M Ed); school administration (Ed D); science education (M Ed); social studies education (M Ed); special education (M Ed); technology education (M Ed). *Accreditation:* NCATE. Part-time and evening/weekend programs available. Terminal master's awarded for partial completion of doctoral program. *Degree requirements:* For doctorate, thesis/dissertation. *Entrance requirements:* For master's, minimum GPA of 2.5; for doctorate, GRE or MAT, minimum GPA of 2.0 (undergraduate), 3.5 (graduate). Electronic applications accepted. *Expenses:* Contact institution. *Faculty research:* Reading and cognition, adult education, technology education, educational leadership, special education.

Wilkes University, College of Graduate and Professional Studies, School of Education, Wilkes-Barre, PA 18766-0002. Offers art and science of teaching (MS Ed); classroom technology (MS Ed); early childhood literacy (MS Ed); educational computing (MS Ed); educational development and strategies (MS Ed); educational leadership (MS Ed); educational technology (Ed D); higher education administration (Ed D); instructional media (MS Ed); instructional technology (MS Ed); K-12 administration (Ed D); online teaching (MS Ed); reading (MS Ed); school business leadership (MS Ed); secondary education (MS Ed), including biology, chemistry, English, history, mathematics; special education (MS Ed); teaching English as a second language (MS Ed); twenty-first century teaching and learning (MS Ed). Part-time and evening/weekend programs available. Postbaccalaureate distance learning degree programs offered (minimal on-campus study). *Students:* 92 full-time (63 women), 2,005 part-time (1,459 women); includes 89 minority (23 Black or African American, non-Hispanic/Latino; 1 American Indian or Alaska Native, non-Hispanic/Latino; 14 Asian, non-Hispanic/Latino; 33 Hispanic/Latino; 1 Native Hawaiian or other Pacific Islander, non-Hispanic/Latino; 17 Two or more races, non-Hispanic/Latino), 6 international. Average age 33. In 2011, 1,150 master's, 3 doctorates awarded. *Entrance requirements:* Additional exam requirements/recommendations for international students: Required—TOEFL (minimum score 550 paper-based; 213 computer-based; 79 iBT). *Application deadline:* Applications are processed on a rolling basis. Application fee: $45. Electronic applications accepted. *Expenses:* Contact institution. *Financial support:* Federal Work-Study and unspecified assistantships available. Financial award application deadline: 3/1; financial award applicants required to submit FAFSA. *Unit head:* Dr. Michael Speziale, Dean, 570-408-4679, Fax: 570-408-4905, E-mail: michael.speziale@wilkes.edu. *Application contact:* Erin Sutzko, Director of Extended Learning, 570-408-4253, Fax: 570-408-7846, E-mail: erin.sutzko@wilkes.edu. Web site: http://www.wilkes.edu/pages/383.asp.

William Carey University, School of Education, Hattiesburg, MS 39401-5499. Offers art education (M Ed); art of teaching (M Ed); elementary education (M Ed, Ed S); English education (M Ed); gifted education (M Ed); history and social science (M Ed); mild/moderate disabilities (M Ed); secondary education (M Ed). Part-time programs available. *Degree requirements:* For master's, comprehensive exam. *Entrance requirements:* For master's, GRE, MAT, minimum GPA of 2.5, Class A teacher's license. Additional exam requirements/recommendations for international students: Required—TOEFL (minimum score 550 paper-based; 213 computer-based).

Worcester State University, Graduate Studies, Program in History, Worcester, MA 01602-2597. Offers MA. Part-time programs available. *Faculty:* 3 full-time (2 women), 1 part-time/adjunct (0 women). *Students:* 4 full-time (0 women), 15 part-time (3 women); includes 1 minority (Black or African American, non-Hispanic/Latino). Average age 36. 25 applicants, 92% accepted, 12 enrolled. In 2011, 19 master's awarded. *Degree requirements:* For master's, comprehensive exam (for some programs), thesis optional. *Entrance requirements:* For master's, GRE General Test or MAT, 18 undergraduate credits in history, including U.S. history and Western civilizations. Additional exam requirements/recommendations for international students: Required—TOEFL (minimum score 500 paper-based; 61 iBT). *Application deadline:* For fall admission, 6/15 for domestic and international students; for spring admission, 4/1 for domestic and international students. Applications are processed on a rolling basis. Application fee: $40. Electronic applications accepted. *Expenses:* Tuition, state resident: full-time $2700; part-time $150 per credit. Tuition, nonresident: full-time $2700; part-time $150 per credit. *Required fees:* $2016; $112 per credit. *Financial support:* In 2011–12, 2 students received support, including 2 research assistantships with full and partial tuition reimbursements available (averaging $4,000 per year); career-related internships or fieldwork, scholarships/grants, and unspecified assistantships also available. Financial award application deadline: 3/1; financial award applicants required to submit FAFSA. *Faculty research:* Labor history, Middle East politics, American-Russian relations, American-East Asian relations. *Unit head:* Dr. Charlotte Haller, Coordinator, 508-929-8046, Fax: 508-929-8155, E-mail: challer1@worcester.edu. *Application contact:* Sara Grady, Assistant Dean of Graduate and Continuing Education, 508-929-8787, Fax: 508-929-8100, E-mail: sara.grady@worcester.edu.

Vocational and Technical Education

Alabama Agricultural and Mechanical University, School of Graduate Studies, School of Engineering and Technology, Department of Industrial Technology, Huntsville, AL 35811. Offers M Ed, MS. *Accreditation:* NCATE. Part-time and evening/weekend programs available. *Degree requirements:* For master's, comprehensive exam, thesis optional. *Entrance requirements:* For master's, GRE General Test. Additional exam requirements/recommendations for international students: Required—TOEFL (minimum score 500 paper-based; 173 computer-based; 61 iBT). Electronic applications accepted. *Faculty research:* Ionized gases, hypersonic flow, phenomenology, robotic systems development.

Alcorn State University, School of Graduate Studies, Department of Advanced Technologies, Alcorn State, MS 39096-7500. Offers workforce education leadership (MS).

Alcorn State University, School of Graduate Studies, School of Psychology and Education, Alcorn State, MS 39096-7500. Offers agricultural education (MS Ed); elementary education (MS Ed, Ed S); guidance and counseling (MS Ed); industrial education (MS Ed); secondary education (MS Ed), including health and physical education; special education (MS Ed). *Accreditation:* NCATE. *Degree requirements:* For master's, thesis optional.

Appalachian State University, Cratis D. Williams Graduate School, Department of Technology, Boone, NC 28608. Offers appropriate technology (MS); renewable energy engineering (MS). Part-time programs available. *Faculty:* 18 full-time (5 women), 4 part-time/adjunct (1 woman). *Students:* 38 full-time (7 women), 5 part-time (1 woman); includes 3 minority (1 Black or African American, non-Hispanic/Latino; 1 American Indian or Alaska Native, non-Hispanic/Latino; 1 Asian, non-Hispanic/Latino), 1 international. 28 applicants, 82% accepted, 12 enrolled. In 2011, 19 master's awarded. *Degree requirements:* For master's, comprehensive exam, thesis optional. *Entrance requirements:* For master's, GRE General Test, 3 letters of recommendation. Additional exam requirements/recommendations for international students: Required—TOEFL (minimum score 550 paper-based; 230 computer-based; 79 iBT), IELTS (minimum score 6.5). *Application deadline:* For fall admission, 3/15 priority date for domestic students, 2/1 for international students; for spring admission, 11/1 for domestic students, 7/1 for international students. Applications are processed on a rolling basis. Application fee: $55. Electronic applications accepted. *Expenses:* Tuition, state resident: full-time $4040; part-time $180 per semester hour. Tuition, nonresident: full-time $15,900; part-time $760 per semester hour. *Required fees:* $2500; $20 per semester hour. Tuition and fees vary according to campus/location. *Financial support:* In 2011–12, 14 research assistantships (averaging $9,000 per year) were awarded; fellowships, teaching assistantships, career-related internships or fieldwork, Federal Work-Study, institutionally sponsored loans, scholarships/grants, and unspecified assistantships also available. Financial award application deadline: 4/1; financial award applicants required to submit FAFSA. *Faculty research:* Wind power, biofuels, green construction, solar energy production. *Total annual research expenditures:* $322,000. *Unit head:* Dr. Jeff Tiller, Chair, 828-262-6351, E-mail: tillerjs@appstate.edu. *Application contact:* Dr. Marie Hoepfl, Graduate Program Director, 828-262-6351, E-mail: hoepflmc@appstate.edu. Web site: http://www.tec.appstate.edu.

Ball State University, Graduate School, College of Applied Science and Technology, Department of Industry and Technology, Muncie, IN 47306-1099. Offers MA, MAE. *Accreditation:* NCATE (one or more programs are accredited). *Faculty:* 11 full-time (3 women). *Students:* 9 full-time (3 women), 53 part-time (11 women); includes 3 minority (1 Black or African American, non-Hispanic/Latino; 2 Two or more races, non-Hispanic/Latino). Average age 38. 22 applicants, 82% accepted, 13 enrolled. In 2011, 33 master's awarded. Application fee: $25 ($35 for international students). Tuition and fees vary according to program and reciprocity agreements. *Financial support:* In 2011–12, 5 students received support, including 5 teaching assistantships with full tuition reimbursements available (averaging $5,923 per year). Financial award application deadline: 3/1. *Unit head:* Dr. Samuel Cotton, Chairperson, 765-285-5641, Fax: 765-285-2162. Web site: http://www.bsu.edu/cast/itech/.

Bowling Green State University, Graduate College, College of Technology, Program in Career and Technology Education, Bowling Green, OH 43403. Offers career and technology education (M Ed), including technology. Part-time programs available. *Degree requirements:* For master's, thesis or alternative. *Entrance requirements:* For master's, GRE General Test. Additional exam requirements/recommendations for international students: Required—TOEFL. Electronic applications accepted. *Faculty research:* Curriculum in technology education.

Buffalo State College, State University of New York, The Graduate School, Faculty of Applied Science and Education, Department of Educational Foundations, Program in Career and Technical Education, Buffalo, NY 14222-1095. Offers MS Ed. *Accreditation:* NCATE. Part-time and evening/weekend programs available. *Degree requirements:* For master's, thesis or project. *Entrance requirements:* For master's, minimum GPA of 2.5 in last 60 hours, New York teaching certificate. Additional exam requirements/recommendations for international students: Required—TOEFL (minimum score 550 paper-based; 213 computer-based).

Buffalo State College, State University of New York, The Graduate School, Faculty of Applied Science and Education, Department of Technology, Program in Technology Education, Buffalo, NY 14222-1095. Offers MS Ed. *Accreditation:* NCATE. *Degree requirements:* For master's, thesis or project. *Entrance requirements:* For master's, minimum GPA of 2.5 in last 60 hours, New York teaching certificate. Additional exam requirements/recommendations for international students: Required—TOEFL (minimum score 550 paper-based; 213 computer-based).

California Baptist University, Program in Education, Riverside, CA 92504-3206. Offers educational leadership for faith-based instruction (MS); educational leadership for public institutions (MS); educational technology (MS); instructional computer applications (MS); international education (MS); reading (MS); school counseling (MS); school psychology (MS); special education (MS); special education in mild/moderate disabilities (MS); special education in moderate/severe disabilities (MS); teaching (MS); teaching and learning with induction program (MS Ed). Part-time and evening/weekend programs available. *Faculty:* 16 full-time (10 women), 1 (woman) part-time/adjunct. *Students:* 380 full-time (323 women); includes 149 minority (28 Black or African American, non-Hispanic/Latino; 2 American Indian or Alaska Native, non-Hispanic/Latino; 13 Asian, non-Hispanic/Latino; 100 Hispanic/Latino; 2 Native Hawaiian or other Pacific Islander, non-Hispanic/Latino; 4 Two or more races, non-Hispanic/Latino). Average age 32. 181 applicants, 70% accepted, 111 enrolled. In 2011, 82 master's awarded. *Degree requirements:* For master's, comprehensive exam or thesis. *Entrance requirements:* For master's, minimum undergraduate GPA of 3.0; 18 semester units of prerequisite course work in education; three recommendations; essay; interview. Additional exam requirements/recommendations for international students: Required—TOEFL (minimum score 575 paper-based; 230 computer-based; 89 iBT). *Application deadline:* For fall admission, 8/1 priority date for domestic students, 7/1 for international students; for spring admission, 12/1 priority date for domestic students, 11/1 for international students. Applications are processed on a rolling basis. Application fee: $45. Electronic applications accepted. *Expenses:* Contact institution. *Financial support:* In 2011–12, 4 students received support. Federal Work-Study and institutionally sponsored loans available. Financial award applicants required to submit FAFSA. *Faculty research:* Special education, neurosciences and education, cultural influences on behavior, faith-based school leadership, social and philosophical contexts of education. *Unit head:* Dr. John Shoup, Dean, School of Education, 951-343-4205, Fax: 951-343-4516, E-mail: jshoup@calbaptist.edu. *Application contact:* Dr. James Heyman, Director, Master of Science Program in Education, 951-343-4243, Fax: 951-343-5095, E-mail: jheyman@calbaptist.edu. Web site: http://www.calbaptist.edu/mastersined/.

California State University, Sacramento, Office of Graduate Studies, College of Education, Department of Special Education, Rehabilitation, and School Psychology, Sacramento , CA 95819-6079. Offers school psychology (MS); special education (MA); vocational rehabilitation (MS). *Accreditation:* CORE. Part-time programs available. *Faculty:* 17 full-time (11 women), 16 part-time/adjunct (13 women). *Students:* 204 full-time, 93 part-time; includes 81 minority (24 Black or African American, non-Hispanic/Latino; 7 American Indian or Alaska Native, non-Hispanic/Latino; 15 Asian, non-Hispanic/Latino; 24 Hispanic/Latino; 8 Native Hawaiian or other Pacific Islander, non-Hispanic/Latino; 3 Two or more races, non-Hispanic/Latino), 2 international. Average age 36. 210 applicants, 86% accepted, 130 enrolled. In 2011, 86 master's awarded. *Entrance requirements:* For master's, minimum GPA of 2.5. Additional exam requirements/recommendations for international students: Required—TOEFL. *Application deadline:* For fall admission, 3/1 for domestic and international students; for spring admission, 9/15 for domestic students, 9/30 for international students. Applications are processed on a rolling basis. Application fee: $55. Electronic applications accepted. *Financial support:* Career-related internships or fieldwork and Federal Work-Study available. Support available to part-time students. Financial award application deadline: 3/1; financial award applicants required to submit FAFSA. *Faculty research:* Reading and learning disabilities; vocational rehabilitation counseling issues and implementation; school-based crisis intervention; posttraumatic stress disorder; attention-deficit/hyperactivity disorder; school based suicide prevention, intervention, and postvention; autism spectrum disorders; special education technology, strategies and assessment. *Unit head:* Ostertag A. Bruce, Chair, 916-278-6622, Fax: 916-278-3498, E-mail: ostertag@csus.edu. *Application contact:* Jose Martinez, Outreach and Graduate Diversity Coordinator, 916-278-6470, Fax: 916-278-5669, E-mail: martinj@skymail.csus.edu. Web site: http://www.edweb.csus.edu/eds.

California State University, San Bernardino, Graduate Studies, College of Education, Program in Vocational and Career Education, San Bernardino, CA 92407-2397. Offers MA. *Accreditation:* NCATE. Part-time and evening/weekend programs available. *Students:* 1 full-time (0 women), 2 part-time (both women); includes 1 minority (Black or African American, non-Hispanic/Latino). Average age 37. In 2011, 11 master's awarded. *Degree requirements:* For master's, thesis. *Entrance requirements:* For master's, minimum GPA of 3.0 in education, vocational teaching credential. *Application deadline:* For fall admission, 8/31 priority date for domestic students. Application fee: $55. *Expenses:* Tuition, state resident: full-time $7356. Tuition, nonresident: full-time $7356. *Required fees:* $1077. Tuition and fees vary according to program. *Financial support:* Career-related internships or fieldwork and Federal Work-Study available. Support available to part-time students. *Unit head:* Dr. Herbert Brunkhorst, Coordinator, Designated Subjects, 909-537-5613. *Application contact:* Sandra Kamusikiri, Associate Vice-President/Dean of Graduate Studies, 909-537-5058, E-mail: skamusik@csusb.edu.

California University of Pennsylvania, School of Graduate Studies and Research, College of Education and Human Services, Program in Technology Education, California, PA 15419-1394. Offers M Ed. *Accreditation:* NCATE. Part-time and evening/weekend programs available. *Degree requirements:* For master's, comprehensive exam, thesis optional. *Entrance requirements:* For master's, MAT, minimum GPA of 3.0, teaching experience in industrial arts. Additional exam requirements/recommendations for international students: Required—TOEFL (minimum score 550 paper-based; 213 computer-based; 80 iBT). Electronic applications accepted. *Faculty research:* Curriculum, trends in technology, standards-based assessment.

Central Connecticut State University, School of Graduate Studies, School of Technology, Department of Technology Engineering Education, New Britain, CT 06050-4010. Offers MS, Certificate. Part-time and evening/weekend programs available. *Faculty:* 5 full-time (1 woman), 1 part-time/adjunct (0 women). *Students:* 3 full-time (2 women), 19 part-time (1 woman); includes 4 minority (1 Black or African American, non-Hispanic/Latino; 1 Asian, non-Hispanic/Latino; 1 Hispanic/Latino; 1 Two or more races, non-Hispanic/Latino). Average age 35. 11 applicants, 82% accepted, 4 enrolled. In 2011, 8 master's, 2 other advanced degrees awarded. *Degree requirements:* For master's, comprehensive exam, thesis or alternative; for Certificate, qualifying exam. *Entrance requirements:* For master's, minimum undergraduate GPA of 2.7. Additional exam requirements/recommendations for international students: Required—TOEFL (minimum score 550 paper-based; 213 computer-based). *Application deadline:* For fall admission, 6/1 for domestic students, 5/1 for international students; for spring admission, 11/1 for domestic and international students. Applications are processed on a rolling basis. Application fee: $50. Electronic applications accepted. *Expenses: Tuition, area resident:* Full-time $5137; part-time $482 per credit. Tuition, state resident: full-time $7707; part-time $494 per credit. Tuition, nonresident: full-time $14,311; part-time $494 per credit. *Required fees:* $3865. One-time fee: $62 part-time. *Financial support:* In 2011–12, 1 student received support, including 1 research assistantship; career-related internships or fieldwork, Federal Work-Study, scholarships/grants, and unspecified assistantships also available. Support available to part-time students. Financial award application deadline: 4/15; financial award applicants required to submit FAFSA. *Faculty research:* Instruction, curriculum development, administration, occupational training. *Unit head:* Dr. James DeLaura, Chair, 860-832-1850, E-mail: delaura@ccsu.edu. *Application contact:* Patricia Gardner, Associate Director of Graduate Studies, 860-832-2350, Fax: 860-832-2352, E-mail: graduateadmissions@ccsu.edu. Web site: http://www.ccsu.edu/page.cfm?p=6498.

Central Washington University, Graduate Studies and Research, College of Education and Professional Studies, Department of Family and Consumer Sciences, Ellensburg, WA 98926. Offers career and technical education (MS); family and consumer sciences education (MS); family studies (MS). Part-time programs available. *Faculty:* 15 full-time (10 women). *Students:* 14 full-time (10 women), 6 part-time (all women); includes 3 minority (all Hispanic/Latino). 12 applicants, 83% accepted, 8 enrolled. In 2011, 12 master's awarded. *Degree requirements:* For master's, thesis or alternative. *Entrance requirements:* For master's, minimum GPA of 3.0. Additional exam requirements/recommendations for international students: Required—TOEFL (minimum score 550 paper-based; 213 computer-based; 79 iBT). *Application deadline:* For fall admission, 2/1 priority date for domestic students; for winter admission, 10/1 for domestic students; for spring admission, 1/1 for domestic students. Applications are processed on a rolling basis. Application fee: $50. Electronic applications accepted. *Expenses:* Tuition, state resident: full-time $8112; part-time $270 per credit. Tuition, nonresident: full-time $18,069; part-time $602 per credit. *Required fees:* $924. *Financial support:* In 2011–12, research assistantships with full and partial tuition reimbursements (averaging $9,234 per year), 3 teaching assistantships (averaging $9,234 per year) were awarded; Federal Work-Study, health care benefits, and unspecified assistantships also available. Financial award application deadline: 3/1; financial award applicants required to submit FAFSA. *Unit head:* Dr. Robert Perkins, Professor of Leadership and Family and Consumer Sciences Professional Core, 509-963-1292, E-mail: perkinsr@cwu.edu. *Application contact:* Justine Eason, Admissions Program Coordinator, 509-963-3103, Fax: 509-963-1799, E-mail: masters@cwu.edu. Web site: http://www.cwu.edu/~fandcs/.

Chicago State University, School of Graduate and Professional Studies, College of Education, Department of Technology and Education, Chicago, IL 60628. Offers secondary education (MAT); technology and education (MS Ed). Postbaccalaureate distance learning degree programs offered. *Degree requirements:* For master's, thesis optional. *Entrance requirements:* For master's, minimum GPA of 2.75.

Clarion University of Pennsylvania, Office of Graduate Programs, Master of Education Program, Clarion, PA 16214. Offers curriculum and instruction (M Ed); early childhood (M Ed, Certificate); English (M Ed); instructional technology specialist (K-12) (Certificate); literacy (M Ed); mathematics education (M Ed); reading specialist (M Ed, Certificate); science education (M Ed); special education (M Ed); technology (M Ed); world language (M Ed). *Accreditation:* NCATE. Part-time programs available. *Students:* 14 full-time (11 women), 207 part-time (163 women); includes 3 minority (1 Black or African American, non-Hispanic/Latino; 2 Hispanic/Latino). Average age 31. In 2011, 96 master's awarded. *Degree requirements:* For master's, thesis or alternative. *Entrance requirements:* For master's, minimum QPA of 3.0. *Application deadline:* Applications are processed on a rolling basis. *Expenses:* Tuition, state resident: part-time $429 per credit. Tuition, nonresident: part-time $644 per credit. *Financial support:* Research assistantships with full and partial tuition reimbursements and career-related internships or fieldwork available. Support available to part-time students. Financial award application deadline: 3/1. *Unit head:* Dr. John Groves, Dean, 814-393-2146, Fax: 514-393-2446. *Application contact:* Dr. Brenda Sanders Dede, Assistant Vice President for Academic Affairs, 814-393-2337, Fax: 814-393-2030, E-mail: bdede@clarion.edu. Web site: http://www.clarion.edu/25887/.

Colorado State University, Graduate School, College of Applied Human Sciences, School of Education, Fort Collins, CO 80523-1588. Offers adult education and training (M Ed); community college leadership (PhD); counseling and career development (M Ed); education and human resource studies (M Ed, PhD); educational leadership (M Ed, PhD); interdisciplinary studies (PhD); organizational performance and change (M Ed, PhD); student affairs in higher education (MS). *Accreditation:* ACA; Teacher Education Accreditation Council. Part-time and evening/weekend programs available. *Faculty:* 18 full-time (11 women), 1 part-time/adjunct (0 women). *Students:* 161 full-time (106 women), 491 part-time (291 women); includes 130 minority (28 Black or African American, non-Hispanic/Latino; 5 American Indian or Alaska Native, non-Hispanic/Latino; 12 Asian, non-Hispanic/Latino; 68 Hispanic/Latino; 3 Native Hawaiian or other Pacific Islander, non-Hispanic/Latino; 14 Two or more races, non-Hispanic/Latino), 29 international. Average age 38. 468 applicants, 31% accepted, 112 enrolled. In 2011, 192 master's, 30 doctorates awarded. *Degree requirements:* For master's, comprehensive exam (for some programs), thesis optional; for doctorate, comprehensive exam, thesis/dissertation, minimum of 60 credits. *Entrance requirements:* For master's, GRE, minimum undergraduate GPA of 3.0, 3 letters of recommendation, curriculum vitae/resume; for doctorate, minimum GPA of 3.0, 3 letters of recommendation, curriculum vitae. Additional exam requirements/recommendations for international students: Required—TOEFL (minimum score 550 paper-based; 213 computer-based; 80 iBT). *Application deadline:* For fall admission, 2/15 priority date for domestic students, 2/15 for international students; for spring admission, 9/1 priority date for domestic students, 9/1 for international students. Applications are processed on a rolling basis. Application fee: $50. Electronic applications accepted. *Expenses:* Tuition, state resident: full-time $7992. Tuition, nonresident: full-time $19,592. *Required fees:* $1735; $58 per credit. *Financial support:* In 2011–12, 11 students received support, including 1 fellowship (averaging $37,500 per year), 3 research assistantships with full tuition reimbursements available (averaging $8,911 per year), 7 teaching assistantships with full tuition reimbursements available (averaging $12,691 per year); Federal Work-Study, scholarships/grants, and unspecified assistantships also available. Financial award application deadline: 2/15; financial award applicants required to submit FAFSA. *Faculty research:* Innovative instruction, diverse learners, transition, scientifically-based evaluation methods, leadership and organizational development, research methodology. *Total annual research expenditures:* $455,133. *Unit head:* Dr. Kevin Oltjenbruns, Interim Director, 970-491-6316, Fax: 970-491-1317, E-mail: kevin.oltjenbruns@colostate.edu. *Application contact:* Kathy Lucas, Graduate Contact, 970-491-1963, Fax: 970-491-1317, E-mail: kplucas@cahs.colostate.edu. Web site: http://www.soe.cahs.colostate.edu/.

East Carolina University, Graduate School, College of Education, Department of Business and Information Technologies Education, Greenville, NC 27858-4353. Offers business education (MA Ed); elementary education (MAT); English education (MAT); family and consumer science (MAT); health education (MAT); Hispanic studies (MAT); history education (MAT); marketing education (MA Ed); middle grades education (MAT); music education (MAT); physical education (MAT); science education (MAT); special education (MAT), including general curriculum; vocation education (MS). *Accreditation:* NCATE. Part-time and evening/weekend programs available. Postbaccalaureate distance learning degree programs offered (no on-campus study). *Degree requirements:* For master's, comprehensive exam, thesis optional. *Entrance requirements:* For master's, GRE or MAT, minimum GPA of 2.5, bachelor's degree in related field, teaching license (MA Ed). Additional exam requirements/recommendations for international students: Required—TOEFL. *Application deadline:* For fall admission, 6/1 priority date for domestic students. Applications are processed on a rolling basis. Application fee: $50. *Expenses:* Tuition, state resident: full-time $3557; part-time $444.63 per semester hour. Tuition, nonresident: full-time $14,351; part-time $1793.88 per semester hour. *Required fees:* $2016; $252 per semester hour. Part-time tuition and fees vary according to course load, campus/location and program. *Financial support:* Federal Work-Study available. Support available to part-time students. Financial award application deadline: 6/1. *Unit head:* Dr. Ivan G. Wallace, Chair, 252-328-6983, Fax: 252-328-6835, E-mail: wallacei@ecu.edu. *Application contact:* Dean of Graduate School, 252-328-6012, Fax: 252-328-6071, E-mail: gradschool@ecu.edu. Web site: http://www.ecu.edu/cs-educ/bite/index.cfm.

Eastern Kentucky University, The Graduate School, College of Business and Technology, Department of Technology, Program in Industrial Education, Richmond, KY 40475-3102. Offers occupational training and development (MS); technical administration (MS); technology education (MS). *Accreditation:* NCATE. Part-time programs available. *Entrance requirements:* For master's, GRE General Test, minimum GPA of 2.5.

Eastern Kentucky University, The Graduate School, College of Education, Department of Curriculum and Instruction, Program in Secondary and Higher Education, Richmond, KY 40475-3102. Offers secondary education (MA Ed), including agricultural education, art education, biological sciences education, business education, English education, geography education, history education, home economics education, industrial education, mathematical sciences education, physical education, school health education. *Accreditation:* NCATE. Part-time programs available. *Entrance requirements:* For master's, GRE General Test, minimum GPA of 2.5.

Eastern Michigan University, Graduate School, College of Technology, School of Technology Studies, Program in Career, Technical and Workforce Education, Ypsilanti, MI 48197. Offers MS. Part-time and evening/weekend programs available. Postbaccalaureate distance learning degree programs offered (minimal on-campus study). In 2011, 2 degrees awarded. *Entrance requirements:* Additional exam requirements/recommendations for international students: Required—TOEFL. *Application deadline:* Applications are processed on a rolling basis. Application fee: $35. *Expenses:* Tuition, state resident: full-time $10,367; part-time $432 per credit hour. Tuition, nonresident: full-time $20,435; part-time $851 per credit hour. *Required fees:* $39 per credit hour. $46 per semester. One-time fee: $100. Tuition and fees vary according to course level, degree level and reciprocity agreements. *Financial support:* Fellowships, research assistantships with full tuition reimbursements, teaching assistantships with full tuition reimbursements, career-related internships or fieldwork, Federal Work-Study, institutionally sponsored loans, scholarships/grants, tuition waivers (partial), and unspecified assistantships available. Support available to part-time students. Financial award applicants required to submit FAFSA. *Unit head:* Dr. Ronald Fulkert, Program Coordinator, 734-487-1161, Fax: 734-487-7690, E-mail: rfulkert@emich.edu. *Application contact:* Graduate Admissions, 734-487-2400, Fax: 734-487-6559, E-mail: graduate.admissions@emich.edu.

Eastern New Mexico University, Graduate School, College of Education and Technology, Department of Curriculum and Instruction, Portales, NM 88130. Offers bilingual education (M Ed); educational technology (M Ed); elementary education (M Ed); English as a second language (M Ed); pedagogy and learning (M Ed); professional technical education (M Ed); reading/literacy (M Ed). Part-time programs available. Postbaccalaureate distance learning degree programs offered (minimal on-campus study). *Degree requirements:* For master's, comprehensive exam, thesis optional. *Entrance requirements:* For master's, minimum GPA of 3.0, photocopy of teaching license, writing assessment, letter of recommendation. Additional exam requirements/recommendations for international students: Required—TOEFL (minimum score 550 paper-based; 213 computer-based; 79 iBT), IELTS (minimum score 6). Electronic applications accepted.

Fitchburg State University, Division of Graduate and Continuing Education, Program in Occupational Education, Fitchburg, MA 01420-2697. Offers M Ed. *Accreditation:* NCATE. Part-time and evening/weekend programs available. *Students:* 36 part-time (21 women); includes 1 minority (Black or African American, non-Hispanic/Latino). Average age 45. 9 applicants, 100% accepted, 9 enrolled. In 2011, 4 master's awarded. *Entrance requirements:* Additional exam requirements/recommendations for international students: Required—TOEFL (minimum score 550 paper-based; 213 computer-based; 79 iBT). *Application deadline:* For fall admission, 7/15 for international students; for spring admission, 12/1 for international students. Applications are processed on a rolling basis. Application fee: $25 ($50 for international students). Electronic applications accepted. *Expenses:* Tuition, state resident: full-time $2700; part-time $150 per credit. Tuition, nonresident: full-time $2700; part-time $150 per credit. *Required fees:* $2286; $127 per credit. *Financial support:* In 2011–12, research assistantships with partial tuition reimbursements (averaging $5,500 per year) were awarded; Federal Work-Study, scholarships/grants, and unspecified assistantships also available. Support available to part-time students. Financial award application deadline: 3/1; financial award applicants required to submit FAFSA. *Unit head:* Dr. James Alicata, Chair, 978-665-3047, Fax: 978-665-3658, E-mail: gce@fitchburgstate.edu. *Application contact:* Kay Reynolds, Director of Admissions, 978-665-3144, Fax: 978-665-4540, E-mail: admissions@fitchburgstate.edu. Web site: http://www.fitchburgstate.edu.

Fitchburg State University, Division of Graduate and Continuing Education, Program in Technology Education, Fitchburg, MA 01420-2697. Offers M Ed. *Accreditation:* NCATE. Part-time and evening/weekend programs available. *Students:* 5 part-time (0 women). Average age 41. 1 applicant, 100% accepted, 1 enrolled. In 2011, 1 master's awarded. *Entrance requirements:* Additional exam requirements/recommendations for international students: Required—TOEFL (minimum score 550 paper-based; 213 computer-based; 79 iBT). *Application deadline:* For fall admission, 7/15 for international students; for spring admission, 12/1 for international students. Applications are processed on a rolling basis. Application fee: $25 ($50 for international students). Electronic applications accepted. *Expenses:* Tuition, state resident: full-time $2700; part-time $150 per credit. Tuition, nonresident: full-time $2700; part-time $150 per credit. *Required fees:* $2286; $127 per credit. *Financial support:* In 2011–12, research assistantships with partial tuition reimbursements (averaging $5,500 per year) were awarded; Federal Work-Study, scholarships/grants, and unspecified assistantships also available. Support available to part-time students. Financial award application deadline: 3/1; financial award applicants required to submit FAFSA. *Unit head:* Wayne Whitfield, Chair, 978-665-4807, Fax: 978-665-3658, E-mail: gce@fitchburgstate.edu. *Application contact:* Kay Reynolds, Director of Admissions, 978-665-3144, Fax: 978-665-4540, E-mail: admissions@fitchburgstate.edu. Web site: http://www.fitchburgstate.edu.

Florida Agricultural and Mechanical University, Division of Graduate Studies, Research, and Continuing Education, College of Education, Department of Vocational Education, Tallahassee, FL 32307-3200. Offers business education (MBE); industrial education (M Ed, MS Ed). *Accreditation:* NCATE. *Degree requirements:* For master's, thesis (for some programs). *Entrance requirements:* For master's, GRE General Test, minimum GPA of 3.0. Additional exam requirements/recommendations for international students: Required—TOEFL.

The George Washington University, Graduate School of Education and Human Development, Department of Counseling and Human Development, Program in Career and Workforce Development, Washington, DC 20052. Offers Graduate Certificate.

The George Washington University, Graduate School of Education and Human Development, Department of Counseling and Human Development, Program in Job Development and Placement, Washington, DC 20052. Offers Graduate Certificate. Postbaccalaureate distance learning degree programs offered.

Idaho State University, Office of Graduate Studies, College of Technology, Department of Human Resource Training and Development, Pocatello, ID 83209-8380. Offers MTD. Part-time and evening/weekend programs available. *Degree requirements:* For master's, comprehensive exam, thesis optional, statistical procedures. *Entrance requirements:* For master's, GRE or MAT, minimum GPA of 3.0 in upper-division courses. Additional exam requirements/recommendations for international students: Required—TOEFL (minimum score 550 paper-based; 213 computer-based; 80 iBT). Electronic applications accepted. *Faculty research:* Learning styles, instructional methodology, leadership administration.

Indiana State University, College of Graduate and Professional Studies, College of Technology, Department of Industrial Technology Education, Terre Haute, IN 47809. Offers career and technical education (MS); human resource development (MS); technology education (MS); MA/MS. *Accreditation:* NCATE (one or more programs are accredited). *Entrance requirements:* For master's, bachelor's degree in industrial technology or related field. Additional exam requirements/recommendations for international students: Required—TOEFL. Electronic applications accepted.

Indiana University of Pennsylvania, School of Graduate Studies and Research, Eberly College of Business and Information Technology, Department of Technology Support and Training, Program in Business/Administrative, Indiana, PA 15705-1087. Offers M Ed. Part-time programs available. *Faculty:* 3 full-time (2 women). *Students:* 6 part-time (1 woman). Average age 41. 11 applicants, 18% accepted, 2 enrolled. In 2011, 1 master's awarded. *Entrance requirements:* Additional exam requirements/recommendations for international students: Required—TOEFL (minimum score 540 paper-based; 207 computer-based). *Application deadline:* Applications are processed on a rolling basis. Application fee: $50. Electronic applications accepted. *Expenses:* Tuition, state resident: full-time $7488; part-time $416 per credit. Tuition, nonresident: full-time $11,232; part-time $624 per credit. *Required fees:* $2070; $192.20 per credit. $90 per semester. *Financial support:* Application deadline: 4/15; applicants required to submit FAFSA. *Unit head:* Dr. Linda Szul, Chairperson, 724-357-3003, E-mail: lfszul@iup.edu. *Application contact:* Dr. Dawn Woodland, Graduate Coordinator, 724-357-5736, E-mail: woodland@iup.edu. Web site: http://www.iup.edu/upper.aspx?id=49407.

Inter American University of Puerto Rico, Metropolitan Campus, Graduate Programs, Program in Occupational Education, San Juan, PR 00919-1293. Offers MA. *Degree requirements:* For master's, comprehensive exam. *Entrance requirements:* For master's, GRE or EXADEP, interview. Electronic applications accepted.

Iowa State University of Science and Technology, Program in Industrial Agriculture and Technology, Ames, IA 50011-3130. Offers MS, PhD. In 2011, 5 master's, 1 doctorate awarded. *Entrance requirements:* For master's and doctorate, GRE General Test. Additional exam requirements/recommendations for international students: Required—TOEFL (minimum score 550 paper-based; 79 iBT), IELTS (minimum score 6.5). *Application deadline:* For fall admission, 2/1 priority date for domestic students, 2/1 for international students; for spring admission, 7/1 for domestic and international students. Application fee: $40 ($90 for international students). Electronic applications accepted. *Faculty research:* Industrial technology, technology education, training and development, technical education. *Unit head:* Dr. Steve Hoff, Director of Graduate Education, 515-294-1033. *Application contact:* Kris Bell, Application Contact, 515-294-1033, E-mail: kabell@iastate.edu. Web site: http://www.abe.iastate.edu.

Jackson State University, Graduate School, College of Science, Engineering and Technology, Department of Technology, Jackson, MS 39217. Offers hazardous materials management (MS); technology education (MS Ed). Part-time and evening/weekend programs available. *Degree requirements:* For master's, comprehensive exam, thesis or alternative. *Entrance requirements:* For master's, GRE General Test. Additional exam requirements/recommendations for international students: Required—TOEFL (minimum score 520 paper-based; 195 computer-based; 67 iBT).

James Madison University, The Graduate School, College of Education, Adult Education Department, Program in Adult Education/Human Resource Development, Harrisonburg, VA 22807. Offers MS Ed. *Accreditation:* NCATE. Part-time and evening/weekend programs available. *Students:* 26 full-time (17 women), 11 part-time (10 women); includes 10 minority (9 Black or African American, non-Hispanic/Latino; 1 Asian, non-Hispanic/Latino). Average age 27. In 2011, 12 master's awarded. *Entrance requirements:* For master's, GRE General Test. Additional exam requirements/recommendations for international students: Required—TOEFL. *Application deadline:* For fall admission, 5/1 priority date for domestic students; for spring admission, 9/1 priority date for domestic students. Applications are processed on a rolling basis. Application fee: $55. Electronic applications accepted. *Expenses:* Tuition, state resident: full-time $8016; part-time $334 per credit hour. Tuition, nonresident: full-time $22,656; part-time $944 per credit hour. *Financial support:* In 2011–12, 16 students received support. 15 graduate assistantships ($7382), 1 athletic assistantship ($8664) available. Financial award application deadline: 3/1; financial award applicants required to submit FAFSA. *Unit head:* Dr. Diane Foucar-Szocki, Academic Unit Head, 540-568-6794. *Application contact:* Lynette M. Bible, Director of Graduate Admissions, 540-568-6395, Fax: 540-568-7860, E-mail: biblelm@jmu.edu.

Kansas State University, Graduate School, College of Education, Department of Curriculum and Instruction, Manhattan, KS 66506. Offers career and technical education (Ed D, PhD); curriculum studies (Ed D, PhD); digital teaching and learning (MS); educational computing, design and online learning (MS); educational technology (Ed D, PhD); elementary/middle level (MS); English as a second language (MS); language/diversity education (Ed D, PhD); literacy education (Ed D, PhD); mathematics education (Ed D, PhD); middle level/secondary (MS); reading and language arts (MS); reading specialist endorsement (MS); science education (Ed D, PhD); social science education (Ed D, PhD); teacher education (Ed D, PhD); teacher leader/school improvement (MS, Ed D). *Accreditation:* NCATE. Part-time programs available. Postbaccalaureate distance learning degree programs offered (minimal on-campus study). *Faculty:* 15 full-time (12 women), 3 part-time/adjunct (2 women). *Students:* 37 full-time (30 women), 113 part-time (91 women); includes 14 minority (4 Black or African American, non-Hispanic/Latino; 1 American Indian or Alaska Native, non-Hispanic/Latino; 1 Asian, non-Hispanic/Latino; 7 Hispanic/Latino; 1 Two or more races, non-Hispanic/Latino), 15 international. Average age 37. 75 applicants, 51% accepted, 9 enrolled. In 2011, 48 master's, 14 doctorates awarded. *Degree requirements:* For master's, comprehensive exam, portfolio, project, report or thesis; for doctorate, comprehensive exam, thesis/dissertation, preliminary exam. *Entrance requirements:* For master's, minimum GPA of 3.0; for doctorate, GRE, minimum GPA of 3.0. Additional exam requirements/recommendations for international students: Required—TOEFL. *Application deadline:* For fall admission, 2/1 priority date for domestic students, 2/1 for international students; for spring admission, 8/1 priority date for domestic students, 8/1 for international students. Applications are processed on a rolling basis. Application fee: $40 ($55 for international students). Electronic applications accepted. *Financial support:* In 2011–12, 1 research assistantship (averaging $16,900 per year), 8 teaching assistantships (averaging $12,466 per year) were awarded; career-related internships or fieldwork, institutionally sponsored loans, and scholarships/grants also available. Support available to part-time students. Financial award application deadline: 3/1; financial award applicants required to submit FAFSA. *Faculty research:* Literacy and technology, critical race theory and diversity, achievement gaps, school improvement, teacher education. *Total annual research expenditures:* $510,907. *Unit head:* Dr. Gail Shroyer, Chair, 785-532-5550, Fax: 785-532-7304, E-mail: gshroyer@ksu.edu. *Application contact:* Dona Deam, Application Contact, 785-532-5595, Fax: 785-532-7304, E-mail: ddeam@ksu.edu. Web site: http://coe.k-state.edu/departments/currin/curringrad.htm.

Kansas State University, Graduate School, College of Education, Department of Educational Leadership, Manhattan, KS 66506. Offers adult, occupational and continuing education (MS, Ed D, PhD); educational leadership (MS, Ed D). *Accreditation:* NCATE. *Faculty:* 10 full-time (5 women), 1 part-time/adjunct (0 women). *Students:* 43 full-time (21 women), 185 part-time (91 women); includes 37 minority (14 Black or African American, non-Hispanic/Latino; 1 American Indian or Alaska Native, non-Hispanic/Latino; 4 Asian, non-Hispanic/Latino; 16 Hispanic/Latino; 2 Two or more races, non-Hispanic/Latino), 1 international. Average age 40. 96 applicants, 59% accepted, 37 enrolled. In 2011, 74 master's, 8 doctorates awarded. *Degree requirements:* For master's, comprehensive exam; for doctorate, comprehensive exam, thesis/dissertation. *Entrance requirements:* For master's, minimum undergraduate GPA of 3.0; for doctorate, GRE General Test, minimum GPA of 3.0 in last 60 hours. Additional exam requirements/recommendations for international students: Required—TOEFL. *Application deadline:* For fall admission, 2/1 priority date for domestic students, 2/1 for international students; for spring admission, 8/1 priority date for domestic students, 8/1 for international students. Applications are processed on a rolling basis. Application fee: $40 ($55 for international students). Electronic applications accepted. *Financial support:* Career-related internships or fieldwork, institutionally sponsored loans, and scholarships/grants available. Support available to part-time students. Financial award application deadline: 3/1; financial award applicants required to submit FAFSA. *Faculty research:* Educational law, school finance, school facilities, organizational leadership, adult learning, distance learning/education. *Total annual research expenditures:* $5,648. *Unit head:* David C. Thompson, Head, 785-532-5535, Fax: 785-532-7304, E-mail: thomsond@ksu.edu. *Application contact:* Dona Deam, Applications Contact, 785-532-5595, Fax: 785-532-7304, E-mail: ddeam@ksu.edu. Web site: http://coe.k-state.edu/departments/edlea/index.htm.

Kent State University, Graduate School of Education, Health, and Human Services, School of Teaching, Learning and Curriculum Studies, Program in Career Technical Teacher Education, Kent, OH 44242-0001. Offers M Ed. Part-time and evening/weekend programs available. *Faculty:* 2 full-time, 3 part-time/adjunct (2 women). *Students:* 19 part-time (12 women); includes 2 minority (both Black or African American, non-Hispanic/Latino). 5 applicants, 60% accepted. In 2011, 13 master's awarded. *Entrance requirements:* For master's, 2 letters of reference, goals statement. Additional exam requirements/recommendations for international students: Required—TOEFL (minimum score 550 paper-based; 213 computer-based; 80 iBT). *Application deadline:* Applications are processed on a rolling basis. Application fee: $30 ($60 for international students). Electronic applications accepted. *Expenses:* Tuition, state resident: full-time $8136; part-time $452 per credit hour. Tuition, nonresident: full-time $14,292; part-time $794 per credit hour. *Financial support:* Research assistantships with full tuition reimbursements, Federal Work-Study, scholarships/grants, and unspecified assistantships available. Financial award application deadline: 4/1; financial award applicants required to submit FAFSA. *Faculty research:* Workforce education/development, adult education, training and organizational change. *Unit head:* Dr. Patrick O'Connor, Coordinator, 330-672-0689, E-mail: poconnor@kent.edu. *Application contact:* Nancy Miller, Academic Program Coordinator, Office of Graduate Student Services, 330-672-2576, Fax: 330-672-9162, E-mail: ogs@kent.edu.

Louisiana State University and Agricultural and Mechanical College, Graduate School, College of Agriculture, School of Human Resource Education and Workforce Development, Baton Rouge, LA 70803. Offers agriculture and extension education and youth development (MS, PhD); career and technical education (MS, PhD); comprehensive vocational education (MS, PhD); extension and international education (MS, PhD); human resource and leadership development (MS, PhD); industrial education (MS); vocational agriculture education (MS, PhD); vocational business education (MS); vocational home economics education (MS). *Accreditation:* NCATE. Part-time programs available. *Faculty:* 9 full-time (5 women), 3 part-time/adjunct (0 women). *Students:* 51 full-time (36 women), 85 part-time (59 women); includes 28 minority (23 Black or African American, non-Hispanic/Latino; 1 Asian, non-Hispanic/Latino; 4 Hispanic/Latino), 3 international. Average age 36. 29 applicants, 83% accepted, 20 enrolled. In 2011, 15 master's, 17 doctorates awarded. Terminal master's awarded for partial completion of doctoral program. *Degree requirements:* For master's, thesis (for some programs); for doctorate, thesis/dissertation. *Entrance requirements:* For master's and doctorate, GRE General Test, minimum GPA of 3.0. Additional exam requirements/recommendations for international students: Required—TOEFL (minimum score 550 paper-based; 213 computer-based; 79 iBT) or IELTS (minimum score 6.5). *Application deadline:* For fall admission, 1/25 priority date for domestic students, 5/15 for international students; for spring admission, 10/15 for international students. Applications are processed on a rolling basis. Application fee: $50 ($70 for international students). Electronic applications accepted. *Financial support:* In 2011–12, 84 students received support, including 3 fellowships with full and partial tuition reimbursements available (averaging $14,986 per year), 4 research assistantships with full and partial tuition reimbursements available (averaging $12,000 per year), 11 teaching assistantships with partial tuition reimbursements available (averaging $13,300 per year); career-related internships or fieldwork, Federal Work-Study, institutionally sponsored loans, health care benefits, tuition waivers (full and partial), and unspecified assistantships also available. Financial award application deadline: 3/1; financial award applicants required to submit FAFSA. *Faculty research:* Adult education, history and philosophy of vocational education, curriculum and instruction, career decision-making. *Unit head:* Dr. Michael F. Burnett, Director, 225-578-5748, Fax: 225-578-2526, E-mail: vocbur@lsu.edu. Web site: http://www.lsu.edu/hrleader/.

Marshall University, Academic Affairs Division, Graduate School of Education and Professional Development, Division of Adult and Technical Education, Huntington, WV 25755. Offers MS. *Accreditation:* NCATE. Evening/weekend programs available. *Students:* 40 full-time (19 women), 67 part-time (49 women); includes 11 minority (9 Black or African American, non-Hispanic/Latino; 2 Asian, non-Hispanic/Latino), 6 international. Average age 38. In 2011, 65 master's awarded. *Degree requirements:* For master's, thesis optional, comprehensive assessment. Application fee: $40. *Unit head:* Dr. Lee Olson, Program Coordinator, 304-696-6757, E-mail: olsonl@marshall.edu. *Application contact:* Graduate Admission.

Middle Tennessee State University, College of Graduate Studies, College of Basic and Applied Sciences, Department of Engineering Technology and Industrial Studies, Murfreesboro, TN 37132. Offers engineering technology (MS). Part-time and evening/weekend programs available. Postbaccalaureate distance learning degree programs offered. *Faculty:* 10 full-time (1 woman). *Students:* 3 full-time (0 women), 22 part-time (4 women); includes 11 minority (2 Black or African American, non-Hispanic/Latino; 5 Asian, non-Hispanic/Latino; 2 Hispanic/Latino; 2 Two or more races, non-Hispanic/Latino). Average age 31. 30 applicants, 47% accepted. In 2011, 6 master's awarded. *Degree requirements:* For master's, comprehensive exam. *Entrance requirements:* For master's, GRE. Additional exam requirements/recommendations for international students: Required—TOEFL (minimum score 525 paper-based; 195 computer-based; 71 iBT) or IELTS (minimum score 6). *Application deadline:* For fall admission, 6/1 for domestic and international students. Applications are processed on a rolling basis. Application fee: $25 ($30 for international students). Electronic applications accepted. *Expenses:* Tuition, state resident: full-time $10,008. Tuition, nonresident: full-time $25,056. *Financial support:* In 2011–12, 9 students received support. Tuition waivers available. Support available to part-time students. Financial award application deadline: 5/1; financial award applicants required to submit FAFSA. *Faculty research:* Solar energy, alternative fuels. *Unit head:* Dr. Walter Boles, Chair, 615-898-2776, Fax: 615-898-5697, E-mail: walter.boles@mtsu.edu. *Application contact:* Dr. Michael D. Allen, Dean and Vice Provost for Research, 615-898-2840, Fax: 615-904-8020, E-mail: michael.allen@mtsu.edu.

Millersville University of Pennsylvania, College of Graduate and Professional Studies, School of Education, Department of Applied Engineering, Safety, and Technology, Millersville, PA 17551-0302. Offers technology education (M Ed). *Accreditation:* NCATE. Part-time and evening/weekend programs available. *Faculty:* 13 full-time (2 women), 13 part-time/adjunct (1 woman). *Students:* 1 full-time (0 women), 6 part-time (0 women); includes 1 minority (Asian, non-Hispanic/Latino). Average age 35. In 2011, 4 master's awarded. *Degree requirements:* For master's, thesis optional. *Entrance requirements:* For master's, GRE or MAT, 3 letters of recommendation. Additional exam requirements/recommendations for international students: Required—TOEFL (minimum score 500 paper-based; 183 computer-based; 65 iBT). *Application deadline:* For fall admission, 1/15 priority date for domestic students, 1/15 for international students; for winter admission, 10/1 priority date for domestic students, 10/1 for international students; for spring admission, 10/1 priority date for domestic students, 10/1 for international students. Applications are processed on a rolling basis. Application fee: $40 ($50 for international students). Electronic applications accepted. *Expenses:* Tuition, state resident: full-time $3744; part-time $416 per credit. Tuition, nonresident: full-time $5616; part-time $624 per credit. *Required fees:* $1130; $125.50 per credit. Tuition and fees vary according to course load. *Financial support:* In 2011–12, 1 student received support, including 2 research assistantships with full tuition reimbursements available (averaging $2,131 per year); institutionally sponsored loans and unspecified assistantships also available. Support available to part-time students. Financial award application deadline: 3/15; financial award applicants required to submit FAFSA. *Faculty research:* Building energy conservation, alternative energy, creativity and design in technology education, CAD teaching and learning, spatial visualization, rapid prototyping, designing and building light structures, friction stir welding: mechanics of dental implants . *Unit head:* Dr. Barry G. David, Chair, 717-872-3327, Fax: 717-872-3318, E-mail: barry.david@millersville.edu. *Application contact:* Dr. Victor S. DeSantis, Dean, College of Graduate and Professional Studies, 717-872-3099, Fax: 717-872-3453, E-mail: victor.desantis@millersville.edu. Web site: http://www.millersville.edu/itec/.

Montana State University, College of Graduate Studies, College of Education, Health, and Human Development, Department of Education, Bozeman, MT 59717. Offers adult and higher education (Ed D); curriculum and instruction (M Ed, Ed D), including professional educator (M Ed), technology education (M Ed); education (M Ed), including adult and higher education, educational leadership, school counseling; educational leadership (Ed D, Ed S). *Accreditation:* Teacher Education Accreditation Council. Part-time programs available. Postbaccalaureate distance learning degree programs offered (minimal on-campus study). *Degree requirements:* For master's, comprehensive exam; for doctorate, comprehensive exam, thesis/dissertation. *Entrance requirements:* For master's, GRE, 3 letters of reference, essays, BA transcripts; for doctorate, GRE, MAT, 3 letters of reference, essay, BA and M Ed transcripts; for Ed S, PRAXIS. Additional exam requirements/recommendations for international students: Required—TOEFL (minimum score 550 paper-based; 213 computer-based). Electronic applications accepted. *Faculty research:* Critical literacy; standards-based education; school Improvement, organizational change, leadership in rural education, leadership in Indian education; student Learning; multicultural/culturally responsive education for social justice Native American indigenous education, community-centered education teacher preparation.

Morehead State University, Graduate Programs, College of Science and Technology, Department of Industrial and Engineering Technology, Morehead, KY 40351. Offers career and technical education (MS); engineering technology (MS). Part-time and evening/weekend programs available. *Degree requirements:* For master's, completion and defense of thesis or written and oral comprehensive exit exams. *Entrance requirements:* For master's, GRE, minimum undergraduate GPA of 3.0 in major. Additional exam requirements/recommendations for international students: Required—TOEFL (minimum score 500 paper-based; 173 computer-based). Electronic applications accepted.

Murray State University, College of Education, Department of Adolescent, Career and Special Education, Program in Industrial and Technical Education, Murray, KY 42071. Offers MS. *Accreditation:* NCATE. Part-time programs available. *Degree requirements:* For master's, thesis (for some programs), portfolio. *Entrance requirements:* For master's, GRE General Test. Additional exam requirements/recommendations for international students: Required—TOEFL.

North Carolina Agricultural and Technical State University, School of Graduate Studies, School of Technology, Department of Graphic Communication Systems and Technological Studies, Greensboro, NC 27411. Offers graphic communication systems (MSTM); technology education (MAT). *Accreditation:* NCATE (one or more programs are accredited). Part-time and evening/weekend programs available. *Degree requirements:* For master's, comprehensive exam, thesis or alternative, qualifying exam. *Entrance requirements:* For master's, GRE General Test, minimum GPA of 3.0.

North Dakota State University, College of Graduate and Interdisciplinary Studies, College of Human Development and Education, School of Education, Fargo, ND 58108. Offers agricultural education (M Ed, MS), including agricultural education, agricultural extension education (MS); counseling (M Ed, MS, PhD); curriculum and instruction (M Ed, MS), including pedagogy, physical education and athletic administration; education (PhD); educational leadership (M Ed, MS, Ed S); family and consumer sciences education (M Ed, MS); history education (M Ed, MS); institutional analysis (Ed D); mathematics education (M Ed, MS); music education (M Ed, MS); occupational and adult education (Ed D); science education (M Ed, MS). *Accreditation:* NCATE. Part-time and evening/weekend programs available. Postbaccalaureate distance learning degree programs offered (minimal on-campus study). *Faculty:* 24 full-time (10 women), 2 part-time/adjunct (1 woman). *Students:* 91 full-time (64 women), 114 part-time (78 women); includes 13 minority (4 Black or African American, non-Hispanic/Latino; 5 American Indian or Alaska Native, non-Hispanic/Latino; 1 Hispanic/Latino; 3 Two or more races, non-Hispanic/Latino), 8 international. 88 applicants, 67% accepted, 56 enrolled. In 2011, 43 master's, 12 doctorates awarded. *Degree requirements:* For master's, comprehensive exam; for doctorate, thesis/dissertation; for Ed S, thesis. *Entrance requirements:* For degree, GRE General Test, master's degree, minimum GPA of 3.25. Additional exam requirements/recommendations for international students:

Vocational and Technical Education

Required—TOEFL. *Application deadline:* Applications are processed on a rolling basis. Application fee: $45 ($60 for international students). *Financial support:* Research assistantships, teaching assistantships, career-related internships or fieldwork, Federal Work-Study, institutionally sponsored loans, and tuition waivers (full) available. Financial award application deadline: 4/15. *Unit head:* Dr. William Martin, Chair, 701-231-7202, Fax: 701-231-7416, E-mail: william.martin@ndsu.edu. *Application contact:* Sonya Goergen, Marketing, Recruitment, and Public Relations Coordinator, 701-231-7033, Fax: 701-231-6524. Web site: http://www.ndsu.nodak.edu/school_of_education/.

Northern Arizona University, Graduate College, College of Education, Department of Educational Specialties, Flagstaff , AZ 86011. Offers autism spectrum disorders (Certificate); bilingual/multicultural education (M Ed), including bilingual education, ESL education; career and technical education (M Ed, Certificate); curriculum and instruction (Ed D); early childhood special education (M Ed); early intervention (Certificate); educational technology (M Ed, Certificate); special education (M Ed). *Faculty:* 28 full-time (19 women). *Students:* 113 full-time (91 women), 206 part-time (158 women); includes 104 minority (8 Black or African American, non-Hispanic/Latino; 17 American Indian or Alaska Native, non-Hispanic/Latino; 6 Asian, non-Hispanic/Latino; 65 Hispanic/Latino; 2 Native Hawaiian or other Pacific Islander, non-Hispanic/Latino; 6 Two or more races, non-Hispanic/Latino), 3 international. Average age 30. 141 applicants, 75% accepted, 76 enrolled. In 2011, 167 master's, 7 Certificates awarded. *Degree requirements:* For master's, comprehensive exam (for some programs), thesis (for some programs). *Entrance requirements:* For master's, minimum GPA of 3.0. Additional exam requirements/recommendations for international students: Required—TOEFL (minimum score 550 paper-based; 213 computer-based; 80 iBT), IELTS (minimum score 7). *Application deadline:* For fall admission, 3/1 for international students; for spring admission, 9/15 for international students. Applications are processed on a rolling basis. Application fee: $65. Electronic applications accepted. *Expenses:* Tuition, state resident: full-time $7190; part-time $355 per credit hour. Tuition, nonresident: full-time $18,092; part-time $1005 per credit hour. *Required fees:* $818; $328 per semester. *Financial support:* Applicants required to submit FAFSA. *Unit head:* Dr. Jennifer Prior, Chair, 928-523-5064, Fax: 928-523-1929, E-mail: jennifer.prior@nau.edu. *Application contact:* Shirley Robinson, Coordinator, 928-523-4348, Fax: 928-523-8950, E-mail: shirley.robinson@nau.edu. Web site: http://nau.edu/coe/ed-specialties/.

Old Dominion University, Darden College of Education, Programs in Occupational and Technical Studies, Norfolk, VA 23529. Offers business and industry training (MS); career and technical education (MS, PhD); community college teaching (MS); human resources training (PhD); STEM education (MS); technology education (PhD). *Accreditation:* NCATE (one or more programs are accredited). Part-time and evening/weekend programs available. Postbaccalaureate distance learning degree programs offered (minimal on-campus study). *Faculty:* 7 full-time (1 woman), 8 part-time/adjunct (3 women). *Students:* 14 full-time (10 women), 59 part-time (33 women); includes 28 minority (18 Black or African American, non-Hispanic/Latino; 1 American Indian or Alaska Native, non-Hispanic/Latino; 2 Asian, non-Hispanic/Latino; 6 Hispanic/Latino; 1 Two or more races, non-Hispanic/Latino), 1 international. Average age 42. 44 applicants, 95% accepted, 37 enrolled. In 2011, 27 master's, 5 doctorates awarded. *Degree requirements:* For master's, comprehensive exam, thesis optional, writing exam, candidacy exam; for doctorate, comprehensive exam, thesis/dissertation, writing exam, candidacy exam. *Entrance requirements:* For master's, GRE General Test or MAT, minimum GPA of 2.8, 2 letters of reference; for doctorate, GRE, minimum GPA of 3.0, 3 letters of reference. Additional exam requirements/recommendations for international students: Required—TOEFL. *Application deadline:* For fall admission, 6/1 priority date for domestic students, 6/1 for international students; for winter admission, 11/1 priority date for domestic students, 11/1 for international students; for spring admission, 3/1 priority date for domestic students, 3/1 for international students. Applications are processed on a rolling basis. Application fee: $50. Electronic applications accepted. *Expenses:* Tuition, state resident: full-time $9096; part-time $379 per credit. Tuition, nonresident: full-time $23,064; part-time $961 per credit. *Required fees:* $127 per semester. One-time fee: $50. *Financial support:* In 2011–12, 19 students received support, including 1 fellowship with full tuition reimbursement available (averaging $15,000 per year), 2 research assistantships with partial tuition reimbursements available (averaging $9,000 per year), 4 teaching assistantships with partial tuition reimbursements available (averaging $15,000 per year); career-related internships or fieldwork, scholarships/grants, tuition waivers (partial), and unspecified assistantships also available. Support available to part-time students. Financial award application deadline: 2/15; financial award applicants required to submit FAFSA. *Faculty research:* Training and development, marketing, technology, special populations, STEM education. *Total annual research expenditures:* $799,773. *Unit head:* Dr. John M. Ritz, Graduate Program Director, 757-683-5226, Fax: 757-683-5227, E-mail: jritz@odu.edu. *Application contact:* William Heffelfinger, Director of Graduate Admissions, 757-683-5554, Fax: 757-683-3255, E-mail: gradadmit@odu.edu. Web site: http://education.odu.edu/ots/.

Our Lady of the Lake University of San Antonio, School of Professional Studies, Program in Curriculum and Instruction, San Antonio, TX 78207-4689. Offers bilingual (M Ed); early childhood education (M Ed); English as a second language (M Ed); integrated math teaching (M Ed); integrated science teaching (M Ed); master reading teacher (M Ed); master technology teacher (M Ed); reading specialist (M Ed).

Penn State University Park, Graduate School, College of Education, Department of Learning and Performance Systems, State College, University Park, PA 16802-1503. Offers adult education (M Ed, D Ed, PhD, Certificate); instructional systems (M Ed, MS, D Ed, PhD); workforce education and development (M Ed, MS, PhD). *Unit head:* Dr. David H. Monk, Dean, 814-865-2526, Fax: 814-865-0555, E-mail: dhm6@psu.edu. *Application contact:* Cynthia E. Nicosia, Director, Graduate Enrollment Services, 814-865-1834, E-mail: cey1@psu.edu. Web site: http://www.ed.psu.edu/educ/lps/dept-lps.

Pittsburg State University, Graduate School, College of Technology, Department of Technology and Workforce Learning, Pittsburg, KS 66762. Offers career and technical education (MS); human resource development (MS); technology (MS), including printing management; workforce development and education (Ed S). *Degree requirements:* For master's, thesis or alternative.

Purdue University, Graduate School, College of Education, Department of Curriculum and Instruction, West Lafayette, IN 47907. Offers agricultural and extension education (PhD, Ed S); agriculture and extension education (MS, MS Ed); art education (PhD); consumer and family sciences and extension education (MS Ed, PhD, Ed S); curriculum studies (MS Ed, PhD, Ed S); educational technology (MS Ed, PhD, Ed S); elementary education (MS Ed); foreign language education (MS Ed, PhD, Ed S); industrial technology (PhD, Ed S); language arts (MS Ed, PhD, Ed S); literacy (MS Ed, PhD, Ed S); mathematics/science education (MS, MS Ed, PhD, Ed S); social studies (MS Ed, PhD); social studies education (Ed S); vocational/industrial education (MS Ed, PhD, Ed S); vocational/technical education (MS Ed, PhD, Ed S). *Accreditation:* NCATE. Part-time and evening/weekend programs available. *Faculty:* 30 full-time (21 women), 1 (woman) part-time/adjunct. *Students:* 89 full-time (64 women), 134 part-time (84 women); includes 31 minority (12 Black or African American, non-Hispanic/Latino; 3 American Indian or Alaska Native, non-Hispanic/Latino; 7 Asian, non-Hispanic/Latino; 9 Hispanic/Latino), 49 international. Average age 36. 136 applicants, 83% accepted, 72 enrolled. In 2011, 26 master's, 13 doctorates awarded. *Degree requirements:* For master's, thesis optional; for doctorate, thesis/dissertation, oral and written exams; for Ed S, oral presentation, project. *Entrance requirements:* For master's, GRE general test is required if undergraduate GPA is below 3.0, minimum undergraduate GPA of 3.0 or equivalent; for doctorate, GRE General Test, a combined GRE verbal and quantitative score of 1000 (300 for revised GRE Test) or more is expected, minimum undergraduate GPA of 3.0 or equivalent; master's degree with minimum GPA of 3.0 or equivalent; for Ed S, GRE general test, a combined GRE verbal and quantitative score of 1000 (300 for revised GRE Test) or more is expected, minimum undergraduate GPA of 3.0 or equivalent; master's degree. Additional exam requirements/recommendations for international students: Required—TOEFL (minimum score 550 paper-based; 77 iBT). *Application deadline:* For fall admission, 12/15 priority date for domestic students, 3/1 for international students; for spring admission, 9/15 for domestic students, 8/1 for international students. Application fee: $60 ($75 for international students). Electronic applications accepted. *Financial support:* Fellowships with full tuition reimbursements, research assistantships with full tuition reimbursements, teaching assistantships with full tuition reimbursements, career-related internships or fieldwork, and tuition waivers (full) available. Support available to part-time students. Financial award application deadline: 3/1; financial award applicants required to submit FAFSA. *Faculty research:* Literacy acquisition and development, teacher beliefs and knowledge, recruitment and retention of underrepresented students, economic education, literacy discourse. *Unit head:* Dr. Philip J. VanFossen, Head, 765-494-7935, Fax: 765-496-1622, E-mail: vanfoss@purdue.edu. *Application contact:* Sarah N. Prater, Graduate Contact, 765-494-2345, Fax: 765-494-5832, E-mail: prater0@purdue.edu. Web site: http://www.edci.purdue.edu/.

Purdue University, Graduate School, College of Technology, Graduate Program in Industrial Technology, West Lafayette, IN 47907. Offers MS. Part-time and evening/weekend programs available. Postbaccalaureate distance learning degree programs offered (minimal on-campus study). *Faculty:* 143 full-time (21 women). *Students:* 11 full-time (2 women), 1 part-time (0 women); includes 1 minority (Black or African American, non-Hispanic/Latino), 6 international. Average age 26. 17 applicants, 53% accepted, 5 enrolled. In 2011, 3 master's awarded. *Degree requirements:* For master's, thesis optional. *Entrance requirements:* For master's, GRE General Test, minimum GPA of 3.0. Additional exam requirements/recommendations for international students: Required—TOEFL (minimum score 550 paper-based; 213 computer-based). *Application deadline:* For fall admission, 4/1 for domestic and international students; for spring admission, 10/1 priority date for domestic students, 10/1 for international students. Applications are processed on a rolling basis. Application fee: $60 ($75 for international students). Electronic applications accepted. *Financial support:* Fellowships and teaching assistantships available. Support available to part-time students. Financial award applicants required to submit FAFSA. *Unit head:* Dr. Ragu Athinarayanan, Head, 765-494-0940, E-mail: rathinar@purdue.edu. *Application contact:* Jill S. Albrecht, Graduate Contact, 765-494-1088. Web site: http://www.tech.purdue.edu/graduate.

South Carolina State University, School of Graduate Studies, Department of Education, Orangeburg, SC 29117-0001. Offers counseling education (M Ed); early childhood and special education (M Ed); early childhood education (MAT); educational leadership (Ed D, Ed S); elementary education (M Ed, MAT); engineering (MAT); general science (MAT); mathematics (MAT); secondary education (M Ed), including biology education, business education, counselor education, English education, home economics education, industrial education, mathematics education, science education, social studies education; special education (M Ed), including emotionally handicapped, learning disabilities, mentally handicapped. *Accreditation:* NCATE. Part-time and evening/weekend programs available. *Faculty:* 9 full-time (6 women), 6 part-time/adjunct (2 women). *Students:* 34 full-time (29 women), 50 part-time (40 women); includes 74 minority (72 Black or African American, non-Hispanic/Latino; 1 Asian, non-Hispanic/Latino; 1 Hispanic/Latino). Average age 34. 23 applicants, 91% accepted, 14 enrolled. In 2011, 11 master's awarded. *Degree requirements:* For master's, thesis optional, departmental qualifying exam. *Entrance requirements:* For master's, GRE General Test, NTE, interview, teaching certificate. *Application deadline:* For fall admission, 6/15 priority date for domestic students, 6/15 for international students; for spring admission, 11/1 for domestic and international students. Applications are processed on a rolling basis. Application fee: $25. Electronic applications accepted. *Expenses:* Tuition, state resident: full-time $8688; part-time $514 per credit hour. Tuition, nonresident: full-time $17,600; part-time $1009 per credit hour. *Required fees:* $570. *Financial support:* In 2011–12, 3 fellowships (averaging $5,020 per year) were awarded; career-related internships or fieldwork, Federal Work-Study, and institutionally sponsored loans also available. Financial award application deadline: 6/1. *Faculty research:* Critical thinking, child abuse, stress, test-taking skills, conflict resolution, mainstreaming. *Unit head:* Dr. Charlie Spell, Interim Chair, 803-536-7098, Fax: 803-516-4568, E-mail: cspell@scsu.edu. *Application contact:* Annette Hazzard-Jones, Program Coordinator II, 803-536-8809, Fax: 803-536-8812, E-mail: zs_ahazzard@scsu.edu.

Southern Illinois University Carbondale, Graduate School, College of Education and Human Services, Department of Workforce Education and Development, Carbondale, IL 62901-4701. Offers MS Ed, PhD. *Accreditation:* NCATE. Part-time programs available. *Faculty:* 15 full-time (6 women), 1 part-time/adjunct (0 women). *Students:* 80 full-time (40 women), 114 part-time (58 women); includes 55 minority (41 Black or African American, non-Hispanic/Latino; 1 American Indian or Alaska Native, non-Hispanic/Latino; 3 Asian, non-Hispanic/Latino; 10 Hispanic/Latino), 17 international. Average age 32. 54 applicants, 81% accepted, 16 enrolled. In 2011, 62 master's, 6 doctorates awarded. *Degree requirements:* For master's, thesis; for doctorate, thesis/dissertation. *Entrance requirements:* For master's, minimum GPA of 2.7; for doctorate, GRE General Test, minimum GPA of 3.25. Additional exam requirements/recommendations for international students: Required—TOEFL. *Application deadline:* Applications are processed on a rolling basis. Application fee: $20. *Financial support:* In 2011–12, 38 students received support, including 4 research assistantships with full tuition reimbursements available, 10 teaching assistantships with full tuition reimbursements available; fellowships with full tuition reimbursements available, career-related internships or fieldwork, Federal Work-Study, institutionally sponsored loans, tuition waivers (full), and unspecified assistantships also available. Support available to part-time students. *Faculty research:* Career education, technical training, curriculum development, competency-based instruction, impact of technology on workplace and workforce. *Unit head:* Dr. Keith Waugh, Chair, 618-453-3321, Fax: 618-453-1909, E-mail: ckwaugh@siu.edu. *Application contact:* Dr. Marcia Anderson, Coordinator, 618-453-3321, Fax: 618-453-1909, E-mail: mandersn@siu.edu. Web site: http://wed.siu.edu/.

Southern New Hampshire University, School of Education, Manchester, NH 03106-1045. Offers business education (MS); child development (M Ed); computer technology education (Certificate); curriculum and instruction (M Ed); education (M Ed, CAS); elementary education (M Ed); general special education (Certificate); school business administrator (Certificate); secondary education (M Ed); training and development (Certificate). Part-time and evening/weekend programs available. Postbaccalaureate distance learning degree programs offered (no on-campus study). *Degree requirements:* For master's, comprehensive exam (for some programs), thesis or alternative. *Entrance requirements:* For master's, PRAXIS I, minimum GPA of 2.75. Additional exam requirements/recommendations for international students: Required—TOEFL (minimum score 550 paper-based; 213 computer-based). Electronic applications accepted. *Expenses:* Contact institution.

State University of New York at Oswego, Graduate Studies, School of Education, Department of Technology, Oswego, NY 13126. Offers MS Ed. *Accreditation:* NCATE. Part-time programs available. *Degree requirements:* For master's, thesis optional, departmental exam. *Entrance requirements:* For master's, provisional teaching certificate in technology education. Additional exam requirements/recommendations for international students: Required—TOEFL (minimum score 560 paper-based; 220 computer-based). *Faculty research:* Curriculum development, microcomputer applications.

State University of New York at Oswego, Graduate Studies, School of Education, Department of Vocational Teacher Preparation, Oswego, NY 13126. Offers agriculture (MS Ed); business and marketing (MS Ed); family and consumer sciences (MS Ed); health careers (MS Ed); technical education (MS Ed); trade education (MS Ed). *Accreditation:* NCATE. Part-time and evening/weekend programs available. *Degree requirements:* For master's, comprehensive exam, thesis or alternative. *Entrance requirements:* Additional exam requirements/recommendations for international students: Required—TOEFL (minimum score 560 paper-based; 220 computer-based).

Temple University, College of Education, Department of Curriculum, Instruction, and Technology in Education, Philadelphia, PA 19122-6096. Offers applied behavioral analysis (MS Ed); career and technical education (MS Ed); early childhood education and elementary education (MS Ed); English education (MS Ed); language arts education (Ed D); math/science education (Ed D); mathematics education (MS Ed); science education (MS Ed); second and foreign language education (MS Ed); special education (MS Ed); teaching English as a second language (MS Ed). Part-time and evening/weekend programs available. *Faculty:* 19 full-time (12 women). *Students:* 30 full-time (23 women), 86 part-time (69 women); includes 12 minority (4 Black or African American, non-Hispanic/Latino; 2 Asian, non-Hispanic/Latino; 5 Hispanic/Latino; 1 Two or more races, non-Hispanic/Latino), 5 international. 82 applicants, 71% accepted, 51 enrolled. In 2011, 181 master's, 16 doctorates awarded. Terminal master's awarded for partial completion of doctoral program. *Degree requirements:* For master's, thesis or alternative; for doctorate, thesis/dissertation. *Entrance requirements:* For master's and doctorate, GRE General Test or MAT, minimum GPA of 3.0. Additional exam requirements/recommendations for international students: Required—TOEFL (minimum score 550 paper-based; 213 computer-based; 79 iBT). *Application deadline:* For fall admission, 4/1 for domestic students, 12/15 for international students; for spring admission, 10/1 for domestic students, 8/1 for international students. Application fee: $50. Electronic applications accepted. *Expenses:* Tuition, state resident: full-time $12,366; part-time $687 per credit hour. Tuition, nonresident: full-time $17,298; part-time $961 per credit hour. *Required fees:* $590; $213 per year. *Financial support:* Fellowships, research assistantships with full tuition reimbursements, and teaching assistantships with full tuition reimbursements available. Financial award application deadline: 1/15; financial award applicants required to submit FAFSA. *Faculty research:* School improvement, problem-solving, literacy, language development. *Unit head:* Dr. Michael W. Smith, Chair, 215-204-6387, Fax: 215-204-1414, E-mail: mwsmith@temple.edu. *Application contact:* Dr. Margo Greicar, Director for Graduate Academic and Student Affairs, 215-204-8011, Fax: 215-204-4383, E-mail: margo.greicar@temple.edu. Web site: http://www.temple.edu/education/cite/.

Texas State University–San Marcos, Graduate School, College of Applied Arts, Program in Management of Technical Education, San Marcos, TX 78666. Offers M Ed. Part-time and evening/weekend programs available. *Faculty:* 3 full-time (0 women). *Students:* 5 full-time (all women), 8 part-time (4 women); includes 9 minority (2 Black or African American, non-Hispanic/Latino; 6 Hispanic/Latino; 1 Two or more races, non-Hispanic/Latino). Average age 37. 8 applicants, 50% accepted, 2 enrolled. In 2011, 9 master's awarded. *Degree requirements:* For master's, comprehensive exam. *Entrance requirements:* For master's, minimum GPA of 2.75 in last 60 hours of course work. Additional exam requirements/recommendations for international students: Required—TOEFL (minimum score 550 paper-based; 213 computer-based; 78 iBT). *Application deadline:* For fall admission, 6/15 for domestic students, 6/1 for international students; for spring admission, 10/15 for domestic students, 10/1 for international students. Applications are processed on a rolling basis. Application fee: $40 ($90 for international students). Electronic applications accepted. *Expenses:* Tuition, state resident: full-time $6408; part-time $3204 per semester. Tuition, nonresident: full-time $14,832; part-time $7416 per semester. *Required fees:* $1824; $912 per semester. Tuition and fees vary according to course load. *Financial support:* In 2011–12, 6 students received support. Research assistantships, teaching assistantships, career-related internships or fieldwork, Federal Work-Study, and institutionally sponsored loans available. Support available to part-time students. Financial award application deadline: 4/1; financial award applicants required to submit FAFSA. *Unit head:* Dr. Stephen Springer, Director, 512-245-2115, E-mail: ss01@txstate.edu. *Application contact:* Dr. J. Michael Willoughby, Dean of Graduate School, 512-245-2581, Fax: 512-245-8365, E-mail: gradcollege@txstate.edu. Web site: http://www.oced.txstate.edu.

Texas State University–San Marcos, Graduate School, Interdisciplinary Studies Program in Occupational Education, San Marcos, TX 78666. Offers M Ed, MSIS. *Faculty:* 4 full-time (0 women). *Students:* 10 full-time (6 women), 39 part-time (25 women); includes 23 minority (7 Black or African American, non-Hispanic/Latino; 1 Asian, non-Hispanic/Latino; 15 Hispanic/Latino). Average age 42. 18 applicants, 56% accepted, 7 enrolled. In 2011, 15 master's awarded. *Degree requirements:* For master's, comprehensive exam, thesis optional. *Entrance requirements:* For master's, minimum GPA of 2.75 for undergraduate work, statement of personal goals. Additional exam requirements/recommendations for international students: Required—TOEFL (minimum score 550 paper-based; 213 computer-based; 78 iBT). *Application deadline:* For fall admission, 6/15 priority date for domestic students, 6/1 for international students; for spring admission, 10/15 priority date for domestic students, 10/1 for international students. Applications are processed on a rolling basis. Application fee: $40 ($90 for international students). Electronic applications accepted. *Expenses:* Tuition, state resident: full-time $6408; part-time $3204 per semester. Tuition, nonresident: full-time $14,832; part-time $7416 per semester. *Required fees:* $1824; $912 per semester. Tuition and fees vary according to course load. *Financial support:* Research assistantships, teaching assistantships, Federal Work-Study, institutionally sponsored loans, scholarships/grants, health care benefits, and unspecified assistantships available. Support available to part-time students. Financial award application deadline: 4/1; financial award applicants required to submit FAFSA. *Unit head:* Dr. Stephen Springer, Director, 512-245-2115, E-mail: ss01@txstate.edu. *Application contact:* Dr. J. Michael Willoughby, Dean of Graduate School, 512-245-2581, Fax: 512-245-8365, E-mail: gradcollege@txstate.edu. Web site: http://www.OCED.txstate.edu/.

The University of Akron, Graduate School, College of Education, Department of Educational Foundations and Leadership, Program in Technical Education, Akron, OH 44325. Offers MS. *Accreditation:* NCATE. *Students:* 8 full-time (5 women), 46 part-time (37 women); includes 10 minority (7 Black or African American, non-Hispanic/Latino; 1 Asian, non-Hispanic/Latino; 1 Hispanic/Latino; 1 Two or more races, non-Hispanic/Latino), 6 international. Average age 41. 5 applicants, 40% accepted, 2 enrolled. In 2011, 5 master's awarded. *Degree requirements:* For master's, comprehensive exam, cumulative portfolio. *Entrance requirements:* For master's, minimum GPA of 2.75. Additional exam requirements/recommendations for international students: Required—TOEFL (minimum score 550 paper-based; 213 computer-based; 79 iBT). *Application deadline:* Applications are processed on a rolling basis. Application fee: $30 ($40 for international students). Electronic applications accepted. *Expenses:* Tuition, state resident: full-time $7038; part-time $391 per credit hour. Tuition, nonresident: full-time $12,051; part-time $670 per credit hour. *Required fees:* $1274; $34 per credit hour. *Financial support:* Fellowships, research assistantships, and teaching assistantships available. *Unit head:* Dr. Susan Olson, Chair, 330-972-8223, E-mail: solson@uakron.edu. *Application contact:* Dr. Mark Tausig, Associate Dean, 330-972-6266, Fax: 330-972-6475, E-mail: mtausig@uakron.edu.

University of Arkansas, Graduate School, College of Education and Health Professions, Department of Rehabilitation, Human Resources and Communication Disorders, Program in Workforce Development Education, Fayetteville, AR 72701-1201. Offers M Ed, Ed D. Part-time and evening/weekend programs available. Postbaccalaureate distance learning degree programs offered. *Students:* 27 full-time (13 women), 145 part-time (114 women); includes 47 minority (36 Black or African American, non-Hispanic/Latino; 2 American Indian or Alaska Native, non-Hispanic/Latino; 7 Hispanic/Latino; 2 Two or more races, non-Hispanic/Latino), 3 international. In 2011, 32 master's, 3 doctorates awarded. *Application deadline:* For fall admission, 4/1 for international students; for spring admission, 10/1 for international students. Applications are processed on a rolling basis. Electronic applications accepted. *Financial support:* Fellowships, research assistantships, teaching assistantships, career-related internships or fieldwork, and Federal Work-Study available. Support available to part-time students. Financial award application deadline: 4/1; financial award applicants required to submit FAFSA. *Unit head:* Dr. Fran Hagstrom, Departmental Chairperson, 479-575-4758, Fax: 479-575-2492, E-mail: fhagstr@uark.edu. *Application contact:* Dr. Brent Williams, Graduate Coordinator, 479-575-4758, E-mail: btwilli@uark.edu. Web site: http://rhrc.uark.edu.

The University of British Columbia, Faculty of Education, Department of Curriculum and Pedagogy, Vancouver, BC V6T 1Z4, Canada. Offers art education (M Ed, MA); business education (MA); curriculum studies (M Ed, MA, PhD); home economics education (M Ed, MA); math education (M Ed, MA); music education (M Ed, MA); physical education (M Ed, MA); science education (M Ed, MA); social studies education (M Ed, MA); technology studies education (M Ed, MA). Part-time programs available. *Degree requirements:* For master's, thesis (MA); for doctorate, comprehensive exam, thesis/dissertation. *Entrance requirements:* Additional exam requirements/recommendations for international students: Required—TOEFL (minimum score 580 paper-based; 237 computer-based; 92 iBT). Electronic applications accepted. *Expenses:* Contact institution. *Faculty research:* School subjects, teaching and learning.

University of Calgary, Faculty of Graduate Studies, Faculty of Education, Graduate Division of Educational Research, Calgary, AB T2N 1N4, Canada. Offers community rehabilitation and disability studies (M Ed, M Sc, Ed D, PhD, Graduate Certificate, Graduate Diploma); curriculum, teaching and learning (M Ed, M Sc, MA, Ed D, PhD, Graduate Certificate, Graduate Diploma); educational contexts (M Ed, MA, Ed D, PhD, Graduate Certificate, Graduate Diploma); educational leadership (M Ed, MA, Ed D, PhD, Graduate Certificate, Graduate Diploma); educational technology (M Ed, M Sc, MA, Ed D, PhD, Graduate Certificate, Graduate Diploma); gifted education (M Sc, MA, Ed D, PhD, Graduate Certificate, Graduate Diploma); higher education administration (Ed D); interpretive studies in education (M Ed, M Sc, MA, Ed D, PhD, Graduate Certificate, Graduate Diploma); second language teaching (M Ed, Ed D, PhD, Graduate Certificate, Graduate Diploma); teaching English as a second language (M Ed, M Sc, MA, Ed D, PhD, Graduate Certificate, Graduate Diploma); workplace and adult learning (M Ed, MA, Ed D, PhD, Graduate Certificate, Graduate Diploma). Ed D in both higher education administration and educational leadership offered via distance delivery. Part-time and evening/weekend programs available. Postbaccalaureate distance learning degree programs offered (minimal on-campus study). *Degree requirements:* For master's, thesis (for some programs); for doctorate, thesis/dissertation, candidacy exam. *Entrance requirements:* For master's, minimum GPA of 3.0, 3 letters of reference; for doctorate, minimum GPA of 3.5, 3 letters of reference; for other advanced degree, minimum GPA of 3.0. Additional exam requirements/recommendations for international students: Required—TOEFL, IELTS. Electronic applications accepted. *Faculty research:* Curriculum, leadership, technology, contexts, gifted, second language teaching, work place and adult learning.

University of Central Florida, College of Education, Department of Educational and Human Sciences, Program in Career and Technical Education, Orlando, FL 32816. Offers MA. *Accreditation:* NCATE. Part-time and evening/weekend programs available. *Students:* 19 full-time (14 women), 55 part-time (49 women); includes 31 minority (21 Black or African American, non-Hispanic/Latino; 1 Asian, non-Hispanic/Latino; 7 Hispanic/Latino; 2 Two or more races, non-Hispanic/Latino). Average age 40. 30 applicants, 87% accepted, 21 enrolled. In 2011, 12 master's awarded. *Entrance requirements:* For master's, GRE General Test. Additional exam requirements/recommendations for international students: Required—TOEFL. *Application deadline:* For fall admission, 7/15 for domestic students; for spring admission, 12/1 for domestic students. Electronic applications accepted. *Expenses:* Tuition, state resident: part-time $277.08 per credit hour. Tuition, nonresident: part-time $277.08 per credit hour. Part-time tuition and fees vary according to degree level and program. *Financial support:* Fellowships with partial tuition reimbursements, research assistantships with partial tuition reimbursements, teaching assistantships with partial tuition reimbursements, career-related internships or fieldwork, Federal Work-Study, institutionally sponsored loans, tuition waivers (partial), and unspecified assistantships available. Financial award application deadline: 3/1; financial award applicants required to submit FAFSA. *Unit head:* Dr. Jo Ann M. Whiteman, Program Coordinator, 407-823-2848, E-mail: joann.whiteman@ucf.edu. *Application contact:* Barbara Rodriguez Lamas, Director, Admissions and Registration, 407-823-2766, Fax: 407-823-6442, E-mail: gradadmissions@ucf.edu.

University of Central Missouri, The Graduate School, College of Education, Warrensburg, MO 64093. Offers career and technical education administration (MS); career and technical education industry training (MS); career and technical education leadership/teaching (MS); college student personnel administration (MS); counseling (MS); curriculum and instruction (Ed S); educational leadership (Ed D); educational technology (MS); elementary education/educational foundations and literacy (MSE); elementary school administration (MSE); elementary school principalship (Ed S); human services/learning resources (Ed S); human services/professional counseling (Ed S); human services/special education (Ed S); human services/technology and occupational education (Ed S); K-12 education/educational foundations and literacy (MSE); K-12 special education (MSE); library science and information services (MS); literacy education (MSE); secondary education/educational foundations & literacy (MSE); secondary school administration (MSE); secondary school principalship (Ed S); superintendency (Ed S); teaching (MAT). Ed D offered jointly with University of Missouri. Part-time programs available. Postbaccalaureate distance learning degree programs offered. *Entrance requirements:* Additional exam requirements/recommendations for

international students: Required—TOEFL (minimum score 550 paper-based; 79 computer-based). Electronic applications accepted.

University of Georgia, College of Education, Department of Workforce Education, Leadership and Social Foundations, Athens, GA 30602. Offers educational leadership (Ed D); human resources and organization design (M Ed); occupational studies (MAT, Ed D, PhD, Ed S); social foundations of education (PhD). *Accreditation:* NCATE. *Faculty:* 14 full-time (7 women). *Students:* 27 full-time (15 women), 70 part-time (46 women); includes 24 minority (23 Black or African American, non-Hispanic/Latino; 1 Native Hawaiian or other Pacific Islander, non-Hispanic/Latino), 5 international. Average age 37. 40 applicants, 63% accepted, 8 enrolled. In 2011, 16 master's, 23 doctorates, 5 other advanced degrees awarded. *Entrance requirements:* For master's, GRE General Test, MAT; for doctorate, GRE General Test; for Ed S, GRE General Test or MAT. *Application deadline:* For fall admission, 7/1 priority date for domestic students; for spring admission, 11/15 for domestic students. Application fee: $50. Electronic applications accepted. *Financial support:* Fellowships, research assistantships, teaching assistantships, and unspecified assistantships available. *Unit head:* Dr. Roger B. Hill, Interim Head, 706-542-4100, Fax: 706-542-4054, E-mail: rbhill@uga.edu. *Application contact:* Dr. Robert C. Wicklein, Graduate Coordinator, 706-542-4503, Fax: 706-542-4054, E-mail: wickone@uga.edu. Web site: http://www.coe.uga.edu/welsf/.

University of Illinois at Urbana–Champaign, Graduate College, College of Education, Department of Human Resource Education, Champaign, IL 61820. Offers Ed M, MS, Ed D, PhD, CAS, MBA/M Ed. Part-time and evening/weekend programs available. Postbaccalaureate distance learning degree programs offered (no on-campus study). *Faculty:* 6 full-time (1 woman). *Students:* 48 full-time (21 women), 118 part-time (81 women); includes 30 minority (19 Black or African American, non-Hispanic/Latino; 6 Asian, non-Hispanic/Latino; 5 Hispanic/Latino), 38 international. 104 applicants, 63% accepted, 29 enrolled. In 2011, 87 master's, 9 doctorates, 3 other advanced degrees awarded. *Entrance requirements:* For master's, minimum GPA of 3.0; for doctorate, GRE, minimum GPA of 3.0. Additional exam requirements/recommendations for international students: Required—TOEFL (minimum score 96 iBT). *Application deadline:* Applications are processed on a rolling basis. Application fee: $75 ($90 for international students). Electronic applications accepted. *Financial support:* In 2011–12, 3 fellowships, 8 research assistantships, 11 teaching assistantships were awarded; tuition waivers (full and partial) also available. *Unit head:* James D. Anderson, Head, 217-333-7404, Fax: 217-244-5632, E-mail: janders@illinois.edu. *Application contact:* Laura Ketchum, Secretary, 217-333-0807, Fax: 217-244-5632, E-mail: lirle@illinois.edu. Web site: http://education.illinois.edu/hre/index.html.

University of Kentucky, Graduate School, College of Agriculture, Program in Career, Technology and Leadership Education, Lexington, KY 40506-0032. Offers MS. *Accreditation:* NCATE. Terminal master's awarded for partial completion of doctoral program. *Degree requirements:* For master's, comprehensive exam, thesis optional. *Entrance requirements:* For master's, GRE General Test, minimum undergraduate GPA of 2.75. Additional exam requirements/recommendations for international students: Required—TOEFL (minimum score 550 paper-based; 213 computer-based). Electronic applications accepted.

University of Maryland Eastern Shore, Graduate Programs, Department of Technology, Princess Anne, MD 21853-1299. Offers career and technology education (M Ed). Part-time and evening/weekend programs available. *Degree requirements:* For master's, comprehensive exam, seminar paper. *Entrance requirements:* For master's, PRAXIS, writing sample. Additional exam requirements/recommendations for international students: Required—TOEFL (minimum score 213 computer-based; 80 iBT). Electronic applications accepted. *Faculty research:* Doppler Radar study.

University of Minnesota, Twin Cities Campus, Graduate School, College of Education and Human Development, Department of Organizational Leadership, Policy and Development, Minneapolis, MN 55455-0213. Offers adult education (M Ed, MA, Ed D, PhD, Certificate); agricultural, food and environmental education (M Ed, MA, Ed D, PhD); business and industry education (M Ed, MA, Ed D, PhD); business education (M Ed); comparative and international development education (MA, PhD); disability policy and services (Certificate); educational administration (MA, Ed D, PhD); evaluation studies (MA, PhD); higher education (MA, PhD); human resource development (M Ed, MA, Ed D, PhD, Certificate); marketing education (M Ed); postsecondary administration (Ed D); program evaluation (Certificate); school-to-work (Certificate); staff development (Certificate); teacher leadership (M Ed); technical education (Certificate); technology education (M Ed, MA); work and human resource education (M Ed, MA, Ed D, PhD); youth development leadership (M Ed). *Faculty:* 28 full-time (12 women). *Students:* 265 full-time (183 women), 196 part-time (43 women); includes 97 minority (48 Black or African American, non-Hispanic/Latino; 5 American Indian or Alaska Native, non-Hispanic/Latino; 30 Asian, non-Hispanic/Latino; 14 Hispanic/Latino), 75 international. Average age 38. 419 applicants, 68% accepted, 202 enrolled. In 2011, 140 master's, 48 doctorates, 149 other advanced degrees awarded. Application fee: $55. *Financial support:* In 2011–12, 2 fellowships (averaging $14,581 per year), 46 research assistantships with full tuition reimbursements (averaging $8,130 per year), 14 teaching assistantships with full tuition reimbursements (averaging $8,800 per year) were awarded. *Faculty research:* Organizational change in schools, universities, and other organizations; international education and development; program evaluation to facilitate organizational reform; international human resource development and change; interactions of gender and race/ethnicity on learning and leadership; development of initiatives to develop intercultural sensitivity and global awareness; leadership theory and development in educational, work-based, and other organizations. *Total annual research expenditures:* $787,672. *Unit head:* Dr. Rebecca Ropers-Huilman, Chair, 612-624-1006, Fax: 612-624-3377, E-mail: ropers@umn.edu. *Application contact:* Dr. Jennifer Engler, Assistant Dean, 612-626-2887, Fax: 612-626-7496, E-mail: engle009@umn.edu. Web site: http://www.education.umn.edu/edpa/.

University of Missouri, Graduate School, College of Education, Department of Learning, Teaching and Curriculum, Columbia, MO 65211. Offers agricultural education (M Ed, PhD, Ed S); art education (M Ed, PhD, Ed S); business and office education (M Ed, PhD, Ed S); early childhood education (M Ed, PhD, Ed S); elementary education (M Ed, PhD, Ed S); English education (M Ed, PhD, Ed S); foreign language education (M Ed, PhD, Ed S); health education and promotion (M Ed, PhD); learning and instruction (M Ed); marketing education (M Ed, PhD, Ed S); mathematics education (M Ed, PhD, Ed S); music education (M Ed, PhD, Ed S); reading education (M Ed, PhD, Ed S); science education (M Ed, PhD, Ed S); social studies education (M Ed, PhD, Ed S); vocational education (M Ed, PhD, Ed S). Part-time programs available. *Faculty:* 26 full-time (16 women), 3 part-time/adjunct (2 women). *Students:* 184 full-time (145 women), 276 part-time (215 women); includes 34 minority (10 Black or African American, non-Hispanic/Latino; 1 American Indian or Alaska Native, non-Hispanic/Latino; 7 Asian, non-Hispanic/Latino; 8 Hispanic/Latino; 8 Two or more races, non-Hispanic/Latino), 39 international. Average age 32. 309 applicants, 76% accepted, 204 enrolled. In 2011, 232 master's, 8 doctorates, 2 other advanced degrees awarded. Terminal master's awarded for partial completion of doctoral program. *Degree requirements:* For doctorate, thesis/dissertation. *Entrance requirements:* For master's and Ed S, GRE General Test or MAT, minimum GPA of 3.0; for doctorate, GRE General Test, minimum GPA of 3.0. Additional exam requirements/recommendations for international students: Required—TOEFL (minimum score 600 paper-based; 250 computer-based; 100 iBT). Application fee: $55 ($75 for international students). Electronic applications accepted. *Expenses:* Tuition, state resident: full-time $5881. Tuition, nonresident: full-time $15,183. *Required fees:* $952. Tuition and fees vary according to campus/location and program. *Financial support:* Fellowships, research assistantships, teaching assistantships, and institutionally sponsored loans available. *Application contact:* Fran Colley, 573-882-6462, E-mail: colleyf@missouri.edu. Web site: http://education.missouri.edu/LTC/.

University of Nebraska–Lincoln, Graduate College, College of Education and Human Sciences, Department of Teaching, Learning and Teacher Education, Lincoln, NE 68588. Offers adult and continuing education (MA); educational studies (Ed D, PhD), including special education (Ed D); teaching, learning and teacher education (M Ed, MA, MST, Ed D, PhD); vocational and adult education (M Ed, MA). *Accreditation:* NCATE. *Degree requirements:* For master's, thesis optional. *Entrance requirements:* Additional exam requirements/recommendations for international students: Required—TOEFL (minimum score 550 paper-based; 213 computer-based). Electronic applications accepted. *Faculty research:* Teacher education, instructional leadership, literacy education, technology, improvement of school curriculum.

University of Northern Iowa, Graduate College, College of Humanities, Arts and Sciences, Department of Industrial Technology, Cedar Falls, IA 50614. Offers MS, PSM, DIT. *Students:* 19 full-time (1 woman), 27 part-time (5 women), 20 international. 41 applicants, 61% accepted, 14 enrolled. In 2011, 3 master's, 1 doctorate awarded. *Degree requirements:* For master's, comprehensive exam, thesis or alternative; for doctorate, thesis/dissertation. *Entrance requirements:* For master's, GRE, minimum GPA of 3.0, 3 professional references; for doctorate, GRE, minimum GPA of 3.5. Additional exam requirements/recommendations for international students: Required—TOEFL (minimum score 600 paper-based; 250 computer-based; 100 iBT). *Application deadline:* For fall admission, 8/1 priority date for domestic students. Applications are processed on a rolling basis. Application fee: $50 ($70 for international students). Electronic applications accepted. *Expenses:* Tuition, state resident: full-time $7476. Tuition, nonresident: full-time $16,410. *Required fees:* $942. *Financial support:* Teaching assistantships, career-related internships or fieldwork, Federal Work-Study, scholarships/grants, and tuition waivers (full and partial) available. Support available to part-time students. Financial award application deadline: 2/1. *Unit head:* Dr. James Maxwell, Department Head/Director, 319-273-2563, Fax: 319-273-5818, E-mail: james.maxwell@uni.edu. *Application contact:* Laurie S. Russell, Record Analyst, 319-273-2623, Fax: 319-273-2885, E-mail: laurie.russell@uni.edu. Web site: http://www.uni.edu/indtech/.

University of North Texas, Toulouse Graduate School, College of Information, Department of Learning Technologies, Program in Applied Technology, Training and Development, Denton, TX 76203. Offers M Ed, MS, Ed D, PhD. *Accreditation:* NCATE. *Degree requirements:* For doctorate, one foreign language, thesis/dissertation, internship. *Entrance requirements:* For master's, GRE General Test; for doctorate, GRE General Test, admissions exam. Additional exam requirements/recommendations for international students: Recommended—TOEFL (minimum score 550 paper-based; 213 computer-based; 79 iBT). *Expenses:* Tuition, state resident: part-time $100 per credit hour. Tuition, nonresident: part-time $413 per credit hour.

University of North Texas, Toulouse Graduate School, College of Information, Department of Library and Information Sciences, Denton, TX 76203. Offers information science (MS, PhD); learning technologies (M Ed, Ed D), including applied technology, training and development (M Ed), computer education and cognitive systems, educational computing; library science (MS). *Accreditation:* ALA (one or more programs are accredited). Part-time and evening/weekend programs available. *Degree requirements:* For master's, comprehensive exam; for doctorate, comprehensive exam, thesis/dissertation. *Entrance requirements:* For master's, GRE General Test, MAT; for doctorate, GRE General Test. Additional exam requirements/recommendations for international students: Recommended—TOEFL (minimum score 550 paper-based; 213 computer-based; 79 iBT). Electronic applications accepted. *Expenses:* Tuition, state resident: part-time $100 per credit hour. Tuition, nonresident: part-time $413 per credit hour. *Faculty research:* Information resources and services, information management and retrieval, computer-based information systems, human information behavior.

University of Phoenix–Phoenix Main Campus, College of Education, Tempe, AZ 85282-2371. Offers administration and supervision (MA Ed); adult education and training (MA Ed); curriculum and instruction reading (MA Ed); curriculum instruction (MA Ed); early childhood education (MA Ed); education studies (MA Ed); elementary teacher education (MA Ed); secondary teacher education (MA Ed); special education (MA Ed); teacher leadership (MA Ed). Evening/weekend programs available. Postbaccalaureate distance learning degree programs offered. *Students:* 297 full-time (203 women); includes 53 minority (19 Black or African American, non-Hispanic/Latino; 1 American Indian or Alaska Native, non-Hispanic/Latino; 6 Asian, non-Hispanic/Latino; 21 Hispanic/Latino; 2 Native Hawaiian or other Pacific Islander, non-Hispanic/Latino; 4 Two or more races, non-Hispanic/Latino), 3 international. Average age 35. *Entrance requirements:* Additional exam requirements/recommendations for international students: Required—TOEFL, TOEIC (Test of English as an International Communication), Berlitz Online English Proficiency Exam, Pearson Test of English, or IELTS. *Application deadline:* Applications are processed on a rolling basis. Application fee: $45. Electronic applications accepted. *Expenses:* Contact institution. *Financial support:* Scholarships/grants available. Financial award applicants required to submit FAFSA. *Application contact:* 866-766-0766. Web site: http://www.phoenix.edu/colleges_divisions/education.html.

University of South Africa, Institute for Science and Technology Education, Pretoria, South Africa. Offers mathematics, science and technology education (M Sc, PhD).

University of Southern Mississippi, Graduate School, College of Education and Psychology, Department of Technology Education, Hattiesburg, MS 39406-0001. Offers business technology education (MS); instructional technology (MS); technical occupational education (MS). Part-time programs available. *Faculty:* 6 full-time (3 women). *Students:* 7 full-time (4 women), 22 part-time (16 women); includes 5 minority (all Black or African American, non-Hispanic/Latino), 2 international. Average age 37. 15 applicants, 53% accepted, 6 enrolled. In 2011, 13 degrees awarded. *Degree requirements:* For master's, comprehensive exam, thesis (for some programs). *Entrance requirements:* For master's, GRE General Test, MAT, minimum GPA of 2.75 in last 60 hours. Additional exam requirements/recommendations for international students: Required—TOEFL. *Application deadline:* For fall admission, 3/1 priority date for domestic students, 3/1 for international students. Applications are processed on a rolling basis. Application fee: $50. *Financial support:* In 2011–12, 2 research assistantships with full tuition reimbursements (averaging $9,000 per year), 1 teaching assistantship with full tuition reimbursement (averaging $10,000 per year) were awarded; Federal Work-Study also available. Financial award application deadline: 3/15; financial award applicants required to submit FAFSA. *Faculty research:* Occupational competency, professional development for vocational-technical. *Total annual research expenditures:* $166,068. *Unit head:* Dr. Edward C. Mann, Chair, 601-266-4446, Fax: 601-266-5957, E-mail: edward.mann@usm.edu. *Application contact:* Shonna Breland, Manager of

Graduate Admissions, 601-266-6563, Fax: 601-266-5138. Web site: http://www.usm.edu/technologyeducation.

University of South Florida, Graduate School, College of Education, Department of Adult, Career and Higher Education, Tampa, FL 33620-9951. Offers adult education (MA, Ed D, PhD, Ed S); career and technical education (MA); career and workforce education (PhD); higher education/community college teaching (MA, Ed D, PhD); vocational education (Ed S). Part-time programs available. Postbaccalaureate distance learning degree programs offered (minimal on-campus study). *Faculty:* 9 full-time (3 women), 4 part-time/adjunct (3 women). *Students:* 38 full-time (21 women), 169 part-time (115 women); includes 59 minority (37 Black or African American, non-Hispanic/Latino; 5 Asian, non-Hispanic/Latino; 14 Hispanic/Latino; 3 Two or more races, non-Hispanic/Latino), 6 international. Average age 44. 98 applicants, 70% accepted, 42 enrolled. In 2011, 33 master's, 13 doctorates awarded. *Median time to degree:* Of those who began their doctoral program in fall 2003, 50% received their degree in 8 years or less. *Degree requirements:* For master's, comprehensive exam; for doctorate, comprehensive exam, thesis/dissertation, philosophies of inquiry; multiple research methods; for Ed S, comprehensive exam, thesis. *Entrance requirements:* For master's, minimum GPA of 3.0 in last 60 hours of course work; for doctorate and Ed S, GRE General Test, GRE Writing Test. Additional exam requirements/recommendations for international students: Required—TOEFL (minimum score 500 paper-based; 213 computer-based; 91 iBT). *Application deadline:* For fall admission, 2/15 for domestic students, 1/2 for international students; for spring admission, 10/15 for domestic students, 6/1 for international students. Applications are processed on a rolling basis. Application fee: $30. Electronic applications accepted. *Financial support:* In 2011–12, 5 students received support, including 5 teaching assistantships with full tuition reimbursements available (averaging $15,000 per year); career-related internships or fieldwork, scholarships/grants, and unspecified assistantships also available. Financial award applicants required to submit FAFSA. *Faculty research:* Community college leadership; integration of academic, career and technical education; competency-based education; continuing education administration; adult learning and development. *Total annual research expenditures:* $9,807. *Unit head:* Dr. Ann Cranston-Gingras, Chairperson, 813-974-6036, Fax: 813-974-3366, E-mail: cranston@usf.edu. *Application contact:* Dr. William Young, Program Director, 813-974-1861, Fax: 813-974-3366, E-mail: williamyoung@usf.edu.

The University of Texas at Tyler, College of Business and Technology, School of Human Resource Development and Technology, Tyler, TX 75799-0001. Offers human resource development (MS, PhD); industrial management (MS). Part-time and evening/weekend programs available. Postbaccalaureate distance learning degree programs offered (no on-campus study). *Degree requirements:* For master's, comprehensive exam. *Entrance requirements:* For master's, GRE General Test or MAT. Additional exam requirements/recommendations for international students: Required—TOEFL (minimum score 79 computer-based). Electronic applications accepted. *Faculty research:* Human resource development.

The University of Toledo, College of Graduate Studies, Judith Herb College of Education, Health Science and Human Service, Department of Curriculum and Instruction, Toledo, OH 43606-3390. Offers art education (ME); career and technical education (ME); curriculum and instruction (ME, PhD, Ed S); education and anthropology (MAE); education and biology (MES); education and chemistry (MES); education and classics (MAE); education and economics (MAE); education and English (MAE); education and French (MAE); education and geography (MAE); education and geology (MES); education and German (MAE); education and history (MAE); education and mathematics (MAE, MES); education and physics (MES); education and political science (MAE); education and sociology (MAE); education and Spanish (MAE); educational media (PhD); educational technology (ME); English as a second language (MAE); gifted and talented (PhD); middle childhood education licensure (ME); music education (MME); secondary education (PhD); secondary education licensure (ME). *Accreditation:* NCATE. Part-time and evening/weekend programs available. *Faculty:* 24. *Students:* 60 full-time (31 women), 211 part-time (161 women); includes 23 minority (21 Black or African American, non-Hispanic/Latino; 2 Hispanic/Latino), 20 international. Average age 35. 115 applicants, 73% accepted, 74 enrolled. In 2011, 105 master's, 3 doctorates, 4 other advanced degrees awarded. *Degree requirements:* For master's, comprehensive exam, thesis or alternative; for doctorate, comprehensive exam, thesis/dissertation; for Ed S, thesis optional. *Entrance requirements:* For master's, doctorate, and Ed S, minimum cumulative GPA of 2.7 for all previous academic work, letters of recommendation. Additional exam requirements/recommendations for international students: Required—TOEFL (minimum score 550 paper-based; 213 computer-based; 80 iBT), IELTS (minimum score 6.5). *Application deadline:* For fall admission, 1/15 priority date for domestic students, 1/15 for international students. Applications are processed on a rolling basis. Application fee: $45 ($75 for international students). Electronic applications accepted. *Financial support:* In 2011–12, 9 research assistantships with full and partial tuition reimbursements (averaging $7,184 per year), 12 teaching assistantships with full and partial tuition reimbursements (averaging $8,425 per year) were awarded; career-related internships or fieldwork, Federal Work-Study, institutionally sponsored loans, scholarships/grants, tuition waivers (full and partial), unspecified assistantships, and administrative assistantships also available. Support available to part-time students. *Unit head:* Dr. Leigh Chiarelott, Chair, 419-530-5371, E-mail: eigh.chiarelott@utoledo.edu. *Application contact:* Graduate School Office, 419-530-4723, Fax: 419-530-4724, E-mail: grdsch@utnet.utoledo.edu. Web site: http://www.utoledo.edu/eduhshs/.

University of Victoria, Faculty of Graduate Studies, Faculty of Education, Department of Curriculum and Instruction, Victoria, BC V8W 2Y2, Canada. Offers art education (M Ed, PhD); curriculum studies (M Ed, MA, PhD); early childhood education (M Ed, PhD); educational studies (PhD); language and literacy (M Ed, MA, PhD); mathematics (M Ed, MA, PhD); music education (M Ed, MA, PhD); science (M Ed, MA, PhD); social studies (M Ed, MA); social, cultural and foundational studies (MA, PhD); technology and environmental education (PhD). Part-time programs available. *Degree requirements:* For master's, thesis, project (M Ed); for doctorate, comprehensive exam, thesis/dissertation. *Entrance requirements:* For master's, minimum B average. Additional exam requirements/recommendations for international students: Required—TOEFL (minimum score 575 paper-based; 233 computer-based), IELTS (minimum score 7). Electronic applications accepted. *Faculty research:* Elementary and secondary English, language arts, curriculum theory and practice, educational media and technology, educational administration and leadership, history and philosophy of education.

University of West Florida, College of Professional Studies, Department of Applied Science, Technology and Administration, Pensacola, FL 32514-5750. Offers career and technical education (M Ed); curriculum and instruction (Ed S); curriculum and instruction: instructional technology (Ed D); educational leadership (M Ed), including education and training management; instructional technology (M Ed), including educational leadership, instructional technology. *Faculty:* 10 full-time (4 women), 5 part-time/adjunct (2 women). *Students:* 44 full-time (33 women), 188 part-time (113 women); includes 72 minority (38 Black or African American, non-Hispanic/Latino; 4 American Indian or Alaska Native, non-Hispanic/Latino; 4 Asian, non-Hispanic/Latino; 19 Hispanic/Latino; 2 Native Hawaiian or other Pacific Islander, non-Hispanic/Latino; 5 Two or more races, non-Hispanic/Latino), 2 international. Average age 35. 126 applicants, 58% accepted, 49 enrolled. In 2011, 81 degrees awarded. *Entrance requirements:* For master's, GRE, GMAT, or MAT, letter of intent, names of references. Additional exam requirements/recommendations for international students: Required—TOEFL (minimum score 550 paper-based; 213 computer-based). *Application deadline:* For fall admission, 6/1 for domestic and international students; for spring admission, 10/1 for domestic and international students. Applications are processed on a rolling basis. Electronic applications accepted. *Expenses:* Tuition, state resident: full-time $5729; part-time $302 per credit hour. Tuition, nonresident: full-time $20,059; part-time $961 per credit hour. *Required fees:* $1509; $63 per credit hour. *Financial support:* In 2011–12, 17 fellowships (averaging $200 per year), 11 research assistantships with partial tuition reimbursements, 3 teaching assistantships with partial tuition reimbursements were awarded; unspecified assistantships also available. *Unit head:* Dr. Karen Rasmussen, Chair, 850-474-2300, E-mail: krasmuss@uwf.edu. *Application contact:* Terry McCray, Assistant Director of Graduate Admissions, 850-473-7718, Fax: 850-473-7714, E-mail: gradadmissions@uwf.edu. Web site: http://uwf.edu/ect/.

University of Wisconsin–Stout, Graduate School, School of Education, Program in Career and Technical Education, Menomonie, WI 54751. Offers MS, Ed S. Part-time programs available. *Degree requirements:* For master's and Ed S, thesis. *Entrance requirements:* For master's, minimum GPA of 2.75; for Ed S, minimum GPA of 3.25. Additional exam requirements/recommendations for international students: Required—TOEFL (minimum score 500 paper-based; 173 computer-based; 61 iBT). Electronic applications accepted. *Faculty research:* Needs assessment, task analysis, instructional development, learning technologies.

University of Wisconsin–Stout, Graduate School, School of Education, Program in Industrial/Technology Education, Menomonie, WI 54751. Offers MS. Part-time programs available. *Degree requirements:* For master's, thesis. *Entrance requirements:* For master's, minimum GPA of 2.75. Additional exam requirements/recommendations for international students: Required—TOEFL (minimum score 500 paper-based; 173 computer-based; 61 iBT). Electronic applications accepted. *Faculty research:* Gender equity, instructional design, cognitive processes, socio-cultural impacts.

Utah State University, School of Graduate Studies, College of Engineering, Department of Engineering and Technology Education, Logan, UT 84322. Offers industrial technology (MS). Part-time and evening/weekend programs available. *Degree requirements:* For master's, thesis optional. *Entrance requirements:* For master's, GRE General Test, MAT, minimum GPA of 3.0 in last 30 hours of course work. Additional exam requirements/recommendations for international students: Required—TOEFL. *Faculty research:* Computer-aided design drafting, technology and the public school, materials, electronics, aviation.

Valley City State University, Online Master of Education Program, Valley City, ND 58072. Offers library and information technologies (M Ed); teaching and technology (M Ed); teaching English language learners (ELL) (M Ed); technology education (M Ed). *Accreditation:* NCATE. Part-time and evening/weekend programs available. Postbaccalaureate distance learning degree programs offered (no on-campus study). *Faculty:* 25 full-time (18 women), 2 part-time/adjunct (both women). *Students:* 4 full-time (3 women), 147 part-time (99 women); includes 6 minority (1 Black or African American, non-Hispanic/Latino; 1 American Indian or Alaska Native, non-Hispanic/Latino; 2 Asian, non-Hispanic/Latino; 2 Hispanic/Latino). Average age 34. 40 applicants, 83% accepted, 30 enrolled. In 2011, 30 master's awarded. *Degree requirements:* For master's, action research report, comprehensive portfolio. *Entrance requirements:* For master's, GRE, MAT, PRAXIS II or National Teaching Board for Professional Standards (if GPA less than 3.0). Additional exam requirements/recommendations for international students: Required—TOEFL (minimum score 525 paper-based; 70 iBT). *Application deadline:* For fall admission, 5/23 priority date for domestic students, 5/23 for international students; for spring admission, 4/20 priority date for domestic students, 4/23 for international students. Applications are processed on a rolling basis. Application fee: $35. Electronic applications accepted. *Expenses:* Tuition, state resident: full-time $4533.30; part-time $251.85 per credit hour. Tuition, nonresident: full-time $4533; part-time $251.85 per credit hour. *Required fees:* $1239.48; $68.86 per credit hour. *Financial support:* In 2011–12, 27 students received support. Tuition waivers (full and partial) available. Financial award application deadline: 5/15; financial award applicants required to submit FAFSA. *Faculty research:* Academically at-risk students in higher education, communication pedagogy and technology, gender communication, computer-mediated communication, creativity in music. *Total annual research expenditures:* $26,000. *Unit head:* Dr. Gary Thompson, Dean, 701-845-7197, E-mail: gary.thompson@vcsu.edu. *Application contact:* Misty Lindgren, 701-845-7303, Fax: 701-845-7305, E-mail: misty.lindgren@vcsu.edu. Web site: http://www.vcsu.edu/graduate.

Virginia Polytechnic Institute and State University, Graduate School, College of Liberal Arts and Human Sciences, School of Education, Department of Teaching and Learning, Blacksburg, VA 24061. Offers career and technical education (MS Ed, Ed D, PhD, Ed S); cognition and education (Certificate); counselor education (MA, PhD); curriculum and instruction (MA Ed, Ed D, PhD, Ed S); educational research, evaluation (PhD); higher education administration (Certificate); integrative STEM education (Certificate). *Accreditation:* NCATE. Postbaccalaureate distance learning degree programs offered (no on-campus study). Terminal master's awarded for partial completion of doctoral program. *Degree requirements:* For master's, comprehensive exam (for some programs), thesis (for some programs); for doctorate, comprehensive exam (for some programs), thesis/dissertation (for some programs). *Entrance requirements:* For master's and doctorate, GRE. Additional exam requirements/recommendations for international students: Required—TOEFL (minimum score 550 paper-based; 213 computer-based). *Application deadline:* For fall admission, 7/1 for domestic and international students; for spring admission, 12/1 for domestic and international students. Applications are processed on a rolling basis. Application fee: $65. Electronic applications accepted. *Expenses:* Tuition, state resident: full-time $10,048; part-time $558.25 per credit hour. Tuition, nonresident: full-time $19,497; part-time $1083.25 per credit hour. *Required fees:* $405 per semester. Tuition and fees vary according to course load, campus/location and program. *Financial support:* Career-related internships or fieldwork, Federal Work-Study, scholarships/grants, health care benefits, and unspecified assistantships available. Financial award application deadline: 1/15. *Faculty research:* Instructional technology, teacher evaluation, school change, literacy, teaching strategies. *Unit head:* Dr. Daisy L. Stewart, Unit Head, 540-231-8180, Fax: 540-231-3717, E-mail: daisys@vt.edu. *Application contact:* Daisy Stewart, Contact, 540-231-8180, Fax: 540-231-3717, E-mail: daisys@vt.edu. Web site: http://www.soe.vt.edu/.

Virginia Polytechnic Institute and State University, VT Online, Blacksburg, VA 24061. Offers advanced transportation systems (Certificate); aerospace engineering (MS); agricultural and life sciences (MSLFS); business information systems (Graduate Certificate); career and technical education (MS); civil engineering (MS); computer engineering (M Eng, MS); decision support systems (Graduate Certificate); eLearning leadership (MA); electrical engineering (M Eng, MS); engineering administration (MEA); environmental engineering (Certificate); environmental politics and policy (Graduate Certificate); environmental sciences and engineering (MS); foundations of political analysis (Graduate Certificate); health product risk management (Graduate Certificate);

industrial and systems engineering (MS); information policy and society (Graduate Certificate); information security (Graduate Certificate); information technology (MIT); instructional technology (MA); integrative STEM education (MA Ed); liberal arts (Graduate Certificate); life sciences: health product risk management (MS); natural resources (MNR, Graduate Certificate); networking (Graduate Certificate); nonprofit and nongovernmental organization management (Graduate Certificate); ocean engineering (MS); political science (MA); security studies (Graduate Certificate); software development (Graduate Certificate). *Expenses:* Tuition, state resident: full-time $10,048; part-time $558.25 per credit hour. Tuition, nonresident: full-time $19,497; part-time $1083.25 per credit hour. *Required fees:* $405 per semester. Tuition and fees vary according to course load, campus/location and program. *Application contact:* Graduate School Applications General Assistance, 540-231-8636, Fax: 540-231-2039, E-mail: gradappl@vt.edu. Web site: http://www.vto.vt.edu/.

Virginia State University, School of Graduate Studies, Research, and Outreach, School of Liberal Arts and Education, Department of Graduate Professional Education Programs, Program in Career and Technical Studies, Petersburg, VA 23806-0001. Offers M Ed, MS, CAGS. *Degree requirements:* For master's, thesis (for some programs).

Wayne State College, School of Education and Counseling, Department of Educational Foundations and Leadership, Program in Curriculum and Instruction, Wayne, NE 68787. Offers alternative education (MSE); business and information technology education (MSE); communication arts education (MSE); early childhood education (MSE); elementary education (MSE); English as a second language (MSE); English education (MSE); family and consumer sciences education (MSE); industrial technology and vocational education (MSE); learning communities (MSE); mathematics education (MSE); music education (MSE); science education (MSE); social science education (MSE). *Accreditation:* NCATE. Part-time and evening/weekend programs available. *Degree requirements:* For master's, comprehensive exam, thesis optional. *Entrance requirements:* For master's, GRE General Test. Additional exam requirements/recommendations for international students: Required—TOEFL (minimum score 550 paper-based; 213 computer-based).

Wayne State University, College of Education, Division of Teacher Education, Detroit, MI 48202. Offers art education (M Ed), including art therapy; bilingual/bicultural education (M Ed); career and technical education (M Ed); curriculum and instruction (Ed D, PhD, Ed S), including art education (PhD), bilingual education (Ed D, Ed S), bilingual-bicultural education (PhD), career and technical education (MAT, Ed D, PhD, Ed S), early childhood education (MAT, Ed D, PhD, Ed S), elementary education, English as a second language (MAT, Ed D, Ed S), English education (MAT, Ed D, PhD, Ed S), foreign language education (MAT, PhD), K-12 curriculum, mathematics education (MAT, Ed D, PhD, Ed S), science education (MAT, Ed D, PhD, Ed S), secondary education, social studies education (MAT, Ed S), social studies education: secondary (Ed D, PhD); elementary education (MAT), including special education; elementary education (M Ed, MAT), including children's literature (MAT), early childhood education (MAT, Ed D, PhD, Ed S), general elementary education (MAT); elementary or secondary education (MAT), including bilingual/bicultural education, English as a second language (MAT, Ed D, Ed S), mathematics education (MAT, Ed D, PhD, Ed S), science education (MAT, Ed D, PhD, Ed S), social studies education (MAT, Ed S); English education-secondary (M Ed); foreign language education (M Ed); mathematics education (M Ed); reading (M Ed, Ed S); reading, languages and literature (Ed D); science education (M Ed); secondary education (MAT), including art education (K-12), career and technical education (MAT, Ed D, PhD, Ed S), English education (MAT, Ed D, PhD, Ed S), foreign language education (MAT, PhD), kinesiology; social studies education secondary (M Ed); special education (M Ed, Ed D, PhD, Ed S). *Students:* 216 full-time (154 women), 626 part-time (478 women); includes 289 minority (227 Black or African American, non-Hispanic/Latino; 4 American Indian or Alaska Native, non-Hispanic/Latino; 27 Asian, non-Hispanic/Latino; 21 Hispanic/Latino; 1 Native Hawaiian or other Pacific Islander, non-Hispanic/Latino; 9 Two or more races, non-Hispanic/Latino), 14 international. Average age 37. 347 applicants, 37% accepted, 93 enrolled. In 2011, 226 master's, 12 doctorates, 46 other advanced degrees awarded. *Degree requirements:* For master's, thesis (for some programs), thesis, essay or project (for some M Ed programs), professional field experience (for MAT programs); for doctorate, thesis/dissertation. *Entrance requirements:* For master's, Michigan Basic Skills Test (MA in teaching); for doctorate, minimum undergraduate GPA of 3.0, graduate 3.5; interview, curriculum vitae; references. Additional exam requirements/recommendations for international students: Required—TOEFL (minimum score 550 paper-based; 213 computer-based), TWE (minimum score 5.5). *Application deadline:* For fall admission, 6/1 priority date for domestic students, 5/1 for international students; for winter admission, 10/1 priority date for domestic students, 9/1 for international students; for spring admission, 2/1 priority date for domestic students, 1/1 for international students. Applications are processed on a rolling basis. Application fee: $50. Electronic applications accepted. *Expenses:* Tuition, state resident: part-time $512.85 per credit. Tuition, nonresident: part-time $1132.65 per credit. *Required fees:* $26.60 per credit. $199.65 per semester. Tuition and fees vary according to course load and program. *Financial support:* In 2011–12, 42 students received support. Fellowships, research assistantships with tuition reimbursements available, teaching assistantships, scholarships/grants, and unspecified assistantships available. *Faculty research:* Reading and writing literacy and literature. *Total annual research expenditures:* $264,016. *Unit head:* Dr. Craig Roney, Assistant Dean, 313-577-0902, E-mail: rroney@wayne.edu. Web site: http://coe.wayne.edu/ted/index.php.

Western Michigan University, Graduate College, College of Education and Human Development, Department of Family and Consumer Sciences, Program in Career and Technical Education, Kalamazoo, MI 49008. Offers MA. *Accreditation:* NCATE.

Westfield State University, Division of Graduate and Continuing Education, Department of Education, Program in Occupational Education, Westfield, MA 01086. Offers M Ed, CAGS. *Accreditation:* NCATE. Part-time and evening/weekend programs available. *Degree requirements:* For master's, comprehensive exam. *Entrance requirements:* For master's, GRE General Test or MAT, minimum undergraduate GPA of 2.7.

Wilmington University, College of Education, New Castle, DE 19720-6491. Offers applied technology in education (M Ed); career and technical education (M Ed); educational leadership (Ed D); elementary and secondary school counseling (M Ed); elementary studies (M Ed); ESOL literacy (M Ed); higher education leadership (Ed D); instruction: gifted and talented (M Ed); instruction: teacher of reading (M Ed); instruction: teaching and learning (M Ed); organizational leadership (Ed D); school leadership (M Ed); secondary education (MAT); special education (M Ed). *Accreditation:* NCATE. Part-time and evening/weekend programs available. *Faculty:* 7 full-time (4 women). *Students:* 638 full-time (425 women), 2,014 part-time (1,635 women). Average age 33. *Entrance requirements:* For master's, 2 letters of recommendation, interview. Additional exam requirements/recommendations for international students: Required—TOEFL (minimum score 500 paper-based; 173 computer-based). *Application deadline:* For fall admission, 4/30 for domestic students. Applications are processed on a rolling basis. Application fee: $35. Electronic applications accepted. *Expenses: Tuition:* Part-time $534 per credit hour. *Required fees:* $25 per term. *Financial support:* Applicants required to submit FAFSA. *Unit head:* Dr. John C. Gray, Dean, 302-295-1139. *Application contact:* Chris Ferguson, Director of Admissions, 302-356-4636 Ext. 256, Fax: 302-328-5164, E-mail: inquire@wilmcoll.edu. Web site: http://www.wilmu.edu/education/.

Wright State University, School of Graduate Studies, College of Education and Human Services, Department of Educational Leadership, Programs in Educational Leadership, Dayton, OH 45435. Offers curriculum and instruction: teacher leader (MA); educational administrative specialist: teacher leader (M Ed); educational administrative specialist: vocational education administration (M Ed, MA); student affairs in higher education-administration (M Ed, MA). *Accreditation:* NCATE. *Degree requirements:* For master's, thesis (for some programs). *Entrance requirements:* For master's, GRE General Test, MAT. Additional exam requirements/recommendations for international students: Required—TOEFL.

Wright State University, School of Graduate Studies, College of Education and Human Services, Department of Teacher Education, Programs in Workforce Education, Dayton, OH 45435. Offers career, technology and vocational education (M Ed, MA); computer/technology education (M Ed, MA); library/media (M Ed, MA); vocational education (M Ed, MA). *Accreditation:* NCATE. *Degree requirements:* For master's, thesis (for some programs). *Entrance requirements:* For master's, GRE General Test, MAT. Additional exam requirements/recommendations for international students: Required—TOEFL.

ACADEMIC AND PROFESSIONAL PROGRAMS IN LAW

Section 27
Law

This section contains a directory of institutions offering graduate work in law, followed by an in-depth entry submitted by an institution that chose to prepare a detailed program description. Additional information about programs listed in the directory but not augmented by an in-depth entry may be obtained by writing directly to the dean of a graduate school or chair of a department at the address given in the directory.

For programs offering related work, see also in this book *Business Administration and Management* and *Social Work.* In the other guides in this series:

Graduate Programs in the Humanities, Arts & Social Sciences

See *Criminology and Forensics; Public, Regional, and Industrial Affairs; Economics;* and *Political Science and International Affairs*

Graduate Programs in the Physical Sciences, Mathematics, Agricultural Sciences, the Environment & Natural Resources

See *Environmental Sciences and Management*

Graduate Programs in Engineering & Applied Sciences

See *Management of Engineering and Technology*

CONTENTS

Program Directories

Display and Close-Up

Environmental Law

Chapman University, School of Law, Orange, CA 92866. Offers advocacy and dispute resolution (JD); entertainment and media law (LL M); entertainment law (JD); environmental, land use, and real estate (JD); international law (JD); law (JD); prosecutorial science (LL M); tax law (JD); taxation (LL M); trial advocacy (LL M); JD/MBA; JD/MFA. *Accreditation:* ABA. Part-time and evening/weekend programs available. *Faculty:* 49 full-time (20 women), 26 part-time/adjunct (6 women). *Students:* 526 full-time (265 women), 58 part-time (25 women); includes 139 minority (4 Black or African American, non-Hispanic/Latino; 2 American Indian or Alaska Native, non-Hispanic/Latino; 68 Asian, non-Hispanic/Latino; 45 Hispanic/Latino; 2 Native Hawaiian or other Pacific Islander, non-Hispanic/Latino; 18 Two or more races, non-Hispanic/Latino), 11 international. Average age 26. 2,823 applicants, 34% accepted, 160 enrolled. In 2011, 43 master's, 177 doctorates awarded. *Entrance requirements:* For doctorate, LSAT, minimum undergraduate GPA of 2.75. Additional exam requirements/recommendations for international students: Required—TOEFL (minimum score 600 paper-based; 213 computer-based; 80 iBT). *Application deadline:* For fall admission, 4/15 priority date for domestic students. Applications are processed on a rolling basis. Application fee: $65. Electronic applications accepted. *Expenses:* Contact institution. *Financial support:* Fellowships, Federal Work-Study, and scholarships/grants available. Financial award applicants required to submit FAFSA. *Unit head:* Dr. Tom Campbell, Dean, 714-628-2500. *Application contact:* Marissa Vargas, Assistant Director of Admission and Financial Aid, 877-CHAPLAW, E-mail: mvargas@chapman.edu. Web site: http://www.chapman.edu/law/.

Florida State University, College of Law, Tallahassee, FL 32306-1601. Offers American law for foreign lawyers (LL M); environmental law and policy (LL M); law (JD); JD/MBA; JD/MPA; JD/MS; JD/MSP; JD/MSW. *Accreditation:* ABA. *Faculty:* 55 full-time (27 women), 31 part-time/adjunct (8 women). *Students:* 736 full-time (290 women), 3 part-time (0 women); includes 72 minority (34 Black or African American, non-Hispanic/Latino; 1 American Indian or Alaska Native, non-Hispanic/Latino; 11 Asian, non-Hispanic/Latino; 26 Hispanic/Latino), 2 international. Average age 24. 2,824 applicants, 29% accepted, 252 enrolled. In 2011, 1 master's, 271 doctorates awarded. *Entrance requirements:* For doctorate, LSAT. Additional exam requirements/recommendations for international students: Required—TOEFL (minimum score 600 paper-based; 250 computer-based; 100 iBT). *Application deadline:* For fall admission, 3/15 priority date for domestic students, 3/15 for international students. Applications are processed on a rolling basis. Application fee: $30. Electronic applications accepted. *Expenses:* Contact institution. *Financial support:* In 2011–12, 290 students received support, including 1 fellowship with full tuition reimbursement available (averaging $20,250 per year), 55 research assistantships (averaging $1,183 per year), 11 teaching assistantships (averaging $1,835 per year); scholarships/grants and unspecified assistantships also available. Financial award application deadline: 6/30; financial award applicants required to submit FAFSA. *Faculty research:* Law and business, environmental and land use, international, criminal. *Total annual research expenditures:* $156,374. *Unit head:* Donald J. Weidner, Dean, 850-644-3400, Fax: 850-644-5487, E-mail: dweidner@law.fsu.edu. *Application contact:* Jennifer L. Kessinger, Director of Admissions and Records, 850-644-3787, Fax: 850-644-7284, E-mail: jkessing@law.fsu.edu. Web site: http://www.law.fsu.edu/.

Golden Gate University, School of Law, San Francisco, CA 94105-2968. Offers environmental law (LL M); intellectual property law (LL M); international legal studies (LL M, SJD); law (JD); taxation (LL M); U. S. legal studies (LL M); JD/MBA; JD/PhD. *Accreditation:* ABA. Part-time and evening/weekend programs available. *Degree requirements:* For doctorate, thesis/dissertation (for some programs). *Entrance requirements:* For doctorate, LSAT (for JD). Additional exam requirements/recommendations for international students: Required—TOEFL (minimum score 600 paper-based; 250 computer-based). Electronic applications accepted. *Expenses:* Contact institution. *Faculty research:* International law, intellectual property law, environmental law, real estate, civil rights.

Lehigh University, College of Arts and Sciences, Program in Environmental Initiative, Bethlehem, PA 18015. Offers environmental law and policy (Graduate Certificate); environmental policy design (MA). Part-time programs available. *Students:* 4 full-time (all women), 2 part-time (both women). Average age 26. 2 applicants, 100% accepted, 1 enrolled. In 2011, 10 degrees awarded. *Degree requirements:* For master's, thesis optional, thesis or additional course work. *Entrance requirements:* For master's, minimum GPA of 2.75, 3.0 for last two undergraduate semesters. Additional exam requirements/recommendations for international students: Required—TOEFL. *Application deadline:* For fall admission, 1/15 for domestic and international students; for spring admission, 12/1 for domestic and international students. Applications are processed on a rolling basis. Application fee: $75. Electronic applications accepted. *Financial support:* In 2011–12, 1 teaching assistantship with full tuition reimbursement (averaging $17,900 per year) was awarded; scholarships/grants and tuition waivers (partial) also available. Financial award application deadline: 1/15; financial award applicants required to submit FAFSA. *Faculty research:* Environmental law, politics, sustainability, policy (national and local). *Unit head:* Dr. John Gilroy, Director, 610-758-5964, Fax: 610-758-6377, E-mail: ei@lehigh.edu. *Application contact:* Terry Harnett, Academic Coordinator, 610-758-4745, Fax: 610-758-6232, E-mail: mth204@lehigh.edu. Web site: http://www.ei.lehigh.edu.

Lewis & Clark College, Lewis & Clark Law School, Portland, OR 97219. Offers environmental and natural resources law (LL M); law (JD). *Accreditation:* ABA. Part-time and evening/weekend programs available. *Entrance requirements:* For doctorate, LSAT. Additional exam requirements/recommendations for international students: Recommended—TOEFL (minimum score 600 paper-based; 250 computer-based). Electronic applications accepted. *Expenses:* Contact institution.

Pace University, Pace Law School, White Plains, NY 10603. Offers comparative legal studies (LL M); environmental law (LL M, SJD), including climate change (LL M), land use and sustainability (LL M); law (JD); JD/LL M; JD/MA; JD/MBA; JD/MEM; JD/MPA; JD/MS. JD/MA offered jointly with Sarah Lawrence College; JD/MEM offered jointly with Yale University School of Forestry and Environmental Studies. *Accreditation:* ABA. Part-time programs available. *Degree requirements:* For master's, writing sample; for doctorate, thesis/dissertation (for some programs), extensive thesis proposal (for SJD). *Entrance requirements:* For doctorate, LSAT (for JD). Additional exam requirements/recommendations for international students: Required—TOEFL (minimum score 600 paper-based; 250 computer-based); Recommended—TWE. Electronic applications accepted. *Expenses:* Contact institution. *Faculty research:* Reform of energy regulations, international law, land use law, prosecutorial misconduct, corporation law, international sale of goods.

Thomas M. Cooley Law School, JD and LL M Programs, Lansing, MI 48901-3038. Offers administrative law (public law) (JD); business transactions (JD); Canadian law (JD); Constitutional law and civil rights (public law) (JD); corporate law and finance (LL M); environmental law (public law) (JD); general practice (JD); insurance (LL M); intellectual property (LL M, JD); international law (JD); litigation (JD); self-directed (LL M, JD); taxation (LL M, JD); U.S. law for foreign attorneys (LL M); JD/MBA; JD/MPA; JD/MSW. *Accreditation:* ABA. Part-time and evening/weekend programs available. Postbaccalaureate distance learning degree programs offered (no on-campus study). *Faculty:* 131 full-time (55 women), 286 part-time/adjunct (93 women). *Students:* 781 full-time (368 women), 2,964 part-time (1,450 women); includes 1,055 minority (543 Black or African American, non-Hispanic/Latino; 19 American Indian or Alaska Native, non-Hispanic/Latino; 179 Asian, non-Hispanic/Latino; 205 Hispanic/Latino; 9 Native Hawaiian or other Pacific Islander, non-Hispanic/Latino; 100 Two or more races, non-Hispanic/Latino), 220 international. Average age 30. 4,032 applicants, 80% accepted, 1161 enrolled. In 2011, 40 master's, 999 doctorates awarded. *Degree requirements:* For master's, thesis optional; for doctorate, minimum of 3 credits of clinical experience. *Entrance requirements:* For master's, JD or LL B; for doctorate, LSAT. Additional exam requirements/recommendations for international students: Required—TOEFL. *Application deadline:* For fall admission, 9/1 for domestic and international students; for winter admission, 1/1 for domestic and international students; for spring admission, 5/1 for domestic and international students. Applications are processed on a rolling basis. Electronic applications accepted. *Expenses: Tuition:* Full-time $34,300; part-time $1225 per credit hour. *Required fees:* $40; $40 per year. Tuition and fees vary according to degree level and student level. *Financial support:* In 2011–12, 2,324 students received support. Career-related internships or fieldwork, Federal Work-Study, scholarships/grants, traineeships, and unspecified assistantships available. Support available to part-time students. Financial award applicants required to submit FAFSA. *Faculty research:* Wrongful convictions, civil rights, environmental law, litigation techniques, data mining, intellectual property, practical and skills-based legal education. *Unit head:* Don LeDuc, President and Dean, 517-371-5140 Ext. 2009, Fax: 517-334-5152. *Application contact:* Dr. Paul Zelenski, Associate Dean of Enrollment and Student Services, 517-371-5140 Ext. 2244, Fax: 517-334-5718, E-mail: admissions@cooley.edu. Web site: http://www.cooley.edu/.

University of Calgary, Faculty of Law, Programs in Natural Resources, Energy and Environmental Law, Calgary, AB T2N 1N4, Canada. Offers LL M, Postbaccalaureate Certificate. Part-time and evening/weekend programs available. *Degree requirements:* For master's, thesis optional. *Entrance requirements:* For master's, JD or LL B. Additional exam requirements/recommendations for international students: Required—TOEFL (minimum score 100 iBT), IELTS (minimum score 7). Electronic applications accepted. *Faculty research:* Natural resources law and regulations; environmental law, ethics and policies; oil and gas and energy law; water and municipal law; Aboriginal law.

University of Colorado Denver, School of Public Affairs, Program in Public Affairs and Administration, Denver, CO 80127. Offers public administration (MPA), including domestic violence, emergency management and homeland security, environmental policy, management and law, homeland security and defense, local government, nonprofit management, public administration; public affairs (PhD). *Accreditation:* NASPAA. Part-time and evening/weekend programs available. Postbaccalaureate distance learning degree programs offered (no on-campus study). *Faculty:* 19 full-time (9 women), 14 part-time/adjunct (5 women). *Students:* 264 full-time (158 women), 177 part-time (100 women); includes 54 minority (17 Black or African American, non-Hispanic/Latino; 2 American Indian or Alaska Native, non-Hispanic/Latino; 11 Asian, non-Hispanic/Latino; 22 Hispanic/Latino; 2 Two or more races, non-Hispanic/Latino), 31 international. Average age 34. 215 applicants, 67% accepted, 96 enrolled. In 2011, 155 master's, 4 doctorates awarded. *Degree requirements:* For master's, thesis or alternative, 36-39 credit hours; for doctorate, comprehensive exam, thesis/dissertation, minimum of 66 semester hours, including at least 30 hours of doctoral dissertation. *Entrance requirements:* For master's and doctorate, GRE, resume, essay, transcripts, recommendations. Additional exam requirements/recommendations for international students: Required—TOEFL (minimum score 550 paper-based; 223 computer-based). *Application deadline:* For fall admission, 2/1 for domestic students; for spring admission, 10/15 priority date for domestic students. Application fee: $50 ($75 for international students). Electronic applications accepted. *Expenses:* Contact institution. *Financial support:* Fellowships with partial tuition reimbursements, research assistantships with partial tuition reimbursements, teaching assistantships with partial tuition reimbursements, Federal Work-Study, and scholarships/grants available. Support available to part-time students. Financial award application deadline: 4/1; financial award applicants required to submit FAFSA. *Faculty research:* Housing, education and the social and economic issues of vulnerable populations; nonprofit governance and management; education finance, effectiveness and reform; P-20 education initiatives; municipal government accountability. *Unit head:* Dr. Kathleen Beatty, Director of Executive MPA Program, 303-315-2485, Fax: 303-315-2229, E-mail: kathleen.beatty@ucdenver.edu. *Application contact:* Annie Davies, Director of Marketing, Community Outreach and Alumni Affairs, 303-315-2896, Fax: 303-315-2229, E-mail: annie.davies@ucdenver.edu. Web site: http://www.ucdenver.edu/academics/colleges/SPA/Academics/programs/PublicAffairsAdmin/Pages/index.aspx.

University of Florida, Levin College of Law, Gainesville, FL 32611. Offers comparative law (LL M); environmental law (LL M); international taxation (LL M); law (JD); taxation (LL M, SJD). *Accreditation:* ABA. *Faculty:* 77 full-time (37 women), 36 part-time/adjunct (10 women). *Students:* 1,111 full-time (476 women); includes 257 minority (68 Black or African American, non-Hispanic/Latino; 14 American Indian or Alaska Native, non-Hispanic/Latino; 57 Asian, non-Hispanic/Latino; 118 Hispanic/Latino), 45 international. Average age 24. 3,024 applicants, 29% accepted, 295 enrolled. In 2011, 406 doctorates awarded. *Entrance requirements:* For doctorate, LSAT (for JD). Additional exam requirements/recommendations for international students: Required—TOEFL (minimum score 250 computer-based; 100 iBT). *Application deadline:* For fall admission, 3/15 for domestic and international students. Applications are processed on a rolling basis. Application fee: $30. Electronic applications accepted. *Financial support:* In 2011–12, 291 students received support, including 34 research assistantships (averaging $9,867 per year); Federal Work-Study, institutionally sponsored loans, scholarships/grants, health care benefits, and unspecified assistantships also available. Financial award application deadline: 4/15; financial award applicants required to submit FAFSA. *Faculty research:* Environmental and land use law, taxation, dispute resolution, family law, Constitutional law. *Unit head:* Robert Jerry, Dean, 352-273-0600, Fax: 352-392-8727, E-mail: jerryr@law.ufl.edu. *Application contact:* Michelle Adorno, Assistant Dean for Admissions, 352-273-0890, Fax: 352-392-4087, E-mail: madorno@law.ufl.edu. Web site: http://www.law.ufl.edu/.

University of Houston, Law Center, Houston, TX 77204-6060. Offers energy, environment, and natural resources (LL M); health law (LL M); intellectual property and information law (LL M); international law (LL M); law (LL M, JD); tax law (LL M). *Accreditation:* ABA. Part-time and evening/weekend programs available. *Entrance requirements:* For doctorate, LSAT. Additional exam requirements/recommendations for international students: Required—TOEFL (minimum score 600 paper-based; 100 iBT). Electronic applications accepted. *Expenses:* Contact institution. *Faculty research:* Health law, international, tax, environmental/energy, information law/intellectual property.

University of Idaho, College of Law, Moscow, ID 83844-2321. Offers law (JD); litigation and alternative dispute resolution (JD); Native American law (JD); natural resources and environmental law (JD). *Accreditation:* ABA. *Faculty:* 20 full-time, 1 part-time/adjunct. *Students:* 358 full-time, 4 part-time. Average age 29. *Entrance requirements:* For doctorate, LSAT, Law School Admission Council Credential Assembly Service (CAS) Report. *Application deadline:* For fall admission, 2/15 for domestic students. Applications are processed on a rolling basis. Application fee: $50 ($60 for international students). Electronic applications accepted. *Expenses:* Tuition, state resident: full-time $3874; part-time $334 per credit hour. Tuition, nonresident: full-time $16,394; part-time $861 per credit hour. *Required fees:* $2808; $99 per credit hour. Tuition and fees vary according to program. *Financial support:* Career-related internships or fieldwork, Federal Work-Study, and institutionally sponsored loans available. Financial award applicants required to submit FAFSA. *Faculty research:* Transboundary river governance, tribal protection and stewardship, regional water issues, environmental law. *Unit head:* Donald L. Burnett, Jr., Dean, 208-885-4977, E-mail: uilaw@uidaho.edu. *Application contact:* Dr. Nilsa A. Bosque-Perez, Interim Dean of the College of Graduate Studies, 208-885-6243, Fax: 208-885-6198, E-mail: uigrad@uidaho.edu. Web site: http://www.uidaho.edu/law/.

University of Pittsburgh, School of Law, Master of Studies in Law Program, Pittsburgh, PA 15260. Offers business law (MSL), including commercial law, corporate law, general business law, international business, tax law; constitutional law (MSL); criminal law and justice (MSL); disabilities law (MSL); dispute resolution (MSL); education law (MSL); elder and estate planning law (MSL); employment and labor law (MSL); environment and real estate law (MSL); family law (MSL); general law and jurisprudence (MSL); health law (MSL); intellectual property and technology (MSL); international and comparative law (MSL); personal injury and civil litigation (MSL); regulatory law (MSL); self-designed (MSL); sports and entertainment law (MSL). Part-time programs available. *Faculty:* 43 full-time (16 women), 104 part-time/adjunct (30 women). *Students:* 5 full-time (3 women), 16 part-time (12 women); includes 6 minority (all Black or African American, non-Hispanic/Latino). Average age 31. 19 applicants, 58% accepted, 11 enrolled. In 2011, 6 master's awarded. *Entrance requirements:* Additional exam requirements/recommendations for international students: Required—TOEFL (minimum score 600 paper-based; 250 computer-based; 100 iBT). *Application deadline:* For fall admission, 6/30 for domestic students, 5/1 for international students. Applications are processed on a rolling basis. Application fee: $0. *Expenses:* Tuition, state resident: full-time $18,774; part-time $760 per credit. Tuition, nonresident: full-time $30,736; part-time $1258 per credit. *Required fees:* $740; $200 per term. Tuition and fees vary according to program. *Faculty research:* Law, health law, business law, contracts, intellectual property. *Unit head:* Prof. Alan Meisel, Director, 412-648-1384, Fax: 412-648-2649, E-mail: meisel@pitt.edu. *Application contact:* Bethann Pischke, Administrative Coordinator, 412-648-7120, Fax: 412-648-2649, E-mail: pischke@pitt.edu. Web site: http://www.law.pitt.edu/academics/msl.

University of Pittsburgh, School of Law, Program in Environmental Law, Science and Policy, Pittsburgh, PA 15260. Offers Certificate. *Faculty:* 46 full-time (19 women), 108 part-time/adjunct (30 women). *Students:* 23 full-time (11 women). *Expenses:* Tuition, state resident: full-time $18,774; part-time $760 per credit. Tuition, nonresident: full-time $30,736; part-time $1258 per credit. *Required fees:* $740; $200 per term. Tuition and fees vary according to program. *Unit head:* Emily Collins, Director, 412-648-8549, Fax: 412-648-1992, E-mail: eac50@pitt.edu. *Application contact:* Charmaine McCall, Assistant Dean of Admissions and Financial Aid, 412-648-1413, Fax: 412-648-1318, E-mail: cmccall@pitt.edu.

University of Tulsa, College of Law, Tulsa, OK 74104. Offers American Indian and indigenous law (LL M); American law for foreign students (LL M), including energy law concentration; comparative and international law (Certificate); entrepreneurial law (Certificate); health law (Certificate); Indian law (online) (MJ); law (JD); Native American law (Certificate); public policy (Certificate); resources, energy, and environmental law (Certificate); JD/M Tax; JD/MA; JD/MBA; JD/MS. *Accreditation:* ABA. Part-time programs available. Postbaccalaureate distance learning degree programs offered (no on-campus study). *Faculty:* 27 full-time (12 women), 26 part-time/adjunct (8 women). *Students:* 326 full-time (122 women), 50 part-time (27 women); includes 86 minority (11 Black or African American, non-Hispanic/Latino; 40 American Indian or Alaska Native, non-Hispanic/Latino; 5 Asian, non-Hispanic/Latino; 10 Hispanic/Latino; 20 Two or more races, non-Hispanic/Latino), 2 international. Average age 27. 1,525 applicants, 38% accepted, 108 enrolled. In 2011, 4 master's, 126 doctorates awarded. *Degree requirements:* For master's, thesis optional. *Entrance requirements:* For master's, JD from an ABA-approved U.S. law school or a JD equivalent from non-U.S. university; for doctorate, LSAT, BS or BA from 4-year regionally-accredited college/university; for Certificate, BS or BA from 4-year regionally-accredited college/university. Additional exam requirements/recommendations for international students: Required—TOEFL (minimum score 570 paper-based; 230 computer-based; 90 iBT), IELTS (minimum score 7). *Application deadline:* For fall admission, 2/1 priority date for domestic students, 2/1 for international students; for spring admission, 12/5 priority date for domestic students, 12/5 for international students. Applications are processed on a rolling basis. Application fee: $30. Electronic applications accepted. *Expenses:* Contact institution. *Financial support:* In 2011–12, 190 students received support. Career-related internships or fieldwork, Federal Work-Study, and scholarships/grants available. Support available to part-time students. Financial award application deadline: 8/1; financial award applicants required to submit FAFSA. *Faculty research:* International law, Native American law, criminal law, commercial speech, copyright law. *Unit head:* Janet Levit, Dean, 918-631-2400, Fax: 918-631-3126, E-mail: janet-levit@utulsa.edu. *Application contact:* April M. Fox, Assistant Dean of Admissions and Financial Aid, 918-631-2406, Fax: 918-631-3630, E-mail: april-fox@utulsa.edu. Web site: http://www.utulsa.edu/law/.

Vermont Law School, Law School, Environmental Law Center, South Royalton, VT 05068-0096. Offers LL M, MELP, JD/MELP. Part-time programs available. *Faculty:* 15 full-time (6 women), 10 part-time/adjunct (9 women). *Students:* 55 full-time (33 women); includes 12 minority (4 Black or African American, non-Hispanic/Latino; 1 American Indian or Alaska Native, non-Hispanic/Latino; 3 Asian, non-Hispanic/Latino; 1 Hispanic/Latino; 3 Two or more races, non-Hispanic/Latino). Average age 30. 148 applicants, 83% accepted, 41 enrolled. In 2011, 53 master's awarded. *Entrance requirements:* Additional exam requirements/recommendations for international students: Required—TOEFL. *Application deadline:* For fall admission, 3/1 priority date for domestic students. Applications are processed on a rolling basis. Application fee: $60. *Financial support:* In 2011–12, 2 fellowships with full tuition reimbursements (averaging $5,000 per year) were awarded; career-related internships or fieldwork, Federal Work-Study, institutionally sponsored loans, scholarships/grants, and tuition waivers (partial) also available. Support available to part-time students. Financial award application deadline: 3/1; financial award applicants required to submit FAFSA. *Faculty research:* Environment and technology; takings; international environmental law; interaction among science, law, and environmental policy; air pollution. *Total annual research expenditures:* $52,000. *Unit head:* Marc Mihaly, Associate Dean, 802-831-1342, Fax: 802-763-2490, E-mail: admiss@vermontlaw.edu. *Application contact:* Anne Mansfield, Associate Director, 802-831-1338, Fax: 802-763-2940, E-mail: admiss@vermontlaw.edu. Web site: http://www.vermontlaw.edu/.

Health Law

Boston University, School of Public Health, Health Law, Bioethics and Human Rights Department, Boston, MA 02118. Offers MPH. Part-time and evening/weekend programs available. *Faculty:* 5 full-time, 16 part-time/adjunct. *Students:* 10 full-time (8 women), 8 part-time (all women); includes 5 minority (1 Black or African American, non-Hispanic/Latino; 1 Asian, non-Hispanic/Latino; 1 Hispanic/Latino; 1 Native Hawaiian or other Pacific Islander, non-Hispanic/Latino; 1 Two or more races, non-Hispanic/Latino). Average age 28. 86 applicants, 56% accepted, 9 enrolled. *Entrance requirements:* For master's, GRE, MCAT, LSAT, GMAT, DAT. Additional exam requirements/recommendations for international students: Required—TOEFL (minimum score 600 paper-based; 250 computer-based; 100 iBT) or IELTS (minimum score 6). *Application deadline:* For fall admission, 2/1 priority date for domestic students, 2/1 for international students; for spring admission, 10/15 priority date for domestic students, 10/15 for international students. Applications are processed on a rolling basis. Application fee: $115. Electronic applications accepted. *Expenses: Tuition:* Full-time $40,848; part-time $1276 per credit hour. *Required fees:* $572; $286 per semester. *Financial support:* In 2011–12, 1 fellowship was awarded; career-related internships or fieldwork, Federal Work-Study, institutionally sponsored loans, scholarships/grants, and tuition waivers (partial) also available. Support available to part-time students. Financial award application deadline: 3/1; financial award applicants required to submit FAFSA. *Unit head:* Prof. George Annas, Chair, 617-638-4626, E-mail: hld@bu.edu. *Application contact:* LePhan Quan, Associate Director of Admissions, 617-638-4640, Fax: 617-638-5299, E-mail: asksph@bu.edu. Web site: http://sph.bu.edu.

DePaul University, College of Law, Chicago, IL 60604-2287. Offers health law (LL M); intellectual property law (LL M); international law (LL M); law (JD); tax law (LL M); JD/MAIS; JD/MBA; JD/MPS; JD/MS. *Accreditation:* ABA. Part-time and evening/weekend programs available. *Faculty:* 54 full-time (21 women), 65 part-time/adjunct (21 women). *Students:* 853 full-time (404 women), 220 part-time (109 women); includes 234 minority (65 Black or African American, non-Hispanic/Latino; 6 American Indian or Alaska Native, non-Hispanic/Latino; 73 Asian, non-Hispanic/Latino; 90 Hispanic/Latino), 13 international. Average age 24. 4,743 applicants, 42% accepted, 298 enrolled. In 2011, 7 master's, 319 doctorates awarded. *Entrance requirements:* For doctorate, LSAT. Additional exam requirements/recommendations for international students: Recommended—TOEFL (minimum score 577 paper-based; 233 computer-based; 90 iBT), IELTS (minimum score 6.5). *Application deadline:* For fall admission, 3/1 for domestic and international students. Applications are processed on a rolling basis. Application fee: $60. Electronic applications accepted. *Expenses:* Contact institution. *Financial support:* In 2011–12, 640 students received support, including 23 fellowships with partial tuition reimbursements available (averaging $5,000 per year), 75 research assistantships (averaging $1,964 per year); career-related internships or fieldwork, scholarships/grants, and tuition waivers (partial) also available. Support available to part-time students. Financial award application deadline: 3/1; financial award applicants required to submit FAFSA. *Faculty research:* Aviation law, intellectual property law, international law, Constitutional law, human rights law, church-state studies. *Total annual research expenditures:* $142,134. *Unit head:* Gregory Mark, Dean, 312-362-5595, E-mail: gmark@depaul.edu. *Application contact:* Michael S. Burns, Director of Law Admission and Associate Dean, 312-362-6831, Fax: 312-362-5280, E-mail: lawinfo@depaul.edu. Web site: http://www.law.depaul.edu/.

DePaul University, School of Public Service, Chicago, IL 60604. Offers administrative foundations (Certificate); community development (Certificate); financial administration management (Certificate); health administration (Certificate); health law and policy (MS); international public services (MS); leadership and policy studies (MS); metropolitan planning (Certificate); nonprofit leadership (Certificate); nonprofit management (MNM); public administration (MPA); public service management (MS), including association management, fundraising and philanthropy, healthcare administration, higher education administration, metropolitan planning; public services (Certificate); JD/MS. Part-time and evening/weekend programs available. Postbaccalaureate distance learning degree programs offered (minimal on-campus study). *Faculty:* 14 full-time (3 women), 43 part-time/adjunct (24 women). *Students:* 366 full-time (266 women), 316 part-time (216 women); includes 283 minority (143 Black or African American, non-Hispanic/Latino; 1 American Indian or Alaska Native, non-Hispanic/Latino; 35 Asian, non-Hispanic/Latino; 88 Hispanic/Latino; 16 Two or more races, non-Hispanic/Latino), 13 international. Average age 29. 162 applicants, 100% accepted, 94 enrolled. In 2011, 108 master's awarded. *Degree requirements:* For master's, thesis or integrative seminar. *Entrance requirements:* For master's, minimum GPA of 2.7. Additional exam requirements/recommendations for international students: Required—TOEFL (minimum score 550 paper-based; 213 computer-based; 80 iBT), IELTS (minimum score 6.5). *Application deadline:* Applications are processed on a rolling basis. Application fee: $40. Electronic applications accepted. *Financial support:* In 2011–12, 60 students received support, including 3 research assistantships with full tuition reimbursements available (averaging $7,000 per year); career-related internships or fieldwork, Federal Work-Study, institutionally sponsored loans, scholarships/grants, tuition waivers (partial), and unspecified assistantships also available. Support available to part-time students. Financial award application deadline: 7/1; financial award applicants required to submit FAFSA. *Faculty research:* Government financing, transportation, leadership, health care, volunteerism and organizational behavior, non-profit organizations. *Total annual research expenditures:* $20,000. *Unit head:* Dr. J. Patrick Murphy, Director, 312-362-5608, Fax: 312-362-5506, E-mail: jpmurphy@depaul.edu. *Application contact:* Megan B.

Balderston, Director of Admissions and Marketing, 312-362-5565, Fax: 312-362-5506, E-mail: pubserv@depaul.edu. Web site: http://las.depaul.edu/sps/.

Georgetown University, Law Center, Washington, DC 20001. Offers global health law (LL M); individualized study (LL M); international business and economic law (LL M); law (JD, SJD); national security law (LL M); securities and financial regulation (LL M); taxation (LL M); JD/LL M; JD/MA; JD/MBA; JD/MPH; JD/PhD. *Accreditation:* ABA. Part-time and evening/weekend programs available. *Degree requirements:* For master's, thesis; for doctorate, thesis/dissertation (for some programs). *Entrance requirements:* For master's, JD, LL B, or first law degree earned in country of origin; for doctorate, LSAT (for JD). Additional exam requirements/recommendations for international students: Required—TOEFL. *Expenses:* Contact institution. *Faculty research:* Constitutional law, legal history, jurisprudence.

Loyola University Chicago, School of Law, Chicago, IL 60611. Offers advocacy (LL M); business and corporate governance law (MJ); business law (LL M, MJ); child and family law (LL M); children's law and policy (MJ); health law (LL M, MJ); health law and policy (D Law, SJD); international law (LL M); law (JD); rule of law development (LL M); tax law (LL M); U. S. law for foreign lawyers (LL M); JD/MA; JD/MBA; JD/MSW; MJ/MSW. *Accreditation:* ABA. Part-time and evening/weekend programs available. Postbaccalaureate distance learning degree programs offered (minimal on-campus study). *Faculty:* 48 full-time (17 women), 129 part-time/adjunct (60 women). *Students:* 857 full-time (434 women), 9 part-time (3 women); includes 201 minority (77 Black or African American, non-Hispanic/Latino; 1 American Indian or Alaska Native, non-Hispanic/Latino; 40 Asian, non-Hispanic/Latino; 63 Hispanic/Latino; 20 Two or more races, non-Hispanic/Latino), 11 international. Average age 25. 5,040 applicants, 34% accepted, 271 enrolled. *Entrance requirements:* Additional exam requirements/recommendations for international students: Required—TOEFL (minimum score 550 paper-based; 79 iBT), IELTS (minimum score 6.5). *Application deadline:* For fall admission, 3/1 for domestic students. Applications are processed on a rolling basis. Application fee: $0. Electronic applications accepted. *Expenses: Tuition:* Full-time $15,660; part-time $870 per credit hour. *Required fees:* $125 per semester. Tuition and fees vary according to course load and program. *Unit head:* Pamela Bloomquist, Assistant Dean for Admission and Financial Assistance, Law School, 312-915-7170, Fax: 312-915-7906, E-mail: ploom@luc.edu. *Application contact:* Ronald P. Martin, Associate Director, Graduate and Professional Enrollment Management Operations, 312-915-8951, E-mail: rmarti7@luc.edu. Web site: http://www.luc.edu/law/.

Nova Southeastern University, Shepard Broad Law Center, Fort Lauderdale, FL 33314. Offers education law (MS, Certificate); employment law (MS); health law (MS); law (JD); JD/MBA; JD/MS; JD/MURP. JD/MURP offered jointly with Florida Atlantic University. *Accreditation:* ABA. Part-time and evening/weekend programs available. Postbaccalaureate distance learning degree programs offered (minimal on-campus study). *Students:* 1,055 full-time (547 women), 166 part-time (130 women); includes 434 minority (115 Black or African American, non-Hispanic/Latino; 3 American Indian or Alaska Native, non-Hispanic/Latino; 48 Asian, non-Hispanic/Latino; 252 Hispanic/Latino; 4 Native Hawaiian or other Pacific Islander, non-Hispanic/Latino; 12 Two or more races, non-Hispanic/Latino), 28 international. Average age 29. In 2011, 46 master's, 305 doctorates awarded. *Degree requirements:* For doctorate, thesis/dissertation. *Application deadline:* For fall admission, 3/1 priority date for domestic students. Applications are processed on a rolling basis. Application fee: $50. Electronic applications accepted. *Expenses:* Contact institution. *Financial support:* In 2011–12, 58 fellowships were awarded; research assistantships, teaching assistantships, Federal Work-Study, scholarships/grants, tuition waivers (full and partial), and unspecified assistantships also available. Support available to part-time students. Financial award application deadline: 4/15; financial award applicants required to submit FAFSA. *Faculty research:* Legal issues in family law, civil rights, business associations, criminal law, law and popular culture. *Unit head:* Althornia Steele, Dean, 954-262-6100, Fax: 954-262-3834, E-mail: asteele@nova.edu. *Application contact:* Beth Hall, Assistant Dean of Admissions, 954-262-6121, Fax: 954-262-3844, E-mail: hallb@nsu.law.nova.edu. Web site: http://www.nsulaw.nova.edu/.

Quinnipiac University, School of Law, Hamden, CT 06518-1940. Offers health law (LL M); law (JD); JD/MBA. *Accreditation:* ABA. Part-time and evening/weekend programs available. *Faculty:* 38 full-time (16 women), 34 part-time/adjunct (8 women). *Students:* 356 full-time (173 women), 82 part-time (38 women); includes 59 minority (8 Black or African American, non-Hispanic/Latino; 2 American Indian or Alaska Native, non-Hispanic/Latino; 23 Asian, non-Hispanic/Latino; 20 Hispanic/Latino; 6 Two or more races, non-Hispanic/Latino), 1 international. Average age 24. 2,037 applicants, 47% accepted, 123 enrolled. In 2011, 134 doctorates awarded. *Entrance requirements:* For doctorate, LSAT. Additional exam requirements/recommendations for international students: Recommended—TOEFL. *Application deadline:* For fall admission, 3/1 priority date for domestic students. Applications are processed on a rolling basis. Application fee: $65. Electronic applications accepted. *Expenses:* Contact institution. *Financial support:* In 2011–12, 309 students received support, including 32 fellowships (averaging $1,560 per year), 55 research assistantships (averaging $1,800 per year); career-related internships or fieldwork, Federal Work-Study, and scholarships/grants also available. Support available to part-time students. Financial award application deadline: 4/15; financial award applicants required to submit FAFSA. *Faculty research:* Tax, health, public interest, corporate law, dispute resolution, intellectual property. *Unit head:* Brad Saxton, Dean, 203-582-3200, Fax: 203-582-3209, E-mail: ladm@quinnipiac.edu. *Application contact:* Edwin Wilkes, Associate Vice-President/Dean of Law School Admissions, 203-582-3400, Fax: 203-582-3339, E-mail: ladm@quinnipiac.edu. Web site: http://law.quinnipiac.edu/.

Seton Hall University, School of Law, Newark, NJ 07102-5210. Offers health law (LL M, JD); intellectual property (LL M, JD); law (MSJ); JD/MADIR; JD/MBA; MD/JD; MD/MSJ. MD/JD, MD/MSJ offered jointly with University of Medicine and Dentistry of New Jersey. *Accreditation:* ABA. Part-time and evening/weekend programs available. *Degree requirements:* For master's, thesis optional. *Entrance requirements:* For master's, professional experience, letters of recommendation; for doctorate, LSAT, active LSDAS registration, letters of recommendation. Additional exam requirements/recommendations for international students: Recommended—TOEFL. Electronic applications accepted. *Expenses:* Contact institution. *Faculty research:* Health law, intellectual property law, science and the law, international law and employment/labor law.

Southern Illinois University Carbondale, School of Law, Program in Legal Studies, Carbondale, IL 62901-4701. Offers general law (MLS); health law and policy (MLS). *Students:* 5 full-time (2 women), 4 part-time (all women); includes 3 minority (all Black or African American, non-Hispanic/Latino), 1 international. 9 applicants, 78% accepted, 3 enrolled. In 2011, 3 master's awarded. *Unit head:* Thomas Britton, Director, 618-453-8980, E-mail: llmadmit@siu.edu. *Application contact:* Barb Smith, Office Specialist, 618-453-8858, E-mail: mlsadmit@siu.edu.

Suffolk University, Law School, Boston, MA 02108. Offers business law and financial services (JD); civil litigation (JD); global law and technology (LL M); health and biomedical law (JD); intellectual property law (JD); international law (JD); JD/MBA; JD/MPA; JD/MSCJ; JD/MSF; JD/MSIE. *Accreditation:* ABA. Part-time and evening/weekend programs available. *Degree requirements:* For master's, legal writing. *Entrance requirements:* For master's, 2 letters of recommendation, resume, personal statement; for doctorate, LSAT, LSDAS, dean's certification, recommendation. Additional exam requirements/recommendations for international students: Required—TOEFL (minimum score 600 paper-based; 250 computer-based; 100 iBT). *Application deadline:* For fall admission, 3/1 for domestic and international students. Applications are processed on a rolling basis. Application fee: $60. Electronic applications accepted. *Expenses:* Contact institution. *Financial support:* Career-related internships or fieldwork, Federal Work-Study, institutionally sponsored loans, and scholarships/grants available. Support available to part-time students. Financial award application deadline: 3/1; financial award applicants required to submit FAFSA. *Faculty research:* Civil law, international law, health/biomedical law, business and finance, intellectual property. *Unit head:* Gail N. Ellis, Dean of Admissions, 617-573-8144, Fax: 617-523-1367, E-mail: gellis@suffolk.edu. *Application contact:* Ian A. Menchini, Director of Electronic Marketing and Enrollment Management, 617-573-8144, Fax: 617-523-1367, E-mail: imenchin@suffolk.edu. Web site: http://www.law.suffolk.edu/.

Union Graduate College, Center for Bioethics and Clinical Leadership, Schenectady, NY 12308-3107. Offers bioethics (MS); clinical ethics (AC); clinical leadership in health management (MS); health, policy and law (AC). Part-time and evening/weekend programs available. Postbaccalaureate distance learning degree programs offered (minimal on-campus study). *Faculty:* 2 full-time (0 women), 10 part-time/adjunct (7 women). *Students:* 7 full-time (4 women), 92 part-time (52 women); includes 38 minority (6 Black or African American, non-Hispanic/Latino; 26 Asian, non-Hispanic/Latino; 4 Hispanic/Latino; 2 Two or more races, non-Hispanic/Latino), 3 international. Average age 32. 32 applicants, 78% accepted, 21 enrolled. In 2011, 21 master's, 3 other advanced degrees awarded. *Entrance requirements:* For master's, letters of recommendation. Additional exam requirements/recommendations for international students: Required—TOEFL (minimum score 550 paper-based; 213 computer-based). *Application deadline:* Applications are processed on a rolling basis. Application fee: $60. Electronic applications accepted. *Expenses:* Contact institution. *Financial support:* In 2011–12, 10 students received support. Federal Work-Study, scholarships/grants, health care benefits, and tuition waivers (partial) available. Support available to part-time students. Financial award applicants required to submit FAFSA. *Faculty research:* Bioethics education, clinical ethics consultation, research ethics, history of biomedical ethics, international bioethics/research ethics. *Unit head:* Dr. Robert B. Baker, Director, 518-631-9860, Fax: 518-631-9903, E-mail: bakerr@union.edu. *Application contact:* Ann Nolte, Assistant Director, 518-631-9860, Fax: 518-631-9903, E-mail: noltea@uniongraduatecollege.edu.

Université de Sherbrooke, Faculty of Law, Sherbrooke, QC J1K 2R1, Canada. Offers alternative dispute resolution (LL M, Diploma); business law (Diploma); health law (LL M, Diploma); law (JD, LL D); legal management (Diploma); notarial law (DDN); transnational law (Diploma). Part-time and evening/weekend programs available. *Degree requirements:* For master's, thesis; for other advanced degree, one foreign language. *Entrance requirements:* For master's and other advanced degree, LL B. Electronic applications accepted.

University of California, San Diego, Office of Graduate Studies, Program in Health Law, La Jolla, CA 92093. Offers MAS. Program offered jointly with School of Medicine and California Western School of Law. Part-time programs available. *Degree requirements:* For master's, capstone project. *Entrance requirements:* For master's, undergraduate degree in healthcare, law, or related field; 3 years work experience; 3 letters of recommendation; resume.

University of Denver, University College, Denver, CO 80208. Offers arts and culture (MLS, Certificate), including art, literature, and culture, arts development and program management (Certificate), creative writing; environmental policy and management (MAS, Certificate), including energy and sustainability (Certificate), environmental assessment of nuclear power (Certificate), environmental health and safety (Certificate), environmental management, natural resource management (Certificate); geographic information systems (MAS, Certificate); global affairs (MLS, Certificate), including translation studies, world history and culture; healthcare leadership (MPH, Certificate), including healthcare policy, law, and ethics, medical and healthcare information technologies, strategic management of healthcare; information and communications technology (MCIS, Certificate), including database design and administration (Certificate), geographic information systems (MCIS), information security systems security (Certificate), information systems security (MCIS), project management (MCIS, MPS, Certificate), software design and administration (Certificate), software design and programming (MCIS), technology management, telecommunications technology (MCIS), Web design and development; leadership and organizations (MPS, Certificate), including human capital in organizations, philanthropic leadership, project management (MCIS, MPS, Certificate), strategic innovation and change; organizational and professional communication (MPS, Certificate), including alternative dispute resolution, organizational communication, organizational development and training, public relations and marketing; security management (MAS, Certificate), including emergency planning and response, information security (MAS), organizational security; strategic human resource management (MPS, Certificate), including global human resources (MPS), human resource management and development (MPS). Part-time and evening/weekend programs available. Postbaccalaureate distance learning degree programs offered (no on-campus study). *Faculty:* 204 part-time/adjunct (80 women). *Students:* 56 full-time (26 women), 1,096 part-time (647 women); includes 196 minority (81 Black or African American, non-Hispanic/Latino; 7 American Indian or Alaska Native, non-Hispanic/Latino; 30 Asian, non-Hispanic/Latino; 66 Hispanic/Latino; 3 Native Hawaiian or other Pacific Islander, non-Hispanic/Latino; 9 Two or more races, non-Hispanic/Latino), 76 international. Average age 36. 572 applicants, 95% accepted, 410 enrolled. In 2011, 404 master's, 123 other advanced degrees awarded. *Degree requirements:* For master's, capstone project. *Entrance requirements:* For master's, two letters of recommendation, personal statement, resume. Additional exam requirements/recommendations for international students: Required—TOEFL (minimum score 550 paper-based; 80 iBT). *Application deadline:* For fall admission, 7/20 priority date for domestic students, 6/8 for international students; for winter admission, 10/26 priority date for domestic students, 9/14 for international students; for spring admission, 2/1 priority date for domestic students, 12/14 for international students. Applications are processed on a rolling basis. Application fee: $75. Electronic applications accepted. *Expenses:* Contact institution. *Financial support:* Applicants required to submit FAFSA. *Unit head:* Dr. James Davis, Dean, 303-871-2291, Fax: 303-871-4047, E-mail: jdavis@du.edu. *Application contact:* Information Contact, 303-871-3155, Fax: 303-871-4047, E-mail: ucolinfo@du.edu. Web site: http://www.universitycollege.du.edu/.

University of Houston, Law Center, Houston, TX 77204-6060. Offers energy, environment, and natural resources (LL M); health law (LL M); intellectual property and information law (LL M); international law (LL M); law (LL M, JD); tax law (LL M). *Accreditation:* ABA. Part-time and evening/weekend programs available. *Entrance requirements:* For doctorate, LSAT. Additional exam requirements/recommendations for international students: Required—TOEFL (minimum score 600 paper-based; 100 iBT). Electronic applications accepted. *Expenses:* Contact institution. *Faculty research:* Health law, international, tax, environmental/energy, information law/intellectual property.

The University of Manchester, School of Law, Manchester, United Kingdom. Offers bioethics and medical jurisprudence (PhD); criminology (M Phil, PhD); law (M Phil, PhD).

University of Pittsburgh, School of Law, Master of Studies in Law Program, Pittsburgh, PA 15260. Offers business law (MSL), including commercial law, corporate law, general business law, international business, tax law; constitutional law (MSL); criminal law and justice (MSL); disabilities law (MSL); dispute resolution (MSL); education law (MSL); elder and estate planning law (MSL); employment and labor law (MSL); environment and real estate law (MSL); family law (MSL); general law and jurisprudence (MSL); health law (MSL); intellectual property and technology (MSL); international and comparative law (MSL); personal injury and civil litigation (MSL); regulatory law (MSL); self-designed (MSL); sports and entertainment law (MSL). Part-time programs available. *Faculty:* 43 full-time (16 women), 104 part-time/adjunct (30 women). *Students:* 5 full-time (3 women), 16 part-time (12 women); includes 6 minority (all Black or African American, non-Hispanic/Latino). Average age 31. 19 applicants, 58% accepted, 11 enrolled. In 2011, 6 master's awarded. *Entrance requirements:* Additional exam requirements/recommendations for international students: Required—TOEFL (minimum score 600 paper-based; 250 computer-based; 100 iBT). *Application deadline:* For fall admission, 6/30 for domestic students, 5/1 for international students. Applications are processed on a rolling basis. Application fee: $0. *Expenses:* Tuition, state resident: full-time $18,774; part-time $760 per credit. Tuition, nonresident: full-time $30,736; part-time $1258 per credit. *Required fees:* $740; $200 per term. Tuition and fees vary according to program. *Faculty research:* Law, health law, business law, contracts, intellectual property. *Unit head:* Prof. Alan Meisel, Director, 412-648-1384, Fax: 412-648-2649, E-mail: meisel@pitt.edu. *Application contact:* Bethann Pischke, Administrative Coordinator, 412-648-7120, Fax: 412-648-2649, E-mail: pischke@pitt.edu. Web site: http://www.law.pitt.edu/academics/msl.

University of Pittsburgh, School of Law, Program in Health Law, Pittsburgh, PA 15260. Offers Certificate. *Faculty:* 46 full-time (19 women), 108 part-time/adjunct (30 women). *Students:* 35 full-time (16 women). *Application deadline:* For spring admission, 7/31 for domestic students. Applications are processed on a rolling basis. *Expenses:* Tuition, state resident: full-time $18,774; part-time $760 per credit. Tuition, nonresident: full-time $30,736; part-time $1258 per credit. *Required fees:* $740; $200 per term. Tuition and fees vary according to program. *Unit head:* Prof. Alan Meisel, Professor/Director, 412-648-1384, Fax: 412-648-2649, E-mail: meisel@pitt.edu. *Application contact:* Bethann Pischke, Program Administrator, 412-648-7120, Fax: 412-648-2649, E-mail: pischke@pitt.edu.

University of Tulsa, College of Law, Tulsa, OK 74104. Offers American Indian and indigenous law (LL M); American law for foreign students (LL M), including energy law concentration; comparative and international law (Certificate); entrepreneurial law (Certificate); health law (Certificate); Indian law (online) (MJ); law (JD); Native American law (Certificate); public policy (Certificate); resources, energy, and environmental law (Certificate); JD/M Tax; JD/MA; JD/MBA; JD/MS. *Accreditation:* ABA. Part-time programs available. Postbaccalaureate distance learning degree programs offered (no on-campus study). *Faculty:* 27 full-time (12 women), 26 part-time/adjunct (8 women). *Students:* 326 full-time (122 women), 50 part-time (27 women); includes 86 minority (11 Black or African American, non-Hispanic/Latino; 40 American Indian or Alaska Native, non-Hispanic/Latino; 5 Asian, non-Hispanic/Latino; 10 Hispanic/Latino; 20 Two or more races, non-Hispanic/Latino), 2 international. Average age 27. 1,525 applicants, 38% accepted, 108 enrolled. In 2011, 4 master's, 126 doctorates awarded. *Degree requirements:* For master's, thesis optional. *Entrance requirements:* For master's, JD from an ABA-approved U.S. law school or a JD equivalent from non-U.S. university; for doctorate, LSAT, BS or BA from 4-year regionally-accredited college/university; for Certificate, BS or BA from 4-year regionally-accredited college/university. Additional exam requirements/recommendations for international students: Required—TOEFL (minimum score 570 paper-based; 230 computer-based; 90 iBT), IELTS (minimum score 7). *Application deadline:* For fall admission, 2/1 priority date for domestic students, 2/1 for international students; for spring admission, 12/5 priority date for domestic students, 12/5 for international students. Applications are processed on a rolling basis. Application fee: $30. Electronic applications accepted. *Expenses:* Contact institution. *Financial support:* In 2011–12, 190 students received support. Career-related internships or fieldwork, Federal Work-Study, and scholarships/grants available. Support available to part-time students. Financial award application deadline: 8/1; financial award applicants required to submit FAFSA. *Faculty research:* International law, Native American law, criminal law, commercial speech, copyright law. *Unit head:* Janet Levit, Dean, 918-631-2400, Fax: 918-631-3126, E-mail: janet-levit@utulsa.edu. *Application contact:* April M. Fox, Assistant Dean of Admissions and Financial Aid, 918-631-2406, Fax: 918-631-3630, E-mail: april-fox@utulsa.edu. Web site: http://www.utulsa.edu/law/.

Widener University, School of Law at Wilmington, Wilmington, DE 19803-0474. Offers corporate law and finance (LL M); health law (LL M, MJ, D Law); juridical science (SJD); law (JD). *Accreditation:* ABA. Part-time programs available. *Degree requirements:* For doctorate, thesis/dissertation (for some programs). *Entrance requirements:* For master's, GMAT.

Xavier University, College of Social Sciences, Health and Education, School of Nursing, Cincinnati, OH 45207. Offers clinical nurse leader (MSN); education (MSN); forensic nursing (MSN); healthcare law (MSN); informatics (MSN); nursing administration (MSN); school nursing (MSN); MSN/M Ed; MSN/MBA; MSN/MS. *Accreditation:* AACN. Part-time and evening/weekend programs available. *Faculty:* 13 full-time (all women), 10 part-time/adjunct (all women). *Students:* 69 full-time (66 women), 158 part-time (156 women); includes 30 minority (19 Black or African American, non-Hispanic/Latino; 2 American Indian or Alaska Native, non-Hispanic/Latino; 4 Asian, non-Hispanic/Latino; 3 Hispanic/Latino; 2 Two or more races, non-Hispanic/Latino). Average age 38. 117 applicants, 81% accepted, 71 enrolled. In 2011, 63 master's awarded. *Degree requirements:* For master's, thesis, scholarly project. *Entrance requirements:* For master's, GRE. Additional exam requirements/recommendations for international students: Required—TOEFL. *Application deadline:* Applications are processed on a rolling basis. Application fee: $35. Electronic applications accepted. *Expenses: Tuition:* Part-time $576 per credit hour. *Financial support:* In 2011–12, 88 students received support. Applicants required to submit FAFSA. *Faculty research:* Clinical nurse leader, simulation, employment satisfaction, nontraditional students, holistic nursing. *Unit head:* Dr. Susan M. Schmidt, Director, 513-745-3815, Fax: 513-745-1087, E-mail: schmidt@xavier.edu. *Application contact:* Marilyn Volk Gomez, Director of Nursing Student Services, 513-745-4392, Fax: 513-745-1087, E-mail: gomez@xavier.edu. Web site: http://www.xavier.edu/msn/.

Intellectual Property Law

Boston University, School of Law, Boston, MA 02215. Offers American law (LL M); banking (LL M); intellectual property law (LL M); law (JD); taxation (LL M); JD/LL M; JD/MA; JD/MBA; JD/MPH; JD/MS. *Accreditation:* ABA. *Faculty:* 55 full-time (26 women), 88 part-time/adjunct (25 women). *Students:* 971 full-time (496 women), 62 part-time (27 women); includes 224 minority (38 Black or African American, non-Hispanic/Latino; 2 American Indian or Alaska Native, non-Hispanic/Latino; 85 Asian, non-Hispanic/Latino; 72 Hispanic/Latino; 27 Two or more races, non-Hispanic/Latino), 156 international. Average age 26. 7,073 applicants, 20% accepted, 242 enrolled. In 2011, 169 master's, 271 doctorates awarded. *Degree requirements:* For master's, thesis (for some programs); for doctorate, thesis/dissertation, research project resulting in a paper. *Entrance requirements:* For master's, JD; for doctorate, LSAT. Additional exam requirements/recommendations for international students: Required—TOEFL (minimum score 600 paper-based; 250 computer-based; 100 iBT). *Application deadline:* For fall admission, 3/1 for domestic and international students. Applications are processed on a rolling basis. Application fee: $75. Electronic applications accepted. *Expenses: Tuition:* Full-time $40,848; part-time $1276 per credit hour. *Required fees:* $572; $286 per semester. *Financial support:* In 2011–12, 533 students received support. Career-related internships or fieldwork, Federal Work-Study, institutionally sponsored loans, and scholarships/grants available. Financial award application deadline: 3/1; financial award applicants required to submit FAFSA. *Faculty research:* Litigation and dispute resolution, intellectual property law, business organizations and finance law, international law, health law. *Unit head:* Maureen A. O'Rourke, Dean, 617-353-3112, Fax: 617-353-7400, E-mail: lawdean@bu.edu. *Application contact:* Alissa Leonard, Director of Admissions and Financial Aid, 617-353-3100, Fax: 617-353-0578, E-mail: bulawadm@bu.edu. Web site: http://www.bu.edu/law/.

Case Western Reserve University, School of Law, Cleveland, OH 44106. Offers intellectual property (LL M); international business law (LL M); international criminal law (LL M); law (JD); U. S. legal studies (LL M); JD/CNM; JD/MA; JD/MBA; JD/MD; JD/MPH; JD/MS; JD/MSSA. *Accreditation:* ABA. Part-time programs available. *Faculty:* 48 full-time (15 women), 54 part-time/adjunct (16 women). *Students:* 600 full-time (260 women), 5 part-time (2 women); includes 110 minority (30 Black or African American, non-Hispanic/Latino; 4 American Indian or Alaska Native, non-Hispanic/Latino; 57 Asian, non-Hispanic/Latino; 17 Hispanic/Latino; 2 Two or more races, non-Hispanic/Latino), 48 international. Average age 24. 1,651 applicants, 47% accepted, 192 enrolled. In 2011, 49 master's, 203 doctorates awarded. *Entrance requirements:* For doctorate, LSAT, LSDAS. Additional exam requirements/recommendations for international students: Required—TOEFL. *Application deadline:* For fall admission, 4/1 priority date for domestic students, 4/1 for international students. Applications are processed on a rolling basis. Application fee: $40. Electronic applications accepted. Application fee is waived when completed online. *Expenses:* Contact institution. *Financial support:* In 2011–12, 440 students received support. Career-related internships or fieldwork, Federal Work-Study, institutionally sponsored loans, and scholarships/grants available. Financial award application deadline: 5/1; financial award applicants required to submit FAFSA. *Unit head:* Lawrence E. Mitchell, Dean, 216-368-3283. *Application contact:* Kelli Curtis, Assistant Dean for Admissions, 216-368-3600, Fax: 216-368-0185, E-mail: lawadmissions@case.edu. Web site: http://law.case.edu/.

DePaul University, College of Law, Chicago, IL 60604-2287. Offers health law (LL M); intellectual property law (LL M); international law (LL M); law (JD); tax law (LL M); JD/MAIS; JD/MBA; JD/MPS; JD/MS. *Accreditation:* ABA. Part-time and evening/weekend programs available. *Faculty:* 54 full-time (21 women), 65 part-time/adjunct (21 women). *Students:* 853 full-time (404 women), 220 part-time (109 women); includes 234 minority (65 Black or African American, non-Hispanic/Latino; 6 American Indian or Alaska Native, non-Hispanic/Latino; 73 Asian, non-Hispanic/Latino; 90 Hispanic/Latino), 13 international. Average age 24. 4,743 applicants, 42% accepted, 298 enrolled. In 2011, 7 master's, 319 doctorates awarded. *Entrance requirements:* For doctorate, LSAT. Additional exam requirements/recommendations for international students: Recommended—TOEFL (minimum score 577 paper-based; 233 computer-based; 90 iBT), IELTS (minimum score 6.5). *Application deadline:* For fall admission, 3/1 for domestic and international students. Applications are processed on a rolling basis. Application fee: $60. Electronic applications accepted. *Expenses:* Contact institution. *Financial support:* In 2011–12, 640 students received support, including 23 fellowships with partial tuition reimbursements available (averaging $5,000 per year), 75 research assistantships (averaging $1,964 per year); career-related internships or fieldwork, scholarships/grants, and tuition waivers (partial) also available. Support available to part-time students. Financial award application deadline: 3/1; financial award applicants required to submit FAFSA. *Faculty research:* Aviation law, intellectual property law, international law, Constitutional law, human rights law, church-state studies. *Total annual research expenditures:* $142,134. *Unit head:* Gregory Mark, Dean, 312-362-5595, E-mail: gmark@depaul.edu. *Application contact:* Michael S. Burns, Director of Law Admission and Associate Dean, 312-362-6831, Fax: 312-362-5280, E-mail: lawinfo@depaul.edu. Web site: http://www.law.depaul.edu/.

Fordham University, School of Law, New York, NY 10023. Offers banking, corporate and finance law (LL M); intellectual property and information law (LL M); international business and trade law (LL M); law (JD); JD/MA; JD/MBA; JD/MSW. *Accreditation:* ABA. Part-time and evening/weekend programs available. *Entrance requirements:* For doctorate, LSAT. Additional exam requirements/recommendations for international students: Required—TOEFL. Electronic applications accepted. *Expenses:* Contact institution. *Faculty research:* Intellectual property, business law, international law.

Golden Gate University, School of Law, San Francisco, CA 94105-2968. Offers environmental law (LL M); intellectual property law (LL M); international legal studies (LL M, SJD); law (JD); taxation (LL M); U. S. legal studies (LL M); JD/MBA; JD/PhD. *Accreditation:* ABA. Part-time and evening/weekend programs available. *Degree requirements:* For doctorate, thesis/dissertation (for some programs). *Entrance requirements:* For doctorate, LSAT (for JD). Additional exam requirements/recommendations for international students: Required—TOEFL (minimum score 600 paper-based; 250 computer-based). Electronic applications accepted. *Expenses:* Contact institution. *Faculty research:* International law, intellectual property law, environmental law, real estate, civil rights.

Intellectual Property Law

John Marshall Law School, Graduate and Professional Programs, Chicago, IL 60604-3968. Offers employee benefits (LL M, MS); global legal studies (LL M); information technology (MS); information technology and privacy law (LL M); intellectual property (LL M, MS); international business and trade (LL M); law (JD); real estate (LL M, MS); taxation (LL M, MS); trial advocacy (LL M); JD/LL M; JD/MA; JD/MBA; JD/MPA. JD/MBA offered jointly with Dominican University; JD/MA and JD/MPA with Roosevelt University. *Accreditation:* ABA. Part-time and evening/weekend programs available. *Faculty:* 69 full-time (22 women), 133 part-time/adjunct (40 women). *Students:* 1,305 full-time (598 women), 368 part-time (180 women); includes 385 minority (148 Black or African American, non-Hispanic/Latino; 15 American Indian or Alaska Native, non-Hispanic/Latino; 108 Asian, non-Hispanic/Latino; 110 Hispanic/Latino; 2 Native Hawaiian or other Pacific Islander, non-Hispanic/Latino; 2 Two or more races, non-Hispanic/Latino), 40 international. Average age 27. 3,513 applicants, 48% accepted, 365 enrolled. In 2011, 86 master's, 403 doctorates awarded. *Degree requirements:* For master's, 24 credits; for doctorate, 90 credits. *Entrance requirements:* For master's, JD; for doctorate, LSAT. Additional exam requirements/recommendations for international students: Required—TOEFL. *Application deadline:* For fall admission, 3/1 priority date for domestic students, 3/1 for international students; for spring admission, 10/15 priority date for domestic students, 10/15 for international students. Applications are processed on a rolling basis. Application fee: $0. Electronic applications accepted. *Expenses:* Contact institution. *Financial support:* In 2011–12, 1,350 students received support. Scholarships/grants and tuition waivers (full and partial) available. Support available to part-time students. Financial award application deadline: 6/1; financial award applicants required to submit FAFSA. *Unit head:* John Corkery, Dean, 312-427-2737. *Application contact:* William B. Powers, Associate Dean of Admission and Student Affairs, 800-537-4280, Fax: 312-427-5136, E-mail: admission@jmls.edu.

Montclair State University, The Graduate School, College of Humanities and Social Sciences, MA Program in Law and Governance, Montclair, NJ 07043-1624. Offers conflict management and peace studies (MA); governance, compliance and regulation (MA); intellectual property (MA); law and governance (MA); legal management (MA). Part-time and evening/weekend programs available. *Faculty:* 13 full-time (6 women), 25 part-time/adjunct (8 women). *Students:* 11 full-time (6 women), 23 part-time (13 women); includes 17 minority (8 Black or African American, non-Hispanic/Latino; 2 Asian, non-Hispanic/Latino; 5 Hispanic/Latino; 2 Two or more races, non-Hispanic/Latino), 2 international. Average age 30. 32 applicants, 44% accepted, 10 enrolled. In 2011, 16 master's awarded. *Degree requirements:* For master's, thesis or comprehensive exam. *Entrance requirements:* For master's, GRE General Test, minimum cumulative GPA of 2.75 for undergraduate work, 2 letters of recommendation, essay. Additional exam requirements/recommendations for international students: Required—TOEFL (minimum score 83 iBT) or IELTS (minimum score 6.5). *Application deadline:* Applications are processed on a rolling basis. Application fee: $60. Electronic applications accepted. *Financial support:* In 2011–12, 1 research assistantship with full tuition reimbursement (averaging $7,000 per year) was awarded; Federal Work-Study, scholarships/grants, and unspecified assistantships also available. Support available to part-time students. Financial award application deadline: 3/1; financial award applicants required to submit FAFSA. *Unit head:* Dr. William Berlin, Chair, 973-655-7576, E-mail: berlinw@mail.montclair.edu. *Application contact:* Amy Aiello, Director of Graduate Admissions and Operations, 973-655-5147, Fax: 973-655-7869, E-mail: graduate.school@montclair.edu. Web site: http://www.montclair.edu/graduate/programs-of-study/law-and-governance/.

Santa Clara University, School of Law, Santa Clara, CA 95053. Offers high technology law (Certificate); intellectual property law (LL M); international and comparative law (LL M); international high tech law (Certificate); international law (Certificate); law (JD); public interest and social justice law (Certificate); U. S. law for foreign lawyers (LL M); JD/MBA. *Accreditation:* ABA. Part-time and evening/weekend programs available. *Faculty:* 65 full-time (32 women), 49 part-time/adjunct (23 women). *Students:* 928 full-time (441 women), 67 part-time (36 women); includes 392 minority (22 Black or African American, non-Hispanic/Latino; 7 American Indian or Alaska Native, non-Hispanic/Latino; 238 Asian, non-Hispanic/Latino; 88 Hispanic/Latino; 3 Native Hawaiian or other Pacific Islander, non-Hispanic/Latino; 34 Two or more races, non-Hispanic/Latino), 56 international. Average age 28. 3,887 applicants, 37% accepted, 335 enrolled. In 2011, 25 master's, 296 doctorates awarded. *Degree requirements:* For master's, comprehensive exam, thesis; for doctorate, comprehensive exam, thesis/dissertation, 86 units. *Entrance requirements:* For master's and doctorate, LSAT, transcript, personal statement, letters of recommendation. *Application deadline:* For fall admission, 2/1 priority date for domestic students, 2/1 for international students. Applications are processed on a rolling basis. Application fee: $75. Electronic applications accepted. *Expenses:* Contact institution. *Financial support:* In 2011–12, 446 students received support. Fellowships with full and partial tuition reimbursements available, Federal Work-Study, and scholarships/grants available. Financial award application deadline: 2/1; financial award applicants required to submit FAFSA. *Faculty research:* Intellectual property, international human rights, privacy rights, wrongful convictions, shareholder and firm governance. *Unit head:* Donald Polden, Dean, 408-554-4362. *Application contact:* Jeannette Leach, Director of Admissions, 408-554-5048. Web site: http://www.scu.edu/law/.

Suffolk University, Law School, Boston, MA 02108. Offers business law and financial services (JD); civil litigation (JD); global law and technology (LL M); health and biomedical law (JD); intellectual property law (JD); international law (JD); JD/MBA; JD/MPA; JD/MSCJ; JD/MSF; JD/MSIE. *Accreditation:* ABA. Part-time and evening/weekend programs available. *Degree requirements:* For master's, legal writing. *Entrance requirements:* For master's, 2 letters of recommendation, resume, personal statement; for doctorate, LSAT, LSDAS, dean's certification, recommendation. Additional exam requirements/recommendations for international students: Required—TOEFL (minimum score 600 paper-based; 250 computer-based; 100 iBT). *Application deadline:* For fall admission, 3/1 for domestic and international students. Applications are processed on a rolling basis. Application fee: $60. Electronic applications accepted. *Expenses:* Contact institution. *Financial support:* Career-related internships or fieldwork, Federal Work-Study, institutionally sponsored loans, and scholarships/grants available. Support available to part-time students. Financial award application deadline: 3/1; financial award applicants required to submit FAFSA. *Faculty research:* Civil law, international law, health/biomedical law, business and finance, intellectual property. *Unit head:* Gail N. Ellis, Dean of Admissions, 617-573-8144, Fax: 617-523-1367, E-mail: gellis@suffolk.edu. *Application contact:* Ian A. Menchini, Director of Electronic Marketing and Enrollment Management, 617-573-8144, Fax: 617-523-1367, E-mail: imenchin@suffolk.edu. Web site: http://www.law.suffolk.edu/.

Thomas M. Cooley Law School, JD and LL M Programs, Lansing, MI 48901-3038. Offers administrative law (public law) (JD); business transactions (JD); Canadian law (JD); Constitutional law and civil rights (public law) (JD); corporate law and finance (LL M); environmental law (public law) (JD); general practice (JD); insurance (LL M); intellectual property (LL M, JD); international law (JD); litigation (JD); self-directed (LL M, JD); taxation (LL M, JD); U.S. law for foreign attorneys (LL M); JD/MBA; JD/MPA; JD/MSW. *Accreditation:* ABA. Part-time and evening/weekend programs available. Postbaccalaureate distance learning degree programs offered (no on-campus study). *Faculty:* 131 full-time (55 women), 286 part-time/adjunct (93 women). *Students:* 781 full-time (368 women), 2,964 part-time (1,450 women); includes 1,055 minority (543 Black or African American, non-Hispanic/Latino; 19 American Indian or Alaska Native, non-Hispanic/Latino; 179 Asian, non-Hispanic/Latino; 205 Hispanic/Latino; 9 Native Hawaiian or other Pacific Islander, non-Hispanic/Latino; 100 Two or more races, non-Hispanic/Latino), 220 international. Average age 30. 4,032 applicants, 80% accepted, 1161 enrolled. In 2011, 40 master's, 999 doctorates awarded. *Degree requirements:* For master's, thesis optional; for doctorate, minimum of 3 credits of clinical experience. *Entrance requirements:* For master's, JD or LL B; for doctorate, LSAT. Additional exam requirements/recommendations for international students: Required—TOEFL. *Application deadline:* For fall admission, 9/1 for domestic and international students; for winter admission, 1/1 for domestic and international students; for spring admission, 5/1 for domestic and international students. Applications are processed on a rolling basis. Electronic applications accepted. *Expenses: Tuition:* Full-time $34,300; part-time $1225 per credit hour. *Required fees:* $40; $40 per year. Tuition and fees vary according to degree level and student level. *Financial support:* In 2011–12, 2,324 students received support. Career-related internships or fieldwork, Federal Work-Study, scholarships/grants, traineeships, and unspecified assistantships available. Support available to part-time students. Financial award applicants required to submit FAFSA. *Faculty research:* Wrongful convictions, civil rights, environmental law, litigation techniques, data mining, intellectual property, practical and skills-based legal education. *Unit head:* Don LeDuc, President and Dean, 517-371-5140 Ext. 2009, Fax: 517-334-5152. *Application contact:* Dr. Paul Zelenski, Associate Dean of Enrollment and Student Services, 517-371-5140 Ext. 2244, Fax: 517-334-5718, E-mail: admissions@cooley.edu. Web site: http://www.cooley.edu/.

University of Houston, Law Center, Houston, TX 77204-6060. Offers energy, environment, and natural resources (LL M); health law (LL M); intellectual property and information law (LL M); international law (LL M); law (LL M, JD); tax law (LL M). *Accreditation:* ABA. Part-time and evening/weekend programs available. *Entrance requirements:* For doctorate, LSAT. Additional exam requirements/recommendations for international students: Required—TOEFL (minimum score 600 paper-based; 100 iBT). Electronic applications accepted. *Expenses:* Contact institution. *Faculty research:* Health law, international, tax, environmental/energy, information law/intellectual property.

University of Pittsburgh, School of Law, Master of Studies in Law Program, Pittsburgh, PA 15260. Offers business law (MSL), including commercial law, corporate law, general business law, international business, tax law; constitutional law (MSL); criminal law and justice (MSL); disabilities law (MSL); dispute resolution (MSL); education law (MSL); elder and estate planning law (MSL); employment and labor law (MSL); environment and real estate law (MSL); family law (MSL); general law and jurisprudence (MSL); health law (MSL); intellectual property and technology (MSL); international and comparative law (MSL); personal injury and civil litigation (MSL); regulatory law (MSL); self-designed (MSL); sports and entertainment law (MSL). Part-time programs available. *Faculty:* 43 full-time (16 women), 104 part-time/adjunct (30 women). *Students:* 5 full-time (3 women), 16 part-time (12 women); includes 6 minority (all Black or African American, non-Hispanic/Latino). Average age 31. 19 applicants, 58% accepted, 11 enrolled. In 2011, 6 master's awarded. *Entrance requirements:* Additional exam requirements/recommendations for international students: Required—TOEFL (minimum score 600 paper-based; 250 computer-based; 100 iBT). *Application deadline:* For fall admission, 6/30 for domestic students, 5/1 for international students. Applications are processed on a rolling basis. Application fee: $0. *Expenses:* Tuition, state resident: full-time $18,774; part-time $760 per credit. Tuition, nonresident: full-time $30,736; part-time $1258 per credit. *Required fees:* $740; $200 per term. Tuition and fees vary according to program. *Faculty research:* Law, health law, business law, contracts, intellectual property. *Unit head:* Prof. Alan Meisel, Director, 412-648-1384, Fax: 412-648-2649, E-mail: meisel@pitt.edu. *Application contact:* Bethann Pischke, Administrative Coordinator, 412-648-7120, Fax: 412-648-2649, E-mail: pischke@pitt.edu. Web site: http://www.law.pitt.edu/academics/msl.

University of Pittsburgh, School of Law, Program in Intellectual Property and Technology Law, Pittsburgh, PA 15260. Offers Certificate. *Faculty:* 3 full-time (0 women), 10 part-time/adjunct (2 women). *Students:* 16 full-time (5 women). *Expenses:* Tuition, state resident: full-time $18,774; part-time $760 per credit. Tuition, nonresident: full-time $30,736; part-time $1258 per credit. *Required fees:* $740; $200 per term. Tuition and fees vary according to program. *Faculty research:* Patent, copyright, trademark, cyberspace, biotechnology. *Unit head:* Prof. George H. Pike, Assistant Professor and Interim Director, 412-648-1322, Fax: 412-648-1352, E-mail: gpike@pitt.edu. *Application contact:* Charmaine McCall, Assistant Dean of Admissions and Financial Aid, 412-648-1413, Fax: 412-648-1318, E-mail: cmccall@pitt.edu. Web site: http://www.law.pitt.edu/academics/programs/ip/index.html.

University of San Francisco, School of Law, Master of Law Program, San Francisco, CA 94117-1080. Offers intellectual property and technology law (LL M); international transactions and comparative law (LL M). *Faculty:* 15 full-time (7 women), 49 part-time/adjunct (18 women). *Students:* 15 full-time (7 women), 3 part-time (2 women), 14 international. Average age 30. 125 applicants, 62% accepted, 17 enrolled. In 2011, 23 master's awarded. *Entrance requirements:* For master's, law degree from U.S. or foreign school (intellectual property and technology law), law degree from foreign school (international transactions and comparative law). Application fee: $60. *Expenses: Tuition:* Full-time $20,070; part-time $1115 per unit. Tuition and fees vary according to course load, campus/location and program. *Financial support:* In 2011–12, 13 students received support. *Unit head:* Eldon Reiley, Director, Fax: 415-422-5440. *Application contact:* Program Assistant, 415-422-5100, E-mail: masterlaws@usfca.edu.

University of Washington, Graduate School, School of Law, Seattle, WA 98195-3020. Offers Asian law (LL M, PhD); intellectual property law and policy (LL M); law (JD); law of sustainable international development (LL M); taxation (LL M); JD/LL M; JD/MA; JD/MAIS; JD/MBA; JD/MPA; JD/MS; JD/PhD. *Accreditation:* ABA. *Degree requirements:* For master's, thesis; for doctorate, thesis/dissertation (for some programs). *Entrance requirements:* For master's, language proficiency (LL M in Asian law); for doctorate, LSAT (for JD). Additional exam requirements/recommendations for international students: Required—TOEFL. *Expenses:* Contact institution. *Faculty research:* Asian, international and comparative law, intellectual property law, health law, environmental law, taxation.

Webster University, College of Arts and Sciences, Department of Behavioral and Social Sciences, St. Louis, MO 63119-3194. Offers counseling (MA); gerontology (MA, Certificate); intellectual property paralegal studies (Certificate); legal analysis (MA); legal studies (MA); paralegal studies (Certificate); patent agency (MA). Part-time programs available. Postbaccalaureate distance learning degree programs offered (no on-campus study). *Degree requirements:* For master's, comprehensive exam (for some programs), thesis (for some programs). *Expenses: Tuition:* Full-time $10,890; part-time $605 per credit hour. Tuition and fees vary according to campus/location and program.

Yeshiva University, Benjamin N. Cardozo School of Law, New York, NY 10003-4301. Offers comparative legal thought (LL M); dispute resolution and advocacy (LL M); general studies (LL M); intellectual property law (LL M); law (JD). *Accreditation:* ABA. Part-time programs available. *Faculty:* 58 full-time (23 women), 107 part-time/adjunct (41 women). *Students:* 1,114 full-time (585 women), 114 part-time (62 women); includes

250 minority (55 Black or African American, non-Hispanic/Latino; 2 American Indian or Alaska Native, non-Hispanic/Latino; 48 Asian, non-Hispanic/Latino; 84 Hispanic/Latino; 40 Native Hawaiian or other Pacific Islander, non-Hispanic/Latino; 21 Two or more races, non-Hispanic/Latino), 17 international. Average age 24. 5,058 applicants, 32% accepted, 325 enrolled. In 2011, 66 master's, 383 doctorates awarded. *Entrance requirements:* For doctorate, LSAT, 2 letters of recommendation. *Application deadline:* For fall admission, 4/1 priority date for domestic students; for spring admission, 12/1 priority date for domestic students. Applications are processed on a rolling basis. Application fee: $75. Electronic applications accepted. *Expenses:* Contact institution. *Financial support:* In 2011–12, 965 students received support, including 140 research assistantships; career-related internships or fieldwork, Federal Work-Study, institutionally sponsored loans, scholarships/grants, health care benefits, and tuition waivers (full and partial) also available. Support available to part-time students. Financial award application deadline: 3/1; financial award applicants required to submit FAFSA. *Faculty research:* Corporate and commercial law, intellectual property law, criminal law and litigation, Constitutional law, legal theory and jurisprudence. *Unit head:* David G. Martinidez, Dean of Admissions, 212-790-0274, Fax: 212-790-0482, E-mail: lawinfo@yu.edu. *Application contact:* Michael Kranzler, Director of Admissions, 212-960-5277, Fax: 212-960-0086. Web site: http://www.cardozo.yu.edu/.

Law

Albany Law School, Professional Program, Albany, NY 12208-3494. Offers LL M, JD, JD/MBA, JD/MPA, JD/MRP, JD/MS, JD/MSW. JD/MBA offered jointly with The College of Saint Rose, The Sage Colleges, Union Graduate College, and University at Albany, State University of New York; JD/MPA, JD/MRP, and JD/MSW offered jointly with University at Albany, State University of New York. *Accreditation:* ABA. Part-time programs available. *Faculty:* 55 full-time (27 women), 52 part-time/adjunct (13 women). *Students:* 672 full-time (301 women), 24 part-time (12 women); includes 94 minority (20 Black or African American, non-Hispanic/Latino; 1 American Indian or Alaska Native, non-Hispanic/Latino; 33 Asian, non-Hispanic/Latino; 20 Hispanic/Latino; 20 Two or more races, non-Hispanic/Latino), 11 international. 2,153 applicants, 52% accepted, 235 enrolled. In 2011, 3 master's, 239 doctorates awarded. *Entrance requirements:* For master's, GRE or LSAT; for doctorate, LSAT. Additional exam requirements/recommendations for international students: Recommended—TOEFL (minimum score 600 paper-based; 250 computer-based). *Application deadline:* For fall admission, 3/1 priority date for domestic students. Applications are processed on a rolling basis. Application fee: $60. *Expenses:* Contact institution. *Financial support:* Research assistantships, career-related internships or fieldwork, Federal Work-Study, institutionally sponsored loans, scholarships/grants, health care benefits, and tuition waivers (full and partial) available. Support available to part-time students. Financial award applicants required to submit FAFSA. *Faculty research:* Federal tax, constitutional law, secured transactions, international law, American politics. *Unit head:* Connie Mayer, Interim President and Dean, 518-445-2321, Fax: 518-472-5865. *Application contact:* Nadia F. Castriota, Director of Admissions, 518-445-2326, Fax: 518-445-2369, E-mail: ncast@albanylaw.edu.

Alliant International University–San Francisco, San Francisco Law School, JD Program, San Francisco, CA 94133-1221. Offers JD. Part-time and evening/weekend programs available. *Faculty:* 2 full-time (1 woman), 15 part-time/adjunct (3 women). *Students:* 60 full-time (31 women), 1 (woman) part-time; includes 33 minority (9 Black or African American, non-Hispanic/Latino; 10 Asian, non-Hispanic/Latino; 8 Hispanic/Latino; 6 Two or more races, non-Hispanic/Latino). Average age 35. *Entrance requirements:* For doctorate, LSAT, personal statement, interview. *Application deadline:* Applications are processed on a rolling basis. Application fee: $75. Electronic applications accepted. *Financial support:* Application deadline: 2/15; applicants required to submit FAFSA. *Unit head:* Jane Gamp, Dean, 415-626-5550, Fax: 415-626-5584, E-mail: admissions@alliant.edu. *Application contact:* Margaret Havey, Director of Admissions, 415-626-5550, E-mail: admissions@alliant.edu. Web site: http://www.alliant.edu/sfls/sfls-program-and-coursework/index.php.

American University, Washington College of Law, Program in International Legal Studies, Washington, DC 20016-8181. Offers LL M, Certificate. Part-time and evening/weekend programs available. *Students:* 40 full-time (25 women), 113 part-time (72 women); includes 11 minority (4 Black or African American, non-Hispanic/Latino; 1 American Indian or Alaska Native, non-Hispanic/Latino; 1 Asian, non-Hispanic/Latino; 5 Hispanic/Latino), 121 international. Average age 27. 381 applicants, 62% accepted, 76 enrolled. In 2011, 100 master's awarded. *Entrance requirements:* For master's, JD, 2 recommendations. Additional exam requirements/recommendations for international students: Required—TOEFL (minimum score 580 paper-based; 237 computer-based; 92 iBT), IELTS (minimum score 6.5). *Application deadline:* For fall admission, 6/1 for domestic students; for spring admission, 11/1 for domestic students. Applications are processed on a rolling basis. Application fee: $55. *Expenses:* Contact institution. *Financial support:* Fellowships, research assistantships, teaching assistantships, career-related internships or fieldwork, and tuition waivers (partial) available. Financial award application deadline: 2/15; financial award applicants required to submit FAFSA. *Unit head:* Claudio M. Grossman, Director, 202-274-4004, Fax: 202-274-4005, E-mail: grossman@wcl.american.edu. *Application contact:* Akira Shiroma, Assistant Dean of Admissions, 202-274-4101, Fax: 202-274-4107, E-mail: shiroma@wcl.american.edu. Web site: http://www.wcl.american.edu/.

American University, Washington College of Law, Program in Law, Washington, DC 20016-8001. Offers JD, JD/MA, JD/MBA, JD/MS. *Accreditation:* ABA. Part-time and evening/weekend programs available. *Students:* 1,245 full-time (707 women), 255 part-time (125 women); includes 527 minority (136 Black or African American, non-Hispanic/Latino; 7 American Indian or Alaska Native, non-Hispanic/Latino; 119 Asian, non-Hispanic/Latino; 229 Hispanic/Latino; 2 Native Hawaiian or other Pacific Islander, non-Hispanic/Latino; 34 Two or more races, non-Hispanic/Latino), 45 international. Average age 26. 7,561 applicants, 26% accepted, 380 enrolled. In 2011, 466 doctorates awarded. *Entrance requirements:* For doctorate, LSAT, registration with LSDAS, 2 recommendations. *Application deadline:* For fall admission, 3/1 for domestic students. Applications are processed on a rolling basis. Application fee: $55. *Expenses:* Contact institution. *Financial support:* Fellowships, career-related internships or fieldwork, Federal Work-Study, institutionally sponsored loans, and tuition waivers (partial) available. Support available to part-time students. Financial award application deadline: 2/15. *Unit head:* Claudio Grossman, Assistant Dean of Admissions and Financial Aid, 202-274-4004, Fax: 202-274-4005, E-mail: grossman@wcl.american.edu. *Application contact:* Akira Shiroma, Assistant Dean of Admissions, 202-274-4101, Fax: 202-274-4107, E-mail: shiroma@wcl.american.edu. Web site: http://www.wcl.american.edu/.

American University, Washington College of Law, Program in Law and Government, Washington, DC 20016-8001. Offers LL M. *Students:* 21 full-time (9 women), 41 part-time (25 women); includes 15 minority (11 Black or African American, non-Hispanic/Latino; 1 American Indian or Alaska Native, non-Hispanic/Latino; 1 Asian, non-Hispanic/Latino; 2 Hispanic/Latino), 7 international. Average age 33. 77 applicants, 77% accepted, 33 enrolled. In 2011, 37 master's awarded. *Degree requirements:* For master's, thesis optional. *Entrance requirements:* For master's, JD, 2 recommendations. Additional exam requirements/recommendations for international students: Required—TOEFL (minimum score 300 paper-based; 250 computer-based). *Application deadline:* For fall admission, 6/1 priority date for domestic students; for spring admission, 11/1 priority date for domestic students. Applications are processed on a rolling basis. Application fee: $55. *Expenses:* Contact institution. *Financial support:* Fellowships with partial tuition reimbursements, career-related internships or fieldwork, and institutionally sponsored loans available. Support available to part-time students. Financial award application deadline: 2/15. *Unit head:* Claudio Grossman, Dean, 202-274-4004, Fax: 202-274-4005, E-mail: grossman@wcl.american.edu. *Application contact:* Akira Shiroma, Assistant Dean of Admissions, 202-274-4101, Fax: 202-274-4107, E-mail: shiroma@wcl.american.edu. Web site: http://www.wcl.american.edu/.

The American University in Cairo, School of Global Affairs and Public Policy, Department of Law, Cairo, Egypt. Offers international and comparative law (LL M); international human rights law (MA). *Expenses: Tuition:* Part-time $932 per credit hour. Tuition and fees vary according to course load, degree level and program. *Unit head:* Thomas Skouteris, Chair, 20-2-2615-3119, E-mail: tskouteris@aucegypt.edu. *Application contact:* Wesley Clark, Director of North American Admissions and Financial Aid, 212-646-810-9433 Ext. 4547, E-mail: wclark@aucnyo.edu. Web site: http://www.aucegypt.edu/GAPP/law/.

The American University of Paris, Graduate Programs, Paris, France. Offers cross-cultural and sustainable business management (MA); cultural translation (MA); global communications (MA); global communications and civil society (MA); international affairs, conflict resolution and civil society development (MA); Middle East and Islamic studies (MA); Middle East and Islamic studies and international affairs (MA); public policy and international affairs (MA); public policy and international law (MA). *Faculty:* 14 full-time (3 women). *Students:* 142 full-time (98 women), 59 part-time (41 women). *Degree requirements:* For master's, thesis. *Entrance requirements:* For master's, minimum undergraduate GPA of 3.0. Additional exam requirements/recommendations for international students: Recommended—TOEFL, IELTS. *Application deadline:* For fall admission, 4/15 for international students; for spring admission, 11/15 for international students. Applications are processed on a rolling basis. Application fee: $75. Electronic applications accepted. Tuition and fees charges are reported in euros. *Expenses: Tuition:* Full-time 25,060 euros; part-time 784 euros per credit. *Required fees:* 784 euros per credit. *Financial support:* Scholarships/grants available. Financial award applicants required to submit FAFSA. *Unit head:* Dr. Celeste Schenck, President, 33 1 40 62 06 59, E-mail: president@aup.fr. *Application contact:* International Admissions Counselor, 33-1 40 62 07 20, Fax: 33-1 47 05 34 32, E-mail: admissions@aup.edu. Web site: http://aup.edu/main/academics/graduate.htm.

Appalachian School of Law, Professional Program in Law, Grundy, VA 24614. Offers JD. *Accreditation:* ABA. *Faculty:* 15 full-time (4 women), 1 part-time/adjunct (0 women). *Students:* 332 full-time (119 women); includes 46 minority (17 Black or African American, non-Hispanic/Latino; 8 Asian, non-Hispanic/Latino; 14 Hispanic/Latino; 7 Two or more races, non-Hispanic/Latino). Average age 26. 1,177 applicants, 77% accepted, 146 enrolled. In 2011, 93 doctorates awarded. *Entrance requirements:* For doctorate, LSAT, bachelor's degree from accredited institution. *Application deadline:* For fall admission, 6/1 for domestic students. Applications are processed on a rolling basis. Application fee: $60. Electronic applications accepted. *Expenses: Tuition:* Full-time $29,500. *Required fees:* $325. *Financial support:* Research assistantships, career-related internships or fieldwork, Federal Work-Study, institutionally sponsored loans, scholarships/grants, and tuition waivers (full and partial) available. Financial award application deadline: 7/1; financial award applicants required to submit FAFSA. *Faculty research:* Natural resources, alternative dispute resolution, Constitutional law, professional ethics, intellectual property. *Unit head:* Clinton W. Shinn, Dean, 276-935-4349, Fax: 276-935-8261, E-mail: wshinn@asl.edu. *Application contact:* Mary Ragland, Director of Student Services and Recruiting, 276-935-4349 Ext. 1224, Fax: 276-935-8496, E-mail: mragland@asl.edu. Web site: http://www.asl.edu/.

Arizona State University, Sandra Day O'Connor College of Law, Tempe, AZ 85287-7906. Offers biotechnology and genomics (LL M); global legal studies (LL M); law (JD); law (customized) (LL M); legal studies (MLS); tribal policy, law and government (LL M); JD/MBA; JD/MD; JD/PhD. JD/MD offered jointly with Mayo Medical School. *Accreditation:* ABA. *Faculty:* 62 full-time (23 women), 68 part-time/adjunct (18 women). *Students:* 615 full-time (247 women), 32 part-time (17 women); includes 148 minority (11 Black or African American, non-Hispanic/Latino; 31 American Indian or Alaska Native, non-Hispanic/Latino; 22 Asian, non-Hispanic/Latino; 67 Hispanic/Latino; 17 Two or more races, non-Hispanic/Latino), 11 international. Average age 28. 2,334 applicants, 28% accepted, 168 enrolled. In 2011, 19 master's, 200 doctorates awarded. *Degree requirements:* For doctorate, papers. *Entrance requirements:* For master's, bachelor's degree and JD (for LL M); for doctorate, LSAT, bachelor's degree. Additional exam requirements/recommendations for international students: Required—TOEFL (minimum score 550 paper-based; 80 iBT). *Application deadline:* For fall admission, 2/1 priority date for domestic students, 2/1 for international students. Applications are processed on a rolling basis. Application fee: $60. Electronic applications accepted. *Expenses:* Contact institution. *Financial support:* In 2011–12, 322 students received support. Research assistantships, teaching assistantships, career-related internships or fieldwork, Federal Work-Study, institutionally sponsored loans, scholarships/grants, tuition waivers (full and partial), and unspecified assistantships available. Financial award application deadline: 3/15; financial award applicants required to submit FAFSA. *Faculty research:* Emerging technologies and the law, Indian law, law and philosophy, international law, intellectual property. *Total annual research expenditures:* $925,469. *Unit head:* Douglas Sylvester, Dean/Professor, 480-965-6188, Fax: 480-965-6521, E-mail: douglas.sylvester@asu.edu. *Application contact:* Chitra Damania, Director of Operations, 480-965-1474, Fax: 480-727-7930, E-mail: law.admissions@asu.edu. Web site: http://www.law.asu.edu/.

Atlanta's John Marshall Law School, JD and LL M Programs, Atlanta, GA 30309. Offers American legal studies (LL M); employment law (LL M); law (JD). *Accreditation:*

Law

ABA. Part-time and evening/weekend programs available. Postbaccalaureate distance learning degree programs offered (minimal on-campus study). *Faculty:* 45 full-time (26 women), 29 part-time/adjunct (8 women). *Students:* 528 full-time (259 women), 226 part-time (120 women); includes 282 minority (177 Black or African American, non-Hispanic/Latino; 11 American Indian or Alaska Native, non-Hispanic/Latino; 9 Asian, non-Hispanic/Latino; 39 Hispanic/Latino; 46 Native Hawaiian or other Pacific Islander, non-Hispanic/Latino), 3 international. Average age 24. 1,867 applicants, 49% accepted, 264 enrolled. In 2011, 132 doctorates awarded. *Entrance requirements:* For master's, JD from accredited law school or bar admission; for doctorate, LSAT, LSDAS report, personal statement, two letters of reference. Additional exam requirements/recommendations for international students: Required—TOEFL. *Application deadline:* Applications are processed on a rolling basis. Application fee: $50. Electronic applications accepted. *Expenses: Tuition:* Full-time $33,840; part-time $1128 per credit hour. *Required fees:* $165; $165 per year. *Financial support:* In 2011–12, 117 students received support. Scholarships/grants available. Financial award application deadline: 6/12; financial award applicants required to submit FAFSA. *Faculty research:* Tort reform, terrorism and the use of the U. S. military, Title VII's referral and deferral scheme, public utilities, eminent domain and land use regulations, recent films and their visions of law in Western society. *Unit head:* Kevin Cieply, Associate Dean for Academic Affairs, 404-872-3593 Ext. 264, Fax: 404-873-3802, E-mail: kcieply@johnmarshall.edu. *Application contact:* Crystal Ridgley, Assistant Director of Admissions, 404-872-3593 Ext. 265, Fax: 404-873-3802, E-mail: cridgley@johnmarshall.edu.

Ave Maria School of Law, School of Law, Naples, FL 34119. Offers JD. *Accreditation:* ABA. *Faculty:* 32 full-time (11 women), 13 part-time/adjunct (4 women). *Students:* 489 full-time (221 women); includes 103 minority (22 Black or African American, non-Hispanic/Latino; 2 American Indian or Alaska Native, non-Hispanic/Latino; 7 Asian, non-Hispanic/Latino; 62 Hispanic/Latino; 10 Two or more races, non-Hispanic/Latino), 4 international. Average age 26. 1,633 applicants, 54% accepted, 210 enrolled. In 2011, 87 doctorates awarded. *Entrance requirements:* For doctorate, LSAT, 2 letters of recommendation, LSDAS, personal statement. Additional exam requirements/recommendations for international students: Required—TOEFL (minimum score 600 paper-based; 250 computer-based). *Application deadline:* For fall admission, 4/1 priority date for domestic students, 4/1 for international students. Applications are processed on a rolling basis. Application fee: $50. Electronic applications accepted. *Expenses: Tuition:* Full-time $35,948. *Required fees:* $500. *Financial support:* In 2011–12, 193 students received support. Career-related internships or fieldwork, Federal Work-Study, and scholarships/grants available. Financial award application deadline: 6/1; financial award applicants required to submit FAFSA. *Unit head:* Eugene R. Milhizer, President/Dean, 239-687-5300. *Application contact:* Monique McCarthy, Assistant Dean for Admissions, 239-687-5420, Fax: 239-352-2890, E-mail: info@avemarialaw.edu. Web site: http://www.avemarialaw.edu/.

Barry University, Dwayne O. Andreas School of Law, Orlando, FL 32807. Offers JD, JD/MS. *Accreditation:* ABA. *Entrance requirements:* For doctorate, LSAT.

Baylor University, School of Law, Waco, TX 76798-7288. Offers JD, JD/MBA, JD/MPPA, JD/MT. *Accreditation:* ABA. *Faculty:* 27 full-time (6 women), 13 part-time/adjunct (2 women). *Students:* 435 full-time (228 women), 7 part-time (2 women); includes 78 minority (8 Black or African American, non-Hispanic/Latino; 1 American Indian or Alaska Native, non-Hispanic/Latino; 20 Asian, non-Hispanic/Latino; 25 Hispanic/Latino; 24 Two or more races, non-Hispanic/Latino), 6 international. Average age 25. 2,360 applicants, 32% accepted, 86 enrolled. In 2011, 158 doctorates awarded. *Entrance requirements:* For doctorate, LSAT. *Application deadline:* For fall admission, 5/1 for domestic students; for spring admission, 11/1 for domestic students. Applications are processed on a rolling basis. Application fee: $40. Electronic applications accepted. *Expenses:* Contact institution. *Financial support:* In 2011–12, 400 students received support. Career-related internships or fieldwork, Federal Work-Study, institutionally sponsored loans, and scholarships/grants available. Financial award application deadline: 2/1; financial award applicants required to submit FAFSA. *Unit head:* Dr. Bradley J. B. Toben, Dean, 254-710-1911, Fax: 254-710-2316. *Application contact:* Nicole Masciopinto, Director of Admissions and Student Recruitment, 254-710-1911, Fax: 254-710-2316, E-mail: nicole_masciopinto@baylor.edu. Web site: http://law.baylor.edu/.

Belmont University, College of Law, Nashville, TN 37212-3757. Offers JD. *Faculty:* 9 full-time (4 women), 3 part-time/adjunct (1 woman). *Students:* 131 full-time (74 women), 1 part-time (0 women); includes 23 minority (14 Black or African American, non-Hispanic/Latino; 1 American Indian or Alaska Native, non-Hispanic/Latino; 1 Asian, non-Hispanic/Latino; 3 Hispanic/Latino; 4 Two or more races, non-Hispanic/Latino). Average age 26. 438 applicants, 39% accepted, 132 enrolled. *Expenses: Tuition:* Full-time $28,500; part-time $900 per hour. *Required fees:* $790; $165 per semester. Tuition and fees vary according to course level, degree level and program. *Unit head:* Jeff Kinsler, Dean, 615-460-6320, E-mail: jeff.kinsler@belmont.edu. *Application contact:* David Mee, Dean of Enrollment Services, 615-460-6785, Fax: 615-460-5434, E-mail: david.mee@belmont.edu. Web site: http://www.belmont.edu/law/.

Boston College, Law School, Newton, MA 02459. Offers JD, JD/MA, JD/MBA, JD/MSW. *Accreditation:* ABA. *Entrance requirements:* For doctorate, LSAT. Additional exam requirements/recommendations for international students: Required—TOEFL. Electronic applications accepted. *Expenses:* Contact institution. *Faculty research:* Commercial law, labor law, legal history, comparative law, international law, business law, intellectual property law, tax law, environmental law.

Boston University, School of Law, Boston, MA 02215. Offers American law (LL M); banking (LL M); intellectual property law (LL M); law (JD); taxation (LL M); JD/LL M; JD/MA; JD/MBA; JD/MPH; JD/MS. *Accreditation:* ABA. *Faculty:* 55 full-time (26 women), 88 part-time/adjunct (25 women). *Students:* 971 full-time (496 women), 62 part-time (27 women); includes 224 minority (38 Black or African American, non-Hispanic/Latino; 2 American Indian or Alaska Native, non-Hispanic/Latino; 85 Asian, non-Hispanic/Latino; 72 Hispanic/Latino; 27 Two or more races, non-Hispanic/Latino), 156 international. Average age 26. 7,073 applicants, 20% accepted, 242 enrolled. In 2011, 169 master's, 271 doctorates awarded. *Degree requirements:* For master's, thesis (for some programs); for doctorate, thesis/dissertation, research project resulting in a paper. *Entrance requirements:* For master's, JD; for doctorate, LSAT. Additional exam requirements/recommendations for international students: Required—TOEFL (minimum score 600 paper-based; 250 computer-based; 100 iBT). *Application deadline:* For fall admission, 3/1 for domestic and international students. Applications are processed on a rolling basis. Application fee: $75. Electronic applications accepted. *Expenses: Tuition:* Full-time $40,848; part-time $1276 per credit hour. *Required fees:* $572; $286 per semester. *Financial support:* In 2011–12, 533 students received support. Career-related internships or fieldwork, Federal Work-Study, institutionally sponsored loans, and scholarships/grants available. Financial award application deadline: 3/1; financial award applicants required to submit FAFSA. *Faculty research:* Litigation and dispute resolution, intellectual property law, business organizations and finance law, international law, health law. *Unit head:* Maureen A. O'Rourke, Dean, 617-353-3112, Fax: 617-353-7400, E-mail: lawdean@bu.edu. *Application contact:* Alissa Leonard, Director of Admissions and Financial Aid, 617-353-3100, Fax: 617-353-0578, E-mail: bulawadm@bu.edu. Web site: http://www.bu.edu/law/.

Brigham Young University, Graduate Studies, J. Reuben Clark Law School, Provo, UT 84602-8000. Offers LL M, JD, JD/M Acc, JD/M Ed, JD/MBA, JD/MPA, JD/MPP. *Accreditation:* ABA. *Faculty:* 43 full-time (14 women), 40 part-time/adjunct (11 women). *Students:* 443 full-time (165 women); includes 73 minority (5 Black or African American, non-Hispanic/Latino; 5 American Indian or Alaska Native, non-Hispanic/Latino; 18 Asian, non-Hispanic/Latino; 31 Hispanic/Latino; 14 Native Hawaiian or other Pacific Islander, non-Hispanic/Latino), 5 international. Average age 26. 755 applicants, 27% accepted, 146 enrolled. In 2011, 8 master's, 145 doctorates awarded. *Entrance requirements:* For doctorate, LSAT. Additional exam requirements/recommendations for international students: Required—TOEFL (minimum score 590 paper-based; 243 computer-based; 96 iBT), IELTS (minimum score 7). *Application deadline:* For fall admission, 3/1 priority date for domestic students. Applications are processed on a rolling basis. Application fee: $50. Electronic applications accepted. *Expenses:* Contact institution. *Financial support:* In 2011–12, 155 students received support, including 155 fellowships (averaging $6,229 per year); research assistantships, teaching assistantships, career-related internships or fieldwork, institutionally sponsored loans, scholarships/grants, and health care benefits also available. Financial award application deadline: 6/1; financial award applicants required to submit FAFSA. *Faculty research:* International law, federal taxation, real property law, constitutional law, business organization law. *Unit head:* James R. Rasband, Dean, 801-422-6383, Fax: 801-422-0389, E-mail: rasbandj@law.byu.edu. *Application contact:* GaeLynn Kuchar, Admissions Director, 801-422-4277, Fax: 801-422-0389, E-mail: kucharg@lawgate.byu.edu. Web site: http://www.law2.byu.edu/.

Brooklyn Law School, Professional Program, Brooklyn, NY 11201-3798. Offers JD, JD/MA, JD/MBA, JD/MS, JD/MUP. JD/MBA offered jointly with Bernard M. Baruch College of the City University of New York; JD/MS with Pratt Institute; JD/MUP with Hunter College of the City University of New York; and JD/MA with Brooklyn College of the City University of New York. *Accreditation:* ABA. Part-time and evening/weekend programs available. *Entrance requirements:* For doctorate, LSAT, dean's certification, 2 faculty letters of evaluation. Additional exam requirements/recommendations for international students: Required—TOEFL and TWE required for Foreign Trained Lawyers Program; Recommended—TOEFL (minimum score 600 paper-based; 250 computer-based; 100 iBT), TWE. Electronic applications accepted. *Faculty research:* Civil procedure, securities regulation, family law, corporate finance, international business and law, health law.

California Western School of Law, Graduate and Professional Programs, San Diego, CA 92101-3090. Offers law (LL M, JD); JD/MBA; JD/MSW; JD/PhD; MCL/LL M. JD/MSW and JD/MBA offered jointly with San Diego State University; JD/PhD with University of California, San Diego. *Accreditation:* ABA. Part-time programs available. *Entrance requirements:* For doctorate, LSAT. Additional exam requirements/recommendations for international students: Required—TOEFL. Electronic applications accepted. *Faculty research:* Biotechnology, child and family law, international law, labor and employment law, sports law.

Campbell University, Graduate and Professional Programs, Norman Adrian Wiggins School of Law, Buies Creek, NC 27506. Offers JD, JD/MPA. Dual degree offered in partnership with North Carolina State University. *Accreditation:* ABA. *Entrance requirements:* For doctorate, LSAT, interview. Additional exam requirements/recommendations for international students: Recommended—TOEFL. Electronic applications accepted. *Expenses:* Contact institution. *Faculty research:* Interdisciplinary approaches to legal problems, management and planning for lawyers, church/state constitutional problems, basic research in substantive legal areas.

Capital University, Law School, Columbus, OH 43215-3200. Offers LL M, MT, JD, JD/LL M, JD/MBA, JD/MSA, JD/MSN, JD/MTS. *Accreditation:* ABA. Part-time and evening/weekend programs available. *Degree requirements:* For master's, thesis or alternative. *Entrance requirements:* For master's, previous course work in accounting, business law, and taxation; for doctorate, LSAT, LSDAS. Additional exam requirements/recommendations for international students: Required—TOEFL. Electronic applications accepted. *Expenses:* Contact institution. *Faculty research:* Dispute resolution, remedies, taxation, commercial law, election law.

Case Western Reserve University, School of Law, Cleveland, OH 44106. Offers intellectual property (LL M); international business law (LL M); international criminal law (LL M); law (JD); U. S. legal studies (LL M); JD/CNM; JD/MA; JD/MBA; JD/MD; JD/MPH; JD/MS; JD/MSSA. *Accreditation:* ABA. Part-time programs available. *Faculty:* 48 full-time (15 women), 54 part-time/adjunct (16 women). *Students:* 600 full-time (260 women), 5 part-time (2 women); includes 110 minority (30 Black or African American, non-Hispanic/Latino; 4 American Indian or Alaska Native, non-Hispanic/Latino; 57 Asian, non-Hispanic/Latino; 17 Hispanic/Latino; 2 Two or more races, non-Hispanic/Latino), 48 international. Average age 24. 1,651 applicants, 47% accepted, 192 enrolled. In 2011, 49 master's, 203 doctorates awarded. *Entrance requirements:* For doctorate, LSAT, LSDAS. Additional exam requirements/recommendations for international students: Required—TOEFL. *Application deadline:* For fall admission, 4/1 priority date for domestic students, 4/1 for international students. Applications are processed on a rolling basis. Application fee: $40. Electronic applications accepted. Application fee is waived when completed online. *Expenses:* Contact institution. *Financial support:* In 2011–12, 440 students received support. Career-related internships or fieldwork, Federal Work-Study, institutionally sponsored loans, and scholarships/grants available. Financial award application deadline: 5/1; financial award applicants required to submit FAFSA. *Unit head:* Lawrence E. Mitchell, Dean, 216-368-3283. *Application contact:* Kelli Curtis, Assistant Dean for Admissions, 216-368-3600, Fax: 216-368-0185, E-mail: lawadmissions@case.edu. Web site: http://law.case.edu/.

The Catholic University of America, Columbus School of Law, Washington, DC 20064. Offers JD, JD/JCL, JD/MA, JD/MLS, JD/MSW. *Accreditation:* ABA. Part-time and evening/weekend programs available. *Entrance requirements:* For doctorate, LSAT. Additional exam requirements/recommendations for international students: Required—TOEFL. Electronic applications accepted. *Expenses:* Contact institution.

Central European University, Graduate Studies, Department of Legal Studies, Budapest, Hungary. Offers comparative Constitutional law (LL M); human rights (LL M, MA); international business law (LL M); law and economics (LL M, MA); legal studies (SJD). *Faculty:* 7 full-time (2 women), 31 part-time/adjunct (8 women). *Students:* 104 full-time (58 women). Average age 27. 474 applicants, 22% accepted, 80 enrolled. In 2011, 36 master's, 7 doctorates awarded. Terminal master's awarded for partial completion of doctoral program. *Degree requirements:* For master's, one foreign language, thesis; for doctorate, one foreign language, comprehensive exam, thesis/dissertation. *Entrance requirements:* For master's and doctorate, LSAT, CEU admissions exams. Additional exam requirements/recommendations for international students: Required—TOEFL (minimum score 570 paper-based; 230 computer-based); Recommended—IELTS (minimum score 6.5). *Application deadline:* For fall admission, 1/24 for domestic and international students. Application fee: $0. Electronic applications accepted. *Expenses:* Contact institution. *Financial support:* In 2011–12, 85 students received support, including 88 fellowships with full and partial tuition reimbursements available (averaging $6,100 per year); career-related internships or fieldwork, institutionally sponsored loans, scholarships/grants, and tuition waivers (full and partial) also available. Financial award application deadline: 1/5. *Faculty research:* Institutional, constitutional and human rights in European Union law; biomedical law and reproductive rights; data protection law; Islamic banking and finance. *Unit head:* Dr. Stefan Messmann, Head, 361-327-3274, Fax: 361-327-3198, E-mail: legalst@ceu.hu. *Application contact:* Maria Balla, Coordinator, 361-327-3204, Fax: 361-327-3198, E-mail: ballam@ceu.hu. Web site: http://www.ceu.hu/legal/.

Champlain College, Graduate Studies, Burlington, VT 05402-0670. Offers business (MBA); digital forensic management (MS); education (M Ed); emergent media (MFA); health care management (MS); law (MS); managing innovation and information technology (MS); mediation and applied conflict studies (MS). Part-time programs available. Postbaccalaureate distance learning degree programs offered (no on-campus study). *Faculty:* 11 full-time (1 woman), 26 part-time/adjunct (11 women). *Students:* 328 full-time (213 women), 66 part-time (36 women); includes 17 minority (11 Black or African American, non-Hispanic/Latino; 1 Asian, non-Hispanic/Latino; 4 Hispanic/Latino; 1 Two or more races, non-Hispanic/Latino). Average age 37. 132 applicants, 90% accepted, 102 enrolled. In 2011, 8 master's awarded. *Degree requirements:* For master's, capstone project. *Entrance requirements:* Additional exam requirements/recommendations for international students: Required—TOEFL. *Application deadline:* For fall admission, 8/1 priority date for domestic students, 8/1 for international students; for spring admission, 1/1 priority date for domestic students, 1/1 for international students. Applications are processed on a rolling basis. Application fee: $50. Electronic applications accepted. *Expenses: Tuition:* Part-time $746 per credit. Tuition and fees vary according to program. *Financial support:* Applicants required to submit FAFSA. *Unit head:* Dr. Donald Haggerty, Associate Provost, 802-865-6403, Fax: 802-865-6447. *Application contact:* Jon Walsh, Assistant Vice President, Graduate Admission, 800-570-5858, E-mail: walsh@champlain.edu. Web site: http://www.champlain.edu/master/.

Chapman University, School of Law, Orange, CA 92866. Offers advocacy and dispute resolution (JD); entertainment and media law (LL M); entertainment law (JD); environmental, land use, and real estate (JD); international law (JD); law (JD); prosecutorial science (LL M); tax law (JD); taxation (LL M); trial advocacy (LL M); JD/MBA; JD/MFA. *Accreditation:* ABA. Part-time and evening/weekend programs available. *Faculty:* 49 full-time (20 women), 26 part-time/adjunct (6 women). *Students:* 526 full-time (265 women), 58 part-time (25 women); includes 139 minority (4 Black or African American, non-Hispanic/Latino; 2 American Indian or Alaska Native, non-Hispanic/Latino; 68 Asian, non-Hispanic/Latino; 45 Hispanic/Latino; 2 Native Hawaiian or other Pacific Islander, non-Hispanic/Latino; 18 Two or more races, non-Hispanic/Latino), 11 international. Average age 26. 2,823 applicants, 34% accepted, 160 enrolled. In 2011, 43 master's, 177 doctorates awarded. *Entrance requirements:* For doctorate, LSAT, minimum undergraduate GPA of 2.75. Additional exam requirements/recommendations for international students: Required—TOEFL (minimum score 600 paper-based; 213 computer-based; 80 iBT). *Application deadline:* For fall admission, 4/15 priority date for domestic students. Applications are processed on a rolling basis. Application fee: $65. Electronic applications accepted. *Expenses:* Contact institution. *Financial support:* Fellowships, Federal Work-Study, and scholarships/grants available. Financial award applicants required to submit FAFSA. *Unit head:* Dr. Tom Campbell, Dean, 714-628-2500. *Application contact:* Marissa Vargas, Assistant Director of Admission and Financial Aid, 877-CHAPLAW, E-mail: mvargas@chapman.edu. Web site: http://www.chapman.edu/law/.

Charlotte School of Law, Professional Program, Charlotte, NC 28204. Offers JD.

City University of New York School of Law, Professional Program, Flushing, NY 11367-1358. Offers JD. *Accreditation:* ABA. *Faculty:* 49 full-time (34 women), 10 part-time/adjunct (5 women). *Students:* 471 full-time (293 women), 1 (woman) part-time; includes 189 minority (39 Black or African American, non-Hispanic/Latino; 1 American Indian or Alaska Native, non-Hispanic/Latino; 53 Asian, non-Hispanic/Latino; 80 Hispanic/Latino; 1 Native Hawaiian or other Pacific Islander, non-Hispanic/Latino; 15 Two or more races, non-Hispanic/Latino), 5 international. Average age 27. 1,883 applicants, 30% accepted, 171 enrolled. In 2011, 111 doctorates awarded. *Entrance requirements:* For doctorate, LSAT, CAS Report, bachelor's degree. Additional exam requirements/recommendations for international students: Recommended—TOEFL. *Application deadline:* For fall admission, 3/15 priority date for domestic students. Applications are processed on a rolling basis. Application fee: $60. Electronic applications accepted. *Expenses:* Tuition, state resident: full-time $11,420; part-time $475 per credit. Tuition, nonresident: full-time $18,980; part-time $795 per credit. *Required fees:* $1711; $60 per credit. $85.85 per semester. *Financial support:* In 2011–12, 68 students received support, including 68 fellowships (averaging $8,063 per year), 34 research assistantships (averaging $1,762 per year), 34 teaching assistantships (averaging $11,245 per year); career-related internships or fieldwork, Federal Work-Study, scholarships/grants, and tuition waivers (partial) also available. Financial award application deadline: 5/2; financial award applicants required to submit FAFSA. *Unit head:* Michelle J. Anderson, Dean/Professor of Law, 718-340-4201, Fax: 718-340-4482. *Application contact:* Helena Quon, Director of Admissions, 718-340-4210, Fax: 718-340-4435, E-mail: admissions@mail.law.cuny.edu. Web site: http://www.law.cuny.edu/.

Cleveland State University, Cleveland-Marshall College of Law, Cleveland, OH 44115. Offers business law (JD); civil litigation and dispute resolution (JD); criminal law (JD); employment labor law (JD); international and comparative law (JD); law (LL M); JD/MAES; JD/MBA; JD/MPA; JD/MSES; JD/MUPDD. *Accreditation:* ABA. Part-time and evening/weekend programs available. *Faculty:* 38 full-time (20 women), 30 part-time/adjunct (9 women). *Students:* 391 full-time (162 women), 170 part-time (82 women); includes 87 minority (53 Black or African American, non-Hispanic/Latino; 1 American Indian or Alaska Native, non-Hispanic/Latino; 14 Asian, non-Hispanic/Latino; 17 Hispanic/Latino; 2 Two or more races, non-Hispanic/Latino), 6 international. Average age 27. 1,655 applicants, 38% accepted, 173 enrolled. In 2011, 3 master's, 183 doctorates awarded. *Degree requirements:* For master's, thesis (for graduates of U.S. law schools); for doctorate, 90 credits (41 in required courses). *Entrance requirements:* For master's, JD or LL B; for doctorate, LSAT, bachelor's degree. Additional exam requirements/recommendations for international students: Required—TOEFL (minimum score 600 paper-based; 250 computer-based; 100 iBT). *Application deadline:* For fall admission, 5/1 for domestic and international students. Applications are processed on a rolling basis. Application fee: $0. Electronic applications accepted. *Expenses:* Contact institution. *Financial support:* In 2011–12, 206 students received support, including 23 fellowships (averaging $2,400 per year), 50 research assistantships (averaging $900 per year), 8 teaching assistantships with partial tuition reimbursements available (averaging $1,650 per year); career-related internships or fieldwork, Federal Work-Study, scholarships/grants, tuition waivers (full and partial), and unspecified assistantships also available. Support available to part-time students. Financial award application deadline: 5/1; financial award applicants required to submit FAFSA. *Faculty research:* Health law, international law, Constitutional law, commercial law, business organizations. *Unit head:* Phyllis L. Crocker, Dean, 216-687-2300, Fax: 216-687-6881, E-mail: phyllis.crocker@law.csuohio.edu. *Application contact:* Christopher Lucak, Assistant Dean for Admissions, 216-687-4692, Fax: 216-687-6881, E-mail: christopher.lucak@law.csuohio.edu. Web site: http://www.law.csuohio.edu/.

Cleveland State University, College of Graduate Studies, Maxine Goodman Levin College of Urban Affairs, Program in Urban Studies, Cleveland, OH 44115. Offers law and public policy (MS); public finance (MS); urban economic development (Certificate); urban policy analysis (MS); urban real estate development (MS); urban real estate development and finance (Certificate). PhD program offered jointly with The University of Akron. Part-time and evening/weekend programs available. *Faculty:* 26 full-time (10 women), 20 part-time/adjunct (11 women). *Students:* 16 full-time (10 women), 35 part-time (18 women); includes 7 minority (all Black or African American, non-Hispanic/Latino), 17 international. Average age 37. 63 applicants, 49% accepted, 18 enrolled. In 2011, 7 master's, 5 doctorates, 6 other advanced degrees awarded. *Degree requirements:* For master's, thesis or alternative, exit project; for doctorate, comprehensive exam, thesis/dissertation. *Entrance requirements:* For master's, GRE General Test, minimum GPA of 3.0; for doctorate, GRE General Test, minimum GPA of 3.5. Additional exam requirements/recommendations for international students: Required—TOEFL (minimum score 525 paper-based; 197 computer-based; 65 iBT). *Application deadline:* For fall admission, 1/15 priority date for domestic students, 1/15 for international students. Applications are processed on a rolling basis. Application fee: $30. Electronic applications accepted. *Expenses:* Tuition, state resident: full-time $6416; part-time $494 per credit hour. Tuition, nonresident: full-time $12,074; part-time $929 per credit hour. *Financial support:* In 2011–12, 15 students received support, including 8 research assistantships with full and partial tuition reimbursements available (averaging $9,000 per year), 7 teaching assistantships with full and partial tuition reimbursements available (averaging $2,400 per year); career-related internships or fieldwork, scholarships/grants, traineeships, and unspecified assistantships also available. Support available to part-time students. Financial award application deadline: 3/1; financial award applicants required to submit FAFSA. *Faculty research:* Environmental issues, economic development, urban and public policy, public management. *Unit head:* Dr. Mittie Davis Jones, Director, 216-687-3861, Fax: 216-687-9342, E-mail: m.d.jones97@csuohio.edu. *Application contact:* Joan Demko, Graduate Academic Program Specialist, 216-523-7522, Fax: 216-687-5398, E-mail: urbanprograms@csuohio.edu. Web site: http://urban.csuohio.edu/academics/graduate/msus/.

The College of William and Mary, William and Mary Law School, Williamsburg, VA 23187-8795. Offers LL M, JD, JD/MA, JD/MBA, JD/MPP. *Accreditation:* ABA. *Faculty:* 39 full-time (14 women), 49 part-time/adjunct (12 women). *Students:* 654 full-time (335 women), 18 part-time (8 women); includes 129 minority (74 Black or African American, non-Hispanic/Latino; 27 Asian, non-Hispanic/Latino; 17 Hispanic/Latino; 1 Native Hawaiian or other Pacific Islander, non-Hispanic/Latino; 10 Two or more races, non-Hispanic/Latino), 30 international. Average age 25. 6,151 applicants, 23% accepted, 256 enrolled. In 2011, 19 master's, 202 doctorates awarded. *Degree requirements:* For doctorate, major paper. *Entrance requirements:* For master's, LL B, references; for doctorate, LSAT, baccalaureate degree, references. Additional exam requirements/recommendations for international students: Required—TOEFL (minimum score 600 paper-based; 250 computer-based; 100 iBT). *Application deadline:* For fall admission, 3/1 priority date for domestic students, 3/1 for international students. Application fee: $50. Electronic applications accepted. *Expenses:* Contact institution. *Financial support:* In 2011–12, 371 students received support, including 184 fellowships with partial tuition reimbursements available (averaging $4,000 per year), 79 research assistantships (averaging $1,530 per year), 38 teaching assistantships (averaging $4,000 per year); career-related internships or fieldwork, scholarships/grants, and unspecified assistantships also available. Financial award application deadline: 2/15; financial award applicants required to submit FAFSA. *Faculty research:* Constitutional law, criminal law, corporate law, international law, legal skills/trial advocacy. *Total annual research expenditures:* $28,157. *Unit head:* Davison M. Douglas, Dean/Professor, 757-221-3790, Fax: 757-221-3261, E-mail: dmdoug@wm.edu. *Application contact:* Faye F. Shealy, Associate Dean for Admission, 757-221-3785, Fax: 757-221-3261, E-mail: ffshea@wm.edu. Web site: http://law.wm.edu/.

Columbia University, School of Law, New York, NY 10027. Offers LL M, JD, JSD, JD/M Phil, JD/MA, JD/MBA, JD/MFA, JD/MIA, JD/MPA, JD/MPH, JD/MSW. *Accreditation:* ABA. *Entrance requirements:* For doctorate, LSAT (for JD). Electronic applications accepted. *Expenses:* Contact institution. *Faculty research:* Human rights, law and philosophy, corporate governance, regulation of the workplace, death penalty.

Concord Law School, Program in Law, Los Angeles, CA 90024. Offers EJD, JD. Part-time and evening/weekend programs available. Postbaccalaureate distance learning degree programs offered (no on-campus study). *Degree requirements:* For doctorate, comprehensive exam. *Entrance requirements:* For doctorate, online admissions test. Additional exam requirements/recommendations for international students: Required—TOEFL (minimum score 520 paper-based). Electronic applications accepted.

Cornell University, Cornell Law School, Ithaca, NY 14853-4901. Offers LL M, JD, JSD, JD/DESS, JD/LL M, JD/MA, JD/MBA, JD/MILR, JD/MLLP, JD/MLP, JD/MPA, JD/MRP, JD/Maitrise en Droit, JD/PhD. JD/MLLP offered jointly with Humboldt University, Berlin; JD/DESS offered jointly with Institut d'etudes Politiques de Paris ("Sciences Po") and Paris I. *Accreditation:* ABA. *Entrance requirements:* For doctorate, LSAT (for JD). Electronic applications accepted. *Expenses:* Contact institution. *Faculty research:* International law, Constitutional law, corporate laws, public interest law, feminist legal theory.

Cornell University, Graduate School, Graduate Field of Law, Ithaca, NY 14853. Offers JSD. *Faculty:* 48 full-time (13 women). *Students:* 14 full-time (7 women); includes 2 minority (1 Black or African American, non-Hispanic/Latino; 1 Hispanic/Latino), 10 international. Average age 32. 5 applicants, 20% accepted, 1 enrolled. In 2011, 3 doctorates awarded. *Entrance requirements:* For doctorate, JD, LL M, or equivalent; 2 letters of recommendation. Additional exam requirements/recommendations for international students: Required—TOEFL (minimum score 550 paper-based; 213 computer-based). *Application deadline:* For fall admission, 5/1 for domestic students. Application fee: $95. Electronic applications accepted. *Expenses:* Contact institution. *Financial support:* In 2011–12, 11 fellowships with full tuition reimbursements were awarded; research assistantships with full tuition reimbursements, teaching assistantships with full tuition reimbursements, institutionally sponsored loans, scholarships/grants, health care benefits, tuition waivers (full and partial), and unspecified assistantships also available. Financial award applicants required to submit FAFSA. *Faculty research:* International economic integration (WTO and EU), international commercial arbitration, feminist jurisprudence, human rights. *Unit head:* Director of Graduate Studies, 607-255-5141. *Application contact:* Graduate Field Assistant, 607-255-5141, E-mail: gradlaw@law.mail.cornell.edu. Web site: http://www.gradschool.cornell.edu/fields.php?id-89&a-2.

Creighton University, School of Law, Omaha, NE 68178-0001. Offers MS, JD, Certificate, JD/MA, JD/MBA, JD/MS. *Accreditation:* ABA. Part-time programs available. *Faculty:* 33 full-time (9 women), 35 part-time/adjunct (13 women). *Students:* 431 full-time (161 women), 11 part-time (4 women); includes 47 minority (13 Black or African American, non-Hispanic/Latino; 15 Asian, non-Hispanic/Latino; 17 Hispanic/Latino; 2 Two or more races, non-Hispanic/Latino), 7 international. Average age 25. 1,232 applicants, 57% accepted, 135 enrolled. In 2011, 153 doctorates awarded. *Entrance requirements:* For doctorate, LSAT, bachelor's degree. Additional exam requirements/recommendations for international students: Recommended—TOEFL (minimum score 600 paper-based). *Application deadline:* For fall admission, 5/1 priority date for domestic students, 5/1 for international students. Applications are processed on a rolling basis.

Application fee: $50. Electronic applications accepted. *Expenses:* Contact institution. *Financial support:* In 2011–12, 211 students received support. Career-related internships or fieldwork, institutionally sponsored loans, and scholarships/grants available. Support available to part-time students. Financial award application deadline: 7/1; financial award applicants required to submit FAFSA. *Faculty research:* Conflict of laws, international law, evidence, cyber warfare, Constitutional law. *Unit head:* Marianne B. Culhane, Dean and Professor of Law, 402-280-2874, Fax: 402-280-3161. *Application contact:* Andrea D. Bashara, Assistant Dean, 402-280-2586, Fax: 402-280-3161, E-mail: bashara@creighton.edu. Web site: http://www.creighton.edu/law.

Dalhousie University, Faculty of Graduate Studies, Dalhousie Law School, Halifax, NS B3H 4H9, Canada. Offers LL M, JSD, LL B/MBA, LL B/MLIS, LL B/MPA. Part-time programs available. *Degree requirements:* For master's, thesis or alternative; for doctorate, thesis/dissertation. *Entrance requirements:* For master's, LL B; for doctorate, LL M. Additional exam requirements/recommendations for international students: Required—1 of 5 approved tests: TOEFL, IELTS, CANTEST, CAEL, Michigan English Language Assessment Battery. Electronic applications accepted. *Expenses:* Contact institution. *Faculty research:* Marine and environmental law, health law, the family law program.

DePaul University, College of Law, Chicago, IL 60604-2287. Offers health law (LL M); intellectual property law (LL M); international law (LL M); law (JD); tax law (LL M); JD/MAIS; JD/MBA; JD/MPS; JD/MS. *Accreditation:* ABA. Part-time and evening/weekend programs available. *Faculty:* 54 full-time (21 women), 65 part-time/adjunct (21 women). *Students:* 853 full-time (404 women), 220 part-time (109 women); includes 234 minority (65 Black or African American, non-Hispanic/Latino; 6 American Indian or Alaska Native, non-Hispanic/Latino; 73 Asian, non-Hispanic/Latino; 90 Hispanic/Latino), 13 international. Average age 24. 4,743 applicants, 42% accepted, 298 enrolled. In 2011, 7 master's, 319 doctorates awarded. *Entrance requirements:* For doctorate, LSAT. Additional exam requirements/recommendations for international students: Recommended—TOEFL (minimum score 577 paper-based; 233 computer-based; 90 iBT), IELTS (minimum score 6.5). *Application deadline:* For fall admission, 3/1 for domestic and international students. Applications are processed on a rolling basis. Application fee: $60. Electronic applications accepted. *Expenses:* Contact institution. *Financial support:* In 2011–12, 640 students received support, including 23 fellowships with partial tuition reimbursements available (averaging $5,000 per year), 75 research assistantships (averaging $1,964 per year); career-related internships or fieldwork, scholarships/grants, and tuition waivers (partial) also available. Support available to part-time students. Financial award application deadline: 3/1; financial award applicants required to submit FAFSA. *Faculty research:* Aviation law, intellectual property law, international law, Constitutional law, human rights law, church-state studies. *Total annual research expenditures:* $142,134. *Unit head:* Gregory Mark, Dean, 312-362-5595, E-mail: gmark@depaul.edu. *Application contact:* Michael S. Burns, Director of Law Admission and Associate Dean, 312-362-6831, Fax: 312-362-5280, E-mail: lawinfo@depaul.edu. Web site: http://www.law.depaul.edu/.

Drake University, Law School, Des Moines, IA 50311-4516. Offers JD, JD/MA, JD/MBA, JD/MPA, JD/MS, JD/MSW, JD/Pharm D. JD/MA and JD/MS offered jointly with Iowa State University of Science and Technology; JD/MSW with The University of Iowa. *Accreditation:* ABA. *Faculty:* 29 full-time (10 women), 14 part-time/adjunct (6 women). *Students:* 426 full-time (193 women), 14 part-time (11 women); includes 51 minority (18 Black or African American, non-Hispanic/Latino; 8 Asian, non-Hispanic/Latino; 22 Hispanic/Latino; 3 Two or more races, non-Hispanic/Latino), 5 international. Average age 26. 1,009 applicants, 55% accepted, 142 enrolled. In 2011, 159 doctorates awarded. *Degree requirements:* For doctorate, 2 internships. *Entrance requirements:* For doctorate, LSAT, LSDAS report. Additional exam requirements/recommendations for international students: Required—TOEFL (minimum score 560 paper-based; 220 computer-based), TWE. *Application deadline:* For fall admission, 4/1 priority date for domestic students, 4/1 for international students. Applications are processed on a rolling basis. Application fee: $40. Electronic applications accepted. *Expenses:* Contact institution. *Financial support:* In 2011–12, 20 research assistantships (averaging $757 per year), 6 teaching assistantships (averaging $2,142 per year) were awarded; career-related internships or fieldwork, Federal Work-Study, institutionally sponsored loans, scholarships/grants, and tuition waivers (full and partial) also available. Support available to part-time students. Financial award application deadline: 3/1; financial award applicants required to submit FAFSA. *Faculty research:* Constitutional law, environmental law, agricultural law, computers and the law, bioethics and health law. *Total annual research expenditures:* $167,107. *Unit head:* David Walker, Dean, 515-271-1805, Fax: 515-271-4118, E-mail: david.walker@drake.edu. *Application contact:* Jason Allen, Director of Admission, 515-271-2040, Fax: 515-271-2530, E-mail: jason.allen@drake.edu. Web site: http://www.law.drake.edu/.

Duke University, School of Law, Durham, NC 27708. Offers LL M, MLS, JD, SJD, JD/AM, JD/LL M, JD/MA, JD/MBA, JD/MEM, JD/MPP, JD/MS, JD/MTS, JD/PhD, MD/JD. LL M and SJD offered only to international students. *Accreditation:* ABA. *Degree requirements:* For doctorate, thesis/dissertation (for some programs). *Entrance requirements:* For doctorate, LSAT (for JD). Additional exam requirements/recommendations for international students: Required—TOEFL (minimum score 600 paper-based). Electronic applications accepted. *Expenses:* Contact institution. *Faculty research:* International and comparative law; constitutional and public law; intellectual property, science and technology; business, finance, and corporate law; environmental law and policy.

Duquesne University, Bayer School of Natural and Environmental Sciences, Program in Forensic Science and Law, Pittsburgh, PA 15282-0001. Offers MS. *Faculty:* 4 full-time (2 women), 7 part-time/adjunct (4 women). *Students:* 14 full-time (11 women); includes 2 minority (both Asian, non-Hispanic/Latino). Average age 22. 14 applicants, 100% accepted, 14 enrolled. In 2011, 14 master's awarded. *Degree requirements:* For master's, comprehensive exam. *Entrance requirements:* For master's, SAT or ACT, 1 recommendation form; minimum total QPA of 3.0, 2.5 in math and science. *Application deadline:* For fall admission, 7/1 for domestic and international students. Applications are processed on a rolling basis. Application fee: $50. Electronic applications accepted. *Expenses: Tuition:* Full-time $16,596; part-time $922 per credit. *Required fees:* $1584; $88 per credit. Tuition and fees vary according to program. *Financial support:* In 2011–12, 7 students received support. Career-related internships or fieldwork and unspecified assistantships available. Financial award application deadline: 5/1. *Faculty research:* Extraction protocols, mass spectrometry, synthetic fiber analysis, synthetic polymer characterization, trace analysis, amplification of DNA, methods for labeling DNA, construction of a genetic profile, experiential exploration of mitochondrial DNA, the Y-chromosome, and amelogenin. *Unit head:* Dr. Federick W. Fochtman, Director, 412-396-6373, E-mail: fochtman@duq.edu. *Application contact:* Val Lijewski, Academic Advisor, 412-396-1084, Fax: 412-396-1402, E-mail: lijewski@duq.edu. Web site: http://www.science.duq.edu/.

Duquesne University, School of Law, Pittsburgh, PA 15282-0700. Offers LL M, JD, JD/M Div, JD/MBA, JD/MS, JD/MSEM. JD/M Div offered jointly with Pittsburgh Theological Seminary. *Accreditation:* ABA. Part-time and evening/weekend programs available. *Faculty:* 26 full-time (4 women), 51 part-time/adjunct (11 women). *Students:* 640 full-time (277 women); includes 44 minority (11 Black or African American, non-Hispanic/Latino; 1 American Indian or Alaska Native, non-Hispanic/Latino; 16 Asian, non-Hispanic/Latino; 13 Hispanic/Latino; 3 Two or more races, non-Hispanic/Latino), 2 international. Average age 26. In 2011, 1 master's, 205 doctorates awarded. *Entrance requirements:* For doctorate, LSAT, minimum GPA of 3.25. Additional exam requirements/recommendations for international students: Required—TOEFL (minimum score 600 paper-based). *Application deadline:* For fall admission, 4/1 for domestic students. Applications are processed on a rolling basis. Application fee: $60. *Expenses:* Contact institution. *Financial support:* In 2011–12, 267 students received support. Research assistantships, teaching assistantships, career-related internships or fieldwork, Federal Work-Study, scholarships/grants, and tuition waivers (partial) available. Support available to part-time students. Financial award application deadline: 5/31. *Faculty research:* Clinical legal education, litigation/trial advocacy. *Total annual research expenditures:* $100,000. *Unit head:* Ken Gormley, Interim Dean, 412-396-6300, Fax: 412-396-6659, E-mail: gormley@duq.edu. *Application contact:* Joseph P. Campion, Director, Admissions, 412-396-6296, Fax: 412-396-6659, E-mail: campion@duq.edu. Web site: http://www.law.duq.edu/.

Elon University, Program in Law, Elon, NC 27244-2010. Offers JD. *Faculty:* 28 full-time (10 women), 17 part-time/adjunct (3 women). *Students:* 368 full-time (168 women); includes 46 minority (31 Black or African American, non-Hispanic/Latino; 5 American Indian or Alaska Native, non-Hispanic/Latino; 6 Asian, non-Hispanic/Latino; 4 Hispanic/Latino), 1 international. Average age 26. 836 applicants, 48% accepted, 129 enrolled. In 2011, 98 doctorates awarded. *Entrance requirements:* For doctorate, LSAT, LSDAS. Additional exam requirements/recommendations for international students: Required—TOEFL (minimum score 550 paper-based; 213 computer-based; 79 iBT). *Application deadline:* For spring admission, 4/1 priority date for domestic students. Applications are processed on a rolling basis. Application fee: $50. Electronic applications accepted. *Expenses:* Contact institution. *Financial support:* In 2011–12, 275 students received support. Federal Work-Study and scholarships/grants available. Financial award applicants required to submit FAFSA. *Faculty research:* Quality of life and job satisfaction, civil procedure, damages, assessment for development of instruments, psychological types. *Unit head:* George Johnson, Dean, 336-279-9201, E-mail: gjohnson8@elon.edu. *Application contact:* Alan Woodlief, Associate Dean of School of Law/Director of Law School Admissions, 336-279-9203, E-mail: awoodlief@elon.edu. Web site: http://www.elon.edu/law.

Emory University, School of Law, Atlanta, GA 30322-2770. Offers LL M, JD, Certificate, JD/Certificate, JD/LL M, JD/M Div, JD/MA, JD/MBA, JD/MPH, JD/MTS, JD/PhD. *Accreditation:* ABA. *Faculty:* 67 full-time (30 women), 49 part-time/adjunct (7 women). *Students:* 810 full-time (350 women); includes 221 minority (42 Black or African American, non-Hispanic/Latino; 6 American Indian or Alaska Native, non-Hispanic/Latino; 86 Asian, non-Hispanic/Latino; 65 Hispanic/Latino; 22 Two or more races, non-Hispanic/Latino), 33 international. Average age 24. 3,951 applicants, 33% accepted, 246 enrolled. In 2011, 255 doctorates, 9 Certificates awarded. *Entrance requirements:* For doctorate, LSAT, 2 letters of recommendation. Additional exam requirements/recommendations for international students: Required—TOEFL (minimum score 600 paper-based; 250 computer-based). *Application deadline:* For fall admission, 3/1 for domestic and international students. Applications are processed on a rolling basis. Application fee: $70. Electronic applications accepted. *Expenses:* Contact institution. *Financial support:* In 2011–12, 529 students received support, including 26 fellowships (averaging $9,000 per year), 57 research assistantships (averaging $9,880 per year); career-related internships or fieldwork, Federal Work-Study, institutionally sponsored loans, scholarships/grants, and tuition waivers (full and partial) also available. Financial award application deadline: 3/1; financial award applicants required to submit FAFSA. *Faculty research:* Law and economics, law and religion, international law, human rights, feminism and legal theory. *Total annual research expenditures:* $201,645. *Unit head:* Robert Schapiro, Dean, 404-712-8815, Fax: 404-727-0866, E-mail: david.partlett@emory.edu. *Application contact:* Ethan Rosenzweig, Assistant Dean for Admission, 404-727-6802, Fax: 404-727-2477, E-mail: lawinfo@law.emory.edu.

Facultad de derecho Eugenio María de Hostos, School of Law, Mayagüez, PR 00681. Offers JD. *Entrance requirements:* For doctorate, EXADEP, LSAT, 2 letters of recommendation.

Faulkner University, Thomas Goode Jones School of Law, Montgomery, AL 36109-3398. Offers JD. *Accreditation:* ABA. *Entrance requirements:* For doctorate, LSAT. Additional exam requirements/recommendations for international students: Recommended—TOEFL. Electronic applications accepted.

Florida Agricultural and Mechanical University, College of Law, Tallahassee, FL 32307-3200. Offers JD. *Accreditation:* ABA. Part-time and evening/weekend programs available. *Entrance requirements:* For doctorate, LSAT, LSDAS, 2 letters of recommendation. Additional exam requirements/recommendations for international students: Required—TOEFL. *Expenses:* Contact institution.

Florida Coastal School of Law, Professional Program, Jacksonville, FL 32256. Offers JD. *Accreditation:* ABA. Part-time programs available. *Entrance requirements:* For doctorate, LSAT. Additional exam requirements/recommendations for international students: Recommended—TOEFL (minimum score 600 paper-based; 250 computer-based). Electronic applications accepted. *Expenses:* Contact institution. *Faculty research:* Law and business, law technology and intellectual property, juvenile justice and family law, constitutional law, labor law.

Florida International University, College of Law, Miami, FL 33199. Offers JD. *Accreditation:* ABA. Part-time and evening/weekend programs available. *Entrance requirements:* For doctorate, LSAT, 3 letters of recommendation. Additional exam requirements/recommendations for international students: Recommended—TOEFL. Electronic applications accepted. *Expenses:* Contact institution.

Florida State University, College of Law, Tallahassee, FL 32306-1601. Offers American law for foreign lawyers (LL M); environmental law and policy (LL M); law (JD); JD/MBA; JD/MPA; JD/MS; JD/MSP; JD/MSW. *Accreditation:* ABA. *Faculty:* 55 full-time (27 women), 31 part-time/adjunct (8 women). *Students:* 736 full-time (290 women), 3 part-time (0 women); includes 72 minority (34 Black or African American, non-Hispanic/Latino; 1 American Indian or Alaska Native, non-Hispanic/Latino; 11 Asian, non-Hispanic/Latino; 26 Hispanic/Latino), 2 international. Average age 24. 2,824 applicants, 29% accepted, 252 enrolled. In 2011, 1 master's, 271 doctorates awarded. *Entrance requirements:* For doctorate, LSAT. Additional exam requirements/recommendations for international students: Required—TOEFL (minimum score 600 paper-based; 250 computer-based; 100 iBT). *Application deadline:* For fall admission, 3/15 priority date for domestic students, 3/15 for international students. Applications are processed on a rolling basis. Application fee: $30. Electronic applications accepted. *Expenses:* Contact institution. *Financial support:* In 2011–12, 290 students received support, including 1 fellowship with full tuition reimbursement available (averaging $20,250 per year), 55 research assistantships (averaging $1,183 per year), 11 teaching assistantships (averaging $1,835 per year); scholarships/grants and unspecified assistantships also available. Financial award application deadline: 6/30; financial award applicants required to submit FAFSA. *Faculty research:* Law and business, environmental and land use, international, criminal. *Total annual research expenditures:* $156,374. *Unit head:* Donald J. Weidner, Dean, 850-644-3400, Fax: 850-644-5487, E-mail: dweidner@law.fsu.edu.

Application contact: Jennifer L. Kessinger, Director of Admissions and Records, 850-644-3787, Fax: 850-644-7284, E-mail: jkessing@law.fsu.edu. Web site: http://www.law.fsu.edu/.

Fordham University, School of Law, New York, NY 10023. Offers banking, corporate and finance law (LL M); intellectual property and information law (LL M); international business and trade law (LL M); law (JD); JD/MA; JD/MBA; JD/MSW. *Accreditation:* ABA. Part-time and evening/weekend programs available. *Entrance requirements:* For doctorate, LSAT. Additional exam requirements/recommendations for international students: Required—TOEFL. Electronic applications accepted. *Expenses:* Contact institution. *Faculty research:* Intellectual property, business law, international law.

Friends University, Graduate School, Wichita, KS 67213. Offers accounting (MBA); business administration (MBA); business law (MBL); Christian ministry (MACM); environment science (MSES); family therapy (MSFT); global leadership and management (MA); health care leadership (MHCL); management information systems (MMIS); operations management (MSOM); organization development (MSOD); teaching (MAT). Part-time and evening/weekend programs available. Postbaccalaureate distance learning degree programs offered (no on-campus study). *Faculty:* 14 full-time (5 women), 2 part-time/adjunct (1 woman). *Students:* 158 full-time (114 women), 616 part-time (367 women); includes 159 minority (83 Black or African American, non-Hispanic/Latino; 12 American Indian or Alaska Native, non-Hispanic/Latino; 26 Asian, non-Hispanic/Latino; 22 Hispanic/Latino; 2 Native Hawaiian or other Pacific Islander, non-Hispanic/Latino; 14 Two or more races, non-Hispanic/Latino). Average age 36. 497 applicants, 68% accepted, 256 enrolled. In 2011, 341 degrees awarded. *Degree requirements:* For master's, research project. *Entrance requirements:* For master's, bachelor's degree from accredited institution, official transcripts from institution granting bachelor's degree, interview with program director, letter(s) of recommendation. Additional exam requirements/recommendations for international students: Required—TOEFL (minimum score 560 paper-based; 220 computer-based). *Application deadline:* Applications are processed on a rolling basis. Application fee: $45 ($65 for international students). Electronic applications accepted. *Expenses: Tuition:* Part-time $601 per credit hour. One-time fee: $45 full-time. Tuition and fees vary according to campus/location and program. *Financial support:* Applicants required to submit FAFSA. *Unit head:* Dr. Evelyn Hume, Dean, 800-794-6945 Ext. 5859, Fax: 316-295-5040, E-mail: evelyn_hume@friends.edu. *Application contact:* Jeanette Hanson, Executive Director of Adult Recruitment, 800-794-6945, Fax: 316-295-5050, E-mail: jeanette@friends.edu. Web site: http://www.friends.edu.

George Mason University, School of Law, Arlington, VA 22201. Offers intellectual property (LL M); law (JD); law and economics (LL M); JD/MA; JD/MPP; JD/PhD. *Accreditation:* ABA. Part-time and evening/weekend programs available. *Faculty:* 36 full-time (8 women), 81 part-time/adjunct (22 women). *Students:* 510 full-time (218 women), 210 part-time (88 women); includes 105 minority (7 Black or African American, non-Hispanic/Latino; 6 American Indian or Alaska Native, non-Hispanic/Latino; 66 Asian, non-Hispanic/Latino; 23 Hispanic/Latino; 3 Two or more races, non-Hispanic/Latino), 13 international. Average age 25. 4,514 applicants, 24% accepted, 186 enrolled. In 2011, 2 master's, 231 doctorates awarded. *Entrance requirements:* For master's, JD or international equivalent; for doctorate, LSAT, baccalaureate degree. Additional exam requirements/recommendations for international students: Required—TOEFL (minimum score 600 paper-based; 250 computer-based; 100 iBT), IELTS. *Application deadline:* For fall admission, 4/1 for domestic and international students. Applications are processed on a rolling basis. Application fee: $35. Electronic applications accepted. Application fee is waived when completed online. *Expenses:* Contact institution. *Financial support:* In 2011–12, 1 fellowship with full tuition reimbursement (averaging $38,112 per year) was awarded; career-related internships or fieldwork, scholarships/grants, health care benefits, and tuition waivers (partial) also available. Support available to part-time students. Financial award applicants required to submit FAFSA. *Faculty research:* Law and economics; neuroeconomics; infrastructure protection, including homeland and national security; intellectual property. *Unit head:* Daniel D. Polsby, Dean, 703-993-8006, Fax: 703-993-8088. *Application contact:* Alison H. Price, Associate Dean/Director of Admission, 703-993-8010, Fax: 703-993-8088, E-mail: lawadmit@gmu.edu. Web site: http://www.law.gmu.edu/.

Georgetown University, Graduate School of Arts and Sciences, Department of Government, Washington, DC 20057. Offers American government (MA, PhD); comparative government (PhD); conflict resolution (MA); democracy and governance (MA); international law and government (MA); international relations (PhD); political theory (PhD); MA/PhD. Terminal master's awarded for partial completion of doctoral program. *Degree requirements:* For master's, one foreign language, comprehensive exam; for doctorate, one foreign language, comprehensive exam, thesis/dissertation. *Entrance requirements:* For master's, GRE General Test, minimum B average; for doctorate, GRE General Test, MA. Additional exam requirements/recommendations for international students: Required—TOEFL. *Faculty research:* Western Europe, Latin America, the Middle East, political theory, international relations and law, methodology, American politics and institutions.

Georgetown University, Law Center, Washington, DC 20001. Offers global health law (LL M); individualized study (LL M); international business and economic law (LL M); law (JD, SJD); national security law (LL M); securities and financial regulation (LL M); taxation (LL M); JD/LL M; JD/MA; JD/MBA; JD/MPH; JD/PhD. *Accreditation:* ABA. Part-time and evening/weekend programs available. *Degree requirements:* For master's, thesis; for doctorate, thesis/dissertation (for some programs). *Entrance requirements:* For master's, JD, LL B, or first law degree earned in country of origin; for doctorate, LSAT (for JD). Additional exam requirements/recommendations for international students: Required—TOEFL. *Expenses:* Contact institution. *Faculty research:* Constitutional law, legal history, jurisprudence.

The George Washington University, Law School, Washington, DC 20052. Offers LL M, JD, SJD, JD/MA, JD/MBA, JD/MPA, JD/MPH, LL M/MA, LL M/MPH. *Accreditation:* ABA. Part-time and evening/weekend programs available. *Faculty:* 84 full-time (33 women), 197 part-time/adjunct (59 women). *Students:* 1,659 full-time (773 women), 435 part-time (153 women); includes 461 minority (115 Black or African American, non-Hispanic/Latino; 6 American Indian or Alaska Native, non-Hispanic/Latino; 187 Asian, non-Hispanic/Latino; 144 Hispanic/Latino; 5 Native Hawaiian or other Pacific Islander, non-Hispanic/Latino; 4 Two or more races, non-Hispanic/Latino), 121 international. Average age 27. 9,510 applicants, 30% accepted, 685 enrolled. In 2011, 224 master's, 517 doctorates awarded. *Degree requirements:* For doctorate, thesis/dissertation (for some programs). *Entrance requirements:* For master's, JD or equivalent; for doctorate, LSAT (for JD), LL M or equivalent (for SJD). *Application deadline:* For fall admission, 3/1 for domestic students. Applications are processed on a rolling basis. Application fee: $75. *Expenses:* Contact institution. *Financial support:* Research assistantships, career-related internships or fieldwork, Federal Work-Study, institutionally sponsored loans, scholarships/grants, and tuition waivers (full and partial) available. Support available to part-time students. Financial award application deadline: 3/1; financial award applicants required to submit CSS PROFILE or FAFSA. *Unit head:* Frederick M. Lawrence, Dean, 202-994-6288, Fax: 202-994-5157, E-mail: flawrence@law.gwu.edu. *Application contact:* Robert V. Stanek, Assistant Dean of Admissions and Financial Aid, 202-739-0648, Fax: 202-739-0624, E-mail: jd@admit.nlc.gwu.edu. Web site: http://www.law.gwu.edu/.

Georgia State University, College of Law, Atlanta, GA 30302-4037. Offers JD, JD/MA, JD/MBA, JD/MCRP, JD/MHA, JD/MPA, JD/MSHA. *Accreditation:* ABA. Part-time and evening/weekend programs available. *Entrance requirements:* For doctorate, LSAT, LSDAS, 2 letters of recommendation. Additional exam requirements/recommendations for international students: Recommended—TOEFL (minimum score 630 paper-based). Electronic applications accepted. *Expenses:* Contact institution. *Faculty research:* Tax law, criminal law, constitutional law, health law, metropolitan growth.

Golden Gate University, School of Law, San Francisco, CA 94105-2968. Offers environmental law (LL M); intellectual property law (LL M); international legal studies (LL M, SJD); law (JD); taxation (LL M); U. S. legal studies (LL M); JD/MBA; JD/PhD. *Accreditation:* ABA. Part-time and evening/weekend programs available. *Degree requirements:* For doctorate, thesis/dissertation (for some programs). *Entrance requirements:* For doctorate, LSAT (for JD). Additional exam requirements/recommendations for international students: Required—TOEFL (minimum score 600 paper-based; 250 computer-based). Electronic applications accepted. *Expenses:* Contact institution. *Faculty research:* International law, intellectual property law, environmental law, real estate, civil rights.

Gonzaga University, School of Law, Spokane, WA 99220-3528. Offers JD, JD/M Acc, JD/MBA. *Accreditation:* ABA. Part-time programs available. *Entrance requirements:* For doctorate, LSAT. *Expenses:* Contact institution. *Faculty research:* Environmental law, business law, public interest law, tax law.

Hamline University, School of Law, St. Paul, MN 55104-1284. Offers LL M, JD, JD/MANM, JD/MAOL, JD/MAPA, JD/MBA, JD/MFA, JD/MLIS. JD/MAOL offered jointly with St. Catherine University. *Accreditation:* ABA. Part-time and evening/weekend programs available. *Faculty:* 42 full-time (19 women), 52 part-time/adjunct (27 women). *Students:* 482 full-time (258 women), 135 part-time (78 women); includes 69 minority (18 Black or African American, non-Hispanic/Latino; 2 American Indian or Alaska Native, non-Hispanic/Latino; 21 Asian, non-Hispanic/Latino; 22 Hispanic/Latino; 6 Two or more races, non-Hispanic/Latino). Average age 29. 1,232 applicants, 60% accepted, 205 enrolled. In 2011, 2 master's, 110 doctorates awarded. *Entrance requirements:* For doctorate, LSAT, 2 letters of recommendation. Additional exam requirements/recommendations for international students: Required—TOEFL (minimum score 100 iBT). *Application deadline:* For fall admission, 5/1 priority date for domestic students, 5/1 for international students. Applications are processed on a rolling basis. Application fee: $35. Electronic applications accepted. *Expenses:* Contact institution. *Financial support:* In 2011–12, 366 students received support, including 30 fellowships with full and partial tuition reimbursements available (averaging $2,200 per year); career-related internships or fieldwork, Federal Work-Study, and scholarships/grants also available. Support available to part-time students. Financial award applicants required to submit FAFSA. *Faculty research:* Alternative dispute resolution, intellectual property, health law, business law, ethics/public law. *Unit head:* Donald M. Lewis, Dean, 651-523-2968, Fax: 651-523-2435, E-mail: dlewis02@hamline.edu. *Application contact:* Robin C. Ingli, Director of Admissions, 800-388-3688, Fax: 651-523-3064, E-mail: ringli@hamline.edu. Web site: http://www.hamline.edu/law/.

Harvard University, Law School, Graduate Programs in Law, Cambridge, MA 02138. Offers LL M, SJD. *Degree requirements:* For master's, thesis optional; for doctorate, thesis/dissertation. *Entrance requirements:* Additional exam requirements/recommendations for international students: Required—TOEFL. *Expenses: Tuition:* Full-time $36,304. *Required fees:* $1186. Full-time tuition and fees vary according to program. *Faculty research:* Corporation finance, national and international law, legal ethics, family law, criminal law, administrative law, constitutional law.

Harvard University, Law School, Professional Programs in Law, Cambridge, MA 02138. Offers international and comparative law (JD); law and business (JD); law and government (JD); law and social change (JD); law, science and technology (JD); JD/MALD; JD/MBA; JD/MPH; JD/MPP; JD/PhD. *Accreditation:* ABA. *Degree requirements:* For doctorate, 3rd-year paper. *Entrance requirements:* For doctorate, LSAT. *Expenses: Tuition:* Full-time $36,304. *Required fees:* $1186. Full-time tuition and fees vary according to program. *Faculty research:* Constitutional law, voting rights law, cyber law.

Hofstra University, School of Law, Hempstead, NY 11549. Offers American legal studies (LL M); family law (LL M); law (JD); JD/MBA. *Accreditation:* ABA. Part-time programs available. *Faculty:* 57 full-time (21 women), 37 part-time/adjunct (5 women). *Students:* 1,020 full-time (468 women), 76 part-time (40 women); includes 330 minority (98 Black or African American, non-Hispanic/Latino; 3 American Indian or Alaska Native, non-Hispanic/Latino; 126 Asian, non-Hispanic/Latino; 102 Hispanic/Latino; 1 Two or more races, non-Hispanic/Latino), 53 international. Average age 25. In 2011, 1 master's, 306 doctorates awarded. *Entrance requirements:* For doctorate, LSAT, letter of recommendation, personal statement, undergraduate transcripts. Additional exam requirements/recommendations for international students: Recommended—TOEFL (minimum score 600 paper-based; 250 computer-based; 100 iBT). *Application deadline:* For fall admission, 4/15 priority date for domestic students, 4/15 for international students. Applications are processed on a rolling basis. Application fee: $70 ($75 for international students). Electronic applications accepted. *Expenses:* Contact institution. *Financial support:* In 2011–12, 562 students received support, including 531 fellowships with full and partial tuition reimbursements available (averaging $23,980 per year), 1 research assistantship with full and partial tuition reimbursement available (averaging $6,075 per year); Federal Work-Study, institutionally sponsored loans, scholarships/grants, tuition waivers (full and partial), and unspecified assistantships also available. Support available to part-time students. Financial award applicants required to submit FAFSA. *Faculty research:* Commercial and corporate law, health law, gender and LGBT issues, international and comparative law, child and family advocacy. *Unit head:* Eric Lane, Interim Dean, 516-463-5854, Fax: 516-463-6264, E-mail: lawezl@hofstra.edu. *Application contact:* John Chalmers, Director of Law School Enrollment Operations, 516-463-5791, Fax: 516-463-6264, E-mail: lawadmissions@hofstra.edu. Web site: http://law.hofstra.edu/.

Howard University, School of Law, Washington, DC 20008. Offers LL M, JD, JD/MBA. *Accreditation:* ABA. *Degree requirements:* For master's, one foreign language, thesis; for doctorate, thesis/dissertation (for some programs). *Entrance requirements:* For doctorate, LSAT. Additional exam requirements/recommendations for international students: Required—TOEFL. Electronic applications accepted. *Expenses:* Contact institution. *Faculty research:* Criminal law, family law, telecommunications, religion, antitrust.

Humphreys College, Laurence Drivon School of Law, Stockton, CA 95207-3896. Offers JD. Part-time and evening/weekend programs available. *Entrance requirements:* For doctorate, LSAT, minimum GPA of 2.5. Electronic applications accepted.

Illinois Institute of Technology, Chicago-Kent College of Law, Chicago, IL 60661-3691. Offers family law (LL M); financial services (LL M); international intellectual property (LL M); international law (LL M); law (JD); taxation (LL M); JD/LL M; JD/MBA; JD/MPA; JD/MPH; JD/MS. *Accreditation:* ABA. Part-time and evening/weekend programs available. *Entrance requirements:* For doctorate, LSAT, LSDAS. Additional exam requirements/recommendations for international students: Required—TOEFL (minimum score 600 paper-based; 250 computer-based; 100 iBT); Recommended—IELTS (minimum score 7). Electronic applications accepted. *Expenses:* Contact institution. *Faculty research:* Constitutional law, bioethics, environmental law.

Indiana University Bloomington, Maurer School of Law, Bloomington, IN 47405-7000. Offers comparative law (MCL); juridical science (SJD); law (LL M, JD); law and social sciences (PhD); legal studies (Certificate); JD/MA; JD/MBA; JD/MLS; JD/MPA; JD/MS; JD/MSES. PhD offered through University Graduate School. *Accreditation:* ABA. *Faculty:* 72 full-time (28 women), 14 part-time/adjunct (4 women). *Students:* 762 full-time (290 women), 43 part-time (16 women); includes 109 minority (41 Black or African American, non-Hispanic/Latino; 1 American Indian or Alaska Native, non-Hispanic/Latino; 27 Asian, non-Hispanic/Latino; 38 Hispanic/Latino; 2 Two or more races, non-Hispanic/Latino), 142 international. Average age 26. 2,171 applicants, 23% accepted, 228 enrolled. In 2011, 76 master's, 185 doctorates, 1 other advanced degree awarded. *Degree requirements:* For master's, thesis or practicum; for doctorate, thesis/dissertation (for some programs), research seminar (for JD). *Entrance requirements:* For master's, LSAT, 3 letters of recommendation, law degree or license to practice; for doctorate, LSAT. Additional exam requirements/recommendations for international students: Required—TOEFL (minimum score 560 paper-based; 213 computer-based; 80 iBT). *Application deadline:* For fall admission, 3/1 priority date for domestic students, 3/1 for international students. Applications are processed on a rolling basis. Application fee: $55 ($65 for international students). Electronic applications accepted. *Financial support:* In 2011–12, 301 students received support, including 278 fellowships (averaging $16,000 per year), 1 research assistantship (averaging $15,217 per year), 2 teaching assistantships (averaging $14,000 per year); career-related internships or fieldwork, Federal Work-Study, institutionally sponsored loans, scholarships/grants, health care benefits, and unspecified assistantships also available. Financial award application deadline: 3/1; financial award applicants required to submit FAFSA. *Faculty research:* Environmental risk assessment and policy analysis, information privacy and security, judicial independence, accountability, ethics. *Total annual research expenditures:* $1.4 million. *Unit head:* Lauren K. Robel, Dean, 812-855-8885, Fax: 812-855-7057, E-mail: lrobel@indiana.edu. *Application contact:* Kelly M. Compton, Director of Admissions, 812-855-2704, Fax: 812-855-0555, E-mail: kmcompto@indiana.edu. Web site: http://www.law.indiana.edu/.

Indiana University–Purdue University Indianapolis, School of Law, Indianapolis, IN 46202-2896. Offers LL M, JD, SJD, JD/M Phil, JD/MBA, JD/MHA, JD/MLS, JD/MPA, JD/MPH, JD/MSW. *Accreditation:* ABA. *Faculty:* 1 (woman) full-time. *Students:* 685 full-time (301 women), 389 part-time (170 women); includes 151 minority (62 Black or African American, non-Hispanic/Latino; 2 American Indian or Alaska Native, non-Hispanic/Latino; 44 Asian, non-Hispanic/Latino; 31 Hispanic/Latino; 12 Two or more races, non-Hispanic/Latino), 123 international. Average age 28. 530 applicants, 88% accepted, 316 enrolled. In 2011, 120 master's, 247 doctorates awarded. *Entrance requirements:* Additional exam requirements/recommendations for international students: Required—TOEFL. Application fee: $55 ($65 for international students). *Financial support:* Fellowships, research assistantships with full and partial tuition reimbursements, Federal Work-Study, institutionally sponsored loans, and scholarships/grants available. Support available to part-time students. Financial award applicants required to submit FAFSA. *Unit head:* Susanah M. Mead, Interim Dean, 317-274-8523. *Application contact:* Patricia Kinney, Director of Admissions, 317-274-2459, Fax: 317-278-4780, E-mail: pkkinney@iupui.edu. Web site: http://indylaw.indiana.edu.

Instituto Tecnológico y de Estudios Superiores de Monterrey, Campus Ciudad de México, School of Humanities and Social Sciences, Ciudad de Mexico, Mexico. Offers LL B. Part-time and evening/weekend programs available. *Entrance requirements:* For degree, Instituto entrance exam. Additional exam requirements/recommendations for international students: Required—TOEFL. *Faculty research:* Law; politics; international relations.

Inter American University of Puerto Rico School of Law, Professional Program, San Juan, PR 00936-8351. Offers JD. *Accreditation:* ABA. Part-time and evening/weekend programs available. *Entrance requirements:* For doctorate, LSAT, PAEG, minimum GPA of 2.5. *Expenses:* Contact institution.

John F. Kennedy University, School of Law, Pleasant Hill, CA 94523-4817. Offers JD. Part-time and evening/weekend programs available. *Entrance requirements:* For doctorate, LSAT, interview. Additional exam requirements/recommendations for international students: Required—TOEFL. *Expenses:* Contact institution.

John Marshall Law School, Graduate and Professional Programs, Chicago, IL 60604-3968. Offers employee benefits (LL M, MS); global legal studies (LL M); information technology (MS); information technology and privacy law (LL M); intellectual property (LL M, MS); international business and trade (LL M); law (JD); real estate (LL M, MS); taxation (LL M, MS); trial advocacy (LL M); JD/LL M; JD/MA; JD/MBA; JD/MPA. JD/MBA offered jointly with Dominican University; JD/MA and JD/MPA with Roosevelt University. *Accreditation:* ABA. Part-time and evening/weekend programs available. *Faculty:* 69 full-time (22 women), 133 part-time/adjunct (40 women). *Students:* 1,305 full-time (598 women), 368 part-time (180 women); includes 385 minority (148 Black or African American, non-Hispanic/Latino; 15 American Indian or Alaska Native, non-Hispanic/Latino; 108 Asian, non-Hispanic/Latino; 110 Hispanic/Latino; 2 Native Hawaiian or other Pacific Islander, non-Hispanic/Latino; 2 Two or more races, non-Hispanic/Latino), 40 international. Average age 27. 3,513 applicants, 48% accepted, 365 enrolled. In 2011, 86 master's, 403 doctorates awarded. *Degree requirements:* For master's, 24 credits; for doctorate, 90 credits. *Entrance requirements:* For master's, JD; for doctorate, LSAT. Additional exam requirements/recommendations for international students: Required—TOEFL. *Application deadline:* For fall admission, 3/1 priority date for domestic students, 3/1 for international students; for spring admission, 10/15 priority date for domestic students, 10/15 for international students. Applications are processed on a rolling basis. Application fee: $0. Electronic applications accepted. *Expenses:* Contact institution. *Financial support:* In 2011–12, 1,350 students received support. Scholarships/grants and tuition waivers (full and partial) available. Support available to part-time students. Financial award application deadline: 6/1; financial award applicants required to submit FAFSA. *Unit head:* John Corkery, Dean, 312-427-2737. *Application contact:* William B. Powers, Associate Dean of Admission and Student Affairs, 800-537-4280, Fax: 312-427-5136, E-mail: admission@jmls.edu.

The Judge Advocate General's School, U.S. Army, Graduate Programs, Charlottesville, VA 22903-1781. Offers military law (LL M). Only active duty military lawyers attend this school. *Accreditation:* ABA. *Degree requirements:* For master's, thesis optional. *Entrance requirements:* For master's, active duty military lawyer, international military officer, or DOD civilian attorney, JD or LL B. *Faculty research:* Criminal law, administrative and civil law, contract law, international law, legal research and writing.

Kaplan University, Davenport Campus, School of Criminal Justice, Davenport, IA 52807-2095. Offers corrections (MSCJ); global issues in criminal justice (MSCJ); law (MSCJ); leadership and executive management (MSCJ); policing (MSCJ). Part-time and evening/weekend programs available. Postbaccalaureate distance learning degree programs offered (no on-campus study). *Entrance requirements:* Additional exam requirements/recommendations for international students: Required—TOEFL (minimum score 550 paper-based; 218 computer-based; 80 iBT). Electronic applications accepted.

Lewis & Clark College, Lewis & Clark Law School, Portland, OR 97219. Offers environmental and natural resources law (LL M); law (JD). *Accreditation:* ABA. Part-time and evening/weekend programs available. *Entrance requirements:* For doctorate, LSAT. Additional exam requirements/recommendations for international students: Recommended—TOEFL (minimum score 600 paper-based; 250 computer-based). Electronic applications accepted. *Expenses:* Contact institution.

Liberty University, School of Law, Lynchburg, VA 24502. Offers JD. *Accreditation:* ABA. *Students:* 289 full-time (101 women); includes 27 minority (7 Black or African American, non-Hispanic/Latino; 1 American Indian or Alaska Native, non-Hispanic/Latino; 6 Asian, non-Hispanic/Latino; 5 Hispanic/Latino; 1 Native Hawaiian or other Pacific Islander, non-Hispanic/Latino; 7 Two or more races, non-Hispanic/Latino), 7 international. Average age 28. *Entrance requirements:* For doctorate, LSAT, 2 letters of recommendation, interview, subscription to LSDAS. Additional exam requirements/recommendations for international students: Required—TOEFL (minimum score 600 paper-based; 250 computer-based; 100 iBT). *Application deadline:* For fall admission, 6/1 for domestic students. Application fee: $50. Electronic applications accepted. *Unit head:* Mathew D. Staver, Dean, 434-592-5300, Fax: 434-592-5400, E-mail: law@liberty.edu. *Application contact:* Joleen Thaxton, Assistant Director of Admissions, 434-592-5300, Fax: 434-592-5400, E-mail: lawadmissions@liberty.edu.

Lincoln Memorial University, Duncan School of Law, Harrogate, TN 37752-1901. Offers JD. Part-time programs available. *Entrance requirements:* For doctorate, LSAT. Additional exam requirements/recommendations for international students: Required—TOEFL (minimum score 500 paper-based). Electronic applications accepted. *Expenses:* Contact institution.

Louisiana State University and Agricultural and Mechanical College, Paul M. Hebert Law Center, Baton Rouge, LA 70803. Offers LL M, JD. *Accreditation:* ABA; SACS. *Faculty:* 46 full-time (14 women), 52 part-time/adjunct (5 women). *Students:* 676 full-time (298 women), 19 part-time (5 women); includes 152 minority (71 Black or African American, non-Hispanic/Latino; 5 American Indian or Alaska Native, non-Hispanic/Latino; 21 Asian, non-Hispanic/Latino; 43 Hispanic/Latino; 12 Two or more races, non-Hispanic/Latino), 9 international. Average age 26. 1,437 applicants, 44% accepted, 239 enrolled. In 2011, 7 master's, 173 doctorates awarded. *Degree requirements:* For master's, thesis. *Entrance requirements:* For doctorate, LSAT. Additional exam requirements/recommendations for international students: Required—TOEFL (minimum score 600 paper-based; 250 computer-based; 100 iBT). *Application deadline:* For fall admission, 3/1 priority date for domestic students, 3/1 for international students. Applications are processed on a rolling basis. Application fee: $50. Electronic applications accepted. *Expenses:* Contact institution. *Financial support:* Scholarships/grants and tuition waivers (full and partial) available. Financial award applicants required to submit FAFSA. *Unit head:* Jack M. Weiss, Chancellor, 225-578-8491, Fax: 225-578-8202, E-mail: jack.weiss@law.lsu.edu. *Application contact:* Jake T. Henry, III, Director of Admissions, 225-578-8646, Fax: 225-578-8647, E-mail: jake.henry@law.lsu.edu. Web site: http://www.law.lsu.edu/.

Loyola Marymount University, College of Business Administration, MBA/JD Program, Los Angeles, CA 90045-2659. Offers MBA/JD. Part-time programs available. *Faculty:* 42 full-time (13 women), 11 part-time/adjunct (2 women). *Students:* 2 full-time (0 women), 7 part-time (1 woman); includes 2 minority (1 Black or African American, non-Hispanic/Latino; 1 Hispanic/Latino). Average age 25. 8 applicants, 63% accepted, 5 enrolled. *Entrance requirements:* Additional exam requirements/recommendations for international students: Required—TOEFL (minimum score 600 paper-based; 250 computer-based; 100 iBT). *Application deadline:* For spring admission, 6/30 for domestic students. Application fee: $75. Electronic applications accepted. *Expenses:* Contact institution. *Financial support:* In 2011–12, 2 students received support. Scholarships/grants and unspecified assistantships available. Financial award application deadline: 6/30; financial award applicants required to submit FAFSA. *Unit head:* Dr. Dennis Draper, Dean, 310-338-7504, E-mail: ddraper@lmu.edu. *Application contact:* Chake H. Kouyoumjian, Associate Dean of the Graduate Division, 310-338-2721, E-mail: ckouyoum@lmu.edu. Web site: http://www.lls.edu/academics/jd/jdmba.html.

Loyola Marymount University, Loyola Law School Los Angeles, Los Angeles, CA 90015. Offers law (JD); taxation (LL M); JD/LL M; JD/MBA. *Accreditation:* ABA. Part-time and evening/weekend programs available. *Faculty:* 74 full-time (35 women), 55 part-time/adjunct (13 women). *Students:* 1,021 full-time (533 women), 258 part-time (106 women); includes 953 minority (51 Black or African American, non-Hispanic/Latino; 8 American Indian or Alaska Native, non-Hispanic/Latino; 259 Asian, non-Hispanic/Latino; 163 Hispanic/Latino; 4 Native Hawaiian or other Pacific Islander, non-Hispanic/Latino; 468 Two or more races, non-Hispanic/Latino). Average age 26. 6,781 applicants, 24% accepted, 391 enrolled. In 2011, 23 master's, 403 doctorates awarded. *Entrance requirements:* For master's, JD; for doctorate, LSAT. *Application deadline:* For fall admission, 2/1 for domestic and international students. Applications are processed on a rolling basis. Application fee: $65. Electronic applications accepted. *Financial support:* Research assistantships, Federal Work-Study, and scholarships/grants available. Financial award application deadline: 3/11; financial award applicants required to submit FAFSA. *Unit head:* Victor Gold, Dean, 213-736-1062, Fax: 213-487-6736, E-mail: victor.gold@lls.edu. *Application contact:* Jannell Lundy Roberts, Assistant Dean, Admissions, 213-736-1074, Fax: 213-736-6523, E-mail: admissions@lls.edu. Web site: http://www.lls.edu/.

Loyola University Chicago, School of Law, Chicago, IL 60611. Offers advocacy (LL M); business and corporate governance law (MJ); business law (LL M, MJ); child and family law (LL M); children's law and policy (MJ); health law (LL M, MJ); health law and policy (D Law, SJD); international law (LL M); law (JD); rule of law development (LL M); tax law (LL M); U. S. law for foreign lawyers (LL M); JD/MA; JD/MBA; JD/MSW; MJ/MSW. *Accreditation:* ABA. Part-time and evening/weekend programs available. Postbaccalaureate distance learning degree programs offered (minimal on-campus study). *Faculty:* 48 full-time (17 women), 129 part-time/adjunct (60 women). *Students:* 857 full-time (434 women), 9 part-time (3 women); includes 201 minority (77 Black or African American, non-Hispanic/Latino; 1 American Indian or Alaska Native, non-Hispanic/Latino; 40 Asian, non-Hispanic/Latino; 63 Hispanic/Latino; 20 Two or more races, non-Hispanic/Latino), 11 international. Average age 25. 5,040 applicants, 34% accepted, 271 enrolled. *Entrance requirements:* Additional exam requirements/recommendations for international students: Required—TOEFL (minimum score 550 paper-based; 79 iBT), IELTS (minimum score 6.5). *Application deadline:* For fall admission, 3/1 for domestic students. Applications are processed on a rolling basis. Application fee: $0. Electronic applications accepted. *Expenses: Tuition:* Full-time $15,660; part-time $870 per credit hour. *Required fees:* $125 per semester. Tuition and fees vary according to course load and program. *Unit head:* Pamela Bloomquist, Assistant Dean for Admission and Financial Assistance, Law School, 312-915-7170, Fax: 312-915-7906, E-mail: ploom@luc.edu. *Application contact:* Ronald P. Martin, Associate Director, Graduate and Professional Enrollment Management Operations, 312-915-8951, E-mail: rmarti7@luc.edu. Web site: http://www.luc.edu/law/.

Loyola University New Orleans, College of Law, New Orleans, LA 70118. Offers LL M, JD, JD/MBA, JD/MPA, JD/MURP. *Accreditation:* ABA. Part-time and evening/weekend programs available. *Students:* 695 full-time (357 women), 129 part-time (55 women); includes 233 minority (101 Black or African American, non-Hispanic/Latino; 9 American Indian or Alaska Native, non-Hispanic/Latino; 25 Asian, non-Hispanic/Latino; 87 Hispanic/Latino; 1 Native Hawaiian or other Pacific Islander, non-Hispanic/Latino; 10 Two or more races, non-Hispanic/Latino), 6 international. Average age 27. 1,811 applicants, 46% accepted, 197 enrolled. In 2011, 5 master's, 260 doctorates awarded. *Entrance requirements:* For doctorate, LSAT, letters of recommendation, interview, resume. Additional exam requirements/recommendations for international students: Recommended—TOEFL (minimum score 550 paper-based; 213 computer-based). *Application deadline:* For fall admission, 2/1 priority date for domestic students, 2/1 for international students. Applications are processed on a rolling basis. Application fee: $40. Electronic applications accepted. *Expenses:* Contact institution. *Financial support:* Research assistantships, teaching assistantships, career-related internships or fieldwork, and scholarships/grants available. Support available to part-time students. Financial award application deadline: 5/1; financial award applicants required to submit FAFSA. *Faculty research:* Louisiana civil code, international law, commercial law, comparative law. *Unit head:* Dr. Maria Lopez, Dean of the College of Law, 504-861-5405, Fax: 504-861-5739, E-mail: mlopez@loyno.edu. *Application contact:* Michele K. Allison-Davis, Assistant Dean, Admissions, 504-861-5575, Fax: 504-861-5772, E-mail: maldavis@loyno.edu. Web site: http://www.loyno.edu/law/.

Marquette University, Law School, Milwaukee, WI 53201-1881. Offers JD, JD/Certificate, JD/MA, JD/MBA. *Accreditation:* ABA. Part-time and evening/weekend programs available. *Faculty:* 41 full-time (18 women), 26 part-time/adjunct (12 women). *Students:* 608 full-time (255 women), 121 part-time (63 women); includes 132 minority (37 Black or African American, non-Hispanic/Latino; 2 American Indian or Alaska Native, non-Hispanic/Latino; 25 Asian, non-Hispanic/Latino; 51 Hispanic/Latino; 2 Native Hawaiian or other Pacific Islander, non-Hispanic/Latino; 15 Two or more races, non-Hispanic/Latino), 2 international. Average age 27. 2,005 applicants, 21% accepted, 213 enrolled. In 2011, 230 doctorates awarded. *Entrance requirements:* For doctorate, LSAT, subscription to LSAC's Credential Assembly Service. Additional exam requirements/recommendations for international students: Required—TOEFL. *Application deadline:* For fall admission, 4/1 for domestic students. Applications are processed on a rolling basis. Application fee: $50. Electronic applications accepted. *Expenses:* Contact institution. *Financial support:* Career-related internships or fieldwork, Federal Work-Study, and scholarships/grants available. Support available to part-time students. Financial award application deadline: 3/1; financial award applicants required to submit FAFSA. *Faculty research:* Constitutional law, sports law, dispute resolution, intellectual property, legal ethics. *Unit head:* Joseph D. Kearney, Dean, 414-288-7090, Fax: 414-288-6403, E-mail: joseph.kearney@marquette.edu. *Application contact:* Sean Reilly, Assistant Dean for Admissions, 414-288-6767, Fax: 414-288-0676, E-mail: sean.reilly@marquette.edu. Web site: http://law.marquette.edu/.

Massachusetts School of Law at Andover, Professional Program, Andover, MA 01810. Offers JD. Part-time and evening/weekend programs available. *Entrance requirements:* For doctorate, Massachusetts School of Law Aptitude Test (MSLAT), interview. Additional exam requirements/recommendations for international students: Recommended—TOEFL. Electronic applications accepted.

McGill University, Faculty of Graduate and Postdoctoral Studies, Faculty of Law, Department of Law, Montréal, QC H3A 2T5, Canada. Offers LL M, DCL.

McGill University, Faculty of Graduate and Postdoctoral Studies, Faculty of Law, Institute of Air and Space Law, Montréal, QC H3A 2T5, Canada. Offers LL M, DCL, Graduate Certificate.

McGill University, Faculty of Graduate and Postdoctoral Studies, Faculty of Law, Institute of Comparative Law, Montréal, QC H3A 2T5, Canada. Offers LL M, DCL, Graduate Certificate.

Mercer University, Walter F. George School of Law, Macon, GA 31207. Offers JD, JD/MBA. *Accreditation:* ABA. Part-time programs available. *Entrance requirements:* For doctorate, LSAT. Electronic applications accepted. *Expenses:* Contact institution. *Faculty research:* Legal ethics, environmental law, employment discrimination, statutory law, legal writing.

Michigan State University College of Law, Professional Program, East Lansing, MI 48824-1300. Offers American legal system (LL M); intellectual property (LL M); jurisprudence (MJ); law (JD). *Accreditation:* ABA. Part-time programs available. *Faculty:* 56 full-time (26 women), 80 part-time/adjunct (20 women). *Students:* 769 full-time (364 women), 199 part-time (99 women); includes 193 minority (71 Black or African American, non-Hispanic/Latino; 17 American Indian or Alaska Native, non-Hispanic/Latino; 32 Asian, non-Hispanic/Latino; 45 Hispanic/Latino; 4 Native Hawaiian or other Pacific Islander, non-Hispanic/Latino; 24 Two or more races, non-Hispanic/Latino), 97 international. Average age 26. 3,732 applicants, 32% accepted, 307 enrolled. In 2011, 302 doctorates awarded. *Entrance requirements:* For doctorate, LSAT. Additional exam requirements/recommendations for international students: Required—TOEFL (minimum score 600 paper-based; 250 computer-based). *Application deadline:* For fall admission, 4/30 priority date for domestic students, 7/1 for international students. Applications are processed on a rolling basis. Application fee: $60. Electronic applications accepted. *Expenses:* Contact institution. *Financial support:* In 2011–12, 351 students received support, including 300 fellowships (averaging $29,712 per year); career-related internships or fieldwork, Federal Work-Study, institutionally sponsored loans, scholarships/grants, and tuition waivers (full) also available. Support available to part-time students. Financial award application deadline: 4/15; financial award applicants required to submit FAFSA. *Faculty research:* International, Constitutional, health, tax and environmental law; intellectual property, trial practice, corporate law. *Unit head:* Joan W. Howarth, Dean and Professor of Law, 517-432-6993, Fax: 517-432-6801, E-mail: howarth@law.msu.edu. *Application contact:* Charles Roboski, Assistant Dean of Admissions, 517-432-0222, Fax: 517-432-0098, E-mail: roboski@law.msu.edu. Web site: http://www.law.msu.edu/.

Mississippi College, School of Law, Jackson, MS 39201. Offers civil law studies (Certificate); law (JD); JD/MBA. *Accreditation:* ABA. *Degree requirements:* For doctorate, thesis/dissertation. *Entrance requirements:* For doctorate, LSAT, LDAS report. Additional exam requirements/recommendations for international students: Recommended—TOEFL, IELTS. Electronic applications accepted. *Expenses:* Contact institution.

Montclair State University, The Graduate School, College of Humanities and Social Sciences, MA Program in Law and Governance, Montclair, NJ 07043-1624. Offers conflict management and peace studies (MA); governance, compliance and regulation (MA); intellectual property (MA); law and governance (MA); legal management (MA). Part-time and evening/weekend programs available. *Faculty:* 13 full-time (6 women), 25 part-time/adjunct (8 women). *Students:* 11 full-time (6 women), 23 part-time (13 women); includes 17 minority (8 Black or African American, non-Hispanic/Latino; 2 Asian, non-Hispanic/Latino; 5 Hispanic/Latino; 2 Two or more races, non-Hispanic/Latino), 2 international. Average age 30. 32 applicants, 44% accepted, 10 enrolled. In 2011, 16 master's awarded. *Degree requirements:* For master's, thesis or comprehensive exam. *Entrance requirements:* For master's, GRE General Test, minimum cumulative GPA of 2.75 for undergraduate work, 2 letters of recommendation, essay. Additional exam requirements/recommendations for international students: Required—TOEFL (minimum score 83 iBT) or IELTS (minimum score 6.5). *Application deadline:* Applications are processed on a rolling basis. Application fee: $60. Electronic applications accepted. *Financial support:* In 2011–12, 1 research assistantship with full tuition reimbursement (averaging $7,000 per year) was awarded; Federal Work-Study, scholarships/grants, and unspecified assistantships also available. Support available to part-time students. Financial award application deadline: 3/1; financial award applicants required to submit FAFSA. *Unit head:* Dr. William Berlin, Chair, 973-655-7576, E-mail: berlinw@mail.montclair.edu. *Application contact:* Amy Aiello, Director of Graduate Admissions and Operations, 973-655-5147, Fax: 973-655-7869, E-mail: graduate.school@montclair.edu. Web site: http://www.montclair.edu/graduate/programs-of-study/law-and-governance/.

New England Law–Boston, Professional Program, Boston, MA 02116-5687. Offers advanced legal studies (LL M); law (JD). *Accreditation:* ABA. Part-time and evening/weekend programs available. *Faculty:* 34 full-time (10 women), 72 part-time/adjunct (27 women). *Students:* 810 full-time (477 women), 321 part-time (165 women); includes 113 minority (16 Black or African American, non-Hispanic/Latino; 49 Asian, non-Hispanic/Latino; 26 Hispanic/Latino; 22 Two or more races, non-Hispanic/Latino), 7 international. 2,934 applicants, 72% accepted, 385 enrolled. *Entrance requirements:* For doctorate, LSAT, LSDAS. Additional exam requirements/recommendations for international students: Required—TOEFL (minimum score 600 paper-based; 250 computer-based; 100 iBT). *Application deadline:* For fall admission, 3/15 for domestic students. Applications are processed on a rolling basis. Application fee: $65. Electronic applications accepted. *Expenses: Tuition:* Full-time $40,904; part-time $30,680 per year. *Required fees:* $80 per year. Tuition and fees vary according to class time and student level. *Financial support:* In 2011–12, 654 students received support. Federal Work-Study, scholarships/grants, and tuition waivers (full and partial) available. Support available to part-time students. Financial award application deadline: 3/25; financial award applicants required to submit FAFSA. *Unit head:* John F. O'Brien, Dean, 617-422-7221, Fax: 617-422-7333. *Application contact:* Michelle L'Etoile, Director of Admissions, 617-422-7210, Fax: 617-422-7201, E-mail: admit@nesl.edu.

New York Law School, Graduate Programs, New York, NY 10013. Offers financial services (LL M); law (JD); mental disability law (MA); real estate (LL M); taxation (LL M); JD/MA; JD/MBA. JD/MBA offered jointly with Bernard M. Baruch College of the City University of New York; JD/MA in forensic psychology offered jointly with John Jay College of Criminal Justice of the City University of New York. *Accreditation:* ABA. Part-time and evening/weekend programs available. Postbaccalaureate distance learning degree programs offered (minimal on-campus study). *Faculty:* 103 full-time (45 women), 118 part-time/adjunct (42 women). *Students:* 1,416 full-time (760 women), 456 part-time (204 women); includes 476 minority (134 Black or African American, non-Hispanic/Latino; 5 American Indian or Alaska Native, non-Hispanic/Latino; 74 Asian, non-Hispanic/Latino; 243 Hispanic/Latino; 1 Native Hawaiian or other Pacific Islander, non-Hispanic/Latino; 19 Two or more races, non-Hispanic/Latino). Average age 27. 6,058 applicants, 44% accepted, 519 enrolled. In 2011, 37 master's, 515 doctorates awarded. *Entrance requirements:* For master's, JD (for LL M ; for doctorate, LSAT, letters of recommendation, resume. Additional exam requirements/recommendations for international students: Recommended—TOEFL (minimum score 600 paper-based; 250 computer-based; 100 iBT). *Application deadline:* For fall admission, 4/1 priority date for domestic students, 4/1 for international students. Applications are processed on a rolling basis. Application fee: $0. Electronic applications accepted. *Expenses: Tuition:* Full-time $46,200; part-time $35,600 per year. *Required fees:* $1600; $1300 per year. Tuition and fees vary according to degree level and student level. *Financial support:* In 2011–12, 588 students received support, including 34 fellowships (averaging $3,010 per year), 229 research assistantships (averaging $4,322 per year), 17 teaching assistantships (averaging $4,278 per year); career-related internships or fieldwork, Federal Work-Study, institutionally sponsored loans, and scholarships/grants also available. Support available to part-time students. Financial award application deadline: 4/1; financial award applicants required to submit FAFSA. *Unit head:* Carol A. Buckler, Interim Dean, 212-431-2840, Fax: 212-219-3752, E-mail: cbuckler@nyls.edu. *Application contact:* Susan W. Gross, Senior Director of Admissions and Financial Aid, 212-431-2888, Fax: 212-966-1522, E-mail: sgross@nyls.edu. Web site: http://www.nyls.edu.

See Display on next page and Close-Up on page 1627.

New York University, School of Law, New York, NY 10012-1019. Offers law (LL M, JD, JSD); law and business (Advanced Certificate); taxation (Advanced Certificate); JD/LL B; JD/LL M; JD/MA; JD/MBA; JD/MPA; JD/MPP; JD/MSW; JD/MUP; JD/PhD. *Accreditation:* ABA. Part-time programs available. *Entrance requirements:* For doctorate, LSAT (for JD). Electronic applications accepted. *Expenses:* Contact institution. *Faculty research:* International law, environmental law, corporate law, globalization of law, philosophy of law.

North Carolina Central University, Division of Academic Affairs, School of Law, Durham, NC 27707. Offers JD, JD/MLS. *Accreditation:* ABA. Part-time and evening/weekend programs available. *Entrance requirements:* For doctorate, LSAT, LSDAS. Additional exam requirements/recommendations for international students: Required—TOEFL. *Expenses:* Contact institution.

Northeastern University, School of Law, Boston, MA 02115-5005. Offers JD, JD/MA, JD/MBA, JD/MPH, JD/MS/MBA, JD/PhD. JD/MPH offered jointly with Tufts University; JD/MS/MBA with Graduate School of Professional Accounting; JD/PhD with Program in Law, Policy, and Society; JD with Vermont Law School and Brandeis University. *Accreditation:* ABA. *Faculty:* 35 full-time (18 women), 33 part-time/adjunct (15 women). *Students:* 629 full-time (375 women). Average age 26. 4,316 applicants, 32% accepted, 220 enrolled. In 2011, 192 doctorates awarded. *Degree requirements:* For doctorate, recommendation of faculty, 103 quarter hours of academic credit, four quarters of cooperative work under the supervision of an attorney, fulfillment of the public interest graduation requirement. *Entrance requirements:* For doctorate, LSAT, personal statement; resume; two recommendations; current CAS report (including transcripts from all academic institutions attended). Additional exam requirements/recommendations for international students: Required—TOEFL (minimum score 600 paper-based; 100 iBT). *Application deadline:* For fall admission, 3/1 for domestic and international students. Applications are processed on a rolling basis. Application fee: $75. Electronic applications accepted. *Expenses:* Contact institution. *Financial support:* In 2011–12, 534 students received support, including 48 fellowships (averaging $3,000 per year), 18 research assistantships (averaging $869 per year), 18 teaching assistantships (averaging $565 per year); career-related internships or fieldwork, Federal Work-Study, institutionally sponsored loans, scholarships/grants, and tuition waivers (full and partial) also available. Financial award application deadline: 2/15; financial award applicants required to submit FAFSA. *Faculty research:* Human rights, health, criminal, corporate/finance, international. *Unit head:* Emily A. Spieler, Dean, 617-373-3307, Fax: 617-373-8793, E-mail: e.spieler@neu.edu. *Application contact:* Information Contact, 617-373-2395, Fax: 617-373-8865, E-mail: lawadmissions@neu.edu. Web site: http://www.northeastern.edu/law/.

Northern Illinois University, College of Law, De Kalb, IL 60115-2854. Offers JD. *Accreditation:* ABA. Part-time programs available. *Faculty:* 22 full-time (11 women). *Students:* 318 full-time (138 women), 1 part-time; includes 67 minority (27 Black or African American, non-Hispanic/Latino; 1 American Indian or Alaska Native, non-Hispanic/Latino; 10 Asian, non-Hispanic/Latino; 24 Hispanic/Latino; 2 Native Hawaiian or other Pacific Islander, non-Hispanic/Latino; 3 Two or more races, non-Hispanic/Latino), 1 international. Average age 26. 1,074 applicants, 44% accepted, 103 enrolled. In 2011, 87 doctorates awarded. *Entrance requirements:* For doctorate, LSAT. Additional exam requirements/recommendations for international students: Required—TOEFL. *Application deadline:* For fall admission, 5/15 priority date for domestic students, 5/15 for international students. Applications are processed on a rolling basis. Application fee: $50. Electronic applications accepted. *Expenses:* Contact institution. *Financial support:* In 2011–12, 4 teaching assistantships were awarded; research assistantships, career-related internships or fieldwork, Federal Work-Study, tuition waivers (full and partial), and unspecified assistantships also available. Support available to part-time students. Financial award application deadline: 3/1; financial award applicants required to submit FAFSA. *Faculty research:* Feminist legal theory, environment law, agricultural law, administrative law, Constitutional law. *Unit head:* Jennifer L. Rosato, Dean, 815-753-1380, Fax: 815-753-8552, E-mail: jrosato@niu.edu. *Application contact:* Judith L. Malen, Director of Admissions and Financial Aid, 815-753-1420, E-mail: jmalen@niu.edu. Web site: http://law.niu.edu/.

Northern Kentucky University, Chase College of Law, Highland Heights, KY 41099. Offers JD, JD/MBA, JD/MBI, JD/MHI. *Accreditation:* ABA. Part-time and evening/weekend programs available. *Faculty:* 37 full-time (15 women), 25 part-time/adjunct (13 women). *Students:* 355 full-time (133 women), 219 part-time (91 women); includes 43 minority (20 Black or African American, non-Hispanic/Latino; 3 American Indian or Alaska Native, non-Hispanic/Latino; 10 Asian, non-Hispanic/Latino; 8 Hispanic/Latino; 1 Native Hawaiian or other Pacific Islander, non-Hispanic/Latino; 1 Two or more races, non-Hispanic/Latino). Average age 24. 891 applicants, 52% accepted, 180 enrolled. In 2011, 193 doctorates awarded. *Entrance requirements:* For doctorate, LSAT. Additional exam requirements/recommendations for international students: Required—TOEFL. *Application deadline:* For fall admission, 4/1 priority date for domestic students, 4/1 for international students. Applications are processed on a rolling basis. Application fee: $40. Electronic applications accepted. *Expenses:* Contact institution. *Financial support:* In 2011–12, 218 students received support, including 21 fellowships (averaging $2,500 per year), 38 research assistantships (averaging $1,000 per year); career-related internships or fieldwork, Federal Work-Study, scholarships/grants, and unspecified assistantships also available. Support available to part-time students. Financial award application deadline: 3/1; financial award applicants required to submit FAFSA. *Faculty research:* Employment and employment discrimination law, tort law, constitutional and criminal law, art law, business law. *Unit head:* Dennis R. Honabach, Dean, 859-572-6406, Fax: 859-572-6183, E-mail: honabachd1@nku.edu. *Application contact:* Ashley Folger Gray, Director of Admissions, 859-572-5841, Fax: 859-572-6081, E-mail: graya4@nku.edu. Web site: http://chaselaw.nku.edu.

Northwestern University, The Graduate School, Program in Law and Social Science, Evanston, IL 60208. Offers Certificate. *Degree requirements:* For Certificate, research project. *Faculty research:* Law and social science.

Northwestern University, Law School, Chicago, IL 60611-3069. Offers international human rights (LL M); law (JD); law and business (LL M); tax (LL M in Tax); JD/LL M; JD/MBA; JD/PhD; LL M/Certificate. Executive LL M programs offered in Madrid (Spain), Seoul (South Korea), and Tel Aviv (Israel). *Accreditation:* ABA. *Entrance requirements:* For master's, law degree or equivalent, letter of recommendation, resume; for doctorate, LSAT, 1 letter of recommendation, resume. Additional exam requirements/recommendations for international students: Required—TOEFL. Electronic applications accepted. *Expenses:* Contact institution. *Faculty research:* Constitutional law, corporate law, international law, law and social policy, ethical studies.

Nova Southeastern University, Shepard Broad Law Center, Fort Lauderdale, FL 33314. Offers education law (MS, Certificate); employment law (MS); health law (MS); law (JD); JD/MBA; JD/MS; JD/MURP. JD/MURP offered jointly with Florida Atlantic University. *Accreditation:* ABA. Part-time and evening/weekend programs available. Postbaccalaureate distance learning degree programs offered (minimal on-campus study). *Students:* 1,055 full-time (547 women), 166 part-time (130 women); includes 434 minority (115 Black or African American, non-Hispanic/Latino; 3 American Indian or Alaska Native, non-Hispanic/Latino; 48 Asian, non-Hispanic/Latino; 252 Hispanic/Latino; 4 Native Hawaiian or other Pacific Islander, non-Hispanic/Latino; 12 Two or more races, non-Hispanic/Latino), 28 international. Average age 29. In 2011, 46 master's, 305 doctorates awarded. *Degree requirements:* For doctorate, thesis/dissertation. *Application deadline:* For fall admission, 3/1 priority date for domestic students. Applications are processed on a rolling basis. Application fee: $50. Electronic applications accepted. *Expenses:* Contact institution. *Financial support:* In 2011–12, 58 fellowships were awarded; research assistantships, teaching assistantships, Federal Work-Study, scholarships/grants, tuition waivers (full and partial), and unspecified assistantships also available. Support available to part-time students. Financial award application deadline: 4/15; financial award applicants required to submit FAFSA. *Faculty research:* Legal issues in family law, civil rights, business associations, criminal law, law and popular culture. *Unit head:* Althornia Steele, Dean, 954-262-6100, Fax: 954-262-3834, E-mail: asteele@nova.edu. *Application contact:* Beth Hall, Assistant Dean of Admissions, 954-262-6121, Fax: 954-262-3844, E-mail: hallb@nsu.law.nova.edu. Web site: http://www.nsulaw.nova.edu/.

Ohio Northern University, Claude W. Pettit College of Law, Ada, OH 45810-1599. Offers LL M, JD. *Accreditation:* ABA. *Faculty:* 28 full-time (12 women), 9 part-time/adjunct (2 women). *Students:* 317 full-time (131 women), 3 part-time (1 woman); includes 35 minority (18 Black or African American, non-Hispanic/Latino; 1 American Indian or Alaska Native, non-Hispanic/Latino; 6 Asian, non-Hispanic/Latino; 5 Hispanic/Latino; 5 Two or more races, non-Hispanic/Latino), 9 international. Average age 26. 1,228 applicants, 41% accepted, 111 enrolled. In 2011, 11 master's, 101 doctorates awarded. *Entrance requirements:* For doctorate, LSAT. Additional exam requirements/recommendations for international students: Required—TOEFL. *Application deadline:* Applications are processed on a rolling basis. Electronic applications accepted. *Expenses:* Contact institution. *Financial support:* Career-related internships or fieldwork, Federal Work-Study, institutionally sponsored loans, and scholarships/grants available. Financial award applicants required to submit FAFSA. *Faculty research:* Constitutional law, environmental law, business law and taxation, criminal law, public interest law, death penalty for women and juveniles, international human rights, sports violence. *Unit head:* Dr. David C. Crago, Dean, 419-772-2205, Fax: 419-772-1875, E-mail: c-crago@onu.edu. *Application contact:* Linda English, Assistant Dean and Director of Law Admissions, 419-772-2210, Fax: 419-772-3042, E-mail: l-english@onu.edu. Web site: http://www.law.onu.edu/.

The Ohio State University, Moritz College of Law, Columbus, OH 43210. Offers LL M, MSL, JD, JD/MA, JD/MBA, JD/MD, JD/MHA, JD/MPH. *Accreditation:* ABA. Electronic applications accepted. *Expenses:* Contact institution. *Faculty research:* Alternative dispute resolution, law and policy, clinical programs, criminal law, intellectual property, cyberlaw.

Oklahoma City University, School of Law, Oklahoma City, OK 73106-1402. Offers JD, JD/MBA. *Accreditation:* ABA. Part-time and evening/weekend programs available. *Faculty:* 30 full-time (16 women), 22 part-time/adjunct (17 women). *Students:* 568 full-time (234 women), 37 part-time (17 women); includes 124 minority (21 Black or African American, non-Hispanic/Latino; 29 American Indian or Alaska Native, non-Hispanic/Latino; 16 Asian, non-Hispanic/Latino; 33 Hispanic/Latino; 25 Two or more races, non-Hispanic/Latino), 11 international. Average age 28. 1,208 applicants, 53% accepted, 204 enrolled. In 2011, 177 doctorates awarded. *Entrance requirements:* For doctorate, LSAT. *Application deadline:* Applications are processed on a rolling basis. Application fee: $50 ($70 for international students). Electronic applications accepted. *Expenses:* Contact institution. *Financial support:* Career-related internships or fieldwork, Federal Work-Study, institutionally sponsored loans, scholarships/grants, and tuition waivers available. Support available to part-time students. Financial award application deadline: 3/1; financial award applicants required to submit FAFSA. *Faculty research:* Family law, environmental law, consumer law, alternative dispute resolution, criminal law and procedure. *Unit head:* Dr. Valerie K. Couch, Dean, 405-208-5440, Fax: 405-208-6041, E-mail: vcouch@okcu.edu. *Application contact:* Dr. Laurie W. Jones, Interim Associate Director, Law School Admissions, 405-208-5354, Fax: 405-208-5814, E-mail: ljones@okcu.edu. Web site: http://www.okcu.edu/law/.

Pace University, Pace Law School, White Plains, NY 10603. Offers comparative legal studies (LL M); environmental law (LL M, SJD), including climate change (LL M), land use and sustainability (LL M); law (JD); JD/LL M; JD/MA; JD/MBA; JD/MEM; JD/MPA; JD/MS. JD/MA offered jointly with Sarah Lawrence College; JD/MEM offered jointly with Yale University School of Forestry and Environmental Studies. *Accreditation:* ABA. Part-time programs available. *Degree requirements:* For master's, writing sample; for doctorate, thesis/dissertation (for some programs), extensive thesis proposal (for SJD). *Entrance requirements:* For doctorate, LSAT (for JD). Additional exam requirements/recommendations for international students: Required—TOEFL (minimum score 600 paper-based; 250 computer-based); Recommended—TWE. Electronic applications accepted. *Expenses:* Contact institution. *Faculty research:* Reform of energy regulations, international law, land use law, prosecutorial misconduct, corporation law, international sale of goods.

Park University, College of Graduate and Professional Studies, Kansas City, MO 54105. Offers adult education (M Ed); at-risk students (M Ed); disaster and emergency management (MPA); educational administration (M Ed); entrepreneurship (MBA); general business (MBA); general education (M Ed); government/business relations (MPA); healthcare/services management (MBA, MPA); international business (MBA); K-12 certification (MAT); management information systems (MBA); management of information systems (MPA); middle school certification (MAT); multi-cultural education (M Ed); nonprofit management (MPA); public management (MPA); school law (M Ed); secondary school certification (MAT); special education (M Ed). Part-time and evening/weekend programs available. Postbaccalaureate distance learning degree programs offered (no on-campus study). *Degree requirements:* For master's, comprehensive exam, thesis (for some programs). *Entrance requirements:* For master's, GRE, GMAT, teacher certification (M Ed). Additional exam requirements/recommendations for international students: Required—TOEFL (minimum score 550 paper-based). Electronic applications accepted. *Faculty research:* Literacy, leadership, brain based research, multicultural education, diversity.

Penn State Dickinson School of Law, Graduate and Professional Programs, Carlisle, PA 17013-2899. Offers comparative law (LL M); law (JD). *Accreditation:* ABA. Part-time programs available. *Students:* 592 full-time (259 women), 3 part-time (2 women). In 2011, 18 master's awarded. *Entrance requirements:* For doctorate, employment record, 2 letters of recommendation. Additional exam requirements/recommendations for international students: Required—TOEFL for JD. *Application deadline:* For fall admission, 3/1 priority date for domestic students. Applications are processed on a rolling basis. Application fee: $60. Electronic applications accepted. *Financial support:* Research assistantships, Federal Work-Study, institutionally sponsored loans, and scholarships/grants available. Support available to part-time students. Financial award application deadline: 3/1; financial award applicants required to submit FAFSA. *Faculty research:* Arbitration, sports law, international human rights law, alternate dispute resolution. *Unit head:* Philip J. McConnaughay, Dean, 814-863-1521, E-mail: pjm30@psu.edu. *Application contact:* Barbara W. Guillaume, Director, Law Admissions, 717-240-5207, Fax: 717-241-3503, E-mail: bwg1@psu.edu. Web site: http://www.dsl.psu.edu/.

Pepperdine University, School of Law, Juris Doctor Program, Malibu, CA 90263. Offers JD, JD/MBA. *Accreditation:* ABA. *Faculty:* 35 full-time (12 women), 40 part-time/adjunct (5 women). *Students:* 628 full-time (318 women), 1 part-time (0 women); includes 135 minority (20 Black or African American, non-Hispanic/Latino; 49 Asian, non-Hispanic/Latino; 40 Hispanic/Latino; 26 Two or more races, non-Hispanic/Latino), 13 international. 3,422 applicants, 28% accepted, 222 enrolled. *Entrance requirements:* For doctorate, LSAT, 2 letters of recommendation, resume, personal statement, registration with the Credential Assembly Service (CAS). *Application deadline:* For fall admission, 3/1 priority date for domestic students, 3/1 for international students. Applications are processed on a rolling basis. Application fee: $60. *Expenses:* Contact institution. *Financial support:* Federal Work-Study, institutionally sponsored loans, and scholarships/grants available. Financial award application deadline: 4/1; financial award applicants required to submit FAFSA. *Unit head:* Dr. Timothy L. Perrin, Vice Dean, School of Law, 310-506-4662, E-mail: timothy.perrin@pepperdine.edu. *Application contact:* Shannon Phillips, Director of Admissions and Records, 310-506-4631, Fax: 310-506-4266, E-mail: shannon.phillips@pepperdine.edu. Web site: http://law.pepperdine.edu/academics/juris-doctor/.

Pontifical Catholic University of Puerto Rico, School of Law, Ponce, PR 00717-0777. Offers JD. *Accreditation:* ABA. Part-time and evening/weekend programs available. *Entrance requirements:* For doctorate, LSAT, PAEG, 3 letters of recommendation.

Pontificia Universidad Catolica Madre y Maestra, Graduate School, Faculty of Social and Administrative Sciences, Santiago, Dominican Republic. Offers business administration (MBA), including business development, finance, international business, management skills (M Mgmt, MBA), marketing, operations, strategic cost management, strategy, tourist destination planning and management; law (LL M), including civil law, corporate business law, criminal law, international relations, real estate law; management (M Mgmt), including higher financial management, insurance program administration, management skills (M Mgmt, MBA); psychology (MA), including clinical child and adolescent psychology, forensic psychology; strategic human resources (EMBA).

Queen's University at Kingston, Faculty of Law, Kingston, ON K7L 3N6, Canada. Offers LL M, JD, JD/MBA, JD/MIR, JD/MPA. Part-time programs available. *Degree requirements:* For master's, thesis. *Entrance requirements:* For doctorate, LSAT, minimum 2 years of college. Additional exam requirements/recommendations for international students: Required—TOEFL, TWE. *Faculty research:* Labor relations law, tax law and policy, criminal law and policy, critical legal theories, international legal relations.

Quinnipiac University, School of Law, Hamden, CT 06518-1940. Offers health law (LL M); law (JD); JD/MBA. *Accreditation:* ABA. Part-time and evening/weekend programs available. *Faculty:* 38 full-time (16 women), 34 part-time/adjunct (8 women). *Students:* 356 full-time (173 women), 82 part-time (38 women); includes 59 minority (8 Black or African American, non-Hispanic/Latino; 2 American Indian or Alaska Native, non-Hispanic/Latino; 23 Asian, non-Hispanic/Latino; 20 Hispanic/Latino; 6 Two or more races, non-Hispanic/Latino), 1 international. Average age 24. 2,037 applicants, 47% accepted, 123 enrolled. In 2011, 134 doctorates awarded. *Entrance requirements:* For doctorate, LSAT. Additional exam requirements/recommendations for international students: Recommended—TOEFL. *Application deadline:* For fall admission, 3/1 priority date for domestic students. Applications are processed on a rolling basis. Application fee: $65. Electronic applications accepted. *Expenses:* Contact institution. *Financial support:* In 2011–12, 309 students received support, including 32 fellowships (averaging $1,560 per year), 55 research assistantships (averaging $1,800 per year); career-related internships or fieldwork, Federal Work-Study, and scholarships/grants also available. Support available to part-time students. Financial award application deadline: 4/15; financial award applicants required to submit FAFSA. *Faculty research:* Tax, health, public interest, corporate law, dispute resolution, intellectual property. *Unit head:* Brad Saxton, Dean, 203-582-3200, Fax: 203-582-3209, E-mail: ladm@quinnipiac.edu. *Application contact:* Edwin Wilkes, Associate Vice-President/Dean of Law School Admissions, 203-582-3400, Fax: 203-582-3339, E-mail: ladm@quinnipiac.edu. Web site: http://law.quinnipiac.edu/.

Regent University, Graduate School, School of Law, Virginia Beach, VA 23464-9800. Offers American legal studies (LL M); law (JD); JD/MA; JD/MBA. *Accreditation:* ABA. Part-time programs available. *Faculty:* 29 full-time (8 women), 48 part-time/adjunct (13 women). *Students:* 426 full-time (200 women), 79 part-time (46 women); includes 74 minority (22 Black or African American, non-Hispanic/Latino; 9 American Indian or Alaska Native, non-Hispanic/Latino; 23 Asian, non-Hispanic/Latino; 20 Hispanic/Latino), 73 international. Average age 28. 1,239 applicants, 34% accepted, 149 enrolled. In 2011, 121 doctorates awarded. *Entrance requirements:* For doctorate, LSAT, minimum undergraduate GPA of 2.75, 3 letters of recommendation, resume. Additional exam requirements/recommendations for international students: Required—TOEFL (minimum score 600 paper-based; 250 computer-based). *Application deadline:* For fall admission, 3/1 for domestic students. Applications are processed on a rolling basis. Application fee: $50. Electronic applications accepted. *Expenses:* Contact institution. *Financial support:* Career-related internships or fieldwork, scholarships/grants, and tuition waivers (full and partial) available. Support available to part-time students. Financial award application deadline: 2/1; financial award applicants required to submit FAFSA. *Faculty research:* Family law, Constitutional law, law and culture, evidence and practice, intellectual property. *Unit head:* Jeffrey Brauch, Dean, 757-352-4040, Fax: 757-352-4595, E-mail: jeffbra@regent.edu. *Application contact:* Matthew Chadwick, Director of Enrollment Support Services, 800-373-5504, Fax: 757-352-4381, E-mail: admissions@regent.edu. Web site: http://www.regent.edu/law/.

Roger Williams University, School of Law, Bristol, RI 02809-5171. Offers JD, JD/MLRHR, JD/MMA, JD/MSCJ. JD/MMA and JD/MLRHR offered jointly with University of Rhode Island; JD/MSCJ with School of Justice Studies. *Accreditation:* ABA. Part-time programs available. *Faculty:* 36 full-time (19 women), 30 part-time/adjunct (5 women). *Students:* 555 full-time (278 women); includes 78 minority (17 Black or African American, non-Hispanic/Latino; 2 American Indian or Alaska Native, non-Hispanic/Latino; 14 Asian, non-Hispanic/Latino; 37 Hispanic/Latino; 8 Two or more races, non-Hispanic/Latino), 5 international. Average age 26. 1,388 applicants, 66% accepted, 194 enrolled. In 2011, 152 doctorates awarded. *Entrance requirements:* For doctorate, LSAT. Additional exam requirements/recommendations for international students: Required—TOEFL (minimum score 600 paper-based; 250 computer-based; 100 iBT). *Application deadline:* For fall admission, 3/15 priority date for domestic students, 3/15 for international students. Applications are processed on a rolling basis. Application fee: $60. Electronic applications accepted. *Financial support:* In 2011–12, 262 students received support, including 11 fellowships (averaging $671 per year), 65 research assistantships (averaging $806 per year); career-related internships or fieldwork, Federal Work-Study, scholarships/grants, and tuition waivers (full and partial) also available. Financial award application deadline: 2/15; financial award applicants required to submit FAFSA. *Faculty research:* Civil rights, admiralty, labor, intellectual property, international and comparative law. *Unit head:* David A. Logan, Dean, 401-254-4500, Fax: 401-254-3525, E-mail: dlogan@rwu.edu. *Application contact:* Michael W. Donnelly-Boylen, Assistant Dean of Admissions, 800-633-2727, Fax: 401-254-4516, E-mail: mdonnelly-boylen@rwu.edu. Web site: http://law.rwu.edu.

Rutgers, The State University of New Jersey, Camden, School of Law, Camden, NJ 08102. Offers JD, JD/DO, JD/MA, JD/MBA, JD/MCRP, JD/MD, JD/MPA, JD/MPH, JD/MS, JD/MSW. JD/MCRP, JD/MA, JD/MPA, JD/MSW, JD/MS offered jointly with Rutgers, The State University of New Jersey, New Brunswick; JD/MPA, JD/MD, JD/DO with University of Medicine and Dentistry of New Jersey. *Accreditation:* ABA. Part-time and evening/weekend programs available. *Entrance requirements:* For doctorate, LSAT. Additional exam requirements/recommendations for international students: Recommended—TOEFL. Electronic applications accepted. *Expenses:* Contact institution. *Faculty research:* International law, commercial law, public law, health law, constitutional law, jurisprudence.

Rutgers, The State University of New Jersey, Newark, School of Law, Newark, NJ 07102-3094. Offers JD, JD/MA, JD/MBA, JD/MCRP, JD/MD, JD/MSW, JD/PhD. JD/MCRP, JD/PhD offered jointly with Rutgers, The State University of New Jersey, New Brunswick. *Accreditation:* ABA. Part-time and evening/weekend programs available. *Entrance requirements:* For doctorate, LSAT. *Expenses:* Contact institution. *Faculty research:* Civil rights and liberties, women and the law, international human rights and world order, corporate law, employment law.

St. John's University, School of Law, Program in Law, Queens, NY 11439. Offers JD, JD/LL M, MA/JD, MBA/JD. *Students:* 787 full-time (324 women), 149 part-time (76 women); includes 227 minority (42 Black or African American, non-Hispanic/Latino; 72 Asian, non-Hispanic/Latino; 89 Hispanic/Latino; 24 Two or more races, non-Hispanic/Latino), 11 international. Average age 25. 4,056 applicants, 40% accepted, 287 enrolled. In 2011, 276 doctorates awarded. *Entrance requirements:* For doctorate, LSAT. Additional exam requirements/recommendations for international students: Required—TOEFL (minimum score 600 paper-based; 250 computer-based; 100 iBT), IELTS (minimum score 5.5). *Application deadline:* For fall admission, 4/1 priority date for domestic students, 4/1 for international students. Applications are processed on a rolling basis. Application fee: $60. Electronic applications accepted. *Expenses: Tuition:* Full-time $18,000; part-time $1000 per credit. *Required fees:* $170 per semester. Tuition and fees vary according to program. *Unit head:* Michael A. Simons, Dean, 718-990-6601, Fax: 718-990-6694, E-mail: simonsm@stjohns.edu. *Application contact:* Robert Harrison, Assistant Dean and Director of Admissions, 718-990-6474, Fax: 718-990-6699, E-mail: lawinfo@stjohns.edu.

Saint Joseph's University, College of Arts and Sciences, Department of Criminal Justice, Philadelphia, PA 19131-1395. Offers administration/police executive (MS); behavior analysis (MS, Post-Master's Certificate); criminal justice (MS, Post-Master's Certificate); criminology (MS); federal law (MS); intelligence and crime (MS); probation, parole, and corrections (MS). Part-time and evening/weekend programs available. Postbaccalaureate distance learning degree programs offered (no on-campus study). *Faculty:* 5 full-time (all women), 44 part-time/adjunct (14 women). *Students:* 43 full-time (27 women), 436 part-time (286 women); includes 145 minority (107 Black or African American, non-Hispanic/Latino; 4 American Indian or Alaska Native, non-Hispanic/Latino; 5 Asian, non-Hispanic/Latino; 26 Hispanic/Latino; 3 Two or more races, non-Hispanic/Latino), 2 international. Average age 32. 193 applicants, 85% accepted, 140 enrolled. In 2011, 144 master's, 10 other advanced degrees awarded. *Degree requirements:* For master's, thesis. *Entrance requirements:* For master's, GRE General Test or minimum GPA of 3.0, 2 letters of recommendation. Additional exam requirements/recommendations for international students: Required—TOEFL (minimum score 550 paper-based; 213 computer-based; 79 iBT). *Application deadline:* For fall admission, 7/15 priority date for domestic students, 4/15 for international students; for winter admission, 1/15 for international students; for spring admission, 11/15 priority date for domestic students, 10/15 for international students. Applications are processed on a rolling basis. Application fee: $35. Electronic applications accepted. *Expenses: Tuition:* Part-time $735 per credit hour. Tuition and fees vary according to degree level and program. *Financial support:* Career-related internships or fieldwork and unspecified assistantships available. Financial award applicants required to submit FAFSA. *Unit head:* Patricia Griffin, Director, 610-660-1294, E-mail: pgriffin@sju.edu. *Application contact:* Kate McConnell, Director, Graduate College of Arts and Sciences Admissions and Retention, 610-660-3184, Fax: 610-660-3230, E-mail: kate.mconnell@sju.edu. Web site: http://www.sju.edu/academics/cas/grad/criminaljustice/index.html.

Saint Louis University, School of Law, St. Louis, MO 63108. Offers LL M, JD. *Accreditation:* ABA. Part-time and evening/weekend programs available. *Degree requirements:* For master's, thesis (for some programs). *Entrance requirements:* For master's, JD or equivalent; for doctorate, LSAT, letters of recommendation, resume, personal statement, LSDAS. Additional exam requirements/recommendations for international students: Required—TOEFL (minimum score 590 paper-based; 194 computer-based). Electronic applications accepted. *Expenses:* Contact institution. *Faculty research:* Health law, employment law, international comparative law, lawyering skills (clinical).

St. Mary's University, School of Law, San Antonio, TX 78228-8602. Offers JD, JD/MA, JD/MBA, JD/MPA, JD/MS. *Accreditation:* ABA. *Entrance requirements:* For doctorate, LSAT. Additional exam requirements/recommendations for international students: Required—TOEFL (minimum score 600 paper-based; 213 computer-based). Electronic applications accepted. *Expenses:* Contact institution. *Faculty research:* Ethics, church and state, exclusionary rule, civil rights, tort law.

St. Thomas University, School of Law, Miami Gardens, FL 33054-6459. Offers international human rights (LL M); international taxation (LL M); law (JD); JD/MBA; JD/MS. *Accreditation:* ABA. Postbaccalaureate distance learning degree programs offered (no on-campus study). *Degree requirements:* For master's, thesis (international taxation). *Entrance requirements:* For doctorate, LSAT. Electronic applications accepted. *Expenses:* Contact institution.

Samford University, Cumberland School of Law, Birmingham, AL 35229. Offers MCL, JD, JD/M Acc, JD/M Div, JD/MBA, JD/MPA, JD/MPH, JD/MSEM, JD/MTS. JD/MPH and JD/MPA offered jointly with The University of Alabama at Birmingham. *Accreditation:* ABA. Part-time programs available. *Faculty:* 25 full-time (7 women), 16 part-time/adjunct (7 women). *Students:* 479 full-time (198 women), 3 part-time (1 woman); includes 53 minority (22 Black or African American, non-Hispanic/Latino; 3 American Indian or Alaska Native, non-Hispanic/Latino; 7 Asian, non-Hispanic/Latino; 8 Hispanic/Latino; 1 Native Hawaiian or other Pacific Islander, non-Hispanic/Latino; 12 Two or more races, non-Hispanic/Latino). Average age 25. 1,405 applicants, 42% accepted, 153 enrolled. In 2011, 3 master's, 150 doctorates awarded. *Entrance requirements:* For doctorate, LSAT. Additional exam requirements/recommendations for international students: Required—TOEFL (minimum score 550 paper-based; 213 computer-based). *Application deadline:* For fall admission, 2/28 priority date for domestic students, 2/28 for international students. Applications are processed on a rolling basis. Application fee: $50. Electronic applications accepted. *Expenses:* Contact institution. *Financial support:* In 2011–12, 170 students received support. Career-related internships or fieldwork, Federal Work-Study, institutionally sponsored loans, and scholarships/grants available. Financial award application deadline: 3/1; financial award applicants required to submit FAFSA. *Faculty research:* Constitutional law (commerce clause), law and literature, legal history, law and ethics, evidence. *Unit head:* John L. Carroll, Dean, 205-726-2704, Fax: 205-726-4107, E-mail: jlcarrol@samford.edu. *Application contact:* Jennifer Y. Sims, Assistant Dean of Admissions, 205-726-2702, Fax: 205-726-2057, E-mail: law.admissions@samford.edu. Web site: http://cumberland.samford.edu/.

San Joaquin College of Law, Law Program, Clovis, CA 93612-1312. Offers JD. Part-time and evening/weekend programs available. *Entrance requirements:* For doctorate, LSAT.

Santa Clara University, School of Law, Santa Clara, CA 95053. Offers high technology law (Certificate); intellectual property law (LL M); international and comparative law (LL M); international high tech law (Certificate); international law (Certificate); law (JD); public interest and social justice law (Certificate); U. S. law for foreign lawyers (LL M); JD/MBA. *Accreditation:* ABA. Part-time and evening/weekend programs available. *Faculty:* 65 full-time (32 women), 49 part-time/adjunct (23 women). *Students:* 928 full-time (441 women), 67 part-time (36 women); includes 392 minority (22 Black or African American, non-Hispanic/Latino; 7 American Indian or Alaska Native, non-Hispanic/Latino; 238 Asian, non-Hispanic/Latino; 88 Hispanic/Latino; 3 Native Hawaiian or other Pacific Islander, non-Hispanic/Latino; 34 Two or more races, non-Hispanic/Latino), 56 international. Average age 28. 3,887 applicants, 37% accepted, 335 enrolled. In 2011, 25 master's, 296 doctorates awarded. *Degree requirements:* For master's, comprehensive exam, thesis; for doctorate, comprehensive exam, thesis/dissertation, 86 units. *Entrance requirements:* For master's and doctorate, LSAT, transcript, personal statement, letters of recommendation. *Application deadline:* For fall admission, 2/1 priority date for domestic students, 2/1 for international students. Applications are processed on a rolling basis. Application fee: $75. Electronic applications accepted. *Expenses:* Contact institution. *Financial support:* In 2011–12, 446 students received support. Fellowships with full and partial tuition reimbursements available, Federal Work-Study, and scholarships/grants available. Financial award application deadline: 2/1; financial award applicants required to submit FAFSA. *Faculty research:* Intellectual property, international human rights, privacy rights, wrongful convictions, shareholder and firm governance. *Unit head:* Donald Polden, Dean, 408-554-4362. *Application contact:* Jeannette Leach, Director of Admissions, 408-554-5048. Web site: http://www.scu.edu/law/.

Seattle University, School of Law, Seattle, WA 98122-4340. Offers JD, JD/MATL, JD/MBA, JD/MCJ, JD/MIB, JD/MPA, JD/MSAL, JD/MSF, JD/MSL. *Accreditation:* ABA. Part-time programs available. *Faculty:* 61 full-time (29 women), 49 part-time/adjunct (14 women). *Students:* 806 full-time (408 women), 194 part-time (101 women); includes 250 minority (30 Black or African American, non-Hispanic/Latino; 11 American Indian or Alaska Native, non-Hispanic/Latino; 97 Asian, non-Hispanic/Latino; 59 Hispanic/Latino; 6 Native Hawaiian or other Pacific Islander, non-Hispanic/Latino; 47 Two or more races, non-Hispanic/Latino), 9 international. Average age 27. 2,226 applicants, 46% accepted, 322 enrolled. In 2011, 314 doctorates awarded. *Entrance requirements:* For doctorate, LSAT. Additional exam requirements/recommendations for international students: Required—TOEFL (minimum score 600 paper-based; 250 computer-based; 100 iBT). *Application deadline:* For fall admission, 3/1 priority date for domestic students, 3/1 for international students. Applications are processed on a rolling basis. Application fee: $60. Electronic applications accepted. *Expenses:* Contact institution. *Financial support:* In 2011–12, 482 students received support. Career-related internships or fieldwork, Federal Work-Study, scholarships/grants, and non-federal work-study available. Support available to part-time students. Financial award application deadline: 2/15; financial award applicants required to submit FAFSA. *Faculty research:* Race, postcolonial theory, and U. S. civil rights; secrecy and democratic decisions; linguistic features of police culture and the coercive impact of police officer swearing in police-citizen interaction; the imprisoned parent: differential power in same-sex families based on legal and cultural understandings of parentage; theology in public reason and legal discourse: a case for the preferential option for the poor. *Total annual research expenditures:* $454,000. *Unit head:* Mark C. Niles, Dean, 206-398-4300, Fax: 206-398-4310, E-mail: nilesm@seattleu.edu. *Application contact:* Carol T. Cochran, Assistant Dean for Admission, 206-398-4206, Fax: 206-398-4058, E-mail: ccochran@seattleu.edu. Web site: http://www.law.seattleu.edu/.

Seton Hall University, School of Law, Newark, NJ 07102-5210. Offers health law (LL M, JD); intellectual property (LL M, JD); law (MSJ); JD/MADIR; JD/MBA; MD/JD; MD/MSJ. MD/JD, MD/MSJ offered jointly with University of Medicine and Dentistry of New Jersey. *Accreditation:* ABA. Part-time and evening/weekend programs available. *Degree requirements:* For master's, thesis optional. *Entrance requirements:* For master's, professional experience, letters of recommendation; for doctorate, LSAT, active LSDAS registration, letters of recommendation. Additional exam requirements/recommendations for international students: Recommended—TOEFL. Electronic applications accepted. *Expenses:* Contact institution. *Faculty research:* Health law, intellectual property law, science and the law, international law and employment/labor law.

Southern Illinois University Carbondale, School of Law, Carbondale, IL 62901-6804. Offers general law (LL M); health law and policy (LL M); law (JD); legal studies (MLS), including general law, health law and policy; JD/M Acc; JD/MBA; JD/MD; JD/MPA; JD/MSW; JD/PhD. *Accreditation:* ABA. Part-time programs available. *Faculty:* 23 full-time (11 women), 12 part-time/adjunct (6 women). *Students:* 380 full-time (143 women), 3 part-time (1 woman); includes 29 minority (9 Black or African American, non-Hispanic/Latino; 1 American Indian or Alaska Native, non-Hispanic/Latino; 12 Asian, non-Hispanic/Latino; 7 Hispanic/Latino), 2 international. Average age 27. 802 applicants, 50% accepted, 158 enrolled. In 2011, 107 doctorates awarded. *Entrance requirements:* For doctorate, LSAT. Additional exam requirements/recommendations for international students: Required—TOEFL (minimum score 600 paper-based). *Application deadline:* For fall admission, 3/1 for domestic and international students. Applications are processed on a rolling basis. Application fee: $50. Electronic applications accepted. *Expenses:* Contact institution. *Financial support:* In 2011–12, 326 students received support. Career-related internships or fieldwork, Federal Work-Study, institutionally sponsored loans, scholarships/grants, and health care benefits available. Support available to part-time students. Financial award application deadline: 4/1; financial award applicants required to submit FAFSA. *Faculty research:* Health care law, criminal law, environmental law, international law, tort reform. *Unit head:* Peter C. Alexander, Dean, 618-453-8761, Fax: 618-453-8769. *Application contact:* Michael P. Ruiz, Assistant Dean for Admissions, 618-453-8858, Fax: 618-453-8769, E-mail: lawadmit@siu.edu. Web site: http://www.law.siu.edu/.

Southern Methodist University, Dedman School of Law, Dallas, TX 75275-0110. Offers foreign law school graduates (LL M); law (JD, SJD); law-general (LL M); taxation (LL M); JD/MA; JD/MBA. *Accreditation:* ABA. Part-time and evening/weekend programs available. *Degree requirements:* For master's, thesis optional; for doctorate, thesis/dissertation (for some programs), 30 hours of public service (for JD). *Entrance requirements:* For master's, JD; for doctorate, LSAT (for JD). Additional exam requirements/recommendations for international students: Required—TOEFL (minimum score 575 paper-based; 233 computer-based; 91 iBT). Electronic applications accepted. *Expenses:* Contact institution. *Faculty research:* Corporate law, intellectual property, international law, commercial law, dispute resolution.

Southern University and Agricultural and Mechanical College, Southern University Law Center, Baton Rouge, LA 70813. Offers JD. *Accreditation:* ABA; SACS. Part-time and evening/weekend programs available. *Entrance requirements:* For doctorate, LSAT. Additional exam requirements/recommendations for international students: Recommended—TOEFL. Electronic applications accepted. *Expenses:* Contact institution. *Faculty research:* Civil law, comparative law, constitutional law, civil rights law.

South Texas College of Law, Professional Program, Houston, TX 77002-7000. Offers JD. *Accreditation:* ABA. Part-time and evening/weekend programs available. *Faculty:* 55 full-time (20 women), 41 part-time/adjunct (13 women). *Students:* 996 full-time (445 women), 271 part-time (138 women); includes 397 minority (48 Black or African American, non-Hispanic/Latino; 5 American Indian or Alaska Native, non-Hispanic/Latino; 111 Asian, non-Hispanic/Latino; 196 Hispanic/Latino; 2 Native Hawaiian or other Pacific Islander, non-Hispanic/Latino; 35 Two or more races, non-Hispanic/Latino), 3 international. Average age 27. 2,307 applicants, 44% accepted, 424 enrolled. In 2011, 399 doctorates awarded. *Degree requirements:* For doctorate, completion of 90 hours within 7 years of enrollment. *Entrance requirements:* For doctorate, LSAT (taken within last 4 years), degree from accredited 4-year institution. *Application deadline:* For fall admission, 2/15 for domestic and international students; for spring admission, 10/1 for domestic and international students. Application fee: $55. Electronic applications accepted. *Expenses: Tuition:* Full-time $26,250; part-time $17,500 per year. *Required fees:* $600; $600 per year. *Financial support:* In 2011–12, 1,035 students received support. Federal Work-Study, scholarships/grants, and tuition waivers (full and partial) available. Support available to part-time students. Financial award application deadline: 5/1; financial award applicants required to submit FAFSA. *Unit head:* Donald J. Guter, President and Dean, 713-646-1819, Fax: 713-646-2909, E-mail: dguter@stcl.edu. *Application contact:* Alicia K. Cramer, Assistant Dean of Admissions, 713-646-1810, Fax: 713-646-2906, E-mail: admissions@stcl.edu. Web site: http://www.stcl.edu/.

Southwestern Law School, Graduate Programs, Los Angeles, CA 90010. Offers entertainment and media law (LL M); general studies (LL M); law (JD). *Accreditation:* ABA. Part-time and evening/weekend programs available. Postbaccalaureate distance learning degree programs offered. *Entrance requirements:* For master's, JD; for doctorate, LSAT, LSDAS. Additional exam requirements/recommendations for international students: Required—TOEFL. Electronic applications accepted. *Faculty research:* International trade and law, mediation/arbitration, land use and urban planning, antitrust law, entertainment and media law.

Stanford University, Law School, Stanford, CA 94305-8610. Offers JSM, MLS, JD, JSD, JD/MBA, JD/PhD. *Accreditation:* ABA. *Degree requirements:* For doctorate, thesis/dissertation (for some programs). *Entrance requirements:* For doctorate, LSAT (for JD). Electronic applications accepted. *Expenses:* Contact institution.

Stetson University, College of Law, Gulfport, FL 33707-3299. Offers LL M, JD, JD/MBA. *Accreditation:* ABA. *Students:* 968 full-time (494 women), 153 part-time (70 women); includes 226 minority (56 Black or African American, non-Hispanic/Latino; 3 American Indian or Alaska Native, non-Hispanic/Latino; 19 Asian, non-Hispanic/Latino; 121 Hispanic/Latino; 1 Native Hawaiian or other Pacific Islander, non-Hispanic/Latino; 26 Two or more races, non-Hispanic/Latino), 26 international. Average age 27. In 2011, 23 master's, 315 doctorates awarded. *Entrance requirements:* For doctorate, LSAT, LSDAS. *Application deadline:* For fall admission, 3/1 priority date for domestic students; for spring admission, 9/1 for domestic students. Application fee: $50. *Expenses:* Contact institution. *Financial support:* Research assistantships, teaching assistantships, career-related internships or fieldwork, institutionally sponsored loans, and scholarships/grants available. Financial award application deadline: 4/1; financial award applicants required to submit FAFSA. *Unit head:* Dr. Christopher Pietruszkiewicz, Dean, 727-562-7810. *Application contact:* Laura Zuppo, Executive Director of Admissions and Financial Aid, 727-562-7802, E-mail: lawadmit@law.stetson.edu. Web site: http://www.law.stetson.edu/.

Suffolk University, Law School, Boston, MA 02108. Offers business law and financial services (JD); civil litigation (JD); global law and technology (LL M); health and biomedical law (JD); intellectual property law (JD); international law (JD); JD/MBA; JD/MPA; JD/MSCJ; JD/MSF; JD/MSIE. *Accreditation:* ABA. Part-time and evening/weekend programs available. *Degree requirements:* For master's, legal writing. *Entrance requirements:* For master's, 2 letters of recommendation, resume, personal statement; for doctorate, LSAT, LSDAS, dean's certification, recommendation. Additional exam requirements/recommendations for international students: Required—TOEFL (minimum score 600 paper-based; 250 computer-based; 100 iBT). *Application deadline:* For fall admission, 3/1 for domestic and international students. Applications are processed on a rolling basis. Application fee: $60. Electronic applications accepted. *Expenses:* Contact institution. *Financial support:* Career-related internships or fieldwork, Federal Work-Study, institutionally sponsored loans, and scholarships/grants available. Support available to part-time students. Financial award application deadline: 3/1; financial award applicants required to submit FAFSA. *Faculty research:* Civil law, international law, health/biomedical law, business and finance, intellectual property. *Unit head:* Gail N. Ellis, Dean of Admissions, 617-573-8144, Fax: 617-523-1367, E-mail: gellis@suffolk.edu. *Application contact:* Ian A. Menchini, Director of Electronic Marketing and Enrollment Management, 617-573-8144, Fax: 617-523-1367, E-mail: imenchin@suffolk.edu. Web site: http://www.law.suffolk.edu/.

Syracuse University, College of Law, Syracuse, NY 13244-1030. Offers JD, JD/MA, JD/MBA, JD/MLS, JD/MPA, JD/MPS, JD/MS, JD/MS Acct, JD/MSW, JD/PhD. *Accreditation:* ABA. Part-time programs available. *Faculty:* 43 full-time (17 women), 31 part-time/adjunct (12 women). *Students:* 643 full-time (276 women), 5 part-time (3 women); includes 122 minority (18 Black or African American, non-Hispanic/Latino; 3 American Indian or Alaska Native, non-Hispanic/Latino; 50 Asian, non-Hispanic/Latino; 36 Hispanic/Latino; 1 Native Hawaiian or other Pacific Islander, non-Hispanic/Latino; 14 Two or more races, non-Hispanic/Latino), 17 international. Average age 25. 2,484 applicants, 48% accepted, 256 enrolled. In 2011, 191 doctorates awarded. *Entrance requirements:* For doctorate, LSAT. Additional exam requirements/recommendations for international students: Required—TOEFL (minimum score 600 paper-based; 250 computer-based), TWE. *Application deadline:* For fall admission, 4/1 priority date for domestic students, 4/1 for international students. Applications are processed on a rolling basis. Application fee: $70. Electronic applications accepted. *Expenses:* Contact institution. *Financial support:* In 2011–12, 487 students received support. Fellowships, research assistantships, career-related internships or fieldwork, Federal Work-Study, institutionally sponsored loans, scholarships/grants, and tuition waivers (partial) available. Support available to part-time students. Financial award application deadline: 2/15; financial award applicants required to submit FAFSA. *Faculty research:* Interdisciplinary legal studies, law and technology, international law, advocacy training, family law. *Unit head:* Hannah Arterian, Dean, 315-443-2524, Fax: 315-443-4213. *Application contact:* Nikki Laubenstein, Director of Admissions, 315-443-1962, Fax: 315-443-9568, E-mail: admissions@law.syr.edu. Web site: http://www.law.syr.edu/.

Taft Law School, Graduate Programs, Santa Ana, CA 92704-6954. Offers American jurisprudence (LL M); law (JD); taxation (LL M).

Temple University, James E. Beasley School of Law, Philadelphia, PA 19122. Offers law (JD); legal education (SJD); taxation (LL M); transnational law (LL M); trial advocacy (LL M); JD/LL M; JD/MBA. *Accreditation:* ABA. Part-time and evening/weekend programs available. *Entrance requirements:* For doctorate, LSAT (for JD). Additional exam requirements/recommendations for international students: Recommended—TOEFL. Electronic applications accepted. *Expenses:* Contact institution. *Faculty research:* Evidence, gender issues, health care law, immigration law, and intellectual property law .

Texas Southern University, Thurgood Marshall School of Law, Houston, TX 77004-4584. Offers JD. *Accreditation:* ABA. *Entrance requirements:* For doctorate, LSAT. Electronic applications accepted. *Expenses:* Contact institution. *Faculty research:* Sports law, civil rights and minors, international economics regulation, contracts principle, standards of judicial review.

Texas Tech University, Graduate School, School of Law, Lubbock, TX 79409-0004. Offers LL M, JD, JD/M Engr, JD/MBA, JD/MD, JD/MPA, JD/MS, JD/MSA. *Accreditation:* ABA. *Faculty:* 31 full-time (9 women), 3 part-time/adjunct (2 women). *Students:* 687 full-time (301 women), 11 part-time (1 woman); includes 176 minority (16 Black or African American, non-Hispanic/Latino; 4 American Indian or Alaska Native, non-Hispanic/Latino; 40 Asian, non-Hispanic/Latino; 111 Hispanic/Latino; 5 Two or more races, non-Hispanic/Latino), 17 international. Average age 25. 1,463 applicants, 46% accepted, 233 enrolled. In 2011, 202 doctorates awarded. *Entrance requirements:* For doctorate, LSAT. Additional exam requirements/recommendations for international students: Required—TOEFL (minimum score 550 paper-based; 213 computer-based; 79 iBT), IELTS (minimum score 6.5). *Application deadline:* For fall admission, 2/1 priority date for domestic students, 2/1 for international students. Applications are processed on a rolling basis. Application fee: $50. Electronic applications accepted. *Expenses:* Contact institution. *Financial support:* In 2011–12, 446 students received support. Federal Work-Study and scholarships/grants available. Financial award application deadline: 4/15; financial award applicants required to submit FAFSA. *Faculty research:* Bioterrorism, advocacy, military law and policy, oil and gas law, international law. *Total annual research expenditures:* $182,550. *Unit head:* Darby Dickerson, Dean, 806-742-3990, Fax: 806-742-1629, E-mail: darby.dickerson@ttu.edu. *Application contact:* Stephen Perez, Assistant Dean of Admissions and Recruitment, 806-742-3990 Ext. 273, Fax: 806-742-4617, E-mail: stephen.perez@ttu.edu. Web site: http://www.law.ttu.edu/.

Texas Wesleyan University, School of Law, Fort Worth, TX 76102. Offers JD. *Accreditation:* ABA. Part-time and evening/weekend programs available. *Faculty:* 42 full-time (19 women), 22 part-time/adjunct (6 women). *Students:* 438 full-time (196 women), 297 part-time (141 women); includes 170 minority (32 Black or African American, non-Hispanic/Latino; 6 American Indian or Alaska Native, non-Hispanic/Latino; 31 Asian, non-Hispanic/Latino; 85 Hispanic/Latino; 1 Native Hawaiian or other Pacific Islander, non-Hispanic/Latino; 15 Two or more races, non-Hispanic/Latino), 7 international. Average age 29. 1,977 applicants, 44% accepted, 735 enrolled. In 2011, 229 doctorates awarded. *Entrance requirements:* For doctorate, LSAT, LSDAS report, 2 letters of recommendation. Additional exam requirements/recommendations for international students: Required—TOEFL. *Application deadline:* For fall admission, 3/31 priority date for domestic students. Applications are processed on a rolling basis. Application fee: $55. Electronic applications accepted. *Expenses:* Contact institution. *Financial support:* Career-related internships or fieldwork, scholarships/grants, and tuition waivers (full and partial) available. Support available to part-time students. Financial award application deadline: 3/15; financial award applicants required to submit FAFSA. *Unit head:* Frederic White, Dean and Professor of Law, 817-212-4100, Fax: 817-212-4199. *Application contact:* Sherolyn Hurst, Assistant Dean of Admissions and Scholarships, 817-212-4040, Fax: 817-212-4141, E-mail: lawadmissions@law.txwes.edu. Web site: http://www.law.txwes.edu/.

Thomas Jefferson School of Law, Graduate and Professional Programs, San Diego, CA 92110-2905. Offers JD. JD/MBA offered in partnership with San Diego State University. *Accreditation:* ABA. Part-time and evening/weekend programs available. *Faculty:* 43 full-time (21 women), 41 part-time/adjunct (10 women). *Students:* 892 full-time (385 women), 366 part-time (168 women). Average age 26. *Entrance requirements:* For doctorate, LSAT. Additional exam requirements/recommendations for international students: Required—TOEFL. *Application deadline:* For fall admission, 12/1 priority date for domestic students; for spring admission, 10/1 priority date for domestic students. Applications are processed on a rolling basis. Application fee: $50. Electronic applications accepted. *Expenses: Tuition:* Full-time $41,000; part-time $30,000 per year. *Required fees:* $1730; $1730 per year. One-time fee: $50. *Financial support:* Fellowships with full and partial tuition reimbursements, career-related internships or fieldwork, Federal Work-Study, scholarships/grants, and tuition waivers available. Support available to part-time students. Financial award application deadline: 4/30; financial award applicants required to submit FAFSA. *Faculty research:* Tenant's rights, fetal rights/medical ethics, bilateral treaties/international law, sexual harassment and gender treatment. *Unit head:* Rudolph C. Hasl, Dean and President, 619-297-9700 Ext. 1404, E-mail: hasl@tjsl.edu. *Application contact:* M. Elizabeth Kransberger, Associate Dean for Student Services, 619-297-9700 Ext. 1600, Fax: 619-294-4713, E-mail: bkransberger@tjsl.edu. Web site: http://www.tjsl.edu.

Thomas M. Cooley Law School, JD and LL M Programs, Lansing, MI 48901-3038. Offers administrative law (public law) (JD); business transactions (JD); Canadian law (JD); Constitutional law and civil rights (public law) (JD); corporate law and finance (LL M); environmental law (public law) (JD); general practice (JD); insurance (LL M); intellectual property (LL M, JD); international law (JD); litigation (JD); self-directed (LL M, JD); taxation (LL M, JD); U.S. law for foreign attorneys (LL M); JD/MBA; JD/MPA; JD/MSW. *Accreditation:* ABA. Part-time and evening/weekend programs available. Postbaccalaureate distance learning degree programs offered (no on-campus study). *Faculty:* 131 full-time (55 women), 286 part-time/adjunct (93 women). *Students:* 781 full-time (368 women), 2,964 part-time (1,450 women); includes 1,055 minority (543 Black or African American, non-Hispanic/Latino; 19 American Indian or Alaska Native, non-Hispanic/Latino; 179 Asian, non-Hispanic/Latino; 205 Hispanic/Latino; 9 Native Hawaiian or other Pacific Islander, non-Hispanic/Latino; 100 Two or more races, non-Hispanic/Latino), 220 international. Average age 30. 4,032 applicants, 80% accepted, 1161 enrolled. In 2011, 40 master's, 999 doctorates awarded. *Degree requirements:* For master's, thesis optional; for doctorate, minimum of 3 credits of clinical experience. *Entrance requirements:* For master's, JD or LL B; for doctorate, LSAT. Additional exam requirements/recommendations for international students: Required—TOEFL. *Application deadline:* For fall admission, 9/1 for domestic and international students; for winter admission, 1/1 for domestic and international students; for spring admission, 5/1 for domestic and international students. Applications are processed on a rolling basis. Electronic applications accepted. *Expenses: Tuition:* Full-time $34,300; part-time $1225 per credit hour. *Required fees:* $40; $40 per year. Tuition and fees vary according to degree level and student level. *Financial support:* In 2011–12, 2,324 students received support. Career-related internships or fieldwork, Federal Work-Study, scholarships/grants, traineeships, and unspecified assistantships available. Support available to part-time students. Financial award applicants required to submit FAFSA. *Faculty research:* Wrongful convictions, civil rights, environmental law, litigation techniques, data mining, intellectual property, practical and skills-based legal education. *Unit head:* Don LeDuc, President and Dean, 517-371-5140 Ext. 2009, Fax: 517-334-5152. *Application contact:* Dr. Paul Zelenski, Associate Dean of Enrollment and Student Services, 517-371-5140 Ext. 2244, Fax: 517-334-5718, E-mail: admissions@cooley.edu. Web site: http://www.cooley.edu/.

Touro College, Jacob D. Fuchsberg Law Center, Central Islip, NY 11722. Offers general law (LL M); law (JD); U. S. legal studies (LL M); JD/MBA; JD/MSW. *Accreditation:* ABA. Part-time and evening/weekend programs available. *Entrance requirements:* For doctorate, LSAT. *Application deadline:* Applications are processed on a rolling basis. Application fee: $60. *Expenses:* Contact institution. *Financial support:* Fellowships, career-related internships or fieldwork, and Federal Work-Study available. Support available to part-time students. Financial award application deadline: 5/1. *Faculty research:* Business law, civil rights, international law, criminal justice. *Unit head:* Lawrence Raful, Dean, 516-421-2244. *Application contact:* Office of Admissions, 516-421-2244 Ext. 314. Web site: http://www.tourolaw.edu/.

Trinity International University, Trinity Law School, Santa Ana, CA 92705. Offers JD. Part-time and evening/weekend programs available. *Entrance requirements:* For doctorate, LSAT. Additional exam requirements/recommendations for international students: Required—TOEFL (minimum score 580 paper-based). *Expenses:* Contact institution.

Tufts University, Fletcher School of Law and Diplomacy, Medford, MA 02155. Offers LL M, MA, MALD, MIB, PhD, DVM/MA, JD/MALD, MALD/MA, MALD/MBA, MALD/MS, MD/MA. Postbaccalaureate distance learning degree programs offered (minimal on-campus study). *Degree requirements:* For master's, one foreign language, thesis; for doctorate, one foreign language, comprehensive exam, thesis/dissertation, dissertation defense. *Entrance requirements:* For master's and doctorate, GMAT or GRE General Test. Additional exam requirements/recommendations for international students: Required—TOEFL (minimum score 600 paper-based; 250 computer-based; 100 iBT), IELTS (minimum score 7). Electronic applications accepted. *Expenses:* Contact institution. *Faculty research:* Negotiation and conflict resolution, international organizations, international business and economic law, security studies, development economics.

Tulane University, School of Law, New Orleans, LA 70118. Offers admiralty (LL M); American business law (LL M); energy and environment (LL M); international and comparative law (LL M); law (LL M, JD, SJD); JD/M Acct; JD/MA; JD/MBA; JD/MHA; JD/MPH; JD/MS; JD/MSW. *Accreditation:* ABA. *Degree requirements:* For doctorate, thesis/dissertation (for some programs). *Entrance requirements:* For doctorate, LSAT (for JD). Additional exam requirements/recommendations for international students: Required—TOEFL (minimum score 575 paper-based; 233 computer-based). Electronic applications accepted. *Expenses:* Contact institution. *Faculty research:* Civil law.

Universidad Autonoma de Guadalajara, Graduate Programs, Guadalajara, Mexico. Offers administrative law and justice (LL M); advertising and corporate communications (MA); architecture (M Arch); business (MBA); computational science (MCC); education

(Ed M, Ed D); English-Spanish translation (MA); entrepreneurship and management (MBA); integrated management of digital animation (MA); international business (MIB); international corporate law (LL M); internet technologies (MS); manufacturing systems (MMS); occupational health (MS); philosophy (MA, PhD); power electronics (MS); quality systems (MQS); renewable energy (MS); social evaluation of projects (MBA); strategic market research (MBA); tax law (MA); teaching mathematics (MA).

Universidad Central del Este, Law School, San Pedro de Macoris, Dominican Republic. Offers JD.

Universidad Iberoamericana, Graduate School, Santo Domingo D.N., Dominican Republic. Offers business administration (MBA, PMBA); constitutional law (LL M); dentistry (DMD); educational management (MA); integrated marketing communication (MA); psychopedagogical intervention (M Ed); real estate law (LL M); strategic management of human talent (MM).

Université de Montréal, Faculty of Law, Montréal, QC H3C 3J7, Canada. Offers business law (DESS); common law (North America) (JD); international law (DESS); law (LL M, LL D, DDN, DESS, LL B); tax law (LL M). Part-time programs available. *Degree requirements:* For master's, thesis; for doctorate, thesis/dissertation, project; for other advanced degree, thesis (for some programs). Electronic applications accepted. *Faculty research:* Legal theory; constitutional, private, and public law.

Université de Sherbrooke, Faculty of Law, Sherbrooke, QC J1K 2R1, Canada. Offers alternative dispute resolution (LL M, Diploma); business law (Diploma); health law (LL M, Diploma); law (JD, LL D); legal management (Diploma); notarial law (DDN); transnational law (Diploma). Part-time and evening/weekend programs available. *Degree requirements:* For master's, thesis; for other advanced degree, one foreign language. *Entrance requirements:* For master's and other advanced degree, LL B. Electronic applications accepted.

Université du Québec à Montréal, Graduate Programs, Program in Social and Labor Law, Montréal, QC H3C 3P8, Canada. Offers Certificate.

Université Laval, Faculty of Law, Programs in Law, Québec, QC G1K 7P4, Canada. Offers environment, sustainable development and food safety (LL M); international and transnational law (LL M, Diploma); law (LL M, LL D); law of business (LL M, Diploma). Part-time programs available. Terminal master's awarded for partial completion of doctoral program. *Degree requirements:* For master's, thesis (for some programs); for doctorate, thesis/dissertation. *Entrance requirements:* For master's, doctorate, and Diploma, knowledge of French and English. Electronic applications accepted.

University at Buffalo, the State University of New York, Graduate School, Law School, Buffalo, NY 14260. Offers criminal law (LL M); general law (LL M); law (JD); JD/MA; JD/MBA; JD/MLS; JD/MPH; JD/MSW; JD/MUP; JD/PhD; JD/Pharm D. *Accreditation:* ABA. *Faculty:* 60 full-time (28 women), 123 part-time/adjunct (43 women). *Students:* 658 full-time (307 women), 5 part-time (4 women); includes 93 minority (30 Black or African American, non-Hispanic/Latino; 4 American Indian or Alaska Native, non-Hispanic/Latino; 24 Asian, non-Hispanic/Latino; 18 Hispanic/Latino; 17 Two or more races, non-Hispanic/Latino), 22 international. Average age 26. 1,619 applicants, 39% accepted, 175 enrolled. In 2011, 14 master's, 244 doctorates awarded. *Entrance requirements:* For master's, JD; for doctorate, LSAT, minimum undergraduate GPA of 2.5. Additional exam requirements/recommendations for international students: Required—TOEFL (minimum score 650 paper-based; 280 computer-based; 114 iBT). *Application deadline:* For fall admission, 3/15 priority date for domestic students, 3/15 for international students. Applications are processed on a rolling basis. Application fee: $75. Electronic applications accepted. *Expenses:* Contact institution. *Financial support:* In 2011–12, 660 students received support, including 6 fellowships with full tuition reimbursements available (averaging $16,010 per year), 21 research assistantships; career-related internships or fieldwork, Federal Work-Study, institutionally sponsored loans, scholarships/grants, tuition waivers (full and partial), and unspecified assistantships also available. Financial award application deadline: 3/1; financial award applicants required to submit FAFSA. *Faculty research:* Criminal law, environmental law, international law, human rights, labor and employment law. *Total annual research expenditures:* $91,478. *Unit head:* Dr. Makau Mutua, Dean, 716-645-2311, Fax: 716-645-2064, E-mail: mutua@buffalo.edu. *Application contact:* Lillie V. Wiley-Upshaw, Vice Dean/Director of Admissions and Financial Aid, 716-645-2907, Fax: 716-645-6676, E-mail: law-admissions@buffalo.edu. Web site: http://www.law.buffalo.edu/.

The University of Akron, School of Law, Akron, OH 44325. Offers intellectual property (LL M); law (JD); JD/M Tax; JD/MAP; JD/MBA; JD/MPA; JD/MSMHR. *Accreditation:* ABA. Part-time and evening/weekend programs available. *Faculty:* 36 full-time (14 women), 17 part-time/adjunct (4 women). *Students:* 322 full-time (125 women), 224 part-time (108 women); includes 80 minority (32 Black or African American, non-Hispanic/Latino; 2 American Indian or Alaska Native, non-Hispanic/Latino; 21 Asian, non-Hispanic/Latino; 20 Hispanic/Latino; 5 Two or more races, non-Hispanic/Latino), 1 international. Average age 28. 1,876 applicants, 39% accepted, 202 enrolled. In 2011, 109 doctorates awarded. *Entrance requirements:* For doctorate, LSAT, LSDAS. Additional exam requirements/recommendations for international students: Required—TOEFL (minimum score 650 paper-based; 230 computer-based; 115 iBT). *Application deadline:* For fall admission, 3/1 priority date for domestic students, 3/1 for international students. Applications are processed on a rolling basis. Application fee: $0. Electronic applications accepted. *Expenses:* Contact institution. *Financial support:* In 2011–12, 171 students received support. Career-related internships or fieldwork, scholarships/grants, and tuition waivers (full and partial) available. Support available to part-time students. Financial award applicants required to submit FAFSA. *Faculty research:* Intellectual property; law and science; trust and elder law, including taxation and retirement benefits; professional responsibility and judicial ethics; constitutional law, theory, and process. *Total annual research expenditures:* $79,015. *Unit head:* Martin H. Belsky, Dean, 330-972-6359, Fax: 330-258-2343, E-mail: belsky@uakron.edu. *Application contact:* Lauri S. File, Assistant Dean of Admission and Financial Aid, 330-972-7331, Fax: 330-258-2343, E-mail: lfile@uakron.edu. Web site: http://www.uakron.edu/law/index.dot.

The University of Alabama, School of Law, Tuscaloosa, AL 35487. Offers LL M, LL M in Tax, JD, JD/MBA. *Accreditation:* ABA. *Faculty:* 32 full-time (12 women), 45 part-time/adjunct (7 women). *Students:* 524 full-time (210 women), 136 part-time (61 women); includes 111 minority (60 Black or African American, non-Hispanic/Latino; 6 American Indian or Alaska Native, non-Hispanic/Latino; 20 Asian, non-Hispanic/Latino; 17 Hispanic/Latino; 8 Two or more races, non-Hispanic/Latino), 4 international. Average age 28. 2,063 applicants, 30% accepted, 235 enrolled. In 2011, 94 master's, 162 doctorates awarded. *Degree requirements:* For doctorate, 90 hours, including 3 hours of professional skills, 1 seminar, and 35 required hours. *Entrance requirements:* For doctorate, LSAT, undergraduate degree. Additional exam requirements/recommendations for international students: Required—TOEFL, IELTS. *Application deadline:* Applications are processed on a rolling basis. Application fee: $50 ($60 for international students). Electronic applications accepted. *Expenses:* Contact institution. *Financial support:* In 2011–12, 383 students received support. Applicants required to submit FAFSA. *Faculty research:* Public interest law, Constitutional law, civil rights, international law, tax law. *Unit head:* Aaron V. Latham, Dean, 205-348-5195, Fax: 205-348-6397, E-mail: alatham@law.ua.edu. *Application contact:* Page Thead Pulliam, Assistant Director for Admissions, 205-348-7945, Fax: 205-348-3917, E-mail: ppulliam@law.ua.edu. Web site: http://www.law.ua.edu/.

University of Alberta, Faculty of Law, Edmonton, AB T6G 2E1, Canada. Offers LL M, PhD. Part-time programs available. *Degree requirements:* For master's, thesis. *Entrance requirements:* For master's, minimum GPA of 3.0, curriculum vitae, 3 letters of recommendation; for doctorate, LSAT. Additional exam requirements/recommendations for international students: Required—TOEFL (minimum score 600 paper-based; 250 computer-based). Electronic applications accepted. *Faculty research:* Health law, environmental law, native law issues, constitutional law, human rights.

The University of Arizona, James E. Rogers College of Law, Tucson, AZ 85721-0176. Offers indigenous peoples law and policy (LL M); international trade and business law (LL M); law (JD); JD/MA; JD/MBA; JD/MPA; JD/PhD. *Accreditation:* ABA. *Degree requirements:* For doctorate, publishable paper. *Entrance requirements:* For doctorate, LSAT, LSDAS, resume, 2 letters of recommendation. Additional exam requirements/recommendations for international students: Required—TOEFL. Electronic applications accepted. *Expenses:* Contact institution. *Faculty research:* Tax law, employment law, corporate law, torts, trial practice and skills, constitutional law, Indian law, family law, estates and trusts.

University of Arkansas, School of Law, Fayetteville, AR 72701. Offers agricultural law (LL M); law (JD). *Accreditation:* ABA. *Students:* 413 full-time (177 women); includes 70 minority (34 Black or African American, non-Hispanic/Latino; 5 American Indian or Alaska Native, non-Hispanic/Latino; 9 Asian, non-Hispanic/Latino; 19 Hispanic/Latino; 1 Native Hawaiian or other Pacific Islander, non-Hispanic/Latino; 2 Two or more races, non-Hispanic/Latino), 2 international. In 2011, 6 master's, 122 doctorates awarded. *Entrance requirements:* For doctorate, LSAT. *Application deadline:* For fall admission, 4/1 for domestic students. Applications are processed on a rolling basis. Application fee: $0. *Expenses:* Contact institution. *Financial support:* In 2011–12, fellowships with full tuition reimbursements (averaging $6,000 per year), 8 research assistantships (averaging $2,500 per year) were awarded; teaching assistantships, career-related internships or fieldwork, Federal Work-Study, and scholarships/grants also available. Support available to part-time students. Financial award application deadline: 4/1; financial award applicants required to submit FAFSA. *Unit head:* Cynthia Nance, Dean, 479-575-5601, Fax: 479-575-3320, E-mail: cnance@uark.edu. *Application contact:* James K. Miller, Associate Dean for Students, 479-575-3102, E-mail: jkmiller@uark.edu. Web site: http://www.law.uark.edu/.

University of Arkansas at Little Rock, William H. Bowen School of Law, Little Rock, AR 72202-5142. Offers JD, JD/MPS. *Accreditation:* ABA. Part-time and evening/weekend programs available. *Entrance requirements:* For doctorate, LSAT. Electronic applications accepted. *Expenses:* Contact institution. *Faculty research:* Employment discrimination, uniform commercial code, Arkansas legal history, scientific evidence, mediation.

University of Atlanta, Graduate Programs, Atlanta, GA 30360. Offers business (MS); business administration (Exec MBA, MBA); computer science (MS); educational leadership (MS, Ed D); healthcare administration (MS, D Sc, Graduate Certificate); information technology for management (Graduate Certificate); international project management (Graduate Certificate); law (JD); managerial science (DBA); project management (Graduate Certificate); social science (MS). Postbaccalaureate distance learning degree programs offered. *Entrance requirements:* For master's, minimum cumulative GPA of 2.5.

University of Baltimore, School of Law, Baltimore, MD 21201-5779. Offers law (JD); law of the United States (LL M); taxation (LL M); JD/LL M; JD/MBA; JD/MPA; JD/MS; JD/PhD. JD/MS offered jointly with Division of Criminology, Criminal Justice, and Social Policy; JD/PhD with University of Maryland, Baltimore. *Accreditation:* ABA. Part-time and evening/weekend programs available. *Faculty:* 76 full-time (36 women), 102 part-time/adjunct (31 women). *Students:* 738 full-time (370 women), 360 part-time (172 women); includes 203 minority (89 Black or African American, non-Hispanic/Latino; 1 American Indian or Alaska Native, non-Hispanic/Latino; 56 Asian, non-Hispanic/Latino; 39 Hispanic/Latino; 1 Native Hawaiian or other Pacific Islander, non-Hispanic/Latino; 17 Two or more races, non-Hispanic/Latino), 2 international. Average age 27. 2,105 applicants, 41% accepted, 328 enrolled. In 2011, 297 degrees awarded. *Entrance requirements:* For doctorate, LSAT. *Application deadline:* For fall admission, 4/1 priority date for domestic students, 4/1 for international students. Applications are processed on a rolling basis. Application fee: $60. Electronic applications accepted. *Expenses:* Contact institution. *Financial support:* In 2011–12, 192 students received support. Research assistantships, teaching assistantships, career-related internships or fieldwork, Federal Work-Study, institutionally sponsored loans, and scholarships/grants available. Support available to part-time students. Financial award application deadline: 4/1; financial award applicants required to submit FAFSA. *Faculty research:* Plain view doctrine, statute of limitations, bankruptcy, family law, international and comparative law, Constitutional law. *Unit head:* Ronald Weich, Dean, 410-837-4458. *Application contact:* Jeffrey L. Zavrotny, Assistant Dean for Admissions, 410-837-5809, Fax: 410-837-4188, E-mail: jzavrotny@ubalt.edu. Web site: http://law.ubalt.edu/.

The University of British Columbia, Faculty of Law, Vancouver, BC V6T 1Z1, Canada. Offers LL M, LL M CL, PhD. Part-time programs available. *Degree requirements:* For master's, variable foreign language requirement, thesis, seminar; for doctorate, variable foreign language requirement, comprehensive exam, thesis/dissertation, seminar. *Entrance requirements:* For master's, LL B or JD, thesis proposal, 3 letters of reference; for doctorate, LL B or JD, LL M, thesis proposal, 3 letters of reference. Additional exam requirements/recommendations for international students: Required—TOEFL (minimum score 600 paper-based; 250 computer-based; 100 iBT), IELTS (minimum score 7). Electronic applications accepted. *Faculty research:* Aboriginal rights/native law, Asian legal studies, criminal law, environmental law, international law, corporate, human rights, intellectual property, dispute resolution, entertainment.

University of Calgary, Faculty of Law, Calgary, AB T2N 1N4, Canada. Offers LL M, JD, Postbaccalaureate Certificate. *Entrance requirements:* For doctorate, LSAT. Additional exam requirements/recommendations for international students: Required—TOEFL (minimum score 600 paper-based; 250 computer-based; 100 iBT). *Expenses:* Contact institution.

University of California, Berkeley, Graduate Division, Haas School of Business and School of Law, Concurrent JD/MBA Program, Berkeley, CA 94720-1500. Offers JD/MBA. *Accreditation:* AACSB; ABA. *Faculty:* 77 full-time (18 women), 152 part-time/adjunct (24 women). *Students:* 2 full-time (0 women). *Entrance requirements:* Additional exam requirements/recommendations for international students: Required—TOEFL. Application fee: $200. Electronic applications accepted. *Financial support:* Application deadline: 3/1; applicants required to submit FAFSA. *Unit head:* Julia Hwang, Director, MBA Program, 510-642-1405, Fax: 510-643-6659, E-mail: julia_hwang@haas.berkeley.edu. *Application contact:* Office of Admissions, 510-642-1405, Fax: 510-643-6659, E-mail: admissions@boalt.berkeley.edu. Web site: http://mba.haas.berkeley.edu/academics/concurrentdegrees.html.

University of California, Berkeley, School of Law, Berkeley, CA 94720-7200. Offers jurisprudence and social policy (PhD); law (LL M, JD, JSD); JD/MA; JD/MBA; JD/MCP; JD/MJ; JD/MPP; JD/MSW. *Accreditation:* ABA. Terminal master's awarded for partial completion of doctoral program. *Degree requirements:* For master's, thesis; for doctorate, variable foreign language requirement, thesis/dissertation (for some programs). *Entrance requirements:* For master's and doctorate, letters of recommendation. Additional exam requirements/recommendations for international students: Required—TOEFL. *Expenses:* Contact institution. *Faculty research:* Law and technology; social justice; environmental law; business, law and economics; international/comparative law.

University of California, Davis, School of Law, Davis, CA 95616-5201. Offers LL M, JD, JD/MA, JD/MBA. *Accreditation:* ABA. *Entrance requirements:* For doctorate, LSAT. Electronic applications accepted. *Expenses:* Contact institution. *Faculty research:* International law, intellectual property, immigration, environmental law, public interest law.

University of California, Hastings College of the Law, Graduate Programs, San Francisco, CA 94102-4978. Offers LL M, MSL, JD. *Accreditation:* ABA. *Faculty:* 73 full-time (33 women), 62 part-time/adjunct (22 women). *Students:* 1,241 full-time (669 women), 3 part-time (1 woman); includes 412 minority (39 Black or African American, non-Hispanic/Latino; 6 American Indian or Alaska Native, non-Hispanic/Latino; 288 Asian, non-Hispanic/Latino; 79 Hispanic/Latino), 18 international. *Entrance requirements:* For doctorate, LSAT, LSDAS, 2 letters of recommendation. *Application deadline:* For fall admission, 3/1 priority date for domestic students, 3/1 for international students. Applications are processed on a rolling basis. Application fee: $75. Electronic applications accepted. *Expenses:* Tuition, state resident: full-time $40,836. Tuition, nonresident: full-time $49,336. *Financial support:* Career-related internships or fieldwork, Federal Work-Study, institutionally sponsored loans, and scholarships/grants available. Support available to part-time students. Financial award application deadline: 3/2; financial award applicants required to submit FAFSA. *Faculty research:* Immigration and refugee law, civil procedure and evidence, taxation law, environmental law and policy, Constitutional law and civil rights. *Application contact:* Greg Canada, Assistant Dean of Admissions, 415-565-4623, Fax: 415-565-4863, E-mail: canadag@uchastings.edu. Web site: http://www.uchastings.edu/.

University of California, Irvine, School of Law, Irvine, CA 92697. Offers JD. *Degree requirements:* For doctorate, project. *Unit head:* Erwin Chemerinsky, Dean, 949-824-7722, E-mail: echemerinsky@law.uci.edu. Web site: http://www.law.uci.edu/.

University of California, Los Angeles, School of Law, Los Angeles, CA 90095. Offers LL M, JD, SJD, JD/MA, JD/MBA, JD/MPH, JD/MPP, JD/MSW, JD/MURP, JD/PhD. *Accreditation:* ABA. *Faculty:* 111 full-time (41 women), 63 part-time/adjunct (18 women). *Students:* 1,089 full-time (519 women); includes 318 minority (39 Black or African American, non-Hispanic/Latino; 18 American Indian or Alaska Native, non-Hispanic/Latino; 148 Asian, non-Hispanic/Latino; 85 Hispanic/Latino; 1 Native Hawaiian or other Pacific Islander, non-Hispanic/Latino; 27 Two or more races, non-Hispanic/Latino), 94 international. Average age 25. 7,328 applicants, 20% accepted, 321 enrolled. In 2011, 74 master's, 342 doctorates awarded. *Entrance requirements:* For doctorate, LSAT (for JD). Additional exam requirements/recommendations for international students: Required—TOEFL for LL M. *Application deadline:* For fall admission, 2/1 for domestic students. Applications are processed on a rolling basis. Application fee: $75. Electronic applications accepted. *Expenses:* Contact institution. *Financial support:* In 2011–12, 739 students received support. Career-related internships or fieldwork, scholarships/grants, health care benefits, tuition waivers (full and partial), and unspecified assistantships available. Financial award application deadline: 3/2. *Faculty research:* Business law and policy; critical race studies, entertainment; media, and intellectual property law; law and philosophy; public interest law and policy. *Unit head:* Rachel F. Moran, Dean/Professor of Law, 310-825-8202. *Application contact:* Admissions Office, 310-825-2080. Web site: http://www.law.ucla.edu/.

University of California, San Diego, Office of Graduate Studies, Program in Health Law, La Jolla, CA 92093. Offers MAS. Program offered jointly with School of Medicine and California Western School of Law. Part-time programs available. *Degree requirements:* For master's, capstone project. *Entrance requirements:* For master's, undergraduate degree in healthcare, law, or related field; 3 years work experience; 3 letters of recommendation; resume.

University of Chicago, The Law School, Chicago, IL 60637. Offers LL M, MCL, DCL, JD, JSD, JD/AM, JD/MBA, JD/MPP. *Accreditation:* ABA. *Faculty:* 70 full-time (21 women). *Students:* 624 full-time (276 women); includes 174 minority (39 Black or African American, non-Hispanic/Latino; 1 American Indian or Alaska Native, non-Hispanic/Latino; 55 Asian, non-Hispanic/Latino; 46 Hispanic/Latino; 33 Two or more races, non-Hispanic/Latino), 16 international. Average age 24. 4,783 applicants, 17% accepted, 191 enrolled. In 2011, 67 master's, 201 doctorates awarded. *Entrance requirements:* For doctorate, LSAT (for JD). Additional exam requirements/recommendations for international students: Required—TOEFL. *Application deadline:* For fall admission, 2/1 priority date for domestic students. Applications are processed on a rolling basis. Application fee: $75. Electronic applications accepted. *Expenses:* Contact institution. *Financial support:* In 2011–12, 294 students received support. Fellowships, research assistantships, career-related internships or fieldwork, institutionally sponsored loans, and scholarships/grants available. Financial award application deadline: 3/1; financial award applicants required to submit FAFSA. *Unit head:* Michael Schill, Dean, 773-702-9494, Fax: 773-834-4409. *Application contact:* Ann K. Perry, Associate Dean of Admissions, 773-834-4425, Fax: 773-834-0942, E-mail: admissions@law.uchicago.edu. Web site: http://www.law.uchicago.edu/.

University of Cincinnati, College of Law, Cincinnati, OH 45221-0040. Offers JD, JD/MA, JD/MBA, JD/MCP, JD/MSW. *Accreditation:* ABA. *Faculty:* 32 full-time, 34 part-time/adjunct. *Students:* 409 full-time (167 women); includes 65 minority (28 Black or African American, non-Hispanic/Latino; 25 Asian, non-Hispanic/Latino; 12 Hispanic/Latino), 2 international. Average age 25. 1,572 applicants, 47% accepted, 119 enrolled. In 2011, 120 degrees awarded. *Entrance requirements:* For doctorate, LSAT. Additional exam requirements/recommendations for international students: Required—TOEFL (minimum score 520 paper-based; 190 computer-based; 68 iBT). *Application deadline:* For fall admission, 3/1 priority date for domestic students. Applications are processed on a rolling basis. Application fee: $35. Electronic applications accepted. *Expenses:* Contact institution. *Financial support:* In 2011–12, 288 students received support, including 288 fellowships (averaging $7,151 per year); research assistantships, career-related internships or fieldwork, Federal Work-Study, scholarships/grants, tuition waivers (full and partial), and unspecified assistantships also available. Financial award application deadline: 3/1; financial award applicants required to submit FAFSA. *Faculty research:* International human rights, corporate law, intellectual property law, criminal law, law and psychiatry. *Unit head:* Louis D. Bilionis, Dean, 513-556-0121, Fax: 513-556-2391, E-mail: louis.bilionis@uc.edu. *Application contact:* Al Watson, Assistant Dean and Director of Admissions, 513-556-0077, Fax: 513-556-2391, E-mail: alfred.watson@uc.edu. Web site: http://www.law.uc.edu/.

University of Colorado Boulder, School of Law, Boulder, CO 80309-0401. Offers JD, JD/MBA, JD/MPA, JD/MS, JD/PhD. *Accreditation:* ABA. *Faculty:* 35 full-time (14 women). *Students:* 519 full-time (253 women), 14 part-time (7 women); includes 124 minority (15 Black or African American, non-Hispanic/Latino; 14 American Indian or Alaska Native, non-Hispanic/Latino; 38 Asian, non-Hispanic/Latino; 52 Hispanic/Latino; 5 Two or more races, non-Hispanic/Latino), 6 international. Average age 27. 972 applicants, 99% accepted, 162 enrolled. In 2011, 180 doctorates awarded. *Entrance requirements:* For doctorate, LSAT, minimum undergraduate GPA of 2.75. *Application deadline:* For fall admission, 2/15 for domestic students. Applications are processed on a rolling basis. Application fee: $50 ($60 for international students). Electronic applications accepted. *Expenses:* Contact institution. *Financial support:* In 2011–12, 24 students received support, including 13 fellowships (averaging $7,657 per year), 10 teaching assistantships with full and partial tuition reimbursements available (averaging $1,595 per year); institutionally sponsored loans, scholarships/grants, health care benefits, and unspecified assistantships also available. Financial award applicants required to submit FAFSA. *Total annual research expenditures:* $1.2 million. *Application contact:* E-mail: lawadmin@colorado.edu. Web site: http://www.colorado.edu/Law/.

University of Connecticut, School of Law, Hartford, CT 06105. Offers JD, JD/LL M, JD/MBA, JD/MLS, JD/MPA, JD/MPH, JD/MSW. *Accreditation:* ABA. Part-time programs available. *Faculty:* 44 full-time (20 women), 75 part-time/adjunct (17 women). *Students:* 490 full-time (221 women), 207 part-time (85 women); includes 144 minority (25 Black or African American, non-Hispanic/Latino; 4 American Indian or Alaska Native, non-Hispanic/Latino; 63 Asian, non-Hispanic/Latino; 51 Hispanic/Latino; 1 Native Hawaiian or other Pacific Islander, non-Hispanic/Latino), 48 international. Average age 25. 2,025 applicants, 34% accepted, 181 enrolled. In 2011, 177 degrees awarded. *Degree requirements:* For doctorate, extensive research paper. *Entrance requirements:* For doctorate, LSAT, undergraduate degree. Additional exam requirements/recommendations for international students: Required—TOEFL. *Application deadline:* For fall admission, 3/15 for domestic and international students. Applications are processed on a rolling basis. Application fee: $60. Electronic applications accepted. *Expenses:* Contact institution. *Financial support:* In 2011–12, 294 students received support. Federal Work-Study, scholarships/grants, and tuition waivers (full and partial) available. Financial award application deadline: 3/15; financial award applicants required to submit FAFSA. *Faculty research:* International law, intellectual property, human rights, taxation, energy and environmental law. *Unit head:* Jeremy Paul, Dean, 860-570-5127, Fax: 860-570-5218. *Application contact:* Karen Lynn DeMeola, Assistant Dean for Admissions and Student Finance, 860-570-5162, Fax: 860-570-5153, E-mail: karen.demeola@law.uconn.edu. Web site: http://www.law.uconn.edu/.

University of Dayton, School of Law, Dayton, OH 45469-1300. Offers LL M, MSL, JD, JD/M Ed, JD/MBA, JD/MS Ed. *Accreditation:* ABA. *Faculty:* 25 full-time (10 women), 21 part-time/adjunct (3 women). *Students:* 484 full-time (203 women), 9 part-time (5 women); includes 43 minority (26 Black or African American, non-Hispanic/Latino; 3 American Indian or Alaska Native, non-Hispanic/Latino; 8 Asian, non-Hispanic/Latino; 6 Hispanic/Latino), 1 international. Average age 25. 1,751 applicants, 70% accepted, 177 enrolled. In 2011, 2 master's, 154 doctorates awarded. *Entrance requirements:* For master's, GRE, GMAT, MSL; for doctorate, LSAT, accredited bachelor's degree or foreign equivalent. Additional exam requirements/recommendations for international students: Recommended—TOEFL (minimum score 550 paper-based; 213 computer-based; 80 iBT). *Application deadline:* For fall admission, 5/1 priority date for domestic students, 5/1 for international students; for spring admission, 3/1 priority date for domestic students, 3/1 for international students. Applications are processed on a rolling basis. Application fee: $0 ($50 for international students). Electronic applications accepted. *Expenses:* Contact institution. *Financial support:* In 2011–12, 296 students received support. Career-related internships or fieldwork, institutionally sponsored loans, scholarships/grants, and tuition waivers (partial) available. Financial award application deadline: 3/1; financial award applicants required to submit FAFSA. *Faculty research:* Bankruptcy, criminal procedure, torts, computer law, intellectual property. *Unit head:* Paul McGreal, Dean, 937-229-3795, Fax: 937-229-2469. *Application contact:* Janet L. Hein, Assistant Dean/Director of Admissions and Financial Aid, 937-229-3555, Fax: 937-229-4194, E-mail: lawinfo@udayton.edu. Web site: http://www.udayton.edu/law.

University of Denver, College of Law, Professional Program, Denver, CO 80208. Offers JD. *Accreditation:* ABA. Part-time and evening/weekend programs available. *Faculty:* 80 full-time (39 women), 80 part-time/adjunct (27 women). *Students:* 921 full-time (455 women), 25 part-time (12 women); includes 152 minority (22 Black or African American, non-Hispanic/Latino; 9 American Indian or Alaska Native, non-Hispanic/Latino; 27 Asian, non-Hispanic/Latino; 70 Hispanic/Latino; 24 Two or more races, non-Hispanic/Latino), 6 international. Average age 28. 2,496 applicants, 41% accepted, 332 enrolled. In 2011, 285 degrees awarded. *Median time to degree:* Of those who began their doctoral program in fall 2003, 100% received their degree in 8 years or less. *Entrance requirements:* For doctorate, LSAT. Additional exam requirements/recommendations for international students: Required—TOEFL (minimum score 587 paper-based; 95 iBT). *Application deadline:* For fall admission, 3/1 priority date for domestic students. Applications are processed on a rolling basis. Application fee: $60. Electronic applications accepted. *Financial support:* In 2011–12, 394 students received support. Career-related internships or fieldwork, Federal Work-Study, institutionally sponsored loans, and tutorships available. Support available to part-time students. Financial award application deadline: 2/15; financial award applicants required to submit FAFSA. *Faculty research:* Lawyering skills, international and legal studies, natural resources law (domestic and international), transportation law, public interest law, business and commercial law. *Unit head:* Martin Katz, Dean, 303-871-6103, Fax: 303-871-6992, E-mail: martin.katz@du.edu. *Application contact:* Wende Best Conway, Assistant Director of Admissions, 303-871-6135, Fax: 303-871-6992, E-mail: admissions@law.du.edu. Web site: http://www.law.du.edu/.

University of Denver, College of Law, Programs in American and Comparative Law and International Natural Resources Law, Denver, CO 80208. Offers American and comparative law (LL M); international natural resources law (LL M, MRLS). *Faculty:* 80 full-time (39 women), 80 part-time/adjunct (27 women). *Students:* 31 full-time (15 women), 30 part-time (15 women); includes 3 minority (1 Black or African American, non-Hispanic/Latino; 1 Asian, non-Hispanic/Latino; 1 Two or more races, non-Hispanic/Latino), 15 international. Average age 31. 66 applicants, 89% accepted, 38 enrolled. In 2011, 35 degrees awarded. *Degree requirements:* For master's, internship. *Entrance requirements:* For master's, JD from U.S. institution. Additional exam requirements/recommendations for international students: Required—TOEFL (minimum score 550 paper-based; 80 iBT). *Application deadline:* Applications are processed on a rolling basis. Application fee: $60. Electronic applications accepted. *Financial support:* In 2011–12, 17 students received support. Federal Work-Study and institutionally sponsored loans available. Support available to part-time students. Financial award application deadline: 2/15; financial award applicants required to submit FAFSA. *Unit head:* Don Smith, Director, 303-871-6052, E-mail: don.smith@du.edu. *Application contact:* Lucy Daberkow, Assistant Director, 303-871-6324, Fax: 303-871-6711, E-mail: ldaberkow@law.du.edu.

University of Denver, Morgridge College of Education, Denver, CO 80208. Offers advanced study in law librarianship (Certificate); child and family studies (MA, PhD); counseling psychology (MA, PhD); curriculum and instruction (MA, PhD, Certificate); educational leadership (Ed D, PhD); educational leadership and policy studies (MA, Certificate); higher education (MA, PhD); library and information science (MLIS); research methods and statistics (MA, PhD); school administration (PhD); school psychology (Ed S). *Accreditation:* ALA; APA (one or more programs are accredited). Part-time and evening/weekend programs available. Postbaccalaureate distance learning degree programs offered (no on-campus study). *Faculty:* 34 full-time (25 women), 70 part-time/adjunct (54 women). *Students:* 385 full-time (289 women), 386 part-time (303 women); includes 168 minority (49 Black or African American, non-Hispanic/Latino; 8 American Indian or Alaska Native, non-Hispanic/Latino; 25 Asian, non-Hispanic/Latino; 71 Hispanic/Latino; 1 Native Hawaiian or other Pacific Islander, non-Hispanic/Latino; 14 Two or more races, non-Hispanic/Latino), 17 international. Average age 33. 668 applicants, 72% accepted, 256 enrolled. In 2011, 308 master's, 43 doctorates, 55 other advanced degrees awarded. Terminal master's awarded for partial completion of doctoral program. *Degree requirements:* For master's, comprehensive exam; for doctorate, 2 foreign languages, comprehensive exam, thesis/dissertation. *Entrance requirements:* For master's and doctorate, GRE General Test or GMAT. Additional exam requirements/recommendations for international students: Required—TOEFL (minimum score 550 paper-based; 80 iBT). *Application deadline:* Applications are processed on a rolling basis. Application fee: $60. Electronic applications accepted. *Financial support:* In 2011–12, 72 teaching assistantships with full and partial tuition reimbursements (averaging $9,049 per year) were awarded; career-related internships or fieldwork, Federal Work-Study, institutionally sponsored loans, scholarships/grants, and unspecified assistantships also available. Support available to part-time students. Financial award application deadline: 2/15; financial award applicants required to submit FAFSA. *Faculty research:* Parkinson's disease, personnel training, development and assessments, gifted education, service-learning, transportation, public schools. *Unit head:* Dr. Gregory M. Anderson, Dean, 303-871-3665, E-mail: gregory.m.anderson@du.edu. *Application contact:* Chris Dowen, Director, MCE Admission Office, 303-871-2783, E-mail: chris.dowen@du.edu. Web site: http://www.du.edu/education/.

University of Detroit Mercy, School of Law, Detroit, MI 48226. Offers JD, JD/LL B, JD/MBA. *Accreditation:* ABA. Part-time programs available. *Entrance requirements:* For doctorate, LSAT. *Expenses:* Contact institution.

University of Florida, Levin College of Law, Gainesville, FL 32611. Offers comparative law (LL M); environmental law (LL M); international taxation (LL M); law (JD); taxation (LL M, SJD). *Accreditation:* ABA. *Faculty:* 77 full-time (37 women), 36 part-time/adjunct (10 women). *Students:* 1,111 full-time (476 women); includes 257 minority (68 Black or African American, non-Hispanic/Latino; 14 American Indian or Alaska Native, non-Hispanic/Latino; 57 Asian, non-Hispanic/Latino; 118 Hispanic/Latino), 45 international. Average age 24. 3,024 applicants, 29% accepted, 295 enrolled. In 2011, 406 doctorates awarded. *Entrance requirements:* For doctorate, LSAT (for JD). Additional exam requirements/recommendations for international students: Required—TOEFL (minimum score 250 computer-based; 100 iBT). *Application deadline:* For fall admission, 3/15 for domestic and international students. Applications are processed on a rolling basis. Application fee: $30. Electronic applications accepted. *Financial support:* In 2011–12, 291 students received support, including 34 research assistantships (averaging $9,867 per year); Federal Work-Study, institutionally sponsored loans, scholarships/grants, health care benefits, and unspecified assistantships also available. Financial award application deadline: 4/15; financial award applicants required to submit FAFSA. *Faculty research:* Environmental and land use law, taxation, dispute resolution, family law, Constitutional law. *Unit head:* Robert Jerry, Dean, 352-273-0600, Fax: 352-392-8727, E-mail: jerryr@law.ufl.edu. *Application contact:* Michelle Adorno, Assistant Dean for Admissions, 352-273-0890, Fax: 352-392-4087, E-mail: madorno@law.ufl.edu. Web site: http://www.law.ufl.edu/.

University of Georgia, School of Law, Athens, GA 30602. Offers LL M, JD, JD/M Acc, JD/MBA. *Accreditation:* ABA. *Students:* 9 full-time (5 women), 2 part-time (both women); includes 1 minority (Black or African American, non-Hispanic/Latino), 7 international. Average age 28. 60 applicants, 37% accepted, 9 enrolled. In 2011, 13 master's, 229 doctorates awarded. *Degree requirements:* For master's, thesis. *Entrance requirements:* For doctorate, LSAT. Additional exam requirements/recommendations for international students: Required—TOEFL (minimum score 600 paper-based; 250 computer-based). *Application deadline:* For fall admission, 7/1 priority date for domestic students; for spring admission, 11/15 for domestic students. Application fee: $50. Electronic applications accepted. *Expenses:* Contact institution. *Financial support:* Fellowships, research assistantships, teaching assistantships, Federal Work-Study, institutionally sponsored loans, tuition waivers (partial), and unspecified assistantships available. Financial award application deadline: 1/31. *Unit head:* Rebecca H. White, Dean, 706-542-7140, Fax: 706-542-5283, E-mail: rhwhite@uga.edu. *Application contact:* Paul M. Kurtz, Associate Dean for Academic and Student Affairs, 706-542-7140, E-mail: pmkurtz@uga.edu. Web site: http://www.law.uga.edu/.

University of Hawaii at Manoa, William S. Richardson School of Law, Honolulu, HI 96822-2328. Offers LL M, JD, Graduate Certificate, JD/Certificate, JD/MA, JD/MBA, JD/MLI Sc, JD/MS, JD/MURP, JD/PhD. *Accreditation:* ABA. *Degree requirements:* For doctorate, 6 semesters of full-time residency. *Entrance requirements:* For doctorate, LSAT. Additional exam requirements/recommendations for international students: Required—TOEFL. *Expenses:* Contact institution. *Faculty research:* Law of the sea, Asian and Pacific comparative law, native Hawaiian rights, environmental law.

University of Houston, Law Center, Houston, TX 77204-6060. Offers energy, environment, and natural resources (LL M); health law (LL M); intellectual property and information law (LL M); international law (LL M); law (LL M, JD); tax law (LL M). *Accreditation:* ABA. Part-time and evening/weekend programs available. *Entrance requirements:* For doctorate, LSAT. Additional exam requirements/recommendations for international students: Required—TOEFL (minimum score 600 paper-based; 100 iBT). Electronic applications accepted. *Expenses:* Contact institution. *Faculty research:* Health law, international, tax, environmental/energy, information law/intellectual property.

University of Idaho, College of Law, Moscow, ID 83844-2321. Offers law (JD); litigation and alternative dispute resolution (JD); Native American law (JD); natural resources and environmental law (JD). *Accreditation:* ABA. *Faculty:* 20 full-time, 1 part-time/adjunct. *Students:* 358 full-time, 4 part-time. Average age 29. *Entrance requirements:* For doctorate, LSAT, Law School Admission Council Credential Assembly Service (CAS) Report. *Application deadline:* For fall admission, 2/15 for domestic students. Applications are processed on a rolling basis. Application fee: $50 ($60 for international students). Electronic applications accepted. *Expenses:* Tuition, state resident: full-time $3874; part-time $334 per credit hour. Tuition, nonresident: full-time $16,394; part-time $861 per credit hour. *Required fees:* $2808; $99 per credit hour. Tuition and fees vary according to program. *Financial support:* Career-related internships or fieldwork, Federal Work-Study, and institutionally sponsored loans available. Financial award applicants required to submit FAFSA. *Faculty research:* Transboundary river governance, tribal protection and stewardship, regional water issues, environmental law. *Unit head:* Donald L. Burnett, Jr., Dean, 208-885-4977, E-mail: uilaw@uidaho.edu. *Application contact:* Dr. Nilsa A. Bosque-Perez, Interim Dean of the College of Graduate Studies, 208-885-6243, Fax: 208-885-6198, E-mail: uigrad@uidaho.edu. Web site: http://www.uidaho.edu/law/.

University of Illinois at Urbana–Champaign, College of Law, Champaign, IL 61820. Offers LL M, MCL, JD, JSD, JD/DVM, JD/MBA, JD/MCS, JD/MHRIR, JD/MS, JD/MUP, MAS/JD, MD/JD. *Accreditation:* ABA. *Faculty:* 51 full-time (21 women), 29 part-time/adjunct (10 women). *Students:* 726 full-time (324 women), 1 part-time (0 women); includes 188 minority (49 Black or African American, non-Hispanic/Latino; 2 American Indian or Alaska Native, non-Hispanic/Latino; 62 Asian, non-Hispanic/Latino; 58 Hispanic/Latino; 2 Native Hawaiian or other Pacific Islander, non-Hispanic/Latino; 15 Two or more races, non-Hispanic/Latino), 113 international. 1,128 applicants, 35% accepted, 283 enrolled. In 2011, 82 master's, 191 doctorates awarded. *Entrance requirements:* For master's, minimum GPA of 3.0; for doctorate, LSAT (for JD), minimum GPA of 3.0 (for JSD). Additional exam requirements/recommendations for international students: Required—TOEFL (minimum score 550 paper-based; 250 computer-based; 79 iBT) or IELTS (minimum score 7). *Application deadline:* Applications are processed on a rolling basis. Application fee: $75 ($90 for international students). Electronic applications accepted. *Expenses:* Contact institution. *Financial support:* In 2011–12, 2 fellowships, 1 research assistantship, 5 teaching assistantships were awarded; tuition waivers (full and partial) also available. *Unit head:* Bruce Smith, Dean, 217-244-8446, Fax: 217-244-1478, E-mail: smithb@illinois.edu. *Application contact:* Christine Renshaw, Assistant Director, 217-333-6066, Fax: 217-244-1478, E-mail: renshaw@illinois.edu. Web site: http://www.law.illinois.edu/.

The University of Iowa, College of Law, Iowa City, IA 52242. Offers LL M, JD, JD/MA, JD/MBA, JD/MD, JD/MHA, JD/MPH, JD/MS, JD/PhD. *Accreditation:* ABA. *Faculty:* 48 full-time (17 women), 26 part-time/adjunct (11 women). *Students:* 550 full-time (234 women); includes 91 minority (15 Black or African American, non-Hispanic/Latino; 6 American Indian or Alaska Native, non-Hispanic/Latino; 39 Asian, non-Hispanic/Latino; 30 Hispanic/Latino; 1 Native Hawaiian or other Pacific Islander, non-Hispanic/Latino), 8 international. Average age 24. 1,872 applicants, 39% accepted, 180 enrolled. In 2011, 5 master's, 183 doctorates awarded. *Entrance requirements:* For doctorate, LSAT. Additional exam requirements/recommendations for international students: Required—TOEFL or IELTS. *Application deadline:* For fall admission, 3/1 for domestic and international students. Applications are processed on a rolling basis. Application fee: $60 ($85 for international students). Electronic applications accepted. *Expenses:* Contact institution. *Financial support:* In 2011–12, 364 students received support, including 284 fellowships with full and partial tuition reimbursements available (averaging $16,238 per year), 145 research assistantships with partial tuition reimbursements available (averaging $2,175 per year); career-related internships or fieldwork, Federal Work-Study, institutionally sponsored loans, scholarships/grants, health care benefits, and unspecified assistantships also available. Financial award applicants required to submit FAFSA. *Faculty research:* International and comparative law, health law, business law, intellectual property law, antitrust law. *Total annual research expenditures:* $491,559. *Unit head:* Gail Agrawal, Dean, 319-335-9034, E-mail: gail-agrawal@uiowa.edu. *Application contact:* Collins Byrd, Assistant Dean of Admissions, 319-335-9095, Fax: 319-335-9646, E-mail: law-admissions@uiowa.edu. Web site: http://www.law.uiowa.edu/.

The University of Kansas, School of Law, Lawrence, KS 66045-7608. Offers JD, JD/MA, JD/MBA, JD/MHSA, JD/MPA, JD/MS, JD/MSW, JD/MUP. *Accreditation:* ABA. *Faculty:* 39 full-time (17 women), 19 part-time/adjunct (5 women). *Students:* 463 full-time (179 women), 27 part-time (5 women); includes 81 minority (13 Black or African American, non-Hispanic/Latino; 9 American Indian or Alaska Native, non-Hispanic/Latino; 16 Asian, non-Hispanic/Latino; 32 Hispanic/Latino; 11 Two or more races, non-Hispanic/Latino), 29 international. Average age 26. 819 applicants, 49% accepted, 134 enrolled. In 2011, 160 doctorates awarded. *Entrance requirements:* For doctorate, LSAT, 2 letters of recommendation. Additional exam requirements/recommendations for international students: Required—TOEFL. *Application deadline:* For fall admission, 5/1 for domestic and international students. Applications are processed on a rolling basis. Application fee: $55. Electronic applications accepted. *Expenses:* Contact institution. *Financial support:* In 2011–12, 7 fellowships (averaging $3,000 per year), 40 research assistantships, 9 teaching assistantships (averaging $3,600 per year) were awarded; career-related internships or fieldwork, Federal Work-Study, institutionally sponsored loans, and scholarships/grants also available. Financial award application deadline: 2/15; financial award applicants required to submit FAFSA. *Faculty research:* International law, business law, criminal law, elder law, law and public policy. *Unit head:* Stephen W. Mazza, Dean, 785-864-4550, Fax: 785-864-5054. *Application contact:* Steven Freedman, Assistant Dean for Admissions, 866-220-3654, E-mail: admitlaw@ku.edu. Web site: http://www.law.ku.edu/.

University of Kentucky, College of Law, Lexington, KY 40506-0048. Offers JD, JD/MA, JD/MBA, JD/MPA. *Accreditation:* ABA. *Entrance requirements:* For doctorate, LSAT, LSDAS. Additional exam requirements/recommendations for international students: Required—TOEFL. Electronic applications accepted. *Expenses:* Contact institution. *Faculty research:* Health law, education law, advocacy, business law, white collar crime, international trade law, corporate mergers, taxation of Internet transactions.

University of La Verne, College of Law, Ontario, CA 91764. Offers JD. Part-time and evening/weekend programs available. *Entrance requirements:* For doctorate, LSAT. Additional exam requirements/recommendations for international students: Recommended—TOEFL. Electronic applications accepted. *Expenses:* Contact institution.

University of Louisville, Louis D. Brandeis School of Law, Louisville, KY 40208. Offers JD, JD/M Div, JD/MAH, JD/MAPS, JD/MBA, JD/MSSW, JD/MUP. *Accreditation:* ABA. Part-time programs available. *Faculty:* 30 full-time (12 women), 16 part-time/adjunct (6 women). *Students:* 372 full-time (169 women), 28 part-time (9 women); includes 30 minority (15 Black or African American, non-Hispanic/Latino; 3 Asian, non-Hispanic/Latino; 9 Hispanic/Latino; 3 Two or more races, non-Hispanic/Latino), 3 international. Average age 26. 1,500 applicants, 33% accepted, 132 enrolled. In 2011, 143 doctorates awarded. *Degree requirements:* For doctorate, 30 work hours of pro bono service. *Entrance requirements:* For doctorate, LSAT. Additional exam requirements/recommendations for international students: Required—TOEFL (minimum score 550 paper-based; 220 computer-based). *Application deadline:* For fall admission, 3/15 for domestic and international students. Applications are processed on a rolling basis. Application fee: $50. Electronic applications accepted. *Expenses:* Contact institution. *Financial support:* In 2011–12, 146 students received support. Fellowships, research assistantships, teaching assistantships, career-related internships or fieldwork, scholarships/grants, and tuition waivers (partial) available. Support available to part-time students. Financial award application deadline: 6/1; financial award applicants required to submit FAFSA. *Faculty research:* Intellectual property, environmental law, corporate law, taxation, health law, disability law. *Unit head:* James Ming Chen, Dean, 502-852-6879, Fax: 502-852-0862, E-mail: jim.chen@louisville.edu. *Application contact:* Brandon L. Hamilton, Assistant Dean for Admission and Financial Aid, 502-852-6365, Fax: 502-852-8971, E-mail: lawadmissions@louisville.edu. Web site: http://www.law.louisville.edu/.

The University of Manchester, School of Law, Manchester, United Kingdom. Offers bioethics and medical jurisprudence (PhD); criminology (M Phil, PhD); law (M Phil, PhD).

University of Manitoba, Faculty of Graduate Studies, Faculty of Law, Winnipeg, MB R3T 2N2, Canada. Offers LL M. *Degree requirements:* For master's, thesis. *Entrance requirements:* For master's, LL B, minimum GPA of 3.0. Additional exam requirements/recommendations for international students: Required—TOEFL (minimum score 600 paper-based; 240 computer-based). Electronic applications accepted. *Faculty research:* Constitutional law, alternative dispute resolution, human rights law, international trade law, corporate law.

University of Maryland, Baltimore, Francis King Carey School of Law, Baltimore, MD 21201. Offers LL M, JD, JD/MA, JD/MBA, JD/MCP, JD/MPH, JD/MPM, JD/MPP, JD/MS, JD/MSN, JD/MSW, JD/PhD, JD/Pharm D. *Accreditation:* ABA. Part-time and evening/weekend programs available. *Faculty:* 68 full-time (36 women), 51 part-time/adjunct (15 women). *Students:* 740 full-time (361 women), 221 part-time (104 women); includes 305 minority (98 Black or African American, non-Hispanic/Latino; 2 American Indian or Alaska Native, non-Hispanic/Latino; 93 Asian, non-Hispanic/Latino; 86 Hispanic/Latino; 1 Native Hawaiian or other Pacific Islander, non-Hispanic/Latino; 25 Two or more races, non-Hispanic/Latino), 11 international. Average age 27. 3,994 applicants, 20% accepted, 276 enrolled. In 2011, 6 master's, 297 doctorates awarded. *Degree requirements:* For master's, thesis; for doctorate, writing certification. *Entrance requirements:* For doctorate, LSAT, LSDAS. Additional exam requirements/recommendations for international students: Required—TOEFL (minimum score 550 paper-based; 80 iBT). *Application deadline:* For fall admission, 4/1 priority date for domestic students, 4/1 for international students. Applications are processed on a rolling basis. Application fee: $70. Electronic applications accepted. *Expenses:* Contact institution. *Financial support:* In 2011–12, 515 students received support, including 35 fellowships (averaging $4,000 per year); Federal Work-Study, institutionally sponsored loans, and scholarships/grants also available. Support available to part-time students. Financial award application deadline: 3/1; financial award applicants required to submit FAFSA. *Faculty research:* Environmental regulation, health care policy, intellectual property, civil rights and race history and policy, international and comparative law. *Total annual research expenditures:* $5.7 million. *Unit head:* Phoebe A. Haddon, Dean/Professor, 410-706-7214, Fax: 410-706-4045, E-mail: phaddon@law.umaryland.edu. *Application contact:* Connie Beals, Assistant Dean for Admissions and Student Recruiting, 410-706-3492, Fax: 410-706-1793, E-mail: admissions@law.umaryland.edu. Web site: http://www.law.umaryland.edu/.

University of Maryland, College Park, Academic Affairs, Robert H. Smith School of Business, Program in Business Management/Law, College Park, MD 20742. Offers JD/MBA. *Accreditation:* AACSB. *Students:* 1 full-time (0 women), 3 part-time (2 women); includes 1 minority (Asian, non-Hispanic/Latino). 2 applicants, 50% accepted, 1 enrolled. *Entrance requirements:* Additional exam requirements/recommendations for international students: Required—TOEFL. *Application deadline:* For fall admission, 5/1 for domestic students, 2/1 for international students; for spring admission, 11/30 for domestic students, 6/1 for international students. Applications are processed on a rolling basis. Application fee: $75. *Expenses: Tuition, area resident:* Part-time $525 per credit hour. Tuition, state resident: part-time $525 per credit hour. Tuition, nonresident: part-time $1131 per credit hour. *Required fees:* $386.31 per term. Tuition and fees vary according to program. *Financial support:* Applicants required to submit FAFSA. *Unit head:* Dr. Anand Anandalingam, Dean, 301-405-0582, E-mail: ganand@umd.edu. *Application contact:* Dr. Charles A. Caramello, Dean of Graduate School, 301-405-0358, Fax: 301-314-9305.

University of Maryland, College Park, Academic Affairs, School of Public Policy, Joint Program in Public Policy/Law, College Park, MD 20742. Offers JD/MPM. *Students:* 3 full-time (1 woman), 1 part-time (0 women). 17 applicants, 29% accepted, 1 enrolled. *Application deadline:* For fall admission, 4/1 for domestic students, 2/1 for international students; for spring admission, 10/15 for domestic students, 6/1 for international students. Applications are processed on a rolling basis. Application fee: $75. Electronic applications accepted. *Expenses: Tuition, area resident:* Part-time $525 per credit hour. Tuition, state resident: part-time $525 per credit hour. Tuition, nonresident: part-time $1131 per credit hour. *Required fees:* $386.31 per term. Tuition and fees vary according to program. *Financial support:* In 2011–12, 2 teaching assistantships (averaging $14,633 per year) were awarded. Financial award applicants required to submit FAFSA. *Unit head:* Dr. Donald Kettl, Dean, 301-405-6356, E-mail: kettl@umd.edu. *Application contact:* Dr. Charles A. Caramello, Dean of Graduate School, 301-405-0358, Fax: 301-314-9305.

University of Massachusetts Dartmouth, Graduate School, University of Massachusetts School of Law at Dartmouth, North Dartmouth, MA 02747-2300. Offers JD. Part-time and evening/weekend programs available. *Faculty:* 18 full-time (9 women), 26 part-time/adjunct (10 women). *Students:* 212 full-time (100 women), 123 part-time (71 women); includes 99 minority (42 Black or African American, non-Hispanic/Latino; 2 American Indian or Alaska Native, non-Hispanic/Latino; 18 Asian, non-Hispanic/Latino; 24 Hispanic/Latino; 13 Two or more races, non-Hispanic/Latino), 3 international. Average age 30. 359 applicants, 75% accepted, 113 enrolled. In 2011, 47 doctorates awarded. *Entrance requirements:* For doctorate, LSAT, CAS report, 2 letters of recommendation, resume, statement of intent. Additional exam requirements/recommendations for international students: Required—TOEFL (minimum score 533 paper-based; 200 computer-based; 72 iBT). *Application deadline:* For fall admission, 6/30 for domestic students, 5/30 for international students. Applications are processed on a rolling basis. Application fee: $50. *Expenses:* Tuition, state resident: full-time $2071; part-time $86.29 per credit. Tuition, nonresident: full-time $8099; part-time $337.46 per credit. *Required fees:* $438.58 per credit. Part-time tuition and fees vary according to class time, course load, degree level and reciprocity agreements. *Financial support:* Research assistantships, scholarships/grants, tuition waivers (full and partial), and summer stipends available. Support available to part-time students. Financial award application deadline: 6/30; financial award applicants required to submit FAFSA. *Faculty research:* Legal history, legal philosophy, apology statutes. *Unit head:* Michael Hillinger, Interim Dean, 508-985-1119, Fax: 508-985-1104, E-mail: mhillinger@umassd.edu. *Application contact:* Nancy Fitzsimmons Hebert, Director of Admission, 508-998-9400 Ext. 113, Fax: 508-998-9561, E-mail: nhebert@umassd.edu. Web site: http://www.umassd.edu/law.

University of Memphis, Cecil C. Humphreys School of Law, Memphis, TN 38103-2189. Offers JD, JD/MA, JD/MBA, JD/MPH. *Accreditation:* ABA. Part-time programs available. *Faculty:* 24 full-time (10 women), 44 part-time/adjunct (13 women). *Students:* 394 full-time (162 women), 27 part-time (12 women); includes 60 minority (40 Black or African American, non-Hispanic/Latino; 3 American Indian or Alaska Native, non-Hispanic/Latino; 10 Asian, non-Hispanic/Latino; 7 Hispanic/Latino). Average age 26. 861 applicants, 35% accepted, 144 enrolled. In 2011, 126 degrees awarded. *Entrance requirements:* For doctorate, LSAT, CAS report, letters of recommendation, or evaluations. Additional exam requirements/recommendations for international students: Required—TOEFL. *Application deadline:* For fall admission, 3/1 priority date for domestic students, 3/1 for international students. Applications are processed on a rolling basis. Application fee: $25 ($40 for international students). Electronic applications accepted. *Expenses:* Contact institution. *Financial support:* In 2011–12, 133 students received support, including 24 research assistantships with full and partial tuition reimbursements available (averaging $3,000 per year), 2 teaching assistantships (averaging $3,000 per year); career-related internships or fieldwork, Federal Work-Study, scholarships/grants, tuition waivers (partial), and unspecified assistantships also available. Support available to part-time students. Financial award application deadline: 4/1; financial award applicants required to submit FAFSA. *Faculty research:* Legal education, shareholder rights, tort law, evidence law, employment law. *Total annual research expenditures:* $40,000. *Unit head:* Dr. Kevin H. Smith, Dean, 901-678-2421, Fax: 901-678-5210, E-mail: ksmith@memphis.edu. *Application contact:* Dr. Sue Ann McClellan, Assistant Dean for Law Admissions, Recruiting and Scholarships, 901-678-5403, Fax: 901-678-5210, E-mail: smcclell@memphis.edu. Web site: http://www.memphis.edu/law/.

University of Miami, Graduate School, School of Law, Coral Gables, FL 33124-8087. Offers business and financial law (Certificate); employment, labor and immigration law (JD); estate planning (LL M); international law (LL M), including general international law, inter-American law, international arbitration, U.S. transnational law for foreign lawyers; law (JD); ocean and coastal law (LL M); real property development (real estate) (LL M); taxation (LL M); JD/LL M; JD/LL M/MBA; JD/MA; JD/MBA; JD/MD; JD/MM; JD/MPH; JD/MPS. *Accreditation:* ABA. *Faculty:* 82 full-time (37 women), 107 part-time/adjunct (41 women). *Students:* 1,348 full-time (588 women), 135 part-time (58 women); includes 395 minority (90 Black or African American, non-Hispanic/Latino; 9 American Indian or Alaska Native, non-Hispanic/Latino; 49 Asian, non-Hispanic/Latino; 236 Hispanic/Latino; 1 Native Hawaiian or other Pacific Islander, non-Hispanic/Latino; 10 Two or more races, non-Hispanic/Latino), 56 international. Average age 24. 4,729 applicants, 46% accepted, 447 enrolled. In 2011, 96 master's, 385 doctorates awarded. *Entrance requirements:* For doctorate, LSAT, 2 letters of recommendation. Additional exam requirements/recommendations for international students: Required—TOEFL (minimum score 580 paper-based; 237 computer-based; 92 iBT). *Application deadline:* For fall admission, 1/6 priority date for domestic students, 1/6 for international students. Applications are processed on a rolling basis. Application fee: $60. Electronic applications accepted. *Expenses:* Contact institution. *Financial support:* Fellowships, research assistantships, career-related internships or fieldwork, Federal Work-Study, institutionally sponsored loans, scholarships/grants, and unspecified assistantships available. Financial award application deadline: 3/1; financial award applicants required to submit FAFSA. *Faculty research:* National security law, international finance, Internet law/law of electronic commerce, law of the seas, art law/cultural heritage law. *Unit head:* Michael Goodnight, Associate Dean of Admissions and Enrollment Management, 305-284-2527, Fax: 305-284-3084, E-mail: mgoodnig@law.miami.edu. *Application contact:* Therese Lambert, Director of Student Recruitment, 305-284-6746, Fax: 305-284-3084, E-mail: tlambert@law.miami.edu. Web site: http://www.law.miami.edu/.

University of Michigan, Law School, Ann Arbor, MI 48109-1215. Offers comparative law (MCL); international tax (LL M); law (LL M, JD, SJD); JD/MA; JD/MBA; JD/MHSA; JD/MPH; JD/MPP; JD/MS; JD/MSI; JD/MSW; JD/MUP; JD/PhD. *Accreditation:* ABA. *Faculty:* 94 full-time (33 women), 36 part-time/adjunct (10 women). *Students:* 1,149 full-time (534 women); includes 242 minority (42 Black or African American, non-Hispanic/Latino; 17 American Indian or Alaska Native, non-Hispanic/Latino; 129 Asian, non-Hispanic/Latino; 53 Hispanic/Latino; 1 Native Hawaiian or other Pacific Islander, non-Hispanic/Latino), 30 international. 5,424 applicants, 21% accepted, 359 enrolled. In 2011, 36 master's, 383 doctorates awarded. *Entrance requirements:* For master's and doctorate, LSAT. Additional exam requirements/recommendations for international students: Required—TOEFL. *Application deadline:* For fall admission, 2/15 for domestic students. Applications are processed on a rolling basis. Application fee: $75. Electronic applications accepted. *Expenses:* Contact institution. *Financial support:* In 2011–12, 838 students received support. Career-related internships or fieldwork, Federal Work-Study, institutionally sponsored loans, and scholarships/grants available. Financial award applicants required to submit FAFSA. *Unit head:* Evan H. Caminker, Dean, 734-764-1358. *Application contact:* Sarah C. Zearfoss, Assistant Dean and Director of Admissions, 734-764-0537, Fax: 734-647-3218, E-mail: law.jd.admissions@umich.edu. Web site: http://www.law.umich.edu/.

University of Minnesota, Twin Cities Campus, Law School, Minneapolis, MN 55455. Offers LL M, JD, JD/MA, JD/MBA, JD/MBT, JD/MCS, JD/MD, JD/MHA, JD/MP, JD/MPA, JD/MPP, JD/MS, JD/MURP, JD/PhD. *Accreditation:* ABA. *Entrance requirements:* For doctorate, LSAT. Additional exam requirements/recommendations for international students: Required—TOEFL. Electronic applications accepted. *Expenses:* Contact institution. *Faculty research:* International and comparative law; law, science, and technology; criminal justice; law and business.

University of Mississippi, School of Law, Oxford, University, MS 38677. Offers JD, JD/MBA. *Accreditation:* ABA. *Students:* 528 full-time (241 women), 3 part-time (1 woman); includes 89 minority (62 Black or African American, non-Hispanic/Latino; 5 American Indian or Alaska Native, non-Hispanic/Latino; 6 Asian, non-Hispanic/Latino; 15 Hispanic/Latino; 1 Two or more races, non-Hispanic/Latino). Average age 24. 1,069 applicants, 42% accepted, 160 enrolled. In 2011, 149 doctorates awarded. *Entrance requirements:* For doctorate, LSAT, LSDAS. Additional exam requirements/recommendations for international students: Required—TOEFL. *Application deadline:* For fall admission, 4/1 for domestic students. Application fee: $40. *Expenses:* Contact institution. *Financial support:* Fellowships, research assistantships, teaching assistantships, career-related internships or fieldwork, Federal Work-Study, institutionally sponsored loans, and scholarships/grants available. Support available to part-time students. Financial award application deadline: 3/1; financial award applicants required to submit FAFSA. *Unit head:* Dr. Ira Richard Gershon, Dean, 662-915-6900, Fax: 662-915-6895, E-mail: igershon@olemiss.edu. *Application contact:* Barbara Vinson, Director of Admissions and Recruiting, 662-915-7361, E-mail: bvinson@olemiss.edu.

University of Missouri, School of Law, Columbia, MO 65211. Offers LL M, JD, JD/MA, JD/MBA, JD/MPA. *Accreditation:* ABA. *Faculty:* 35 full-time (13 women), 14 part-time/adjunct (7 women). *Students:* 445 full-time (176 women), 22 part-time (10 women); includes 70 minority (28 Black or African American, non-Hispanic/Latino; 7 American Indian or Alaska Native, non-Hispanic/Latino; 22 Asian, non-Hispanic/Latino; 13 Hispanic/Latino), 4 international. Average age 26. In 2011, 144 degrees awarded. *Entrance requirements:* For doctorate, LSAT. Additional exam requirements/recommendations for international students: Required—TOEFL. *Application deadline:* For fall admission, 3/1 priority date for domestic students. Applications are processed on a rolling basis. *Expenses:* Contact institution. *Financial support:* Fellowships, Federal Work-Study, and institutionally sponsored loans available. Financial award application deadline: 3/1; financial award applicants required to submit FAFSA. *Unit head:* Dr. R. Lawrence Dessem, Dean, 573-882-3246, E-mail: dessemrl@law.missouri.edu. *Application contact:* Tracy Gonzalez, Assistant Dean for Admissions, Career Development and Student Services, 573-884-2979, E-mail: gonzalezt@missouri.edu. Web site: http://www.law.missouri.edu/.

University of Missouri–Kansas City, School of Law, Kansas City, MO 64110-2499. Offers law (LL M, JD), including general (LL M), taxation (LL M); JD/LL M; JD/MBA; JD/MPA; LL M/MPA. *Accreditation:* ABA. Part-time programs available. *Faculty:* 32 full-time (13 women), 7 part-time/adjunct (3 women). *Students:* 452 full-time (162 women), 55 part-time (24 women); includes 56 minority (22 Black or African American, non-Hispanic/Latino; 3 American Indian or Alaska Native, non-Hispanic/Latino; 14 Asian, non-Hispanic/Latino; 16 Hispanic/Latino; 1 Two or more races, non-Hispanic/Latino), 25 international. Average age 28. 929 applicants, 21% accepted, 172 enrolled. In 2011, 30 master's, 156 doctorates awarded. *Degree requirements:* For master's, thesis (for general). *Entrance requirements:* For master's, LSAT, minimum GPA of 3.0 (for general), 2.7 (for taxation); for doctorate, LSAT. Additional exam requirements/

recommendations for international students: Required—TOEFL (minimum score 550 paper-based; 213 computer-based; 80 iBT). *Application deadline:* For fall admission, 3/1 priority date for domestic students, 3/1 for international students. Applications are processed on a rolling basis. Application fee: $50. Electronic applications accepted. *Expenses:* Contact institution. *Financial support:* In 2011–12, 40 teaching assistantships with partial tuition reimbursements (averaging $2,327 per year) were awarded; career-related internships or fieldwork, Federal Work-Study, institutionally sponsored loans, scholarships/grants, and tuition waivers (full and partial) also available. Support available to part-time students. Financial award application deadline: 3/1; financial award applicants required to submit FAFSA. *Faculty research:* Family and children's issues, litigation, estate planning, urban law, business, tax entrepreneurial law. *Unit head:* Ellen Y. Suni, Dean, 816-235-1007, Fax: 816-235-5276, E-mail: sunie@umkc.edu. *Application contact:* Debbie Brooks, Director of Admissions, 816-235-1672, Fax: 816-235-5276, E-mail: brooksdv@umkc.edu. Web site: http://www.law.umkc.edu/.

The University of Montana, School of Law, Missoula, MT 59812. Offers JD, JD/MBA, JD/MPA. *Accreditation:* ABA. *Degree requirements:* For doctorate, oral presentation, paper. *Entrance requirements:* For doctorate, LSAT. *Expenses:* Contact institution. *Faculty research:* Legal education curriculum, business and probate law reform, rules of civil procedure reform, tribal courts, women's issues.

University of Nebraska–Lincoln, College of Law, Lincoln, NE 68583-0902. Offers law (JD); legal studies (MLS); space and telecommunications law (LL M); JD/MA; JD/MBA; JD/MCRP; JD/MPA; JD/PhD. *Accreditation:* ABA. *Entrance requirements:* For doctorate, LSAT. Electronic applications accepted. *Expenses:* Contact institution. *Faculty research:* Law and medicine, constitutional law, criminal procedure, international trade.

University of Nevada, Las Vegas, William S. Boyd School of Law, Las Vegas, NV 89154-1003. Offers JD, JD/MBA, JD/MSW, JD/PhD. *Accreditation:* ABA. Part-time and evening/weekend programs available. *Faculty:* 42 full-time (20 women), 15 part-time/adjunct (4 women). *Entrance requirements:* For doctorate, LSAT, resume, personal statement, letter of recommendation, LSDAS report. *Application deadline:* For fall admission, 3/15 for domestic and international students. Applications are processed on a rolling basis. Application fee: $50. Electronic applications accepted. *Expenses:* Contact institution. *Financial support:* Career-related internships or fieldwork and scholarships/grants available. Support available to part-time students. Financial award application deadline: 2/1; financial award applicants required to submit FAFSA. *Faculty research:* Civil procedure, Constitutional law, federal courts, professional responsibility, juvenile justice. *Unit head:* John V. White, Dean, 702-895-3671, Fax: 702-895-1095. *Application contact:* Elizabeth M. Karl, Admissions and Records Assistant III, 702-895-2424, Fax: 702-895-2414, E-mail: elizabeth.karl@unlv.edu. Web site: http://www.law.unlv.edu/.

University of New Hampshire, Professional Program, Durham, NH 03824. Offers intellectual property (Diploma); intellectual property, commerce and technology (LL M, MIP); law (JD); JD/MIP. Diploma awarded as part of Intellectual Property Summer Institute. *Accreditation:* ABA. *Entrance requirements:* For doctorate, LSAT. Additional exam requirements/recommendations for international students: Required—TOEFL (minimum score 600 paper-based; 250 computer-based). *Application deadline:* For fall admission, 5/1 priority date for domestic students. Applications are processed on a rolling basis. Electronic applications accepted. *Expenses:* Contact institution. *Financial support:* Application deadline: 4/15. *Faculty research:* Legal applications of artificial intelligence, intellectual property. *Unit head:* John D. Hutson, President and Dean, 603-228-1541, Fax: 603-228-1074, E-mail: jhutson@piercelaw.edu. *Application contact:* Katie McDonald, Assistant Dean, 603-228-9217, Fax: 603-224-4661, E-mail: kmcdonald@piercelaw.edu. Web site: http://law.unh.edu/.

University of New Mexico, School of Law, Albuquerque, NM 87131-0001. Offers JD, JD/MA, JD/MBA, JD/MPA, JD/MS, JD/PhD. *Accreditation:* ABA. *Faculty:* 35 full-time (20 women), 36 part-time/adjunct (18 women). *Students:* 362 full-time (172 women); includes 151 minority (10 Black or African American, non-Hispanic/Latino; 30 American Indian or Alaska Native, non-Hispanic/Latino; 9 Asian, non-Hispanic/Latino; 100 Hispanic/Latino; 1 Native Hawaiian or other Pacific Islander, non-Hispanic/Latino; 1 Two or more races, non-Hispanic/Latino), 1 international. 921 applicants, 26% accepted, 113 enrolled. In 2011, 106 doctorates awarded. *Degree requirements:* For doctorate, advanced writing piece, clinic. *Entrance requirements:* For doctorate, LSAT, bachelor's degree. Additional exam requirements/recommendations for international students: Required—TOEFL (minimum score 600 paper-based; 250 computer-based; 100 iBT). *Application deadline:* For fall admission, 2/15 priority date for domestic students, 2/15 for international students. Applications are processed on a rolling basis. Application fee: $50. Electronic applications accepted. *Expenses:* Contact institution. *Financial support:* Career-related internships or fieldwork, Federal Work-Study, and scholarships/grants available. Financial award application deadline: 3/1; financial award applicants required to submit FAFSA. *Unit head:* Kevin Washburn, Dean, 505-277-4700, Fax: 505-277-9558, E-mail: washburn@law.unm.edu. *Application contact:* Susan L. Mitchell, Assistant Dean for Admissions and Financial Aid, 505-277-0959, Fax: 505-277-9958, E-mail: mitchell@law.unm.edu. Web site: http://lawschool.unm.edu/.

The University of North Carolina at Chapel Hill, School of Law, Chapel Hill, NC 27599-3380. Offers JD, JD/MAMC, JD/MAPPS, JD/MASA, JD/MBA, JD/MPA, JD/MPH, JD/MRP, JD/MSIS, JD/MSLS, JD/MSW. JD/MAPPS offered jointly with Duke University. *Accreditation:* ABA. *Entrance requirements:* For doctorate, LSAT. Additional exam requirements/recommendations for international students: Required—TOEFL (minimum score 650 paper-based; 260 computer-based; 100 iBT). Electronic applications accepted. *Expenses:* Contact institution. *Faculty research:* Death penalty, feminist legal theory, urban reform risk-based environmental policy, state and U.S. constitutional law, health law policy.

University of North Dakota, School of Law, Grand Forks, ND 58202. Offers JD. *Accreditation:* ABA. *Entrance requirements:* For doctorate, LSAT. *Expenses:* Contact institution.

University of Notre Dame, Law School, Notre Dame, IN 46556-0780. Offers human rights (LL M, JSD); international and comparative law (LL M); law (JD). *Accreditation:* ABA. *Faculty:* 61 full-time (20 women), 47 part-time/adjunct (18 women). *Students:* 586 full-time (247 women); includes 172 minority (33 Black or African American, non-Hispanic/Latino; 9 American Indian or Alaska Native, non-Hispanic/Latino; 47 Asian, non-Hispanic/Latino; 70 Hispanic/Latino; 13 Two or more races, non-Hispanic/Latino), 32 international. 3,059 applicants, 21% accepted, 183 enrolled. In 2011, 22 master's, 190 doctorates awarded. *Degree requirements:* For master's, thesis, 1-year residency; for doctorate, thesis/dissertation, 2-year residency (for JSD). *Entrance requirements:* For doctorate, LSAT (for JD), LL M (for JSD). Additional exam requirements/recommendations for international students: Required—TOEFL. *Application deadline:* For fall admission, 11/1 priority date for domestic students; for winter admission, 2/28 for domestic students. Applications are processed on a rolling basis. Application fee: $65. Electronic applications accepted. *Expenses:* Contact institution. *Financial support:* In 2011–12, 422 students received support, including 422 fellowships with tuition reimbursements available (averaging $16,849 per year); research assistantships, teaching assistantships, career-related internships or fieldwork, Federal Work-Study, institutionally sponsored loans, scholarships/grants, health care benefits, unspecified assistantships, and university dormitory rector assistants also available. Financial award application deadline: 2/28; financial award applicants required to submit FAFSA. *Unit head:* Nell Jessup Newton, Dean, 574-631-6789, Fax: 574-631-8400, E-mail: nell.newton@nd.edu. *Application contact:* Melissa Ann Fruscione, Director of Admissions and Financial Aid, 574-631-6626, Fax: 574-631-5474, E-mail: lawadmit@nd.edu. Web site: http://www.law.nd.edu/.

University of Oklahoma, College of Law, Norman, OK 73019. Offers LL M, JD, JD/MA, JD/MBA, JD/MPH, JD/MS. *Accreditation:* ABA. *Faculty:* 40 full-time (14 women), 15 part-time/adjunct (4 women). *Students:* 530 full-time (232 women); includes 109 minority (23 Black or African American, non-Hispanic/Latino; 43 American Indian or Alaska Native, non-Hispanic/Latino; 20 Asian, non-Hispanic/Latino; 21 Hispanic/Latino; 1 Native Hawaiian or other Pacific Islander, non-Hispanic/Latino; 1 Two or more races, non-Hispanic/Latino), 1 international. Average age 25. 1,105 applicants, 31% accepted, 153 enrolled. In 2011, 163 doctorates awarded. *Entrance requirements:* For master's, JD or equivalent; for doctorate, LSAT. Additional exam requirements/recommendations for international students: Required—TOEFL (minimum score 550 paper-based; 213 computer-based; 79 iBT). *Application deadline:* For fall admission, 3/15 for domestic students, 4/1 for international students. Applications are processed on a rolling basis. Application fee: $50 ($90 for international students). Electronic applications accepted. *Expenses:* Contact institution. *Financial support:* In 2011–12, 408 students received support. Career-related internships or fieldwork, Federal Work-Study, institutionally sponsored loans, scholarships/grants, and tuition waivers (full and partial) available. Financial award application deadline: 3/1; financial award applicants required to submit FAFSA. *Unit head:* Joseph Harroz, Jr., Dean, 405-325-4884, Fax: 405-325-7712, E-mail: jharroz@ou.edu. *Application contact:* Vicki Ferguson, Admissions Coordinator, 405-325-4728, Fax: 405-325-0502, E-mail: admissions@law.ou.edu. Web site: http://www.law.ou.edu/.

University of Oregon, School of Law, Eugene, OR 97403. Offers MA, MS, JD, JD/MBA, JD/MS. *Accreditation:* ABA. *Entrance requirements:* For doctorate, LSAT. *Expenses:* Contact institution.

University of Ottawa, Faculty of Graduate and Postdoctoral Studies, Faculty of Law, Ottawa, ON K1N 6N5, Canada. Offers LL M, LL D. Part-time and evening/weekend programs available. *Degree requirements:* For master's, thesis or alternative; for doctorate, thesis/dissertation. *Entrance requirements:* For master's, minimum B average, LL B; for doctorate, LL M, minimum B+ average. Electronic applications accepted. *Faculty research:* International law, human rights law, family law.

University of Pennsylvania, Law School, Philadelphia, PA 19104. Offers LL CM, LL M, JD, SJD, JD/AM, JD/LL M, JD/M Bioethics, JD/MA, JD/MBA, JD/MCP, JD/MD, JD/MES, JD/MPA, JD/MPH, JD/MS, JD/MS Ed, JD/MSSP, JD/MSW, JD/PhD. *Accreditation:* ABA. *Faculty:* 70 full-time (22 women), 45 part-time/adjunct (12 women). *Students:* 805 full-time (382 women), 1 part-time (0 women); includes 246 minority (59 Black or African American, non-Hispanic/Latino; 1 American Indian or Alaska Native, non-Hispanic/Latino; 118 Asian, non-Hispanic/Latino; 32 Hispanic/Latino; 1 Native Hawaiian or other Pacific Islander, non-Hispanic/Latino; 35 Two or more races, non-Hispanic/Latino), 30 international. Average age 24. 4,952 applicants, 17% accepted, 266 enrolled. In 2011, 95 master's, 273 doctorates awarded. *Degree requirements:* For master's, thesis optional; for doctorate, thesis/dissertation. *Entrance requirements:* For master's, prior law degree (for LL M); for doctorate, LSAT (for JD), LL M (for SJD). Additional exam requirements/recommendations for international students: Recommended—TOEFL (minimum score 600 paper-based; 250 computer-based; 100 iBT), IELTS (minimum score 7). *Application deadline:* For fall admission, 3/1 for domestic students, 2/1 for international students. Applications are processed on a rolling basis. Application fee: $80. Electronic applications accepted. *Expenses:* Contact institution. *Financial support:* In 2011–12, 354 students received support, including 1 fellowship (averaging $23,000 per year), 22 teaching assistantships (averaging $2,500 per year); research assistantships, career-related internships or fieldwork, Federal Work-Study, institutionally sponsored loans, and scholarships/grants also available. Financial award application deadline: 3/1; financial award applicants required to submit FAFSA. *Faculty research:* Administrative law and regulation, business and corporate law, civil procedure, Constitutional law, criminal law, environmental law, health law, intellectual property and technology law, international and comparative law, law and economics, legal history, philosophy, tax law and policy. *Total annual research expenditures:* $416,772. *Unit head:* Michael A. Fitts, Dean, 215-898-7463, Fax: 215-573-2025. *Application contact:* Renee Post, Associate Dean of Admissions and Financial Aid, 215-898-7400, Fax: 215-898-9606, E-mail: contactadmissions@law.upenn.edu. Web site: http://www.law.upenn.edu/.

University of Pittsburgh, Katz Graduate School of Business, MBA/Juris Doctor Program, Pittsburgh, PA 15260. Offers MBA/JD. *Faculty:* 62 full-time (17 women), 21 part-time/adjunct (4 women). *Students:* 13 full-time (5 women); includes 2 minority (1 Black or African American, non-Hispanic/Latino; 1 Hispanic/Latino). Average age 28. 19 applicants, 95% accepted, 7 enrolled. *Entrance requirements:* Additional exam requirements/recommendations for international students: Required—TOEFL (minimum score 600 paper, 250 computer, 100 iBT) or IELTS. *Application deadline:* For fall admission, 4/1 priority date for domestic students, 2/1 for international students. Application fee: $50. Electronic applications accepted. *Expenses:* Tuition, state resident: full-time $18,774; part-time $760 per credit. Tuition, nonresident: full-time $30,736; part-time $1258 per credit. *Required fees:* $740; $200 per term. Tuition and fees vary according to program. *Financial support:* In 2011–12, 5 students received support. Career-related internships or fieldwork and scholarships/grants available. Financial award application deadline: 3/1; financial award applicants required to submit FAFSA. *Faculty research:* Accounting statements and reporting, corporate finance, information systems processes, structures and decision-making, consumer behavior and marketing models. *Unit head:* William T. Valenta, Assistant Dean/Director, 412-648-1610, Fax: 412-648-1659, E-mail: wtvalenta@katz.pitt.edu. *Application contact:* Thomas Keller, Director of MBA Admissions, 412-648-1700, Fax: 412-648-1659, E-mail: mba@katz.pitt.edu. Web site: http://www.business.pitt.edu/katz/mba/academics/programs/mba-jd.php.

University of Pittsburgh, School of Law, Certificate in International and Comparative Law, Pittsburgh, PA 15260. Offers Certificate. *Faculty:* 46 full-time (19 women), 108 part-time/adjunct (30 women). *Students:* 41 full-time (14 women); includes 8 minority (4 Black or African American, non-Hispanic/Latino; 2 Asian, non-Hispanic/Latino; 2 Hispanic/Latino), 1 international. Average age 24. *Expenses:* Tuition, state resident: full-time $18,774; part-time $760 per credit. Tuition, nonresident: full-time $30,736; part-time $1258 per credit. *Required fees:* $740; $200 per term. Tuition and fees vary according to program. *Unit head:* Prof. Ronald A. Brand, Director, Center for International Legal Education, 412-648-7023, Fax: 412-648-2648, E-mail: rbrand@pitt.edu. *Application contact:* Gina Huggins, Program Administrator, 412-648-2023, Fax: 412-648-2648, E-mail: cile@pitt.edu.

University of Pittsburgh, School of Law, John P. Gismondi Civil Litigation Certificate Program, Pittsburgh, PA 15260. Offers Certificate. *Faculty:* 8 full-time (5 women), 36 part-time/adjunct (9 women). *Students:* 86 full-time (33 women). *Expenses:* Tuition, state resident: full-time $18,774; part-time $760 per credit. Tuition, nonresident: full-time $30,736; part-time $1258 per credit. *Required fees:* $740; $200 per term. Tuition and fees vary according to program. *Unit head:* Martha Mannix, Clinical Associate Professor of Law/Director, 412-648-1390, Fax: 412-648-1947, E-mail: mmannix@pitt.edu. *Application contact:* Charmaine McCall, Assistant Dean of Admissions and Financial Aid, 412-648-1413, Fax: 412-648-1318, E-mail: cmccall@pitt.edu.

University of Pittsburgh, School of Law, LL M Program for Foreign Lawyers, Pittsburgh, PA 15260. Offers LL M. Program offered to international students only. *Faculty:* 46 full-time (19 women), 108 part-time/adjunct (30 women). *Students:* 14 full-time (8 women), 1 (woman) part-time; includes 1 minority (Hispanic/Latino), 13 international. Average age 25. 74 applicants, 61% accepted, 15 enrolled. In 2011, 15 master's awarded. *Degree requirements:* For master's, seminar paper. *Entrance requirements:* For master's, law degree from foreign university. Additional exam requirements/recommendations for international students: Required—TOEFL (minimum score 600 paper-based; 250 computer-based; 100 iBT); Recommended—IELTS (minimum score 7). *Application deadline:* For fall admission, 3/31 for international students. Applications are processed on a rolling basis. Application fee: $0 ($55 for international students). *Expenses:* Contact institution. *Financial support:* In 2011–12, 9 students received support, including 9 fellowships with partial tuition reimbursements available (averaging $15,000 per year); career-related internships or fieldwork and scholarships/grants also available. *Faculty research:* International arbitration, private international law, Islamic law, environmental criminal and comparative law. *Unit head:* Prof. Ronald A. Brand, Director, Center for International Legal Education, 412-648-7023, Fax: 412-648-2648, E-mail: rbrand@pitt.edu. *Application contact:* Gina Huggins, Program Administrator, 412-648-7023, Fax: 412-648-2648, E-mail: cile@pitt.edu. Web site: http://www.law.pitt.edu/academics/international-lawyers-programs/llm.

University of Pittsburgh, School of Law, Professional Programs in Law, Pittsburgh, PA 15260. Offers JD, JD/MA, JD/MAM, JD/MBA, JD/MID, JD/MPA, JD/MPH, JD/MPIA, JD/MSPPM, JD/MSW. *Accreditation:* ABA. *Faculty:* 46 full-time (19 women), 108 part-time/adjunct (30 women). *Students:* 701 full-time (291 women), 18 part-time (6 women); includes 103 minority (58 Black or African American, non-Hispanic/Latino; 1 American Indian or Alaska Native, non-Hispanic/Latino; 25 Asian, non-Hispanic/Latino; 16 Hispanic/Latino; 3 Two or more races, non-Hispanic/Latino). 2,476 applicants, 37% accepted, 254 enrolled. In 2011, 254 doctorates awarded. *Entrance requirements:* For doctorate, LSAT. Additional exam requirements/recommendations for international students: Required—TOEFL. *Application deadline:* For fall admission, 3/1 for domestic students. Applications are processed on a rolling basis. Application fee: $65. Electronic applications accepted. *Expenses:* Contact institution. *Financial support:* In 2011–12, 380 students received support, including 36 research assistantships (averaging $5,440 per year), 13 teaching assistantships (averaging $1,200 per year); career-related internships or fieldwork, Federal Work-Study, scholarships/grants, and unspecified assistantships also available. Financial award application deadline: 3/1; financial award applicants required to submit FAFSA. *Faculty research:* Civil and criminal justice, Constitutional law, health law, international law, law and society. *Total annual research expenditures:* $397,636. *Unit head:* Mary Crossley, Dean, 412-648-1401, Fax: 412-648-2647, E-mail: crossley@pitt.edu. *Application contact:* Charmaine McCall, Assistant Dean of Admissions and Financial Aid, 412-648-1413, Fax: 412-648-1318, E-mail: cmccall@pitt.edu. Web site: http://www.law.pitt.edu/.

University of Puerto Rico, Río Piedras, School of Law, San Juan, PR 00931-3349. Offers LL M, JD. *Accreditation:* ABA. Part-time and evening/weekend programs available. *Entrance requirements:* For master's, LSAT, minimum GPA of 3.0, letter of recommendation; for doctorate, GMAT, GRE, LSAT, EXADEP, minimum GPA of 3.0. Additional exam requirements/recommendations for international students: Required—TOEFL. *Faculty research:* Civil code; Puerto Rico constitutional law; professional behavior, rules and regulations; international law; expert testimony.

University of Richmond, School of Law, Richmond, University of Richmond, VA 23173. Offers JD, JD/MA, JD/MBA, JD/MHA, JD/MPA, JD/MS, JD/MSW, JD/MURP. JD/MSW, JD/MHA, JD/MPA offered jointly with Virginia Commonwealth University; JD/MURP with Virginia Commonwealth University; JD/MA with Department of History; JD/MS with Department of Biology. *Accreditation:* ABA. *Entrance requirements:* For doctorate, LSAT. Electronic applications accepted. *Expenses:* Contact institution.

University of St. Thomas, Graduate Studies, School of Law, Minneapolis, MN 55403-2015. Offers JD, JD/MA, JD/MBA, JD/MSW. *Accreditation:* ABA. *Faculty:* 42 full-time (18 women), 64 part-time/adjunct (19 women). *Students:* 489 full-time (210 women), 2 part-time (1 woman); includes 66 minority (12 Black or African American, non-Hispanic/Latino; 4 American Indian or Alaska Native, non-Hispanic/Latino; 25 Asian, non-Hispanic/Latino; 18 Hispanic/Latino; 1 Native Hawaiian or other Pacific Islander, non-Hispanic/Latino; 6 Two or more races, non-Hispanic/Latino), 2 international. Average age 27. 1,283 applicants, 55% accepted, 171 enrolled. In 2011, 134 doctorates awarded. *Degree requirements:* For doctorate, mentor externship, public service. *Entrance requirements:* For doctorate, LSAT, 2 letters of recommendation. Additional exam requirements/recommendations for international students: Required—TOEFL (minimum score 550 paper-based; 213 computer-based), IELTS (minimum score 6.5), or Michigan English Language Assessment Battery (minimum score 80). *Application deadline:* For fall admission, 7/1 priority date for domestic students, 7/1 for international students. Applications are processed on a rolling basis. Application fee: $0. Electronic applications accepted. *Financial support:* In 2011–12, 277 students received support. Scholarships/grants available. Financial award application deadline: 7/1; financial award applicants required to submit FAFSA. *Faculty research:* Business law, Constitutional law, criminal law, legal ethics, international law. *Unit head:* Thomas M. Mengler, Dean, 651-962-4880, Fax: 651-962-4881, E-mail: tmmengler@stthomas.edu. *Application contact:* Cari Haaland, Assistant Dean for Admissions and International Programs, 651-962-4895, Fax: 651-962-4876, E-mail: lawschool@stthomas.edu. Web site: http://www.stthomas.edu/law/.

University of San Diego, School of Law, San Diego, CA 92110-2492. Offers business and corporate law (LL M); comparative law (LL M); general studies (LL M); international law (LL M); law (JD); taxation (LL M, Diploma); JD/IMBA; JD/MA; JD/MBA. *Accreditation:* ABA. Part-time and evening/weekend programs available. *Faculty:* 55 full-time (19 women), 71 part-time/adjunct (21 women). *Students:* 896 full-time (445 women), 177 part-time (79 women); includes 341 minority (15 Black or African American, non-Hispanic/Latino; 4 American Indian or Alaska Native, non-Hispanic/Latino; 159 Asian, non-Hispanic/Latino; 114 Hispanic/Latino; 2 Native Hawaiian or other Pacific Islander, non-Hispanic/Latino; 47 Two or more races, non-Hispanic/Latino), 31 international. Average age 36. 4,314 applicants, 38% accepted, 300 enrolled. In 2011, 71 master's, 322 doctorates awarded. *Entrance requirements:* For master's, JD, LL B or equivalent from an ABA-accredited law school; for doctorate, LSAT, bachelor's degree. Additional exam requirements/recommendations for international students: Required—TOEFL (minimum score 600 paper-based; 250 computer-based; 98 iBT). *Application deadline:* For fall admission, 2/1 priority date for domestic students. Applications are processed on a rolling basis. Application fee: $50. Electronic applications accepted. *Expenses:* Contact institution. *Financial support:* In 2011–12, 627 students received support. Career-related internships or fieldwork, Federal Work-Study, institutionally sponsored loans, and scholarships/grants available. Support available to part-time students. Financial award application deadline: 3/1; financial award applicants required to submit FAFSA. *Unit head:* Dr. Stephen C. Ferruolo, Dean, 619-260-2330, Fax: 619-260-2218. *Application contact:* Jorge Garcia, Director of Admissions and Financial Aid, 619-260-4528, Fax: 619-260-2218, E-mail: jdinfo@sandiego.edu. Web site: http://www.sandiego.edu/usdlaw/.

University of San Francisco, School of Law, San Francisco, CA 94117-1080. Offers law (LL M, JD), including intellectual property and technology law (LL M), international transactions and comparative law (LL M); JD/MBA. *Accreditation:* ABA. Part-time and evening/weekend programs available. *Faculty:* 27 full-time (13 women), 49 part-time/adjunct (18 women). *Students:* 596 full-time (331 women), 138 part-time (69 women); includes 285 minority (54 Black or African American, non-Hispanic/Latino; 3 American Indian or Alaska Native, non-Hispanic/Latino; 92 Asian, non-Hispanic/Latino; 91 Hispanic/Latino; 2 Native Hawaiian or other Pacific Islander, non-Hispanic/Latino; 43 Two or more races, non-Hispanic/Latino), 23 international. Average age 27. 4,428 applicants, 39% accepted, 270 enrolled. In 2011, 23 master's, 221 doctorates awarded. *Entrance requirements:* For doctorate, LSAT, minimum undergraduate GPA of 3.2. *Application deadline:* For fall admission, 4/1 for domestic students. Applications are processed on a rolling basis. *Expenses:* Contact institution. *Financial support:* In 2011–12, 277 students received support. Career-related internships or fieldwork, Federal Work-Study, and institutionally sponsored loans available. Support available to part-time students. Financial award application deadline: 3/2; financial award applicants required to submit FAFSA. *Unit head:* Jeffrey Brand, Dean, 415-422-6304. *Application contact:* Alan P. Guerrero, Director of Admissions, 415-422-2975, E-mail: lawadmissions@usfca.edu. Web site: http://www.law.usfca.edu/.

University of Saskatchewan, College of Graduate Studies and Research, College of Law, Saskatoon, SK S7N 5A2, Canada. Offers LL M, JD. Part-time programs available. *Degree requirements:* For master's, thesis. *Entrance requirements:* For master's, LL B; for doctorate, LSAT. Additional exam requirements/recommendations for international students: Required—TOEFL. *Faculty research:* Cooperative, native/aboriginal, constitutional, commercial, consumer, and natural resource law; criminal justice; human rights.

University of South Africa, College of Law, Pretoria, South Africa. Offers correctional services management (M Tech); criminology (MA, PhD); law (LL M, LL D); penology (MA, PhD); police science (MA, PhD); policing (M Tech); security risk management (M Tech); social science in criminology (MA).

University of South Carolina, School of Law, Columbia, SC 29208. Offers JD, JD/IMBA, JD/M Acc, JD/MCJ, JD/MEERM, JD/MHA, JD/MHR, JD/MIBS, JD/MPA, JD/MSEL, JD/MSW. *Accreditation:* ABA. *Degree requirements:* For doctorate, thesis/dissertation. *Entrance requirements:* For doctorate, LSAT. *Expenses:* Contact institution.

The University of South Dakota, Graduate School, School of Law, Vermillion, SD 57069-2390. Offers JD, JD/MA, JD/MBA, JD/MP Acc, JD/MPA, JD/MS. *Accreditation:* ABA. Part-time programs available. *Entrance requirements:* For doctorate, LSAT. Additional exam requirements/recommendations for international students: Required—TOEFL (minimum score 600 paper-based; 250 computer-based). Electronic applications accepted. *Expenses:* Contact institution. *Faculty research:* Indian law, skills training, international law, family law, evidence.

University of Southern California, Graduate School, Gould School of Law, Los Angeles, CA 90089. Offers comparative law for foreign attorneys (MCL); law (JD); law for foreign-educated attorneys (LL M); JD/MA; JD/MBA; JD/MBT; JD/MPA; JD/MPP; JD/MRED; JD/MS; JD/MSW; JD/PhD; JD/Pharm D. *Accreditation:* ABA. *Entrance requirements:* For doctorate, LSAT. Additional exam requirements/recommendations for international students: Required—TOEFL. *Faculty research:* Intellectual property law, tax law, criminal law, law and philosophy, law and history.

University of Southern Maine, University of Maine School of Law, Portland, ME 04102. Offers JD, JD/MBA. *Accreditation:* ABA. Part-time programs available. *Faculty:* 16 full-time (4 women), 13 part-time/adjunct (4 women). *Students:* 270 full-time (133 women), 10 part-time (2 women); includes 28 minority (4 Black or African American, non-Hispanic/Latino; 3 American Indian or Alaska Native, non-Hispanic/Latino; 2 Asian, non-Hispanic/Latino; 10 Hispanic/Latino; 9 Native Hawaiian or other Pacific Islander, non-Hispanic/Latino), 3 international. Average age 28. 988 applicants, 48% accepted, 91 enrolled. In 2011, 90 degrees awarded. *Entrance requirements:* For doctorate, LSAT. Additional exam requirements/recommendations for international students: Required—TOEFL. *Application deadline:* For fall admission, 3/1 for domestic and international students. Applications are processed on a rolling basis. Application fee: $50. Electronic applications accepted. Application fee is waived when completed online. *Expenses:* Contact institution. *Financial support:* In 2011–12, 87 students received support, including 15 fellowships (averaging $3,000 per year), 21 research assistantships (averaging $1,200 per year), 8 teaching assistantships (averaging $1,400 per year); Federal Work-Study and scholarships/grants also available. Financial award application deadline: 2/15; financial award applicants required to submit FAFSA. *Faculty research:* Commercial law aspects of intellectual property; domestic violence; race, gender, and law; environmental law and climate change; bankruptcy and predatory lending. *Unit head:* Peter R. Pitegoff, Dean, 207-780-4344, Fax: 207-780-4239. *Application contact:* Nicole Vinal, Interim Director of Admissions/Director of Finance and Administration, 207-228-8442, Fax: 207-780-4239, E-mail: mainelaw@usm.maine.edu. Web site: http://mainelaw.maine.edu/.

The University of Tennessee, College of Law, Knoxville, TN 37996-1810. Offers business transactions (JD); law (JD); trial advocacy and dispute resolution (JD); JD/MBA; JD/MPA. *Accreditation:* ABA. *Faculty:* 44 full-time (20 women), 36 part-time/adjunct (15 women). *Students:* 487 full-time (212 women); includes 121 minority (49 Black or African American, non-Hispanic/Latino; 2 American Indian or Alaska Native, non-Hispanic/Latino; 20 Asian, non-Hispanic/Latino; 30 Hispanic/Latino; 1 Native Hawaiian or other Pacific Islander, non-Hispanic/Latino; 19 Two or more races, non-Hispanic/Latino), 2 international. Average age 23. 1,277 applicants, 34% accepted, 160 enrolled. In 2011, 146 doctorates awarded. *Entrance requirements:* For doctorate, LSAT. Additional exam requirements/recommendations for international students: Recommended—TOEFL. *Application deadline:* For fall admission, 2/15 priority date for domestic students, 2/15 for international students. Applications are processed on a rolling basis. Application fee: $15. Electronic applications accepted. *Expenses:* Contact institution. *Financial support:* In 2011–12, 299 students received support, including 8 research assistantships with full tuition reimbursements available (averaging $5,400 per year); career-related internships or fieldwork, Federal Work-Study, institutionally sponsored loans, scholarships/grants, and unspecified assistantships also available. Support available to part-time students. Financial award application deadline: 3/1; financial award applicants required to submit FAFSA. *Faculty research:* Legal expert systems, medical malpractice remedies, professional ethics, insanity defense. *Unit head:* Dr. Karen R. Britton, Director of Admissions, Financial Aid and Career Services, 865-974-4131, Fax: 865-974-1572, E-mail: lawadmit@utk.edu. *Application contact:* Janet S. Hatcher, Admissions and Financial Aid Advisor, 865-974-4131, Fax: 865-974-1572, E-mail: hatcher@utk.edu. Web site: http://www.law.utk.edu/.

The University of Texas at Austin, Graduate School, College of Liberal Arts, Teresa Lozano Long Institute of Latin American Studies, Austin, TX 78712-1111. Offers cultural politics of Afro-Latin and indigenous peoples (MA); development studies (MA);

environmental studies (MA); human rights (MA); Latin American and international law (LL M); JD/MA; MA/MA; MBA/MA; MP Aff/MA; MSCRP/MA. LL M offered jointly with The University of Texas School of Law. *Entrance requirements:* For master's, GRE General Test. Application fee: $50 ($75 for international students). *Financial support:* Fellowships available. Financial award application deadline: 2/1. *Unit head:* Charles R. Hale, Director, 512-471-7530, E-mail: crhale@mail.utexas.edu. *Application contact:* Dr. Henry Dietz, Graduate Adviser, 512-471-8770, E-mail: dietz@mail.utexas.edu. Web site: http://www.utexas.edu/cola/insts/llilas/.

The University of Texas at Austin, School of Law, Austin, TX 78705-3224. Offers LL M, JD, JD/MA, JD/MBA, JD/MGPS, JD/MP Aff, JD/MSCRP. *Accreditation:* ABA. *Faculty:* 136 full-time (46 women), 64 part-time/adjunct (22 women). *Students:* 1,212 full-time (561 women); includes 318 minority (54 Black or African American, non-Hispanic/Latino; 5 American Indian or Alaska Native, non-Hispanic/Latino; 59 Asian, non-Hispanic/Latino; 171 Hispanic/Latino; 1 Native Hawaiian or other Pacific Islander, non-Hispanic/Latino; 28 Two or more races, non-Hispanic/Latino), 21 international. Average age 24. 4,759 applicants, 27% accepted, 370 enrolled. In 2011, 47 master's, 382 doctorates awarded. *Entrance requirements:* For doctorate, LSAT, minimum GPA of 2.2. *Application deadline:* For fall admission, 11/1 for domestic students; for spring admission, 2/1 for domestic students. Application fee: $70. Electronic applications accepted. *Expenses:* Contact institution. *Financial support:* In 2011–12, 750 students received support, including 100 research assistantships, 32 teaching assistantships (averaging $3,900 per year); career-related internships or fieldwork, scholarships/grants, and tuition waivers (full) also available. Financial award application deadline: 3/15; financial award applicants required to submit FAFSA. *Faculty research:* Constitutional law, corporate law, environmental law, employment and labor law, intellectual property law. *Unit head:* Stefanie Lindquist, Dean, 512-232-1120, Fax: 512-471-6987, E-mail: slindquist@law.utexas.edu. *Application contact:* 512-232-1200, Fax: 512-471-2765, E-mail: admissions@law.utexas.edu. Web site: http://www.utexas.edu/law/.

The University of Texas at Dallas, School of Economic, Political and Policy Sciences, Program in Political Science, Richardson, TX 75080. Offers constitutional law (MA); legislative studies (MA); political science (MA, PhD). Part-time and evening/weekend programs available. *Faculty:* 13 full-time (3 women). *Students:* 36 full-time (16 women), 22 part-time (12 women); includes 25 minority (9 Black or African American, non-Hispanic/Latino; 1 American Indian or Alaska Native, non-Hispanic/Latino; 7 Asian, non-Hispanic/Latino; 6 Hispanic/Latino; 2 Two or more races, non-Hispanic/Latino), 3 international. Average age 32. 69 applicants, 45% accepted, 22 enrolled. In 2011, 24 master's, 3 doctorates awarded. Terminal master's awarded for partial completion of doctoral program. *Degree requirements:* For master's, thesis optional, independent study; for doctorate, thesis/dissertation, practicum research. *Entrance requirements:* For master's, GRE (minimum combined verbal and quantitative score of 1100), minimum undergraduate GPA of 3.0; for doctorate, GRE (minimum combined verbal and quantitative score of 1200, writing 4.5), minimum undergraduate GPA of 3.2. Additional exam requirements/recommendations for international students: Required—TOEFL (minimum score 550 paper-based; 215 computer-based). *Application deadline:* For fall admission, 7/15 for domestic students, 5/1 for international students; for spring admission, 11/15 for domestic students, 9/1 for international students. Applications are processed on a rolling basis. Application fee: $50 ($100 for international students). Electronic applications accepted. *Expenses:* Tuition, state resident: full-time $11,170; part-time $620.56 per credit hour. Tuition, nonresident: full-time $20,212; part-time $1122.89 per credit hour. *Financial support:* In 2011–12, 25 students received support, including 4 research assistantships with partial tuition reimbursements available (averaging $16,650 per year), 15 teaching assistantships with partial tuition reimbursements available (averaging $11,700 per year); career-related internships or fieldwork, Federal Work-Study, institutionally sponsored loans, and scholarships/grants also available. Support available to part-time students. Financial award application deadline: 4/30; financial award applicants required to submit FAFSA. *Faculty research:* Terrorism and democratic stability, redistricting and representation, trust and social exchange, how economic ideas impact political thought and public policy. *Unit head:* Dr. Robert C. Lowry, Program Head, 972-883-6720, Fax: 972-883-2735, E-mail: robert.lowry@utdallas.edu. *Application contact:* Dr. Linda Keith, Associate Program Head, 972-883-6481, Fax: 972-883-2735, E-mail: linda.keith@utdallas.edu. Web site: http://www.utdallas.edu/epps/political-science/.

University of the District of Columbia, David A. Clarke School of Law, Washington, DC 20008. Offers clinical teaching and social justice (LL M); law (JD). *Accreditation:* ABA. Part-time and evening/weekend programs available. *Degree requirements:* For doctorate, 90 credits, advanced legal writing. *Entrance requirements:* For doctorate, LSAT. Additional exam requirements/recommendations for international students: Recommended—TOEFL. Electronic applications accepted. *Expenses:* Contact institution. *Faculty research:* HIV law, juvenile law, legislative law, community development, small business, immigration and human rights.

University of the Pacific, McGeorge School of Law, Sacramento, CA 95817. Offers advocacy (JD); criminal justice (JD); experiential law teaching (LL M); intellectual property (JD); international legal studies (JD); international water resources law (LL M, JSD); law (JD); public law and policy (JD); public policy and law (LL M); tax (JD); transnational business practice (LL M); JD/MBA; JD/MPPA. *Accreditation:* ABA. Part-time and evening/weekend programs available. *Faculty:* 48 full-time (20 women), 59 part-time/adjunct (18 women). *Students:* 704 full-time (325 women), 255 part-time (122 women); includes 254 minority (19 Black or African American, non-Hispanic/Latino; 19 American Indian or Alaska Native, non-Hispanic/Latino; 151 Asian, non-Hispanic/Latino; 65 Hispanic/Latino), 41 international. Average age 27. 3,564 applicants, 38% accepted, 228 enrolled. In 2011, 36 master's, 307 doctorates awarded. *Degree requirements:* For master's, thesis (for some programs); for doctorate, thesis/dissertation (for some programs). *Entrance requirements:* For master's, JD; for doctorate, LSAT (for JD), LL M (for JSD). Additional exam requirements/recommendations for international students: Required—TOEFL (minimum score 600 paper-based; 250 computer-based; 100 iBT). *Application deadline:* For fall admission, 3/15 priority date for domestic students. Applications are processed on a rolling basis. Application fee: $50. Electronic applications accepted. *Expenses:* Contact institution. *Financial support:* Fellowships, research assistantships, teaching assistantships, career-related internships or fieldwork, Federal Work-Study, institutionally sponsored loans, and scholarships/grants available. Support available to part-time students. Financial award applicants required to submit FAFSA. *Faculty research:* International legal studies, public policy and law, advocacy, intellectual property law, taxation, criminal law. *Unit head:* Elizabeth Rindskopf Parker, Dean, 916-739-7151, E-mail: elizabeth@pacific.edu. *Application contact:* 916-739-7105, Fax: 916-739-7301, E-mail: mcgeorge@pacific.edu. Web site: http://www.mcgeorge.edu/.

The University of Toledo, College of Law, Toledo, OH 43606-3390. Offers JD, JD/MACJ, JD/MBA, JD/MPA, JD/MSE. *Accreditation:* ABA. Part-time and evening/weekend programs available. *Faculty:* 32 full-time (14 women), 17 part-time/adjunct (5 women). *Students:* 357 full-time (140 women), 80 part-time (35 women); includes 44 minority (16 Black or African American, non-Hispanic/Latino; 3 American Indian or Alaska Native, non-Hispanic/Latino; 11 Asian, non-Hispanic/Latino; 14 Hispanic/Latino), 6 international. Average age 27. 1,440 applicants, 43% accepted, 137 enrolled. In 2011, 116 doctorates awarded. *Entrance requirements:* For doctorate, LSAT, completion of bachelor's degree prior to first day of law classes. Additional exam requirements/recommendations for international students: Required—TOEFL (minimum score 600 paper-based; 250 computer-based; 100 iBT). *Application deadline:* For fall admission, 7/31 priority date for domestic students, 7/31 for international students. Applications are processed on a rolling basis. Application fee: $0. Electronic applications accepted. *Expenses:* Contact institution. *Financial support:* In 2011–12, 197 students received support, including 23 research assistantships (averaging $584 per year), 19 teaching assistantships; career-related internships or fieldwork, Federal Work-Study, and scholarships/grants also available. Support available to part-time students. Financial award application deadline: 8/1; financial award applicants required to submit FAFSA. *Faculty research:* Theories of land reform, judicial functions of trademarks, federal sentencing/theories of punishment, class action claims in consumer bankruptcy, originalism and the Aristotelian tradition. *Total annual research expenditures:* $84,000. *Unit head:* Daniel J. Steinbock, Dean, 419-530-2379, Fax: 419-530-4526, E-mail: daniel.steinbock@utoledo.edu. *Application contact:* Jessica Mehl, Assistant Dean of Law Admissions, 419-530-4131, Fax: 419-530-4345, E-mail: law.admissions@utoledo.edu. Web site: http://www.law.utoledo.edu.

University of Toronto, School of Graduate Studies, Faculty of Law and School of Graduate Studies, Graduate Programs in Law, Toronto, ON M5S 1A1, Canada. Offers LL M, MSL, SJD. *Degree requirements:* For master's, thesis (for some programs); for doctorate, thesis/dissertation. *Entrance requirements:* Additional exam requirements/recommendations for international students: Required—TOEFL (minimum score 600 paper-based; 100 iBT), TWE (minimum score 5). Electronic applications accepted.

University of Toronto, School of Graduate Studies, Faculty of Law, Professional Program in Law, Toronto, ON M5S 1A1, Canada. Offers JD, JD/Certificate, JD/MA, JD/MBA, JD/MI, JD/MSW, JD/PhD. *Entrance requirements:* For doctorate, LSAT. *Expenses:* Contact institution.

University of Tulsa, College of Law, Tulsa, OK 74104. Offers American Indian and indigenous law (LL M); American law for foreign students (LL M), including energy law concentration; comparative and international law (Certificate); entrepreneurial law (Certificate); health law (Certificate); Indian law (online) (MJ); law (JD); Native American law (Certificate); public policy (Certificate); resources, energy, and environmental law (Certificate); JD/M Tax; JD/MA; JD/MBA; JD/MS. *Accreditation:* ABA. Part-time programs available. Postbaccalaureate distance learning degree programs offered (no on-campus study). *Faculty:* 27 full-time (12 women), 26 part-time/adjunct (8 women). *Students:* 326 full-time (122 women), 50 part-time (27 women); includes 86 minority (11 Black or African American, non-Hispanic/Latino; 40 American Indian or Alaska Native, non-Hispanic/Latino; 5 Asian, non-Hispanic/Latino; 10 Hispanic/Latino; 20 Two or more races, non-Hispanic/Latino), 2 international. Average age 27. 1,525 applicants, 38% accepted, 108 enrolled. In 2011, 4 master's, 126 doctorates awarded. *Degree requirements:* For master's, thesis optional. *Entrance requirements:* For master's, JD from an ABA-approved U.S. law school or a JD equivalent from non-U.S. university; for doctorate, LSAT, BS or BA from 4-year regionally-accredited college/university; for Certificate, BS or BA from 4-year regionally-accredited college/university. Additional exam requirements/recommendations for international students: Required—TOEFL (minimum score 570 paper-based; 230 computer-based; 90 iBT), IELTS (minimum score 7). *Application deadline:* For fall admission, 2/1 priority date for domestic students, 2/1 for international students; for spring admission, 12/5 priority date for domestic students, 12/5 for international students. Applications are processed on a rolling basis. Application fee: $30. Electronic applications accepted. *Expenses:* Contact institution. *Financial support:* In 2011–12, 190 students received support. Career-related internships or fieldwork, Federal Work-Study, and scholarships/grants available. Support available to part-time students. Financial award application deadline: 8/1; financial award applicants required to submit FAFSA. *Faculty research:* International law, Native American law, criminal law, commercial speech, copyright law. *Unit head:* Janet Levit, Dean, 918-631-2400, Fax: 918-631-3126, E-mail: janet-levit@utulsa.edu. *Application contact:* April M. Fox, Assistant Dean of Admissions and Financial Aid, 918-631-2406, Fax: 918-631-3630, E-mail: april-fox@utulsa.edu. Web site: http://www.utulsa.edu/law/.

University of Utah, S. J. Quinney College of Law, Salt Lake City, UT 84112-0730. Offers LL M, JD, JD/MBA, JD/MPA, JD/MPP, JD/MSW. *Accreditation:* ABA. *Faculty:* 36 full-time (11 women), 14 part-time/adjunct (4 women). *Students:* 394 full-time (168 women), 8 part-time (2 women); includes 42 minority (3 Black or African American, non-Hispanic/Latino; 1 American Indian or Alaska Native, non-Hispanic/Latino; 14 Asian, non-Hispanic/Latino; 19 Hispanic/Latino; 5 Two or more races, non-Hispanic/Latino), 2 international. Average age 28. 1,230 applicants, 31% accepted, 114 enrolled. In 2011, 140 doctorates awarded. *Entrance requirements:* For doctorate, LSAT, bachelor's degree from accredited college/university. Additional exam requirements/recommendations for international students: Required—TOEFL (minimum score 600 paper-based; 250 computer-based). *Application deadline:* For fall admission, 2/15 for domestic and international students. Applications are processed on a rolling basis. Application fee: $60. *Expenses:* Contact institution. *Financial support:* In 2011–12, 205 students received support, including 192 fellowships with full and partial tuition reimbursements available (averaging $3,134 per year), 14 research assistantships with partial tuition reimbursements available (averaging $6,000 per year); career-related internships or fieldwork, Federal Work-Study, institutionally sponsored loans, and scholarships/grants also available. Financial award application deadline: 4/1; financial award applicants required to submit FAFSA. *Faculty research:* Environmental law, family law, international law, criminal law, business law. *Total annual research expenditures:* $891,533. *Unit head:* Hiram E. Chodosh, Dean, 801-581-6833, Fax: 801-581-6897. *Application contact:* Reyes Aguilar, Associate Dean for Admission and Financial Aid, 801-581-7479, Fax: 801-581-6897, E-mail: aguilarr@law.utah.edu. Web site: http://www.law.utah.edu.

University of Victoria, Faculty of Law, Victoria, BC V8W 2Y2, Canada. Offers LL M, JD, PhD, MBA/JD, MPA/JD. Part-time programs available. *Degree requirements:* For master's, thesis; for doctorate, thesis/dissertation (for some programs), major research paper (for JD). *Entrance requirements:* For master's, LL B or JD; for doctorate, LSAT (for JD), LL B or JD (for PhD); minimum 3 years of full-time study or part-time equivalent leading toward a bachelor's degree (for JD). Additional exam requirements/recommendations for international students: Required—TOEFL (minimum score 600 paper-based; 250 computer-based; 100 iBT). Electronic applications accepted. *Expenses:* Contact institution. *Faculty research:* Environmental law and policy, international law, alternative dispute resolution, intellectual property law, Aboriginal law.

University of Virginia, School of Law, Charlottesville, VA 22903-1789. Offers LL M, JD, SJD, JD/MA, JD/MBA, JD/MP, JD/MPH, JD/MS, JD/MUEP. *Accreditation:* ABA. *Faculty:* 86 full-time (22 women), 4 part-time/adjunct (1 woman). *Students:* 1,132 full-time (500 women); includes 283 minority (77 Black or African American, non-Hispanic/Latino; 5 American Indian or Alaska Native, non-Hispanic/Latino; 119 Asian, non-Hispanic/Latino; 53 Hispanic/Latino; 29 Two or more races, non-Hispanic/Latino), 44 international. Average age 25. 8,015 applicants, 31% accepted, 406 enrolled. In 2011, 21 master's, 378 doctorates awarded. *Degree requirements:* For doctorate, thesis/dissertation (for some programs), oral exam (for SJD). *Entrance requirements:* For master's, 2 letters of recommendation; personal statement; for doctorate, LSAT (for JD). Additional exam requirements/recommendations for international students: Required—TOEFL. *Application deadline:* For fall admission, 3/1 priority date for domestic students, 3/2 for international students. Applications are processed on a rolling basis. Application fee: $75. Electronic applications accepted. *Expenses:* Contact institution. *Financial support:* Fellowships, career-related internships or fieldwork, Federal Work-Study, and institutionally sponsored loans available. Financial award application deadline: 3/1; financial award applicants required to submit FAFSA. *Unit head:* Paul G. Mahoney, Jr., Dean, 434-924-7351, Fax: 434-982-2128, E-mail: lawadmit@virginia.edu. *Application contact:* Anne M. Richard, Senior Assistant Dean for Admissions, 434-243-1456, Fax: 434-982-2128, E-mail: lawadmit@virginia.edu. Web site: http://www.law.virginia.edu/.

University of Washington, Graduate School, School of Law, Seattle, WA 98195-3020. Offers Asian law (LL M, PhD); intellectual property law and policy (LL M); law (JD); law of sustainable international development (LL M); taxation (LL M); JD/LL M; JD/MA; JD/MAIS; JD/MBA; JD/MPA; JD/MS; JD/PhD. *Accreditation:* ABA. *Degree requirements:* For master's, thesis; for doctorate, thesis/dissertation (for some programs). *Entrance requirements:* For master's, language proficiency (LL M in Asian law); for doctorate, LSAT (for JD). Additional exam requirements/recommendations for international students: Required—TOEFL. *Expenses:* Contact institution. *Faculty research:* Asian, international and comparative law, intellectual property law, health law, environmental law, taxation.

The University of Western Ontario, Faculty of Law, London, ON N6A 5B8, Canada. Offers LL M, MLS, JD, Diploma. *Entrance requirements:* For master's, B+ average in BA, sample of legal academic writing; for doctorate, LSAT. Additional exam requirements/recommendations for international students: Required—TOEFL. *Expenses:* Contact institution. *Faculty research:* Taxation, administrative law, torts, drug and alcohol law and policy, property.

University of Wisconsin–Madison, Law School, Graduate Programs in Law, Madison, WI 53706-1380. Offers LL M, SJD. *Faculty:* 43 full-time (17 women), 11 part-time/adjunct (2 women). *Students:* 98 full-time (63 women), 7 part-time (5 women); includes 6 minority (4 Black or African American, non-Hispanic/Latino; 2 Asian, non-Hispanic/Latino), 99 international. Average age 28. 121 applicants, 79% accepted, 51 enrolled. In 2011, 54 master's, 3 doctorates awarded. *Degree requirements:* For master's, thesis (for some programs); for doctorate, thesis/dissertation. *Entrance requirements:* Additional exam requirements/recommendations for international students: Required—TOEFL (minimum score 580 paper-based; 237 computer-based; 92 iBT). *Application deadline:* For fall admission, 3/1 for domestic and international students; for spring admission, 10/1 for domestic students, 10/15 for international students. Applications are processed on a rolling basis. Application fee: $56. Electronic applications accepted. *Expenses:* Tuition, state resident: full-time $10,296; part-time $643.51 per credit. Tuition, nonresident: full-time $24,054; part-time $1503.40 per credit. *Required fees:* $70.06 per credit. Tuition and fees vary according to course load, campus/location, program and reciprocity agreements. *Financial support:* In 2011–12, 5 fellowships with full tuition reimbursements (averaging $12,000 per year) were awarded; scholarships/grants and tuition waivers (partial) also available. *Faculty research:* Tax policy in emerging economics, international trade law, anti-trust law and regulation, Asian comparative law and legal history, intellectual property in business organization. *Unit head:* 608-262-9120. *Application contact:* Jason Smith, Graduate Programs Coordinator, 608-262-9120, Fax: 608-265-2253, E-mail: gradprog@law.wisc.edu. Web site: http://www.law.wisc.edu/grad/.

University of Wisconsin–Madison, Law School, Law Program, Madison, WI 53706. Offers JD. Part-time programs available. *Faculty:* 73 full-time (35 women), 70 part-time/adjunct (33 women). *Students:* 846 full-time (389 women), 51 part-time (26 women); includes 181 minority (55 Black or African American, non-Hispanic/Latino; 14 American Indian or Alaska Native, non-Hispanic/Latino; 42 Asian, non-Hispanic/Latino; 57 Hispanic/Latino; 2 Native Hawaiian or other Pacific Islander, non-Hispanic/Latino; 11 Two or more races, non-Hispanic/Latino), 127 international. Average age 24. 2,870 applicants, 26% accepted, 242 enrolled. In 2011, 58 doctorates awarded. *Entrance requirements:* For doctorate, LSAT. Additional exam requirements/recommendations for international students: Required—TOEFL. *Application deadline:* For fall admission, 3/1 for domestic and international students. Applications are processed on a rolling basis. Application fee: $56. Electronic applications accepted. *Expenses:* Tuition, state resident: full-time $10,296; part-time $643.51 per credit. Tuition, nonresident: full-time $24,054; part-time $1503.40 per credit. *Required fees:* $70.06 per credit. Tuition and fees vary according to course load, campus/location, program and reciprocity agreements. *Financial support:* In 2011–12, 341 students received support, including 62 fellowships with partial tuition reimbursements available (averaging $13,481 per year), 1 research assistantship with full tuition reimbursement available (averaging $12,000 per year); teaching assistantships with full tuition reimbursements available, career-related internships or fieldwork, Federal Work-Study, institutionally sponsored loans, scholarships/grants, tuition waivers (partial), and unspecified assistantships also available. Support available to part-time students. Financial award application deadline: 4/1; financial award applicants required to submit FAFSA. *Unit head:* Margaret Raymond, Dean, 608-262-0618, Fax: 608-262-5485. *Application contact:* Rebecca L. Scheller, Assistant Dean for Admissions and Financial Aid, 608-262-5914, Fax: 608-263-3190, E-mail: admissions@law.wisc.edu. Web site: http://www.law.wisc.edu.

University of Wyoming, College of Law, Laramie, WY 82071. Offers JD, JD/MPA. *Accreditation:* ABA. *Entrance requirements:* For doctorate, LSAT. Additional exam requirements/recommendations for international students: Required—TOEFL. Electronic applications accepted. *Expenses:* Contact institution. *Faculty research:* Environmental, public land, constitutional, securities law, criminal law.

Valparaiso University, School of Law, Valparaiso, IN 46383-4945. Offers LL M, JD, JD/MA, JD/MALS, JD/MBA, JD/MS, JD/MSSA. *Accreditation:* ABA. Part-time programs available. *Faculty:* 38 full-time (14 women), 27 part-time/adjunct (13 women). *Students:* 546 full-time (251 women), 27 part-time (10 women); includes 163 minority (65 Black or African American, non-Hispanic/Latino; 5 American Indian or Alaska Native, non-Hispanic/Latino; 27 Asian, non-Hispanic/Latino; 50 Hispanic/Latino; 3 Native Hawaiian or other Pacific Islander, non-Hispanic/Latino; 13 Two or more races, non-Hispanic/Latino), 11 international. 1,391 applicants, 71% accepted, 218 enrolled. *Entrance requirements:* For doctorate, LSAT. Additional exam requirements/recommendations for international students: Required—TOEFL (minimum score 600 paper-based; 95 iBT). *Application deadline:* For fall admission, 3/1 priority date for domestic students. Applications are processed on a rolling basis. Application fee: $60. Electronic applications accepted. *Expenses:* Contact institution. *Financial support:* In 2011–12, 136 students received support, including 47 research assistantships, 10 teaching assistantships (averaging $2,400 per year); career-related internships or fieldwork, Federal Work-Study, institutionally sponsored loans, scholarships/grants, and tuition waivers (partial) also available. Support available to part-time students. Financial award application deadline: 3/1; financial award applicants required to submit FAFSA. *Faculty research:* International law, jurisprudence, Constitutional law, animal law. *Total annual research expenditures:* $128,000. *Unit head:* Jay Conison, Dean, 219-465-7834, Fax: 219-465-7872, E-mail: jay.conison@valpo.edu. *Application contact:* Michael Ramian, Assistant Director of Admissions, 219-465-7821, Fax: 219-465-7975, E-mail: law.admissions@valpo.edu. Web site: http://www.valpo.edu/law/.

Vanderbilt University, Vanderbilt Law School, Nashville, TN 37203. Offers law (LL M, JD); law and economics (PhD); JD/M Div; JD/MA; JD/MBA; JD/MD; JD/MPP; JD/MTS; JD/PhD; LL M/MA. *Accreditation:* ABA. *Faculty:* 46 full-time (18 women), 75 part-time/adjunct (22 women). *Students:* 586 full-time (267 women); includes 110 minority (48 Black or African American, non-Hispanic/Latino; 1 American Indian or Alaska Native, non-Hispanic/Latino; 32 Asian, non-Hispanic/Latino; 25 Hispanic/Latino; 4 Two or more races, non-Hispanic/Latino), 24 international. Average age 23. 3,987 applicants, 26% accepted, 193 enrolled. In 2011, 22 master's, 199 doctorates awarded. *Degree requirements:* For doctorate, comprehensive exam (for some programs), thesis/dissertation (for some programs), 72 hours of coursework and research (for PhD). *Entrance requirements:* For master's, foreign law degree (for LL M); for doctorate, GRE (for PhD), LSAT, advanced undergraduate economics (for PhD). Additional exam requirements/recommendations for international students: Required—TOEFL. *Application deadline:* For fall admission, 3/15 for domestic and international students. Applications are processed on a rolling basis. Application fee: $50. Electronic applications accepted. *Expenses:* Contact institution. *Financial support:* In 2011–12, 434 students received support. Career-related internships or fieldwork, Federal Work-Study, institutionally sponsored loans, scholarships/grants, and health care benefits available. Financial award application deadline: 2/15; financial award applicants required to submit FAFSA. *Unit head:* G. Todd Morton, Assistant Dean of Admissions, 615-322-6452, Fax: 615-322-1531, E-mail: admissions@law.vanderbilt.edu. *Application contact:* Admissions Office, 615-322-6452, Fax: 615-322-1531, E-mail: admissions@law.vanderbilt.edu. Web site: http://law.vanderbilt.edu/.

Vermont Law School, Law School, Professional Program, South Royalton, VT 05068-0096. Offers JD, JD/MELP. *Accreditation:* ABA. *Faculty:* 43 full-time (23 women), 19 part-time/adjunct (9 women). *Students:* 566 full-time (282 women); includes 58 minority (12 Black or African American, non-Hispanic/Latino; 5 American Indian or Alaska Native, non-Hispanic/Latino; 19 Asian, non-Hispanic/Latino; 15 Hispanic/Latino; 7 Two or more races, non-Hispanic/Latino). Average age 26. 1,020 applicants, 69% accepted, 151 enrolled. In 2011, 174 doctorates awarded. *Entrance requirements:* For doctorate, LSAT, LSDAS/registration, resume. Additional exam requirements/recommendations for international students: Required—TOEFL (minimum score 600 paper-based). *Application deadline:* For fall admission, 3/1 priority date for domestic students; for spring admission, 11/15 priority date for domestic students. Applications are processed on a rolling basis. Application fee: $60. Electronic applications accepted. *Expenses:* Contact institution. *Financial support:* Career-related internships or fieldwork, Federal Work-Study, institutionally sponsored loans, scholarships/grants, and tuition waivers (partial) available. Financial award application deadline: 3/1; financial award applicants required to submit FAFSA. *Faculty research:* Environmental law, national security, law and medicine. *Unit head:* Geoffrey B. Shields, President and Dean, 802-831-1237, Fax: 802-763-2663, E-mail: hmccarthy@vermontlaw.edu. *Application contact:* Kathy Hartman, Associate Dean for Enrollment Management, 802-831-1239, Fax: 802-831-1174, E-mail: admiss@vermontlaw.edu. Web site: http://www.vermontlaw.edu/.

Villanova University, School of Law, Program in Law, Villanova, PA 19085-1699. Offers JD, JD/LL M, JD/MBA. *Entrance requirements:* For doctorate, LSAT. Electronic applications accepted. *Expenses:* Contact institution. *Faculty research:* International law (public and private), criminal law and procedure sentencing, clinical/pro bono, tax, law and religion.

Wake Forest University, School of Law, Winston-Salem, NC 27109. Offers LL M, JD, SJD, JD/M Div, JD/MA, JD/MBA. LL M for foreign law graduates in American law. *Accreditation:* ABA. *Entrance requirements:* For doctorate, LSAT (for JD). Additional exam requirements/recommendations for international students: Required—TOEFL. Electronic applications accepted. *Expenses:* Contact institution. *Faculty research:* Constitutional law, family law, land use planning, torts, taxation.

Walden University, Graduate Programs, School of Public Policy and Administration, Minneapolis, MN 55401. Offers criminal justice (MPA, MPP, MS), including emergency management (MS, PhD), homeland security policy (MS, PhD), homeland security policy and coordination (MS, PhD), law and public policy (MS, PhD), policy analysis (MS, PhD), public management and leadership (MS, PhD), self-designed (MS), terrorism, mediation, and peace (MS, PhD); criminal justice leadership and executive management (MS), including emergency management (MS, PhD), homeland security policy (MS, PhD), homeland security policy and coordination (MS, PhD), law and public policy (MS, PhD), policy analysis (MS, PhD), public management and leadership (MS, PhD), self-designed, terrorism, mediation, and peace (MS, PhD); emergency management (MPA, MPP, MS), including criminal justice (MS, PhD), homeland security (MS), public management and leadership (MS, PhD), terrorism and emergency management (MS); government management (Postbaccalaureate Certificate); health policy (MPA); homeland security policy (MPA, MPP); homeland security policy and coordination (MPA, MPP); interdisciplinary policy studies (MPA, MPP); international nongovernmental organizations (MPA, MPP); law and public policy (MPA, MPP); local government management for sustainable communities (MPA, MPP); nonprofit management (Postbaccalaureate Certificate); nonprofit management and leadership (MPA, MPP, MS); policy analysis (MPA); public management and leadership (MPA, MPP); public policy and administration (PhD), including criminal justice (MS, PhD), emergency management (MS, PhD), health policy, homeland security policy (MS, PhD), homeland security policy and coordination (MS, PhD), interdisciplinary policy studies, international nongovernmental organizations, law and public policy (MS, PhD), local government management for sustainable communities, nonprofit management and leadership, policy analysis (MS, PhD), public management and leadership (MS, PhD), terrorism, mediation, and peace (MS, PhD); terrorism, mediation, and peace (MPA, MPP). Part-time and evening/weekend programs available. Postbaccalaureate distance learning degree programs offered (minimal on-campus study). *Faculty:* 9 full-time (3 women), 90 part-time/adjunct (41 women). *Students:* 1,396 full-time (886 women), 902 part-time (581 women); includes 1,392 minority (1,205 Black or African American, non-Hispanic/Latino; 11 American Indian or Alaska Native, non-Hispanic/Latino; 35 Asian, non-Hispanic/Latino; 95 Hispanic/Latino; 2 Native Hawaiian or other Pacific Islander, non-Hispanic/Latino; 44 Two or more races, non-Hispanic/Latino), 82 international. Average age 41. In 2011, 265 master's, 34 doctorates, 13 other advanced degrees awarded. *Degree requirements:* For doctorate, thesis/dissertation, residency. *Entrance requirements:* For master's, bachelor's degree or equivalent in related field, minimum GPA of 2.5; for doctorate, master's degree or equivalent in related field; minimum GPA of 3.0; official transcripts; three years of related professional/academic experience (preferred); access to computer and Internet. Additional exam requirements/recommendations for international students: Required—TOEFL (minimum score 550 paper-based; 213 computer-based), IELTS (minimum score 6.5), or Michigan English Language Assessment Battery (minimum score 82). *Application deadline:* Applications are processed on a rolling basis. Application fee: $50. Electronic applications accepted. *Financial support:* Federal Work-Study, scholarships/grants, unspecified assistantships, and family tuition reduction, active duty/veteran tuition reduction, group tuition reduction, interest-free payment plans, employee tuition reduction available. Support available to part-time students. Financial award applicants required to submit FAFSA. *Unit head:* Dr.

Mark Gordon, Associate Dean, 800-925-3368. *Application contact:* Jennifer Hall, Vice President of Enrollment Management, 866-4-WALDEN, E-mail: info@waldenu.edu. Web site: http://www.waldenu.edu/Colleges-and-Schools/College-of-Social-and-Behavioral-Sciences/School-of-Public-Policy-and-Administration.htm.

Washburn University, School of Law, Topeka, KS 66621. Offers JD. *Accreditation:* ABA. *Faculty:* 30 full-time (12 women), 29 part-time/adjunct (12 women). *Students:* 413 full-time (157 women); includes 57 minority (17 Black or African American, non-Hispanic/Latino; 12 American Indian or Alaska Native, non-Hispanic/Latino; 10 Asian, non-Hispanic/Latino; 17 Hispanic/Latino; 1 Native Hawaiian or other Pacific Islander, non-Hispanic/Latino), 8 international. Average age 26. 883 applicants, 40% accepted, 124 enrolled. *Entrance requirements:* For doctorate, LSAT. Additional exam requirements/recommendations for international students: Recommended—TOEFL (minimum score 550 paper-based; 213 computer-based). *Application deadline:* For fall admission, 4/1 priority date for domestic students, 4/1 for international students; for spring admission, 11/1 priority date for domestic students, 11/1 for international students. Applications are processed on a rolling basis. Application fee: $40. Electronic applications accepted. *Expenses:* Contact institution. *Financial support:* In 2011–12, 221 students received support. Career-related internships or fieldwork and scholarships/grants available. Financial award applicants required to submit FAFSA. *Faculty research:* Constitutional law, family law, energy law, banking and securities law, oil and gas. *Unit head:* Thomas J. Romig, Dean, 785-670-1662, Fax: 785-670-3249, E-mail: thomas.romig@washburn.edu. *Application contact:* Karla Whitaker, Director of Admissions, 785-670-1185, Fax: 785-670-1120, E-mail: karla.whitaker@washburn.edu. Web site: http://washburnlaw.edu/.

Washington and Lee University, School of Law, Lexington, VA 24450. Offers law (JD); U. S. law (LL M). *Accreditation:* ABA. *Faculty:* 35 full-time (12 women), 25 part-time/adjunct (4 women). *Students:* 395 full-time (181 women); includes 55 minority (27 Black or African American, non-Hispanic/Latino; 12 Asian, non-Hispanic/Latino; 10 Hispanic/Latino; 6 Two or more races, non-Hispanic/Latino), 4 international. Average age 24. 3,972 applicants, 24% accepted, 121 enrolled. In 2011, 123 doctorates awarded. *Entrance requirements:* For doctorate, LSAT. Additional exam requirements/recommendations for international students: Required—TOEFL (minimum score 600 paper-based; 250 computer-based; 100 iBT). *Application deadline:* For fall admission, 3/1 priority date for domestic students. Applications are processed on a rolling basis. Electronic applications accepted. *Expenses: Tuition:* Full-time $40,820. *Required fees:* $1127. *Financial support:* In 2011–12, 261 students received support. Fellowships, research assistantships, career-related internships or fieldwork, Federal Work-Study, institutionally sponsored loans, and scholarships/grants available. Financial award application deadline: 2/15; financial award applicants required to submit FAFSA. *Unit head:* Mark H. Grunewald, Dean, 540-458-8502, Fax: 540-458-8488, E-mail: grunewaldm@wlu.edu. *Application contact:* Stephen Brett Twitty, Director of Admissions, 540-458-8503, Fax: 540-458-8586, E-mail: twittys@wlu.edu. Web site: http://law.wlu.edu/.

Washington University in St. Louis, School of Law, St. Louis, MO 63130-4899. Offers LL M, MJS, JD, JSD, JD/MA, JD/MBA, JD/MHA, JD/MS, JD/MSW, JD/PhD. *Accreditation:* ABA. *Entrance requirements:* For doctorate, LSAT (for JD). Electronic applications accepted. *Expenses:* Contact institution. *Faculty research:* International law, environmental law, employment discrimination, reproductive rights, bankruptcy and white-collar crime.

Wayne State University, Law School, Detroit, MI 48202. Offers corporate and finance law (LL M); labor and employment law (LL M); law (JD, PhD); taxation (LL M); United States law (LL M); JD/MA; JD/MADR; JD/MBA. *Accreditation:* ABA. Part-time and evening/weekend programs available. *Faculty:* 40 full-time (16 women), 21 part-time/adjunct (4 women). *Students:* 504 full-time (212 women), 96 part-time (45 women); includes 94 minority (36 Black or African American, non-Hispanic/Latino; 3 American Indian or Alaska Native, non-Hispanic/Latino; 38 Asian, non-Hispanic/Latino; 17 Hispanic/Latino), 14 international. Average age 27. 1,164 applicants, 45% accepted, 196 enrolled. In 2011, 17 master's, 198 doctorates awarded. *Degree requirements:* For master's, essay. *Entrance requirements:* For master's, JD; for doctorate, LSAT, LDAS report with LSAT scores, bachelor's degree from accredited institution, personal statement, transcripts from all U.S. undergraduate schools attended and an analysis and summary of the transcripts; letter of recommendation (up to two are accepted). Additional exam requirements/recommendations for international students: Required—TOEFL (minimum score 600 paper-based); Recommended—TWE. *Application deadline:* For fall admission, 3/15 priority date for domestic students, 3/15 for international students. Applications are processed on a rolling basis. Application fee: $50. Electronic applications accepted. *Expenses:* Contact institution. *Financial support:* Federal Work-Study and scholarships/grants available. Support available to part-time students. Financial award application deadline: 3/15; financial award applicants required to submit FAFSA. *Faculty research:* Constitutional law, intellectual property, commercial law, health law, tax law. *Total annual research expenditures:* $160,129. *Unit head:* Robert Ackerman, Dean, 313-577-9016, E-mail: ackerman@wayne.edu. *Application contact:* Erica M. Jackson, Assistant Dean of Admissions, 313-577-3937, E-mail: lawinquire@wayne.edu. Web site: http://www.law.wayne.edu/.

Wayne State University, School of Library and Information Science, Detroit, MI 48202. Offers archival administration (MLIS, Certificate); arts and museum librarianship (Certificate); general librarianship (MLIS); health sciences librarianship (MLIS); information management for librarians (Certificate); information science (MLIS); law librarianship (MLIS); library and information science (MLIS, Spec), including academic libraries (MLIS); organization of information (MLIS); public libraries (MLIS); public library services to children and young adults (MLIS, Certificate); records and information management (Certificate); records management (MLIS); references services (MLIS); school library media (Spec); school library media specialist endorsement (MLIS); special libraries (MLIS); urban librarianship (Certificate); urban libraries (MLIS); MLIS/MA. *Accreditation:* ALA (one or more programs are accredited). Part-time and evening/weekend programs available. Postbaccalaureate distance learning degree programs offered (no on-campus study). *Faculty:* 13 full-time (8 women), 25 part-time/adjunct (19 women). *Students:* 121 full-time (93 women), 447 part-time (346 women); includes 57 minority (37 Black or African American, non-Hispanic/Latino; 1 American Indian or Alaska Native, non-Hispanic/Latino; 4 Asian, non-Hispanic/Latino; 7 Hispanic/Latino; 8 Two or more races, non-Hispanic/Latino), 4 international. Average age 33. 336 applicants, 62% accepted, 135 enrolled. In 2011, 212 master's, 38 other advanced degrees awarded. *Entrance requirements:* For master's and other advanced degree, GRE or MAT (if undergraduate GPA is between 2.5 and 2.99), minimum undergraduate GPA of 3.0 or graduate degree, personal statement, new student orientation. Additional exam requirements/recommendations for international students: Required—TOEFL (minimum score 550 paper-based; 213 computer-based); Recommended—TWE (minimum score 5.5). *Application deadline:* For fall admission, 7/1 for domestic students, 5/1 for international students; for winter admission, 10/1 for domestic students, 9/1 for international students; for spring admission, 3/15 for domestic students, 1/1 for international students. Applications are processed on a rolling basis. Application fee: $50. Electronic applications accepted. *Expenses:* Tuition, state resident: part-time $512.85 per credit. Tuition, nonresident: part-time $1132.65 per credit. *Required fees:* $26.60 per credit. $199.65 per semester. Tuition and fees vary according to course load and program. *Financial support:* In 2011–12, 1 research assistantship with tuition reimbursement (averaging $12,250 per year) was awarded; fellowships with tuition reimbursements, career-related internships or fieldwork, Federal Work-Study, institutionally sponsored loans, scholarships/grants, and unspecified assistantships also available. Support available to part-time students. Financial award application deadline: 5/15. *Faculty research:* Convergence of academic libraries and other academic services, competitive intelligence and data mining, impact of digitization on libraries, international librarianship, consumer health information, urban library issues, human-computer interaction, universal access to libraries and instructional support services. *Unit head:* Dr. Sandra Yee, Dean, 313-577-4059, Fax: 313-577-7563, E-mail: aj0533@wayne.edu. *Application contact:* Dr. Stephen Fredericks, Associate Dean and Director, 313-577-7563, E-mail: bajjaly@wayne.edu. Web site: http://www.lisp.wayne.edu/.

Western New England University, School of Law, Springfield, MA 01119. Offers estate planning/elder law (LL M); law (JD). *Accreditation:* ABA. Part-time and evening/weekend programs available. *Students:* 318 full-time (163 women), 189 part-time (111 women); includes 56 minority (22 Black or African American, non-Hispanic/Latino; 3 American Indian or Alaska Native, non-Hispanic/Latino; 18 Asian, non-Hispanic/Latino; 13 Hispanic/Latino), 1 international. 1,170 applicants, 51% accepted, 109 enrolled. In 2011, 34 master's, 148 doctorates awarded. *Entrance requirements:* For doctorate, LSAT, letters of recommendation. *Application deadline:* For fall admission, 3/15 priority date for domestic students. Applications are processed on a rolling basis. Application fee: $50. Electronic applications accepted. *Expenses:* Contact institution. *Financial support:* Career-related internships or fieldwork, Federal Work-Study, institutionally sponsored loans, and scholarships/grants available. Support available to part-time students. Financial award application deadline: 4/1; financial award applicants required to submit FAFSA. *Unit head:* Arthur R. Gaudio, Dean, 413-782-2201, E-mail: agaudio@wne.edu. *Application contact:* Michael A. Johnson, Director of Admissions, 413-782-1406, E-mail: admissions@law.wne.edu. Web site: http://www.law.wne.edu/.

Western State University College of Law, Professional Program, Fullerton, CA 92831-3000. Offers JD. *Accreditation:* ABA. Part-time and evening/weekend programs available. *Entrance requirements:* For doctorate, LSAT, 2 letters of recommendation. Additional exam requirements/recommendations for international students: Required—TOEFL (minimum score 550 paper-based; 213 computer-based; 80 iBT). Electronic applications accepted. *Faculty research:* Criminal law and practice, entrepreneurship, teaching effectiveness and student success, learning theory and legal education.

West Virginia University, College of Law, Morgantown, WV 26506-6130. Offers JD, JD/MBA, JD/MPA. *Accreditation:* ABA. Part-time programs available. *Entrance requirements:* For doctorate, LSAT. Additional exam requirements/recommendations for international students: Required—TOEFL. Electronic applications accepted. *Expenses:* Contact institution. *Faculty research:* Constitutional law, public interest law, corporate law, environment and natural resources innocence project, professional skills, leadership, intellectual property, entrepreneurship, labor, sustainable development, family law, IR human rights, immigration.

Whittier College, Whittier Law School, Costa Mesa, CA 92626. Offers foreign legal studies (LL M); law (JD). *Accreditation:* ABA. Part-time and evening/weekend programs available. *Entrance requirements:* For master's, first degree in law; for doctorate, LSAT. Additional exam requirements/recommendations for international students: Required—TOEFL (minimum score 600 paper-based; 250 computer-based). Electronic applications accepted. *Expenses:* Contact institution. *Faculty research:* Intellectual property, international law, health law, children's rights.

Widener University, School of Human Service Professions, Institute for Graduate Clinical Psychology, Law-Psychology Program, Chester, PA 19013-5792. Offers JD/Psy D. Electronic applications accepted.

Widener University, School of Law at Harrisburg, Harrisburg, PA 17106-9381. Offers JD. *Accreditation:* ABA. Part-time programs available. *Entrance requirements:* For doctorate, LSAT. Electronic applications accepted. *Expenses:* Contact institution. *Faculty research:* Health law, toxic torts, constitutional law, intellectual property, corporate law.

Widener University, School of Law at Wilmington, Wilmington, DE 19803-0474. Offers corporate law and finance (LL M); health law (LL M, MJ, D Law); juridical science (SJD); law (JD). *Accreditation:* ABA. Part-time programs available. *Degree requirements:* For doctorate, thesis/dissertation (for some programs). *Entrance requirements:* For master's, GMAT.

Willamette University, College of Law, Salem, OR 97301-3922. Offers LL M, JD, JD/MBA. *Accreditation:* ABA. *Faculty:* 37 full-time (13 women), 19 part-time/adjunct (4 women). *Students:* 407 full-time (172 women), 2 part-time (1 woman); includes 60 minority (2 Black or African American, non-Hispanic/Latino; 8 American Indian or Alaska Native, non-Hispanic/Latino; 27 Asian, non-Hispanic/Latino; 23 Hispanic/Latino), 9 international. Average age 27. 1,092 applicants, 49% accepted, 141 enrolled. In 2011, 2 master's, 128 doctorates awarded. *Degree requirements:* For master's, thesis; for doctorate, thesis/dissertation. *Entrance requirements:* For doctorate, LSAT. Additional exam requirements/recommendations for international students: Required—TOEFL (minimum score 600 paper-based; 250 computer-based; 100 iBT); Recommended—IELTS (minimum score 7.5). *Application deadline:* For fall admission, 3/1 priority date for domestic students, 3/1 for international students. Applications are processed on a rolling basis. Application fee: $50. Electronic applications accepted. *Expenses:* Contact institution. *Financial support:* In 2011–12, 268 students received support. Fellowships with partial tuition reimbursements available, research assistantships with partial tuition reimbursements available, Federal Work-Study, scholarships/grants, and tuition waivers (full and partial) available. Financial award application deadline: 3/1; financial award applicants required to submit FAFSA. *Faculty research:* Dispute resolution, international law, business law, law and government. *Total annual research expenditures:* $130,000. *Unit head:* Peter V. Letsou, Dean, 503-370-6024, Fax: 503-370-6828, E-mail: pletsou@willamette.edu. *Application contact:* Carolyn Dennis, Director of Admission, 503-370-6282, Fax: 503-370-6087, E-mail: law-admission@willamette.edu. Web site: http://www.willamette.edu/wucl/.

William Mitchell College of Law, Professional Program, St. Paul, MN 55105-3076. Offers LL M, JD. *Accreditation:* ABA. Part-time and evening/weekend programs available. *Faculty:* 41 full-time (18 women), 281 part-time/adjunct (143 women). *Students:* 698 full-time (330 women), 306 part-time (159 women); includes 131 minority (23 Black or African American, non-Hispanic/Latino; 7 American Indian or Alaska Native, non-Hispanic/Latino; 37 Asian, non-Hispanic/Latino; 28 Hispanic/Latino; 18 Native Hawaiian or other Pacific Islander, non-Hispanic/Latino; 18 Two or more races, non-Hispanic/Latino), 9 international. Average age 29. 1,327 applicants, 70% accepted, 309 enrolled. In 2011, 282 doctorates awarded. *Entrance requirements:* For doctorate, LSAT. Additional exam requirements/recommendations for international students: Required—TOEFL (minimum score 250 computer-based; 100 iBT). *Application deadline:* For spring admission, 8/1 for domestic and international students. Applications are processed on a rolling basis. Application fee: $0. Electronic applications accepted. *Expenses: Tuition:* Full-time $35,710; part-time $25,840 per year. *Required fees:* $50; $50 per year. *Financial support:* In 2011–12, 720 students received support, including

111 research assistantships (averaging $2,000 per year); Federal Work-Study and scholarships/grants also available. Financial award application deadline: 3/15; financial award applicants required to submit FAFSA. *Faculty research:* Child protection, domestic violence, elder law, intellectual property law, preventive detention and post-release civil commitment. *Total annual research expenditures:* $65,000. *Unit head:* Eric S. Janus, President/Dean, 651-290-6310, Fax: 651-290-6426. *Application contact:* Kendra Dane, Assistant Dean and Director of Admissions, 651-290-6343, Fax: 651-290-7535, E-mail: admissions@wmitchell.edu. Web site: http://www.wmitchell.edu/.

Yale University, Yale Law School, New Haven, CT 06520-8215. Offers LL M, MSL, JD, JSD, JD/MA, JD/MAR, JD/MBA, JD/MD, JD/MES, JD/PhD. *Accreditation:* ABA. *Faculty:* 64 full-time, 54 part-time/adjunct. *Students:* 638 full-time (315 women). Average age 24. 3,173 applicants, 8% accepted, 205 enrolled. In 2011, 29 master's, 13 doctorates awarded. *Entrance requirements:* For doctorate, LSAT (for JD). Additional exam requirements/recommendations for international students: Required—TOEFL (minimum score 600 paper-based; 250 computer-based). *Application deadline:* For fall admission, 2/15 for domestic students. Applications are processed on a rolling basis. Application fee: $75. Electronic applications accepted. *Expenses:* Contact institution. *Financial support:* Application deadline: 3/15; applicants required to submit FAFSA. *Unit head:* Robert Post, Dean, 203-432-1660. *Application contact:* Asha Rangappa, Associate Dean, 203-432-4995, E-mail: admissions.law@yale.edu. Web site: http://www.law.yale.edu/.

Yeshiva University, Benjamin N. Cardozo School of Law, New York, NY 10003-4301. Offers comparative legal thought (LL M); dispute resolution and advocacy (LL M); general studies (LL M); intellectual property law (LL M); law (JD). *Accreditation:* ABA. Part-time programs available. *Faculty:* 58 full-time (23 women), 107 part-time/adjunct (41 women). *Students:* 1,114 full-time (585 women), 114 part-time (62 women); includes 250 minority (55 Black or African American, non-Hispanic/Latino; 2 American Indian or Alaska Native, non-Hispanic/Latino; 48 Asian, non-Hispanic/Latino; 84 Hispanic/Latino; 40 Native Hawaiian or other Pacific Islander, non-Hispanic/Latino; 21 Two or more races, non-Hispanic/Latino), 17 international. Average age 24. 5,058 applicants, 32% accepted, 325 enrolled. In 2011, 66 master's, 383 doctorates awarded. *Entrance requirements:* For doctorate, LSAT, 2 letters of recommendation. *Application deadline:* For fall admission, 4/1 priority date for domestic students; for spring admission, 12/1 priority date for domestic students. Applications are processed on a rolling basis. Application fee: $75. Electronic applications accepted. *Expenses:* Contact institution. *Financial support:* In 2011–12, 965 students received support, including 140 research assistantships; career-related internships or fieldwork, Federal Work-Study, institutionally sponsored loans, scholarships/grants, health care benefits, and tuition waivers (full and partial) also available. Support available to part-time students. Financial award application deadline: 3/1; financial award applicants required to submit FAFSA. *Faculty research:* Corporate and commercial law, intellectual property law, criminal law and litigation, Constitutional law, legal theory and jurisprudence. *Unit head:* David G. Martinidez, Dean of Admissions, 212-790-0274, Fax: 212-790-0482, E-mail: lawinfo@yu.edu. *Application contact:* Michael Kranzler, Director of Admissions, 212-960-5277, Fax: 212-960-0086. Web site: http://www.cardozo.yu.edu/.

York University, Faculty of Graduate Studies, Atkinson Faculty of Liberal and Professional Studies, Program in Public Policy, Administration and Law, Toronto, ON M3J 1P3, Canada. Offers MPPAL.

York University, Faculty of Graduate Studies, Osgoode Hall Law School, Toronto, ON M3J 1P3, Canada. Offers LL M, JD, PhD. Part-time and evening/weekend programs available. *Degree requirements:* For master's, thesis; for doctorate, comprehensive exam, thesis/dissertation. *Entrance requirements:* For doctorate, LSAT. Electronic applications accepted.

Legal and Justice Studies

American Public University System, AMU/APU Graduate Programs, Charles Town, WV 25414. Offers accounting (MBA, MS); administration and supervision (M Ed); criminal justice (MA); emergency and disaster management (MA); entrepreneurship (MBA); environmental policy and management (MS), including environmental planning, environmental sustainability, fish and wildlife management, general (MA, MS), global environmental management; finance (MBA); general (MBA); global business management (MBA); guidance and counseling (M Ed); history (MA), including American history, ancient and classical history, European history, global history, military and diplomatic history, public history; homeland security (MA); homeland security resource allocation (MBA); humanities (MA); information technology (MS), including digital forensics, enterprise software development, information assurance and security, IT project management; information technology management (MBA); intelligence studies (MA), including criminal intelligence, general (MA, MS), homeland security, intelligence analysis, intelligence collection, intelligence operations, terrorism studies; international relations and conflict resolution (MA), including comparative and security issues, conflict resolution, international and transnational security issues, peacekeeping; legal studies (MA); management (MA), including defense management, general (MA, MS), human resource management, organizational leadership, public administration, reverse logistics, strategic consulting; marketing (MBA); military history (MA), including American military history, American revolution, civil war, war since 1946, World War II; military studies (MA), including air warfare, asymmetrical warfare, joint warfare, land warfare, naval warfare, strategic leadership; national security studies (MA), including general (MA, MS), homeland security, regional security studies, security and intelligence analysis, terrorism studies; nonprofit management (MBA); political science (MA), including American politics and government, comparative government and development, public policy; psychology (MA); public administration (MA, MPA), including disaster management (MPA), environmental policy (MA), health policy (MPA), human resources (MPA), national security (MPA), organizational management (MPA), security management (MPA); public health (MA, MPH), including emergency management (MPH), environmental health (MPH), public administration (MA); reverse logistics management (MA); security management (MA); space studies (MS), including aerospace science, planetary science; sports and health sciences (MS); sports management (MS), including coaching theory and strategy, sports administration; teaching (M Ed), including curriculum and instruction for elementary teachers, elementary, elementary reading, English language learners, instructional leadership, online learning, secondary social sciences, special education; transportation and logistics management (MA), including maritime engineering management. Programs offered via distance learning only. Part-time and evening/weekend programs available. Postbaccalaureate distance learning degree programs offered (no on-campus study). *Faculty:* 445 full-time (241 women), 1,360 part-time/adjunct (617 women). *Students:* 688 full-time (338 women), 10,168 part-time (3,706 women); includes 3,130 minority (1,007 Black or African American, non-Hispanic/Latino; 103 American Indian or Alaska Native, non-Hispanic/Latino; 825 Asian, non-Hispanic/Latino; 810 Hispanic/Latino; 51 Native Hawaiian or other Pacific Islander, non-Hispanic/Latino; 334 Two or more races, non-Hispanic/Latino), 134 international. Average age 35. In 2011, 2,386 master's awarded. *Degree requirements:* For master's, comprehensive exam or practicum. *Entrance requirements:* For master's, official transcript showing earned bachelor's degree from institution accredited by recognized accrediting body. Additional exam requirements/recommendations for international students: Required—TOEFL (minimum score 550 paper-based; 213 computer-based), IELTS (minimum score 6.5). *Application deadline:* Applications are processed on a rolling basis. Application fee: $0. Electronic applications accepted. *Expenses: Tuition:* Part-time $325 per credit hour. *Financial support:* Applicants required to submit FAFSA. *Faculty research:* Military history, criminal justice, management performance, national security. *Unit head:* Dr. Karan Powell, Executive Vice President and Provost, 877-468-6268, Fax: 304-724-3780. *Application contact:* Terry Grant, Vice President of Enrollment Management, 877-468-6268, Fax: 304-724-3780, E-mail: info@apus.edu. Web site: http://www.apus.edu.

American University, Washington College of Law, Humphrey Fellows Program in Human Rights and the Law, Washington, DC 20016-8181. Offers Certificate. *Students:* 11 full-time (8 women). Average age 37. *Entrance requirements:* For degree, JD. *Expenses:* Contact institution. *Unit head:* Claudio M. Grossman, Dean, 202-274-4004, Fax: 202-274-4005, E-mail: grossman@wcl.american.edu. *Application contact:* Akira Shiroma, Assistant Dean of Admissions, 202-274-4101, Fax: 202-274-4107, E-mail: shiroma@wcl.american.edu. Web site: http://www.wcl.american.edu/.

American University, Washington College of Law, Program in International Legal Studies, Washington, DC 20016-8181. Offers LL M, Certificate. Part-time and evening/weekend programs available. *Students:* 40 full-time (25 women), 113 part-time (72 women); includes 11 minority (4 Black or African American, non-Hispanic/Latino; 1 American Indian or Alaska Native, non-Hispanic/Latino; 1 Asian, non-Hispanic/Latino; 5 Hispanic/Latino), 121 international. Average age 27. 381 applicants, 62% accepted, 76 enrolled. In 2011, 100 master's awarded. *Entrance requirements:* For master's, JD, 2 recommendations. Additional exam requirements/recommendations for international students: Required—TOEFL (minimum score 580 paper-based; 237 computer-based; 92 iBT), IELTS (minimum score 6.5). *Application deadline:* For fall admission, 6/1 for domestic students; for spring admission, 11/1 for domestic students. Applications are processed on a rolling basis. Application fee: $55. *Expenses:* Contact institution. *Financial support:* Fellowships, research assistantships, teaching assistantships, career-related internships or fieldwork, and tuition waivers (partial) available. Financial award application deadline: 2/15; financial award applicants required to submit FAFSA. *Unit head:* Claudio M. Grossman, Director, 202-274-4004, Fax: 202-274-4005, E-mail: grossman@wcl.american.edu. *Application contact:* Akira Shiroma, Assistant Dean of Admissions, 202-274-4101, Fax: 202-274-4107, E-mail: shiroma@wcl.american.edu. Web site: http://www.wcl.american.edu/.

American University, Washington College of Law, Program in Judicial Sciences, Washington, DC 20016-8001. Offers SJD. *Students:* 4 full-time (2 women), 15 part-time (10 women); includes 1 minority (Black or African American, non-Hispanic/Latino), 16 international. Average age 38. *Entrance requirements:* For doctorate, JD, LL M or LL B. Additional exam requirements/recommendations for international students: Required—TOEFL (minimum score 250 computer-based; 100 iBT). *Application deadline:* Applications are processed on a rolling basis. Application fee: $55. *Expenses:* Contact institution. *Unit head:* Claudio Grossman, Dean, 202-274-4004, Fax: 202-274-4005, E-mail: grossman@wcl.american.edu. *Application contact:* Akira Shiroma, Assistant Dean of Admissions, 202-274-4101, Fax: 202-274-4107, E-mail: shiroma@wcl.american.edu. Web site: http://www.wcl.american.edu/.

American University, Washington College of Law, Program in Law and Government, Washington, DC 20016-8001. Offers LL M. *Students:* 21 full-time (9 women), 41 part-time (25 women); includes 15 minority (11 Black or African American, non-Hispanic/Latino; 1 American Indian or Alaska Native, non-Hispanic/Latino; 1 Asian, non-Hispanic/Latino; 2 Hispanic/Latino), 7 international. Average age 33. 77 applicants, 77% accepted, 33 enrolled. In 2011, 37 master's awarded. *Degree requirements:* For master's, thesis optional. *Entrance requirements:* For master's, JD, 2 recommendations. Additional exam requirements/recommendations for international students: Required—TOEFL (minimum score 300 paper-based; 250 computer-based). *Application deadline:* For fall admission, 6/1 priority date for domestic students; for spring admission, 11/1 priority date for domestic students. Applications are processed on a rolling basis. Application fee: $55. *Expenses:* Contact institution. *Financial support:* Fellowships with partial tuition reimbursements, career-related internships or fieldwork, and institutionally sponsored loans available. Support available to part-time students. Financial award application deadline: 2/15. *Unit head:* Claudio Grossman, Dean, 202-274-4004, Fax: 202-274-4005, E-mail: grossman@wcl.american.edu. *Application contact:* Akira Shiroma, Assistant Dean of Admissions, 202-274-4101, Fax: 202-274-4107, E-mail: shiroma@wcl.american.edu. Web site: http://www.wcl.american.edu/.

Arizona State University, College of Liberal Arts and Sciences, School of Justice and Social Inquiry, Tempe, AZ 85287-4902. Offers African American diaspora studies (Graduate Certificate); gender studies (PhD, Graduate Certificate); justice studies (MS, PhD); socio-economic justice (Graduate Certificate); PhD/JD. Part-time programs available. Terminal master's awarded for partial completion of doctoral program. *Degree requirements:* For master's, thesis or alternative, interactive Program of Study (iPOS) submitted before completing 50 percent of required credit hours; for doctorate, comprehensive exam, thesis/dissertation, interactive Program of Study (iPOS) submitted before completing 50 percent of required credit hours. *Entrance requirements:* For master's, GRE or LSAT, minimum GPA of 3.0 or equivalent in last 2 years of work leading to bachelor's degree; for doctorate, GRE or LSAT (for justice studies program), minimum GPA of 3.0 or equivalent in last 2 years of work leading to bachelor's degree. Additional exam requirements/recommendations for international students: Required—TOEFL (minimum score 80 iBT), TOEFL, IELTS, or Pearson Test of English. Electronic applications accepted.

Arizona State University, New College of Interdisciplinary Arts and Sciences, Program in Social Justice and Human Rights, Phoenix, AZ 85069-7100. Offers MA. Fall admission only. Part-time and evening/weekend programs available. *Degree requirements:* For master's, thesis or applied project, interactive Program of Study (iPOS) submitted before completing 50 percent of required credit hours. *Entrance* *requirements:* For master's, GRE, minimum GPA of 3.0 or equivalent in last 2 years of work leading to bachelor's degree, 2 letters of recommendation, official transcripts, writing sample, personal statement, resume. Additional exam requirements/recommendations for international students: Required—TOEFL (minimum score 80 iBT), TOEFL, IELTS, or Pearson Test of English. Electronic applications accepted. *Faculty research:* Social movements, violence against women, globalization, innovative uses of human rights law, environmental ethics, social justice and art, women and international development, slavery, genocide, metropolitan studies, urban culture and social space, fair trade, citizenship; immigration.

Arizona State University, Sandra Day O'Connor College of Law, Tempe, AZ 85287-7906. Offers biotechnology and genomics (LL M); global legal studies (LL M); law (JD); law (customized) (LL M); legal studies (MLS); tribal policy, law and government (LL M); JD/MBA; JD/MD; JD/PhD. JD/MD offered jointly with Mayo Medical School. *Accreditation:* ABA. *Faculty:* 62 full-time (23 women), 68 part-time/adjunct (18 women). *Students:* 615 full-time (247 women), 32 part-time (17 women); includes 148 minority (11 Black or African American, non-Hispanic/Latino; 31 American Indian or Alaska Native, non-Hispanic/Latino; 22 Asian, non-Hispanic/Latino; 67 Hispanic/Latino; 17 Two or more races, non-Hispanic/Latino), 11 international. Average age 28. 2,334 applicants, 28% accepted, 168 enrolled. In 2011, 19 master's, 200 doctorates awarded. *Degree requirements:* For doctorate, papers. *Entrance requirements:* For master's, bachelor's degree and JD (for LL M); for doctorate, LSAT, bachelor's degree. Additional exam requirements/recommendations for international students: Required—TOEFL (minimum score 550 paper-based; 80 iBT). *Application deadline:* For fall admission, 2/1 priority date for domestic students, 2/1 for international students. Applications are processed on a rolling basis. Application fee: $60. Electronic applications accepted. *Expenses:* Contact institution. *Financial support:* In 2011–12, 322 students received support. Research assistantships, teaching assistantships, career-related internships or fieldwork, Federal Work-Study, institutionally sponsored loans, scholarships/grants, tuition waivers (full and partial), and unspecified assistantships available. Financial award application deadline: 3/15; financial award applicants required to submit FAFSA. *Faculty research:* Emerging technologies and the law, Indian law, law and philosophy, international law, intellectual property. *Total annual research expenditures:* $925,469. *Unit head:* Douglas Sylvester, Dean/Professor, 480-965-6188, Fax: 480-965-6521, E-mail: douglas.sylvester@asu.edu. *Application contact:* Chitra Damania, Director of Operations, 480-965-1474, Fax: 480-727-7930, E-mail: law.admissions@asu.edu. Web site: http://www.law.asu.edu/.

Boston University, School of Public Health, Health Law, Bioethics and Human Rights Department, Boston, MA 02118. Offers MPH. Part-time and evening/weekend programs available. *Faculty:* 5 full-time, 16 part-time/adjunct. *Students:* 10 full-time (8 women), 8 part-time (all women); includes 5 minority (1 Black or African American, non-Hispanic/Latino; 1 Asian, non-Hispanic/Latino; 1 Hispanic/Latino; 1 Native Hawaiian or other Pacific Islander, non-Hispanic/Latino; 1 Two or more races, non-Hispanic/Latino). Average age 28. 86 applicants, 56% accepted, 9 enrolled. *Entrance requirements:* For master's, GRE, MCAT, LSAT, GMAT, DAT. Additional exam requirements/recommendations for international students: Required—TOEFL (minimum score 600 paper-based; 250 computer-based; 100 iBT) or IELTS (minimum score 6). *Application deadline:* For fall admission, 2/1 priority date for domestic students, 2/1 for international students; for spring admission, 10/15 priority date for domestic students, 10/15 for international students. Applications are processed on a rolling basis. Application fee: $115. Electronic applications accepted. *Expenses: Tuition:* Full-time $40,848; part-time $1276 per credit hour. *Required fees:* $572; $286 per semester. *Financial support:* In 2011–12, 1 fellowship was awarded; career-related internships or fieldwork, Federal Work-Study, institutionally sponsored loans, scholarships/grants, and tuition waivers (partial) also available. Support available to part-time students. Financial award application deadline: 3/1; financial award applicants required to submit FAFSA. *Unit head:* Prof. George Annas, Chair, 617-638-4626, E-mail: hld@bu.edu. *Application contact:* LePhan Quan, Associate Director of Admissions, 617-638-4640, Fax: 617-638-5299, E-mail: asksph@bu.edu. Web site: http://sph.bu.edu.

Brock University, Faculty of Graduate Studies, Faculty of Social Sciences, Program in Social Justice and Equity Studies, St. Catharines, ON L2S 3A1, Canada. Offers MA. Part-time programs available. *Degree requirements:* For master's, thesis optional. *Entrance requirements:* For master's, honors degree. Additional exam requirements/recommendations for international students: Required—TOEFL (minimum score 550 paper-based; 213 computer-based; 80 iBT), IELTS (minimum score 6.5), TWE (minimum score 4). Electronic applications accepted. *Faculty research:* Social inequality, social movements, gender, racism, environmental justice.

California University of Pennsylvania, School of Graduate Studies and Research, Department of Professional Studies, California, PA 15419-1394. Offers legal studies (MS), including homeland security, law and public policy. Part-time and evening/weekend programs available. Postbaccalaureate distance learning degree programs offered (no on-campus study). *Degree requirements:* For master's, thesis optional. *Entrance requirements:* For master's, interview, minimum QPA of 3.0. Additional exam requirements/recommendations for international students: Required—TOEFL (minimum score 550 paper-based; 213 computer-based; 80 iBT). Electronic applications accepted. *Faculty research:* Ethics in political practice, ethics and law, law and morality, St. Thomas Aquinas and crime, police policy.

Capital University, School of Nursing, Columbus, OH 43209-2394. Offers administration (MSN); legal studies (MSN); theological studies (MSN); JD/MSN; MBA/MSN; MSN/MTS. *Accreditation:* AACN. Part-time and evening/weekend programs available. *Degree requirements:* For master's, thesis or alternative. *Entrance requirements:* For master's, BSN, current RN license, minimum GPA of 3.0, undergraduate courses in statistics and research. Additional exam requirements/recommendations for international students: Required—TOEFL (minimum score 550 paper-based). *Expenses:* Contact institution. *Faculty research:* Bereavement, wellness/health promotion, emergency cardiac care, critical thinking, complementary and alternative healthcare.

Carleton University, Faculty of Graduate Studies, Faculty of Public Affairs and Management, Department of Law, Ottawa, ON K1S 5B6, Canada. Offers conflict resolution (Certificate); legal studies (MA). *Degree requirements:* For master's, thesis. *Entrance requirements:* For master's, honors degree. Additional exam requirements/recommendations for international students: Required—TOEFL. *Faculty research:* Legal and social theory; women, law, and gender relations; law, crime, and social order; political economy of law; international law.

Case Western Reserve University, School of Law, Cleveland, OH 44106. Offers intellectual property (LL M); international business law (LL M); international criminal law (LL M); law (JD); U. S. legal studies (LL M); JD/CNM; JD/MA; JD/MBA; JD/MD; JD/MPH; JD/MS; JD/MSSA. *Accreditation:* ABA. Part-time programs available. *Faculty:* 48 full-time (15 women), 54 part-time/adjunct (16 women). *Students:* 600 full-time (260 women), 5 part-time (2 women); includes 110 minority (30 Black or African American, non-Hispanic/Latino; 4 American Indian or Alaska Native, non-Hispanic/Latino; 57 Asian, non-Hispanic/Latino; 17 Hispanic/Latino; 2 Two or more races, non-Hispanic/Latino), 48 international. Average age 24. 1,651 applicants, 47% accepted, 192 enrolled. In 2011, 49 master's, 203 doctorates awarded. *Entrance requirements:* For doctorate, LSAT, LSDAS. Additional exam requirements/recommendations for international students: Required—TOEFL. *Application deadline:* For fall admission, 4/1 priority date for domestic students, 4/1 for international students. Applications are processed on a rolling basis. Application fee: $40. Electronic applications accepted. Application fee is waived when completed online. *Expenses:* Contact institution. *Financial support:* In 2011–12, 440 students received support. Career-related internships or fieldwork, Federal Work-Study, institutionally sponsored loans, and scholarships/grants available. Financial award application deadline: 5/1; financial award applicants required to submit FAFSA. *Unit head:* Lawrence E. Mitchell, Dean, 216-368-3283. *Application contact:* Kelli Curtis, Assistant Dean for Admissions, 216-368-3600, Fax: 216-368-0185, E-mail: lawadmissions@case.edu. Web site: http://law.case.edu/.

The Catholic University of America, School of Canon Law, Washington, DC 20064. Offers JCD, JCL, JD/JCL. Part-time programs available. *Faculty:* 7 full-time (1 woman). *Students:* 29 full-time (5 women), 45 part-time (6 women); includes 12 minority (1 Black or African American, non-Hispanic/Latino; 4 Asian, non-Hispanic/Latino; 6 Hispanic/Latino; 1 Two or more races, non-Hispanic/Latino), 5 international. Average age 40. 36 applicants, 78% accepted, 24 enrolled. In 2011, 2 doctorates awarded. *Degree requirements:* For doctorate, 2 foreign languages, thesis/dissertation, fluency in canonical Latin. *Entrance requirements:* For doctorate, GRE General Test, minimum A-avergae, JCL. Additional exam requirements/recommendations for international students: Required—TOEFL (minimum score 580 paper-based; 237 computer-based). *Application deadline:* For fall admission, 8/1 priority date for domestic students, 7/15 for international students; for spring admission, 12/1 priority date for domestic students, 10/15 for international students. Applications are processed on a rolling basis. Application fee: $55. Electronic applications accepted. *Expenses: Tuition:* Full-time $35,260; part-time $1380 per credit. *Required fees:* $80; $40 per semester hour. One-time fee: $425. *Financial support:* Fellowships, research assistantships, teaching assistantships, Federal Work-Study, scholarships/grants, tuition waivers (full and partial), and unspecified assistantships available. Financial award application deadline: 2/1; financial award applicants required to submit FAFSA. *Faculty research:* Ecclesiology and the Sacrament of Orders, procedural law, temporal goods, matrimonial jurisprudence, sacramental and liturgical law. *Unit head:* Rev. Robert Kaslyn, SJ, Dean, 202-319-5492, Fax: 202-319-4187, E-mail: cua-canonlaw@cua.edu. *Application contact:* Andrew Woodall, Director of Graduate Admissions, 202-319-5057, Fax: 202-319-6533, E-mail: cua-admissions@cua.edu. Web site: http://canonlaw.cua.edu.

Central European University, Graduate Studies, Department of Legal Studies, Budapest, Hungary. Offers comparative Constitutional law (LL M); human rights (LL M, MA); international business law (LL M); law and economics (LL M, MA); legal studies (SJD). *Faculty:* 7 full-time (2 women), 31 part-time/adjunct (8 women). *Students:* 104 full-time (58 women). Average age 27. 474 applicants, 22% accepted, 80 enrolled. In 2011, 36 master's, 7 doctorates awarded. Terminal master's awarded for partial completion of doctoral program. *Degree requirements:* For master's, one foreign language, thesis; for doctorate, one foreign language, comprehensive exam, thesis/dissertation. *Entrance requirements:* For master's and doctorate, LSAT, CEU admissions exams. Additional exam requirements/recommendations for international students: Required—TOEFL (minimum score 570 paper-based; 230 computer-based); Recommended—IELTS (minimum score 6.5). *Application deadline:* For fall admission, 1/24 for domestic and international students. Application fee: $0. Electronic applications accepted. *Expenses:* Contact institution. *Financial support:* In 2011–12, 85 students received support, including 88 fellowships with full and partial tuition reimbursements available (averaging $6,100 per year); career-related internships or fieldwork, institutionally sponsored loans, scholarships/grants, and tuition waivers (full and partial) also available. Financial award application deadline: 1/5. *Faculty research:* Institutional, constitutional and human rights in European Union law; biomedical law and reproductive rights; data protection law; Islamic banking and finance. *Unit head:* Dr. Stefan Messmann, Head, 361-327-3274, Fax: 361-327-3198, E-mail: legalst@ceu.hu. *Application contact:* Maria Balla, Coordinator, 361-327-3204, Fax: 361-327-3198, E-mail: ballam@ceu.hu. Web site: http://www.ceu.hu/legal/.

Fielding Graduate University, Graduate Programs, School of Human and Organization Development, Santa Barbara, CA 93105-3538. Offers evidence-based coaching (Certificate); human and organizational systems (PhD), including aging, culture and society, information society and knowledge organizations, transformative learning for social justice; human development (PhD), including aging, culture and society, information society and knowledge organizations, transformative learning for social justice; integral studies (Certificate); organization management and development (MA, Certificate). Postbaccalaureate distance learning degree programs offered (minimal on-campus study). *Faculty:* 25 full-time (11 women), 11 part-time/adjunct (4 women). *Students:* 422 full-time (304 women), 130 part-time (91 women); includes 119 minority (67 Black or African American, non-Hispanic/Latino; 5 American Indian or Alaska Native, non-Hispanic/Latino; 14 Asian, non-Hispanic/Latino; 22 Hispanic/Latino; 11 Two or more races, non-Hispanic/Latino), 63 international. Average age 49. 133 applicants, 97% accepted, 85 enrolled. In 2011, 46 master's, 34 doctorates, 69 other advanced degrees awarded. Terminal master's awarded for partial completion of doctoral program. *Degree requirements:* For master's, thesis or alternative; for doctorate, comprehensive exam, thesis/dissertation. *Entrance requirements:* For master's, minimum GPA of 2.5, letter of recommendation; for doctorate, 2 letters of recommendation, writing sample, resume, self-assessment statement. *Application deadline:* For fall admission, 3/1 for domestic and international students; for spring admission, 9/1 for domestic and international students. Application fee: $75. Electronic applications accepted. *Expenses:* Contact institution. *Financial support:* In 2011–12, 38 students received support. Scholarships/grants and health care benefits available. Support available to part-time students. Financial award applicants required to submit FAFSA. *Unit head:* Dr. Charles McClintock, Dean, 805-898-2930, Fax: 805-687-4590, E-mail: cmcclintock@fielding.edu. *Application contact:* Carmen Kuchera, Admission Counselor, 800-340-1099 Ext. 4098, Fax: 805-687-9793, E-mail: hodadmissions@fielding.edu. Web site: http://www.fielding.edu/programs/hod/default.aspx.

The George Washington University, College of Professional Studies, Paralegal Studies Programs, Washington, DC 20052. Offers MPS, Graduate Certificate. *Students:* 26 full-time (22 women), 179 part-time (149 women); includes 78 minority (54 Black or African American, non-Hispanic/Latino; 2 American Indian or Alaska Native, non-Hispanic/Latino; 4 Asian, non-Hispanic/Latino; 15 Hispanic/Latino; 1 Native Hawaiian or other Pacific Islander, non-Hispanic/Latino; 2 Two or more races, non-Hispanic/Latino), 1 international. Average age 38. 175 applicants, 79% accepted, 81 enrolled. In 2011, 72 master's, 21 other advanced degrees awarded. *Application deadline:* For fall admission, 4/1 for domestic and international students; for spring admission, 10/1 for domestic and international students. Electronic applications accepted. *Unit head:* Toni Marsh, Director, 202-994-2844, E-mail: marsht01@gwu.edu. *Application contact:* Kristin Williams, Assistant Vice President for Graduate and Special Enrollment Management, 202-994-0467, Fax: 202-994-0371, E-mail: ksw@gwu.edu. Web site: http://nearyou.gwu.edu/plx/

The George Washington University, College of Professional Studies, Program in Law Firm Management, Washington, DC 20052. Offers MPS, Graduate Certificate. Program offered in partnership with The Hildebrandt Institute and held at Alexandria, VA education center. Postbaccalaureate distance learning degree programs offered. *Students:* 18 part-time (9 women); includes 3 minority (2 Black or African American, non-Hispanic/Latino; 1 Asian, non-Hispanic/Latino), 1 international. Average age 42. 18 applicants, 100% accepted, 12 enrolled. In 2011, 14 master's, 2 other advanced degrees awarded. *Entrance requirements:* For master's, resume, 2 references. Additional exam requirements/recommendations for international students: Required—TOEFL. *Application deadline:* For fall admission, 4/1 for domestic and international students. Electronic applications accepted. *Unit head:* Kathleen M. Burke, Dean, 202-994-9711. *Application contact:* Kristin Williams, Assistant Vice President for Graduate and Special Enrollment Management, 202-994-0467, Fax: 202-994-0371, E-mail: ksw@gwu.edu. Web site: http://nearyou.gwu.edu/lawfirm/.

Golden Gate University, School of Law, San Francisco, CA 94105-2968. Offers environmental law (LL M); intellectual property law (LL M); international legal studies (LL M, SJD); law (JD); taxation (LL M); U. S. legal studies (LL M); JD/MBA; JD/PhD. *Accreditation:* ABA. Part-time and evening/weekend programs available. *Degree requirements:* For doctorate, thesis/dissertation (for some programs). *Entrance requirements:* For doctorate, LSAT (for JD). Additional exam requirements/recommendations for international students: Required—TOEFL (minimum score 600 paper-based; 250 computer-based). Electronic applications accepted. *Expenses:* Contact institution. *Faculty research:* International law, intellectual property law, environmental law, real estate, civil rights.

Governors State University, College of Arts and Sciences, Program in Political and Justice Studies, University Park, IL 60484. Offers MA. Part-time and evening/weekend programs available. *Students:* 13 full-time (7 women), 41 part-time (23 women); includes 36 minority (32 Black or African American, non-Hispanic/Latino; 1 Asian, non-Hispanic/Latino; 3 Hispanic/Latino), 1 international. Average age 35. *Degree requirements:* For master's, thesis or alternative. *Entrance requirements:* For master's, bachelor's degree in related field. *Application deadline:* For fall admission, 7/15 priority date for domestic students; for spring admission, 11/10 for domestic students. Applications are processed on a rolling basis. Application fee: $25. *Financial support:* Research assistantships, Federal Work-Study, institutionally sponsored loans, and scholarships/grants available. Support available to part-time students. Financial award application deadline: 5/1. *Unit head:* Dr. James Howley, Chair, Division of Liberal Arts, 708-534-7893. *Application contact:* Yakeea Daniels, Director of Admission, 708-534-4510, E-mail: ydaniels@govst.edu.

Harrison Middleton University, Graduate Program, Tempe, AZ 85282. Offers education (MA, Ed D); humanities (MA); imaginative literature (MA); interdisciplinary studies (DA); jurisprudence (MA); natural science (MA); philosophy and religion (MA); social science (MA). Part-time and evening/weekend programs available. Postbaccalaureate distance learning degree programs offered (no on-campus study). *Faculty:* 18 full-time (7 women), 14 part-time/adjunct (6 women). *Students:* 53 full-time (20 women). 4 applicants, 100% accepted, 4 enrolled. In 2011, 4 master's awarded. *Degree requirements:* For master's and doctorate, capstone project. *Entrance requirements:* For doctorate, 2 academic letters of reference, interview. Additional exam requirements/recommendations for international students: Required—TOEFL (minimum score 550 paper-based; 80 iBT). *Application deadline:* Applications are processed on a rolling basis. Application fee: $50. Electronic applications accepted. One-time fee: $400 full-time. Full-time tuition and fees vary according to course load and degree level. *Faculty research:* Japanese animation, educational leadership, war art, John Muir's wilderness. *Unit head:* Susan Chiaramonte, Director of Accreditation and Licensure, 877-248-6724, Fax: 800-762-1622, E-mail: schiaramonte@hmu.edu. *Application contact:* Dr. Deborah Deacon, Dean of Graduate Studies, 877-248-6724, Fax: 800-762-1622, E-mail: ddeacon@hmu.edu. Web site: http://www.hmu.edu.

Harvard University, Law School, Professional Programs in Law, Cambridge, MA 02138. Offers international and comparative law (JD); law and business (JD); law and government (JD); law and social change (JD); law, science and technology (JD); JD/MALD; JD/MBA; JD/MPH; JD/MPP; JD/PhD. *Accreditation:* ABA. *Degree requirements:* For doctorate, 3rd-year paper. *Entrance requirements:* For doctorate, LSAT. *Expenses: Tuition:* Full-time $36,304. *Required fees:* $1186. Full-time tuition and fees vary according to program. *Faculty research:* Constitutional law, voting rights law, cyber law.

Hodges University, Graduate Programs, Naples, FL 34119. Offers business administration (MBA); criminal justice (MS); education (MPS); information systems management (MIS); legal studies (MS); management (MSM); mental health counseling (MS); public administration (MPA). Part-time and evening/weekend programs available. Postbaccalaureate distance learning degree programs offered (no on-campus study). *Faculty:* 22 full-time (9 women), 3 part-time/adjunct (2 women). *Students:* 28 full-time (21 women), 237 part-time (156 women); includes 76 minority (35 Black or African American, non-Hispanic/Latino; 5 Asian, non-Hispanic/Latino; 36 Hispanic/Latino). Average age 36. 92 applicants, 91% accepted, 81 enrolled. *Degree requirements:* For master's, comprehensive exam (for some programs), thesis (for some programs). *Entrance requirements:* For master's, in-house entrance exam. Additional exam requirements/recommendations for international students: Recommended—TOEFL. *Application deadline:* Applications are processed on a rolling basis. Application fee: $50. Electronic applications accepted. *Expenses: Tuition:* Full-time $11,340; part-time $630 per credit hour. *Required fees:* $250 per term. *Financial support:* In 2011–12, 200 students received support. Federal Work-Study and scholarships/grants available. Financial award application deadline: 7/9; financial award applicants required to submit FAFSA. *Unit head:* Terry McMahan, President, 239-513-1122, Fax: 239-598-6253, E-mail: tmcmahan@hodges.edu. *Application contact:* Rita Lampus, Vice President of Student Enrollment Management, 239-513-1122, Fax: 239-598-6253, E-mail: rlampus@hodges.edu.

Hofstra University, School of Law, Hempstead, NY 11549. Offers American legal studies (LL M); family law (LL M); law (JD); JD/MBA. *Accreditation:* ABA. Part-time programs available. *Faculty:* 57 full-time (21 women), 37 part-time/adjunct (5 women). *Students:* 1,020 full-time (468 women), 76 part-time (40 women); includes 330 minority (98 Black or African American, non-Hispanic/Latino; 3 American Indian or Alaska Native, non-Hispanic/Latino; 126 Asian, non-Hispanic/Latino; 102 Hispanic/Latino; 1 Two or more races, non-Hispanic/Latino), 53 international. Average age 25. In 2011, 1 master's, 306 doctorates awarded. *Entrance requirements:* For doctorate, LSAT, letter of recommendation, personal statement, undergraduate transcripts. Additional exam requirements/recommendations for international students: Recommended—TOEFL (minimum score 600 paper-based; 250 computer-based; 100 iBT). *Application deadline:* For fall admission, 4/15 priority date for domestic students, 4/15 for international students. Applications are processed on a rolling basis. Application fee: $70 ($75 for international students). Electronic applications accepted. *Expenses:* Contact institution. *Financial support:* In 2011–12, 562 students received support, including 531 fellowships with full and partial tuition reimbursements available (averaging $23,980 per year), 1 research assistantship with full and partial tuition reimbursement available (averaging $6,075 per year); Federal Work-Study, institutionally sponsored loans, scholarships/grants, tuition waivers (full and partial), and unspecified assistantships also available. Support available to part-time students. Financial award applicants required to submit FAFSA. *Faculty research:* Commercial and corporate law, health law, gender and LGBT issues, international and comparative law, child and family advocacy. *Unit head:* Eric Lane, Interim Dean, 516-463-5854, Fax: 516-463-6264, E-mail: lawezl@hofstra.edu. *Application contact:* John Chalmers, Director of Law School Enrollment Operations, 516-463-5791, Fax: 516-463-6264, E-mail: lawadmissions@hofstra.edu. Web site: http://law.hofstra.edu/.

Hollins University, Graduate Programs, Program in Liberal Studies, Roanoke, VA 24020-1603. Offers humanities (MALS); interdisciplinary studies (MALS); justice and legal studies (MALS); liberal studies (CAS); social science (MALS); visual and performing arts (MALS). Part-time and evening/weekend programs available. *Degree requirements:* For master's, thesis. *Entrance requirements:* For master's, letters of recommendation, interview. Additional exam requirements/recommendations for international students: Required—TOEFL (minimum score 550 paper-based; 213 computer-based; 79 iBT). Electronic applications accepted. *Faculty research:* Elderly blacks, film, feminist economics, US voting patterns, Wagner, diversity.

John Jay College of Criminal Justice of the City University of New York, Graduate Studies, Programs in Criminal Justice, New York, NY 10019-1093. Offers criminal justice (MA, PhD); criminology and deviance (PhD); forensic psychology (PhD); forensic science (PhD); law and philosophy (PhD); organizational behavior (PhD); public policy (PhD). Part-time and evening/weekend programs available. Terminal master's awarded for partial completion of doctoral program. *Degree requirements:* For master's, thesis or alternative; for doctorate, one foreign language, thesis/dissertation. *Entrance requirements:* For master's, GRE General Test, minimum B average; for doctorate, GRE General Test. Additional exam requirements/recommendations for international students: Required—TOEFL (minimum score 500 paper-based; 173 computer-based).

John Marshall Law School, Graduate and Professional Programs, Chicago, IL 60604-3968. Offers employee benefits (LL M, MS); global legal studies (LL M); information technology (MS); information technology and privacy law (LL M); intellectual property (LL M, MS); international business and trade (LL M); law (JD); real estate (LL M, MS); taxation (LL M, MS); trial advocacy (LL M); JD/LL M; JD/MA; JD/MBA; JD/MPA. JD/MBA offered jointly with Dominican University; JD/MA and JD/MPA with Roosevelt University. *Accreditation:* ABA. Part-time and evening/weekend programs available. *Faculty:* 69 full-time (22 women), 133 part-time/adjunct (40 women). *Students:* 1,305 full-time (598 women), 368 part-time (180 women); includes 385 minority (148 Black or African American, non-Hispanic/Latino; 15 American Indian or Alaska Native, non-Hispanic/Latino; 108 Asian, non-Hispanic/Latino; 110 Hispanic/Latino; 2 Native Hawaiian or other Pacific Islander, non-Hispanic/Latino; 2 Two or more races, non-Hispanic/Latino), 40 international. Average age 27. 3,513 applicants, 48% accepted, 365 enrolled. In 2011, 86 master's, 403 doctorates awarded. *Degree requirements:* For master's, 24 credits; for doctorate, 90 credits. *Entrance requirements:* For master's, JD; for doctorate, LSAT. Additional exam requirements/recommendations for international students: Required—TOEFL. *Application deadline:* For fall admission, 3/1 priority date for domestic students, 3/1 for international students; for spring admission, 10/15 priority date for domestic students, 10/15 for international students. Applications are processed on a rolling basis. Application fee: $0. Electronic applications accepted. *Expenses:* Contact institution. *Financial support:* In 2011–12, 1,350 students received support. Scholarships/grants and tuition waivers (full and partial) available. Support available to part-time students. Financial award application deadline: 6/1; financial award applicants required to submit FAFSA. *Unit head:* John Corkery, Dean, 312-427-2737. *Application contact:* William B. Powers, Associate Dean of Admission and Student Affairs, 800-537-4280, Fax: 312-427-5136, E-mail: admission@jmls.edu.

Kaplan University, Davenport Campus, School of Legal Studies, Davenport, IA 52807-2095. Offers health care delivery (MS); pathway to paralegal (Postbaccalaureate Certificate); state and local government (MS). Part-time and evening/weekend programs available. Postbaccalaureate distance learning degree programs offered (no on-campus study). *Entrance requirements:* Additional exam requirements/recommendations for international students: Required—TOEFL (minimum score 550 paper-based; 218 computer-based; 80 iBT).

Loyola University Chicago, Institute of Pastoral Studies, Master of Arts in Social Justice and Community Development Program, Chicago, IL 60611. Offers MA, MSW/MA. *Students:* 29 full-time (23 women), 21 part-time (14 women); includes 14 minority (9 Black or African American, non-Hispanic/Latino; 5 Hispanic/Latino), 3 international. Average age 31. 34 applicants, 76% accepted, 18 enrolled. In 2011, 21 degrees awarded. *Degree requirements:* For master's, internship. *Entrance requirements:* Additional exam requirements/recommendations for international students: Required—TOEFL. *Expenses: Tuition:* Full-time $15,660; part-time $870 per credit hour. *Required fees:* $125 per semester. Tuition and fees vary according to course load and program. *Unit head:* Dr. Melissa Browning, Graduate Program Director, 312-915-7453, Fax: 312-915-7410, E-mail: mbrowning@luc.edu. *Application contact:* Rachel D. Gibbons, Assistant Director, 312-915-7450, Fax: 312-915-7410, E-mail: rgibbon@luc.edu.

Marlboro College, Graduate School, Program in Teaching for Social Justice, Brattleboro, VT 05301. Offers MAT. *Degree requirements:* For master's, 32 credits including teaching internship. *Entrance requirements:* For master's, letter of intent, 2 letters of recommendation, transcripts, interview. Electronic applications accepted.

Marygrove College, Graduate Division, Program in Social Justice, Detroit, MI 48221-2599. Offers MA.

Marymount University, School of Business Administration, Program in Legal Administration, Arlington, VA 22207-4299. Offers legal administration (MA); paralegal studies (Certificate). Part-time and evening/weekend programs available. *Faculty:* 1 full-time (0 women), 4 part-time/adjunct (1 woman). *Students:* 5 full-time (all women), 21 part-time (15 women); includes 11 minority (3 Black or African American, non-Hispanic/Latino; 2 Asian, non-Hispanic/Latino; 4 Hispanic/Latino; 2 Two or more races, non-Hispanic/Latino), 2 international. Average age 31. 9 applicants, 100% accepted, 7 enrolled. In 2011, 4 master's awarded. *Degree requirements:* For master's, thesis or alternative. *Entrance requirements:* For master's, GMAT or GRE General Test, resume; for Certificate, resume. Additional exam requirements/recommendations for international students: Required—TOEFL (minimum score 600 paper-based; 250 computer-based; 96 iBT), IELTS (minimum score 6.5). *Application deadline:* For fall admission, 7/1 priority date for domestic students, 7/1 for international students; for spring admission, 11/15 for domestic students, 11/16 for international students. Applications are processed on a rolling basis. Application fee: $40. Electronic applications accepted. *Expenses: Tuition:* Part-time $770 per credit hour. *Required fees:* $8 per credit hour. One-time fee: $180 full-time. *Financial support:* Research assistantships with full tuition reimbursements, career-related internships or fieldwork, Federal Work-Study, scholarships/grants, and unspecified assistantships available. Support available to part-time students. Financial award applicants required to submit FAFSA. *Unit head:* Susan Ninassi, Director, 703-284-5934, Fax: 703-527-3830, E-mail: susanne.ninassi@marymount.edu. *Application contact:* Francesca Reed, Director, Graduate Admissions, 703-284-5901, Fax: 703-527-3815, E-mail: grad.admissions@marymount.edu. Web site: http://www.marymount.edu/academics/programs/legalAdmin.

Michigan State University College of Law, Professional Program, East Lansing, MI 48824-1300. Offers American legal system (LL M); intellectual property (LL M); jurisprudence (MJ); law (JD). *Accreditation:* ABA. Part-time programs available. *Faculty:* 56 full-time (26 women), 80 part-time/adjunct (20 women). *Students:* 769 full-time (364 women), 199 part-time (99 women); includes 193 minority (71 Black or African American, non-Hispanic/Latino; 17 American Indian or Alaska Native, non-Hispanic/Latino; 32 Asian, non-Hispanic/Latino; 45 Hispanic/Latino; 4 Native Hawaiian or other Pacific Islander, non-Hispanic/Latino; 24 Two or more races, non-Hispanic/Latino), 97 international. Average age 26. 3,732 applicants, 32% accepted, 307 enrolled. In 2011, 302 doctorates awarded. *Entrance requirements:* For doctorate, LSAT. Additional exam requirements/recommendations for international students: Required—TOEFL (minimum score 600 paper-based; 250 computer-based). *Application deadline:* For fall admission, 4/30 priority date for domestic students, 7/1 for international students. Applications are processed on a rolling basis. Application fee: $60. Electronic applications accepted. *Expenses:* Contact institution. *Financial support:* In 2011–12, 351 students received support, including 300 fellowships (averaging $29,712 per year); career-related internships or fieldwork, Federal Work-Study, institutionally sponsored loans, scholarships/grants, and tuition waivers (full) also available. Support available to part-time students. Financial award application deadline: 4/15; financial award applicants required to submit FAFSA. *Faculty research:* International, Constitutional, health, tax and environmental law; intellectual property, trial practice, corporate law. *Unit head:* Joan W. Howarth, Dean and Professor of Law, 517-432-6993, Fax: 517-432-6801, E-mail: howarth@law.msu.edu. *Application contact:* Charles Roboski, Assistant Dean of Admissions, 517-432-0222, Fax: 517-432-0098, E-mail: roboski@law.msu.edu. Web site: http://www.law.msu.edu/.

Mississippi College, Graduate School, College of Arts and Sciences, School of Humanities and Social Sciences, Department of History, Political Science, Administration of Justice, and Paralegal Studies, Clinton, MS 39058. Offers administration of justice (MSS); history (M Ed, MA, MSS); paralegal studies (Certificate); political science (MSS); social sciences (M Ed, MSS). Part-time programs available. *Degree requirements:* For master's, one foreign language, comprehensive exam, thesis (for some programs). *Entrance requirements:* For master's, GRE or NTE, minimum GPA of 2.5. Additional exam requirements/recommendations for international students: Recommended—TOEFL, IELTS. Electronic applications accepted.

Montclair State University, The Graduate School, College of Humanities and Social Sciences, Paralegal Studies Certificate Program, Montclair, NJ 07043-1624. Offers Certificate. Part-time and evening/weekend programs available. *Students:* 10 full-time (7 women), 15 part-time (11 women); includes 12 minority (2 Black or African American, non-Hispanic/Latino; 3 Asian, non-Hispanic/Latino; 7 Hispanic/Latino). Average age 33. 31 applicants, 58% accepted, 12 enrolled. In 2011, 11 Certificates awarded. *Entrance requirements:* For degree, 2 letters of recommendation, essay. Additional exam requirements/recommendations for international students: Required—TOEFL (minimum score 83 iBT) or IELTS. *Application deadline:* For fall admission, 6/1 for international students; for spring admission, 10/1 for international students. Applications are processed on a rolling basis. Application fee: $60. Electronic applications accepted. *Financial support:* Federal Work-Study and scholarships/grants available. Support available to part-time students. Financial award application deadline: 3/1; financial award applicants required to submit FAFSA. *Unit head:* Dr. Norma Connolly, Chairperson, 973-655-4152, E-mail: connolyn@mail.montclair.edu. *Application contact:* Amy Aiello, Director of Graduate Admissions and Operations, 973-655-4000, E-mail: graduate.school@montclair.edu.

New York University, Graduate School of Arts and Science and School of Law, Institute for Law and Society, New York, NY 10012-1019. Offers MA, PhD, JD/MA, JD/PhD. *Faculty:* 3 full-time (1 woman). *Students:* 11 full-time (5 women); includes 1 minority (Hispanic/Latino), 1 international. Average age 32. In 2011, 1 master's, 1 doctorate awarded. *Degree requirements:* For doctorate, one foreign language, thesis/dissertation. *Entrance requirements:* For doctorate, GRE. Additional exam requirements/recommendations for international students: Required—TOEFL. Application fee: $90. *Financial support:* Fellowships with tuition reimbursements, teaching assistantships with tuition reimbursements, career-related internships or fieldwork, Federal Work-Study, institutionally sponsored loans, scholarships/grants, health care benefits, and unspecified assistantships available. Financial award applicants required to submit FAFSA. *Faculty research:* Politics of law, law and social policy, law in comparative global perspective, rights and social movements. *Unit head:* Malcolm Semple, Acting Dean, 212-998-8040. *Application contact:* Roberta Popik, Associate Dean of Enrollment, 212-998-8050, Fax: 212-995-4557, E-mail: gsas.admissions@nyu.edu. Web site: http://www.law.nyu.edu/ils/.

Northeastern University, College of Social Sciences and Humanities, School of Public Policy and Urban Affairs, Program in Law and Public Policy, Boston, MA 02115-5096. Offers MS, PhD, JD/PhD. Part-time and evening/weekend programs available. *Faculty:* 33 full-time (18 women), 18 part-time/adjunct (6 women). *Students:* 40 full-time (21 women), 22 part-time (14 women). Average age 40. 39 applicants, 51% accepted, 6 enrolled. In 2011, 5 master's, 6 doctorates awarded. *Degree requirements:* For master's, comprehensive exam; for doctorate, comprehensive exam, thesis/dissertation. *Entrance requirements:* For master's, GRE General Test; for doctorate, GRE General Test or LSAT. Additional exam requirements/recommendations for international students: Required—TOEFL. *Application deadline:* For fall admission, 2/1 for domestic students. Application fee: $50. *Financial support:* In 2011–12, teaching assistantships with tuition reimbursements (averaging $14,035 per year) were awarded; fellowships with tuition reimbursements, research assistantships with tuition reimbursements, tuition waivers (full and partial), and unspecified assistantships also available. Financial award application deadline: 2/1; financial award applicants required to submit FAFSA. *Faculty research:* Policy issues in health, crime, and labor; urban studies; education; law and environmental issues; economic development; international trade and law. *Unit head:* Dr. Joan Fitzgerald, Director, 617-373-3644, Fax: 617-373-4691, E-mail: jo.fitzgerald@neu.edu. *Application contact:* Jo-Anne Dickinson, Graduate Admissions Contact, 617-373-5990, Fax: 617-373-7281, E-mail: gsas@neu.edu. Web site: http://www.neu.edu/lpp.

Nova Southeastern University, Shepard Broad Law Center, Fort Lauderdale, FL 33314. Offers education law (MS, Certificate); employment law (MS); health law (MS); law (JD); JD/MBA; JD/MS; JD/MURP. JD/MURP offered jointly with Florida Atlantic University. *Accreditation:* ABA. Part-time and evening/weekend programs available. Postbaccalaureate distance learning degree programs offered (minimal on-campus study). *Students:* 1,055 full-time (547 women), 166 part-time (130 women); includes 434 minority (115 Black or African American, non-Hispanic/Latino; 3 American Indian or Alaska Native, non-Hispanic/Latino; 48 Asian, non-Hispanic/Latino; 252 Hispanic/Latino; 4 Native Hawaiian or other Pacific Islander, non-Hispanic/Latino; 12 Two or more races, non-Hispanic/Latino), 28 international. Average age 29. In 2011, 46 master's, 305 doctorates awarded. *Degree requirements:* For doctorate, thesis/dissertation. *Application deadline:* For fall admission, 3/1 priority date for domestic students. Applications are processed on a rolling basis. Application fee: $50. Electronic applications accepted. *Expenses:* Contact institution. *Financial support:* In 2011–12, 58 fellowships were awarded; research assistantships, teaching assistantships, Federal Work-Study, scholarships/grants, tuition waivers (full and partial), and unspecified assistantships also available. Support available to part-time students. Financial award application deadline: 4/15; financial award applicants required to submit FAFSA. *Faculty research:* Legal issues in family law, civil rights, business associations, criminal law, law and popular culture. *Unit head:* Althornia Steele, Dean, 954-262-6100, Fax: 954-262-3834, E-mail: asteele@nova.edu. *Application contact:* Beth Hall, Assistant Dean of Admissions, 954-262-6121, Fax: 954-262-3844, E-mail: hallb@nsu.law.nova.edu. Web site: http://www.nsulaw.nova.edu/.

Pace University, Pace Law School, White Plains, NY 10603. Offers comparative legal studies (LL M); environmental law (LL M, SJD), including climate change (LL M), land use and sustainability (LL M); law (JD); JD/LL M; JD/MA; JD/MBA; JD/MEM; JD/MPA; JD/MS. JD/MA offered jointly with Sarah Lawrence College; JD/MEM offered jointly with Yale University School of Forestry and Environmental Studies. *Accreditation:* ABA. Part-time programs available. *Degree requirements:* For master's, writing sample; for doctorate, thesis/dissertation (for some programs), extensive thesis proposal (for SJD). *Entrance requirements:* For doctorate, LSAT (for JD). Additional exam requirements/recommendations for international students: Required—TOEFL (minimum score 600 paper-based; 250 computer-based); Recommended—TWE. Electronic applications accepted. *Expenses:* Contact institution. *Faculty research:* Reform of energy regulations, international law, land use law, prosecutorial misconduct, corporation law, international sale of goods.

Prairie View A&M University, College of Juvenile Justice and Psychology, Prairie View, TX 77446-0519. Offers clinical adolescent psychology (PhD); juvenile forensic psychology (MSJFP); juvenile justice (MSJJ, PhD). Part-time and evening/weekend programs available. *Degree requirements:* For master's, comprehensive exam (for some programs), thesis (for some programs); for doctorate, comprehensive exam, thesis/dissertation. *Entrance requirements:* For master's, GRE, minimum GPA of 2.75; for doctorate, GRE, previous course work in clinical adolescent psychology, minimum GPA of 3.5. Additional exam requirements/recommendations for international students: Required—TOEFL. *Faculty research:* Juvenile justice, juvenile forensic psychology, teen court, graduate education, capital punishment.

Queen's University at Kingston, School of Graduate Studies and Research, Faculty of Arts and Sciences, Department of Sociology, Kingston, ON K7L 3N6, Canada. Offers communication and Information technology (MA, PhD); feminist sociology (MA, PhD); socio-legal studies (MA, PhD); sociological theory (MA, PhD). Part-time programs available. *Degree requirements:* For master's, thesis; for doctorate, comprehensive exam, thesis/dissertation. *Entrance requirements:* For master's, honors bachelors degree in sociology; for doctorate, honors bachelors degree, masters degree in sociology. Additional exam requirements/recommendations for international students: Required—TOEFL. *Faculty research:* Social change and modernization, social control, deviance and criminology, surveillance.

Regent University, Graduate School, School of Law, Virginia Beach, VA 23464-9800. Offers American legal studies (LL M); law (JD); JD/MA; JD/MBA. *Accreditation:* ABA. Part-time programs available. *Faculty:* 29 full-time (8 women), 48 part-time/adjunct (13 women). *Students:* 426 full-time (200 women), 79 part-time (46 women); includes 74 minority (22 Black or African American, non-Hispanic/Latino; 9 American Indian or Alaska Native, non-Hispanic/Latino; 23 Asian, non-Hispanic/Latino; 20 Hispanic/Latino), 73 international. Average age 28. 1,239 applicants, 34% accepted, 149 enrolled. In 2011, 121 doctorates awarded. *Entrance requirements:* For doctorate, LSAT, minimum undergraduate GPA of 2.75, 3 letters of recommendation, resume. Additional exam requirements/recommendations for international students: Required—TOEFL (minimum score 600 paper-based; 250 computer-based). *Application deadline:* For fall admission, 3/1 for domestic students. Applications are processed on a rolling basis. Application fee: $50. Electronic applications accepted. *Expenses:* Contact institution. *Financial support:* Career-related internships or fieldwork, scholarships/grants, and tuition waivers (full and partial) available. Support available to part-time students. Financial award application deadline: 2/1; financial award applicants required to submit FAFSA. *Faculty research:* Family law, Constitutional law, law and culture, evidence and practice, intellectual property. *Unit head:* Jeffrey Brauch, Dean, 757-352-4040, Fax: 757-352-4595, E-mail: jeffbra@regent.edu. *Application contact:* Matthew Chadwick, Director of Enrollment Support Services, 800-373-5504, Fax: 757-352-4381, E-mail: admissions@regent.edu. Web site: http://www.regent.edu/law/.

Rutgers, The State University of New Jersey, New Brunswick, Graduate School-New Brunswick, Department of Political Science, Piscataway, NJ 08854-8097. Offers American politics (PhD); comparative politics (PhD); international relations (PhD); political theory (PhD); public law (PhD); women and politics (PhD). *Degree requirements:* For doctorate, one foreign language, comprehensive exam, thesis/dissertation. *Entrance requirements:* For doctorate, GRE General Test. Additional exam requirements/recommendations for international students: Required—TOEFL.

St. John's University, College of Professional Studies, Department of Criminal Justice and Legal Studies, Queens, NY 11439. Offers MPS. Part-time and evening/weekend programs available. Postbaccalaureate distance learning degree programs offered (no on-campus study). *Students:* 24 full-time (13 women), 32 part-time (20 women); includes 25 minority (9 Black or African American, non-Hispanic/Latino; 3 Asian, non-Hispanic/Latino; 12 Hispanic/Latino; 1 Two or more races, non-Hispanic/Latino). Average age 28. 47 applicants, 83% accepted, 19 enrolled. In 2011, 31 master's awarded. *Degree requirements:* For master's, comprehensive exam, thesis optional, capstone project. *Entrance requirements:* For master's, bachelor's degree from regionally-accredited college or university, minimum overall GPA of 3.0, 2 letters of recommendation, 300-word essay. Additional exam requirements/recommendations for international students: Required—TOEFL (minimum score 600 paper-based; 250 computer-based; 100 iBT), IELTS (minimum score 5.5). *Application deadline:* For fall admission, 5/1 priority date for domestic students, 5/1 for international students; for spring admission, 11/1 priority date for domestic students, 11/1 for international students. Applications are processed on a rolling basis. Application fee: $70. Electronic applications accepted. *Expenses: Tuition:* Full-time $18,000; part-time $1000 per credit. *Required fees:* $170 per semester. Tuition and fees vary according to program. *Financial support:* Research assistantships available. *Faculty research:* Fire litigation, forensic psychology, organized crime, probation and parole, leadership studies, criminal justice ethics and integration control. *Unit head:* Dr. Keith Carrington, Chair, 718-390-2042, E-mail: carringk@stjohns.edu. *Application contact:* Robert Medrano, Director of Graduate Admission, 718-990-1601, Fax: 718-990-5686, E-mail: gradhelp@stjohns.edu.

St. John's University, St. John's College of Liberal Arts and Sciences, Program in Global Development and Social Justice, Queens, NY 11439. Offers MA. Program offered in collaboration with Unicaritas. Part-time programs available. Postbaccalaureate distance learning degree programs offered. *Students:* 5 full-time (4 women), 33 part-time (24 women); includes 7 minority (1 Black or African American, non-Hispanic/Latino; 2 Asian, non-Hispanic/Latino; 4 Hispanic/Latino), 1 international. Average age 32. 68 applicants, 62% accepted, 18 enrolled. In 2011, 14 master's awarded. *Degree requirements:* For master's, capstone project. *Entrance requirements:* For master's, 2 letters of recommendation, personal essay. Additional exam requirements/recommendations for international students: Required—TOEFL (minimum score 600 paper-based; 250 computer-based; 100 iBT), IELTS (minimum score 5.5). *Application deadline:* For fall admission, 5/1 priority date for domestic students, 5/1 for international students; for spring admission, 11/1 priority date for domestic students, 11/1 for international students. Applications are processed on a rolling basis. Application fee: $70. Electronic applications accepted. *Expenses: Tuition:* Full-time $18,000; part-time $1000 per credit. *Required fees:* $170 per semester. Tuition and fees vary according to program. *Unit head:* Dr. Annalisa Sacca, Director of the Center for Global Development, 718-990-5204, E-mail: saccaa@stjohns.edu. *Application contact:* Robert Medrano, Director of Graduate Admissions, 718-990-1601, E-mail: gradhelp@stjohns.edu. Web site: http://www.stjohns.edu/academics/graduate/liberalarts/departments/cgd/ma_gdsj.

St. John's University, School of Law, Program in U.S. Legal Studies for Foreign Law School Graduates, Queens, NY 11439. Offers LL M. Part-time programs available. *Students:* 9 full-time (5 women), 6 part-time (4 women); includes 7 minority (3 Black or African American, non-Hispanic/Latino; 2 Asian, non-Hispanic/Latino; 2 Hispanic/Latino), 4 international. Average age 37. 38 applicants, 47% accepted, 12 enrolled. In 2011, 15 master's awarded. *Entrance requirements:* For master's, law degree from non-U.S. law school, resume, 2 letters of recommendation, writing sample, interview, personal statement. Additional exam requirements/recommendations for international students: Required—TOEFL (minimum score 600 paper-based; 250 computer-based; 100 iBT), IELTS (minimum score 7), TWE. *Application deadline:* For fall admission, 4/1 priority date for domestic students, 4/1 for international students. Applications are processed on a rolling basis. Application fee: $100. Electronic applications accepted. *Expenses: Tuition:* Full-time $18,000; part-time $1000 per credit. *Required fees:* $170 per semester. Tuition and fees vary according to program. *Unit head:* Luca Melchionna, Director of Transitional Programming, 718-990-6948, E-mail: melchiol@stjohns.edu. *Application contact:* Robert Harrison, Assistant Dean and Director of Admissions, 718-990-6474, Fax: 718-990-6699, E-mail: lawinfo@stjohns.edu. Web site: http://www.stjohns.edu/academics/graduate/law/academics/llm/usls.

Saint Leo University, Graduate Studies in Criminal Justice, Saint Leo, FL 33574-6665. Offers corrections (MS); criminal justice (MS); critical incident management (MS); forensic psychology (MS); forensic science (MS); legal studies (MS). Part-time and evening/weekend programs available. Postbaccalaureate distance learning degree programs offered (minimal on-campus study). *Faculty:* 7 full-time (1 woman), 15 part-time/adjunct (3 women). *Students:* 522 full-time (313 women); includes 222 minority (183 Black or African American, non-Hispanic/Latino; 4 American Indian or Alaska Native, non-Hispanic/Latino; 1 Asian, non-Hispanic/Latino; 28 Hispanic/Latino; 1 Native Hawaiian or other Pacific Islander, non-Hispanic/Latino; 5 Two or more races, non-Hispanic/Latino). Average age 37. In 2011, 102 master's awarded. *Degree requirements:* For master's, comprehensive project. *Entrance requirements:* For master's, bachelor's degree with minimum GPA of 3.0 from regionally-accredited college or university. Additional exam requirements/recommendations for international students: Required—TOEFL (minimum score 550 paper-based; 213 computer-based; 80 iBT). *Application deadline:* For fall admission, 7/1 priority date for domestic students, 7/1 for international students; for spring admission, 11/1 priority date for domestic students, 11/1 for international students. Applications are processed on a rolling basis. Application fee: $80. Electronic applications accepted. *Expenses:* Contact institution. *Financial support:* In 2011–12, 11 students received support. Federal Work-Study, scholarships/grants, and health care benefits available. Financial award applicants required to submit FAFSA. *Unit head:* Dr. Robert Diemer, Director, 352-588-8974, Fax: 352-588-8289, E-mail: robert.diemer@saintleo.edu. *Application contact:* Jared Welling, Director of Graduate Admission, 800-707-8846, Fax: 352-588-7873, E-mail: grad.admissions@saintleo.edu. Web site: http://www.saintleo.edu/Academics/School-of-Education-Social-Services/Graduate-Degree-Programs.

San Francisco State University, Division of Graduate Studies, College of Education, Department of Administration and Interdisciplinary Studies, Program in Equity and Social Justice in Education, San Francisco, CA 94132-1722. Offers MA. *Unit head:* Dr. Marilyn Stepney, Chair, 415-338-1653, E-mail: mstepney@sfsu.edu. *Application contact:* Dr. Doris Flowers, Graduate Coordinator, 415-338-2614, E-mail: dflowers@sfsu.edu. Web site: http://coe.sfsu.edu/dais.

Southern Illinois University Carbondale, School of Law, Program in Legal Studies, Carbondale, IL 62901-4701. Offers general law (MLS); health law and policy (MLS). *Students:* 5 full-time (2 women), 4 part-time (all women); includes 3 minority (all Black or African American, non-Hispanic/Latino), 1 international. 9 applicants, 78% accepted, 3 enrolled. In 2011, 3 master's awarded. *Unit head:* Thomas Britton, Director, 618-453-8980, E-mail: llmadmit@siu.edu. *Application contact:* Barb Smith, Office Specialist, 618-453-8858, E-mail: mlsadmit@siu.edu.

State University of New York at Binghamton, Graduate School, School of Arts and Sciences, Program in Social, Political, Ethical and Legal Philosophy, Binghamton, NY 13902-6000. Offers MA, PhD. *Students:* 22 full-time (10 women), 15 part-time (5 women); includes 9 minority (2 Black or African American, non-Hispanic/Latino; 1 American Indian or Alaska Native, non-Hispanic/Latino; 4 Hispanic/Latino; 2 Native Hawaiian or other Pacific Islander, non-Hispanic/Latino), 4 international. Average age 29. 34 applicants, 47% accepted, 7 enrolled. In 2011, 7 master's, 6 doctorates awarded. Application fee: $60. *Financial support:* In 2011–12, 25 students received support, including 2 fellowships with full tuition reimbursements available (averaging $14,500 per year), 20 teaching assistantships with full tuition reimbursements available (averaging $14,500 per year); career-related internships or fieldwork, Federal Work-Study, institutionally sponsored loans, scholarships/grants, health care benefits, tuition waivers (full and partial), and unspecified assistantships also available. Financial award application deadline: 2/15; financial award applicants required to submit FAFSA. *Unit head:* Dr. Max Pensky, Chairperson, 607-777-4163, E-mail: mpensky@binghamton.edu. *Application contact:* Catherine Smith, Recruiting and Admissions Coordinator, 607-777-2151, Fax: 607-777-2501, E-mail: cmsmith@binghamton.edu. Web site: http://philosophy.binghamton.edu.

Taft Law School, Graduate Programs, Santa Ana, CA 92704-6954. Offers American jurisprudence (LL M); law (JD); taxation (LL M).

Temple University, James E. Beasley School of Law, Philadelphia, PA 19122. Offers law (JD); legal education (SJD); taxation (LL M); transnational law (LL M); trial advocacy (LL M); JD/LL M; JD/MBA. *Accreditation:* ABA. Part-time and evening/weekend programs available. *Entrance requirements:* For doctorate, LSAT (for JD). Additional exam requirements/recommendations for international students: Recommended—TOEFL. Electronic applications accepted. *Expenses:* Contact institution. *Faculty research:* Evidence, gender issues, health care law, immigration law, and intellectual property law .

Texas State University–San Marcos, Graduate School, College of Liberal Arts, Department of Political Science, Program in Legal Studies, San Marcos, TX 78666. Offers MA. *Faculty:* 5 full-time (2 women). *Students:* 25 full-time (19 women), 42 part-time (32 women); includes 27 minority (8 Black or African American, non-Hispanic/Latino; 1 Asian, non-Hispanic/Latino; 16 Hispanic/Latino; 2 Two or more races, non-Hispanic/Latino), 1 international. Average age 34. 27 applicants, 63% accepted, 12 enrolled. In 2011, 32 master's awarded. *Degree requirements:* For master's, comprehensive exam. *Entrance requirements:* For master's, GRE General Test (minimum score 900, 4 analytical preferred) or LSAT, minimum GPA of 2.75 in last 60 hours of undergraduate work. Additional exam requirements/recommendations for international students: Required—TOEFL (minimum score 550 paper-based; 213 computer-based; 78 iBT). *Application deadline:* For fall admission, 6/15 priority date for domestic students, 6/1 for international students; for spring admission, 10/15 priority date for domestic students, 10/1 for international students. Applications are processed on a rolling basis. Application fee: $90 ($140 for international students). Electronic applications accepted. *Expenses:* Tuition, state resident: full-time $6408; part-time $3204 per semester. Tuition, nonresident: full-time $14,832; part-time $7416 per semester. *Required fees:* $1824; $912 per semester. Tuition and fees vary according to course load. *Financial support:* In 2011–12, 33 students received support, including 2 teaching assistantships (averaging $10,152 per year); research assistantships, Federal Work-Study, institutionally sponsored loans, scholarships/grants, health care benefits, and unspecified assistantships also available. Financial award application deadline: 4/1; financial award applicants required to submit FAFSA. *Unit head:* Dr. Lynn Crossett, Graduate Advisor, 512-245-2233, Fax: 512-245-7815, E-mail: th10@txstate.edu. *Application contact:* Dr. J. Michael Willoughby, Dean of Graduate School, 512-245-2581, Fax: 512-245-8365, E-mail: gradcollege@txstate.edu. Web site: http://www.polisci.txstate.edu/.

Thomas M. Cooley Law School, JD and LL M Programs, Lansing, MI 48901-3038. Offers administrative law (public law) (JD); business transactions (JD); Canadian law (JD); Constitutional law and civil rights (public law) (JD); corporate law and finance (LL M); environmental law (public law) (JD); general practice (JD); insurance (LL M); intellectual property (LL M, JD); international law (JD); litigation (JD); self-directed (LL M, JD); taxation (LL M, JD); U.S. law for foreign attorneys (LL M); JD/MBA; JD/MPA; JD/MSW. *Accreditation:* ABA. Part-time and evening/weekend programs available. Postbaccalaureate distance learning degree programs offered (no on-campus study). *Faculty:* 131 full-time (55 women), 286 part-time/adjunct (93 women). *Students:* 781 full-time (368 women), 2,964 part-time (1,450 women); includes 1,055 minority (543 Black or African American, non-Hispanic/Latino; 19 American Indian or Alaska Native, non-Hispanic/Latino; 179 Asian, non-Hispanic/Latino; 205 Hispanic/Latino; 9 Native Hawaiian or other Pacific Islander, non-Hispanic/Latino; 100 Two or more races, non-Hispanic/Latino), 220 international. Average age 30. 4,032 applicants, 80% accepted, 1161 enrolled. In 2011, 40 master's, 999 doctorates awarded. *Degree requirements:* For master's, thesis optional; for doctorate, minimum of 3 credits of clinical experience. *Entrance requirements:* For master's, JD or LL B; for doctorate, LSAT. Additional exam requirements/recommendations for international students: Required—TOEFL. *Application deadline:* For fall admission, 9/1 for domestic and international students; for winter admission, 1/1 for domestic and international students; for spring admission, 5/1 for domestic and international students. Applications are processed on a rolling basis. Electronic applications accepted. *Expenses: Tuition:* Full-time $34,300; part-time $1225 per credit hour. *Required fees:* $40; $40 per year. Tuition and fees vary according to degree level and student level. *Financial support:* In 2011–12, 2,324 students received support. Career-related internships or fieldwork, Federal Work-Study, scholarships/grants, traineeships, and unspecified assistantships available. Support available to part-time students. Financial award applicants required to submit FAFSA. *Faculty research:* Wrongful convictions, civil rights, environmental law, litigation techniques, data mining, intellectual property, practical and skills-based legal education. *Unit head:* Don LeDuc, President and Dean, 517-371-5140 Ext. 2009, Fax: 517-334-5152. *Application contact:* Dr. Paul Zelenski, Associate Dean of Enrollment and Student Services, 517-371-5140 Ext. 2244, Fax: 517-334-5718, E-mail: admissions@cooley.edu. Web site: http://www.cooley.edu/.

Touro College, Jacob D. Fuchsberg Law Center, Central Islip, NY 11722. Offers general law (LL M); law (JD); U. S. legal studies (LL M); JD/MBA; JD/MSW. *Accreditation:* ABA. Part-time and evening/weekend programs available. *Entrance requirements:* For doctorate, LSAT. *Application deadline:* Applications are processed on a rolling basis. Application fee: $60. *Expenses:* Contact institution. *Financial support:* Fellowships, career-related internships or fieldwork, and Federal Work-Study available. Support available to part-time students. Financial award application deadline: 5/1. *Faculty research:* Business law, civil rights, international law, criminal justice. *Unit head:* Lawrence Raful, Dean, 516-421-2244. *Application contact:* Office of Admissions, 516-421-2244 Ext. 314. Web site: http://www.tourolaw.edu/.

Trident University International, College of Health Sciences, Program in Health Sciences, Cypress, CA 90630. Offers clinical research administration (MS, Certificate); emergency and disaster management (MS, Certificate); environmental health science (Certificate); health care administration (PhD); health care management (MS), including health informatics; health education (MS, Certificate); health informatics (Certificate); health sciences (PhD); international health (MS); international health: educator or researcher option (PhD); international health: practitioner option (PhD); law and expert witness studies (MS, Certificate); public health (MS); quality assurance (Certificate). Part-time and evening/weekend programs available. Postbaccalaureate distance learning degree programs offered (no on-campus study). *Degree requirements:* For doctorate, comprehensive exam, thesis/dissertation, defense of dissertation. *Entrance requirements:* For master's, minimum GPA of 2.5 (students with GPA 3.0 or greater may transfer up to 30% of graduate level credits); for doctorate, minimum GPA of 3.4, curriculum vitae, course work in research methods or statistics. Additional exam requirements/recommendations for international students: Required—TOEFL. Electronic applications accepted.

Universidad Autonoma de Guadalajara, Graduate Programs, Guadalajara, Mexico. Offers administrative law and justice (LL M); advertising and corporate communications (MA); architecture (M Arch); business (MBA); computational science (MCC); education (Ed M, Ed D); English-Spanish translation (MA); entrepreneurship and management (MBA); integrated management of digital animation (MA); international business (MIB); international corporate law (LL M); internet technologies (MS); manufacturing systems (MMS); occupational health (MS); philosophy (MA, PhD); power electronics (MS); quality systems (MQS); renewable energy (MS); social evaluation of projects (MBA); strategic market research (MBA); tax law (MA); teaching mathematics (MA).

Université Laval, Faculty of Law, Program in Notarial Law, Québec, QC G1K 7P4, Canada. Offers Diploma. Part-time programs available. *Entrance requirements:* For degree, knowledge of French. Electronic applications accepted.

University of Baltimore, Graduate School, The Yale Gordon College of Liberal Arts, Program in Legal and Ethical Studies, Baltimore, MD 21201-5779. Offers MA. Part-time and evening/weekend programs available. *Degree requirements:* For master's, thesis optional. *Entrance requirements:* For master's, minimum GPA of 3.0. Additional exam requirements/recommendations for international students: Required—TOEFL (minimum score 550 paper-based; 213 computer-based). Electronic applications accepted. *Faculty research:* Morality in law and economics, religion in lawmaking, comparative legal history, law and social change, critical issues in constitutional law, theories of justice.

University of Calgary, Faculty of Law, Programs in Natural Resources, Energy and Environmental Law, Calgary, AB T2N 1N4, Canada. Offers LL M, Postbaccalaureate Certificate. Part-time and evening/weekend programs available. *Degree requirements:* For master's, thesis optional. *Entrance requirements:* For master's, JD or LL B. Additional exam requirements/recommendations for international students: Required—TOEFL (minimum score 100 iBT), IELTS (minimum score 7). Electronic applications accepted. *Faculty research:* Natural resources law and regulations; environmental law, ethics and policies; oil and gas and energy law; water and municipal law; Aboriginal law.

Legal and Justice Studies

University of California, Berkeley, School of Law, Program in Jurisprudence and Social Policy, Berkeley, CA 94720-1500. Offers PhD. *Degree requirements:* For doctorate, one foreign language, thesis/dissertation, oral qualifying exam. *Entrance requirements:* For doctorate, GRE General Test, sample of written work, letters of recommendation. Electronic applications accepted. *Expenses:* Contact institution. *Faculty research:* Law and philosophy, legal history, law and economics, law and political science, law and sociology.

University of California, San Diego, Office of Graduate Studies, Program in Health Law, La Jolla, CA 92093. Offers MAS. Program offered jointly with School of Medicine and California Western School of Law. Part-time programs available. *Degree requirements:* For master's, capstone project. *Entrance requirements:* For master's, undergraduate degree in healthcare, law, or related field; 3 years work experience; 3 letters of recommendation; resume.

University of Charleston, Executive Master of Forensic Accounting Program, Charleston, WV 25304-1099. Offers EMFA. Part-time and evening/weekend programs available. *Entrance requirements:* For master's, undergraduate degree from regionally-accredited institution; minimum GPA of 3.0 in undergraduate work (recommended); three years of work experience since receiving undergraduate degree (recommended); minimum of two professional recommendations, one from current employer, addressing career potential and ability to do graduate work. Additional exam requirements/recommendations for international students: Required—TOEFL. *Application deadline:* Applications are processed on a rolling basis. Electronic applications accepted. *Financial support:* In 2011–12, 1 student received support. Applicants required to submit FAFSA. *Application contact:* Linda Anderson, Administrative Assistant, 304-357-4870, Fax: 304-357-4872, E-mail: lindaanderson@ucwv.edu. Web site: http://www.ucwv.edu/Forensic-Accounting/.

University of Denver, College of Law, Program in Legal Administration, Denver, CO 80208. Offers MSLA, Certificate. Part-time and evening/weekend programs available. *Faculty:* 80 full-time (39 women), 80 part-time/adjunct (27 women). *Students:* 9 full-time (3 women), 29 part-time (24 women); includes 9 minority (3 Black or African American, non-Hispanic/Latino; 1 Asian, non-Hispanic/Latino; 5 Hispanic/Latino). Average age 33. 25 applicants, 100% accepted, 14 enrolled. In 2011, 19 master's, 1 Certificate awarded. *Degree requirements:* For master's, internship. *Entrance requirements:* For master's, GRE General Test, GMAT, or LSAT. Additional exam requirements/recommendations for international students: Required—TOEFL (minimum score 570 paper-based; 88 iBT). *Application deadline:* Applications are processed on a rolling basis. Application fee: $60. Electronic applications accepted. *Financial support:* Career-related internships or fieldwork and Federal Work-Study available. Support available to part-time students. Financial award application deadline: 2/15; financial award applicants required to submit FAFSA. *Unit head:* Hope Kentnor, Director, 305-871-6308, Fax: 303-871-6333, E-mail: hope.kentor@du.edu. *Application contact:* Lucy Daberkow, Associate Director of Admissions, 303-871-6324, Fax: 303-871-6378, E-mail: msln@law.du.edu. Web site: http://www.law.du.edu/index.php/msla.

University of Illinois at Springfield, Graduate Programs, College of Public Affairs and Administration, Program in Legal Studies, Springfield, IL 62703-5407. Offers MA. Part-time and evening/weekend programs available. Postbaccalaureate distance learning degree programs offered (no on-campus study). *Faculty:* 2 full-time (both women). *Students:* 6 full-time (2 women), 39 part-time (24 women); includes 6 minority (3 Black or African American, non-Hispanic/Latino; 1 Asian, non-Hispanic/Latino; 1 Hispanic/Latino; 1 Two or more races, non-Hispanic/Latino). Average age 36. 47 applicants, 45% accepted, 16 enrolled. In 2011, 7 master's awarded. *Degree requirements:* For master's, thesis or seminar. *Entrance requirements:* For master's, minimum undergraduate GPA of 3.0 (for on-campus program), 3.25 (for online program); demonstration of writing ability. Additional exam requirements/recommendations for international students: Required—TOEFL (minimum score 600 paper-based; 250 computer-based; 100 iBT). *Application deadline:* Applications are processed on a rolling basis. Application fee: $50 ($60 for international students). Electronic applications accepted. *Expenses:* Tuition, state resident: full-time $6978; part-time $290.75 per credit hour. Tuition, nonresident: full-time $15,282; part-time $636.75 per credit hour. *Required fees:* $2106; $87.75 per credit hour. *Financial support:* In 2011–12, fellowships with full tuition reimbursements (averaging $8,550 per year), research assistantships with full tuition reimbursements (averaging $8,550 per year), teaching assistantships with full tuition reimbursements (averaging $8,550 per year) were awarded; career-related internships or fieldwork, Federal Work-Study, scholarships/grants, health care benefits, and unspecified assistantships also available. Support available to part-time students. Financial award application deadline: 11/15; financial award applicants required to submit FAFSA. *Unit head:* Kathryn E. Eisenhart, Program Administrator, 217-206-7882, Fax: 217-206-7807, E-mail: eisenhart.kathryn@uis.edu. *Application contact:* Dr. Lynn Pardie, Office of Graduate Studies, 800-252-8533, Fax: 217-206-7623, E-mail: lpard1@uis.edu. Web site: http://www.uis.edu/legalstudies/.

University of Mississippi, Graduate School, School of Applied Sciences, Department of Legal Studies, Oxford, University, MS 38677. Offers MS. *Students:* 25 full-time (12 women), 13 part-time (2 women); includes 7 minority (6 Black or African American, non-Hispanic/Latino; 1 Two or more races, non-Hispanic/Latino), 1 international. In 2011, 4 degrees awarded. *Unit head:* Dr. David McElreath, Chair, 662-915-1635, E-mail: dhmcel@olemiss.edu. *Application contact:* Dr. Christy M. Wyandt, Associate Dean, 662-915-7474, Fax: 662-915-7577, E-mail: cwyandt@olemiss.edu. Web site: http://www.olemiss.edu/depts/legalstudies/.

University of Nebraska–Lincoln, College of Law, Program in Legal Studies, Lincoln, NE 68588. Offers MLS. *Entrance requirements:* For master's, GRE or LSAT. Additional exam requirements/recommendations for international students: Required—TOEFL (minimum score 600 paper-based; 250 computer-based). Electronic applications accepted.

University of Nevada, Reno, Graduate School, College of Liberal Arts, School of Social Research and Justice Studies, Program in Judicial Studies, Reno, NV 89557. Offers MJS, PhD. Offered jointly with the National Judicial College and the National Council of Juvenile and Family Court Judges. Part-time programs available. Terminal master's awarded for partial completion of doctoral program. *Degree requirements:* For master's, thesis; for doctorate, thesis/dissertation. *Entrance requirements:* For master's and doctorate, sitting judge, law degree from an accredited school. Additional exam requirements/recommendations for international students: Required—TOEFL (minimum score 500 paper-based; 173 computer-based; 61 iBT), IELTS (minimum score 6). Electronic applications accepted. *Expenses:* Contact institution. *Faculty research:* Jury research, capital punishment, expert testimony, environmental law, medical issues.

University of New Hampshire, Graduate School, College of Liberal Arts, Program in Justice Studies, Durham, NH 03824. Offers MA. Program offered in summer only. Part-time programs available. *Faculty:* 22 full-time (11 women). *Students:* 14 full-time (8 women), 6 part-time (3 women). Average age 27. In 2011, 16 master's awarded. *Degree requirements:* For master's, thesis optional. *Entrance requirements:* For master's, GRE. Additional exam requirements/recommendations for international students: Required—TOEFL (minimum score 550 paper-based; 213 computer-based; 80 iBT); Recommended—TWE. *Application deadline:* For fall admission, 3/1 for domestic and international students. Applications are processed on a rolling basis. Application fee: $65. Electronic applications accepted. *Expenses:* Tuition, state resident: full-time $12,360; part-time $687 per credit hour. Tuition, nonresident: full-time $25,680; part-time $1058 per credit hour. *International tuition:* $29,550 full-time. *Required fees:* $1666; $833 per course. $416.50 per semester. Tuition and fees vary according to course load and degree level. *Financial support:* In 2011–12, 3 students received support, including 1 research assistantship, 2 teaching assistantships; fellowships, career-related internships or fieldwork, Federal Work-Study, scholarships/grants, and tuition waivers (full and partial) also available. Support available to part-time students. Financial award application deadline: 3/1. *Unit head:* Dr. Ellen Cohn, Chairperson, 603-862-3197, E-mail: ellen.cohn@unh.edu. *Application contact:* Deborah Briand, Administrative Assistant, 603-862-1716, E-mail: justice.studies@unh.edu. Web site: http://www.unh.edu/justice-studies/.

University of Oklahoma, College of Arts and Sciences, Department of Human Relations, Norman, OK 73019. Offers human relations (MHR), including affirmative action, chemical addictions counseling, family relations, general, human resources, juvenile justice; human relations licensure (Graduate Certificate). Part-time and evening/weekend programs available. Postbaccalaureate distance learning degree programs offered (minimal on-campus study). *Faculty:* 27 full-time (18 women), 2 part-time/adjunct (1 woman). *Students:* 327 full-time (207 women), 537 part-time (328 women); includes 343 minority (203 Black or African American, non-Hispanic/Latino; 42 American Indian or Alaska Native, non-Hispanic/Latino; 22 Asian, non-Hispanic/Latino; 45 Hispanic/Latino; 31 Two or more races, non-Hispanic/Latino), 15 international. Average age 34. 317 applicants, 90% accepted, 201 enrolled. In 2011, 310 degrees awarded. *Degree requirements:* For master's, thesis optional. *Entrance requirements:* For master's, minimum GPA of 3.0 in last 60 hours of undergraduate course work, resume, 3 letters of reference. Additional exam requirements/recommendations for international students: Required—TOEFL (minimum score 550 paper-based; 79 iBT). *Application deadline:* For fall admission, 4/1 priority date for domestic students, 3/1 for international students; for spring admission, 11/1 for domestic students, 9/1 for international students. Applications are processed on a rolling basis. Application fee: $40 ($90 for international students). Electronic applications accepted. *Expenses:* Tuition, state resident: full-time $4087; part-time $170.30 per credit hour. Tuition, nonresident: full-time $14,875; part-time $619.80 per credit hour. *Required fees:* $2659; $100.25 per credit hour. Tuition and fees vary according to course load and degree level. *Financial support:* In 2011–12, 358 students received support, including 12 research assistantships with partial tuition reimbursements available (averaging $11,021 per year), 5 teaching assistantships (averaging $11,124 per year); career-related internships or fieldwork, scholarships/grants, and unspecified assistantships also available. Financial award applicants required to submit FAFSA. *Faculty research:* Non-profit organizations, high risk youth, trauma, women's studies, impact of war on women and children. *Total annual research expenditures:* $62,927. *Unit head:* Dr. Susan Marcus-Mendoza, Chair, 405-325-1756, Fax: 405-325-4402, E-mail: smmendoza@ou.edu. *Application contact:* Lawana Miller, Admissions Coordinator, 405-325-1756, Fax: 405-325-4402, E-mail: lmiller@ou.edu. Web site: http://www.ou.edu/cas/hr.

University of Pennsylvania, Wharton School, Legal Studies and Business Ethics Department, Philadelphia, PA 19104. Offers MBA, PhD. *Expenses: Tuition:* Full-time $26,660; part-time $4944 per course. *Required fees:* $2318; $291 per course. Tuition and fees vary according to course load, degree level and program.

University of Pittsburgh, School of Law, Master of Studies in Law Program, Pittsburgh, PA 15260. Offers business law (MSL), including commercial law, corporate law, general business law, international business, tax law; constitutional law (MSL); criminal law and justice (MSL); disabilities law (MSL); dispute resolution (MSL); education law (MSL); elder and estate planning law (MSL); employment and labor law (MSL); environment and real estate law (MSL); family law (MSL); general law and jurisprudence (MSL); health law (MSL); intellectual property and technology (MSL); international and comparative law (MSL); personal injury and civil litigation (MSL); regulatory law (MSL); self-designed (MSL); sports and entertainment law (MSL). Part-time programs available. *Faculty:* 43 full-time (16 women), 104 part-time/adjunct (30 women). *Students:* 5 full-time (3 women), 16 part-time (12 women); includes 6 minority (all Black or African American, non-Hispanic/Latino). Average age 31. 19 applicants, 58% accepted, 11 enrolled. In 2011, 6 master's awarded. *Entrance requirements:* Additional exam requirements/recommendations for international students: Required—TOEFL (minimum score 600 paper-based; 250 computer-based; 100 iBT). *Application deadline:* For fall admission, 6/30 for domestic students, 5/1 for international students. Applications are processed on a rolling basis. Application fee: $0. *Expenses:* Tuition, state resident: full-time $18,774; part-time $760 per credit hour. Tuition, nonresident: full-time $30,736; part-time $1258 per credit. *Required fees:* $740; $200 per term. Tuition and fees vary according to program. *Faculty research:* Law, health law, business law, contracts, intellectual property. *Unit head:* Prof. Alan Meisel, Director, 412-648-1384, Fax: 412-648-2649, E-mail: meisel@pitt.edu. *Application contact:* Bethann Pischke, Administrative Coordinator, 412-648-7120, Fax: 412-648-2649, E-mail: pischke@pitt.edu. Web site: http://www.law.pitt.edu/academics/msl.

University of Pittsburgh, School of Law, Program in Health Law, Pittsburgh, PA 15260. Offers Certificate. *Faculty:* 46 full-time (19 women), 108 part-time/adjunct (30 women). *Students:* 35 full-time (16 women). *Application deadline:* For spring admission, 7/31 for domestic students. Applications are processed on a rolling basis. *Expenses:* Tuition, state resident: full-time $18,774; part-time $760 per credit. Tuition, nonresident: full-time $30,736; part-time $1258 per credit. *Required fees:* $740; $200 per term. Tuition and fees vary according to program. *Unit head:* Prof. Alan Meisel, Professor/Director, 412-648-1384, Fax: 412-648-2649, E-mail: meisel@pitt.edu. *Application contact:* Bethann Pischke, Program Administrator, 412-648-7120, Fax: 412-648-2649, E-mail: pischke@pitt.edu.

University of San Diego, School of Law, San Diego, CA 92110-2492. Offers business and corporate law (LL M); comparative law (LL M); general studies (LL M); international law (LL M); law (JD); taxation (LL M, Diploma); JD/IMBA; JD/MA; JD/MBA. *Accreditation:* ABA. Part-time and evening/weekend programs available. *Faculty:* 55 full-time (19 women), 71 part-time/adjunct (21 women). *Students:* 896 full-time (445 women), 177 part-time (79 women); includes 341 minority (15 Black or African American, non-Hispanic/Latino; 4 American Indian or Alaska Native, non-Hispanic/Latino; 159 Asian, non-Hispanic/Latino; 114 Hispanic/Latino; 2 Native Hawaiian or other Pacific Islander, non-Hispanic/Latino; 47 Two or more races, non-Hispanic/Latino), 31 international. Average age 36. 4,314 applicants, 38% accepted, 300 enrolled. In 2011, 71 master's, 322 doctorates awarded. *Entrance requirements:* For master's, JD, LL B or equivalent from an ABA-accredited law school; for doctorate, LSAT, bachelor's degree. Additional exam requirements/recommendations for international students: Required—TOEFL (minimum score 600 paper-based; 250 computer-based; 98 iBT). *Application deadline:* For fall admission, 2/1 priority date for domestic students. Applications are processed on a rolling basis. Application fee: $50. Electronic applications accepted. *Expenses:* Contact institution. *Financial support:* In 2011–12, 627 students received support. Career-related internships or fieldwork, Federal Work-Study, institutionally sponsored loans, and scholarships/grants available. Support available to part-time students. Financial award application deadline: 3/1; financial award applicants required to submit FAFSA. *Unit head:* Dr. Stephen C. Ferruolo, Dean, 619-260-2330, Fax: 619-260-2218. *Application contact:* Jorge Garcia, Director of Admissions and Financial Aid, 619-260-4528, Fax: 619-260-2218, E-mail: jdinfo@sandiego.edu. Web site: http://www.sandiego.edu/usdlaw/.

University of the District of Columbia, David A. Clarke School of Law, Washington, DC 20008. Offers clinical teaching and social justice (LL M); law (JD). *Accreditation:* ABA. Part-time and evening/weekend programs available. *Degree requirements:* For doctorate, 90 credits, advanced legal writing. *Entrance requirements:* For doctorate, LSAT. Additional exam requirements/recommendations for international students: Recommended—TOEFL. Electronic applications accepted. *Expenses:* Contact institution. *Faculty research:* HIV law, juvenile law, legislative law, community development, small business, immigration and human rights.

University of the Pacific, McGeorge School of Law, Sacramento, CA 95817. Offers advocacy (JD); criminal justice (JD); experiential law teaching (LL M); intellectual property (JD); international legal studies (JD); international water resources law (LL M, JSD); law (JD); public law and policy (JD); public policy and law (LL M); tax (JD); transnational business practice (LL M); JD/MBA; JD/MPPA. *Accreditation:* ABA. Part-time and evening/weekend programs available. *Faculty:* 48 full-time (20 women), 59 part-time/adjunct (18 women). *Students:* 704 full-time (325 women), 255 part-time (122 women); includes 254 minority (19 Black or African American, non-Hispanic/Latino; 19 American Indian or Alaska Native, non-Hispanic/Latino; 151 Asian, non-Hispanic/Latino; 65 Hispanic/Latino), 41 international. Average age 27. 3,564 applicants, 38% accepted, 228 enrolled. In 2011, 36 master's, 307 doctorates awarded. *Degree requirements:* For master's, thesis (for some programs); for doctorate, thesis/dissertation (for some programs). *Entrance requirements:* For master's, JD; for doctorate, LSAT (for JD), LL M (for JSD). Additional exam requirements/recommendations for international students: Required—TOEFL (minimum score 600 paper-based; 250 computer-based; 100 iBT). *Application deadline:* For fall admission, 3/15 priority date for domestic students. Applications are processed on a rolling basis. Application fee: $50. Electronic applications accepted. *Expenses:* Contact institution. *Financial support:* Fellowships, research assistantships, teaching assistantships, career-related internships or fieldwork, Federal Work-Study, institutionally sponsored loans, and scholarships/grants available. Support available to part-time students. Financial award applicants required to submit FAFSA. *Faculty research:* International legal studies, public policy and law, advocacy, intellectual property law, taxation, criminal law. *Unit head:* Elizabeth Rindskopf Parker, Dean, 916-739-7151, E-mail: elizabeth@pacific.edu. *Application contact:* 916-739-7105, Fax: 916-739-7301, E-mail: mcgeorge@pacific.edu. Web site: http://www.mcgeorge.edu/.

University of the Sacred Heart, Graduate Programs, Program in Systems of Justice, San Juan, PR 00914-0383. Offers human rights and anti-discriminatory processes (MASJ); mediation and transformation of conflicts (MASJ).

University of Washington, Graduate School, School of Law, Seattle, WA 98195-3020. Offers Asian law (LL M, PhD); intellectual property law and policy (LL M); law (JD); law of sustainable international development (LL M); taxation (LL M); JD/LL M; JD/MA; JD/MAIS; JD/MBA; JD/MPA; JD/MS; JD/PhD. *Accreditation:* ABA. *Degree requirements:* For master's, thesis; for doctorate, thesis/dissertation (for some programs). *Entrance requirements:* For master's, language proficiency (LL M in Asian law); for doctorate, LSAT (for JD). Additional exam requirements/recommendations for international students: Required—TOEFL. *Expenses:* Contact institution. *Faculty research:* Asian, international and comparative law, intellectual property law, health law, environmental law, taxation.

University of Windsor, Faculty of Graduate Studies, Faculty of Arts and Social Sciences, Department of Communication Studies, Windsor, ON N9B 3P4, Canada. Offers communication and social justice (MA). *Degree requirements:* For master's, thesis. *Entrance requirements:* For master's, writing sample/media production or multimedia portfolio. Additional exam requirements/recommendations for international students: Required—TOEFL (minimum score 600 paper-based; 250 computer-based). Electronic applications accepted. *Faculty research:* Sociology of news, media ownership and control, communication networks and social movements, issues of media representation.

University of Wisconsin–Madison, Law School, Graduate Programs in Law, Madison, WI 53706-1380. Offers LL M, SJD. *Faculty:* 43 full-time (17 women), 11 part-time/adjunct (2 women). *Students:* 98 full-time (63 women), 7 part-time (5 women); includes 6 minority (4 Black or African American, non-Hispanic/Latino; 2 Asian, non-Hispanic/Latino), 99 international. Average age 28. 121 applicants, 79% accepted, 51 enrolled. In 2011, 54 master's, 3 doctorates awarded. *Degree requirements:* For master's, thesis (for some programs); for doctorate, thesis/dissertation. *Entrance requirements:* Additional exam requirements/recommendations for international students: Required—TOEFL (minimum score 580 paper-based; 237 computer-based; 92 iBT). *Application deadline:* For fall admission, 3/1 for domestic and international students; for spring admission, 10/1 for domestic students, 10/15 for international students. Applications are processed on a rolling basis. Application fee: $56. Electronic applications accepted. *Expenses:* Tuition, state resident: full-time $10,296; part-time $643.51 per credit. Tuition, nonresident: full-time $24,054; part-time $1503.40 per credit. *Required fees:* $70.06 per credit. Tuition and fees vary according to course load, campus/location, program and reciprocity agreements. *Financial support:* In 2011–12, 5 fellowships with full tuition reimbursements (averaging $12,000 per year) were awarded; scholarships/grants and tuition waivers (partial) also available. *Faculty research:* Tax policy in emerging economics, international trade law, anti-trust law and regulation, Asian comparative law and legal history, intellectual property in business organization. *Unit head:* 608-262-9120. *Application contact:* Jason Smith, Graduate Programs Coordinator, 608-262-9120, Fax: 608-265-2253, E-mail: gradprog@law.wisc.edu. Web site: http://www.law.wisc.edu/grad/.

Valparaiso University, Graduate School, Program in Legal Studies and Principles, Valparaiso, IN 46383. Offers Certificate. Part-time and evening/weekend programs available. In 2011, 1 Certificate awarded. *Entrance requirements:* Additional exam requirements/recommendations for international students: Required—TOEFL (minimum score 550 paper-based; 213 computer-based; 80 iBT). *Application deadline:* Applications are processed on a rolling basis. Application fee: $30 ($50 for international students). Electronic applications accepted. *Expenses: Tuition:* Part-time $560 per credit hour. Tuition and fees vary according to course load and program. *Financial support:* Available to part-time students. Applicants required to submit FAFSA. *Unit head:* Dr. David L. Rowland, Dean, Graduate School and Continuing Education/Associate Provost, 219-464-5313, Fax: 219-464-5381, E-mail: david.rowland@valpo.edu. *Application contact:* Dustin Jesch, Coordinator, U.S. Student Engagement, 219-464-5313, Fax: 219-464-5381, E-mail: dustin.jesch@valpo.edu. Web site: http://valpo.edu/grad/programs/lawcert.php.

Vermont Law School, Law School, Environmental Law Center, South Royalton, VT 05068-0096. Offers LL M, MELP, JD/MELP. Part-time programs available. *Faculty:* 15 full-time (6 women), 10 part-time/adjunct (9 women). *Students:* 55 full-time (33 women); includes 12 minority (4 Black or African American, non-Hispanic/Latino; 1 American Indian or Alaska Native, non-Hispanic/Latino; 3 Asian, non-Hispanic/Latino; 1 Hispanic/Latino; 3 Two or more races, non-Hispanic/Latino). Average age 30. 148 applicants, 83% accepted, 41 enrolled. In 2011, 53 master's awarded. *Entrance requirements:* Additional exam requirements/recommendations for international students: Required—TOEFL. *Application deadline:* For fall admission, 3/1 priority date for domestic students. Applications are processed on a rolling basis. Application fee: $60. *Financial support:* In 2011–12, 2 fellowships with full tuition reimbursements (averaging $5,000 per year) were awarded; career-related internships or fieldwork, Federal Work-Study, institutionally sponsored loans, scholarships/grants, and tuition waivers (partial) also available. Support available to part-time students. Financial award application deadline: 3/1; financial award applicants required to submit FAFSA. *Faculty research:* Environment and technology; takings; international environmental law; interaction among science, law, and environmental policy; air pollution. *Total annual research expenditures:* $52,000. *Unit head:* Marc Mihaly, Associate Dean, 802-831-1342, Fax: 802-763-2490, E-mail: admiss@vermontlaw.edu. *Application contact:* Anne Mansfield, Associate Director, 802-831-1338, Fax: 802-763-2940, E-mail: admiss@vermontlaw.edu. Web site: http://www.vermontlaw.edu/.

Weber State University, College of Social and Behavioral Sciences, Program in Criminal Justice, Ogden, UT 84408-1001. Offers MCJ. Part-time and evening/weekend programs available. *Entrance requirements:* For master's, GRE General Test, resume.

Webster University, College of Arts and Sciences, Department of Behavioral and Social Sciences, Program in Legal Analysis, St. Louis, MO 63119-3194. Offers MA. Part-time programs available. *Entrance requirements:* Additional exam requirements/recommendations for international students: Required—TOEFL. *Expenses: Tuition:* Full-time $10,890; part-time $605 per credit hour. Tuition and fees vary according to campus/location and program.

Webster University, College of Arts and Sciences, Department of Behavioral and Social Sciences, Program in Legal Studies, St. Louis, MO 63119-3194. Offers MA. Part-time and evening/weekend programs available. *Degree requirements:* For master's, thesis optional. *Entrance requirements:* Additional exam requirements/recommendations for international students: Required—TOEFL. *Expenses: Tuition:* Full-time $10,890; part-time $605 per credit hour. Tuition and fees vary according to campus/location and program. *Faculty research:* Intellectual property rights, emerging torts, death penalty, juvenile justice, confidentiality issues in banking.

Webster University, College of Arts and Sciences, Department of Behavioral and Social Sciences, Program in Patent Agency, St. Louis, MO 63119-3194. Offers MA. Part-time and evening/weekend programs available. *Entrance requirements:* Additional exam requirements/recommendations for international students: Required—TOEFL. *Expenses: Tuition:* Full-time $10,890; part-time $605 per credit hour. Tuition and fees vary according to campus/location and program. *Faculty research:* Intellectual property rights, emerging torts, death penalty, juvenile justice, confidentiality issues in banking.

West Virginia University, Eberly College of Arts and Sciences, School of Applied Social Sciences, Division of Public Administration, Morgantown, WV 26506. Offers legal studies (MLS); public administration (MPA); JD/MPA; MSW/MPA. *Accreditation:* NASPAA. Part-time programs available. *Degree requirements:* For master's, internship. *Entrance requirements:* For master's, GRE General Test, minimum GPA of 2.75. Additional exam requirements/recommendations for international students: Required—TOEFL. Electronic applications accepted. *Faculty research:* Public management and organization, conflict resolution, work satisfaction, health administration, social policy and welfare.

Whittier College, Whittier Law School, Costa Mesa, CA 92626. Offers foreign legal studies (LL M); law (JD). *Accreditation:* ABA. Part-time and evening/weekend programs available. *Entrance requirements:* For master's, first degree in law; for doctorate, LSAT. Additional exam requirements/recommendations for international students: Required—TOEFL (minimum score 600 paper-based; 250 computer-based). Electronic applications accepted. *Expenses:* Contact institution. *Faculty research:* Intellectual property, international law, health law, children's rights.

Wilfrid Laurier University, Faculty of Graduate and Postdoctoral Studies, School of International Policy and Governance, Global Governance Program, Waterloo, ON N2L 3C5, Canada. Offers conflict and security (PhD); global environment (PhD); global justice and human rights (PhD); global political economy (PhD); global social governance (PhD); multilateral institutions and diplomacy (PhD). Offered jointly with University of Waterloo. *Degree requirements:* For doctorate, thesis/dissertation. *Entrance requirements:* For doctorate, MA in political science, history, economics, international development studies, international peace studies, globalization studies, environmental studies or related field with minimum A-. Additional exam requirements/recommendations for international students: Required—TOEFL (minimum score 89 iBT). Electronic applications accepted. *Faculty research:* Global political economy, global environment, conflict and security, global justice and human rights, multilateral institutions and diplomacy.

NEW YORK LAW SCHOOL

NEW YORK LAW SCHOOL

Master of Arts in Mental Disability Law Studies
Certificate in Advanced Mental Disability Law Studies

Program of Study

New York Law School has created the nation's first online mental disability law program, offering a Master of Arts in mental disability law studies and a certificate in advanced mental disability law studies. This diverse program provides psychologists, psychiatrists, other mental health professionals, criminologists, criminal justice specialists, advocates, activists, human rights workers, social workers, and attorneys with advanced training in an important, growing field. It is the only program of its kind offered by an American Bar Association–approved law school and delivered directly through the convenience of distance learning.

Students advance their professional status and legal literacy by learning about the complexities of the law and how court decisions affect the way they handle cases, conduct research, or advocate on behalf of persons with mental disabilities. Along the way, students develops the skills required as an expert witness, administrator, clinician, researcher, advocate, or attorney in order to bring about meaningful change in the lives and treatment of persons with mental disabilities.

Designed and taught by renowned Professor Michael L. Perlin, the online mental disability law program provides the most up-to-date information and interpretation of civil, criminal, constitutional, and international human rights law via high-quality instruction and academic guidance in a multidimensional distance-learning environment. Students who are currently engaged in professional careers can further their education while maintaining their current employment since all classes meet at night and on weekends. The program utilizes the latest and most effective online learning technologies to easily disseminate legal-based education to professionals and advanced learners who may otherwise be unable to gain access to this training.

The majority of course content is completed online, where students have access to a virtual community of fellow students. Each fourteen-week course is taught by experienced, distinguished scholars and practitioners. Courses include weekly recorded lectures; weekly reading assignments; personalized e-mail access to the program's faculty and staff members; weekly synchronous classes in a virtual classroom via chat sessions where students and faculty meet in real time; weekly asynchronous threaded question-and-answer discussions through message boards; two daylong weekend seminars held at New York Law School, where students meet with professors to discuss topics addressed during the course and to emphasize skills training; and a short take-home midterm and final exam.

The Master of Arts in mental disability law studies is a 30-credit degree-bearing program that can be completed in eighteen months or up to five years, depending on whether the student is enrolled full- or part-time. Candidates are required to successfully complete six courses of the core curriculum, three elective courses, and an independent writing project supervised by the program director and/or program faculty member. (All courses are 3 credits.) To earn the M.A. degree, a candidate must have a minimum cumulative GPA of 2.5.

The certificate in advanced mental disability law studies provides the opportunity to pursue graduate studies with a shorter 15-credit certificate, which can be completed in ten to eighteen months, depending on whether the student is enrolled full- or part-time. Candidates must successfully complete one required course and four elective courses. (All courses are 3 credits.) To receive the certificate, a candidate must have a minimum cumulative GPA of 2.5.

Research Facilities

The Mendik Library at New York Law School has a sizable collection in disciplines related to the area of mental disability law and provides ample staff research and reference support to the program. Resources include materials from international, federal, all fifty states, and local New York jurisdictions. The library's collection is augmented by a sophisticated range of computer research services and other technological enhancements. The online public access catalog, automated acquisitions, serials, and circulation control systems provide easy and comprehensive access to the collection. Reference librarians assist users in locating materials outside the Law School's collection and in arranging access to the most convenient sources. To maximize the range of materials and facilities available to students and faculty, the library has joined several library consortia providing access to New York metropolitan area libraries, and international and comparative law materials. Using the bibliographic databases, librarians can locate and arrange for the interlibrary loan of materials from academic, court, public, and private libraries throughout New York and the United States. The library also subscribes to e-journals and JSTOR, a resource to full articles in nonlegal, multidiscipline areas. All students have Lexis and Westlaw accounts for access to the latest state, federal, and regulatory decisions in cases related to their studies, as well as journals and newspaper resources. Although hard copy publications are available to students in the program, most of the research sources and tools used will be electronic. The combination of the library's holdings, borrowing policies, and student access to Lexis and Westlaw is allows for successful completion of student research in the program.

Financial Aid

M.A. students may be eligible for private loans. Veterans may be able to use their G.I. bill benefits. For information, contact the Office of Admissions and Financial Aid at 212-431-2828 or e-mail financialaid@nyls.edu.

Cost of Study

Tuition for students in Master of Arts degree and Certificate programs is $2400 per course for the 2012–13 academic year. For students who work for nonprofit organizations or government agencies, the tuition is $1500 per course for the year.

Student Group

New York Law School reflects the cosmopolitan nature of its urban setting in New York City. The total number of J.D. students enrolled in all divisions, all classes, is approximately 1,765. There are approximately 95 students enrolled in the School's advanced-degree programs in financial services law, real estate, taxation, and mental disability law. The student body represents 235 undergraduate schools, thirty-six states and territories, twenty-one other countries, and several international institutions. The student body (entering class of 2011) is 54 percent female; 32 percent identify themselves as members of minority groups. In addition to the M.A. degree and certificate programs, the Law School offers Master of Laws (LL.M.) degrees in American business law, financial services law, real estate, and taxation.

Discrimination and harassment interfere with the educational purpose of New York Law School and negatively affect all members of the Law School community. Faculty, staff, and students have a right to be free from discrimination and harassment based on race, color, ethnicity, ancestry, citizenship, religion, sex, pregnancy, sexual orientation, gender identity, gender expression, national origin, age, disability, AIDS, predisposing genetic characteristics, marital or parental status, military status, domestic violence victim status, or any other classification protected by local, state, or federal law ("Protected Classification"). Discrimination or harassment directed at any member of the Law School community within the context of the Law School or Law School–sponsored activities will not be permitted, and complaints will be investigated promptly and thoroughly. New York Law School is proud of its policy of maintaining a work, academic, and residential environment that encourages tolerance and respect for the dignity of each individual.

For many years, New York Law School has had a human rights policy barring employers who practice discrimination in employment from using the services of the School's Office of Career Services. This policy has, in the past, been applied to bar military recruiters from campus because of the military's employment policies that discriminate on the basis of sexual orientation. Following the recent Supreme Court decision upholding the constitutionality of the Solomon Amendment, a federal appropriations provision threatening loss of federal funds to schools that exclude military recruiters, the faculty decided to allow the military on campus for recruitment purposes, while still encouraging and supporting efforts in the law school community to express disapproval of sexual orientation discrimination in general and the military's policy in particular. New York Law School continues to oppose the practice of discrimination in employment by all employers including discrimination on the basis of sexual orientation.

New York Law School complies with the Americans with Disabilities Act of 1990 as amended and with Section 504 of the Rehabilitation Act of 1973 as amended. The Law School's Office of Student Life and Office of Academic Affairs formulate general policy on disability issues and make decisions on individual accommodation requests.

Location

New York Law School is located in the heart of Manhattan's Tribeca district—home of the city's legal, government, and corporate headquarters, as well as a thriving cultural scene. In addition, New York Law School's first-rate campus has evolved to meet the changing needs of its students. In spring 2009, the School opened a new, state-of-the-art academic building that has nearly doubled the size of the campus. The glass-enclosed, 235,000-square-foot building extends five stories above ground and four below. With this sleek new facility, combined with the School's existing three structures, the campus reflects the Law School's past and future, symbolizing the growth and renewal of Tribeca and all of lower Manhattan. The new building is almost exclusively student-centered, with classrooms, lounges, study rooms, dining facilities, and the library all housed within the building's central core. Students attend classes in rooms designed to maximize teaching and learning opportunities, with cutting-edge technology, top-notch lighting and acoustics, and tiered seating that promotes the open exchange of ideas.

The Law School

New York Law School, one of the oldest independent law schools in the United States, was founded in 1891 by the faculty, students, and alumni of Columbia College Law School, led by their founding dean, Theodore Dwight, a major figure in the history of legal education. In 1894, the Law School established one of the nation's first evening divisions to provide a flexible alternative to full-time legal studies to those in the workforce or with family obligations.

From its inception, New York Law School's lower Manhattan location, in the midst of the country's largest concentration of government agencies, courts, law firms, banks, corporate headquarters, and securities exchanges, has made immersion in the legal life of a great city an essential part of the School's identity and curriculum.

The Law School offers a course of study leading to the J.D. degree through full-time day and part-time evening divisions. It offers a J.D./M.B.A., with Baruch College, City University of New York; and joint bachelor's/J.D. programs with Stevens Institute of Technology, Adelphi University, New England College, and Southern Vermont College. In fall 2012 the Law School began offering a J.D./M.A. dual-degree forensic psychology program with a focus on mental disability law, in partnership with John Jay College of Criminal Justice. In fall 2003 the Law School began offering the Master of Laws (LL.M.) in taxation. In 2009, the School also began offering a Master of Arts degree in mental disability law studies, a certificate in advanced mental disability law studies, an LL.M. in real estate, and an LL.M. in financial services Law. In 2012, the Law School started offering the LL.M. in American business law.

Applying

Priority consideration is given to applications received and completed by the following dates: December 1 for spring admission; April 30 for summer admission; and June 28 for fall admission. Applications received or completed after these priority deadlines are considered only if space is available.

All candidates for the M.A. in mental disability law studies must have earned, at a minimum, an undergraduate degree from a qualifying institution prior to enrollment in the online mental disability law program. Applicants generally must have the equivalent of a B average in their undergraduate careers or in subsequent graduate work; however, applicants whose GPA is less than a 3.0 are considered on a case-by-case basis if their resumes or curricula vitae indicate a significant amount of professional experience in the field. Candidates who have completed any part of their education outside the United States may satisfy this degree requirement on the basis of an equivalent degree earned in an international jurisdiction. Applications for certification and evaluation requirements are posted on the New York Law School Web site at http://www.nyls.edu/mdl.

Applicants for whom English is a second language and who have not studied law at an institution where English is the primary language of instruction are required to take the Test of English as a Foreign Language (TOEFL). Results of the TOEFL must be forwarded to the Admissions Office for review. The minimum score requirement is 600 on the paper-based exam (with a minimum score of 60 in each of the three sections) and 250 on the computer-based scale (with a minimum score of 25 in each of the subsections.) Applicants taking the Internet-based TOEFL (iBT) must achieve a minimum score of 100, a minimum score of 26 on the reading and listening sections, and a minimum score of 22 on the writing subsection.

Applicants must submit the following: a completed and signed M.A. in mental disability law studies or certificate in advanced mental disability law studies application form; all previous post-secondary education degree transcripts; personal statement; resume or curriculum vitae; and two letters of recommendation. No graduate test examination is required for admissions.

Correspondence and Information

The Online Mental Disability Law Program
Master of Arts Degree and Certificate

New York Law School
185 West Broadway
New York, New York 10013-2921
Phone: 212-431-2125
Fax: 212-343-2039
E-mail: mdl@nyls.edu
Web site: http://www.nyls.edu/mdl

Office of Admissions and Financial Aid
New York Law School
185 West Broadway
New York, New York 10013-2921
United States
Phone: 212-431-2888
Fax: 212-966-1522
E-mail: admissions@nyls.edu
Web site: http://www.nyls.edu/mdl

THE FACULTY AND THEIR RESEARCH

Michael L. Perlin is Professor of Law, Director of the Online Mental Disability Law program, and Director of the International Mental Disability Law Reform Project of the Law School's Justice Action Center. Professor Perlin holds teaching appointments as adjunct professor of psychiatry and law at the University of Rochester Medical Center and at NYU School of Medicine. He is a former director of the Division of Mental Health Advocacy in the New Jersey Department of the Public Advocate and former deputy public defender in charge of the Mercer County Office of the Public Defender. He now serves on the board of advisors of Disability Rights International (DRI) and on the advisory board of the Centre for the Advancement of Law and Mental Health; for many years, he sat on the board of directors of the International Academy of Law and Mental Health. In conjunction with DRI, a Washington, D.C.–based human rights advocacy organization, he has presented mental disability law training workshops in Hungary, Estonia, Latvia, Bulgaria, and Uruguay. He has been a visiting fellow at the European University Institute–Law in Florence, Italy; a visiting professor at Abo Akademi University/Turku University Law School in Turku, Finland; a visiting scholar at Hebrew University in Jerusalem, Israel; and has taught at Stockholm University Law School and National Taipei University. As a Fulbright Senior Specialist, he has taught in the Global Legal Studies program in Haifa, Israel. In October 2012 he will be teaching (via the Fulbright Program) at the Islamic University in Yogyakarta, Indonesia, where he will be helping to create a disability rights law clinic. He has consulted extensively with the China Office of the American Bar Association's Rule of Law Initiative–Asia and has been the recipient of the Eve Sellye Family Trust Fellowship at the University of Auckland where he has also been designated a Distinguished Visiting Scholar. Previously, Professor Perlin was an adjunct professor of law and psychology at the California School of Professional Psychology in Fresno, California; the Pfizer Distinguished Visiting Professor at Wright State University School of Medicine; and the Ida Beem Distinguished Visiting Scholar at the University of Iowa Law School and Medical College. Professor Perlin is the creator of the first Internet-based mental disability law courses to be offered by an American law school; the online program now includes thirteen courses, a master's degree program, and an advanced certificate program. International sections of survey of mental disability law, New York Law School's initial online course, have been offered in Japan and Nicaragua; sections of the international human rights and mental disability law course have been offered in Finland and in Israel. He is now involved in efforts to create a Disability Rights Tribunal for Asia and the Pacific; under his leadership, the Disability Rights Information Center for Asia and the Pacific will be housed at New York Law School. Professor Perlin's three-volume treatise, *Mental Disability Law, Civil and Criminal,* won the 1990 Walter Jeffords Writing Prize and was expanded into a five-volume second edition that was the recipient of the 2003 Otto Walter Writing Prize; he is currently at work on a seven-volume third edition. His most recent book is *International Human Rights and Mental Disability Law: When the Silenced are Heard* (Oxford University Press); later in 2012, his next book, *Mental Disability and the Death Penalty: The Shame of the Criminal Justice System*, is slated to be published (Rowman Littlefield). His book *The Jurisprudence of the Insanity Defense* won the Manfred Guttmacher Award of the American Psychiatric Association and the American Academy of Psychiatry and Law as the best book of the year in law and forensic psychiatry in 1994–95. Another book, *The Hidden Prejudice: Mental Disability on Trial*, was published in 2000 as part of the American Psychological Association Press's Law, Society, and Psychology series, and also received the Otto Walter Writing Prize. He has published multiple casebooks, including *Mental Disability Law: Cases and Materials* (second edition, 2005), *International Human Rights and Comparative Mental Disability Law* (2006), *Lawyering Skills in the Representation of Persons with Mental Disabilities* (2006), and *Mental Health Issues in Jails and Prisons* (2008). He has written more than 250 articles on all aspects of mental disability law. In 1988, Professor Perlin was given the American Academy of Psychiatry and Law's Amicus Award. He graduated *magna cum laude* from Rutgers University and from Columbia University Law School, where he was a Harlan Fiske Stone Scholar.

Adjunct Faculty

Emily Campbell, Adjunct Professor; J.D., Nebraska–Lincoln, 1991; Ph.D., Nebraska–Lincoln, 1996. Principle: The Campbell Firm PLLC.

Pamela S. Cohen, Adjunct Professor; J.D., Columbia, 1987. Staff attorney, Disability Rights California.

Heather Ellis Cucolo, Adjunct Professor; J.D., New York Law, 2003. Acting Director, Online Mental Disability Law program (2012).

Bruce David, Adjunct Professor; D.O., Southeastern College of Osteopathic Medicine, 1988; J.D., New York Law, 1992. Director of Forensic Psychiatry, Nassau University Medical Center. Course: Forensic Reports, Experts and Forensic Ethics.

Henry A. Dlugacz, Adjunct Professor; M.S.W., CUNY, Hunter, 1981; J.D., New York Law, 1991. Attorney and expert consultant, private practice.

Deborah Dorfman, Adjunct Professor; M.A., NYU, 1989; J.D., New York Law, 1992. Senior Attorney, Center for Public Representation.

Richard Friedman, Adjunct Professor; M.S.W., Michigan; J.D., Rutgers. Managing Attorney/Deputy Public Defender, New Jersey Office of the Public Defender, Division of Mental Health Advocacy.

Michelle Galietta, Adjunct Professor, Ph.D., Fordham, 1994. Director of Ph.D. program in forensic psychology, Director of Clinical Training, and Associate Professor at John Jay College.

James Gilson, Adjunct Professor, J.D., New York Law, 1989. In-house expert for sexual assault cases throughout New Jersey, New Jersey Office of the Public Defender. Attorney, New Jersey Office of the Public Defender.

Sarah Kerr, Adjunct Professor; J.D., Pittsburgh, 1987. Attorney, Prisoner's Rights Project, Legal Aid Society.

Kathryn A. LaFortune, Adjunct Professor; J.D., Tulsa, 1983; Ph.D., Tulsa, 1997. Chief of Forensic Services and Psychological Services, Oklahoma Indigent Defense System. Adjunct Professor, University of Tulsa College of Law, University of Tulsa Department of Psychology, and the Oklahoma State University College of Osteopathic Medicine-College of Health Sciences.

Shelley Mitchell, Adjunct Professor; J.D., Florida, 1984. Sole practitioner.

Patrick Reilly, Adjunct Professor; Ph.D., NYU, 1976; J.D., Seton Hall, 1986. Director, Division of Mental Health Advocacy, New Jersey Office of the Public Defender.

Beth Ribet, Adjunct Professor; Ph.D., California, Irvine, 2005; J.D., UCLA, 2009.

Andrea Risoli, Adjunct Professor; J.D., New York Law, 2000. Sole practitioner.

Lisa Schatz-Vance, Adjunct Professor; J.D., New York Law, 1997. Executive Director, Senior Citizens Law Office, New Mexico.

David Shapiro, Adjunct Professor; Ph.D., Michigan, 1972. Associate Professor of Psychology, Center for Psychological Studies, Nova Southeastern University.

Eva Szeli, Adjunct Professor; Ph.D., 1994, J.D., 1999, Miami. Senior Lecturer, Arizona State University.

Karen Talley, Adjunct Professor; J.D. 1995, New York Law, 1995. Supervising Attorney, Private Counsel Unit, Committee for Public Counsel Services, Mental Health Litigation Division.

New York Law School's state-of-the-art academic building, which extends five stories above ground and four below.

ACADEMIC AND PROFESSIONAL PROGRAMS IN LIBRARY AND INFORMATION STUDIES

Section 28
Library and Information Studies

This section contains a directory of institutions offering graduate work in library and information studies, followed by in-depth entries submitted by institutions that chose to prepare detailed program descriptions. Additional information about programs listed in the directory but not augmented by an in-depth entry may be obtained by writing directly to the dean of a graduate school or chair of a department at the address given in the directory.

For programs offering related work, see also in this book *Education*. In another guide in this series:

Graduate Programs in Engineering & Applied Sciences
See *Computer Science and Information Technology*

CONTENTS

Program Directories

Displays and Close-Ups

Archives/Archival Administration

Claremont Graduate University, Graduate Programs, School of Arts and Humanities, Department of History, Claremont, CA 91711-6160. Offers Africana history (Certificate); American studies and U. S. history (MA, PhD); archival studies (MA); early modern studies (MA, PhD); European studies (MA, PhD); oral history (MA, PhD); MBA/MA; MBA/PhD. *Faculty:* 4 full-time (2 women), 1 part-time/adjunct (0 women). *Students:* 66 full-time (30 women), 9 part-time (3 women); includes 22 minority (3 Black or African American, non-Hispanic/Latino; 1 American Indian or Alaska Native, non-Hispanic/Latino; 4 Asian, non-Hispanic/Latino; 8 Hispanic/Latino; 1 Native Hawaiian or other Pacific Islander, non-Hispanic/Latino; 5 Two or more races, non-Hispanic/Latino), 2 international. Average age 36. In 2011, 4 master's, 3 doctorates awarded. Terminal master's awarded for partial completion of doctoral program. *Entrance requirements:* For master's and doctorate, GRE General Test. Additional exam requirements/recommendations for international students: Required—TOEFL (minimum score 550 paper-based; 213 computer-based; 80 iBT). *Application deadline:* For fall admission, 2/1 priority date for domestic students. Applications are processed on a rolling basis. Application fee: $60. Electronic applications accepted. *Expenses: Tuition:* Full-time $36,374; part-time $1581 per unit. *Required fees:* $165 per semester. *Financial support:* Fellowships, research assistantships, Federal Work-Study, institutionally sponsored loans, and scholarships/grants available. Support available to part-time students. Financial award application deadline: 2/15; financial award applicants required to submit FAFSA. *Faculty research:* Intellectual and social history, cultural studies, gender studies, Western history, Chicano history. *Unit head:* Robert Dawidoff, Chair, 909-607-3332, Fax: 909-621-8609, E-mail: robert.dawidoff@cgu.edu. *Application contact:* Susan Hampson, Admissions Coordinator, 909-607-1278, E-mail: humanities@cgu.edu. Web site: http://www.cgu.edu/pages/369.asp.

Clayton State University, School of Graduate Studies, Program in Archival Studies, Morrow, GA 30260-0285. Offers MAS. Postbaccalaureate distance learning degree programs offered (no on-campus study). *Faculty:* 2 full-time (0 women), 5 part-time/adjunct (4 women). *Students:* 7 full-time (4 women), 11 part-time (6 women); includes 7 minority (all Black or African American, non-Hispanic/Latino). Average age 39. 17 applicants, 94% accepted, 14 enrolled. *Entrance requirements:* For master's, GRE, 2 official transcripts; 3 letters of recommendation; statement of purpose. Additional exam requirements/recommendations for international students: Required—TOEFL (minimum score 550 paper-based; 213 computer-based). *Application deadline:* For fall admission, 6/15 priority date for domestic students, 5/1 for international students. Applications are processed on a rolling basis. Application fee: $75. Electronic applications accepted. *Expenses:* Tuition, state resident: full-time $3528; part-time $196 per credit hour. Tuition, nonresident: full-time $13,176; part-time $732 per credit hour. *Required fees:* $1404; $552 per semester. Tuition and fees vary according to course load and campus/location. *Unit head:* Richard Pearce-Moses, Program Director, Master of Archival Studies, 678-466-4400, Fax: 678-466-4459, E-mail: archivalstudies@mail.clayton.edu. *Application contact:* Elizabeth Taylor, Assistant to the Dean of Graduate Studies, 678-466-4113, Fax: 678-466-4119, E-mail: elizabethtaylor@clayton.edu. Web site: http://cims.clayton.edu/mas/.

Columbia University, School of Continuing Education, Program in Information and Archive Management, New York, NY 10027. Offers MS. Part-time programs available. *Entrance requirements:* For master's, minimum undergraduate GPA of 3.0. Additional exam requirements/recommendations for international students: Required—American Language Program placement test. Electronic applications accepted. *Faculty research:* Library science technology, information systems.

Drexel University, The iSchool at Drexel, College of Information Science and Technology, Master of Science in Library and Information Science Program, Philadelphia, PA 19104-2875. Offers archival studies (MS); competitive intelligence and knowledge management (MS); digital libraries (MS); library and information services (MS); school library media (MS); youth services (MS). Part-time and evening/weekend programs available. Postbaccalaureate distance learning degree programs offered (no on-campus study). *Faculty:* 30 full-time (20 women), 29 part-time/adjunct (15 women). *Students:* 198 full-time (155 women), 437 part-time (353 women); includes 79 minority (30 Black or African American, non-Hispanic/Latino; 6 American Indian or Alaska Native, non-Hispanic/Latino; 20 Asian, non-Hispanic/Latino; 23 Hispanic/Latino), 15 international. Average age 33. 464 applicants, 72% accepted, 202 enrolled. In 2011, 261 master's awarded. *Entrance requirements:* For master's, GRE General Test. Additional exam requirements/recommendations for international students: Required—TOEFL (minimum score 600 paper-based; 250 computer-based; 100 iBT). *Application deadline:* For fall admission, 8/1 for domestic and international students; for spring admission, 2/1 for domestic and international students. Applications are processed on a rolling basis. Electronic applications accepted. *Expenses:* Contact institution. *Financial support:* In 2011–12, 217 students received support, including 252 fellowships with partial tuition reimbursements available (averaging $22,500 per year); institutionally sponsored loans and scholarships/grants also available. Support available to part-time students. Financial award application deadline: 3/1; financial award applicants required to submit FAFSA. *Faculty research:* Library and information resources and services, knowledge organization and representation, information retrieval/information visualization/bibliometrics, information needs and behaviors, digital libraries. *Total annual research expenditures:* $2 million. *Unit head:* Dr. David E. Fenske, Dean/Professor of Information Science, 215-895-2475, Fax: 215-895-6378, E-mail: fenske@drexel.edu. *Application contact:* Matthew Lechtenberg, Graduate Admissions Manager, 215-895-1951, Fax: 215-895-2303, E-mail: ml333@drexel.edu.

East Tennessee State University, School of Graduate Studies, School of Continuing Studies and Academic Outreach, Johnson City, TN 37614. Offers archival studies (MALS, Postbaccalaureate Certificate); gender and diversity (MALS); strategic leadership (MPS); training and development (MPS). Part-time programs available. Postbaccalaureate distance learning degree programs offered (no on-campus study). *Faculty:* 7 full-time (3 women), 1 (woman) part-time/adjunct. *Students:* 28 full-time (21 women), 50 part-time (40 women); includes 13 minority (6 Black or African American, non-Hispanic/Latino; 1 American Indian or Alaska Native, non-Hispanic/Latino; 2 Hispanic/Latino; 4 Two or more races, non-Hispanic/Latino). Average age 41. 49 applicants, 55% accepted, 24 enrolled. In 2011, 14 master's, 2 other advanced degrees awarded. *Degree requirements:* For master's, comprehensive exam, thesis optional, professional project. *Entrance requirements:* For master's, GRE General Test, minimum GPA of 2.75, professional portfolio, three letters of recommendation, interview, writing sample; for Postbaccalaureate Certificate, minimum GPA of 2.5, three letters of recommendation, interview. Additional exam requirements/recommendations for international students: Required—TOEFL (minimum score 550 paper-based; 213 computer-based; 79 iBT). *Application deadline:* For fall admission, 6/1 for domestic students, 4/30 for international students; for spring admission, 11/1 for domestic students, 9/30 for international students. Application fee: $35 ($45 for international students). Electronic applications accepted. *Expenses:* Tuition, state resident: full-time $7312; part-time $350 per credit hour. Tuition, nonresident: full-time $18,490; part-time $621 per credit hour. *Required fees:* $63 per credit hour. Tuition and fees vary according to course load and program. *Financial support:* In 2011–12, 20 students received support, including 6 research assistantships with full tuition reimbursements available (averaging $6,000 per year); institutionally sponsored loans, scholarships/grants, and unspecified assistantships also available. Financial award application deadline: 7/1; financial award applicants required to submit FAFSA. *Faculty research:* Appalachian studies, women's and gender studies, interdisciplinary theory, regional and Southern cultures. *Unit head:* Dr. Rick E. Osborn, Dean, 423-439-4223, Fax: 423-439-7091, E-mail: osbornr@etsu.edu. *Application contact:* Mary Duncan, Graduate Specialist, 423-439-4302, Fax: 423-439-5624, E-mail: duncanm@etsu.edu.

Emporia State University, Graduate School, School of Library and Information Management, Emporia, KS 66801-5087. Offers archives studies (Certificate); legal information management (Certificate); library and information management (MLS, PhD, Certificate). *Accreditation:* ALA (one or more programs are accredited). Part-time and evening/weekend programs available. Postbaccalaureate distance learning degree programs offered (minimal on-campus study). *Faculty:* 8 full-time (4 women). *Students:* 22 full-time (19 women), 326 part-time (258 women); includes 31 minority (4 Black or African American, non-Hispanic/Latino; 1 American Indian or Alaska Native, non-Hispanic/Latino; 9 Asian, non-Hispanic/Latino; 10 Hispanic/Latino; 4 Native Hawaiian or other Pacific Islander, non-Hispanic/Latino; 3 Two or more races, non-Hispanic/Latino), 3 international. 125 applicants, 77% accepted, 78 enrolled. In 2011, 133 master's, 1 doctorate, 7 other advanced degrees awarded. *Degree requirements:* For master's, comprehensive exam, thesis optional; for doctorate, thesis/dissertation. *Entrance requirements:* For master's, GRE General Test, interview, minimum undergraduate GPA of 3.0, letters of recommendation; for doctorate, GRE General Test, interview, minimum graduate GPA of 3.5. Additional exam requirements/recommendations for international students: Required—TOEFL (minimum score 520 paper-based; 133 computer-based; 68 iBT). *Application deadline:* For fall admission, 8/15 priority date for domestic students. Applications are processed on a rolling basis. Application fee: $30 ($75 for international students). Electronic applications accepted. *Expenses:* Tuition, state resident: full-time $2342; part-time $195 per credit hour. Tuition, nonresident: full-time $7254; part-time $605 per credit hour. *Required fees:* $66 per credit hour. Tuition and fees vary according to campus/location. *Financial support:* In 2011–12, 9 research assistantships with full tuition reimbursements (averaging $7,059 per year), 2 teaching assistantships with full tuition reimbursements (averaging $7,059 per year) were awarded; Federal Work-Study, institutionally sponsored loans, and unspecified assistantships also available. Financial award application deadline: 3/15; financial award applicants required to submit FAFSA. *Unit head:* Dr. Gwen Alexander, Interim Dean, 620-341-5203, Fax: 620-341-5233, E-mail: galexan1@emporia.edu. *Application contact:* Candace Boardman, Director, Kansas MLS Program, 620-341-6159, E-mail: cboardma@emporia.edu. Web site: http://www.emporia.edu/las/index.html.

Long Island University–C. W. Post Campus, College of Information and Computer Science, Palmer School of Library and Information Science, Brookville, NY 11548-1300. Offers archives and records management (Certificate); information studies (PhD); library and information science (MS); library media specialist (MS); public library management (Certificate). *Accreditation:* ALA (one or more programs are accredited). Part-time and evening/weekend programs available. Postbaccalaureate distance learning degree programs offered (minimal on-campus study). *Degree requirements:* For master's, thesis optional, internship; for doctorate, thesis/dissertation, qualifying exam. *Entrance requirements:* For master's, GRE or MAT, minimum undergraduate GPA of 3.0, resume. Electronic applications accepted. *Faculty research:* Information retrieval, digital libraries, scientometric and infometric studies, preservation/archiving and electronic records.

Montclair State University, The Graduate School, School of the Arts, Department of Art and Design, Program in Fine Art, Montclair, NJ 07043-1624. Offers museum management (MA); studio (MA). Part-time and evening/weekend programs available. *Students:* 10 full-time (7 women), 23 part-time (16 women); includes 6 minority (1 Black or African American, non-Hispanic/Latino; 1 Asian, non-Hispanic/Latino; 2 Hispanic/Latino; 2 Two or more races, non-Hispanic/Latino). Average age 34. 18 applicants, 39% accepted, 6 enrolled. In 2011, 13 master's awarded. *Degree requirements:* For master's, project. *Entrance requirements:* For master's, GRE or MAT, 2 letters of recommendation, essay. *Application deadline:* Applications are processed on a rolling basis. Application fee: $60. Electronic applications accepted. *Financial support:* Federal Work-Study, scholarships/grants, and unspecified assistantships available. Support available to part-time students. Financial award application deadline: 3/1; financial award applicants required to submit FAFSA. *Unit head:* Dr. Scott Gordley, Chairperson, 973-655-7295. *Application contact:* Amy Aiello, Director of Graduate Admissions and Operations, 973-655-5147, E-mail: graduate.school@montclair.edu. Web site: http://www.montclair.edu/Arts/.

New York University, Graduate School of Arts and Science, Department of History, New York, NY 10012-1019. Offers African diaspora (PhD); African history (PhD); archival management and historical editing (Advanced Certificate); Atlantic history (PhD); French studies/history (PhD); Hebrew and Judaic studies/history (PhD); history (MA, PhD), including Europe (PhD), Latin America and the Caribbean (PhD), United States (PhD), women's history (MA); Middle Eastern history (MA); Middle Eastern studies/history (PhD); public history (Advanced Certificate); world history (MA); JD/MA; MA/Advanced Certificate. Part-time programs available. *Faculty:* 43 full-time (19 women). *Students:* 119 full-time (74 women), 33 part-time (23 women); includes 31 minority (16 Black or African American, non-Hispanic/Latino; 3 Asian, non-Hispanic/Latino; 11 Hispanic/Latino; 1 Two or more races, non-Hispanic/Latino), 34 international. Average age 31. 488 applicants, 19% accepted, 30 enrolled. In 2011, 27 master's, 14 doctorates, 1 other advanced degree awarded. Terminal master's awarded for partial completion of doctoral program. *Degree requirements:* For master's, seminar paper; for doctorate, one foreign language, thesis/dissertation, oral and written exams; for Advanced Certificate, internship. *Entrance requirements:* For master's, GRE General Test, minimum GPA of 3.0, writing sample; for doctorate, GRE. Additional exam requirements/recommendations for international students: Required—TOEFL. *Application deadline:* For fall admission, 12/18 for domestic and international students. Application fee: $90. *Financial support:* Fellowships with tuition reimbursements, research assistantships, teaching assistantships with tuition reimbursements, career-related internships or fieldwork, Federal Work-Study, institutionally sponsored loans, scholarships/grants, health care benefits, and unspecified assistantships available. Financial award application deadline: 12/18; financial award applicants required to submit FAFSA. *Faculty research:* African, East Asian, medieval, early modern, and modern European history; U. S. history; African and African diaspora; Latin American history; Atlantic world. *Unit head:* Joanna Waley-Cohen, Chair, 212-998-8600, Fax: 212-995-4017, E-mail: graduate.history@nyu.edu. *Application contact:* Fiona Griffiths,

Director of Graduate Studies, 212-998-8600, Fax: 212-995-4017, E-mail: graduate.history@nyu.edu. Web site: http://www.nyu.edu/gsas/dept/history/.

New York University, Tisch School of the Arts and Graduate School of Arts and Science, Department of Cinema Studies, Program in Moving Image Archiving and Preservation, New York, NY 10012-1019. Offers MA. *Faculty:* 2 full-time, 4 part-time/adjunct. *Students:* 16 full-time (6 women), 1 (woman) part-time; includes 1 minority (Hispanic/Latino). Average age 28. 15 applicants, 87% accepted, 7 enrolled. In 2011, 6 master's awarded. *Degree requirements:* For master's, internship. *Entrance requirements:* For master's, GRE. Additional exam requirements/recommendations for international students: Required—TOEFL or IELTS. *Application deadline:* For fall admission, 12/1 for domestic and international students. Application fee: $60. Electronic applications accepted. *Financial support:* In 2011–12, 11 students received support, including 5 fellowships with full and partial tuition reimbursements available; tuition waivers (partial) also available. Financial award application deadline: 2/15. *Unit head:* Howard Besser, Head, 212-998-1618. *Application contact:* Dan Sandford, Director of Graduate Admissions, 212-998-1918, Fax: 212-995-4060, E-mail: tisch.gradadmissions@nyu.edu. Web site: http://www.cinema.tisch.nyu.edu/.

Pratt Institute, School of Information and Library Science, New York, NY 10011. Offers archives (Adv C); library and information science (MS, Adv C); library and information science media specialist (MS); library media specialist (Adv C); museum libraries (Adv C); JD/MS. *Accreditation:* ALA. Part-time programs available. *Faculty:* 9 full-time (6 women), 27 part-time/adjunct (15 women). *Students:* 131 full-time (106 women), 184 part-time (151 women); includes 72 minority (21 Black or African American, non-Hispanic/Latino; 19 Asian, non-Hispanic/Latino; 26 Hispanic/Latino; 6 Two or more races, non-Hispanic/Latino), 3 international. Average age 32. 207 applicants, 93% accepted, 81 enrolled. In 2011, 111 master's, 1 other advanced degree awarded. *Degree requirements:* For master's, thesis. *Entrance requirements:* Additional exam requirements/recommendations for international students: Required—TOEFL (minimum score 600 paper-based; 250 computer-based; 100 iBT). *Application deadline:* For fall admission, 1/5 for domestic and international students; for spring admission, 10/1 for domestic and international students. Application fee: $50 ($90 for international students). Electronic applications accepted. *Expenses:* Contact institution. *Financial support:* Career-related internships or fieldwork, Federal Work-Study, institutionally sponsored loans, scholarships/grants, health care benefits, and unspecified assistantships available. Support available to part-time students. Financial award application deadline: 2/1; financial award applicants required to submit FAFSA. *Faculty research:* Development of urban libraries and information centers, medical and law librarianship, information management. *Unit head:* Dr. Tula Giannini, Dean, 212-647-7682, E-mail: giannini@pratt.edu. *Application contact:* Young Hah, Director of Graduate Admissions, 718-636-3683, Fax: 718-399-4242, E-mail: yhah@pratt.edu. Web site: http://www.pratt.edu/academics/information_and_library_sciences.

See Display on page 1636 and Close-Up on page 1651.

Simmons College, Graduate School of Library and Information Science, Boston, MA 02115. Offers archives management (MS, Certificate); instructional technology licensure (Certificate); library and information science (MS, PhD); managerial leadership in the informational professions (PhD); school library teacher (MS, Certificate); MS/MA. *Accreditation:* ALA (one or more programs are accredited). *Unit head:* Dr. Michele V. Cloonan, Dean, 617-521-2806, Fax: 617-521-3192, E-mail: michele.cloonan@simmons.edu. *Application contact:* Sarah Petrakos, Assistant Dean, Admission and Recruitment, 617-521-2868, Fax: 617-521-3192, E-mail: gslisadm@simmons.edu. Web site: http://www.simmons.edu/gslis/.

The University of British Columbia, Faculty of Arts, School of Library, Archival and Information Studies, Master of Archival Studies Program, Vancouver, BC V6T 1Z1, Canada. Offers MAS. *Degree requirements:* For master's, thesis optional. *Entrance requirements:* For master's, minimum B+ average or minimum GPA of 3.3 in undergraduate upper-division courses. Additional exam requirements/recommendations for international students: Required—TOEFL (minimum score 600 paper-based; 250 computer-based; 100 iBT). Electronic applications accepted. *Faculty research:* Diplomatics, electronic record, appraisal, descriptive standards, preservation.

The University of British Columbia, Faculty of Arts, School of Library, Archival and Information Studies, PhD Program in Library, Archival and Information Studies, Vancouver, BC V6T 1Z1, Canada. Offers PhD. *Degree requirements:* For doctorate, thesis/dissertation. *Entrance requirements:* For doctorate, GRE, minimum GPA of 3.3 in MAS or MLIS (other master's degrees may be considered). Additional exam requirements/recommendations for international students: Required—TOEFL (minimum score 600 paper-based; 250 computer-based; 100 iBT). Electronic applications accepted. *Faculty research:* Computer systems/database design; library and archival management; archival description and organization; children's literature and youth services; interactive information retrieval.

University of California, Los Angeles, Graduate Division, Graduate School of Education and Information Studies, Department of Information Studies, Los Angeles, CA 90095-1521. Offers archival studies (MLIS); informatics (MLIS); information studies (PhD); library and information science (Certificate); library studies (MLIS); moving image archive studies (MA); MBA/MLIS; MLIS/MA. *Accreditation:* ALA (one or more programs are accredited). *Faculty:* 13 full-time (7 women), 10 part-time/adjunct (8 women). *Students:* 141 full-time (118 women), 22 part-time (16 women); includes 62 minority (10 Black or African American, non-Hispanic/Latino; 2 American Indian or Alaska Native, non-Hispanic/Latino; 38 Asian, non-Hispanic/Latino; 12 Hispanic/Latino), 3 international. Average age 27. 171 applicants, 77% accepted, 82 enrolled. In 2011, 69 master's, 8 doctorates awarded. Terminal master's awarded for partial completion of doctoral program. *Degree requirements:* For master's, thesis or alternative, professional portfolio; for doctorate, thesis/dissertation, oral and written qualifying exams. *Entrance requirements:* For master's, GRE General Test, previous course work in statistics; for doctorate, GRE General Test, previous course work in statistics, 2 samples of research writing in English. Additional exam requirements/recommendations for international students: Required—TOEFL (minimum score 613 paper-based; 220 computer-based; 87 iBT), IELTS (minimum score 7). *Application deadline:* For fall admission, 11/30 for domestic students, 10/30 for international students. Applications are processed on a rolling basis. Application fee: $80 ($90 for international students). Electronic applications accepted. *Financial support:* In 2011–12, 44 students received support, including 29 fellowships with full and partial tuition reimbursements available (averaging $10,505 per year), 7 research assistantships with partial tuition reimbursements available (averaging $29,061 per year), 12 teaching assistantships with partial tuition reimbursements available (averaging $18,984 per year); career-related internships or fieldwork, Federal Work-Study, institutionally sponsored loans, scholarships/grants, and unspecified assistantships also available. Financial award application deadline: 3/1; financial award applicants required to submit FAFSA. *Faculty research:* Multimedia, digital libraries, archives and electronic records, interface design, information technology and preservation, preservation, access. *Unit head:* Dr. Gregory H. Leazer, Associate Professor and Chair, 310-825-8799, E-mail: gleazer@ucla.edu. *Application contact:* Susan S. Abler, Student Affairs Officer, 310-825-5269, Fax: 310-206-4460, E-mail: abler@gseis.ucla.edu. Web site: http://is.gseis.ucla.edu/.

University of California, Los Angeles, Graduate Division, School of Theater, Film and Television, Interdepartmental Program in Moving Image Archive Studies, Los Angeles, CA 90095. Offers MA. *Students:* 18 full-time (11 women); includes 5 minority (1 Asian, non-Hispanic/Latino; 3 Hispanic/Latino; 1 Two or more races, non-Hispanic/Latino). Average age 28. 43 applicants, 40% accepted, 8 enrolled. In 2011, 8 master's awarded. Application fee: $70 ($90 for international students). Electronic applications accepted. *Financial support:* In 2011–12, 14 fellowships, 1 teaching assistantship were awarded; research assistantships, Federal Work-Study, scholarships/grants, and unspecified assistantships also available. *Unit head:* Nick Browne, Chair, 310-825-4089, E-mail: browne@ucla.edu. *Application contact:* Departmental Office, 310-206-4966, E-mail: lwatsky@tft.ucla.edu. Web site: http://www.mias.ucla.edu/.

University of California, Riverside, Graduate Division, Department of History, Riverside, CA 92521-0102. Offers archival management (MA); historic preservation (MA); history (MA, PhD); museum curatorship (MA). Part-time programs available. *Faculty:* 28 full-time (12 women). *Students:* 79 full-time (34 women), 2 part-time (both women); includes 18 minority (2 Black or African American, non-Hispanic/Latino; 2 American Indian or Alaska Native, non-Hispanic/Latino; 7 Asian, non-Hispanic/Latino; 6 Hispanic/Latino; 1 Native Hawaiian or other Pacific Islander, non-Hispanic/Latino), 1 international. Average age 31. 69 applicants, 29% accepted, 9 enrolled. In 2011, 22 master's, 3 doctorates awarded. Terminal master's awarded for partial completion of doctoral program. *Degree requirements:* For master's, one foreign language, comprehensive exam, internship report and oral exams, or thesis; for doctorate, 2 foreign languages, thesis/dissertation, qualifying exams. *Entrance requirements:* For master's and doctorate, GRE General Test, minimum GPA of 3.2. Additional exam requirements/recommendations for international students: Required—TOEFL (minimum score 550 paper-based; 213 computer-based; 80 iBT). *Application deadline:* For fall admission, 12/15 priority date for domestic students, 12/15 for international students. Applications are processed on a rolling basis. Application fee: $80 ($100 for international students). Electronic applications accepted. *Financial support:* In 2011–12, 56 students received support, including fellowships with full tuition reimbursements available (averaging $10,129 per year), research assistantships with partial tuition reimbursements available (averaging $16,169 per year), teaching assistantships with partial tuition reimbursements available (averaging $17,310 per year); career-related internships or fieldwork, Federal Work-Study, institutionally sponsored loans, scholarships/grants, traineeships, health care benefits, tuition waivers (full and partial), and unspecified assistantships also available. Financial award application deadline: 12/15; financial award applicants required to submit FAFSA. *Faculty research:* Native American history, United States, public history, Europe, Latin America. *Unit head:* Dr. Thomas Cogswell, Chair, 951-827-1437, Fax: 951-827-5299, E-mail: history@ucr.edu. *Application contact:* Graduate Admissions, 951-827-3313, Fax: 951-827-2238, E-mail: grdadmis@ucr.edu. Web site: http://history.ucr.edu/.

University of Manitoba, Faculty of Graduate Studies, Faculty of Arts, Department of History, Winnipeg, MB R3T 2N2, Canada. Offers archival studies (MA); history (MA, PhD). MA offered jointly with The University of Winnipeg. *Degree requirements:* For master's, thesis; for doctorate, one foreign language, thesis/dissertation.

University of Massachusetts Boston, Office of Graduate Studies, College of Liberal Arts, Program in History, Boston, MA 02125-3393. Offers archival methods (MA); historical archaeology (MA); history (MA). Part-time and evening/weekend programs available. *Degree requirements:* For master's, thesis, oral exam. *Entrance requirements:* For master's, minimum GPA of 2.75. *Faculty research:* European intellectual history, American labor and social history in 19th century, colonial American Revolution, Afro-American Cold War.

University of Michigan, Horace H. Rackham School of Graduate Studies, School of Information, Ann Arbor, MI 48109-1285. Offers archives and records management (MSI); community informatics (MSI); health informatics (MS); human computer interaction (MSI); information (PhD); information analysis and retrieval (MSI); information economics for management (MSI); information policy (MSI); library and information science (MSI); preservation of information (MSI); school library media (MSI); social computing (MSI). *Accreditation:* ALA (one or more programs are accredited). *Entrance requirements:* For master's and doctorate, GRE General Test. Additional exam requirements/recommendations for international students: Required—TOEFL (minimum score 600 paper-based; 100 iBT). Electronic applications accepted.

University of South Carolina, The Graduate School, College of Arts and Sciences, Department of History, Program in Public History, Columbia, SC 29208. Offers archives (MA); historic preservation (MA); museum (MA); museum management (Certificate); MLIS/MA. *Degree requirements:* For master's, one foreign language, thesis, internship. *Entrance requirements:* For master's, GRE General Test, writing sample. Additional exam requirements/recommendations for international students: Required—TOEFL. Electronic applications accepted. *Faculty research:* Museum studies, historic preservation, archives administration.

University of Wisconsin–Milwaukee, Graduate School, School of Information Studies, Milwaukee, WI 53201-0413. Offers advanced studies in library and information science (CAS); archives and records administration (CAS); digital libraries (Certificate); information studies (MLIS, PhD); MLIS/MA; MLIS/MM; MLIS/MS. *Accreditation:* ALA (one or more programs are accredited). Part-time programs available. *Faculty:* 22 full-time (11 women). *Students:* 173 full-time (136 women), 426 part-time (339 women); includes 60 minority (16 Black or African American, non-Hispanic/Latino; 1 American Indian or Alaska Native, non-Hispanic/Latino; 14 Asian, non-Hispanic/Latino; 8 Hispanic/Latino; 21 Two or more races, non-Hispanic/Latino), 30 international. Average age 34. 291 applicants, 73% accepted, 122 enrolled. In 2011, 182 master's awarded. *Entrance requirements:* For master's, GRE General Test or MAT; for doctorate, GRE. Additional exam requirements/recommendations for international students: Required—TOEFL (minimum score 550 paper-based; 213 computer-based), IELTS (minimum score 6.5). *Application deadline:* For fall admission, 1/1 priority date for domestic students; for spring admission, 9/1 for domestic students. Applications are processed on a rolling basis. Application fee: $56 ($96 for international students). Electronic applications accepted. One-time fee: $506.10 full-time. Tuition and fees vary according to course load and reciprocity agreements. *Financial support:* In 2011–12, 4 teaching assistantships were awarded; fellowships, research assistantships, career-related internships or fieldwork, Federal Work-Study, health care benefits, unspecified assistantships, and project assistantships also available. Support available to part-time students. Financial award application deadline: 4/15; financial award applicants required to submit FAFSA. *Total annual research expenditures:* $302,657. *Unit head:* Dietmar Wolfram, Interim Dean, 414-229-4709, E-mail: dwolfram@uwm.edu. *Application contact:* Hur-Li Lee, Representative, 414-229-6838, E-mail: hurli@uwm.edu. Web site: http://www.uwm.edu/Dept/SLIS/.

Wayne State University, College of Liberal Arts and Sciences, Department of History, Detroit, MI 48202. Offers archival administration (Graduate Certificate); history (MA, PhD); world history (Graduate Certificate); JD/MA; M Ed/MA; MLIS/MA. Application deadline for PhD is February 15. Evening/weekend programs available. *Students:* 18 full-time (8 women), 30 part-time (5 women); includes 3 minority (2 Black or African American, non-Hispanic/Latino; 1 Two or more races, non-Hispanic/Latino), 1 international. Average age 40. 37 applicants, 35% accepted, 6 enrolled. In 2011, 6 master's, 3 doctorates awarded. *Degree requirements:* For master's, thesis (for some programs), final oral exam on thesis or essay; for doctorate, 2 foreign languages, thesis/dissertation, qualifying exam in 4 fields of history. *Entrance requirements:* For master's, GRE General Test, minimum GPA of 3.25 in history, 3.0 overall; foreign language; letter of intent; research paper; at least two letters of recommendation from former instructors; for doctorate, GRE General Test, minimum GPA of 3.0; letter of intent; research paper; at least three letters of recommendation from former professors. Additional exam requirements/recommendations for international students: Required—TOEFL (minimum score 550 paper-based; 213 computer-based); Recommended—TWE (minimum score 5.5). *Application deadline:* For fall admission, 5/1 for domestic and international students; for winter admission, 11/1 for domestic students, 10/1 for international students; for spring admission, 3/15 for domestic students, 1/1 for international students. Applications are processed on a rolling basis. Application fee: $50. Electronic applications accepted. *Expenses:* Tuition, state resident: part-time $512.85 per credit. Tuition, nonresident: part-time $1132.65 per credit. *Required fees:* $26.60 per credit. $199.65 per semester. Tuition and fees vary according to course load and program. *Financial support:* In 2011–12, 13 students received support, including 2 fellowships with tuition reimbursements available (averaging $16,875 per year), 1 research assistantship with tuition reimbursement available (averaging $17,453 per year), 6 teaching assistantships with tuition reimbursements available (averaging $15,713 per year); institutionally sponsored loans, scholarships/grants, health care benefits, and unspecified assistantships also available. Support available to part-time students. Financial award application deadline: 3/1. *Faculty research:* Labor and social history, citizenship and governance, modern U. S. history, early modern and modern European history, African-American history. *Total annual research expenditures:* $16,861. *Unit head:* Dr. Marc Kruman, Chair, 313-577-2593, E-mail: m.kruman@wayne.edu. *Application contact:* Mel Small, Graduate Director, 313-577-6138, E-mail: m.small@wayne.edu. Web site: http://clasweb.clas.wayne.edu/history.

Wayne State University, School of Library and Information Science, Detroit, MI 48202. Offers archival administration (MLIS, Certificate); arts and museum librarianship (Certificate); general librarianship (MLIS); health sciences librarianship (MLIS); information management for librarians (Certificate); information science (MLIS); law librarianship (MLIS); library and information science (MLIS, Spec), including academic libraries (MLIS); organization of information (MLIS); public libraries (MLIS); public library services to children and young adults (MLIS, Certificate); records and information management (Certificate); records management (MLIS); references services (MLIS); school library media (Spec); school library media specialist endorsement (MLIS); special libraries (MLIS); urban librarianship (Certificate); urban libraries (MLIS); MLIS/MA. *Accreditation:* ALA (one or more programs are accredited). Part-time and evening/weekend programs available. Postbaccalaureate distance learning degree programs offered (no on-campus study). *Faculty:* 13 full-time (8 women), 25 part-time/adjunct (19 women). *Students:* 121 full-time (93 women), 447 part-time (346 women); includes 57 minority (37 Black or African American, non-Hispanic/Latino; 1 American Indian or Alaska Native, non-Hispanic/Latino; 4 Asian, non-Hispanic/Latino; 7 Hispanic/Latino; 8 Two or more races, non-Hispanic/Latino), 4 international. Average age 33. 336 applicants, 62% accepted, 135 enrolled. In 2011, 212 master's, 38 other advanced degrees awarded. *Entrance requirements:* For master's and other advanced degree, GRE or MAT (if undergraduate GPA is between 2.5 and 2.99), minimum undergraduate GPA of 3.0 or graduate degree, personal statement, new student orientation. Additional exam requirements/recommendations for international students: Required—TOEFL (minimum score 550 paper-based; 213 computer-based); Recommended—TWE (minimum score 5.5). *Application deadline:* For fall admission, 7/1 for domestic students, 5/1 for international students; for winter admission, 10/1 for domestic students, 9/1 for international students; for spring admission, 3/15 for domestic students, 1/1 for international students. Applications are processed on a rolling basis. Application fee: $50. Electronic applications accepted. *Expenses:* Tuition, state resident: part-time $512.85 per credit. Tuition, nonresident: part-time $1132.65 per credit. *Required fees:* $26.60 per credit. $199.65 per semester. Tuition and fees vary according to course load and program. *Financial support:* In 2011–12, 1 research assistantship with tuition reimbursement (averaging $12,250 per year) was awarded; fellowships with tuition reimbursements, career-related internships or fieldwork, Federal Work-Study, institutionally sponsored loans, scholarships/grants, and unspecified assistantships also available. Support available to part-time students. Financial award application deadline: 5/15. *Faculty research:* Convergence of academic libraries and other academic services, competitive intelligence and data mining, impact of digitization on libraries, international librarianship, consumer health information, urban library issues, human-computer interaction, universal access to libraries and instructional support services. *Unit head:* Dr. Sandra Yee, Dean, 313-577-4059, Fax: 313-577-7563, E-mail: aj0533@wayne.edu. *Application contact:* Dr. Stephen Fredericks, Associate Dean and Director, 313-577-7563, E-mail: bajjaly@wayne.edu. Web site: http://www.lisp.wayne.edu/.

Information Studies

The Catholic University of America, School of Library and Information Science, Washington, DC 20064. Offers MSLS, JD/MSLS, MSLS/MA, MSLS/MS. *Accreditation:* ALA (one or more programs are accredited). Part-time programs available. *Faculty:* 7 full-time (5 women), 16 part-time/adjunct (7 women). *Students:* 31 full-time (25 women), 182 part-time (128 women); includes 58 minority (33 Black or African American, non-Hispanic/Latino; 8 Asian, non-Hispanic/Latino; 12 Hispanic/Latino; 1 Native Hawaiian or other Pacific Islander, non-Hispanic/Latino; 4 Two or more races, non-Hispanic/Latino), 3 international. Average age 34. 147 applicants, 82% accepted, 58 enrolled. In 2011, 83 degrees awarded. *Degree requirements:* For master's, comprehensive exam. *Entrance requirements:* For master's, statement of purpose, official copies of academic transcripts, three letters of recommendation, interview. Additional exam requirements/recommendations for international students: Required—TOEFL (minimum score 580 paper-based; 237 computer-based). *Application deadline:* For fall admission, 8/1 priority date for domestic students, 7/15 for international students; for spring admission, 11/1 priority date for domestic students, 10/15 for international students. Applications are processed on a rolling basis. Application fee: $55. Electronic applications accepted. *Expenses:* Contact institution. *Financial support:* Fellowships, research assistantships, teaching assistantships, Federal Work-Study, scholarships/grants, tuition waivers (full and partial), and unspecified assistantships available. Financial award application deadline: 2/1; financial award applicants required to submit FAFSA. *Faculty research:* Digital collections, library and information science education, information design and architecture, information system design and evaluation. *Total annual research expenditures:* $5,870. *Unit head:* Dr. Ingrid Hsieh-Yee, Acting Dean, 202-319-5085, Fax: 202-319-5574, E-mail: hsiehyee@cua.edu. *Application contact:* Andrew Woodall, Director of Graduate Admissions, 202-319-5057, Fax: 202-319-6533, E-mail: cua-admissions@cua.edu. Web site: http://slis.cua.edu/.

Central Connecticut State University, School of Graduate Studies, School of Arts and Sciences, Department of Information Design, New Britain, CT 06050-4010. Offers graphic information design (MA). Part-time and evening/weekend programs available. *Faculty:* 4 full-time (2 women), 3 part-time/adjunct (2 women). *Students:* 10 full-time (5 women), 5 part-time (all women); includes 1 minority (Black or African American, non-Hispanic/Latino), 3 international. Average age 30. 9 applicants, 78% accepted, 7 enrolled. In 2011, 3 master's awarded. *Degree requirements:* For master's, thesis or alternative. *Entrance requirements:* For master's, portfolio, minimum undergraduate GPA of 3.0, essay. Additional exam requirements/recommendations for international students: Required—TOEFL (minimum score 550 paper-based; 213 computer-based). *Application deadline:* For fall admission, 6/1 for domestic students, 5/1 for international students; for spring admission, 11/1 for domestic and international students. Applications are processed on a rolling basis. Application fee: $50. Electronic applications accepted. *Expenses: Tuition, area resident:* Full-time $5137; part-time $482 per credit. Tuition, state resident: full-time $7707; part-time $494 per credit. Tuition, nonresident: full-time $14,311; part-time $494 per credit. *Required fees:* $3865. One-time fee: $62 part-time. *Financial support:* In 2011–12, 3 students received support, including 3 research assistantships; career-related internships or fieldwork, Federal Work-Study, scholarships/grants, and unspecified assistantships also available. Support available to part-time students. Financial award application deadline: 4/15; financial award applicants required to submit FAFSA. *Unit head:* Dr. Eleanor Thornton, Chair, 860-832-2564, E-mail: thorntone@ccsu.edu. *Application contact:* Patricia Gardner, Associate Director of Graduate Studies, 860-832-2350, Fax: 860-832-2352, E-mail: graduateadmissions@ccsu.edu. Web site: http://www.design.ccsu.edu/.

Columbia University, School of Continuing Education, Program in Information and Archive Management, New York, NY 10027. Offers MS. Part-time programs available. *Entrance requirements:* For master's, minimum undergraduate GPA of 3.0. Additional exam requirements/recommendations for international students: Required—American Language Program placement test. Electronic applications accepted. *Faculty research:* Library science technology, information systems.

Cornell University, Graduate School, Graduate Fields of Arts and Sciences, Field of Information Science, Ithaca, NY 14853-0001. Offers cognition (PhD); human computer interaction (PhD); information systems (PhD); social aspects of information (PhD). *Faculty:* 38 full-time (11 women). *Students:* 31 full-time (12 women); includes 3 minority (1 Black or African American, non-Hispanic/Latino; 2 Asian, non-Hispanic/Latino), 18 international. Average age 27. 152 applicants, 14% accepted, 17 enrolled. In 2011, 3 doctorates awarded. *Degree requirements:* For doctorate, comprehensive exam, thesis/dissertation. *Entrance requirements:* For doctorate, GRE General Test, 3 letters of recommendation. Additional exam requirements/recommendations for international students: Required—TOEFL (minimum score 550 paper-based; 213 computer-based; 77 iBT). *Application deadline:* For fall admission, 1/1 for domestic students. Application fee: $95. Electronic applications accepted. *Financial support:* In 2011–12, 2 fellowships with full tuition reimbursements, 8 research assistantships with full tuition reimbursements, 6 teaching assistantships with full tuition reimbursements were awarded; institutionally sponsored loans, scholarships/grants, tuition waivers (full and partial), and unspecified assistantships also available. Financial award applicants required to submit FAFSA. *Faculty research:* Digital libraries, game theory, data mining, human-computer interaction, computational linguistics. *Unit head:* Director of Graduate Studies, 607-255-5925. *Application contact:* Graduate Field Assistant, 607-255-5925, E-mail: info@infosci.cornell.edu. Web site: http://www.gradschool.cornell.edu/fields.php?id-9A&a-2.

Dalhousie University, Faculty of Management, School of Information Management, Halifax, NS B3H 3J5, Canada. Offers MIM, MLIS, LL B/MLIS, MBA/MLIS, MLIS/MPA, MLIS/MREM. *Accreditation:* ALA (one or more programs are accredited). Part-time programs available. *Degree requirements:* For master's, one foreign language, thesis optional. *Entrance requirements:* For master's, resume, interview. Additional exam requirements/recommendations for international students: Required—TOEFL, IELTS, CANTEST, CAEL, or Michigan English Language Assessment Battery. Electronic applications accepted. *Faculty research:* Information-seeking behavior, electronic text design, browsing in digital environments, information diffusion among scientists.

Dominican University, Graduate School of Library and Information Science, River Forest, IL 60305-1099. Offers library and information science (MLIS, PhD); special studies (CSS); MBA/MLIS; MLIS/M Div; MLIS/MA; MLIS/MM. MLIS/M Div offered jointly with McCormick Theological Seminary; MLIS/MA with Loyola University Chicago; and MLIS/MM with Northwestern University. *Accreditation:* ALA (one or more programs are accredited). Part-time and evening/weekend programs available. Postbaccalaureate distance learning degree programs offered (minimal on-campus study). *Faculty:* 15 full-time (10 women), 24 part-time/adjunct (17 women). *Students:* 140 full-time (104 women), 312 part-time (247 women); includes 81 minority (26 Black or African American, non-Hispanic/Latino; 2 American Indian or Alaska Native, non-Hispanic/Latino; 10 Asian, non-Hispanic/Latino; 31 Hispanic/Latino; 1 Native Hawaiian or other Pacific Islander, non-Hispanic/Latino; 11 Two or more races, non-Hispanic/Latino), 4 international. Average age 33. 155 applicants, 95% accepted, 139 enrolled. In 2011, 214 master's awarded. *Entrance requirements:* For master's, minimum GPA of 3.0, GRE General Test, or MAT. Additional exam requirements/recommendations for international students: Required—TOEFL. *Application deadline:* For fall admission, 6/1 priority date for domestic students; for winter admission, 3/1 priority date for domestic students; for spring admission, 10/1 priority date for domestic students. Applications are processed on a rolling basis. Application fee: $25. *Expenses:* Contact institution. *Financial support:* Fellowships, research assistantships, career-related internships or fieldwork, Federal Work-Study, scholarships/grants, and tuition waivers (partial) available. Support available to part-time students. Financial award application deadline: 4/15; financial award applicants required to submit FAFSA. *Faculty research:* Productivity and the information environment, bibliometrics, library history, subject access, library materials and services for children. *Unit head:* Dr. Susan Roman, Dean, 708-524-6986, Fax: 708-524-6657, E-mail: sroman@dom.edu. *Application contact:* Raymond Kennelly, Senior Vice President of Enrollment Management, 708-524-6544, E-mail: rkennelly@dom.edu. Web site: http://www.dom.edu/gslis.

Drexel University, The iSchool at Drexel, College of Information Science and Technology, Master of Science in Information Systems Program, Philadelphia, PA

19104-2875. Offers MSIS. Part-time and evening/weekend programs available. Postbaccalaureate distance learning degree programs offered (no on-campus study). *Faculty:* 30 full-time (20 women), 29 part-time/adjunct (15 women). *Students:* 20 full-time (10 women), 132 part-time (36 women); includes 33 minority (18 Black or African American, non-Hispanic/Latino; 2 American Indian or Alaska Native, non-Hispanic/Latino; 8 Asian, non-Hispanic/Latino; 5 Hispanic/Latino), 14 international. Average age 34. 82 applicants, 76% accepted, 48 enrolled. In 2011, 113 master's awarded. *Entrance requirements:* For master's, GRE General Test. Additional exam requirements/recommendations for international students: Required—TOEFL (minimum score 600 paper-based; 250 computer-based; 100 iBT). *Application deadline:* For fall admission, 8/1 for domestic and international students; for spring admission, 2/1 for domestic and international students. Applications are processed on a rolling basis. Electronic applications accepted. *Expenses:* Contact institution. *Financial support:* In 2011–12, 25 students received support, including 26 fellowships with partial tuition reimbursements available (averaging $22,500 per year); institutionally sponsored loans and scholarships/grants also available. Support available to part-time students. Financial award applicants required to submit FAFSA. *Faculty research:* Information retrieval/information visualization/bibliometrics, human-computer interaction, digital libraries, databases, text/data mining. *Total annual research expenditures:* $2 million. *Unit head:* Dr. David E. Fenske, Dean/Professor of Information Science, 215-895-2475, Fax: 215-895-6378, E-mail: fenske@drexel.edu. *Application contact:* Matthew Lechtenberg, Graduate Admissions Manager, 215-895-1951, Fax: 215-895-2303, E-mail: ml333@drexel.edu.

Emporia State University, Graduate School, School of Library and Information Management, Emporia, KS 66801-5087. Offers archives studies (Certificate); legal information management (Certificate); library and information management (MLS, PhD, Certificate). *Accreditation:* ALA (one or more programs are accredited). Part-time and evening/weekend programs available. Postbaccalaureate distance learning degree programs offered (minimal on-campus study). *Faculty:* 8 full-time (4 women). *Students:* 22 full-time (19 women), 326 part-time (258 women); includes 31 minority (4 Black or African American, non-Hispanic/Latino; 1 American Indian or Alaska Native, non-Hispanic/Latino; 9 Asian, non-Hispanic/Latino; 10 Hispanic/Latino; 4 Native Hawaiian or other Pacific Islander, non-Hispanic/Latino; 3 Two or more races, non-Hispanic/Latino), 3 international. 125 applicants, 77% accepted, 78 enrolled. In 2011, 133 master's, 1 doctorate, 7 other advanced degrees awarded. *Degree requirements:* For master's, comprehensive exam, thesis optional; for doctorate, thesis/dissertation. *Entrance requirements:* For master's, GRE General Test, interview, minimum undergraduate GPA of 3.0, letters of recommendation; for doctorate, GRE General Test, interview, minimum graduate GPA of 3.5. Additional exam requirements/recommendations for international students: Required—TOEFL (minimum score 520 paper-based; 133 computer-based; 68 iBT). *Application deadline:* For fall admission, 8/15 priority date for domestic students. Applications are processed on a rolling basis. Application fee: $30 ($75 for international students). Electronic applications accepted. *Expenses:* Tuition, state resident: full-time $2342; part-time $195 per credit hour. Tuition, nonresident: full-time $7254; part-time $605 per credit hour. *Required fees:* $66 per credit hour. Tuition and fees vary according to campus/location. *Financial support:* In 2011–12, 9 research assistantships with full tuition reimbursements (averaging $7,059 per year), 2 teaching assistantships with full tuition reimbursements (averaging $7,059 per year) were awarded; Federal Work-Study, institutionally sponsored loans, and unspecified assistantships also available. Financial award application deadline: 3/15; financial award applicants required to submit FAFSA. *Unit head:* Dr. Gwen Alexander, Interim Dean, 620-341-5203, Fax: 620-341-5233, E-mail: galexan1@emporia.edu. *Application contact:* Candace Boardman, Director, Kansas MLS Program, 620-341-6159, E-mail: cboardma@emporia.edu. Web site: http://www.emporia.edu/las/index.html.

Florida State University, The Graduate School, College of Communication and Information, School of Library and Information Studies, Tallahassee, FL 32306-2100. Offers MA, MS, PhD, Specialist. *Accreditation:* ALA (one or more programs are accredited). Part-time and evening/weekend programs available. Postbaccalaureate distance learning degree programs offered (no on-campus study). *Faculty:* 31 full-time (17 women), 16 part-time/adjunct (8 women). *Students:* 13 full-time (10 women), 532 part-time (395 women); includes 135 minority (47 Black or African American, non-Hispanic/Latino; 1 American Indian or Alaska Native, non-Hispanic/Latino; 29 Asian, non-Hispanic/Latino; 57 Hispanic/Latino; 1 Two or more races, non-Hispanic/Latino). Average age 35. 235 applicants, 82% accepted, 138 enrolled. In 2011, 216 master's, 10 doctorates, 3 other advanced degrees awarded. *Degree requirements:* For master's, thesis optional, minimum GPA of 3.0, 36 hours; for doctorate, comprehensive exam, thesis/dissertation, dissertation defense, manuscript clearance, minimum GPA of 3.0; for Specialist, minimum GPA of 3.0, 30 hours. *Entrance requirements:* For master's, GRE (minimum percentile of at least 50 on each of the verbal and quantitative portions and writing score of 4.0), minimum GPA of 3.0 on last 2 years of baccalaureate degree, resume, statement of goals, two letters of recommendation, two official transcripts from every college-level institution attended; for doctorate, GRE (minimum percentile of at least 50 on each of the verbal and quantitative portions and writing score of 4.0), minimum GPA of 3.0 on last degree program, resume, 3 letters of recommendation, personal/goals statement, writing sample, brief digital video, two official transcripts from all college-level institutions attended; for Specialist, GRE (minimum percentile of at least 50 on each of the verbal and quantitative portions and writing score of 4.0), minimum graduate GPA of 3.2, resume, statement of goals, 2 letters of recommendation, writing sample, two official transcripts from every college-level institution attended. Additional exam requirements/recommendations for international students: Required—TOEFL (minimum score 585 paper-based; 94 iBT), IELTS (minimum score 6.5). *Application deadline:* For fall admission, 7/1 for domestic and international students; for spring admission, 11/1 for domestic and international students. Applications are processed on a rolling basis. Application fee: $30. Electronic applications accepted. *Expenses:* Contact institution. *Financial support:* In 2011–12, 263 students received support, including 3 fellowships with full tuition reimbursements available, 70 research assistantships with full tuition reimbursements available, 51 teaching assistantships with full tuition reimbursements available; career-related internships or fieldwork, Federal Work-Study, scholarships/grants, health care benefits, unspecified assistantships, and reduced tuition program for out-of-state students also available. Financial award application deadline: 3/1; financial award applicants required to submit FAFSA. *Faculty research:* Needs assessment, social informatics, usability analysis, human information behavior, youth services. *Unit head:* Dr. Corinne Jorgensen, Director/Associate Dean, 850-644-8126, Fax: 850-644-9763, E-mail: corinne.jorgensen@cci.fsu.edu. *Application contact:* Graduate Student Services, 850-645-3280, Fax: 850-644-9763, E-mail: slisgradadmissions@admin.fsu.edu. Web site: http://slis.fsu.edu/.

Indiana University Bloomington, School of Library and Information Science, Bloomington, IN 47405-3907. Offers MIS, MLS, PhD, Sp LIS, JD/MLS, MIS/MA, MLS/MA, MPA/MIS, MPA/MLS. *Accreditation:* ALA (one or more programs are accredited). Part-time programs available. *Faculty:* 16 full-time (7 women). *Students:* 256 full-time (176 women), 67 part-time (49 women); includes 46 minority (13 Black or African American, non-Hispanic/Latino; 2 American Indian or Alaska Native, non-Hispanic/Latino; 23 Asian, non-Hispanic/Latino; 4 Hispanic/Latino; 4 Two or more races, non-Hispanic/Latino), 28 international. Average age 29. 286 applicants, 79% accepted, 101 enrolled. In 2011, 143 master's, 7 doctorates, 2 other advanced degrees awarded. *Degree requirements:* For doctorate, thesis/dissertation. *Entrance requirements:* For master's and doctorate, GRE General Test, 3 letters of reference. Additional exam requirements/recommendations for international students: Required—TOEFL (minimum score 600 paper-based; 250 computer-based; 100 iBT). *Application deadline:* For fall admission, 5/15 priority date for domestic students, 12/1 for international students; for spring admission, 10/15 priority date for domestic students, 9/1 for international students. Applications are processed on a rolling basis. Application fee: $55 ($65 for international students). Electronic applications accepted. *Expenses:* Contact institution. *Financial support:* Fellowships with full and partial tuition reimbursements, research assistantships with full and partial tuition reimbursements, career-related internships or fieldwork, Federal Work-Study, institutionally sponsored loans, scholarships/grants, tuition waivers (partial), and unspecified assistantships available. Support available to part-time students. Financial award application deadline: 1/15. *Faculty research:* Scholarly communication, interface design, library and management policy, computer-mediated communication, information retrieval. *Application contact:* Rhonda Spencer, Director of Admissions, 812-855-2018, Fax: 812-855-6166, E-mail: slis@indiana.edu. Web site: http://www.slis.indiana.edu/.

Long Island University–C. W. Post Campus, College of Information and Computer Science, Palmer School of Library and Information Science, Brookville, NY 11548-1300. Offers archives and records management (Certificate); information studies (PhD); library and information science (MS); library media specialist (MS); public library management (Certificate). *Accreditation:* ALA (one or more programs are accredited). Part-time and evening/weekend programs available. Postbaccalaureate distance learning degree programs offered (minimal on-campus study). *Degree requirements:* For master's, thesis optional, internship; for doctorate, thesis/dissertation, qualifying exam. *Entrance requirements:* For master's, GRE or MAT, minimum undergraduate GPA of 3.0, resume. Electronic applications accepted. *Faculty research:* Information retrieval, digital libraries, scientometric and infometric studies, preservation/archiving and electronic records.

Long Island University–Hudson at Westchester, Program in Library and Information Science, Purchase, NY 10577. Offers MS. Part-time and evening/weekend programs available.

Louisiana State University and Agricultural and Mechanical College, Graduate School, School of Library and Information Science, Baton Rouge, LA 70803. Offers MLIS. *Accreditation:* ALA. Part-time and evening/weekend programs available. Postbaccalaureate distance learning degree programs offered (no on-campus study). *Faculty:* 10 full-time (8 women). *Students:* 68 full-time (53 women), 99 part-time (83 women); includes 20 minority (16 Black or African American, non-Hispanic/Latino; 1 American Indian or Alaska Native, non-Hispanic/Latino; 2 Asian, non-Hispanic/Latino; 1 Two or more races, non-Hispanic/Latino), 8 international. Average age 33. 55 applicants, 78% accepted, 37 enrolled. In 2011, 63 master's awarded. *Degree requirements:* For master's, comprehensive exam, thesis optional. *Entrance requirements:* For master's, GRE General Test, minimum GPA of 3.0. Additional exam requirements/recommendations for international students: Required—TOEFL (minimum score 550 paper-based; 213 computer-based; 79 iBT) or IELTS (minimum score 6.5). *Application deadline:* For fall admission, 1/25 priority date for domestic students, 5/15 for international students; for spring admission, 10/15 for international students. Applications are processed on a rolling basis. Application fee: $50 ($70 for international students). Electronic applications accepted. *Financial support:* In 2011–12, 95 students received support, including 5 fellowships (averaging $19,807 per year), 7 research assistantships with partial tuition reimbursements available (averaging $12,343 per year), 12 teaching assistantships with partial tuition reimbursements available (averaging $12,475 per year); career-related internships or fieldwork, Federal Work-Study, institutionally sponsored loans, scholarships/grants, health care benefits, and unspecified assistantships also available. Support available to part-time students. Financial award applicants required to submit FAFSA. *Faculty research:* Information retrieval, management, collection development, public libraries. *Total annual research expenditures:* $37,299. *Unit head:* Dr. Beth M. Paskoff, Dean, 225-578-3158, Fax: 225-578-4581, E-mail: bpaskoff@lsu.edu. *Application contact:* LaToya Joseph, Administrative Assistant, 225-578-3150, Fax: 225-578-4581, E-mail: lcjoseph@lsu.edu. Web site: http://slis.lsu.edu/.

Mansfield University of Pennsylvania, Graduate Studies, Program in School Library and Information Technologies, Mansfield, PA 16933. Offers library science (M Ed). Part-time and evening/weekend programs available. Postbaccalaureate distance learning degree programs offered. *Degree requirements:* For master's, comprehensive exam, thesis optional. *Entrance requirements:* For master's, minimum GPA of 3.0. Additional exam requirements/recommendations for international students: Required—TOEFL (minimum score 550 paper-based; 220 computer-based). Electronic applications accepted. *Expenses:* Contact institution.

McGill University, Faculty of Graduate and Postdoctoral Studies, Faculty of Education, School of Information Studies, Montréal, QC H3A 2T5, Canada. Offers MLIS, PhD, Certificate, Diploma. *Accreditation:* ALA (one or more programs are accredited).

Metropolitan State University, College of Management, St. Paul, MN 55106-5000. Offers business administration (MBA, DBA); database administration (Graduate Certificate); healthcare information technology management (Graduate Certificate); information assurance security (Graduate Certificate); management information systems (MMIS); MIS generalist (Graduate Certificate); MIS systems analysis and design (Graduate Certificate); project management (Graduate Certificate); public and nonprofit administration (MPNA). Part-time and evening/weekend programs available. *Students:* 63 full-time (41 women), 409 part-time (192 women); includes 94 minority (38 Black or African American, non-Hispanic/Latino; 33 Asian, non-Hispanic/Latino; 14 Hispanic/Latino; 9 Two or more races, non-Hispanic/Latino), 61 international. Average age 35. *Degree requirements:* For master's, thesis optional, computer language (MMIS). *Entrance requirements:* For master's, GMAT (MBA), resume. Additional exam requirements/recommendations for international students: Required—TOEFL (minimum score 550 paper-based; 213 computer-based). *Application deadline:* For fall admission, 7/15 for international students; for winter admission, 11/15 for international students; for spring admission, 3/15 for international students. Applications are processed on a rolling basis. Application fee: $20. Electronic applications accepted. *Expenses:* Tuition, state resident: full-time $5799.06; part-time $322.17 per credit. Tuition, nonresident: full-time $11,411; part-time $633.92 per credit. Tuition and fees vary according to degree level, program and reciprocity agreements. *Financial support:* Research assistantships with partial tuition reimbursements, career-related internships or fieldwork, and Federal Work-Study available. Support available to part-time students. Financial award applicants required to submit FAFSA. *Faculty research:* Yugoslav economic system, workers' cooperatives, participative management and job enrichment, global business systems. *Unit head:* Dr. Paul Huo, Dean, 612-659-7271, Fax: 612-659-7268, E-mail: paul.huo@metrostate.edu. Web site: http://choose.metrostate.edu/comgradprograms.

North Carolina Central University, Division of Academic Affairs, School of Library and Information Sciences, Durham, NC 27707-3129. Offers MIS, MLS. *Accreditation:* ALA (one or more programs are accredited). Part-time and evening/weekend programs available. *Degree requirements:* For master's, one foreign language, thesis, research paper, or project. *Entrance requirements:* For master's, GRE, 90 hours in liberal arts. Additional exam requirements/recommendations for international students: Required—

TOEFL. *Faculty research:* African-American resources, planning and evaluation, analysis of economic and physical resources, geography of information, artificial intelligence.

Pratt Institute, School of Information and Library Science, New York, NY 10011. Offers archives (Adv C); library and information science (MS, Adv C); library and information science media specialist (MS); library media specialist (Adv C); museum libraries (Adv C); JD/MS. *Accreditation:* ALA. Part-time programs available. *Faculty:* 9 full-time (6 women), 27 part-time/adjunct (15 women). *Students:* 131 full-time (106 women), 184 part-time (151 women); includes 72 minority (21 Black or African American, non-Hispanic/Latino; 19 Asian, non-Hispanic/Latino; 26 Hispanic/Latino; 6 Two or more races, non-Hispanic/Latino), 3 international. Average age 32. 207 applicants, 93% accepted, 81 enrolled. In 2011, 111 master's, 1 other advanced degree awarded. *Degree requirements:* For master's, thesis. *Entrance requirements:* Additional exam requirements/recommendations for international students: Required—TOEFL (minimum score 600 paper-based; 250 computer-based; 100 iBT). *Application deadline:* For fall admission, 1/5 for domestic and international students; for spring admission, 10/1 for domestic and international students. Application fee: $50 ($90 for international students). Electronic applications accepted. *Expenses:* Contact institution. *Financial support:* Career-related internships or fieldwork, Federal Work-Study, institutionally sponsored loans, scholarships/grants, health care benefits, and unspecified assistantships available. Support available to part-time students. Financial award application deadline: 2/1; financial award applicants required to submit FAFSA. *Faculty research:* Development of urban libraries and information centers, medical and law librarianship, information management. *Unit head:* Dr. Tula Giannini, Dean, 212-647-7682, E-mail: giannini@pratt.edu. *Application contact:* Young Hah, Director of Graduate Admissions, 718-636-3683, Fax: 718-399-4242, E-mail: yhah@pratt.edu. Web site: http://www.pratt.edu/academics/information_and_library_sciences.

See Display on this page and Close-Up on page 1651.

Queens College of the City University of New York, Division of Graduate Studies, Social Science Division, Graduate School of Library and Information Studies, Flushing, NY 11367-1597. Offers MLS, AC. *Accreditation:* ALA (one or more programs are accredited). Part-time and evening/weekend programs available. *Faculty:* 17 full-time (11 women). *Students:* 35 full-time (25 women), 433 part-time (305 women); includes 91 minority (25 Black or African American, non-Hispanic/Latino; 2 American Indian or Alaska Native, non-Hispanic/Latino; 23 Asian, non-Hispanic/Latino; 41 Hispanic/Latino), 3 international. 322 applicants, 64% accepted, 166 enrolled. In 2011, 200 master's awarded. *Degree requirements:* For master's, thesis; for AC, thesis optional. *Entrance requirements:* For master's, minimum GPA of 3.0; for AC, master's degree or equivalent. Additional exam requirements/recommendations for international students: Required—TOEFL. *Application deadline:* For fall admission, 4/1 for domestic students; for spring admission, 11/1 for domestic students. Applications are processed on a rolling basis. Application fee: $125. *Expenses:* Tuition, state resident: part-time $345 per credit. Tuition, nonresident: part-time $640 per credit. *Required fees:* $145.25 per semester. *Financial support:* Career-related internships or fieldwork, Federal Work-Study, institutionally sponsored loans, and tuition waivers (partial) available. Support available to part-time students. Financial award application deadline: 4/1; financial award applicants required to submit FAFSA. *Faculty research:* Multimedia and video studies, ethnicity and librarianship, information science and computer applications. *Unit head:* Dr. Virgil Blake, Director/Chair, 718-997-3790. *Application contact:* Dr. Karen Smith, Graduate Adviser, 718-997-3790, E-mail: karen_smith@qc.edu.

Queen's University at Kingston, School of Graduate Studies and Research, Faculty of Arts and Sciences, Department of Sociology, Kingston, ON K7L 3N6, Canada. Offers communication and Information technology (MA, PhD); feminist sociology (MA, PhD); socio-legal studies (MA, PhD); sociological theory (MA, PhD). Part-time programs available. *Degree requirements:* For master's, thesis; for doctorate, comprehensive exam, thesis/dissertation. *Entrance requirements:* For master's, honors bachelors degree in sociology; for doctorate, honors bachelors degree, masters degree in sociology. Additional exam requirements/recommendations for international students: Required—TOEFL. *Faculty research:* Social change and modernization, social control, deviance and criminology, surveillance.

Rutgers, The State University of New Jersey, New Brunswick, School of Communication, Information and Library Studies, Program in Communication and Information Studies, Piscataway, NJ 08854-8097. Offers MCIS. Part-time programs available. *Entrance requirements:* For master's, GRE General Test. Additional exam requirements/recommendations for international students: Required—TOEFL. Electronic applications accepted. *Faculty research:* Communication processes and systems, information process and systems, human information and communication behavior.

Rutgers, The State University of New Jersey, New Brunswick, School of Communication, Information and Library Studies, Program in Communication, Library and Information Science and Media Studies, Piscataway, NJ 08854-8097. Offers PhD. Part-time programs available. *Degree requirements:* For doctorate, comprehensive exam, thesis/dissertation, qualifying exams. *Entrance requirements:* For doctorate, GRE General Test, proficiency in statistics. Additional exam requirements/recommendations for international students: Required—TOEFL (minimum score 600 paper-based; 250 computer-based). Electronic applications accepted. *Faculty research:* Information science, media studies.

St. Catherine University, Graduate Programs, Program in Library and Information Science, St. Paul, MN 55105. Offers MLIS. Part-time and evening/weekend programs available. *Degree requirements:* For master's, microcomputer competency. *Entrance requirements:* For master's, GRE or MAT, minimum GPA of 3.2 or GRE. Additional exam requirements/recommendations for international students: Required—Michigan English Language Assessment Battery or TOEFL (minimum score 600 paper-based; 250 computer-based; 100 iBT). *Expenses: Required fees:* $30 per semester. Tuition and fees vary according to program.

St. John's University, St. John's College of Liberal Arts and Sciences, Division of Library and Information Science, Queens, NY 11439. Offers MLS, Adv C, MA/MLS, MS/MLS. *Accreditation:* ALA (one or more programs are accredited). Part-time and evening/weekend programs available. Postbaccalaureate distance learning degree programs offered (no on-campus study). *Students:* 24 full-time (19 women), 55 part-time (50 women); includes 20 minority (10 Black or African American, non-Hispanic/Latino; 2 Asian, non-Hispanic/Latino; 8 Hispanic/Latino). Average age 33. 62 applicants, 90% accepted, 26 enrolled. In 2011, 86 master's awarded. *Degree requirements:* For master's, comprehensive exam, internship. *Entrance requirements:* For master's, interview, minimum GPA of 3.0, 2 letters of recommendation, essay. Additional exam requirements/recommendations for international students: Required—TOEFL (minimum score 600 paper-based; 250 computer-based; 100 iBT), IELTS (minimum score 5.5). *Application deadline:* For fall admission, 5/1 priority date for domestic students, 5/1 for international students; for spring admission, 11/1 priority date for domestic students, 11/1 for international students. Applications are processed on a rolling basis. Application fee: $70. Electronic applications accepted. *Expenses:* Contact institution. *Financial support:* Research assistantships, career-related internships or fieldwork, and scholarships/grants available. Support available to part-time students. Financial award application deadline: 3/1; financial award applicants required to submit FAFSA. *Faculty research:* Indexes and metatags, information use and users, competitive intelligence, knowledge management, database theory, young adult and children services, school media services, archives, oral history. *Unit head:* Dr. Jeffrey Olson, Director, 718-990-5705, E-mail: olsonj@stjohns.edu. *Application contact:* Robert Medrano, Director of Graduate Admissions, 718-990-1601, Fax: 718-990-5686, E-mail: gradhelp@stjohns.edu.

San Jose State University, Graduate Studies and Research, College of Applied Sciences and Arts, School of Library and Information Science, San Jose, CA 95192-0001. Offers MLIS, PhD. *Accreditation:* ALA (one or more programs are accredited). Part-time and evening/weekend programs available. *Degree requirements:* For master's, comprehensive exam. *Entrance requirements:* Additional exam requirements/recommendations for international students: Required—TOEFL (minimum score 600 paper-based). Electronic applications accepted. *Faculty research:* Evaluation of information services online, search strategy, organizational behavior.

Simmons College, Graduate School of Library and Information Science, Boston, MA 02115. Offers archives management (MS, Certificate); instructional technology licensure (Certificate); library and information science (MS, PhD); managerial leadership in the informational professions (PhD); school library teacher (MS, Certificate); MS/MA. *Accreditation:* ALA (one or more programs are accredited). *Unit head:* Dr. Michele V. Cloonan, Dean, 617-521-2806, Fax: 617-521-3192, E-mail: michele.cloonan@simmons.edu. *Application contact:* Sarah Petrakos, Assistant Dean, Admission and Recruitment, 617-521-2868, Fax: 617-521-3192, E-mail: gslisadm@simmons.edu. Web site: http://www.simmons.edu/gslis/.

Southern Connecticut State University, School of Graduate Studies, School of Education, Department of Information and Library Science, New Haven, CT 06515-1355. Offers library science (MLS); library/information studies (Diploma); JD/MLS; MLS/MA; MLS/MS. *Accreditation:* ALA. Part-time and evening/weekend programs available. Postbaccalaureate distance learning degree programs offered (no on-campus study). *Faculty:* 9 full-time (5 women), 3 part-time/adjunct (all women). *Students:* 44 full-time (35 women), 200 part-time (171 women); includes 17 minority (6 Black or African American, non-Hispanic/Latino; 3 Asian, non-Hispanic/Latino; 4 Hispanic/Latino; 4 Two or more races, non-Hispanic/Latino), 1 international. 465 applicants, 12% accepted, 42 enrolled. In 2011, 84 master's, 5 other advanced degrees awarded. *Degree requirements:* For master's and Diploma, thesis or alternative. *Entrance requirements:* For master's, GRE General Test, interview, minimum QPA of 2.7, introductory computer science course; for Diploma, master's degree in library science or information science. *Application deadline:* For fall admission, 7/15 priority date for domestic students. Applications are processed on a rolling basis. Application fee: $50. Electronic applications accepted. *Expenses:* Tuition, state resident: full-time $5137; part-time $413 per credit. *Required fees:* $4008; $55 per term. *Financial support:* Research assistantships available. Financial award application deadline: 4/15; financial award applicants required to submit FAFSA. *Unit head:* Dr. Chang Suk Kim, Chairperson, 203-392-5191, Fax: 203-392-5780, E-mail: kimc1@southernct.edu. *Application contact:* Dr. Elsie Okobi, Graduate Coordinator, 203-392-5709, E-mail: okobie1@southernct.edu.

Syracuse University, School of Information Studies, Program in Information Management, Syracuse, NY 13244. Offers MS, DPS. Part-time and evening/weekend programs available. Postbaccalaureate distance learning degree programs offered (minimal on-campus study). *Students:* 199 full-time (69 women), 146 part-time (40 women); includes 85 minority (29 Black or African American, non-Hispanic/Latino; 2 American Indian or Alaska Native, non-Hispanic/Latino; 16 Asian, non-Hispanic/Latino; 31 Hispanic/Latino; 7 Two or more races, non-Hispanic/Latino), 144 international. Average age 29. 606 applicants, 54% accepted, 130 enrolled. In 2011, 123 master's, 2 doctorates awarded. *Entrance requirements:* For master's, GRE General Test. Additional exam requirements/recommendations for international students: Required—TOEFL (minimum score 100 iBT). *Application deadline:* For fall admission, 2/15 priority date for domestic students, 2/15 for international students; for spring admission, 10/15 priority date for domestic students, 10/15 for international students. Applications are processed on a rolling basis. Application fee: $75. Electronic applications accepted. *Expenses: Tuition:* Part-time $1206 per credit. *Financial support:* Fellowships with tuition reimbursements, research assistantships with partial tuition reimbursements, teaching assistantships with partial tuition reimbursements, and scholarships/grants available. Financial award application deadline: 1/1; financial award applicants required to submit FAFSA. *Unit head:* David Dischiave, Director, 315-443-4681, Fax: 315-443-6886, E-mail: ddischia@syr.edu. *Application contact:* Susan Corieri, Director of Enrollment Management, 315-443-2575, E-mail: ischool@syr.edu. Web site: http://ischool.syr.edu/.

See Display below and Close-Up on page 1653.

Universidad del Turabo, Graduate Programs, Programs in Education, Program in Library Service and Information Technology, Gurabo, PR 00778-3030. Offers M Ed. *Students:* 31 full-time (26 women), 26 part-time (22 women); includes 45 minority (all Hispanic/Latino). Average age 34. 36 applicants, 89% accepted, 22 enrolled. In 2011, 43 master's awarded. *Unit head:* Angela Candelario, Dean, 787-743-7979 Ext. 4126. *Application contact:* Virginia Gonzalez, Admissions Officer, 787-746-3009.

Université de Montréal, Faculty of Arts and Sciences, School of Library and Information Sciences, Montréal, QC H3C 3J7, Canada. Offers information sciences (MIS, PhD). *Accreditation:* ALA (one or more programs are accredited). *Degree requirements:* For master's, thesis optional. *Entrance requirements:* For master's, interview, master's degree in library and information science or equivalent. Electronic applications accepted.

University at Albany, State University of New York, College of Computing and Information, Department of Information Studies, Albany, NY 12222-0001. Offers information science (MS, CAS). *Faculty research:* Electronic information across technologies system dynamics modeling archives, records administration.

University at Buffalo, the State University of New York, Graduate School, Graduate School of Education, Department of Library and Information Studies, Buffalo, NY 14260. Offers library and information studies (MLS, Certificate); library and information studies (online) (MLS); library media specialist (online) (MLS). *Accreditation:* ALA (one or more programs are accredited). Part-time programs available. Postbaccalaureate distance learning degree programs offered (no on-campus study). *Faculty:* 11 full-time (8 women), 26 part-time/adjunct (14 women). *Students:* 115 full-time (84 women), 218 part-time (167 women); includes 31 minority (15 Black or African American, non-Hispanic/Latino; 1 American Indian or Alaska Native, non-Hispanic/Latino; 8 Asian, non-Hispanic/Latino; 7 Hispanic/Latino), 5 international. Average age 34. 250 applicants, 57% accepted, 137 enrolled. In 2011, 112 master's, 4 other advanced degrees awarded. *Degree requirements:* For master's, thesis optional; for Certificate, thesis. *Entrance requirements:* For master's, minimum GPA of 3.0. Additional exam requirements/recommendations for international students: Required—TOEFL (minimum score 550 paper-based; 79 iBT). *Application deadline:* For fall admission, 4/1 priority date for domestic students, 4/1 for international students; for spring admission, 10/15 priority date for domestic students, 10/15 for international students. Applications are processed on a rolling basis. Application fee: $50. Electronic applications accepted. *Financial support:* In 2011–12, 14 fellowships (averaging $5,115 per year), 6 research assistantships (averaging $9,000 per year) were awarded; teaching assistantships, career-related internships or fieldwork, Federal Work-Study, institutionally sponsored

loans, and unspecified assistantships also available. Support available to part-time students. Financial award application deadline: 3/1; financial award applicants required to submit FAFSA. *Faculty research:* Information-seeking behavior, thesauri, impact of technology, questioning behaviors, educational informatics. *Unit head:* Dr. Dagobert Soergel, Chair, 716-645-2412, Fax: 716-645-3775, E-mail: dsoergel@buffalo.edu. *Application contact:* Dr. Radhika Suresh, Director of Graduate Admissions and Student Services, 716-645-2110, Fax: 716-645-7937, E-mail: gse-info@buffalo.edu. Web site: http://www.gse.buffalo.edu/lis/.

The University of Alabama, Graduate School, College of Communication and Information Sciences, School of Library and Information Studies, Tuscaloosa, AL 35487-0252. Offers book arts (MFA); library and information studies (MLIS, PhD). *Accreditation:* ALA (one or more programs are accredited). Part-time and evening/weekend programs available. Postbaccalaureate distance learning degree programs offered (minimal on-campus study). *Faculty:* 11 full-time (5 women), 2 part-time/adjunct (both women). *Students:* 86 full-time (70 women), 197 part-time (151 women); includes 27 minority (10 Black or African American, non-Hispanic/Latino; 1 American Indian or Alaska Native, non-Hispanic/Latino; 3 Asian, non-Hispanic/Latino; 9 Hispanic/Latino; 4 Two or more races, non-Hispanic/Latino), 4 international. Average age 34. 224 applicants, 55% accepted, 85 enrolled. In 2011, 128 degrees awarded. *Degree requirements:* For master's, comprehensive exam (for some programs), thesis optional; for doctorate, comprehensive exam, thesis/dissertation. *Entrance requirements:* For master's, GRE General Test or MAT, minimum GPA of 3.0; for doctorate, GRE. Additional exam requirements/recommendations for international students: Required—TOEFL. *Application deadline:* For fall admission, 7/1 priority date for domestic students, 7/1 for international students; for spring admission, 11/1 priority date for domestic students, 11/1 for international students. Applications are processed on a rolling basis. Application fee: $50 ($60 for international students). Electronic applications accepted. *Expenses:* Tuition, state resident: full-time $8600. Tuition, nonresident: full-time $21,900. *Financial support:* In 2011–12, 64 students received support, including 3 fellowships with full tuition reimbursements available (averaging $15,000 per year), 18 research assistantships with full and partial tuition reimbursements available (averaging $6,003 per year), 12 teaching assistantships with full and partial tuition reimbursements available (averaging $6,003 per year); career-related internships or fieldwork, scholarships/grants, health care benefits, unspecified assistantships, and 15 additional grant-funded fellowships, full tuition waiver, professional travel also available. Support available to part-time students. Financial award application deadline: 3/15. *Faculty research:* Library administration, user services, digital libraries, book arts, evaluation. *Unit head:* Dr. Heidi Julien, Director and Professor, 205-348-4610, Fax: 205-348-3746, E-mail: hjulien@slis.ua.edu. *Application contact:* Beth Riggs, Assistant to the Director, 205-348-1527, Fax: 205-3483746, E-mail: briggs@slis.ua.edu. Web site: http://www.slis.ua.edu/.

University of Alberta, Faculty of Graduate Studies and Research, School of Library and Information Studies, Edmonton, AB T6G 2E1, Canada. Offers MLIS. *Accreditation:* ALA. *Entrance requirements:* Additional exam requirements/recommendations for international students: Required—TOEFL, Canadian Academic English Language Assessment. Electronic applications accepted. *Faculty research:* Intellectual freedom, materials for children and young adults, library classification, multi-media literacy.

The University of Arizona, College of Social and Behavioral Sciences, School of Information Resources and Library Science, Tucson, AZ 85721. Offers MA, PhD. *Accreditation:* ALA (one or more programs are accredited). Part-time programs available. *Faculty:* 9 full-time (6 women). *Students:* 95 full-time (71 women), 146 part-time (114 women); includes 44 minority (4 Black or African American, non-Hispanic/Latino; 1 American Indian or Alaska Native, non-Hispanic/Latino; 2 Asian, non-Hispanic/Latino; 26 Hispanic/Latino; 11 Two or more races, non-Hispanic/Latino), 5 international. Average age 37. 22 applicants, 36% accepted, 7 enrolled. In 2011, 104 master's awarded. *Degree requirements:* For master's, proficiency in disk operating system (DOS); for doctorate, thesis/dissertation. *Entrance requirements:* For master's and doctorate, GRE General Test, 3 letters of recommendation, resume. Additional exam requirements/recommendations for international students: Required—TOEFL (minimum score 550 paper-based; 213 computer-based; 79 iBT). *Application deadline:* For spring admission, 9/1 for domestic and international students. Applications are processed on a rolling basis. Application fee: $65. Electronic applications accepted. *Expenses:* Tuition, state resident: full-time $10,840. Tuition, nonresident: full-time $25,802. *Financial support:* In 2011–12, 17 research assistantships with full tuition reimbursements (averaging $20,288 per year), 13 teaching assistantships with full tuition reimbursements (averaging $20,288 per year) were awarded; career-related internships or fieldwork, Federal Work-Study, institutionally sponsored loans, scholarships/grants, health care benefits, tuition waivers (full and partial), and unspecified assistantships also available. Financial award application deadline: 3/1. *Faculty research:* Microcomputer applications; quantitative methods systems; information transfer, planning, evaluation, and technology. *Total annual research expenditures:* $1.1 million. *Unit head:* Dr. Jana Bradley, Director, 520-621-3565, Fax: 520-621-3279, E-mail: janabrad@email.arizona.edu. *Application contact:* Geraldine Fragoso, Program Manager, 520-621-3565, Fax: 520-621-3279, E-mail: gfragoso@email.arizona.edu. Web site: http://www.sirls.arizona.edu/.

The University of British Columbia, Faculty of Arts, School of Library, Archival and Information Studies, Dual Master of Archival Studies/Master of Library and Information Studies Program, Vancouver, BC V6T 1Z1, Canada. Offers MLIS/MAS. *Entrance requirements:* Additional exam requirements/recommendations for international students: Required—TOEFL (minimum score 600 paper-based; 250 computer-based; 100 iBT). Electronic applications accepted. *Faculty research:* Computer systems/database design, information-seeking behaviour, archives and records management, children's literature and services, digital libraries and archives.

The University of British Columbia, Faculty of Arts, School of Library, Archival and Information Studies, Master of Library and Information Studies Program, Vancouver, BC V6T 1Z1, Canada. Offers MLIS. Part-time programs available. *Degree requirements:* For master's, thesis optional. *Entrance requirements:* For master's, minimum GPA of 3.3 in undergraduate upper-division courses. Additional exam requirements/recommendations for international students: Required—TOEFL (minimum score 600 paper-based; 250 computer-based; 100 iBT). Electronic applications accepted. *Faculty research:* Computer systems/database design; digital libraries; metadata/classification; human-computer interaction; children's literature and services.

The University of British Columbia, Faculty of Arts, School of Library, Archival and Information Studies, PhD Program in Library, Archival and Information Studies, Vancouver, BC V6T 1Z1, Canada. Offers PhD. *Degree requirements:* For doctorate, thesis/dissertation. *Entrance requirements:* For doctorate, GRE, minimum GPA of 3.3 in MAS or MLIS (other master's degrees may be considered). Additional exam requirements/recommendations for international students: Required—TOEFL (minimum score 600 paper-based; 250 computer-based; 100 iBT). Electronic applications accepted. *Faculty research:* Computer systems/database design; library and archival management; archival description and organization; children's literature and youth services; interactive information retrieval.

University of California, Berkeley, Graduate Division, School of Information Management and Systems, Berkeley, CA 94720-1500. Offers MIMS, PhD. *Degree requirements:* For doctorate, thesis/dissertation, qualifying exam. *Entrance requirements:* For master's, GRE General Test, minimum GPA of 3.0, previous course work in java or C programming, 3 letters of recommendation; for doctorate, GRE General Test, minimum GPA of 3.0. Additional exam requirements/recommendations for international students: Required—TOEFL. *Faculty research:* Information retrieval research, design and evaluation of information systems, work practice-based design of information systems, economics of information, intellectual property law.

University of California, Los Angeles, Graduate Division, Graduate School of Education and Information Studies, Department of Information Studies, Los Angeles, CA 90095-1521. Offers archival studies (MLIS); informatics (MLIS); information studies (PhD); library and information science (Certificate); library studies (MLIS); moving image archive studies (MA); MBA/MLIS; MLIS/MA. *Accreditation:* ALA (one or more programs are accredited). *Faculty:* 13 full-time (7 women), 10 part-time/adjunct (8 women). *Students:* 141 full-time (118 women), 22 part-time (16 women); includes 62 minority (10 Black or African American, non-Hispanic/Latino; 2 American Indian or Alaska Native, non-Hispanic/Latino; 38 Asian, non-Hispanic/Latino; 12 Hispanic/Latino), 3 international. Average age 27. 171 applicants, 77% accepted, 82 enrolled. In 2011, 69 master's, 8 doctorates awarded. Terminal master's awarded for partial completion of doctoral program. *Degree requirements:* For master's, thesis or alternative, professional portfolio; for doctorate, thesis/dissertation, oral and written qualifying exams. *Entrance requirements:* For master's, GRE General Test, previous course work in statistics; for doctorate, GRE General Test, previous course work in statistics, 2 samples of research writing in English. Additional exam requirements/recommendations for international students: Required—TOEFL (minimum score 613 paper-based; 220 computer-based; 87 iBT), IELTS (minimum score 7). *Application deadline:* For fall admission, 11/30 for domestic students, 10/30 for international students. Applications are processed on a rolling basis. Application fee: $80 ($90 for international students). Electronic applications accepted. *Financial support:* In 2011–12, 44 students received support, including 29 fellowships with full and partial tuition reimbursements available (averaging $10,505 per year), 7 research assistantships with partial tuition reimbursements available (averaging $29,061 per year), 12 teaching assistantships with partial tuition reimbursements available (averaging $18,984 per year); career-related internships or fieldwork, Federal Work-Study, institutionally sponsored loans, scholarships/grants, and unspecified assistantships also available. Financial award application deadline: 3/1; financial award applicants required to submit FAFSA. *Faculty research:* Multimedia, digital libraries, archives and electronic records, interface design, information technology and preservation, preservation, access. *Unit head:* Dr. Gregory H. Leazer, Associate Professor and Chair, 310-825-8799, E-mail: gleazer@ucla.edu. *Application contact:* Susan S. Abler, Student Affairs Officer, 310-825-5269, Fax: 310-206-4460, E-mail: abler@gseis.ucla.edu. Web site: http://is.gseis.ucla.edu/.

University of Hawaii at Manoa, Graduate Division, College of Natural Sciences, Department of Information and Computer Sciences, Library and Information Science Program, Honolulu, HI 96822-2233. Offers advanced library and information science (Graduate Certificate); library and information science (MLI Sc). *Accreditation:* ALA (one or more programs are accredited). Part-time programs available. *Degree requirements:* For master's, comprehensive exam, thesis optional. *Entrance requirements:* For master's, GRE General Test. Additional exam requirements/recommendations for international students: Required—TOEFL (minimum score 600 paper-based; 250 computer-based). Electronic applications accepted. *Faculty research:* Information behavior, evaluation of electronic information sources, online learning, history of libraries, information literacy.

University of Illinois at Urbana–Champaign, Graduate College, Graduate School of Library and Information Science, Champaign, IL 61820. Offers bioinformatics (MS); digital libraries (CAS); library and information science (MS, PhD, CAS). *Accreditation:* ALA (one or more programs are accredited). Postbaccalaureate distance learning degree programs offered. *Faculty:* 25 full-time (12 women), 5 part-time/adjunct (4 women). *Students:* 349 full-time (256 women), 353 part-time (276 women); includes 125 minority (30 Black or African American, non-Hispanic/Latino; 1 American Indian or Alaska Native, non-Hispanic/Latino; 37 Asian, non-Hispanic/Latino; 40 Hispanic/Latino; 1 Native Hawaiian or other Pacific Islander, non-Hispanic/Latino; 16 Two or more races, non-Hispanic/Latino), 27 international. 606 applicants, 68% accepted, 250 enrolled. In 2011, 245 master's, 6 doctorates, 8 other advanced degrees awarded. *Entrance requirements:* For master's, GRE General Test, minimum GPA of 3.0; for doctorate, minimum GPA of 3.0; for CAS, master's degree in library and information science or related field with minimum GPA of 3.0. Additional exam requirements/recommendations for international students: Required—TOEFL (minimum score 620 paper-based; 260 computer-based; 105 iBT) or IELTS (minimum score 7). *Application deadline:* Applications are processed on a rolling basis. Application fee: $75 ($90 for international students). Electronic applications accepted. *Financial support:* In 2011–12, 24 fellowships, 39 research assistantships, 44 teaching assistantships were awarded; tuition waivers (full and partial) also available. *Unit head:* Allen Renear, Dean, 217-265-5216, Fax: 217-244-3302, E-mail: renear@illinois.edu. *Application contact:* Valerie Youngen, Admissions and Records Representative, 217-333-0734, Fax: 217-244-3302, E-mail: vyoungen@llinois.edu. Web site: http://www.lis.illinois.edu.

The University of Iowa, Graduate College, School of Library and Information Science, Iowa City, IA 52242-1316. Offers MA, MA/Certificate, MBA/MA. *Accreditation:* ALA (one or more programs are accredited). *Degree requirements:* For master's, thesis optional, exam, portfolio. *Entrance requirements:* For master's, GRE General Test, minimum GPA of 3.0. Additional exam requirements/recommendations for international students: Required—TOEFL (minimum score 550 paper-based; 213 computer-based; 81 iBT). Electronic applications accepted.

University of Maryland, College Park, Academic Affairs, College of Information Studies, College Park, MD 20742. Offers MIM, MLS, PhD, MA/MLS. *Accreditation:* ALA (one or more programs are accredited). Part-time and evening/weekend programs available. *Faculty:* 27 full-time (12 women), 21 part-time/adjunct (16 women). *Students:* 242 full-time (175 women), 223 part-time (164 women); includes 85 minority (32 Black or African American, non-Hispanic/Latino; 2 American Indian or Alaska Native, non-Hispanic/Latino; 21 Asian, non-Hispanic/Latino; 17 Hispanic/Latino; 13 Two or more races, non-Hispanic/Latino), 47 international. 759 applicants, 59% accepted, 171 enrolled. In 2011, 210 master's, 1 doctorate awarded. Terminal master's awarded for partial completion of doctoral program. *Degree requirements:* For master's, thesis optional; for doctorate, comprehensive exam, thesis/dissertation, 1-year residency. *Entrance requirements:* For master's and doctorate, GRE General Test, minimum GPA of 3.0, 3 letters of recommendation. Additional exam requirements/recommendations for international students: Required—TOEFL. *Application deadline:* For fall admission, 12/1 for domestic students, 11/1 for international students. Applications are processed on a rolling basis. Application fee: $75. Electronic applications accepted. *Expenses: Tuition, area resident:* Part-time $525 per credit hour. Tuition, state resident: part-time $525 per credit hour. Tuition, nonresident: part-time $1131 per credit hour. *Required fees:* $386.31 per term. Tuition and fees vary according to program. *Financial support:* In 2011–12, 33 fellowships with full and partial tuition reimbursements (averaging $10,677 per year), 2 research assistantships (averaging $16,706 per year), 74 teaching assistantships (averaging $16,207 per year) were awarded; career-related internships or fieldwork, Federal Work-Study, scholarships/grants, and tuition waivers (full and partial) also available. Support available to part-time students. Financial award application deadline: 2/1; financial award applicants required to submit FAFSA. *Total annual research expenditures:* $3 million. *Unit head:* Dr. Jennifer Preece, Dean, 301-405-2036, Fax: 301-314-9145, E-mail: preece@umd.edu. *Application contact:* Dr. Charles A. Caramello, Dean of Graduate School, 301-405-0358, Fax: 301-314-9305.

University of Michigan, Horace H. Rackham School of Graduate Studies, School of Information, Ann Arbor, MI 48109-1285. Offers archives and records management (MSI); community informatics (MSI); health informatics (MS); human computer interaction (MSI); information (PhD); information analysis and retrieval (MSI); information economics for management (MSI); information policy (MSI); library and information science (MSI); preservation of information (MSI); school library media (MSI); social computing (MSI). *Accreditation:* ALA (one or more programs are accredited). *Entrance requirements:* For master's and doctorate, GRE General Test. Additional exam requirements/recommendations for international students: Required—TOEFL (minimum score 600 paper-based; 100 iBT). Electronic applications accepted.

University of Missouri, Graduate School, College of Education, School of Information Science and Learning Technologies, Columbia, MO 65211. Offers educational technology (M Ed, Ed S); information science and learning technology (PhD); library science (MA). *Accreditation:* ALA (one or more programs are accredited). Part-time and evening/weekend programs available. *Faculty:* 16 full-time (11 women), 1 (woman) part-time/adjunct. *Students:* 125 full-time (89 women), 296 part-time (214 women); includes 19 minority (6 Black or African American, non-Hispanic/Latino; 1 American Indian or Alaska Native, non-Hispanic/Latino; 3 Asian, non-Hispanic/Latino; 8 Hispanic/Latino; 1 Two or more races, non-Hispanic/Latino), 22 international. Average age 34. 159 applicants, 66% accepted, 78 enrolled. In 2011, 154 master's, 3 doctorates, 20 other advanced degrees awarded. *Entrance requirements:* For master's, GRE General Test or MAT, minimum GPA of 3.0. Additional exam requirements/recommendations for international students: Required—TOEFL (minimum score 540 paper-based; 207 computer-based; 76 iBT). *Application deadline:* For fall admission, 3/1 priority date for domestic students; for winter admission, 10/1 priority date for domestic students; for spring admission, 3/1 priority date for domestic students. Applications are processed on a rolling basis. Application fee: $55 ($75 for international students). *Expenses:* Tuition, state resident: full-time $5881. Tuition, nonresident: full-time $15,183. *Required fees:* $952. Tuition and fees vary according to campus/location and program. *Financial support:* Fellowships and teaching assistantships available. *Faculty research:* Problem-based learning, technology usability in classrooms, computer-based performance support tools for children and youth with learning disabilities and/or emotional/behavioral disorders, engineering education collaboration environment , effectiveness of activities designed to recruit and retain women in engineering and science. *Unit head:* Dr. John Wedman, Director, E-mail: wedmanj@missouri.edu. *Application contact:* Amy Adam, 573-884-1391, E-mail: adamae@missouri.edu. Web site: http://education.missouri.edu/SISLT/.

The University of North Carolina at Chapel Hill, Graduate School, School of Information and Library Science, Chapel Hill, NC 27599. Offers MSIS, MSLS, PhD, CAS. *Accreditation:* ALA (one or more programs are accredited). Part-time programs available. Terminal master's awarded for partial completion of doctoral program. *Degree requirements:* For master's, comprehensive exam, paper or project; for doctorate, comprehensive exam, thesis/dissertation. *Entrance requirements:* For master's and doctorate, GRE General Test. Additional exam requirements/recommendations for international students: Required—TOEFL (minimum score 625 paper-based; 263 computer-based). Electronic applications accepted. *Faculty research:* Information retrieval and management, digital libraries, management of information resources, archives and records management, health informatics.

The University of North Carolina at Greensboro, Graduate School, School of Education, Department of Library and Information Studies, Greensboro, NC 27412-5001. Offers MLIS. *Accreditation:* ALA. Part-time and evening/weekend programs available. Postbaccalaureate distance learning degree programs offered (no on-campus study). *Degree requirements:* For master's, portfolio. *Entrance requirements:* For master's, GRE General Test. Additional exam requirements/recommendations for international students: Required—TOEFL (minimum score 550 paper-based; 213 computer-based), IELTS (minimum score 6.5). Electronic applications accepted. *Faculty research:* Library history, gender studies, children's literature, web design, homeless, technical services.

University of North Texas, Toulouse Graduate School, College of Information, Department of Library and Information Sciences, Denton, TX 76203. Offers information science (MS, PhD); learning technologies (M Ed, Ed D), including applied technology, training and development (M Ed), computer education and cognitive systems, educational computing; library science (MS). *Accreditation:* ALA (one or more programs are accredited). Part-time and evening/weekend programs available. *Degree requirements:* For master's, comprehensive exam; for doctorate, comprehensive exam, thesis/dissertation. *Entrance requirements:* For master's, GRE General Test, MAT; for doctorate, GRE General Test. Additional exam requirements/recommendations for international students: Recommended—TOEFL (minimum score 550 paper-based; 213 computer-based; 79 iBT). Electronic applications accepted. *Expenses:* Tuition, state resident: part-time $100 per credit hour. Tuition, nonresident: part-time $413 per credit hour. *Faculty research:* Information resources and services, information management and retrieval, computer-based information systems, human information behavior.

University of Oklahoma, College of Arts and Sciences, School of Library and Information Studies, Program in Library and Information Studies, Norman, OK 73019-0390. Offers library and information studies (MLIS); library information studies (Graduate Certificate); M Ed/MLIS; MBA/MLIS. Part-time and evening/weekend programs available. Postbaccalaureate distance learning degree programs offered. *Students:* 60 full-time (47 women), 121 part-time (97 women); includes 32 minority (8 Black or African American, non-Hispanic/Latino; 13 American Indian or Alaska Native, non-Hispanic/Latino; 4 Asian, non-Hispanic/Latino; 3 Hispanic/Latino; 4 Two or more races, non-Hispanic/Latino), 3 international. Average age 33. 77 applicants, 94% accepted, 47 enrolled. In 2011, 59 degrees awarded. *Degree requirements:* For master's, comprehensive exam (MLIS). *Entrance requirements:* For master's, GRE, minimum GPA of 3.2 in last 60 hours or 3.0 overall. Additional exam requirements/recommendations for international students: Required—TOEFL (minimum score 550 paper-based; 213 computer-based; 79 iBT). *Application deadline:* For fall admission, 3/1 priority date for domestic students, 4/1 for international students; for spring admission, 10/15 for domestic students, 9/1 for international students. Applications are processed on a rolling basis. Application fee: $40 ($90 for international students). Electronic applications accepted. *Expenses:* Tuition, state resident: full-time $4087; part-time $170.30 per credit hour. Tuition, nonresident: full-time $14,875; part-time $619.80 per credit hour. *Required fees:* $2659; $100.25 per credit hour. Tuition and fees vary according to course load and degree level. *Financial support:* In 2011–12, 88 students received support. Federal Work-Study, scholarships/grants, health care benefits, and unspecified assistantships available. Support available to part-time students. Financial award applicants required to submit FAFSA. *Faculty research:* Equity of access, information services to special populations, information use in the digital age, library services and materials for young people, pluralization of archival theory and education. *Unit head:* Cecelia Brown, Director, 405-325-3921, Fax: 405-325-7648, E-mail: cbrown@ou.edu. *Application contact:* Maggie Ryan, Coordinator of Admissions, 405-325-3921, Fax: 405-325-7648, E-mail: mryan@ou.edu.

University of Pittsburgh, School of Information Sciences, Library and Information Science Program, Pittsburgh, PA 15260. Offers health sciences librarianship (Certificate); library and information science (MLIS, PhD). *Accreditation:* ALA (one or more programs are accredited). Part-time and evening/weekend programs available. Postbaccalaureate distance learning degree programs offered (minimal on-campus study). *Faculty:* 9 full-time (5 women), 6 part-time/adjunct (5 women). *Students:* 167 full-time (133 women), 177 part-time (145 women); includes 35 minority (11 Black or African American, non-Hispanic/Latino; 1 American Indian or Alaska Native, non-Hispanic/Latino; 7 Asian, non-Hispanic/Latino; 11 Hispanic/Latino; 5 Two or more races, non-Hispanic/Latino), 15 international. 382 applicants, 85% accepted, 154 enrolled. In 2011, 217 master's, 5 doctorates, 11 other advanced degrees awarded. *Degree requirements:* For master's, thesis optional; for doctorate, comprehensive exam, thesis/dissertation. *Entrance requirements:* For master's, GRE General Test or MAT, bachelor's degree from accredited university; minimum GPA of 3.0; for doctorate, GRE General Test, minimum GPA of 3.5; for Certificate, MLIS, MSIS with minimum GPA of 3.0. Additional exam requirements/recommendations for international students: Required—TOEFL (minimum score 550 paper-based; 80 iBT). *Application deadline:* For fall admission, 1/15 priority date for domestic students, 1/15 for international students. Applications are processed on a rolling basis. Application fee: $50. Electronic applications accepted. *Expenses:* Contact institution. *Financial support:* Fellowships with full tuition reimbursements, research assistantships with full and partial tuition reimbursements, teaching assistantships with full and partial tuition reimbursements, career-related internships or fieldwork, scholarships/grants, health care benefits, tuition waivers (full and partial), and unspecified assistantships available. Financial award application deadline: 1/15; financial award applicants required to submit FAFSA. *Faculty research:* Archives and preservation management, children's resources and services, digital libraries, cross-lingual information retrieval, cyberscholarship and cyberinfrastructure. *Unit head:* Dr. Martin Weiss, Chair, 412-624-9430, Fax: 412-624-5231, E-mail: mbw@pitt.edu. *Application contact:* Brandi Belleau Liskey, Student Recruiting Coordinator, 412-648-3108, Fax: 412-624-5231, E-mail: lisinq@sis.pitt.edu. Web site: http://www.ischool.pitt.edu/lis.

University of Puerto Rico, Río Piedras, Graduate School of Information Sciences and Technologies, San Juan, PR 00931-3300. Offers administration of academic libraries (PMC); administration of public libraries (PMC); administration of special libraries (PMC); consultant in information services (PMC); documents and files administration (Post-Graduate Certificate); electronic information resources analyst (Post-Graduate Certificate); information science (MIS); librarianship and information services (MLS); school librarian (Post-Graduate Certificate); school librarian distance education mode (Post-Graduate Certificate); specialist in legal information (PMC). *Accreditation:* ALA. Part-time programs available. *Degree requirements:* For master's, comprehensive exam, thesis, portfolio. *Entrance requirements:* For master's, PAEG, GRE, interview, minimum GPA of 3.0, 3 letters of recommendation; for other advanced degree, PAEG, GRE, minimum GPA of 3.0, IST master's degree. *Faculty research:* Investigating the users needs and preferences for a specialized environmental library.

University of Rhode Island, Graduate School, College of Arts and Sciences, Graduate School of Library and Information Studies, Kingston, RI 02881. Offers MLIS, MLIS/MA, MLIS/MPA. *Accreditation:* ALA (one or more programs are accredited). Part-time programs available. *Faculty:* 3 full-time (all women), 6 part-time/adjunct (4 women). *Students:* 40 full-time (29 women), 89 part-time (74 women); includes 5 minority (2 Asian, non-Hispanic/Latino; 2 Hispanic/Latino; 1 Two or more races, non-Hispanic/Latino). In 2011, 62 master's awarded. *Degree requirements:* For master's, comprehensive exam. *Entrance requirements:* For master's, GRE or MAT (if undergraduate GPA less than 3.0), 2 letters of recommendation. Additional exam requirements/recommendations for international students: Required—TOEFL (minimum score 550 paper-based; 213 computer-based). *Application deadline:* For fall admission, 6/15 for domestic students, 2/1 for international students; for spring admission, 10/15 for domestic students, 7/15 for international students. Application fee: $65. Electronic applications accepted. *Expenses:* Tuition, state resident: full-time $10,432; part-time $580 per credit hour. Tuition, nonresident: full-time $23,130; part-time $1285 per credit hour. *Required fees:* $1362; $36 per credit hour. $35 per semester. One-time fee: $130. *Financial support:* Application deadline: 1/15; applicants required to submit FAFSA. *Unit head:* Dr. Gale Eaton, Director, 401-874-4641, Fax: 401-874-4964, E-mail: geaton@uri.edu. *Application contact:* Nasser H. Zawia, Dean of the Graduate School, 401-874-5909, Fax: 401-874-5787, E-mail: nzawia@uri.edu. Web site: http://www.uri.edu/artsci/lsc/.

University of South Carolina, The Graduate School, College of Mass Communications and Information Studies, School of Library and Information Science, Columbia, SC 29208. Offers MLIS, PhD, Certificate, Specialist, MLIS/MA. *Accreditation:* ALA (one or more programs are accredited). Part-time programs available. Postbaccalaureate distance learning degree programs offered (no on-campus study). *Degree requirements:* For master's, end of program portfolio; for doctorate, comprehensive exam, thesis/dissertation. *Entrance requirements:* For master's and other advanced degree, GRE General Test or MAT; for doctorate, GTE, writing sample. Additional exam requirements/recommendations for international students: Required—TOEFL (minimum score 570 paper-based; 230 computer-based; 75 iBT). Electronic applications accepted. *Faculty research:* Information technology management, distance education, library services for children and young adults, special libraries.

University of South Florida, Graduate School, College of Arts and Sciences, School of Information, Tampa, FL 33620-9951. Offers library and information science (MA). *Accreditation:* ALA. Part-time and evening/weekend programs available. Postbaccalaureate distance learning degree programs offered (minimal on-campus study). *Faculty:* 12 full-time (8 women), 19 part-time/adjunct (12 women). *Students:* 106 full-time (87 women), 188 part-time (166 women); includes 60 minority (16 Black or African American, non-Hispanic/Latino; 2 American Indian or Alaska Native, non-Hispanic/Latino; 8 Asian, non-Hispanic/Latino; 32 Hispanic/Latino; 2 Two or more races, non-Hispanic/Latino), 2 international. Average age 34. 137 applicants, 55% accepted, 50 enrolled. In 2011, 152 master's awarded. *Degree requirements:* For master's, comprehensive exam, thesis optional. *Entrance requirements:* For master's, GRE, minimum GPA of 3.25 in upper-division course work, personal statement, writing sample. Additional exam requirements/recommendations for international students: Required—TOEFL (minimum score 550 paper-based; 213 computer-based; 79 iBT) or IELTS (minimum score 6.5). *Application deadline:* For fall admission, 6/1 for domestic students, 1/2 for international students; for spring admission, 10/15 for domestic students, 6/1 for international students. Applications are processed on a rolling basis. Application fee: $30. Electronic applications accepted. *Financial support:* Unspecified assistantships available. Financial award application deadline: 6/30. *Faculty research:* Youth services in libraries, community engagement and libraries, information architecture, biomedical informatics. *Total annual research expenditures:* $11,976. *Unit head:* Jim Andrews, Director, 813-974-2108, Fax: 813-974-6840, E-mail: jandrews@cas.usf.edu. *Application contact:* Sylvia Gardner, Administrative Assistant, 813-974-0853, Fax: 813-974-5911, E-mail: gardner@cas.usf.edu. Web site: http://si.usf.edu/.

The University of Texas at Austin, Graduate School, School of Information, Austin, TX 78712-1111. Offers MSIS, PhD, MSIS/MA. *Accreditation:* ALA (one or more programs are accredited). Part-time programs available. *Degree requirements:* For doctorate, 2 foreign languages, thesis/dissertation. *Entrance requirements:* For master's and doctorate, GRE General Test. *Application deadline:* For fall admission, 2/1 priority date for domestic students; for winter admission, 4/1 for domestic students; for spring admission, 10/1 for domestic students. Applications are processed on a rolling basis. Application fee: $50 ($75 for international students). Electronic applications accepted. *Financial support:* Fellowships, research assistantships, teaching assistantships, career-related internships or fieldwork, Federal Work-Study, and tuition waivers (partial) available. Support available to part-time students. Financial award application deadline: 2/1. *Faculty research:* Information retrieval and artificial intelligence, library history and administration, classification and cataloguing. *Unit head:* Andrew I. Dillon, Dean, 512-471-3821, Fax: 512-471-3971, E-mail: adillion@ischool.utexas.edu. *Application contact:* Dr. Philip Doty, Associate Dean, 512-471-3746, Fax: 512-471-3971, E-mail: pdoty@ischool.utexas.edu. Web site: http://www.ischool.utexas.edu/.

University of Toronto, School of Graduate Studies, Faculty of Information Studies, Toronto, ON M5S 1A1, Canada. Offers information (MI, PhD); museum studies (MM St); JD/MI. *Accreditation:* ALA (one or more programs are accredited). Part-time programs available. *Degree requirements:* For master's, thesis optional; for doctorate, thesis/dissertation, oral exam/thesis defense. *Entrance requirements:* For master's, 2 letters of reference; for doctorate, 3 letters of reference, minimum B+ average. Additional exam requirements/recommendations for international students: Required—TOEFL (minimum score 600 paper-based; 100 iBT), IELTS (minimum score 8), TWE (minimum score 5.5), or Michigan English Language Assessment Battery (minimum score 95). Application fee: $125 Canadian dollars. Electronic applications accepted. *Expenses:* Contact institution. *Unit head:* Prof. Seamus Ross, Dean, 416-978-3202, Fax: 416-978-5762. *Application contact:* Secretary, 416-978-3234, Fax: 416-978-5762, E-mail: inquire.ischool@utoronto.ca. Web site: http://www.ischool.utoronto.ca/.

The University of Western Ontario, Faculty of Graduate Studies, Faculty of Information and Media Studies, Programs in Library and Information Science, London, ON N6A 5B8, Canada. Offers MLIS, PhD. Program conducted on a trimester basis. *Accreditation:* ALA (one or more programs are accredited). Part-time and evening/weekend programs available. *Degree requirements:* For doctorate, comprehensive exam, thesis/dissertation. *Entrance requirements:* For master's, honors degree, minimum B average during previous 2 years of course work; for doctorate, MLIS or equivalent. Additional exam requirements/recommendations for international students: Required—TOEFL (minimum score 625 paper-based; 263 computer-based), TWE (minimum score 5). Electronic applications accepted. *Faculty research:* Information, individuals, and society; information systems, policy, power, and institutions.

University of Wisconsin–Madison, Graduate School, College of Letters and Science, School of Library and Information Studies, Madison, WI 53706-1380. Offers MA, PhD. *Accreditation:* ALA (one or more programs are accredited). Part-time programs available. *Degree requirements:* For doctorate, comprehensive exam, thesis/dissertation. Electronic applications accepted. *Expenses:* Tuition, state resident: full-time $10,296; part-time $643.51 per credit. Tuition, nonresident: full-time $24,054; part-time $1503.40 per credit. *Required fees:* $70.06 per credit. Tuition and fees vary according to course load, campus/location, program and reciprocity agreements. *Faculty research:* Intellectual freedom, children's literature, print culture history, information systems design and evaluation, school library media centers.

University of Wisconsin–Milwaukee, Graduate School, School of Information Studies, Milwaukee, WI 53201-0413. Offers advanced studies in library and information science (CAS); archives and records administration (CAS); digital libraries (Certificate); information studies (MLIS, PhD); MLIS/MA; MLIS/MM; MLIS/MS. *Accreditation:* ALA (one or more programs are accredited). Part-time programs available. *Faculty:* 22 full-time (11 women). *Students:* 173 full-time (136 women), 426 part-time (339 women); includes 60 minority (16 Black or African American, non-Hispanic/Latino; 1 American Indian or Alaska Native, non-Hispanic/Latino; 14 Asian, non-Hispanic/Latino; 8 Hispanic/Latino; 21 Two or more races, non-Hispanic/Latino), 30 international. Average age 34. 291 applicants, 73% accepted, 122 enrolled. In 2011, 182 master's awarded. *Entrance requirements:* For master's, GRE General Test or MAT; for doctorate, GRE. Additional exam requirements/recommendations for international students: Required—TOEFL (minimum score 550 paper-based; 213 computer-based), IELTS (minimum score 6.5). *Application deadline:* For fall admission, 1/1 priority date for domestic students; for spring admission, 9/1 for domestic students. Applications are processed on a rolling basis. Application fee: $56 ($96 for international students). Electronic applications accepted. One-time fee: $506.10 full-time. Tuition and fees vary according to course load and reciprocity agreements. *Financial support:* In 2011–12, 4 teaching assistantships were awarded; fellowships, research assistantships, career-related internships or fieldwork, Federal Work-Study, health care benefits, unspecified assistantships, and project assistantships also available. Support available to part-time students. Financial award application deadline: 4/15; financial award applicants required to submit FAFSA. *Total annual research expenditures:* $302,657. *Unit head:* Dietmar Wolfram, Interim Dean, 414-229-4709, E-mail: dwolfram@uwm.edu. *Application contact:* Hur-Li Lee, Representative, 414-229-6838, E-mail: hurli@uwm.edu. Web site: http://www.uwm.edu/Dept/SLIS/.

Valdosta State University, Program in Library and Information Science, Valdosta, GA 31698. Offers MLIS. *Accreditation:* ALA. Postbaccalaureate distance learning degree programs offered (minimal on-campus study). *Faculty:* 7 full-time (3 women). *Students:* 22 full-time (15 women), 213 part-time (170 women); includes 54 minority (32 Black or African American, non-Hispanic/Latino; 6 Asian, non-Hispanic/Latino; 16 Two or more races, non-Hispanic/Latino). Average age 30. 91 applicants, 62% accepted, 37 enrolled. In 2011, 48 master's awarded. *Degree requirements:* For master's, comprehensive exam. *Entrance requirements:* For master's, two essays, resume, three recommendations. Additional exam requirements/recommendations for international students: Required—TOEFL (minimum score 523 paper-based; 193 computer-based). *Application deadline:* For fall admission, 4/14 for domestic students, 4/15 for international students. Application fee: $35. *Expenses:* Tuition, state resident: full-time $7098; part-time $217 per hour. Tuition, nonresident: full-time $20,630; part-time $780 per hour. *Financial support:* In 2011–12, 4 students received support, including 4 research assistantships with full tuition reimbursements available (averaging $3,652 per year); institutionally sponsored loans, scholarships/grants, and unspecified assistantships also available. Support available to part-time students. Financial award application deadline: 7/1; financial award applicants required to submit FAFSA. *Unit head:* Dr. Wallace Koehler, Director, 229-245-3732, Fax: 229-333-5862, E-mail: wkoehler@valdosta.edu. *Application contact:* Jessica DeVane, Admissions Specialist, 229-333-5694, Fax: 229-245-3853, E-mail: jldevane@valdosta.edu.

Wayne State University, School of Library and Information Science, Detroit, MI 48202. Offers archival administration (MLIS, Certificate); arts and museum librarianship (Certificate); general librarianship (MLIS); health sciences librarianship (MLIS); information management for librarians (Certificate); information science (MLIS); law librarianship (MLIS); library and information science (MLIS, Spec), including academic libraries (MLIS); organization of information (MLIS); public libraries (MLIS); public library services to children and young adults (MLIS, Certificate); records and information management (Certificate); records management (MLIS); references services (MLIS); school library media (Spec); school library media specialist endorsement (MLIS); special libraries (MLIS); urban librarianship (Certificate); urban libraries (MLIS); MLIS/MA. *Accreditation:* ALA (one or more programs are accredited). Part-time and evening/weekend programs available. Postbaccalaureate distance learning degree programs offered (no on-campus study). *Faculty:* 13 full-time (8 women), 25 part-time/adjunct (19 women). *Students:* 121 full-time (93 women), 447 part-time (346 women); includes 57 minority (37 Black or African American, non-Hispanic/Latino; 1 American Indian or Alaska Native, non-Hispanic/Latino; 4 Asian, non-Hispanic/Latino; 7 Hispanic/Latino; 8 Two or more races, non-Hispanic/Latino), 4 international. Average age 33. 336 applicants, 62% accepted, 135 enrolled. In 2011, 212 master's, 38 other advanced degrees awarded. *Entrance requirements:* For master's and other advanced degree, GRE or MAT (if undergraduate GPA is between 2.5 and 2.99), minimum undergraduate GPA of 3.0 or graduate degree, personal statement, new student orientation. Additional exam requirements/recommendations for international students: Required—TOEFL (minimum score 550 paper-based; 213 computer-based); Recommended—TWE (minimum score 5.5). *Application deadline:* For fall admission, 7/1 for domestic students, 5/1 for international students; for winter admission, 10/1 for domestic students, 9/1 for international students; for spring admission, 3/15 for domestic students, 1/1 for international students. Applications are processed on a rolling basis. Application fee: $50. Electronic applications accepted. *Expenses:* Tuition, state resident: part-time $512.85 per credit. Tuition, nonresident: part-time $1132.65 per credit. *Required fees:* $26.60 per credit. $199.65 per semester. Tuition and fees vary according to course load and program. *Financial support:* In 2011–12, 1 research assistantship with tuition reimbursement (averaging $12,250 per year) was awarded; fellowships with tuition reimbursements, career-related internships or fieldwork, Federal Work-Study, institutionally sponsored loans, scholarships/grants, and unspecified assistantships also available. Support available to part-time students. Financial award application deadline: 5/15. *Faculty research:* Convergence of academic libraries and other academic services, competitive intelligence and data mining, impact of digitization on libraries, international librarianship, consumer health information, urban library issues, human-computer interaction, universal access to libraries and instructional support services. *Unit head:* Dr. Sandra Yee, Dean, 313-577-4059, Fax: 313-577-7563, E-mail: aj0533@wayne.edu. *Application contact:* Dr. Stephen Fredericks, Associate Dean and Director, 313-577-7563, E-mail: bajjaly@wayne.edu. Web site: http://www.lisp.wayne.edu/.

Library Science

Appalachian State University, Cratis D. Williams Graduate School, Department of Leadership and Educational Studies, Boone, NC 28608. Offers educational administration (Ed S); educational media (MA); higher education (MA, Ed S); library science (MLS); school administration (MSA). Part-time and evening/weekend programs available. Postbaccalaureate distance learning degree programs offered (no on-campus study). *Faculty:* 35 full-time (15 women), 1 (woman) part-time/adjunct. *Students:* 35 full-time (27 women), 369 part-time (293 women); includes 31 minority (26 Black or African American, non-Hispanic/Latino; 1 Asian, non-Hispanic/Latino; 4 Hispanic/Latino). 196 applicants, 83% accepted, 117 enrolled. In 2011, 195 master's, 32 other advanced degrees awarded. *Degree requirements:* For master's and Ed S, comprehensive exam, thesis optional. *Entrance requirements:* For master's and Ed S, GRE or MAT, 3 letters of recommendation. Additional exam requirements/recommendations for international students: Required—TOEFL (minimum score 570 paper-based; 230 computer-based; 79 iBT), IELTS (minimum score 6.5). *Application deadline:* For fall admission, 3/14 priority date for domestic students, 2/1 for international students; for spring admission, 11/1 for domestic students, 7/1 for international students. Applications are processed on a rolling basis. Application fee: $55. Electronic applications accepted. *Expenses:* Tuition, state resident: full-time $4040; part-time $180 per semester hour. Tuition, nonresident: full-time $15,900; part-time $760 per semester hour. *Required fees:* $2500; $20 per semester hour. Tuition and fees vary according to campus/location. *Financial support:* In 2011–12, 10 research assistantships (averaging $8,000 per year) were awarded; career-related internships or fieldwork, scholarships/grants, and unspecified assistantships also available. Financial award application deadline: 4/1; financial award applicants required to submit FAFSA. *Faculty research:* Brain, learning and meditation; leadership of teaching and learning. *Total annual research expenditures:* $515,000. *Unit head:* Dr. Robert Sanders, Interim Director, 828-262-3112, E-mail: sandersrl@appstate.edu. *Application contact:* Lori Dean, Graduate Student Coordinator, 828-262-6041, E-mail: deanlk@appstate.edu. Web site: http://www.les.appstate.edu.

Azusa Pacific University, School of Education, Department of Advanced Studies, Program in School Librarianship, Azusa, CA 91702-7000. Offers MA.

Azusa Pacific University, School of Education, Department of Advanced Studies, Program in Teacher Librarian Services, Azusa, CA 91702-7000. Offers Credential. Postbaccalaureate distance learning degree programs offered (no on-campus study).

The Catholic University of America, School of Library and Information Science, Washington, DC 20064. Offers MSLS, JD/MSLS, MSLS/MA, MSLS/MS. *Accreditation:* ALA (one or more programs are accredited). Part-time programs available. *Faculty:* 7 full-time (5 women), 16 part-time/adjunct (7 women). *Students:* 31 full-time (25 women), 182 part-time (128 women); includes 58 minority (33 Black or African American, non-Hispanic/Latino; 8 Asian, non-Hispanic/Latino; 12 Hispanic/Latino; 1 Native Hawaiian or other Pacific Islander, non-Hispanic/Latino; 4 Two or more races, non-Hispanic/Latino), 3 international. Average age 34. 147 applicants, 82% accepted, 58 enrolled. In 2011, 83 degrees awarded. *Degree requirements:* For master's, comprehensive exam. *Entrance requirements:* For master's, statement of purpose, official copies of academic transcripts, three letters of recommendation, interview. Additional exam requirements/recommendations for international students: Required—TOEFL (minimum score 580 paper-based; 237 computer-based). *Application deadline:* For fall admission, 8/1 priority date for domestic students, 7/15 for international students; for spring admission, 11/1 priority date for domestic students, 10/15 for international students. Applications are processed on a rolling basis. Application fee: $55. Electronic applications accepted. *Expenses:* Contact institution. *Financial support:* Fellowships, research assistantships, teaching assistantships, Federal Work-Study, scholarships/grants, tuition waivers (full and partial), and unspecified assistantships available. Financial award application deadline: 2/1; financial award applicants required to submit FAFSA. *Faculty research:* Digital collections, library and information science education, information design and architecture, information system design and evaluation. *Total annual research expenditures:* $5,870. *Unit head:* Dr. Ingrid Hsieh-Yee, Acting Dean, 202-319-5085, Fax: 202-319-5574, E-mail: hsiehyee@cua.edu. *Application contact:* Andrew Woodall, Director of Graduate Admissions, 202-319-5057, Fax: 202-319-6533, E-mail: cua-admissions@cua.edu. Web site: http://slis.cua.edu/.

Chicago State University, School of Graduate and Professional Studies, College of Education, Department of Reading, Elementary Education, Library Information and Media Studies, Program in Library Information and Media Studies, Chicago, IL 60628. Offers MS Ed. *Entrance requirements:* For master's, minimum GPA of 2.75.

Clarion University of Pennsylvania, Office of Graduate Programs, Master of Science in Library Science Program, Clarion, PA 16214. Offers MSLS, CAS. *Accreditation:* ALA (one or more programs are accredited). Part-time programs available. *Students:* 120 full-time (91 women), 389 part-time (331 women); includes 30 minority (9 Black or African American, non-Hispanic/Latino; 5 Asian, non-Hispanic/Latino; 11 Hispanic/Latino; 1 Native Hawaiian or other Pacific Islander, non-Hispanic/Latino; 4 Two or more races, non-Hispanic/Latino), 7 international. Average age 35. In 2011, 296 master's awarded. *Degree requirements:* For master's, thesis or alternative. *Entrance requirements:* For master's, minimum QPA of 3.0. Additional exam requirements/recommendations for international students: Required—TOEFL (minimum score 550 paper-based; 213 computer-based; 80 iBT). *Application deadline:* For fall admission, 8/1 priority date for domestic students, 4/15 for international students; for spring admission, 12/1 priority date for domestic students, 9/15 for international students. Applications are processed on a rolling basis. Application fee: $30. Electronic applications accepted. *Expenses:* Tuition, state resident: part-time $429 per credit. Tuition, nonresident: part-time $644 per credit. *Financial support:* Research assistantships with partial tuition reimbursements available. Financial award application deadline: 3/1. *Unit head:* Dr. Janice Krueger, Chair, 814-393-2271, Fax: 814-393-2150. *Application contact:* Dr. Brenda Sanders Dede, Assistant Vice President for Academic Affairs, 814-393-2337, Fax: 814-393-2030, E-mail: bdede@clarion.edu. Web site: http://www.clarion.edu/1095/.

Dalhousie University, Faculty of Management, School of Information Management, Halifax, NS B3H 3J5, Canada. Offers MIM, MLIS, LL B/MLIS, MBA/MLIS, MLIS/MPA, MLIS/MREM. *Accreditation:* ALA (one or more programs are accredited). Part-time programs available. *Degree requirements:* For master's, one foreign language, thesis optional. *Entrance requirements:* For master's, resume, interview. Additional exam requirements/recommendations for international students: Required—TOEFL, IELTS, CANTEST, CAEL, or Michigan English Language Assessment Battery. Electronic applications accepted. *Faculty research:* Information-seeking behavior, electronic text design, browsing in digital environments, information diffusion among scientists.

Dominican University, Graduate School of Library and Information Science, River Forest, IL 60305-1099. Offers library and information science (MLIS, PhD); special studies (CSS); MBA/MLIS; MLIS/M Div; MLIS/MA; MLIS/MM. MLIS/M Div offered jointly with McCormick Theological Seminary; MLIS/MA with Loyola University Chicago; and MLIS/MM with Northwestern University. *Accreditation:* ALA (one or more programs are accredited). Part-time and evening/weekend programs available. Postbaccalaureate distance learning degree programs offered (minimal on-campus study). *Faculty:* 15 full-time (10 women), 24 part-time/adjunct (17 women). *Students:* 140 full-time (104 women), 312 part-time (247 women); includes 81 minority (26 Black or African American, non-Hispanic/Latino; 2 American Indian or Alaska Native, non-Hispanic/Latino; 10 Asian, non-Hispanic/Latino; 31 Hispanic/Latino; 1 Native Hawaiian or other Pacific Islander, non-Hispanic/Latino; 11 Two or more races, non-Hispanic/Latino), 4 international. Average age 33. 155 applicants, 95% accepted, 139 enrolled. In 2011, 214 master's awarded. *Entrance requirements:* For master's, minimum GPA of 3.0, GRE General Test, or MAT. Additional exam requirements/recommendations for international students: Required—TOEFL. *Application deadline:* For fall admission, 6/1 priority date for domestic students; for winter admission, 3/1 priority date for domestic students; for spring admission, 10/1 priority date for domestic students. Applications are processed on a rolling basis. Application fee: $25. *Expenses:* Contact institution. *Financial support:* Fellowships, research assistantships, career-related internships or fieldwork, Federal Work-Study, scholarships/grants, and tuition waivers (partial) available. Support available to part-time students. Financial award application deadline: 4/15; financial award applicants required to submit FAFSA. *Faculty research:* Productivity and the information environment, bibliometrics, library history, subject access, library materials and services for children. *Unit head:* Dr. Susan Roman, Dean, 708-524-6986, Fax: 708-524-6657, E-mail: sroman@dom.edu. *Application contact:* Raymond Kennelly, Senior Vice President of Enrollment Management, 708-524-6544, E-mail: rkennelly@dom.edu. Web site: http://www.dom.edu/gslis.

Drexel University, The iSchool at Drexel, College of Information Science and Technology, Philadelphia, PA 19104-2875. Offers MS, MSIS, MSSE, PhD, Advanced Certificate, Certificate, PMC. *Accreditation:* ALA (one or more programs are accredited). Part-time and evening/weekend programs available. Postbaccalaureate distance learning degree programs offered (no on-campus study). *Faculty:* 30 full-time (20 women), 29 part-time/adjunct (15 women). *Students:* 259 full-time (182 women), 643 part-time (433 women); includes 128 minority (53 Black or African American, non-Hispanic/Latino; 8 American Indian or Alaska Native, non-Hispanic/Latino; 37 Asian, non-Hispanic/Latino; 30 Hispanic/Latino), 56 international. Average age 34. 652 applicants, 69% accepted, 288 enrolled. In 2011, 332 master's, 9 doctorates, 16 other advanced degrees awarded. *Degree requirements:* For doctorate, thesis/dissertation. *Entrance requirements:* For master's and doctorate, GRE General Test. Additional exam requirements/recommendations for international students: Required—TOEFL (minimum score 600 paper-based; 250 computer-based; 100 iBT). *Application deadline:* For fall admission, 9/1 for domestic and international students; for spring admission, 3/4 for domestic students, 2/15 for international students. Applications are processed on a rolling basis. Electronic applications accepted. *Expenses:* Contact institution. *Financial support:* In 2011–12, 282 students received support, including 282 fellowships with partial tuition reimbursements available (averaging $22,500 per year), 25 research assistantships with full tuition reimbursements available (averaging $22,500 per year), 10 teaching assistantships with full tuition reimbursements available (averaging $22,250 per year); institutionally sponsored loans, scholarships/grants, health care benefits, tuition waivers (partial), and unspecified assistantships also available. Support available to part-time students. Financial award application deadline: 3/1; financial award applicants required to submit FAFSA. *Faculty research:* Information retrieval/information visualization/bibliometrics, human-computer interaction, digital libraries, databases, text/data mining. *Total annual research expenditures:* $2 million. *Unit head:* Dr. David E. Fenske, Dean/Professor of Information Science, 215-895-2475, Fax: 215-895-6378, E-mail: fenske@drexel.edu. *Application contact:* Matthew Lechtenberg, Graduate Admissions Manager, 215-895-1951, Fax: 215-895-2303, E-mail: ml333@drexel.edu. Web site: http://www.ischool.drexel.edu/.

East Carolina University, Graduate School, College of Education, Department of Library Science, Greenville, NC 27858-4353. Offers MLS. *Accreditation:* NCATE. Part-time and evening/weekend programs available. Postbaccalaureate distance learning degree programs offered (no on-campus study). *Degree requirements:* For master's, comprehensive exam, thesis optional. *Entrance requirements:* For master's, GRE General Test or MAT, interview, minimum GPA of 2.5, bachelor's degree in related field, teaching license (MA Ed). Additional exam requirements/recommendations for international students: Required—TOEFL. *Application deadline:* For fall admission, 6/1 priority date for domestic students. Applications are processed on a rolling basis. Application fee: $50. *Expenses:* Tuition, state resident: full-time $3557; part-time $444.63 per semester hour. Tuition, nonresident: full-time $14,351; part-time $1793.88 per semester hour. *Required fees:* $2016; $252 per semester hour. Part-time tuition and fees vary according to course load, campus/location and program. *Financial support:* Research assistantships, teaching assistantships, and Federal Work-Study available. Support available to part-time students. Financial award application deadline: 6/1. *Unit head:* John B. Harer, Interim Chair, 252-328-4389, E-mail: harerj@ecu.edu. *Application contact:* Dean of Graduate School, 252-328-6012, Fax: 252-328-6071, E-mail: gradschool@ecu.edu. Web site: http://www.ecu.edu/cs-educ/libs/index.cfm.

Eastern Kentucky University, The Graduate School, College of Education, Department of Curriculum and Instruction, Richmond, KY 40475-3102. Offers elementary education (MA Ed), including early elementary education, reading; library science (MA Ed); music education (MA Ed); secondary and higher education (MA Ed), including secondary education; teaching (MAT). *Accreditation:* NCATE. Part-time programs available. *Degree requirements:* For master's, portfolio is part of exam. *Entrance requirements:* For master's, GRE General Test, PRAXIS II (KY), minimum GPA of 2.5. *Faculty research:* Technology in education, reading instruction, e-portfolios, induction to teacher education, dispositions of teachers.

East Tennessee State University, School of Graduate Studies, College of Education, Department of Curriculum and Instruction, Johnson City, TN 37614. Offers educational media/educational technology (M Ed), including educational communications and technology, school library media; elementary education (M Ed); reading (MA), including reading education, storytelling; school library professional (Post-Master's Certificate); secondary education (M Ed), including classroom technology, secondary education (M Ed, MAT); storytelling (Postbaccalaureate Certificate); teacher education with multiple levels (initial licensure) (MAT), including elementary education, middle grades education, secondary education (M Ed, MAT). *Accreditation:* NCATE. Part-time and evening/weekend programs available. Postbaccalaureate distance learning degree programs offered (no on-campus study). *Faculty:* 20 full-time (13 women), 3 part-time/adjunct (all women). *Students:* 108 full-time (76 women), 107 part-time (97 women); includes 9 minority (4 Black or African American, non-Hispanic/Latino; 1 Asian, non-Hispanic/Latino; 2 Hispanic/Latino; 2 Two or more races, non-Hispanic/Latino), 2 international. Average age 33. 141 applicants, 57% accepted, 79 enrolled. In 2011, 129 master's awarded. *Degree requirements:* For master's, comprehensive exam, thesis optional, student teaching, practicum; for other advanced degree, field work (school library); culminating experience (storytelling). *Entrance requirements:* For master's, GRE, SAT, ACT, PRAXIS, minimum GPA of 3.0; for other advanced degree, master's degree, TN teaching license (school library professional post-master's certificate); three letters of recommendation (storytelling certificate). Additional exam requirements/recommendations for international students: Required—TOEFL (minimum score 550 paper-based; 213 computer-based; 79 iBT). *Application deadline:* For fall admission, 6/1 for domestic students, 4/30 for international students; for spring admission, 11/1 for domestic students, 4/30 for international students. Application fee: $35 ($45 for international students). Electronic applications accepted. *Expenses:* Tuition, state resident: full-time $7312; part-time $350 per credit hour. Tuition, nonresident: full-time $18,490; part-time $621 per credit hour. *Required fees:* $63 per credit hour. Tuition and fees vary according to course load and program. *Financial support:* In 2011–12, 60 students received support, including 7 research assistantships with full tuition reimbursements available (averaging $6,000 per year), 11 teaching assistantships with full tuition reimbursements available (averaging $6,000 per year); career-related internships or fieldwork, institutionally sponsored loans, scholarships/grants, and unspecified assistantships also available. Financial award application deadline: 7/1; financial award applicants required to submit FAFSA. *Faculty research:* Critical thinking; curriculum development in reading, math, and science education; cultural diversity; cognitive processes; effective teaching strategies. *Unit head:* Dr. Rhona Hurwitz, Chair, 423-439-7598, Fax: 423-439-8362, E-mail: hurwitz@etsu.edu. *Application contact:* Fiona Goodyear, Graduate Specialist, 423-439-6148, Fax: 423-439-5624, E-mail: goodyear@etsu.edu.

Emporia State University, Graduate School, School of Library and Information Management, Emporia, KS 66801-5087. Offers archives studies (Certificate); legal information management (Certificate); library and information management (MLS, PhD, Certificate). *Accreditation:* ALA (one or more programs are accredited). Part-time and evening/weekend programs available. Postbaccalaureate distance learning degree programs offered (minimal on-campus study). *Faculty:* 8 full-time (4 women). *Students:* 22 full-time (19 women), 326 part-time (258 women); includes 31 minority (4 Black or African American, non-Hispanic/Latino; 1 American Indian or Alaska Native, non-Hispanic/Latino; 9 Asian, non-Hispanic/Latino; 10 Hispanic/Latino; 4 Native Hawaiian or other Pacific Islander, non-Hispanic/Latino; 3 Two or more races, non-Hispanic/Latino), 3 international. 125 applicants, 77% accepted, 78 enrolled. In 2011, 133 master's, 1 doctorate, 7 other advanced degrees awarded. *Degree requirements:* For master's, comprehensive exam, thesis optional; for doctorate, thesis/dissertation. *Entrance requirements:* For master's, GRE General Test, interview, minimum undergraduate GPA of 3.0, letters of recommendation; for doctorate, GRE General Test, interview, minimum graduate GPA of 3.5. Additional exam requirements/recommendations for international students: Required—TOEFL (minimum score 520 paper-based; 133 computer-based; 68 iBT). *Application deadline:* For fall admission, 8/15 priority date for domestic students. Applications are processed on a rolling basis. Application fee: $30 ($75 for international students). Electronic applications accepted. *Expenses:* Tuition, state resident: full-time $2342; part-time $195 per credit hour. Tuition, nonresident: full-time $7254; part-time $605 per credit hour. *Required fees:* $66 per credit hour. Tuition and fees vary according to campus/location. *Financial support:* In 2011–12, 9 research assistantships with full tuition reimbursements (averaging $7,059 per year), 2 teaching assistantships with full tuition reimbursements (averaging $7,059 per year) were awarded; Federal Work-Study, institutionally sponsored loans, and unspecified assistantships also available. Financial award application deadline: 3/15; financial award applicants required to submit FAFSA. *Unit head:* Dr. Gwen Alexander, Interim Dean, 620-341-5203, Fax: 620-341-5233, E-mail: galexan1@emporia.edu. *Application* *contact:* Candace Boardman, Director, Kansas MLS Program, 620-341-6159, E-mail: cboardma@emporia.edu. Web site: http://www.emporia.edu/las/index.html.

Florida State University, The Graduate School, College of Communication and Information, School of Library and Information Studies, Tallahassee, FL 32306-2100. Offers MA, MS, PhD, Specialist. *Accreditation:* ALA (one or more programs are accredited). Part-time and evening/weekend programs available. Postbaccalaureate distance learning degree programs offered (no on-campus study). *Faculty:* 31 full-time (17 women), 16 part-time/adjunct (8 women). *Students:* 13 full-time (10 women), 532 part-time (395 women); includes 135 minority (47 Black or African American, non-Hispanic/Latino; 1 American Indian or Alaska Native, non-Hispanic/Latino; 29 Asian, non-Hispanic/Latino; 57 Hispanic/Latino; 1 Two or more races, non-Hispanic/Latino). Average age 35. 235 applicants, 82% accepted, 138 enrolled. In 2011, 216 master's, 10 doctorates, 3 other advanced degrees awarded. *Degree requirements:* For master's, thesis optional, minimum GPA of 3.0, 36 hours; for doctorate, comprehensive exam, thesis/dissertation, dissertation defense, manuscript clearance, minimum GPA of 3.0; for Specialist, minimum GPA of 3.0, 30 hours. *Entrance requirements:* For master's, GRE (minimum percentile of at least 50 on each of the verbal and quantitative portions and writing score of 4.0), minimum GPA of 3.0 on last 2 years of baccalaureate degree, resume, statement of goals, two letters of recommendation, two official transcripts from every college-level institution attended; for doctorate, GRE (minimum percentile of at least 50 on each of the verbal and quantitative portions and writing score of 4.0), minimum GPA of 3.0 on last degree program, resume, 3 letters of recommendation, personal/goals statement, writing sample, brief digital video, two official transcripts from all college-level institutions attended; for Specialist, GRE (minimum percentile of at least 50 on each of the verbal and quantitative portions and writing score of 4.0), minimum graduate GPA of 3.2, resume, statement of goals, 2 letters of recommendation, writing sample, two official transcripts from every college-level institution attended. Additional exam requirements/recommendations for international students: Required—TOEFL (minimum score 585 paper-based; 94 iBT), IELTS (minimum score 6.5). *Application deadline:* For fall admission, 7/1 for domestic and international students; for spring admission, 11/1 for domestic and international students. Applications are processed on a rolling basis. Application fee: $30. Electronic applications accepted. *Expenses:* Contact institution. *Financial support:* In 2011–12, 263 students received support, including 3 fellowships with full tuition reimbursements available, 70 research assistantships with full tuition reimbursements available, 51 teaching assistantships with full tuition reimbursements available; career-related internships or fieldwork, Federal Work-Study, scholarships/grants, health care benefits, unspecified assistantships, and reduced tuition program for out-of-state students also available. Financial award application deadline: 3/1; financial award applicants required to submit FAFSA. *Faculty research:* Needs assessment, social informatics, usability analysis, human information behavior, youth services. *Unit head:* Dr. Corinne Jorgensen, Director/Associate Dean, 850-644-8126, Fax: 850-644-9763, E-mail: corinne.jorgensen@cci.fsu.edu. *Application contact:* Graduate Student Services, 850-645-3280, Fax: 850-644-9763, E-mail: slisgradadmissions@admin.fsu.edu. Web site: http://slis.fsu.edu/.

Georgia College & State University, Graduate School, The John H. Lounsbury College of Education, Department of Foundations and Secondary Education, Milledgeville, GA 31061. Offers curriculum and instruction (Ed S), including secondary education; educational technology (M Ed), including library media; educational technology (M Ed), including instructional technology; secondary education (M Ed, MAT). *Accreditation:* NCATE. Part-time and evening/weekend programs available. *Students:* 84 full-time (47 women), 120 part-time (98 women); includes 51 minority (43 Black or African American, non-Hispanic/Latino; 2 Asian, non-Hispanic/Latino; 4 Hispanic/Latino; 2 Two or more races, non-Hispanic/Latino), 1 international. Average age 31. 69 applicants, 51% accepted, 28 enrolled. In 2011, 105 master's, 33 other advanced degrees awarded. *Degree requirements:* For master's, comprehensive exam; for Ed S, comprehensive exam, electronic portfolio presentation. *Entrance requirements:* For master's, on-site writing assessment, 2 letters of recommendation, level 4 teaching certificate; for Ed S, on-site writing assessment, master's degree, 2 letters of recommendation, 2 years of teaching experience, level 5 teacher certification. Additional exam requirements/recommendations for international students: Recommended—TOEFL (minimum score 550 paper-based; 213 computer-based; 79 iBT). *Application deadline:* For fall admission, 7/1 priority date for domestic students, 4/1 for international students; for spring admission, 11/15 priority date for domestic students, 9/1 for international students. Applications are processed on a rolling basis. Application fee: $40. Electronic applications accepted. *Expenses:* Tuition, state resident: full-time $4806; part-time $267 per credit hour. Tuition, nonresident: full-time $17,802; part-time $989 per credit hour. *Required fees:* $936 per semester. Tuition and fees vary according to course load and campus/location. *Financial support:* In 2011–12, 12 research assistantships with full tuition reimbursements were awarded; career-related internships or fieldwork and Federal Work-Study also available. Support available to part-time students. Financial award applicants required to submit FAFSA. *Unit head:* Dr. Brian Mumma, Interim Chair, 478-445-2517, E-mail: brian.mumma@gcsu.edu. *Application contact:* Shanda Brand, Graduate Advisor, 478-445-1383, E-mail: shanda.brand@gcsu.edu.

Indiana University Bloomington, School of Library and Information Science, Bloomington, IN 47405-3907. Offers MIS, MLS, PhD, Sp LIS, JD/MLS, MIS/MA, MLS/MA, MPA/MIS, MPA/MLS. *Accreditation:* ALA (one or more programs are accredited). Part-time programs available. *Faculty:* 16 full-time (7 women). *Students:* 256 full-time (176 women), 67 part-time (49 women); includes 46 minority (13 Black or African American, non-Hispanic/Latino; 2 American Indian or Alaska Native, non-Hispanic/Latino; 23 Asian, non-Hispanic/Latino; 4 Hispanic/Latino; 4 Two or more races, non-Hispanic/Latino), 28 international. Average age 29. 286 applicants, 79% accepted, 101 enrolled. In 2011, 143 master's, 7 doctorates, 2 other advanced degrees awarded. *Degree requirements:* For doctorate, thesis/dissertation. *Entrance requirements:* For master's and doctorate, GRE General Test, 3 letters of reference. Additional exam requirements/recommendations for international students: Required—TOEFL (minimum score 600 paper-based; 250 computer-based; 100 iBT). *Application deadline:* For fall admission, 5/15 priority date for domestic students, 12/1 for international students; for spring admission, 10/15 priority date for domestic students, 9/1 for international students. Applications are processed on a rolling basis. Application fee: $55 ($65 for international students). Electronic applications accepted. *Expenses:* Contact institution. *Financial support:* Fellowships with full and partial tuition reimbursements, research assistantships with full and partial tuition reimbursements, career-related internships or fieldwork, Federal Work-Study, institutionally sponsored loans, scholarships/grants, tuition waivers (partial), and unspecified assistantships available. Support available to part-time students. Financial award application deadline: 1/15. *Faculty research:* Scholarly communication, interface design, library and management policy, computer-mediated communication, information retrieval. *Application contact:* Rhonda Spencer, Director of Admissions, 812-855-2018, Fax: 812-855-6166, E-mail: slis@indiana.edu. Web site: http://www.slis.indiana.edu/.

Indiana University–Purdue University Indianapolis, School of Library and Information Science, Indianapolis, IN 46202-2896. Offers MLS. Part-time and evening/weekend programs available. *Faculty:* 3 full-time (2 women). *Students:* 66 full-time (46 women), 169 part-time (133 women); includes 21 minority (11 Black or African American, non-Hispanic/Latino; 2 Asian, non-Hispanic/Latino; 5 Hispanic/Latino; 3 Two or more races, non-Hispanic/Latino). Average age 34. 53 applicants, 96% accepted, 33 enrolled. In 2011, 110 master's awarded. *Entrance requirements:* For master's, GRE General Test. Additional exam requirements/recommendations for international students: Required—TOEFL (minimum score 600 paper-based). *Application deadline:* For fall admission, 7/15 priority date for domestic students; for spring admission, 11/15 priority date for domestic students. Applications are processed on a rolling basis. Application fee: $55 ($65 for international students). *Financial support:* In 2011–12, teaching assistantships (averaging $9,500 per year) were awarded; career-related internships or fieldwork, Federal Work-Study, institutionally sponsored loans, and scholarships/grants also available. Support available to part-time students. *Unit head:* Dr. Daniel Collison, Executive Associate Dean, 317-278-2375, Fax: 317-278-1807, E-mail: slisindy@iupui.edu. *Application contact:* Dr. Sherry Queener, Director, Graduate Studies and Associate Dean, 317-274-1577, Fax: 317-278-2380. Web site: http://www.slis.indiana.edu/.

Indiana University–Purdue University Indianapolis, School of Public and Environmental Affairs, Indianapolis, IN 46202. Offers criminal justice and public safety (MS); homeland security and emergency management (Graduate Certificate); library management (Graduate Certificate); nonprofit management (Graduate Certificate); public affairs (MPA); public management (Graduate Certificate); social entrepreneurship: nonprofit and public benefit organizations (Graduate Certificate); JD/MPA; MLS/NMC; MLS/PMC; MPA/MA. *Accreditation:* CAHME (one or more programs are accredited); NASPAA. Part-time and evening/weekend programs available. Postbaccalaureate distance learning degree programs offered (no on-campus study). *Faculty:* 24 full-time (8 women), 10 part-time/adjunct (2 women). *Students:* 204 full-time (124 women), 109 part-time (74 women); includes 61 minority (45 Black or African American, non-Hispanic/Latino; 1 American Indian or Alaska Native, non-Hispanic/Latino; 7 Asian, non-Hispanic/Latino; 8 Hispanic/Latino), 11 international. Average age 31. 214 applicants, 83% accepted, 147 enrolled. In 2011, 55 master's, 43 other advanced degrees awarded. *Entrance requirements:* For master's, GRE General Test, GMAT or LSAT, minimum GPA of 3.0 (preferred). *Application deadline:* For fall admission, 5/15 priority date for domestic students, 2/1 for international students; for spring admission, 2/15 priority date for domestic students, 9/15 for international students. Applications are processed on a rolling basis. Application fee: $60. Electronic applications accepted. *Financial support:* In 2011–12, 12 research assistantships with full tuition reimbursements (averaging $12,000 per year) were awarded; fellowships, teaching assistantships, career-related internships or fieldwork, Federal Work-Study, institutionally sponsored loans, and scholarships/grants also available. Support available to part-time students. Financial award application deadline: 3/1; financial award applicants required to submit FAFSA. *Faculty research:* Nonprofit and public management, public policy, urban policy, sustainability policy, disaster preparedness and recovery, vehicular safety, homicide, offender rehabilitation and re-entry. *Total annual research expenditures:* $1.6 million. *Unit head:* Dr. Terry L. Baumer, Executive Associate Dean, 317-274-2016, Fax: 317-274-5153, E-mail: tebaumer@iupui.edu. *Application contact:* Luke Bickel, Director of Graduate Programs, 317-274-4656, Fax: 317-278-9668, E-mail: lbickel@iupui.edu. Web site: http://www.spea.iupui.edu/.

Instituto Tecnológico y de Estudios Superiores de Monterrey, Campus Irapuato, Graduate Programs, Irapuato, Mexico. Offers administration (MBA); administration of information technology (MAIT); administration of telecommunications (MAT); architecture (M Arch); computer science (MCS); education (M Ed); educational administration (MEA); educational innovation and technology (DEIT); educational technology (MET); electronic commerce (MBA); environmental administration and planning (MEAP); environmental systems (MES); finances (MBA); humanistic studies (MHS); international management for Latin American executives (MIMLAE); library and information science (MLIS); manufacturing quality management (MMQM); marketing research (MBA).

Inter American University of Puerto Rico, Barranquitas Campus, Program in Education, Barranquitas, PR 00794. Offers curriculum and teaching (M Ed), including biology education, English as a second language, history education, mathematics education, Spanish; educational leadership and management (MA); elementary education (M Ed); information and library service technology (M Ed); special education (MA). *Degree requirements:* For master's, comprehensive exam, thesis optional. *Entrance requirements:* For master's, EXADEP, letter of recommendation. Electronic applications accepted.

Inter American University of Puerto Rico, San Germán Campus, Graduate Studies Center, Program in Library Sciences, San Germán, PR 00683-5008. Offers MLS. Part-time and evening/weekend programs available. *Degree requirements:* For master's, comprehensive exam. *Entrance requirements:* For master's, GRE General Test or EXADEP, minimum GPA of 3.0. *Application deadline:* For fall admission, 4/30 priority date for domestic students; for spring admission, 11/15 for domestic students. Applications are processed on a rolling basis. Application fee: $31. *Expenses: Required fees:* $213 per semester. *Financial support:* Teaching assistantships, Federal Work-Study, and unspecified assistantships available. *Unit head:* Dr. Elba T. Irizarry, Director of Graduate Studies Center, 787-264-1912 Ext. 7357, Fax: 787-892-6350, E-mail: elbat@sg.inter.edu.

Kent State University, College of Communication and Information, School of Library and Information Science, Kent, OH 44242-0001. Offers MLIS. *Accreditation:* ALA. *Degree requirements:* For master's, thesis optional. *Entrance requirements:* For master's, GRE General Test, minimum GPA of 2.75. *Expenses:* Tuition, state resident: full-time $8136; part-time $452 per credit hour. Tuition, nonresident: full-time $14,292; part-time $794 per credit hour.

Kutztown University of Pennsylvania, College of Education, Program in Library Science, Kutztown, PA 19530-0730. Offers MLS. Part-time and evening/weekend programs available. *Faculty:* 6 full-time (5 women). *Students:* 7 full-time (5 women), 17 part-time (16 women). Average age 33. 10 applicants, 70% accepted, 5 enrolled. In 2011, 17 master's awarded. *Degree requirements:* For master's, comprehensive exam. *Entrance requirements:* For master's, GRE General Test. Additional exam requirements/recommendations for international students: Required—TOEFL (minimum score 550 paper-based; 79 iBT). *Application deadline:* For fall admission, 8/1 priority date for domestic students, 8/1 for international students; for spring admission, 12/1 priority date for domestic students, 12/1 for international students. Applications are processed on a rolling basis. Application fee: $35. Electronic applications accepted. *Expenses:* Tuition, state resident: full-time $7488; part-time $416 per credit. Tuition, nonresident: full-time $11,232; part-time $624 per credit. *Financial support:* Career-related internships or fieldwork, Federal Work-Study, scholarships/grants, and unspecified assistantships available. Financial award application deadline: 3/1; financial award applicants required to submit FAFSA. *Unit head:* Dr. Eloise Long, Chairperson, 610-683-4302, Fax: 610-683-1326, E-mail: long@kutztown.edu. *Application contact:* Kelly D. Burr, Associate Director, Graduate Admissions, 610-683-4200, Fax: 610-683-1393, E-mail: graduate@kutztown.edu.

Long Island University–C. W. Post Campus, College of Information and Computer Science, Palmer School of Library and Information Science, Brookville, NY 11548-1300. Offers archives and records management (Certificate); information studies (PhD); library and information science (MS); library media specialist (MS); public library management (Certificate). *Accreditation:* ALA (one or more programs are accredited). Part-time and evening/weekend programs available. Postbaccalaureate distance learning degree programs offered (minimal on-campus study). *Degree requirements:* For master's, thesis optional, internship; for doctorate, thesis/dissertation, qualifying exam. *Entrance requirements:* For master's, GRE or MAT, minimum undergraduate GPA of 3.0, resume. Electronic applications accepted. *Faculty research:* Information retrieval, digital libraries, scientometric and infometric studies, preservation/archiving and electronic records.

Long Island University–Hudson at Westchester, Program in Library and Information Science, Purchase, NY 10577. Offers MS. Part-time and evening/weekend programs available.

Louisiana State University and Agricultural and Mechanical College, Graduate School, School of Library and Information Science, Baton Rouge, LA 70803. Offers MLIS. *Accreditation:* ALA. Part-time and evening/weekend programs available. Postbaccalaureate distance learning degree programs offered (no on-campus study). *Faculty:* 10 full-time (8 women). *Students:* 68 full-time (53 women), 99 part-time (83 women); includes 20 minority (16 Black or African American, non-Hispanic/Latino; 1 American Indian or Alaska Native, non-Hispanic/Latino; 2 Asian, non-Hispanic/Latino; 1 Two or more races, non-Hispanic/Latino), 8 international. Average age 33. 55 applicants, 78% accepted, 37 enrolled. In 2011, 63 master's awarded. *Degree requirements:* For master's, comprehensive exam, thesis optional. *Entrance requirements:* For master's, GRE General Test, minimum GPA of 3.0. Additional exam requirements/recommendations for international students: Required—TOEFL (minimum score 550 paper-based; 213 computer-based; 79 iBT) or IELTS (minimum score 6.5). *Application deadline:* For fall admission, 1/25 priority date for domestic students, 5/15 for international students; for spring admission, 10/15 for international students. Applications are processed on a rolling basis. Application fee: $50 ($70 for international students). Electronic applications accepted. *Financial support:* In 2011–12, 95 students received support, including 5 fellowships (averaging $19,807 per year), 7 research assistantships with partial tuition reimbursements available (averaging $12,343 per year), 12 teaching assistantships with partial tuition reimbursements available (averaging $12,475 per year); career-related internships or fieldwork, Federal Work-Study, institutionally sponsored loans, scholarships/grants, health care benefits, and unspecified assistantships also available. Support available to part-time students. Financial award applicants required to submit FAFSA. *Faculty research:* Information retrieval, management, collection development, public libraries. *Total annual research expenditures:* $37,299. *Unit head:* Dr. Beth M. Paskoff, Dean, 225-578-3158, Fax: 225-578-4581, E-mail: bpaskoff@lsu.edu. *Application contact:* LaToya Joseph, Administrative Assistant, 225-578-3150, Fax: 225-578-4581, E-mail: lcjoseph@lsu.edu. Web site: http://slis.lsu.edu/.

Mansfield University of Pennsylvania, Graduate Studies, Program in School Library and Information Technologies, Mansfield, PA 16933. Offers library science (M Ed). Part-time and evening/weekend programs available. Postbaccalaureate distance learning degree programs offered. *Degree requirements:* For master's, comprehensive exam, thesis optional. *Entrance requirements:* For master's, minimum GPA of 3.0. Additional exam requirements/recommendations for international students: Required—TOEFL (minimum score 550 paper-based; 220 computer-based). Electronic applications accepted. *Expenses:* Contact institution.

McDaniel College, Graduate and Professional Studies, Program in Media/Library Science, Westminster, MD 21157-4390. Offers MS. Part-time and evening/weekend programs available. *Degree requirements:* For master's, comprehensive exam, thesis optional. *Entrance requirements:* For master's, GRE General Test, MAT, or NTE/PRAXIS I, letters of reference (3). Additional exam requirements/recommendations for international students: Required—TOEFL (minimum score 213 computer-based).

McGill University, Faculty of Graduate and Postdoctoral Studies, Faculty of Education, School of Information Studies, Montréal, QC H3A 2T5, Canada. Offers MLIS, PhD, Certificate, Diploma. *Accreditation:* ALA (one or more programs are accredited).

North Carolina Central University, Division of Academic Affairs, School of Library and Information Sciences, Durham, NC 27707-3129. Offers MIS, MLS. *Accreditation:* ALA (one or more programs are accredited). Part-time and evening/weekend programs available. *Degree requirements:* For master's, one foreign language, thesis, research paper, or project. *Entrance requirements:* For master's, GRE, 90 hours in liberal arts. Additional exam requirements/recommendations for international students: Required—TOEFL. *Faculty research:* African-American resources, planning and evaluation, analysis of economic and physical resources, geography of information, artificial intelligence.

Old Dominion University, Darden College of Education, Program in Elementary/Middle Education, Norfolk, VA 23529. Offers elementary education (MS Ed); instructional technology (MS Ed); library science (MS Ed); middle school education (MS Ed). *Accreditation:* NCATE. Part-time and evening/weekend programs available. Postbaccalaureate distance learning degree programs offered (no on-campus study). *Faculty:* 18 full-time (16 women), 34 part-time/adjunct (27 women). *Students:* 151 full-time (140 women), 118 part-time (96 women); includes 53 minority (27 Black or African American, non-Hispanic/Latino; 3 Asian, non-Hispanic/Latino; 10 Hispanic/Latino; 2 Native Hawaiian or other Pacific Islander, non-Hispanic/Latino; 11 Two or more races, non-Hispanic/Latino). Average age 31. 291 applicants, 50% accepted, 123 enrolled. In 2011, 167 master's awarded. *Degree requirements:* For master's, comprehensive exam. *Entrance requirements:* For master's, GRE General Test or MAT; PRAXIS I, SAT or ACT, minimum GPA of 2.8. Additional exam requirements/recommendations for international students: Required—TOEFL (minimum score 600 paper-based; 250 computer-based). *Application deadline:* For fall admission, 6/1 priority date for domestic students; for winter admission, 11/1 priority date for domestic students; for spring admission, 3/1 priority date for domestic students. Applications are processed on a rolling basis. Application fee: $50. Electronic applications accepted. *Expenses:* Tuition, state resident: full-time $9096; part-time $379 per credit. Tuition, nonresident: full-time $23,064; part-time $961 per credit. *Required fees:* $127 per semester. One-time fee: $50. *Financial support:* In 2011–12, 180 students received support, including teaching assistantships (averaging $9,000 per year); career-related internships or fieldwork, Federal Work-Study, institutionally sponsored loans, and scholarships/grants also available. Support available to part-time students. Financial award application deadline: 2/15; financial award applicants required to submit FAFSA. *Faculty research:* Education pre-K to 6, school librarianship. *Unit head:* Dr. Lea Lee, Graduate Program Director, 757-683-4801, Fax: 757-683-5862, E-mail: lxlee@odu.edu. *Application contact:* William Heffelfinger, Director of Graduate Admissions, 757-683-5554, Fax: 757-683-3255, E-mail: gradadmit@odu.edu. Web site: http://education.odu.edu/eci/.

Old Dominion University, Darden College of Education, Programs in Secondary Education, Norfolk, VA 23529. Offers biology (MS Ed); chemistry (MS Ed); English (MS Ed); instructional technology (MS Ed); library science (MS Ed); secondary education (MS Ed). *Accreditation:* NCATE. Part-time and evening/weekend programs available. Postbaccalaureate distance learning degree programs offered (minimal on-campus study). *Faculty:* 20 full-time (16 women). *Students:* 82 full-time (49 women), 95 part-time (63 women); includes 37 minority (21 Black or African American, non-Hispanic/Latino; 3 Asian, non-Hispanic/Latino; 8 Hispanic/Latino; 5 Two or more races, non-Hispanic/Latino), 1 international. Average age 32. 67 applicants, 79% accepted, 53 enrolled. In 2011, 84 degrees awarded. *Degree requirements:* For master's, comprehensive exam, thesis. *Entrance requirements:* For master's, GRE General Test or MAT, PRAXIS I (for licensure), minimum GPA of 2.8, teaching certificate. Additional exam requirements/recommendations for international students: Required—TOEFL. *Application deadline:* For fall admission, 6/1 for domestic and international students; for winter admission, 11/1 for domestic and international students; for spring admission, 3/1 for domestic and international students. Applications are processed on a rolling basis. Application fee: $50. Electronic applications accepted. *Expenses:* Tuition, state resident: full-time $9096; part-time $379 per credit. Tuition, nonresident: full-time $23,064; part-time $961 per credit. *Required fees:* $127 per semester. One-time fee: $50. *Financial support:* In 2011–12, 56 students received support, including fellowships (averaging $15,000 per year), 2 research assistantships with tuition reimbursements available (averaging $9,000 per year), 3 teaching assistantships with tuition reimbursements available (averaging $12,500 per year); career-related internships or fieldwork, Federal Work-Study, institutionally sponsored loans, scholarships/grants, and tuition waivers (partial) also available. Support available to part-time students. Financial award application deadline: 2/15; financial award applicants required to submit FAFSA. *Faculty research:* Use of technology, writing project for teachers, geography teaching, reading. *Unit head:* Dr. Robert Lucking, Graduate Program Director, 757-683-5545, Fax: 757-683-5862, E-mail: rlucking@odu.edu. *Application contact:* William Heffelfinger, Director of Graduate Admissions, 757-683-5554, Fax: 757-683-3255, E-mail: gradadmit@odu.edu. Web site: http://education.odu.edu/eci/secondary/.

Olivet Nazarene University, Graduate School, Division of Education, Program in Library Information Specialist, Bourbonnais, IL 60914. Offers MAE.

Pratt Institute, School of Information and Library Science, New York, NY 10011. Offers archives (Adv C); library and information science (MS, Adv C); library and information science media specialist (MS); library media specialist (Adv C); museum libraries (Adv C); JD/MS. *Accreditation:* ALA. Part-time programs available. *Faculty:* 9 full-time (6 women), 27 part-time/adjunct (15 women). *Students:* 131 full-time (106 women), 184 part-time (151 women); includes 72 minority (21 Black or African American, non-Hispanic/Latino; 19 Asian, non-Hispanic/Latino; 26 Hispanic/Latino; 6 Two or more races, non-Hispanic/Latino), 3 international. Average age 32. 207 applicants, 93% accepted, 81 enrolled. In 2011, 111 master's, 1 other advanced degree awarded. *Degree requirements:* For master's, thesis. *Entrance requirements:* Additional exam requirements/recommendations for international students: Required—TOEFL (minimum score 600 paper-based; 250 computer-based; 100 iBT). *Application deadline:* For fall admission, 1/5 for domestic and international students; for spring admission, 10/1 for domestic and international students. Application fee: $50 ($90 for international students). Electronic applications accepted. *Expenses:* Contact institution. *Financial support:* Career-related internships or fieldwork, Federal Work-Study, institutionally sponsored loans, scholarships/grants, health care benefits, and unspecified assistantships available. Support available to part-time students. Financial award application deadline: 2/1; financial award applicants required to submit FAFSA. *Faculty research:* Development of urban libraries and information centers, medical and law librarianship, information management. *Unit head:* Dr. Tula Giannini, Dean, 212-647-7682, E-mail: giannini@pratt.edu. *Application contact:* Young Hah, Director of Graduate Admissions, 718-636-3683, Fax: 718-399-4242, E-mail: yhah@pratt.edu. Web site: http://www.pratt.edu/academics/information_and_library_sciences.

See Display on page 1636 and Close-Up on page 1651.

Queens College of the City University of New York, Division of Graduate Studies, Social Science Division, Graduate School of Library and Information Studies, Flushing, NY 11367-1597. Offers MLS, AC. *Accreditation:* ALA (one or more programs are accredited). Part-time and evening/weekend programs available. *Faculty:* 17 full-time (11 women). *Students:* 35 full-time (25 women), 433 part-time (305 women); includes 91 minority (25 Black or African American, non-Hispanic/Latino; 2 American Indian or Alaska Native, non-Hispanic/Latino; 23 Asian, non-Hispanic/Latino; 41 Hispanic/Latino), 3 international. 322 applicants, 64% accepted, 166 enrolled. In 2011, 200 master's awarded. *Degree requirements:* For master's, thesis; for AC, thesis optional. *Entrance requirements:* For master's, minimum GPA of 3.0; for AC, master's degree or equivalent. Additional exam requirements/recommendations for international students: Required—TOEFL. *Application deadline:* For fall admission, 4/1 for domestic students; for spring admission, 11/1 for domestic students. Applications are processed on a rolling basis. Application fee: $125. *Expenses:* Tuition, state resident: part-time $345 per credit. Tuition, nonresident: part-time $640 per credit. *Required fees:* $145.25 per semester. *Financial support:* Career-related internships or fieldwork, Federal Work-Study, institutionally sponsored loans, and tuition waivers (partial) available. Support available to part-time students. Financial award application deadline: 4/1; financial award applicants required to submit FAFSA. *Faculty research:* Multimedia and video studies, ethnicity and librarianship, information science and computer applications. *Unit head:* Dr. Virgil Blake, Director/Chair, 718-997-3790. *Application contact:* Dr. Karen Smith, Graduate Adviser, 718-997-3790, E-mail: karen_smith@qc.edu.

Rowan University, Graduate School, College of Education, Department of Special Educational Services/Instruction, Program in School and Public Librarianship, Glassboro, NJ 08028-1701. Offers MA. *Accreditation:* NCATE. Part-time and evening/weekend programs available. *Degree requirements:* For master's, comprehensive exam, thesis. *Entrance requirements:* For master's, GRE General Test, minimum GPA of 2.8. Additional exam requirements/recommendations for international students: Required—TOEFL. Electronic applications accepted.

Rutgers, The State University of New Jersey, New Brunswick, School of Communication, Information and Library Studies, Department of Library and Information Science, Piscataway, NJ 08854-8097. Offers MLS. *Accreditation:* ALA. Part-time programs available. Postbaccalaureate distance learning degree programs offered (no on-campus study). *Entrance requirements:* For master's, GRE General Test. Additional exam requirements/recommendations for international students: Required—TOEFL. Electronic applications accepted. *Faculty research:* Information science, library services, management of information services.

Rutgers, The State University of New Jersey, New Brunswick, School of Communication, Information and Library Studies, Program in Communication, Library and Information Science and Media Studies, Piscataway, NJ 08854-8097. Offers PhD. Part-time programs available. *Degree requirements:* For doctorate, comprehensive exam, thesis/dissertation, qualifying exams. *Entrance requirements:* For doctorate, GRE General Test, proficiency in statistics. Additional exam requirements/recommendations for international students: Required—TOEFL (minimum score 600 paper-based; 250 computer-based). Electronic applications accepted. *Faculty research:* Information science, media studies.

St. Catherine University, Graduate Programs, Program in Library and Information Science, St. Paul, MN 55105. Offers MLIS. Part-time and evening/weekend programs available. *Degree requirements:* For master's, microcomputer competency. *Entrance requirements:* For master's, GRE or MAT, minimum GPA of 3.2 or GRE. Additional exam requirements/recommendations for international students: Required—Michigan

English Language Assessment Battery or TOEFL (minimum score 600 paper-based; 250 computer-based; 100 iBT). *Expenses: Required fees:* $30 per semester. Tuition and fees vary according to program.

St. John's University, St. John's College of Liberal Arts and Sciences, Division of Library and Information Science, Queens, NY 11439. Offers MLS, Adv C, MA/MLS, MS/MLS. *Accreditation:* ALA (one or more programs are accredited). Part-time and evening/weekend programs available. Postbaccalaureate distance learning degree programs offered (no on-campus study). *Students:* 24 full-time (19 women), 55 part-time (50 women); includes 20 minority (10 Black or African American, non-Hispanic/Latino; 2 Asian, non-Hispanic/Latino; 8 Hispanic/Latino). Average age 33. 62 applicants, 90% accepted, 26 enrolled. In 2011, 86 master's awarded. *Degree requirements:* For master's, comprehensive exam, internship. *Entrance requirements:* For master's, interview, minimum GPA of 3.0, 2 letters of recommendation, essay. Additional exam requirements/recommendations for international students: Required—TOEFL (minimum score 600 paper-based; 250 computer-based; 100 iBT), IELTS (minimum score 5.5). *Application deadline:* For fall admission, 5/1 priority date for domestic students, 5/1 for international students; for spring admission, 11/1 priority date for domestic students, 11/1 for international students. Applications are processed on a rolling basis. Application fee: $70. Electronic applications accepted. *Expenses:* Contact institution. *Financial support:* Research assistantships, career-related internships or fieldwork, and scholarships/grants available. Support available to part-time students. Financial award application deadline: 3/1; financial award applicants required to submit FAFSA. *Faculty research:* Indexes and metatags, information use and users, competitive intelligence, knowledge management, database theory, young adult and children services, school media services, archives, oral history. *Unit head:* Dr. Jeffrey Olson, Director, 718-990-5705, E-mail: olsonj@stjohns.edu. *Application contact:* Robert Medrano, Director of Graduate Admissions, 718-990-1601, Fax: 718-990-5686, E-mail: gradhelp@stjohns.edu.

Sam Houston State University, College of Education, Department of Library Science, Huntsville, TX 77341. Offers MLS. Part-time and evening/weekend programs available. *Faculty:* 7 full-time (all women), 4 part-time/adjunct (all women). *Students:* 196 part-time (186 women); includes 73 minority (7 Black or African American, non-Hispanic/Latino; 66 Hispanic/Latino). Average age 38. 75 applicants, 76% accepted, 24 enrolled. In 2011, 167 master's awarded. *Entrance requirements:* For master's, GRE General Test, minimum GPA of 2.8. Additional exam requirements/recommendations for international students: Required—TOEFL (minimum score 550 paper-based; 213 computer-based; 79 iBT). *Application deadline:* For fall admission, 8/1 for domestic students, 6/25 for international students; for spring admission, 12/1 for domestic students, 11/12 for international students. Applications are processed on a rolling basis. Application fee: $45 ($75 for international students). Electronic applications accepted. *Expenses:* Tuition, state resident: full-time $4420; part-time $221 per credit hour. Tuition, nonresident: full-time $10,680; part-time $534 per credit hour. *Required fees:* $329 per credit hour. *Financial support:* Teaching assistantships, career-related internships or fieldwork, and Federal Work-Study available. Support available to part-time students. Financial award application deadline: 5/31; financial award applicants required to submit FAFSA. *Unit head:* Dr. Holly Weimar, Acting Chair, 936-294-1151, Fax: 936-294-1153, E-mail: haw001@shsu.edu. *Application contact:* Molly Doughtie, Advisor, 936-294-1105, E-mail: edu_mxd@shsu.edu. Web site: http://www.shsu.edu/~lis_www/.

San Jose State University, Graduate Studies and Research, College of Applied Sciences and Arts, School of Library and Information Science, San Jose, CA 95192-0001. Offers MLIS, PhD. *Accreditation:* ALA (one or more programs are accredited). Part-time and evening/weekend programs available. *Degree requirements:* For master's, comprehensive exam. *Entrance requirements:* Additional exam requirements/recommendations for international students: Required—TOEFL (minimum score 600 paper-based). Electronic applications accepted. *Faculty research:* Evaluation of information services online, search strategy, organizational behavior.

Simmons College, Graduate School of Library and Information Science, Boston, MA 02115. Offers archives management (MS, Certificate); instructional technology licensure (Certificate); library and information science (MS, PhD); managerial leadership in the informational professions (PhD); school library teacher (MS, Certificate); MS/MA. *Accreditation:* ALA (one or more programs are accredited). *Unit head:* Dr. Michele V. Cloonan, Dean, 617-521-2806, Fax: 617-521-3192, E-mail: michele.cloonan@simmons.edu. *Application contact:* Sarah Petrakos, Assistant Dean, Admission and Recruitment, 617-521-2868, Fax: 617-521-3192, E-mail: gslisadm@simmons.edu. Web site: http://www.simmons.edu/gslis/.

Southern Arkansas University–Magnolia, Graduate Programs, Magnolia, AR 71754. Offers agriculture (MS); business administration (MBA); computer and information sciences (MS); education (M Ed), including counseling and development, curriculum and instruction, educational administration and supervision, elementary education, middle level, reading, secondary education, TESOL; kinesiology (M Ed); library media and information specialist (M Ed); mental health and clinical counseling (MS); public administration (MPA); school counseling (M Ed); teaching (MAT). *Accreditation:* NCATE. Part-time and evening/weekend programs available. Postbaccalaureate distance learning degree programs offered. *Faculty:* 34 full-time (15 women), 8 part-time/adjunct (5 women). *Students:* 87 full-time (62 women), 320 part-time (224 women); includes 116 minority (111 Black or African American, non-Hispanic/Latino; 2 American Indian or Alaska Native, non-Hispanic/Latino; 2 Asian, non-Hispanic/Latino; 1 Hispanic/Latino), 25 international. Average age 33. 201 applicants, 98% accepted, 156 enrolled. In 2011, 162 master's awarded. *Degree requirements:* For master's, comprehensive exam (for some programs), thesis optional. *Entrance requirements:* For master's, GRE, MAT or GMAT, minimum GPA of 2.5. Additional exam requirements/recommendations for international students: Required—TOEFL (minimum score 173 computer-based). *Application deadline:* For fall admission, 7/15 for domestic and international students; for winter admission, 12/1 for domestic and international students; for spring admission, 12/1 for domestic and international students. Applications are processed on a rolling basis. Application fee: $25 ($35 for international students). Electronic applications accepted. *Expenses:* Tuition, state resident: part-time $232 per credit. Tuition, nonresident: part-time $339 per credit. *Required fees:* $44 per credit. Part-time tuition and fees vary according to course load. *Financial support:* Career-related internships or fieldwork, Federal Work-Study, scholarships/grants, tuition waivers (full), and unspecified assistantships available. Financial award applicants required to submit FAFSA. *Faculty research:* Alternative certification for teachers, supervision of instruction, instructional leadership, counseling. *Unit head:* Dr. Kim Bloss, Dean, School of Graduate Studies, 870-235-4150, Fax: 870-235-5227, E-mail: kkbloss@saumag.edu. *Application contact:* Gaye Calhoun, Admissions Specialist, 870-235-4150, Fax: 870-235-5227, E-mail: glcalhoun@saumag.edu. Web site: http://www.saumag.edu/graduate.

Southern Connecticut State University, School of Graduate Studies, School of Education, Department of Information and Library Science, New Haven, CT 06515-1355. Offers library science (MLS); library/information studies (Diploma); JD/MLS; MLS/MA; MLS/MS. *Accreditation:* ALA. Part-time and evening/weekend programs available. Postbaccalaureate distance learning degree programs offered (no on-campus study). *Faculty:* 9 full-time (5 women), 3 part-time/adjunct (all women). *Students:* 44 full-time (35 women), 200 part-time (171 women); includes 17 minority (6 Black or African American, non-Hispanic/Latino; 3 Asian, non-Hispanic/Latino; 4 Hispanic/Latino; 4 Two or more races, non-Hispanic/Latino), 1 international. 465 applicants, 12% accepted, 42 enrolled. In 2011, 84 master's, 5 other advanced degrees awarded. *Degree requirements:* For master's and Diploma, thesis or alternative. *Entrance requirements:* For master's, GRE General Test, interview, minimum QPA of 2.7, introductory computer science course; for Diploma, master's degree in library science or information science. *Application deadline:* For fall admission, 7/15 priority date for domestic students. Applications are processed on a rolling basis. Application fee: $50. Electronic applications accepted. *Expenses:* Tuition, state resident: full-time $5137; part-time $413 per credit. *Required fees:* $4008; $55 per term. *Financial support:* Research assistantships available. Financial award application deadline: 4/15; financial award applicants required to submit FAFSA. *Unit head:* Dr. Chang Suk Kim, Chairperson, 203-392-5191, Fax: 203-392-5780, E-mail: kimc1@southernct.edu. *Application contact:* Dr. Elsie Okobi, Graduate Coordinator, 203-392-5709, E-mail: okobie1@southernct.edu.

Syracuse University, School of Information Studies, Program in Digital Libraries, Syracuse, NY 13244. Offers CAS. Part-time and evening/weekend programs available. Postbaccalaureate distance learning degree programs offered (minimal on-campus study). *Students:* 1 (woman) full-time, 6 part-time (4 women); includes 2 minority (both Black or African American, non-Hispanic/Latino). Average age 39. 6 applicants, 100% accepted, 2 enrolled. In 2011, 12 degrees awarded. *Entrance requirements:* Additional exam requirements/recommendations for international students: Required—TOEFL (minimum score 100 iBT). *Application deadline:* For fall admission, 2/1 priority date for domestic students, 2/1 for international students; for spring admission, 10/15 priority date for domestic students, 10/15 for international students. Applications are processed on a rolling basis. Application fee: $75. Electronic applications accepted. *Expenses: Tuition:* Part-time $1206 per credit. *Financial support:* Fellowships, research assistantships, teaching assistantships, and scholarships/grants available. Financial award application deadline: 1/1; financial award applicants required to submit FAFSA. *Unit head:* Prof. Jian Qin, Head, 315-443-2911, E-mail: dlibcas@syr.edu. *Application contact:* Susan Corieri, Director of Enrollment Management, 315-443-2575, E-mail: ischool@syr.edu. Web site: http://ischool.syr.edu/.

See Display on page 1637 and Close-Up on page 1653.

Syracuse University, School of Information Studies, Program in Library and Information Science, Syracuse, NY 13244. Offers MS. *Accreditation:* ALA. Part-time and evening/weekend programs available. Postbaccalaureate distance learning degree programs offered (minimal on-campus study). *Students:* 15 full-time (all women), 34 part-time (32 women); includes 4 minority (1 Black or African American, non-Hispanic/Latino; 1 Asian, non-Hispanic/Latino; 2 Two or more races, non-Hispanic/Latino). Average age 34. 22 applicants, 82% accepted, 14 enrolled. In 2011, 23 degrees awarded. *Degree requirements:* For master's, fieldwork or research paper. *Entrance requirements:* For master's, GRE General Test. Additional exam requirements/recommendations for international students: Required—TOEFL (minimum score 100 iBT). *Application deadline:* For fall admission, 2/1 priority date for domestic students, 2/1 for international students; for spring admission, 10/15 priority date for domestic students, 10/15 for international students. Application fee: $75. Electronic applications accepted. *Expenses: Tuition:* Part-time $1206 per credit. *Financial support:* Fellowships with full tuition reimbursements available. Financial award application deadline: 1/1; financial award applicants required to submit FAFSA. *Unit head:* R. David Lankes, Head, 315-443-2911, Fax: 315-443-6886, E-mail: rdlankes@iis.syr.edu. *Application contact:* Susan Corieri, Director of Enrollment Management, 315-443-2575, E-mail: ischool@syr.edu. Web site: http://ischool.syr.edu/.

See Display on page 1637 and Close-Up on page 1653.

Tennessee Technological University, Graduate School, College of Education, Department of Curriculum and Instruction, Program in Library Science, Cookeville, TN 38505. Offers MA. Part-time and evening/weekend programs available. *Students:* 7 full-time (all women), 11 part-time (10 women). 4 applicants, 100% accepted, 3 enrolled. In 2011, 4 master's awarded. *Degree requirements:* For master's, comprehensive exam, thesis or alternative. *Entrance requirements:* For master's, MAT or GRE. Additional exam requirements/recommendations for international students: Required—TOEFL (minimum score 550 paper-based; 71 iBT), IELTS (minimum score 5.5), Pearson Test of English Academic. *Application deadline:* For fall admission, 8/1 for domestic students, 5/1 for international students; for spring admission, 12/1 for domestic students, 10/1 for international students. Application fee: $25 ($30 for international students). Electronic applications accepted. *Expenses:* Tuition, state resident: full-time $8094; part-time $422 per credit hour. Tuition, nonresident: full-time $20,574; part-time $1046 per credit hour. *Financial support:* In 2011–12, research assistantships (averaging $4,000 per year), 2 teaching assistantships (averaging $4,000 per year) were awarded. Financial award application deadline: 4/1. *Unit head:* Dr. Susan Gord, Interim Chairperson, 931-372-3181, Fax: 931-372-6270, E-mail: sgore@tntech.edu. *Application contact:* Shelia K. Kendrick, Coordinator of Graduate Admissions, 931-372-3808, Fax: 931-372-3497, E-mail: skendrick@tntech.edu.

Texas Woman's University, Graduate School, College of Professional Education, School of Library and Information Studies, Denton, TX 76201. Offers library science (MA, MLS, PhD). *Accreditation:* ALA (one or more programs are accredited). Part-time and evening/weekend programs available. Postbaccalaureate distance learning degree programs offered (minimal on-campus study). *Faculty:* 18 full-time (13 women), 3 part-time/adjunct (2 women). *Students:* 75 full-time (69 women), 391 part-time (372 women); includes 123 minority (44 Black or African American, non-Hispanic/Latino; 2 American Indian or Alaska Native, non-Hispanic/Latino; 7 Asian, non-Hispanic/Latino; 70 Hispanic/Latino). Average age 37. 127 applicants, 86% accepted, 84 enrolled. In 2011, 166 master's, 2 doctorates awarded. *Degree requirements:* For master's, comprehensive exam, thesis or alternative; for doctorate, comprehensive exam, thesis/dissertation. *Entrance requirements:* For master's, GRE (preferred), GMAT, MCAT, MAT, 3 letters of recommendation, 2-page statement of intent, resume; for doctorate, GRE (preferred), GMAT, MCAT, MAT, curriculum vitae/resume, 3 letters of reference, essay. Additional exam requirements/recommendations for international students: Required—TOEFL (minimum score 550 paper-based; 213 computer-based; 79 iBT). *Application deadline:* For fall admission, 2/15 priority date for domestic students, 2/15 for international students. Applications are processed on a rolling basis. Application fee: $50 ($75 for international students). Electronic applications accepted. *Expenses:* Tuition, state resident: full-time $3834; part-time $213 per credit hour. Tuition, nonresident: full-time $9468; part-time $526 per credit hour. *Required fees:* $213 per credit hour. Tuition and fees vary according to course load. *Financial support:* In 2011–12, 89 students received support, including 15 research assistantships (averaging $10,746 per year), teaching assistantships (averaging $10,746 per year); career-related internships or fieldwork, Federal Work-Study, institutionally sponsored loans, scholarships/grants, traineeships, health care benefits, and unspecified assistantships also available. Support available to part-time students. Financial award application deadline: 3/1; financial award applicants required to submit FAFSA. *Faculty research:* Children's literature, health information, information needs analysis, school library leadership, library management and assessment. *Unit head:* Dr. Ling Hwey Jeng, Director, 940-898-2602, Fax: 940-898-2611, E-mail: slis@twu.edu. *Application contact:* Dr. Samuel Wheeler, Assistant Director of Admissions, 940-898-3188, Fax: 940-898-3081, E-mail: wheelersr@twu.edu. Web site: http://www.twu.edu/slis/.

Trevecca Nazarene University, College of Lifelong Learning, School of Education, Major in Library and Information Science, Nashville, TN 37210-2877. Offers MLI Sc. Part-time and evening/weekend programs available. *Students:* 19 full-time (16 women), 6 part-time (all women); includes 2 minority (1 Asian, non-Hispanic/Latino; 1 Two or more races, non-Hispanic/Latino). Average age 36. In 2011, 28 master's awarded. *Degree requirements:* For master's, exit assessment. *Entrance requirements:* For master's, GRE General Test, MAT, technology pre-assessment, minimum GPA of 2.7, 2 reference forms. Additional exam requirements/recommendations for international students: Required—TOEFL (minimum score 550 paper-based; 213 computer-based). *Application deadline:* Applications are processed on a rolling basis. Application fee: $25. *Expenses:* Contact institution. *Financial support:* Applicants required to submit FAFSA. *Unit head:* Dr. Esther Swink, Dean, School of Education/Director of Graduate Education Program, 615-248-1201, Fax: 615-248-1597, E-mail: admissions_ged@trevecca.edu. *Application contact:* Melanie Eaton, Admissions, 615-248-1498, E-mail: admissions_ged@trevecca.edu. Web site: http://www.trevecca.edu/.

Universidad del Turabo, Graduate Programs, Programs in Education, Program in Administration of School Libraries, Gurabo, PR 00778-3030. Offers M Ed, Certificate. *Students:* 2 full-time (1 woman), 1 (woman) part-time; all minorities (all Hispanic/Latino). Average age 34. 2 applicants, 100% accepted, 1 enrolled. *Unit head:* Angela Candelario, Dean, 787-743-7979 Ext. 4126. *Application contact:* Virginia Gonzalez, Admissions Officer, 787-746-3009.

Universidad del Turabo, Graduate Programs, Programs in Education, Program in Library Service and Information Technology, Gurabo, PR 00778-3030. Offers M Ed. *Students:* 31 full-time (26 women), 26 part-time (22 women); includes 45 minority (all Hispanic/Latino). Average age 34. 36 applicants, 89% accepted, 22 enrolled. In 2011, 43 master's awarded. *Unit head:* Angela Candelario, Dean, 787-743-7979 Ext. 4126. *Application contact:* Virginia Gonzalez, Admissions Officer, 787-746-3009.

Université de Montréal, Faculty of Arts and Sciences, School of Library and Information Sciences, Montréal, QC H3C 3J7, Canada. Offers information sciences (MIS, PhD). *Accreditation:* ALA (one or more programs are accredited). *Degree requirements:* For master's, thesis optional. *Entrance requirements:* For master's, interview, master's degree in library and information science or equivalent. Electronic applications accepted.

University at Buffalo, the State University of New York, Graduate School, Graduate School of Education, Department of Library and Information Studies, Buffalo, NY 14260. Offers library and information studies (MLS, Certificate); library and information studies (online) (MLS); library media specialist (online) (MLS). *Accreditation:* ALA (one or more programs are accredited). Part-time programs available. Postbaccalaureate distance learning degree programs offered (no on-campus study). *Faculty:* 11 full-time (8 women), 26 part-time/adjunct (14 women). *Students:* 115 full-time (84 women), 218 part-time (167 women); includes 31 minority (15 Black or African American, non-Hispanic/Latino; 1 American Indian or Alaska Native, non-Hispanic/Latino; 8 Asian, non-Hispanic/Latino; 7 Hispanic/Latino), 5 international. Average age 34. 250 applicants, 57% accepted, 137 enrolled. In 2011, 112 master's, 4 other advanced degrees awarded. *Degree requirements:* For master's, thesis optional; for Certificate, thesis. *Entrance requirements:* For master's, minimum GPA of 3.0. Additional exam requirements/recommendations for international students: Required—TOEFL (minimum score 550 paper-based; 79 iBT). *Application deadline:* For fall admission, 4/1 priority date for domestic students, 4/1 for international students; for spring admission, 10/15 priority date for domestic students, 10/15 for international students. Applications are processed on a rolling basis. Application fee: $50. Electronic applications accepted. *Financial support:* In 2011–12, 14 fellowships (averaging $5,115 per year), 6 research assistantships (averaging $9,000 per year) were awarded; teaching assistantships, career-related internships or fieldwork, Federal Work-Study, institutionally sponsored loans, and unspecified assistantships also available. Support available to part-time students. Financial award application deadline: 3/1; financial award applicants required to submit FAFSA. *Faculty research:* Information-seeking behavior, thesauri, impact of technology, questioning behaviors, educational informatics. *Unit head:* Dr. Dagobert Soergel, Chair, 716-645-2412, Fax: 716-645-3775, E-mail: dsoergel@buffalo.edu. *Application contact:* Dr. Radhika Suresh, Director of Graduate Admissions and Student Services, 716-645-2110, Fax: 716-645-7937, E-mail: gse-info@buffalo.edu. Web site: http://www.gse.buffalo.edu/lis/.

The University of Alabama, Graduate School, College of Communication and Information Sciences, School of Library and Information Studies, Tuscaloosa, AL 35487-0252. Offers book arts (MFA); library and information studies (MLIS, PhD). *Accreditation:* ALA (one or more programs are accredited). Part-time and evening/weekend programs available. Postbaccalaureate distance learning degree programs offered (minimal on-campus study). *Faculty:* 11 full-time (5 women), 2 part-time/adjunct (both women). *Students:* 86 full-time (70 women), 197 part-time (151 women); includes 27 minority (10 Black or African American, non-Hispanic/Latino; 1 American Indian or Alaska Native, non-Hispanic/Latino; 3 Asian, non-Hispanic/Latino; 9 Hispanic/Latino; 4 Two or more races, non-Hispanic/Latino), 4 international. Average age 34. 224 applicants, 55% accepted, 85 enrolled. In 2011, 128 degrees awarded. *Degree requirements:* For master's, comprehensive exam (for some programs), thesis optional; for doctorate, comprehensive exam, thesis/dissertation. *Entrance requirements:* For master's, GRE General Test or MAT, minimum GPA of 3.0; for doctorate, GRE. Additional exam requirements/recommendations for international students: Required—TOEFL. *Application deadline:* For fall admission, 7/1 priority date for domestic students, 7/1 for international students; for spring admission, 11/1 priority date for domestic students, 11/1 for international students. Applications are processed on a rolling basis. Application fee: $50 ($60 for international students). Electronic applications accepted. *Expenses:* Tuition, state resident: full-time $8600. Tuition, nonresident: full-time $21,900. *Financial support:* In 2011–12, 64 students received support, including 3 fellowships with full tuition reimbursements available (averaging $15,000 per year), 18 research assistantships with full and partial tuition reimbursements available (averaging $6,003 per year), 12 teaching assistantships with full and partial tuition reimbursements available (averaging $6,003 per year); career-related internships or fieldwork, scholarships/grants, health care benefits, unspecified assistantships, and 15 additional grant-funded fellowships, full tuition waiver, professional travel also available. Support available to part-time students. Financial award application deadline: 3/15. *Faculty research:* Library administration, user services, digital libraries, book arts, evaluation. *Unit head:* Dr. Heidi Julien, Director and Professor, 205-348-4610, Fax: 205-348-3746, E-mail: hjulien@slis.ua.edu. *Application contact:* Beth Riggs, Assistant to the Director, 205-348-1527, Fax: 205-3483746, E-mail: briggs@slis.ua.edu. Web site: http://www.slis.ua.edu/.

University of Alberta, Faculty of Graduate Studies and Research, School of Library and Information Studies, Edmonton, AB T6G 2E1, Canada. Offers MLIS. *Accreditation:* ALA. *Entrance requirements:* Additional exam requirements/recommendations for international students: Required—TOEFL, Canadian Academic English Language Assessment. Electronic applications accepted. *Faculty research:* Intellectual freedom, materials for children and young adults, library classification, multi-media literacy.

The University of Arizona, College of Social and Behavioral Sciences, School of Information Resources and Library Science, Tucson, AZ 85721. Offers MA, PhD. *Accreditation:* ALA (one or more programs are accredited). Part-time programs available. *Faculty:* 9 full-time (6 women). *Students:* 95 full-time (71 women), 146 part-time (114 women); includes 44 minority (4 Black or African American, non-Hispanic/Latino; 1 American Indian or Alaska Native, non-Hispanic/Latino; 2 Asian, non-Hispanic/Latino; 26 Hispanic/Latino; 11 Two or more races, non-Hispanic/Latino), 5 international. Average age 37. 22 applicants, 36% accepted, 7 enrolled. In 2011, 104 master's awarded. *Degree requirements:* For master's, proficiency in disk operating system (DOS); for doctorate, thesis/dissertation. *Entrance requirements:* For master's and doctorate, GRE General Test, 3 letters of recommendation, resume. Additional exam requirements/recommendations for international students: Required—TOEFL (minimum score 550 paper-based; 213 computer-based; 79 iBT). *Application deadline:* For spring admission, 9/1 for domestic and international students. Applications are processed on a rolling basis. Application fee: $65. Electronic applications accepted. *Expenses:* Tuition, state resident: full-time $10,840. Tuition, nonresident: full-time $25,802. *Financial support:* In 2011–12, 17 research assistantships with full tuition reimbursements (averaging $20,288 per year), 13 teaching assistantships with full tuition reimbursements (averaging $20,288 per year) were awarded; career-related internships or fieldwork, Federal Work-Study, institutionally sponsored loans, scholarships/grants, health care benefits, tuition waivers (full and partial), and unspecified assistantships also available. Financial award application deadline: 3/1. *Faculty research:* Microcomputer applications; quantitative methods systems; information transfer, planning, evaluation, and technology. *Total annual research expenditures:* $1.1 million. *Unit head:* Dr. Jana Bradley, Director, 520-621-3565, Fax: 520-621-3279, E-mail: janabrad@email.arizona.edu. *Application contact:* Geraldine Fragoso, Program Manager, 520-621-3565, Fax: 520-621-3279, E-mail: gfragoso@email.arizona.edu. Web site: http://www.sirls.arizona.edu/.

The University of British Columbia, Faculty of Arts, School of Library, Archival and Information Studies, Dual Master of Archival Studies/Master of Library and Information Studies Program, Vancouver, BC V6T 1Z1, Canada. Offers MLIS/MAS. *Entrance requirements:* Additional exam requirements/recommendations for international students: Required—TOEFL (minimum score 600 paper-based; 250 computer-based; 100 iBT). Electronic applications accepted. *Faculty research:* Computer systems/database design, information-seeking behaviour, archives and records management, children's literature and services, digital libraries and archives.

The University of British Columbia, Faculty of Arts, School of Library, Archival and Information Studies, Master of Library and Information Studies Program, Vancouver, BC V6T 1Z1, Canada. Offers MLIS. Part-time programs available. *Degree requirements:* For master's, thesis optional. *Entrance requirements:* For master's, minimum GPA of 3.3 in undergraduate upper-division courses. Additional exam requirements/recommendations for international students: Required—TOEFL (minimum score 600 paper-based; 250 computer-based; 100 iBT). Electronic applications accepted. *Faculty research:* Computer systems/database design; digital libraries; metadata/classification; human-computer interaction; children's literature and services.

The University of British Columbia, Faculty of Arts, School of Library, Archival and Information Studies, PhD Program in Library, Archival and Information Studies, Vancouver, BC V6T 1Z1, Canada. Offers PhD. *Degree requirements:* For doctorate, thesis/dissertation. *Entrance requirements:* For doctorate, GRE, minimum GPA of 3.3 in MAS or MLIS (other master's degrees may be considered). Additional exam requirements/recommendations for international students: Required—TOEFL (minimum score 600 paper-based; 250 computer-based; 100 iBT). Electronic applications accepted. *Faculty research:* Computer systems/database design; library and archival management; archival description and organization; children's literature and youth services; interactive information retrieval.

University of California, Los Angeles, Graduate Division, Graduate School of Education and Information Studies, Department of Information Studies, Los Angeles, CA 90095-1521. Offers archival studies (MLIS); informatics (MLIS); information studies (PhD); library and information science (Certificate); library studies (MLIS); moving image archive studies (MA); MBA/MLIS; MLIS/MA. *Accreditation:* ALA (one or more programs are accredited). *Faculty:* 13 full-time (7 women), 10 part-time/adjunct (8 women). *Students:* 141 full-time (118 women), 22 part-time (16 women); includes 62 minority (10 Black or African American, non-Hispanic/Latino; 2 American Indian or Alaska Native, non-Hispanic/Latino; 38 Asian, non-Hispanic/Latino; 12 Hispanic/Latino), 3 international. Average age 27. 171 applicants, 77% accepted, 82 enrolled. In 2011, 69 master's, 8 doctorates awarded. Terminal master's awarded for partial completion of doctoral program. *Degree requirements:* For master's, thesis or alternative, professional portfolio; for doctorate, thesis/dissertation, oral and written qualifying exams. *Entrance requirements:* For master's, GRE General Test, previous course work in statistics; for doctorate, GRE General Test, previous course work in statistics, 2 samples of research writing in English. Additional exam requirements/recommendations for international students: Required—TOEFL (minimum score 613 paper-based; 220 computer-based; 87 iBT), IELTS (minimum score 7). *Application deadline:* For fall admission, 11/30 for domestic students, 10/30 for international students. Applications are processed on a rolling basis. Application fee: $80 ($90 for international students). Electronic applications accepted. *Financial support:* In 2011–12, 44 students received support, including 29 fellowships with full and partial tuition reimbursements available (averaging $10,505 per year), 7 research assistantships with partial tuition reimbursements available (averaging $29,061 per year), 12 teaching assistantships with partial tuition reimbursements available (averaging $18,984 per year); career-related internships or fieldwork, Federal Work-Study, institutionally sponsored loans, scholarships/grants, and unspecified assistantships also available. Financial award application deadline: 3/1; financial award applicants required to submit FAFSA. *Faculty research:* Multimedia, digital libraries, archives and electronic records, interface design, information technology and preservation, preservation, access. *Unit head:* Dr. Gregory H. Leazer, Associate Professor and Chair, 310-825-8799, E-mail: gleazer@ucla.edu. *Application contact:* Susan S. Abler, Student Affairs Officer, 310-825-5269, Fax: 310-206-4460, E-mail: abler@gseis.ucla.edu. Web site: http://is.gseis.ucla.edu/.

University of Central Arkansas, Graduate School, College of Education, Department of Leadership Studies, Program in Library Media and Information Technology, Conway, AR 72035-0001. Offers MS. Part-time programs available. *Students:* 5 full-time (4 women), 87 part-time (all women); includes 8 minority (2 Black or African American, non-Hispanic/Latino; 5 American Indian or Alaska Native, non-Hispanic/Latino; 1 Hispanic/Latino). Average age 36. 29 applicants, 100% accepted, 26 enrolled. In 2011, 49 master's awarded. *Degree requirements:* For master's, comprehensive exam. *Entrance requirements:* For master's, GRE General Test, minimum GPA of 2.7. Additional exam requirements/recommendations for international students: Required—TOEFL (minimum score 550 paper-based; 213 computer-based). *Application deadline:* For fall admission, 3/1 priority date for domestic students, 3/1 for international students; for spring admission, 10/1 priority date for domestic students, 10/1 for international students. Applications are processed on a rolling basis. Application fee: $25 ($50 for international students). *Expenses:* Tuition, state resident: full-time $4834; part-time $398.35 per credit hour. Tuition, nonresident: full-time $8686. *Financial support:*

Federal Work-Study, scholarships/grants, and tuition waivers (partial) available. Financial award application deadline: 2/15; financial award applicants required to submit FAFSA. *Unit head:* Stephanie Huffman, Head, 501-450-5430, Fax: 501-450-5680, E-mail: steph@uca.edu. *Application contact:* Susan Wood, Administrative Specialist, 501-450-3124, Fax: 501-450-5678, E-mail: swood@uca.edu.

University of Central Missouri, The Graduate School, College of Education, Warrensburg, MO 64093. Offers career and technical education administration (MS); career and technical education industry training (MS); career and technical education leadership/teaching (MS); college student personnel administration (MS); counseling (MS); curriculum and instruction (Ed S); educational leadership (Ed D); educational technology (MS); elementary education/educational foundations and literacy (MSE); elementary school administration (MSE); elementary school principalship (Ed S); human services/learning resources (Ed S); human services/professional counseling (Ed S); human services/special education (Ed S); human services/technology and occupational education (Ed S); K-12 education/educational foundations and literacy (MSE); K-12 special education (MSE); library science and information services (MS); literacy education (MSE); secondary education/educational foundations & literacy (MSE); secondary school administration (MSE); secondary school principalship (Ed S); superintendency (Ed S); teaching (MAT). Ed D offered jointly with University of Missouri. Part-time programs available. Postbaccalaureate distance learning degree programs offered. *Entrance requirements:* Additional exam requirements/recommendations for international students: Required—TOEFL (minimum score 550 paper-based; 79 computer-based). Electronic applications accepted.

University of Central Oklahoma, College of Graduate Studies and Research, College of Education and Professional Studies, Department of Advanced Professional and Special Services, Program in Library Media Education, Edmond, OK 73034-5209. Offers M Ed. *Accreditation:* NCATE. Part-time programs available. *Entrance requirements:* For master's, GRE General Test. Additional exam requirements/recommendations for international students: Required—TOEFL (minimum score 550 paper-based; 213 computer-based). *Application deadline:* For fall admission, 7/1 for international students; for spring admission, 11/1 for international students. Applications are processed on a rolling basis. Application fee: $25. Electronic applications accepted. *Expenses:* Tuition, state resident: full-time $3901; part-time $218.30 per credit hour. Tuition, nonresident: full-time $9198; part-time $511.20 per credit hour. Tuition and fees vary according to program. *Financial support:* Unspecified assistantships available. Financial award application deadline: 3/31; financial award applicants required to submit FAFSA. *Unit head:* Dr. Pat Couts, Adviser, 405-974-5888, Fax: 405-974-3822. *Application contact:* Dr. Richard Bernard, Dean, Jackson College of Graduate Studies, 405-974-3493, Fax: 405-974-3852, E-mail: gradcoll@uco.edu. Web site: http://www.uco.edu/ceps/dept/apss/instructional-media/index.asp.

University of Denver, Morgridge College of Education, Denver, CO 80208. Offers advanced study in law librarianship (Certificate); child and family studies (MA, PhD); counseling psychology (MA, PhD); curriculum and instruction (MA, PhD, Certificate); educational leadership (Ed D, PhD); educational leadership and policy studies (MA, Certificate); higher education (MA, PhD); library and information science (MLIS); research methods and statistics (MA, PhD); school administration (PhD); school psychology (Ed S). *Accreditation:* ALA; APA (one or more programs are accredited). Part-time and evening/weekend programs available. Postbaccalaureate distance learning degree programs offered (no on-campus study). *Faculty:* 34 full-time (25 women), 70 part-time/adjunct (54 women). *Students:* 385 full-time (289 women), 386 part-time (303 women); includes 168 minority (49 Black or African American, non-Hispanic/Latino; 8 American Indian or Alaska Native, non-Hispanic/Latino; 25 Asian, non-Hispanic/Latino; 71 Hispanic/Latino; 1 Native Hawaiian or other Pacific Islander, non-Hispanic/Latino; 14 Two or more races, non-Hispanic/Latino), 17 international. Average age 33. 668 applicants, 72% accepted, 256 enrolled. In 2011, 308 master's, 43 doctorates, 55 other advanced degrees awarded. Terminal master's awarded for partial completion of doctoral program. *Degree requirements:* For master's, comprehensive exam; for doctorate, 2 foreign languages, comprehensive exam, thesis/dissertation. *Entrance requirements:* For master's and doctorate, GRE General Test or GMAT. Additional exam requirements/recommendations for international students: Required—TOEFL (minimum score 550 paper-based; 80 iBT). *Application deadline:* Applications are processed on a rolling basis. Application fee: $60. Electronic applications accepted. *Financial support:* In 2011–12, 72 teaching assistantships with full and partial tuition reimbursements (averaging $9,049 per year) were awarded; career-related internships or fieldwork, Federal Work-Study, institutionally sponsored loans, scholarships/grants, and unspecified assistantships also available. Support available to part-time students. Financial award application deadline: 2/15; financial award applicants required to submit FAFSA. *Faculty research:* Parkinson's disease, personnel training, development and assessments, gifted education, service-learning, transportation, public schools. *Unit head:* Dr. Gregory M. Anderson, Dean, 303-871-3665, E-mail: gregory.m.anderson@du.edu. *Application contact:* Chris Dowen, Director, MCE Admission Office, 303-871-2783, E-mail: chris.dowen@du.edu. Web site: http://www.du.edu/education/.

University of Hawaii at Manoa, Graduate Division, College of Natural Sciences, Department of Information and Computer Sciences, Library and Information Science Program, Honolulu, HI 96822-2233. Offers advanced library and information science (Graduate Certificate); library and information science (MLI Sc). *Accreditation:* ALA (one or more programs are accredited). Part-time programs available. *Degree requirements:* For master's, comprehensive exam, thesis optional. *Entrance requirements:* For master's, GRE General Test. Additional exam requirements/recommendations for international students: Required—TOEFL (minimum score 600 paper-based; 250 computer-based). Electronic applications accepted. *Faculty research:* Information behavior, evaluation of electronic information sources, online learning, history of libraries, information literacy.

University of Houston–Clear Lake, School of Education, Program in Curriculum and Instruction, Houston, TX 77058-1098. Offers curriculum and instruction (MS); early childhood education (MS); reading (MS); school library and information science (MS). Part-time and evening/weekend programs available. *Degree requirements:* For master's, thesis (for some programs). *Entrance requirements:* For master's, GRE or minimum GPA of 3.0 in last 60 hours. Additional exam requirements/recommendations for international students: Required—TOEFL (minimum score 550 paper-based; 213 computer-based). Electronic applications accepted.

University of Illinois at Urbana–Champaign, Graduate College, Graduate School of Library and Information Science, Champaign, IL 61820. Offers bioinformatics (MS); digital libraries (CAS); library and information science (MS, PhD, CAS). *Accreditation:* ALA (one or more programs are accredited). Postbaccalaureate distance learning degree programs offered. *Faculty:* 25 full-time (12 women), 5 part-time/adjunct (4 women). *Students:* 349 full-time (256 women), 353 part-time (276 women); includes 125 minority (30 Black or African American, non-Hispanic/Latino; 1 American Indian or Alaska Native, non-Hispanic/Latino; 37 Asian, non-Hispanic/Latino; 40 Hispanic/Latino; 1 Native Hawaiian or other Pacific Islander, non-Hispanic/Latino; 16 Two or more races, non-Hispanic/Latino), 27 international. 606 applicants, 68% accepted, 250 enrolled. In 2011, 245 master's, 6 doctorates, 8 other advanced degrees awarded. *Entrance requirements:* For master's, GRE General Test, minimum GPA of 3.0; for doctorate, minimum GPA of 3.0; for CAS, master's degree in library and information science or related field with minimum GPA of 3.0. Additional exam requirements/recommendations for international students: Required—TOEFL (minimum score 620 paper-based; 260 computer-based; 105 iBT) or IELTS (minimum score 7). *Application deadline:* Applications are processed on a rolling basis. Application fee: $75 ($90 for international students). Electronic applications accepted. *Financial support:* In 2011–12, 24 fellowships, 39 research assistantships, 44 teaching assistantships were awarded; tuition waivers (full and partial) also available. *Unit head:* Allen Renear, Dean, 217-265-5216, Fax: 217-244-3302, E-mail: renear@illinois.edu. *Application contact:* Valerie Youngen, Admissions and Records Representative, 217-333-0734, Fax: 217-244-3302, E-mail: vyoungen@llinois.edu. Web site: http://www.lis.illinois.edu.

The University of Iowa, Graduate College, School of Library and Information Science, Iowa City, IA 52242-1316. Offers MA, MA/Certificate, MBA/MA. *Accreditation:* ALA (one or more programs are accredited). *Degree requirements:* For master's, thesis optional, exam, portfolio. *Entrance requirements:* For master's, GRE General Test, minimum GPA of 3.0. Additional exam requirements/recommendations for international students: Required—TOEFL (minimum score 550 paper-based; 213 computer-based; 81 iBT). Electronic applications accepted.

University of Kentucky, Graduate School, College of Communications and Information Studies, Program in Library and Information Science, Lexington, KY 40506-0032. Offers MA, MSLS. *Accreditation:* ALA (one or more programs are accredited). Part-time programs available. *Degree requirements:* For master's, variable foreign language requirement, comprehensive exam. *Entrance requirements:* For master's, GRE General Test, minimum undergraduate GPA of 2.75. Additional exam requirements/recommendations for international students: Required—TOEFL (minimum score 550 paper-based; 213 computer-based). *Faculty research:* Information retrieval systems, information-seeking behavior, organizational behavior, computer cataloging, library resource sharing.

See Display on next page and Close-Up on page 1655.

University of Maryland, College Park, Academic Affairs, Program in History, Library, and Information Services, College Park, MD 20742. Offers MA/MLS. *Students:* 18 full-time (16 women), 2 part-time (both women); includes 2 minority (1 Black or African American, non-Hispanic/Latino; 1 Asian, non-Hispanic/Latino). 32 applicants, 25% accepted, 5 enrolled. *Entrance requirements:* Additional exam requirements/recommendations for international students: Required—TOEFL. *Application deadline:* For fall admission, 12/15 for domestic and international students. Applications are processed on a rolling basis. Application fee: $75. Electronic applications accepted. *Expenses: Tuition, area resident:* Part-time $525 per credit hour. Tuition, state resident: part-time $525 per credit hour. Tuition, nonresident: part-time $1131 per credit hour. *Required fees:* $386.31 per term. Tuition and fees vary according to program. *Financial support:* In 2011–12, 10 teaching assistantships (averaging $16,395 per year) were awarded; fellowships and research assistantships also available. Financial award applicants required to submit FAFSA. *Unit head:* Dr. David Sicilia, Associate Professor/Associate Director, 301-405-4628, E-mail: dsicilia@umd.edu. *Application contact:* Dr. Charles A. Caramello, Dean of Graduate School, 301-405-0358, Fax: 301-314-9305.

University of Michigan, Horace H. Rackham School of Graduate Studies, School of Information, Ann Arbor, MI 48109-1285. Offers archives and records management (MSI); community informatics (MSI); health informatics (MS); human computer interaction (MSI); information (PhD); information analysis and retrieval (MSI); information economics for management (MSI); information policy (MSI); library and information science (MSI); preservation of information (MSI); school library media (MSI); social computing (MSI). *Accreditation:* ALA (one or more programs are accredited). *Entrance requirements:* For master's and doctorate, GRE General Test. Additional exam requirements/recommendations for international students: Required—TOEFL (minimum score 600 paper-based; 100 iBT). Electronic applications accepted.

University of Missouri, Graduate School, College of Education, School of Information Science and Learning Technologies, Columbia, MO 65211. Offers educational technology (M Ed, Ed S); information science and learning technology (PhD); library science (MA). *Accreditation:* ALA (one or more programs are accredited). Part-time and evening/weekend programs available. *Faculty:* 16 full-time (11 women), 1 (woman) part-time/adjunct. *Students:* 125 full-time (89 women), 296 part-time (214 women); includes 19 minority (6 Black or African American, non-Hispanic/Latino; 1 American Indian or Alaska Native, non-Hispanic/Latino; 3 Asian, non-Hispanic/Latino; 8 Hispanic/Latino; 1 Two or more races, non-Hispanic/Latino), 22 international. Average age 34. 159 applicants, 66% accepted, 78 enrolled. In 2011, 154 master's, 3 doctorates, 20 other advanced degrees awarded. *Entrance requirements:* For master's, GRE General Test or MAT, minimum GPA of 3.0. Additional exam requirements/recommendations for international students: Required—TOEFL (minimum score 540 paper-based; 207 computer-based; 76 iBT). *Application deadline:* For fall admission, 3/1 priority date for domestic students; for winter admission, 10/1 priority date for domestic students; for spring admission, 3/1 priority date for domestic students. Applications are processed on a rolling basis. Application fee: $55 ($75 for international students). *Expenses:* Tuition, state resident: full-time $5881. Tuition, nonresident: full-time $15,183. *Required fees:* $952. Tuition and fees vary according to campus/location and program. *Financial support:* Fellowships and teaching assistantships available. *Faculty research:* Problem-based learning, technology usability in classrooms, computer-based performance support tools for children and youth with learning disabilities and/or emotional/behavioral disorders, engineering education collaboration environment , effectiveness of activities designed to recruit and retain women in engineering and science. *Unit head:* Dr. John Wedman, Director, E-mail: wedmanj@missouri.edu. *Application contact:* Amy Adam, 573-884-1391, E-mail: adamae@missouri.edu. Web site: http://education.missouri.edu/SISLT/.

The University of North Carolina at Chapel Hill, Graduate School, School of Information and Library Science, Chapel Hill, NC 27599. Offers MSIS, MSLS, PhD, CAS. *Accreditation:* ALA (one or more programs are accredited). Part-time programs available. Terminal master's awarded for partial completion of doctoral program. *Degree requirements:* For master's, comprehensive exam, paper or project; for doctorate, comprehensive exam, thesis/dissertation. *Entrance requirements:* For master's and doctorate, GRE General Test. Additional exam requirements/recommendations for international students: Required—TOEFL (minimum score 625 paper-based; 263 computer-based). Electronic applications accepted. *Faculty research:* Information retrieval and management, digital libraries, management of information resources, archives and records management, health informatics.

The University of North Carolina at Greensboro, Graduate School, School of Education, Department of Library and Information Studies, Greensboro, NC 27412-5001. Offers MLIS. *Accreditation:* ALA. Part-time and evening/weekend programs available. Postbaccalaureate distance learning degree programs offered (no on-campus study). *Degree requirements:* For master's, portfolio. *Entrance requirements:* For master's, GRE General Test. Additional exam requirements/recommendations for international students: Required—TOEFL (minimum score 550 paper-based; 213 computer-based), IELTS (minimum score 6.5). Electronic applications accepted. *Faculty* *research:* Library history, gender studies, children's literature, web design, homeless, technical services.

University of Northern Colorado, Graduate School, College of Education and Behavioral Sciences, Department of Educational Technology, Program in School Library Education, Greeley, CO 80639. Offers MA. Part-time programs available. Electronic applications accepted.

University of North Texas, Toulouse Graduate School, College of Information, Department of Library and Information Sciences, Denton, TX 76203. Offers information science (MS, PhD); learning technologies (M Ed, Ed D), including applied technology, training and development (M Ed), computer education and cognitive systems, educational computing; library science (MS). *Accreditation:* ALA (one or more programs are accredited). Part-time and evening/weekend programs available. *Degree requirements:* For master's, comprehensive exam; for doctorate, comprehensive exam, thesis/dissertation. *Entrance requirements:* For master's, GRE General Test, MAT; for doctorate, GRE General Test. Additional exam requirements/recommendations for international students: Recommended—TOEFL (minimum score 550 paper-based; 213 computer-based; 79 iBT). Electronic applications accepted. *Expenses:* Tuition, state resident: part-time $100 per credit hour. Tuition, nonresident: part-time $413 per credit hour. *Faculty research:* Information resources and services, information management and retrieval, computer-based information systems, human information behavior.

University of Oklahoma, College of Arts and Sciences, School of Library and Information Studies, Program in Library and Information Studies, Norman, OK 73019-0390. Offers library and information studies (MLIS); library information studies (Graduate Certificate); M Ed/MLIS; MBA/MLIS. Part-time and evening/weekend programs available. Postbaccalaureate distance learning degree programs offered. *Students:* 60 full-time (47 women), 121 part-time (97 women); includes 32 minority (8 Black or African American, non-Hispanic/Latino; 13 American Indian or Alaska Native, non-Hispanic/Latino; 4 Asian, non-Hispanic/Latino; 3 Hispanic/Latino; 4 Two or more races, non-Hispanic/Latino), 3 international. Average age 33. 77 applicants, 94% accepted, 47 enrolled. In 2011, 59 degrees awarded. *Degree requirements:* For master's, comprehensive exam (MLIS). *Entrance requirements:* For master's, GRE, minimum GPA of 3.2 in last 60 hours or 3.0 overall. Additional exam requirements/recommendations for international students: Required—TOEFL (minimum score 550 paper-based; 213 computer-based; 79 iBT). *Application deadline:* For fall admission, 3/1 priority date for domestic students, 4/1 for international students; for spring admission, 10/15 for domestic students, 9/1 for international students. Applications are processed on a rolling basis. Application fee: $40 ($90 for international students). Electronic applications accepted. *Expenses:* Tuition, state resident: full-time $4087; part-time $170.30 per credit hour. Tuition, nonresident: full-time $14,875; part-time $619.80 per credit hour. *Required fees:* $2659; $100.25 per credit hour. Tuition and fees vary according to course load and degree level. *Financial support:* In 2011–12, 88 students received support. Federal Work-Study, scholarships/grants, health care benefits, and unspecified assistantships available. Support available to part-time students. Financial award applicants required to submit FAFSA. *Faculty research:* Equity of access, information services to special populations, information use in the digital age, library services and materials for young people, pluralization of archival theory and education. *Unit head:* Cecelia Brown, Director, 405-325-3921, Fax: 405-325-7648, E-mail: cbrown@ou.edu. *Application contact:* Maggie Ryan, Coordinator of Admissions, 405-325-3921, Fax: 405-325-7648, E-mail: mryan@ou.edu.

University of Pittsburgh, School of Information Sciences, Library and Information Science Program, Pittsburgh, PA 15260. Offers health sciences librarianship (Certificate); library and information science (MLIS, PhD). *Accreditation:* ALA (one or more programs are accredited). Part-time and evening/weekend programs available. Postbaccalaureate distance learning degree programs offered (minimal on-campus study). *Faculty:* 9 full-time (5 women), 6 part-time/adjunct (5 women). *Students:* 167 full-time (133 women), 177 part-time (145 women); includes 35 minority (11 Black or African American, non-Hispanic/Latino; 1 American Indian or Alaska Native, non-Hispanic/Latino; 7 Asian, non-Hispanic/Latino; 11 Hispanic/Latino; 5 Two or more races, non-Hispanic/Latino), 15 international. 382 applicants, 85% accepted, 154 enrolled. In 2011, 217 master's, 5 doctorates, 11 other advanced degrees awarded. *Degree requirements:* For master's, thesis optional; for doctorate, comprehensive exam, thesis/dissertation. *Entrance requirements:* For master's, GRE General Test or MAT, bachelor's degree from accredited university; minimum GPA of 3.0; for doctorate, GRE General Test, minimum GPA of 3.5; for Certificate, MLIS, MSIS with minimum GPA of 3.0. Additional exam requirements/recommendations for international students: Required—TOEFL (minimum score 550 paper-based; 80 iBT). *Application deadline:* For fall admission, 1/15 priority date for domestic students, 1/15 for international students. Applications are processed on a rolling basis. Application fee: $50. Electronic applications accepted. *Expenses:* Contact institution. *Financial support:* Fellowships with full tuition reimbursements, research assistantships with full and partial tuition reimbursements, teaching assistantships with full and partial tuition reimbursements, career-related internships or fieldwork, scholarships/grants, health care benefits, tuition waivers (full and partial), and unspecified assistantships available. Financial award application deadline: 1/15; financial award applicants required to submit FAFSA. *Faculty research:* Archives and preservation management, children's resources and services, digital libraries, cross-lingual information retrieval, cyberscholarship and cyberinfrastructure. *Unit head:* Dr. Martin Weiss, Chair, 412-624-9430, Fax: 412-624-5231, E-mail: mbw@pitt.edu. *Application contact:* Brandi Belleau Liskey, Student Recruiting Coordinator, 412-648-3108, Fax: 412-624-5231, E-mail: lisinq@sis.pitt.edu. Web site: http://www.ischool.pitt.edu/lis.

University of Puerto Rico, Río Piedras, Graduate School of Information Sciences and Technologies, San Juan, PR 00931-3300. Offers administration of academic libraries (PMC); administration of public libraries (PMC); administration of special libraries (PMC); consultant in information services (PMC); documents and files administration (Post-Graduate Certificate); electronic information resources analyst (Post-Graduate Certificate); information science (MIS); librarianship and information services (MLS); school librarian (Post-Graduate Certificate); school librarian distance education mode (Post-Graduate Certificate); specialist in legal information (PMC). *Accreditation:* ALA. Part-time programs available. *Degree requirements:* For master's, comprehensive exam, thesis, portfolio. *Entrance requirements:* For master's, PAEG, GRE, interview, minimum GPA of 3.0, 3 letters of recommendation; for other advanced degree, PAEG, GRE, minimum GPA of 3.0, IST master's degree. *Faculty research:* Investigating the users needs and preferences for a specialized environmental library.

University of Rhode Island, Graduate School, College of Arts and Sciences, Graduate School of Library and Information Studies, Kingston, RI 02881. Offers MLIS, MLIS/MA, MLIS/MPA. *Accreditation:* ALA (one or more programs are accredited). Part-time programs available. *Faculty:* 3 full-time (all women), 6 part-time/adjunct (4 women). *Students:* 40 full-time (29 women), 89 part-time (74 women); includes 5 minority (2 Asian, non-Hispanic/Latino; 2 Hispanic/Latino; 1 Two or more races, non-Hispanic/Latino). In 2011, 62 master's awarded. *Degree requirements:* For master's, comprehensive exam. *Entrance requirements:* For master's, GRE or MAT (if undergraduate GPA less than 3.0), 2 letters of recommendation. Additional exam requirements/recommendations for international students: Required—TOEFL (minimum score 550 paper-based; 213 computer-based). *Application deadline:* For fall admission, 6/15 for domestic students, 2/1 for international students; for spring admission, 10/15 for domestic students, 7/15 for international students. Application fee: $65. Electronic applications accepted. *Expenses:* Tuition, state resident: full-time $10,432; part-time $580 per credit hour. Tuition, nonresident: full-time $23,130; part-time $1285 per credit hour. *Required fees:* $1362; $36 per credit hour. $35 per semester. One-time fee: $130. *Financial support:* Application deadline: 1/15; applicants required to submit FAFSA. *Unit head:* Dr. Gale Eaton, Director, 401-874-4641, Fax: 401-874-4964, E-mail: geaton@uri.edu. *Application contact:* Nasser H. Zawia, Dean of the Graduate School, 401-874-5909, Fax: 401-874-5787, E-mail: nzawia@uri.edu. Web site: http://www.uri.edu/artsci/lsc/.

University of South Carolina, The Graduate School, College of Mass Communications and Information Studies, School of Library and Information Science, Columbia, SC 29208. Offers MLIS, PhD, Certificate, Specialist, MLIS/MA. *Accreditation:* ALA (one or more programs are accredited). Part-time programs available. Postbaccalaureate distance learning degree programs offered (no on-campus study). *Degree requirements:* For master's, end of program portfolio; for doctorate, comprehensive exam, thesis/dissertation. *Entrance requirements:* For master's and other advanced degree, GRE General Test or MAT; for doctorate, GTE, writing sample. Additional exam requirements/recommendations for international students: Required—TOEFL (minimum score 570 paper-based; 230 computer-based; 75 iBT). Electronic applications accepted. *Faculty research:* Information technology management, distance education, library services for children and young adults, special libraries.

University of Southern Mississippi, Graduate School, College of Education and Psychology, School of Library and Information Science, Hattiesburg, MS 39406-0001. Offers MLIS. *Accreditation:* ALA. Part-time and evening/weekend programs available. Postbaccalaureate distance learning degree programs offered (minimal on-campus study). *Faculty:* 8 full-time (7 women), 1 part-time/adjunct (0 women). *Students:* 34 full-time (31 women), 122 part-time (99 women); includes 24 minority (18 Black or African American, non-Hispanic/Latino; 1 Hispanic/Latino; 5 Two or more races, non-Hispanic/Latino), 2 international. Average age 37. 52 applicants, 81% accepted, 31 enrolled. In 2011, 60 degrees awarded. *Degree requirements:* For master's, comprehensive exam, thesis. *Entrance requirements:* For master's, GRE General Test, minimum GPA of 3.0. Additional exam requirements/recommendations for international students: Required—TOEFL, IELTS. *Application deadline:* For fall admission, 3/15 priority date for domestic students, 3/15 for international students; for spring admission, 1/10 priority date for domestic students, 1/10 for international students. Applications are processed on a rolling basis. Application fee: $50. Electronic applications accepted. *Financial support:* In 2011–12, 8 students received support, including 6 research assistantships with full tuition reimbursements available (averaging $7,200 per year), 1 teaching assistantship with full tuition reimbursement available (averaging $7,200 per year); fellowships with tuition reimbursements available, career-related internships or fieldwork, Federal Work-Study, institutionally sponsored loans, scholarships/grants, health care benefits, and unspecified assistantships also available. Financial award application deadline: 3/15; financial award applicants required to submit FAFSA. *Faculty research:* Printing, library history, children's literature, telecommunications, management. *Total annual research expenditures:* $14,185. *Unit head:* Dr. Melanie J. Norton, Director, 601-266-4228, Fax: 601-266-5774. *Application contact:* Dr. Melanie J. Norton, Director, 601-266-4228, Fax: 601-266-5774. Web site: http://www.usm.edu/graduateschool/table.php.

University of South Florida, Graduate School, College of Arts and Sciences, School of Information, Tampa, FL 33620-9951. Offers library and information science (MA). *Accreditation:* ALA. Part-time and evening/weekend programs available. Postbaccalaureate distance learning degree programs offered (minimal on-campus study). *Faculty:* 12 full-time (8 women), 19 part-time/adjunct (12 women). *Students:* 106 full-time (87 women), 188 part-time (166 women); includes 60 minority (16 Black or African American, non-Hispanic/Latino; 2 American Indian or Alaska Native, non-Hispanic/Latino; 8 Asian, non-Hispanic/Latino; 32 Hispanic/Latino; 2 Two or more races, non-Hispanic/Latino), 2 international. Average age 34. 137 applicants, 55% accepted, 50 enrolled. In 2011, 152 master's awarded. *Degree requirements:* For master's, comprehensive exam, thesis optional. *Entrance requirements:* For master's, GRE, minimum GPA of 3.25 in upper-division course work, personal statement, writing sample. Additional exam requirements/recommendations for international students: Required—TOEFL (minimum score 550 paper-based; 213 computer-based; 79 iBT) or IELTS (minimum score 6.5). *Application deadline:* For fall admission, 6/1 for domestic students, 1/2 for international students; for spring admission, 10/15 for domestic students, 6/1 for international students. Applications are processed on a rolling basis. Application fee: $30. Electronic applications accepted. *Financial support:* Unspecified assistantships available. Financial award application deadline: 6/30. *Faculty research:* Youth services in libraries, community engagement and libraries, information architecture, biomedical informatics. *Total annual research expenditures:* $11,976. *Unit head:* Jim Andrews, Director, 813-974-2108, Fax: 813-974-6840, E-mail: jandrews@cas.usf.edu. *Application contact:* Sylvia Gardner, Administrative Assistant, 813-974-0853, Fax: 813-974-5911, E-mail: gardner@cas.usf.edu. Web site: http://si.usf.edu/.

University of Washington, Graduate School, The Information School, Seattle, WA 98195. Offers information management (MSIM); information science (PhD); library and information science (MLIS). *Accreditation:* ALA (one or more programs are accredited). Part-time and evening/weekend programs available. Postbaccalaureate distance learning degree programs offered (minimal on-campus study). *Faculty:* 37 full-time (17 women), 17 part-time/adjunct (10 women). *Students:* 282 full-time (185 women), 257 part-time (184 women); includes 93 minority (9 Black or African American, non-Hispanic/Latino; 7 American Indian or Alaska Native, non-Hispanic/Latino; 54 Asian, non-Hispanic/Latino; 20 Hispanic/Latino; 3 Native Hawaiian or other Pacific Islander, non-Hispanic/Latino), 72 international. Average age 31. 775 applicants, 61% accepted, 239 enrolled. In 2011, 219 master's, 5 doctorates awarded. Terminal master's awarded for partial completion of doctoral program. *Degree requirements:* For master's, comprehensive exam (for some programs), thesis optional, culminating experience project (thesis, capstone or portfolio), internship; for doctorate, comprehensive exam, thesis/dissertation. *Entrance requirements:* For master's, GRE General Test, GMAT, minimum GPA of 3.0; for doctorate, GRE General Test, minimum GPA of 3.0. Additional exam requirements/recommendations for international students: Required—TOEFL (minimum score 580 paper-based; 237 computer-based; 92 iBT), IELTS (minimum score 7), MLT (minimum score 90). *Application deadline:* For fall admission, 12/1 priority date for domestic students, 12/1 for international students. Application fee: $75. Electronic applications accepted. *Expenses:* Contact institution. *Financial support:* In 2011–12, 57 students received support, including 8 fellowships with full tuition reimbursements available (averaging $12,942 per year), 19 research assistantships with full and partial tuition reimbursements available (averaging $11,270 per year), 18 teaching assistantships with full and partial tuition reimbursements available (averaging $18,205 per year); career-related internships or fieldwork, Federal Work-Study, institutionally sponsored loans, scholarships/grants, health care benefits, tuition waivers (full and partial), unspecified assistantships, and graduate assistantships (17 awards averaging $14,090) also available. Support available to part-time students. Financial award application deadline: 2/28; financial award applicants required to submit FAFSA. *Faculty research:* Human/computer interaction, information policy and ethics, knowledge organization, information literacy and access, information assurance and cyber security. *Total annual research expenditures:* $4.5 million. *Unit head:* Dr. Harry Bruce, Dean, 206-616-0985, E-mail: harryb@uw.edu. *Application contact:* Kari Brothers, Admissions Counselor, 206-616-5541, Fax: 206-616-3152, E-mail: kari683@uw.edu. Web site: http://ischool.uw.edu/.

The University of Western Ontario, Faculty of Graduate Studies, Faculty of Information and Media Studies, Programs in Library and Information Science, London, ON N6A 5B8, Canada. Offers MLIS, PhD. Program conducted on a trimester basis. *Accreditation:* ALA (one or more programs are accredited). Part-time and evening/weekend programs available. *Degree requirements:* For doctorate, comprehensive exam, thesis/dissertation. *Entrance requirements:* For master's, honors degree, minimum B average during previous 2 years of course work; for doctorate, MLIS or equivalent. Additional exam requirements/recommendations for international students: Required—TOEFL (minimum score 625 paper-based; 263 computer-based), TWE (minimum score 5). Electronic applications accepted. *Faculty research:* Information, individuals, and society; information systems, policy, power, and institutions.

University of Wisconsin–Eau Claire, College of Education and Human Sciences, Program in Secondary Education, Eau Claire, WI 54702-4004. Offers professional development (MEPD), including initial teacher, library science, professional development, professional educator. Part-time and evening/weekend programs available. Postbaccalaureate distance learning degree programs offered (minimal on-campus study). *Faculty:* 13 full-time (9 women). *Students:* 3 full-time (1 woman), 34 part-time (29 women); includes 5 minority (2 American Indian or Alaska Native, non-Hispanic/Latino; 1 Asian, non-Hispanic/Latino; 2 Hispanic/Latino). Average age 34. 8 applicants, 88% accepted, 6 enrolled. In 2011, 10 master's awarded. *Degree requirements:* For master's, comprehensive exam, thesis, research paper, portfolio or written exam; oral exam. *Entrance requirements:* For master's, certification to teach, minimum GPA of 2.75. Additional exam requirements/recommendations for international students: Required—TOEFL (minimum score 550 paper-based; 213 computer-based; 79 iBT); Recommended—IELTS (minimum score 7). *Application deadline:* For fall admission, 7/1 priority date for domestic students, 6/1 for international students; for spring admission, 12/1 priority date for domestic students, 11/1 for international students. Applications are processed on a rolling basis. Application fee: $56. *Expenses:* Tuition, state resident: full-time $7312; part-time $406 per credit. Tuition, nonresident: full-time $16,771; part-time $932 per credit. *Required fees:* $1101; $61 per credit. *Financial support:* In 2011–12, 8 students received support. Federal Work-Study and unspecified assistantships available. Financial award application deadline: 3/1; financial award applicants required to submit FAFSA. *Unit head:* Dr. Jill Pastrana, Chair, 715-836-2013, Fax: 715-836-4868, E-mail: pastrajp@uwec.edu. *Application contact:* Dr. Sherry Macaul, Coordinator, 715-836-5735, E-mail: macaulsl@uwec.edu. Web site: http://www.uwec.edu/ES/programs/graduateprograms.htm.

University of Wisconsin–Madison, Graduate School, College of Letters and Science, School of Library and Information Studies, Madison, WI 53706-1380. Offers MA, PhD. *Accreditation:* ALA (one or more programs are accredited). Part-time programs available. *Degree requirements:* For doctorate, comprehensive exam, thesis/dissertation. Electronic applications accepted. *Expenses:* Tuition, state resident: full-time $10,296; part-time $643.51 per credit. Tuition, nonresident: full-time $24,054; part-time $1503.40 per credit. *Required fees:* $70.06 per credit. Tuition and fees vary according to course load, campus/location, program and reciprocity agreements. *Faculty research:* Intellectual freedom, children's literature, print culture history, information systems design and evaluation, school library media centers.

University of Wisconsin–Milwaukee, Graduate School, School of Information Studies, Milwaukee, WI 53201-0413. Offers advanced studies in library and information science (CAS); archives and records administration (CAS); digital libraries (Certificate); information studies (MLIS, PhD); MLIS/MA; MLIS/MM; MLIS/MS. *Accreditation:* ALA (one or more programs are accredited). Part-time programs available. *Faculty:* 22 full-time (11 women). *Students:* 173 full-time (136 women), 426 part-time (339 women); includes 60 minority (16 Black or African American, non-Hispanic/Latino; 1 American Indian or Alaska Native, non-Hispanic/Latino; 14 Asian, non-Hispanic/Latino; 8 Hispanic/Latino; 21 Two or more races, non-Hispanic/Latino), 30 international. Average age 34. 291 applicants, 73% accepted, 122 enrolled. In 2011, 182 master's awarded. *Entrance requirements:* For master's, GRE General Test or MAT; for doctorate, GRE. Additional exam requirements/recommendations for international students: Required—TOEFL (minimum score 550 paper-based; 213 computer-based), IELTS (minimum score 6.5). *Application deadline:* For fall admission, 1/1 priority date for domestic students; for spring admission, 9/1 for domestic students. Applications are processed on a rolling basis. Application fee: $56 ($96 for international students). Electronic applications accepted. One-time fee: $506.10 full-time. Tuition and fees vary according to course load and reciprocity agreements. *Financial support:* In 2011–12, 4 teaching assistantships were awarded; fellowships, research assistantships, career-related internships or fieldwork, Federal Work-Study, health care benefits, unspecified assistantships, and project assistantships also available. Support available to part-time students. Financial award application deadline: 4/15; financial award applicants required to submit FAFSA. *Total annual research expenditures:* $302,657. *Unit head:* Dietmar Wolfram, Interim Dean, 414-229-4709, E-mail: dwolfram@uwm.edu. *Application contact:* Hur-Li Lee, Representative, 414-229-6838, E-mail: hurli@uwm.edu. Web site: http://www.uwm.edu/Dept/SLIS/.

University of Wisconsin–Whitewater, School of Graduate Studies, College of Education and Professional Studies, Department of Curriculum and Instruction, Whitewater, WI 53190-1790. Offers professional development (MS), including bilingual education, challenging advanced learners, curriculum and instruction, educational leadership, health, human performance and recreation, health, physical education and coaching, information technologies and libraries, reading. *Accreditation:* NCATE. Part-time and evening/weekend programs available. Postbaccalaureate distance learning degree programs offered. *Students:* 25 full-time (12 women), 68 part-time (51 women); includes 26 minority (15 Black or African American, non-Hispanic/Latino; 3 Asian, non-Hispanic/Latino; 8 Hispanic/Latino). Average age 33. 29 applicants, 86% accepted, 16 enrolled. In 2011, 44 master's awarded. *Degree requirements:* For master's, thesis or integrated project. *Entrance requirements:* Additional exam requirements/recommendations for international students: Required—TOEFL (minimum score 550 paper-based; 213 computer-based; 80 iBT), IELTS (minimum score 6). *Application deadline:* For fall admission, 7/15 priority date for domestic students, 7/15 for international students; for spring admission, 12/1 priority date for domestic students, 12/1 for international students. Applications are processed on a rolling basis. Application fee: $56. Electronic applications accepted. *Expenses:* Tuition, state resident: full-time $4088. Tuition, nonresident: full-time $8817. Tuition and fees vary according to program. *Financial support:* Research assistantships, Federal Work-Study, unspecified assistantships, and out-of-state fee waivers available. Support available to part-time students. Financial award application deadline: 3/15; financial award applicants required to submit FAFSA. *Faculty research:* Hybrid of exercise physiology and psychology; gender equity; education, pedagogy, and technology; comprehensive school health education. *Unit head:* Dr. John Zbikowski, Coordinator, 262-472-4860, Fax: 262-472-

1988, E-mail: zbikowskij@uww.edu. *Application contact:* Sally A. Lange, School of Graduate Studies, 262-472-1006, Fax: 262-472-5027, E-mail: gradschl@uww.edu.

Valdosta State University, Program in Library and Information Science, Valdosta, GA 31698. Offers MLIS. *Accreditation:* ALA. Postbaccalaureate distance learning degree programs offered (minimal on-campus study). *Faculty:* 7 full-time (3 women). *Students:* 22 full-time (15 women), 213 part-time (170 women); includes 54 minority (32 Black or African American, non-Hispanic/Latino; 6 Asian, non-Hispanic/Latino; 16 Two or more races, non-Hispanic/Latino). Average age 30. 91 applicants, 62% accepted, 37 enrolled. In 2011, 48 master's awarded. *Degree requirements:* For master's, comprehensive exam. *Entrance requirements:* For master's, two essays, resume, three recommendations. Additional exam requirements/recommendations for international students: Required—TOEFL (minimum score 523 paper-based; 193 computer-based). *Application deadline:* For fall admission, 4/14 for domestic students, 4/15 for international students. Application fee: $35. *Expenses:* Tuition, state resident: full-time $7098; part-time $217 per hour. Tuition, nonresident: full-time $20,630; part-time $780 per hour. *Financial support:* In 2011–12, 4 students received support, including 4 research assistantships with full tuition reimbursements available (averaging $3,652 per year); institutionally sponsored loans, scholarships/grants, and unspecified assistantships also available. Support available to part-time students. Financial award application deadline: 7/1; financial award applicants required to submit FAFSA. *Unit head:* Dr. Wallace Koehler, Director, 229-245-3732, Fax: 229-333-5862, E-mail: wkoehler@valdosta.edu. *Application contact:* Jessica DeVane, Admissions Specialist, 229-333-5694, Fax: 229-245-3853, E-mail: jldevane@valdosta.edu.

Valley City State University, Online Master of Education Program, Valley City, ND 58072. Offers library and information technologies (M Ed); teaching and technology (M Ed); teaching English language learners (ELL) (M Ed); technology education (M Ed). *Accreditation:* NCATE. Part-time and evening/weekend programs available. Postbaccalaureate distance learning degree programs offered (no on-campus study). *Faculty:* 25 full-time (18 women), 2 part-time/adjunct (both women). *Students:* 4 full-time (3 women), 147 part-time (99 women); includes 6 minority (1 Black or African American, non-Hispanic/Latino; 1 American Indian or Alaska Native, non-Hispanic/Latino; 2 Asian, non-Hispanic/Latino; 2 Hispanic/Latino). Average age 34. 40 applicants, 83% accepted, 30 enrolled. In 2011, 30 master's awarded. *Degree requirements:* For master's, action research report, comprehensive portfolio. *Entrance requirements:* For master's, GRE, MAT, PRAXIS II or National Teaching Board for Professional Standards (if GPA less than 3.0). Additional exam requirements/recommendations for international students: Required—TOEFL (minimum score 525 paper-based; 70 iBT). *Application deadline:* For fall admission, 5/23 priority date for domestic students, 5/23 for international students; for spring admission, 4/20 priority date for domestic students, 4/23 for international students. Applications are processed on a rolling basis. Application fee: $35. Electronic applications accepted. *Expenses:* Tuition, state resident: full-time $4533.30; part-time $251.85 per credit hour. Tuition, nonresident: full-time $4533; part-time $251.85 per credit hour. *Required fees:* $1239.48; $68.86 per credit hour. *Financial support:* In 2011–12, 27 students received support. Tuition waivers (full and partial) available. Financial award application deadline: 5/15; financial award applicants required to submit FAFSA. *Faculty research:* Academically at-risk students in higher education, communication pedagogy and technology, gender communication, computer-mediated communication, creativity in music. *Total annual research expenditures:* $26,000. *Unit head:* Dr. Gary Thompson, Dean, 701-845-7197, E-mail: gary.thompson@vcsu.edu. *Application contact:* Misty Lindgren, 701-845-7303, Fax: 701-845-7305, E-mail: misty.lindgren@vcsu.edu. Web site: http://www.vcsu.edu/graduate.

Wayne State University, School of Library and Information Science, Detroit, MI 48202. Offers archival administration (MLIS, Certificate); arts and museum librarianship (Certificate); general librarianship (MLIS); health sciences librarianship (MLIS); information management for librarians (Certificate); information science (MLIS); law librarianship (MLIS); library and information science (MLIS, Spec), including academic libraries (MLIS); organization of information (MLIS); public libraries (MLIS); public library services to children and young adults (MLIS, Certificate); records and information management (Certificate); records management (MLIS); references services (MLIS); school library media (Spec); school library media specialist endorsement (MLIS); special libraries (MLIS); urban librarianship (Certificate); urban libraries (MLIS); MLIS/MA. *Accreditation:* ALA (one or more programs are accredited). Part-time and evening/weekend programs available. Postbaccalaureate distance learning degree programs offered (no on-campus study). *Faculty:* 13 full-time (8 women), 25 part-time/adjunct (19 women). *Students:* 121 full-time (93 women), 447 part-time (346 women); includes 57 minority (37 Black or African American, non-Hispanic/Latino; 1 American Indian or Alaska Native, non-Hispanic/Latino; 4 Asian, non-Hispanic/Latino; 7 Hispanic/Latino; 8 Two or more races, non-Hispanic/Latino), 4 international. Average age 33. 336 applicants, 62% accepted, 135 enrolled. In 2011, 212 master's, 38 other advanced degrees awarded. *Entrance requirements:* For master's and other advanced degree, GRE or MAT (if undergraduate GPA is between 2.5 and 2.99), minimum undergraduate GPA of 3.0 or graduate degree, personal statement, new student orientation. Additional exam requirements/recommendations for international students: Required—TOEFL (minimum score 550 paper-based; 213 computer-based); Recommended—TWE (minimum score 5.5). *Application deadline:* For fall admission, 7/1 for domestic students, 5/1 for international students; for winter admission, 10/1 for domestic students, 9/1 for international students; for spring admission, 3/15 for domestic students, 1/1 for international students. Applications are processed on a rolling basis. Application fee: $50. Electronic applications accepted. *Expenses:* Tuition, state resident: part-time $512.85 per credit. Tuition, nonresident: part-time $1132.65 per credit. *Required fees:* $26.60 per credit. $199.65 per semester. Tuition and fees vary according to course load and program. *Financial support:* In 2011–12, 1 research assistantship with tuition reimbursement (averaging $12,250 per year) was awarded; fellowships with tuition reimbursements, career-related internships or fieldwork, Federal Work-Study, institutionally sponsored loans, scholarships/grants, and unspecified assistantships also available. Support available to part-time students. Financial award application deadline: 5/15. *Faculty research:* Convergence of academic libraries and other academic services, competitive intelligence and data mining, impact of digitization on libraries, international librarianship, consumer health information, urban library issues, human-computer interaction, universal access to libraries and instructional support services. *Unit head:* Dr. Sandra Yee, Dean, 313-577-4059, Fax: 313-577-7563, E-mail: aj0533@wayne.edu. *Application contact:* Dr. Stephen Fredericks, Associate Dean and Director, 313-577-7563, E-mail: bajjaly@wayne.edu. Web site: http://www.lisp.wayne.edu/.

Wright State University, School of Graduate Studies, College of Education and Human Services, Department of Teacher Education, Programs in Workforce Education, Dayton, OH 45435. Offers career, technology and vocational education (M Ed, MA); computer/technology education (M Ed, MA); library/media (M Ed, MA); vocational education (M Ed, MA). *Accreditation:* NCATE. *Degree requirements:* For master's, thesis (for some programs). *Entrance requirements:* For master's, GRE General Test, MAT. Additional exam requirements/recommendations for international students: Required—TOEFL.

PRATT INSTITUTE

School of Information and Library Science

Programs of Study

Distinguished as the only ALA-accredited graduate school of information and library science based in Manhattan and the oldest library and information science (LIS) school in North America, Pratt's School of Information and Library Science (SILS) was established in 1890 and has been continuously accredited since 1923, when accreditation was first introduced to the field.

Building upon Pratt's national reputation as a leading school in art and design, Pratt brings creativity and innovation to library science education to offer students exciting and cutting-edge programs and courses from archives and digital libraries, to special libraries and school library media.

In addition to the 36-credit Master of Science in Library and Information Science (M.S.L.I.S.) degree, Pratt offers three joint-degree programs, one with Pratt's History of Art Department (M.S.L.I.S./M.S. in history of art, 60 credits), one with Pratt's Digital Arts M.F.A. (M.S.L.I.S./M.F.A. in digital arts, 75 credits), and one with the Brooklyn Law School (M.S.L.I.S./J.D., 86 credits); a 12-credit Archives Certificate Program within the M.S.L.I.S.; a 12-credit Museum Libraries Certificate; and an M.S. with Library Media Specialist certification.

The School of Information and Library Science prepares students for leadership positions in the information professions, including special opportunities in arts and humanities librarianship for students pursuing careers in academic and research libraries, art and museum libraries, and archives and special collections. The program combines a core curriculum (information professions, information services and sources, information technologies, and knowledge organization) with elective courses, such as advanced Web design, digital libraries, human information behavior, information architecture, information policy, and projects in digital archives. Some courses are taught on location in museums and libraries, such as the New York Public Library, the Watson Library, and the Metropolitan Museum of Art. Other courses are held on the Brooklyn Campus in the Pratt Library, and students in the library and media specialist (LMS) studies program take courses in the Art and Design Education Department. SILS maintains a dean's office in North Hall. Students carry out practicum internships at many of New York's leading cultural institutions. Students may choose from a number of program concentrations, depending on their interests and career goals, including business, cultural informatics, digital technology and knowledge organization, legal and health information, library media specialist studies, management and leadership, public urban libraries, and reference and information literacy.

The master's program may be completed in as little as two semesters and one summer and must be completed within four years of enrollment. Courses are offered in the evening, during the day, and on Saturday and Sunday to accommodate students who work.

Research Facilities

The program's teaching and research facilities occupy the entire sixth floor of a seven-story facility in its home at 144 West 14th Street, Manhattan, in a beautifully restored landmark building, designated the Pratt Manhattan Center (PMC). Here, students find faculty and staff offices, smart classrooms, large computer labs, an elegant conference room, and the student cyber place. The fifth-floor computer lab adds to SILS resources, and a separate scanning lab supports digital library projects. The fourth floor is home to the PMC library, containing extensive LIS collections of books, journals, and full-text online databases. Special SILS events and lectures are held in a 150-person lecture hall adjoining the second-floor gallery space. This rich complex of facilities, all with wireless access and convenient to students and faculty members, adds greatly to effective operations and enhances the learning environment.

Financial Aid

Graduate scholarships ranging in amount are awarded to all eligible applicants. There is no application required. Financial aid is available through a variety of programs funded by institutions, New York State, and the federal government. These include the Federal Perkins Loan and the Federal Work-Study Program, the Tuition Assistance Program of New York State, and Pratt scholarships, loans, and student aid. Continuing students in all departments may apply for fellowships and assistantships on a competitive basis. Special alumni-sponsored fellowships are also available.

Cost of Study

In 2012–13, tuition is $1126 per credit for the M.S.L.I.S. degree, and student fees are approximately $1740 per year. The cost of books and supplies varies widely among the different programs.

Living and Housing Costs

Housing is available for single students on the Brooklyn Campus. The cost averages $13,086 (room and board $16,866) per year. The Office of Residential Life maintains listings of off-campus housing to help students find suitable accommodations.

Student Group

Graduate students at Pratt are drawn from all parts of the United States (forty-one states) and fifty-five other countries. The SILS graduate program average age is 32, with most students working full-time while taking M.S.L.I.S. courses. The employment outlook for Pratt graduates is bright. At present, more than 95 percent of the graduates obtain positions in a broad range of work environments from academic libraries and museums, to special libraries, including those in the corporate, business, and medical fields. The growth potential of the job market is seemingly unlimited. Job opportunities have been increasing for graduates of the information and library science program.

Location

Pratt-SILS is headquartered in the heart of Manhattan. Here, most SILS courses are offered at times convenient to those students who wish to work and pursue their M.S.L.I.S. The main campus of Pratt Institute is located in the Clinton Hill section of Brooklyn. Some courses are offered there to support programs such as the joint degree with Brooklyn Law School and program courses in urban librarianship at Brooklyn Public Library. In Manhattan, courses are taught at Cornell Medical Center for health sciences specialization and the New York Public Library/Research Libraries for special collections.

Pratt Institute

SILS students enjoy the advantages of New York's position as a world center for the information professions. Students also benefit from the wealth of professional experience and expertise that complements their formal study. A vast variety of cultural and recreational activities are available in the neighborhood, in Brooklyn, in the city, and in the region. Pratt has a parklike campus in a quiet neighborhood of Victorian buildings set in the midst of one of the most vibrant cities in the world.

The Institute

A private, nonsectarian institute of higher education, Pratt was founded in 1887 by industrialist and philanthropist Charles Pratt. Changing with the requirements of the professions for which it educates, Pratt today prepares a student body of approximately 4,700 undergraduate and graduate students for a wide range of careers in architecture and planning, design and fine arts, and information science.

Applying

Applications should be submitted by January 5 for anticipated entrance in the fall semester and by October 1 for anticipated entrance in the spring semester. Applications received after these deadlines are considered if there is available space. Information and application forms may be obtained from the Graduate Admissions Office or the Web site. Applications may also be submitted online at http://www.pratt.edu/admiss/apply.

Correspondence and Information

Graduate Admissions Office
Pratt Institute
200 Willoughby Avenue
Brooklyn, New York 11205
Phone: 718-636-3514
800-331-0834 (toll-free)
Fax: 718-399-4242
Web site: http://www.pratt.edu/admissions

School of Information and Library Science
Pratt Institute
144 West 14th Street, 6th Floor
New York, New York 10011
Phone: 212-647-7682
E-mail: infosils@pratt.edu
Web site: http://www.pratt.edu/sils

THE FACULTY

Tula Giannini, Dean; Ph.D., Bryn Mawr.
Amy Azzarito, Visiting Assistant Professor; M.L.S., Pratt.
Virginia L. Bartow, Visiting Assistant Professor; M.L.S., Columbia.
Jason Baumann, Visiting Assistant Professor; M.L.S., CUNY, Queens.
John Berry, Visiting Professor; M.L.S., Simmons.
Helen-Ann Brown, Visiting Assistant Professor; M.L.S., Maryland, College Park.
Gilok Choi, Assistant Professor; Ph.D., Texas at Austin.
Anthony Cocciolo, Assistant Professor; Ed.D., Columbia.
Anthony M. Cucchiara, Visiting Assistant Professor; M.L.S., Pratt.
Joseph Dalton, Visiting Assistant Professor; M.S.in L.I.S., Illinois at Urbana-Champaign.
Deirdre Donohue, Visiting Assistant Professor; M.L.S., Pratt.
Richard Eiger, Visiting Professor; M.B.A., NYU.
Rebecca Federman, Visiting Assistant Professor; M.L.S., Pratt.
Judith Freeman, Visiting Professor; M.L.S., Rutgers.
Nancy Friedland, Visiting Associate Professor; M.L.S., Rutgers.
Barbara Genco, Visiting Associate Professor; M.L.S., Pratt.
Sharareh Goldsmith, Visiting Assistant Professor; M.L.S., Pratt.
Alexis Hagadorn, Visiting Assistant Professor; M.L.S., Columbia.
Susan Hamson, Visiting Assistant Professor; Ph.D., Temple.
Denise Hibay, Visiting Associate Professor; M.L.S., Pittsburgh.
Jessica Lee Hochman, Assistant Professor; M.A., Columbia.
Jennifer Hubert-Swan, Visiting Assistant Professor; M.L.S. Wayne State (Michigan).
Michael Inman, Visiting Assistant Professor; M.L.S., Pratt.
Elyssa Kroski, Visiting Assistant Professor; M.S.L.I.S., LIU, C.W. Post.
Irene Lopatovska, Assistant Professor; M.L.S., North Texas.
Ellen Loughran, Assistant Professor; B.A., Marymount Manhattan.
Amy Lucker, Visiting Assistant Professor; M.S.L.I.S., Simmons College.
Hillias Martin, Visting Assistant Professor; M.L.I.S., Pratt.
Seoud M. Matta, Dean Emeritus; D.L.S., Columbia.
Elena Dana Neacsu, Visiting Assistant Professor; M.L.S., CUNY, Queens.
Maria Cristina Pattuelli, Assistant Professor; Ph.D., North Carolina at Chapel Hill.
Slava Polishchuk, Visiting Assistant Professor; M.F.A., CUNY, Brooklyn.
Deborah Rabina, Assistant Professor; Ph.D., Rutgers.
Lee Robinson, Visiting Associate Professor; M.L.S., Columbia.
Pamela Rollo, Visiting Professor; M.L.S., Columbia.
Caroline Romans, Visiting Professor; M.L.S., Drexel.
Charles Rubenstein, Professor; Ph.D., Polytechnic of NYU.
Nasser Sharify, Dean Emeritus, Distinguished Professor of Library and Information Science; D.L.S., Columbia.
Kenneth Soehner, Visiting Associate Professor; M.L.S., Columbia.
Chris Alen Sula, Assistant Professor; Ph.D., CUNY Graduate Center.
Kevin B. Winkler, Visiting Assistant Professor; M.L.S., Columbia.
Philip Yockey, Visiting Associate Professor; M.L.S., Columbia.

SYRACUSE UNIVERSITY

School of Information Studies
Master of Science in Information Management
Master of Science in Library and Information Science
Master of Science in Telecommunications and Network Management

Programs of Study

The Syracuse University School of Information Studies (iSchool) offers M.S. degree programs in three areas to prepare students for a growing number of dynamic careers that involve the management and use of information: digital librarianship, data science, global enterprise technologies, social media, virtual environments, databases, information security and IT governance, information and communication technologies, wireless networks, mobile and Web applications, and telecommunications technologies. Students can earn any of these degrees on campus or online with limited residency requirements.

Ranked number one in information systems by *U.S. News & World Report,* the iSchool offers an M.S. in information management (IM), which requires the completion of 42 credit hours. Each student completes course work in management approaches and strategies, user information needs, technological infrastructures, and elective subjects. There is also an exit requirement. The program provides an integrated approach to the effective management and use of information and communication technologies within organizations. Many IM students concurrently pursue a Certificate of Advanced Study in information security management.

The iSchool also offers a 30-credit executive track for the M.S. in information management, geared toward midcareer professionals looking to advance their organizations and their job prospects. This track can be completed online or on campus.

Accredited by the American Library Association (ALA), the M.S. in library and information science (LIS) program requires the completion of 36 credit hours. The program is dedicated to educating students to become leaders in the evolution of the library and information profession. LIS students work with interdisciplinary faculty advisers to plan their programs of study, which may include course work in other academic areas. The program offers a concentration in school media and certificates of advanced study in digital libraries and school media, which were ranked fourth in the 2009 *U.S. News & World Report* rankings, as well as a certificate in cultural heritage preservation and data science.

The M.S. in telecommunications and network management (TNM) requires the completion of 36 credit hours. It provides an integrated approach to the effective management, operation, and implementation of telecommunication systems, including voice, data, and wireless networks, within organizations. Faculty members engage students in research and classroom lessons in a wide variety of areas, including international telecommunications policy and Internet governance, information assurance/security, e-collaboration, enterprise architecture, wireless systems, information policy, information systems management, online retrieval systems, project management, strategic planning, and telecommunications management. Many TNM students also pursue a Certificate of Advanced Study in information systems and telecommunications management.

All three degree programs focus on employing technology and digital tools to find, evaluate, organize, and use information for the betterment of people. Graduates of the iSchool at Syracuse work in a broad range of managerial and technical positions in business, government, education, health care, and other fields.

The iSchool also offers two doctoral-level programs: a research-oriented Ph.D. in information science and technology for those individuals interested in becoming researchers, professors, and consultants (i.e., more theoretically oriented positions) and the Doctorate of Professional Studies in information management, a part-time distance-learning executive degree program for working professionals who are interested in the applied aspects of the information field.

The iSchool's Certificates of Advanced Study have broad appeal and attract students across disciplines. Options include information security management, information systems and telecommunications management, e-government management and leadership, cultural heritage and preservation, digital libraries, school media, global enterprise technologies, data science, and information innovation: social media. These certificates can be earned on campus or online, and provide a valuable development opportunity both for emerging and experienced professionals in the information field.

Research Facilities

Ranked as one of the most connected campuses by Princeton Review/forbes.com and a 2010 Campus Technology Innovator award recipient, Syracuse University offers wireless capabilities from most buildings and public spaces on campus and provides students with hundreds of computer workstations in public clusters. The School of Information Studies is located in a recently renovated building, Hinds Hall, in the heart of the University's Main Campus Quad. The facility features the latest technologies and innovative instructional and meeting spaces to encourage collaborative and interactive learning. The iSchool's research and development centers, which have achieved national and international distinction, allow students to apply classroom lessons to authentic problems, sometimes using technologies that have not yet made it to market.

The University's library system includes collections of 3.1 million volumes, more than 24,000 online and print journals, and extensive collections of microforms, maps, images, music scores, videos, rare books, and manuscripts. Many of these resources can be accessed from academic and residence hall computer clusters. Among its special collections is the Belfer Audio Laboratory and Archive, which contains more than 340,000 historical sound recordings in all formats, including a collection of 22,000 cylinder records, the largest held by any private institution in North America.

Financial Aid

Fellowships, scholarships, and assistantships are available to full-time students both on campus and online. The most prestigious and competitive are Syracuse University graduate fellowships, which include a scholarship and a stipend for the academic year. University scholarships provide 24 credit hours of tuition, and graduate assistantships provide tuition and a stipend for the academic year. The University also participates in the federal Scholarship for Service program, which awards full scholarships plus a stipend and paid internship opportunities to U.S. citizens who are interested in earning graduate degrees in fields related to information assurance and security. Syracuse also offers fellowships through the McNair Scholars program and Graduate Education for Minorities (GEM) program. Tuition scholarships and other small scholarships are available to part-time students.

Loans are available through the University financial aid office. For Federal Work-Study Program contracts, students work through the University student employment office. Financial aid is awarded according to federal financial need guidelines.

Cost of Study

Tuition for 2012–13 is $1249 per graduate credit hour.

Living and Housing Costs

Academic-year living expenses are about $17,870 for single students. The University has residence hall rooms and on-campus apartments for single and married graduate students. Many graduate students choose to live off campus.

Student Group

Syracuse University has about 12,000 students, including about 4,500 graduate students. Approximately 650 graduate students are enrolled in the School of Information Studies. Thirty percent are international students, with the remainder coming from all parts of the United States. Students have diverse backgrounds, with undergraduate majors in the liberal arts, natural sciences, fine arts, business administration, computer science, and engineering. They participate in more than 300 student groups and extracurricular activities, including Women in Information Technology, Information Studies Graduate Organization, Black and Latino Information Studies Support, iOrange Toastmasters, iVenture Upstate, and chapters of national information and library associations.

Student Outcomes

Career opportunities for graduates of the programs are excellent. Information management graduates find lucrative professional positions in a wide variety of organizations, with responsibilities ranging from information systems analysis, database design, and consulting, to risk assessment, social media strategy, and systems management. Library and information science graduates not only work in library settings, but also hold professional positions in corporations, media and communications outlets, museums, government agencies, and universities. Telecommunications and network management graduates find success in four main sectors of industry: information systems positions within organizations requiring data and voice network management and strategies; telecommunications organizations involved in voice, data, or video transmissions; large voice and data network communication vendors such as Cisco and Nortel; and large consulting companies.

Location

The Syracuse metropolitan area is home to more than a half million people and is the commercial, industrial, medical, and cultural center of central New York State. The 200-acre Main Campus is spacious and attractive, and new University facilities extend the campus into the heart of downtown Syracuse, which is only a 20-minute walk from the University. Winters are snowy and summers are pleasant. Lake Ontario, the Finger Lakes, and the Adirondack and Catskill Mountains are nearby. Boston, Toronto, New York, and Philadelphia are within a 5-hour drive.

The School

The School of Information Studies is a leading center for innovative graduate programs in information fields. The school's focus on information users and understanding user information needs sets it apart from other institutions that offer computer science, management, and related programs. The interdisciplinary faculty combines expertise in information science, telecommunications, public administration, education, school media, business management and management information systems, social science, design, linguistics, computer science, library science, and communications. The iSchool also offers a unique undergraduate degree program in information management and technology.

Applying

Applicants for the master's degree programs must have a bachelor's degree from an accredited undergraduate institution and an academic record that is satisfactory for admission to the graduate school. Two letters of recommendation, a resume,

Syracuse University

and an essay on academic plans and professional goals are also required. Applicants for the master's degree and doctoral programs are required to submit scores from the Graduate Record Examinations (GRE). Whenever possible, an interview is recommended. International students should plan to take the Test of English as a Foreign Language (TOEFL); a score of at least 90 on the internet-based test is expected. Students interested in University fellowships must apply by January 8. Other financial aid applicants must submit all materials by February 1.

For additional information, please visit the School of Information Studies Web site, http://ischool.syr.edu or e-mail iGrad@syr.edu. Follow the School on Facebook or Twitter at http://facebook.com/su.ischool and http://twitter.com/ischoolsu. Videos about the School can be found at http://www.youtube.com/user/syracuseischool.

Correspondence and Information

School of Information Studies
343 Hinds Hall
Syracuse University
Syracuse, New York 13244-4100
United States
Phone: 315-443-2911
E-mail: iGrad@syr.edu
Web site: http://ischool.syr.edu
http://facebook.com/su.ischool (Facebook)
http://twitter.com/ischoolsu (Twitter)

THE FACULTY AND THEIR RESEARCH

Marilyn Arnone, Research Associate Professor; Ph.D. (instructional design, development, and evaluation), Syracuse. Information literacy education, children's learning and curiosity in interactive multimedia environments.

Bahram Attaie, Assistant Professor of Practice. Microsoft and Cisco certification, business information technology, networking and database programming for the corporate world.

Susan Bonzi, Director of Instructional Quality and Associate Professor; Ph.D. (library and information science), Illinois. Image retrieval systems, bibliometrics, linguistics applications in information science. Received the first Information Science Doctoral Dissertation Award from the American Society for Information Science (ASIS), 1982.

Carlos E. Caicedo, Assistant Professor; Ph.D. (telecommunications), Pittsburgh. Security in future data environments, spectrum trading markets and technology, security management, telecommunication and network systems management.

Derrick L. Cogburn, Associate Professor; Ph.D. (political science), Howard. Global information and communication technology (ICT) policy, global governance, use of ICTs for socioeconomic development.

Kevin Crowston, Professor; Ph.D. (information technologies), MIT. Organizational implications of technology, free/libre open source software development, coordination in distributed teams, ICT in real estate.

Jason Dedrick, Associate Professor; Ph.D. (management information systems), California, Irvine. Globalization of information technology, national technology policy, offshoring of knowledge work, personal computing industry, green information technologies.

Michael D'Eredita, Assistant Professor; Ph.D. (experimental/cognitive psychology), Syracuse. Enterprise skill acquisition, collective expertise, virtual apprenticeship, organizational behavior, collaboration.

David Dischiave, Assistant Professor of Practice; M.S. (computer information technology), Regis. Systems analysis and design, database management and design, project management, computer hardware and operating system architecture.

Susan Dischiave, Assistant Professor of Practice; M.B.A. (business administration), Le Moyne. Enterprise systems analysis and design, database management and design, application development.

Renee Franklin, Assistant Professor; Ph.D. (information studies), Florida State. School library media, intellectual freedom in K–12 schools, increasing the level of participation of underrepresented ethnic groups in library and information science education.

Paul Gandel, Professor; Ph.D. (information studies), Syracuse. Digital libraries; digital services; information organization and retrieval; information technology and development; information, organizations, and society knowledge.

Martha A. Garcia-Murillo, Associate Professor; Ph.D. (international political economy and telecommunications), USC. Digital divide, economics of the information industry, information and communications policy and regulations.

Robert Heckman, Senior Associate Dean; Ph.D. (information systems), Pittsburgh. Strategy and planning for information resources, teaching and learning strategies for professionals, collaboration in virtual communities and teams, open source software development.

Jill Hurst-Wahl, Assistant Professor of Practice; M.L.S., Maryland. Digitization, digital libraries, copyright, online social networking, Web 2.0, virtual worlds.

Michelle Lynn Kaarst-Brown, Associate Professor; Ph.D. (organizational theory and management information systems), York. Information technology culture, strategic alignment of information technology with business strategy, perceptions of risk and opportunity in IT adoption, influences on IT governance, Internet-based business.

Bruce Kingma, Professor and Associate Provost for Innovation and Entrepreneurship; Ph.D. (economics), Rochester. Economics of online education, digital libraries, scholarly publishing, library and nonprofit management.

Barbara Kwasnik, Professor; Ph.D. (library and information studies), Rutgers. Classification research, knowledge representation and organization, research methods, information-related behavior.

R. David Lankes, Associate Professor; Ph.D. (information transfer), Syracuse. Participatory librarianship, digital reference, digital libraries, credibility.

Kenneth Lavender, Assistant Professor of Practice; Ph.D. (English), California, Santa Barbara. Digital reference, rare books, archives, preservation of cultural heritage, distance education pedagogy, context of information services.

Elizabeth D. Liddy, Dean and Trustee Professor; Ph.D. (information transfer), Syracuse. Indexing, data mining, natural-language processing, information retrieval.

Ian MacInnes, Associate Dean for Academic Affairs; Ph.D. (political economy and public policy), USC. Electronic commerce, competition policy, information technology and globalization, public policy, standardization, network economics, microeconomics.

Nancy McCracken, Research Associate Professor; Ph.D. (computer and information science), Syracuse. Computational linguistics, natural language processing, data mining, information extraction and retrieval, question answering, knowledge representation.

Lee McKnight, Associate Professor; Ph.D. (political science, communication, and international relations), MIT. Wireless grids, nomadicity, social networking of devices, Internet economics and policy, national and international technology policy.

David Molta, Assistant Dean, Technology Integration; M.P.A., North Texas. Mobile and wireless information systems; interoperability and performance testing; impact of mobile communications technologies on individuals, organizations, and society.

Milton L. Mueller, Professor; Ph.D. (telecommunication), Pennsylvania. Internet governance, telecommunication policy, transnational civil society, global governance institutions in communication and information, digital identity, digital convergence.

Scott Nicholson, Associate Professor; Ph.D. (information studies), North Texas. Gaming in libraries, evaluation and assessment of library services, data mining for libraries, Web search tools.

Michael Nilan, Associate Professor; Ph.D. (communication research), Washington (Seattle). Virtual communities, cognitive behavior, information seeking and using, information system design and evaluation, user-based research methods.

Megan Oakleaf, Assistant Professor; Ph.D. (information and library science), North Carolina at Chapel Hill. Evolution and assessment of information services, outcomes-based assessment, evidence-based decision making, digital reference, digital libraries, information services.

Carsten Osterlund, Associate Professor; Ph.D. (organization studies and behavioral policy science), MIT. Medical informatics, documenting work, distributed work, organizational implications of information technology, indoor tracking systems, qualitative research techniques.

Joon S. Park, Associate Professor; Ph.D. (information technology and information security), George Mason. Information and systems security; security policies, models, mechanisms, evaluation, survivability, and applications.

Jian Qin, Associate Professor; Ph.D. (library and information science), Illinois at Urbana-Champaign. Knowledge organization, information organization, information technology applications in managing knowledge and information.

Anthony Rotolo, Assistant Professor of Practice and Social Media Strategist; M.S. (information management), Syracuse. Social media and Web 2.0. instructional technologies, online safety, augmented reality, e-democracy, social implications of technology.

Jeffrey Rubin, Assistant Professor of Practice; M.S. (telecommunications and network management), Syracuse. Managing Web sites, e-business, content management systems, information architecture, designing Internet services, Web analytics.

Steven B. Sawyer, Associate Professor; D.B.A. (management information systems), Boston. Social informatics, design and development of information systems, project management, role of information and communication technologies relative to organizational and social change.

Ruth V. Small, Meredith Professor; Ph.D. (instructional design, development, and evaluation), Syracuse. Motivational aspects of information literacy, design and use of information and information technologies in education, role of school media specialist, information components of inventive thinking.

Jeffrey Stanton, Associate Dean for Research and Doctoral Programs; Ph.D. (information studies), Connecticut. Organizational psychology and data collection; behavioral information security; statistical models to predict attitudes, motivation, and behavior; interactions between people and technology.

Zixiang (Alex) Tan, Associate Professor; Ph.D. (telecommunications management and policy), Rutgers. Telecommunications policy and regulations, new technology development and applications, industry restructure and competition.

Arthur Thomas, Assistant Professor of Practice; Ph.D. (research and evaluation/instructional systems design and management), SUNY at Buffalo. Performance improvement, project management, data networking engineering, instructional design, information systems management.

Howard Turtle, Associate Research Professor; Ph.D. (computer science), Massachusetts Amherst. Design and implementation of retrieval systems, operating system support for large databases, text representation techniques, automatic classification, text and data mining, and automated inference techniques.

Murali Venkatesh, Associate Professor; Ph.D. (management), Indiana. Civic network design, group-based decision support systems, sociological analyses of administrative documents, human-computer interaction, telecommunications.

Carlos Villalba, Assistant Professor of Practice; Ph.D. candidate (instructional design, development, and evaluation), Syracuse. Oracle database administration, IT security, open source application development, search engine optimization, e-commerce.

Jun Wang, Assistant Research Professor; Ph.D. (library and information science), Illinois at Urbana-Champaign. Human computation, machine learning, computational neuroscience, computational language evolution.

Ozgur Yilmazel, Assistant Research Professor; Ph.D. (electrical engineering), Syracuse. Natural language processing, information retrieval, text categorization, software engineering.

Bei Yu, Assistant Professor; Ph.D. (library and information science), Illinois at Urbana-Champaign. Text classification and analysis, natural language processing, political linguistics, language and social behavior, automated language extraction and classification development.

Ping Zhang, Professor; Ph.D. (information systems), Texas at Austin. Human computer interaction, information management, intellectual development of information-related fields.

The iSchool is located on the Main Campus Quad in the heart of the Syracuse University campus.

UNIVERSITY OF KENTUCKY

Program in Library and Information Science

Programs of Study

The University of Kentucky's School of Library and Information Science (UK SLIS) offers the only ALA-accredited master's degree program in Kentucky. The program includes a wide array of courses for students who choose to pursue a master's degree. UK SLIS is a member of the iSchools, a collective of information schools dedicated to advancing the information field in the twenty-first century.

The M.S. degree is a 36-hour program: 15 hours of core courses for general preparation and the remainder customized to the student's interests. Course tracks include school library certification, health information, information technology, academic libraries, public libraries, and others. Students complete a program portfolio in their final semester. A 42-hour M.A. with thesis option is also available.

Licensed school teachers can earn a school library certification as they work on a master's degree. Certification and the master's course are combined for a total of 36 credit hours.

Students can complete all course work online, with no required face-to-face meetings. Students taking only online courses are charged in-state (resident) tuition rates, which are significantly lower than out-of-state tuition. Students may also opt to complete the program with a mix of online and face-to-face courses, with the program's required courses being offered in a face-to-face format.

Beginning in spring 2013, students at UK SLIS can apply for an alternative spring break program at the Library of Congress, the National Library of Medicine, or the National Archives. All offer students an excellent opportunity for real-world application of theory learned in classes.

Research Facilities

The University's Library System, one of the nation's top research libraries, contains more than 3.7 million volumes and 26,000 linear feet of manuscripts. In addition, UK serves as the Regional Depository as part of the Federal Depository Library Program.

Financial Aid

All applicants are encouraged to submit the FAFSA form. In addition, assistantships and scholarships are available through the program. Information on assistantships is available online at http://www.research.uky.edu/gs/StudentFunding/assistantships.html. Information on program scholarships is available at http://cis.uky.edu/lis/content/funding-your-education.

Cost of Study

Students taking only online courses are charged in-state tuition. Information about full tuition charges can be found online at http://www.uky.edu/registrar/tuition-fees.

Living and Housing Costs

Students who choose to pursue their degree on campus can apply for a limited number of efficiency, one-bedroom, and two-bedroom apartments designated for graduate student and family housing. Additional information is available at http://www.uky.edu/Housing/graduate.

Student Group

UK SLIS has an active student group, LISSO, in charge of student activities. There are also student chapters of the American Library Association (ALA), Special Library Association (SLA), and Society of American Archivisits (SAA).

Location

The University is located in Lexington, a metropolitan area with a population of approximately 295,000. Lexington is located in the heart of the famous Bluegrass region of central Kentucky, about 85 miles from both Louisville, Kentucky, and Cincinnati, Ohio. Lexington has numerous theaters, concert halls, and restaurants and more than 400 horse farms—the city is often referred to as the Horse Capital of the World. There are many opportunities for outdoor recreation, including a readily accessible network of state parks with opportunities for hiking and canoeing. In addition, the University has recreational facilities and offers a variety of artistic presentations. Lexington's downtown area is within walking distance of the University campus.

The University

The University of Kentucky was established in 1865 as the Agricultural and Mechanical College of the Kentucky University. Today, it is a public, research-extensive, land-grant university with an enrollment of more than 27,000 and an annual budget of $2.6 billion. The University is also Kentucky's ninth-largest organization. The University has more than eighty national rankings for academic excellence, and it ranks tenth in the nation among all universities for the number of start-up companies formed per $10 million in research spending.

Applying

The application deadline is July 1 for the fall term, November 15 for the spring term, and May 1 for the summer term. Applicants must apply to the University of Kentucky Graduate School and separately to the UK SLIS. Requirements include a completed application for admission (available online), one official transcript from each previous school attended (an undergraduate GPA of at least 3.0 is required), an official score report of GRE results (requirements: 150 verbal, 140 quantitative or 4.0 for the analytical section), a personal statement, and three letters of recommendation. Additional information regarding application to the Graduate School can be found at http://www.rgs.uky.edu/gs.

For additional details, applicants may contact Will Buntin at will.buntin@uky.edu or sign up for the University of Kentucky SLIS prospective student newsletter at http://cis.uky.edu/lis/content/online-information-session.

University of Kentucky

Correspondence and Information

Will Buntin, Assistant Director for Student Affairs
School of Library and Information Science
University of Kentucky
327 LCLI
Lexington, Kentucky 40506-0055
Phone: 859-257-3317
Fax: 859-257-4205
E-mail: ukslis@uky.edu
Web site: http://cis.uky.edu/lis/

THE FACULTY AND THEIR RESEARCH

Members of the University of Kentucky SLIS faculty are a varied group with a wide range of interests. Complete faculty profiles are available online at http://cis.uky.edu/lis/content/faculty.

Participants in the first alternative spring break program at UK.

ACADEMIC AND PROFESSIONAL PROGRAMS IN PHYSICAL EDUCATION, SPORTS, AND RECREATION

Section 29
Leisure Studies and Recreation

This section contains a directory of institutions offering graduate work in leisure studies and recreation. Additional information about programs listed in the directory but not augmented by an in-depth entry may be obtained by writing directly to the dean of a graduate school or chair of a department at the address given in the directory.

In the other guides in this series:

Graduate Programs in the Humanities, Arts & Social Sciences
See *Performing Arts*

Graduate Programs in the Physical Sciences, Mathematics, Agricultural Sciences, the Environment & Natural Resources
See *Natural Resources*

CONTENTS

Program Directories

Leisure Studies

Bowling Green State University, Graduate College, College of Education and Human Development, School of Human Movement, Sport, and Leisure Studies, Bowling Green, OH 43403. Offers developmental kinesiology (M Ed); recreation and leisure (M Ed); sport administration (M Ed). Part-time programs available. *Degree requirements:* For master's, thesis or alternative. *Entrance requirements:* For master's, GRE General Test, minimum GPA of 2.7. Additional exam requirements/recommendations for international students: Required—TOEFL. Electronic applications accepted. *Faculty research:* Teacher-learning process, travel and tourism, sport marketing and management, exercise physiology and sport psychology, life-span motor development.

California State University, Long Beach, Graduate Studies, College of Health and Human Services, Department of Recreation and Leisure Studies, Long Beach, CA 90840. Offers recreation administration (MS). Part-time programs available. *Faculty:* 2 full-time (both women), 1 (woman) part-time/adjunct. *Students:* 5 full-time (4 women), 7 part-time (5 women); includes 3 minority (1 Black or African American, non-Hispanic/Latino; 1 Hispanic/Latino; 1 Two or more races, non-Hispanic/Latino), 2 international. Average age 30. 16 applicants, 63% accepted, 6 enrolled. In 2011, 7 master's awarded. *Degree requirements:* For master's, comprehensive exam or thesis. *Entrance requirements:* For master's, GRE General Test. *Application deadline:* For fall admission, 7/1 for domestic students. Applications are processed on a rolling basis. Application fee: $55. Electronic applications accepted. *Financial support:* Federal Work-Study, institutionally sponsored loans, and scholarships/grants available. Financial award application deadline: 3/2. *Unit head:* Dr. Maridith Janssen, Chair, 562-985-4079, Fax: 562-985-8154, E-mail: mjanssen@csulb.edu. *Application contact:* Dr. Katherine James, Graduate Advisor, 562-985-8077, Fax: 562-985-8154, E-mail: kjames@csulb.edu.

Central Michigan University, College of Graduate Studies, College of Education and Human Services, Department of Recreation, Parks, and Leisure Services Administration, Mount Pleasant, MI 48859. Offers recreation and park administration (MA); therapeutic recreation (MA). Part-time programs available. *Degree requirements:* For master's, thesis or alternative. Electronic applications accepted. *Faculty research:* Commercial recreation and facilities management, study of ethics in parks and recreation professionals, computer touch-tone information services at visitor centers, creative play spaces for children, therapeutic recreation.

The College at Brockport, State University of New York, School of Health and Human Performance, Department of Recreation and Leisure Studies, Brockport, NY 14420-2997. Offers recreation and leisure service management (MS). Part-time programs available. *Students:* 10 full-time (8 women), 10 part-time (4 women); includes 3 minority (1 Black or African American, non-Hispanic/Latino; 1 Asian, non-Hispanic/Latino; 1 Hispanic/Latino). 8 applicants, 75% accepted, 4 enrolled. In 2011, 12 master's awarded. *Degree requirements:* For master's, thesis or alternative. *Entrance requirements:* For master's, minimum GPA of 3.0, letters of recommendation, written critical analysis; statement of objectives. Additional exam requirements/recommendations for international students: Required—TOEFL (minimum score 550 paper-based; 213 computer-based; 79 iBT). *Application deadline:* For fall admission, 5/30 priority date for domestic students, 5/30 for international students; for spring admission, 11/15 priority date for domestic students, 11/15 for international students. Application fee: $50. Electronic applications accepted. *Financial support:* Federal Work-Study, scholarships/grants, and unspecified assistantships available. Support available to part-time students. Financial award application deadline: 3/15; financial award applicants required to submit FAFSA. *Faculty research:* Leisure service delivery systems; therapeutic recreation; international issues in recreation and leisure; tourism; customer service, customer behavior and perceived value/satisfaction; leisure motivation among Baby Boomers. *Unit head:* Arthur Graham, Chairperson, 585-395-2643, Fax: 585-395-5246, E-mail: jfrater@brockport.edu. *Application contact:* Dr. Lynda Sperazza, Graduate Director, 585-395-5490, Fax: 585-395-5246, E-mail: lsperazza@brockport.edu. Web site: http://www.brockport.edu/graduate/.

Dalhousie University, Faculty of Health Professions, School of Health and Human Performance, Program in Leisure Studies, Halifax, NS B3H 1T8, Canada. Offers MA. Part-time programs available. *Degree requirements:* For master's, thesis. *Entrance requirements:* For master's, minimum GPA of 3.3. Additional exam requirements/recommendations for international students: Required—TOEFL, IELTS, CANTEST, CAEL, or Michigan English Language Assessment Battery. Electronic applications accepted. *Faculty research:* Leisure and lifestyles of social groups such as older adults, women, and persons with health problems or disabilities; historical analysis of leisure; sport and leisure administration.

East Carolina University, Graduate School, College of Health and Human Performance, Department of Recreation and Leisure Studies, Greenville, NC 27858-4353. Offers aquatic therapy (Certificate); biofeedback (Certificate); recreation and park administration (MS), including generalist, recreational sports management; recreational therapy administration (MS). Part-time and evening/weekend programs available. Postbaccalaureate distance learning degree programs offered (minimal on-campus study). *Degree requirements:* For master's, comprehensive exam, thesis optional. *Entrance requirements:* For master's, GRE General Test or MAT. Additional exam requirements/recommendations for international students: Required—TOEFL. *Application deadline:* For fall admission, 6/1 priority date for domestic students. Applications are processed on a rolling basis. Application fee: $50. *Expenses:* Tuition, state resident: full-time $3557; part-time $444.63 per semester hour. Tuition, nonresident: full-time $14,351; part-time $1793.88 per semester hour. *Required fees:* $2016; $252 per semester hour. Part-time tuition and fees vary according to course load, campus/location and program. *Financial support:* Research assistantships and teaching assistantships with partial tuition reimbursements available. Financial award application deadline: 6/1. *Faculty research:* Therapeutic recreation, stress and coping behavior, medicine carrying capacity, choice behavior, tourism preferences. *Unit head:* Dr. Deb Jordan, Chair, 252-737-2990, E-mail: jordand@ecu.edu. *Application contact:* Dr. Sharon Knight, Director of Graduate Studies, 252-328-4637, Fax: 252-328-4655, E-mail: knights@ecu.edu. Web site: http://www.ecu.edu/rcls/.

Howard University, Graduate School, Department of Health, Human Performance and Leisure Studies, Washington, DC 20059-0002. Offers exercise physiology (MS); health education (MS); sports studies (MS), including sociology of sports, sports management; urban recreation (MS), including leisure studies. Part-time and evening/weekend programs available. *Degree requirements:* For master's, comprehensive exam, thesis. *Entrance requirements:* For master's, BS in human performance or related field. Additional exam requirements/recommendations for international students: Recommended—TOEFL. Electronic applications accepted. *Faculty research:* Health promotion, cardiovascular hypertension, physical activity, sport and human rights issues.

Indiana University Bloomington, School of Health, Physical Education and Recreation, Department of Recreation, Park, and Tourism Studies, Bloomington, IN 47405-7000. Offers leisure behavior (PhD); outdoor recreation (MS); recreation administration (MS); recreational sports administration (MS); therapeutic recreation (MS); tourism management (MS). *Faculty:* 16 full-time (6 women), 2 part-time/adjunct (both women). *Students:* 61 full-time (32 women), 22 part-time (20 women); includes 9 minority (4 Black or African American, non-Hispanic/Latino; 1 Asian, non-Hispanic/Latino; 1 Hispanic/Latino; 3 Two or more races, non-Hispanic/Latino), 22 international. Average age 31. 48 applicants, 73% accepted, 18 enrolled. In 2011, 17 master's, 6 doctorates awarded. Terminal master's awarded for partial completion of doctoral program. *Degree requirements:* For master's, thesis optional; for doctorate, thesis/dissertation. *Entrance requirements:* For master's, GRE General Test, minimum GPA of 2.8; for doctorate, GRE General Test, minimum GPA of 3.0 (undergraduate), 3.5 (graduate). Additional exam requirements/recommendations for international students: Required—TOEFL. *Application deadline:* For fall admission, 1/1 for international students; for spring admission, 9/1 for international students. Applications are processed on a rolling basis. Application fee: $55 ($65 for international students). *Financial support:* Fellowships, research assistantships, teaching assistantships with partial tuition reimbursements, career-related internships or fieldwork, Federal Work-Study, institutionally sponsored loans, scholarships/grants, tuition waivers (partial), unspecified assistantships, and fee remissions available. Financial award application deadline: 3/1. *Faculty research:* Leisure counseling, gerontology, special populations, planning and development. *Unit head:* Bryan McCormick, Chair, 812-855-3482, E-mail: bmccormi@indiana.edu. *Application contact:* Program Office, 812-855-4711, Fax: 812-855-3998, E-mail: recpark@indiana.edu. Web site: http://www.indiana.edu/~recpark/.

Murray State University, College of Health Sciences and Human Services, Department of Wellness and Therapeutic Sciences, Program in Exercise and Leisure Studies, Murray, KY 42071. Offers MS. Part-time programs available. *Degree requirements:* For master's, thesis optional. *Entrance requirements:* For master's, GRE General Test or MAT. Additional exam requirements/recommendations for international students: Required—TOEFL. *Faculty research:* Exercise and cancer recovery.

Penn State University Park, Graduate School, College of Health and Human Development, Department of Recreation, Park and Tourism Management, State College, University Park, PA 16802-1503. Offers M Ed, MS, PhD. *Unit head:* Dr. Ann C. Crouter, Dean, 814-865-1428, Fax: 814-865-3282, E-mail: ac1@psu.edu. *Application contact:* Cynthia E. Nicosia, Director, Graduate Enrollment Services, 814-865-1795, Fax: 814-865-4627, E-mail: cey1@psu.edu. Web site: http://www.hhdev.psu.edu/rptm/.

Prescott College, Graduate Programs, Program in Adventure Education/Wilderness Leadership, Prescott, AZ 86301. Offers adventure education (MA); adventure-based environmental education (MA); student-directed concentrations (MA). Part-time programs available. Postbaccalaureate distance learning degree programs offered (minimal on-campus study). *Faculty:* 1 (woman) full-time, 19 part-time/adjunct (14 women). *Students:* 5 full-time (0 women), 24 part-time (14 women); includes 2 minority (1 American Indian or Alaska Native, non-Hispanic/Latino; 1 Two or more races, non-Hispanic/Latino), 4 international. Average age 31. 13 applicants, 100% accepted, 4 enrolled. In 2011, 9 master's awarded. *Degree requirements:* For master's, thesis, fieldwork or internship, practicum. *Entrance requirements:* For master's, 2 letters of recommendation, resume. Additional exam requirements/recommendations for international students: Required—TOEFL (minimum score 500 paper-based; 173 computer-based). *Application deadline:* For fall admission, 4/15 priority date for domestic students, 4/15 for international students; for spring admission, 9/15 priority date for domestic students, 9/15 for international students. Applications are processed on a rolling basis. Application fee: $40. Electronic applications accepted. *Expenses:* *Tuition:* Full-time $16,440; part-time $685 per credit. *Required fees:* $150 per semester. One-time fee: $350. *Financial support:* Career-related internships or fieldwork, Federal Work-Study, and scholarships/grants available. Financial award applicants required to submit FAFSA. *Unit head:* Denise Mitten, Chair, 303-350-1004, E-mail: dmitten@prescott.edu. *Application contact:* Kerstin Alicki, Admissions Counselor, 928-350-2100, Fax: 928-776-5242, E-mail: admissions@prescott.edu.

San Francisco State University, Division of Graduate Studies, College of Health and Human Services, Department of Recreation and Leisure Studies, San Francisco, CA 94132-1722. Offers recreation (MS). Part-time programs available. *Application deadline:* Applications are processed on a rolling basis. *Financial support:* Career-related internships or fieldwork available. *Unit head:* Dr. Patrick Tierney, Chair, 415-338-2030, E-mail: ptierney@sfsu.edu. *Application contact:* Christina Alcantara, Office Manager, 415-338-3327, E-mail: cba@sfsu.edu. Web site: http://recdept.sfsu.edu/.

Southeast Missouri State University, School of Graduate Studies, Department of Health, Human Performance and Recreation, Cape Girardeau, MO 63701-4799. Offers nutrition and exercise science (MS). Part-time and evening/weekend programs available. *Faculty:* 7 full-time (1 woman), 2 part-time/adjunct (1 woman). *Students:* 17 full-time (6 women), 7 part-time (4 women), 10 international. Average age 26. 20 applicants, 95% accepted, 8 enrolled. In 2011, 4 master's awarded. *Degree requirements:* For master's, comprehensive exam, thesis optional, internship. *Entrance requirements:* For master's, GRE General Test (minimum combined score of 950), minimum undergraduate GPA of 3.0, minimum B grade in prerequisite courses. Additional exam requirements/recommendations for international students: Required—TOEFL (minimum score 550 paper-based; 213 computer-based; 79 iBT); Recommended—IELTS (minimum score 6). *Application deadline:* For fall admission, 8/1 for domestic students, 7/1 for international students; for spring admission, 11/21 for domestic students, 11/1 for international students. Applications are processed on a rolling basis. Application fee: $30 ($40 for international students). Electronic applications accepted. *Expenses:* Tuition, state resident: full-time $4896; part-time $272 per credit hour. Tuition, nonresident: full-time $8649; part-time $480.50 per credit hour. *Financial support:* In 2011–12, 16 students received support, including 4 teaching assistantships with full tuition reimbursements available (averaging $7,600 per year); career-related internships or fieldwork, Federal Work-Study, scholarships/grants, tuition waivers (full), and unspecified assistantships also available. Financial award application deadline: 6/30; financial award applicants required to submit FAFSA. *Faculty research:* Health issues of athletes, body composition assessment, exercise testing, exercise training, perceptual responses to physical activity. *Unit head:* Dr. Joe Pujol, Chairperson, 573-651-2664, Fax: 573-651-5150, E-mail: jpujol@semo.edu. *Application contact:* Alisa Aleen McFerron, Assistant Director of Admissions for Operations, 573-651-5937, Fax: 573-651-5936, E-mail: amcferron@semo.edu. Web site: http://www.semo.edu/health/.

Southern Connecticut State University, School of Graduate Studies, School of Health and Human Services, Department of Recreation and Leisure Studies, New Haven, CT 06515-1355. Offers MS. Part-time and evening/weekend programs available. *Faculty:* 3 full-time (2 women), 3 part-time/adjunct (1 woman). *Students:* 14 full-time (10 women), 35 part-time (21 women); includes 8 minority (4 Black or African American, non-Hispanic/Latino; 3 Hispanic/Latino; 1 Two or more races, non-Hispanic/Latino). 32

applicants, 66% accepted, 21 enrolled. In 2011, 7 master's awarded. *Degree requirements:* For master's, thesis or alternative. *Entrance requirements:* For master's, interview, minimum undergraduate QPA of 3.0 in graduate major field or 2.5 overall. *Application deadline:* For fall admission, 7/15 priority date for domestic students. Applications are processed on a rolling basis. Application fee: $50. Electronic applications accepted. *Expenses:* Tuition, state resident: full-time $5137; part-time $413 per credit. *Required fees:* $4008; $55 per term. *Financial support:* In 2011–12, 1 teaching assistantship was awarded; career-related internships or fieldwork also available. Financial award application deadline: 4/15; financial award applicants required to submit FAFSA. *Unit head:* Dr. James MacGregor, Chairperson, 203-392-6385, Fax: 203-392-6965, E-mail: macgregorj1@southernct.edu. *Application contact:* Dr. Jan Louise Jones, Graduate Coordinator, 203-392-8837, Fax: 203-392-6147, E-mail: jonesj39@southernct.edu.

Temple University, School of Tourism and Hospitality Management, Program in Sport and Recreation Administration, Philadelphia, PA 19122-6096. Offers Ed M. Part-time and evening/weekend programs available. *Faculty:* 6 full-time (2 women). *Students:* 37 full-time (14 women), 11 part-time (3 women); includes 5 minority (3 Black or African American, non-Hispanic/Latino; 1 Asian, non-Hispanic/Latino; 1 Two or more races, non-Hispanic/Latino), 3 international. Average age 25. 63 applicants, 75% accepted, 24 enrolled. In 2011, 16 master's awarded. *Entrance requirements:* For master's, GRE General Test or MAT, minimum undergraduate GPA of 3.0. Additional exam requirements/recommendations for international students: Required—TOEFL (minimum score 550 paper-based; 213 computer-based; 79 iBT). *Application deadline:* For fall admission, 4/15 priority date for domestic students, 12/15 for international students; for spring admission, 9/30 priority date for domestic students, 8/1 for international students. Application fee: $50. Electronic applications accepted. *Expenses:* Tuition, state resident: full-time $12,366; part-time $687 per credit hour. Tuition, nonresident: full-time $17,298; part-time $961 per credit hour. *Required fees:* $590; $213 per year. *Financial support:* Teaching assistantships available. Financial award application deadline: 1/15; financial award applicants required to submit FAFSA. *Unit head:* Dr. Elizabeth H. Barber, Associate Dean, 215-204-6294, E-mail: elizabeth.barber@temple.edu. *Application contact:* Tara Schumacher, Coordinator of Outreach, 215-204-6575, Fax: 215-204-8781, E-mail: tara.schumacher@temple.edu. Web site: http://sthm.temple.edu/grad/explore-ma-sports.html.

Texas State University–San Marcos, Graduate School, College of Education, Department of Health and Human Performance, Program in Recreation and Leisure Services, San Marcos, TX 78666. Offers MSRLS. *Faculty:* 4 full-time (3 women), 1 (woman) part-time/adjunct. *Students:* 34 full-time (23 women), 25 part-time (11 women); includes 24 minority (3 Black or African American, non-Hispanic/Latino; 1 Asian, non-Hispanic/Latino; 18 Hispanic/Latino; 2 Two or more races, non-Hispanic/Latino). Average age 28. 57 applicants, 81% accepted, 23 enrolled. In 2011, 26 master's awarded. *Degree requirements:* For master's, comprehensive exam, thesis optional. *Entrance requirements:* For master's, GRE General Test, minimum GPA of 2.75 in last 60 hours of course work. Additional exam requirements/recommendations for international students: Required—TOEFL (minimum score 550 paper-based; 213 computer-based; 78 iBT). *Application deadline:* For fall admission, 6/15 priority date for domestic students, 6/1 for international students; for spring admission, 10/15 priority date for domestic students, 10/1 for international students. Applications are processed on a rolling basis. Application fee: $40 ($90 for international students). Electronic applications accepted. *Expenses:* Tuition, state resident: full-time $6408; part-time $3204 per semester. Tuition, nonresident: full-time $14,832; part-time $7416 per semester. *Required fees:* $1824; $912 per semester. Tuition and fees vary according to course load. *Financial support:* In 2011–12, 19 students received support, including 6 research assistantships (averaging $10,089 per year), 5 teaching assistantships (averaging $10,692 per year). Financial award application deadline: 4/1; financial award applicants required to submit FAFSA. *Unit head:* Dr. Janet Hodges, Graduate Advisor, 512-245-2561, Fax: 512-245-8678, E-mail: jh223@txstate.edu. *Application contact:* Amy Galle, Head, 512-245-2561, Fax: 512-245-8678, E-mail: ag04@txstate.edu. Web site: http://www.hhp.txstate.edu/Degree-Plans/Graduate.html.

Universidad Metropolitana, School of Education, Program in Managing Recreation and Sports Services, San Juan, PR 00928-1150. Offers M Ed. Part-time programs available. *Degree requirements:* For master's, thesis or alternative. *Entrance requirements:* For master's, EXADEP, interview. Electronic applications accepted.

Université du Québec à Trois-Rivières, Graduate Programs, Program in Leisure, Culture and Tourism Sciences, Trois-Rivières, QC G9A 5H7, Canada. Offers MA, DESS. Part-time programs available. *Degree requirements:* For master's, thesis optional. *Entrance requirements:* For master's, appropriate bachelor's degree, proficiency in French.

University of Connecticut, Graduate School, Neag School of Education, Department of Kinesiology, Program in Sport Management and Sociology, Storrs, CT 06269. Offers MA, PhD. Terminal master's awarded for partial completion of doctoral program. *Degree requirements:* For master's, comprehensive exam, thesis or alternative; for doctorate, thesis/dissertation. *Entrance requirements:* For doctorate, GRE General Test. Additional exam requirements/recommendations for international students: Required—TOEFL (minimum score 550 paper-based; 213 computer-based). Electronic applications accepted.

University of Georgia, College of Education, Department of Counseling and Human Development Services, Athens, GA 30602. Offers college student affairs administration (M Ed, PhD); counseling and student personnel (PhD); counseling psychology (PhD); professional counseling (M Ed); professional school counseling (Ed S); recreation and leisure studies (M Ed, MA, PhD). *Accreditation:* ACA (one or more programs are accredited); APA (one or more programs are accredited); NCATE. *Faculty:* 23 full-time (14 women). *Students:* 173 full-time (126 women), 78 part-time (46 women); includes 82 minority (70 Black or African American, non-Hispanic/Latino; 3 Asian, non-Hispanic/Latino; 7 Hispanic/Latino; 1 Native Hawaiian or other Pacific Islander, non-Hispanic/Latino; 1 Two or more races, non-Hispanic/Latino), 1 international. Average age 30. 375 applicants, 26% accepted, 53 enrolled. In 2011, 48 master's, 27 doctorates, 14 other advanced degrees awarded. *Degree requirements:* For master's, thesis (MA); for doctorate, variable foreign language requirement, thesis/dissertation. *Entrance requirements:* For master's, GRE General Test or MAT; for doctorate, GRE General Test. *Application deadline:* For fall admission, 7/1 priority date for domestic students; for spring admission, 11/15 for domestic students. Application fee: $50. Electronic applications accepted. *Financial support:* Fellowships, research assistantships, teaching assistantships, and unspecified assistantships available. *Unit head:* Dr. Rosemary E. Phelps, Head, 706-542-4221, Fax: 706-542-4130, E-mail: rephelps@uga.edu. *Application contact:* Dr. Corey W. Johnson, Graduate Coordinator, 706-542-4335, Fax: 706-542-4130, E-mail: cwjohns@uga.edu. Web site: http://www.coe.uga.edu/chds/.

University of Illinois at Urbana–Champaign, Graduate College, College of Applied Health Sciences, Department of Recreation, Sport and Tourism, Champaign, IL 61820. Offers MS, PhD. Part-time and evening/weekend programs available. Postbaccalaureate distance learning degree programs offered (no on-campus study). *Faculty:* 11 full-time (8 women). *Students:* 32 full-time (11 women), 100 part-time (58 women); includes 15 minority (7 Black or African American, non-Hispanic/Latino; 1 American Indian or Alaska Native, non-Hispanic/Latino; 5 Hispanic/Latino; 2 Two or more races, non-Hispanic/Latino), 17 international. 129 applicants, 51% accepted, 47 enrolled. In 2011, 23 master's, 8 doctorates awarded. *Entrance requirements:* For master's, GRE General Test, minimum GPA of 3.0; for doctorate, GRE, minimum GPA of 3.0. Additional exam requirements/recommendations for international students: Required—TOEFL (minimum score 600 paper-based; 250 computer-based). *Application deadline:* Applications are processed on a rolling basis. Application fee: $75 ($90 for international students). Electronic applications accepted. *Financial support:* In 2011–12, 1 fellowship, 15 research assistantships, 15 teaching assistantships were awarded; tuition waivers (full and partial) also available. *Unit head:* Cary D. McDonald, Head, 217-333-4410, Fax: 217-244-1935, E-mail: carym@illinois.edu. *Application contact:* Jill M. Gurke, Secretary, 217-244-8243, Fax: 217-244-1935, E-mail: jgurke@illinois.edu. Web site: http://www.rst.illinois.edu.

The University of Iowa, Graduate College, College of Liberal Arts and Sciences, Program in Leisure Studies, Iowa City, IA 52242-1316. Offers leisure and recreational sport management (MA); therapeutic recreation (MA). *Degree requirements:* For master's, thesis optional, exam. *Entrance requirements:* For master's, minimum GPA of 3.0. Additional exam requirements/recommendations for international students: Required—TOEFL (minimum score 550 paper-based; 213 computer-based; 81 iBT). Electronic applications accepted.

University of Memphis, Graduate School, College of Education, Department of Health and Sport Sciences, Memphis, TN 38152. Offers clinical nutrition (MS); exercise and sport science (MS); health promotion (MS); physical education teacher education (MS), including teacher education; sport and leisure commerce (MS). Part-time and evening/weekend programs available. *Degree requirements:* For master's, comprehensive exam, thesis. *Entrance requirements:* For master's, GRE General Test or GMAT (sport and leisure commerce). *Faculty research:* Sport marketing and consumer analysis, health psychology, smoking cessation, psychosocial aspects of cardiovascular disease, global health promotion.

University of Minnesota, Twin Cities Campus, Graduate School, College of Education and Human Development, School of Kinesiology, Division of Recreation, Park, and Leisure Studies, Minneapolis, MN 55455-0213. Offers M Ed, MA, PhD. Part-time programs available. *Students:* 1 (woman) full-time, 1 part-time (0 women). Average age 52. In 2011, 5 master's, 1 doctorate awarded. Terminal master's awarded for partial completion of doctoral program. *Degree requirements:* For master's, thesis (for some programs), final oral exam; for doctorate, thesis/dissertation, preliminary written/oral exam, final oral exam. *Entrance requirements:* For master's, GRE or MAT, minimum GPA of 3.0; for doctorate, GRE or MAT, minimum GPA of 3.0, writing sample. *Application deadline:* For fall admission, 7/15 for domestic students; for spring admission, 12/15 for domestic students. Applications are processed on a rolling basis. Application fee: $55. *Financial support:* Fellowships, research assistantships, teaching assistantships, career-related internships or fieldwork, Federal Work-Study, institutionally sponsored loans, and tuition waivers (full and partial) available. Support available to part-time students. *Unit head:* Dr. Li Li Ji, Director, 612-642-9809, Fax: 612-626-7700, E-mail: llji@umn.edu. *Application contact:* Dr. Jennifer Engler, Assistant Dean, 612-626-2887, Fax: 612-626-7496, E-mail: engle009@umn.edu. Web site: http://www.cehd.umn.edu/kin/recreation.

University of Mississippi, Graduate School, School of Applied Sciences, Department of Health, Exercise Science, and Recreation Management, Oxford, University, MS 38677. Offers exercise science (MS); exercise science and leisure management (PhD); park and recreation management (MA); wellness (MS). *Students:* 50 full-time (32 women), 13 part-time (7 women); includes 6 minority (all Black or African American, non-Hispanic/Latino), 9 international. In 2011, 9 master's, 1 doctorate awarded. *Degree requirements:* For master's, thesis (for some programs); for doctorate, thesis/dissertation. *Entrance requirements:* For master's, GRE General Test, minimum GPA of 3.0; for doctorate, GRE General Test. Additional exam requirements/recommendations for international students: Required—TOEFL. *Application deadline:* For fall admission, 4/1 for domestic students; for spring admission, 10/1 for domestic students. Applications are processed on a rolling basis. Application fee: $25. *Financial support:* Scholarships/grants available. Financial award application deadline: 3/1; financial award applicants required to submit FAFSA. *Unit head:* Dr. Mark Loftin, Interim Chair, 662-915-5844, Fax: 662-915-5525, E-mail: mloftin@olemiss.edu. *Application contact:* Dr. Christy M. Wyandt, Associate Dean, 662-915-7474, Fax: 662-915-7577, E-mail: cwyandt@olemiss.edu.

University of Nevada, Las Vegas, Graduate College, William F. Harrah College of Hotel Administration, Department of Leisure Studies, Las Vegas, NV 89154-6013. Offers sport and leisure services management (MS). Part-time programs available. *Faculty:* 6 full-time (2 women). *Students:* 8 full-time (1 woman), 7 part-time (4 women); includes 2 minority (1 Black or African American, non-Hispanic/Latino; 1 Asian, non-Hispanic/Latino), 2 international. Average age 28. 13 applicants, 23% accepted, 0 enrolled. In 2011, 9 master's awarded. *Degree requirements:* For master's, thesis (for some programs), professional paper. *Entrance requirements:* For master's, GRE General Test. Additional exam requirements/recommendations for international students: Required—TOEFL (minimum score 550 paper-based; 213 computer-based; 80 iBT), IELTS (minimum score 7). *Application deadline:* For fall admission, 5/1 for international students; for spring admission, 10/1 for international students. Applications are processed on a rolling basis. Application fee: $60 ($95 for international students). Electronic applications accepted. *Financial support:* In 2011–12, 3 students received support, including 3 teaching assistantships with partial tuition reimbursements available (averaging $11,667 per year); institutionally sponsored loans, scholarships/grants, health care benefits, and unspecified assistantships also available. Financial award application deadline: 3/1. *Faculty research:* Tourism and destination management, convention and meeting planning and administration, hospitality accounting and finance, hospitality real property asset management, hospitality marketing and services management. *Total annual research expenditures:* $5,750. *Unit head:* Dr. Pearl Brewer, Chair/Professor, 702-895-3643, Fax: 702-895-4872, E-mail: pearl.brewer@unlv.edu. *Application contact:* Graduate College Admissions Evaluator, 702-895-3320, Fax: 702-895-4180, E-mail: gradcollege@unlv.edu.

University of Northern Iowa, Graduate College, College of Education, School of Health, Physical Education, and Leisure Services, Program in Leisure, Youth, and Human Services, Cedar Falls, IA 50614. Offers leisure services (Ed D); youth and human services (MA). *Students:* 32 full-time (19 women), 19 part-time (11 women); includes 12 minority (8 Black or African American, non-Hispanic/Latino; 3 Asian, non-Hispanic/Latino; 1 Hispanic/Latino), 4 international. 32 applicants, 75% accepted, 11 enrolled. In 2011, 23 master's, 4 doctorates awarded. *Degree requirements:* For master's, comprehensive exam, thesis or alternative; for doctorate, thesis/dissertation. *Entrance requirements:* For master's, minimum GPA of 3.0; for doctorate, GRE, minimum GPA of 3.5. Additional exam requirements/recommendations for international students: Required—TOEFL (minimum score 500 paper-based; 180 computer-based; 61 iBT). *Application deadline:* Applications are processed on a rolling basis. Application fee: $50 ($70 for international students). Electronic applications accepted. *Expenses:* Tuition, state resident: full-time $7476. Tuition, nonresident: full-time $16,410. *Required fees:* $942. *Financial support:* Career-related internships or fieldwork, Federal Work-

Study, institutionally sponsored loans, tuition waivers (full), and unspecified assistantships available. Financial award application deadline: 2/1. *Unit head:* Dr. Samuel Lankford, Interim Director, 319-273-6840, Fax: 319-273-5958, E-mail: sam.lankford@uni.edu. *Application contact:* Laurie S. Russell, Record Analyst, 319-273-2623, Fax: 319-273-2885, E-mail: laurie.russell@uni.edu. Web site: http://www.uni.edu/coe/departments/school-health-physical-education-leisure-services/leisure-youth-and-human-services-0.

University of North Texas, Toulouse Graduate School, College of Education, Department of Kinesiology, Health Promotion, and Recreation, Program in Recreation and Leisure Studies, Denton, TX 76203. Offers recreation and leisure studies (MS); recreation management (Certificate). Part-time programs available. *Degree requirements:* For master's, thesis or alternative, culminating project or field placement. *Entrance requirements:* For master's, GRE General Test or MAT, resume, 2 letters of reference, 300-word statement. Additional exam requirements/recommendations for international students: Recommended—TOEFL (minimum score 550 paper-based; 213 computer-based). Electronic applications accepted. *Expenses:* Tuition, state resident: part-time $100 per credit hour. Tuition, nonresident: part-time $413 per credit hour. *Faculty research:* Physically active leisure, trail use, community recreation programming, inclusion of persons with disabilities, therapeutic recreation.

University of South Alabama, Graduate School, College of Education, Department of Health, Physical Education and Leisure Services, Mobile, AL 36688-0002. Offers exercise science (MS); health education (M Ed); physical education (M Ed); therapeutic recreation (MS). *Accreditation:* NCATE (one or more programs are accredited). Part-time programs available. *Faculty:* 10 full-time (2 women). *Students:* 27 full-time (15 women), 4 part-time (all women); includes 5 minority (4 Black or African American, non-Hispanic/Latino; 1 Asian, non-Hispanic/Latino), 4 international. 29 applicants, 52% accepted, 12 enrolled. In 2011, 17 master's awarded. *Degree requirements:* For master's, comprehensive exam. *Entrance requirements:* For master's, GRE General Test or MAT. *Application deadline:* For fall admission, 7/15 priority date for domestic students, 6/15 for international students; for spring admission, 12/1 priority date for domestic students, 11/1 for international students. Applications are processed on a rolling basis. Application fee: $35. *Expenses:* Tuition, state resident: full-time $7968; part-time $332 per credit hour. Tuition, nonresident: full-time $15,936; part-time $664 per credit hour. *Financial support:* In 2011–12, 10 teaching assistantships were awarded; career-related internships or fieldwork also available. Support available to part-time students. Financial award application deadline: 4/1. *Unit head:* Dr. Frederick M. Scaffidi, Chair, 251-460-7131. *Application contact:* Dr. Abigail Baxter, Director of Graduate Studies, 231-460-7131.

University of Southern Mississippi, Graduate School, College of Health, School of Human Performance and Recreation, Hattiesburg, MS 39406-0001. Offers human performance (MS, PhD), including exercise physiology (PhD), human performance (MS), physical education (MS); interscholastic athletic administration (MS); recreation and leisure management (MS); sport administration (MS); sport and coaching education (MS); sport management (MS). Part-time and evening/weekend programs available. *Faculty:* 13 full-time (5 women). *Students:* 59 full-time (20 women), 38 part-time (12 women); includes 16 minority (12 Black or African American, non-Hispanic/Latino; 1 Asian, non-Hispanic/Latino; 2 Hispanic/Latino; 1 Two or more races, non-Hispanic/Latino), 9 international. Average age 29. 49 applicants, 73% accepted, 33 enrolled. In 2011, 44 master's, 1 doctorate awarded. *Degree requirements:* For master's, comprehensive exam, thesis optional; for doctorate, comprehensive exam, thesis/dissertation. *Entrance requirements:* For master's, GRE General Test, minimum GPA of 2.75 in last 60 hours; for doctorate, GRE General Test, minimum GPA of 3.5. Additional exam requirements/recommendations for international students: Required—TOEFL, IELTS. *Application deadline:* For fall admission, 3/1 priority date for domestic students, 3/1 for international students; for spring admission, 1/10 priority date for domestic students, 1/10 for international students. Applications are processed on a rolling basis. Application fee: $50. Electronic applications accepted. *Financial support:* In 2011–12, 1 fellowship (averaging $16,000 per year), 6 research assistantships with full tuition reimbursements (averaging $7,492 per year), 5 teaching assistantships with full tuition reimbursements (averaging $7,330 per year) were awarded; career-related internships or fieldwork, Federal Work-Study, institutionally sponsored loans, scholarships/grants, health care benefits, and unspecified assistantships also available. Financial award application deadline: 3/15; financial award applicants required to submit FAFSA. *Faculty research:* Exercise physiology, health behaviors, resource management, activity interaction, site development. *Unit head:* Dr. Frederick Green, Director, 601-266-5379, Fax: 601-266-4445. *Application contact:* Dr. Trenton Gould, Graduate Coordinator, 601-266-5379, Fax: 601-266-4445. Web site: http://www.usm.edu/graduateschool/table.php.

The University of Tennessee, Graduate School, College of Education, Health and Human Sciences, Department of Exercise, Sport, and Leisure Studies, Knoxville, TN 37996. Offers exercise science (MS, PhD), including biomechanics/sports medicine, exercise physiology; recreation and leisure studies (MS); sport management (MS); sport studies (MS, PhD); therapeutic recreation (MS). Part-time and evening/weekend programs available. *Degree requirements:* For master's, thesis optional. *Entrance requirements:* For master's, minimum GPA of 2.7. Additional exam requirements/recommendations for international students: Required—TOEFL. Electronic applications accepted. *Expenses:* Tuition, state resident: full-time $8332; part-time $464 per credit hour. Tuition, nonresident: full-time $25,174; part-time $1400 per credit hour. *Required fees:* $1162; $56 per credit hour. Tuition and fees vary according to program.

The University of Toledo, College of Graduate Studies, Judith Herb College of Education, Health Science and Human Service, Department of Health and Recreation, Toledo, OH 43606-3390. Offers health education (ME, PhD); health promotions and education (MPH); recreation and leisure studies (MA). Part-time programs available. *Students:* 20 full-time (16 women), 30 part-time (21 women); includes 5 minority (4 Black or African American, non-Hispanic/Latino; 1 Asian, non-Hispanic/Latino), 2 international. Average age 34. 26 applicants, 65% accepted, 12 enrolled. In 2011, 11 master's, 5 doctorates awarded. *Degree requirements:* For master's, comprehensive exam, thesis; for doctorate, thesis/dissertation. *Entrance requirements:* For master's and doctorate, minimum cumulative GPA of 2.7 for all previous academic work, letters of recommendation. Additional exam requirements/recommendations for international students: Required—TOEFL (minimum score 550 paper-based; 213 computer-based; 80 iBT), IELTS (minimum score 6.5). *Application deadline:* For fall admission, 1/15 priority date for domestic students, 1/15 for international students. Applications are processed on a rolling basis. Application fee: $45 ($75 for international students). Electronic applications accepted. *Financial support:* In 2011–12, 11 teaching assistantships with full and partial tuition reimbursements (averaging $9,682 per year) were awarded; career-related internships or fieldwork, Federal Work-Study, institutionally sponsored loans, scholarships/grants, tuition waivers (full and partial), and unspecified assistantships also available. Support available to part-time students. *Unit head:* Joseph Dake, Chair, 419-530-2767, E-mail: joseph.dake@utoledo.edu. *Application contact:* Graduate School Office, 419-530-4723, Fax: 419-530-4724, E-mail: grdsch@utnet.utoledo.edu. Web site: http://www.utoledo.edu/eduhshs/.

University of Utah, Graduate School, College of Health, Department of Parks, Recreation, and Tourism, Salt Lake City, UT 84112. Offers M Phil, MS, Ed D, PhD. *Faculty:* 10 full-time (4 women), 1 part-time/adjunct (0 women). *Students:* 32 full-time (19 women), 17 part-time (9 women); includes 1 minority (Hispanic/Latino), 6 international. Average age 32. 29 applicants, 45% accepted, 12 enrolled. In 2011, 8 master's, 5 doctorates awarded. Terminal master's awarded for partial completion of doctoral program. *Median time to degree:* Of those who began their doctoral program in fall 2003, 100% received their degree in 8 years or less. *Degree requirements:* For master's, comprehensive exam, thesis or alternative; for doctorate, comprehensive exam, thesis/dissertation. *Entrance requirements:* For master's, minimum GPA of 3.0; for doctorate, GRE General Test, minimum GPA of 3.2. Additional exam requirements/recommendations for international students: Required—TOEFL (minimum score 500 paper-based; 173 computer-based). *Application deadline:* For fall admission, 3/1 for domestic students, 2/15 for international students; for spring admission, 10/1 for domestic students. Application fee: $55 ($65 for international students). Electronic applications accepted. *Financial support:* In 2011–12, 3 research assistantships with full tuition reimbursements, 7 teaching assistantships with full tuition reimbursements were awarded; career-related internships or fieldwork, scholarships/grants, health care benefits, and unspecified assistantships also available. Financial award application deadline: 2/15; financial award applicants required to submit FAFSA. *Faculty research:* Therapeutic, community, and outdoor recreation; tourism, youth development. *Total annual research expenditures:* $39,469. *Unit head:* Dr. Daniel L. Dustin, Chair, 801-581-7560, E-mail: daniel.dustin@health.utah.edu. *Application contact:* Dr. Jim Sibthorp, Director of Graduate Studies, 801-581-5940, Fax: 801-581-4930, E-mail: kim.sibthorp@health.utah.edu. Web site: http://www.health.utah.edu/prt/.

University of Victoria, Faculty of Graduate Studies, Faculty of Education, School of Exercise Science, Physical, and Health Education, Victoria, BC V8W 2Y2, Canada. Offers coaching studies (co-operative education) (M Ed); kinesiology (M Sc, MA); leisure service administration (MA); physical education (MA). Part-time programs available. *Degree requirements:* For master's, comprehensive exam (for some programs), thesis (for some programs). *Entrance requirements:* For master's, minimum B average. Additional exam requirements/recommendations for international students: Required—TOEFL (minimum score 575 paper-based; 233 computer-based), IELTS (minimum score 7). Electronic applications accepted. *Faculty research:* Children and exercise, mental skills in sports, teaching effectiveness, neural control of human movement, physical performance and health.

University of Waterloo, Graduate Studies, Faculty of Applied Health Sciences, Department of Recreation and Leisure Studies, Waterloo, ON N2L 3G1, Canada. Offers MA, PhD. Part-time programs available. *Degree requirements:* For master's, thesis; for doctorate, comprehensive exam, thesis/dissertation. *Entrance requirements:* For master's, honors degree, minimum B average, writing sample, resume; for doctorate, GRE (recommended), master's degree, minimum B average, writing sample, resumé. Additional exam requirements/recommendations for international students: Required—TOEFL, TWE. Electronic applications accepted. *Faculty research:* Tourism, leisure behavior, special populations, leisure service management, outdoor resources, aging, health and well-being, work and health.

University of West Florida, College of Professional Studies, Department of Health, Leisure, and Exercise Science, Program in Health, Leisure, and Exercise Science, Pensacola, FL 32514-5750. Offers exercise science (MS); physical education (MS). Part-time and evening/weekend programs available. *Faculty:* 6 full-time (2 women), 1 (woman) part-time/adjunct. *Students:* 14 full-time (10 women), 16 part-time (7 women); includes 6 minority (2 Black or African American, non-Hispanic/Latino; 1 Asian, non-Hispanic/Latino; 2 Hispanic/Latino; 1 Native Hawaiian or other Pacific Islander, non-Hispanic/Latino), 2 international. Average age 28. 22 applicants, 55% accepted, 7 enrolled. In 2011, 20 master's awarded. *Degree requirements:* For master's, thesis or alternative. *Entrance requirements:* For master's, GRE or MAT, official transcripts; minimum GPA of 3.0; letter of intent; two personal references; work experience. Additional exam requirements/recommendations for international students: Required—TOEFL (minimum score 550 paper-based; 213 computer-based). *Application deadline:* For fall admission, 6/1 for domestic and international students; for spring admission, 10/1 for domestic and international students. Applications are processed on a rolling basis. Application fee: $30. Electronic applications accepted. *Expenses:* Tuition, state resident: full-time $5729; part-time $302 per credit hour. Tuition, nonresident: full-time $20,059; part-time $961 per credit hour. *Required fees:* $1509; $63 per credit hour. *Financial support:* Career-related internships or fieldwork, Federal Work-Study, scholarships/grants, and tuition waivers (partial) available. Support available to part-time students. Financial award application deadline: 4/15; financial award applicants required to submit FAFSA. *Unit head:* Dr. John Todorovich, Chairperson, 850-473-7248, Fax: 850-474-2106. *Application contact:* Terry McCray, Assistant Director of Graduate Admissions, 850-473-7718, Fax: 850-473-7714, E-mail: gradadmissions@uwf.edu.

Recreation and Park Management

Acadia University, Faculty of Professional Studies, School of Recreation Management and Kinesiology, Wolfville, NS B4P 2R6, Canada. Offers MR. *Degree requirements:* For master's, thesis. *Entrance requirements:* Additional exam requirements/recommendations for international students: Required—TOEFL (minimum score 580 paper-based; 237 computer-based; 93 iBT), IELTS (minimum score 6.5).

Arizona State University, College of Public Programs, School of Community Resources and Development, Phoenix, AZ 85004-0685. Offers community resources and development (PhD); nonprofit leadership and management (Graduate Certificate); nonprofit studies (MNpS); recreation and tourism studies (MS). Part-time and evening/weekend programs available. Terminal master's awarded for partial completion of doctoral program. *Degree requirements:* For master's, thesis or alternative, interactive Program of Study (iPOS) submitted before completing 50 percent of required credit hours; for doctorate, comprehensive exam, thesis/dissertation, interactive Program of Study (iPOS) submitted before completing 50 percent of required credit hours. *Entrance* *requirements:* For master's and doctorate, GRE, minimum GPA of 3.0 or equivalent in last 2 years of work leading to bachelor's degree. Additional exam requirements/recommendations for international students: Required—TOEFL (minimum score 80 iBT), TOEFL, IELTS, or Pearson Test of English. Electronic applications accepted. *Expenses:* Contact institution.

Aurora University, George Williams College, Aurora, IL 60506-4892. Offers MS. Part-time and evening/weekend programs available. *Entrance requirements:* Additional exam requirements/recommendations for international students: Required—TOEFL (minimum score 550 paper-based; 213 computer-based). Electronic applications accepted.

Bowling Green State University, Graduate College, College of Education and Human Development, School of Human Movement, Sport, and Leisure Studies, Bowling Green, OH 43403. Offers developmental kinesiology (M Ed); recreation and leisure (M Ed); sport administration (M Ed). Part-time programs available. *Degree requirements:* For master's, thesis or alternative. *Entrance requirements:* For master's, GRE General Test, minimum GPA of 2.7. Additional exam requirements/recommendations for international students: Required—TOEFL. Electronic applications accepted. *Faculty research:* Teacher-learning process, travel and tourism, sport marketing and management, exercise physiology and sport psychology, life-span motor development.

Brigham Young University, Graduate Studies, Marriott School of Management, Department of Recreation Management and Youth Leadership, Provo , UT 84602. Offers youth and family recreation (MS). *Faculty:* 10 full-time (1 woman), 15 part-time/adjunct (6 women). *Students:* 16 full-time (8 women); includes 3 minority (1 Asian, non-Hispanic/Latino; 1 Hispanic/Latino; 1 Native Hawaiian or other Pacific Islander, non-Hispanic/Latino). Average age 29. 7 applicants, 57% accepted, 4 enrolled. In 2011, 2 master's awarded. *Degree requirements:* For master's, thesis, oral defense. *Entrance requirements:* For master's, GRE General Test, minimum GPA of 3.0 in last 60 hours. Additional exam requirements/recommendations for international students: Required—TOEFL (minimum score 580 paper-based; 237 computer-based; 85 iBT), IELTS (minimum score 7). *Application deadline:* For fall admission, 2/1 priority date for domestic students, 2/1 for international students. Application fee: $50. Electronic applications accepted. *Expenses:* Contact institution. *Financial support:* In 2011–12, 9 research assistantships with full tuition reimbursements (averaging $2,200 per year) were awarded; fellowships, teaching assistantships with tuition reimbursements, career-related internships or fieldwork, institutionally sponsored loans, scholarships/grants, tuition waivers (full and partial), unspecified assistantships, and administrative aides also available. Support available to part-time students. Financial award application deadline: 3/1. *Faculty research:* Family recreation, adolescent development, leisure behavior, families with child with disability inclusive and adaptive recreation. *Unit head:* Dr. Patti Ann Freeman, Chair, 801-422-1286, Fax: 801-422-0609, E-mail: patti_freeman@byu.edu. *Application contact:* Dr. Brian Jack Hill, Graduate Coordinator, 801-422-1287, Fax: 801-422-0609, E-mail: brian_hill@byu.edu. Web site: http://www.rmyl.byu.edu/graduate.html.

California State University, Chico, Office of Graduate Studies, College of Communication and Education, Department of Recreation, Hospitality and Parks Management, Chico, CA 95929-0722. Offers recreation administration (MA). Part-time programs available. *Faculty:* 2 full-time (both women). *Students:* 6 full-time (4 women), 2 part-time (1 woman), 1 international. Average age 27. 9 applicants, 44% accepted, 4 enrolled. In 2011, 9 master's awarded. *Degree requirements:* For master's, thesis or alternative. *Entrance requirements:* For master's, GRE General Test, 3 letters of recommendation, statement of purpose, resume. Additional exam requirements/recommendations for international students: Required—TOEFL (minimum score 550 paper-based; 213 computer-based; 80 iBT), IELTS (minimum score 6.5). *Application deadline:* For fall admission, 3/1 priority date for domestic students, 3/1 for international students; for spring admission, 9/15 priority date for domestic students, 9/15 for international students. Application fee: $55. Electronic applications accepted. Tuition and fees vary according to class time, course load and degree level. *Financial support:* Fellowships, career-related internships or fieldwork, scholarships/grants, and traineeships available. Financial award application deadline: 3/1; financial award applicants required to submit FAFSA. *Unit head:* Dr. Morgan Geddie, Chair, 530-898-6408, Fax: 530-898-6557, E-mail: recr@csuchico.edu. *Application contact:* Judy L. Rice, Graduate Admissions Coordinator, 530-898-5416, Fax: 530-898-3342, E-mail: jlrice@csuchico.edu. Web site: http://www.csuchico.edu/recr/.

California State University, East Bay, Office of Academic Programs and Graduate Studies, College of Education and Allied Studies, Department of Hospitality, Recreation and Tourism, Hayward, CA 94542-3000. Offers recreation and tourism (MS). Part-time and evening/weekend programs available. Postbaccalaureate distance learning degree programs offered (no on-campus study). *Faculty:* 3 full-time (2 women), 1 (woman) part-time/adjunct. *Students:* 32 full-time (21 women), 22 part-time (13 women); includes 16 minority (5 Black or African American, non-Hispanic/Latino; 5 Asian, non-Hispanic/Latino; 4 Hispanic/Latino; 2 Two or more races, non-Hispanic/Latino). Average age 36. 38 applicants, 74% accepted, 24 enrolled. In 2011, 11 master's awarded. *Degree requirements:* For master's, thesis optional. *Entrance requirements:* For master's, minimum GPA of 2.75; 2 years' related work experience; 3 letters of recommendation; resume; baccalaureate degree. Additional exam requirements/recommendations for international students: Required—TOEFL (minimum score 550 paper-based; 237 computer-based). *Application deadline:* For fall admission, 6/30 for domestic and international students. Applications are processed on a rolling basis. Application fee: $55. Electronic applications accepted. *Expenses:* Tuition, state resident: full-time $6738; part-time $1302 per quarter. Tuition, nonresident: full-time $12,690; part-time $2294 per quarter. *Required fees:* $449 per quarter. Tuition and fees vary according to degree level, program and reciprocity agreements. *Financial support:* Federal Work-Study, institutionally sponsored loans, and scholarships/grants available. Support available to part-time students. Financial award application deadline: 3/2; financial award applicants required to submit FAFSA. *Faculty research:* Leisure, online vs. F2F learning, risk management, leadership, tourism consumer behavior. *Unit head:* Dr. Melany Spielman, Chair/Recreation Graduate Advisor, 510-885-3043, E-mail: melany.spielman@csueastbay.edu. Web site: http://www20.csueastbay.edu/ceas/departments/hrt/.

California State University, Long Beach, Graduate Studies, College of Health and Human Services, Department of Recreation and Leisure Studies, Long Beach, CA 90840. Offers recreation administration (MS). Part-time programs available. *Faculty:* 2 full-time (both women), 1 (woman) part-time/adjunct. *Students:* 5 full-time (4 women), 7 part-time (5 women); includes 3 minority (1 Black or African American, non-Hispanic/Latino; 1 Hispanic/Latino; 1 Two or more races, non-Hispanic/Latino), 2 international. Average age 30. 16 applicants, 63% accepted, 6 enrolled. In 2011, 7 master's awarded. *Degree requirements:* For master's, comprehensive exam or thesis. *Entrance requirements:* For master's, GRE General Test. *Application deadline:* For fall admission, 7/1 for domestic students. Applications are processed on a rolling basis. Application fee: $55. Electronic applications accepted. *Financial support:* Federal Work-Study, institutionally sponsored loans, and scholarships/grants available. Financial award application deadline: 3/2. *Unit head:* Dr. Maridith Janssen, Chair, 562-985-4079, Fax: 562-985-8154, E-mail: mjanssen@csulb.edu. *Application contact:* Dr. Katherine James, Graduate Advisor, 562-985-8077, Fax: 562-985-8154, E-mail: kjames@csulb.edu.

California State University, Northridge, Graduate Studies, College of Health and Human Development, Department of Recreation and Tourism Management, Northridge, CA 91330. Offers hospitality and tourism (MS); recreational sport management/campus recreation (MS). *Degree requirements:* For master's, thesis (for some programs). *Entrance requirements:* For master's, GRE (if cumulative undergraduate GPA less than 3.0). Additional exam requirements/recommendations for international students: Required—TOEFL.

California State University, Sacramento, Office of Graduate Studies, College of Health and Human Services, Department of Recreation and Leisure Studies, Sacramento, CA 95819-6110. Offers recreation administration (MS). Part-time programs available. *Faculty:* 8 full-time (4 women), 7 part-time/adjunct (5 women). *Students:* 6 full-time, 9 part-time; includes 2 minority (1 American Indian or Alaska Native, non-Hispanic/Latino; 1 Asian, non-Hispanic/Latino). Average age 29. 14 applicants, 71% accepted, 5 enrolled. In 2011, 11 master's awarded. *Degree requirements:* For master's, thesis or project; writing proficiency exam. *Entrance requirements:* Additional exam requirements/recommendations for international students: Required—TOEFL. *Application deadline:* For fall admission, 3/1 for domestic and international students; for spring admission, 9/30 for international students. Applications are processed on a rolling basis. Application fee: $55. Electronic applications accepted. *Financial support:* Research assistantships, teaching assistantships, career-related internships or fieldwork, and Federal Work-Study available. Support available to part-time students. Financial award application deadline: 3/1; financial award applicants required to submit FAFSA. *Unit head:* Greg Shaw, Chair, 916-278-6752, Fax: 916-278-5053, E-mail: shaw@csus.edu. *Application contact:* Jose Martinez, Outreach and Graduate Diversity Coordinator, 916-278-6470, Fax: 916-278-5669, E-mail: martinj@skymail.csus.edu. Web site: http://www.csus.edu/hhs/rpta.

Central Michigan University, College of Graduate Studies, College of Education and Human Services, Department of Recreation, Parks, and Leisure Services Administration, Mount Pleasant, MI 48859. Offers recreation and park administration (MA); therapeutic recreation (MA). Part-time programs available. *Degree requirements:* For master's, thesis or alternative. Electronic applications accepted. *Faculty research:* Commercial recreation and facilities management, study of ethics in parks and recreation professionals, computer touch-tone information services at visitor centers, creative play spaces for children, therapeutic recreation.

Central Michigan University, College of Graduate Studies, Interdisciplinary Administration Programs, Mount Pleasant, MI 48859. Offers acquisitions administration (MSA, Graduate Certificate); general administration (MSA, Graduate Certificate); health services administration (MSA, Graduate Certificate); human resource administration (Graduate Certificate); human resources administration (MSA); information resource management (MSA, Graduate Certificate); international administration (MSA, Graduate Certificate); leadership (MSA, Graduate Certificate); organizational communication (MSA, Graduate Certificate); public administration (MSA, Graduate Certificate); recreation and park administration (MSA); sport administration (MSA). *Accreditation:* AACSB. Part-time and evening/weekend programs available. Postbaccalaureate distance learning degree programs offered (no on-campus study). *Degree requirements:* For master's, thesis or alternative. *Entrance requirements:* For master's, bachelor's degree with minimum GPA of 2.7. Electronic applications accepted. *Faculty research:* Interdisciplinary studies in acquisitions administration, health services administration, sport administration, recreation and park administration, and international administration.

Clemson University, Graduate School, College of Health, Education, and Human Development, Department of Parks, Recreation, and Tourism Management, Clemson, SC 29634. Offers MS, PhD. Part-time programs available. Postbaccalaureate distance learning degree programs offered (no on-campus study). *Faculty:* 17 full-time (7 women). *Students:* 61 full-time (29 women), 7 part-time (6 women); includes 1 minority (Hispanic/Latino), 21 international. Average age 32. 116 applicants, 80% accepted, 26 enrolled. In 2011, 6 master's, 5 doctorates awarded. *Degree requirements:* For master's, thesis (for some programs); for doctorate, thesis/dissertation. *Entrance requirements:* For master's, GRE General Test, minimum undergraduate GPA of 3.0; for doctorate, GRE General Test, minimum graduate GPA of 3.0. Additional exam requirements/recommendations for international students: Required—TOEFL. *Application deadline:* For fall admission, 5/1 priority date for domestic students; for spring admission, 10/1 for domestic students. Applications are processed on a rolling basis. Application fee: $70 ($80 for international students). Electronic applications accepted. *Financial support:* In 2011–12, 50 students received support, including 2 research assistantships with partial tuition reimbursements available (averaging $9,400 per year), 66 teaching assistantships with partial tuition reimbursements available (averaging $5,350 per year); fellowships with full and partial tuition reimbursements available, career-related internships or fieldwork, scholarships/grants, health care benefits, tuition waivers (partial), and unspecified assistantships also available. Support available to part-time students. Financial award application deadline: 1/15; financial award applicants required to submit FAFSA. *Faculty research:* Recreation resource management, leisure behavior, therapeutic recreation, community leisure . *Total annual research expenditures:* $380,421. *Unit head:* Dr. Brett A. Wright, Chair, 864-656-3036, Fax: 864-656-2226, E-mail: wright@clemson.edu. *Application contact:* Dr. Denise M. Anderson, Graduate Coordinator, 864-656-5679, Fax: 864-656-2226, E-mail: dander2@clemson.edu. Web site: http://www.hehd.clemson.edu/prtm/.

The College at Brockport, State University of New York, School of Health and Human Performance, Department of Recreation and Leisure Studies, Brockport, NY 14420-2997. Offers recreation and leisure service management (MS). Part-time programs available. *Students:* 10 full-time (8 women), 10 part-time (4 women); includes 3 minority (1 Black or African American, non-Hispanic/Latino; 1 Asian, non-Hispanic/Latino; 1 Hispanic/Latino). 8 applicants, 75% accepted, 4 enrolled. In 2011, 12 master's awarded. *Degree requirements:* For master's, thesis or alternative. *Entrance requirements:* For master's, minimum GPA of 3.0, letters of recommendation, written critical analysis; statement of objectives. Additional exam requirements/recommendations for international students: Required—TOEFL (minimum score 550 paper-based; 213 computer-based; 79 iBT). *Application deadline:* For fall admission, 5/30 priority date for domestic students, 5/30 for international students; for spring admission, 11/15 priority date for domestic students, 11/15 for international students. Application fee: $50. Electronic applications accepted. *Financial support:* Federal Work-Study, scholarships/grants, and unspecified assistantships available. Support available to part-time students. Financial award application deadline: 3/15; financial award applicants required to submit FAFSA. *Faculty research:* Leisure service delivery systems; therapeutic recreation; international issues in recreation and leisure; tourism; customer service, customer behavior and perceived value/satisfaction; leisure motivation among Baby Boomers. *Unit head:* Arthur Graham, Chairperson, 585-395-2643, Fax: 585-395-5246, E-mail: jfrater@brockport.edu. *Application contact:* Dr. Lynda Sperazza, Graduate Director, 585-395-5490, Fax: 585-395-5246, E-mail: lsperazza@brockport.edu. Web site: http://www.brockport.edu/graduate/.

Recreation and Park Management

Colorado State University, Graduate School, Warner College of Natural Resources, Department of Human Dimensions of Natural Resources, Fort Collins, CO 80523-1480. Offers MS, PhD. Part-time programs available. Postbaccalaureate distance learning degree programs offered. *Faculty:* 11 full-time (3 women). *Students:* 43 full-time (24 women), 16 part-time (8 women); includes 8 minority (1 Black or African American, non-Hispanic/Latino; 6 Hispanic/Latino; 1 Two or more races, non-Hispanic/Latino), 6 international. Average age 31. 16 applicants, 50% accepted, 7 enrolled. In 2011, 10 master's, 2 doctorates awarded. Terminal master's awarded for partial completion of doctoral program. *Degree requirements:* For master's, comprehensive exam, thesis; for doctorate, comprehensive exam, thesis/dissertation. *Entrance requirements:* For master's, GRE General Test, minimum GPA of 3.0, 3 letters of recommendation, statement of interest; for doctorate, GRE General Test (combined minimum score of 1000 on the Verbal and Quantitative sections), minimum GPA of 3.0, 3 letters of recommendation, copy of master's thesis or professional paper, interview, statement of interest. Additional exam requirements/recommendations for international students: Required—TOEFL (minimum score 550 paper-based; 213 computer-based; 80 iBT). *Application deadline:* For fall admission, 2/1 priority date for domestic students, 2/1 for international students. Application fee: $50. Electronic applications accepted. *Expenses:* Tuition, state resident: full-time $7992. Tuition, nonresident: full-time $19,592. *Required fees:* $1735; $58 per credit. *Financial support:* In 2011–12, 27 students received support, including 2 fellowships (averaging $14,054 per year), 18 research assistantships with tuition reimbursements available (averaging $14,762 per year), 7 teaching assistantships with tuition reimbursements available (averaging $11,227 per year); career-related internships or fieldwork, Federal Work-Study, scholarships/grants, traineeships, and unspecified assistantships also available. Support available to part-time students. Financial award application deadline: 2/15; financial award applicants required to submit FAFSA. *Faculty research:* International tourism, wilderness preservation, resource interpretation, human dimensions in natural resources, protected areas management. *Total annual research expenditures:* $1.5 million. *Unit head:* Dr. Michael J. Manfredo, Head, 970-491-0474, Fax: 970-491-2255, E-mail: manfredo@cnr.colostate.edu. *Application contact:* Jacqie Hasan, Graduate Contact, 970-491-6591, Fax: 970-491-2255, E-mail: jacqie.hasan@colostate.edu. Web site: http://warnercnr.colostate.edu/hdnr-home.

Delta State University, Graduate Programs, College of Education, Division of Health, Physical Education, and Recreation, Cleveland, MS 38733-0001. Offers health, physical education, and recreation (M Ed); sport and human performance (MS). Part-time and evening/weekend programs available. *Degree requirements:* For master's, thesis optional. *Entrance requirements:* For master's, GRE General Test or MAT, Class A teaching certificate. *Expenses:* Tuition, state resident: full-time $4702; part-time $294 per credit hour. Tuition, nonresident: full-time $12,516; part-time $760 per credit hour. *Required fees:* $586. *Faculty research:* Blood pressure, body fat, power and reaction time, learning disorders for athletes, effects of walking.

East Carolina University, Graduate School, College of Health and Human Performance, Department of Recreation and Leisure Studies, Greenville, NC 27858-4353. Offers aquatic therapy (Certificate); biofeedback (Certificate); recreation and park administration (MS), including generalist, recreational sports management; recreational therapy administration (MS). Part-time and evening/weekend programs available. Postbaccalaureate distance learning degree programs offered (minimal on-campus study). *Degree requirements:* For master's, comprehensive exam, thesis optional. *Entrance requirements:* For master's, GRE General Test or MAT. Additional exam requirements/recommendations for international students: Required—TOEFL. *Application deadline:* For fall admission, 6/1 priority date for domestic students. Applications are processed on a rolling basis. Application fee: $50. *Expenses:* Tuition, state resident: full-time $3557; part-time $444.63 per semester hour. Tuition, nonresident: full-time $14,351; part-time $1793.88 per semester hour. *Required fees:* $2016; $252 per semester hour. Part-time tuition and fees vary according to course load, campus/location and program. *Financial support:* Research assistantships and teaching assistantships with partial tuition reimbursements available. Financial award application deadline: 6/1. *Faculty research:* Therapeutic recreation, stress and coping behavior, medicine carrying capacity, choice behavior, tourism preferences. *Unit head:* Dr. Deb Jordan, Chair, 252-737-2990, E-mail: jordand@ecu.edu. *Application contact:* Dr. Sharon Knight, Director of Graduate Studies, 252-328-4637, Fax: 252-328-4655, E-mail: knights@ecu.edu. Web site: http://www.ecu.edu/rcls/.

Eastern Kentucky University, The Graduate School, College of Health Sciences, Department of Recreation and Park Administration, Richmond, KY 40475-3102. Offers MS. Part-time programs available. *Degree requirements:* For master's, comprehensive exam, thesis optional. *Entrance requirements:* For master's, GRE General Test, MAT, minimum GPA of 2.5. *Faculty research:* Marketing, at risk youth, outdoor education, event planning, TR in schools.

Eastern Washington University, Graduate Studies, College of Arts, Letters and Education, Department of Physical Education, Health and Recreation, Cheney, WA 99004-2431. Offers exercise science (MS); sports and recreation administration (MS). *Faculty:* 14 full-time (5 women). *Students:* 28 full-time (9 women), 4 part-time (2 women); includes 4 minority (3 Black or African American, non-Hispanic/Latino; 1 Hispanic/Latino). Average age 29. 50 applicants, 48% accepted, 14 enrolled. In 2011, 7 master's awarded. *Degree requirements:* For master's, comprehensive exam, thesis or alternative. *Entrance requirements:* For master's, minimum GPA of 3.0. *Application deadline:* For fall admission, 4/1 priority date for domestic students; for spring admission, 1/15 for domestic students. Applications are processed on a rolling basis. Application fee: $50. *Financial support:* In 2011–12, 10 teaching assistantships with partial tuition reimbursements (averaging $6,624 per year) were awarded; career-related internships or fieldwork, Federal Work-Study, institutionally sponsored loans, and scholarships/grants also available. Support available to part-time students. Financial award application deadline: 2/1; financial award applicants required to submit FAFSA. *Unit head:* John Cogley, Chair, 509-359-2486, E-mail: john.cogley@mail.ewu.edu. *Application contact:* Dr. Jeni McNeal, Professor of Physical Education, Health and Recreation, 509-359-2872, Fax: 509-359-4833, E-mail: jeni_mcneal@hotmail.com.

Florida Agricultural and Mechanical University, Division of Graduate Studies, Research, and Continuing Education, College of Education, Department of Health, Physical Education, and Recreation, Tallahassee, FL 32307-3200. Offers M Ed, MS Ed. *Accreditation:* NCATE. Part-time and evening/weekend programs available. *Degree requirements:* For master's, thesis optional. *Entrance requirements:* For master's, GRE General Test, minimum GPA of 3.0. Additional exam requirements/recommendations for international students: Required—TOEFL. *Faculty research:* Administration/curriculum, work behavior, psychology.

Florida International University, College of Education, Department of Educational Leadership and Policy Studies, Miami, FL 33199. Offers adult education (MS); adult education in human resource development (Ed D); clinical mental health counseling (MS); conflict resolution and consensus building (Certificate); counselor education (MS); educational administration and supervision (Ed D); educational leadership (MS, Certificate, Ed S); higher education (Ed D); higher education administration (MS); human resource development (MS); instruction in urban settings (MS); international/intercultural education (MS); learning technologies (MS); multicultural-bilingual (MS); multicultural-TESOL (MS); recreation and sport management (MS); recreation therapy (MS); rehabilitation counseling (MS); school counseling (MS); school psychology (Ed S); urban education (MS). Part-time and evening/weekend programs available. *Degree requirements:* For doctorate, thesis/dissertation. *Entrance requirements:* For master's, minimum GPA of 3.0; for doctorate and other advanced degree, GRE General Test. Additional exam requirements/recommendations for international students: Required—TOEFL (minimum score 550 paper-based; 213 computer-based; 80 iBT), IELTS (minimum score 6.3). Electronic applications accepted.

Florida State University, The Graduate School, College of Education, Department of Sport Management, Tallahassee, FL 32306. Offers MS, Ed D, PhD, Certificate. *Faculty:* 9 full-time (2 women). *Students:* 105 full-time (35 women), 36 part-time (18 women); includes 18 minority (9 Black or African American, non-Hispanic/Latino; 4 Asian, non-Hispanic/Latino; 5 Hispanic/Latino), 30 international. Average age 30. 176 applicants, 58% accepted, 62 enrolled. In 2011, 68 master's, 8 doctorates awarded. *Degree requirements:* For master's and Certificate, comprehensive exam, thesis optional; for doctorate, comprehensive exam, thesis/dissertation. *Entrance requirements:* For master's, doctorate, and Certificate, GRE General Test, minimum GPA of 3.0. Additional exam requirements/recommendations for international students: Required—TOEFL (minimum score 550 paper-based; 213 computer-based; 80 iBT). *Application deadline:* For fall admission, 7/1 for domestic and international students; for winter admission, 11/1 for domestic and international students; for spring admission, 3/1 for domestic and international students. Application fee: $30. Electronic applications accepted. *Expenses:* Tuition, state resident: full-time $9474; part-time $350.88 per credit hour. Tuition, nonresident: full-time $16,236; part-time $601.34 per credit hour. *Required fees:* $630 per semester. One-time fee: $20. Tuition and fees vary according to course load and campus/location. *Financial support:* In 2011–12, 2 research assistantships with full and partial tuition reimbursements, 54 teaching assistantships with full and partial tuition reimbursements were awarded; fellowships with full and partial tuition reimbursements, career-related internships or fieldwork, Federal Work-Study, scholarships/grants, health care benefits, and unspecified assistantships also available. Financial award application deadline: 1/15; financial award applicants required to submit FAFSA. *Faculty research:* Sport marketing, gender issues in sport, finances in sport industry, coaching. *Total annual research expenditures:* $48,242. *Unit head:* Dr. Jeffrey D. James, Chair, 850-644-9214, Fax: 850-644-0975, E-mail: jdjames@fsu.edu. *Application contact:* Sandra Auguste, Program Assistant, 850-644-4813, Fax: 850-644-0975, E-mail: sauguste@fsu.edu. Web site: http://www.fsu.edu/~smrmpe/.

Frostburg State University, Graduate School, College of Education, Program in Parks and Recreational Management, Frostburg, MD 21532-1099. Offers MS. Part-time and evening/weekend programs available. *Degree requirements:* For master's, thesis. *Entrance requirements:* For master's, resume. Additional exam requirements/recommendations for international students: Required—TOEFL. Electronic applications accepted.

George Mason University, College of Education and Human Development, School of Recreation, Health and Tourism, Manassas , VA 20110. Offers exercise, fitness, and health promotion (MS); sport and recreation studies (MS). *Faculty:* 34 full-time (15 women), 59 part-time/adjunct (32 women). *Students:* 18 full-time (10 women), 25 part-time (11 women); includes 5 minority (2 Black or African American, non-Hispanic/Latino; 1 Asian, non-Hispanic/Latino; 1 Hispanic/Latino; 1 Two or more races, non-Hispanic/Latino). Average age 29. 58 applicants, 60% accepted, 22 enrolled. In 2011, 7 degrees awarded. *Degree requirements:* For master's, thesis (for some programs). *Entrance requirements:* For master's, GRE General Test or MAT, 3 letters of recommendation; official transcripts; expanded goals statement; undergraduate course in statistics and minimum GPA of 3.0 in last 60 credit hours and overall (for MS in sport and recreation studies); baccalaureate degree related to kinesiology, exercise science or athletic training (for MS in exercise, fitness and health promotion). Additional exam requirements/recommendations for international students: Required—TOEFL (minimum score 570 paper-based; 230 computer-based; 88 iBT), IELTS, Pearson Test of English. *Application deadline:* For fall admission, 4/1 priority date for domestic students; for spring admission, 11/1 priority date for domestic students. Application fee: $65 ($80 for international students). Electronic applications accepted. *Expenses:* Tuition, state resident: full-time $8750; part-time $364.58 per credit. Tuition, nonresident: full-time $24,092; part-time $1003.83 per credit. *Required fees:* $2514; $104.75 per credit. *Financial support:* In 2011–12, 7 students received support, including 7 research assistantships with full and partial tuition reimbursements available (averaging $6,675 per year); career-related internships or fieldwork, Federal Work-Study, scholarships/grants, unspecified assistantships, and health care benefits (full-time research or teaching assistantship recipients) also available. Support available to part-time students. Financial award application deadline: 3/1; financial award applicants required to submit FAFSA. *Faculty research:* Informing policy; promoting economic development; advocating stewardship of natural resources; improving the quality of life of individuals, families, and communities at the local, national and international levels. *Total annual research expenditures:* $553,053. *Unit head:* David Wiggins, Director, 703-993-2057, Fax: 703-993-2025, E-mail: dwiggin1@gmu.edu. *Application contact:* Dr. Pierre Rodgers, Associate Professor/Co-Coordinator of Graduate Programs, 703-993-8317, Fax: 703-993-2025, E-mail: prodgers@gmu.edu. Web site: http://rht.gmu.edu/grad/.

Georgia College & State University, Graduate School, College of Health Sciences, Department of Kinesiology, Milledgeville, GA 31061. Offers health promotion (M Ed); human performance (M Ed); kinesiology (MAT); outdoor education (M Ed). *Accreditation:* NCATE (one or more programs are accredited). Part-time and evening/weekend programs available. *Students:* 31 full-time (13 women), 11 part-time (7 women); includes 8 minority (6 Black or African American, non-Hispanic/Latino; 2 Hispanic/Latino), 1 international. Average age 27. 32 applicants, 69% accepted, 16 enrolled. In 2011, 12 master's awarded. *Degree requirements:* For master's, comprehensive exam, thesis optional. *Entrance requirements:* For master's, GRE General Test or MAT, minimum GPA of 2.75 in upper-level undergraduate courses, 2 letters of reference. Additional exam requirements/recommendations for international students: Recommended—TOEFL (minimum score 550 paper-based; 213 computer-based; 79 iBT). *Application deadline:* For fall admission, 7/1 priority date for domestic students, 4/1 for international students; for spring admission, 11/15 priority date for domestic students, 9/1 for international students. Applications are processed on a rolling basis. Application fee: $40. Electronic applications accepted. *Expenses:* Tuition, state resident: full-time $4806; part-time $267 per credit hour. Tuition, nonresident: full-time $17,802; part-time $989 per credit hour. *Required fees:* $936 per semester. Tuition and fees vary according to course load and campus/location. *Financial support:* In 2011–12, 25 research assistantships with full tuition reimbursements were awarded; career-related internships or fieldwork and unspecified assistantships also available. Support available to part-time students. Financial award applicants required to submit FAFSA. *Unit head:* Dr. Lisa Griffin, Interim Chair, 478-445-4072, Fax: 478-445-1790, E-mail: lisa.griffin@gcsu.edu. *Application contact:* 800-342-0471, E-mail: grad-admit@gcsu.edu.

Hardin-Simmons University, Graduate School, Irvin School of Education, Department of Fitness and Sport Sciences, Program in Kinesiology, Sport, and Recreation, Abilene, TX 79698-0001. Offers M Ed. Part-time programs available. *Faculty:* 6 full-time (3 women), 2 part-time/adjunct (0 women). *Students:* 7 full-time (0 women), 15 part-time (5 women); includes 4 minority (1 Black or African American, non-Hispanic/Latino; 3 Hispanic/Latino). Average age 25. 12 applicants, 83% accepted, 6 enrolled. In 2011, 10 master's awarded. *Degree requirements:* For master's, comprehensive exam, thesis optional, internship, project. *Entrance requirements:* For master's, minimum undergraduate GPA of 3.0 in major, 2.7 overall; interview; writing sample; letters of recommendation; resume. Additional exam requirements/recommendations for international students: Required—TOEFL (minimum score 550 paper-based; 213 computer-based; 75 iBT). *Application deadline:* For fall admission, 8/15 priority date for domestic students, 4/1 for international students; for spring admission, 1/5 priority date for domestic students, 9/1 for international students. Applications are processed on a rolling basis. Application fee: $50. *Expenses: Tuition:* Full-time $12,870; part-time $715 per credit hour. *Required fees:* $650; $110 per semester. Tuition and fees vary according to degree level. *Financial support:* In 2011–12, 12 fellowships (averaging $1,667 per year) were awarded; career-related internships or fieldwork, scholarships/grants, and recreation assistantships also available. Support available to part-time students. Financial award application deadline: 6/30; financial award applicants required to submit FAFSA. *Unit head:* Dr. Robert Moore, Director, 325-670-1265, Fax: 325-670-1218, E-mail: bemoore@hsutx.edu. *Application contact:* Dr. Nancy Kucinski, Dean of Graduate Studies, 325-670-1298, Fax: 325-670-1564, E-mail: gradoff@hsutx.edu. Web site: http://www.hsutx.edu/academics/irvin/graduate/kinesiology.

Indiana University Bloomington, School of Health, Physical Education and Recreation, Department of Recreation, Park, and Tourism Studies, Bloomington, IN 47405-7000. Offers leisure behavior (PhD); outdoor recreation (MS); recreation administration (MS); recreational sports administration (MS); therapeutic recreation (MS); tourism management (MS). *Faculty:* 16 full-time (6 women), 2 part-time/adjunct (both women). *Students:* 61 full-time (32 women), 22 part-time (20 women); includes 9 minority (4 Black or African American, non-Hispanic/Latino; 1 Asian, non-Hispanic/Latino; 1 Hispanic/Latino; 3 Two or more races, non-Hispanic/Latino), 22 international. Average age 31. 48 applicants, 73% accepted, 18 enrolled. In 2011, 17 master's, 6 doctorates awarded. Terminal master's awarded for partial completion of doctoral program. *Degree requirements:* For master's, thesis optional; for doctorate, thesis/dissertation. *Entrance requirements:* For master's, GRE General Test, minimum GPA of 2.8; for doctorate, GRE General Test, minimum GPA of 3.0 (undergraduate), 3.5 (graduate). Additional exam requirements/recommendations for international students: Required—TOEFL. *Application deadline:* For fall admission, 1/1 for international students; for spring admission, 9/1 for international students. Applications are processed on a rolling basis. Application fee: $55 ($65 for international students). *Financial support:* Fellowships, research assistantships, teaching assistantships with partial tuition reimbursements, career-related internships or fieldwork, Federal Work-Study, institutionally sponsored loans, scholarships/grants, tuition waivers (partial), unspecified assistantships, and fee remissions available. Financial award application deadline: 3/1. *Faculty research:* Leisure counseling, gerontology, special populations, planning and development. *Unit head:* Bryan McCormick, Chair, 812-855-3482, E-mail: bmccormi@indiana.edu. *Application contact:* Program Office, 812-855-4711, Fax: 812-855-3998, E-mail: recpark@indiana.edu. Web site: http://www.indiana.edu/~recpark/.

Kent State University, Graduate School of Education, Health, and Human Services, School of Foundations, Leadership and Administration, Sports Recreation and Management Program, Kent, OH 44242-0001. Offers sport and recreation management (MA); sports studies (MA). *Faculty:* 9 full-time (5 women), 17 part-time/adjunct (8 women). *Students:* 42 full-time (10 women), 16 part-time (6 women); includes 7 minority (4 Black or African American, non-Hispanic/Latino; 3 Asian, non-Hispanic/Latino). 60 applicants, 77% accepted. In 2011, 24 master's awarded. *Degree requirements:* For master's, thesis optional. *Entrance requirements:* For master's, GRE required if undergraduate GPA below 3.0, goals statement, 2 letters of recommendation. Additional exam requirements/recommendations for international students: Required—TOEFL (minimum score 550 paper-based; 213 computer-based; 80 iBT). Application fee: $30 ($60 for international students). *Expenses:* Tuition, state resident: full-time $8136; part-time $452 per credit hour. Tuition, nonresident: full-time $14,292; part-time $794 per credit hour. *Financial support:* In 2011–12, 6 research assistantships (averaging $8,500 per year) were awarded; fellowships, teaching assistantships, Federal Work-Study, scholarships/grants, unspecified assistantships, and 1 administrative assistantship (averaging $8,500 per year) also available. *Unit head:* Mark Lyberger, Coordinator, 330-672-0228, E-mail: mlyberge@kent.edu. *Application contact:* Nancy Miller, Academic Program Coordinator, Office of Graduate Student Services, 330-672-2576, Fax: 330-672-9162, E-mail: ogs@kent.edu.

Lehman College of the City University of New York, Division of Natural and Social Sciences, Department of Health Sciences, Program in Recreation, Bronx, NY 10468-1589. Offers recreation education (MA, MS Ed). Part-time and evening/weekend programs available. *Degree requirements:* For master's, comprehensive exam, thesis or alternative. *Entrance requirements:* For master's, minimum GPA of 2.7. *Faculty research:* Therapeutic recreation philosophy, curriculum, current approaches to treatment, impact of societal trends, ethical issues.

Michigan State University, The Graduate School, College of Agriculture and Natural Resources, Department of Community, Agriculture, Recreation, and Resource Studies, East Lansing, MI 48824. Offers MS, PhD. *Entrance requirements:* Additional exam requirements/recommendations for international students: Required—TOEFL. Electronic applications accepted.

Middle Tennessee State University, College of Graduate Studies, College of Behavioral and Health Sciences, Department of Health and Human Performance, Program in Health, Physical Education and Recreation, Murfreesboro, TN 37132. Offers MS. Part-time and evening/weekend programs available. Postbaccalaureate distance learning degree programs offered. *Faculty:* 24 full-time (9 women), 5 part-time/adjunct (3 women). *Students:* 5 full-time (3 women), 68 part-time (29 women); includes 26 minority (24 Black or African American, non-Hispanic/Latino; 1 Hispanic/Latino; 1 Two or more races, non-Hispanic/Latino). 66 applicants, 83% accepted. In 2011, 31 master's awarded. *Degree requirements:* For master's, comprehensive exam, thesis optional. *Entrance requirements:* For master's, GRE. Additional exam requirements/recommendations for international students: Required—TOEFL (minimum score 525 paper-based; 195 computer-based; 71 iBT) or IELTS (minimum score 6). *Application deadline:* For fall admission, 6/1 for domestic and international students. Applications are processed on a rolling basis. Application fee: $25 ($30 for international students). *Expenses:* Tuition, state resident: full-time $10,008. Tuition, nonresident: full-time $25,056. *Financial support:* In 2011–12, 14 students received support. Tuition waivers available. Support available to part-time students. Financial award application deadline: 5/1. *Faculty research:* Kinesiometrics, leisure behavior, health, lifestyles. *Unit head:* Dr. Harold D. Whiteside, Interim Dean, 615-898-2900, Fax: 615-494-7704, E-mail: harold.whiteside@mtsu.edu. *Application contact:* Dr. Michael D. Allen, Dean and Vice Provost for Research, 615-898-2840, Fax: 615-904-8020, E-mail: michael.allen@mtsu.edu.

Naropa University, Graduate Programs, Program in Transpersonal Counseling Psychology, Concentration in Wilderness Therapy, Boulder, CO 80302-6697. Offers MA. *Faculty:* 9 full-time (6 women), 27 part-time/adjunct (16 women). *Students:* 30 full-time (20 women), 14 part-time (9 women); includes 3 minority (all Hispanic/Latino), 1 international. Average age 30. 54 applicants, 39% accepted, 16 enrolled. In 2011, 15 master's awarded. *Degree requirements:* For master's, internship, field work. *Entrance requirements:* For master's, in-person interview, outdoor experience, course work in psychology, resume, letter of interest, 3 letters of recommendation. Additional exam requirements/recommendations for international students: Required—TOEFL (minimum score 600 paper-based; 250 computer-based). *Application deadline:* For fall admission, 1/15 priority date for domestic students, 1/15 for international students. Applications are processed on a rolling basis. Application fee: $60. Electronic applications accepted. *Expenses: Tuition:* Full-time $20,400; part-time $850 per credit. *Required fees:* $660; $250 per semester. *Financial support:* In 2011–12, 5 students received support, including 3 research assistantships with partial tuition reimbursements available (averaging $2,500 per year); teaching assistantships with partial tuition reimbursements available, career-related internships or fieldwork, Federal Work-Study, scholarships/grants, health care benefits, tuition waivers (partial), and unspecified assistantships also available. Support available to part-time students. Financial award application deadline: 3/1; financial award applicants required to submit FAFSA. *Unit head:* Dr. MacAndrew Jack, Director, Graduate School of Psychology, 303-245-4752, E-mail: mjack@naropa.edu. *Application contact:* Krista Stuchlik, Senior Graduate Admissions Counselor, 303-546-3528, Fax: 303-546-3583, E-mail: kstuchlik@naropa.edu.

New England College, Program in Sports and Recreation Management: Coaching, Henniker, NH 03242-3293. Offers MS. *Entrance requirements:* For master's, resume, 2 letters of reference.

North Carolina Central University, Division of Academic Affairs, College of Behavioral and Social Sciences, Department of Physical Education and Recreation, Durham, NC 27707-3129. Offers athletic administration (MS); physical education (MS); recreation administration (MS); therapeutic recreation (MS). Part-time and evening/weekend programs available. *Degree requirements:* For master's, one foreign language, comprehensive exam, thesis. *Entrance requirements:* For master's, GRE, minimum GPA of 3.0 in major, 2.5 overall. Additional exam requirements/recommendations for international students: Required—TOEFL. *Faculty research:* Physical activity patterns of children with disabilities, physical fitness test of North Carolina school children, exercise physiology, motor learning/development.

North Carolina State University, Graduate School, College of Natural Resources, Department of Parks, Recreation and Tourism Management, Raleigh, NC 27695. Offers natural resource management (MPRTM, MS); park and recreation management (MPRTM, MS); parks, recreation and tourism management (PhD); recreational sport management (MPRTM, MS); spatial information science (MPRTM, MS); tourism policy and development (MPRTM, MS). *Degree requirements:* For master's, thesis (for some programs); for doctorate, thesis/dissertation. *Entrance requirements:* For master's and doctorate, GRE General Test. Additional exam requirements/recommendations for international students: Required—TOEFL. Electronic applications accepted. *Faculty research:* Tourism policy and development, spatial information systems, natural resource management, recreational sports management, park and recreation management.

Northwest Missouri State University, Graduate School, College of Education and Human Services, Department of Health, Physical Education, Recreation and Dance, Maryville, MO 64468-6001. Offers applied health science (MS); health and physical education (MS Ed); recreation (MS). *Accreditation:* NCATE. Part-time programs available. *Faculty:* 10 full-time (4 women). *Students:* 31 full-time (13 women), 10 part-time (4 women); includes 5 minority (2 Black or African American, non-Hispanic/Latino; 2 Hispanic/Latino; 1 Two or more races, non-Hispanic/Latino), 2 international. 25 applicants, 100% accepted, 17 enrolled. In 2011, 22 master's awarded. *Degree requirements:* For master's, comprehensive exam. *Entrance requirements:* For master's, GRE General Test, minimum undergraduate GPA of 2.75, teaching certificate, writing sample. Additional exam requirements/recommendations for international students: Required—TOEFL (minimum score 550 paper-based; 213 computer-based). *Application deadline:* For fall admission, 7/1 for domestic and international students; for spring admission, 11/15 for domestic and international students. Applications are processed on a rolling basis. Application fee: $0 ($50 for international students). *Financial support:* In 2011–12, 35 teaching assistantships with full tuition reimbursements (averaging $6,000 per year) were awarded; unspecified assistantships also available. Financial award application deadline: 4/1; financial award applicants required to submit FAFSA. *Unit head:* Dr. Terry Robertson, Chairperson, 660-562-1781. *Application contact:* Dr. Gregory Haddock, Dean of Graduate School, 660-562-1145, Fax: 660-562-1096, E-mail: gradsch@nwmissouri.edu.

Ohio University, Graduate College, Gladys W. and David H. Patton College of Education and Human Services, Department of Recreation and Sport Pedagogy, Program in Recreation Studies, Athens, OH 45701-2979. Offers MS. Part-time programs available. *Students:* 7 full-time (3 women), 1 part-time (0 women); includes 1 minority (Black or African American, non-Hispanic/Latino), 1 international. 9 applicants, 78% accepted, 5 enrolled. In 2011, 14 master's awarded. *Degree requirements:* For master's, thesis or alternative. *Entrance requirements:* For master's, GRE. Additional exam requirements/recommendations for international students: Required—TOEFL (minimum score 550 paper-based; 80 iBT) or IELTS (minimum score 6.5). *Application deadline:* For fall admission, 3/1 priority date for domestic students, 3/1 for international students; for winter admission, 11/1 priority date for domestic students, 11/1 for international students; for spring admission, 1/1 priority date for domestic students, 1/1 for international students. Application fee: $50 ($55 for international students). Electronic applications accepted. *Financial support:* In 2011–12, teaching assistantships with full tuition reimbursements (averaging $7,900 per year) were awarded; Federal Work-Study, scholarships/grants, tuition waivers (full), and unspecified assistantships also available. Financial award application deadline: 3/15. *Faculty research:* Recreation, leisure studies, physical education, national parks. *Total annual research expenditures:* $7,500. *Unit head:* Dr. Beth VanDerveer, Chair, 740-593-4656, Fax: 740-593-0284, E-mail: vanderve@ohio.edu. *Application contact:* Dr. Bruce Martin, Assistant Professor, 740-593-4647, E-mail: martinc2@ohio.edu. Web site: http://www.ohio.edu/graduate/programinfo/RecStudies-Info.cfm.

Old Dominion University, Darden College of Education, Program in Physical Education, Recreation and Tourism Studies Emphasis, Norfolk, VA 23529. Offers MS Ed. Part-time and evening/weekend programs available. Postbaccalaureate distance learning degree programs offered (minimal on-campus study). *Faculty:* 1 full-time (0 women). *Students:* 3 part-time (2 women); includes 2 minority (both Black or African American, non-Hispanic/Latino). Average age 28. 10 applicants, 60% accepted, 3 enrolled. In 2011, 9 master's awarded. *Degree requirements:* For master's, comprehensive exam, thesis or alternative, internship, research project. *Entrance requirements:* For master's, GRE, minimum GPA of 2.8 overall, 3.0 in major. Additional exam requirements/recommendations for international students: Required—TOEFL (minimum score 500 paper-based; 200 computer-based). *Application deadline:* For fall admission, 6/1 for domestic students. Application fee: $50. Electronic applications accepted. *Expenses:* Tuition, state resident: full-time $9096; part-time $379 per credit. Tuition, nonresident: full-time $23,064; part-time $961 per credit. *Required fees:* $127 per semester. One-time fee: $50. *Financial support:* In 2011–12, 1 student received support, including 1 research assistantship with partial tuition reimbursement available (averaging $9,000 per year); career-related internships or fieldwork, scholarships/grants, and unspecified assistantships also available. Financial award application deadline: 3/1; financial award applicants required to submit FAFSA. *Faculty research:* Ethnicity and recreation, recreation programming, recreation and resiliency, tourism development, dog parks, sense of community and urban parks. *Total annual research expenditures:* $12,000. *Unit head:* Dr. Edwin Gomez, Graduate Program Director, 757-683-4995, Fax: 757-683-4270, E-mail: egomez@odu.edu. *Application contact:* Nechell Bonds, Director of Admissions, 757-683-3685, Fax: 757-683-3255, E-mail: gradadmit@odu.edu.

Penn State University Park, Graduate School, College of Health and Human Development, Department of Recreation, Park and Tourism Management, State College, University Park, PA 16802-1503. Offers M Ed, MS, PhD. *Unit head:* Dr. Ann C. Crouter, Dean, 814-865-1428, Fax: 814-865-3282, E-mail: ac1@psu.edu. *Application contact:* Cynthia E. Nicosia, Director, Graduate Enrollment Services, 814-865-1795, Fax: 814-865-4627, E-mail: cey1@psu.edu. Web site: http://www.hhdev.psu.edu/rptm/.

San Francisco State University, Division of Graduate Studies, College of Health and Human Services, Department of Recreation and Leisure Studies, San Francisco, CA 94132-1722. Offers recreation (MS). Part-time programs available. *Application deadline:* Applications are processed on a rolling basis. *Financial support:* Career-related internships or fieldwork available. *Unit head:* Dr. Patrick Tierney, Chair, 415-338-2030, E-mail: ptierney@sfsu.edu. *Application contact:* Christina Alcantara, Office Manager, 415-338-3327, E-mail: cba@sfsu.edu. Web site: http://recdept.sfsu.edu/.

San Jose State University, Graduate Studies and Research, College of Applied Sciences and Arts, Department of Hospitality, Recreation and Tourism Management, San Jose, CA 95192-0001. Offers recreation (MS). Electronic applications accepted.

Slippery Rock University of Pennsylvania, Graduate Studies (Recruitment), College of Health, Environment, and Science, Department of Parks, Recreation, and Environmental Education, Slippery Rock, PA 16057-1383. Offers environmental education (M Ed); park and resource management (MS). Part-time and evening/weekend programs available. Postbaccalaureate distance learning degree programs offered (no on-campus study). *Faculty:* 3 full-time (1 woman), 3 part-time/adjunct (2 women). *Students:* 20 full-time (10 women), 75 part-time (38 women); includes 2 minority (1 Hispanic/Latino; 1 Two or more races, non-Hispanic/Latino), 1 international. Average age 30. 66 applicants, 77% accepted, 32 enrolled. In 2011, 49 degrees awarded. *Degree requirements:* For master's, comprehensive exam (for some programs), thesis (for some programs), internship. *Entrance requirements:* For master's, GRE General Test, MAT, minimum GPA of 2.75. Additional exam requirements/recommendations for international students: Required—TOEFL (minimum score 550 paper-based; 213 computer-based; 80 iBT). *Application deadline:* For fall admission, 3/1 priority date for domestic students, 5/1 for international students; for spring admission, 10/1 priority date for domestic students, 9/1 for international students. Applications are processed on a rolling basis. Application fee: $25 ($30 for international students). Electronic applications accepted. *Expenses:* Contact institution. *Financial support:* Career-related internships or fieldwork, Federal Work-Study, institutionally sponsored loans, scholarships/grants, tuition waivers (partial), and unspecified assistantships available. Support available to part-time students. Financial award application deadline: 5/1; financial award applicants required to submit FAFSA. *Unit head:* Dr. Daniel Dziubek, Graduate Coordinator, 724-738-2958, Fax: 724-738-2938, E-mail: daniel.dziubek@sru.edu. *Application contact:* Angela Barrett, Director of Graduate Admissions, 724-738-2051, Fax: 724-738-2146, E-mail: graduate.admissions@sru.edu.

South Dakota State University, Graduate School, College of Education and Human Sciences, Department of Health, Physical Education and Recreation, Brookings, SD 57007. Offers MS. Part-time programs available. *Degree requirements:* For master's, thesis, oral and written exams. *Entrance requirements:* Additional exam requirements/recommendations for international students: Required—TOEFL (minimum score 550 paper-based; 213 computer-based; 71 iBT). *Faculty research:* Effective teaching behaviors in physical education, sports nutrition, muscle/bone interaction, hormonal response to exercise.

Southern Adventist University, School of Business and Management, Collegedale, TN 37315-0370. Offers accounting (MBA); church administration (MSA); church and nonprofit leadership (MBA); financial management (MFM); healthcare administration (MBA); management (MBA); marketing management (MBA); outdoor education (MSA). Part-time and evening/weekend programs available. Postbaccalaureate distance learning degree programs offered (no on-campus study). *Entrance requirements:* For master's, GMAT. Additional exam requirements/recommendations for international students: Required—TOEFL (minimum score 600 paper-based; 250 computer-based; 100 iBT). Electronic applications accepted.

Southern Connecticut State University, School of Graduate Studies, School of Health and Human Services, Department of Recreation and Leisure Studies, New Haven, CT 06515-1355. Offers MS. Part-time and evening/weekend programs available. *Faculty:* 3 full-time (2 women), 3 part-time/adjunct (1 woman). *Students:* 14 full-time (10 women), 35 part-time (21 women); includes 8 minority (4 Black or African American, non-Hispanic/Latino; 3 Hispanic/Latino; 1 Two or more races, non-Hispanic/Latino). 32 applicants, 66% accepted, 21 enrolled. In 2011, 7 master's awarded. *Degree requirements:* For master's, thesis or alternative. *Entrance requirements:* For master's, interview, minimum undergraduate QPA of 3.0 in graduate major field or 2.5 overall. *Application deadline:* For fall admission, 7/15 priority date for domestic students. Applications are processed on a rolling basis. Application fee: $50. Electronic applications accepted. *Expenses:* Tuition, state resident: full-time $5137; part-time $413 per credit. *Required fees:* $4008; $55 per term. *Financial support:* In 2011–12, 1 teaching assistantship was awarded; career-related internships or fieldwork also available. Financial award application deadline: 4/15; financial award applicants required to submit FAFSA. *Unit head:* Dr. James MacGregor, Chairperson, 203-392-6385, Fax: 203-392-6965, E-mail: macgregorj1@southernct.edu. *Application contact:* Dr. Jan Louise Jones, Graduate Coordinator, 203-392-8837, Fax: 203-392-6147, E-mail: jonesj39@southernct.edu.

Southern Illinois University Carbondale, Graduate School, College of Education and Human Services, Department of Health Education and Recreation, Program in Recreation, Carbondale, IL 62901-4701. Offers MS Ed. Part-time programs available. *Faculty:* 5 full-time (2 women). *Students:* 18 full-time (7 women), 12 part-time (4 women); includes 4 minority (2 Black or African American, non-Hispanic/Latino; 1 Asian, non-Hispanic/Latino; 1 Hispanic/Latino), 2 international. Average age 26. 10 applicants, 80% accepted, 5 enrolled. In 2011, 15 master's awarded. *Degree requirements:* For master's, thesis. *Entrance requirements:* For master's, minimum GPA of 2.7. Additional exam requirements/recommendations for international students: Required—TOEFL. *Application deadline:* Applications are processed on a rolling basis. Application fee: $20. *Financial support:* In 2011–12, 15 students received support, including 4 research assistantships with full tuition reimbursements available, 4 teaching assistantships with full tuition reimbursements available; fellowships with full tuition reimbursements available, career-related internships or fieldwork, Federal Work-Study, institutionally sponsored loans, and tuition waivers (full) also available. Support available to part-time students. Financial award application deadline: 2/1. *Faculty research:* Leisure across the life span, outdoor recreation, recreation therapy, leisure service administration. *Unit head:* Dr. David Birch, Chair, 618-453-2777, Fax: 618-453-1829, E-mail: dabirch@siu.edu. *Application contact:* Carol Reynolds, Administrative Assistant, 618-453-2415, Fax: 618-453-1829, E-mail: creynolds@siu.edu. Web site: http://web.coehs.siu.edu/Public/her/grad/healthedgraduate.php.

Southern University and Agricultural and Mechanical College, Graduate School, College of Education, Program in Leisure and Recreation Studies, Baton Rouge, LA 70813. Offers therapeutic recreation (MS). *Degree requirements:* For master's, comprehensive exam, thesis optional. *Entrance requirements:* For master's, GMAT or GRE General Test. Additional exam requirements/recommendations for international students: Required—TOEFL (minimum score 525 paper-based; 193 computer-based).

Southwestern Oklahoma State University, College of Professional and Graduate Studies, School of Behavioral Sciences and Education, Specialization in Parks and Recreation Management, Weatherford, OK 73096-3098. Offers M Ed.

Springfield College, Graduate Programs, Programs in Sport Management and Recreation, Springfield, MA 01109-3797. Offers recreational management (M Ed, MS); sport management (M Ed, MS); therapeutic recreational management (M Ed, MS). Part-time programs available. *Degree requirements:* For master's, comprehensive exam, research project. *Entrance requirements:* Additional exam requirements/recommendations for international students: Required—TOEFL (minimum score 550 paper-based; 213 computer-based). Electronic applications accepted.

State University of New York College at Cortland, Graduate Studies, School of Professional Studies, Department of Recreation and Leisure Studies, Cortland, NY 13045. Offers MS, MS Ed. Part-time and evening/weekend programs available. *Degree requirements:* For master's, comprehensive exam, thesis (for some programs). *Entrance requirements:* Additional exam requirements/recommendations for international students: Required—TOEFL.

Temple University, Health Sciences Center, College of Health Professions and Social Work, Program in Therapeutic Recreation, Philadelphia, PA 19122-6096. Offers health ecology (PhD); recreation therapy (MS). Part-time and evening/weekend programs available. *Faculty:* 3 full-time (1 woman). *Students:* 7 full-time (all women), 4 part-time (all women); includes 2 minority (both Black or African American, non-Hispanic/Latino), 1 international. Average age 29. 13 applicants, 62% accepted, 5 enrolled. In 2011, 3 master's awarded. *Degree requirements:* For master's, comprehensive exam, thesis optional. *Entrance requirements:* For master's, GRE or MAT. Additional exam requirements/recommendations for international students: Required—TOEFL (minimum score 550 paper-based; 213 computer-based; 79 iBT). *Application deadline:* For fall admission, 6/1 for domestic students, 12/15 for international students; for spring admission, 10/15 for domestic students, 8/1 for international students. Applications are processed on a rolling basis. Application fee: $60. Electronic applications accepted. *Expenses:* Tuition, state resident: full-time $12,366; part-time $687 per credit hour. Tuition, nonresident: full-time $17,298; part-time $961 per credit hour. *Required fees:* $590; $213 per year. *Financial support:* Application deadline: 1/15; applicants required to submit FAFSA. *Faculty research:* Quality of life, curriculum issues, disability issues, adaptive equipment/technology. *Unit head:* John Shank, Graduate Chairperson, 215-204-6278, E-mail: jshank@temple.edu. *Application contact:* Tara Schumacher, Coordinator of Outreach, 215-204-6575, Fax: 215-204-8781, E-mail: tara.schumacher@temple.edu. Web site: http://chpsw.temple.edu/rs/therapeutic-recreation.

Temple University, School of Tourism and Hospitality Management, Program in Sport and Recreation Administration, Philadelphia, PA 19122-6096. Offers Ed M. Part-time and evening/weekend programs available. *Faculty:* 6 full-time (2 women). *Students:* 37 full-time (14 women), 11 part-time (3 women); includes 5 minority (3 Black or African American, non-Hispanic/Latino; 1 Asian, non-Hispanic/Latino; 1 Two or more races, non-Hispanic/Latino), 3 international. Average age 25. 63 applicants, 75% accepted, 24 enrolled. In 2011, 16 master's awarded. *Entrance requirements:* For master's, GRE General Test or MAT, minimum undergraduate GPA of 3.0. Additional exam requirements/recommendations for international students: Required—TOEFL (minimum score 550 paper-based; 213 computer-based; 79 iBT). *Application deadline:* For fall admission, 4/15 priority date for domestic students, 12/15 for international students; for spring admission, 9/30 priority date for domestic students, 8/1 for international students. Application fee: $50. Electronic applications accepted. *Expenses:* Tuition, state resident: full-time $12,366; part-time $687 per credit hour. Tuition, nonresident: full-time $17,298; part-time $961 per credit hour. *Required fees:* $590; $213 per year. *Financial support:* Teaching assistantships available. Financial award application deadline: 1/15; financial award applicants required to submit FAFSA. *Unit head:* Dr. Elizabeth H. Barber, Associate Dean, 215-204-6294, E-mail: elizabeth.barber@temple.edu. *Application contact:* Tara Schumacher, Coordinator of Outreach, 215-204-6575, Fax: 215-204-8781, E-mail: tara.schumacher@temple.edu. Web site: http://sthm.temple.edu/grad/explore-ma-sports.html.

Texas A&M University, College of Agriculture and Life Sciences, Department of Recreation, Park and Tourism Sciences, College Station, TX 77843. Offers natural resources development (M Agr); recreation resources development (M Agr); recreation, park, and tourism sciences (MS, PhD). *Faculty:* 17. *Students:* 58 full-time (32 women), 19 part-time (11 women); includes 10 minority (5 Black or African American, non-Hispanic/Latino; 1 Asian, non-Hispanic/Latino; 3 Hispanic/Latino; 1 Two or more races, non-Hispanic/Latino), 30 international. Average age 28. In 2011, 12 master's, 6 doctorates awarded. *Degree requirements:* For master's, thesis (for some programs), internship and professional paper (M Agr); for doctorate, thesis/dissertation. *Entrance requirements:* For master's and doctorate, GRE General Test. Additional exam requirements/recommendations for international students: Required—TOEFL. *Application deadline:* For fall admission, 4/15 priority date for domestic students; for spring admission, 10/15 priority date for domestic students. Applications are processed on a rolling basis. Application fee: $50 ($75 for international students). Electronic applications accepted. *Expenses:* Tuition, state resident: full-time $5437; part-time $226.55 per credit hour. Tuition, nonresident: full-time $12,949; part-time $539.55 per credit hour. *Required fees:* $2741. *Financial support:* Fellowships, research assistantships, teaching assistantships, career-related internships or fieldwork, institutionally sponsored loans, and scholarships/grants available. Financial award application deadline: 4/15; financial award applicants required to submit FAFSA. *Faculty research:* Administration and tourism, outdoor recreation, commercial recreation, environmental law, system planning. *Unit head:* Dr. Gary Ellis, Head, 979-845-7324. *Application contact:* Graduate Admissions, 979-845-1044, E-mail: admissions@tamu.edu. Web site: http://rpts.tamu.edu/.

Texas State University–San Marcos, Graduate School, College of Education, Department of Health and Human Performance, Program in Recreation and Leisure Services, San Marcos, TX 78666. Offers MSRLS. *Faculty:* 4 full-time (3 women), 1 (woman) part-time/adjunct. *Students:* 34 full-time (23 women), 25 part-time (11 women); includes 24 minority (3 Black or African American, non-Hispanic/Latino; 1 Asian, non-Hispanic/Latino; 18 Hispanic/Latino; 2 Two or more races, non-Hispanic/Latino). Average age 28. 57 applicants, 81% accepted, 23 enrolled. In 2011, 26 master's awarded. *Degree requirements:* For master's, comprehensive exam, thesis optional.

Entrance requirements: For master's, GRE General Test, minimum GPA of 2.75 in last 60 hours of course work. Additional exam requirements/recommendations for international students: Required—TOEFL (minimum score 550 paper-based; 213 computer-based; 78 iBT). *Application deadline:* For fall admission, 6/15 priority date for domestic students, 6/1 for international students; for spring admission, 10/15 priority date for domestic students, 10/1 for international students. Applications are processed on a rolling basis. Application fee: $40 ($90 for international students). Electronic applications accepted. *Expenses:* Tuition, state resident: full-time $6408; part-time $3204 per semester. Tuition, nonresident: full-time $14,832; part-time $7416 per semester. *Required fees:* $1824; $912 per semester. Tuition and fees vary according to course load. *Financial support:* In 2011–12, 19 students received support, including 6 research assistantships (averaging $10,089 per year), 5 teaching assistantships (averaging $10,692 per year). Financial award application deadline: 4/1; financial award applicants required to submit FAFSA. *Unit head:* Dr. Janet Hodges, Graduate Advisor, 512-245-2561, Fax: 512-245-8678, E-mail: jh223@txstate.edu. *Application contact:* Amy Galle, Head, 512-245-2561, Fax: 512-245-8678, E-mail: ag04@txstate.edu. Web site: http://www.hhp.txstate.edu/Degree-Plans/Graduate.html.

Texas State University–San Marcos, Graduate School, Interdisciplinary Studies Program in Health, Physical Education, and Recreation, San Marcos, TX 78666. Offers MAIS. Part-time and evening/weekend programs available. *Students:* 2 applicants, 50% accepted. *Degree requirements:* For master's, comprehensive exam, thesis optional. *Entrance requirements:* For master's, GRE General Test, minimum GPA of 2.75 in last 60 hours of course work. Additional exam requirements/recommendations for international students: Required—TOEFL (minimum score 550 paper-based; 213 computer-based; 78 iBT). *Application deadline:* For fall admission, 6/15 priority date for domestic students, 6/1 for international students; for spring admission, 10/15 priority date for domestic students, 10/1 for international students. Applications are processed on a rolling basis. Application fee: $40 ($90 for international students). *Expenses:* Tuition, state resident: full-time $6408; part-time $3204 per semester. Tuition, nonresident: full-time $14,832; part-time $7416 per semester. *Required fees:* $1824; $912 per semester. Tuition and fees vary according to course load. *Financial support:* Teaching assistantships, career-related internships or fieldwork, Federal Work-Study, institutionally sponsored loans, scholarships/grants, health care benefits, and unspecified assistantships available. Support available to part-time students. Financial award application deadline: 4/1; financial award applicants required to submit FAFSA. *Unit head:* Dr. Karen Meaney, Graduate Advisor, 512-245-2952, Fax: 512-245-8678, E-mail: km66@txstate.edu. *Application contact:* Dr. J. Michael Willoughby, Dean of Graduate School, 512-245-2581, Fax: 512-245-8365, E-mail: gradcollege@txstate.edu. Web site: http://www.hhp.txstate.edu/.

Universidad Metropolitana, School of Education, Program in Managing Recreation and Sports Services, San Juan, PR 00928-1150. Offers M Ed. Part-time programs available. *Degree requirements:* For master's, thesis or alternative. *Entrance requirements:* For master's, EXADEP, interview. Electronic applications accepted.

University of Alberta, Faculty of Graduate Studies and Research, Department of Physical Education and Recreation, Edmonton, AB T6G 2E1, Canada. Offers physical education (M Sc); recreation and physical education (MA, PhD). Part-time programs available. Terminal master's awarded for partial completion of doctoral program. *Degree requirements:* For master's, thesis (for some programs); for doctorate, thesis/dissertation. *Entrance requirements:* For master's, bachelor's degree in related field; for doctorate, master's degree in related field with thesis. Additional exam requirements/recommendations for international students: Required—TOEFL. *Faculty research:* Motivation and adherence to physical ability, performance enhancement, adapted physical activity, exercise physiology, sport administration, tourism.

University of Arkansas, Graduate School, College of Education and Health Professions, Department of Health Science, Kinesiology, Recreation and Dance, Program in Recreation, Fayetteville, AR 72701-1201. Offers M Ed, Ed D. *Students:* 26 full-time (9 women), 37 part-time (7 women); includes 16 minority (10 Black or African American, non-Hispanic/Latino; 1 American Indian or Alaska Native, non-Hispanic/Latino; 1 Asian, non-Hispanic/Latino; 2 Hispanic/Latino; 2 Two or more races, non-Hispanic/Latino), 2 international. In 2011, 15 master's, 2 doctorates awarded. *Degree requirements:* For master's, thesis optional; for doctorate, thesis/dissertation. *Entrance requirements:* For doctorate, GRE General Test. *Application deadline:* For fall admission, 4/1 for international students; for spring admission, 10/1 for international students. Applications are processed on a rolling basis. Application fee: $40 ($50 for international students). Electronic applications accepted. *Financial support:* In 2011–12, 8 research assistantships, 10 teaching assistantships were awarded; fellowships with tuition reimbursements, career-related internships or fieldwork, and Federal Work-Study also available. Support available to part-time students. Financial award application deadline: 4/1; financial award applicants required to submit FAFSA. *Unit head:* Dr. Bart Hammig, Department Chairperson, 479-575-2857, Fax: 479-575-5728, E-mail: bhammig@uark.edu. *Application contact:* Dr. Dean Gorman, Coordinator of Graduate Studies, 479-575-2890, E-mail: dgorman@uark.edu. Web site: http://recr.uark.edu/.

University of Florida, Graduate School, College of Health and Human Performance, Department of Tourism, Recreation and Sport Management, Gainesville, FL 32611. Offers health and human performance (PhD), including natural resource recreation (MS, PhD), sport management (MS, PhD), tourism; recreational studies (MS), including campus recreation programming and administration, natural resource recreation (MS, PhD), recreation administration and supervision, sport management (MS, PhD), tourism and commercial recreation. *Degree requirements:* For master's, comprehensive exam (for some programs), thesis (for some programs); for doctorate, comprehensive exam, thesis/dissertation. *Entrance requirements:* For master's and doctorate, GRE General Test, minimum GPA of 3.0. Additional exam requirements/recommendations for international students: Required—TOEFL (minimum score 550 paper-based; 213 computer-based; 80 iBT), IELTS (minimum score 6). Electronic applications accepted. *Faculty research:* Hospitality, natural resource management, sport management, sport management, tourism.

University of Idaho, College of Graduate Studies, College of Education, Department of Movement Sciences, Program in Movement and Leisure Sciences, Moscow, ID 83844-2401. Offers MS. *Students:* 16 full-time, 5 part-time. Average age 28. In 2011, 7 master's awarded. *Entrance requirements:* For master's, minimum GPA of 2.8. *Application deadline:* For fall admission, 8/1 for domestic students; for spring admission, 12/15 for domestic students. Applications are processed on a rolling basis. Application fee: $60. Electronic applications accepted. *Expenses:* Tuition, state resident: full-time $3874; part-time $334 per credit hour. Tuition, nonresident: full-time $16,394; part-time $861 per credit hour. *Required fees:* $2808; $99 per credit hour. Tuition and fees vary according to program. *Financial support:* Research assistantships available. Financial award applicants required to submit FAFSA. *Unit head:* Dr. Kathy Browder, Chair, 208-885-2192, E-mail: hperd@uidaho.edu. *Application contact:* Erick Larson, Director of Graduate Admissions, 208-885-4723, E-mail: gadms@uidaho.edu. Web site: http://www.uidaho.edu/ed/movementsciences/recreation-ms.

The University of Iowa, Graduate College, College of Liberal Arts and Sciences, Program in Leisure Studies, Iowa City, IA 52242-1316. Offers leisure and recreational sport management (MA); therapeutic recreation (MA). *Degree requirements:* For master's, thesis optional, exam. *Entrance requirements:* For master's, minimum GPA of 3.0. Additional exam requirements/recommendations for international students: Required—TOEFL (minimum score 550 paper-based; 213 computer-based; 81 iBT). Electronic applications accepted.

University of Manitoba, Faculty of Graduate Studies, Faculty of Kinesiology and Recreation Management, Winnipeg, MB R3T 2N2, Canada. Offers kinesiology and recreation (M Sc, MA).

University of Minnesota, Twin Cities Campus, Graduate School, College of Education and Human Development, School of Kinesiology, Division of Recreation, Park, and Leisure Studies, Minneapolis, MN 55455-0213. Offers M Ed, MA, PhD. Part-time programs available. *Students:* 1 (woman) full-time, 1 part-time (0 women). Average age 52. In 2011, 5 master's, 1 doctorate awarded. Terminal master's awarded for partial completion of doctoral program. *Degree requirements:* For master's, thesis (for some programs), final oral exam; for doctorate, thesis/dissertation, preliminary written/oral exam, final oral exam. *Entrance requirements:* For master's, GRE or MAT, minimum GPA of 3.0; for doctorate, GRE or MAT, minimum GPA of 3.0, writing sample. *Application deadline:* For fall admission, 7/15 for domestic students; for spring admission, 12/15 for domestic students. Applications are processed on a rolling basis. Application fee: $55. *Financial support:* Fellowships, research assistantships, teaching assistantships, career-related internships or fieldwork, Federal Work-Study, institutionally sponsored loans, and tuition waivers (full and partial) available. Support available to part-time students. *Unit head:* Dr. Li Li Ji, Director, 612-642-9809, Fax: 612-626-7700, E-mail: llji@umn.edu. *Application contact:* Dr. Jennifer Engler, Assistant Dean, 612-626-2887, Fax: 612-626-7496, E-mail: engle009@umn.edu. Web site: http://www.cehd.umn.edu/kin/recreation.

University of Mississippi, Graduate School, School of Applied Sciences, Department of Health, Exercise Science, and Recreation Management, Oxford, University, MS 38677. Offers exercise science (MS); exercise science and leisure management (PhD); park and recreation management (MA); wellness (MS). *Students:* 50 full-time (32 women), 13 part-time (7 women); includes 6 minority (all Black or African American, non-Hispanic/Latino), 9 international. In 2011, 9 master's, 1 doctorate awarded. *Degree requirements:* For master's, thesis (for some programs); for doctorate, thesis/dissertation. *Entrance requirements:* For master's, GRE General Test, minimum GPA of 3.0; for doctorate, GRE General Test. Additional exam requirements/recommendations for international students: Required—TOEFL. *Application deadline:* For fall admission, 4/1 for domestic students; for spring admission, 10/1 for domestic students. Applications are processed on a rolling basis. Application fee: $25. *Financial support:* Scholarships/grants available. Financial award application deadline: 3/1; financial award applicants required to submit FAFSA. *Unit head:* Dr. Mark Loftin, Interim Chair, 662-915-5844, Fax: 662-915-5525, E-mail: mloftin@olemiss.edu. *Application contact:* Dr. Christy M. Wyandt, Associate Dean, 662-915-7474, Fax: 662-915-7577, E-mail: cwyandt@olemiss.edu.

University of Missouri, Graduate School, School of Natural Resources, Department of Parks, Recreation and Tourism, Columbia, MO 65211. Offers MS. *Faculty:* 6 full-time (3 women), 1 part-time/adjunct (0 women). *Students:* 11 full-time (7 women), 1 part-time (0 women); includes 1 minority (Hispanic/Latino), 7 international. Average age 26. 5 applicants, 60% accepted, 3 enrolled. In 2011, 3 degrees awarded. *Entrance requirements:* For master's, GRE General Test, minimum GPA of 3.0. Additional exam requirements/recommendations for international students: Required—TOEFL (minimum score 500 paper-based; 173 computer-based; 61 iBT). *Application deadline:* Applications are processed on a rolling basis. Application fee: $55 ($75 for international students). *Expenses:* Tuition, state resident: full-time $5881. Tuition, nonresident: full-time $15,183. *Required fees:* $952. Tuition and fees vary according to campus/location and program. *Financial support:* Research assistantships, teaching assistantships, institutionally sponsored loans, and scholarships/grants available. *Faculty research:* Rural and cultural tourism, agriculture entrepreneurship, marketing research in commercial recreation, therapeutic recreation, social aspects of natural resource management, education and outreach, human dimensions of natural resource management with an emphasis in the social psychological aspects of outdoor recreation. *Unit head:* Dr. David Vaught, Department Chair, E-mail: vaughtd@missouri.edu. *Application contact:* Dr. Mark Morgan, Director of Graduate Studies, 573-882-9525, E-mail: morganm@missouri.edu. Web site: http://www.snr.missouri.edu/prt/academics/graduate-program.php.

The University of Montana, Graduate School, College of Forestry and Conservation, Missoula, MT 59812-0002. Offers ecosystem management (MEM, MS); fish and wildlife biology (PhD); forestry (MS, PhD); recreation management (MS); resource conservation (MS); wildlife biology (MS). *Degree requirements:* For doctorate, thesis/dissertation. *Entrance requirements:* For master's and doctorate, GRE General Test. Additional exam requirements/recommendations for international students: Required—TOEFL (minimum score 575 paper-based; 213 computer-based).

University of Nebraska at Omaha, Graduate Studies, College of Education, School of Health, Physical Education, and Recreation, Omaha, NE 68182. Offers athletic training (MA); health, physical education, and recreation (MA, MS). Part-time and evening/weekend programs available. *Faculty:* 13 full-time (4 women). *Students:* 37 full-time (15 women), 40 part-time (25 women); includes 4 minority (1 Black or African American, non-Hispanic/Latino; 2 Hispanic/Latino; 1 Two or more races, non-Hispanic/Latino), 2 international. Average age 27. 27 applicants, 67% accepted, 15 enrolled. In 2011, 33 master's awarded. *Degree requirements:* For master's, comprehensive exam, thesis (for some programs). *Entrance requirements:* For master's, minimum GPA of 3.0, statement of purpose, letters of recommendation. Additional exam requirements/recommendations for international students: Required—TOEFL (minimum score 550 paper-based; 213 computer-based; 80 iBT). *Application deadline:* For fall admission, 7/1 priority date for domestic students; for spring admission, 12/1 priority date for domestic students. Applications are processed on a rolling basis. Application fee: $45. Electronic applications accepted. *Financial support:* In 2011–12, 40 students received support, including 25 research assistantships with tuition reimbursements available, 10 teaching assistantships with tuition reimbursements available; fellowships, Federal Work-Study, institutionally sponsored loans, scholarships/grants, tuition waivers (full), and unspecified assistantships also available. Support available to part-time students. Financial award application deadline: 3/1; financial award applicants required to submit FAFSA. *Unit head:* Dr. Dan Blanke, Director, 402-554-2670. *Application contact:* Dr. Kris Berg, 402-554-2341, Fax: 402-554-3143, E-mail: graduate@unomaha.edu.

University of New Brunswick Fredericton, School of Graduate Studies, Faculty of Kinesiology, Fredericton, NB E3B 5A3, Canada. Offers exercise and sport science (M Sc); sport and recreation management (MBA); sport and recreation studies (MA). Part-time programs available. *Faculty:* 15 full-time (7 women). *Students:* 39 full-time (15 women), 6 part-time (4 women). In 2011, 7 master's awarded. *Degree requirements:* For master's, thesis (for some programs). *Entrance requirements:* For master's, minimum GPA of 3.0, written statement of research goals and interests. Additional exam requirements/recommendations for international students: Required—TOEFL (minimum score 600 paper-based; 250 computer-based), TWE (minimum score 4). *Application deadline:* For winter admission, 1/31 for domestic students; for spring admission, 3/31 for domestic students. Applications are processed on a rolling basis. Application fee: $50 Canadian dollars. Electronic applications accepted. *Financial support:* In 2011–12,

38 fellowships with tuition reimbursements, 3 research assistantships, 56 teaching assistantships were awarded; career-related internships or fieldwork and scholarships/grants also available. *Unit head:* Dr. Tim McGarry, Acting Director of Graduate Studies, 506-458-7109, Fax: 506-453-3511, E-mail: tmcgarry@unb.ca. *Application contact:* Leslie Harquail, Graduate Secretary, 506-453-4575, Fax: 506-453-3511, E-mail: harquail@unb.ca. Web site: http://www.unbf.ca/kinesiology/.

University of New Hampshire, Graduate School, School of Health and Human Services, Department of Recreation Management and Policy, Durham, NH 03824. Offers recreation administration (MS); therapeutic recreation (MS). Part-time programs available. *Faculty:* 4 full-time (3 women). *Students:* 9 full-time (3 women), 7 part-time (3 women). Average age 27. 14 applicants, 79% accepted, 8 enrolled. In 2011, 5 master's awarded. *Degree requirements:* For master's, thesis optional. *Entrance requirements:* For master's, GRE. Additional exam requirements/recommendations for international students: Required—TOEFL (minimum score 550 paper-based; 213 computer-based; 80 iBT); Recommended—TWE. *Application deadline:* For fall admission, 6/1 priority date for domestic students, 4/1 for international students; for spring admission, 12/1 for domestic students. Application fee: $65. Electronic applications accepted. *Expenses:* Tuition, state resident: full-time $12,360; part-time $687 per credit hour. Tuition, nonresident: full-time $25,680; part-time $1058 per credit hour. *International tuition:* $29,550 full-time. *Required fees:* $1666; $833 per course. $416.50 per semester. Tuition and fees vary according to course load and degree level. *Financial support:* In 2011–12, 10 students received support, including 8 teaching assistantships; fellowships and research assistantships also available. *Unit head:* Dr. Janet Sable, Chairperson, 603-862-3401. *Application contact:* Linda Noon, Administrative Assistant, 603-862-2391, E-mail: rmp.graduate@unh.edu. Web site: http://chhs.unh.edu/rmp/index.

The University of North Carolina at Greensboro, Graduate School, School of Health and Human Performance, Department of Recreation, Tourism, and Hospitality Management, Greensboro, NC 27412-5001. Offers parks and recreation management (MS). *Degree requirements:* For master's, thesis. *Entrance requirements:* For master's, GRE General Test. Additional exam requirements/recommendations for international students: Required—TOEFL. Electronic applications accepted.

University of North Texas, Toulouse Graduate School, College of Education, Department of Kinesiology, Health Promotion, and Recreation, Program in Recreation and Leisure Studies, Denton, TX 76203. Offers recreation and leisure studies (MS); recreation management (Certificate). Part-time programs available. *Degree requirements:* For master's, thesis or alternative, culminating project or field placement. *Entrance requirements:* For master's, GRE General Test or MAT, resume, 2 letters of reference, 300-word statement. Additional exam requirements/recommendations for international students: Recommended—TOEFL (minimum score 550 paper-based; 213 computer-based). Electronic applications accepted. *Expenses:* Tuition, state resident: part-time $100 per credit hour. Tuition, nonresident: part-time $413 per credit hour. *Faculty research:* Physically active leisure, trail use, community recreation programming, inclusion of persons with disabilities, therapeutic recreation.

University of Rhode Island, Graduate School, College of Human Science and Services, Department of Kinesiology, Kingston, RI 02881. Offers cultural studies of sport and physical culture (MS); exercise science (MS); physical education pedagogy (MS); psychosocial/behavioral aspects of physical activity (MS). *Accreditation:* NCATE. Part-time programs available. *Faculty:* 13 full-time (7 women). *Students:* 11 full-time (7 women), 7 part-time (2 women); includes 1 minority (Hispanic/Latino). In 2011, 10 master's awarded. *Degree requirements:* For master's, thesis optional. *Entrance requirements:* For master's, GRE, 2 letters of recommendation. Additional exam requirements/recommendations for international students: Required—TOEFL (minimum score 550 paper-based; 213 computer-based). *Application deadline:* For fall admission, 4/15 for domestic students, 2/1 for international students; for spring admission, 11/15 for domestic students, 7/15 for international students. Application fee: $65. Electronic applications accepted. *Expenses:* Tuition, state resident: full-time $10,432; part-time $580 per credit hour. Tuition, nonresident: full-time $23,130; part-time $1285 per credit hour. *Required fees:* $1362; $36 per credit hour. $35 per semester. One-time fee: $130. *Financial support:* In 2011–12, 5 teaching assistantships with full and partial tuition reimbursements (averaging $8,250 per year) were awarded. Financial award application deadline: 4/15; financial award applicants required to submit FAFSA. *Faculty research:* Strength training and older adults, interventions to promote a healthy lifestyle as well as analysis of the psychosocial outcomes of those interventions, effects of exercise and nutrition on skeletal muscle of aging healthy adults with CVD and other metabolic related diseases, physical activity and fitness of deaf children and youth. *Unit head:* Dr. Deborah Riebe, Chair, 401-874-5444, Fax: 401-874-4215, E-mail: debriebe@uri.edu. *Application contact:* Dr. Lori Ciccomascolo, Director of Graduate Studies, 401-874-5454, Fax: 401-874-4215, E-mail: lecicco@uri.edu. Web site: http://www.uri.edu/hss/physical_education/.

University of South Alabama, Graduate School, College of Education, Department of Health, Physical Education and Leisure Services, Mobile, AL 36688-0002. Offers exercise science (MS); health education (M Ed); physical education (M Ed); therapeutic recreation (MS). *Accreditation:* NCATE (one or more programs are accredited). Part-time programs available. *Faculty:* 10 full-time (2 women). *Students:* 27 full-time (15 women), 4 part-time (all women); includes 5 minority (4 Black or African American, non-Hispanic/Latino; 1 Asian, non-Hispanic/Latino), 4 international. 29 applicants, 52% accepted, 12 enrolled. In 2011, 17 master's awarded. *Degree requirements:* For master's, comprehensive exam. *Entrance requirements:* For master's, GRE General Test or MAT. *Application deadline:* For fall admission, 7/15 priority date for domestic students, 6/15 for international students; for spring admission, 12/1 priority date for domestic students, 11/1 for international students. Applications are processed on a rolling basis. Application fee: $35. *Expenses:* Tuition, state resident: full-time $7968; part-time $332 per credit hour. Tuition, nonresident: full-time $15,936; part-time $664 per credit hour. *Financial support:* In 2011–12, 10 teaching assistantships were awarded; career-related internships or fieldwork also available. Support available to part-time students. Financial award application deadline: 4/1. *Unit head:* Dr. Frederick M. Scaffidi, Chair, 251-460-7131. *Application contact:* Dr. Abigail Baxter, Director of Graduate Studies, 231-460-7131.

University of Southern Mississippi, Graduate School, College of Health, School of Human Performance and Recreation, Hattiesburg, MS 39406-0001. Offers human performance (MS, PhD), including exercise physiology (PhD), human performance (MS), physical education (MS); interscholastic athletic administration (MS); recreation and leisure management (MS); sport administration (MS); sport and coaching education (MS); sport management (MS). Part-time and evening/weekend programs available. *Faculty:* 13 full-time (5 women). *Students:* 59 full-time (20 women), 38 part-time (12 women); includes 16 minority (12 Black or African American, non-Hispanic/Latino; 1 Asian, non-Hispanic/Latino; 2 Hispanic/Latino; 1 Two or more races, non-Hispanic/Latino), 9 international. Average age 29. 49 applicants, 73% accepted, 33 enrolled. In 2011, 44 master's, 1 doctorate awarded. *Degree requirements:* For master's, comprehensive exam, thesis optional; for doctorate, comprehensive exam, thesis/dissertation. *Entrance requirements:* For master's, GRE General Test, minimum GPA of 2.75 in last 60 hours; for doctorate, GRE General Test, minimum GPA of 3.5. Additional exam requirements/recommendations for international students: Required—TOEFL, IELTS. *Application deadline:* For fall admission, 3/1 priority date for domestic students, 3/1 for international students; for spring admission, 1/10 priority date for domestic students, 1/10 for international students. Applications are processed on a rolling basis. Application fee: $50. Electronic applications accepted. *Financial support:* In 2011–12, 1 fellowship (averaging $16,000 per year), 6 research assistantships with full tuition reimbursements (averaging $7,492 per year), 5 teaching assistantships with full tuition reimbursements (averaging $7,330 per year) were awarded; career-related internships or fieldwork, Federal Work-Study, institutionally sponsored loans, scholarships/grants, health care benefits, and unspecified assistantships also available. Financial award application deadline: 3/15; financial award applicants required to submit FAFSA. *Faculty research:* Exercise physiology, health behaviors, resource management, activity interaction, site development. *Unit head:* Dr. Frederick Green, Director, 601-266-5379, Fax: 601-266-4445. *Application contact:* Dr. Trenton Gould, Graduate Coordinator, 601-266-5379, Fax: 601-266-4445. Web site: http://www.usm.edu/graduateschool/table.php.

The University of Tennessee, Graduate School, College of Education, Health and Human Sciences, Department of Exercise, Sport, and Leisure Studies, Knoxville, TN 37996. Offers exercise science (MS, PhD), including biomechanics/sports medicine, exercise physiology; recreation and leisure studies (MS); sport management (MS); sport studies (MS, PhD); therapeutic recreation (MS). Part-time and evening/weekend programs available. *Degree requirements:* For master's, thesis optional. *Entrance requirements:* For master's, minimum GPA of 2.7. Additional exam requirements/recommendations for international students: Required—TOEFL. Electronic applications accepted. *Expenses:* Tuition, state resident: full-time $8332; part-time $464 per credit hour. Tuition, nonresident: full-time $25,174; part-time $1400 per credit hour. *Required fees:* $1162; $56 per credit hour. Tuition and fees vary according to program.

The University of Toledo, College of Graduate Studies, Judith Herb College of Education, Health Science and Human Service, Department of Health and Recreation, Toledo, OH 43606-3390. Offers health education (ME, PhD); health promotions and education (MPH); recreation and leisure studies (MA). Part-time programs available. *Students:* 20 full-time (16 women), 30 part-time (21 women); includes 5 minority (4 Black or African American, non-Hispanic/Latino; 1 Asian, non-Hispanic/Latino), 2 international. Average age 34. 26 applicants, 65% accepted, 12 enrolled. In 2011, 11 master's, 5 doctorates awarded. *Degree requirements:* For master's, comprehensive exam, thesis; for doctorate, thesis/dissertation. *Entrance requirements:* For master's and doctorate, minimum cumulative GPA of 2.7 for all previous academic work, letters of recommendation. Additional exam requirements/recommendations for international students: Required—TOEFL (minimum score 550 paper-based; 213 computer-based; 80 iBT), IELTS (minimum score 6.5). *Application deadline:* For fall admission, 1/15 priority date for domestic students, 1/15 for international students. Applications are processed on a rolling basis. Application fee: $45 ($75 for international students). Electronic applications accepted. *Financial support:* In 2011–12, 11 teaching assistantships with full and partial tuition reimbursements (averaging $9,682 per year) were awarded; career-related internships or fieldwork, Federal Work-Study, institutionally sponsored loans, scholarships/grants, tuition waivers (full and partial), and unspecified assistantships also available. Support available to part-time students. *Unit head:* Joseph Dake, Chair, 419-530-2767, E-mail: joseph.dake@utoledo.edu. *Application contact:* Graduate School Office, 419-530-4723, Fax: 419-530-4724, E-mail: grdsch@utnet.utoledo.edu. Web site: http://www.utoledo.edu/eduhshs/.

University of Utah, Graduate School, College of Health, Department of Parks, Recreation, and Tourism, Salt Lake City, UT 84112. Offers M Phil, MS, Ed D, PhD. *Faculty:* 10 full-time (4 women), 1 part-time/adjunct (0 women). *Students:* 32 full-time (19 women), 17 part-time (9 women); includes 1 minority (Hispanic/Latino), 6 international. Average age 32. 29 applicants, 45% accepted, 12 enrolled. In 2011, 8 master's, 5 doctorates awarded. Terminal master's awarded for partial completion of doctoral program. *Median time to degree:* Of those who began their doctoral program in fall 2003, 100% received their degree in 8 years or less. *Degree requirements:* For master's, comprehensive exam, thesis or alternative; for doctorate, comprehensive exam, thesis/dissertation. *Entrance requirements:* For master's, minimum GPA of 3.0; for doctorate, GRE General Test, minimum GPA of 3.2. Additional exam requirements/recommendations for international students: Required—TOEFL (minimum score 500 paper-based; 173 computer-based). *Application deadline:* For fall admission, 3/1 for domestic students, 2/15 for international students; for spring admission, 10/1 for domestic students. Application fee: $55 ($65 for international students). Electronic applications accepted. *Financial support:* In 2011–12, 3 research assistantships with full tuition reimbursements, 7 teaching assistantships with full tuition reimbursements were awarded; career-related internships or fieldwork, scholarships/grants, health care benefits, and unspecified assistantships also available. Financial award application deadline: 2/15; financial award applicants required to submit FAFSA. *Faculty research:* Therapeutic, community, and outdoor recreation; tourism, youth development. *Total annual research expenditures:* $39,469. *Unit head:* Dr. Daniel L. Dustin, Chair, 801-581-7560, E-mail: daniel.dustin@health.utah.edu. *Application contact:* Dr. Jim Sibthorp, Director of Graduate Studies, 801-581-5940, Fax: 801-581-4930, E-mail: kim.sibthorp@health.utah.edu. Web site: http://www.health.utah.edu/prt/.

University of Waterloo, Graduate Studies, Faculty of Applied Health Sciences, Department of Recreation and Leisure Studies, Waterloo, ON N2L 3G1, Canada. Offers MA, PhD. Part-time programs available. *Degree requirements:* For master's, thesis; for doctorate, comprehensive exam, thesis/dissertation. *Entrance requirements:* For master's, honors degree, minimum B average, writing sample, resume; for doctorate, GRE (recommended), master's degree, minimum B average, writing sample, resumé. Additional exam requirements/recommendations for international students: Required—TOEFL, TWE. Electronic applications accepted. *Faculty research:* Tourism, leisure behavior, special populations, leisure service management, outdoor resources, aging, health and well-being, work and health.

University of Wisconsin–La Crosse, Office of University Graduate Studies, College of Science and Health, Department of Recreation Management and Therapeutic Recreation, La Crosse, WI 54601-3742. Offers recreation management (MS); therapeutic recreation (MS). Part-time programs available. *Faculty:* 5 full-time (3 women), 2 part-time/adjunct (0 women). *Students:* 28 full-time (20 women), 8 part-time (7 women); includes 1 minority (Black or African American, non-Hispanic/Latino), 5 international. Average age 28. 49 applicants, 82% accepted, 22 enrolled. In 2011, 12 master's awarded. *Degree requirements:* For master's, thesis or alternative, project or internship. *Entrance requirements:* Additional exam requirements/recommendations for international students: Required—TOEFL (minimum score 550 paper-based; 213 computer-based; 79 iBT). *Application deadline:* For fall admission, 3/15 priority date for domestic students. Applications are processed on a rolling basis. Application fee: $56. Electronic applications accepted. *Expenses:* Tuition, state resident: full-time $8391; part-time $481.17 per credit. Tuition, nonresident: full-time $17,850; part-time $1006.68 per credit. *Required fees:* $2 per credit. $18.25 per semester. Tuition and fees vary according to course load, program, reciprocity agreements and student level. *Financial support:* In 2011–12, 8 research assistantships with partial tuition reimbursements (averaging $7,137 per year) were awarded; Federal Work-Study, scholarships/grants, health care benefits, and tuition waivers (partial) also available. Support available to part-time students. Financial award application deadline: 3/15; financial award applicants required to submit FAFSA. *Unit head:* Dr. Jearold Holland, Program Director, 608-785-8214, Fax: 608-785-8206, E-mail: jholland@uwlax.edu. *Application contact:* Kathryn Kiefer, Director of Admissions, 608-785-8939, E-mail: admissions@uwlax.edu. Web site: http://www.uwlax.edu/sah/rmtr/.

University of Wisconsin–Milwaukee, Graduate School, College of Health Sciences, Department of Occupational Science and Technology, Milwaukee, WI 53201-0413. Offers ergonomics (Certificate); occupational therapy (MS); therapeutic recreation (Certificate). *Accreditation:* AOTA. *Faculty:* 11 full-time (6 women), 1 (woman) part-time/adjunct. *Students:* 36 full-time (30 women), 11 part-time (7 women), 3 international. Average age 30. 16 applicants, 31% accepted, 0 enrolled. In 2011, 29 degrees awarded. *Degree requirements:* For master's, thesis or alternative. *Entrance requirements:* Additional exam requirements/recommendations for international students: Required—TOEFL (minimum score 550 paper-based; 79 iBT), IELTS (minimum score 6.5). *Application deadline:* For fall admission, 1/1 priority date for domestic students; for spring admission, 9/1 for domestic students. Applications are processed on a rolling basis. Application fee: $45 ($75 for international students). One-time fee: $506.10 full-time. Tuition and fees vary according to course load and reciprocity agreements. *Financial support:* Fellowships, research assistantships, teaching assistantships, and unspecified assistantships available. Support available to part-time students. Financial award application deadline: 4/15. *Total annual research expenditures:* $21,103. *Unit head:* Carol Haertlein Sells, Department Chair, 414-229-6933, E-mail: chaert@uwm.edu. *Application contact:* Roger O. Smith, General Information Contact, 414-229-6697, Fax: 414-229-6697, E-mail: smithro@uwm.edu. Web site: http://www4.uwm.edu/chs/academics/occupational_therapy/.

Utah State University, School of Graduate Studies, College of Natural Resources, Department of Environment and Society, Logan, UT 84322. Offers bioregional planning (MS); geography (MA, MS); human dimensions of ecosystem science and management (MS, PhD); recreation resource management (MS, PhD). *Degree requirements:* For master's, comprehensive exam, thesis (for some programs). *Entrance requirements:* For master's and doctorate, GRE General Test, minimum GPA of 3.0. Additional exam requirements/recommendations for international students: Required—TOEFL. Electronic applications accepted. *Faculty research:* Geographic information systems/geographic and environmental education, bioregional planning, natural resource and environmental policy, outdoor recreation and tourism, natural resource and environmental management.

Virginia Commonwealth University, Graduate School, School of Education, Program in Sport Leadership, Richmond, VA 23284-9005. Offers MS. *Entrance requirements:* For master's, GRE General Test or MAT. Additional exam requirements/recommendations for international students: Required—TOEFL (minimum score 600 paper-based; 250 computer-based; 100 iBT). Electronic applications accepted. *Expenses:* Tuition, state resident: full-time $9133; part-time $507 per credit. Tuition, nonresident: full-time $18,777; part-time $1043 per credit. *Required fees:* $77 per credit. Tuition and fees vary according to degree level, campus/location, program and student level.

Western Illinois University, School of Graduate Studies, College of Education and Human Services, Department of Recreation, Park, and Tourism Administration, Macomb, IL 61455-1390. Offers MS. Part-time programs available. *Students:* 28 full-time (16 women), 9 part-time (4 women); includes 3 minority (2 Black or African American, non-Hispanic/Latino; 1 Asian, non-Hispanic/Latino), 4 international. Average age 28. 25 applicants, 80% accepted. In 2011, 28 master's awarded. *Degree requirements:* For master's, thesis or alternative. *Entrance requirements:* Additional exam requirements/recommendations for international students: Required—TOEFL (minimum score 550 paper-based; 213 computer-based; 80 iBT). *Application deadline:* Applications are processed on a rolling basis. Application fee: $30. Electronic applications accepted. *Expenses:* Tuition, state resident: part-time $281.16 per credit hour. Tuition, nonresident: part-time $562.32 per credit hour. Part-time tuition and fees vary according to campus/location and reciprocity agreements. *Financial support:* In 2011–12, 23 students received support, including 23 research assistantships with full tuition reimbursements available (averaging $7,360 per year). Financial award applicants required to submit FAFSA. *Unit head:* Dr. K. Dale Adkins, Chairperson, 309-298-1967. *Application contact:* Dr. Nancy Parsons, Assistant Director of Graduate Studies, 309-298-1806, Fax: 309-298-2345, E-mail: grad-office@wiu.edu. Web site: http://www.wiu.edu/rpta.

Western Kentucky University, Graduate Studies, College of Health and Human Services, Department of Kinesiology, Recreation and Sport, Bowling Green, KY 42101. Offers athletic administration and coaching (MS); physical education (MS); recreation and sport administration (MS). Part-time and evening/weekend programs available. Postbaccalaureate distance learning degree programs offered. *Degree requirements:* For master's, comprehensive exam, thesis optional. *Entrance requirements:* For master's, GRE General Test, minimum GPA of 2.75. Additional exam requirements/recommendations for international students: Required—TOEFL (minimum score 555 paper-based; 213 computer-based; 79 iBT). *Faculty research:* Orthopedic rehabilitation, fitness center coordination, heat acclimation, biomechanical and physiological parameters.

West Virginia University, Davis College of Agriculture, Forestry and Consumer Sciences, Division of Forestry, Program in Recreation, Parks and Tourism Resources, Morgantown, WV 26506. Offers MS. Part-time programs available. *Degree requirements:* For master's, thesis (for some programs). *Entrance requirements:* For master's, GRE, minimum GPA of 3.0. Additional exam requirements/recommendations for international students: Required—TOEFL. *Faculty research:* Attitudes, use patterns and impacts of outdoor recreation in West Virginia.

Winona State University, College of Education, Department of Education Leadership, Winona, MN 55987. Offers educational leadership (Ed S), including general superintendency, K-12 principalship; general school leadership (MS); K-12 principalship (MS); outdoor education/adventure-based leadership (MS); sports management (MS); teacher leadership (MS). *Accreditation:* NCATE. Part-time and evening/weekend programs available. *Students:* 52 full-time (24 women), 57 part-time (18 women); includes 8 minority (5 Black or African American, non-Hispanic/Latino; 1 Asian, non-Hispanic/Latino; 1 Hispanic/Latino; 1 Two or more races, non-Hispanic/Latino), 3 international. Average age 34. In 2011, 17 master's, 10 other advanced degrees awarded. *Degree requirements:* For master's, comprehensive exam, thesis optional; for Ed S, thesis optional. *Application deadline:* For fall admission, 8/8 for domestic students; for spring admission, 12/10 for domestic students. Applications are processed on a rolling basis. Application fee: $20. *Financial support:* Federal Work-Study available. Support available to part-time students. Financial award applicants required to submit FAFSA. *Unit head:* Dr. George P. Morrow, Chair, 507-457-5346, Fax: 507-457-5882, E-mail: gmorrow@winona.edu. *Application contact:* Dr. George P. Morrow, 507-457-5346, Fax: 507-457-5882, E-mail: gmorrow@winona.edu. Web site: http://www.winona.edu/educationleadership/.

Wright State University, School of Graduate Studies, College of Education and Human Services, Department of Health, Physical Education, and Recreation, Dayton, OH 45435. Offers M Ed, MA. *Accreditation:* NCATE. *Degree requirements:* For master's, comprehensive exam, thesis (for some programs). *Entrance requirements:* For master's, GRE General Test, MAT. Additional exam requirements/recommendations for international students: Required—TOEFL. *Faculty research:* Motor learning, motor development, exercise physiology, adapted physical education.

Section 30
Physical Education and Kinesiology

This section contains a directory of institutions offering graduate work in physical education and kinesiology. Additional information about programs listed in the directory but not augmented by an in-depth entry may be obtained by writing directly to the dean of a graduate school or chair of a department at the address given in the directory.

For programs offering related work, see also in this book *Business Administration and Management, Education,* and *Sports Management.* In another guide in this series:

Graduate Programs in the Humanities, Arts & Social Sciences
See *Performing Arts*

CONTENTS

Program Directories

Athletic Training and Sports Medicine

Armstrong Atlantic State University, School of Graduate Studies, Program in Sports Medicine, Savannah, GA 31419-1997. Offers sports health sciences (MSSM). Part-time programs available. *Faculty:* 3 full-time (1 woman), 1 part-time/adjunct (0 women). *Students:* 17 full-time (8 women), 8 part-time (5 women); includes 5 minority (1 Black or African American, non-Hispanic/Latino; 3 Hispanic/Latino; 1 Two or more races, non-Hispanic/Latino), 2 international. Average age 25. 26 applicants, 50% accepted, 11 enrolled. In 2011, 8 master's awarded. *Degree requirements:* For master's, comprehensive exam, thesis optional, project. *Entrance requirements:* For master's, GRE General Test, MAT, GMAT, minimum GPA of 2.5. Additional exam requirements/recommendations for international students: Required—TOEFL (minimum score 523 paper-based; 193 computer-based). *Application deadline:* For fall admission, 7/1 priority date for domestic students, 5/1 for international students; for spring admission, 11/15 priority date for domestic students, 9/15 for international students. Application fee: $30. *Expenses:* Tuition, state resident: full-time $3402. Tuition, nonresident: full-time $12,636. *Financial support:* In 2011–12, research assistantships with full tuition reimbursements (averaging $5,000 per year) were awarded; scholarships/grants, tuition waivers (full), and unspecified assistantships also available. Financial award applicants required to submit FAFSA. *Unit head:* Dr. James Streater, Department Head, 912-921-2548, Fax: 912-344-3490, E-mail: sandy.streater@armstrong.edu. *Application contact:* Brian Riemann, Graduate Coordinator, 912-344-2934, Fax: 912-344-3490, E-mail: brian.riemann@armstrong.edu. Web site: http://www.sportsmedicine.armstrong.edu/.

A.T. Still University of Health Sciences, Arizona School of Health Sciences, Mesa, AZ 85206. Offers advanced occupational therapy (MS); advanced physician assistant (MS); athletic training (MS); audiology (Au D); health sciences (DHSc); human movement (MS); occupational therapy (MS); physical therapy (DPT); physician assistant (MS); transitional audiology (Au D); transitional physical therapy (DPT). *Accreditation:* AOTA (one or more programs are accredited); ASHA. Part-time and evening/weekend programs available. Postbaccalaureate distance learning degree programs offered (minimal on-campus study). *Faculty:* 44 full-time (27 women), 235 part-time/adjunct (141 women). *Students:* 410 full-time (275 women), 1,010 part-time (675 women); includes 320 minority (73 Black or African American, non-Hispanic/Latino; 18 American Indian or Alaska Native, non-Hispanic/Latino; 158 Asian, non-Hispanic/Latino; 62 Hispanic/Latino; 9 Two or more races, non-Hispanic/Latino), 6 international. Average age 35. 4,395 applicants, 18% accepted, 694 enrolled. In 2011, 221 master's, 406 doctorates awarded. *Median time to degree:* Of those who began their doctoral program in fall 2003, 98% received their degree in 8 years or less. *Degree requirements:* For master's, thesis (for some programs); for doctorate, thesis/dissertation (for some programs). *Entrance requirements:* For master's, GRE General Test; for doctorate, GRE, Evaluation of Practicing Audiologists Capabilities (Au D), Physical Therapist Evaluation Tool (DPT), current state licensure, master's degree or equivalent (Au D). Additional exam requirements/recommendations for international students: Required—TOEFL (minimum score 550 paper-based; 213 computer-based; 80 iBT). *Application deadline:* For fall admission, 8/1 priority date for domestic students, 8/1 for international students. Applications are processed on a rolling basis. Application fee: $60. *Expenses:* Contact institution. *Financial support:* In 2011–12, 272 students received support, including 14 fellowships (averaging $16,000 per year); Federal Work-Study and scholarships/grants also available. Financial award application deadline: 5/1; financial award applicants required to submit FAFSA. *Faculty research:* Physical therapy: metabolism during exercise and activity; neuromuscular function after injury, prevention of lifestyle diseases, prevention and treatment of overuse injuries; athletic training: pediatric sport-related concussion, adolescent athlete health-related quality of life; occupational therapy: spirituality and health disparities, geriatric and pediatric well-being, pain management for participation. *Total annual research expenditures:* $75,682. *Unit head:* Dr. Randy Danielsen, Dean, 480-219-6000, Fax: 480-219-6110, E-mail: rdanielsen@atsu.edu. *Application contact:* Donna Sparks, Associate Director, Admissions Processing, 660-626-2117, Fax: 660-626-2969, E-mail: admissions@atsu.edu. Web site: http://www.atsu.edu/ashs.

Barry University, School of Human Performance and Leisure Sciences, Programs in Movement Science, Specialization in Athletic Training, Miami Shores, FL 33161-6695. Offers MS. Part-time and evening/weekend programs available. *Degree requirements:* For master's, comprehensive exam, project or thesis. *Entrance requirements:* For master's, GRE General Test, minimum GPA of 3.0. Electronic applications accepted. *Faculty research:* Pain management, prevention and injury analysis, low energy static magnetic field therapy, upper extremity biomechanics.

Bloomsburg University of Pennsylvania, School of Graduate Studies, College of Science and Technology, Department of Exercise Science, Bloomsburg, PA 17815-1301. Offers clinical athletic training (MS); exercise science (MS). *Degree requirements:* For master's, thesis, practical clinical experience. *Entrance requirements:* For master's, GRE General Test or MAT, minimum QPA of 3.0. Additional exam requirements/recommendations for international students: Required—TOEFL (minimum score 550 paper-based; 213 computer-based; 79 iBT). Electronic applications accepted.

Boston University, College of Health and Rehabilitation Sciences: Sargent College, Department of Physical Therapy and Athletic Training, Boston, MA 02215. Offers physical therapy (DPT); rehabilitation sciences (D Sc). *Accreditation:* APTA (one or more programs are accredited). Postbaccalaureate distance learning degree programs offered (minimal on-campus study). *Faculty:* 13 full-time (10 women), 26 part-time/adjunct (12 women). *Students:* 142 full-time (107 women), 53 part-time (33 women); includes 28 minority (2 Black or African American, non-Hispanic/Latino; 2 American Indian or Alaska Native, non-Hispanic/Latino; 16 Asian, non-Hispanic/Latino; 5 Hispanic/Latino; 1 Native Hawaiian or other Pacific Islander, non-Hispanic/Latino; 2 Two or more races, non-Hispanic/Latino), 6 international. Average age 28. 542 applicants, 26% accepted, 38 enrolled. In 2011, 97 doctorates awarded. *Degree requirements:* For doctorate, comprehensive exam, thesis/dissertation. *Entrance requirements:* For doctorate, GRE General Test, master's degree (for Sc D), bachelor's degree (for DPT). Additional exam requirements/recommendations for international students: Required—TOEFL (minimum score 550 paper-based; 84 computer-based). *Application deadline:* For fall admission, 1/7 priority date for domestic students, 1/7 for international students. Applications are processed on a rolling basis. Application fee: $120. Electronic applications accepted. *Expenses: Tuition:* Full-time $40,848; part-time $1276 per credit hour. *Required fees:* $572; $286 per semester. *Financial support:* In 2011–12, 125 students received support, including 14 fellowships (averaging $16,000 per year), 10 teaching assistantships with partial tuition reimbursements available (averaging $3,000 per year); career-related internships or fieldwork, Federal Work-Study, institutionally sponsored loans, scholarships/grants, and tuition waivers (partial) also available. Financial award application deadline: 4/15; financial award applicants required to submit FAFSA. *Faculty research:* Gait, balance, motor control, dynamic systems analysis, spinal cord injury. *Total annual research expenditures:* $1.3 million. *Unit head:* Dr. Melanie Matthies, Chairman, 617-353-2724, E-mail: pt@bu.edu. *Application contact:* Sharon Sankey, Director, Student Services, 617-353-2713, Fax: 617-353-7500, E-mail: ssankey@bu.edu. Web site: http://www.bu.edu/sargent/.

Brigham Young University, Graduate Studies, College of Life Sciences, Department of Exercise Sciences, Provo, UT 84602. Offers athletic training (MS); exercise physiology (MS, PhD); exercise science (MS); health promotion (MS, PhD); physical medicine and rehabilitation (PhD). *Faculty:* 21 full-time (3 women), 3 part-time/adjunct (0 women). *Students:* 17 full-time (10 women), 35 part-time (20 women); includes 4 minority (2 Asian, non-Hispanic/Latino; 1 Hispanic/Latino; 1 Native Hawaiian or other Pacific Islander, non-Hispanic/Latino), 1 international. Average age 29. 28 applicants, 43% accepted, 7 enrolled. In 2011, 14 master's, 1 doctorate awarded. *Degree requirements:* For master's, thesis, oral defense; for doctorate, comprehensive exam, thesis/dissertation, oral defense, oral and written exams. *Entrance requirements:* For master's, GRE General Test, minimum GPA of 3.2 in last 60 hours of course work; for doctorate, GRE General Test, minimum GPA of 3.5 in last 60 hours of course work. Additional exam requirements/recommendations for international students: Required—TOEFL (minimum score 580 paper-based; 237 computer-based; 85 iBT), IELTS (minimum score 7). *Application deadline:* For fall admission, 2/1 for domestic and international students. Application fee: $50. Electronic applications accepted. *Expenses: Tuition:* Full-time $5760; part-time $320 per credit. Tuition and fees vary according to student's religious affiliation. *Financial support:* In 2011–12, 52 students received support, including 15 research assistantships with partial tuition reimbursements available (averaging $5,615 per year), 34 teaching assistantships with partial tuition reimbursements available (averaging $10,106 per year); fellowships, career-related internships or fieldwork, institutionally sponsored loans, scholarships/grants, tuition waivers (partial), unspecified assistantships, and 10 PhD fulltTuition scholarships also available. Financial award application deadline: 3/1. *Faculty research:* Injury prevention and rehabilitation, human skeletal muscle adaptation, cardiovascular health and fitness, lifestyle modification and health promotion. *Total annual research expenditures:* $2,888. *Unit head:* Dr. Gary Mack, Chair, 801-422-2466, Fax: 801-422-0555, E-mail: gary_mack@byu.edu. *Application contact:* Dr. Jeffrey Brent Feland, Graduate Coordinator, 801-422-1182, Fax: 801-422-0555, E-mail: brent_feland@byu.edu. Web site: http://www.exsc.byu.edu.

California Baptist University, Program in Athletic Training, Riverside, CA 92504-3206. Offers MS. Part-time programs available. *Faculty:* 6 full-time (2 women), 1 part-time/adjunct (0 women). *Students:* 40 full-time (28 women); includes 23 minority (5 Black or African American, non-Hispanic/Latino; 1 American Indian or Alaska Native, non-Hispanic/Latino; 4 Asian, non-Hispanic/Latino; 9 Hispanic/Latino; 2 Native Hawaiian or other Pacific Islander, non-Hispanic/Latino; 2 Two or more races, non-Hispanic/Latino). Average age 25. 52 applicants, 46% accepted, 17 enrolled. In 2011, 9 master's awarded. *Entrance requirements:* For master's, minimum GPA of 2.75; three recommendations; comprehensive essay; CPR Certification; 150 hours of clinical observation; interview. Additional exam requirements/recommendations for international students: Required—TOEFL (minimum score 575 paper-based; 230 computer-based; 89 iBT). *Application deadline:* For fall admission, 8/1 priority date for domestic students, 7/1 for international students; for spring admission, 12/1 priority date for domestic students, 11/1 for international students. Applications are processed on a rolling basis. Application fee: $45. Electronic applications accepted. *Expenses:* Contact institution. *Financial support:* Federal Work-Study and institutionally sponsored loans available. Financial award applicants required to submit FAFSA. *Faculty research:* Musculoskeletal injury and examination, sudden death in young athletes, thermoregulation, carbohydrate oxidation, cardiovascular morbidity and mortality. *Unit head:* Dr. Chuck Sands, Dean of the College of Allied Health, 951-343-4619, E-mail: csands@calbaptist.edu. *Application contact:* Dr. Nicole MacDonald, Director, Athletic Training Program, 951-343-4379, E-mail: nmacdona@calbaptist.edu. Web site: http://www.calbaptist.edu/at/.

California State University, Long Beach, Graduate Studies, College of Health and Human Services, Department of Kinesiology, Long Beach, CA 90840. Offers adapted physical education (MA); coaching and student athlete development (MA); exercise physiology and nutrition (MS); exercise science (MS); individualized studies (MA); kinesiology (MA); pedagogical studies (MA); sport and exercise psychology (MS); sport management (MA); sports medicine and injury studies (MS). Part-time programs available. *Faculty:* 9 full-time (5 women), 5 part-time/adjunct (4 women). *Students:* 48 full-time (27 women), 39 part-time (13 women); includes 38 minority (5 Black or African American, non-Hispanic/Latino; 2 American Indian or Alaska Native, non-Hispanic/Latino; 7 Asian, non-Hispanic/Latino; 18 Hispanic/Latino; 6 Two or more races, non-Hispanic/Latino), 2 international. Average age 28. 214 applicants, 50% accepted, 32 enrolled. In 2011, 69 master's awarded. *Degree requirements:* For master's, oral and written comprehensive exams or thesis. *Entrance requirements:* For master's, GRE General Test, minimum GPA of 2.75 during previous 2 years of course work. *Application deadline:* For fall admission, 6/1 for domestic students. Applications are processed on a rolling basis. Application fee: $55. Electronic applications accepted. *Financial support:* Federal Work-Study, institutionally sponsored loans, and scholarships/grants available. Financial award application deadline: 3/2. *Faculty research:* Pulmonary functioning, feedback and practice structure, strength training, history and politics of sports, special population research issues. *Unit head:* Dr. Sharon R. Guthrie, Chair, 562-985-7487, Fax: 562-985-8067, E-mail: guthrie@csulb.edu. *Application contact:* Dr. Grant Hill, Graduate Advisor, 562-985-8856, Fax: 562-985-8067, E-mail: ghill@csulb.edu.

California University of Pennsylvania, School of Graduate Studies and Research, College of Education and Human Services, Department of Health Science, California, PA 15419-1394. Offers athletic training (MS). *Degree requirements:* For master's, comprehensive exam, thesis. *Entrance requirements:* For master's, minimum GPA of 3.0. Additional exam requirements/recommendations for international students: Required—TOEFL (minimum score 550 paper-based; 213 computer-based; 80 iBT). *Faculty research:* Exercise physiology, pedagogy, athletic training, biomechanical engineering, case studies in injury and athletic medicine.

East Carolina University, Graduate School, College of Health and Human Performance, Department of Health Education and Promotion, Greenville, NC 27858-4353. Offers athletic training (MS); environmental health (MS); health education (MA, MA Ed). *Accreditation:* NCATE. *Degree requirements:* For master's, comprehensive exam, thesis optional. *Entrance requirements:* For master's, GRE General Test or MAT. Additional exam requirements/recommendations for international students: Required—TOEFL. *Application deadline:* For fall admission, 6/1 priority date for domestic students. Applications are processed on a rolling basis. Application fee: $50. *Expenses:* Tuition, state resident: full-time $3557; part-time $444.63 per semester hour. Tuition, nonresident: full-time $14,351; part-time $1793.88 per semester hour. *Required fees:* $2016; $252 per semester hour. Part-time tuition and fees vary according to course load, campus/location and program. *Financial support:* Fellowships, research assistantships, teaching assistantships, and career-related internships or fieldwork available. Support available to part-time students. Financial award application deadline: 6/1. *Faculty research:* Community health education, worksite health promotion, school health education, environmental health. *Unit head:* Dr. Tim Kelley, Chair, 252-737-2225, E-mail: kelleyt@ecu.edu. Web site: http://www.ecu.edu/hlth/.

Eastern Michigan University, Graduate School, College of Health and Human Services, School of Health Promotion and Human Performance, Programs in Exercise Physiology, Ypsilanti, MI 48197. Offers exercise physiology (MS); sports medicine-biomechanics (MS); sports medicine-corporate adult fitness (MS); sports medicine-exercise physiology (MS). Part-time and evening/weekend programs available. *Students:* 22 full-time (16 women), 42 part-time (18 women); includes 8 minority (4 Black or African American, non-Hispanic/Latino; 2 American Indian or Alaska Native, non-Hispanic/Latino; 1 Hispanic/Latino; 1 Two or more races, non-Hispanic/Latino), 4 international. Average age 30. 59 applicants, 68% accepted, 22 enrolled. In 2011, 20 degrees awarded. *Degree requirements:* For master's, comprehensive exam, thesis or 450-hour internship. *Entrance requirements:* Additional exam requirements/recommendations for international students: Required—TOEFL. *Application deadline:* For fall admission, 8/1 for domestic students, 5/1 for international students; for winter admission, 12/1 for domestic students, 10/1 for international students; for spring admission, 3/15 for domestic students, 3/1 for international students. Application fee: $35. *Expenses:* Tuition, state resident: full-time $10,367; part-time $432 per credit hour. Tuition, nonresident: full-time $20,435; part-time $851 per credit hour. *Required fees:* $39 per credit hour. $46 per semester. One-time fee: $100. Tuition and fees vary according to course level, degree level and reciprocity agreements. *Unit head:* Dr. Steve McGregor, Program Coordinator, 734-487-0090, Fax: 734-487-2024, E-mail: stephen.mcgregor@emich.edu. *Application contact:* Dr. Brenda Riemer, Chair, Graduate Programs, 734-487-0090 Ext. 2745, Fax: 734-487-2024, E-mail: briemer@emich.edu.

Eastern Michigan University, Graduate School, College of Health and Human Services, School of Health Promotion and Human Performance, Programs in Orthotics and Prosthetics, Ypsilanti, MI 48197. Offers orthotics (Graduate Certificate); orthotics/prosthetics (MS); prosthetics (Graduate Certificate). *Students:* 35 full-time (24 women), 4 part-time (3 women); includes 4 minority (2 Black or African American, non-Hispanic/Latino; 1 Asian, non-Hispanic/Latino; 1 Hispanic/Latino), 2 international. Average age 26. 49 applicants, 53% accepted, 20 enrolled. In 2011, 20 master's, 2 other advanced degrees awarded. *Degree requirements:* For master's, comprehensive exam, thesis or project, 500 hours of clinicals. *Entrance requirements:* For master's, MAT. Additional exam requirements/recommendations for international students: Required—TOEFL. *Application deadline:* For fall admission, 5/1 for domestic and international students. Applications are processed on a rolling basis. Application fee: $35. *Expenses:* Tuition, state resident: full-time $10,367; part-time $432 per credit hour. Tuition, nonresident: full-time $20,435; part-time $851 per credit hour. *Required fees:* $39 per credit hour. $46 per semester. One-time fee: $100. Tuition and fees vary according to course level, degree level and reciprocity agreements. *Financial support:* Fellowships, research assistantships with full tuition reimbursements, teaching assistantships with full tuition reimbursements, career-related internships or fieldwork, Federal Work-Study, institutionally sponsored loans, scholarships/grants, tuition waivers (partial), and unspecified assistantships available. Support available to part-time students. Financial award applicants required to submit FAFSA. *Unit head:* Robert Rhodes, Program Coordinator, 734-487-7120 Ext. 2724, Fax: 734-487-2024, E-mail: rrhodes4@emich.edu. *Application contact:* Dr. Brenda Riemer, Chair, Graduate Programs, 734-487-0090 Ext. 2745, Fax: 734-487-2024, E-mail: briemer@emich.edu.

Florida International University, College of Nursing and Health Sciences, Department of Athletic Training, Miami, FL 33199. Offers MS. *Degree requirements:* For master's, 800 clinical education hours. *Entrance requirements:* For master's, bachelor's degree from accredited institution; minimum GPA of 3.0 overall and in last 60 credits of upper-division courses of the bachelor's degree; three letters of recommendation; resume; personal statement of professional/educational goals. Additional exam requirements/recommendations for international students: Required—TOEFL (minimum score 550 paper-based; 80 iBT). Electronic applications accepted. *Expenses:* Contact institution. *Faculty research:* Continuing professional education, leadership styles and outcomes, professionalism and professional Image.

Georgia State University, College of Education, Department of Kinesiology and Health, Program in Sports Medicine, Atlanta, GA 30302-3083. Offers MS. *Degree requirements:* For master's, comprehensive exam. *Entrance requirements:* For master's, GRE General Test, minimum GPA of 2.5. *Faculty research:* Athletic training.

Humboldt State University, Academic Programs, College of Professional Studies, Department of Kinesiology and Recreation Administration, Arcata, CA 95521-8299. Offers athletic training education (MS); exercise science/wellness management (MS); pre-physical therapy (MS); teaching/coaching (MS). *Students:* 11 full-time (7 women), 10 part-time (6 women); includes 4 minority (1 American Indian or Alaska Native, non-Hispanic/Latino; 2 Hispanic/Latino; 1 Two or more races, non-Hispanic/Latino). Average age 28. 9 applicants, 100% accepted, 6 enrolled. In 2011, 7 master's awarded. *Degree requirements:* For master's, thesis or alternative. *Entrance requirements:* For master's, GMAT, minimum GPA of 2.5. Additional exam requirements/recommendations for international students: Required—TOEFL. *Application deadline:* For fall admission, 6/1 for domestic students; for spring admission, 12/2 for domestic students. Applications are processed on a rolling basis. Application fee: $55. *Expenses:* Tuition, state resident: full-time $6734. Tuition, nonresident: full-time $15,662; part-time $372 per credit. *Required fees:* $903. Tuition and fees vary according to program. *Financial support:* Teaching assistantships, career-related internships or fieldwork, Federal Work-Study, and institutionally sponsored loans available. Financial award application deadline: 3/1; financial award applicants required to submit FAFSA. *Faculty research:* Human performance, adapted physical education, physical therapy. *Unit head:* Dr. Chris Hooper, Chair, 707-826-3853, Fax: 707-826-5451, E-mail: cah3@humboldt.edu. *Application contact:* Dr. Rock Braithwaite, Coordinator, 707-826-4543, Fax: 707-826-5451, E-mail: reb22@humboldt.edu. Web site: http://www.humboldt.edu/kra/.

Indiana State University, College of Graduate and Professional Studies, College of Nursing, Health and Human Services, Department of Athletic Training, Terre Haute, IN 47809. Offers MS. *Degree requirements:* For master's, thesis or alternative. *Entrance requirements:* For master's, GRE General Test. Electronic applications accepted.

Indiana University Bloomington, School of Health, Physical Education and Recreation, Department of Kinesiology, Bloomington, IN 47405-7000. Offers adapted physical education (MS); applied sport science (MS); athletic administration/sport management (MS); athletic training (MS); biomechanics (MS); ergonomics (MS); exercise physiology (MS); human performance (PhD), including adapted physical education, biomechanics, exercise physiology, motor learning/control, sport management; motor learning/control (MS); physical activity, fitness and wellness (MS). Part-time programs available. *Faculty:* 28 full-time (11 women). *Students:* 150 full-time (59 women), 22 part-time (9 women); includes 20 minority (12 Black or African American, non-Hispanic/Latino; 1 American Indian or Alaska Native, non-Hispanic/Latino; 1 Asian, non-Hispanic/Latino; 4 Hispanic/Latino; 2 Two or more races, non-Hispanic/Latino), 33 international. Average age 28. 211 applicants, 60% accepted, 62 enrolled. In 2011, 67 master's, 7 doctorates awarded. Terminal master's awarded for partial completion of doctoral program. *Degree requirements:* For master's, thesis optional; for doctorate, variable foreign language requirement, thesis/dissertation. *Entrance requirements:* For master's, GRE General Test, minimum GPA of 2.8; for doctorate, GRE General Test, minimum graduate GPA of 3.5, undergraduate 3.0. *Application deadline:* For fall admission, 1/1 for international students; for spring admission, 9/1 for international students. Applications are processed on a rolling basis. Application fee: $55 ($65 for international students). *Financial support:* Fellowships, research assistantships with full tuition reimbursements, teaching assistantships with full tuition reimbursements, career-related internships or fieldwork, Federal Work-Study, institutionally sponsored loans, scholarships/grants, tuition waivers (partial), and fee remissions available. Financial award application deadline: 3/1. *Faculty research:* Exercise physiology and biochemistry, sports biomechanics, human motor control, adaptation of fitness and exercise to special populations. *Unit head:* Dr. David M. Koceja, Chairperson, 812-855-5523, Fax: 812-855-3193, E-mail: koceja@indiana.edu. *Application contact:* Kristine M. Wasson, Administrative Assistant for Graduate Studies, 812-855-5523, Fax: 812-855-3193, E-mail: ktanksle@indiana.edu. Web site: http://www.indiana.edu/~kines/.

Inter American University of Puerto Rico, Metropolitan Campus, Graduate Programs, Program in Physical Education, San Juan, PR 00919-1293. Offers teaching of physical education (MA); training and sport performance (MA). *Degree requirements:* For master's, comprehensive exam. *Entrance requirements:* For master's, GRE or EXADEP, interview. Electronic applications accepted.

Kent State University, Graduate School of Education, Health, and Human Services, School of Health Sciences, Program in Athletic Training, Kent, OH 44242-0001. Offers MA. *Faculty:* 5 full-time (3 women). *Students:* 8 full-time (5 women), 4 part-time (2 women); includes 1 minority (Asian, non-Hispanic/Latino). 10 applicants, 90% accepted. In 2011, 3 master's awarded. Application fee: $30 ($60 for international students). *Expenses:* Tuition, state resident: full-time $8136; part-time $452 per credit hour. Tuition, nonresident: full-time $14,292; part-time $794 per credit hour. *Financial support:* In 2011–12, 3 fellowships (averaging $8,313 per year), research assistantships (averaging $8,313 per year) were awarded; Federal Work-Study, scholarships/grants, and unspecified assistantships also available. *Unit head:* Dr. Kimberly Peer, Coordinator, 330-672-9785, E-mail: kpeer@kent.edu. *Application contact:* Nancy Miller, Academic Program Coordinator, Office of Graduate Student Services, 330-672-2576, Fax: 330-672-9162, E-mail: ogs@kent.edu.

Kent State University, Graduate School of Education, Health, and Human Services, School of Health Sciences, Program in Exercise Physiology, Kent, OH 44242-0001. Offers athletic training (MS); exercise physiology (MS, PhD). *Faculty:* 10 full-time (5 women), 1 part-time/adjunct (0 women). *Students:* 39 full-time (19 women), 12 part-time (3 women); includes 3 minority (2 Asian, non-Hispanic/Latino; 1 Hispanic/Latino). 63 applicants, 60% accepted. In 2011, 20 master's, 3 doctorates awarded. *Degree requirements:* For doctorate, comprehensive exam, thesis/dissertation. *Entrance requirements:* For master's, GRE, 2 letters of reference, goals statement; for doctorate, GRE, 2 letters of reference, goals statement, minimum master's-level GPA of 3.0. Additional exam requirements/recommendations for international students: Required—TOEFL (minimum score 550 paper-based; 213 computer-based; 80 iBT). Application fee: $30 ($60 for international students). *Expenses:* Tuition, state resident: full-time $8136; part-time $452 per credit hour. Tuition, nonresident: full-time $14,292; part-time $794 per credit hour. *Financial support:* In 2011–12, 4 fellowships (averaging $8,500 per year), 12 research assistantships (averaging $11,417 per year) were awarded; teaching assistantships, Federal Work-Study, scholarships/grants, and unspecified assistantships also available. *Unit head:* Ellen Glickman, Coordinator, 330-672-2930, E-mail: eglickma@kent.edu. *Application contact:* Nancy Miller, Academic Program Coordinator, Office of Graduate Student Services, 330-672-2576, Fax: 330-672-9162, E-mail: ogs@kent.edu.

Lenoir-Rhyne University, Graduate Programs, School of Health, Exercise and Sport Science, Hickory, NC 28601. Offers athletic training (MS).

Long Island University–Brooklyn Campus, School of Health Professions, Division of Sports Sciences, Brooklyn, NY 11201-8423. Offers adapted physical education (MS); athletic training and sports sciences (MS); exercise physiology (MS); health sciences (MS). Part-time and evening/weekend programs available. *Entrance requirements:* For master's, 2 letters of recommendation. Additional exam requirements/recommendations for international students: Required—TOEFL (minimum score 500 paper-based; 173 computer-based). Electronic applications accepted.

Manchester College, Graduate Programs, Program in Athletic Training, North Manchester, IN 46962-1225. Offers MAT. *Faculty:* 6 full-time (1 woman), 1 (woman) part-time/adjunct. *Students:* 8 full-time (3 women). 7 applicants, 86% accepted, 6 enrolled. *Degree requirements:* For master's, 51 semester hours; minimum cumulative GPA of 3.0, 2.0 in each required course; completion of all required didactic and clinical courses. *Entrance requirements:* For master's, baccalaureate degree from regionally-accredited institution; minimum cumulative undergraduate GPA of 3.0; certification in first aid and CPR; completion of the published technical standards for the program; letters of recommendation. Additional exam requirements/recommendations for international students: Required—TOEFL (minimum score 550 paper-based; 213 computer-based; 79 iBT). *Application deadline:* For fall admission, 2/1 priority date for domestic students. Applications are processed on a rolling basis. Electronic applications accepted. *Financial support:* In 2011–12, 8 students received support. Application deadline: 5/1; applicants required to submit FAFSA. *Unit head:* Mark Huntington, Associate Dean for Academic Affairs/Director, 260-982-5033, E-mail: mwhuntington@manchester.edu. Web site: http://graduateprograms.manchester.edu/AT/index.htm.

Montana State University Billings, College of Allied Health Professions, Department of Health and Human Performance, Program in Athletic Training, Billings, MT 59101-0298. Offers MS.

Ohio University, Graduate College, College of Health Sciences and Professions, School of Applied Health Sciences and Wellness, Program in Athletic Training, Athens, OH 45701-2979. Offers MS. *Students:* 33 full-time (21 women); includes 4 minority (1 Black or African American, non-Hispanic/Latino; 1 Asian, non-Hispanic/Latino; 2 Hispanic/Latino). 17 applicants, 0% accepted, 0 enrolled. In 2011, 21 master's awarded. *Entrance requirements:* For master's, GRE. Additional exam requirements/recommendations for international students: Required—TOEFL (minimum score 550 paper-based; 80 iBT) or IELTS (minimum score 7.5). Application fee: $50 ($55 for international students). *Financial support:* In 2011–12, teaching assistantships with full tuition reimbursements (averaging $9,000 per year) were awarded; Federal Work-Study and unspecified assistantships also available. Financial award application deadline: 2/15. *Faculty research:* Athletic training, heart, injuries, health, muscles, exercise, sport. *Unit head:* Dr. Chad Starkey, Coordinator, 740-593-1217, Fax: 740-593-0284, E-mail: starkeyc@ohio.edu. *Application contact:* Marnie Miller, Graduate Admissions, 740-593-2800, Fax: 740-593-4625, E-mail: graduate@ohio.edu. Web site: http://www.ohio.edu/chsp/ahsw/academics/atg.cfm.

Old Dominion University, Darden College of Education, Program in Physical Education, Athletic Training Emphasis, Norfolk, VA 23529. Offers MS Ed. Part-time programs available. *Faculty:* 1 (woman) full-time. *Students:* 24 full-time (18 women);

includes 3 minority (all Black or African American, non-Hispanic/Latino). Average age 23. 40 applicants, 33% accepted, 13 enrolled. In 2011, 11 master's awarded. *Degree requirements:* For master's, comprehensive exam, thesis or research project. *Entrance requirements:* For master's, GRE, minimum GPA of 3.0. Additional exam requirements/recommendations for international students: Required—TOEFL (minimum score 500 paper-based; 200 computer-based). *Application deadline:* For spring admission, 2/1 priority date for domestic students, 2/1 for international students. Applications are processed on a rolling basis. Application fee: $50. Electronic applications accepted. *Expenses:* Tuition, state resident: full-time $9096; part-time $379 per credit. Tuition, nonresident: full-time $23,064; part-time $961 per credit. *Required fees:* $127 per semester. One-time fee: $50. *Financial support:* In 2011–12, 23 research assistantships with partial tuition reimbursements (averaging $12,000 per year), 1 teaching assistantship with partial tuition reimbursement (averaging $9,000 per year) were awarded; career-related internships or fieldwork, scholarships/grants, and unspecified assistantships also available. Financial award application deadline: 4/15; financial award applicants required to submit FAFSA. *Faculty research:* ACL injury prevention, lower extremity biomechanical program satisfaction, manual therapy, evidence-based practice in education. *Unit head:* Dr. Bonnie L. Van Lunen, Graduate Program Director, 757-683-3516, Fax: 757-683-4270, E-mail: bvanlune@odu.edu. *Application contact:* William Heffelfinger, Director of Graduate Admissions, 757-683-5554, Fax: 757-683-3255, E-mail: gradadmit@odu.edu. Web site: http://education.odu.edu/esper/academics/athletic/graduate.shtml.

Plymouth State University, College of Graduate Studies, Graduate Studies in Education, Program in Athletic Training, Plymouth, NH 03264-1595. Offers M Ed, MS. Part-time and evening/weekend programs available. *Entrance requirements:* For master's, MAT, GRE General Test.

Rocky Mountain University of Health Professions, PhD Program in Athletic Training, Provo, UT 84606. Offers PhD. *Degree requirements:* For doctorate, thesis/dissertation.

Saint Louis University, Graduate Education, Doisy College of Health Sciences, Department of Physical Therapy, St. Louis, MO 63103-2097. Offers athletic training (MAT); physical therapy (DPT). *Accreditation:* APTA. Part-time programs available. *Entrance requirements:* Additional exam requirements/recommendations for international students: Required—TOEFL (minimum score 525 paper-based; 194 computer-based; 55 iBT). Electronic applications accepted. *Faculty research:* Patellofemoral pain and associated risk factors; prevalence of disordered eating in physical therapy students; effects of selected interventions for children with cerebral palsy on gait and posture: hippotherapy, ankle strengthening, supported treadmill training, spirituality in physical therapy/patient care, risk factors for exercise-related leg pain in running athletes.

Seton Hall University, School of Health and Medical Sciences, Program in Athletic Training, South Orange, NJ 07079-2697. Offers MS. *Degree requirements:* For master's, research project. *Entrance requirements:* Additional exam requirements/recommendations for international students: Required—TOEFL. Electronic applications accepted. *Expenses: Tuition:* Part-time $1033 per credit hour. *Required fees:* $85 per semester. *Faculty research:* Electrotherapy.

Shenandoah University, School of Health Professions, Division of Athletic Training, Winchester, VA 22601-5195. Offers athletic training (MS); performing arts medicine (Certificate). *Faculty:* 3 full-time (2 women), 1 (woman) part-time/adjunct. *Students:* 21 full-time (11 women), 6 part-time (all women); includes 7 minority (2 Black or African American, non-Hispanic/Latino; 5 Hispanic/Latino). Average age 25. 31 applicants, 87% accepted, 27 enrolled. In 2011, 16 master's awarded. *Degree requirements:* For master's, clinical field experience. *Entrance requirements:* For master's, SAT or GRE General Test, minimum GPA of 2.8, interview, athletic experience, 3 letters of recommendation, essay. Additional exam requirements/recommendations for international students: Required—TOEFL (minimum score 550 paper-based; 213 computer-based; 79 iBT), IELTS (minimum score 6.5). *Application deadline:* Applications are processed on a rolling basis. Application fee: $30. Electronic applications accepted. *Expenses:* Contact institution. *Financial support:* In 2011–12, 4 students received support. Application deadline: 3/15; applicants required to submit FAFSA. *Unit head:* Dr. Rose A. Schmieg, Director, 540-545-7385, Fax: 540-545-7387, E-mail: rschmieg@su.edu. *Application contact:* David Anthony, Dean of Admissions, 540-665-4581, Fax: 540-665-4627, E-mail: admit@su.edu.

Springfield College, Graduate Programs, Programs in Exercise Science and Sport Studies, Springfield, MA 01109-3797. Offers athletic training (MS); exercise physiology (MS), including clinical exercise physiology, science and research; exercise science and sport studies (PhD); health promotion and disease prevention (MS); sport psychology (MS). Part-time programs available. Terminal master's awarded for partial completion of doctoral program. *Degree requirements:* For master's, comprehensive exam, research project or thesis; for doctorate, comprehensive exam, thesis/dissertation. *Entrance requirements:* For master's and doctorate, GRE General Test. Additional exam requirements/recommendations for international students: Required—TOEFL (minimum score 550 paper-based; 213 computer-based). Electronic applications accepted.

Stephen F. Austin State University, Graduate School, College of Education, Department of Kinesiology and Health Science, Nacogdoches, TX 75962. Offers athletic training (MS); kinesiology (M Ed). *Degree requirements:* For master's, comprehensive exam. *Entrance requirements:* For master's, GRE General Test. Additional exam requirements/recommendations for international students: Required—TOEFL.

Texas State University–San Marcos, Graduate School, College of Education, Department of Health and Human Performance, Program in Athletic Training, San Marcos, TX 78666. Offers MS. *Faculty:* 2 full-time (1 woman), 1 part-time/adjunct (0 women). *Students:* 19 full-time (11 women); includes 4 minority (1 Black or African American, non-Hispanic/Latino; 1 Asian, non-Hispanic/Latino; 2 Hispanic/Latino). Average age 25. 24 applicants, 54% accepted, 9 enrolled. In 2011, 4 master's awarded. *Degree requirements:* For master's, comprehensive exam, thesis optional. *Entrance requirements:* For master's, athletic trainer certification or eligibility for certification exam. Additional exam requirements/recommendations for international students: Required—TOEFL (minimum score 550 paper-based; 213 computer-based; 78 iBT). *Application deadline:* For fall admission, 6/15 for domestic students, 6/1 for international students; for spring admission, 10/15 for domestic students, 10/1 for international students. Application fee: $40 ($90 for international students). *Expenses:* Tuition, state resident: full-time $6408; part-time $3204 per semester. Tuition, nonresident: full-time $14,832; part-time $7416 per semester. *Required fees:* $1824; $912 per semester. Tuition and fees vary according to course load. *Financial support:* In 2011–12, 14 students received support, including 15 research assistantships (averaging $8,892 per year), 10 teaching assistantships (averaging $7,470 per year). *Unit head:* Dr. Jack Ransone, Coordinator, 512-245-8176, E-mail: jr41@txstate.edu. *Application contact:* Amy Galle, Head, 512-245-2561, Fax: 512-245-8678, E-mail: ag04@txstate.edu. Web site: http://www.hhp.txstate.edu/Degree-Plans/Graduate.html.

Texas Tech University Health Sciences Center, School of Allied Health Sciences, Program in Athletic Training, Lubbock, TX 79430. Offers MAT. *Faculty:* 4 full-time (2 women). *Students:* 40 full-time (20 women), 4 part-time (all women); includes 15 minority (3 Black or African American, non-Hispanic/Latino; 3 Asian, non-Hispanic/Latino; 8 Hispanic/Latino; 1 Native Hawaiian or other Pacific Islander, non-Hispanic/Latino). Average age 29. 70 applicants, 34% accepted, 24 enrolled. In 2011, 21 master's awarded. *Entrance requirements:* Additional exam requirements/recommendations for international students: Required—TOEFL, IELTS. *Application deadline:* For fall admission, 10/15 priority date for domestic students; for spring admission, 2/1 priority date for domestic students. Application fee: $35. Electronic applications accepted. *Financial support:* Career-related internships or fieldwork, institutionally sponsored loans, and scholarships/grants available. Financial award applicants required to submit FAFSA. *Unit head:* Dr. Steve Sawyer, Chair, 806-743-3226, Fax: 806-743-3249, E-mail: steve.sawyer@ttuhsc.edu. *Application contact:* Jeri Moravcik, Assistant Director of Admissions and Student Affairs, 806-743-3220, Fax: 806-743-2994, E-mail: jeri.moravcik@ttuhsc.edu. Web site: http://www.ttuhsc.edu/sah/mat/.

United States Sports Academy, Graduate Programs, Program in Sports Medicine, Daphne, AL 36526-7055. Offers MSS. Part-time programs available. Postbaccalaureate distance learning degree programs offered (no on-campus study). *Degree requirements:* For master's, comprehensive exam, thesis optional. *Entrance requirements:* For master's, GRE General Test, GMAT, or MAT, minimum GPA of 2.5, 3 letters of recommendation, resume. Additional exam requirements/recommendations for international students: Required—TOEFL (minimum score 500 paper-based; 213 computer-based). Electronic applications accepted. *Faculty research:* Psychiatric aspects of injury rehabilitation, geriatric exercises and mobility.

Universidad del Turabo, Graduate Programs, Programs in Education, Program in Athletic Training, Gurabo, PR 00778-3030. Offers MPHE. *Students:* 18 full-time (4 women), 7 part-time (2 women); includes 22 minority (all Hispanic/Latino). Average age 30. 15 applicants, 87% accepted, 8 enrolled. In 2011, 9 master's awarded. *Unit head:* Angela Candelario, Dean, 787-743-7979 Ext. 4126. *Application contact:* Virginia Gonzalez, Admissions Officer, 787-746-3009.

University of Arkansas, Graduate School, College of Education and Health Professions, Department of Health Science, Kinesiology, Recreation and Dance, Program in Athletic Training, Fayetteville, AR 72701-1201. Offers MAT. *Students:* 29 full-time (18 women); includes 5 minority (3 Black or African American, non-Hispanic/Latino; 1 Asian, non-Hispanic/Latino; 1 Two or more races, non-Hispanic/Latino), 1 international. In 2011, 12 master's awarded. *Application deadline:* For fall admission, 4/1 for international students; for spring admission, 10/1 for international students. Applications are processed on a rolling basis. Electronic applications accepted. *Financial support:* In 2011–12, 2 research assistantships were awarded; teaching assistantships also available. *Unit head:* Dr. Bart Hammig, Department Head, 479-575-2858, Fax: 479-575-2487, E-mail: bhammig@uark.edu. *Application contact:* Dr. Dean Gorman, Coordinator of Graduate Studies, 479-575-2890, Fax: 479-575-2487, E-mail: dgorman@uark.edu. Web site: http://kins.uark.edu/.

University of Central Oklahoma, College of Graduate Studies and Research, College of Education and Professional Studies, Department of Kinesiology and Health Studies, Edmond, OK 73034-5209. Offers athletic training (MS); wellness management (MS). *Students:* 48 full-time (28 women), 39 part-time (28 women); includes 29 minority (11 Black or African American, non-Hispanic/Latino; 5 American Indian or Alaska Native, non-Hispanic/Latino; 3 Asian, non-Hispanic/Latino; 5 Hispanic/Latino; 5 Two or more races, non-Hispanic/Latino), 11 international. Average age 29. In 2011, 18 master's awarded. *Expenses:* Tuition, state resident: full-time $3901; part-time $218.30 per credit hour. Tuition, nonresident: full-time $9198; part-time $511.20 per credit hour. Tuition and fees vary according to program. *Unit head:* Jeff McKibbin, Program Director, 405-974-2959, Fax: 405-974-3805, E-mail: jmckibbin@uco.edu. *Application contact:* Dr. Richard Bernard, Dean, Graduate College, 405-974-3493, Fax: 405-974-3852, E-mail: gradcoll@uco.edu. Web site: http://www.ucogradat.net.

University of Colorado at Colorado Springs, College of Letters, Arts and Sciences, Master of Sciences Program, Colorado Springs, CO 80933-7150. Offers applied science - bioscience (M Sc); applied science - physics (M Sc); biology (M Sc); chemistry (M Sc); health promotion (M Sc); mathematics (M Sc); physics (M Sc); sports medicine (M Sc); sports nutrition (M Sc). Part-time programs available. *Students:* 13 full-time (5 women), 11 part-time (6 women); includes 3 minority (2 Asian, non-Hispanic/Latino; 1 Hispanic/Latino). Average age 33. 15 applicants, 53% accepted, 3 enrolled. In 2011, 39 degrees awarded. *Degree requirements:* For master's, thesis or alternative. *Entrance requirements:* For master's, minimum GPA of 2.75. Additional exam requirements/recommendations for international students: Recommended—TOEFL. *Application deadline:* For fall admission, 6/1 priority date for domestic students; for spring admission, 12/1 for domestic students. Application fee: $60 ($75 for international students). *Expenses:* Contact institution. *Financial support:* In 2011–12, 5 students received support. Fellowships, research assistantships, teaching assistantships, career-related internships or fieldwork, Federal Work-Study, and scholarships/grants available. Support available to part-time students. Financial award application deadline: 3/1; financial award applicants required to submit FAFSA. *Faculty research:* Biomechanics and physiology of elite athletic training, genetic engineering in yeast and bacteria including phage display and DNA repair, immunology and cell biology, synthetic organic chemistry. *Unit head:* Dr. Tom Christensen, Dean, 719-255-4550, Fax: 719-255-4200, E-mail: tchriste@uccs.edu. *Application contact:* Taryn Bailey, Information Contact, 719-255-3702, Fax: 719-255-3037, E-mail: gradinfo@uccs.edu.

The University of Findlay, Graduate and Professional Studies, College of Health Professions, Master of Athletic Training Program, Findlay, OH 45840-3653. Offers MAT. *Faculty:* 2 full-time (1 woman), 5 part-time/adjunct (4 women). *Students:* 19 full-time (11 women); includes 1 minority (Hispanic/Latino). Average age 22. 20 applicants, 80% accepted, 11 enrolled. In 2011, 8 master's awarded. *Entrance requirements:* For master's, bachelor's degree from accredited institution, minimum GPA of 3.0, 75 hours of supervised clinical experience, 3 letters of recommendation. Additional exam requirements/recommendations for international students: Required—TOEFL (minimum score 550 paper-based; 213 computer-based; 80 iBT). *Application deadline:* For fall admission, 2/1 for domestic and international students. Applications are processed on a rolling basis. Application fee: $25. Electronic applications accepted. *Expenses: Tuition:* Full-time $6300; part-time $700 per semester hour. *Required fees:* $35 per semester hour. One-time fee: $25. Tuition and fees vary according to course load, degree level and program. *Financial support:* Federal Work-Study, health care benefits, and unspecified assistantships available. Financial award applicants required to submit FAFSA. *Unit head:* Dr. Susan Stevens, Chair, Department of Health and Human Performance, 419-434-6739. *Application contact:* Heather Riffle, Assistant Director, Graduate and Professional Studies, 419-434-4640, Fax: 419-434-5517, E-mail: riffle@findlay.edu.

University of Florida, Graduate School, College of Health and Human Performance, Department of Applied Physiology and Kinesiology, Gainesville, FL 32611. Offers athletic training/sport medicine (MS); biobehavioral science (MS, PhD); clinical exercise physiology (MS); exercise physiology (MS, PhD); health and human performance (PhD); human performance (MS). *Degree requirements:* For master's, comprehensive exam, thesis (for some programs); for doctorate, comprehensive exam, thesis/dissertation. *Entrance requirements:* For doctorate, GRE General Test. Additional exam requirements/recommendations for international students: Required—TOEFL (minimum score 550 paper-based; 213 computer-based; 80 iBT), IELTS (minimum score 6).

Electronic applications accepted. *Faculty research:* Cardiovascular disease; basic mechanisms that underlie exercise-induced changes in the body at the organ, tissue, cellular and molecular level; development of rehabilitation techniques for regaining motor control after stroke or as a consequence of Parkinson's disease; maintaining optimal health and delaying age-related declines in physiological function; psychomotor mechanisms impacting health and performance across the life span.

University of Idaho, College of Graduate Studies, College of Education, Department of Movement Sciences, Moscow , ID 83844-2401. Offers athletic training (DAT); movement and leisure sciences (MS); physical education (M Ed, MS). *Faculty:* 11 full-time, 1 part-time/adjunct. *Students:* 30 full-time, 9 part-time. Average age 28. In 2011, 17 master's awarded. *Degree requirements:* For doctorate, thesis/dissertation. *Entrance requirements:* For master's, minimum GPA of 2.8; for doctorate, minimum undergraduate GPA of 2.8, graduate 3.0. *Application deadline:* For fall admission, 8/1 for domestic students; for spring admission, 12/15 for domestic students. Applications are processed on a rolling basis. Application fee: $60. Electronic applications accepted. *Expenses:* Tuition, state resident: full-time $3874; part-time $334 per credit hour. Tuition, nonresident: full-time $16,394; part-time $861 per credit hour. *Required fees:* $2808; $99 per credit hour. Tuition and fees vary according to program. *Financial support:* Research assistantships and teaching assistantships available. Financial award applicants required to submit FAFSA. *Unit head:* Dr. Kathy Browder, Chair, 208-885-2192, E-mail: hperd@uidaho.edu. *Application contact:* Erick Larson, Director of Graduate Admissions, 208-885-4723, E-mail: gadms@uidaho.edu. Web site: http://www.uidaho.edu/ed/movementsciences.

University of Miami, Graduate School, School of Education and Human Development, Department of Kinesiology and Sport Sciences, Program in Exercise Physiology, Coral Gables, FL 33124. Offers exercise physiology (MS Ed, PhD); strength and conditioning (MS Ed). Part-time and evening/weekend programs available. *Faculty:* 4 full-time (1 woman). *Students:* 34 full-time (16 women), 4 part-time (1 woman); includes 15 minority (2 Black or African American, non-Hispanic/Latino; 1 Asian, non-Hispanic/Latino; 11 Hispanic/Latino; 1 Two or more races, non-Hispanic/Latino), 7 international. Average age 28. 48 applicants, 67% accepted, 15 enrolled. In 2011, 9 master's, 5 doctorates awarded. Terminal master's awarded for partial completion of doctoral program. *Degree requirements:* For master's, comprehensive exam (for some programs), thesis optional, special project; for doctorate, thesis/dissertation, qualifying exam. *Entrance requirements:* For master's and doctorate, GRE General Test. Additional exam requirements/recommendations for international students: Required—TOEFL (minimum score 550 paper-based; 80 iBT); Recommended—IELTS (minimum score 6.5). *Application deadline:* For fall admission, 10/15 for international students. Applications are processed on a rolling basis. Application fee: $65. Electronic applications accepted. *Financial support:* In 2011–12, 31 students received support. Health care benefits and unspecified assistantships available. Support available to part-time students. Financial award application deadline: 3/1; financial award applicants required to submit FAFSA. *Faculty research:* Women's health, cardiovascular health, aging, metabolism, obesity. *Unit head:* Dr. Arlette Perry, Department Chairperson, 305-284-3024, Fax: 305-284-5168, E-mail: aperry@miami.edu. *Application contact:* Lois Heffernan, Graduate Admissions Coordinator, 305-284-2167, Fax: 305-284-9395, E-mail: lheffernan@miami.edu.

University of Miami, Graduate School, School of Education and Human Development, Department of Kinesiology and Sport Sciences, Program in Sports Medicine, Coral Gables, FL 33124. Offers athletic training (MS Ed). Part-time and evening/weekend programs available. *Faculty:* 2 full-time (1 woman). *Students:* 5 full-time (2 women); includes 1 minority (Black or African American, non-Hispanic/Latino). Average age 24. 16 applicants, 63% accepted, 3 enrolled. In 2011, 1 master's awarded. *Degree requirements:* For master's, thesis optional, special project. *Entrance requirements:* For master's, GRE General Test. Additional exam requirements/recommendations for international students: Required—TOEFL (minimum score 550 paper-based; 80 iBT); Recommended—IELTS (minimum score 6.5). *Application deadline:* Applications are processed on a rolling basis. Application fee: $65. Electronic applications accepted. *Financial support:* In 2011–12, 5 students received support. Available to part-time students. Application deadline: 3/1; applicants required to submit FAFSA. *Faculty research:* Care, prevention, and treatment of athletic injuries. *Unit head:* Dr. Joseph Signorile, Professor, 305-284-4078, Fax: 305-284-5168, E-mail: jsignorile@miami.edu. *Application contact:* Lois Heffernan, Graduate Admissions Coordinator, 305-284-2167, Fax: 305-284-9395, E-mail: lheffernan@miami.edu.

University of Nebraska at Omaha, Graduate Studies, College of Education, School of Health, Physical Education, and Recreation, Omaha, NE 68182. Offers athletic training (MA); health, physical education, and recreation (MA, MS). Part-time and evening/weekend programs available. *Faculty:* 13 full-time (4 women). *Students:* 37 full-time (15 women), 40 part-time (25 women); includes 4 minority (1 Black or African American, non-Hispanic/Latino; 2 Hispanic/Latino; 1 Two or more races, non-Hispanic/Latino), 2 international. Average age 27. 27 applicants, 67% accepted, 15 enrolled. In 2011, 33 master's awarded. *Degree requirements:* For master's, comprehensive exam, thesis (for some programs). *Entrance requirements:* For master's, minimum GPA of 3.0, statement of purpose, letters of recommendation. Additional exam requirements/recommendations for international students: Required—TOEFL (minimum score 550 paper-based; 213 computer-based; 80 iBT). *Application deadline:* For fall admission, 7/1 priority date for domestic students; for spring admission, 12/1 priority date for domestic students. Applications are processed on a rolling basis. Application fee: $45. Electronic applications accepted. *Financial support:* In 2011–12, 40 students received support, including 25 research assistantships with tuition reimbursements available, 10 teaching assistantships with tuition reimbursements available; fellowships, Federal Work-Study, institutionally sponsored loans, scholarships/grants, tuition waivers (full), and unspecified assistantships also available. Support available to part-time students. Financial award application deadline: 3/1; financial award applicants required to submit FAFSA. *Unit head:* Dr. Dan Blanke, Director, 402-554-2670. *Application contact:* Dr. Kris Berg, 402-554-2341, Fax: 402-554-3143, E-mail: graduate@unomaha.edu.

The University of North Carolina at Chapel Hill, Graduate School, College of Arts and Sciences, Department of Exercise and Sport Science, Chapel Hill, NC 27599. Offers athletic training (MA); exercise physiology (MA); sport administration (MA). *Degree requirements:* For master's, comprehensive exam, thesis. *Entrance requirements:* For master's, GRE General Test, minimum GPA of 3.0. Additional exam requirements/recommendations for international students: Required—TOEFL (minimum score 550 paper-based). Electronic applications accepted. *Faculty research:* Mild head injury in sport, endocrine system's response to exercise, obesity and children, effect of aerobic exercise on cerebral bloodflow in elderly population.

University of Northern Iowa, Graduate College, College of Education, School of Health, Physical Education, and Leisure Services, Program in Athletic Training, Cedar Falls, IA 50614. Offers athletic training (MS); rehabilitation studies (Ed D). Part-time and evening/weekend programs available. *Students:* 13 full-time (9 women), 5 part-time (3 women). 26 applicants, 62% accepted, 6 enrolled. In 2011, 5 degrees awarded. *Degree requirements:* For master's, comprehensive exam. *Entrance requirements:* Additional exam requirements/recommendations for international students: Required—TOEFL (minimum score 550 paper-based; 213 computer-based; 79 iBT). *Application deadline:* For fall admission, 4/1 for international students; for winter admission, 10/1 for international students. Applications are processed on a rolling basis. Application fee: $50 ($70 for international students). Electronic applications accepted. *Expenses:* Tuition, state resident: full-time $7476. Tuition, nonresident: full-time $16,410. *Required fees:* $942. *Financial support:* Unspecified assistantships available. Financial award application deadline: 2/1; financial award applicants required to submit FAFSA. *Unit head:* Jody Brucker, Coordinator, 319-273-6477, Fax: 319-273-5958, E-mail: jody.brucker@uni.edu. *Application contact:* Laurie S. Russell, Record Analyst, 319-273-2623, Fax: 319-273-6792, E-mail: laurie.russell@uni.edu. Web site: http://www.uni.edu/coe/departments/school-health-physical-education-leisure-services/athletic-training.

University of Pittsburgh, School of Health and Rehabilitation Sciences, Master's Programs in Health and Rehabilitation Sciences, Pittsburgh, PA 15260. Offers health and rehabilitation sciences (MS), including clinical dietetics and nutrition, health care supervision and management, health information systems, occupational therapy, physical therapy, rehabilitation counseling, rehabilitation science and technology, sports medicine, wellness and human performance. *Accreditation:* APTA. Part-time and evening/weekend programs available. *Faculty:* 22 full-time (16 women), 4 part-time/adjunct (2 women). *Students:* 144 full-time (91 women), 35 part-time (23 women); includes 23 minority (8 Black or African American, non-Hispanic/Latino; 8 Asian, non-Hispanic/Latino; 3 Hispanic/Latino; 4 Two or more races, non-Hispanic/Latino), 74 international. Average age 28. 399 applicants, 61% accepted, 121 enrolled. In 2011, 86 master's awarded. *Degree requirements:* For master's, comprehensive exam (for some programs), thesis optional. *Entrance requirements:* For master's, minimum GPA of 3.0. Additional exam requirements/recommendations for international students: Required—TOEFL (minimum score 550 paper-based; 213 computer-based; 80 iBT), IELTS (minimum score 6.5). *Application deadline:* For fall admission, 3/1 for international students; for spring admission, 7/31 for international students. Applications are processed on a rolling basis. Application fee: $50. Electronic applications accepted. *Expenses:* Contact institution. *Financial support:* Research assistantships, teaching assistantships, Federal Work-Study, institutionally sponsored loans, traineeships, and unspecified assistantships available. Financial award applicants required to submit FAFSA. *Faculty research:* Assistive technology, seating and wheeled mobility, cellular neurophysiology, low back syndrome, augmentative communication. *Total annual research expenditures:* $7.8 million. *Unit head:* Dr. Clifford E. Brubaker, Dean, 412-383-6560, Fax: 412-383-6535, E-mail: cliffb@pitt.edu. *Application contact:* Shameem Gangjee, Director of Admissions, 412-383-6558, Fax: 412-383-6535, E-mail: admissions@shrs.pitt.edu. Web site: http://www.shrs.pitt.edu/.

The University of Tennessee, Graduate School, College of Education, Health and Human Sciences, Department of Exercise, Sport, and Leisure Studies, Program in Exercise Science, Knoxville, TN 37996. Offers biomechanics/sports medicine (MS, PhD); exercise physiology (MS, PhD). *Accreditation:* CEPH (one or more programs are accredited). Part-time programs available. *Degree requirements:* For master's, thesis optional. *Entrance requirements:* For master's, minimum GPA of 2.7. Additional exam requirements/recommendations for international students: Required—TOEFL. Electronic applications accepted. *Expenses:* Tuition, state resident: full-time $8332; part-time $464 per credit hour. Tuition, nonresident: full-time $25,174; part-time $1400 per credit hour. *Required fees:* $1162; $56 per credit hour. Tuition and fees vary according to program.

The University of Tennessee at Chattanooga, Graduate School, College of Health, Education and Professional Studies, Department of Health and Human Performance, Chattanooga, TN 37403. Offers athletic training (MSAT); health and human performance (MS). *Faculty:* 6 full-time (1 woman), 1 (woman) part-time/adjunct. *Students:* 43 full-time (31 women), 3 part-time (2 women); includes 6 minority (4 Black or African American, non-Hispanic/Latino; 2 Hispanic/Latino), 1 international. Average age 25. 11 applicants, 64% accepted, 4 enrolled. In 2011, 17 degrees awarded. *Degree requirements:* For master's, thesis or alternative, clinical rotations. *Entrance requirements:* For master's, GRE General Test or MAT, minimum GPA of 2.75 overall or 3.0 in last 60 hours; CPR and First Aid certification. Additional exam requirements/recommendations for international students: Required—TOEFL (minimum score 550 paper-based; 213 computer-based; 79 iBT), IELTS (minimum score 6). *Application deadline:* For fall admission, 8/1 priority date for domestic students, 6/1 for international students; for spring admission, 12/1 priority date for domestic students, 10/1 for international students. Applications are processed on a rolling basis. Application fee: $35. Electronic applications accepted. *Expenses:* Tuition, state resident: full-time $6472; part-time $359 per credit hour. Tuition, nonresident: full-time $20,006; part-time $1111 per credit hour. *Required fees:* $1320; $160 per credit hour. *Financial support:* Career-related internships or fieldwork, scholarships/grants, and unspecified assistantships available. Support available to part-time students. *Faculty research:* Therapeutic exercise, lumbar spine biomechanics, physical activity epidemiology, functional rehabilitation outcomes, metabolic health. *Unit head:* Dr. Leroy Fanning, Head, 423-425-4432, Fax: 423-425-4457, E-mail: gatp@utc.edu. *Application contact:* Dr. Jerald Ainsworth, Dean of Graduate Studies, 423-425-4478, Fax: 423-425-5223, E-mail: jerald-ainsworth@utc.edu. Web site: https://www.utc.edu/Academic/HealthAndHumanPerformance/.

University of Wisconsin–La Crosse, Office of University Graduate Studies, College of Science and Health, Department of Exercise and Sport Science, Program in Human Performance, La Crosse, WI 54601-3742. Offers applied sport science (MS); strength and conditioning (MS). Part-time programs available. *Faculty:* 4 full-time (1 woman). *Students:* 18 full-time (7 women), 6 part-time (3 women); includes 1 minority (Hispanic/Latino), 1 international. Average age 24. 32 applicants, 66% accepted, 13 enrolled. In 2011, 10 master's awarded. *Degree requirements:* For master's, comprehensive exam (for some programs), thesis optional. *Entrance requirements:* For master's, GRE, course work in anatomy, physiology, biomechanics, and exercise physiology. Additional exam requirements/recommendations for international students: Required—TOEFL (minimum score 550 paper-based; 213 computer-based; 79 iBT). *Application deadline:* For fall admission, 2/1 priority date for domestic students, 2/1 for international students. Application fee: $56. Electronic applications accepted. *Expenses:* Tuition, state resident: full-time $8391; part-time $481.17 per credit. Tuition, nonresident: full-time $17,850; part-time $1006.68 per credit. *Required fees:* $2 per credit. $18.25 per semester. Tuition and fees vary according to course load, program, reciprocity agreements and student level. *Financial support:* Federal Work-Study, scholarships/grants, health care benefits, and tuition waivers (partial) available. Support available to part-time students. Financial award application deadline: 3/15; financial award applicants required to submit FAFSA. *Faculty research:* Anaerobic metabolism, power development, strength training, biomechanics, athletic performance. *Unit head:* Dr. Glenn Wright, Director, 608-785-8689, Fax: 608-785-8172, E-mail: wright.glen@uwlax.edu. *Application contact:* Kathryn Kiefer, Director of Admissions, 608-785-8939, E-mail: admissions@uwlax.edu. Web site: http://www.uwlax.edu/sah/ess/hp/.

Virginia Commonwealth University, Graduate School, School of Education, Department of Health and Human Performance, Program in Athletic Training, Richmond, VA 23284-9005. Offers MSAT. Electronic applications accepted. *Expenses:* Tuition, state resident: full-time $9133; part-time $507 per credit. Tuition, nonresident:

full-time $18,777; part-time $1043 per credit. *Required fees:* $77 per credit. Tuition and fees vary according to degree level, campus/location, program and student level.

Weber State University, Jerry and Vickie Moyes College of Education, Program in Athletic Training, Ogden, UT 84408-1001. Offers MSAT. Part-time programs available. *Degree requirements:* For master's, thesis. *Entrance requirements:* For master's, GRE (if GPA less than 3.0), physical, immunizations. Additional exam requirements/recommendations for international students: Required—TOEFL (minimum score 550 paper-based; 213 computer-based). *Faculty research:* Pedagogy, heat illness, electrical stimulation.

West Chester University of Pennsylvania, College of Health Sciences, Department of Kinesiology, West Chester, PA 19383. Offers exercise/sport physiology (MS), including athletic training; physical education (MS); sport management and athletics (MPA). *Faculty:* 7 part-time/adjunct (3 women). *Students:* 19 full-time (10 women), 14 part-time (7 women); includes 5 minority (all Black or African American, non-Hispanic/Latino). Average age 26. 37 applicants, 35% accepted, 10 enrolled. In 2011, 12 degrees awarded. *Degree requirements:* For master's, thesis or report (MS), 2 internships (MPA). *Entrance requirements:* For master's, GRE with minimum score of 1000 (for MS), 2 letters of recommendation, transcripts, and statement of professional goals (for MS); 2 letters of reference, resume, career goal statement (for MPA). Additional exam requirements/recommendations for international students: Required—TOEFL (minimum score 550 paper-based; 213 computer-based; 80 iBT). *Application deadline:* For fall admission, 4/15 priority date for domestic students, 3/15 for international students; for spring admission, 10/15 priority date for domestic students, 9/1 for international students. Applications are processed on a rolling basis. Application fee: $45. Electronic applications accepted. *Expenses:* Tuition, state resident: full-time $7488; part-time $416 per credit. Tuition, nonresident: full-time $11,232; part-time $624 per credit. *Required fees:* $1784.64; $67.59 per credit. Tuition and fees vary according to program. *Financial support:* Unspecified assistantships available. Support available to part-time students. Financial award application deadline: 2/15; financial award applicants required to submit FAFSA. *Faculty research:* Metabolism during exercise, biomechanics, rating of perceived exertion, motor learning. *Unit head:* Dr. Frank Fry, Chair and Graduate Coordinator for the MS in General Physical Education Program, 610-436-2610, Fax: 610-436-2860, E-mail: ffry@wcupa.edu. *Application contact:* Dr. Sheri Melton, Graduate Coordinator for the Exercise and Sport Physiology Programs, 610-436-2260, Fax: 610-436-2860, E-mail: smelton@wcupa.edu. Web site: http://www.wcupa.edu/_academics/sch_shs.hpe/.

Western Michigan University, Graduate College, College of Education and Human Development, Department of Health, Physical Education and Recreation, Kalamazoo, MI 49008. Offers exercise and sports medicine (MS), including athletic training, exercise physiology; physical education (MA), including coaching sport performance, pedagogy, special physical education, sport management.

West Virginia University, School of Physical Education, Morgantown, WV 26506. Offers athletic coaching education (MS); athletic training (MS); physical education/teacher education (MS, PhD), including curriculum and instruction (PhD), motor behavior (PhD), physical education supervision (PhD); sport and exercise psychology (PhD); sport management (MS). *Degree requirements:* For doctorate, comprehensive exam, thesis/dissertation, oral exam. *Entrance requirements:* For master's, GRE or MAT, minimum GPA of 3.0; for doctorate, GRE General Test or MAT, minimum GPA of 3.5. Additional exam requirements/recommendations for international students: Required—TOEFL (minimum score 550 paper-based; 213 computer-based). Electronic applications accepted. *Faculty research:* Sport psychosociology, teacher education, exercise psychology, counseling.

West Virginia Wesleyan College, Department of Exercise Science, Buckhannon, WV 26201. Offers athletic training (MS).

Exercise and Sports Science

American Public University System, AMU/APU Graduate Programs, Charles Town, WV 25414. Offers accounting (MBA, MS); administration and supervision (M Ed); criminal justice (MA); emergency and disaster management (MA); entrepreneurship (MBA); environmental policy and management (MS), including environmental planning, environmental sustainability, fish and wildlife management, general (MA, MS), global environmental management; finance (MBA); general (MBA); global business management (MBA); guidance and counseling (M Ed); history (MA), including American history, ancient and classical history, European history, global history, military and diplomatic history, public history; homeland security (MA); homeland security resource allocation (MBA); humanities (MA); information technology (MS), including digital forensics, enterprise software development, information assurance and security, IT project management; information technology management (MBA); intelligence studies (MA), including criminal intelligence, general (MA, MS), homeland security, intelligence analysis, intelligence collection, intelligence operations, terrorism studies; international relations and conflict resolution (MA), including comparative and security issues, conflict resolution, international and transnational security issues, peacekeeping; legal studies (MA); management (MA), including defense management, general (MA, MS), human resource management, organizational leadership, public administration, reverse logistics, strategic consulting; marketing (MBA); military history (MA), including American military history, American revolution, civil war, war since 1946, World War II; military studies (MA), including air warfare, asymmetrical warfare, joint warfare, land warfare, naval warfare, strategic leadership; national security studies (MA), including general (MA, MS), homeland security, regional security studies, security and intelligence analysis, terrorism studies; nonprofit management (MBA); political science (MA), including American politics and government, comparative government and development, public policy; psychology (MA); public administration (MA, MPA), including disaster management (MPA), environmental policy (MA), health policy (MPA), human resources (MPA), national security (MPA), organizational management (MPA), security management (MPA); public health (MA, MPH), including emergency management (MPH), environmental health (MPH), public administration (MA); reverse logistics management (MA); security management (MA); space studies (MS), including aerospace science, planetary science; sports and health sciences (MS); sports management (MS), including coaching theory and strategy, sports administration; teaching (M Ed), including curriculum and instruction for elementary teachers, elementary, elementary reading, English language learners, instructional leadership, online learning, secondary social sciences, special education; transportation and logistics management (MA), including maritime engineering management. Programs offered via distance learning only. Part-time and evening/weekend programs available. Postbaccalaureate distance learning degree programs offered (no on-campus study). *Faculty:* 445 full-time (241 women), 1,360 part-time/adjunct (617 women). *Students:* 688 full-time (338 women), 10,168 part-time (3,706 women); includes 3,130 minority (1,007 Black or African American, non-Hispanic/Latino; 103 American Indian or Alaska Native, non-Hispanic/Latino; 825 Asian, non-Hispanic/Latino; 810 Hispanic/Latino; 51 Native Hawaiian or other Pacific Islander, non-Hispanic/Latino; 334 Two or more races, non-Hispanic/Latino), 134 international. Average age 35. In 2011, 2,386 master's awarded. *Degree requirements:* For master's, comprehensive exam or practicum. *Entrance requirements:* For master's, official transcript showing earned bachelor's degree from institution accredited by recognized accrediting body. Additional exam requirements/recommendations for international students: Required—TOEFL (minimum score 550 paper-based; 213 computer-based), IELTS (minimum score 6.5). *Application deadline:* Applications are processed on a rolling basis. Application fee: $0. Electronic applications accepted. *Expenses: Tuition:* Part-time $325 per credit hour. *Financial support:* Applicants required to submit FAFSA. *Faculty research:* Military history, criminal justice, management performance, national security. *Unit head:* Dr. Karan Powell, Executive Vice President and Provost, 877-468-6268, Fax: 304-724-3780. *Application contact:* Terry Grant, Vice President of Enrollment Management, 877-468-6268, Fax: 304-724-3780, E-mail: info@apus.edu. Web site: http://www.apus.edu.

American University, College of Arts and Sciences, School of Education, Teaching, and Health, Program in Health Promotion Management, Washington, DC 20016-8001. Offers MS, Certificate. *Students:* 20 full-time (17 women), 30 part-time (23 women); includes 5 minority (2 Black or African American, non-Hispanic/Latino; 1 Asian, non-Hispanic/Latino; 1 Hispanic/Latino; 1 Two or more races, non-Hispanic/Latino), 1 international. Average age 28. 35 applicants, 69% accepted, 15 enrolled. In 2011, 11 master's awarded. *Degree requirements:* For master's, comprehensive exam, thesis or alternative, tools of research. *Entrance requirements:* For master's, GRE, interview (recommended). Application fee: $80. *Expenses: Tuition:* Full-time $24,264; part-time $1348 per credit hour. *Required fees:* $430. Tuition and fees vary according to course load and program. *Unit head:* Dr. Sarah Irvine-Belson, Director, 202-885-3714, Fax: 202-885-1187, E-mail: educate@american.edu. *Application contact:* Kathleen Clowery, Director, Graduate Admissions, 202-885-3621, Fax: 202-885-1505, E-mail: clowery@american.edu. Web site: http://www.american.edu/cas/seth/.

Appalachian State University, Cratis D. Williams Graduate School, Department of Health, Leisure, and Exercise Science, Boone, NC 28608. Offers exercise science (MS), including clinical exercise physiology, research, strength and conditioning. *Faculty:* 22 full-time (5 women), 3 part-time/adjunct (1 woman). *Students:* 28 full-time (14 women), 2 part-time (0 women); includes 2 minority (1 Asian, non-Hispanic/Latino; 1 Hispanic/Latino). 54 applicants, 50% accepted, 14 enrolled. In 2011, 14 master's awarded. *Degree requirements:* For master's, comprehensive exam, thesis optional. *Entrance requirements:* For master's, GRE General Test, 3 letters of recommendation. Additional exam requirements/recommendations for international students: Required—TOEFL (minimum score 570 paper-based; 230 computer-based; 79 iBT), IELTS (minimum score 6.5). *Application deadline:* For fall admission, 3/1 priority date for domestic students, 2/1 for international students; for spring admission, 11/1 for domestic students, 7/1 for international students. Applications are processed on a rolling basis. Application fee: $55. Electronic applications accepted. *Expenses:* Tuition, state resident: full-time $4040; part-time $180 per semester hour. Tuition, nonresident: full-time $15,900; part-time $760 per semester hour. *Required fees:* $2500; $20 per semester hour. Tuition and fees vary according to campus/location. *Financial support:* In 2011–12, 20 research assistantships (averaging $9,500 per year) were awarded; career-related internships or fieldwork, Federal Work-Study, scholarships/grants, and unspecified assistantships also available. Financial award application deadline: 4/1; financial award applicants required to submit FAFSA. *Faculty research:* Exercise immunology, biomechanics, exercise and chronic disease, muscle damage, strength and conditioning. *Total annual research expenditures:* $1 million. *Unit head:* Dr. Paul Gaskill, Head, 828-262-6336, E-mail: gaskillpl@appstate.edu. *Application contact:* Dr. Jeff McBride, Director, 828-262-7148, E-mail: mcbridejm@appstate.edu. Web site: http://www.hles.appstate.edu.

Arizona State University, College of Nursing and Health Innovation, Phoenix, AZ 85004. Offers advanced nursing practice (DNP); child/family mental health nurse practitioner (Graduate Certificate); clinical research management (MS); community and public health practice (Graduate Certificate); community health (MS); exercise and wellness (MS), including exercise and wellness; family nurse practitioner (Graduate Certificate); healthcare innovation (MHI); international health for healthcare (Graduate Certificate); kinesiology (MS, PhD); nursing (MS, Graduate Certificate); nursing and healthcare innovation (PhD); nutrition (MS); physical activity nutrition and wellness (PhD), including physical activity, nutrition and wellness; public health (MPH); regulatory science and health safety (MS). *Accreditation:* AACN. Postbaccalaureate distance learning degree programs offered (minimal on-campus study). *Degree requirements:* For master's, comprehensive exam (for some programs), thesis (for some programs), interactive Program of Study (iPOS) submitted before completing 50 percent of required credit hours; for doctorate, comprehensive exam, thesis/dissertation, interactive Program of Study (iPOS) submitted before completing 50 percent of required credit hours. *Entrance requirements:* For master's and doctorate, GRE, minimum GPA of 3.0 or equivalent in last 2 years of work leading to bachelor's degree. Additional exam requirements/recommendations for international students: Required—TOEFL (minimum score 80 iBT), TOEFL, IELTS, or Pearson Test of English. Electronic applications accepted. *Expenses:* Contact institution.

Arkansas State University, Graduate School, College of Education, Department of Health, Physical Education, and Sport Sciences, Jonesboro, State University, AR 72467. Offers exercise science (MS); physical education (MSE, SCCT); sports administration (MS). Part-time programs available. *Faculty:* 9 full-time (3 women). *Students:* 22 full-time (8 women), 22 part-time (9 women); includes 6 minority (5 Black or African American, non-Hispanic/Latino; 1 Hispanic/Latino), 9 international. Average age 25. 44 applicants, 70% accepted, 20 enrolled. In 2011, 11 master's awarded. *Degree requirements:* For master's, comprehensive exam, thesis or alternative; for SCCT, comprehensive exam. *Entrance requirements:* For master's, GRE General Test or MAT, appropriate bachelor's degree, official transcripts, immunization records, statement of goals, letters of recommendation; for SCCT, GRE General Test or MAT, interview, master's degree, official transcript, immunization records. Additional exam requirements/recommendations for international students: Required—TOEFL (minimum score 550 paper-based; 213 computer-based; 79 iBT), IELTS (minimum score 6), Pearson Test of English Academic (minimum score 56). *Application deadline:* For fall admission, 7/1 for domestic and international students; for spring admission, 11/15 for domestic students, 11/14 for international students. Applications are processed on a rolling basis. Application fee: $30 ($40 for international students). Electronic applications accepted. *Expenses:* Tuition, state resident: full-time $4044; part-time $225 per credit hour. Tuition, nonresident: full-time $8087; part-time $449 per credit hour. *Required fees:* $936; $52 per credit hour. $25 per term. One-time fee: $30. Tuition and fees vary according to course load and program. *Financial support:* In 2011–12, 20 students received support. Teaching assistantships, career-related internships or fieldwork, scholarships/grants, and unspecified assistantships available. Financial award application deadline: 7/1; financial award applicants required to submit FAFSA. *Unit head:* Dr. Jim Stillwell, Chair, 870-972-3066, Fax: 870-972-3096, E-mail: jstillwel@astate.edu. *Application contact:* Dr. Andrew Sustich, Dean of the Graduate School, 870-972-3029, Fax: 870-972-3857, E-mail: sustich@astate.edu. Web site: http://www.astate.edu/a/education/hpess/index.dot.

Armstrong Atlantic State University, School of Graduate Studies, Program in Sports Medicine, Savannah, GA 31419-1997. Offers sports health sciences (MSSM). Part-time programs available. *Faculty:* 3 full-time (1 woman), 1 part-time/adjunct (0 women). *Students:* 17 full-time (8 women), 8 part-time (5 women); includes 5 minority (1 Black or African American, non-Hispanic/Latino; 3 Hispanic/Latino; 1 Two or more races, non-Hispanic/Latino), 2 international. Average age 25. 26 applicants, 50% accepted, 11 enrolled. In 2011, 8 master's awarded. *Degree requirements:* For master's, comprehensive exam, thesis optional, project. *Entrance requirements:* For master's, GRE General Test, MAT, GMAT, minimum GPA of 2.5. Additional exam requirements/recommendations for international students: Required—TOEFL (minimum score 523 paper-based; 193 computer-based). *Application deadline:* For fall admission, 7/1 priority date for domestic students, 5/1 for international students; for spring admission, 11/15 priority date for domestic students, 9/15 for international students. Application fee: $30. *Expenses:* Tuition, state resident: full-time $3402. Tuition, nonresident: full-time $12,636. *Financial support:* In 2011–12, research assistantships with full tuition reimbursements (averaging $5,000 per year) were awarded; scholarships/grants, tuition waivers (full), and unspecified assistantships also available. Financial award applicants required to submit FAFSA. *Unit head:* Dr. James Streater, Department Head, 912-921-2548, Fax: 912-344-3490, E-mail: sandy.streater@armstrong.edu. *Application contact:* Brian Riemann, Graduate Coordinator, 912-344-2934, Fax: 912-344-3490, E-mail: brian.riemann@armstrong.edu. Web site: http://www.sportsmedicine.armstrong.edu/.

Ashland University, Dwight Schar College of Education, Department of Sport Sciences, Ashland, OH 44805-3702. Offers adapted physical education (M Ed); applied exercise science (M Ed); sport education (M Ed); sport management (M Ed). Part-time programs available. *Faculty:* 11 full-time (5 women). *Students:* 15 full-time (1 woman), 21 part-time (9 women); includes 4 minority (2 Black or African American, non-Hispanic/Latino; 1 Hispanic/Latino; 1 Two or more races, non-Hispanic/Latino), 1 international. Average age 29. In 2011, 20 master's awarded. *Degree requirements:* For master's, practicum, inquiry seminar, thesis, or internship. *Entrance requirements:* For master's, teaching certificate or license, bachelor's degree, minimum cumulative GPA of 2.75. Additional exam requirements/recommendations for international students: Required—TOEFL. *Application deadline:* For fall admission, 8/27 for domestic students; for spring admission, 1/15 for domestic students. Applications are processed on a rolling basis. Application fee: $30. *Expenses: Tuition:* Full-time $5580; part-time $465 per credit hour. *Financial support:* In 2011–12, 1 student received support. Teaching assistantships, institutionally sponsored loans, and scholarships/grants available. Financial award application deadline: 4/15. *Faculty research:* Coaching, legal issues, strength and conditioning, sport management rating of perceived exertion, youth fitness, geriatric exercise science. *Unit head:* Dr. Randall F. Gearhart, Chair, 419-289-6198, E-mail: rgearhar@ashland.edu. *Application contact:* Dr. Linda Billman, Director and Chair, Graduate Studies in Education/Associate Dean, 419-289-5369, Fax: 419-289-5331, E-mail: lbillman@ashland.edu.

Auburn University, Graduate School, College of Education, Department of Kinesiology, Auburn University, AL 36849. Offers exercise science (M Ed, MS, PhD); health promotion (M Ed, MS); kinesiology (PhD); physical education/teacher education (M Ed, MS, Ed D, Ed S). *Accreditation:* NCATE. Part-time programs available. *Faculty:* 15 full-time (8 women). *Students:* 60 full-time (30 women), 33 part-time (15 women); includes 17 minority (14 Black or African American, non-Hispanic/Latino; 1 Asian, non-Hispanic/Latino; 2 Hispanic/Latino), 6 international. Average age 27. 116 applicants, 61% accepted, 41 enrolled. In 2011, 48 master's, 4 doctorates awarded. *Degree requirements:* For master's, thesis (for some programs); for doctorate, thesis/dissertation; for Ed S, exam, field project. *Entrance requirements:* For master's, GRE General Test; for doctorate and Ed S, GRE General Test, interview, master's degree. *Application deadline:* For fall admission, 7/7 for domestic students; for spring admission, 11/24 for domestic students. Applications are processed on a rolling basis. Application fee: $50 ($60 for international students). Electronic applications accepted. *Expenses:* Tuition, state resident: full-time $7290; part-time $405 per credit hour. Tuition, nonresident: full-time $21,870; part-time $1215 per credit hour. *International tuition:* $22,000 full-time. *Required fees:* $1402. *Financial support:* Research assistantships, teaching assistantships, and Federal Work-Study available. Support available to part-time students. Financial award application deadline: 3/15; financial award applicants required to submit FAFSA. *Faculty research:* Biomechanics, exercise physiology, motor skill learning, school health, curriculum development. *Unit head:* Dr. Mary E. Rudisill, Head, 334-844-1458. *Application contact:* Dr. George Flowers, Dean of the Graduate School, 334-844-2125.

Austin Peay State University, College of Graduate Studies, College of Behavioral and Health Sciences, Department of Health and Human Performance, Clarksville, TN 37044. Offers health leadership (MS). Part-time and evening/weekend programs available. Postbaccalaureate distance learning degree programs offered (no on-campus study). *Faculty:* 6 full-time (3 women). *Students:* 21 full-time (16 women), 45 part-time (32 women); includes 28 minority (19 Black or African American, non-Hispanic/Latino; 6 Hispanic/Latino; 3 Two or more races, non-Hispanic/Latino). Average age 30. 58 applicants, 86% accepted, 38 enrolled. In 2011, 24 master's awarded. *Degree requirements:* For master's, comprehensive exam, thesis optional. *Entrance requirements:* For master's, GRE General Test, 3 letters of recommendation, minimum undergraduate GPA of 2.5. Additional exam requirements/recommendations for international students: Required—TOEFL (minimum score 500 paper-based; 173 computer-based). *Application deadline:* For fall admission, 8/1 priority date for domestic students. Applications are processed on a rolling basis. Application fee: $25. Electronic applications accepted. *Expenses:* Tuition, state resident: part-time $350 per credit hour. Tuition, nonresident: full-time $20,644; part-time $971 per credit hour. *Required fees:* $1224; $61.20 per credit hour. *Financial support:* In 2011–12, research assistantships with full tuition reimbursements (averaging $5,184 per year) were awarded; career-related internships or fieldwork, Federal Work-Study, institutionally sponsored loans, scholarships/grants, and unspecified assistantships also available. Support available to part-time students. Financial award application deadline: 3/1; financial award applicants required to submit FAFSA. *Unit head:* Dr. Marcy Maurer, Chair, 931-221-6105, Fax: 931-221-7040, E-mail: maurerm@apsu.edu. *Application contact:* Kendra Bryant, Graduate Admissions, 800-844-2778, Fax: 931-221-6188, E-mail: admissionsweb@apsu.edu. Web site: http://www.apsu.edu/hhp/.

Ball State University, Graduate School, College of Applied Science and Technology, Interdepartmental Program in Human Bioenergetics, Muncie, IN 47306-1099. Offers PhD. *Students:* 2 full-time (1 woman), 5 part-time (1 woman), 1 international. 15 applicants, 20% accepted, 2 enrolled. In 2011, 3 degrees awarded. *Degree requirements:* For doctorate, thesis/dissertation. *Entrance requirements:* For doctorate, GRE General Test, interview, minimum graduate GPA of 3.2, resume. Application fee: $50. Tuition and fees vary according to program and reciprocity agreements. *Financial support:* In 2011–12, 8 students received support, including 8 research assistantships with full tuition reimbursements available (averaging $17,359 per year). Financial award application deadline: 3/1. *Unit head:* Dr. Scott Trappe, Director, 765-285-1145, Fax: 765-285-8596. Web site: http://cms.bsu.edu/Academics/CentersandInstitutes/HPL/GraduatePrograms/HumanBioenergetics.aspx.

Barry University, School of Human Performance and Leisure Sciences, Programs in Movement Science, Specialization in Exercise Science, Miami Shores, FL 33161-6695. Offers MS. *Degree requirements:* For master's, comprehensive exam, thesis. *Entrance requirements:* For master's, GRE, minimum GPA of 3.0. Electronic applications accepted. *Faculty research:* Physiological adaptations to exercise.

Baylor University, Graduate School, School of Education, Department of Health, Human Performance and Recreation, Waco, TX 76798. Offers exercise, nutrition and preventive health (PhD); health, human performance and recreation (MS Ed). *Accreditation:* NCATE. Part-time programs available. *Faculty:* 13 full-time (5 women), 3 part-time/adjunct (1 woman). *Students:* 64 full-time (41 women), 28 part-time (10 women); includes 16 minority (5 Black or African American, non-Hispanic/Latino; 1 Asian, non-Hispanic/Latino; 7 Hispanic/Latino; 3 Two or more races, non-Hispanic/Latino), 8 international. 30 applicants, 87% accepted. In 2011, 42 degrees awarded. *Degree requirements:* For master's, thesis optional. *Entrance requirements:* For master's, GRE General Test. *Application deadline:* For fall admission, 4/1 priority date for domestic students; for spring admission, 10/1 for domestic students. Applications are processed on a rolling basis. Application fee: $25. Electronic applications accepted. *Financial support:* In 2011–12, 35 students received support, including 22 teaching assistantships; career-related internships or fieldwork, Federal Work-Study, institutionally sponsored loans, tuition waivers (partial), and recreation supplements also available. *Faculty research:* Behavior change theory, pedagogy, nutrition and enzyme therapy, exercise testing, health planning. *Unit head:* Dr. Glenn Miller, Graduate Program Director, 254-710-4001, Fax: 254-710-3527, E-mail: glenn_miller@baylor.edu. *Application contact:* Eva Berger-Rhodes, Administrative Assistant, 254-710-4945, Fax: 254-710-3870, E-mail: eva_rhodes@baylor.edu. Web site: http://www.baylor.edu/HHPR/.

Benedictine University, Graduate Programs, Program in Clinical Exercise Physiology, Lisle, IL 60532-0900. Offers MS. Part-time programs available. *Faculty:* 1 full-time (0 women), 3 part-time/adjunct (1 woman). *Students:* 5 full-time (2 women), 25 part-time (17 women); includes 5 minority (1 Black or African American, non-Hispanic/Latino; 1 Asian, non-Hispanic/Latino; 3 Hispanic/Latino). Average age 28. 22 applicants, 73% accepted, 12 enrolled. In 2011, 13 master's awarded. *Entrance requirements:* Additional exam requirements/recommendations for international students: Required—TOEFL (minimum score 550 paper-based; 213 computer-based). *Application deadline:* For fall admission, 9/1 for domestic students; for winter admission, 12/1 for domestic students; for spring admission, 2/15 for domestic students. Applications are processed on a rolling basis. Application fee: $40. Electronic applications accepted. *Financial support:* Career-related internships or fieldwork and health care benefits available. Support available to part-time students. *Faculty research:* Protein synthesis cell signaling control, aging. *Unit head:* Dr. Allison Wilson, Director of New Faculty Mentoring Program, 630-829-6520, E-mail: awilson@ben.edu. *Application contact:* Kari Gibbons, Associate Vice President, Enrollment Center, 630-829-6200, Fax: 630-829-6584, E-mail: kgibbons@ben.edu.

Bloomsburg University of Pennsylvania, School of Graduate Studies, College of Science and Technology, Department of Exercise Science, Bloomsburg, PA 17815-1301. Offers clinical athletic training (MS); exercise science (MS). *Degree requirements:* For master's, thesis, practical clinical experience. *Entrance requirements:* For master's, GRE General Test or MAT, minimum QPA of 3.0. Additional exam requirements/recommendations for international students: Required—TOEFL (minimum score 550 paper-based; 213 computer-based; 79 iBT). Electronic applications accepted.

Boise State University, Graduate College, College of Education, Department of Kinesiology, Program in Exercise and Sports Studies, Boise, ID 83725-0399. Offers MS. Part-time programs available. *Degree requirements:* For master's, thesis. *Entrance requirements:* For master's, minimum GPA of 3.0. Electronic applications accepted.

Brigham Young University, Graduate Studies, College of Life Sciences, Department of Exercise Sciences, Provo, UT 84602. Offers athletic training (MS); exercise physiology (MS, PhD); exercise science (MS); health promotion (MS, PhD); physical medicine and rehabilitation (PhD). *Faculty:* 21 full-time (3 women), 3 part-time/adjunct (0 women). *Students:* 17 full-time (10 women), 35 part-time (20 women); includes 4 minority (2 Asian, non-Hispanic/Latino; 1 Hispanic/Latino; 1 Native Hawaiian or other Pacific Islander, non-Hispanic/Latino), 1 international. Average age 29. 28 applicants, 43% accepted, 7 enrolled. In 2011, 14 master's, 1 doctorate awarded. *Degree requirements:* For master's, thesis, oral defense; for doctorate, comprehensive exam, thesis/dissertation, oral defense, oral and written exams. *Entrance requirements:* For master's, GRE General Test, minimum GPA of 3.2 in last 60 hours of course work; for doctorate, GRE General Test, minimum GPA of 3.5 in last 60 hours of course work. Additional exam requirements/recommendations for international students: Required—TOEFL (minimum score 580 paper-based; 237 computer-based; 85 iBT), IELTS (minimum score 7). *Application deadline:* For fall admission, 2/1 for domestic and international students. Application fee: $50. Electronic applications accepted. *Expenses: Tuition:* Full-time $5760; part-time $320 per credit. Tuition and fees vary according to student's religious affiliation. *Financial support:* In 2011–12, 52 students received support, including 15 research assistantships with partial tuition reimbursements available (averaging $5,615 per year), 34 teaching assistantships with partial tuition reimbursements available (averaging $10,106 per year); fellowships, career-related internships or fieldwork, institutionally sponsored loans, scholarships/grants, tuition waivers (partial), unspecified assistantships, and 10 PhD fulltTuition scholarships also available. Financial award application deadline: 3/1. *Faculty research:* Injury prevention and rehabilitation, human skeletal muscle adaptation, cardiovascular health and fitness, lifestyle modification and health promotion. *Total annual research expenditures:* $2,888. *Unit head:* Dr. Gary Mack, Chair, 801-422-2466, Fax: 801-422-0555, E-mail: gary_mack@byu.edu. *Application contact:* Dr. Jeffrey Brent Feland, Graduate Coordinator, 801-422-1182, Fax: 801-422-0555, E-mail: brent_feland@byu.edu. Web site: http://www.exsc.byu.edu.

Brooklyn College of the City University of New York, Division of Graduate Studies, Department of Physical Education and Exercise Science, Brooklyn, NY 11210-2889. Offers exercise science and rehabilitation (MS); physical education (MS), including sports management. Part-time programs available. *Degree requirements:* For master's, comprehensive exam or thesis. *Entrance requirements:* For master's, previous course work in physical education and education, minimum GPA of 3.0, 2 letters of recommendation, essay. Additional exam requirements/recommendations for international students; Required—TOEFL (minimum score 500 paper-based; 173 computer-based; 61 iBT). Electronic applications accepted. *Faculty research:* Exercise physiology, motor learning, sports psychology, women in athletics.

California Baptist University, Program in Kinesiology, Riverside, CA 92504-3206. Offers exercise science (MS); physical education pedagogy (MS); sport management (MS). Part-time and evening/weekend programs available. *Faculty:* 6 full-time (2 women), 1 part-time/adjunct (0 women). *Students:* 42 full-time (20 women); includes 11 minority (6 Black or African American, non-Hispanic/Latino; 2 Asian, non-Hispanic/Latino; 2 Hispanic/Latino; 1 Two or more races, non-Hispanic/Latino), 14 international. Average age 27. 47 applicants, 70% accepted, 18 enrolled. In 2011, 25 master's awarded. *Degree requirements:* For master's, comprehensive exam or thesis. *Entrance requirements:* For master's, minimum undergraduate GPA of 2.75; three recommendations; comprehensive essay; resume; interview. Additional exam requirements/recommendations for international students: Required—TOEFL (minimum score 575 paper-based; 230 computer-based; 89 iBT). *Application deadline:* For fall admission, 8/1 priority date for domestic students, 7/1 for international students; for spring admission, 12/1 priority date for domestic students, 11/1 for international students. Applications are processed on a rolling basis. Application fee: $45. Electronic applications accepted. *Expenses:* Contact institution. *Financial support:* In 2011–12, 2 students received support, including 2 teaching assistantships (averaging $6,450 per year); Federal Work-Study, institutionally sponsored loans, and unspecified assistantships also available. Financial award applicants required to submit FAFSA. *Faculty research:* Musculoskeletal injury and examination, thermoregulation, immune function, carbohydrate oxidation, cardiovascular morbidity and mortality. *Unit head:* Dr. Chuck Sands, Dean, College of Allied Health, 951-343-4619, E-mail: csands@calbaptist.edu. *Application contact:* Dr. Sean Sullivan, Chair, Department of Kinesiology, 951-343-4528, Fax: 951-343-5095, E-mail: ssullivan@calbaptist.edu. Web site: http://www.calbaptist.edu/mskin/.

California State University, Fresno, Division of Graduate Studies, College of Health and Human Services, Department of Kinesiology, Fresno, CA 93740-8027. Offers exercise science (MA); sport psychology (MA). Part-time and evening/weekend programs available. *Degree requirements:* For master's, thesis or alternative. *Entrance requirements:* For master's, GRE General Test, minimum GPA of 2.7. Additional exam requirements/recommendations for international students: Required—TOEFL. Electronic applications accepted. *Faculty research:* Refugee education, homeless, geriatrics, fitness.

California State University, Long Beach, Graduate Studies, College of Health and Human Services, Department of Kinesiology, Long Beach, CA 90840. Offers adapted physical education (MA); coaching and student athlete development (MA); exercise physiology and nutrition (MS); exercise science (MS); individualized studies (MA); kinesiology (MA); pedagogical studies (MA); sport and exercise psychology (MS); sport management (MA); sports medicine and injury studies (MS). Part-time programs available. *Faculty:* 9 full-time (5 women), 5 part-time/adjunct (4 women). *Students:* 48 full-time (27 women), 39 part-time (13 women); includes 38 minority (5 Black or African American, non-Hispanic/Latino; 2 American Indian or Alaska Native, non-Hispanic/Latino; 7 Asian, non-Hispanic/Latino; 18 Hispanic/Latino; 6 Two or more races, non-Hispanic/Latino), 2 international. Average age 28. 214 applicants, 50% accepted, 32 enrolled. In 2011, 69 master's awarded. *Degree requirements:* For master's, oral and written comprehensive exams or thesis. *Entrance requirements:* For master's, GRE General Test, minimum GPA of 2.75 during previous 2 years of course work. *Application deadline:* For fall admission, 6/1 for domestic students. Applications are processed on a rolling basis. Application fee: $55. Electronic applications accepted. *Financial support:* Federal Work-Study, institutionally sponsored loans, and scholarships/grants available. Financial award application deadline: 3/2. *Faculty research:* Pulmonary functioning, feedback and practice structure, strength training, history and politics of sports, special population research issues. *Unit head:* Dr. Sharon R. Guthrie, Chair, 562-985-7487, Fax: 562-985-8067, E-mail: guthrie@csulb.edu. *Application contact:* Dr. Grant Hill, Graduate Advisor, 562-985-8856, Fax: 562-985-8067, E-mail: ghill@csulb.edu.

California University of Pennsylvania, School of Graduate Studies and Research, College of Education and Human Services, Program in Exercise Science and Health Promotion, California, PA 15419-1394. Offers performance enhancement and injury prevention (MS); rehabilitation science (MS); sport psychology (MS); wellness and fitness (MS). Part-time and evening/weekend programs available. Postbaccalaureate distance learning degree programs offered (no on-campus study). *Degree requirements:* For master's, comprehensive exam, thesis optional. *Entrance requirements:* For master's, minimum QPA of 3.0. Additional exam requirements/recommendations for international students: Required—TOEFL (minimum score 550 paper-based; 213 computer-based; 80 iBT). Electronic applications accepted. *Expenses:* Contact institution. *Faculty research:* Reducing obesity in children, sport performance, creating unique biomechanical assessment techniques, Web-based training for fitness professionals, Webcams.

Central Connecticut State University, School of Graduate Studies, School of Education and Professional Studies, Department of Physical Education and Human Performance, New Britain, CT 06050-4010. Offers physical education (MS, Certificate). Part-time and evening/weekend programs available. *Faculty:* 16 full-time (8 women), 30 part-time/adjunct (20 women). *Students:* 22 full-time (7 women), 32 part-time (10 women); includes 1 minority (Two or more races, non-Hispanic/Latino). Average age 28. 27 applicants, 70% accepted, 11 enrolled. In 2011, 19 master's, 1 other advanced degree awarded. *Degree requirements:* For master's, comprehensive exam, thesis or alternative; for Certificate, qualifying exam. *Entrance requirements:* For master's, minimum GPA of 2.7, bachelor's degree in physical education (preferred). Additional exam requirements/recommendations for international students: Required—TOEFL (minimum score 550 paper-based; 213 computer-based). *Application deadline:* For fall admission, 6/1 for domestic students, 5/1 for international students; for spring admission, 11/1 for domestic and international students. Applications are processed on a rolling basis. Application fee: $50. Electronic applications accepted. *Expenses: Tuition, area resident:* Full-time $5137; part-time $482 per credit. Tuition, state resident: full-time $7707; part-time $494 per credit. Tuition, nonresident: full-time $14,311; part-time $494 per credit. *Required fees:* $3865. One-time fee: $62 part-time. *Financial support:* In 2011–12, 8 students received support, including 3 research assistantships; career-related internships or fieldwork, Federal Work-Study, scholarships/grants, and unspecified assistantships also available. Support available to part-time students. Financial award application deadline: 4/15; financial award applicants required to submit FAFSA. *Faculty research:* Exercise science, athletic training, preparation of physical education for schools. *Unit head:* Dr. David Harackiewicz, Chair, 860-832-2155, E-mail: harackiewicz@ccsu.edu. *Application contact:* Patricia Gardner, Associate Director of Graduate Studies, 860-832-2350, Fax: 860-832-2352, E-mail: graduateadmissions@ccsu.edu. Web site: http://www.education.ccsu.edu/Departments/Physical_Education_and_Human_Performance/.

Central Michigan University, College of Graduate Studies, The Herbert H. and Grace A. Dow College of Health Professions, Department of Physical Education and Sport, Mount Pleasant, MI 48859. Offers physical education (MA), including athletic administration, coaching, exercise science, teaching; sport administration (MA). Part-time programs available. *Degree requirements:* For master's, thesis or alternative. Electronic applications accepted. *Faculty research:* Athletic administration and sport management, performance enhancing substance use in sport, computer applications for sport managers, mental skill development for ultimate performance, teaching methods.

Central Michigan University, College of Graduate Studies, The Herbert H. and Grace A. Dow College of Health Professions, School of Health Sciences, Mount Pleasant, MI 48859. Offers exercise science (MA); health administration (DHA). Part-time and evening/weekend programs available. Postbaccalaureate distance learning degree programs offered (no on-campus study). *Degree requirements:* For doctorate, comprehensive exam, thesis/dissertation. *Entrance requirements:* For doctorate, accredited master's or doctoral degree, 5 years related work experience. Electronic applications accepted.

Central Washington University, Graduate Studies and Research, College of Education and Professional Studies, Department of Nutrition, Exercise and Health Services, Ellensburg, WA 98926. Offers exercise science (MS); nutrition (MS). Part-time programs available. *Faculty:* 19 full-time (7 women). *Students:* 15 full-time (11 women), 1 part-time (0 women). 20 applicants, 55% accepted, 11 enrolled. In 2011, 16 master's awarded. *Degree requirements:* For master's, thesis or alternative. *Entrance requirements:* For master's, GRE, minimum GPA of 3.0; writing sample (for exercise students). Additional exam requirements/recommendations for international students: Required—TOEFL (minimum score 550 paper-based; 213 computer-based; 79 iBT). *Application deadline:* For fall admission, 2/1 priority date for domestic students; for winter admission, 10/1 for domestic students; for spring admission, 1/1 for domestic students. Applications are processed on a rolling basis. Application fee: $50. Electronic applications accepted. *Expenses:* Tuition, state resident: full-time $8112; part-time $270 per credit. Tuition, nonresident: full-time $18,069; part-time $602 per credit. *Required fees:* $924. *Financial support:* In 2011–12, 2 research assistantships (averaging $9,234 per year), 15 teaching assistantships with full and partial tuition reimbursements (averaging $9,234 per year) were awarded; Federal Work-Study and health care benefits also available. Financial award application deadline: 3/1; financial award applicants required to submit FAFSA. *Unit head:* Dr. Leo D'Acquisto, Graduate Coordinator, 509-963-1911. *Application contact:* Justine Eason, Admissions Program Coordinator, 509-963-3103, Fax: 509-963-1799, E-mail: masters@cwu.edu. Web site: http://www.cwu.edu/~nehs/.

Cleveland State University, College of Graduate Studies, College of Education and Human Services, Department of Health, Physical Education, Recreation and Dance, Cleveland, OH 44115. Offers community health education (M Ed); exercise science (M Ed); human performance (M Ed); physical education pedagogy (M Ed); public health (MPH); school health education (M Ed); sport and exercise psychology (M Ed); sports management (M Ed). Part-time programs available. *Faculty:* 7 full-time (4 women), 3 part-time/adjunct (2 women). *Students:* 40 full-time (22 women), 91 part-time (48 women); includes 17 minority (15 Black or African American, non-Hispanic/Latino; 1 Asian, non-Hispanic/Latino; 1 Hispanic/Latino), 17 international. Average age 28. 138 applicants, 80% accepted, 60 enrolled. In 2011, 30 master's awarded. *Degree requirements:* For master's, comprehensive exam, thesis optional. *Entrance requirements:* For master's, GRE General Test or MAT (if undergraduate GPA less than 2.75), minimum undergraduate GPA of 2.75. Additional exam requirements/recommendations for international students: Required—TOEFL (minimum score 525 paper-based; 197 computer-based), IELTS (minimum score 6). *Application deadline:* For fall admission, 7/15 priority date for domestic students; for spring admission, 12/15 priority date for domestic students. Applications are processed on a rolling basis. Application fee: $30. Electronic applications accepted. *Expenses:* Tuition, state resident: full-time $6416; part-time $494 per credit hour. Tuition, nonresident: full-time $12,074; part-time $929 per credit hour. *Financial support:* In 2011–12, 6 research assistantships with full and partial tuition reimbursements (averaging $3,480 per year), 1 teaching assistantship with full and partial tuition reimbursement (averaging $3,480 per year) were awarded; career-related internships or fieldwork, tuition waivers (full), and unspecified assistantships also available. Financial award application deadline: 3/15. *Faculty research:* Bone density, marketing fitness centers, motor development of disabled, online learning and survey research. *Unit head:* Dr. Sheila M. Patterson, Chairperson, 216-687-4870, Fax: 216-687-5410, E-mail: s.m.patterson@csuohio.edu. *Application contact:* Deborah L. Brown, Interim Assistant Director, Graduate Admissions, 216-523-7572, Fax: 216-687-5400, E-mail: d.l.brown@csuohio.edu. Web site: http://www.csuohio.edu/coehs/departments/hperd.

The College of St. Scholastica, Graduate Studies, Department of Exercise Physiology, Duluth, MN 55811-4199. Offers MA. Part-time programs available. *Faculty:* 3 full-time (0 women). *Students:* 15 full-time (6 women), 2 part-time (0 women); includes 1 minority (Hispanic/Latino). Average age 25. 25 applicants, 76% accepted, 15 enrolled. In 2011, 16 master's awarded. *Degree requirements:* For master's, thesis (for some programs). *Entrance requirements:* For master's, minimum GPA of 2.7. Additional exam requirements/recommendations for international students: Required—TOEFL (minimum score 550 paper-based; 213 computer-based; 79 iBT). *Application deadline:* For fall admission, 8/1 priority date for domestic students, 8/1 for international students; for spring admission, 11/15 priority date for domestic students, 11/15 for international students. Applications are processed on a rolling basis. Application fee: $50. Electronic applications accepted. *Financial support:* In 2011–12, 17 students received support, including 9 teaching assistantships (averaging $1,865 per year); Federal Work-Study and scholarships/grants also available. Support available to part-time students. Financial award applicants required to submit FAFSA. *Faculty research:* Cardiovascular and metabolic responses, cardiorespiratory effects, orthostatic intolerance, lower extremity asymmetry. *Unit head:* Dr. Larry Birnbaum, Director, 218-723-6297, Fax: 218-723-5991. *Application contact:* Lindsay Lahti, Director of Graduate and Extended Studies Recruitment, 218-733-2240, Fax: 218-733-2275, E-mail: gradstudies@css.edu. Web site: http://www.css.edu/Academics/School-of-Health-Sciences/Exercise-Physiology.html.

Colorado State University, Graduate School, College of Applied Human Sciences, Department of Health and Exercise Science, Fort Collins, CO 80523-1582. Offers exercise science and nutrition (MS); health and exercise science (MS); human bioenergetics (PhD). Part-time programs available. *Faculty:* 13 full-time (3 women), 1 part-time/adjunct (0 women). *Students:* 21 full-time (13 women), 13 part-time (6 women); includes 1 minority (Hispanic/Latino), 2 international. Average age 29. 48 applicants, 21% accepted, 7 enrolled. In 2011, 4 master's, 2 doctorates awarded. *Degree requirements:* For master's, thesis; for doctorate, comprehensive exam, thesis/dissertation, mentored teaching. *Entrance requirements:* For master's, GRE General Test, minimum GPA of 3.0; for doctorate, bachelor's or master's degree. Additional exam requirements/recommendations for international students: Required—TOEFL (minimum score 550 paper-based; 213 computer-based; 80 iBT). *Application deadline:* For fall admission, 1/31 priority date for domestic students, 1/31 for international students; for spring admission, 9/30 priority date for domestic students, 9/30 for international students. Application fee: $50. Electronic applications accepted. *Expenses:* Tuition, state resident: full-time $7992. Tuition, nonresident: full-time $19,592. *Required fees:* $1735; $58 per credit. *Financial support:* In 2011–12, 26 students received support, including 10 research assistantships with full tuition reimbursements available (averaging $14,137 per year), 16 teaching assistantships with full tuition reimbursements available (averaging $12,700 per year); fellowships and unspecified assistantships also available. Financial award application deadline: 1/31; financial award applicants required to submit FAFSA. *Faculty research:* Metabolism and metabolic disease, obesity, diabetes, hypertension, physical activity and health across the lifespan, bioenergetics. *Total annual research expenditures:* $2.4 million. *Unit head:* Dr. Richard Gay Israel, Department Head, 970-491-3785, Fax: 970-491-0216, E-mail: richard.israel@colostate.edu. *Application contact:* Robin Noehl, Department Operations, 970-491-7161, Fax: 970-491-0445, E-mail: robin.noehl@colostate.edu. Web site: http://www.hes.cahs.colostate.edu/.

Concordia University, School of Graduate Studies, Faculty of Arts and Science, Department of Exercise Science, Montréal, QC H3G 1M8, Canada. Offers M Sc.

Concordia University Chicago, College of Graduate and Innovative Programs, Program in Human Services, River Forest, IL 60305-1499. Offers human services (MA), including administration, exercise science. Part-time and evening/weekend programs available. *Degree requirements:* For master's, comprehensive exam, thesis. *Entrance requirements:* For master's, minimum GPA of 2.9. Additional exam requirements/recommendations for international students: Required—TOEFL (minimum score 550 paper-based; 195 computer-based). Electronic applications accepted.

Delaware State University, Graduate Programs, College of Education, Health and Public Policy, Department of Sport Sciences, Dover, DE 19901-2277. Offers sport administration (MS). *Entrance requirements:* Additional exam requirements/recommendations for international students: Required—TOEFL (minimum score 550 paper-based). Electronic applications accepted.

Delta State University, Graduate Programs, College of Education, Division of Health, Physical Education, and Recreation, Cleveland, MS 38733-0001. Offers health, physical education, and recreation (M Ed); sport and human performance (MS). Part-time and evening/weekend programs available. *Degree requirements:* For master's, thesis optional. *Entrance requirements:* For master's, GRE General Test or MAT, Class A teaching certificate. *Expenses:* Tuition, state resident: full-time $4702; part-time $294 per credit hour. Tuition, nonresident: full-time $12,516; part-time $760 per credit hour. *Required fees:* $586. *Faculty research:* Blood pressure, body fat, power and reaction time, learning disorders for athletes, effects of walking.

East Carolina University, Graduate School, College of Health and Human Performance, Department of Kinesiology, Greenville, NC 27858-4353. Offers adapted physical education (MA Ed, MS); bioenergetics and exercise science (PhD); biomechanics (MS); exercise physiology (MS); physical activity promotion (MS); physical education (MA Ed, MAT); physical education clinical supervision (Certificate); physical education pedagogy (MA Ed, MS); sport and exercise psychology (MS); sport management (Certificate). *Degree requirements:* For master's, comprehensive exam, thesis optional; for doctorate, comprehensive exam, thesis/dissertation. *Entrance requirements:* For master's, GRE General Test or MAT; for doctorate, GRE. Additional exam requirements/recommendations for international students: Required—TOEFL. *Application deadline:* For fall admission, 2/1 priority date for domestic students, 2/1 for international students. Applications are processed on a rolling basis. Application fee: $50. *Expenses:* Tuition, state resident: full-time $3557; part-time $444.63 per semester hour. Tuition, nonresident: full-time $14,351; part-time $1793.88 per semester hour. *Required fees:* $2016; $252 per semester hour. Part-time tuition and fees vary according to course load, campus/location and program. *Financial support:* Research assistantships with tuition reimbursements and teaching assistantships available. Support available to part-time students. Financial award application deadline: 2/1. *Faculty research:* Diabetes metabolism, pediatric obesity, biomechanics of arthritis, physical activity measurement. *Unit head:* Dr. Stacey Altman, Chair, 252-328-2973, E-mail: altmans@ecu.edu.

Eastern Illinois University, Graduate School, College of Education and Professional Studies, Department of Kinesiology and Sports Studies, Charleston, IL 61920-3099. Offers MS. Part-time programs available. *Expenses:* Tuition, state resident: part-time $279 per credit hour. Tuition, nonresident: part-time $670 per credit hour. *Required fees:* $179.07 per credit hour. $1253 per semester.

Eastern Michigan University, Graduate School, College of Health and Human Services, School of Health Promotion and Human Performance, Programs in Exercise Physiology, Ypsilanti, MI 48197. Offers exercise physiology (MS); sports medicine-biomechanics (MS); sports medicine-corporate adult fitness (MS); sports medicine-exercise physiology (MS). Part-time and evening/weekend programs available. *Students:* 22 full-time (16 women), 42 part-time (18 women); includes 8 minority (4 Black or African American, non-Hispanic/Latino; 2 American Indian or Alaska Native, non-Hispanic/Latino; 1 Hispanic/Latino; 1 Two or more races, non-Hispanic/Latino), 4 international. Average age 30. 59 applicants, 68% accepted, 22 enrolled. In 2011, 20 degrees awarded. *Degree requirements:* For master's, comprehensive exam, thesis or 450-hour internship. *Entrance requirements:* Additional exam requirements/recommendations for international students: Required—TOEFL. *Application deadline:* For fall admission, 8/1 for domestic students, 5/1 for international students; for winter admission, 12/1 for domestic students, 10/1 for international students; for spring admission, 3/15 for domestic students, 3/1 for international students. Application fee: $35. *Expenses:* Tuition, state resident: full-time $10,367; part-time $432 per credit hour. Tuition, nonresident: full-time $20,435; part-time $851 per credit hour. *Required fees:* $39 per credit hour. $46 per semester. One-time fee: $100. Tuition and fees vary according to course level, degree level and reciprocity agreements. *Unit head:* Dr. Steve McGregor, Program Coordinator, 734-487-0090, Fax: 734-487-2024, E-mail: stephen.mcgregor@emich.edu. *Application contact:* Dr. Brenda Riemer, Chair, Graduate Programs, 734-487-0090 Ext. 2745, Fax: 734-487-2024, E-mail: briemer@emich.edu.

Eastern New Mexico University, Graduate School, College of Education and Technology, Department of Health and Physical Education, Portales, NM 88130. Offers physical education (MS), including sport administration, sport science. Part-time programs available. *Degree requirements:* For master's, comprehensive exam, thesis optional. *Entrance requirements:* For master's, minimum GPA of 3.0, 15 hours leveling courses without bachelor's degree in physical education, two references. Additional exam requirements/recommendations for international students: Required—TOEFL (minimum score 550 paper-based; 213 computer-based; 79 iBT), IELTS (minimum score 6). Electronic applications accepted.

Eastern Washington University, Graduate Studies, College of Arts, Letters and Education, Department of Physical Education, Health and Recreation, Cheney, WA 99004-2431. Offers exercise science (MS); sports and recreation administration (MS). *Faculty:* 14 full-time (5 women). *Students:* 28 full-time (9 women), 4 part-time (2 women); includes 4 minority (3 Black or African American, non-Hispanic/Latino; 1 Hispanic/Latino). Average age 29. 50 applicants, 48% accepted, 14 enrolled. In 2011, 7 master's awarded. *Degree requirements:* For master's, comprehensive exam, thesis or alternative. *Entrance requirements:* For master's, minimum GPA of 3.0. *Application deadline:* For fall admission, 4/1 priority date for domestic students; for spring admission, 1/15 for domestic students. Applications are processed on a rolling basis. Application fee: $50. *Financial support:* In 2011–12, 10 teaching assistantships with partial tuition reimbursements (averaging $6,624 per year) were awarded; career-related internships or fieldwork, Federal Work-Study, institutionally sponsored loans, and scholarships/grants also available. Support available to part-time students. Financial award application deadline: 2/1; financial award applicants required to submit FAFSA. *Unit head:* John Cogley, Chair, 509-359-2486, E-mail: john.cogley@mail.ewu.edu. *Application contact:* Dr. Jeni McNeal, Professor of Physical Education, Health and Recreation, 509-359-2872, Fax: 509-359-4833, E-mail: jeni_mcneal@hotmail.com.

East Stroudsburg University of Pennsylvania, Graduate School, College of Health Sciences, Department of Exercise Science, East Stroudsburg, PA 18301-2999. Offers cardiac rehabilitation and exercise science (MS). Part-time and evening/weekend programs available. *Degree requirements:* For master's, comprehensive exam, thesis or alternative, computer literacy. *Entrance requirements:* Additional exam requirements/recommendations for international students: Required—TOEFL (minimum score 560 paper-based; 220 computer-based; 83 iBT).

East Tennessee State University, School of Graduate Studies, College of Education, Department of Kinesiology, Leisure and Sport Sciences, Johnson City, TN 37614. Offers exercise physiology and performance (MA); sport management (MA); sport physiology and performance (PhD), including sport performance, sport physiology. Part-time and evening/weekend programs available. *Faculty:* 10 full-time (1 woman). *Students:* 83 full-time (26 women), 8 part-time (2 women); includes 6 minority (2 Black or African American, non-Hispanic/Latino; 2 Asian, non-Hispanic/Latino; 2 Two or more races, non-Hispanic/Latino), 8 international. Average age 25. 113 applicants, 51% accepted, 57 enrolled. In 2011, 26 master's awarded. Terminal master's awarded for partial completion of doctoral program. *Degree requirements:* For master's, comprehensive exam, thesis optional, thesis or internship; for doctorate, comprehensive exam, thesis/dissertation, 2 semesters of full-time residency. *Entrance requirements:* For master's, GRE General Test, major or minor in physical education or equivalent, interview, minimum GPA of 2.7, resume, three letters of recommendation; for doctorate, GRE General Test, minimum GPA of 3.4 (for applicants with master's degree) or 3.0 (for applicants with bachelor's degree), curriculum vitae or resume, interview, four letters of recommendation. Additional exam requirements/recommendations for international students: Required—TOEFL (minimum score 550 paper-based; 213 computer-based; 79 iBT). *Application deadline:* For fall admission, 6/1 for domestic students, 4/30 for international students; for spring admission, 11/1 for domestic students, 9/30 for international students. Application fee: $35 ($45 for international students). Electronic applications accepted. *Expenses:* Tuition, state resident: full-time $7312; part-time $350 per credit hour. Tuition, nonresident: full-time $18,490; part-time $621 per credit hour. *Required fees:* $63 per credit hour. Tuition and fees vary according to course load and program. *Financial support:* In 2011–12, 52 students received support, including 6 fellowships with full tuition reimbursements available (averaging $17,250 per year), 2 research assistantships with full tuition reimbursements available (averaging $11,250 per year), 14 teaching assistantships with full tuition reimbursements available (averaging $6,000 per year); career-related internships or fieldwork, institutionally sponsored loans, scholarships/grants, and unspecified assistantships also available. Financial award application deadline: 7/1; financial award applicants required to submit FAFSA. *Faculty research:* Methods of training for individual and team sports, enhancing acute sport performance, fatigue management in athletes, risk management, facilities management, motorsport. *Total annual research expenditures:* $500. *Unit head:* Dr. Christopher Ayers, Chair, 423-439-4265, Fax: 423-439-7560, E-mail: ayersc@etsu.edu. *Application contact:* Linda Raines, Graduate Specialist, 423-439-6158, Fax: 423-439-5624, E-mail: raineslt@etsu.edu.

Fairmont State University, Programs in Education, Fairmont, WV 26554. Offers digital media, new literacies and learning (M Ed); education (MAT); exercise science, fitness and wellness (M Ed); leadership studies (M Ed); online learning (M Ed); professional studies (M Ed); reading (M Ed); special education (M Ed). *Accreditation:* NCATE. Part-time and evening/weekend programs available. Postbaccalaureate distance learning degree programs offered. *Faculty:* 16 part-time/adjunct (10 women). *Students:* 103 full-time (72 women), 142 part-time (103 women); includes 11 minority (2 Black or African American, non-Hispanic/Latino; 1 American Indian or Alaska Native, non-Hispanic/Latino; 6 Hispanic/Latino; 2 Two or more races, non-Hispanic/Latino), 2 international. Average age 33. 71 applicants, 85% accepted. In 2011, 58 master's awarded. *Entrance requirements:* For master's, GRE. *Application deadline:* For fall admission, 5/1 for domestic and international students. Applications are processed on a rolling basis. Application fee: $40. *Expenses:* Tuition, state resident: full-time $5900. Tuition, nonresident: full-time $12,596. *Unit head:* Dr. Van O. Dempsey, III, Dean, School of Education, 304-367-4241, Fax: 304-367-4599, E-mail: vdempsey@fairmontstate.edu. Web site: http://www.fairmontstate.edu/graduatestudies/default.asp.

Florida Atlantic University, College of Education, Department of Exercise Science and Health Promotion, Boca Raton, FL 33431-0991. Offers MS. Part-time and evening/weekend programs available. *Faculty:* 9 full-time (3 women), 14 part-time/adjunct (10 women). *Students:* 43 full-time (21 women), 20 part-time (9 women); includes 12 minority (5 Black or African American, non-Hispanic/Latino; 1 Asian, non-Hispanic/Latino; 4 Hispanic/Latino; 2 Two or more races, non-Hispanic/Latino), 2 international. Average age 26. 78 applicants, 51% accepted, 7 enrolled. In 2011, 23 master's awarded. *Degree requirements:* For master's, comprehensive exam, thesis optional. *Entrance requirements:* For master's, GRE General Test, minimum GPA of 3.0 during last 60 hours of course work. Additional exam requirements/recommendations for international students: Required—TOEFL (minimum score 500 paper-based). *Application deadline:* For fall admission, 7/1 priority date for domestic students, 2/15 for international students; for spring admission, 11/1 priority date for domestic students, 7/15 for international students. Applications are processed on a rolling basis. Application fee: $30. *Expenses: Tuition, area resident:* Part-time $343.02 per credit hour. Tuition, state resident: full-time $8232. Tuition, nonresident: full-time $23,931; part-time $997.14 per credit hour. *Financial support:* Research assistantships with partial tuition reimbursements, teaching assistantships with partial tuition reimbursements, and career-related internships or fieldwork available. *Faculty research:* Pulmonary limitations during exercise, metabolism regulation, determinants of performance, age-related change in functional mobility and geriatric exercise, behavioral change aimed at promoting active lifestyles. *Unit head:* Dr. Sue Graves, Chair, 954-236-1261, Fax: 954-236-1259. *Application contact:* Dr. Joseph A. O'Kroy, Graduate Coordinator, 954-236-1266, Fax: 954-236-1259, E-mail: okroy@fau.edu. Web site: http://www.coe.fau.edu/academicdepartments/eshp/.

Florida State University, The Graduate School, College of Human Sciences, Department of Nutrition, Food and Exercise Sciences, Tallahassee, FL 32306-1493. Offers exercise physiology (PhD); nutrition and food science (MS, PhD), including clinical nutrition (MS), food science, human nutrition (PhD), nutrition education and health promotion (MS), nutrition science (MS), sports nutrition (MS); sports sciences (MS). Part-time programs available. *Faculty:* 18 full-time (10 women). *Students:* 88 full-time (56 women), 15 part-time (5 women); includes 24 minority (9 Black or African American, non-Hispanic/Latino; 4 Asian, non-Hispanic/Latino; 10 Hispanic/Latino; 1 Native Hawaiian or other Pacific Islander, non-Hispanic/Latino), 21 international. Average age 26. 172 applicants, 51% accepted, 32 enrolled. In 2011, 38 master's, 7 doctorates awarded. *Degree requirements:* For master's, comprehensive exam (for some programs), thesis optional; for doctorate, thesis/dissertation. *Entrance requirements:* For master's, GRE General Test, minimum upper-division GPA of 3.0; for doctorate, GRE General Test, minimum upper-division GPA of 3.0, MS. Additional exam requirements/recommendations for international students: Required—TOEFL (minimum score 550 paper-based; 80 iBT). *Application deadline:* For fall admission, 7/1 for domestic students, 3/1 for international students; for spring admission, 11/1 for domestic students, 5/1 for international students. Applications are processed on a rolling basis. Application fee: $30. Electronic applications accepted. *Expenses:* Tuition, state resident: full-time $9474; part-time $350.88 per credit hour. Tuition, nonresident: full-time $16,236; part-time $601.34 per credit hour. *Required fees:* $630 per semester. One-time fee: $20. Tuition and fees vary according to course load and campus/location. *Financial support:* In 2011–12, 59 students received support, including fellowships with partial tuition reimbursements available (averaging $10,000 per year), 17 research assistantships with partial tuition reimbursements available (averaging $8,000 per year), 47 teaching assistantships with partial tuition reimbursements available (averaging $8,000 per year); career-related internships or fieldwork, Federal Work-Study, institutionally sponsored loans, scholarships/grants, and unspecified assistantships also available. Financial award application deadline: 1/15; financial award applicants required to submit FAFSA. *Faculty research:* Body composition, functional food, chronic disease and aging response; food safety, food allergy, and safety/quality detection methods; sports nutrition, energy and human performance; strength training, functional performance, cardiovascular physiology, sarcopenia . *Unit head:* Dr. Bahram H. Arjmandi, Professor/Chair, 850-645-1517, Fax: 850-645-5000, E-mail: barjmandi@fsu.edu. *Application contact:* Joseph J. Carroll, Administrative Support Assistant, 850-644-4800, Fax: 850-645-5000, E-mail: jjcarroll@admin.fsu.edu. Web site: http://www.chs.fsu.edu/.

Gardner-Webb University, Graduate School, Department of Physical Education, Wellness, and Sport Studies, Boiling Springs, NC 28017. Offers sport science and pedagogy (MA). Part-time and evening/weekend programs available. *Faculty:* 2 full-time (1 woman). *Students:* 15 part-time (4 women); includes 5 minority (all Black or African American, non-Hispanic/Latino). Average age 25. 11 applicants, 100% accepted, 11 enrolled. In 2011, 3 master's awarded. *Degree requirements:* For master's, comprehensive exam. *Entrance requirements:* For master's, GRE General Test or NTE, PRAXIS, minimum GPA of 2.5. *Application deadline:* For fall admission, 8/1 priority date for domestic students. Applications are processed on a rolling basis. Application fee: $40. Electronic applications accepted. *Expenses: Tuition:* Full-time $6300; part-time $350 per credit hour. *Financial support:* Unspecified assistantships available. *Unit head:* Dr. Ken Baker, Chair, 704-406-4481, Fax: 704-406-4739. *Application contact:* Office of Graduate Admissions, 877-498-4723, Fax: 704-406-3895, E-mail: gradinfo@gardner-webb.edu.

George Mason University, College of Education and Human Development, School of Recreation, Health and Tourism, Manassas , VA 20110. Offers exercise, fitness, and health promotion (MS); sport and recreation studies (MS). *Faculty:* 34 full-time (15 women), 59 part-time/adjunct (32 women). *Students:* 18 full-time (10 women), 25 part-time (11 women); includes 5 minority (2 Black or African American, non-Hispanic/Latino; 1 Asian, non-Hispanic/Latino; 1 Hispanic/Latino; 1 Two or more races, non-Hispanic/Latino). Average age 29. 58 applicants, 60% accepted, 22 enrolled. In 2011, 7 degrees awarded. *Degree requirements:* For master's, thesis (for some programs). *Entrance requirements:* For master's, GRE General Test or MAT, 3 letters of recommendation; official transcripts; expanded goals statement; undergraduate course in statistics and minimum GPA of 3.0 in last 60 credit hours and overall (for MS in sport and recreation studies); baccalaureate degree related to kinesiology, exercise science or athletic training (for MS in exercise, fitness and health promotion). Additional exam requirements/recommendations for international students: Required—TOEFL (minimum score 570 paper-based; 230 computer-based; 88 iBT), IELTS, Pearson Test of English. *Application deadline:* For fall admission, 4/1 priority date for domestic students; for spring admission, 11/1 priority date for domestic students. Application fee: $65 ($80 for international students). Electronic applications accepted. *Expenses:* Tuition, state resident: full-time $8750; part-time $364.58 per credit. Tuition, nonresident: full-time $24,092; part-time $1003.83 per credit. *Required fees:* $2514; $104.75 per credit. *Financial support:* In 2011–12, 7 students received support, including 7 research assistantships with full and partial tuition reimbursements available (averaging $6,675 per year); career-related internships or fieldwork, Federal Work-Study, scholarships/grants, unspecified assistantships, and health care benefits (full-time research or teaching assistantship recipients) also available. Support available to part-time students. Financial award application deadline: 3/1; financial award applicants required to submit FAFSA. *Faculty research:* Informing policy; promoting economic development; advocating stewardship of natural resources; improving the quality of life of individuals, families, and communities at the local, national and international levels. *Total annual research expenditures:* $553,053. *Unit head:* David Wiggins, Director, 703-993-2057, Fax: 703-993-2025, E-mail: dwiggin1@gmu.edu. *Application contact:* Dr. Pierre Rodgers, Associate Professor/Co-Coordinator of Graduate Programs, 703-993-8317, Fax: 703-993-2025, E-mail: prodgers@gmu.edu. Web site: http://rht.gmu.edu/grad/.

George Mason University, College of Health and Human Services, Program in Health Science, Fairfax, VA 22030. Offers MS. *Degree requirements:* For master's, comprehensive exam, thesis optional. *Expenses:* Tuition, state resident: full-time $8750; part-time $364.58 per credit. Tuition, nonresident: full-time $24,092; part-time $1003.83 per credit. *Required fees:* $2514; $104.75 per credit. *Financial support:* Applicants required to submit FAFSA.

The George Washington University, School of Public Health and Health Services, Department of Exercise Science, Washington, DC 20052. Offers MS. *Faculty:* 9 full-time (5 women), 69 part-time/adjunct (40 women). *Students:* 25 full-time (13 women), 17 part-time (15 women); includes 8 minority (4 Black or African American, non-Hispanic/Latino; 1 Asian, non-Hispanic/Latino; 3 Two or more races, non-Hispanic/Latino), 2 international. Average age 27. 41 applicants, 90% accepted, 18 enrolled. In 2011, 25 master's awarded. *Degree requirements:* For master's, comprehensive exam, thesis. *Entrance requirements:* For master's, GRE General Test or MAT. Additional exam requirements/recommendations for international students: Required—TOEFL. *Application deadline:* For fall admission, 4/15 priority date for domestic students, 4/15 for international students; for spring admission, 11/1 for domestic and international students. Applications are processed on a rolling basis. Application fee: $75. *Financial support:* In 2011–12, 12 students received support. Tuition waivers available. Financial award application deadline: 2/15. *Faculty research:* Fitness and cardiac rehabilitation, exercise testing, women in exercise. *Unit head:* Dr. Loretta DiPietro, Chair, 202-994-4910, Fax: 202-994-1420, E-mail: esclxd@gwumc.edu. *Application contact:* Jane Smith, Director of Admissions, 202-994-0248, Fax: 202-994-1860, E-mail: sphhsinfo@gwumc.edu.

Georgia College & State University, Graduate School, College of Health Sciences, Department of Kinesiology, Milledgeville, GA 31061. Offers health promotion (M Ed); human performance (M Ed); kinesiology (MAT); outdoor education (M Ed). *Accreditation:* NCATE (one or more programs are accredited). Part-time and evening/weekend programs available. *Students:* 31 full-time (13 women), 11 part-time (7 women); includes 8 minority (6 Black or African American, non-Hispanic/Latino; 2 Hispanic/Latino), 1 international. Average age 27. 32 applicants, 69% accepted, 16 enrolled. In 2011, 12 master's awarded. *Degree requirements:* For master's, comprehensive exam, thesis optional. *Entrance requirements:* For master's, GRE General Test or MAT, minimum GPA of 2.75 in upper-level undergraduate courses, 2 letters of reference. Additional exam requirements/recommendations for international students: Recommended—TOEFL (minimum score 550 paper-based; 213 computer-based; 79 iBT). *Application deadline:* For fall admission, 7/1 priority date for domestic students, 4/1 for international students; for spring admission, 11/15 priority date for domestic students, 9/1 for international students. Applications are processed on a rolling basis. Application fee: $40. Electronic applications accepted. *Expenses:* Tuition, state resident: full-time $4806; part-time $267 per credit hour. Tuition, nonresident: full-time $17,802; part-time $989 per credit hour. *Required fees:* $936 per semester. Tuition and fees vary according to course load and campus/location. *Financial support:* In 2011–12, 25 research assistantships with full tuition reimbursements were awarded; career-related internships or fieldwork and unspecified assistantships also available. Support available to part-time students. Financial award applicants required to submit FAFSA. *Unit head:* Dr. Lisa Griffin, Interim Chair, 478-445-4072, Fax: 478-445-1790, E-mail: lisa.griffin@gcsu.edu. *Application contact:* 800-342-0471, E-mail: grad-admit@gcsu.edu.

Georgia State University, College of Education, Department of Kinesiology and Health, Program in Exercise Science, Atlanta, GA 30302-3083. Offers MS. *Degree requirements:* For master's, comprehensive exam. *Entrance requirements:* For master's, GRE General Test, minimum GPA of 2.5. *Faculty research:* Aging, exercise metabolism, biomechanics and ergonomics, blood pressure regulation, exercise performance.

Hofstra University, School of Education, Health, and Human Services, Department of Physical Education and Sports Sciences, Hempstead, NY 11549. Offers adventure education (Advanced Certificate); health education (MS), including PK-12 teaching certification; physical education (MA, MS), including adventure education, curriculum (MA), strength and conditioning; sport science (MS), including adventure education (MA, MS), strength and conditioning (MA, MS). Part-time and evening/weekend programs available. *Students:* 81 full-time (34 women), 56 part-time (25 women); includes 12 minority (9 Black or African American, non-Hispanic/Latino; 1 Asian, non-Hispanic/Latino; 2 Hispanic/Latino), 1 international. Average age 27. 52 applicants, 96% accepted, 31 enrolled. In 2011, 80 master's awarded. *Degree requirements:* For master's, one foreign language, electronic portfolio, capstone project, minimum GPA of 3.0. *Entrance requirements:* For master's, interview, 2 letters of recommendation, essay. Additional exam requirements/recommendations for international students: Required—TOEFL (minimum score 550 paper-based; 213 computer-based; 80 iBT). *Application deadline:* Applications are processed on a rolling basis. Application fee: $70 ($75 for international students). Electronic applications accepted. *Expenses: Tuition:* Full-time $18,990; part-time $1055 per credit hour. *Required fees:* $970. Tuition and fees vary according to program. *Financial support:* In 2011–12, 49 students received support, including 19 fellowships with full and partial tuition reimbursements available (averaging $3,216 per year), 3 research assistantships with full and partial tuition reimbursements available (averaging $18,529 per year); Federal Work-Study, institutionally sponsored loans, scholarships/grants, tuition waivers (full and partial), and unspecified assistantships also available. Support available to part-time students. Financial award applicants required to submit FAFSA. *Faculty research:* After school programming, skill development and health behavior, energy expenditures in physical activities, cultural competence and health education, childhood obesity. *Unit head:* Dr. Carol L. Alberts, Chairperson, 516-463-5809, Fax: 516-463-6275, E-mail: hprcla@hofstra.edu. *Application contact:* Carol Drummer, Dean of Graduate Admissions, 516-463-4876, Fax: 516-463-4664, E-mail: gradstudent@hofstra.edu. Web site: http://www.hofstra.edu/education/.

Howard University, Graduate School, Department of Health, Human Performance and Leisure Studies, Washington, DC 20059-0002. Offers exercise physiology (MS); health education (MS); sports studies (MS), including sociology of sports, sports management; urban recreation (MS), including leisure studies. Part-time and evening/weekend programs available. *Degree requirements:* For master's, comprehensive exam, thesis. *Entrance requirements:* For master's, BS in human performance or related field. Additional exam requirements/recommendations for international students: Recommended—TOEFL. Electronic applications accepted. *Faculty research:* Health promotion, cardiovascular hypertension, physical activity, sport and human rights issues.

Humboldt State University, Academic Programs, College of Professional Studies, Department of Kinesiology and Recreation Administration, Arcata, CA 95521-8299. Offers athletic training education (MS); exercise science/wellness management (MS); pre-physical therapy (MS); teaching/coaching (MS). *Students:* 11 full-time (7 women), 10 part-time (6 women); includes 4 minority (1 American Indian or Alaska Native, non-Hispanic/Latino; 2 Hispanic/Latino; 1 Two or more races, non-Hispanic/Latino). Average age 28. 9 applicants, 100% accepted, 6 enrolled. In 2011, 7 master's awarded. *Degree requirements:* For master's, thesis or alternative. *Entrance requirements:* For master's, GMAT, minimum GPA of 2.5. Additional exam requirements/recommendations for international students: Required—TOEFL. *Application deadline:* For fall admission, 6/1 for domestic students; for spring admission, 12/2 for domestic students. Applications are processed on a rolling basis. Application fee: $55. *Expenses:* Tuition, state resident: full-time $6734. Tuition, nonresident: full-time $15,662; part-time $372 per credit. *Required fees:* $903. Tuition and fees vary according to program. *Financial support:* Teaching assistantships, career-related internships or fieldwork, Federal Work-Study, and institutionally sponsored loans available. Financial award application deadline: 3/1; financial award applicants required to submit FAFSA. *Faculty research:* Human performance, adapted physical education, physical therapy. *Unit head:* Dr. Chris Hooper, Chair, 707-826-3853, Fax: 707-826-5451, E-mail: cah3@humboldt.edu. *Application contact:* Dr. Rock Braithwaite, Coordinator, 707-826-4543, Fax: 707-826-5451, E-mail: reb22@humboldt.edu. Web site: http://www.humboldt.edu/kra/.

Indiana State University, College of Graduate and Professional Studies, College of Nursing, Health and Human Services, Department of Physical Education, Terre Haute, IN 47809. Offers adult fitness (MA, MS); coaching (MA, MS); exercise science (MA, MS). *Degree requirements:* For master's, thesis (for some programs). *Entrance requirements:* For master's, minor in physical education. Electronic applications accepted. *Faculty research:* Exercise science.

Indiana University Bloomington, School of Health, Physical Education and Recreation, Department of Kinesiology, Bloomington, IN 47405-7000. Offers adapted physical education (MS); applied sport science (MS); athletic administration/sport management (MS); athletic training (MS); biomechanics (MS); ergonomics (MS); exercise physiology (MS); human performance (PhD), including adapted physical education, biomechanics, exercise physiology, motor learning/control, sport management; motor learning/control (MS); physical activity, fitness and wellness (MS). Part-time programs available. *Faculty:* 28 full-time (11 women). *Students:* 150 full-time (59 women), 22 part-time (9 women); includes 20 minority (12 Black or African American, non-Hispanic/Latino; 1 American Indian or Alaska Native, non-Hispanic/Latino; 1 Asian, non-Hispanic/Latino; 4 Hispanic/Latino; 2 Two or more races, non-

Hispanic/Latino), 33 international. Average age 28. 211 applicants, 60% accepted, 62 enrolled. In 2011, 67 master's, 7 doctorates awarded. Terminal master's awarded for partial completion of doctoral program. *Degree requirements:* For master's, thesis optional; for doctorate, variable foreign language requirement, thesis/dissertation. *Entrance requirements:* For master's, GRE General Test, minimum GPA of 2.8; for doctorate, GRE General Test, minimum graduate GPA of 3.5, undergraduate 3.0. *Application deadline:* For fall admission, 1/1 for international students; for spring admission, 9/1 for international students. Applications are processed on a rolling basis. Application fee: $55 ($65 for international students). *Financial support:* Fellowships, research assistantships with full tuition reimbursements, teaching assistantships with full tuition reimbursements, career-related internships or fieldwork, Federal Work-Study, institutionally sponsored loans, scholarships/grants, tuition waivers (partial), and fee remissions available. Financial award application deadline: 3/1. *Faculty research:* Exercise physiology and biochemistry, sports biomechanics, human motor control, adaptation of fitness and exercise to special populations. *Unit head:* Dr. David M. Koceja, Chairperson, 812-855-5523, Fax: 812-855-3193, E-mail: koceja@indiana.edu. *Application contact:* Kristine M. Wasson, Administrative Assistant for Graduate Studies, 812-855-5523, Fax: 812-855-3193, E-mail: ktanksle@indiana.edu. Web site: http://www.indiana.edu/~kines/.

Indiana University of Pennsylvania, School of Graduate Studies and Research, College of Health and Human Services, Department of Health and Physical Education, MS Program in Sport Science/Exercise Science, Indiana, PA 15705-1087. Offers MS. Part-time programs available. *Faculty:* 10 full-time (6 women). *Students:* 12 full-time (7 women), 4 part-time (2 women), 3 international. Average age 24. 36 applicants, 56% accepted, 11 enrolled. In 2011, 10 master's awarded. *Degree requirements:* For master's, thesis optional. *Entrance requirements:* For master's, 2 letters of recommendation. Additional exam requirements/recommendations for international students: Required—TOEFL (minimum score 540 paper-based; 207 computer-based). *Application deadline:* Applications are processed on a rolling basis. Application fee: $50. Electronic applications accepted. *Expenses:* Tuition, state resident: full-time $7488; part-time $416 per credit. Tuition, nonresident: full-time $11,232; part-time $624 per credit. *Required fees:* $2070; $192.20 per credit. $90 per semester. *Financial support:* In 2011–12, 3 research assistantships (averaging $5,440 per year) were awarded; fellowships also available. Financial award application deadline: 4/15; financial award applicants required to submit FAFSA. *Unit head:* Dr. Robert Kostelnik, 724-357-7645, E-mail: robert.kostelnik@iup.edu. *Application contact:* Dr. Jacqueline Beck, Associate Dean, 724-357-2560, E-mail: jbeck@iup.edu. Web site: http://www.iup.edu/page.aspx?id=12277.

Indiana University of Pennsylvania, School of Graduate Studies and Research, College of Health and Human Services, Department of Health and Physical Education, Program in Sports Science/Sport Studies, Indiana, PA 15705-1087. Offers MS. *Faculty:* 10 full-time (6 women). *Students:* 10 full-time (3 women), 1 part-time (0 women); includes 6 minority (3 Black or African American, non-Hispanic/Latino; 1 American Indian or Alaska Native, non-Hispanic/Latino; 1 Asian, non-Hispanic/Latino; 1 Two or more races, non-Hispanic/Latino). Average age 28. 16 applicants, 75% accepted, 9 enrolled. In 2011, 4 master's awarded. *Entrance requirements:* For master's, MAT. Additional exam requirements/recommendations for international students: Required—TOEFL (minimum score 540 paper-based; 207 computer-based). *Application deadline:* Applications are processed on a rolling basis. Application fee: $50. Electronic applications accepted. *Expenses:* Tuition, state resident: full-time $7488; part-time $416 per credit. Tuition, nonresident: full-time $11,232; part-time $624 per credit. *Required fees:* $2070; $192.20 per credit. $90 per semester. *Financial support:* In 2011–12, 4 research assistantships with full and partial tuition reimbursements (averaging $4,080 per year) were awarded. Financial award application deadline: 4/15; financial award applicants required to submit FAFSA. *Unit head:* Dr. Elaine Blair, Chairperson, 724-357-2770, E-mail: eblair@iup.edu. *Application contact:* Dr. Jacqueline Beck, Associate Dean, 724-357-2560, E-mail: jbeck@iup.edu. Web site: http://www.iup.edu/upper.aspx?id=49407.

Inter American University of Puerto Rico, Metropolitan Campus, Graduate Programs, Program in Physical Education, San Juan, PR 00919-1293. Offers teaching of physical education (MA); training and sport performance (MA). *Degree requirements:* For master's, comprehensive exam. *Entrance requirements:* For master's, GRE or EXADEP, interview. Electronic applications accepted.

Iowa State University of Science and Technology, Program in Diet and Exercise, Ames, IA 50011-1123. Offers MS. *Entrance requirements:* For master's, GRE, minimum GPA of 3.5, 3 letters of recommendation. Additional exam requirements/recommendations for international students: Required—TOEFL (minimum score 550 paper-based; 79 iBT), IELTS (minimum score 6.5). *Financial support:* Unspecified assistantships available. *Unit head:* Ruth Litchfield, Director of Graduate Education, 515-294-9484, Fax: 515-294-6193, E-mail: litch@iastate.edu. *Application contact:* Ruth Litchfield, Application Contact, 515-294-9484, Fax: 515-294-6193, E-mail: litch@iastate.edu. Web site: http://www.hs.iastate.edu/dietandexercise/.

Ithaca College, Division of Graduate and Professional Studies, School of Health Sciences and Human Performance, Program in Exercise and Sport Sciences, Ithaca, NY 14850. Offers MS. Part-time programs available. *Faculty:* 9 full-time (4 women). *Students:* 25 full-time (11 women), 11 part-time (7 women); includes 2 minority (1 Black or African American, non-Hispanic/Latino; 1 Two or more races, non-Hispanic/Latino), 6 international. Average age 24. 86 applicants, 53% accepted, 18 enrolled. In 2011, 19 master's awarded. *Degree requirements:* For master's, comprehensive exam (for some programs), thesis optional. *Entrance requirements:* For master's, GRE General Test, minimum GPA of 3.0. Additional exam requirements/recommendations for international students: Required—TOEFL (minimum score 550 paper-based; 213 computer-based; 80 iBT). *Application deadline:* For fall admission, 3/1 priority date for domestic students, 3/1 for international students. Applications are processed on a rolling basis. Application fee: $40. Electronic applications accepted. *Expenses: Tuition:* Part-time $663 per credit hour. *Required fees:* $663 per credit hour. *Financial support:* In 2011–12, 21 students received support, including 21 teaching assistantships (averaging $12,907 per year); career-related internships or fieldwork, Federal Work-Study, scholarships/grants, and unspecified assistantships also available. Support available to part-time students. Financial award application deadline: 3/1; financial award applicants required to submit CSS PROFILE or FAFSA. *Faculty research:* Coach and athlete behavior and performance, strength and conditioning for athletes, exercise physiology across the age spectrum, psychophysiology, sport psychology. *Unit head:* Dr. Jeff Ives, Chairperson, 607-274-3143, Fax: 607-274-1263, E-mail: gps@ithaca.edu. *Application contact:* Gerard Turbide, Director, Office of Admission, 607-274-3143, Fax: 607-274-1263, E-mail: gps@ithaca.edu. Web site: http://www.ithaca.edu/gps/gradprograms/programsites/ess.

Kean University, College of Education, Program in Exercise Science, Union, NJ 07083. Offers MS. *Faculty:* 16 full-time (10 women). *Students:* 6 full-time (0 women), 17 part-time (8 women); includes 6 minority (3 Black or African American, non-Hispanic/Latino; 1 Asian, non-Hispanic/Latino; 2 Hispanic/Latino), 2 international. Average age 26. 18 applicants, 100% accepted, 7 enrolled. *Degree requirements:* For master's, thesis, research component. *Entrance requirements:* For master's, GRE General Test, minimum GPA of 3.0, interview, 2 letters of recommendation, minimum B average in undergraduate prerequisites, official transcripts, personal statement, interview, resume. Additional exam requirements/recommendations for international students: Required—TOEFL (minimum score 79 iBT). *Application deadline:* For fall admission, 6/1 for domestic and international students; for spring admission, 12/1 for domestic and international students. Applications are processed on a rolling basis. Application fee: $75 ($150 for international students). Electronic applications accepted. *Expenses:* Tuition, state resident: full-time $11,302; part-time $550 per credit. Tuition, nonresident: full-time $15,318; part-time $674 per credit. *Required fees:* $2849; $130 per credit. Tuition and fees vary according to degree level. *Financial support:* In 2011–12, 3 research assistantships with full tuition reimbursements (averaging $3,263 per year) were awarded; unspecified assistantships also available. Financial award applicants required to submit FAFSA. *Unit head:* Dr. Walter D. Andzel, Program Coordinator, 908-737-0662, E-mail: wandzel@kean.edu. *Application contact:* Steven Koch, Admissions Counselor, 908-737-5924, Fax: 908-737-5925, E-mail: skoch@kean.edu. Web site: http://www.kean.edu/KU/Exercise-Science.

Kennesaw State University, College of Health and Human Services, Program in Applied Exercise and Health Science, Kennesaw, GA 30144-5591. Offers MS. Part-time and evening/weekend programs available. *Students:* 9 full-time (4 women), 14 part-time (7 women); includes 6 minority (4 Black or African American, non-Hispanic/Latino; 1 American Indian or Alaska Native, non-Hispanic/Latino; 1 Two or more races, non-Hispanic/Latino), 1 international. Average age 27. 22 applicants, 68% accepted, 8 enrolled. In 2011, 12 master's awarded. *Entrance requirements:* For master's, GRE, resume. Additional exam requirements/recommendations for international students: Required—TOEFL (minimum score 550 paper-based; 218 computer-based; 80 iBT), IELTS (minimum score 6). *Application deadline:* For fall admission, 3/1 for domestic and international students; for winter admission, 10/1 for domestic and international students; for spring admission, 3/1 for domestic and international students. Applications are processed on a rolling basis. Application fee: $60. Electronic applications accepted. *Expenses:* Tuition, state resident: full-time $3000; part-time $250 per semester hour. Tuition, nonresident: full-time $10,836; part-time $903 per semester hour. *Required fees:* $774 per semester. *Financial support:* In 2011–12, 2 research assistantships (averaging $4,000 per year) were awarded. Financial award application deadline: 4/1; financial award applicants required to submit FAFSA. *Unit head:* Dr. J. C. Bradbury, Program Director, 678-797-2369, E-mail: jbradbu2@kennesaw.edu. *Application contact:* Tamara Hutto, Admissions Counselor, 770-420-4377, Fax: 770-423-6885, E-mail: vmarquez@kennesaw.edu.

Kent State University, Graduate School of Education, Health, and Human Services, School of Foundations, Leadership and Administration, Sports Recreation and Management Program, Kent, OH 44242-0001. Offers sport and recreation management (MA); sports studies (MA). *Faculty:* 9 full-time (5 women), 17 part-time/adjunct (8 women). *Students:* 42 full-time (10 women), 16 part-time (6 women); includes 7 minority (4 Black or African American, non-Hispanic/Latino; 3 Asian, non-Hispanic/Latino). 60 applicants, 77% accepted. In 2011, 24 master's awarded. *Degree requirements:* For master's, thesis optional. *Entrance requirements:* For master's, GRE required if undergraduate GPA below 3.0, goals statement, 2 letters of recommendation. Additional exam requirements/recommendations for international students: Required—TOEFL (minimum score 550 paper-based; 213 computer-based; 80 iBT). Application fee: $30 ($60 for international students). *Expenses:* Tuition, state resident: full-time $8136; part-time $452 per credit hour. Tuition, nonresident: full-time $14,292; part-time $794 per credit hour. *Financial support:* In 2011–12, 6 research assistantships (averaging $8,500 per year) were awarded; fellowships, teaching assistantships, Federal Work-Study, scholarships/grants, unspecified assistantships, and 1 administrative assistantship (averaging $8,500 per year) also available. *Unit head:* Mark Lyberger, Coordinator, 330-672-0228, E-mail: mlyberge@kent.edu. *Application contact:* Nancy Miller, Academic Program Coordinator, Office of Graduate Student Services, 330-672-2576, Fax: 330-672-9162, E-mail: ogs@kent.edu.

Kent State University, Graduate School of Education, Health, and Human Services, School of Health Sciences, Program in Exercise Physiology, Kent, OH 44242-0001. Offers athletic training (MS); exercise physiology (MS, PhD). *Faculty:* 10 full-time (5 women), 1 part-time/adjunct (0 women). *Students:* 39 full-time (19 women), 12 part-time (3 women); includes 3 minority (2 Asian, non-Hispanic/Latino; 1 Hispanic/Latino). 63 applicants, 60% accepted. In 2011, 20 master's, 3 doctorates awarded. *Degree requirements:* For doctorate, comprehensive exam, thesis/dissertation. *Entrance requirements:* For master's, GRE, 2 letters of reference, goals statement; for doctorate, GRE, 2 letters of reference, goals statement, minimum master's-level GPA of 3.0. Additional exam requirements/recommendations for international students: Required—TOEFL (minimum score 550 paper-based; 213 computer-based; 80 iBT). Application fee: $30 ($60 for international students). *Expenses:* Tuition, state resident: full-time $8136; part-time $452 per credit hour. Tuition, nonresident: full-time $14,292; part-time $794 per credit hour. *Financial support:* In 2011–12, 4 fellowships (averaging $8,500 per year), 12 research assistantships (averaging $11,417 per year) were awarded; teaching assistantships, Federal Work-Study, scholarships/grants, and unspecified assistantships also available. *Unit head:* Ellen Glickman, Coordinator, 330-672-2930, E-mail: eglickma@kent.edu. *Application contact:* Nancy Miller, Academic Program Coordinator, Office of Graduate Student Services, 330-672-2576, Fax: 330-672-9162, E-mail: ogs@kent.edu.

Lakehead University, Graduate Studies, School of Kinesiology, Thunder Bay, ON P7B 5E1, Canada. Offers kinesiology (M Sc); kinesiology and gerontology (M Sc). Part-time programs available. *Degree requirements:* For master's, thesis. *Entrance requirements:* For master's, minimum B average. Additional exam requirements/recommendations for international students: Required—TOEFL. *Faculty research:* Social psychology and physical education, sport history, sports medicine, exercise physiology, gerontology.

Liberty University, School of Education, Lynchburg, VA 24502. Offers administration and supervision (M Ed); curriculum and instruction (M Ed); early childhood education (M Ed); educational leadership (Ed D, Ed S); educational technology and online instruction (M Ed); elementary education (M Ed, MAT); gifted education (M Ed); math specialist (M Ed); middle grades (M Ed); outdoor adventure sport (MS); reading specialist (M Ed); school counseling (M Ed); secondary education (M Ed, MAT); special education (M Ed, MAT); sports administration (MS); teaching and learning (Ed D, Ed S). *Accreditation:* NCATE. Part-time programs available. Postbaccalaureate distance learning degree programs offered (minimal on-campus study). *Students:* 2,245 full-time (1,572 women), 3,500 part-time (2,558 women); includes 1,141 minority (888 Black or African American, non-Hispanic/Latino; 19 American Indian or Alaska Native, non-Hispanic/Latino; 21 Asian, non-Hispanic/Latino; 123 Hispanic/Latino; 9 Native Hawaiian or other Pacific Islander, non-Hispanic/Latino; 81 Two or more races, non-Hispanic/Latino), 76 international. Average age 37. In 2011, 760 master's, 48 doctorates, 321 other advanced degrees awarded. *Degree requirements:* For doctorate, comprehensive exam, thesis/dissertation. *Entrance requirements:* For master's, GRE General Test or MAT (if taken in or before 1999), 2 letters of recommendation, minimum undergraduate GPA of 3.0, curriculum vitae; for doctorate, GRE General Test or MAT (if taken before 1999), minimum master's GPA of 3.0, 3 years of teacher experience; for Ed S, GRE General Test or MAT (if taken before 1999), minimum master's GPA of 3.0, 3 years of teaching experience. Additional exam requirements/recommendations for international students: Required—TOEFL (minimum score 600 paper-based; 250 computer-based). *Application deadline:* For fall admission, 6/1 priority date for domestic students; for spring admission, 11/1 for domestic students. Applications are processed on a rolling basis. Application fee: $50. Electronic applications accepted. *Expenses:* Contact institution. *Financial support:* Federal Work-Study and tuition waivers (partial) available. *Faculty research:* Self-determination, character education, bibliotherapy, learning styles, distance education. *Unit head:* Dr. Karen L. Parker, Dean, 434-582-2195, Fax: 434-582-2468, E-mail: kparker@liberty.edu. *Application contact:* Jay Bridge, Director of Graduate Admissions, 800-424-9595, Fax: 800-628-7977, E-mail: gradadmissions@liberty.edu. Web site: http://www.liberty.edu/academics/education/graduate/.

Life University, College of Arts and Sciences, Program in Sport Health Science, Marietta, GA 30060-2903. Offers chiropractic sport science (MS); exercise and sport science (MS); sport coaching (MS); sport injury management (MS). Part-time programs available. *Degree requirements:* For master's, comprehensive exam (for some programs), thesis optional. *Entrance requirements:* For master's, GRE General Test or MAT, minimum GPA of 3.0, 3 letters of recommendation. Additional exam requirements/recommendations for international students: Required—TOEFL (minimum score 500 paper-based; 173 computer-based). *Application deadline:* For fall admission, 4/1 priority date for domestic students, 4/1 for international students; for winter admission, 12/1 priority date for domestic students, 12/1 for international students; for spring admission, 3/1 priority date for domestic students, 3/1 for international students. Applications are processed on a rolling basis. Application fee: $50. Electronic applications accepted. *Financial support:* Career-related internships or fieldwork, Federal Work-Study, and tuition waivers (full and partial) available. Support available to part-time students. Financial award application deadline: 9/1; financial award applicants required to submit FAFSA. *Unit head:* Dr. Jerry Hardee, Academic Dean, 770-426-2697, Fax: 770-426-2790, E-mail: jhardee@life.edu. *Application contact:* Dr. Deborah Heairlston, Director of New Student Development, 770-426-2703, Fax: 770-426-2895, E-mail: drdeb@life.edu. Web site: http://www.life.edu/enrollment/admissions/graduate-admissions.

Lipscomb University, Program in Exercise and Nutrition Science, Nashville, TN 37204-3951. Offers MS. Part-time and evening/weekend programs available. *Faculty:* 5 full-time (4 women), 1 part-time/adjunct (0 women). *Students:* 31 full-time (27 women), 24 part-time (15 women); includes 5 minority (3 Black or African American, non-Hispanic/Latino; 1 Asian, non-Hispanic/Latino; 1 Hispanic/Latino), 1 international. Average age 26. 44 applicants, 57% accepted, 19 enrolled. In 2011, 15 master's awarded. *Degree requirements:* For master's, comprehensive exam (for some programs), thesis (for some programs). *Entrance requirements:* For master's, GRE (minimum score of 800), minimum GPA of 2.75 on all undergraduate work; 2 letters of recommendation; resume. Additional exam requirements/recommendations for international students: Required—TOEFL (minimum score 570 paper-based; 230 computer-based). *Application deadline:* For fall admission, 6/1 for domestic students; for spring admission, 12/1 for domestic students. Applications are processed on a rolling basis. Application fee: $50 ($75 for international students). Electronic applications accepted. *Expenses: Tuition:* Full-time $16,830; part-time $935 per credit hour. Tuition and fees vary according to degree level and program. *Financial support:* Applicants required to submit FAFSA. *Unit head:* Dr. Karen Robichaud, Director, 615-966-5602, E-mail: karen.robichaud@lipscomb.edu. Web site: http://exns.lipscomb.edu/.

Logan University–College of Chiropractic, University Programs, Chesterfield, MO 63006-1065. Offers nutrition and human performance (MS); sports science and rehabilitation (MS). *Faculty:* 10 full-time (6 women), 16 part-time/adjunct (6 women). *Students:* 27 full-time (12 women), 39 part-time (10 women); includes 12 minority (7 Black or African American, non-Hispanic/Latino; 4 Asian, non-Hispanic/Latino; 1 Hispanic/Latino). Average age 26. 45 applicants, 98% accepted, 34 enrolled. In 2011, 51 master's awarded. *Degree requirements:* For master's, comprehensive exam. *Entrance requirements:* For master's, GRE or National Board of Chiropractic Examiners test, minimum GPA of 2.5. Additional exam requirements/recommendations for international students: Required—TOEFL (minimum score 79 iBT). *Application deadline:* For fall admission, 7/15 priority date for domestic students, 7/15 for international students; for winter admission, 11/15 priority date for domestic students, 11/15 for international students; for spring admission, 3/15 priority date for domestic students, 3/15 for international students. Application fee: $50. *Expenses:* Contact institution. *Financial support:* In 2011–12, 35 students received support. Federal Work-Study and scholarships/grants available. Support available to part-time students. Financial award applicants required to submit FAFSA. *Faculty research:* Ankle injury prevention in high school athletes, low back pain in college football players, short arc banding and low back pain, the effects of enzymes on inflammatory blood markers, gait analysis in high school and college athletes. *Unit head:* Dr. Elizabeth A. Goodman, Dean, 636-227-2100, Fax: 636-207-2431, E-mail: elizabeth.goodman@logan.edu. *Application contact:* Steve Held, Director of Admissions, 636-227-2100 Ext. 1754, Fax: 636-207-2425, E-mail: loganadm@logan.edu.

Long Island University–Brooklyn Campus, School of Health Professions, Division of Sports Sciences, Brooklyn, NY 11201-8423. Offers adapted physical education (MS); athletic training and sports sciences (MS); exercise physiology (MS); health sciences (MS). Part-time and evening/weekend programs available. *Entrance requirements:* For master's, 2 letters of recommendation. Additional exam requirements/recommendations for international students: Required—TOEFL (minimum score 500 paper-based; 173 computer-based). Electronic applications accepted.

Louisiana Tech University, Graduate School, College of Education, Department of Health and Exercise Sciences, Ruston, LA 71272. Offers MS. *Accreditation:* NCATE. Part-time programs available. *Degree requirements:* For master's, thesis or alternative. *Entrance requirements:* For master's, GRE General Test.

Manhattanville College, Graduate Studies, School of Education, Program in Physical Education and Sport Pedagogy, Purchase, NY 10577-2132. Offers MAT. Part-time and evening/weekend programs available. *Entrance requirements:* Additional exam requirements/recommendations for international students: Required—TOEFL. Electronic applications accepted.

Marshall University, Academic Affairs Division, College of Health Professions, School of Kinesiology, Program in Exercise Science, Huntington, WV 25755. Offers MS. *Students:* 41 full-time (23 women), 2 part-time (both women); includes 5 minority (4 Black or African American, non-Hispanic/Latino; 1 Hispanic/Latino), 2 international. Average age 26. In 2011, 14 master's awarded. *Degree requirements:* For master's, thesis optional, comprehensive assessment. *Entrance requirements:* For master's, GRE General Test. Application fee: $40. *Unit head:* Dr. William Marley, Director, Human Performance Laboratory Programs, 304-696-2936, E-mail: marley@marshall.edu. *Application contact:* Information Contact, 304-746-1900, Fax: 304-746-1902, E-mail: services@marshall.edu.

Marywood University, Academic Affairs, College of Health and Human Services, Department of Nutrition and Dietetics, Program in Sports Nutrition and Exercise Science, Scranton, PA 18509-1598. Offers MS. *Entrance requirements:* Additional exam requirements/recommendations for international students: Required—TOEFL (minimum score 550 paper-based; 213 computer-based; 79 iBT). *Application deadline:* For fall admission, 4/1 priority date for domestic students, 3/31 for international students; for spring admission, 11/1 priority date for domestic students, 8/31 for international students. Applications are processed on a rolling basis. Application fee: $35. Electronic applications accepted. *Financial support:* Career-related internships or fieldwork, scholarships/grants, and unspecified assistantships available. Support available to part-time students. Financial award application deadline: 6/30; financial award applicants required to submit FAFSA. *Faculty research:* Lung function studies (pulmonary diffusing capacity of nitric oxide). *Unit head:* Dr. Lee Harrison, Chair, 570-348-6211 Ext. 2303, E-mail: harrisonl@marywood.edu. Web site: http://www.marywood.edu/nutrition/graduate-programs/sports-nutrition/.

McNeese State University, Doré School of Graduate Studies, Burton College of Education, Department of Health and Human Performance, Lake Charles, LA 70609. Offers exercise physiology (MS); health promotion (MS); nutrition and wellness (MS). *Accreditation:* NCATE. Evening/weekend programs available. *Faculty:* 5 full-time (2 women). *Students:* 42 full-time (28 women), 11 part-time (8 women); includes 14 minority (11 Black or African American, non-Hispanic/Latino; 1 Asian, non-Hispanic/Latino; 1 Hispanic/Latino; 1 Two or more races, non-Hispanic/Latino), 5 international. In 2011, 23 master's awarded. *Entrance requirements:* For master's, GRE, undergraduate major or minor in health and human performance or related field of study. *Application deadline:* For fall admission, 5/15 priority date for domestic students, 5/15 for international students; for spring admission, 10/15 priority date for domestic students, 10/15 for international students. Applications are processed on a rolling basis. Application fee: $20 ($30 for international students). *Expenses:* Tuition, state resident: part-time $519 per credit hour. Tuition and fees vary according to course load. *Financial support:* Application deadline: 5/1. *Unit head:* Dr. Michael Soileau, Head, 337-475-5374, Fax: 337-475-5947, E-mail: msoileau@mcneese.edu. *Application contact:* Dr. George F. Mead, Jr., Interim Dean of Dore' School of Graduate Studies, 337-475-5396, Fax: 337-475-5397, E-mail: admissions@mcneese.edu.

Memorial University of Newfoundland, School of Graduate Studies, School of Human Kinetics and Recreation, St. John's, NL A1C 5S7, Canada. Offers administration, curriculum and supervision (MPE); biomechanics/ergonomics (MS Kin); exercise and work physiology (MS Kin); sport psychology (MS Kin). Part-time programs available. *Degree requirements:* For master's, thesis optional, seminars, thesis presentations. *Entrance requirements:* For master's, bachelor's degree in a related field, minimum B average. Electronic applications accepted. *Faculty research:* Administration, sociology of sports, kinesiology, physiology/recreation.

Mercyhurst College, Graduate Studies, Program in Exercise Science, Erie, PA 16546. Offers MS. *Faculty:* 1 (woman) full-time, 1 part-time/adjunct. *Students:* 7 full-time (4 women); includes 1 minority (Black or African American, non-Hispanic/Latino), 3 international. Average age 23. 2 applicants, 100% accepted, 1 enrolled. *Degree requirements:* For master's, comprehensive exam. *Entrance requirements:* For master's, GRE, resume, essay, three professional references, transcripts from accredited institution. Additional exam requirements/recommendations for international students: Required—TOEFL. *Application deadline:* For fall admission, 8/1 for domestic and international students. Application fee: $35. Application fee is waived when completed online. *Expenses: Tuition:* Part-time $570 per credit. *Required fees:* $90 per term. Tuition and fees vary according to program. *Financial support:* In 2011–12, 2 research assistantships with full and partial tuition reimbursements were awarded. Financial award applicants required to submit FAFSA. *Unit head:* Dr. Christine Lo-Bue Estes, Assistant Professor, 814-824-3609, Fax: 814-824-2098, E-mail: clobueestes@mercyhurst.edu. *Application contact:* Sarah Murphy, Academic Coordinator, 814-824-2297, Fax: 814-824-2055, E-mail: smurphy@mercyhurst.edu. Web site: http://graduate.mercyhurst.edu/academics/graduate-degrees/exercise-science/.

Miami University, School of Education and Allied Professions, Department of Kinesiology and Health, Oxford, OH 45056. Offers exercise and health studies (MS); sport studies (MS). Part-time programs available. *Students:* 47 full-time (28 women), 6 part-time (3 women); includes 4 minority (1 Black or African American, non-Hispanic/Latino; 2 Asian, non-Hispanic/Latino; 1 Hispanic/Latino), 4 international. Average age 24. In 2011, 22 master's awarded. *Entrance requirements:* For master's, GRE or MAT, minimum undergraduate GPA of 3.0 during previous 2 years or 2.75 overall. Additional exam requirements/recommendations for international students: Required—TOEFL. *Application deadline:* Applications are processed on a rolling basis. Application fee: $50. Electronic applications accepted. *Expenses:* Tuition, state resident: full-time $12,023; part-time $501 per credit hour. Tuition, nonresident: full-time $26,554; part-time $1107 per credit hour. *Required fees:* $528. *Financial support:* Fellowships with full tuition reimbursements, research assistantships, teaching assistantships, Federal Work-Study, health care benefits, tuition waivers (full), and unspecified assistantships available. Financial award application deadline: 2/1; financial award applicants required to submit FAFSA. *Unit head:* Dr. Helaine Alessio, Chair, 513-529-2700, E-mail: alessih@muohio.edu. *Application contact:* Dr. Rose Marie Ward, Coordinator, Graduate Program, 513-529-9355, E-mail: wardrm1@muohio.edu. Web site: http://www.units.muohio.edu/eap/knh/.

Middle Tennessee State University, College of Graduate Studies, College of Behavioral and Health Sciences, Department of Health and Human Performance, Program in Exercise Science, Murfreesboro, TN 37132. Offers MS. Part-time and evening/weekend programs available. Postbaccalaureate distance learning degree programs offered. *Faculty:* 24 full-time (9 women), 5 part-time/adjunct (3 women). *Students:* 2 full-time (1 woman), 20 part-time (12 women); includes 10 minority (6 Black or African American, non-Hispanic/Latino; 1 Asian, non-Hispanic/Latino; 2 Hispanic/Latino; 1 Two or more races, non-Hispanic/Latino). 37 applicants, 81% accepted. In 2011, 12 master's awarded. *Degree requirements:* For master's, comprehensive exam, thesis optional. *Entrance requirements:* For master's, GRE. Additional exam requirements/recommendations for international students: Required—TOEFL (minimum score 525 paper-based; 195 computer-based; 71 iBT) or IELTS (minimum score 6). *Application deadline:* For fall admission, 6/1 for domestic and international students. Applications are processed on a rolling basis. Application fee: $25 ($30 for international students). *Expenses:* Tuition, state resident: full-time $10,008. Tuition, nonresident: full-time $25,056. *Financial support:* Application deadline: 5/1. *Faculty research:* Kinesiometrics, leisure behavior, health, lifestyles. *Unit head:* Dr. Harold D. Whiteside, Interim Dean, 615-898-2900, Fax: 615-494-7704, E-mail: harold.whiteside@mtsu.edu. *Application contact:* Dr. Michael D. Allen, Dean and Vice Provost for Research, 615-898-2840, Fax: 615-904-8020, E-mail: michael.allen@mtsu.edu.

Middle Tennessee State University, College of Graduate Studies, College of Behavioral and Health Sciences, Department of Health and Human Performance, Program in Human Performance, Murfreesboro, TN 37132. Offers PhD. Part-time and evening/weekend programs available. Postbaccalaureate distance learning degree programs offered. *Faculty:* 24 full-time (9 women), 5 part-time/adjunct (3 women). *Students:* 2 full-time (1 woman), 33 part-time (17 women); includes 8 minority (3 Black or African American, non-Hispanic/Latino; 4 Asian, non-Hispanic/Latino; 1 Two or more races, non-Hispanic/Latino). 17 applicants, 100% accepted. In 2011, 7 doctorates awarded. *Degree requirements:* For doctorate, comprehensive exam, thesis/dissertation. *Entrance requirements:* For doctorate, GRE. Additional exam requirements/recommendations for international students: Required—TOEFL (minimum score 525 paper-based; 195 computer-based; 71 iBT) or IELTS (minimum score 6).

Application deadline: For fall admission, 6/1 for domestic and international students. Applications are processed on a rolling basis. Application fee: $25 ($30 for international students). *Expenses:* Tuition, state resident: full-time $10,008. Tuition, nonresident: full-time $25,056. *Financial support:* In 2011–12, 15 students received support. Tuition waivers available. Support available to part-time students. Financial award application deadline: 5/1. *Faculty research:* Kinesiometrics, leisure behavior, health/lifestyles. *Unit head:* Dr. Harold D. Whiteside, Interim Dean, 615-898-2900, Fax: 615-494-7704, E-mail: harold.whiteside@mtsu.edu. *Application contact:* Dr. Michael D. Allen, Dean and Vice Provost for Research, 615-898-2840, Fax: 615-904-8020, E-mail: michael.allen@mtsu.edu.

Montclair State University, The Graduate School, College of Education and Human Services, Department of Exercise Science and Physical Education, Nutrition and Exercise Science Certificate Program, Montclair, NJ 07043-1624. Offers Certificate. *Students:* 2 full-time (both women), 7 part-time (6 women); includes 2 minority (both Hispanic/Latino), 1 international. Average age 31. 7 applicants, 100% accepted, 6 enrolled. In 2011, 3 degrees awarded. *Application deadline:* Applications are processed on a rolling basis. Application fee: $60. Electronic applications accepted. *Financial support:* Federal Work-Study and scholarships/grants available. Support available to part-time students. *Unit head:* Dr. Susana Juniu, Chairperson, 973-655-7093. *Application contact:* Amy Aliello, Executive Director of The Graduate School, 973-655-5147, Fax: 973-655-7869, E-mail: graduate.school@montclair.edu. Web site: http://cehs.montclair.edu/academic/es/programs/nutritionexercert.shtml.

Montclair State University, The Graduate School, College of Education and Human Services, Department of Exercise Science and Physical Education, Program in Exercise Science and Physical Education, Montclair, NJ 07043-1624. Offers exercise science (MA); sports administration and coaching (MA); teaching and supervision in physical education (MA). Part-time and evening/weekend programs available. *Students:* 8 full-time (6 women), 35 part-time (14 women); includes 4 minority (1 Black or African American, non-Hispanic/Latino; 1 Asian, non-Hispanic/Latino; 2 Hispanic/Latino), 1 international. Average age 31. 25 applicants, 44% accepted, 10 enrolled. In 2011, 14 master's awarded. *Degree requirements:* For master's, comprehensive exam, thesis or alternative. *Entrance requirements:* For master's, GRE General Test, essay, 2 letters of recommendation. Additional exam requirements/recommendations for international students: Required—TOEFL (minimum score 83 iBT), IELTS (minimum score 6.5). *Application deadline:* Applications are processed on a rolling basis. Application fee: $60. Electronic applications accepted. *Financial support:* Federal Work-Study, scholarships/grants, and unspecified assistantships available. Support available to part-time students. Financial award application deadline: 3/1; financial award applicants required to submit FAFSA. *Unit head:* Dr. Robert Horn, Chairperson, 973-655-5253, E-mail: hornr@mail.montclair.edu. *Application contact:* Amy Aliello, Executive Director of The Graduate School, 973-655-5147, Fax: 973-655-7869, E-mail: graduate.school@montclair.edu. Web site: http://cehs.montclair.edu/academic/es/programs/master_physed.shtml.

Morehead State University, Graduate Programs, College of Science and Technology, Department of Health, Wellness and Human Performance, Morehead, KY 40351. Offers health/physical education (MA). *Accreditation:* NCATE. Part-time and evening/weekend programs available. *Degree requirements:* For master's, comprehensive exam, thesis, oral exam, written core exam. *Entrance requirements:* For master's, GRE General Test or MAT, minimum GPA of 2.5; undergraduate major/minor in health, physical education, or recreation. Additional exam requirements/recommendations for international students: Required—TOEFL (minimum score 500 paper-based; 173 computer-based). Electronic applications accepted. *Faculty research:* Child growth and performance, instructional strategies, outdoor leadership qualities, exercise science, athletic training.

Murray State University, College of Health Sciences and Human Services, Department of Wellness and Therapeutic Sciences, Program in Exercise and Leisure Studies, Murray, KY 42071. Offers MS. Part-time programs available. *Degree requirements:* For master's, thesis optional. *Entrance requirements:* For master's, GRE General Test or MAT. Additional exam requirements/recommendations for international students: Required—TOEFL. *Faculty research:* Exercise and cancer recovery.

New Mexico Highlands University, Graduate Studies, School of Education, Department of Exercise and Sport Sciences, Las Vegas, NM 87701. Offers human performance and sport (MA); sports administration (MA); teacher education (MA). Part-time programs available. *Faculty:* 5 full-time (3 women). *Students:* 20 full-time (4 women), 27 part-time (9 women); includes 25 minority (7 Black or African American, non-Hispanic/Latino; 17 Hispanic/Latino; 1 Native Hawaiian or other Pacific Islander, non-Hispanic/Latino), 1 international. Average age 30. 17 applicants, 94% accepted, 13 enrolled. In 2011, 19 master's awarded. *Degree requirements:* For master's, comprehensive exam, thesis or alternative. *Entrance requirements:* For master's, minimum undergraduate GPA of 3.0. Additional exam requirements/recommendations for international students: Required—TOEFL (minimum score 540 paper-based; 207 computer-based). *Application deadline:* For fall admission, 8/1 priority date for domestic students. Applications are processed on a rolling basis. Application fee: $15. *Expenses:* Tuition, state resident: full-time $2767; part-time $146 per credit hour. Tuition, nonresident: full-time $4879; part-time $234 per credit hour. *International tuition:* $5436 full-time. *Required fees:* $737. *Financial support:* In 2011–12, 6 students received support. Career-related internships or fieldwork, Federal Work-Study, institutionally sponsored loans, scholarships/grants, tuition waivers (partial), and unspecified assistantships available. Support available to part-time students. Financial award application deadline: 3/1; financial award applicants required to submit FAFSA. *Faculty research:* Child obesity and physical inactivity, body composition and fitness assessment, motor development, sport marketing, sport finance. *Unit head:* Yongseek Kim, Department Head, 505-454-3490, E-mail: ykim@nmhu.edu. *Application contact:* Diane Trujillo, Administrative Assistant, Graduate Studies, 505-454-3266, Fax: 505-426-2117, E-mail: dtrujillo@nmhu.edu.

North Dakota State University, College of Graduate and Interdisciplinary Studies, College of Human Development and Education, Department of Health, Nutrition, and Exercise Sciences, Fargo, ND 58108. Offers dietetics (MS); entry level athletic training (MS); exercise science (MS); nutrition science (MS); public health (MS); sport pedagogy (MS); sports recreation management (MS). Part-time and evening/weekend programs available. Postbaccalaureate distance learning degree programs offered (no on-campus study). *Faculty:* 15 full-time (8 women). *Students:* 10 full-time (4 women). 37 applicants, 84% accepted, 10 enrolled. In 2011, 15 master's awarded. *Degree requirements:* For master's, thesis (for some programs). *Entrance requirements:* For master's, minimum GPA of 3.0. Additional exam requirements/recommendations for international students: Required—TOEFL (minimum score 525 paper-based; 197 computer-based; 71 iBT). *Application deadline:* For fall admission, 3/1 priority date for domestic students, 3/1 for international students. Applications are processed on a rolling basis. Application fee: $35. Electronic applications accepted. *Financial support:* In 2011–12, 18 teaching assistantships with full tuition reimbursements (averaging $6,500 per year) were awarded. Financial award application deadline: 3/31. *Faculty research:* Biomechanics, sport specialization, recreation, nutrition, athletic training. *Unit head:* Dr. Margaret Fitzgerald, Head, 701-231-7474, Fax: 701-231-8872, E-mail: margaret.fitzgerald@ndsu.edu. *Application contact:* Dr. Gary Liguori, Graduate Coordinator, 701-231-7474, Fax: 701-231-6524. Web site: http://www.ndsu.edu/hnes/.

Northeastern University, Bouvé College of Health Sciences, Program in Exercise Science, Boston, MA 02115-5096. Offers physical activity and public health (MS). Part-time and evening/weekend programs available. *Students:* 26 full-time (17 women). 36 applicants, 69% accepted, 13 enrolled. In 2011, 8 master's awarded. *Degree requirements:* For master's, comprehensive exam, thesis optional. *Entrance requirements:* For master's, GRE General Test. Additional exam requirements/recommendations for international students: Required—TOEFL (minimum score 100 iBT). *Application deadline:* For fall admission, 6/1 for domestic students. Applications are processed on a rolling basis. Application fee: $50. Electronic applications accepted. *Financial support:* Research assistantships with tuition reimbursements, teaching assistantships with tuition reimbursements, career-related internships or fieldwork, Federal Work-Study, scholarships/grants, tuition waivers (partial), and unspecified assistantships available. Support available to part-time students. Financial award application deadline: 3/1; financial award applicants required to submit FAFSA. *Faculty research:* Exercise in cardiovascular pulmonary and metabolic diseases, mechanisms related to lactate and ventilation threshold, body composition assessment techniques. *Unit head:* Prof. Carmen C. Sceppa, Director, Graduate Program in Exercise Science, 617-373-5543, Fax: 617-373-2968, E-mail: c.sceppa@neu.edu. *Application contact:* Margaret Schnabel, Director of Graduate Admissions, 617-373-2708, E-mail: bouvegrad@neu.edu. Web site: http://www.northeastern.edu/graduate/programs/exercise-science/.

Northern Michigan University, College of Graduate Studies, College of Professional Studies, Department of Health, Physical Education and Recreation, Marquette, MI 49855-5301. Offers exercise science (MS). Part-time programs available. *Degree requirements:* For master's, thesis or alternative. *Entrance requirements:* For master's, GRE General Test, minimum GPA of 3.0 in major, 2.75 overall; 9 hours of course work in human anatomy, physiology, kinesiology.

Oakland University, Graduate Study and Lifelong Learning, School of Health Sciences, Program in Exercise Science, Rochester, MI 48309-4401. Offers MS, Certificate. *Degree requirements:* For master's, thesis (for some programs). *Entrance requirements:* For master's, minimum GPA of 3.0 for unconditional admission. Additional exam requirements/recommendations for international students: Required—TOEFL (minimum score 550 paper-based; 213 computer-based). Electronic applications accepted. *Expenses:* Contact institution.

Ohio University, Graduate College, College of Arts and Sciences, Department of Biological Sciences, Athens, OH 45701-2979. Offers biological sciences (MS, PhD); cell biology and physiology (MS, PhD); ecology and evolutionary biology (MS, PhD); exercise physiology and muscle biology (MS, PhD); microbiology (MS, PhD); neuroscience (MS, PhD). *Students:* 35 full-time (12 women), 4 part-time (1 woman), 14 international. 62 applicants, 10% accepted, 5 enrolled. In 2011, 2 master's, 8 doctorates awarded. Terminal master's awarded for partial completion of doctoral program. *Degree requirements:* For master's, comprehensive exam, thesis, 1 quarter of teaching experience; for doctorate, comprehensive exam, thesis/dissertation, 2 quarters of teaching experience. *Entrance requirements:* For master's, GRE General Test, names of three faculty members whose research interests most closely match the applicant's interest; for doctorate, GRE General Test, essay concerning prior training, research interest and career goals, plus names of three faculty members whose research interests most closely match the applicant's interest. Additional exam requirements/recommendations for international students: Required—TOEFL (minimum score 620 paper-based; 105 iBT) or IELTS (minimum score 7.5). *Application deadline:* For fall admission, 1/15 for domestic and international students. Application fee: $50 ($55 for international students). Electronic applications accepted. *Financial support:* In 2011–12, 1 fellowship with full tuition reimbursement (averaging $18,957 per year), 10 research assistantships with full tuition reimbursements (averaging $18,957 per year), 42 teaching assistantships with full tuition reimbursements (averaging $18,957 per year) were awarded; Federal Work-Study and institutionally sponsored loans also available. Financial award application deadline: 1/15. *Faculty research:* Ecology and evolutionary biology, exercise physiology and muscle biology, neurobiology, cell biology, physiology. *Total annual research expenditures:* $2.8 million. *Unit head:* Dr. Ralph DiCaprio, Chair, 740-593-2290, Fax: 740-593-0300, E-mail: dicapri@ohio.edu. *Application contact:* Dr. Patrick Hassett, Graduate Chair, 740-593-4793, Fax: 740-593-0300, E-mail: hassett@ohio.edu. Web site: http://www.biosci.ohiou.edu/.

Ohio University, Graduate College, College of Health Sciences and Professions, School of Applied Health Sciences and Wellness, Program in Physiology of Exercise, Athens, OH 45701-2979. Offers MS. *Students:* 14 full-time (10 women), 1 part-time (0 women). 8 applicants, 38% accepted, 3 enrolled. In 2011, 7 master's awarded. *Degree requirements:* For master's, thesis or alternative. *Entrance requirements:* For master's, GRE, minimum GPA of 3.0. Additional exam requirements/recommendations for international students: Required—TOEFL (minimum score 550 paper-based; 80 iBT) or IELTS (minimum score 6.5). *Application deadline:* For fall admission, 3/1 priority date for domestic students, 3/1 for international students. Application fee: $50 ($55 for international students). Electronic applications accepted. *Financial support:* In 2011–12, research assistantships with tuition reimbursements (averaging $8,577 per year), teaching assistantships with full tuition reimbursements (averaging $8,577 per year) were awarded; Federal Work-Study, institutionally sponsored loans, and scholarships/grants also available. Financial award application deadline: 3/15. *Faculty research:* Blood pressure, heart rate, health skeleton, muscles, training. *Unit head:* Dr. Roger Gilders, Coordinator, 740-593-0101, Fax: 740-593-0285, E-mail: gilders@ohio.edu. *Application contact:* Graduate Records. Web site: http://bios.ohio.edu/graduate/integrative-physiology-and-neuroscience/comparative-exercise-physiology.

Old Dominion University, Darden College of Education, Program in Physical Education, Exercise and Wellness Emphasis, Norfolk, VA 23529. Offers MS Ed. Part-time and evening/weekend programs available. *Faculty:* 7 full-time (4 women). *Students:* 22 full-time (16 women), 9 part-time (all women); includes 8 minority (5 Black or African American, non-Hispanic/Latino; 1 American Indian or Alaska Native, non-Hispanic/Latino; 1 Asian, non-Hispanic/Latino; 1 Two or more races, non-Hispanic/Latino), 3 international. Average age 27. 12 applicants, 100% accepted, 10 enrolled. In 2011, 13 master's awarded. *Degree requirements:* For master's, comprehensive exam, thesis or alternative, internship, research project. *Entrance requirements:* For master's, GRE, minimum GPA of 2.8 overall, 3.0 in major. Additional exam requirements/recommendations for international students: Required—TOEFL (minimum score 550 paper-based; 200 computer-based; 79 iBT). *Application deadline:* For fall admission, 7/1 for domestic students; for spring admission, 11/1 for domestic students. Applications are processed on a rolling basis. Application fee: $40. *Expenses:* Tuition, state resident: full-time $9096; part-time $379 per credit. Tuition, nonresident: full-time $23,064; part-time $961 per credit. *Required fees:* $127 per semester. One-time fee: $50. *Financial support:* In 2011–12, 1 teaching assistantship (averaging $9,000 per year) was awarded; career-related internships or fieldwork and scholarships/grants also available. Financial award application deadline: 4/15. *Faculty research:* Diabetes, exercise prescription, gait and balance. *Total annual research expenditures:* $105,000. *Unit head:* Dr. David Swain, Graduate Program Director, 757-683-6028, E-mail: dswain@odu.edu. *Application contact:* William Heffelfinger, Director of Graduate Admissions,

Exercise and Sports Science

757-683-5554, Fax: 757-683-3255, E-mail: gradadmit@odu.edu. Web site: http://education.odu.edu/esper/academics/exsci/graduate.shtml.

Oregon State University, Graduate School, College of Public Health and Human Sciences, Programs in Exercise and Sport Science, Program in Exercise Physiology, Corvallis, OR 97331. Offers MS.

Oregon State University, Graduate School, College of Public Health and Human Sciences, Programs in Exercise and Sport Science, Program in Neuromechanics, Corvallis, OR 97331. Offers MS, PhD.

Purdue University, Graduate School, College of Health and Human Sciences, Department of Health and Kinesiology, West Lafayette, IN 47907. Offers athletic training education administration (MS); exercise, human physiology of movement and sport (PhD); health education (MS, PhD); motor control and development (MS, PhD); physical education pedagogy (MS, PhD); sport and exercise psychology (MS, PhD). Part-time programs available. *Faculty:* 20 full-time (9 women), 14 part-time/adjunct (4 women). *Students:* 53 full-time (27 women), 19 part-time (9 women); includes 9 minority (3 Black or African American, non-Hispanic/Latino; 1 American Indian or Alaska Native, non-Hispanic/Latino; 2 Asian, non-Hispanic/Latino; 1 Hispanic/Latino; 2 Two or more races, non-Hispanic/Latino), 14 international. Average age 30. 108 applicants, 48% accepted, 29 enrolled. In 2011, 17 master's, 6 doctorates awarded. *Degree requirements:* For master's, thesis optional; for doctorate, comprehensive exam, thesis/dissertation, Qualifying Examination, Preliminary Examination. *Entrance requirements:* For master's, GRE General Test, minimum score 1000 combined verbal and quantitative scores, minimum undergraduate GPA of 3.0 or equivalent; for doctorate, GRE General Test, minimum score 1100 combined verbal and quantitative scores, minimum undergraduate GPA of 3.0 or equivalent; master's degree with minimum GPA of 3.25 (recommended). Additional exam requirements/recommendations for international students: Required—TOEFL (minimum score 550 computer-based; 77 iBT); Recommended—TWE. *Application deadline:* For fall admission, 4/30 for domestic and international students; for spring admission, 10/15 for domestic and international students. Applications are processed on a rolling basis. Application fee: $60 ($75 for international students). Electronic applications accepted. *Financial support:* Fellowships with partial tuition reimbursements, research assistantships with partial tuition reimbursements, teaching assistantships with partial tuition reimbursements, and Federal Work-Study available. Support available to part-time students. Financial award applicants required to submit FAFSA. *Faculty research:* Wellness, motivation, teaching effectiveness, learning and development. *Unit head:* Dr. Larry J. Leverenz, Interim Head, 765-494-0865, Fax: 765-494-496-1239, E-mail: llevere@purdue.edu. *Application contact:* Lisa Duncan, Graduate Contact, 765-494-3162, E-mail: llduncan@purdue.edu. Web site: http://www.purdue.edu/hhs/hk/.

Queens College of the City University of New York, Division of Graduate Studies, Mathematics and Natural Sciences Division, Department of Family, Nutrition and Exercise Sciences, Flushing, NY 11367-1597. Offers home economics (MS Ed); physical education and exercise sciences (MS Ed). Part-time and evening/weekend programs available. *Faculty:* 12 full-time (7 women). *Students:* 15 full-time (14 women), 66 part-time (53 women); includes 31 minority (7 Black or African American, non-Hispanic/Latino; 19 Asian, non-Hispanic/Latino; 5 Hispanic/Latino), 4 international. 58 applicants, 78% accepted, 25 enrolled. In 2011, 14 master's awarded. *Degree requirements:* For master's, research project. *Entrance requirements:* For master's, minimum GPA of 3.0. Additional exam requirements/recommendations for international students: Required—TOEFL. *Application deadline:* For fall admission, 4/1 for domestic students; for spring admission, 11/1 for domestic students. Applications are processed on a rolling basis. Application fee: $125. *Expenses:* Tuition, state resident: part-time $345 per credit. Tuition, nonresident: part-time $640 per credit. *Required fees:* $145.25 per semester. *Financial support:* Career-related internships or fieldwork, Federal Work-Study, institutionally sponsored loans, and tuition waivers (partial) available. Support available to part-time students. Financial award application deadline: 4/1; financial award applicants required to submit FAFSA. *Faculty research:* Exercise and environmental physiology, interdisciplinary approaches to school curricula using outdoor education, program development in cardiac rehabilitation and adult fitness, nutrition education. *Unit head:* Dr. Elizabeth Lowe, Chairperson, 718-997-4168. *Application contact:* Mario Caruso, Director of Graduate Admissions, 718-997-5200, Fax: 718-997-5193, E-mail: graduate_admissions@qc.edu.

Queen's University at Kingston, School of Graduate Studies and Research, School of Kinesiology and Health Studies, Kingston, ON K7L 3N6, Canada. Offers applied exercise science (PhD); biomechanics/ergonomics (M Sc); exercise physiology (M Sc); social psychology of sport and exercise rehabilitation (MA); sociology of sport (MA). Part-time programs available. *Degree requirements:* For master's, thesis (for some programs); for doctorate, comprehensive exam, thesis/dissertation. *Entrance requirements:* For master's and doctorate, minimum B+ average. Additional exam requirements/recommendations for international students: Required—TOEFL. Electronic applications accepted. *Faculty research:* Expert performance ergonomics, obesity research, pregnancy and exercise, gender and sport participation.

Rocky Mountain University of Health Professions, Program in Orthopaedic and Sports Science, Provo, UT 84606. Offers PhD. *Degree requirements:* For doctorate, thesis/dissertation.

Sacred Heart University, Graduate Programs, College of Health Professions, Program in Exercise Science and Nutrition, Fairfield, CT 06825-1000. Offers MS.

St. Cloud State University, School of Graduate Studies, School of Education, Department of Health, Physical Education, Recreation, and Sport Science, St. Cloud, MN 56301-4498. Offers exercise science (MS); physical education (MS); sports management (MS). *Degree requirements:* For master's, thesis or alternative. *Entrance requirements:* For master's, GRE General Test, minimum GPA of 2.75. Additional exam requirements/recommendations for international students: Required—Michigan English Language Assessment Battery; Recommended—TOEFL (minimum score 550 paper-based; 213 computer-based), IELTS (minimum score 6.5). Electronic applications accepted.

Saint Mary's College of California, School of Liberal Arts, Department of Kinesiology, Moraga, CA 94556. Offers sport management (MA); sport studies (MA). Part-time programs available. *Faculty:* 6 full-time (1 woman), 5 part-time/adjunct (3 women). *Students:* 3 full-time (0 women), 22 part-time (13 women); includes 6 minority (3 Black or African American, non-Hispanic/Latino; 3 Asian, non-Hispanic/Latino). Average age 27. 23 applicants, 65% accepted, 14 enrolled. In 2011, 7 master's awarded. *Degree requirements:* For master's, thesis or special project. *Entrance requirements:* For master's, minimum GPA of 2.75, BA in physical education or related field, or professional experience. Application fee: $25. Electronic applications accepted. *Expenses:* Contact institution. *Financial support:* In 2011–12, 15 students received support, including research assistantships (averaging $6,000 per year); career-related internships or fieldwork, institutionally sponsored loans, scholarships/grants, tuition waivers (partial), and unspecified assistantships also available. Support available to part-time students. Financial award applicants required to submit FAFSA. *Faculty research:* Moral development in sport, applied motor learning, achievement motivation, sport history. *Total annual research expenditures:* $1,500. *Unit head:* William Manning, Chair, 925-631-4969, Fax: 925-631-4965, E-mail: wmanning@stmarys-ca.edu. *Application contact:* Jeanne Abate, Administrative Assistant, 925-631-4377, Fax: 925-631-4965, E-mail: jabate@stmarys-ca.edu. Web site: http://www.stmarys-ca.edu/graduate-kinesiology.

San Diego State University, Graduate and Research Affairs, College of Health and Human Services, School of Exercise and Nutritional Sciences, Program in Exercise Physiology, San Diego, CA 92182. Offers MS, MS/MS. *Degree requirements:* For master's, thesis. *Entrance requirements:* For master's, GRE General Test, 2 letters of reference. Additional exam requirements/recommendations for international students: Required—TOEFL. Electronic applications accepted.

San Francisco State University, Division of Graduate Studies, College of Health and Human Services, Department of Kinesiology, San Francisco, CA 94132-1722. Offers exercise physiology (MS); movement science (MS); physical activity: social scientific perspectives (MS). *Application deadline:* Applications are processed on a rolling basis. *Unit head:* Dr. Marialice Kern, Chair, 415-338-2244, E-mail: mkern@sfsu.edu. *Application contact:* Maria Allain, Academic Office Coordinator, 415-338-2244, E-mail: meallain@sfsu.edu. Web site: http://kin.sfsu.edu/.

Smith College, Graduate and Special Programs, Department of Exercise and Sport Studies, Northampton, MA 01063. Offers MS. Part-time programs available. *Faculty:* 4 full-time (2 women), 1 part-time/adjunct (0 women). *Students:* 18 full-time (16 women); includes 3 minority (1 Asian, non-Hispanic/Latino; 1 Hispanic/Latino; 1 Two or more races, non-Hispanic/Latino), 2 international. Average age 25. 28 applicants, 46% accepted, 9 enrolled. In 2011, 11 master's awarded. *Degree requirements:* For master's, thesis or special studies. *Entrance requirements:* For master's, GRE General Test. Additional exam requirements/recommendations for international students: Required—TOEFL (minimum score 590 paper-based; 243 computer-based; 97 iBT). *Application deadline:* For fall admission, 4/1 for domestic students, 1/15 for international students; for spring admission, 12/1 for domestic students. Application fee: $60. *Expenses: Tuition:* Full-time $14,925; part-time $1245 per credit. *Financial support:* In 2011–12, 18 students received support, including 11 teaching assistantships with full tuition reimbursements available (averaging $12,090 per year); career-related internships or fieldwork, institutionally sponsored loans, scholarships/grants, and tuition waivers (partial) also available. Support available to part-time students. Financial award application deadline: 1/15; financial award applicants required to submit CSS PROFILE or FAFSA. *Faculty research:* Women in sport, perceived exertion, motor programming, race in sport, stress management. *Unit head:* Don Siegel, Graduate Student Adviser, 413-585-3977, E-mail: dsiegel@smith.edu. *Application contact:* Ruth Morgan, Administrative Assistant, 413-585-3050, Fax: 413-585-3054, E-mail: rmorgan@smith.edu. Web site: http://www.smith.edu/ess/.

Southeast Missouri State University, School of Graduate Studies, Department of Health, Human Performance and Recreation, Cape Girardeau, MO 63701-4799. Offers nutrition and exercise science (MS). Part-time and evening/weekend programs available. *Faculty:* 7 full-time (1 woman), 2 part-time/adjunct (1 woman). *Students:* 17 full-time (6 women), 7 part-time (4 women), 10 international. Average age 26. 20 applicants, 95% accepted, 8 enrolled. In 2011, 4 master's awarded. *Degree requirements:* For master's, comprehensive exam, thesis optional, internship. *Entrance requirements:* For master's, GRE General Test (minimum combined score of 950), minimum undergraduate GPA of 3.0, minimum B grade in prerequisite courses. Additional exam requirements/recommendations for international students: Required—TOEFL (minimum score 550 paper-based; 213 computer-based; 79 iBT); Recommended—IELTS (minimum score 6). *Application deadline:* For fall admission, 8/1 for domestic students, 7/1 for international students; for spring admission, 11/21 for domestic students, 11/1 for international students. Applications are processed on a rolling basis. Application fee: $30 ($40 for international students). Electronic applications accepted. *Expenses:* Tuition, state resident: full-time $4896; part-time $272 per credit hour. Tuition, nonresident: full-time $8649; part-time $480.50 per credit hour. *Financial support:* In 2011–12, 16 students received support, including 4 teaching assistantships with full tuition reimbursements available (averaging $7,600 per year); career-related internships or fieldwork, Federal Work-Study, scholarships/grants, tuition waivers (full), and unspecified assistantships also available. Financial award application deadline: 6/30; financial award applicants required to submit FAFSA. *Faculty research:* Health issues of athletes, body composition assessment, exercise testing, exercise training, perceptual responses to physical activity. *Unit head:* Dr. Joe Pujol, Chairperson, 573-651-2664, Fax: 573-651-5150, E-mail: jpujol@semo.edu. *Application contact:* Alisa Aleen McFerron, Assistant Director of Admissions for Operations, 573-651-5937, Fax: 573-651-5936, E-mail: amcferron@semo.edu. Web site: http://www.semo.edu/health/.

Southern Connecticut State University, School of Graduate Studies, School of Education, Department of Exercise Science, New Haven, CT 06515-1355. Offers human performance (MS); physical education (MS); school health education (MS); sport psychology (MS). Part-time and evening/weekend programs available. *Faculty:* 8 full-time (4 women). *Students:* 10 full-time (5 women), 20 part-time (9 women); includes 3 minority (1 Black or African American, non-Hispanic/Latino; 1 Asian, non-Hispanic/Latino; 1 Hispanic/Latino). 132 applicants, 20% accepted, 19 enrolled. In 2011, 6 master's awarded. *Degree requirements:* For master's, thesis or alternative. *Entrance requirements:* For master's, interview. *Application deadline:* For fall admission, 7/15 priority date for domestic students. Applications are processed on a rolling basis. Application fee: $50. Electronic applications accepted. *Expenses:* Tuition, state resident: full-time $5137; part-time $413 per credit. *Required fees:* $4008; $55 per term. *Financial support:* Application deadline: 4/15; applicants required to submit FAFSA. *Unit head:* Dr. Daniel Swartz, Chairperson, 203-392-8721, Fax: 203-392-6911, E-mail: swartzd1@southernct.edu. *Application contact:* Dr. Robert Axtell, Coordinator, 203-392-6037, Fax: 203-392-6093, E-mail: axtell@southernct.edu.

Southern Utah University, Program in Sports Conditioning, Cedar City, UT 84720-2498. Offers MS. *Students:* 3 full-time (2 women), 40 part-time (11 women); includes 7 minority (2 Black or African American, non-Hispanic/Latino; 1 American Indian or Alaska Native, non-Hispanic/Latino; 1 Hispanic/Latino; 3 Native Hawaiian or other Pacific Islander, non-Hispanic/Latino). Average age 33. 10 applicants, 100% accepted, 9 enrolled. In 2011, 18 master's awarded. *Application deadline:* For fall admission, 7/15 for domestic students; for spring admission, 10/15 for domestic students. Applications are processed on a rolling basis. Application fee: $50 ($65 for international students). Electronic applications accepted. *Unit head:* Dr. Deb Hill, Dean, 435-865-8628, Fax: 435-865-8485, E-mail: hilld@suu.edu. *Application contact:* Joan Anderson, Administrative Assistant, 435-586-7816, Fax: 435-865-8057, E-mail: anderson_j@suu.edu.

Springfield College, Graduate Programs, Programs in Exercise Science and Sport Studies, Springfield, MA 01109-3797. Offers athletic training (MS); exercise physiology (MS), including clinical exercise physiology, science and research; exercise science and sport studies (PhD); health promotion and disease prevention (MS); sport psychology (MS). Part-time programs available. Terminal master's awarded for partial completion of doctoral program. *Degree requirements:* For master's, comprehensive exam, research project or thesis; for doctorate, comprehensive exam, thesis/dissertation. *Entrance requirements:* For master's and doctorate, GRE General Test. Additional exam

requirements/recommendations for international students: Required—TOEFL (minimum score 550 paper-based; 213 computer-based). Electronic applications accepted.

State University of New York College at Cortland, Graduate Studies, School of Professional Studies, Department of Exercise Science and Sport Studies, Cortland, NY 13045. Offers MS.

Syracuse University, School of Education, Program in Exercise Science, Syracuse, NY 13244. Offers MS. Part-time programs available. *Students:* 16 full-time (8 women); includes 1 minority (Black or African American, non-Hispanic/Latino), 2 international. Average age 24. 36 applicants, 92% accepted, 11 enrolled. In 2011, 9 degrees awarded. *Degree requirements:* For master's, thesis or alternative. *Entrance requirements:* For master's, GRE, resume. Additional exam requirements/recommendations for international students: Required—TOEFL (minimum score 100 iBT). *Application deadline:* For fall admission, 2/1 priority date for domestic students, 2/1 for international students; for spring admission, 10/15 priority date for domestic students, 10/15 for international students. Applications are processed on a rolling basis. Application fee: $75. Electronic applications accepted. *Expenses: Tuition:* Part-time $1206 per credit. *Financial support:* Fellowships, research assistantships with full and partial tuition reimbursements, and teaching assistantships with full and partial tuition reimbursements available. Financial award application deadline: 1/1; financial award applicants required to submit FAFSA. *Faculty research:* Bone density, obesity in females, cardiovascular functioning, attitudes toward physical education, sports management and psychology. *Unit head:* Dr. Tom Brutsaert, Chair, 315-443-2114, E-mail: tdbrutsa@syr.edu. *Application contact:* Laurie Deyo, Graduate Recruiter, School of Education, 315-443-2505, E-mail: e-gradrcrt@syr.edu. Web site: http://soeweb.syr.edu/exsci/exercisescience.html.

Tennessee State University, The School of Graduate Studies and Research, College of Education, Department of Human Performance and Sports Science, Nashville, TN 37209-1561. Offers MA Ed. *Degree requirements:* For master's, thesis optional. *Entrance requirements:* For master's, GRE General Test or MAT.

Texas A&M University–Commerce, Graduate School, College of Education and Human Services, Department of Health and Human Performance, Commerce, TX 75429-3011. Offers exercise physiology (MS); health and human performance (M Ed); health promotion (MS); health, kinesiology and sports studies (Ed D); motor performance (MS); sport studies (MS). Part-time programs available. *Degree requirements:* For master's, comprehensive exam, thesis (for some programs). *Entrance requirements:* For master's, GRE General Test. Electronic applications accepted. *Faculty research:* Teaching, physical fitness.

Texas Tech University, Graduate School, College of Arts and Sciences, Department of Health, Exercise and Sport Sciences, Lubbock, TX 79409. Offers exercise and sport sciences (MS). Part-time programs available. *Faculty:* 17 full-time (8 women). *Students:* 66 full-time (25 women), 17 part-time (2 women); includes 10 minority (5 Black or African American, non-Hispanic/Latino; 1 Asian, non-Hispanic/Latino; 4 Hispanic/Latino), 17 international. Average age 25. 67 applicants, 57% accepted, 28 enrolled. In 2011, 40 master's awarded. *Degree requirements:* For master's, comprehensive exam (for some programs), thesis optional. *Entrance requirements:* For master's, GRE General Test. Additional exam requirements/recommendations for international students: Required—TOEFL (minimum score 550 paper-based; 213 computer-based; 79 iBT). *Application deadline:* For fall admission, 6/1 priority date for domestic students, 1/15 for international students; for spring admission, 9/1 priority date for domestic students, 6/15 for international students. Applications are processed on a rolling basis. Application fee: $50 ($75 for international students). Electronic applications accepted. *Expenses:* Tuition, state resident: full-time $5899; part-time $245.80 per credit hour. Tuition, nonresident: full-time $13,411; part-time $558.80 per credit hour. *Required fees:* $2680.60; $86.50 per credit hour. $920.30 per semester. *Financial support:* In 2011–12, 15 students received support. Application deadline: 4/15; applicants required to submit FAFSA. *Faculty research:* Cardiopulmonary physiology, physical activity in children, motivation for exercise participation, muscle physiology, sport injury, aging and movement control. *Total annual research expenditures:* $46,976. *Unit head:* Dr. Noreen L. Goggin, Chairperson, 806-742-3371, Fax: 806-742-1688, E-mail: noreen.goggin@ttu.edu. *Application contact:* Monica Luna, Graduate Program Secretary, 806-742-3371, Fax: 806-742-1688. Web site: http://www.hess.ttu.edu/.

Texas Woman's University, Graduate School, College of Health Sciences, Department of Kinesiology, Denton, TX 76201. Offers adapted physical education (MS, PhD); biomechanics (MS, PhD); coaching (MS); exercise physiology (MS, PhD); pedagogy (MS); sport management (MS, PhD). Part-time and evening/weekend programs available. *Faculty:* 12 full-time (6 women), 1 part-time/adjunct (0 women). *Students:* 55 full-time (38 women), 104 part-time (69 women); includes 35 minority (24 Black or African American, non-Hispanic/Latino; 1 American Indian or Alaska Native, non-Hispanic/Latino; 10 Hispanic/Latino), 23 international. Average age 31. 86 applicants, 73% accepted, 38 enrolled. In 2011, 25 master's, 7 doctorates awarded. Terminal master's awarded for partial completion of doctoral program. *Degree requirements:* For master's, comprehensive exam, thesis or alternative; for doctorate, comprehensive exam, thesis/dissertation, qualifying exam. *Entrance requirements:* For master's, GRE General Test (biomechanics emphasis only), 2 letters of reference, curriculum vitae, interview (adapted physical education emphasis only); for doctorate, GRE General Test (biomechanics emphasis only), interview, 3 letters of reference, curriculum vitae. Additional exam requirements/recommendations for international students: Required—TOEFL (minimum score 550 paper-based; 213 computer-based; 79 iBT). *Application deadline:* For fall admission, 7/1 priority date for domestic students, 3/1 for international students; for spring admission, 11/1 priority date for domestic students, 7/1 for international students. Applications are processed on a rolling basis. Application fee: $50 ($75 for international students). Electronic applications accepted. *Expenses:* Tuition, state resident: full-time $3834; part-time $213 per credit hour. Tuition, nonresident: full-time $9468; part-time $526 per credit hour. *Required fees:* $213 per credit hour. Tuition and fees vary according to course load. *Financial support:* In 2011–12, 46 students received support, including 7 research assistantships (averaging $10,746 per year), 14 teaching assistantships (averaging $10,746 per year); career-related internships or fieldwork, Federal Work-Study, institutionally sponsored loans, scholarships/grants, traineeships, health care benefits, and unspecified assistantships also available. Support available to part-time students. Financial award application deadline: 3/1; financial award applicants required to submit FAFSA. *Faculty research:* Exercise and Type 2 diabetes risk, bone mineral density and exercise in special populations, obesity in children, factors influencing sport consumer behavior and loyalty, roles and responsibilities of paraeducators in adapted physical education. *Total annual research expenditures:* $19,544. *Unit head:* Dr. David Nichols, Chair, 940-898-2575, Fax: 940-898-2581, E-mail: dnichols@twu.edu. *Application contact:* Dr. Samuel Wheeler, Assistant Director of Admissions, 940-898-3188, Fax: 940-898-3081, E-mail: wheelersr@twu.edu. Web site: http://www.twu.edu/kinesiology/.

Texas Woman's University, Graduate School, College of Health Sciences, Department of Nutrition and Food Sciences, Program in Exercise and Sports Nutrition, Denton, TX 76201. Offers MS. Part-time programs available. *Students:* 11 full-time (10 women), 8 part-time (5 women); includes 5 minority (4 Black or African American, non-Hispanic/Latino; 1 Hispanic/Latino). Average age 29. 6 applicants, 83% accepted, 4 enrolled. In 2011, 11 master's awarded. *Degree requirements:* For master's, comprehensive exam, thesis or alternative. *Entrance requirements:* For master's, GRE General Test (preferred minimum score 153 [500 old version] Verbal, 140 [400 old version] Quantitative), 9 hours each of chemistry, nutrition, and kinesiology; 3 hours of human physiology; minimum GPA of 3.0 in last 60 hours; resume; 2 letters of recommendation. Additional exam requirements/recommendations for international students: Required—TOEFL (minimum score 550 paper-based; 213 computer-based; 79 iBT). *Application deadline:* For fall admission, 7/1 priority date for domestic students, 3/1 for international students; for spring admission, 11/1 priority date for domestic students, 7/1 for international students. Applications are processed on a rolling basis. Application fee: $50 ($75 for international students). Electronic applications accepted. *Expenses:* Tuition, state resident: full-time $3834; part-time $213 per credit hour. Tuition, nonresident: full-time $9468; part-time $526 per credit hour. *Required fees:* $213 per credit hour. Tuition and fees vary according to course load. *Financial support:* In 2011–12, 8 students received support, including 6 research assistantships (averaging $11,520 per year), teaching assistantships (averaging $11,520 per year); career-related internships or fieldwork, Federal Work-Study, institutionally sponsored loans, scholarships/grants, traineeships, health care benefits, and unspecified assistantships also available. Support available to part-time students. Financial award application deadline: 3/1; financial award applicants required to submit FAFSA. *Faculty research:* Metabolism of lipoproteins, bone metabolism, osteoporosis, adult and childhood obesity. *Unit head:* Dr. Chandan Prasad, Program Director, 940-898-2636, Fax: 940-898-2634, E-mail: nutrfdsci@twu.edu. *Application contact:* Dr. Samuel Wheeler, Assistant Director of Admissions, 940-898-3188, Fax: 940-898-3081, E-mail: wheelersr@twu.edu. Web site: http://www.twu.edu/nutrition-food-sciences/.

Troy University, Graduate School, College of Education, Program in Postsecondary Education, Troy, AL 36082. Offers adult education (M Ed); biology (M Ed); criminal justice (M Ed); English (M Ed); foundations of education (M Ed); general science (M Ed); higher education administration (M Ed); history (M Ed); instructional technology (M Ed); mathematics (M Ed); music industry (M Ed); physical fitness (M Ed); political science (M Ed); public administration (M Ed); social science (M Ed); teaching English (M Ed). *Accreditation:* NCATE. Part-time and evening/weekend programs available. *Faculty:* 53 full-time (21 women), 22 part-time/adjunct (8 women). *Students:* 74 full-time (51 women), 166 part-time (121 women); includes 148 minority (143 Black or African American, non-Hispanic/Latino; 1 American Indian or Alaska Native, non-Hispanic/Latino; 2 Hispanic/Latino; 2 Two or more races, non-Hispanic/Latino). Average age 34. 174 applicants, 82% accepted, 88 enrolled. In 2011, 221 master's awarded. *Degree requirements:* For master's, comprehensive exam, thesis. *Entrance requirements:* For master's, MAT (minimum score 385), minimum GPA of 2.5. Additional exam requirements/recommendations for international students: Required—TOEFL (minimum score 523 paper-based; 193 computer-based; 70 iBT), IELTS (minimum score 6), or ACT COMPASS ESL (minimum listening, reading, and grammar score 270). *Application deadline:* Applications are processed on a rolling basis. Application fee: $50. Electronic applications accepted. *Expenses:* Tuition, state resident: full-time $6960; part-time $290 per credit hour. Tuition, nonresident: full-time $13,920; part-time $580 per credit hour. *Required fees:* $386 per term. *Financial support:* Available to part-time students. Applicants required to submit FAFSA. *Unit head:* Dr. Jan Oliver, Associate Professor, 334-670-3444, Fax: 334-670-3296, E-mail: oliver@troy.edu. *Application contact:* Brenda K. Campbell, Director of Graduate Admissions, 334-670-3178, Fax: 334-670-3733, E-mail: bcamp@troy.edu.

United States Sports Academy, Graduate Programs, Program in Sports Fitness and Health, Daphne, AL 36526-7055. Offers MSS. Part-time programs available. Postbaccalaureate distance learning degree programs offered (no on-campus study). *Degree requirements:* For master's, comprehensive exam, thesis optional. *Entrance requirements:* For master's, GRE General Test, GMAT, or MAT, minimum GPA of 2.5, 3 letters of recommendation, resume. Additional exam requirements/recommendations for international students: Required—TOEFL (minimum score 500 paper-based; 213 computer-based). Electronic applications accepted. *Faculty research:* Exercise physiology, conditioning.

United States Sports Academy, Graduate Programs, Program in Sport Studies, Daphne, AL 36526-7055. Offers MSS. Part-time programs available. Postbaccalaureate distance learning degree programs offered (no on-campus study). *Degree requirements:* For master's, comprehensive exam, thesis optional. *Entrance requirements:* For master's, GRE General Test, GMAT, or MAT, minimum GPA of 2.5, 3 letters of recommendation, resume. Additional exam requirements/recommendations for international students: Required—TOEFL (minimum score 500 paper-based; 213 computer-based). Electronic applications accepted.

University at Buffalo, the State University of New York, Graduate School, School of Public Health and Health Professions, Department of Exercise and Nutrition Sciences, Buffalo, NY 14260. Offers exercise science (MS, PhD); nutrition (MS, Advanced Certificate). Part-time programs available. *Faculty:* 11 full-time (2 women). *Students:* 87 full-time (54 women), 1 part-time (0 women); includes 11 minority (1 Black or African American, non-Hispanic/Latino; 1 American Indian or Alaska Native, non-Hispanic/Latino; 9 Asian, non-Hispanic/Latino), 22 international. Average age 24. 131 applicants, 48% accepted, 37 enrolled. In 2011, 28 master's, 3 doctorates, 13 other advanced degrees awarded. *Degree requirements:* For master's, comprehensive exam or thesis; for doctorate, comprehensive exam, thesis/dissertation. *Entrance requirements:* For master's, GRE General Test (exercise science and nutrition), minimum GPA of 3.0; for doctorate, GRE General Test, minimum GPA of 3.0 (PhD). Additional exam requirements/recommendations for international students: Required—TOEFL (minimum score 550 paper-based; 213 computer-based; 79 iBT), IELTS (minimum score 6.5). *Application deadline:* For fall admission, 4/1 for domestic students, 2/1 for international students; for spring admission, 8/15 for international students. Applications are processed on a rolling basis. Application fee: $50. Electronic applications accepted. *Financial support:* In 2011–12, 10 students received support, including 1 research assistantship with tuition reimbursement available (averaging $18,000 per year), 9 teaching assistantships with full and partial tuition reimbursements available (averaging $11,000 per year); career-related internships or fieldwork, Federal Work-Study, institutionally sponsored loans, scholarships/grants, health care benefits, tuition waivers (full and partial), unspecified assistantships, and stipends also available. Financial award application deadline: 3/15; financial award applicants required to submit FAFSA. *Faculty research:* Cardiovascular disease-diet and exercise, respiratory control and muscle function, plasticity of connective and neural tissue, exercise nutrition, diet and cancer. *Unit head:* Dr. David Pendergast, Chair, 716-829-6795, Fax: 716-829-2979, E-mail: dpenderg@buffalo.edu. *Application contact:* Dr. Gaspar Farkas, Director of Graduate Studies, 716-829-6756, Fax: 716-829-2428, E-mail: farkas@buffalo.edu. Web site: http://phhp.buffalo.edu/ens/.

The University of Akron, Graduate School, College of Education, Department of Sport Science and Wellness Education, Program in Exercise Physiology/Adult Fitness, Akron, OH 44325. Offers MA, MS. *Students:* 30 full-time (18 women), 18 part-time (9 women); includes 2 minority (both Black or African American, non-Hispanic/Latino), 2 international. Average age 29. 43 applicants, 72% accepted, 21 enrolled. In 2011, 22 master's awarded. *Degree requirements:* For master's, comprehensive exam, thesis optional. *Entrance requirements:* For master's, minimum GPA of 2.75, two letters of recommendation, statement of purpose. Additional exam requirements/recommendations for international students: Required—TOEFL (minimum score 550 paper-based; 213 computer-based; 79 iBT). *Application deadline:* Applications are processed on a rolling basis. Application fee: $30 ($40 for international students). Electronic applications accepted. *Expenses:* Tuition, state resident: full-time $7038; part-time $391 per credit hour. Tuition, nonresident: full-time $12,051; part-time $670 per credit hour. *Required fees:* $1274; $34 per credit hour. *Unit head:* Dr. Ron Otterstetter, Coordinator, 330-972-7738, E-mail: ro5@uakron.edu. *Application contact:* Dr. Mark Tausig, Associate Dean, 330-972-6266, Fax: 330-972-6475, E-mail: mtausig@uakron.edu.

The University of Akron, Graduate School, College of Education, Department of Sport Science and Wellness Education, Program in Sports Science/Coaching, Akron, OH 44325. Offers MA, MS. *Students:* 44 full-time (11 women), 29 part-time (8 women); includes 12 minority (9 Black or African American, non-Hispanic/Latino; 1 Hispanic/Latino; 2 Two or more races, non-Hispanic/Latino), 1 international. Average age 28. 57 applicants, 72% accepted, 29 enrolled. In 2011, 27 master's awarded. *Degree requirements:* For master's, comprehensive exam, thesis optional. *Entrance requirements:* For master's, minimum GPA of 2.75, three letters of recommendation, statement of purpose. Additional exam requirements/recommendations for international students: Required—TOEFL (minimum score 550 paper-based; 213 computer-based; 79 iBT). *Application deadline:* Applications are processed on a rolling basis. Application fee: $30 ($40 for international students). Electronic applications accepted. *Expenses:* Tuition, state resident: full-time $7038; part-time $391 per credit hour. Tuition, nonresident: full-time $12,051; part-time $670 per credit hour. *Required fees:* $1274; $34 per credit hour. *Unit head:* Dr. Alan Kornspan, Program Coordinator, 330-972-8145, E-mail: alan3@uakron.edu. *Application contact:* Dr. Mark Tausig, Associate Dean, 330-972-6266, Fax: 330-972-6475, E-mail: mtausig@uakron.edu.

The University of Alabama, Graduate School, College of Education, Department of Kinesiology, Tuscaloosa, AL 35487. Offers alternative sport pedagogy (MA); exercise science (MA, PhD); human performance (MA); sport management (MA); sport pedagogy (MA, PhD). Part-time programs available. *Faculty:* 8 full-time (1 woman). *Students:* 59 full-time (22 women), 22 part-time (14 women); includes 11 minority (7 Black or African American, non-Hispanic/Latino; 1 Asian, non-Hispanic/Latino; 2 Hispanic/Latino; 1 Two or more races, non-Hispanic/Latino), 7 international. Average age 30. 50 applicants, 78% accepted, 20 enrolled. In 2011, 23 master's, 6 doctorates awarded. *Median time to degree:* Of those who began their doctoral program in fall 2003, 100% received their degree in 8 years or less. *Degree requirements:* For master's, comprehensive exam, thesis optional; for doctorate, comprehensive exam, thesis/dissertation. *Entrance requirements:* For master's and doctorate, GRE, MAT, minimum GPA of 3.0. Additional exam requirements/recommendations for international students: Required—TOEFL. *Application deadline:* Applications are processed on a rolling basis. Application fee: $50 ($60 for international students). Electronic applications accepted. *Expenses:* Tuition, state resident: full-time $8600. Tuition, nonresident: full-time $21,900. *Financial support:* In 2011–12, 14 students received support, including 13 teaching assistantships with full tuition reimbursements available (averaging $8,678 per year). *Faculty research:* Race, gender and sexuality in sports; physical education teacher socialization; disability sports; physical activity and health; environmental physiology. *Total annual research expenditures:* $19,866. *Unit head:* Dr. Matt Curtner-Smith, Department Head and Professor, 205-348-9209, Fax: 205-348-0867, E-mail: msmith@bamaed.ua.edu. *Application contact:* Dr. Kathy S. Wetzel, Assistant Dean for Student Services, 205-348-1154, Fax: 205-348-0080, E-mail: kwetzel@bamaed.ua.edu. Web site: http://www.kinesiology.ua.edu/.

University of Alberta, Faculty of Graduate Studies and Research, Department of Physical Education and Recreation, Edmonton, AB T6G 2E1, Canada. Offers physical education (M Sc); recreation and physical education (MA, PhD). Part-time programs available. Terminal master's awarded for partial completion of doctoral program. *Degree requirements:* For master's, thesis (for some programs); for doctorate, thesis/dissertation. *Entrance requirements:* For master's, bachelor's degree in related field; for doctorate, master's degree in related field with thesis. Additional exam requirements/recommendations for international students: Required—TOEFL. *Faculty research:* Motivation and adherence to physical ability, performance enhancement, adapted physical activity, exercise physiology, sport administration, tourism.

University of Calgary, Faculty of Graduate Studies, Faculty of Kinesiology, Calgary, AB T2N 1N4, Canada. Offers biomedical engineering (M Sc, PhD); kinesiology (M Kin, M Sc, PhD), including biomechanics (PhD), health and exercise physiology (PhD). *Degree requirements:* For master's, thesis (M Sc); for doctorate, thesis/dissertation. *Entrance requirements:* Additional exam requirements/recommendations for international students: Required—TOEFL. Electronic applications accepted. *Faculty research:* Load acting on the human body, muscle mechanics and physiology, optimizing high performance athlete performance, eye movement in sports, analysis of body composition.

University of California, Davis, Graduate Studies, Graduate Group in Exercise Science, Davis, CA 95616. Offers MS. *Degree requirements:* For master's, thesis. *Entrance requirements:* For master's, GRE, minimum GPA of 3.25. Additional exam requirements/recommendations for international students: Required—TOEFL (minimum score 550 paper-based; 213 computer-based). Electronic applications accepted.

University of Central Florida, College of Education, Department of Child, Family and Community Sciences, Program in Sport and Exercise Science, Orlando, FL 32816. Offers MS. Part-time and evening/weekend programs available. *Students:* 43 full-time (15 women), 40 part-time (16 women); includes 17 minority (13 Black or African American, non-Hispanic/Latino; 3 Hispanic/Latino; 1 Two or more races, non-Hispanic/Latino), 1 international. Average age 25. 67 applicants, 58% accepted, 25 enrolled. In 2011, 34 master's awarded. *Entrance requirements:* For master's, GRE General Test. Additional exam requirements/recommendations for international students: Required—TOEFL. *Application deadline:* For fall admission, 7/15 for domestic students; for spring admission, 12/1 for domestic students. Application fee: $30. Electronic applications accepted. *Expenses:* Tuition, state resident: part-time $277.08 per credit hour. Tuition, nonresident: part-time $277.08 per credit hour. Part-time tuition and fees vary according to degree level and program. *Financial support:* In 2011–12, 7 students received support, including 1 fellowship with partial tuition reimbursement available (averaging $1,300 per year), 4 research assistantships with partial tuition reimbursements available (averaging $6,900 per year), 3 teaching assistantships with partial tuition reimbursements available (averaging $5,700 per year); career-related internships or fieldwork, Federal Work-Study, institutionally sponsored loans, tuition waivers (partial), and unspecified assistantships also available. Financial award application deadline: 3/1; financial award applicants required to submit FAFSA. *Unit head:* Dr. Jay Hoffman, Chair, 407-823-1151, E-mail: jay.hoffman@ucf.edu. *Application contact:* Barbara Rodriguez, Director, Admissions and Registration, 407-823-2766, Fax: 407-823-6442, E-mail: gradadmissions@ucf.edu.

University of Central Florida, College of Education, Education Doctoral Programs, Orlando, FL 32816. Offers communication sciences and disorders (PhD); counselor education (PhD); education (Ed D); elementary education (PhD); exceptional education (PhD); exercise physiology (PhD); higher education (PhD); hospitality education (PhD); instructional technology (PhD); mathematics education (PhD); reading education (PhD); science education (PhD); social science education (PhD); TESOL (PhD). *Students:* 135 full-time (87 women), 73 part-time (51 women); includes 49 minority (21 Black or African American, non-Hispanic/Latino; 4 Asian, non-Hispanic/Latino; 20 Hispanic/Latino; 4 Two or more races, non-Hispanic/Latino), 18 international. Average age 39. 125 applicants, 46% accepted, 46 enrolled. In 2011, 43 doctorates awarded. Application fee: $30. Electronic applications accepted. *Expenses:* Tuition, state resident: part-time $277.08 per credit hour. Tuition, nonresident: part-time $277.08 per credit hour. Part-time tuition and fees vary according to degree level and program. *Financial support:* In 2011–12, 85 students received support, including 48 fellowships with partial tuition reimbursements available (averaging $5,900 per year), 36 research assistantships with partial tuition reimbursements available (averaging $6,900 per year), 59 teaching assistantships with partial tuition reimbursements available (averaging $6,900 per year). *Unit head:* Dr. Rex Culp, Associate Dean, 407-823-5391, E-mail: rex.culp@ucf.edu. *Application contact:* Barbara Rodriguez, Associate Director, Admissions and Registration, 407-823-2766, Fax: 407-823-6442, E-mail: gradadmissions@ucf.edu. Web site: http://education.ucf.edu/departments.cfm.

University of Central Missouri, The Graduate School, College of Health and Human Services, Warrensburg, MO 64093. Offers criminal justice (MS); industrial hygiene (MS); occupational safety management (MS); physical education/exercise and sport science (MS); rural family nursing (MS); social gerontology (MS); sociology (MA); speech language pathology and audiology (MS). *Accreditation:* NCATE. Part-time programs available. Postbaccalaureate distance learning degree programs offered. *Entrance requirements:* Additional exam requirements/recommendations for international students: Required—TOEFL (minimum score 550 paper-based; 79 computer-based). Electronic applications accepted.

University of Connecticut, Graduate School, Neag School of Education, Department of Kinesiology, Program in Exercise Science, Storrs, CT 06269. Offers MA, PhD. Terminal master's awarded for partial completion of doctoral program. *Degree requirements:* For master's, comprehensive exam, thesis or alternative; for doctorate, thesis/dissertation. *Entrance requirements:* For doctorate, GRE General Test. Additional exam requirements/recommendations for international students: Required—TOEFL (minimum score 550 paper-based; 213 computer-based). Electronic applications accepted.

University of Dayton, Department of Health and Sport Science, Dayton, OH 45469-1300. Offers exercise science (MS Ed); physical therapy (DPT). Part-time programs available. *Faculty:* 16 full-time (7 women). *Students:* 113 full-time (70 women), 4 part-time (1 woman); includes 4 minority (all Black or African American, non-Hispanic/Latino), 5 international. Average age 36. 195 applicants, 43% accepted, 41 enrolled. In 2011, 3 master's, 34 doctorates awarded. *Degree requirements:* For master's, thesis; for doctorate, thesis/dissertation. *Entrance requirements:* For master's, GRE General Test, MAT, minimum GPA of 2.75; for doctorate, GRE General Test, minimum GPA of 3.0, 80 observation hours. Additional exam requirements/recommendations for international students: Required—TOEFL (minimum score 550 paper-based; 213 computer-based; 80 iBT). *Application deadline:* For fall admission, 2/15 priority date for domestic students, 3/1 for international students; for winter admission, 7/1 for international students; for spring admission, 1/1 for international students. Applications are processed on a rolling basis. Application fee: $0 ($50 for international students). Electronic applications accepted. *Expenses: Tuition:* Full-time $8400; part-time $700 per credit hour. *Required fees:* $25 per semester. Tuition and fees vary according to degree level. *Financial support:* In 2011–12, 4 students received support, including 8 research assistantships with partial tuition reimbursements available (averaging $4,800 per year), 5 teaching assistantships with full tuition reimbursements available (averaging $8,550 per year); career-related internships or fieldwork, institutionally sponsored loans, health care benefits, and unspecified assistantships also available. Financial award applicants required to submit FAFSA. *Faculty research:* Energy expenditure, strength, training, teaching nutrition and calcium intake for children and families in Head-Start. *Unit head:* Dr. Lloyd Laubach, Interim Chair, 937-229-4240, Fax: 937-229-4244, E-mail: llaubach1@udayton.edu. *Application contact:* Laura Greger, Administrative Assistant, 937-229-4225, E-mail: lgreger1@udayton.edu.

University of Florida, Graduate School, College of Health and Human Performance, Department of Applied Physiology and Kinesiology, Gainesville, FL 32611. Offers athletic training/sport medicine (MS); biobehavioral science (MS, PhD); clinical exercise physiology (MS); exercise physiology (MS, PhD); health and human performance (PhD); human performance (MS). *Degree requirements:* For master's, comprehensive exam, thesis (for some programs); for doctorate, comprehensive exam, thesis/dissertation. *Entrance requirements:* For doctorate, GRE General Test. Additional exam requirements/recommendations for international students: Required—TOEFL (minimum score 550 paper-based; 213 computer-based; 80 iBT), IELTS (minimum score 6). Electronic applications accepted. *Faculty research:* Cardiovascular disease; basic mechanisms that underlie exercise-induced changes in the body at the organ, tissue, cellular and molecular level; development of rehabilitation techniques for regaining motor control after stroke or as a consequence of Parkinson's disease; maintaining optimal health and delaying age-related declines in physiological function; psychomotor mechanisms impacting health and performance across the life span.

University of Houston, College of Liberal Arts and Social Sciences, Department of Health and Human Performance, Houston, TX 77204. Offers exercise science (MS); human nutrition (MS); human space exploration sciences (MS); kinesiology (PhD); physical education (M Ed). *Accreditation:* NCATE (one or more programs are accredited). Part-time and evening/weekend programs available. *Degree requirements:* For master's, comprehensive exam (for some programs), thesis (for some programs); for doctorate, comprehensive exam, thesis/dissertation, qualifying exam, candidacy paper. *Entrance requirements:* For master's, GRE (minimum 35th percentile on each section), minimum cumulative GPA of 3.0; for doctorate, GRE (minimum 35th percentile on each section), minimum cumulative GPA of 3.3. Additional exam requirements/recommendations for international students: Required—TOEFL (minimum score 550 paper-based; 79 iBT). Electronic applications accepted. *Faculty research:* Biomechanics, exercise physiology, obesity, nutrition, space exploration science.

University of Houston–Clear Lake, School of Human Sciences and Humanities, Programs in Human Sciences, Houston, TX 77058-1098. Offers behavioral sciences (MA), including criminology, cross cultural studies, general psychology, sociology; clinical psychology (MA); criminology (MA); cross cultural studies (MA); family therapy (MA); fitness and human performance (MA); school psychology (MA). *Accreditation:* AAMFT/COAMFTE. Part-time and evening/weekend programs available. Postbaccalaureate distance learning degree programs offered (minimal on-campus study). *Degree requirements:* For master's, thesis or alternative. *Entrance requirements:* For master's, GRE General Test. Additional exam requirements/recommendations for international students: Required—TOEFL (minimum score 550 paper-based; 213 computer-based). Electronic applications accepted. *Faculty research:* Smoking cessation, adolescent sexuality, white collar crime, serial murder, human factors/human computer interaction.

The University of Iowa, Graduate College, College of Liberal Arts and Sciences, Department of Health and Sport Studies, Iowa City, IA 52242-1316. Offers psychology of sport and physical activity (MA, PhD); sports studies (MA, PhD). *Degree requirements:* For master's, thesis optional, exam; for doctorate, comprehensive exam, thesis/dissertation. *Entrance requirements:* For master's and doctorate, GRE General Test, minimum GPA of 3.0. Additional exam requirements/recommendations for international students: Required—TOEFL (minimum score 600 paper-based; 250 computer-based; 100 iBT). Electronic applications accepted.

The University of Iowa, Graduate College, College of Liberal Arts and Sciences, Department of Integrative Physiology, Iowa City, IA 52242-1316. Offers exercise science (MS); integrative physiology (PhD). *Degree requirements:* For master's, thesis optional, exam; for doctorate, comprehensive exam, thesis/dissertation. *Entrance requirements:* For master's and doctorate, GRE General Test, minimum GPA of 3.0. Additional exam requirements/recommendations for international students: Required—TOEFL (minimum score 550 paper-based; 213 computer-based; 81 iBT). Electronic applications accepted.

University of Kentucky, Graduate School, College of Education, Program in Kinesiology and Health Promotion, Lexington, KY 40506-0032. Offers exercise science (PhD); kinesiology (MS, Ed D). Terminal master's awarded for partial completion of doctoral program. *Degree requirements:* For master's, comprehensive exam, thesis optional; for doctorate, comprehensive exam, thesis/dissertation. *Entrance requirements:* For master's, GRE General Test, minimum undergraduate GPA of 2.75; for doctorate, GRE General Test, minimum graduate GPA of 3.0. Additional exam requirements/recommendations for international students: Required—TOEFL (minimum score 550 paper-based; 213 computer-based). Electronic applications accepted.

University of Lethbridge, School of Graduate Studies, Lethbridge, AB T1K 3M4, Canada. Offers accounting (MScM); addictions counseling (M Sc); agricultural biotechnology (M Sc); agricultural studies (M Sc, MA); anthropology (MA); archaeology (MA); art (MA, MFA); biochemistry (M Sc); biological sciences (M Sc); biomolecular science (PhD); biosystems and biodiversity (PhD); Canadian studies (MA); chemistry (M Sc); computer science (M Sc); computer science and geographical information science (M Sc); counseling psychology (M Ed); dramatic arts (MA); earth, space, and physical science (PhD); economics (MA); educational leadership (M Ed); English (MA); environmental science (M Sc); evolution and behavior (PhD); exercise science (M Sc); finance (MScM); French (MA); French/German (MA); French/Spanish (MA); general education (M Ed); general management (MScM); geography (M Sc, MA); German (MA); health science (M Sc); history (MA); human resource management and labour relations (MScM); individualized multidisciplinary (M Sc, MA); information systems (MScM); international management (MScM); kinesiology (M Sc, MA); management (M Sc, MA); marketing (MScM); mathematics (M Sc); music (M Mus, MA); Native American studies (MA); neuroscience (M Sc, PhD); new media (MA); nursing (M Sc); philosophy (MA); physics (M Sc); policy and strategy (MScM); political science (MA); psychology (M Sc, MA); religious studies (MA); social sciences (MA); sociology (MA); theatre and dramatic arts (MFA); theoretical and computational science (PhD); urban and regional studies (MA); women's studies (MA). Part-time and evening/weekend programs available. *Degree requirements:* For doctorate, comprehensive exam, thesis/dissertation. *Entrance requirements:* For master's, GMAT (M Sc in management), bachelor's degree in related field, minimum GPA of 3.0 during previous 20 graded semester courses, 2 years teaching or related experience (M Ed); for doctorate, master's degree, minimum graduate GPA of 3.5. Additional exam requirements/recommendations for international students: Required—TOEFL. *Faculty research:* Movement and brain plasticity, gibberellin physiology, photosynthesis, carbon cycling, molecular properties of main-group ring components.

University of Louisiana at Monroe, Graduate School, College of Education and Human Development, Department of Kinesiology, Monroe, LA 71209-0001. Offers applied exercise physiology (MS); clinical exercise physiology (MS). Part-time and evening/weekend programs available. *Faculty:* 4 full-time (0 women). *Students:* 15 full-time (4 women), 8 part-time (4 women); includes 6 minority (4 Black or African American, non-Hispanic/Latino; 1 American Indian or Alaska Native, non-Hispanic/Latino; 1 Hispanic/Latino), 2 international. Average age 24. 13 applicants, 92% accepted, 9 enrolled. In 2011, 15 master's awarded. *Degree requirements:* For master's, comprehensive exam, thesis, 6-hour internship. *Entrance requirements:* For master's, GRE General Test. Additional exam requirements/recommendations for international students: Required—TOEFL (minimum score 500 paper-based; 173 computer-based; 61 iBT). *Application deadline:* For fall admission, 8/24 priority date for domestic students, 7/1 for international students; for winter admission, 12/14 priority date for domestic students; for spring admission, 1/19 for domestic students, 11/1 for international students. Applications are processed on a rolling basis. Application fee: $20 ($30 for international students). Electronic applications accepted. *Expenses:* Tuition, state resident: full-time $3436; part-time $240 per credit hour. Tuition, nonresident: full-time $3436; part-time $240 per credit hour. *International tuition:* $10,733 full-time. *Required fees:* $1460.90. *Financial support:* In 2011–12, 4 research assistantships with full tuition reimbursements (averaging $2,500 per year) were awarded; career-related internships or fieldwork, Federal Work-Study, and unspecified assistantships also available. Financial award application deadline: 4/1; financial award applicants required to submit FAFSA. *Faculty research:* Cardiovascular disease risk factors; exercise and immunological system; attitude, exercise, and the aged. *Unit head:* Dr. Ken Alford, Department Head, 318-342-1306, E-mail: alford@ulm.edu. *Application contact:* Dr. Tommie Church, Director of Graduate Studies, 318-342-1321, E-mail: church@ulm.edu. Web site: http://www.ulm.edu/kinesiology/.

University of Louisville, Graduate School, College of Education and Human Development, Department of Health and Sport Sciences, Louisville, KY 40292-0001. Offers community health education (M Ed); exercise physiology (MS); health and physical education (MAT); sport administration (MS). Part-time and evening/weekend programs available. *Entrance requirements:* For master's, GRE General Test. Additional exam requirements/recommendations for international students: Required—TOEFL (minimum score 560 paper-based; 210 computer-based; 83 iBT). Electronic applications accepted. *Expenses:* Tuition, state resident: full-time $9692; part-time $539 per credit hour. Tuition, nonresident: full-time $20,168; part-time $1121 per credit hour. Tuition and fees vary according to program and reciprocity agreements. *Faculty research:* Impact of sports and sport marketing on society, factors associated with school and community health, cardiac and pulmonary rehabilitation, impact of participation in activities on student retention and graduation, strength and conditioning.

University of Maine, Graduate School, College of Education and Human Development, Program in Kinesiology and Physical Education, Orono, ME 04469. Offers curriculum and instruction (M Ed); exercise science (MS). Part-time and evening/weekend programs available. *Students:* 10 full-time (3 women), 2 part-time (1 woman); includes 2 minority (1 Hispanic/Latino; 1 Two or more races, non-Hispanic/Latino). Average age 29. 16 applicants, 69% accepted, 9 enrolled. In 2011, 8 degrees awarded. *Degree requirements:* For master's, thesis or alternative. *Entrance requirements:* For master's, MAT. Additional exam requirements/recommendations for international students: Required—TOEFL. *Application deadline:* For fall admission, 2/1 priority date for domestic students. Applications are processed on a rolling basis. Application fee: $65. Electronic applications accepted. *Expenses:* Tuition, state resident: full-time $5016. Tuition, nonresident: full-time $14,424. *Financial support:* Career-related internships or fieldwork, Federal Work-Study, institutionally sponsored loans, tuition waivers (full and partial), and unspecified assistantships available. Support available to part-time students. Financial award application deadline: 3/1. *Unit head:* Dr. Janet Spector, Coordinator, 207-581-2444, Fax: 207-581-2423. *Application contact:* Scott G. Delcourt, Associate Dean of the Graduate School, 207-581-3291, Fax: 207-581-3232, E-mail: graduate@maine.edu. Web site: http://www2umaine.edu/graduate/.

University of Memphis, Graduate School, College of Education, Department of Health and Sport Sciences, Memphis, TN 38152. Offers clinical nutrition (MS); exercise and sport science (MS); health promotion (MS); physical education teacher education (MS), including teacher education; sport and leisure commerce (MS). Part-time and evening/weekend programs available. *Degree requirements:* For master's, comprehensive exam, thesis. *Entrance requirements:* For master's, GRE General Test or GMAT (sport and leisure commerce). *Faculty research:* Sport marketing and consumer analysis, health psychology, smoking cessation, psychosocial aspects of cardiovascular disease, global health promotion.

University of Miami, Graduate School, School of Education and Human Development, Department of Kinesiology and Sport Sciences, Program in Exercise Physiology, Coral Gables, FL 33124. Offers exercise physiology (MS Ed, PhD); strength and conditioning (MS Ed). Part-time and evening/weekend programs available. *Faculty:* 4 full-time (1 woman). *Students:* 34 full-time (16 women), 4 part-time (1 woman); includes 15 minority (2 Black or African American, non-Hispanic/Latino; 1 Asian, non-Hispanic/Latino; 11 Hispanic/Latino; 1 Two or more races, non-Hispanic/Latino), 7 international. Average age 28. 48 applicants, 67% accepted, 15 enrolled. In 2011, 9 master's, 5 doctorates awarded. Terminal master's awarded for partial completion of doctoral program. *Degree requirements:* For master's, comprehensive exam (for some programs), thesis optional, special project; for doctorate, thesis/dissertation, qualifying exam. *Entrance requirements:* For master's and doctorate, GRE General Test. Additional exam requirements/recommendations for international students: Required—TOEFL (minimum score 550 paper-based; 80 iBT); Recommended—IELTS (minimum score 6.5). *Application deadline:* For fall admission, 10/15 for international students. Applications are processed on a rolling basis. Application fee: $65. Electronic applications accepted. *Financial support:* In 2011–12, 31 students received support. Health care benefits and unspecified assistantships available. Support available to part-time students. Financial award application deadline: 3/1; financial award applicants required to submit FAFSA. *Faculty research:* Women's health, cardiovascular health, aging, metabolism, obesity. *Unit head:* Dr. Arlette Perry, Department Chairperson, 305-284-3024, Fax: 305-284-5168, E-mail: aperry@miami.edu. *Application contact:* Lois Heffernan, Graduate Admissions Coordinator, 305-284-2167, Fax: 305-284-9395, E-mail: lheffernan@miami.edu.

University of Minnesota, Twin Cities Campus, Graduate School, College of Education and Human Development, School of Kinesiology, Minneapolis, MN 55455-0213. Offers adapted physical education (MA, PhD); biomechanics (MA); biomechanics and neural control (PhD); coaching (Certificate); developmental adapted physical education (M Ed); exercise physiology (MA, PhD); human factors/ergonomics (MA, PhD); international/comparative sport (MA, PhD); kinesiology (M Ed, MA, PhD); leisure services/management (MA, PhD); motor development (MA, PhD); motor learning/control (MA, PhD); outdoor education/recreation (MA, PhD); physical education (M Ed); recreation, park, and leisure studies (M Ed, MA, PhD); sport and exercise science (M Ed); sport management (M Ed, MA, PhD); sport psychology (MA, PhD); sport sociology (MA, PhD); therapeutic recreation (MA, PhD). Part-time programs available. *Faculty:* 15 full-time (7 women). *Students:* 144 full-time (72 women), 49 part-time (19 women); includes 20 minority (9 Black or African American, non-Hispanic/Latino; 3 American Indian or Alaska Native, non-Hispanic/Latino; 4 Asian, non-Hispanic/Latino; 2 Hispanic/Latino; 2 Native Hawaiian or other Pacific Islander, non-Hispanic/Latino), 18 international. Average age 29. 198 applicants, 42% accepted, 77 enrolled. In 2011, 74 master's, 11 doctorates, 19 other advanced degrees awarded. Terminal master's awarded for partial completion of doctoral program. *Degree requirements:* For master's, final oral exam; for doctorate, thesis/dissertation, preliminary written/oral exam, final oral exam. *Entrance requirements:* For master's, GRE or MAT, minimum GPA of 3.0; for doctorate, GRE or MAT, minimum GPA of 3.0, writing sample. Application fee: $55. *Financial support:* In 2011–12, 1 fellowship (averaging $60,000 per year), 4 research assistantships with full tuition reimbursements (averaging $99,992 per year), 48 teaching assistantships with full tuition reimbursements (averaging $12,534 per year) were awarded; career-related internships or fieldwork, Federal Work-Study, institutionally sponsored loans, and tuition waivers (full and partial) also available. Support available to part-time students. *Faculty research:* Exercise physiology; biochemical, molecular and nutritional aspects of exercise; sport training and performance; sport and exercise psychology; behavioral aspects of physical activity; youth sport science; gender and sport sociology; sports management; sports policy, marketing and law; motor development and disabilities; movement perception and action; movement neuroscience. *Total annual research expenditures:* $369,026. *Unit head:* Dr. Li Li Ji, Director, 612-624-9809, Fax: 612-626-7700, E-mail: llji@umn.edu. *Application contact:* Dr. Jennifer Engler, Assistant Dean, 612-626-2887, Fax: 612-626-7496, E-mail: engle009@umn.edu.

University of Mississippi, Graduate School, School of Applied Sciences, Department of Health, Exercise Science, and Recreation Management, Oxford, University, MS 38677. Offers exercise science (MS); exercise science and leisure management (PhD); park and recreation management (MA); wellness (MS). *Students:* 50 full-time (32 women), 13 part-time (7 women); includes 6 minority (all Black or African American, non-Hispanic/Latino), 9 international. In 2011, 9 master's, 1 doctorate awarded. *Degree requirements:* For master's, thesis (for some programs); for doctorate, thesis/dissertation. *Entrance requirements:* For master's, GRE General Test, minimum GPA of 3.0; for doctorate, GRE General Test. Additional exam requirements/recommendations for international students: Required—TOEFL. *Application deadline:* For fall admission, 4/1 for domestic students; for spring admission, 10/1 for domestic students. Applications are processed on a rolling basis. Application fee: $25. *Financial support:* Scholarships/grants available. Financial award application deadline: 3/1; financial award applicants required to submit FAFSA. *Unit head:* Dr. Mark Loftin, Interim Chair, 662-915-5844, Fax: 662-915-5525, E-mail: mloftin@olemiss.edu. *Application contact:* Dr. Christy M. Wyandt, Associate Dean, 662-915-7474, Fax: 662-915-7577, E-mail: cwyandt@olemiss.edu.

University of Missouri, Graduate School, College of Human Environmental Sciences, Department of Nutritional Sciences, Columbia, MO 65211. Offers exercise physiology (MA, PhD); nutritional sciences (MS, PhD). *Faculty:* 10 full-time (7 women). *Students:* 7 full-time (5 women), 8 part-time (4 women), 2 international. Average age 26. 27 applicants, 15% accepted, 4 enrolled. In 2011, 3 master's, 4 doctorates awarded. *Degree requirements:* For doctorate, thesis/dissertation. *Entrance requirements:* For master's and doctorate, GRE General Test, minimum GPA of 3.0. Additional exam requirements/recommendations for international students: Required—TOEFL (minimum score 500 paper-based; 173 computer-based; 61 iBT). *Application deadline:* Applications are processed on a rolling basis. Application fee: $55 ($75 for international students). *Expenses:* Tuition, state resident: full-time $5881. Tuition, nonresident: full-time $15,183. *Required fees:* $952. Tuition and fees vary according to campus/location and program. *Financial support:* Fellowships, research assistantships, teaching assistantships, and institutionally sponsored loans available. *Faculty research:* Fitness and wellness; body composition research; child care provider workforce development; childhood overweight: etiology and outcomes; development during infancy and early childhood; regulation and organization of glycolysis; metabolomics; diabetes and smooth muscle metabolism; lipid metabolism and lipotoxicity - mitochondrial dysfunction in diabetes, atherosclerosis, and cell phenotype transformation; magnetic resonance measures of cellular metabolism; smooth muscle physiology/pathophysiology. *Application contact:* Twila J. Stokes, 573-882-4136, E-mail: stokest@missouri.edu. Web site: http://ns.missouri.edu/.

The University of Montana, Graduate School, Phyllis J. Washington College of Education and Human Sciences, Department of Health and Human Performance, Missoula, MT 59812-0002. Offers exercise science (MS); health and human performance (MS); health promotion (MS). Part-time programs available. *Entrance requirements:* For master's, GRE General Test. Additional exam requirements/recommendations for international students: Required—TOEFL. *Faculty research:* Exercise physiology, performance psychology, nutrition, pre-employment physical screening, program evaluation.

University of Nebraska at Kearney, Graduate Studies, College of Education, Department of Health, Physical Education, Recreation, and Leisure Studies, Kearney, NE 68849-0001. Offers adapted physical education (MA Ed); exercise science (MA Ed); master teacher (MA Ed). Part-time and evening/weekend programs available. *Degree requirements:* For master's, comprehensive exam, thesis optional. *Entrance requirements:* For master's, GRE General Test. Additional exam requirements/recommendations for international students: Required—TOEFL (minimum score 550 paper-based; 213 computer-based). Electronic applications accepted. *Faculty research:* Ergonomic aids, nutrition, motor development, sports pedagogy, applied behavior analysis.

University of Nebraska–Lincoln, Graduate College, College of Education and Human Sciences, Department of Nutrition and Health Sciences, Lincoln, NE 68588. Offers community nutrition and health promotion (MS); nutrition (MS, PhD); nutrition and exercise (MS); nutrition and health sciences (MS, PhD). *Degree requirements:* For master's, thesis optional. *Entrance requirements:* For master's, GRE General Test. Additional exam requirements/recommendations for international students: Required—TOEFL (minimum score 550 paper-based; 213 computer-based). Electronic applications accepted. *Faculty research:* Foods/food service administration, community nutrition science, diet-health relationships.

University of Nevada, Las Vegas, Graduate College, School of Allied Health Sciences, Department of Kinesiology, Las Vegas, NV 89154-3034. Offers exercise physiology (MS); kinesiology (MS). Part-time programs available. *Faculty:* 10 full-time (4 women), 1 part-time/adjunct (0 women). *Students:* 18 full-time (9 women), 25 part-time (8 women); includes 11 minority (1 Black or African American, non-Hispanic/Latino; 3 Asian, non-Hispanic/Latino; 5 Hispanic/Latino; 2 Two or more races, non-Hispanic/Latino), 2 international. Average age 27. 38 applicants, 79% accepted, 9 enrolled. In 2011, 18 master's awarded. *Degree requirements:* For master's, comprehensive exam (for some programs), thesis (for some programs). *Entrance requirements:* For master's, GRE General Test. Additional exam requirements/recommendations for international students: Required—TOEFL (minimum score 550 paper-based; 213 computer-based; 80 iBT), IELTS (minimum score 7). *Application deadline:* For fall admission, 6/15 priority date for domestic students, 5/1 for international students; for spring admission, 11/15 priority date for domestic students, 10/1 for international students. Applications are processed on a rolling basis. Application fee: $60 ($95 for international students). Electronic applications accepted. *Financial support:* In 2011–12, 21 students received support, including 6 research assistantships with partial tuition reimbursements available (averaging $12,792 per year), 15 teaching assistantships with partial tuition reimbursements available (averaging $8,617 per year); institutionally sponsored loans, scholarships/grants, health care benefits, and unspecified assistantships also available. Financial award application deadline: 3/1. *Faculty research:* Biomechanics of gait, factors in motor skill acquisition and performance, nutritional supplements and performance, lipoprotein chemistry, body composition methods. *Total annual research expenditures:* $131,409. *Unit head:* Dr. John Young, Chair/Professor, 702-895-4626, Fax: 702-895-1500, E-mail: john.young@unlv.edu. *Application contact:* Graduate College Admissions Evaluator, 702-895-3320, Fax: 702-895-4180, E-mail: gradcollege@unlv.edu. Web site: http://kinesiology.unlv.edu/.

University of New Brunswick Fredericton, School of Graduate Studies, Faculty of Kinesiology, Fredericton, NB E3B 5A3, Canada. Offers exercise and sport science (M Sc); sport and recreation management (MBA); sport and recreation studies (MA). Part-time programs available. *Faculty:* 15 full-time (7 women). *Students:* 39 full-time (15 women), 6 part-time (4 women). In 2011, 7 master's awarded. *Degree requirements:* For master's, thesis (for some programs). *Entrance requirements:* For master's, minimum GPA of 3.0, written statement of research goals and interests. Additional exam requirements/recommendations for international students: Required—TOEFL (minimum score 600 paper-based; 250 computer-based), TWE (minimum score 4). *Application deadline:* For winter admission, 1/31 for domestic students; for spring admission, 3/31 for domestic students. Applications are processed on a rolling basis. Application fee: $50 Canadian dollars. Electronic applications accepted. *Financial support:* In 2011–12, 38 fellowships with tuition reimbursements, 3 research assistantships, 56 teaching assistantships were awarded; career-related internships or fieldwork and scholarships/grants also available. *Unit head:* Dr. Tim McGarry, Acting Director of Graduate Studies, 506-458-7109, Fax: 506-453-3511, E-mail: tmcgarry@unb.ca. *Application contact:* Leslie Harquail, Graduate Secretary, 506-453-4575, Fax: 506-453-3511, E-mail: harquail@unb.ca. Web site: http://www.unbf.ca/kinesiology/.

University of New Mexico, Graduate School, College of Education, Department of Health, Exercise and Sports Sciences, Program in Physical Education, Albuquerque, NM 87131-2039. Offers adapted physical education (MS); curriculum and instruction (MS); exercise science (MS); generalist (MS); sports administration (MS). Part-time programs available. *Faculty:* 56 full-time (32 women), 41 part-time/adjunct (29 women). *Students:* 45 full-time (25 women), 44 part-time (10 women); includes 42 minority (4 Black or African American, non-Hispanic/Latino; 2 American Indian or Alaska Native, non-Hispanic/Latino; 2 Asian, non-Hispanic/Latino; 31 Hispanic/Latino; 3 Two or more races, non-Hispanic/Latino), 9 international. Average age 29. 65 applicants, 58% accepted, 29 enrolled. In 2011, 27 degrees awarded. Terminal master's awarded for partial completion of doctoral program. *Degree requirements:* For master's, comprehensive exam, thesis optional. *Entrance requirements:* For master's, GRE, 3 letters of reference, minimum cumulative GPA of 3.0 in last 2 years of bachelor's degree, letter of intent. Additional exam requirements/recommendations for international students: Required—TOEFL (minimum score 550 paper-based; 213 computer-based). *Application deadline:* For fall admission, 3/1 priority date for domestic students; for spring admission, 11/1 priority date for domestic students. Application fee: $50. Electronic applications accepted. *Financial support:* In 2011–12, 57 students received support, including 1 fellowship (averaging $2,290 per year), 1 teaching assistantship with full tuition reimbursement available (averaging $11,294 per year); career-related internships or fieldwork, Federal Work-Study, institutionally sponsored loans, scholarships/grants, health care benefits, tuition waivers, and unspecified assistantships also available. Financial award application deadline: 3/1; financial award applicants required to submit FAFSA. *Faculty research:* Physical education pedagogy, sports psychology, sports administration, cardiac rehabilitation, sports physiology, physical fitness assessment, exercise prescription. *Total annual research expenditures:* $17,400. *Unit head:* Dr. Gloria Napper-Owen, Chair, 505-277-8173, Fax: 505-277-6227, E-mail: napperow@unm.edu. *Application contact:* Carol Catania, Department Office, 505-277-5151, Fax: 505-277-6227, E-mail: catania@unm.edu. Web site: http://coe.unm.edu/departments/hess/pe-teacher-education.html.

University of New Mexico, Graduate School, College of Education, Department of Health, Exercise and Sports Sciences, Program in Physical Education, Sports and Exercise Science, Albuquerque, NM 87131-2039. Offers curriculum and instruction (PhD); exercise science (PhD); sports administration (PhD). Part-time programs available. *Students:* 26 full-time (12 women), 25 part-time (7 women); includes 17 minority (4 Black or African American, non-Hispanic/Latino; 3 Asian, non-Hispanic/Latino; 8 Hispanic/Latino; 1 Native Hawaiian or other Pacific Islander, non-Hispanic/Latino; 1 Two or more races, non-Hispanic/Latino), 11 international. Average age 34. 31 applicants, 45% accepted, 8 enrolled. In 2011, 4 degrees awarded. *Degree requirements:* For doctorate, comprehensive exam, thesis/dissertation, inquiry skills, 24 credits in supporting area. *Entrance requirements:* For doctorate, GRE, letter of intent, 3 letters of reference, minimum cumulative GPA of 3.0 in last 2 years of bachelor's degree. Additional exam requirements/recommendations for international students: Required—TOEFL (minimum score 550 paper-based; 213 computer-based). *Application deadline:* For fall admission, 3/1 priority date for domestic students; for spring admission, 11/1 priority date for domestic students. Application fee: $50. Electronic applications accepted. *Financial support:* In 2011–12, 33 students received support, including 3 fellowships (averaging $2,290 per year), 16 teaching assistantships with full tuition reimbursements available (averaging $10,987 per year); career-related internships or fieldwork, Federal Work-Study, institutionally sponsored loans, scholarships/grants, health care benefits, tuition waivers, and unspecified assistantships also available. Financial award application deadline: 3/1; financial award applicants required to submit FAFSA. *Faculty research:* Facility risk management, physical education pedagogy practices, physiological adaptations to exercise, physiological adaptations to heat. *Total annual research expenditures:* $17,400. *Unit head:* Dr. Gloria Napper-Owen, Chair, 505-277-8173, Fax: 505-277-6227, E-mail: napperow@unm.edu. *Application contact:* Carol Catania, Program Office, 505-277-5151, Fax: 505-277-6227, E-mail: catania@unm.edu. Web site: http://coe.unm.edu/index.php/hess/hess-programs/pe-teacher-education/degree-endorsement-programs/physical-education-sports-and-exercise-science-phd.ht.

University of North Alabama, College of Education, Department of Health, Physical Education, and Recreation, FLORENCE, AL 35632-0001. Offers health and human performance (MS), including exercise science, kinesiology, wellness and health promotion; P-12 physical education (MA Ed). *Faculty:* 3 full-time (2 women), 2 part-time/adjunct (0 women). *Students:* 11 full-time (4 women), 4 part-time (1 woman); includes 3 minority (2 Black or African American, non-Hispanic/Latino; 1 Two or more races, non-Hispanic/Latino), 2 international. Average age 24. In 2011, 4 master's awarded. *Unit head:* Dr. Thomas E. Coates, Chair, 256-765-4377. *Application contact:* Kim Mauldin, Director of Admissions, 256-765-4608, Fax: 256-765-4960, E-mail: komauldin@una.edu. Web site: http://www.una.edu/hper/docs/HPERThesisGuideliens.pdf.

The University of North Carolina at Chapel Hill, Graduate School, College of Arts and Sciences, Department of Exercise and Sport Science, Chapel Hill, NC 27599. Offers athletic training (MA); exercise physiology (MA); sport administration (MA). *Degree requirements:* For master's, comprehensive exam, thesis. *Entrance requirements:* For master's, GRE General Test, minimum GPA of 3.0. Additional exam requirements/recommendations for international students: Required—TOEFL (minimum score 550 paper-based). Electronic applications accepted. *Faculty research:* Mild head injury in sport, endocrine system's response to exercise, obesity and children, effect of aerobic exercise on cerebral bloodflow in elderly population.

The University of North Carolina at Charlotte, Graduate School, College of Health and Human Services, Department of Kinesiology, Charlotte, NC 28223-0001. Offers clinical exercise physiology (MS). Part-time programs available. *Faculty:* 8 full-time (4 women). *Students:* 12 full-time (all women), 13 part-time (7 women); includes 3 minority (1 Black or African American, non-Hispanic/Latino; 1 American Indian or Alaska Native, non-Hispanic/Latino; 1 Asian, non-Hispanic/Latino). Average age 26. 33 applicants, 73% accepted, 12 enrolled. In 2011, 12 master's awarded. *Degree requirements:* For master's, thesis or practicum. *Entrance requirements:* For master's, GRE or MAT. Additional exam requirements/recommendations for international students: Required—TOEFL (minimum score 557 paper-based; 220 computer-based; 83 iBT). *Application deadline:* For fall admission, 7/1 for domestic students, 5/1 for international students; for spring admission, 11/1 for domestic students, 10/1 for international students. Applications are processed on a rolling basis. Application fee: $65 ($75 for international students). Electronic applications accepted. *Expenses:* Tuition, state resident: full-time $3689. Tuition, nonresident: full-time $15,226. *Required fees:* $2198. Tuition and fees vary according to course load and program. *Financial support:* In 2011–12, 6 students received support, including 2 research assistantships (averaging $1,083 per year), 4 teaching assistantships (averaging $10,000 per year); career-related internships or fieldwork, institutionally sponsored loans, scholarships/grants, traineeships, and unspecified assistantships also available. Support available to part-time students. Financial award application deadline: 4/1; financial award applicants required to submit FAFSA. *Faculty research:* Genetic determinants of physical activity, cardiac muscle apoptosis with aging, sensorimotor deficits in knee osteoarthritis, mechanical laxity in functional ankle instability. *Total annual research expenditures:* $31,091. *Unit head:* Dr. Mitchell L. Cordova, Chair, 704-687-4695, Fax: 704-687-3180, E-mail: mcordova@uncc.edu. *Application contact:* Kathy B. Giddings, Director of Graduate Admissions, 704-687-5503, Fax: 704-687-3279, E-mail: gradadm@uncc.edu. Web site: http://www.health.uncc.edu/.

The University of North Carolina at Greensboro, Graduate School, School of Health and Human Performance, Department of Exercise and Sports Science, Greensboro, NC 27412-5001. Offers M Ed, MS, Ed D, PhD. *Degree requirements:* For master's, thesis (for some programs); for doctorate, thesis/dissertation. *Entrance requirements:* For master's and doctorate, GRE General Test. Additional exam requirements/recommendations for international students: Required—TOEFL. Electronic applications accepted.

University of Northern Colorado, Graduate School, College of Natural and Health Sciences, School of Sport and Exercise Science, Greeley, CO 80639. Offers exercise science (MS, PhD); sport administration (MS, PhD); sport pedagogy (MS, PhD). Part-time and evening/weekend programs available. *Degree requirements:* For master's, comprehensive exam; for doctorate, comprehensive exam, thesis/dissertation. *Entrance requirements:* For master's, 2 letters of recommendation, resume; for doctorate, GRE General Test, 3 letters of recommendation, resume. Electronic applications accepted.

University of North Florida, Brooks College of Health, Department of Clinical and Applied Movement Sciences, Jacksonville, FL 32224. Offers exercise science and chronic disease (MSH); physical therapy (DPT). *Accreditation:* APTA. Part-time and evening/weekend programs available. *Faculty:* 14 full-time (9 women), 2 part-time/adjunct (0 women). *Students:* 87 full-time (52 women); includes 10 minority (2 Black or African American, non-Hispanic/Latino; 1 Asian, non-Hispanic/Latino; 5 Hispanic/Latino; 2 Two or more races, non-Hispanic/Latino), 2 international. Average age 25. 303 applicants, 17% accepted, 27 enrolled. In 2011, 24 doctorates awarded. *Degree requirements:* For master's, internship. *Entrance requirements:* For master's, GRE General Test, minimum GPA of 3.0 in last 60 hours, volunteer/observation experience. Additional exam requirements/recommendations for international students: Required—TOEFL (minimum score 500 paper-based; 173 computer-based). *Application deadline:* For fall admission, 2/15 for domestic students, 1/15 for international students. Application fee: $30. Electronic applications accepted. *Expenses:* Tuition, state resident: full-time $8793; part-time $366.38 per credit hour. Tuition, nonresident: full-time $23,502; part-time $979.24 per credit hour. *Required fees:* $1384; $57.66 per credit hour. Tuition and fees vary according to course load and program. *Financial support:* In 2011–12, 35 students received support. Teaching assistantships, career-related internships or fieldwork, Federal Work-Study, scholarships/grants, and tuition waivers (partial) available. Support available to part-time students. Financial award application deadline: 4/1; financial award applicants required to submit FAFSA. *Faculty research:* Clinical outcomes related to orthopedic physical therapy interventions, instructional multimedia in physical therapy education, effect of functional electrical stimulation orthostatic hypotension in acute complete spinal cord injury individuals. *Total annual research expenditures:* $72,169. *Unit head:* Dr. Lillia Loriz, Chair, 904-620-2841, E-mail: lloriz@unf.edu. *Application contact:* Beth Dibble, Program Director, 904-620-2418, E-mail: ptadmissions@unf.edu. Web site: http://www.unf.edu/brooks/movement_science/.

University of Oklahoma, College of Arts and Sciences, Department of Health and Exercise Science, Norman, OK 73019. Offers health and exercise science (MS, PhD), including exercise physiology, general (MS), health promotion. *Faculty:* 8 full-time (2 women). *Students:* 35 full-time (15 women), 3 part-time (all women); includes 5 minority (1 Black or African American, non-Hispanic/Latino; 1 American Indian or Alaska Native, non-Hispanic/Latino; 1 Hispanic/Latino; 2 Two or more races, non-Hispanic/Latino), 8 international. Average age 28. 33 applicants, 33% accepted, 4 enrolled. In 2011, 8 master's, 4 doctorates awarded. *Degree requirements:* For master's, comprehensive exam (for some programs), thesis. *Entrance requirements:* For master's, GRE General Test, minimum GPA of 3.0 in last 60 hours of undergraduate course work, interview, 3 letters of recommendation; for doctorate, GRE General Test, 3 letters of recommendation, curriculum vitae. Additional exam requirements/recommendations for international students: Required—TOEFL (minimum score 550 paper-based; 79 iBT). *Application deadline:* For fall admission, 4/1 priority date for domestic students, 3/1 for international students; for spring admission, 11/1 for domestic students, 9/1 for international students. Applications are processed on a rolling basis. Application fee: $40 ($90 for international students). Electronic applications accepted. *Expenses:* Tuition, state resident: full-time $4087; part-time $170.30 per credit hour. Tuition, nonresident: full-time $14,875; part-time $619.80 per credit hour. *Required fees:* $2659; $100.25 per credit hour. Tuition and fees vary according to course load and degree level. *Financial support:* In 2011–12, 38 students received support, including 35 teaching assistantships with partial tuition reimbursements available (averaging $13,224 per year); career-related internships or fieldwork, scholarships/grants, health care benefits, and unspecified assistantships also available. Financial award applicants required to submit FAFSA. *Faculty research:* Neuromuscular function and performance, aging, bone health and endocrine function, childhood obesity, physical performance. *Total annual research expenditures:* $387,349. *Unit head:* Michael Bemben, Chair, 405-325-5211, Fax: 405-325-0594, E-mail: mgbemben@ou.edu. *Application contact:* Dr. Laurette Taylor, Graduate Liaison, 405-325-1372, Fax: 405-325-0594, E-mail: eltaylr@ou.edu. Web site: http://hes.ou.edu.

University of Pittsburgh, School of Education, Department of Health and Physical Activity, Program in Developmental Movement, Pittsburgh, PA 15260. Offers MS. *Students:* 3 full-time (1 woman), 1 (woman) part-time; includes 1 minority (Black or African American, non-Hispanic/Latino). Average age 30. 1 applicant, 100% accepted, 1 enrolled. In 2011, 7 master's awarded. *Degree requirements:* For master's, thesis. *Entrance requirements:* Additional exam requirements/recommendations for international students: Required—TOEFL. *Application deadline:* For fall admission, 2/1 for domestic students. Application fee: $50. Electronic applications accepted. *Expenses:* Tuition, state resident: full-time $18,774; part-time $760 per credit. Tuition, nonresident: full-time $30,736; part-time $1258 per credit. *Required fees:* $740; $200 per term. Tuition and fees vary according to program. *Financial support:* Traineeships and unspecified assistantships available. Financial award application deadline: 3/1; financial award applicants required to submit FAFSA. *Unit head:* Dr. John M. Jakicic, Chair, 412-648-8914, E-mail: jjakicic@pitt.edu. *Application contact:* Dr. Marjie Schermer, Graduate Enrollment Manager, 412-648-2230, Fax: 412-648-1899, E-mail: soeinfo@pitt.edu.

University of Pittsburgh, School of Education, Department of Health and Physical Activity, Program in Exercise Physiology, Pittsburgh, PA 15260. Offers MS, PhD. *Students:* 50 full-time (31 women), 24 part-time (16 women); includes 7 minority (5 Black or African American, non-Hispanic/Latino; 1 Hispanic/Latino; 1 Two or more races, non-Hispanic/Latino), 2 international. Average age 29. 57 applicants, 82% accepted, 37 enrolled. In 2011, 27 master's, 6 doctorates awarded. *Entrance requirements:* Additional exam requirements/recommendations for international students: Required—TOEFL (minimum score 550 paper-based; 213 computer-based; 80 iBT). *Application deadline:* Applications are processed on a rolling basis. Application fee: $50. Electronic applications accepted. *Expenses:* Tuition, state resident: full-time $18,774; part-time $760 per credit. Tuition, nonresident: full-time $30,736; part-time $1258 per credit. *Required fees:* $740; $200 per term. Tuition and fees vary according to program. *Unit head:* Dr. John M. Jakicic, Chair, 412-648-8914, E-mail: jjakicic@pitt.edu. *Application contact:* Dr. Marjie Schermer, Graduate Enrollment Manager, 412-648-2230, Fax: 412-648-1899, E-mail: soeinfo@pitt.edu.

University of Puerto Rico, Río Piedras, College of Education, Program in Exercise Sciences, San Juan, PR 00931-3300. Offers MS. *Entrance requirements:* For master's, PAEG or GRE, minimum GPA of 3.0.

University of Rhode Island, Graduate School, College of Human Science and Services, Department of Kinesiology, Kingston, RI 02881. Offers cultural studies of sport and physical culture (MS); exercise science (MS); physical education pedagogy (MS); psychosocial/behavioral aspects of physical activity (MS). *Accreditation:* NCATE. Part-time programs available. *Faculty:* 13 full-time (7 women). *Students:* 11 full-time (7 women), 7 part-time (2 women); includes 1 minority (Hispanic/Latino). In 2011, 10 master's awarded. *Degree requirements:* For master's, thesis optional. *Entrance requirements:* For master's, GRE, 2 letters of recommendation. Additional exam requirements/recommendations for international students: Required—TOEFL (minimum score 550 paper-based; 213 computer-based). *Application deadline:* For fall admission, 4/15 for domestic students, 2/1 for international students; for spring admission, 11/15 for domestic students, 7/15 for international students. Application fee: $65. Electronic applications accepted. *Expenses:* Tuition, state resident: full-time $10,432; part-time $580 per credit hour. Tuition, nonresident: full-time $23,130; part-time $1285 per credit hour. *Required fees:* $1362; $36 per credit hour. $35 per semester. One-time fee: $130. *Financial support:* In 2011–12, 5 teaching assistantships with full and partial tuition reimbursements (averaging $8,250 per year) were awarded. Financial award application deadline: 4/15; financial award applicants required to submit FAFSA. *Faculty research:* Strength training and older adults, interventions to promote a healthy lifestyle as well as analysis of the psychosocial outcomes of those interventions, effects of exercise and nutrition on skeletal muscle of aging health adults with CVD and other metabolic related diseases, physical activity and fitness of deaf children and youth. *Unit head:* Dr. Deborah Riebe, Chair, 401-874-5444, Fax: 401-874-4215, E-mail: debriebe@uri.edu. *Application contact:* Dr. Lori Ciccomascolo, Director of Graduate Studies, 401-874-5454, Fax: 401-874-4215, E-mail: lecicco@uri.edu. Web site: http://www.uri.edu/hss/physical_education/.

University of South Alabama, Graduate School, College of Education, Department of Health, Physical Education and Leisure Services, Mobile, AL 36688-0002. Offers exercise science (MS); health education (M Ed); physical education (M Ed); therapeutic recreation (MS). *Accreditation:* NCATE (one or more programs are accredited). Part-time programs available. *Faculty:* 10 full-time (2 women). *Students:* 27 full-time (15 women), 4 part-time (all women); includes 5 minority (4 Black or African American, non-Hispanic/Latino; 1 Asian, non-Hispanic/Latino), 4 international. 29 applicants, 52% accepted, 12 enrolled. In 2011, 17 master's awarded. *Degree requirements:* For master's, comprehensive exam. *Entrance requirements:* For master's, GRE General Test or MAT. *Application deadline:* For fall admission, 7/15 priority date for domestic students, 6/15 for international students; for spring admission, 12/1 priority date for domestic students, 11/1 for international students. Applications are processed on a rolling basis. Application fee: $35. *Expenses:* Tuition, state resident: full-time $7968; part-time $332 per credit hour. Tuition, nonresident: full-time $15,936; part-time $664 per credit hour. *Financial support:* In 2011–12, 10 teaching assistantships were awarded; career-related internships or fieldwork also available. Support available to part-time students. Financial award application deadline: 4/1. *Unit head:* Dr. Frederick M. Scaffidi, Chair, 251-460-7131. *Application contact:* Dr. Abigail Baxter, Director of Graduate Studies, 231-460-7131.

University of South Carolina, The Graduate School, Arnold School of Public Health, Department of Exercise Science, Columbia, SC 29208. Offers MS, DPT, PhD. Part-time programs available. *Degree requirements:* For master's, comprehensive exam, thesis (for some programs), project; for doctorate, comprehensive exam, thesis/dissertation. *Entrance requirements:* For master's and doctorate, GRE General Test. Additional exam requirements/recommendations for international students: Required—TOEFL (minimum score 570 paper-based; 230 computer-based). Electronic applications accepted. *Faculty research:* Effects of acute and chronic exercise on human function and health, motor control.

The University of South Dakota, Graduate School, School of Education, Division of Kinesiology and Sport Science, Vermillion, SD 57069-2390. Offers MA. *Accreditation:* NCATE. Part-time programs available. *Degree requirements:* For master's, comprehensive exam, thesis or alternative. *Entrance requirements:* For master's, GRE General Test, MAT, minimum GPA of 2.7. Additional exam requirements/recommendations for international students: Required—TOEFL (minimum score 550 paper-based; 213 computer-based; 79 iBT). Electronic applications accepted. *Expenses:* Tuition, state resident: full-time $3118.50; part-time $173.25 per credit hour. Tuition, nonresident: full-time $6601; part-time $366.70 per credit hour. *Required fees:* $2268; $126 per credit hour. Tuition and fees vary according to program.

University of Southern Mississippi, Graduate School, College of Health, School of Human Performance and Recreation, Hattiesburg, MS 39406-0001. Offers human performance (MS, PhD), including exercise physiology (PhD), human performance (MS), physical education (MS); interscholastic athletic administration (MS); recreation and leisure management (MS); sport administration (MS); sport and coaching education (MS); sport management (MS). Part-time and evening/weekend programs available. *Faculty:* 13 full-time (5 women). *Students:* 59 full-time (20 women), 38 part-time (12 women); includes 16 minority (12 Black or African American, non-Hispanic/Latino; 1 Asian, non-Hispanic/Latino; 2 Hispanic/Latino; 1 Two or more races, non-Hispanic/Latino), 9 international. Average age 29. 49 applicants, 73% accepted, 33 enrolled. In 2011, 44 master's, 1 doctorate awarded. *Degree requirements:* For master's, comprehensive exam, thesis optional; for doctorate, comprehensive exam, thesis/dissertation. *Entrance requirements:* For master's, GRE General Test, minimum GPA of 2.75 in last 60 hours; for doctorate, GRE General Test, minimum GPA of 3.5. Additional exam requirements/recommendations for international students: Required—TOEFL, IELTS. *Application deadline:* For fall admission, 3/1 priority date for domestic students, 3/1 for international students; for spring admission, 1/10 priority date for domestic students, 1/10 for international students. Applications are processed on a rolling basis. Application fee: $50. Electronic applications accepted. *Financial support:* In 2011–12, 1 fellowship (averaging $16,000 per year), 6 research assistantships with full tuition reimbursements (averaging $7,492 per year), 5 teaching assistantships with full tuition reimbursements (averaging $7,330 per year) were awarded; career-related internships or fieldwork, Federal Work-Study, institutionally sponsored loans, scholarships/grants, health care benefits, and unspecified assistantships also available. Financial award application deadline: 3/15; financial award applicants required to submit FAFSA. *Faculty research:* Exercise physiology, health behaviors, resource management, activity interaction, site development. *Unit head:* Dr. Frederick Green, Director, 601-266-5379, Fax: 601-266-4445. *Application contact:* Dr. Trenton Gould, Graduate Coordinator, 601-266-5379, Fax: 601-266-4445. Web site: http://www.usm.edu/graduateschool/table.php.

University of South Florida, Graduate School, College of Education, School of Physical Education and Exercise Science, Tampa, FL 33620-9951. Offers exercise science (MA); physical education teacher preparation (MA). Part-time and evening/weekend programs available. Postbaccalaureate distance learning degree programs offered (no on-campus study). *Faculty:* 9 full-time (6 women). *Students:* 30 full-time (10 women), 76 part-time (27 women); includes 26 minority (10 Black or African American, non-Hispanic/Latino; 4 American Indian or Alaska Native, non-Hispanic/Latino; 2 Asian, non-Hispanic/Latino; 10 Hispanic/Latino), 1 international. Average age 33. 128 applicants, 71% accepted, 51 enrolled. In 2011, 51 master's awarded. *Degree requirements:* For master's, comprehensive exam, thesis optional. *Entrance requirements:* For master's, GRE General Test, minimum GPA of 3.0 in last 60 hours of coursework. Additional exam requirements/recommendations for international students: Required—TOEFL (minimum score 500 paper-based; 213 computer-based). *Application deadline:* For fall admission, 2/15 for domestic students, 1/2 for international students; for spring admission, 10/15 for domestic students, 6/1 for international students. Applications are processed on a rolling basis. Application fee: $30. Electronic applications accepted. *Financial support:* In 2011–12, 5 teaching assistantships with full tuition reimbursements (averaging $9,200 per year) were awarded; unspecified assistantships also available. Financial award application deadline: 7/1; financial award applicants required to submit FAFSA. *Faculty research:* Physical education pedagogy, active gaming, exercise motivation, heat stress research, strength and nutrition research, physical activity risk management. *Total annual research expenditures:* $20,482. *Unit head:* Dr. Steve Sanders, Director, 813-974-4871, Fax: 813-974-4979,

E-mail: sanders@usf.edu. *Application contact:* Dr. Steve Sanders, Director, 813-974-4871, Fax: 813-974-4979, E-mail: sanders@usf.edu. Web site: http://www.coedu.usf.edu/main/departments/physed/programs.html.

The University of Tennessee, Graduate School, College of Education, Health and Human Sciences, Department of Exercise, Sport, and Leisure Studies, Program in Exercise Science, Knoxville, TN 37996. Offers biomechanics/sports medicine (MS, PhD); exercise physiology (MS, PhD). *Accreditation:* CEPH (one or more programs are accredited). Part-time programs available. *Degree requirements:* For master's, thesis optional. *Entrance requirements:* For master's, minimum GPA of 2.7. Additional exam requirements/recommendations for international students: Required—TOEFL. Electronic applications accepted. *Expenses:* Tuition, state resident: full-time $8332; part-time $464 per credit hour. Tuition, nonresident: full-time $25,174; part-time $1400 per credit hour. *Required fees:* $1162; $56 per credit hour. Tuition and fees vary according to program.

The University of Tennessee, Graduate School, College of Education, Health and Human Sciences, Program in Education, Knoxville, TN 37996. Offers art education (MS); counseling education (PhD); cultural studies in education (PhD); curriculum (MS, Ed S); curriculum, educational research and evaluation (Ed D, PhD); early childhood education (PhD); early childhood special education (MS); education of deaf and hard of hearing (MS); educational administration and policy studies (Ed D, PhD); educational administration and supervision (Ed S); educational psychology (Ed D, PhD); elementary education (MS, Ed S); elementary teaching (MS); English education (MS, Ed S); exercise science (PhD); foreign language/ESL education (MS, Ed S); instructional technology (MS, Ed D, PhD, Ed S); literacy, language and ESL education (PhD); literacy, language education, and ESL education (Ed D); mathematics education (MS, Ed S); modified and comprehensive special education (MS); reading education (MS, Ed S); school counseling (Ed S); school psychology (PhD, Ed S); science education (MS, Ed S); secondary teaching (MS); social foundations (MS); social science education (MS, Ed S); socio-cultural foundations of sports and education (PhD); special education (Ed S); teacher education (Ed D, PhD). *Accreditation:* NCATE. Part-time and evening/weekend programs available. *Degree requirements:* For master's and Ed S, thesis optional; for doctorate, variable foreign language requirement, thesis/dissertation. *Entrance requirements:* For master's, minimum GPA of 2.7; for doctorate and Ed S, GRE General Test, minimum GPA of 2.7. Additional exam requirements/recommendations for international students: Required—TOEFL. Electronic applications accepted. *Expenses:* Tuition, state resident: full-time $8332; part-time $464 per credit hour. Tuition, nonresident: full-time $25,174; part-time $1400 per credit hour. *Required fees:* $1162; $56 per credit hour. Tuition and fees vary according to program.

The University of Texas at Arlington, Graduate School, College of Education and Health Professions, Department of Kinesiology, Arlington, TX 76019. Offers exercise science (MS). *Faculty:* 8 full-time (0 women), 5 part-time/adjunct (0 women). *Students:* 23 full-time (6 women), 5 part-time (3 women); includes 5 minority (2 Black or African American, non-Hispanic/Latino; 1 Asian, non-Hispanic/Latino; 1 Hispanic/Latino; 1 Two or more races, non-Hispanic/Latino), 5 international. 37 applicants, 97% accepted, 13 enrolled. In 2011, 6 degrees awarded. *Degree requirements:* For master's, 36 hours with at least 21 hours in kinesiology. *Entrance requirements:* For master's, GRE (minimum quantitative score of 144 [500 on old scale] and verbal of 153 [500 on old scale]), undergraduate and/or graduate course work in exercise science, kinesiology, or physical education (preferred); minimum GPA of 3.0 overall and/or in last 60 undergraduate hours; 3 letters of reference. *Financial support:* In 2011–12, 6 students received support, including 4 research assistantships (averaging $8,000 per year), 6 teaching assistantships with tuition reimbursements available (averaging $11,000 per year); teaching assistantships also available. *Unit head:* Dr. Louise A. Fincher, Chair, 817-272-3107, E-mail: lfincher@uta.edu. *Application contact:* Dr. Mark Ricard, Professor and Graduate Coordinator, 817-272-0764, E-mail: ricard@uta.edu. Web site: http://www.uta.edu/coehp/kinesiology/.

The University of Texas at Austin, Graduate School, College of Education, Department of Kinesiology and Health Education, Austin, TX 78712-1111. Offers behavioral health (PhD); exercise and sport psychology (M Ed, MA); exercise science (M Ed, MS, PhD); health education (M Ed, MS, Ed D, PhD). Part-time programs available. Terminal master's awarded for partial completion of doctoral program. *Degree requirements:* For master's, thesis (for some programs); for doctorate, thesis/dissertation. *Entrance requirements:* For master's and doctorate, GRE General Test. Additional exam requirements/recommendations for international students: Required—TOEFL. *Application deadline:* For fall admission, 2/1 priority date for domestic students; for spring admission, 10/1 for domestic students. Applications are processed on a rolling basis. Application fee: $50 ($75 for international students). Electronic applications accepted. *Financial support:* Fellowships, research assistantships, teaching assistantships, career-related internships or fieldwork, and Federal Work-Study available. Financial award application deadline: 2/1; financial award applicants required to submit FAFSA. *Faculty research:* Health promotion, human performance and exercise biochemistry, motor behavior and biomechanics, sport management, aging and pediatric development. *Unit head:* Dr. John L. Ivy, Chair, 512-471-1273, Fax: 512-471-8914, E-mail: johnivy@mail.utexas.edu. *Application contact:* Dr. Darla Castelli, Graduate Advisor, 512-232-7636, Fax: 512-232-5334, E-mail: dcastelli@mail.utexas.edu. Web site: http://www.edb.utexas.edu/education/departments/khe/.

University of the Pacific, College of the Pacific, Department of Sport Sciences, Stockton, CA 95211-0197. Offers MA. *Faculty:* 9 full-time (3 women), 1 (woman) part-time/adjunct. *Students:* 1 full-time (0 women), 15 part-time (10 women); includes 3 minority (1 Black or African American, non-Hispanic/Latino; 1 Asian, non-Hispanic/Latino; 1 Hispanic/Latino). Average age 25. 23 applicants, 65% accepted, 8 enrolled. In 2011, 2 master's awarded. *Degree requirements:* For master's, comprehensive exam (for some programs), thesis (for some programs). *Entrance requirements:* For master's, GRE General Test. Additional exam requirements/recommendations for international students: Required—TOEFL (minimum score 475 paper-based; 150 computer-based). *Application deadline:* For fall admission, 3/1 priority date for domestic students; for spring admission, 10/1 for domestic students. Applications are processed on a rolling basis. Application fee: $75. *Expenses: Tuition:* Full-time $18,900; part-time $1181 per unit. *Required fees:* $949. *Financial support:* In 2011–12, 7 teaching assistantships were awarded; institutionally sponsored loans also available. Support available to part-time students. Financial award application deadline: 3/1; financial award applicants required to submit FAFSA. *Unit head:* Dr. Christopher Snell, Chairperson, 209-946-2703, E-mail: csnell@pacific.edu. *Application contact:* Information Contact, 209-946-2261.

The University of Toledo, College of Graduate Studies, Judith Herb College of Education, Health Science and Human Service, Department of Kinesiology, Toledo, OH 43606-3390. Offers exercise science (MSX, PhD). Part-time programs available. *Faculty:* 13. *Students:* 45 full-time (24 women), 4 part-time (1 woman); includes 5 minority (3 Asian, non-Hispanic/Latino; 1 Hispanic/Latino; 1 Two or more races, non-Hispanic/Latino), 2 international. Average age 25. 72 applicants, 38% accepted, 25 enrolled. In 2011, 15 master's, 3 doctorates awarded. *Degree requirements:* For master's, comprehensive exam, thesis; for doctorate, comprehensive exam, thesis/dissertation. *Entrance requirements:* For master's and doctorate, minimum cumulative GPA of 2.7 for all previous academic work, letters of recommendation. Additional exam requirements/recommendations for international students: Required—TOEFL (minimum score 550 paper-based; 213 computer-based; 80 iBT), IELTS (minimum score 6.5). *Application deadline:* For fall admission, 1/15 priority date for domestic students, 1/15 for international students. Applications are processed on a rolling basis. Application fee: $45 ($75 for international students). Electronic applications accepted. *Financial support:* In 2011–12, 3 research assistantships with full and partial tuition reimbursements (averaging $6,333 per year), 19 teaching assistantships with full and partial tuition reimbursements (averaging $13,290 per year) were awarded; career-related internships or fieldwork, Federal Work-Study, institutionally sponsored loans, scholarships/grants, tuition waivers (full and partial), and unspecified assistantships also available. *Unit head:* Dr. Barry Scheuermann, Chair, 419-530-2692. *Application contact:* Graduate School Office, 419-530-4723, Fax: 419-530-4724, E-mail: grdsch@utnet.utoledo.edu. Web site: http://www.utoledo.edu/eduhshs/.

University of Utah, Graduate School, College of Health, Department of Exercise and Sport Science, Salt Lake City, UT 84112. Offers MS, PhD. *Faculty:* 15 full-time (8 women), 2 part-time/adjunct (1 woman). *Students:* 73 full-time (30 women), 8 part-time (3 women); includes 7 minority (4 Asian, non-Hispanic/Latino; 1 Hispanic/Latino; 1 Native Hawaiian or other Pacific Islander, non-Hispanic/Latino; 1 Two or more races, non-Hispanic/Latino), 6 international. Average age 30. 133 applicants, 40% accepted, 36 enrolled. In 2011, 22 master's, 5 doctorates awarded. Terminal master's awarded for partial completion of doctoral program. *Median time to degree:* Of those who began their doctoral program in fall 2003, 80% received their degree in 8 years or less. *Degree requirements:* For master's, comprehensive exam, thesis (for some programs); for doctorate, comprehensive exam, thesis/dissertation. *Entrance requirements:* For master's and doctorate, GRE General Test, curriculum vitae, 2 letters of recommendation, minimum GPA of 3.0. Additional exam requirements/recommendations for international students: Required—TOEFL (minimum score 500 paper-based; 173 computer-based; 61 iBT). *Application deadline:* For fall admission, 12/1 for domestic and international students. Application fee: $55 ($65 for international students). Electronic applications accepted. *Financial support:* In 2011–12, 44 students received support, including 1 fellowship with full and partial tuition reimbursement available (averaging $14,000 per year), 13 research assistantships with full and partial tuition reimbursements available (averaging $13,000 per year), 32 teaching assistantships with full and partial tuition reimbursements available (averaging $12,000 per year); career-related internships or fieldwork, scholarships/grants, traineeships, health care benefits, and unspecified assistantships also available. Financial award application deadline: 4/15; financial award applicants required to submit FAFSA. *Faculty research:* Exercise physiology, psychosocial aspects of sports and physical education, special physical education, elementary/secondary physical education. *Total annual research expenditures:* $231,623. *Unit head:* Dr. Barry B. Shultz, Chair, 801-581-4440, Fax: 801-585-3992, E-mail: barry.shultz@health.utah.edu. *Application contact:* Dr. James C. Hannon, Director of Graduate Studies, 801-581-7646, Fax: 801-585-3992, E-mail: james.hannon@hsc.utah.edu. Web site: http://www.health.utah.edu/ess/.

University of West Florida, College of Professional Studies, Department of Applied Science, Technology and Administration, Program in Administration, Pensacola, FL 32514-5750. Offers acquisition and contract administration (MSA); biomedical/pharmaceutical (MSA); criminal justice administration (MSA); database administration (MSA); education leadership (MSA); healthcare administration (MSA); human performance technology (MSA); leadership (MSA); nursing administration (MSA); public administration (MSA); software engineering administration (MSA). Part-time and evening/weekend programs available. Postbaccalaureate distance learning degree programs offered (no on-campus study). *Students:* 36 full-time (28 women), 158 part-time (95 women); includes 61 minority (31 Black or African American, non-Hispanic/Latino; 4 American Indian or Alaska Native, non-Hispanic/Latino; 4 Asian, non-Hispanic/Latino; 17 Hispanic/Latino; 2 Native Hawaiian or other Pacific Islander, non-Hispanic/Latino; 3 Two or more races, non-Hispanic/Latino), 1 international. Average age 34. 102 applicants, 59% accepted, 40 enrolled. In 2011, 62 master's awarded. *Entrance requirements:* For master's, GRE General Test, letter of intent, names of references. Additional exam requirements/recommendations for international students: Required—TOEFL (minimum score 550 paper-based; 213 computer-based). *Application deadline:* For fall admission, 6/1 for domestic and international students; for spring admission, 10/1 for domestic and international students. Applications are processed on a rolling basis. Application fee: $30. *Expenses:* Tuition, state resident: full-time $5729; part-time $302 per credit hour. Tuition, nonresident: full-time $20,059; part-time $961 per credit hour. *Required fees:* $1509; $63 per credit hour. *Financial support:* Unspecified assistantships available. Financial award application deadline: 4/15; financial award applicants required to submit FAFSA. *Unit head:* Dr. Karen Rasmussen, Chairperson, 850-474-2301, Fax: 850-474-2804, E-mail: krasmuss@uwf.edu. *Application contact:* Terry McCray, Assistant Director of Graduate Admissions, 850-473-7718, Fax: 850-473-7714, E-mail: gradadmissions@uwf.edu. Web site: http://uwf.edu/msaprogram/.

University of West Florida, College of Professional Studies, Department of Health, Leisure, and Exercise Science, Program in Health, Leisure, and Exercise Science, Pensacola, FL 32514-5750. Offers exercise science (MS); physical education (MS). Part-time and evening/weekend programs available. *Faculty:* 6 full-time (2 women), 1 (woman) part-time/adjunct. *Students:* 14 full-time (10 women), 16 part-time (7 women); includes 6 minority (2 Black or African American, non-Hispanic/Latino; 1 Asian, non-Hispanic/Latino; 2 Hispanic/Latino; 1 Native Hawaiian or other Pacific Islander, non-Hispanic/Latino), 2 international. Average age 28. 22 applicants, 55% accepted, 7 enrolled. In 2011, 20 master's awarded. *Degree requirements:* For master's, thesis or alternative. *Entrance requirements:* For master's, GRE or MAT, official transcripts; minimum GPA of 3.0; letter of intent; two personal references; work experience. Additional exam requirements/recommendations for international students: Required—TOEFL (minimum score 550 paper-based; 213 computer-based). *Application deadline:* For fall admission, 6/1 for domestic and international students; for spring admission, 10/1 for domestic and international students. Applications are processed on a rolling basis. Application fee: $30. Electronic applications accepted. *Expenses:* Tuition, state resident: full-time $5729; part-time $302 per credit hour. Tuition, nonresident: full-time $20,059; part-time $961 per credit hour. *Required fees:* $1509; $63 per credit hour. *Financial support:* Career-related internships or fieldwork, Federal Work-Study, scholarships/grants, and tuition waivers (partial) available. Support available to part-time students. Financial award application deadline: 4/15; financial award applicants required to submit FAFSA. *Unit head:* Dr. John Todorovich, Chairperson, 850-473-7248, Fax: 850-474-2106. *Application contact:* Terry McCray, Assistant Director of Graduate Admissions, 850-473-7718, Fax: 850-473-7714, E-mail: gradadmissions@uwf.edu.

University of West Florida, College of Professional Studies, Department of Research and Applied Studies, Pensacola, FL 32514-5750. Offers administration (MSA), including acquisition and contract administration, biomedical/pharmaceutical, criminal justice administration, database administration, education leadership, healthcare administration, human performance technology, leadership, nursing administration, public administration, software engineering and administration; college student personnel administration (M Ed), including college personnel administration, guidance and counseling; curriculum and instruction (M Ed, Ed S); educational leadership (M Ed); middle and secondary level education and ESOL (M Ed). Part-time and evening/

weekend programs available. *Faculty:* 2 full-time (both women), 3 part-time/adjunct (2 women). *Students:* 26 full-time (15 women), 13 part-time (9 women); includes 8 minority (4 Black or African American, non-Hispanic/Latino; 2 American Indian or Alaska Native, non-Hispanic/Latino; 1 Hispanic/Latino; 1 Two or more races, non-Hispanic/Latino), 1 international. Average age 26. 51 applicants, 51% accepted, 16 enrolled. In 2011, 17 master's, 49 Ed Ss awarded. *Entrance requirements:* For master's, GRE or MAT, official transcripts; minimum undergraduate GPA of 3.0; letter of intent; three letters of recommendation; resume. Additional exam requirements/recommendations for international students: Required—TOEFL (minimum score 550 paper-based; 213 computer-based). *Application deadline:* For fall admission, 6/1 for domestic and international students; for spring admission, 10/1 for domestic and international students. Applications are processed on a rolling basis. Application fee: $30. *Expenses:* Tuition, state resident: full-time $5729; part-time $302 per credit hour. Tuition, nonresident: full-time $20,059; part-time $961 per credit hour. *Required fees:* $1509; $63 per credit hour. *Financial support:* In 2011–12, 33 fellowships (averaging $860 per year), 10 research assistantships (averaging $3,280 per year), 2 teaching assistantships (averaging $3,760 per year) were awarded; unspecified assistantships also available. Financial award application deadline: 4/15; financial award applicants required to submit FAFSA. *Unit head:* Dr. Joyce Nichols, Chairperson, 850-857-6042, E-mail: jcoleman0@uwf.edu. *Application contact:* Terry McCray, Assistant Director of Graduate Admissions, 850-473-7718, Fax: 850-473-7714, E-mail: gradadmissions@uwf.edu. Web site: http://uwf.edu/pcl/.

University of Wisconsin–La Crosse, Office of University Graduate Studies, College of Science and Health, Department of Exercise and Sport Science, Program in Clinical Exercise Physiology, La Crosse, WI 54601-3742. Offers MS. *Students:* 16 full-time (10 women); includes 2 minority (1 Asian, non-Hispanic/Latino; 1 Hispanic/Latino), 1 international. Average age 24. 1 applicant, 0% accepted, 0 enrolled. In 2011, 14 master's awarded. *Degree requirements:* For master's, thesis optional. *Entrance requirements:* Additional exam requirements/recommendations for international students: Required—TOEFL (minimum score 550 paper-based; 213 computer-based; 79 iBT). *Application deadline:* For fall admission, 2/1 priority date for domestic students, 2/1 for international students. Application fee: $56. Electronic applications accepted. *Expenses:* Tuition, state resident: full-time $8391; part-time $481.17 per credit. Tuition, nonresident: full-time $17,850; part-time $1006.68 per credit. *Required fees:* $2 per credit. $18.25 per semester. Tuition and fees vary according to course load, program, reciprocity agreements and student level. *Financial support:* Federal Work-Study, scholarships/grants, health care benefits, and tuition waivers (partial) available. Support available to part-time students. Financial award application deadline: 3/15; financial award applicants required to submit FAFSA. *Unit head:* Dr. John Porcari, Director, 608-785-8684, Fax: 608-785-8686, E-mail: porcari.john@uwlax.edu. *Application contact:* Kathryn Kiefer, Director of Admissions, 608-785-8939, E-mail: admissions@uwlax.edu. Web site: http://www.uwlax.edu/sah/ess/cep/.

University of Wisconsin–La Crosse, Office of University Graduate Studies, College of Science and Health, Department of Exercise and Sport Science, Program in Human Performance, La Crosse, WI 54601-3742. Offers applied sport science (MS); strength and conditioning (MS). Part-time programs available. *Faculty:* 4 full-time (1 woman). *Students:* 18 full-time (7 women), 6 part-time (3 women); includes 1 minority (Hispanic/Latino), 1 international. Average age 24. 32 applicants, 66% accepted, 13 enrolled. In 2011, 10 master's awarded. *Degree requirements:* For master's, comprehensive exam (for some programs), thesis optional. *Entrance requirements:* For master's, GRE, course work in anatomy, physiology, biomechanics, and exercise physiology. Additional exam requirements/recommendations for international students: Required—TOEFL (minimum score 550 paper-based; 213 computer-based; 79 iBT). *Application deadline:* For fall admission, 2/1 priority date for domestic students, 2/1 for international students. Application fee: $56. Electronic applications accepted. *Expenses:* Tuition, state resident: full-time $8391; part-time $481.17 per credit. Tuition, nonresident: full-time $17,850; part-time $1006.68 per credit. *Required fees:* $2 per credit. $18.25 per semester. Tuition and fees vary according to course load, program, reciprocity agreements and student level. *Financial support:* Federal Work-Study, scholarships/grants, health care benefits, and tuition waivers (partial) available. Support available to part-time students. Financial award application deadline: 3/15; financial award applicants required to submit FAFSA. *Faculty research:* Anaerobic metabolism, power development, strength training, biomechanics, athletic performance. *Unit head:* Dr. Glenn Wright, Director, 608-785-8689, Fax: 608-785-8172, E-mail: wright.glen@uwlax.edu. *Application contact:* Kathryn Kiefer, Director of Admissions, 608-785-8939, E-mail: admissions@uwlax.edu. Web site: http://www.uwlax.edu/sah/ess/hp/.

University of Wisconsin–Whitewater, School of Graduate Studies, College of Education and Professional Studies, Department of Curriculum and Instruction, Whitewater, WI 53190-1790. Offers professional development (MS), including bilingual education, challenging advanced learners, curriculum and instruction, educational leadership, health, human performance and recreation, health, physical education and coaching, information technologies and libraries, reading. *Accreditation:* NCATE. Part-time and evening/weekend programs available. Postbaccalaureate distance learning degree programs offered. *Students:* 25 full-time (12 women), 68 part-time (51 women); includes 26 minority (15 Black or African American, non-Hispanic/Latino; 3 Asian, non-Hispanic/Latino; 8 Hispanic/Latino). Average age 33. 29 applicants, 86% accepted, 16 enrolled. In 2011, 44 master's awarded. *Degree requirements:* For master's, thesis or integrated project. *Entrance requirements:* Additional exam requirements/recommendations for international students: Required—TOEFL (minimum score 550 paper-based; 213 computer-based; 80 iBT), IELTS (minimum score 6). *Application deadline:* For fall admission, 7/15 priority date for domestic students, 7/15 for international students; for spring admission, 12/1 priority date for domestic students, 12/1 for international students. Applications are processed on a rolling basis. Application fee: $56. Electronic applications accepted. *Expenses:* Tuition, state resident: full-time $4088. Tuition, nonresident: full-time $8817. Tuition and fees vary according to program. *Financial support:* Research assistantships, Federal Work-Study, unspecified assistantships, and out-of-state fee waivers available. Support available to part-time students. Financial award application deadline: 3/15; financial award applicants required to submit FAFSA. *Faculty research:* Hybrid of exercise physiology and psychology; gender equity; education, pedagogy, and technology; comprehensive school health education. *Unit head:* Dr. John Zbikowski, Coordinator, 262-472-4860, Fax: 262-472-1988, E-mail: zbikowskij@uww.edu. *Application contact:* Sally A. Lange, School of Graduate Studies, 262-472-1006, Fax: 262-472-5027, E-mail: gradschl@uww.edu.

University of Wyoming, College of Health Sciences, Division of Kinesiology and Health, Laramie, WY 82070. Offers MS. *Accreditation:* NCATE. Part-time programs available. Postbaccalaureate distance learning degree programs offered (no on-campus study). *Degree requirements:* For master's, comprehensive exam (for some programs), thesis (for some programs). *Entrance requirements:* For master's, GRE General Test, minimum GPA of 3.0. Additional exam requirements/recommendations for international students: Required—TOEFL. Electronic applications accepted. *Faculty research:* Teacher effectiveness, effects of exercising on heart function, physiological responses of overtraining, psychological benefits of physical activity, health behavior.

Virginia Commonwealth University, Graduate School, School of Education, Department of Health and Human Performance, Program in Health and Movement Sciences, Richmond, VA 23284-9005. Offers MS. *Entrance requirements:* For master's, GRE or MAT. Additional exam requirements/recommendations for international students: Required—TOEFL (minimum score 600 paper-based; 250 computer-based; 100 iBT). Electronic applications accepted. *Expenses:* Tuition, state resident: full-time $9133; part-time $507 per credit. Tuition, nonresident: full-time $18,777; part-time $1043 per credit. *Required fees:* $77 per credit. Tuition and fees vary according to degree level, campus/location, program and student level.

Wake Forest University, Graduate School of Arts and Sciences, Department of Health and Exercise Science, Winston-Salem, NC 27109. Offers MS. *Degree requirements:* For master's, one foreign language, thesis. *Entrance requirements:* For master's, GRE General Test, resume. Additional exam requirements/recommendations for international students: Required—TOEFL (minimum score 213 computer-based; 79 iBT). Electronic applications accepted. *Faculty research:* Cardiac rehabilitation, biomechanics, health psychology, exercise physiology.

Washington State University, Graduate School, College of Education, Department of Teaching and Learning, Pullman, WA 99164. Offers curriculum and instruction (Ed D, PhD); diverse languages (M Ed, MA); elementary education (M Ed, MA, MIT); exercise science (MS); literacy education (M Ed, MA, PhD); math education (PhD); secondary education (M Ed, MA). *Accreditation:* NCATE. *Faculty:* 20. *Students:* 79 full-time (51 women), 40 part-time (31 women); includes 24 minority (3 Black or African American, non-Hispanic/Latino; 5 Asian, non-Hispanic/Latino; 13 Hispanic/Latino; 1 Native Hawaiian or other Pacific Islander, non-Hispanic/Latino; 2 Two or more races, non-Hispanic/Latino), 43 international. Average age 34. 106 applicants, 47% accepted, 43 enrolled. In 2011, 34 master's, 3 doctorates awarded. *Degree requirements:* For master's, comprehensive exam (for some programs), thesis (for some programs), oral or written exam; for doctorate, comprehensive exam, thesis/dissertation, oral and written exam. *Entrance requirements:* For master's and doctorate, GRE General Test, minimum GPA of 3.0, 3 letters of recommendation. Additional exam requirements/recommendations for international students: Required—TOEFL. *Application deadline:* For fall admission, 2/1 for domestic students, 3/1 for international students; for spring admission, 9/1 for domestic students, 7/1 for international students. Applications are processed on a rolling basis. Application fee: $75. *Financial support:* In 2011–12, 130 teaching assistantships with partial tuition reimbursements (averaging $18,204 per year) were awarded; career-related internships or fieldwork, Federal Work-Study, institutionally sponsored loans, tuition waivers (partial), unspecified assistantships, and staff assistantships, teaching associateships also available. Financial award application deadline: 4/1. *Faculty research:* Evolution of middle school education, issues in special education, computer-assisted language learning. *Total annual research expenditures:* $324,000. *Unit head:* Dr. Dawn Shinew, Interim Chair, 509-335-5027, E-mail: dshinew@wsu.edu. *Application contact:* Graduate School Admissions, 800-GRADWSU, Fax: 509-335-1949, E-mail: gradsch@wsu.edu. Web site: http://www.educ.wsu.edu/TL/overview.htm.

Washington State University Spokane, Graduate Programs, Program in Exercise Science, Spokane, WA 99210-1495. Offers MS. *Faculty:* 4. *Students:* 17 full-time (16 women), 3 part-time (1 woman); includes 3 minority (1 Black or African American, non-Hispanic/Latino; 1 Asian, non-Hispanic/Latino; 1 Hispanic/Latino), 1 international. Average age 26. 15 applicants, 100% accepted, 15 enrolled. *Degree requirements:* For master's, comprehensive exam, thesis optional. *Entrance requirements:* For master's, GRE, minimum GPA of 3.0. Additional exam requirements/recommendations for international students: Required—TOEFL (minimum score 550 paper-based; 213 computer-based). *Application deadline:* For fall admission, 7/15 priority date for domestic students, 3/1 for international students; for spring admission, 10/15 priority date for domestic students, 7/1 for international students. Application fee: $75. *Financial support:* In 2011–12, 4 students received support, including 3 research assistantships with full and partial tuition reimbursements available (averaging $13,917 per year), teaching assistantships with full and partial tuition reimbursements available (averaging $13,056 per year); career-related internships or fieldwork, Federal Work-Study, scholarships/grants, health care benefits, and unspecified assistantships also available. *Faculty research:* Experimental exercise physiology, cellular and molecular mechanisms. *Unit head:* Dr. Sally Blank, Associate Professor/Director, 509-358-7633, E-mail: seblank@wsu.edu. *Application contact:* Graduate School Admissions, 800-GRADWSU, Fax: 509-335-1949, E-mail: gradsch@wsu.edu. Web site: http://www.pharmacy.wsu.edu/NEP/index.html.

Wayne State College, Department of Health, Human Performance and Sport, Wayne, NE 68787. Offers exercise science (MSE); organizational management (MS), including sport management. Part-time and evening/weekend programs available. *Degree requirements:* For master's, comprehensive exam, thesis optional. *Entrance requirements:* For master's, GRE General Test, minimum GPA of 3.0. Additional exam requirements/recommendations for international students: Required—TOEFL (minimum score 550 paper-based; 213 computer-based). Electronic applications accepted.

Wayne State University, College of Education, Division of Kinesiology, Health and Sports Studies, Detroit, MI 48202. Offers exercise and sport science (M Ed); health education (M Ed); kinesiology (M Ed, PhD); physical education (M Ed); sports administration (MA); wellness clinician/research (M Ed). *Students:* 39 full-time (23 women), 68 part-time (31 women); includes 36 minority (31 Black or African American, non-Hispanic/Latino; 1 Asian, non-Hispanic/Latino; 1 Hispanic/Latino; 1 Native Hawaiian or other Pacific Islander, non-Hispanic/Latino; 2 Two or more races, non-Hispanic/Latino), 3 international. Average age 31. 115 applicants, 39% accepted, 27 enrolled. In 2011, 39 master's, 1 doctorate awarded. *Degree requirements:* For master's, thesis (for some programs). *Entrance requirements:* Additional exam requirements/recommendations for international students: Required—TOEFL; Recommended—TWE (minimum score 6). *Application deadline:* For fall admission, 6/1 priority date for domestic students, 5/1 for international students; for winter admission, 10/1 priority date for domestic students, 9/1 for international students; for spring admission, 2/1 priority date for domestic students, 1/1 for international students. Applications are processed on a rolling basis. Application fee: $50. Electronic applications accepted. *Expenses:* Tuition, state resident: part-time $512.85 per credit. Tuition, nonresident: part-time $1132.65 per credit. *Required fees:* $26.60 per credit. $199.65 per semester. Tuition and fees vary according to course load and program. *Financial support:* In 2011–12, 6 research assistantships with tuition reimbursements (averaging $16,061 per year) were awarded; teaching assistantships with tuition reimbursements, career-related internships or fieldwork, scholarships/grants, health care benefits, and unspecified assistantships also available. *Faculty research:* Fitness in urban children, motor development of crack babies, effects of caffeine on metabolism/exercise, body composition of elite youth sports participants, systematic observation of teaching. *Unit head:* Dr. Mariane Fahlman, Assistant Dean, 313-577-5066, Fax: 313-577-9301, E-mail: m.fahlman@wayne.edu. *Application contact:* John Wirth, Assistant Professor, 313-993-7972, Fax: 313-577-5999, E-mail: johnwirth@wayne.edu. Web site: http://coe.wayne.edu/kinesiology/index.php.

West Chester University of Pennsylvania, College of Health Sciences, Department of Kinesiology, West Chester, PA 19383. Offers exercise/sport physiology (MS), including athletic training; physical education (MS); sport management and athletics (MPA). *Faculty:* 7 part-time/adjunct (3 women). *Students:* 19 full-time (10 women), 14 part-time (7 women); includes 5 minority (all Black or African American, non-Hispanic/Latino). Average age 26. 37 applicants, 35% accepted, 10 enrolled. In 2011, 12 degrees awarded. *Degree requirements:* For master's, thesis or report (MS), 2 internships (MPA). *Entrance requirements:* For master's, GRE with minimum score of 1000 (for MS), 2 letters of recommendation, transcripts, and statement of professional goals (for MS); 2 letters of reference, resume, career goal statement (for MPA). Additional exam requirements/recommendations for international students: Required—TOEFL (minimum score 550 paper-based; 213 computer-based; 80 iBT). *Application deadline:* For fall admission, 4/15 priority date for domestic students, 3/15 for international students; for spring admission, 10/15 priority date for domestic students, 9/1 for international students. Applications are processed on a rolling basis. Application fee: $45. Electronic applications accepted. *Expenses:* Tuition, state resident: full-time $7488; part-time $416 per credit. Tuition, nonresident: full-time $11,232; part-time $624 per credit. *Required fees:* $1784.64; $67.59 per credit. Tuition and fees vary according to program. *Financial support:* Unspecified assistantships available. Support available to part-time students. Financial award application deadline: 2/15; financial award applicants required to submit FAFSA. *Faculty research:* Metabolism during exercise, biomechanics, rating of perceived exertion, motor learning. *Unit head:* Dr. Frank Fry, Chair and Graduate Coordinator for the MS in General Physical Education Program, 610-436-2610, Fax: 610-436-2860, E-mail: ffry@wcupa.edu. *Application contact:* Dr. Sheri Melton, Graduate Coordinator for the Exercise and Sport Physiology Programs, 610-436-2260, Fax: 610-436-2860, E-mail: smelton@wcupa.edu. Web site: http://www.wcupa.edu/_academics/sch_shs.hpe/.

Western Michigan University, Graduate College, College of Education and Human Development, Department of Health, Physical Education and Recreation, Kalamazoo, MI 49008. Offers exercise and sports medicine (MS), including athletic training, exercise physiology; physical education (MA), including coaching sport performance, pedagogy, special physical education, sport management.

Western Washington University, Graduate School, College of Humanities and Social Sciences, Department of Physical Education, Health, and Recreation, Bellingham, WA 98225-5996. Offers exercise science (MS); sport psychology (MS). Part-time programs available. *Degree requirements:* For master's, thesis. *Entrance requirements:* For master's, GRE General Test, minimum GPA of 3.0 in last 60 semester hours or last 90 quarter hours. Additional exam requirements/recommendations for international students: Required—TOEFL (minimum score 567 paper-based; 227 computer-based). Electronic applications accepted. *Faculty research:* Spinal motor control, biomechanics/kinesiology, biomechanics of aging, mobility of older adults, fall prevention, exercise interventions and function, magnesium and inspiratory muscle training (IMT).

West Texas A&M University, College of Education and Social Sciences, Department of Sports and Exercise Science, Canyon, TX 79016-0001. Offers MS. Part-time and evening/weekend programs available. *Degree requirements:* For master's, comprehensive exam, thesis or alternative. *Entrance requirements:* For master's, GRE General Test, minimum GPA of 3.0. Additional exam requirements/recommendations for international students: Required—TOEFL (minimum score 550 paper-based). Electronic applications accepted. *Faculty research:* Coronary heart disease, athletic performance, pain coping, cardiovascular fitness, nutritional status of NCAA athletes.

West Virginia University, School of Medicine, Graduate Programs at the Health Sciences Center, Interdisciplinary Graduate Programs in Biomedical Sciences, Exercise Physiology Program, Morgantown, WV 26506. Offers MS, PhD, MD/PhD. *Degree requirements:* For doctorate, comprehensive exam, thesis/dissertation. *Entrance requirements:* For doctorate, GRE General Test, minimum GPA of 3.0. Additional exam requirements/recommendations for international students: Required—TOEFL. Electronic applications accepted. *Faculty research:* Cardiovascular function in health and disease, circulatory adaptations to exercise training, aging, microgravity, muscle adaptation and injury.

West Virginia University, School of Physical Education, Morgantown, WV 26506. Offers athletic coaching education (MS); athletic training (MS); physical education/teacher education (MS, PhD), including curriculum and instruction (PhD), motor behavior (PhD), physical education supervision (PhD); sport and exercise psychology (PhD); sport management (MS). *Degree requirements:* For doctorate, comprehensive exam, thesis/dissertation, oral exam. *Entrance requirements:* For master's, GRE or MAT, minimum GPA of 3.0; for doctorate, GRE General Test or MAT, minimum GPA of 3.5. Additional exam requirements/recommendations for international students: Required—TOEFL (minimum score 550 paper-based; 213 computer-based). Electronic applications accepted. *Faculty research:* Sport psychosociology, teacher education, exercise psychology, counseling.

Wichita State University, Graduate School, College of Education, Department of Human Performance Studies, Wichita, KS 67260. Offers exercise science (M Ed). Part-time programs available. *Expenses:* Tuition, state resident: full-time $4746; part-time $263.65 per credit. Tuition, nonresident: full-time $11,669; part-time $648.30 per credit. *Unit head:* Dr. Mike Rogers, Chairperson, 316-978-3340, Fax: 316-978-3302, E-mail: mike.rogers@wichita.edu. *Application contact:* Carrie C. Henderson, Admissions Coordinator, 316-978-3095, Fax: 316-978-3253, E-mail: carrie.henderson@wichita.edu. Web site: http://www.wichita.edu/.

Kinesiology and Movement Studies

Acadia University, Faculty of Professional Studies, School of Recreation Management and Kinesiology, Wolfville, NS B4P 2R6, Canada. Offers MR. *Degree requirements:* For master's, thesis. *Entrance requirements:* Additional exam requirements/recommendations for international students: Required—TOEFL (minimum score 580 paper-based; 237 computer-based; 93 iBT), IELTS (minimum score 6.5).

Arizona State University, College of Nursing and Health Innovation, Phoenix, AZ 85004. Offers advanced nursing practice (DNP); child/family mental health nurse practitioner (Graduate Certificate); clinical research management (MS); community and public health practice (Graduate Certificate); community health (MS); exercise and wellness (MS), including exercise and wellness; family nurse practitioner (Graduate Certificate); healthcare innovation (MHI); international health for healthcare (Graduate Certificate); kinesiology (MS, PhD); nursing (MS, Graduate Certificate); nursing and healthcare innovation (PhD); nutrition (MS); physical activity nutrition and wellness (PhD), including physical activity, nutrition and wellness; public health (MPH); regulatory science and health safety (MS). *Accreditation:* AACN. Postbaccalaureate distance learning degree programs offered (minimal on-campus study). *Degree requirements:* For master's, comprehensive exam (for some programs), thesis (for some programs), interactive Program of Study (iPOS) submitted before completing 50 percent of required credit hours; for doctorate, comprehensive exam, thesis/dissertation, interactive Program of Study (iPOS) submitted before completing 50 percent of required credit hours. *Entrance requirements:* For master's and doctorate, GRE, minimum GPA of 3.0 or equivalent in last 2 years of work leading to bachelor's degree. Additional exam requirements/recommendations for international students: Required—TOEFL (minimum score 80 iBT), TOEFL, IELTS, or Pearson Test of English. Electronic applications accepted. *Expenses:* Contact institution.

A.T. Still University of Health Sciences, Arizona School of Health Sciences, Mesa, AZ 85206. Offers advanced occupational therapy (MS); advanced physician assistant (MS); athletic training (MS); audiology (Au D); health sciences (DHSc); human movement (MS); occupational therapy (MS); physical therapy (DPT); physician assistant (MS); transitional audiology (Au D); transitional physical therapy (DPT). *Accreditation:* AOTA (one or more programs are accredited); ASHA. Part-time and evening/weekend programs available. Postbaccalaureate distance learning degree programs offered (minimal on-campus study). *Faculty:* 44 full-time (27 women), 235 part-time/adjunct (141 women). *Students:* 410 full-time (275 women), 1,010 part-time (675 women); includes 320 minority (73 Black or African American, non-Hispanic/Latino; 18 American Indian or Alaska Native, non-Hispanic/Latino; 158 Asian, non-Hispanic/Latino; 62 Hispanic/Latino; 9 Two or more races, non-Hispanic/Latino), 6 international. Average age 35. 4,395 applicants, 18% accepted, 694 enrolled. In 2011, 221 master's, 406 doctorates awarded. *Median time to degree:* Of those who began their doctoral program in fall 2003, 98% received their degree in 8 years or less. *Degree requirements:* For master's, thesis (for some programs); for doctorate, thesis/dissertation (for some programs). *Entrance requirements:* For master's, GRE General Test; for doctorate, GRE, Evaluation of Practicing Audiologists Capabilities (Au D), Physical Therapist Evaluation Tool (DPT), current state licensure, master's degree or equivalent (Au D). Additional exam requirements/recommendations for international students: Required—TOEFL (minimum score 550 paper-based; 213 computer-based; 80 iBT). *Application deadline:* For fall admission, 8/1 priority date for domestic students, 8/1 for international students. Applications are processed on a rolling basis. Application fee: $60. *Expenses:* Contact institution. *Financial support:* In 2011–12, 272 students received support, including 14 fellowships (averaging $16,000 per year); Federal Work-Study and scholarships/grants also available. Financial award application deadline: 5/1; financial award applicants required to submit FAFSA. *Faculty research:* Physical therapy: metabolism during exercise and activity; neuromuscular function after injury, prevention of lifestyle diseases, prevention and treatment of overuse injuries; athletic training: pediatric sport-related concussion, adolescent athlete health-related quality of life; occupational therapy: spirituality and health disparities, geriatric and pediatric well-being, pain management for participation. *Total annual research expenditures:* $75,682. *Unit head:* Dr. Randy Danielsen, Dean, 480-219-6000, Fax: 480-219-6110, E-mail: rdanielsen@atsu.edu. *Application contact:* Donna Sparks, Associate Director, Admissions Processing, 660-626-2117, Fax: 660-626-2969, E-mail: admissions@atsu.edu. Web site: http://www.atsu.edu/ashs.

Auburn University, Graduate School, College of Education, Department of Kinesiology, Auburn University, AL 36849. Offers exercise science (M Ed, MS, PhD); health promotion (M Ed, MS); kinesiology (PhD); physical education/teacher education (M Ed, MS, Ed D, Ed S). *Accreditation:* NCATE. Part-time programs available. *Faculty:* 15 full-time (8 women). *Students:* 60 full-time (30 women), 33 part-time (15 women); includes 17 minority (14 Black or African American, non-Hispanic/Latino; 1 Asian, non-Hispanic/Latino; 2 Hispanic/Latino), 6 international. Average age 27. 116 applicants, 61% accepted, 41 enrolled. In 2011, 48 master's, 4 doctorates awarded. *Degree requirements:* For master's, thesis (for some programs); for doctorate, thesis/dissertation; for Ed S, exam, field project. *Entrance requirements:* For master's, GRE General Test; for doctorate and Ed S, GRE General Test, interview, master's degree. *Application deadline:* For fall admission, 7/7 for domestic students; for spring admission, 11/24 for domestic students. Applications are processed on a rolling basis. Application fee: $50 ($60 for international students). Electronic applications accepted. *Expenses:* Tuition, state resident: full-time $7290; part-time $405 per credit hour. Tuition, nonresident: full-time $21,870; part-time $1215 per credit hour. *International tuition:* $22,000 full-time. *Required fees:* $1402. *Financial support:* Research assistantships, teaching assistantships, and Federal Work-Study available. Support available to part-time students. Financial award application deadline: 3/15; financial award applicants required to submit FAFSA. *Faculty research:* Biomechanics, exercise physiology, motor skill learning, school health, curriculum development. *Unit head:* Dr. Mary E. Rudisill, Head, 334-844-1458. *Application contact:* Dr. George Flowers, Dean of the Graduate School, 334-844-2125.

Barry University, School of Human Performance and Leisure Sciences, Programs in Movement Science, General Movement Science Program, Miami Shores, FL 33161-6695. Offers MS.

Barry University, School of Human Performance and Leisure Sciences, Programs in Movement Science, Specialization in Biomechanics, Miami Shores, FL 33161-6695. Offers MS. *Entrance requirements:* For master's, GRE General Test, minimum GPA of 3.0. Electronic applications accepted. *Faculty research:* Upper extremity biomechanics, orthopedic biomechanics.

Bowling Green State University, Graduate College, College of Education and Human Development, School of Human Movement, Sport, and Leisure Studies, Bowling Green, OH 43403. Offers developmental kinesiology (M Ed); recreation and leisure (M Ed); sport administration (M Ed). Part-time programs available. *Degree requirements:* For master's, thesis or alternative. *Entrance requirements:* For master's, GRE General Test, minimum GPA of 2.7. Additional exam requirements/recommendations for international students: Required—TOEFL. Electronic applications accepted. *Faculty research:* Teacher-learning process, travel and tourism, sport marketing and management, exercise physiology and sport psychology, life-span motor development.

California Polytechnic State University, San Luis Obispo, College of Science and Mathematics, Department of Kinesiology, San Luis Obispo, CA 93407. Offers MS. Part-time programs available. *Faculty:* 2 part-time/adjunct (both women). *Students:* 8 full-time (5 women), 7 part-time (4 women); includes 3 minority (2 Hispanic/Latino; 1 Two or more races, non-Hispanic/Latino), 1 international. Average age 25. 23 applicants, 57% accepted, 6 enrolled. In 2011, 12 master's awarded. *Degree requirements:* For master's, comprehensive exam (for some programs), thesis (for some programs). *Entrance requirements:* For master's, minimum GPA of 2.75 in last 90 quarter units of course work; letters of recommendation. Additional exam requirements/recommendations for international students: Required—TOEFL (minimum score 550 paper-based; 213 computer-based) or IELTS (minimum score 6). *Application deadline:* For fall admission, 4/1 for domestic students, 11/30 for international students; for winter admission, 9/1 for domestic students, 6/30 for international students. Applications are processed on a rolling basis. Application fee: $55. Electronic applications accepted. *Expenses:* Tuition, state resident: full-time $6738. Tuition, nonresident: full-time $17,898. *Required fees:* $2449. *Financial support:* Fellowships, research assistantships, teaching assistantships, career-related internships or fieldwork, Federal Work-Study, and scholarships/grants available. Support available to part-time students. Financial award application deadline: 3/2; financial award applicants required to submit FAFSA. *Faculty research:* Biomechanics, motor learning and control, physiology of exercise, commercial fitness, cardiac rehabilitation. *Unit head:* Dr. Kris Jankovitz, Graduate Coordinator, 805-756-2534, Fax: 805-756-7273, E-mail: kjankovi@calpoly.edu. *Application contact:* Dr. James Maraviglia, Associate Vice Provost for Marketing and Enrollment Development, 805-756-2311, Fax: 805-756-5400, E-mail: admissions@calpoly.edu. Web site: http://www.kinesiology.calpoly.edu/degrees/ms/index.html.

California State Polytechnic University, Pomona, Academic Affairs, College of Science, Program in Kinesiology, Pomona, CA 91768-2557. Offers MS. Part-time programs available. *Students:* 1 (woman) full-time, 20 part-time (12 women); includes 12 minority (3 Asian, non-Hispanic/Latino; 8 Hispanic/Latino; 1 Two or more races, non-Hispanic/Latino), 1 international. Average age 28. 23 applicants, 48% accepted, 3 enrolled. In 2011, 11 master's awarded. *Degree requirements:* For master's, thesis or alternative. *Application deadline:* For fall admission, 5/1 priority date for domestic students; for winter admission, 10/15 priority date for domestic students; for spring admission, 1/20 priority date for domestic students. Applications are processed on a rolling basis. Application fee: $55. Electronic applications accepted. *Expenses:* Tuition, state resident: full-time $6738. Tuition, nonresident: full-time $12,300. *Required fees:* $657. Tuition and fees vary according to course load and program. *Financial support:* Federal Work-Study and institutionally sponsored loans available. Support available to part-time students. Financial award application deadline: 3/2; financial award applicants required to submit FAFSA. *Unit head:* Dr. Perky F. Vetter, Chair, Kinesiology and Health Promotion Department, 909-869-2764, E-mail: pvetter@csupomona.edu. *Application contact:* Deborah L. Brandon, Executive Director, Admissions and Outreach, 909-869-3427, Fax: 909-869-5315, E-mail: dlbrandon@csupomona.edu. Web site: http://www.csupomona.edu/~kin/programs.html.

California State University, Chico, Office of Graduate Studies, College of Communication and Education, Department of Kinesiology, Chico, CA 95929-0722. Offers MA. Part-time programs available. *Faculty:* 8 full-time (4 women), 2 part-time/adjunct (1 woman). *Students:* 38 full-time (15 women), 12 part-time (4 women); includes 12 minority (1 Black or African American, non-Hispanic/Latino; 4 Asian, non-Hispanic/Latino; 7 Hispanic/Latino), 3 international. Average age 26. 32 applicants, 69% accepted, 19 enrolled. In 2011, 31 master's awarded. *Degree requirements:* For master's, comprehensive examination or thesis and project. *Entrance requirements:* For master's, GRE General Test, 2 letters of recommendation, statement of purpose. Additional exam requirements/recommendations for international students: Required—TOEFL (minimum score 550 paper-based; 213 computer-based; 80 iBT), IELTS (minimum score 6.5), Pearson Test of English (minimum score 59). *Application deadline:* For fall admission, 3/1 priority date for domestic students, 3/1 for international students; for spring admission, 9/15 priority date for domestic students, 9/15 for international students. Application fee: $55. Electronic applications accepted. Tuition and fees vary according to class time, course load and degree level. *Financial support:* Fellowships, teaching assistantships, career-related internships or fieldwork, scholarships/grants, and unspecified assistantships available. Financial award application deadline: 3/1; financial award applicants required to submit FAFSA. *Unit head:* Rebecca Lytle, Chair, 530-898-6373, Fax: 530-898-4932, E-mail: phed@csuchico.edu. *Application contact:* Judy L. Rice, Graduate Admissions Coordinator, 530-898-5416, Fax: 530-898-3342, E-mail: grin@csuchico.edu. Web site: http://www.csuchico.edu/kine.

California State University, Fresno, Division of Graduate Studies, College of Health and Human Services, Department of Kinesiology, Fresno, CA 93740-8027. Offers exercise science (MA); sport psychology (MA). Part-time and evening/weekend programs available. *Degree requirements:* For master's, thesis or alternative. *Entrance requirements:* For master's, GRE General Test, minimum GPA of 2.7. Additional exam requirements/recommendations for international students: Required—TOEFL. Electronic applications accepted. *Faculty research:* Refugee education, homeless, geriatrics, fitness.

California State University, Long Beach, Graduate Studies, College of Health and Human Services, Department of Kinesiology, Long Beach, CA 90840. Offers adapted physical education (MA); coaching and student athlete development (MA); exercise physiology and nutrition (MS); exercise science (MS); individualized studies (MA); kinesiology (MA); pedagogical studies (MA); sport and exercise psychology (MS); sport management (MA); sports medicine and injury studies (MS). Part-time programs available. *Faculty:* 9 full-time (5 women), 5 part-time/adjunct (4 women). *Students:* 48 full-time (27 women), 39 part-time (13 women); includes 38 minority (5 Black or African American, non-Hispanic/Latino; 2 American Indian or Alaska Native, non-Hispanic/Latino; 7 Asian, non-Hispanic/Latino; 18 Hispanic/Latino; 6 Two or more races, non-Hispanic/Latino), 2 international. Average age 28. 214 applicants, 50% accepted, 32 enrolled. In 2011, 69 master's awarded. *Degree requirements:* For master's, oral and written comprehensive exams or thesis. *Entrance requirements:* For master's, GRE General Test, minimum GPA of 2.75 during previous 2 years of course work. *Application deadline:* For fall admission, 6/1 for domestic students. Applications are processed on a rolling basis. Application fee: $55. Electronic applications accepted. *Financial support:* Federal Work-Study, institutionally sponsored loans, and scholarships/grants available. Financial award application deadline: 3/2. *Faculty research:* Pulmonary functioning, feedback and practice structure, strength training, history and politics of sports, special population research issues. *Unit head:* Dr. Sharon R. Guthrie, Chair, 562-985-7487, Fax: 562-985-8067, E-mail: guthrie@csulb.edu. *Application contact:* Dr. Grant Hill, Graduate Advisor, 562-985-8856, Fax: 562-985-8067, E-mail: ghill@csulb.edu.

California State University, Los Angeles, Graduate Studies, College of Health and Human Services, Department of Kinesiology and Nutritional Sciences, Los Angeles, CA 90032-8530. Offers nutritional science (MS); physical education and kinesiology (MA, MS). *Accreditation:* AND. Part-time and evening/weekend programs available. *Faculty:* 5 full-time (3 women), 2 part-time/adjunct (1 woman). *Students:* 96 full-time (84 women), 40 part-time (34 women); includes 70 minority (6 Black or African American, non-Hispanic/Latino; 1 American Indian or Alaska Native, non-Hispanic/Latino; 36 Asian, non-Hispanic/Latino; 24 Hispanic/Latino; 3 Two or more races, non-Hispanic/Latino), 12 international. Average age 31. 152 applicants, 51% accepted, 44 enrolled. In 2011, 38 master's awarded. *Degree requirements:* For master's, comprehensive exam, project or thesis. *Entrance requirements:* For master's, minimum GPA of 2.75. Additional exam requirements/recommendations for international students: Required—TOEFL (minimum score 500 paper-based; 173 computer-based). *Application deadline:* For fall admission, 5/1 for domestic and international students. Applications are processed on a rolling basis. Application fee: $55. *Expenses:* Tuition, state resident: full-time $8225. *Financial support:* Federal Work-Study available. Support available to part-time students. Financial award application deadline: 3/1. *Unit head:* Dr. Nazareth Khodiguian, Chair, 323-343-4650, Fax: 323-343-6482, E-mail: nkhodig@calstatela.edu. *Application contact:* Dr. Karin Brown, Acting Associate Dean of Graduate Studies, 323-343-3820, Fax: 323-343-5653, E-mail: kbrown5@calstatela.edu. Web site: http://www.calstatela.edu/dept/pe/.

California State University, Northridge, Graduate Studies, College of Health and Human Development, Department of Kinesiology, Northridge, CA 91330. Offers MS. Part-time and evening/weekend programs available. *Degree requirements:* For master's, thesis or alternative. *Entrance requirements:* For master's, GRE General Test or minimum GPA of 3.0, 3 letters of recommendation. Additional exam requirements/recommendations for international students: Required—TOEFL.

California State University, San Bernardino, Graduate Studies, College of Natural Sciences, Department of Kinesiology, San Bernardino, CA 92407-2397. Offers MA Ed. Part-time and evening/weekend programs available. *Students:* 6 full-time (0 women), 1 part-time (0 women); includes 1 minority (Black or African American, non-Hispanic/Latino), 4 international. Average age 29. *Degree requirements:* For master's, advancement to candidacy. *Entrance requirements:* For master's, minimum GPA of 3.0. *Application deadline:* Applications are processed on a rolling basis. Application fee: $55. *Expenses:* Tuition, state resident: full-time $7356. Tuition, nonresident: full-time $7356. *Required fees:* $1077. Tuition and fees vary according to program. *Financial support:* Career-related internships or fieldwork, Federal Work-Study, and institutionally sponsored loans available. Support available to part-time students. *Unit head:* Dr. Terry Rizzo, Chair, 909-537-5355, Fax: 909-537-2397, E-mail: trizzo@csusb.edu. *Application contact:* Sandra Kamusikiri, Associate Vice-President/Dean of Graduate Studies, 909-537-5058, E-mail: skamusik@csusb.edu.

Canisius College, Graduate Division, School of Education and Human Services, Department of Kinesiology, Buffalo, NY 14208-1098. Offers health and human performance (MS Ed); physical education (MS Ed); physical education birth -12 (MS Ed). Part-time and evening/weekend programs available. Postbaccalaureate distance learning degree programs offered (minimal on-campus study). *Faculty:* 11 full-time (1 woman), 14 part-time/adjunct (4 women). *Students:* 78 full-time (35 women), 159 part-time (61 women); includes 13 minority (7 Black or African American, non-Hispanic/Latino; 2 American Indian or Alaska Native, non-Hispanic/Latino; 1 Asian, non-Hispanic/Latino; 3 Two or more races, non-Hispanic/Latino), 23 international. Average age 29. 107 applicants, 80% accepted, 66 enrolled. In 2011, 106 master's awarded. *Degree requirements:* For master's, research project. *Entrance requirements:* For master's, GRE if cumulative GPA less than 2.7, transcripts, two letters of recommendation. Additional exam requirements/recommendations for international students: Required—TOEFL. *Application deadline:* Applications are processed on a rolling basis. Application fee: $25. Electronic applications accepted. *Financial support:* Career-related internships or fieldwork, Federal Work-Study, scholarships/grants, tuition waivers (partial), and unspecified assistantships available. Support available to part-time students. Financial award application deadline: 4/30; financial award applicants required to submit FAFSA. *Unit head:* Dr. Jeffrey Lindauer, Chair/Professor, Department of Kinesiology, 716-888-2196, E-mail: lindaue@canisius.edu. *Application contact:* Jim Bagwell, Director of Graduate Recruitment and Admissions, 716-888-2544, Fax: 716-888-3290, E-mail: bagwellj@canisius.edu. Web site: http://www.canisius.edu/newsevents/display_story.asp?iNewsID=6477.

Columbia University, College of Physicians and Surgeons, Programs in Occupational Therapy, New York, NY 10032. Offers movement science (Ed D), including occupational therapy; occupational therapy (professional) (MS); occupational therapy administration or education (post-professional) (MS); MPH/MS. *Accreditation:* AOTA. *Degree requirements:* For master's, project, 6 months of fieldwork, thesis (for post-professional students); for doctorate, comprehensive exam, thesis/dissertation. *Entrance requirements:* For master's, undergraduate course work in anatomy, physiology, statistics, psychology, social sciences, humanities, English composition; NBCOT eligibility; for doctorate, NBCOT certification, MS. Additional exam requirements/recommendations for international students: Required—TOEFL (minimum score 250 computer-based; 100 iBT), TWE (minimum score 4). Electronic applications accepted. *Expenses:* Contact institution. *Faculty research:* Community mental health, developmental tasks of late life, infant play, cognition, obesity, motor learning.

Dalhousie University, Faculty of Health Professions, School of Health and Human Performance, Program in Kinesiology, Halifax, NS B3H 3J5, Canada. Offers M Sc. Part-time programs available. *Degree requirements:* For master's, thesis. *Entrance requirements:* Additional exam requirements/recommendations for international students: Required—TOEFL, IELTS, CANTEST, CAEL, or Michigan English Language Assessment Battery. Electronic applications accepted. *Faculty research:* Sport science, fitness, neuromuscular physiology, biomechanics, ergonomics, sport psychology.

Dallas Baptist University, Dorothy M. Bush College of Education, Program in Kinesiology, Dallas, TX 75211-9299. Offers M Ed. *Entrance requirements:* For master's, GRE General Test, minimum GPA of 3.0. Additional exam requirements/recommendations for international students: Required—TOEFL, IELTS. Application fee: $25. *Expenses: Tuition:* Full-time $12,060; part-time $670 per credit hour. *Required fees:* $100; $50 per semester. *Financial support:* Federal Work-Study, institutionally sponsored loans, scholarships/grants, and tuition waivers (full and partial) available. Support available to part-time students. Financial award applicants required to submit FAFSA. *Unit head:* Dr. Ray Galloway, Director, 214-333-5414, Fax: 214-333-5306, E-mail: rayg@dbu.edu. *Application contact:* Kit Montgomery, Director of Graduate Programs, 214-333-5242, Fax: 214-333-5579, E-mail: graduate@dbu.edu. Web site: http://www3.dbu.edu/graduate/kinesiology.asp.

East Carolina University, Graduate School, College of Health and Human Performance, Department of Kinesiology, Greenville, NC 27858-4353. Offers adapted physical education (MA Ed, MS); bioenergetics and exercise science (PhD); biomechanics (MS); exercise physiology (MS); physical activity promotion (MS); physical education (MA Ed, MAT); physical education clinical supervision (Certificate); physical education pedagogy (MA Ed, MS); sport and exercise psychology (MS); sport management (Certificate). *Degree requirements:* For master's, comprehensive exam, thesis optional; for doctorate, comprehensive exam, thesis/dissertation. *Entrance requirements:* For master's, GRE General Test or MAT; for doctorate, GRE. Additional exam requirements/recommendations for international students: Required—TOEFL. *Application deadline:* For fall admission, 2/1 priority date for domestic students, 2/1 for international students. Applications are processed on a rolling basis. Application fee: $50. *Expenses:* Tuition, state resident: full-time $3557; part-time $444.63 per semester hour. Tuition, nonresident: full-time $14,351; part-time $1793.88 per semester hour. *Required fees:* $2016; $252 per semester hour. Part-time tuition and fees vary according to course load, campus/location and program. *Financial support:* Research assistantships with tuition reimbursements and teaching assistantships available. Support available to part-time students. Financial award application deadline: 2/1. *Faculty research:* Diabetes metabolism, pediatric obesity, biomechanics of arthritis, physical activity measurement. *Unit head:* Dr. Stacey Altman, Chair, 252-328-2973, E-mail: altmans@ecu.edu.

Kinesiology and Movement Studies

Eastern Illinois University, Graduate School, College of Education and Professional Studies, Department of Kinesiology and Sports Studies, Charleston, IL 61920-3099. Offers MS. Part-time programs available. *Expenses:* Tuition, state resident: part-time $279 per credit hour. Tuition, nonresident: part-time $670 per credit hour. *Required fees:* $179.07 per credit hour. $1253 per semester.

Eastern Michigan University, Graduate School, College of Health and Human Services, School of Health Promotion and Human Performance, Programs in Exercise Physiology, Ypsilanti, MI 48197. Offers exercise physiology (MS); sports medicine-biomechanics (MS); sports medicine-corporate adult fitness (MS); sports medicine-exercise physiology (MS). Part-time and evening/weekend programs available. *Students:* 22 full-time (16 women), 42 part-time (18 women); includes 8 minority (4 Black or African American, non-Hispanic/Latino; 2 American Indian or Alaska Native, non-Hispanic/Latino; 1 Hispanic/Latino; 1 Two or more races, non-Hispanic/Latino), 4 international. Average age 30. 59 applicants, 68% accepted, 22 enrolled. In 2011, 20 degrees awarded. *Degree requirements:* For master's, comprehensive exam, thesis or 450-hour internship. *Entrance requirements:* Additional exam requirements/recommendations for international students: Required—TOEFL. *Application deadline:* For fall admission, 8/1 for domestic students, 5/1 for international students; for winter admission, 12/1 for domestic students, 10/1 for international students; for spring admission, 3/15 for domestic students, 3/1 for international students. Application fee: $35. *Expenses:* Tuition, state resident: full-time $10,367; part-time $432 per credit hour. Tuition, nonresident: full-time $20,435; part-time $851 per credit hour. *Required fees:* $39 per credit hour. $46 per semester. One-time fee: $100. Tuition and fees vary according to course level, degree level and reciprocity agreements. *Unit head:* Dr. Steve McGregor, Program Coordinator, 734-487-0090, Fax: 734-487-2024, E-mail: stephen.mcgregor@emich.edu. *Application contact:* Dr. Brenda Riemer, Chair, Graduate Programs, 734-487-0090 Ext. 2745, Fax: 734-487-2024, E-mail: briemer@emich.edu.

Fresno Pacific University, Graduate Programs, Program in Kinesiology, Fresno, CA 93702-4709. Offers MA. *Entrance requirements:* Additional exam requirements/recommendations for international students: Required—TOEFL (minimum score 550 paper-based; 213 computer-based).

Georgia College & State University, Graduate School, College of Health Sciences, Department of Kinesiology, Milledgeville, GA 31061. Offers health promotion (M Ed); human performance (M Ed); kinesiology (MAT); outdoor education (M Ed). *Accreditation:* NCATE (one or more programs are accredited). Part-time and evening/weekend programs available. *Students:* 31 full-time (13 women), 11 part-time (7 women); includes 8 minority (6 Black or African American, non-Hispanic/Latino; 2 Hispanic/Latino), 1 international. Average age 27. 32 applicants, 69% accepted, 16 enrolled. In 2011, 12 master's awarded. *Degree requirements:* For master's, comprehensive exam, thesis optional. *Entrance requirements:* For master's, GRE General Test or MAT, minimum GPA of 2.75 in upper-level undergraduate courses, 2 letters of reference. Additional exam requirements/recommendations for international students: Recommended—TOEFL (minimum score 550 paper-based; 213 computer-based; 79 iBT). *Application deadline:* For fall admission, 7/1 priority date for domestic students, 4/1 for international students; for spring admission, 11/15 priority date for domestic students, 9/1 for international students. Applications are processed on a rolling basis. Application fee: $40. Electronic applications accepted. *Expenses:* Tuition, state resident: full-time $4806; part-time $267 per credit hour. Tuition, nonresident: full-time $17,802; part-time $989 per credit hour. *Required fees:* $936 per semester. Tuition and fees vary according to course load and campus/location. *Financial support:* In 2011–12, 25 research assistantships with full tuition reimbursements were awarded; career-related internships or fieldwork and unspecified assistantships also available. Support available to part-time students. Financial award applicants required to submit FAFSA. *Unit head:* Dr. Lisa Griffin, Interim Chair, 478-445-4072, Fax: 478-445-1790, E-mail: lisa.griffin@gcsu.edu. *Application contact:* 800-342-0471, E-mail: grad-admit@gcsu.edu.

Georgia Southern University, Jack N. Averitt College of Graduate Studies, College of Health and Human Sciences, Department of Health and Kinesiology, Statesboro, GA 30460. Offers MS. Part-time and evening/weekend programs available. Postbaccalaureate distance learning degree programs offered. *Students:* 61 full-time (32 women), 51 part-time (13 women); includes 21 minority (17 Black or African American, non-Hispanic/Latino; 1 Asian, non-Hispanic/Latino; 3 Hispanic/Latino), 2 international. Average age 27. 70 applicants, 59% accepted, 29 enrolled. In 2011, 64 master's awarded. *Degree requirements:* For master's, comprehensive exam (for some programs), thesis optional. *Entrance requirements:* For master's, GRE, minimum GPA of 2.75, resume, letters of reference. Additional exam requirements/recommendations for international students: Required—TOEFL (minimum score 550 paper-based; 213 computer-based; 80 iBT). *Application deadline:* For fall admission, 3/1 priority date for domestic students, 3/1 for international students; for spring admission, 10/1 priority date for domestic students, 10/1 for international students. Applications are processed on a rolling basis. Application fee: $50. Electronic applications accepted. *Expenses:* Tuition, state resident: full-time $6300; part-time $263 per semester hour. Tuition, nonresident: full-time $25,174; part-time $1049 per semester hour. *Required fees:* $1872. *Financial support:* In 2011–12, 55 students received support, including research assistantships with partial tuition reimbursements available (averaging $7,200 per year), teaching assistantships with partial tuition reimbursements available (averaging $7,200 per year); tuition waivers (partial) and unspecified assistantships also available. Financial award application deadline: 4/15; financial award applicants required to submit FAFSA. *Faculty research:* Concussions and postural control, overtraining in athletes, sport supplements and performance, mental training and performance. *Total annual research expenditures:* $60,648. *Unit head:* Dr. Barry A. Joyner, Chair, 912-478-0495, Fax: 912-478-0381, E-mail: joyner@georgiasouthern.edu. *Application contact:* Amanda Gilliland, Coordinator for Graduate Student Recruitment, 912-478-5384, Fax: 912-478-0740, E-mail: gradadmissions@georgiasouthern.edu. Web site: http://www.georgiasouthernhealthscience.com/html.

Georgia State University, College of Education, Department of Kinesiology and Health, Program in Kinesiology, Atlanta, GA 30302-3083. Offers PhD. *Degree requirements:* For doctorate, comprehensive exam, thesis/dissertation. *Entrance requirements:* For doctorate, GRE General Test or MAT, minimum GPA of 3.3. *Faculty research:* Aging, exercise metabolism, biomechanics and ergonomics, blood pressure regulation, exercise performance.

Hardin-Simmons University, Graduate School, Irvin School of Education, Department of Fitness and Sport Sciences, Program in Kinesiology, Sport, and Recreation, Abilene, TX 79698-0001. Offers M Ed. Part-time programs available. *Faculty:* 6 full-time (3 women), 2 part-time/adjunct (0 women). *Students:* 7 full-time (0 women), 15 part-time (5 women); includes 4 minority (1 Black or African American, non-Hispanic/Latino; 3 Hispanic/Latino). Average age 25. 12 applicants, 83% accepted, 6 enrolled. In 2011, 10 master's awarded. *Degree requirements:* For master's, comprehensive exam, thesis optional, internship, project. *Entrance requirements:* For master's, minimum undergraduate GPA of 3.0 in major, 2.7 overall; interview; writing sample; letters of recommendation; resume. Additional exam requirements/recommendations for international students: Required—TOEFL (minimum score 550 paper-based; 213 computer-based; 75 iBT). *Application deadline:* For fall admission, 8/15 priority date for domestic students, 4/1 for international students; for spring admission, 1/5 priority date for domestic students, 9/1 for international students. Applications are processed on a rolling basis. Application fee: $50. *Expenses: Tuition:* Full-time $12,870; part-time $715 per credit hour. *Required fees:* $650; $110 per semester. Tuition and fees vary according to degree level. *Financial support:* In 2011–12, 12 fellowships (averaging $1,667 per year) were awarded; career-related internships or fieldwork, scholarships/grants, and recreation assistantships also available. Support available to part-time students. Financial award application deadline: 6/30; financial award applicants required to submit FAFSA. *Unit head:* Dr. Robert Moore, Director, 325-670-1265, Fax: 325-670-1218, E-mail: bemoore@hsutx.edu. *Application contact:* Dr. Nancy Kucinski, Dean of Graduate Studies, 325-670-1298, Fax: 325-670-1564, E-mail: gradoff@hsutx.edu. Web site: http://www.hsutx.edu/academics/irvin/graduate/kinesiology.

Humboldt State University, Academic Programs, College of Professional Studies, Department of Kinesiology and Recreation Administration, Arcata, CA 95521-8299. Offers athletic training education (MS); exercise science/wellness management (MS); pre-physical therapy (MS); teaching/coaching (MS). *Students:* 11 full-time (7 women), 10 part-time (6 women); includes 4 minority (1 American Indian or Alaska Native, non-Hispanic/Latino; 2 Hispanic/Latino; 1 Two or more races, non-Hispanic/Latino). Average age 28. 9 applicants, 100% accepted, 6 enrolled. In 2011, 7 master's awarded. *Degree requirements:* For master's, thesis or alternative. *Entrance requirements:* For master's, GMAT, minimum GPA of 2.5. Additional exam requirements/recommendations for international students: Required—TOEFL. *Application deadline:* For fall admission, 6/1 for domestic students; for spring admission, 12/2 for domestic students. Applications are processed on a rolling basis. Application fee: $55. *Expenses:* Tuition, state resident: full-time $6734. Tuition, nonresident: full-time $15,662; part-time $372 per credit. *Required fees:* $903. Tuition and fees vary according to program. *Financial support:* Teaching assistantships, career-related internships or fieldwork, Federal Work-Study, and institutionally sponsored loans available. Financial award application deadline: 3/1; financial award applicants required to submit FAFSA. *Faculty research:* Human performance, adapted physical education, physical therapy. *Unit head:* Dr. Chris Hooper, Chair, 707-826-3853, Fax: 707-826-5451, E-mail: cah3@humboldt.edu. *Application contact:* Dr. Rock Braithwaite, Coordinator, 707-826-4543, Fax: 707-826-5451, E-mail: reb22@humboldt.edu. Web site: http://www.humboldt.edu/kra/.

Indiana University Bloomington, School of Health, Physical Education and Recreation, Department of Kinesiology, Bloomington, IN 47405-7000. Offers adapted physical education (MS); applied sport science (MS); athletic administration/sport management (MS); athletic training (MS); biomechanics (MS); ergonomics (MS); exercise physiology (MS); human performance (PhD), including adapted physical education, biomechanics, exercise physiology, motor learning/control, sport management; motor learning/control (MS); physical activity, fitness and wellness (MS). Part-time programs available. *Faculty:* 28 full-time (11 women). *Students:* 150 full-time (59 women), 22 part-time (9 women); includes 20 minority (12 Black or African American, non-Hispanic/Latino; 1 American Indian or Alaska Native, non-Hispanic/Latino; 1 Asian, non-Hispanic/Latino; 4 Hispanic/Latino; 2 Two or more races, non-Hispanic/Latino), 33 international. Average age 28. 211 applicants, 60% accepted, 62 enrolled. In 2011, 67 master's, 7 doctorates awarded. Terminal master's awarded for partial completion of doctoral program. *Degree requirements:* For master's, thesis optional; for doctorate, variable foreign language requirement, thesis/dissertation. *Entrance requirements:* For master's, GRE General Test, minimum GPA of 2.8; for doctorate, GRE General Test, minimum graduate GPA of 3.5, undergraduate 3.0. *Application deadline:* For fall admission, 1/1 for international students; for spring admission, 9/1 for international students. Applications are processed on a rolling basis. Application fee: $55 ($65 for international students). *Financial support:* Fellowships, research assistantships with full tuition reimbursements, teaching assistantships with full tuition reimbursements, career-related internships or fieldwork, Federal Work-Study, institutionally sponsored loans, scholarships/grants, tuition waivers (partial), and fee remissions available. Financial award application deadline: 3/1. *Faculty research:* Exercise physiology and biochemistry, sports biomechanics, human motor control, adaptation of fitness and exercise to special populations. *Unit head:* Dr. David M. Koceja, Chairperson, 812-855-5523, Fax: 812-855-3193, E-mail: koceja@indiana.edu. *Application contact:* Kristine M. Wasson, Administrative Assistant for Graduate Studies, 812-855-5523, Fax: 812-855-3193, E-mail: ktanksle@indiana.edu. Web site: http://www.indiana.edu/~kines/.

Inter American University of Puerto Rico, San Germán Campus, Graduate Studies Center, Program in Health and Physical Education, San Germán, PR 00683-5008. Offers MA. Part-time and evening/weekend programs available. *Degree requirements:* For master's, comprehensive exam. *Entrance requirements:* For master's, GRE General Test or EXADEP, minimum GPA of 3.0. *Application deadline:* For fall admission, 4/30 priority date for domestic students; for spring admission, 11/15 for domestic students. Applications are processed on a rolling basis. Application fee: $31. *Expenses: Required fees:* $213 per semester. *Financial support:* Teaching assistantships available. *Unit head:* Dr. Elba T. Irizarry, Director of Graduate Studies Center, 787-264-1912 Ext. 7357, Fax: 787-892-6350, E-mail: elbat@sg.inter.edu.

Iowa State University of Science and Technology, Department of Kinesiology, Ames, IA 50011-1160. Offers MS, PhD. *Entrance requirements:* For master's and doctorate, GRE General Test. Additional exam requirements/recommendations for international students: Required—TOEFL (minimum score 560 paper-based; 79 iBT), IELTS (minimum score 6.5). *Application deadline:* For fall admission, 1/1 priority date for domestic students, 1/1 for international students. Application fee: $40 ($90 for international students). Electronic applications accepted. *Unit head:* Dr. Ann Smiley-Oyen, Director of Graduate Education, 515-294-6459, Fax: 515-294-8740, E-mail: asmiley@iastate.edu. *Application contact:* Dr. Ann Smiley-Oyen, Application Contact, 515-294-6459, Fax: 515-294-8740, E-mail: asmiley@iastate.edu. Web site: http://www.kin.hs.iastate.edu/graduate/.

James Madison University, The Graduate School, College of Integrated Science and Technology, Department of Kinesiology, Harrisonburg, VA 22807. Offers MS. Part-time and evening/weekend programs available. *Faculty:* 9 full-time (2 women), 1 part-time/adjunct (0 women). *Students:* 84 full-time (47 women), 5 part-time (2 women); includes 7 minority (5 Black or African American, non-Hispanic/Latino; 1 American Indian or Alaska Native, non-Hispanic/Latino; 1 Two or more races, non-Hispanic/Latino). Average age 27. In 2011, 42 master's awarded. *Degree requirements:* For master's, thesis or alternative. *Entrance requirements:* For master's, GRE General Test. Additional exam requirements/recommendations for international students: Required—TOEFL. *Application deadline:* For fall admission, 5/1 priority date for domestic students; for spring admission, 9/1 priority date for domestic students. Applications are processed on a rolling basis. Application fee: $55. Electronic applications accepted. *Expenses:* Tuition, state resident: full-time $8016; part-time $334 per credit hour. Tuition, nonresident: full-time $22,656; part-time $944 per credit hour. *Financial support:* In 2011–12, 46 students received support, including 14 teaching assistantships with full tuition reimbursements available (averaging $8,664 per year); Federal Work-Study and 13 athletic assistantships ($8664), 5 service assistantships ($7382), 14 graduate assistantships ($7382) also available. Financial award application deadline: 3/1;

financial award applicants required to submit FAFSA. *Unit head:* Dr. Christopher J. Womack, Academic Unit Head, 540-568-6145, E-mail: womackex@jmu.edu. *Application contact:* Dr. M. Kent Todd, Graduate Coordinator, 540-568-3947, E-mail: toddmk@jmu.edu.

Kansas State University, Graduate School, College of Arts and Sciences, Department of Kinesiology, Manhattan, KS 66506. Offers MS. Part-time programs available. *Faculty:* 7 full-time (2 women), 2 part-time/adjunct (0 women). *Students:* 15 full-time (4 women), 4 part-time (0 women); includes 3 minority (1 Asian, non-Hispanic/Latino; 1 Hispanic/Latino; 1 Two or more races, non-Hispanic/Latino), 2 international. Average age 24. 27 applicants, 44% accepted, 7 enrolled. In 2011, 4 master's awarded. *Degree requirements:* For master's, thesis optional. *Entrance requirements:* For master's, GRE General Test, bachelor's degree in kinesiology or exercise science, minimum GPA of 3.0. Additional exam requirements/recommendations for international students: Required—TOEFL. *Application deadline:* For fall admission, 2/1 priority date for domestic students, 2/1 for international students; for spring admission, 8/1 priority date for domestic students, 8/1 for international students. Applications are processed on a rolling basis. Application fee: $40 ($55 for international students). Electronic applications accepted. *Financial support:* In 2011–12, 9 teaching assistantships (averaging $10,000 per year) were awarded; tuition waivers (full) also available. Financial award application deadline: 3/1; financial award applicants required to submit FAFSA. *Faculty research:* Exercise physiology, vascular function, cardiorespiratory disease, physical inactivity, exercise adherence and compliance, public health/physical activity. *Total annual research expenditures:* $218,220. *Unit head:* Prof. David Dzewaltowski, Head, 785-532-7795, Fax: 785-532-6486, E-mail: dadx@ksu.edu. *Application contact:* Prof. Thomas J. Barstow, Graduate Program Coordinator, 785-532-0712, Fax: 785-532-6486, E-mail: tbarsto@ksu.edu. Web site: http://www.k-state.edu/kines/.

Lakehead University, Graduate Studies, School of Kinesiology, Thunder Bay, ON P7B 5E1, Canada. Offers kinesiology (M Sc); kinesiology and gerontology (M Sc). Part-time programs available. *Degree requirements:* For master's, thesis. *Entrance requirements:* For master's, minimum B average. Additional exam requirements/recommendations for international students: Required—TOEFL. *Faculty research:* Social psychology and physical education, sport history, sports medicine, exercise physiology, gerontology.

Lamar University, College of Graduate Studies, College of Education and Human Development, Department of Health and Kinesiology, Beaumont, TX 77710. Offers kinesiology (MS). *Faculty:* 7 full-time (1 woman). *Students:* 28 full-time (13 women), 13 part-time (5 women); includes 15 minority (12 Black or African American, non-Hispanic/Latino; 1 Asian, non-Hispanic/Latino; 2 Hispanic/Latino), 8 international. Average age 26. 25 applicants, 92% accepted, 12 enrolled. In 2011, 8 master's awarded. *Degree requirements:* For master's, comprehensive exam (for some programs), thesis optional. *Entrance requirements:* For master's, GRE General Test, minimum GPA of 2.5. Additional exam requirements/recommendations for international students: Required—TOEFL. *Application deadline:* For fall admission, 8/1 for domestic students; for spring admission, 12/1 for domestic students. Applications are processed on a rolling basis. Application fee: $25. *Expenses:* Tuition, state resident: full-time $5430; part-time $272 per credit hour. Tuition, nonresident: full-time $11,540; part-time $577 per credit hour. *Required fees:* $1916. *Financial support:* In 2011–12, 4 teaching assistantships (averaging $7,500 per year) were awarded. Financial award application deadline: 4/1. *Faculty research:* Motor learning, exercise physiology, pedagogy. *Unit head:* Dr. Charles L. Nix, Chair, 409-880-2226, Fax: 409-880-1761, E-mail: nixcl@hal.lamar.edu. *Application contact:* Dr. Daniel R. Chilek, Graduate Coordinator, 409-880-8090, Fax: 409-880-1761, E-mail: chilekdr@hal.lamar.edu.

Louisiana State University and Agricultural and Mechanical College, Graduate School, College of Education, Department of Kinesiology, Baton Rouge, LA 70803. Offers MS, PhD. PhD offered jointly with Louisiana State University in Shreveport. *Faculty:* 22 full-time (8 women). *Students:* 73 full-time (34 women), 28 part-time (14 women); includes 13 minority (12 Black or African American, non-Hispanic/Latino; 1 Hispanic/Latino), 5 international. Average age 26. 96 applicants, 63% accepted, 35 enrolled. In 2011, 42 master's, 6 doctorates awarded. Terminal master's awarded for partial completion of doctoral program. *Degree requirements:* For master's, thesis (for some programs); for doctorate, one foreign language, thesis/dissertation, residency. *Entrance requirements:* For master's and doctorate, GRE General Test, minimum GPA of 3.0. Additional exam requirements/recommendations for international students: Required—TOEFL (minimum score 550 paper-based; 213 computer-based; 79 iBT) or IELTS (minimum score 6.5). *Application deadline:* For fall admission, 1/25 priority date for domestic students, 5/15 for international students; for spring admission, 10/15 for international students. Applications are processed on a rolling basis. Application fee: $50 ($70 for international students). Electronic applications accepted. *Financial support:* In 2011–12, 80 students received support, including 3 fellowships with full and partial tuition reimbursements available (averaging $19,853 per year), 25 teaching assistantships with full and partial tuition reimbursements available (averaging $9,895 per year); research assistantships with full and partial tuition reimbursements available, career-related internships or fieldwork, Federal Work-Study, health care benefits, tuition waivers (full and partial), and unspecified assistantships also available. Financial award applicants required to submit FAFSA. *Faculty research:* Physical activity promotion in schools, wellness centers, hospitals and sports settings, healthy aging, rehabilitation studies. *Total annual research expenditures:* $252,445. *Unit head:* Dr. Melinda Solmon, Chair, 225-578-2036, Fax: 225-578-3680, E-mail: msolmo1@lsu.edu. *Application contact:* Dr. Melinda Solmon, Coordinator of Graduate Studies, 225-578-2639, Fax: 225-578-3680, E-mail: msolmo1@lsu.edu. Web site: http://uiswcmsweb.prod.lsu.edu/kinesiology/.

Louisiana State University in Shreveport, College of Business, Education, and Human Development, Program in Kinesiology and Wellness, Shreveport, LA 71115-2399. Offers MS. Part-time and evening/weekend programs available. *Students:* 5 full-time (2 women), 2 part-time (1 woman); includes 2 minority (both Asian, non-Hispanic/Latino), 1 international. Average age 26. 3 applicants, 100% accepted, 0 enrolled. In 2011, 4 master's awarded. *Entrance requirements:* For master's, GRE, baccalaureate degree with minimum GPA of 2.5 or 2.75 on last 60 credit hours attempted in degree program. Additional exam requirements/recommendations for international students: Required—TOEFL (minimum score 550 paper-based; 213 computer-based; 80 iBT). *Application deadline:* For fall admission, 6/30 for domestic and international students; for spring admission, 11/30 for domestic and international students. Application fee: $10 ($20 for international students). *Financial support:* Unspecified assistantships available. Financial award applicants required to submit FAFSA. *Unit head:* Dr. Timothy P. Winter, Program Director, 318-797-5264, Fax: 318-797-5386, E-mail: timothy.winter@lsus.edu. *Application contact:* Christianne Wojcik, Director of Academic Services, 318-797-5247, Fax: 318-798-4120, E-mail: christianne.wojcik@lsus.edu.

McGill University, Faculty of Graduate and Postdoctoral Studies, Faculty of Education, Department of Kinesiology and Physical Education, Montréal, QC H3A 2T5, Canada. Offers M Sc, MA, PhD, Certificate, Diploma.

McMaster University, School of Graduate Studies, Faculty of Social Sciences, Department of Kinesiology, Hamilton, ON L8S 4M2, Canada. Offers human biodynamics (M Sc, PhD). *Degree requirements:* For master's, thesis. *Entrance requirements:* For master's, minimum B+ average in undergraduate course work. Additional exam requirements/recommendations for international students: Required—TOEFL (minimum score 580 paper-based; 237 computer-based). *Faculty research:* Motor learning and control, neuromuscular physiology, exercise rehabilitation, cellular responses to exercise, management.

Memorial University of Newfoundland, School of Graduate Studies, School of Human Kinetics and Recreation, St. John's, NL A1C 5S7, Canada. Offers administration, curriculum and supervision (MPE); biomechanics/ergonomics (MS Kin); exercise and work physiology (MS Kin); sport psychology (MS Kin). Part-time programs available. *Degree requirements:* For master's, thesis optional, seminars, thesis presentations. *Entrance requirements:* For master's, bachelor's degree in a related field, minimum B average. Electronic applications accepted. *Faculty research:* Administration, sociology of sports, kinesiology, physiology/recreation.

Michigan State University, The Graduate School, College of Education, Department of Kinesiology, East Lansing, MI 48824. Offers MS, PhD. *Entrance requirements:* Additional exam requirements/recommendations for international students: Required—TOEFL. Electronic applications accepted.

Midwestern State University, Graduate Studies, College of Health Sciences and Human Services, Program in Kinesiology, Wichita Falls, TX 76308. Offers MSK. Part-time programs available. *Degree requirements:* For master's, comprehensive exam, thesis optional. *Entrance requirements:* For master's, GRE General Test or MAT. Additional exam requirements/recommendations for international students: Required—TOEFL (minimum score 550 paper-based; 213 computer-based). Electronic applications accepted. *Faculty research:* Exercise adherence, muscular tissue remodeling during hypertrophy, student engagement and success, operational paradigms of the exercise sciences.

Mississippi College, Graduate School, School of Education, Department of Kinesiology, Clinton, MS 39058. Offers athletic administration (MS). *Degree requirements:* For master's, comprehensive exam, thesis optional. *Entrance requirements:* For master's, GRE, GMAT, or PRAXIS, minimum GPA of 2.5. Additional exam requirements/recommendations for international students: Recommended—TOEFL, IELTS. Electronic applications accepted.

Mississippi State University, College of Education, Department of Kinesiology, Mississippi State, MS 39762. Offers MS. Part-time programs available. Postbaccalaureate distance learning degree programs offered (minimal on-campus study). *Faculty:* 6 full-time (1 woman). *Students:* 58 full-time (23 women), 15 part-time (6 women); includes 11 minority (7 Black or African American, non-Hispanic/Latino; 1 Hispanic/Latino; 3 Two or more races, non-Hispanic/Latino), 1 international. Average age 25. 55 applicants, 47% accepted, 21 enrolled. In 2011, 37 master's awarded. *Degree requirements:* For master's, comprehensive exam, thesis optional. *Entrance requirements:* For master's, GRE General Test, minimum GPA of 3.0. Additional exam requirements/recommendations for international students: Required—TOEFL (minimum score 550 paper-based; 213 computer-based; 79 iBT); Recommended—IELTS (minimum score 6.5). *Application deadline:* For fall admission, 7/1 for domestic students, 5/1 for international students; for spring admission, 11/1 for domestic students, 9/1 for international students. Applications are processed on a rolling basis. Application fee: $40. Electronic applications accepted. *Expenses:* Tuition, state resident: full-time $5805; part-time $322.50 per credit hour. Tuition, nonresident: full-time $14,670; part-time $815 per credit hour. *Financial support:* In 2011–12, 5 teaching assistantships (averaging $8,772 per year) were awarded; career-related internships or fieldwork, Federal Work-Study, institutionally sponsored loans, and unspecified assistantships also available. Financial award application deadline: 4/1; financial award applicants required to submit FAFSA. *Faculty research:* Static balance and stepping performance of older adults, organizational justice, public health, strength training and recovery drinks, high risk drinking perceptions and behaviors. *Unit head:* Dr. Stanley Brown, Professor and Department Head, 662-325-7229, Fax: 662-325-4525, E-mail: spb107@msstate.edu. *Application contact:* Dr. John G. Lamberth, Associate Professor and Graduate Coordinator, 662-325-0906, Fax: 662-325-4525, E-mail: jgl@ra.msstate.edu. Web site: http://www.kinesiology.msstate.edu/.

New York University, Steinhardt School of Culture, Education, and Human Development, Department of Physical Therapy, New York, NY 10010-5615. Offers orthopedic physical therapy (Advanced Certificate); physical therapy (MA, DPT), including pathokinesiology (MA); physical therapy for practicing physical therapists (DPT); research in physical therapy (PhD). *Accreditation:* APTA (one or more programs are accredited). Part-time programs available. *Faculty:* 10 full-time (6 women), 9 part-time/adjunct (4 women). *Students:* 96 full-time (72 women), 19 part-time (13 women); includes 34 minority (4 Black or African American, non-Hispanic/Latino; 22 Asian, non-Hispanic/Latino; 6 Hispanic/Latino; 1 Native Hawaiian or other Pacific Islander, non-Hispanic/Latino; 1 Two or more races, non-Hispanic/Latino), 12 international. Average age 26. 391 applicants, 27% accepted, 42 enrolled. In 2011, 5 master's, 42 doctorates awarded. *Degree requirements:* For master's, thesis (for some programs); for doctorate, thesis/dissertation. *Entrance requirements:* For master's, physical therapy certificate; for doctorate, GRE General Test, interview, physical therapy certificate. Additional exam requirements/recommendations for international students: Required—TOEFL. *Application deadline:* For fall admission, 12/1 priority date for domestic students, 12/1 for international students; for spring admission, 11/1 for domestic and international students. Applications are processed on a rolling basis. Application fee: $75. Electronic applications accepted. *Financial support:* Fellowships with full and partial tuition reimbursements, research assistantships with full and partial tuition reimbursements, career-related internships or fieldwork, Federal Work-Study, scholarships/grants, tuition waivers (partial), and unspecified assistantships available. Support available to part-time students. Financial award application deadline: 2/1; financial award applicants required to submit FAFSA. *Faculty research:* Motor learning and control, neuromuscular disorders, biomechanics and ergonomics, movement analysis, exercise physiology, neurocognitive function in joint instability, pathomechanics. *Unit head:* Dr. Wen K. Ling, Chairperson, 212-998-9400, Fax: 212-995-4190. *Application contact:* 212-998-5030, Fax: 212-995-4328, E-mail: steinhardt.gradadmissions@nyu.edu. Web site: http://steinhardt.nyu.edu/pt.

Northwestern University, Northwestern University Feinberg School of Medicine, Department of Physical Therapy and Human Movement Sciences, Chicago, IL 60611-2814. Offers movement and rehabilitation science (PhD); physical therapy (DPT). *Accreditation:* APTA. *Faculty:* 24 full-time (14 women), 4 part-time/adjunct (3 women). *Students:* 211 full-time (170 women); includes 27 minority (4 Black or African American, non-Hispanic/Latino; 8 Asian, non-Hispanic/Latino; 11 Hispanic/Latino; 1 Native Hawaiian or other Pacific Islander, non-Hispanic/Latino; 3 Two or more races, non-Hispanic/Latino). Average age 24. 486 applicants, 44% accepted, 81 enrolled. *Degree requirements:* For doctorate, synthesis research project. *Entrance requirements:* For doctorate, GRE General Test (DPT), baccalaureate degree with minimum GPA of 3.0 in required course work (DPT). Additional exam requirements/recommendations for international students: Required—TOEFL (minimum score 265 computer-based). *Application deadline:* For fall admission, 10/1 for domestic and international students. Applications are processed on a rolling basis. Application fee: $40. Electronic applications accepted. *Expenses:* Contact institution. *Financial support:* In 2011–12, 184 students received support. Federal Work-Study, institutionally sponsored loans, and scholarships/grants available. Financial award application deadline: 2/15; financial award applicants required to submit FAFSA. *Faculty research:* Motor control, robotics, neuromuscular imaging, student performance (academic/professional), clinical outcomes. *Total annual research expenditures:* $3.8 million. *Unit head:* Dr. Julius P. A. Dewald, Professor and Chair, 312-908-6788, Fax: 312-908-0741, E-mail: j-dewald@northwestern.edu. *Application contact:* Dr. Jane Sullivan, Associate Professor and Assistant Chair for Recruitment and Admissions, 312-908-6789, Fax: 312-908-0741, E-mail: j-sullivan@northwestern.edu.

Old Dominion University, Darden College of Education, Program in Human Movement Science, Norfolk, VA 23529. Offers PhD. *Faculty:* 2 full-time (both women). *Students:* 7 full-time (5 women), 5 part-time (3 women); includes 2 minority (both Black or African American, non-Hispanic/Latino). Average age 33. 9 applicants, 44% accepted, 4 enrolled. In 2011, 2 doctorates awarded. *Degree requirements:* For doctorate, comprehensive exam, thesis/dissertation. *Entrance requirements:* For doctorate, GRE, minimum GPA of 3.0. Additional exam requirements/recommendations for international students: Required—TOEFL. *Application deadline:* For spring admission, 2/1 priority date for domestic students, 2/1 for international students. Applications are processed on a rolling basis. Application fee: $40. Electronic applications accepted. *Expenses:* Tuition, state resident: full-time $9096; part-time $379 per credit. Tuition, nonresident: full-time $23,064; part-time $961 per credit. *Required fees:* $127 per semester. One-time fee: $50. *Financial support:* In 2011–12, 6 students received support, including 1 fellowship with full tuition reimbursement available (averaging $15,000 per year), 4 teaching assistantships with full tuition reimbursements available (averaging $15,000 per year); career-related internships or fieldwork, scholarships/grants, and unspecified assistantships also available. Financial award application deadline: 5/1. *Faculty research:* Prevention of ACL injury, lower extremity mechanics, manual therapy, athletic training education, evidence-based practice outcomes. *Total annual research expenditures:* $10,000. *Unit head:* Dr. Bonnie L. Van Lunen, Graduate Program Director, 757-683-3516, Fax: 757-683-4270, E-mail: bvanlune@odu.edu. *Application contact:* Alice McAdory, Director of Admissions, 757-683-3685, Fax: 757-683-3255, E-mail: gradadmit@odu.edu. Web site: http://education.odu.edu/esper/academics/phd/.

Oregon State University, Graduate School, College of Public Health and Human Sciences, Programs in Exercise and Sport Science, Program in Movement Studies in Disability, Corvallis, OR 97331. Offers MS, PhD. *Degree requirements:* For master's, thesis. *Entrance requirements:* For master's, minimum GPA of 3.0 in last 90 hours. Additional exam requirements/recommendations for international students: Required—TOEFL. *Faculty research:* Fitness testing of disabled, biomechanics of disabled, assessment of disabled athletes, biomechanics of wheeling, energy cost of wheeling.

Oregon State University, Graduate School, College of Public Health and Human Sciences, Programs in Exercise and Sport Science, Program in Physical Activity and Public Health, Corvallis, OR 97331. Offers MS.

Penn State University Park, Graduate School, College of Health and Human Development, Department of Kinesiology, State College, University Park, PA 16802-1503. Offers MS, PhD, Certificate. *Unit head:* Dr. Ann C. Crouter, Dean, 814-865-1428, Fax: 814-865-3282, E-mail: ac1@psu.edu. *Application contact:* Cynthia E. Nicosia, Director, Graduate Enrollment Services, 814-865-1795, Fax: 814-865-4627, E-mail: cey1@psu.edu. Web site: http://www.hhdev.psu.edu/kines/.

Purdue University, Graduate School, College of Health and Human Sciences, Department of Health and Kinesiology, West Lafayette, IN 47907. Offers athletic training education administration (MS); exercise, human physiology of movement and sport (PhD); health education (MS, PhD); motor control and development (MS, PhD); physical education pedagogy (MS, PhD); sport and exercise psychology (MS, PhD). Part-time programs available. *Faculty:* 20 full-time (9 women), 14 part-time/adjunct (4 women). *Students:* 53 full-time (27 women), 19 part-time (9 women); includes 9 minority (3 Black or African American, non-Hispanic/Latino; 1 American Indian or Alaska Native, non-Hispanic/Latino; 2 Asian, non-Hispanic/Latino; 1 Hispanic/Latino; 2 Two or more races, non-Hispanic/Latino), 14 international. Average age 30. 108 applicants, 48% accepted, 29 enrolled. In 2011, 17 master's, 6 doctorates awarded. *Degree requirements:* For master's, thesis optional; for doctorate, comprehensive exam, thesis/dissertation, Qualifying Examination, Preliminary Examination. *Entrance requirements:* For master's, GRE General Test, minimum score 1000 combined verbal and quantitative scores, minimum undergraduate GPA of 3.0 or equivalent; for doctorate, GRE General Test, minimum score 1100 combined verbal and quantitative scores, minimum undergraduate GPA of 3.0 or equivalent; master's degree with minimum GPA of 3.25 (recommended). Additional exam requirements/recommendations for international students: Required—TOEFL (minimum score 550 computer-based; 77 iBT); Recommended—TWE. *Application deadline:* For fall admission, 4/30 for domestic and international students; for spring admission, 10/15 for domestic and international students. Applications are processed on a rolling basis. Application fee: $60 ($75 for international students). Electronic applications accepted. *Financial support:* Fellowships with partial tuition reimbursements, research assistantships with partial tuition reimbursements, teaching assistantships with partial tuition reimbursements, and Federal Work-Study available. Support available to part-time students. Financial award applicants required to submit FAFSA. *Faculty research:* Wellness, motivation, teaching effectiveness, learning and development. *Unit head:* Dr. Larry J. Leverenz, Interim Head, 765-494-0865, Fax: 765-494-496-1239, E-mail: llevere@purdue.edu. *Application contact:* Lisa Duncan, Graduate Contact, 765-494-3162, E-mail: llduncan@purdue.edu. Web site: http://www.purdue.edu/hhs/hk/.

Saint Mary's College of California, School of Liberal Arts, Department of Kinesiology, Moraga, CA 94556. Offers sport management (MA); sport studies (MA). Part-time programs available. *Faculty:* 6 full-time (1 woman), 5 part-time/adjunct (3 women). *Students:* 3 full-time (0 women), 22 part-time (13 women); includes 6 minority (3 Black or African American, non-Hispanic/Latino; 3 Asian, non-Hispanic/Latino). Average age 27. 23 applicants, 65% accepted, 14 enrolled. In 2011, 7 master's awarded. *Degree requirements:* For master's, thesis or special project. *Entrance requirements:* For master's, minimum GPA of 2.75, BA in physical education or related field, or professional experience. Application fee: $25. Electronic applications accepted. *Expenses:* Contact institution. *Financial support:* In 2011–12, 15 students received support, including research assistantships (averaging $6,000 per year); career-related internships or fieldwork, institutionally sponsored loans, scholarships/grants, tuition waivers (partial), and unspecified assistantships also available. Support available to part-time students. Financial award applicants required to submit FAFSA. *Faculty research:* Moral development in sport, applied motor learning, achievement motivation, sport history. *Total annual research expenditures:* $1,500. *Unit head:* William Manning, Chair, 925-631-4969, Fax: 925-631-4965, E-mail: wmanning@stmarys-ca.edu. *Application contact:* Jeanne Abate, Administrative Assistant, 925-631-4377, Fax: 925-631-4965, E-mail: jabate@stmarys-ca.edu. Web site: http://www.stmarys-ca.edu/graduate-kinesiology.

Sam Houston State University, College of Education, Department of Health and Kinesiology, Huntsville, TX 77341. Offers health (MA); kinesiology (MA). Part-time and evening/weekend programs available. *Faculty:* 11 full-time (4 women). *Students:* 35 full-time (16 women), 33 part-time (20 women); includes 24 minority (18 Black or African American, non-Hispanic/Latino; 1 American Indian or Alaska Native, non-Hispanic/Latino; 5 Hispanic/Latino), 2 international. Average age 27. 54 applicants, 59% accepted, 32 enrolled. In 2011, 26 master's awarded. *Entrance requirements:* For master's, GRE, MAT. Additional exam requirements/recommendations for international students: Required—TOEFL (minimum score 550 paper-based; 213 computer-based; 79 iBT). *Application deadline:* For fall admission, 8/1 for domestic students, 6/25 for international students; for spring admission, 12/1 for domestic students, 11/12 for international students. Applications are processed on a rolling basis. Application fee: $45 ($75 for international students). Electronic applications accepted. *Expenses:* Tuition, state resident: full-time $4420; part-time $221 per credit hour. Tuition, nonresident: full-time $10,680; part-time $534 per credit hour. *Required fees:* $329 per credit hour. *Financial support:* Research assistantships, teaching assistantships, career-related internships or fieldwork, Federal Work-Study, and institutionally sponsored loans available. Financial award application deadline: 5/31; financial award applicants required to submit FAFSA. *Unit head:* Dr. Alice Fisher, Chair, 936-294-1165, Fax: 936-294-3891. *Application contact:* Molly Doughtie, Advisor, 936-294-1105, E-mail: edu_mxd@shsu.edu. Web site: http://www.shsu.edu/~hpe_www/.

San Diego State University, Graduate and Research Affairs, College of Health and Human Services, School of Exercise and Nutritional Sciences, Program in Kinesiology, San Diego, CA 92182. Offers MA. *Degree requirements:* For master's, thesis. *Entrance requirements:* For master's, GRE General Test, 2 letters of reference. Additional exam requirements/recommendations for international students: Required—TOEFL. Electronic applications accepted.

San Francisco State University, Division of Graduate Studies, College of Health and Human Services, Department of Kinesiology, San Francisco, CA 94132-1722. Offers exercise physiology (MS); movement science (MS); physical activity: social scientific perspectives (MS). *Application deadline:* Applications are processed on a rolling basis. *Unit head:* Dr. Marialice Kern, Chair, 415-338-2244, E-mail: mkern@sfsu.edu. *Application contact:* Maria Allain, Academic Office Coordinator, 415-338-2244, E-mail: meallain@sfsu.edu. Web site: http://kin.sfsu.edu/.

San Jose State University, Graduate Studies and Research, College of Applied Sciences and Arts, Department of Kinesiology, San Jose, CA 95192-0001. Offers MA. *Degree requirements:* For master's, comprehensive exam. *Entrance requirements:* For master's, bachelor's degree in physical education. Electronic applications accepted.

Simon Fraser University, Graduate Studies, Faculty of Applied Sciences, School of Kinesiology, Burnaby, BC V5A 1S6, Canada. Offers M Sc, PhD. *Degree requirements:* For master's, thesis; for doctorate, thesis/dissertation. *Entrance requirements:* For master's, minimum GPA of 3.0; for doctorate, minimum GPA of 3.5. Additional exam requirements/recommendations for international students: Required—TOEFL or IELTS. *Faculty research:* Biomechanics, human factors/ergonomics, behavioral neuroscience/motor control, cardiovascular/respiratory physiology, endocrine and immune systems.

Sonoma State University, School of Science and Technology, Department of Kinesiology, Rohnert Park, CA 94928-3609. Offers MA. Part-time programs available. *Faculty:* 2 full-time (both women). *Students:* 10 part-time (2 women); includes 1 minority (Two or more races, non-Hispanic/Latino). Average age 32. 12 applicants, 17% accepted, 2 enrolled. *Degree requirements:* For master's, thesis, oral exam. *Entrance requirements:* For master's, minimum GPA of 2.8. Additional exam requirements/recommendations for international students: Required—TOEFL (minimum score 500 paper-based; 173 computer-based). *Application deadline:* For fall admission, 11/30 for domestic students; for spring admission, 9/1 for domestic students. Applications are processed on a rolling basis. Application fee: $55. *Financial support:* Career-related internships or fieldwork available. Financial award application deadline: 3/2; financial award applicants required to submit FAFSA. *Unit head:* Dr. Elaine McHugh, Chair, 707-664-2660, E-mail: elaine.mchugh@sonoma.edu. *Application contact:* Dr. Lauren Morimoto, Graduate Coordinator, 707-664-2479, E-mail: morimoto@sonoma.edu. Web site: http://www.sonoma.edu/kinesiology/nsf/ma_program.shtml.

Southeastern Louisiana University, College of Nursing and Health Sciences, Department of Kinesiology and Health Studies, Hammond, LA 70402. Offers health and kinesiology (MA), including exercise science, health promotion and exercise science, health studies, kinesiology. *Accreditation:* NCATE. Part-time programs available. *Faculty:* 7 full-time (2 women), 1 (woman) part-time/adjunct. *Students:* 40 full-time (26 women), 25 part-time (17 women); includes 15 minority (11 Black or African American, non-Hispanic/Latino; 1 Asian, non-Hispanic/Latino; 1 Hispanic/Latino; 2 Two or more races, non-Hispanic/Latino), 4 international. Average age 27. 27 applicants, 100% accepted, 19 enrolled. In 2011, 24 degrees awarded. *Degree requirements:* For master's, comprehensive exam (for some programs), thesis (for some programs). *Entrance requirements:* For master's, GRE General Test (minimum score 800), undergraduate human anatomy and physiology course. Additional exam requirements/recommendations for international students: Required—TOEFL (minimum score 500 paper-based; 173 computer-based; 61 iBT). *Application deadline:* For fall admission, 7/15 priority date for domestic students, 6/1 for international students; for spring admission, 12/1 priority date for domestic students, 10/1 for international students. Applications are processed on a rolling basis. Application fee: $20 ($30 for international students). Electronic applications accepted. *Expenses:* Tuition, state resident: full-time $3977; part-time $283 per semester hour. Tuition, nonresident: full-time $13,482; part-time $811 per semester hour. *Financial support:* In 2011–12, 2 fellowships (averaging $10,800 per year), 8 research assistantships (averaging $9,500 per year), 3 teaching assistantships (averaging $9,000 per year) were awarded; career-related internships or fieldwork, Federal Work-Study, institutionally sponsored loans, scholarships/grants, and unspecified assistantships also available. Support available to part-time students. Financial award application deadline: 5/1; financial award applicants required to submit FAFSA. *Faculty research:* Exercise endocrinology, perceptions of exercise intensity and pain, spirituality and health, alternative health practices, use of podcasting and other technology to promote healthy behaviors. *Unit head:* Dr. Edward Hebert, Department Head, 985-549-2129, Fax: 985-549-5119, E-mail: ehebert@selu.edu. *Application contact:* Sandra Meyers, Graduate Admissions Analyst, 985-549-5620, Fax: 985-549-5632, E-mail: admissions@selu.edu. Web site: http://www.selu.edu/acad_research/depts/kin_hs.

Southern Arkansas University–Magnolia, Graduate Programs, Magnolia, AR 71754. Offers agriculture (MS); business administration (MBA); computer and information sciences (MS); education (M Ed), including counseling and development, curriculum and instruction, educational administration and supervision, elementary education, middle level, reading, secondary education, TESOL; kinesiology (M Ed); library media and information specialist (M Ed); mental health and clinical counseling (MS); public administration (MPA); school counseling (M Ed); teaching (MAT). *Accreditation:* NCATE. Part-time and evening/weekend programs available. Postbaccalaureate distance learning degree programs offered. *Faculty:* 34 full-time (15 women), 8 part-time/adjunct (5 women). *Students:* 87 full-time (62 women), 320 part-time (224 women); includes 116 minority (111 Black or African American, non-Hispanic/Latino; 2 American Indian or Alaska Native, non-Hispanic/Latino; 2 Asian, non-Hispanic/Latino; 1 Hispanic/Latino), 25 international. Average age 33. 201 applicants, 98% accepted, 156 enrolled. In 2011, 162 master's awarded. *Degree requirements:* For master's, comprehensive exam (for some programs), thesis optional. *Entrance requirements:* For master's, GRE, MAT or GMAT, minimum GPA of 2.5. Additional exam requirements/recommendations for international students: Required—TOEFL (minimum score 173 computer-based). *Application deadline:* For fall admission, 7/15 for domestic and international students; for winter admission, 12/1 for domestic and international students; for spring admission, 12/1 for domestic and international students. Applications are processed on a rolling basis. Application fee: $25 ($35 for international students). Electronic applications accepted. *Expenses:* Tuition, state resident: part-time $232 per credit. Tuition, nonresident: part-time $339 per credit. *Required fees:* $44 per credit. Part-time tuition and fees vary according to course load. *Financial support:* Career-related internships or fieldwork, Federal Work-Study, scholarships/grants, tuition waivers (full), and unspecified assistantships available. Financial award applicants required to submit FAFSA. *Faculty research:* Alternative certification for teachers, supervision of instruction, instructional leadership, counseling. *Unit head:* Dr. Kim Bloss, Dean, School of Graduate Studies, 870-235-4150, Fax: 870-235-5227, E-mail: kkbloss@saumag.edu. *Application contact:* Gaye Calhoun, Admissions Specialist, 870-235-4150, Fax: 870-235-5227, E-mail: glcalhoun@saumag.edu. Web site: http://www.saumag.edu/graduate.

Southern Illinois University Edwardsville, Graduate School, School of Education, Department of Kinesiology and Health Education, Edwardsville, IL 62026. Offers kinesiology (MS Ed), including kinesiology, physical education and sport pedagogy. *Accreditation:* NCATE. Part-time and evening/weekend programs available. *Faculty:* 12 full-time (5 women). *Students:* 31 full-time (16 women), 45 part-time (18 women); includes 17 minority (10 Black or African American, non-Hispanic/Latino; 2 Asian, non-Hispanic/Latino; 5 Hispanic/Latino), 1 international. 70 applicants, 59% accepted. In 2011, 35 master's awarded. *Degree requirements:* For master's, comprehensive exam (for some programs), thesis (for some programs). *Entrance requirements:* Additional exam requirements/recommendations for international students: Required—TOEFL (minimum score 550 paper-based; 213 computer-based; 79 iBT), IELTS (minimum score 6.5). *Application deadline:* For fall admission, 7/22 for domestic students, 6/1 for international students; for spring admission, 12/9 for domestic students, 10/1 for international students. Applications are processed on a rolling basis. Application fee: $30. Electronic applications accepted. Tuition and fees vary according to course load and program. *Financial support:* In 2011–12, 6 teaching assistantships with full tuition reimbursements (averaging $9,927 per year) were awarded; fellowships, research assistantships with full tuition reimbursements, institutionally sponsored loans, scholarships/grants, and unspecified assistantships also available. Financial award application deadline: 3/1; financial award applicants required to submit FAFSA. *Unit head:* Dr. Curt Lox, Director, 618-650-2938, E-mail: clox@siue.edu. *Application contact:* Dr. Erik Kirk, Program Director, 618-650-2718, E-mail: ekirk@siue.edu. Web site: http://www.siue.edu/education/khe.

Southwestern Oklahoma State University, College of Professional and Graduate Studies, School of Behavioral Sciences and Education, Specialization in Kinesiology, Weatherford, OK 73096-3098. Offers M Ed. Part-time programs available. *Degree requirements:* For master's, exam. *Entrance requirements:* For master's, GRE General Test or minimum undergraduate GPA of 3.0. Additional exam requirements/recommendations for international students: Required—TOEFL.

Stephen F. Austin State University, Graduate School, College of Education, Department of Kinesiology and Health Science, Nacogdoches, TX 75962. Offers athletic training (MS); kinesiology (M Ed). *Degree requirements:* For master's, comprehensive exam. *Entrance requirements:* For master's, GRE General Test. Additional exam requirements/recommendations for international students: Required—TOEFL.

Teachers College, Columbia University, Graduate Faculty of Education, Department of Biobehavioral Studies, Program in Kinesiology, New York, NY 10027. Offers PhD. *Faculty:* 5 full-time (2 women), 2 part-time/adjunct (1 woman). *Degree requirements:* For doctorate, comprehensive exam, thesis/dissertation. *Application deadline:* For fall admission, 12/15 priority date for domestic students. Applications are processed on a rolling basis. Application fee: $65. *Faculty research:* Modulators of autonomic outflow, the effects of aerobic improvements on autonomic and blood pressure regulation, the role of physical activity in the prevention and treatment of chronic diseases, rehabilitation and cerebral palsy. *Unit head:* Prof. Andrew Gordon, Program Coordinator, 212-678-3325, E-mail: msnsprogram@tc.edu. *Application contact:* Morgan Oakes, Admissions Contact, 212-678-3710. Web site: http://www.tc.edu/bbs/Movement/.

Teachers College, Columbia University, Graduate Faculty of Education, Department of Biobehavioral Studies, Program in Motor Learning/Movement Science, New York, NY 10027-6696. Offers Ed M, MA, Ed D. Part-time and evening/weekend programs available. *Faculty:* 5 full-time (2 women), 2 part-time/adjunct (1 woman). *Students:* 3 full-time (2 women), 23 part-time (17 women); includes 7 minority (1 Black or African American, non-Hispanic/Latino; 4 Asian, non-Hispanic/Latino; 2 Hispanic/Latino), 5 international. Average age 33. 54 applicants, 57% accepted, 15 enrolled. In 2011, 8 master's, 3 doctorates awarded. Terminal master's awarded for partial completion of doctoral program. *Degree requirements:* For master's, integrative paper; for doctorate, thesis/dissertation, teaching assistantship. *Application deadline:* For fall admission, 1/2 priority date for domestic students. Applications are processed on a rolling basis. Application fee: $65. *Financial support:* Teaching assistantships, career-related internships or fieldwork, Federal Work-Study, institutionally sponsored loans, traineeships, and tuition waivers (full and partial) available. Support available to part-time students. Financial award application deadline: 2/1. *Faculty research:* Motor control, analysis of tasks, biomechanical aspect of learning, skill acquisition, recovery of motor behavior. *Unit head:* Prof. Andrew Gordon, Program Coordinator, 212-678-3325, E-mail: agordona@tc.edu. *Application contact:* Morgan Oakes, Assistant Director of Admission, 212-678-3710, Fax: 212-678-4171, E-mail: tcinfo@tc.edu.

Temple University, Health Sciences Center, College of Health Professions and Social Work, Department of Kinesiology, Philadelphia, PA 19122-6096. Offers kinesiology (Ed M, PhD), including behavioral sciences, somatic sciences. Part-time programs available. *Faculty:* 9 full-time (3 women). *Students:* 53 full-time (38 women), 12 part-time (3 women); includes 7 minority (6 Black or African American, non-Hispanic/Latino; 1 Hispanic/Latino), 12 international. Average age 28. 34 applicants, 85% accepted, 21 enrolled. In 2011, 16 master's, 5 doctorates awarded. Terminal master's awarded for partial completion of doctoral program. *Degree requirements:* For master's, thesis; for doctorate, thesis/dissertation. *Entrance requirements:* For master's, GRE General Test or MAT, minimum undergraduate GPA of 3.0; for doctorate, GRE General Test, minimum undergraduate GPA of 3.0. Additional exam requirements/recommendations for international students: Required—TOEFL (minimum score 550 paper-based; 213 computer-based; 79 iBT). *Application deadline:* For fall admission, 1/15 for domestic students, 12/15 for international students; for spring admission, 10/1 for domestic students, 8/1 for international students. Application fee: $50. *Expenses:* Tuition, state resident: full-time $12,366; part-time $687 per credit hour. Tuition, nonresident: full-time $17,298; part-time $961 per credit hour. *Required fees:* $590; $213 per year. *Financial support:* Fellowships, research assistantships with full tuition reimbursements, teaching assistantships with full tuition reimbursements, career-related internships or fieldwork, and Federal Work-Study available. Financial award application deadline: 1/15; financial award applicants required to submit FAFSA. *Unit head:* Dr. Michael Sachs, Interim Chair, 214-204-8707, E-mail: msachs@temple.edu. *Application contact:* Tara Schumacher, Coordinator of Outreach, 215-204-6575, Fax: 215-204-8781, E-mail: tara.schumacher@temple.edu. Web site: http://www.temple.edu/chp/departments/kinesiology/.

Tennessee Technological University, Graduate School, College of Education, Department of Exercise Science, Physical Education and Wellness, Cookeville, TN 38505. Offers MA. *Accreditation:* NCATE. Part-time programs available. Postbaccalaureate distance learning degree programs offered (no on-campus study). *Faculty:* 7 full-time (0 women). *Students:* 21 full-time (15 women), 24 part-time (13 women). Average age 27. 32 applicants, 72% accepted, 19 enrolled. In 2011, 21 master's awarded. *Degree requirements:* For master's, comprehensive exam, thesis or alternative. *Entrance requirements:* For master's, MAT or GRE. Additional exam requirements/recommendations for international students: Required—TOEFL (minimum score 527 paper-based; 71 iBT), IELTS (minimum score 5.5), Pearson Test of English Academic. *Application deadline:* For fall admission, 8/1 for domestic students, 5/1 for international students; for spring admission, 12/1 for domestic students, 10/1 for international students. Application fee: $25 ($30 for international students). Electronic applications accepted. *Expenses:* Tuition, state resident: full-time $8094; part-time $422 per credit hour. Tuition, nonresident: full-time $20,574; part-time $1046 per credit hour. *Financial support:* In 2011–12, fellowships (averaging $8,000 per year), 3 research assistantships (averaging $4,000 per year), 4 teaching assistantships (averaging $4,000 per year) were awarded; career-related internships or fieldwork also available. Financial award application deadline: 4/1. *Unit head:* Dr. J. P. Barfield, Interim Chairperson, 931-372-3467, Fax: 931-372-6319, E-mail: jpbarfield@tntech.edu. *Application contact:* Shelia K. Kendrick, Coordinator of Graduate Admissions, 931-372-3808, Fax: 931-372-3497, E-mail: skendrick@tntech.edu.

Texas A&M University, College of Education and Human Development, Department of Health and Kinesiology, College Station, TX 77843. Offers health education (MS, PhD); kinesiology (MS, PhD); physical education (M Ed); sport management (MS). Part-time programs available. *Faculty:* 37. *Students:* 171 full-time (80 women), 38 part-time (22 women); includes 60 minority (21 Black or African American, non-Hispanic/Latino; 8 Asian, non-Hispanic/Latino; 29 Hispanic/Latino; 2 Two or more races, non-Hispanic/Latino), 35 international. Average age 23. In 2011, 54 master's, 17 doctorates awarded. *Degree requirements:* For master's, thesis (for some programs); for doctorate, comprehensive exam, thesis/dissertation. *Entrance requirements:* For master's and doctorate, GRE General Test. Additional exam requirements/recommendations for international students: Required—TOEFL. *Application deadline:* Applications are processed on a rolling basis. Application fee: $50 ($75 for international students). Electronic applications accepted. *Expenses:* Tuition, state resident: full-time $5437; part-time $226.55 per credit hour. Tuition, nonresident: full-time $12,949; part-time $539.55 per credit hour. *Required fees:* $2741. *Financial support:* Fellowships with partial tuition reimbursements, research assistantships, teaching assistantships, career-related internships or fieldwork, and institutionally sponsored loans available. Financial award application deadline: 2/15; financial award applicants required to submit FAFSA. *Unit head:* Dr. Richard Kreider, Head, 979-845-1333, Fax: 979-847-8987, E-mail: rkreider@hlkn.tamu.edu. *Application contact:* Dr. Becky Carr, Assistant Dean for Administrative Services, 979-862-1342, Fax: 979-845-6129, E-mail: bcarr@tamu.edu. Web site: http://hlknweb.tamu.edu/.

Texas A&M University–Commerce, Graduate School, College of Education and Human Services, Department of Health and Human Performance, Commerce, TX 75429-3011. Offers exercise physiology (MS); health and human performance (M Ed); health promotion (MS); health, kinesiology and sports studies (Ed D); motor performance (MS); sport studies (MS). Part-time programs available. *Degree requirements:* For master's, comprehensive exam, thesis (for some programs). *Entrance requirements:* For master's, GRE General Test. Electronic applications accepted. *Faculty research:* Teaching, physical fitness.

Texas A&M University–Corpus Christi, Graduate Studies and Research, College of Education, Corpus Christi, TX 78412-5503. Offers counseling (MS, PhD), including counseling (MS), counselor education (PhD); curriculum and instruction (MS, Ed D); early childhood education (MS); educational administration (MS); educational leadership (Ed D); educational technology (MS); elementary education (MS); kinesiology (MS); reading (MS); secondary education (MS); special education (MS). Part-time and evening/weekend programs available. *Degree requirements:* For master's, comprehensive exam, thesis (for some programs); for doctorate, comprehensive exam, thesis/dissertation. *Entrance requirements:* For master's, GRE General Test. Additional exam requirements/recommendations for international students: Required—TOEFL. Electronic applications accepted.

Texas A&M University–Kingsville, College of Graduate Studies, College of Education, Department of Health and Kinesiology, Kingsville, TX 78363. Offers MA, MS. Part-time programs available. *Degree requirements:* For master's, comprehensive exam, thesis or alternative. *Entrance requirements:* For master's, GRE General Test, minimum GPA of 3.0. *Faculty research:* Body composition, electromyography.

Texas A&M University–San Antonio, Department of Curriculum and Kinesiology, San Antonio, TX 78224. Offers bilingual education (MA); early childhood education (M Ed); kinesiology (MS); reading (MS); special education (M Ed), including educational diagnostician, instructional specialist. Part-time and evening/weekend programs available. *Students:* 76 full-time (51 women), 240 part-time (180 women). Average age 37. *Degree requirements:* For master's, comprehensive exam, thesis or alternative. *Entrance requirements:* For master's, MAT. Additional exam requirements/recommendations for international students: Required—TOEFL (minimum score 550 paper-based; 213 computer-based; 80 iBT), IELTS (minimum score 6). *Application deadline:* For fall admission, 8/15 priority date for domestic students, 6/1 for international students; for spring admission, 12/15 priority date for domestic students, 10/1 for international students. Applications are processed on a rolling basis. Application fee: $35 ($50 for international students). Electronic applications accepted. *Expenses:* Tuition, state resident: part-time $691.11 per course. Tuition, nonresident: part-time $1621.11 per course. *Financial support:* Application deadline: 3/31; applicants required to submit FAFSA. *Unit head:* Dr. Samuel Garcia, Department Chair, 210-784-2505, E-mail: samuel.garcia@tamusa.tamus.edu. *Application contact:* Jennifer M. Dovalina, Graduate Admissions Specialist, 210-784-1380, E-mail: graduateadmissions@tamusa.tamus.edu. Web site: http://www.tamusa.tamus.edu/education/index.html.

Texas Christian University, Harris College of Nursing and Health Sciences, Department of Kinesiology, Fort Worth, TX 76129-0002. Offers MS. Part-time programs available. *Faculty:* 6 full-time (4 women), 1 part-time/adjunct. *Students:* 13 full-time (7 women), 6 part-time (3 women); includes 3 minority (1 Black or African American, non-Hispanic/Latino; 2 Hispanic/Latino). Average age 23. 26 applicants, 92% accepted, 13 enrolled. In 2011, 1 master's awarded. *Degree requirements:* For master's, thesis. *Entrance requirements:* For master's, GRE General Test, course work in kinesiology. Additional exam requirements/recommendations for international students: Required—TOEFL. *Application deadline:* For fall admission, 3/1 for domestic and international students; for spring admission, 12/1 for domestic and international students. Applications are processed on a rolling basis. Application fee: $60. *Expenses:* *Tuition:* Full-time $20,250; part-time $1125 per credit hour. Part-time tuition and fees vary according to course load and program. *Financial support:* In 2011–12, 8 research assistantships with full tuition reimbursements (averaging $7,500 per year), 3 teaching assistantships were awarded; unspecified assistantships also available. Financial award application deadline: 3/1. *Unit head:* Dr. Joel Mitchell, Chairperson, 817-257-7665, E-mail: j.mitchell@tcu.edu. *Application contact:* Admissions, TCU Graduate Studies Office, 817-257-7515, Fax: 817-257-7484, E-mail: frogmail@tcu.edu. Web site: http://www.kinesiology.tcu.edu.

Texas Woman's University, Graduate School, College of Health Sciences, Department of Kinesiology, Denton, TX 76201. Offers adapted physical education (MS, PhD); biomechanics (MS, PhD); coaching (MS); exercise physiology (MS, PhD); pedagogy (MS); sport management (MS, PhD). Part-time and evening/weekend programs available. *Faculty:* 12 full-time (6 women), 1 part-time/adjunct (0 women). *Students:* 55 full-time (38 women), 104 part-time (69 women); includes 35 minority (24 Black or African American, non-Hispanic/Latino; 1 American Indian or Alaska Native, non-Hispanic/Latino; 10 Hispanic/Latino), 23 international. Average age 31. 86 applicants, 73% accepted, 38 enrolled. In 2011, 25 master's, 7 doctorates awarded. Terminal master's awarded for partial completion of doctoral program. *Degree requirements:* For master's, comprehensive exam, thesis or alternative; for doctorate, comprehensive exam, thesis/dissertation, qualifying exam. *Entrance requirements:* For master's, GRE General Test (biomechanics emphasis only), 2 letters of reference, curriculum vitae, interview (adapted physical education emphasis only); for doctorate, GRE General Test (biomechanics emphasis only), interview, 3 letters of reference, curriculum vitae. Additional exam requirements/recommendations for international students: Required—TOEFL (minimum score 550 paper-based; 213 computer-based; 79 iBT). *Application deadline:* For fall admission, 7/1 priority date for domestic students, 3/1 for international students; for spring admission, 11/1 priority date for domestic students, 7/1 for international students. Applications are processed on a rolling basis. Application fee: $50 ($75 for international students). Electronic applications accepted. *Expenses:* Tuition, state resident: full-time $3834; part-time $213 per credit hour. Tuition, nonresident: full-time $9468; part-time $526 per credit hour. *Required fees:* $213 per credit hour. Tuition and fees vary according to course load. *Financial support:* In 2011–12, 46 students received support, including 7 research assistantships (averaging $10,746 per year), 14 teaching assistantships (averaging $10,746 per year); career-related internships or fieldwork, Federal Work-Study, institutionally sponsored loans, scholarships/grants, traineeships, health care benefits, and unspecified assistantships also available. Support available to part-time students. Financial award application deadline: 3/1; financial award applicants required to submit FAFSA. *Faculty research:* Exercise and Type 2 diabetes risk, bone mineral density and exercise in special populations, obesity in children, factors influencing sport consumer behavior and loyalty, roles and responsibilities of paraeducators in adapted physical education. *Total annual research expenditures:* $19,544. *Unit head:* Dr. David Nichols, Chair, 940-898-2575, Fax: 940-898-2581, E-mail: dnichols@twu.edu. *Application contact:* Dr. Samuel Wheeler, Assistant Director of Admissions, 940-898-3188, Fax: 940-898-3081, E-mail: wheelersr@twu.edu. Web site: http://www.twu.edu/kinesiology/.

Towson University, Program in Kinesiology, Towson, MD 21252-0001. Offers MS. *Students:* 11 part-time (4 women); includes 2 minority (both Black or African American, non-Hispanic/Latino). *Expenses:* Tuition, state resident: part-time $337 per credit. Tuition, nonresident: part-time $709 per credit. *Required fees:* $99 per credit. *Unit head:* Heather Crowe, Graduate Program Director, 410-704-4399.

Université de Montréal, Department of Kinesiology, Montréal, QC H3C 3J7, Canada. Offers kinesiology (M Sc, DESS); physical activity (M Sc, PhD). *Degree requirements:* For master's, one foreign language, thesis (for some programs); for doctorate, one foreign language, thesis/dissertation, general exam. Electronic applications accepted. *Faculty research:* Physiology of exercise, psychology of sports, biomechanics, dance, sociology of sports.

Université de Sherbrooke, Faculty of Physical Education and Sports, Program in Physical Education, Sherbrooke, QC J1K 2R1, Canada. Offers kinanthropology (M Sc); physical activity (Diploma). *Degree requirements:* For master's, thesis. *Entrance requirements:* For master's, minimum GPA of 2.7; for Diploma, bachelor's degree in physical education. *Faculty research:* Physical fitness, nutrition, human factors, sociology, teaching.

Université du Québec à Montréal, Graduate Programs, Program in Human Movement Studies, Montréal, QC H3C 3P8, Canada. Offers M Sc. Part-time programs available. *Degree requirements:* For master's, thesis optional. *Entrance requirements:* For master's, appropriate bachelor's degree or equivalent and proficiency in French.

Université Laval, Faculty of Medicine, Graduate Programs in Medicine, Programs in Kinesiology, Québec, QC G1K 7P4, Canada. Offers M Sc, PhD. Terminal master's awarded for partial completion of doctoral program. *Degree requirements:* For master's, thesis; for doctorate, comprehensive exam, thesis/dissertation. *Entrance requirements:* For master's and doctorate, French exam, knowledge of French, comprehension of written English. Electronic applications accepted.

The University of Alabama, Graduate School, College of Education, Department of Kinesiology, Tuscaloosa, AL 35487. Offers alternative sport pedagogy (MA); exercise science (MA, PhD); human performance (MA); sport management (MA); sport pedagogy (MA, PhD). Part-time programs available. *Faculty:* 8 full-time (1 woman). *Students:* 59 full-time (22 women), 22 part-time (14 women); includes 11 minority (7 Black or African American, non-Hispanic/Latino; 1 Asian, non-Hispanic/Latino; 2 Hispanic/Latino; 1 Two or more races, non-Hispanic/Latino), 7 international. Average age 30. 50 applicants, 78% accepted, 20 enrolled. In 2011, 23 master's, 6 doctorates awarded. *Median time to degree:* Of those who began their doctoral program in fall 2003, 100% received their degree in 8 years or less. *Degree requirements:* For master's, comprehensive exam, thesis optional; for doctorate, comprehensive exam, thesis/dissertation. *Entrance requirements:* For master's and doctorate, GRE, MAT, minimum GPA of 3.0. Additional exam requirements/recommendations for international students: Required—TOEFL. *Application deadline:* Applications are processed on a rolling basis. Application fee: $50 ($60 for international students). Electronic applications accepted. *Expenses:* Tuition, state resident: full-time $8600. Tuition, nonresident: full-time $21,900. *Financial support:* In 2011–12, 14 students received support, including 13 teaching assistantships with full tuition reimbursements available (averaging $8,678 per year). *Faculty research:* Race, gender and sexuality in sports; physical education teacher socialization; disability sports; physical activity and health; environmental physiology. *Total annual research expenditures:* $19,866. *Unit head:* Dr. Matt Curtner-Smith, Department Head and Professor, 205-348-9209, Fax: 205-348-0867, E-mail: msmith@bamaed.ua.edu. *Application contact:* Dr. Kathy S. Wetzel, Assistant Dean for Student Services, 205-348-1154, Fax: 205-348-0080, E-mail: kwetzel@bamaed.ua.edu. Web site: http://www.kinesiology.ua.edu/.

University of Arkansas, Graduate School, College of Education and Health Professions, Department of Health Science, Kinesiology, Recreation and Dance, Program in Kinesiology, Fayetteville, AR 72701-1201. Offers MS, PhD. *Students:* 31 full-time (21 women), 25 part-time (9 women); includes 6 minority (1 Black or African American, non-Hispanic/Latino; 3 American Indian or Alaska Native, non-Hispanic/Latino; 1 Hispanic/Latino; 1 Two or more races, non-Hispanic/Latino), 4 international. In 2011, 10 master's, 6 doctorates awarded. *Degree requirements:* For doctorate, thesis/dissertation. *Entrance requirements:* For doctorate, GRE General Test. *Application deadline:* For fall admission, 4/1 for international students; for spring admission, 10/1 for international students. Applications are processed on a rolling basis. Application fee: $40 ($50 for international students). Electronic applications accepted. *Financial support:* Fellowships with tuition reimbursements, research assistantships, teaching assistantships, career-related internships or fieldwork, and Federal Work-Study available. Support available to part-time students. Financial award application deadline: 4/1; financial award applicants required to submit FAFSA. *Unit head:* Dr. Bart Hammig, Departmental Chairperson, 479-575-2857, Fax: 479-575-5778, E-mail: bhammig@uark.edu. *Application contact:* Dr. Dean Gorman, Coordinator of Graduate Studies, 479-575-2890, E-mail: dgorman@uark.edu. Web site: http://kins.uark.edu/.

The University of British Columbia, Faculty of Education, School of Human Kinetics, Vancouver, BC V6T 1Z1, Canada. Offers M Sc, MA, MHK, PhD. Part-time programs available. *Degree requirements:* For master's, thesis (for some programs); for doctorate, comprehensive exam, thesis/dissertation. *Entrance requirements:* For doctorate, thesis-based master's degree. Additional exam requirements/recommendations for international students: Required—TOEFL (minimum score 550 paper-based; 213 computer-based), IELTS. Electronic applications accepted. *Faculty research:* Exercise physiology, biomechanics, motor learning, natural sciences, socio-managerial.

University of Calgary, Faculty of Graduate Studies, Faculty of Kinesiology, Calgary, AB T2N 1N4, Canada. Offers biomedical engineering (M Sc, PhD); kinesiology (M Kin, M Sc, PhD), including biomechanics (PhD), health and exercise physiology (PhD). *Degree requirements:* For master's, thesis (M Sc); for doctorate, thesis/dissertation. *Entrance requirements:* Additional exam requirements/recommendations for international students: Required—TOEFL. Electronic applications accepted. *Faculty research:* Load acting on the human body, muscle mechanics and physiology, optimizing high performance athlete performance, eye movement in sports, analysis of body composition.

University of Central Arkansas, Graduate School, College of Health and Behavioral Sciences, Department of Kinesiology, Conway, AR 72035-0001. Offers MS. *Faculty:* 3 full-time (1 woman), 1 (woman) part-time/adjunct. *Students:* 8 full-time (2 women), 2 part-time (0 women); includes 1 minority (Black or African American, non-Hispanic/Latino). Average age 25. 3 applicants, 100% accepted, 2 enrolled. In 2011, 6 master's awarded. *Degree requirements:* For master's, comprehensive exam, thesis optional. *Entrance requirements:* For master's, GRE General Test, minimum GPA of 2.7. Additional exam requirements/recommendations for international students: Required—TOEFL (minimum score 550 paper-based; 213 computer-based). *Application deadline:* For fall admission, 3/1 priority date for domestic students; for spring admission, 10/1 for domestic students. Applications are processed on a rolling basis. Application fee: $25 ($50 for international students). *Expenses:* Tuition, state resident: full-time $4834; part-time $398.35 per credit hour. Tuition, nonresident: full-time $8686. *Financial support:* Federal Work-Study, scholarships/grants, tuition waivers (partial), and unspecified assistantships available. Financial award application deadline: 2/15; financial award applicants required to submit FAFSA. *Unit head:* Dr. Deborah Howell, Chairperson, 501-450-3148, Fax: 501-450-5503, E-mail: debbieh@uca.edu. *Application contact:* Sandy Burks, Administrative Specialist, 501-450-3124, Fax: 501-450-5678, E-mail: slburks@uca.edu. Web site: http://www.uca.edu/divisions/academic/kped/.

University of Colorado Boulder, Graduate School, College of Arts and Sciences, Department of Integrative Physiology, Boulder, CO 80309. Offers MS, PhD. *Faculty:* 21 full-time (7 women). *Students:* 66 full-time (24 women), 7 part-time (2 women); includes 8 minority (1 American Indian or Alaska Native, non-Hispanic/Latino; 3 Asian, non-Hispanic/Latino; 3 Hispanic/Latino; 1 Two or more races, non-Hispanic/Latino), 3 international. Average age 27. 83 applicants, 25% accepted, 17 enrolled. In 2011, 20 master's, 3 doctorates awarded. Terminal master's awarded for partial completion of doctoral program. *Median time to degree:* Of those who began their doctoral program in fall 2003, 67% received their degree in 8 years or less. *Degree requirements:* For master's, comprehensive exam, thesis or alternative; for doctorate, thesis/dissertation. *Entrance requirements:* For master's, GRE General Test, minimum undergraduate GPA of 2.75. *Application deadline:* For fall admission, 1/15 for domestic students, 12/15 for international students. Applications are processed on a rolling basis. Application fee: $50 ($60 for international students). Electronic applications accepted. *Financial support:* In 2011–12, 106 students received support, including 28 fellowships (averaging $7,566 per year), 37 research assistantships with full and partial tuition reimbursements available (averaging $15,350 per year), 41 teaching assistantships with full and partial tuition reimbursements available (averaging $16,968 per year); institutionally sponsored loans, scholarships/grants, health care benefits, and unspecified assistantships also available. Financial award application deadline: 2/1; financial award applicants required to submit FAFSA. *Faculty research:* Integrative or cellular kinesiology. *Total annual research expenditures:* $9.2 million. *Application contact:* E-mail: iphygrad@colorado.edu. Web site: http://www.colorado.edu/intphys/.

University of Delaware, College of Arts and Sciences, Interdisciplinary Program in Biomechanics and Movement Science, Newark, DE 19716. Offers MS, PhD. Part-time programs available. Terminal master's awarded for partial completion of doctoral program. *Degree requirements:* For master's, thesis; for doctorate, thesis/dissertation. *Entrance requirements:* For master's and doctorate, GRE General Test, minimum undergraduate GPA of 3.0. Additional exam requirements/recommendations for international students: Required—TOEFL (minimum score 550 paper-based; 213 computer-based). Electronic applications accepted. *Faculty research:* Muscle modeling, gait, motor control, human movement.

University of Delaware, College of Health Sciences, Department of Kinesiology and Applied Physiology, Newark, DE 19716. Offers MS, PhD.

University of Florida, Graduate School, College of Health and Human Performance, Department of Applied Physiology and Kinesiology, Gainesville, FL 32611. Offers athletic training/sport medicine (MS); biobehavioral science (MS, PhD); clinical exercise physiology (MS); exercise physiology (MS, PhD); health and human performance (PhD); human performance (MS). *Degree requirements:* For master's, comprehensive exam, thesis (for some programs); for doctorate, comprehensive exam, thesis/dissertation. *Entrance requirements:* For doctorate, GRE General Test. Additional exam requirements/recommendations for international students: Required—TOEFL (minimum score 550 paper-based; 213 computer-based; 80 iBT), IELTS (minimum score 6). Electronic applications accepted. *Faculty research:* Cardiovascular disease; basic mechanisms that underlie exercise-induced changes in the body at the organ, tissue, cellular and molecular level; development of rehabilitation techniques for regaining motor control after stroke or as a consequence of Parkinson's disease; maintaining optimal health and delaying age-related declines in physiological function; psychomotor mechanisms impacting health and performance across the life span.

University of Georgia, College of Education, Department of Kinesiology, Athens, GA 30602. Offers MS, PhD. *Faculty:* 20 full-time (5 women). *Students:* 127 full-time (56 women), 18 part-time (7 women); includes 21 minority (13 Black or African American, non-Hispanic/Latino; 1 Asian, non-Hispanic/Latino; 4 Hispanic/Latino; 3 Two or more races, non-Hispanic/Latino), 20 international. Average age 27. 225 applicants, 36% accepted, 50 enrolled. In 2011, 35 master's, 9 doctorates awarded. *Entrance requirements:* For master's, GRE General Test or MAT; for doctorate, GRE General

Test. Additional exam requirements/recommendations for international students: Required—TOEFL. *Application deadline:* For fall admission, 7/1 priority date for domestic students; for spring admission, 11/15 for domestic students. Application fee: $50. Electronic applications accepted. *Unit head:* Dr. Kirk J. Cureton, Head, 706-542-4387, Fax: 706-542-3148, E-mail: kcureton@uga.edu. *Application contact:* Dr. Michael Schmidt, Graduate Coordinator, 706-542-6577, Fax: 706-542-3148, E-mail: schmidtm@uga.edu. Web site: http://www.coe.uga.edu/kinesiology.

University of Hawaii at Manoa, Graduate Division, College of Education, Department of Kinesiology and Rehabilitation Science, Honolulu, HI 96822. Offers kinesiology (MS). Part-time programs available. *Degree requirements:* For master's, thesis optional. *Entrance requirements:* For master's, GRE General Test. Additional exam requirements/recommendations for international students: Required—TOEFL (minimum score 540 paper-based; 207 computer-based; 76 iBT), IELTS (minimum score 5).

University of Hawaii at Manoa, Graduate Division, College of Education, PhD in Education Program, Honolulu, HI 96822. Offers curriculum and instruction (PhD); educational administration (PhD); educational foundations (PhD); educational policy studies (PhD); educational technology (PhD); exceptionalities (PhD); kinesiology (PhD). Part-time and evening/weekend programs available. *Degree requirements:* For doctorate, thesis/dissertation. *Entrance requirements:* For doctorate, GRE General Test, sample of written work. Additional exam requirements/recommendations for international students: Required—TOEFL (minimum score 600 paper-based; 250 computer-based; 100 iBT), IELTS (minimum score 7).

University of Houston, College of Liberal Arts and Social Sciences, Department of Health and Human Performance, Houston, TX 77204. Offers exercise science (MS); human nutrition (MS); human space exploration sciences (MS); kinesiology (PhD); physical education (M Ed). *Accreditation:* NCATE (one or more programs are accredited). Part-time and evening/weekend programs available. *Degree requirements:* For master's, comprehensive exam (for some programs), thesis (for some programs); for doctorate, comprehensive exam, thesis/dissertation, qualifying exam, candidacy paper. *Entrance requirements:* For master's, GRE (minimum 35th percentile on each section), minimum cumulative GPA of 3.0; for doctorate, GRE (minimum 35th percentile on each section), minimum cumulative GPA of 3.3. Additional exam requirements/recommendations for international students: Required—TOEFL (minimum score 550 paper-based; 79 iBT). Electronic applications accepted. *Faculty research:* Biomechanics, exercise physiology, obesity, nutrition, space exploration science.

University of Illinois at Chicago, Graduate College, College of Applied Health Sciences, Program in Kinesiology, Chicago, IL 60607-7128. Offers MS, PhD. Part-time programs available. *Degree requirements:* For master's, thesis. *Entrance requirements:* For master's, GRE General Test, minimum GPA of 2.75. Additional exam requirements/recommendations for international students: Required—TOEFL. Electronic applications accepted. *Faculty research:* Mitochondrial biogenesis, glucocorticoid lipid metabolism, at-risk youth, motor control.

University of Illinois at Urbana–Champaign, Graduate College, College of Applied Health Sciences, Department of Kinesiology and Community Health, Champaign, IL 61820. Offers community health (MS, MSPH, PhD); kinesiology (MS, PhD); public health (MPH); rehabilitation (MS). *Faculty:* 25 full-time (12 women). *Students:* 137 full-time (83 women), 10 part-time (8 women); includes 35 minority (16 Black or African American, non-Hispanic/Latino; 14 Asian, non-Hispanic/Latino; 3 Hispanic/Latino; 2 Two or more races, non-Hispanic/Latino), 38 international. 167 applicants, 40% accepted, 45 enrolled. In 2011, 22 master's, 11 doctorates awarded. *Entrance requirements:* For master's, GRE, minimum GPA of 3.0; for doctorate, GRE, minimum graduate GPA of 3.5. Additional exam requirements/recommendations for international students: Required—TOEFL. *Application deadline:* Applications are processed on a rolling basis. Application fee: $75 ($90 for international students). Electronic applications accepted. *Financial support:* In 2011–12, 15 fellowships, 37 research assistantships, 71 teaching assistantships were awarded; tuition waivers (full and partial) also available. *Unit head:* Wojciech Chodzko-Zajko, Head, 217-244-0823, Fax: 217-244-7322, E-mail: wojtek@illinois.edu. *Application contact:* Tina M. Candler, Office Manager, 217-333-1083, Fax: 217-244-7322, E-mail: tcandler@illinois.edu. Web site: http://www.kch.illinois.edu/.

University of Kentucky, Graduate School, College of Education, Program in Kinesiology and Health Promotion, Lexington, KY 40506-0032. Offers exercise science (PhD); kinesiology (MS, Ed D). Terminal master's awarded for partial completion of doctoral program. *Degree requirements:* For master's, comprehensive exam, thesis optional; for doctorate, comprehensive exam, thesis/dissertation. *Entrance requirements:* For master's, GRE General Test, minimum undergraduate GPA of 2.75; for doctorate, GRE General Test, minimum graduate GPA of 3.0. Additional exam requirements/recommendations for international students: Required—TOEFL (minimum score 550 paper-based; 213 computer-based). Electronic applications accepted.

University of Lethbridge, School of Graduate Studies, Lethbridge, AB T1K 3M4, Canada. Offers accounting (MScM); addictions counseling (M Sc); agricultural biotechnology (M Sc); agricultural studies (M Sc, MA); anthropology (MA); archaeology (MA); art (MA, MFA); biochemistry (M Sc); biological sciences (M Sc); biomolecular science (PhD); biosystems and biodiversity (PhD); Canadian studies (MA); chemistry (M Sc); computer science (M Sc); computer science and geographical information science (M Sc); counseling psychology (M Ed); dramatic arts (MA); earth, space, and physical science (PhD); economics (MA); educational leadership (M Ed); English (MA); environmental science (M Sc); evolution and behavior (PhD); exercise science (M Sc); finance (MScM); French (MA); French/German (MA); French/Spanish (MA); general education (M Ed); general management (MScM); geography (M Sc, MA); German (MA); health science (M Sc); history (MA); human resource management and labour relations (MScM); individualized multidisciplinary (M Sc, MA); information systems (MScM); international management (MScM); kinesiology (M Sc, MA); management (M Sc, MA); marketing (MScM); mathematics (M Sc); music (M Mus, MA); Native American studies (MA); neuroscience (M Sc, PhD); new media (MA); nursing (M Sc); philosophy (MA); physics (M Sc); policy and strategy (MScM); political science (MA); psychology (M Sc, MA); religious studies (MA); social sciences (MA); sociology (MA); theatre and dramatic arts (MFA); theoretical and computational science (PhD); urban and regional studies (MA); women's studies (MA). Part-time and evening/weekend programs available. *Degree requirements:* For doctorate, comprehensive exam, thesis/dissertation. *Entrance requirements:* For master's, GMAT (M Sc in management), bachelor's degree in related field, minimum GPA of 3.0 during previous 20 graded semester courses, 2 years teaching or related experience (M Ed); for doctorate, master's degree, minimum graduate GPA of 3.5. Additional exam requirements/recommendations for international students: Required—TOEFL. *Faculty research:* Movement and brain plasticity, gibberellin physiology, photosynthesis, carbon cycling, molecular properties of main-group ring components.

University of Maine, Graduate School, College of Education and Human Development, Program in Kinesiology and Physical Education, Orono, ME 04469. Offers curriculum and instruction (M Ed); exercise science (MS). Part-time and evening/weekend programs available. *Students:* 10 full-time (3 women), 2 part-time (1 woman); includes 2 minority (1 Hispanic/Latino; 1 Two or more races, non-Hispanic/Latino). Average age 29. 16 applicants, 69% accepted, 9 enrolled. In 2011, 8 degrees awarded. *Degree requirements:* For master's, thesis or alternative. *Entrance requirements:* For master's, MAT. Additional exam requirements/recommendations for international students: Required—TOEFL. *Application deadline:* For fall admission, 2/1 priority date for domestic students. Applications are processed on a rolling basis. Application fee: $65. Electronic applications accepted. *Expenses:* Tuition, state resident: full-time $5016. Tuition, nonresident: full-time $14,424. *Financial support:* Career-related internships or fieldwork, Federal Work-Study, institutionally sponsored loans, tuition waivers (full and partial), and unspecified assistantships available. Support available to part-time students. Financial award application deadline: 3/1. *Unit head:* Dr. Janet Spector, Coordinator, 207-581-2444, Fax: 207-581-2423. *Application contact:* Scott G. Delcourt, Associate Dean of the Graduate School, 207-581-3291, Fax: 207-581-3232, E-mail: graduate@maine.edu. Web site: http://www2umaine.edu/graduate/.

University of Manitoba, Faculty of Graduate Studies, Faculty of Kinesiology and Recreation Management, Winnipeg, MB R3T 2N2, Canada. Offers kinesiology and recreation (M Sc, MA).

University of Maryland, College Park, Academic Affairs, School of Public Health, Department of Kinesiology, College Park, MD 20742. Offers MA, PhD. Part-time and evening/weekend programs available. *Faculty:* 38 full-time (12 women), 8 part-time/adjunct (3 women). *Students:* 48 full-time (20 women), 4 part-time (3 women); includes 6 minority (2 Black or African American, non-Hispanic/Latino; 2 Asian, non-Hispanic/Latino; 2 Hispanic/Latino), 12 international. 75 applicants, 5% accepted, 4 enrolled. In 2011, 7 master's, 3 doctorates awarded. *Degree requirements:* For master's, thesis optional; for doctorate, thesis/dissertation. *Entrance requirements:* For master's, GRE General Test, minimum GPA of 3.0, 3 letters of recommendation; for doctorate, GRE General Test, minimum GPA of 3.5, 3 letters of recommendation. *Application deadline:* For fall admission, 1/15 for domestic and international students; for spring admission, 10/1 for domestic students, 6/1 for international students. Applications are processed on a rolling basis. Application fee: $75. Electronic applications accepted. *Expenses: Tuition, area resident:* Part-time $525 per credit hour. Tuition, state resident: part-time $525 per credit hour. Tuition, nonresident: part-time $1131 per credit hour. *Required fees:* $386.31 per term. Tuition and fees vary according to program. *Financial support:* In 2011–12, 8 fellowships with full and partial tuition reimbursements (averaging $17,100 per year), 4 research assistantships (averaging $15,878 per year), 17 teaching assistantships (averaging $15,987 per year) were awarded; career-related internships or fieldwork, Federal Work-Study, and scholarships/grants also available. Support available to part-time students. Financial award applicants required to submit CSS PROFILE or FAFSA. *Faculty research:* Sports, biophysical and professional studies, cognitive motor behavior, exercise physiology. *Total annual research expenditures:* $1.5 million. *Unit head:* Bradley Hatfield, Chair, 301-405-2450, Fax: 301-405-5578, E-mail: bhatfiel@umd.edu. *Application contact:* Dr. Charles A. Caramello, Dean of Graduate School, 301-405-0358, Fax: 301-314-9305.

University of Massachusetts Amherst, Graduate School, School of Public Health and Health Sciences, Department of Kinesiology, Amherst, MA 01003. Offers MS, PhD. Part-time programs available. *Faculty:* 17 full-time (7 women). *Students:* 39 full-time (25 women), 5 part-time (2 women); includes 6 minority (2 Black or African American, non-Hispanic/Latino; 1 Asian, non-Hispanic/Latino; 3 Hispanic/Latino), 4 international. Average age 29. 72 applicants, 17% accepted, 10 enrolled. In 2011, 4 master's, 7 doctorates awarded. Terminal master's awarded for partial completion of doctoral program. *Degree requirements:* For master's, comprehensive exam (for some programs), thesis optional; for doctorate, comprehensive exam, thesis/dissertation. *Entrance requirements:* For master's and doctorate, GRE General Test. Additional exam requirements/recommendations for international students: Required—TOEFL (minimum score 550 paper-based; 213 computer-based; 80 iBT), IELTS (minimum score 6.5). *Application deadline:* For fall admission, 2/1 for domestic and international students. Applications are processed on a rolling basis. Application fee: $50 ($65 for international students). Electronic applications accepted. Tuition and fees vary according to course load, campus/location and program. *Financial support:* Fellowships with full and partial tuition reimbursements, research assistantships with full and partial tuition reimbursements, teaching assistantships with full and partial tuition reimbursements, career-related internships or fieldwork, Federal Work-Study, scholarships/grants, traineeships, health care benefits, tuition waivers (full and partial), and unspecified assistantships available. Support available to part-time students. Financial award application deadline: 2/1. *Unit head:* Dr. Jane Kent-Braun, Graduate Program Director, 413-545-6070, Fax: 413-545-2906. *Application contact:* Lindsay DeSantis, Interim Supervisor of Admissions, 413-545-0722, Fax: 413-577-0010, E-mail: gradadm@grad.umass.edu. Web site: http://www.umass.edu/sphhs/kinesiology/.

University of Medicine and Dentistry of New Jersey, School of Health Related Professions, Department of Interdisciplinary Studies, Program in Health Sciences, Newark, NJ 07107-1709. Offers cardiopulmonary sciences (PhD); clinical laboratory sciences (PhD); health sciences (MS); interdisciplinary studies (PhD); nutrition (PhD); physical therapy/movement science (PhD). Part-time and evening/weekend programs available. Postbaccalaureate distance learning degree programs offered (no on-campus study). *Faculty:* 4 full-time (all women), 10 part-time/adjunct (7 women). *Students:* 3 full-time, 130 part-time; includes 32 minority (10 Black or African American, non-Hispanic/Latino; 10 Asian, non-Hispanic/Latino; 11 Hispanic/Latino; 1 Native Hawaiian or other Pacific Islander, non-Hispanic/Latino). Average age 41. 132 applicants, 51% accepted, 51 enrolled. In 2011, 17 master's, 4 doctorates awarded. *Degree requirements:* For doctorate, thesis/dissertation. *Entrance requirements:* For master's, BS, 2 reference letters, statement of career goals, curriculum vitae; for doctorate, GRE, interview, writing sample, 3 reference letters, curriculum vitae. Additional exam requirements/recommendations for international students: Required—TOEFL. *Application deadline:* For fall admission, 3/1 for domestic students. Applications are processed on a rolling basis. Application fee: $75. Electronic applications accepted. *Unit head:* Dr. Bob Denmark, Director, 973-972-5410, Fax: 973-972-7403, E-mail: ms-phd-hs@umdnj.edu. *Application contact:* Diane Hanrahan, Manager of Admissions, 973-972-5336, Fax: 973-972-7463, E-mail: shrpadm@umdnj.edu.

University of Michigan, Horace H. Rackham School of Graduate Studies, School of Kinesiology, Ann Arbor, MI 48109. Offers kinesiology (MS, PhD); sport management (AM). *Faculty:* 30 full-time (11 women). *Students:* 74 full-time (39 women); includes 23 minority (2 Black or African American, non-Hispanic/Latino; 17 Asian, non-Hispanic/Latino; 4 Hispanic/Latino), 23 international. 120 applicants, 44% accepted, 24 enrolled. In 2011, 20 master's, 4 doctorates awarded. Terminal master's awarded for partial completion of doctoral program. *Degree requirements:* For master's, thesis (for some programs); for doctorate, comprehensive exam, thesis/dissertation, oral defense of dissertation. *Entrance requirements:* For master's and doctorate, GRE General Test. Additional exam requirements/recommendations for international students: Required—TOEFL. *Application deadline:* For fall admission, 1/15 priority date for domestic students, 1/15 for international students. Applications are processed on a rolling basis. Application fee: $60 ($75 for international students). Electronic applications accepted. *Expenses:* Contact institution. *Financial support:* In 2011–12, 13 fellowships, 10 research assistantships, 14 teaching assistantships were awarded; Federal Work-Study, scholarships/grants, health care benefits, and unspecified assistantships also available. Financial award application deadline: 1/15. *Faculty research:* Motor development, exercise physiology, biomechanics, sport medicine, sport management. *Unit head:* Dr. Ketra L. Armstrong, Associate Dean for Graduate Programs and Faculty Affairs, 734-647-3027, Fax: 734-647-2808, E-mail: ketra@umich.edu. *Application contact:* Charlene F. Ruloff, Graduate Program Coordinator, 734-764-1343, Fax: 734-647-2808, E-mail: cruloff@umich.edu. Web site: http://www.kines.umich.edu/.

University of Minnesota, Twin Cities Campus, Graduate School, College of Education and Human Development, School of Kinesiology, Division of Kinesiology, Minneapolis, MN 55455-0213. Offers M Ed, MA, PhD. Part-time programs available. *Students:* 144 full-time (72 women), 48 part-time (19 women); includes 20 minority (9 Black or African American, non-Hispanic/Latino; 3 American Indian or Alaska Native, non-Hispanic/Latino; 4 Asian, non-Hispanic/Latino; 2 Hispanic/Latino; 2 Native Hawaiian or other Pacific Islander, non-Hispanic/Latino), 18 international. Average age 29. 198 applicants, 42% accepted, 77 enrolled. In 2011, 69 master's, 10 doctorates awarded. Terminal master's awarded for partial completion of doctoral program. *Degree requirements:* For master's, thesis (for some programs), final oral exam; for doctorate, thesis/dissertation, preliminary written/oral exam, final oral exam. *Entrance requirements:* For master's, GRE or MAT, minimum GPA of 3.0; for doctorate, GRE or MAT, minimum GPA of 3.0, writing sample. *Application deadline:* Applications are processed on a rolling basis. Application fee: $55. *Financial support:* Fellowships, research assistantships, teaching assistantships, career-related internships or fieldwork, Federal Work-Study, institutionally sponsored loans, and tuition waivers (full and partial) available. Support available to part-time students. *Unit head:* Dr. Li Li Ji, Director, 612-624-9809, Fax: 612-626-7700, E-mail: llji@umn.edu. *Application contact:* Dr. Jennifer Engler, Assistant Dean, 612-626-2887, Fax: 612-626-7496, E-mail: engle009@umn.edu. Web site: http://www.cehd.umn.edu/kin/kinesiology.

University of Nevada, Las Vegas, Graduate College, School of Allied Health Sciences, Department of Kinesiology, Las Vegas, NV 89154-3034. Offers exercise physiology (MS); kinesiology (MS). Part-time programs available. *Faculty:* 10 full-time (4 women), 1 part-time/adjunct (0 women). *Students:* 18 full-time (9 women), 25 part-time (8 women); includes 11 minority (1 Black or African American, non-Hispanic/Latino; 3 Asian, non-Hispanic/Latino; 5 Hispanic/Latino; 2 Two or more races, non-Hispanic/Latino), 2 international. Average age 27. 38 applicants, 79% accepted, 9 enrolled. In 2011, 18 master's awarded. *Degree requirements:* For master's, comprehensive exam (for some programs), thesis (for some programs). *Entrance requirements:* For master's, GRE General Test. Additional exam requirements/recommendations for international students: Required—TOEFL (minimum score 550 paper-based; 213 computer-based; 80 iBT), IELTS (minimum score 7). *Application deadline:* For fall admission, 6/15 priority date for domestic students, 5/1 for international students; for spring admission, 11/15 priority date for domestic students, 10/1 for international students. Applications are processed on a rolling basis. Application fee: $60 ($95 for international students). Electronic applications accepted. *Financial support:* In 2011–12, 21 students received support, including 6 research assistantships with partial tuition reimbursements available (averaging $12,792 per year), 15 teaching assistantships with partial tuition reimbursements available (averaging $8,617 per year); institutionally sponsored loans, scholarships/grants, health care benefits, and unspecified assistantships also available. Financial award application deadline: 3/1. *Faculty research:* Biomechanics of gait, factors in motor skill acquisition and performance, nutritional supplements and performance, lipoprotein chemistry, body composition methods. *Total annual research expenditures:* $131,409. *Unit head:* Dr. John Young, Chair/Professor, 702-895-4626, Fax: 702-895-1500, E-mail: john.young@unlv.edu. *Application contact:* Graduate College Admissions Evaluator, 702-895-3320, Fax: 702-895-4180, E-mail: gradcollege@unlv.edu. Web site: http://kinesiology.unlv.edu/.

University of New Hampshire, Graduate School, School of Health and Human Services, Department of Kinesiology, Durham, NH 03824. Offers adapted physical education (Postbaccalaureate Certificate); kinesiology (MS). Part-time programs available. *Faculty:* 13 full-time (3 women). *Students:* 2 full-time (1 woman), 10 part-time (6 women). Average age 28. 27 applicants, 59% accepted, 8 enrolled. In 2011, 6 master's, 1 other advanced degree awarded. *Degree requirements:* For master's, thesis or alternative. *Entrance requirements:* For master's, GRE General Test. Additional exam requirements/recommendations for international students: Required—TOEFL (minimum score 550 paper-based; 213 computer-based; 80 iBT). *Application deadline:* For fall admission, 6/1 priority date for domestic students, 4/1 for international students; for spring admission, 12/1 for domestic students. Applications are processed on a rolling basis. Application fee: $65. *Expenses:* Tuition, state resident: full-time $12,360; part-time $687 per credit hour. Tuition, nonresident: full-time $25,680; part-time $1058 per credit hour. *International tuition:* $29,550 full-time. *Required fees:* $1666; $833 per course. $416.50 per semester. Tuition and fees vary according to course load and degree level. *Financial support:* In 2011–12, 4 students received support, including 4 teaching assistantships; fellowships, research assistantships, career-related internships or fieldwork, Federal Work-Study, scholarships/grants, and tuition waivers (full and partial) also available. Support available to part-time students. Financial award application deadline: 2/15. *Faculty research:* Exercise specialist, sports studies, special physical education, pediatric exercises and motor behavior. *Unit head:* Dr. Ron Croce, Chairperson, 603-862-2080. *Application contact:* Allison Dwyer, Administrative Assistant, 603-862-2071, E-mail: kinesiology.dept@unh.edu. Web site: http://chhs.unh.edu/kin/index.

University of North Alabama, College of Education, Department of Health, Physical Education, and Recreation, FLORENCE, AL 35632-0001. Offers health and human performance (MS), including exercise science, kinesiology, wellness and health promotion; P-12 physical education (MA Ed). *Faculty:* 3 full-time (2 women), 2 part-time/adjunct (0 women). *Students:* 11 full-time (4 women), 4 part-time (1 woman); includes 3 minority (2 Black or African American, non-Hispanic/Latino; 1 Two or more races, non-Hispanic/Latino), 2 international. Average age 24. In 2011, 4 master's awarded. *Unit head:* Dr. Thomas E. Coates, Chair, 256-765-4377. *Application contact:* Kim Mauldin, Director of Admissions, 256-765-4608, Fax: 256-765-4960, E-mail: komauldin@una.edu. Web site: http://www.una.edu/hper/docs/HPERThesisGuideliens.pdf.

The University of North Carolina at Chapel Hill, School of Medicine and Graduate School, Graduate Programs in Medicine, Chapel Hill, NC 27599. Offers allied health sciences (MPT, MS, Au D, DPT, PhD), including human movement science (MS, PhD), occupational science (MS, PhD), physical therapy (MPT, MS, DPT), rehabilitation counseling and psychology (MS), speech and hearing sciences (MS, Au D, PhD); biochemistry and biophysics (MS, PhD); bioinformatics and computational biology (PhD); biomedical engineering (MS, PhD); cell and developmental biology (PhD); cell and molecular physiology (PhD); genetics and molecular biology (PhD); microbiology and immunology (MS, PhD), including immunology, microbiology; neurobiology (PhD); pathology and laboratory medicine (PhD), including experimental pathology; pharmacology (PhD); MD/PhD. Postbaccalaureate distance learning degree programs offered. Terminal master's awarded for partial completion of doctoral program. *Degree requirements:* For master's, comprehensive exam; for doctorate, thesis/dissertation. Electronic applications accepted. *Expenses:* Contact institution.

The University of North Carolina at Chapel Hill, School of Medicine and Graduate School, Graduate Programs in Medicine, Department of Allied Health Sciences, Curriculum in Human Movement Science, Chapel Hill, NC 27599. Offers PhD. *Degree requirements:* For doctorate, comprehensive exam, thesis/dissertation or alternative. *Entrance requirements:* For doctorate, GRE General Test, curriculum vitae, minimum GPA of 3.0. Additional exam requirements/recommendations for international students: Required—TOEFL (minimum score 550 paper-based; 79 computer-based). Electronic applications accepted. *Faculty research:* Orthopaedics, neuromuscular, biomedical endocrinology, postural control developmental disabilities.

The University of North Carolina at Chapel Hill, School of Medicine and Graduate School, Graduate Programs in Medicine, Department of Allied Health Sciences, Program in Human Movement Science, Chapel Hill, NC 27599. Offers PhD. *Entrance requirements:* Additional exam requirements/recommendations for international students: Required—TOEFL (minimum score 550 paper-based; 79 computer-based). Electronic applications accepted.

The University of North Carolina at Charlotte, Graduate School, College of Health and Human Services, Department of Kinesiology, Charlotte, NC 28223-0001. Offers clinical exercise physiology (MS). Part-time programs available. *Faculty:* 8 full-time (4 women). *Students:* 12 full-time (all women), 13 part-time (7 women); includes 3 minority (1 Black or African American, non-Hispanic/Latino; 1 American Indian or Alaska Native, non-Hispanic/Latino; 1 Asian, non-Hispanic/Latino). Average age 26. 33 applicants, 73% accepted, 12 enrolled. In 2011, 12 master's awarded. *Degree requirements:* For master's, thesis or practicum. *Entrance requirements:* For master's, GRE or MAT. Additional exam requirements/recommendations for international students: Required—TOEFL (minimum score 557 paper-based; 220 computer-based; 83 iBT). *Application deadline:* For fall admission, 7/1 for domestic students, 5/1 for international students; for spring admission, 11/1 for domestic students, 10/1 for international students. Applications are processed on a rolling basis. Application fee: $65 ($75 for international students). Electronic applications accepted. *Expenses:* Tuition, state resident: full-time $3689. Tuition, nonresident: full-time $15,226. *Required fees:* $2198. Tuition and fees vary according to course load and program. *Financial support:* In 2011–12, 6 students received support, including 2 research assistantships (averaging $1,083 per year), 4 teaching assistantships (averaging $10,000 per year); career-related internships or fieldwork, institutionally sponsored loans, scholarships/grants, traineeships, and unspecified assistantships also available. Support available to part-time students. Financial award application deadline: 4/1; financial award applicants required to submit FAFSA. *Faculty research:* Genetic determinants of physical activity, cardiac muscle apoptosis with aging, sensorimotor deficits in knee osteoarthritis, mechanical laxity in functional ankle instability. *Total annual research expenditures:* $31,091. *Unit head:* Dr. Mitchell L. Cordova, Chair, 704-687-4695, Fax: 704-687-3180, E-mail: mcordova@uncc.edu. *Application contact:* Kathy B. Giddings, Director of Graduate Admissions, 704-687-5503, Fax: 704-687-3279, E-mail: gradadm@uncc.edu. Web site: http://www.health.uncc.edu/.

University of North Dakota, Graduate School, College of Education and Human Development, Department of Kinesiology, Grand Forks, ND 58202. Offers MS. Part-time programs available. *Degree requirements:* For master's, thesis or alternative, final or comprehensive examination. *Entrance requirements:* For master's, GRE General Test, minimum GPA of 3.0. Additional exam requirements/recommendations for international students: Required—TOEFL (minimum score 550 paper-based; 213 computer-based; 79 iBT), IELTS (minimum score 6.5). Electronic applications accepted. *Faculty research:* Exercise physiology, exercise biomechanics, anatomy and physiology, exercise psychology.

University of Northern Iowa, Graduate College, College of Education, School of Health, Physical Education, and Leisure Services, Program in Physical Education, Cedar Falls, IA 50614. Offers kinesiology (MA); physical education (MA); teaching/coaching (MA). Part-time and evening/weekend programs available. *Students:* 18 full-time (5 women), 6 part-time (1 woman); includes 3 minority (2 Black or African American, non-Hispanic/Latino; 1 Hispanic/Latino), 1 international. 25 applicants, 68% accepted, 12 enrolled. In 2011, 32 master's awarded. *Degree requirements:* For master's, comprehensive exam, thesis or alternative. *Entrance requirements:* For master's, minimum GPA of 3.0. Additional exam requirements/recommendations for international students: Required—TOEFL (minimum score 500 paper-based; 180 computer-based; 61 iBT). *Application deadline:* For fall admission, 8/1 priority date for domestic students. Applications are processed on a rolling basis. Application fee: $50 ($70 for international students). Electronic applications accepted. *Expenses:* Tuition, state resident: full-time $7476. Tuition, nonresident: full-time $16,410. *Required fees:* $942. *Financial support:* Career-related internships or fieldwork, Federal Work-Study, and tuition waivers (full and partial) available. Support available to part-time students. Financial award application deadline: 2/1. *Unit head:* Dr. Forest Dolgener, Coordinator, 319-273-6479, Fax: 319-273-5958, E-mail: forrest.dolgener@uni.edu. *Application contact:* Laurie S. Russell, Record Analyst, 319-273-2623, Fax: 319-273-2885, E-mail: laurie.russell@uni.edu. Web site: http://www.uni.edu/coe/hpels/Academic/master_degrees.shtml.

University of North Texas, Toulouse Graduate School, College of Education, Department of Kinesiology, Health Promotion, and Recreation, Program in Kinesiology, Denton, TX 76203. Offers MS. Part-time programs available. *Degree requirements:* For master's, comprehensive exam, thesis optional. *Entrance requirements:* For master's, GRE General Test, GMAT or MAT, minimum overall GPA of 2.8, 300-word essay. Additional exam requirements/recommendations for international students: Recommended—TOEFL (minimum score 550 paper-based; 213 computer-based; 79 iBT). Electronic applications accepted. *Expenses:* Tuition, state resident: part-time $100 per credit hour. Tuition, nonresident: part-time $413 per credit hour. *Faculty research:* Exercise science, sports psychology, sport management, health fitness management, physical activity.

University of Ottawa, Faculty of Graduate and Postdoctoral Studies, Faculty of Health Sciences, School of Human Kinetics, Ottawa, ON K1N 6N5, Canada. Offers MA. *Degree requirements:* For master's, thesis or alternative. *Entrance requirements:* For master's, honors degree or equivalent, minimum B average. Electronic applications accepted. *Faculty research:* Psychosocial sciences, physical and health administration of sport and physical activity, intervention and consultation in sport, physical activity and health.

University of Regina, Faculty of Graduate Studies and Research, Faculty of Kinesiology and Health Studies, Regina, SK S4S 0A2, Canada. Offers M Sc, PhD. *Faculty:* 17 full-time (7 women), 1 (woman) part-time/adjunct. *Students:* 22 full-time (11 women), 7 part-time (4 women). 15 applicants, 67% accepted. In 2011, 5 degrees awarded. *Degree requirements:* For master's, thesis; for doctorate, thesis/dissertation. *Entrance requirements:* Additional exam requirements/recommendations for international students: Required—TOEFL (minimum score 580 paper-based; 80 iBT), IELTS (minimum score 6.5). *Application deadline:* Applications are processed on a rolling basis. Application fee: $100. Electronic applications accepted. *Financial support:* In 2011–12, 3 fellowships (averaging $6,000 per year), 4 teaching assistantships (averaging $2,298 per year) were awarded; research assistantships and scholarships/grants also available. Financial award application deadline: 6/15. *Faculty research:* Social psychology of physical activity and health, social science of physical activity and recreation, recreation and leisure, sport management, exercise science. *Unit head:* Dr. Craig Chamberlin, Dean, 306-585-4535, Fax: 306-585-5441, E-mail: shanthi.johnson@

uregina.ca. *Application contact:* Dr. Shanthi Johnson, Graduate Program Coordinator, 306-585-3180, Fax: 306-585-5693, E-mail: shanthi.johnson@uregina.ca.

University of Saskatchewan, College of Graduate Studies and Research, College of Kinesiology, Saskatoon, SK S7N 5A2, Canada. Offers M Sc, PhD, Diploma. *Degree requirements:* For master's, thesis; for doctorate, thesis/dissertation. *Entrance requirements:* Additional exam requirements/recommendations for international students: Required—TOEFL.

The University of South Dakota, Graduate School, School of Education, Division of Kinesiology and Sport Science, Vermillion, SD 57069-2390. Offers MA. *Accreditation:* NCATE. Part-time programs available. *Degree requirements:* For master's, comprehensive exam, thesis or alternative. *Entrance requirements:* For master's, GRE General Test, MAT, minimum GPA of 2.7. Additional exam requirements/recommendations for international students: Required—TOEFL (minimum score 550 paper-based; 213 computer-based; 79 iBT). Electronic applications accepted. *Expenses:* Tuition, state resident: full-time $3118.50; part-time $173.25 per credit hour. Tuition, nonresident: full-time $6601; part-time $366.70 per credit hour. *Required fees:* $2268; $126 per credit hour. Tuition and fees vary according to program.

University of Southern California, Graduate School, Herman Ostrow School of Dentistry, Division of Biokinesiology and Physical Therapy, Los Angeles, CA 90089. Offers biokinesiology (MS, PhD); physical therapy (DPT). *Accreditation:* APTA (one or more programs are accredited). *Degree requirements:* For master's, comprehensive exam; for doctorate, thesis/dissertation. *Entrance requirements:* For master's and doctorate, GRE (minimum combined score 1200, verbal 600, quantitative 600). Additional exam requirements/recommendations for international students: Required—TOEFL. Electronic applications accepted. *Expenses:* Contact institution. *Faculty research:* Exercise and aging biomechanics, musculoskeletal biomechanics, exercise and hormones related to muscle wasting, computational neurorehabilitation, motor behavior and neurorehabilitation, motor development, infant motor performance.

The University of Tennessee, Graduate School, College of Education, Health and Human Sciences, Department of Exercise, Sport, and Leisure Studies, Program in Exercise Science, Knoxville, TN 37996. Offers biomechanics/sports medicine (MS, PhD); exercise physiology (MS, PhD). *Accreditation:* CEPH (one or more programs are accredited). Part-time programs available. *Degree requirements:* For master's, thesis optional. *Entrance requirements:* For master's, minimum GPA of 2.7. Additional exam requirements/recommendations for international students: Required—TOEFL. Electronic applications accepted. *Expenses:* Tuition, state resident: full-time $8332; part-time $464 per credit hour. Tuition, nonresident: full-time $25,174; part-time $1400 per credit hour. *Required fees:* $1162; $56 per credit hour. Tuition and fees vary according to program.

The University of Texas at Austin, Graduate School, College of Education, Department of Kinesiology and Health Education, Austin, TX 78712-1111. Offers behavioral health (PhD); exercise and sport psychology (M Ed, MA); exercise science (M Ed, MS, PhD); health education (M Ed, MS, Ed D, PhD). Part-time programs available. Terminal master's awarded for partial completion of doctoral program. *Degree requirements:* For master's, thesis (for some programs); for doctorate, thesis/dissertation. *Entrance requirements:* For master's and doctorate, GRE General Test. Additional exam requirements/recommendations for international students: Required—TOEFL. *Application deadline:* For fall admission, 2/1 priority date for domestic students; for spring admission, 10/1 for domestic students. Applications are processed on a rolling basis. Application fee: $50 ($75 for international students). Electronic applications accepted. *Financial support:* Fellowships, research assistantships, teaching assistantships, career-related internships or fieldwork, and Federal Work-Study available. Financial award application deadline: 2/1; financial award applicants required to submit FAFSA. *Faculty research:* Health promotion, human performance and exercise biochemistry, motor behavior and biomechanics, sport management, aging and pediatric development. *Unit head:* Dr. John L. Ivy, Chair, 512-471-1273, Fax: 512-471-8914, E-mail: johnivy@mail.utexas.edu. *Application contact:* Dr. Darla Castelli, Graduate Advisor, 512-232-7636, Fax: 512-232-5334, E-mail: dcastelli@mail.utexas.edu. Web site: http://www.edb.utexas.edu/education/departments/khe/.

The University of Texas at El Paso, Graduate School, College of Health Sciences, Department of Kinesiology, El Paso, TX 79968-0001. Offers kinesiology (MS); kinesiology on-line (MS). Part-time and evening/weekend programs available. Postbaccalaureate distance learning degree programs offered. *Students:* 20 (12 women); includes 9 minority (all Hispanic/Latino), 1 international. Average age 34. 14 applicants, 71% accepted, 8 enrolled. In 2011, 2 master's awarded. *Degree requirements:* For master's, thesis optional. *Entrance requirements:* For master's, GRE. Additional exam requirements/recommendations for international students: Required—TOEFL; Recommended—IELTS. *Application deadline:* For fall admission, 8/1 priority date for domestic students, 3/1 for international students; for spring admission, 11/1 priority date for domestic students, 9/1 for international students. Applications are processed on a rolling basis. Application fee: $45 ($80 for international students). Electronic applications accepted. *Financial support:* In 2011–12, research assistantships (averaging $18,825 per year), teaching assistantships with partial tuition reimbursements (averaging $18,000 per year) were awarded; fellowships with tuition reimbursements, institutionally sponsored loans, scholarships/grants, health care benefits, tuition waivers (partial), and unspecified assistantships also available. Support available to part-time students. Financial award application deadline: 3/15; financial award applicants required to submit FAFSA. *Unit head:* Dr. Darla Smith, Chair, 915-747-7245, Fax: 915-747-8211, E-mail: darsmith@utep.edu. *Application contact:* Dr. Benjamin Flores, Interim Dean of the Graduate School, 915-747-5491, Fax: 915-747-5788, E-mail: bflores@utep.edu. Web site: http://kinesiology.utep.edu/.

The University of Texas at San Antonio, College of Education and Human Development, Department of Health and Kinesiology, San Antonio, TX 78249-0617. Offers MS. Part-time and evening/weekend programs available. *Faculty:* 12 full-time (5 women). *Students:* 62 full-time (33 women), 68 part-time (45 women); includes 83 minority (9 Black or African American, non-Hispanic/Latino; 1 American Indian or Alaska Native, non-Hispanic/Latino; 2 Asian, non-Hispanic/Latino; 69 Hispanic/Latino; 1 Native Hawaiian or other Pacific Islander, non-Hispanic/Latino; 1 Two or more races, non-Hispanic/Latino), 5 international. Average age 29. 70 applicants, 79% accepted, 47 enrolled. In 2011, 40 master's awarded. *Entrance requirements:* For master's, GRE or GMAT, bachelor's degree with minimum GPA of 3.0 in last 60 hours of coursework; resume; statement of purpose; two letters of recommendation. Additional exam requirements/recommendations for international students: Required—TOEFL (minimum score 500 paper-based; 61 iBT), IELTS (minimum score 5). *Application deadline:* For fall admission, 7/1 for domestic students, 4/1 for international students; for spring admission, 11/1 for domestic students, 9/1 for international students. Application fee: $45 ($85 for international students). *Expenses:* Tuition, state resident: full-time $3148; part-time $2176 per semester. Tuition, nonresident: full-time $8782; part-time $5932 per semester. *Required fees:* $719 per semester. *Faculty research:* Motor behavior, motor skills, exercise and nutrition, athlete efficacy, diabetes prevention. *Unit head:* Dr. Wan Xiang Yao, Chair, 210-458-6224, Fax: 210-452-5873, E-mail: wanxiang.yao@utsa.edu. *Application contact:* Dr. Alberto Cordova, Graduate Advisor of Record, 210-458-6226, Fax: 210-458-5873, E-mail: alberto.cordova@utsa.edu. Web site: http://education.utsa.edu/health_and_kinesiology.

The University of Texas at Tyler, College of Nursing and Health Sciences, Department of Health and Kinesiology, Tyler, TX 75799-0001. Offers health and kinesiology (M Ed, MA); health sciences (MS); kinesiology (MS). *Accreditation:* Teacher Education Accreditation Council. Part-time programs available. Postbaccalaureate distance learning degree programs offered. *Degree requirements:* For master's, comprehensive exam (for some programs), thesis (for some programs). *Entrance requirements:* Additional exam requirements/recommendations for international students: Required—TOEFL (minimum score 79 computer-based). Electronic applications accepted. *Faculty research:* Osteoporosis, muscle soreness, economy of locomotion, adoption of rehabilitation programs, effect of inactivity and aging on muscle blood vessels, territoriality.

The University of Texas of the Permian Basin, Office of Graduate Studies, College of Arts and Sciences, Department of Kinesiology, Odessa, TX 79762-0001. Offers MS. Part-time and evening/weekend programs available. Postbaccalaureate distance learning degree programs offered (no on-campus study). *Degree requirements:* For master's, comprehensive exam (for some programs), thesis (for some programs). *Entrance requirements:* For master's, GRE General Test, minimum GPA of 2.5. Additional exam requirements/recommendations for international students: Required—TOEFL (minimum score 550 paper-based; 213 computer-based).

The University of Texas–Pan American, College of Education, Department of Health and Kinesiology, Edinburg, TX 78539. Offers MS. Part-time and evening/weekend programs available. Postbaccalaureate distance learning degree programs offered (no on-campus study). *Degree requirements:* For master's, comprehensive exam, thesis optional, oral exam. *Entrance requirements:* For master's, minimum GPA of 3.0 in last 60 hours. *Application deadline:* For fall admission, 7/17 for domestic students; for spring admission, 11/16 for domestic students. Application fee: $0. Tuition and fees vary according to course load, program and student level. *Financial support:* Teaching assistantships, institutionally sponsored loans, and unspecified assistantships available. Financial award application deadline: 4/15. *Faculty research:* History, physiology of exercise, fitness levels, Mexican-American children, winter tourist profiles, sports psychology. *Unit head:* Dr. Paul Villas, Chair, 956-665-3501, Fax: 956-665-3502, E-mail: pvillas@utpa.edu. *Application contact:* Dr. Layne W. Jorgenson, Graduate Program Coordinator, 956-665-3506, Fax: 956-665-3502, E-mail: lj85f0@utpa.edu. Web site: http://portal.utpa.edu/utpa_main/daa_home/coed_home/heak_home.

University of the Incarnate Word, School of Graduate Studies and Research, Dreeben School of Education, Programs in Education, San Antonio, TX 78209-6397. Offers adult education (M Ed, MA); cross-cultural education (M Ed, MA); early childhood literacy (M Ed, MA); general education (M Ed, MA); higher education (PhD); instructional technology (M Ed, MA); international education and entrepreneurship (PhD); kinesiology (M Ed, MA); literacy (M Ed, MA); organizational leadership (PhD); organizational learning and learning (M Ed, MA); reading (M Ed, MA); special education (M Ed, MA); teacher leadership (M Ed, MA). Part-time and evening/weekend programs available. *Faculty:* 14 full-time (8 women), 10 part-time/adjunct (9 women). *Students:* 13 full-time (7 women), 197 part-time (129 women); includes 111 minority (23 Black or African American, non-Hispanic/Latino; 2 American Indian or Alaska Native, non-Hispanic/Latino; 1 Asian, non-Hispanic/Latino; 85 Hispanic/Latino), 26 international. Average age 41. 78 applicants, 79% accepted, 34 enrolled. In 2011, 21 master's, 12 doctorates awarded. *Degree requirements:* For master's, capstone; for doctorate, thesis/dissertation, qualifying exam. *Entrance requirements:* For master's, baccalaureate degree; minimum foundation GPA of 2.5; interview; for doctorate, master's degree; interview; supervised writing sample. Additional exam requirements/recommendations for international students: Required—TOEFL (minimum score 560 paper-based; 220 computer-based; 83 iBT). *Application deadline:* Applications are processed on a rolling basis. Application fee: $20. Electronic applications accepted. *Expenses: Tuition:* Part-time $725 per credit hour. Tuition and fees vary according to degree level. *Financial support:* In 2011–12, 5 research assistantships were awarded; Federal Work-Study and scholarships/grants also available. Financial award applicants required to submit FAFSA. *Unit head:* Dr. Denise Staudt, Dean, Dreeben School of Education, 210-829-2762, E-mail: staudt@uiwtx.edu. *Application contact:* Andrea Cyterski-Acosta, Dean of Enrollment, 210-829-6005, Fax: 210-829-3921, E-mail: admis@uiwtx.edu. Web site: http://www.uiw.edu/education/index.htm.

University of the Incarnate Word, School of Graduate Studies and Research, School of Nursing and Health Professions, Programs in Kinesiology, San Antonio, TX 78209-6397. Offers MS. Part-time and evening/weekend programs available. *Faculty:* 1 full-time (0 women). *Students:* 7 full-time (5 women), 6 part-time (2 women); includes 5 minority (1 Black or African American, non-Hispanic/Latino; 4 Hispanic/Latino), 1 international. Average age 26. 5 applicants, 100% accepted, 4 enrolled. In 2011, 11 master's awarded. *Degree requirements:* For master's, capstone. *Entrance requirements:* For master's, GRE, master's and baccalaureate degrees in kinesiology or related field; teacher certification in physical education or other teaching field plus athletic coaching experience, or letter of recommendation from professional in field. Additional exam requirements/recommendations for international students: Required—TOEFL (minimum score 560 paper-based; 220 computer-based; 83 iBT). *Application deadline:* Applications are processed on a rolling basis. Application fee: $20. Electronic applications accepted. *Expenses: Tuition:* Part-time $725 per credit hour. Tuition and fees vary according to degree level. *Financial support:* Federal Work-Study and scholarships/grants available. *Unit head:* Dr. William Carleton, Chair, 210-829-3966, Fax: 210-829-3174, E-mail: carleton@uiwtx.edu. *Application contact:* Andrea Cyterski-Acosta, Dean of Enrollment, 210-829-6005, Fax: 210-829-3921, E-mail: admis@uiwtx.edu. Web site: http://www.uiw.edu/gradstudies/documents/mskinesiology.pdf.

University of Victoria, Faculty of Graduate Studies, Faculty of Education, School of Exercise Science, Physical, and Health Education, Victoria, BC V8W 2Y2, Canada. Offers coaching studies (co-operative education) (M Ed); kinesiology (M Sc, MA); leisure service administration (MA); physical education (MA). Part-time programs available. *Degree requirements:* For master's, comprehensive exam (for some programs), thesis (for some programs). *Entrance requirements:* For master's, minimum B average. Additional exam requirements/recommendations for international students: Required—TOEFL (minimum score 575 paper-based; 233 computer-based), IELTS (minimum score 7). Electronic applications accepted. *Faculty research:* Children and exercise, mental skills in sports, teaching effectiveness, neural control of human movement, physical performance and health.

University of Virginia, Curry School of Education, Department of Human Services, Program in Health and Physical Education, Charlottesville, VA 22903. Offers M Ed, Ed D. *Students:* 35 full-time (21 women), 1 (woman) part-time; includes 3 minority (1 Black or African American, non-Hispanic/Latino; 1 Asian, non-Hispanic/Latino; 1 Hispanic/Latino), 3 international. Average age 24. 5 applicants, 100% accepted, 5 enrolled. In 2011, 36 master's awarded. *Entrance requirements:* For master's and doctorate, GRE General Test, 2 letters of recommendation. Additional exam requirements/recommendations for international students: Required—TOEFL (minimum score 600 paper-based; 250 computer-based; 90 iBT), IELTS (minimum score 7). *Application deadline:* Applications are processed on a rolling basis. Application fee: $60.

Kinesiology and Movement Studies

Electronic applications accepted. *Financial support:* Applicants required to submit FAFSA. *Unit head:* Luke E. Kelly, Program Coordinator, 434-924-6207. *Application contact:* Lynn Renfroe, Information Contact, 434-924-6254, E-mail: ldr9t@virginia.edu. Web site: http://curry.virginia.edu/academics/degrees/postgraduate-master-in-teaching/pg-mt-in-health-physical-education.

University of Virginia, Curry School of Education, Program in Education, Charlottesville, VA 22903. Offers administration and supervision (PhD); applied developmental science (PhD); counselor education (PhD); curriculum and instruction (PhD); early childhood-developmental risk (MT); education evaluation (PhD); educational psychology (PhD); educational research (PhD); elementary (MT, PhD); English education (MT, PhD); foreign language education (MT); higher education (PhD); instructional technology (PhD); kinesiology (MT, PhD); math education (PhD); reading education (PhD); research statistics and evaluation (PhD); school psychology (PhD); science education (PhD); social studies education (MT, PhD); special education (PhD); world languages education (MT). *Students:* 299 full-time (216 women), 60 part-time (33 women); includes 46 minority (18 Black or African American, non-Hispanic/Latino; 17 Asian, non-Hispanic/Latino; 7 Hispanic/Latino; 4 Two or more races, non-Hispanic/Latino), 23 international. Average age 30. 307 applicants, 42% accepted, 80 enrolled. In 2011, 113 master's, 62 doctorates awarded. *Degree requirements:* For master's, comprehensive exam (for some programs), field project; for doctorate, comprehensive exam, thesis/dissertation. *Entrance requirements:* For doctorate, GRE General Test. Additional exam requirements/recommendations for international students: Required—TOEFL (minimum score 600 paper-based; 250 computer-based; 90 iBT), IELTS (minimum score 7). *Application deadline:* Applications are processed on a rolling basis. Application fee: $60. Electronic applications accepted. *Financial support:* Fellowships, research assistantships, and teaching assistantships available. Financial award application deadline: 1/5; financial award applicants required to submit FAFSA. *Unit head:* Robert C. Pianta, Dean, 434-924-3334. *Application contact:* Joanne McNergney, Assistant Dean for Admissions and Student Services, 434-924-3334, E-mail: curry-admissions@virginia.edu.

University of Waterloo, Graduate Studies, Faculty of Applied Health Sciences, Department of Kinesiology, Waterloo, ON N2L 3G1, Canada. Offers M Sc, PhD. Part-time programs available. *Degree requirements:* For master's, thesis; for doctorate, comprehensive exam, thesis/dissertation. *Entrance requirements:* For master's, honors degree, minimum B average, writing sample; for doctorate, GRE (recommended), master's degree, minimum B average, writing sample. Additional exam requirements/recommendations for international students: Required—TOEFL, TWE. Electronic applications accepted. *Faculty research:* Work physiology, biomechanics and neural control of human movement, psychomotor learning and performance, aging, health and well-being, work and health.

The University of Western Ontario, Faculty of Graduate Studies, Health Sciences Division, School of Kinesiology, London, ON N6A 5B8, Canada. Offers M Sc, MA, PhD. *Degree requirements:* For master's, thesis optional; for doctorate, comprehensive exam, thesis/dissertation. *Entrance requirements:* For doctorate, MA in physical education or kinesiology. Additional exam requirements/recommendations for international students: Required—Michigan English Language Assessment Battery, TOEFL or IELTS. *Faculty research:* Exercise physiology/biochemistry, sports injuries, sport psychology, sport history, sport philosophy.

University of Windsor, Faculty of Graduate Studies, Faculty of Human Kinetics, Windsor, ON N9B 3P4, Canada. Offers MHK. Part-time programs available. *Degree requirements:* For master's, thesis optional. *Entrance requirements:* For master's, minimum B average. Additional exam requirements/recommendations for international students: Required—TOEFL (minimum score 600 paper-based; 250 computer-based). Electronic applications accepted. *Faculty research:* Movement sciences, sport and lifestyle management, historical and sociological studies of sport.

University of Wisconsin–Madison, Graduate School, School of Education, Department of Kinesiology, Madison, WI 53706-1380. Offers kinesiology (MS, PhD); occupational therapy (MS, PhD); therapeutic science (MS). *Accreditation:* AOTA. *Degree requirements:* For doctorate, thesis/dissertation. *Entrance requirements:* For master's and doctorate, GRE General Test. Application fee: $56. Electronic applications accepted. *Expenses:* Tuition, state resident: full-time $10,296; part-time $643.51 per credit. Tuition, nonresident: full-time $24,054; part-time $1503.40 per credit. *Required fees:* $70.06 per credit. Tuition and fees vary according to course load, campus/location, program and reciprocity agreements. *Financial support:* Fellowships with full tuition reimbursements, research assistantships with full tuition reimbursements, teaching assistantships with full tuition reimbursements, and project assistantships available. *Unit head:* Dr. Dorothy Edwards, Chair, 608-262-1654, E-mail: dfedwards@education.wisc.edu. *Application contact:* 608-262-2433, Fax: 608-262-5134, E-mail: gradadmiss@mail.bascom.wisc.edu. Web site: http://www.education.wisc.edu/kinesiology.

University of Wisconsin–Milwaukee, Graduate School, College of Health Sciences, Program in Kinesiology/Human Movement Sciences, Milwaukee, WI 53201-0413. Offers MS. Part-time programs available. *Faculty:* 8 full-time (4 women), 1 part-time/adjunct (0 women). *Students:* 15 full-time (8 women), 9 part-time (3 women); includes 2 minority (1 Asian, non-Hispanic/Latino; 1 Two or more races, non-Hispanic/Latino), 1 international. Average age 29. 28 applicants, 50% accepted, 8 enrolled. In 2011, 7 degrees awarded. *Degree requirements:* For master's, comprehensive exam, thesis optional. *Entrance requirements:* For master's, GRE General Test. Additional exam requirements/recommendations for international students: Required—TOEFL (minimum score 550 paper-based; 79 iBT), IELTS (minimum score 6.5). *Application deadline:* For fall admission, 1/1 priority date for domestic students; for spring admission, 9/1 for domestic students. Applications are processed on a rolling basis. Application fee: $56 ($96 for international students). One-time fee: $506.10 full-time. Tuition and fees vary according to course load and reciprocity agreements. *Financial support:* In 2011–12, 2 fellowships, 7 teaching assistantships were awarded; research assistantships, career-related internships or fieldwork, unspecified assistantships, and project assistantships also available. Support available to part-time students. Financial award application deadline: 4/15. *Total annual research expenditures:* $619,482. *Unit head:* Barbara Meyer, Department Chair, 414-4591, E-mail: bbmeyer@uwm.edu. Web site: http://www4.uwm.edu/chs/academics/human_movement_sci/kinesiology_masters/.

University of Wyoming, College of Health Sciences, Division of Kinesiology and Health, Laramie, WY 82070. Offers MS. *Accreditation:* NCATE. Part-time programs available. Postbaccalaureate distance learning degree programs offered (no on-campus study). *Degree requirements:* For master's, comprehensive exam (for some programs), thesis (for some programs). *Entrance requirements:* For master's, GRE General Test, minimum GPA of 3.0. Additional exam requirements/recommendations for international students: Required—TOEFL. Electronic applications accepted. *Faculty research:* Teacher effectiveness, effects of exercising on heart function, physiological responses of overtraining, psychological benefits of physical activity, health behavior.

Washington University in St. Louis, School of Medicine, Graduate Programs in Medicine, Interdisciplinary Program in Movement Science, St. Louis, MO 63130-4899. Offers PhD. *Degree requirements:* For doctorate, thesis/dissertation. *Entrance requirements:* For doctorate, GRE General Test. Electronic applications accepted.

Wayne State University, College of Education, Division of Kinesiology, Health and Sports Studies, Detroit, MI 48202. Offers exercise and sport science (M Ed); health education (M Ed); kinesiology (M Ed, PhD); physical education (M Ed); sports administration (MA); wellness clinician/research (M Ed). *Students:* 39 full-time (23 women), 68 part-time (31 women); includes 36 minority (31 Black or African American, non-Hispanic/Latino; 1 Asian, non-Hispanic/Latino; 1 Hispanic/Latino; 1 Native Hawaiian or other Pacific Islander, non-Hispanic/Latino; 2 Two or more races, non-Hispanic/Latino), 3 international. Average age 31. 115 applicants, 39% accepted, 27 enrolled. In 2011, 39 master's, 1 doctorate awarded. *Degree requirements:* For master's, thesis (for some programs). *Entrance requirements:* Additional exam requirements/recommendations for international students: Required—TOEFL; Recommended—TWE (minimum score 6). *Application deadline:* For fall admission, 6/1 priority date for domestic students, 5/1 for international students; for winter admission, 10/1 priority date for domestic students, 9/1 for international students; for spring admission, 2/1 priority date for domestic students, 1/1 for international students. Applications are processed on a rolling basis. Application fee: $50. Electronic applications accepted. *Expenses:* Tuition, state resident: part-time $512.85 per credit. Tuition, nonresident: part-time $1132.65 per credit. *Required fees:* $26.60 per credit. $199.65 per semester. Tuition and fees vary according to course load and program. *Financial support:* In 2011–12, 6 research assistantships with tuition reimbursements (averaging $16,061 per year) were awarded; teaching assistantships with tuition reimbursements, career-related internships or fieldwork, scholarships/grants, health care benefits, and unspecified assistantships also available. *Faculty research:* Fitness in urban children, motor development of crack babies, effects of caffeine on metabolism/exercise, body composition of elite youth sports participants, systematic observation of teaching. *Unit head:* Dr. Mariane Fahlman, Assistant Dean, 313-577-5066, Fax: 313-577-9301, E-mail: m.fahlman@wayne.edu. *Application contact:* John Wirth, Assistant Professor, 313-993-7972, Fax: 313-577-5999, E-mail: johnwirth@wayne.edu. Web site: http://coe.wayne.edu/kinesiology/index.php.

Wayne State University, College of Education, Division of Teacher Education, Detroit, MI 48202. Offers art education (M Ed), including art therapy; bilingual/bicultural education (M Ed); career and technical education (M Ed); curriculum and instruction (Ed D, PhD, Ed S), including art education (PhD), bilingual education (Ed D, Ed S), bilingual-bicultural education (PhD), career and technical education (MAT, Ed D, PhD, Ed S), early childhood education (MAT, Ed D, PhD, Ed S), elementary education, English as a second language (MAT, Ed D, Ed S), English education (MAT, Ed D, PhD, Ed S), foreign language education (MAT, PhD), K-12 curriculum, mathematics education (MAT, Ed D, PhD, Ed S), science education (MAT, Ed D, PhD, Ed S), secondary education, social studies education (MAT, Ed S), social studies education: secondary (Ed D, PhD); elementary education (MAT), including special education; elementary education (M Ed, MAT), including children's literature (MAT), early childhood education (MAT, Ed D, PhD, Ed S), general elementary education (MAT); elementary or secondary education (MAT), including bilingual/bicultural education, English as a second language (MAT, Ed D, Ed S), mathematics education (MAT, Ed D, PhD, Ed S), science education (MAT, Ed D, PhD, Ed S), social studies education (MAT, Ed S); English education-secondary (M Ed); foreign language education (M Ed); mathematics education (M Ed); reading (M Ed, Ed S); reading, languages and literature (Ed D); science education (M Ed); secondary education (MAT), including art education (K-12), career and technical education (MAT, Ed D, PhD, Ed S), English education (MAT, Ed D, PhD, Ed S), foreign language education (MAT, PhD), kinesiology; social studies education secondary (M Ed); special education (M Ed, Ed D, PhD, Ed S). *Students:* 216 full-time (154 women), 626 part-time (478 women); includes 289 minority (227 Black or African American, non-Hispanic/Latino; 4 American Indian or Alaska Native, non-Hispanic/Latino; 27 Asian, non-Hispanic/Latino; 21 Hispanic/Latino; 1 Native Hawaiian or other Pacific Islander, non-Hispanic/Latino; 9 Two or more races, non-Hispanic/Latino), 14 international. Average age 37. 347 applicants, 37% accepted, 93 enrolled. In 2011, 226 master's, 12 doctorates, 46 other advanced degrees awarded. *Degree requirements:* For master's, thesis (for some programs), thesis, essay or project (for some M Ed programs), professional field experience (for MAT programs); for doctorate, thesis/dissertation. *Entrance requirements:* For master's, Michigan Basic Skills Test (MA in teaching); for doctorate, minimum undergraduate GPA of 3.0, graduate 3.5; interview, curriculum vitae; references. Additional exam requirements/recommendations for international students: Required—TOEFL (minimum score 550 paper-based; 213 computer-based), TWE (minimum score 5.5). *Application deadline:* For fall admission, 6/1 priority date for domestic students, 5/1 for international students; for winter admission, 10/1 priority date for domestic students, 9/1 for international students; for spring admission, 2/1 priority date for domestic students, 1/1 for international students. Applications are processed on a rolling basis. Application fee: $50. Electronic applications accepted. *Expenses:* Tuition, state resident: part-time $512.85 per credit. Tuition, nonresident: part-time $1132.65 per credit. *Required fees:* $26.60 per credit. $199.65 per semester. Tuition and fees vary according to course load and program. *Financial support:* In 2011–12, 42 students received support. Fellowships, research assistantships with tuition reimbursements available, teaching assistantships, scholarships/grants, and unspecified assistantships available. *Faculty research:* Reading and writing literacy and literature. *Total annual research expenditures:* $264,016. *Unit head:* Dr. Craig Roney, Assistant Dean, 313-577-0902, E-mail: rroney@wayne.edu. Web site: http://coe.wayne.edu/ted/index.php.

West Chester University of Pennsylvania, College of Health Sciences, Department of Kinesiology, West Chester, PA 19383. Offers exercise/sport physiology (MS), including athletic training; physical education (MS); sport management and athletics (MPA). *Faculty:* 7 part-time/adjunct (3 women). *Students:* 19 full-time (10 women), 14 part-time (7 women); includes 5 minority (all Black or African American, non-Hispanic/Latino). Average age 26. 37 applicants, 35% accepted, 10 enrolled. In 2011, 12 degrees awarded. *Degree requirements:* For master's, thesis or report (MS), 2 internships (MPA). *Entrance requirements:* For master's, GRE with minimum score of 1000 (for MS), 2 letters of recommendation, transcripts, and statement of professional goals (for MS); 2 letters of reference, resume, career goal statement (for MPA). Additional exam requirements/recommendations for international students: Required—TOEFL (minimum score 550 paper-based; 213 computer-based; 80 iBT). *Application deadline:* For fall admission, 4/15 priority date for domestic students, 3/15 for international students; for spring admission, 10/15 priority date for domestic students, 9/1 for international students. Applications are processed on a rolling basis. Application fee: $45. Electronic applications accepted. *Expenses:* Tuition, state resident: full-time $7488; part-time $416 per credit. Tuition, nonresident: full-time $11,232; part-time $624 per credit. *Required fees:* $1784.64; $67.59 per credit. Tuition and fees vary according to program. *Financial support:* Unspecified assistantships available. Support available to part-time students. Financial award application deadline: 2/15; financial award applicants required to submit FAFSA. *Faculty research:* Metabolism during exercise, biomechanics, rating of perceived exertion, motor learning. *Unit head:* Dr. Frank Fry, Chair and Graduate Coordinator for the MS in General Physical Education Program, 610-436-2610, Fax: 610-436-2860, E-mail: ffry@wcupa.edu. *Application contact:* Dr. Sheri Melton, Graduate Coordinator for the Exercise and Sport Physiology Programs, 610-436-2260, Fax: 610-

436-2860, E-mail: smelton@wcupa.edu. Web site: http://www.wcupa.edu/_academics/sch_shs.hpe/.

Western Illinois University, School of Graduate Studies, College of Education and Human Services, Department of Kinesiology, Program in Kinesiology, Macomb, IL 61455-1390. Offers MS. Part-time programs available. *Students:* 36 full-time (19 women), 4 part-time (3 women); includes 5 minority (2 Black or African American, non-Hispanic/Latino; 2 Hispanic/Latino; 1 Two or more races, non-Hispanic/Latino), 7 international. Average age 24. 48 applicants, 67% accepted. In 2011, 20 master's awarded. *Entrance requirements:* For master's, minimum GPA of 3.0. Additional exam requirements/recommendations for international students: Required—TOEFL (minimum score 550 paper-based; 213 computer-based; 80 iBT). *Application deadline:* Applications are processed on a rolling basis. Application fee: $30. Electronic applications accepted. *Expenses:* Tuition, state resident: part-time $281.16 per credit hour. Tuition, nonresident: part-time $562.32 per credit hour. Part-time tuition and fees vary according to campus/location and reciprocity agreements. *Financial support:* In 2011–12, 21 students received support, including 12 research assistantships with full tuition reimbursements available (averaging $7,360 per year), 9 teaching assistantships with full tuition reimbursements available (averaging $8,480 per year). Financial award applicants required to submit FAFSA. *Unit head:* Dr. Cynthia Piletic, Graduate Committee Chairperson, 309-298-1981. *Application contact:* Dr. Nancy Parsons, Interim Associate Provost and Director of Graduate Studies, 309-298-1806, Fax: 309-298-2345, E-mail: grad-office@wiu.edu. Web site: http://wiu.edu/kinesiology.

Wilfrid Laurier University, Faculty of Graduate and Postdoctoral Studies, Faculty of Science, Department of Kinesiology and Physical Education, Waterloo, ON N2L 3C5, Canada. Offers physical activity and health (M Sc). *Degree requirements:* For master's, thesis. *Entrance requirements:* For master's, honours degree in kinesiology, health, physical education with a minimum B+ in kinesiology and health-related courses. Additional exam requirements/recommendations for international students: Required—TOEFL (minimum score 89 iBT). Electronic applications accepted. *Faculty research:* Biomechanics, health, exercise physiology, motor control, sport psychology.

York University, Faculty of Graduate Studies, Faculty of Health, Program in Kinesiology and Health Science, Toronto, ON M3J 1P3, Canada. Offers M Sc, MA, PhD. Part-time programs available. *Degree requirements:* For master's, thesis or alternative; for doctorate, comprehensive exam, thesis/dissertation. Electronic applications accepted.

Physical Education

Adams State University, The Graduate School, Department of Human Performance and Physical Education, Alamosa, CO 81102. Offers MA. *Accreditation:* Teacher Education Accreditation Council. Part-time programs available. *Degree requirements:* For master's, comprehensive exam. *Entrance requirements:* For master's, GRE General Test or MAT, minimum undergraduate GPA of 2.75.

Adelphi University, Ruth S. Ammon School of Education, Program in Physical Education and Human Performance Science, Garden City, NY 11530-0701. Offers aging (Certificate); physical/educational human performance science (MA). Part-time and evening/weekend programs available. *Students:* 51 full-time (15 women), 44 part-time (21 women); includes 18 minority (7 Black or African American, non-Hispanic/Latino; 2 Asian, non-Hispanic/Latino; 9 Hispanic/Latino). Average age 29. In 2011, 50 master's awarded. *Degree requirements:* For master's, internship. *Entrance requirements:* For master's, 3 letters of recommendation, resume. Additional exam requirements/recommendations for international students: Required—TOEFL (minimum score 550 paper-based; 213 computer-based; 80 iBT). *Application deadline:* For fall admission, 4/1 for international students; for spring admission, 11/1 for international students. Applications are processed on a rolling basis. Application fee: $50. Electronic applications accepted. *Expenses: Tuition:* Full-time $29,600; part-time $930 per credit. *Required fees:* $1100. *Financial support:* Fellowships, research assistantships with full and partial tuition reimbursements, teaching assistantships, career-related internships or fieldwork, Federal Work-Study, institutionally sponsored loans, and tuition waivers (full) available. Support available to part-time students. Financial award application deadline: 2/15; financial award applicants required to submit FAFSA. *Faculty research:* Physical education for the handicapped, sport sociology, sport pedagogy. *Unit head:* Dr. Ronald S. Feingold, Chair, 516-877-4764, E-mail: feingold@adelphi.edu. *Application contact:* Christine Murphy, Director of Admissions, 516-877-3050, Fax: 516-877-3039, E-mail: graduateadmissions@adelphi.edu.

Alabama Agricultural and Mechanical University, School of Graduate Studies, School of Education, Area in Health and Physical Education, Huntsville, AL 35811. Offers physical education (M Ed, MS). Part-time and evening/weekend programs available. *Degree requirements:* For master's, comprehensive exam. *Entrance requirements:* For master's, GRE General Test. Additional exam requirements/recommendations for international students: Required—TOEFL (minimum score 500 paper-based; 173 computer-based; 61 iBT). Electronic applications accepted. *Faculty research:* Cardiorespiratory assessment.

Alabama State University, Department of Health, Physical Education, and Recreation, Montgomery, AL 36101-0271. Offers health education (M Ed); physical education (M Ed). Part-time programs available. *Faculty:* 4 full-time (all women), 1 part-time/adjunct (0 women). *Students:* 58 full-time (48 women), 1 (woman) part-time; includes 42 minority (all Black or African American, non-Hispanic/Latino). Average age 27. 166 applicants, 25% accepted, 22 enrolled. In 2011, 1 master's awarded. *Degree requirements:* For master's, comprehensive exam. *Entrance requirements:* For master's, GRE General Test, MAT, graduate writing competency test. Additional exam requirements/recommendations for international students: Required—TOEFL (minimum score 500 paper-based; 173 computer-based). *Application deadline:* For fall admission, 7/15 for domestic students; for spring admission, 12/15 for domestic students. Applications are processed on a rolling basis. Application fee: $10. *Financial support:* In 2011–12, research assistantships (averaging $9,450 per year) were awarded. *Faculty research:* Risk factors for heart disease in the college-age population, cardiovascular reactivity for the Cold Pressor Test. *Unit head:* Dr. Doris Screws, Chair, 334-229-4504, Fax: 334-229-4928. *Application contact:* Dr. Doris Screws, Dean of Graduate Studies, 334-229-4274, Fax: 334-229-4928, E-mail: dscrews@alasu.edu. Web site: http://www.alasu.edu/academics/colleges—departments/college-of-education/health-physical-education—recreation/index.aspx.

Albany State University, College of Education, Albany, GA 31705-2717. Offers early childhood education (M Ed); education specialist (Ed S); educational leadership and administration (M Ed); health, physical education and recreation (M Ed); middle grades education (M Ed); school counseling (M Ed); special education (M Ed). *Accreditation:* NCATE. Part-time and evening/weekend programs available. Postbaccalaureate distance learning degree programs offered (minimal on-campus study). *Faculty:* 19 full-time (13 women), 7 part-time/adjunct (5 women). *Students:* 90 full-time (69 women), 118 part-time (92 women); includes 152 minority (151 Black or African American, non-Hispanic/Latino; 1 American Indian or Alaska Native, non-Hispanic/Latino), 1 international. Average age 35. 93 applicants, 78% accepted, 38 enrolled. In 2011, 43 master's, 8 Ed Ss awarded. *Degree requirements:* For master's, comprehensive exam, internship, GACE Content Exam. *Entrance requirements:* For master's, GRE or MAT. *Application deadline:* For fall admission, 6/1 for domestic students, 5/1 for international students; for spring admission, 11/1 for domestic students, 10/1 for international students. Applications are processed on a rolling basis. Application fee: $20. Electronic applications accepted. *Expenses:* Tuition, state resident: full-time $3204; part-time $178 per credit hour. Tuition, nonresident: full-time $12,816; part-time $712 per credit hour. *Required fees:* $379 per semester. *Financial support:* Scholarships/grants available. Financial award application deadline: 4/15; financial award applicants required to submit FAFSA. *Faculty research:* GACE preparation, STEM (science, technology, engineering, and mathematics), technology education, special education; professional teacher development, health implications liberation philosophy, NET-Q, learning community, disabled or at-risk students. *Total annual research expenditures:* $252,502. *Unit head:* Dr. Kimberly King-Jupiter, Dean, 229-430-1718, Fax: 229-430-4993, E-mail: kimberly.king-jupiter@asurams.edu. *Application contact:* Jeffrey Pierce, II, Graduate Admissions Counselor, 229-430-4646, Fax: 229-430-4105, E-mail: jeffrey.pierce@asurams.edu. Web site: http://asu-sacs.asurams.edu/ASUCatalog/Graduate/index.html.

Alcorn State University, School of Graduate Studies, School of Psychology and Education, Alcorn State, MS 39096-7500. Offers agricultural education (MS Ed); elementary education (MS Ed, Ed S); guidance and counseling (MS Ed); industrial education (MS Ed); secondary education (MS Ed), including health and physical education; special education (MS Ed). *Accreditation:* NCATE. *Degree requirements:* For master's, thesis optional.

American University of Puerto Rico, Program in Education, Bayamón, PR 00960-2037. Offers art education (M Ed); elementary education 4-6 (M Ed); elementary education K-3 (M Ed); general science education (M Ed); physical education (M Ed); special education (M Ed). *Entrance requirements:* For master's, EXADEP, GRE, or MAT, 2 letters of recommendation, minimum GPA of 2.5. *Application deadline:* For fall admission, 8/1 for domestic students; for winter admission, 10/18 for domestic students; for spring admission, 3/15 for domestic students. Applications are processed on a rolling basis. Application fee: $50. *Expenses: Tuition:* Part-time $190 per credit. *Required fees:* $48.33 per credit. Tuition and fees vary according to course load and program. *Application contact:* Information Contact, 787-620-2040, E-mail: oficnaadmisiones@aupr.edu.

Arizona State University, Mary Lou Fulton Teachers College, Program in Curriculum and Instruction, Phoenix, AZ 85069. Offers curriculum and instruction (M Ed, MA, PhD); elementary education (M Ed); physical education (MPE); secondary education (M Ed). Part-time and evening/weekend programs available. Postbaccalaureate distance learning degree programs offered (minimal on-campus study). Terminal master's awarded for partial completion of doctoral program. *Degree requirements:* For master's, thesis or alternative, applied project, interactive Program of Study (iPOS) submitted before completing 50 percent of required credit hours; for doctorate, comprehensive exam, thesis/dissertation, interactive Program of Study (iPOS) submitted before completing 50 percent of required credit hours. *Entrance requirements:* For master's, GRE or GMAT (for some programs), minimum GPA of 3.0 or equivalent in last 2 years of work leading to bachelor's degree, 3 letters of recommendation, personal statement describing research and career goals, curriculum vitae or resume, IVP fingerprint clearance card (for those seeking Arizona certification); for doctorate, GRE or GMAT (depending on program), minimum GPA of 3.0 or equivalent in last 2 years of work leading to bachelor's degree, 3 letters of recommendation, personal statement describing research and career goals, curriculum vitae or resume. Additional exam requirements/recommendations for international students: Required—TOEFL, IELTS, or Pearson Test of English. Electronic applications accepted. *Expenses:* Contact institution. *Faculty research:* Early childhood, media and computers, elementary education, secondary education, English education, bilingual education, language and literacy, science education, engineering education, exercise and wellness education.

Arkansas State University, Graduate School, College of Education, Department of Health, Physical Education, and Sport Sciences, Jonesboro, State University, AR 72467. Offers exercise science (MS); physical education (MSE, SCCT); sports administration (MS). Part-time programs available. *Faculty:* 9 full-time (3 women). *Students:* 22 full-time (8 women), 22 part-time (9 women); includes 6 minority (5 Black or African American, non-Hispanic/Latino; 1 Hispanic/Latino), 9 international. Average age 25. 44 applicants, 70% accepted, 20 enrolled. In 2011, 11 master's awarded. *Degree requirements:* For master's, comprehensive exam, thesis or alternative; for SCCT, comprehensive exam. *Entrance requirements:* For master's, GRE General Test or MAT, appropriate bachelor's degree, official transcripts, immunization records, statement of goals, letters of recommendation; for SCCT, GRE General Test or MAT, interview, master's degree, official transcript, immunization records. Additional exam requirements/recommendations for international students: Required—TOEFL (minimum score 550 paper-based; 213 computer-based; 79 iBT), IELTS (minimum score 6), Pearson Test of English Academic (minimum score 56). *Application deadline:* For fall admission, 7/1 for domestic and international students; for spring admission, 11/15 for domestic students, 11/14 for international students. Applications are processed on a rolling basis. Application fee: $30 ($40 for international students). Electronic applications accepted. *Expenses:* Tuition, state resident: full-time $4044; part-time $225 per credit hour. Tuition, nonresident: full-time $8087; part-time $449 per credit hour. *Required fees:* $936; $52 per credit hour. $25 per term. One-time fee: $30. Tuition and fees vary according to course load and program. *Financial support:* In 2011–12, 20 students received support. Teaching assistantships, career-related internships or fieldwork, scholarships/grants, and unspecified assistantships available. Financial award application deadline: 7/1; financial award applicants required to submit FAFSA. *Unit head:* Dr. Jim Stillwell, Chair, 870-972-3066, Fax: 870-972-3096, E-mail: jstillwel@astate.edu. *Application contact:* Dr. Andrew Sustich, Dean of the Graduate School, 870-972-3029, Fax: 870-972-3857, E-mail: sustich@astate.edu. Web site: http://www.astate.edu/a/education/hpess/index.dot.

Physical Education

Arkansas Tech University, Center for Leadership and Learning, College of Education, Russellville, AR 72801. Offers college student personnel (MS); educational leadership (Ed S); elementary education (M Ed); instructional improvement (M Ed); instructional technology (M Ed); physical education (M Ed); school counseling and leadership (M Ed); teaching (MAT). *Accreditation:* NCATE. Part-time and evening/weekend programs available. Postbaccalaureate distance learning degree programs offered (no on-campus study). *Students:* 70 full-time (44 women), 247 part-time (189 women); includes 57 minority (38 Black or African American, non-Hispanic/Latino; 1 American Indian or Alaska Native, non-Hispanic/Latino; 8 Asian, non-Hispanic/Latino; 4 Hispanic/Latino; 6 Two or more races, non-Hispanic/Latino), 3 international. Average age 31. In 2011, 58 master's awarded. *Degree requirements:* For master's, comprehensive exam, thesis optional, action research project. *Entrance requirements:* Additional exam requirements/recommendations for international students: Required—TOEFL (minimum score 550 paper-based; 213 computer-based; 79 iBT), IELTS (minimum score 6.5). *Application deadline:* For fall admission, 3/1 priority date for domestic students, 5/1 for international students; for spring admission, 10/1 priority date for domestic students, 10/1 for international students. Applications are processed on a rolling basis. Application fee: $25 ($75 for international students). Electronic applications accepted. *Expenses:* Tuition, state resident: full-time $4968; part-time $207 per credit hour. Tuition, nonresident: full-time $9936; part-time $414 per credit hour. *Required fees:* $375 per semester. Tuition and fees vary according to course load. *Financial support:* In 2011–12, teaching assistantships with full tuition reimbursements (averaging $4,800 per year) were awarded; research assistantships with full tuition reimbursements, career-related internships or fieldwork, Federal Work-Study, scholarships/grants, health care benefits, and unspecified assistantships also available. Support available to part-time students. Financial award application deadline: 4/15; financial award applicants required to submit FAFSA. *Unit head:* Dr. Eldon G. Clary, Jr., Dean, 479-968-0350, Fax: 479-968-0350, E-mail: eclary@atu.edu. *Application contact:* Dr. Mary B. Gunter, Dean of Graduate College, 479-968-0398, Fax: 479-964-0542, E-mail: gradcollege@atu.edu. Web site: http://www.atu.edu/education/.

Ashland University, Dwight Schar College of Education, Department of Sport Sciences, Ashland, OH 44805-3702. Offers adapted physical education (M Ed); applied exercise science (M Ed); sport education (M Ed); sport management (M Ed). Part-time programs available. *Faculty:* 11 full-time (5 women). *Students:* 15 full-time (1 woman), 21 part-time (9 women); includes 4 minority (2 Black or African American, non-Hispanic/Latino; 1 Hispanic/Latino; 1 Two or more races, non-Hispanic/Latino), 1 international. Average age 29. In 2011, 20 master's awarded. *Degree requirements:* For master's, practicum, inquiry seminar, thesis, or internship. *Entrance requirements:* For master's, teaching certificate or license, bachelor's degree, minimum cumulative GPA of 2.75. Additional exam requirements/recommendations for international students: Required—TOEFL. *Application deadline:* For fall admission, 8/27 for domestic students; for spring admission, 1/15 for domestic students. Applications are processed on a rolling basis. Application fee: $30. *Expenses: Tuition:* Full-time $5580; part-time $465 per credit hour. *Financial support:* In 2011–12, 1 student received support. Teaching assistantships, institutionally sponsored loans, and scholarships/grants available. Financial award application deadline: 4/15. *Faculty research:* Coaching, legal issues, strength and conditioning, sport management rating of perceived exertion, youth fitness, geriatric exercise science. *Unit head:* Dr. Randall F. Gearhart, Chair, 419-289-6198, E-mail: rgearhar@ashland.edu. *Application contact:* Dr. Linda Billman, Director and Chair, Graduate Studies in Education/Associate Dean, 419-289-5369, Fax: 419-289-5331, E-mail: lbillman@ashland.edu.

Auburn University, Graduate School, College of Education, Department of Kinesiology, Auburn University, AL 36849. Offers exercise science (M Ed, MS, PhD); health promotion (M Ed, MS); kinesiology (PhD); physical education/teacher education (M Ed, MS, Ed D, Ed S). *Accreditation:* NCATE. Part-time programs available. *Faculty:* 15 full-time (8 women). *Students:* 60 full-time (30 women), 33 part-time (15 women); includes 17 minority (14 Black or African American, non-Hispanic/Latino; 1 Asian, non-Hispanic/Latino; 2 Hispanic/Latino), 6 international. Average age 27. 116 applicants, 61% accepted, 41 enrolled. In 2011, 48 master's, 4 doctorates awarded. *Degree requirements:* For master's, thesis (for some programs); for doctorate, thesis/dissertation; for Ed S, exam, field project. *Entrance requirements:* For master's, GRE General Test; for doctorate and Ed S, GRE General Test, interview, master's degree. *Application deadline:* For fall admission, 7/7 for domestic students; for spring admission, 11/24 for domestic students. Applications are processed on a rolling basis. Application fee: $50 ($60 for international students). Electronic applications accepted. *Expenses:* Tuition, state resident: full-time $7290; part-time $405 per credit hour. Tuition, nonresident: full-time $21,870; part-time $1215 per credit hour. *International tuition:* $22,000 full-time. *Required fees:* $1402. *Financial support:* Research assistantships, teaching assistantships, and Federal Work-Study available. Support available to part-time students. Financial award application deadline: 3/15; financial award applicants required to submit FAFSA. *Faculty research:* Biomechanics, exercise physiology, motor skill learning, school health, curriculum development. *Unit head:* Dr. Mary E. Rudisill, Head, 334-844-1458. *Application contact:* Dr. George Flowers, Dean of the Graduate School, 334-844-2125.

Auburn University Montgomery, School of Education, Department of Foundations, Secondary, and Physical Education, Montgomery, AL 36124-4023. Offers physical education (M Ed); secondary education (M Ed, Ed S). *Accreditation:* NCATE. Part-time and evening/weekend programs available. *Degree requirements:* For master's and Ed S, comprehensive exam, thesis optional. *Entrance requirements:* For master's, GRE General Test or MAT, certification, BS in teaching; for Ed S, GRE General Test or MAT, certification. Electronic applications accepted. *Expenses:* Tuition, state resident: full-time $5076. Tuition, nonresident: full-time $15,228.

Augusta State University, Graduate Studies, College of Education, Program in Health and Physical Education, Augusta, GA 30904-2200. Offers M Ed. *Faculty:* 2 full-time (both women). *Students:* 1 full-time (0 women), 6 part-time (3 women); includes 3 minority (all Black or African American, non-Hispanic/Latino). Average age 31. 1 applicant, 100% accepted, 1 enrolled. In 2011, 7 master's awarded. *Entrance requirements:* For master's, GRE, MAT, minimum GPA of 2.5. Application fee: $20. *Financial support:* Career-related internships or fieldwork, Federal Work-Study, institutionally sponsored loans, and unspecified assistantships available. Support available to part-time students. *Unit head:* Dr. Paula J. Dohoney, Chair, 706-731-7922, Fax: 706-667-4140, E-mail: pdohoney@aug.edu. *Application contact:* Andrea M. Scott, Secretary to the Dean, 706-737-1499, Fax: 706-667-4706, E-mail: ascott@aug.edu.

Austin College, Program in Education, Sherman, TX 75090-4400. Offers art education (MA); elementary education (MA); middle school education (MA); music education (MA); physical education and coaching (MA); secondary education (MA); theatre education (MA). Part-time programs available. *Faculty:* 5 full-time (4 women). *Students:* 21 full-time (13 women), 2 part-time (both women). Average age 23. In 2011, 24 master's awarded. *Degree requirements:* For master's, one foreign language, thesis or alternative. *Entrance requirements:* For master's, Texas Academic Skills Program Test. *Application deadline:* For fall admission, 5/1 priority date for domestic students; for spring admission, 1/15 priority date for domestic students. Applications are processed on a rolling basis. Application fee: $35. Electronic applications accepted. *Expenses: Tuition:* Full-time $38,445. *Required fees:* $160. *Financial support:* Career-related internships or fieldwork, Federal Work-Study, scholarships/grants, and unspecified assistantships available. Support available to part-time students. Financial award application deadline: 4/1; financial award applicants required to submit FAFSA. *Unit head:* Dr. Barbara Sylvester, Director of Teaching Program, 903-813-2327, E-mail: bsylvester@austincollege.edu. *Application contact:* Dr. Barbara Sylvester, Director of Teaching Program, 903-813-2327, E-mail: bsylvester@austincollege.edu. Web site: http://www.austincollege.edu/.

Azusa Pacific University, School of Education, Department of Advanced Studies, Program in Physical Education, Azusa, CA 91702-7000. Offers M Ed. Evening/weekend programs available. *Degree requirements:* For master's, core exams, oral exam, oral presentation. *Entrance requirements:* For master's, BA in physical education or 12 units of course work in education, minimum GPA of 3.0.

Ball State University, Graduate School, College of Applied Science and Technology, School of Physical Education, Muncie, IN 47306-1099. Offers MA, MAE, MS, PhD. *Faculty:* 23 full-time (8 women), 5 part-time/adjunct (2 women). *Students:* 61 full-time (25 women), 65 part-time (24 women); includes 6 minority (2 Black or African American, non-Hispanic/Latino; 4 Hispanic/Latino), 2 international. Average age 24. 143 applicants, 45% accepted, 47 enrolled. In 2011, 77 degrees awarded. *Degree requirements:* For doctorate, thesis/dissertation. *Entrance requirements:* For master's, resume; for doctorate, GRE General Test, minimum graduate GPA of 3.2. Application fee: $50. Tuition and fees vary according to program and reciprocity agreements. *Financial support:* In 2011–12, 71 students received support, including 68 teaching assistantships with full tuition reimbursements available (averaging $10,841 per year); research assistantships also available. Financial award application deadline: 3/1. *Unit head:* Dr. Mitchell Whaley, Director, 765-285-1748, Fax: 765-285-8254. *Application contact:* Dr. Robert Morris, Associate Provost for Research and Dean of the Graduate School, 765-285-5723, Fax: 765-285-1328, E-mail: rmorris@bsu.edu. Web site: http://cms.bsu.edu/Academics/CollegesandDepartments/PhysicalEducation.aspx.

Baylor University, Graduate School, School of Education, Department of Health, Human Performance and Recreation, Waco, TX 76798. Offers exercise, nutrition and preventive health (PhD); health, human performance and recreation (MS Ed). *Accreditation:* NCATE. Part-time programs available. *Faculty:* 13 full-time (5 women), 3 part-time/adjunct (1 woman). *Students:* 64 full-time (41 women), 28 part-time (10 women); includes 16 minority (5 Black or African American, non-Hispanic/Latino; 1 Asian, non-Hispanic/Latino; 7 Hispanic/Latino; 3 Two or more races, non-Hispanic/Latino), 8 international. 30 applicants, 87% accepted. In 2011, 42 degrees awarded. *Degree requirements:* For master's, thesis optional. *Entrance requirements:* For master's, GRE General Test. *Application deadline:* For fall admission, 4/1 priority date for domestic students; for spring admission, 10/1 for domestic students. Applications are processed on a rolling basis. Application fee: $25. Electronic applications accepted. *Financial support:* In 2011–12, 35 students received support, including 22 teaching assistantships; career-related internships or fieldwork, Federal Work-Study, institutionally sponsored loans, tuition waivers (partial), and recreation supplements also available. *Faculty research:* Behavior change theory, pedagogy, nutrition and enzyme therapy, exercise testing, health planning. *Unit head:* Dr. Glenn Miller, Graduate Program Director, 254-710-4001, Fax: 254-710-3527, E-mail: glenn_miller@baylor.edu. *Application contact:* Eva Berger-Rhodes, Administrative Assistant, 254-710-4945, Fax: 254-710-3870, E-mail: eva_rhodes@baylor.edu. Web site: http://www.baylor.edu/HHPR/.

Boise State University, Graduate College, College of Education, Department of Kinesiology, Program in Physical Education, Boise, ID 83725-0399. Offers MS. Part-time programs available. *Degree requirements:* For master's, thesis. *Entrance requirements:* For master's, minimum GPA of 3.0. Electronic applications accepted.

Bridgewater State University, School of Graduate Studies, School of Education and Allied Studies, Department of Movement Arts, Health Promotion, and Leisure Studies, Program in Physical Education, Bridgewater, MA 02325-0001. Offers MS. Part-time and evening/weekend programs available. *Degree requirements:* For master's, thesis or alternative. *Entrance requirements:* For master's, GRE General Test.

Brooklyn College of the City University of New York, Division of Graduate Studies, Department of Physical Education and Exercise Science, Brooklyn, NY 11210-2889. Offers exercise science and rehabilitation (MS); physical education (MS), including sports management. Part-time programs available. *Degree requirements:* For master's, comprehensive exam or thesis. *Entrance requirements:* For master's, previous course work in physical education and education, minimum GPA of 3.0, 2 letters of recommendation, essay. Additional exam requirements/recommendations for international students: Required—TOEFL (minimum score 500 paper-based; 173 computer-based; 61 iBT). Electronic applications accepted. *Faculty research:* Exercise physiology, motor learning, sports psychology, women in athletics.

Brooklyn College of the City University of New York, Division of Graduate Studies, School of Education, Program in Adolescence Education and Special Subjects, Brooklyn, NY 11210-2889. Offers adolescence science education (MAT); art teacher (MA); biology teacher (MA); chemistry teacher (MA); earth science teacher (MAT); English teacher (MA); French teacher (MA); health and nutrition sciences: health teacher (MS Ed); mathematics teacher (MA); music education (CAS); music teacher (MA); physical education teacher (MS Ed); physics teacher (MA); social studies teacher (MA); Spanish teacher (MA). Part-time and evening/weekend programs available. *Degree requirements:* For master's, comprehensive exam (for some programs), thesis (for some programs). *Entrance requirements:* For master's, LAST, previous course work in education, resume, 2 letters of recommendation, essay. Additional exam requirements/recommendations for international students: Required—TOEFL (minimum score 500 paper-based; 173 computer-based; 61 iBT). Electronic applications accepted. *Faculty research:* Interdisciplinary education, semiotics, discourse analysis, autobiography, teacher identity.

California Baptist University, Program in Kinesiology, Riverside, CA 92504-3206. Offers exercise science (MS); physical education pedagogy (MS); sport management (MS). Part-time and evening/weekend programs available. *Faculty:* 6 full-time (2 women), 1 part-time/adjunct (0 women). *Students:* 42 full-time (20 women); includes 11 minority (6 Black or African American, non-Hispanic/Latino; 2 Asian, non-Hispanic/Latino; 2 Hispanic/Latino; 1 Two or more races, non-Hispanic/Latino), 14 international. Average age 27. 47 applicants, 70% accepted, 18 enrolled. In 2011, 25 master's awarded. *Degree requirements:* For master's, comprehensive exam or thesis. *Entrance requirements:* For master's, minimum undergraduate GPA of 2.75; three recommendations; comprehensive essay; resume; interview. Additional exam requirements/recommendations for international students: Required—TOEFL (minimum score 575 paper-based; 230 computer-based; 89 iBT). *Application deadline:* For fall admission, 8/1 priority date for domestic students, 7/1 for international students; for spring admission, 12/1 priority date for domestic students, 11/1 for international students. Applications are processed on a rolling basis. Application fee: $45. Electronic applications accepted. *Expenses:* Contact institution. *Financial support:* In 2011–12, 2 students received support, including 2 teaching assistantships (averaging $6,450 per year); Federal Work-Study, institutionally sponsored loans, and unspecified assistantships also available. Financial award applicants required to submit FAFSA. *Faculty research:* Musculoskeletal injury and examination, thermoregulation, immune function, carbohydrate oxidation, cardiovascular morbidity and mortality. *Unit head:* Dr. Chuck Sands, Dean, College of Allied Health, 951-343-4619, E-mail: csands@calbaptist.edu. *Application contact:* Dr. Sean Sullivan, Chair, Department of Kinesiology, 951-343-4528, Fax: 951-343-5095, E-mail: ssullivan@calbaptist.edu. Web site: http://www.calbaptist.edu/mskin/.

California State University, Dominguez Hills, College of Professional Studies, School of Health and Human Services, Program in Physical Education Administration, Carson, CA 90747-0001. Offers MA. Part-time programs available. *Faculty:* 2 full-time (1 woman). *Students:* 1 full-time (0 women), 7 part-time (4 women); includes 7 minority (3 Black or African American, non-Hispanic/Latino; 4 Hispanic/Latino). Average age 36. 22 applicants, 95% accepted, 5 enrolled. In 2011, 16 master's awarded. *Degree requirements:* For master's, comprehensive exam. *Entrance requirements:* For master's, minimum GPA of 2.75. Additional exam requirements/recommendations for international students: Required—TOEFL, IELTS. *Application deadline:* For fall admission, 6/1 for domestic students. Applications are processed on a rolling basis. Application fee: $55. *Faculty research:* Teaching pedagogy, physical activity. *Unit head:* Dr. Ben Zhou, Chair, 310-243-2223, E-mail: bzhou@csudh.edu. *Application contact:* 310-243-3600. Web site: http://www.csudh.edu/cps/hhs/kr/index.htm.

California State University, East Bay, Office of Academic Programs and Graduate Studies, College of Education and Allied Studies, Department of Kinesiology, Hayward, CA 94542-3000. Offers MS. *Faculty:* 9 full-time (8 women), 1 (woman) part-time/adjunct. *Students:* 22 full-time (8 women), 3 part-time (2 women); includes 12 minority (1 Black or African American, non-Hispanic/Latino; 2 Asian, non-Hispanic/Latino; 7 Hispanic/Latino; 2 Two or more races, non-Hispanic/Latino), 1 international. Average age 31. 28 applicants, 54% accepted, 12 enrolled. In 2011, 17 master's awarded. *Degree requirements:* For master's, exam or thesis. *Entrance requirements:* For master's, BA in kinesiology or related discipline, minimum major course work GPA of 3.0. Additional exam requirements/recommendations for international students: Required—TOEFL (minimum score 550 paper-based; 213 computer-based). *Application deadline:* For fall admission, 6/30 for domestic and international students. Applications are processed on a rolling basis. Application fee: $55. Electronic applications accepted. *Expenses:* Tuition, state resident: full-time $6738; part-time $1302 per quarter. Tuition, nonresident: full-time $12,690; part-time $2294 per quarter. *Required fees:* $449 per quarter. Tuition and fees vary according to degree level, program and reciprocity agreements. *Financial support:* Fellowships, Federal Work-Study, institutionally sponsored loans, and scholarships/grants available. Support available to part-time students. Financial award application deadline: 3/2; financial award applicants required to submit FAFSA. *Faculty research:* Physiology, psychology of sport/movement, skill acquisition, cultural influence on physical activity. *Unit head:* Dr. Penny McCullagh, Chair, 510-885-3061, Fax: 510-885-2423, E-mail: penny.mccullagh@csueastbay.edu. *Application contact:* Prof. Cathy Inouye, Kinesiology Graduate Advisor, 510-885-3048, Fax: 510-885-2423, E-mail: cathy.inouye@csueastbay.edu. Web site: http://www20.csueastbay.edu/ecat/graduate-chapters/g-kin.html.

California State University, Fullerton, Graduate Studies, College of Health and Human Development, Department of Kinesiology, Fullerton, CA 92834-9480. Offers MS. Part-time programs available. *Students:* 46 full-time (23 women), 60 part-time (26 women); includes 52 minority (1 Black or African American, non-Hispanic/Latino; 14 Asian, non-Hispanic/Latino; 30 Hispanic/Latino; 7 Two or more races, non-Hispanic/Latino), 4 international. Average age 27. 107 applicants, 52% accepted, 39 enrolled. In 2011, 51 master's awarded. *Degree requirements:* For master's, project or thesis. *Entrance requirements:* For master's, minimum GPA of 3.0 in field, 2.5 overall. Application fee: $55. *Financial support:* Career-related internships or fieldwork, Federal Work-Study, institutionally sponsored loans, and scholarships/grants available. Support available to part-time students. Financial award application deadline: 3/1; financial award applicants required to submit FAFSA. *Unit head:* Dr. Stephen Walk, Head, 657-278-3320. *Application contact:* Admissions/Applications, 657-278-2371.

California State University, Long Beach, Graduate Studies, College of Health and Human Services, Department of Kinesiology, Long Beach, CA 90840. Offers adapted physical education (MA); coaching and student athlete development (MA); exercise physiology and nutrition (MS); exercise science (MS); individualized studies (MA); kinesiology (MA); pedagogical studies (MA); sport and exercise psychology (MS); sport management (MA); sports medicine and injury studies (MS). Part-time programs available. *Faculty:* 9 full-time (5 women), 5 part-time/adjunct (4 women). *Students:* 48 full-time (27 women), 39 part-time (13 women); includes 38 minority (5 Black or African American, non-Hispanic/Latino; 2 American Indian or Alaska Native, non-Hispanic/Latino; 7 Asian, non-Hispanic/Latino; 18 Hispanic/Latino; 6 Two or more races, non-Hispanic/Latino), 2 international. Average age 28. 214 applicants, 50% accepted, 32 enrolled. In 2011, 69 master's awarded. *Degree requirements:* For master's, oral and written comprehensive exams or thesis. *Entrance requirements:* For master's, GRE General Test, minimum GPA of 2.75 during previous 2 years of course work. *Application deadline:* For fall admission, 6/1 for domestic students. Applications are processed on a rolling basis. Application fee: $55. Electronic applications accepted. *Financial support:* Federal Work-Study, institutionally sponsored loans, and scholarships/grants available. Financial award application deadline: 3/2. *Faculty research:* Pulmonary functioning, feedback and practice structure, strength training, history and politics of sports, special population research issues. *Unit head:* Dr. Sharon R. Guthrie, Chair, 562-985-7487, Fax: 562-985-8067, E-mail: guthrie@csulb.edu. *Application contact:* Dr. Grant Hill, Graduate Advisor, 562-985-8856, Fax: 562-985-8067, E-mail: ghill@csulb.edu.

California State University, Los Angeles, Graduate Studies, College of Health and Human Services, Department of Kinesiology and Nutritional Sciences, Los Angeles, CA 90032-8530. Offers nutritional science (MS); physical education and kinesiology (MA, MS). *Accreditation:* AND. Part-time and evening/weekend programs available. *Faculty:* 5 full-time (3 women), 2 part-time/adjunct (1 woman). *Students:* 96 full-time (84 women), 40 part-time (34 women); includes 70 minority (6 Black or African American, non-Hispanic/Latino; 1 American Indian or Alaska Native, non-Hispanic/Latino; 36 Asian, non-Hispanic/Latino; 24 Hispanic/Latino; 3 Two or more races, non-Hispanic/Latino), 12 international. Average age 31. 152 applicants, 51% accepted, 44 enrolled. In 2011, 38 master's awarded. *Degree requirements:* For master's, comprehensive exam, project or thesis. *Entrance requirements:* For master's, minimum GPA of 2.75. Additional exam requirements/recommendations for international students: Required—TOEFL (minimum score 500 paper-based; 173 computer-based). *Application deadline:* For fall admission, 5/1 for domestic and international students. Applications are processed on a rolling basis. Application fee: $55. *Expenses:* Tuition, state resident: full-time $8225. *Financial support:* Federal Work-Study available. Support available to part-time students. Financial award application deadline: 3/1. *Unit head:* Dr. Nazareth Khodiguian, Chair, 323-343-4650, Fax: 323-343-6482, E-mail: nkhodig@calstatela.edu. *Application contact:* Dr. Karin Brown, Acting Associate Dean of Graduate Studies, 323-343-3820, Fax: 323-343-5653, E-mail: kbrown5@calstatela.edu. Web site: http://www.calstatela.edu/dept/pe/.

California State University, Sacramento, Office of Graduate Studies, College of Health and Human Services, Department of Kinesiology and Health Science, Sacramento, CA 95819-6073. Offers physical education (MS). *Accreditation:* APTA. Part-time programs available. *Faculty:* 20 full-time (7 women), 35 part-time/adjunct (22 women). *Students:* 7 full-time, 32 part-time; includes 10 minority (1 Black or African American, non-Hispanic/Latino; 2 Asian, non-Hispanic/Latino; 3 Hispanic/Latino; 2 Native Hawaiian or other Pacific Islander, non-Hispanic/Latino; 2 Two or more races, non-Hispanic/Latino). Average age 28. 47 applicants, 51% accepted, 15 enrolled. In 2011, 10 master's awarded. *Degree requirements:* For master's, thesis or project; writing proficiency exam. *Entrance requirements:* Additional exam requirements/recommendations for international students: Required—TOEFL. *Application deadline:* For fall admission, 1/28 for domestic students, 3/1 for international students; for spring admission, 9/30 for international students. Applications are processed on a rolling basis. Application fee: $55. Electronic applications accepted. *Financial support:* Research assistantships, teaching assistantships, career-related internships or fieldwork, and Federal Work-Study available. Support available to part-time students. Financial award application deadline: 3/1; financial award applicants required to submit FAFSA. *Unit head:* Joan Neide, Chair, 916-278-5383, Fax: 916-278-7664, E-mail: neidej@csus.edu. *Application contact:* Jose Martinez, Outreach and Graduate Diversity Coordinator, 916-278-6470, Fax: 916-278-5669, E-mail: martinj@skymail.csus.edu. Web site: http://www.csus.edu/hhs/khs.

California State University, Stanislaus, College of Education, Program in Education (MA), Turlock, CA 95382. Offers curriculum and instruction (MA), including education technology, elementary education, multilingual education, physical education, reading, secondary education, special education; school administration (MA); school counseling (MA). Part-time and evening/weekend programs available. *Degree requirements:* For master's, comprehensive exam (for some programs), thesis (for some programs). *Entrance requirements:* For master's, MAT, GRE, or CBEST (varies by concentration), 3 letters of recommendation, personal statement. Additional exam requirements/recommendations for international students: Required—TOEFL (minimum score 550 paper-based; 213 computer-based). *Application deadline:* For fall admission, 5/1 for domestic students; for spring admission, 1/7 for domestic students. Application fee: $55. Electronic applications accepted. *Expenses: Required fees:* $4616 per year. *Financial support:* Federal Work-Study available. Financial award application deadline: 3/1; financial award applicants required to submit FAFSA. *Faculty research:* Children's perspectives on historical events, method elementary schools dual language education, K-12 reading and CYRM programs. *Unit head:* Dr. Kathy Norman, Dean, College of Education, 209-667-3652, Fax: 209-664-6613, E-mail: coe@csustan.edu. *Application contact:* Graduate School, 209-667-3129, Fax: 209-664-7025, E-mail: graduate_school@csustan.edu. Web site: http://www.csustan.edu/COE/.

Campbell University, Graduate and Professional Programs, School of Education, Buies Creek, NC 27506. Offers administration (MSA); community counseling (MA); elementary education (M Ed); English education (M Ed); interdisciplinary studies (M Ed); mathematics education (M Ed); middle grades education (M Ed); physical education (M Ed); school counseling (M Ed); secondary education (M Ed); social science education (M Ed). *Accreditation:* NCATE. Part-time and evening/weekend programs available. *Degree requirements:* For master's, comprehensive exam. *Entrance requirements:* For master's, GRE General Test, minimum GPA of 2.7. *Faculty research:* Spiritual values and wellness issues in counseling, stress and professional burnout among counselors, thinking strategies, leadership, adaptive technology.

Canisius College, Graduate Division, School of Education and Human Services, Department of Kinesiology, Buffalo, NY 14208-1098. Offers health and human performance (MS Ed); physical education (MS Ed); physical education birth -12 (MS Ed). Part-time and evening/weekend programs available. Postbaccalaureate distance learning degree programs offered (minimal on-campus study). *Faculty:* 11 full-time (1 woman), 14 part-time/adjunct (4 women). *Students:* 78 full-time (35 women), 159 part-time (61 women); includes 13 minority (7 Black or African American, non-Hispanic/Latino; 2 American Indian or Alaska Native, non-Hispanic/Latino; 1 Asian, non-Hispanic/Latino; 3 Two or more races, non-Hispanic/Latino), 23 international. Average age 29. 107 applicants, 80% accepted, 66 enrolled. In 2011, 106 master's awarded. *Degree requirements:* For master's, research project. *Entrance requirements:* For master's, GRE if cumulative GPA less than 2.7, transcripts, two letters of recommendation. Additional exam requirements/recommendations for international students: Required—TOEFL. *Application deadline:* Applications are processed on a rolling basis. Application fee: $25. Electronic applications accepted. *Financial support:* Career-related internships or fieldwork, Federal Work-Study, scholarships/grants, tuition waivers (partial), and unspecified assistantships available. Support available to part-time students. Financial award application deadline: 4/30; financial award applicants required to submit FAFSA. *Unit head:* Dr. Jeffrey Lindauer, Chair/Professor, Department of Kinesiology, 716-888-2196, E-mail: lindaue@canisius.edu. *Application contact:* Jim Bagwell, Director of Graduate Recruitment and Admissions, 716-888-2544, Fax: 716-888-3290, E-mail: bagwellj@canisius.edu. Web site: http://www.canisius.edu/newsevents/display_story.asp?iNewsID=6477.

Caribbean University, Graduate School, Bayamón, PR 00960-0493. Offers administration and supervision (MA Ed); criminal justice (MA); curriculum and instruction (MA Ed, PhD), including elementary education (MA Ed), English education (MA Ed), history education (MA Ed), mathematics education (MA Ed), primary education (MA Ed), science education (MA Ed), Spanish education (MA Ed); educational technology in instructional systems (MA Ed); gerontology (MSN); human resources (MBA); museology, archiving and art history (MA Ed); neonatal pediatrics (MSN); physical education (MA Ed); special education (MA Ed). *Entrance requirements:* For master's, interview, minimum GPA of 2.5.

Central Connecticut State University, School of Graduate Studies, School of Education and Professional Studies, Department of Physical Education and Human Performance, New Britain, CT 06050-4010. Offers physical education (MS, Certificate). Part-time and evening/weekend programs available. *Faculty:* 16 full-time (8 women), 30 part-time/adjunct (20 women). *Students:* 22 full-time (7 women), 32 part-time (10 women); includes 1 minority (Two or more races, non-Hispanic/Latino). Average age 28. 27 applicants, 70% accepted, 11 enrolled. In 2011, 19 master's, 1 other advanced degree awarded. *Degree requirements:* For master's, comprehensive exam, thesis or alternative; for Certificate, qualifying exam. *Entrance requirements:* For master's, minimum GPA of 2.7, bachelor's degree in physical education (preferred). Additional exam requirements/recommendations for international students: Required—TOEFL (minimum score 550 paper-based; 213 computer-based). *Application deadline:* For fall admission, 6/1 for domestic students, 5/1 for international students; for spring admission, 11/1 for domestic and international students. Applications are processed on a rolling basis. Application fee: $50. Electronic applications accepted. *Expenses: Tuition, area resident:* Full-time $5137; part-time $482 per credit. Tuition, state resident: full-time $7707; part-time $494 per credit. Tuition, nonresident: full-time $14,311; part-time $494 per credit. *Required fees:* $3865. One-time fee: $62 part-time. *Financial support:* In 2011–12, 8 students received support, including 3 research assistantships; career-related internships or fieldwork, Federal Work-Study, scholarships/grants, and unspecified assistantships also available. Support available to part-time students. Financial award application deadline: 4/15; financial award applicants required to submit FAFSA. *Faculty research:* Exercise science, athletic training, preparation of physical education for schools. *Unit head:* Dr. David Harackiewicz, Chair, 860-832-2155, E-mail: harackiewicz@ccsu.edu. *Application contact:* Patricia Gardner, Associate Director of Graduate Studies, 860-832-2350, Fax: 860-832-2352, E-mail: graduateadmissions@ccsu.edu. Web site: http://www.education.ccsu.edu/Departments/Physical_Education_and_Human_Performance/.

Central Michigan University, College of Graduate Studies, The Herbert H. and Grace A. Dow College of Health Professions, Department of Physical Education and Sport, Mount Pleasant, MI 48859. Offers physical education (MA), including athletic administration, coaching, exercise science, teaching; sport administration (MA). Part-time programs available. *Degree requirements:* For master's, thesis or alternative. Electronic applications accepted. *Faculty research:* Athletic administration and sport management, performance enhancing substance use in sport, computer applications for sport managers, mental skill development for ultimate performance, teaching methods.

Central Washington University, Graduate Studies and Research, College of Education and Professional Studies, Department of Physical Education, School and Public Health, Ellensburg, WA 98926. Offers athletic administration (MS); health and physical education (MS). Part-time programs available. *Faculty:* 15 full-time (7 women). *Students:* 12 full-time (2 women), 12 part-time (4 women); includes 1 minority (Hispanic/Latino). 4 applicants, 75% accepted, 3 enrolled. In 2011, 12 master's awarded. *Application deadline:* For fall admission, 2/1 priority date for domestic students; for winter admission, 10/1 for domestic students; for spring admission, 1/1 for domestic students. Applications are processed on a rolling basis. Application fee: $50. Electronic applications accepted. *Expenses:* Tuition, state resident: full-time $8112; part-time $270 per credit. Tuition, nonresident: full-time $18,069; part-time $602 per credit. *Required fees:* $924. *Financial support:* In 2011–12, 5 teaching assistantships (averaging $9,234 per year) were awarded; career-related internships or fieldwork, Federal Work-Study, scholarships/grants, health care benefits, and unspecified assistantships also available. Financial award applicants required to submit FAFSA. *Unit head:* Dr. Kirk Mathias, Graduate Coordinator, 509-963-1911. *Application contact:* Justine Eason, Admissions Program Coordinator, 509-963-3103, Fax: 509-963-1799, E-mail: masters@cwu.edu. Web site: http://www.cwu.edu/~pesph/.

Chicago State University, School of Graduate and Professional Studies, College of Education, Department of Health, Physical Education and Recreation, Chicago, IL 60628. Offers physical education (MS Ed). Part-time and evening/weekend programs available. Postbaccalaureate distance learning degree programs offered. *Degree requirements:* For master's, thesis optional. *Entrance requirements:* For master's, minimum GPA of 2.75. *Faculty research:* Sports psychology, recreation and leisure studies administration.

The Citadel, The Military College of South Carolina, Citadel Graduate College, Department of Health, Exercise, and Sport Science, Charleston, SC 29409. Offers health, exercise, and sport science (MS); physical education (MAT). *Accreditation:* NCATE. Part-time and evening/weekend programs available. *Faculty:* 7 full-time (2 women). *Students:* 13 full-time (7 women), 42 part-time (18 women); includes 11 minority (8 Black or African American, non-Hispanic/Latino; 2 Hispanic/Latino; 1 Two or more races, non-Hispanic/Latino), 1 international. Average age 26. In 2011, 21 master's awarded. *Degree requirements:* For master's, comprehensive exam, thesis optional. *Entrance requirements:* For master's, GRE (minimum score 900) or MAT (minimum score 396), minimum undergraduate GPA of 2.5, 3 letters of recommendation, resume detailing previous work experience (for MS only). Additional exam requirements/recommendations for international students: Required—TOEFL (minimum score 550 paper-based; 213 computer-based; 79 iBT). *Application deadline:* Applications are processed on a rolling basis. Application fee: $30. Electronic applications accepted. *Expenses: Tuition, area resident:* Part-time $501 per credit hour. Tuition, state resident: part-time $501 per credit hour. Tuition, nonresident: part-time $824 per credit hour. *Required fees:* $40 per term. One-time fee: $30. *Financial support:* Career-related internships or fieldwork, health care benefits, and unspecified assistantships available. Support available to part-time students. Financial award application deadline: 7/1; financial award applicants required to submit FAFSA. *Faculty research:* Risk management in sport and physical activity programs, school-wide physical activity programs, exercise intervention among HIV-infected individuals, factors influencing motor skill in SC physical education programs, effect of mouthpiece use on human performance. *Unit head:* Dr. Dena Garner, Interim Department Head, 843-953-5060, Fax: 843-953-6798, E-mail: dena.garner@citadel.edu. *Application contact:* Dr. Steve A. Nida, Associate Provost, The Citadel Graduate College, 843-953-5089, Fax: 843-953-7630, E-mail: cgc@citadel.edu. Web site: http://www.citadel.edu/hess/index.htm.

The Citadel, The Military College of South Carolina, Citadel Graduate College, School of Education, Program in Secondary Education, Charleston, SC 29409. Offers biology (MAT); English language arts (MAT); mathematics (MAT); mathematics education (MAE); physical education (MAT); social studies (MAT). *Accreditation:* NCATE. Part-time and evening/weekend programs available. *Faculty:* 12 full-time (8 women), 9 part-time/adjunct (4 women). *Students:* 21 full-time (11 women), 51 part-time (25 women); includes 10 minority (7 Black or African American, non-Hispanic/Latino; 2 Asian, non-Hispanic/Latino; 1 Hispanic/Latino). Average age 31. In 2011, 34 master's awarded. *Degree requirements:* For master's, comprehensive exam, internship. *Entrance requirements:* For master's, GRE (minimum score 900) or MAT (minimum score 396), minimum undergraduate GPA of 2.5. Additional exam requirements/recommendations for international students: Required—TOEFL (minimum score 550 paper-based; 213 computer-based). *Application deadline:* Applications are processed on a rolling basis. Application fee: $30. Electronic applications accepted. *Expenses: Tuition, area resident:* Part-time $501 per credit hour. Tuition, state resident: part-time $501 per credit hour. Tuition, nonresident: part-time $824 per credit hour. *Required fees:* $40 per term. One-time fee: $30. *Financial support:* Career-related internships or fieldwork, health care benefits, and unspecified assistantships available. Support available to part-time students. Financial award application deadline: 7/1; financial award applicants required to submit FAFSA. *Unit head:* Dr. Kathryn A. Richardson-Jones, Coordinator, 843-953-3163, Fax: 843-953-7258, E-mail: kathryn.jones@citadel.edu. *Application contact:* Dr. Steve A. Nida, Associate Provost, The Citadel Graduate College, 843-953-5089, Fax: 843-953-7630, E-mail: cgc@citadel.edu. Web site: http://www.citadel.edu/education/teacher-education/mat-master-of-arts-in-teaching.html.

Cleveland State University, College of Graduate Studies, College of Education and Human Services, Department of Health, Physical Education, Recreation and Dance, Cleveland, OH 44115. Offers community health education (M Ed); exercise science (M Ed); human performance (M Ed); physical education pedagogy (M Ed); public health (MPH); school health education (M Ed); sport and exercise psychology (M Ed); sports management (M Ed). Part-time programs available. *Faculty:* 7 full-time (4 women), 3 part-time/adjunct (2 women). *Students:* 40 full-time (22 women), 91 part-time (48 women); includes 17 minority (15 Black or African American, non-Hispanic/Latino; 1 Asian, non-Hispanic/Latino; 1 Hispanic/Latino), 17 international. Average age 28. 138 applicants, 80% accepted, 60 enrolled. In 2011, 30 master's awarded. *Degree requirements:* For master's, comprehensive exam, thesis optional. *Entrance requirements:* For master's, GRE General Test or MAT (if undergraduate GPA less than 2.75), minimum undergraduate GPA of 2.75. Additional exam requirements/recommendations for international students: Required—TOEFL (minimum score 525 paper-based; 197 computer-based), IELTS (minimum score 6). *Application deadline:* For fall admission, 7/15 priority date for domestic students; for spring admission, 12/15 priority date for domestic students. Applications are processed on a rolling basis. Application fee: $30. Electronic applications accepted. *Expenses:* Tuition, state resident: full-time $6416; part-time $494 per credit hour. Tuition, nonresident: full-time $12,074; part-time $929 per credit hour. *Financial support:* In 2011–12, 6 research assistantships with full and partial tuition reimbursements (averaging $3,480 per year), 1 teaching assistantship with full and partial tuition reimbursement (averaging $3,480 per year) were awarded; career-related internships or fieldwork, tuition waivers (full), and unspecified assistantships also available. Financial award application deadline: 3/15. *Faculty research:* Bone density, marketing fitness centers, motor development of disabled, online learning and survey research. *Unit head:* Dr. Sheila M. Patterson, Chairperson, 216-687-4870, Fax: 216-687-5410, E-mail: s.m.patterson@csuohio.edu. *Application contact:* Deborah L. Brown, Interim Assistant Director, Graduate Admissions, 216-523-7572, Fax: 216-687-5400, E-mail: d.l.brown@csuohio.edu. Web site: http://www.csuohio.edu/coehs/departments/hperd.

The College at Brockport, State University of New York, School of Health and Human Performance, Department of Kinesiology, Sports Studies and Physical Education, Brockport, NY 14420-2997. Offers adapted physical education (AGC); physical education (MS Ed), including adapted physical education, athletic administration, teacher education/pedagogy. Part-time programs available. *Students:* 17 full-time (14 women), 45 part-time (16 women); includes 2 minority (both Hispanic/Latino). 42 applicants, 69% accepted, 21 enrolled. In 2011, 41 master's awarded. *Degree requirements:* For master's, thesis or alternative. *Entrance requirements:* For master's, minimum GPA of 3.0; statement of objectives. Additional exam requirements/recommendations for international students: Required—TOEFL (minimum score 550 paper-based; 213 computer-based; 79 iBT). *Application deadline:* For fall admission, 4/15 priority date for domestic students, 4/15 for international students; for spring admission, 11/15 priority date for domestic students, 11/15 for international students. Application fee: $80. Electronic applications accepted. *Financial support:* In 2011–12, 1 research assistantship with full tuition reimbursement (averaging $6,200 per year), 5 teaching assistantships with full tuition reimbursements (averaging $6,000 per year) were awarded; Federal Work-Study, scholarships/grants, and unspecified assistantships also available. Support available to part-time students. Financial award application deadline: 3/15; financial award applicants required to submit FAFSA. *Faculty research:* Athletic administration, adapted physical education, physical education curriculum, physical education teaching/coaching, children's physical activity. *Unit head:* Dr. Susan C. Petersen, Chairperson, 585-395-5332, Fax: 585-395-2771, E-mail: speterse@brockport.edu. *Application contact:* Dr. Cathy Houston-Wilson, Graduate Program Director, 585-395-5352, Fax: 585-395-2771, E-mail: chouston@brockport.edu. Web site: http://www.brockport.edu/graduate/.

The College of New Jersey, Graduate Studies, School of Nursing, Health and Exercise Science, Department of Health and Exercise Science, Program in Health Education, Ewing, NJ 08628. Offers health (MAT); physical education (M Ed). *Accreditation:* NCATE. Part-time programs available. *Degree requirements:* For master's, comprehensive exam. *Entrance requirements:* For master's, GRE, minimum GPA of 3.0 in field or 2.75 overall. Additional exam requirements/recommendations for international students: Required—TOEFL. Electronic applications accepted.

The College of New Jersey, Graduate Studies, School of Nursing, Health and Exercise Science, Department of Health and Exercise Science, Program in Physical Education, Ewing, NJ 08628. Offers M Ed, MAT. Part-time programs available. *Degree requirements:* For master's, comprehensive exam. *Entrance requirements:* For master's, GRE, minimum GPA of 2.75 overall or 3.0 in field. Additional exam requirements/recommendations for international students: Required—TOEFL. Electronic applications accepted.

Colorado State University–Pueblo, College of Education, Engineering and Professional Studies, Education Program, Pueblo, CO 81001-4901. Offers art education (M Ed); foreign language education (M Ed); health and physical education (M Ed); instructional technology (M Ed); linguistically diverse education (M Ed); music education (M Ed); special education (M Ed). *Accreditation:* Teacher Education Accreditation Council. Part-time programs available. *Degree requirements:* For master's, portfolio. *Entrance requirements:* For master's, 3 recommendations, teaching license. Additional exam requirements/recommendations for international students: Required—TOEFL (minimum score 500 paper-based; 173 computer-based). Electronic applications accepted. *Faculty research:* Portfolio assessment, math education, science education.

Columbus State University, Graduate Studies, College of Education and Health Professions, Department of Teacher Education, Columbus, GA 31907-5645. Offers accomplished teaching (M Ed); early childhood education (M Ed, MAT, Ed S); health and physical education (M Ed, MAT); middle grades education (M Ed, MAT, Ed S); school library media (M Ed, MAT); secondary education (M Ed, MAT, Ed S), including English/language arts (M Ed, Ed S), general science (M Ed), mathematics (M Ed), social science (M Ed); special education (M Ed, Ed S), including general curriculum (M Ed). *Accreditation:* NCATE. Part-time and evening/weekend programs available. Postbaccalaureate distance learning degree programs offered (minimal on-campus study). *Degree requirements:* For master's, thesis, exit exam; for Ed S, thesis or alternative. *Entrance requirements:* For master's, GRE General Test, minimum GPA of 2.75; for Ed S, GRE General Test. Additional exam requirements/recommendations for international students: Required—TOEFL (minimum score 550 paper-based; 213 computer-based; 79 iBT). Electronic applications accepted.

Concordia University, School of Arts and Sciences, Irvine, CA 92612-3299. Offers coaching and athletic administration (MA). Part-time and evening/weekend programs available. Postbaccalaureate distance learning degree programs offered (no on-campus study). *Faculty:* 7 full-time (2 women), 18 part-time/adjunct (2 women). *Students:* 353 full-time (81 women), 226 part-time (50 women); includes 134 minority (72 Black or African American, non-Hispanic/Latino; 1 American Indian or Alaska Native, non-Hispanic/Latino; 7 Asian, non-Hispanic/Latino; 42 Hispanic/Latino; 3 Native Hawaiian or other Pacific Islander, non-Hispanic/Latino; 9 Two or more races, non-Hispanic/Latino). Average age 34. 168 applicants, 100% accepted, 156 enrolled. In 2011, 228 master's awarded. *Degree requirements:* For master's, culminating project. *Entrance requirements:* For master's, official college/university transcript(s); signed statement of intent. Additional exam requirements/recommendations for international students: Required—TOEFL (minimum score 550 paper-based; 213 computer-based; 79 iBT). *Application deadline:* For fall admission, 8/10 for domestic students, 6/1 for international students; for spring admission, 2/15 for domestic students, 10/1 for international students. Application fee: $50 ($125 for international students). Electronic applications accepted. *Expenses:* Contact institution. *Financial support:* In 2011–12, 15 students received support. Tuition waivers (full and partial) and unspecified assistantships available. Financial award applicants required to submit FAFSA. *Unit head:* Dr. Timothy Preuss, Dean, 949-214-3286, E-mail: tim.preuss@cui.edu. *Application contact:* Chris Lewis, Associate Director of Graduate Admissions, 949-214-3025, Fax: 949-854-6894, E-mail: chris.lewis@cui.edu. Web site: http://www.cui.edu.

Delta State University, Graduate Programs, College of Education, Division of Health, Physical Education, and Recreation, Cleveland, MS 38733-0001. Offers health, physical education, and recreation (M Ed); sport and human performance (MS). Part-time and evening/weekend programs available. *Degree requirements:* For master's, thesis optional. *Entrance requirements:* For master's, GRE General Test or MAT, Class A teaching certificate. *Expenses:* Tuition, state resident: full-time $4702; part-time $294 per credit hour. Tuition, nonresident: full-time $12,516; part-time $760 per credit hour. *Required fees:* $586. *Faculty research:* Blood pressure, body fat, power and reaction time, learning disorders for athletes, effects of walking.

DePaul University, College of Education, Chicago, IL 60106. Offers bilingual bicultural education (M Ed, MA); counseling (M Ed, MA), including college student development, community counseling, school counseling; curriculum studies (M Ed, MA, Ed D); early childhood education (M Ed, MA); educational leadership (M Ed, MA, Ed D), including administration and supervision (M Ed, MA), physical education (M Ed, MA); middle school mathematics education (MS); reading specialist (M Ed, MA); social and cultural foundations in education (M Ed, MA), including curriculum studies/development (MA); special education (M Ed, MA); teaching and learning (M Ed, MA), including elementary education, secondary education; world languages education (M Ed, MA). Part-time and evening/weekend programs available. *Faculty:* 49 full-time (28 women), 94 part-time/adjunct (60 women). *Students:* 894 full-time (707 women), 473 part-time (361 women); includes 349 minority (159 Black or African American, non-Hispanic/Latino; 3 American Indian or Alaska Native, non-Hispanic/Latino; 45 Asian, non-Hispanic/Latino; 115 Hispanic/Latino; 2 Native Hawaiian or other Pacific Islander, non-Hispanic/Latino; 25 Two or more races, non-Hispanic/Latino), 21 international. Average age 30. 872 applicants, 64% accepted, 325 enrolled. In 2011, 499 master's, 10 doctorates awarded. *Median time to degree:* Of those who began their doctoral program in fall 2003, 32% received their degree in 8 years or less. *Degree requirements:* For master's, thesis/dissertation (for MA); capstone course or paper (for M Ed); for doctorate, thesis/dissertation. *Entrance requirements:* For master's, interview, minimum GPA of 2.75, 2 letters of recommendation, bachelor's degree conferred by accredited college or university; for doctorate, interview, master's degree, writing sample, 3 letters of recommendation. Additional exam requirements/recommendations for international students: Required—TOEFL (minimum score 550 paper-based; 213 computer-based; 80 iBT). *Application deadline:* For fall admission, 8/15 priority date for domestic students; for winter admission, 12/1 priority date for domestic students; for spring admission, 3/1 priority date for domestic students. Applications are processed on a rolling basis. Application fee: $40. Electronic applications accepted. *Financial support:* In 2011–12, 163 students received support, including 15 research assistantships with full tuition reimbursements available (averaging $6,375 per year); career-related internships or fieldwork, Federal Work-Study, scholarships/grants, and unspecified assistantships also available. Support available to part-time students. Financial award application deadline: 12/31; financial award applicants required to submit FAFSA. *Faculty research:* Reflective teaching, children at risk, loss, ethnicity, urban education. *Total annual research expenditures:* $916,310. *Unit head:* Dr. Paul Zionts, Dean, 773-325-7581, Fax: 773-325-7713, E-mail: pzionts@depaul.edu. *Application contact:* Brandon Washington, Enrollment Management Coordinator, 773-325-1152, Fax: 773-325-2270, E-mail: bwashin3@depaul.edu. Web site: http://education.depaul.edu.

East Carolina University, Graduate School, College of Education, Department of Business and Information Technologies Education, Greenville, NC 27858-4353. Offers business education (MA Ed); elementary education (MAT); English education (MAT); family and consumer science (MAT); health education (MAT); Hispanic studies (MAT); history education (MAT); marketing education (MA Ed); middle grades education (MAT); music education (MAT); physical education (MAT); science education (MAT); special education (MAT), including general curriculum; vocation education (MS). *Accreditation:* NCATE. Part-time and evening/weekend programs available. Postbaccalaureate distance learning degree programs offered (no on-campus study). *Degree requirements:* For master's, comprehensive exam, thesis optional. *Entrance requirements:* For master's, GRE or MAT, minimum GPA of 2.5, bachelor's degree in related field, teaching license (MA Ed). Additional exam requirements/recommendations for international students: Required—TOEFL. *Application deadline:* For fall admission, 6/1 priority date for domestic students. Applications are processed on a rolling basis. Application fee: $50. *Expenses:* Tuition, state resident: full-time $3557; part-time $444.63 per semester hour. Tuition, nonresident: full-time $14,351; part-time $1793.88 per semester hour. *Required fees:* $2016; $252 per semester hour. Part-time tuition and fees vary according to course load, campus/location and program. *Financial support:* Federal Work-Study available. Support available to part-time students. Financial award application deadline: 6/1. *Unit head:* Dr. Ivan G. Wallace, Chair, 252-328-6983, Fax: 252-328-6835, E-mail: wallacei@ecu.edu. *Application contact:* Dean of Graduate School, 252-328-6012, Fax: 252-328-6071, E-mail: gradschool@ecu.edu. Web site: http://www.ecu.edu/cs-educ/bite/index.cfm.

East Carolina University, Graduate School, College of Health and Human Performance, Department of Kinesiology, Greenville, NC 27858-4353. Offers adapted physical education (MA Ed, MS); bioenergetics and exercise science (PhD); biomechanics (MS); exercise physiology (MS); physical activity promotion (MS); physical education (MA Ed, MAT); physical education clinical supervision (Certificate); physical education pedagogy (MA Ed, MS); sport and exercise psychology (MS); sport management (Certificate). *Degree requirements:* For master's, comprehensive exam, thesis optional; for doctorate, comprehensive exam, thesis/dissertation. *Entrance requirements:* For master's, GRE General Test or MAT; for doctorate, GRE. Additional exam requirements/recommendations for international students: Required—TOEFL. *Application deadline:* For fall admission, 2/1 priority date for domestic students, 2/1 for international students. Applications are processed on a rolling basis. Application fee: $50. *Expenses:* Tuition, state resident: full-time $3557; part-time $444.63 per semester hour. Tuition, nonresident: full-time $14,351; part-time $1793.88 per semester hour. *Required fees:* $2016; $252 per semester hour. Part-time tuition and fees vary according to course load, campus/location and program. *Financial support:* Research assistantships with tuition reimbursements and teaching assistantships available. Support available to part-time students. Financial award application deadline: 2/1. *Faculty research:* Diabetes metabolism, pediatric obesity, biomechanics of arthritis, physical activity measurement. *Unit head:* Dr. Stacey Altman, Chair, 252-328-2973, E-mail: altmans@ecu.edu.

Eastern Kentucky University, The Graduate School, College of Education, Department of Curriculum and Instruction, Program in Secondary and Higher Education, Richmond, KY 40475-3102. Offers secondary education (MA Ed), including agricultural education, art education, biological sciences education, business education, English education, geography education, history education, home economics education, industrial education, mathematical sciences education, physical education, school health education. *Accreditation:* NCATE. Part-time programs available. *Entrance requirements:* For master's, GRE General Test, minimum GPA of 2.5.

Eastern Kentucky University, The Graduate School, College of Health Sciences, Department of Exercise and Sport Science, Richmond, KY 40475-3102. Offers exercise and sport science (MS); exercise and wellness (MS); sports administration (MS). Part-time programs available. *Entrance requirements:* For master's, GRE General Test (minimum score 700 verbal and quantitative), minimum GPA of 2.5 (for most), minimum GPA of 3.0 (analytical writing). *Faculty research:* Nutrition and exercise.

Eastern Michigan University, Graduate School, College of Health and Human Services, School of Health Promotion and Human Performance, Programs in Physical Education, Ypsilanti, MI 48197. Offers adapted physical education (MS); physical education pedagogy (MS). Part-time and evening/weekend programs available. Postbaccalaureate distance learning degree programs offered (minimal on-campus study). *Students:* 8 part-time (3 women); includes 1 minority (Black or African American, non-Hispanic/Latino). Average age 32. 1 applicant, 100% accepted, 1 enrolled. In 2011, 2 degrees awarded. *Degree requirements:* For master's, thesis or independent study project and comprehensive exams. *Entrance requirements:* Additional exam requirements/recommendations for international students: Required—TOEFL. *Application deadline:* For fall admission, 8/1 for domestic students, 5/1 for international students; for winter admission, 12/1 for domestic students, 10/1 for international students; for spring admission, 4/15 for domestic students, 3/1 for international students. Applications are processed on a rolling basis. Application fee: $35. *Expenses:* Tuition, state resident: full-time $10,367; part-time $432 per credit hour. Tuition, nonresident: full-time $20,435; part-time $851 per credit hour. *Required fees:* $39 per credit hour. $46 per semester. One-time fee: $100. Tuition and fees vary according to course level, degree level and reciprocity agreements. *Financial support:* Fellowships, research assistantships with full tuition reimbursements, teaching assistantships with full tuition reimbursements, career-related internships or fieldwork, Federal Work-Study, institutionally sponsored loans, scholarships/grants, tuition waivers (partial), and unspecified assistantships available. Support available to part-time students. Financial award applicants required to submit FAFSA. *Unit head:* Prof. Laura Sweet, Program Coordinator, 734-487-7120 Ext. 2722, Fax: 734-487-2024, E-mail: lsweet1@emich.edu. *Application contact:* Dr. Brenda Riemer, Chair, Graduate Programs, 734-487-0090 Ext. 2745, Fax: 734-487-2024, E-mail: briemer@emich.edu.

Eastern New Mexico University, Graduate School, College of Education and Technology, Department of Health and Physical Education, Portales, NM 88130. Offers physical education (MS), including sport administration, sport science. Part-time programs available. *Degree requirements:* For master's, comprehensive exam, thesis optional. *Entrance requirements:* For master's, minimum GPA of 3.0, 15 hours leveling courses without bachelor's degree in physical education, two references. Additional exam requirements/recommendations for international students: Required—TOEFL (minimum score 550 paper-based; 213 computer-based; 79 iBT), IELTS (minimum score 6). Electronic applications accepted.

Eastern Washington University, Graduate Studies, College of Arts, Letters and Education, Department of Physical Education, Health and Recreation, Cheney, WA 99004-2431. Offers exercise science (MS); sports and recreation administration (MS). *Faculty:* 14 full-time (5 women). *Students:* 28 full-time (9 women), 4 part-time (2 women); includes 4 minority (3 Black or African American, non-Hispanic/Latino; 1 Hispanic/Latino). Average age 29. 50 applicants, 48% accepted, 14 enrolled. In 2011, 7 master's awarded. *Degree requirements:* For master's, comprehensive exam, thesis or alternative. *Entrance requirements:* For master's, minimum GPA of 3.0. *Application deadline:* For fall admission, 4/1 priority date for domestic students; for spring admission, 1/15 for domestic students. Applications are processed on a rolling basis. Application fee: $50. *Financial support:* In 2011–12, 10 teaching assistantships with partial tuition reimbursements (averaging $6,624 per year) were awarded; career-related internships or fieldwork, Federal Work-Study, institutionally sponsored loans, and scholarships/grants also available. Support available to part-time students. Financial award application deadline: 2/1; financial award applicants required to submit FAFSA. *Unit head:* John Cogley, Chair, 509-359-2486, E-mail: john.cogley@mail.ewu.edu. *Application contact:* Dr. Jeni McNeal, Professor of Physical Education, Health and Recreation, 509-359-2872, Fax: 509-359-4833, E-mail: jeni_mcneal@hotmail.com.

East Stroudsburg University of Pennsylvania, Graduate School, College of Health Sciences, Department of Exercise Science, East Stroudsburg, PA 18301-2999. Offers cardiac rehabilitation and exercise science (MS). Part-time and evening/weekend programs available. *Degree requirements:* For master's, comprehensive exam, thesis or alternative, computer literacy. *Entrance requirements:* Additional exam requirements/recommendations for international students: Required—TOEFL (minimum score 560 paper-based; 220 computer-based; 83 iBT).

East Stroudsburg University of Pennsylvania, Graduate School, College of Health Sciences, Department of Physical Education, East Stroudsburg, PA 18301-2999. Offers health and physical education (M Ed). *Degree requirements:* For master's, computer literacy, portfolio exhibition as exiting research project. *Entrance requirements:* For master's, teacher certification in physical education or health and physical education. Additional exam requirements/recommendations for international students: Required—TOEFL (minimum score 560 paper-based; 220 computer-based; 83 iBT) or IELTS.

East Tennessee State University, School of Graduate Studies, College of Education, Department of Kinesiology, Leisure and Sport Sciences, Johnson City, TN 37614. Offers exercise physiology and performance (MA); sport management (MA); sport physiology and performance (PhD), including sport performance, sport physiology. Part-time and evening/weekend programs available. *Faculty:* 10 full-time (1 woman). *Students:* 83 full-time (26 women), 8 part-time (2 women); includes 6 minority (2 Black or African American, non-Hispanic/Latino; 2 Asian, non-Hispanic/Latino; 2 Two or more races, non-Hispanic/Latino), 8 international. Average age 25. 113 applicants, 51% accepted, 57 enrolled. In 2011, 26 master's awarded. Terminal master's awarded for partial completion of doctoral program. *Degree requirements:* For master's, comprehensive exam, thesis optional, thesis or internship; for doctorate, comprehensive exam, thesis/dissertation, 2 semesters of full-time residency. *Entrance requirements:* For master's, GRE General Test, major or minor in physical education or equivalent, interview, minimum GPA of 2.7, resume, three letters of recommendation; for doctorate, GRE General Test, minimum GPA of 3.4 (for applicants with master's degree) or 3.0 (for applicants with bachelor's degree), curriculum vitae or resume, interview, four letters of recommendation. Additional exam requirements/recommendations for international students: Required—TOEFL (minimum score 550 paper-based; 213 computer-based; 79 iBT). *Application deadline:* For fall admission, 6/1 for domestic students, 4/30 for international students; for spring admission, 11/1 for domestic students, 9/30 for international students. Application fee: $35 ($45 for international students). Electronic applications accepted. *Expenses:* Tuition, state resident: full-time $7312; part-time $350 per credit hour. Tuition, nonresident: full-time $18,490; part-time $621 per credit hour. *Required fees:* $63 per credit hour. Tuition and fees vary according to course load and program. *Financial support:* In 2011–12, 52 students received support, including 6 fellowships with full tuition reimbursements available (averaging $17,250 per year), 2 research assistantships with full tuition reimbursements available (averaging $11,250 per year), 14 teaching assistantships with full tuition reimbursements available (averaging $6,000 per year); career-related internships or fieldwork, institutionally sponsored loans, scholarships/grants, and unspecified assistantships also available. Financial award application deadline: 7/1; financial award applicants required to submit FAFSA. *Faculty research:* Methods of training for individual and team sports, enhancing acute sport performance, fatigue management in athletes, risk management, facilities management, motorsport. *Total annual research expenditures:* $500. *Unit head:* Dr.

Physical Education

Christopher Ayers, Chair, 423-439-4265, Fax: 423-439-7560, E-mail: ayersc@etsu.edu. *Application contact:* Linda Raines, Graduate Specialist, 423-439-6158, Fax: 423-439-5624, E-mail: raineslt@etsu.edu.

Emporia State University, Graduate School, Teachers College, Department of Health, Physical Education and Recreation, Emporia, KS 66801-5087. Offers physical education (MS). Part-time programs available. Postbaccalaureate distance learning degree programs offered (no on-campus study). *Faculty:* 19 full-time (13 women). *Students:* 23 full-time (9 women), 160 part-time (61 women); includes 21 minority (8 Black or African American, non-Hispanic/Latino; 1 Asian, non-Hispanic/Latino; 9 Hispanic/Latino; 1 Native Hawaiian or other Pacific Islander, non-Hispanic/Latino; 2 Two or more races, non-Hispanic/Latino), 1 international. 47 applicants, 66% accepted, 30 enrolled. In 2011, 92 master's awarded. *Degree requirements:* For master's, comprehensive exam or thesis. *Entrance requirements:* For master's, bachelor's degree in physical education, health, and recreation; letters of recommendation. Additional exam requirements/recommendations for international students: Required—TOEFL (minimum score 520 paper-based; 133 computer-based; 68 iBT). *Application deadline:* For fall admission, 8/15 priority date for domestic students. Applications are processed on a rolling basis. Application fee: $30 ($75 for international students). Electronic applications accepted. *Expenses:* Tuition, state resident: full-time $2342; part-time $195 per credit hour. Tuition, nonresident: full-time $7254; part-time $605 per credit hour. *Required fees:* $66 per credit hour. Tuition and fees vary according to campus/location. *Financial support:* In 2011–12, 5 teaching assistantships with full tuition reimbursements (averaging $7,059 per year) were awarded; career-related internships or fieldwork, Federal Work-Study, institutionally sponsored loans, health care benefits, and unspecified assistantships also available. Financial award application deadline: 3/15; financial award applicants required to submit FAFSA. *Unit head:* Dr. Joan Brewer, Chair, 620-341-5926, E-mail: jbrewer@emporia.edu. *Application contact:* Mary Sewell, Admissions Coordinator, 800-950-GRAD, Fax: 620-341-5909, E-mail: msewell@emporia.edu. Web site: http://www.emporia.edu/hper/.

Florida Agricultural and Mechanical University, Division of Graduate Studies, Research, and Continuing Education, College of Education, Department of Health, Physical Education, and Recreation, Tallahassee, FL 32307-3200. Offers M Ed, MS Ed. *Accreditation:* NCATE. Part-time and evening/weekend programs available. *Degree requirements:* For master's, thesis optional. *Entrance requirements:* For master's, GRE General Test, minimum GPA of 3.0. Additional exam requirements/recommendations for international students: Required—TOEFL. *Faculty research:* Administration/curriculum, work behavior, psychology.

Florida International University, College of Education, Department of Curriculum and Instruction, Miami, FL 33199. Offers art education (MAT, MS, Ed D); curriculum and instruction (Ed S); curriculum development (MS); curriculum studies (PhD); early childhood education (MS, Ed D); elementary education (MS, Ed D); English education (MAT, MS, Ed D); foreign language education - teaching English to speakers of other languages (TESOL) (MS, Certificate), including foreign language education (Certificate), teaching English (MS); French education - initial teacher preparation (MAT); international and intercultural development education (Ed D); international and intercultural developmental education (MS); language, literacy and culture (PhD); learning technologies (MS, Ed D, PhD); mathematics education (MAT, MS, Ed D, PhD); modern language education/bilingual education (MS, Ed D); physical education (MS); reading education (MS, Ed D); science education (MAT, MS, Ed D, PhD); social studies education (MAT, MS, Ed D); Spanish education - initial teacher preparation (MAT); special education (MS). Part-time and evening/weekend programs available. *Degree requirements:* For doctorate, comprehensive exam, thesis/dissertation. *Entrance requirements:* For master's, GRE General Test, Florida General Knowledge Test or Florida College Level Academic Skills Test; for doctorate and other advanced degree, GRE General Test. Additional exam requirements/recommendations for international students: Required—TOEFL (minimum score 550 paper-based; 213 computer-based; 80 iBT), IELTS (minimum score 6.3). Electronic applications accepted.

Florida State University, The Graduate School, College of Education, Department of Sport Management, Tallahassee, FL 32306. Offers MS, Ed D, PhD, Certificate. *Faculty:* 9 full-time (2 women). *Students:* 105 full-time (35 women), 36 part-time (18 women); includes 18 minority (9 Black or African American, non-Hispanic/Latino; 4 Asian, non-Hispanic/Latino; 5 Hispanic/Latino), 30 international. Average age 30. 176 applicants, 58% accepted, 62 enrolled. In 2011, 68 master's, 8 doctorates awarded. *Degree requirements:* For master's and Certificate, comprehensive exam, thesis optional; for doctorate, comprehensive exam, thesis/dissertation. *Entrance requirements:* For master's, doctorate, and Certificate, GRE General Test, minimum GPA of 3.0. Additional exam requirements/recommendations for international students: Required—TOEFL (minimum score 550 paper-based; 213 computer-based; 80 iBT). *Application deadline:* For fall admission, 7/1 for domestic and international students; for winter admission, 11/1 for domestic and international students; for spring admission, 3/1 for domestic and international students. Application fee: $30. Electronic applications accepted. *Expenses:* Tuition, state resident: full-time $9474; part-time $350.88 per credit hour. Tuition, nonresident: full-time $16,236; part-time $601.34 per credit hour. *Required fees:* $630 per semester. One-time fee: $20. Tuition and fees vary according to course load and campus/location. *Financial support:* In 2011–12, 2 research assistantships with full and partial tuition reimbursements, 54 teaching assistantships with full and partial tuition reimbursements were awarded; fellowships with full and partial tuition reimbursements, career-related internships or fieldwork, Federal Work-Study, scholarships/grants, health care benefits, and unspecified assistantships also available. Financial award application deadline: 1/15; financial award applicants required to submit FAFSA. *Faculty research:* Sport marketing, gender issues in sport, finances in sport industry, coaching. *Total annual research expenditures:* $48,242. *Unit head:* Dr. Jeffrey D. James, Chair, 850-644-9214, Fax: 850-644-0975, E-mail: jdjames@fsu.edu. *Application contact:* Sandra Auguste, Program Assistant, 850-644-4813, Fax: 850-644-0975, E-mail: sauguste@fsu.edu. Web site: http://www.fsu.edu/~smrmpe/.

Fort Hays State University, Graduate School, College of Health and Life Sciences, Department of Health and Human Performance, Hays, KS 67601-4099. Offers MS. Part-time programs available. *Degree requirements:* For master's, comprehensive exam, thesis optional. *Entrance requirements:* For master's, GRE General Test or MAT. Additional exam requirements/recommendations for international students: Required—TOEFL (minimum score 550 paper-based; 213 computer-based). Electronic applications accepted. *Faculty research:* Isoproterenol hydrochloride and exercise, dehydrogenase and high-density lipoprotein levels in athletics, venous blood parameters to adipose fat.

Gardner-Webb University, Graduate School, Department of Physical Education, Wellness, and Sport Studies, Boiling Springs, NC 28017. Offers sport science and pedagogy (MA). Part-time and evening/weekend programs available. *Faculty:* 2 full-time (1 woman). *Students:* 15 part-time (4 women); includes 5 minority (all Black or African American, non-Hispanic/Latino). Average age 25. 11 applicants, 100% accepted, 11 enrolled. In 2011, 3 master's awarded. *Degree requirements:* For master's, comprehensive exam. *Entrance requirements:* For master's, GRE General Test or NTE, PRAXIS, minimum GPA of 2.5. *Application deadline:* For fall admission, 8/1 priority date for domestic students. Applications are processed on a rolling basis. Application fee: $40. Electronic applications accepted. *Expenses: Tuition:* Full-time $6300; part-time $350 per credit hour. *Financial support:* Unspecified assistantships available. *Unit head:* Dr. Ken Baker, Chair, 704-406-4481, Fax: 704-406-4739. *Application contact:* Office of Graduate Admissions, 877-498-4723, Fax: 704-406-3895, E-mail: gradinfo@gardner-webb.edu.

Georgia College & State University, Graduate School, College of Health Sciences, Department of Kinesiology, Milledgeville, GA 31061. Offers health promotion (M Ed); human performance (M Ed); kinesiology (MAT); outdoor education (M Ed). *Accreditation:* NCATE (one or more programs are accredited). Part-time and evening/weekend programs available. *Students:* 31 full-time (13 women), 11 part-time (7 women); includes 8 minority (6 Black or African American, non-Hispanic/Latino; 2 Hispanic/Latino), 1 international. Average age 27. 32 applicants, 69% accepted, 16 enrolled. In 2011, 12 master's awarded. *Degree requirements:* For master's, comprehensive exam, thesis optional. *Entrance requirements:* For master's, GRE General Test or MAT, minimum GPA of 2.75 in upper-level undergraduate courses, 2 letters of reference. Additional exam requirements/recommendations for international students: Recommended—TOEFL (minimum score 550 paper-based; 213 computer-based; 79 iBT). *Application deadline:* For fall admission, 7/1 priority date for domestic students, 4/1 for international students; for spring admission, 11/15 priority date for domestic students, 9/1 for international students. Applications are processed on a rolling basis. Application fee: $40. Electronic applications accepted. *Expenses:* Tuition, state resident: full-time $4806; part-time $267 per credit hour. Tuition, nonresident: full-time $17,802; part-time $989 per credit hour. *Required fees:* $936 per semester. Tuition and fees vary according to course load and campus/location. *Financial support:* In 2011–12, 25 research assistantships with full tuition reimbursements were awarded; career-related internships or fieldwork and unspecified assistantships also available. Support available to part-time students. Financial award applicants required to submit FAFSA. *Unit head:* Dr. Lisa Griffin, Interim Chair, 478-445-4072, Fax: 478-445-1790, E-mail: lisa.griffin@gcsu.edu. *Application contact:* 800-342-0471, E-mail: grad-admit@gcsu.edu.

Georgia Southwestern State University, Graduate Studies, School of Education, Americus, GA 31709-4693. Offers early childhood education (M Ed, Ed S); health and physical education (M Ed); middle grades education (M Ed, Ed S); reading (M Ed); secondary education (M Ed); special education (M Ed). *Accreditation:* NCATE. *Degree requirements:* For master's, comprehensive exam. *Entrance requirements:* For master's, GRE General Test or MAT, minimum GPA of 2.5; for Ed S, GRE General Test or MAT, minimum graduate GPA of 3.25, M Ed from accredited college or university, 3 years teaching experience. Electronic applications accepted.

Georgia State University, College of Education, Department of Kinesiology and Health, Program in Health and Physical Education, Atlanta, GA 30302-3083. Offers M Ed. Part-time and evening/weekend programs available. *Degree requirements:* For master's, comprehensive exam. *Entrance requirements:* For master's, GRE General Test, minimum GPA of 2.5. *Faculty research:* Exercise science, teacher behavior.

Henderson State University, Graduate Studies, Teachers College, Department of Health, Physical Education, Recreation and Athletic Training, Arkadelphia, AR 71999-0001. Offers recreation (MS); sports administration (MS). Part-time programs available. *Entrance requirements:* For master's, GRE General Test or MAT, minimum GPA of 2.7. Additional exam requirements/recommendations for international students: Required—TOEFL (minimum score 550 paper-based; 213 computer-based); Recommended—IELTS (minimum score 6). Electronic applications accepted.

Hofstra University, School of Education, Health, and Human Services, Department of Physical Education and Sports Sciences, Hempstead, NY 11549. Offers adventure education (Advanced Certificate); health education (MS), including PK-12 teaching certification; physical education (MA, MS), including adventure education, curriculum (MA), strength and conditioning; sport science (MS), including adventure education (MA, MS), strength and conditioning (MA, MS). Part-time and evening/weekend programs available. *Students:* 81 full-time (34 women), 56 part-time (25 women); includes 12 minority (9 Black or African American, non-Hispanic/Latino; 1 Asian, non-Hispanic/Latino; 2 Hispanic/Latino), 1 international. Average age 27. 52 applicants, 96% accepted, 31 enrolled. In 2011, 80 master's awarded. *Degree requirements:* For master's, one foreign language, electronic portfolio, capstone project, minimum GPA of 3.0. *Entrance requirements:* For master's, interview, 2 letters of recommendation, essay. Additional exam requirements/recommendations for international students: Required—TOEFL (minimum score 550 paper-based; 213 computer-based; 80 iBT). *Application deadline:* Applications are processed on a rolling basis. Application fee: $70 ($75 for international students). Electronic applications accepted. *Expenses: Tuition:* Full-time $18,990; part-time $1055 per credit hour. *Required fees:* $970. Tuition and fees vary according to program. *Financial support:* In 2011–12, 49 students received support, including 19 fellowships with full and partial tuition reimbursements available (averaging $3,216 per year), 3 research assistantships with full and partial tuition reimbursements available (averaging $18,529 per year); Federal Work-Study, institutionally sponsored loans, scholarships/grants, tuition waivers (full and partial), and unspecified assistantships also available. Support available to part-time students. Financial award applicants required to submit FAFSA. *Faculty research:* After school programming, skill development and health behavior, energy expenditures in physical activities, cultural competence and health education, childhood obesity. *Unit head:* Dr. Carol L. Alberts, Chairperson, 516-463-5809, Fax: 516-463-6275, E-mail: hprcla@hofstra.edu. *Application contact:* Carol Drummer, Dean of Graduate Admissions, 516-463-4876, Fax: 516-463-4664, E-mail: gradstudent@hofstra.edu. Web site: http://www.hofstra.edu/education/.

Howard University, Graduate School, Department of Health, Human Performance and Leisure Studies, Washington, DC 20059-0002. Offers exercise physiology (MS); health education (MS); sports studies (MS), including sociology of sports, sports management; urban recreation (MS), including leisure studies. Part-time and evening/weekend programs available. *Degree requirements:* For master's, comprehensive exam, thesis. *Entrance requirements:* For master's, BS in human performance or related field. Additional exam requirements/recommendations for international students: Recommended—TOEFL. Electronic applications accepted. *Faculty research:* Health promotion, cardiovascular hypertension, physical activity, sport and human rights issues.

Humboldt State University, Academic Programs, College of Professional Studies, Department of Kinesiology and Recreation Administration, Arcata, CA 95521-8299. Offers athletic training education (MS); exercise science/wellness management (MS); pre-physical therapy (MS); teaching/coaching (MS). *Students:* 11 full-time (7 women), 10 part-time (6 women); includes 4 minority (1 American Indian or Alaska Native, non-Hispanic/Latino; 2 Hispanic/Latino; 1 Two or more races, non-Hispanic/Latino). Average age 28. 9 applicants, 100% accepted, 6 enrolled. In 2011, 7 master's awarded. *Degree requirements:* For master's, thesis or alternative. *Entrance requirements:* For master's, GMAT, minimum GPA of 2.5. Additional exam requirements/recommendations for international students: Required—TOEFL. *Application deadline:* For fall admission, 6/1 for domestic students; for spring admission, 12/2 for domestic students. Applications are processed on a rolling basis. Application fee: $55. *Expenses:* Tuition, state resident: full-time $6734. Tuition, nonresident: full-time $15,662; part-time $372 per credit. *Required fees:* $903. Tuition and fees vary according to program. *Financial support:*

Teaching assistantships, career-related internships or fieldwork, Federal Work-Study, and institutionally sponsored loans available. Financial award application deadline: 3/1; financial award applicants required to submit FAFSA. *Faculty research:* Human performance, adapted physical education, physical therapy. *Unit head:* Dr. Chris Hooper, Chair, 707-826-3853, Fax: 707-826-5451, E-mail: cah3@humboldt.edu. *Application contact:* Dr. Rock Braithwaite, Coordinator, 707-826-4543, Fax: 707-826-5451, E-mail: reb22@humboldt.edu. Web site: http://www.humboldt.edu/kra/.

Idaho State University, Office of Graduate Studies, College of Education, Department of Sports Science and Physical Education, Pocatello, ID 83209-8105. Offers physical education (MPE). Part-time programs available. *Degree requirements:* For master's, comprehensive exam (for some programs), thesis optional, internship, oral defense of dissertation, or written exams. *Entrance requirements:* For master's, MAT or GRE General Test, minimum GPA of 3.0 in upper division classes. Additional exam requirements/recommendations for international students: Required—TOEFL (minimum score 550 paper-based; 213 computer-based; 80 iBT). Electronic applications accepted. *Faculty research:* Gender and diversity; concussion awareness/sports medicine; legal aspects of athletic health care; sports psychology; exercise physiology; sports management and leadership; adapted activities; fitness, wellness, and nutrition; coaching perspectives; critical features of athletic activities.

Illinois State University, Graduate School, College of Applied Science and Technology, School of Kinesiology and Recreation, Normal, IL 61790-2200. Offers health education (MS); physical education (MS). *Degree requirements:* For master's, thesis or alternative. *Entrance requirements:* For master's, GRE General Test, minimum GPA of 2.6 in last 60 hours of course work. *Faculty research:* Influences on positive youth development through sport, country-wide health fitness project, graduate practicum in athletic training, perceived exertion and self-selected intensity during resistance exercise in younger and older.

Indiana State University, College of Graduate and Professional Studies, College of Nursing, Health and Human Services, Department of Physical Education, Terre Haute, IN 47809. Offers adult fitness (MA, MS); coaching (MA, MS); exercise science (MA, MS). *Degree requirements:* For master's, thesis (for some programs). *Entrance requirements:* For master's, minor in physical education. Electronic applications accepted. *Faculty research:* Exercise science.

Indiana University Bloomington, School of Health, Physical Education and Recreation, Department of Kinesiology, Bloomington, IN 47405-7000. Offers adapted physical education (MS); applied sport science (MS); athletic administration/sport management (MS); athletic training (MS); biomechanics (MS); ergonomics (MS); exercise physiology (MS); human performance (PhD), including adapted physical education, biomechanics, exercise physiology, motor learning/control, sport management; motor learning/control (MS); physical activity, fitness and wellness (MS). Part-time programs available. *Faculty:* 28 full-time (11 women). *Students:* 150 full-time (59 women), 22 part-time (9 women); includes 20 minority (12 Black or African American, non-Hispanic/Latino; 1 American Indian or Alaska Native, non-Hispanic/Latino; 1 Asian, non-Hispanic/Latino; 4 Hispanic/Latino; 2 Two or more races, non-Hispanic/Latino), 33 international. Average age 28. 211 applicants, 60% accepted, 62 enrolled. In 2011, 67 master's, 7 doctorates awarded. Terminal master's awarded for partial completion of doctoral program. *Degree requirements:* For master's, thesis optional; for doctorate, variable foreign language requirement, thesis/dissertation. *Entrance requirements:* For master's, GRE General Test, minimum GPA of 2.8; for doctorate, GRE General Test, minimum graduate GPA of 3.5, undergraduate 3.0. *Application deadline:* For fall admission, 1/1 for international students; for spring admission, 9/1 for international students. Applications are processed on a rolling basis. Application fee: $55 ($65 for international students). *Financial support:* Fellowships, research assistantships with full tuition reimbursements, teaching assistantships with full tuition reimbursements, career-related internships or fieldwork, Federal Work-Study, institutionally sponsored loans, scholarships/grants, tuition waivers (partial), and fee remissions available. Financial award application deadline: 3/1. *Faculty research:* Exercise physiology and biochemistry, sports biomechanics, human motor control, adaptation of fitness and exercise to special populations. *Unit head:* Dr. David M. Koceja, Chairperson, 812-855-5523, Fax: 812-855-3193, E-mail: koceja@indiana.edu. *Application contact:* Kristine M. Wasson, Administrative Assistant for Graduate Studies, 812-855-5523, Fax: 812-855-3193, E-mail: ktanksle@indiana.edu. Web site: http://www.indiana.edu/~kines/.

Indiana University of Pennsylvania, School of Graduate Studies and Research, College of Health and Human Services, Department of Health and Physical Education, Program in Health and Physical Education, Indiana, PA 15705-1087. Offers M Ed. *Faculty:* 10 full-time (6 women). *Students:* 20 full-time (9 women), 10 part-time (6 women); includes 2 minority (1 Hispanic/Latino; 1 Two or more races, non-Hispanic/Latino). Average age 26. 23 applicants, 61% accepted, 10 enrolled. In 2011, 23 master's awarded. *Entrance requirements:* Additional exam requirements/recommendations for international students: Required—TOEFL (minimum score 540 paper-based; 207 computer-based). *Application deadline:* Applications are processed on a rolling basis. Application fee: $50. Electronic applications accepted. *Expenses:* Tuition, state resident: full-time $7488; part-time $416 per credit. Tuition, nonresident: full-time $11,232; part-time $624 per credit. *Required fees:* $2070; $192.20 per credit. $90 per semester. *Financial support:* In 2011–12, 7 research assistantships with full and partial tuition reimbursements (averaging $5,051 per year) were awarded. Financial award application deadline: 4/15; financial award applicants required to submit FAFSA. *Unit head:* Dr. Elaine Blair, Chairperson, 724-357-2770, E-mail: eblair@iup.edu. *Application contact:* Dr. Jacqueline Beck, Associate Dean, 724-357-2560, E-mail: jbeck@iup.edu. Web site: http://www.iup.edu/upper.aspx?id=49407.

Indiana University–Purdue University Indianapolis, School of Physical Education and Tourism Management, Indianapolis, IN 46202-2896. Offers physical education (MS). *Faculty:* 4 full-time (2 women). *Students:* 17 full-time (7 women), 11 part-time (6 women); includes 2 minority (both Black or African American, non-Hispanic/Latino), 3 international. Average age 28. 21 applicants, 52% accepted, 8 enrolled. In 2011, 7 master's awarded. Application fee: $55 ($65 for international students). *Financial support:* Career-related internships or fieldwork, Federal Work-Study, institutionally sponsored loans, and scholarships/grants available. Support available to part-time students. *Application contact:* Dr. Sherry Queener, Director, Graduate Studies and Associate Dean, 317-274-1577, Fax: 317-278-2380. Web site: http://www.iupui.edu/~indyhper/.

Inter American University of Puerto Rico, Metropolitan Campus, Graduate Programs, Program in Physical Education, San Juan, PR 00919-1293. Offers teaching of physical education (MA); training and sport performance (MA). *Degree requirements:* For master's, comprehensive exam. *Entrance requirements:* For master's, GRE or EXADEP, interview. Electronic applications accepted.

Inter American University of Puerto Rico, San Germán Campus, Graduate Studies Center, Program in Health and Physical Education, San Germán, PR 00683-5008. Offers MA. Part-time and evening/weekend programs available. *Degree requirements:* For master's, comprehensive exam. *Entrance requirements:* For master's, GRE General Test or EXADEP, minimum GPA of 3.0. *Application deadline:* For fall admission, 4/30 priority date for domestic students; for spring admission, 11/15 for domestic students. Applications are processed on a rolling basis. Application fee: $31. *Expenses: Required fees:* $213 per semester. *Financial support:* Teaching assistantships available. *Unit head:* Dr. Elba T. Irizarry, Director of Graduate Studies Center, 787-264-1912 Ext. 7357, Fax: 787-892-6350, E-mail: elbat@sg.inter.edu.

Ithaca College, Division of Graduate and Professional Studies, School of Health Sciences and Human Performance, Program in Physical Education, Ithaca, NY 14850. Offers MS. Part-time programs available. *Faculty:* 10 full-time (8 women). *Students:* 3 full-time (1 woman), 1 international. Average age 26. 3 applicants, 67% accepted, 2 enrolled. In 2011, 1 master's awarded. *Entrance requirements:* For master's, minimum GPA of 3.0. Additional exam requirements/recommendations for international students: Required—TOEFL (minimum score 550 paper-based; 213 computer-based; 80 iBT). *Application deadline:* For fall admission, 3/1 priority date for domestic students, 3/1 for international students; for spring admission, 12/1 for domestic and international students. Applications are processed on a rolling basis. Application fee: $40. Electronic applications accepted. *Expenses:* Contact institution. *Financial support:* In 2011–12, 3 students received support, including 3 teaching assistantships (averaging $4,856 per year); career-related internships or fieldwork, Federal Work-Study, scholarships/grants, and unspecified assistantships also available. Support available to part-time students. Financial award application deadline: 3/1; financial award applicants required to submit CSS PROFILE or FAFSA. *Faculty research:* Needs assessment evaluation of health education programs, minority health (includes diversity), employee health assessment and program planning, youth at risk/families, multicultural/international health, program planning/health behaviors, sexuality education in the family and school setting, parent-teacher and student-teacher relationships, attitude/interest/motivation, teaching effectiveness, student learning/achievement. *Unit head:* Dr. Srijana Bajracharya, Chairperson, 607-274-3143, Fax: 607-274-1263, E-mail: gps@ithaca.edu. *Application contact:* Gerard Turbide, Director, Office of Admission, 607-274-3143, Fax: 607-274-1263, E-mail: gps@ithaca.edu. Web site: http://www.ithaca.edu/gps/gradprograms/programsites/hppe/programs/physed.

Jackson State University, Graduate School, College of Education and Human Development, Department of Health, Physical Education and Recreation, Jackson, MS 39217. Offers MS Ed. *Accreditation:* NCATE. Part-time and evening/weekend programs available. *Degree requirements:* For master's, comprehensive exam, thesis or alternative. *Entrance requirements:* For master's, GRE General Test. Additional exam requirements/recommendations for international students: Required—TOEFL (minimum score 520 paper-based; 195 computer-based; 67 iBT).

Jacksonville State University, College of Graduate Studies and Continuing Education, College of Education and Professional Studies, Program in Physical Education, Jacksonville, AL 36265-1602. Offers MS Ed, Ed S. *Accreditation:* NCATE. Part-time and evening/weekend programs available. *Degree requirements:* For master's, comprehensive exam, thesis (for some programs). *Entrance requirements:* For master's, GRE General Test or MAT. Electronic applications accepted. *Expenses:* Tuition, state resident: part-time $336 per hour. Tuition, nonresident: part-time $672 per hour. Part-time tuition and fees vary according to degree level.

Lindenwood University, Graduate Programs, School of Education, St. Charles, MO 63301-1695. Offers education (MA); educational administration (MA, Ed D, Ed S); human performance (MS); instructional leadership (Ed D, Ed S); library media (MA); professional and school counseling (MA); professional counseling (MA); school administration (Ed S); school counseling (MA); teaching (MA); teaching English to speakers of other languages (MA). Part-time and evening/weekend programs available. *Faculty:* 33 full-time (13 women), 176 part-time/adjunct (83 women). *Students:* 472 full-time (353 women), 1,772 part-time (1,373 women); includes 666 minority (605 Black or African American, non-Hispanic/Latino; 15 American Indian or Alaska Native, non-Hispanic/Latino; 5 Asian, non-Hispanic/Latino; 2 Hispanic/Latino; 4 Native Hawaiian or other Pacific Islander, non-Hispanic/Latino; 35 Two or more races, non-Hispanic/Latino), 24 international. Average age 36. 472 applicants, 87% accepted, 366 enrolled. In 2011, 747 master's, 42 doctorates, 69 other advanced degrees awarded. *Degree requirements:* For master's, thesis (for some programs), minimum GPA of 3.0; for doctorate, thesis/dissertation, minimum GPA of 3.0; for Ed S, comprehensive exam, project, minimum GPA of 3.0. *Entrance requirements:* For master's, interview, minimum GPA of 3.0, writing sample, letter of recommendation; for doctorate, GRE, minimum graduate GPA of 3.4, resume, interview, writing sample, 4 letters of recommendation; for Ed S, master's degree in education, relevant work experience. Additional exam requirements/recommendations for international students: Required—TOEFL (minimum score 550 paper-based; 213 computer-based; 80 iBT). *Application deadline:* For fall admission, 8/26 priority date for domestic students, 8/26 for international students; for spring admission, 1/27 priority date for domestic students, 1/27 for international students. Applications are processed on a rolling basis. Application fee: $30 ($100 for international students). Electronic applications accepted. *Expenses: Tuition:* Full-time $13,650; part-time $395 per credit hour. *Required fees:* $150 per semester. Tuition and fees vary according to course level and course load. *Financial support:* In 2011–12, 153 students received support. Career-related internships or fieldwork, institutionally sponsored loans, tuition waivers (partial), and unspecified assistantships available. Financial award application deadline: 6/30; financial award applicants required to submit FAFSA. *Unit head:* Dr. Cynthia Bice, Dean, 636-949-4618, Fax: 636-949-4197, E-mail: cbice@lindenwood.edu. *Application contact:* Brett Barger, Dean of Evening Admissions and Extension Campuses, 636-949-4934, Fax: 636-949-4109, E-mail: adultadmissions@lindenwood.edu.

Long Island University–Brooklyn Campus, School of Health Professions, Division of Sports Sciences, Brooklyn, NY 11201-8423. Offers adapted physical education (MS); athletic training and sports sciences (MS); exercise physiology (MS); health sciences (MS). Part-time and evening/weekend programs available. *Entrance requirements:* For master's, 2 letters of recommendation. Additional exam requirements/recommendations for international students: Required—TOEFL (minimum score 500 paper-based; 173 computer-based). Electronic applications accepted.

Louisiana Tech University, Graduate School, College of Education, Department of Curriculum, Instruction and Leadership, Ruston, LA 71272. Offers curriculum and instruction (MS, Ed D); educational leadership (Ed D); secondary education (M Ed), including business education, English education, foreign language education, health and physical education, mathematics education, science education, social studies education, speech education. *Accreditation:* NCATE. Part-time programs available. *Degree requirements:* For doctorate, thesis/dissertation. *Entrance requirements:* For master's and doctorate, GRE General Test.

McDaniel College, Graduate and Professional Studies, Program in Physical Education, Westminster, MD 21157-4390. Offers MS. Part-time and evening/weekend programs available. *Degree requirements:* For master's, comprehensive exam, thesis optional. *Entrance requirements:* For master's, letters of reference (3). Additional exam requirements/recommendations for international students: Required—TOEFL (minimum score 213 computer-based).

Physical Education

McGill University, Faculty of Graduate and Postdoctoral Studies, Faculty of Education, Department of Kinesiology and Physical Education, Montréal, QC H3A 2T5, Canada. Offers M Sc, MA, PhD, Certificate, Diploma.

Memorial University of Newfoundland, School of Graduate Studies, School of Human Kinetics and Recreation, St. John's, NL A1C 5S7, Canada. Offers administration, curriculum and supervision (MPE); biomechanics/ergonomics (MS Kin); exercise and work physiology (MS Kin); sport psychology (MS Kin). Part-time programs available. *Degree requirements:* For master's, thesis optional, seminars, thesis presentations. *Entrance requirements:* For master's, bachelor's degree in a related field, minimum B average. Electronic applications accepted. *Faculty research:* Administration, sociology of sports, kinesiology, physiology/recreation.

Middle Tennessee State University, College of Graduate Studies, College of Behavioral and Health Sciences, Department of Health and Human Performance, Program in Health, Physical Education and Recreation, Murfreesboro, TN 37132. Offers MS. Part-time and evening/weekend programs available. Postbaccalaureate distance learning degree programs offered. *Faculty:* 24 full-time (9 women), 5 part-time/adjunct (3 women). *Students:* 5 full-time (3 women), 68 part-time (29 women); includes 26 minority (24 Black or African American, non-Hispanic/Latino; 1 Hispanic/Latino; 1 Two or more races, non-Hispanic/Latino). 66 applicants, 83% accepted. In 2011, 31 master's awarded. *Degree requirements:* For master's, comprehensive exam, thesis optional. *Entrance requirements:* For master's, GRE. Additional exam requirements/recommendations for international students: Required—TOEFL (minimum score 525 paper-based; 195 computer-based; 71 iBT) or IELTS (minimum score 6). *Application deadline:* For fall admission, 6/1 for domestic and international students. Applications are processed on a rolling basis. Application fee: $25 ($30 for international students). *Expenses:* Tuition, state resident: full-time $10,008. Tuition, nonresident: full-time $25,056. *Financial support:* In 2011–12, 14 students received support. Tuition waivers available. Support available to part-time students. Financial award application deadline: 5/1. *Faculty research:* Kinesiometrics, leisure behavior, health, lifestyles. *Unit head:* Dr. Harold D. Whiteside, Interim Dean, 615-898-2900, Fax: 615-494-7704, E-mail: harold.whiteside@mtsu.edu. *Application contact:* Dr. Michael D. Allen, Dean and Vice Provost for Research, 615-898-2840, Fax: 615-904-8020, E-mail: michael.allen@mtsu.edu.

Minnesota State University Mankato, College of Graduate Studies, College of Allied Health and Nursing, Department of Human Performance, Mankato, MN 56001. Offers MA, MS. Part-time programs available. *Students:* 54 full-time (26 women), 61 part-time (20 women). *Degree requirements:* For master's, comprehensive exam, thesis. *Entrance requirements:* For master's, minimum GPA of 3.0 during previous 2 years. Additional exam requirements/recommendations for international students: Required—TOEFL. *Application deadline:* For fall admission, 3/1 priority date for domestic students, 3/1 for international students. Applications are processed on a rolling basis. Application fee: $40. *Financial support:* Research assistantships with full tuition reimbursements, teaching assistantships with full tuition reimbursements, career-related internships or fieldwork, Federal Work-Study, institutionally sponsored loans, and unspecified assistantships available. Support available to part-time students. Financial award application deadline: 3/15; financial award applicants required to submit FAFSA. *Faculty research:* Exercise physiology. *Unit head:* Dr. Cindra Kamphoff, Graduate Coordinator, 507-389-6313. *Application contact:* 507-389-2321, E-mail: grad@mnsu.edu. Web site: http://ahn.mnsu.edu/hp/.

Mississippi State University, College of Education, Department of Kinesiology, Mississippi State, MS 39762. Offers MS. Part-time programs available. Postbaccalaureate distance learning degree programs offered (minimal on-campus study). *Faculty:* 6 full-time (1 woman). *Students:* 58 full-time (23 women), 15 part-time (6 women); includes 11 minority (7 Black or African American, non-Hispanic/Latino; 1 Hispanic/Latino; 3 Two or more races, non-Hispanic/Latino), 1 international. Average age 25. 55 applicants, 47% accepted, 21 enrolled. In 2011, 37 master's awarded. *Degree requirements:* For master's, comprehensive exam, thesis optional. *Entrance requirements:* For master's, GRE General Test, minimum GPA of 3.0. Additional exam requirements/recommendations for international students: Required—TOEFL (minimum score 550 paper-based; 213 computer-based; 79 iBT); Recommended—IELTS (minimum score 6.5). *Application deadline:* For fall admission, 7/1 for domestic students, 5/1 for international students; for spring admission, 11/1 for domestic students, 9/1 for international students. Applications are processed on a rolling basis. Application fee: $40. Electronic applications accepted. *Expenses:* Tuition, state resident: full-time $5805; part-time $322.50 per credit hour. Tuition, nonresident: full-time $14,670; part-time $815 per credit hour. *Financial support:* In 2011–12, 5 teaching assistantships (averaging $8,772 per year) were awarded; career-related internships or fieldwork, Federal Work-Study, institutionally sponsored loans, and unspecified assistantships also available. Financial award application deadline: 4/1; financial award applicants required to submit FAFSA. *Faculty research:* Static balance and stepping performance of older adults, organizational justice, public health, strength training and recovery drinks, high risk drinking perceptions and behaviors. *Unit head:* Dr. Stanley Brown, Professor and Department Head, 662-325-7229, Fax: 662-325-4525, E-mail: spb107@msstate.edu. *Application contact:* Dr. John G. Lamberth, Associate Professor and Graduate Coordinator, 662-325-0906, Fax: 662-325-4525, E-mail: jgl@ra.msstate.edu. Web site: http://www.kinesiology.msstate.edu/.

Missouri State University, Graduate College, College of Health and Human Services, Department of Health, Physical Education, and Recreation, Springfield, MO 65897. Offers health promotion and wellness management (MS); secondary education (MS Ed), including physical education. Part-time programs available. *Faculty:* 12 full-time (5 women). *Students:* 11 full-time (8 women), 8 part-time (5 women); includes 2 minority (1 Black or African American, non-Hispanic/Latino; 1 Asian, non-Hispanic/Latino). Average age 28. 14 applicants, 100% accepted, 9 enrolled. In 2011, 10 master's awarded. *Degree requirements:* For master's, comprehensive exam, thesis or alternative. *Entrance requirements:* For master's, GRE (MS), minimum GPA of 2.8 (MS); 9-12 teaching certification (MS Ed). Additional exam requirements/recommendations for international students: Required—TOEFL (minimum score 550 paper-based; 213 computer-based; 79 iBT). *Application deadline:* For fall admission, 7/20 priority date for domestic students, 5/1 for international students; for spring admission, 12/20 priority date for domestic students, 9/1 for international students. Applications are processed on a rolling basis. Application fee: $35 ($50 for international students). Electronic applications accepted. *Expenses:* Tuition, state resident: full-time $4086; part-time $227 per credit hour. Tuition, nonresident: full-time $8172; part-time $454 per credit hour. *Required fees:* $275 per semester. Tuition and fees vary according to course load, campus/location and program. *Financial support:* In 2011–12, 7 teaching assistantships with full tuition reimbursements (averaging $8,988 per year) were awarded; Federal Work-Study, institutionally sponsored loans, scholarships/grants, and unspecified assistantships also available. Financial award application deadline: 3/31; financial award applicants required to submit FAFSA. *Unit head:* Dr. Sarah McCallister, Acting Head, 417-836-6582, Fax: 417-836-5371, E-mail: sarahmccallister@missouristate.edu. *Application contact:* Misty Stewart, Coordinator of Graduate Admissions and Recruitment, 417-836-6079, Fax: 417-836-6200, E-mail: mistystewart@missouristate.edu. Web site: http://www.missouristate.edu/HPER/.

Montana State University Billings, College of Allied Health Professions, Department of Health and Human Performance, Billings, MT 59101-0298. Offers athletic training (MS); sport management (MS). *Degree requirements:* For master's, thesis optional. *Entrance requirements:* For master's, GRE General Test, minimum undergraduate GPA of 3.0.

Montclair State University, The Graduate School, College of Education and Human Services, Department of Curriculum and Teaching, Program in Teaching in Content Area, Montclair, NJ 07043-1624. Offers art (MAT); biology (MAT); chemistry (MAT); earth science (MAT); English (MAT); French (MAT); health and physical education (MAT); health education (MAT); mathematics (MAT); music (MAT); physical education (MAT); physical science (MAT); social studies (MAT); Spanish (MAT); teacher of English as a second language (MAT). *Students:* 162 full-time (90 women), 47 part-time (29 women); includes 37 minority (4 Black or African American, non-Hispanic/Latino; 11 Asian, non-Hispanic/Latino; 18 Hispanic/Latino; 4 Two or more races, non-Hispanic/Latino), 5 international. Average age 31. 145 applicants, 41% accepted, 56 enrolled. In 2011, 229 master's awarded. *Degree requirements:* For master's, comprehensive exam, thesis or alternative. *Entrance requirements:* For master's, GRE General Test, interview, 2 letters of recommendation. Additional exam requirements/recommendations for international students: Required—TOEFL (minimum score 83 iBT), IELTS (minimum score 6.5). *Application deadline:* Applications are processed on a rolling basis. Application fee: $60. Electronic applications accepted. *Financial support:* Federal Work-Study, scholarships/grants, and unspecified assistantships available. Support available to part-time students. Financial award application deadline: 3/1; financial award applicants required to submit FAFSA. *Unit head:* Dr. David Schwarzer, Chairperson, 973-655-5187. *Application contact:* Amy Aiello, Executive Director of The Graduate School, 973-655-5147, Fax: 973-655-7869, E-mail: graduate.school@montclair.edu.

Montclair State University, The Graduate School, College of Education and Human Services, Department of Exercise Science and Physical Education, Program in Exercise Science and Physical Education, Montclair, NJ 07043-1624. Offers exercise science (MA); sports administration and coaching (MA); teaching and supervision in physical education (MA). Part-time and evening/weekend programs available. *Students:* 8 full-time (6 women), 35 part-time (14 women); includes 4 minority (1 Black or African American, non-Hispanic/Latino; 1 Asian, non-Hispanic/Latino; 2 Hispanic/Latino), 1 international. Average age 31. 25 applicants, 44% accepted, 10 enrolled. In 2011, 14 master's awarded. *Degree requirements:* For master's, comprehensive exam, thesis or alternative. *Entrance requirements:* For master's, GRE General Test, essay, 2 letters of recommendation. Additional exam requirements/recommendations for international students: Required—TOEFL (minimum score 83 iBT), IELTS (minimum score 6.5). *Application deadline:* Applications are processed on a rolling basis. Application fee: $60. Electronic applications accepted. *Financial support:* Federal Work-Study, scholarships/grants, and unspecified assistantships available. Support available to part-time students. Financial award application deadline: 3/1; financial award applicants required to submit FAFSA. *Unit head:* Dr. Robert Horn, Chairperson, 973-655-5253, E-mail: hornr@mail.montclair.edu. *Application contact:* Amy Aiello, Executive Director of The Graduate School, 973-655-5147, Fax: 973-655-7869, E-mail: graduate.school@montclair.edu. Web site: http://cehs.montclair.edu/academic/es/programs/master_physed.shtml.

Montclair State University, The Graduate School, College of Education and Human Services, Department of Exercise Science and Physical Education, Program in Teaching Physical Education, Montclair, NJ 07043-1624. Offers MAT. *Students:* 4 full-time (0 women), 2 part-time (0 women); includes 1 minority (Black or African American, non-Hispanic/Latino). Average age 31. 14 applicants, 50% accepted, 6 enrolled. *Degree requirements:* For master's, comprehensive exam, thesis or alternative. *Entrance requirements:* For master's, GRE General Test, interview, essay, 2 letters of recommendation. Additional exam requirements/recommendations for international students: Required—TOEFL (minimum score 83 iBT), IELTS (minimum score 6.5). *Application deadline:* Applications are processed on a rolling basis. Application fee: $60. Electronic applications accepted. *Financial support:* Application deadline: 3/1; applicants required to submit FAFSA. *Unit head:* Dr. Robert Horn, Chairperson, 973-655-5253. *Application contact:* Amy Aiello, Executive Director of The Graduate School, 973-655-5147, Fax: 973-655-7869, E-mail: graduate.school@montclair.edu. Web site: http://www.montclair.edu/cehs/academics/programs/mat-physed/.

Morehead State University, Graduate Programs, College of Education, Department of Middle Grades and Secondary Education, Morehead, KY 40351. Offers business and marketing education (MAT); English/language arts 5-9 (MAT); French (MAT); health P-12 (MAT); mathematics 5-9 (MAT); physical education P-12 (MAT); science 5-9 (MAT); secondary biology (MAT); secondary chemistry (MAT); secondary earth science (MAT); secondary English (MAT); secondary math (MAT); secondary physics (MAT); secondary social studies (MAT); social studies 5-9 (MAT); Spanish (MAT). Part-time and evening/weekend programs available. *Degree requirements:* For master's, portfolio. *Entrance requirements:* For master's, GRE or PRAXIS II content exam, minimum overall undergraduate GPA of 2.5. Additional exam requirements/recommendations for international students: Required—TOEFL (minimum score 500 paper-based; 173 computer-based). Electronic applications accepted.

Morehead State University, Graduate Programs, College of Science and Technology, Department of Health, Wellness and Human Performance, Morehead, KY 40351. Offers health/physical education (MA). *Accreditation:* NCATE. Part-time and evening/weekend programs available. *Degree requirements:* For master's, comprehensive exam, thesis, oral exam, written core exam. *Entrance requirements:* For master's, GRE General Test or MAT, minimum GPA of 2.5; undergraduate major/minor in health, physical education, or recreation. Additional exam requirements/recommendations for international students: Required—TOEFL (minimum score 500 paper-based; 173 computer-based). Electronic applications accepted. *Faculty research:* Child growth and performance, instructional strategies, outdoor leadership qualities, exercise science, athletic training.

Murray State University, College of Education, Department of Adolescent, Career and Special Education, Murray, KY 42071. Offers health, physical education, and recreation (MA), including physical education; industrial and technical education (MS); middle school education (MA Ed, Ed S); secondary education (MA Ed, Ed S); special education (MA Ed), including advanced learning behavior disorders, learning disabilities, moderate/severe disorders. *Accreditation:* NCATE. Part-time programs available. *Entrance requirements:* Additional exam requirements/recommendations for international students: Required—TOEFL.

North Carolina Agricultural and Technical State University, School of Graduate Studies, School of Education, Department of Human Performance and Leisure Studies, Greensboro, NC 27411. Offers physical education (MAT, MS). *Accreditation:* NCATE. Part-time and evening/weekend programs available. *Degree requirements:* For master's, comprehensive exam, thesis or alternative, qualifying exam. *Entrance requirements:* For master's, GRE General Test or MAT.

North Carolina Central University, Division of Academic Affairs, College of Behavioral and Social Sciences, Department of Physical Education and Recreation, Durham, NC 27707-3129. Offers athletic administration (MS); physical education (MS); recreation administration (MS); therapeutic recreation (MS). Part-time and evening/weekend programs available. *Degree requirements:* For master's, one foreign language, comprehensive exam, thesis. *Entrance requirements:* For master's, GRE, minimum GPA of 3.0 in major, 2.5 overall. Additional exam requirements/recommendations for international students: Required—TOEFL. *Faculty research:* Physical activity patterns of children with disabilities, physical fitness test of North Carolina school children, exercise physiology, motor learning/development.

North Dakota State University, College of Graduate and Interdisciplinary Studies, College of Human Development and Education, School of Education, Program in Curriculum and Instruction, Fargo, ND 58108. Offers pedagogy (M Ed, MS); physical education and athletic administration (M Ed, MS). *Students:* 23 full-time (14 women), 70 part-time (50 women); includes 8 minority (2 Black or African American, non-Hispanic/Latino; 4 American Indian or Alaska Native, non-Hispanic/Latino; 1 Hispanic/Latino; 1 Two or more races, non-Hispanic/Latino), 6 international. Average age 27. 19 applicants, 74% accepted, 6 enrolled. *Degree requirements:* For master's, comprehensive exam, thesis (for some programs). *Entrance requirements:* For master's, Cooperative English Test, GRE General Test, MAT. Additional exam requirements/recommendations for international students: Required—TOEFL. *Application deadline:* For fall admission, 5/1 for domestic students. Applications are processed on a rolling basis. Application fee: $35. *Financial support:* Teaching assistantships, career-related internships or fieldwork, Federal Work-Study, institutionally sponsored loans, and tuition waivers (full) available. Financial award application deadline: 4/15. *Unit head:* Dr. William Martin, Chair, 701-231-7202, Fax: 701-231-7416, E-mail: william.martin@ndsu.edu. *Application contact:* Dr. Justin Wageman, Associate Professor, 701-231-7108, Fax: 701-231-9685, E-mail: justin.wageman@ndsu.edu.

Northern Illinois University, Graduate School, College of Education, Department of Kinesiology and Physical Education, De Kalb, IL 60115-2854. Offers physical education (MS Ed); sport management (MS). Part-time and evening/weekend programs available. *Faculty:* 21 full-time (12 women). *Students:* 63 full-time (24 women), 71 part-time (34 women); includes 26 minority (10 Black or African American, non-Hispanic/Latino; 5 Asian, non-Hispanic/Latino; 8 Hispanic/Latino; 3 Two or more races, non-Hispanic/Latino), 5 international. Average age 27. 66 applicants, 73% accepted, 26 enrolled. In 2011, 55 master's awarded. *Degree requirements:* For master's, comprehensive exam, thesis optional. *Entrance requirements:* For master's, GRE General Test, minimum GPA of 2.75, undergraduate major in related area. Additional exam requirements/recommendations for international students: Required—TOEFL (minimum score 550 paper-based; 213 computer-based). *Application deadline:* For fall admission, 6/1 for domestic students, 5/1 for international students; for spring admission, 11/1 for domestic students, 10/1 for international students. Applications are processed on a rolling basis. Application fee: $40. Electronic applications accepted. *Financial support:* In 2011–12, 1 research assistantship with full tuition reimbursement, 35 teaching assistantships with full tuition reimbursements were awarded; fellowships with full tuition reimbursements, career-related internships or fieldwork, Federal Work-Study, scholarships/grants, tuition waivers (full), and unspecified assistantships also available. Support available to part-time students. Financial award applicants required to submit FAFSA. *Faculty research:* Leadership in athletic training, motor development, dance education, gait analysis, fat phobia. *Unit head:* Dr. Paul Carpenter, Chair, 815-753-8284, Fax: 815-753-1413, E-mail: knpe@niu.edu. *Application contact:* Dr. Laurie Zittel, Director, Graduate Studies, 815-753-1425, E-mail: lzape@niu.edu. Web site: http://cedu.niu.edu/knpe/.

Northern State University, Division of Graduate Studies in Education, Program in Teaching and Learning, Aberdeen, SD 57401-7198. Offers educational studies (MS Ed); elementary classroom teaching (MS Ed); health, physical education, and coaching (MS Ed); secondary classroom teaching (MS Ed). *Accreditation:* NCATE. Part-time and evening/weekend programs available. *Degree requirements:* For master's, thesis optional. *Entrance requirements:* For master's, minimum GPA of 2.75. Additional exam requirements/recommendations for international students: Required—TOEFL (minimum score 550 paper-based; 213 computer-based; 76 iBT), IELTS (minimum score 6). Electronic applications accepted.

North Georgia College & State University, School of Education, Dahlonega, GA 30597. Offers art education (MAT); early childhood education (M Ed); English education (MAT); history education (MAT); math education (MAT); middle grades education (M Ed, MAT); physical education (MS); school leadership (Ed S); secondary education (M Ed), including English education, history education, mathematics education, physical education; teacher education (MAT). *Accreditation:* NCATE. Part-time and evening/weekend programs available. Postbaccalaureate distance learning degree programs offered (no on-campus study). *Faculty:* 23 full-time (14 women), 16 part-time/adjunct (11 women). *Students:* 19 full-time (17 women), 199 part-time (147 women); includes 7 minority (3 Black or African American, non-Hispanic/Latino; 1 Asian, non-Hispanic/Latino; 3 Hispanic/Latino), 1 international. Average age 34. 259 applicants, 66% accepted, 112 enrolled. In 2011, 100 master's, 16 other advanced degrees awarded. *Degree requirements:* For master's, comprehensive exam, thesis optional. *Entrance requirements:* For master's, GRE or MAT, GACE, minimum GPA of 2.75; for Ed S, GRE General Test or MAT, 3 years of teaching experience, master's degree, minimum graduate GPA of 3.25, leadership position in the school. Additional exam requirements/recommendations for international students: Required—TOEFL (minimum score 550 paper-based; 213 computer-based; 79 iBT), IELTS (minimum score 6.5). *Application deadline:* For fall admission, 8/1 priority date for domestic students, 7/1 for international students; for spring admission, 12/1 priority date for domestic students, 11/1 for international students. Applications are processed on a rolling basis. Application fee: $40. Electronic applications accepted. *Expenses:* Tuition, state resident: full-time $3528; part-time $196 per credit hour. Tuition, nonresident: full-time $14,094; part-time $783 per credit hour. *Required fees:* $1718; $859 per semester. Tuition and fees vary according to course load, campus/location and program. *Financial support:* Teaching assistantships, career-related internships or fieldwork, scholarships/grants, and unspecified assistantships available. Financial award application deadline: 5/1; financial award applicants required to submit CSS PROFILE or FAFSA. *Faculty research:* Identification of professional development school structures supporting P-12 student achievement, impact of diverse field placement settings in teacher belief development among preservice teachers, use of inquiry methodology in social studies teaching with English language learners, use of instructional differentiation in the middle grades classroom, effects of international school placements on preservice teacher beliefs and attitudes. *Unit head:* Dr. Bob Michael, Dean, School of Education, 706-864-1998, Fax: 706-867-2850, E-mail: bmichael@northgeorgia.edu. *Application contact:* Susan L. Perry, Graduate Admissions Coordinator, 706-864-1543, Fax: 706-867-2795, E-mail: slperry@northgeorgia.edu. Web site: http://www.northgeorgia.edu/soe/.

Northwest Missouri State University, Graduate School, College of Education and Human Services, Department of Health, Physical Education, Recreation and Dance, Maryville, MO 64468-6001. Offers applied health science (MS); health and physical education (MS Ed); recreation (MS). *Accreditation:* NCATE. Part-time programs available. *Faculty:* 10 full-time (4 women). *Students:* 31 full-time (13 women), 10 part-time (4 women); includes 5 minority (2 Black or African American, non-Hispanic/Latino; 2 Hispanic/Latino; 1 Two or more races, non-Hispanic/Latino), 2 international. 25 applicants, 100% accepted, 17 enrolled. In 2011, 22 master's awarded. *Degree requirements:* For master's, comprehensive exam. *Entrance requirements:* For master's, GRE General Test, minimum undergraduate GPA of 2.75, teaching certificate, writing sample. Additional exam requirements/recommendations for international students: Required—TOEFL (minimum score 550 paper-based; 213 computer-based). *Application deadline:* For fall admission, 7/1 for domestic and international students; for spring admission, 11/15 for domestic and international students. Applications are processed on a rolling basis. Application fee: $0 ($50 for international students). *Financial support:* In 2011–12, 35 teaching assistantships with full tuition reimbursements (averaging $6,000 per year) were awarded; unspecified assistantships also available. Financial award application deadline: 4/1; financial award applicants required to submit FAFSA. *Unit head:* Dr. Terry Robertson, Chairperson, 660-562-1781. *Application contact:* Dr. Gregory Haddock, Dean of Graduate School, 660-562-1145, Fax: 660-562-1096, E-mail: gradsch@nwmissouri.edu.

The Ohio State University, Graduate School, College of Education and Human Ecology, School of Physical Activity and Educational Services, Columbus, OH 43210. Offers M Ed, MA, PhD. Part-time programs available. *Faculty:* 36. *Students:* 160 full-time (98 women), 92 part-time (65 women); includes 35 minority (16 Black or African American, non-Hispanic/Latino; 1 American Indian or Alaska Native, non-Hispanic/Latino; 6 Asian, non-Hispanic/Latino; 8 Hispanic/Latino; 4 Two or more races, non-Hispanic/Latino), 19 international. Average age 31. In 2011, 26 master's, 38 doctorates awarded. *Degree requirements:* For master's, thesis optional; for doctorate, thesis/dissertation. *Entrance requirements:* Additional exam requirements/recommendations for international students: Required—TOEFL (minimum score 600 paper-based; 250 computer-based), Michigan English Language Assessment Battery (minimum score 82). *Application deadline:* For fall admission, 8/15 priority date for domestic students, 7/1 for international students; for winter admission, 12/1 priority date for domestic students, 11/1 for international students; for spring admission, 3/1 priority date for domestic students, 2/1 for international students. Applications are processed on a rolling basis. Application fee: $40 ($50 for international students). Electronic applications accepted. *Expenses:* Tuition, state resident: full-time $11,400. Tuition, nonresident: full-time $28,125. Tuition and fees vary according to course load, degree level, campus/location and program. *Financial support:* Fellowships, research assistantships, teaching assistantships, Federal Work-Study, and institutionally sponsored loans available. Support available to part-time students. *Unit head:* Donna Pastore, Director, 614-292-6787, Fax: 614-292-7229, E-mail: pastore.3@osu.edu. *Application contact:* Graduate Admissions, 614-292-6031, Fax: 614-292-3656, E-mail: gradadmissions@osu.edu. Web site: http://ehe.osu.edu/paes/.

Ohio University, Graduate College, Gladys W. and David H. Patton College of Education and Human Services, Department of Recreation and Sport Pedagogy, Program in Coaching Education, Athens, OH 45701-2979. Offers MS. *Students:* 21 full-time (4 women), 212 part-time (26 women); includes 50 minority (32 Black or African American, non-Hispanic/Latino; 1 American Indian or Alaska Native, non-Hispanic/Latino; 1 Asian, non-Hispanic/Latino; 13 Hispanic/Latino; 3 Two or more races, non-Hispanic/Latino), 11 international. 99 applicants, 82% accepted, 74 enrolled. In 2011, 43 master's awarded. *Entrance requirements:* For master's, GRE. Additional exam requirements/recommendations for international students: Required—TOEFL (minimum score 550 paper-based; 80 iBT) or IELTS (minimum score 6.5). *Application deadline:* For fall admission, 3/1 priority date for domestic students, 3/1 for international students. Applications are processed on a rolling basis. Application fee: $50 ($55 for international students). Electronic applications accepted. *Financial support:* In 2011–12, research assistantships with full tuition reimbursements (averaging $8,835 per year), teaching assistantships with full tuition reimbursements (averaging $8,835 per year) were awarded; scholarships/grants and stipends also available. Financial award application deadline: 3/1. *Faculty research:* Sports, physical activity, athletes. *Unit head:* Dr. Beth VanDerveer, Assistant Professor and Coordinator, 740-593-4656, Fax: 740-593-0284, E-mail: vanderve@ohio.edu. *Application contact:* Dr. David Carr, Assistant Professor and Coordinator, 740-593-4651, Fax: 740-593-0284, E-mail: carrd@ohio.edu. Web site: http://www.cehs.ohio.edu/academics/rsp/mce/index.htm.

Old Dominion University, Darden College of Education, Program in Physical Education, Norfolk, VA 23529. Offers athletic training (MS Ed); curriculum and instruction (MS Ed); exercise and wellness (MS Ed); physical education (MS Ed); recreation and tourism studies (MS Ed); sport management (MS Ed). Part-time and evening/weekend programs available. *Faculty:* 12 full-time (6 women), 6 part-time/adjunct (4 women). *Students:* 69 full-time (46 women), 37 part-time (19 women); includes 21 minority (16 Black or African American, non-Hispanic/Latino; 1 American Indian or Alaska Native, non-Hispanic/Latino; 1 Asian, non-Hispanic/Latino; 1 Native Hawaiian or other Pacific Islander, non-Hispanic/Latino; 2 Two or more races, non-Hispanic/Latino), 5 international. Average age 26. 105 applicants, 72% accepted, 55 enrolled. In 2011, 54 master's awarded. *Degree requirements:* For master's, comprehensive exam, thesis or alternative, internship, research project. *Entrance requirements:* For master's, GRE General Test, minimum GPA of 2.8. Additional exam requirements/recommendations for international students: Required—TOEFL (minimum score 500 paper-based; 200 computer-based). *Application deadline:* For fall admission, 7/1 for domestic students; for spring admission, 11/1 for domestic students. Applications are processed on a rolling basis. Application fee: $50. *Expenses:* Tuition, state resident: full-time $9096; part-time $379 per credit. Tuition, nonresident: full-time $23,064; part-time $961 per credit. *Required fees:* $127 per semester. One-time fee: $50. *Financial support:* In 2011–12, 1 fellowship (averaging $1,500 per year), 2 research assistantships with partial tuition reimbursements (averaging $9,000 per year), 5 teaching assistantships with tuition reimbursements (averaging $9,000 per year) were awarded; career-related internships or fieldwork and scholarships/grants also available. Financial award application deadline: 4/15; financial award applicants required to submit FAFSA. *Faculty research:* Exercise physiology, nutrition and sports, motion analysis, sports management. *Total annual research expenditures:* $183,251. *Unit head:* Robert Spina, Chair, 757-683-6029, Fax: 757-683-4270, E-mail: rspina@odu.edu. *Application contact:* William Heffelfinger, Director of Graduate Admissions, 757-683-5554, Fax: 757-683-3255, E-mail: gradadmit@odu.edu. Web site: http://education.odu.edu/esper/.

Oregon State University, Graduate School, College of Public Health and Human Sciences, Programs in Exercise and Sport Science, Corvallis, OR 97331. Offers exercise physiology (MS); movement studies in disability (MS, PhD); neuromechanics (MS, PhD); physical activity and public health (MS); physical education teacher education (MS); sport and exercise psychology (MS, PhD). Terminal master's awarded for partial completion of doctoral program. *Degree requirements:* For master's, thesis; for doctorate, thesis/dissertation. *Entrance requirements:* For master's and doctorate, minimum GPA of 3.0 in last 90 hours. Additional exam requirements/recommendations for international students: Required—TOEFL. *Faculty research:* Motor control, sports medicine, exercise physiology, sport psychology, biomechanics.

Pittsburg State University, Graduate School, College of Education, Department of Health, Physical Education and Recreation, Pittsburg, KS 66762. Offers physical education (MS). *Degree requirements:* For master's, thesis or alternative. *Faculty research:* Personality of athletes, fitness activities for children, aerobic conditioning, fitness evaluation.

Prairie View A&M University, College of Education, Department of Health and Human Performance, Prairie View, TX 77446-0519. Offers health education (M Ed, MS); physical education (M Ed, MS). *Accreditation:* NCATE. Part-time and evening/weekend programs available. *Entrance requirements:* For master's, GRE General Test. Additional exam requirements/recommendations for international students: Required—TOEFL.

Purdue University, Graduate School, College of Health and Human Sciences, Department of Health and Kinesiology, West Lafayette, IN 47907. Offers athletic training education administration (MS); exercise, human physiology of movement and sport (PhD); health education (MS, PhD); motor control and development (MS, PhD); physical education pedagogy (MS, PhD); sport and exercise psychology (MS, PhD). Part-time programs available. *Faculty:* 20 full-time (9 women), 14 part-time/adjunct (4 women). *Students:* 53 full-time (27 women), 19 part-time (9 women); includes 9 minority (3 Black or African American, non-Hispanic/Latino; 1 American Indian or Alaska Native, non-Hispanic/Latino; 2 Asian, non-Hispanic/Latino; 1 Hispanic/Latino; 2 Two or more races, non-Hispanic/Latino), 14 international. Average age 30. 108 applicants, 48% accepted, 29 enrolled. In 2011, 17 master's, 6 doctorates awarded. *Degree requirements:* For master's, thesis optional; for doctorate, comprehensive exam, thesis/dissertation, Qualifying Examination, Preliminary Examination. *Entrance requirements:* For master's, GRE General Test, minimum score 1000 combined verbal and quantitative scores, minimum undergraduate GPA of 3.0 or equivalent; for doctorate, GRE General Test, minimum score 1100 combined verbal and quantitative scores, minimum undergraduate GPA of 3.0 or equivalent; master's degree with minimum GPA of 3.25 (recommended). Additional exam requirements/recommendations for international students: Required—TOEFL (minimum score 550 computer-based; 77 iBT); Recommended—TWE. *Application deadline:* For fall admission, 4/30 for domestic and international students; for spring admission, 10/15 for domestic and international students. Applications are processed on a rolling basis. Application fee: $60 ($75 for international students). Electronic applications accepted. *Financial support:* Fellowships with partial tuition reimbursements, research assistantships with partial tuition reimbursements, teaching assistantships with partial tuition reimbursements, and Federal Work-Study available. Support available to part-time students. Financial award applicants required to submit FAFSA. *Faculty research:* Wellness, motivation, teaching effectiveness, learning and development. *Unit head:* Dr. Larry J. Leverenz, Interim Head, 765-494-0865, Fax: 765-494-496-1239, E-mail: llevere@purdue.edu. *Application contact:* Lisa Duncan, Graduate Contact, 765-494-3162, E-mail: lduncan@purdue.edu. Web site: http://www.purdue.edu/hhs/hk/.

Rhode Island College, School of Graduate Studies, Feinstein School of Education and Human Development, Department of Health and Physical Education, Providence, RI 02908-1991. Offers health education (M Ed); physical education (CGS). *Accreditation:* NCATE. Part-time and evening/weekend programs available. *Faculty:* 2 full-time (1 woman). *Students:* 14 part-time (12 women); includes 1 minority (Hispanic/Latino). Average age 38. In 2011, 10 master's awarded. *Degree requirements:* For master's, comprehensive assessment. *Entrance requirements:* For master's, GRE General Test or MAT, undergraduate transcripts; minimum undergraduate GPA of 3.0; 3 letters of recommendation; for CGS, GRE or MAT (for most programs), undergraduate transcripts; minimum undergraduate GPA of 3.0; 3 letters of recommendation. Additional exam requirements/recommendations for international students: Recommended—TOEFL (minimum score 550 paper-based; 213 computer-based; 79 iBT). *Application deadline:* For fall admission, 3/1 for domestic students; for spring admission, 11/1 for domestic students. Applications are processed on a rolling basis. Application fee: $50. *Expenses:* Tuition, state resident: full-time $8592; part-time $358 per credit hour. Tuition, nonresident: full-time $16,800; part-time $700 per credit hour. *Required fees:* $602; $22 per credit. $72 per term. *Financial support:* Teaching assistantships with full tuition reimbursements, Federal Work-Study, scholarships/grants, health care benefits, and unspecified assistantships available. Support available to part-time students. Financial award application deadline: 5/15; financial award applicants required to submit FAFSA. *Unit head:* Dr. Betty Rauhe, Chair, 401-456-8046. *Application contact:* Graduate Studies, 401-456-8700. Web site: http://www.ric.edu/healthPhysicalEducation/.

Saginaw Valley State University, College of Education, Program in Adapted Physical Activity, University Center, MI 48710. Offers MAT. Part-time and evening/weekend programs available. *Students:* 2 part-time (1 woman). Average age 32. *Degree requirements:* For master's, capstone course. *Entrance requirements:* For master's, minimum GPA of 3.0. Additional exam requirements/recommendations for international students: Required—TOEFL (minimum score 525 paper-based; 197 computer-based; 71 iBT). *Application deadline:* Applications are processed on a rolling basis. Application fee: $25. Electronic applications accepted. *Expenses:* Tuition, state resident: full-time $8300; part-time $5333 per year. Tuition, nonresident: full-time $15,613; part-time $10,209 per year. *International tuition:* $15,631 full-time. *Financial support:* Federal Work-Study and scholarships/grants available. Support available to part-time students. Financial award applicants required to submit FAFSA. *Unit head:* Dr. Steve P. Barbus, Jr., Dean, 989-964-6067, Fax: 989-790-4385, E-mail: barbus@svsu.edu. *Application contact:* Kathy Lopez, Certification Officer, 989-964-4661, Fax: 989-964-4385, E-mail: klopez@svsu.edu.

St. Cloud State University, School of Graduate Studies, School of Education, Department of Health, Physical Education, Recreation, and Sport Science, St. Cloud, MN 56301-4498. Offers exercise science (MS); physical education (MS); sports management (MS). *Degree requirements:* For master's, thesis or alternative. *Entrance requirements:* For master's, GRE General Test, minimum GPA of 2.75. Additional exam requirements/recommendations for international students: Required—Michigan English Language Assessment Battery; Recommended—TOEFL (minimum score 550 paper-based; 213 computer-based), IELTS (minimum score 6.5). Electronic applications accepted.

Salem State University, School of Graduate Studies, Program in Physical Education, Salem, MA 01970-5353. Offers M Ed. Part-time and evening/weekend programs available. *Entrance requirements:* For master's, GRE or MAT. Additional exam requirements/recommendations for international students: Required—TOEFL (minimum score 550 paper-based; 80 iBT) or IELTS (minimum score 5.5).

Slippery Rock University of Pennsylvania, Graduate Studies (Recruitment), College of Education, Department of Physical Education, Slippery Rock, PA 16057-1383. Offers adapted physical activity (MS). Part-time and evening/weekend programs available. *Faculty:* 7 full-time (2 women), 1 (woman) part-time/adjunct. *Students:* 15 full-time (9 women), 3 part-time (2 women); includes 1 minority (Hispanic/Latino), 1 international. Average age 25. 30 applicants, 73% accepted, 15 enrolled. In 2011, 24 degrees awarded. *Degree requirements:* For master's, internship. *Entrance requirements:* For master's, GRE General Test, MAT, minimum GPA of 2.75, two letters of recommendation, essay, official transcripts. Additional exam requirements/recommendations for international students: Required—TOEFL (minimum score 550 paper-based; 213 computer-based; 80 iBT). *Application deadline:* For fall admission, 3/1 priority date for domestic students, 5/1 for international students. Applications are processed on a rolling basis. Application fee: $25 ($30 for international students). Electronic applications accepted. *Expenses:* Tuition, state resident: full-time $7488; part-time $416 per credit. Tuition, nonresident: full-time $11,232; part-time $624 per credit. *International tuition:* $11,146 full-time. *Required fees:* $2722; $140 per credit. Tuition and fees vary according to degree level and program. *Financial support:* Career-related internships or fieldwork, Federal Work-Study, institutionally sponsored loans, scholarships/grants, tuition waivers (partial), and unspecified assistantships available. Support available to part-time students. Financial award application deadline: 5/1; financial award applicants required to submit FAFSA. *Unit head:* Dr. Robert Arnhold, Graduate Coordinator, 724-738-2847, Fax: 724-738-4987, E-mail: robert.arnhold@sru.edu. *Application contact:* Angela Barrett, Director of Graduate Admissions, 724-738-2051, Fax: 724-738-2146, E-mail: graduate.admissions@sru.edu.

South Dakota State University, Graduate School, College of Education and Human Sciences, Department of Health, Physical Education and Recreation, Brookings, SD 57007. Offers MS. Part-time programs available. *Degree requirements:* For master's, thesis, oral and written exams. *Entrance requirements:* Additional exam requirements/recommendations for international students: Required—TOEFL (minimum score 550 paper-based; 213 computer-based; 71 iBT). *Faculty research:* Effective teaching behaviors in physical education, sports nutrition, muscle/bone interaction, hormonal response to exercise.

Southern Connecticut State University, School of Graduate Studies, School of Education, Department of Exercise Science, New Haven, CT 06515-1355. Offers human performance (MS); physical education (MS); school health education (MS); sport psychology (MS). Part-time and evening/weekend programs available. *Faculty:* 8 full-time (4 women). *Students:* 10 full-time (5 women), 20 part-time (9 women); includes 3 minority (1 Black or African American, non-Hispanic/Latino; 1 Asian, non-Hispanic/Latino; 1 Hispanic/Latino). 132 applicants, 20% accepted, 19 enrolled. In 2011, 6 master's awarded. *Degree requirements:* For master's, thesis or alternative. *Entrance requirements:* For master's, interview. *Application deadline:* For fall admission, 7/15 priority date for domestic students. Applications are processed on a rolling basis. Application fee: $50. Electronic applications accepted. *Expenses:* Tuition, state resident: full-time $5137; part-time $413 per credit. *Required fees:* $4008; $55 per term. *Financial support:* Application deadline: 4/15; applicants required to submit FAFSA. *Unit head:* Dr. Daniel Swartz, Chairperson, 203-392-8721, Fax: 203-392-6911, E-mail: swartzd1@southernct.edu. *Application contact:* Dr. Robert Axtell, Coordinator, 203-392-6037, Fax: 203-392-6093, E-mail: axtell@southernct.edu.

Southern Illinois University Carbondale, Graduate School, College of Education and Human Services, Department of Physical Education, Carbondale, IL 62901-4701. Offers physical education (MS Ed). Part-time programs available. *Faculty:* 6 full-time (2 women). *Students:* 39 full-time (17 women), 23 part-time (9 women); includes 10 minority (9 Black or African American, non-Hispanic/Latino; 1 Asian, non-Hispanic/Latino), 2 international. Average age 25. 29 applicants, 66% accepted, 10 enrolled. In 2011, 30 master's awarded. *Degree requirements:* For master's, thesis. *Entrance requirements:* For master's, GRE, minimum GPA of 2.7. Additional exam requirements/recommendations for international students: Required—TOEFL. *Application deadline:* Applications are processed on a rolling basis. Application fee: $20. *Financial support:* In 2011–12, 17 students received support, including 10 teaching assistantships; fellowships, research assistantships, career-related internships or fieldwork, Federal Work-Study, institutionally sponsored loans, and tuition waivers (full) also available. Support available to part-time students. *Faculty research:* Caffeine and exercise effects, ground reaction forces in walking and running, social psychology of sports. *Unit head:* Dr. E. William Vogler, Chairperson, 618-536-2431, E-mail: wvogler@siu.edu. *Application contact:* Chasity Jack, Administrative Clerk, 618-453-3134, E-mail: cjack@siu.edu. Web site: http://kin.ehs.siu.edu/.

Southern Illinois University Edwardsville, Graduate School, School of Education, Department of Kinesiology and Health Education, Edwardsville, IL 62026. Offers kinesiology (MS Ed), including kinesiology, physical education and sport pedagogy. *Accreditation:* NCATE. Part-time and evening/weekend programs available. *Faculty:* 12 full-time (5 women). *Students:* 31 full-time (16 women), 45 part-time (18 women); includes 17 minority (10 Black or African American, non-Hispanic/Latino; 2 Asian, non-Hispanic/Latino; 5 Hispanic/Latino), 1 international. 70 applicants, 59% accepted. In 2011, 35 master's awarded. *Degree requirements:* For master's, comprehensive exam (for some programs), thesis (for some programs). *Entrance requirements:* Additional exam requirements/recommendations for international students: Required—TOEFL (minimum score 550 paper-based; 213 computer-based; 79 iBT), IELTS (minimum score 6.5). *Application deadline:* For fall admission, 7/22 for domestic students, 6/1 for international students; for spring admission, 12/9 for domestic students, 10/1 for international students. Applications are processed on a rolling basis. Application fee: $30. Electronic applications accepted. Tuition and fees vary according to course load and program. *Financial support:* In 2011–12, 6 teaching assistantships with full tuition reimbursements (averaging $9,927 per year) were awarded; fellowships, research assistantships with full tuition reimbursements, institutionally sponsored loans, scholarships/grants, and unspecified assistantships also available. Financial award application deadline: 3/1; financial award applicants required to submit FAFSA. *Unit head:* Dr. Curt Lox, Director, 618-650-2938, E-mail: clox@siue.edu. *Application contact:* Dr. Erik Kirk, Program Director, 618-650-2718, E-mail: ekirk@siue.edu. Web site: http://www.siue.edu/education/khe.

Springfield College, Graduate Programs, Programs in Physical Education, Springfield, MA 01109-3797. Offers adapted physical education (M Ed, MPE, MS); advanced level coaching (M Ed, MPE, MS); athletic administration (M Ed, MPE, MS); general physical education (PhD, CAGS); health education licensure (MPE, MS); health education licensure program (M Ed); physical education licensure (MPE, MS); physical education licensure program (M Ed); teaching and administration (MS). Part-time programs available. *Degree requirements:* For master's, comprehensive exam, thesis (for some programs). *Entrance requirements:* For master's and doctorate, GRE General Test. Additional exam requirements/recommendations for international students: Required—TOEFL (minimum score 550 paper-based; 213 computer-based). Electronic applications accepted.

State University of New York College at Cortland, Graduate Studies, School of Professional Studies, Department of Physical Education, Cortland, NY 13045. Offers MS Ed. Part-time and evening/weekend programs available. *Entrance requirements:* Additional exam requirements/recommendations for international students: Required—TOEFL.

Stony Brook University, State University of New York, School of Professional Development, Stony Brook, NY 11794. Offers biology-grade 7-12 (MAT); chemistry-grade 7-12 (MAT); coaching (Graduate Certificate); coaching online (Graduate Certificate); computer integrated engineering (Graduate Certificate); earth science-grade 7-12 (MAT); educational computing (Graduate Certificate); educational leadership (Advanced Certificate); English-grade 7-12 (MAT); environmental management (Graduate Certificate); environmental/occupational health and safety (Graduate Certificate); French-grade 7-12 (MAT); German-grade 7-12 (MAT); human resource management (Graduate Certificate); human resource management online (Graduate Certificate); information systems management (Graduate Certificate); Italian-grade 7-12 (MAT); liberal studies (MA); liberal studies online (MAT); mathematics-grade 7-12 (MAT); operation research (Graduate Certificate); physics-grade 7-12 (MAT); professional studies online (MPS); school administration and supervision (Graduate Certificate); school building leadership (Graduate Certificate); school district administration (Graduate Certificate); school district business leadership (Advanced Certificate); school district leadership (Graduate Certificate); social science and the professions (MPS), including environmental waste management, human resource management; social studies-grade 7-12 (MAT); Spanish-grade 7-12 (MAT); waste management (Graduate Certificate). Part-time and evening/weekend programs available. Postbaccalaureate distance learning degree programs offered. *Degree requirements:* For master's, one foreign language, thesis or alternative.

Sul Ross State University, School of Professional Studies, Department of Physical Education, Alpine, TX 79832. Offers M Ed. Part-time programs available. *Entrance requirements:* For master's, GMAT or GRE General Test, minimum GPA of 2.5 in last 60 hours of undergraduate work.

Tarleton State University, College of Graduate Studies, College of Education, Department of Kinesiology, Stephenville, TX 76402. Offers physical education (M Ed). Part-time and evening/weekend programs available. *Faculty:* 9 full-time (4 women). *Students:* 9 full-time (2 women), 45 part-time (17 women); includes 15 minority (6 Black or African American, non-Hispanic/Latino; 1 American Indian or Alaska Native, non-Hispanic/Latino; 7 Hispanic/Latino; 1 Two or more races, non-Hispanic/Latino). Average age 24. 26 applicants, 96% accepted, 19 enrolled. In 2011, 20 master's awarded. *Degree requirements:* For master's, comprehensive exam, thesis optional. *Entrance requirements:* For master's, GRE General Test, minimum GPA of 3.0. Additional exam requirements/recommendations for international students: Required—TOEFL (minimum score 550 paper-based; 213 computer-based; 80 iBT). *Application deadline:* For fall admission, 8/5 priority date for domestic students; for spring admission, 12/1 for domestic students. Applications are processed on a rolling basis. Application fee: $30 ($130 for international students). Electronic applications accepted. *Expenses:* Tuition, state resident: full-time $3131.46; part-time $174 per credit hour. Tuition, nonresident: full-time $8225; part-time $457 per credit hour. *Required fees:* $1446. Tuition and fees vary according to course load and campus/location. *Financial support:* Research assistantships, teaching assistantships with partial tuition reimbursements, career-related internships or fieldwork, Federal Work-Study, and institutionally sponsored loans available. Support available to part-time students. Financial award application deadline: 5/1; financial award applicants required to submit FAFSA. *Unit head:* Dr. Steve Crews, Head, 254-968-9377, Fax: 254-968-9831, E-mail: crews@tarleton.edu. *Application contact:* Information Contact, 254-968-9104, Fax: 254-968-9670, E-mail: gradoffice@tarleton.edu. Web site: http://www.tarleton.edu/kinesiology/index.html.

Teachers College, Columbia University, Graduate Faculty of Education, Department of Biobehavioral Studies, Program in Curriculum and Teaching in Physical Education, New York, NY 10027-6696. Offers Ed M, MA, Ed D. Part-time and evening/weekend programs available. *Faculty:* 5 full-time (2 women), 2 part-time/adjunct (1 woman). *Students:* 7 full-time (3 women), 23 part-time (8 women); includes 12 minority (7 Black or African American, non-Hispanic/Latino; 1 Asian, non-Hispanic/Latino; 4 Hispanic/Latino), 2 international. Average age 34. 9 applicants, 67% accepted, 4 enrolled. In 2011, 9 master's, 1 doctorate awarded. Terminal master's awarded for partial completion of doctoral program. *Degree requirements:* For master's, integrative paper; for doctorate, thesis/dissertation. *Entrance requirements:* For doctorate, writing sample, prior formal training and/or teaching experience in physical education. *Application deadline:* For fall admission, 1/15 priority date for domestic students. Applications are processed on a rolling basis. Application fee: $65. *Financial support:* Career-related internships or fieldwork, Federal Work-Study, institutionally sponsored loans, and tuition waivers (full and partial) available. Support available to part-time students. Financial award application deadline: 2/1. *Faculty research:* Analysis of teaching, teacher performance, program development, data bank project in physical education. *Unit head:* Prof. Stephen Silverman, Program Coordinator, 212-678-3324, E-mail: ss928@columbia.edu. *Application contact:* Morgan Oakes, Assistant Counselor, 212-678-3710, Fax: 212-678-4171, E-mail: tcinfo@tc.edu.

Temple University, Health Sciences Center, College of Health Professions and Social Work, Department of Kinesiology, Philadelphia, PA 19122-6096. Offers kinesiology (Ed M, PhD), including behavioral sciences, somatic sciences. Part-time programs available. *Faculty:* 9 full-time (3 women). *Students:* 53 full-time (38 women), 12 part-time (3 women); includes 7 minority (6 Black or African American, non-Hispanic/Latino; 1 Hispanic/Latino), 12 international. Average age 28. 34 applicants, 85% accepted, 21 enrolled. In 2011, 16 master's, 5 doctorates awarded. Terminal master's awarded for partial completion of doctoral program. *Degree requirements:* For master's, thesis; for doctorate, thesis/dissertation. *Entrance requirements:* For master's, GRE General Test or MAT, minimum undergraduate GPA of 3.0; for doctorate, GRE General Test, minimum undergraduate GPA of 3.0. Additional exam requirements/recommendations for international students: Required—TOEFL (minimum score 550 paper-based; 213 computer-based; 79 iBT). *Application deadline:* For fall admission, 1/15 for domestic students, 12/15 for international students; for spring admission, 10/1 for domestic students, 8/1 for international students. Application fee: $50. *Expenses:* Tuition, state resident: full-time $12,366; part-time $687 per credit hour. Tuition, nonresident: full-time $17,298; part-time $961 per credit hour. *Required fees:* $590; $213 per year. *Financial support:* Fellowships, research assistantships with full tuition reimbursements, teaching assistantships with full tuition reimbursements, career-related internships or fieldwork, and Federal Work-Study available. Financial award application deadline: 1/15; financial award applicants required to submit FAFSA. *Unit head:* Dr. Michael Sachs, Interim Chair, 214-204-8707, E-mail: msachs@temple.edu. *Application contact:* Tara Schumacher, Coordinator of Outreach, 215-204-6575, Fax: 215-204-8781, E-mail: tara.schumacher@temple.edu. Web site: http://www.temple.edu/chp/departments/kinesiology/.

Tennessee State University, The School of Graduate Studies and Research, College of Education, Department of Human Performance and Sports Science, Nashville, TN 37209-1561. Offers MA Ed. *Degree requirements:* For master's, thesis optional. *Entrance requirements:* For master's, GRE General Test or MAT.

Tennessee Technological University, Graduate School, College of Education, Department of Exercise Science, Physical Education and Wellness, Cookeville, TN 38505. Offers MA. *Accreditation:* NCATE. Part-time programs available. Postbaccalaureate distance learning degree programs offered (no on-campus study). *Faculty:* 7 full-time (0 women). *Students:* 21 full-time (15 women), 24 part-time (13 women). Average age 27. 32 applicants, 72% accepted, 19 enrolled. In 2011, 21 master's awarded. *Degree requirements:* For master's, comprehensive exam, thesis or alternative. *Entrance requirements:* For master's, MAT or GRE. Additional exam requirements/recommendations for international students: Required—TOEFL (minimum score 527 paper-based; 71 iBT), IELTS (minimum score 5.5), Pearson Test of English Academic. *Application deadline:* For fall admission, 8/1 for domestic students, 5/1 for international students; for spring admission, 12/1 for domestic students, 10/1 for international students. Application fee: $25 ($30 for international students). Electronic applications accepted. *Expenses:* Tuition, state resident: full-time $8094; part-time $422 per credit hour. Tuition, nonresident: full-time $20,574; part-time $1046 per credit hour. *Financial support:* In 2011–12, fellowships (averaging $8,000 per year), 3 research assistantships (averaging $4,000 per year), 4 teaching assistantships (averaging $4,000 per year) were awarded; career-related internships or fieldwork also available. Financial award application deadline: 4/1. *Unit head:* Dr. J. P. Barfield, Interim Chairperson, 931-372-3467, Fax: 931-372-6319, E-mail: jpbarfield@tntech.edu. *Application contact:* Shelia K. Kendrick, Coordinator of Graduate Admissions, 931-372-3808, Fax: 931-372-3497, E-mail: skendrick@tntech.edu.

Texas A&M University, College of Education and Human Development, Department of Health and Kinesiology, College Station, TX 77843. Offers health education (MS, PhD); kinesiology (MS, PhD); physical education (M Ed); sport management (MS). Part-time programs available. *Faculty:* 37. *Students:* 171 full-time (80 women), 38 part-time (22 women); includes 60 minority (21 Black or African American, non-Hispanic/Latino; 8 Asian, non-Hispanic/Latino; 29 Hispanic/Latino; 2 Two or more races, non-Hispanic/Latino), 35 international. Average age 23. In 2011, 54 master's, 17 doctorates awarded. *Degree requirements:* For master's, thesis (for some programs); for doctorate, comprehensive exam, thesis/dissertation. *Entrance requirements:* For master's and doctorate, GRE General Test. Additional exam requirements/recommendations for international students: Required—TOEFL. *Application deadline:* Applications are processed on a rolling basis. Application fee: $50 ($75 for international students). Electronic applications accepted. *Expenses:* Tuition, state resident: full-time $5437; part-time $226.55 per credit hour. Tuition, nonresident: full-time $12,949; part-time $539.55 per credit hour. *Required fees:* $2741. *Financial support:* Fellowships with partial tuition reimbursements, research assistantships, teaching assistantships, career-related internships or fieldwork, and institutionally sponsored loans available. Financial award application deadline: 2/15; financial award applicants required to submit FAFSA. *Unit head:* Dr. Richard Kreider, Head, 979-845-1333, Fax: 979-847-8987, E-mail: rkreider@hlkn.tamu.edu. *Application contact:* Dr. Becky Carr, Assistant Dean for Administrative Services, 979-862-1342, Fax: 979-845-6129, E-mail: bcarr@tamu.edu. Web site: http://hlknweb.tamu.edu/.

Texas A&M University–Commerce, Graduate School, College of Education and Human Services, Department of Health and Human Performance, Commerce, TX 75429-3011. Offers exercise physiology (MS); health and human performance (M Ed); health promotion (MS); health, kinesiology and sports studies (Ed D); motor performance (MS); sport studies (MS). Part-time programs available. *Degree requirements:* For master's, comprehensive exam, thesis (for some programs). *Entrance requirements:* For master's, GRE General Test. Electronic applications accepted. *Faculty research:* Teaching, physical fitness.

Texas Southern University, College of Education, Department of Health and Kinesiology, Houston, TX 77004-4584. Offers health education (MS); human performance (MS). Part-time and evening/weekend programs available. *Degree requirements:* For master's, comprehensive exam, thesis optional. *Entrance requirements:* For master's, GRE General Test, minimum GPA of 2.5. Additional exam requirements/recommendations for international students: Required—TOEFL. Electronic applications accepted.

Texas State University–San Marcos, Graduate School, College of Education, Department of Health and Human Performance, Program in Physical Education, San Marcos, TX 78666. Offers M Ed. Part-time and evening/weekend programs available. *Faculty:* 11 full-time (4 women), 1 (woman) part-time/adjunct. *Students:* 52 full-time (19 women), 43 part-time (16 women); includes 45 minority (9 Black or African American, non-Hispanic/Latino; 1 Asian, non-Hispanic/Latino; 35 Hispanic/Latino), 2 international. Average age 27. 56 applicants, 80% accepted, 25 enrolled. In 2011, 38 master's awarded. *Degree requirements:* For master's, comprehensive exam, thesis optional. *Entrance requirements:* For master's, GRE General Test, minimum GPA of 2.75 in last 60 hours of course work. Additional exam requirements/recommendations for international students: Required—TOEFL (minimum score 550 paper-based; 213 computer-based; 78 iBT). *Application deadline:* For fall admission, 6/15 priority date for domestic students, 6/1 for international students; for spring admission, 10/15 priority date for domestic students, 10/1 for international students. Applications are processed on a rolling basis. Application fee: $40 ($90 for international students). Electronic applications accepted. *Expenses:* Tuition, state resident: full-time $6408; part-time $3204 per semester. Tuition, nonresident: full-time $14,832; part-time $7416 per semester. *Required fees:* $1824; $912 per semester. Tuition and fees vary according to course load. *Financial support:* In 2011–12, 37 students received support, including 6 research assistantships (averaging $11,367 per year), 15 teaching assistantships (averaging $10,350 per year); career-related internships or fieldwork, Federal Work-Study, and institutionally sponsored loans also available. Support available to part-time students. Financial award application deadline: 4/1; financial award applicants required to submit FAFSA. *Faculty research:* AIDS education, employee wellness, isometric strength evaluation. *Unit head:* Dr. Karen Meaney, Graduate Advisor, 512-245-2561, Fax: 512-245-8678, E-mail: km66@txstate.edu. *Application contact:* Amy Galle, Head, 512-245-2561, Fax: 512-245-8678, E-mail: ag04@txstate.edu. Web site: http://www.hhp.txstate.edu/Degree-Plans/Graduate.html.

Texas State University–San Marcos, Graduate School, Interdisciplinary Studies Program in Health, Physical Education, and Recreation, San Marcos, TX 78666. Offers MAIS. Part-time and evening/weekend programs available. *Students:* 2 applicants, 50% accepted. *Degree requirements:* For master's, comprehensive exam, thesis optional. *Entrance requirements:* For master's, GRE General Test, minimum GPA of 2.75 in last 60 hours of course work. Additional exam requirements/recommendations for international students: Required—TOEFL (minimum score 550 paper-based; 213 computer-based; 78 iBT). *Application deadline:* For fall admission, 6/15 priority date for domestic students, 6/1 for international students; for spring admission, 10/15 priority date for domestic students, 10/1 for international students. Applications are processed on a rolling basis. Application fee: $40 ($90 for international students). *Expenses:* Tuition, state resident: full-time $6408; part-time $3204 per semester. Tuition, nonresident: full-time $14,832; part-time $7416 per semester. *Required fees:* $1824; $912 per semester. Tuition and fees vary according to course load. *Financial support:* Teaching assistantships, career-related internships or fieldwork, Federal Work-Study, institutionally sponsored loans, scholarships/grants, health care benefits, and unspecified assistantships available. Support available to part-time students. Financial award application deadline: 4/1; financial award applicants required to submit FAFSA. *Unit head:* Dr. Karen Meaney, Graduate Advisor, 512-245-2952, Fax: 512-245-8678, E-mail: km66@txstate.edu. *Application contact:* Dr. J. Michael Willoughby, Dean of Graduate School, 512-245-2581, Fax: 512-245-8365, E-mail: gradcollege@txstate.edu. Web site: http://www.hhp.txstate.edu/.

Texas Woman's University, Graduate School, College of Health Sciences, Department of Kinesiology, Denton, TX 76201. Offers adapted physical education (MS, PhD); biomechanics (MS, PhD); coaching (MS); exercise physiology (MS, PhD); pedagogy (MS); sport management (MS, PhD). Part-time and evening/weekend programs available. *Faculty:* 12 full-time (6 women), 1 part-time/adjunct (0 women). *Students:* 55 full-time (38 women), 104 part-time (69 women); includes 35 minority (24 Black or African American, non-Hispanic/Latino; 1 American Indian or Alaska Native, non-Hispanic/Latino; 10 Hispanic/Latino), 23 international. Average age 31. 86 applicants, 73% accepted, 38 enrolled. In 2011, 25 master's, 7 doctorates awarded. Terminal master's awarded for partial completion of doctoral program. *Degree requirements:* For master's, comprehensive exam, thesis or alternative; for doctorate, comprehensive exam, thesis/dissertation, qualifying exam. *Entrance requirements:* For master's, GRE General Test (biomechanics emphasis only), 2 letters of reference, curriculum vitae, interview (adapted physical education emphasis only); for doctorate, GRE General Test (biomechanics emphasis only), interview, 3 letters of reference, curriculum vitae. Additional exam requirements/recommendations for international students: Required—TOEFL (minimum score 550 paper-based; 213 computer-based; 79 iBT). *Application deadline:* For fall admission, 7/1 priority date for domestic students, 3/1 for international students; for spring admission, 11/1 priority date for domestic students, 7/1 for international students. Applications are processed on a rolling basis. Application fee: $50 ($75 for international students). Electronic applications accepted. *Expenses:* Tuition, state resident: full-time $3834; part-time $213 per credit hour. Tuition, nonresident: full-time $9468; part-time $526 per credit hour. *Required fees:* $213 per credit hour. Tuition and fees vary according to course load. *Financial support:* In 2011–12, 46 students received support, including 7 research assistantships (averaging $10,746 per year), 14 teaching assistantships (averaging $10,746 per year); career-related internships or fieldwork, Federal Work-Study, institutionally sponsored loans, scholarships/grants, traineeships, health care benefits, and unspecified assistantships also available. Support available to part-time students. Financial award application deadline: 3/1; financial award applicants required to submit FAFSA. *Faculty research:* Exercise and Type 2 diabetes risk, bone mineral density and exercise in special populations, obesity in children, factors influencing sport consumer behavior and loyalty, roles and responsibilities of paraeducators in adapted physical education. *Total annual research expenditures:* $19,544. *Unit head:* Dr. David Nichols, Chair, 940-898-2575, Fax: 940-898-2581, E-mail: dnichols@twu.edu. *Application contact:* Dr. Samuel Wheeler, Assistant Director of Admissions, 940-898-3188, Fax: 940-898-3081, E-mail: wheelersr@twu.edu. Web site: http://www.twu.edu/kinesiology/.

Troy University, Graduate School, College of Education, Program in Teacher Education-Multiple Levels, Troy, AL 36082. Offers art education (MS); gifted education (MS); instrumental (MS); physical education (MS); reading specialist (MS); vocal/choral (MS). Part-time and evening/weekend programs available. *Faculty:* 6 full-time (4 women). *Students:* 6 full-time (4 women), 20 part-time (10 women); includes 3 minority (all Black or African American, non-Hispanic/Latino). Average age 30. 12 applicants, 83% accepted, 5 enrolled. In 2011, 13 master's awarded. *Degree requirements:* For master's, comprehensive exam, thesis. *Entrance requirements:* For master's, minimum GPA of 2.5. Additional exam requirements/recommendations for international students: Required—TOEFL (minimum score 523 paper-based; 193 computer-based; 70 iBT), IELTS (minimum score 6). *Application deadline:* Applications are processed on a rolling basis. Application fee: $50. Electronic applications accepted. *Expenses:* Tuition, state resident: full-time $6960; part-time $290 per credit hour. Tuition, nonresident: full-time $13,920; part-time $580 per credit hour. *Required fees:* $386 per term. *Financial support:* Available to part-time students. Applicants required to submit FAFSA. *Unit head:* Dr. Charlotte S. Minnick, Director, Teacher Education, 334-670-3544, Fax: 334-670-3548, E-mail: csminnick@troy.edu. *Application contact:* Brenda K. Campbell, Director of Graduate Admissions, 334-670-3178, Fax: 334-670-3733, E-mail: bcamp@troy.edu.

Union College, Graduate Programs, Department of Education, Barbourville, KY 40906-1499. Offers elementary education (MA); health and physical education (MA); middle grades (MA); music education (MA); principalship (MA); reading specialist (MA); secondary education (MA); special education (MA). *Degree requirements:* For master's, thesis optional. *Entrance requirements:* For master's, GRE General Test, NTE.

United States Sports Academy, Graduate Programs, Program in Sports Coaching, Daphne, AL 36526-7055. Offers MSS. Part-time programs available. Postbaccalaureate distance learning degree programs offered (no on-campus study). *Degree requirements:* For master's, comprehensive exam, thesis optional. *Entrance requirements:* For master's, GRE General Test, GMAT, or MAT, minimum GPA of 2.5, 3 letters of recommendation, resume. Additional exam requirements/recommendations for international students: Required—TOEFL (minimum score 500 paper-based; 213 computer-based). Electronic applications accepted. *Faculty research:* Effect of attentional skill on sports performance, survey of coaching qualifications, coaching certification.

Universidad del Turabo, Graduate Programs, Programs in Education, Program in Coaching, Gurabo, PR 00778-3030. Offers MPHE. *Students:* 20 full-time (10 women), 6 part-time (1 woman); includes 20 minority (all Hispanic/Latino). Average age 26. 16 applicants, 88% accepted, 13 enrolled. In 2011, 13 master's awarded. *Unit head:* Angela Candelario, Dean, 787-743-7979 Ext. 4126. *Application contact:* Virginia Gonzalez, Admissions Officer, 787-746-3009.

Universidad Metropolitana, School of Education, Program in Teaching of Physical Education, San Juan, PR 00928-1150. Offers teaching of adult physical education (M Ed); teaching of elementary physical education (M Ed); teaching of secondary physical education (M Ed). *Degree requirements:* For master's, thesis or alternative. *Entrance requirements:* For master's, EXADEP, interview. Electronic applications accepted.

Université de Montréal, Department of Kinesiology, Montréal, QC H3C 3J7, Canada. Offers kinesiology (M Sc, DESS); physical activity (M Sc, PhD). *Degree requirements:* For master's, one foreign language, thesis (for some programs); for doctorate, one foreign language, thesis/dissertation, general exam. Electronic applications accepted. *Faculty research:* Physiology of exercise, psychology of sports, biomechanics, dance, sociology of sports.

Université de Sherbrooke, Faculty of Physical Education and Sports, Program in Physical Education, Sherbrooke, QC J1K 2R1, Canada. Offers kinanthropology (M Sc); physical activity (Diploma). *Degree requirements:* For master's, thesis. *Entrance requirements:* For master's, minimum GPA of 2.7; for Diploma, bachelor's degree in physical education. *Faculty research:* Physical fitness, nutrition, human factors, sociology, teaching.

Université du Québec à Trois-Rivières, Graduate Programs, Program in Physical Education, Trois-Rivières, QC G9A 5H7, Canada. Offers M Sc. Part-time programs available. *Degree requirements:* For master's, thesis. *Entrance requirements:* For master's, appropriate bachelor's degree, proficiency in French.

The University of Akron, Graduate School, College of Education, Department of Sport Science and Wellness Education, Program in Sports Science/Coaching, Akron, OH 44325. Offers MA, MS. *Students:* 44 full-time (11 women), 29 part-time (8 women); includes 12 minority (9 Black or African American, non-Hispanic/Latino; 1 Hispanic/Latino; 2 Two or more races, non-Hispanic/Latino), 1 international. Average age 28. 57 applicants, 72% accepted, 29 enrolled. In 2011, 27 master's awarded. *Degree requirements:* For master's, comprehensive exam, thesis optional. *Entrance requirements:* For master's, minimum GPA of 2.75, three letters of recommendation, statement of purpose. Additional exam requirements/recommendations for international students: Required—TOEFL (minimum score 550 paper-based; 213 computer-based; 79 iBT). *Application deadline:* Applications are processed on a rolling basis. Application fee: $30 ($40 for international students). Electronic applications accepted. *Expenses:* Tuition, state resident: full-time $7038; part-time $391 per credit hour. Tuition, nonresident: full-time $12,051; part-time $670 per credit hour. *Required fees:* $1274; $34 per credit hour. *Unit head:* Dr. Alan Kornspan, Program Coordinator, 330-972-8145, E-mail: alan3@uakron.edu. *Application contact:* Dr. Mark Tausig, Associate Dean, 330-972-6266, Fax: 330-972-6475, E-mail: mtausig@uakron.edu.

The University of Alabama, Graduate School, College of Education, Department of Kinesiology, Tuscaloosa, AL 35487. Offers alternative sport pedagogy (MA); exercise science (MA, PhD); human performance (MA); sport management (MA); sport pedagogy (MA, PhD). Part-time programs available. *Faculty:* 8 full-time (1 woman). *Students:* 59 full-time (22 women), 22 part-time (14 women); includes 11 minority (7 Black or African American, non-Hispanic/Latino; 1 Asian, non-Hispanic/Latino; 2 Hispanic/Latino; 1 Two or more races, non-Hispanic/Latino), 7 international. Average age 30. 50 applicants, 78% accepted, 20 enrolled. In 2011, 23 master's, 6 doctorates awarded. *Median time to degree:* Of those who began their doctoral program in fall 2003, 100% received their degree in 8 years or less. *Degree requirements:* For master's, comprehensive exam, thesis optional; for doctorate, comprehensive exam, thesis/dissertation. *Entrance requirements:* For master's and doctorate, GRE, MAT, minimum GPA of 3.0. Additional exam requirements/recommendations for international students: Required—TOEFL. *Application deadline:* Applications are processed on a rolling basis. Application fee: $50 ($60 for international students). Electronic applications accepted. *Expenses:* Tuition, state resident: full-time $8600. Tuition, nonresident: full-time $21,900. *Financial support:* In 2011–12, 14 students received support, including 13 teaching assistantships with full tuition reimbursements available (averaging $8,678 per year). *Faculty research:* Race, gender and sexuality in sports; physical education teacher socialization; disability sports; physical activity and health; environmental physiology. *Total annual research expenditures:* $19,866. *Unit head:* Dr. Matt Curtner-Smith, Department Head and Professor, 205-348-9209, Fax: 205-348-0867, E-mail: msmith@bamaed.ua.edu. *Application contact:* Dr. Kathy S. Wetzel, Assistant Dean for Student Services, 205-348-1154, Fax: 205-348-0080, E-mail: kwetzel@bamaed.ua.edu. Web site: http://www.kinesiology.ua.edu/.

The University of Alabama at Birmingham, College of Arts and Sciences, School of Education, Program in Physical Education, Birmingham, AL 35294. Offers MA Ed. Evening/weekend programs available. *Degree requirements:* For master's, thesis optional. *Entrance requirements:* For master's, GRE General Test, MAT, or NTE, minimum GPA of 3.0. *Application deadline:* Applications are processed on a rolling basis. Electronic applications accepted. *Expenses:* Tuition, state resident: full-time $5922; part-time $309 per hour. Tuition, nonresident: full-time $13,428; part-time $726 per hour. Tuition and fees vary according to program. *Unit head:* Dr. Kristi S. Menear, 205-975-7409, E-mail: kmenear@uab.edu. Web site: http://www.uab.edu/humanstudies/physicaleducation.

University of Alberta, Faculty of Graduate Studies and Research, Department of Physical Education and Recreation, Edmonton, AB T6G 2E1, Canada. Offers physical education (M Sc); recreation and physical education (MA, PhD). Part-time programs available. Terminal master's awarded for partial completion of doctoral program. *Degree requirements:* For master's, thesis (for some programs); for doctorate, thesis/dissertation. *Entrance requirements:* For master's, bachelor's degree in related field; for doctorate, master's degree in related field with thesis. Additional exam requirements/recommendations for international students: Required—TOEFL. *Faculty research:* Motivation and adherence to physical ability, performance enhancement, adapted physical activity, exercise physiology, sport administration, tourism.

University of Arkansas, Graduate School, College of Education and Health Professions, Department of Health Science, Kinesiology, Recreation and Dance, Program in Physical Education, Fayetteville, AR 72701-1201. Offers M Ed, MAT. *Students:* 11 part-time (2 women); includes 3 minority (2 Black or African American, non-Hispanic/Latino; 1 Two or more races, non-Hispanic/Latino). In 2011, 9 master's awarded. *Degree requirements:* For master's, thesis optional. *Application deadline:* For fall admission, 4/1 for international students; for spring admission, 10/1 for international students. Applications are processed on a rolling basis. Application fee: $40 ($50 for international students). Electronic applications accepted. *Financial support:* Fellowships with tuition reimbursements, research assistantships, teaching assistantships, career-related internships or fieldwork, and Federal Work-Study available. Support available to part-time students. Financial award application deadline: 4/1; financial award applicants required to submit FAFSA. *Unit head:* Dr. Bart Hammig, Department Chairperson, 479-575-2890, Fax: 479-575-5778, E-mail: bhammig@uark.edu. *Application contact:* Dr. Dean Gorman, Coordinator of Graduate Studies, 479-575-2890, E-mail: dgorman@uark.edu. Web site: http://hkrd.uark.edu/.

University of Arkansas at Pine Bluff, School of Education, Pine Bluff, AR 71601-2799. Offers early childhood education (M Ed); secondary education (M Ed), including English education, mathematics education, physical education, science education, social studies education; teaching (MAT). *Accreditation:* NCATE. Part-time and evening/weekend programs available. *Degree requirements:* For master's, comprehensive exam. *Entrance requirements:* For master's, GRE, minimum GPA of 2.75, NTE or Standard Arkansas Teaching Certificate. *Faculty research:* Teacher certification, accreditation, assessment, standards, portfolio development, rehabilitation, technology.

The University of British Columbia, Faculty of Education, Department of Curriculum and Pedagogy, Vancouver, BC V6T 1Z4, Canada. Offers art education (M Ed, MA); business education (MA); curriculum studies (M Ed, MA, PhD); home economics education (M Ed, MA); math education (M Ed, MA); music education (M Ed, MA); physical education (M Ed, MA); science education (M Ed, MA); social studies education (M Ed, MA); technology studies education (M Ed, MA). Part-time programs available. *Degree requirements:* For master's, thesis (MA); for doctorate, comprehensive exam, thesis/dissertation. *Entrance requirements:* Additional exam requirements/recommendations for international students: Required—TOEFL (minimum score 580 paper-based; 237 computer-based; 92 iBT). Electronic applications accepted. *Expenses:* Contact institution. *Faculty research:* School subjects, teaching and learning.

University of Central Missouri, The Graduate School, College of Health and Human Services, Warrensburg, MO 64093. Offers criminal justice (MS); industrial hygiene (MS); occupational safety management (MS); physical education/exercise and sport science (MS); rural family nursing (MS); social gerontology (MS); sociology (MA); speech language pathology and audiology (MS). *Accreditation:* NCATE. Part-time programs available. Postbaccalaureate distance learning degree programs offered. *Entrance requirements:* Additional exam requirements/recommendations for international students: Required—TOEFL (minimum score 550 paper-based; 79 computer-based). Electronic applications accepted.

University of Dayton, Department of Health and Sport Science, Dayton, OH 45469-1300. Offers exercise science (MS Ed); physical therapy (DPT). Part-time programs available. *Faculty:* 16 full-time (7 women). *Students:* 113 full-time (70 women), 4 part-time (1 woman); includes 4 minority (all Black or African American, non-Hispanic/Latino), 5 international. Average age 36. 195 applicants, 43% accepted, 41 enrolled. In 2011, 3 master's, 34 doctorates awarded. *Degree requirements:* For master's, thesis; for doctorate, thesis/dissertation. *Entrance requirements:* For master's, GRE General Test, MAT, minimum GPA of 2.75; for doctorate, GRE General Test, minimum GPA of 3.0, 80 observation hours. Additional exam requirements/recommendations for international students: Required—TOEFL (minimum score 550 paper-based; 213 computer-based; 80 iBT). *Application deadline:* For fall admission, 2/15 priority date for domestic students, 3/1 for international students; for winter admission, 7/1 for international students; for spring admission, 1/1 for international students. Applications are processed on a rolling basis. Application fee: $0 ($50 for international students). Electronic applications accepted. *Expenses: Tuition:* Full-time $8400; part-time $700 per credit hour. *Required fees:* $25 per semester. Tuition and fees vary according to degree level. *Financial support:* In 2011–12, 4 students received support, including 8 research assistantships with partial tuition reimbursements available (averaging $4,800 per year), 5 teaching assistantships with full tuition reimbursements available (averaging $8,550 per year); career-related internships or fieldwork, institutionally sponsored loans, health care benefits, and unspecified assistantships also available. Financial award applicants required to submit FAFSA. *Faculty research:* Energy expenditure, strength, training, teaching nutrition and calcium intake for children and families in Head-Start. *Unit head:* Dr. Lloyd Laubach, Interim Chair, 937-229-4240, Fax: 937-229-4244, E-mail: llaubach1@udayton.edu. *Application contact:* Laura Greger, Administrative Assistant, 937-229-4225, E-mail: lgreger1@udayton.edu.

University of Florida, Graduate School, College of Health and Human Performance, Department of Applied Physiology and Kinesiology, Gainesville, FL 32611. Offers athletic training/sport medicine (MS); biobehavioral science (MS, PhD); clinical exercise physiology (MS); exercise physiology (MS, PhD); health and human performance (PhD); human performance (MS). *Degree requirements:* For master's, comprehensive exam, thesis (for some programs); for doctorate, comprehensive exam, thesis/dissertation. *Entrance requirements:* For doctorate, GRE General Test. Additional exam requirements/recommendations for international students: Required—TOEFL (minimum score 550 paper-based; 213 computer-based; 80 iBT), IELTS (minimum score 6). Electronic applications accepted. *Faculty research:* Cardiovascular disease; basic mechanisms that underlie exercise-induced changes in the body at the organ, tissue, cellular and molecular level; development of rehabilitation techniques for regaining motor control after stroke or as a consequence of Parkinson's disease; maintaining optimal health and delaying age-related declines in physiological function; psychomotor mechanisms impacting health and performance across the life span.

University of Georgia, College of Education, Department of Kinesiology, Athens, GA 30602. Offers MS, PhD. *Faculty:* 20 full-time (5 women). *Students:* 127 full-time (56 women), 18 part-time (7 women); includes 21 minority (13 Black or African American, non-Hispanic/Latino; 1 Asian, non-Hispanic/Latino; 4 Hispanic/Latino; 3 Two or more races, non-Hispanic/Latino), 20 international. Average age 27. 225 applicants, 36% accepted, 50 enrolled. In 2011, 35 master's, 9 doctorates awarded. *Entrance requirements:* For master's, GRE General Test or MAT; for doctorate, GRE General Test. Additional exam requirements/recommendations for international students: Required—TOEFL. *Application deadline:* For fall admission, 7/1 priority date for domestic students; for spring admission, 11/15 for domestic students. Application fee: $50. Electronic applications accepted. *Unit head:* Dr. Kirk J. Cureton, Head, 706-542-4387, Fax: 706-542-3148, E-mail: kcureton@uga.edu. *Application contact:* Dr. Michael Schmidt, Graduate Coordinator, 706-542-6577, Fax: 706-542-3148, E-mail: schmidtm@uga.edu. Web site: http://www.coe.uga.edu/kinesiology.

University of Houston, College of Liberal Arts and Social Sciences, Department of Health and Human Performance, Houston, TX 77204. Offers exercise science (MS); human nutrition (MS); human space exploration sciences (MS); kinesiology (PhD); physical education (M Ed). *Accreditation:* NCATE (one or more programs are accredited). Part-time and evening/weekend programs available. *Degree requirements:* For master's, comprehensive exam (for some programs), thesis (for some programs); for doctorate, comprehensive exam, thesis/dissertation, qualifying exam, candidacy paper. *Entrance requirements:* For master's, GRE (minimum 35th percentile on each section), minimum cumulative GPA of 3.0; for doctorate, GRE (minimum 35th percentile on each section), minimum cumulative GPA of 3.3. Additional exam requirements/recommendations for international students: Required—TOEFL (minimum score 550 paper-based; 79 iBT). Electronic applications accepted. *Faculty research:* Biomechanics, exercise physiology, obesity, nutrition, space exploration science.

University of Idaho, College of Graduate Studies, College of Education, Department of Movement Sciences, Program in Physical Education, Moscow, ID 83844-2401. Offers M Ed, MS. *Students:* 7 full-time, 4 part-time. Average age 26. In 2011, 10 master's awarded. *Entrance requirements:* For master's, minimum GPA of 2.8. *Application deadline:* For fall admission, 8/1 for domestic students; for spring admission, 12/15 for domestic students. Applications are processed on a rolling basis. Application fee: $60. Electronic applications accepted. *Expenses:* Tuition, state resident: full-time $3874; part-time $334 per credit hour. Tuition, nonresident: full-time $16,394; part-time $861 per credit hour. *Required fees:* $2808; $99 per credit hour. Tuition and fees vary according to program. *Financial support:* Research assistantships and teaching assistantships available. Financial award applicants required to submit FAFSA. *Unit head:* Dr. Kathy Browder, Chair, 208-885-2192, E-mail: hperd@uidaho.edu. *Application contact:* Erick Larson, Director of Graduate Admissions, 208-885-4723, E-mail: gadms@uidaho.edu. Web site: http://www.uidaho.edu/ed/movementsciences.

University of Indianapolis, Graduate Programs, School of Education, Indianapolis, IN 46227-3697. Offers art education (MAT); biology (MAT); chemistry (MAT); curriculum and instruction (MA); earth sciences (MAT); education (MA, MAT); educational leadership (MA); elementary education (MA); English (MAT); French (MAT); math (MAT); physical education (MAT); physics (MAT); secondary education (MA), including art education, education, English education, social studies education; social studies (MAT); Spanish (MAT). *Accreditation:* NCATE. Part-time and evening/weekend programs available. *Faculty:* 3 full-time (2 women), 3 part-time/adjunct (2 women). *Students:* 32 full-time (18 women), 97 part-time (56 women); includes 22 minority (20 Black or African American, non-Hispanic/Latino; 1 Asian, non-Hispanic/Latino; 1 Hispanic/Latino), 3 international. Average age 33. In 2011, 78 master's awarded. *Entrance requirements:* For master's, GRE Subject Test, PRAXIS I, minimum GPA of 2.5, 3 letters of recommendation, interview, writing exercise. Additional exam requirements/recommendations for international students: Required—TOEFL (minimum score 550 paper-based; 213 computer-based). *Application deadline:* Applications are processed on a rolling basis. Application fee: $50. Tuition and fees vary according to degree level and program. *Financial support:* Federal Work-Study available. Financial award application deadline: 5/1; financial award applicants required to submit FAFSA. *Faculty research:* Assessment of teacher education, perceptions of prospective teachers by parents. *Unit head:* Dr. Kathy Moran, Dean, 317-788-3285, Fax: 317-788-3300, E-mail: kmoran@uindy.edu. *Application contact:* Jeni Kirby, 317-788-2113, E-mail: kirbyj@uindy.edu. Web site: http://education.uindy.edu/.

The University of Iowa, Graduate College, College of Liberal Arts and Sciences, Department of Health and Sport Studies, Iowa City, IA 52242-1316. Offers psychology of sport and physical activity (MA, PhD); sports studies (MA, PhD). *Degree requirements:* For master's, thesis optional, exam; for doctorate, comprehensive exam, thesis/dissertation. *Entrance requirements:* For master's and doctorate, GRE General Test, minimum GPA of 3.0. Additional exam requirements/recommendations for international students: Required—TOEFL (minimum score 600 paper-based; 250 computer-based; 100 iBT). Electronic applications accepted.

The University of Kansas, Graduate Studies, School of Education, Department of Health, Sport, and Exercise Sciences, Lawrence, KS 66045. Offers health and physical education (MS Ed, Ed D, PhD). *Accreditation:* NCATE. Part-time and evening/weekend programs available. *Faculty:* 11 full-time (4 women), 2 part-time/adjunct (0 women). *Students:* 43 full-time (20 women), 20 part-time (10 women); includes 8 minority (2 Asian, non-Hispanic/Latino; 3 Hispanic/Latino; 3 Two or more races, non-Hispanic/Latino), 3 international. Average age 29. 63 applicants, 46% accepted, 22 enrolled. In 2011, 34 master's, 1 doctorate awarded. *Degree requirements:* For master's, comprehensive exam (for some programs), thesis (for some programs); for doctorate, variable foreign language requirement, comprehensive exam, thesis/dissertation. *Entrance requirements:* For master's, GRE General Test (minimum score 1000, 450 verbal, 450 quantitative, 4.0 analytical), minimum GPA of 3.0; for doctorate, GRE General Test (minimum score 1100: verbal 500, quantitative 500, analytical 4.5), minimum graduate GPA of 3.5, undergraduate 3.0. Additional exam requirements/recommendations for international students: Required—TOEFL (minimum score 570 paper-based; 230 computer-based). *Application deadline:* For fall admission, 3/15 priority date for domestic students; for spring admission, 10/15 priority date for domestic students. Applications are processed on a rolling basis. Application fee: $55 ($65 for international students). Electronic applications accepted. Tuition and fees vary according to course load, campus/location, program and reciprocity agreements. *Financial support:* Research assistantships with full and partial tuition reimbursements and teaching assistantships with full and partial tuition reimbursements available. Financial award application deadline: 4/1. *Faculty research:* Exercise and sport psychology, obesity prevention, sexuality health, sport ethics, skeletal muscle cell signaling and performance. *Unit head:* Dr. Andrew Fry, Chair, 785-864-0784, Fax: 785-864-3343, E-mail: acfry@ku.edu. *Application contact:* Dr. Keith D. Tennant, Graduate Coordinator, 785-864-4656, Fax: 785-864-3343, E-mail: ktennant@ku.edu. Web site: http://www.soe.ku.edu/hses/.

University of Louisville, Graduate School, College of Education and Human Development, Department of Health and Sport Sciences, Louisville, KY 40292-0001. Offers community health education (M Ed); exercise physiology (MS); health and physical education (MAT); sport administration (MS). Part-time and evening/weekend programs available. *Entrance requirements:* For master's, GRE General Test. Additional exam requirements/recommendations for international students: Required—TOEFL (minimum score 560 paper-based; 210 computer-based; 83 iBT). Electronic applications accepted. *Expenses:* Tuition, state resident: full-time $9692; part-time $539 per credit hour. Tuition, nonresident: full-time $20,168; part-time $1121 per credit hour. Tuition and fees vary according to program and reciprocity agreements. *Faculty research:* Impact of sports and sport marketing on society, factors associated with school and community health, cardiac and pulmonary rehabilitation, impact of participation in activities on student retention and graduation, strength and conditioning.

University of Maine, Graduate School, College of Education and Human Development, Program in Kinesiology and Physical Education, Orono, ME 04469. Offers curriculum and instruction (M Ed); exercise science (MS). Part-time and evening/weekend programs available. *Students:* 10 full-time (3 women), 2 part-time (1 woman); includes 2 minority (1 Hispanic/Latino; 1 Two or more races, non-Hispanic/Latino). Average age 29. 16 applicants, 69% accepted, 9 enrolled. In 2011, 8 degrees awarded. *Degree requirements:* For master's, thesis or alternative. *Entrance requirements:* For master's, MAT. Additional exam requirements/recommendations for international students: Required—TOEFL. *Application deadline:* For fall admission, 2/1 priority date for domestic students. Applications are processed on a rolling basis. Application fee: $65. Electronic applications accepted. *Expenses:* Tuition, state resident: full-time $5016. Tuition, nonresident: full-time $14,424. *Financial support:* Career-related internships or fieldwork, Federal Work-Study, institutionally sponsored loans, tuition waivers (full and partial), and unspecified assistantships available. Support available to part-time students. Financial award application deadline: 3/1. *Unit head:* Dr. Janet Spector, Coordinator, 207-581-2444, Fax: 207-581-2423. *Application contact:* Scott G. Delcourt, Associate Dean of the Graduate School, 207-581-3291, Fax: 207-581-3232, E-mail: graduate@maine.edu. Web site: http://www2umaine.edu/graduate/.

University of Manitoba, Faculty of Graduate Studies, Faculty of Kinesiology and Recreation Management, Winnipeg, MB R3T 2N2, Canada. Offers kinesiology and recreation (M Sc, MA).

University of Memphis, Graduate School, College of Education, Department of Health and Sport Sciences, Memphis, TN 38152. Offers clinical nutrition (MS); exercise and sport science (MS); health promotion (MS); physical education teacher education (MS), including teacher education; sport and leisure commerce (MS). Part-time and evening/weekend programs available. *Degree requirements:* For master's, comprehensive exam, thesis. *Entrance requirements:* For master's, GRE General Test or GMAT (sport and leisure commerce). *Faculty research:* Sport marketing and consumer analysis, health psychology, smoking cessation, psychosocial aspects of cardiovascular disease, global health promotion.

University of Minnesota, Twin Cities Campus, Graduate School, College of Education and Human Development, School of Kinesiology, Minneapolis, MN 55455-0213. Offers adapted physical education (MA, PhD); biomechanics (MA); biomechanics and neural control (PhD); coaching (Certificate); developmental adapted physical education (M Ed); exercise physiology (MA, PhD); human factors/ergonomics (MA, PhD); international/comparative sport (MA, PhD); kinesiology (M Ed, MA, PhD); leisure services/management (MA, PhD); motor development (MA, PhD); motor learning/control (MA, PhD); outdoor education/recreation (MA, PhD); physical education (M Ed); recreation, park, and leisure studies (M Ed, MA, PhD); sport and exercise science (M Ed); sport management (M Ed, MA, PhD); sport psychology (MA, PhD); sport sociology (MA, PhD); therapeutic recreation (MA, PhD). Part-time programs available. *Faculty:* 15 full-time (7 women). *Students:* 144 full-time (72 women), 49 part-time (19 women); includes 20 minority (9 Black or African American, non-Hispanic/Latino; 3 American Indian or Alaska Native, non-Hispanic/Latino; 4 Asian, non-Hispanic/Latino; 2 Hispanic/Latino; 2 Native Hawaiian or other Pacific Islander, non-Hispanic/Latino), 18 international. Average age 29. 198 applicants, 42% accepted, 77 enrolled. In 2011, 74 master's, 11 doctorates, 19 other advanced degrees awarded. Terminal master's awarded for partial completion of doctoral program. *Degree requirements:* For master's, final oral exam; for doctorate, thesis/dissertation, preliminary written/oral exam, final oral exam. *Entrance requirements:* For master's, GRE or MAT, minimum GPA of 3.0; for doctorate, GRE or MAT, minimum GPA of 3.0, writing sample. Application fee: $55. *Financial support:* In 2011–12, 1 fellowship (averaging $60,000 per year), 4 research assistantships with full tuition reimbursements (averaging $99,992 per year), 48 teaching assistantships with full tuition reimbursements (averaging $12,534 per year) were awarded; career-related internships or fieldwork, Federal Work-Study, institutionally sponsored loans, and tuition waivers (full and partial) also available. Support available to part-time students. *Faculty research:* Exercise physiology; biochemical, molecular and nutritional aspects of exercise; sport training and performance; sport and exercise psychology; behavioral aspects of physical activity; youth sport science; gender and sport sociology; sports management; sports policy, marketing and law; motor development and disabilities; movement perception and action; movement neuroscience. *Total annual research expenditures:* $369,026. *Unit head:* Dr. Li Li Ji, Director, 612-624-9809, Fax: 612-626-7700, E-mail: llji@umn.edu. *Application contact:* Dr. Jennifer Engler, Assistant Dean, 612-626-2887, Fax: 612-626-7496, E-mail: engle009@umn.edu.

The University of Montana, Graduate School, Phyllis J. Washington College of Education and Human Sciences, Department of Health and Human Performance,

Missoula, MT 59812-0002. Offers exercise science (MS); health and human performance (MS); health promotion (MS). Part-time programs available. *Entrance requirements:* For master's, GRE General Test. Additional exam requirements/recommendations for international students: Required—TOEFL. *Faculty research:* Exercise physiology, performance psychology, nutrition, pre-employment physical screening, program evaluation.

University of Nebraska at Kearney, Graduate Studies, College of Education, Department of Health, Physical Education, Recreation, and Leisure Studies, Kearney, NE 68849-0001. Offers adapted physical education (MA Ed); exercise science (MA Ed); master teacher (MA Ed). Part-time and evening/weekend programs available. *Degree requirements:* For master's, comprehensive exam, thesis optional. *Entrance requirements:* For master's, GRE General Test. Additional exam requirements/recommendations for international students: Required—TOEFL (minimum score 550 paper-based; 213 computer-based). Electronic applications accepted. *Faculty research:* Ergonomic aids, nutrition, motor development, sports pedagogy, applied behavior analysis.

University of Nebraska at Omaha, Graduate Studies, College of Education, School of Health, Physical Education, and Recreation, Omaha, NE 68182. Offers athletic training (MA); health, physical education, and recreation (MA, MS). Part-time and evening/weekend programs available. *Faculty:* 13 full-time (4 women). *Students:* 37 full-time (15 women), 40 part-time (25 women); includes 4 minority (1 Black or African American, non-Hispanic/Latino; 2 Hispanic/Latino; 1 Two or more races, non-Hispanic/Latino), 2 international. Average age 27. 27 applicants, 67% accepted, 15 enrolled. In 2011, 33 master's awarded. *Degree requirements:* For master's, comprehensive exam, thesis (for some programs). *Entrance requirements:* For master's, minimum GPA of 3.0, statement of purpose, letters of recommendation. Additional exam requirements/recommendations for international students: Required—TOEFL (minimum score 550 paper-based; 213 computer-based; 80 iBT). *Application deadline:* For fall admission, 7/1 priority date for domestic students; for spring admission, 12/1 priority date for domestic students. Applications are processed on a rolling basis. Application fee: $45. Electronic applications accepted. *Financial support:* In 2011–12, 40 students received support, including 25 research assistantships with tuition reimbursements available, 10 teaching assistantships with tuition reimbursements available; fellowships, Federal Work-Study, institutionally sponsored loans, scholarships/grants, tuition waivers (full), and unspecified assistantships also available. Support available to part-time students. Financial award application deadline: 3/1; financial award applicants required to submit FAFSA. *Unit head:* Dr. Dan Blanke, Director, 402-554-2670. *Application contact:* Dr. Kris Berg, 402-554-2341, Fax: 402-554-3143, E-mail: graduate@unomaha.edu.

University of Nevada, Las Vegas, Graduate College, College of Education, Department of Sports Education Leadership, Las Vegas, NV 89154-3031. Offers physical education (M Ed, MS); sports education leadership (PhD). *Faculty:* 8 full-time (5 women), 12 part-time/adjunct (5 women). *Students:* 2 full-time (0 women), 13 part-time (6 women); includes 5 minority (all Black or African American, non-Hispanic/Latino). Average age 31. 2 applicants, 0% accepted, 0 enrolled. In 2011, 19 master's, 3 doctorates awarded. *Degree requirements:* For doctorate, comprehensive exam, thesis/dissertation, scholarly product. *Entrance requirements:* For master's and doctorate, GRE General Test. Additional exam requirements/recommendations for international students: Required—TOEFL (minimum score 550 paper-based; 213 computer-based; 80 iBT), IELTS (minimum score 7). *Application deadline:* For fall admission, 5/1 for international students; for spring admission, 10/1 for international students. Applications are processed on a rolling basis. Application fee: $60 ($95 for international students). Electronic applications accepted. *Financial support:* In 2011–12, 10 students received support, including 2 research assistantships (averaging $6,750 per year), 8 teaching assistantships (averaging $9,614 per year); institutionally sponsored loans, scholarships/grants, health care benefits, and unspecified assistantships also available. Financial award application deadline: 3/1. *Total annual research expenditures:* $45,038. *Unit head:* Dr. Monica Lounsbery, Chair/Associate Professor, 702-895-5057, Fax: 702-895-5056, E-mail: monica.lounsbery@unlv.edu. *Application contact:* Graduate College Admissions Evaluator, 702-895-3320, Fax: 702-895-4180, E-mail: gradcollege@unlv.edu. Web site: http://education.unlv.edu/sel/index.html.

University of New Brunswick Fredericton, School of Graduate Studies, Faculty of Kinesiology, Fredericton, NB E3B 5A3, Canada. Offers exercise and sport science (M Sc); sport and recreation management (MBA); sport and recreation studies (MA). Part-time programs available. *Faculty:* 15 full-time (7 women). *Students:* 39 full-time (15 women), 6 part-time (4 women). In 2011, 7 master's awarded. *Degree requirements:* For master's, thesis (for some programs). *Entrance requirements:* For master's, minimum GPA of 3.0, written statement of research goals and interests. Additional exam requirements/recommendations for international students: Required—TOEFL (minimum score 600 paper-based; 250 computer-based), TWE (minimum score 4). *Application deadline:* For winter admission, 1/31 for domestic students; for spring admission, 3/31 for domestic students. Applications are processed on a rolling basis. Application fee: $50 Canadian dollars. Electronic applications accepted. *Financial support:* In 2011–12, 38 fellowships with tuition reimbursements, 3 research assistantships, 56 teaching assistantships were awarded; career-related internships or fieldwork and scholarships/grants also available. *Unit head:* Dr. Tim McGarry, Acting Director of Graduate Studies, 506-458-7109, Fax: 506-453-3511, E-mail: tmcgarry@unb.ca. *Application contact:* Leslie Harquail, Graduate Secretary, 506-453-4575, Fax: 506-453-3511, E-mail: harquail@unb.ca. Web site: http://www.unbf.ca/kinesiology/.

University of New Hampshire, Graduate School, School of Health and Human Services, Department of Kinesiology, Durham, NH 03824. Offers adapted physical education (Postbaccalaureate Certificate); kinesiology (MS). Part-time programs available. *Faculty:* 13 full-time (3 women). *Students:* 2 full-time (1 woman), 10 part-time (6 women). Average age 28. 27 applicants, 59% accepted, 8 enrolled. In 2011, 6 master's, 1 other advanced degree awarded. *Degree requirements:* For master's, thesis or alternative. *Entrance requirements:* For master's, GRE General Test. Additional exam requirements/recommendations for international students: Required—TOEFL (minimum score 550 paper-based; 213 computer-based; 80 iBT). *Application deadline:* For fall admission, 6/1 priority date for domestic students, 4/1 for international students; for spring admission, 12/1 for domestic students. Applications are processed on a rolling basis. Application fee: $65. *Expenses:* Tuition, state resident: full-time $12,360; part-time $687 per credit hour. Tuition, nonresident: full-time $25,680; part-time $1058 per credit hour. *International tuition:* $29,550 full-time. *Required fees:* $1666; $833 per course. $416.50 per semester. Tuition and fees vary according to course load and degree level. *Financial support:* In 2011–12, 4 students received support, including 4 teaching assistantships; fellowships, research assistantships, career-related internships or fieldwork, Federal Work-Study, scholarships/grants, and tuition waivers (full and partial) also available. Support available to part-time students. Financial award application deadline: 2/15. *Faculty research:* Exercise specialist, sports studies, special physical education, pediatric exercises and motor behavior. *Unit head:* Dr. Ron Croce, Chairperson, 603-862-2080. *Application contact:* Allison Dwyer, Administrative Assistant, 603-862-2071, E-mail: kinesiology.dept@unh.edu. Web site: http://chhs.unh.edu/kin/index.

University of New Mexico, Graduate School, College of Education, Department of Health, Exercise and Sports Sciences, Program in Physical Education, Albuquerque, NM 87131-2039. Offers adapted physical education (MS); curriculum and instruction (MS); exercise science (MS); generalist (MS); sports administration (MS). Part-time programs available. *Faculty:* 56 full-time (32 women), 41 part-time/adjunct (29 women). *Students:* 45 full-time (25 women), 44 part-time (10 women); includes 42 minority (4 Black or African American, non-Hispanic/Latino; 2 American Indian or Alaska Native, non-Hispanic/Latino; 2 Asian, non-Hispanic/Latino; 31 Hispanic/Latino; 3 Two or more races, non-Hispanic/Latino), 9 international. Average age 29. 65 applicants, 58% accepted, 29 enrolled. In 2011, 27 degrees awarded. Terminal master's awarded for partial completion of doctoral program. *Degree requirements:* For master's, comprehensive exam, thesis optional. *Entrance requirements:* For master's, GRE, 3 letters of reference, minimum cumulative GPA of 3.0 in last 2 years of bachelor's degree, letter of intent. Additional exam requirements/recommendations for international students: Required—TOEFL (minimum score 550 paper-based; 213 computer-based). *Application deadline:* For fall admission, 3/1 priority date for domestic students; for spring admission, 11/1 priority date for domestic students. Application fee: $50. Electronic applications accepted. *Financial support:* In 2011–12, 57 students received support, including 1 fellowship (averaging $2,290 per year), 1 teaching assistantship with full tuition reimbursement available (averaging $11,294 per year); career-related internships or fieldwork, Federal Work-Study, institutionally sponsored loans, scholarships/grants, health care benefits, tuition waivers, and unspecified assistantships also available. Financial award application deadline: 3/1; financial award applicants required to submit FAFSA. *Faculty research:* Physical education pedagogy, sports psychology, sports administration, cardiac rehabilitation, sports physiology, physical fitness assessment, exercise prescription. *Total annual research expenditures:* $17,400. *Unit head:* Dr. Gloria Napper-Owen, Chair, 505-277-8173, Fax: 505-277-6227, E-mail: napperow@unm.edu. *Application contact:* Carol Catania, Department Office, 505-277-5151, Fax: 505-277-6227, E-mail: catania@unm.edu. Web site: http://coe.unm.edu/departments/hess/pe-teacher-education.html.

University of New Mexico, Graduate School, College of Education, Department of Health, Exercise and Sports Sciences, Program in Physical Education, Sports and Exercise Science, Albuquerque, NM 87131-2039. Offers curriculum and instruction (PhD); exercise science (PhD); sports administration (PhD). Part-time programs available. *Students:* 26 full-time (12 women), 25 part-time (7 women); includes 17 minority (4 Black or African American, non-Hispanic/Latino; 3 Asian, non-Hispanic/Latino; 8 Hispanic/Latino; 1 Native Hawaiian or other Pacific Islander, non-Hispanic/Latino; 1 Two or more races, non-Hispanic/Latino), 11 international. Average age 34. 31 applicants, 45% accepted, 8 enrolled. In 2011, 4 degrees awarded. *Degree requirements:* For doctorate, comprehensive exam, thesis/dissertation, inquiry skills, 24 credits in supporting area. *Entrance requirements:* For doctorate, GRE, letter of intent, 3 letters of reference, minimum cumulative GPA of 3.0 in last 2 years of bachelor's degree. Additional exam requirements/recommendations for international students: Required—TOEFL (minimum score 550 paper-based; 213 computer-based). *Application deadline:* For fall admission, 3/1 priority date for domestic students; for spring admission, 11/1 priority date for domestic students. Application fee: $50. Electronic applications accepted. *Financial support:* In 2011–12, 33 students received support, including 3 fellowships (averaging $2,290 per year), 16 teaching assistantships with full tuition reimbursements available (averaging $10,987 per year); career-related internships or fieldwork, Federal Work-Study, institutionally sponsored loans, scholarships/grants, health care benefits, tuition waivers, and unspecified assistantships also available. Financial award application deadline: 3/1; financial award applicants required to submit FAFSA. *Faculty research:* Facility risk management, physical education pedagogy practices, physiological adaptations to exercise, physiological adaptations to heat. *Total annual research expenditures:* $17,400. *Unit head:* Dr. Gloria Napper-Owen, Chair, 505-277-8173, Fax: 505-277-6227, E-mail: napperow@unm.edu. *Application contact:* Carol Catania, Program Office, 505-277-5151, Fax: 505-277-6227, E-mail: catania@unm.edu. Web site: http://coe.unm.edu/index.php/hess/hess-programs/pe-teacher-education/degree-endorsement-programs/physical-education-sports-and-exercise-science-phd.ht.

University of North Alabama, College of Education, Department of Health, Physical Education, and Recreation, FLORENCE, AL 35632-0001. Offers health and human performance (MS), including exercise science, kinesiology, wellness and health promotion; P-12 physical education (MA Ed). *Faculty:* 3 full-time (2 women), 2 part-time/adjunct (0 women). *Students:* 11 full-time (4 women), 4 part-time (1 woman); includes 3 minority (2 Black or African American, non-Hispanic/Latino; 1 Two or more races, non-Hispanic/Latino), 2 international. Average age 24. In 2011, 4 master's awarded. *Unit head:* Dr. Thomas E. Coates, Chair, 256-765-4377. *Application contact:* Kim Mauldin, Director of Admissions, 256-765-4608, Fax: 256-765-4960, E-mail: komauldin@una.edu. Web site: http://www.una.edu/hper/docs/HPERThesisGuideliens.pdf.

The University of North Carolina at Chapel Hill, Graduate School, College of Arts and Sciences, Department of Exercise and Sport Science, Chapel Hill, NC 27599. Offers athletic training (MA); exercise physiology (MA); sport administration (MA). *Degree requirements:* For master's, comprehensive exam, thesis. *Entrance requirements:* For master's, GRE General Test, minimum GPA of 3.0. Additional exam requirements/recommendations for international students: Required—TOEFL (minimum score 550 paper-based). Electronic applications accepted. *Faculty research:* Mild head injury in sport, endocrine system's response to exercise, obesity and children, effect of aerobic exercise on cerebral bloodflow in elderly population.

The University of North Carolina at Pembroke, Graduate Studies, Department of Health, Physical Education, and Recreation, Pembroke, NC 28372-1510. Offers physical education (MA, MAT). Part-time and evening/weekend programs available. *Degree requirements:* For master's, comprehensive exam, thesis optional. *Entrance requirements:* For master's, MAT or GRE, minimum GPA of 3.0 in major, 2.5 overall. Additional exam requirements/recommendations for international students: Required—TOEFL.

University of Northern Colorado, Graduate School, College of Natural and Health Sciences, School of Sport and Exercise Science, Greeley, CO 80639. Offers exercise science (MS, PhD); sport administration (MS, PhD); sport pedagogy (MS, PhD). Part-time and evening/weekend programs available. *Degree requirements:* For master's, comprehensive exam; for doctorate, comprehensive exam, thesis/dissertation. *Entrance requirements:* For master's, 2 letters of recommendation, resume; for doctorate, GRE General Test, 3 letters of recommendation, resume. Electronic applications accepted.

University of Northern Iowa, Graduate College, College of Education, School of Health, Physical Education, and Leisure Services, Program in Physical Education, Cedar Falls, IA 50614. Offers kinesiology (MA); physical education (MA); teaching/coaching (MA). Part-time and evening/weekend programs available. *Students:* 18 full-time (5 women), 6 part-time (1 woman); includes 3 minority (2 Black or African American, non-Hispanic/Latino; 1 Hispanic/Latino), 1 international. 25 applicants, 68% accepted, 12 enrolled. In 2011, 32 master's awarded. *Degree requirements:* For master's, comprehensive exam, thesis or alternative. *Entrance requirements:* For master's, minimum GPA of 3.0. Additional exam requirements/recommendations for international students: Required—TOEFL (minimum score 500 paper-based; 180

computer-based; 61 iBT). *Application deadline:* For fall admission, 8/1 priority date for domestic students. Applications are processed on a rolling basis. Application fee: $50 ($70 for international students). Electronic applications accepted. *Expenses:* Tuition, state resident: full-time $7476. Tuition, nonresident: full-time $16,410. *Required fees:* $942. *Financial support:* Career-related internships or fieldwork, Federal Work-Study, and tuition waivers (full and partial) available. Support available to part-time students. Financial award application deadline: 2/1. *Unit head:* Dr. Forest Dolgener, Coordinator, 319-273-6479, Fax: 319-273-5958, E-mail: forrest.dolgener@uni.edu. *Application contact:* Laurie S. Russell, Record Analyst, 319-273-2623, Fax: 319-273-2885, E-mail: laurie.russell@uni.edu. Web site: http://www.uni.edu/coe/hpels/Academic/master_degrees.shtml.

University of Puerto Rico, Mayagüez Campus, Graduate Studies, College of Arts and Sciences, Department of Physical Education, Mayagüez, PR 00681-9000. Offers MA. Part-time programs available. *Students:* 12 full-time (6 women), 2 part-time (1 woman); includes 13 minority (all Hispanic/Latino), 1 international. 12 applicants, 50% accepted, 4 enrolled. *Degree requirements:* For master's, thesis optional. *Entrance requirements:* For master's, EXADEP, minimum GPA of 2.5. *Application deadline:* For fall admission, 2/15 for domestic and international students; for spring admission, 9/15 for domestic and international students. Applications are processed on a rolling basis. Tuition and fees vary according to course level and course load. *Financial support:* In 2011–12, 10 students received support, including 10 teaching assistantships (averaging $8,500 per year); institutionally sponsored loans and unspecified assistantships also available. *Unit head:* Dr. Eduardo Soltero, Interim Director, 787-832-4040 Ext. 3841, Fax: 787-833-4825, E-mail: eduardo.soltero@upr.edu. *Application contact:* Nancy Damiani, Secretary, 787-832-4040 Ext. 3828, Fax: 787-265-1225, E-mail: nancyi.damiani@upr.edu.

University of Rhode Island, Graduate School, College of Human Science and Services, Department of Kinesiology, Kingston, RI 02881. Offers cultural studies of sport and physical culture (MS); exercise science (MS); physical education pedagogy (MS); psychosocial/behavioral aspects of physical activity (MS). *Accreditation:* NCATE. Part-time programs available. *Faculty:* 13 full-time (7 women). *Students:* 11 full-time (7 women), 7 part-time (2 women); includes 1 minority (Hispanic/Latino). In 2011, 10 master's awarded. *Degree requirements:* For master's, thesis optional. *Entrance requirements:* For master's, GRE, 2 letters of recommendation. Additional exam requirements/recommendations for international students: Required—TOEFL (minimum score 550 paper-based; 213 computer-based). *Application deadline:* For fall admission, 4/15 for domestic students, 2/1 for international students; for spring admission, 11/15 for domestic students, 7/15 for international students. Application fee: $65. Electronic applications accepted. *Expenses:* Tuition, state resident: full-time $10,432; part-time $580 per credit hour. Tuition, nonresident: full-time $23,130; part-time $1285 per credit hour. *Required fees:* $1362; $36 per credit hour. $35 per semester. One-time fee: $130. *Financial support:* In 2011–12, 5 teaching assistantships with full and partial tuition reimbursements (averaging $8,250 per year) were awarded. Financial award application deadline: 4/15; financial award applicants required to submit FAFSA. *Faculty research:* Strength training and older adults, interventions to promote a healthy lifestyle as well as analysis of the psychosocial outcomes of those interventions, effects of exercise and nutrition on skeletal muscle of aging healthy adults with CVD and other metabolic related diseases, physical activity and fitness of deaf children and youth. *Unit head:* Dr. Deborah Riebe, Chair, 401-874-5444, Fax: 401-874-4215, E-mail: debriebe@uri.edu. *Application contact:* Dr. Lori Ciccomascolo, Director of Graduate Studies, 401-874-5454, Fax: 401-874-4215, E-mail: lecicco@uri.edu. Web site: http://www.uri.edu/hss/physical_education/.

University of South Alabama, Graduate School, College of Education, Department of Health, Physical Education and Leisure Services, Mobile, AL 36688-0002. Offers exercise science (MS); health education (M Ed); physical education (M Ed); therapeutic recreation (MS). *Accreditation:* NCATE (one or more programs are accredited). Part-time programs available. *Faculty:* 10 full-time (2 women). *Students:* 27 full-time (15 women), 4 part-time (all women); includes 5 minority (4 Black or African American, non-Hispanic/Latino; 1 Asian, non-Hispanic/Latino), 4 international. 29 applicants, 52% accepted, 12 enrolled. In 2011, 17 master's awarded. *Degree requirements:* For master's, comprehensive exam. *Entrance requirements:* For master's, GRE General Test or MAT. *Application deadline:* For fall admission, 7/15 priority date for domestic students, 6/15 for international students; for spring admission, 12/1 priority date for domestic students, 11/1 for international students. Applications are processed on a rolling basis. Application fee: $35. *Expenses:* Tuition, state resident: full-time $7968; part-time $332 per credit hour. Tuition, nonresident: full-time $15,936; part-time $664 per credit hour. *Financial support:* In 2011–12, 10 teaching assistantships were awarded; career-related internships or fieldwork also available. Support available to part-time students. Financial award application deadline: 4/1. *Unit head:* Dr. Frederick M. Scaffidi, Chair, 251-460-7131. *Application contact:* Dr. Abigail Baxter, Director of Graduate Studies, 231-460-7131.

University of South Carolina, The Graduate School, College of Education, Department of Physical Education, Columbia, SC 29208. Offers IMA, MAT, MS, PhD. Part-time programs available. *Degree requirements:* For master's, comprehensive exam, thesis (for some programs); for doctorate, comprehensive exam, thesis/dissertation. *Entrance requirements:* For master's, GRE General Test, or Miller Analogies Test, writing sample, letter of intent, letters of recommendation; for doctorate, GRE General Test or Miller Analogies Test, writing sample, interview, letter of intent, letters of recommendation. *Faculty research:* Teaching/learning processes, anthropometric measurement, growth and development, motor development.

University of Southern Mississippi, Graduate School, College of Health, School of Human Performance and Recreation, Hattiesburg, MS 39406-0001. Offers human performance (MS, PhD), including exercise physiology (PhD), human performance (MS), physical education (MS); interscholastic athletic administration (MS); recreation and leisure management (MS); sport administration (MS); sport and coaching education (MS); sport management (MS). Part-time and evening/weekend programs available. *Faculty:* 13 full-time (5 women). *Students:* 59 full-time (20 women), 38 part-time (12 women); includes 16 minority (12 Black or African American, non-Hispanic/Latino; 1 Asian, non-Hispanic/Latino; 2 Hispanic/Latino; 1 Two or more races, non-Hispanic/Latino), 9 international. Average age 29. 49 applicants, 73% accepted, 33 enrolled. In 2011, 44 master's, 1 doctorate awarded. *Degree requirements:* For master's, comprehensive exam, thesis optional; for doctorate, comprehensive exam, thesis/dissertation. *Entrance requirements:* For master's, GRE General Test, minimum GPA of 2.75 in last 60 hours; for doctorate, GRE General Test, minimum GPA of 3.5. Additional exam requirements/recommendations for international students: Required—TOEFL, IELTS. *Application deadline:* For fall admission, 3/1 priority date for domestic students, 3/1 for international students; for spring admission, 1/10 priority date for domestic students, 1/10 for international students. Applications are processed on a rolling basis. Application fee: $50. Electronic applications accepted. *Financial support:* In 2011–12, 1 fellowship (averaging $16,000 per year), 6 research assistantships with full tuition reimbursements (averaging $7,492 per year), 5 teaching assistantships with full tuition reimbursements (averaging $7,330 per year) were awarded; career-related internships or fieldwork, Federal Work-Study, institutionally sponsored loans, scholarships/grants, health care benefits, and unspecified assistantships also available. Financial award application deadline: 3/15; financial award applicants required to submit FAFSA. *Faculty research:* Exercise physiology, health behaviors, resource management, activity interaction, site development. *Unit head:* Dr. Frederick Green, Director, 601-266-5379, Fax: 601-266-4445. *Application contact:* Dr. Trenton Gould, Graduate Coordinator, 601-266-5379, Fax: 601-266-4445. Web site: http://www.usm.edu/graduateschool/table.php.

University of South Florida, Graduate School, College of Education, School of Physical Education and Exercise Science, Tampa, FL 33620-9951. Offers exercise science (MA); physical education teacher preparation (MA). Part-time and evening/weekend programs available. Postbaccalaureate distance learning degree programs offered (no on-campus study). *Faculty:* 9 full-time (6 women). *Students:* 30 full-time (10 women), 76 part-time (27 women); includes 26 minority (10 Black or African American, non-Hispanic/Latino; 4 American Indian or Alaska Native, non-Hispanic/Latino; 2 Asian, non-Hispanic/Latino; 10 Hispanic/Latino), 1 international. Average age 33. 128 applicants, 71% accepted, 51 enrolled. In 2011, 51 master's awarded. *Degree requirements:* For master's, comprehensive exam, thesis optional. *Entrance requirements:* For master's, GRE General Test, minimum GPA of 3.0 in last 60 hours of coursework. Additional exam requirements/recommendations for international students: Required—TOEFL (minimum score 500 paper-based; 213 computer-based). *Application deadline:* For fall admission, 2/15 for domestic students, 1/2 for international students; for spring admission, 10/15 for domestic students, 6/1 for international students. Applications are processed on a rolling basis. Application fee: $30. Electronic applications accepted. *Financial support:* In 2011–12, 5 teaching assistantships with full tuition reimbursements (averaging $9,200 per year) were awarded; unspecified assistantships also available. Financial award application deadline: 7/1; financial award applicants required to submit FAFSA. *Faculty research:* Physical education pedagogy, active gaming, exercise motivation, heat stress research, strength and nutrition research, physical activity risk management. *Total annual research expenditures:* $20,482. *Unit head:* Dr. Steve Sanders, Director, 813-974-4871, Fax: 813-974-4979, E-mail: sanders@usf.edu. *Application contact:* Dr. Steve Sanders, Director, 813-974-4871, Fax: 813-974-4979, E-mail: sanders@usf.edu. Web site: http://www.coedu.usf.edu/main/departments/physed/programs.html.

The University of Tennessee at Chattanooga, Graduate School, College of Health, Education and Professional Studies, Department of Health and Human Performance, Chattanooga, TN 37403. Offers athletic training (MSAT); health and human performance (MS). *Faculty:* 6 full-time (1 woman), 1 (woman) part-time/adjunct. *Students:* 43 full-time (31 women), 3 part-time (2 women); includes 6 minority (4 Black or African American, non-Hispanic/Latino; 2 Hispanic/Latino), 1 international. Average age 25. 11 applicants, 64% accepted, 4 enrolled. In 2011, 17 degrees awarded. *Degree requirements:* For master's, thesis or alternative, clinical rotations. *Entrance requirements:* For master's, GRE General Test or MAT, minimum GPA of 2.75 overall or 3.0 in last 60 hours; CPR and First Aid certification. Additional exam requirements/recommendations for international students: Required—TOEFL (minimum score 550 paper-based; 213 computer-based; 79 iBT), IELTS (minimum score 6). *Application deadline:* For fall admission, 8/1 priority date for domestic students, 6/1 for international students; for spring admission, 12/1 priority date for domestic students, 10/1 for international students. Applications are processed on a rolling basis. Application fee: $35. Electronic applications accepted. *Expenses:* Tuition, state resident: full-time $6472; part-time $359 per credit hour. Tuition, nonresident: full-time $20,006; part-time $1111 per credit hour. *Required fees:* $1320; $160 per credit hour. *Financial support:* Career-related internships or fieldwork, scholarships/grants, and unspecified assistantships available. Support available to part-time students. *Faculty research:* Therapeutic exercise, lumbar spine biomechanics, physical activity epidemiology, functional rehabilitation outcomes, metabolic health. *Unit head:* Dr. Leroy Fanning, Head, 423-425-4432, Fax: 423-425-4457, E-mail: gatp@utc.edu. *Application contact:* Dr. Jerald Ainsworth, Dean of Graduate Studies, 423-425-4478, Fax: 423-425-5223, E-mail: jerald-ainsworth@utc.edu. Web site: https://www.utc.edu/Academic/HealthAndHumanPerformance/.

The University of Texas at Austin, Graduate School, College of Education, Department of Curriculum and Instruction, Austin, TX 78712-1111. Offers bilingual/bicultural education (M Ed, MA, PhD); cultural studies in education (M Ed, MA, PhD); early childhood education (M Ed, MA, PhD); language and literacy studies (M Ed, PhD); learning technologies (M Ed, MA, PhD); physical education (M Ed, MA, PhD). Terminal master's awarded for partial completion of doctoral program. *Degree requirements:* For doctorate, thesis/dissertation. *Entrance requirements:* For master's and doctorate, GRE General Test. *Application deadline:* For fall admission, 3/1 for domestic students; for spring admission, 10/1 for domestic students. Applications are processed on a rolling basis. Application fee: $50 ($75 for international students). Electronic applications accepted. *Financial support:* Fellowships and teaching assistantships with partial tuition reimbursements available. Financial award application deadline: 2/1. *Unit head:* Betty Maloch, Chair, 512-232-4262, E-mail: bmaloch@austin.utexas.edu. *Application contact:* Stephen Flynn, Graduate Coordinator, 512-471-3747, E-mail: sflynn@austin.utexas.edu. Web site: http://www.edb.utexas.edu/coe/depts/ci/cti.html.

University of the Incarnate Word, School of Graduate Studies and Research, School of Nursing and Health Professions, Programs in Sports Management, San Antonio, TX 78209-6397. Offers sport management (MS, Certificate); sport pedagogy (Certificate). Part-time and evening/weekend programs available. *Faculty:* 2 full-time (0 women), 1 (woman) part-time/adjunct. *Students:* 11 full-time (6 women), 5 part-time (2 women); includes 9 minority (3 Black or African American, non-Hispanic/Latino; 6 Hispanic/Latino), 2 international. Average age 25. 10 applicants, 100% accepted, 7 enrolled. In 2011, 4 master's awarded. *Degree requirements:* For master's, internship. *Entrance requirements:* For master's, GRE, letter of recommendation from professional in field. Additional exam requirements/recommendations for international students: Required—TOEFL (minimum score 560 paper-based; 220 computer-based; 83 iBT). *Application deadline:* Applications are processed on a rolling basis. Application fee: $20. Electronic applications accepted. *Expenses: Tuition:* Part-time $725 per credit hour. Tuition and fees vary according to degree level. *Financial support:* Federal Work-Study and scholarships/grants available. Financial award applicants required to submit FAFSA. *Unit head:* Dr. Randall Griffiths, Assistant Professor, 210-829-2795, Fax: 210-829-3174, E-mail: rgriffit@uiwtx.edu. *Application contact:* Andrea Cyterski-Acosta, Dean of Enrollment, 210-829-6005, Fax: 210-829-3921, E-mail: admis@uiwtx.edu. Web site: http://www.uiw.edu/gradstudies/documents/mssportsmanagement.pdf.

The University of Toledo, College of Graduate Studies, Judith Herb College of Education, Health Science and Human Service, Department of Early Childhood, Physical and Special Education, Toledo, OH 43606-3390. Offers early childhood education (ME, PhD); physical education (ME); special education (ME, PhD). Part-time programs available. *Faculty:* 15. *Students:* 29 full-time (20 women), 125 part-time (102 women); includes 15 minority (10 Black or African American, non-Hispanic/Latino; 2 Asian, non-Hispanic/Latino; 3 Hispanic/Latino), 3 international. Average age 32. 61 applicants, 67% accepted, 34 enrolled. In 2011, 55 master's awarded. *Degree requirements:* For master's, thesis. *Entrance requirements:* For master's, minimum cumulative GPA of 2.7 for all previous academic work, letters of recommendation. Additional exam requirements/recommendations for international students: Required—

TOEFL (minimum score 550 paper-based; 213 computer-based; 80 iBT), IELTS (minimum score 6.5). *Application deadline:* For fall admission, 1/15 priority date for domestic students, 1/15 for international students. Applications are processed on a rolling basis. Application fee: $45 ($75 for international students). Electronic applications accepted. *Financial support:* In 2011–12, 13 teaching assistantships with full and partial tuition reimbursements (averaging $4,974 per year) were awarded; career-related internships or fieldwork, Federal Work-Study, institutionally sponsored loans, scholarships/grants, tuition waivers (full and partial), and unspecified assistantships also available. Support available to part-time students. *Unit head:* Dr. Richard Welsch, Interim Chair, 419-530-2468, E-mail: richard.welsch@utoledo.edu. *Application contact:* Graduate School Office, 419-530-4723, Fax: 419-530-4724, E-mail: grdsch@utnet.utoledo.edu. Web site: http://www.utoledo.edu/eduhshs/.

University of Toronto, School of Graduate Studies, Faculty of Physical Education and Health, Toronto, ON M5S 1A1, Canada. Offers M Sc, PhD. *Degree requirements:* For master's, thesis, oral defense of thesis; for doctorate, comprehensive exam, defense of thesis. *Entrance requirements:* For master's, background in physical education and health, minimum B+ average in final year of undergraduate study, 2 letters of reference, resume, 2 writing samples; for doctorate, master's degree with successful defense of thesis, background in exercise sciences, minimum A- average, 2 letters of reference. Additional exam requirements/recommendations for international students: Required—TOEFL (minimum score 580 paper-based; 93 iBT), TWE (minimum score 5). Electronic applications accepted.

University of Victoria, Faculty of Graduate Studies, Faculty of Education, School of Exercise Science, Physical, and Health Education, Victoria, BC V8W 2Y2, Canada. Offers coaching studies (co-operative education) (M Ed); kinesiology (M Sc, MA); leisure service administration (MA); physical education (MA). Part-time programs available. *Degree requirements:* For master's, comprehensive exam (for some programs), thesis (for some programs). *Entrance requirements:* For master's, minimum B average. Additional exam requirements/recommendations for international students: Required—TOEFL (minimum score 575 paper-based; 233 computer-based), IELTS (minimum score 7). Electronic applications accepted. *Faculty research:* Children and exercise, mental skills in sports, teaching effectiveness, neural control of human movement, physical performance and health.

University of Virginia, Curry School of Education, Department of Human Services, Program in Health and Physical Education, Charlottesville, VA 22903. Offers M Ed, Ed D. *Students:* 35 full-time (21 women), 1 (woman) part-time; includes 3 minority (1 Black or African American, non-Hispanic/Latino; 1 Asian, non-Hispanic/Latino; 1 Hispanic/Latino), 3 international. Average age 24. 5 applicants, 100% accepted, 5 enrolled. In 2011, 36 master's awarded. *Entrance requirements:* For master's and doctorate, GRE General Test, 2 letters of recommendation. Additional exam requirements/recommendations for international students: Required—TOEFL (minimum score 600 paper-based; 250 computer-based; 90 iBT), IELTS (minimum score 7). *Application deadline:* Applications are processed on a rolling basis. Application fee: $60. Electronic applications accepted. *Financial support:* Applicants required to submit FAFSA. *Unit head:* Luke E. Kelly, Program Coordinator, 434-924-6207. *Application contact:* Lynn Renfroe, Information Contact, 434-924-6254, E-mail: ldr9t@virginia.edu. Web site: http://curry.virginia.edu/academics/degrees/postgraduate-master-in-teaching/pg-mt-in-health-physical-education.

University of Washington, Graduate School, College of Education, Seattle, WA 98195. Offers curriculum and instruction (M Ed, Ed D, PhD), including educational technology, general curriculum (Ed D, PhD), language, literacy, and culture, mathematics education, multicultural education, reading and language arts education (Ed D), science education, social studies education, teaching and curriculum (M Ed); educational leadership and policy studies (M Ed, Ed D, PhD), including administration (Ed D), educational policy, organization, and leadership (M Ed, PhD), higher education, leadership for learning (Ed D), social and cultural foundations of education (M Ed, PhD); educational psychology (M Ed, PhD), including educational psychology (PhD), human development and cognition (M Ed), learning sciences, measurement, statistics and research design (M Ed), school psychology (M Ed); instructional leadership (M Ed); intercollegiate athletic leadership (M Ed); special education (M Ed, Ed D, PhD), including early childhood special education (M Ed), emotional and behavioral disabilities (M Ed), learning disabilities (M Ed), low-incidence disabilities (M Ed), severe disabilities (M Ed), special education (Ed D, PhD); teacher education (MIT). *Accreditation:* APA. Part-time and evening/weekend programs available. *Degree requirements:* For master's, thesis optional; for doctorate, thesis/dissertation. *Entrance requirements:* For master's and doctorate, GRE General Test, minimum GPA of 3.0. Additional exam requirements/recommendations for international students: Required—TOEFL. Electronic applications accepted. *Faculty research:* School restructuring/effective schools, special education interventions, literacy and writing, technology, school partnerships, teacher preparation.

University of West Florida, College of Professional Studies, Department of Health, Leisure, and Exercise Science, Program in Health, Leisure, and Exercise Science, Pensacola, FL 32514-5750. Offers exercise science (MS); physical education (MS). Part-time and evening/weekend programs available. *Faculty:* 6 full-time (2 women), 1 (woman) part-time/adjunct. *Students:* 14 full-time (10 women), 16 part-time (7 women); includes 6 minority (2 Black or African American, non-Hispanic/Latino; 1 Asian, non-Hispanic/Latino; 2 Hispanic/Latino; 1 Native Hawaiian or other Pacific Islander, non-Hispanic/Latino), 2 international. Average age 28. 22 applicants, 55% accepted, 7 enrolled. In 2011, 20 master's awarded. *Degree requirements:* For master's, thesis or alternative. *Entrance requirements:* For master's, GRE or MAT, official transcripts; minimum GPA of 3.0; letter of intent; two personal references; work experience. Additional exam requirements/recommendations for international students: Required—TOEFL (minimum score 550 paper-based; 213 computer-based). *Application deadline:* For fall admission, 6/1 for domestic and international students; for spring admission, 10/1 for domestic and international students. Applications are processed on a rolling basis. Application fee: $30. Electronic applications accepted. *Expenses:* Tuition, state resident: full-time $5729; part-time $302 per credit hour. Tuition, nonresident: full-time $20,059; part-time $961 per credit hour. *Required fees:* $1509; $63 per credit hour. *Financial support:* Career-related internships or fieldwork, Federal Work-Study, scholarships/grants, and tuition waivers (partial) available. Support available to part-time students. Financial award application deadline: 4/15; financial award applicants required to submit FAFSA. *Unit head:* Dr. John Todorovich, Chairperson, 850-473-7248, Fax: 850-474-2106. *Application contact:* Terry McCray, Assistant Director of Graduate Admissions, 850-473-7718, Fax: 850-473-7714, E-mail: gradadmissions@uwf.edu.

University of West Florida, College of Professional Studies, Ed D Programs, Specialization in Curriculum and Instruction: Physical Education and Health, Pensacola, FL 32514-5750. Offers Ed D. Part-time and evening/weekend programs available. *Students:* 1 full-time, 12 part-time (9 women); includes 11 minority (8 Black or African American, non-Hispanic/Latino; 2 Asian, non-Hispanic/Latino; 1 Native Hawaiian or other Pacific Islander, non-Hispanic/Latino), 2 international. Average age 38. 6 applicants, 67% accepted, 3 enrolled. *Degree requirements:* For doctorate, comprehensive exam, thesis/dissertation. *Entrance requirements:* For doctorate, GRE, MAT, or GMAT, letter of intent; writing sample; three letters of recommendation; two completed disposition assessment forms; written statement of goals; interview with admissions committee. Additional exam requirements/recommendations for international students: Required—TOEFL (minimum score 550 paper-based; 213 computer-based). *Application deadline:* For fall admission, 6/1 for domestic and international students; for spring admission, 10/1 for domestic students. Applications are processed on a rolling basis. Application fee: $30. *Expenses:* Tuition, state resident: full-time $5729; part-time $302 per credit hour. Tuition, nonresident: full-time $20,059; part-time $961 per credit hour. *Required fees:* $1509; $63 per credit hour. *Unit head:* Dr. Pam Northrup, Interim Dean, 850-474-2769, Fax: 850-474-3205. *Application contact:* Terry McCray, Assistant Director of Graduate Admissions, 850-473-7718, Fax: 850-473-7714, E-mail: gradadmissions@uwf.edu. Web site: http://uwf.edu/edd/physicaled_health.cfm.

University of West Georgia, College of Education, Department of Leadership and Applied Instruction, Carrollton, GA 30118. Offers art education (M Ed); art teacher education (Ed S); biology - secondary education (M Ed); biology/secondary education (Ed S); business education (M Ed, Ed S); chemistry/secondary education (Ed S); earth science/secondary education (Ed S); economics/secondary education (Ed S); educational leadership (M Ed, Ed S); English teacher education (M Ed, Ed S); French teacher education (M Ed, Ed S); history teacher education (Ed S); mathematics teacher education (M Ed, Ed S); middle grades education (M Ed, Ed S); physical education and recreation (Ed S); physical education teaching and coaching (M Ed); physics/secondary education (Ed S); science teacher education (M Ed, Ed S); secondary education (M Ed); social science - secondary education (M Ed); social science teacher education (M Ed); Spanish (M Ed); Spanish teacher education (M Ed, Ed S); sports management (M Ed). *Accreditation:* NCATE. Part-time and evening/weekend programs available. *Faculty:* 18 full-time (9 women). *Students:* 75 full-time (49 women), 169 part-time (109 women); includes 90 minority (85 Black or African American, non-Hispanic/Latino; 3 Hispanic/Latino; 2 Two or more races, non-Hispanic/Latino), 1 international. Average age 36. 115 applicants, 67% accepted, 19 enrolled. In 2011, 73 master's, 53 Ed Ss awarded. *Degree requirements:* For master's, internship; for Ed S, research project. *Entrance requirements:* For master's, GRE General Test, minimum GPA of 2.7; for Ed S, GRE General Test, master's degree, minimum graduate GPA of 3.0, district appointment. Additional exam requirements/recommendations for international students: Required—TOEFL (minimum score 523 paper-based; 193 computer-based; 69 iBT); Recommended—IELTS (minimum score 6). *Application deadline:* For fall admission, 7/21 for domestic students, 6/1 for international students; for spring admission, 11/30 for domestic students, 10/15 for international students. Applications are processed on a rolling basis. Application fee: $30. Electronic applications accepted. *Expenses:* Tuition, state resident: full-time $4336; part-time $181 per credit hour. Tuition, nonresident: full-time $17,362; part-time $724 per credit hour. Tuition and fees vary according to course load, degree level, campus/location and program. *Financial support:* In 2011–12, 1 research assistantship with full tuition reimbursement (averaging $7,444 per year) was awarded; career-related internships or fieldwork, scholarships/grants, and unspecified assistantships also available. Support available to part-time students. Financial award application deadline: 7/1; financial award applicants required to submit FAFSA. *Total annual research expenditures:* $5,000. *Unit head:* Dr. Frank Butts, Chair, 678-839-6530, Fax: 678-839-6195, E-mail: fbutts@westga.edu. *Application contact:* Deanna Richards, Coordinator, Graduate Studies, 678-839-5946, E-mail: drichard@westga.edu. Web site: http://www.westga.edu/coelai.

University of Wisconsin–La Crosse, Office of University Graduate Studies, College of Science and Health, Department of Exercise and Sport Science, Program in Physical Education Teaching, La Crosse, WI 54601-3742. Offers adapted physical education (MS); adventure education (MS). Part-time and evening/weekend programs available. *Students:* 19 full-time (8 women), 4 part-time (3 women); includes 3 minority (1 Asian, non-Hispanic/Latino; 1 Hispanic/Latino; 1 Two or more races, non-Hispanic/Latino), 1 international. Average age 27. 18 applicants, 50% accepted, 6 enrolled. In 2011, 14 master's awarded. *Degree requirements:* For master's, thesis optional. *Entrance requirements:* For master's, minimum GPA of 3.0 during previous 2 years, 2.85 overall; BA in physical education. Additional exam requirements/recommendations for international students: Required—TOEFL (minimum score 550 paper-based; 213 computer-based; 79 iBT). *Application deadline:* Applications are processed on a rolling basis. Application fee: $56. Electronic applications accepted. *Expenses:* Tuition, state resident: full-time $8391; part-time $481.17 per credit. Tuition, nonresident: full-time $17,850; part-time $1006.68 per credit. *Required fees:* $2 per credit. $18.25 per semester. Tuition and fees vary according to course load, program, reciprocity agreements and student level. *Financial support:* Federal Work-Study, scholarships/grants, health care benefits, and tuition waivers (partial) available. Support available to part-time students. Financial award application deadline: 3/15; financial award applicants required to submit FAFSA. *Unit head:* Dr. Jeff Steffen, Director, 608-785-6535, E-mail: steffen.jeff@uwlax.edu. *Application contact:* Kathryn Kiefer, Director of Admissions, 608-785-8939, E-mail: admissions@uwlax.edu. Web site: http://www.uwlax.edu/sah/ess/pe/.

University of Wisconsin–Whitewater, School of Graduate Studies, College of Education and Professional Studies, Department of Curriculum and Instruction, Whitewater, WI 53190-1790. Offers professional development (MS), including bilingual education, challenging advanced learners, curriculum and instruction, educational leadership, health, human performance and recreation, health, physical education and coaching, information technologies and libraries, reading. *Accreditation:* NCATE. Part-time and evening/weekend programs available. Postbaccalaureate distance learning degree programs offered. *Students:* 25 full-time (12 women), 68 part-time (51 women); includes 26 minority (15 Black or African American, non-Hispanic/Latino; 3 Asian, non-Hispanic/Latino; 8 Hispanic/Latino). Average age 33. 29 applicants, 86% accepted, 16 enrolled. In 2011, 44 master's awarded. *Degree requirements:* For master's, thesis or integrated project. *Entrance requirements:* Additional exam requirements/recommendations for international students: Required—TOEFL (minimum score 550 paper-based; 213 computer-based; 80 iBT), IELTS (minimum score 6). *Application deadline:* For fall admission, 7/15 priority date for domestic students, 7/15 for international students; for spring admission, 12/1 priority date for domestic students, 12/1 for international students. Applications are processed on a rolling basis. Application fee: $56. Electronic applications accepted. *Expenses:* Tuition, state resident: full-time $4088. Tuition, nonresident: full-time $8817. Tuition and fees vary according to program. *Financial support:* Research assistantships, Federal Work-Study, unspecified assistantships, and out-of-state fee waivers available. Support available to part-time students. Financial award application deadline: 3/15; financial award applicants required to submit FAFSA. *Faculty research:* Hybrid of exercise physiology and psychology; gender equity; education, pedagogy, and technology; comprehensive school health education. *Unit head:* Dr. John Zbikowski, Coordinator, 262-472-4860, Fax: 262-472-1988, E-mail: zbikowskij@uww.edu. *Application contact:* Sally A. Lange, School of Graduate Studies, 262-472-1006, Fax: 262-472-5027, E-mail: gradschl@uww.edu.

University of Wyoming, College of Health Sciences, Division of Kinesiology and Health, Laramie, WY 82070. Offers MS. *Accreditation:* NCATE. Part-time programs available. Postbaccalaureate distance learning degree programs offered (no on-campus study). *Degree requirements:* For master's, comprehensive exam (for some programs), thesis (for some programs). *Entrance requirements:* For master's, GRE General Test, minimum GPA of 3.0. Additional exam requirements/recommendations for international students: Required—TOEFL. Electronic applications accepted. *Faculty research:* Teacher effectiveness, effects of exercising on heart function, physiological responses of overtraining, psychological benefits of physical activity, health behavior.

Utah State University, School of Graduate Studies, Emma Eccles Jones College of Education and Human Services, Department of Health, Physical Education and Recreation, Logan, UT 84322. Offers M Ed, MS. Part-time and evening/weekend programs available. Postbaccalaureate distance learning degree programs offered (minimal on-campus study). *Degree requirements:* For master's, thesis (for some programs). *Entrance requirements:* For master's, GRE General Test or MAT, minimum GPA of 3.0. Additional exam requirements/recommendations for international students: Required—TOEFL. *Faculty research:* Sport psychology intervention, motor learning biomechanics, pedagogy, physiology.

Virginia Commonwealth University, Graduate School, School of Education, Department of Health and Human Performance, Richmond, VA 23284-9005. Offers athletic training (MSAT); health and movement sciences (MS); rehabilitation and movement science (PhD). *Entrance requirements:* For master's, GRE General Test or MAT. Additional exam requirements/recommendations for international students: Required—TOEFL (minimum score 600 paper-based; 250 computer-based; 100 iBT); Recommended—IELTS (minimum score 6.5). Electronic applications accepted. *Expenses:* Tuition, state resident: full-time $9133; part-time $507 per credit. Tuition, nonresident: full-time $18,777; part-time $1043 per credit. *Required fees:* $77 per credit. Tuition and fees vary according to degree level, campus/location, program and student level.

Virginia Commonwealth University, Graduate School, School of Education, Program in Teaching and Learning, Richmond, VA 23284-9005. Offers early and elementary education (MT); health and physical education (MT); secondary 6-12 education (MT); secondary education (Certificate). *Accreditation:* NCATE. Part-time programs available. *Entrance requirements:* For master's, GRE General Test or MAT. Additional exam requirements/recommendations for international students: Required—TOEFL (minimum score 600 paper-based; 250 computer-based; 100 iBT). Electronic applications accepted. *Expenses:* Tuition, state resident: full-time $9133; part-time $507 per credit. Tuition, nonresident: full-time $18,777; part-time $1043 per credit. *Required fees:* $77 per credit. Tuition and fees vary according to degree level, campus/location, program and student level.

Wayne State College, Department of Health, Human Performance and Sport, Wayne, NE 68787. Offers exercise science (MSE); organizational management (MS), including sport management. Part-time and evening/weekend programs available. *Degree requirements:* For master's, comprehensive exam, thesis optional. *Entrance requirements:* For master's, GRE General Test, minimum GPA of 3.0. Additional exam requirements/recommendations for international students: Required—TOEFL (minimum score 550 paper-based; 213 computer-based). Electronic applications accepted.

Wayne State University, College of Education, Division of Kinesiology, Health and Sports Studies, Detroit, MI 48202. Offers exercise and sport science (M Ed); health education (M Ed); kinesiology (M Ed, PhD); physical education (M Ed); sports administration (MA); wellness clinician/research (M Ed). *Students:* 39 full-time (23 women), 68 part-time (31 women); includes 36 minority (31 Black or African American, non-Hispanic/Latino; 1 Asian, non-Hispanic/Latino; 1 Hispanic/Latino; 1 Native Hawaiian or other Pacific Islander, non-Hispanic/Latino; 2 Two or more races, non-Hispanic/Latino), 3 international. Average age 31. 115 applicants, 39% accepted, 27 enrolled. In 2011, 39 master's, 1 doctorate awarded. *Degree requirements:* For master's, thesis (for some programs). *Entrance requirements:* Additional exam requirements/recommendations for international students: Required—TOEFL; Recommended—TWE (minimum score 6). *Application deadline:* For fall admission, 6/1 priority date for domestic students, 5/1 for international students; for winter admission, 10/1 priority date for domestic students, 9/1 for international students; for spring admission, 2/1 priority date for domestic students, 1/1 for international students. Applications are processed on a rolling basis. Application fee: $50. Electronic applications accepted. *Expenses:* Tuition, state resident: part-time $512.85 per credit. Tuition, nonresident: part-time $1132.65 per credit. *Required fees:* $26.60 per credit. $199.65 per semester. Tuition and fees vary according to course load and program. *Financial support:* In 2011–12, 6 research assistantships with tuition reimbursements (averaging $16,061 per year) were awarded; teaching assistantships with tuition reimbursements, career-related internships or fieldwork, scholarships/grants, health care benefits, and unspecified assistantships also available. *Faculty research:* Fitness in urban children, motor development of crack babies, effects of caffeine on metabolism/exercise, body composition of elite youth sports participants, systematic observation of teaching. *Unit head:* Dr. Mariane Fahlman, Assistant Dean, 313-577-5066, Fax: 313-577-9301, E-mail: m.fahlman@wayne.edu. *Application contact:* John Wirth, Assistant Professor, 313-993-7972, Fax: 313-577-5999, E-mail: johnwirth@wayne.edu. Web site: http://coe.wayne.edu/kinesiology/index.php.

West Chester University of Pennsylvania, College of Health Sciences, Department of Kinesiology, West Chester, PA 19383. Offers exercise/sport physiology (MS), including athletic training; physical education (MS); sport management and athletics (MPA). *Faculty:* 7 part-time/adjunct (3 women). *Students:* 19 full-time (10 women), 14 part-time (7 women); includes 5 minority (all Black or African American, non-Hispanic/Latino). Average age 26. 37 applicants, 35% accepted, 10 enrolled. In 2011, 12 degrees awarded. *Degree requirements:* For master's, thesis or report (MS), 2 internships (MPA). *Entrance requirements:* For master's, GRE with minimum score of 1000 (for MS), 2 letters of recommendation, transcripts, and statement of professional goals (for MS); 2 letters of reference, resume, career goal statement (for MPA). Additional exam requirements/recommendations for international students: Required—TOEFL (minimum score 550 paper-based; 213 computer-based; 80 iBT). *Application deadline:* For fall admission, 4/15 priority date for domestic students, 3/15 for international students; for spring admission, 10/15 priority date for domestic students, 9/1 for international students. Applications are processed on a rolling basis. Application fee: $45. Electronic applications accepted. *Expenses:* Tuition, state resident: full-time $7488; part-time $416 per credit. Tuition, nonresident: full-time $11,232; part-time $624 per credit. *Required fees:* $1784.64; $67.59 per credit. Tuition and fees vary according to program. *Financial support:* Unspecified assistantships available. Support available to part-time students. Financial award application deadline: 2/15; financial award applicants required to submit FAFSA. *Faculty research:* Metabolism during exercise, biomechanics, rating of perceived exertion, motor learning. *Unit head:* Dr. Frank Fry, Chair and Graduate Coordinator for the MS in General Physical Education Program, 610-436-2610, Fax: 610-436-2860, E-mail: ffry@wcupa.edu. *Application contact:* Dr. Sheri Melton, Graduate Coordinator for the Exercise and Sport Physiology Programs, 610-436-2260, Fax: 610-436-2860, E-mail: smelton@wcupa.edu. Web site: http://www.wcupa.edu/_academics/sch_shs.hpe/.

Western Carolina University, Graduate School, College of Education and Allied Professions, School of Teaching and Learning, Cullowhee, NC 28723. Offers community college and higher education (MA Ed), including community college administration, community college teaching; comprehensive education (MA Ed, MAT); educational leadership (MA Ed, MSA, Ed D, Ed S), including educational leadership (MSA, Ed D, Ed S), educational supervision (MA Ed); teaching (MA Ed, MAT), including comprehensive education (MA Ed), physical education (MA Ed), teaching (MAT). *Accreditation:* NCATE. Part-time and evening/weekend programs available. Postbaccalaureate distance learning degree programs offered. *Students:* 40 full-time (24 women), 150 part-time (133 women); includes 13 minority (6 Black or African American, non-Hispanic/Latino; 2 American Indian or Alaska Native, non-Hispanic/Latino; 4 Hispanic/Latino; 1 Two or more races, non-Hispanic/Latino), 9 international. Average age 32. 96 applicants, 90% accepted, 71 enrolled. In 2011, 86 master's, 13 doctorates, 5 other advanced degrees awarded. *Degree requirements:* For master's, comprehensive exam; for doctorate, comprehensive exam, thesis/dissertation. *Entrance requirements:* For master's, GRE, appropriate undergraduate degree, 3 letters of recommendation; for doctorate, GRE General Test, minimum graduate GPA of 3.5, appropriate master's degree; for other advanced degree, GRE General Test, minimum graduate GPA of 3.5, work experience, appropriate master's degree. Additional exam requirements/recommendations for international students: Required—TOEFL (minimum score 550 paper-based; 270 computer-based; 79 iBT). *Application deadline:* For fall admission, 2/1 for domestic students; for spring admission, 9/1 priority date for domestic students. Applications are processed on a rolling basis. Application fee: $50. *Expenses:* Tuition, state resident: full-time $3348. Tuition, nonresident: full-time $12,933. *Required fees:* $3155. *Financial support:* In 2011–12, 2 fellowships were awarded; research assistantships with full and partial tuition reimbursements, teaching assistantships with full and partial tuition reimbursements, career-related internships or fieldwork, institutionally sponsored loans, scholarships/grants, and unspecified assistantships also available. Financial award application deadline: 3/31; financial award applicants required to submit FAFSA. *Faculty research:* Educational leadership, special education, rural education, organizational theory and practice, interinstitutional partnership, program evaluation. *Unit head:* Dr. William Dee Nichols, Department Head, 828-227-7108, Fax: 828-227-7607, E-mail: wdnichols@wcu.edu. *Application contact:* Admissions Specialist for Educational Leadership and Foundations, 828-227-7398, Fax: 828-227-7480, E-mail: gradsch@email.wcu.edu. Web site: http://www.wcu.edu/3067.asp.

Western Kentucky University, Graduate Studies, College of Health and Human Services, Department of Kinesiology, Recreation and Sport, Bowling Green, KY 42101. Offers athletic administration and coaching (MS); physical education (MS); recreation and sport administration (MS). Part-time and evening/weekend programs available. Postbaccalaureate distance learning degree programs offered. *Degree requirements:* For master's, comprehensive exam, thesis optional. *Entrance requirements:* For master's, GRE General Test, minimum GPA of 2.75. Additional exam requirements/recommendations for international students: Required—TOEFL (minimum score 555 paper-based; 213 computer-based; 79 iBT). *Faculty research:* Orthopedic rehabilitation, fitness center coordination, heat acclimation, biomechanical and physiological parameters.

Western Michigan University, Graduate College, College of Education and Human Development, Department of Health, Physical Education and Recreation, Kalamazoo, MI 49008. Offers exercise and sports medicine (MS), including athletic training, exercise physiology; physical education (MA), including coaching sport performance, pedagogy, special physical education, sport management.

Western Washington University, Graduate School, College of Humanities and Social Sciences, Department of Physical Education, Health, and Recreation, Bellingham, WA 98225-5996. Offers exercise science (MS); sport psychology (MS). Part-time programs available. *Degree requirements:* For master's, thesis. *Entrance requirements:* For master's, GRE General Test, minimum GPA of 3.0 in last 60 semester hours or last 90 quarter hours. Additional exam requirements/recommendations for international students: Required—TOEFL (minimum score 567 paper-based; 227 computer-based). Electronic applications accepted. *Faculty research:* Spinal motor control, biomechanics/kinesiology, biomechanics of aging, mobility of older adults, fall prevention, exercise interventions and function, magnesium and inspiratory muscle training (IMT).

Westfield State University, Division of Graduate and Continuing Education, Department of Movement Science, Sport, and Leisure, Westfield, MA 01086. Offers physical education (M Ed). Part-time and evening/weekend programs available. *Degree requirements:* For master's, comprehensive exam. *Entrance requirements:* For master's, GRE General Test or MAT, minimum GPA of 2.7.

West Virginia University, School of Physical Education, Morgantown, WV 26506. Offers athletic coaching education (MS); athletic training (MS); physical education/teacher education (MS, PhD), including curriculum and instruction (PhD), motor behavior (PhD), physical education supervision (PhD); sport and exercise psychology (PhD); sport management (MS). *Degree requirements:* For doctorate, comprehensive exam, thesis/dissertation, oral exam. *Entrance requirements:* For master's, GRE or MAT, minimum GPA of 3.0; for doctorate, GRE General Test or MAT, minimum GPA of 3.5. Additional exam requirements/recommendations for international students: Required—TOEFL (minimum score 550 paper-based; 213 computer-based). Electronic applications accepted. *Faculty research:* Sport psychosociology, teacher education, exercise psychology, counseling.

Wilfrid Laurier University, Faculty of Graduate and Postdoctoral Studies, Faculty of Science, Department of Kinesiology and Physical Education, Waterloo, ON N2L 3C5, Canada. Offers physical activity and health (M Sc). *Degree requirements:* For master's, thesis. *Entrance requirements:* For master's, honours degree in kinesiology, health, physical education with a minimum B+ in kinesiology and health-related courses. Additional exam requirements/recommendations for international students: Required—TOEFL (minimum score 89 iBT). Electronic applications accepted. *Faculty research:* Biomechanics, health, exercise physiology, motor control, sport psychology.

William Woods University, Graduate and Adult Studies, Fulton, MO 65251-1098. Offers administration (Ed S); agriculture (MBA); athletic/activities administration (M Ed); curriculum and instruction (M Ed); curriculum leadership (Ed S); elementary administration (M Ed); health management (MBA); human resources (MBA); principalship (Ed S); secondary administration (M Ed); special education director (M Ed). Evening/weekend programs available. *Degree requirements:* For master's, capstone course (MBA), action research (M Ed); for Ed S, field experience. *Entrance requirements:* For master's, 2 recommendations, resumé, BA/BS; teaching certification (M Ed); course work in economics and accounting (MBA); for Ed S, M Ed, 2 letters of recommendation, resume, teaching certification. Additional exam requirements/recommendations for international students: Required—TOEFL (minimum score 550 paper-based). Electronic applications accepted.

Wingate University, Thayer School of Education, Wingate, NC 28174-0159. Offers community college leadership (Ed D); educational leadership (MA Ed, Ed D); elementary education (MA Ed, MAT); health and physical education (MA Ed); sport administration (MA Ed). *Accreditation:* NCATE. Part-time and evening/weekend programs available. *Faculty:* 5 full-time (3 women), 10 part-time/adjunct (3 women). *Students:* 7 full-time (4 women), 251 part-time (152 women); includes 68 minority (63 Black or African American, non-Hispanic/Latino; 1 American Indian or Alaska Native, non-Hispanic/Latino; 1 Asian, non-Hispanic/Latino; 3 Hispanic/Latino), 2 international. Average age 35. In 2011, 29 master's awarded. *Degree requirements:* For master's, portfolio. *Entrance requirements:* For master's, GRE General Test or MAT, teaching certificate (MA Ed). *Application deadline:* For fall admission, 8/15 priority date for domestic students; for spring admission, 12/15 for domestic students. Applications are processed on a rolling basis. Application fee: $0. *Expenses: Tuition:* Part-time $455 per credit hour. Part-time tuition and fees vary according to degree level and program. *Financial support:* In 2011–12, 20 students received support. Scholarships/grants available. Support available to part-time students. Financial award applicants required to submit FAFSA. *Unit head:* Dr. Sarah Harrison-Burns, Dean, 704-233-8128, E-mail: shburns@wingate.edu. *Application contact:* Theresa Hopkins, Secretary, 704-321-1470, Fax: 704-233-8273, E-mail: t.hopkins@wingate.edu.

Winthrop University, College of Education, Program in Physical Education, Rock Hill, SC 29733. Offers MS. Part-time programs available. *Degree requirements:* For master's, comprehensive exam, thesis optional. *Entrance requirements:* For master's, GRE General Test or PRAXIS. Electronic applications accepted.

Wright State University, School of Graduate Studies, College of Education and Human Services, Department of Health, Physical Education, and Recreation, Dayton, OH 45435. Offers M Ed, MA. *Accreditation:* NCATE. *Degree requirements:* For master's, comprehensive exam, thesis (for some programs). *Entrance requirements:* For master's, GRE General Test, MAT. Additional exam requirements/recommendations for international students: Required—TOEFL. *Faculty research:* Motor learning, motor development, exercise physiology, adapted physical education.

Section 31
Sports Management

This section contains a directory of institutions offering graduate work in sports management. Additional information about programs listed in the directory but not augmented by an in-depth entry may be obtained by writing directly to the dean of a graduate school or chair of a department at the address given in the directory.

For programs offering related work, see also in this book *Business Administration and Management, Education,* and *Physical Education and Kinesiology.*

CONTENTS

Program Directory

Sports Management

American Public University System, AMU/APU Graduate Programs, Charles Town, WV 25414. Offers accounting (MBA, MS); administration and supervision (M Ed); criminal justice (MA); emergency and disaster management (MA); entrepreneurship (MBA); environmental policy and management (MS), including environmental planning, environmental sustainability, fish and wildlife management, general (MA, MS), global environmental management; finance (MBA); general (MBA); global business management (MBA); guidance and counseling (M Ed); history (MA), including American history, ancient and classical history, European history, global history, military and diplomatic history, public history; homeland security (MA); homeland security resource allocation (MBA); humanities (MA); information technology (MS), including digital forensics, enterprise software development, information assurance and security, IT project management; information technology management (MBA); intelligence studies (MA), including criminal intelligence, general (MA, MS), homeland security, intelligence analysis, intelligence collection, intelligence operations, terrorism studies; international relations and conflict resolution (MA), including comparative and security issues, conflict resolution, international and transnational security issues, peacekeeping; legal studies (MA); management (MA), including defense management, general (MA, MS), human resource management, organizational leadership, public administration, reverse logistics, strategic consulting; marketing (MBA); military history (MA), including American military history, American revolution, civil war, war since 1946, World War II; military studies (MA), including air warfare, asymmetrical warfare, joint warfare, land warfare, naval warfare, strategic leadership; national security studies (MA), including general (MA, MS), homeland security, regional security studies, security and intelligence analysis, terrorism studies; nonprofit management (MBA); political science (MA), including American politics and government, comparative government and development, public policy; psychology (MA); public administration (MA, MPA), including disaster management (MPA), environmental policy (MA), health policy (MPA), human resources (MPA), national security (MPA), organizational management (MPA), security management (MPA); public health (MA, MPH), including emergency management (MPH), environmental health (MPH), public administration (MA); reverse logistics management (MA); security management (MA); space studies (MS), including aerospace science, planetary science; sports and health sciences (MS); sports management (MS), including coaching theory and strategy, sports administration; teaching (M Ed), including curriculum and instruction for elementary teachers, elementary, elementary reading, English language learners, instructional leadership, online learning, secondary social sciences, special education; transportation and logistics management (MA), including maritime engineering management. Programs offered via distance learning only. Part-time and evening/weekend programs available. Postbaccalaureate distance learning degree programs offered (no on-campus study). *Faculty:* 445 full-time (241 women), 1,360 part-time/adjunct (617 women). *Students:* 688 full-time (338 women), 10,168 part-time (3,706 women); includes 3,130 minority (1,007 Black or African American, non-Hispanic/Latino; 103 American Indian or Alaska Native, non-Hispanic/Latino; 825 Asian, non-Hispanic/Latino; 810 Hispanic/Latino; 51 Native Hawaiian or other Pacific Islander, non-Hispanic/Latino; 334 Two or more races, non-Hispanic/Latino), 134 international. Average age 35. In 2011, 2,386 master's awarded. *Degree requirements:* For master's, comprehensive exam or practicum. *Entrance requirements:* For master's, official transcript showing earned bachelor's degree from institution accredited by recognized accrediting body. Additional exam requirements/recommendations for international students: Required—TOEFL (minimum score 550 paper-based; 213 computer-based), IELTS (minimum score 6.5). *Application deadline:* Applications are processed on a rolling basis. Application fee: $0. Electronic applications accepted. *Expenses: Tuition:* Part-time $325 per credit hour. *Financial support:* Applicants required to submit FAFSA. *Faculty research:* Military history, criminal justice, management performance, national security. *Unit head:* Dr. Karan Powell, Executive Vice President and Provost, 877-468-6268, Fax: 304-724-3780. *Application contact:* Terry Grant, Vice President of Enrollment Management, 877-468-6268, Fax: 304-724-3780, E-mail: info@apus.edu. Web site: http://www.apus.edu.

Angelo State University, College of Graduate Studies, College of Education, Department of Kinesiology, San Angelo, TX 76909. Offers coaching, sport, recreation and fitness administration (M Ed). Part-time and evening/weekend programs available. *Faculty:* 3 full-time (0 women). *Students:* 5 full-time (2 women), 32 part-time (9 women); includes 11 minority (5 Black or African American, non-Hispanic/Latino; 6 Hispanic/Latino), 3 international. Average age 24. 22 applicants, 77% accepted, 16 enrolled. In 2011, 3 master's awarded. *Degree requirements:* For master's, comprehensive exam. *Entrance requirements:* Additional exam requirements/recommendations for international students: Required—TOEFL or IELTS. *Application deadline:* For fall admission, 7/15 priority date for domestic students, 6/10 for international students; for spring admission, 12/1 priority date for domestic students, 11/1 for international students. Applications are processed on a rolling basis. Application fee: $40 ($50 for international students). Electronic applications accepted. *Financial support:* In 2011–12, 2 teaching assistantships (averaging $10,251 per year) were awarded; career-related internships or fieldwork, Federal Work-Study, scholarships/grants, and unspecified assistantships also available. Support available to part-time students. Financial award application deadline: 3/1; financial award applicants required to submit FAFSA. *Unit head:* Dr. Doyle Carter, Department Head, 325-942-2365 Ext. 225, Fax: 325-942-2129, E-mail: doyle.carter@angelo.edu. *Application contact:* Dr. Warren Simpson, Graduate Advisor, 325-942-2173 Ext. 224, Fax: 325-942-2129, E-mail: warren.simpson@angelo.edu. Web site: http://www.angelo.edu/dept/kinesiology/.

Arkansas State University, Graduate School, College of Education, Department of Health, Physical Education, and Sport Sciences, Jonesboro, State University, AR 72467. Offers exercise science (MS); physical education (MSE, SCCT); sports administration (MS). Part-time programs available. *Faculty:* 9 full-time (3 women). *Students:* 22 full-time (8 women), 22 part-time (9 women); includes 6 minority (5 Black or African American, non-Hispanic/Latino; 1 Hispanic/Latino), 9 international. Average age 25. 44 applicants, 70% accepted, 20 enrolled. In 2011, 11 master's awarded. *Degree requirements:* For master's, comprehensive exam, thesis or alternative; for SCCT, comprehensive exam. *Entrance requirements:* For master's, GRE General Test or MAT, appropriate bachelor's degree, official transcripts, immunization records, statement of goals, letters of recommendation; for SCCT, GRE General Test or MAT, interview, master's degree, official transcript, immunization records. Additional exam requirements/recommendations for international students: Required—TOEFL (minimum score 550 paper-based; 213 computer-based; 79 iBT), IELTS (minimum score 6), Pearson Test of English Academic (minimum score 56). *Application deadline:* For fall admission, 7/1 for domestic and international students; for spring admission, 11/15 for domestic students, 11/14 for international students. Applications are processed on a rolling basis. Application fee: $30 ($40 for international students). Electronic applications accepted. *Expenses:* Tuition, state resident: full-time $4044; part-time $225 per credit hour. Tuition, nonresident: full-time $8087; part-time $449 per credit hour. *Required fees:* $936; $52 per credit hour. $25 per term. One-time fee: $30. Tuition and fees vary according to course load and program. *Financial support:* In 2011–12, 20 students received support. Teaching assistantships, career-related internships or fieldwork, scholarships/grants, and unspecified assistantships available. Financial award application deadline: 7/1; financial award applicants required to submit FAFSA. *Unit head:* Dr. Jim Stillwell, Chair, 870-972-3066, Fax: 870-972-3096, E-mail: jstillwel@astate.edu. *Application contact:* Dr. Andrew Sustich, Dean of the Graduate School, 870-972-3029, Fax: 870-972-3857, E-mail: sustich@astate.edu. Web site: http://www.astate.edu/a/education/hpess/index.dot.

Ashland University, Dwight Schar College of Education, Department of Sport Sciences, Ashland, OH 44805-3702. Offers adapted physical education (M Ed); applied exercise science (M Ed); sport education (M Ed); sport management (M Ed). Part-time programs available. *Faculty:* 11 full-time (5 women). *Students:* 15 full-time (1 woman), 21 part-time (9 women); includes 4 minority (2 Black or African American, non-Hispanic/Latino; 1 Hispanic/Latino; 1 Two or more races, non-Hispanic/Latino), 1 international. Average age 29. In 2011, 20 master's awarded. *Degree requirements:* For master's, practicum, inquiry seminar, thesis, or internship. *Entrance requirements:* For master's, teaching certificate or license, bachelor's degree, minimum cumulative GPA of 2.75. Additional exam requirements/recommendations for international students: Required—TOEFL. *Application deadline:* For fall admission, 8/27 for domestic students; for spring admission, 1/15 for domestic students. Applications are processed on a rolling basis. Application fee: $30. *Expenses: Tuition:* Full-time $5580; part-time $465 per credit hour. *Financial support:* In 2011–12, 1 student received support. Teaching assistantships, institutionally sponsored loans, and scholarships/grants available. Financial award application deadline: 4/15. *Faculty research:* Coaching, legal issues, strength and conditioning, sport management rating of perceived exertion, youth fitness, geriatric exercise science. *Unit head:* Dr. Randall F. Gearhart, Chair, 419-289-6198, E-mail: rgearhar@ashland.edu. *Application contact:* Dr. Linda Billman, Director and Chair, Graduate Studies in Education/Associate Dean, 419-289-5369, Fax: 419-289-5331, E-mail: lbillman@ashland.edu.

Augustana College, Program in Sports Administration and Leadership, Sioux Falls, SD 57197. Offers MA. Part-time programs available. *Faculty:* 8 full-time (4 women), 1 (woman) part-time/adjunct. *Students:* 17 part-time (6 women); includes 1 minority (Black or African American, non-Hispanic/Latino). 5 applicants, 60% accepted, 3 enrolled. In 2011, 5 master's awarded. *Degree requirements:* For master's, thesis, synthesis portfolio, research paper, oral and summary exam. *Entrance requirements:* For master's, minimum cumulative undergraduate GPA of 3.0 for last 60 semester hours; appropriate bachelor's degree; 2-3 page essay discussing academic interests, education goals, and plans for graduate study. Additional exam requirements/recommendations for international students: Required—TOEFL. *Application deadline:* For fall admission, 6/1 priority date for domestic students, 6/1 for international students. Applications are processed on a rolling basis. Application fee: $50. Electronic applications accepted. *Expenses: Tuition:* Full-time $28,240; part-time $480 per credit. *Required fees:* $340. *Financial support:* In 2011–12, 11 students received support, including 11 teaching assistantships; career-related internships or fieldwork, Federal Work-Study, institutionally sponsored loans, scholarships/grants, tuition waivers, and unspecified assistantships also available. Financial award application deadline: 3/1; financial award applicants required to submit FAFSA. *Unit head:* Dr. Sherry Barkley, Sports Administration and Leadership Master's Program Director, 605-274-4312, E-mail: sherry.barkley@augie.edu. *Application contact:* Nancy Wright, Administrative Assistant, Graduate Education, 605-274-5417, Fax: 605-274-4450, E-mail: nancy.wright@augie.edu.

Barry University, School of Human Performance and Leisure Sciences, Program in Sport Management, Miami Shores, FL 33161-6695. Offers MS. Part-time and evening/weekend programs available. *Degree requirements:* For master's, comprehensive exam, project or thesis. *Entrance requirements:* For master's, GMAT or GRE General Test, minimum GPA of 3.0. Electronic applications accepted. *Faculty research:* Economic impact of professional sports, sport marketing.

Barry University, School of Human Performance and Leisure Sciences and Andreas School of Business, Program in Sport Management and Business Administration, Miami Shores, FL 33161-6695. Offers MS/MBA. Part-time and evening/weekend programs available. Electronic applications accepted. *Faculty research:* Economic impact of professional sports, sport marketing.

Belmont University, College of Arts and Sciences, Department of Education, Nashville, TN 37212-3757. Offers education (M Ed); elementary education (MAT), including early childhood education, elementary education, language arts education; English (MAT); history (MAT); mathematics (MAT); middle grade education (MAT); science (MAT); secondary education (MAT); special education (MAT); sports administration (MSA). *Accreditation:* NCATE. Part-time and evening/weekend programs available. *Faculty:* 11 full-time (8 women), 23 part-time/adjunct (12 women). *Students:* 83 full-time (77 women), 205 part-time (162 women); includes 50 minority (36 Black or African American, non-Hispanic/Latino; 1 American Indian or Alaska Native, non-Hispanic/Latino; 1 Asian, non-Hispanic/Latino; 7 Hispanic/Latino; 5 Two or more races, non-Hispanic/Latino), 2 international. Average age 30. 83 applicants, 67% accepted, 35 enrolled. In 2011, 169 master's awarded. *Degree requirements:* For master's, thesis (for some programs). *Entrance requirements:* For master's, MAT or GRE and/or GMAT, minimum GPA of 2.75. Additional exam requirements/recommendations for international students: Required—TOEFL. *Application deadline:* For fall admission, 8/1 priority date for domestic students, 6/1 for international students; for spring admission, 12/1 priority date for domestic students, 10/1 for international students. Applications are processed on a rolling basis. Application fee: $50. *Expenses:* Contact institution. *Financial support:* In 2011–12, 30 students received support. Fellowships with partial tuition reimbursements available, teaching assistantships with partial tuition reimbursements available, institutionally sponsored loans, tuition waivers (partial), and unspecified assistantships available. Financial award application deadline: 4/15; financial award applicants required to submit FAFSA. *Faculty research:* Improving secondary literacy, Montessori, classroom management strategies, teacher residency programs, online professional development, mentoring, leadership, faculty development. *Total annual research expenditures:* $2,500. *Unit head:* Dr. Cynthia R. Watkins, Associate Dean, 615-460-6053, Fax: 615-460-5556, E-mail: cynthia.watkins@belmont.edu. *Application contact:* Andrea McClain, Admission/Licensure Officer, 615-460-5483, Fax: 615-460-5556, E-mail: andrea.mcclain@belmont.edu.

Belmont University, College of Arts and Sciences, Department of Sport Administration, Nashville, TN 37212-3757. Offers MSA. Part-time programs available. *Faculty:* 2 full-time (1 woman), 1 part-time/adjunct (0 women). *Students:* 5 full-time (1 woman), 57 part-time (30 women); includes 3 minority (all Black or African American, non-Hispanic/Latino), 1 international. Average age 24. 103 applicants, 45% accepted, 34 enrolled. In 2011, 35 master's awarded. *Degree requirements:* For master's, comprehensive exam (for some programs), culminating portfolio. *Entrance requirements:* For master's, GRE and/or GMAT. *Application deadline:* For fall admission, 3/1 priority date for domestic students. Application fee: $50. *Expenses: Tuition:* Full-time $28,500; part-time $900 per hour. *Required fees:* $790; $165 per semester. Tuition and fees vary according to course level, degree level and program. *Financial support:* In 2011–12, 4 students received support. Fellowships with partial tuition reimbursements available, teaching assistantships with partial tuition reimbursements available, institutionally sponsored loans, tuition waivers (partial), and unspecified assistantships available. Financial award applicants required to submit FAFSA. *Unit head:* Dr. Amy Baker, Director, 615-460-6978, Fax: 615-460-6157, E-mail: amy.baker@belmont.edu. *Application contact:* Kim Godwin, Program Assistant, 615-460-6189, Fax: 615-460-6157, E-mail: kim.godwin@belmont.edu. Web site: http://www.belmont.edu/sa/index.html.

Bowling Green State University, Graduate College, College of Education and Human Development, School of Human Movement, Sport, and Leisure Studies, Bowling Green, OH 43403. Offers developmental kinesiology (M Ed); recreation and leisure (M Ed); sport administration (M Ed). Part-time programs available. *Degree requirements:* For master's, thesis or alternative. *Entrance requirements:* For master's, GRE General Test, minimum GPA of 2.7. Additional exam requirements/recommendations for international students: Required—TOEFL. Electronic applications accepted. *Faculty research:* Teacher-learning process, travel and tourism, sport marketing and management, exercise physiology and sport psychology, life-span motor development.

Brooklyn College of the City University of New York, Division of Graduate Studies, Department of Physical Education and Exercise Science, Brooklyn, NY 11210-2889. Offers exercise science and rehabilitation (MS); physical education (MS), including sports management. Part-time programs available. *Degree requirements:* For master's, comprehensive exam or thesis. *Entrance requirements:* For master's, previous course work in physical education and education, minimum GPA of 3.0, 2 letters of recommendation, essay. Additional exam requirements/recommendations for international students: Required—TOEFL (minimum score 500 paper-based; 173 computer-based; 61 iBT). Electronic applications accepted. *Faculty research:* Exercise physiology, motor learning, sports psychology, women in athletics.

California Baptist University, Program in Kinesiology, Riverside, CA 92504-3206. Offers exercise science (MS); physical education pedagogy (MS); sport management (MS). Part-time and evening/weekend programs available. *Faculty:* 6 full-time (2 women), 1 part-time/adjunct (0 women). *Students:* 42 full-time (20 women); includes 11 minority (6 Black or African American, non-Hispanic/Latino; 2 Asian, non-Hispanic/Latino; 2 Hispanic/Latino; 1 Two or more races, non-Hispanic/Latino), 14 international. Average age 27. 47 applicants, 70% accepted, 18 enrolled. In 2011, 25 master's awarded. *Degree requirements:* For master's, comprehensive exam or thesis. *Entrance requirements:* For master's, minimum undergraduate GPA of 2.75; three recommendations; comprehensive essay; resume; interview. Additional exam requirements/recommendations for international students: Required—TOEFL (minimum score 575 paper-based; 230 computer-based; 89 iBT). *Application deadline:* For fall admission, 8/1 priority date for domestic students, 7/1 for international students; for spring admission, 12/1 priority date for domestic students, 11/1 for international students. Applications are processed on a rolling basis. Application fee: $45. Electronic applications accepted. *Expenses:* Contact institution. *Financial support:* In 2011–12, 2 students received support, including 2 teaching assistantships (averaging $6,450 per year); Federal Work-Study, institutionally sponsored loans, and unspecified assistantships also available. Financial award applicants required to submit FAFSA. *Faculty research:* Musculoskeletal injury and examination, thermoregulation, immune function, carbohydrate oxidation, cardiovascular morbidity and mortality. *Unit head:* Dr. Chuck Sands, Dean, College of Allied Health, 951-343-4619, E-mail: csands@calbaptist.edu. *Application contact:* Dr. Sean Sullivan, Chair, Department of Kinesiology, 951-343-4528, Fax: 951-343-5095, E-mail: ssullivan@calbaptist.edu. Web site: http://www.calbaptist.edu/mskin/.

California State University, Long Beach, Graduate Studies, College of Health and Human Services, Department of Kinesiology, Long Beach, CA 90840. Offers adapted physical education (MA); coaching and student athlete development (MA); exercise physiology and nutrition (MS); exercise science (MS); individualized studies (MA); kinesiology (MA); pedagogical studies (MA); sport and exercise psychology (MS); sport management (MA); sports medicine and injury studies (MS). Part-time programs available. *Faculty:* 9 full-time (5 women), 5 part-time/adjunct (4 women). *Students:* 48 full-time (27 women), 39 part-time (13 women); includes 38 minority (5 Black or African American, non-Hispanic/Latino; 2 American Indian or Alaska Native, non-Hispanic/Latino; 7 Asian, non-Hispanic/Latino; 18 Hispanic/Latino; 6 Two or more races, non-Hispanic/Latino), 2 international. Average age 28. 214 applicants, 50% accepted, 32 enrolled. In 2011, 69 master's awarded. *Degree requirements:* For master's, oral and written comprehensive exams or thesis. *Entrance requirements:* For master's, GRE General Test, minimum GPA of 2.75 during previous 2 years of course work. *Application deadline:* For fall admission, 6/1 for domestic students. Applications are processed on a rolling basis. Application fee: $55. Electronic applications accepted. *Financial support:* Federal Work-Study, institutionally sponsored loans, and scholarships/grants available. Financial award application deadline: 3/2. *Faculty research:* Pulmonary functioning, feedback and practice structure, strength training, history and politics of sports, special population research issues. *Unit head:* Dr. Sharon R. Guthrie, Chair, 562-985-7487, Fax: 562-985-8067, E-mail: guthrie@csulb.edu. *Application contact:* Dr. Grant Hill, Graduate Advisor, 562-985-8856, Fax: 562-985-8067, E-mail: ghill@csulb.edu.

California University of Pennsylvania, School of Graduate Studies and Research, College of Education and Human Services, Program in Sport Management Studies, California, PA 15419-1394. Offers intercollegiate athletic administration (MS); sport management (MS); sports counseling (MS). Postbaccalaureate distance learning degree programs offered.

Canisius College, Graduate Division, School of Education and Human Services, Program in Sport Administration, Buffalo, NY 14208-1098. Offers sports administration (MS Ed); sports administration online (MS Ed). Postbaccalaureate distance learning degree programs offered (no on-campus study). *Faculty:* 2 full-time (0 women), 11 part-time/adjunct (3 women). *Students:* 87 full-time (28 women), 123 part-time (40 women); includes 28 minority (15 Black or African American, non-Hispanic/Latino; 1 American Indian or Alaska Native, non-Hispanic/Latino; 2 Asian, non-Hispanic/Latino; 4 Hispanic/Latino; 6 Two or more races, non-Hispanic/Latino), 11 international. Average age 27. 127 applicants, 81% accepted, 65 enrolled. In 2011, 64 master's awarded. *Entrance requirements:* For master's, transcripts, essay, minimum GPA of 2.7. Additional exam requirements/recommendations for international students: Required—TOEFL. *Application deadline:* Applications are processed on a rolling basis. Application fee: $25. Electronic applications accepted. *Financial support:* Career-related internships or fieldwork, Federal Work-Study, scholarships/grants, and unspecified assistantships available. Support available to part-time students. Financial award application deadline: 4/30; financial award applicants required to submit FAFSA. *Unit head:* Dr. Shawn O'Rourke, Associate Dean, 716-888-3179, E-mail: orourke1@canisius.edu. *Application contact:* Jim Bagwell, Director of Graduate Recruitment and Admissions, 716-888-2544, E-mail: bagwellj@canisius.edu. Web site: http://www.canisius.edu/masters-in-sport-administration/.

Cardinal Stritch University, College of Arts and Sciences, Program in Sport Management, Milwaukee, WI 53217-3985. Offers MS.

Central Michigan University, Central Michigan University Global Campus, Program in Sport Administration, Mount Pleasant, MI 48859. Offers MA. Part-time and evening/weekend programs available. *Entrance requirements:* For master's, minimum GPA of 3.0. *Unit head:* Scott J. Smith, Director, 989-774-6525, E-mail: smith5sj@cmich.edu. *Application contact:* 877-268-4636, E-mail: cmuglobal@cmich.edu.

Central Michigan University, College of Graduate Studies, The Herbert H. and Grace A. Dow College of Health Professions, Department of Physical Education and Sport, Mount Pleasant, MI 48859. Offers physical education (MA), including athletic administration, coaching, exercise science, teaching; sport administration (MA). Part-time programs available. *Degree requirements:* For master's, thesis or alternative. Electronic applications accepted. *Faculty research:* Athletic administration and sport management, performance enhancing substance use in sport, computer applications for sport managers, mental skill development for ultimate performance, teaching methods.

Central Michigan University, College of Graduate Studies, Interdisciplinary Administration Programs, Mount Pleasant, MI 48859. Offers acquisitions administration (MSA, Graduate Certificate); general administration (MSA, Graduate Certificate); health services administration (MSA, Graduate Certificate); human resource administration (Graduate Certificate); human resources administration (MSA); information resource management (MSA, Graduate Certificate); international administration (MSA, Graduate Certificate); leadership (MSA, Graduate Certificate); organizational communication (MSA, Graduate Certificate); public administration (MSA, Graduate Certificate); recreation and park administration (MSA); sport administration (MSA). *Accreditation:* AACSB. Part-time and evening/weekend programs available. Postbaccalaureate distance learning degree programs offered (no on-campus study). *Degree requirements:* For master's, thesis or alternative. *Entrance requirements:* For master's, bachelor's degree with minimum GPA of 2.7. Electronic applications accepted. *Faculty research:* Interdisciplinary studies in acquisitions administration, health services administration, sport administration, recreation and park administration, and international administration.

Central Washington University, Graduate Studies and Research, College of Education and Professional Studies, Department of Physical Education, School and Public Health, Ellensburg, WA 98926. Offers athletic administration (MS); health and physical education (MS). Part-time programs available. *Faculty:* 15 full-time (7 women). *Students:* 12 full-time (2 women), 12 part-time (4 women); includes 1 minority (Hispanic/Latino). 4 applicants, 75% accepted, 3 enrolled. In 2011, 12 master's awarded. *Application deadline:* For fall admission, 2/1 priority date for domestic students; for winter admission, 10/1 for domestic students; for spring admission, 1/1 for domestic students. Applications are processed on a rolling basis. Application fee: $50. Electronic applications accepted. *Expenses:* Tuition, state resident: full-time $8112; part-time $270 per credit. Tuition, nonresident: full-time $18,069; part-time $602 per credit. *Required fees:* $924. *Financial support:* In 2011–12, 5 teaching assistantships (averaging $9,234 per year) were awarded; career-related internships or fieldwork, Federal Work-Study, scholarships/grants, health care benefits, and unspecified assistantships also available. Financial award applicants required to submit FAFSA. *Unit head:* Dr. Kirk Mathias, Graduate Coordinator, 509-963-1911. *Application contact:* Justine Eason, Admissions Program Coordinator, 509-963-3103, Fax: 509-963-1799, E-mail: masters@cwu.edu. Web site: http://www.cwu.edu/~pesph/.

Cleveland State University, College of Graduate Studies, College of Education and Human Services, Department of Health, Physical Education, Recreation and Dance, Cleveland, OH 44115. Offers community health education (M Ed); exercise science (M Ed); human performance (M Ed); physical education pedagogy (M Ed); public health (MPH); school health education (M Ed); sport and exercise psychology (M Ed); sports management (M Ed). Part-time programs available. *Faculty:* 7 full-time (4 women), 3 part-time/adjunct (2 women). *Students:* 40 full-time (22 women), 91 part-time (48 women); includes 17 minority (15 Black or African American, non-Hispanic/Latino; 1 Asian, non-Hispanic/Latino; 1 Hispanic/Latino), 17 international. Average age 28. 138 applicants, 80% accepted, 60 enrolled. In 2011, 30 master's awarded. *Degree requirements:* For master's, comprehensive exam, thesis optional. *Entrance requirements:* For master's, GRE General Test or MAT (if undergraduate GPA less than 2.75), minimum undergraduate GPA of 2.75. Additional exam requirements/recommendations for international students: Required—TOEFL (minimum score 525 paper-based; 197 computer-based), IELTS (minimum score 6). *Application deadline:* For fall admission, 7/15 priority date for domestic students; for spring admission, 12/15 priority date for domestic students. Applications are processed on a rolling basis. Application fee: $30. Electronic applications accepted. *Expenses:* Tuition, state resident: full-time $6416; part-time $494 per credit hour. Tuition, nonresident: full-time $12,074; part-time $929 per credit hour. *Financial support:* In 2011–12, 6 research assistantships with full and partial tuition reimbursements (averaging $3,480 per year), 1 teaching assistantship with full and partial tuition reimbursement (averaging $3,480 per year) were awarded; career-related internships or fieldwork, tuition waivers (full), and unspecified assistantships also available. Financial award application deadline: 3/15. *Faculty research:* Bone density, marketing fitness centers, motor development of disabled, online learning and survey research. *Unit head:* Dr. Sheila M. Patterson, Chairperson, 216-687-4870, Fax: 216-687-5410, E-mail: s.m.patterson@csuohio.edu. *Application contact:* Deborah L. Brown, Interim Assistant Director, Graduate Admissions, 216-523-7572, Fax: 216-687-5400, E-mail: d.l.brown@csuohio.edu. Web site: http://www.csuohio.edu/coehs/departments/hperd.

The College at Brockport, State University of New York, School of Health and Human Performance, Department of Kinesiology, Sports Studies and Physical Education, Brockport, NY 14420-2997. Offers adapted physical education (AGC); physical education (MS Ed), including adapted physical education, athletic administration, teacher education/pedagogy. Part-time programs available. *Students:* 17 full-time (14 women), 45 part-time (16 women); includes 2 minority (both Hispanic/Latino). 42 applicants, 69% accepted, 21 enrolled. In 2011, 41 master's awarded. *Degree requirements:* For master's, thesis or alternative. *Entrance requirements:* For master's, minimum GPA of 3.0; statement of objectives. Additional exam requirements/recommendations for international students: Required—TOEFL (minimum score 550 paper-based; 213 computer-based; 79 iBT). *Application deadline:* For fall admission, 4/15 priority date for domestic students, 4/15 for international students; for spring admission, 11/15 priority date for domestic students, 11/15 for international students. Application fee: $80. Electronic applications accepted. *Financial support:* In 2011–12, 1 research assistantship with full tuition reimbursement (averaging $6,200 per year), 5 teaching assistantships with full tuition reimbursements (averaging $6,000 per year) were awarded; Federal Work-Study, scholarships/grants, and unspecified assistantships also available. Support available to part-time students. Financial award application deadline: 3/15; financial award applicants required to submit FAFSA. *Faculty research:* Athletic administration, adapted physical education, physical education curriculum, physical education teaching/coaching, children's physical activity. *Unit head:* Dr. Susan C. Petersen, Chairperson, 585-395-5332, Fax: 585-395-2771, E-mail: speterse@brockport.edu. *Application contact:* Dr. Cathy Houston-Wilson, Graduate Program

Director, 585-395-5352, Fax: 585-395-2771, E-mail: chouston@brockport.edu. Web site: http://www.brockport.edu/graduate/.

Columbia University, School of Continuing Education, Program in Sports Management, New York, NY 10027. Offers MS. Part-time programs available. *Entrance requirements:* For master's, minimum GPA of 3.0, 2 letters of recommendation, professional resume. Electronic applications accepted.

Concordia University, School of Arts and Sciences, Irvine, CA 92612-3299. Offers coaching and athletic administration (MA). Part-time and evening/weekend programs available. Postbaccalaureate distance learning degree programs offered (no on-campus study). *Faculty:* 7 full-time (2 women), 18 part-time/adjunct (2 women). *Students:* 353 full-time (81 women), 226 part-time (50 women); includes 134 minority (72 Black or African American, non-Hispanic/Latino; 1 American Indian or Alaska Native, non-Hispanic/Latino; 7 Asian, non-Hispanic/Latino; 42 Hispanic/Latino; 3 Native Hawaiian or other Pacific Islander, non-Hispanic/Latino; 9 Two or more races, non-Hispanic/Latino). Average age 34. 168 applicants, 100% accepted, 156 enrolled. In 2011, 228 master's awarded. *Degree requirements:* For master's, culminating project. *Entrance requirements:* For master's, official college/university transcript(s); signed statement of intent. Additional exam requirements/recommendations for international students: Required—TOEFL (minimum score 550 paper-based; 213 computer-based; 79 iBT). *Application deadline:* For fall admission, 8/10 for domestic students, 6/1 for international students; for spring admission, 2/15 for domestic students, 10/1 for international students. Application fee: $50 ($125 for international students). Electronic applications accepted. *Expenses:* Contact institution. *Financial support:* In 2011–12, 15 students received support. Tuition waivers (full and partial) and unspecified assistantships available. Financial award applicants required to submit FAFSA. *Unit head:* Dr. Timothy Preuss, Dean, 949-214-3286, E-mail: tim.preuss@cui.edu. *Application contact:* Chris Lewis, Associate Director of Graduate Admissions, 949-214-3025, Fax: 949-854-6894, E-mail: chris.lewis@cui.edu. Web site: http://www.cui.edu.

Concordia University, School of Graduate Studies, John Molson School of Business, Montréal, QC H3G 1M8, Canada. Offers administration (M Sc, Diploma); aviation management (Certificate, Diploma); business administration (MBA, UA Undergraduate Associate, PhD), including international aviation (UA Undergraduate Associate); chartered accountancy (Diploma); community organizational development (Certificate); event management and fundraising (Certificate); executive business administration (EMBA); investment management (Diploma); investment management option (MBA); management accounting (Certificate); management of healthcare organizations (Certificate); sport administration (Diploma). PhD program offered jointly with HEC Montreal, McGill University, and Université du Québec à Montréal. *Accreditation:* AACSB. Part-time and evening/weekend programs available. *Degree requirements:* For master's, one foreign language, thesis (for some programs), research project; for doctorate, one foreign language, thesis/dissertation; for other advanced degree, one foreign language. *Entrance requirements:* For master's and doctorate, GMAT. Additional exam requirements/recommendations for international students: Required—TOEFL. *Expenses:* Contact institution. *Faculty research:* General business, capital markets, international business.

Concordia University, St. Paul, College of Education, St. Paul, MN 55104-5494. Offers curriculum and instruction (MA Ed), including K-12 reading endorsement; differentiated instruction (MA Ed); early childhood education (MA Ed); educational leadership (MA Ed); educational technology (MA Ed); family life education (MA); K-12 reading endorsement (Certificate); special education (Certificate); sports management (MA). *Accreditation:* NCATE. Evening/weekend programs available. Postbaccalaureate distance learning degree programs offered (minimal on-campus study). *Faculty:* 7 full-time (3 women), 64 part-time/adjunct (42 women). *Students:* 617 full-time (495 women), 9 part-time (6 women); includes 57 minority (30 Black or African American, non-Hispanic/Latino; 2 American Indian or Alaska Native, non-Hispanic/Latino; 17 Asian, non-Hispanic/Latino; 5 Hispanic/Latino; 1 Native Hawaiian or other Pacific Islander, non-Hispanic/Latino; 2 Two or more races, non-Hispanic/Latino). Average age 36. 302 applicants, 83% accepted, 210 enrolled. In 2011, 320 master's, 68 other advanced degrees awarded. *Application deadline:* Applications are processed on a rolling basis. Application fee: $50. Electronic applications accepted. *Expenses: Tuition:* Full-time $8100; part-time $435 per credit. Tuition and fees vary according to program. *Financial support:* Applicants required to submit FAFSA. *Unit head:* Dr. Donald Helmstetter, Dean, 651-641-8227, Fax: 651-641-8807, E-mail: helmstetter@csp.edu. *Application contact:* Kimberly Craig, Director of Graduate and Cohort Admission, 651-603-6223, Fax: 651-603-6320, E-mail: craig@csp.edu.

Defiance College, Program in Business Administration, Defiance, OH 43512-1610. Offers criminal justice (MBA); health care (MBA); leadership (MBA); sport management (MBA). Part-time and evening/weekend programs available. *Faculty:* 3 full-time (0 women), 2 part-time/adjunct (1 woman). *Students:* 49 part-time (21 women); includes 2 minority (both Hispanic/Latino). *Degree requirements:* For master's, thesis. *Entrance requirements:* For master's, minimum GPA of 2.5. Additional exam requirements/recommendations for international students: Recommended—TOEFL. *Application deadline:* For fall admission, 8/1 for domestic and international students. Applications are processed on a rolling basis. Application fee: $25. *Expenses: Tuition:* Full-time $10,800; part-time $450 per credit hour. *Required fees:* $95; $35 per semester. *Unit head:* Dr. Susan Wajert, Coordinator, 419-783-2372, Fax: 419-784-0426, E-mail: swajert@definance.edu. *Application contact:* Sally Bissell, Director of Continuing Education, 419-783-2350, Fax: 419-784-0426, E-mail: sbissell@defiance.edu. Web site: http://www.defiance.edu.

Dowling College, Graduate Programs in Education, Oakdale, NY 11769-1999. Offers adolescence education with middle childhood extension (MS); advanced certificate in gifted education (AC); childhood and early childhood education (MS); childhood and gifted education (MS); computers in education (AC); early childhood education (MS); educational administration (Ed D); educational technology leadership (MS); educational technology specialist (AC); literacy education (MS); literary education (AC); school building leader (AC); school district business leader (MBA, AC); school district leader (AC); special education (MS); sports management (MS). *Accreditation:* NCATE. Part-time and evening/weekend programs available. Postbaccalaureate distance learning degree programs offered (minimal on-campus study). *Faculty:* 23 full-time (12 women), 70 part-time/adjunct (44 women). *Students:* 336 full-time (245 women), 631 part-time (485 women); includes 83 minority (29 Black or African American, non-Hispanic/Latino; 2 American Indian or Alaska Native, non-Hispanic/Latino; 7 Asian, non-Hispanic/Latino; 45 Hispanic/Latino). Average age 32. 280 applicants, 85% accepted, 167 enrolled. In 2011, 425 master's, 27 doctorates, 40 other advanced degrees awarded. *Degree requirements:* For master's and AC, comprehensive exam; for doctorate, thesis/dissertation. *Entrance requirements:* For master's, minimum GPA of 3.0; for doctorate, GRE, master's degree; for AC, teaching certificate. Additional exam requirements/recommendations for international students: Required—TOEFL (minimum score 550 paper-based). *Application deadline:* For fall admission, 9/1 priority date for domestic students; for winter admission, 1/1 priority date for domestic students; for spring admission, 2/1 priority date for domestic students. Applications are processed on a rolling basis. Application fee: $50. Electronic applications accepted. *Expenses: Tuition:* Full-time $19,162; part-time $933 per credit. *Required fees:* $1330; $700 per year. Tuition and fees vary according to course load. *Financial support:* Career-related internships or fieldwork and Federal Work-Study available. Support available to part-time students. Financial award application deadline: 6/30; financial award applicants required to submit FAFSA. *Faculty research:* Natural readers, Korean styles and learning strategies, mothers of children with disabilities, computers in instruction, cultural background and organizational roadblocks to problem solving. *Unit head:* Carol Pulsonetti, Director of Operations, School of Education, 631-244-3243, E-mail: pulsonec@dowling.edu. *Application contact:* Ronnie S. Macdonald, Assistant Vice President for Enrollment Services/Dean of Admissions, 631-244-3357, Fax: 631-244-1059, E-mail: macdonar@dowling.edu.

Dowling College, School of Business, Oakdale, NY 11769-1999. Offers aviation management (MBA, Certificate); banking and finance (MBA, Certificate); corporate finance (MBA); financial planning (Certificate); health care management (MBA, Certificate); human resource management (Certificate); information systems management (MBA); management and leadership (MBA); marketing (Certificate); project management (Certificate); public management (MBA, Certificate); sport, event and entertainment management (Certificate); JD/MBA. Part-time and evening/weekend programs available. Postbaccalaureate distance learning degree programs offered (minimal on-campus study). *Faculty:* 10 full-time (4 women), 54 part-time/adjunct (6 women). *Students:* 237 full-time (99 women), 403 part-time (199 women); includes 186 minority (95 Black or African American, non-Hispanic/Latino; 62 Asian, non-Hispanic/Latino; 28 Hispanic/Latino; 1 Native Hawaiian or other Pacific Islander, non-Hispanic/Latino), 1 international. Average age 35. 345 applicants, 83% accepted, 193 enrolled. In 2011, 350 master's, 7 other advanced degrees awarded. *Degree requirements:* For master's, comprehensive exam, thesis optional. *Entrance requirements:* For master's, minimum GPA of 2.8, 2 letters of recommendation, courses or seminar in accounting and finance, resume. Additional exam requirements/recommendations for international students: Required—TOEFL (minimum score 550 paper-based). *Application deadline:* For fall admission, 9/1 priority date for domestic students; for winter admission, 1/1 priority date for domestic students; for spring admission, 2/1 priority date for domestic students. Applications are processed on a rolling basis. Application fee: $50. Electronic applications accepted. *Expenses: Tuition:* Full-time $19,162; part-time $933 per credit. *Required fees:* $1330; $700 per year. Tuition and fees vary according to course load. *Financial support:* Career-related internships or fieldwork and Federal Work-Study available. Support available to part-time students. Financial award application deadline: 6/30; financial award applicants required to submit FAFSA. *Faculty research:* International finance, computer applications, labor relations, executive development. *Unit head:* Antonia Loschiavo, Assistant Dean, 631-244-3266, Fax: 631-244-1018, E-mail: loschiat@dowling.edu. *Application contact:* Ronnie S. Macdonald, Assistant Vice President for Enrollment Services/Dean of Admissions, 631-244-3357, Fax: 631-244-1059, E-mail: macdonar@dowling.edu.

Drexel University, Goodwin College of Professional Studies, School of Technology and Professional Studies, Philadelphia, PA 19104-2875. Offers construction management (MS); engineering technology (MS); food science (MS); hospitality management (MS); professional studies: creativity studies (MS); professional studies: e-learning leadership (MS); professional studies: homeland security management (MS); project management (MS); property management (MS); sport management (MS). Postbaccalaureate distance learning degree programs offered.

Duquesne University, School of Leadership and Professional Advancement, Pittsburgh, PA 15282-0001. Offers leadership (MS), including business ethics, community leadership, global leadership, information technology, leadership, liberal studies, professional administration, sports leadership. Part-time and evening/weekend programs available. Postbaccalaureate distance learning degree programs offered (no on-campus study). *Faculty:* 1 full-time (0 women), 88 part-time/adjunct (39 women). *Students:* 311 full-time (134 women), 151 part-time (68 women); includes 109 minority (69 Black or African American, non-Hispanic/Latino; 3 American Indian or Alaska Native, non-Hispanic/Latino; 11 Asian, non-Hispanic/Latino; 19 Hispanic/Latino; 1 Native Hawaiian or other Pacific Islander, non-Hispanic/Latino; 6 Two or more races, non-Hispanic/Latino), 9 international. Average age 35. 172 applicants, 73% accepted, 107 enrolled. In 2011, 67 degrees awarded. *Degree requirements:* For master's, capstone course. *Entrance requirements:* For master's, professional work experience, 500-word essay, resume, interview. Additional exam requirements/recommendations for international students: Required—TOEFL (minimum score 80 iBT). *Application deadline:* Applications are processed on a rolling basis. Application fee: $0. Electronic applications accepted. Application fee is waived when completed online. *Expenses: Tuition:* Full-time $16,596; part-time $922 per credit. *Required fees:* $1584; $88 per credit. Tuition and fees vary according to program. *Financial support:* Applicants required to submit FAFSA. *Unit head:* Dr. Dorothy Bassett, Dean, 412-396-2141, Fax: 412-396-4711, E-mail: bassettd@duq.edu. *Application contact:* Marianne Leister, Director of Student Services, 412-396-4933, Fax: 412-396-5072, E-mail: leister@duq.edu. Web site: http://www.duq.edu/leadership.

East Carolina University, Graduate School, College of Health and Human Performance, Department of Kinesiology, Greenville, NC 27858-4353. Offers adapted physical education (MA Ed, MS); bioenergetics and exercise science (PhD); biomechanics (MS); exercise physiology (MS); physical activity promotion (MS); physical education (MA Ed, MAT); physical education clinical supervision (Certificate); physical education pedagogy (MA Ed, MS); sport and exercise psychology (MS); sport management (Certificate). *Degree requirements:* For master's, comprehensive exam, thesis optional; for doctorate, comprehensive exam, thesis/dissertation. *Entrance requirements:* For master's, GRE General Test or MAT; for doctorate, GRE. Additional exam requirements/recommendations for international students: Required—TOEFL. *Application deadline:* For fall admission, 2/1 priority date for domestic students, 2/1 for international students. Applications are processed on a rolling basis. Application fee: $50. *Expenses:* Tuition, state resident: full-time $3557; part-time $444.63 per semester hour. Tuition, nonresident: full-time $14,351; part-time $1793.88 per semester hour. *Required fees:* $2016; $252 per semester hour. Part-time tuition and fees vary according to course load, campus/location and program. *Financial support:* Research assistantships with tuition reimbursements and teaching assistantships available. Support available to part-time students. Financial award application deadline: 2/1. *Faculty research:* Diabetes metabolism, pediatric obesity, biomechanics of arthritis, physical activity measurement. *Unit head:* Dr. Stacey Altman, Chair, 252-328-2973, E-mail: altmans@ecu.edu.

East Carolina University, Graduate School, College of Health and Human Performance, Department of Recreation and Leisure Studies, Greenville, NC 27858-4353. Offers aquatic therapy (Certificate); biofeedback (Certificate); recreation and park administration (MS), including generalist, recreational sports management; recreational therapy administration (MS). Part-time and evening/weekend programs available. Postbaccalaureate distance learning degree programs offered (minimal on-campus study). *Degree requirements:* For master's, comprehensive exam, thesis optional. *Entrance requirements:* For master's, GRE General Test or MAT. Additional exam requirements/recommendations for international students: Required—TOEFL. *Application deadline:* For fall admission, 6/1 priority date for domestic students. Applications are processed on a rolling basis. Application fee: $50. *Expenses:* Tuition, state resident: full-time $3557; part-time $444.63 per semester hour. Tuition, nonresident: full-time $14,351; part-time $1793.88 per semester hour. *Required fees:* $2016; $252 per semester hour. Part-time tuition and fees vary according to course load, campus/location and program. *Financial support:* Research assistantships and teaching assistantships with partial tuition reimbursements available. Financial award application deadline: 6/1. *Faculty research:* Therapeutic recreation, stress and coping behavior, medicine carrying capacity, choice behavior, tourism preferences. *Unit head:* Dr. Deb Jordan, Chair, 252-737-2990, E-mail: jordand@ecu.edu. *Application contact:* Dr. Sharon Knight, Director of Graduate Studies, 252-328-4637, Fax: 252-328-4655, E-mail: knights@ecu.edu. Web site: http://www.ecu.edu/rcls/.

Eastern Kentucky University, The Graduate School, College of Health Sciences, Department of Exercise and Sport Science, Richmond, KY 40475-3102. Offers exercise and sport science (MS); exercise and wellness (MS); sports administration (MS). Part-time programs available. *Entrance requirements:* For master's, GRE General Test (minimum score 700 verbal and quantitative), minimum GPA of 2.5 (for most), minimum GPA of 3.0 (analytical writing). *Faculty research:* Nutrition and exercise.

Eastern Michigan University, Graduate School, College of Health and Human Services, School of Health Promotion and Human Performance, Program in Sports Management, Ypsilanti, MI 48197. Offers MS. Part-time and evening/weekend programs available. *Students:* 14 full-time (4 women), 46 part-time (13 women); includes 11 minority (7 Black or African American, non-Hispanic/Latino; 1 American Indian or Alaska Native, non-Hispanic/Latino; 2 Hispanic/Latino; 1 Native Hawaiian or other Pacific Islander, non-Hispanic/Latino), 1 international. Average age 27. 69 applicants, 74% accepted, 25 enrolled. In 2011, 28 degrees awarded. *Degree requirements:* For master's, comprehensive exams or thesis. *Entrance requirements:* For master's, minimum GPA of 2.75. Additional exam requirements/recommendations for international students: Required—TOEFL. *Application deadline:* For fall admission, 8/1 for domestic students, 5/1 for international students; for winter admission, 12/1 for domestic students, 10/1 for international students; for spring admission, 4/15 for domestic students, 3/1 for international students. Applications are processed on a rolling basis. Application fee: $35. *Expenses:* Tuition, state resident: full-time $10,367; part-time $432 per credit hour. Tuition, nonresident: full-time $20,435; part-time $851 per credit hour. *Required fees:* $39 per credit hour. $46 per semester. One-time fee: $100. Tuition and fees vary according to course level, degree level and reciprocity agreements. *Financial support:* Fellowships, research assistantships with full tuition reimbursements, teaching assistantships with full tuition reimbursements, career-related internships or fieldwork, Federal Work-Study, institutionally sponsored loans, scholarships/grants, tuition waivers (partial), and unspecified assistantships available. Support available to part-time students. Financial award applicants required to submit FAFSA. *Unit head:* Dr. Brenda Riemer, Coordinator, 734-487-7120 Ext. 2745, Fax: 734-487-2024, E-mail: briemer@emich.edu. *Application contact:* Dr. Brenda Riemer, Chair, Graduate Programs, 734-487-0090 Ext. 2745, Fax: 734-487-2024, E-mail: briemer@emich.edu.

Eastern New Mexico University, Graduate School, College of Education and Technology, Department of Health and Physical Education, Portales, NM 88130. Offers physical education (MS), including sport administration, sport science. Part-time programs available. *Degree requirements:* For master's, comprehensive exam, thesis optional. *Entrance requirements:* For master's, minimum GPA of 3.0, 15 hours leveling courses without bachelor's degree in physical education, two references. Additional exam requirements/recommendations for international students: Required—TOEFL (minimum score 550 paper-based; 213 computer-based; 79 iBT), IELTS (minimum score 6). Electronic applications accepted.

Eastern Washington University, Graduate Studies, College of Arts, Letters and Education, Department of Physical Education, Health and Recreation, Cheney, WA 99004-2431. Offers exercise science (MS); sports and recreation administration (MS). *Faculty:* 14 full-time (5 women). *Students:* 28 full-time (9 women), 4 part-time (2 women); includes 4 minority (3 Black or African American, non-Hispanic/Latino; 1 Hispanic/Latino). Average age 29. 50 applicants, 48% accepted, 14 enrolled. In 2011, 7 master's awarded. *Degree requirements:* For master's, comprehensive exam, thesis or alternative. *Entrance requirements:* For master's, minimum GPA of 3.0. *Application deadline:* For fall admission, 4/1 priority date for domestic students; for spring admission, 1/15 for domestic students. Applications are processed on a rolling basis. Application fee: $50. *Financial support:* In 2011–12, 10 teaching assistantships with partial tuition reimbursements (averaging $6,624 per year) were awarded; career-related internships or fieldwork, Federal Work-Study, institutionally sponsored loans, and scholarships/grants also available. Support available to part-time students. Financial award application deadline: 2/1; financial award applicants required to submit FAFSA. *Unit head:* John Cogley, Chair, 509-359-2486, E-mail: john.cogley@mail.ewu.edu. *Application contact:* Dr. Jeni McNeal, Professor of Physical Education, Health and Recreation, 509-359-2872, Fax: 509-359-4833, E-mail: jeni_mcneal@hotmail.com.

East Stroudsburg University of Pennsylvania, Graduate School, College of Business and Management, Department of Sport Management, East Stroudsburg, PA 18301-2999. Offers management and leadership (MS); sports management (MS). Part-time and evening/weekend programs available. *Degree requirements:* For master's, comprehensive exam. *Entrance requirements:* For master's, GRE and/or GMAT. Additional exam requirements/recommendations for international students: Required—TOEFL (minimum score 560 paper-based; 220 computer-based; 83 iBT) or IELTS.

East Tennessee State University, School of Graduate Studies, College of Education, Department of Kinesiology, Leisure and Sport Sciences, Johnson City, TN 37614. Offers exercise physiology and performance (MA); sport management (MA); sport physiology and performance (PhD), including sport performance, sport physiology. Part-time and evening/weekend programs available. *Faculty:* 10 full-time (1 woman). *Students:* 83 full-time (26 women), 8 part-time (2 women); includes 6 minority (2 Black or African American, non-Hispanic/Latino; 2 Asian, non-Hispanic/Latino; 2 Two or more races, non-Hispanic/Latino), 8 international. Average age 25. 113 applicants, 51% accepted, 57 enrolled. In 2011, 26 master's awarded. Terminal master's awarded for partial completion of doctoral program. *Degree requirements:* For master's, comprehensive exam, thesis optional, thesis or internship; for doctorate, comprehensive exam, thesis/dissertation, 2 semesters of full-time residency. *Entrance requirements:* For master's, GRE General Test, major or minor in physical education or equivalent, interview, minimum GPA of 2.7, resume, three letters of recommendation; for doctorate, GRE General Test, minimum GPA of 3.4 (for applicants with master's degree) or 3.0 (for applicants with bachelor's degree), curriculum vitae or resume, interview, four letters of recommendation. Additional exam requirements/recommendations for international students: Required—TOEFL (minimum score 550 paper-based; 213 computer-based; 79 iBT). *Application deadline:* For fall admission, 6/1 for domestic students, 4/30 for international students; for spring admission, 11/1 for domestic students, 9/30 for international students. Application fee: $35 ($45 for international students). Electronic applications accepted. *Expenses:* Tuition, state resident: full-time $7312; part-time $350 per credit hour. Tuition, nonresident: full-time $18,490; part-time $621 per credit hour. *Required fees:* $63 per credit hour. Tuition and fees vary according to course load and program. *Financial support:* In 2011–12, 52 students received support, including 6 fellowships with full tuition reimbursements available (averaging $17,250 per year), 2 research assistantships with full tuition reimbursements available (averaging $11,250 per year), 14 teaching assistantships with full tuition reimbursements available (averaging $6,000 per year); career-related internships or fieldwork, institutionally sponsored loans, scholarships/grants, and unspecified assistantships also available. Financial award application deadline: 7/1; financial award applicants required to submit FAFSA. *Faculty research:* Methods of training for individual and team sports, enhancing acute sport performance, fatigue management in athletes, risk management, facilities management, motorsport. *Total annual research expenditures:* $500. *Unit head:* Dr. Christopher Ayers, Chair, 423-439-4265, Fax: 423-439-7560, E-mail: ayersc@etsu.edu. *Application contact:* Linda Raines, Graduate Specialist, 423-439-6158, Fax: 423-439-5624, E-mail: rainesl t@etsu.edu.

Endicott College, Van Loan School of Graduate and Professional Studies, Program in Athletic Administration, Beverly, MA 01915-2096. Offers M Ed. Part-time and evening/weekend programs available. *Faculty:* 1 full-time (0 women), 10 part-time/adjunct (2 women). *Students:* 34 full-time (8 women), 28 part-time (7 women); includes 1 minority (Black or African American, non-Hispanic/Latino), 1 international. Average age 30. 23 applicants, 70% accepted, 13 enrolled. In 2011, 43 master's awarded. *Degree requirements:* For master's, thesis, practicum. *Entrance requirements:* For master's, GRE or MAT, two letters of recommendation. Additional exam requirements/recommendations for international students: Required—TOEFL. *Application deadline:* Applications are processed on a rolling basis. Application fee: $50. Electronic applications accepted. *Expenses:* Contact institution. *Financial support:* Applicants required to submit FAFSA. *Unit head:* Richard Benedetto, Associate Dean of Graduate School, 978-232-2744, Fax: 978-232-3000, E-mail: rbenedet@endicott.edu.

Fairleigh Dickinson University, College at Florham, Anthony J. Petrocelli College of Continuing Studies, Program in Sports Administration, Madison, NJ 07940-1099. Offers MSA.

Fairleigh Dickinson University, Metropolitan Campus, Anthony J. Petrocelli College of Continuing Studies, Department of Sports Administration, Program in Sports Administration, Teaneck, NJ 07666-1914. Offers MSA.

Florida International University, College of Education, Department of Educational Leadership and Policy Studies, Miami, FL 33199. Offers adult education (MS); adult education in human resource development (Ed D); clinical mental health counseling (MS); conflict resolution and consensus building (Certificate); counselor education (MS); educational administration and supervision (Ed D); educational leadership (MS, Certificate, Ed S); higher education (Ed D); higher education administration (MS); human resource development (MS); instruction in urban settings (MS); international/intercultural education (MS); learning technologies (MS); multicultural-bilingual (MS); multicultural-TESOL (MS); recreation and sport management (MS); recreation therapy (MS); rehabilitation counseling (MS); school counseling (MS); school psychology (Ed S); urban education (MS). Part-time and evening/weekend programs available. *Degree requirements:* For doctorate, thesis/dissertation. *Entrance requirements:* For master's, minimum GPA of 3.0; for doctorate and other advanced degree, GRE General Test. Additional exam requirements/recommendations for international students: Required—TOEFL (minimum score 550 paper-based; 213 computer-based; 80 iBT), IELTS (minimum score 6.3). Electronic applications accepted.

Florida State University, The Graduate School, College of Education, Department of Sport Management, Tallahassee, FL 32306. Offers MS, Ed D, PhD, Certificate. *Faculty:* 9 full-time (2 women). *Students:* 105 full-time (35 women), 36 part-time (18 women); includes 18 minority (9 Black or African American, non-Hispanic/Latino; 4 Asian, non-Hispanic/Latino; 5 Hispanic/Latino), 30 international. Average age 30. 176 applicants, 58% accepted, 62 enrolled. In 2011, 68 master's, 8 doctorates awarded. *Degree requirements:* For master's and Certificate, comprehensive exam, thesis optional; for doctorate, comprehensive exam, thesis/dissertation. *Entrance requirements:* For master's, doctorate, and Certificate, GRE General Test, minimum GPA of 3.0. Additional exam requirements/recommendations for international students: Required—TOEFL (minimum score 550 paper-based; 213 computer-based; 80 iBT). *Application deadline:* For fall admission, 7/1 for domestic and international students; for winter admission, 11/1 for domestic and international students; for spring admission, 3/1 for domestic and international students. Application fee: $30. Electronic applications accepted. *Expenses:* Tuition, state resident: full-time $9474; part-time $350.88 per credit hour. Tuition, nonresident: full-time $16,236; part-time $601.34 per credit hour. *Required fees:* $630 per semester. One-time fee: $20. Tuition and fees vary according to course load and campus/location. *Financial support:* In 2011–12, 2 research assistantships with full and partial tuition reimbursements, 54 teaching assistantships with full and partial tuition reimbursements were awarded; fellowships with full and partial tuition reimbursements, career-related internships or fieldwork, Federal Work-Study, scholarships/grants, health care benefits, and unspecified assistantships also available. Financial award application deadline: 1/15; financial award applicants required to submit FAFSA. *Faculty research:* Sport marketing, gender issues in sport, finances in sport industry, coaching. *Total annual research expenditures:* $48,242. *Unit head:* Dr. Jeffrey D. James, Chair, 850-644-9214, Fax: 850-644-0975, E-mail: jdjames@fsu.edu. *Application contact:* Sandra Auguste, Program Assistant, 850-644-4813, Fax: 850-644-0975, E-mail: sauguste@fsu.edu. Web site: http://www.fsu.edu/~smrmpe/.

Franklin Pierce University, Graduate Studies, Rindge, NH 03461-0060. Offers curriculum and instruction (M Ed); emerging network technologies (Graduate Certificate); energy and sustainability studies (MBA); health administration (MBA, Graduate Certificate); human resource management (MBA, Graduate Certificate); information technology (MBA); information technology management (MS); leadership (MBA, DA); nursing (MS); physical therapy (DPT); physician assistant studies (MPAS); special education (M Ed); sports management (MBA). *Accreditation:* APTA. Part-time programs available. Postbaccalaureate distance learning degree programs offered (no on-campus study). *Degree requirements:* For master's, concentrated original research projects; student teaching; fieldwork and/or internship; leadership project; PRAXIS I and II (for M Ed); for doctorate, concentrated original research projects, clinical fieldwork and/or internship, leadership project. *Entrance requirements:* For master's, minimum GPA of 2.5, 3 letters of recommendation; competencies in accounting, economics, statistics, and computer skills through life experience or undergraduate coursework (for MBA); certification/e-portfolio, minimum C grade in all education courses (for M Ed); license to practice as RN (for MS in nursing); for doctorate, GRE, BA/BS, 3 letters of recommendation, personal mission statement, interview, writing sample, minimum cumulative GPA of 2.8, master's degree (for DA); 80 hours of observation/work in PT settings, completion of anatomy, chemistry, physics, and statistics, minimum GPA of 3.0 (for DPT). Additional exam requirements/recommendations for international students: Required—TOEFL (minimum score 550 paper-based; 195 computer-based; 61 iBT). Electronic applications accepted. *Faculty research:* Evidence-based practice in sports physical therapy, human resource management in economic crisis, leadership in nursing, innovation in sports facility management, differentiated learning and understanding by design.

George Mason University, College of Education and Human Development, School of Recreation, Health and Tourism, Manassas , VA 20110. Offers exercise, fitness, and health promotion (MS); sport and recreation studies (MS). *Faculty:* 34 full-time (15 women), 59 part-time/adjunct (32 women). *Students:* 18 full-time (10 women), 25 part-time (11 women); includes 5 minority (2 Black or African American, non-Hispanic/Latino;

1 Asian, non-Hispanic/Latino; 1 Hispanic/Latino; 1 Two or more races, non-Hispanic/Latino). Average age 29. 58 applicants, 60% accepted, 22 enrolled. In 2011, 7 degrees awarded. *Degree requirements:* For master's, thesis (for some programs). *Entrance requirements:* For master's, GRE General Test or MAT, 3 letters of recommendation; official transcripts; expanded goals statement; undergraduate course in statistics and minimum GPA of 3.0 in last 60 credit hours and overall (for MS in sport and recreation studies); baccalaureate degree related to kinesiology, exercise science or athletic training (for MS in exercise, fitness and health promotion). Additional exam requirements/recommendations for international students: Required—TOEFL (minimum score 570 paper-based; 230 computer-based; 88 iBT), IELTS, Pearson Test of English. *Application deadline:* For fall admission, 4/1 priority date for domestic students; for spring admission, 11/1 priority date for domestic students. Application fee: $65 ($80 for international students). Electronic applications accepted. *Expenses:* Tuition, state resident: full-time $8750; part-time $364.58 per credit. Tuition, nonresident: full-time $24,092; part-time $1003.83 per credit. *Required fees:* $2514; $104.75 per credit. *Financial support:* In 2011–12, 7 students received support, including 7 research assistantships with full and partial tuition reimbursements available (averaging $6,675 per year); career-related internships or fieldwork, Federal Work-Study, scholarships/grants, unspecified assistantships, and health care benefits (full-time research or teaching assistantship recipients) also available. Support available to part-time students. Financial award application deadline: 3/1; financial award applicants required to submit FAFSA. *Faculty research:* Informing policy; promoting economic development; advocating stewardship of natural resources; improving the quality of life of individuals, families, and communities at the local, national and international levels. *Total annual research expenditures:* $553,053. *Unit head:* David Wiggins, Director, 703-993-2057, Fax: 703-993-2025, E-mail: dwiggin1@gmu.edu. *Application contact:* Dr. Pierre Rodgers, Associate Professor/Co-Coordinator of Graduate Programs, 703-993-8317, Fax: 703-993-2025, E-mail: prodgers@gmu.edu. Web site: http://rht.gmu.edu/grad/.

Georgetown University, Graduate School of Arts and Sciences, School of Continuing Studies, Washington, DC 20057. Offers American studies (MALS); Catholic studies (MALS); classical civilizations (MALS); disability studies (MPS); ethics and the professions (MALS); human resources management (MPS); humanities (MALS); individualized study (MALS); international affairs (MALS); Islam and Muslim-Christian relations (MALS); journalism (MPS); liberal studies (DLS); literature and society (MALS); medieval and early modern European studies (MALS); public relations and corporate communications (MPS); real estate (MPS); religious studies (MALS); social and public policy (MALS); sports industry management (MPS); the theory and practice of American democracy (MALS); visual culture (MALS). *Entrance requirements:* Additional exam requirements/recommendations for international students: Required—TOEFL.

The George Washington University, School of Business, Department of Tourism and Hospitality Management, Washington, DC 20052. Offers event and meeting management (MTA); event management (Professional Certificate); hospitality management (MTA, Professional Certificate); sport management (MTA); sports business management (Professional Certificate); sustainable tourism destination management (MTA); tourism administration (MTA); tourism and hospitality management (MBA); tourism destination management (Professional Certificate). Part-time programs available. Postbaccalaureate distance learning degree programs offered. *Faculty:* 9 full-time (5 women), 11 part-time/adjunct (5 women). *Students:* 84 full-time (62 women), 107 part-time (77 women); includes 43 minority (27 Black or African American, non-Hispanic/Latino; 2 American Indian or Alaska Native, non-Hispanic/Latino; 5 Asian, non-Hispanic/Latino; 9 Hispanic/Latino), 38 international. Average age 30. 152 applicants, 74% accepted, 56 enrolled. In 2011, 69 master's awarded. *Degree requirements:* For master's, comprehensive exam, thesis. *Entrance requirements:* For master's, GRE General Test. Additional exam requirements/recommendations for international students: Required—TOEFL. *Application deadline:* For fall admission, 4/1 priority date for domestic students; for spring admission, 10/1 for domestic students. Applications are processed on a rolling basis. Application fee: $75. *Financial support:* In 2011–12, 32 students received support. Fellowships, teaching assistantships, career-related internships or fieldwork, Federal Work-Study, institutionally sponsored loans, and tuition waivers (partial) available. Financial award application deadline: 4/1. *Faculty research:* Tourism policy, tourism impact forecasting, geotourism. *Unit head:* Susan M. Phillips, Dean, 202-994-6380, E-mail: gwsbdean@gwu.edu. *Application contact:* Kristin Williams, Assistant Vice President for Graduate and Special Enrollment Management, 202-994-0467, Fax: 202-994-0371, E-mail: ksw@gwu.edu. Web site: http://business.gwu.edu/tourism/.

Georgia Southern University, Jack N. Averitt College of Graduate Studies, College of Health and Human Sciences, Department of Hospitality, Tourism, and Family and Consumer Sciences, Program in Sport Management, Statesboro, GA 30460. Offers MS. Part-time programs available. *Students:* 3 full-time (2 women), 27 part-time (5 women); includes 10 minority (6 Black or African American, non-Hispanic/Latino; 2 Hispanic/Latino; 2 Two or more races, non-Hispanic/Latino), 1 international. Average age 28. 20 applicants, 80% accepted, 9 enrolled. In 2011, 14 master's awarded. *Degree requirements:* For master's, terminal exam. *Entrance requirements:* For master's, GMAT, GRE, resume. Additional exam requirements/recommendations for international students: Required—TOEFL (minimum score 550 paper-based; 213 computer-based; 80 iBT). *Application deadline:* For fall admission, 3/1 priority date for domestic students, 3/1 for international students; for spring admission, 10/1 priority date for domestic students, 10/1 for international students. Applications are processed on a rolling basis. Application fee: $50. Electronic applications accepted. *Expenses:* Tuition, state resident: full-time $6300; part-time $263 per semester hour. Tuition, nonresident: full-time $25,174; part-time $1049 per semester hour. *Required fees:* $1872. *Financial support:* In 2011–12, 6 students received support. Career-related internships or fieldwork, Federal Work-Study, scholarships/grants, and tuition waivers (partial) available. Support available to part-time students. Financial award application deadline: 4/15; financial award applicants required to submit FAFSA. *Faculty research:* Outsourcing sport marketing, international integration of North American sports, sport law, sport financing, sport economics. *Unit head:* Dr. Sam Todd, Coordinator, 912-478-5054, Fax: 912-478-0386, E-mail: sytodd@georgiasouthern.edu. *Application contact:* Amanda Gilliland, Coordinator for Graduate Student Recruitment, 912-478-5384, Fax: 912-478-0740, E-mail: gradadmissions@georgiasouthern.edu.

Georgia State University, College of Education, Department of Kinesiology and Health, Program in Sports Administration, Atlanta, GA 30302-3083. Offers MS. *Degree requirements:* For master's, comprehensive exam. *Entrance requirements:* For master's, GRE General Test, minimum GPA of 2.5. *Faculty research:* Sports marketing.

Gonzaga University, School of Education, Program in Sports and Athletic Administration, Spokane, WA 99258. Offers MASPAA. *Degree requirements:* For master's, comprehensive exam. *Entrance requirements:* Additional exam requirements/recommendations for international students: Required—TOEFL.

Grambling State University, School of Graduate Studies and Research, College of Education, Department of Kinesiology, Sports and Leisure Studies, Grambling, LA 71245. Offers sports administration (MS). Part-time programs available. *Degree requirements:* For master's, comprehensive exam. *Entrance requirements:* For master's, GRE General Test, minimum GPA of 2.5 on last degree. Additional exam requirements/recommendations for international students: Required—TOEFL (minimum score 500 paper-based; 173 computer-based; 61 iBT). Electronic applications accepted. *Expenses:* Tuition, state resident: full-time $3546; part-time $192 per credit hour. Tuition, nonresident: full-time $3456; part-time $192 per credit hour. *Required fees:* $1829; $1829 per semester hour. *Faculty research:* Administrative relations and organization, measuring human performance, sport history from ancient times through current date, learning dynamics of personality and sports selection.

Henderson State University, Graduate Studies, Teachers College, Department of Health, Physical Education, Recreation and Athletic Training, Arkadelphia, AR 71999-0001. Offers recreation (MS); sports administration (MS). Part-time programs available. *Entrance requirements:* For master's, GRE General Test or MAT, minimum GPA of 2.7. Additional exam requirements/recommendations for international students: Required—TOEFL (minimum score 550 paper-based; 213 computer-based); Recommended—IELTS (minimum score 6). Electronic applications accepted.

Hofstra University, Frank G. Zarb School of Business, Department of Management, Entrepreneurship and General Management, Hempstead, NY 11549. Offers business administration (MBA), including health services management, management, sports and entertainment management; general management (Advanced Certificate); human resource management (MS, Advanced Certificate). Part-time and evening/weekend programs available. Postbaccalaureate distance learning degree programs offered (minimal on-campus study). *Faculty:* 7 full-time (2 women), 8 part-time/adjunct (1 woman). *Students:* 92 full-time (36 women), 151 part-time (62 women); includes 58 minority (25 Black or African American, non-Hispanic/Latino; 23 Asian, non-Hispanic/Latino; 10 Hispanic/Latino), 24 international. Average age 32. 227 applicants, 72% accepted, 93 enrolled. In 2011, 74 master's awarded. *Degree requirements:* For master's, thesis optional, capstone course (for MBA); thesis (for MS); minimum GPA of 3.0. *Entrance requirements:* For master's, GMAT/GRE, 2 letters of recommendation; resume; essay. Additional exam requirements/recommendations for international students: Required—TOEFL (minimum score 550 paper-based; 213 computer-based; 80 iBT); Recommended—IELTS (minimum score 6). *Application deadline:* Applications are processed on a rolling basis. Application fee: $70 ($75 for international students). Electronic applications accepted. *Expenses:* Contact institution. *Financial support:* In 2011–12, 23 students received support, including 18 fellowships with full and partial tuition reimbursements available (averaging $5,605 per year), 1 research assistantship with full and partial tuition reimbursement available (averaging $11,370 per year); career-related internships or fieldwork, Federal Work-Study, institutionally sponsored loans, scholarships/grants, tuition waivers (full and partial), and unspecified assistantships also available. Support available to part-time students. Financial award applicants required to submit FAFSA. *Faculty research:* Business/personal ethics, sustainability, innovation, decision-making, supply chain management, learning and pedagogical issues, family business, small business, entrepreneurship. *Unit head:* Dr. Li-Lian Gao, Chairperson, 516-463-5729, Fax: 516-463-4834, E-mail: mgblzg@hofstra.edu. *Application contact:* Carol Drummer, Dean of Graduate Admissions, 516-463-4876, Fax: 516-463-4664, E-mail: gradstudent@hofstra.edu. Web site: http://www.hofstra.edu/Academics/Colleges/Zarb/MGMT/.

Holy Names University, Graduate Division, Department of Business, Oakland, CA 94619-1699. Offers energy and environment management (MBA); finance (MBA); management and leadership (MBA); marketing (MBA); sports management (MBA). Part-time and evening/weekend programs available. *Entrance requirements:* For master's, minimum undergraduate GPA of 2.6 overall, 3.0 in major. Additional exam requirements/recommendations for international students: Required—TOEFL (minimum score 550 paper-based; 213 computer-based; 80 iBT). *Faculty research:* Business ethics, sustainable economics, accounting models, cross-cultural management, diversity in organizations.

Howard University, Graduate School, Department of Health, Human Performance and Leisure Studies, Washington, DC 20059-0002. Offers exercise physiology (MS); health education (MS); sports studies (MS), including sociology of sports, sports management; urban recreation (MS), including leisure studies. Part-time and evening/weekend programs available. *Degree requirements:* For master's, comprehensive exam, thesis. *Entrance requirements:* For master's, BS in human performance or related field. Additional exam requirements/recommendations for international students: Recommended—TOEFL. Electronic applications accepted. *Faculty research:* Health promotion, cardiovascular hypertension, physical activity, sport and human rights issues.

Indiana State University, College of Graduate and Professional Studies, College of Nursing, Health and Human Services, Department of Physical Education, Terre Haute, IN 47809. Offers adult fitness (MA, MS); coaching (MA, MS); exercise science (MA, MS). *Degree requirements:* For master's, thesis (for some programs). *Entrance requirements:* For master's, minor in physical education. Electronic applications accepted. *Faculty research:* Exercise science.

Indiana State University, College of Graduate and Professional Studies, College of Nursing, Health and Human Services, Department of Recreation and Sport Management, Terre Haute, IN 47809. Offers MA, MS. *Degree requirements:* For master's, comprehensive exam (for some programs), thesis (for some programs). *Entrance requirements:* For master's, GRE General Test, undergraduate major in related field. Electronic applications accepted.

Indiana University Bloomington, School of Health, Physical Education and Recreation, Department of Kinesiology, Bloomington, IN 47405-7000. Offers adapted physical education (MS); applied sport science (MS); athletic administration/sport management (MS); athletic training (MS); biomechanics (MS); ergonomics (MS); exercise physiology (MS); human performance (PhD), including adapted physical education, biomechanics, exercise physiology, motor learning/control, sport management; motor learning/control (MS); physical activity, fitness and wellness (MS). Part-time programs available. *Faculty:* 28 full-time (11 women). *Students:* 150 full-time (59 women), 22 part-time (9 women); includes 20 minority (12 Black or African American, non-Hispanic/Latino; 1 American Indian or Alaska Native, non-Hispanic/Latino; 1 Asian, non-Hispanic/Latino; 4 Hispanic/Latino; 2 Two or more races, non-Hispanic/Latino), 33 international. Average age 28. 211 applicants, 60% accepted, 62 enrolled. In 2011, 67 master's, 7 doctorates awarded. Terminal master's awarded for partial completion of doctoral program. *Degree requirements:* For master's, thesis optional; for doctorate, variable foreign language requirement, thesis/dissertation. *Entrance requirements:* For master's, GRE General Test, minimum GPA of 2.8; for doctorate, GRE General Test, minimum graduate GPA of 3.5, undergraduate 3.0. *Application deadline:* For fall admission, 1/1 for international students; for spring admission, 9/1 for international students. Applications are processed on a rolling basis. Application fee: $55 ($65 for international students). *Financial support:* Fellowships, research assistantships with full tuition reimbursements, teaching assistantships with full tuition reimbursements, career-related internships or fieldwork, Federal Work-Study, institutionally sponsored loans, scholarships/grants, tuition waivers (partial), and fee remissions available. Financial award application deadline: 3/1. *Faculty research:* Exercise physiology and biochemistry, sports biomechanics, human motor control, adaptation of fitness and exercise to special populations. *Unit head:* Dr. David M. Koceja, Chairperson, 812-855-5523, Fax: 812-855-3193, E-mail: koceja@indiana.edu.

Application contact: Kristine M. Wasson, Administrative Assistant for Graduate Studies, 812-855-5523, Fax: 812-855-3193, E-mail: ktanksle@indiana.edu. Web site: http://www.indiana.edu/~kines/.

Indiana University Bloomington, School of Health, Physical Education and Recreation, Department of Recreation, Park, and Tourism Studies, Bloomington, IN 47405-7000. Offers leisure behavior (PhD); outdoor recreation (MS); recreation administration (MS); recreational sports administration (MS); therapeutic recreation (MS); tourism management (MS). *Faculty:* 16 full-time (6 women), 2 part-time/adjunct (both women). *Students:* 61 full-time (32 women), 22 part-time (20 women); includes 9 minority (4 Black or African American, non-Hispanic/Latino; 1 Asian, non-Hispanic/Latino; 1 Hispanic/Latino; 3 Two or more races, non-Hispanic/Latino), 22 international. Average age 31. 48 applicants, 73% accepted, 18 enrolled. In 2011, 17 master's, 6 doctorates awarded. Terminal master's awarded for partial completion of doctoral program. *Degree requirements:* For master's, thesis optional; for doctorate, thesis/dissertation. *Entrance requirements:* For master's, GRE General Test, minimum GPA of 2.8; for doctorate, GRE General Test, minimum GPA of 3.0 (undergraduate), 3.5 (graduate). Additional exam requirements/recommendations for international students: Required—TOEFL. *Application deadline:* For fall admission, 1/1 for international students; for spring admission, 9/1 for international students. Applications are processed on a rolling basis. Application fee: $55 ($65 for international students). *Financial support:* Fellowships, research assistantships, teaching assistantships with partial tuition reimbursements, career-related internships or fieldwork, Federal Work-Study, institutionally sponsored loans, scholarships/grants, tuition waivers (partial), unspecified assistantships, and fee remissions available. Financial award application deadline: 3/1. *Faculty research:* Leisure counseling, gerontology, special populations, planning and development. *Unit head:* Bryan McCormick, Chair, 812-855-3482, E-mail: bmccormi@indiana.edu. *Application contact:* Program Office, 812-855-4711, Fax: 812-855-3998, E-mail: recpark@indiana.edu. Web site: http://www.indiana.edu/~recpark/.

Indiana University of Pennsylvania, School of Graduate Studies and Research, College of Health and Human Services, Department of Health and Physical Education, Program in Sport Science/Sport Management, Indiana, PA 15705-1087. Offers MS. *Faculty:* 10 full-time (6 women). *Students:* 15 full-time (4 women), 2 part-time (1 woman); includes 2 minority (both Black or African American, non-Hispanic/Latino), 1 international. Average age 24. 31 applicants, 61% accepted, 14 enrolled. In 2011, 7 master's awarded. *Degree requirements:* For master's, thesis or internship. *Entrance requirements:* Additional exam requirements/recommendations for international students: Required—TOEFL (minimum score 540 paper-based; 207 computer-based). Application fee: $50. *Expenses:* Tuition, state resident: full-time $7488; part-time $416 per credit. Tuition, nonresident: full-time $11,232; part-time $624 per credit. *Required fees:* $2070; $192.20 per credit. $90 per semester. *Financial support:* In 2011–12, 1 research assistantship with full and partial tuition reimbursement (averaging $5,440 per year) was awarded. Financial award application deadline: 4/15; financial award applicants required to submit FAFSA. *Unit head:* Dr. Elaine Blair, Chairperson, 724-357-2770, E-mail: eblair@iup.edu. *Application contact:* Dr. Jacqueline Beck, Associate Dean, 724-357-2560, E-mail: jbeck@iup.edu. Web site: http://www.iup.edu/upper.aspx?id=49407.

Ithaca College, Division of Graduate and Professional Studies, School of Health Sciences and Human Performance, Program in Sport Management, Ithaca, NY 14850. Offers MS. Part-time programs available. *Faculty:* 5 full-time (2 women). *Students:* 19 full-time (5 women), 6 part-time (4 women); includes 4 minority (1 Black or African American, non-Hispanic/Latino; 2 Asian, non-Hispanic/Latino; 1 Hispanic/Latino), 4 international. Average age 24. 47 applicants, 81% accepted, 19 enrolled. In 2011, 16 master's awarded. *Degree requirements:* For master's, thesis optional. *Entrance requirements:* For master's, GRE General Test, minimum GPA of 3.0. Additional exam requirements/recommendations for international students: Required—TOEFL (minimum score 550 paper-based; 213 computer-based; 80 iBT). *Application deadline:* For fall admission, 3/1 priority date for domestic students, 3/1 for international students; for spring admission, 12/1 for domestic and international students. Applications are processed on a rolling basis. Application fee: $40. Electronic applications accepted. *Expenses: Tuition:* Part-time $663 per credit hour. *Required fees:* $663 per credit hour. *Financial support:* In 2011–12, 11 students received support, including 11 teaching assistantships (averaging $8,340 per year); career-related internships or fieldwork, Federal Work-Study, scholarships/grants, and unspecified assistantships also available. Support available to part-time students. Financial award application deadline: 3/1; financial award applicants required to submit CSS PROFILE or FAFSA. *Faculty research:* Consumer behavior in sport, legal issues in sport, Title IX and gender equity in sport, college sport finances, policy and governance, American Indians and sport. *Unit head:* Dr. Ellen Staurowsky, Chairperson, 607-274-3527, Fax: 607-274-1263, E-mail: gps@ithaca.edu. *Application contact:* Rob Gearhart, Dean, Graduate and Professional Studies, 607-274-3527, Fax: 607-274-1263, E-mail: gps@ithaca.edu. Web site: http://www.ithaca.edu/hshp/grad/sportmgmt.

Jacksonville University, School of Education, Jacksonville, FL 32211. Offers educational leadership (M Ed); instructional leadership and organizational development (M Ed); sport management and leadership (M Ed). Part-time and evening/weekend programs available. *Degree requirements:* For master's, comprehensive exam. *Entrance requirements:* For master's, GRE General Test, minimum GPA of 3.0. Additional exam requirements/recommendations for international students: Required—TOEFL (minimum score 550 paper-based), TWE. *Expenses:* Contact institution.

Kansas Wesleyan University, Program in Business Administration, Salina, KS 67401-6196. Offers business administration (MBA); sports management (MBA). Part-time and evening/weekend programs available. *Entrance requirements:* For master's, GMAT, minimum graduate GPA of 3.0 or undergraduate GPA of 3.25.

Kent State University, Graduate School of Education, Health, and Human Services, School of Foundations, Leadership and Administration, Sports Recreation and Management Program, Kent, OH 44242-0001. Offers sport and recreation management (MA); sports studies (MA). *Faculty:* 9 full-time (5 women), 17 part-time/adjunct (8 women). *Students:* 42 full-time (10 women), 16 part-time (6 women); includes 7 minority (4 Black or African American, non-Hispanic/Latino; 3 Asian, non-Hispanic/Latino). 60 applicants, 77% accepted. In 2011, 24 master's awarded. *Degree requirements:* For master's, thesis optional. *Entrance requirements:* For master's, GRE required if undergraduate GPA below 3.0, goals statement, 2 letters of recommendation. Additional exam requirements/recommendations for international students: Required—TOEFL (minimum score 550 paper-based; 213 computer-based; 80 iBT). Application fee: $30 ($60 for international students). *Expenses:* Tuition, state resident: full-time $8136; part-time $452 per credit hour. Tuition, nonresident: full-time $14,292; part-time $794 per credit hour. *Financial support:* In 2011–12, 6 research assistantships (averaging $8,500 per year) were awarded; fellowships, teaching assistantships, Federal Work-Study, scholarships/grants, unspecified assistantships, and 1 administrative assistantship (averaging $8,500 per year) also available. *Unit head:* Mark Lyberger, Coordinator, 330-672-0228, E-mail: mlyberge@kent.edu. *Application contact:* Nancy Miller, Academic Program Coordinator, Office of Graduate Student Services, 330-672-2576, Fax: 330-672-9162, E-mail: ogs@kent.edu.

Lasell College, Graduate and Professional Studies in Sport Management, Newton, MA 02466-2709. Offers sport hospitality management (MS, Graduate Certificate); sport leadership (MS, Graduate Certificate); sport non-profit management (MS, Graduate Certificate). Part-time programs available. Postbaccalaureate distance learning degree programs offered (no on-campus study). *Faculty:* 1 (woman) full-time, 4 part-time/adjunct (3 women). *Students:* 13 full-time (5 women), 20 part-time (10 women); includes 10 minority (4 Black or African American, non-Hispanic/Latino; 2 American Indian or Alaska Native, non-Hispanic/Latino; 4 Hispanic/Latino). Average age 28. 30 applicants, 63% accepted, 9 enrolled. *Entrance requirements:* For master's and Graduate Certificate, bachelor's degree from an accredited institution. Additional exam requirements/recommendations for international students: Required—TOEFL (minimum score 550 paper-based; 213 computer-based; 79 iBT), IELTS. *Application deadline:* For fall admission, 8/31 priority date for domestic students, 6/30 for international students; for spring admission, 12/31 priority date for domestic students, 10/31 for international students. Applications are processed on a rolling basis. Electronic applications accepted. *Expenses: Tuition:* Part-time $575 per credit. *Required fees:* $70 per semester. *Financial support:* Available to part-time students. Application deadline: 8/31; applicants required to submit FAFSA. *Unit head:* Dr. Joan Dolamore, Dean of Graduate and Professional Studies, 617-243-2485, Fax: 617-243-2450, E-mail: gradinfo@lasell.edu. *Application contact:* Adrienne Franciosi, Director of Graduate Admission, 617-243-2214, Fax: 617-243-2450, E-mail: gradinfo@lasell.edu. Web site: http://www.lasell.edu/Academics/Graduate-and-Professional-Studies/MS-in-Sport-Management-.html.

Liberty University, School of Education, Lynchburg, VA 24502. Offers administration and supervision (M Ed); curriculum and instruction (M Ed); early childhood education (M Ed); educational leadership (Ed D, Ed S); educational technology and online instruction (M Ed); elementary education (M Ed, MAT); gifted education (M Ed); math specialist (M Ed); middle grades (M Ed); outdoor adventure sport (MS); reading specialist (M Ed); school counseling (M Ed); secondary education (M Ed, MAT); special education (M Ed, MAT); sports administration (MS); teaching and learning (Ed D, Ed S). *Accreditation:* NCATE. Part-time programs available. Postbaccalaureate distance learning degree programs offered (minimal on-campus study). *Students:* 2,245 full-time (1,572 women), 3,500 part-time (2,558 women); includes 1,141 minority (888 Black or African American, non-Hispanic/Latino; 19 American Indian or Alaska Native, non-Hispanic/Latino; 21 Asian, non-Hispanic/Latino; 123 Hispanic/Latino; 9 Native Hawaiian or other Pacific Islander, non-Hispanic/Latino; 81 Two or more races, non-Hispanic/Latino), 76 international. Average age 37. In 2011, 760 master's, 48 doctorates, 321 other advanced degrees awarded. *Degree requirements:* For doctorate, comprehensive exam, thesis/dissertation. *Entrance requirements:* For master's, GRE General Test or MAT (if taken in or before 1999), 2 letters of recommendation, minimum undergraduate GPA of 3.0, curriculum vitae; for doctorate, GRE General Test or MAT (if taken before 1999), minimum master's GPA of 3.0, 3 years of teacher experience; for Ed S, GRE General Test or MAT (if taken before 1999), minimum master's GPA of 3.0, 3 years of teaching experience. Additional exam requirements/recommendations for international students: Required—TOEFL (minimum score 600 paper-based; 250 computer-based). *Application deadline:* For fall admission, 6/1 priority date for domestic students; for spring admission, 11/1 for domestic students. Applications are processed on a rolling basis. Application fee: $50. Electronic applications accepted. *Expenses:* Contact institution. *Financial support:* Federal Work-Study and tuition waivers (partial) available. *Faculty research:* Self-determination, character education, bibliotherapy, learning styles, distance education. *Unit head:* Dr. Karen L. Parker, Dean, 434-582-2195, Fax: 434-582-2468, E-mail: kparker@liberty.edu. *Application contact:* Jay Bridge, Director of Graduate Admissions, 800-424-9595, Fax: 800-628-7977, E-mail: gradadmissions@liberty.edu. Web site: http://www.liberty.edu/academics/education/graduate/.

Lindenwood University, Graduate Programs, School of Business and Entrepreneurship, St. Charles, MO 63301-1695. Offers accounting (MBA, MS); business administration (MBA); entrepreneurial studies (MBA, MS); finance (MBA, MS); human resource management (MBA); human resources (MS); international business (MBA, MS); management (MBA, MS); management information systems (MBA, MS); marketing (MBA, MS); public management (MBA, MS); sport management (MA); supply chain management (MBA). *Accreditation:* ACBSP. Part-time and evening/weekend programs available. *Faculty:* 20 full-time (8 women), 17 part-time/adjunct (5 women). *Students:* 165 full-time (66 women), 223 part-time (100 women); includes 59 minority (48 Black or African American, non-Hispanic/Latino; 4 Asian, non-Hispanic/Latino; 2 Native Hawaiian or other Pacific Islander, non-Hispanic/Latino; 5 Two or more races, non-Hispanic/Latino), 140 international. Average age 29. 156 applicants, 76% accepted, 103 enrolled. In 2011, 205 degrees awarded. *Degree requirements:* For master's, comprehensive exam (for some programs), thesis (for some programs). *Entrance requirements:* For master's, interview, minimum GPA of 3.0, letter of recommendation. Additional exam requirements/recommendations for international students: Required—TOEFL (minimum score 550 paper-based; 213 computer-based; 80 iBT). *Application deadline:* For fall admission, 8/15 priority date for domestic students, 8/15 for international students; for winter admission, 1/9 priority date for domestic students, 1/9 for international students; for spring admission, 3/12 priority date for domestic students, 3/12 for international students. Applications are processed on a rolling basis. Application fee: $30 ($100 for international students). Electronic applications accepted. *Expenses: Tuition:* Full-time $13,650; part-time $395 per credit hour. *Required fees:* $150 per semester. Tuition and fees vary according to course level and course load. *Financial support:* In 2011–12, 206 students received support. Career-related internships or fieldwork, Federal Work-Study, institutionally sponsored loans, and tuition waivers (partial) available. Financial award application deadline: 6/30; financial award applicants required to submit FAFSA. *Unit head:* Roger Ellis, Dean, 636-949-4839, E-mail: rellis@lindenwood.edu. *Application contact:* Brett Barger, Dean of Evening Admissions and Extension Campuses, 636-949-4934, Fax: 636-949-4109, E-mail: adultadmissions@lindenwood.edu. Web site: http://www.lindenwood.edu.

Lipscomb University, College of Business, Nashville, TN 37204-3951. Offers accounting (MBA); business administration (general) (MBA); conflict management (MBA); financial services (MBA); healthcare management (MBA); human resources (MHR); leadership (MBA); nonprofit management (MBA); sports management (MBA); sustainability (MBA). *Accreditation:* ACBSP. Part-time and evening/weekend programs available. *Faculty:* 13 full-time (3 women), 7 part-time/adjunct (1 woman). *Students:* 51 full-time (21 women), 83 part-time (48 women); includes 20 minority (16 Black or African American, non-Hispanic/Latino; 3 Asian, non-Hispanic/Latino; 1 Hispanic/Latino), 1 international. Average age 33. 190 applicants, 43% accepted, 54 enrolled. In 2011, 85 master's awarded. *Entrance requirements:* For master's, GMAT, interview, 2 references, resume. Additional exam requirements/recommendations for international students: Required—TOEFL (minimum score 570 paper-based; 230 computer-based). *Application deadline:* For fall admission, 6/15 for domestic students, 2/1 for international students; for winter admission, 6/1 for international students; for spring admission, 11/15 for domestic students. Applications are processed on a rolling basis. Application fee: $50 ($75 for international students). Electronic applications accepted. *Expenses:* Contact institution. *Financial support:* Career-related internships or fieldwork, scholarships/grants, tuition waivers (partial), and unspecified assistantships available. Support available to part-time students. Financial award application deadline: 7/1; financial award applicants required to submit FAFSA. *Faculty research:* Impact of spirituality on organization commitment, leadership, psychological empowerment, training. *Unit head:* Dr. Mike Kendrick, Associate Dean of Graduate Business Programs, 615-966-1833, Fax: 615-966-1818, E-mail: mikekendrick@lipscomb.edu. *Application contact:* Lisa Shacklett, Executive Director of Enrollment and Marketing, 615-966-5968, E-mail: lisa.shacklett@lipscomb.edu. Web site: http://mba.lipscomb.edu.

Lynn University, College of Business and Management, Boca Raton, FL 33431-5598. Offers aviation management (MBA); financial valuation and investment management (MBA); hospitality management (MBA); international business (MBA); marketing (MBA); mass communication and media management (MBA); sports and athletics administration (MBA). Part-time and evening/weekend programs available. Postbaccalaureate distance learning degree programs offered. *Degree requirements:* For master's, project. *Entrance requirements:* For master's, GMAT or GRE, minimum undergraduate GPA of 3.0, resume, 2 letters of recommendation. Additional exam requirements/recommendations for international students: Required—TOEFL (minimum score 550 paper-based; 213 computer-based). Electronic applications accepted. *Faculty research:* Labor relations, dynamic balance in leisure-time skills, ethics in athletics, hotel development.

Manhattanville College, Graduate Studies, Humanities and Social Sciences Programs, Program in Sport Business Management, Purchase, NY 10577-2132. Offers MS. Part-time and evening/weekend programs available. *Entrance requirements:* Additional exam requirements/recommendations for international students: Required—TOEFL.

Marquette University, Graduate School, College of Professional Studies, Milwaukee, WI 53201-1881. Offers criminal justice administration (MLS); dispute resolution (MDR, MLS); engineering (MLS); health care administration (MLS); law enforcement leadership and management (Certificate); leadership studies (Certificate); non-profit sector (MLS); public service (MAPS, MLS); sports leadership (MLS). Part-time and evening/weekend programs available. Postbaccalaureate distance learning degree programs offered (no on-campus study). *Faculty:* 9 full-time (8 women), 10 part-time/adjunct (5 women). *Students:* 26 full-time (13 women), 142 part-time (90 women); includes 29 minority (19 Black or African American, non-Hispanic/Latino; 1 American Indian or Alaska Native, non-Hispanic/Latino; 3 Asian, non-Hispanic/Latino; 5 Hispanic/Latino; 1 Two or more races, non-Hispanic/Latino), 3 international. Average age 37. 88 applicants, 78% accepted, 36 enrolled. In 2011, 36 master's, 29 Certificates awarded. *Degree requirements:* For master's, comprehensive exam (for some programs). *Entrance requirements:* For master's, GRE General Test (preferred), GMAT, or LSAT, official transcripts from all current and previous colleges/universities except Marquette, three letters of recommendation, statement of purpose. Additional exam requirements/recommendations for international students: Required—TOEFL. *Application deadline:* Applications are processed on a rolling basis. Application fee: $50. Electronic applications accepted. *Expenses: Tuition:* Full-time $17,010; part-time $945 per credit hour. Tuition and fees vary according to program. *Financial support:* In 2011–12, 9 students received support, including 8 fellowships with full tuition reimbursements available (averaging $16,247 per year). Financial award application deadline: 2/15. *Unit head:* Dr. Johnette Caulfield, Adjunct Assistant Professor/Director, 414-288-5556, E-mail: jay.caulfield@marquette.edu. *Application contact:* Craig Pierce, Assistant Director for Recruitment, 414-288-5740, Fax: 414-288-1902, E-mail: craig.pierce@marquette.edu.

Marquette University, Graduate School of Management, Executive MBA Program, Milwaukee, WI 53201-1881. Offers economics (MBA); finance (MBA); human resources (MBA); international business (MBA); management information systems (MBA); marketing (MBA); operations and supply chain management (MBA); sports business (MBA). *Accreditation:* AACSB. *Students:* 50 full-time (15 women); includes 4 minority (1 Black or African American, non-Hispanic/Latino; 3 Asian, non-Hispanic/Latino), 3 international. Average age 37. 37 applicants, 81% accepted, 29 enrolled. In 2011, 36 master's awarded. *Degree requirements:* For master's, international trip. *Entrance requirements:* For master's, GMAT or GRE, two letters of recommendation, official transcripts from current and previous colleges/universities. Additional exam requirements/recommendations for international students: Required—TOEFL (minimum score 550 paper-based; 85 computer-based; 88 iBT), IELTS (minimum score 6.5), Pearson Test of English. *Application deadline:* For fall admission, 2/15 for domestic and international students. Application fee: $50. Electronic applications accepted. *Expenses:* Contact institution. *Financial support:* Application deadline: 2/15. *Faculty research:* International trade and finance, customer relationship management, consumer satisfaction, customer service . *Unit head:* Dr. Jeanne Simmons, Graduate Director, 414-288-7145, Fax: 414-288-1660, E-mail: jeanne.simmons@marquette.edu. *Application contact:* Debra Leutermann, Admissions Coordinator, 414-288-7145, Fax: 414-288-8078, E-mail: debra.leutermann@marquette.edu. Web site: http://www.busadm.mu.edu/emba/.

Marquette University, Graduate School of Management, Program in Business Administration, Milwaukee, WI 53201-1881. Offers business administration (MBA); economics (MBA); entrepreneurship (Certificate); finance (MBA); human resources (MBA); international business (MBA); management information systems (MBA); marketing (MBA); operations and supply chain management (MBA); sports business (MBA); JD/MBA; MBA/MA; MBA/MSN. *Accreditation:* AACSB. Part-time and evening/weekend programs available. *Students:* 42 full-time (14 women), 335 part-time (94 women); includes 24 minority (5 Black or African American, non-Hispanic/Latino; 1 American Indian or Alaska Native, non-Hispanic/Latino; 15 Asian, non-Hispanic/Latino; 3 Hispanic/Latino), 29 international. Average age 31. 182 applicants, 59% accepted, 103 enrolled. In 2011, 128 master's awarded. *Degree requirements:* For Certificate, business plan. *Entrance requirements:* For master's, GMAT or GRE, letters of recommendation. Additional exam requirements/recommendations for international students: Required—TOEFL (minimum score 550 paper-based; 85 computer-based; 88 iBT), IELTS (minimum score 6.5), Pearson Test of English. *Application deadline:* For fall admission, 2/15 for domestic and international students. Applications are processed on a rolling basis. Application fee: $50. Electronic applications accepted. *Expenses: Tuition:* Full-time $17,010; part-time $945 per credit hour. Tuition and fees vary according to program. *Financial support:* In 2011–12, 4 fellowships, 11 teaching assistantships were awarded; research assistantships, Federal Work-Study, institutionally sponsored loans, scholarships/grants, and tuition waivers (full and partial) also available. Support available to part-time students. Financial award application deadline: 2/15. *Faculty research:* Ethics in the professions, services marketing, technology impact on decision-making, mentoring. *Unit head:* Dr. Jeanne Simmons, Graduate Director, 414-288-7145, Fax: 414-288-1660, E-mail: jeanne.simmons@marquette.edu. *Application contact:* Debra Leutermann, Admissions Coordinator, 414-288-8064, Fax: 414-288-1902, E-mail: debra.leutermann@marquette.edu. Web site: http://business.marquette.edu/academics/mba.

Marshall University, Academic Affairs Division, College of Health Professions, School of Kinesiology, Program in Sport Administration, Huntington, WV 25755. Offers MS. *Students:* 26 full-time (8 women), 2 part-time (1 woman); includes 2 minority (1 Asian, non-Hispanic/Latino; 1 Two or more races, non-Hispanic/Latino), 2 international. Average age 24. In 2011, 14 master's awarded. *Degree requirements:* For master's, thesis optional, comprehensive assessment. *Entrance requirements:* For master's, GRE General Test. Application fee: $40. *Unit head:* Dr. Jennifer Mak, Director, 304-696-2927, E-mail: mak@marshall.edu. *Application contact:* Information Contact, 304-746-1900, Fax: 304-746-1902, E-mail: services@marshall.edu.

Maryville University of Saint Louis, The John E. Simon School of Business, St. Louis, MO 63141-7299. Offers accounting (MBA, PGC); business studies (PGC); management (MBA, PGC); marketing (MBA, PGC); process and project management (MBA, PGC); sport and entertainment management (MBA, PGC). *Accreditation:* ACBSP. Part-time and evening/weekend programs available. *Faculty:* 8 full-time (3 women), 14 part-time/adjunct (5 women). *Students:* 19 full-time (10 women), 114 part-time (56 women); includes 13 minority (7 Black or African American, non-Hispanic/Latino; 3 Asian, non-Hispanic/Latino; 2 Hispanic/Latino; 1 Two or more races, non-Hispanic/Latino), 3 international. Average age 31. In 2011, 56 master's awarded. *Entrance requirements:* For master's, GMAT (unless applicant possesses undergraduate business degree with minimum cumulative GPA of 3.0, or has completed master's degree from accredited university or one early access course prior to undergraduate degree). Additional exam requirements/recommendations for international students: Required—TOEFL (minimum score 85 iBT). *Application deadline:* Applications are processed on a rolling basis. Application fee: $40 ($60 for international students). Electronic applications accepted. *Expenses: Tuition:* Full-time $21,922; part-time $675 per credit hour. *Required fees:* $233.75 per semester. *Financial support:* Career-related internships or fieldwork, Federal Work-Study, tuition waivers (partial), and campus employment available. Financial award application deadline: 3/1; financial award applicants required to submit FAFSA. *Faculty research:* International business, e-marketing, strategic planning, interpersonal management skills, financial analysis. *Unit head:* Dr. Pamela Horwitz, Dean, 314-529-9418, Fax: 314-529-9975, E-mail: horwitz@maryville.edu. *Application contact:* Kathy Dougherty, Director of MBA Programs, 314-529-9382, Fax: 314-529-9975, E-mail: business@maryville.edu. Web site: http://www.maryville.edu/academics-bu-mba.

Mercyhurst College, Graduate Studies, Program in Organizational Leadership, Erie, PA 16546. Offers accounting (MS); entrepreneurship (MS); higher education administration (MS); human resources (MS); nonprofit management (MS); organizational leadership (Certificate); sports leadership (MS). Part-time and evening/weekend programs available. *Faculty:* 1 full-time (0 women), 11 part-time/adjunct (4 women). *Students:* 42 full-time (16 women), 22 part-time (15 women); includes 5 minority (3 Black or African American, non-Hispanic/Latino; 1 American Indian or Alaska Native, non-Hispanic/Latino; 1 Hispanic/Latino), 9 international. Average age 30. 60 applicants, 62% accepted, 25 enrolled. In 2011, 27 master's, 2 other advanced degrees awarded. *Degree requirements:* For master's, thesis. *Entrance requirements:* For master's, GRE General Test or MAT, interview, resume, essay, three professional references, transcripts. Additional exam requirements/recommendations for international students: Required—TOEFL. *Application deadline:* For fall admission, 8/1 priority date for domestic students, 7/1 for international students; for winter admission, 11/1 for domestic students, 10/1 for international students; for spring admission, 2/1 for domestic students, 1/1 for international students. Applications are processed on a rolling basis. Application fee: $35. Electronic applications accepted. *Expenses: Tuition:* Part-time $570 per credit. *Required fees:* $90 per term. Tuition and fees vary according to program. *Financial support:* In 2011–12, 16 students received support, including 112 research assistantships with full and partial tuition reimbursements available (averaging $6,000 per year); career-related internships or fieldwork and unspecified assistantships also available. Support available to part-time students. Financial award application deadline: 5/1; financial award applicants required to submit FAFSA. *Faculty research:* Leadership training, organizational communication, leadership pedagogy. *Unit head:* Dr. Gilbert Jacobs, Director, 814-824-2390, E-mail: gjacobs@mercyhurst.edu. *Application contact:* Sarah Murphy, Academic Coordinator, 814-824-2297, Fax: 814-824-2055, E-mail: smurphy@mercyhurst.edu.

Messiah College, Program in Higher Education, Mechanicsburg, PA 17055. Offers college athletics management (MA); self-designed concentration (MA); student affairs (MA). Part-time programs available. *Faculty:* 2 full-time (1 woman), 3 part-time/adjunct (2 women). *Students:* 2 full-time (1 woman), 2 part-time (both women). Average age 25. *Application deadline:* For fall admission, 6/1 priority date for domestic students; for winter admission, 11/1 priority date for domestic students; for spring admission, 11/1 priority date for domestic students. Applications are processed on a rolling basis. Application fee: $30. Electronic applications accepted. *Expenses: Tuition:* Full-time $9648; part-time $536 per credit hour. *Required fees:* $150; $25 per course. *Financial support:* Federal Work-Study and unspecified assistantships available. Financial award applicants required to submit FAFSA. *Faculty research:* College athletics management, assessment and student learning outcomes, the life and legacy of Ernest L. Boyer, common learning, student affairs practice. *Unit head:* Dr. Cynthia Wells, Assistant Professor of Higher Education/Program Coordinator, 717-766-2511 Ext. 7378, E-mail: cwells@messiah.edu. *Application contact:* Jackie Gehman, Graduate Enrollment Coordinator, 717-796-5061, Fax: 717-691-2386, E-mail: jgehman@messiah.edu. Web site: http://www.messiah.edu/academics/graduate_studies/Higher-Ed/.

Millersville University of Pennsylvania, College of Graduate and Professional Studies, School of Education, Department of Wellness and Sport Science, Program in Sport Management, Millersville, PA 17551-0302. Offers athletic coaching (M Ed); athletic management (M Ed). Part-time and evening/weekend programs available. *Faculty:* 10 full-time (4 women). *Students:* 16 full-time (6 women), 37 part-time (11 women); includes 5 minority (4 Black or African American, non-Hispanic/Latino; 1 Hispanic/Latino). Average age 28. 26 applicants, 88% accepted, 12 enrolled. In 2011, 17 master's awarded. *Degree requirements:* For master's, comprehensive exam, thesis optional. *Entrance requirements:* For master's, GRE, MAT, or GMAT, 3 letters of recommendation. Additional exam requirements/recommendations for international students: Required—TOEFL (minimum score 500 paper-based; 183 computer-based; 65 iBT). *Application deadline:* For fall admission, 1/15 priority date for domestic students, 1/15 for international students; for winter admission, 10/1 priority date for domestic students, 10/1 for international students; for spring admission, 10/1 priority date for domestic students, 10/1 for international students. Applications are processed on a rolling basis. Application fee: $40 ($50 for international students). Electronic applications accepted. *Expenses:* Tuition, state resident: full-time $3744; part-time $416 per credit. Tuition, nonresident: full-time $5616; part-time $624 per credit. *Required fees:* $1130; $125.50 per credit. Tuition and fees vary according to course load. *Financial support:* In 2011–12, 12 students received support, including 12 research assistantships with full tuition reimbursements available (averaging $4,208 per year); institutionally sponsored loans and unspecified assistantships also available. Support available to part-time students. Financial award application deadline: 3/15; financial award applicants required to submit FAFSA. *Unit head:* Dr. Rebecca J. Mowrey, Coordinator, 717-872-3794, Fax: 717-871-2393, E-mail: rebecca.mowrey@millersville.edu. *Application contact:* Dr. Victor S. DeSantis, Dean, College of Graduate and Professional Studies, 717-872-3099, Fax: 717-872-3453, E-mail: victor.desantis@millersville.edu. Web site: http://www.millersville.edu/wssd/graduate/index.php.

Missouri State University, Graduate College, Interdisciplinary Program in Administrative Studies, Springfield, MO 65897. Offers applied communication (MS); criminal justice (MS); environmental management (MS); homeland security (MS); project management (MS); sports management (MS). Part-time and evening/weekend programs available. Postbaccalaureate distance learning degree programs offered (no on-campus study). *Students:* 22 full-time (12 women), 61 part-time (28 women); includes 14 minority (5 Black or African American, non-Hispanic/Latino; 2 Asian, non-Hispanic/Latino; 4 Hispanic/Latino; 3 Two or more races, non-Hispanic/Latino). Average age 32. 31 applicants, 97% accepted, 18 enrolled. In 2011, 31 master's awarded. *Degree requirements:* For master's, comprehensive exam, thesis or alternative. *Entrance requirements:* For master's, GRE, GMAT, 3 years of work experience. Additional exam requirements/recommendations for international students: Required—TOEFL (minimum score 550 paper-based; 213 computer-based; 79 iBT). *Application deadline:* For fall admission, 7/20 priority date for domestic students; for spring admission, 12/20 priority date for domestic students. Applications are processed on a rolling basis. Application fee: $35 ($50 for international students). Electronic applications accepted. *Expenses:* Tuition, state resident: full-time $4086; part-time $227 per credit hour. Tuition, nonresident: full-time $8172; part-time $454 per credit hour. *Required fees:* $275 per semester. Tuition and fees vary according to course load, campus/location and program. *Financial support:* Career-related internships or fieldwork, Federal Work-Study, institutionally sponsored loans, scholarships/grants, and unspecified assistantships available. Support available to part-time students. Financial award application deadline: 3/31; financial award applicants required to submit FAFSA. *Unit head:* Dr. Thomas Tomasi, Interim Program Director, 417-836-5335, Fax: 417-836-6888, E-mail: tomtomasi@missouristate.edu. *Application contact:* Misty Stewart, Coordinator of Graduate Recruitment, 417-836-6079, Fax: 417-836-6200, E-mail: mistystewart@missouristate.edu. Web site: http://msas.missouristate.edu.

Montana State University Billings, College of Allied Health Professions, Department of Health and Human Performance, Billings, MT 59101-0298. Offers athletic training (MS); sport management (MS). *Degree requirements:* For master's, thesis optional. *Entrance requirements:* For master's, GRE General Test, minimum undergraduate GPA of 3.0.

Montclair State University, The Graduate School, College of Education and Human Services, Department of Exercise Science and Physical Education, Program in Exercise Science and Physical Education, Montclair, NJ 07043-1624. Offers exercise science (MA); sports administration and coaching (MA); teaching and supervision in physical education (MA). Part-time and evening/weekend programs available. *Students:* 8 full-time (6 women), 35 part-time (14 women); includes 4 minority (1 Black or African American, non-Hispanic/Latino; 1 Asian, non-Hispanic/Latino; 2 Hispanic/Latino), 1 international. Average age 31. 25 applicants, 44% accepted, 10 enrolled. In 2011, 14 master's awarded. *Degree requirements:* For master's, comprehensive exam, thesis or alternative. *Entrance requirements:* For master's, GRE General Test, essay, 2 letters of recommendation. Additional exam requirements/recommendations for international students: Required—TOEFL (minimum score 83 iBT), IELTS (minimum score 6.5). *Application deadline:* Applications are processed on a rolling basis. Application fee: $60. Electronic applications accepted. *Financial support:* Federal Work-Study, scholarships/grants, and unspecified assistantships available. Support available to part-time students. Financial award application deadline: 3/1; financial award applicants required to submit FAFSA. *Unit head:* Dr. Robert Horn, Chairperson, 973-655-5253, E-mail: hornr@mail.montclair.edu. *Application contact:* Amy Aliello, Executive Director of The Graduate School, 973-655-5147, Fax: 973-655-7869, E-mail: graduate.school@montclair.edu. Web site: http://cehs.montclair.edu/academic/es/programs/master_physed.shtml.

Morehead State University, Graduate Programs, College of Business and Public Affairs, School of Business Administration, Morehead, KY 40351. Offers business administration (MBA); information systems (MSIS); sport management (MA). Part-time and evening/weekend programs available. *Entrance requirements:* For master's, GRE or GMAT. Additional exam requirements/recommendations for international students: Required—TOEFL (minimum score 500 paper-based; 173 computer-based). Electronic applications accepted.

Neumann University, Program in Sports Management, Aston, PA 19014-1298. Offers MS. Part-time programs available. *Degree requirements:* For master's, thesis or alternative, experiential component. Electronic applications accepted.

New England College, Program in Sports and Recreation Management: Coaching, Henniker, NH 03242-3293. Offers MS. *Entrance requirements:* For master's, resume, 2 letters of reference.

New Mexico Highlands University, Graduate Studies, School of Education, Department of Exercise and Sport Sciences, Las Vegas, NM 87701. Offers human performance and sport (MA); sports administration (MA); teacher education (MA). Part-time programs available. *Faculty:* 5 full-time (3 women). *Students:* 20 full-time (4 women), 27 part-time (9 women); includes 25 minority (7 Black or African American, non-Hispanic/Latino; 17 Hispanic/Latino; 1 Native Hawaiian or other Pacific Islander, non-Hispanic/Latino), 1 international. Average age 30. 17 applicants, 94% accepted, 13 enrolled. In 2011, 19 master's awarded. *Degree requirements:* For master's, comprehensive exam, thesis or alternative. *Entrance requirements:* For master's, minimum undergraduate GPA of 3.0. Additional exam requirements/recommendations for international students: Required—TOEFL (minimum score 540 paper-based; 207 computer-based). *Application deadline:* For fall admission, 8/1 priority date for domestic students. Applications are processed on a rolling basis. Application fee: $15. *Expenses:* Tuition, state resident: full-time $2767; part-time $146 per credit hour. Tuition, nonresident: full-time $4879; part-time $234 per credit hour. *International tuition:* $5436 full-time. *Required fees:* $737. *Financial support:* In 2011–12, 6 students received support. Career-related internships or fieldwork, Federal Work-Study, institutionally sponsored loans, scholarships/grants, tuition waivers (partial), and unspecified assistantships available. Support available to part-time students. Financial award application deadline: 3/1; financial award applicants required to submit FAFSA. *Faculty research:* Child obesity and physical inactivity, body composition and fitness assessment, motor development, sport marketing, sport finance. *Unit head:* Yongseek Kim, Department Head, 505-454-3490, E-mail: ykim@nmhu.edu. *Application contact:* Diane Trujillo, Administrative Assistant, Graduate Studies, 505-454-3266, Fax: 505-426-2117, E-mail: dtrujillo@nmhu.edu.

New York University, School of Continuing and Professional Studies, The Preston Robert Tisch Center for Hospitality, Tourism, and Sports Management, Program in Sports Business, New York, NY 10012-1019. Offers collegiate and professional sports operations (MS); marketing and media (MS); sports business (Advanced Certificate). Part-time and evening/weekend programs available. *Faculty:* 13 full-time (5 women), 26 part-time/adjunct (8 women). *Students:* 27 full-time (8 women), 41 part-time (18 women); includes 5 minority (3 Black or African American, non-Hispanic/Latino; 1 American Indian or Alaska Native, non-Hispanic/Latino; 1 Hispanic/Latino), 11 international. Average age 29. 140 applicants, 49% accepted, 22 enrolled. In 2011, 38 master's, 5 other advanced degrees awarded. *Degree requirements:* For master's, thesis. *Entrance requirements:* For master's, GRE/GMAT only upon request, relevant professional work, internship or volunteer experience. Additional exam requirements/recommendations for international students: Required—TOEFL (minimum score 600 paper-based; 250 computer-based; 100 iBT), IELTS (minimum score 7). *Application deadline:* For fall admission, 2/1 priority date for domestic students, 2/1 for international students; for spring admission, 10/15 priority date for domestic students, 8/15 for international students. Applications are processed on a rolling basis. Application fee: $150. Electronic applications accepted. *Financial support:* In 2011–12, 47 students received support, including 43 fellowships (averaging $3,033 per year); scholarships/grants also available. Support available to part-time students. Financial award application deadline: 2/15. *Faculty research:* Implications of college football's bowl coalition series from a legal, economic, and academic perspective; social history of sports. *Application contact:* Admissions Office, 212-998-7100, E-mail: scps.gradadmissions@nyu.edu. Web site: http://www.scps.nyu.edu/areas-of-study/tisch/graduate-programs/ms-sports-business/.

Nichols College, Graduate Program in Business Administration, Dudley, MA 01571-5000. Offers business administration (MBA, MOL); security management (MBA); sport management (MBA). Part-time and evening/weekend programs available. Postbaccalaureate distance learning degree programs offered (no on-campus study). *Entrance requirements:* For master's, 2 letters of recommendation. Additional exam requirements/recommendations for international students: Required—TOEFL (minimum score 500 paper-based; 213 computer-based). Electronic applications accepted.

North Carolina Central University, Division of Academic Affairs, College of Behavioral and Social Sciences, Department of Physical Education and Recreation, Durham, NC 27707-3129. Offers athletic administration (MS); physical education (MS); recreation administration (MS); therapeutic recreation (MS). Part-time and evening/weekend programs available. *Degree requirements:* For master's, one foreign language, comprehensive exam, thesis. *Entrance requirements:* For master's, GRE, minimum GPA of 3.0 in major, 2.5 overall. Additional exam requirements/recommendations for international students: Required—TOEFL. *Faculty research:* Physical activity patterns of children with disabilities, physical fitness test of North Carolina school children, exercise physiology, motor learning/development.

North Carolina State University, Graduate School, College of Natural Resources, Department of Parks, Recreation and Tourism Management, Raleigh, NC 27695. Offers natural resource management (MPRTM, MS); park and recreation management (MPRTM, MS); parks, recreation and tourism management (PhD); recreational sport management (MPRTM, MS); spatial information science (MPRTM, MS); tourism policy and development (MPRTM, MS). *Degree requirements:* For master's, thesis (for some programs); for doctorate, thesis/dissertation. *Entrance requirements:* For master's and doctorate, GRE General Test. Additional exam requirements/recommendations for international students: Required—TOEFL. Electronic applications accepted. *Faculty research:* Tourism policy and development, spatial information systems, natural resource management, recreational sports management, park and recreation management.

North Central College, Graduate and Continuing Education Programs, Program in Leadership Studies, Naperville, IL 60566-7063. Offers higher education leadership (MLS); professional leadership (MLS); social entrepreneurship (MLS); sports leadership (MLS). Part-time and evening/weekend programs available. *Faculty:* 9 full-time (1 woman), 11 part-time/adjunct (5 women). *Students:* 44 full-time (28 women), 32 part-time (20 women); includes 16 minority (9 Black or African American, non-Hispanic/Latino; 6 Hispanic/Latino; 1 Two or more races, non-Hispanic/Latino), 1 international. Average age 29. 69 applicants, 74% accepted, 32 enrolled. In 2011, 20 master's awarded. *Degree requirements:* For master's, thesis optional, project. *Entrance requirements:* For master's, interview. Additional exam requirements/recommendations for international students: Required—TOEFL (minimum score 570 paper-based; 233 computer-based; 90 iBT). *Application deadline:* For fall admission, 8/15 for domestic students; for winter admission, 12/1 for domestic students; for spring admission, 2/1 for domestic students. Applications are processed on a rolling basis. Application fee: $25. *Expenses:* Contact institution. *Financial support:* In 2011–12, 1 student received support. Scholarships/grants available. Support available to part-time students. *Unit head:* Dr. Thomas Cavenagh, Program Coordinator, Leadership Studies, 630-637-5285. *Application contact:* Wendy Kulpinski, Director of Graduate and Continuing Education Admission, 630-637-5808, Fax: 630-637-5844, E-mail: wekulpinski@noctrl.edu.

North Dakota State University, College of Graduate and Interdisciplinary Studies, College of Human Development and Education, Department of Health, Nutrition, and Exercise Sciences, Fargo, ND 58108. Offers dietetics (MS); entry level athletic training (MS); exercise science (MS); nutrition science (MS); public health (MS); sport pedagogy (MS); sports recreation management (MS). Part-time and evening/weekend programs available. Postbaccalaureate distance learning degree programs offered (no on-campus study). *Faculty:* 15 full-time (8 women). *Students:* 10 full-time (4 women). 37 applicants, 84% accepted, 10 enrolled. In 2011, 15 master's awarded. *Degree requirements:* For master's, thesis (for some programs). *Entrance requirements:* For master's, minimum GPA of 3.0. Additional exam requirements/recommendations for international students: Required—TOEFL (minimum score 525 paper-based; 197 computer-based; 71 iBT). *Application deadline:* For fall admission, 3/1 priority date for domestic students, 3/1 for international students. Applications are processed on a rolling basis. Application fee: $35. Electronic applications accepted. *Financial support:* In 2011–12, 18 teaching assistantships with full tuition reimbursements (averaging $6,500 per year) were awarded. Financial award application deadline: 3/31. *Faculty research:* Biomechanics, sport specialization, recreation, nutrition, athletic training. *Unit head:* Dr. Margaret Fitzgerald, Head, 701-231-7474, Fax: 701-231-8872, E-mail: margaret.fitzgerald@ndsu.edu. *Application contact:* Dr. Gary Liguori, Graduate Coordinator, 701-231-7474, Fax: 701-231-6524. Web site: http://www.ndsu.edu/hnes/.

North Dakota State University, College of Graduate and Interdisciplinary Studies, College of Human Development and Education, School of Education, Program in Curriculum and Instruction, Fargo, ND 58108. Offers pedagogy (M Ed, MS); physical education and athletic administration (M Ed, MS). *Students:* 23 full-time (14 women), 70 part-time (50 women); includes 8 minority (2 Black or African American, non-Hispanic/Latino; 4 American Indian or Alaska Native, non-Hispanic/Latino; 1 Hispanic/Latino; 1 Two or more races, non-Hispanic/Latino), 6 international. Average age 27. 19 applicants, 74% accepted, 6 enrolled. *Degree requirements:* For master's, comprehensive exam, thesis (for some programs). *Entrance requirements:* For master's, Cooperative English Test, GRE General Test, MAT. Additional exam requirements/recommendations for international students: Required—TOEFL. *Application deadline:* For fall admission, 5/1 for domestic students. Applications are processed on a rolling basis. Application fee: $35. *Financial support:* Teaching assistantships, career-related internships or fieldwork, Federal Work-Study, institutionally sponsored loans, and tuition waivers (full) available. Financial award application deadline: 4/15. *Unit head:* Dr. William Martin, Chair, 701-231-7202, Fax: 701-231-7416, E-mail: william.martin@ndsu.edu. *Application contact:* Dr. Justin Wageman, Associate Professor, 701-231-7108, Fax: 701-231-9685, E-mail: justin.wageman@ndsu.edu.

Northern Illinois University, Graduate School, College of Education, Department of Kinesiology and Physical Education, De Kalb, IL 60115-2854. Offers physical education (MS Ed); sport management (MS). Part-time and evening/weekend programs available. *Faculty:* 21 full-time (12 women). *Students:* 63 full-time (24 women), 71 part-time (34 women); includes 26 minority (10 Black or African American, non-Hispanic/Latino; 5 Asian, non-Hispanic/Latino; 8 Hispanic/Latino; 3 Two or more races, non-Hispanic/Latino), 5 international. Average age 27. 66 applicants, 73% accepted, 26 enrolled. In 2011, 55 master's awarded. *Degree requirements:* For master's, comprehensive exam, thesis optional. *Entrance requirements:* For master's, GRE General Test, minimum GPA of 2.75, undergraduate major in related area. Additional exam requirements/ recommendations for international students: Required—TOEFL (minimum score 550 paper-based; 213 computer-based). *Application deadline:* For fall admission, 6/1 for domestic students, 5/1 for international students; for spring admission, 11/1 for domestic students, 10/1 for international students. Applications are processed on a rolling basis. Application fee: $40. Electronic applications accepted. *Financial support:* In 2011–12, 1 research assistantship with full tuition reimbursement, 35 teaching assistantships with full tuition reimbursements were awarded; fellowships with full tuition reimbursements, career-related internships or fieldwork, Federal Work-Study, scholarships/grants, tuition waivers (full), and unspecified assistantships also available. Support available to part-time students. Financial award applicants required to submit FAFSA. *Faculty research:* Leadership in athletic training, motor development, dance education, gait analysis, fat phobia. *Unit head:* Dr. Paul Carpenter, Chair, 815-753-8284, Fax: 815-753-1413, E-mail: knpe@niu.edu. *Application contact:* Dr. Laurie Zittel, Director, Graduate Studies, 815-753-1425, E-mail: lzape@niu.edu. Web site: http://cedu.niu.edu/knpe/.

Northwestern University, School of Continuing Studies, Program in Sports Administration, Evanston, IL 60208. Offers sports management (MA); sports marketing and public relations (MA).

Ohio University, Graduate College, College of Business, Department of Sports Administration, Athens, OH 45701-2979. Offers athletic administration (MS); sports administration (MSA). Postbaccalaureate distance learning degree programs offered (minimal on-campus study). *Students:* 16 full-time (6 women), 195 part-time (156 women); includes 32 minority (20 Black or African American, non-Hispanic/Latino; 7 Hispanic/Latino; 5 Two or more races, non-Hispanic/Latino), 3 international. 103 applicants, 74% accepted, 68 enrolled. In 2011, 27 master's awarded. *Degree requirements:* For master's, 11-week internship. *Entrance requirements:* For master's, interview. Additional exam requirements/recommendations for international students: Required—TOEFL (minimum score 600 paper-based; 250 computer-based; 100 iBT) or IELTS (minimum score 7.5). *Application deadline:* For fall admission, 2/1 for domestic and international students. Application fee: $50 ($55 for international students). Electronic applications accepted. *Financial support:* Fellowships with full tuition reimbursements, research assistantships with full and partial tuition reimbursements, Federal Work-Study, institutionally sponsored loans, scholarships/grants, tuition waivers (partial), and stipends available. Financial award application deadline: 2/1. *Faculty research:* Sport management, sport marketing, sports and technology, career development. *Unit head:* Dr. Ming Li, Chair, 740-593-0597, Fax: 740-593-0284, E-mail: lim1@ohio.edu. *Application contact:* Teresa Tedrow, Administrative Coordinator, 740-593-4666, Fax: 740-593-0539, E-mail: tedrow@ohio.edu. Web site: http://ohiou.edu/sportadmin/.

Ohio University, Graduate College, Gladys W. and David H. Patton College of Education and Human Services, Department of Recreation and Sport Pedagogy, Program in Coaching Education, Athens, OH 45701-2979. Offers MS. *Students:* 21 full-time (4 women), 212 part-time (26 women); includes 50 minority (32 Black or African American, non-Hispanic/Latino; 1 American Indian or Alaska Native, non-Hispanic/Latino; 1 Asian, non-Hispanic/Latino; 13 Hispanic/Latino; 3 Two or more races, non-Hispanic/Latino), 11 international. 99 applicants, 82% accepted, 74 enrolled. In 2011, 43 master's awarded. *Entrance requirements:* For master's, GRE. Additional exam requirements/recommendations for international students: Required—TOEFL (minimum score 550 paper-based; 80 iBT) or IELTS (minimum score 6.5). *Application deadline:* For fall admission, 3/1 priority date for domestic students, 3/1 for international students. Applications are processed on a rolling basis. Application fee: $50 ($55 for international students). Electronic applications accepted. *Financial support:* In 2011–12, research assistantships with full tuition reimbursements (averaging $8,835 per year), teaching assistantships with full tuition reimbursements (averaging $8,835 per year) were awarded; scholarships/grants and stipends also available. Financial award application deadline: 3/1. *Faculty research:* Sports, physical activity, athletes. *Unit head:* Dr. Beth VanDerveer, Assistant Professor and Coordinator, 740-593-4656, Fax: 740-593-0284, E-mail: vanderve@ohio.edu. *Application contact:* Dr. David Carr, Assistant Professor and Coordinator, 740-593-4651, Fax: 740-593-0284, E-mail: carrd@ohio.edu. Web site: http://www.cehs.ohio.edu/academics/rsp/mce/index.htm.

Old Dominion University, Darden College of Education, Program in Physical Education, Sport Management Emphasis, Norfolk, VA 23529. Offers MS Ed. Part-time and evening/weekend programs available. Postbaccalaureate distance learning degree programs offered. *Faculty:* 5 full-time (2 women), 2 part-time/adjunct (both women). *Students:* 14 full-time (6 women), 17 part-time (4 women); includes 6 minority (5 Black or African American, non-Hispanic/Latino; 1 Two or more races, non-Hispanic/Latino), 2 international. Average age 25. 42 applicants, 60% accepted, 20 enrolled. In 2011, 23 master's awarded. *Degree requirements:* For master's, comprehensive exam, thesis or alternative, internship, research project. *Entrance requirements:* For master's, GRE, minimum GPA of 2.8 overall, 3.0 in major. Additional exam requirements/ recommendations for international students: Required—TOEFL (minimum score 500 paper-based; 200 computer-based). *Application deadline:* For fall admission, 7/1 for domestic students; for spring admission, 11/1 for domestic students. Applications are processed on a rolling basis. Application fee: $50. *Expenses:* Tuition, state resident: full-time $9096; part-time $379 per credit. Tuition, nonresident: full-time $23,064; part-time $961 per credit. *Required fees:* $127 per semester. One-time fee: $50. *Financial support:* In 2011–12, fellowships (averaging $15,000 per year), 1 research assistantship with partial tuition reimbursement (averaging $10,000 per year), teaching assistantships with partial tuition reimbursements (averaging $10,000 per year) were awarded; career-related internships or fieldwork and scholarships/grants also available. Financial award application deadline: 4/15; financial award applicants required to submit FAFSA. *Faculty research:* Leadership, fan motives, sport communications, curriculum development in sport management, violence in sport. *Total annual research expenditures:* $185,000. *Unit head:* Robert Case, Graduate Program Director, 757-683-5962, Fax: 757-683-4270, E-mail: rcase@odu.edu. *Application contact:* William Heffelfinger, Director of Graduate Admissions, 757-683-5554, Fax: 757-683-3255, E-mail: gradadmit@odu.edu. Web site: http://education.odu.edu/esper/academics/sportsman/graduate/graduate.shtml.

Purdue University, Graduate School, College of Health and Human Sciences, Department of Health and Kinesiology, West Lafayette, IN 47907. Offers athletic training education administration (MS); exercise, human physiology of movement and sport (PhD); health education (MS, PhD); motor control and development (MS, PhD); physical education pedagogy (MS, PhD); sport and exercise psychology (MS, PhD). Part-time programs available. *Faculty:* 20 full-time (9 women), 14 part-time/adjunct (4 women). *Students:* 53 full-time (27 women), 19 part-time (9 women); includes 9 minority (3 Black or African American, non-Hispanic/Latino; 1 American Indian or Alaska Native, non-Hispanic/Latino; 2 Asian, non-Hispanic/Latino; 1 Hispanic/Latino; 2 Two or more races, non-Hispanic/Latino), 14 international. Average age 30. 108 applicants, 48% accepted, 29 enrolled. In 2011, 17 master's, 6 doctorates awarded. *Degree requirements:* For master's, thesis optional; for doctorate, comprehensive exam, thesis/dissertation, Qualifying Examination, Preliminary Examination. *Entrance requirements:* For master's, GRE General Test, minimum score 1000 combined verbal and quantitative scores, minimum undergraduate GPA of 3.0 or equivalent; for doctorate, GRE General Test, minimum score 1100 combined verbal and quantitative scores, minimum undergraduate GPA of 3.0 or equivalent; master's degree with minimum GPA of 3.25 (recommended). Additional exam requirements/recommendations for international students: Required—TOEFL (minimum score 550 computer-based; 77 iBT); Recommended—TWE. *Application deadline:* For fall admission, 4/30 for domestic and international students; for spring admission, 10/15 for domestic and international students. Applications are processed on a rolling basis. Application fee: $60 ($75 for international students). Electronic applications accepted. *Financial support:* Fellowships with partial tuition reimbursements, research assistantships with partial tuition reimbursements, teaching assistantships with partial tuition reimbursements, and Federal Work-Study available. Support available to part-time students. Financial award applicants required to submit FAFSA. *Faculty research:* Wellness, motivation, teaching effectiveness, learning and development. *Unit head:* Dr. Larry J. Leverenz, Interim Head, 765-494-0865, Fax: 765-494-496-1239, E-mail: llevere@purdue.edu. *Application contact:* Lisa Duncan, Graduate Contact, 765-494-3162, E-mail: lduncan@purdue.edu. Web site: http://www.purdue.edu/hhs/hk/.

Robert Morris University, Graduate Studies, School of Education and Social Sciences, Moon Township, PA 15108-1189. Offers business education (MS); education (Postbaccalaureate Certificate); instructional leadership (MS), including education, sport management; instructional management and leadership (PhD). *Accreditation:* Teacher Education Accreditation Council. Part-time and evening/weekend programs available. Postbaccalaureate distance learning degree programs offered (no on-campus study). *Faculty:* 14 full-time (3 women), 11 part-time/adjunct (6 women). *Students:* 326 part-time (217 women); includes 24 minority (21 Black or African American, non-Hispanic/Latino; 1 Asian, non-Hispanic/Latino; 2 Hispanic/Latino), 1 international. *Degree requirements:* For doctorate, thesis/dissertation. *Entrance requirements:* Additional exam requirements/recommendations for international students: Required—TOEFL (minimum score 550 paper-based; 213 computer-based; 79 iBT). *Application deadline:* For fall admission, 7/1 priority date for domestic students, 7/1 for international students; for spring admission, 11/1 priority date for domestic students, 11/1 for international students. Applications are processed on a rolling basis. Application fee: $35. Electronic applications accepted. *Expenses:* Contact institution. *Unit head:* Dr. John E. Graham, Dean, 412-397-6022, Fax: 412-397-2524, E-mail: graham@rmu.edu. *Application contact:* Debra Roach, Assistant Dean, Graduate Admissions, 412-397-5200, Fax: 412-397-2425, E-mail: graduateadmissions@rmu.edu. Web site: http://www.rmu.edu/web/cms/schools/sess/.

Robert Morris University Illinois, Morris Graduate School of Management, Chicago, IL 60605. Offers accounting (MBA); accounting/finance (MBA); design and media (MM); health care administration (MM); higher education administration (MM); human resource management (MBA); information systems (MIS); law enforcement administration (MM); management (MBA); management/finance (MIS); management/human resource management (MBA); sports administration (MM). Part-time and evening/weekend programs available. *Faculty:* 7 full-time (1 woman), 21 part-time/adjunct (5 women). *Students:* 296 full-time (172 women), 216 part-time (136 women); includes 273 minority (160 Black or African American, non-Hispanic/Latino; 1 American Indian or Alaska Native, non-Hispanic/Latino; 32 Asian, non-Hispanic/Latino; 78 Hispanic/Latino; 2 Two or more races, non-Hispanic/Latino), 28 international. Average age 32. 247 applicants, 69% accepted, 152 enrolled. In 2011, 244 master's awarded. *Entrance requirements:* Additional exam requirements/recommendations for international students: Required—TOEFL (minimum score 550 paper-based; 173 computer-based). *Application deadline:* Applications are processed on a rolling basis. Application fee: $20 ($100 for international students). Electronic applications accepted. *Expenses: Tuition:* Full-time $13,800; part-time $2300 per course. *Financial support:* In 2011–12, 643 students received support. Federal Work-Study, scholarships/grants, tuition waivers, and leadership and athletic scholarships available. Support available to part-time students. Financial award applicants required to submit FAFSA. *Unit head:* Kayed Akkawi, Dean, 312-935-6025, Fax: 312-935-6020, E-mail: kakkawi@robertmorris.edu. *Application contact:* Fernando Villeda, Dean of Morris Graduate School of Management, 312-935-6050, Fax: 312-935-6020, E-mail: fvilleda@robertmorris.edu.

St. Cloud State University, School of Graduate Studies, School of Education, Department of Health, Physical Education, Recreation, and Sport Science, St. Cloud, MN 56301-4498. Offers exercise science (MS); physical education (MS); sports management (MS). *Degree requirements:* For master's, thesis or alternative. *Entrance requirements:* For master's, GRE General Test, minimum GPA of 2.75. Additional exam requirements/recommendations for international students: Required—Michigan English Language Assessment Battery; Recommended—TOEFL (minimum score 550 paper-based; 213 computer-based), IELTS (minimum score 6.5). Electronic applications accepted.

St. Edward's University, School of Education, Program in Teaching, Austin, TX 78704. Offers curriculum leadership (Certificate); instructional technology (Certificate); mediation (Certificate); mentoring and supervision (Certificate); special education (Certificate); sports management (Certificate); teaching (MA), including conflict resolution, initial teacher certification, liberal arts, special education, sports management, teacher leadership. Part-time and evening/weekend programs available. *Students:* 1 full-time (0 women), 32 part-time (22 women); includes 14 minority (2 Black or African American, non-Hispanic/Latino; 1 Asian, non-Hispanic/Latino; 10 Hispanic/Latino; 1 Two or more races, non-Hispanic/Latino), 1 international. Average age 32. 8 applicants, 75% accepted, 6 enrolled. In 2011, 13 master's awarded. *Degree requirements:* For master's, minimum of 24 resident hours. *Entrance requirements:* For master's, GRE General Test, minimum GPA of 3.0 in last 60 hours or 2.75 overall. Additional exam requirements/recommendations for international students: Required—TOEFL (minimum score 550 paper-based; 213 computer-based; 79 iBT) or IELTS (minimum score 6). *Application deadline:* For fall admission, 7/1 for domestic and international students; for spring admission, 11/1 for domestic and international students. Applications are processed on a rolling basis. Application fee: $45 ($50 for international students). Electronic applications accepted. *Expenses: Tuition:* Full-time $17,550; part-time $975 per credit hour. *Required fees:* $50 per trimester. Full-time tuition and fees vary according to course load and program. *Unit head:* Dr. David Hollier, Director, 512-448-8666, Fax: 512-428-1372, E-mail: davidrh@stedwards.edu. *Application contact:* Sarah Hennes, Graduate Admission Coordinator, 512-448-8600, Fax: 512-428-1032, E-mail: sarahhe@stedwards.edu. Web site: http://www.stedwards.edu.

St. John's University, College of Professional Studies, Department of Sport Management, Queens, NY 11439. Offers MPS. Part-time and evening/weekend programs available. *Students:* 45 full-time (13 women), 21 part-time (6 women); includes 18 minority (7 Black or African American, non-Hispanic/Latino; 1 Asian, non-Hispanic/Latino; 7 Hispanic/Latino; 3 Two or more races, non-Hispanic/Latino), 9 international. Average age 25. 107 applicants, 76% accepted, 30 enrolled. In 2011, 18 master's awarded. *Degree requirements:* For master's, comprehensive exam, thesis optional, capstone project, internship. *Entrance requirements:* For master's, bachelor's degree from regionally-accredited college or university, minimum GPA of 3.0, 2 letters of recommendation, 300-word essay. Additional exam requirements/recommendations for international students: Required—TOEFL (minimum score 600 paper-based; 250

computer-based; 100 iBT), IELTS (minimum score 5.5). *Application deadline:* For fall admission, 5/1 priority date for domestic students, 5/1 for international students; for spring admission, 11/1 priority date for domestic students, 11/1 for international students. Applications are processed on a rolling basis. Application fee: $70. Electronic applications accepted. *Expenses: Tuition:* Full-time $18,000; part-time $1000 per credit. *Required fees:* $170 per semester. Tuition and fees vary according to program. *Faculty research:* The Olympic Movement, sports economics, administration of intercollegiate athletics, sport management education. *Unit head:* Prof. Glenn Gerstner, Director, Graduate Program, 718-990-7474, E-mail: gerstneg@stjohns.edu. *Application contact:* Robert Medrano, Director of Graduate Admissions, 718-990-1601, Fax: 718-990-5686, E-mail: gradhelp@stjohns.edu.

Saint Leo University, Graduate Business Studies, Saint Leo, FL 33574-6665. Offers accounting (MBA); business (MBA); health services management (MBA); human resource management (MBA); information security management (MBA); marketing (MBA); sport business (MBA). Part-time and evening/weekend programs available. Postbaccalaureate distance learning degree programs offered (no on-campus study). *Faculty:* 39 full-time (7 women), 56 part-time/adjunct (17 women). *Students:* 1,506 full-time (901 women); includes 620 minority (480 Black or African American, non-Hispanic/Latino; 5 American Indian or Alaska Native, non-Hispanic/Latino; 21 Asian, non-Hispanic/Latino; 100 Hispanic/Latino; 1 Native Hawaiian or other Pacific Islander, non-Hispanic/Latino; 13 Two or more races, non-Hispanic/Latino), 20 international. Average age 38. In 2011, 574 master's awarded. *Entrance requirements:* For master's, GMAT (minimum score 500 if applicant does not have 5 years of professional work experience), bachelor's degree with minimum GPA of 3.0 in the last 60 hours of coursework from regionally-accredited college or university; 5 years of professional work experience; resume; 2 letters of recommendation. Additional exam requirements/recommendations for international students: Required—TOEFL (minimum score 550 paper-based; 213 computer-based; 80 iBT). *Application deadline:* For fall admission, 7/1 priority date for domestic students, 7/1 for international students; for spring admission, 11/12 priority date for domestic students, 11/1 for international students. Applications are processed on a rolling basis. Application fee: $80. Electronic applications accepted. *Expenses: Tuition:* Full-time $11,340; part-time $630 per semester hour. Tuition and fees vary according to campus/location and program. *Financial support:* In 2011–12, 72 students received support. Career-related internships or fieldwork, Federal Work-Study, scholarships/grants, and health care benefits available. Financial award application deadline: 3/1; financial award applicants required to submit FAFSA. *Unit head:* Dr. Lorrie McGovern, Director, 352-588-7390, Fax: 352-588-8585, E-mail: mbaslu@saintleo.edu. *Application contact:* Jared Welling, Director of Graduate Admission, 800-707-8846, Fax: 352-588-7873, E-mail: grad.admissions@saintleo.edu. Web site: http://www.saintleo.edu/Academics/School-of-Business/Graduate-Degree-Programs.

Saint Mary's College of California, School of Liberal Arts, Department of Kinesiology, Moraga, CA 94556. Offers sport management (MA); sport studies (MA). Part-time programs available. *Faculty:* 6 full-time (1 woman), 5 part-time/adjunct (3 women). *Students:* 3 full-time (0 women), 22 part-time (13 women); includes 6 minority (3 Black or African American, non-Hispanic/Latino; 3 Asian, non-Hispanic/Latino). Average age 27. 23 applicants, 65% accepted, 14 enrolled. In 2011, 7 master's awarded. *Degree requirements:* For master's, thesis or special project. *Entrance requirements:* For master's, minimum GPA of 2.75, BA in physical education or related field, or professional experience. Application fee: $25. Electronic applications accepted. *Expenses:* Contact institution. *Financial support:* In 2011–12, 15 students received support, including research assistantships (averaging $6,000 per year); career-related internships or fieldwork, institutionally sponsored loans, scholarships/grants, tuition waivers (partial), and unspecified assistantships also available. Support available to part-time students. Financial award applicants required to submit FAFSA. *Faculty research:* Moral development in sport, applied motor learning, achievement motivation, sport history. *Total annual research expenditures:* $1,500. *Unit head:* William Manning, Chair, 925-631-4969, Fax: 925-631-4965, E-mail: wmanning@stmarys-ca.edu. *Application contact:* Jeanne Abate, Administrative Assistant, 925-631-4377, Fax: 925-631-4965, E-mail: jabate@stmarys-ca.edu. Web site: http://www.stmarys-ca.edu/graduate-kinesiology.

St. Thomas University, School of Business, Department of Management, Miami Gardens, FL 33054-6459. Offers accounting (MBA); general management (MSM, Certificate); health management (MBA, MSM, Certificate); human resource management (MBA, MSM, Certificate); international business (MBA, MIB, MSM, Certificate); justice administration (MSM, Certificate); management accounting (MSM, Certificate); public management (MSM, Certificate); sports administration (MS). Part-time and evening/weekend programs available. *Degree requirements:* For master's, comprehensive exam. *Entrance requirements:* For master's, interview, minimum GPA of 3.0 or GMAT. Additional exam requirements/recommendations for international students: Required—TOEFL (minimum score 550 paper-based; 213 computer-based; 79 iBT). Electronic applications accepted.

San Diego State University, Graduate and Research Affairs, College of Business Administration, Sports Business Management Program, San Diego, CA 92182. Offers MBA.

Seattle University, College of Arts and Sciences, Center for the Study of Sport and Exercise, Seattle, WA 98122-1090. Offers MSAL. Part-time and evening/weekend programs available. *Faculty:* 2 full-time (1 woman), 3 part-time/adjunct (1 woman). *Students:* 2 full-time (1 woman), 46 part-time (19 women); includes 9 minority (1 Black or African American, non-Hispanic/Latino; 1 American Indian or Alaska Native, non-Hispanic/Latino; 2 Asian, non-Hispanic/Latino; 3 Hispanic/Latino; 1 Native Hawaiian or other Pacific Islander, non-Hispanic/Latino; 1 Two or more races, non-Hispanic/Latino), 2 international. Average age 25. *Degree requirements:* For master's, thesis or applied inquiry. *Entrance requirements:* For master's, GRE (Verbal, Quantitative, and Analytical), minimum GPA of 3.0. Additional exam requirements/recommendations for international students: Required—TOEFL, IELTS. *Application deadline:* For fall admission, 2/15 for domestic and international students. Application fee: $55. Electronic applications accepted. *Financial support:* Applicants required to submit FAFSA. *Faculty research:* Sport consumer behavior, strategic management of sport organizations, leadership in sport, organizational behavior, lifestyle sports. *Total annual research expenditures:* $1,000. *Unit head:* Dr. Galen Trail, Director, 206-398-4605, E-mail: trailg@seattleu.edu. *Application contact:* Janet Shandley, Associate Dean of Graduate Admissions, 206-296-5900, Fax: 206-298-5656, E-mail: grad_admissions@seattleu.edu.

Seton Hall University, Stillman School of Business, Programs in Business Administration, South Orange, NJ 07079-2697. Offers accounting (MBA); finance (MBA); information technology management (MBA); international business (MBA); management (MBA); marketing (MBA); sport management (MBA); supply chain management (MBA). Part-time and evening/weekend programs available. *Faculty:* 37 full-time (9 women), 19 part-time/adjunct (1 woman). *Students:* 166 full-time (65 women), 284 part-time (131 women); includes 113 minority (21 Black or African American, non-Hispanic/Latino; 81 Asian, non-Hispanic/Latino; 9 Hispanic/Latino; 2 Native Hawaiian or other Pacific Islander, non-Hispanic/Latino). Average age 29. 459 applicants, 59% accepted, 208 enrolled. In 2011, 210 master's awarded. *Degree requirements:* For master's, 20 hours of community service (Social Responsibility Project). *Entrance requirements:* For master's, GMAT, GRE or CPA, advanced degree from AACSB institution, MS in a business discipline, professional degree (MD, JD, PhD, DVM, DDS, etc.), minimum undergraduate GPA of 3.0. Additional exam requirements/recommendations for international students: Required—TOEFL (minimum score 102 iBT), IELTS or Pearson Test of English. *Application deadline:* For fall admission, 5/31 priority date for domestic students, 3/31 for international students; for spring admission, 10/31 priority date for domestic students, 9/30 for international students. Applications are processed on a rolling basis. Application fee: $75. Electronic applications accepted. *Expenses: Tuition:* Part-time $1033 per credit hour. *Required fees:* $85 per semester. *Financial support:* In 2011–12, research assistantships with full tuition reimbursements (averaging $35,610 per year) were awarded; career-related internships or fieldwork, Federal Work-Study, scholarships/grants, and unspecified assistantships also available. Support available to part-time students. Financial award application deadline: 6/30; financial award applicants required to submit FAFSA. *Faculty research:* Financial, hedge funds, international business, legal issues, disclosure and branding. *Unit head:* Dr. Joyce A. Strawser, Dean, 973-761-9013, Fax: 973-761-9217, E-mail: joyce.strawser@shu.edu. *Application contact:* Catherine Bianchi, Director of Graduate Admissions, 973-761-9262, Fax: 973-761-9208, E-mail: catherine.bianchi@shu.edu. Web site: http://www.shu.edu/academics/business.

Southeast Missouri State University, School of Graduate Studies, Harrison College of Business, Cape Girardeau, MO 63701-4799. Offers accounting (MBA); entrepreneurship (MBA); financial management (MBA); general management (MBA); health administration (MBA); industrial management (MBA); international business (MBA); sport management (MBA). *Accreditation:* AACSB. Part-time and evening/weekend programs available. Postbaccalaureate distance learning degree programs offered (no on-campus study). *Faculty:* 31 full-time (10 women). *Students:* 49 full-time (23 women), 77 part-time (30 women); includes 5 minority (1 Black or African American, non-Hispanic/Latino; 1 American Indian or Alaska Native, non-Hispanic/Latino; 2 Hispanic/Latino; 1 Two or more races, non-Hispanic/Latino), 35 international. Average age 27. 78 applicants, 69% accepted, 43 enrolled. In 2011, 47 master's awarded. *Degree requirements:* For master's, variable foreign language requirement, comprehensive exam, applied research project related to field. *Entrance requirements:* For master's, GMAT (minimum score of 450), minimum undergraduate GPA of 2.5, C or better in prerequisite courses. Additional exam requirements/recommendations for international students: Required—TOEFL (minimum score 550 paper-based; 213 computer-based; 79 iBT); Recommended—IELTS (minimum score 6). *Application deadline:* For fall admission, 8/1 for domestic students, 7/1 for international students; for spring admission, 11/21 for domestic students, 11/1 for international students. Applications are processed on a rolling basis. Application fee: $30 ($40 for international students). Electronic applications accepted. *Expenses:* Tuition, state resident: full-time $4896; part-time $272 per credit hour. Tuition, nonresident: full-time $8649; part-time $480.50 per credit hour. *Financial support:* In 2011–12, 46 students received support, including 12 teaching assistantships with full tuition reimbursements available (averaging $7,600 per year); career-related internships or fieldwork, Federal Work-Study, scholarships/grants, tuition waivers (full), and unspecified assistantships also available. Financial award application deadline: 6/30; financial award applicants required to submit FAFSA. *Faculty research:* Human resources, laws impacting accounting, advertising. *Unit head:* Dr. Kenneth A. Heischmidt, Director, Graduate Programs in Business, 573-651-5116, Fax: 573-651-5032, E-mail: kheischmidt@semo.edu. *Application contact:* Gail Amick, Administrative Secretary, 573-651-2049, Fax: 573-651-2001, E-mail: gamick@semo.edu. Web site: http://www.semo.edu/mba.

Southern New Hampshire University, School of Business, Manchester, NH 03106-1045. Offers accounting (MS); business administration (MBA, Certificate), including accounting (Certificate), business administration (MBA), finance (Certificate), forensic accounting (Certificate), human resources management (Certificate), international business (Certificate), international sport management (Certificate), leadership of not for profit organizations (Certificate), marketing (Certificate), operations management (Certificate), sport management (Certificate), taxation (Certificate); finance (MS); hospitality and tourism leadership (Certificate); information technology (MS, Certificate); information technology/international business (Certificate); integrated marketing communications (Certificate); international business (MS, DBA); marketing (MS); operations and project management (MS); organizational leadership (MS); project management (Certificate); sport management (MS); MBA/Certificate. *Accreditation:* ACBSP. Part-time and evening/weekend programs available. Postbaccalaureate distance learning degree programs offered (no on-campus study). Terminal master's awarded for partial completion of doctoral program. *Degree requirements:* For master's, one foreign language, comprehensive exam (for some programs), thesis or alternative; for doctorate, one foreign language, comprehensive exam, thesis/dissertation. *Entrance requirements:* For master's, minimum GPA of 2.5; for doctorate, GMAT. Additional exam requirements/recommendations for international students: Required—TOEFL (minimum score 500 paper-based). Electronic applications accepted.

Springfield College, Graduate Programs, Programs in Physical Education, Springfield, MA 01109-3797. Offers adapted physical education (M Ed, MPE, MS); advanced level coaching (M Ed, MPE, MS); athletic administration (M Ed, MPE, MS); general physical education (PhD, CAGS); health education licensure (MPE, MS); health education licensure program (M Ed); physical education licensure (MPE, MS); physical education licensure program (M Ed); teaching and administration (MS). Part-time programs available. *Degree requirements:* For master's, comprehensive exam, thesis (for some programs). *Entrance requirements:* For master's and doctorate, GRE General Test. Additional exam requirements/recommendations for international students: Required—TOEFL (minimum score 550 paper-based; 213 computer-based). Electronic applications accepted.

Springfield College, Graduate Programs, Programs in Sport Management and Recreation, Springfield, MA 01109-3797. Offers recreational management (M Ed, MS); sport management (M Ed, MS); therapeutic recreational management (M Ed, MS). Part-time programs available. *Degree requirements:* For master's, comprehensive exam, research project. *Entrance requirements:* Additional exam requirements/recommendations for international students: Required—TOEFL (minimum score 550 paper-based; 213 computer-based). Electronic applications accepted.

State University of New York College at Cortland, Graduate Studies, School of Professional Studies, Department of Sport Management, Cortland, NY 13045. Offers international sport management (MS); sport management (MS). *Entrance requirements:* For master's, GMAT or GRE, 2 letters of recommendation.

Syracuse University, Falk College of Sport and Human Dynamics, Program in Sport Venue and Event Management, Syracuse, NY 13244. Offers MS. *Entrance requirements:* For master's, GRE, undergraduate transcripts, three recommendations, resume, personal statement. Additional exam requirements/recommendations for international students: Required—TOEFL. *Expenses: Tuition:* Part-time $1206 per credit. *Unit head:* Dr. Diane Lyden Murphy, Dean, 315-443-5582, Fax: 315-443-2562, E-mail: falk@syr.edu. *Application contact:* Felecia Otero, Director of College Admissions, 315-443-5555, Fax: 315-443-2562, E-mail: falk@syr.edu. Web site: http://falk.syr.edu/SportManagement/Default.aspx.

Sports Management

Temple University, Fox School of Business, Doctoral Programs in Business, Philadelphia, PA 19122-6096. Offers accounting (PhD); entrepreneurship (PhD); finance (PhD); international business (PhD); management information systems (PhD); marketing (PhD); risk management and insurance (PhD); statistics (PhD); strategic management (PhD); tourism and sport (PhD). *Accreditation:* AACSB. *Degree requirements:* For doctorate, thesis/dissertation. *Entrance requirements:* For doctorate, GRE General Test, GMAT, minimum GPA of 3.0, master's degree. Additional exam requirements/recommendations for international students: Required—TOEFL (minimum score 600 paper-based; 250 computer-based; 100 iBT), IELTS (minimum score 7.5). Electronic applications accepted. *Expenses:* Tuition, state resident: full-time $12,366; part-time $687 per credit hour. Tuition, nonresident: full-time $17,298; part-time $961 per credit hour. *Required fees:* $590; $213 per year.

Temple University, School of Tourism and Hospitality Management, Program in Sport and Recreation Administration, Philadelphia, PA 19122-6096. Offers Ed M. Part-time and evening/weekend programs available. *Faculty:* 6 full-time (2 women). *Students:* 37 full-time (14 women), 11 part-time (3 women); includes 5 minority (3 Black or African American, non-Hispanic/Latino; 1 Asian, non-Hispanic/Latino; 1 Two or more races, non-Hispanic/Latino), 3 international. Average age 25. 63 applicants, 75% accepted, 24 enrolled. In 2011, 16 master's awarded. *Entrance requirements:* For master's, GRE General Test or MAT, minimum undergraduate GPA of 3.0. Additional exam requirements/recommendations for international students: Required—TOEFL (minimum score 550 paper-based; 213 computer-based; 79 iBT). *Application deadline:* For fall admission, 4/15 priority date for domestic students, 12/15 for international students; for spring admission, 9/30 priority date for domestic students, 8/1 for international students. Application fee: $50. Electronic applications accepted. *Expenses:* Tuition, state resident: full-time $12,366; part-time $687 per credit hour. Tuition, nonresident: full-time $17,298; part-time $961 per credit hour. *Required fees:* $590; $213 per year. *Financial support:* Teaching assistantships available. Financial award application deadline: 1/15; financial award applicants required to submit FAFSA. *Unit head:* Dr. Elizabeth H. Barber, Associate Dean, 215-204-6294, E-mail: elizabeth.barber@temple.edu. *Application contact:* Tara Schumacher, Coordinator of Outreach, 215-204-6575, Fax: 215-204-8781, E-mail: tara.schumacher@temple.edu. Web site: http://sthm.temple.edu/grad/explore-ma-sports.html.

Texas A&M University, College of Education and Human Development, Department of Health and Kinesiology, College Station, TX 77843. Offers health education (MS, PhD); kinesiology (MS, PhD); physical education (M Ed); sport management (MS). Part-time programs available. *Faculty:* 37. *Students:* 171 full-time (80 women), 38 part-time (22 women); includes 60 minority (21 Black or African American, non-Hispanic/Latino; 8 Asian, non-Hispanic/Latino; 29 Hispanic/Latino; 2 Two or more races, non-Hispanic/Latino), 35 international. Average age 23. In 2011, 54 master's, 17 doctorates awarded. *Degree requirements:* For master's, thesis (for some programs); for doctorate, comprehensive exam, thesis/dissertation. *Entrance requirements:* For master's and doctorate, GRE General Test. Additional exam requirements/recommendations for international students: Required—TOEFL. *Application deadline:* Applications are processed on a rolling basis. Application fee: $50 ($75 for international students). Electronic applications accepted. *Expenses:* Tuition, state resident: full-time $5437; part-time $226.55 per credit hour. Tuition, nonresident: full-time $12,949; part-time $539.55 per credit hour. *Required fees:* $2741. *Financial support:* Fellowships with partial tuition reimbursements, research assistantships, teaching assistantships, career-related internships or fieldwork, and institutionally sponsored loans available. Financial award application deadline: 2/15; financial award applicants required to submit FAFSA. *Unit head:* Dr. Richard Kreider, Head, 979-845-1333, Fax: 979-847-8987, E-mail: rkreider@hlkn.tamu.edu. *Application contact:* Dr. Becky Carr, Assistant Dean for Administrative Services, 979-862-1342, Fax: 979-845-6129, E-mail: bcarr@tamu.edu. Web site: http://hlknweb.tamu.edu/.

Texas Woman's University, Graduate School, College of Health Sciences, Department of Kinesiology, Denton, TX 76201. Offers adapted physical education (MS, PhD); biomechanics (MS, PhD); coaching (MS); exercise physiology (MS, PhD); pedagogy (MS); sport management (MS, PhD). Part-time and evening/weekend programs available. *Faculty:* 12 full-time (6 women), 1 part-time/adjunct (0 women). *Students:* 55 full-time (38 women), 104 part-time (69 women); includes 35 minority (24 Black or African American, non-Hispanic/Latino; 1 American Indian or Alaska Native, non-Hispanic/Latino; 10 Hispanic/Latino), 23 international. Average age 31. 86 applicants, 73% accepted, 38 enrolled. In 2011, 25 master's, 7 doctorates awarded. Terminal master's awarded for partial completion of doctoral program. *Degree requirements:* For master's, comprehensive exam, thesis or alternative; for doctorate, comprehensive exam, thesis/dissertation, qualifying exam. *Entrance requirements:* For master's, GRE General Test (biomechanics emphasis only), 2 letters of reference, curriculum vitae, interview (adapted physical education emphasis only); for doctorate, GRE General Test (biomechanics emphasis only), interview, 3 letters of reference, curriculum vitae. Additional exam requirements/recommendations for international students: Required—TOEFL (minimum score 550 paper-based; 213 computer-based; 79 iBT). *Application deadline:* For fall admission, 7/1 priority date for domestic students, 3/1 for international students; for spring admission, 11/1 priority date for domestic students, 7/1 for international students. Applications are processed on a rolling basis. Application fee: $50 ($75 for international students). Electronic applications accepted. *Expenses:* Tuition, state resident: full-time $3834; part-time $213 per credit hour. Tuition, nonresident: full-time $9468; part-time $526 per credit hour. *Required fees:* $213 per credit hour. Tuition and fees vary according to course load. *Financial support:* In 2011–12, 46 students received support, including 7 research assistantships (averaging $10,746 per year), 14 teaching assistantships (averaging $10,746 per year); career-related internships or fieldwork, Federal Work-Study, institutionally sponsored loans, scholarships/grants, traineeships, health care benefits, and unspecified assistantships also available. Support available to part-time students. Financial award application deadline: 3/1; financial award applicants required to submit FAFSA. *Faculty research:* Exercise and Type 2 diabetes risk, bone mineral density and exercise in special populations, obesity in children, factors influencing sport consumer behavior and loyalty, roles and responsibilities of paraeducators in adapted physical education. *Total annual research expenditures:* $19,544. *Unit head:* Dr. David Nichols, Chair, 940-898-2575, Fax: 940-898-2581, E-mail: dnichols@twu.edu. *Application contact:* Dr. Samuel Wheeler, Assistant Director of Admissions, 940-898-3188, Fax: 940-898-3081, E-mail: wheelersr@twu.edu. Web site: http://www.twu.edu/kinesiology/.

Tiffin University, Program in Business Administration, Tiffin, OH 44883-2161. Offers finance (MBA); general management (MBA); healthcare administration (MBA); human resources (MBA); international business (MBA); leadership (MBA); marketing (MBA); sports management (MBA). *Accreditation:* ACBSP. Part-time and evening/weekend programs available. Postbaccalaureate distance learning degree programs offered (no on-campus study). *Faculty:* 30 full-time (15 women), 22 part-time/adjunct (6 women). *Students:* 209 full-time (107 women), 340 part-time (172 women); includes 112 minority (91 Black or African American, non-Hispanic/Latino; 4 Asian, non-Hispanic/Latino; 17 Hispanic/Latino), 71 international. Average age 31. 237 applicants, 76% accepted. In 2011, 170 master's awarded. *Entrance requirements:* For master's, minimum undergraduate GPA of 2.5, work experience. Additional exam requirements/recommendations for international students: Required—TOEFL (minimum score 550 paper-based; 213 computer-based; 79 iBT). *Application deadline:* For fall admission, 8/15 for domestic students, 8/1 for international students; for spring admission, 1/9 for domestic students, 12/1 for international students. Applications are processed on a rolling basis. Electronic applications accepted. *Expenses: Tuition:* Full-time $11,200; part-time $700 per credit. Tuition and fees vary according to program. *Financial support:* Available to part-time students. Application deadline: 7/31; applicants required to submit FAFSA. *Faculty research:* Small business, executive development operations, research and statistical analysis, market research, management information systems. *Unit head:* Dr. Lillian Schumacher, Dean of the School of Business, 419-448-3053, Fax: 419-443-5002, E-mail: schumacherlb@tiffin.edu. *Application contact:* Nikki Hintze, Director of Graduate Admissions and Student Services, 800-968-6446 Ext. 3445, Fax: 419-443-5002, E-mail: hintzenm@tiffin.edu. Web site: http://www.tiffin.edu/graduateprograms/.

Troy University, Graduate School, College of Health and Human Services, Program in Sport and Fitness Management, Troy, AL 36082. Offers MS. Part-time and evening/weekend programs available. *Faculty:* 11 full-time (3 women), 1 part-time/adjunct (0 women). *Students:* 34 full-time (9 women), 56 part-time (21 women); includes 35 minority (32 Black or African American, non-Hispanic/Latino; 3 Hispanic/Latino). Average age 27. 73 applicants, 81% accepted, 34 enrolled. In 2011, 37 master's awarded. *Degree requirements:* For master's, comprehensive exam, minimum GPA of 3.0, candidacy, research course. *Entrance requirements:* For master's, GRE (minimum score of 850) or MAT, minimum undergraduate GPA of 2.5. Additional exam requirements/recommendations for international students: Required—TOEFL (minimum score 523 paper-based; 193 computer-based; 70 iBT), IELTS (minimum score 6), or ACT COMPASS ESL (minimum listening, reading, and grammar score 270). *Application deadline:* Applications are processed on a rolling basis. Application fee: $50. Electronic applications accepted. *Expenses:* Tuition, state resident: full-time $6960; part-time $290 per credit hour. Tuition, nonresident: full-time $13,920; part-time $580 per credit hour. *Required fees:* $386 per term. *Financial support:* Career-related internships or fieldwork and unspecified assistantships available. *Faculty research:* Sport marketing, fitness, sport law. *Unit head:* Dr. Candice Howard-Shaughnessy, Chairman, 334-670-3443, Fax: 334-670-3936, E-mail: choward@troy.edu. *Application contact:* Brenda K. Campbell, Director of Graduate Admissions, 334-670-3178, Fax: 334-670-3733, E-mail: bcamp@troy.edu.

United States Sports Academy, Graduate Programs, Program in Sport Management, Daphne, AL 36526-7055. Offers MSS, Ed D. Part-time programs available. Postbaccalaureate distance learning degree programs offered (no on-campus study). *Degree requirements:* For master's, comprehensive exam, thesis optional; for doctorate, comprehensive exam, thesis/dissertation. *Entrance requirements:* For master's, GRE General Test, GMAT, or MAT, minimum GPA of 2.5, 3 letters of recommendation, resume; for doctorate, GRE General Test, GMAT, or MAT, master's degree, 3 letters of recommendation, resume. Additional exam requirements/recommendations for international students: Required—TOEFL (minimum score 500 paper-based; 213 computer-based). Electronic applications accepted. *Faculty research:* Sport law, leadership behavior, personnel evaluation.

The University of Alabama, Graduate School, College of Education, Department of Kinesiology, Tuscaloosa, AL 35487. Offers alternative sport pedagogy (MA); exercise science (MA, PhD); human performance (MA); sport management (MA); sport pedagogy (MA, PhD). Part-time programs available. *Faculty:* 8 full-time (1 woman). *Students:* 59 full-time (22 women), 22 part-time (14 women); includes 11 minority (7 Black or African American, non-Hispanic/Latino; 1 Asian, non-Hispanic/Latino; 2 Hispanic/Latino; 1 Two or more races, non-Hispanic/Latino), 7 international. Average age 30. 50 applicants, 78% accepted, 20 enrolled. In 2011, 23 master's, 6 doctorates awarded. *Median time to degree:* Of those who began their doctoral program in fall 2003, 100% received their degree in 8 years or less. *Degree requirements:* For master's, comprehensive exam, thesis optional; for doctorate, comprehensive exam, thesis/dissertation. *Entrance requirements:* For master's and doctorate, GRE, MAT, minimum GPA of 3.0. Additional exam requirements/recommendations for international students: Required—TOEFL. *Application deadline:* Applications are processed on a rolling basis. Application fee: $50 ($60 for international students). Electronic applications accepted. *Expenses:* Tuition, state resident: full-time $8600. Tuition, nonresident: full-time $21,900. *Financial support:* In 2011–12, 14 students received support, including 13 teaching assistantships with full tuition reimbursements available (averaging $8,678 per year). *Faculty research:* Race, gender and sexuality in sports; physical education teacher socialization; disability sports; physical activity and health; environmental physiology. *Total annual research expenditures:* $19,866. *Unit head:* Dr. Matt Curtner-Smith, Department Head and Professor, 205-348-9209, Fax: 205-348-0867, E-mail: msmith@bamaed.ua.edu. *Application contact:* Dr. Kathy S. Wetzel, Assistant Dean for Student Services, 205-348-1154, Fax: 205-348-0080, E-mail: kwetzel@bamaed.ua.edu. Web site: http://www.kinesiology.ua.edu/.

The University of Alabama, Graduate School, College of Human Environmental Sciences, Program in Human Environmental Science, Tuscaloosa, AL 35487. Offers family financial planning and counseling (MS); interactive technology (MS); quality management (MS); restaurant and meeting management (MS); rural community health (MS); sport management (MS). *Faculty:* 1 full-time (0 women). *Students:* 80 full-time (53 women), 93 part-time (55 women); includes 51 minority (42 Black or African American, non-Hispanic/Latino; 3 American Indian or Alaska Native, non-Hispanic/Latino; 3 Hispanic/Latino; 3 Two or more races, non-Hispanic/Latino), 1 international. Average age 33. 118 applicants, 79% accepted, 75 enrolled. In 2011, 83 degrees awarded. *Degree requirements:* For master's, comprehensive exam. *Entrance requirements:* For master's, GRE (for some specializations), minimum GPA of 3.0. Additional exam requirements/recommendations for international students: Required—TOEFL. *Application deadline:* Applications are processed on a rolling basis. Application fee: $50 ($60 for international students). Electronic applications accepted. *Expenses:* Tuition, state resident: full-time $8600. Tuition, nonresident: full-time $21,900. *Faculty research:* Hospitality management, sports medicine education, technology and education. *Unit head:* Dr. Milla D. Boschung, Dean, 205-348-6250, Fax: 205-348-1786, E-mail: mboschun@ches.ua.edu. *Application contact:* Dr. Stuart Usdan, Associate Dean, 205-348-6150, Fax: 205-348-3789, E-mail: susdan@ches.ua.edu.

University of Alberta, Faculty of Graduate Studies and Research, Program in Business Administration, Edmonton, AB T6G 2E1, Canada. Offers international business (MBA); leisure and sport management (MBA); natural resources and energy (MBA); technology commercialization (MBA); MBA/LL B; MBA/M Ag; MBA/M Eng; MBA/MF; MBA/PhD. *Accreditation:* AACSB. Part-time and evening/weekend programs available. *Degree requirements:* For master's, thesis or alternative. *Entrance requirements:* For master's, GMAT. Additional exam requirements/recommendations for international students: Required—TOEFL (minimum score 600 paper-based; 250 computer-based). Electronic applications accepted. *Faculty research:* Natural resources and energy/management and policy/family enterprise/international business/healthcare research management.

University of Central Florida, College of Business Administration, Program in Sport Business Management, Orlando, FL 32816. Offers MSBM. *Faculty:* 7 full-time (0 women), 1 (woman) part-time/adjunct. *Students:* 57 full-time (23 women), 2 part-time (0 women); includes 25 minority (18 Black or African American, non-Hispanic/Latino; 2 Asian, non-Hispanic/Latino; 3 Hispanic/Latino; 2 Two or more races, non-Hispanic/

Latino), 5 international. Average age 25. 105 applicants, 33% accepted, 27 enrolled. In 2011, 25 master's awarded. *Degree requirements:* For master's, thesis or alternative, internship. *Entrance requirements:* For master's, GMAT, minimum GPA of 3.0, letters of recommendation. Additional exam requirements/recommendations for international students: Required—TOEFL. *Application deadline:* For fall admission, 2/15 priority date for domestic students. Application fee: $30. Electronic applications accepted. *Expenses:* Tuition, state resident: part-time $277.08 per credit hour. Tuition, nonresident: part-time $277.08 per credit hour. Part-time tuition and fees vary according to degree level and program. *Financial support:* In 2011–12, 43 students received support, including 8 fellowships with partial tuition reimbursements available (averaging $4,000 per year), 39 research assistantships with partial tuition reimbursements available (averaging $5,000 per year), 4 teaching assistantships (averaging $7,000 per year). *Unit head:* Dr. Richard Lapchick, Director, 407-823-4887, E-mail: richard.lapchick@bus.ucf.edu. *Application contact:* Judy Ryder, Director, Graduate Admissions, 407-823-2364, Fax: 407-823-0219, E-mail: jryder@bus.ucf.edu. Web site: http://www.bus.ucf.edu/sportbusiness/.

University of Colorado Denver, Business School, Master of Business Administration Program, Denver, CO 80217. Offers business intelligence (MBA); business strategy (MBA); business to business marketing (MBA); business to consumer marketing (MBA); change management (MBA); corporate financial management (MBA); enterprise technology management (MBA); entrepreneurship (MBA); health administration (MBA), including financial management, health administration, health information technologies, international health management and policy; human resources management (MBA); investment management (MBA); managing for sustainability (MBA); services management (MBA); sports and entertainment management (MBA). *Accreditation:* AACSB. Part-time and evening/weekend programs available. Postbaccalaureate distance learning degree programs offered (no on-campus study). *Students:* 784 full-time (306 women), 203 part-time (81 women); includes 135 minority (18 Black or African American, non-Hispanic/Latino; 5 American Indian or Alaska Native, non-Hispanic/Latino; 50 Asian, non-Hispanic/Latino; 58 Hispanic/Latino; 4 Two or more races, non-Hispanic/Latino), 38 international. Average age 31. 433 applicants, 76% accepted, 212 enrolled. In 2011, 326 master's awarded. *Degree requirements:* For master's, 48 semester hours, including 30 of core courses, 3 in international business, and 15 in electives from over 50 other graduate business courses. *Entrance requirements:* For master's, GMAT, resume, official transcripts, essay, two letters of recommendation, financial statements (for international applicants). Additional exam requirements/recommendations for international students: Required—TOEFL (minimum score 560 paper-based; 197 computer-based; 83 iBT). *Application deadline:* For fall admission, 4/15 priority date for domestic students, 3/15 for international students; for spring admission, 10/15 priority date for domestic students, 10/1 for international students. Applications are processed on a rolling basis. Application fee: $50 ($75 for international students). Electronic applications accepted. *Expenses:* Contact institution. *Financial support:* Scholarships/grants available. Support available to part-time students. Financial award application deadline: 4/1; financial award applicants required to submit FAFSA. *Faculty research:* Marketing, management, entrepreneurship, finance, health administration. *Unit head:* Elizabeth Cooperman, Professor of Finance and Managing for Sustainability/MBA Program Director, 303-315-8422, E-mail: elizabeth.cooperman@ucdenver.edu. *Application contact:* Shelly Townley, Admissions Director, Graduate Programs, 303-315-8202, E-mail: shelly.townley@ucdenver.edu. Web site: http://www.ucdenver.edu/academics/colleges/business/degrees/ms/accounting/Pages/Accounting.aspx.

University of Colorado Denver, Business School, Program in Management and Organization, Denver, CO 80217. Offers communications management (MS); entrepreneurship and innovation (MS); global management (MS); human resources management (MS); leadership and management (MS); sports and entertainment management (MS). *Accreditation:* AACSB. Part-time and evening/weekend programs available. Postbaccalaureate distance learning degree programs offered (no on-campus study). *Students:* 29 full-time (14 women), 14 part-time (10 women); includes 3 minority (2 Asian, non-Hispanic/Latino; 1 Hispanic/Latino), 5 international. Average age 31. 32 applicants, 63% accepted, 14 enrolled. In 2011, 22 master's awarded. *Degree requirements:* For master's, 30 semester hours (12 of required courses, 12 of management electives, and 6 of free electives). *Entrance requirements:* For master's, GMAT, resume, two letters of recommendation, essay, financial statements (for international applicants). Additional exam requirements/recommendations for international students: Required—TOEFL (minimum score 525 paper-based; 197 computer-based; 71 iBT). *Application deadline:* For fall admission, 4/15 priority date for domestic students, 3/15 for international students; for spring admission, 10/15 priority date for domestic students, 10/1 for international students. Applications are processed on a rolling basis. Application fee: $50 ($75 for international students). Electronic applications accepted. *Expenses:* Contact institution. *Financial support:* Federal Work-Study and scholarships/grants available. Support available to part-time students. Financial award application deadline: 4/1; financial award applicants required to submit FAFSA. *Faculty research:* Human resource management, management of catastrophe, turnaround strategies. *Unit head:* Dr. Kenneth Bettenhausen, Associate Professor/Director of MS in Management, 303-315-8425, E-mail: kenneth.bettenhausen@ucdenver.edu. *Application contact:* Shelly Townley, Admissions Director, Graduate Programs, 303-315-8202, E-mail: shelly.townley@ucdenver.edu. Web site: http://www.ucdenver.edu/academics/colleges/business/degrees/ms/management/Pages/Management.aspx.

University of Dallas, Graduate School of Management, Irving, TX 75062-4736. Offers accounting (MBA, MM, MS); business management (MBA, MM); corporate finance (MBA, MM); financial services (MBA); global business (MBA, MM); health services management (MBA, MM); human resource management (MBA, MM); information assurance (MBA, MM, MS); information technology (MBA, MM, MS); information technology service management (MBA, MM, MS); marketing management (MBA, MM); organization development (MBA, MM); project management (MBA, MM); sports and entertainment management (MBA, MM); strategic leadership (MBA, MM); supply chain management (MBA); supply chain management and market logistics (MM). *Accreditation:* ACBSP. Part-time and evening/weekend programs available. Postbaccalaureate distance learning degree programs offered (no on-campus study). *Entrance requirements:* Additional exam requirements/recommendations for international students: Required—TOEFL. Electronic applications accepted. *Expenses:* Contact institution.

University of Florida, Graduate School, College of Health and Human Performance, Department of Tourism, Recreation and Sport Management, Gainesville, FL 32611. Offers health and human performance (PhD), including natural resource recreation (MS, PhD), sport management (MS, PhD), tourism; recreational studies (MS), including campus recreation programming and administration, natural resource recreation (MS, PhD), recreation administration and supervision, sport management (MS, PhD), tourism and commercial recreation. *Degree requirements:* For master's, comprehensive exam (for some programs), thesis (for some programs); for doctorate, comprehensive exam, thesis/dissertation. *Entrance requirements:* For master's and doctorate, GRE General Test, minimum GPA of 3.0. Additional exam requirements/recommendations for international students: Required—TOEFL (minimum score 550 paper-based; 213 computer-based; 80 iBT), IELTS (minimum score 6). Electronic applications accepted. *Faculty research:* Hospitality, natural resource management, sport management, sport management, tourism.

University of Florida, Graduate School, Warrington College of Business Administration, Hough Graduate School of Business, Programs in Business Administration, Gainesville, FL 32611. Offers accounting (MBA); arts administration (MBA); business strategy and public policy (MBA); competitive strategy (MBA); decision and information sciences (MBA); electronic commerce (MBA); finance (MBA); general business (MBA); global management (MBA); Graham-Buffett security analysis (MBA); health administration (MBA); human resources management (MBA); international studies (MBA); Latin American business (MBA); management (MBA); marketing (MBA); sports administration (MBA); JD/MBA; MBA/MS; MBA/PhD; MBA/Pharm D; MD/MBA. *Accreditation:* AACSB. Part-time and evening/weekend programs available. *Faculty:* 71 full-time (10 women). *Students:* 412 full-time (111 women), 467 part-time (135 women); includes 235 minority (39 Black or African American, non-Hispanic/Latino; 7 American Indian or Alaska Native, non-Hispanic/Latino; 79 Asian, non-Hispanic/Latino; 109 Hispanic/Latino; 1 Native Hawaiian or other Pacific Islander, non-Hispanic/Latino), 44 international. Average age 32. 589 applicants, 52% accepted, 247 enrolled. In 2011, 505 master's awarded. *Degree requirements:* For master's, capstone course. *Entrance requirements:* For master's, GMAT, minimum GPA of 3.0, interview. Additional exam requirements/recommendations for international students: Required—TOEFL (minimum score 550 paper-based; 213 computer-based; 80 iBT), IELTS (minimum score 6). *Application deadline:* For fall admission, 7/1 for domestic students, 1/1 for international students; for spring admission, 12/1 for domestic and international students. Applications are processed on a rolling basis. Application fee: $30. Electronic applications accepted. *Financial support:* Teaching assistantships, career-related internships or fieldwork, scholarships/grants, and unspecified assistantships available. Support available to part-time students. Financial award applicants required to submit FAFSA. *Faculty research:* Accounting, finance, insurance, management, real estate, urban analysis marketing. *Unit head:* Prof. Alexander D. Sevilla, Assistant Dean/Director, 352-273-3252 Ext. 1206, E-mail: alex.sevilla@warrington.ufl.edu. *Application contact:* Prof. Kelli Gust, Associate Director, 352-273-3255, Fax: 352-392-8791, E-mail: kelly.gust@warrington.ufl.edu. Web site: http://www.floridamba.ufl.edu/.

The University of Iowa, Graduate College, College of Liberal Arts and Sciences, Program in Leisure Studies, Iowa City, IA 52242-1316. Offers leisure and recreational sport management (MA); therapeutic recreation (MA). *Degree requirements:* For master's, thesis optional, exam. *Entrance requirements:* For master's, minimum GPA of 3.0. Additional exam requirements/recommendations for international students: Required—TOEFL (minimum score 550 paper-based; 213 computer-based; 81 iBT). Electronic applications accepted.

University of Louisville, Graduate School, College of Education and Human Development, Department of Health and Sport Sciences, Louisville, KY 40292-0001. Offers community health education (M Ed); exercise physiology (MS); health and physical education (MAT); sport administration (MS). Part-time and evening/weekend programs available. *Entrance requirements:* For master's, GRE General Test. Additional exam requirements/recommendations for international students: Required—TOEFL (minimum score 560 paper-based; 210 computer-based; 83 iBT). Electronic applications accepted. *Expenses:* Tuition, state resident: full-time $9692; part-time $539 per credit hour. Tuition, nonresident: full-time $20,168; part-time $1121 per credit hour. Tuition and fees vary according to program and reciprocity agreements. *Faculty research:* Impact of sports and sport marketing on society, factors associated with school and community health, cardiac and pulmonary rehabilitation, impact of participation in activities on student retention and graduation, strength and conditioning.

University of Massachusetts Amherst, Graduate School, Interdisciplinary Programs, Dual Degree Program in Business Administration and Sport Management, Amherst, MA 01003. Offers MBA/MS. Part-time programs available. *Students:* 18 full-time (7 women); includes 2 minority (1 Asian, non-Hispanic/Latino; 1 Hispanic/Latino), 2 international. Average age 27. 83 applicants, 22% accepted, 10 enrolled. *Entrance requirements:* Additional exam requirements/recommendations for international students: Required—TOEFL (minimum score 600 paper-based; 250 computer-based; 100 iBT), IELTS (minimum score 7). *Application deadline:* For fall admission, 2/1 for domestic and international students; for spring admission, 10/1 for domestic and international students. Applications are processed on a rolling basis. Application fee: $50 ($65 for international students). Electronic applications accepted. Tuition and fees vary according to course load, campus/location and program. *Financial support:* Career-related internships or fieldwork, Federal Work-Study, scholarships/grants, traineeships, health care benefits, tuition waivers (full), and unspecified assistantships available. Support available to part-time students. Financial award application deadline: 2/1; financial award applicants required to submit FAFSA. *Unit head:* Dr. Stephen M. McKelvey, Graduate Program Director, 413-545-0471, Fax: 413-545-0642. *Application contact:* Lindsay DeSantis, Interim Supervisor of Admissions, 413-545-0722, Fax: 413-577-0010, E-mail: gradadm@grad.umass.edu. Web site: http://www.isenberg.umass.edu/MBA/Full-Time_MBA/Dual_Degree_Programs/.

University of Massachusetts Amherst, Graduate School, Isenberg School of Management, Department of Sport Management, Amherst, MA 01003. Offers MS, MBA/MS. Part-time programs available. *Faculty:* 13 full-time (4 women). *Students:* 17 full-time (6 women), 2 part-time (0 women); includes 4 minority (1 Black or African American, non-Hispanic/Latino; 1 Asian, non-Hispanic/Latino; 2 Hispanic/Latino), 4 international. Average age 25. 97 applicants, 18% accepted, 16 enrolled. In 2011, 16 master's awarded. Terminal master's awarded for partial completion of doctoral program. *Degree requirements:* For master's, thesis or alternative. *Entrance requirements:* For master's, GMAT. Additional exam requirements/recommendations for international students: Required—TOEFL (minimum score 550 paper-based; 213 computer-based; 80 iBT), IELTS (minimum score 6.5). *Application deadline:* For fall admission, 2/1 for domestic and international students. Applications are processed on a rolling basis. Application fee: $50 ($65 for international students). Electronic applications accepted. Tuition and fees vary according to course load, campus/location and program. *Financial support:* Fellowships with full and partial tuition reimbursements, research assistantships with full and partial tuition reimbursements, teaching assistantships with full and partial tuition reimbursements, career-related internships or fieldwork, Federal Work-Study, scholarships/grants, traineeships, health care benefits, tuition waivers (full and partial), and unspecified assistantships available. Support available to part-time students. Financial award application deadline: 2/1. *Unit head:* Dr. Stephen McKelvey, Graduate Program Director, 413-545-0471, Fax: 413-577-0642. *Application contact:* Lindsay DeSantis, Interim Supervisor of Admissions, 413-545-0722, Fax: 413-577-0010, E-mail: gradadm@grad.umass.edu. Web site: http://www.isenberg.umass.edu/sportmgt/.

University of Massachusetts Amherst, Graduate School, Isenberg School of Management, Program in Management, Amherst, MA 01003. Offers accounting (PhD); business administration (MBA); business administration/sport management (MBA/MS); finance (PhD); hospitality and tourism management (PhD); management science (PhD); marketing (PhD); organization studies (PhD); sport management (PhD); strategic management (PhD); MBA/MS; MPH/MPPA. *Accreditation:* AACSB. Part-time programs available. *Faculty:* 61 full-time (14 women). *Students:* 92 full-time (34 women), 9 part-time (3 women); includes 8 minority (1 Black or African American, non-Hispanic/Latino;

Sports Management

4 Asian, non-Hispanic/Latino; 3 Hispanic/Latino), 47 international. Average age 33. 340 applicants, 15% accepted, 29 enrolled. In 2011, 31 master's, 13 doctorates awarded. Terminal master's awarded for partial completion of doctoral program. *Degree requirements:* For doctorate, comprehensive exam, thesis/dissertation. *Entrance requirements:* For master's and doctorate, GMAT. Additional exam requirements/recommendations for international students: Required—TOEFL (minimum score 550 paper-based; 213 computer-based; 80 iBT), IELTS (minimum score 6.5). *Application deadline:* For fall admission, 1/20 for domestic and international students. Applications are processed on a rolling basis. Application fee: $50 ($65 for international students). Electronic applications accepted. Tuition and fees vary according to course load, campus/location and program. *Financial support:* Fellowships with full and partial tuition reimbursements, research assistantships with full and partial tuition reimbursements, teaching assistantships with full and partial tuition reimbursements, career-related internships or fieldwork, Federal Work-Study, scholarships/grants, traineeships, health care benefits, tuition waivers (full and partial), and unspecified assistantships available. Support available to part-time students. Financial award application deadline: 1/20. *Unit head:* Dr. William Woodridge, Chair, 413-545-5675, Fax: 413-577-2234. *Application contact:* Lindsay DeSantis, Interim Supervisor of Admissions, 413-545-0722, Fax: 413-577-0010, E-mail: gradadm@grad.umass.edu. Web site: http://www.isenberg.umass.edu/.

University of Miami, Graduate School, School of Education and Human Development, Department of Kinesiology and Sport Sciences, Program in Sport Administration, Coral Gables, FL 33124. Offers MS Ed. Part-time and evening/weekend programs available. *Faculty:* 2 full-time (1 woman). *Students:* 20 full-time (8 women), 9 part-time (3 women); includes 6 minority (2 Black or African American, non-Hispanic/Latino; 1 Asian, non-Hispanic/Latino; 3 Hispanic/Latino), 6 international. Average age 24. 87 applicants, 41% accepted, 19 enrolled. In 2011, 22 master's awarded. *Degree requirements:* For master's, special project. *Entrance requirements:* For master's, GRE General Test. Additional exam requirements/recommendations for international students: Required—TOEFL (minimum score 550 paper-based; 80 iBT); Recommended—IELTS (minimum score 6.5). *Application deadline:* Applications are processed on a rolling basis. Application fee: $65. Electronic applications accepted. *Financial support:* In 2011–12, 13 students received support. Institutionally sponsored loans and scholarships/grants available. Financial award application deadline: 3/1; financial award applicants required to submit FAFSA. *Faculty research:* Constitutional procedural due process, legal liability, tort law, moral development in sports administration, ethics intervention. *Unit head:* Dr. Warren Whisenant, Associate Department Chairperson, 305-284-5622, Fax: 305-284-5168, E-mail: wwhisenant@miami.edu. *Application contact:* Lois Heffernan, Graduate Admissions Coordinator, 305-284-2167, Fax: 305-284-9395, E-mail: lheffernan@miami.edu.

University of Michigan, Horace H. Rackham School of Graduate Studies, School of Kinesiology, Ann Arbor, MI 48109. Offers kinesiology (MS, PhD); sport management (AM). *Faculty:* 30 full-time (11 women). *Students:* 74 full-time (39 women); includes 23 minority (2 Black or African American, non-Hispanic/Latino; 17 Asian, non-Hispanic/Latino; 4 Hispanic/Latino), 23 international. 120 applicants, 44% accepted, 24 enrolled. In 2011, 20 master's, 4 doctorates awarded. Terminal master's awarded for partial completion of doctoral program. *Degree requirements:* For master's, thesis (for some programs); for doctorate, comprehensive exam, thesis/dissertation, oral defense of dissertation. *Entrance requirements:* For master's and doctorate, GRE General Test. Additional exam requirements/recommendations for international students: Required—TOEFL. *Application deadline:* For fall admission, 1/15 priority date for domestic students, 1/15 for international students. Applications are processed on a rolling basis. Application fee: $60 ($75 for international students). Electronic applications accepted. *Expenses:* Contact institution. *Financial support:* In 2011–12, 13 fellowships, 10 research assistantships, 14 teaching assistantships were awarded; Federal Work-Study, scholarships/grants, health care benefits, and unspecified assistantships also available. Financial award application deadline: 1/15. *Faculty research:* Motor development, exercise physiology, biomechanics, sport medicine, sport management. *Unit head:* Dr. Ketra L. Armstrong, Associate Dean for Graduate Programs and Faculty Affairs, 734-647-3027, Fax: 734-647-2808, E-mail: ketra@umich.edu. *Application contact:* Charlene F. Ruloff, Graduate Program Coordinator, 734-764-1343, Fax: 734-647-2808, E-mail: cruloff@umich.edu. Web site: http://www.kines.umich.edu/.

University of Minnesota, Twin Cities Campus, Graduate School, College of Education and Human Development, School of Kinesiology, Minneapolis, MN 55455-0213. Offers adapted physical education (MA, PhD); biomechanics (MA); biomechanics and neural control (PhD); coaching (Certificate); developmental adapted physical education (M Ed); exercise physiology (MA, PhD); human factors/ergonomics (MA, PhD); international/comparative sport (MA, PhD); kinesiology (M Ed, MA, PhD); leisure services/management (MA, PhD); motor development (MA, PhD); motor learning/control (MA, PhD); outdoor education/recreation (MA, PhD); physical education (M Ed); recreation, park, and leisure studies (M Ed, MA, PhD); sport and exercise science (M Ed); sport management (M Ed, MA, PhD); sport psychology (MA, PhD); sport sociology (MA, PhD); therapeutic recreation (MA, PhD). Part-time programs available. *Faculty:* 15 full-time (7 women). *Students:* 144 full-time (72 women), 49 part-time (19 women); includes 20 minority (9 Black or African American, non-Hispanic/Latino; 3 American Indian or Alaska Native, non-Hispanic/Latino; 4 Asian, non-Hispanic/Latino; 2 Hispanic/Latino; 2 Native Hawaiian or other Pacific Islander, non-Hispanic/Latino), 18 international. Average age 29. 198 applicants, 42% accepted, 77 enrolled. In 2011, 74 master's, 11 doctorates, 19 other advanced degrees awarded. Terminal master's awarded for partial completion of doctoral program. *Degree requirements:* For master's, final oral exam; for doctorate, thesis/dissertation, preliminary written/oral exam, final oral exam. *Entrance requirements:* For master's, GRE or MAT, minimum GPA of 3.0; for doctorate, GRE or MAT, minimum GPA of 3.0, writing sample. Application fee: $55. *Financial support:* In 2011–12, 1 fellowship (averaging $60,000 per year), 4 research assistantships with full tuition reimbursements (averaging $99,992 per year), 48 teaching assistantships with full tuition reimbursements (averaging $12,534 per year) were awarded; career-related internships or fieldwork, Federal Work-Study, institutionally sponsored loans, and tuition waivers (full and partial) also available. Support available to part-time students. *Faculty research:* Exercise physiology; biochemical, molecular and nutritional aspects of exercise; sport training and performance; sport and exercise psychology; behavioral aspects of physical activity; youth sport science; gender and sport sociology; sports management; sports policy, marketing and law; motor development and disabilities; movement perception and action; movement neuroscience. *Total annual research expenditures:* $369,026. *Unit head:* Dr. Li Li Ji, Director, 612-624-9809, Fax: 612-626-7700, E-mail: llji@umn.edu. *Application contact:* Dr. Jennifer Engler, Assistant Dean, 612-626-2887, Fax: 612-626-7496, E-mail: engle009@umn.edu.

University of Nevada, Las Vegas, Graduate College, College of Education, Department of Sports Education Leadership, Las Vegas, NV 89154-3031. Offers physical education (M Ed, MS); sports education leadership (PhD). *Faculty:* 8 full-time (5 women), 12 part-time/adjunct (5 women). *Students:* 2 full-time (0 women), 13 part-time (6 women); includes 5 minority (all Black or African American, non-Hispanic/Latino). Average age 31. 2 applicants, 0% accepted, 0 enrolled. In 2011, 19 master's, 3 doctorates awarded. *Degree requirements:* For doctorate, comprehensive exam, thesis/dissertation, scholarly product. *Entrance requirements:* For master's and doctorate, GRE General Test. Additional exam requirements/recommendations for international students: Required—TOEFL (minimum score 550 paper-based; 213 computer-based; 80 iBT), IELTS (minimum score 7). *Application deadline:* For fall admission, 5/1 for international students; for spring admission, 10/1 for international students. Applications are processed on a rolling basis. Application fee: $60 ($95 for international students). Electronic applications accepted. *Financial support:* In 2011–12, 10 students received support, including 2 research assistantships (averaging $6,750 per year), 8 teaching assistantships (averaging $9,614 per year); institutionally sponsored loans, scholarships/grants, health care benefits, and unspecified assistantships also available. Financial award application deadline: 3/1. *Total annual research expenditures:* $45,038. *Unit head:* Dr. Monica Lounsbery, Chair/Associate Professor, 702-895-5057, Fax: 702-895-5056, E-mail: monica.lounsbery@unlv.edu. *Application contact:* Graduate College Admissions Evaluator, 702-895-3320, Fax: 702-895-4180, E-mail: gradcollege@unlv.edu. Web site: http://education.unlv.edu/sel/index.html.

University of New Brunswick Fredericton, School of Graduate Studies, Faculty of Business Administration, Fredericton, NB E3B 5A3, Canada. Offers business administration (MBA); engineering management (MBA); entrepreneurship (MBA); sports and recreation management (MBA); MBA/LL B. Part-time programs available. *Faculty:* 23 full-time (3 women), 5 part-time/adjunct (2 women). *Students:* 50 full-time (10 women), 27 part-time (12 women). In 2011, 46 master's awarded. *Degree requirements:* For master's, thesis optional. *Entrance requirements:* For master's, GMAT (minimum score 550), minimum GPA of 3.0; 3-5 years work experience. Additional exam requirements/recommendations for international students: Required—TOEFL (minimum score 580 paper-based; 92 iBT) or IELTS (minimum score 7). *Application deadline:* For fall admission, 3/1 priority date for domestic students. Applications are processed on a rolling basis. Application fee: $50 Canadian dollars. *Financial support:* In 2011–12, 7 fellowships, 1 research assistantship (averaging $4,500 per year), 17 teaching assistantships (averaging $2,250 per year) were awarded. *Faculty research:* Accounting and auditing practices, human resource management, the non-profit sector, marketing, strategic management, entrepreneurship, investment practices, supply chain management, operations management. *Unit head:* Judy Roy, Director of Graduate Studies, 506-458-7307, Fax: 506-453-3561, E-mail: jroy@unb.ca. *Application contact:* Marilyn Davis, Acting Graduate Secretary, 506-453-4766, Fax: 506-453-3561, E-mail: mbacontact@unb.ca. Web site: http://www.business.unbf.ca.

University of New Brunswick Fredericton, School of Graduate Studies, Faculty of Kinesiology, Fredericton, NB E3B 5A3, Canada. Offers exercise and sport science (M Sc); sport and recreation management (MBA); sport and recreation studies (MA). Part-time programs available. *Faculty:* 15 full-time (7 women). *Students:* 39 full-time (15 women), 6 part-time (4 women). In 2011, 7 master's awarded. *Degree requirements:* For master's, thesis (for some programs). *Entrance requirements:* For master's, minimum GPA of 3.0, written statement of research goals and interests. Additional exam requirements/recommendations for international students: Required—TOEFL (minimum score 600 paper-based; 250 computer-based), TWE (minimum score 4). *Application deadline:* For winter admission, 1/31 for domestic students; for spring admission, 3/31 for domestic students. Applications are processed on a rolling basis. Application fee: $50 Canadian dollars. Electronic applications accepted. *Financial support:* In 2011–12, 38 fellowships with tuition reimbursements, 3 research assistantships, 56 teaching assistantships were awarded; career-related internships or fieldwork and scholarships/grants also available. *Unit head:* Dr. Tim McGarry, Acting Director of Graduate Studies, 506-458-7109, Fax: 506-453-3511, E-mail: tmcgarry@unb.ca. *Application contact:* Leslie Harquail, Graduate Secretary, 506-453-4575, Fax: 506-453-3511, E-mail: harquail@unb.ca. Web site: http://www.unbf.ca/kinesiology/.

University of New Haven, Graduate School, School of Business, Program in Business Administration, West Haven, CT 06516-1916. Offers accounting (MBA, Certificate), including CPA (MBA); business management (Certificate); business policy and strategy (MBA); finance (MBA), including CFA; global marketing (MBA); human resource management (Certificate); human resources management (MBA); international business (Certificate); marketing (Certificate); sports management (MBA); telecommunications management (Certificate); MBA/MPA. Part-time and evening/weekend programs available. *Students:* 215 full-time (106 women), 182 part-time (87 women); includes 73 minority (38 Black or African American, non-Hispanic/Latino; 2 American Indian or Alaska Native, non-Hispanic/Latino; 22 Asian, non-Hispanic/Latino; 11 Hispanic/Latino), 129 international. 179 applicants, 97% accepted, 93 enrolled. In 2011, 197 master's, 28 other advanced degrees awarded. *Degree requirements:* For master's, thesis or alternative. *Entrance requirements:* For master's, GMAT. Additional exam requirements/recommendations for international students: Required—TOEFL (minimum score 520 paper-based; 190 computer-based; 70 iBT), IELTS (minimum score 5.5). *Application deadline:* For fall admission, 5/31 for international students; for winter admission, 10/15 for international students; for spring admission, 1/15 for international students. Applications are processed on a rolling basis. Application fee: $50. Electronic applications accepted. *Expenses:* Contact institution. *Financial support:* Research assistantships with partial tuition reimbursements, teaching assistantships with partial tuition reimbursements, Federal Work-Study, scholarships/grants, health care benefits, tuition waivers, and unspecified assistantships available. Support available to part-time students. Financial award applicants required to submit FAFSA. *Unit head:* Charles Coleman, Chairman, 203-932-7375. *Application contact:* Eloise Gormley, Director of Graduate Admissions, 203-932-7449, Fax: 203-932-7137, E-mail: gradinfo@newhaven.edu. Web site: http://www.newhaven.edu/7433/.

University of New Haven, Graduate School, School of Business, Program in Sports Management, West Haven, CT 06516-1916. Offers facility management (MS); management of sports industries (Certificate); sports management (MS). *Students:* 23 full-time (6 women), 9 part-time (2 women); includes 4 minority (2 Black or African American, non-Hispanic/Latino; 1 Hispanic/Latino; 1 Two or more races, non-Hispanic/Latino), 4 international. Average age 27. 16 applicants, 100% accepted, 13 enrolled. In 2011, 30 master's, 1 other advanced degree awarded. *Entrance requirements:* For master's, GMAT, minimum GPA of 2.7. Additional exam requirements/recommendations for international students: Required—TOEFL (minimum score 520 paper-based; 190 computer-based; 70 iBT); Recommended—IELTS (minimum score 5.5). *Application deadline:* For fall admission, 5/31 for international students; for winter admission, 10/15 for international students; for spring admission, 1/15 for international students. Applications are processed on a rolling basis. Application fee: $50. Electronic applications accepted. *Expenses: Tuition:* Part-time $750 per credit. *Financial support:* Research assistantships with partial tuition reimbursements, teaching assistantships with partial tuition reimbursements, career-related internships or fieldwork, Federal Work-Study, scholarships/grants, tuition waivers, and unspecified assistantships available. Support available to part-time students. Financial award applicants required to submit FAFSA. *Unit head:* Dr. Gil B. Fried, Head, 203-932-7081. *Application contact:* Eloise Gormley, Director of Graduate Admissions, 203-932-7449, Fax: 203-932-7137, E-mail: gradinfo@newhaven.edu. Web site: http://www.newhaven.edu/6851/.

University of New Mexico, Graduate School, College of Education, Department of Health, Exercise and Sports Sciences, Program in Physical Education, Albuquerque, NM 87131-2039. Offers adapted physical education (MS); curriculum and instruction

(MS); exercise science (MS); generalist (MS); sports administration (MS). Part-time programs available. *Faculty:* 56 full-time (32 women), 41 part-time/adjunct (29 women). *Students:* 45 full-time (25 women), 44 part-time (10 women); includes 42 minority (4 Black or African American, non-Hispanic/Latino; 2 American Indian or Alaska Native, non-Hispanic/Latino; 2 Asian, non-Hispanic/Latino; 31 Hispanic/Latino; 3 Two or more races, non-Hispanic/Latino), 9 international. Average age 29. 65 applicants, 58% accepted, 29 enrolled. In 2011, 27 degrees awarded. Terminal master's awarded for partial completion of doctoral program. *Degree requirements:* For master's, comprehensive exam, thesis optional. *Entrance requirements:* For master's, GRE, 3 letters of reference, minimum cumulative GPA of 3.0 in last 2 years of bachelor's degree, letter of intent. Additional exam requirements/recommendations for international students: Required—TOEFL (minimum score 550 paper-based; 213 computer-based). *Application deadline:* For fall admission, 3/1 priority date for domestic students; for spring admission, 11/1 priority date for domestic students. Application fee: $50. Electronic applications accepted. *Financial support:* In 2011–12, 57 students received support, including 1 fellowship (averaging $2,290 per year), 1 teaching assistantship with full tuition reimbursement available (averaging $11,294 per year); career-related internships or fieldwork, Federal Work-Study, institutionally sponsored loans, scholarships/grants, health care benefits, tuition waivers, and unspecified assistantships also available. Financial award application deadline: 3/1; financial award applicants required to submit FAFSA. *Faculty research:* Physical education pedagogy, sports psychology, sports administration, cardiac rehabilitation, sports physiology, physical fitness assessment, exercise prescription. *Total annual research expenditures:* $17,400. *Unit head:* Dr. Gloria Napper-Owen, Chair, 505-277-8173, Fax: 505-277-6227, E-mail: napperow@unm.edu. *Application contact:* Carol Catania, Department Office, 505-277-5151, Fax: 505-277-6227, E-mail: catania@unm.edu. Web site: http://coe.unm.edu/departments/hess/pe-teacher-education.html.

University of New Mexico, Graduate School, College of Education, Department of Health, Exercise and Sports Sciences, Program in Physical Education, Sports and Exercise Science, Albuquerque, NM 87131-2039. Offers curriculum and instruction (PhD); exercise science (PhD); sports administration (PhD). Part-time programs available. *Students:* 26 full-time (12 women), 25 part-time (7 women); includes 17 minority (4 Black or African American, non-Hispanic/Latino; 3 Asian, non-Hispanic/Latino; 8 Hispanic/Latino; 1 Native Hawaiian or other Pacific Islander, non-Hispanic/Latino; 1 Two or more races, non-Hispanic/Latino), 11 international. Average age 34. 31 applicants, 45% accepted, 8 enrolled. In 2011, 4 degrees awarded. *Degree requirements:* For doctorate, comprehensive exam, thesis/dissertation, inquiry skills, 24 credits in supporting area. *Entrance requirements:* For doctorate, GRE, letter of intent, 3 letters of reference, minimum cumulative GPA of 3.0 in last 2 years of bachelor's degree. Additional exam requirements/recommendations for international students: Required—TOEFL (minimum score 550 paper-based; 213 computer-based). *Application deadline:* For fall admission, 3/1 priority date for domestic students; for spring admission, 11/1 priority date for domestic students. Application fee: $50. Electronic applications accepted. *Financial support:* In 2011–12, 33 students received support, including 3 fellowships (averaging $2,290 per year), 16 teaching assistantships with full tuition reimbursements available (averaging $10,987 per year); career-related internships or fieldwork, Federal Work-Study, institutionally sponsored loans, scholarships/grants, health care benefits, tuition waivers, and unspecified assistantships also available. Financial award application deadline: 3/1; financial award applicants required to submit FAFSA. *Faculty research:* Facility risk management, physical education pedagogy practices, physiological adaptations to exercise, physiological adaptations to heat. *Total annual research expenditures:* $17,400. *Unit head:* Dr. Gloria Napper-Owen, Chair, 505-277-8173, Fax: 505-277-6227, E-mail: napperow@unm.edu. *Application contact:* Carol Catania, Program Office, 505-277-5151, Fax: 505-277-6227, E-mail: catania@unm.edu. Web site: http://coe.unm.edu/index.php/hess/hess-programs/pe-teacher-education/degree-endorsement-programs/physical-education-sports-and-exercise-science-phd.ht.

The University of North Carolina at Chapel Hill, Graduate School, College of Arts and Sciences, Department of Exercise and Sport Science, Chapel Hill, NC 27599. Offers athletic training (MA); exercise physiology (MA); sport administration (MA). *Degree requirements:* For master's, comprehensive exam, thesis. *Entrance requirements:* For master's, GRE General Test, minimum GPA of 3.0. Additional exam requirements/recommendations for international students: Required—TOEFL (minimum score 550 paper-based). Electronic applications accepted. *Faculty research:* Mild head injury in sport, endocrine system's response to exercise, obesity and children, effect of aerobic exercise on cerebral bloodflow in elderly population.

University of Northern Colorado, Graduate School, College of Natural and Health Sciences, School of Sport and Exercise Science, Greeley, CO 80639. Offers exercise science (MS, PhD); sport administration (MS, PhD); sport pedagogy (MS, PhD). Part-time and evening/weekend programs available. *Degree requirements:* For master's, comprehensive exam; for doctorate, comprehensive exam, thesis/dissertation. *Entrance requirements:* For master's, 2 letters of recommendation, resume; for doctorate, GRE General Test, 3 letters of recommendation, resume. Electronic applications accepted.

University of North Florida, College of Education and Human Services, Department of Leadership, School Counseling and Sport Management, Jacksonville, FL 32224. Offers counselor education (M Ed), including school counseling; educational leadership (M Ed, Ed D), including athletic administration (M Ed), educational leadership (Ed D), educational leadership (certification) (M Ed), educational technology (M Ed); instructional leadership (M Ed). Part-time and evening/weekend programs available. *Faculty:* 15 full-time (9 women). *Students:* 48 full-time (35 women), 200 part-time (135 women); includes 67 minority (47 Black or African American, non-Hispanic/Latino; 2 American Indian or Alaska Native, non-Hispanic/Latino; 6 Asian, non-Hispanic/Latino; 10 Hispanic/Latino; 2 Two or more races, non-Hispanic/Latino), 2 international. Average age 36. 97 applicants, 48% accepted, 41 enrolled. In 2011, 84 master's, 6 doctorates awarded. *Degree requirements:* For doctorate, thesis/dissertation. *Entrance requirements:* For master's, GRE General Test, minimum GPA of 3.0 in last 60 hours, interview, 3 letters of recommendation; for doctorate, GRE General Test, master's degree, interview, 3 letters of recommendation, writing sample. Additional exam requirements/recommendations for international students: Required—TOEFL (minimum score 500 paper-based; 173 computer-based). *Application deadline:* For fall admission, 7/1 priority date for domestic students, 5/1 for international students; for spring admission, 11/1 priority date for domestic students, 10/1 for international students. Applications are processed on a rolling basis. Application fee: $30. Electronic applications accepted. *Expenses:* Tuition, state resident: full-time $8793; part-time $366.38 per credit hour. Tuition, nonresident: full-time $23,502; part-time $979.24 per credit hour. *Required fees:* $1384; $57.66 per credit hour. Tuition and fees vary according to course load and program. *Financial support:* In 2011–12, 68 students received support, including 2 research assistantships (averaging $6,200 per year), 2 teaching assistantships (averaging $6,250 per year); career-related internships or fieldwork, Federal Work-Study, scholarships/grants, tuition waivers (partial), and unspecified assistantships also available. Support available to part-time students. Financial award application deadline: 4/1; financial award applicants required to submit FAFSA. *Faculty research:* Counseling: ethics; lesbian, bisexual and transgender issues; educational leadership: school culture and climate; educational assessment and accountability; school safety and student discipline. *Total annual research expenditures:* $137,500. *Unit head:* Dr. Edgar N. Jackson, Jr., Chair, 904-620-1829, E-mail: newton.jackson@unf.edu. *Application contact:* Lillith Richardson, Assistant Director, The Graduate School, 904-620-1360, Fax: 904-620-1362, E-mail: graduateschool@unf.edu. Web site: http://www.unf.edu/coehs/lscsm/.

University of San Francisco, College of Arts and Sciences, Sport Management Program, San Francisco, CA 94117-1080. Offers MA. Evening/weekend programs available. *Faculty:* 5 full-time (1 woman), 13 part-time/adjunct (2 women). *Students:* 196 full-time (71 women), 10 part-time (6 women); includes 66 minority (8 Black or African American, non-Hispanic/Latino; 1 American Indian or Alaska Native, non-Hispanic/Latino; 18 Asian, non-Hispanic/Latino; 27 Hispanic/Latino; 12 Two or more races, non-Hispanic/Latino), 17 international. Average age 26. 252 applicants, 36% accepted, 69 enrolled. In 2011, 95 master's awarded. *Degree requirements:* For master's, thesis or alternative. *Entrance requirements:* For master's, interview, minimum GPA of 2.75. *Application deadline:* For fall admission, 3/31 priority date for domestic students. Applications are processed on a rolling basis. Application fee: $55 ($65 for international students). *Expenses: Tuition:* Full-time $20,070; part-time $1115 per unit. Tuition and fees vary according to course load, campus/location and program. *Financial support:* In 2011–12, 28 students received support. Career-related internships or fieldwork, Federal Work-Study, and institutionally sponsored loans available. Financial award application deadline: 3/2; financial award applicants required to submit FAFSA. *Faculty research:* Media and sports, sports marketing, sports law, management and organization. *Unit head:* Dr. Stan Fasci, Graduate Director, 415-422-2678, Fax: 415-422-6267. *Application contact:* Information Contact, 415-422-5135, Fax: 415-422-2217, E-mail: asgraduate@usfca.edu. Web site: http://www.usfca.edu/artsci/sm/.

University of South Carolina, The Graduate School, College of Hospitality, Retail, and Sport Management, Department of Sport and Entertainment Management, Columbia, SC 29208. Offers live sport and entertainment events (MS); public assembly facilities management (MS). Part-time programs available. *Degree requirements:* For master's, comprehensive exam, thesis optional. *Entrance requirements:* For master's, GRE General Test or GMAT (preferred), minimum GPA of 3.0. Additional exam requirements/recommendations for international students: Required—TOEFL (minimum score 570 paper-based; 230 computer-based; 70 iBT). Electronic applications accepted. *Expenses:* Contact institution. *Faculty research:* Public assembly marketing, operations, box office, booking and scheduling, law/economic impacts.

University of Southern Maine, School of Education and Human Development, Educational Leadership Program, Portland, ME 04104-9300. Offers assistant principal (Certificate); athletic administration (Certificate); educational leadership (MS Ed, CAS); middle-level education (Certificate). Part-time and evening/weekend programs available. Postbaccalaureate distance learning degree programs offered (minimal on-campus study). *Degree requirements:* For master's, thesis or alternative, practicum, internship; for other advanced degree, thesis or alternative. *Entrance requirements:* For master's, three years of documented teaching; for other advanced degree, master's degree. Additional exam requirements/recommendations for international students: Required—TOEFL (minimum score 550 paper-based; 213 computer-based; 79 iBT). Electronic applications accepted.

University of Southern Mississippi, Graduate School, College of Health, School of Human Performance and Recreation, Hattiesburg, MS 39406-0001. Offers human performance (MS, PhD), including exercise physiology (PhD), human performance (MS), physical education (MS); interscholastic athletic administration (MS); recreation and leisure management (MS); sport administration (MS); sport and coaching education (MS); sport management (MS). Part-time and evening/weekend programs available. *Faculty:* 13 full-time (5 women). *Students:* 59 full-time (20 women), 38 part-time (12 women); includes 16 minority (12 Black or African American, non-Hispanic/Latino; 1 Asian, non-Hispanic/Latino; 2 Hispanic/Latino; 1 Two or more races, non-Hispanic/Latino), 9 international. Average age 29. 49 applicants, 73% accepted, 33 enrolled. In 2011, 44 master's, 1 doctorate awarded. *Degree requirements:* For master's, comprehensive exam, thesis optional; for doctorate, comprehensive exam, thesis/dissertation. *Entrance requirements:* For master's, GRE General Test, minimum GPA of 2.75 in last 60 hours; for doctorate, GRE General Test, minimum GPA of 3.5. Additional exam requirements/recommendations for international students: Required—TOEFL, IELTS. *Application deadline:* For fall admission, 3/1 priority date for domestic students, 3/1 for international students; for spring admission, 1/10 priority date for domestic students, 1/10 for international students. Applications are processed on a rolling basis. Application fee: $50. Electronic applications accepted. *Financial support:* In 2011–12, 1 fellowship (averaging $16,000 per year), 6 research assistantships with full tuition reimbursements (averaging $7,492 per year), 5 teaching assistantships with full tuition reimbursements (averaging $7,330 per year) were awarded; career-related internships or fieldwork, Federal Work-Study, institutionally sponsored loans, scholarships/grants, health care benefits, and unspecified assistantships also available. Financial award application deadline: 3/15; financial award applicants required to submit FAFSA. *Faculty research:* Exercise physiology, health behaviors, resource management, activity interaction, site development. *Unit head:* Dr. Frederick Green, Director, 601-266-5379, Fax: 601-266-4445. *Application contact:* Dr. Trenton Gould, Graduate Coordinator, 601-266-5379, Fax: 601-266-4445. Web site: http://www.usm.edu/graduateschool/table.php.

The University of Tennessee, Graduate School, College of Education, Health and Human Sciences, Department of Exercise, Sport, and Leisure Studies, Knoxville, TN 37996. Offers exercise science (MS, PhD), including biomechanics/sports medicine, exercise physiology; recreation and leisure studies (MS); sport management (MS); sport studies (MS, PhD); therapeutic recreation (MS). Part-time and evening/weekend programs available. *Degree requirements:* For master's, thesis optional. *Entrance requirements:* For master's, minimum GPA of 2.7. Additional exam requirements/recommendations for international students: Required—TOEFL. Electronic applications accepted. *Expenses:* Tuition, state resident: full-time $8332; part-time $464 per credit hour. Tuition, nonresident: full-time $25,174; part-time $1400 per credit hour. *Required fees:* $1162; $56 per credit hour. Tuition and fees vary according to program.

University of the Incarnate Word, School of Graduate Studies and Research, H-E-B School of Business and Administration, Programs in Administration, San Antonio, TX 78209-6397. Offers adult education (MAA); applied administration (MAA); communication arts (MAA); healthcare administration (MAA); instructional technology (MAA); international business (Certificate); nutrition (MAA); organizational development (MAA, Certificate); project management (Certificate); sports management (MAA). Part-time and evening/weekend programs available. Postbaccalaureate distance learning degree programs offered (no on-campus study). *Faculty:* 23 full-time (10 women), 26 part-time/adjunct (12 women). *Students:* 25 full-time (18 women), 54 part-time (33 women); includes 50 minority (10 Black or African American, non-Hispanic/Latino; 40 Hispanic/Latino), 5 international. Average age 34. 35 applicants, 94% accepted, 19 enrolled. In 2011, 38 master's awarded. *Degree requirements:* For master's, capstone. *Entrance requirements:* For master's, GRE, GMAT, undergraduate degree, minimum GPA of 2.5. Additional exam requirements/recommendations for international students: Required—TOEFL (minimum score 560 paper-based; 220 computer-based; 83 iBT). *Application deadline:* Applications are processed on a rolling basis. Application fee: $20.

Electronic applications accepted. *Expenses: Tuition:* Part-time $725 per credit hour. Tuition and fees vary according to degree level. *Financial support:* Federal Work-Study and scholarships/grants available. Financial award applicants required to submit FAFSA. *Unit head:* Dr. Mark Teachout, MAA Programs Director, 210-829-3177, Fax: 210-805-3564, E-mail: teachout@uiwtx.edu. *Application contact:* Andrea Cyterski-Acosta, Dean of Enrollment, 210-829-6005, Fax: 210-829-3921, E-mail: admis@uiwtx.edu. Web site: http://www.uiw.edu/maa/index.htm and http://www.uiw.edu/maa/admissions.html.

University of the Incarnate Word, School of Graduate Studies and Research, H-E-B School of Business and Administration, Programs in Business Administration, San Antonio, TX 78209-6397. Offers general business (MBA); international business (MBA); international business strategy (MBA); sports management (MBA). *Accreditation:* ACBSP. Part-time and evening/weekend programs available. Postbaccalaureate distance learning degree programs offered. *Faculty:* 23 full-time (10 women), 26 part-time/adjunct (12 women). *Students:* 78 full-time (38 women), 93 part-time (46 women); includes 85 minority (11 Black or African American, non-Hispanic/Latino; 5 Asian, non-Hispanic/Latino; 68 Hispanic/Latino; 1 Native Hawaiian or other Pacific Islander, non-Hispanic/Latino), 42 international. Average age 28. 114 applicants, 96% accepted, 40 enrolled. In 2011, 83 master's awarded. *Degree requirements:* For master's, capstone. *Entrance requirements:* For master's, GMAT (minimum score 450), undergraduate degree with minimum overall GPA of 2.5. Additional exam requirements/recommendations for international students: Required—TOEFL (minimum score 560 paper-based; 220 computer-based; 83 iBT). *Application deadline:* Applications are processed on a rolling basis. Application fee: $20. Electronic applications accepted. *Expenses: Tuition:* Part-time $725 per credit hour. Tuition and fees vary according to degree level. *Financial support:* Federal Work-Study and scholarships/grants available. Financial award applicants required to submit FAFSA. *Unit head:* Dr. Jeannie Scott, Acting Dean, 210-283-5002, Fax: 210-805-3564, E-mail: scott@uiwtx.edu. *Application contact:* Andrea Cyterski-Acosta, Dean of Enrollment, 210-829-6005, Fax: 210-829-3921, E-mail: admis@uiwtx.edu. Web site: http://www.uiw.edu/mba/index.htm and http://www.uiw.edu/mba/admission.html.

University of the Incarnate Word, School of Graduate Studies and Research, School of Nursing and Health Professions, Programs in Sports Management, San Antonio, TX 78209-6397. Offers sport management (MS, Certificate); sport pedagogy (Certificate). Part-time and evening/weekend programs available. *Faculty:* 2 full-time (0 women), 1 (woman) part-time/adjunct. *Students:* 11 full-time (6 women), 5 part-time (2 women); includes 9 minority (3 Black or African American, non-Hispanic/Latino; 6 Hispanic/Latino), 2 international. Average age 25. 10 applicants, 100% accepted, 7 enrolled. In 2011, 4 master's awarded. *Degree requirements:* For master's, internship. *Entrance requirements:* For master's, GRE, letter of recommendation from professional in field. Additional exam requirements/recommendations for international students: Required—TOEFL (minimum score 560 paper-based; 220 computer-based; 83 iBT). *Application deadline:* Applications are processed on a rolling basis. Application fee: $20. Electronic applications accepted. *Expenses: Tuition:* Part-time $725 per credit hour. Tuition and fees vary according to degree level. *Financial support:* Federal Work-Study and scholarships/grants available. Financial award applicants required to submit FAFSA. *Unit head:* Dr. Randall Griffiths, Assistant Professor, 210-829-2795, Fax: 210-829-3174, E-mail: rgriffit@uiwtx.edu. *Application contact:* Andrea Cyterski-Acosta, Dean of Enrollment, 210-829-6005, Fax: 210-829-3921, E-mail: admis@uiwtx.edu. Web site: http://www.uiw.edu/gradstudies/documents/mssportsmanagement.pdf.

University of the Southwest, Graduate Programs, Hobbs, NM 88240-9129. Offers business administration (MBA); curriculum and instruction (MSE); curriculum and instruction: bilingual (MSE); curriculum and instruction: TESOL (MSE); early childhood education (MSE); educational administration (MSE); mental health counseling (MSE); school counseling (MSE); special education (MSE); sports management (MBA). Part-time and evening/weekend programs available. Postbaccalaureate distance learning degree programs offered (no on-campus study). *Faculty:* 13 full-time (6 women), 28 part-time/adjunct (17 women). *Students:* 76 full-time (63 women), 229 part-time (194 women); includes 104 minority (50 Black or African American, non-Hispanic/Latino; 2 American Indian or Alaska Native, non-Hispanic/Latino; 8 Asian, non-Hispanic/Latino; 44 Hispanic/Latino). Average age 38. 173 applicants, 71% accepted, 101 enrolled. In 2011, 75 master's awarded. *Degree requirements:* For master's, comprehensive exam, thesis (for some programs). *Entrance requirements:* Additional exam requirements/recommendations for international students: Recommended—TOEFL. *Application deadline:* Applications are processed on a rolling basis. Application fee: $50. Electronic applications accepted. *Expenses: Tuition:* Full-time $12,288; part-time $512 per credit hour. One-time fee: $50. Tuition and fees vary according to course load. *Financial support:* In 2011–12, 47 students received support. Federal Work-Study available. Financial award application deadline: 4/1; financial award applicants required to submit FAFSA. *Unit head:* Dr. Mary Harris, Dean of Education, 575-492-2162, Fax: 575-392-6006, E-mail: mharris@usw.edu. *Application contact:* Melissa Mitchell, Senior Online Program Advisor, 575-492-2142, Fax: 575-392-6006, E-mail: mmitchell@usw.edu. Web site: http://www.usw.edu/admissions/graduate_admission/graduate_admissions.

University of West Georgia, College of Education, Department of Leadership and Applied Instruction, Carrollton, GA 30118. Offers art education (M Ed); art teacher education (Ed S); biology - secondary education (M Ed); biology/secondary education (Ed S); business education (M Ed, Ed S); chemistry/secondary education (Ed S); earth science/secondary education (Ed S); economics/secondary education (Ed S); educational leadership (M Ed, Ed S); English teacher education (M Ed, Ed S); French teacher education (M Ed, Ed S); history teacher education (Ed S); mathematics teacher education (M Ed, Ed S); middle grades education (M Ed, Ed S); physical education and recreation (Ed S); physical education teaching and coaching (M Ed); physics/secondary education (Ed S); science teacher education (M Ed, Ed S); secondary education (M Ed); social science - secondary education (M Ed); social science teacher education (M Ed); Spanish (M Ed); Spanish teacher education (M Ed, Ed S); sports management (M Ed). *Accreditation:* NCATE. Part-time and evening/weekend programs available. *Faculty:* 18 full-time (9 women). *Students:* 75 full-time (49 women), 169 part-time (109 women); includes 90 minority (85 Black or African American, non-Hispanic/Latino; 3 Hispanic/Latino; 2 Two or more races, non-Hispanic/Latino), 1 international. Average age 36. 115 applicants, 67% accepted, 19 enrolled. In 2011, 73 master's, 53 Ed Ss awarded. *Degree requirements:* For master's, internship; for Ed S, research project. *Entrance requirements:* For master's, GRE General Test, minimum GPA of 2.7; for Ed S, GRE General Test, master's degree, minimum graduate GPA of 3.0, district appointment. Additional exam requirements/recommendations for international students: Required—TOEFL (minimum score 523 paper-based; 193 computer-based; 69 iBT); Recommended—IELTS (minimum score 6). *Application deadline:* For fall admission, 7/21 for domestic students, 6/1 for international students; for spring admission, 11/30 for domestic students, 10/15 for international students. Applications are processed on a rolling basis. Application fee: $30. Electronic applications accepted. *Expenses:* Tuition, state resident: full-time $4336; part-time $181 per credit hour. Tuition, nonresident: full-time $17,362; part-time $724 per credit hour. Tuition and fees vary according to course load, degree level, campus/location and program. *Financial support:* In 2011–12, 1 research assistantship with full tuition reimbursement (averaging $7,444 per year) was awarded; career-related internships or fieldwork, scholarships/grants, and unspecified assistantships also available. Support available to part-time students. Financial award application deadline: 7/1; financial award applicants required to submit FAFSA. *Total annual research expenditures:* $5,000. *Unit head:* Dr. Frank Butts, Chair, 678-839-6530, Fax: 678-839-6195, E-mail: fbutts@westga.edu. *Application contact:* Deanna Richards, Coordinator, Graduate Studies, 678-839-5946, E-mail: drichard@westga.edu. Web site: http://www.westga.edu/coelai.

Valparaiso University, Graduate School, Program in Sports Administration, Valparaiso, IN 46383. Offers MS, JD/MS. Part-time and evening/weekend programs available. *Students:* 20 full-time (7 women), 11 part-time (4 women); includes 5 minority (2 Black or African American, non-Hispanic/Latino; 1 American Indian or Alaska Native, non-Hispanic/Latino; 1 Hispanic/Latino; 1 Two or more races, non-Hispanic/Latino), 3 international. Average age 26. In 2011, 19 master's awarded. *Entrance requirements:* For master's, minimum GPA of 3.0. Additional exam requirements/recommendations for international students: Required—TOEFL (minimum score 550 paper-based; 213 computer-based; 80 iBT). *Application deadline:* Applications are processed on a rolling basis. Application fee: $30 ($50 for international students). Electronic applications accepted. *Expenses: Tuition:* Part-time $560 per credit hour. Tuition and fees vary according to course load and program. *Financial support:* Available to part-time students. Applicants required to submit FAFSA. *Unit head:* Dr. David L. Rowland, Dean, Graduate School and Continuing Education/Associate Provost, 219-464-5313, Fax: 219-464-5381, E-mail: david.rowland@valpo.edu. *Application contact:* Dustin Jesch, Coordinator, U.S. Student Engagement, 219-464-5313, Fax: 219-464-5381, E-mail: dustin.jesch@valpo.edu. Web site: http://valpo.edu/grad/sportsad/index.php.

Washington State University, Graduate School, College of Education, Department of Educational Leadership and Counseling Psychology, Pullman, WA 99164. Offers counseling psychology (Ed M, MA, PhD, Certificate), including counseling psychology (Ed M, MA, PhD), school psychologist (Certificate); educational leadership (M Ed, MA, Ed D, PhD); educational psychology (Ed M, MA, PhD); higher education (Ed M, MA, Ed D, PhD), including higher education administration (PhD), sport management (PhD), student affairs (PhD); higher education with sport management (Ed M). *Accreditation:* NCATE. *Faculty:* 12. *Students:* 103 full-time (68 women), 59 part-time (29 women); includes 36 minority (6 Black or African American, non-Hispanic/Latino; 10 Asian, non-Hispanic/Latino; 16 Hispanic/Latino; 4 Two or more races, non-Hispanic/Latino), 18 international. Average age 30. 244 applicants, 29% accepted, 45 enrolled. In 2011, 44 master's, 11 doctorates awarded. Terminal master's awarded for partial completion of doctoral program. *Degree requirements:* For master's, comprehensive exam (for some programs), thesis (for some programs), oral or written exam; for doctorate, comprehensive exam, thesis/dissertation, oral and written exams. *Entrance requirements:* For master's and doctorate, GRE General Test, minimum GPA of 3.0, 3 letters of recommendation. Additional exam requirements/recommendations for international students: Required—TOEFL (minimum score 550 paper-based; 213 computer-based). *Application deadline:* For fall admission, 3/1 for domestic and international students; for spring admission, 10/1 for domestic students, 7/1 for international students. Application fee: $75. *Financial support:* In 2011–12, 1 research assistantship (averaging $18,204 per year), 4 teaching assistantships (averaging $18,204 per year) were awarded; career-related internships or fieldwork, Federal Work-Study, institutionally sponsored loans, scholarships/grants, tuition waivers (partial), and unspecified assistantships also available. Financial award application deadline: 4/1; financial award applicants required to submit FAFSA. *Faculty research:* Attentional processes, cross-cultural psychology, faculty development in higher education. *Total annual research expenditures:* $554,000. *Unit head:* Dr. Phyllis Erdman, Associate Dean, 509-335-9117, E-mail: perdman@wsu.edu. *Application contact:* Graduate School Admissions, 800-GRADWSU, Fax: 509-335-1949, E-mail: gradsch@wsu.edu. Web site: http://www.educ.wsu.edu/elcp/.

Wayne State College, Department of Health, Human Performance and Sport, Wayne, NE 68787. Offers exercise science (MSE); organizational management (MS), including sport management. Part-time and evening/weekend programs available. *Degree requirements:* For master's, comprehensive exam, thesis optional. *Entrance requirements:* For master's, GRE General Test, minimum GPA of 3.0. Additional exam requirements/recommendations for international students: Required—TOEFL (minimum score 550 paper-based; 213 computer-based). Electronic applications accepted.

Wayne State University, College of Education, Division of Kinesiology, Health and Sports Studies, Detroit, MI 48202. Offers exercise and sport science (M Ed); health education (M Ed); kinesiology (M Ed, PhD); physical education (M Ed); sports administration (MA); wellness clinician/research (M Ed). *Students:* 39 full-time (23 women), 68 part-time (31 women); includes 36 minority (31 Black or African American, non-Hispanic/Latino; 1 Asian, non-Hispanic/Latino; 1 Hispanic/Latino; 1 Native Hawaiian or other Pacific Islander, non-Hispanic/Latino; 2 Two or more races, non-Hispanic/Latino), 3 international. Average age 31. 115 applicants, 39% accepted, 27 enrolled. In 2011, 39 master's, 1 doctorate awarded. *Degree requirements:* For master's, thesis (for some programs). *Entrance requirements:* Additional exam requirements/recommendations for international students: Required—TOEFL; Recommended—TWE (minimum score 6). *Application deadline:* For fall admission, 6/1 priority date for domestic students, 5/1 for international students; for winter admission, 10/1 priority date for domestic students, 9/1 for international students; for spring admission, 2/1 priority date for domestic students, 1/1 for international students. Applications are processed on a rolling basis. Application fee: $50. Electronic applications accepted. *Expenses:* Tuition, state resident: part-time $512.85 per credit. Tuition, nonresident: part-time $1132.65 per credit. *Required fees:* $26.60 per credit. $199.65 per semester. Tuition and fees vary according to course load and program. *Financial support:* In 2011–12, 6 research assistantships with tuition reimbursements (averaging $16,061 per year) were awarded; teaching assistantships with tuition reimbursements, career-related internships or fieldwork, scholarships/grants, health care benefits, and unspecified assistantships also available. *Faculty research:* Fitness in urban children, motor development of crack babies, effects of caffeine on metabolism/exercise, body composition of elite youth sports participants, systematic observation of teaching. *Unit head:* Dr. Mariane Fahlman, Assistant Dean, 313-577-5066, Fax: 313-577-9301, E-mail: m.fahlman@wayne.edu. *Application contact:* John Wirth, Assistant Professor, 313-993-7972, Fax: 313-577-5999, E-mail: johnwirth@wayne.edu. Web site: http://coe.wayne.edu/kinesiology/index.php.

Webber International University, Graduate School of Business, Babson Park, FL 33827-0096. Offers accounting (MBA); management (MBA); security management (MBA); sports management (MBA). Part-time and evening/weekend programs available. *Degree requirements:* For master's, thesis or alternative. *Entrance requirements:* For master's, previous course work in financial and managerial accounting. Additional exam requirements/recommendations for international students: Required—TOEFL. *Faculty research:* Finance strategy, market research, investments, intranet.

West Chester University of Pennsylvania, College of Health Sciences, Department of Kinesiology, West Chester, PA 19383. Offers exercise/sport physiology (MS), including athletic training; physical education (MS); sport management and athletics (MPA). *Faculty:* 7 part-time/adjunct (3 women). *Students:* 19 full-time (10 women), 14 part-time (7 women); includes 5 minority (all Black or African American, non-Hispanic/Latino). Average age 26. 37 applicants, 35% accepted, 10 enrolled. In 2011, 12 degrees awarded. *Degree requirements:* For master's, thesis or report (MS), 2 internships (MPA). *Entrance requirements:* For master's, GRE with minimum score of 1000 (for MS), 2 letters of recommendation, transcripts, and statement of professional goals (for MS); 2 letters of reference, resume, career goal statement (for MPA). Additional exam requirements/recommendations for international students: Required—TOEFL (minimum score 550 paper-based; 213 computer-based; 80 iBT). *Application deadline:* For fall admission, 4/15 priority date for domestic students, 3/15 for international students; for spring admission, 10/15 priority date for domestic students, 9/1 for international students. Applications are processed on a rolling basis. Application fee: $45. Electronic applications accepted. *Expenses:* Tuition, state resident: full-time $7488; part-time $416 per credit. Tuition, nonresident: full-time $11,232; part-time $624 per credit. *Required fees:* $1784.64; $67.59 per credit. Tuition and fees vary according to program. *Financial support:* Unspecified assistantships available. Support available to part-time students. Financial award application deadline: 2/15; financial award applicants required to submit FAFSA. *Faculty research:* Metabolism during exercise, biomechanics, rating of perceived exertion, motor learning. *Unit head:* Dr. Frank Fry, Chair and Graduate Coordinator for the MS in General Physical Education Program, 610-436-2610, Fax: 610-436-2860, E-mail: ffry@wcupa.edu. *Application contact:* Dr. Sheri Melton, Graduate Coordinator for the Exercise and Sport Physiology Programs, 610-436-2260, Fax: 610-436-2860, E-mail: smelton@wcupa.edu. Web site: http://www.wcupa.edu/_academics/sch_shs.hpe/.

Western Illinois University, School of Graduate Studies, College of Education and Human Services, Department of Kinesiology, Program in Sport Management, Macomb, IL 61455-1390. Offers MS. Part-time programs available. *Students:* 42 full-time (14 women), 5 part-time (0 women); includes 8 minority (6 Black or African American, non-Hispanic/Latino; 1 Hispanic/Latino; 1 Two or more races, non-Hispanic/Latino), 1 international. Average age 24. 42 applicants, 76% accepted. In 2011, 19 master's awarded. *Entrance requirements:* For master's, minimum GPA of 3.0. Additional exam requirements/recommendations for international students: Required—TOEFL (minimum score 550 paper-based; 213 computer-based; 80 iBT). *Application deadline:* Applications are processed on a rolling basis. Application fee: $30. Electronic applications accepted. *Expenses:* Tuition, state resident: part-time $281.16 per credit hour. Tuition, nonresident: part-time $562.32 per credit hour. Part-time tuition and fees vary according to campus/location and reciprocity agreements. *Financial support:* In 2011–12, 18 students received support, including 18 research assistantships with full tuition reimbursements available (averaging $7,360 per year); teaching assistantships also available. *Unit head:* Dr. Darlene Young, Graduate Committee Chairperson, 309-298-1981. *Application contact:* Dr. Nancy Parsons, Interim Associate Provost and Director of Graduate Studies, 309-298-1806, Fax: 309-298-2345, E-mail: grad-office@wiu.edu. Web site: http://wiu.edu/kinesiology.

Western Kentucky University, Graduate Studies, College of Health and Human Services, Department of Kinesiology, Recreation and Sport, Bowling Green, KY 42101. Offers athletic administration and coaching (MS); physical education (MS); recreation and sport administration (MS). Part-time and evening/weekend programs available. Postbaccalaureate distance learning degree programs offered. *Degree requirements:* For master's, comprehensive exam, thesis optional. *Entrance requirements:* For master's, GRE General Test, minimum GPA of 2.75. Additional exam requirements/recommendations for international students: Required—TOEFL (minimum score 555 paper-based; 213 computer-based; 79 iBT). *Faculty research:* Orthopedic rehabilitation, fitness center coordination, heat acclimation, biomechanical and physiological parameters.

Western Michigan University, Graduate College, College of Education and Human Development, Department of Health, Physical Education and Recreation, Kalamazoo, MI 49008. Offers exercise and sports medicine (MS), including athletic training, exercise physiology; physical education (MA), including coaching sport performance, pedagogy, special physical education, sport management.

Western New England University, College of Business, Program in Business Administration (General), Springfield, MA 01119. Offers general business (MBA); sport management (MBA). *Accreditation:* AACSB. Part-time and evening/weekend programs available. *Students:* 111 part-time (51 women); includes 12 minority (6 Black or African American, non-Hispanic/Latino; 1 Asian, non-Hispanic/Latino; 3 Hispanic/Latino; 2 Two or more races, non-Hispanic/Latino), 1 international. *Entrance requirements:* For master's, GMAT, 2 letters of reference, resume. *Application deadline:* Applications are processed on a rolling basis. Application fee: $30. *Financial support:* Available to part-time students. Applicants required to submit FAFSA. *Unit head:* Dr. Julie Siciliano, Jr., Dean, 413-782-1231. *Application contact:* Matt Fox, Director of Recruiting and Marketing for Adult Learners, 413-782-1249, Fax: 413-782-1779, E-mail: learn@wne.edu. Web site: http://www1.wne.edu/business/index.cfm?selection-doc.1279.

West Virginia University, School of Physical Education, Morgantown, WV 26506. Offers athletic coaching education (MS); athletic training (MS); physical education/teacher education (MS, PhD), including curriculum and instruction (PhD), motor behavior (PhD), physical education supervision (PhD); sport and exercise psychology (PhD); sport management (MS). *Degree requirements:* For doctorate, comprehensive exam, thesis/dissertation, oral exam. *Entrance requirements:* For master's, GRE or MAT, minimum GPA of 3.0; for doctorate, GRE General Test or MAT, minimum GPA of 3.5. Additional exam requirements/recommendations for international students: Required—TOEFL (minimum score 550 paper-based; 213 computer-based). Electronic applications accepted. *Faculty research:* Sport psychosociology, teacher education, exercise psychology, counseling.

Wichita State University, Graduate School, College of Education, Department of Sport Management, Wichita, KS 67260. Offers M Ed. *Expenses:* Tuition, state resident: full-time $4746; part-time $263.65 per credit. Tuition, nonresident: full-time $11,669; part-time $648.30 per credit. *Unit head:* Dr. G. Clayton Stoldt, Chair, 316-978-5445, Fax: 316-978-5451. *Application contact:* Dr. Mark Vermillion, Graduate Coordinator, 316-978-5444, Fax: 316-978-5451, E-mail: mark.vermillion@wichita.edu. Web site: http://www.wichita.edu/sportmanagement.

Wingate University, Thayer School of Education, Wingate, NC 28174-0159. Offers community college leadership (Ed D); educational leadership (MA Ed, Ed D); elementary education (MA Ed, MAT); health and physical education (MA Ed); sport administration (MA Ed). *Accreditation:* NCATE. Part-time and evening/weekend programs available. *Faculty:* 5 full-time (3 women), 10 part-time/adjunct (3 women). *Students:* 7 full-time (4 women), 251 part-time (152 women); includes 68 minority (63 Black or African American, non-Hispanic/Latino; 1 American Indian or Alaska Native, non-Hispanic/Latino; 1 Asian, non-Hispanic/Latino; 3 Hispanic/Latino), 2 international. Average age 35. In 2011, 29 master's awarded. *Degree requirements:* For master's, portfolio. *Entrance requirements:* For master's, GRE General Test or MAT, teaching certificate (MA Ed). *Application deadline:* For fall admission, 8/15 priority date for domestic students; for spring admission, 12/15 for domestic students. Applications are processed on a rolling basis. Application fee: $0. *Expenses: Tuition:* Part-time $455 per credit hour. Part-time tuition and fees vary according to degree level and program. *Financial support:* In 2011–12, 20 students received support. Scholarships/grants available. Support available to part-time students. Financial award applicants required to submit FAFSA. *Unit head:* Dr. Sarah Harrison-Burns, Dean, 704-233-8128, E-mail: shburns@wingate.edu. *Application contact:* Theresa Hopkins, Secretary, 704-321-1470, Fax: 704-233-8273, E-mail: t.hopkins@wingate.edu.

Winona State University, College of Education, Department of Education Leadership, Winona, MN 55987. Offers educational leadership (Ed S), including general superintendency, K-12 principalship; general school leadership (MS); K-12 principalship (MS); outdoor education/adventure-based leadership (MS); sports management (MS); teacher leadership (MS). *Accreditation:* NCATE. Part-time and evening/weekend programs available. *Students:* 52 full-time (24 women), 57 part-time (18 women); includes 8 minority (5 Black or African American, non-Hispanic/Latino; 1 Asian, non-Hispanic/Latino; 1 Hispanic/Latino; 1 Two or more races, non-Hispanic/Latino), 3 international. Average age 34. In 2011, 17 master's, 10 other advanced degrees awarded. *Degree requirements:* For master's, comprehensive exam, thesis optional; for Ed S, thesis optional. *Application deadline:* For fall admission, 8/8 for domestic students; for spring admission, 12/10 for domestic students. Applications are processed on a rolling basis. Application fee: $20. *Financial support:* Federal Work-Study available. Support available to part-time students. Financial award applicants required to submit FAFSA. *Unit head:* Dr. George P. Morrow, Chair, 507-457-5346, Fax: 507-457-5882, E-mail: gmorrow@winona.edu. *Application contact:* Dr. George P. Morrow, 507-457-5346, Fax: 507-457-5882, E-mail: gmorrow@winona.edu. Web site: http://www.winona.edu/educationleadership/.

Xavier University, College of Social Sciences, Health and Education, Department of Sports Studies, Cincinnati, OH 45207. Offers sport administration (M Ed). Part-time and evening/weekend programs available. *Faculty:* 3 full-time (1 woman), 7 part-time/adjunct (1 woman). *Students:* 26 full-time (7 women), 38 part-time (11 women); includes 12 minority (9 Black or African American, non-Hispanic/Latino; 2 Asian, non-Hispanic/Latino; 1 Hispanic/Latino), 1 international. Average age 27. 47 applicants, 91% accepted, 20 enrolled. In 2011, 33 master's awarded. *Degree requirements:* For master's, thesis optional, internship. *Entrance requirements:* For master's, GRE or MAT. Additional exam requirements/recommendations for international students: Required—TOEFL. *Application deadline:* For fall admission, 2/15 priority date for domestic students, 2/15 for international students; for spring admission, 9/15 priority date for domestic students, 9/15 for international students. Applications are processed on a rolling basis. Application fee: $35. Electronic applications accepted. *Expenses: Tuition:* Part-time $576 per credit hour. *Financial support:* In 2011–12, 51 students received support. Applicants required to submit FAFSA. *Faculty research:* Coaching education, brand equity, strategic management, economic impact, place marketing. *Unit head:* Dr. Douglas Olberding, Chair, 513-745-1085, Fax: 513-745-4291, E-mail: olberdin@xavier.edu. *Application contact:* Roger Bosse, Graduate Services Director, 513-745-3357, Fax: 513-745-1048, E-mail: bosse@xavier.edu. Web site: http://www.xavier.edu/sport-administration/.

Yorktown University, School of Business, Denver, CO 80246. Offers entrepreneurship (MBA); sport management (MBA).

ACADEMIC AND PROFESSIONAL PROGRAMS IN SOCIAL WORK

Section 32
Social Work

This section contains a directory of institutions offering graduate work in social work, followed by in-depth entries submitted by institutions that chose to prepare detailed program descriptions. Additional information about programs listed in the directory but not augmented by an in-depth entry may be obtained by writing directly to the dean of a graduate school or chair of a department at the address given in the directory.

For programs offering related work, see also in this book *Allied Health* and *Education.* In another guide in this series:

Graduate Programs in the Humanities, Arts & Social Sciences

See *Criminology and Forensics, Family and Consumer Sciences, Psychology and Counseling,* and *Sociology, Anthropology, and Archaeology*

CONTENTS

Program Directories

Displays and Close-Ups

Human Services

Abilene Christian University, Graduate School, College of Education and Human Services, Abilene, TX 79699-9100. Offers M Ed, MS, MSSW, Certificate, Post-Master's Certificate. *Faculty:* 5 full-time (1 woman), 14 part-time/adjunct (7 women). *Students:* 77 full-time (67 women), 182 part-time (127 women); includes 70 minority (37 Black or African American, non-Hispanic/Latino; 2 Asian, non-Hispanic/Latino; 27 Hispanic/Latino; 4 Two or more races, non-Hispanic/Latino), 6 international. 221 applicants, 44% accepted, 64 enrolled. In 2011, 125 master's awarded. *Degree requirements:* For master's, comprehensive exam (for some programs), thesis (for some programs), practicum. *Entrance requirements:* For master's, GRE. Additional exam requirements/recommendations for international students: Required—TOEFL (minimum score 550 paper-based; 213 computer-based; 80 iBT), IELTS (minimum score 6). *Application deadline:* For fall admission, 8/15 priority date for domestic students; for winter admission, 10/1 priority date for domestic students; for spring admission, 12/15 priority date for domestic students. Applications are processed on a rolling basis. Application fee: $50. Electronic applications accepted. *Expenses: Tuition:* Full-time $14,168; part-time $787 per hour. *Required fees:* $82 per hour. $10 per term. *Financial support:* In 2011–12, 46 students received support. Career-related internships or fieldwork and scholarships/grants available. Financial award application deadline: 4/1; financial award applicants required to submit FAFSA. *Total annual research expenditures:* $154. *Unit head:* Dr. Donnie Snider, Interim Dean, 325-674-2700, E-mail: dcs03b@acu.edu. *Application contact:* David Pittman, Graduate Admissions Counselor, 325-674-2656, Fax: 325-674-6717, E-mail: gradinfo@acu.edu.

Albertus Magnus College, Master of Science in Human Services Program, New Haven, CT 06511-1189. Offers MS. Evening/weekend programs available. *Faculty:* 3 full-time (1 woman), 8 part-time/adjunct (5 women). *Students:* 26 full-time (25 women), 10 part-time (all women); includes 20 minority (17 Black or African American, non-Hispanic/Latino; 3 Hispanic/Latino). 14 applicants, 86% accepted, 9 enrolled. In 2011, 25 master's awarded. *Degree requirements:* For master's, thesis, internship, capstone thesis. *Entrance requirements:* For master's, minimum GPA of 2.8. *Application deadline:* For fall admission, 8/15 for domestic students; for spring admission, 1/15 for domestic students. Application fee: $50. Electronic applications accepted. *Financial support:* Applicants required to submit FAFSA. *Unit head:* Dr. Sean O'Connell, Interim Vice President for Academic Affairs, 203-777-8539, Fax: 203-777-3701, E-mail: soconnell@albertus.edu. *Application contact:* Dr. Ragaa Mazen, Director of Human Services Program, 203-777-8574, Fax: 203-777-3701, E-mail: rmazen@albertus.edu. Web site: http://www.albertus.edu/masters-degrees/human-services/.

Andrews University, School of Graduate Studies, College of Arts and Sciences, Department of Behavioral Science, Berrien Springs, MI 49104. Offers international development (MSA). *Students:* 11 full-time (9 women), 8 part-time (7 women); includes 12 minority (7 Black or African American, non-Hispanic/Latino; 1 American Indian or Alaska Native, non-Hispanic/Latino; 2 Hispanic/Latino; 1 Native Hawaiian or other Pacific Islander, non-Hispanic/Latino; 1 Two or more races, non-Hispanic/Latino), 3 international. Average age 34. 15 applicants, 53% accepted, 7 enrolled. In 2011, 4 master's awarded. *Entrance requirements:* For master's, GRE. Additional exam requirements/recommendations for international students: Required—TOEFL (minimum score 550 paper-based). Application fee: $40. *Unit head:* Dr. Duane C. McBride, Chair, 269-471-3152. *Application contact:* Carolyn Hurst, Supervisor of Graduate Admission, 800-253-2874, Fax: 269-471-6321, E-mail: graduate@andrews.edu.

Bellevue University, Graduate School, College of Arts and Sciences, Bellevue, NE 68005-3098. Offers clinical counseling (MS); healthcare administration (MHA); human services (MA); international security and intelligence studies (MS); managerial communication (MA). Postbaccalaureate distance learning degree programs offered.

Boricua College, Program in Human Services (Brooklyn Campus), New York, NY 10032-1560. Offers MS. Evening/weekend programs available. *Degree requirements:* For master's, thesis. *Entrance requirements:* For master's, interview by the faculty.

Boricua College, Program in Human Services (Manhattan Campus), New York, NY 10032-1560. Offers MS. Evening/weekend programs available. *Degree requirements:* For master's, thesis. *Entrance requirements:* For master's, interview by the faculty.

Brandeis University, The Heller School for Social Policy and Management, Program in Nonprofit Management, Waltham, MA 02454-9110. Offers child, youth, and family management (MBA); health care management (MBA); social impact management (MBA); social policy and management (MBA); sustainable development (MBA); MBA/MA; MBA/MD. MBA/MD program offered in conjunction with Tufts University School of Medicine. *Accreditation:* AACSB. Part-time programs available. *Students:* 82 full-time (50 women), 7 part-time (5 women); includes 8 minority (2 Black or African American, non-Hispanic/Latino; 4 Asian, non-Hispanic/Latino; 2 Hispanic/Latino), 5 international. Average age 27. 130 applicants, 73% accepted, 56 enrolled. In 2011, 47 master's awarded. *Degree requirements:* For master's, team consulting project. *Entrance requirements:* For master's, GMAT (preferred) or GRE, 2 letters of recommendation, problem statement analysis, 3-5 years of professional experience. Additional exam requirements/recommendations for international students: Required—TOEFL (minimum score 600 paper-based; 250 computer-based; 100 iBT). *Application deadline:* For fall admission, 3/15 for domestic and international students. Applications are processed on a rolling basis. Application fee: $55. Electronic applications accepted. *Expenses:* Contact institution. *Financial support:* In 2011–12, 89 students received support. Career-related internships or fieldwork, scholarships/grants, and tuition waivers (partial) available. Support available to part-time students. Financial award application deadline: 3/15; financial award applicants required to submit FAFSA. *Faculty research:* Health care; children and families; elder and disabled services; social impact management; organizations in the non-profit, for-profit, or public sector. *Unit head:* Dr. Brenda Anderson, Program Director, 781-736-8423, E-mail: banderson@brandeis.edu. *Application contact:* Shana Sconyers, Assistant Director for Admissions and Financial Aid, 781-736-4229, E-mail: sconyers@brandeis.edu. Web site: http://heller.brandeis.edu/academic/mba.html.

California State University, Sacramento, Office of Graduate Studies, College of Health and Human Services, Division of Social Work, Sacramento, CA 95819-6090. Offers family and children's services (MSW); health care (MSW); mental health (MSW); social justice and corrections (MSW). *Accreditation:* CSWE. *Faculty:* 23 full-time (12 women), 16 part-time/adjunct (8 women). *Students:* 235 full-time, 17 part-time; includes 106 minority (20 Black or African American, non-Hispanic/Latino; 1 American Indian or Alaska Native, non-Hispanic/Latino; 8 Asian, non-Hispanic/Latino; 58 Hispanic/Latino; 2 Native Hawaiian or other Pacific Islander, non-Hispanic/Latino; 17 Two or more races, non-Hispanic/Latino). Average age 33. 436 applicants, 48% accepted, 133 enrolled. In 2011, 155 master's awarded. *Degree requirements:* For master's, thesis, research project, or comprehensive exam; writing proficiency exam. *Entrance requirements:* For master's, minimum GPA of 2.5 during previous 2 years of course work. Additional exam requirements/recommendations for international students: Required—TOEFL. *Application deadline:* For fall admission, 1/18 for domestic students, 3/1 for international students; for spring admission, 9/30 for international students. Applications are processed on a rolling basis. Application fee: $55. Electronic applications accepted. *Financial support:* Career-related internships or fieldwork and Federal Work-Study available. Support available to part-time students. Financial award application deadline: 3/1; financial award applicants required to submit FAFSA. *Unit head:* Dr. Robin Kennedy, Chair, 916-278-6913, Fax: 916-278-7167, E-mail: kennedyr@csus.edu. *Application contact:* Jose Martinez, Outreach and Graduate Diversity Coordinator, 916-278-6470, Fax: 916-278-5669, E-mail: martinj@skymail.csus.edu. Web site: http://www.csus.edu/hhs/sw.

Capella University, School of Human Services, Minneapolis, MN 55402. Offers addictions counseling (Certificate); counseling studies (MS, PhD); criminal justice (MS, PhD, Certificate); diversity studies (Certificate); general human services (MS, PhD); health care administration (MS, PhD, Certificate); management of nonprofit agencies (MS, PhD, Certificate); marital, couple and family counseling/therapy (MS); marriage and family services (Certificate); mental health counseling (MS); professional counseling (Certificate); social and community services (MS, PhD, Certificate). Part-time and evening/weekend programs available. Postbaccalaureate distance learning degree programs offered (minimal on-campus study). Terminal master's awarded for partial completion of doctoral program. *Degree requirements:* For master's, thesis optional, integrative project; for doctorate, comprehensive exam, thesis/dissertation. *Entrance requirements:* Additional exam requirements/recommendations for international students: Required—TOEFL (minimum score 550 paper-based; 213 computer-based), TWE (minimum score 4). Electronic applications accepted. *Faculty research:* Compulsive and addictive behaviors, substance abuse, assessment of psychopathology and neuropsychology.

Capella University, School of Public Service Leadership, Minneapolis, MN 55402. Offers criminal justice (MS, PhD); emergency management (MS, PhD); general human services (MS, PhD); general public administration (MPA, DPA); gerontology (MS); health care administration (MS, PhD); health management and policy (MSPH); management of nonprofit agencies (MS, PhD); nurse educator (MS); public safety leadership (MS, PhD); social and community services (MS, PhD); social behavioral sciences (MSPH).

Chestnut Hill College, School of Graduate Studies, Program in Administration of Human Services, Philadelphia, PA 19118-2693. Offers MS, CAS. Part-time and evening/weekend programs available. *Faculty:* 3 full-time (all women), 7 part-time/adjunct (5 women). *Students:* 13 full-time (12 women), 30 part-time (27 women); includes 22 minority (20 Black or African American, non-Hispanic/Latino; 2 Hispanic/Latino). Average age 36. 13 applicants, 92% accepted. In 2011, 21 master's awarded. *Degree requirements:* For master's, special projects or internship. *Entrance requirements:* For master's, GRE General Test or MAT, 100 volunteer hours or 1 year work-related human services experience, statement of professional goals, writing sample, letters of recommendation. Additional exam requirements/recommendations for international students: Required—TOEFL (minimum score 500 paper-based; 213 computer-based). *Application deadline:* For fall admission, 7/17 priority date for domestic students, 7/15 for international students; for spring admission, 12/15 priority date for domestic students, 12/15 for international students. Applications are processed on a rolling basis. Application fee: $55. *Expenses: Tuition:* Part-time $555 per credit hour. One-time fee: $55 part-time. Part-time tuition and fees vary according to degree level and program. *Financial support:* Institutionally sponsored loans and unspecified assistantships available. *Faculty research:* Best practices and trends in adult education degree programs, middle and late adulthood development, quality of living issues for older persons. *Unit head:* Dr. Elaine Green, Chair, 215-248-7172, Fax: 215-248-7065, E-mail: green@chc.edu. *Application contact:* Amy Boorse, Application Manager, School of Graduate Studies, 215-248-7097, Fax: 215-248-7161, E-mail: gradadmissions@chc.edu. Web site: http://www.chc.edu/Graduate/Programs/Masters/Administration_of_Human_Services/.

Concordia University Chicago, College of Graduate and Innovative Programs, Program in Human Services, River Forest, IL 60305-1499. Offers human services (MA), including administration, exercise science. Part-time and evening/weekend programs available. *Degree requirements:* For master's, comprehensive exam, thesis. *Entrance requirements:* For master's, minimum GPA of 2.9. Additional exam requirements/recommendations for international students: Required—TOEFL (minimum score 550 paper-based; 195 computer-based). Electronic applications accepted.

Concordia University Wisconsin, Graduate Programs, School of Human Services, Mequon, WI 53097-2402. Offers MOT, MSN, MSPT, MSRS, DPT. *Students:* 236 full-time (188 women), 374 part-time (356 women); includes 59 minority (23 Black or African American, non-Hispanic/Latino; 2 American Indian or Alaska Native, non-Hispanic/Latino; 13 Asian, non-Hispanic/Latino; 10 Hispanic/Latino; 11 Two or more races, non-Hispanic/Latino), 4 international. Average age 34. *Application contact:* Bill V. Mueller, Graduate Admissions Counselor, 262-243-4551, Fax: 262-243-4428, E-mail: williamvmueller@cuw.edu.

Coppin State University, Division of Graduate Studies, Division of Arts and Sciences, Department of Social Sciences, Baltimore, MD 21216-3698. Offers human services administration (MS). Part-time and evening/weekend programs available. *Entrance requirements:* For master's, resume, references, interview.

Drury University, Graduate Programs in Education, Springfield, MO 65802. Offers elementary education (M Ed); gifted education (M Ed); human services (M Ed); instructional mathematics K-8 (M Ed); instructional technology (M Ed); middle school teaching (M Ed); secondary education (M Ed); special education (M Ed); special reading (M Ed). *Accreditation:* NCATE. Part-time and evening/weekend programs available. *Degree requirements:* For master's, thesis. *Entrance requirements:* For master's, GRE or MAT, minimum GPA of 2.75. Additional exam requirements/recommendations for international students: Required—TOEFL. Electronic applications accepted. *Faculty research:* Cultural enrichment, research skills, parental involvement relating to reading skills, reading strategies for mainstreaming children.

Eastern Michigan University, Graduate School, College of Health and Human Services, Interdisciplinary Program in Health and Human Services, Ypsilanti, MI 48197. Offers community building (Graduate Certificate). Part-time and evening/weekend programs available. *Students:* 4 part-time (3 women); includes 1 minority (Hispanic/Latino). Average age 42. 2 applicants, 50% accepted, 1 enrolled. In 2011, 3 Graduate Certificates awarded. *Entrance requirements:* Additional exam requirements/recommendations for international students: Required—TOEFL. Application fee: $35. *Expenses:* Tuition, state resident: full-time $10,367; part-time $432 per credit hour. Tuition, nonresident: full-time $20,435; part-time $851 per credit hour. *Required fees:* $39 per credit hour. $46 per semester. One-time fee: $100. Tuition and fees vary according to course level, degree level and reciprocity agreements. *Unit head:* Dr.

Marcia Bombyk, Program Coordinator, 734-487-4173, Fax: 734-487-8536, E-mail: marcia.bombyk@emich.edu. *Application contact:* Graduate Admissions, 734-487-2400, Fax: 734-487-6559, E-mail: graduate.admissions@emich.edu.

Eastern New Mexico University, Graduate School, College of Liberal Arts and Sciences, Department of Health and Human Services, Portales, NM 88130. Offers speech pathology and audiology (MS). *Accreditation:* ASHA. Part-time programs available. Postbaccalaureate distance learning degree programs offered (minimal on-campus study). *Faculty:* 4 full-time (2 women), 1 (woman) part-time/adjunct. *Students:* 22 full-time (20 women), 71 part-time (66 women); includes 41 minority (5 Black or African American, non-Hispanic/Latino; 1 Asian, non-Hispanic/Latino; 34 Hispanic/Latino; 1 Two or more races, non-Hispanic/Latino), 1 international. Average age 29. 49 applicants, 96% accepted, 28 enrolled. In 2011, 14 master's awarded. *Degree requirements:* For master's, thesis optional, oral and written comprehensive exam, oral presentation of professional portfolio. *Entrance requirements:* For master's, GRE, three letters of recommendation, resume, two essays. Additional exam requirements/recommendations for international students: Required—TOEFL (minimum score 550 paper-based; 213 computer-based; 79 iBT), IELTS (minimum score 6). *Application deadline:* For fall admission, 3/1 priority date for domestic students, 3/1 for international students. Applications are processed on a rolling basis. Application fee: $10. Electronic applications accepted. *Financial support:* In 2011–12, 11 research assistantships with partial tuition reimbursements (averaging $4,250 per year) were awarded; scholarships/grants and unspecified assistantships also available. Support available to part-time students. Financial award applicants required to submit FAFSA. *Unit head:* Dr. Suzanne Swift, Chair/Interim Graduate Coordinator, 575-562-2724, Fax: 575-562-2380, E-mail: suzanne.swift@enmu.edu. *Application contact:* Wendy Turner, Department Secretary, 575-562-2156, Fax: 575-562-2380, E-mail: wendy.turner@enmu.edu. Web site: http://liberal-arts.enmu.edu/health/cdis/graduate-cdis.shtml.

Fairmont State University, Program in Human Services, Fairmont, WV 26554. Offers human and community service administration (MS). Part-time and evening/weekend programs available. Postbaccalaureate distance learning degree programs offered. *Faculty:* 2 part-time/adjunct (1 woman). *Students:* 1 full-time (0 women), 2 part-time (both women); includes 2 minority (both Black or African American, non-Hispanic/Latino). Average age 42. *Degree requirements:* For master's, comprehensive exam, 400-hour supervised internship. *Entrance requirements:* For master's, GRE, minimum undergraduate cumulative GPA of 3.0; 3 letters of reference; baccalaureate degree in psychology, sociology, or similar social/behavioral field. *Application deadline:* For fall admission, 5/1 for domestic and international students. Applications are processed on a rolling basis. Application fee: $40. *Expenses:* Tuition, state resident: full-time $5900. Tuition, nonresident: full-time $12,596. *Unit head:* Dr. Clarence Rohrbaugh, Chair, Department of Behavioral Science, 304-367-4669, Fax: 304-367-4785, E-mail: crohrbaugh1@fairmontstate.edu. Web site: http://www.fairmontstate.edu/graduatestudies/HSServiceProgram.asp.

Ferris State University, College of Education and Human Services, Big Rapids, MI 49307. Offers M Ed, MSCJ, MSCTE. Part-time and evening/weekend programs available. Postbaccalaureate distance learning degree programs offered (minimal on-campus study). *Faculty:* 16 full-time (10 women), 9 part-time/adjunct (6 women). *Students:* 24 full-time (15 women), 186 part-time (107 women); includes 37 minority (26 Black or African American, non-Hispanic/Latino; 2 American Indian or Alaska Native, non-Hispanic/Latino; 7 Hispanic/Latino; 2 Two or more races, non-Hispanic/Latino), 5 international. Average age 33. 38 applicants, 95% accepted, 18 enrolled. In 2011, 74 master's awarded. *Entrance requirements:* For master's, minimum GPA of 3.0 (MSCJ), 2.75 (MSCTE, M Ed). Additional exam requirements/recommendations for international students: Required—TOEFL (minimum score 500 paper-based; 173 computer-based; 61 iBT). *Application deadline:* For fall admission, 7/1 priority date for domestic students, 7/1 for international students; for winter admission, 12/15 for domestic and international students; for spring admission, 11/1 priority date for domestic students, 11/1 for international students. Applications are processed on a rolling basis. Application fee: $30. Electronic applications accepted. Application fee is waived when completed online. *Financial support:* In 2011–12, 2 research assistantships (averaging $4,850 per year) were awarded; career-related internships or fieldwork, Federal Work-Study, scholarships/grants, and unspecified assistantships also available. Support available to part-time students. Financial award applicants required to submit FAFSA. *Faculty research:* Competency testing, teaching methodologies, assessment of teaching effectiveness, suicide prevention, women in education, special needs. *Unit head:* Michelle Johnston, Dean, 231-591-3646, Fax: 231-592-3792, E-mail: michelle_johnston@ferris.edu. *Application contact:* Dr. Kristen Salomonson, Dean, Enrollment Services/Director, Admissions and Records, 231-591-2100, Fax: 231-591-3944, E-mail: admissions@ferris.edu.

Georgia State University, College of Health and Human Sciences, School of Social Work, Atlanta, GA 30294. Offers community partnerships (MSW). *Accreditation:* CSWE. Part-time programs available. *Degree requirements:* For master's, community project. *Entrance requirements:* For master's, GRE General Test. Additional exam requirements/recommendations for international students: Required—TOEFL (minimum score 550 paper-based; 213 computer-based). Electronic applications accepted. *Faculty research:* Child welfare, labor unions and child care workers, secondary victimization in death penalty cases, aging.

Kansas State University, Graduate School, College of Human Ecology, School of Family Studies and Human Services, Manhattan, KS 66506. Offers communication sciences and disorders (MS); early childhood education (MS); family studies (MS); life span human development (MS); marriage and family therapy (MS). *Accreditation:* AAMFT/COAMFTE; ASHA. Part-time programs available. *Faculty:* 28 full-time (18 women), 4 part-time/adjunct (3 women). *Students:* 56 full-time (47 women), 158 part-time (100 women); includes 34 minority (19 Black or African American, non-Hispanic/Latino; 3 American Indian or Alaska Native, non-Hispanic/Latino; 4 Asian, non-Hispanic/Latino; 7 Hispanic/Latino; 1 Two or more races, non-Hispanic/Latino), 2 international. Average age 32. 195 applicants, 41% accepted, 46 enrolled. In 2011, 56 master's awarded. *Degree requirements:* For master's, thesis or alternative, oral exam, residency. *Entrance requirements:* For master's, GRE, minimum GPA of 3.0 in last 2 years of undergraduate study. Additional exam requirements/recommendations for international students: Required—TOEFL (minimum score 600 paper-based; 250 computer-based). *Application deadline:* For fall admission, 2/1 priority date for domestic students, 2/1 for international students; for spring admission, 8/1 priority date for domestic students, 8/1 for international students. Applications are processed on a rolling basis. Application fee: $40 ($55 for international students). Electronic applications accepted. *Financial support:* In 2011–12, 27 research assistantships (averaging $12,839 per year), 17 teaching assistantships with full and partial tuition reimbursements (averaging $12,771 per year) were awarded; Federal Work-Study, institutionally sponsored loans, scholarships/grants, and unspecified assistantships also available. Support available to part-time students. Financial award application deadline: 3/1; financial award applicants required to submit FAFSA. *Faculty research:* Health and security of military families, personal and family risk assessment and evaluation, disorders of communication and swallowing, families and health. *Total annual research expenditures:* $13.5 million. *Unit head:* Dr. Maurice McDonald, Head, 785-532-5510, Fax: 785-532-5505, E-mail: morey@ksu.edu. *Application contact:* Connie Fechter, Administrative Specialist, 785-532-5510, Fax: 785-532-5505, E-mail: fechter@ksu.edu. Web site: http://www.he.k-state.edu/fshs/.

Kent State University, Graduate School of Education, Health, and Human Services, Kent, OH 44242-0001. Offers M Ed, MA, MAT, MPH, MS, Au D, PhD, Ed S. *Accreditation:* NCATE. Part-time and evening/weekend programs available. Postbaccalaureate distance learning degree programs offered. *Faculty:* 271 full-time (165 women), 220 part-time/adjunct (160 women). *Students:* 981 full-time (754 women), 671 part-time (514 women); includes 152 minority (94 Black or African American, non-Hispanic/Latino; 1 American Indian or Alaska Native, non-Hispanic/Latino; 35 Asian, non-Hispanic/Latino; 21 Hispanic/Latino; 1 Native Hawaiian or other Pacific Islander, non-Hispanic/Latino). 1,343 applicants, 44% accepted. In 2011, 543 master's, 35 doctorates, 35 other advanced degrees awarded. *Degree requirements:* For master's, thesis (for some programs); for doctorate, comprehensive exam, thesis/dissertation. *Entrance requirements:* For doctorate and Ed S, GRE General Test. Additional exam requirements/recommendations for international students: Required—TOEFL (minimum score 525 paper-based; 197 computer-based; 65 iBT). *Application deadline:* Applications are processed on a rolling basis. Application fee: $30 ($60 for international students). Electronic applications accepted. *Expenses:* Tuition, state resident: full-time $8136; part-time $452 per credit hour. Tuition, nonresident: full-time $14,292; part-time $794 per credit hour. *Financial support:* In 2011–12, 32 fellowships with full tuition reimbursements (averaging $11,219 per year), 92 research assistantships with full tuition reimbursements (averaging $10,701 per year) were awarded; teaching assistantships, Federal Work-Study, scholarships/grants, unspecified assistantships, and 24 administrative assistantships (averaging $9,229 per year) also available. Financial award application deadline: 4/1; financial award applicants required to submit FAFSA. *Unit head:* Dr. Daniel Mahony, Dean, 330-672-2202, Fax: 330-672-3407, E-mail: dmahony@kent.edu. *Application contact:* Nancy Miller, Academic Program Coordinator, Office of Graduate Student Services, 330-672-2576, Fax: 330-672-9162, E-mail: nmiller1@kent.edu. Web site: http://www.educ.kent.edu/.

Lehigh University, College of Education, Program in Counseling Psychology, Bethlehem, PA 18015. Offers counseling and human services (M Ed); counseling psychology (PhD); elementary counseling with certification (M Ed); international counseling (M Ed, Certificate); secondary school counseling with certification (M Ed). *Accreditation:* APA (one or more programs are accredited). Part-time and evening/weekend programs available. Postbaccalaureate distance learning degree programs offered (minimal on-campus study). *Faculty:* 4 full-time (3 women), 9 part-time/adjunct (7 women). *Students:* 52 full-time (49 women), 31 part-time (27 women); includes 8 minority (5 Black or African American, non-Hispanic/Latino; 2 Asian, non-Hispanic/Latino; 1 Hispanic/Latino), 6 international. Average age 28. 193 applicants, 31% accepted, 19 enrolled. In 2011, 26 master's, 9 doctorates awarded. *Degree requirements:* For doctorate, comprehensive exam, thesis/dissertation. *Entrance requirements:* For master's, minimum GPA of 3.0, 2 letters of recommendation, essay, transcript; for doctorate, GRE General Test (Verbal and Quantitative), 2 letters of recommendation, transcript, essay; for Certificate, minimum GPA of 3.0. Additional exam requirements/recommendations for international students: Required—TOEFL (minimum score 600 paper-based; 250 computer-based; 93 iBT). *Application deadline:* For fall admission, 3/1 for domestic students, 11/15 for international students; for winter admission, 2/1 for international students. Application fee: $65. Electronic applications accepted. Application fee is waived when completed online. *Financial support:* In 2011–12, 21 students received support, including 1 research assistantship with full and partial tuition reimbursement available (averaging $16,000 per year); fellowships with full and partial tuition reimbursements available, career-related internships or fieldwork, Federal Work-Study, institutionally sponsored loans, scholarships/grants, tuition waivers (full and partial), and unspecified assistantships also available. Financial award application deadline: 2/15; financial award applicants required to submit FAFSA. *Faculty research:* Supervision, violence prevention, multicultural training and counseling, career development and health interventions, intersection of identities. *Unit head:* Dr. Arpana Inman, Coordinator, 610-758-4443, Fax: 610-758-3227, E-mail: agi2@lehigh.edu. *Application contact:* Donna M. Johnson, Coordinator, 610-758-3231, Fax: 610-758-6223, E-mail: dmj4@lehigh.edu.

Liberty University, College of Arts and Sciences, Lynchburg, VA 24502. Offers counseling (MA); human services (MA); nursing (MSN); pastoral care and counseling (PhD); professional counseling (PhD). *Accreditation:* AACN. Part-time programs available. Postbaccalaureate distance learning degree programs offered (minimal on-campus study). *Students:* 2,550 full-time (2,026 women), 5,408 part-time (4,324 women); includes 2,079 minority (1,619 Black or African American, non-Hispanic/Latino; 24 American Indian or Alaska Native, non-Hispanic/Latino; 46 Asian, non-Hispanic/Latino; 231 Hispanic/Latino; 11 Native Hawaiian or other Pacific Islander, non-Hispanic/Latino; 148 Two or more races, non-Hispanic/Latino), 155 international. Average age 36. In 2011, 1,179 master's, 5 doctorates awarded. *Degree requirements:* For master's, comprehensive exam (for some programs); for doctorate, comprehensive exam, thesis/dissertation. *Entrance requirements:* For master's, GRE General Test (MSN), minimum undergraduate GPA of 3.0; for doctorate, GRE General Test, minimum master's GPA of 3.25. Additional exam requirements/recommendations for international students: Required—TOEFL (minimum score 600 paper-based; 250 computer-based; 100 iBT). *Application deadline:* For fall admission, 6/1 priority date for domestic students; for spring admission, 11/1 priority date for domestic students. Applications are processed on a rolling basis. Application fee: $50. Electronic applications accepted. *Financial support:* Teaching assistantships with tuition reimbursements and Federal Work-Study available. *Faculty research:* God concept and adult attachment, building marital strength, image of God and gender, breastfeeding behavior among adolescent mothers, osteoporosis. *Unit head:* Dr. Ronald E. Hawkins, Dean, 434-592-4030, Fax: 434-522-0416, E-mail: rehawkin@liberty.edu. *Application contact:* Jay Bridge, Director of Graduate Admissions, 800-424-9595, Fax: 800-628-7977, E-mail: gradadmissions@liberty.edu.

Lincoln University, Graduate Center, Lincoln University, PA 19352. Offers administration (MSA), including finance, human resources management; early childhood education (M Ed); elementary education (M Ed); human services (M Hum Svcs); reading (MSR). Evening/weekend programs available. *Degree requirements:* For master's, thesis. *Entrance requirements:* For master's, 5 years of work experience in human services. *Faculty research:* Gerontology/minority aging, computers in composition instruction.

Lindenwood University, Graduate Programs, School of Human Services, St. Charles, MO 63301-1695. Offers nonprofit administration (MA); public administration (MPA). Part-time programs available. *Faculty:* 2 full-time (1 woman), 9 part-time/adjunct (4 women). *Students:* 2 full-time (1 woman), 36 part-time (29 women); includes 20 minority (18 Black or African American, non-Hispanic/Latino; 1 American Indian or Alaska Native, non-Hispanic/Latino; 1 Two or more races, non-Hispanic/Latino). Average age 34. 19 applicants, 74% accepted, 13 enrolled. In 2011, 11 degrees awarded. *Degree requirements:* For master's, minimum cumulative GPA of 3.0, directed internship, capstone project. *Entrance requirements:* Additional exam requirements/recommendations for international students: Required—TOEFL (minimum score 550 paper-based; 213 computer-based; 80 iBT). *Application deadline:* For fall admission, 8/26 priority date for domestic students, 8/26 for international students; for spring admission, 1/27 priority date for domestic students, 1/27 for international students. Applications are processed on a rolling basis. Application fee: $30 ($100 for international students). Electronic applications accepted. *Expenses: Tuition:* Full-time $13,650; part-time $395 per credit hour. *Required fees:* $150 per semester. Tuition and fees vary according to course level and course load. *Financial support:* In 2011–12, 12 students received support. Career-related internships or fieldwork, institutionally sponsored loans, tuition waivers, and unspecified assistantships available. Financial award application deadline: 6/30; financial award applicants required to submit FAFSA. *Unit head:* Carla Mueller, Dean, 636-949-4731, E-mail: cmueller@lindenwood.edu. *Application contact:* Brett Barger, Dean of Evening Admissions and Extension Campuses, 636-949-4934, Fax: 636-949-4109, E-mail: adultadmissions@lindenwood.edu. Web site: http://www.lindenwood.edu/humanServices/.

Louisiana State University in Shreveport, College of Business, Education, and Human Development, Program in Human Services Administration, Shreveport, LA 71115-2399. Offers MS. Part-time and evening/weekend programs available. Postbaccalaureate distance learning degree programs offered (no on-campus study). *Students:* 6 full-time (5 women), 20 part-time (16 women); includes 6 minority (5 Black or African American, non-Hispanic/Latino; 1 Hispanic/Latino). Average age 29. 16 applicants, 100% accepted, 8 enrolled. In 2011, 10 master's awarded. *Degree requirements:* For master's, final project. *Entrance requirements:* For master's, GRE, minimum GPA of 3.0 in last 2 undergraduate years, interview, recommendations. Additional exam requirements/recommendations for international students: Required—TOEFL (minimum score 550 paper-based; 213 computer-based; 80 iBT). *Application deadline:* For fall admission, 6/30 for domestic and international students; for spring admission, 11/30 for domestic and international students. Applications are processed on a rolling basis. Application fee: $10 ($20 for international students). *Financial support:* In 2011–12, 2 research assistantships (averaging $3,780 per year) were awarded. *Unit head:* Dr. Helen Wise, Program Director, 318-797-5333, Fax: 318-797-5358, E-mail: helen.wise@lsus.edu. *Application contact:* Christianne Wojcik, Director of Academic Services, 318-797-5247, Fax: 318-798-4120, E-mail: christianne.wojcik@lsus.edu.

McDaniel College, Graduate and Professional Studies, Program in Human Services Management in Special Education, Westminster, MD 21157-4390. Offers MS. *Accreditation:* NCATE. Evening/weekend programs available. *Degree requirements:* For master's, internship. *Entrance requirements:* For master's, letters of reference (3). Additional exam requirements/recommendations for international students: Required—TOEFL (minimum score 213 computer-based).

Minnesota State University Mankato, College of Graduate Studies, College of Social and Behavioral Sciences, Department of Sociology and Corrections, Mankato, MN 56001. Offers sociology (MA); sociology: college teaching option (MA); sociology: corrections (MS); sociology: human services planning and administration (MS). Part-time programs available. *Students:* 12 full-time (9 women), 33 part-time (20 women). *Degree requirements:* For master's, comprehensive exam, thesis or alternative. *Entrance requirements:* For master's, minimum GPA of 3.0 during previous 2 years, 3 letters of reference, resume. Additional exam requirements/recommendations for international students: Required—TOEFL. *Application deadline:* For fall admission, 7/1 priority date for domestic students; for spring admission, 11/1 for domestic students. Applications are processed on a rolling basis. Application fee: $40. Electronic applications accepted. *Financial support:* Research assistantships with full tuition reimbursements, teaching assistantships with full tuition reimbursements, career-related internships or fieldwork, Federal Work-Study, institutionally sponsored loans, and unspecified assistantships available. Support available to part-time students. Financial award application deadline: 3/15; financial award applicants required to submit FAFSA. *Faculty research:* Women's suffrage movements. *Unit head:* Dr. Barbara Carson, Chairperson, 507-389-1562. *Application contact:* 507-389-2321, E-mail: grad@mnsu.edu. Web site: http://sbs.mnsu.edu/soccorr/.

Minnesota State University Moorhead, Graduate Studies, College of Education and Human Services, Moorhead, MN 56563-0002. Offers counseling and student affairs (MS); curriculum and instruction (MS); educational leadership (MS, Ed S); nursing (MS); reading (MS); special education (MS); speech-language pathology (MS). *Accreditation:* NCATE. Part-time and evening/weekend programs available. *Degree requirements:* For master's, comprehensive exam, final oral exam, project or thesis. *Entrance requirements:* Additional exam requirements/recommendations for international students: Required—TOEFL. Electronic applications accepted.

Minnesota State University Moorhead, Graduate Studies, College of Social and Natural Sciences, Program in Public, Human Services, and Health Administration, Moorhead, MN 56563-0002. Offers MS. Part-time and evening/weekend programs available. *Degree requirements:* For master's, final oral exam, final project paper or thesis. *Entrance requirements:* For master's, GRE General Test, minimum GPA of 2.75. Additional exam requirements/recommendations for international students: Required—TOEFL (minimum score 550 paper-based; 213 computer-based). Electronic applications accepted.

Montana State University Billings, College of Allied Health Professions, Department of Rehabilitation and Human Services, Billings, MT 59101-0298. Offers MSRC. *Accreditation:* CORE. Part-time programs available. *Degree requirements:* For master's, thesis or professional paper and/or field experience. *Entrance requirements:* For master's, GRE General Test or MAT, minimum GPA of 3.0.

Murray State University, College of Education, Department of Educational Studies, Leadership and Counseling, Program in Human Development and Leadership, Murray, KY 42071. Offers MS. Part-time programs available. *Degree requirements:* For master's, thesis optional. *Entrance requirements:* Additional exam requirements/recommendations for international students: Required—TOEFL.

National Louis University, College of Arts and Sciences, Chicago, IL 60603. Offers adult education (Ed D); counseling and human services (MS); language and academic development (M Ed, Certificate); psychology (MA, PhD, Certificate); public policy (MA); written communication (MS, Certificate). Part-time and evening/weekend programs available. Postbaccalaureate distance learning degree programs offered (minimal on-campus study). *Students:* 33 full-time (25 women), 466 part-time (388 women); includes 233 minority (176 Black or African American, non-Hispanic/Latino; 1 American Indian or Alaska Native, non-Hispanic/Latino; 12 Asian, non-Hispanic/Latino; 41 Hispanic/Latino; 3 Two or more races, non-Hispanic/Latino). Average age 38. In 2011, 196 master's, 7 doctorates, 48 other advanced degrees awarded. *Degree requirements:* For master's and Certificate, comprehensive exam (for some programs), thesis (for some programs); for doctorate, thesis/dissertation. *Entrance requirements:* For master's, MAT or GRE, 3 professional or academic references, interview, minimum GPA of 3.0; for doctorate, GRE General Test, MAT, or Watson-Glaser Critical Thinking Appraisal, three professional or academic references, statement of academic and professional goals, 3 years of experience in field, interview, master's degree, resume, writing sample; for Certificate, GRE, MAT, or Watson-Glaser Critical Thinking Appraisal, three professional or academic references, statement of academic and professional goals, interview, minimum GPA of 3.0. Additional exam requirements/recommendations for international students: Required—Department of Language Studies Assessment or TOEFL (minimum score 550 paper-based; 213 computer-based; 79 iBT). *Application deadline:* Applications are processed on a rolling basis. Application fee: $40. Electronic applications accepted. *Financial support:* Career-related internships or fieldwork, Federal Work-Study, institutionally sponsored loans, scholarships/grants, and tuition waivers available. Support available to part-time students. Financial award applicants required to submit FAFSA. *Unit head:* Dr. Walter Roettger, Interim Dean, 312-261-3073, Fax: 312-261-3073, E-mail: walter.roettger@nl.edu. *Application contact:* Dr. Ken Kasprzak, Director of Admissions, 888-658-8632, Fax: 847-947-5575, E-mail: kkasprzak@nl.edu.

National University, Academic Affairs, School of Health and Human Services, La Jolla, CA 92037-1011. Offers MHA, MPH, MS, Certificate. Part-time and evening/weekend programs available. Postbaccalaureate distance learning degree programs offered (no on-campus study). *Degree requirements:* For master's, thesis. *Entrance requirements:* For master's, interview, minimum GPA of 2.5. Additional exam requirements/recommendations for international students: Required—TOEFL (minimum score 550 paper-based; 213 computer-based; 79 iBT), IELTS (minimum score 6). *Application deadline:* Applications are processed on a rolling basis. Application fee: $60 ($65 for international students). Electronic applications accepted. *Financial support:* Career-related internships or fieldwork, institutionally sponsored loans, and scholarships/grants available. Support available to part-time students. Financial award application deadline: 6/30; financial award applicants required to submit FAFSA. *Faculty research:* Nursing education, obesity prevention, workforce diversity. *Unit head:* Dr. Michael Lacourse, Dean, 858-309-3472, Fax: 858-309-3480, E-mail: mlacourse@nu.edu. *Application contact:* Dominick Giovanniello, Associate Regional Dean, 800-NAT-UNIV, Fax: 858-541-7792, E-mail: dgiovann@nu.edu. Web site: http://www.nu.edu/OurPrograms/SchoolOfHealthAndHumanServices.html.

New England College, Program in Community Mental Health Counseling, Henniker, NH 03242-3293. Offers human services (MS); mental health counseling (MS). Part-time and evening/weekend programs available. *Degree requirements:* For master's, internship.

Nova Southeastern University, Institute for the Study of Human Service, Health and Justice, Fort Lauderdale, FL 33314-7796. Offers child protection (MHS); criminal justice (MS, PhD); developmental disabilities (MS); gerontology (MA). Part-time programs available. Postbaccalaureate distance learning degree programs offered (no on-campus study). *Faculty:* 41 part-time/adjunct (7 women). *Students:* 65 full-time (47 women), 291 part-time (230 women); includes 250 minority (187 Black or African American, non-Hispanic/Latino; 2 American Indian or Alaska Native, non-Hispanic/Latino; 4 Asian, non-Hispanic/Latino; 51 Hispanic/Latino; 1 Native Hawaiian or other Pacific Islander, non-Hispanic/Latino; 5 Two or more races, non-Hispanic/Latino). Average age 33. 41 applicants, 73% accepted, 30 enrolled. In 2011, 65 master's awarded. *Degree requirements:* For master's, thesis optional. *Entrance requirements:* For master's, minimum GPA of 2.5, 3 letters of recommendation, 150-300 word personal statement. *Application deadline:* For fall admission, 8/4 for domestic and international students; for winter admission, 12/1 for domestic and international students; for spring admission, 4/15 for domestic students, 4/14 for international students. Applications are processed on a rolling basis. Application fee: $50. Electronic applications accepted. *Financial support:* Applicants required to submit FAFSA. *Unit head:* Dr. Tammy Kushner, Executive Associate Dean, 954-262-7001, Fax: 954-262-7005, E-mail: kushner@nova.edu. *Application contact:* Russell Garner, Program Coordinator, 954-262-7001, E-mail: cji@nova.edu. Web site: http://www.nova.edu/humanservices/.

Pontifical Catholic University of Puerto Rico, College of Graduate Studies in Behavioral Science and Community Affairs, Ponce, PR 00717-0777. Offers clinical psychology (PhD, Psy D); clinical social work (MSW); criminology (MA); industrial psychology (PhD); psychology (PhD); public administration (MSS); rehabilitation counseling (MA). Part-time and evening/weekend programs available. *Degree requirements:* For master's, thesis; for doctorate, comprehensive exam, thesis/dissertation. *Entrance requirements:* For master's, EXADEP, GRE General Test, 3 letters of recommendation, interview, minimum GPA of 2.75.

Post University, Program in Human Services, Waterbury, CT 06723-2540. Offers human services (MS); human services/clinical (MS); human services/management (MS). Part-time programs available. Postbaccalaureate distance learning degree programs offered.

Purdue University Calumet, Graduate Studies Office, School of Education, Program in Counseling, Hammond, IN 46323-2094. Offers human services (MS Ed); mental health counseling (MS Ed); school counseling (MS Ed). *Entrance requirements:* Additional exam requirements/recommendations for international students: Required—TOEFL.

Roberts Wesleyan College, Division of Social Work, Rochester, NY 14624-1997. Offers child and family practice (MSW); congregational and community practice (MSW); mental health practice (MSW). *Accreditation:* CSWE. *Entrance requirements:* For master's, minimum GPA of 2.75. *Faculty research:* Religion and social work, family studies, values and ethics.

Rosemont College, Schools of Graduate and Professional Studies, Counseling Psychology Program, Rosemont, PA 19010-1699. Offers human services (MA); school counseling (MA). Part-time and evening/weekend programs available. *Faculty:* 2 full-time (both women), 13 part-time/adjunct (6 women). *Students:* 44 full-time (37 women), 85 part-time (70 women); includes 44 minority (38 Black or African American, non-Hispanic/Latino; 4 Asian, non-Hispanic/Latino; 2 Hispanic/Latino), 1 international. Average age 34. 23 applicants, 96% accepted. In 2011, 36 master's awarded. *Degree requirements:* For master's, thesis or alternative, practicum. *Entrance requirements:* For master's, minimum undergraduate GPA of 3.0, 3 letters of recommendation. Additional exam requirements/recommendations for international students: Required—TOEFL. *Application deadline:* Applications are processed on a rolling basis. Application fee: $50. Electronic applications accepted. Application fee is waived when completed online. *Expenses:* Contact institution. *Financial support:* Institutionally sponsored loans and unspecified assistantships available. Financial award applicants required to submit FAFSA. *Faculty research:* Addictions counseling. *Unit head:* Dr. Leslie Smith, Director, 610-527-0200 Ext. 2302, Fax: 610-526-2964, E-mail: leslie.smith@rosemont.edu. *Application contact:* Meghan Mellinger, Graduate Admissions Counselor, 610-527-0200 Ext. 2596, Fax: 610-520-4399, E-mail: gpsadmissions@rosemont.edu. Web site: http://www.rosemont.edu/.

St. Joseph's College, New York, Graduate Programs, Program in Human Services Management and Leadership, Brooklyn, NY 11205-3688. Offers MS.

See Display on next page and Close-Up on page 1775.

St. Mary's University, Graduate School, Department of Counseling and Human Services, San Antonio, TX 78228-8507. Offers community counseling (MA); counseling (Sp C); counseling education and supervision (PhD); marriage and family relations (Certificate); marriage and family therapy (MA, PhD); mental health (MA); mental health and substance abuse counseling (Certificate); substance abuse (MA). *Accreditation:* AAMFT/COAMFTE (one or more programs are accredited); ACA (one or more programs are accredited). Postbaccalaureate distance learning degree programs offered (minimal on-campus study). *Degree requirements:* For master's, comprehensive exam, internship; for doctorate, comprehensive exam, thesis/dissertation, internship. *Entrance requirements:* For master's, GRE General Test, MAT; for doctorate, GRE General Test, recommendation from employers, admissions committee and department faculty. Additional exam requirements/recommendations for international students: Required—TOEFL (minimum score 550 paper-based; 213 computer-based; 80 iBT). Electronic applications accepted. *Expenses:* Contact institution.

Sojourner-Douglass College, Graduate Program, Baltimore, MD 21205-1814. Offers human services (MASS); public administration (MASS); urban education (reading) (MASS). Part-time and evening/weekend programs available. *Degree requirements:* For master's, comprehensive exam, written proposal oral defense. *Entrance requirements:* For master's, Graduate Examination.

South Carolina State University, School of Graduate Studies, Department of Human Services, Orangeburg, SC 29117-0001. Offers counselor education (M Ed); orientation and mobility (Graduate Certificate); rehabilitation counseling (MA). *Accreditation:* CORE. Part-time and evening/weekend programs available. *Faculty:* 9 full-time (6 women), 9 part-time/adjunct (7 women). *Students:* 149 full-time (124 women), 57 part-time (46 women); includes 190 minority (all Black or African American, non-Hispanic/Latino), 2 international. Average age 34. 114 applicants, 98% accepted, 92 enrolled. In 2011, 56 master's awarded. *Degree requirements:* For master's, comprehensive exam (for some programs), departmental qualifying exam, internship. *Entrance requirements:* For master's, GRE, MAT, minimum GPA of 2.7. *Application deadline:* For fall admission, 6/15 priority date for domestic students, 6/15 for international students; for spring admission, 11/1 for domestic and international students. Applications are processed on a rolling basis. Application fee: $25. Electronic applications accepted. *Expenses:* Tuition, state resident: full-time $8688; part-time $514 per credit hour. Tuition, nonresident: full-time $17,600; part-time $1009 per credit hour. *Required fees:* $570. *Financial support:* In 2011–12, 35 students received support, including 14 fellowships (averaging $5,730 per year); career-related internships or fieldwork, institutionally sponsored loans, and unspecified assistantships also available. Financial award application deadline: 6/1. *Faculty research:* Handicap, disability, rehabilitation evaluation, vocation. *Unit head:* Dr. Cassandra Sligh Conway, Chair, 803-536-7075, Fax: 803-533-3636, E-mail: csligh-dewalt@scsu.edu. *Application contact:* Annette Hazzard-Jones, Program Coordinator II, 803-536-8809, Fax: 803-536-8812, E-mail: zs_ahazzard@scsu.edu.

Southeastern University, Department of Behavioral and Social Sciences, Lakeland, FL 33801-6099. Offers human services (MA); professional counseling (MS); school counseling (MS). Evening/weekend programs available.

Springfield College, Graduate Programs, Program in Human Services, Springfield, MA 01109-3797. Offers human services (MS), including community counseling psychology, mental health counseling, organizational management and leadership. Part-time programs available. *Degree requirements:* For master's, comprehensive exam, thesis (for some programs), research project. *Entrance requirements:* For master's, GRE. Additional exam requirements/recommendations for international students: Required—TOEFL (minimum score 550 paper-based; 213 computer-based). Electronic applications accepted. *Expenses:* Contact institution.

Texas Southern University, College of Liberal Arts and Behavioral Sciences, Department of Human Services and Consumer Sciences, Houston, TX 77004-4584. Offers MS. Part-time and evening/weekend programs available. *Degree requirements:* For master's, comprehensive exam, thesis (for some programs). *Entrance requirements:* For master's, GRE General Test, minimum GPA of 2.5. Additional exam requirements/recommendations for international students: Required—TOEFL. Electronic applications accepted. *Faculty research:* Food radiation/food for space travel, adolescent parenting, gerontology/grandparenting.

Thomas University, Department of Human Services, Thomasville, GA 31792-7499. Offers community counseling (MSCC); rehabilitation counseling (MRC). *Accreditation:* CORE. Part-time programs available. *Entrance requirements:* For master's, resume, 3 academic/professional references. Additional exam requirements/recommendations for international students: Required—TOEFL (minimum score 600 paper-based; 250 computer-based). Electronic applications accepted.

Universidad del Turabo, Graduate Programs, School of Social Sciences and Humanities, Programs in Public Affairs, Program in Human Services Administration, Gurabo, PR 00778-3030. Offers MPA. *Students:* 18 full-time (16 women), 13 part-time (11 women); includes 27 minority (all Hispanic/Latino). Average age 32. 25 applicants, 84% accepted, 15 enrolled. In 2011, 13 master's awarded. *Entrance requirements:* For master's, GRE, EXADEP, interview. *Application deadline:* For fall admission, 8/5 for domestic students. Application fee: $25. *Unit head:* Dr. Marco A. Gil Dela Madrid, Dean, 787-743-7979. *Application contact:* Virginia Gonzalez, Admissions Officer, 787-746-3009.

Université de Montréal, Faculty of Arts and Sciences, Programs in Applied Human Sciences, Montréal, QC H3C 3J7, Canada. Offers PhD. *Degree requirements:* For doctorate, thesis/dissertation, general exam. Electronic applications accepted.

University of Baltimore, Graduate School, The Yale Gordon College of Liberal Arts, Program in Human Services Administration, Baltimore, MD 21201-5779. Offers MS. Part-time and evening/weekend programs available. *Entrance requirements:* For master's, interview. Additional exam requirements/recommendations for international students: Required—TOEFL (minimum score 550 paper-based; 213 computer-based). Electronic applications accepted.

University of Bridgeport, School of Arts and Sciences, Department of Counseling, Bridgeport, CT 06604. Offers clinical mental health counseling (MS); college student personnel (MS); community counseling (MS); human resource development (MS); human service (MS). Part-time and evening/weekend programs available. *Faculty:* 7 full-time (4 women), 13 part-time/adjunct (7 women). *Students:* 26 full-time (22 women), 98 part-time (73 women); includes 76 minority (52 Black or African American, non-Hispanic/Latino; 1 Asian, non-Hispanic/Latino; 18 Hispanic/Latino; 5 Two or more races, non-Hispanic/Latino), 2 international. Average age 36. 99 applicants, 47% accepted, 34 enrolled. In 2011, 23 master's awarded. *Degree requirements:* For master's, thesis, project. *Entrance requirements:* Additional exam requirements/recommendations for international students: Recommended—TOEFL (minimum score 550 paper-based; 213 computer-based; 80 iBT), IELTS (minimum score 6.5). *Application deadline:* For fall admission, 8/1 priority date for domestic students, 8/1 for international students; for spring admission, 12/1 priority date for domestic students, 12/1 for international students. Applications are processed on a rolling basis. Application fee: $50. Electronic applications accepted. *Expenses: Tuition:* Full-time $22,880; part-time $700 per credit. *Required fees:* $1870; $95 per semester. Tuition and fees vary according to course load and program. *Financial support:* In 2011–12, 27 students received support. Fellowships, research assistantships, teaching assistantships, career-related internships or fieldwork, Federal Work-Study, and institutionally sponsored loans available. Support available to part-time students. Financial award application deadline: 6/1; financial award applicants required to submit FAFSA. *Faculty research:* Corporate elder care programs. *Unit head:* Dr. Sara L. Connolly, Director, Division of Counseling and Human Resources, 203-576-4183, Fax: 203-576-4219, E-mail: sconnoll@bridgeport.edu. *Application contact:* Karissa Peckham, Dean of Admissions, 203-576-4552, Fax: 203-576-4941, E-mail: admit@bridgeport.edu.

Human Services

University of Central Missouri, The Graduate School, College of Education, Warrensburg, MO 64093. Offers career and technical education administration (MS); career and technical education industry training (MS); career and technical education leadership/teaching (MS); college student personnel administration (MS); counseling (MS); curriculum and instruction (Ed S); educational leadership (Ed D); educational technology (MS); elementary education/educational foundations and literacy (MSE); elementary school administration (MSE); elementary school principalship (Ed S); human services/learning resources (Ed S); human services/professional counseling (Ed S); human services/special education (Ed S); human services/technology and occupational education (Ed S); K-12 education/educational foundations and literacy (MSE); K-12 special education (MSE); library science and information services (MS); literacy education (MSE); secondary education/educational foundations & literacy (MSE); secondary school administration (MSE); secondary school principalship (Ed S); superintendency (Ed S); teaching (MAT). Ed D offered jointly with University of Missouri. Part-time programs available. Postbaccalaureate distance learning degree programs offered. *Entrance requirements:* Additional exam requirements/recommendations for international students: Required—TOEFL (minimum score 550 paper-based; 79 computer-based). Electronic applications accepted.

University of Colorado at Colorado Springs, College of Education, Colorado Springs, CO 80933-7150. Offers counseling and human services (MA); curriculum and instruction (MA); educational administration (MA); educational leadership (MA, PhD); special education (MA). *Accreditation:* ACA; NCATE. Part-time and evening/weekend programs available. Postbaccalaureate distance learning degree programs offered (minimal on-campus study). *Faculty:* 26 full-time (16 women), 9 part-time/adjunct (5 women). *Students:* 307 full-time (203 women), 115 part-time (92 women); includes 82 minority (24 Black or African American, non-Hispanic/Latino; 3 American Indian or Alaska Native, non-Hispanic/Latino; 12 Asian, non-Hispanic/Latino; 36 Hispanic/Latino; 1 Native Hawaiian or other Pacific Islander, non-Hispanic/Latino; 6 Two or more races, non-Hispanic/Latino), 1 international. Average age 36. 99 applicants, 86% accepted, 61 enrolled. In 2011, 165 master's, 6 doctorates awarded. *Degree requirements:* For master's, comprehensive exam, thesis or alternative, microcomputer proficiency; for doctorate, comprehensive exam, thesis/dissertation, research lab. *Entrance requirements:* For master's, GRE General Test. Additional exam requirements/recommendations for international students: Recommended—TOEFL. *Application deadline:* For fall admission, 2/28 priority date for domestic students, 2/28 for international students; for spring admission, 10/15 for domestic and international students. Applications are processed on a rolling basis. Application fee: $60 ($75 for international students). *Expenses:* Tuition, state resident: part-time $660 per credit hour. Tuition, nonresident: part-time $1133 per credit hour. Tuition and fees vary according to degree level, program and student level. *Financial support:* In 2011–12, 57 students received support. Career-related internships or fieldwork, Federal Work-Study, and scholarships/grants available. Support available to part-time students. Financial award application deadline: 3/1; financial award applicants required to submit FAFSA. *Faculty research:* Job training for special populations, materials development for classroom. *Total annual research expenditures:* $1.6 million. *Unit head:* Dr. Mary Snyder, Dean, 719-255-3701, Fax: 719-262-4133, E-mail: msnyder3@uccs.edu. *Application contact:* Juliane Field, Director, 719-255-4526, Fax: 719-255-4110, E-mail: jfield@uccs.edu. Web site: http://www.uccs.edu/coe.

University of Great Falls, Graduate Studies, Program in Organization Management, Great Falls, MT 59405. Offers human development (MSM); management (MSM). Part-time and evening/weekend programs available. Postbaccalaureate distance learning degree programs offered (minimal on-campus study). *Degree requirements:* For master's, thesis optional. *Entrance requirements:* For master's, GRE General Test or MAT, 3 letters of recommendation. Additional exam requirements/recommendations for international students: Required—TOEFL (minimum score 500 paper-based; 205 computer-based). Electronic applications accepted.

University of Illinois at Springfield, Graduate Programs, College of Education and Human Services, Program in Human Services, Springfield, IL 62703-5407. Offers alcoholism and substance abuse (MA); child and family services (MA); gerontology (MA); social services administration (MA). Part-time and evening/weekend programs available. Postbaccalaureate distance learning degree programs offered (no on-campus study). *Faculty:* 6 full-time (4 women), 2 part-time/adjunct (1 woman). *Students:* 16 full-time (15 women), 90 part-time (83 women); includes 32 minority (26 Black or African American, non-Hispanic/Latino; 1 American Indian or Alaska Native, non-Hispanic/Latino; 1 Asian, non-Hispanic/Latino; 3 Hispanic/Latino; 1 Two or more races, non-Hispanic/Latino). Average age 34. 55 applicants, 31% accepted, 11 enrolled. In 2011, 32 master's awarded. *Degree requirements:* For master's, internship; project or thesis. *Entrance requirements:* For master's, minimum undergraduate GPA of 3.0, 2 letters of recommendation, statement of intent. Additional exam requirements/recommendations for international students: Required—TOEFL (minimum score 500 paper-based; 176 computer-based; 61 iBT). Application fee: $50 ($60 for international students). Electronic applications accepted. *Expenses:* Tuition, state resident: full-time $6978; part-time $290.75 per credit hour. Tuition, nonresident: full-time $15,282; part-time $636.75 per credit hour. *Required fees:* $2106; $87.75 per credit hour. *Financial support:* In 2011–12, fellowships with full tuition reimbursements (averaging $8,550 per year), research assistantships with full tuition reimbursements (averaging $8,550 per year), teaching assistantships with full tuition reimbursements (averaging $8,550 per year) were awarded; career-related internships or fieldwork, Federal Work-Study, scholarships/grants, health care benefits, and unspecified assistantships also available. Support available to part-time students. Financial award application deadline: 11/15. *Unit head:* Dr. Carolyn Peck, Program Administrator, 217-206-7577, Fax: 217-206-6775, E-mail: peck.carolyn@uis.edu. *Application contact:* Dr. Lynn Pardie, Office of Graduate Studies, 800-252-8533, Fax: 217-206-7623, E-mail: lpard1@uis.edu. Web site: http://www.uis.edu/humanservices.

University of Maryland, Baltimore County, Graduate School, College of Arts, Humanities and Social Sciences, Department of Psychology, Program in Human Services Psychology, Baltimore, MD 21250. Offers MA, PhD. *Faculty:* 17 full-time (5 women), 11 part-time/adjunct (4 women). *Students:* 80 full-time (65 women), 16 part-time (9 women); includes 23 minority (11 Black or African American, non-Hispanic/Latino; 4 Asian, non-Hispanic/Latino; 6 Hispanic/Latino; 2 Native Hawaiian or other Pacific Islander, non-Hispanic/Latino). Average age 25. 142 applicants, 32% accepted, 12 enrolled. In 2011, 24 master's, 8 doctorates awarded. Terminal master's awarded for partial completion of doctoral program. *Degree requirements:* For master's, thesis; for doctorate, comprehensive exam, thesis/dissertation. *Entrance requirements:* For master's, GRE General Test, minimum GPA of 3.0; for doctorate, GRE General Test, GRE Subject Test, minimum GPA of 3.0. Additional exam requirements/recommendations for international students: Required—TOEFL. *Application deadline:* For fall admission, 12/1 for domestic and international students. Application fee: $70. Electronic applications accepted. *Financial support:* In 2011–12, 3 students received support, including 1 fellowship with full and partial tuition reimbursement available (averaging $26,000 per year), 22 research assistantships with full and partial tuition reimbursements available (averaging $14,857 per year), 20 teaching assistantships with full and partial tuition reimbursements available (averaging $14,857 per year); career-related internships or fieldwork, Federal Work-Study, scholarships/grants, health care benefits, tuition waivers, and unspecified assistantships also available. Financial award application deadline: 3/1; financial award applicants required to submit FAFSA. *Faculty research:* Addictive behaviors, cardiovascular and cerebrovascular disease, family violence, pediatric psychology, community prevention. *Total annual research expenditures:* $1.5 million. *Unit head:* Dr. Carlo C. DiClememte, Director, 410-455-2567, Fax: 410-455-1055, E-mail: diclemen@umbc.edu. *Application contact:* Nicole Mooney, Program Management Specialist, 410-455-2567, Fax: 410-455-1055, E-mail: psycdept@umbc.edu.

University of Massachusetts Boston, Office of Graduate Studies, College of Public and Community Service, Program in Human Services, Boston, MA 02125-3393. Offers MS. Part-time and evening/weekend programs available. *Degree requirements:* For master's, practicum, final project. *Entrance requirements:* For master's, MAT, GRE, minimum GPA of 2.75. *Faculty research:* Institutional and policy context of human services, ethics and social policy, public law and human services, social welfare, politics and human services.

University of Northern Iowa, Graduate College, College of Education, School of Health, Physical Education, and Leisure Services, Program in Leisure, Youth, and Human Services, Cedar Falls, IA 50614. Offers leisure services (Ed D); youth and human services (MA). *Students:* 32 full-time (19 women), 19 part-time (11 women); includes 12 minority (8 Black or African American, non-Hispanic/Latino; 3 Asian, non-Hispanic/Latino; 1 Hispanic/Latino), 4 international. 32 applicants, 75% accepted, 11 enrolled. In 2011, 23 master's, 4 doctorates awarded. *Degree requirements:* For master's, comprehensive exam, thesis or alternative; for doctorate, thesis/dissertation. *Entrance requirements:* For master's, minimum GPA of 3.0; for doctorate, GRE, minimum GPA of 3.5. Additional exam requirements/recommendations for international students: Required—TOEFL (minimum score 500 paper-based; 180 computer-based; 61 iBT). *Application deadline:* Applications are processed on a rolling basis. Application fee: $50 ($70 for international students). Electronic applications accepted. *Expenses:* Tuition, state resident: full-time $7476. Tuition, nonresident: full-time $16,410. *Required fees:* $942. *Financial support:* Career-related internships or fieldwork, Federal Work-Study, institutionally sponsored loans, tuition waivers (full), and unspecified assistantships available. Financial award application deadline: 2/1. *Unit head:* Dr. Samuel Lankford, Interim Director, 319-273-6840, Fax: 319-273-5958, E-mail: sam.lankford@uni.edu. *Application contact:* Laurie S. Russell, Record Analyst, 319-273-2623, Fax: 319-273-2885, E-mail: laurie.russell@uni.edu. Web site: http://www.uni.edu/coe/departments/school-health-physical-education-leisure-services/leisure-youth-and-human-services-0.

University of Oklahoma, College of Arts and Sciences, Department of Human Relations, Norman, OK 73019. Offers human relations (MHR), including affirmative action, chemical addictions counseling, family relations, general, human resources, juvenile justice; human relations licensure (Graduate Certificate). Part-time and evening/weekend programs available. Postbaccalaureate distance learning degree programs offered (minimal on-campus study). *Faculty:* 27 full-time (18 women), 2 part-time/adjunct (1 woman). *Students:* 327 full-time (207 women), 537 part-time (328 women); includes 343 minority (203 Black or African American, non-Hispanic/Latino; 42 American Indian or Alaska Native, non-Hispanic/Latino; 22 Asian, non-Hispanic/Latino; 45 Hispanic/Latino; 31 Two or more races, non-Hispanic/Latino), 15 international. Average age 34. 317 applicants, 90% accepted, 201 enrolled. In 2011, 310 degrees awarded. *Degree requirements:* For master's, thesis optional. *Entrance requirements:* For master's, minimum GPA of 3.0 in last 60 hours of undergraduate course work, resume, 3 letters of reference. Additional exam requirements/recommendations for international students: Required—TOEFL (minimum score 550 paper-based; 79 iBT). *Application deadline:* For fall admission, 4/1 priority date for domestic students, 3/1 for international students; for spring admission, 11/1 for domestic students, 9/1 for international students. Applications are processed on a rolling basis. Application fee: $40 ($90 for international students). Electronic applications accepted. *Expenses:* Tuition, state resident: full-time $4087; part-time $170.30 per credit hour. Tuition, nonresident: full-time $14,875; part-time $619.80 per credit hour. *Required fees:* $2659; $100.25 per credit hour. Tuition and fees vary according to course load and degree level. *Financial support:* In 2011–12, 358 students received support, including 12 research assistantships with partial tuition reimbursements available (averaging $11,021 per year), 5 teaching assistantships (averaging $11,124 per year); career-related internships or fieldwork, scholarships/grants, and unspecified assistantships also available. Financial award applicants required to submit FAFSA. *Faculty research:* Non-profit organizations, high risk youth, trauma, women's studies, impact of war on women and children. *Total annual research expenditures:* $62,927. *Unit head:* Dr. Susan Marcus-Mendoza, Chair, 405-325-1756, Fax: 405-325-4402, E-mail: smmendoza@ou.edu. *Application contact:* Lawana Miller, Admissions Coordinator, 405-325-1756, Fax: 405-325-4402, E-mail: lmiller@ou.edu. Web site: http://www.ou.edu/cas/hr.

University of Phoenix–Minneapolis/St. Louis Park Campus, College of Human Services, St. Louis Park, MN 55426. Offers community counseling (MSC).

University of Phoenix–Puerto Rico Campus, College of Human Services, Guaynabo, PR 00968. Offers marriage and family counseling (MSC); mental health counseling (MSC). Evening/weekend programs available. *Degree requirements:* For master's, thesis (for some programs). *Entrance requirements:* For master's, Counselor Preparation Comprehensive Examination, minimum undergraduate GPA of 2.5, 3 years work experience. Additional exam requirements/recommendations for international students: Required—TOEFL (minimum score 550 paper-based; 213 computer-based; 79 iBT). Electronic applications accepted.

Upper Iowa University, Online Master's Programs, Fayette, IA 52142-1857. Offers accounting (MBA); corporate financial management (MBA); global business (MBA); health and human services (MPA); higher education administration (MHEA); homeland security (MPA); human resources management (MBA); justice administration (MPA); organizational development (MBA); public personnel management (MPA); quality management (MBA). MBA also available at Madison, WI campus. Part-time programs available. Postbaccalaureate distance learning degree programs offered (no on-campus study). *Degree requirements:* For master's, research project. *Entrance requirements:* For master's, GMAT, GRE, or minimum GPA of 2.7 during last 60 hours. Additional exam requirements/recommendations for international students: Required—TOEFL (minimum score 570 paper-based; 230 computer-based). Electronic applications accepted. *Faculty research:* Total quality management, CQI, teams, organization culture and climate, management.

Walden University, Graduate Programs, School of Counseling and Social Service, Minneapolis, MN 55401. Offers career counseling (MS); counselor education and supervision (PhD), including consultation, counseling and social change, forensic mental health counseling, general program, nonprofit management and leadership, trauma and crisis; human services (PhD), including clinical social work, criminal justice, disaster, crisis and intervention, family studies and intervention strategies, general program, human services administration, public health, social policy analysis and planning; marriage, couple, and family counseling (MS), including forensic counseling, trauma and crisis counseling; mental health counseling (MS), including forensic counseling, trauma and crisis counseling. Part-time and evening/weekend programs available. Postbaccalaureate distance learning degree programs offered (minimal on-campus study). *Faculty:* 26 full-time (19 women), 252 part-time/adjunct (178 women). *Students:* 3,089 full-time (2,614 women), 1,044 part-time (907 women); includes 2,109 minority (1,718 Black or African American, non-Hispanic/Latino; 31 American Indian or Alaska Native, non-Hispanic/Latino; 43 Asian, non-Hispanic/Latino; 236 Hispanic/Latino; 2 Native Hawaiian or other Pacific Islander, non-Hispanic/Latino; 79 Two or more races, non-Hispanic/Latino), 55 international. Average age 39. In 2011, 180 master's, 15 doctorates awarded. *Degree requirements:* For master's, residency (for some programs); for doctorate, thesis/dissertation, residency. *Entrance requirements:* For master's, bachelor's degree or equivalent in related field, minimum GPA of 2.5; for doctorate, master's degree or equivalent in related field; minimum GPA of 3.0; official transcripts; three years' related professional/academic experience (preferred); access to computer and Internet. Additional exam requirements/recommendations for international students: Required—TOEFL (minimum score 550 paper-based; 213 computer-based), IELTS (minimum score 6.5), or Michigan English Language Assessment Battery (minimum score 82). *Application deadline:* Applications are processed on a rolling basis. Application fee: $50. Electronic applications accepted. *Financial support:* Federal Work-Study, scholarships/grants, unspecified assistantships, and family tuition reduction, active duty/veteran tuition reduction, group tuition reduction, interest-free payment plans, employee tuition reduction available. Support available to part-time students. Financial award applicants required to submit FAFSA. *Unit head:* Dr. Savitri Dixon-Saxon, Associate Dean, 800-925-3368. *Application contact:* Jennifer Hall, Vice President of Enrollment Management, 866-4-WALDEN, E-mail: info@waldenu.edu. Web site: http://www.waldenu.edu/Colleges-and-Schools/College-of-Social-and-Behavioral-Sciences/School-of-Counseling-and-Social-Service.htm.

West Virginia University, Eberly College of Arts and Sciences, School of Applied Social Sciences, Division of Social Work, Morgantown, WV 26506. Offers aging and health care (MSW); children and families (MSW); community mental health (MSW); community organization and social administration (MSW); direct (clinical) social work practice (MSW). *Accreditation:* CSWE. Part-time programs available. *Degree requirements:* For master's, fieldwork. *Entrance requirements:* For master's, GRE, minimum GPA of 2.75, 2 letters of reference. Additional exam requirements/recommendations for international students: Required—TOEFL. *Faculty research:* Rural and small town social work practice, gerontology, health and mental health, welfare reform, child welfare.

Wichita State University, Graduate School, Fairmount College of Liberal Arts and Sciences, School of Community Affairs, Wichita, KS 67260. Offers criminal justice (MA). Part-time programs available. *Expenses:* Tuition, state resident: full-time $4746; part-time $263.65 per credit. Tuition, nonresident: full-time $11,669; part-time $648.30 per credit. *Unit head:* Dr. Michael Birzer, Director, 316-978-7200, Fax: 316-978-3626, E-mail: michael.birzer@wichita.edu. *Application contact:* Carrie C. Henderson, Admissions Coordinator, 316-978-3095, Fax: 316-978-3253, E-mail: carrie.henderson@wichita.edu.

Wilmington University, College of Social and Behavioral Sciences, New Castle, DE 19720-6491. Offers administration of human services (MS); administration of justice (MS); clinical mental health counseling (MS); homeland security (MS). *Accreditation:* ACA. Part-time and evening/weekend programs available. *Faculty:* 3 full-time (1 woman). *Students:* 79 full-time (53 women), 290 part-time (241 women). Average age 35. *Entrance requirements:* Additional exam requirements/recommendations for international students: Required—TOEFL (minimum score 500 paper-based; 173 computer-based). *Application deadline:* Applications are processed on a rolling basis. Application fee: $35. Electronic applications accepted. *Expenses: Tuition:* Part-time $534 per credit hour. *Required fees:* $25 per term. *Financial support:* Applicants required to submit FAFSA. *Unit head:* Dr. Christian A. Trowbridge, Dean, 302-295-1151, Fax: 302-328-5164. *Application contact:* Chris Ferguson, Director of Admissions, 302-356-4636 Ext. 256, Fax: 302-328-5164, E-mail: inquire@wilmcoll.edu. Web site: http://www.wilmu.edu/behavioralscience/.

Youngstown State University, Graduate School, Bitonte College of Health and Human Services, Department of Health Professions, Youngstown, OH 44555-0001. Offers health and human services (MHHS); public health (MPH). *Accreditation:* NAACLS. Part-time and evening/weekend programs available. *Degree requirements:* For master's, thesis optional. *Entrance requirements:* For master's, GRE General Test, minimum GPA of 3.0. Additional exam requirements/recommendations for international students: Required—TOEFL. *Faculty research:* Drug prevention, multiskilling in health care, organizational behavior, health care management, health behaviors, research management.

Social Work

Abilene Christian University, Graduate School, College of Education and Human Services, School of Social Work, Abilene, TX 79699-9100. Offers MSSW. *Accreditation:* CSWE. Part-time programs available. *Faculty:* 6 part-time/adjunct (2 women). *Students:* 27 full-time (24 women), 4 part-time (all women); includes 9 minority (3 Black or African American, non-Hispanic/Latino; 6 Hispanic/Latino), 1 international. 29 applicants, 59% accepted, 17 enrolled. In 2011, 19 master's awarded. *Degree requirements:* For master's, thesis. *Entrance requirements:* For master's, GRE if undergraduate GPA less than 3.0. Additional exam requirements/recommendations for international students: Required—TOEFL (minimum score 550 paper-based; 213 computer-based; 80 iBT), IELTS (minimum score 6). *Application deadline:* For fall admission, 2/16 priority date for domestic students; for spring admission, 11/1 for domestic students. Applications are processed on a rolling basis. Application fee: $50. Electronic applications accepted. *Expenses: Tuition:* Full-time $14,168; part-time $787 per hour. *Required fees:* $82 per hour. $10 per term. *Financial support:* In 2011–12, 16 students received support, including 2 research assistantships with partial tuition reimbursements available (averaging $5,800 per year); career-related internships or fieldwork, Federal Work-Study, and tuition waivers (partial) also available. Financial award application deadline: 4/1; financial award applicants required to submit FAFSA. *Unit head:* Dr. Wayne Paris, MSSW Graduate Director, 325-674-2072, Fax: 325-674-6525, E-mail: socialwork@acu.edu. *Application contact:* David Pittman, Graduate Admissions Counselor, 325-674-2656, Fax: 325-674-6717, E-mail: gradinfo@acu.edu. Web site: http://www.acu.edu/socialwork.

Adelphi University, School of Social Work, Garden City, NY 11530-0701. Offers social welfare (DSW); social work (MSW, PhD). *Accreditation:* CSWE (one or more programs are accredited). Part-time and evening/weekend programs available. *Faculty:* 29 full-time (20 women), 103 part-time/adjunct (77 women). *Students:* 506 full-time (451 women), 355 part-time (306 women); includes 403 minority (259 Black or African American, non-Hispanic/Latino; 1 American Indian or Alaska Native, non-Hispanic/Latino; 15 Asian, non-Hispanic/Latino; 117 Hispanic/Latino; 2 Native Hawaiian or other Pacific Islander, non-Hispanic/Latino; 9 Two or more races, non-Hispanic/Latino), 5 international. Average age 34. 658 applicants, 73% accepted, 322 enrolled. In 2011, 335 master's, 7 doctorates awarded. *Degree requirements:* For master's, field internships; for doctorate, thesis/dissertation. *Entrance requirements:* For master's, minimum undergraduate GPA of 3.0, paid or volunteer work experience, 3 letters of recommendation, interview; for doctorate, GRE, MSW with minimum GPA of 3.3, 3 years post-MSW work experience, 3 letters of reference, 3 examples of professional writing. Additional exam requirements/recommendations for international students: Required—TOEFL (minimum score 550 paper-based; 213 computer-based; 80 iBT). *Application deadline:* For fall admission, 4/1 for international students; for spring admission, 12/1 for domestic students, 11/1 for international students. Application fee: $50. Electronic applications accepted. *Expenses: Tuition:* Full-time $29,600; part-time $930 per credit. *Required fees:* $1100. *Financial support:* In 2011–12, 27 research assistantships (averaging $5,446 per year) were awarded; career-related internships or fieldwork, Federal Work-Study, institutionally sponsored loans, scholarships/grants, traineeships, tuition waivers (full and partial), and unspecified assistantships also available. Financial award application deadline: 2/15; financial award applicants required to submit FAFSA. *Faculty research:* Services for rape victims, immigrant research methods, remarriage and step families, social health indicators. *Unit head:* Dr. Andrew Safyer, Dean, 516-877-4300, E-mail: asafyer@adelphi.edu. *Application contact:* Christine Murphy, Director of Admissions, 516-877-3050, Fax: 516-877-3039, E-mail: graduateadmissions@adelphi.edu. Web site: http://socialwork.adelphi.edu/.

See Display on next page and Close-Up on page 1771.

Alabama Agricultural and Mechanical University, School of Graduate Studies, School of Arts and Sciences, Department of Social Work, Huntsville, AL 35811. Offers MSW. *Accreditation:* CSWE. *Degree requirements:* For master's, thesis. *Entrance requirements:* For master's, GRE General Test, portfolio. Additional exam requirements/recommendations for international students: Required—TOEFL (minimum score 500 paper-based; 173 computer-based; 61 iBT). Electronic applications accepted.

Albany State University, College of Arts and Humanities, Albany, GA 31705-2717. Offers English education (M Ed); public administration (MPA), including community and economic development administration, criminal justice administration, general administration, health administration and policy, human resources management, public policy, water resources management; social work (MSW). Part-time programs available. *Faculty:* 13 full-time (6 women). *Students:* 47 full-time (38 women), 38 part-time (22 women); includes 77 minority (all Black or African American, non-Hispanic/Latino), 1 international. Average age 35. 43 applicants, 70% accepted, 23 enrolled. In 2011, 20 master's awarded. *Degree requirements:* For master's, comprehensive exam, professional portfolio (for MPA), internship, capstone report. *Entrance requirements:* For master's, GRE, MAT, minimum GPA of 3.0, official transcript, pre-medical record/certificate of immunization, letters of reference. *Application deadline:* For fall admission, 6/1 for domestic students, 5/1 for international students; for spring admission, 11/1 for domestic students, 10/1 for international students. Applications are processed on a rolling basis. Application fee: $20. Electronic applications accepted. *Expenses:* Tuition, state resident: full-time $3204; part-time $178 per credit hour. Tuition, nonresident: full-time $12,816; part-time $712 per credit hour. *Required fees:* $379 per semester. *Financial support:* Application deadline: 4/15; applicants required to submit FAFSA. *Faculty research:* HIV prevention for minority students . *Total annual research expenditures:* $2,000. *Unit head:* Dr. Leroy Bynum, Dean, 229-430-1877, Fax: 229-430-4296, E-mail: leroy.bynum@asurams.edu. *Application contact:* Jeffrey Pierce, II, Graduate Admissions Counselor, 229-430-4646, Fax: 229-430-4105, E-mail: jeffrey.pierce@asurams.edu. Web site: http://asu-sacs.asurams.edu/ASUCatalog/Graduate/index.html.

American Jewish University, Graduate School of Nonprofit Management, Program in Jewish Communal Studies, Bel Air, CA 90077-1599. Offers MAJCS. *Degree requirements:* For master's, thesis. *Entrance requirements:* For master's, GMAT or GRE General Test, interview.

Andrews University, School of Graduate Studies, College of Arts and Sciences, Department of Social Work, Berrien Springs, MI 49104. Offers MSW. *Accreditation:* CSWE. *Students:* 31 full-time (22 women), 5 part-time (all women); includes 22 minority (13 Black or African American, non-Hispanic/Latino; 1 American Indian or Alaska Native, non-Hispanic/Latino; 2 Asian, non-Hispanic/Latino; 5 Hispanic/Latino; 1 Two or more races, non-Hispanic/Latino), 2 international. Average age 33. 72 applicants, 61% accepted, 20 enrolled. In 2011, 13 master's awarded. *Entrance requirements:* For master's, GRE. Additional exam requirements/recommendations for international students: Required—TOEFL (minimum score 550 paper-based). *Application deadline:* Applications are processed on a rolling basis. Application fee: $40. *Unit head:* Dr. Curtis VanderWaal, Chair, 269-471-6196. *Application contact:* Carolyn Hurst, Supervisor of Graduate Admission, 800-253-2874, Fax: 269-471-6321, E-mail: graduate@andrews.edu.

Appalachian State University, Cratis D. Williams Graduate School, Department of Social Work, Boone, NC 28608. Offers MSW. *Accreditation:* CSWE. Part-time and evening/weekend programs available. Postbaccalaureate distance learning degree programs offered (no on-campus study). *Faculty:* 8 full-time (7 women), 3 part-time/adjunct (2 women). *Students:* 31 full-time (29 women), 20 part-time (19 women); includes 1 minority (Black or African American, non-Hispanic/Latino). 84 applicants, 63% accepted, 17 enrolled. In 2011, 11 master's awarded. *Degree requirements:* For master's, comprehensive exam. *Entrance requirements:* For master's, GRE General Test, 3 letters of recommendation. Additional exam requirements/recommendations for international students: Required—TOEFL (minimum score 550 paper-based; 230 computer-based; 79 iBT), IELTS (minimum score 6.5). *Application deadline:* For fall admission, 3/1 for domestic students, 2/1 for international students; for spring admission, 7/1 for international students. Applications are processed on a rolling basis. Application fee: $55. Electronic applications accepted. *Expenses:* Tuition, state resident: full-time $4040; part-time $180 per semester hour. Tuition, nonresident: full-time $15,900; part-time $760 per semester hour. *Required fees:* $2500; $20 per semester hour. Tuition and fees vary according to campus/location. *Financial support:* In 2011–12, 6 research assistantships (averaging $8,000 per year) were awarded; career-related internships or fieldwork, Federal Work-Study, scholarships/grants, and unspecified assistantships also available. Financial award application deadline: 4/1; financial award applicants required to submit FAFSA. *Faculty research:* Community and organizational practice, individual and family. *Unit head:* Dr. Gail Leedy, Chairperson, 800-355-4084 Ext. 2299, E-mail: leedyg@appstate.edu. Web site: http://www.socialwork.appstate.edu/.

Arizona State University, College of Public Programs, School of Social Work, Phoenix, AZ 85004-0689. Offers assessment of integrative health modalities (Graduate Certificate); gerontology and geriatric care (Graduate Certificate); Latino cultural competency (Graduate Certificate); social work (PhD); social work (advanced direct practice) (MSW); social work (planning, administration and community practice) (MSW); trauma and bereavement (Graduate Certificate); MPA/MSW. *Accreditation:* CSWE (one or more programs are accredited). Part-time programs available. Terminal master's awarded for partial completion of doctoral program. *Degree requirements:* For master's, thesis or alternative, capstone project, interactive Program of Study (iPOS) submitted before completing 50 percent of required credit hours; for doctorate, comprehensive exam, thesis/dissertation, interactive Program of Study (iPOS) submitted before completing 50 percent of required credit hours. *Entrance requirements:* For master's, GRE or MAT, minimum GPA of 3.2 or equivalent in last 2 years of work leading to bachelor's degree; for doctorate, GRE, minimum GPA of 3.0 or equivalent in last 2 years of work leading to bachelor's degree, 3 letters of recommendation, resume, samples of professional writing, personal statement. Additional exam requirements/recommendations for international students: Required—TOEFL, IELTS, or Pearson Test of English. Electronic applications accepted. *Expenses:* Contact institution.

Arkansas State University, Graduate School, College of Nursing and Health Professions, Department of Social Work, Jonesboro, State University, AR 72467. Offers addiction studies (Certificate); social work (MSW). Part-time programs available. *Faculty:* 7 full-time (5 women). *Students:* 39 full-time (28 women), 42 part-time (37 women); includes 16 minority (15 Black or African American, non-Hispanic/Latino; 1 Hispanic/Latino). Average age 35. 66 applicants, 70% accepted, 44 enrolled. In 2011, 45 master's awarded. *Degree requirements:* For master's, comprehensive exam, thesis (for some programs). *Entrance requirements:* For master's, GRE or MAT, appropriate bachelor's degree, letters of reference, personal statement, resume, official transcript, immunization records. Additional exam requirements/recommendations for international students: Required—TOEFL (minimum score 550 paper-based; 213 computer-based; 79 iBT), IELTS (minimum score 6), Pearson Test of English Academic (minimum score 56). *Application deadline:* Applications are processed on a rolling basis. Application fee: $30 ($40 for international students). Electronic applications accepted. *Expenses:* Contact institution. *Financial support:* In 2011–12, 3 students received support. Career-related internships or fieldwork, scholarships/grants, and unspecified assistantships available. Financial award application deadline: 7/1; financial award applicants required to submit FAFSA. *Unit head:* Dr. Loretta Brewer, Interim Chair, 870-972-3984, Fax: 870-972-3987, E-mail: lbrewer@astate.edu. *Application contact:* Dr. Andrew Sustich, Dean of the Graduate School, 870-972-3029, Fax: 870-972-3857, E-mail: sustich@astate.edu. Web site: http://www.astate.edu/a/conhp/socialwork/index.dot.

Asbury University, School of Graduate and Professional Studies, Master of Social Work Program, Wilmore, KY 40390-1198. Offers child and family services (MSW). *Accreditation:* CSWE. *Degree requirements:* For master's, comprehensive exam, 954 praticum hours completed in agency. *Entrance requirements:* For master's, prerequisite courses in psychology, sociology, and statistics. Additional exam requirements/recommendations for international students: Required—TOEFL. Electronic applications accepted. *Expenses:* Contact institution. *Faculty research:* Integration of faith and practice, survivors of family violence, program evaluation, cross-cultural counseling.

Assumption College, Graduate Studies, School Counseling Program, Worcester, MA 01609-1296. Offers school counseling (MA, CAGS); social worker/adjustment counselor (CAGS). Part-time and evening/weekend programs available. *Faculty:* 3 full-time (1 woman), 7 part-time/adjunct (4 women). *Students:* 59 full-time (49 women), 22 part-time (20 women); includes 6 minority (2 Black or African American, non-Hispanic/Latino; 3 Hispanic/Latino; 1 Two or more races, non-Hispanic/Latino). Average age 28. 76 applicants, 66% accepted, 38 enrolled. In 2011, 26 master's, 5 other advanced degrees awarded. *Degree requirements:* For master's, comprehensive exam, internship, practicum; for CAGS, comprehensive exam, practicum. *Entrance requirements:* For master's, 3 letters of recommendation, resume, interview, essay; for CAGS, 3 letters of recommendation, resume, essay, interview. Additional exam requirements/recommendations for international students: Required—TOEFL (minimum score 540 paper-based; 200 computer-based; 76 iBT), IELTS (minimum score 6). *Application deadline:* For winter admission, 2/1 for domestic and international students. Application fee: $30. Electronic applications accepted. *Expenses: Tuition:* Full-time $9414; part-time $523 per credit. *Required fees:* $20 per term. Full-time tuition and fees vary according to course load and program. *Financial support:* In 2011–12, 2 students received support. Tuition waivers (partial) and unspecified assistantships available. Financial award application deadline: 5/1; financial award applicants required to submit FAFSA. *Faculty research:* Low dose stress reduction interventions for elementary school teachers. *Unit head:* Dr. Mary Ann Mariani, Director, 508-767-7087, Fax: 508-767-7263, E-mail: mmariani@assumption.edu. *Application contact:* Laura Lawrence, Graduate Programs Operations Manager, 508-767-7387, Fax: 508-767-7030, E-mail: graduate@assumption.edu. Web site: http://graduate.assumption.edu/school-counseling/ma-school-counseling.

Augsburg College, Program in Social Work, Minneapolis, MN 55454-1351. Offers MSW. *Accreditation:* CSWE. Part-time and evening/weekend programs available. *Degree requirements:* For master's, thesis optional. *Entrance requirements:* For master's, previous course work in human biology and statistics.

Aurora University, College of Professional Studies, School of Social Work, Aurora, IL 60506-4892. Offers MSW, DSW. *Accreditation:* CSWE. Part-time and evening/weekend programs available. *Degree requirements:* For master's, thesis optional; for doctorate, comprehensive exam, thesis/dissertation. *Entrance requirements:* For master's, minimum GPA of 3.0; for doctorate, GRE, MSW from CSWE-accredited school; minimum GPA of 3.0; at least 3 years of post-MSW social work experience; 3 letters of recommendation; writing sample in the area of clinical social work; personal interview. Additional exam requirements/recommendations for international students: Required—TOEFL (minimum score 550 paper-based; 213 computer-based). Electronic applications accepted. *Expenses:* Contact institution.

Austin Peay State University, College of Graduate Studies, College of Behavioral and Health Sciences, Department of Social Work, Clarksville, TN 37044. Offers MSW. Part-time and evening/weekend programs available. *Faculty:* 3 full-time (1 woman). *Students:* 22 full-time (21 women), 11 part-time (all women); includes 13 minority (7 Black or African American, non-Hispanic/Latino; 1 Asian, non-Hispanic/Latino; 1 Hispanic/Latino; 4 Two or more races, non-Hispanic/Latino). Average age 33. 28 applicants, 86% accepted, 21 enrolled. In 2011, 8 master's awarded. *Degree requirements:* For master's, internship of 400-500 hours. *Entrance requirements:* For master's, GRE General Test, letters of recommendation. Additional exam requirements/recommendations for international students: Required—TOEFL (minimum score 500 paper-based; 173 computer-based). *Application deadline:* For fall admission, 8/1 priority date for domestic students. Application fee: $25. *Expenses:* Tuition, state resident: part-time $350 per credit hour. Tuition, nonresident: full-time $20,644; part-time $971 per credit hour. *Required fees:* $1224; $61.20 per credit hour. *Financial support:* In 2011–12, research assistantships (averaging $5,184 per year) were awarded; career-related internships or fieldwork, Federal Work-Study, institutionally sponsored loans, scholarships/grants, and unspecified assistantships also available. Support available to part-time students. Financial award application deadline: 3/1; financial award applicants required to submit FAFSA. *Unit head:* Mary Fran Davis, Chair, 931-221-7730, Fax: 931-221-6440, E-mail: davism@apsu.edu. *Application contact:* Kendra Bryant, Graduate Admissions, 800-844-2778, Fax: 931-221-6188, E-mail: admissionsweb@apsu.edu. Web site: http://www.apsu.edu/socialwork/.

Azusa Pacific University, School of Behavioral and Applied Sciences, Department of Social Work, Azusa, CA 91702-7000. Offers MSW. *Accreditation:* CSWE.

Barry University, School of Social Work, Doctoral Program in Social Work, Miami Shores, FL 33161-6695. Offers PhD. Part-time and evening/weekend programs available. *Degree requirements:* For doctorate, thesis/dissertation. *Entrance requirements:* For doctorate, GRE, MSW from an accredited school of social work, 2 years of professional experience. Electronic applications accepted. *Faculty research:* Family and children services, homelessness, gerontology, school social work.

Barry University, School of Social Work, Master's Program in Social Work, Miami Shores, FL 33161-6695. Offers MSW. *Accreditation:* CSWE. Part-time and evening/weekend programs available. *Degree requirements:* For master's, fieldwork. *Entrance requirements:* For master's, minimum GPA of 3.0, minimum of 30 liberal arts credits. Additional exam requirements/recommendations for international students: Required—TOEFL (minimum score 550 paper-based; 173 computer-based). Electronic applications accepted. *Faculty research:* Family and children services, homelessness, gerontology, school social work.

Baylor University, School of Social Work, Waco, TX 76798-7320. Offers MSW, M Div/MSW, MTS/MSW. *Accreditation:* CSWE. Part-time programs available. *Faculty:* 11 full-time (5 women), 13 part-time/adjunct (7 women). *Students:* 79 full-time (70 women), 4 part-time (3 women); includes 28 minority (15 Black or African American, non-Hispanic/Latino; 1 American Indian or Alaska Native, non-Hispanic/Latino; 3 Asian, non-Hispanic/Latino; 7 Hispanic/Latino; 2 Two or more races, non-Hispanic/Latino), 8 international. Average age 27. 190 applicants, 72% accepted. In 2011, 60 master's awarded. *Degree requirements:* For master's, research project. *Entrance requirements:* For master's, writing sample. Additional exam requirements/recommendations for international students: Required—TOEFL (minimum score 550 paper-based; 213 computer-based; 80 iBT) or IELTS (minimum score 6.5). *Application deadline:* For spring admission, 3/15 for domestic and international students. Applications are processed on a rolling basis. Application fee: $45. Electronic applications accepted. *Financial support:* In 2011–12, 12 research assistantships with tuition reimbursements (averaging $6,800 per year) were awarded; career-related internships or fieldwork, Federal Work-Study, institutionally sponsored loans, scholarships/grants, traineeships, tuition waivers (full and partial), and unspecified assistantships also available. Support available to part-time students. Financial award application deadline: 6/1; financial award applicants required to submit FAFSA. *Faculty research:* Healthy marriage, family literacy, Alzheimer's and grief, congregational community service, clergy sexual abuse, older volunteers. *Total annual research expenditures:* $533,412. *Unit head:* Dr. Dennis Myers, Associate Dean for Graduate Studies, 254-710-6404, E-mail: dennis_myers@baylor.edu. *Application contact:* Tracey Kelley, Director of Recruitment and Career Services, 254-710-4479, Fax: 254-710-6455, E-mail: tracey_kelley@baylor.edu. Web site: http://www.baylor.edu/social_work/?_buref=661-48570.

Boise State University, Graduate College, College of Social Sciences and Public Affairs, School of Social Work, Boise, ID 83725-0399. Offers MSW. *Accreditation:* CSWE. Part-time programs available. *Entrance requirements:* For master's, GRE General Test, minimum GPA of 3.0. Electronic applications accepted.

Boston College, Graduate School of Social Work, Chestnut Hill, MA 02467-3800. Offers MSW, PhD, JD/MSW, MSW/MA, MSW/MBA. *Accreditation:* CSWE (one or more programs are accredited). *Faculty:* 19 full-time (9 women), 27 part-time/adjunct (19 women). *Students:* 447 full-time (391 women), 67 part-time (63 women); includes 122 minority (38 Black or African American, non-Hispanic/Latino; 5 American Indian or Alaska Native, non-Hispanic/Latino; 27 Asian, non-Hispanic/Latino; 36 Hispanic/Latino; 9 Native Hawaiian or other Pacific Islander, non-Hispanic/Latino; 7 Two or more races, non-Hispanic/Latino), 20 international. 916 applicants, 55% accepted, 207 enrolled. In 2011, 195 master's, 5 doctorates awarded. *Degree requirements:* For master's, 2 internships; for doctorate, comprehensive exam, thesis/dissertation. *Entrance requirements:* For doctorate, GRE. Additional exam requirements/recommendations for international students: Required—TOEFL (minimum score 550 paper-based; 213 computer-based; 80 iBT). *Application deadline:* For fall admission, 3/1 for domestic students. Application fee: $40. Electronic applications accepted. *Expenses:* Contact institution. *Financial support:* In 2011–12, 313 students received support, including 19 fellowships with full tuition reimbursements available (averaging $18,000 per year); career-related internships or fieldwork, Federal Work-Study, institutionally sponsored loans, scholarships/grants, traineeships, tuition waivers (partial), and unspecified assistantships also available. Support available to part-time students. Financial award applicants required to submit FAFSA. *Faculty research:* Well-being of children and families, health and mental health issues, aging and work, consumer-directed services, international social work practice. *Total annual research expenditures:* $4 million. *Application contact:* Dr. William Howard, Director of Admissions, 617-552-4024, Fax: 617-552-1690, E-mail: william.howard@bc.edu. Web site: http://www.bc.edu/schools/gssw/.

Boston University, Graduate School of Arts and Sciences, Interdisciplinary Program in Sociology and Social Work, Boston, MA 02215. Offers PhD. *Students:* 17 full-time (13 women), 6 part-time (all women); includes 5 minority (1 Black or African American, non-Hispanic/Latino; 2 Asian, non-Hispanic/Latino; 2 Hispanic/Latino), 2 international. Average age 37. 39 applicants, 28% accepted, 5 enrolled. *Degree requirements:* For doctorate, one foreign language, comprehensive exam, thesis/dissertation, critical essay. *Entrance requirements:* For doctorate, GRE General Test or MAT, sample of written work. Additional exam requirements/recommendations for international students: Required—TOEFL. *Application deadline:* For fall admission, 1/15 for domestic and international students. Application fee: $70. Electronic applications accepted. *Expenses: Tuition:* Full-time $40,848; part-time $1276 per credit hour. *Required fees:* $572; $286 per semester. *Financial support:* In 2011–12, 11 students received support, including 1 research assistantship with full tuition reimbursement available (averaging $19,300 per year); career-related internships or fieldwork, Federal Work-Study, and scholarships/grants also available. Support available to part-time students. Financial award application deadline: 1/15; financial award applicants required to submit FAFSA. *Faculty research:* Mental health, child welfare, aging, substance abuse. *Unit head:* Sara Bachman, Director, 617-353-1415, Fax: 617-353-5612, E-mail: sbachman@bu.edu. *Application contact:* Dustin Stonecipher, Staff Coordinator, 617-353-9675, Fax: 617-353-5612, E-mail: dtstone@bu.edu. Web site: http://www.bu.edu/ssw/academics/phd/.

Boston University, School of Social Work, Boston, MA 02215. Offers clinical practice with individuals, families, and groups (MSW); macro social work practice (MSW); social work (MSW); social work and sociology (PhD); D Min/MSW; M Div/MSW; MSW/Ed D; MSW/Ed M; MSW/MPH; MSW/MTS. *Accreditation:* CSWE (one or more programs are accredited). Part-time and evening/weekend programs available. Postbaccalaureate distance learning degree programs offered (minimal on-campus study). *Faculty:* 29 full-time (21 women), 36 part-time/adjunct (27 women). *Students:* 200 full-time (187 women), 212 part-time (186 women); includes 67 minority (22 Black or African American, non-Hispanic/Latino; 2 American Indian or Alaska Native, non-Hispanic/Latino; 7 Asian, non-Hispanic/Latino; 29 Hispanic/Latino; 7 Two or more races, non-Hispanic/Latino), 6 international. Average age 30. 937 applicants, 64% accepted, 179 enrolled. In 2011, 155 degrees awarded. *Degree requirements:* For doctorate, one foreign language, thesis/dissertation, critical essay. *Entrance requirements:* For master's, GRE General Test or MAT (if GPA below 3.0), minimum GPA of 3.0; for doctorate, GRE General Test or MAT, writing sample. Additional exam requirements/recommendations for international students: Required—TOEFL (minimum score 577 paper-based; 233 computer-based; 91 iBT), IELTS (minimum score 6.5). *Application deadline:* For fall admission, 3/1 for domestic and international students. Applications are processed on a rolling basis. Application fee: $70. Electronic applications accepted. *Expenses:* Contact institution. *Financial support:* In 2011–12, 160 students received support. Career-related internships or fieldwork, Federal Work-Study, institutionally sponsored loans, scholarships/grants, and Graduate Research Assistant Scholarship Program (GRASP) available. Support available to part-time students. Financial award application deadline: 3/1; financial award applicants required to submit FAFSA. *Faculty research:* Aging, children and families, substance abuse and HIV, trauma and mental health, public health social work. *Total annual research expenditures:* $2.4 million. *Unit head:* Gail Steketee, Dean, 617-353-3760, Fax: 617-353-5612. *Application contact:* Alison McAlear, Associate Dean for Enrollment Services and External Relations, 617-353-3750, Fax: 617-353-5612, E-mail: busswad@bu.edu. Web site: http://www.bu.edu/ssw/.

Bridgewater State University, School of Graduate Studies, School of Arts and Sciences, Department of Social Work, Bridgewater, MA 02325-0001. Offers MSW. *Accreditation:* CSWE.

Brigham Young University, Graduate Studies, College of Family, Home, and Social Sciences, School of Social Work, Provo, UT 84602. Offers clinical social work (MSW), including research. *Accreditation:* CSWE. *Faculty:* 10 full-time (5 women), 4 part-time/adjunct (3 women). *Students:* 74 full-time (55 women); includes 9 minority (1 Black or African American, non-Hispanic/Latino; 1 American Indian or Alaska Native, non-Hispanic/Latino; 2 Asian, non-Hispanic/Latino; 2 Hispanic/Latino; 2 Native Hawaiian or other Pacific Islander, non-Hispanic/Latino; 1 Two or more races, non-Hispanic/Latino). Average age 29. 155 applicants, 30% accepted, 40 enrolled. In 2011, 35 master's awarded. *Degree requirements:* For master's, thesis optional. *Entrance requirements:* Additional exam requirements/recommendations for international students: Required—TOEFL (minimum score 580 paper-based; 237 computer-based; 85 iBT), IELTS (minimum score 7). *Application deadline:* For fall admission, 1/15 for domestic and international students. Application fee: $50. Electronic applications accepted. *Expenses: Tuition:* Full-time $5760; part-time $320 per credit. Tuition and fees vary according to student's religious affiliation. *Financial support:* In 2011–12, 21 students received support, including 23 fellowships with full and partial tuition reimbursements available (averaging $1,777 per year), 20 research assistantships (averaging $2,800 per year), 2 teaching assistantships (averaging $2,880 per year); career-related internships or fieldwork, tuition waivers (partial), and administrative aides, paid field practicum, AmeriCorps education awards also available. Financial award application deadline: 1/15. *Faculty research:* Poverty, adoptions, depression, spirituality, child welfare, marriage and family, American Indian child welfare, health care, mental health, mood disorders, substance abuse, women and gender. *Total annual research expenditures:* $100,000. *Unit head:* Dr. Gordon E. Limb, Director, 801-422-3282, Fax: 801-422-0624, E-mail: socialwork@byu.edu. *Application contact:* Lisa Willey, Graduate Secretary, 801-422-5681, Fax: 801-422-0624, E-mail: msw@byu.edu. Web site: https://socialwork.byu.edu/Pages/Home.aspx.

Bryn Mawr College, Graduate School of Social Work and Social Research, Bryn Mawr, PA 19010. Offers MLSP, MSS, PhD. *Accreditation:* CSWE (one or more programs are accredited). Part-time and evening/weekend programs available. *Faculty:* 14 full-time (7 women), 16 part-time/adjunct (2 women). *Students:* 170 full-time (146 women), 67 part-time (62 women); includes 58 minority (32 Black or African American, non-Hispanic/Latino; 9 Asian, non-Hispanic/Latino; 6 Hispanic/Latino; 11 Two or more races, non-Hispanic/Latino), 2 international. Average age 34. 223 applicants, 69% accepted, 84 enrolled. In 2011, 82 master's, 1 doctorate awarded. *Degree requirements:* For master's, fieldwork; for doctorate, comprehensive exam, thesis/dissertation. *Entrance requirements:* For master's, interview, 3 letters of reference; for doctorate, GRE General Test, interview, 3 letters of reference, master's degree. Additional exam requirements/recommendations for international students: Required—TOEFL (minimum score 620 paper-based). *Application deadline:* For fall admission, 3/31 priority date for domestic students, 3/31 for international students. Applications are processed on a rolling basis. Application fee: $50. Electronic applications accepted. *Expenses:* Contact institution. *Financial support:* In 2011–12, 183 students received support, including 29 fellowships with full and partial tuition reimbursements available (averaging $2,517 per year), 1 research assistantship with full and partial tuition reimbursement available (averaging $9,333 per year), 7 teaching assistantships with full and partial tuition reimbursements available (averaging $8,680 per year); career-related internships or fieldwork, Federal Work-Study, institutionally sponsored loans, scholarships/grants, tuition waivers (full and partial), and dissertation award (PhD) also available. Support available to part-time students. Financial award application deadline: 3/1; financial award applicants required to submit FAFSA. *Faculty research:* Ethical issues, children and adolescents, poverty, mental health, child and family welfare. *Total annual research expenditures:* $7.1 million. *Unit head:* Dr. Darlyne Bailey, Dean, 610-520-2610, Fax: 610-520-2613, E-mail: dbailey01@brynmawr.edu. *Application contact:* Diane D. Craw, Assistant to the Dean and Administrative Director, Social Work, 610-520-2612, Fax: 610-520-2613, E-mail: dcraw@brynmawr.edu. Web site: http://www.brynmawr.edu/socialwork.

California State University, Bakersfield, Division of Graduate Studies, School of Social Sciences and Education, Program in Social Work, Bakersfield, CA 93311. Offers MSW. *Accreditation:* CSWE. *Application deadline:* Applications are processed on a rolling basis. Application fee: $55. *Expenses: Required fees:* $1302 per unit. Part-time tuition and fees vary according to course load and program. *Unit head:* Dr. Debra Morrison-Orton, Director, 661-664-2089, Fax: 661-665-6928, E-mail: dmorrison_orton@csub.edu. Web site: http://www.csub.edu/socialwork/program_info.shtml.

California State University, Chico, Office of Graduate Studies, College of Behavioral and Social Sciences, School of Social Work, Chico, CA 95929-0722. Offers MSW. *Accreditation:* CSWE. Evening/weekend programs available. *Faculty:* 8 full-time (5 women), 13 part-time/adjunct (9 women). *Students:* 102 full-time (81 women), 5 part-time (4 women); includes 30 minority (2 Black or African American, non-Hispanic/Latino; 3 American Indian or Alaska Native, non-Hispanic/Latino; 7 Asian, non-Hispanic/Latino; 18 Hispanic/Latino), 1 international. Average age 34. 122 applicants, 38% accepted, 29 enrolled. In 2011, 57 master's awarded. *Degree requirements:* For master's, thesis or project. *Entrance requirements:* For master's, 3 letters of recommendation on departmental form, statement of purpose. Additional exam requirements/recommendations for international students: Required—TOEFL (minimum score 550 paper-based; 213 computer-based; 80 iBT), IELTS (minimum score 6.5), Pearson Test of English (minimum score 59). *Application deadline:* For fall admission, 3/1 for domestic and international students. Application fee: $55. Electronic applications accepted. Tuition and fees vary according to class time, course load and degree level. *Financial support:* Application deadline: 3/1; applicants required to submit FAFSA. *Unit head:* Celeste A. Jones, Director, 530-898-6204, Fax: 530-898-5574, E-mail: swrk@csuchico.edu. *Application contact:* Judy L. Rice, Graduate Admissions Coordinator, 530-898-6880, Fax: 530-898-6889, E-mail: jlrice@csuchico.edu. Web site: http://www.csuchico.edu/swrk.

California State University, Dominguez Hills, College of Professional Studies, School of Health and Human Services, Program in Social Work, Carson, CA 90747-0001. Offers MSW. *Accreditation:* CSWE. Part-time and evening/weekend programs available. *Faculty:* 9 full-time (7 women), 7 part-time/adjunct (6 women). *Students:* 53 full-time (43 women), 74 part-time (63 women); includes 102 minority (40 Black or African American, non-Hispanic/Latino; 15 Asian, non-Hispanic/Latino; 44 Hispanic/Latino; 3 Two or more races, non-Hispanic/Latino), 1 international. Average age 33. 358 applicants, 29% accepted, 47 enrolled. In 2011, 53 master's awarded. *Degree requirements:* For master's, thesis. *Entrance requirements:* For master's, minimum GPA of 2.75 in last 60 units; 3 courses in behavioral science, 2 in humanities, 1 each in English composition, elementary statistics, and human biology. *Application deadline:* For fall admission, 4/30 for domestic students. Applications are processed on a rolling basis. *Faculty research:* HIV/AIDS, community capacity, program evaluation. *Unit head:* Dr. Mekada Graham-Gallegan, Professor and Director, 310-243-2521, E-mail: mgraham@csudh.edu. *Application contact:* Susan Nakaoka, Director of Admissions, 310-243-2181, Fax: 310-217-6800, E-mail: snakaoka@csudh.edu. Web site: http://www.csudh.edu/cps/hhs/sw/.

California State University, East Bay, Office of Academic Programs and Graduate Studies, College of Letters, Arts, and Social Sciences, Department of Social Work, Hayward, CA 94542-3000. Offers children, youth, family service (MSW); community mental health (MSW). *Accreditation:* CSWE. *Faculty:* 4 full-time (3 women), 13 part-time/adjunct (11 women). *Students:* 152 full-time (127 women), 4 part-time (all women); includes 93 minority (27 Black or African American, non-Hispanic/Latino; 28 Asian, non-Hispanic/Latino; 31 Hispanic/Latino; 7 Two or more races, non-Hispanic/Latino), 1 international. Average age 31. 452 applicants, 52% accepted, 96 enrolled. In 2011, 115 master's awarded. *Degree requirements:* For master's, comprehensive exam. *Entrance requirements:* For master's, minimum GPA of 2.8; courses in statistics and either human biology, physiology, or anatomy; liberal arts or social science baccalaureate; 3 letters of recommendation; personal statement; consent to criminal background check; student professional liability insurance. Additional exam requirements/recommendations for international students: Required—TOEFL (minimum score 550 paper-based; 213 computer-based). *Application deadline:* For fall admission, 3/15 for domestic and international students. Applications are processed on a rolling basis. Application fee: $55. Electronic applications accepted. *Expenses:* Tuition, state resident: full-time $6738; part-time $1302 per quarter. Tuition, nonresident: full-time $12,690; part-time $2294 per quarter. *Required fees:* $449 per quarter. Tuition and fees vary according to degree level, program and reciprocity agreements. *Financial support:* Fellowships, career-related internships or fieldwork, Federal Work-Study, institutionally sponsored loans, and scholarships/grants available. Support available to part-time students. Financial award application deadline: 3/2; financial award applicants required to submit FAFSA. *Unit head:* Dr. Evaon Wong-Kim, Chair/Social Work Graduate Advisor, 510-885-4916, Fax: 510-885-7580, E-mail: evaon.wongkim@csueastbay.edu. *Application contact:* Dr. Dianne Rush Woods, Graduate Advisor for MSW Special Session, 510-885-2535, Fax: 510-885-7580, E-mail: dianne.woods@csueastbay.edu. Web site: http://www20.csueastbay.edu/class/departments/socialwork/.

California State University, Fresno, Division of Graduate Studies, College of Health and Human Services, Department of Social Work Education, Fresno, CA 93740-8027. Offers MSW. *Accreditation:* CSWE. Part-time and evening/weekend programs available. *Degree requirements:* For master's, thesis or alternative. *Entrance requirements:* For master's, GRE General Test, minimum GPA of 2.5. Additional exam requirements/recommendations for international students: Required—TOEFL. Electronic applications accepted. *Faculty research:* Children at risk, international cooperation, child welfare training, nutrition.

California State University, Fullerton, Graduate Studies, College of Health and Human Development, Program of Social Work, Fullerton, CA 92834-9480. Offers MSW. *Accreditation:* CSWE. Part-time programs available. *Students:* 81 full-time (69 women), 1 (woman) part-time; includes 54 minority (6 Black or African American, non-Hispanic/Latino; 14 Asian, non-Hispanic/Latino; 31 Hispanic/Latino; 3 Two or more races, non-Hispanic/Latino). Average age 27. 208 applicants, 32% accepted, 41 enrolled. In 2011, 44 master's awarded. *Entrance requirements:* For master's, minimum GPA of 3.0 for last 60 semester or 90 quarter units. Application fee: $55. *Financial support:* Career-related internships or fieldwork, Federal Work-Study, institutionally sponsored loans, and scholarships/grants available. Support available to part-time students. Financial award application deadline: 3/1; financial award applicants required to submit FAFSA. *Unit head:* Dr. David Cherin, Director, 657-278-2790. *Application contact:* Admissions/Applications, 657-278-2371. Web site: http://hhd.fullerton.edu/msw.

California State University, Long Beach, Graduate Studies, College of Health and Human Services, Department of Social Work, Long Beach, CA 90840. Offers MSW. *Accreditation:* CSWE. Part-time and evening/weekend programs available. Postbaccalaureate distance learning degree programs offered (no on-campus study). *Faculty:* 24 full-time (15 women), 12 part-time/adjunct (9 women). *Students:* 225 full-time (206 women), 155 part-time (135 women); includes 282 minority (35 Black or African American, non-Hispanic/Latino; 4 American Indian or Alaska Native, non-Hispanic/Latino; 47 Asian, non-Hispanic/Latino; 186 Hispanic/Latino; 1 Native Hawaiian or other Pacific Islander, non-Hispanic/Latino; 9 Two or more races, non-Hispanic/Latino), 5 international. Average age 32. 1,163 applicants, 20% accepted, 172 enrolled. In 2011, 220 master's awarded. *Degree requirements:* For master's, thesis. *Application deadline:* For fall admission, 3/1 for domestic students. Applications are processed on a rolling basis. Application fee: $55. Electronic applications accepted. *Financial support:* Federal Work-Study, institutionally sponsored loans, and scholarships/grants available. Financial award application deadline: 3/2. *Unit head:* Dr. John Oliver, Director, 562-985-5655, Fax: 562-985-5514, E-mail: joliver@csulb.edu. *Application contact:* Dr. Rebecca Lopez, Coordinator of Academic Programs, 562-985-5655, Fax: 562-985-5514, E-mail: rlopez@csulb.edu.

California State University, Los Angeles, Graduate Studies, College of Health and Human Services, School of Social Work, Los Angeles, CA 90032-8530. Offers MSW. *Accreditation:* CSWE. *Faculty:* 11 full-time (7 women), 24 part-time/adjunct (16 women). *Students:* 195 full-time (153 women), 46 part-time (35 women); includes 185 minority (19 Black or African American, non-Hispanic/Latino; 2 American Indian or Alaska Native, non-Hispanic/Latino; 22 Asian, non-Hispanic/Latino; 137 Hispanic/Latino; 5 Two or more races, non-Hispanic/Latino), 7 international. Average age 32. 805 applicants, 21% accepted, 112 enrolled. In 2011, 123 master's awarded. *Entrance requirements:* Additional exam requirements/recommendations for international students: Required—TOEFL (minimum score 500 paper-based; 173 computer-based). *Application deadline:* For fall admission, 5/1 for domestic and international students. Applications are processed on a rolling basis. Application fee: $55. *Expenses:* Tuition, state resident: full-time $8225. *Financial support:* Application deadline: 3/1. *Unit head:* Dr. Dale Weaver, Chair, 323-343-4680, Fax: 323-343-5009, E-mail: dweaver@calstatela.edu. *Application contact:* Dr. Karin Brown, Acting Associate Dean of Graduate Studies, 323-343-3820, Fax: 323-343-5653, E-mail: kbrown5@calstatela.edu. Web site: http://www.calstatela.edu/dept/soc_work/index.htm.

California State University, Monterey Bay, College of Professional Studies, Health, Human Services and Public Policy Department, Seaside, CA 93955-8001. Offers public policy (MPP); social work (MSW). Part-time programs available. *Degree requirements:* For master's, internship. *Entrance requirements:* For master's, GRE, curriculum vitae, recommendations. Additional exam requirements/recommendations for international students: Required—TOEFL (minimum score 525 paper-based; 213 computer-based; 71 iBT). Electronic applications accepted. *Faculty research:* Social policy, health policy, politics and government.

California State University, Northridge, Graduate Studies, College of Social and Behavioral Sciences, Department of Social Work, Northridge, CA 91330. Offers MSW. Part-time programs available. *Entrance requirements:* For master's, GRE (if cumulative undergraduate GPA less than 3.0).

California State University, Sacramento, Office of Graduate Studies, College of Health and Human Services, Division of Social Work, Sacramento, CA 95819-6090. Offers family and children's services (MSW); health care (MSW); mental health (MSW); social justice and corrections (MSW). *Accreditation:* CSWE. *Faculty:* 23 full-time (12 women), 16 part-time/adjunct (8 women). *Students:* 235 full-time, 17 part-time; includes 106 minority (20 Black or African American, non-Hispanic/Latino; 1 American Indian or Alaska Native, non-Hispanic/Latino; 8 Asian, non-Hispanic/Latino; 58 Hispanic/Latino; 2 Native Hawaiian or other Pacific Islander, non-Hispanic/Latino; 17 Two or more races, non-Hispanic/Latino). Average age 33. 436 applicants, 48% accepted, 133 enrolled. In 2011, 155 master's awarded. *Degree requirements:* For master's, thesis, research project, or comprehensive exam; writing proficiency exam. *Entrance requirements:* For master's, minimum GPA of 2.5 during previous 2 years of course work. Additional exam requirements/recommendations for international students: Required—TOEFL. *Application deadline:* For fall admission, 1/18 for domestic students, 3/1 for international students; for spring admission, 9/30 for international students. Applications are processed on a rolling basis. Application fee: $55. Electronic applications accepted. *Financial support:* Career-related internships or fieldwork and Federal Work-Study available. Support available to part-time students. Financial award application deadline: 3/1; financial award applicants required to submit FAFSA. *Unit head:* Dr. Robin Kennedy, Chair, 916-278-6913, Fax: 916-278-7167, E-mail: kennedyr@csus.edu. *Application contact:* Jose Martinez, Outreach and Graduate Diversity Coordinator, 916-278-6470, Fax: 916-278-5669, E-mail: martinj@skymail.csus.edu. Web site: http://www.csus.edu/hhs/sw.

California State University, San Bernardino, Graduate Studies, College of Social and Behavioral Sciences, Department of Social Work, San Bernardino, CA 92407-2397. Offers MSW. *Accreditation:* CSWE. Part-time and evening/weekend programs available. *Students:* 27 full-time (21 women), 130 part-time (117 women); includes 91 minority (23 Black or African American, non-Hispanic/Latino; 1 American Indian or Alaska Native, non-Hispanic/Latino; 6 Asian, non-Hispanic/Latino; 56 Hispanic/Latino; 5 Two or more races, non-Hispanic/Latino). Average age 29. 229 applicants, 36% accepted, 67 enrolled. In 2011, 69 master's awarded. *Degree requirements:* For master's, field practicum, research project. *Entrance requirements:* For master's, minimum GPA of 2.75 in last 2 years of course work, liberal arts background. *Application deadline:* For fall admission, 8/31 priority date for domestic students. Application fee: $55. *Expenses:* Tuition, state resident: full-time $7356. Tuition, nonresident: full-time $7356. *Required fees:* $1077. Tuition and fees vary according to program. *Financial support:* Fellowships, research assistantships, career-related internships or fieldwork, Federal Work-Study, institutionally sponsored loans, and stipends for practicum available. Support available to part-time students. Financial award application deadline: 5/1. *Faculty research:* Addiction, computers in social work practice, minority issues, gerontology. *Unit head:* Laurie Smith, Director/Associate Professor/Graduate Coordinator, 909-537-3837, Fax: 909-537-7029, E-mail: lasmith@csusb.edu. *Application contact:* Sandra Kamusikiri, Associate Vice-President/Dean of Graduate Studies, 909-537-5058, E-mail: skamusik@csusb.edu.

California State University, Stanislaus, College of Human and Health Sciences, Program in Social Work (MSW), Turlock, CA 95382. Offers MSW. *Accreditation:* CSWE. *Degree requirements:* For master's, thesis. *Entrance requirements:* For master's, minimum GPA of 3.0, 3 letters of reference, personal statement. *Application deadline:* For fall admission, 2/28 for domestic students. Application fee: $55. Electronic applications accepted. *Expenses: Required fees:* $4616 per year. *Financial support:* Career-related internships or fieldwork and Federal Work-Study available. Financial award application deadline: 3/1; financial award applicants required to submit FAFSA. *Faculty research:* Mental health supervision, health issues on adulthood and aging, geriatric social work, effects of violence on children, rural mental health. *Unit head:* Dr. Robin Ringstad, Department Chair, 209-667-3355, E-mail: rringstad@csustan.edu. *Application contact:* Graduate School, 209-667-3129, Fax: 209-664-7025, E-mail: graduate_school@csustan.edu. Web site: http://www.csustan.edu/social_work/.

California University of Pennsylvania, School of Graduate Studies and Research, College of Education and Human Services, Department of Social Work, California, PA 15419-1394. Offers MSW. *Accreditation:* CSWE. Part-time programs available. *Degree requirements:* For master's, comprehensive exam. *Entrance requirements:* For master's, GRE, letters of reference. Additional exam requirements/recommendations for international students: Required—TOEFL. Electronic applications accepted. *Faculty research:* Social welfare and policy, housing and community development, health and mental health, Black Appalachian, aging.

Campbellsville University, Carver School of Social Work, Campbellsville, KY 42718-2799. Offers M Ed/MLIS. Evening/weekend programs available. *Students:* 50 full-time (41 women), 35 part-time (27 women); includes 19 minority (15 Black or African American, non-Hispanic/Latino; 4 Hispanic/Latino), 1 international. Application fee: $25. Electronic applications accepted. *Expenses: Tuition:* Full-time $6030; part-time $335 per credit hour. *Financial support:* Applicants required to submit FAFSA. *Unit head:* Dr. Darlene F. Eastridge, Program Director, 270-789-5178, Fax: 270-789-5542, E-mail: dfeastridge@campbellsville.edu. *Application contact:* Monica Bamwine, Assistant Director of Admissions, 270-789-5221, Fax: 270-789-5071, E-mail: mkbamwine@campbellsville.edu.

Carleton University, Faculty of Graduate Studies, Faculty of Public Affairs and Management, School of Social Work, Ottawa, ON K1S 5B6, Canada. Offers MSW. Part-time programs available. *Degree requirements:* For master's, thesis optional. *Entrance requirements:* For master's, basic research methods course. Additional exam requirements/recommendations for international students: Required—TOEFL. *Faculty research:* Social administration, program evaluation, history of Canadian social welfare, women's issues, education in social work.

Case Western Reserve University, Mandel School of Applied Social Sciences, Cleveland, OH 44106. Offers social administration (MSSA); social welfare (PhD); JD/MSSA; MSSA/MA; MSSA/MBA; MSSA/MNO. *Accreditation:* CSWE (one or more programs are accredited). Evening/weekend programs available. *Degree requirements:* For master's, fieldwork; for doctorate, thesis/dissertation. *Entrance requirements:* For master's, GRE General Test, MAT, or minimum GPA of 2.7; for doctorate, GRE General Test. Additional exam requirements/recommendations for international students: Required—TOEFL (minimum score 550 paper-based; 213 computer-based; 79 iBT). Electronic applications accepted. *Expenses:* Contact institution. *Faculty research:* Urban poverty, community social development, substance abuse, health, child welfare, aging, mental health.

The Catholic University of America, National Catholic School of Social Service, Washington, DC 20064. Offers MSW, PhD, MSW/JD. *Accreditation:* CSWE (one or more programs are accredited). Part-time programs available. *Faculty:* 18 full-time (15 women), 26 part-time/adjunct (20 women). *Students:* 151 full-time (137 women), 176 part-time (150 women); includes 92 minority (38 Black or African American, non-Hispanic/Latino; 7 Asian, non-Hispanic/Latino; 12 Hispanic/Latino; 1 Native Hawaiian or other Pacific Islander, non-Hispanic/Latino; 34 Two or more races, non-Hispanic/Latino), 4 international. Average age 34. 324 applicants, 69% accepted, 111 enrolled. In 2011, 122 master's, 6 doctorates awarded. *Degree requirements:* For master's, comprehensive exam, thesis or alternative; for doctorate, comprehensive exam, thesis/dissertation, minimum GPA of 3.0. *Entrance requirements:* For master's, GRE or MAT if undergraduate GPA less than 3.0, statement of purpose, official copies of academic transcripts, three letters of recommendation, resume; for doctorate, GRE, statement of purpose, official copies of academic transcripts, three letters of recommendation, resume, writing sample. Additional exam requirements/recommendations for international students: Required—TOEFL (minimum score 600 paper-based; 250 computer-based). *Application deadline:* For fall admission, 7/15 priority date for domestic students, 7/15 for international students; for spring admission, 12/1 priority date for domestic students, 10/15 for international students. Applications are processed on a rolling basis. Application fee: $55. Electronic applications accepted. *Expenses:* Contact institution. *Financial support:* Fellowships, research assistantships, teaching assistantships, Federal Work-Study, scholarships/grants, tuition waivers (full and partial), and unspecified assistantships available. Financial award application deadline: 2/1; financial award applicants required to submit FAFSA. *Faculty research:* International social development; spirituality and social work; advancement of children, youth, and families; global aging; community development and social justice; promotion of health; mental health well-being. *Total annual research expenditures:* $185,164. *Unit head:* Dr. James R. Zabora, Dean, 202-319-5454, Fax: 202-319-5093, E-mail: zabora@cua.edu. *Application contact:* Andrew Woodall, Director of Graduate Admissions, 202-319-5057, Fax: 202-319-6533, E-mail: cua-admissions@cua.edu. Web site: http://ncsss.cua.edu.

Chicago State University, School of Graduate and Professional Studies, College of Arts and Sciences, Program in Social Work, Chicago, IL 60628. Offers MSW. *Accreditation:* CSWE. Electronic applications accepted.

Clark Atlanta University, School of Social Work, Atlanta, GA 30314. Offers MSW, PhD. *Accreditation:* CSWE (one or more programs are accredited). Part-time programs available. *Faculty:* 9 full-time (6 women), 19 part-time/adjunct (10 women). *Students:* 178 full-time (155 women), 71 part-time (56 women); includes 232 minority (231 Black or African American, non-Hispanic/Latino; 1 Hispanic/Latino), 1 international. Average age 32. 179 applicants, 97% accepted, 116 enrolled. In 2011, 50 master's, 4 doctorates awarded. Terminal master's awarded for partial completion of doctoral program. *Degree requirements:* For master's, one foreign language; for doctorate, one foreign language, comprehensive exam, thesis/dissertation. *Entrance requirements:* For master's, GRE General Test, minimum undergraduate GPA of 3.0; for doctorate, GRE General Test. Additional exam requirements/recommendations for international students: Required—TOEFL (minimum score 500 paper-based; 173 computer-based; 61 iBT). *Application deadline:* For fall admission, 4/1 for domestic and international students; for spring admission, 11/1 for domestic and international students. Applications are processed on a rolling basis. Application fee: $40 ($55 for international students). Electronic applications accepted. *Expenses: Tuition:* Full-time $13,572; part-time $754 per credit hour. *Required fees:* $806; $403 per semester. *Financial support:* Career-related internships or fieldwork, Federal Work-Study, scholarships/grants, and unspecified assistantships available. Support available to part-time students. Financial award application deadline: 4/30; financial award applicants required to submit FAFSA. *Unit head:* Dr. Vimala Pillari, Interim Dean, 404-880-8006, E-mail: rlyle@cau.edu. *Application contact:* Michelle Clark-Davis, Graduate Program Admissions, 404-880-6605, E-mail: cauadmissions@cau.edu.

Cleveland State University, College of Graduate Studies, College of Liberal Arts and Social Sciences, School of Social Work, Cleveland, OH 44115. Offers MSW. Program offered jointly with The University of Akron. *Accreditation:* CSWE. Part-time and evening/weekend programs available. Postbaccalaureate distance learning degree programs offered (no on-campus study). *Faculty:* 10 full-time (2 women), 8 part-time/adjunct (5 women). *Students:* 126 full-time (102 women), 67 part-time (59 women); includes 75 minority (69 Black or African American, non-Hispanic/Latino; 1 Asian, non-Hispanic/Latino; 5 Hispanic/Latino). Average age 35. 197 applicants, 55% accepted, 76 enrolled. In 2011, 58 master's awarded. *Entrance requirements:* For master's, 3 letters of reference. Additional exam requirements/recommendations for international students: Required—TOEFL (minimum score 525 paper-based; 197 computer-based); Recommended—IELTS (minimum score 6). *Application deadline:* For fall admission, 2/28 for domestic students. Application fee: $30. *Expenses:* Tuition, state resident: full-time $6416; part-time $494 per credit hour. Tuition, nonresident: full-time $12,074; part-time $929 per credit hour. *Financial support:* In 2011–12, 15 students received support, including 10 research assistantships with full and partial tuition reimbursements available (averaging $3,480 per year); tuition waivers (full) also available. Financial award applicants required to submit FAFSA. *Faculty research:* Mental health, aging. *Total annual research expenditures:* $1.2 million. *Unit head:* Dr. Maggie Jackson, Director, 216-687-4599, Fax: 216-687-5590, E-mail: m.jackson@csuohio.edu. *Application contact:* Deborah L. Brown, Interim Assistant Director, Graduate Admissions, 216-523-7572, Fax: 216-687-5400, E-mail: d.l.brown@csuohio.edu. Web site: http://www.csuohio.edu/socialwork/.

The College at Brockport, State University of New York, School of Education and Human Services, Greater Rochester Collaborative Master of Social Work Program, Brockport, NY 14420-2997. Offers social work (MSW), including family and community practice, interdisciplinary health practice. Program offered jointly with Nazareth College of Rochester. *Accreditation:* CSWE. Part-time programs available. *Students:* 51 full-time (47 women), 74 part-time (61 women); includes 26 minority (17 Black or African American, non-Hispanic/Latino; 4 Asian, non-Hispanic/Latino; 4 Hispanic/Latino; 1 Native Hawaiian or other Pacific Islander, non-Hispanic/Latino). 114 applicants, 47% accepted, 36 enrolled. In 2011, 58 master's awarded. *Degree requirements:* For master's, thesis or alternative. *Entrance requirements:* For master's, minimum GPA of 3.0, letters of recommendation; statement of objectives. Additional exam requirements/recommendations for international students: Required—TOEFL (minimum score 550 paper-based; 213 computer-based; 79 iBT). *Application deadline:* For fall admission, 3/15 priority date for domestic students, 3/15 for international students. Application fee: $50. Electronic applications accepted. *Expenses:* Contact institution. *Financial support:* Federal Work-Study, scholarships/grants, and unspecified assistantships available. Support available to part-time students. Financial award application deadline: 3/15; financial award applicants required to submit FAFSA. *Faculty research:* Caregiving, child welfare, gerontological social work, home-school-community partnerships, domestic violence. *Unit head:* Dr. Jason Dauenhauer, Director, 585-395-8450, Fax: 585-395-8603, E-mail: grcmsw@brockport.edu. *Application contact:* Brad Snyder, Coordinator of Admissions, 585-395-3845, Fax: 585-395-8603, E-mail: bsnyder@brockport.edu. Web site: http://www.brockport.edu/graduate/.

Colorado State University, Graduate School, College of Applied Human Sciences, School of Social Work, Fort Collins, CO 80523-1586. Offers MSW. *Accreditation:* CSWE. Part-time programs available. Postbaccalaureate distance learning degree programs offered (minimal on-campus study). *Faculty:* 6 full-time (5 women), 2 part-time/adjunct (1 woman). *Students:* 73 full-time (65 women), 88 part-time (81 women); includes 19 minority (2 American Indian or Alaska Native, non-Hispanic/Latino; 15 Hispanic/Latino; 2 Two or more races, non-Hispanic/Latino), 1 international. Average age 33. 112 applicants, 36% accepted, 25 enrolled. In 2011, 50 master's awarded. *Degree requirements:* For master's, variable foreign language requirement, thesis optional. *Entrance requirements:* For master's, minimum GPA of 3.0; 18 credits of course work in social or behavioral science, human biology, statistics, and human development; 450 hours of verifiable human service work and/or volunteer experience; bachelor's degree. Additional exam requirements/recommendations for international students: Required—TOEFL (minimum score 550 paper-based; 213 computer-based; 80 iBT). *Application deadline:* For fall admission, 1/2 priority date for domestic students, 1/2 for international students. Application fee: $50. Electronic applications accepted. *Expenses:* Contact institution. *Financial support:* In 2011–12, 3 students received support, including 2 research assistantships with partial tuition reimbursements available (averaging $15,755 per year), 1 teaching assistantship with partial tuition reimbursement available (averaging $10,275 per year); fellowships with partial tuition reimbursements available, career-related internships or fieldwork, scholarships/grants, and unspecified assistantships also available. Financial award application deadline: 12/15; financial award applicants required to submit FAFSA. *Faculty research:* Environmental health, child welfare, mental health, international social work, disabilities, social advocacy. *Total annual research expenditures:* $1.3 million. *Unit head:* Dr. Deborah P. Valentine, Director, 970-491-1893, Fax: 970-491-7280, E-mail: deborah.valentine@colostate.edu. *Application contact:* Peter Friedrichsen, MSW Program Coordinator, 970-491-2536, Fax: 970-491-7280, E-mail: peter.friedrichsen@colostate.edu. Web site: http://www.cahs.colostate.edu/ssw/.

Columbia University, School of Social Work, New York, NY 10027. Offers MSSW, PhD, JD/MS, MBA/MS, MPA/MS, MPH/MS, MS/M Div, MS/MA, MS/MS, MS/MS Ed. MS/MS Ed offered jointly with Bank Street College of Education; MS/M Div with Union Theological Seminary in the City of New York; MS/MA with The Jewish Theological Seminary. *Accreditation:* CSWE (one or more programs are accredited). *Degree requirements:* For doctorate, thesis/dissertation. *Entrance requirements:* For master's, 3 letters of reference; for doctorate, GRE General Test, 3 letters of recommendation. Additional exam requirements/recommendations for international students: Required—TOEFL, TWE. Electronic applications accepted. *Expenses:* Contact institution.

Cornell University, Graduate School, Graduate Fields of Human Ecology, Field of Policy Analysis and Management, Ithaca, NY 14853-0001. Offers consumer policy (PhD); evaluation (PhD); family and social welfare policy (PhD); health administration (MHA); health management and policy (PhD). *Faculty:* 33 full-time (13 women). *Students:* 63 full-time (36 women); includes 15 minority (6 Black or African American, non-Hispanic/Latino; 1 American Indian or Alaska Native, non-Hispanic/Latino; 8 Asian, non-Hispanic/Latino), 7 international. Average age 25. 137 applicants, 35% accepted, 29 enrolled. In 2011, 33 master's, 1 doctorate awarded. *Degree requirements:* For master's, thesis; for doctorate, thesis/dissertation. *Entrance requirements:* For master's, GRE General Test or GMAT, 2 letters of recommendation; for doctorate, GRE General Test, 2 letters of recommendation. Additional exam requirements/recommendations for international students: Required—TOEFL (minimum score 550 paper-based; 213 computer-based; 77 iBT). *Application deadline:* For fall admission, 1/15 for domestic students. Application fee: $95. Electronic applications accepted. *Financial support:* In 2011–12, 17 students received support, including 2 fellowships with full and partial tuition reimbursements available, 6 research assistantships with full and partial tuition reimbursements available, 7 teaching assistantships with full and partial tuition reimbursements available; institutionally sponsored loans, scholarships/grants, health care benefits, tuition waivers (full and partial), and unspecified assistantships also available. Financial award applicants required to submit FAFSA. *Faculty research:* Health policy, family policy, social welfare policy, program evaluation, consumer policy. *Unit head:* Director of Graduate Studies, 607-255-7772. *Application contact:* Graduate Field Assistant, 607-255-7772, Fax: 607-255-4071, E-mail: pam_phd@cornell.edu. Web site: http://www.gradschool.cornell.edu/fields.php?id-69&a-2.

Dalhousie University, Faculty of Health Professions, School of Social Work, Halifax, NS B3H3J5, Canada. Offers MSW. Part-time programs available. Postbaccalaureate distance learning degree programs offered (minimal on-campus study). *Degree requirements:* For master's, thesis optional, field placement. *Entrance requirements:* For master's, bachelor's degree in social work, 2 years work experience in social work, minimum GPA of 3.0. Additional exam requirements/recommendations for international students: Required—TOEFL, IELTS, CANTEST, CAEL, or Michigan English Language Assessment Battery. Electronic applications accepted. *Expenses:* Contact institution. *Faculty research:* Family and child welfare, physical and mental health, public policy, elder abuse, violence against women, community practice.

Delaware State University, Graduate Programs, College of Education, Health and Public Policy, Department of Social Work, Program in Social Work, Dover, DE 19901-2277. Offers MSW. *Accreditation:* CSWE. Evening/weekend programs available. *Entrance requirements:* For master's, GRE, minimum GPA of 3.0 in major, 2.75 overall. Additional exam requirements/recommendations for international students: Required—TOEFL. Electronic applications accepted. *Faculty research:* Gerontology, human behavior, corrections, child welfare, adolescent behavior policy.

DePaul University, College of Liberal Arts and Sciences, Program in Social Work, Chicago, IL 60604-2287. Offers MSW. *Application contact:* Ann Spittle, Director of Graduate Admission, 773-325-7315, Fax: 773-476-3244, E-mail: graduatelas@depaul.edu.

Dominican University, Graduate School of Social Work, River Forest, IL 60305. Offers MSW. *Accreditation:* CSWE. Part-time programs available. *Faculty:* 6 full-time (4 women), 10 part-time/adjunct (5 women). *Students:* 105 full-time (89 women), 71 part-time (61 women); includes 74 minority (37 Black or African American, non-Hispanic/Latino; 1 Asian, non-Hispanic/Latino; 29 Hispanic/Latino; 7 Two or more races, non-Hispanic/Latino), 2 international. Average age 32. 69 applicants, 91% accepted, 57 enrolled. In 2011, 74 master's awarded. *Entrance requirements:* For master's, minimum GPA of 2.75 for regular standing, 3.0 for advanced standing. Additional exam requirements/recommendations for international students: Required—TOEFL (minimum score 83 iBT); Recommended—IELTS (minimum score 7). *Application deadline:* For fall admission, 7/1 for domestic and international students; for spring admission, 11/1 for domestic and international students. Applications are processed on a rolling basis.

Application fee: $25. Electronic applications accepted. *Expenses: Tuition:* Full-time $16,632; part-time $792 per credit hour. *Required fees:* $15 per semester. Tuition and fees vary according to degree level, campus/location and program. *Financial support:* In 2011–12, 4 research assistantships (averaging $4,000 per year) were awarded; Federal Work-Study, scholarships/grants, and unspecified assistantships also available. Financial award applicants required to submit FAFSA. *Faculty research:* Human trafficking, domestic violence, gerontology, school social work, child welfare. *Unit head:* Dr. Charles Stoops, Dean, 708-366-3316, E-mail: cstoops@dom.edu. *Application contact:* Felicia L. Townsend, Assistant Dean of Recruitment, Admissions and Marketing, 708-771-5298, Fax: 708-366-3446, E-mail: ftownsend@dom.edu. Web site: http://www.socialwork.dom.edu.

East Carolina University, Graduate School, College of Human Ecology, School of Social Work, Greenville, NC 27858-4353. Offers gerontology (Certificate); social work (MSW); substance abuse (Certificate). *Accreditation:* CSWE. Postbaccalaureate distance learning degree programs offered (no on-campus study). *Degree requirements:* For master's, comprehensive exam. *Entrance requirements:* For master's, GRE or MAT. Additional exam requirements/recommendations for international students: Required—TOEFL. *Application deadline:* For fall admission, 2/1 priority date for domestic students, 2/1 for international students. Application fee: $50. *Expenses:* Tuition, state resident: full-time $3557; part-time $444.63 per semester hour. Tuition, nonresident: full-time $14,351; part-time $1793.88 per semester hour. *Required fees:* $2016; $252 per semester hour. Part-time tuition and fees vary according to course load, campus/location and program. *Financial support:* Fellowships and research assistantships available. Financial award application deadline: 6/1. *Faculty research:* Social research, gerontology, women's issues, social services in schools, human behavior. *Unit head:* Dr. Shelia Bunch, Director, 252-328-4202, E-mail: bunchs@ecu.edu. *Application contact:* Dean of Graduate School, 252-328-6012, Fax: 252-328-6071, E-mail: gradschool@ecu.edu. Web site: http://www.ecu.edu/che/socw/.

Eastern Michigan University, Graduate School, College of Health and Human Services, School of Social Work, Ypsilanti, MI 48197. Offers family and children's services (MSW); mental health and chemical dependency (MSW); services to the aging (MSW). *Accreditation:* CSWE. Part-time and evening/weekend programs available. *Faculty:* 20 full-time (16 women). *Students:* 13 full-time (11 women), 192 part-time (170 women); includes 77 minority (70 Black or African American, non-Hispanic/Latino; 5 Hispanic/Latino; 2 Two or more races, non-Hispanic/Latino). Average age 36. 283 applicants, 40% accepted, 78 enrolled. In 2011, 56 master's awarded. *Entrance requirements:* Additional exam requirements/recommendations for international students: Required—TOEFL. *Application deadline:* For fall admission, 1/15 priority date for domestic students. Applications are processed on a rolling basis. Application fee: $35. *Expenses:* Tuition, state resident: full-time $10,367; part-time $432 per credit hour. Tuition, nonresident: full-time $20,435; part-time $851 per credit hour. *Required fees:* $39 per credit hour. $46 per semester. One-time fee: $100. Tuition and fees vary according to course level, degree level and reciprocity agreements. *Financial support:* Fellowships, research assistantships with full tuition reimbursements, teaching assistantships with full tuition reimbursements, career-related internships or fieldwork, Federal Work-Study, institutionally sponsored loans, scholarships/grants, tuition waivers (partial), and unspecified assistantships available. Support available to part-time students. Financial award applicants required to submit FAFSA. *Unit head:* Dr. Ann Alvarez, Director, 734-487-0393, Fax: 734-487-6832, E-mail: aalvare4@emich.edu. *Application contact:* Julie Harkema, Admissions Director, 734-487-4206, Fax: 734-487-6832, E-mail: jharkema@emich.edu. Web site: http://www.emich.edu/sw.

Eastern Washington University, Graduate Studies, College of Social and Behavioral Sciences and Social Work, Masters in Social Work, Cheney, WA 99004-2431. Offers MSW, MPA/MSW. *Accreditation:* CSWE. Part-time programs available. *Faculty:* 23 full-time (13 women). *Students:* 136 full-time (106 women), 166 part-time (136 women); includes 28 minority (6 Black or African American, non-Hispanic/Latino; 4 American Indian or Alaska Native, non-Hispanic/Latino; 7 Asian, non-Hispanic/Latino; 11 Hispanic/Latino), 1 international. Average age 36. 154 applicants, 36% accepted, 51 enrolled. In 2011, 173 master's awarded. *Degree requirements:* For master's, comprehensive exam. *Entrance requirements:* For master's, minimum GPA of 3.0. *Application deadline:* Applications are processed on a rolling basis. Application fee: $50. *Financial support:* In 2011–12, 23 teaching assistantships with partial tuition reimbursements (averaging $7,000 per year) were awarded; career-related internships or fieldwork, Federal Work-Study, institutionally sponsored loans, scholarships/grants, health care benefits, tuition waivers (partial), and unspecified assistantships also available. Support available to part-time students. Financial award application deadline: 2/1; financial award applicants required to submit FAFSA. *Unit head:* Dr. Jim Perez, Interim Dean, 509-359-4863. *Application contact:* Diane Somerday, Program Coordinator, 509-359-6482. Web site: http://www.ewu.edu/Locations/Off-Campus-Degree-Programs/Clark/MSW.xml.

East Tennessee State University, School of Graduate Studies, College of Arts and Sciences, Department of Social Work, Johnson City, TN 37614. Offers MSW. *Accreditation:* CSWE. *Faculty:* 10 full-time (7 women), 1 (woman) part-time/adjunct. *Students:* 56 full-time (48 women), 16 part-time (all women); includes 9 minority (6 Black or African American, non-Hispanic/Latino; 1 Asian, non-Hispanic/Latino; 1 Hispanic/Latino; 1 Two or more races, non-Hispanic/Latino). Average age 33. 96 applicants, 45% accepted, 23 enrolled. In 2011, 35 master's awarded. *Degree requirements:* For master's, comprehensive exam, field practicum. *Entrance requirements:* For master's, minimum GPA of 2.75, 3.0 for last 60 hours; three letters of recommendation; resume. Additional exam requirements/recommendations for international students: Required—TOEFL (minimum score 550 paper-based; 213 computer-based; 79 iBT). *Application deadline:* For fall admission, 2/1 for domestic and international students. Application fee: $35 ($45 for international students). Electronic applications accepted. *Expenses:* Tuition, state resident: full-time $7312; part-time $350 per credit hour. Tuition, nonresident: full-time $18,490; part-time $621 per credit hour. *Required fees:* $63 per credit hour. Tuition and fees vary according to course load and program. *Financial support:* In 2011–12, 16 students received support, including 9 research assistantships with full tuition reimbursements available (averaging $6,000 per year), 2 teaching assistantships with full tuition reimbursements available (averaging $6,000 per year); career-related internships or fieldwork, institutionally sponsored loans, scholarships/grants, and unspecified assistantships also available. Financial award application deadline: 7/1; financial award applicants required to submit FAFSA. *Unit head:* Dr. Michael Smith, Chair, 423-439-6006, Fax: 423-439-6010, E-mail: smithml1@etsu.edu. *Application contact:* Bethany Glassbrenner, Graduate Specialist, 423-439-6165, Fax: 423-439-5624, E-mail: glassbrenner@etsu.edu.

Edinboro University of Pennsylvania, College of Arts and Sciences, Department of Social Work, Edinboro, PA 16444. Offers MSW. *Accreditation:* CSWE. Evening/weekend programs available. *Faculty:* 4 full-time (3 women), 1 (woman) part-time/adjunct. *Students:* 51 full-time (46 women), 83 part-time (70 women); includes 8 minority (5 Black or African American, non-Hispanic/Latino; 1 American Indian or Alaska Native, non-Hispanic/Latino; 2 Hispanic/Latino). Average age 34. In 2011, 32 master's awarded. *Degree requirements:* For master's, competency exam. *Application deadline:* Applications are processed on a rolling basis. Application fee: $30. Electronic applications accepted. *Financial support:* In 2011–12, 5 research assistantships with full and partial tuition reimbursements (averaging $4,050 per year) were awarded; career-related internships or fieldwork, Federal Work-Study, scholarships/grants, and unspecified assistantships also available. Support available to part-time students. Financial award application deadline: 2/15; financial award applicants required to submit FAFSA. *Unit head:* Dr. Rosie Scaggs, Program Head, 814-732-1658, E-mail: rscaggs@edinboro.edu. *Application contact:* Dr. Alan Biel, Dean, 814-732-2752, Fax: 814-732-2268, E-mail: abiel@edinboro.edu. Web site: http://www.edinboro.edu/departments/social_work/msw_program.dot.

Fayetteville State University, Graduate School, Program in Social Work, Fayetteville, NC 28301-4298. Offers MSW. *Accreditation:* CSWE. *Faculty:* 12 full-time (7 women), 7 part-time/adjunct (2 women). *Students:* 78 full-time (62 women), 54 part-time (36 women); includes 79 minority (67 Black or African American, non-Hispanic/Latino; 4 American Indian or Alaska Native, non-Hispanic/Latino; 6 Hispanic/Latino; 2 Two or more races, non-Hispanic/Latino). Average age 35. 68 applicants, 100% accepted, 68 enrolled. In 2011, 25 master's awarded. *Application deadline:* For fall admission, 1/15 for domestic students. Application fee: $35. *Unit head:* Dr. Terri Moore-Brown, Department Chair, 910-672-1853, E-mail: tmbrown@uncfsu.edu. *Application contact:* Katrina Hoffman, Graduate Admissions Officer, 910-672-1374, Fax: 910-672-1470, E-mail: khoffma1@uncfsu.edu.

Florida Agricultural and Mechanical University, Division of Graduate Studies, Research, and Continuing Education, College of Arts and Sciences, Department of History and Political Science, Program in Applied Social Science, Tallahassee, FL 32307-3200. Offers African American history (MASS); criminal justice (MASS); economics (MASS); history (MASS); political science (MASS); public administration (MASS); public management (MASS); social work (MASS); sociology (MASS). Part-time programs available. *Degree requirements:* For master's, thesis optional. *Entrance requirements:* For master's, GRE General Test, minimum GPA of 3.0. *Faculty research:* Southern history, black history, election trends, presidential history.

Florida Agricultural and Mechanical University, Division of Graduate Studies, Research, and Continuing Education, College of Arts and Sciences, Department of History and Political Science, Program in Social Work, Tallahassee, FL 32307-3200. Offers MSW. *Accreditation:* CSWE. *Entrance requirements:* For master's, GRE General Test, minimum GPA of 3.0, 3 letters of recommendation. Additional exam requirements/recommendations for international students: Required—TOEFL.

Florida Atlantic University, College of Design and Social Inquiry, School of Social Work, Boca Raton, FL 33431-0991. Offers MSW. *Accreditation:* CSWE. Part-time and evening/weekend programs available. *Faculty:* 17 full-time (9 women), 20 part-time/adjunct (17 women). *Students:* 114 full-time (96 women), 102 part-time (91 women); includes 87 minority (38 Black or African American, non-Hispanic/Latino; 2 American Indian or Alaska Native, non-Hispanic/Latino; 5 Asian, non-Hispanic/Latino; 39 Hispanic/Latino; 3 Two or more races, non-Hispanic/Latino). Average age 34. 289 applicants, 51% accepted, 70 enrolled. In 2011, 58 master's awarded. *Application deadline:* For fall admission, 5/1 priority date for domestic students, 2/15 for international students. Applications are processed on a rolling basis. Application fee: $30. *Expenses: Tuition, area resident:* Part-time $343.02 per credit hour. Tuition, state resident: full-time $8232. Tuition, nonresident: full-time $23,931; part-time $997.14 per credit hour. *Financial support:* Fellowships with tuition reimbursements, research assistantships with tuition reimbursements, career-related internships or fieldwork, Federal Work-Study, institutionally sponsored loans, and tuition waivers (partial) available. Financial award application deadline: 4/1. *Faculty research:* Child welfare, special work education. *Unit head:* Dr. Michele Hawkins, Director, 561-297-3234, Fax: 561-297-2866, E-mail: mhawkins@fau.edu. *Application contact:* Dr. Elwood Hamlin, II, Coordinator, 501-297-3234, E-mail: ehamlin@fau.edu. Web site: http://www.fau.edu/ssw/.

Florida Gulf Coast University, College of Professional Studies, Program in Social Work, Fort Myers, FL 33965-6565. Offers MSW. *Accreditation:* CSWE. Part-time and evening/weekend programs available. *Faculty:* 37 full-time (15 women), 38 part-time/adjunct (12 women). *Students:* 33 full-time (30 women), 25 part-time (21 women); includes 16 minority (6 Black or African American, non-Hispanic/Latino; 1 Asian, non-Hispanic/Latino; 9 Hispanic/Latino), 1 international. Average age 33. 54 applicants, 70% accepted, 28 enrolled. In 2011, 38 master's awarded. *Entrance requirements:* For master's, GRE General Test, MAT, minimum GPA of 3.0. Additional exam requirements/recommendations for international students: Required—TOEFL (minimum score 550 paper-based; 213 computer-based). *Application deadline:* For fall admission, 4/1 priority date for domestic students. Applications are processed on a rolling basis. Application fee: $30. Electronic applications accepted. *Expenses:* Tuition, state resident: full-time $8289. Tuition, nonresident: full-time $28,895. *Required fees:* $1831. One-time fee: $30 full-time. *Financial support:* In 2011–12, 6 research assistantships were awarded; career-related internships or fieldwork and tuition waivers (partial) also available. Support available to part-time students. *Faculty research:* Gerontology, clinical case management, domestic violence, homelessness, migrant workers. *Unit head:* Dr. Mary Hart, Director/Assistant Professor, 239-590-7839, Fax: 239-590-7842, E-mail: mhart@fgcu.edu. *Application contact:* Laura Althouse, Executive Secretary, 239-590-7825, Fax: 239-590-7843, E-mail: lalthouse@fgcu.edu.

Florida International University, Robert Stempel College of Public Health and Social Work, School of Social Work, Miami, FL 33199. Offers social welfare (PhD); social work (MSW). *Accreditation:* CSWE (one or more programs are accredited). Part-time and evening/weekend programs available. *Degree requirements:* For doctorate, comprehensive exam, thesis/dissertation. *Entrance requirements:* For master's, minimum undergraduate GPA of 3.0 in upper-level coursework; letters of recommendation; undergraduate courses in biology (including human biology), statistics, and social/behavioral science (12 credits); BSW from accredited program; for doctorate, GRE, minimum graduate GPA of 3.5, 3 letters of recommendation, resume, writing samples, 2 examples of scholarly work. Additional exam requirements/recommendations for international students: Required—TOEFL (minimum score 550 paper-based; 80 iBT). Electronic applications accepted.

Florida State University, The Graduate School, College of Social Work, Tallahassee, FL 32306. Offers clinical social work (MSW); social policy and administration (MSW); social work (PhD); JD/MSW; MPA/MSW; MS/MSW; MSW/MBA. *Accreditation:* CSWE (one or more programs are accredited). Part-time and evening/weekend programs available. Postbaccalaureate distance learning degree programs offered (no on-campus study). *Faculty:* 35 full-time (22 women). *Students:* 277 full-time (241 women), 218 part-time (194 women); includes 151 minority (110 Black or African American, non-Hispanic/Latino; 3 American Indian or Alaska Native, non-Hispanic/Latino; 11 Asian, non-Hispanic/Latino; 21 Hispanic/Latino; 1 Native Hawaiian or other Pacific Islander, non-Hispanic/Latino; 5 Two or more races, non-Hispanic/Latino), 6 international. Average age 28. 499 applicants, 72% accepted, 289 enrolled. In 2011, 177 master's, 5 doctorates awarded. *Degree requirements:* For doctorate, comprehensive exam, thesis/dissertation. *Entrance requirements:* For master's, GRE General Test, minimum GPA of 3.0; for doctorate, GRE General Test, minimum GPA of 3.0. Additional exam requirements/recommendations for international students: Required—TOEFL (minimum score 80 iBT). *Application deadline:* For fall admission, 5/1 priority date for domestic students, 5/1 for international students; for winter admission, 3/1 priority date for domestic students, 3/1 for international students; for spring admission, 10/1 priority date for domestic students, 10/1 for international students. Applications are processed on a rolling basis. Application fee: $30. Electronic applications accepted. *Expenses:* Tuition, state resident: full-time $9474; part-time $350.88 per credit hour. Tuition, nonresident: full-time $16,236; part-time $601.34 per credit hour. *Required fees:* $630 per semester. One-time fee: $20. Tuition and fees vary according to course load and campus/location. *Financial support:* In 2011–12, 36 students received support, including 1 fellowship with full tuition reimbursement available (averaging $22,000 per year), 35 research assistantships with partial tuition reimbursements available (averaging $3,500 per year), 20 teaching assistantships with full tuition reimbursements available (averaging $15,000 per year); career-related internships or fieldwork, Federal Work-Study, institutionally sponsored loans, scholarships/grants, traineeships, health care benefits, tuition waivers (partial), and unspecified assistantships also available. Support available to part-time students. Financial award application deadline: 3/1; financial award applicants required to submit FAFSA. *Faculty research:* Family violence, AIDS/HIV, aging, family therapy, substance abuse, criminal justice. *Total annual research expenditures:* $2.6 million. *Unit head:* Dr. Nicholas Mazza, Dean, 850-644-4752, Fax: 850-644-9750, E-mail: nfmazza@fsu.edu. *Application contact:* Craig Stanley, Director of the MSW Program, 800-378-9550, Fax: 850-644-1201, E-mail: grad@csw.fsu.edu. Web site: http://csw.fsu.edu/.

Fordham University, Graduate School of Social Service, New York, NY 10023. Offers social work (MSW, PhD); JD/MSW. *Accreditation:* CSWE (one or more programs are accredited). Part-time and evening/weekend programs available. Postbaccalaureate distance learning degree programs offered (no on-campus study). *Degree requirements:* For master's, 1200 hours of field placement; for doctorate, comprehensive exam, thesis/dissertation. *Entrance requirements:* For master's, BA in liberal arts; for doctorate, GRE, master's degree in social work or related field. Additional exam requirements/recommendations for international students: Required—TOEFL (minimum score 575 paper-based; 231 computer-based; 90 iBT). Electronic applications accepted. *Expenses:* Contact institution. *Faculty research:* Aging, children and family, healthcare, domestic violence, substance abuse.

Gallaudet University, The Graduate School, Washington, DC 20002-3625. Offers audiology (Au D); clinical psychology (PhD); critical studies in the education of deaf learners (PhD); deaf and hard of hearing infants, toddlers, and their families (Certificate); deaf education (Ed S); deaf education: advanced studies (MA); deaf education: special programs in deaf education (MA); deaf history (Certificate); deaf studies (MA, Certificate); education deaf students with disabilities (Certificate); education: teacher preparation (MA), including deaf education, early childhood education and deaf education, elementary education and deaf education, secondary education and deaf education; hearing, speech and language sciences (MS, PhD); international development (MA); interpretation (MA, PhD); linguistics (MA, PhD); mental health counseling (MA); public administration (MA); school counseling (MA); school psychology (Psy S); sign language teaching (MA); social work (MSW); speech-language pathology (MS). Part-time programs available. *Faculty:* 62 full-time (44 women). *Students:* 300 full-time (246 women), 110 part-time (82 women); includes 80 minority (27 Black or African American, non-Hispanic/Latino; 1 American Indian or Alaska Native, non-Hispanic/Latino; 11 Asian, non-Hispanic/Latino; 25 Hispanic/Latino; 1 Native Hawaiian or other Pacific Islander, non-Hispanic/Latino; 15 Two or more races, non-Hispanic/Latino), 24 international. Average age 30. 498 applicants, 45% accepted, 168 enrolled. In 2011, 129 master's, 24 doctorates, 19 other advanced degrees awarded. Terminal master's awarded for partial completion of doctoral program. *Degree requirements:* For master's, comprehensive exam (for some programs), thesis optional; for doctorate, comprehensive exam, thesis/dissertation. *Entrance requirements:* For master's and doctorate, GRE General Test or MAT, letters of recommendation, interviews, goals statement, ASL proficiency interview, written English competency. Additional exam requirements/recommendations for international students: Required—TOEFL. *Application deadline:* For fall admission, 2/15 for domestic students. Applications are processed on a rolling basis. Application fee: $50. Electronic applications accepted. *Expenses: Tuition:* Full-time $12,770; part-time $710 per credit. *Required fees:* $376. *Financial support:* In 2011–12, 287 students received support. Fellowships, research assistantships, teaching assistantships, career-related internships or fieldwork, Federal Work-Study, scholarships/grants, tuition waivers (partial), and unspecified assistantships available. Support available to part-time students. Financial award applicants required to submit FAFSA. *Faculty research:* Bimodal bilingualism development, audiology, telecommunications access, early childhood education, linguistics, visual language and visual learning, rehabilitation and hearing enhancement. *Unit head:* Dr. Carol J. Erting, Dean, 202-651-5520, Fax: 202-651-5027, E-mail: carol.erting@gallaudet.edu. *Application contact:* Wednesday Luria, Coordinator of Prospective Graduate Student Services, 202-651-5400, Fax: 202-651-5295, E-mail: graduate.school@gallaudet.edu. Web site: http://www.gallaudet.edu/x26696.xml.

George Mason University, College of Health and Human Services, Department of Social Work, Fairfax, VA 22030. Offers MSW. *Accreditation:* CSWE. *Faculty:* 15 full-time (11 women), 32 part-time/adjunct (29 women). *Students:* 137 full-time (123 women), 30 part-time (29 women); includes 50 minority (33 Black or African American, non-Hispanic/Latino; 6 Asian, non-Hispanic/Latino; 9 Hispanic/Latino; 2 Two or more races, non-Hispanic/Latino). Average age 30. 251 applicants, 71% accepted, 95 enrolled. In 2011, 50 degrees awarded. *Entrance requirements:* For master's, 2 official transcripts; expanded goals statement; resume; bachelor's degree with minimum GPA of 3.0; 30 undergraduate credits in liberal arts with English composition; history or government, social sciences and statistics; 3 letters of recommendation. Additional exam requirements/recommendations for international students: Required—TOEFL (minimum score 575 paper-based; 230 computer-based; 88 iBT), IELTS, Pearson Test of English. *Application deadline:* For fall admission, 1/15 priority date for domestic students. Application fee: $65 ($80 for international students). Electronic applications accepted. *Expenses:* Tuition, state resident: full-time $8750; part-time $364.58 per credit. Tuition, nonresident: full-time $24,092; part-time $1003.83 per credit. *Required fees:* $2514; $104.75 per credit. *Financial support:* In 2011–12, 6 students received support, including 4 research assistantships with full and partial tuition reimbursements available (averaging $22,369 per year), 2 teaching assistantships with full and partial tuition reimbursements available (averaging $15,000 per year); career-related internships or fieldwork, Federal Work-Study, scholarships/grants, unspecified assistantships, and health care benefits (full-time research or teaching assistantship recipients) also available. Financial award application deadline: 3/1; financial award applicants required to submit FAFSA. *Faculty research:* Social work methods, child welfare, social work ethics, field education, supervision. *Total annual research expenditures:* $67,438. *Unit head:* Cathleen Lewandowski, Chair, 703-993-7017, Fax: 703-993-2193, E-mail: clewando@gmu.edu. *Application contact:* Nimao Abdi, Administrative Support Specialist, Master's Program in Social Work, 703-993-4247, Fax: 703-993-2193, E-mail: nabdi1@gmu.edu. Web site: http://chhs.gmu.edu/socialwork/.

Georgia State University, College of Health and Human Sciences, School of Social Work, Atlanta, GA 30294. Offers community partnerships (MSW). *Accreditation:* CSWE. Part-time programs available. *Degree requirements:* For master's, community project. *Entrance requirements:* For master's, GRE General Test. Additional exam requirements/recommendations for international students: Required—TOEFL (minimum score 550 paper-based; 213 computer-based). Electronic applications accepted. *Faculty research:* Child welfare, labor unions and child care workers, secondary victimization in death penalty cases, aging.

Governors State University, College of Health Professions, Program in Social Work, University Park, IL 60484. Offers MSW. *Accreditation:* CSWE. *Students:* 57 full-time (49 women), 69 part-time (57 women); includes 83 minority (69 Black or African American, non-Hispanic/Latino; 1 American Indian or Alaska Native, non-Hispanic/Latino; 3 Asian, non-Hispanic/Latino; 7 Hispanic/Latino; 1 Native Hawaiian or other Pacific Islander, non-Hispanic/Latino; 2 Two or more races, non-Hispanic/Latino). Average age 34. 73 applicants, 84% accepted, 32 enrolled. *Application deadline:* For fall admission, 2/15 for domestic students. Application fee: $25. *Financial support:* Application deadline: 5/1. *Unit head:* Dr. Elizabeth Cada, Dean, 708-235-7295. *Application contact:* Yakeea Daniels, Director of Admission, 708-534-4510, E-mail: ydaniels@govst.edu.

Graduate School and University Center of the City University of New York, Graduate Studies, Program in Social Welfare, New York, NY 10016-4039. Offers DSW, PhD. *Degree requirements:* For doctorate, thesis/dissertation, project, qualifying exam. *Entrance requirements:* For doctorate, MSW or equivalent, 3 years of post-master's work experience. Additional exam requirements/recommendations for international students: Required—TOEFL. Electronic applications accepted.

Grambling State University, School of Graduate Studies and Research, College of Professional Studies, School of Social Work, Grambling, LA 71245. Offers MSW. *Accreditation:* CSWE. Part-time programs available. *Degree requirements:* For master's, comprehensive exam, research project or thesis. *Entrance requirements:* For master's, GRE, minimum GPA of 3.0 on last degree, 36 hours in liberal arts, autobiography, interview. Additional exam requirements/recommendations for international students: Required—TOEFL (minimum score 500 paper-based; 173 computer-based; 61 iBT). Electronic applications accepted. *Expenses:* Tuition, state resident: full-time $3546; part-time $192 per credit hour. Tuition, nonresident: full-time $3456; part-time $192 per credit hour. *Required fees:* $1829; $1829 per semester hour. *Faculty research:* Welfare history, aging, end of life issues, stress and child abuse; African-American families, rurality.

Grand Valley State University, College of Community and Public Service, School of Social Work, Allendale, MI 49401-9403. Offers MSW. *Accreditation:* CSWE. Part-time programs available. *Entrance requirements:* Additional exam requirements/recommendations for international students: Required—TOEFL. Electronic applications accepted. *Faculty research:* Drug addiction, aging, management, effectiveness of therapy.

Gratz College, Graduate Programs, Program in Jewish Communal Service, Melrose Park, PA 19027. Offers MA, Certificate, MSW/Certificate. MSW/Certificate offered jointly with University of Pennsylvania. Part-time and evening/weekend programs available. Postbaccalaureate distance learning degree programs offered. *Faculty:* 8 full-time (4 women), 11 part-time/adjunct (7 women). *Students:* 4 full-time, 12 part-time. Average age 25. In 2011, 3 master's, 2 other advanced degrees awarded. *Degree requirements:* For master's, one foreign language, internship. *Application deadline:* Applications are processed on a rolling basis. Application fee: $50. *Financial support:* Fellowships, career-related internships or fieldwork, Federal Work-Study, and unspecified assistantships available. Support available to part-time students. Financial award application deadline: 4/15. *Unit head:* Dr. Jerome Kutnick, Dean for Academic Affairs, 215-635-7300 Ext. 137, Fax: 215-635-7320, E-mail: jkutnick@gratz.edu. *Application contact:* Joanna Boeing Bratton, Director of Admissions, 215-635-7300 Ext. 140, Fax: 215-635-7399, E-mail: admissions@gratz.edu.

Hawai`i Pacific University, College of Humanities and Social Sciences, Program in Social Work, Honolulu, HI 96813. Offers MSW. *Accreditation:* CSWE. Part-time and evening/weekend programs available. *Faculty:* 6 full-time (3 women), 2 part-time/adjunct (0 women). *Students:* 90 full-time (70 women), 15 part-time (11 women); includes 45 minority (11 Black or African American, non-Hispanic/Latino; 1 Asian, non-Hispanic/Latino; 14 Hispanic/Latino; 3 Native Hawaiian or other Pacific Islander, non-Hispanic/Latino; 16 Two or more races, non-Hispanic/Latino). 107 applicants, 84% accepted, 51 enrolled. In 2011, 11 master's awarded. *Expenses: Tuition:* Full-time $13,230; part-time $735 per credit. Tuition and fees vary according to course load and program. *Financial support:* In 2011–12, 18 students received support. Career-related internships or fieldwork, Federal Work-Study, scholarships/grants, tuition waivers, and unspecified assistantships available. *Unit head:* Dr. William Potter, Associate Vice President and Dean, 808-544-0228, Fax: 808-544-1424, E-mail: wpotter@hpu.edu. *Application contact:* Chad Schempp, Director of Graduate Admissions, 808-543-8035, Fax: 808-544-0280, E-mail: graduate@hpu.edu.

See Display on next page and Close-Up on page 1773.

Howard University, School of Social Work, Washington, DC 20059. Offers MSW, PhD. *Accreditation:* CSWE (one or more programs are accredited). Part-time programs available. *Degree requirements:* For doctorate, comprehensive exam, thesis/dissertation, qualifying exam. *Entrance requirements:* For master's, minimum GPA of 2.5; for doctorate, GRE General Test, minimum GPA of 3.3, MSW or master's in related field. Additional exam requirements/recommendations for international students: Required—TOEFL. *Faculty research:* Infant mortality, child and family services, displaced populations, social work practice, domestic violence, black males, mental health.

Humboldt State University, Academic Programs, College of Professional Studies, Department of Social Work, Arcata, CA 95521-8299. Offers MSW. *Accreditation:* CSWE. *Students:* 43 full-time (30 women), 1 (woman) part-time; includes 12 minority (4 American Indian or Alaska Native, non-Hispanic/Latino; 1 Asian, non-Hispanic/Latino; 4 Hispanic/Latino; 3 Two or more races, non-Hispanic/Latino). Average age 35. 65 applicants, 65% accepted, 26 enrolled. In 2011, 40 master's awarded. *Entrance requirements:* For master's, 3 letters of recommendation. Additional exam requirements/recommendations for international students: Required—TOEFL (minimum score 500 paper-based; 173 computer-based). *Application deadline:* For fall admission, 3/15 for domestic and international students. Applications are processed on a rolling basis. Application fee: $55. *Expenses:* Tuition, state resident: full-time $6734. Tuition, nonresident: full-time $15,662; part-time $372 per credit. *Required fees:* $903. Tuition and fees vary according to program. *Financial support:* Application deadline: 3/1; applicants required to submit FAFSA. *Unit head:* Dr. Ronnie Swartz, Chair, 707-826-4443, Fax: 707-826-4418, E-mail: rjs19@humboldt.edu. *Application contact:* Dr. Michael Yellow Bird, Coordinator, 707-826-5346, Fax: 707-826-4418, E-mail: mjy9@humboldt.edu. Web site: http://www.humboldt.edu/~swp/mswhomepage.shtml.

Hunter College of the City University of New York, Graduate School, School of Social Work, New York, NY 10021-5085. Offers MSW, DSW. DSW offered jointly with Graduate School and University Center of the City University of New York. *Accreditation:* CSWE (one or more programs are accredited). *Faculty:* 30 full-time (16 women), 63 part-time/adjunct (58 women). *Students:* 778 full-time (658 women), 257 part-time (205 women); includes 472 minority (227 Black or African American, non-Hispanic/Latino; 2 American Indian or Alaska Native, non-Hispanic/Latino; 47 Asian, non-Hispanic/Latino; 196 Hispanic/Latino), 14 international. Average age 33. 1,374 applicants, 42% accepted, 343 enrolled. In 2011, 466 master's awarded. *Degree* requirements: For master's, major paper. *Entrance requirements:* Additional exam requirements/recommendations for international students: Required—TOEFL. *Application deadline:* For fall admission, 1/15 for domestic and international students. Applications are processed on a rolling basis. Application fee: $125. *Expenses:* Tuition, state resident: full-time $8210; part-time $345 per credit. Tuition, nonresident: full-time $15,360; part-time $640 per credit. *Required fees:* $280 per semester. One-time fee: $125. Tuition and fees vary according to class time, campus/location and program. *Financial support:* In 2011–12, 120 fellowships (averaging $1,000 per year) were awarded; career-related internships or fieldwork, Federal Work-Study, and tuition waivers (partial) also available. Support available to part-time students. *Faculty research:* Child welfare, AIDS, homeless, aging, mental health. *Unit head:* Dr. Jacqueline B. Mondros, Dean/Professor, 212-452-7085, Fax: 212-452-7150, E-mail: jmondros@hunter.cuny.edu. *Application contact:* Raymond Montero, Coordinator of Admissions, 212-452-7005, E-mail: grad.socworkadvisor@hunter.cuny.edu. Web site: http://www.hunter.cuny.edu/socwork/.

Illinois State University, Graduate School, College of Arts and Sciences, School of Social Work, Normal, IL 61790-2200. Offers MSW. *Accreditation:* CSWE. *Faculty research:* Developing professional careers in child welfare, research and policy work for the Evan B. Donaldson Adoption Institute, evidence-based practice training pilot evaluation.

Indiana University East, School of Social Work, Richmond, IN 47374-1289. Offers MSW.

Indiana University Northwest, Division of Social Work, Gary, IN 46408-1197. Offers MSW. Part-time and evening/weekend programs available. *Faculty:* 1 full-time (0 women). *Students:* 42 full-time (38 women), 74 part-time (67 women); includes 49 minority (34 Black or African American, non-Hispanic/Latino; 1 American Indian or Alaska Native, non-Hispanic/Latino; 14 Hispanic/Latino). Average age 37. 24 applicants, 100% accepted, 20 enrolled. In 2011, 31 master's awarded. *Entrance requirements:* For master's, minimum GPA of 3.0. *Application deadline:* For fall admission, 2/1 for domestic students. Application fee: $25. *Expenses:* Contact institution. *Financial support:* Career-related internships or fieldwork, Federal Work-Study, and tuition waivers (partial) available. Support available to part-time students. Financial award application deadline: 6/1; financial award applicants required to submit FAFSA. *Faculty research:* Educational outcomes, generalist practice, homelessness. *Total annual research expenditures:* $1,000. *Unit head:* Dr. Frank Caucci, Director, 219-985-4286, Fax: 219-981-4264, E-mail: fcaucci@iun.edu. *Application contact:* Admissions Counselor, 219-980-6760, Fax: 219-980-7103. Web site: http://www.iun.edu/~socialwk/.

Indiana University–Purdue University Indianapolis, School of Social Work, Indianapolis, IN 46202-2896. Offers MSW, PhD, Certificate. *Accreditation:* CSWE (one or more programs are accredited). Part-time and evening/weekend programs available. *Faculty:* 40 full-time. *Students:* 255 full-time (223 women), 262 part-time (219 women); includes 83 minority (52 Black or African American, non-Hispanic/Latino; 3 Asian, non-Hispanic/Latino; 16 Hispanic/Latino; 1 Native Hawaiian or other Pacific Islander, non-Hispanic/Latino; 11 Two or more races, non-Hispanic/Latino). Average age 32. 362 applicants, 65% accepted, 172 enrolled. In 2011, 195 degrees awarded. Terminal master's awarded for partial completion of doctoral program. *Degree requirements:* For master's, field practicum; for doctorate, thesis/dissertation, residential internship. *Entrance requirements:* For master's, minimum GPA of 2.5; course work in social behavior, statistics, research methodology, and human biology; for doctorate, GRE General Test. Additional exam requirements/recommendations for international students: Required—TOEFL. Application fee: $55 ($65 for international students). *Expenses:* Contact institution. *Financial support:* Fellowships with full tuition reimbursements, research assistantships with partial tuition reimbursements, teaching assistantships, Federal Work-Study, institutionally sponsored loans, scholarships/grants, and tuition waivers (partial) available. Support available to part-time students. Financial award applicants required to submit FAFSA. *Faculty research:* Social justice, institutional child welfare, mental health, aging, AIDS/HIV disease. *Total annual research expenditures:* $145,580. *Unit head:* Dr. Margaret Adamek, Dean, 317-274-6730, Fax: 317-274-8630. *Application contact:* Susan Larimer, Information Contact for MSW, 317-274-6966, Fax: 317-274-8630. Web site: http://iussw.iupui.edu/.

Indiana University South Bend, School of Social Work, South Bend, IN 46634-7111. Offers MSW. Part-time and evening/weekend programs available. *Faculty:* 4 full-time (2 women). *Students:* 55 full-time (46 women), 70 part-time (62 women); includes 21 minority (20 Black or African American, non-Hispanic/Latino; 1 Hispanic/Latino). Average age 35. 44 applicants, 77% accepted, 27 enrolled. In 2011, 28 master's awarded. *Application deadline:* For fall admission, 2/1 priority date for domestic students. Application fee: $50 ($60 for international students). *Expenses:* Contact institution. *Financial support:* Career-related internships or fieldwork and Federal Work-Study available. Support available to part-time students. Financial award application deadline: 3/1; financial award applicants required to submit FAFSA. *Unit head:* Dr. Marilynne Ramsey, Program Director, 574-520-4880, Fax: 574-520-4876, E-mail: mjramsey@iusb.edu. *Application contact:* Admissions Counselor, 574-520-4839, Fax: 574-520-4834, E-mail: graduate@iusb.edu.

Institute for Clinical Social Work, Graduate Programs, Chicago, IL 60601. Offers PhD. Part-time programs available. *Degree requirements:* For doctorate, thesis/dissertation, supervised practicum. *Entrance requirements:* For doctorate, 2 years of experience. *Faculty research:* Impact of AIDS on partners, effects of learning disabilities on children and families, clinical social work issues.

Inter American University of Puerto Rico, Metropolitan Campus, Graduate Programs, Program in Social Work, San Juan, PR 00919-1293. Offers advanced clinical services (MSW); advanced social work administration (MSW); clinical services (MSW); social work administration (MSW). *Accreditation:* CSWE. Evening/weekend programs available. *Degree requirements:* For master's, comprehensive exam. *Entrance requirements:* For master's, GRE or EXADEP, interview. Electronic applications accepted.

Jackson State University, Graduate School, School of Social Work, Jackson, MS 39217. Offers MSW, PhD. *Accreditation:* CSWE (one or more programs are accredited). Evening/weekend programs available. *Degree requirements:* For master's, comprehensive exam; for doctorate, comprehensive exam, thesis/dissertation. *Entrance requirements:* For master's, GRE General Test; for doctorate, MAT. Additional exam requirements/recommendations for international students: Required—TOEFL (minimum score 520 paper-based; 195 computer-based; 67 iBT).

Kean University, Nathan Weiss Graduate College, Program in Social Work, Union, NJ 07083. Offers advanced standing (MSW); social work (MSW). *Accreditation:* CSWE. *Faculty:* 4 full-time (all women). *Students:* 138 full-time (120 women), 12 part-time (10 women); includes 94 minority (61 Black or African American, non-Hispanic/Latino; 2 Asian, non-Hispanic/Latino; 29 Hispanic/Latino; 2 Two or more races, non-Hispanic/Latino), 1 international. Average age 30. 246 applicants, 67% accepted, 91 enrolled. In 2011, 54 master's awarded. *Degree requirements:* For master's, field work. *Entrance requirements:* For master's, BSW with minimum GPA of 3.0 overall and in BSW courses, including research; undergraduate course work in social sciences; 3 letters of recommendation; transcripts; personal statement; completion of at least 425 hours of field education, MSW supplemental application. Additional exam requirements/recommendations for international students: Required—TOEFL (minimum score 79 iBT). *Application deadline:* For fall admission, 3/15 for domestic and international students. Applications are processed on a rolling basis. Application fee: $75 ($150 for international students). Electronic applications accepted. *Expenses:* Tuition, state resident: full-time $11,302; part-time $550 per credit. Tuition, nonresident: full-time $15,318; part-time $674 per credit. *Required fees:* $2849; $130 per credit. Tuition and fees vary according to degree level. *Financial support:* In 2011–12, 3 research assistantships with full tuition reimbursements (averaging $3,263 per year) were awarded; unspecified assistantships also available. Financial award applicants required to submit FAFSA. *Unit head:* Dr. Josephine Norward, Program Coordinator, 908-737-4033, E-mail: jnorwar@kean.edu. *Application contact:* Steven Koch, Admissions Counselor, 908-737-5924, E-mail: skoch@kean.edu. Web site: http://www.kean.edu/KU/Social-Work-M-S-W-.

Kennesaw State University, College of Health and Human Services, Program in Social Work, Kennesaw, GA 30144-5591. Offers MSW. *Accreditation:* CSWE. *Students:* 81 full-time (72 women), 1 (woman) part-time; includes 26 minority (20 Black or African American, non-Hispanic/Latino; 6 Hispanic/Latino), 1 international. Average age 32. 108 applicants, 72% accepted, 48 enrolled. In 2011, 30 master's awarded. *Entrance requirements:* For master's, GRE, criminal history check, minimum GPA of 2.75, 3 letters of recommendation, resume. Additional exam requirements/recommendations for international students: Required—TOEFL (minimum score 550 paper-based; 213 computer-based; 80 iBT), IELTS (minimum score 6). *Application deadline:* For fall admission, 3/15 for domestic and international students. Application fee: $60. Electronic applications accepted. *Expenses:* Tuition, state resident: full-time $3000; part-time $250 per semester hour. Tuition, nonresident: full-time $10,836; part-time $903 per semester hour. *Required fees:* $774 per semester. *Financial support:* In 2011–12, 2 research assistantships (averaging $4,000 per year) were awarded; unspecified assistantships also available. Financial award applicants required to submit FAFSA. *Unit head:* Dr. Alan Kirk, Department Chair, 770-423-6630, E-mail: akirk@kennesaw.edu. *Application contact:* Tamara Hutto, Admissions Counselor, 770-420-4377, Fax: 770-423-6885, E-mail: vmarquez@kennesaw.edu. Web site: http://www.kennesaw.edu.

Kutztown University of Pennsylvania, College of Liberal Arts and Sciences, Program in Social Work, Kutztown, PA 19530-0730. Offers MSW. *Accreditation:* CSWE. Part-time and evening/weekend programs available. *Faculty:* 11 full-time (5 women). *Students:* 48 full-time (40 women), 15 part-time (9 women); includes 16 minority (10 Black or African American, non-Hispanic/Latino; 4 Hispanic/Latino; 2 Two or more races, non-Hispanic/Latino), 1 international. Average age 31. 43 applicants, 79% accepted, 30 enrolled. In 2011, 21 master's awarded. *Degree requirements:* For master's, comprehensive exam. *Entrance requirements:* For master's, GRE. Additional exam requirements/recommendations for international students: Required—TOEFL (minimum score 550 paper-based; 79 iBT). *Application deadline:* For fall admission, 8/1 priority date for domestic students, 8/1 for international students; for spring admission, 12/1 priority date for domestic students, 12/1 for international students. Applications are processed on a rolling basis. Application fee: $35. Electronic applications accepted. *Expenses:* Tuition, state resident: full-time $7488; part-time $416 per credit. Tuition, nonresident: full-time $11,232; part-time $624 per credit. *Financial support:* Career-related internships or fieldwork, Federal Work-Study, scholarships/grants, and unspecified assistantships available. Financial award application deadline: 3/1; financial award applicants required to submit FAFSA. *Unit head:* Dr. John Vafeas, Chairperson, 610-683-4235, E-mail: vafeas@kutztown.edu. *Application contact:* Kelly D. Burr, Associate Director, Graduate Admissions, 610-683-4200, Fax: 610-683-1393, E-mail: graduate@kutztown.edu.

Lakehead University, Graduate Studies, Gerontology Collaborative Program-Northern Educational Center for Aging and Health, Thunder Bay, ON P7B 5E1, Canada. Offers gerontology (M Ed, M Sc, MA, MSW). Part-time programs available. *Degree requirements:* For master's, thesis (for some programs). *Entrance requirements:* Additional exam requirements/recommendations for international students: Required—TOEFL. *Faculty research:* Integrated health information systems.

Lakehead University, Graduate Studies, School of Social Work, Thunder Bay, ON P7B 5E1, Canada. Offers gerontology (MSW); social work (MSW); women's studies (MSW). Part-time programs available. *Degree requirements:* For master's, thesis or project. *Entrance requirements:* For master's, minimum B average. Additional exam requirements/recommendations for international students: Required—TOEFL. *Faculty research:* Clinical psychology, social work and practice theory, long-term care, health care for frail elderly, women's studies.

Laurentian University, School of Graduate Studies and Research, School of Social Work, Sudbury, ON P3E 2C6, Canada. Offers MSW. Open only to French-speaking students. Part-time programs available. *Degree requirements:* For master's, thesis. *Faculty research:* Income security, poverty, violence against women, child poverty, effects of economic crisis on families.

Loma Linda University, School of Science and Technology, Department of Social Work and Social Ecology, Loma Linda, CA 92350. Offers social policy and research (PhD); social work (MSW). *Accreditation:* CSWE. *Degree requirements:* For master's, comprehensive exam, thesis optional; for doctorate, comprehensive exam, thesis/dissertation. *Entrance requirements:* For master's and doctorate, GRE General Test. Additional exam requirements/recommendations for international students: Required—TOEFL, Michigan English Language Assessment Battery. Electronic applications accepted.

Long Island University–C. W. Post Campus, School of Health Professions and Nursing, Master of Social Work Program, Brookville, NY 11548-1300. Offers alcohol and substance abuse (MSW); child and family welfare (MSW); forensic social work (MSW); gerontology (MSW); nonprofit management (MSW). *Accreditation:* CSWE.

Louisiana State University and Agricultural and Mechanical College, Graduate School, School of Social Work, Baton Rouge, LA 70803. Offers MSW, PhD. *Accreditation:* CSWE (one or more programs are accredited). Part-time programs available. *Faculty:* 11 full-time (8 women). *Students:* 193 full-time (173 women), 54 part-time (46 women); includes 65 minority (55 Black or African American, non-Hispanic/Latino; 1 American Indian or Alaska Native, non-Hispanic/Latino; 1 Asian, non-Hispanic/Latino; 5 Hispanic/Latino; 3 Two or more races, non-Hispanic/Latino), 4 international. Average age 29. 146 applicants, 87% accepted, 81 enrolled. In 2011, 76 master's, 4 doctorates awarded. *Degree requirements:* For master's, thesis, field instruction; for doctorate, comprehensive exam, thesis/dissertation. *Entrance requirements:* For master's and doctorate, GRE General Test, minimum GPA of 3.0. Additional exam requirements/recommendations for international students: Required—TOEFL (minimum score 550 paper-based; 213 computer-based; 79 iBT) or IELTS (minimum score 6.5). *Application deadline:* For fall admission, 2/15 for domestic and international students. Application fee: $50 ($70 for international students). Electronic applications accepted. *Financial support:* In 2011–12, 177 students received support, including 7 research assistantships with partial tuition reimbursements available (averaging $13,393 per year), 16 teaching assistantships with partial tuition reimbursements available (averaging $11,646 per year); fellowships, career-related internships or fieldwork, Federal Work-Study, scholarships/grants, health care benefits, and unspecified assistantships also available. Support available to part-time students. Financial award applicants required to submit FAFSA. *Faculty research:* Child welfare, gerontology, addictions, mental health. *Total annual research expenditures:* $112,631. *Unit head:* Dr. Daphne Cain, Dean, 225-578-0433, Fax: 225-578-1357, E-mail: dscain@lsu.edu. *Application contact:* Denise Chiasson, Assistant Dean, 225-578-1234, Fax: 225-578-1357, E-mail: dchiass@lsu.edu. Web site: http://www.socialwork.lsu.edu/.

Loyola University Chicago, School of Social Work, Chicago, IL 60660. Offers MSW, PhD, PGC, JD/MSW, M Div/MSW, MJ/MSW, MSW/MA. *Accreditation:* CSWE (one or more programs are accredited). Part-time programs available. *Degree requirements:* For doctorate, comprehensive exam, thesis/dissertation. *Entrance requirements:* For master's, GRE; for doctorate, GRE or MAT. Additional exam requirements/recommendations for international students: Required—TOEFL (minimum score 550 paper-based; 79 computer-based; 79 iBT). *Expenses: Tuition:* Full-time $15,660; part-time $870 per credit hour. *Required fees:* $125 per semester. Tuition and fees vary according to course load and program. *Faculty research:* Aging, trauma, migration, poverty, substance abuse.

Marywood University, Academic Affairs, College of Health and Human Services, School of Social Work and Administrative Services, Scranton, PA 18509-1598. Offers gerontology (MS); health services administration (MHSA); public administration (MPA), including nonprofit management; social work (MSW). *Accreditation:* CSWE. *Faculty:* 18 full-time (12 women). *Students:* 181 full-time (161 women), 140 part-time (127 women); includes 31 minority (10 Black or African American, non-Hispanic/Latino; 1 Asian, non-Hispanic/Latino; 20 Hispanic/Latino). Average age 33. In 2011, 125 degrees awarded. *Entrance requirements:* Additional exam requirements/recommendations for international students: Required—TOEFL (minimum score 550 paper-based; 213 computer-based; 79 iBT). *Application deadline:* For fall admission, 4/1 priority date for domestic students, 3/31 for international students; for spring admission, 11/1 priority date for domestic students, 8/31 for international students. Applications are processed on a rolling basis. Application fee: $35. Electronic applications accepted. *Expenses:* Contact institution. *Financial support:* Research assistantships, career-related internships or fieldwork, scholarships/grants, and unspecified assistantships available. Support available to part-time students. Financial award application deadline: 6/30; financial award applicants required to submit FAFSA. *Faculty research:* Impaired professionals, ethics, child welfare, communities, professional gatekeeping. *Unit head:* Dr. Lloyd Lyter, Director, 570-348-6211 Ext. 2388, E-mail: lyter@marywood.edu. *Application contact:* Tammy Manka, Assistant Director of Graduate Admissions, 866-279-9663, E-mail: tmanka@marywood.edu. Web site: http://www.marywood.edu/academics/gradcatalog/.

Marywood University, Academic Affairs, Reap College of Education and Human Development, Department of Human Development, Emphasis in Social Work, Scranton, PA 18509-1598. Offers PhD. *Entrance requirements:* Additional exam requirements/recommendations for international students: Required—TOEFL (minimum score 550 paper-based; 213 computer-based; 79 iBT). *Application deadline:* For fall admission, 1/30 priority date for domestic students, 1/30 for international students. Application fee: $35. Electronic applications accepted. *Expenses:* Contact institution. *Financial support:* Career-related internships or fieldwork, scholarships/grants, and unspecified assistantships available. Support available to part-time students. Financial award application deadline: 6/30; financial award applicants required to submit FAFSA. *Unit head:* Dr. Brook Cannon, Director, 570-348-6211 Ext. 2324, E-mail: cannonb@marywood.edu. *Application contact:* Tammy Manka, Assistant Director of Graduate Admissions, 570-348-6211 Ext. 2322, E-mail: tmanka@marywood.edu. Web site: http://www.marywood.edu/phd/specializations.html.

McGill University, Faculty of Graduate and Postdoctoral Studies, Faculty of Arts, School of Social Work, Montréal, QC H3A 2T5, Canada. Offers MSW, PhD, Diploma, MSW/LL B. PhD offered jointly with Université de Montréal.

McMaster University, School of Graduate Studies, Faculty of Social Sciences, School of Social Work, Hamilton, ON L8S 4M2, Canada. Offers analysis of social welfare policy (MSW); analysis of social work practice (MSW). Part-time programs available. *Entrance requirements:* For master's, minimum B+ average in final year, BSW from accredited program, half course each in introductory statistics and introductory social research methods. Additional exam requirements/recommendations for international students: Required—TOEFL (minimum score 580 paper-based; 237 computer-based). *Faculty research:* Health policy, income maintenance, child welfare, native issues, immigration policies, racism.

Memorial University of Newfoundland, School of Graduate Studies, School of Social Work, St. John's, NL A1C 5S7, Canada. Offers MSW. Part-time and evening/weekend programs available. *Degree requirements:* For master's, thesis optional, internship. *Entrance requirements:* For master's, BSW with a minimum of 2nd-class standing or equivalent. Electronic applications accepted. *Faculty research:* Violence, child abuse, sexual abuse, social policy, gerontology.

Michigan State University, The Graduate School, College of Social Science, School of Social Work, East Lansing, MI 48824. Offers clinical social work (MSW); organizational and community practice (MSW); social work (PhD). *Accreditation:* CSWE. Part-time programs available. Postbaccalaureate distance learning degree programs offered (minimal on-campus study). *Entrance requirements:* Additional exam requirements/recommendations for international students: Required—TOEFL. Electronic applications accepted.

Middle Tennessee State University, College of Graduate Studies, College of Behavioral and Health Sciences, Department of Social Work, Murfreesboro, TN 37132. Offers MSW. *Students:* 19 full-time (14 women), 21 part-time (18 women); includes 13 minority (10 Black or African American, non-Hispanic/Latino; 1 Hispanic/Latino; 2 Two or more races, non-Hispanic/Latino). Average age 35. 67 applicants, 76% accepted. In 2011, 6 master's awarded. *Entrance requirements:* Additional exam requirements/recommendations for international students: Required—TOEFL (minimum score 525 paper-based; 195 computer-based; 71 iBT), IELTS (minimum score 6). *Expenses:* Tuition, state resident: full-time $10,008. Tuition, nonresident: full-time $25,056. *Unit head:* Dr. Rebecca Smith, Chair, 615-898-2868, Fax: 615-898-5428, E-mail: rebecca.smith@mtsu.edu. *Application contact:* Dr. Michael D. Allen, Dean and Vice Provost for Research, 615-898-2840, Fax: 615-904-8020, E-mail: michael.allen@mtsu.edu. Web site: http://www.mtsu.edu/socialwork/.

Millersville University of Pennsylvania, College of Graduate and Professional Studies, School of Humanities and Social Sciences, Department of Social Work, Millersville, PA 17551-0302. Offers MSW. *Accreditation:* CSWE. Part-time programs available. *Faculty:* 8 full-time (7 women), 12 part-time/adjunct (9 women). *Students:* 36 full-time (32 women), 65 part-time (62 women); includes 12 minority (4 Black or African American, non-Hispanic/Latino; 1 American Indian or Alaska Native, non-Hispanic/Latino; 1 Asian, non-Hispanic/Latino; 5 Hispanic/Latino; 1 Two or more races, non-Hispanic/Latino). Average age 31. 54 applicants, 100% accepted, 54 enrolled. In 2011, 32 master's awarded. *Degree requirements:* For master's, field practicum. *Entrance requirements:* For master's, GRE or MAT (if GPA less than 2.8), 3 letters of recommendation, resume. Additional exam requirements/recommendations for international students: Required—TOEFL (minimum score 500 paper-based; 183 computer-based; 65 iBT). *Application deadline:* For fall admission, 2/1 for domestic and international students. Application fee: $40 ($50 for international students). Electronic applications accepted. *Expenses:* Tuition, state resident: full-time $3744; part-time $416 per credit. Tuition, nonresident: full-time $5616; part-time $624 per credit. *Required* fees: $1130; $125.50 per credit. Tuition and fees vary according to course load. *Financial support:* In 2011–12, 12 students received support, including 13 research assistantships with full tuition reimbursements available (averaging $3,945 per year); institutionally sponsored loans and unspecified assistantships also available. Support available to part-time students. Financial award application deadline: 3/15; financial award applicants required to submit FAFSA. *Faculty research:* Culturally competent social work practice, enhancing undergraduate students writing skills, enhancing youth in foster care, social work group skills, program evaluation of GOTR. *Total annual research expenditures:* $500. *Unit head:* Dr. Kathryn A. Gregoire, Chairperson, 717-871-2475, Fax: 717-872-3959, E-mail: kathryn.gregoire@millersville.edu. *Application contact:* Dr. Victor S. DeSantis, Dean, College of Graduate and Professional Studies, 717-872-3099, Fax: 717-872-3453, E-mail: victor.desantis@millersville.edu. Web site: http://www.millersville.edu/socialwork/grad/.

Minnesota State University Mankato, College of Graduate Studies, College of Social and Behavioral Sciences, Department of Social Work, Mankato, MN 56001. Offers MSW. *Accreditation:* CSWE. *Students:* 23 full-time (21 women), 22 part-time (all women). *Entrance requirements:* Additional exam requirements/recommendations for international students: Required—TOEFL. *Application deadline:* For fall admission, 3/1 for domestic students. *Unit head:* Dr. Nancy Fitzsimons, Graduate Coordinator, 507-389-1287. *Application contact:* 507-389-2321, E-mail: grad@mnsu.edu.

Missouri State University, Graduate College, College of Health and Human Services, School of Social Work, Springfield, MO 65897. Offers MSW. *Accreditation:* CSWE. Part-time programs available. *Faculty:* 7 full-time (6 women), 10 part-time/adjunct (8 women). *Students:* 31 full-time (26 women), 53 part-time (44 women); includes 10 minority (1 Black or African American, non-Hispanic/Latino; 2 American Indian or Alaska Native, non-Hispanic/Latino; 2 Asian, non-Hispanic/Latino; 4 Hispanic/Latino; 1 Two or more races, non-Hispanic/Latino). Average age 32. 54 applicants, 61% accepted, 28 enrolled. In 2011, 39 master's awarded. *Degree requirements:* For master's, comprehensive exam, thesis or alternative. *Entrance requirements:* For master's, GRE, minimum GPA of 3.0. Additional exam requirements/recommendations for international students: Required—TOEFL (minimum score 550 paper-based; 213 computer-based; 79 iBT). *Application deadline:* For fall admission, 2/15 priority date for domestic students, 2/15 for international students. Application fee: $35 ($50 for international students). Electronic applications accepted. *Expenses:* Tuition, state resident: full-time $4086; part-time $227 per credit hour. Tuition, nonresident: full-time $8172; part-time $454 per credit hour. *Required fees:* $275 per semester. Tuition and fees vary according to course load, campus/location and program. *Financial support:* In 2011–12, 3 research assistantships with full tuition reimbursements (averaging $8,000 per year), 1 teaching assistantship with full tuition reimbursement (averaging $8,000 per year) were awarded; Federal Work-Study, institutionally sponsored loans, scholarships/grants, and unspecified assistantships also available. Financial award application deadline: 3/31; financial award applicants required to submit FAFSA. *Faculty research:* Child and family therapy, rural social work, adolescent social issues, domestic violence. *Unit head:* Dr. Susan Dollar, Acting Director, 417-836-6967, Fax: 417-836-7688, E-mail: socialwork@missouristate.edu. *Application contact:* Misty Stewart, Coordinator of Graduate Recruitment, 417-836-6079, Fax: 417-836-6200, E-mail: mistystewart@missouristate.edu. Web site: http://www.missouristate.edu/swk/.

Molloy College, Graduate Social Work Program, Rockville Centre, NY 11571-5002. Offers MSW. *Unit head:* Jennifer S. McKinnon, Coordinator, 516-678-5000 Ext. 6957, E-mail: jmckinnon@molloy.edu. *Application contact:* Alina Haitz, Assistant Director of Graduate Admissions, 516-678-5000 Ext. 6399, Fax: 516-256-2247, E-mail: ahaitz@molloy.edu. Web site: http://www.molloy.edu/academics/graduate-degree-programs/graduate-social-work-.xml.

Monmouth University, The Graduate School, School of Social Work, West Long Branch, NJ 07764-1898. Offers clinical practice with families and children (MSW); international and community development (MSW); play therapy (Post-Master's Certificate). *Accreditation:* CSWE. Part-time and evening/weekend programs available. *Faculty:* 9 full-time (7 women), 25 part-time/adjunct (17 women). *Students:* 157 full-time (142 women), 87 part-time (76 women); includes 53 minority (26 Black or African American, non-Hispanic/Latino; 1 American Indian or Alaska Native, non-Hispanic/Latino; 4 Asian, non-Hispanic/Latino; 20 Hispanic/Latino; 2 Two or more races, non-Hispanic/Latino), 3 international. Average age 30. 237 applicants, 96% accepted, 127 enrolled. In 2011, 105 master's awarded. *Degree requirements:* For master's, thesis, internship. *Entrance requirements:* For master's, minimum GPA of 3.0 in major, 2.75 overall. Additional exam requirements/recommendations for international students: Required—TOEFL (minimum score 550 paper-based; 213 computer-based; 79 iBT), IELTS (minimum score 5) or Michigan English Language Assessment Battery (minimum score 77), Cambridge A, B, C. *Application deadline:* For fall admission, 3/15 priority date for domestic students, 3/15 for international students. Applications are processed on a rolling basis. Application fee: $50. Electronic applications accepted. *Financial support:* In 2011–12, 127 students received support, including 127 fellowships (averaging $3,566 per year), 7 research assistantships (averaging $8,921 per year); career-related internships or fieldwork, scholarships/grants, and unspecified assistantships also available. Support available to part-time students. Financial award applicants required to submit FAFSA. *Faculty research:* Child welfare citizen participation, cultural diversity, diversity issues, employee help. *Unit head:* Dr. Rosemary Barbera, Program Director, 732-571-3606, Fax: 732-263-5217, E-mail: swdept@monmouth.edu. *Application contact:* Kevin Roane, Director, Office of Graduate Admission, 732-571-3452, Fax: 732-263-5123, E-mail: gradadm@monmouth.edu. Web site: http://www.monmouth.edu/academics/schools/social_work/default.asp.

Morgan State University, School of Graduate Studies, School of Education and Urban Studies, Department of Social Work, Baltimore, MD 21251. Offers MSW, PhD. *Accreditation:* CSWE. *Entrance requirements:* For doctorate, GRE.

Nazareth College of Rochester, Graduate Studies, Department of Social Work, Rochester, NY 14618-3790. Offers MSW. Program offered jointly with The College at Brockport, State University of New York. *Accreditation:* CSWE. *Entrance requirements:* For master's, minimum GPA of 3.0.

Newman University, School of Social Work, Wichita, KS 67213-2097. Offers MSW. *Accreditation:* CSWE. Postbaccalaureate distance learning degree programs offered (no on-campus study). *Faculty:* 9 full-time (5 women), 3 part-time/adjunct (2 women). *Students:* 64 full-time (56 women), 75 part-time (66 women); includes 45 minority (16 Black or African American, non-Hispanic/Latino; 3 American Indian or Alaska Native, non-Hispanic/Latino; 3 Asian, non-Hispanic/Latino; 17 Hispanic/Latino; 6 Two or more races, non-Hispanic/Latino), 1 international. Average age 37. 129 applicants, 55% accepted, 60 enrolled. In 2011, 64 master's awarded. *Degree requirements:* For master's, comprehensive exam (for some programs), thesis optional, fieldwork. *Entrance requirements:* For master's, minimum GPA of 3.0, 3 letters of reference. Additional exam requirements/recommendations for international students: Required—TOEFL (minimum score 600 paper-based; 250 computer-based; 100 iBT). *Application deadline:* For fall admission, 8/15 for domestic students, 7/15 for international students. Applications are processed on a rolling basis. Application fee: $25 ($40 for international students). *Expenses: Tuition:* Full-time $8262; part-time $459 per credit hour. *Required fees:* $15 per credit hour. One-time fee: $25 part-time. Tuition and fees vary according to program. *Financial support:* Federal Work-Study and scholarships/grants available. Financial award application deadline: 8/15; financial award applicants required to submit FAFSA. *Unit head:* Dr. Kevin Brown, Director, 316-942-4291 Ext. 2458, Fax: 316-942-4483, E-mail: brownke@newmanu.edu. *Application contact:* Linda Kay Sabala, Director of Graduate Admissions, 316-942-4291 Ext. 2230, Fax: 316-942-4483, E-mail: sabalal@newmanu.edu.

New Mexico Highlands University, Graduate Studies, School of Social Work, Las Vegas, NM 87701. Offers bilingual/bicultural social work practice (MSW); clinical practice (MSW); government non-profit management (MSW). *Accreditation:* CSWE. Part-time programs available. *Faculty:* 19 full-time (8 women). *Students:* 266 full-time (231 women), 82 part-time (68 women); includes 188 minority (15 Black or African American, non-Hispanic/Latino; 24 American Indian or Alaska Native, non-Hispanic/Latino; 2 Asian, non-Hispanic/Latino; 143 Hispanic/Latino; 1 Native Hawaiian or other Pacific Islander, non-Hispanic/Latino; 3 Two or more races, non-Hispanic/Latino), 7 international. Average age 36. 233 applicants, 88% accepted, 136 enrolled. In 2011, 151 master's awarded. *Degree requirements:* For master's, comprehensive exam, thesis or alternative. *Entrance requirements:* For master's, minimum undergraduate GPA of 3.0. Additional exam requirements/recommendations for international students: Required—TOEFL (minimum score 540 paper-based; 207 computer-based). *Application deadline:* For fall admission, 8/1 priority date for domestic students. Applications are processed on a rolling basis. Application fee: $15. *Expenses:* Tuition, state resident: full-time $2767; part-time $146 per credit hour. Tuition, nonresident: full-time $4879; part-time $234 per credit hour. *International tuition:* $5436 full-time. *Required fees:* $737. *Financial support:* In 2011–12, 17 students received support. Career-related internships or fieldwork, Federal Work-Study, institutionally sponsored loans, scholarships/grants, tuition waivers (partial), and unspecified assistantships available. Support available to part-time students. Financial award application deadline: 3/1; financial award applicants required to submit FAFSA. *Faculty research:* Treatment attrition among domestic violence batterers, children's health and mental health, Dejando Huellas: meeting the bilingual/bicultural needs of the Latino mental health patient, impact of culture on the therapeutic process, effects of generational gang involvement on adolescents' future. *Unit head:* Dr. Alfredo Garcia, Dean, 505-891-9053, Fax: 505-454-3290, E-mail: a_garcia@nmhu.edu. *Application contact:* LouAnn Romero, Administrative Assistant, Graduate Studies, 505-454-3087, E-mail: laromero@nmhu.edu.

New Mexico State University, Graduate School, College of Health and Social Services, School of Social Work, Las Cruces, NM 88003-8001. Offers MSW. *Accreditation:* CSWE. Part-time and evening/weekend programs available. *Faculty:* 9 full-time (4 women). *Students:* 107 full-time (87 women), 37 part-time (32 women); includes 86 minority (2 Black or African American, non-Hispanic/Latino; 5 American Indian or Alaska Native, non-Hispanic/Latino; 75 Hispanic/Latino; 1 Native Hawaiian or other Pacific Islander, non-Hispanic/Latino; 3 Two or more races, non-Hispanic/Latino), 1 international. Average age 34. 125 applicants, 57% accepted, 49 enrolled. In 2011, 51 master's awarded. *Degree requirements:* For master's, comprehensive exam, thesis optional, research project, oral exam. *Entrance requirements:* For master's, minimum GPA of 3.0. Additional exam requirements/recommendations for international students: Required—TOEFL (minimum score 637 paper-based; 270 computer-based; 79 iBT), IELTS (minimum score 6.5). *Application deadline:* For fall admission, 1/15 priority date for domestic students, 1/15 for international students. Applications are processed on a rolling basis. Application fee: $40 ($50 for international students). Electronic applications accepted. *Expenses:* Tuition, state resident: full-time $5004; part-time $208.50 per credit. Tuition, nonresident: full-time $17,446; part-time $726.90 per credit. *Financial support:* In 2011–12, 16 teaching assistantships with tuition reimbursements (averaging $10,344 per year) were awarded; fellowships, research assistantships, career-related internships or fieldwork, traineeships, health care benefits, and unspecified assistantships also available. Financial award application deadline: 3/1. *Faculty research:* Attachment issues, border issues, substance abuse, sexual orientation, family diversity. *Unit head:* Dr. Tina Hancock, Head, 575-646-3043, Fax: 575-646-4343, E-mail: thancock@nmsu.edu. *Application contact:* Dr. Ivan de la Rosa, Graduate Program Coordinator, 575-646-2143, Fax: 575-646-4116, E-mail: lilo@nmsu.edu. Web site: http://socialwork.nmsu.edu.

New York University, Silver School of Social Work, New York, NY 10003. Offers MSW, PhD, MSW/JD, MSW/MA, MSW/MPA, MSW/MPH. *Accreditation:* CSWE (one or more programs are accredited). Part-time and evening/weekend programs available. *Faculty:* 50 full-time (39 women), 163 part-time/adjunct (47 women). *Students:* 805 full-time (690 women), 393 part-time (334 women); includes 286 minority (98 Black or African American, non-Hispanic/Latino; 3 American Indian or Alaska Native, non-Hispanic/Latino; 69 Asian, non-Hispanic/Latino; 93 Hispanic/Latino; 3 Native Hawaiian or other Pacific Islander, non-Hispanic/Latino; 20 Two or more races, non-Hispanic/Latino), 80 international. Average age 27. 1,778 applicants, 75% accepted, 498 enrolled. In 2011, 520 master's, 9 doctorates awarded. *Degree requirements:* For doctorate, comprehensive exam, thesis/dissertation. *Entrance requirements:* For master's, bachelor's degree; for doctorate, GRE or MAT, MSW. Additional exam requirements/recommendations for international students: Required—TOEFL, IELTS, TWE. *Application deadline:* For fall admission, 2/6 priority date for domestic students, 2/6 for international students; for spring admission, 11/1 priority date for domestic students, 11/1 for international students. Applications are processed on a rolling basis. Application fee: $60. Electronic applications accepted. *Expenses:* Contact institution. *Financial support:* In 2011–12, 1,104 students received support. Career-related internships or fieldwork, Federal Work-Study, scholarships/grants, health care benefits, tuition waivers (partial), and unspecified assistantships available. Support available to part-time students. Financial award application deadline: 3/1; financial award applicants required to submit FAFSA. *Faculty research:* Social welfare policies, public health, aging, mental health, substance abuse. *Unit head:* Dr. Lynn Videka, Dean, 212-998-5959, Fax: 212-995-4172. *Application contact:* Robert W. Sommo, Jr., Assistant Dean for Enrollment Services, 212-998-5910, Fax: 212-995-4171, E-mail: ssw.admissions@nyu.edu. Web site: http://www.socialwork.nyu.edu/.

Norfolk State University, School of Graduate Studies, School of Social Work, Norfolk, VA 23504. Offers MSW, PhD. *Accreditation:* CSWE (one or more programs are accredited). Part-time programs available. *Degree requirements:* For doctorate, thesis/dissertation. *Entrance requirements:* For master's, minimum GPA of 2.7. Additional exam requirements/recommendations for international students: Required—TOEFL.

North Carolina Agricultural and Technical State University, School of Graduate Studies, College of Arts and Sciences, Department of Sociology and Social Work, Greensboro, NC 27411. Offers MSW. Joint program with The University of North Carolina at Greensboro. *Accreditation:* CSWE. Part-time and evening/weekend programs available. *Degree requirements:* For master's, comprehensive exam, qualifying exam. *Entrance requirements:* For master's, GRE General Test.

North Carolina State University, Graduate School, College of Humanities and Social Sciences, Department of Social Work, Raleigh, NC 27695. Offers MSW. *Accreditation:* CSWE.

Northern Kentucky University, Office of Graduate Programs, College of Education and Human Services, Program in Social Work, Highland Heights, KY 41099. Offers MSW. Part-time and evening/weekend programs available. *Students:* 61 full-time (53 women), 4 part-time (all women); includes 12 minority (11 Black or African American, non-Hispanic/Latino; 1 Asian, non-Hispanic/Latino). Average age 32. 78 applicants, 65% accepted, 48 enrolled. *Degree requirements:* For master's, capstone project. *Entrance requirements:* For master's, GRE (minimum score of 1000), minimum GPA of 3.0; undergraduate courses in psychology, sociology, and statistics with minimum B average; 3 letters of recommendation; essay; letter of intent; resume; interview. Additional exam requirements/recommendations for international students: Required—TOEFL (minimum score 550 paper-based; 213 computer-based; 79 iBT); Recommended—IELTS (minimum score 6.5). *Application deadline:* For fall admission, 8/1 for domestic students, 6/1 for international students. Application fee: $40. Electronic applications accepted. *Expenses:* Tuition, state resident: full-time $7614; part-time $423 per credit hour. Tuition, nonresident: full-time $13,104; part-time $728 per credit hour. Tuition and fees vary according to degree level and reciprocity agreements. *Financial support:* Unspecified assistantships available. Financial award application deadline: 5/1. *Faculty research:* Mentoring at-risk adolescents, homeless children and families, family directed structural therapy, campus climate, using PhotoVoice with adolescents. *Unit head:* Heidi Waters, CSWL Graduate Coordinator, 859-572-7892, Fax: 859-572-6592, E-mail: watersh2@nku.edu. *Application contact:* Dr. Peg Griffin, Director of Graduate Programs, 859-572-6934, Fax: 859-572-6670, E-mail: griffinp@nku.edu. Web site: http://coehs.nku.edu/gradprograms/current/degree/msw/index.php.

Northwest Nazarene University, Graduate Studies, Program in Social Work, Nampa, ID 83686-5897. Offers addiction studies (MSW); clinical gerontological practice with mature and older adults (MSW); community mental health practice (MSW); management, community planning and social administration (MSW). *Accreditation:* CSWE. Part-time programs available. Postbaccalaureate distance learning degree programs offered (no on-campus study). *Faculty:* 10 full-time (7 women), 4 part-time/adjunct (2 women). *Students:* 117 full-time (89 women), 15 part-time (11 women); includes 17 minority (2 American Indian or Alaska Native, non-Hispanic/Latino; 1 Asian, non-Hispanic/Latino; 14 Hispanic/Latino). Average age 36. 70 applicants, 93% accepted, 54 enrolled. In 2011, 42 master's awarded. *Degree requirements:* For master's, comprehensive exam. *Application deadline:* Applications are processed on a rolling basis. Application fee: $25. Electronic applications accepted. *Unit head:* Dr. Mary Curran, Director, 208-467-8679, E-mail: msw@nnu.edu. *Application contact:* Nancy Gibson, Program Assistant, 208-467-8679, Fax: 208-467-8879, E-mail: nkgibson@nnu.edu.

The Ohio State University, Graduate School, College of Social Work, Columbus, OH 43210. Offers MSW, PhD. *Accreditation:* CSWE (one or more programs are accredited). Part-time programs available. *Faculty:* 27. *Students:* 321 full-time (283 women), 188 part-time (163 women); includes 85 minority (53 Black or African American, non-Hispanic/Latino; 7 Asian, non-Hispanic/Latino; 18 Hispanic/Latino; 7 Two or more races, non-Hispanic/Latino), 5 international. Average age 33. In 2011, 99 master's, 11 doctorates awarded. *Degree requirements:* For master's, thesis optional; for doctorate, thesis/dissertation. *Entrance requirements:* Additional exam requirements/recommendations for international students: Required—TOEFL (minimum score 550 paper-based; 213 computer-based), IELTS (minimum score 6.5), or Michigan English Language Assessment Battery (minimum score 82). *Application deadline:* For fall admission, 8/15 priority date for domestic students, 7/1 for international students; for winter admission, 12/1 priority date for domestic students, 11/1 for international students; for spring admission, 3/1 priority date for domestic students, 2/1 for international students. Applications are processed on a rolling basis. Application fee: $40 ($50 for international students). Electronic applications accepted. *Expenses:* Tuition, state resident: full-time $11,400. Tuition, nonresident: full-time $28,125. Tuition and fees vary according to course load, degree level, campus/location and program. *Financial support:* Fellowships, research assistantships, teaching assistantships, Federal Work-Study, institutionally sponsored loans, and unspecified assistantships available. Support available to part-time students. *Unit head:* Tom Gregoire, Dean, 614-292-9426, Fax: 614-292-6940, E-mail: gregoire.5@osu.edu. *Application contact:* Graduate Admissions, 614-292-6031, Fax: 614-292-3656, E-mail: gradadmissions@osu.edu. Web site: http://www.csw.ohio-state.edu/.

The Ohio State University at Lima, Graduate Programs, Lima, OH 45804. Offers early childhood education (M Ed); education (MA); middle childhood education (M Ed); social work (MSW). Part-time programs available. *Faculty:* 41. *Students:* 27 full-time (13 women), 39 part-time (33 women); includes 3 minority (1 Black or African American, non-Hispanic/Latino; 2 Two or more races, non-Hispanic/Latino). Average age 34. Terminal master's awarded for partial completion of doctoral program. *Degree requirements:* For master's, comprehensive exam (for some programs), thesis (for some programs). *Entrance requirements:* For master's, GRE, minimum GPA of 3.0. Additional exam requirements/recommendations for international students: Required—TOEFL (minimum score 550 paper-based; 79 iBT), Michigan English Language Assessment Battery (minimum score 82); Recommended—IELTS (minimum score 7), TWE. *Application deadline:* For fall admission, 6/1 priority date for domestic students, 6/1 for international students; for spring admission, 10/15 priority date for domestic students, 10/15 for international students. Applications are processed on a rolling basis. Application fee: $40 ($50 for international students). Electronic applications accepted. *Expenses:* Tuition, state resident: full-time $11,130. Tuition, nonresident: full-time $27,855. *Financial support:* Application deadline: 2/1. *Unit head:* Dr. John Snyder, Dean/Director, 419-995-8481, E-mail: snyder.4@osu.edu. *Application contact:* Graduate Admissions, 614-292-9444, Fax: 614-292-3895, E-mail: domestic.grad@osu.edu.

The Ohio State University–Mansfield Campus, Graduate Programs, Mansfield, OH 44906-1599. Offers early childhood education (M Ed); education (MA); middle childhood education (M Ed); social work (MSW). Part-time programs available. *Faculty:* 41. *Students:* 21 full-time (15 women), 57 part-time (48 women); includes 5 minority (2 Black or African American, non-Hispanic/Latino; 1 Asian, non-Hispanic/Latino; 1 Hispanic/Latino; 1 Two or more races, non-Hispanic/Latino), 1 international. Average age 33. *Degree requirements:* For master's, comprehensive exam (for some programs), thesis (for some programs). *Entrance requirements:* For master's, GRE, minimum GPA of 3.0. Additional exam requirements/recommendations for international students: Required—TOEFL (minimum score 550 paper-based; 79 iBT), Michigan English Language Assessment Battery (minimum score 82); Recommended—IELTS (minimum score 7). *Application deadline:* For fall admission, 6/1 priority date for domestic students, 6/1 for international students; for spring admission, 10/15 priority date for domestic students, 10/15 for international students. Applications are processed on a rolling basis. Application fee: $40 ($50 for international students). Electronic applications accepted. *Expenses:* Tuition, state resident: full-time $11,130. Tuition, nonresident: full-time $27,855. Tuition and fees vary according to course load. *Financial support:* Teaching assistantships with full tuition reimbursements, Federal Work-Study, and scholarships/grants available. Support available to part-time students. Financial award application deadline: 2/1. *Unit head:* Dr. Stephen M. Gavazzi, Dean and Director, 419-755-4221, Fax: 419-755-4241, E-mail: gavazzi.1@osu.edu. *Application contact:* Graduate Admissions, 614-292-9444, Fax: 614-292-3895, E-mail: domestic.grad@osu.edu.

The Ohio State University–Newark Campus, Graduate Programs, Newark, OH 43055-1797. Offers early/middle childhood education (M Ed); education - teaching and learning (MA); social work (MSW). Part-time programs available. *Faculty:* 56. *Students:* 63 full-time (55 women), 46 part-time (39 women); includes 6 minority (1 Black or African American, non-Hispanic/Latino; 1 Asian, non-Hispanic/Latino; 3 Hispanic/Latino; 1 Two or more races, non-Hispanic/Latino). Average age 31. Terminal master's awarded for partial completion of doctoral program. *Degree requirements:* For master's, comprehensive exam (for some programs), thesis (for some programs). *Entrance requirements:* For master's, GRE, minimum GPA of 3.0. Additional exam requirements/recommendations for international students: Required—Michigan English Language Assessment Battery (minimum score 82); Recommended—TOEFL (minimum score 550 paper-based; 79 iBT), IELTS (minimum score 7). *Application deadline:* For fall admission, 6/1 priority date for domestic students, 6/1 for international students; for spring admission, 10/15 priority date for domestic students, 2/1 for international students. Applications are processed on a rolling basis. Application fee: $40 ($50 for international students). Electronic applications accepted. *Unit head:* Dr. William L. MacDonald, Dean/Director, 740-366-9333 Ext. 330, E-mail: macdonald.24@osu.edu. *Application contact:* Graduate Admissions, 614-292-9444, Fax: 614-292-3985, E-mail: domestic.grad@osu.edu.

Ohio University, Graduate College, College of Health Sciences and Professions, Department of Social and Public Health, Program in Social Work, Athens, OH 45701-2979. Offers MSW. *Accreditation:* CSWE. Part-time programs available. *Students:* 21 full-time (18 women), 10 part-time (9 women); includes 5 minority (2 Black or African American, non-Hispanic/Latino; 1 Hispanic/Latino; 2 Two or more races, non-Hispanic/Latino), 1 international. 32 applicants, 63% accepted, 12 enrolled. In 2011, 15 master's awarded. *Degree requirements:* For master's, fieldwork. *Entrance requirements:* For master's, GRE General Test or minimum GPA of 3.0, liberal arts background with coursework in human biology, statistics, and three social science areas; paid or volunteer work in human services. Additional exam requirements/recommendations for international students: Required—TOEFL (minimum score 620 paper-based; 105 iBT) or IELTS (minimum score 7.5). *Application deadline:* For fall admission, 2/1 for domestic students, 8/15 for international students. Application fee: $50 ($55 for international students). Electronic applications accepted. *Financial support:* In 2011–12, teaching assistantships with full tuition reimbursements (averaging $9,000 per year) were awarded; research assistantships with full tuition reimbursements, career-related internships or fieldwork, Federal Work-Study, tuition waivers (partial), and unspecified assistantships also available. Financial award application deadline: 2/1; financial award applicants required to submit FAFSA. *Faculty research:* Violence, families, rural life. *Total annual research expenditures:* $100,000. *Unit head:* Dr. Susan Kiss Sarnoff, Chair, 740-593-1301, Fax: 740-593-0427, E-mail: sarnoff@ohio.edu. *Application contact:* Dr. Freve Pace, Graduate Chair, 740-593-1321, E-mail: pace@ohio.edu. Web site: http://www.socialwork.ohiou.edu/.

Our Lady of the Lake University of San Antonio, Worden School of Social Service, San Antonio, TX 78207-4689. Offers MSW. *Accreditation:* CSWE. Part-time programs available. *Degree requirements:* For master's, thesis optional, practicum. *Entrance requirements:* For master's, GRE General Test or MAT. Additional exam requirements/recommendations for international students: Required—TOEFL. Electronic applications accepted. *Faculty research:* Cross-cultural social work practice, mental health, adult literacy, spirituality, maternal health care, experiential learning.

Phillips Theological Seminary, Programs in Theology, Tulsa, OK 74116. Offers administration of church agencies (M Div); campus ministry (M Div); church-related social work (M Div); college and seminary teaching (M Div); global mission work (M Div); institutional chaplaincy (M Div); ministerial vocations in Christian education (M Div); ministry (D Min), including parish ministry, pastoral counseling, practices of ministry; ministry and culture (MAMC), including Christian education, congregational leadership, history and practice of Christian spirituality, theology, ethics, and culture; ministry of music (M Div); pastoral care and counseling (M Div); pastoral ministry (M Div); theological studies (MTS). *Accreditation:* ATS. Part-time programs available. Postbaccalaureate distance learning degree programs offered (minimal on-campus study). *Degree requirements:* For master's, thesis (for some programs); for doctorate, thesis/dissertation. *Entrance requirements:* For master's, minimum GPA of 2.5; for doctorate, M Div, minimum GPA of 3.0. *Faculty research:* Biblical studies, historical studies, theology and culture, practical theology, theology and film.

Pontifical Catholic University of Puerto Rico, College of Graduate Studies in Behavioral Science and Community Affairs, Program in Clinical Social Work, Ponce, PR 00717-0777. Offers MSW. Part-time and evening/weekend programs available. *Entrance requirements:* For master's, EXADEP, 3 letters of recommendation, interview, minimum GPA of 2.75.

Portland State University, Graduate Studies, School of Social Work, Portland, OR 97207-0751. Offers social work (MSW); social work and social research (PhD). *Accreditation:* CSWE (one or more programs are accredited). Part-time programs available. *Degree requirements:* For doctorate, comprehensive exam, thesis/dissertation, residency. *Entrance requirements:* For master's, minimum GPA of 3.0 in upper-division course work or 2.75 overall; for doctorate, GRE General Test, 4 references. Additional exam requirements/recommendations for international students: Required—TOEFL (minimum score 550 paper-based; 213 computer-based). *Faculty research:* Child welfare; child mental health; social welfare policies and services; work, family, and dependent care; adult mental health.

Radford University, College of Graduate and Professional Studies, Waldron College of Health and Human Services, School of Social Work, Radford, VA 24142. Offers MSW. *Accreditation:* CSWE. Part-time programs available. *Faculty:* 9 full-time (8 women), 9 part-time/adjunct (7 women). *Students:* 56 full-time (48 women), 41 part-time (32 women); includes 15 minority (14 Black or African American, non-Hispanic/Latino; 1 Hispanic/Latino). Average age 33. 57 applicants, 86% accepted, 26 enrolled. In 2011, 37 master's awarded. *Degree requirements:* For master's, comprehensive exam. *Entrance requirements:* For master's, minimum GPA of 2.75; 3 letters of reference, personal essay, previous experience in the field of human services, resume, official transcripts. Additional exam requirements/recommendations for international students: Required—TOEFL (minimum score 550 paper-based; 213 computer-based; 79 iBT). *Application deadline:* For fall admission, 2/15 priority date for domestic students, 12/1 for international students; for spring admission, 7/1 for international students. Applications are processed on a rolling basis. Application fee: $50. Electronic applications accepted. *Expenses:* Tuition, state resident: full-time $6262; part-time $261 per credit hour. Tuition, nonresident: full-time $14,540; part-time $606 per credit hour. *Required fees:* $2812; $117 per credit hour. Tuition and fees vary according to program. *Financial support:* In 2011–12, 18 students received support, including 8 research assistantships (averaging $4,781 per year), 2 teaching assistantships with partial tuition reimbursements available (averaging $8,420 per year); career-related internships or fieldwork, Federal Work-Study, institutionally sponsored loans, scholarships/grants, and unspecified assistantships also available. Financial award application deadline: 3/1; financial award applicants required to submit FAFSA. *Unit head:* Dr. Elise M. Fullmer, Director, 540-831-7691, Fax: 540-831-7670, E-mail: efullmer@radford.edu. *Application contact:* Rebecca Conner, Graduate Admissions, 540-831-5431, Fax: 540-831-6061, E-mail: gradcollege@radford.edu. Web site: http://www.radford.edu/content/wchs/home/social-work.html.

Social Work

Rhode Island College, School of Graduate Studies, School of Social Work, Providence, RI 02908-1991. Offers MSW. *Accreditation:* CSWE. Part-time programs available. *Faculty:* 8 full-time (6 women), 7 part-time/adjunct (5 women). *Students:* 83 full-time (73 women), 91 part-time (79 women); includes 31 minority (21 Black or African American, non-Hispanic/Latino; 9 Hispanic/Latino; 1 Two or more races, non-Hispanic/Latino). Average age 34. In 2011, 69 master's awarded. *Entrance requirements:* For master's, official transcripts, personal statement, 3 letters of recommendation. Additional exam requirements/recommendations for international students: Recommended—TOEFL (minimum score 550 paper-based; 213 computer-based; 79 iBT). *Application deadline:* For fall admission, 2/1 for domestic students. Applications are processed on a rolling basis. Application fee: $50. *Expenses:* Contact institution. *Financial support:* Career-related internships or fieldwork, Federal Work-Study, scholarships/grants, health care benefits, and unspecified assistantships available. Support available to part-time students. Financial award application deadline: 5/15; financial award applicants required to submit FAFSA. *Unit head:* Dr. Sue Pearlmutter, Dean, 401-456-8042, E-mail: spearlmutter@ric.edu. *Application contact:* Graduate Studies, 401-456-8700. Web site: http://www.ric.edu/socialWork/.

The Richard Stockton College of New Jersey, School of Graduate and Continuing Studies, Program in Social Work, Pomona, NJ 08240-0195. Offers MSW. Evening/weekend programs available. *Faculty:* 7 full-time (5 women), 2 part-time/adjunct (1 woman). *Students:* 45 full-time (37 women), 1 (woman) part-time; includes 18 minority (11 Black or African American, non-Hispanic/Latino; 1 Asian, non-Hispanic/Latino; 5 Hispanic/Latino; 1 Two or more races, non-Hispanic/Latino). Average age 35. 88 applicants, 64% accepted, 33 enrolled. In 2011, 19 master's awarded. *Degree requirements:* For master's, thesis optional, field work. *Entrance requirements:* Additional exam requirements/recommendations for international students: Required—TOEFL. *Application deadline:* For fall admission, 3/1 for domestic and international students. Application fee: $50. Electronic applications accepted. *Expenses:* Tuition, state resident: full-time $13,035; part-time $543 per credit. Tuition, nonresident: full-time $20,065; part-time $836 per credit. *Required fees:* $3920; $163 per credit. Tuition and fees vary according to degree level. *Financial support:* In 2011–12, 12 students received support, including 8 research assistantships; fellowships, Federal Work-Study, scholarships/grants, and unspecified assistantships also available. Financial award application deadline: 3/1; financial award applicants required to submit FAFSA. *Unit head:* Dr. Diane Falk, Program Director, 609-626-3640, E-mail: gradschool@stockton.edu. *Application contact:* Tara Williams, Assistant Director of Graduate Enrollment Management, 609-626-3640, Fax: 609-626-6050, E-mail: gradschool@stockton.edu. Web site: http://www.stockton.edu/grad.

Roberts Wesleyan College, Division of Social Work, Rochester, NY 14624-1997. Offers child and family practice (MSW); congregational and community practice (MSW); mental health practice (MSW). *Accreditation:* CSWE. *Entrance requirements:* For master's, minimum GPA of 2.75. *Faculty research:* Religion and social work, family studies, values and ethics.

Rutgers, The State University of New Jersey, New Brunswick, School of Social Work, Piscataway, NJ 08854-8097. Offers MSW, PhD, JD/MSW, M Div/MSW. *Accreditation:* CSWE (one or more programs are accredited). Part-time programs available. *Degree requirements:* For doctorate, comprehensive exam, thesis/dissertation. *Entrance requirements:* For doctorate, GRE General Test. Additional exam requirements/recommendations for international students: Required—TOEFL. Electronic applications accepted. *Faculty research:* Family theory, adolescent development, child and adolescent mental health delivery systems, poverty and employment policy.

St. Ambrose University, College of Arts and Sciences, Program in Social Work, Davenport, IA 52803-2898. Offers MSW. *Accreditation:* CSWE. Part-time and evening/weekend programs available. *Faculty:* 7 full-time (3 women), 3 part-time/adjunct (all women). *Students:* 64 full-time (54 women), 19 part-time (16 women); includes 8 minority (4 Black or African American, non-Hispanic/Latino; 1 American Indian or Alaska Native, non-Hispanic/Latino; 1 Hispanic/Latino; 2 Two or more races, non-Hispanic/Latino). Average age 28. 81 applicants, 84% accepted, 35 enrolled. In 2011, 37 master's awarded. *Degree requirements:* For master's, comprehensive exam (for some programs), thesis or alternative, integration projects. *Entrance requirements:* For master's, minimum GPA of 3.0, course work in statistics, bachelor's degree in liberal arts. Additional exam requirements/recommendations for international students: Required—TOEFL. *Application deadline:* For fall admission, 8/1 priority date for domestic students; for winter admission, 12/15 priority date for domestic students; for spring admission, 1/1 priority date for domestic students. Applications are processed on a rolling basis. Application fee: $25. Electronic applications accepted. *Expenses: Tuition:* Full-time $13,770; part-time $765 per credit hour. *Required fees:* $60 per semester. Tuition and fees vary according to degree level, program and reciprocity agreements. *Financial support:* In 2011–12, 72 students received support, including 8 research assistantships with partial tuition reimbursements available (averaging $3,600 per year); career-related internships or fieldwork, scholarships/grants, tuition waivers (partial), and unspecified assistantships also available. Financial award application deadline: 8/15; financial award applicants required to submit FAFSA. *Faculty research:* Social work practice, cults/sects, family therapy, developmental disabilities. *Unit head:* Dr. Katherine VanBlair, Associate Director, 563-333-6484, Fax: 563-333-6243, E-mail: vanblairkatherine@sau.edu. *Application contact:* Tonita M. Wamsley, Administrative Assistant and Admissions Coordinator, 563-333-6379, Fax: 563-333-6243, E-mail: wamsleytonitam@sau.edu. Web site: http://web.sau.edu/msw/.

St. Catherine University, Graduate Programs, Program in Social Work, St. Paul, MN 55105. Offers MSW. Program offered jointly with University of St. Thomas. *Accreditation:* CSWE. Part-time and evening/weekend programs available. *Degree requirements:* For master's, clinical research paper. *Entrance requirements:* For master's, minimum GPA of 3.0. Additional exam requirements/recommendations for international students: Required—Michigan English Language Assessment Battery or TOEFL (minimum score 600 paper-based; 250 computer-based; 100 iBT). *Expenses:* Contact institution.

St. Cloud State University, School of Graduate Studies, College of Public Affairs, Department of Social Work, St. Cloud, MN 56301-4498. Offers MSW. *Accreditation:* CSWE. *Entrance requirements:* For master's, GRE General Test, minimum GPA of 2.75.

Saint Leo University, Graduate Studies in Social Work, Saint Leo, FL 33574-6665. Offers advanced clinical practice (MSW). Postbaccalaureate distance learning degree programs offered (minimal on-campus study). *Faculty:* 5 full-time (4 women), 5 part-time/adjunct (4 women). *Students:* 43 full-time (40 women), 23 part-time (20 women); includes 29 minority (22 Black or African American, non-Hispanic/Latino; 5 Hispanic/Latino; 2 Two or more races, non-Hispanic/Latino). Average age 37. *Entrance requirements:* For master's, GRE (minimum score 1000) or MAT (minimum score 410) if undergraduate GPA less than 3.0, 3 recommendations; minimum GPA of 3.0 in undergraduate work, resume (for regular two-year full-time MSW); BSW from CSWE-accredited program with minimum GPA of 3.25 in social work completed in the last 5 years, minimum B average in upper-level social work courses (for one-year full-time advanced standing MSW). *Application deadline:* For fall admission, 3/15 for domestic and international students. Application fee: $80. Electronic applications accepted. *Expenses:* Contact institution. *Financial support:* In 2011–12, 1 student received support. Career-related internships or fieldwork, Federal Work-Study, and health care benefits available. *Unit head:* Dr. Cindy Lee, Director, 352-588-8869, Fax: 352-588-8289, E-mail: cindy.lee@saintleo.edu. *Application contact:* Jared Welling, Director of Graduate Admission, 800-707-8846, Fax: 352-588-7873, E-mail: grad.admissions@saintleo.edu. Web site: http://www.saintleo.edu/Academics/School-of-Education-Social-Services/Graduate-Degree-Programs/Master-of-Social-Work.

Saint Louis University, Graduate Education, College of Education and Public Service, School of Social Work, St. Louis, MO 63103-2097. Offers MSW. *Accreditation:* CSWE. Part-time programs available. *Entrance requirements:* For master's, minimum GPA of 3.0, letters of recommendation. Additional exam requirements/recommendations for international students: Required—TOEFL (minimum score 550 paper-based; 215 computer-based). *Expenses:* Contact institution. *Faculty research:* Gerontology, mental health issues, child welfare (especially abuse and neglect), social justice, and peace making, homelessness.

Salem State University, School of Graduate Studies, Program in Social Work, Salem, MA 01970-5353. Offers MSW. *Accreditation:* CSWE. Part-time and evening/weekend programs available. *Entrance requirements:* For master's, GRE, MAT. Additional exam requirements/recommendations for international students: Required—TOEFL (minimum score 550 paper-based; 80 iBT) or IELTS (minimum score 5.5).

Salisbury University, Graduate Division, Program in Social Work, Salisbury, MD 21801-6837. Offers MSW. *Accreditation:* CSWE. Part-time and evening/weekend programs available. Postbaccalaureate distance learning degree programs offered (no on-campus study). *Faculty:* 15 full-time (13 women), 11 part-time/adjunct (8 women). *Students:* 147 full-time (125 women), 37 part-time (34 women); includes 46 minority (37 Black or African American, non-Hispanic/Latino; 1 American Indian or Alaska Native, non-Hispanic/Latino; 3 Asian, non-Hispanic/Latino; 2 Hispanic/Latino; 3 Two or more races, non-Hispanic/Latino), 1 international. Average age 31. 74 applicants, 73% accepted, 54 enrolled. In 2011, 54 master's awarded. *Degree requirements:* For master's, field practicum. *Entrance requirements:* For master's, baccalaureate degree, minimum undergraduate GPA of 3.0 on last 60 credits, 3 recommendations (one from academic source, and two from an employer, a professional colleague or community associate), resume, 3 personal statements. Additional exam requirements/recommendations for international students: Required—TOEFL (minimum score 550 paper-based; 79 iBT). *Application deadline:* For fall admission, 2/2 for domestic students. Applications are processed on a rolling basis. Application fee: $45. Electronic applications accepted. *Expenses: Tuition, area resident:* Part-time $306 per credit hour. Tuition, state resident: part-time $306 per credit hour. Tuition, nonresident: part-time $595 per credit hour. *Required fees:* $68 per credit hour. *Financial support:* In 2011–12, 128 students received support. Career-related internships or fieldwork, institutionally sponsored loans, and unspecified assistantships available. Support available to part-time students. Financial award application deadline: 3/1; financial award applicants required to submit FAFSA. *Faculty research:* Title IV Public Child Welfare Program, PNC Science Program, Lower Shore Early Intervention Program at WELC. *Total annual research expenditures:* $380,878. *Unit head:* Dr. Vicki Root, Director, 410-677-3948, E-mail: vbroot@salisbury.edu. *Application contact:* Susan Mareski, MSW Program Assistant, 410-677-5363, E-mail: smmareski@salisbury.edu. Web site: http://www.salisbury.edu/socialwork/programs-msw.html.

San Diego State University, Graduate and Research Affairs, College of Health and Human Services, School of Social Work, San Diego, CA 92182. Offers MSW, JD/MSW, MSW/MPH. JD/MSW offered jointly with California Western School of Law. *Accreditation:* CSWE. Part-time programs available. *Degree requirements:* For master's, comprehensive exam, thesis optional. *Entrance requirements:* For master's, GRE General Test. Additional exam requirements/recommendations for international students: Required—TOEFL. Electronic applications accepted. *Faculty research:* Child maltreatment, substance abuse, neighborhood studies, child welfare.

San Francisco State University, Division of Graduate Studies, College of Health and Human Services, School of Social Work, San Francisco, CA 94132-1722. Offers MSW. *Accreditation:* CSWE. Part-time programs available. *Students:* Average age 33. *Degree requirements:* For master's, thesis optional. *Application deadline:* Applications are processed on a rolling basis. *Financial support:* Career-related internships or fieldwork and Federal Work-Study available. *Unit head:* Prof. Eileen Levy, Director, 415-405-4084, E-mail: efl@sfsu.edu. *Application contact:* Sonja Lenz-Rashid, Graduate Coordinator, 415-405-2459, E-mail: srlenz@sfsu.edu. Web site: http://socwork.sfsu.edu/.

San Jose State University, Graduate Studies and Research, College of Applied Sciences and Arts, School of Social Work, San Jose, CA 95192-0001. Offers MSW, Certificate. *Accreditation:* CSWE. Electronic applications accepted.

Savannah State University, Master of Social Work Program, Savannah, GA 31404. Offers MSW. *Accreditation:* CSWE. *Entrance requirements:* For master's, GRE General Test. Additional exam requirements/recommendations for international students: Required—TOEFL. *Faculty research:* Clinical and administrative social work.

Shippensburg University of Pennsylvania, School of Graduate Studies, College of Education and Human Services, Department of Social Work and Gerontology, Shippensburg, PA 17257-2299. Offers social work (MSW). *Accreditation:* CSWE. Part-time and evening/weekend programs available. *Faculty:* 4 full-time (3 women), 4 part-time/adjunct (3 women). *Students:* 22 full-time (all women), 22 part-time (20 women); includes 5 minority (4 Black or African American, non-Hispanic/Latino; 1 Two or more races, non-Hispanic/Latino). Average age 31. 60 applicants, 62% accepted, 23 enrolled. In 2011, 25 master's awarded. *Degree requirements:* For master's, thesis, practicum. *Entrance requirements:* For master's, GRE or MAT (if GPA is below 2.8), 3 professional references; resume; written academic and professional statement; course work in human biology, economics, government/political science, psychology, sociology/anthropology and statistics. Additional exam requirements/recommendations for international students: Required—TOEFL (minimum score 580 paper-based; 237 computer-based); Recommended—IELTS (minimum score 6). *Application deadline:* For fall admission, 4/30 for international students; for spring admission, 9/30 for international students. Applications are processed on a rolling basis. Application fee: $30. Electronic applications accepted. *Expenses: Tuition, area resident:* Part-time $416 per credit. Tuition, state resident: part-time $416 per credit. Tuition, nonresident: part-time $624 per credit. *Required fees:* $119 per credit. *Financial support:* In 2011–12, 7 research assistantships with full tuition reimbursements (averaging $5,000 per year) were awarded; career-related internships or fieldwork, scholarships/grants, unspecified assistantships, and resident hall director and student payroll positions also available. Support available to part-time students. Financial award application deadline: 3/1; financial award applicants required to submit FAFSA. *Unit head:* Dr. Marita N. Flagler, Co-Director, MU-SU Master of Social Work Program, 717-477-1717, Fax: 717-477-4051, E-mail: mnflagler@ship.edu. *Application contact:* Jeremy R. Goshorn, Assistant Dean of Graduate Admissions, 717-477-1231, Fax: 717-477-4016, E-mail: jrgoshorn@ship.edu. Web site: http://www.ship.edu/social_work/.

Simmons College, School of Social Work, Boston, MA 02115. Offers relational and multi-contextual treatment of trauma (Certificate); social work (MSW, PhD); treatment of trauma (Certificate). *Accreditation:* CSWE (one or more programs are accredited). *Unit head:* Dr. Stefan Krug, Dean, 617-521-3929, Fax: 617-521-3980, E-mail: stefan.krug@simmons.edu. *Application contact:* Carlos Frontado, Director of Admissions, 617-521-3920, Fax: 617-521-3980, E-mail: carlos.frontado@simmons.edu. Web site: http://www.simmons.edu/ssw/.

Smith College, School for Social Work, Northampton, MA 01063. Offers MSW, PhD. *Accreditation:* CSWE (one or more programs are accredited). *Faculty:* 16 full-time (12 women), 177 part-time/adjunct (141 women). *Students:* 379 full-time (335 women), 54 part-time (44 women); includes 95 minority (29 Black or African American, non-Hispanic/Latino; 1 American Indian or Alaska Native, non-Hispanic/Latino; 14 Asian, non-Hispanic/Latino; 23 Hispanic/Latino; 28 Two or more races, non-Hispanic/Latino), 5 international. Average age 31. 476 applicants, 58% accepted, 148 enrolled. In 2011, 106 master's, 5 doctorates awarded. *Degree requirements:* For master's, thesis; for doctorate, thesis/dissertation. *Entrance requirements:* For doctorate, MAT. Additional exam requirements/recommendations for international students: Required—TOEFL. *Application deadline:* For fall admission, 2/21 for domestic students. Applications are processed on a rolling basis. Application fee: $60. *Expenses:* Contact institution. *Financial support:* In 2011–12, 237 students received support. Career-related internships or fieldwork, institutionally sponsored loans, and scholarships/grants available. Financial award application deadline: 3/20; financial award applicants required to submit FAFSA. *Faculty research:* Social work practice, human behavior in the social environment, social welfare policy, social work research. *Unit head:* Dr. Carolyn Jacobs, Dean/Professor, 413-585-7977, E-mail: cjacobs@smith.edu. *Application contact:* Irene Rodriguez Martin, Director of Enrollment Management and Continuing Education, 413-585-7960, Fax: 413-585-7994, E-mail: imartin@smith.edu. Web site: http://www.smith.edu/ssw/.

Southern Adventist University, School of Social Work, Collegedale, TN 37315-0370. Offers MSW. Postbaccalaureate distance learning degree programs offered.

Southern Connecticut State University, School of Graduate Studies, School of Health and Human Services, Department of Social Work, New Haven, CT 06515-1355. Offers MSW, MSW/MS. *Accreditation:* CSWE. Part-time and evening/weekend programs available. *Faculty:* 15 full-time (7 women), 17 part-time/adjunct (11 women). *Students:* 135 full-time (119 women), 40 part-time (35 women); includes 50 minority (24 Black or African American, non-Hispanic/Latino; 1 Asian, non-Hispanic/Latino; 21 Hispanic/Latino; 4 Two or more races, non-Hispanic/Latino). 542 applicants, 12% accepted, 50 enrolled. In 2011, 54 master's awarded. *Degree requirements:* For master's, thesis. *Entrance requirements:* For master's, minimum undergraduate QPA of 3.0 in graduate major field, interview. *Application deadline:* For fall admission, 3/1 for domestic students; for spring admission, 12/1 for domestic students. Application fee: $50. Electronic applications accepted. *Expenses:* Tuition, state resident: full-time $5137; part-time $413 per credit. *Required fees:* $4008; $55 per term. *Financial support:* Application deadline: 4/15; applicants required to submit FAFSA. *Faculty research:* Social work practice; social service development; services for women, the aging, children, and families in educational and health care systems. *Unit head:* Dr. Todd Rofuth, Chairperson, 203-392-6557, Fax: 203-392-6580, E-mail: rofutht1@southernct.edu. *Application contact:* Dr. Barbara Worden, Graduate Coordinator, 203-392-6563, Fax: 203-392-6580, E-mail: wordenb1@southernct.edu.

Southern Illinois University Carbondale, Graduate School, College of Education and Human Services, School of Social Work, Carbondale, IL 62901-4701. Offers MSW, JD/MSW. *Accreditation:* CSWE. *Faculty:* 10 full-time (6 women). *Students:* 94 full-time (80 women), 18 part-time (15 women); includes 37 minority (30 Black or African American, non-Hispanic/Latino; 1 American Indian or Alaska Native, non-Hispanic/Latino; 2 Asian, non-Hispanic/Latino; 4 Hispanic/Latino), 3 international. Average age 30. 50 applicants, 62% accepted, 15 enrolled. In 2011, 54 master's awarded. *Entrance requirements:* For master's, GRE General Test, minimum GPA of 2.7. Additional exam requirements/recommendations for international students: Required—TOEFL. *Application deadline:* For fall admission, 3/1 for domestic students. Applications are processed on a rolling basis. Application fee: $20. *Financial support:* In 2011–12, 19 students received support, including 6 research assistantships with full tuition reimbursements available; fellowships with full tuition reimbursements available, teaching assistantships with full tuition reimbursements available, career-related internships or fieldwork, and tuition waivers (full) also available. Financial award application deadline: 5/1. *Faculty research:* Service delivery systems, comparative race relations, advocacy research, gerontology, child welfare and health. *Unit head:* Dr. Mizanur Miah, Director, 618-453-2243. *Application contact:* Judy Wright, Assistant to Graduate Director, 618-453-1202, Fax: 618-453-1219, E-mail: mmmjw@siu.edu. Web site: http://socialwork.siu.edu/.

Southern Illinois University Edwardsville, Graduate School, College of Arts and Sciences, Department of Social Work, Edwardsville, IL 62026. Offers school social work (MSW); social work (MSW). *Accreditation:* CSWE. Part-time and evening/weekend programs available. *Faculty:* 9 full-time (4 women). *Students:* 40 full-time (37 women), 25 part-time (all women); includes 10 minority (9 Black or African American, non-Hispanic/Latino; 1 Hispanic/Latino). 118 applicants, 34% accepted. In 2011, 35 master's awarded. *Degree requirements:* For master's, final exam. *Entrance requirements:* Additional exam requirements/recommendations for international students: Required—TOEFL (minimum score 550 paper-based; 213 computer-based; 79 iBT), IELTS (minimum score 6.5). *Application deadline:* For fall admission, 2/15 for domestic and international students. Application fee: $30. Electronic applications accepted. Tuition and fees vary according to course load and program. *Financial support:* In 2011–12, 1 fellowship with full tuition reimbursement (averaging $8,370 per year), 2 research assistantships with full tuition reimbursements (averaging $9,927 per year), 5 teaching assistantships with full tuition reimbursements (averaging $9,927 per year) were awarded; institutionally sponsored loans, scholarships/grants, and unspecified assistantships also available. Financial award application deadline: 3/1; financial award applicants required to submit FAFSA. *Unit head:* Dr. Larry Kreuger, Chair, 618-650-5758, E-mail: lkreuge@siue.edu. *Application contact:* Dr. Kathleen Tunney, Director, 618-650-5428, E-mail: ktunney@siue.edu. Web site: http://www.siue.edu/artsandsciences/socialwork.

Southern University at New Orleans, School of Graduate Studies, New Orleans, LA 70126-1009. Offers criminal justice (MA); management information systems (MS); museum studies (MA); social work (MSW). *Accreditation:* CSWE. Part-time and evening/weekend programs available. *Faculty:* 28 full-time (12 women), 3 part-time/adjunct (2 women). *Students:* 230 full-time (180 women), 210 part-time (174 women); includes 393 minority (385 Black or African American, non-Hispanic/Latino; 2 American Indian or Alaska Native, non-Hispanic/Latino; 4 Asian, non-Hispanic/Latino; 2 Hispanic/Latino). Average age 35. In 2011, 157 master's awarded. *Degree requirements:* For master's, thesis. *Entrance requirements:* For master's, GRE/GMAT. Additional exam requirements/recommendations for international students: Required—TOEFL. *Application deadline:* Applications are processed on a rolling basis. Application fee: $25 ($35 for international students). *Expenses:* Tuition, state resident: part-time $747 per credit hour. Tuition, nonresident: part-time $747 per credit hour. *Financial support:* Fellowships, career-related internships or fieldwork, and institutionally sponsored loans available. *Application contact:* Deidrea Hazure, Administrative Specialist/Graduate Studies Admissions Coordinator, 504-284-5486, Fax: 504-284-5506, E-mail: dhazure@suno.edu. Web site: http://www.suno.edu/Colleges/Graduate_Studies/.

Spalding University, Graduate Studies, College of Social Sciences and Humanities, School of Social Work, Louisville, KY 40203-2188. Offers MSW. *Accreditation:* CSWE. Evening/weekend programs available. *Faculty:* 7 full-time (5 women), 9 part-time/adjunct (6 women). *Students:* 32 full-time (29 women), 7 part-time (6 women); includes 13 minority (11 Black or African American, non-Hispanic/Latino; 1 Hispanic/Latino; 1 Two or more races, non-Hispanic/Latino). Average age 33. 51 applicants, 29% accepted, 13 enrolled. In 2011, 26 master's awarded. *Degree requirements:* For master's, thesis or alternative, project presentation. *Entrance requirements:* For master's, GRE General Test (if undergraduate GPA less than 2.8), 18 hours of course work in social sciences including statistics, human biology. Additional exam requirements/recommendations for international students: Required—TOEFL (minimum score 535 paper-based; 203 computer-based). *Application deadline:* For fall admission, 5/15 priority date for domestic students. Applications are processed on a rolling basis. Application fee: $30. Electronic applications accepted. *Expenses: Tuition:* Full-time $12,438. Tuition and fees vary according to course load, degree level and program. *Financial support:* Career-related internships or fieldwork, Federal Work-Study, and scholarships/grants available. Financial award application deadline: 3/15; financial award applicants required to submit FAFSA. *Faculty research:* Addictions, spirituality, feminist studies, mental retardation, action research. *Unit head:* Dr. Phyllis Platt, Chair, 502-873-4482 Ext. 2281, E-mail: pplatt@spalding.edu. *Application contact:* Mary Grace, Administrative Assistant, 502-588-7183, Fax: 502-585-7158, E-mail: sgrace@spalding.edu. Web site: http://spalding.edu/academics/social-work/.

Springfield College, Graduate Programs, School of Social Work, Springfield, MA 01109-3797. Offers advanced generalist (weekday and weekend) (MSW); advanced standing (MSW); JD/MSW. *Accreditation:* CSWE. Part-time programs available. *Degree requirements:* For master's, comprehensive exam. *Entrance requirements:* Additional exam requirements/recommendations for international students: Required—TOEFL (minimum score 550 paper-based; 213 computer-based). Electronic applications accepted.

State University of New York at Binghamton, Graduate School, College of Community and Public Affairs, Department of Social Work, Binghamton, NY 13902-6000. Offers MSW, MSW/MPA. MSW/MPA offered jointly with University at Albany, State University of New York. *Accreditation:* CSWE. Part-time and evening/weekend programs available. *Faculty:* 8 full-time (6 women), 8 part-time/adjunct (4 women). *Students:* 70 full-time (53 women), 64 part-time (53 women); includes 21 minority (10 Black or African American, non-Hispanic/Latino; 1 American Indian or Alaska Native, non-Hispanic/Latino; 4 Asian, non-Hispanic/Latino; 5 Hispanic/Latino; 1 Native Hawaiian or other Pacific Islander, non-Hispanic/Latino), 3 international. Average age 33. 154 applicants, 51% accepted, 51 enrolled. In 2011, 55 master's awarded. *Degree requirements:* For master's, thesis. *Entrance requirements:* For master's, GRE General Test. Additional exam requirements/recommendations for international students: Required—TOEFL (minimum score 550 paper-based; 213 computer-based; 80 iBT). *Application deadline:* For fall admission, 2/1 priority date for domestic students, 2/1 for international students. Applications are processed on a rolling basis. Application fee: $60. Electronic applications accepted. *Financial support:* In 2011–12, 29 students received support, including 14 fellowships with full tuition reimbursements available (averaging $10,000 per year), 1 research assistantship with full tuition reimbursement available (averaging $10,000 per year); career-related internships or fieldwork, Federal Work-Study, institutionally sponsored loans, scholarships/grants, health care benefits, and unspecified assistantships also available. Financial award application deadline: 2/15; financial award applicants required to submit FAFSA. *Unit head:* Dr. Laura Bronstein, Chairperson, 607-777-9162, E-mail: lbronst@binghamton.edu. *Application contact:* Catherine Smith, Recruiting and Admissions Coordinator, 607-777-2151, Fax: 607-777-2501, E-mail: cmsmith@binghamton.edu.

Stephen F. Austin State University, Graduate School, College of Applied Arts and Science, School of Social Work, Nacogdoches, TX 75962. Offers MSW. *Accreditation:* CSWE. *Degree requirements:* For master's, comprehensive exam, thesis optional. *Entrance requirements:* For master's, GRE General Test, interview. Additional exam requirements/recommendations for international students: Required—TOEFL (minimum score 550 paper-based).

Stony Brook University, State University of New York, Stony Brook University Medical Center, Health Sciences Center, School of Social Welfare, Doctoral Program in Social Welfare, Stony Brook, NY 11794. Offers PhD. *Degree requirements:* For doctorate, thesis/dissertation. *Entrance requirements:* For doctorate, GRE General Test.

Stony Brook University, State University of New York, Stony Brook University Medical Center, Health Sciences Center, School of Social Welfare, Master's Program in Social Work, Stony Brook, NY 11794. Offers MSW. *Accreditation:* CSWE. *Degree requirements:* For master's, project or thesis. *Entrance requirements:* For master's, interview.

Syracuse University, Falk College of Sport and Human Dynamics, Program in Social Work, Syracuse, NY 13244. Offers MSW. *Accreditation:* CSWE. Part-time and evening/weekend programs available. *Students:* 126 full-time (109 women), 96 part-time (86 women); includes 37 minority (22 Black or African American, non-Hispanic/Latino; 5 American Indian or Alaska Native, non-Hispanic/Latino; 7 Hispanic/Latino; 3 Two or more races, non-Hispanic/Latino), 3 international. Average age 31. 27 applicants, 74% accepted, 12 enrolled. In 2011, 80 master's awarded. *Entrance requirements:* Additional exam requirements/recommendations for international students: Required—TOEFL (minimum score 100 iBT). *Application deadline:* For fall admission, 3/15 for domestic and international students. Applications are processed on a rolling basis. Application fee: $75. Electronic applications accepted. *Expenses: Tuition:* Part-time $1206 per credit. *Financial support:* Fellowships with full tuition reimbursements, research assistantships with full and partial tuition reimbursements, teaching assistantships with full and partial tuition reimbursements, and tuition waivers available. Financial award application deadline: 1/1; financial award applicants required to submit FAFSA. *Faculty research:* Aging policy, healthcare, criminal justice, disability, rights of passage. *Unit head:* Dr. Carrie Smith, Acting Director, 315-443-5555, E-mail: falk@syr.edu. *Application contact:* Felicia Otero Otero, Information Contact, 315-443-5555, E-mail: falk@syr.edu. Web site: http://falk.syr.edu/SocialWork/Default.aspx.

Temple University, Health Sciences Center, College of Health Professions and Social Work, School of Social Work, Philadelphia, PA 19122-6096. Offers MSW. *Accreditation:* CSWE. Part-time and evening/weekend programs available. *Faculty:* 13 full-time (6 women). *Students:* 390 full-time (343 women), 157 part-time (133 women); includes 188 minority (137 Black or African American, non-Hispanic/Latino; 4 American Indian or Alaska Native, non-Hispanic/Latino; 12 Asian, non-Hispanic/Latino; 24 Hispanic/Latino; 11 Two or more races, non-Hispanic/Latino), 5 international. Average age 32. 234 applicants, 90% accepted, 120 enrolled. In 2011, 200 master's awarded. *Entrance requirements:* For master's, minimum GPA of 3.0. Additional exam requirements/recommendations for international students: Required—TOEFL (minimum score 550 paper-based; 213 computer-based; 79 iBT). *Application deadline:*

Social Work

For fall admission, 2/15 priority date for domestic students, 12/15 for international students; for spring admission, 11/1 priority date for domestic students, 8/1 for international students. Applications are processed on a rolling basis. Application fee: $50. Electronic applications accepted. *Expenses:* Tuition, state resident: full-time $12,366; part-time $687 per credit hour. Tuition, nonresident: full-time $17,298; part-time $961 per credit hour. *Required fees:* $590; $213 per year. *Financial support:* Fellowships with tuition reimbursements, research assistantships with tuition reimbursements, teaching assistantships with tuition reimbursements, career-related internships or fieldwork, Federal Work-Study, institutionally sponsored loans, scholarships/grants, traineeships, tuition waivers (partial), unspecified assistantships, and field assistantships available. Financial award application deadline: 1/15; financial award applicants required to submit FAFSA. *Faculty research:* Child welfare, alcoholism, social work practice, developmental disabilities, human sexuality. *Unit head:* Dr. Jeffrey Draine, Chair, 215-204-5443, Fax: 215-204-9606, E-mail: jeffdraine@temple.edu. *Application contact:* Tara Schumacher, Coordinator of Outreach, 215-204-6575, Fax: 215-204-8781, E-mail: tara.schumacher@temple.edu. Web site: http://chpsw.temple.edu/ssa/.

Texas A&M University–Commerce, Graduate School, College of Education and Human Services, Department of Social Work, Commerce, TX 75429-3011. Offers MSW. *Accreditation:* CSWE. *Entrance requirements:* For master's, GRE General Test.

Texas State University–San Marcos, Graduate School, College of Applied Arts, School of Social Work, San Marcos, TX 78666. Offers MSW. *Accreditation:* CSWE. *Faculty:* 13 full-time (10 women), 4 part-time/adjunct (all women). *Students:* 95 full-time (85 women), 127 part-time (114 women); includes 98 minority (23 Black or African American, non-Hispanic/Latino; 2 American Indian or Alaska Native, non-Hispanic/Latino; 3 Asian, non-Hispanic/Latino; 69 Hispanic/Latino; 1 Two or more races, non-Hispanic/Latino). Average age 32. 194 applicants, 46% accepted, 79 enrolled. In 2011, 57 master's awarded. *Degree requirements:* For master's, comprehensive exam. *Entrance requirements:* For master's, minimum GPA of 3.0 in last 60 hours of course work, 3 recommendation forms, curriculum vitae. Additional exam requirements/recommendations for international students: Required—TOEFL (minimum score 550 paper-based; 213 computer-based; 78 iBT). *Application deadline:* For fall admission, 6/15 priority date for domestic students, 6/1 for international students. Applications are processed on a rolling basis. Application fee: $40 ($90 for international students). Electronic applications accepted. *Expenses:* Tuition, state resident: full-time $6408; part-time $3204 per semester. Tuition, nonresident: full-time $14,832; part-time $7416 per semester. *Required fees:* $1824; $912 per semester. Tuition and fees vary according to course load. *Financial support:* In 2011–12, 183 students received support, including 4 research assistantships (averaging $11,493 per year), 2 teaching assistantships (averaging $10,152 per year); career-related internships or fieldwork, Federal Work-Study, institutionally sponsored loans, and unspecified assistantships also available. Support available to part-time students. Financial award application deadline: 4/1; financial award applicants required to submit FAFSA. *Unit head:* Dr. Dorinda Noble, Program Advisor, 512-245-2592, E-mail: dn12@txstate.edu. *Application contact:* Dr. J. Michael Willoughby, Dean of Graduate School, 512-245-2581, Fax: 512-245-8365, E-mail: gradcollege@txstate.edu. Web site: http://www.socialwork.txstate.edu.

Thompson Rivers University, Program in Social Work, Kamloops, BC V2C 5N3, Canada. Offers MSW.

Touro College, Graduate School of Social Work, New York, NY 10010. Offers MSW. *Students:* 197 full-time (124 women), 7 part-time (all women); includes 91 minority (63 Black or African American, non-Hispanic/Latino; 1 American Indian or Alaska Native, non-Hispanic/Latino; 3 Asian, non-Hispanic/Latino; 24 Hispanic/Latino). *Unit head:* Dr. Steven Huberman, Dean, 212-463-0400 Ext. 5269, E-mail: msw@touro.edu. Web site: http://www.touro.edu/msw/.

Troy University, Graduate School, College of Education, Program in Counseling and Psychology, Troy, AL 36082. Offers agency counseling (Ed S); clinical mental health (MS); community counseling (MS, Ed S); corrections counseling (MS); rehabilitation counseling (MS); school psychology (MS, Ed S); school psychometry (MS); social service counseling (MS); student affairs counseling (MS); substance abuse counseling (MS). *Accreditation:* ACA; CORE; NCATE. Part-time and evening/weekend programs available. *Faculty:* 38 full-time (21 women), 40 part-time/adjunct (21 women). *Students:* 299 full-time (239 women), 672 part-time (557 women); includes 604 minority (358 Black or African American, non-Hispanic/Latino; 2 American Indian or Alaska Native, non-Hispanic/Latino; 188 Asian, non-Hispanic/Latino; 50 Hispanic/Latino; 1 Native Hawaiian or other Pacific Islander, non-Hispanic/Latino; 5 Two or more races, non-Hispanic/Latino). Average age 34. 384 applicants, 83% accepted, 196 enrolled. In 2011, 242 master's, 1 other advanced degree awarded. *Degree requirements:* For master's, comprehensive exam, thesis. *Entrance requirements:* For master's, MAT, minimum GPA of 2.5. Additional exam requirements/recommendations for international students: Required—TOEFL (minimum score 523 paper-based; 193 computer-based; 70 iBT), IELTS (minimum score 6). *Application deadline:* Applications are processed on a rolling basis. Application fee: $50. Electronic applications accepted. *Expenses:* Tuition, state resident: full-time $6960; part-time $290 per credit hour. Tuition, nonresident: full-time $13,920; part-time $580 per credit hour. *Required fees:* $386 per term. *Unit head:* Dr. Andrew Creamer, Chair, 334-670-3350, Fax: 334-670-32961, E-mail: drcreamer@troy.edu. *Application contact:* Brenda K. Campbell, Director of Graduate Admissions, 334-670-3178, Fax: 334-670-3733, E-mail: bcamp@troy.edu.

Tulane University, School of Social Work, New Orleans, LA 70118-5669. Offers MSW, JD/MSW, MSW/MPH. *Accreditation:* CSWE (one or more programs are accredited). Part-time programs available. *Degree requirements:* For master's, thesis. *Entrance requirements:* Additional exam requirements/recommendations for international students: Required—TOEFL. Electronic applications accepted.

Universidad del Este, Graduate School, Carolina, PR 00984. Offers accounting (MBA); adult education (M Ed); agribusiness (MBA); criminal justice and criminology (MA); curriculum and instruction - early education (M Ed); curriculum and instruction - elementary (M Ed); curriculum and instruction - English (M Ed); curriculum and instruction - Spanish (M Ed); human resources (MBA); information security management (MBA); information technology and Web business development (MBA); management (MBA); public policy (MPA); social work (MA), including clinical social work; special education (M Ed); strategic leadership (MBA).

Université de Moncton, Faculty of Arts and Social Sciences, School of Social Work, Moncton, NB E1A 3E9, Canada. Offers MSW. *Degree requirements:* For master's, one foreign language, major paper. *Entrance requirements:* For master's, minimum GPA of 3.0. *Faculty research:* Burnout and education, mental health (institutionalization), unemployment's effect on youth, women and health services.

Université de Montréal, Faculty of Arts and Sciences, School of Social Service, Program in Social Administration, Montréal, QC H3C 3J7, Canada. Offers DESS. Electronic applications accepted.

Université de Sherbrooke, Faculty of Letters and Human Sciences, Department of Social Service, Sherbrooke, QC J1K 2R1, Canada. Offers MSS.

Université du Québec à Montréal, Graduate Programs, Program in Social Intervention, Montréal, QC H3C 3P8, Canada. Offers MA. Part-time programs available. *Degree requirements:* For master's, thesis. *Entrance requirements:* For master's, appropriate bachelor's degree or equivalent, proficiency in French.

Université du Québec en Abitibi-Témiscamingue, Graduate Programs, Program in Social Work, Rouyn-Noranda, QC J9X 5E4, Canada. Offers MSW.

Université du Québec en Outaouais, Graduate Programs, Program in Social Work, Gatineau, QC J8X 3X7, Canada. Offers MA. *Students:* 22 full-time, 22 part-time. *Degree requirements:* For master's, thesis (for some programs). *Application deadline:* For fall admission, 6/1 priority date for domestic students, 3/1 for international students; for winter admission, 11/1 priority date for domestic students, 10/1 for international students. Application fee: $30 Canadian dollars. *Financial support:* Research assistantships available. *Unit head:* Annie Devault, Director, 819-595-3900 Ext. 2506, Fax: 819-595-2384, E-mail: annie.devault@uqo.ca. *Application contact:* Registrar's Office, 819-773-1850, Fax: 819-773-1835, E-mail: registraire@ugo.ca.

Université Laval, Faculty of Social Sciences, School of Social Work, Programs in Social Work, Québec, QC G1K 7P4, Canada. Offers M Serv Soc, PhD. Terminal master's awarded for partial completion of doctoral program. *Degree requirements:* For master's, thesis (for some programs); for doctorate, comprehensive exam, thesis/dissertation. *Entrance requirements:* For master's and doctorate, knowledge of French, comprehension of written English. Electronic applications accepted.

University at Albany, State University of New York, School of Social Welfare, Albany, NY 12222-0001. Offers MSW, PhD, MSW/MA. *Accreditation:* CSWE (one or more programs are accredited). Part-time and evening/weekend programs available. *Degree requirements:* For doctorate, thesis/dissertation. *Entrance requirements:* For doctorate, GRE General Test. Additional exam requirements/recommendations for international students: Required—TOEFL (minimum score 550 paper-based; 213 computer-based). Electronic applications accepted. *Faculty research:* Welfare reform, homelessness, children and families, mental health, substance abuse.

University at Buffalo, the State University of New York, Graduate School, School of Social Work, Buffalo, NY 14260. Offers social welfare (PhD); social work (MSW); JD/MSW; MBA/MSW; MPH/MSW. *Accreditation:* CSWE (one or more programs are accredited). Part-time programs available. *Faculty:* 25 full-time (18 women), 33 part-time/adjunct (21 women). *Students:* 260 full-time (219 women), 167 part-time (135 women); includes 68 minority (45 Black or African American, non-Hispanic/Latino; 2 American Indian or Alaska Native, non-Hispanic/Latino; 9 Asian, non-Hispanic/Latino; 10 Hispanic/Latino; 2 Native Hawaiian or other Pacific Islander, non-Hispanic/Latino), 20 international. Average age 29. 478 applicants, 60% accepted, 193 enrolled. In 2011, 188 master's, 5 doctorates awarded. *Degree requirements:* For master's, 900 hours of field work; for doctorate, comprehensive exam, thesis/dissertation. *Entrance requirements:* For master's, 24 credits of course work in liberal arts; for doctorate, GRE General Test, MSW or equivalent. Additional exam requirements/recommendations for international students: Required—TOEFL (minimum score 600 paper-based; 250 computer-based; 100 iBT). *Application deadline:* For fall admission, 3/1 priority date for domestic students, 3/1 for international students. Applications are processed on a rolling basis. Application fee: $50. Electronic applications accepted. *Financial support:* In 2011–12, 97 students received support, including 4 fellowships with full tuition reimbursements available (averaging $7,500 per year), 6 research assistantships with full tuition reimbursements available (averaging $15,000 per year), 6 teaching assistantships with full tuition reimbursements available (averaging $3,000 per year); Federal Work-Study, scholarships/grants, health care benefits, tuition waivers (partial), unspecified assistantships, and instructorships and research grants (PhD) also available. Financial award application deadline: 4/30; financial award applicants required to submit FAFSA. *Faculty research:* Trauma, substance abuse, child welfare, aging, human rights. *Unit head:* Dr. Nancy J. Smyth, Dean, 716-645-3381, Fax: 716-645-3883, E-mail: sw-dean@buffalo.edu. *Application contact:* Maria Carey, Admissions Processor, 716-645-3381, Fax: 716-645-3456, E-mail: sw-info@buffalo.edu. Web site: http://www.socialwork.buffalo.edu/.

See Display on next page and Close-Up on page 1777.

The University of Akron, Graduate School, College of Health Sciences and Human Services, School of Social Work, Akron, OH 44325. Offers MS. *Accreditation:* CSWE. *Faculty:* 9 full-time (7 women), 48 part-time/adjunct (26 women). *Students:* 92 full-time (82 women), 21 part-time (20 women); includes 20 minority (13 Black or African American, non-Hispanic/Latino; 2 American Indian or Alaska Native, non-Hispanic/Latino; 2 Hispanic/Latino; 3 Two or more races, non-Hispanic/Latino), 1 international. Average age 31. 106 applicants, 62% accepted, 47 enrolled. In 2011, 45 master's awarded. *Entrance requirements:* For master's, undergraduate major in social work or related field, three letters of recommendation, essay. Additional exam requirements/recommendations for international students: Required—TOEFL (minimum score 550 paper-based; 213 computer-based; 79 iBT). *Application deadline:* For fall admission, 2/15 for domestic and international students. Application fee: $30 ($40 for international students). Electronic applications accepted. *Expenses:* Tuition, state resident: full-time $7038; part-time $391 per credit hour. Tuition, nonresident: full-time $12,051; part-time $670 per credit hour. *Required fees:* $1274; $34 per credit hour. *Financial support:* In 2011–12, 5 teaching assistantships with full tuition reimbursements were awarded; research assistantships and Federal Work-Study also available. *Faculty research:* Spirituality and alternative healing, child welfare education and training, ethics and social work practice, evidence-based social work practice, social work continuing education. *Unit head:* Dr. Timothy McCarragher, Director, 330-972-5976, E-mail: mccarra@uakron.edu. Web site: http://www.uakron.edu/socialwork/.

The University of Alabama, Graduate School, School of Social Work, Tuscaloosa, AL 35487-0314. Offers MSW, PhD. *Accreditation:* CSWE (one or more programs are accredited). Postbaccalaureate distance learning degree programs offered (no on-campus study). *Faculty:* 21 full-time (14 women). *Students:* 281 full-time (255 women), 76 part-time (70 women); includes 158 minority (135 Black or African American, non-Hispanic/Latino; 1 Asian, non-Hispanic/Latino; 11 Hispanic/Latino; 11 Two or more races, non-Hispanic/Latino), 5 international. Average age 31. 336 applicants, 79% accepted, 192 enrolled. In 2011, 143 master's, 2 doctorates awarded. *Median time to degree:* Of those who began their doctoral program in fall 2003, 83% received their degree in 8 years or less. *Degree requirements:* For doctorate, comprehensive exam, thesis/dissertation. *Entrance requirements:* For master's, GRE or MAT (if GPA less than 3.0), minimum GPA of 2.5; for doctorate, GRE, minimum GPA of 3.0. Additional exam requirements/recommendations for international students: Required—TOEFL, IELTS. *Application deadline:* For fall admission, 2/1 priority date for domestic students; for spring admission, 9/1 priority date for domestic students. Applications are processed on a rolling basis. Application fee: $50 ($60 for international students). Electronic applications accepted. *Expenses:* Tuition, state resident: full-time $8600. Tuition, nonresident: full-time $21,900. *Financial support:* In 2011–12, 113 students received support, including 4 fellowships (averaging $3,750 per year), 9 research assistantships with full tuition reimbursements available (averaging $9,394 per year), 3 teaching assistantships with full tuition reimbursements available (averaging $9,396 per year); career-related internships or fieldwork, scholarships/grants, health care benefits, tuition waivers (partial), and unspecified assistantships also available. Financial award application deadline: 2/1; financial award applicants required to submit FAFSA. *Faculty research:* Children, adolescents, and their families; gerontology; juvenile justice; addictions; health. *Total annual research expenditures:* $182,152. *Unit head:* Dr. James A. Hall, Dean, 205-348-3924, Fax: 205-348-9419, E-mail: jhall1@sw.ua.edu. *Application contact:* Casey Barnes, Admissions Coordinator, 205-348-8413, Fax: 205-348-9419, E-mail: credmill@sw.ua.edu. Web site: http://www.socialwork.ua.edu/.

University of Alaska Anchorage, College of Health, School of Social Work, Anchorage, AK 99508. Offers clinical social work practice (Certificate); social work (MSW); social work management (Certificate). *Accreditation:* CSWE. Part-time and evening/weekend programs available. Postbaccalaureate distance learning degree programs offered (no on-campus study). *Degree requirements:* For master's, comprehensive exam (for some programs), thesis or alternative, research project. *Entrance requirements:* For master's, GRE General Test, writing sample. Additional exam requirements/recommendations for international students: Required—TOEFL (minimum score 550 paper-based; 213 computer-based). Electronic applications accepted. *Expenses:* Contact institution.

University of Arkansas, Graduate School, J. William Fulbright College of Arts and Sciences, School of Social Work, Fayetteville, AR 72701-1201. Offers MSW. *Accreditation:* CSWE. *Students:* 36 full-time (29 women), 2 part-time (1 woman); includes 6 minority (2 Black or African American, non-Hispanic/Latino; 1 American Indian or Alaska Native, non-Hispanic/Latino; 2 Asian, non-Hispanic/Latino; 1 Hispanic/Latino). In 2011, 13 master's awarded. *Entrance requirements:* For master's, GRE General Test. *Application deadline:* For fall admission, 4/1 for international students; for spring admission, 10/1 for international students. Applications are processed on a rolling basis. Application fee: $40 ($50 for international students). Electronic applications accepted. *Financial support:* In 2011–12, 4 research assistantships were awarded; fellowships with tuition reimbursements and teaching assistantships also available. *Unit head:* Dr. Yvette Murphy-Erby, Departmental Chairperson, 479-575-5039, Fax: 479-575-4145, E-mail: ymurphy@uark.edu. *Application contact:* Dr. Glenda House, Graduate Coordinator, 479-575-3783, E-mail: ghouse@uark.edu. Web site: http://socialwork.uark.edu/.

University of Arkansas at Little Rock, Graduate School, College of Professional Studies, School of Social Work, Program in Social Work, Little Rock, AR 72204-1099. Offers advanced direct practice (MSW); management and community practice (MSW). *Accreditation:* CSWE. *Entrance requirements:* For master's, GRE General Test or MAT.

The University of British Columbia, Faculty of Arts and Faculty of Graduate Studies, School of Social Work, Vancouver, BC V6T 1Z2, Canada. Offers MSW, PhD. *Degree requirements:* For master's, thesis or essay; for doctorate, comprehensive exam, thesis/dissertation. *Entrance requirements:* For master's, BSW; for doctorate, MSW. Additional exam requirements/recommendations for international students: Required—TOEFL (minimum score 580 paper-based; 237 computer-based; 93 iBT). Electronic applications accepted. *Faculty research:* Gerontology, family resources, diversity, social inequality.

University of Calgary, Faculty of Graduate Studies, Faculty of Social Work, Calgary, AB T2N 1N4, Canada. Offers MSW, PhD, Postgraduate Diploma. *Degree requirements:* For master's, thesis (for some programs); for doctorate, thesis/dissertation, candidacy exam. *Entrance requirements:* For master's, BSW, minimum undergraduate GPA of 3.4 (1 year program), minimum GPA of 3.5 (2 year program); for doctorate, minimum graduate GPA of 3.5, MSW (preferred); for Postgraduate Diploma, MSW, minimum graduate GPA of 3.5. Additional exam requirements/recommendations for international students: Required—TOEFL (paper-based 550; computer-based 213) or IELTS (paper-based 7). Electronic applications accepted. *Faculty research:* Family violence, direct practice, gerontology, child welfare, community development.

University of California, Berkeley, Graduate Division, School of Social Welfare, Berkeley, CA 94720-1500. Offers MSW, PhD, MSW/PhD. *Accreditation:* CSWE (one or more programs are accredited). Terminal master's awarded for partial completion of doctoral program. *Degree requirements:* For master's, thesis optional; for doctorate, thesis/dissertation, qualifying exam. *Entrance requirements:* For master's and doctorate, GRE General Test, minimum GPA of 3.0, 3 letters of recommendation. Additional exam requirements/recommendations for international students: Required—TOEFL, TWE. *Faculty research:* Child welfare, law and social welfare, minority mental health, social welfare policy analysis, health services.

University of California, Los Angeles, Graduate Division, School of Public Affairs, Program in Social Welfare, Los Angeles, CA 90095. Offers MSW, PhD, JD/MSW. *Accreditation:* CSWE (one or more programs are accredited). *Degree requirements:* For master's, comprehensive exam, research project; for doctorate, thesis/dissertation, oral and written qualifying exams. *Entrance requirements:* For master's, GRE General Test, minimum GPA of 3.0; for doctorate, GRE General Test, minimum undergraduate GPA of 3.0. Additional exam requirements/recommendations for international students: Required—TOEFL. Electronic applications accepted.

University of Central Florida, College of Health and Public Affairs, School of Social Work, Orlando, FL 32816. Offers children's services (Certificate); social work (MSW); social work administration (Certificate). *Accreditation:* CSWE. Part-time and evening/weekend programs available. *Faculty:* 19 full-time (17 women), 21 part-time/adjunct (15 women). *Students:* 181 full-time (156 women), 159 part-time (133 women); includes 132 minority (70 Black or African American, non-Hispanic/Latino; 1 American Indian or Alaska Native, non-Hispanic/Latino; 7 Asian, non-Hispanic/Latino; 50 Hispanic/Latino; 4 Two or more races, non-Hispanic/Latino), 1 international. Average age 32. 326 applicants, 67% accepted, 163 enrolled. In 2011, 133 master's, 4 other advanced degrees awarded. *Degree requirements:* For master's, thesis or alternative, field education. *Entrance requirements:* For master's, resume. Additional exam requirements/recommendations for international students: Required—TOEFL. *Application deadline:* For fall admission, 3/1 for domestic students. Application fee: $30. Electronic applications accepted. *Expenses:* Tuition, state resident: part-time $277.08 per credit hour. Tuition, nonresident: part-time $277.08 per credit hour. Part-time tuition and fees vary according to degree level and program. *Financial support:* In 2011–12, 1 student received support, including 1 research assistantship with partial tuition reimbursement available (averaging $8,000 per year); fellowships with partial tuition reimbursements available, career-related internships or fieldwork, Federal Work-Study, institutionally sponsored loans, and unspecified assistantships also available. Financial award application deadline: 3/1; financial award applicants required to submit FAFSA. *Unit head:* Dr. Sophia Dziegielewski, Interim Director, 407-823-2208, E-mail: sophia.dziegielewski@ucf.edu. *Application contact:* Barbara Rodriguez, Director, Admissions and Registration, 407-823-2766, Fax: 407-823-6442, E-mail: gradadmissions@ucf.edu. Web site: http://www.cohpa.ucf.edu/social/.

University of Chicago, School of Social Service Administration, Chicago, IL 60637. Offers social service administration (PhD); social work (AM); AM/M Div; MBA/AM; MPP/AM. *Accreditation:* CSWE (one or more programs are accredited). Part-time and evening/weekend programs available. *Degree requirements:* For master's, 2 field placements; for doctorate, comprehensive exam, thesis/dissertation. *Entrance requirements:* For master's, 4 letters of recommendation; for doctorate, writing sample, 4 letters of recommendation. Additional exam requirements/recommendations for international students: Required—TOEFL (minimum score 600 paper-based; 250 computer-based). Electronic applications accepted. *Expenses:* Contact institution. *Faculty research:* Family treatment, mental health, the aged, child welfare, health administration.

Social Work

University of Cincinnati, Graduate School, School of Social Work, Cincinnati, OH 45221. Offers MSW. *Accreditation:* CSWE. Part-time programs available. *Entrance requirements:* Additional exam requirements/recommendations for international students: Required—TOEFL. Electronic applications accepted. *Faculty research:* Fatherhood, mediation, mental illness, child welfare, elderly.

University of Denver, Graduate School of Social Work, Denver, CO 80208. Offers adoption competent practice (Certificate); animals and human health (Certificate); social work (MSW, PhD). *Accreditation:* CSWE (one or more programs are accredited). Part-time and evening/weekend programs available. *Faculty:* 27 full-time (18 women), 167 part-time/adjunct (131 women). *Students:* 435 full-time (392 women), 10 part-time (8 women); includes 71 minority (9 Black or African American, non-Hispanic/Latino; 10 American Indian or Alaska Native, non-Hispanic/Latino; 13 Asian, non-Hispanic/Latino; 25 Hispanic/Latino; 1 Native Hawaiian or other Pacific Islander, non-Hispanic/Latino; 13 Two or more races, non-Hispanic/Latino), 5 international. Average age 28. In 2011, 236 master's, 4 doctorates, 98 other advanced degrees awarded. *Degree requirements:* For doctorate, comprehensive exam, thesis/dissertation. *Entrance requirements:* For master's, 20 semester/quarter hours in undergraduate course work in the arts and humanities, social/behavioral sciences, and biological sciences; one course in English composition; for doctorate, GRE General Test, master's degree in social work or social sciences with substantial professional experience in the social work field. Additional exam requirements/recommendations for international students: Required—TOEFL (minimum score 587 paper-based; 95 iBT). *Application deadline:* For fall admission, 1/15 priority date for domestic students. Applications are processed on a rolling basis. Application fee: $60. Electronic applications accepted. *Financial support:* In 2011–12, 405 students received support, including 1 research assistantship with full and partial tuition reimbursement available (averaging $19,636 per year), 13 teaching assistantships with full and partial tuition reimbursements available (averaging $13,615 per year); Federal Work-Study, scholarships/grants, and unspecified assistantships also available. Support available to part-time students. Financial award application deadline: 2/15; financial award applicants required to submit FAFSA. *Faculty research:* Children, youth, and families; mental health; drug dependency; gerontology; child welfare. *Unit head:* Dr. James Herbert Williams, Dean, 303-871-2203, E-mail: james.herbert@du.edu. *Application contact:* Colin Schneider, Director of Admission and Financial Aid, 303-871-2841, Fax: 303-871-2845, E-mail: gssw-admission@du.edu. Web site: http://www.du.edu/socialwork/.

University of Georgia, School of Social Work, Athens, GA 30602. Offers MA, MSW, PhD, Certificate. *Accreditation:* CSWE (one or more programs are accredited). Part-time and evening/weekend programs available. *Faculty:* 20 full-time (13 women), 1 part-time/adjunct (0 women). *Students:* 300 full-time (256 women), 39 part-time (32 women); includes 83 minority (66 Black or African American, non-Hispanic/Latino; 5 Asian, non-Hispanic/Latino; 7 Hispanic/Latino; 5 Two or more races, non-Hispanic/Latino), 10 international. Average age 30. 397 applicants, 58% accepted, 160 enrolled. In 2011, 160 master's, 4 doctorates awarded. *Degree requirements:* For master's, thesis or alternative; for doctorate, one foreign language, thesis/dissertation. *Entrance requirements:* For master's and doctorate, GRE General Test. *Application deadline:* For fall admission, 7/1 priority date for domestic students, 7/1 for international students; for spring admission, 11/15 for domestic and international students. Applications are processed on a rolling basis. Application fee: $50. Electronic applications accepted. *Financial support:* In 2011–12, 39 students received support, including 4 fellowships (averaging $25,000 per year), 35 research assistantships with tuition reimbursements available (averaging $7,500 per year); teaching assistantships with tuition reimbursements available, career-related internships or fieldwork, Federal Work-Study, scholarships/grants, tuition waivers (full and partial), and unspecified assistantships also available. Support available to part-time students. Financial award application deadline: 2/10; financial award applicants required to submit FAFSA. *Faculty research:* Juvenile justice, substance abuse, civil rights and social justice, gerontology, social policy. *Total annual research expenditures:* $2.6 million. *Unit head:* Dr. Maurice C. Daniels, Dean, 706-542-5424, Fax: 706-542-3282, E-mail: daniels@uga.edu. *Application contact:* Dr. Jerome Schiele, Graduate Coordinator, 706-542-5429, Fax: 706-542-3282, E-mail: fschiele@uga.edu. Web site: http://www.ssw.uga.edu/.

University of Guam, Office of Graduate Studies, College of Natural and Applied Sciences, Program in Social Work, Mangilao, GU 96923. Offers MSW.

University of Hawaii at Manoa, Graduate Division, School of Social Work, Honolulu, HI 96822. Offers social welfare (PhD); social work (MSW). *Accreditation:* CSWE (one or more programs are accredited). Part-time programs available. *Degree requirements:* For doctorate, comprehensive exam, thesis/dissertation. *Entrance requirements:* For doctorate, master's degree (MSW preferred), minimum GPA of 3.0. Additional exam requirements/recommendations for international students: Required—TOEFL (minimum score 560 paper-based; 220 computer-based; 83 iBT), IELTS (minimum score 5). *Faculty research:* Health, mental health, AIDS, substance abuse, rural health, community-based research, social policy.

University of Houston, Graduate School of Social Work, Houston, TX 77204. Offers MSW, PhD. *Accreditation:* CSWE (one or more programs are accredited). Part-time programs available. *Degree requirements:* For master's, 900 clock hours of field experience, integrative paper. *Entrance requirements:* For master's, GRE, minimum GPA of 3.0 in last 60 hours, bachelor's degree. Additional exam requirements/recommendations for international students: Required—TOEFL (minimum score 550 paper-based; 79 iBT). *Faculty research:* Health care, gerontology, political social work, mental health, children and families.

University of Illinois at Chicago, Graduate College, Jane Addams College of Social Work, Chicago, IL 60607-7128. Offers MSW, PhD. *Accreditation:* CSWE (one or more programs are accredited). Part-time programs available. Terminal master's awarded for partial completion of doctoral program. *Degree requirements:* For doctorate, thesis/dissertation. *Entrance requirements:* For master's, GMAT, minimum GPA of 2.75; for doctorate, GRE General Test or MAT, minimum GPA of 2.75. Additional exam requirements/recommendations for international students: Required—TOEFL. Electronic applications accepted.

University of Illinois at Urbana–Champaign, Graduate College, School of Social Work, Champaign, IL 61820. Offers advocacy, leadership, and social change (MSW); children, youth and family services (MSW); social work (PhD); MS/MSW. *Accreditation:* CSWE (one or more programs are accredited). *Faculty:* 17 full-time (12 women), 1 (woman) part-time/adjunct. *Students:* 238 full-time (204 women), 57 part-time (48 women); includes 68 minority (33 Black or African American, non-Hispanic/Latino; 9 Asian, non-Hispanic/Latino; 19 Hispanic/Latino; 7 Two or more races, non-Hispanic/Latino), 18 international. 314 applicants, 42% accepted, 117 enrolled. In 2011, 113 master's, 2 doctorates awarded. *Entrance requirements:* For master's and doctorate, minimum GPA of 3.0. Additional exam requirements/recommendations for international students: Required—TOEFL (minimum score 580 paper-based; 237 computer-based). *Application deadline:* Applications are processed on a rolling basis. Application fee: $75 ($90 for international students). Electronic applications accepted. *Financial support:* In 2011–12, 4 fellowships, 13 research assistantships, 4 teaching assistantships were awarded; tuition waivers (full and partial) also available. *Unit head:* Wynne S. Korr, Dean, 217-333-2260, Fax: 217-244-5220, E-mail: wkorr@illinois.edu. *Application contact:* Cheryl M. Street, Admissions and Records Officer, 217-333-2261, Fax: 217-244-5220, E-mail: street@illinois.edu. Web site: http://www.socialwork.illinois.edu.

The University of Iowa, Graduate College, College of Liberal Arts and Sciences, School of Social Work, Iowa City, IA 52242-1316. Offers MSW, PhD, JD/MSW, MSW/MA, MSW/MS, MSW/PhD. *Accreditation:* CSWE. *Degree requirements:* For master's, thesis optional; for doctorate, comprehensive exam, thesis/dissertation. *Entrance requirements:* For master's, minimum GPA of 3.0; for doctorate, GRE General Test, minimum GPA of 3.0. Additional exam requirements/recommendations for international students: Required—TOEFL (minimum score 600 paper-based; 250 computer-based; 100 iBT). Electronic applications accepted.

The University of Kansas, Graduate Studies and The University of Kansas, School of Social Welfare, Lawrence, KS 66045. Offers social welfare (MSW); social work (PhD); JD/MSW. *Accreditation:* CSWE (one or more programs are accredited). Part-time programs available. Postbaccalaureate distance learning degree programs offered (minimal on-campus study). *Faculty:* 10 full-time (6 women), 28 part-time/adjunct (17 women). *Students:* 332 full-time (284 women), 74 part-time (66 women); includes 64 minority (26 Black or African American, non-Hispanic/Latino; 4 American Indian or Alaska Native, non-Hispanic/Latino; 5 Asian, non-Hispanic/Latino; 19 Hispanic/Latino; 10 Two or more races, non-Hispanic/Latino), 9 international. Average age 32. 364 applicants, 77% accepted, 187 enrolled. In 2011, 138 master's, 3 doctorates awarded. *Degree requirements:* For doctorate, thesis/dissertation. *Entrance requirements:* For master's, minimum GPA of 3.0, social work related experience; for doctorate, GRE General Test, minimum B average in statistics. Additional exam requirements/recommendations for international students: Required—TOEFL for Ph D and MSW, IELTS for MSW. *Application deadline:* For fall admission, 2/1 for domestic and international students. Application fee: $45 ($55 for international students). Electronic applications accepted. Tuition and fees vary according to course load, campus/location, program and reciprocity agreements. *Financial support:* Fellowships, research assistantships with full and partial tuition reimbursements, teaching assistantships with full and partial tuition reimbursements, Federal Work-Study, scholarships/grants, and tuition waivers (partial) available. Support available to part-time students. Financial award applicants required to submit FAFSA. *Faculty research:* Chronic mental illness, social work practice, emotionally disturbed children, child welfare, community development. *Unit head:* Mary Ellen Kondrat, Dean, 785-864-4720, Fax: 785-864-5277. *Application contact:* Becky Hofer, Director of Admissions, 785-864-8956, Fax: 785-864-5277, E-mail: bhofer@ku.edu. Web site: http://www.socwel.ku.edu/.

University of Kentucky, Graduate School, College of Social Work, Program in Social Work, Lexington, KY 40506-0032. Offers MSW, PhD. *Accreditation:* CSWE (one or more programs are accredited). *Degree requirements:* For master's, comprehensive exam; for doctorate, comprehensive exam, thesis/dissertation. *Entrance requirements:* For master's, GRE General Test, minimum undergraduate GPA of 2.75; for doctorate, GRE General Test, minimum undergraduate GPA of 3.0. Additional exam requirements/recommendations for international students: Required—TOEFL (minimum score 550 paper-based; 213 computer-based). Electronic applications accepted. *Faculty research:* Aging, family and children, domestic violence, delinquency, health and mental health.

University of Louisville, Graduate School, Raymond A. Kent School of Social Work, Louisville, KY 40292-0001. Offers marriage and family therapy (PMC), including mental health; social work (MSSW, PhD), including alcohol and drug counseling (MSSW), gerontology (MSSW), marriage and family (PhD), school social work (MSSW). *Accreditation:* AAMFT/COAMFTE; CSWE (one or more programs are accredited). Part-time and evening/weekend programs available. *Degree requirements:* For doctorate, comprehensive exam, thesis/dissertation. *Entrance requirements:* For master's, GRE or minimum GPA of 2.75; for doctorate, GRE General Test, interview, writing sample. Additional exam requirements/recommendations for international students: Required—TOEFL (minimum score 550 paper-based; 213 computer-based; 79 iBT). Electronic applications accepted. *Expenses:* Tuition, state resident: full-time $9692; part-time $539 per credit hour. Tuition, nonresident: full-time $20,168; part-time $1121 per credit hour. Tuition and fees vary according to program and reciprocity agreements. *Faculty research:* Child welfare, substance abuse, gerontology, family functioning, health behavior.

University of Maine, Graduate School, College of Business, Public Policy and Health, School of Social Work, Orono, ME 04469. Offers MSW. *Accreditation:* CSWE. *Faculty:* 7 full-time (5 women), 8 part-time/adjunct (all women). *Students:* 103 full-time (81 women), 10 part-time (9 women); includes 7 minority (1 Black or African American, non-Hispanic/Latino; 6 American Indian or Alaska Native, non-Hispanic/Latino), 3 international. Average age 38. 49 applicants, 76% accepted, 32 enrolled. In 2011, 42 master's awarded. *Entrance requirements:* For master's, GRE General Test. Additional exam requirements/recommendations for international students: Required—TOEFL. *Application deadline:* For fall admission, 2/1 priority date for domestic students. Applications are processed on a rolling basis. Application fee: $65. Electronic applications accepted. *Expenses:* Tuition, state resident: full-time $5016. Tuition, nonresident: full-time $14,424. *Financial support:* Application deadline: 3/1. *Total annual research expenditures:* $33,360. *Unit head:* Dr. Gail Werrbach, Director, 207-581-2386, Fax: 207-581-2396. *Application contact:* Scott G. Delcourt, Associate Dean of the Graduate School, 207-581-3291, Fax: 207-581-3232, E-mail: graduate@maine.edu. Web site: http://www2.umaine.edu/graduate/.

The University of Manchester, School of Nursing, Midwifery and Social Work, Manchester, United Kingdom. Offers nursing (M Phil, PhD); social work (M Phil, PhD).

University of Manitoba, Faculty of Graduate Studies, Faculty of Social Work, Winnipeg, MB R3T 2N2, Canada. Offers MSW, PhD. *Degree requirements:* For master's, thesis or alternative.

University of Maryland, Baltimore, Graduate School, School of Social Work, Doctoral Program in Social Work, Baltimore, MD 21201. Offers PhD. Part-time programs available. *Degree requirements:* For doctorate, thesis/dissertation. *Entrance requirements:* For doctorate, GRE General Test, minimum GPA of 3.5, MSW. *Faculty research:* Social work research, social work teaching.

University of Maryland, Baltimore, Graduate School, School of Social Work, Master's Program in Social Work, Baltimore, MD 21201. Offers MSW, MBA/MSW, MSW/JD, MSW/MA, MSW/MPH. MSW/MA offered jointly with Baltimore Hebrew University; MBA/MSU with University of Maryland, College Park; MSW/MPH with The Johns Hopkins University. *Accreditation:* CSWE. *Entrance requirements:* For master's, minimum GPA of 3.0. Additional exam requirements/recommendations for international students: Required—TOEFL. Electronic applications accepted. *Faculty research:* Aging, families and children, health, mental health, social action and community development.

University of Maryland, College Park, Academic Affairs, Robert H. Smith School of Business, Combined MSW/MBA Program, College Park, MD 20742. Offers MSW/MBA. *Accreditation:* AACSB. *Students:* 1 (woman) full-time, all international. 3 applicants, 33% accepted, 0 enrolled. *Entrance requirements:* Additional exam requirements/recommendations for international students: Required—TOEFL. *Application deadline:* For fall admission, 5/1 priority date for domestic students, 2/1 for international students; for spring admission, 11/30 for domestic students, 6/1 for international students. Application fee: $75. *Expenses: Tuition, area resident:* Part-time $525 per credit hour.

Tuition, state resident: part-time $525 per credit hour. Tuition, nonresident: part-time $1131 per credit hour. *Required fees:* $386.31 per term. Tuition and fees vary according to program. *Financial support:* In 2011–12, 1 teaching assistantship (averaging $14,772 per year) was awarded; fellowships and research assistantships also available. *Unit head:* Dr. Anand Anandalingam, Dean, 301-405-0582, E-mail: ganand@umd.edu. *Application contact:* Dr. Charles A. Caramello, Dean of Graduate School, 301-405-0358, Fax: 301-314-9305.

University of Michigan, School of Social Work, Ann Arbor, MI 48109-1106. Offers MSW, PhD, MSW/JD, MSW/MBA, MSW/MPH, MSW/MPP, MSW/MSI, MSW/MUP. PhD offered through the Horace H. Rackham School of Graduate Studies. *Accreditation:* CSWE (one or more programs are accredited). *Faculty:* 59 full-time (35 women), 37 part-time/adjunct (21 women). *Students:* 614 full-time (537 women), 22 part-time (16 women); includes 165 minority (73 Black or African American, non-Hispanic/Latino; 2 American Indian or Alaska Native, non-Hispanic/Latino; 30 Asian, non-Hispanic/Latino; 37 Hispanic/Latino; 23 Two or more races, non-Hispanic/Latino), 18 international. Average age 28. 1,123 applicants, 68% accepted, 361 enrolled. In 2011, 322 master's, 10 doctorates awarded. *Degree requirements:* For doctorate, oral defense of dissertation, preliminary exam. *Entrance requirements:* For master's, minimum of 20 academic semester credits in psychology, sociology, anthropology, economics, history, political science, government, and/or languages; for doctorate, GRE General Test. Additional exam requirements/recommendations for international students: Required—TOEFL (minimum score 600 paper-based; 250 computer-based; 100 iBT), IELTS (minimum score 7), Michigan English Language Assessment Battery (minimum score 85). *Application deadline:* For fall admission, 3/1 priority date for domestic students, 2/1 for international students. Applications are processed on a rolling basis. Application fee: $50. Electronic applications accepted. *Expenses:* Contact institution. *Financial support:* In 2011–12, 573 students received support. Career-related internships or fieldwork, Federal Work-Study, scholarships/grants, traineeships, and unspecified assistantships available. Financial award application deadline: 3/15; financial award applicants required to submit FAFSA. *Faculty research:* Children and families, aging, community organization, health and mental health, policy and evaluation. *Total annual research expenditures:* $3.7 million. *Unit head:* Laura Lein, Dean, 734-764-5347, Fax: 734-764-9954, E-mail: leinl@umich.edu. *Application contact:* Timothy Colenback, Assistant Dean for Student Services, 734-936-0961, Fax: 734-936-1961, E-mail: timot@umich.edu. Web site: http://www.ssw.umich.edu/.

University of Minnesota, Duluth, Graduate School, College of Education and Human Service Professions, Department of Social Work, Duluth, MN 55812-2496. Offers MSW. *Accreditation:* CSWE. Part-time and evening/weekend programs available. Postbaccalaureate distance learning degree programs offered (minimal on-campus study). *Entrance requirements:* For master's, minimum GPA of 3.0. Additional exam requirements/recommendations for international students: Required—TOEFL (minimum score 550 paper-based; 213 computer-based). *Faculty research:* Domestic abuse, substance abuse, minority health, child welfare, gerontology.

University of Minnesota, Twin Cities Campus, Graduate School, College of Education and Human Development, School of Social Work, Minneapolis, MN 55455-0213. Offers MSW, PhD. *Accreditation:* CSWE (one or more programs are accredited). Part-time and evening/weekend programs available. Postbaccalaureate distance learning degree programs offered. *Faculty:* 22 full-time (12 women). *Students:* 226 full-time (192 women), 4,762 part-time (4,743 women); includes 60 minority (22 Black or African American, non-Hispanic/Latino; 7 American Indian or Alaska Native, non-Hispanic/Latino; 22 Asian, non-Hispanic/Latino; 9 Hispanic/Latino), 15 international. Average age 31. 430 applicants, 44% accepted, 121 enrolled. In 2011, 151 master's, 6 doctorates awarded. *Degree requirements:* For doctorate, thesis/dissertation. *Entrance requirements:* For master's, minimum GPA of 3.0, 1 year of work experience; for doctorate, GRE, minimum GPA of 3.0, MSW. *Application deadline:* For fall admission, 1/15 for domestic students. Application fee: $55. *Financial support:* In 2011–12, 142 students received support, including 2 fellowships (averaging $22,500 per year), 36 research assistantships (averaging $11,025 per year); teaching assistantships, career-related internships or fieldwork, Federal Work-Study, institutionally sponsored loans, and tuition waivers (full and partial) also available. Support available to part-time students. Financial award applicants required to submit FAFSA. *Faculty research:* Mental health, clinical mental health, aging and disability, work with youth, family and community violence prevention, new American and immigrant populations, child welfare, youth leadership, community engagement, mediation and restitution, social Justice. *Total annual research expenditures:* $3.6 million. *Unit head:* Dr. James Reinardy, Director, 612-624-3673, Fax: 612-624-3746, E-mail: jreinard@umn.edu. *Application contact:* Dr. Jennifer Engler, Assistant Dean, 612-626-2887, Fax: 612-626-7496, E-mail: engle009@umn.edu. Web site: http://ssw.cehd.umn.edu.

University of Mississippi, Graduate School, School of Applied Sciences, Department of Social Work, Oxford, University, MS 38677. Offers MSW. *Students:* 17 full-time (16 women), 17 part-time (12 women); includes 15 minority (all Black or African American, non-Hispanic/Latino). *Unit head:* Dr. Carol Minor Boyd, Chair, 662-915-7336, Fax: 662-915-1288, E-mail: socialwk@olemiss.edu. *Application contact:* Dr. Christy M. Wyandt, Associate Dean, 662-915-7474, Fax: 662-915-7577, E-mail: cwyandt@olemiss.edu. Web site: http://www.olemiss.edu/depts/socialwork/.

University of Missouri, Graduate School, School of Social Work, Columbia, MO 65211. Offers MSW. *Accreditation:* CSWE. Part-time programs available. *Faculty:* 15 full-time (9 women). *Students:* 145 full-time (133 women), 77 part-time (70 women); includes 26 minority (11 Black or African American, non-Hispanic/Latino; 2 American Indian or Alaska Native, non-Hispanic/Latino; 7 Hispanic/Latino; 1 Native Hawaiian or other Pacific Islander, non-Hispanic/Latino; 5 Two or more races, non-Hispanic/Latino), 3 international. Average age 30. 159 applicants, 62% accepted, 78 enrolled. In 2011, 51 master's awarded. *Entrance requirements:* For master's, GRE General Test, minimum GPA of 3.0. Additional exam requirements/recommendations for international students: Required—TOEFL (minimum score 500 paper-based; 173 computer-based; 61 iBT). *Application deadline:* For fall admission, 1/15 priority date for domestic students. Applications are processed on a rolling basis. Application fee: $55 ($75 for international students). *Expenses:* Tuition, state resident: full-time $5881. Tuition, nonresident: full-time $15,183. *Required fees:* $952. Tuition and fees vary according to campus/location and program. *Financial support:* Fellowships, research assistantships, teaching assistantships, and institutionally sponsored loans available. *Faculty research:* Assessment of risk and resiliency factors in trauma populations, retirement, child welfare, parenting education, adolescent mood disorders, gerontology, rural practice, employee empowerment and involvement, children and youth, field education, substance use disorders in women, child welfare services and organization, maternal and child health, youth development and community betterment, international social work issues, epidemiology, etiology, prevention of health risk behaviors. *Unit head:* Dr. Marjorie Sable, Director, E-mail: sablem@missouri.edu. *Application contact:* Crystal Null, 573-884-9385, E-mail: nullc@missouri.edu. Web site: http://ssw.missouri.edu/.

University of Missouri–Kansas City, College of Arts and Sciences, School of Social Work, Kansas City, MO 64110-2499. Offers MSW. *Accreditation:* CSWE. Part-time and evening/weekend programs available. *Faculty:* 11 full-time (8 women), 11 part-time/adjunct (7 women). *Students:* 118 full-time (97 women), 65 part-time (55 women); includes 38 minority (32 Black or African American, non-Hispanic/Latino; 5 Hispanic/Latino; 1 Two or more races, non-Hispanic/Latino), 2 international. Average age 34. 105 applicants, 45% accepted, 45 enrolled. In 2011, 73 master's awarded. *Entrance requirements:* For master's, minimum GPA of 3.0, 3 letters of reference. Additional exam requirements/recommendations for international students: Recommended—TOEFL (minimum score 550 paper-based; 213 computer-based; 80 iBT). *Application deadline:* For fall admission, 4/30 for domestic and international students; for spring admission, 12/1 for domestic and international students. Applications are processed on a rolling basis. Application fee: $45 ($50 for international students). *Expenses:* Tuition, state resident: full-time $5798; part-time $322.10 per credit hour. Tuition, nonresident: full-time $14,969; part-time $831.60 per credit hour. *Required fees:* $93.51 per credit hour. *Financial support:* In 2011–12, 5 research assistantships with partial tuition reimbursements (averaging $11,280 per year) were awarded; career-related internships or fieldwork and institutionally sponsored loans also available. Financial award application deadline: 3/1; financial award applicants required to submit FAFSA. *Faculty research:* Social justice, LGBT issues, deinstitutionalization, community collaboration and partnerships, evaluation of strengths model with addiction model. *Unit head:* Dr. Monica Nandan, Program Director, 816-235-2203, E-mail: soc-wk@umkc.edu. *Application contact:* Doretta Kidd, Acting Director of Admissions, 816-235-1111, Fax: 816-235-5544, E-mail: admit@umkc.edu. Web site: http://cas.umkc.edu/socialwork/.

University of Missouri–St. Louis, College of Arts and Sciences, School of Social Work, St. Louis, MO 63121. Offers gerontology (MS); long term care administration (Certificate); social work (MSW). *Accreditation:* CSWE. *Faculty:* 11 full-time (9 women), 9 part-time/adjunct (7 women). *Students:* 67 full-time (58 women), 65 part-time (60 women); includes 26 minority (22 Black or African American, non-Hispanic/Latino; 2 Asian, non-Hispanic/Latino; 1 Hispanic/Latino; 1 Two or more races, non-Hispanic/Latino), 1 international. Average age 31. 143 applicants, 45% accepted, 45 enrolled. In 2011, 49 degrees awarded. *Entrance requirements:* For master's, 3 letters of recommendation. Additional exam requirements/recommendations for international students: Required—TOEFL (minimum score 550 paper-based; 213 computer-based). *Application deadline:* For fall admission, 2/15 for domestic and international students. Application fee: $35 ($40 for international students). Electronic applications accepted. *Expenses:* Tuition, state resident: full-time $6273; part-time $3866 per year. Tuition, nonresident: full-time $14,969; part-time $9980 per year. *Required fees:* $315 per year. *Financial support:* In 2011–12, 10 teaching assistantships with full and partial tuition reimbursements (averaging $8,000 per year) were awarded. Financial award applicants required to submit FAFSA. *Faculty research:* Family violence, child abuse/neglect, immigration, community economic development. *Unit head:* Dr. Lois Pierce, Graduate Program Director, 314-516-6364, Fax: 314-516-5816, E-mail: socialwork@umsl.edu. *Application contact:* 314-516-5458, Fax: 314-516-6996, E-mail: gradadm@umsl.edu. Web site: http://www.umsl.edu/~socialwk/.

The University of Montana, Graduate School, College of Health Professions and Biomedical Sciences, School of Social Work, Missoula, MT 59812-0002. Offers MSW. *Accreditation:* CSWE.

University of Nebraska at Omaha, Graduate Studies, College of Public Affairs and Community Service, School of Social Work, Omaha, NE 68182. Offers MSW. *Accreditation:* CSWE. *Faculty:* 12 full-time (10 women). *Students:* 104 full-time (93 women), 58 part-time (54 women); includes 25 minority (10 Black or African American, non-Hispanic/Latino; 3 Asian, non-Hispanic/Latino; 10 Hispanic/Latino; 2 Two or more races, non-Hispanic/Latino). Average age 30. 129 applicants, 44% accepted, 53 enrolled. In 2011, 46 master's awarded. *Degree requirements:* For master's, comprehensive exam, thesis (for some programs). *Entrance requirements:* For master's, minimum GPA of 3.0, letters of recommendation, resume, statement of purpose. Additional exam requirements/recommendations for international students: Required—TOEFL (minimum score 500 paper-based; 173 computer-based; 61 iBT). *Application deadline:* For fall admission, 1/15 for domestic students. Applications are processed on a rolling basis. Application fee: $45. Electronic applications accepted. *Financial support:* In 2011–12, 4 students received support, including 4 research assistantships with tuition reimbursements available; fellowships, career-related internships or fieldwork, Federal Work-Study, institutionally sponsored loans, scholarships/grants, tuition waivers (full), and unspecified assistantships also available. Support available to part-time students. Financial award application deadline: 3/1; financial award applicants required to submit FAFSA. *Unit head:* Dr. Theresa Barron-McKeagney, Director, 402-554-2791. *Application contact:* Jeanette Harder, 402-554-2341, Fax: 402-554-3143, E-mail: graduate@unomaha.edu.

University of Nevada, Las Vegas, Graduate College, Greenspun College of Urban Affairs, School of Social Work, Las Vegas, NV 89154-5032. Offers forensic social work (Advanced Certificate); social work (MSW); MSW/JD. *Accreditation:* CSWE. *Faculty:* 13 full-time (9 women). *Students:* 127 full-time (104 women), 55 part-time (46 women); includes 81 minority (24 Black or African American, non-Hispanic/Latino; 1 American Indian or Alaska Native, non-Hispanic/Latino; 13 Asian, non-Hispanic/Latino; 32 Hispanic/Latino; 5 Native Hawaiian or other Pacific Islander, non-Hispanic/Latino; 6 Two or more races, non-Hispanic/Latino), 10 international. Average age 34. 194 applicants, 65% accepted, 81 enrolled. In 2011, 70 master's, 2 other advanced degrees awarded. *Degree requirements:* For master's, comprehensive exam, thesis optional. *Entrance requirements:* Additional exam requirements/recommendations for international students: Required—TOEFL (minimum score 550 paper-based; 231 computer-based; 80 iBT), IELTS (minimum score 7). *Application deadline:* For fall admission, 4/10 priority date for domestic students, 5/1 for international students; for spring admission, 10/1 for international students. Applications are processed on a rolling basis. Application fee: $60 ($95 for international students). Electronic applications accepted. *Financial support:* In 2011–12, 13 students received support, including 6 research assistantships with partial tuition reimbursements available (averaging $8,318 per year), 7 teaching assistantships with partial tuition reimbursements available (averaging $8,662 per year); institutionally sponsored loans, scholarships/grants, health care benefits, and unspecified assistantships also available. Financial award application deadline: 3/1. *Faculty research:* Child welfare and juvenile justice, health and mental health, poverty and social justice, substance abuse, public policy. *Total annual research expenditures:* $473,309. *Unit head:* Dr. Joanne Thompson, Director/Professor, 702-895-0521, Fax: 702-895-4079, E-mail: joanne.thompson@unlv.edu. *Application contact:* Graduate College Admissions Evaluator, 702-895-3320, Fax: 702-895-4180, E-mail: gradcollege@unlv.edu. Web site: http://socialwork.unlv.edu/.

University of Nevada, Reno, Graduate School, Division of Health Sciences, School of Social Work, Reno, NV 89557. Offers MSW. *Accreditation:* CSWE. *Degree requirements:* For master's, thesis optional. *Entrance requirements:* For master's, GRE General Test, minimum GPA of 2.75, statistics course. Additional exam requirements/recommendations for international students: Required—TOEFL (minimum score 500 paper-based; 173 computer-based; 61 iBT), IELTS (minimum score 6). Electronic applications accepted. *Faculty research:* Policy practice, poverty, women's issues, race and diversity, vulnerable family, social justice, social change, diversity.

University of New England, Westbrook College of Health Professions, School of Social Work, Biddeford, ME 04005-9526. Offers addictions counseling (Certificate); gerontology (Certificate); social work (MSW). *Accreditation:* CSWE. Part-time programs available. *Faculty:* 18 full-time, 23 part-time/adjunct. *Students:* 506 full-time (466 women), 142 part-time (130 women). In 2011, 48 master's awarded. *Degree requirements:* For master's, field internships. *Entrance requirements:* Additional exam requirements/recommendations for international students: Required—TOEFL (minimum score 550 paper-based; 213 computer-based). *Application deadline:* For fall admission, 1/15 priority date for domestic students; for spring admission, 3/31 priority date for domestic students, 3/31 for international students. Applications are processed on a rolling basis. Application fee: $40. Electronic applications accepted. *Financial support:* Scholarships/grants and tuition waivers (partial) available. Financial award application deadline: 5/1; financial award applicants required to submit FAFSA. *Faculty research:* Domestic violence, solution-focused practice, empowerment models, adverse childhood experiences. *Unit head:* Martha Wilson, Director, 207-221-4513, E-mail: mwilson@une.edu. *Application contact:* Stacy Gato, Assistant Director of Graduate Admissions, 207-221-4225, Fax: 207-221-4898, E-mail: gradadmissions@une.edu.

University of New Hampshire, Graduate School Manchester Campus, Manchester, NH 03101. Offers business administration (MBA); counseling (M Ed); education (M Ed, MAT); educational administration and supervision (M Ed, Ed S); information technology (MS); management of technology (MS); public administration (MPA); public health (MPH, Certificate); social work (MSW); software systems engineering (Certificate). Part-time and evening/weekend programs available. *Students:* 78 full-time (50 women), 130 part-time (65 women); includes 62 minority (2 Black or African American, non-Hispanic/Latino; 56 Asian, non-Hispanic/Latino; 4 Hispanic/Latino), 4 international. Average age 34. 132 applicants, 55% accepted, 57 enrolled. In 2011, 66 master's, 9 other advanced degrees awarded. *Degree requirements:* For master's, thesis or alternative. *Entrance requirements:* Additional exam requirements/recommendations for international students: Required—TOEFL (minimum score 550 paper-based; 213 computer-based; 80 iBT). *Application deadline:* For fall admission, 6/1 for domestic students, 4/1 for international students; for spring admission, 12/1 for domestic students. Applications are processed on a rolling basis. Application fee: $65. Electronic applications accepted. *Expenses:* Tuition, state resident: full-time $12,360; part-time $687 per credit hour. Tuition, nonresident: full-time $25,680; part-time $1058 per credit hour. *International tuition:* $29,550 full-time. *Required fees:* $1666; $833 per course. $416.50 per semester. Tuition and fees vary according to course load and degree level. *Financial support:* In 2011–12, 11 students received support, including 2 teaching assistantships; fellowships, research assistantships, Federal Work-Study, scholarships/grants, health care benefits, and unspecified assistantships also available. Support available to part-time students. Financial award application deadline: 3/1; financial award applicants required to submit FAFSA. *Unit head:* Candice Brown, Director, 603-641-4313, E-mail: unhm.gradcenter@unh.edu. *Application contact:* Graduate Admissions Office, 603-862-3000, Fax: 603-862-0275, E-mail: grad.school@unh.edu. Web site: http://www.gradschool.unh.edu/manchester/.

University of New Hampshire, Graduate School, School of Health and Human Services, Department of Social Work, Durham, NH 03824. Offers MSW, Postbaccalaureate Certificate. *Accreditation:* CSWE. Part-time programs available. *Faculty:* 11 full-time (8 women). *Students:* 124 full-time (104 women), 22 part-time (20 women); includes 4 minority (3 American Indian or Alaska Native, non-Hispanic/Latino; 1 Hispanic/Latino), 4 international. Average age 30. 168 applicants, 63% accepted, 65 enrolled. In 2011, 38 degrees awarded. *Entrance requirements:* Additional exam requirements/recommendations for international students: Required—TOEFL (minimum score 550 paper-based; 213 computer-based; 80 iBT). *Application deadline:* For fall admission, 2/1 for domestic and international students. Applications are processed on a rolling basis. Application fee: $65. Electronic applications accepted. *Expenses:* Tuition, state resident: full-time $12,360; part-time $687 per credit hour. Tuition, nonresident: full-time $25,680; part-time $1058 per credit hour. *International tuition:* $29,550 full-time. *Required fees:* $1666; $833 per course. $416.50 per semester. Tuition and fees vary according to course load and degree level. *Financial support:* In 2011–12, 16 students received support, including 6 teaching assistantships; fellowships, research assistantships, career-related internships or fieldwork, Federal Work-Study, and scholarships/grants also available. Support available to part-time students. Financial award application deadline: 2/15. *Unit head:* Dr. Anne Broussard, Chairperson, 603-862-3953. *Application contact:* Karen Frarie, Application Contact, 603-862-0215, E-mail: kfrarie@cisunix.unh.edu. Web site: http://chhs.unh.edu/sw/gradsw.html.

The University of North Carolina at Chapel Hill, Graduate School, School of Social Work, Chapel Hill, NC 27599. Offers MSW, PhD, JD/MSW, MHA/MCRP, MPA/MSW, MSPH/MSW. *Accreditation:* CSWE (one or more programs are accredited). Part-time programs available. Terminal master's awarded for partial completion of doctoral program. *Degree requirements:* For doctorate, thesis/dissertation, qualifying exam. *Entrance requirements:* For master's and doctorate, GRE General Test, minimum GPA of 3.0. Electronic applications accepted. *Faculty research:* School success, risk and resiliency, welfare reform, aging, substance abuse.

The University of North Carolina at Charlotte, Graduate School, College of Health and Human Services, Department of Social Work, Charlotte, NC 28223-0001. Offers MSW. *Accreditation:* CSWE. Part-time programs available. *Faculty:* 14 full-time (9 women), 8 part-time/adjunct (6 women). *Students:* 100 full-time (87 women), 6 part-time (5 women); includes 27 minority (16 Black or African American, non-Hispanic/Latino; 3 Asian, non-Hispanic/Latino; 6 Hispanic/Latino; 2 Two or more races, non-Hispanic/Latino), 1 international. Average age 29. 133 applicants, 71% accepted, 51 enrolled. In 2011, 35 master's awarded. *Degree requirements:* For master's, thesis or alternative. *Entrance requirements:* For master's, GRE, minimum GPA of 2.7 overall, 3.0 in last 30 hours of course work. Additional exam requirements/recommendations for international students: Required—TOEFL (minimum score 557 paper-based; 220 computer-based; 83 iBT). *Application deadline:* For fall admission, 7/1 for domestic students, 5/1 for international students; for spring admission, 11/1 for domestic students, 10/1 for international students. Applications are processed on a rolling basis. Application fee: $65 ($75 for international students). Electronic applications accepted. *Expenses:* Tuition, state resident: full-time $3689. Tuition, nonresident: full-time $15,226. *Required fees:* $2198. Tuition and fees vary according to course load and program. *Financial support:* In 2011–12, 7 students received support, including 7 research assistantships (averaging $3,422 per year); career-related internships or fieldwork, Federal Work-Study, institutionally sponsored loans, scholarships/grants, unspecified assistantships, and administrative assistantship also available. Support available to part-time students. Financial award application deadline: 4/1; financial award applicants required to submit FAFSA. *Faculty research:* Social work practice with lesbian and gay youth, aging, welfare reform, non-custodial fathers, grandparents as caregivers of grandchildren. *Total annual research expenditures:* $281,108. *Unit head:* Dr. Dennis Long, Interim Chair, 704-687-7935, Fax: 704-687-2343, E-mail: ddlong@uncc.edu. *Application contact:* Kathy B. Giddings, Director of Graduate Admissions, 704-687-5503, Fax: 704-687-3279, E-mail: gradadm@uncc.edu.

The University of North Carolina at Greensboro, Graduate School, School of Human Environmental Sciences, Department of Social Work, Greensboro, NC 27412-5001. Offers MSW. Program offered jointly with North Carolina Agricultural and Technical State University. *Accreditation:* CSWE. *Entrance requirements:* For master's, GRE General Test. Additional exam requirements/recommendations for international students: Required—TOEFL. Electronic applications accepted.

The University of North Carolina Wilmington, School of Social Work, Wilmington, NC 28403-3297. Offers MSW. *Accreditation:* CSWE. *Degree requirements:* For master's, comprehensive exam, thesis or alternative. *Entrance requirements:* For master's, GMAT, GRE General Test. Additional exam requirements/recommendations for international students: Required—TOEFL (minimum score 550 paper-based; 217 computer-based; 79 iBT), IELTS (minimum score 6.5).

University of North Dakota, Graduate School, College of Education and Human Development, School of Social Work, Grand Forks, ND 58202. Offers MSW. *Accreditation:* CSWE. *Degree requirements:* For master's, comprehensive exam, thesis or alternative. *Entrance requirements:* For master's, minimum GPA of 3.0. Additional exam requirements/recommendations for international students: Required—TOEFL (minimum score 550 paper-based; 213 computer-based; 79 iBT), IELTS (minimum score 6.5). Electronic applications accepted. *Faculty research:* Mental health, gerontology, chemical abuse, children and families.

University of Northern British Columbia, Office of Graduate Studies, Prince George, BC V2N 4Z9, Canada. Offers business administration (Diploma); community health science (M Sc); disability management (MA); education (M Ed); first nations studies (MA); gender studies (MA); history (MA); interdisciplinary studies (MA); international studies (MA); mathematical, computer and physical sciences (M Sc); natural resources and environmental studies (M Sc, MA, MNRES, PhD); political science (MA); psychology (M Sc, PhD); social work (MSW). Part-time and evening/weekend programs available. Postbaccalaureate distance learning degree programs offered (no on-campus study). *Degree requirements:* For master's, thesis; for doctorate, thesis/dissertation. *Entrance requirements:* For master's, GRE, minimum B average in undergraduate course work; for doctorate, candidacy exam, minimum A average in graduate course work.

University of Northern Iowa, Graduate College, College of Social and Behavioral Sciences, Department of Social Work, Cedar Falls, IA 50614. Offers MSW. *Accreditation:* CSWE. *Students:* 48 full-time (43 women), 5 part-time (all women); includes 3 minority (2 Black or African American, non-Hispanic/Latino; 1 Hispanic/Latino). 74 applicants, 32% accepted, 12 enrolled. In 2011, 41 master's awarded. *Entrance requirements:* For master's, minimum GPA of 3.0; department application; 3 letters of recommendation; personal autobiographical statement. Additional exam requirements/recommendations for international students: Required—TOEFL (minimum score 500 paper-based; 180 computer-based; 61 iBT). *Application deadline:* For fall admission, 8/1 priority date for domestic students. Applications are processed on a rolling basis. Application fee: $50 ($70 for international students). Electronic applications accepted. *Expenses:* Tuition, state resident: full-time $7476. Tuition, nonresident: full-time $16,410. *Required fees:* $942. *Financial support:* Application deadline: 2/1. *Unit head:* Dr. Cindy Juby, III, Program Director, 319-273-5845, Fax: 319-273-6976, E-mail: cynthia.juby@uni.edu. *Application contact:* Laurie S. Russell, Record Analyst, 319-273-2623, Fax: 319-273-2885, E-mail: laurie.russell@uni.edu. Web site: http://www.uni.edu/socialwork/.

University of Oklahoma, College of Arts and Sciences, School of Social Work, Norman, OK 73019. Offers social work (MSW), including administrative and community practice, direct practice. *Accreditation:* CSWE. Part-time programs available. *Faculty:* 22 full-time (12 women), 7 part-time/adjunct (6 women). *Students:* 201 full-time (174 women), 129 part-time (103 women); includes 93 minority (37 Black or African American, non-Hispanic/Latino; 19 American Indian or Alaska Native, non-Hispanic/Latino; 3 Asian, non-Hispanic/Latino; 26 Hispanic/Latino; 8 Two or more races, non-Hispanic/Latino), 2 international. Average age 33. 153 applicants, 80% accepted, 98 enrolled. In 2011, 131 degrees awarded. *Entrance requirements:* For master's, GRE, minimum GPA of 3.0, 3 letters of reference. Additional exam requirements/recommendations for international students: Required—TOEFL (minimum score 550 paper-based; 79 iBT). *Application deadline:* For fall admission, 3/1 priority date for domestic students, 3/1 for international students; for spring admission, 11/1 for domestic students, 9/1 for international students. Application fee: $40 ($90 for international students). Electronic applications accepted. *Expenses:* Tuition, state resident: full-time $4087; part-time $170.30 per credit hour. Tuition, nonresident: full-time $14,875; part-time $619.80 per credit hour. *Required fees:* $2659; $100.25 per credit hour. Tuition and fees vary according to course load and degree level. *Financial support:* In 2011–12, 118 students received support, including 1 fellowship with full tuition reimbursement available (averaging $2,500 per year), 17 research assistantships with partial tuition reimbursements available (averaging $9,868 per year); career-related internships or fieldwork, institutionally sponsored loans, scholarships/grants, tuition waivers (full), and unspecified assistantships also available. Financial award application deadline: 3/1; financial award applicants required to submit FAFSA. *Faculty research:* HIV/AIDS, child welfare, American Indian mental health, human trafficking, poverty. *Total annual research expenditures:* $174,024. *Unit head:* Dr. Donald R. Baker, Director, 405-325-2821, Fax: 405-325-7072, E-mail: drralph@ou.edu. *Application contact:* Dr. Anthony Natale, Graduate Coordinator, 405-325-1408, Fax: 405-325-4683, E-mail: anatale@ou.edu. Web site: http://socialwork.ou.edu.

University of Ottawa, Faculty of Graduate and Postdoctoral Studies, Faculty of Social Sciences, School of Social Work, Ottawa, ON K1N 6N5, Canada. Offers MSS. Program offered in French. *Degree requirements:* For master's, thesis or alternative. *Entrance requirements:* For master's, honors bachelor's degree or equivalent, minimum B average. Electronic applications accepted. *Faculty research:* Family-children, health.

University of Pennsylvania, School of Social Policy and Practice, Graduate Group on Social Welfare, Philadelphia, PA 19104. Offers PhD. *Degree requirements:* For doctorate, thesis/dissertation. *Entrance requirements:* For doctorate, GRE General Test, MSW or master's degree in related field. Additional exam requirements/recommendations for international students: Required—TOEFL (minimum score 600 paper-based; 213 computer-based; 100 iBT). Electronic applications accepted. *Expenses: Tuition:* Full-time $26,660; part-time $4944 per course. *Required fees:* $2318; $291 per course. Tuition and fees vary according to course load, degree level and program. *Faculty research:* Mental health, child welfare, organizational behavior, urban poverty, comparative social welfare.

University of Pennsylvania, School of Social Policy and Practice, Program in Social Work, Philadelphia, PA 19104. Offers MSW, DSW, JD/MSW, MSW/Certificate, MSW/MBA, MSW/MBE, MSW/MCP, MSW/MGA, MSW/MPH, MSW/MS Ed, MSW/MSC, MSW/PhD. *Accreditation:* CSWE. Part-time programs available. Terminal master's awarded for partial completion of doctoral program. *Degree requirements:* For master's, fieldwork. *Entrance requirements:* For doctorate, GRE General Test, MSW or master's degree in related field. Additional exam requirements/recommendations for international students: Required—TOEFL (minimum score 600 paper-based; 213 computer-based; 100 iBT). Electronic applications accepted. *Expenses: Tuition:* Full-time $26,660; part-time $4944 per course. *Required fees:* $2318; $291 per course. Tuition and fees vary according to course load, degree level and program. *Faculty research:* Homelessness, juvenile justice, mental health/children's mental health, child welfare, domestic and family violence.

University of Pittsburgh, School of Social Work, Pittsburgh, PA 15260. Offers gerontology (Certificate); social work (MSW, PhD); M Div/MSW; MPA/MSW; MPH/PhD; MPIA/MSW; MSW/JD; MSW/MPH. *Accreditation:* CSWE (one or more programs are accredited). Part-time programs available. *Faculty:* 35 full-time (22 women), 47 part-time/adjunct (32 women). *Students:* 387 full-time (322 women), 175 part-time (144 women); includes 142 minority (82 Black or African American, non-Hispanic/Latino; 30 Asian, non-Hispanic/Latino; 15 Hispanic/Latino; 15 Two or more races, non-Hispanic/Latino). Average age 28. 597 applicants, 72% accepted, 221 enrolled. In 2011, 226 master's, 1 doctorate awarded. *Degree requirements:* For master's, practicum; for doctorate, comprehensive exam, thesis/dissertation; for Certificate, thesis. *Entrance requirements:* For master's, minimum QPA of 3.0, course work in statistics; for doctorate, GRE, MSW or related degree, course work in statistics. Additional exam requirements/recommendations for international students: Required—TOEFL (minimum score 550 paper-based; 213 computer-based; 100 iBT). *Application deadline:* For fall admission, 12/31 priority date for domestic students, 12/31 for international students. Applications are processed on a rolling basis. Application fee: $40. Electronic applications accepted. *Expenses:* Tuition, state resident: full-time $18,774; part-time $760 per credit. Tuition, nonresident: full-time $30,736; part-time $1258 per credit. *Required fees:* $740; $200 per term. Tuition and fees vary according to program. *Financial support:* In 2011–12, 212 students received support, including 1 research assistantship with full tuition reimbursement available (averaging $12,920 per year), 3 teaching assistantships with full tuition reimbursements available (averaging $15,830 per year); fellowships, career-related internships or fieldwork, institutionally sponsored loans, scholarships/grants, traineeships, tuition waivers (full), and unspecified assistantships also available. Financial award application deadline: 3/31; financial award applicants required to submit FAFSA. *Faculty research:* Mental health services research, child abuse and neglect, geriatrics, criminal justice race issues. *Unit head:* Dr. Larry E. Davis, Dean, 412-624-6304, Fax: 412-624-6323, E-mail: ledavis@pitt.edu. *Application contact:* Philip Mack, Director of Admissions, 412-624-6346, Fax: 412-624-6323, E-mail: psm8@pitt.edu. Web site: http://www.socialwork.pitt.edu.

University of Puerto Rico, Río Piedras, College of Social Sciences, Graduate School of Social Work, San Juan, PR 00931-3300. Offers MSW, PhD. *Accreditation:* CSWE. Part-time programs available. *Degree requirements:* For master's, comprehensive exam, thesis; for doctorate, comprehensive exam, thesis/dissertation. *Entrance requirements:* For master's, PAEG or GRE, interview, minimum GPA of 3.0, letter of recommendation; for doctorate, PAEG or GRE, interview, minimum GPA of 3.0, 3 letters of recommendation, social work experience. *Faculty research:* Social work in Puerto Rico, Cuba, and the Dominican Republic; migration; poverty in Puerto Rico.

University of Regina, Faculty of Graduate Studies and Research, Faculty of Social Work, Regina, SK S4S 0A2, Canada. Offers Aboriginal social work (MASW); social work (MSW). Part-time programs available. *Faculty:* 16 full-time (8 women), 1 (woman) part-time/adjunct. *Students:* 21 full-time (20 women), 41 part-time (37 women). 52 applicants, 65% accepted. In 2011, 19 degrees awarded. *Degree requirements:* For master's, thesis. *Entrance requirements:* For master's, BSW. Additional exam requirements/recommendations for international students: Required—TOEFL (minimum score 580 paper-based; 80 iBT), IELTS (minimum score 6.5). *Application deadline:* For fall admission, 1/31 for domestic and international students. Application fee: $100. Electronic applications accepted. *Expenses:* Contact institution. *Financial support:* In 2011–12, 2 fellowships (averaging $6,000 per year), 8 teaching assistantships (averaging $2,298 per year) were awarded; research assistantships, career-related internships or fieldwork, and scholarships/grants also available. Financial award application deadline: 6/15. *Faculty research:* Social policy analysis; social justice, human rights, and social work; family and child policies and programs; aging, society, and human service work; work, welfare, and social justice. *Unit head:* Dr. Craig Chamberlin, Dean, 306-585-4037, E-mail: craig.chamberlin@uregina.ca. *Application contact:* Dr. Judy White, Graduate Program Coordinator, 306-664-7375, E-mail: judy.white@uregina.ca.

University of St. Francis, College of Arts and Sciences, Joliet, IL 60435-6169. Offers advanced generalist forensic social work (Post-Master's Certificate); physician assistant practice (MS); social work (MSW). *Faculty:* 8 full-time (6 women). *Students:* 94 full-time (67 women), 23 part-time (22 women); includes 43 minority (15 Black or African American, non-Hispanic/Latino; 6 Asian, non-Hispanic/Latino; 17 Hispanic/Latino; 2 Native Hawaiian or other Pacific Islander, non-Hispanic/Latino; 3 Two or more races, non-Hispanic/Latino), 2 international. Average age 31. 62 applicants, 61% accepted, 26 enrolled. In 2011, 41 degrees awarded. *Entrance requirements:* For degree, minimum undergraduate GPA of 3.0, 2 letters recommendation, personal statement. Additional exam requirements/recommendations for international students: Required—TOEFL (minimum score 550 paper-based; 213 computer-based). *Application deadline:* Applications are processed on a rolling basis. Application fee: $30. Electronic applications accepted. *Expenses: Tuition:* Part-time $656 per credit hour. Part-time tuition and fees vary according to degree level, campus/location and program. *Financial support:* In 2011–12, 12 students received support. Scholarships/grants, tuition waivers (partial), and unspecified assistantships available. Support available to part-time students. Financial award applicants required to submit FAFSA. *Unit head:* Dr. Robert Kase, Dean, 815-740-3367, Fax: 815-740-6366. *Application contact:* Sandra Sloka, Director of Admissions for Graduate and Degree Completion Programs, 800-735-7500, Fax: 815-740-5032, E-mail: ssloka@stfrancis.edu.

University of St. Thomas, Graduate Studies, School of Social Work, St. Paul, MN 55105-1096. Offers MSW. *Accreditation:* CSWE. Part-time and evening/weekend programs available. Postbaccalaureate distance learning degree programs offered (minimal on-campus study). *Faculty:* 17 full-time (13 women), 21 part-time/adjunct (15 women). *Students:* 212 full-time (188 women), 147 part-time (138 women); includes 26 minority (6 Black or African American, non-Hispanic/Latino; 4 Asian, non-Hispanic/Latino; 6 Hispanic/Latino; 10 Two or more races, non-Hispanic/Latino), 2 international. Average age 32. 293 applicants, 80% accepted, 147 enrolled. In 2011, 146 master's awarded. *Degree requirements:* For master's, thesis, fieldwork. *Entrance requirements:* For master's, previous course work in developmental psychology, human biology, and statistics/methods. Additional exam requirements/recommendations for international students: Required—TOEFL (minimum score 600 paper-based; 250 computer-based; 100 iBT). *Application deadline:* For fall admission, 1/10 for domestic students. Application fee: $35. Electronic applications accepted. *Expenses:* Contact institution. *Financial support:* In 2011–12, 350 students received support, including 8 fellowships, 15 research assistantships; career-related internships or fieldwork, Federal Work-Study, institutionally sponsored loans, scholarships/grants, and unspecified assistantships also available. Support available to part-time students. Financial award application deadline: 7/1; financial award applicants required to submit FAFSA. *Faculty research:* Clinical supervision and practice, group work, child welfare and social work. *Unit head:* Dr. Barbara W. Shank, Dean and Professor, 651-962-5801, Fax: 651-962-5819, E-mail: bwshank@stthomas.edu. *Application contact:* Lisa Dalsin, Program Manager, 651-962-5810, Fax: 651-962-5819, E-mail: msw@stthomas.edu. Web site: http://www.stthomas.edu/socialwork/.

University of South Africa, College of Human Sciences, Pretoria, South Africa. Offers adult education (M Ed); African languages (MA, PhD); African politics (MA, PhD); Afrikaans (MA, PhD); ancient history (MA, PhD); ancient Near Eastern studies (MA, PhD); anthropology (MA, PhD); applied linguistics (MA); Arabic (MA, PhD); archaeology (MA); art history (MA); Biblical archaeology (MA); Biblical studies (M Th, D Th, PhD); Christian spirituality (M Th, D Th); church history (M Th, D Th); classical studies (MA, PhD); clinical psychology (MA); communication (MA, PhD); comparative education (M Ed, Ed D); consulting psychology (D Admin, D Com, PhD); curriculum studies (M Ed, Ed D); development studies (M Admin, MA, D Admin, PhD); didactics (M Ed, Ed D); education (M Tech); education management (M Ed, Ed D); educational psychology (M Ed); English (MA); environmental education (M Ed); French (MA, PhD); German (MA, PhD); Greek (MA); guidance and counseling (M Ed); health studies (MA, PhD), including health sciences education (MA), health services management (MA), medical and surgical nursing science (critical care general) (MA), midwifery and neonatal nursing science (MA), trauma and emergency care (MA); history (MA, PhD); history of education (Ed D); inclusive education (M Ed, Ed D); information and communications technology policy and regulation (MA); information science (MA, MIS, PhD); international politics (MA, PhD); Islamic studies (MA, PhD); Italian (MA, PhD); Judaica (MA, PhD); linguistics (MA, PhD); mathematical education (M Ed); mathematics education (MA); missiology (M Th, D Th); modern Hebrew (MA, PhD); musicology (MA, MMus, D Mus, PhD); natural science education (M Ed); New Testament (M Th, D Th); Old Testament (D Th); pastoral therapy (M Th, D Th); philosophy (MA); philosophy of education (M Ed, Ed D); politics (MA, PhD); Portuguese (MA, PhD); practical theology (M Th, D Th); psychology (MA, MS, PhD); psychology of education (M Ed, Ed D); public health (MA); religious studies (MA, D Th, PhD); Romance languages (MA); Russian (MA, PhD); Semitic languages (MA, PhD); social behavior studies in HIV/AIDS (MA); social science (mental health) (MA); social science in development studies (MA); social science in psychology (MA); social science in social work (MA); social science in sociology (MA); social work (MSW, DSW, PhD); socio-education (M Ed, Ed D); sociolinguistics (MA); sociology (MA, PhD); Spanish (MA, PhD); systematic theology (M Th, D Th); TESOL (teaching English to speakers of other languages) (MA); theological ethics (M Th, D Th); theory of literature (MA, PhD); urban ministries (D Th); urban ministry (M Th).

University of South Carolina, The Graduate School, College of Social Work, Columbia, SC 29208. Offers MSW, PhD, JD/MSW, MSW/MPA, MSW/MPH. *Accreditation:* CSWE (one or more programs are accredited). Part-time programs available. *Degree requirements:* For master's, comprehensive exam; for doctorate, thesis/dissertation. *Entrance requirements:* For master's, GRE (minimum combined score 800), minimum undergraduate GPA of 3.0. Additional exam requirements/recommendations for international students: Required—TOEFL (minimum score 570 paper-based; 230 computer-based). Electronic applications accepted. *Expenses:* Contact institution. *Faculty research:* Victimization, child abuse and neglect, families.

University of Southern California, Graduate School, School of Social Work, Los Angeles, CA 90089. Offers community organization, planning and administration (MSW); families and children (MSW); health (MSW); mental health (MSW); military social work and veterans services (MSW); older adults (MSW); public child welfare (MSW); school settings (MSW); social work (MSW, PhD); systems of mental illness recovery (MSW); work and life (MSW); JD/MSW; M Pl/MSW; MPA/MSW; MSW/MAJCS; MSW/MBA; MSW/MS. *Accreditation:* CSWE (one or more programs are accredited). *Degree requirements:* For doctorate, comprehensive exam, thesis/dissertation, qualifying exam/publishable paper. *Entrance requirements:* For doctorate, GRE General Test. Additional exam requirements/recommendations for international students: Required—TOEFL (minimum score 600 paper-based; 250 computer-based; 100 iBT), ESL exam. Electronic applications accepted. *Faculty research:* Department of Defense Educational Activity, detection/treatment of depression among older adults, health/aging, psychosocial adaptation to extreme environments/man made disasters; mental health needs of older adults.

University of Southern Indiana, Graduate Studies, College of Liberal Arts, Program in Social Work, Evansville, IN 47712-3590. Offers MSW. *Accreditation:* CSWE. Part-time and evening/weekend programs available. *Faculty:* 10 full-time (4 women), 2 part-time/adjunct (both women). *Students:* 76 full-time (68 women), 22 part-time (18 women); includes 8 minority (4 Black or African American, non-Hispanic/Latino; 3 Asian, non-Hispanic/Latino; 1 Hispanic/Latino). Average age 30. 66 applicants, 98% accepted, 53 enrolled. In 2011, 36 master's awarded. *Entrance requirements:* For master's, minimum GPA of 2.8. Additional exam requirements/recommendations for international students: Required—TOEFL (minimum score 550 paper-based; 213 computer-based; 79 iBT), IELTS (minimum score 6). *Application deadline:* For fall admission, 1/12 for domestic and international students. Application fee: $35. Electronic applications accepted. *Expenses:* Tuition, state resident: full-time $5044; part-time $280.21 per credit hour. Tuition, nonresident: full-time $9949; part-time $552.71 per credit hour. *Required fees:* $240; $22.75 per term. Tuition and fees vary according to course load and reciprocity agreements. *Financial support:* In 2011–12, 8 students received support. Federal Work-Study, scholarships/grants, tuition waivers (full and partial), and unspecified assistantships available. Financial award application deadline: 3/1; financial award applicants required to submit FAFSA. *Unit head:* Dr. Paul Frazer, Director, 812-465-7103, E-mail: pfrazer@usi.edu. *Application contact:* Dr. Wes Durham, Interim Director, Graduate Studies, 812-465-7015, Fax: 812-464-1956, E-mail: wdurham@usi.edu. Web site: http://www.usi.edu/libarts/socialwork/msw-degree.asp.

University of Southern Maine, College of Arts and Sciences, Program in Social Work, Portland, ME 04104-9300. Offers MSW. *Accreditation:* CSWE. Part-time and evening/weekend programs available. *Entrance requirements:* For master's, GRE or MAT. Electronic applications accepted. *Faculty research:* Social inequality, immigrants and refugees, aging, sexual harassment, service learning, technology and social service.

University of Southern Mississippi, Graduate School, College of Health, School of Social Work, Hattiesburg, MS 39406-0001. Offers MSW. *Accreditation:* CSWE. Part-time programs available. *Faculty:* 13 full-time (7 women). *Students:* 120 full-time (106 women), 45 part-time (42 women); includes 76 minority (72 Black or African American, non-Hispanic/Latino; 1 Asian, non-Hispanic/Latino; 2 Hispanic/Latino; 1 Native Hawaiian or other Pacific Islander, non-Hispanic/Latino). Average age 35. 121 applicants, 47% accepted, 48 enrolled. In 2011, 52 degrees awarded. *Degree requirements:* For master's, comprehensive exam, thesis or alternative, practicum. *Entrance requirements:* For master's, GRE General Test, minimum GPA of 2.75 in last 60 hours. Additional exam requirements/recommendations for international students: Required—TOEFL, IELTS. *Application deadline:* For fall admission, 4/1 priority date for domestic students, 4/1 for international students; for spring admission, 1/10 priority date for domestic students, 1/10 for international students. Applications are processed on a rolling basis. Application fee: $50. Electronic applications accepted. *Financial support:* In 2011–12, 16 research assistantships with tuition reimbursements (averaging $7,600 per year), teaching assistantships with tuition reimbursements (averaging $7,600 per year) were awarded; career-related internships or fieldwork, Federal Work-Study, scholarships/grants, health care benefits, and unspecified assistantships also available. Financial award application deadline: 3/15; financial award applicants required to submit FAFSA. *Faculty research:* Delinquency prevention, risk and resiliency in youth, successful aging, women in social service management, social work and the law. *Unit head:* Dr. Tim Rehner, Director, 601-266-4171, Fax: 601-266-4165, E-mail: tim.rehner@usm.edu. *Application contact:* Dr. Thomas Osowski, Assistant Professor/MSW Coordinator, 601-

266-4171, Fax: 601-266-4165, E-mail: tom.osowski@usm.edu. Web site: http://www.usm.edu/graduateschool/table.php.

University of South Florida, Graduate School, College of Behavioral and Community Sciences, School of Social Work, Tampa, FL 33620-9951. Offers MSW, PhD. *Accreditation:* CSWE. Part-time and evening/weekend programs available. *Faculty:* 13 full-time (11 women), 13 part-time/adjunct (10 women). *Students:* 147 full-time (125 women), 37 part-time (32 women); includes 51 minority (20 Black or African American, non-Hispanic/Latino; 5 Asian, non-Hispanic/Latino; 22 Hispanic/Latino; 4 Two or more races, non-Hispanic/Latino), 2 international. Average age 33. 200 applicants, 55% accepted, 72 enrolled. In 2011, 72 master's, 3 doctorates awarded. *Degree requirements:* For master's, comprehensive exam, thesis; for doctorate, comprehensive exam, thesis/dissertation. *Entrance requirements:* For master's, GRE, minimum GPA of 3.0 in last 60 hours, three letters of recommendation, 750-word biographical sketch; for doctorate, GRE, minimum GPA of 3.0, three letters of recommendation, statement of purpose, professional writing sample, interview. Additional exam requirements/recommendations for international students: Required—TOEFL (minimum score 550 paper-based; 213 computer-based). *Application deadline:* For fall admission, 2/15 priority date for domestic students, 1/2 for international students. Applications are processed on a rolling basis. Application fee: $30. Electronic applications accepted. *Financial support:* In 2011–12, 1 student received support, including 1 research assistantship with tuition reimbursement available (averaging $9,001 per year); unspecified assistantships also available. Financial award application deadline: 3/15; financial award applicants required to submit FAFSA. *Faculty research:* Kinship care, child trauma, juvenile delinquency, end-of-life issues, aging issues, child welfare. *Total annual research expenditures:* $2 million. *Unit head:* Dr. Anne L. Strozier, Chair, 813-974-1379, Fax: 813-974-4675, E-mail: strozier@bcs.usf.edu. *Application contact:* Dr. Robin Ersing, PhD Program Director, 813-974-6572, Fax: 813-974-4675, E-mail: rersing@usf.edu. Web site: http://www.cas.usf.edu/social_work/.

University of South Florida Sarasota-Manatee, College of Arts and Sciences, Sarasota, FL 34243. Offers criminal justice administration (MA); social work (MSW). Part-time and evening/weekend programs available. Postbaccalaureate distance learning degree programs offered (minimal on-campus study). *Faculty:* 3 full-time (1 woman). *Students:* 13 full-time (12 women), 21 part-time (14 women); includes 6 minority (1 Black or African American, non-Hispanic/Latino; 5 Hispanic/Latino). 19 applicants, 58% accepted, 6 enrolled. In 2011, 4 master's awarded. *Degree requirements:* For master's, comprehensive exam (for some programs). *Entrance requirements:* For master's, GRE. Additional exam requirements/recommendations for international students: Required—TOEFL or IELTS. *Application deadline:* For fall admission, 2/15 for domestic students, 1/2 for international students; for spring admission, 10/15 for domestic students, 6/1 for international students. Applications are processed on a rolling basis. Application fee: $30. Electronic applications accepted. *Expenses:* Tuition, state resident: full-time $9301; part-time $387.55 per credit hour. Tuition, nonresident: full-time $19,412; part-time $808.85 per credit hour. *Required fees:* $15; $5 per semester. One-time fee: $30. *Faculty research:* Criminological theories; relationships among race, racism, and crime; law enforcement information sharing; directive communication in gerontological practice; age bias and prejudicial views toward older people. *Unit head:* Dr. Jane Rose, Dean, 941-359-4469, Fax: 941-359-4489, E-mail: jane.rose@sar.usf.edu. *Application contact:* Katrina Anderson, Admissions Counselor, 941-359-4334, E-mail: kjander2@sar.usf.edu. Web site: http://www.sarasota.usf.edu/Academics/CAS/.

The University of Tennessee, Graduate School, College of Social Work, Doctor of Social Work Program, Knoxville, TN 37996. Offers clinical practice and leadership (DSW). *Expenses:* Tuition, state resident: full-time $8332; part-time $464 per credit hour. Tuition, nonresident: full-time $25,174; part-time $1400 per credit hour. *Required fees:* $1162; $56 per credit hour. Tuition and fees vary according to program.

The University of Tennessee, Graduate School, College of Social Work, Master of Science in Social Work Program, Knoxville, TN 37996. Offers evidenced-based interpersonal practice (MSSW); management leadership and community practice (MSSW). Part-time programs available. Postbaccalaureate distance learning degree programs offered (minimal on-campus study). *Expenses:* Tuition, state resident: full-time $8332; part-time $464 per credit hour. Tuition, nonresident: full-time $25,174; part-time $1400 per credit hour. *Required fees:* $1162; $56 per credit hour. Tuition and fees vary according to program.

The University of Tennessee, Graduate School, College of Social Work, PhD in Social Work Program, Knoxville, TN 37996. Offers PhD. *Expenses:* Tuition, state resident: full-time $8332; part-time $464 per credit hour. Tuition, nonresident: full-time $25,174; part-time $1400 per credit hour. *Required fees:* $1162; $56 per credit hour. Tuition and fees vary according to program.

The University of Texas at Arlington, Graduate School, School of Social Work, Arlington, TX 76019. Offers MSSW, PhD. *Accreditation:* CSWE (one or more programs are accredited). Part-time and evening/weekend programs available. Postbaccalaureate distance learning degree programs offered (no on-campus study). *Faculty:* 26 full-time (14 women), 2 part-time/adjunct (1 woman). *Students:* 427 full-time (377 women), 270 part-time (241 women); includes 318 minority (177 Black or African American, non-Hispanic/Latino; 7 American Indian or Alaska Native, non-Hispanic/Latino; 18 Asian, non-Hispanic/Latino; 101 Hispanic/Latino; 2 Native Hawaiian or other Pacific Islander, non-Hispanic/Latino; 13 Two or more races, non-Hispanic/Latino), 12 international. Average age 32. 420 applicants, 70% accepted, 248 enrolled. In 2011, 199 master's, 4 doctorates awarded. *Degree requirements:* For master's, thesis optional; for doctorate, comprehensive exam, thesis/dissertation. *Entrance requirements:* For master's, GRE General Test (if GPA less than 3.0), 3 letters of recommendation; for doctorate, GRE General Test (if GPA is below 3.4), minimum graduate GPA of 3.4. Additional exam requirements/recommendations for international students: Required—TOEFL (minimum score 550 paper-based; 213 computer-based). *Application deadline:* For fall admission, 6/5 for domestic students; for winter admission, 10/15 for domestic students. Applications are processed on a rolling basis. Application fee: $35 ($50 for international students). Electronic applications accepted. *Financial support:* In 2011–12, 106 students received support, including 40 fellowships with full tuition reimbursements available (averaging $10,000 per year), 18 research assistantships (averaging $8,000 per year), 10 teaching assistantships (averaging $9,000 per year); career-related internships or fieldwork, Federal Work-Study, institutionally sponsored loans, scholarships/grants, and unspecified assistantships also available. Support available to part-time students. Financial award application deadline: 6/1. *Faculty research:* Community practice, administrative practice, mental health and children and families. *Total annual research expenditures:* $4.4 million. *Unit head:* Dr. Scott D. Ryan, Dean, 817-272-1491, Fax: 817-272-5229, E-mail: sdryan@uta.edu. *Application contact:* Darlene Santee, Director of Admissions, 817-272-3613, Fax: 817-272-5229. Web site: http://www.uta.edu/ssw/.

The University of Texas at Austin, Graduate School, School of Social Work, Austin, TX 78712-1111. Offers MSSW, PhD. *Accreditation:* CSWE (one or more programs are accredited). Part-time programs available. *Degree requirements:* For doctorate, thesis/dissertation. *Entrance requirements:* For master's and doctorate, GRE General Test. Additional exam requirements/recommendations for international students: Required—TOEFL. *Application deadline:* For fall admission, 2/1 priority date for domestic students, 2/1 for international students; for spring admission, 10/1 for domestic and international students. Applications are processed on a rolling basis. Application fee: $50 ($75 for international students). *Financial support:* Fellowships, career-related internships or fieldwork, Federal Work-Study, institutionally sponsored loans, scholarships/grants, and unspecified assistantships available. Financial award application deadline: 2/1; financial award applicants required to submit FAFSA. *Faculty research:* Substance abuse, child welfare, gerontology, mental health, public policy. *Unit head:* Dr. Barbara White, Dean, 512-471-1937, E-mail: bww@austin.utexas.edu. Web site: http://www.utexas.edu/ssw/.

The University of Texas at El Paso, Graduate School, College of Health Sciences, Social Work Program, El Paso, TX 79968-0001. Offers MSW. *Students:* 52 (45 women); includes 42 minority (all Hispanic/Latino). 1 applicant, 100% accepted, 1 enrolled. In 2011, 7 master's awarded. *Application deadline:* For fall admission, 2/28 for domestic students. *Unit head:* Dr. Candyce S. Berger, Coordinator, 915-747-5737, E-mail: csberger2@utep.edu. *Application contact:* Dr. Benjamin Flores, Interim Dean of the Graduate School, 915-747-5491, Fax: 915-747-5788, E-mail: bflores@utep.edu. Web site: http://socialwork.utep.edu/.

The University of Texas at San Antonio, College of Public Policy, Department of Social Work, San Antonio, TX 78249-0617. Offers MSW. *Accreditation:* CSWE. *Faculty:* 10 full-time (7 women), 2 part-time/adjunct (both women). *Students:* 85 full-time (70 women), 132 part-time (111 women); includes 129 minority (29 Black or African American, non-Hispanic/Latino; 2 American Indian or Alaska Native, non-Hispanic/Latino; 7 Asian, non-Hispanic/Latino; 86 Hispanic/Latino; 5 Two or more races, non-Hispanic/Latino), 2 international. Average age 33. 119 applicants, 76% accepted, 73 enrolled. In 2011, 38 master's awarded. *Entrance requirements:* For master's, GRE, bachelor's degree, three letters of recommendation, statement of purpose. Additional exam requirements/recommendations for international students: Required—TOEFL (minimum score 550 paper-based; 79 iBT), IELTS (minimum score 6.5). *Application deadline:* For fall admission, 7/1 for domestic students, 4/1 for international students; for spring admission, 11/1 for domestic students, 9/1 for international students. Application fee: $45 ($85 for international students). *Expenses:* Tuition, state resident: full-time $3148; part-time $2176 per semester. Tuition, nonresident: full-time $8782; part-time $5932 per semester. *Required fees:* $719 per semester. *Unit head:* Dr. Rosalie Ambrosino, Interim Department Chair, 210-458-3000, Fax: 210-458-3001, E-mail: rosalie.ambrosino@utsa.edu. *Application contact:* Robert Ambrosino, Graduate Advisor of Record, 210-458-2026, Fax: 210-458-2026, E-mail: robert.ambrosino@utsa.edu.

The University of Texas–Pan American, College of Health Sciences and Human Services, Department of Social Work, Edinburg, TX 78539. Offers MSSW. *Accreditation:* CSWE. Part-time programs available. *Entrance requirements:* For master's, minimum GPA of 3.0, basic statistics course completed within 5 years of admission. Additional exam requirements/recommendations for international students: Recommended—TOEFL (minimum score 500 paper-based). *Application deadline:* For fall admission, 3/31 priority date for domestic students, 3/31 for international students. Applications are processed on a rolling basis. Application fee: $35. Tuition and fees vary according to course load, program and student level. *Financial support:* In 2011–12, 4 students received support. Fellowships, research assistantships, teaching assistantships, career-related internships or fieldwork, Federal Work-Study, institutionally sponsored loans, scholarships/grants, and traineeships available. Financial award applicants required to submit FAFSA. *Faculty research:* Child welfare, family violence, social justice, Hispanic traditional healing (curanderismo and spirituality), community development. *Unit head:* Dr. Hector Luis Diaz, Chair, 956-665-2413, E-mail: hdiaz@utpa.edu. *Application contact:* Dr. Alonzo Cavazos, MSSW Program Director, 956-665-2487, E-mail: alonso@panam.edu. Web site: http://www.panam.edu/dept/socialwork/.

The University of Toledo, College of Graduate Studies, Judith Herb College of Education, Health Science and Human Service, Department of Criminal Justice and Social Work, Toledo, OH 43606-3390. Offers child advocacy (Certificate); criminal justice (MA); juvenile justice (Certificate); social work (MSW); JD/MA. *Accreditation:* CSWE. Part-time programs available. *Faculty:* 14. *Students:* 52 full-time (41 women), 63 part-time (47 women); includes 31 minority (20 Black or African American, non-Hispanic/Latino; 1 American Indian or Alaska Native, non-Hispanic/Latino; 2 Asian, non-Hispanic/Latino; 5 Hispanic/Latino; 3 Two or more races, non-Hispanic/Latino). Average age 31. 84 applicants, 60% accepted, 38 enrolled. In 2011, 67 master's, 2 other advanced degrees awarded. *Degree requirements:* For master's, comprehensive exam, thesis. *Entrance requirements:* For master's and Certificate, minimum cumulative GPA of 2.7 for all previous academic work, letters of recommendation. Additional exam requirements/recommendations for international students: Required—TOEFL (minimum score 550 paper-based; 213 computer-based; 80 iBT), IELTS (minimum score 6.5). *Application deadline:* For fall admission, 1/15 priority date for domestic students, 1/15 for international students. Applications are processed on a rolling basis. Application fee: $45 ($75 for international students). Electronic applications accepted. *Financial support:* In 2011–12, 5 research assistantships with full and partial tuition reimbursements (averaging $9,000 per year), 14 teaching assistantships with full and partial tuition reimbursements (averaging $6,000 per year) were awarded; Federal Work-Study, scholarships/grants, tuition waivers (full and partial), and unspecified assistantships also available. *Unit head:* Dr. Morris Jenkins, Chair, 419-530-2142, Fax: 419-530-2153, E-mail: morris.jenkins@utoledo.edu. *Application contact:* Graduate School Office, 419-530-4723, Fax: 419-530-4724, E-mail: grdsch@utnet.utoledo.edu. Web site: http://www.utoledo.edu/eduhshs/.

University of Toronto, School of Graduate Studies, Faculty of Social Work, Toronto, ON M5S 1A1, Canada. Offers MSW, PhD, MH Sc/MSW. Part-time programs available. *Degree requirements:* For doctorate, thesis/dissertation, oral exam/thesis defense. *Entrance requirements:* For master's, minimum mid-B average in final year of full-time study, 3 full courses in social sciences, experience in social services (recommended), 3 letters of reference, resume; for doctorate, MSW or equivalent, minimum B+ average, competency in basic statistical methods. Additional exam requirements/recommendations for international students: Required—TOEFL (minimum score 580 paper-based; 93 iBT); IELTS (minimum score 7), TWE (minimum score 5), or Michigan English Language Assessment Battery (minimum score 85). Electronic applications accepted. *Expenses:* Contact institution.

University of Utah, Graduate School, College of Social Work, Salt Lake City, UT 84112. Offers MSW, PhD, MPA/PhD. *Accreditation:* CSWE (one or more programs are accredited). Part-time programs available. Postbaccalaureate distance learning degree programs offered (minimal on-campus study). *Faculty:* 36 full-time (21 women), 7 part-time/adjunct (4 women). *Students:* 294 full-time (217 women), 86 part-time (60 women); includes 66 minority (10 Black or African American, non-Hispanic/Latino; 8 American Indian or Alaska Native, non-Hispanic/Latino; 3 Asian, non-Hispanic/Latino; 30 Hispanic/Latino; 4 Native Hawaiian or other Pacific Islander, non-Hispanic/Latino; 11 Two or more races, non-Hispanic/Latino), 9 international. Average age 34. 464 applicants, 49% accepted, 168 enrolled. In 2011, 173 master's, 4 doctorates awarded. *Median time to degree:* Of those who began their doctoral program in fall 2003, 100% received their degree in 8 years or less. *Degree requirements:* For master's, thesis or alternative; for doctorate, comprehensive exam, thesis/dissertation. *Entrance requirements:* For master's, GRE General Test, MAT, minimum GPA of 3.0; for doctorate, GRE General

Test. Additional exam requirements/recommendations for international students: Required—TOEFL (minimum score 600 paper-based; 250 computer-based; 100 iBT). *Application deadline:* For fall admission, 11/1 for domestic and international students. Application fee: $55 ($65 for international students). Electronic applications accepted. *Expenses:* Contact institution. *Financial support:* In 2011–12, 25 fellowships with partial tuition reimbursements (averaging $3,500 per year), 24 research assistantships with full and partial tuition reimbursements (averaging $6,000 per year), 6 teaching assistantships with partial tuition reimbursements (averaging $5,000 per year) were awarded; Federal Work-Study and institutionally sponsored loans also available. Support available to part-time students. Financial award application deadline: 3/15; financial award applicants required to submit FAFSA. *Faculty research:* Health, mental health, gerontology, child welfare, forensic social work, instructional social work. *Total annual research expenditures:* $447,445. *Unit head:* Dr. Jannah H. Mather, Dean, 801-581-6194, Fax: 801-585-3219, E-mail: jannah.mather@socwk.utah.edu. *Application contact:* Dr. Hank Liese, Associate Dean, 801-581-8828, Fax: 801-585-3219, E-mail: hank.liese@socwk.utah.edu. Web site: http://www.socwk.utah.edu/.

University of Vermont, Graduate College, College of Education and Social Services, Department of Social Work, Burlington, VT 05405. Offers MSW. *Accreditation:* CSWE. *Students:* 59 (51 women); includes 2 minority (1 Asian, non-Hispanic/Latino; 1 Hispanic/Latino). 80 applicants, 66% accepted, 26 enrolled. In 2011, 31 master's awarded. *Entrance requirements:* For master's, GRE General Test, resume. Additional exam requirements/recommendations for international students: Required—TOEFL (minimum score 550 paper-based; 213 computer-based; 80 iBT). *Application deadline:* For fall admission, 2/1 priority date for domestic students, 2/1 for international students. Applications are processed on a rolling basis. Application fee: $40. Electronic applications accepted. *Financial support:* Application deadline: 2/1. *Unit head:* Gary Widrick, Chair, 802-656-8800. *Application contact:* Susan Roche, Coordinator, 802-656-8800.

University of Victoria, Faculty of Graduate Studies, Faculty of Human and Social Development, School of Social Work, Victoria, BC V8W 2Y2, Canada. Offers MSW. *Entrance requirements:* For master's, BSW. Additional exam requirements/recommendations for international students: Required—TOEFL (minimum score 575 paper-based; 233 computer-based), IELTS (minimum score 7). Electronic applications accepted. *Faculty research:* Women's issues, public policy formation and implementation, child welfare, First Nations, community development.

University of Victoria, Faculty of Graduate Studies, Faculty of Human and Social Development, Studies in Policy and Practice Program, Victoria, BC V8W 2Y2, Canada. Offers MA. Part-time programs available. *Degree requirements:* For master's, thesis. *Entrance requirements:* For master's, resume. Additional exam requirements/recommendations for international students: Required—TOEFL (minimum score 575 paper-based; 233 computer-based), IELTS (minimum score 7). Electronic applications accepted. *Faculty research:* Women's issues, public policy formation and implementation, health promotion and education, children, youth and families.

University of Washington, Graduate School, School of Social Work, Seattle, WA 98195. Offers MSW, PhD, MPH/MSW. *Accreditation:* CSWE (one or more programs are accredited). Evening/weekend programs available. Postbaccalaureate distance learning degree programs offered (minimal on-campus study). *Degree requirements:* For master's, thesis optional; for doctorate, thesis/dissertation. *Entrance requirements:* For master's, GRE General Test, minimum GPA of 3.0; for doctorate, master's degree, sample of scholarly work, minimum GPA of 3.0. Additional exam requirements/recommendations for international students: Required—TOEFL. *Faculty research:* Health and mental health; children, youth, and families; multicultural issues; reducing risk and enhancing protective factors in children; etrology of substance use.

University of Washington, Tacoma, Graduate Programs, Program in Social Work, Tacoma, WA 98402-3100. Offers advanced integrative practice (MSW); social work (MSW). Part-time and evening/weekend programs available. *Degree requirements:* For master's, completion of all 75 required credits with minimum cumulative GPA of 3.0, 2.7 in each course; degree completion within 6 years. *Entrance requirements:* For master's, baccalaureate degree from regionally-accredited institution, minimum GPA of 3.0 on most recent 90 quarter credit hours or 60 semester hours, resume, social service experience form, two essay question responses, criminal/conviction history and background check clearance, three letters of reference. Additional exam requirements/recommendations for international students: Required—TOEFL (minimum score 580 paper-based; 237 computer-based; 70 iBT). Electronic applications accepted. *Faculty research:* Domestic violence and prevention, LGBT issues, gerontological social work, transnational social work, child welfare-mental health.

University of West Florida, College of Professional Studies, School of Justice Studies and Social Work, Department of Social Work, Pensacola, FL 32514-5750. Offers MSW. Part-time and evening/weekend programs available. *Faculty:* 7 full-time (3 women), 6 part-time/adjunct (all women). *Students:* 60 full-time (47 women), 3 part-time (all women); includes 22 minority (16 Black or African American, non-Hispanic/Latino; 5 Hispanic/Latino; 1 Two or more races, non-Hispanic/Latino). Average age 37. 50 applicants, 58% accepted, 16 enrolled. In 2011, 52 master's awarded. *Entrance requirements:* For master's, GRE or MAT, official transcripts; minimum undergraduate cumulative GPA of 3.0; academic preparation as demonstrated by quality and relevance of undergraduate degree major; letter of intent; 3 letters of recommendation; work experience as documented on the Social Work Supplemental Application. Additional exam requirements/recommendations for international students: Required—TOEFL (minimum score 550 paper-based; 213 computer-based). *Application deadline:* For fall admission, 6/1 for domestic and international students; for spring admission, 10/1 for domestic and international students. Applications are processed on a rolling basis. Electronic applications accepted. *Expenses:* Tuition, state resident: full-time $5729; part-time $302 per credit hour. Tuition, nonresident: full-time $20,059; part-time $961 per credit hour. *Required fees:* $1509; $63 per credit hour. *Financial support:* In 2011–12, 11 fellowships (averaging $346 per year), 16 research assistantships with partial tuition reimbursements were awarded; unspecified assistantships also available. *Unit head:* Dr. Glenn Rohrer, Chair, 850-474-2154, E-mail: grohrer@uwf.edu. *Application contact:* Terry McCray, Assistant Director of Graduate Admissions, 850-473-7718, Fax: 850-473-7714, E-mail: gradadmissions@uwf.edu. Web site: http://uwf.edu/socialwork/.

University of Windsor, Faculty of Graduate Studies, Faculty of Arts and Social Sciences, School of Social Work, Windsor, ON N9B 3P4, Canada. Offers MSW. Part-time programs available. *Degree requirements:* For master's, thesis or alternative. *Entrance requirements:* For master's, minimum B+ average in last year of undergraduate study. Additional exam requirements/recommendations for international students: Required—TOEFL (minimum score 600 paper-based; 250 computer-based). Electronic applications accepted. *Faculty research:* Addiction, social policy analysis, gerontology and health care.

University of Wisconsin–Green Bay, Graduate Studies, Program in Social Work, Green Bay, WI 54311-7001. Offers MSW. *Accreditation:* CSWE. *Faculty:* 5 full-time (3 women), 9 part-time/adjunct (6 women). *Students:* 19 full-time (17 women), 32 part-time (26 women); includes 8 minority (1 Black or African American, non-Hispanic/Latino; 4 American Indian or Alaska Native, non-Hispanic/Latino; 1 Asian, non-Hispanic/Latino; 2 Hispanic/Latino). Average age 32. 26 applicants, 100% accepted, 23 enrolled. In 2011, 16 master's awarded. *Degree requirements:* For master's, thesis or alternative. *Entrance requirements:* For master's, GRE, minimum GPA of 2.75. *Application deadline:* For fall admission, 8/1 priority date for domestic students; for spring admission, 11/1 priority date for domestic students. Applications are processed on a rolling basis. Application fee: $56. Electronic applications accepted. *Expenses:* Tuition, state resident: full-time $7312; part-time $406 per credit. Tuition, nonresident: full-time $16,771; part-time $932 per credit. *Required fees:* $1312; $55 per credit. Tuition and fees vary according to reciprocity agreements. *Faculty research:* Child welfare. *Unit head:* Dr. Judith Martin, Coordinator, 920-465-2049, E-mail: martinj@uwgb.edu. *Application contact:* Inga Zile, Graduate Studies Coordinator, 920-465-2143, Fax: 920-465-2043, E-mail: zilei@uwgb.edu. Web site: http://www.uwgb.edu/gradstu.

University of Wisconsin–Madison, Graduate School, College of Letters and Science, School of Social Work, Madison, WI 53706-1380. Offers social welfare (PhD); social work (MSW). *Accreditation:* CSWE (one or more programs are accredited). Terminal master's awarded for partial completion of doctoral program. *Degree requirements:* For doctorate, thesis/dissertation. *Entrance requirements:* For master's, minimum GPA of 3.0 on last 60 credits; for doctorate, GRE General Test, minimum GPA of 3.0 on last 60 credits. Electronic applications accepted. *Expenses:* Contact institution. *Faculty research:* Poverty, caregiving, child welfare, developmental disabilities, mental health, severe mental illnesses, adolescence, family, social policy, child support.

University of Wisconsin–Milwaukee, Graduate School, School of Social Welfare, Department of Social Work, Milwaukee, WI 53201-0413. Offers applied gerontology (Certificate); marriage and family therapy (Certificate); non-profit management (Certificate); social work (MSW, PhD). *Accreditation:* CSWE. Part-time programs available. *Faculty:* 14 full-time (8 women). *Students:* 199 full-time (185 women), 89 part-time (76 women); includes 53 minority (25 Black or African American, non-Hispanic/Latino; 1 American Indian or Alaska Native, non-Hispanic/Latino; 6 Asian, non-Hispanic/Latino; 5 Hispanic/Latino; 16 Two or more races, non-Hispanic/Latino). Average age 30. 316 applicants, 59% accepted, 99 enrolled. In 2011, 105 degrees awarded. *Degree requirements:* For master's, thesis or alternative. *Entrance requirements:* For doctorate, GRE, bachelor's degree. Additional exam requirements/recommendations for international students: Required—TOEFL (minimum score 550 paper-based; 79 iBT), IELTS (minimum score 6.5). *Application deadline:* For fall admission, 1/1 priority date for domestic students; for spring admission, 9/1 for domestic students. Applications are processed on a rolling basis. Application fee: $56 ($96 for international students). Electronic applications accepted. One-time fee: $506.10 full-time. Tuition and fees vary according to course load and reciprocity agreements. *Financial support:* In 2011–12, 5 fellowships, 4 research assistantships, 3 teaching assistantships were awarded; career-related internships or fieldwork, health care benefits, unspecified assistantships, and project assistantships also available. Support available to part-time students. Financial award application deadline: 4/15; financial award applicants required to submit FAFSA. *Total annual research expenditures:* $128,142. *Unit head:* Deborah Padgett, Department Chair, 414-229-6452, E-mail: dpadgett@uwm.edu. *Application contact:* General Information Contact, 414-229-4982, Fax: 414-229-6967, E-mail: gradschool@uwm.edu. Web site: http://www.uwm.edu/Dept/SSW/sw/.

University of Wisconsin–Oshkosh, Graduate Studies, Department of Social Work, Oshkosh, WI 54901. Offers MSW. Program offered jointly with University of Wisconsin–Green Bay. *Accreditation:* CSWE. Part-time programs available. *Entrance requirements:* For master's, GRE, letters of recommendation, previous courses in statistics and human biology, work experience. Additional exam requirements/recommendations for international students: Required—TOEFL (minimum score 550 paper-based; 213 computer-based; 79 iBT).

University of Wyoming, College of Health Sciences, Division of Social Work, Laramie, WY 82070. Offers MSW. *Accreditation:* CSWE. *Degree requirements:* For master's, comprehensive exam, thesis or alternative. *Entrance requirements:* For master's, minimum GPA of 3.0. Additional exam requirements/recommendations for international students: Required—TOEFL. *Expenses:* Contact institution. *Faculty research:* Social work education, child welfare, mental health, diversity, school social work.

Valdosta State University, Division of Social Work, Valdosta, GA 31698. Offers MSW. *Accreditation:* CSWE. Part-time and evening/weekend programs available. Postbaccalaureate distance learning degree programs offered (minimal on-campus study). *Faculty:* 7 full-time (4 women). *Students:* 44 full-time (35 women), 81 part-time (72 women); includes 53 minority (48 Black or African American, non-Hispanic/Latino; 1 American Indian or Alaska Native, non-Hispanic/Latino; 2 Asian, non-Hispanic/Latino; 2 Hispanic/Latino). Average age 25. 102 applicants, 56% accepted, 37 enrolled. In 2011, 32 master's awarded. *Degree requirements:* For master's, comprehensive exam, 5 practica. *Entrance requirements:* For master's, GRE General Test, MAT, minimum GPA of 3.0 in last 2 years of course work. Additional exam requirements/recommendations for international students: Required—TOEFL (minimum score 523 paper-based; 193 computer-based). *Application deadline:* For fall admission, 3/15 for domestic and international students. Applications are processed on a rolling basis. Application fee: $35. *Expenses:* Tuition, state resident: full-time $7098; part-time $217 per hour. Tuition, nonresident: full-time $20,630; part-time $780 per hour. *Financial support:* In 2011–12, 4 students received support, including 2 research assistantships with full tuition reimbursements available (averaging $2,452 per year); career-related internships or fieldwork, institutionally sponsored loans, scholarships/grants, and unspecified assistantships also available. Financial award application deadline: 7/1; financial award applicants required to submit FAFSA. *Unit head:* Dr. Martha Giddings, Director, 229-249-4864, Fax: 229-245-4341, E-mail: mgidding@valdosta.edu. *Application contact:* Rebecca Waters, Coordinator of Graduate Admissions, 229-333-5694, Fax: 229-245-3853, E-mail: rlwaters@valdosta.edu.

Virginia Commonwealth University, Graduate School, School of Social Work, Doctoral Program in Social Work, Richmond, VA 23284-9005. Offers PhD. *Degree requirements:* For doctorate, comprehensive exam, thesis/dissertation. *Entrance requirements:* For doctorate, GRE General Test, MSW or related degree. Additional exam requirements/recommendations for international students: Required—TOEFL (minimum score 600 paper-based; 250 computer-based; 100 iBT). Electronic applications accepted. *Expenses:* Tuition, state resident: full-time $9133; part-time $507 per credit. Tuition, nonresident: full-time $18,777; part-time $1043 per credit. *Required fees:* $77 per credit. Tuition and fees vary according to degree level, campus/location, program and student level.

Virginia Commonwealth University, Graduate School, School of Social Work, Master's Program in Social Work, Richmond, VA 23284-9005. Offers MSW, JD/MSW, MSW/M Div, MSW/MPH. *Accreditation:* CSWE. *Entrance requirements:* Additional exam requirements/recommendations for international students: Required—TOEFL (minimum score 600 paper-based; 250 computer-based; 100 iBT). Electronic applications accepted. *Expenses:* Tuition, state resident: full-time $9133; part-time $507 per credit. Tuition, nonresident: full-time $18,777; part-time $1043 per credit. *Required fees:* $77 per credit. Tuition and fees vary according to degree level, campus/location, program and student level.

Social Work

Walden University, Graduate Programs, School of Counseling and Social Service, Minneapolis, MN 55401. Offers career counseling (MS); counselor education and supervision (PhD), including consultation, counseling and social change, forensic mental health counseling, general program, nonprofit management and leadership, trauma and crisis; human services (PhD), including clinical social work, criminal justice, disaster, crisis and intervention, family studies and intervention strategies, general program, human services administration, public health, social policy analysis and planning; marriage, couple, and family counseling (MS), including forensic counseling, trauma and crisis counseling; mental health counseling (MS), including forensic counseling, trauma and crisis counseling. Part-time and evening/weekend programs available. Postbaccalaureate distance learning degree programs offered (minimal on-campus study). *Faculty:* 26 full-time (19 women), 252 part-time/adjunct (178 women). *Students:* 3,089 full-time (2,614 women), 1,044 part-time (907 women); includes 2,109 minority (1,718 Black or African American, non-Hispanic/Latino; 31 American Indian or Alaska Native, non-Hispanic/Latino; 43 Asian, non-Hispanic/Latino; 236 Hispanic/Latino; 2 Native Hawaiian or other Pacific Islander, non-Hispanic/Latino; 79 Two or more races, non-Hispanic/Latino), 55 international. Average age 39. In 2011, 180 master's, 15 doctorates awarded. *Degree requirements:* For master's, residency (for some programs); for doctorate, thesis/dissertation, residency. *Entrance requirements:* For master's, bachelor's degree or equivalent in related field, minimum GPA of 2.5; for doctorate, master's degree or equivalent in related field; minimum GPA of 3.0; official transcripts; three years' related professional/academic experience (preferred); access to computer and Internet. Additional exam requirements/recommendations for international students: Required—TOEFL (minimum score 550 paper-based; 213 computer-based), IELTS (minimum score 6.5), or Michigan English Language Assessment Battery (minimum score 82). *Application deadline:* Applications are processed on a rolling basis. Application fee: $50. Electronic applications accepted. *Financial support:* Federal Work-Study, scholarships/grants, unspecified assistantships, and family tuition reduction, active duty/veteran tuition reduction, group tuition reduction, interest-free payment plans, employee tuition reduction available. Support available to part-time students. Financial award applicants required to submit FAFSA. *Unit head:* Dr. Savitri Dixon-Saxon, Associate Dean, 800-925-3368. *Application contact:* Jennifer Hall, Vice President of Enrollment Management, 866-4-WALDEN, E-mail: info@waldenu.edu. Web site: http://www.waldenu.edu/Colleges-and-Schools/College-of-Social-and-Behavioral-Sciences/School-of-Counseling-and-Social-Service.htm.

Walla Walla University, Graduate School, Wilma Hepker School of Social Work and Sociology, College Place, WA 99324-1198. Offers social work (MSW). *Accreditation:* CSWE. Part-time programs available. *Entrance requirements:* For master's, minimum GPA of 2.75. Additional exam requirements/recommendations for international students: Required—TOEFL (minimum score 550 paper-based; 213 computer-based; 79 iBT). Electronic applications accepted.

Washburn University, School of Applied Studies, Department of Social Work, Topeka, KS 66621. Offers clinical social work (MSW); JD/MSW. *Accreditation:* CSWE. Part-time and evening/weekend programs available. *Faculty:* 7 full-time (3 women), 1 part-time/adjunct (0 women). *Students:* 76 full-time (71 women), 44 part-time (37 women). Average age 32. In 2011, 48 master's awarded. *Degree requirements:* For master's, practicum. *Entrance requirements:* For master's, coursework in human biology and cultural anthropology (or multiculturalism or human diversity). Additional exam requirements/recommendations for international students: Required—TOEFL (minimum score 550 paper-based; 80 iBT). *Application deadline:* For fall admission, 1/15 priority date for domestic students, 1/15 for international students; for spring admission, 10/15 priority date for domestic students, 10/15 for international students. Applications are processed on a rolling basis. Application fee: $25. *Expenses:* Tuition, state resident: full-time $5346; part-time $297 per credit hour. Tuition, nonresident: full-time $10,908; part-time $606 per credit hour. *Required fees:* $86; $43 per semester. *Financial support:* Career-related internships or fieldwork, Federal Work-Study, institutionally sponsored loans, and scholarships/grants available. Support available to part-time students. Financial award applicants required to submit FAFSA. *Faculty research:* Emotional intelligence, compassion fatigue, school social work, diversity issues, spirituality and social work. *Unit head:* Steve Spyres, Acting Chair, 785-670-2146, Fax: 785-670-1027, E-mail: steve.spyres@washburn.edu. *Application contact:* Dr. Kimberly Harrison, MSW Program Director, 785-670-1957, Fax: 785-670-1027, E-mail: kimberly.harrison@washburn.edu. Web site: http://www.washburn.edu/sas/social-work/.

Washington University in St. Louis, George Warren Brown School of Social Work, St. Louis, MO 63130-4899. Offers public health (MPH); social work (MSW, PhD); JD/MSW; M Arch/MSW; MBA/MSW; MPH/MBA; MSW/M Div; MSW/MAJCS; MSW/MAPS; MSW/MPH. MSW/M Div and MSW/MAPS offered jointly with Eden Theological Seminary. *Accreditation:* CSWE (one or more programs are accredited). *Faculty:* 46 full-time, 82 part-time/adjunct. *Students:* 574 full-time (490 women); includes 127 minority (55 Black or African American, non-Hispanic/Latino; 6 American Indian or Alaska Native, non-Hispanic/Latino; 31 Asian, non-Hispanic/Latino; 12 Hispanic/Latino; 23 Two or more races, non-Hispanic/Latino), 98 international. Average age 27. 746 applicants, 63% accepted, 234 enrolled. In 2011, 235 master's, 6 doctorates awarded. *Degree requirements:* For master's, 60 credit hours (MSW), 45 credit hours (MPH); practicum; for doctorate, comprehensive exam, thesis/dissertation. *Entrance requirements:* For master's, GRE, GMAT, LSAT, or MCAT (public health), minimum GPA of 3.0; for doctorate, GRE, MA or MSW. Additional exam requirements/recommendations for international students: Required—TOEFL (minimum score 575 paper-based; 233 computer-based; 90 iBT). *Application deadline:* For fall admission, 12/15 priority date for domestic students, 12/15 for international students. Applications are processed on a rolling basis. Application fee: $40. Electronic applications accepted. *Expenses:* Contact institution. *Financial support:* In 2011–12, 486 students received support. Federal Work-Study, institutionally sponsored loans, scholarships/grants, health care benefits, tuition waivers (partial), and research assistantships, partial tuition waivers available. Support available to part-time students. Financial award applicants required to submit FAFSA. *Faculty research:* Mental health services, social development, child welfare, at-risk teens, autism, environmental health, health policy, health communications, obesity, violence and injury prevention, chronic disease prevention, poverty, public health, productive aging/gerontology, social work, civic engagement, school social work, program evaluation, health disparities. *Unit head:* Dr. Edward F. Lawlor, Dean/Professor, 314-935-6693, Fax: 314-935-8511, E-mail: elawlor@wustl.edu. *Application contact:* Richard Sigg, Director of Admissions and Recruiting, 314-935-6676, Fax: 314-935-4859, E-mail: rsigg@wustl.edu. Web site: http://gwbweb.wustl.edu/.

Wayne State University, College of Liberal Arts and Sciences, Department of Political Science, Program in Public Administration, Detroit, MI 48202. Offers aging policy and management (MPA); criminal justice policy and management (MPA); economic development policy and management (MPA); health services policy and management (MPA); human resources management (MPA); information technology management (MPA); non-profit management (MPA); organizational behavior and management (MPA); public budgeting and financial management (MPA); public policy analysis and program evaluation (MPA); social welfare policy and management (MPA); urban policy and management (MPA). *Accreditation:* NASPAA. Evening/weekend programs available. *Students:* 22 full-time (17 women), 45 part-time (33 women); includes 19 minority (16 Black or African American, non-Hispanic/Latino; 1 American Indian or Alaska Native, non-Hispanic/Latino; 2 Hispanic/Latino), 1 international. Average age 31. 75 applicants, 28% accepted, 11 enrolled. In 2011, 20 master's awarded. *Degree requirements:* For master's, comprehensive exam. *Entrance requirements:* For master's, GRE General Test. Additional exam requirements/recommendations for international students: Required—TOEFL (minimum score 550 paper-based; 213 computer-based); Recommended—TWE (minimum score 5.5). *Application deadline:* For fall admission, 6/1 priority date for domestic students, 5/1 for international students; for winter admission, 10/1 priority date for domestic students, 9/1 for international students; for spring admission, 2/1 priority date for domestic students, 1/1 for international students. Applications are processed on a rolling basis. Application fee: $50. Electronic applications accepted. *Expenses:* Tuition, state resident: part-time $512.85 per credit. Tuition, nonresident: part-time $1132.65 per credit. *Required fees:* $26.60 per credit. $199.65 per semester. Tuition and fees vary according to course load and program. *Financial support:* In 2011–12, 7 students received support. Scholarships/grants available. *Faculty research:* Urban politics, urban education, state administration. *Unit head:* Dr. Brady Baybeck, Director, 313-577-2630, E-mail: mpa@wayne.edu. Web site: http://clasweb.clas.wayne.edu/mapa.

Wayne State University, School of Social Work, Detroit, MI 48202. Offers alcohol and drug abuse studies (Certificate); disabilities (Certificate); gerontology (Certificate); social welfare research and evaluation (Certificate); social work (MSW, PhD); social work and infant mental health (MSW, PhD); social work practice with families and couples (Certificate). Application deadline for PhD is December 18. *Accreditation:* CSWE (one or more programs are accredited). Part-time and evening/weekend programs available. *Students:* 461 full-time (414 women), 207 part-time (188 women); includes 238 minority (204 Black or African American, non-Hispanic/Latino; 1 American Indian or Alaska Native, non-Hispanic/Latino; 6 Asian, non-Hispanic/Latino; 14 Hispanic/Latino; 13 Two or more races, non-Hispanic/Latino), 16 international. Average age 32. 783 applicants, 36% accepted, 188 enrolled. In 2011, 294 master's, 4 doctorates, 14 other advanced degrees awarded. *Entrance requirements:* For master's, personal interest statement, resume, 3 references; for doctorate, GRE, resume, three letters of reference, personal statement, summary of relevant research and professional experience, writing sample; for Certificate, MSW or actively enrolled in advanced portion of MSW program. Additional exam requirements/recommendations for international students: Required—TOEFL (minimum score 550 paper-based; 213 computer-based); Recommended—TWE (minimum score 6). *Application deadline:* For fall admission, 10/1 for domestic and international students. Application fee: $50. Electronic applications accepted. *Expenses:* Tuition, state resident: part-time $512.85 per credit. Tuition, nonresident: part-time $1132.65 per credit. *Required fees:* $26.60 per credit. $199.65 per semester. Tuition and fees vary according to course load and program. *Financial support:* In 2011–12, 70 students received support, including 3 fellowships with tuition reimbursements available (averaging $19,917 per year), 3 research assistantships with tuition reimbursements available (averaging $17,110 per year), 1 teaching assistantship with tuition reimbursement available (averaging $16,921 per year); career-related internships or fieldwork, institutionally sponsored loans, scholarships/grants, tuition waivers (partial), and unspecified assistantships also available. Support available to part-time students. Financial award applicants required to submit FAFSA. *Faculty research:* Child welfare, interpersonal and relationship violence, aging, homelessness and at-risk youth, community-planning and development, international social work, re-entry and re-integration of ex-offenders. *Total annual research expenditures:* $793,598. *Unit head:* Dr. Cheryl Waites, Dean, 313-577-4400, E-mail: ccwaites@wayne.edu. *Application contact:* 313-577-4409. Web site: http://socialwork.wayne.edu/.

West Chester University of Pennsylvania, College of Business and Public Affairs, Department of Social Work, West Chester, PA 19383. Offers MSW. *Accreditation:* CSWE. Part-time and evening/weekend programs available. *Faculty:* 5 full-time (4 women), 9 part-time/adjunct (7 women). *Students:* 92 full-time (86 women), 25 part-time (24 women); includes 27 minority (20 Black or African American, non-Hispanic/Latino; 3 Hispanic/Latino; 4 Two or more races, non-Hispanic/Latino). Average age 30. 214 applicants, 34% accepted, 67 enrolled. In 2011, 2 degrees awarded. *Degree requirements:* For master's, research paper. *Entrance requirements:* For master's, minimum GPA between 2.8 and 3.0, 3-5-page personal statement, 2 letters of recommendation. Additional exam requirements/recommendations for international students: Required—TOEFL (minimum score 550 paper-based; 213 computer-based; 80 iBT). *Application deadline:* For fall admission, 4/15 priority date for domestic students, 3/15 for international students; for spring admission, 10/15 priority date for domestic students, 9/1 for international students. Applications are processed on a rolling basis. Application fee: $45. Electronic applications accepted. *Expenses:* Tuition, state resident: full-time $7488; part-time $416 per credit. Tuition, nonresident: full-time $11,232; part-time $624 per credit. *Required fees:* $1784.64; $67.59 per credit. Tuition and fees vary according to program. *Financial support:* Unspecified assistantships available. Support available to part-time students. Financial award application deadline: 2/15; financial award applicants required to submit FAFSA. *Faculty research:* Trauma and disaster intervention, mental health, traumatic brain injury, social welfare reform, professional development, social work with older adults. *Unit head:* Dr. Ann Abbott, Chair and Graduate Coordinator, 610-738-0351, Fax: 610-738-0375, E-mail: aabbott@wcupa.edu. *Application contact:* Office of Graduate Studies, 610-436-2943, Fax: 610-436-2763, E-mail: gradstudy@wcupa.edu. Web site: http://www.wcupa.edu/_academics/sch_sba/u-sw.html.

Western Carolina University, Graduate School, College of Health and Human Sciences, Department of Social Work, Cullowhee, NC 28723. Offers MSW. *Accreditation:* CSWE. Part-time programs available. *Students:* 58 full-time (47 women), 2 part-time (both women); includes 8 minority (3 Black or African American, non-Hispanic/Latino; 3 Hispanic/Latino; 2 Two or more races, non-Hispanic/Latino). Average age 30. 65 applicants, 71% accepted, 37 enrolled. In 2011, 21 master's awarded. *Entrance requirements:* For master's, appropriate undergraduate major with minimum GPA of 3.0, 3 recommendations, resume. Additional exam requirements/recommendations for international students: Required—TOEFL (minimum score 550 paper-based; 270 computer-based; 79 iBT). *Application deadline:* For fall admission, 2/1 for domestic students. Applications are processed on a rolling basis. Application fee: $50. *Expenses:* Tuition, state resident: full-time $3348. Tuition, nonresident: full-time $12,933. *Required fees:* $3155. *Financial support:* Fellowships, research assistantships with full and partial tuition reimbursements, teaching assistantships with full and partial tuition reimbursements, institutionally sponsored loans, scholarships/grants, and unspecified assistantships available. Financial award application deadline: 3/31. *Unit head:* Dr. Patricia Morse, Department Head, 828-227-7112, Fax: 828-227-7061, E-mail: pmorse@wcu.edu. *Application contact:* Admissions Specialist for Social Work, 828-227-7398, Fax: 828-227-7480, E-mail: gradsch@email.wcu.edu.

Western Kentucky University, Graduate Studies, College of Health and Human Services, Department of Social Work, Bowling Green, KY 42101. Offers MSW. *Accreditation:* CSWE. *Entrance requirements:* Additional exam requirements/recommendations for international students: Required—TOEFL (minimum score 555 paper-based; 213 computer-based; 79 iBT).

Western Michigan University, Graduate College, College of Health and Human Services, School of Social Work, Kalamazoo, MI 49008. Offers MSW. *Accreditation:* CSWE. Part-time programs available.

Western New Mexico University, Graduate Division, Department of Social Work, Silver City, NM 88062-0680. Offers MSW. Part-time programs available. Postbaccalaureate distance learning degree programs offered. Electronic applications accepted.

West Virginia University, Eberly College of Arts and Sciences, School of Applied Social Sciences, Division of Social Work, Morgantown, WV 26506. Offers aging and health care (MSW); children and families (MSW); community mental health (MSW); community organization and social administration (MSW); direct (clinical) social work practice (MSW). *Accreditation:* CSWE. Part-time programs available. *Degree requirements:* For master's, fieldwork. *Entrance requirements:* For master's, GRE, minimum GPA of 2.75, 2 letters of reference. Additional exam requirements/recommendations for international students: Required—TOEFL. *Faculty research:* Rural and small town social work practice, gerontology, health and mental health, welfare reform, child welfare.

Wheelock College, Graduate Programs, Division of Social Work, Boston, MA 02215-4176. Offers MSW. *Accreditation:* CSWE. *Degree requirements:* For master's, comprehensive exam, thesis. *Entrance requirements:* For master's, minimum GPA of 3.0; undergraduate course work in human biology, statistics. Additional exam requirements/recommendations for international students: Required—TOEFL. Electronic applications accepted.

Wichita State University, Graduate School, Fairmount College of Liberal Arts and Sciences, School of Social Work, Wichita, KS 67260. Offers MSW. *Accreditation:* CSWE. *Expenses:* Tuition, state resident: full-time $4746; part-time $263.65 per credit. Tuition, nonresident: full-time $11,669; part-time $648.30 per credit. *Unit head:* Dr. Brien Bolin, Director, 316-978-7250, Fax: 316-978-3328, E-mail: brien.bolin@wichita.edu. *Application contact:* Carrie C. Henderson, Admissions Coordinator, 316-978-3095, Fax: 316-978-3253, E-mail: carrie.henderson@wichita.edu.

Widener University, School of Human Service Professions, Center for Social Work Education, Chester, PA 19013-5792. Offers MSW, PhD. *Accreditation:* CSWE. Part-time programs available. *Degree requirements:* For master's, field practica. *Entrance requirements:* For master's, minimum GPA of 3.0. Electronic applications accepted. *Expenses:* Contact institution. *Faculty research:* Clinical practice, clinical supervision, gerontology, child welfare, self-psychology.

Wilfrid Laurier University, Faculty of Graduate and Postdoctoral Studies, Lyle S. Hallman Faculty of Social Work, Waterloo, ON N2L 3C5, Canada. Offers Aboriginal studies (MSW); community, policy, planning and organizations (MSW); critical social policy and organizational studies (PhD); individuals, families and groups (MSW); social work practice (individuals, families, groups and communities) (PhD); social work practice: individuals, families, groups and communities (PhD). Part-time programs available. *Degree requirements:* For master's, thesis optional; for doctorate, thesis/dissertation. *Entrance requirements:* For master's, course work in social science, research methodology, and statistics; honors BA with a minimum B average; for doctorate, master's degree in social work, minimum A- average. Additional exam requirements/recommendations for international students: Required—TOEFL (minimum score 89 iBT). Electronic applications accepted. *Expenses:* Contact institution.

Winthrop University, College of Arts and Sciences, Program in Social Work, Rock Hill, SC 29733. Offers MA. *Accreditation:* CSWE. *Entrance requirements:* For master's, GRE or MAT, minimum GPA of 3.0, 3 letters of recommendation, resume. Electronic applications accepted.

Yeshiva University, Wurzweiler School of Social Work, New York, NY 10033-3201. Offers MSW, PhD, MSW/Certificate. *Accreditation:* CSWE (one or more programs are accredited). Part-time and evening/weekend programs available. *Faculty:* 18 full-time (8 women), 28 part-time/adjunct (22 women). *Students:* 188 full-time (144 women), 128 part-time (90 women); includes 113 minority (63 Black or African American, non-Hispanic/Latino; 1 Asian, non-Hispanic/Latino; 49 Hispanic/Latino). Average age 40. 370 applicants, 71% accepted, 198 enrolled. In 2011, 117 master's, 2 doctorates awarded. *Median time to degree:* Of those who began their doctoral program in fall 2003, 75% received their degree in 8 years or less. *Degree requirements:* For master's, thesis, integrative essay; for doctorate, comprehensive exam, thesis/dissertation. *Entrance requirements:* For master's, interview, minimum GPA of 3.0, letters of reference; for doctorate, GRE, interview, letters of reference, writing sample, MSW, minimum 2 years professional social work experience. Additional exam requirements/recommendations for international students: Required—TOEFL (minimum score 577 paper-based; 233 computer-based). *Application deadline:* For fall admission, 5/1 priority date for domestic students; for spring admission, 10/31 for domestic students. Applications are processed on a rolling basis. Application fee: $50. *Expenses:* Contact institution. *Financial support:* In 2011–12, 177 students received support, including 2 teaching assistantships (averaging $5,000 per year); career-related internships or fieldwork, Federal Work-Study, institutionally sponsored loans, and scholarships/grants also available. Financial award application deadline: 4/15; financial award applicants required to submit FAFSA. *Faculty research:* Child abuse, AIDS, day care, non profits, gerontology. *Total annual research expenditures:* $300,000. *Unit head:* Dr. Jade C. Docherty, Assistant Dean, 212-960-0829 Ext. 829, Fax: 212-960-0822, E-mail: docherty@yu.edu. *Application contact:* Dr. Catherine Pearlman, Director of Admissions, 212-960-0811, Fax: 212-960-0822, E-mail: cpearlma@yu.edu.

See Display below and Close-Up on page 1779.

York University, Faculty of Graduate Studies, Atkinson Faculty of Liberal and Professional Studies, Program in Social Work, Toronto, ON M3J 1P3, Canada. Offers MSW, PhD. Part-time and evening/weekend programs available. *Degree requirements:* For master's, thesis or alternative. Electronic applications accepted.

ADELPHI UNIVERSITY

School of Social Work

Programs of Study

The School of Social Work at Adelphi University offers programs leading to a Master of Social Work (M.S.W.), a Ph.D. in social work, and post-master's certificate programs in bilingual school social work and human resource management.

The 64-credit M.S.W. program combines core courses in the foundations of social work with supervised field instruction to give students experience in applying social work theories to professional practice. The program fosters an abiding commitment to professional values and social justice and equips students with knowledge and skills for social work practice with a wide range of clients and diverse communities. All first-year M.S.W. students are required to take ten core courses in a set sequence. The plan of study in the first year includes eight courses plus a minimum of 600 hours of supervised field instruction. In their second year of study, students complete six required courses, two elective courses, plus 600 hours of field instruction in advanced, direct social work practice. In addition, M.S.W. students are eligible to enroll in a joint program with the Robert B. Willumstad School of Business leading to a certificate in human resource management that requires only 9 additional credits beyond the M.S.W.

The 51-credit Ph.D. in Social Work gives practitioners the skills and knowledge to effect significant change in social welfare policy and practice. The program emphasizes critical thinking and prepares students to develop knowledge for all methods of social work practice. Graduates are able to provide leadership in the profession as scholars, educators, researchers, and administrators in social agencies. Candidates can pursue doctoral study while they continue to work. Classes are offered one day a week in the late afternoon and early evening. Students must pass qualifying examinations that test mastery and integration of the first two years of study, and they must complete and successfully defend a dissertation that evidences original, independent research.

The interdisciplinary 16-credit certificate in bilingual education is for M.S.W. graduates who are bilingual and work, or plan to work, in a school setting that requires certification in bilingual education. The program consists of core courses that meet the bilingual certification requirements for pupil personnel service professionals mandated by the New York State Department of Education. Courses are offered jointly by the School of Social Work and the Ruth S. Ammon School of Education.

Research Facilities

The University's primary research holdings are at Swirbul Library and include 600,000 volumes (including bound periodicals and government publications), 806,000 items in microformats, 33,000 audiovisual items, and online access to more than 61,000 electronic journal titles and 221 research databases.

Financial Aid

The School of Social Work offers various ways to help defray the cost of graduate study. These include scholarships, assistantships, agency tuition remission, and field-placement stipends. More information is available at online at http://socialwork.adelphi.edu/scholarships/master.php or from the Office of Student Financial Services at http://ecampus.adelphi.edu/sfs.

Cost of Study

For the 2012–13 academic year, the tuition rate is $965 per credit. University fees range from $315 to $550 per semester.

Living and Housing Costs

The University assists single and married students in finding suitable accommodations whenever possible. The cost of living depends on the location and number of rooms rented.

Location

Located in historic Garden City, New York, 45 minutes from Manhattan and 20 minutes from Queens, Adelphi's 75-acre suburban campus is known for the beauty of its landscape and architecture. The campus is a short walk from the Long Island Rail Road and is convenient to New York's major airports and several major highways. Off-campus centers are located in Manhattan, Hauppauge, and Poughkeepsie.

The University and The School

Founded in 1896, Adelphi is a fully accredited, private university with nearly 8,000 undergraduate, graduate, and returning-adult students in the arts and sciences, business, clinical psychology, education, nursing, and social work. Students come from forty-three states and forty-five countries. The Princeton Review named Adelphi University a Best College in the Northeastern Region, and the *Fiske Guide to Colleges* recognized Adelphi as a Best Buy in higher education for the sixth year in a row. The University is one of only twenty-five private institutions in the nation to earn this recognition.

For more than fifty years, the School of Social Work has trained social work practitioners who are dedicated to improving the lives of individuals, families, groups, and communities. Through its many programs, the School has been a driving force for ethical social work practice and a strong advocate for social justice. The School is committed to the development of new knowledge that can inform the evolution of social policy, the organization and delivery of social services, and the profession's ability to intervene effectively with, and on behalf of, vulnerable, disenfranchised, and marginalized populations. The scholarship, research, and demonstration projects that the faculty members and graduate students are engaged in respond to the exigencies of contemporary life and contribute to social work's capacity to improve individuals' well-being. The School features small classes in a supportive environment that fosters a close and nurturing relationship between faculty members and students. The faculty members have extensive teaching experience and are recognized as leaders in their respective fields. The broad base of diverse students and professionals seeking advanced degrees enhances the classroom learning and enriches the educational experience for all.

Applying

Master's degree applicants should have a bachelor's degree with a strong science and liberal arts background; doctoral applicants should have an M.S.W. and at least three years' experience in the field. All applicants must submit a completed application, a $50 application fee, official college transcripts, and three letters of recommendation. Ph.D. applicants must also submit GRE scores and have a minimum 3.3 GPA. An interview is required. Application deadlines are July 15 for the fall semester and December 1 for the spring semester in the M.S.W. program, and April 1 for doctoral applications. For more information, students should contact the School of Social Work directly.

Correspondence and Information

Dr. Andrew Safyer, Dean
School of Social Work
Social Work Building, Room 201
Adelphi University
One South Avenue
Garden City, New York 11530
Phone: 516-877-4354
Fax: 516-877-4436
E-mail: asafyer@adelphi.edu
Web site: http://socialwork.adelphi.edu

THE FACULTY AND THEIR RESEARCH

Wahiba Abu-Ras, Ph.D., Columbia. Child welfare, oppression and diversity.

Julie Cooper Altman, Ph.D., Chicago. Engagement in child welfare services, client use of agency-initiated services, worker use of knowledge, impact of welfare reform, M.S.W. child welfare training outcomes.

Richard Belson, D.S.W., Adelphi. Marriage and family therapy.

Roni Berger, Ph.D., Hebrew University (Jerusalem). Immigrants and refugees, qualitative and combined research methods, remarriage and stepfamilies, law guardianship.

Matthew Bogenschutz, M.S.W., Minnesota, Twin Cities. History and philosophy of social welfare.

Ellen Bogolub, Ph.D., Rutgers. Families and divorce, child welfare.

Diann Cameron-Kelly, Ph.D., Fordham. Early childhood and family systems, civic engagement and civic duty, child and adolescent development.

Peter Chernack, D.S.W., Adelphi. Evaluation of alternative models of field education, university-community partnerships, higher education leadership development.

Carol Cohen, D.S.W., CUNY. Social work with groups, agency-based practice, organizational and community practice.

CarolAnn Daniel, Ph.D., CUNY. Health, gender and Caribbean diaspora; qualitative methods; critical theory.

Beverly Araujo Dawson, Ph.D., Michigan. Impact of psychosocial stressors (discrimination and language barriers on the mental health of Latino immigrants), development of culturally competent interventions for Latino communities.

Adelphi University

Judy Fenster, Ph.D., NYU. Substance abuse, social work education and curriculum.
Richard Francoeur, Ph.D., Pittsburgh. Social work practice, public health social work, practice evaluation.
Godfrey A. Gregg, Ph.D., NYU. Breast cancer, end-of-life issues, sexual orientation, thanatology.
Patricia Joyce, D.S.W., CUNY, Hunter. Trauma, incest, mental illness, nonoffending mothers of sexually abused children, cultural competence and PTSD, secondary trauma and ethnicity, psychoanalytic theory, professionals' constructions of clients, social welfare rhetoric, social process of treatment planning in agency practice.
Njeri Kagotho, Ph.D., Washington. Social welfare, research.
Tae Kuen Kim, Ph.D., Pennsylvania. Social welfare policy, applied statistics, comparative welfare study.
Stavroula Kyriakakis, Ph.D., Washington (St. Louis). Intimate partner violence in immigrant communities, domestic violence interventions.
Shannon Lane, Ph.D., Connecticut. Political social work, women's issues.
Roger Levin, Ph.D., NYU. Issues In social welfare, history and philosophy of social welfare.
Jennifer McClendon, Ph.D., Washington (St. Louis). Crisis intervention, organizational development.
Elizabeth Palley, Ph.D., Brandeis. Disability and family policy, education policy.
Subadra Panchanadeswaran, Ph.D., Baltimore. Immigrant women's health, mental health and trauma, human behavior and theories.
Marilyn Paul, Ph.D., Adelphi. Psychosocial issues confronting contemporary families, social work practice.
Laura Quiros, Ph.D., CUNY. Addiction and mental health, diversity and oppression, multicultural social work education.
Geoffrey Ream, Ph.D., Cornell. Contextual mediators between adolescent sexuality and negative outcomes.
Ellen Rosenberg, D.S.W., Columbia. Social work assessment and diagnosis.
Philip Rozario, Ph.D., Washington (St. Louis). The well-being of caregivers of frail older adults, meaning in later life; successful and productive aging; long-term care issues of frail older adults.
Andrew Safyer, Ph.D., Michigan. At-risk youths and their families, ego psychology, defense mechanisms, narcissistic personality disorders.
Carol Sussal, D.S.W., Adelphi. Social work practice with gay, lesbian, bisexual, and transgendered persons.
Bradley D. Zodikoff, Ph.D., Columbia. Gerontology, geriatric mental health services, family caregiving, social work practice in healthcare, social work research methods.

School of Social Work Community Partnerships

Adelphi New York Statewide Breast Cancer Hotline and Support Program: The only comprehensive, university-based, breast cancer counseling program in New York State, the program supports, educates, and empowers breast cancer patients, professionals and the community. Director: Hillary Rutter (rutter@adelphi.edu)

Adelphi Hartford Partnership Program for Aging Education (HPPAE): Funded by the John A. Hartford Foundation through the New York Academy of Medicine, the HPPAE prepares master's students for practice and leadership roles in gerontology and geriatric mental health. Principal investigator: Dr. Peter Chernack (chernack@adelphi.edu)

Geriatric Mental Health Needs Assessment Project: With funding from the Long Island Community Foundation, this needs-assessment study helps identify specific barriers to geriatric mental healthcare on Long Island. Principal investigator: Dr. Bradley Zodikoff (zodikoff@adelphi.edu); co-principal investigator: Dr. Peter Chernack (chernack@adelphi.edu)

Immigrant Primary Care Project: Funded by the New York Hospital Medical Center of Queens, this project seeks to increase the ability of primary-care medical residents to competently work cross culturally with immigrant Muslim women. Co-principal investigator: Dr. Tricia Joyce (joyce2@adelphi.edu); co-principal investigator: Dr. Suzanne Michael (michael@adelphi.edu)

Investigators to Investors: Funded by the Department of Health and Human Services, Children's Bureau, this five-year project trains M.S.W. child-welfare professionals from the New York City Administration for Children's Services (ACS). Principal investigator: Dr. Julie Cooper Altman (altman@adelphi.edu)

Long Island Center for Nonprofit Leadership: This University-based, community-driven leadership-development initiative responds to the immediate and long-term leadership crisis facing Long Island's nonprofit sector. Principal investigator: Dr. Peter Chernack (chernack@adelphi.edu); co-principal investigator: Dr. Andrew Safyer (asafyer@adelphi.edu)

Adelphi's campus is located in historic Garden City, Long Island, New York.

A registered arboretum, Adelphi is truly a green campus.

HAWAI'I PACIFIC UNIVERSITY

Program in Social Work

Programs of Study

The mission of Hawai'i Pacific University's (HPU) Master of Social Work (M.S.W.) program is to prepare qualified students, especially working adults, for entry into competent, ethical, effective practice of advanced generalist social work. Utilizing critical thinking and building upon the University's diverse environment, M.S.W. students strive to enhance the social well-being of all people; provide leadership in culturally competent services at the micro, mezzo, and macro levels; advocate for social and economic justice locally, nationally, and globally; and promote multiculturalism through furthering social-work knowledge.

The M.S.W. program requires a minimum of 61 semester hours of graduate work: 12 semester hours of Human Behavior in the Social Environment (HBSE) courses, 19 semester hours of practice, 12 semester hours of practicum, 9 semester hours of research, and 9 semester hours of policy.

Research Facilities

To support graduate studies, HPU's Meader and Atherton libraries offer over 110,000 bound volumes, 350,000 microfiche items, and periodical subscriptions to 1,500 print titles and 30,000 electronic journals. Databases of public and state university libraries, legislative information, and business-oriented statistical data are also available in the library or online. Students can access HPU's library databases, course information, their academic information, and an e-mail account through Pipeline, the University's internal Web site for students. The University's accessible on-campus computer center houses more than 420 computers with specialized software to support graduate academic programs. HPU also provides free Wi-Fi so students have wireless access to Pipeline resources anywhere on campus. A significant number of online courses are available as well.

Financial Aid

The University participates in all federal financial aid programs designated for graduate students. These programs provide aid in the form of subsidized (need-based) and unsubsidized (non-need-based) Federal Stafford Student Loans. Through these loans, funds may be available to cover a student's entire cost of education. To apply for aid, students must submit the Free Application for Federal Student Aid (FAFSA) beginning January 1.

The University also offers several types of institutional graduate scholarships to new full-time, degree-seeking students. U.S. citizens, permanent residents, and international students who have a demonstrated financial need may apply. HPU's graduate scholarships include the Graduate Trustee Scholarship of $6000 ($3000/semester), the Graduate Dean Scholarship of $4000 ($2000/semester), and the Graduate Kokua Scholarship of $2000 ($1000/semester). Factors that may be considered when evaluating requests are previous academic record, community involvement and service, and professional work experience and achievement.

In order to be eligible for the best award package, students should apply by HPU's priority deadline of March 1. Applications received after the priority deadline will be awarded on a funds-available basis. Mailing of student award letters usually begins by the end of March. Applicants will be notified by mail as decisions are made.

Cost of Study

Tuition for graduate students enrolled in fall and spring semesters is determined on a per-credit basis; full-time status for a graduate student is 9 credits. Tuition for the optional winter and summer sessions is also determined on a per-credit basis. For the 2012–13 academic year, full-time tuition is $13,590 for most graduate degree programs, including the M.S.W. program. Other expenses, including books, personal expenses, fees, and a student bus pass are estimated at $3285.

Living and Housing Costs

The University has off-campus housing and an apartment referral service for graduate students. The cost of living in off-campus apartments is approximately $12,482 for a double-occupancy room. Additional graduate housing information is available online at www.hpu.edu/housing.

Student Group

University enrollment currently stands at approximately 8,200, including more than 1,200 graduate students. All fifty states and more than 100 countries are represented at HPU, one of the most culturally diverse universities in America.

Location

Hawai'i Pacific University combines the excitement of an urban, downtown campus with the serenity of a residential campus. The urban campus is ideally located in downtown Honolulu, the business and financial center of the Pacific. The downtown campus comprises seven buildings in the center of Honolulu's business district and is home to the College of Business Administration and the College of Humanities and Social Sciences.

Eight miles away, situated on 135 acres in Kaneohe, the windward Hawai'i Loa campus is the site of the College of Nursing and Health Sciences and the College of Natural and Computational Sciences. The Hawai'i Loa campus has residence halls, dining commons, the Educational Technology Center, a student center, and outdoor recreational facilities, including a soccer field, tennis courts, a softball field, and an exercise room.

HPU is affiliated with the Oceanic Institute, an aquaculture research facility located on a 56-acre site at Makapu'u Point on the windward coast of Oahu, Hawaii. All three sites are linked by HPU shuttle, and easily accessed by public transportation as well.

Notably, the downtown campus location is within walking distance of shopping and dining. Iolani Palace, the only royal palace in the United States, is a few blocks away, as are the State Capitol, City Hall, and the Blaisdell Concert Hall. The Honolulu Academy of Arts, Museum of Contemporary Art, Waikiki Aquarium, Honolulu Zoo, and many other cultural attractions are located nearby.

The University

HPU is a private, nonprofit university with approximately 8,200 students. Founded in 1965, HPU prides itself on maintaining strong academic programs, small class sizes, individual attention to students, and a diverse faculty and student population. HPU is recognized as a Best in the West college by The Princeton Review and *U.S. News & World Report* and a Best Buy by *Barron's* business magazine. HPU offers more than fifty acclaimed undergraduate programs and fourteen distinguished graduate programs. The University has a faculty of more than 500, a student-faculty ratio of 15:1, and an average class size of fewer than 25 students. A wide range of counseling and other student support services are available. There are more than fifty student organizations on campus, including the Graduate Student Organization.

Applying

Students must have a baccalaureate degree from an accredited college or university in the United States or an equivalent degree from another country. Applicants should complete and forward a graduate admissions application, send in the $50 nonrefundable application fee, have official transcripts sent from all colleges or universities previously attended, and forward two letters of recommendation. A resume and personal statement about the applicant's academic and career goals is also required. Applicants who have taken the Graduate Record Examination (GRE) should have their scores sent directly to the Graduate Admissions Office. International students should submit scores of a recognized English proficiency test such as TOEFL. Admissions decisions are made on a rolling basis and applicants are notified between one and two weeks after all documents have been submitted. Applicants are encouraged to submit their applications online.

Correspondence and Information

Graduate Admissions
Hawai'i Pacific University
1164 Bishop Street, #911
Honolulu, Hawaii 96813
Phone: 808-544-1135
866-GRAD-HPU (toll-free)
Fax: 808-544-0280
E-mail: graduate@hpu.edu
Web site: http://www.hpu.edu/hpumsw

THE FACULTY AND THEIR RESEARCH

Lorraine Marais, M.S.W., Ed.D., Associate Professor and Director, School of Social Work.

Patricia Nishimoto, M.S.W., Ph.D., Assistant Professor and Program Director for Master of Social Work.

Margo Bare, M.S.W., Instructor and Director of Field Education.

Mark Fox, M.S.W., Instructor of Social Work.

William "Bill" Hummel, M.S.W., Instructor of Social Work.

Scott Okamoto, M.S.W., Ph.D., Associate Professor of Social Work.

Mary Sheridan, Ph.D., Professor of Social Work.

Paul Tuan Tran, M.S.W., Instructor of Social Work.

ST. JOSEPH'S COLLEGE, NEW YORK

Master of Science in Human Services Leadership

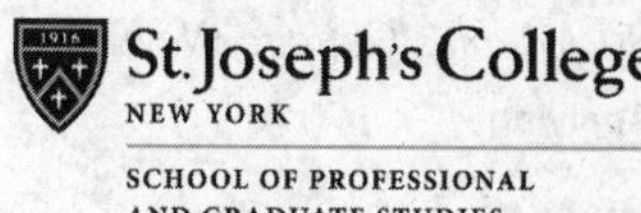

Programs of Study

The 30-credit M.S. in human services leadership program provides human services professionals with a progressive education built on a research-based, groundbreaking leadership development curriculum. Topics include a focus on financial, legal, regulatory, political, social, and historical aspects of the human services industry, all of which are anchored on a contemporary and service-oriented leadership model.

Career opportunities in human services are continuing to expand as is the need for qualified leaders in a field that includes child welfare, mental health, substance abuse, family support, health care, criminal justice and public safety, among others. Whether the goal is a career transition or a promotional opportunity in one of these fields, St. Joseph's graduate program in human services leadership will help students develop the specialized leadership skills necessary to position them as respected professionals in the industry.

The M.S. in human services leadership consists of ten courses developed specifically for this program that incorporate the leadership competencies necessary to develop visionary leaders who will make a positive impact on their organizations and the community at large.

Prospective students who work in the field of human services, whether in a government agency or in a private nonprofit organization, benefit from this degree if they are seeking to develop specialized management skills relevant to their field. As the baby boom generation of manager in this field starts to retire, there is a need for sufficiently prepared new managers to take over. This degree addresses the skills most relevant to successful management and leadership in human services.

Research Facilities

The Callahan Library at the Long Island Campus is a modern, 25,000-square-foot freestanding facility with seating for more than 300 readers. A curriculum library, seminar rooms, administrative offices, and two classrooms are housed in this building. Holdings include more than 105,000 volumes and 307 periodical titles, and they are supplemented by videos and other instructional aids. Patrons have access to the Internet and to several online academic databases. A fully automated library system, Endeavor, ensures the efficient retrieval and management of all library resources. Other resources include the library at St. Joseph's Brooklyn Campus, with more than 109,000 volumes and membership in the Long Island Library Resources Council. This facilitates cooperative associations with the academic and special libraries on Long Island. Internet access, subscriptions to several online full-text databases, and membership in the international bibliographic utility OCLC allow almost limitless access to available information.

McEntegart Hall is a fully air-conditioned five-level structure. Three spacious reading areas with a capacity for 300 readers, including individual study carrels and shelf space for 200,000 volumes, provide an excellent environment for research. In addition, McEntegart Hall houses the College archives, a curriculum library, three computer laboratories, a nursing education laboratory, and a videoconference room. There are eight classrooms, a chapel, a cafeteria, and faculty and student lounges.

A high-speed fiber-optic intracampus network connects all offices, instructional facilities, computer laboratories, and libraries on both the Brooklyn and Long Island Campuses. The network provides Internet access to all students and faculty and staff members. An integrated online library system enables students to search for and check out books at either campus. Online databases and other electronic resources are available to students from either campus or from their home computers. Two wireless laptop classrooms with smart-classroom features provide flexible instruction spaces with the latest technologies. Videoconferencing facilities connect the two campuses, allowing for real-time distance learning in a small-group setting.

Financial Aid

Financial aid programs are available for graduate students. Students should contact the Financial Aid Office for more information (Brooklyn Campus, telephone: 718-940-5700; Long Island Campus, telephone: 631-687-2600).

Cost of Study

In 2012–13, tuition is $19,500 or $715 per credit for graduate programs. The College and technology fees per semester for 12 or more credits totaled $200.

Student Group

The total enrollment for all graduate programs on both campuses is 740.

Location

St. Joseph's College has two campuses—the main campus in the residential Clinton Hill section of Brooklyn and the Long Island branch campus in Patchogue, New York. The main campus offers easy access to all transit lines; to the Long Island Expressway; to all bridges in Brooklyn, Manhattan, and Queens; and to the Verrazano-Narrows Bridge to Staten Island. Within 30 minutes, students leaving St. Joseph's College can find themselves at the Metropolitan Museum of Art, the 42nd Street Library, Carnegie Hall and Lincoln Center, the Broadway theater district, Madison Square Garden, or Shea Stadium. The College itself stands in the center of one of the nation's most diversified academic communities, consisting of six colleges and universities within a 2-mile radius of each other. The 27-acre Long Island Campus, adjacent to Great Patchogue Lake, is an ideal setting for studying, socializing, and partaking in extracurricular activities. Located just off Sunrise Highway, the Long Island Campus is easily accessible from all parts of Long Island.

The College

St. Joseph's College is a fully accredited institution that has been dedicated to providing a diverse population of students in the New York metropolitan area with an affordable education rooted in the liberal arts tradition since 1916. Independent and coeducational, the College provides a strong academic and value-oriented education at the undergraduate and graduate levels. For over a decade, the College has consistently ranked among America's best colleges by *U.S. News & World Report* and *Forbes*.

St. Joseph's College, New York

Applying

All applicants must possess a baccalaureate degree from an accredited institution of higher education with an undergraduate grade point average of 3.0. In addition, applicants typically will be required to be employed in a full-time position and will have substantial work experience involving supervision, program development, specialized training, considerable responsibility and/or independent judgment.

Correspondence and Information

Brooklyn Campus:
St. Joseph's College
245 Clinton Avenue
Brooklyn, New York 11205
Phone: 718-940-5800
E-mail: msmbab@sjcny.edu
Web site:
http://www.sjcny.edu/Academics/MS-in-Human-Services-FAQ/628

Long Island Campus:
St. Joseph's College
155 West Roe Boulevard
Patchogue, New York 11772
Phone: 631-687-4501
E-mail: msmbas@sjcny.edu

THE FACULTY

Carolyn Gallogly, Ph.D., Assistant Professor; Chair, Community Health and Human Services. Long Island Campus: O'Connor Hall, N320A; phone: 631-687-1242; e-mail: cgallogly@sjcny.edu.

K. Candis Best, J.D., M.B.A., Ph.D., Assistant Professor; Associate Chair, Community Health and Human Services. Brooklyn Campus: Lorenzo Hall, third floor; phone: 718-940-5849; e-mail: cbest@sjcny.edu.

Jo Anne Collins, Ph.D., Lecturer. Long Island Campus; e-mail: jcollins@sjcny.edu.

Crystal Harris, Lecturer; Long Island Campus; e-mail: charris@sjcny.edu.

Valerie Cartright, J.D., Lecturer. Long Island Campus; e-mail: vcartright@sjcny.edu.

Michael Chiappone, Lecturer and Adviser. Long Island Campus; e-mail: mchiappone@sjcny.edu.

Joseph Owens, Preceptor. Long Island Campus; e-mail: jowens@sjcny.edu.

Paule T. Pachter, ACSW, LMSW, Instructor. Long Island Campus; e-mail: ppachter@sjcny.edu.

Peggy Regensburg, Ph.D., Preceptor. Long Island Campus; e-mail: pregensburg@sjcny.edu.

UNIVERSITY AT BUFFALO, THE STATE UNIVERSITY OF NEW YORK

School of Social Work

Programs of Study

The University at Buffalo (UB) School of Social Work offers doctoral and master's degree programs that provide value, quality, and dynamic programming at an affordable price.

Ph.D. in Social Welfare: UB's doctoral degree program focuses on interdisciplinary approaches to critical social problems, with the opportunity to develop an individualized course of study that utilizes the extensive resources of the University to meet the student's specific needs and interests.

Master of Social Work (M.S.W.): UB's highly ranked M.S.W. program integrates a trauma-informed and human rights perspective as a transformational lens to focus social work policy and practice. Students create a flexible and individualized advanced-year curriculum, building on the core of their foundation-year courses. The entire curriculum is rooted in an evidence-based practice approach to social work. For this reason, all students learn the critical skills to evaluate their practice in their foundation year.

Students can complete their M.S.W. degree in two years (full-time), or three years (part-time). Those accepted into the advanced standing M.S.W. program (see admission requirements) can complete their M.S.W. degree in one year (full-time), or one-and-a-half years (part-time).

Within the M.S.W. degree program, students complete field placements to help make the transition from student to social work professional. Traditional M.S.W. program students complete two field placements and advanced standing M.S.W. students complete one.

Dual-Degree Options: Joint- and dual-degrees are available in collaboration with the College of Arts and Sciences (B.A./M.S.W.), Law School (J.D./M.S.W.), School of Management (M.B.A./M.S.W.), and the School of Public Health and Health Professions (M.P.H./M.S.W.).

Research Facilities

The Buffalo Center for Social Research is the heart and hub of the knowledge-creation activities for the entire School, resulting in an exciting synergy of people and ideas. Whether it is a team of faculty members and students writing a grant, students analyzing data, interviewers conducting focus groups, student-led teams evaluating agency practice, or ideas being explored in a research seminar, all the work conducted has a common goal: research that makes a real-world impact.

Financial Aid

As a public institution, UB offers a world-class education at an affordable price. There are many sources of funding available to students through federal (FAFSA) and state programs. The University of Buffalo is an approved school under the Canada Student Loans Plan through the Ontario Student Assistance Program. Tuition scholarships, research stipends, and other means of financial support may be available to qualified students. The School of Social Work offers merit-based Dean's Admissions Awards to highly qualified students. A list of these programs, as well as UB scholarship and fellowship opportunities, is available at www.socialwork.buffalo.edu/scholarships.

Cost of Study

Tuition for New York State residents is one third to one quarter the tuition of most private schools; and less than half that of most private schools for non–New York State residents. For the 2012–13 academic year, full-time M.S.W. tuition is $5000 per semester for a New York State resident and $8340 per semester for a non–New York State resident.

Living and Housing Costs

Both on-campus and off-campus housing are available for graduate students. Moderately priced housing is readily available around the Amherst suburban campus. Starting in fall 2012, UB will offer gender-neutral housing in some of its dorms and apartments. More details regarding housing are available online at www.grad.buffalo.edu/life/housing.

Student Group

Rho Kappa is UB School of Social Work's chapter of the Phi Alpha Honor Society for Social Work. Phi Alpha fosters high standards of education for social workers and invites those who have attained excellence in scholarship and achievement in social work to become members. The School of Social Work also has its own Graduate School Association, an active subgroup of the University at Buffalo Graduate Student Association.

Student Outcomes

Over the last three years the average graduation rate for M.S.W. students was 89 percent. The M.S.W. degree automatically entitles graduates to sit for the Licensed Master Social Worker (LMSW) exam. UB alumni who take the New York State LMSW exam have an 89 percent first-time pass rate, and a 94 percent first-time pass rate on the Licensed Clinical Social Worker (LCSW) exam; both of which are above the New York State and national average.

Location

Buffalo is the second-largest city in New York State; it prides itself on being a big city that feels like a small town. The area is a great place to study, work, and live, with world-class art galleries and museums, a comprehensive citywide system of parks and green space, major- and minor-league sports teams, and a wide array of cultural and recreational elements.

University at Buffalo, the State University of New York

The University and The School

UB is a premier, research-intensive public university and a member of the Association of American Universities. As the largest, most comprehensive institution in the sixty-four-campus State University of New York system, UB's research, creative activity, and people seek to positively impact the world. The University at Buffalo School of Social Work is a highly ranked, CSWE-accredited graduate school offering M.S.W. and Ph.D. degrees, as well as continuing professional education.

Applying

For details on the application process for all programs, prospective students should visit www.socialwork.buffalo.edu/admissions.asp.

Correspondence and Information

School of Social Work
685 Baldy Hall
University at Buffalo, the State University of New York
Buffalo, New York 14260-1200
Phone: 716-645-3381 or 1-800-386-6129
Fax: 716-645-3456
E-mail: sw-info@buffalo.edu
Web site: http://www.socialwork.buffalo.edu

THE FACULTY AND THEIR RESEARCH

The faculty consists of a diverse community of scholars, teachers, and activists for change, with interests that span the globe from India to Canada, Pakistan to Korea, and the United States to the United Kingdom. Faculty members share a common passion for community-University partnerships in research and practice.

Faculty areas of interest include:

- Aging
- Children and youth
- Diversity and multicultural issues
- Domestic violence
- Gender and gender issues
- Mental health
- Poverty
- Substance abuse
- Trauma

Living Proof is a podcast series of the University at Buffalo School of Social Work. The purpose of the series is to engage practitioners and researchers in lifelong learning, and to promote research to practice and practice to research. *Living Proof* features conversations with prominent social work professionals, interviews with cutting-edge researchers, and information on emerging trends and best practices in the field of social work. *Living Proof* is available online at http://www.socialwork.buffalo.edu/podcast/index.asp.

YESHIVA UNIVERSITY

Wurzweiler School of Social Work

Programs of Study

The Wurzweiler School of Social Work at Yeshiva University (YU) offers the Master of Social Work (M.S.W.) degree, a Ph.D. degree in social welfare, and Certificates in Jewish Communal Service, Child Welfare Practice, Gerontology, and Social Work Practice with the Military. In fall 2012, the School added a certificate in social work practice with the military. Wurzweiler also offers a joint M.S.W./M.Div. degree with the Yale Divinity School and a joint M.S.W./J.D. program with the Benjamin N. Cardozo School of Law of Yeshiva University.

Wurzweiler's programs are unique as a result of the School's historic emphasis on professional values and ethics, diversity and cultural competence, and religious beliefs and spirituality. Wurzweiler's curriculum is methods-based and offers concentrations in clinical casework, social group work, and community practice.

The M.S.W. program prepares students for advanced social work practice in all fields of practice in the New York City urban environment and internationally. The Ph.D. program, designed for working professionals, furthers their education and quest for scholarly and creative leadership in a wide variety of fields.

Wurzweiler offers studies on two New York campuses, Washington Heights and Midtown Manhattan, and flexible options for all students. These include day, evening, and Sunday classes; fast-track (sixteen months) and extended (three-plus years) programs; and summer block (three summers, two placements) options. In Fall 2012, Wurzweiler inaugurated a new M.S.W./Ph.D. option. At the end of two years of full-time study, students will have earned an M.S.W. degree and completed one full-year of study in the Ph.D. program.

Yeshiva University is accredited by the Commission on Higher Education of the Middle States Association of Colleges and Schools. The Wurzweiler School of Social Work is accredited through 2017 for the M.S.W. program in social work by the Commission on Accreditation of the Council on Social Work Education.

Research Facilities

Yeshiva University's online catalogs describe collections of more than 1 million items in the University's libraries. The YULIS catalog of library holdings at the Wilf and Beren campuses features the option to search and display in Hebrew. The Cardozo and Einstein catalogs describe the University's legal and medical collections. A searchable database of the collection guides users to the archives' rich and diverse holdings of organizational records and personal papers relating to modern Jewish history and culture in the United States and abroad.

Financial Aid

Seventy-eight percent of Wurzweiler students receive some form of financial assistance. Most students find it necessary to finance their education through a combination of sources. Wurzweiler School of Social Work and the University's Office of Student Finance work closely with prospective and current students to access the financial resources to help fund their graduate and postgraduate school education. These include federal student loans, private loans, institutional scholarships, and external scholarships.

Wurzweiler offers need-based and merit scholarships, which are administered by the Wurzweiler Dean's Office. Merit scholarships are awarded to incoming students who demonstrate academic excellence in their undergraduate studies and a strong commitment to the field of social work through their work and/or volunteer experiences. No additional applications are required for these scholarships, and students are notified at the time of acceptance to Wurzweiler. Need-based scholarships are awarded based on a student's demonstration of financial need as determined by the results of the FAFSA filing. Every U.S. citizen or permanent resident seeking financial aid is urged to complete the FAFSA (school code: 002903; campus code: 00).

Cost of Study

Tuition is $990 per credit for the 60-credit M.S.W. program. The tuition is $1165 per credit for the 60-credit Ph.D. degree. More information, including the latest tuition and fee amounts, is available online at http://www.yu.edu/osf/ or from the Yeshiva University's Office of Student Finance (phone: 212-960-5399).

Living and Housing Costs

The School does not provide graduate student housing; however, there are numerous student housing options available in the greater metropolitan area.

Student Group

Yeshiva University has more than 6,400 undergraduate and graduate students at its four New York City campuses. The Wurzweiler School of Social Work currently enrolls 300 M.S.W. and 50 Ph.D. students.

Students at Wurzweiler come from over sixty locations around the world, including Israel, Canada, France, Japan, South America, Eastern Europe, and Africa. The student body includes individuals from every religious and ethnic group. Many are working people who have to balance the demands of school, work, and family and find that Wurzweiler's individual attention and flexible programming help them succeed in their educational pursuits.

Student Outcomes

Since its founding in 1957, the Wurzweiler School of Social Work awarded more than 7,300 master's degrees and 175 doctoral degrees. Its alumni include therapists, managers, administrators, researchers, professors, college deans, and legislators. They are employed in every sector of social services, from neighborhood agencies to the federal government. The School offers a prep class for the LMSW licensing exam and has a dedicated Career Development Office.

Location

Wurzweiler School of Social Work is located in New York City as part of Yeshiva University's Wilf Campus in Washington Heights and on the Beren Campus in Midtown Manhattan. The School offers field internships throughout the United States, including select international placements. A new partnership with the American Jewish World Service is slated to expand placement opportunities in Africa, India, and Thailand. Field placement agencies are selected for their diversity, quality of service to the community, opportunities for learning, expertise of supervisors, and eagerness to collaborate with the School to create a challenging educational venture for its students.

The University

For more than a century, students at Yeshiva University have received a personal, small-college experience while benefitting from the academic rigor of a top-ranked research university. Since its inception YU has been dedicated to melding the ancient traditions of Jewish law and life with the heritage of Western civilization. YU has four New York City campuses: the Wilf Campus, Israel Henry Beren Campus, Brookdale Center, and Jack and Pearl Resnick Campus. The University's graduate and affiliate schools include Albert Einstein College of Medicine, Benjamin N. Cardozo School of Law, Wurzweiler School of Social Work, Ferkauf Gradaute School of Psychology, Azrieli Graduate School of Jewish Education and Administration, Bernard Revel Graduate School of Jewish Studies, and Rabbi Isaac Elchanan Theological Seminary.

Applying

For application information and admissions details prospective students should visit http://yu.edu/wurzweiler.

Correspondence and Information

For the M.S.W. programs:
Wurzweiler School of Social Work
Yeshiva University
2495 Amsterdam Avenue
New York, New York 10033
United States
Phone: 212-960-0810
Web site: http://yu.edu/wurzweiler

For the Ph.D. program:
Wurzweiler School of Social Work
Yeshiva University
2495 Amsterdam Avenue
New York, New York 10033
United States
Phone: 212-960-0840
Web site: http://yu.edu/wurzweiler

THE FACULTY AND THEIR RESEARCH

The Wurzweiler School of Social Work faculty includes experienced social work practitioners and researchers with doctoral degrees who are nationally and internationally respected scholars and leaders. Faculty members serve on national commissions and publish regularly in top professional journals. Eight faculty members have earned Fulbright Specialist Awards in the past five years.

Wurzweiler faculty members advise, advocate, lead community organizations, and present research at international conferences. But most importantly, they are part of the School for their students. More information about the faculty is available online at http://www.yu.edu/wurzweiler/faculty/.

The student body of Wurzweiler is widely diverse in nationality, gender, race, and religion.

The small class size and specialized advising system at Wurzweiler creates an intimate and active classroom experience.

APPENDIXES

Institutional Changes Since the 2012 Edition

Following is an alphabetical listing of institutions that have recently closed, merged with other institutions, or changed their names or status. In the case of a name change, the former name appears first, followed by the new name.

Adams State College (Alamosa, CO): name changed to Adams State University

Andrew Jackson University (Birmingham, AL): name changed to New Charter University

The Art Institute of Atlanta (Atlanta, GA): no longer offers graduate degrees

The Art Institute of Boston at Lesley University (Boston, MA): merged into a single entry for Lesley University (Cambridge, MA)

The Art Institute of California–San Francisco (San Francisco, CA): name changed to The Art Institute of California, a college of Argosy University, San Francisco

Atlantic Union College (South Lancaster, MA): currently not accepting applications

Babel University School of Translation (Honolulu, HI): name changed to Babel University Professional School of Translation

Baldwin-Wallace College (Berea, OH): name changed to Baldwin Wallace University

Baltimore International College (Baltimore, MD): name changed to Stratford University

Bethany University (Scotts Valley, CA): closed

Bethesda Christian University (Anaheim, CA): name changed to Bethesda University of California

Broadview University (West Jordan, UT): name changed to Broadview University–West Jordan

City of Hope National Medical Center/Beckman Research Institute (Duarte, CA): name changed to Irell & Manella Graduate School of Biological Sciences

City University of New York School of Law at Queens College (Flushing, NY): name changed to City University of New York School of Law

Cleveland Chiropractic College–Los Angeles Campus (Los Angeles, CA): closed

College of Notre Dame of Maryland (Baltimore, MD): name changed to Notre Dame of Maryland University

College of the Humanities and Sciences, Harrison Middleton University (Tempe, AZ): name changed to Harrison Middleton University

Colorado Technical University Denver (Greenwood Village, CO): name changed to Colorado Technical University Denver South

Concordia University (Ann Arbor, MI): name changed to Concordia University Ann Arbor

Cornell University, Joan and Sanford I. Weill Medical College and Graduate School of Medical Sciences (New York, NY): name changed to Weill Cornell Medical College

Daniel Webster College–Portsmouth Campus (Portsmouth, NH): closed

Edward Via Virginia College of Osteopathic Medicine (Blacksburg, VA): name changed to Edward Via College of Osteopahtic Medicine–Virginia Campus

Evangelical Theological Seminary (Myerstown, PA): name changed to Evangelical Seminary

Everest University (Lakeland, FL): no longer offers graduate degrees

Faith Evangelical Lutheran Seminary (Tacoma, WA): name changed to Faith Evangelical College & Seminary

Franklin Pierce Law Center (Concord, NH): name changed to University of New Hampshire School of Law

Frontier School of Midwifery and Family Nursing (Hyden, KY): name changed to Frontier Nursing University

Globe University (Woodbury, MN): name changed to Globe University–Woodbury

Harding University Graduate School of Religion (Memphis, TN): name changed to Harding School of Theology

Kol Yaakov Torah Center (Monsey, NY): closed

Long Island University at Riverhead (Riverhead, NY): name changed to Long Island University–Riverhead

Long Island University, Brentwood Campus (Brentwood, NY): name changed to Long Island University–Brentwood Campus

Long Island University, Brooklyn Campus (Brooklyn, NY): name changed to Long Island University–Brooklyn Campus

Long Island University, C.W. Post Campus (Brookville, NY): name changed to Long Island University–C. W. Post Campus

Long Island University, Rockland Graduate Campus (Orangeburg, NY): name changed to Long Island University–Hudson at Rockland

Long Island University, Westchester Graduate Campus (Purchase, NY): name changed to Long Island University–Hudson at Westchester

Lourdes College (Sylvania, OH): name changed to Lourdes University

Lutheran Theological Seminary (Saskatoon, SK, Canada): name changed to Lutheran Theological Seminary Saskatoon

Mars Hill Graduate School (Seattle, WA): name changed to The Seattle School of Theology and Psychology

Mesa State College (Grand Junction, CO): name changed to Colorado Mesa University

Michigan Theological Seminary (Plymouth, MI): name changed to Moody Theological Seminary–Michigan

Midwest University (Wentzville, MO): no longer accredited by agency recognized by USDE or CHEA

National Defense Intelligence College (Washington, DC): name changed to National Intelligence University

National-Louis University (Chicago, IL): name changed to National Louis University

National Theatre Conservatory (Denver, CO): closed

The New School: A University (New York, NY): name changed to The New School

Northeastern Ohio Universities Colleges of Medicine and Pharmacy (Rootstown, OH): name changed to Northeastern Ohio Medical University

Northwest Baptist Seminary (Tacoma, WA): name changed to Corban University School of Ministry

Northwood University (Midland, MI): name changed to Northwood University, Michigan Campus

OGI School of Science & Engineering at Oregon Health & Science University (Beaverton, OR): merged into a single entry for Oregon Health & Science University (Portland, OR) by request from the institution

Parker College of Chiropractic (Dallas, TX): name changed to Parker University

Philadelphia Biblical University (Langhorne, PA): name changed to Cairn University

Piedmont Baptist College and Graduate School (Winston-Salem, NC): name changed to Piedmont International University

Pikeville College (Pikeville, KY): name changed to University of Pikeville

Polytechnic Institute of NYU (Brooklyn, NY): name changed to Polytechnic Institute of New York University

Ponce School of Medicine (Ponce, PR): name changed to Ponce School of Medicine & Health Sciences

Rivier College (Nashua, NH): name changed to Rivier University

Saint Bernard's School of Theology and Ministry (Rochester, NY): name changed to St. Bernard's School of Theology and Ministry

St. Charles Borromeo Seminary, Overbrook (Wynnewood, PA): name changed to Saint Charles Borromeo Seminary, Overbrook

Saint Francis Seminary (St. Francis, WI): name changed to Saint Francis de Sales Seminary

Saint Joseph College (West Hartford, CT): name changed to University of Saint Joseph

Saint Vincent de Paul Regional Seminary (Boynton Beach, FL): name changed to St. Vincent de Paul Regional Seminary

Schiller International University (London, United Kingdom): closed

Silver Lake College (Manitowoc, WI): name changed to Silver Lake College of the Holy Family

Trinity (Washington) University (Washington, DC): name changed to Trinity Washington University

TUI University (Cypress, CA): name changed to Trident University International

University of Phoenix (Phoenix, AZ): name changed to University of Phoenix–Online Campus

University of Phoenix–Phoenix Campus (Phoenix, AZ): name changed to University of Phoenix–Phoenix Main Campus

The University of Tennessee–Oak Ridge National Laboratory Graduate School of Genome Science and Technology (Oak Ridge, TN): name changed to The University of Tennessee–Oak Ridge National Laboratory

The University of Texas Southwestern Medical Center at Dallas (Dallas, TX): name changed to The University of Texas Southwestern Medical Center

University of Trinity College (Toronto, ON, Canada): name changed to Trinity College

Washington Theological Union (Washington, DC): closed

West Virginia University Institute of Technology (Montgomery, WV): no longer offers graduate degrees.

Abbreviations Used in the Guides

The following list includes abbreviations of degree names used in the profiles in the 2013 edition of the guides. Because some degrees (e.g., Doctor of Education) can be abbreviated in more than one way (e.g., D.Ed. or Ed.D.), and because the abbreviations used in the guides reflect the preferences of the individual colleges and universities, the list may include two or more abbreviations for a single degree.

DEGREES

A Mus D — Doctor of Musical Arts
AC — Advanced Certificate
AD — Artist's Diploma
 — Doctor of Arts
ADP — Artist's Diploma
Adv C — Advanced Certificate
Adv M — Advanced Master
AGC — Advanced Graduate Certificate
AGSC — Advanced Graduate Specialist Certificate
ALM — Master of Liberal Arts
AM — Master of Arts
AMBA — Accelerated Master of Business Administration
 — Aviation Master of Business Administration
AMRS — Master of Arts in Religious Studies
APC — Advanced Professional Certificate
APMPH — Advanced Professional Master of Public Health
App Sc — Applied Scientist
App Sc D — Doctor of Applied Science
AstE — Astronautical Engineer
Au D — Doctor of Audiology
B Th — Bachelor of Theology
CAES — Certificate of Advanced Educational Specialization
CAGS — Certificate of Advanced Graduate Studies
CAL — Certificate in Applied Linguistics
CALS — Certificate of Advanced Liberal Studies
CAMS — Certificate of Advanced Management Studies
CAPS — Certificate of Advanced Professional Studies
CAS — Certificate of Advanced Studies
CASPA — Certificate of Advanced Study in Public Administration
CASR — Certificate in Advanced Social Research
CATS — Certificate of Achievement in Theological Studies
CBHS — Certificate in Basic Health Sciences
CBS — Graduate Certificate in Biblical Studies
CCJA — Certificate in Criminal Justice Administration
CCSA — Certificate in Catholic School Administration
CCTS — Certificate in Clinical and Translational Science
CE — Civil Engineer
CEM — Certificate of Environmental Management
CET — Certificate in Educational Technologies
CGS — Certificate of Graduate Studies
Ch E — Chemical Engineer
CM — Certificate in Management
CMH — Certificate in Medical Humanities
CMM — Master of Church Ministries
CMS — Certificate in Ministerial Studies
CNM — Certificate in Nonprofit Management
CPASF — Certificate Program for Advanced Study in Finance
CPC — Certificate in Professional Counseling
 — Certificate in Publication and Communication
CPH — Certificate in Public Health
CPM — Certificate in Public Management
CPS — Certificate of Professional Studies
CScD — Doctor of Clinical Science
CSD — Certificate in Spiritual Direction
CSS — Certificate of Special Studies
CTS — Certificate of Theological Studies
CURP — Certificate in Urban and Regional Planning
D Admin — Doctor of Administration
D Arch — Doctor of Architecture
D Be — Doctor in Bioethics
D Com — Doctor of Commerce
D Couns — Doctor of Counseling
D Div — Doctor of Divinity
D Ed — Doctor of Education
D Ed Min — Doctor of Educational Ministry
D Eng — Doctor of Engineering
D Engr — Doctor of Engineering
D Ent — Doctor of Enterprise
D Env — Doctor of Environment
D Law — Doctor of Law
D Litt — Doctor of Letters
D Med Sc — Doctor of Medical Science
D Min — Doctor of Ministry
D Miss — Doctor of Missiology
D Mus — Doctor of Music
D Mus A — Doctor of Musical Arts
D Phil — Doctor of Philosophy
D Prof — Doctor of Professional Studies
D Ps — Doctor of Psychology
D Sc — Doctor of Science
D Sc D — Doctor of Science in Dentistry
D Sc IS — Doctor of Science in Information Systems
D Sc PA — Doctor of Science in Physician Assistant Studies
D Th — Doctor of Theology
D Th P — Doctor of Practical Theology
DA — Doctor of Accounting
 — Doctor of Arts
DA Ed — Doctor of Arts in Education
DAH — Doctor of Arts in Humanities
DAOM — Doctorate in Acupuncture and Oriental Medicine
DAT — Doctorate of Athletic Training
DATH — Doctorate of Art Therapy
DBA — Doctor of Business Administration
DBH — Doctor of Behavioral Health
DBL — Doctor of Business Leadership
DBS — Doctor of Buddhist Studies
DC — Doctor of Chiropractic
DCC — Doctor of Computer Science
DCD — Doctor of Communications Design
DCL — Doctor of Civil Law
 — Doctor of Comparative Law
DCM — Doctor of Church Music
DCN — Doctor of Clinical Nutrition
DCS — Doctor of Computer Science
DDN — Dipllf.me du Droit Notarial
DDS — Doctor of Dental Surgery
DE — Doctor of Education
 — Doctor of Engineering
DED — Doctor of Economic Development
DEIT — Doctor of Educational Innovation and Technology
DEL — Doctor of Executive Leadership
DEM — Doctor of Educational Ministry
DEPD — Dipllf.me lfEtudes Splfecialislfees
DES — Doctor of Engineering Science
DESS — Dipllf.me lfEtudes Suplferieures Splfecialislfees

DFA	Doctor of Fine Arts
DGP	Diploma in Graduate and Professional Studies
DH Ed	Doctor of Health Education
DH Sc	Doctor of Health Sciences
DHA	Doctor of Health Administration
DHCE	Doctor of Health Care Ethics
DHL	Doctor of Hebrew Letters
	Doctor of Hebrew Literature
DHS	Doctor of Health Science
DHSc	Doctor of Health Science
Dip CS	Diploma in Christian Studies
DIT	Doctor of Industrial Technology
DJ Ed	Doctor of Jewish Education
DJS	Doctor of Jewish Studies
DLS	Doctor of Liberal Studies
DM	Doctor of Management
	Doctor of Music
DMA	Doctor of Musical Arts
DMD	Doctor of Dental Medicine
DME	Doctor of Music Education
DMEd	Doctor of Music Education
DMFT	Doctor of Marital and Family Therapy
DMH	Doctor of Medical Humanities
DML	Doctor of Modern Languages
DMP	Doctorate in Medical Physics
DMPNA	Doctor of Management Practice in Nurse Anesthesia
DN Sc	Doctor of Nursing Science
DNAP	Doctor of Nurse Anesthesia Practice
DNP	Doctor of Nursing Practice
DNP-A	Doctor of Nursing PracticeAnesthesia
DNS	Doctor of Nursing Science
DO	Doctor of Osteopathy
DOT	Doctor of Occupational Therapy
DPA	Doctor of Public Administration
DPC	Doctor of Pastoral Counseling
DPDS	Doctor of Planning and Development Studies
DPH	Doctor of Public Health
DPM	Doctor of Plant Medicine
	Doctor of Podiatric Medicine
DPPD	Doctor of Policy, Planning, and Development
DPS	Doctor of Professional Studies
DPT	Doctor of Physical Therapy
DPTSc	Doctor of Physical Therapy Science
Dr DES	Doctor of Design
Dr NP	Doctor of Nursing Practice
Dr PH	Doctor of Public Health
Dr Sc PT	Doctor of Science in Physical Therapy
DRSc	Doctor of Regulatory Science
DS	Doctor of Science
DS Sc	Doctor of Social Science
DSJS	Doctor of Science in Jewish Studies
DSL	Doctor of Strategic Leadership
DSW	Doctor of Social Work
DTL	Doctor of Talmudic Law
DV Sc	Doctor of Veterinary Science
DVM	Doctor of Veterinary Medicine
DWS	Doctor of Worship Studies
EAA	Engineer in Aeronautics and Astronautics
EASPh D	Engineering and Applied Science Doctor of Philosophy
ECS	Engineer in Computer Science
Ed D	Doctor of Education
Ed DCT	Doctor of Education in College Teaching
Ed L D	Doctor of Education Leadership
Ed M	Master of Education
Ed S	Specialist in Education
Ed Sp	Specialist in Education
EDB	Executive Doctorate in Business
EDM	Executive Doctorate in Management
EE	Electrical Engineer
EJD	Executive Juris Doctor
EMBA	Executive Master of Business Administration
EMFA	Executive Master of Forensic Accounting
EMHA	Executive Master of Health Administration
EMIB	Executive Master of International Business
EML	Executive Master of Leadership
EMPA	Executive Master of Public Administration
EMS	Executive Master of Science
EMTM	Executive Master of Technology Management
Eng	Engineer
Eng Sc D	Doctor of Engineering Science
Engr	Engineer
Ex Doc	Executive Doctor of Pharmacy
Exec Ed D	Executive Doctor of Education
Exec MBA	Executive Master of Business Administration
Exec MPA	Executive Master of Public Administration
Exec MPH	Executive Master of Public Health
Exec MS	Executive Master of Science
G Dip	Graduate Diploma
GBC	Graduate Business Certificate
GCE	Graduate Certificate in Education
GDM	Graduate Diploma in Management
GDPA	Graduate Diploma in Public Administration
GDRE	Graduate Diploma in Religious Education
GEMBA	Global Executive Master of Business Administration
GEMPA	Gulf Executive Master of Public Administration
GM Acc	Graduate Master of Accountancy
GMBA	Global Master of Business Administration
GP LL M	Global Professional Master of Laws
GPD	Graduate Performance Diploma
GSS	Graduate Special Certificate for Students in Special Situations
IEMBA	International Executive Master of Business Administration
IM Acc	Integrated Master of Accountancy
IMA	Interdisciplinary Master of Arts
IMBA	International Master of Business Administration
IMES	International Master's in Environmental Studies
Ingeniero	Engineer
JCD	Doctor of Canon Law
JCL	Licentiate in Canon Law
JD	Juris Doctor
JSD	Doctor of Juridical Science
	Doctor of Jurisprudence
	Doctor of the Science of Law
JSM	Master of Science of Law
L Th	Licenciate in Theology
LL B	Bachelor of Laws
LL CM	Master of Laws in Comparative Law
LL D	Doctor of Laws
LL M	Master of Laws
LL M in Tax	Master of Laws in Taxation
LL M CL	Master of Laws (Common Law)
M Ac	Master of Accountancy
	Master of Accounting
	Master of Acupuncture
M Ac OM	Master of Acupuncture and Oriental Medicine
M Acc	Master of Accountancy
	Master of Accounting
M Acct	Master of Accountancy
	Master of Accounting
M Accy	Master of Accountancy
M Actg	Master of Accounting
M Acy	Master of Accountancy

M Ad	Master of Administration
M Ad Ed	Master of Adult Education
M Adm	Master of Administration
M Adm Mgt	Master of Administrative Management
M Admin	Master of Administration
M ADU	Master of Architectural Design and Urbanism
M Adv	Master of Advertising
M Aero E	Master of Aerospace Engineering
M AEST	Master of Applied Environmental Science and Technology
M Ag	Master of Agriculture
M Ag Ed	Master of Agricultural Education
M Agr	Master of Agriculture
M Anesth Ed	Master of Anesthesiology Education
M App Comp Sc	Master of Applied Computer Science
M App St	Master of Applied Statistics
M Appl Stat	Master of Applied Statistics
M Aq	Master of Aquaculture
M Arc	Master of Architecture
M Arch	Master of Architecture
M Arch I	Master of Architecture I
M Arch II	Master of Architecture II
M Arch E	Master of Architectural Engineering
M Arch H	Master of Architectural History
M Bioethics	Master in Bioethics
M Biomath	Master of Biomathematics
M Ch	Master of Chemistry
M Ch E	Master of Chemical Engineering
M Chem	Master of Chemistry
M Cl D	Master of Clinical Dentistry
M Cl Sc	Master of Clinical Science
M Comp	Master of Computing
M Comp Sc	Master of Computer Science
M Coun	Master of Counseling
M Dent	Master of Dentistry
M Dent Sc	Master of Dental Sciences
M Des	Master of Design
M Des S	Master of Design Studies
M Div	Master of Divinity
M Ec	Master of Economics
M Econ	Master of Economics
M Ed	Master of Education
M Ed T	Master of Education in Teaching
M En	Master of Engineering
	Master of Environmental Science
M En S	Master of Environmental Sciences
M Eng	Master of Engineering
M Eng Mgt	Master of Engineering Management
M Engr	Master of Engineering
M Ent	Master of Enterprise
M Env	Master of Environment
M Env Des	Master of Environmental Design
M Env E	Master of Environmental Engineering
M Env Sc	Master of Environmental Science
M Fin	Master of Finance
M Geo E	Master of Geological Engineering
M Geoenv E	Master of Geoenvironmental Engineering
M Geog	Master of Geography
M Hum	Master of Humanities
M Hum Svcs	Master of Human Services
M IBD	Master of Integrated Building Delivery
M IDST	Master's in Interdisciplinary Studies
M Kin	Master of Kinesiology
M Land Arch	Master of Landscape Architecture
M Litt	Master of Letters
M Mat SE	Master of Material Science and Engineering
M Math	Master of Mathematics
M Mech E	Master of Mechanical Engineering
M Med Sc	Master of Medical Science
M Mgmt	Master of Management
M Mgt	Master of Management
M Min	Master of Ministries
M Mtl E	Master of Materials Engineering
M Mu	Master of Music
M Mus	Master of Music
M Mus Ed	Master of Music Education
M Music	Master of Music
M Nat Sci	Master of Natural Science
M Oc E	Master of Oceanographic Engineering
M Pet E	Master of Petroleum Engineering
M Pharm	Master of Pharmacy
M Phil	Master of Philosophy
M Phil F	Master of Philosophical Foundations
M Pl	Master of Planning
M Plan	Master of Planning
M Pol	Master of Political Science
M Pr Met	Master of Professional Meteorology
M Prob S	Master of Probability and Statistics
M Psych	Master of Psychology
M Pub	Master of Publishing
M Rel	Master of Religion
M Sc	Master of Science
M Sc A	Master of Science (Applied)
M Sc AC	Master of Science in Applied Computing
M Sc AHN	Master of Science in Applied Human Nutrition
M Sc BMC	Master of Science in Biomedical Communications
M Sc CS	Master of Science in Computer Science
M Sc E	Master of Science in Engineering
M Sc Eng	Master of Science in Engineering
M Sc Engr	Master of Science in Engineering
M Sc F	Master of Science in Forestry
M Sc FE	Master of Science in Forest Engineering
M Sc Geogr	Master of Science in Geography
M Sc N	Master of Science in Nursing
M Sc OT	Master of Science in Occupational Therapy
M Sc P	Master of Science in Planning
M Sc Pl	Master of Science in Planning
M Sc PT	Master of Science in Physical Therapy
M Sc T	Master of Science in Teaching
M SEM	Master of Sustainable Environmental Management
M Serv Soc	Master of Social Service
M Soc	Master of Sociology
M Sp Ed	Master of Special Education
M Stat	Master of Statistics
M Sys E	Master of Systems Engineering
M Sys Sc	Master of Systems Science
M Tax	Master of Taxation
M Tech	Master of Technology
M Th	Master of Theology
M Tox	Master of Toxicology
M Trans E	Master of Transportation Engineering
M Urb	Master of Urban Planning
M Vet Sc	Master of Veterinary Science
MA	Master of Accounting
	Master of Administration
	Master of Arts
MA Comm	Master of Arts in Communication
MA Ed	Master of Arts in Education
MA Ed Ad	Master of Arts in Educational Administration
MA Ext	Master of Agricultural Extension
MA Islamic	Master of Arts in Islamic Studies
MA Min	Master of Arts in Ministry
MA Miss	Master of Arts in Missiology
MA Past St	Master of Arts in Pastoral Studies
MA Ph	Master of Arts in Philosophy

MA Psych	Master of Arts in Psychology
MA Sc	Master of Applied Science
MA Sp	Master of Arts (Spirituality)
MA Th	Master of Arts in Theology
MA-R	Master of Arts (Research)
MAA	Master of Administrative Arts
	Master of Applied Anthropology
	Master of Applied Arts
	Master of Arts in Administration
MAAA	Master of Arts in Arts Administration
MAAAP	Master of Arts Administration and Policy
MAAE	Master of Arts in Art Education
MAAT	Master of Arts in Applied Theology
	Master of Arts in Art Therapy
MAB	Master of Agribusiness
MABC	Master of Arts in Biblical Counseling
	Master of Arts in Business Communication
MABE	Master of Arts in Bible Exposition
MABL	Master of Arts in Biblical Languages
MABM	Master of Agribusiness Management
MABMH	bioethics and medical humanities
MABS	Master of Arts in Biblical Studies
MABT	Master of Arts in Bible Teaching
MAC	Master of Accountancy
	Master of Accounting
	Master of Arts in Communication
	Master of Arts in Counseling
MACC	Master of Arts in Christian Counseling
	Master of Arts in Clinical Counseling
MACCM	Master of Arts in Church and Community Ministry
MACCT	Master of Accounting
MACD	Master of Arts in Christian Doctrine
MACE	Master of Arts in Christian Education
MACFM	Master of Arts in Children's and Family Ministry
MACH	Master of Arts in Church History
MACI	Master of Arts in Curriculum and Instruction
MACIS	Master of Accounting and Information Systems
MACJ	Master of Arts in Criminal Justice
MACL	Master of Arts in Christian Leadership
MACM	Master of Arts in Christian Ministries
	Master of Arts in Christian Ministry
	Master of Arts in Church Music
	Master of Arts in Counseling Ministries
MACN	Master of Arts in Counseling
MACO	Master of Arts in Counseling
MAcOM	Master of Acupuncture and Oriental Medicine
MACP	Master of Arts in Christian Practice
	Master of Arts in Counseling Psychology
MACS	Master of Applied Computer Science
	Master of Arts in Catholic Studies
	Master of Arts in Christian Studies
MACSE	Master of Arts in Christian School Education
MACT	Master of Arts in Christian Thought
	Master of Arts in Communications and Technology
MAD	Master in Educational Institution Administration
	Master of Art and Design
MAD-Crit	Master of Arts in Design Criticism
MADR	Master of Arts in Dispute Resolution
MADS	Master of Animal and Dairy Science
	Master of Applied Disability Studies
MAE	Master of Aerospace Engineering
	Master of Agricultural Economics
	Master of Agricultural Education
	Master of Architectural Engineering
	Master of Art Education
	Master of Arts in Education
	Master of Arts in English
MAEd	Master of Arts Education
MAEL	Master of Arts in Educational Leadership
MAEM	Master of Arts in Educational Ministries
MAEN	Master of Arts in English
MAEP	Master of Arts in Economic Policy
MAES	Master of Arts in Environmental Sciences
MAET	Master of Arts in English Teaching
MAF	Master of Arts in Finance
MAFE	Master of Arts in Financial Economics
MAFLL	Master of Arts in Foreign Language and Literature
MAFM	Master of Accounting and Financial Management
MAFS	Master of Arts in Family Studies
MAG	Master of Applied Geography
MAGU	Master of Urban Analysis and Management
MAH	Master of Arts in Humanities
MAHA	Master of Arts in Humanitarian Assistance
	Master of Arts in Humanitarian Studies
MAHCM	Master of Arts in Health Care Mission
MAHG	Master of American History and Government
MAHL	Master of Arts in Hebrew Letters
MAHN	Master of Applied Human Nutrition
MAHSR	Master of Applied Health Services Research
MAIA	Master of Arts in International Administration
	Master of Arts in International Affairs
MAIB	Master of Arts in International Business
MAIDM	Master of Arts in Interior Design and Merchandising
MAIH	Master of Arts in Interdisciplinary Humanities
MAIOP	Master of Arts in Industrial/Organizational Psychology
MAIPCR	Master of Arts in International Peace and Conflict Management
MAIS	Master of Arts in Intercultural Studies
	Master of Arts in Interdisciplinary Studies
	Master of Arts in International Studies
MAIT	Master of Administration in Information Technology
	Master of Applied Information Technology
MAJ	Master of Arts in Journalism
MAJ Ed	Master of Arts in Jewish Education
MAJCS	Master of Arts in Jewish Communal Service
MAJE	Master of Arts in Jewish Education
MAJPS	Master of Arts in Jewish Professional Studies
MAJS	Master of Arts in Jewish Studies
MAL	Master in Agricultural Leadership
MALA	Master of Arts in Liberal Arts
MALD	Master of Arts in Law and Diplomacy
MALER	Master of Arts in Labor and Employment Relations
MALM	Master of Arts in Leadership Evangelical Mobilization
MALP	Master of Arts in Language Pedagogy
MALPS	Master of Arts in Liberal and Professional Studies
MALS	Master of Arts in Liberal Studies
MAM	Master of Acquisition Management
	Master of Agriculture and Management
	Master of Applied Mathematics
	Master of Arts in Ministry
	Master of Arts Management
	Master of Avian Medicine
MAMB	Master of Applied Molecular Biology
MAMC	Master of Arts in Mass Communication
	Master of Arts in Ministry and Culture
	Master of Arts in Ministry for a Multicultural Church
	Master of Arts in Missional Christianity

MAME	Master of Arts in Missions/Evangelism
MAMFC	Master of Arts in Marriage and Family Counseling
MAMFCC	Master of Arts in Marriage, Family, and Child Counseling
MAMFT	Master of Arts in Marriage and Family Therapy
MAMHC	Master of Arts in Mental Health Counseling
MAMI	Master of Arts in Missions
MAMS	Master of Applied Mathematical Sciences
	Master of Arts in Ministerial Studies
	Master of Arts in Ministry and Spirituality
MAMT	Master of Arts in Mathematics Teaching
MAN	Master of Applied Nutrition
MANT	Master of Arts in New Testament
MAOL	Master of Arts in Organizational Leadership
MAOM	Master of Acupuncture and Oriental Medicine
	Master of Arts in Organizational Management
MAOT	Master of Arts in Old Testament
MAP	Master of Applied Psychology
	Master of Arts in Planning
	Master of Psychology
	Master of Public Administration
MAP Min	Master of Arts in Pastoral Ministry
MAPA	Master of Arts in Public Administration
MAPC	Master of Arts in Pastoral Counseling
	Master of Arts in Professional Counseling
MAPE	Master of Arts in Political Economy
MAPM	Master of Arts in Pastoral Ministry
	Master of Arts in Pastoral Music
	Master of Arts in Practical Ministry
MAPP	Master of Arts in Public Policy
MAPPS	Master of Arts in Asia Pacific Policy Studies
MAPS	Master of Arts in Pastoral Counseling/Spiritual Formation
	Master of Arts in Pastoral Studies
	Master of Arts in Public Service
MAPT	Master of Practical Theology
MAPW	Master of Arts in Professional Writing
MAR	Master of Arts in Reading
	Master of Arts in Religion
Mar Eng	Marine Engineer
MARC	Master of Arts in Rehabilitation Counseling
MARE	Master of Arts in Religious Education
MARL	Master of Arts in Religious Leadership
MARS	Master of Arts in Religious Studies
MAS	Master of Accounting Science
	Master of Actuarial Science
	Master of Administrative Science
	Master of Advanced Study
	Master of Aeronautical Science
	Master of American Studies
	Master of Applied Science
	Master of Applied Statistics
	Master of Archival Studies
MASA	Master of Advanced Studies in Architecture
MASD	Master of Arts in Spiritual Direction
MASE	Master of Arts in Special Education
MASF	Master of Arts in Spiritual Formation
MASJ	Master of Arts in Systems of Justice
MASLA	Master of Advanced Studies in Landscape Architecture
MASM	Master of Aging Services Management
	Master of Arts in Specialized Ministries
MASP	Master of Applied Social Psychology
	Master of Arts in School Psychology
MASPAA	Master of Arts in Sports and Athletic Administration
MASS	Master of Applied Social Science
	Master of Arts in Social Science
MAST	Master of Arts in Science Teaching
MASW	Master of Aboriginal Social Work
MAT	Master of Arts in Teaching
	Master of Arts in Theology
	Master of Athletic Training
	Master's in Administration of Telecommunications
Mat E	Materials Engineer
MATCM	Master of Acupuncture and Traditional Chinese Medicine
MATDE	Master of Arts in Theology, Development, and Evangelism
MATDR	Master of Territorial Management and Regional Development
MATE	Master of Arts for the Teaching of English
MATESL	Master of Arts in Teaching English as a Second Language
MATESOL	Master of Arts in Teaching English to Speakers of Other Languages
MATF	Master of Arts in Teaching English as a Foreign Language/Intercultural Studies
MATFL	Master of Arts in Teaching Foreign Language
MATH	Master of Arts in Therapy
MATI	Master of Administration of Information Technology
MATL	Master of Arts in Teacher Leadership
	Master of Arts in Teaching of Languages
	Master of Arts in Transformational Leadership
MATM	Master of Arts in Teaching of Mathematics
MATS	Master of Arts in Theological Studies
	Master of Arts in Transforming Spirituality
MATSL	Master of Arts in Teaching a Second Language
MAUA	Master of Arts in Urban Affairs
MAUD	Master of Arts in Urban Design
MAURP	Master of Arts in Urban and Regional Planning
MAWSHP	Master of Arts in Worship
MAYM	Master of Arts in Youth Ministry
MB	Master of Bioinformatics
	Master of Biology
MBA	Master of Business Administration
MBA-AM	Master of Business Administration in Aviation Management
MBA-EP	Master of Business AdministrationNExperienced Professionals
MBA/MGPS	Master of Business Administration/Master of Global Policy Studies
MBAA	Master of Business Administration in Aviation
MBAE	Master of Biological and Agricultural Engineering
	Master of Biosystems and Agricultural Engineering
MBAH	Master of Business Administration in Health
MBAi	Master of Business AdministrationNInternational
MBAICT	Master of Business Administration in Information and Communication Technology
MBATM	Master of Business Administration in Technology Management
MBC	Master of Building Construction
MBE	Master of Bilingual Education
	Master of Bioengineering
	Master of Bioethics
	Master of Biological Engineering
	Master of Biomedical Engineering
	Master of Business and Engineering
	Master of Business Economics
	Master of Business Education
MBEE	Master in Biotechnology Enterprise and Entrepreneurship
MBET	Master of Business, Entrepreneurship and Technology
MBIOT	Master of Biotechnology

MBiotech	Master of Biotechnology
MBL	Master of Business Law
	Master of Business Leadership
MBLE	Master in Business Logistics Engineering
MBMI	Master of Biomedical Imaging and Signals
MBMSE	Master of Business Management and Software Engineering
MBOE	Master of Business Operational Excellence
MBS	Master of Biblical Studies
	Master of Biological Science
	Master of Biomedical Sciences
	Master of Bioscience
	Master of Building Science
	Master of Business and Science
MBST	Master of Biostatistics
MBT	Master of Biblical and Theological Studies
	Master of Biomedical Technology
	Master of Biotechnology
	Master of Business Taxation
MC	Master of Communication
	Master of Counseling
	Master of Cybersecurity
MC Ed	Master of Continuing Education
MC Sc	Master of Computer Science
MCA	Master of Arts in Applied Criminology
	Master of Commercial Aviation
MCAM	Master of Computational and Applied Mathematics
MCC	Master of Computer Science
MCCS	Master of Crop and Soil Sciences
MCD	Master of Communications Disorders
	Master of Community Development
MCE	Master in Electronic Commerce
	Master of Christian Education
	Master of Civil Engineering
	Master of Control Engineering
MCEM	Master of Construction Engineering Management
MCH	Master of Chemical Engineering
MCHE	Master of Chemical Engineering
MCIS	Master of Communication and Information Studies
	Master of Computer and Information Science
	Master of Computer Information Systems
MCIT	Master of Computer and Information Technology
MCJ	Master of Criminal Justice
MCJA	Master of Criminal Justice Administration
MCL	Master in Communication Leadership
	Master of Canon Law
	Master of Comparative Law
MCM	Master of Christian Ministry
	Master of Church Music
	Master of City Management
	Master of Communication Management
	Master of Community Medicine
	Master of Construction Management
	Master of Contract Management
	Master of Corporate Media
MCMP	Master of City and Metropolitan Planning
MCMS	Master of Clinical Medical Science
MCN	Master of Clinical Nutrition
MCOL	Master of Arts in Community and Organizational Leadership
MCP	Master of City Planning
	Master of Community Planning
	Master of Counseling Psychology
	Master of Cytopathology Practice
	Master of Science in Quality Systems and Productivity
MCPC	Master of Arts in Chaplaincy and Pastoral Care
MCPD	Master of Community Planning and Development
MCR	Master in Clinical Research
MCRP	Master of City and Regional Planning
MCRS	Master of City and Regional Studies
MCS	Master of Christian Studies
	Master of Clinical Science
	Master of Combined Sciences
	Master of Communication Studies
	Master of Computer Science
	Master of Consumer Science
MCSE	Master of Computer Science and Engineering
MCSL	Master of Catholic School Leadership
MCSM	Master of Construction Science/Management
MCST	Master of Science in Computer Science and Information Technology
MCTP	Master of Communication Technology and Policy
MCTS	Master of Clinical and Translational Science
MCVS	Master of Cardiovascular Science
MD	Doctor of Medicine
MDA	Master of Development Administration
	Master of Dietetic Administration
MDB	Master of Design-Build
MDE	Master of Developmental Economics
	Master of Distance Education
	Master of the Education of the Deaf
MDH	Master of Dental Hygiene
MDM	Master of Design Methods
	Master of Digital Media
MDP	Master in Sustainable Development Practice
	Master of Development Practice
MDR	Master of Dispute Resolution
MDS	Master of Dental Surgery
	Master of Design Studies
ME	Master of Education
	Master of Engineering
	Master of Entrepreneurship
	Master of Evangelism
ME Sc	Master of Engineering Science
MEA	Master of Educational Administration
	Master of Engineering Administration
MEAP	Master of Environmental Administration and Planning
MEBT	Master in Electronic Business Technologies
MEC	Master of Electronic Commerce
MECE	Master of Electrical and Computer Engineering
Mech E	Mechanical Engineer
MED	Master of Education of the Deaf
MEDS	Master of Environmental Design Studies
MEE	Master in Education
	Master of Electrical Engineering
	Master of Energy Engineering
	Master of Environmental Engineering
MEEM	Master of Environmental Engineering and Management
MEENE	Master of Engineering in Environmental Engineering
MEEP	Master of Environmental and Energy Policy
MEERM	Master of Earth and Environmental Resource Management
MEH	Master in Humanistic Studies
	Master of Environmental Horticulture
MEHP	Master of Education in the Health Professions
MEHS	Master of Environmental Health and Safety
MEIM	Master of Entertainment Industry Management
MEL	Master of Educational Leadership
	Master of English Literature
MELP	Master of Environmental Law and Policy

MEM Master of Ecosystem Management
Master of Electricity Markets
Master of Engineering Management
Master of Environmental Management
Master of Marketing
MEME Master of Engineering in Manufacturing Engineering
Master of Engineering in Mechanical Engineering
MENG Master of Arts in English
MENVEGR Master of Environmental Engineering
MEP Master of Engineering Physics
MEPC Master of Environmental Pollution Control
MEPD Master of EducationNProfessional Development
Master of Environmental Planning and Design
MER Master of Employment Relations
MERE Master of Entrepreneurial Real Estate
MES Master of Education and Science
Master of Engineering Science
Master of Environment and Sustainability
Master of Environmental Science
Master of Environmental Studies
Master of Environmental Systems
Master of Special Education
MESM Master of Environmental Science and Management
MET Master of Educational Technology
Master of Engineering Technology
Master of Entertainment Technology
Master of Environmental Toxicology
METM Master of Engineering and Technology Management
MEVE Master of Environmental Engineering
MF Master of Finance
Master of Forestry
MFA Master of Fine Arts
MFAM Master in Food Animal Medicine
MFAS Master of Fisheries and Aquatic Science
MFAW Master of Fine Arts in Writing
MFC Master of Forest Conservation
MFCS Master of Family and Consumer Sciences
MFE Master of Financial Economics
Master of Financial Engineering
Master of Forest Engineering
MFG Master of Functional Genomics
MFHD Master of Family and Human Development
MFM Master of Financial Management
Master of Financial Mathematics
MFMS Master's in Food Microbiology and Safety
MFPE Master of Food Process Engineering
MFR Master of Forest Resources
MFRC Master of Forest Resources and Conservation
MFS Master of Food Science
Master of Forensic Sciences
Master of Forest Science
Master of Forest Studies
Master of French Studies
MFST Master of Food Safety and Technology
MFT Master of Family Therapy
Master of Food Technology
MFWB Master of Fishery and Wildlife Biology
MFWCB Master of Fish, Wildlife and Conservation Biology
MFWS Master of Fisheries and Wildlife Sciences
MFYCS Master of Family, Youth and Community Sciences
MG Master of Genetics
MGA Master of Global Affairs
Master of Governmental Administration
MGC Master of Genetic Counseling
MGD Master of Graphic Design
MGE Master of Geotechnical Engineering
MGEM Master of Global Entrepreneurship and Management
MGIS Master of Geographic Information Science
Master of Geographic Information Systems
MGM Master of Global Management
MGP Master of Gestion de Projet
MGPS Master of Global Policy Studies
MGPS/MA Master of Global Policy Studies/Master of Arts
MGPS/MPH Master of Global Policy Studies/Master of Public Health
MGREM Master of Global Real Estate Management
MGS Master of Gerontological Studies
Master of Global Studies
MH Master of Humanities
MH Ed Master of Health Education
MH Sc Master of Health Sciences
MHA Master of Health Administration
Master of Healthcare Administration
Master of Hospital Administration
Master of Hospitality Administration
MHAD Master of Health Administration
MHB Master of Human Behavior
MHCA Master of Health Care Administration
MHCI Master of Health Care Informatics
Master of Human-Computer Interaction
MHCL Master of Health Care Leadership
MHE Master of Health Education
Master of Human Ecology
MHE Ed Master of Home Economics Education
MHEA Master of Higher Education Administration
MHHS Master of Health and Human Services
MHI Master of Health Informatics
Master of Healthcare Innovation
MHIIM Master of Health Informatics and Information Management
MHIS Master of Health Information Systems
MHK Master of Human Kinetics
MHL Master of Hebrew Literature
MHM Master of Healthcare Management
MHMS Master of Health Management Systems
MHP Master of Health Physics
Master of Heritage Preservation
Master of Historic Preservation
MHPA Master of Heath Policy and Administration
MHPE Master of Health Professions Education
MHR Master of Human Resources
MHRD Master in Human Resource Development
MHRIR Master of Human Resources and Industrial Relations
MHRLR Master of Human Resources and Labor Relations
MHRM Master of Human Resources Management
MHS Master of Health Science
Master of Health Sciences
Master of Health Studies
Master of Hispanic Studies
Master of Human Services
Master of Humanistic Studies
MHSA Master of Health Services Administration
MHSM Master of Health Systems Management
MI Master of Information
Master of Instruction
MI Arch Master of Interior Architecture
MIA Master of Interior Architecture
Master of International Affairs

MIAA	Master of International Affairs and Administration
MIAM	Master of International Agribusiness Management
MIAPD	Master of Interior Architecture and Product Design
MIB	Master of International Business
MIBA	Master of International Business Administration
MICM	Master of International Construction Management
MID	Master of Industrial Design
	Master of Industrial Distribution
	Master of Interior Design
	Master of International Development
MIDC	Master of Integrated Design and Construction
MIE	Master of Industrial Engineering
MIH	Master of Integrative Health
MIHTM	Master of International Hospitality and Tourism Management
MIJ	Master of International Journalism
MILR	Master of Industrial and Labor Relations
MiM	Master in Management
MIM	Master of Industrial Management
	Master of Information Management
	Master of International Management
MIMLAE	Master of International Management for Latin American Executives
MIMS	Master of Information Management and Systems
	Master of Integrated Manufacturing Systems
MIP	Master of Infrastructure Planning
	Master of Intellectual Property
	Master of International Policy
MIPA	Master of International Public Affairs
MIPER	Master of International Political Economy of Resources
MIPP	Master of International Policy and Practice
	Master of International Public Policy
MIPS	Master of International Planning Studies
MIR	Master of Industrial Relations
	Master of International Relations
MIRHR	Master of Industrial Relations and Human Resources
MIS	Master of Industrial Statistics
	Master of Information Science
	Master of Information Systems
	Master of Integrated Science
	Master of Interdisciplinary Studies
	Master of International Service
	Master of International Studies
MISE	Master of Industrial and Systems Engineering
MISKM	Master of Information Sciences and Knowledge Management
MISM	Master of Information Systems Management
MIT	Master in Teaching
	Master of Industrial Technology
	Master of Information Technology
	Master of Initial Teaching
	Master of International Trade
	Master of Internet Technology
MITA	Master of Information Technology Administration
MITM	Master of Information Technology and Management
MITO	Master of Industrial Technology and Operations
MJ	Master of Journalism
	Master of Jurisprudence
MJ Ed	Master of Jewish Education
MJA	Master of Justice Administration
MJM	Master of Justice Management
MJS	Master of Judicial Studies
	Master of Juridical Science
MKM	Master of Knowledge Management
ML	Master of Latin
ML Arch	Master of Landscape Architecture
MLA	Master of Landscape Architecture
	Master of Liberal Arts
MLAS	Master of Laboratory Animal Science
	Master of Liberal Arts and Sciences
MLAUD	Master of Landscape Architecture in Urban Development
MLD	Master of Leadership Development
MLE	Master of Applied Linguistics and Exegesis
MLER	Master of Labor and Employment Relations
MLHR	Master of Labor and Human Resources
MLI Sc	Master of Library and Information Science
MLIS	Master of Library and Information Science
	Master of Library and Information Studies
MLM	Master of Library Media
MLRHR	Master of Labor Relations and Human Resources
MLS	Master of Leadership Studies
	Master of Legal Studies
	Master of Liberal Studies
	Master of Library Science
	Master of Life Sciences
MLSP	Master of Law and Social Policy
MLT	Master of Language Technologies
MLTCA	Master of Long Term Care Administration
MM	Master of Management
	Master of Ministry
	Master of Missiology
	Master of Music
MM Ed	Master of Music Education
MM Sc	Master of Medical Science
MM St	Master of Museum Studies
MMA	Master of Marine Affairs
	Master of Media Arts
	Master of Musical Arts
MMAE	Master of Mechanical and Aerospace Engineering
MMAL	Master of Maritime Administration and Logistics
MMAS	Master of Military Art and Science
MMB	Master of Microbial Biotechnology
MMBA	Managerial Master of Business Administration
MMC	Master of Manufacturing Competitiveness
	Master of Mass Communications
	Master of Music Conducting
MMCM	Master of Music in Church Music
MMCSS	Master of Mathematical Computational and Statistical Sciences
MME	Master of Manufacturing Engineering
	Master of Mathematics Education
	Master of Mathematics for Educators
	Master of Mechanical Engineering
	Master of Medical Engineering
	Master of Mining Engineering
	Master of Music Education
MMF	Master of Mathematical Finance
MMFT	Master of Marriage and Family Therapy
MMG	Master of Management
MMH	Master of Management in Hospitality
	Master of Medical Humanities
MMI	Master of Management of Innovation
MMIS	Master of Management Information Systems
MMM	Master of Manufacturing Management
	Master of Marine Management

	Master of Medical Management
MMME	Master of Metallurgical and Materials Engineering
MMP	Master of Management Practice
	Master of Marine Policy
	Master of Medical Physics
	Master of Music Performance
MMPA	Master of Management and Professional Accounting
MMQM	Master of Manufacturing Quality Management
MMR	Master of Marketing Research
MMRM	Master of Marine Resources Management
MMS	Master of Management Science
	Master of Management Studies
	Master of Manufacturing Systems
	Master of Marine Studies
	Master of Materials Science
	Master of Medical Science
	Master of Medieval Studies
MMSE	Master of Manufacturing Systems Engineering
	Multidisciplinary Master of Science in Engineering
MMSM	Master of Music in Sacred Music
MMT	Master in Marketing
	Master of Music Teaching
	Master of Music Therapy
	Master's in Marketing Technology
MMus	Master of Music
MN	Master of Nursing
	Master of Nutrition
MN NP	Master of Nursing in Nurse Practitioner
MNA	Master of Nonprofit Administration
	Master of Nurse Anesthesia
MNAL	Master of Nonprofit Administration and Leadership
MNAS	Master of Natural and Applied Science
MNCM	Master of Network and Communications Management
MNE	Master of Network Engineering
	Master of Nuclear Engineering
MNL	Master in International Business for Latin America
MNM	Master of Nonprofit Management
MNO	Master of Nonprofit Organization
MNPL	Master of Not-for-Profit Leadership
MNpS	Master of Nonprofit Studies
MNR	Master of Natural Resources
MNRES	Master of Natural Resources and Environmental Studies
MNRM	Master of Natural Resource Management
MNRS	Master of Natural Resource Stewardship
MNS	Master of Natural Science
MO	Master of Oceanography
MOD	Master of Organizational Development
MOGS	Master of Oil and Gas Studies
MOH	Master of Occupational Health
MOL	Master of Organizational Leadership
MOM	Master of Oriental Medicine
MOR	Master of Operations Research
MOT	Master of Occupational Therapy
MP	Master of Physiology
	Master of Planning
MP Ac	Master of Professional Accountancy
MP Acc	Master of Professional Accountancy
	Master of Professional Accounting
	Master of Public Accounting
MP Aff	Master of Public Affairs
MP Aff/MPH	Master of Public Affairs/Master of Public Health
MP Th	Master of Pastoral Theology
MPA	Master of Physician Assistant
	Master of Professional Accountancy
	Master of Professional Accounting
	Master of Public Administration
	Master of Public Affairs
MPAC	Master of Professional Accounting
MPAID	Master of Public Administration and International Development
MPAP	Master of Physician Assistant Practice
	Master of Public Affairs and Politics
MPAS	Master of Physician Assistant Science
	Master of Physician Assistant Studies
MPC	Master of Pastoral Counseling
	Master of Professional Communication
	Master of Professional Counseling
MPCU	Master of Planning in Civic Urbanism
MPD	Master of Product Development
	Master of Public Diplomacy
MPDS	Master of Planning and Development Studies
MPE	Master of Physical Education
	Master of Power Engineering
MPEM	Master of Project Engineering and Management
MPH	Master of Public Health
MPHE	Master of Public Health Education
MPHTM	Master of Public Health and Tropical Medicine
MPI	Master of Product Innovation
MPIA	Master in International Affairs
	Master of Public and International Affairs
MPM	Master of Pastoral Ministry
	Master of Pest Management
	Master of Policy Management
	Master of Practical Ministries
	Master of Project Management
	Master of Public Management
MPNA	Master of Public and Nonprofit Administration
MPO	Master of Prosthetics and Orthotics
MPOD	Master of Positive Organizational Development
MPP	Master of Public Policy
MPPA	Master of Public Policy Administration
	Master of Public Policy and Administration
MPPAL	Master of Public Policy, Administration and Law
MPPM	Master of Public and Private Management
	Master of Public Policy and Management
MPPPM	Master of Plant Protection and Pest Management
MPRTM	Master of Parks, Recreation, and Tourism Management
MPS	Master of Pastoral Studies
	Master of Perfusion Science
	Master of Planning Studies
	Master of Political Science
	Master of Preservation Studies
	Master of Professional Studies
	Master of Public Service
MPSA	Master of Public Service Administration
MPSRE	Master of Professional Studies in Real Estate
MPT	Master of Pastoral Theology
	Master of Physical Therapy
	Master of Practical Theology
MPVM	Master of Preventive Veterinary Medicine
MPW	Master of Professional Writing
	Master of Public Works
MQM	Master of Quality Management
MQS	Master of Quality Systems
MR	Master of Recreation
	Master of Retailing
MRA	Master in Research Administration
MRC	Master of Rehabilitation Counseling

MRCP	Master of Regional and City Planning
	Master of Regional and Community Planning
MRD	Master of Rural Development
MRE	Master of Real Estate
	Master of Religious Education
MRED	Master of Real Estate Development
MREM	Master of Resource and Environmental Management
MRLS	Master of Resources Law Studies
MRM	Master of Resources Management
MRP	Master of Regional Planning
MRS	Master of Religious Studies
MRSc	Master of Rehabilitation Science
MS	Master of Science
MS Cmp E	Master of Science in Computer Engineering
MS Kin	Master of Science in Kinesiology
MS Acct	Master of Science in Accounting
MS Accy	Master of Science in Accountancy
MS Aero E	Master of Science in Aerospace Engineering
MS Ag	Master of Science in Agriculture
MS Arch	Master of Science in Architecture
MS Arch St	Master of Science in Architectural Studies
MS Bio E	Master of Science in Bioengineering
	Master of Science in Biomedical Engineering
MS Bm E	Master of Science in Biomedical Engineering
MS Ch E	Master of Science in Chemical Engineering
MS Chem	Master of Science in Chemistry
MS Cp E	Master of Science in Computer Engineering
MS Eco	Master of Science in Economics
MS Econ	Master of Science in Economics
MS Ed	Master of Science in Education
MS El	Master of Science in Educational Leadership and Administration
MS En E	Master of Science in Environmental Engineering
MS Eng	Master of Science in Engineering
MS Engr	Master of Science in Engineering
MS Env E	Master of Science in Environmental Engineering
MS Exp Surg	Master of Science in Experimental Surgery
MS Int A	Master of Science in International Affairs
MS Mat E	Master of Science in Materials Engineering
MS Mat SE	Master of Science in Material Science and Engineering
MS Met E	Master of Science in Metallurgical Engineering
MS Mgt	Master of Science in Management
MS Min	Master of Science in Mining
MS Min E	Master of Science in Mining Engineering
MS Mt E	Master of Science in Materials Engineering
MS Otal	Master of Science in Otalrynology
MS Pet E	Master of Science in Petroleum Engineering
MS Phys	Master of Science in Physics
MS Poly	Master of Science in Polymers
MS Psy	Master of Science in Psychology
MS Pub P	Master of Science in Public Policy
MS Sc	Master of Science in Social Science
MS Sp Ed	Master of Science in Special Education
MS Stat	Master of Science in Statistics
MS Surg	Master of Science in Surgery
MS Tax	Master of Science in Taxation
MS Tc E	Master of Science in Telecommunications Engineering
MS-R	Master of Science (Research)
MS/CAGS	Master of Science/Certificate of Advanced Graduate Studies
MSA	Master of School Administration
	Master of Science Administration
	Master of Science in Accountancy
	Master of Science in Accounting
	Master of Science in Administration
	Master of Science in Aeronautics
	Master of Science in Agriculture
	Master of Science in Anesthesia
	Master of Science in Architecture
	Master of Science in Aviation
	Master of Sports Administration
MSA Phy	Master of Science in Applied Physics
MSAA	Master of Science in Astronautics and Aeronautics
MSAAE	Master of Science in Aeronautical and Astronautical Engineering
MSABE	Master of Science in Agricultural and Biological Engineering
MSAC	Master of Science in Acupuncture
MSACC	Master of Science in Accounting
MSAE	Master of Science in Aeronautical Engineering
	Master of Science in Aerospace Engineering
	Master of Science in Applied Economics
	Master of Science in Applied Engineering
	Master of Science in Architectural Engineering
MSAH	Master of Science in Allied Health
MSAL	Master of Sport Administration and Leadership
MSAM	Master of Science in Applied Mathematics
MSANR	Master of Science in Agriculture and Natural Resources Systems Management
MSAPM	Master of Security Analysis and Portfolio Management
MSAS	Master of Science in Applied Statistics
	Master of Science in Architectural Studies
MSAT	Master of Science in Accounting and Taxation
	Master of Science in Advanced Technology
	Master of Science in Athletic Training
MSB	Master of Science in Bible
	Master of Science in Biotechnology
	Master of Science in Business
	Master of Sustainable Business
MSBA	Master of Science in Business Administration
	Master of Science in Business Analysis
MSBAE	Master of Science in Biological and Agricultural Engineering
	Master of Science in Biosystems and Agricultural Engineering
MSBC	Master of Science in Building Construction
MSBCB	bioinformatics and computational biology
MSBE	Master of Science in Biological Engineering
	Master of Science in Biomedical Engineering
MSBENG	Master of Science in Bioengineering
MSBIT	Master of Science in Business Information Technology
MSBM	Master of Sport Business Management
MSBME	Master of Science in Biomedical Engineering
MSBMS	Master of Science in Basic Medical Science
MSBS	Master of Science in Biomedical Sciences
MSC	Master of Science in Commerce
	Master of Science in Communication
	Master of Science in Computers
	Master of Science in Counseling
	Master of Science in Criminology
MSCC	Master of Science in Christian Counseling
	Master of Science in Community Counseling
MSCD	Master of Science in Communication Disorders
	Master of Science in Community Development
MSCE	Master of Science in Civil Engineering
	Master of Science in Clinical Epidemiology
	Master of Science in Computer Engineering
	Master of Science in Continuing Education
MSCEE	Master of Science in Civil and Environmental Engineering
MSCF	Master of Science in Computational Finance
MSCH	Master of Science in Chemical Engineering

MSChE Master of Science in Chemical Engineering
MSCI Master of Science in Clinical Investigation
Master of Science in Curriculum and Instruction
MSCIS Master of Science in Computer and Information Systems
Master of Science in Computer Information Science
Master of Science in Computer Information Systems
MSCIT Master of Science in Computer Information Technology
MSCJ Master of Science in Criminal Justice
MSCJA Master of Science in Criminal Justice Administration
MSCJS Master of Science in Crime and Justice Studies
MSCLS Master of Science in Clinical Laboratory Studies
MSCM Master of Science in Church Management
Master of Science in Conflict Management
Master of Science in Construction Management
MScM Master of Science in Management
MSCM Master of Supply Chain Management
MSCNU Master of Science in Clinical Nutrition
MSCP Master of Science in Clinical Psychology
Master of Science in Community Psychology
Master of Science in Computer Engineering
Master of Science in Counseling Psychology
MSCPE Master of Science in Computer Engineering
MSCPharm Master of Science in Pharmacy
MSCPI Master in Strategic Planning for Critical Infrastructures
MSCR Master of Science in Clinical Research
MSCRP Master of Science in City and Regional Planning
Master of Science in Community and Regional Planning
MSCRP/MP Aff Master of Science in Community and Regional Planning/Master of Public Affairs
MSCRP/MSSD Master of Science in Community and Regional Planning/Master of Science in Sustainable Design
MSCRP/MSUD Master of Science in Community and Regional Planning/Masters of Science in Urban Design
MSCS Master of Science in Clinical Science
Master of Science in Computer Science
MSCSD Master of Science in Communication Sciences and Disorders
MSCSE Master of Science in Computer Science and Engineering
MSCTE Master of Science in Career and Technical Education
MSD Master of Science in Dentistry
Master of Science in Design
Master of Science in Dietetics
MSE Master of Science Education
Master of Science in Economics
Master of Science in Education
Master of Science in Engineering
Master of Science in Engineering Management
Master of Software Engineering
Master of Special Education
Master of Structural Engineering
MSECE Master of Science in Electrical and Computer Engineering
MSED Master of Sustainable Economic Development
MSEE Master of Science in Electrical Engineering
Master of Science in Environmental Engineering
MSEH Master of Science in Environmental Health
MSEL Master of Science in Educational Leadership
MSEM Master of Science in Engineering Management
Master of Science in Engineering Mechanics
Master of Science in Environmental Management
MSENE Master of Science in Environmental Engineering
MSEO Master of Science in Electro-Optics
MSEP Master of Science in Economic Policy
MSEPA Master of Science in Economics and Policy Analysis
MSES Master of Science in Embedded Software Engineering
Master of Science in Engineering Science
Master of Science in Environmental Science
Master of Science in Environmental Studies
MSESM Master of Science in Engineering Science and Mechanics
MSET Master of Science in Educational Technology
Master of Science in Engineering Technology
MSEV Master of Science in Environmental Engineering
MSEVH Master of Science in Environmental Health and Safety
MSF Master of Science in Finance
Master of Science in Forestry
Master of Spiritual Formation
MSFA Master of Science in Financial Analysis
MSFAM Master of Science in Family Studies
MSFCS Master of Science in Family and Consumer Science
MSFE Master of Science in Financial Engineering
MSFOR Master of Science in Forestry
MSFP Master of Science in Financial Planning
MSFS Master of Science in Financial Sciences
Master of Science in Forensic Science
MSFSB Master of Science in Financial Services and Banking
MSFT Master of Science in Family Therapy
MSGC Master of Science in Genetic Counseling
MSH Master of Science in Health
Master of Science in Hospice
MSHA Master of Science in Health Administration
MSHCA Master of Science in Health Care Administration
MSHCI Master of Science in Human Computer Interaction
MSHCPM Master of Science in Health Care Policy and Management
MSHE Master of Science in Health Education
MSHES Master of Science in Human Environmental Sciences
MSHFID Master of Science in Human Factors in Information Design
MSHFS Master of Science in Human Factors and Systems
MSHI Master of Science in Health Informatics
MSHP Master of Science in Health Professions
Master of Science in Health Promotion
MSHR Master of Science in Human Resources
MSHRL Master of Science in Human Resource Leadership
MSHRM Master of Science in Human Resource Management
MSHROD Master of Science in Human Resources and Organizational Development
MSHS Master of Science in Health Science
Master of Science in Health Services
Master of Science in Health Systems
Master of Science in Homeland Security
MSHT Master of Science in History of Technology
MSI Master of Science in Information
Master of Science in Instruction
Master of System Integration
MSIA Master of Science in Industrial Administration

	Master of Science in Information Assurance and Computer Security
MSIB	Master of Science in International Business
MSIDM	Master of Science in Interior Design and Merchandising
MSIDT	Master of Science in Information Design and Technology
MSIE	Master of Science in Industrial Engineering
	Master of Science in International Economics
MSIEM	Master of Science in Information Engineering and Management
MSIID	Master of Science in Information and Instructional Design
MSIM	Master of Science in Information Management
	Master of Science in International Management
MSIMC	Master of Science in Integrated Marketing Communications
MSIR	Master of Science in Industrial Relations
MSIS	Master of Science in Information Science
	Master of Science in Information Studies
	Master of Science in Information Systems
	Master of Science in Interdisciplinary Studies
MSIS/MA	Master of Science in Information Studies/ Master of Arts
MSISE	Master of Science in Infrastructure Systems Engineering
MSISM	Master of Science in Information Systems Management
MSISPM	Master of Science in Information Security Policy and Management
MSIST	Master of Science in Information Systems Technology
MSIT	Master of Science in Industrial Technology
	Master of Science in Information Technology
	Master of Science in Instructional Technology
MSITM	Master of Science in Information Technology Management
MSJ	Master of Science in Journalism
	Master of Science in Jurisprudence
MSJC	Master of Social Justice and Criminology
MSJE	Master of Science in Jewish Education
MSJFP	Master of Science in Juvenile Forensic Psychology
MSJJ	Master of Science in Juvenile Justice
MSJPS	Master of Science in Justice and Public Safety
MSJS	Master of Science in Jewish Studies
MSK	Master of Science in Kinesiology
MSL	Master of School Leadership
	Master of Science in Leadership
	Master of Science in Limnology
	Master of Strategic Leadership
	Master of Studies in Law
MSLA	Master of Science in Landscape Architecture
	Master of Science in Legal Administration
MSLD	Master of Science in Land Development
MSLFS	Master of Science in Life Sciences
MSLP	Master of Speech-Language Pathology
MSLS	Master of Science in Library Science
MSLSCM	Master of Science in Logistics and Supply Chain Management
MSLT	Master of Second Language Teaching
MSM	Master of Sacred Ministry
	Master of Sacred Music
	Master of School Mathematics
	Master of Science in Management
	Master of Science in Organization Management
	Master of Security Management
MSMA	Master of Science in Marketing Analysis
MSMAE	Master of Science in Materials Engineering
MSMC	Master of Science in Mass Communications
MSME	Master of Science in Mathematics Education
	Master of Science in Mechanical Engineering
MSMFE	Master of Science in Manufacturing Engineering
MSMFT	Master of Science in Marriage and Family Therapy
MSMIS	Master of Science in Management Information Systems
MSMIT	Master of Science in Management and Information Technology
MSMLS	Master of Science in Medical Laboratory Science
MSMOT	Master of Science in Management of Technology
MSMS	Master of Science in Management Science
	Master of Science in Medical Sciences
MSMSE	Master of Science in Manufacturing Systems Engineering
	Master of Science in Material Science and Engineering
	Master of Science in Mathematics and Science Education
MSMT	Master of Science in Management and Technology
MSMus	Master of Sacred Music
MSN	Master of Science in Nursing
MSN-R	Master of Science in Nursing (Research)
MSNA	Master of Science in Nurse Anesthesia
MSNE	Master of Science in Nuclear Engineering
MSNED	Master of Science in Nurse Education
MSNM	Master of Science in Nonprofit Management
MSNS	Master of Science in Natural Science
	Master of Science in Nutritional Science
MSOD	Master of Science in Organizational Development
MSOEE	Master of Science in Outdoor and Environmental Education
MSOES	Master of Science in Occupational Ergonomics and Safety
MSOH	Master of Science in Occupational Health
MSOL	Master of Science in Organizational Leadership
MSOM	Master of Science in Operations Management
	Master of Science in Oriental Medicine
MSOR	Master of Science in Operations Research
MSOT	Master of Science in Occupational Technology
	Master of Science in Occupational Therapy
MSP	Master of Science in Pharmacy
	Master of Science in Planning
	Master of Science in Psychology
	Master of Speech Pathology
MSPA	Master of Science in Physician Assistant
	Master of Science in Professional Accountancy
MSPAS	Master of Science in Physician Assistant Studies
MSPC	Master of Science in Professional Communications
	Master of Science in Professional Counseling
MSPE	Master of Science in Petroleum Engineering
MSPG	Master of Science in Psychology
MSPH	Master of Science in Public Health
MSPHR	Master of Science in Pharmacy
MSPM	Master of Science in Professional Management
	Master of Science in Project Management
MSPNGE	Master of Science in Petroleum and Natural Gas Engineering
MSPS	Master of Science in Pharmaceutical Science
	Master of Science in Political Science
	Master of Science in Psychological Services
MSPT	Master of Science in Physical Therapy
MSpVM	Master of Specialized Veterinary Medicine
MSR	Master of Science in Radiology
	Master of Science in Reading
MSRA	Master of Science in Recreation Administration

MSRC	Master of Science in Resource Conservation
MSRE	Master of Science in Real Estate
	Master of Science in Religious Education
MSRED	Master of Science in Real Estate Development
MSRLS	Master of Science in Recreation and Leisure Studies
MSRMP	Master of Science in Radiological Medical Physics
MSRS	Master of Science in Rehabilitation Science
MSS	Master of Science in Software
	Master of Security Studies
	Master of Social Science
	Master of Social Services
	Master of Software Systems
	Master of Sports Science
	Master of Strategic Studies
MSSA	Master of Science in Social Administration
MSSCP	Master of Science in Science Content and Process
MSSD	Master of Science in Sustainable Design
MSSE	Master of Science in Software Engineering
	Master of Science in Space Education
	Master of Science in Special Education
MSSEM	Master of Science in Systems and Engineering Management
MSSI	Master of Science in Security Informatics
	Master of Science in Strategic Intelligence
MSSL	Master of Science in School Leadership
	Master of Science in Strategic Leadership
MSSLP	Master of Science in Speech-Language Pathology
MSSM	Master of Science in Sports Medicine
MSSP	Master of Science in Social Policy
MSSPA	Master of Science in Student Personnel Administration
MSSS	Master of Science in Safety Science
	Master of Science in Systems Science
MSST	Master of Science in Security Technologies
MSSW	Master of Science in Social Work
MSSWE	Master of Science in Software Engineering
MST	Master of Science and Technology
	Master of Science in Taxation
	Master of Science in Teaching
	Master of Science in Technology
	Master of Science in Telecommunications
	Master of Science Teaching
MSTC	Master of Science in Technical Communication
	Master of Science in Telecommunications
MSTCM	Master of Science in Traditional Chinese Medicine
MSTE	Master of Science in Telecommunications Engineering
	Master of Science in Transportation Engineering
MSTM	Master of Science in Technical Management
	Master of Science in Technology Management
	Master of Science in Transfusion Medicine
MSTOM	Master of Science in Traditional Oriental Medicine
MSUD	Master of Science in Urban Design
MSW	Master of Social Work
MSWE	Master of Software Engineering
MSWREE	Master of Science in Water Resources and Environmental Engineering
MSX	Master of Science in Exercise Science
MT	Master of Taxation
	Master of Teaching
	Master of Technology
	Master of Textiles
MTA	Master of Tax Accounting
	Master of Teaching Arts
	Master of Tourism Administration
MTCM	Master of Traditional Chinese Medicine
MTD	Master of Training and Development
MTE	Master in Educational Technology
MTESOL	Master in Teaching English to Speakers of Other Languages
MTHM	Master of Tourism and Hospitality Management
MTI	Master of Information Technology
MTIM	Master of Trust and Investment Management
MTL	Master of Talmudic Law
MTM	Master of Technology Management
	Master of Telecommunications Management
	Master of the Teaching of Mathematics
MTMH	Master of Tropical Medicine and Hygiene
MTOM	Master of Traditional Oriental Medicine
MTP	Master of Transpersonal Psychology
MTPC	Master of Technical and Professional Communication
MTR	Master of Translational Research
MTS	Master of Theatre Studies
	Master of Theological Studies
MTSC	Master of Technical and Scientific Communication
MTSE	Master of Telecommunications and Software Engineering
MTT	Master in Technology Management
MTX	Master of Taxation
MUA	Master of Urban Affairs
MUCD	Master of Urban and Community Design
MUD	Master of Urban Design
MUDS	Master of Urban Design Studies
MUEP	Master of Urban and Environmental Planning
MUP	Master of Urban Planning
MUPDD	Master of Urban Planning, Design, and Development
MUPP	Master of Urban Planning and Policy
MUPRED	Master of Urban Planning and Real Estate Development
MURP	Master of Urban and Regional Planning
	Master of Urban and Rural Planning
MURPL	Master of Urban and Regional Planning
MUS	Master of Urban Studies
MUSA	Master of Urban Spatial Analytics
MVM	Master of VLSI and Microelectronics
MVP	Master of Voice Pedagogy
MVPH	Master of Veterinary Public Health
MVS	Master of Visual Studies
MWC	Master of Wildlife Conservation
MWE	Master in Welding Engineering
MWPS	Master of Wood and Paper Science
MWR	Master of Water Resources
MWS	Master of Women's Studies
	Master of Worship Studies
MZS	Master of Zoological Science
Nav Arch	Naval Architecture
Naval E	Naval Engineer
ND	Doctor of Naturopathic Medicine
NE	Nuclear Engineer
Nuc E	Nuclear Engineer
OD	Doctor of Optometry
OTD	Doctor of Occupational Therapy
PBME	Professional Master of Biomedical Engineering
PC	Performer's Certificate
PD	Professional Diploma
PGC	Post-Graduate Certificate
PGD	Postgraduate Diploma
Ph L	Licentiate of Philosophy
Pharm D	Doctor of Pharmacy

PhD	Doctor of Philosophy
PhD Otal	Doctor of Philosophy in Otalrynology
PhD Surg	Doctor of Philosophy in Surgery
PhDEE	Doctor of Philosophy in Electrical Engineering
PMBA	Professional Master of Business Administration
PMC	Post Master Certificate
PMD	Post-Master's Diploma
PMS	Professional Master of Science Professional Master's
Post-Doctoral MS	Post-Doctoral Master of Science
Post-MSN Certificate	Post-Master of Science in Nursing Certificate
PPDPT	Postprofessional Doctor of Physical Therapy
Pro-MS	Professional Science Master's
PSM	Professional Master of Science Professional Science Master's
Psy D	Doctor of Psychology
Psy M	Master of Psychology
Psy S	Specialist in Psychology
Psya D	Doctor of Psychoanalysis
Rh D	Doctor of Rehabilitation
S Psy S	Specialist in Psychological Services
Sc D	Doctor of Science
Sc M	Master of Science
SCCT	Specialist in Community College Teaching
ScDPT	Doctor of Physical Therapy Science
SD	Doctor of Science Specialist Degree
SJD	Doctor of Juridical Science
SLPD	Doctor of Speech-Language Pathology
SM	Master of Science
SM Arch S	Master of Science in Architectural Studies
SMACT	Master of Science in Art, Culture and Technology
SMBT	Master of Science in Building Technology
SP	Specialist Degree
Sp C	Specialist in Counseling
Sp Ed	Specialist in Education
Sp LIS	Specialist in Library and Information Science
SPA	Specialist in Arts
SPCM	Specialist in Church Music
Spec	Specialist's Certificate
Spec M	Specialist in Music
SPEM	Specialist in Educational Ministries
Spt	Specialist Degree
SPTH	Specialist in Theology
SSP	Specialist in School Psychology
STB	Bachelor of Sacred Theology
STD	Doctor of Sacred Theology
STL	Licentiate of Sacred Theology
STM	Master of Sacred Theology
TDPT	Transitional Doctor of Physical Therapy
Th D	Doctor of Theology
Th M	Master of Theology
VMD	Doctor of Veterinary Medicine
WEMBA	Weekend Executive Master of Business Administration
XMA	Executive Master of Arts

INDEXES

Displays and Close-Ups

Directories and Subject Areas

Following is an alphabetical listing of directories and subject areas. Also listed are cross-references for subject area names not used in the directory structure of the guides, for example, "City and Regional Planning (*see* Urban and Regional Planning)."

Graduate Programs in the Humanities, Arts & Social Sciences

Graduate Programs in the Biological/ Biomedical Sciences & Health-Related Medical Professions

Biological Oceanography (*see* Marine Biology)
Biophysics
Biopsychology
Botany
Breeding (*see* Botany; Plant Biology; Genetics)
Cancer Biology/Oncology
Cardiovascular Sciences
Cell Biology
Cellular Physiology (*see* Cell Biology; Physiology)
Child-Care Nursing (*see* Maternal and Child/Neonatal Nursing)
Chiropractic
Clinical Laboratory Sciences/Medical Technology
Clinical Research
Community Health
Community Health Nursing
Computational Biology
Conservation (*see* Conservation Biology; Environmental Biology)
Conservation Biology
Crop Sciences (*see* Botany; Plant Biology)
Cytology (*see* Cell Biology)
Dental and Oral Surgery (*see* Oral and Dental Sciences)
Dental Assistant Studies (*see* Dental Hygiene)
Dental Hygiene
Dental Services (*see* Dental Hygiene)
Dentistry
Developmental Biology
Dietetics (*see* Nutrition)
Ecology
Embryology (*see* Developmental Biology)
Emergency Medical Services
Endocrinology (*see* Physiology)
Entomology
Environmental Biology
Environmental and Occupational Health
Epidemiology
Evolutionary Biology
Family Nurse Practitioner Studies
Foods (*see* Nutrition)
Forensic Nursing
Genetics
Genomic Sciences
Gerontological Nursing
Health Physics/Radiological Health
Health Promotion
Health-Related Professions (*see* individual allied health professions)
Health Services Management and Hospital Administration
Health Services Research
Histology (*see* Anatomy; Cell Biology)
HIV/AIDS Nursing
Hospice Nursing
Hospital Administration (*see* Health Services Management and Hospital Administration)
Human Genetics
Immunology
Industrial Hygiene
Infectious Diseases
International Health
Laboratory Medicine (*see* Clinical Laboratory Sciences/Medical Technology; Immunology; Microbiology; Pathology)
Life Sciences (*see* Biological and Biomedical Sciences)
Marine Biology
Maternal and Child Health
Maternal and Child/Neonatal Nursing
Medical Imaging
Medical Microbiology
Medical Nursing (*see* Medical/Surgical Nursing)
Medical Physics
Medical/Surgical Nursing
Medical Technology (*see* Clinical Laboratory Sciences/Medical Technology)
Medical Sciences (*see* Biological and Biomedical Sciences)
Medical Science Training Programs (*see* Biological and Biomedical Sciences)
Medicinal and Pharmaceutical Chemistry
Medicinal Chemistry (*see* Medicinal and Pharmaceutical Chemistry)
Medicine (*see* Allopathic Medicine; Naturopathic Medicine; Osteopathic Medicine; Podiatric Medicine)
Microbiology
Midwifery (*see* Nurse Midwifery)
Molecular Biology
Molecular Biophysics
Molecular Genetics
Molecular Medicine
Molecular Pathogenesis
Molecular Pathology
Molecular Pharmacology
Molecular Physiology
Molecular Toxicology
Naturopathic Medicine
Neural Sciences (*see* Biopsychology; Neurobiology; Neuroscience)
Neurobiology
Neuroendocrinology (*see* Biopsychology; Neurobiology; Neuroscience; Physiology)
Neuropharmacology (*see* Biopsychology; Neurobiology; Neuroscience; Pharmacology)
Neurophysiology (*see* Biopsychology; Neurobiology; Neuroscience; Physiology)
Neuroscience
Nuclear Medical Technology (*see* Clinical Laboratory Sciences/ Medical Technology)
Nurse Anesthesia
Nurse Midwifery
Nurse Practitioner Studies (*see* Family Nurse Practitioner Studies)
Nursing Administration (*see* Nursing and Healthcare Administration)
Nursing and Healthcare Administration
Nursing Education
Nursing—General
Nursing Informatics
Nutrition
Occupational Health (*see* Environmental and Occupational Health; Occupational Health Nursing)
Occupational Health Nursing
Occupational Therapy
Oncology (*see* Cancer Biology/Oncology)
Oncology Nursing
Optometry
Oral and Dental Sciences
Oral Biology (*see* Oral and Dental Sciences)
Oral Pathology (*see* Oral and Dental Sciences)
Organismal Biology (*see* Biological and Biomedical Sciences; Zoology)
Oriental Medicine and Acupuncture (*see* Acupuncture and Oriental Medicine)
Orthodontics (*see* Oral and Dental Sciences)
Osteopathic Medicine
Parasitology
Pathobiology
Pathology
Pediatric Nursing
Pedontics (*see* Oral and Dental Sciences)
Perfusion
Pharmaceutical Administration
Pharmaceutical Chemistry (*see* Medicinal and Pharmaceutical Chemistry)
Pharmaceutical Sciences
Pharmacology
Pharmacy
Photobiology of Cells and Organelles (*see* Botany; Cell Biology; Plant Biology)
Physical Therapy
Physician Assistant Studies
Physiological Optics (*see* Vision Sciences)
Podiatric Medicine
Preventive Medicine (*see* Community Health and Public Health)
Physiological Optics (*see* Physiology)
Physiology
Plant Biology
Plant Molecular Biology
Plant Pathology
Plant Physiology
Pomology (*see* Botany; Plant Biology)
Psychiatric Nursing
Public Health—General
Public Health Nursing (*see* Community Health Nursing)
Psychiatric Nursing
Psychobiology (*see* Biopsychology)
Psychopharmacology (*see* Biopsychology; Neuroscience; Pharmacology)
Radiation Biology
Radiological Health (*see* Health Physics/Radiological Health)
Rehabilitation Nursing
Rehabilitation Sciences
Rehabilitation Therapy (*see* Physical Therapy)
Reproductive Biology
School Nursing
Sociobiology (*see* Evolutionary Biology)
Structural Biology
Surgical Nursing (*see* Medical/Surgical Nursing)
Systems Biology
Teratology
Therapeutics
Theoretical Biology (*see* Biological and Biomedical Sciences)
Therapeutics (*see* Pharmaceutical Sciences; Pharmacology; Pharmacy)

Toxicology
Transcultural Nursing
Translational Biology
Tropical Medicine (*see* Parasitology)
Veterinary Medicine
Veterinary Sciences
Virology
Vision Sciences
Wildlife Biology (*see* Zoology)
Women's Health Nursing
Zoology

Graduate Programs in the Physical Sciences, Mathematics, Agricultural Sciences, the Environment & Natural Resources

Acoustics
Agricultural Sciences
Agronomy and Soil Sciences
Analytical Chemistry
Animal Sciences
Applied Mathematics
Applied Physics
Applied Statistics
Aquaculture
Astronomy
Astrophysical Sciences (*see* Astrophysics; Atmospheric Sciences; Meteorology; Planetary and Space Sciences)
Astrophysics
Atmospheric Sciences
Biological Oceanography (*see* Marine Affairs; Marine Sciences; Oceanography)
Biomathematics
Biometry
Biostatistics
Chemical Physics
Chemistry
Computational Sciences
Condensed Matter Physics
Dairy Science (*see* Animal Sciences)
Earth Sciences (*see* Geosciences)
Environmental Management and Policy
Environmental Sciences
Environmental Studies (*see* Environmental Management and Policy)
Experimental Statistics (*see* Statistics)
Fish, Game, and Wildlife Management
Food Science and Technology
Forestry
General Science (*see* specific topics)
Geochemistry
Geodetic Sciences
Geological Engineering (*see* Geology)
Geological Sciences (*see* Geology)
Geology
Geophysical Fluid Dynamics (*see* Geophysics)
Geophysics
Geosciences
Horticulture
Hydrogeology
Hydrology
Inorganic Chemistry
Limnology
Marine Affairs
Marine Geology
Marine Sciences
Marine Studies (*see* Marine Affairs; Marine Geology; Marine Sciences; Oceanography)
Mathematical and Computational Finance
Mathematical Physics
Mathematical Statistics (*see* Applied Statistics; Statistics)
Mathematics
Meteorology
Mineralogy
Natural Resource Management (*see* Environmental Management and Policy; Natural Resources)
Natural Resources
Nuclear Physics (*see* Physics)
Ocean Engineering (*see* Marine Affairs; Marine Geology; Marine Sciences; Oceanography)
Oceanography
Optical Sciences
Optical Technologies (*see* Optical Sciences)
Optics (*see* Applied Physics; Optical Sciences; Physics)
Organic Chemistry
Paleontology
Paper Chemistry (*see* Chemistry)
Photonics
Physical Chemistry
Physics
Planetary and Space Sciences
Plant Sciences
Plasma Physics
Poultry Science (*see* Animal Sciences)
Radiological Physics (*see* Physics)
Range Management (*see* Range Science)
Range Science
Resource Management (*see* Environmental Management and Policy; Natural Resources)
Solid-Earth Sciences (*see* Geosciences)
Space Sciences (*see* Planetary and Space Sciences)
Statistics
Theoretical Chemistry
Theoretical Physics
Viticulture and Enology
Water Resources

Graduate Programs in Engineering & Applied Sciences

Aeronautical Engineering (*see* Aerospace/Aeronautical Engineering)
Aerospace/Aeronautical Engineering
Aerospace Studies (*see* Aerospace/Aeronautical Engineering)
Agricultural Engineering
Applied Mechanics (*see* Mechanics)
Applied Science and Technology
Architectural Engineering
Artificial Intelligence/Robotics
Astronautical Engineering (*see* Aerospace/Aeronautical Engineering)
Automotive Engineering
Aviation
Biochemical Engineering
Bioengineering
Bioinformatics
Biological Engineering (*see* Bioengineering)
Biomedical Engineering
Biosystems Engineering
Biotechnology
Ceramic Engineering (*see* Ceramic Sciences and Engineering)
Ceramic Sciences and Engineering
Ceramics (*see* Ceramic Sciences and Engineering)
Chemical Engineering
Civil Engineering
Computer and Information Systems Security
Computer Engineering
Computer Science
Computing Technology (*see* Computer Science)
Construction Engineering
Construction Management
Database Systems
Electrical Engineering
Electronic Materials
Electronics Engineering (*see* Electrical Engineering)
Energy and Power Engineering
Energy Management and Policy
Engineering and Applied Sciences
Engineering and Public Affairs (*see* Technology and Public Policy)
Engineering and Public Policy (*see* Energy Management and Policy; Technology and Public Policy)
Engineering Design
Engineering Management
Engineering Mechanics (*see* Mechanics)
Engineering Metallurgy (*see* Metallurgical Engineering and Metallurgy)
Engineering Physics
Environmental Design (*see* Environmental Engineering)
Environmental Engineering
Ergonomics and Human Factors
Financial Engineering
Fire Protection Engineering
Food Engineering (*see* Agricultural Engineering)
Game Design and Development
Gas Engineering (*see* Petroleum Engineering)
Geological Engineering
Geophysics Engineering (*see* Geological Engineering)

Geotechnical Engineering
Hazardous Materials Management
Health Informatics
Health Systems (*see* Safety Engineering; Systems Engineering)
Highway Engineering (*see* Transportation and Highway Engineering)
Human-Computer Interaction
Human Factors (*see* Ergonomics and Human Factors)
Hydraulics
Hydrology (*see* Water Resources Engineering)
Industrial Engineering (*see* Industrial/Management Engineering)
Industrial/Management Engineering
Information Science
Internet Engineering
Macromolecular Science (*see* Polymer Science and Engineering)
Management Engineering (*see* Engineering Management; Industrial/Management Engineering)
Management of Technology
Manufacturing Engineering
Marine Engineering (*see* Civil Engineering)
Materials Engineering
Materials Sciences
Mechanical Engineering
Mechanics
Medical Informatics
Metallurgical Engineering and Metallurgy
Metallurgy (*see* Metallurgical Engineering and Metallurgy)
Mineral/Mining Engineering
Modeling and Simulation
Nanotechnology
Nuclear Engineering
Ocean Engineering
Operations Research
Paper and Pulp Engineering
Petroleum Engineering
Pharmaceutical Engineering
Plastics Engineering (*see* Polymer Science and Engineering)
Polymer Science and Engineering
Public Policy (*see* Energy Management and Policy; Technology and Public Policy)
Reliability Engineering
Robotics (*see* Artificial Intelligence/Robotics)
Safety Engineering
Software Engineering
Solid-State Sciences (*see* Materials Sciences)
Structural Engineering
Surveying Science and Engineering
Systems Analysis (*see* Systems Engineering)
Systems Engineering
Systems Science
Technology and Public Policy
Telecommunications
Telecommunications Management
Textile Sciences and Engineering
Textiles (*see* Textile Sciences and Engineering)
Transportation and Highway Engineering
Urban Systems Engineering (*see* Systems Engineering)
Waste Management (*see* Hazardous Materials Management)
Water Resources Engineering

Graduate Programs in Business, Education, Information Studies, Law & Social Work

Accounting
Actuarial Science
Adult Education
Advertising and Public Relations
Agricultural Education
Alcohol Abuse Counseling (*see* Counselor Education)
Archival Management and Studies
Art Education
Athletics Administration (*see* Kinesiology and Movement Studies)
Athletic Training and Sports Medicine
Audiology (*see* Communication Disorders)
Aviation Management
Banking (*see* Finance and Banking)
Business Administration and Management—General
Business Education
Communication Disorders
Community College Education
Computer Education
Continuing Education (*see* Adult Education)
Counseling (*see* Counselor Education)
Counselor Education
Curriculum and Instruction
Developmental Education
Distance Education Development
Drug Abuse Counseling (*see* Counselor Education)
Early Childhood Education
Educational Leadership and Administration
Educational Measurement and Evaluation
Educational Media/Instructional Technology
Educational Policy
Educational Psychology
Education—General
Education of the Blind (*see* Special Education)
Education of the Deaf (*see* Special Education)
Education of the Gifted
Education of the Hearing Impaired (*see* Special Education)
Education of the Learning Disabled (*see* Special Education)
Education of the Mentally Retarded (*see* Special Education)
Education of the Physically Handicapped (*see* Special Education)
Education of Students with Severe/Multiple Disabilities
Education of the Visually Handicapped (*see* Special Education)
Electronic Commerce
Elementary Education
English as a Second Language
English Education
Entertainment Management
Entrepreneurship
Environmental Education
Environmental Law
Exercise and Sports Science
Exercise Physiology (*see* Kinesiology and Movement Studies)
Facilities and Entertainment Management
Finance and Banking
Food Services Management (*see* Hospitality Management)
Foreign Languages Education
Foundations and Philosophy of Education
Guidance and Counseling (*see* Counselor Education)
Health Education
Health Law
Hearing Sciences (*see* Communication Disorders)
Higher Education
Home Economics Education
Hospitality Management
Hotel Management (*see* Travel and Tourism)
Human Resources Development
Human Resources Management
Human Services
Industrial Administration (*see* Industrial and Manufacturing Management)
Industrial and Manufacturing Management
Industrial Education (*see* Vocational and Technical Education)
Information Studies
Instructional Technology (*see* Educational Media/Instructional Technology)
Insurance
Intellectual Property Law
International and Comparative Education
International Business
International Commerce (*see* International Business)
International Economics (*see* International Business)
International Trade (*see* International Business)
Investment and Securities (*see* Business Administration and Management; Finance and Banking; Investment Management)
Investment Management
Junior College Education (*see* Community College Education)
Kinesiology and Movement Studies
Law
Legal and Justice Studies
Leisure Services (*see* Recreation and Park Management)
Leisure Studies
Library Science
Logistics
Management (*see* Business Administration and Management)
Management Information Systems
Management Strategy and Policy
Marketing
Marketing Research
Mathematics Education
Middle School Education
Movement Studies (*see* Kinesiology and Movement Studies)
Multilingual and Multicultural Education
Museum Education
Music Education
Nonprofit Management
Nursery School Education (*see* Early Childhood Education)
Occupational Education (*see* Vocational and Technical Education)

Organizational Behavior
Organizational Management
Parks Administration (*see* Recreation and Park Management)
Personnel (*see* Human Resources Development; Human Resources Management; Organizational Behavior; Organizational Management; Student Affairs)
Philosophy of Education (*see* Foundations and Philosophy of Education)
Physical Education
Project Management
Public Relations (*see* Advertising and Public Relations)
Quality Management
Quantitative Analysis
Reading Education
Real Estate
Recreation and Park Management
Recreation Therapy (*see* Recreation and Park Management)
Religious Education
Remedial Education (*see* Special Education)
Restaurant Administration (*see* Hospitality Management)
Science Education
Secondary Education
Social Sciences Education
Social Studies Education (*see* Social Sciences Education)
Social Work
Special Education
Speech-Language Pathology and Audiology (*see* Communication Disorders)
Sports Management
Sports Medicine (*see* Athletic Training and Sports Medicine)
Sports Psychology and Sociology (*see* Kinesiology and Movement Studies)
Student Affairs
Substance Abuse Counseling (*see* Counselor Education)
Supply Chain Management
Sustainability Management
Systems Management (*see* Management Information Systems)
Taxation
Teacher Education (*see* specific subject areas)
Teaching English as a Second Language (*see* English as a Second Language)
Technical Education (*see* Vocational and Technical Education)
Transportation Management
Travel and Tourism
Urban Education
Vocational and Technical Education
Vocational Counseling (*see* Counselor Education)

Directories and Subject Areas in This Book

NOTES

NOTES

NOTES